BASEBALL *EXTRA*

A newspaper history of the glorious game from its beginnings to the present

From the Eric C. Caren Collection

CASTLE BOOKS

I would like to dedicate this book to my lifelong childhood friend, Perry Alter
with fond memories of playing catch and running bases, trading baseball cards,
and arguing over which was the best New York team.

This book has special meaning to me in light of the fact that the very first item in my
newspaper collection was the gift of a 1913 sports page I received when I was eleven years old.
—Eric C. Caren

Publisher's Note: Every effort has been made to contact the owners of the papers reprinted herein,
and to obtain permissions where necessary, all of which are acknowledged.
In many cases, the papers are no longer in circulation or have transferred hands many times over.
We regret any inadvertent omissions.

The materials in this book have been reproduced from old and exceedingly rare and valuable newspapers.
We believe that the articles and photographs herein are of such historic importance
that an occasional lapse in the quality of reproduction is justified.

Published by Castle Books
a division of Book Sales, Inc.
114 Northfield Avenue
Edison, NJ 08837, USA

Compiled by Eric C. Caren

ISBN 0-7858-1188-5
Printed and bound in Spain by Bookprint, S.L., Barcelona

Contents

Page	Date	Publication	Articles of interest
59	September 21, 1903	The Inter Ocean (Chicago)	The Chicago Cubs and the New York Giants.
60	September 23, 1903	The Pittsburg Dispatch	A look at John McGraw and his New York team.
61	September 27, 1903	The Pittsburg Dispatch	"The Team Which Will This Week Tackle the Pittsburgs"—in the first World Series.
62	October 7, 1903	The Pittsburg Dispatch	"A Big Crowd Sees Boston Team Downed by the Thrice Champion Pirates."
63	October 8, 1903	Boston Daily Advertiser	Cy Young wins the 5th game of first World Series.
64	October 14, 1903	Boston Daily Advertiser	Boston wins the very first modern World Series.
65	October 8, 1905	The Brooklyn Daily Eagle	A look at the World Series contenders.
66	October 10, 1905	The Philadelphia Inquirer	Christy Mathewson and New York win the first game of the World Series.
67	October 14, 1905	The Evening Sun (NY)	Giants win the World Series.
68	September 2, 1906	The Cleveland Leader	A look at the Chicago White Stockings.
69	October 7, 1906	The World (NY)	A look at some of the great stars of the day.
70	October 9, 1906	The Brooklyn Daily Eagle	"Series For Baseball Championship of World Begins To-Day"
71	October 15, 1906	The World (NY)	White Sox win World Series.
72	October 3, 1907	The Cleveland Leader	Alta Weiss "Girl Tosser Wins Game, Also Fans"
73	September 13, 1908	The World (NY)	"Ty Cobb, His Baseball Career"
74-75	September 24, 1908	The Boston Post	The 'Merkle boner' game. "Merkle's Stupid Play Causes Riot"
76	September 25, 1908	The Boston Post	Perhaps the first old-timers game photo includes T. Bond, J. O'Rourke, A.G. Spalding, and J. Tyng.
77	October 3, 1908	The Boston Post	Addie Joss pitches perfect game.
78	October 9, 1908	The Boston Post	Evers, Chance, and Mordecai Brown are featured.
79	October 11, 1908	The World (NY)	"Manager Hugh Jennings of Detroit Tells Story of His Career"
80	October 14, 1908	The Milwaukee Daily News	"Cubs Again Champions of the World"
81-82	October 9, 1909	The Milwaukee Daily News	A look at the NL champion Pittsburg team, plus a look at some "American League Leaders".
83	October 12, 1909	The Evening Leader (New Haven)	"Hans Wagner, Pittsburg shortstop who made four hits and stole four bases" in World Series game.
84	October 17, 1909	New Haven Sunday Leader	Pittsburg wins the World Series.
	1910's		
85	April 10, 1910	New York Daily Tribune	A look at some of the country's premier ball parks.
86	April 15, 1910	The Evening Star (D.C.)	President Taft is earliest president to throw out the first ball.
87	April 22, 1910	Cleveland Plain Dealer (OH)	"New Ball Park Dedicated Before Immense Throng"
88	August 7, 1910	Boston Sunday Post	An early contest to identify pro baseball players.
89	October 10, 1910	Charlotte Daily Observer (NC)	"How Cubs and Athletics Will Line Up in World's Baseball Series"
90	October 10, 1910	Cleveland Plain Dealer	"Napoleon Lajoie Makes Eight Hits Out of Eight Times at Bat"
91	October 24, 1910	The Providence Journal (RI)	Philadelphia Athletics win the World Series.
92	August 2, 1911	The Detroit Free Press	"Ty Cobb Poses Exclusively for the Detroit Free Press"
93	August 19, 1911	Virginian-Pilot (Norfolk)	"She is Good Baseball Player"
94	October 17, 1911	The Boston Post	"Baker Defeats New Yorkers With a Home Run in the Sixth"
95	October 18, 1911	The Boston Post	"Baker Hits Homer and Athletics Win 3 to 2"
96	May 18, 1912	Los Angeles Evening Herald	"Cobb Team Quits Field— Big Baseball War is On"
97	May 19, 1912	New York Tribune	"Strike in Baseball Now a Stern Reality", amateurs play for Detroit.
98	October 10, 1912	The Boston Post	World Series game ends in a tie.
99	October 16, 1912	The Evening Sun (NY)	Red Sox win World Series.
100-101	October 17, 1912	The Florida Times-Union (Jacksonville)	The Snodgrass error in 10th inning leads to Boston winning the World Series.
102	October 17, 1912	San Francisco Examiner	"Glaring Muff By Snodgrass Brings On Giant's Defeat"
103	January 28, 1913	New York Tribune	"Olympic Hero [Jim Thorpe] to be Stripped of His Honors"
104	April 9, 1913	The Brooklyn Daily Eagle	"Brooklyn Team Starts 1913 Pennant Race"
105	July 16, 1913	The Brooklyn Daily Eagle	"Scenes at the Official Dedication of Ebbets Field"
106	September 7, 1913	The New York Press	"John J. McGraw, the 'Little Napoleon' of Baseball"
107	October 5, 1913	The New York Press	A look at the World Series contenders.
108	October 8, 1913	The Boston Traveler	"Matty and Plank in Pitching Duel"
109	October 9, 1913	Lewiston Evening Journal (ME)	Christy Mathewson hero of the game.
110	October 11, 1913	The Boston Traveler	"Athletics Take World's Series"
111	October 12, 1913	The New York Times	"The Napoleons of Baseball"—John J. McGraw and Connie Mack
112	December 28, 1913	The Detroit Free Press	"Claims Colored Championship of the State"
113	April 13, 1914	The Baltimore News	"New Federal League Opens Season at Terrapin Park..."
114	April 21, 1914	The Baltimore News	A look at Babe Ruth with Baltimore teammates in the International League.
115	July 11, 1914	The Boston Traveler	Boston acquires Babe Ruth from Baltimore.
116	July 12, 1914	Boston Sunday Post	"The Three New Red Sox Players Purchased from Baltimore"
117	July 12, 1914	The Sunday Herald (Boston)	Babe Ruth begins his career with Boston.
118	July 17, 1914	The Boston Post	"Tigers, Incidentally, Remind Ruth the American League is Not the International"
119	July 18, 1914	Los Angeles Examiner	" 'Rube' Marquard Beats Pirates in 21 innings, 3 to 1"
120	October 4, 1914	Boston Sunday Post	A look at the 'Miracle' Braves.
121	October 7, 1914	Lewiston Evening Journal (ME)	A look at some of the World Series contenders.
122	October 13, 1914	The Boston Post	Braves win game 3 of World Series in the 12th inning.
123	October 13, 1914	The Evening Sun (NY)	"Braves Now Champions, Taking Four Straight"
124	August 19, 1915	The Boston Post	"47,000 Storm New Braves Park..."
125	August 21, 1915	The Boston Herald	"White Sox Get Joe Jackson"
126	September 29, 1915	Public Ledger (Philadelphia)	" 'Alexander the Great' and 'Ty' Cobb Are World's Series Reporters for the Public Ledger"
127	October 1, 1915	The Boston Post	"Royal Rooters Get Turn Down" and a look at the AL champion Red Sox with Babe Ruth.
128	October 4, 1915	The Times (Los Angeles)	"Ty Cobb's Record is Greatest Ever Made"

Page	Date	Publication	Articles of interest
129-131	October 10, 1915	Public Ledger (Philadelphia)	Grover Cleveland Alexander, plus a look at the World Series contenders.
132	October 9, 1915	Los Angeles Express	"Ty Cobb 8-Time Batting Champion"
133	October 14, 1915	The Boston Post	Red Sox win World Series.
134	June 4, 1916	New York World Rotogravure	A look at the 1916 New York Giants.
135	October 10, 1916	Morning Tribune (Los Angeles)	Babe Ruth winning pitcher in second game of World Series.
136	October 13, 1916	The Boston Herald	"Red Sox Again World's Baseball Champions"
137	October 22, 1916	The Sunday Herald (Boston)	A look at the world champion Red Sox as well as the defeated Brooklyn Dodgers.
138	May 3, 1917	The Des Moines Register (IA)	"Cubs and Reds Play Nine Hitless, Runless Innings; Reds Victors"
139	June 23, 1917	The Boston Traveler	"Ruth Attacks Umpire"
140	September 28, 1917	The Boston Herald	Babe Ruth and the Red Sox defeat an incredible All-Star team including W. Johnson, J. Jackson, T. Cobb, and T. Speaker.
141	October 7, 1917	The Detroit Free Press	"White Sox Beat Giants in First Game for Title"
142	October 16, 1917	San Francisco Examiner	"White Sox Win the World's Championship"
143	July 20, 1918	The Freeman—An Illustrated Colored Newspaper (Indianapolis)	"Taylor Cleans Cubans—Lose to Rube" in Negro Leagues.
144	September 6, 1918	The Boston Post	"Ruth's Great Pitching Gives Red Sox First" game of the World Series.
145	September 12, 1918	The Boston Post	Red Sox win World Series but share front page space with World War I news.
146	September 9, 1919	The Boston Post	"Now Everybody Can Make a Home Run as Babe Shows How To Do It"
147	September 11, 1919	The Boston Post	"Maker and Breaker of World's Home Run Record"
148	October 9, 1919	The Bulletin (San Francisco)	"Reds Win Series"
	1920's		
149	January 6, 1920	The Boston Post	"Babe Ruth Sold to the Yankees"
150	May 2, 1920	New Haven Union (CT)	"Boston and Brooklyn Set New Record in 26-Inning Game"
151	May 6, 1920	Mid-Week Pictorial (The New York Times)	Managers of major league baseball.
152	June 27, 1920	The Brooklyn Daily Eagle	Lou Gherrig [sic] hits grand slam for his high school.
153	July 20, 1920	The Sun and New York Herald	"Ruth Hits Two More Home Runs, Increasing His Total to 31 and Setting a New High Record"
154	August 17, 1920	The Cleveland News	Ray Chapman is killed by Carl Mays' pitch.
155	September 29, 1920	White Sox Scandal	"Eight White Sox indicted for fraud.
156	October 11, 1920	The Pittsburgh Post	Wambsganss' unassissted triple play in the World Series.
157	October 13, 1920	The Boston Post	Cleveland wins World Series.
158	July 25, 1921	The Chicago Evening Post	"Cicotte and Jackson's Confessing Admitted"
159	August 3, 1921	The Chicago Evening Post	"Landis Bars Acquitted Sox From League Ball"
160	August 3, 1921	San Francisco Chronicle	"Chicago 'Black Sox' Acquitted"
161	October 2, 1921	The Salt Lake Tribune (UT)	A look at the contenders in the 1921 "Subway Series"
162	October 3, 1921	The Boston Post	Experts lined up to cover the World Series.
163	October 13, 1921	The Evening Bulletin (Providence, RI)	"Giants Win World Championship."
164	April 2, 1922	New York Tribune	"The High Cost of Baseball"
165	September 22, 1922	St. Louis Post-Dispatch	George Sisler named AL Most Valuable Player
166	October 2, 1922	St. Louis Post-Dispatch	"Hornsby Finishes Season With .401 Batting Mark"
167	October 5, 1922	Long Branch Daily Record (NJ)	"Darkness Ends Second World Series Struggle on 3 to 3 Tie"
168	October 9, 1922	The Hartford Courant	Giants win World Series
169	April 19, 1923	Los Angeles Examiner	"74,000 See Ruth Smash First Homer" at newly opened Yankee Stadium.
170	October 10, 1923	Los Angeles Evening Herald	"World Series Opened in N.Y."
171	October 11, 1923	Los Angeles Examiner	"Giants Win; Stengel Hero" in first game of World Series.
172	October 12, 1923	Seattle Post-Intelligencer	"Ruth's Two Home Runs Defeat Giants, 4 to 2"
173	October 15, 1923	The Evening Bulletin (Providence, RI)	"Yanks Win World's Baseball Championship", Ruth gets third home run.
174	February 2, 1924	Wisconsin News (Milwaukee)	A look at Rogers Hornsby.
175	October 10, 1924	The San Francisco Call	Senators win World Series
176	October 19, 1924	Chicago Sunday Tribune	A "harmless grounder" turns into "the winning run" for the Senators in the World Series.
177	November 9, 1924	The Detroit News	"Ty Cobb's Perfect Sliding Form"
178	May 6, 1925	The Saratogian (NY)	"Cobb's Hits Net Sixteen Bases; New Record Established"
179	October 7, 1925	The Sun (Philadelphia)	"Senators and Pirates Ready For Opening Tilt of World Series"
180	October 8, 1925	Los Angeles Examiner	"Christy Mathewson, Baseball Star, Dies"
181	October 15, 1925	Brooklyn Daily Eagle	Pirates win the World Series.
182	April 13, 1926	The Chicago Daily News	"Play Ball!" A look at the Chicago White Sox.
183	August 31, 1926	New York American	"Here's Melvin Ott, the 17-year-old recruit of the Giants..."
184	October 7, 1926	The Boston Post	"Babe's Three Homers Lam Spots Off Cards"
185	October 11, 1926	The Boston Post	St. Louis wins the World Series. Alexander strikes out Lazzeri with bases loaded in the 7th.
186	April 4, 1927	Baltimore American	"Cobb Hits Homer; Macks win"
187	June 25, 1927	New York American	"Lou 'Buster' Gehrig"
188	July 19, 1927	The Detroit News	"Ty Cobb Makes 4,000th Hit of His Major League Career"
189	September 8, 1927	Baltimore American	"Ruth's 5 Homers in 3 Games Equals Mark"
190	September 30, 1927	Los Angeles Examiner	"Ruth Equals Record" as he slams his 59th home run of the year.
191	September 30, 1927	Los Angeles Evening Herald	"Ruth Hits 60th Home Run"
192	October 6, 1927	Oakland Tribune	"Murder, Manslaughter and Little OOM Paul Waner"
192	October 8, 1927	Los Angeles Evening Herald	"N.Y. Wins World Series By Beating Pirates, 4-3"
194	October 9, 1927	Oakland Tribune	A look at the 1927 Yankee team that swept the World Series.

Page	Date	Publication	Articles of interest
263	October 1, 1945	Chicago Daily Tribune	Hank Greenberg hits pennant-winning Grand Slam.
264	October 11, 1945	The New York Times	"The Detroit Tigers: They Are the Winners and New Champions of the Baseball World"
265	October 24, 1945	Brooklyn Eagle	Jackie Robinson signs with Montreal, farm team of Dodgers.
266	October 16, 1946	The NewYork Times	Enos Slaughter's famous slide into home wins World Series for Cards.
267	January 21, 1947	The Washington Afro-American	"Josh Gibson Dies.."
268	February 10, 1947	The Detroit Free Press	"Hank [Greenberg] Ready To Quit"
269	April 12, 1947	The Washington Afro-American	"Brooklyn Signs Jackie Robinson"
270	April 22, 1947	The Washington Afro-American	Roy Campanella wins clean-up spot with Montreal Royals.
271	July 8, 1947	The Washington Afro-American	"Doby Plays With Indians"
272	October 4, 1947	The Des Moines Register	Cookie Lavagetto spoils Bill Beven's World Series no-hitter.
273	October 7, 1947	St. Louis Post-Dispatch	"Yanks Win Series", and a look at "The Catch of the Series" by Al Gionfriddo.
274	July 10, 1948	The Washington Afro-American	"At Long Last! Satchel Paige in Big League"
275	August 17, 1948	Daily News (NY)	"Babe Ruth Dies"
276	October 5, 1948	Cleveland Plain Dealer	"Indians Win First Pennant in 28 Years..." Boudreau hits 2 homers.
277	October 12, 1948	San Francisco Chronicle	"Indians Win World Series"
278	October 13, 1948	San Francisco Chronicle	"Casey Stengel New Yankee Pilot"
279	October 8, 1949	The Washington Afro-American	Jackie Robinson, Roy Campanella, and Don Newcombe
280	October 10, 1949	San Antonio Express (TX)	"Yanks Win 10-6 to Capture Series"
	1950's		
281	February 8, 1950	The Boston Herald	Ted Williams signs $100,000 plus contract, setting record.
282	October 2, 1950	The Washington Observer (PA)	"Phils Win Pennant On Dick Sisler's Homer in Tenth"
283	October 5, 1950	Evening Chronicle Extra (Allentown, PA)	DiMaggio home run in 10th inning wins second World Series game.
284	October 8, 1950	Boston Sunday Herald	"Yankees Win, 5-2, For Sixth Sweep"
285	March 23, 1951	The Kansas City Times	"The Mantle Boy is Yankees Joy"
286	April 6, 1951	The Kansas City Star	"The Clipper and His Replacement" (Mickey Mantle)
287	April 15, 1951	The New York Times	Joe DiMaggio and Casey Stengel check out the new rookie, Mickey Mantle.
288	April 18, 1951	The New York Times	Mickey Mantle's first major league game.
289	May 2, 1951	Daily Mirror (NY)	Mickey Mantle hits his first major league home run.
290	May 26, 1951	The New York Times	A look at the Giants new recruit, Willie Mays.
291	August 20, 1951	St. Louis Post-Dispatch	Bill Veeck's most famous novelty act—midget Ed Gaedel pinch-hits and walks.
292	August 25, 1951	St. Louis Post-Dispatch	Another Bill Veeck stunt—grandstand managers.
293	October 4, 1951	The Evening Star (DC)	Giant's Monte Irwin is first to steal home in World Series in last 30 years.
294-295	October 4, 1951	Daily News (NY)	Bobby Thomson hits the "shot heard 'round the world."
296	October 11, 1951	Daily Mirror (NY)	Yankees win World Series.
297	November 1, 1951	New York Herald Tribune	Roy Campanella voted NL MVP for 1951.
298	December 12, 1951	The New York Times	Joe DiMaggio retires.
299	May 1, 1952	Daily Record (Boston)	"Sox Win On Ted's Homer", just before Ted Williams leaves for Korean War.
300	June 27, 1952	Daily News (NY)	Women are barred from minor leagues.
301	October 1, 1952	Daily Mirror (NY)	A look at the Dodger and Yankee stars before opening of World Series.
302	October 4, 1952	Brooklyn Eagle	"We Wuz Ato-mized! Yankees Even World Series"
303	October 8, 1952	New York Herald Tribune	Yankees win 4th Series in a row.
304	October 8, 1952	Brooklyn Eagle	"Yankees Slipped Us a 'Mickey'!" Yankees win World Series over Dodgers.
305	March 6, 1953	Daily Mirror (NY)	Mickey Mantle replaces Joe DiMaggio in cleanup spot.
306	March 19, 1953	Daily Mirror (NY)	The Braves move from Boston to Milwaukee—the first franchise shift in baseball since 1903.
307	April 18, 1953	The New York Times	Mickey Mantle hits fabled 565 foot home run at Griffith Stadium.
308	June 19, 1953	New Haven Journal-Courier	Boston Red Sox break modern major league record for one-inning scoring.
309	October 5, 1953	The New York Times	Mantle hits Grand Slam in World Series game 5.
310	October 5, 1953	Daily Mirror (NY)	Mantle homers in World Series game.
311	October 6, 1953	New York Herald Tribune	Yankees win unprecedented 5th straight World Series.
312	June 4, 1954	Los Angeles Examiner	Hank Thompson ties modern NL record for consecutive homers in a single game.
313	September 30, 1954	The San Francisco News	Willie Mays makes the catch of the century.
314	September 30, 1954	Daily Record (Boston)	"Pinch Homer Paces 5-2 Giant Win"
315	October 3, 1954	Sunday Mirror (NY)	"G-I-A-N-T-S World Champs!"
316	October 27, 1954	Los Angeles Eve. Herald Express	Marilyn Monroe and Joe DiMaggio divorce.
317	April 18, 1955	Los Angeles Examiner	Al Kaline hits three home runs and ties the major league record.
318	August 3, 1955	Chicago Daily Tribune	Ernie Banks ties Grand Slam record.
319	September 28, 1955	The Providence Journal (RI)	A look at World Series contenders—Yankees and Dodgers.
320	September 29, 1955	The Providence Journal (RI)	Jackie Robinson called "safe" in stealing home in controversial first game of the World Series.
321	October 2, 1955	Cleveland Plain Dealer	Dodgers 3 home runs beat Yankees to tie the World Series, 2 games apiece.
322	October 4, 1955	Los Angeles Examiner	Yankees even series at three games apiece.
323	October 5, 1955	The Indianapolis Star	"Bums Are Champs—At Last" Brooklyn wins World Series.
324	October 9, 1956	Daily Mirror (NY)	"Don Wins Perfect Game"
325	October 10, 1956	Evening Chronicle (Allentown, PA)	Yankees win World Series.
326	June 14, 1957	Los Angeles Times	Ted Williams becomes first in the AL to hit 3 home runs in a game, twice in one season.
327	July 21, 1957	This Week Magazine—The Pittsburgh Press	A look at Mickey Mantle.
328	October 9, 1957	New York Herald Tribune	"It's Official—Dodgers Go To Los Angeles"
329	October 11, 1957	Milwaukee Sentinel	Braves win World Series.

Page	Date	Publication	Articles of interest
330	January 28, 1958	Los Angeles Evening Herald Express Extra	"Campanella, Star of Dodgers, Breaks Neck"
331	May 13, 1958	St. Louis Post-Dispatch	Stan Musial gets his 3000th hit.
332	May 27, 1959	The Detroit Free Press	Harvey Haddix pitches 12 perfect innings and loses game.
333	June 11, 1959	Cleveland Press	Rocky Colavito hits four consecutive home runs.
334	October 7, 1959	Los Angeles Herald & Express	World Series action—Dodgers vs. White Sox.
335	October 9, 1959	The Macon News (GA)	"L.A. Dodgers Win World Series"
	1960's		
336	October 13, 1960	New York Post	"Pirates Take it All on Mazeroski's HR"
337	October 13, 1960	The Pittsburgh Press	Mazeroski's dramatic 9th inning home run makes "Pirates World Champs".
338	October 18, 1960	New York Post	"Casey Stengel Fired"
339	April 29, 1961	The Dallas Morning News	Warren Spahn pitches his second no-hitter.
340	July 9, 1961	Sunday News Magazine (NY)	Mickey Mantle portrait.
341	September 27, 1961	The Plain Dealer (Cleveland)	Maris hits 60th home run, ties Babe Ruth's record.
342	October 2, 1961	New York Mirror	Roger Maris hits 61st home run, breaking Babe Ruth's record.
343	October 5, 1961	The Plain Dealer (Cleveland)	Whitey Ford's 3rd straight World Series shutout.
344	October 9, 1961	The Plain Dealer (Cleveland)	Whitey Ford pitches 32 consecutive scoreless innings in World Series breaking Babe Ruth's record.
345	September 24, 1962	Topeka State Journal (KS)	Maury Wills breaks Ty Cobb's single-season stolen base record.
346	October 3, 1962	News Call Bulletin (San Francisco)	Dramatic 9th-inning victory by Giants over Los Angeles to win pennant.
347	October 3, 1963	The Evening Star (DC)	Sandy Koufax World Series strikeout record.
348	October 6, 1963	Sunday News (NY)	Don Drysdale pitches World Series shut-out.
349	October 7, 1963	The New York Times	The Dodgers and Koufax win the World Series.
350	July 7, 1964	Evening Tribune (San Diego)	Johnny Callison hits 9th-inning home run to win All-Star game for the National League.
351	October 16, 1964	New York Post	St. Louis Cardinals win World Series.
352	November 17, 1964	Daily News (NY)	Yogi Berra is made manager of the Mets.
353	September 10, 1965	The Washington Post (DC)	Koufax hurls perfect game.
354	October 6, 1965	New York Post	A look at the World Series combattants.
355	January 21, 1966	Record American (Boston)	Ted Williams inducted into Hall of Fame.
356	June 10, 1966	The Dallas Morning News	Minnesota sets AL mark for home runs in one inning.
357	October 10, 1966	New York Post	The Orioles sweep the World Series in four straight games.
358	July 12, 1967	Chicago Tribune	NL wins All Star game as Tony Perez hits home run in 15th inning.
359	October 2, 1967	Boston Herald Traveler	Red Sox win AL pennant.
360	October 13, 1967	The Macon Telegraph (GA)	"Cards Win World Series"
361	June 9, 1968	Sunday News (NY)	Don Drysdale breaks scoreless-innings-pitched record.
362	October 2, 1968	Daily News (NY)	"World Series Showdown: McLain vs. Gibson"
363	October 3, 1968	Daily News (NY)	Bob Gibson breaks World Series strikeout record.
364	October 11, 1968	Chicago Tribune	Detroit Tigers win World Series.
365	March 2, 1969	The New York Times	Mickey Mantle retires.
366	April 28, 1969	Daily News (NY)	"Durocher, Baseball's Liperace Without Candlelabra"
367	July 17, 1969	New York Post	Rod Carew breaks AL record for steals of home in a season.
368	September 23, 1969	New York Post	Willie Mays hits 600th home run.
369	October 17, 1969	Daily News (NY)	Miracle Mets win World Series.
	1970's		
370	May 18, 1970	Daily News (NY)	"Aaron Joins 3,000-Hit Club"
371	October 14, 1970	The Indianapolis Star	Baltimore pitcher Dave McNally hits World Series grand slam.
372	August 11, 1971	Daily News (NY)	"Killebrew Hits 500th Homer"
373	October 18, 1971	The Washington Post	Clemente and the Pirates win the World Series.
374	October 1, 1972	The News American (Baltimore)	Roberto Clemente gets his 3000th hit.
375	October 24, 1972	New York Post	Jackie Robinson is Dead at 51.
376	September 28, 1973	Daily News (NY)	"Ryan Breaks Koufax SO Record"
377	April 9, 1974	Philadelphia Daily News	Hank Aaron hits 715th home run breaking Ruth's record.
378	October 16, 1974	Daily News (NY)	"A's Top Dodgers, 3-2" and takes 2-1 World Series lead.
379	October 18, 1974	The New York Times	Oakland A's win third straight World Series.
380	September 30, 1975	Daily News (NY)	"Casey Stengel dies at 85"
381	October22, 1975	The Topeka State Journal (KS)	Carlton Fisk hits dramatic game-winning homer in 12th inning to tie up the World Series.
382	October 23, 1975	The Macon News (GA)	"Reds Win World Series"
383	April 16, 1976	Daily News (NY)	The new Yankee Stadium opens.
384	June 29, 1976	The New York Times	Mark "The Bird" Fidrych, 21-year old rookie, is seen on national television for the first time.
385	October 22, 1976	The Minneapolis Star (MN)	Johnny Bench hits two home runs as Reds win World Series.
386	November 5, 1976	The Daily Item (Port Chester, NY)	First mass market free agent negotiation selections.
387	October 19, 1977	Minneapolis Tribune	Reggie Jackson becomes "Mr. October", hitting three home runs in the final World Series game.
388	October 3, 1978	New York Daily Metro	Bucky Dent Home Run gives Yankees A.L. East title.
389	August 3, 1979	The Indianapolis Star	N.Y. Yankees' Thurman Munson Killed.
390	September 13, 1979	New York Post	Carl Yastrzemski gets his 3000th hit.
391	October 18, 1979	The Minneapolis Star (MN)	Willie Stargell stars as Pirates win World Series.

Page	Date	Publication	Articles of interest
	1980's		
392	October 22, 1980	The Philadelphia Inquirer	Phillies win World Series.
393	October 29, 1981	Los Angeles Times	Dodgers win World Series.
394	October 21, 1982	St. Louis Post-Dispatch	Cardinals win World Series.
395	July 25, 1983	New York Post	George Brett pine tar bat game.
396	October 17, 1983	Daily News (NY)	"Orioles Fly Away With Series"
397	October 15, 1984	Detroit Free Press	Tigers win World Series.
398	September 12, 1985	The Cincinnati Enquirer	Pete Rose breaks Ty Cobb's record becoming baseball's all-time leading hitter.
399	October28, 1985	The Kansas City Star	Royals win World Series.
400	October 16, 1986	Daily News (NY)	Mets win Pennant.
401	October 27, 1986	USA Today (DC)	Bill Buckner's famous error on Mookie Wilson's grounder in 6th game of the World Series.
402	June 22, 1987	Daily News (NY)	Tom Seaver retires.
403	October 26, 1987	Star Tribune (Minn./St. Paul)	Twins win World Series.
404	June 24, 1988	New York Post	Billy Martin is fired— again!
405	October 16, 1988	Los Angeles Times	"Gibsons's Shot in the Dark Stuns A's"
406	October 21, 1988	Los Angeles Herald Examiner	"Dodgers Are Champs!"
407	August 23, 1989	New York Post	Nolan Ryan become first pitcher to achieve 5000 stikeouts.
408	August 24, 1989	The Cincinnati Post	Pete Rose banished from baseball.
409	October 18, 1989	Star Tribune (Minn./St. Paul)	Earthquake forces postponement of World Series game # 3.
410	October 29, 1989	Sunday Tribune (Oakland)	A's win World Series.
	1990's		
411	July 2, 1990	Daily News (NY)	Andy Hawkins pitches no-hitter but loses game.
412	August 1, 1990	The Dallas Morning News	"Ryan Wins 3000"
413	October 21, 1990	The Kentucky Enquirer	Cincinnati Reds win World Series.
414	May 2, 1991	Dallas Times Herald	Nolan Ryan pitches his 7th no-hitter.
415	October 28, 1991	Star Tribune (Minn./St. Paul)	Twins win World Series.
416	October 26, 1992	The Globe and Mail (Toronto)	Blue Jays win World Series.
417	April 6, 1993	The Denver Post	Colorado Rockies first game.
418	September 17, 1993	Star Tribune (Minn./St. Paul)	Dave Winfield gets his 3000th hit.
419	October 22, 1993	The New York Times	29 runs scored in game four of the World Series.
420	October 25, 1993	The Globe and Mail (Toronto)	Blue Jays win second straight World Series.
421	February 11, 1994	The Journal (Milwaukee)	Robin Yount retires.
422	August 14, 1995	Daily News (NY)	Death of Mickey Mantle.
423	September 7, 1995	Daily News (NY)	Cal Ripken, Jr. plays 2131st consecutive game, breaking Lou Gehrig's record.
424	October 29, 1995	The New York Times	Braves give Atlanta first major sports championship ever.
425	September 6, 1996	Star Tribune (Minn./St. Paul)	Kirby Puckett souvenir edition.
426	October 27, 1996	Daily News (NY)	Yankees win World Series.
427	October 27, 1997	New York Post	Marlins win World Series.
428	September 9, 1998	St. Louis Post-Dispatch	McGwire breaks Roger Maris' single-season home run record.
429	September 14, 1998	Chicago Sun-Times	Sammy Sosa hits 62nd home run.
430	September 28, 1998	St. Louis Post-Dispatch	McGwire ends season with 70 home runs and new record.
431	October 22, 1998	Daily News (NY)	Yankees win World Series.
432	March 9, 1999	Daily News (NY)	Joe DiMaggio dies.
433	August 7, 1999	The New York Times	Tony Gwinn gets his 3000th hit.
434	August 8, 1999	The New York Times	Wade Boggs gets his 3000th hit.
435	September 19, 1999	The New York Times	Sosa reaches 60th home run a second time.
436	October 28, 1999	The Daily News	Yankees—"Team of the Century"
437	October 8, 1909	The Pittsburg Dispatch (PA)	The Honus Wagner Advertisement. Honus Wagner's 1909 T-206 Baseball card sold for well over $1 million in July 2000 based primarily on the legend that has long been associated with the card. The story has always been that the T-206 Honus Wagner card was incredibly rare due to the fact that Wagner had objected to the use of his likeness and name in association with smoking. The long-told story stated that Mr. Wagner forced the American Tobacco Company to cease production of his own baseball card in the famed T-206 series. Baseball card collectors and dealers felt that this act of morality had kept the supply of Wagner cards limited to the number that had been issued prior to Wagner's demands. This newly-discovered advertisement issued during the now famous Detroit (Cobb) vs. Pittsburgh (Wagner) World Series calls into question the legend as well as the real motives of Honus Wagner. He is clearly shown endorsing a major cigarette company in his own hometown newspaper at World Series time, presumably after the T-206 series had been issued during the regular baseball season. We literally stopped the press to add this last minute acquisition of The Caren Archive to the book. We felt that the importance and rarity of this item justified its placement out of chronological sequence in the book.

Acknowledgments

© ***The Morning Call, Inc.,*** *Allentown, PA*: October 3, 1936; October 5, 1950 (*Evening Chronicle Extra*); October 10, 1956 (*Evening Chronicle*). © ***The Des Moines Register***: May 3, 1917; June 13, 1939; July 9, 1941; July 18, 1941; May 26, 1943; October 4, 1947. © ***The Kansas City Star***: April 6, 1951; October 28, 1985 This One's For You! It was a glorious, crazy season for Miracle Royals (Joe McGuff, photos by Jim McTaggert and Patrick Sullivan); March 23, 1951 (*The Kansas City Times*). © ***Detroit Free Press***: August 21, 1882; August 2, 1911; December 28, 1913; October 7, 1917; September 28, 1938; February 10, 1947; May 27, 1959; October 15, 1984. © ***1986, USA TODAY***: October 27, 1986. © ***The San Francisco Chronicle***: September 29, 1920; August 3, 1921; July 14, 1933; July 15, 1933; July 27, 1933; July 14, 1934; October 4, 1934; May 4, 1936; May 11, 1936; October 12, 1948; October 13, 1948. © ***1965, 1971, The Washington Post***: September 10, 1965; October 18, 1971. © ***New York Daily News, L.P.***: June 3, 1935; June 22, 1939; October 6, 1941; January 17, 1942; October 10, 1944; August 17 1948; October 4, 1951; June 27, 1952; July 9, 1962 (*Sunday News Magazine*); October 6, 1963 (*Sunday News*); November 17, 1964; June 9, 1968 (*Sunday News*); October 2, 1968; October 3, 1968; October 4, 1941; April 28, 1969; October 17, 1969; May 18, 1970; August 11, 1971; September 28, 1973; October 16, 1974; September 30, 1975; April 16, 1976; October 17, 1983; October 16, 1986; June 22, 1987; July 2, 1990; August 14, 1995; September 7, 1995; October 27, 1996; October 22, 1998; March 9, 1999; October 28, 1999. © ***2000 Journal Sentinel Inc.***: (*Milwaukee Sentinel*) October 11, 1957 Best in the World! Burdette Wins 3rd Game, 2nd Shutout (Red Thisted); (*The Milwaukee Journal*) February 11, 1994 Yount caps stellar career (Bob Berghaus), No. 19 gave us years of thrills (Tom Flaherty, photos by Tom Lynn and Karen A. Sherlock). © ***The Detroit News***: November 9, 1924; July 19, 1927. © ***The Globe and Mail***: October 26, 1992; October 25, 1993. ***The New York Post © 2000 NYP Holdings, Inc.***: October 13, 1960; October 18, 1960; October 16, 1964; October 6, 1965; October 10, 1966; July 17, 1969; September 23, 1969; October 24, 1972; September 13, 1979; July 25, 1983; June 24, 1988; August 23, 1989; October 27, 1997. ***The New York Times © 2000 by New York Times Company***: March 18, 1871 (*New York Tribune*); April 10, 1910 (*New York Daily Tribune*); May 19, 1912 (*New York Tribune*); January 28, 1913 (*New York Tribune*); April 2, 1922 (*New York Tribune*); October 9, 1927 (*New York Herald Tribune*); October 2, 1932 (*New York Herald Tribune*); July 11, 1934 (*New York Herald Tri*bune); September 24, 1934 (*New York Herald Tribune*); October 8, 1935 (*New York Herald Tri*bune); October 9, 1939 (*New York Herald Tribune*); September 17, 1940 (*New York Herald Tribune*); November 1, 1951 (*New York Herald Tribune*); October 8, 1952 (*New York Herald Tribune*); October 6, 1953 (*New York Herald Tribune*); October 9, 1957 (*New York Herald Tribune*); July 20, 1920 (*The Sun and New York Herald*); February 7, 1876 ; October 12, 1913; May 6, 1920 (*Mid-Week Pictorial*); October 15, 1927 (*Mid-Week Pictorial*); October 8, 1931; June 4, 1932; July 3, 1941; October 11, 1945; October 16, 1946; April 15, 1951; April 18, 1951; May 26, 1951; December 12, 1951; April 18, 1953; October 7, 1963; March 2, 1969; October 18, 1974; June 29, 1976; October 22, 1993; October 29, 1995; August 7, 1999; August 8, 1999; September 19, 1999. © ***The Bisbee Daily Review* by *Wick Communications,*** *Sierra Vista, AZ.*: July 6, 1933 (*The Bisbee Evening Ore*); October 9, 1940 (*The Bisbee Evening Ore*). © *The Macon Telegraph*: October 9, 1959 (*The Macon News*); October 13, 1967; October 23, 1975 (*The Macon News*). © ***The Daily Freeman,*** *Kingston, N.J.*: May 28, 1945. © ***The Saratogian***: May 6, 1925. © ***The Cincinnati Enquirer***: September 12, 1985 (*The Cincinnati Enquirer*); October 21, 1990 (*The Kentucky Enquirer*). ***The Plain Dealer © 1910-1961***: April 22, 1910; October 10, 1910; October 5, 1948; October 2, 1955; September 27, 1961; October 5, 1961; October 9, 1961. © ***The Washington Observer & Reporter* by *The Observer Publishing Company***: October 2, 1950 (*The Washington Observer*). © ***The Dallas Morning News***: April 29, 1961; June 10, 1966; August 1, 1990. © ***Sun Journal,*** *Lewiston, Maine*: October 9, 1913 (*Lewiston Evening Journal*); October 7, 1914 (*Lewiston Evening Journal*). © ***The St. Louis Post-Dispatch***: September 22, 1922; October 2, 1922; October 7, 1928; October 7, 1947; October 9, 1934; August 20, 1951; August 25, 1951; May 13, 1958; October 21, 1982; September 9, 1998; September 28, 1998. © ***The Washington Afro-American***: January 21, 1947; April 12, 1947; April 22, 1947; July 8, 1947; July 10, 1948; October 8, 1949. © ***The Cincinnati Post***: August 24, 1989. © ***Los Angeles Times***: October 4, 1915; June 14, 1957; October 29, 1981; August 13, 1984; October 16, 1988. © ***San Diego Union Tribune***: July 7, 1964. © ***Pittsburgh Post-Gazette***: October 11, 1920 (*The Pittsburgh Post*); July 21, 1957 (The *Pittsburgh Press: This Week Magazine*); October 13, 1960 (*The Pittsburgh Press*). © ***The Hartford Courant***: October 9, 1922. ***The Chicago Sun-Times, Inc © 2000***: (1) *The Chicago Daily News*: April 13, 1926 (*Photogravure Section*) "Play Ball!" (2) *The Chicago Daily News*: April 12, 1930 (*Photogravure Section*) "Play Ball!" (3) *The Chicago Daily News*: September 14, 1998 (headline) Sosa Slams 62; Articles: Club slugger ties McGwire's Record (Dave Van Dyck, staff reporter); Hyde favors House Hearings (Lynn Sweet, Sun-Times Washington Bureau). © ***The Providence Journal***: October 24, 1884 (*Providence Daily Journal*); October 24, 1910; September 28, 1955; Sept 29, 1955. © ***The Salt Lake Tribune***: October 2, 1921. © ***Brooklyn Daily Eagle***: October 8, 1905; October 9, 1906; April 9, 1913; July 16, 1913; June 27, 1920; October 15, 1925; October 24, 1945; October 4, 1952; October 8, 1952. © ***San Antonio Express News***: October 10, 1949. © ***The Oakland Tribune***: October 6, 1927; October 9, 1927; June 25, 1936; October 29, 1989 (*Oakland Sunday Tribune*). © ***San Francisco Examiner***: October 17, 1912; October 16, 1917; October 8, 1933; November 22, 1934. © ***The Denver Post***: April 6, 1933. © ***New Haven Register***: June 19, 1953 (*New Haven Journal-Courier*). © ***The Florida Times-Union***: October 17, 1912. © ***Honolulu Star-Bulletin***: April 24, 1937. © ***The Indianapolis Star & News***: October 5, 1955; October 1, 1970; August 3, 1979. © ***The Topeka Capital-Journal***: September 24, 1962 *(The Topeka State Journal)*; October 22, 1975 (*The Topeka State Journal*). © ***The Virginian-Pilot***: August 19, 1911. © ***Seattle Post-Intelligencer***: October 12, 1923. © ***The Minneapolis Tribune***: October 19, 1977; October 26, 1987 (*Star Tribune*); October 18, 1989 (*Star Tribune*); October 28, 1991 (*Star Tribune*); September 17, 1993 (*Star Tribune*); September 6, 1996 (*Star Tribune*); October 23, 1976 (*Minneapolis Star*); October 18, 1979 (*Minneapolis Star*). *All AP/Associated Press articles reprinted with permission of* **The Associated Press**. *Any AP or Wide World Photos courtesy of* ***AP/Wide World Photos***. *All UP/UPI articles reprinted with the permission of* **United Press International**. *All UPI images from* **Corbis Images**. © ***The Charlotte Daily Observer***: October 10, 1910. © ***The Chicago Tribune***: September 5, 1891; October 1924 (*Chicago Sunday Tribune*); May 30, 1930 (*Chicago Daily Tribune*); October 26, 1931 (*Chicago Daily Tribune*); September 11, 1933 (*Chicago Daily Tribune*); October 1, 1945 (*Chicago Daily Tribune*); August 3, 1955 (*Chicago Daily Tribune*); July 12, 1967; October 11, 1968; Sept 29, 1938 (*Chicago Daily Tribune*). © ***The Daily Item***: November 5, 1976. © ***The Boston Herald/Traveler***: July 12, 1914 (*The Sunday Herald*); October 13, 1916; October 22, 1916 (*The Sunday Herald*); August 21, 1915; September 28, 1917; July 11, 1934; February 27, 1935; February 8, 1950; October 8, 1950 (*The Sunday Herald*); October 2, 1967; October 8, 1913; October 11, 1913; July 11, 1914; June 23, 1917. © ***The Detroit Journal***: January 29, 1901. © ***The Philadelphia Inquirer***: April 9, 1974; October 10, 1905; May 26, 1935; October 22, 1980. *Reprinted with permission of the* ***Hearst Corporation***: ***The Los Angeles Herald Examiner***: July 18, 1914; April 19,1923; October 8, 1925; September 30, 1927; January 14, 1929; October 16, 1931; October 3, 1932; October 3, 1938; June 4, 1954; April 18, 1955; October 4, 1955; October 21, 1988; ***The Los Angeles Evening Herald***: May 18, 1929; October 9, 1915 (*Los Angeles Express*); October 10, 1923; September 30, 1927; October 27, 1954; January 28, 1958 (*Los Angeles Evening Express Extra*); October 7, 1959 (*Los Angeles Herald & Express*); ***The Chicago Herald and Examiner Sports***: March 30, 1934; ***The Record American***: January 21, 1966; ***The Boston Evening American***: May 24, 1932; ***The Baltimore American***: April 4, 1927; September 8, 1927; ***The News American***: October 1, 1972.

Porter's Spirit of the Times

BRIGHTLY, SC

A Chronicle of the Turf, Field Sports, Literature and the Stage.

OFFICE { Nos. 346 & 348 BROADWAY, CORNER OF LEONARD STREET. | NEW YORK, SATURDAY, SEPTEMBER 12, 1857. | WHOLE NO. 54. } VOL. III.—NO. 2.

CONTENTS OF THIS NUMBER.

TRANSLATED FROM THE FRENCH, EXPRESSLY FOR "PORTER'S SPIRIT."

Meditations and Confessions OF ALPHONSE DE LAMARTINE.

PARIS, July.

INTRODUCTION.

THE first installment of the extraordinary essay, of which the following is a continuation, described the first inception of the passion for literature upon the mind of the great Lamartine. It described the gradual process by which that taste was strengthened, and gave the distinguished writer's first boyish composition, as an illustration of the original character of his mind. It closed with a description of a lofty mountain, called Monsard, near the poet's birth-place, in the south-west of France, which mountain his father used frequently to visit of an afternoon with a book, and occupy, on its very summit, one of three naturally carved cathedral chairs, or stepped niches in the rock, which commanded a view of the plains and lower country for miles and miles. This daily habit on the part of Lamartine's father was shared in by another person, who will now be described.

CHAP. IX.—M. DE VAUDRAN.

The name of this second constant visitor of the mountain was M. de Vaudran.

He was a man of fifty or sixty years of age, and a member of a numerous and respectable family in our country, named De Bruys. The house of this patriarchal family was seen surrounded by terraces and gardens at the foot of Monsard, on the side of a dusty road, around meadows and little groves, with a streamlet on one side.

This family, before the revolution, had placed at Paris many of its sons in the highest offices of the monarchy. The aptness of this family for business and for letters was proverbial in all our country. The daughters were not less famous than the brothers for character and for mind. The youngest of these ladies yet lives, at the age of fifty-five, in the same house that I can now see the white walls of when I write these lines. She has lost none of the graces of her heart, of her smile, of her mind; she has used time, which has not used her. She is a green shoot of the past, left alone on the tomb of her brothers and sisters. All the country loves to find her in the morning where it left her in the evening.

M. de Vaudran had been at the head of one of the most important departments of government at the commencement of the reign of Louis XVI. Intimate with Malesherbes, and with the most important politicians and writers of the age decapitated, in 1793, he had fallen with the monarchy, imprisoned and proscribed. Pardoned by the alternations of revolutionary days, he had at last been left dry on the shore, like a wreck by the tempest, in his paternal domain.

He lived, like a philosopher, with his sisters, his opinions and his recollections keeping him hanging between two ages. Endowed with an exalted mind, with profound erudition, and an eloquence sober and precise as the affairs he had managed, he had sufficient resources in himself to enable him to support idleness, that punishment of all vacant minds.

Of all his property in Paris, he had saved only his library. He had placed it, as his chief treasure, in the upper stories of his sisters' house, and he consoled himself there with the mute consolers which are the best for every wound. Neighborhood and similarity of tastes had united my father and himself by a strong liking. It was not absolutely what is called friendship, but a reciprocal respect, which gave majesty and something of reserve to their emotions. But these two men sought each other out, though they were reserved, like two characters ashamed of their impulses. One day, impelled by the same instinct of solitude and meditation, they met on this lonely place. They passed an hour in agreeable reading and contemplation, and the next day were not surprised to meet again. Thenceforth, without any appointment, they met almost every day.

The face of M. de Vaudran was characteristic of his life. His eyes glowed with a fire deadened by misfortune. His lips were expressive of philosophic disdain. On his face was read the remark of Machiavelli about fortune: "I let its malignity have full sway. I am willing to be trampled under its feet, to be enabled to see if, finally, there be no chorde" in it.

His voice was grave, and his choice of expressions select. His rather elaborate manners recalled the Court of Versailles in a little hamlet of our mountains. His costume denoted a man of distinction, who respected the past in his season of decay. His hair was arranged in crisp and powdered curls over his temples. He had his hat in one hand, with a band of black ribbon fastened by a silver buckle, a gray coat with cut steel buttons, covering a vest of white, with large pockets. His shoes were fastened over his instep by steel buckles, and he carried a gold-headed cane.

Scarcely had he seated himself in the stone chair nearest my father, when I would sometimes hear the lighter step of a third visitor, ascending the mountain slowly, but resolutely. I could soon distinguish against the blue sky the dark frock of a young man, who, under the garb of a priest, had the manly form, expres-

(DRAWN AND ENGRAVED EXPRESSLY FOR "PORTER'S SPIRIT OF THE TIMES.")

BASE BALL IN AMERICA.

THE EAGLES AND GOTHAMS PLAYING THEIR GREAT MATCH AT THE ELYSIAN FIELDS, ON TUESDAY, SEPTEMBER 8TH.

THE CRICKET MATCH PLAYED AT HOBOKEN ON OCTOBER 3–6, 1859, BETWEEN THE ALL ENGLAND ELEVEN AND THE UNITED STATES TWENTY-TWO.

LONG STOP. LONG SLIP. LEG. UMPIRE. SHORT SLIP. WICKET-KEEPER. BAT. OFF SIDE. ON SIDE. MID WICKET. BAT. BOWLER. WICKET. UMPIRE. LONG FIELD OFF. LONG FIELD ON.

A BASE-BALL MATCH AT THE ELYSIAN FIELDS, HOBOKEN

GRAND BASE BALL MATCH FOR THE CHAMPIONSHIP, BETWEEN THE EXCELSIOR AND ATLANTIC CLUBS, OF BROOKLYN, AT THE EXCELSIOR CLUB GROUNDS, SOUTH BROOKLYN, ON THURSDAY, JULY 19.—FROM A SKETCH MADE BY OUR OWN ARTIST.

MATCH BETWEEN THE EXCELSIOR AND ATLANTIC CLUBS.

Right glad are we to find that manly sports and exercises are becoming so popular in America. This is as it should be; and it is good for the public health and morals. Once make Cricket and Base Ball and Quoits and Foot Ball and the rest of them national pastimes, and there will be little room left for big crimes to grow among us. It is bad diseased people who commit murders, and arson, and rapes and robberies—rarely or never, your robust fellow who has a sound stomach, and well-developed muscles. Hence we were glad to hear of the Base Ball match between the Excelsior and Atlantic Clubs, the other day, in Brooklyn, which took place on the grounds of the former Club, and in the presence of at least twelve thousand people.

This contest has been the leading topic of conversation in Base Ball Clubs for the past month and more; and since the return of the Excelsiors from their successful tour through the State, during which they played matches with the principal Ball Clubs of Albany, Troy, Buffalo, Rochester and Newburgh, the excitement has been on the increase, and yesterday it culminated in the collection of the vast assemblage of interested sp ctators that surrounded the ball ground of the Excelsior Club. Their opponents on this occasion have by common consent been for a long time known as the champions of the game, they never having yet been beaten in a series of home and home matches since their organization.

They have at last, however, met their superiors, and the Excelsiors may now take precedence of all as the best players in the State. Among those whose efforts merit special commendation of the victors, we would name Messrs. Leggett, Creighton, Pearsall, Holder and Russell, for their activity and efficiency in the holding department, and J. Whiting for his fine batting; and on the part of the Atlantic, Messrs. Oliver, Joe Oliver and Smith deserve praise for their excellent general play. The admirable arrangements of the Excelsior contributed greatly to make the proceedings pass off creditably. We append the scores:

Atlantic Club. Players.	H. L.	Runs.	Excelsior Club. Players.	H. L.	Runs.
P. O'Brien, l. f.	4	0	Pearsall, 1st b.	5	2
Hamilton, r. f.	4	0	Reynolds, s.	5	1
Pearce, s.	2	1	J. Whiting, 3d b.	0	5
M. O'Brien, 3d b.	4	0	Holder, 2d b.	1	3
Price, pitcher.	3	1	Russell, l. f.	3	2
Smith, catcher.	1	1	Brainard, r. f.	3	2
Joe Oliver, c. f.	2	1	Creighton, pitcher.	4	1
Oliver. 2d b.	3	0	Flanley, c. f.	3	3
F. Seinsoth, 1st b.	4	0	Leggett, catcher.	3	4
Total	27	4	Total	27	23

INNINGS.

Clubs.	1st	2d	3d	4th	5th	6th	7th	8th	9th	Totals.
Atlantic	0	0	1	0	0	0	2	1	0	4
Excelsior	2	2	5	3	1	0	6	3	1	23

Umpire, Mr. R. Barre, of the Pastime Club.
Scorer for the Atlantic Club, Mr. G. W. Moore.
Scorer for the Excelsior Club, Mr. S. S. Gregory.

Sweet are the uses of adversity—especially in the case of lawyers, who thrive in proportion to the number and variety of their trials.

THE METEOR.

Mr. Jarvis, the well-known artist of No. 506 Broadway, this city, was one of the favored few who enjoyed a full nnd unobstructed view of the brilliant meteor which passed over the northern part of the continent on the night of Friday, the 19th inst. He has since shown us a painting, representing this phenomenon as viewed by him after the main body had apparently divided, followed by a comet-like tail of great brilliancy. Whilst a painting can, of course, only do but small justice to a subject like this, Mr. Jarvis has succeeded not alone in conveying a correct idea of the luminous messenger as it sped on its way, but also in rendering it, in spite of the sombre hues of the coloring a most lively and pituresque scene. The painting can be viewed at his studio. Professor Bartlett's theory for the explanation of meteor phenomena is as follows:—"These bodies are of the nature of planets, and circulate about the sun in orbits as unerringly as their larger brethren. When they and the earth come simultaneously to those points of their orbits which are nearest together, the action of the earth often becomes superior to that of the sun, and the small masses are drawn to its surfrce. Plunging with enormous velocity into our atmosphere, these little bodies compress the air in front and rub against it with such violence on the sides, os to produce heat enough to fuse, and light sufficient to illuminate the most refractory and darkest of substances. The exterior and molten crust is swept to the rear by the resisting air; a new surface becomes exposed; this, in its turn, is fused and carried backward, and so on till finally the whole track of the meteor is strewn with groups of disintegrated and scintillating material."

THE NEW YORK CITY GUARD FIRING AT A TARGET WITH THE GUNS AT FORT HAMILTON.

It was an excellent idea of Capt. Lovel that our volunteer troops ought to be drilled for the defence of the forts of New York. These forts mount about 400 guns, which would require at least 2,500 men to serve them. Now we have not so many men to spare, from other arms of the service, to do this most necessary work; hence the value of Capt. Lovel's suggestion, who has not only suggested but acted it out. On Wednesday, the 18th inst., he marshaled his men—the famous and efficient City Guard—for target practice at Fort Hamilton, and the result was satisfactory in the highest degree, and the men won the approbation, very warmly expressed, of Major Anderson, who commanded the garrison at the Fort. The War Department had granted them the use of the guns at Fort Hamilton, and had directed them also to be supplied with ammunition. They left the City in the ferry-boat *Peconic*, which was gratuitously furnished by the Union Ferry Company, accompanied by a deputation from the Chamber of Commerce and several other invited guests, and reached the Fort soon after 1 o'clock. The company numbered about 50 men, and they took charge of six of the barbette 32-pounders upon the Fort—in two divisions, five men being assigned to each gun. The target was an ordinary cask—43 inches across and about 45 long—floating in the water a little over a mile from the Fort. There was a fresh wind and the bay was exceedingly rough, so that the target frequently disappeared entirely from sight. There were three small fishing boats lying nearly in range a little beyond the target, and several sailing-vessels in the immediate vicinity, which delayed the commencement of the firing for some little time. Half-a-dozen blank catridges produced no effect—but the first ball fired, whirling through the air with the strange sound, half roar and half scream, peculiar to the movement, and striking the water in their neighborhood, throwing a dense cloud of spray some ten or fifteen feet into the air, made a decided impression upon the sailing-vessels, and speedily cleared the field. The fishermen, however, remained at their posts during the whole performance.

The men worked the heavy guns, if not with the ease and rapidity of regulars, certainly with a good degree of vigor and efficiency. The six were loaded and sighted at once, and the firing was in succession at the order—the interval between the guns being only sufficient to watch the striking of the ball. The firing was at an elevation at first of four and a half, and after one round, of five degrees. The line of fire is first taken by sighting directly at the target, and then the piece is elevated by a screw so as to bring the top of the marked scale in range with the muzzle. Considerable allowance had to be made for the wind, which blew sharply from the northeast, directly across the range of fire.

Under all these disadvantages the firing of these inexperienced gunners—none of whom had ever before fired a shot—was remarkably good. Out of 36 shots discharged, more than half would have struck the hull of a vessel of ordinary size, stationed where the target was; and at least half a dozen were very close and admirable shots.

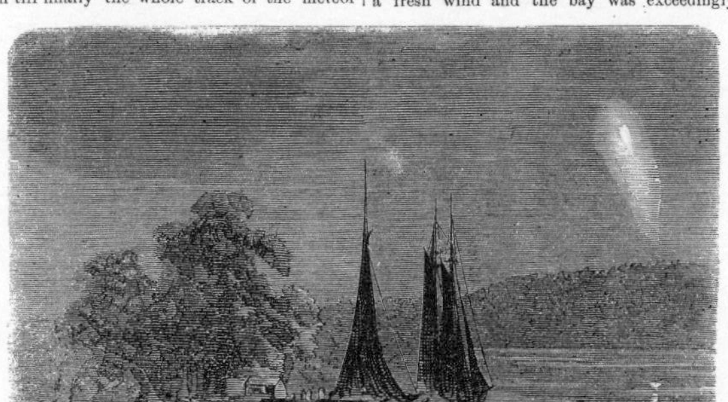

THE GREAT METEOR OF JULY 20—ITS APPEARANCE WHEN IT FIRST AROSE ABOVE THE WESTERN HORIZON.

PALERMO.

Palermo is a large and fine archiepiscopal city, agreeably situated on the northern coast, commanding a beautiful sea view, and in a luxuriously fertile and well-cultivated plain, called La Conca d'Oro, (the golden shell,) which is inclosed on three sides by mountains, and opens on the north to a spacious bay. The houses are all flat-topped, and have balconies, with glass doors, instead of windows. The streets are well laid out, and nearly all terminate at the principal entrances. Several fine public buildings, seven squares, with fine walks, the best of which is the Marina, lying along the shore; a University, several literary establishments, entitle Palermo to rank among the principal cities of Europe.

My rule is, deliberately to consider, before I commence, whether the thing is practicable. If it be not practicable I do not attempt it. If it be practicable, I can accomplish it, if I give sufficient pains to it; and having begun, I never stop till the thing is done. To this rule I owe all my success.—*John Hunter.*

DINNER TO CAPT. JOHN VINE HALL AND PARTY BY CAPT. R. B. COLEMAN, AT THE INTERNATIONAL HOTEL, NIAGARA FALLS.

Prior to the departure of Capt. Hall and party from Niagara, several of the most prominent gentlemen at the Falls were invited to a dinner in honor of Capt. Hall and his party.

The dinner was got up in the most splendid and sumptuous manner, such a dinner as Capt. Coleman only can get up. Capt. Coleman presided, having on his right Capt. Hall, and on his left Capt. Thomason. There were also present Dr. Watson, surgeon of the Great Eastern; Mr. Arthur Rousby, second officer; Mr. Bush, owner of the International, and several other distinguished gentlemen. John J. Sproull, Esq., of the Illinois Central Railroad, was seated in the vice chair. For dinner there were six courses, including soup, fish, meats, game, salads, pastry, and no end of wine. After the edibles had been properly discussed, Mr. Sproull rose and proposed the health of "Capt. Coleman, the man who knows how to keep a hotel."

To this toast the Captain answered with excellent spirit. He alluded to the time, nearly thirty years ago, when he was in command of the largest steamboat that was then afloat. At that time, Capt. Comstock (of the Adriatic) was under him, and with the experience he had, he well knew the hazardous and difficult task his friend Capt. Hall had to perform. I am happy, said he, addressing Capt. Hall, to welcome you to the shores of America; and here, in sight of British dominions, it makes my bosom swell with pride to know that I am able to offer you hospitalities such as cannot, at least, be excelled upon the other side of the river; and he only regretted that no proper demonstration had been made by the authorities of New York city to properly welcome him and those officers with him. We should, continued he, have all been satisfied had they have only for a few hours thrown open the official doors of the city, or visited the Great Eastern in a body, and congratulated you upon your safe arrival. The Captain's remarks were well-timed, and, in concluding, he proposed the health of

"Capt. Hall and the officers of the Great Eastern." He sat down amid loud applause.

Capt. Hall stated that nothing gave him more pleasure than to respond to a toast which seemed to be so unanimously endorsed, and that they had certainly anticipated some little mark of respect from those having charge of the great metropolitan city of America. Not that he at all desired any attention shown himself, but some compliment to the projectors of the great enterprise. He himself was no one; he was merely the driver of the Great Eastern; but he should have been proud to have seen some appreciation shown by the authorities of the great object which had been so successfully accomplished. However, said he, when the authorities failed, the press came forward. The proprietors of one illustrated paper alone tendered to us a banquet such as was a worthy compliment even to a Prince. They had invited to meet us the first legal, mercantile and literary representatives of New York, and every officer on board the Great Eastern, whether absent or present, acknowledged the high compliment conferred on them. Capt. Hall spoke for some time upon the many courtesies and kindnesses extended to him since his arrival, by private parties, and finished by proposing the health of the

"Proprietors of the New York Illustrated News," gentlemen who, believing that we, the officers of the Great Eastern, had not properly been received, gave, as representatives of the Press of America, a banquet, demonstrating at once their appreciation of our labors and their high-toned liberality.

Mr. T. E Rawlings, of the Illustrated News, being present, responded as follows:

Capt. Hall having paid so high a compliment to the proprietors of that journal which I have the honor to represent, I am in duty bound to return thanks in their behalf. The gentlemen alluded to, having duly considered the great feat accomplished by those having charge of the Great Eastern, and how faithfully they had performed the important duties of their mission, felt it were but justice to give them some ovation after their arrival. The result was the banquet given at the La Farge House. Mr. Rawlings said he would not enter into any lengthy remarks upon the success of the New York Illustrated News. Suffice it to say, it was now a permanently established thing—in fact, an institution, without which none of us would be contented, and he felt justified in saying that, although the youngest illustrated paper in this country, the superiority of its illustrations and the management of its literary department over any other, could not be gainsayed.

Several other speeches were made, and at a late hour the party broke up, highly gratified with the evening's entertainment.

In the early part of this week Capt. Hall departed for Toronto, from whence he will return to the Great Eastern, stopping a day at Saratoga on his way back. Correspondent.

THE SAVANNAH REPUBLICAN BLUES.

The Savannah Republican Blues have been spending the last week in the city, at the Lafarge House, as guests of the New York City Guard. On Monday evening a complimentary banquet was given them at the Metropolitan Hotel, under the presidency of Colonel Lovell of the Guard. It was a very magnificent affair. The Blues have also visited most of our public institutions. On Wednesday they departed for home in the steamship Florida. Prior to their departure, they were entertained to a collation by the City Guard, their hosts, when speeches were made and appropriate sentiments expressed The troops then marched down Broadway, and attracted the attention of a large crowd of spectators. They embarked at five o'clock, and in a quarter of an hour after the steamer got under way, amid cheers, firing of cannon, the strains of Dodworth's Band and other demonstrations of an enthusiastic farewell.

QUEEN VICTORIA.

Her Majesty, the Queen of England, is so well known to Americans in all that relates to her political and personal history, that in introducing a new portrait of her, which we do this week, we are hardly called upon to give the old facts about her. It may be as well, however, to say that she was the only daughter of his late Royal Highness, Edward, Duke of Kent, and that she was born May 24, 1819 She succeeded to the throne on the death of her uncle, King William the IV., on the 20th June, 1837, and was crowned June 28th, 1838. She was married February 10th, 1840, to Prince Albert, of Saxe Cobourg and Gotha. Her Majesty has won for herself the reputation of being the best mother in England—and she is certainly the best Queen who has ever wielded the destinies of that mighty Empire.

PRINCE ALBERT.

Prince Albert of Saxe Cobourg and Gotha, was married to the Queen of Great Britain on the 10th Feb. 1840. He was born August 26th, 1819, and is, on the whole, very popular in England. The royal family consists of the following members:—I. Victoria Adelaide Mary Louisa, Princess Royal, *b.* Nov. 21, 1840, *m.* Jan. 23, 1858, Prince Frederick William of Prussia. II. Albert Edward, Prince of Wales, *b.* Nov. 9, 1841. III. Alice Maud Mary, *b.* April 25, 1843. IV. Alfred Ernest Albert, *b.* Aug. 6, 1844. V. Helena Augusta Victoria, *b.* May 25, 1846. VI. Louisa Carolina Alberta, *b.* March 18, 1848. VII. Arthur Patrick William Albert, *b.* May 1, 1850. VIII. Leopold George Duncan Albert, *b.* April 7, 1853. IX. Beatrice Mary Victoria Feodore, *b.* April 14, 1857.

PERSONAL.

Col. Cipriani is now stopping at the Gilmore House, Baltimore. The Baltimore *American* is informed that the original statement that the Colonel is charged with making arrangements for the visit of Prince Napoleon is correct, and that the Prince will arrive here in his yacht before the close of the summer.

A report has been in circulation that President Buchanan has sold his residence near Lancaster, Penn., known as Wheatland, and that he has purchased, or is about to purchase a property in the vicinity of Baltimore. It is also said that a Mr. Potter is the purchaser, to whom the place has many cherished associations, having once been the property of his father.

Mrs. E. C. Kinney, wife of our late Charge at the Court of Turin, Sardinia, is making a short visit to her friends, from whom she has been absent ten years. She also finds her son, E. C. Stedman (the author of the "Diamond Wedding," &c.), grown to be a poet worthy of his mother, who, in the land of song, has both gathered laurels for herself and reflected honor upon her native land.

THE METEOR—AS IT APPEARED IN THE ZENITH PASSING OVER NEW YORK.

GREAT BASE BALL MATCH BETWEEN THE ATLANTIC AND ECKFORD CLUBS OF BROOKLYN, AT THE UNION BASE BALL GROUNDS, B

KLYN, E. D., OCT. 13, WITH PORTRAITS OF THE LEADING PLAYERS OF THE PRINCIPAL CLUBS OF NEW YORK, BROOKYN AND NEWARK.

'CHAMPION NINE" OF THE ATLANTIC BASE-BALL CLUB OF BROOKLYN, L. I., 1865.

THE ATLANTIC BASE-BALL CLUB.

WE give on this page portraits of the nine members of the Atlantic Base-Ball Club in Brooklyn, who were engaged in the recent contests for the championship with the members of the Athletic Club of Philadelphia. The "nine" of the Atlantic were victors in two successive matches—one played in Philadelphia, October 30, of which we gave an illustration in our last paper, the other a week later in Brooklyn. This latter established the claim of the Atlantic Club to the championship until some more successful rival shall arise to dispute it.

EXCURSION TO THE OIL REGIONS.

ON page 740 we publish three interesting illustrations relating to the Oil Regions of Pennsylvania. A short time since invitations were issued by Mr. C. VERNON CULVER to the capitalists of different cities to meet at Meadville for an excursion through the oil region of Pennsylvania. The party, consisting of senators, bankers, capitalists, and a necessary number of the journalistic fraternity, visited Corry, where extensive refining of petroleum is carried on.

Thence *via* the Oil Creek Railroad to Titusville. The next place visited was Schaffer, near which the first oil was discovered. Here horses were in readiness to convey the excursionists to "Pit Hole City." The ride was a merry one despite the rain and mud. The arrival at "Pit Hole" was the signal for the inhabitants to enjoy a joke at the expense of the bespattered excursionists. They were designated as "Bummers," "Do-Boys," "Raiders," etc.

Through the streets, where six months since there were no houses, we rode to the Pit Hole Creek. Here every thing was oil—thousand-barrel wells and hundred-barrel wells were plenty. Here we met men that hardly knew how much they were worth. "But the wells will give out," they said. Vast fortunes have been made by enterprising men who "went in" early. Messrs. DUNCAN and PRATHER associated themselves with several other gentlemen as early as December, 1864, in the purchase of the land interest in the Holden Farm, which contains 171 acres of land, selling the same in December last for one million and a half dollars.

The Second National Petroleum Company of this city bought the M'Kinney Farm, adjoining the H[illegible]den Farm, for $250,000, and soon after [illegible]used $600,000. This land is said to be wonderfully productive. After resting at the "Morey House" during the night the excursionists mounted their steeds for the journey *via* "Cherry Run" to Oil City.

It seems strange that such a common-sense race as our Yankees are should have built in such an impossible spot. Nature left the spot for a few oil wells, but no room for a city. Two miles more and we reach Reno, which place it is designed to make the metropolis of the oil region. Mr. C. VERNON CULVER owns the 1200 acres of land upon which the town is laid out. After a comfortable lunch, Mr. CULVER rose and proposed a very satisfactory scheme for persons desiring to invest their money.

"I propose," said he, "to stock this ground at $10,000,000. The money as paid in for the stock (which will not be sold for less than par) to be placed in the hands of trustees, and by them placed in the United States Treasury. The interest of this money up to $1,000,000 to be expended in developments of the property. I also propose to be ready at all times to return the par value of the stock when it is called for.

"If I can make this stock so satisfactory as to keep it out, which I am more than confident that I can, I shall be in the [illegible]eceipt of $600,000 each year, the interest of the sto[illegible] at six per cent."

The proposition w[illegible] received with great favor by the excursionists, [illegible] soon started in the train in waiting for Frankli[illegible] thence to Meadville, where the comforts of the M[illegible]Ienry House were not to be forgotten.

Explosions are of frequent occurrence in the oil regions. One occurred very recently (on the evening of November 8) at Pit Hole City.

EXECUTION OF WIRZ.

IN accordance with the sentence promulgated on Monday, November 6, Captain WIRZ, the Andersonville jailer, was hung in the yard of the Old Capitol prison at Washington on Friday, the 10th instant. Perhaps in no single instance on record has the execution of any criminal been so clearly demanded by justice. Certainly it is a rare thing for men and women to rend the air with cheers as was the case when WIRZ was hung. In ordinary

THE "ATHLETICS," OF PHILADELPHIA.

THE "ATLANTICS," OF BROOKLYN.

THE "ATLANTIC" BASE-BALL CLUB OF BROOKLYN, AND THE "ATHLETIC" OF PHILADELPHIA.—PHOTOGRAPHED BY CHARLES H. WILLIAMSON, BROOKLYN, L. I.—[SEE PAGE 702.]

THE GREAT CONTEST BETWEEN THE ATLANTIC BASE BALL CLUB OF BROOKLYN, AND THE ATHLETICS OF PHILADELPHIA, AT THE CAPITOLINE GROUNDS, FULTON AVENUE, BROOKLYN, MONDAY, OCT 15TH.—PAGE 103.

The Ball Players' Chronicle.

…y Journal Devoted to the Interests of the American Game of Base Ball and Kindred Sports of the Field.

THOMPSON & PEARSON, Publishers. | NEW YORK, JUNE 6, 1867. | HENRY CHADWICK, Editor, | No. 1.

…ase Ball.

…ME IN THE EAST.

…GAME IN BOSTON—BRIL…TESTS FOR THE SIL…L AND THE NEW …AND CHAM…ONSHIP.

…of the Grand Match, …well, at Medford, …ne 1st, 1867.

…WIN THE BALL.

… we believe, that the …of Base Ball Players …opt a regular code …lar game of ball of …e "Massachusetts … it required great …, at no time ever … as the "National …own in New Eng…."

…NEW ENGLAND.

…ame, as played in …ed into New Eng…ri-Mountain Clubs …ons,—before it be…ular favor, the New …lowing local preju… in selecting the best …rominent among the …ell, of Boston, [illegible] any one indi…itled to the credit of fostering the …e in New England, Mr. Lowell is. …ered a strong party around him, … period, the Lowell Club sprang …, and, ever since, it has been the …ization of the East.

…ow began to attract general atten… it was not long afterwards before …setts game became obsolete, and …e every such club has disbanded, or …dvocate of the National game. The … of base ball as a valuable auxiliary … education soon attracted the atten…eachers of schools and the Faculty of …ding colleges, and as the papers, too, be…gan give it attention, as a matter of public inte…st, the base ball fever soon began to prevail in New England, as it did in other portions of the country. But it was not until the rivalry between the College clubs and the city organizations was commenced that the furore now existing in regard to the game was inaugurated. We have not the scores of the first two or three series of games between the rival clubs, the Harvard College Club and Lowell of Boston, but suffice it to say, that the contests between them proved very attractive, and soon became the events of the season in the way of out-door sports.

THE CHAMPIONSHIP OF NEW ENGLAND.

To add to the interest taken in the game a series of contests for the championship of New England were arranged, and to give eclat to these trials of skill Mr. Lowell, with characteristic liberality, presented a handsome silver ball, valued at one hundred and fifty dollars, as the emblem of the championship, the same to be contested for in accordance with a code of rules, a copy of which we append:

1st. All match games for the championship shall be played in accordance with the rules adopted by the National Association.

2d. The season for play shall commence each year on the first day of May, and continue until the first day of October.

3d. All challenges shall be sent to the chairman of the Silver Ball Committee, who will communicate with the champion club.

4th. The champion club must be prepared to play within fifteen days after receipt of the challenge *from* the Committee. In case it is decided to play a series of games the first game must be played as provided for above, the second game within ten days from the date of the first, and the third game within ten days from the date of the second; and the championship club shall play clubs in the order of the date of their challenges.

5th. The championship club may be allowed the privilege of appointing the time for playing, subject to the conditions of the preceding rule.

6th. The place for playing all champion games shall be mutually agreed upon by the contesting clubs. Should they fail to agree within seven days from receiqt of challenge by the champion club, the matter shall be referred to the Silver Ball Committee, whose decision shall be final.

7th. All expenses of every champion club must be defrayed by the challenging club.

8th. Any club, having held the silver ball for three consecutive years, shall become its rightful owners, and the New England Association shall furnish a new emblem of championship.

9th. In case the champion ball shall change hands during the season, all outstanding matches shall be assumed by the new champions.

10th. No *challenging* club, being defeated, shall challenge again the same champions during the same season.

11th. The champions, being defeated, may challenge immediately after their defeat, and be allowed a match in the order of their challenge.

12th. The champion ball shall remain in the custody of the champion club until the decision of the game or series of games (as may have been mutually arranged), when it shall be placed in the hands of the committee on the champion ball, and by them be awarded to the winning club, immediately and on the spot.

In accordance with the above code several first class contests took place during the season of 1865, but the games of 1866 proved to be the most interesting, for it was in that year that the Harvard Club, desirous of improving their play by contact with the noted clubs of New York, though defeated [illegible] majority of games played, they acquitted themselves so creditably as to win hosts of admirers, not only for their fine manly play, but for their gentlemanly deportment and indomitable pluck as displayed in their contests here. Returning home, however, they found the Lowells still too strong for them [illegible] in July, 1866, they had to succumb to them and yield them the palm of superiority for the season, as will be seen by the following score of the game then played, it being the third game of the series between them:

LOWELL.	O.	R.	HARVARD.	O.	R.
Lovett, p	3	4	Wright, 1st b	1	5
Joslyn, 3d b	1	4	Hunniwell, p	4	2
Alline, c. f	5	2	Watson, 3d b	5	2
Lowell, l. f	4	4	Flagg, c	4	2
Sumner, 2d b	2	6	Ames, 2d b	4	2
Wilder, c	4	4	Abercrombie, c. f	1	4
Gardner, r. f	3	5	Smith, l. f	3	3
Crosby, 1st b	2	5	Parker, s. s	4	2
Burton, s. s	3	3	Sprague, r. f	1	5
Total		37	Total		27

INNINGS.

	1st.	2d.	3d.	4th.	5th.	6th.	7th.	8th.	9th.
Lowell	2	3	4	4	8	1	10	3	2—37
Harvard	4	4	7	2	1	2	3	2	2—27

Umpire—Mr. Warner, of the Pioneer Club of Springfield.

Scorers—Messrs. Fuller and Harris.

Time of game—Three hours and 20 minutes.

Fly catches—Lowell, 12: Harvard, 6.

The last trial of skill between these noted clubs in 1866, was the culmination of the season's play, the Lowells holding the silver emblem of the championship, and the title of the champions of New England.

THE CONTESTS OF 1867.

We now come to the contests of the present season between the Harvard and Lowell Clubs, and more brilliant displays of the most attractive features of the national game, or more manly encounters on the ball fields of New England, were never before witnessed.

THE FIRST GAME OF THE SERIES,

For the silver ball, this year, between the Harvard and Lowell Clubs, was arranged to take place on the Boston Common, on Wednesday, May 13th, and, accordingly on that day, the Common was visited by a large concourse of the admirers of the game, in anticipation of witnessing a fine display of ball playing and a close and exciting contest. The comparative superiority of the Harvards in batting, judging from the standard of the relative scores made by the Harvards and Lowells in their previous games with the Beacon and Somerset Clubs, the Harvards scoring a total of 117 to 24 against them, while the totals of the Lowells stood at 76 to 54 only, led many to anticipate the success of the Harvards in the first encounter; but apparently the Lowells had laid by a reserve stock of skill for special employment against their rivals, for the expected victory was not achieved, the Lowells being the victors in the contest.

The game opened favorably for the Lowells by a score of 3 to 0, and this advantage was increased before the sixth inning, the total at the close of the fifth inning standing at 26 to 7. In the 6th innings, the Harvards rallied well for the lead, pulling up their score to 17, and, in the 7th, they added 8 runs more, the totals at the close of the 7th innings standing at 34 to 25 still in favor of the Lowells. The Harvards had two more innings left to recover their lost ground, in, but they were unable to add more runs to the score than the Lowells did, the final figures being 37 to 28 in favor of the Lowells. We give the score below:

LOWELL.	O.	R.	HARVARD.	O.	R.
Lovett, p	2	5	Hunnewell, p	5	6
Joslyn, 3d b	2	6	Ames, 2d b	3	4
Alline, c. f	3	4	Flagg, c	3	2
Rogers, r. f	3	5	Shaw, 1st	4	1
Lowell, l. f	5	3	Parker, 3d b	3	2
Sumner, 2d b	3	4	Sprague, c. f	2	3
Wilder, c	3	3	Smith, l. f	2	[illegible]
Jewell, 1st b	2	4	Willard, s. s	[illegible]	[illegible]
Thompson, s. s	4	3	Meally, r. f	2	[illegible]
Total		37	Total		[illegible]

INNINGS.

	1st.	2d.	3d.	4th.	5th.	6th.	7th.	8th.	9th.
Lowell	[illegible]	[illegible]	[illegible]	14	[illegible]	[illegible]	[illegible]	0	3—37
Harvard	[illegible]	[illegible]	[illegible]	0	[illegible]	10	8	1	2—28

Umpire—[illegible] the Athletic club, of Philadelphia.

Scorers—Messrs. C. L. Fuller and W. Worthington.

THE SECOND GAME OF THE SERIES.

On Friday, May 24th, the second game of the series was played, the locale of the contest being the ball grounds known as "Jarvis's Field" at East Cambridge. At this game, a very large concourse of spectators were assembled, and this time the Lowells felt very sure of a signal victory, but the Fates decreed otherwise, the final result being the success of the Harvard nine. This game opened very favorably for the Lowells, by a score of 6 to 1, and the close of the third innings saw them in the van by the totals of 15 to 9. In the next two innings, the Harvards rallied prettily for the lead, and they entered upon the sixth innings with the totals standing at 18 to 19, the Lowells leading by one run only. The excitement at this period of the contest was intense, and when the Harvards gained the lead, as they did in the sixth innings by a score of 5 to 2, the Harvard crowd became so elated that they acted like wild people. The ninth inning terminated in favor of the Harvards by a score of 3 to 1, leaving the totals at 32 to 26 in favor of the Collegians, and a more elated party than the majority were on that field that day has seldom been seen. We give the score of the game below:

LOWELL.	O.	R.	HARVARD.	O.	R.
Lovett, p	4	2	Sprague, c. f	4	3
Joselyn, 3d b	5	2	Smith, l. f	4	3
Alline, r. f	3	4	Hunnewell, p	3	2
Rogers, c. f	2	4	Flagg, c	3	2
Lowell, l. f	1	4	Parker, 3d b	4	3
Sumner, 2d b	4	2	Ames, 2d b	4	3
Wilder, c	2	3	McKim, r. f	2	5
Jewell, 1st b	1	4	Shaw, 1st b	1	6
Thompson, s. s	5	1	Willard, s. s	2	5
Total		26	Total		32

INNINGS.

	1st.	2d.	3d.	4th.	5th.	6th.	7th.	8th.	9th.
Lowell	6	2	7	0	4	0	2	4	1—26
Harvard	1	3	5	1	8	2	5	4	3—32

Umpire—E. H. Hayhurst, of the Athletic Club, Philadelphia.

Scorers—W. Worthington, C. L. Fuller.

Time of game—Three hours and ten minutes.

Fly catches—Lowell, 14; Harvard, 8.

We now come to the third of the series of games, and it proved to be the most exciting contest at base ball ever witnessed in New England. Before commenting further on the incidents of the match, we proceed at once to give the full details as taken down in short-hand expressly for this journal.

DETAILS OF THE THIRD AND GRAND MATCH.

First Innings' Play.

At 3:20 P. M., the field having been cleared, as far as four hard-working policemen and the gentlemen of the Olympic Club could possibly effect such object, the game began. The Lowells won the toss and went to the bat. Here, our players generally take the field when they win the choice, in order to have the last chance at the bat. Lovett opened play by sending the ball to Smith at left field, out of reach, Lovett making his second by his hit. Joslyn was next, and he began by hitting a bounder, the style which takes so well on a hard ground, but which on a turfy field like that of the Olympic's can generally be fielded to the bases in time; this time, however, the ball went over Ames's head, and Joslyn thereby secured his first, Lovett reaching his third. Alline followed and he also hit a bounder which ought to have been the means of his retirement; but it was not handled in time and Alline secured his base. Rogers also went in for the bounder business, but Parker field[illegible] ball well to Shaw, the "Brook[illegible] king, not [illegible] sharply to Shaw's [illegible] at first, "out on the first base" was the cry of the [illegible] two outs and three runs, Joslyn [illegible] made, and only come in on hits that had [illegible] ball. Sumner then gave the fielders a chance to dispose of him at first, but it was not accepted, and he secured his base; before he could get further than the second, however, Wilder popped one up near Shaw's position and the Umpire, first crying "foul," followed it with "out on the fly," Shaw capturing the ball in style and closing the innings for three runs. When the game began we took our seat with the scorers and reporters—and every Boston paper was represented—but before the innings was half over we found it would be next to impossible to take a short hand report, while such confusion prevailed as did around the scorers' position, and we therefore took the Umpire's chair, and even then had a difficult task to perform, so noisy were the crowd, sharp, short huzzas and hisses marking the plays and decisions made, the former being excusable, but the latter a disgrace, for the partizans on each side hissed nearly every decision of the Umpire, and we have never seen fewer errors committed or better judgment shown by an Umpire. The yells of derision when errors were committed were only equalled by the jeers of juvenile roughs in New York on similar occasions, and were entirely out of place as emanating from an educated crowds as the bulk of the assemblage seemed to be on this occasion.

The Harvards now went to the bat, Sprague leading off by popping one up, by which Jewell was afforded a good chance for a catch; the ball was dropped, however, and Sprague secured his base. Smith then sent a bounder to Joslyn, but the ball was not handled in time, and Smith also secured his 1st. Hunniwell, not to be behind the rest in liberality, offered Alline a good chance for a catch, but it was not accepted, and another secured base was the result, and Flagg's high long ball to centre field, not only gave him his 1st easily, also sending the two first men home, but, owing to a rather wild throw of Rafens's, Hunniwell reached his 3d; instead of being put out at 3d, and, by a passed ball, got home, four runs being scored, when,

A Weekly Journal Devoted to the Interests of the American Game of Base Ball and Kindred Sports of the Field.

VOL. 1. {THOMPSON & PEARSON, Publishers.} NEW YORK, OCTOBER 17, 1867. {HENRY CHADWICK, Editor.} No. 20.

Base Ball.

THE GAME IN NEW YORK.

THE ATLANTIC AND UNION MATCH.

The Championship Pennant Leaves Brooklyn for the First Time.

Great Excitement in Morrisania.

On Thursday, October 9th, 1867, an event occurred which will be noteworthy as a prominent chapter in the annals of the game in this section of the country, for on that day the laurels of the championship of the United States were wrested for the first time from the Atlantic Club by a club not located in Brooklyn. For ten years past the championship has been held by Brooklyn clubs, the Atlantics being the first champion club of the United States, and the last, up to the 9th of October, 1867. For an interval of two years, however, the title was held by another Brooklyn club—the Eckford Club of the Eastern District, who were champions during 1862 and 1863; but with this exception, the Atlantics have flown the whip pennant, and bravely held their own against all comers for the past ten years.

On the day in question the Union Club became the champion club of the United States, by virtue of the winning of two games in succession of a home-and-home series with the Atlantic Club of Brooklyn, their first game being won at Morrisania, July 31st, by a score of 32 to 19, and the second, Oct. 9th, by a score of 14 to 13—an aggregate of 46 to 32. Before proceeding to give the details of this last game, we propose briefly to review the season's play of the Union Club.

The Unions began play for the season in a regular match game, on the 18th of May, their adversaries being the Atlanta Club of Tremont. This they won by a score of 48 to 10. On the 25th of May they played th Athletes of Washington Heights, and then made the highest score known in the history of the club, the Unions winning by the totals of 101 to 13 in a game of six innings only. On the 4th of June they entered the championship arena, encountering the noted Irvingtons for the first time, and this time met with defeat by a score of 26 to 17. On the 12th of June victory perched upon their banner in a contest with the Eureka Club at Newark, the score being 26 to 12; and on the 15th of June they captured a trophy from the Eclectics by a score of 45 to 10 in a game of seven innings. The return match was played on June 29th, the Unions again winning, but only by a score of 36 to 32. On the 2d of July their return game with the Irvington Club was hastily played, and another defeat was the result, the Irvingtons winning by a score of 26 to 22. They now realized the fact that they were not properly prepared for the championship contest, and they wisely resolved upon a week's tour through the western part of the State for practice; and accordingly they left town, July 7th, and on the 8th played the National Club of Albany, winning easily by a score of 47 to 16. On the 9th they met the noted Unions—ye "Haymakers"—at Lansingburg, and this time they had foemen worthy of their steel, and for the first time the Unions had to yield to a "country club"—the score standing at 51 to 23 against them. This repulse only spurred them to extra exertions, and on the 10th they defeated the Utica Club by a score of 49 to 26, and on the 11th the Excelsiors of Rochester, by a score of 34 to 15—closing their week's play with a victory over the noted Niagaras of Buffalo by a score of 25 to 19. On the 13th they returned home—tired, of course, but greatly improved by the practice, as their play in the next two games fully proved.

On the 31st of July we find them again entering the championship arena, and this time they face the champions themselves, and it being a contest between a nine well practiced in home positions, against a nine entirely out of practice, the result was the signal success of the trained nine of the Unions by a score of 32 to 19. This victory offset the Irvington defeats, and after a practice game with the Atlantas, of Tremont, Aug. 6th, which they won by a score of 31 to 16, they encountered the Mutuals on the 14th of August, at Brooklyn, and it not only proved to be a brilliant victory, but the finest fielding game the two clubs had ever played before, the result being the success of the Unions by a score of 9 to 8. Union stock was now at a high premium, and when their fine nine entered the field, Aug. 19th, to meet the Athletics, and finish their home-and-home game with them, every one anticipated another signal triumph for the gallant Unions. But Dame Fortune, with her usual fickleness, deserted them on this occasion, the result of the contest being their signal defeat by the Philadelphians by a score of 23 to 10, the only consolation being that the Athletics also defeated the Mutuals the next day. The Unions did not again play until Aug. 25th, when they visited Newark and played the Active Club, winning by a score of 22 to 12, and on the 27th they had a close game with the Eckfords, but came off the victors by a score of 25 to 23. On the 31st of Aug. they took another little country trip to get their hands in again, and visiting Norwich played two games there, first with the Pequot Club, winning by the score of 33 to 8, and then with the Riverside Club, score 66 to 17. On Sept. 10th, they defeated the Eurekas again by a score of 33 to 14, and on the 12th polished off the Excelsiors, of Rochester—then visiting New York—by a score of 29 to 21, and on the 17th won another trophy from the Actives, of Newark, by a score of 22 to 11. On the 19th of Sept. they met the Orientals, with four of their nine absent, and this carelessness cost them the game by a score of 42 to 19 against them. Two days after, Sept. 21st, they visited Philadelphia, and again being short-handed, sustained defeat at the hands of the Athletics, but only by a score of 36 to 32. On Sept. 23d, they were defeated by the Mutuals by a score of 20 to 24, thus losing two games out of the series of three between them, and the next day they played their return game with the Unions, of Lansingburgh, at Brooklyn, and were beaten by a score of 26 to 21. On the 28th of September they met the Actives, and after a closely contested game, came off the victors by a score of 15 to 11. This was the last game prior to their meeting with the Atlantics, their total scores in the above matches being 872 against 543. They play one more game before they close the season, and that is their return game with the Athletic Club. Early in the season they notified clubs that their season would close Oct. 16th.

We now come to the contest of Oct. 9th, on which occasion they played their return match with the Atlantic Club, at Brooklyn, in the presence of about three thousand people, the attendance not being as numerous as it would have been had such a fine game and a close contest been anticipated; but in view of the recent defeat of the Mutuals by the Atlantics, and of the Unions by the Haymakers, it was pretty generally expected that the Atlantic Club would have but little trouble in winning a ball, even from the crack club of Morrisania. The uncertainty of ball matches in general and of the result of contests in which the Union Club take part in particular, should have taught the habitues of our leading contests better; but it did not have that effect, and the result was a comparatively slim attendance. The Unions had out the strongest nine on this occasion they ever presented in a match, while the Atlantics were not only minus the services of Charley Smith, but had a nine out which was not as happy a family as it is requisite to have to fully develop the strength of a nine.

The game began at 2.50 P. M. with the Atlantics at the bat, Pearce leading off with a safe hit to centre field, on which he easily secured his base, Start following suit with a safe bounder to right field, both being helped round by passed balls. Galvin then came to the bat, and, banging away at the first ball within reach, sent it high to left field, and it fell very prettily into Smith's hands, Start getting home by the operation, Pearce having preceded him. Crane also sent a high ball to right field, directly into Beals' hands; and as Mills also popped one up for Shelley to take, the innings closed for the two runs scored by Pearce and Start. Smith led off on the Union side, and hit a "corker" to centre field; but Galvin judged the ball finely, and bottled Smith's corker in style. Martin then sent a hot bounder to Crane, which Fred passed to Start, but scarcely in time, the ball certainly not being handled before the striker reached the base; but the umpire thought it had, and Martin had to retire; whereupon up went a regular old Morrisania growl from the Union backers and hisses from the betting men of the crowd who had invested on the Unions. In view of the fact that the two clubs had experienced difficulty in getting any one fo act as umpire, and that the secretary of the National Association—as fair and square a ball player as there is—had undertaken the disagreeable task, common courtesy for the favor done should have led the partisans of the clubs to have held their peace at least, if they could not approve. But betting men do not know the meaning of the word when they have money at stake, and club partisans are no better; and hence both are always down upon the umpire the moment he commits an error of judgment, except when it favors their side. Those who desire to escape insults and abuse would do well to refuse to act as umpire in any match on which the betting crowd have money invested. Let these growlers be taught a lesson, for it is about time they were.

Pabor followed Martin, and he gave Start a chance to field him out, but Joe failed to hold the ball in time, and Pabor made his base, and by passed balls got round to his third; and as Ferguson gave Austin a life on a muffed ball, Pabor scored his run, Akin being third out, by the good fielding of Zettlein to Start. This left the totals of the first innings at 2 to 1 in favor of the Atlantics.

In the second innings Ferguson led off with a high ball to right field, which Beals caught in brilliant style. McDonald then sent a ball to Akin, which was thrown poorly to Goldie, who failed to hold it, and McDonald reached his base. Zettlein was next, and by a bounding ball out of Akin's reach secured his base. Kenney, too, sent one of the same kind to Akin; but the latter stopped it beautifully, and, sending it straight to Goldie, caused Kenney's retirement, McDonald getting home at the same time. Goldie, seeing Zettlein running to third, hastily threw the ball to Shelley, but out of reach, and the "charmer" got in—and just in time, too, for Pearce afterwards retired on a foul fly well taken by Birdsall. This left the Atlantics' total at 4, and the Unions went in to get square. Birdsall led off well with a good bounder to Kenney, on which he secured his first, but, as Kenney let the ball go by him, David ran to his third; and after Shelley had tipped out, David came in on Beals's hit, Tommy being well put out by Zettlein and Start, and Goldie closed the innings by retiring from a ball prettily caught by Crane—the totals standing at 4 to 2 in favor of the Atlantics, the ratio of the first innings' lead being kept up.

Start opened play in the third innings by giving Goldie a chance to field him out, Joe taking a back seat in consequence. Galvin was next, and he hit a beauty to left field, easily making his base, and, Crane following suit well, things began to look favorable for a good score; but Mills failed to come to time, and, giving an easy chance to Martin, became the second hand out. Ferguson, however, came to the rescue with a beautiful grounder to right field, easily getting his base, and sending Galvin in; and as Beals, seeing Crane running home, threw the ball in to Birdsall, Ferguson ran to second, Crane getting home, from the ball being thrown in too high. Although Beals was playing finely in the field, and had played the point correctly, the wind alone taking the ball out of reach, he did not escape the growlers, the find-fault style of thing prevailing too much in the Union Club for their own welfare. Ferguson was on his second, with two runs in, when McDonald gave Austin a chance for a good fly catch, which was well attended to, and the innings was finished, with the Atlantic score at 6—a very poor score from the beginning for Atlantic batting. Smith led off on the Union side, and, hitting what he thought a safe one to right field, took his base; but Kenney ran a long way in for the ball, and took it on the fly in splendid style, it being the best catch on the Atlantic side. Martin tried the same kind of ball, and this time it was a success, and Martin made his base; and Zettlein throwing a ball poorly to Start, Martin got round to his third. Pabor then hit a ball to Start, who fielded it in time to first; but this time the umpire erred on the other side, and, thinking Pabor had reached his base as soon as Start, gave Charley in. The Atlantics looked surprised, but said not a word, and the Union growlers kept quiet, the umpire doing right always when he errs on the side we bet on. This squared things in regard to the errors of judgment complained of, as Martin got in and Pabor had a life given him. Afterwards a muff by Crane helped Pabor round, and Austin's good hit sent him home. Austin, in running to second, was caught napping by Crane, who received the ball from Mills in time to touch Austin, but he failed to reach him, although it must have looked to the umpire as a plain out, for Austin was ten feet off his base when Crane had the ball; but the growlers said it was "rough," and again pitched into the umpire, they complaining of two decisions against them thus far in the game to one in their favor. Two hands were out and two runs were scored when Akin hit a high ball to right field, which was a far less difficult one to catch than the one Kenney had previously held; but this time Kenney dropped it, and Akin made his base, and, Birdsall following with a good hit, two men were on the bases when Shelley gave Kenney another chance for a catch; but it was scarcely within reach, and as it was neither caught nor stopped Shelley made his third base, and Akin and Birdsall got home; and as Beals sent a "corker" to left field and Goldie followed suit, Shelley and Beals got home, four runs being added after Kenney's first mis-catch, Goldie being on the second base when Smith was well put out by

NATIONAL CHRONICLE

JOURNAL OF AMERICAN SPORTS AND AMUSEMENTS.

VOL I., No. 23. SATURDAY, JUNE 12, 1869. PRICE SIX CENTS.

NATIONAL CHRONICLE BULLETIN.

MATCHES TO COME OFF

BASE BALL.

June 14.—Athletic vs. Olympic, 17th and Columbia avenue.
June 17.—Athletic vs. Olympic, 17th and Columbia avenue, (return game).
June 17.—Brown University vs. Lowell, (return game), Providence R. I.
June ——Harvard vs. Lowell, (return game).
June 18.---Cincinnati vs. Eckford of Brooklyn.
June 18.---Atlantic vs. Star, Capitoline Grounds.
June 30.---Yale Sophomore vs. Princeton Sophomore, at New Haven, Conn.
July 1st.---Harvard Sophomore vs. Princeton Sophomore, at Cambridge, Mass.
July 5.—Harvard vs. Yale, at Springfield.
July 5.—Atlantic vs. Athletic, at New York.
July 12.—Atlantic vs. Athletic, at Philadelphia.

CORRECT LIST OF GAMES IN THE CINCINNATI'S TOUR.

June 12.—Cincinnati vs. Harvard, of Boston.
June 13.—Sunday—stop at New Haven.
June 14.—Cincinnati vs. Yale, of New Haven.
June 15.—Cincinnati vs. Eckford, of Brooklyn.
June 16.—Cincinnati vs. Atlantic, of Brooklyn.
June 17.—Cincinnati vs. Mutual, of New York.
June 18.—No game.
June 19.—Cincinnati vs. Olympic, of Philadelphia.
June 20.—Sunday—stop at Philadelphia.
June 21.—Cincinnati vs. Athletic, of Philadelphia.
June 22.—Cincinnati vs. Keystone, of Philadelphia.
June 23.—No game.
June 24.—Cincinnati vs. Maryland, of Baltimore.
June 25.—Cincinnati vs. National, of Washington.
June 26.—Cincinnati vs. Olympic, of Washington.
June 27.—Sunday—stop at Washington.
June 28.—Cincinnati vs. Olympic, of Washington.
June 29.—No game.
June 30.—Cincinnati vs. Baltic, of Wheeling.
July 1.—Home.

For later games see Bulletin Extra, page 94.

AQUATIC.

June 17.—Charlestown Regatta.
June 22.—Stephen Wier and James McConnell, 5 mile race, at Fort Grant, for $100 a side.
June 14.—Annual cruise Altantic Yacht Club, from New York to Whitestone.
July 4.—Boston Regatta.
July 23.—Harvard and Yale, Worcester, Mass.
Aug.—.—Harvard and Oxford, on the Thames, England.
Aug.—.—Harvard and Cambridge, on the Thames, England.

VELOCIPEDE.

June —.—John Higgen and Samuel Wilmen, 2 miles, at Providence, R. I., for $100 a side.
June 23.—Fred Hanlon and Frank Swift, in New York or Brooklyn, for $1,000 a side and the championship.

MR. JAMES CREIGHTON, (The lamented Champion Ball and Cricket Player of America.)

BASE BALL CLUB NINES OF AMERICA.

No. 5.

The Athletic Club of Philadelphia.

John Dickson McBride still remains their (to them) unrivalled pitcher. His style is that of the laborious order, that is, he works continually to win a game. He is one of the swiftest, most dodging and skillful pitchers that ever filled that position. He has been pitcher, and, without fear of contradiction, general issimo and "mainstay" of the Athletic club since 1864, for he is the only man that ever could have brought that club from its then almost obscure rank to that of of the heaviest batting and best fielding clubs in the whole fraternity. Dick wants a man to face him, who, like the famed Achilles, is invulnerable, (since the ball is not apt to touch the heel), for he must be wonderfully toughened to stand Dick's constant volley. From the beginning to the end of the game, no matter how long that may be, he keeps that same swift, "unhittable" pace, becoming swifter, if anything, at the end. Dick, by his constant, untiring disposition, but more so by his unflinching firmness in declining all offers to leave his old club, has acquired the name of being "par excellent" *the* pitcher of the country. His claim to this title will be disputed by both Pratt and Fisher, since both have now fields to support them, fully equal to that possessed by the Athletic club. Dick is regular in his delivery, watches his opponents closely, never gives them a ball where they want it, but so near that both umpire and batsman are deceived. I have seen strike after strike called on batsman when the ball was at least a foot near or from the base, yet being of the right height, completely deceived the umpire—but not such men as Pete O'Brien, Flanly, or Johnnie Grun. He is a plucky fielder in his position, facing the hottest liner, and throws to bases beautifully. He was their short stop when Pratt pitched, and was one of the best in his day; indeed there is not a position which Dick cannot fill finely. As a batsman he was once terriffic, and the safest one could imagine. During the early part of last season Dick was sick, and since then I do not think he either pitches or bats up to his former standard. The way the Mutuals batted him in their last game was a caution; and caused the not complimentary remark, "the bee has lost his sting." The latest advices from Philadelphia report that Dick has fallen off in his delivery, and nothing but the splendid field prevented defeat for them in their game with the Olympics.

Edward Cuthbert has been selected to fill the position of catcher. Very likely he will do with credit, since he performed the same duty for Fisher. Ed. is a plucky, safe, and earnest worker; a good fielder in the position, picking up grounders nicely; facing tips and high fouls: stands well up to the base and throws well to bases. But for all these he is far inferior to Radcliffe, who stood without a rival behind swift pitching last season. Indeed they cannot repair his loss, for he was the only man they ever possessed who could do justice to McBride. The fraternity may rest assured, if it is possible for Ed to fill Radcliffe's position he will exert all his powers to do so. I saw him quite often in the position last year, but noticed a decided change for the worst when he exchanged with Radcliffe. As a first baseman Ed is first-class, that being one of his home positions, being sure and quick in fielding, and unfailing in holding the hottest balls. As an in-fielder he is fine in any position; but in the outfield he cannot be surpassed, and in his regular position, viz, left field, has only two rivals, Jack Chapman and John Hatfield. He is one of the most graceful catchers, a sure guager, and a muff is a rarity with him. As a batsman he is as good as any in the club or in the whole fraternity, while as a base runner few can approach him.

Weston Fisler will be retained at first base. Now West is like Bob Ferguson, one of *the* ball players of the country. He never attempt a position without doing splendidly, and there are few positions he has not filled As first base he is sure in fielding, prompt in picking up a ball, and throwing to base, unfailing in holding all species of hot liners, whether thrown or batted; a good thrower and quick to take advantage of all chances. As second base he is excellent, being a fine fielder, sure thrower, and a superior fly catcher. As short he is one of the most active and expert. As third base he promised to outrival any who have yet assayed the same, being an excellent fielder, a sure, long, and heavy thrower, a fine judge of fly balls in that position. As a fielder he is splendid, both at left and centre, being a fine judge and sure in holding. As a bats man he is the best in the club—if it is possible to make any discrimination between them—and in the Atlantic—Athletic matches generally leads the score.

Al. J. Reach will still remain on second base. Now, Al. is one of our best ball players, and one who can play in most any position effectively, but the position in which he excels is not second base; but first. He is a left-handed player, and is accordingly apt to throw wildly, but at first, where there is very little throwing, he would prove himself equal to the best. At second he is fearless in facing the hottest batted or thrown balls, neat and sure in fielding, but *not* as sure in throwing, although he is a *very* good thrower, and only surpassed by one left-handed player, (Swandell, of the Mutuals.) I have seen Al. play a whole game through without a miss either in fielding, throwing, or fly-catching; and at other times have seen him make some awkward and expensive throws. As a fly catcher he is splendid, *very* sure and *very* active in getting under short field-flies. He covers a large space around the base, but no more than he can manage. Now, this latter expression needs explanation, for there are several basemen who endeavor to imitate that "paragon" of second basemen—Al. Martin, of the Unions, in covering a large space. Now, both Martin and Akin (who played short), were extremely active and quick runners, and would support one another effectively, thus allowing Martin to play farther from his base than he could with a less active short. Now, Reach does not attempt this, but covers just as much *he* can by vigorous work manage to render dangerous. As a first baseman he was one of the *very* best in his day, when the old Eckfords were champions. He is extremely skillful in holding all hard-thrown balls, high, low, or wide, and his play here has never been equalled by that on second. Fisler would make a magnificent second, and with Reach as first, would render those positions the best manned of any of our "Champion" clubs. As third and short he is an excellent fielder, suppports the bases beautifully, but did not throw equally to either Duffy or Devyr, although he was as good, if not superior, in fielding. As a batsman he is very heavy, having led the score for the last two seasons, although his outs are greater in proportion (during '67), to McBride and Sensenderfer, (during '68), to Cuthbert, Foran, Fisher, and Radcliffe. Thus showing that the first striker has an advantage over the others. Now, Reach is like Pike, they both imagine they can play, the one second, the other third, better than, first in the former case, and in the field in latter.

John Foran has been retained and will be located on third base. Foran is a good fielder, and a pretty accurate thrower, and will make his base more effective than Berry has done. He is a good judge of field-flies, and is quite sharp in chance watching. As second base he was considered one of the best in the West, and his play while in the Alleghany club, so impressed the Athletics, that they engaged him for their nine. As a fielder he did not play up to the standard, especially after the fine display Cuthbert had made in the preceding season. As a batsman his average was good in runs, while in outs it was the best in the club; viz., 2.347, while Fisler's was 2.361. He polished off McBride in the Athletic-Alleghany match to the tune of but three runs.

Thomas Berry has been appointed short stop, with the expectation of his eclipsing his third base play. Tom. is essentially an out-fielder, and one of the best in the Quaker City. At third he was not either accurate in throwing, nor sure in fielding, especially for this club. As short he will have to exert himself to fill even Wilkin's place, and will be far inferior to Bob Reach, who wisely took the certain for the uncercertain. As first base he was very poor, and they had to exchange Fisler's and his positions. As a fielder he is very good, being sure in judging and holding. While speaking of Berry it will be well to allude to the present Athletic-Keystone controversy. During the early part of 1867, the Athletics started on a trip to the Eastern States. Their nine was incomplete, and having heard that it would be dangerous policy to play either the Harvard or Lowell clubs with a poor nine, induced this same Berry to leave the Keystone Club, of which he was a member, having played in a match game, May 29th, and join their club, playing him in a match game, June 12th. The Keystone club, not liking such contemptible conduct on his part, promptly dismissed him from the club, and passed a resolution not to engage in a match with any club playing this same Berry. Not long after, thinking it would be better for the game in that city to forget old grudges, they rescinded that resolution, and have engaged in games with them since. Now this season the same thing occurred again, this time the Athletic club being the injured party. They also dismissed Radcliffe, and passed a resolution also, not to engage in any match with a club having Radcliffe in their nine. The Keystones have him and are anxious to play with the Athletics. How can they substantiate their conduct this season without condemning their last season's conduct. They are in a tight box, while the Keystones are triumphant. They are reaping where they have sown, and have a rich harvest. Better do as the Keystone's did—forget and forgive; play a series of games; do their best; the defeated party will be sufficiently punished by being defeated. The controversy now stands, Berry vs. Radcliffe. The Athletics induced the former to leave the Keystone Club, while the Keystones had nothing to do in the leaving of Radcliffe, thus giving them the right, if there is any right, in the case.

John Sensenderfer has again been appointed their left fielder. John is by no means a reliable man; I have seen him play as well as the best, making some most beautiful and difficult catches, and at others muff the easiest flys. As a general thing, he is good and safe, and when in earnest does well. As centre fielder he did better than at left field. The "Count" is a splendid judge, being fully equal to the best in this respect; and when he does muff they are really bad ones, being well judged but bound clean out of his hands. As a batsman he is very heavy and safe, and fully in keeping with the rest of the nine.

John F. McMullen has been engaged as centre fielder. John has been to the West and gained a good reputation as an efficient and reliable player. During the last two years he has filled every position in the field, but only excels in the outer field. He makes a very good catcher and a fine change pitcher, and will

(*Continued on page 96.*)

THE PICKED NINE OF THE "RED STOCKING" BASE-BALL CLUB, CINCINNATI, OHIO.—Phot. by F. L. Huff, 244 Broad Street, Newark, N. J.—[See Page 422.]

THE "RED STOCKING" BASE-BALL CLUB, CINCINNATI.

We give, on page 421, portraits of the picked nine of the "Red Stocking" Base-Ball Club of Cincinnati, Ohio. On the 16th they beat the "Mutuals," and the next day the "Atlantics" of Brooklyn. The latter game was won 32 to 10. If the "Red Stockings" keep on and hold their own, they will be the champion club before the summer is ended. Hurrah for the Porkopolitans!

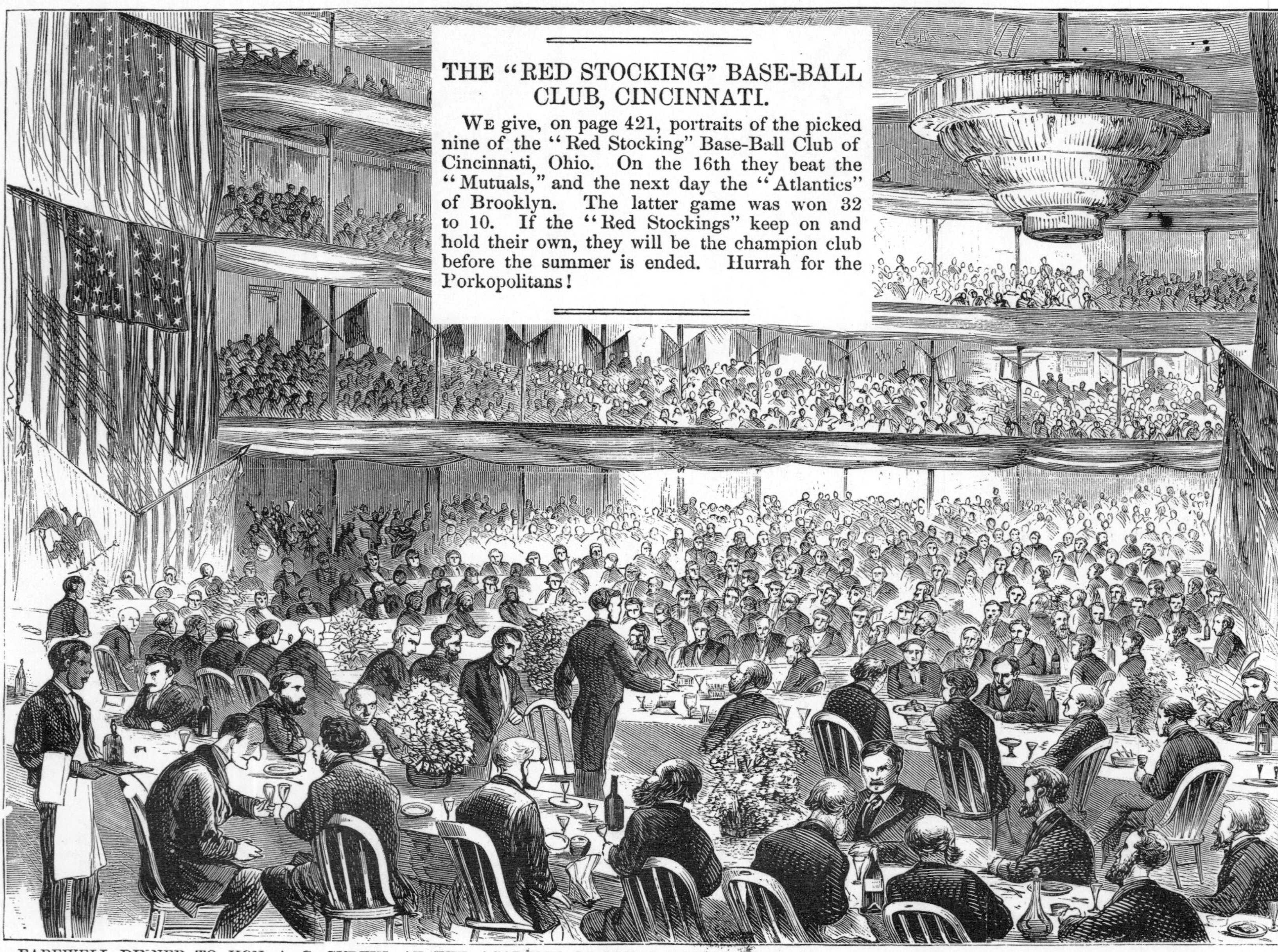

FAREWELL DINNER TO HON. A. G. CURTIN, AT THE ACADEMY OF MUSIC, PHILADELPHIA, June 12, 1869.—Sketched by Theo. R. Davis.—[See Page 422.]

OLIVER OPTIC'S MAGAZINE! 1870.

The Young People's Favorite.

In No, 170 (April 2), commences the publication of an new series of Oliver Optic's, entitled,

THE ONWARD AND UPWARD SERIES.

which will contain Six Stories, embracing the experience of a live boy in six different occupations, as follows :—

1. **Field and Forest**; or, The Fortunes of a Farmer; continued in No. 170.
2. **Plane and Plank**; or, The Mishaps of a Mechanic.
3. **Desk and Debit**; or the Catastrophes of a Clerk.
4. **Cringle and Cross-Tree**; or The Sea Swashes of a Sailor.
- **Bivouac and Battle**; or, the Struggles of a Soldier.
6. **Sea and Shore**; or, The Tramps of a Traveller.

OUR BOYS AND GIRLS for 1870, will contain three of these stories, and their publication in this form presents to the subscribers of the Magazine an opportunity to obtain them at the earliest, and in the cheapest form. It will be seen that such an array of stories for young people cannot be obtained in any other publication.

In addition to the exclusive use of the writings of OLIVER OPTIC, the Publishers invite the attention of the public to other prominent features of the Magazine. All the old favorites will be retained, and many additional writers of eminence have been engaged.

The "Great Triumph," a very beautiful and interesting Fairy Story, by Paul Cobden.

A Continued Story, by Rev. Elijah Kellogg, the popular author of the "Elm Island Stories,"

Letters from Europe, by Oliver Optic, may be expected, one of which will appear every week during his absence abroad.

Historical Sketches, by Samuel Burnham.

Natural History, including frequent articles from Mr. Samuels and Mr. Burleigh, who have already proved their capacity to please and instruct.

Wide Awake Stories, by Sophia May, Mrs. Parker, Mrs. Ballard, Mrs. Moulton, Miss Douglas, Wirt Sikes, Willy Wisp, and others. As during the last year, the Magazine will contain

Twenty-six Original Dialogues, written expressly for our pages by those who have distinguished themselves in this branch, and

Twenty-six Marked Declamations, prepared by a teacher of twenty years experience in the school room.

Our Play Ground. will contain reliable article on the manly sports of America, and reports of all the important matches in base ball and croquet.

The Head-Work, will continue to receive the attention which the unabating interest of the young people inthe subject demands.

Our Letter Bag will still be as spicy and sparkling as ever, affording a medium of communication with our young readers. The Magazine will contain beautiful

Illustrations from Original Designs, by the best artists.

OLIVER OPTICS MAGAZINE is issued **Fifty-two times a Year,** also in Monthly Parts. Subscribers can receive either in weekly or monthly instalments at their option; and furnishes more first-class American reading matter, and at less cost than any similar publication

Terms in dvance.

SINGLE SURSCRIPTIONS, ONE YEAR,	$2 50
ONE VOLUME, SIX MONTHS,	1 25
SINGLE COPIES,	06
THREE SUBSCRIPTIONS, ONE YEAR,	6 50
FIVE SUBSCRIPTIONS, ONE YEAR,	10 00
TEN SUBSCRIPTIONS, ONE YEAR (with an extra copy *free*),	20 00

CLUB RATES WITH OTHER MAGAZINES.

Oliver Optic's Magazine and Harpers Weekly.	$5 00
Oliver Optic's Magazine and Harper's Bazar..	5 00
Oliver Optic's Magazine and Harper's Mag....	5 00
Oliver Optic's Magazine and Galaxy	5 00
Oliver Optic's Mag. and Appleton's Journal...	5 00
Oliver Optic's Magazine and Atlantic Monthly	5 00
Oliver Optic's Magazine and Hours at Home..	5 00
Oliver Optic's Magazine and Old and New.....	5 00
Oliver Optic's Magazine and Lippincott's Mag.	5 00
Oliver Optic's Mag. and Putnam's Monthly...	5 00

A handsome Cloth Cover, with a beautiful gilt design, will be furnished for either year, for..............................50 cents.

Canvrsers and Local Agents wanted in every Town and State.

LEE & SHEPARD, Pu blishers, Boston

mar26

Ayer's Hair Vigor,

For the Renovation of the Hair.

The Great Desideratum of the Age.

A dressing which is at once agreeable, healthy, and effectual for preserving the hair. *Faded or gray hair is soon restored to its original color and the gloss and freshness of youth.* Thin hair is thickened, falling hair checked, and baldness often, though not always, cured by its use. Nothing can restore the hair where the follicles are destroyed, or the glands atrophied and decayed. But such as remain can be saved for usefulness by this application. Instead of fouling the hair with a pasty sediment, it will keep it clean and vigorous. Its occasional use will prevent the hair from turning gray or falling off, and consequently prevent baldness. Free from those deleterious substances which make some preparations dangerous and injurious to the hair, the Vigor can only benefit but not harm it. If wanted merely for a

HAIR DRESSING,

nothing else can be found so desirable. Containing neither oil nor dye, it does not soil white cambric, and yet lasts longer on the hair, giving it a rich glossy lustre and a grateful perfume.

Prepared by Dr. J. C. Ayer & Co.,

PRACTICAL AND ANALYTICAL CHEMISTS,

LOWELL, MASS.

PRICE $1.00.

NOW READY.

CHADWICK'S

BASE BALL MANUAL

FOR 1870

Chadwick's Base Ball Manual.

Chadwick's Base Ball Manual

This work, which has been in preparation since the meeting of the National Association last December, is now ready. It is the the most exhaustive work on the game ever published, and should be in the possession of

EVERY BASE BALL PLAYER IN THE COUNTRY.

IT CONTAINS

AN EDITORIAL PREFACE AND INTRODUCTORY, GIVING A BRIEF SKETCH OF THE HISTORY OF BASE BALL; A COMPLETE HISTORY OF THE

NATIONAL ASSOCIATION,

DETAILING ITS RISE, PROGRESS, AND PRESENT POSITION, WITH A LIST OF ALL THE OFFICERS SINCE ITS FORMATION, AND THE NAMES OF ALL DELEGATES WHO HAVE SERVED ON THE COMMITTEES; A REVIEW OF THE SEASON OF 1869;

THE RULES AND REGULATIONS

as amended at the last meeting of the National Association, with explanatory notes by the editor.

Instructive articles on

UMPIRE'S DUTIES,

PITCHING

BATTING,

FIELDING.

A record of the noteworthy events, regarding the games that have transpired within the past ten years.

AVERAGES OF THE PROFESSIONAL CLUBS!

Together with other matter pertaining to the game, which make it

THE BOOK OF THE SECSON!

The book is for sale by all the news dealers, who are requested to send their orders at once to either of the following News Companies:—

New England News Company,	Boston.
American News Company	New York.
New York News Company,	New York.
Central News Company,	Philadelphia.
Western News Company,	Chicago.
St. Louis News Company,	St. Louis, Mo.
White & Bauer,	San Francisco.

Parties and clubs residing where there are no news dealers, may obtain the book through this office, which will be mailed to them on the receipt of the price of the book, with a two cent stamp to pay the postage.

PRICE 25 CENTS.

CLUB DIRECTORY.

Names of Secretaries of clubs, their address, and time of meetings, whether weekly or monthly, wil be inserted under this head, for the nominal charge of one dollar for the year.

ASSOCIATIONS.

National Association, Rec. Sec'y, Charles E. Coon, P. O. Box 550, Washington, D. C.

National Association of Junior Base Ball Players, S. W. Pearson, Corresponding Secretary, 33 North 2d St., Troy, N. Y.

National Association of Junior Base Ball Players, T. Edwin Leary Recording Secretary, 28 Beach St., New York city.

Alabama Association, Geo. H. Patrick, Secretary, Lock Box 301, Montgomery, Ala.

Louisiana Association, Thomas J. B. Flynn, Jr., Secretary, Steven Plains, Westbrook, Maine.

Massachusetts Association, Charles R. Byram, Rec. Secretary, NATIONAL CHRONICLE Office, Boston.

Massachusetts Junior Base Ball Association, C. R. Smith, Secretary, 15 Broad street, Lynn, Mass

Missouri State Association, George D. Barkloge, Cor. Secretary, care National Loan Bank, St. Louis, Mo.

New York Association, Rec. Sec. M. J. Kelly, "Herald" Office, New York City.

New York Association, Henry W. Garfield, Cor. Sec'y, City Bank, Albany, New York.

Ohio Association, Frank Harvey, Secretary, Box 427, Cincinnati, O.

SENIOR.

Eckford, Charles M. Simonson, 194 South Second St., Brooklyn, E. D. Meetings first Friday of each month.

Empire, St. Louis o. Charles H Stevens, Box 2538

Athletic, A. H. Wright, "Sunday Mercury" Office Philadelphia, Pa.

Buckskin Gloversville, N. Y., A. W. Berry, P. Box 219.

Atlantic, John C. Chapman Corresponding Secretary. Box 214, Brooklyn P. O. Monthly meetings every second Tuesday in the month.

Revere, Boston, Frank W. Wise, Box 3006.

Lowell, Boston, G. N. Briggs, Box 3538.

Clipper, Lowell, Mass., J. W. White, No 3 Central st eet.

Dunderburg, Peekskill, N. Y., C. E: Swift, Box 256.

Irving B. B. Club, Frank A. O'Donnel, Box 5047 N Y. Weekly meetings every Tuesday.

JUNIORS.

Star, Springfield, Mass. Solon S. Roper. Box 875.

Lincoln, West Newton, John F. Kent.

Monitor, Frank H. Sleeper, North Avenue, Cam-Cambridge Mass.

Aquila, Boston, C. A. Lloyd, 36 School street.

Excelsior, W. H. Dillon, 14 Essex St., Boston.

Dirigo, Augusta, Me., W. W. Morse.

Mazeppa, Worcester, Mass., T. S. Courtney.

Una, Charlestown, Mass., J. Hurd Brown, Secretary, 25 Mt. Vernon St.

Emmet, Natick, Mass., David F. Finn.

Somerset, Boston, 10 Somerset street, Boston.

Bay State, Lynn, Mass., Chas. R. Smith, 15 Broad street.

Osceola, L. C. Newhall, Box 81, Lynn, Mass.

CRICKET.

Alpha, Salem, Mass., Charles H. Goss, Box 202.

ADVERTISEMENTS.

BASE BALL.

DON,T BUY YOUR

UNIFORMS, BALLS, BATS

—OR—

ANYTHING IN THE BALL PLAYING LINE,

For the coming season, until you have consulted our

NEW CATALOGUE AND COLORED SAMPLE SHE

ENT FREE. Address

PECK & SNYDER,

22 Ann St., N.Y

BASE BALL 1870.

THE

LEDGER JOB PRINTING

OFFICE,

PHILADELPHIA, PA.,

HAS CONSTANTLY ON HAND A LARGE ASSORTMENT

—OF—

ILLUMINATED ADVERTISING CARDS.

SUITABLE FOR ALL KINDS OF **BUSINESS.**

J. E. JACKSON,

BUSINESS MANAGER.

SCORE CARDS.

GOOD FOR ANY GAME.

FOR SALE

AT

5 HAWLEY STREET,

BOSTON.

BILLIARDS.

RUDOLPHE VS. JOSEPH DION.

Ireland's Billiard Rooms in New York, were thronged last Saturday evening, the attraction being a series of friendly games between Rudolphe and Joseph Dion.

The games were played upon the usual carom tables, with the standard balls and cushions. Three contests took place, all of the French carom game, one hundred points up. The playing was unusually brilliant, and on both sides was characterized by many exquisite shots, calling out the rapturous applause of the auditors. Mr. Rudolphe won the first game, in which he exhibited his marvellous powers in many fancy shots, beating his adversary, when Dion had made but twenty-nine points.

Another trial ensued, and it was here the genuine capacities of the two contestants became apparent. The second trial was easily won by Dion. His execution was graceful, easy and beautifully conceived. Dion seems to possess a self-confidence that even the most embittering adversity cannot disarm. He is always the same—a cavalier as an opponent, a steadfast, determined and undaunted player when he tries to win. He is a consummate artist. No player can excel the delicate touch with which he handles his cue. It is a musical motion, and there is an entire absence of effort and careless manner patent in every shot. This faculty, which is nothing but a keen polish of nerve and a true conception of the player's function, is success itself, as was apparent last evening. To exhibit one's prowess in the midst of excitement and under the gaze of hundreds and still attain maxmium perfection is a rare consummation. Such an opponent had the expert Rudolphe. Dion directed his ball with marvellous *finesse*. A peculiar feature which was his intuitive judgment. It seldom failed. In cushioning, in fine caroms, draws, nursing, the demonstrations of the lookers-on attested his skill by continuous applause.

Rudolphe on the contrary, was not treated to common courtesy. The popular voice was against him, and being a nervous man it doubtless affected his playing. Rudolphe sought too much for precision with his cue and hand—too much mathematics. Accuracy—valuable as it is—does not triumph unless supported by freedom of action. Measurement is part of Mr. Rupolphe's execution—that is, what he does with the balls is more external than spontaneous. Still he made the most difficult and brilliant shots of the evening, and they were duly appreciated.

The second game, when Rudolphe was leading, suddenly turned in favor of Dion, when the latter worked the balls on the right side cushion and effectually locked them near the jaws. He ran 53; this closed the game, while Rudolphe had 32 to make. At this point Dion exhibited his characteristic confidence, and stroke upon stroke fell with rapid certainty.

A third game was desired by Rudolphe, and finally, after some reluctance, was agreed to by Dion. This ended as the second did. In this trial, though Rudolphe was again leading, Dion, amid loud applause and by the most skillful and marvellously facile shots, nursed the balls again towards the side cushion and worked them in the jaws, when he ran the game out by making 51. The following are the scores:—

FIRST. GAME.

Rudolphe—0, 0, 1, 1, 35, 0, 0, 29, 10, 36.
Dion—1, 1, 0, 7, 11, 3, 3, 2, 1.

SECOND GAME.

Rudolphe—0, 0, 0, 0, 0, 4, 0, 0, 0, 0, 0, 4, 2, 7, 0, 9, 6, 5, 0.
Dion—0, 0, 0, 0, 0, 1, 14, 0, 2, 0, 6, 6, 16, 0, 5, 53.

THIRD GAME.

Rudolphe—0, 2, 6, 0, 2, 0, 2, 3, 26, 4, 0, 13, 0, 0, 0, 0, 0, 13.
Dion—6, 1, 6, 1, 3, 4, 3, 1, 0, 2, 0, 2, 1, 4, 5, 2, 7, 1, 51.

BILLIARD SCRATCHES.—An amateur tournament will soon take place at Baltimore. . . . In his match at French caroms, for $100 a side, with John Egan, Benjamin was defeated by 21 points. The game was 300 up, Benjamin giving the odds of 60, and was played at Norwalk, Conn., last Monday night.

BASE BALL IN IOWA.

CEDAR RAPIDS VS. RUSTICS. — The following is the score of a match game of base ball between the Cedar Rapid and the Rustic clubs of Western College, Iowa, played at Western on June 3d.

CEDAR RAPIDS.	O	R	RUSTIC.	O	R
Neill p	3	1	Colby c	1	12
Stevene 2b	4	3	Riggs 3b	4	10
Stewart 1b	4	1	W Drury s s	1	13
Hawley 3b	4	1	Overhalser 1b	4	10
Menehead c	3	3	Shbey lf	2	9
Lahey s s	2	4	Rolland cf	5	9
Ward lf	1	3	Hastings 2b	3	10
Neidig cf	4	2	Wadner rf	5	9
Greene r f	2	3	M Drury p	2	10
	27	21		27	92

Innings	1	2	3	4	5	6	7	8	9
Cedar Rapid	0	0	1	6	2	6	0	0	6—21
Rustic	28	6	24	5	7	3	2	13	4—92

Fly catches—Cedar Rapids 11, Rustic 15.
Umpire—J. H. Allison.
Scorers—Messrs. Gray and Gault.
Time—3:40.

BASE BALL.

ATHLETIC VS. HAYMAKER.

On the afternoon of Wednesday, June 8th, the Haymakers played with the Athletics. The sun shone forth brightly and the weather was all that could be desired. The concourse of spectators who witnessed the game was very large—numbering some five or six thousand. It was generally anticipated that the contest would be a very evenly contested one, but the sequel proved that the Athletics were far superior to their opponents; the defeat being the most signal one on record in a game between two first-class clubs. The Haymakers were confident of victory—feeling assured from the easy manner in which they had punished the pitching of the Atlantics and Keystones, that they would have no trouble in hitting McBride; but the pitching of "Dick," as usual, proved to be so very effective, that it was with difficulty they scored six runs—that being four more than they were entitled to. The Athletics having lost the toss, went first to the bat; Reach hitting a ball clean over the fence at right field, and making a clean home run. This good beginning was greeted with loud applause, which was redoubled when Malone made another hit in the same direction—sending the ball over the right field fence, and making a clean home run. McBride also made a run in this inning, after making his first by a high throw of Penfield. King and Bellan made good fly catches in this inning. Three runs were regarded as a good "send-off" especially as the Haymakers failed to score a run in their three first innings; Bechtel and Schafer making magnificent running fly catches in the second inning, and a pretty double play being made by Reach and Fisler in the third inning. The Athletics, in the second and third innings, scored twelve runs by the most brilliant batting; Al. Reach, in the second in the second inning, duplicating his previous hit over the right field fence, and making a second clean home run.

The totals at the close of the third innings stood 12 to 0 in favor of the Athletics, and all interest in the game ceased, curiosity to see how badly the Haymakers would be beaten alone keeping the vast assemblage present.

The Haymakers scored two runs in their fourth innings, and that was all that they earned during the entire game, errors of fielding on the part of the Athletics giving them four runs in the last five innings. The Haymakers changed positions in almost every innings, but it made no difference, the Athletics, by the most brilliant punishing hitting they have ever exhibited, increasing their score until it reached, at the close, the unprecedented phase of 41 to 6. Schafer made a clean home run in the sixth innings fly a terrific hit over King's head at left field, the hit being the longest of the game. Sensenderfer also made a clean home run in the ninth innings.

The Athletics, with but one exception, fielded superbly, and supported the admirable pitching of McBride in such a manner as to prove them the strongest fielding nine in the country. Their batting in this game, also, was far superior to any they have displayed for a couple of seasons; and the easy manner in which they have punished the very swift pitching of Fisher, must have astonished the Haymakers, to whom Fisher, in previous games, had proved to be their main reliancee.

ATHLETIC	O	R	1B	T	HAYMAKERS	O	R	1B	T
Reach 2b	4	5	4	11	Dick 2c	3	1	1	1
McBride p	2	6	4	4	Hollister 1b	2	2	2	2
Malone c	2	6	3	7	S King l f	4	0	1	1
Fisler 1b	6	1	1	1	Flowers c	5	0	0	0
Sensenderfer cf	3	4	4	7	Woolverton 3	2	1	1	1
Schafer rf	3	4	5	9	Fisher p	2	I	1	1
Radcliff ss	3	5	4	6	Foran r f	3	0	1	1
Bechtel lf	2	5	3	7	Bellan c f	2	1	0	0
Pratt 3b	2	5	3	3	Penfield	4	0	2	2

Innings	1	2	3	4	5	6	7	8	9
Athletic	3	7	2	6	2	3	2	6	10--41
Haymakers	0	0	0	2	1	1	2	0	0-- 6

C. N. Halbach, of the Keystones. Scorers—Messrs. R. W. Benson and J. W. Schofield. Time of Game—3 hours and 5 minutes.

THE GAME IN TENENSSEE.

BLUE STOCKINGS VS. NASHVILLE. — On June 2d the Nashville club played the Blue Stockings a match game of base ball for the championsnip of Tennessee, (which is now held by the Nashville's,) which was won by the Nashvilles by the the following score:

Nashville 26, Blue Stockings 18.

The return game will be played next week

The following is the score:—

NASHVILLE	R	O	BLUE STOCKING	R	O
D Kelly	5	1	Doubillbis	2	3
Teyrell	1	4	Flatter	3	2
Riely	3	2	Haile	3	1
Moses	2	4	Clemmon	2	2
Denham	2	1	Rhea	1	4
Dougherty	2	3	Reddick	2	2
Bosted	4	1	Fowler	2	1
Carroll	3	1	Irvin	2	0
Polmie	3	1	Arnson	1	3
	25	18		18	18

Innings	1	2	3	4	5	6
Nashvilie	2	8	7	0	6	2—25
Blue Stocking	6	0	1	2	4	5--18

Passed balls—Nashville 6, Blue Stocking 14

Called balls—Nashville 3, Blue Stoeking 7.

Umpire—Tom Moors.

Scorer—J. F. Farrell.

Time—2:20.

The Irvings and Lexingtons of New York, both amateur clubs played a grand game last Saturday which resulted in favor of the latter by a score of 26 to 18.

THE JUNIOR CHAMPIONSHIP.

LINCOLN VS. AQUILA.—The second of a series of games for the Junior Championship and Champion Bat, was played between the Lincoln and Aquila clubs, on Boston Common, Saturday June 11th. The fielding was poor on both sides, but the Lincolns obtained another victory the score standing 41 to 15. As the Lincolns won the first game, they are now the holders of the Champion Bat.

Below is the score:—

LINCOLN	O	R	LB	AQUILA	O	R	LB
Wood	1	7	0	Griffin	2	4	0
Scott	3	3	2	Lloyd	3	1	0
Swift	3	5	0	Robinson	2	2	1
Buffum	5	3	0	Sawyer	4	2	0
Kent	2	6	0	Cutter	2	2	2
Watson	1	5	2	Brewster	3	1	1
Hurll	5	3	0	Newman	2	1	1
Warren	4	4	0	Washburn	4	1	0
C Watson	3	5	0	Reynolds	4	1	0
	27	41	4		27	15	5

Innings	1	2	3	4	5	6	7	8	9
Lincoln	5	3	4	4	11	5	1	5	3—41
Aquila	3	0	1	2	1	7	1	0	0—15

Fly catches—Lincoln—Swift 4, Hurll 2, Scott 1, Buffum 1, Kent 1, E. Watson 1—9. Aquila—Cutter 2, Robinson 2, Griffin 1, C. Lloyd 1. Washburn 1, Reynolds 1—9. Home runs—Lincoln—T. Swift 1, C. Watson 1—2. Out on bases—Lincoln 8, Aquila 14. Out on Fouls—Lincoln 9, Aquila 3. Struck out—Aquila 1. Run out—Aquila 1. Umpire—F. S. Clark, Excelsior club. Scorers—H. West, and W. H. Dillon. Time—2.10.

BASE BALL AT TROY.—The Putnams and Champions met on the Haymaker's grounds Friday afternoon, June 10th. Quite a large crowd assembled to witness the game. The game commenced at three o'clock with the Champions at the bat, who, by good batting, secured four runs putting the Putnams out for a blinder, In the second inning, the Putnams by fine batting secured nine runs, they batting very heavy the rest of the game The Champions would give the fielder a chance to put them out most every time, they seeming to be unable to bat Lennay's pitching. Ed. King (a brother of Steve and Mart. King) who played left field, made eight fly-catches, not missing any. Bouker and Warner also did excellently. Of the Champions, Bliven's left field playing was first-class. The umpiring of Mr. Gaffney was very good, being impartial. It is but justice to the Putnams to state they were short of their regular catcher. Ham. Below is the score:

PUTNAMS.	O	R	1B	TB	CHAMPIONS.	O	R	1B	TB
Dakin 3b	3	4	5	8	Lenair 3b	5	2	0	0
Boland r f	6	3	5	9	Powers ss	1	5	6	13
Noxon 1b	2	6	7	13	Bliven l f	4	2	2	4
Warner 2b	3	5	5	9	Cautwell c	3	3	4	4
Lennay p	1	6	7	13	Cornwell c f	3	4	3	3
Bonker c	2	4	5	9	Blacker p	3	3	4	6
M Boland 3b	6	2	2	3	Murphy r f	4	2	0	0
King l j	1	5	6	11	Farrel 1b	3	3	2	2
Bunting c f	3	3	4	8	Levoy 2b	1	4	3	4
Total	27	38	46	83	Total	27	28	24	36

Innings	1	2	3	4	5	6	7	8	9
Putnams	0	9	5	0	5	8	6	4	1--38
Champions	4	3	2	2	1	4	5	6	1--28

Fly cathes—Putnams, 13; Champions, 13. Home runs—Lennay, 1. Umpire—T. A. Gaffney, of Redmond Base Ball Club.

FERGUSON vs THE REPORTERS.

The "little unpleasantness" that has prevailed in New York among the reporters and the captain of the Atlantics has been, we are glad to learn settled in a pleasant manner.

"Chad" interviewed Ferguson last Friday at the close of the Excelsior-Harmonic game, and the "chin music that resulted from it is as follows:" "As soon as the umpire suspended the game on account of the rain, we left the reporters' stand and walked over to where Ferguson stood, and "interviewed" him. As we approached him, instead of attempting to "put a head on us" for our severe criticism of yesterday, Fergy simply said, "How are you, Mr. Chadwick?" at the same time smiling. Walking up to him, the following conversation ensued:

"Look here, Ferguson, I want to have a talk with you about this misunderstanding between you and the reporters, and to learn the facts of the case from you: for this whole matter is injuring the game, the Capitoline Grounds, and the Atlantic Club, and it has proved excessively annoying to all of us."

"Let us sit down here, then, and talk over the matter, and try and get things straight." We responded; and with this we took a seat together, and "buzzed" each other for about an hour. It would be needless to repeat the conversation; suffice it to say that evidence was afforded, which convinced us that both Ferguson and the reporters have been the victims, and in a measure, the catspaws of those who had certain "little games" of their own to play, the one party to induce some one to pounce upon the reporters, and the other to create ill-feeling among the reportorial corps against the Atlantic Club.

Mr. Ferguson authorizes us to state that he has hitherto regarded Mr. Kelly of the *Herald* and Mr. Picott of the *Tribune* among his best press friends, and it was a painful surprise to him when he read what seemed to him an unjust censure of his conduct as captain, especially as his men had told him that they thought he had said or done nothing out of the way on the occasion of the match in question. As for laying hands on either of these gentlemen, he had no such intention at any time, and yesterday he went over to the Union grounds to see Mr. Picott and explain to him this fact.

Now that the animus of the whole thing is understood, and Ferguson has shown himself to be the true, manly ball player we have hitherto held him to be, we trust that all parties will shake hands, take a smile together, and once more have everything go on as pleasantly as before this late unpleasantness. Messrs. Weed and Decker have explained that it was a mistake to suppose that their line of policy towards the reportorial corps would be otherwise than the courteous one it hitherto has been.

The above are our sentiments "to a T" and now let the matter drop.

THE RED STOCKINGS TOUR.

THE CONCLUDING GAMES IN NEW ENGLAND.

THE NEW YORK GAMES THIS WEEK.

They meet their First Defeat for two years at the hands of the Atlantic Club.

FULL DETAILS.

We resume our detailed account of the Red Stockings games, beginning where we left off last week, at the close of their match with the Lowells.

Tuesday, the Red Stockings took the 8:30 A. M., train for Worcester, where they were to meet the Fairmounts of Marlboro. After partaking of dinner at the Bay State House, the boys proceeded to the place of meeting, where everything being in readiness the play began. A very large number of spectators were in attendance. It commenced to rain heavily at the end of the first inning when game was called, the Red Stockings having scored 12 runs to a blank for the Fairmounts. It was decided to play the game Friday, and Wednesday morning the Red Stockings left for Lowell to meet their engagement with the Clippers.

RED STOCKINGS VS. CLIPPERS.

A large number of spectators assembled to witness the game. The Clippers lost the toss and opened the

First Inning.—Whitney had his first given him on called balls, and succeeded in making a run, Conway out on a foul tip to Allison, White at second and Cooledge on three strikes, Carter left. Geo. Wright and Gould scored runs for the Red Stockings, the outs were Waterman at second, H. Wright, and Leonard at first, Allison left on third.

Second Inning.— The Clippers retired in one, two three order; Blood on a foul fly finely caught by Allison, Church on three strikes and Hill at first. Brainard and Sweasy tallied for the Cincinnatis, McVey was forced out at second by George Wright, who was put out at first, a double play. Gould was third hand out.

Third Inning.— Again were the Clippers whitewashed. Davis out on three strikes, Whitney at first by Sweasey to Gould and Conway at second. Waterman and Allison were the run-getters for the Cincinnatis. H. Wright was put out at first, Leonard on a foul bound by Whitney, and Sweasy flyed out to Church, Brainard left.

Fourth Inning.—Another goose egg for the Lowell boys. White at first, Carter in stealing to third and Coolidge on a fly to Geo. Wright. The Red Stockings were also handsomely skunked. Geo. Wright retired at first, Gould on a fly to Hill, and McVey ran on a foul ball and was put out in returning to his base.

Fifth Inning.—Coolidge made the second run of the game for the Clippers in this inning, off a good hit. Blood went out on a foul fly to Waterman. Church on three strikes and Davis at first. Waterman, Allison, Brainard and Sweasey tallied. H. Wright and Leonard out at first and McVey on a fly taken by White.

Sixth Inning.—The whitewashing business resumed, Whitney flyed out to Sweasy, Conway on a fly to H. Wright, and White on a fly to H. Wright and White on a foul to Allison. Gould, Waterman, and Allison scored runs. Geo. Wright retired on a foul fly to Whitney, Brainard on a fly to White, and Sweasy fouled out to Carter.

Seventh Inning.—Carter out on a foul fly to Allison, Coolidge out in stealing to third, and Blood was cut off in stealing to second at the same time, neat double play. This was the big inning for the Cincinnatis, and they scored twelve runs. The outs were George Wright at first, McVey in stealing home and Brainard out to White.

Eighth Inning.—Church forced out at second by Hill, who was also "doubled up" at first. Davis out on three strikes. Geo. Wright and McVey scored the runs in this inning. Sweasy out at first, Waterman at the same place and Allison flyed out to Davis.

Ninth Inning.—Whitney scored a run off a safe hit. Conway ditto, White out at first, Carter on a wild throw to Gould, went to second, and afterwards scored a run. Cooledge flyed out to McVey. Blood at first, Allison to Gould.

The following is the score:—

CINCINNATI.	O	R	1B	TB
G. Wright s s	4	4	4	4
Gould 1b	2	5	5	10
Waterman 3b	3	5	4	4
Allison c	1	5	4	4
H. Wright c f	3	2	2	2
Leonard l f	4	1	3	5
Brainard p	3	3	3	5
Sweasy 2b	3	4	3	5
McVey r f	4	3	4	4
Total	27	32	32	43

CLIPPER.	O	R	1B	TB
Whintey c	2	2	1	1
Conway p	3	1	2	2
White s s	4	0	1	1
Carter 1b	2	1	0	0
Coolidge 3b	4	1	3	2
Blood c f	4	0	1	1
Church r f	3	0	1	1
Hill 2b	2	0	0	0
Davis l f	3	0	0	0
Total	27	5	9	8

Innings	1	2	3	4	5	9	7	8	9
Cincinnati	2	2	2	0	4	3	12	2	5—32
Clippers	1	0	0	0	1	0	0	0	3-- 5

RED STOCKINGS VS. TRIMOUNTAINS.

Thursday the 8th inst., the Red Stockings played their last match in Boston with the Trimountain club. The attendance was not large, their being less than a thousand spectators present, when Mr. Geo. M. Briggs of the Lowell club called the game. The Trimountains won the toss, and Geo. Wright of the Red Stockings went to the bat to begin the

First Inning.—Four runs were made off of good batting by Geo. Wright, Waterman, Allison and H. Wright. Gould went out at first, Barrows to Record, Leonard and Sweasy on foul bounds by Huntley. Sullivan opened the ball for the Trimountains and made two bases on a good hit to right field. Record fell a victim to Sweasy at first. Barrows hit a grounder which Sweasy failed to stop, and Barrows was safe at first, Sullivan who had stole to third coming in, Sanderson and Jackson the next two strikers flyed out, and the inning was closed.

Second Inning. — McVey had his first on called balls. Geo. Wright hit up a sky scraper which Barrows attended to, and McVey who had started for second was put out in returning to first. Gould hit to Jackson who swung the ball in to Record, in his inimitable manner, and a whitewash was placed to the Red Stockings credit. The Trimountains also retired in one two three order; Pratt and Putnam at first, and Huntley on a foul bound to Allison.

Third Inning.—Waterman fell a victim to Jackson at first. Allison hit to left field for two bases, went to third on a passed ball, and in on H. Wright's hit, who scratched his third off a muff by Record, on a ball passed him by Barrows. Leonard sent a messenger through the air to Putnam, who nabbed it, and it was thrown to first putting out H. Wright. Harris out on a foul fly to Allison; Sullivan popped up one which Geo. Wright got under. Record by a safe hit to centre field, secured his first, went to third on passed balls, and in on Barrows hit to left field, who took one base, Sanderson sent up an easy fly between the pitchers plate and the first base. Brainard thought Gould was going for it, while Charley thought it was Asa's huckleberry. So between them both, the striker made his base. Barrows was on the way to third, when Brainard finally got the ball, and threw it to Waterman, but just to late to catch Barrows, who afterwards made his tally on a passed ball. Jackson closed the inning byouling out to Allison. Score 5 to 3.

Fourth Inning.—This Inning should have been a whitewash for the Reds, Leonard hit to Record and was out; Brainard flyed out to Harris and Sweasy gave Record a grounder, which he failed to stop and Sweasy got his first, McVey by a good hit to right field, scored his first, Sweasy going to third, and in on a passed ball, McVey going to second. George Wright by a hit to long left field made two bases, McVey coming in. A wild pitch of Jackson carried George to third, and he came home on Gould's hit, who made two bases on a strike to centre field. Waterman brought Gould home and took second on a safe hit, where he was left, Allison going out at first, Barrows to Record. Pratt fouled out to Gould, Huntley followed at first, Putnam by a safe hit to right field went to second, where he was left, as Harris was third hand out, at first base.

Fifth Inning.—H. Wright had a life given him on a muff by Sullivan, and he came home on Leonard's hit to right field which gave him one base. Brainard hit to Record and was out. Sweasy hit a corker to centre field which Harris caught. McVey made two bases off a safe hit. Geo. Wright sent a hot grounder to Barrows, who threw it poorly to Record, and Geo. went to third. McVey coming in. Gould out at first. Sullivan and Record were out at first, and Barrows on a fly to H. Wright, another whitewash.

Sixth Inning.—Waterman scratched his first off a poor throw by Sullivan to Record, Waterman going to third base; and in on a passed ball. Allison hit to left-field for two bases, and came in on H. Wright's strike to right field who went to second. Leonard fell a victim to Barrows and Record at first. Brainard made second and sent Harry home on a grounder to left-field. Sweasy hit to short field and on a poor throw by Pratt to Record went to second, Brainard coming in. McVey made two bases on his hit to centre, bringing Sweasy in and afterwards came home himself. Geo. Wright and Gould went out at first, Sanderson earned his first on a safe hit to centre field, and an overpitch carried him to third. Jackson drove one through Leonard, Sanderson in, and Jackson going to second. Pratt hit to Brainard who put it to Geo. Wright to cut off Jackson, Waterman finally captured him, Pratt

[*See page* 187]

New-York Tribune.

Vol. XXX.....No. 9,344. NEW-YORK, SATURDAY, MARCH 18, 1871. PRICE FOUR CENTS.

SANTO DOMINGO.

DIPLOMACY EXTRAORDINARY.

HAYTI WARNED BY THE UNITED STATES TO BE NEUTRAL TOWARD SANTO DOMINGO—COMMUNICATIONS FROM ADMIRAL POOR, CONSUL GAUTIER, AND MINISTER BASSETT.

Communications from United States officials referring to the pending negotiations with Santo Domingo, and warning Hayti to remain neutral, have been published in the Haytien journals, and excited a great deal of unpleasant comment. We have received from Port-au-Prince French translations of several of these documents. Copies of the originals have doubtless been sent to Washington by the same mail; but as we have been unable as yet to obtain transcripts of them, we are obliged to render the translations back again into English. Our readers will bear this circumstance in mind in forming an opinion upon the tone of the communication addressed by our officials to the authorities of a friendly Republic. The first is a letter from Admiral Poor to the Provisional President of Hayti:

To President SAGET, *Provisional President Republic. Hayti:*

SIR: The undersigned avails himself of the arrival in this port of the Severn, flag-ship of the United States North Atlantic squadron, to inform your Excellency that he has received instructions from his Government to inform your Excellency that negotiations are now pending between the United States Government and the Government of Santo Domingo, and that during such negotiations the United States Government is determined to use all its power to prevent any meddling on the part of Hayti or any other power with the Dominican Government. Therefore, any interference with, or attack on the Dominicans by ships under the Haytien flag, or any other flag, during the said negotiations will be considered an act of hostility to the United States flag, and will provoke hostilities in return—(*considérée comme un acte d'hostilité au pavillon des Etats Unis et provoquera de hostilité en retour*). I have, &c.,

C. H. POOR, Rear-Admiral, &c.

Port-au-Prince, Feb. 10, 1871.

United States Consul Gautier addresses Gen. Nord Alexis in the following terms:

GENERAL: A large majority of the Dominican people have asked through their representatives to be annexed to the United States; and negotiations with that view have been entered into and still continue. A Commission has been appointed to go to Santo Domingo and make a careful examination, when all who are opposed to annexation will again have an opportunity to make themselves heard. In the meantime the United States have engaged to protect the legitimate Government of ...

INFORMATION FOR EMIGRANTS.

HOW TO GET THERE AND WHAT TO DO—THE PRICE OF LAND, LABOR, ETC.—RAISING COFFEE, FRUIT, ETC.

FOREIGN NEWS.

THE FRENCH CAPITAL.

THE SITUATION AT MONTMARTRE UNCHANGED—AN ATTEMPT TO BE MADE TO SURPRISE THE INSURGENTS—GEN. UHRICH A CANDIDATE FOR THE ASSEMBLY.

GENERAL FRENCH NEWS.

GERMANY.

ITALY.

RUSSIA.

ENGLAND.

THE NEW-DOMINION.

THE OUTRAGE IN MANITOBA.

MISCELLANEOUS CABLE NEWS.

A SERIES OF RAILROAD ACCIDENTS.

THE COAL TROUBLES.

ANOTHER SUPPOSED NATHAN MURDERER.

CRIMES AND CASUALTIES—BY TELEGRAPH.

RAILROAD LABORERS RESISTING A CIVIL PROCESS—BLOODSHED ANTICIPATED.

WASHINGTON.

RESOURCES OF ALASKA.

CURRENCY PROPOSITION.

NOMINATIONS AND CONFIRMATIONS.

PERSONALITIES—BY TELEGRAPH.

TELEGRAPHIC NOTES.

The whole story on the part of the Companies is a lame iteration of the general cry against the miners. It has been conclusively shown, by the most one-sided opposition testimony, that the miners in few cases make over $9 a week, yet in no instance was it shown that operators and railway men failed to receive less than from 35 to 50 per cent on their investments.

THE CONVENTION OF PROFESSIONAL BASE BALL CLUBS.

The meeting of representatives from the professional clubs of the country, last night, resulted in establishing the "National Association of Base Ball Players," and as they adopted the constitution, by-laws, and playing rules of the old National Association, they practically take the place of that institution. The clubs sending delegates included the Mutual of this City; Eckford of Brooklyn; Chicago and Boston Clubs; the Forest City Clubs of Cleveland and Rockford; the Haymakers of Troy, and the Olympic and National of Washington. The Convention adopted a code of rules governing championship contests, and elected the following officers: President, J. N. Kern, Athletic; Vice-President, J. S. Evans, Cleveland; Secretary, N. E. Young, Olympic; Treasurer, J. W. Schofield, Haymakers. The representation was the best ever sent to a Convention by professional clubs, and everything passed off in the most harmonious manner. The Convention adjournned to meet in Cleveland in March, 1872.

"A HEAVY STREAK OF BATTING."

SKETCH FROM THE REAR OF THE CATCHER'S POSITION AT THE GREAT BASE-BALL MATCH BETWEEN THE ATHLETIC AND PHILADELPHIA CLUBS AT PHILADELPHIA.

THE MODOC WAR—ARMY SCOUTS AND FRIENDLY INDIANS STRIKING THE TRAIL OF THE FUGITIVE SAVAGES.

THE BALTIMORE BASE-BALL "NINE."

HALL. PIKE. YORK. RADCLIFFE. CUMMINGS, P. HASTINGS. FORCE. MCVEY. MILLS.

SIR WALTER RALEIGH OUTWITS EARL LEICESTER—LAST SCENE IN THE SECOND ACT OF "AMY ROBSART."

THE DAILY GRAPHIC

AN ILLUSTRATED EVENING NEWSPAPER.

39 & 41 PARK PLACE.

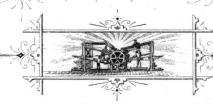

VOL. II.—NO. 106. NEW YORK, SATURDAY, JULY 5, 1873. FIVE CENTS.

THE ATHLETIC BASE-BALL CLUB OF PHILADELPHIA.

THE ATLANTIC BASE-BALL CLUB, OF BROOKLYN.

THE NATIONAL GAME.

THE NEW BANK IN UTAH.

(Description on Seventh Page.)

M'Vey (Right Field). James O'Rourke (First Base). Andrew Leonard (Left Field). Al. Spaulding (Pitcher). George Wright (Short Stop). Harry Wright (Captain—Centre Field). James White (Catcher). George Hall (Substitute). Rosco Barnes (Second Base). Schaffer (Third Base). Thomas Beales (Substitute).

INTERNATIONAL BASE-BALL—THE BOSTON CHAMPIONS.—FROM A PHOTOGRAPH BY J. W. BLACK, BOSTON, MASSACHUSETTS.—[SEE PAGE 537.]

T. MURMAN (2d Substitute). J. E. CLAPP (Captain). A. W. GEANEY (Left field). JNO. J. P. SENSENDERFER (1st Substitute) A. C. ANSON (Right field) A. J. REACH (Manager). J. L. MCBRIDE (Captain and pitcher) E. B. SUTTON (3d Base). WESTON D. FISLER (1st Base). J. V. BATTIN (2d Base). J. F. MCMULLEN (Centre field) W. U. MCGEARY (Short stop).

THE NATIONAL GAME ABROAD.—THE ATHLETIC BASEBALL CLUB OF PHILADELPHIA.—PHOTOGRAPHED BY STODDARDS & FENNIMORE.

INTERNATIONAL BASEBALL.

BOSTON AND PHILADELPHIA CHAMPIONS.

ON this page we present portraits of the members of the Baseball ex-champion Athletics of Philadelphia, and the Boston champion Red Stockings, who visit England this month to play against their English cousins, and to engage in several exhibition games among themselves. Their first public appearance will be made at Lord's Grounds, London, on August 3d. Special accommodations will be provided for American visitors. The Royal Band will play American national airs, and 10,000 persons are expected to be present. The following is a list of the members of the two clubs:

ATHLETICS, PHILADELPHIA, EX-CHAMPIONS.—J. L. McBride, Captain and pitcher; J. E. Clapp, catcher; A. J. Reach, manager; W. U. McGeary, short stop; Weston D. Fisler, first base; Jas. V. Battin, second base; E. B. Sutton, third base; A. W. Geaney, left field; A. C. Anson, right field; J. F. McMullen, centre field; Jno. J. P. Sensenderfer, first substitute; T. Murman, second substitute.

RED STOCKINGS, BOSTON, CHAMPIONS.—Harry Wright, Captain, centre field; James White, catcher; Al. Spaulding, pitcher; George Wright, short stop; James O'Rourke, first base; Roscoe Barnes, second

JAMES O'ROURKE (1st Base). MCVEY (Right field). ANDREW LEONARD (Left field). AL. SPAULDING (Pitcher). GEORGE WRIGHT (Short stop). HARRY WRIGHT (Captain, Centre field). GEORGE HALL (Substitute). JAMES WHITE (Catcher) M. SCHAFFER (3d Base). ROSCOE BARNES (2d Base) THOS. BEALES (Substitute).

THE NATIONAL GAME ABROAD.—THE BOSTON (RED STOCKING) BASEBALL CLUB OF BOSTON.—PHOTOGRAPHED BY J. W. BLACE.

J. D. M'BRIDE (CAPTAIN AND PITCHER).

J. E. CLAPP (CATCHER).

W. M. M'GEARY (SHORT STOP).

J. F. M'MULLEN (CENTRE FIELD).

WESTON D. FISLER (FIRST BASE).

JOSEPH V. BATTIN (SECOND BASE).

E. B. SUTTON (THIRD BASE).

A. W. GEDNEY (LEFT FIELD).

A. C. ANSON (RIGHT FIELD).

INTERNATIONAL BASE-BALL—THE PHILADELPHIA ATHLETICS.—FROM PHOTOGRAPHS BY SUDDARDS & FENNEMORE, PHILADELPHIA.—[SEE PAGE 626.]

BASE-BALL IN ENGLAND—THE MATCH ON LORD'S CRICKET GROUNDS BETWEEN THE RED STOCKINGS AND THE ATHLETICS.—From a Sketch by Abner Crossman.—[See Page 742.]

The New-York Times.

VOL. XXV.......NO. 7612. NEW-YORK, MONDAY, FEBRUARY 7, 1876. PRICE FOUR CENTS.

WASHINGTON.

SEEKING FOR INFORMATION.

DEMOCRATIC INVESTIGATING COMMITTEES LISTENING TO QUESTIONABLE AUTHORITIES—CORRECT KNOWLEDGE SEEMINGLY OF LITTLE CONSEQUENCE.

Special Dispatch to the New-York Times.

WASHINGTON, Feb. 6.—The Democratic committees are seeking information, in their efforts at retrenchment and investigation, from a class of persons that may properly be called discharged employes. There are ex-Consols, ex-clerks, and ex-officers of various kinds, either called before committees as witnesses, or called for private consultation. Now and then witnesses not of this class are examined, but their evidence is not of the kind wanted. The Committee on Appropriations have asked for very little information of any kind. They have set out to reduce the Appropriation bills forty millions, and knowledge is not at all likely to facilitate the reductions. It is a great deal easier to lop away expenditures promiscuously than to study where expenditures can be reduced with least loss to the public service. The committee proposes to reduce the appropriations for Congress, the Courts, and the Executive Departments from five to seven millions; but in respect to the departments, they are calling few, of the responsible officers to ask them what clerks can best be spared, or what salaries can be reduced. They cut away heads of important divisions in the Treasury Department without knowing anything about the nature of the duties performed, or the real value of the officers struck off. Bureaus already so low in the number of clerks that the current work is with great difficulty kept up to date, are slashed away so that at the end of the year the work must be in arrears, to the great annoyance of people interested in the business and to the danger of public losses. The prompt examination of accounts of disbursing officers by the Auditors is of the utmost importance. It was when these accounts accumulated for many months, on account of the lack of clerks to keep up to current dates, that several large defalcations became possible which would have been confined to small amounts if prompt examinations had been possible. In some of the offices the Democratic parsimony and blindness will have the result of making possible just such defalcations again as were discovered in completing the investigations of old accounts which accumulated after the war, and the attempt to save a few clerks for political effect may end, and certainly will have a tendency to end, in the loss of millions. There are doubtless some offices where the heads have managed to retain a larger force than necessary, for all bureau officers, of course, like to control as large a force of clerks as possible. Such offices can by proper inquiry be found out, and the application of the pruning knife would be applauded. But many of the bureaus are now overworked, and could not lose one clerk more without damage to the public service. Treasurer New, who is one of the best executive officers in the departments, finds that he can, of his own accord, make a reduction of fifty clerks. He tells the committee he is willing to go to the very verge in economy in this respect, and he cannot make a greater reduction and surround the great money vaults containing the treasure of the Government with proper safeguards. "Then leave the vaults open," the committee say, "for we are determined not to give you the force you deem necessary." The proposition to reduce salaries without asking how it may best be done is of a similar character. There are here and there clerks and officers who are overpaid, considering the work they do. Probably no immense organization like a department could be kept free of such cases. But all the prominent positions are underpaid, and the reduction of ten per cent. in salaries will create disgust, dampen spirit and enthusiasm for work, and invite to laziness, and even crime, for it is the dissatisfied man that steals. The reductions in force will, so far as their personal and political effects are concerned, react upon the authors of them. The Administration has been by no means proscriptive in its management of the departments, and while few Democrats have been appointed, few have been dismissed because they were Democrats. The clerks to be cut off by order of the Democratic House will be of that class, and they will no doubt, when the time comes for dismissals, be diligently inquired out. They have their Democratic majority to thank for their uncomfortable situation, and they are rapidly becoming good Republicans, if hatred of their natural protectors can make them so. No Democrat has more friends in office, if current rumors can be credited, than Samuel J. Randall, the joint author with Mr. Holman of the proposition to save $40,000,000. He, no doubt, trusts the Senate to save the departments and himself the consequences of the reductions, but many leading Senators express the purpose to advocate the passage of the bills in that body just as the House sends them over for concurrence, and leave the responsibility with the House, which has no desire but to make party capital for next Summer.

THE RESUMPTION ACT.

THE TREASURY DEPARTMENT'S COMMUNICATION TO THE HOUSE—AMOUNT OF COIN PURCHASED AND OF INTEREST-BEARING BONDS SOLD.

Special Dispatch to the New-York Times.

WASHINGTON, Feb. 6.—The Treasury Department will, within a day or two, send two important communications to the House in answer to resolutions of inquiry by that body. One is an answer to the questions propounded by Mr. Kelley as to the amount of silver-coin on hand, the amounts of silver purchased, and of interest-bearing bonds sold under the provisions of the Resumption act. It will be remembered that he presented specific and detailed interrogatories as to the operation of that act. The answer will be given in detail, and will be satisfactory at least in its completeness. Mr. Kelley desires to use the information in favor of the repeal of the law and the passage of a measure of inflation. He will probably learn that purchases of silver have been made in the aggregate amount of about nine millions of dollars, and that interest-bearing bonds have been sold, under the provisions of the law, to the amount of about fifteen millions, for the purpose of paying for silver bullion and retiring legal tenders, as required by the law. The latter statement is the point of Kelley's inquiry, for he wants to show that the enforcement of the law, in addition to the unnumbered woes of contraction which he is ready to depict, is placing additional burdens upon the people in the matter of interest. Of course the interest is the only amount in dispute, for the silver that has been bought is worth as much as the bonds sold; and as the greenbacks are a debt of the Government, their retirement and displacement by bonds is only a change in the form of the debt which the law contemplated. In regard to the circulation of silver coin, it may be said in this connection that fractional currency is now worth a little more in comparison with gold and silver bullion, and if there could be any assurance that there would be no large and permanent rise in gold, silver coin could be safely put in circulation. The department is rapidly accumulating coin, and the time now appears to be not far distant when the fractional currency may be retired; but no step will be taken till the Treasury is fortified against all contingencies. So far as the interest on the $40,000,000 of bonds, which will be required to replace fractional notes, is a part of the debt is concerned, it would be less in amount annually than the present cost of replacing continually the paper that is worn out and rendered unfit for service. The same statement is nearly true of the cost of maintaining the greenback notes in circulation. The specific and authoritative statement will be an interesting document, and will afford facts for much discussion.

CONGRESSIONAL TOPICS.

MR. HEWITT'S RESOLUTION OF INQUIRY TO BE ANSWERED TO-DAY—THE CONTRACTION OF THE CURRENCY—THE PACIFIC RAILROAD SUBSIDY—THE CENTENNIAL BILL.

Special Dispatch to the New-York Times.

WASHINGTON, Feb. 6.—The resolution passed by the House on the motion of Mr. Hewitt, of New-York, will be answered to-morrow. His inquiries did not of themselves disclose the purpose of his resolution, which is explained as requesting information which will show whether legal-tender notes paid into the Treasury by national banks to retire their notes really produce a contraction of the currency. To illustrate: A bank desires to withdraw $50,000 of its own notes, and to reclaim the bonds deposited in the United States Treasury, to secure them; it cannot gather up its scattered notes at once, and instead sends to the Treasury $50,000 legal tenders, and gets back its bonds. Mr. Hewitt wants to know whether the $50,000 is treated by the Treasury as ordinary receipts and is paid out again in course of business for current expenses, or is set apart as a fund by itself, to redeem the notes of the bank as they may be presented. The answer to this inquiry of Mr. Hewitt's, if this be the point of it, is that the legal tenders so received are kept in a fund by themselves for the specific purpose for which they are received, and they do not go into general circulation except as the notes which they are kept to redeem are presented and destroyed. There is therefore a real contraction of the circulation by the amounts of greenbacks paid in for the surrender of bank notes.

The subcommittee of the Committee on Pacific Railroads have agreed to the bill granting Col. Tom Scott a subsidy, and will report it to the full committee at their next meeting. Mr. Atkins has it in charge, and he hopes the full committee will agree to the bill, so that it can be reported to the House on Wednesday, when committees are called. It is now certain that Col. Scott will be able to push his bill to a square vote in the House. There is yet no means of making a satisfactory estimate of the probable vote, but the passage of the bill is generally regarded as very doubtful. Of course, if it fails in the House, the Senate will be spared the opportunity to show how it can resist the tremendous pressure that has been arranged to operate upon it if the bill should get through the House.

The Centennial bill will probably be brought up in the Senate to-morrow, and an effort may be made to set the Pinchback case aside to consider it. It is more likely that it will only gain a place in the morning hour, where it will be taken up daily and discussed a little till the Pinchback case is out of the way. Under the action of the Democratic caucus the vote may be taken without much delay on the Pinchback resolution, but that is after all doubtful. There is now manifested a little stronger opposition than was expected, and the partisans of Pinchback cannot name one Senator of those who were against his admission last Spring who has changed his purpose of opposition. The result of the vote is quite in doubt, and in a full Senate will be close.

Treasurer New proposes to resign his present position at an early day, probably at the close of the present fiscal year. This determination has been caused entirely by his private affairs, his principal partner in the banking business at Indianapolis being forced to retire from the management of his bank in consequence of failing health. Mr. New, when relieved from his present public duties, will return to Indianapolis and assume charge of the bank as its president. The Treasurer has communicated his purpose to resign to Secretary Bristow, who is reluctant to part with him, and indulges the hope that some arrangement will be made by Mr. New which will enable him to continue to serve as Treasurer.

The answer of the Treasury Department to the inquiry of the House as to Customs offices where the Customs receipts are not equal to the cost of maintaining them, is now ready. It shows that the number of such offices is fifty-seven. Sixteen of them are in New-England, and two—Dunkirk and Sag Harbor—are in New-York Three are in New-Jersey. Alexandria and Georgetown, in this District, do not pay the expenses by receipts. Brownsville, Texas, has the largest deficiency. It will be found on examination that most of these offices will have to be maintained to prevent smuggling, but the House will no doubt attempt to abolish some of them, or at least to reduce the expenses.

BILLS IN THE HOUSE.

PROTECTION OF NEW-YORK HARBOR FROM INJURY BY DUMPING REFUSE—USELESS SLAUGHTER OF BUFFALOES.

Special Dispatch to the New-York Times.

WASHINGTON, Feb. 6.—Mr. Schumaker has introduced a bill providing that no street-sweepings, earth, ballast from vessels, ashes, swill, garbage, dead animals, decayed or other fruits or vegetables, or rubbish of any kind, or any articles that will not float shall be dumped or deposited in New-York Bay, or in the rivers adjoining the City of New-York, or in the waters of the Atlantic Ocean within five miles of Sandy Hook, or in the Hudson or East Rivers, or Long Island Sound west of Middle Ground Shoal, under a penalty of from fifty to one thousand dollars for each offense, and imprisonment, two-thirds of the amount of the fine to be paid to the person who furnishes the information which leads to conviction. The bill authorizes the District Attorneys of the Southern and Eastern Districts of New-York to appoint four special officers who shall have power to arrest all persons found violating the law, and gives the same authority to make arrests to the Police of New-York and Brooklyn. The salaries of the four special officers provided for in the bill are not to exceed the salaries of New-York patrolmen.

A bill has been introduced in the House to prevent the useless slaughter of buffaloes within the Territories of the United States. It is made unlawful for any person not an Indian to kill, wound, or in any manner destroy any female buffalo of any age found at large within the Territories. It is also made unlawful for any
person to kill or wound a
male buffaloes than neede
hunter, or than can be used,
for the food of others, or fo
hundred dollars for each bu
prescribed. Western men s
destruction of buffaloes on
necessary some measure fo
animals from annihilation
period.

THE PRESIDENT AN

FALSE RUMORS OF INHAI
THE PRESIDENT AND C

WASHINGTON, Feb. 6.—
several stories put afloat i
regard to a quarrel betwee
Secretary Bristow, and a
Secretary and Senator Conl
forms in which th
been served up would
columns of THE TIMES for
them. They are persisten
some incredulous people ar
lieve that there is serious
net. This makes it seem d
the subject which was said
casion of the trouble in th
mentioned, neither during t
fore nor after it. The stori
ed inventions. The repo
between the Secretary and
in which the latter is said to
retary's office declaring he
it again, is also false. The t
not met for a month, perh
during that time in the Sec
the supposed subject of co
been mentioned between the

NOTES FROM THE

THE MEXICAN RAIDS INTO
IZED SALE OF A LA
TARY AND MEDICAL R

WASHINGTON, Feb. 6.—
been relieved as Special Tre
York, will be assigned to ano
responsible. It is said arran
were commenced before he w
Hale.

Information has recently bee
sentative Hancock to the effe
into Texas continue, but wh
prevented if there were more
border.

By a decree of the District C
the First National Bank is aut
of the claim of the First N
Jay Cooke & Co., amounting t
dividend of five per cent. has
D. Cooke, Jr., for assignment,
Cooke, Jr., for the cancellat
against the bank, amounting t
on which dividends aggregat
cent. have been paid, upon con
to Cook shall be without reco
ceived individually, and shall
the right of Cook to collect or
the five per cent. paid by t
ruptcy, and the assignment
shall not prejudice or affect an
which may be asserted by
against the assets or estate of

A large volume has been iss
the Surgeon General of the N
ters of great importance to all
a profession. Although the p
are seventy-eight, are wholly
cers, much contained in them
est to the merchant marine; a
and mode of administration of
diseases—endemic and epide
pography, source and characte
with tests for its purity, provi
of general interest found in t
trade and principal seaports o
portant question of ventilati
subjects of hygiene pertainin
fully discussed, and many sug
if duly considered and put in
materially to the comfort of a
the greater part of their life a

Messrs. Hammond and Be
three meetings here to-day, series of revival exercises that, it is understood, will continue for several weeks. Intense interest was manifested, and great throngs, notwithstanding the very bad weather, attended the services.

The President has recognized Frederick Ferdinand Myhlertz as Vice Consul of Denmark at Philadelphia.

REGISTER FOR FOREIGN SHIPS.

A BARK SAVED BY TRANSFER TO A FOREIGN FLAG—HER PRESENT DISADVANTAGES.

WASHINGTON, Feb. 6.—Some time ago a petition was presented to the House of Representatives by Charles Brewer & Co., of Boston, asking that an American register be granted to the Hawaiian bark Arctic owned by that firm. The Committee on Commerce, to whom the petition was referred, made a favorable report, and recommended that the bill reported by them be passed, basing their recommendation on the action of the Government in similar cases. The facts of the case are as follows: It appears that the bark was built at Rochester, Mass., in 1850; was purchased by Messrs. Brewer & Co. in 1861, and was used by them in carrying, from New-Bedford and Boston to Honolulu, supplies for the American whaling fleet in the North Pacific. This was a highly important service, and any interruption of it would have caused a serious injury to American interests. In 1863 it was found necessary, in order to prevent the capture and destruction of the vessel by rebel cruisers which then infested the Pacific Ocean, to place her under the Hawaiian flag; and that was accordingly done, although the service and the ownership continued unchanged. It is evident, from what took place immediately after the transfer to a foreign flag, that the vessel would have been captured if the transfer had not been made, thereby depriving the whalers of supplies necessary to the continued pursuit of their vocation. The vessel continued in this business until 1869, when she was fitted at New-Bedford as a whale ship, and from that time to the present has been engaged in the whale fishery, refitting from time to time at Honolulu, and shipping her catch of oil and bone to New-Bedford. Being under a foreign flag, although owned and commanded by American citizens, her oil is subject to a duty of twenty per cent. ad valorem, and she cannot enter an American port without being subject to tonnage dues. The owners, therefore, labor under a serious disadvantage in carrying on their business, and, considering the circumstances which forced them to seek protection under another flag, they feel justified in asking the Government to cure the disability under which they labor by the grant of an American register.

MARINE DISASTERS.

BALTIMORE, Feb. 6.—The revenue cutter Colfax reports schooners H. M. Hisser, Williams, Philadelphia, for Baltimore, in ballast; Starlight, Travers, Cambridge, for Baltimore, with an assorted cargo, and oyster-pungy Great Western, Gallend, Pool's Island, for Baltimore, ashore at Rock Creek. Twelve bay craft are reported ashore in Magothy River. These disasters were caused by the gale of Wednesday morning.

NAVAL INTELLIGENCE.

BALTIMORE, Feb. 6.—The United States steamer Juniata, from Pensacola, to be stationed here as a receiving ship, arrived to-day.

THE WHISKY CONSPIRACIES.

PREPARING FOR THE BABCOCK TRIAL

ST. LOUIS IN A STATE OF EXPECTANCY—THE OPENING ARGUMENTS TO BE MADE BY MR. DYER AND MR. STORRS ON THE RESPECTIVE SIDES—THE DISTRICT ATTORNEY AND THE UNITED STATES MARSHAL

AN EXPLANATION OF THE LETTERS AND DISPATCHES BETWEEN M'DONALD, JOYCE AND BABCOCK.

Dispatch to the Associated Press.

ST. LOUIS, Feb. 6.—Judge John K. Porter, counsel for Gen. Babcock, and C. C. Sniffin, assistant secretary of President Grant, arrived to-day, and are quartered at the Lindell Hotel. It is stated on authority of Judge Krum, that the President will come out here during the trial, and probably be a witness for the defense. The *Times* this morning gives the following, upon high authority, as the manner in which the defense expect to explain the letters and telegrams which passed between McDonald, Joyce, and Babcock, regarding contemplated visits to St. Louis of revenue agents to examine distilleries. These dispatches will be admitted by the defense as genuine, and even the purpose of the dispatches will be admitted; but it will be represented that both McDonald and Joyce were held in the highest esteem as gentlemen and officials by all the Treasury officials and many dignataries at Washington; that their superior officers regarded them as among the most honorable, trustworthy, and efficient revenue officials in the service, as well as true and devoted friends of the Administration; that such confidence was reposed in them by their superiors in office as to induce Gen. Babcock to receive them on terms of intimacy, and even consult them sometimes on important State matters; that they boasted of the powerful political influence they possessed in Missouri, and that they were constantly and earnestly working for the good of the Administration, and were gradually and surely adding to the strength of that party in this State. Under such influences, it will be represented, Gen. Babcock felt safe in complying with almost any request they made of him, being confident that to grant it was for the good of the public service and the Republican Party. That he saw officers, higher in position than himself, yield to the requests and gladly receive and adopt the advice of McDonald especially. Hence he honestly believed he was doing right in advancing any measure Gen. McDonald advocated upon the explanation made by the latter. Under such influences, and honestly believing he was doing right, and giving proper advice to two of the most trustworthy officers of the Government, who would use it with discretion, and for the good of the service, the defense will represent that Gen. Babcock did send certain telegrams of the character named, but will stoutly deny and offer evidence to prove that he never received a dollar from McDonald or Joyce, or imagined that a Whisky Ring existed. Testimony will also be introduced, of course, to sustain the relations of Babcock and McDonald as explained above.

NEW DISCOVERIES IN CHICAGO.

CLOSE ALLIANCE BETWEEN THE CHICAGO AND THE ST. LOUIS RINGS—THE CHICAGO ROGUES KEPT INFORMED BY THOSE IN ST. LOUIS—GEN. BABCOCK'S DEFENSE

h to the New-York Times.
6.—There are several new
icago whisky matters, by
ment has obtained informa-
ve a connection between the
and that in St. Louis. The
be in possession of Govern-
ported to be very conclusive
tending to show by cor-
telegrams between Rehm,
s, in this city, and several
, that both factions worked
devising ways and means to
ment of its revenue. From
lying in the vault of the
office it can be established
re that the conspiracy exist-
idents of the two cities was a
at each assisted the other in
y of the Treasury. From the
om the verbal testimony of
nade confession it can be es-
ight, that the Chicago Ring
ation in regard to the move-
ton officials through the St.
who were in league with
Internal Revenue officials at
asserted that by this and
he payment of various sums
sing" purposes can be traced
rvants in the City of Mag-
The amount stated is over
inety thousand dollars. The
Jury is now paying its atten-
an exactly similar nature.
he Babcock case is so active
s Chicago in the course of
issue. Mr. Hoeffer, law part-
y A. Storrs, is busily engaged
stimony of Chicago witnesses
em on the stand in St. Louis.
tnesses from Chicago will be
ding Hon. J. R. Jones, Col-
and Benjamin H. Campbell,
shal. It is rumored that some
formation has been obtained
esses, and it is understood that
cured several prominent cit-
willing to swear that several
efore the Grand Jury that in-
dmitted to them that they
considerably in giving their
prosecution assured them
es would be light in propor-
gth of their testimony. It is
t these gentlemen are pre-
oath that the same parties
that in many instances
estimony against Gen. Bab-
out for them by the attorneys
ho were determined to have
is further understood that ev-
uced showing, or having a
that the witnesses on whose
dictment against Babcock
their evidence for no
to purchase immunity from
they had adhered to the
nent would have come into
stimony different from what
ot mean to state that the
overnment advised or asked
perjury, but that it was
and part of the agreement
e witnesses among themselves.

W-ORLEANS RING.

INGS SENT TO PARTIES IN
MOBILE.

Feb. 6.—It is reported on the
t certain parties here, mixed
isky transactions, have dis-
ent to Mobile, for the
surmised, either of de-
records deposited there,
dealers who may have
the parties here, of the best
ed in the event of investiga-
ited States District Attorney
has taken steps, to guard against such contingency by telegraphing officials there to keep strict surveillance over the movements of the rectifiers and liquor dealers of that city.

THE COAL MINES.

THE FIVE WEEKS' SUSPENSION TO BEGIN TO-DAY.

SCRANTON, Feb. 6.—To-morrow morning the five weeks' suspension of labor at the mines, ordered by the combined companies at their recent meeting in New-York, takes effect throughout the anthracite coal fields of Pennsylvania, throwing 60,000 men and boys out of employment. The outlook is not regarded very seriously in this region, as the short season of rest is expected to be followed by one of unusual activity. It is expected the suspension will have the effect of clearing the overcrowded coal-yards at tide-water and making room for a good Spring trade. There is a large number of the poor class who will certainly be pinched by the five weeks of enforced idleness upon which they enter to-morrow, but no serious consequences are apprehended.

THE ADVISORY COUNCIL.

BOSTON, Feb. 6.—Bethany Church, at Montpelier, Vt., unanimously declines the invitation to send delegates to the Advisory Council of Plymouth Church.

The First Parish Congregational Church of Dover, N. H., and Elliot Congregational Church of Lawrence, Mass., have voted to send delegates to the Plymouth Church Advisory Council.

WORCESTER, Feb. 6.—The First and Salem Street Churches in this city have voted to accept the invitation to participate in the Plymouth Church Council.

BANGOR, Feb. 6.—The Central Congregational Church will send delegates to the Plymouth Church Advisory Council.

A VICTIM OF "BLACK FRIDAY."

CHICAGO, Feb. 6.—The body of William F. Ward was discovered this afternoon in a closet of a vacant house on the corner of Washington and Union streets, in this city. The body was already partially decomposed, and was entirely nude, but without marks of violence. His clothes lay on the floor beside him. Mr. Ward was formerly a well-known operator in Wall street, New-York, but in the panic of "Black Friday" lost his entire fortune, which is supposed to have been over one million dollars. Since that time he has been living in penury and distress in this city. It is believed he committed suicide.

FOUR PERSONS BURNED TO DEATH.

LA SALLE, Ill., Feb. 6.—News has been received that the dwelling of George Heindle, near Hollowayville, in Bureau County, this State, was burned on Friday night, and Mr. Heindle, his wife, and two children perished in the flames. A daughter, nineteen years old, narrowly escaped by jumping from a second story window.

FRAUDULENT TRANSACTIONS.

LEBANON, N. H., Feb. 6.—Horace Hatch, who was arrested yesterday, it is alleged, borrowed for a few days some bonds of W. C. Bulkley, and used them to raise money for the Sturtevant Manufacturing Company; further, that the owner of the bonds has been unable to get them back, and that Hatch had also indorsed heavily for the Sturtevant Manufacturing Company. It has now transpired that Hatch's property was all transferred three years ago to avoid the payment of the notes, while he has been receiving a percentage for the use of his name. C. S. Sturtevant, President, and W. S. Moses, Treasurer of the company, are, it is said, also to be arrested.

BASE-BALL.

A MEETING OF THE MANAGERS OF THE PROFESSIONAL NINES—THE PHILADELPHIA CLUB EXCLUDED FROM THE CHAMPIONSHIP CONTESTS—NEW RULES.

A meeting of the managers of all the professional base-ball organizations in the country, excepting the Philadelphia Club, was held at the Grand Central Hotel on Wednesday, Feb. 2, at 2 o'clock. The first action was the passage of a resolution preventing two clubs from any one city entering for the championship. As the Athletics were represented at the meeting, and took part in its action, the Philadelphias were, as a consequence, shut out from entering their nine for the whip pennant. The next action was the passage of a resolution preventing any two clubs from playing in a city in which neither of them belongs. This was done for the purpose of "heading off" two or three clubs and preventing their going to Philadelphia during the Exhibition and playing a series of games. This will be a sore disappointment to these clubs, and will doubtless result in the disbanding of more than one of them before the season is half over. The amending of the rules was taken up, and several important changes were made. Among others, a rule allowing the base-runner to run on a foul fly catch, after he has touched his base, the same as on a fair fly-catch, was adopted. Another of the new rules allows a base-runner to return to his base after a foul ball has been hit, without running the risk of being put out, and still another virtually allows the batsman to have four strikes instead of three. After two balls have been called the umpire shall, when the next fair ball has been pitched and the batsman refuses to strike at it, warn the striker, but shall not be allowed to call a strike until still another fair ball has been pitched.

The following clubs entered for the championship: Athletic, Mutual, New-Haven, Hartford, Boston, Chicago, St. Louis, Louisville, and Cincinnati. The association will be known as the National League of Professional Base-ball Clubs, and has nothing whatever to do with the old National Association. The officers are M. G. Buckley, of the Hartford Club, President, and N. E. Young, of Washington, Secretary. The League will be governed by a board of five Directors. Those chosen for the current year are from the Hartford, Louisville, Boston, Mutual, and St. Louis Clubs. This board will sit annually as a Board of Appeals to decide all disputed points, and their decisions will be final. A most wholesome regulation of this League is one to the effect that when a player has been suspended he must wait until the end of the season, or until December, when the Directors meet, before his appeal can be heard. Thus, if a player is expelled from a club, he cannot join another nine and continue in the field, as under the old system. The League will hold its next meeting in March of next year.

LATEST NEWS BY CABLE.

THE TURKISH PROVINCES.

REPLY OF THE PORTE TO THE FOREIGN POWERS—THE LEADING REFORMS SUGGESTED TO BE PUT IN OPERATION.

CONSTANTINOPLE, Feb. 6.—The Porte to-day dispatched to its Ambassadors at the courts of the six guaranteeing powers a reply to Count Andrassy's note. The reply announces that in consequence of negotiations with the Ambassadors of the three Northern Powers, the Porte has resolved to apply in the insurgent districts five leading points of Andrassy's scheme, namely, the establishment of religious liberty, the modification of the system of collecting tithes, the granting of facilities to agriculturalists, the application of a portion of the revenues of the insurgent provinces to local improvements, and the appointment of a mixed commission of Mussulmans and Christians to watch the execution of these reforms.

WARLIKE PREPARATIONS IN ROUMANIA.

LONDON, Feb. 7.—A special dispatch from Vienna to the *Standard* says the news of warlike preparations in Roumania excites uneasiness. It is said Prince Charles wishes to renounce allegiance to Turkey. The Roumanian Army has 140 pieces of artillery and 100,000 Chassepot rifles coming from Prussia.

The *Tagespresses* reports that Roumania has complained to the European powers that the Turkish Compat Widdin is a permanent menace, compelling her to maintain large forces in order to preserve her dignity and independence.

The journals of Pesth complain that Russia is fomenting insurrection in Bulgaria, and assert that a Russian officer on furlough commands one of the rebel bands in Bosnia.

AUSTRIA.

INDICATIONS OF AN EARLY CHANGE OF MINISTRY—AN ULTRAMONTANE CABINET TO BE FORMED.

LONDON, Feb. 7.—The Berlin correspondent of the *Times* says, according to apparently correct intelligence from Prague, the Vienna Cabinet is on the point of resigning, and a Ministry under the Presidency of Count Taaffe, an Ultramontane, and at present Governor of the Tyrol, will take its place. It will be remembered when a change was first rumored some months ago the semi-official journal, the *Provinzial Correspondenz*, apprehended as a consequence a serious estrangement between Germany and Austria. As Count Andrassy remains in office the worst part of these apprehensions is happily unfulfilled. Yet, as the policy of the Austrian Conservatives and Ultramontanes toward Germany and Turkey is very different from that of the outgoing Administration, a new and disturbing element is suddenly added to the political situation.

SPAIN.

THE ALFONSIST CAMPAIGN IN THE NORTH—DENIAL OF A POLITICAL RUMOR.

MADRID, Feb. 6.—An official dispatch, dated Durango, Feb. 5, reports that Gen. Quesada has occupied that city, meeting with no resistance. Gen. Loma has arrived at Guernica. The Carlists have retreated toward Azpeitia and Azcoitia. Gen. Martinez Campos is fortifying his positions at Daucharinea, where he has seized a Carlist cartridge manufactory. Rumors which have prevailed of a *convenio* between Carlos and Alfonso are entirely unfounded.

GREAT BRITAIN.

THE NAVAL FORCE IN CHINESE WATERS TO BE STRENGTHENED—THE PRINCESS OF WALES.

LONDON, Feb. 6.—The London *Observer* says it has reason to believe, in view of the unsettled state of political affairs, the British Government intends to strengthen its naval forces in the Chinese waters.

LONDON, Feb. 7.—The *Observer* states that the British frigates Narcissus, Immortalite, Newcastle, and Topaze will sail from Bombay in a few days for Hong Kong.

The *Standard* to-day says it is definitely announced that the Duke of Edinburgh is to take command of the iron-clad Sultan, now at Devonport, and proceed on a special cruise when she is refitted.

The Princess of Wales arrived at Dover to-day from Denmark via Calais.

FRANCE.

THE FORTHCOMING ELECTIONS FOR DEPUTIES.

PARIS, Feb. 6.—Louis Blanc has announced his intention of being a candidate in the elections for the Chamber of Deputies in the Fifth and Thirteenth Arrondissements of Paris.

Victor Hugo has declined an invitation from the Irreconcilable Radicals to be a candidate in the Ninth Arrondissement against ex-President Thiers.

GERMANY.

CARDINAL LEDOCHOWSKI'S WHEREABOUTS.

LONDON, Feb. 7.—The *Standard's* Vienna dispatch states that Cardinal Ledochowski will remain some time at his brother's castle in Moravia. The Polish members of the Austrian Reichsrath will send a delegation to visit the Cardinal.

EGYPT.

THE PROPOSED SALE OF RAILWAYS TO AN ENGLISH COMPANY.

LONDON, Feb. 7.—A telegram to the *Standard* from Rome says there is reason to believe that the terms of the treaty for the sale of the Egyptian railways to an English company have been settled, and it is said the contract will be signed next week.

BELGIUM.

THE SEARCH FOR THE LIVING AND DEAD IN THE EXPLODED MINE.

ST. ETIENNE, Feb. 6.—So far seventy corpses have been recovered from the Jabin colliery. The earth is constantly falling in, and the search for the living and dead proceeds slowly under circumstances of great danger.

LONDON, Feb. 7.—A dispatch from St. Etienne to the *Daily Telegraph* reports that 200 miners were killed by the explosion in the Jabin colliery.

PARAGUAY.

FOREIGN AUTHORITY APPROACHING AN END—THE TERRITORIAL DISPUTE.

BUENOS AYRES, Feb. 2, via LONDON, Feb. 7—The Argentine and Brazilian Delegates will cease to hold authority over Paraguay in five months. The dispute in regard to territory between Paraguay and the Argentine States has been submitted to President Grant for arbitration.

THE FRENCH ELECTIONS.

COMPLEXION OF THE SENATE.

HOW THE DEPUTIES ARE CHOSEN—EXTENT OF THE REPUBLICAN VICTORIES—POSSIBLE TACTICS OF THE LEFT—AN ADDRESS OF VICTOR HUGO—THE CHEVALIER WEISS.

From Our Own Correspondent.

PARIS, Friday, Jan. 21, 1876.

We have not yet received any reliable report respecting the character of the Senatorial electors chosen on Sunday last, but I have just made a long and careful study of the isolated reports that have been given us, and have been able to form an approximate idea of what the Senate is to be. Let me premise my brief study by saying, what every student of French politics already knows, that the Senators are not elected by universal suffrage, like the Assembly, but by a restricted and special electoral corps. This is composed, 1. Of the Deputies of the departments; 2. Of the members of the Councils General; 3. Of the members of the Councils of the Arrondissements; 4. Of the delegates chosen by the Communes, one delegate for each municipal council, whatever its size or importance. These delegates were elected on Sunday last. The Senatorial electoral corps is thus complete, and is composed of 43,562 electors, comprising those of Algeria, Corsica, and the Colonies; and it is this special corps which is to elect on Sunday after next, the 30th of January, the remaining 225 members of the new Senate. They assemble in the chief town of each department, and the election will be held under the supervision of the Prefect.

I need scarcely remark, perhaps, that this mode of election shows many inequalities, and that the delegates are not chosen proportionally to the number of inhabitants in the communes. The Commune of Paris, with its half a million of voters, has no more influence than the Commune of Fouilly-les-Oies with its fourscore. It follows that the larger electoral colleges are not chosen by such departments as the Seine, the Rhône, and Bouches-du-Rhône, which have in them such populous cities as Paris, Lyons, and Marseilles, but by the departments which are greatly inferior in the matter of population, but which have a larger number of communes. Thus, the Department of the Pas-de-Calais (Calais and Boulogne) has 1,018 electors; the Somme, (Amiens and Abbeville,) 936; Seine-Inferièure, (Rouen,) 879, and Calvados 865—while the more populous Department of the Bouches-du-Rhône (Marseilles) has only 174; the Alpes-Maritimes and the Var, 208; Vaucluse, 213, and the Haut-Rhin, constituted since the cession of Alsace by the City of Belfort and its environs, has only 112 electors. The contrast is best shown by comparing the Pas-de-Calais with the Seine; while Paris and its environs elect but 221 delegates, Calais, Boulogne, and the surrounding villages and hamlets have 1,018. This system was devised mainly for the purpose of neutralizing the radical influence and tendencies of the great cities, and it appears to have succeeded better that was at first supposed, for of the thousand electors of Boulogne and Calais over six hundred are declared Bonapartists.

All these communal delegates have to assemble on Sunday, the 30th of January, to meet the other electors, and to choose the members of the Senate. As the voyage to the chief town might prove onerous to some, mileage is allowed them, but a very modest estimate has been made. Each delegate will receive fifty cents for every five miles traveled, or, to be accurate, for every myriamètre, or 10,000 yards, all fractions above one-half to be counted as a whole myriamètre. This entails upon the Treasury an expense of 850,000 francs. No mileage is allowed for only two miles. The above sum is the official estimate, but I do not think it will be required, for a large majority of the delegates would hardly think of entering a claim upon the Treasury for a sum so insignificant, and the demand has to be made in writing and handed to the presiding officer of the Assembly before its sitting is over.

As I remarked above, we have not yet received any official report concerning the character of these communal delegates, but on studying out the lists I find that the Republicans are less successful than I had at first supposed. It appears that Conservative opinions prevail in over sixty of the eighty-seven departments, and the two parties are pretty nearly equal in at least ten more, leaving not more than fifteen departments in which the Republicans have triumphed. This statement will be deceptive unless I explain that the seventy departments in which Conservative opinions have prevailed may not elect Conservative Senators, for where the electors are composed of a little more than one-third Republicans and two-thirds Conservatives, divided up into three factions, the Republican candidates would be tolerably sure of election. Hence the fact of our finding seventy departments that are Conservative does not indicate with certainty that all will elect Conservative candidates. In trying to make an estimate of the relative strength of the parties a number of details have to be taken into account that would seem unimportant to the foreign reader. As this letter will reach you about the time that you receive the results by telegraph, all prediction is risky in the extreme, but I am inclined to give the Bonapartists about 140 seats in this Senate of 300 members, and the Royalists will have 30 or thereabouts. Thus the Conservatives, if my estimates are anywhere in the vicinity of the truth, will still have a majority, but being composed partly of Bonapartists the Republicans may, by cultivating alliances with the Royalists, succeed in carrying their measures, as they have done in the Assembly. The entire number of seats that I have given to the Bonapartists will not appear in the first dispatches, for there are a number of men actually belonging to that party, to my personal knowledge, who "keep dark" for the moment. An example of what I mean now lies before me. The Bonapartists of Rouen wanted to bring forward M. Ponyer-Quertier, but he came out with a letter protesting against this use of his name. He would be proud to receive the votes of his fellow-citizens, but did not want to be compromised in favor of any party. M. De Fourtou and others are of the same opinion, but when it comes to a vote they will be found opposed to the Republicans. The Eighty-seventh Department of France, which has the smallest of all the electoral colleges, is all that is left of the Haut-Rhin, (now the German Elsass,) and is called the Arrondissement of Belfort. It has but 112 electors. And the smallest college is going to elect the smallest man to the Senate, every one of these 112 votes being already acquired by M. Thiers. No one will come forward to contest the "Arrondissement of Belfort" with him, and is is morally certain that M. Thiers will be the "Senator for Belfort." If my letter should chance to appear before the dispatches give the result of the elections, I advise the reader to take these notes as comments upon the telegrams, and do not doubt that, though some dis-

The Base Ball News.

HOWARD H. GOSHEN, A Paper Devoted to the Interest of Base Ball. EDITOR AND PUBLISHER

VOL. 1. MIFFLINTOWN, PA., THURSDAY, SEPTEMBER 13. 1877, NO. 20.

A TRAGEDY.

BY N. O. V.

"Will you marry me?"

"No, I will not."

He was Dick Sykes, the first baseman of the Shooting Crackers, and Raggettstown's boast.

She was Nancy, the daughter of Peter Colgate, Raggettstown's banker, mayor and bar-keeper.

"All right," said Dick, "next Saturday we play the Sky Rockets, and your pap has bet all the money he's worth on our nine, and if you don't change your mind before that time, you are a pauper's daughter."

Saturday came.

The Shooting Crackers are all in their places ready for the battle.

The Rockets are first at the bat. Nancy was there; all Raggettstown was there.

Dick glanced at Nancy.

Nancy shook her head.

A frown went over his face, and the game proceeded.

It is the ending of the ninth inning.

The score stands 8 to 8, two hands are out, a man is on the third.

The greatest excitement rages.

A fly ball is batted to Dick.

"Catch it!" shouted old Colgate.

"NEVER!" says Dick.

He drops it.

The man on the third comes home. "8 to 9 in favor of the Sky Rockets!" shouts the scorer.

N. B.—Nancy takes in plain sewing now.

The St Louis *Globe-Democrat* is responsible for the following facts obtained by the Globe-Democrat from reliable sources warrant the assertion that the existence of the present Chicago club will terminate at the end of the season. "The big four" having accomplished the mission for which they were lured from Boston, are now seeking engagements in other sections, while Harry Wright smiles with satisfaction at the knowledge that the Whites could only retain the championship during one season, and it was only won because he had only five men to play with. If Chicago places a nine in the field at all next season it will be a second-rate affair.

The base ball profession will at the end of this season lose the best-known and most highly respected of its active members in the person of Mr. A. G. Spalding, Secretary, Manager and Captain of the Chicagos for two years. His retirement from active service is the result of a determination formed at the end of last season, and growing out of the increased needs of his business, which has grown from a small beginning to a size which imperatively demands his attention as well as that of his brother. Mr. Spalding's record of five years in Boston and two in Chicago has never been equaled, and probably never will be, and it is not exceeding the truth to say that no ball player ever had so wide an acquaintance and so deep a respect among all grades and classes of players as has Mr. Spalding.

The Base Ball News.

H. H. GOSHEN, Editor and Publisher.

Mifflintown, Thursday, Sept. 13.

We publish the following, as was handed us, by a gentlemen.

The son of a citizen of Mifflintown is a member of the Baltic base ball club. On Saturday last, two weeks ago, he played with a Scrub nine against the Auroras. The day in question he had his hair cut and oiled, he accoutred for the affray, and his fond mother tied one of her best lace trimmed handkerchiefs around his throat, and put a clean handkerchief, with some cologne on it, in his belt and kissed him, and he went.—About a quarter to five he returned—that is, the most of him—and the following conversation ensued :

"My son, where is the lace handkerchief you had around your neck?"

"Here, ma, tied around this finger, I picked up a daisy cutter. I think the finger is only out of joint, not broken."

"My son, why do you not speak plainer. Surely, surely you have not been drinking?"

"No, ma, but in the latter half of the seventh inning our catcher's hands gave out, and I went behind, and I stopped a foul tip with my teeth, that is all."

"My son, your nice new uniform is all bloody in front. Whatever can you have been doing?"

"Nothing, ma, only I was trying to scoop in a high one at third, and the sun got in my eyes, and I muffed it, and the ball came on my nose, but I put it over to first and got him out."

My son, your blue flannel pants are all dirty behind."

"That, ma, was in the third inning, when I tried to steal to second, and had to throw myself down and slide in. I got the base anyhow, and came in on a two baser by D—— to left field."

"Alas, my son, I fear that you have had an unpleasant day. Let me send for Drs. C—— and B——, and get some arnica, ice water, lint, raw beefsteak, splints, sticking-plaster, vinegar and brown paper, Radway's Ready Relief, Perry Davis' Pain Killer, compresses, slings, leeches, clean clothes, opodeldoc, horse liniment, and in a few days you will not know yourself."

"Oh, ma, it was the bulliest game I ever was in—the score 27 to 7, in favor of the Scrubs; and if I die I give the spikes of my shoes to D—— for ten cents, with fifteen days credit, and I —"

(Exit, led out by the ear. Curtain falls.

League, Professional and Amateur.

SATURDAY, SEPTEMBER 1.

Boston 8, Cincinnati 3, at Boston.

Hartford 4, Louisville 6,Brooklyn.

Stars 1, Chicago 2, at Syracuse.

Allegheny 1, St Louis 0, at Pittsburg, fifteen innings.

Indianapolis 4, Crickets 2, at Binghampton.

Rochester 3, Buffalo 0, at Buffalo.

Athletic 9, Lockner, an amateur nine, 11, at Philadelphia.

MONDAY, SEPTEMBER 3.

Hartford 9, Chelsea 1, at Brooklyn.

Allegheny 3, Louisville 2, Pittsburg.

Crickets 8, Chicago 2, Binghamton.

Boston 14, Cincinnati 0, at Boston.

St Louis 4, Fall River 3, Fall River.

TUESDAY, SEPTEMBER 4.

Hartford 7, Chicago 1, at Brooklyn.

Boston 7, St Louis 1, at Boston.

Allegheny 0, Louisville 3, Pittsburg.

Stars 4, Indianapolis 2, at Syracuse, the latter withdrew at the ending of the fifth inning, they differing with the umpire.

Rochester 8, Cincinnati 5, Rochester.

Auburn 1, Buffalo 0, at Buffalo.

WEDNESDAY, SEPTEMBER 5.

Athletic 6, Chicago 5, at Phila.

Rochester 2, Indianapolis 2, at Rochester, nine innings, a draw.

Buckeye 5, Louisville 2, at Buffalo.

St Louis 3, Live Oaks 0, at Lynn, Mass, ten innings.

THURSDAY, SEPTEMBER 6.

Boston 11, St Louis 2, at Boston.

Cincinnati 1, Louisville 0, Cincinnati.

Stars 6, Crickets 5, at Binghampton.

FRIDAY, SEPTEMBER 7.

Boston 1, Lowell 0, at Boston.

Louisville 3, Cincinnati 2, Cincinnati.

SATURDAY, SEPTEMBER 8.

Cincinnati 6, Louisville 2, at Cincinnati.

Allegheny 1, Rochester 6, at Pittsburgh.

Hartford 15, St. Louis 6, Brooklyn.

Chicago 1, Boston 0, at Boston.

The Championship Record.

The record in the League championship up to Sept.9, inclusive, is as follows :

Clubs	Games won.	Games lost.
Boston	35	18
Hartford	27	22
Chicago	21	24
Cincinnati	11	37
Louisville	29	22
St Louis	24	22
Totals	147	147

The record in the International championship arena up to Sept. 9, inclusive, is as follows;

Clubs,	Games won.	Gamer lost
Allegheny	14	5
Rochester	12	7
Tecumseh	13	4
Buckeye	9	12
Manchester	10	12
Live Oaks	3	12
Maple Leaf	3	11
Totals	64	64

The Base Ball News.

Mifflintown, Thursday, Sept. 13.

SHORT STOPS.

Short stops are scarce.

What has become of the D. P. Sulouff's?

The Champion City Club has disintegrated.

Billy Kulp is the boss trapper in this section, at present.

Barnes is playing his old position, second base, in the Chicago club.

The Louisvilles lost every championship game on their recent Eastern tour.

Did you meet her at Port Royal yet, Billy? We hope she's a trapper.

The Louisville Club's share of gate money in the games at Boston was $1,400.

Hart, of the McVeytown Actives, is a fine second baseman. So says Dietrick.

The rain on the latter part of last week prevented the Auroras from playing ball.

The Hartfords have played three games this season without an error, and the Bostons one.

The Buffalo club have won but three games out of sixteen they have played recently.

When a club breaks up or disbands, it is fashionable now to speak of it as "disintegrating."

The Louisville club refuse to play in Philadelphia unless they are guaranteed $125.

The Indianapolis club, while on its Eastern tour, refused to play in Philadelphia under any circumstances.

In the series of games between the Bostons and Louisvilles, Jim White, of the former, made twenty-four base hits off of Devlin's pitching.

The Athletics defeated a Scrub nine in Patterson on Wednesday by a score of 25 to 18. The full account of the game came too late too publish.

Mitchell and Miller, pitcher and catcher of the Champion City club, have been engaged to play with Cincinnati the balance of the season. This will greatly strength en the Reds.

Patterson Short Stops.

The Baltic Secretary, pro-tem, informs us that as yet he has not heard from the clubs written to in reference to playing during the Fair.

The fraternity has had a respite for some time. Better get to work and make some show during the Fair.

The Baltics are all anxious for a game of ball. Can they not be accommodated?

We suggest that the editors of the BASE BALL NEWS and New Enterprise drop the "toby" question. We will give them each a good one, if they are scarce of the stuff.

"Have your cats all got tails?" asked a member of one of the leading clubs of Mifflin of one of Patterson's fair damsels. We did not wait to hear the answer.

Herman Cramer, pitcher for the Auroras, has been rusticating at Altoona for the past two weeks. YOU KNOW.

We clip the following from the Philadelphia Times: "If Ward had not treated the Athletic management in such an ungentlemanly manner, and could the club have held on to him, Philadelphia would have had next season one of the best pitchers in the country. The Athletics have developed several players this year and other clubs have been quick to snap them up. Ward is playing finely in Janesville. After the game with the Chicagos the other day Spalding tried to hire him as well as Bushong, the catcher, but with out avail. The present Janesville nine will probably be retained next year."

We notice by the Bellefonte Watchman that Ward is a native of Bellefonte. Not having the surplus on hand to finish his education, and being desirous to do the latter he took the above method—pitcher of a base ball club.

The Lewistown Sentinel says: "The Logan base ballers rather took the wind out of the sails of our Independents on a recent occasion, and on Saturday they are coming in to give our boys a chance to win back their sails. The mumleypeg Baltics are invited to witness the performance, tackle the weakest of the clubs, and score a "full" score of defeats."

Your "pet quality," with the Sentinel editor thrown in as pig-tail, have not the moral courage to play the return game with the Baltics, who can wax the Independents, or anything in Lewistown. After the Logans beat them again send them to Mifflin and the Baltics will do likewise. As to your weaker clubs, we refer to the Aurora, the time the Young America club of Lewistown accepted their challenge two hours after the train (which was the Auroras only way of getting up) had left Mifflin. They know what side of their bread is buttered. The Independents, ditto

The grand tourney at Allegheny, between the Indianapolis, Star and Allegheny nines began on Monday last. Each of the three clubs will play two games, the tourney occupying the whole week. We take stock in the Alleghenys.

The many severe injuries sustained by catchers facing swift pitchers in professional nines have led to the recent adoption of the Thayer wire mask by the professionals, the same having been in use by the amateurs for some time past. It is a valuable safeguard, and it should be worn by every catcher who stands close behind the bat in front of swift pitching.

THE HON. GEORGE P. MARSH.
PHOTOGRAPHED BY L. A. ATWOOD.—[SEE PAGE 491.]

1876, when he did so remarkably well that he has ever since played in that position.

JAMES E. O'NEIL is a Canadian, and began playing as pitcher of the Actives of Woodstock, Canada, in 1877. The peculiarity of his pitching is the wonderful swiftness with which he delivers a ball.

JOHN A. DOYLE, the third pitcher of the team, is a Nova Scotian by birth, but has lived for years, and played ball, in Providence, Rhode Island. Last summer he began life as a professional base-ball player, making his first engagement with the Metropolitans.

JOHN REILLY, who replaces EASTERBROOK as first-base man, is a quiet but popular fellow, and a capital man in his place. He was born in Cincinnati, and has been playing base-ball since 1877.

FRANK LARKIN, popularly known as "Terry," is a New-Yorker, began to play in 1873, and played on second base for the Atlantics of Brooklyn so well last season that the Metropolitans engaged him to fill the same position on their team this year.

FRANK HANKINSON, the third-base man, is also a native of this city, and made his first appearance on the "diamond" in 1875, when he played with the Alaska Juniors.

JOHN NELSON, of Brooklyn, is known as one of the very best short stops in the country, and has played in that position with many of the crack clubs, including the Eckfords, whom he joined in 1869, the Mutuals, Troys, Athletics of Philadelphia, Indianapolis, Hudsons, Albanys, Worcester, and Athletics of Brooklyn.

EDWARD KENNEDY, the left fielder, is an extremely popular player, and deserves as well as receives his full share of applause during a game. He is from Carbondale, Pennsylvania, and has been playing since 1875.

THOMAS E. MANSELL, of Auburn, New York, always played catcher as an amateur; but when in 1877 he accepted a professional engagement with the Auburn Club, it was as left fielder, and a fielder he has been ever since. As centre fielder he gives perfect satisfaction to the "Mets."

STEPHEN BRADY, from Hartford, Connecticut, has played right field for the Metropolitans ever since their organization, but is particularly noted for skill at the bat, having stood at the head of the list as a batsman in nearly every club with which he has been connected.

ENGLISH GOSSIP.

[FROM OUR OWN CORRESPONDENT.]

Umbrella Christians.—Two Great Sales.—The Pathway to India.—Professional Assistance.—The First Illustrator of Dickens.

YEARS ago I remember a great preacher and teacher making some remarks from the pulpit about persons who came into his tabernacle, not "to scoff," indeed, but to shelter themselves from a passing shower. He discoursed upon them, considerably to their discomfort, as "umbrella Christians," a term which for a long time was applied in reproach to those who used religion as a convenience. Now, however, we are changing all that. The Baptists, who I suppose can never have too much of water, have started a novelty in open-air missions called "umbrella services," which it seems are largely attended by young people. There may, however, be some reasons for this which do not enter into the pastor's calculations; in the first place, until we have arrived at maturity, we are not afraid of rheumatism, and would just as soon stand in the rain as not; and secondly, "umbrella courtships" are an older institution than "umbrella services," and have always been greatly appreciated by the parties concerned.

The two great sales of late going on in London have presented a remarkable contrast: the one of the effects of the Duke of Hamilton, and the other of the materials of Kensington House, the stately pile, "so royal, rich, and wide," which Baron Grant (the Promoter) built for himself, but never occupied. In the former case everything has been sold for a fancy price. Indifferent things have realized more than good things do elsewhere, and good things have fetched enormous prices. Such a figure as £6000, for example, for a Marie Antoinette table has probably been never reached before. Think of sinking £300 a year forever in a table! How can it ever repay the purchaser? What of profit *can* he get out of it in proportion to the money he has paid? One would not have wondered so much had one of our brand-new millionaires bid for it with his own lips, seen it knocked down with his own eyes, and heard with his own ears the cheers of the by-standers. He would have made a reputation for himself—which would have lasted perhaps a week. But, as it happens, the table has been bought by a dealer, on commission, for some enthusiast in furniture unknown.

Now at Kensington House we see the reverse of all this. Fashion turns its back on it, and everything is disposed of at what seems for once to justify the phrase "a frightful sacrifice." The "grand marble staircase," which only a few years ago cost £11,000, and can hardly be worse for wear, since no one has trodden it, went for £1000! The "fluted Corinthian columns of Italian marble" that cost £1000 the pair were sold for just one-tenth of that money.

The "rapid act" of the *Alaska* in crossing the Atlantic has quickened the energies and raised the hopes of our ship-owners. Mr. Norwood laid before the House of Commons the other day some most remarkable statistics to show that not only were the advantages of the Suez Canal as a highway to India exaggerated, but immensely exaggerated. By the introduction of steel instead of iron, which certain discoveries have now rendered feasible, ships can be built lighter, and therefore larger, than was the case two years ago—ships that can even now reach Calcutta round the Cape almost as quickly (*i. e.*, within three days) as those which go through the canal. These last, of necessity smaller and of lighter draught, have to call so often for coals that what they gain in shortness of distance they almost lose in length of time. Mr. Norwood predicts that in a little while steel ships will be built to run continuously at the rate of twenty knots an hour, when for the conveyance of troops the advantages of the Suez Canal will cease altogether. In case of our being at war with France and Italy, when of course no English vessel could run the gauntlet of the Mediterranean, India would for political purposes be then as near to us as ever, and by establishing a blockade at Gibraltar and at the mouth of the Red Sea, we could "shut up" our enemies pretty completely. That Cyprus which was once thought to be as appropriate as its namesake to crown poor Lord Beaconsfield's tomb has long been acknowledged to be worthless, and now the value of his other acquisition, the Suez Canal, is beginning to be questioned.

COLONEL JOHN C. HAMILTON.
PHOTOGRAPHED BY W. KURTZ.—[SEE PAGE 491.]

There are disclosures in the case of Mr. Belt, the sculptor, which are calculated to make a novelist's mouth water. Without for a moment imputing to him that he got any assistance not customary with persons of his profession, it seems that a good deal of help is customary with sculptors; for all I know, painters get their pictures done on similar co-operative principles, and I wish it was possible to apply them to literature. If one had a name, for instance, as a writer of fiction, how pleasant it would be to suggest the plot of a story to some rising young writer, with instructions to "work it up" into the three-volume form! I think I could write—that is, put my name to them—a good many novels per annum on this system. I would just suggest the course that true love was to take in the tale, and then set some young lady to carry out the description of the hero, and for the legal matters I would engage some briefless barrister to "devil" for me. It seems to me a very good notion.

There must, of course, be some limit to professional assistance. A modest young medical student who had his doubts of being able

John H. Lynch, P. Charles Reipschlager, C. J. E. O'Neil, P. Edward Kennedy, L. F. J. C. Clapp, C. J. A. Doyle, P. Frank Hankinson, 3d B. Stephen Brady, R. F.
Thomas E. Mansell, C. F. Frank Larkin, 2d B. John Nelson, S. S. John Reilly, 1st B.

THE METROPOLITAN BASE-BALL NINE.—FROM A PHOTOGRAPH BY SARONY.

TRI-WEEKLY EDITION.

The Detroit Free Press.

TRI-WEEKLY EDITION.

VOLUME 47. DETROIT, MICHIGAN, MONDAY, AUGUST 21, 1882. NUMBER 307

HAIR AND VANITY.

The Girl Who Dresses Her Hair But Once a Week.

POINTS ON THE PERQUISITES OF PERIPATETIC HAIR-WORKERS.

The Origin of Bangs and High Forehead Ornamentations.

"There goes a girl who hasn't combed her hair since Sunday and who will not, probably, comb it again until next Sunday."

"What's the matter with her?"

"Nothing, only she's a slave to fashion."

"Do you really mean that she combs her hair only once a week?"

"I do, really. She visits the hair dresser's rooms Sunday morning, or has the hairdresser visit her, when she has her hair 'put up' for the week."

This conversation occurred yesterday between a well-known merchant and a reporter for THE FREE PRESS. It prompted the latter to visit a hair store on a tour of investigation, and in response to a request to see the proprietor he was invited into the workshop in the rear of the salesroom.

"I don't know what I can tell you about the business except that it is a regular trade like any other trade," said the proprietress when the reporter had stated the object of his call.

"Can you give the origin and cause of wearing banged hair?"

"I do not know the origin unless it was a revival of an ancient fashion adopted by the nobility of England."

"About how long ago?"

"Well, the two young princes in the tower (did you ever see the picture?) are shown with banged hair, and really I like it on children. It gives a pure, peaceful and pleasing expression to young features."

"And it is probably to gain that expression that the fashion has been adopted by older persons?"

"Probably; but it is a futile effort in a majority of cases."

"May not excessively high foreheads have been the cause in many instances?"

"Undoubtedly; but it is bad taste, for a stiff, precise fringe of hair at right angles with the lines of the eyes, the nose and the mouth, gives a coarse, bold expression to almost any face above 15 years of age."

"What other style could be adopted to lessen the area of a forehead?"

"Many. The natural hair might be combed low, frizzes might be put on, and front pieces used."

"Is it a fact that there are ladies who have their hair 'done up' but once a week?"

"Yes. I have known of a few such cases, but they were generally ladies without good taste and exceedingly fond of presenting a striking appearance."

"How do you——"

"Excuse me, but will you please step into the salesroom a few minutes?" interrupted the proprietress leading the way. She immediately returned to the back room with a lady customer and the reporter was left to pass the time with a clerk in investigating the mysteries of switches, puffs, curls, wigs, front pieces, false mustaches and whiskers.

"Yes, it's a good business, for it is a profitable way for women to earn their living," said the clerk.

"How much can a good hair worker earn per week?"

"The regular hair dressers—those who work permanently in established shops—earn from $6 to $10 a week; but the 'tramps,' as we call them—those who go about from town to town and canvassing from house to house—make $20 to $40, according to their ability to steal hair and cheat in their work."

"Steal hair?"

"Yes; they take a job of combings to be made into a switch, and will steal the best hair therefrom, and in seven out of ten cases prevail on their customers to permit them to cut from their heads a few long hairs for a covering. Then they will steal from one-sixth to one-third of the living hair so obtained."

"I should think the customer would detect the cheat."

"Generally it is impossible. But supposing they do, and supposing they threaten not to pay for the work?"

"Well, what then?"

"Why, the hair worker will not deliver it until it *is* paid for, and if payment is refused will keep the whole thing and perhaps sell it in the next town for double the figure originally put upon it."

"The moral, then, is: Always patronize established institutions at your own home?"

Just then the lady customer who had entered the shop a half an hour before passed out into the street, and the proprietress of the establishment coming into the salesroom, remarked: "There's a dollar quickly earned."

"What did you do for her?"

"Dressed her switches and put up her hair for a party she is going to attend to-night."

"Do you have much of this work to do?"

"Not just now; it's out of the season; but during the season of opera, theaters and balls, we have all we can do."

"Do you not think it injurious to the hair to plaster it with bandoline, soapoline and the like?"

"I do not think bandoline injurious, but I am sure soap is not the proper thing to use on hair."

"Do you think hair thus 'done up' presents an attractive appearance?"

"It depends upon the color of the hair, the face of the wearer and the style in which the hair is done."

"Would you not advise all persons who wish to have their hair looped, twisted and pasted in that fashion to wear wigs which they can fashion into any outlandish shape they desire?"

"It would be a good thing for us if they would. It would make a market for wigs."

"Where does the hair come from of which wigs, switches, curls, etc., are made?"

"From Europe and the larger cities of America."

"Do you ever buy hair? I mean do you buy it at home here?"

"Always. My patrons are of a class who insist upon guarantees as to the quality of the hair they purchase."

"Where do you get it?"

"Why, scarcely a day passes w[...] not have offers of hair cut from li[...] right here in Detroit."

"What reasons do they give for s[...]

"Various. Sometimes it is from [...] start a new growth; often it is b[...] wearer is tired of a heavy head of h[...] sionally it is by the advice of phys[...] once in a while poverty prods them [...]

"But to return to the women who [...] hair only once a week. Why is tha[...]

"I know of no other cause than [...] have already given."

"May not laziness have something [...] it?"

"I think not; but inability to do [...] may be a cause."

"It's genuine nickel-plated, all-w[...] yard-wide vanity, isn't it?"

"To draw it mildly, yes."

THE LOST EXPLORE[R]

Further Particulars of the Sunke[n ...]er.

The Port Huron Tribune has an a[...] the sinking of the schooner Explor[er ...] Huron. The following particulars [...] dition to those formerly publishe[d ...] were related to Charles A. Jex [...] Huron, by Capt. William Taylor, o[f ...] Wales:

A short time after the reported w[...] the Explorer, Capt. Taylor was cru[...] the shore in the vicinity of Tober[...] bor, when he discovered a small sa[...] anchor near the shore. There was [...] charge of her, but on looking acros[...] he saw a camp and on going ash[...] Capt. Waddel there, who said the [...] belonged to him. After a social [...] Taylor returned to his vess[el ...] he noticed that Waddel's boat [...] with casks or barrels, which [...] thought must contain whis[ky ...] when evening came they "put t[...] together to "gobble" one of the b[...] have a "high old time" over its con[...] agine their surprise when the b[...] found to contain not whisky, but th[...] small schooner about the size of the [...] Capt. Taylor was told of the disco[...] out of curiosity went to Waddel's [...] ascertained by rapping on the hea[...] barrels that none of them were [...] liquid, and he firmly believes that [...] tained the rigging and probably a p[...] cargo of the Explorer.

The following card from Duff [...] published as additional evidence tha[...] sel was scuttled:

"I was the first diver engaged in [...] of the Explorer. We found the [...] ninety-six feet of water, about 300 [...] Tobermorry Harbor, and fastened [...] of our wrecking vessel to her win[...] ning the rope through the Explor[er ...] head. We then brought a chain [...] stern and commenced drawing [...] shore. When in about fifty feet of [...] accidentally broke the chain and I [...] to sweep another chain under her s[...] I discovered a dead body in the ope[...] of the cabin just floating out. It w[...] with a checked shirt, gray pants [...] boots, and was badly decomposed [...] sumed the work of hauling her s[...] when in about twelve feet [...] we found it impossible [...] her further without rais[ing ...] stone that had been placed in he[r ...] went down and worked about two [...] ing the stone, when I was taken sic[k ...] G. McCollough, submarine diver [...] Huron, took my place. I am willin[g ...] under oath, if necessary, that the [...] entirely stripped of canvas, rop[...] cargo, and every movable thing; [...] hatches were spiked down, and th[...] had been chopped through [...] head. That her hold contained not [...] twelve tons of stone, and that twel[...] a half and one one-inch hole were [...] her bottom. They were first disc[...] Capt. Hurl, of Tobermorry, and [...] Capt. Jex plugged them up.

DUFF FE[...]

Talleyrand's Mot.

A writer in a British periodical [...] tion to the declaration of Fisher A[...] during the administration of W[...] said that "though America is ris[...] giant's strength, its bones are yet [...] lages." Since then there must have [...] advance in the direction of th[...] Otherwise, the fragments of Ame[...] by this time have become scatter[...] fossil invertebrates that the geo[...] out of the cliffs of Gay Head. Bu[t ...] writer also quotes Burke, who called [...] icans "a nation in the gristle," wh[...] rand, being a Frenchman, must n[...] his mot, and, accordingly, defines [...] States as "un geant sans os ni ner[...] one and all "make no bones" [...] ing us as boneless. As for Tal[...] would have been quite as satisfac[...] had told us less about America [...] about himself; for tradition runs t[...] half American and the son of a [...] the daughter of a fisherman, whose [...] under the shadow of what Whittie[r ...]

The gray and thunder-smitten [...]
Which marks afar the Desert [...]

It is said that Lieut.-Gov. Robbin[s ...] sachusetts, once found him wander[...] at Mount Desert. The testimony [...] ject is at least curious, and when t[...] layed "Memoirs of Talleyrand" [...] may get that information respectin[g ...] life which is now wanting. Possi[...] then have "a bone to pick" with hi[...] zine of American History for Aug[...]

Men's Hats.

Lewis Mealio, of New York, wh[...] cently at the age of nearly four sco[re ...] last of those Broadway hatters wh[...] craft an aristocratic tone. I well [...] his establishment, which then was [...] street, and was one of elegant style. [...] Co. was another aristocratic hat co[...] for a quarter of a century occupie[d ...] the Astor House basement stores. [...] John N. Genin was also an aristocra[...] and succeeded in obtaining the p[...] Jenny Lind, and also that of Kossu[th ...] cured the former by paying the hi[...] at the ticket auction, and this prov[...] class advertisement. The Swedis[h ...] gale honored him with a call, a[...] autograph at his store. Genin [...] time a very profitable trade and go[...] his fortune afterward changed, [...] poor. Knox, who flourished some [...] Genin, also became rich, but he go[...] in speculation and lost every thing [...] Kossuth the permanent use of th[...] which he rendered so popular. [...] the broad-brimmed slouch was lim[...] younger members of journalism.

The True Newspaper Ma[n.]

Some men seem to be born to do [...] work, and they will do it if they have to live on cold hash and button their coat up to their chin while their only shirt is in the wash. And they will be just as happy, too, as the son-in-law of a monopolist with a bad cough. They would never be contented in any other calling, even if it paid them $10,000 a year and firewood. All others should keep out of the journalistic field.—[Middletown Transcript.

SPORTING MATTERS.

The Detroits Beaten in the Greatest Game of Ball Ever Played.

SEVENTEEN INNINGS PLAYED WITHOUT A RUN BEING SCORED.

Base Ball.

The Detroit-Providence game of yesterday is unrivaled in the history of the league, although not in base ball annals. In 1877 the Harvards and Manchesters played a twenty-four-inning game without a run being made. In the same year the Stars of Syracuse and the St. Louis Browns played a scoreless game of fifteen innings, and the Buckeyes and Tecumsehs played a drawn game of eighteen innings, the score being one each.

The league has witnessed some wonderful contests, but nothing like that of yesterday. Soper made a double row of ciphers clear across his blackboard, tacked on a sheet of paper and had sent for a yard of muslin to stretch across Jefferson avenue, when the intelligence came that the game had ended and that the unlucky Detroits had lost it.

THE FREE PRESS special from Providence states that the game eclipsed anything ever before seen there, and was finally won on Radbourne's lucky hit over the left field fence, which would have been a sure out at Recreation Park, and was nearly a foul ball.

In the fourth inning, with no one out, Hanlon attempted to come home on Powell's single to center field, but was thrown out by Hines.

In the seventh, Bennett made a two-bagger, and went to third on a passed ball. Trott flew out to Wright. Knight got a base on called balls. Weidman hit to Farrell, and a double play was made.

In three other innings the Detroits led off with hits, but the batsmen following, although they hit hard, failed to find a safe place for the ball and no runs were scored, double plays being of frequent occurrence.

Denny and Farrell made several wonderful stops, else Ward would have been badly punished. Weidman pitched the greatest of games. Twice did the Providence team have a man on third base with no one out, but so skillfully did the Kid twirl the ball that the side was put out without a run. In the sixteenth inning Wright hit a liner over Wood's head and out of the horse gate, but Wood went outside, got the ball and fielded Wright out at the plate. Whitney did great work at short stop. The following is

THE SCORE:

DETROIT.

	A.B.	R.	B.H.	T.B.	P.O.	A.	E.
Wood, l. f.	7	0	1	1	4	1	0
Hanlon, c. f.	7	0	1	1	4	0	0
Powell, 1 b	7	0	1	1	21	0	1
Bennett, 3 b	7	0	1	2	3	4	2
Trott, c.	7	0	2	2	13	1	1
Knight, r. f.	6	0	0	0	1	1	0
Weidman, p.	6	0	1	2	2	12	0
Whitney, s. s.	6	0	2	2	1	11	0
Foster, 2 b	6	0	0	0	2	4	2
Totals	59	0	9	11	51	34	6

PROVIDENCE.

	A.B.	R.	B.H.	T.B.	P.O.	A.	E.
Hines, c. f.	7	0	1	1	1	1	0
Farrell, 2 b	7	0	1	1	7	9	1
Start, 1 b	7	0	0	0	25	1	1
Ward, p.	7	0	1	1	2	5	0
York, l. f.	7	0	1	1	3	0	0
Radbourne, r. f.	7	1	1	4	1	0	0
Wright, s. s.	6	0	1	3	2	5	1
Denny, 3 b	6	0	2	2	4	11	1
Nava, c.	6	0	0	0	9	1	1
Totals	60	1	8	13	54	33	5

Innings	1	2	3	4	5	6	7	8	9	10	11	12	13	14	15	16	17	18	
Detroit	0	0	0	0	0	0	0	0	0	0	0	0	0	0	0	0	0	0	—0
Prov'ce	0	0	0	0	0	0	0	0	0	0	0	0	0	0	0	0	0	1	—1

Earned runs—Providence, 1.
Home run—Radbourne.
Three-base hit—Wright.
Two-base hits—Bennett, Weidman.
First base on errors—Detroit, 2; Providence, 2.
First base on called balls—Knight.
Passed balls—Trott, 1; Nava, 1.
Struck out—Detroit, 3; Providence, 5.
Muffed fly—Bennett.
Muffed thrown balls—Foster, 2; Powell, Start.
Wild throws—Bennett, Trott, Nava, Wright, Denny.
Umpire—Bradley.
Attendance—1,118.

SARATOGA, August 17.—First race, one mile, Baron Favrot first, Col. Sprague second, Pride third. Time, 1:57½.

Second race, two miles, Eole first, Gen. Monroe second, Granger third. Time, 3:32½.

Third race, five furlongs, Empress first, Tarantella second, Toeda third. Time, 1:06.

Fourth race, three-quarters of a mile, Amazon first, Gus Matthews second, Baby third. Time, 1:17¼.

MONMOUTH PARK RACES.

MONMOUTH PARK, August 17.—The track was very [...]quarters of a mile, [...]no, Neufchatel third.

[...]e race Buckstone won, [...]l. Time, 1:21.

[...]s race Laura Glass [...]azon third. Time, [...]

[...]dles race Checkmate [...] Priam third. Time, [...]

[...]iles race Keno won, [...]hird. Time, 2:19¾.

[...] won, Ninus second.

[...]lle hurdle Guy won, [...]27¾.

[...]ACES.

[...]he unfinished pacing [...]ere made yesterday) [...]na, Lucy third, Buf-[...]

[...] 1 1 1
[...] 3 2 2
[...] 2 4 4
[...] 4 3 3
[...] 5 5 5

[...] 1 2 0 5
[...] 2 4 3 1
[...] 3 5 4 2
[...] 5 3 5 3
[...] 4 1 0 4
[...] 6 6 dr.

[...]ARE RACES.

[...]'s Fireman's Conven[...] [...]dance at the Driving [...]l races as follows:

[...] 1 4 1 1
[...] 2 1 2 2
[...] 3 2 4 3
[...] 4 3 3 4

[...] 3 1 1 1
[...] 1 2 2 2
[...] 2 3 3 3
[...] dr

[...]ACES.

[...]one and one-eighth [...]on, Carolus second, [...]1¾.

[...]e race Tonawanda [...]d..un third. Time, [...]

[...]le race Monk won, [...] Time, 2:02¾.

[...]ecer won, Black Gal [...]l. 2:01¾.

[...]ce race, five hurdles, [...]lde second, Smooth-[...]

[...] DROWNED.

[...]st 17.—The trotting [...]ovan, was drowned [...]gh a covered well. [...]other of $4,000 for the [...]

[...]OURNAMENT AT DAY-[...]

[...] State Archery Field [...] the Soldiers' Home, [...]d continuing three [...]e larger than at any [...]e of the association. [...]dhed within the last [...]are now some twelve [...]o in Kentucky, a [...]l and vicinity. The [...]out the same grounds [...]wn overlooking this [...]eautiful scenery be[...] [...]e city and is consid[...] [...]tournament in the [...]or the meeting have [...] is now in readiness

[...]T AT CRESTLINE, O.

[...] Potter and Scott, two [...]espectively as the Lit[...] [...]lay, according to the [...]rovec rules. Potter [...] the fourth round and [...]cored man in Ohio to [...]n. Two other hard [...]st too: place. The [...]

[...]er.

[...]APLE MATCH.

[...] John Bodine, the [...] captain of the Amer[...] [...]premacy with the [...]will be organized to-[...]

[...]igeon.

[...]TROIT TO TORONTO.

[...]ming pigeon owned [...]istance from Detroit [...] than five hours.

[...]M VS. SYRACUSE.

[...]st inning—Western [...]use, 55. Second in[...] [...] two wickets down.

[...]d Pillows.

[...]without exception, [...]—so much so that [...] to deviate an inch [...] position finds him-[...]

[...]cots, etc., are made [...]never wide enough [...]down but an inch or [...]ress, and it requires [...]ue of an acrobat, [...]r, to keep the bed-[...] [...]r him. And then [...] the pillows, which [...] large or too small. [...]at the only people [...]omfortable pillows, [...]re the Americans. [...]arding-houses here [...] which is about half [...] stuffed out so hard [...]y benefit the tired [...] have it serve as a [...]e sleeps in a sitting [...]

[...] however, found in [...] shaped, of the same [...] and come to a point [...]d. On these, the [...]ts on an inclined [...]ody on one of the [...]ue at Paris with a [...]k it would be dif-[...] [...]country that would [...] or six feet at most [...]t board, and as for [...]t probably none in [...]ee the one I saw [...]n, which is said to [...]gy or Baron of olden [...]ican.

[...]atched Team.

[...]t Saratoga writes: [...] myself away from [...]other horses. First [...]ous beast, who eyed [...]ed all my advances [...] this animal resem-[...] [...]editor, being a cold [...]h an icy smile and [...]ently has no time [...]tillers need apply. [...] horse, 'Lysander's' [...] really forget, [...]rbilt's permission [...]lain.' Well, 'Ab-[...] [...]ch by his flippancy [...]ar. As soon as he [...]uality of an intro-[...] [...]y pitch and toss [...]tied and left him to [...]orses for Mrs. Van-[...] [...] shown. One of them, having plebeian fondness for straw in his stall and a disposition to paw and dash it around, was in disgrace, with his meddlesome nose fastened to an iron ring, where he had to remain for an hour or two until he was thought to be sufficiently punished. I could not leave without another look at the 'Bride of the Wind,' and she asked me to come again as plainly and intelligently as if she had the gift of speech."

MICHIGAN.

Barry County Democratic Convention.

Special Dispatch to The Detroit Free Press.

HASTINGS, August 19.—The Democratic Convention to-day appointed the following delegates:

To the State Convention—H. A. Goodyear, M. H. Clark, E. C. Elliott, Ira Bachelliar, Thos. Mulvaney, W. S. Goodyear, Norman Bailey, John Lattimer, N. F. Clements, Jas. Loucks, Jesse Jordan, M. W. Riker.

Congressional delegates—M. H. Clark, Geo. W. Ingram, O. Rowbeck, John Barry, Thos. McElwain, David G. Robinson, C. W. Crothers, H. F. Peckham, Chas. Murphy, I. B. Hanna, E. Parker, V. Ostroth, L. Hilbert, P. M. Hide.

There was no expression on the subject of a fusion State ticket.

Eaton County Republican Convention.

Special Dispatch to The Detroit Free Press.

CHARLOTTE, August 19.—The Eaton County Republican County Convention, held here to-day, elected delegates to the State and Congressional Conventions, adopted resolutions of commendation of Ferry's services and deprecating Hubbell's recent actions, and favored the submission of a prohibitory constitutional amendment to the people. The delegation is solid for Congressman Lacey.

Barry County Greenback Convention.

Special Dispatch to The Detroit Free Press.

HASTINGS, August 19.—The Greenbackers held a convention here to-day and appointed twenty-four delegates to the State Convention, with John H. Dennis Chairman; also, twenty-four delegates to the Congressional Convention, with John Dawson Chairman.

Marshall Raises a $10,000 Bonus to Secure Agricultural Works.

Special Dispatch to The Detroit Free Press.

MARSHALL, August 19.—The citizens of Marshall to-day subscribed $10,000 bonus to the Williams Agricultural Works, referred to previously, which secures the location of these extensive works here.

The Monroe County Republican Convention.

The Republican County Convention, held at Monroe Saturday, chose the following delegates:

STATE CONVENTION.

First District—R. E. Phinney, city; Joseph Rean, Erie; John Bianch, La Salle; Burton Parker, city; H. C. McLachlin, Summerfield; C. Schmelzer, city.

Second District—W. A. French, Dundee; M. J. Howe, Milan; John F. Colburn, Berlin; Henry Austin, Frenchtown; Alfred Wilkerson, Dundee; Lorenzo F. Rogers, Bedford; Daniel Devee, Landon.

CONGRESSIONAL.

First District—H. A. Conant, J. D. Ronan and George Spalding, city; John Weeman, Erie; J. J. Sumner and J. R. Rogers, Bedford; R. R. Kirby, Summerfield.

Second District—S. C. Randall, Dundee; John Jackson, Jr., Berlin; William Stewart, Exeter; George W. Doty, Raisinville; N. N. Dusten, Dundee; John L. Hunter, Raisinville; Albert Band, Landon.

A County Committee of three was elected, with an auxiliary committee consisting of one member from each ward and township.

The high-handed manner in which the Washtenaw County Republican Convention was run was frequently alluded to in any but commendatory terms, and though the Monroe County Convention was not entirely free from such features, the following very vague resolution, offered by Gen. Spalding, was unanimously adopted:

Resolved, That it is the best sense of this convention that district representation is now one of the tenets of the Republican party, and that no general convention is authorized to override their express will.

The committee for that purpose now produced Congressman Willits before the convention, and he was received with a feeble demonstration of applause. He said he had labored hard during the past nine months—had written 3,000 letters. He had endeavored to answer every letter written him, and if he had forgotten some, as he probably had, he commended himself to the charity of the writers. He may have cast some votes in Congress with which the convention could not agree, but he had a conscience. He had sometimes voted under heavy pressure and trusted his mistakes, if he had made any, were forgiven. Whether or not he be renominated, he pledged his support to the nominee of the convention.

Eaton County Greenback Convention.

The Greenback County Convention for Eaton County was held at Charlotte, Friday, August 18. Delegates to the State Convention, to be held at Grand Rapids, August 23, were chosen as follows: Henry A. Shaw, H. L. Dewey, A. M. Gillette, J. W. Ewing, S. M. Mayer, C. G. Bate, Joseph Shaw, C. S. Torrey, H. J. Hart, W. H. King, A. E. Ellis.

The following were elected delegates to the Congressional Convention at Albion: Fred. Spicer, Caleb Woo pert, J. G. Estelle, B. Bartlette, Daniel Space, C. E. Ells, I. M. Strong, H. A. Hunsiker, P. Whaley, N. G. Watson, G. W. Irish.

The delegates were instructed to favor a plank in the platform of the State Convention submitting the question of temperance to a vote of the people.

A motion to instruct the delegates to favor a combination, provided they were not compelled to sacrifice Greenback principles, was tabled.

Calhoun County Democratic Convention.

At the Calhoun County Democratic Convention, held at Marshall Friday, the following delegates were elected to attend the State Convention: Wm. H. Porter, Marshall City; Albert Collins, Homer; Devillo Hubbard, Marshall Township; A. P. Gardner, Albion; Milo Soule, Marengo; E. V. B. Hyde, Fredonia; G. Ballentine, Clarendon; Hiram Albertson, Eckford; Adam Krenrick, Clarence; J. L. Whitcomb, Battle Creek; Thos. Huffman, Emmet; W. W. Woolnough, Battle Creek; Jonathan Johnson, Emmet; J. M. Caldwell, Wm. Andrus, W. W. Noble, C. E. Thomas, F. M. Rathbun, Battle Creek.

The following delegates were selected to attend the Congressional Convention: L. T. Vanharn, Homer; D. Hubbard, Marshall; H. N. McCormick, Marengo; Geo. W. Briggs, Fredonia; S. S. Lacey, Marshall; James Graves, Albion; T. W. Robertson, Fred. Stebbins, James L. Whitcomb, D. D. Ford, Eli Flagg and Henry Elbertson.

Calhoun County Republican Convention.

At the Republican County Convention held at Marshall Friday, the following delegates were selected to attend the State Conventin: Martin Haven, Rieng Loud, Charles T. Gorham, W. J. Gregg, Solon Robinson, Wm. Cook, C. S. Hamilton, H. Merril, Lewis Townsend, H. H. Hubbard, T. W. Hall, V. P. Collier, W. D. Baker, A. Minges, John Patchen, J. E. Conklin, R. Sanderson, N. J. Kelsey. To the Congressional Convention: Wm. Gibson, Wm. Howard, A. O. Hyde, Jerome Townsend, Curran Bentley, S. A. Flint, John Brown, Dr. Shortliff, E. Twiss, E. C. Nicols, Orson Nicols, Earl Smith, Richard Keeler, James Walkinshaw, G. S. French.

Resolutions were adopted indorsing Senator T. W. Ferry and Representative E. S. Lacey.

Albion.

Harvey Hall was taken in charge Saturday by United States officers and conveyed to Detroit to appear before a commissioner to answer for pension frauds. There are three charges against him. A commissioner was in Albion last Wednesday taking testimony, and the officers arrived Friday night, proceeding to his house, a few miles from Albion, Saturday morning. At the same time, Hall is under bonds to appear before a Justice for resisting an officer, also to the Circuit Court on an appeal from the conviction and sentence on a charge of assault and battery.

Thrashing has commenced in the vicinity of Albion, and those farmers fortunate enough to have their crops secured are blessed with a heavy yield.

Ann Arbor.

Miss Clara L. Conover, principal of the Grammar School of Ann Arbor, and reappointed for the coming school year, has resigned. Miss Marian Brown, principal of the Third Ward School, has followed Miss Conover's example. Vacancies not yet filled.

The Township Board of Ann Arbor Township was in session on Saturday afternoon, considering a petition for a new bridge across the Huron, on the Whitmore Lake road, known as the McMahon bridge. A township meeting will probably be called.

Farwell.

The suits commenced at Farwell by Henry Spring against Sylvester Ross, for criminal assault and civil damages, have been settled without being brought to trial.

Diphtheria has made its appearance in Farwell again, two children of Chas. Briggs and one of T. Arnold being down with the disease and very low.

The Raintall at Grand Rapids.

Since the 1st day of April, 18.63 inches of rain have fallen at Grand Rapids, as against 10.40 during the same period of last year. In April of the present year the fall was 1.44; May, 3.56; June, 6.16; July, 1.42; August (up to and including the 18th), 6.05.

Constantine.

H. H. Riley leaves Constantine for Traverse City next Tuesday to meet the Board of Commissioners of the Northern Asylum for the Insane.

TELLING A STORY.

They were sitting on the veranda after tea, when the man with a story began to tell it.

"By the way," he said, "I heard a good thing in town to-day."

"Was it very warm in town?" asked the woman who stays at home.

He assured her that it was, and then continued:

"I met Jack Rollins—"

"What, little Jack!" exclaimed the old gentleman. "Why, I remember when Jack's father first come to Huckleberryville, long 'fore he married Hulda—she was a Smith, you know, ole Billy Smith's darter. Ole Billy was a curus chap. Did I ever tell yer 'bout that scrape him and me got inter in ther winter of thirty five—no, 'twas thirty-four—yes —no— Well I disremember zactly wich, but anyhow, Billy and me, we—"

"Yes, yes; we know all about it, Uncle Ben," said the man with a story. "As I was saying, I met Jack Rollins, and he and I thought we'd go down on the beach and have a swim—"

"You are getting on swimmingly now," observed the retailer of second-hand puns.

"Well, as I was saying," resumed the man with a story, "Jack and I went down to the beach, and—"

"You had a nice bath," said the woman who interrupts.

"No, I didn't," sharply answered the man with a story; "you see, the tide—"

"Oh, that reminds me of a funny thing that happened to a lot of us fellows when we were in the army!" exclaimed the war veteran. "It was just after the second Bull Run, and the major—"

The war veteran was reminded of a "funny thing" invariably seven evenings a week, and, though he always told it from beginning to end, nobody ever listened to it. It is not necessary, therefore, to repeat it.

After he had finished, however, the man with a story began again:

"The tide, you see, was way out, and Jack said that we might as well go up to the hotel—"

"Oh, tell us!" again interrupted the retailer of second-class puns.

The man with a story frowned on the punster and continued:

"Go up to the hotel and see who was there. Charley Sprague—"

"Is Charley one o' Squire Sprague's boys?" queried the old gentleman. "The squire and me—"

"No, Charley isn't one of the squire's boys, Uncle Ben," was the rather peevish rejoinder of the man with a story. "Charley—"

"Do you remember what a time we had that night, it rained so?" suddenly asked the young lady with the erratic mind.

"It's awful dry," remarked the amateur agriculturist; "if we don't have rain soon, I guess my potatoes won't amount to much."

"What a horrid dress that Boston woman had on, to-day!" said the young lady in the rocking-chair.

"We had a bully time on the river, to-day," interjected the boy in the flannel shirt.

"Shall you go to the mountains before you return?" asked the young gentleman who was doing the agreeable to the young lady with the low forehead.

The man with a story saw it was no use. So he gave it up in despair and walked sadly away, leaving the others to chat at their own sweet will.

But, mark you, he will tell that story to every one of them separately, and, probably, two or three times to most of them. They will come to the conclusion finally, that it would have been much better for them to let the man with a story tell it at once and have done with it.—[Boston Transcript.

The Wine of the Comet Year.

It has always been a favorite theory among the wine-growers of the Rhine that the wine produced during the year of a comet visitation is perceptibly improved in quality and enhanced in value. The wine of such years is called "comet" wine, the years are "comet" years, and the celestial visitor has been honored in having his title recorded and recited. This is a "comet" year, but for once the wine-growers of France and Germany are doomed to disappointment. Late advices from the Rhine vineyards state that the grape harvest will by no means be an average one, and that beer will have to continue the substitute for wine for another year at least.

The Irish Constabulary.

The Irish constabulary, which has just been in semi-mutiny, and on which the preservation of law in Ireland depends, was created in 1814, and was borne equally by the counties and the consolidated fund. In 1846 the whole expense was undertaken by government, and the force made semi-military. It consists of an inspector general, a deputy inspector general, three assistant inspector generals, thirty-five county inspectors, 199 sub-inspectors, 232 head constables and 10,787 constables, acting constables and sub-constables, making a total of 11,255.

An Improvement.

"You have a beautiful residence there," remarked a White Plains man to one of his neighbors just coming out from a handsome, well-trimmed lawn surrounding a snug cottage. "How happy you must be."

"Think so?"

"I do, truly."

"There are one or two little things I'd have altered if I could get time."

"Why, that would be impossible. What would you suggest?"

"Well, in the first place I'd get my mother-in-law's name out of the body of the deed as grantee if I could find time. But I'm terribly rushed just now, and don't see how I'm going to get around it."—[Texas Oddities.

Opera in London.

The Italian opera in London begins at 8:30 o'clock. The price for the best seat, "orchestra stalls," is $6 25; for seats in the balcony, $3 75, and for seats in the highest gallery, sixty-five cents. The prices for the other seats are according to location, $2 60, $1 75 and $1 25.

The Eastern Trouble.

The Hebrew Leader says: "The whole Eastern trouble centers in the persecuted Jew, and it lies back of all the trouble in Europe. The cowardice of the nations in not compelling the provisions of the treaty of Berlin to be carried out by Russia and other Eastern powers will probably in the end involve all Europe in war."

Hank Monk.

Horace Greeley's famous stage-driver, Hank Monk, is now employed on the proposed line of the Northern Pacific, in Montana. A particularly bold but inexperienced road agent undertook to stop his coach the other day, but Hank whipped up his horses and dashed off with five bullets flying after him, one of which struck a horse. The animal did not, however, break down till the stage reached a freighters' camp.

LOST IN THE WOODS.

The Wonderful Story of an Eight Days' Hunt for and Rescue of Four Children Lost in the Wilderness of the Keweenaw Peninsula of Michigan.

A correspondent of the Boston Post writing from Calumet, Lake Superior, Mich., tells the following thrilling story of the modern Babes in the Wood:

I have a wonderful story to tell you, and so strange, yet true in every detail, that I find it difficult to repeat aright. On Friday morning, July 21, 1882, four little children, living at the Allouez mine (which is four miles from the Calumet & Hecla mine), started out with pails and baskets to pick berries. They wandered along the highway for about a quarter of a mile and then turned on to a new road, which leads through the thick woods to the new mine called the Wolverine. All went well until the youngest, a mite of a girl and very small for her age, being but 7 years old, complained of being tired and wanted to go home. Then for the first time in their efforts to retrace their steps they discovered they had strayed from the path and were lost in the thick woods, where in many places the trees are but a foot apart and the underbrush grows as high as five feet. Vainly they sought the right path, till nightfall closed around them—then, bruised and scratched by the bushes, with head, face and limbs bitten and badly swollen by the nip of the wicked black fly, the two oldest children (belonging to the Finn settlement, beyond the Allouez proper), tired and frightened, laid down and cried themselves to sleep and were found by anxious searchers the following day in a woeful condition. When these children were asked for their little companions they replied: "We begged them to stay with us, but the boy said he would go and find the way to the road and then come back for us, but his little sister would not stay without him, so he took her with him," and they pointed the way they had gone. In that direction lay an old mine, deserted years ago, called the Fulton, so in that locality searched a party of men all day, aided by the half-crazed Norwegian father and Finn mother of the lost little ones, and all day the whistles of the Allouez and Wolverine mines blew at intervals of ten minutes to guide them to the settlements. Saturday night came and no children were found. The weary mother must return to her babe. The men were discouraged, but the father, with a few men, returned to the woods, and spent the night in a fruitless search. Sunday, riding to the Allouez, we found the road full of Swedes, Norwegians, Finns, with all other nationalities we have with us well represented, while large parties were in the woods, and the whistles blew all day. Monday came and the Calumet & Hecla joined in the search, sending out about 400 men. Toward night a little footprint was discovered, and a piece of the little girl's dress, but so late that they could be traced little further that night. Tuesday more men were sent and success was thought to be certain, but alas! no children were found. The day was for us in this latitude intensely hot. At evening the sky was full of dense black clouds and at 8 o'clock the lightning began to flash. The sky seemed full of flames and fire. The thunder was awful—never before do I remember such a rainfall and tempest as raged for nearly four hours while the rest of the night and succeeding day was sultry, with drizzling rain, and Wednesday night another tempest. Still the search continued. No hope was now felt by parents or friends that the little ones would be found alive, after the starvation and exposure, together with the fright of so many days in these pathless woods, where grown people become wild in so short a time; still not a humane person could think of the agonized parents and not desire to help them find the little bodies. So every day the shouts of 600 men or more were making the woods alive. Friday morning—one week from the children's disappearance—came, and the Calumet & Hecla mine was closed and the whole force together with the Allouez men were stationed along the road front, five feet apart, with orders to break through the woods in that line as best they could, to search every hollow stump, to remove underbrush, to examine holes and make sure of leaving no spot unexplored, and yet night brought nearly every man back with no trace of the children, and many ridiculous stories were told or surmised as to their fate, while the father and mother were crazed with grief and horror. Some of the men stayed all night at their almost hopeless task, and some—a party of four Swedes—were themselves lost, and here is their wonderful story:

"At 3 o'clock Friday afternoon we sat down by a brook to rest. We were tired and bewildered and shouted loudly for our companions to come to us, when from a heap of bushes came a boy, saying: 'Where are you? Who is it?' We, thinking he belonged to some party of searchers, asked: 'Who are you with?' His answer came, 'My sister.' Up we sprang to our feet, and knew, even in the midst of our amazement, that the lost children were found and alive, and in their right senses, although they had been alone in the dismal wood, amidst lightning and tempest, for eight days, with nothing to eat but berries. And this boy of but 9 years had built huts of brush to cover them at night, had gathered and loaded both himself and sister with great bunches of blueberries where they were to be found, and was trying to follow the tortuous course of the brook, which, he remembered, emptied into Torch Lake. He was still brave. We gave them small pieces of bread at intervals during the afternoon and night, as we walked in or by the sides of the stream as best we could with our joyful burden, or lay down for a little needed rest, each two men with a child between them to give warmth to the little chilled frame."

Saturday morning I sat at my window, about 7:30 o'clock, with my little girl in my lap, when some one in the street shouted to me, "They are found, they are found." I threw up the sash and a party of men were right in front of the house. They had the children with them. I trembled with excitement and called my Swede girl to talk to them. I could not make them understand. They refused food and drink, which she proffered in their language, saying they had just fed them and did not dare to give them more. Both children's eyes looked wild and rolled restlessly, as they clung tightly to the necks of their rescuers; their bodies seemed covered with bruises and the little feet were badly blistered; they were being taken to the hospital for examination. Meanwhile the news spread. Men, women and children rapidly filled the streets, while the wagon-loads of men that had already started for the woods were recalled. The excitement for awhile was intense. I thought surely now the children will die of fright, with the crowds of shouting people about them, but they behaved bravely. Mr. G. telegraphed the Allouez of their safety and Mr. D. (the Assistant Superintendent of the mine and a man with a wonderfully good, kind heart for suffering humanity) rode with headlong speed to tell the parents. The mother wildly clung to him and fainted away, while the father, who has spent every day and part of every night in the woods, was nearly overcome. They were overjoyed, the hope of ever seeing them alive had left them; they for a long time could not seem to realize the great mercy shown them. To-day the force started prepared to stay two days or more if necessary, but happily the search is ended, and when Mr. G. went to the house this afternoon their water-soaked boots had been cut from them, their blistered feet and torn limbs bathed in oil, they had been put to bed and were eating soup, which is allowed them once in two hours.

THE DEMOCRATIC CANDI

There are three points of coincide
selection of the Democratic candidate
ernor and Lieutenant-Governor of th
New York—both men are bachelors
lawyers, and both Mayors.

Grover Cleveland, the nominee for
was born in Caldwell, New Jersey,
1837. After finishing his education a
ton Academy, in Oneida County, New
took a clerkship in this city, but soon
went to Buffalo and studied law, and
ted to the bar. For three years he wa
District Attorney of Erie County, and i
elected Sheriff. Last year he was ele
of Buffalo. He has a large frame, a n
phatic temperament, light complexion
brown hair, with a tendency to baldne
a bachelor, and a man of considerable

The candidate for Lieutenant-Gover
Bennett Hill, is six years younger tha
ciate on the ticket, having been born
He is a native of Havana, then in
County, and his ancestors were New-E
He was educated in the Havana schools
to Elmira in 1862, where he was admi
bar two years later. He was elected
sembly in 1870, and re-elected in 1871
an Alderman for one term, until last sp
he was chosen Mayor of Elmira.

"SOMEBODY BLUNDER

The terrible railroad crash in the tu
of the New York Grand Central Dé
22d of September, by which several
lost and many persons seriously in
clearly the result of official carelessnes
cident to the Montreal express at On
and-twenty-sixth Street early in the mo
blocked the main track, and all the d
following were sent through the we
This occasioned an unusual crowd on t
so that the Portchester train on reac
hundred-and-twenty-sixth Street was
proceed very slowly, and to wait on e
until the block ahead was clear. It w
halted at Eighty-sixth Street, in the da
side tunnel, and immediately afterwa
run into by a Harlem train, which, either through the neglect of a signal-man or through the engineer's neglect of the signals, had been allowed to rush at full speed into the block on which the Portchester train had been halted. The engine of the Harlem train tore through the rear car of the other, literally splitting it open, and rending it to pieces.

The catastrophe was terrible. The car was filled with passengers, many of them pupils of New York schools. They were flung on each side of the track, with the fragments of the car. All the lights had been extinguished by the shock. The air was heavy with steam and smoke. The entire breadth of the tunnel was filled with the wreck of the passenger-car. The engine had gone so far through it that the front of the boiler was within two or three feet of the front of the car. The car was split in two so that the sides fell apart, almost unbroken, against the walls of the tunnel. The smoke-stack, sand-box, and cab of the engine were torn off by the roof of the car, and were jammed in between the tender and the top of the tunnel. The broken seats and flooring of the car were packed around the driving-wheels of the battered locomotive. In this débris, and under the sides of the
the gutters beside the track, were wedged
a score of wounded passengers. The
escaping from the broken boiler badly
some of them.

stance came promptly. Detachments of
nd firemen were soon on the spot, groping
aid of lanterns among the fragments of
in for the dead and wounded passengers.
ene was awful. Providentially, the hor-
fire were not added to the fearful details
wreck. Had the train burned, as in the
the collision at Spuyten Duyvil Creek, few
rhaps none of the wounded passengers
have escaped.

sorrowful details of this awful catastrophe
ot be repeated here. That it was due to
sness admits of no doubt. There are block
at Fifty-ninth, Seventy-second, Eighty-
Ninety-eighth, One-hundred-and-tenth, One-
d-and-twenty-fifth, and One-hundred-and-
ighth streets, and at Mott Haven. These
are all under the control of the man who
his lofty office in the north end of the
Central Dépôt. They have also telegraph-
munication with each other, as well as a
of communication by automatic electric
When, for instance, a train has passed
ast the signal-man at Ninety-eighth Street,
t display a signal to stop the next train
g until the block between Ninety-eighth
ghty-sixth streets is clear. When the first
asses the man at Eighty-sixth Street, he,
lectric button, must raise the danger tar-
Ninety-eighth Street, to signify that the
clear. Meantime, the first train having
down from Eighty-sixth Street, the block
s displayed there until it is released by
nal-man at Seventy-second Street upon the
of the train there.

terrible blunder in this case appears to lie
n the two stations at Eighty-sixth and
eighth streets. If the engineer of the
train was allowed to pass the Ninety-
Street signal before the preceding train
ssed Eighty-sixth Street, he could hardly
ected, in the darkness of the tunnel and
n the blinding smoke which always hangs
air there, to distinguish red lights on the
the train ahead. If it be true, as report-
on the day of the collision the block sys-
d been practically abandoned during the
continuance of the temporary blockade in the single-track down-town tunnel, and that the trains were allowed to follow one another down closely, with the idea that they would run cautiously and keep in sight of each other, a fearful responsibility rests upon the officials who sanctioned that abandonment.

It rests with the authorities to fix the blame on those who are responsible for this disaster. There should be no delay; the investigation should be most thorough and searching, and the persons on whom the guilt rests should receive speedy and severe punishment.

THE PROVIDENCE BASE-BALL CLUB.

Foremost among the League clubs is the Providence Base-ball Club of Providence, Rhode Island, the "Grays," as they generally term themselves, whose portraits are given on page 621. This club was formed in 1878, won the League championship the following year, and has run the closest kind of a race with the Chicago Club for the same honor this year. During the early part of the season, and until the middle of the present month, the Providence men headed the list of League clubs, and were deemed certain winners of the pennant of 1882; but three brilliant victories scored by the Chicago team week before last placed the two clubs side by side, each having then won forty-nine of their eighty-four games.

The membership of the Providence Club is as follows: Henry B. Winship, president; Harry Wright, manager; Charles Radbourn and J. M. Ward, pitchers and right fielders; B. Gilligan and A. Nava, catchers; Joseph Start, first-base man; John Farrell, second-base man; Jeremiah Denny, third-base man; Thomas York, left fielder; Paul A. Hines, centre fielder; and George Wright, short stop.

Of this strong team the last mentioned, George Wright, is probably the best known and most brilliant player. He is a man thirty-five years of age, and has been a base-ball player for the past twenty years. Born in Harlem, he played with many of the amateur clubs of this city and vicinity from 1862 until 1867, when he joined the Nationals of Washington. In 1869 he played with the Cincinnati Red Stockings, and shared with them the victories of that famous season. In 1871 he joined the Boston Club, and remained with them until 1879, when he joined the Providence Club, with which he has since been identified.

Mr. Harry Wright, brother of George, has devoted himself to the management of base-ball clubs rather than to active work in the field, and has met with such signal success in this department that his name is almost uniformly associated with victory and championship pennants. For ten seasons he managed the Boston Club, and before that the Cincinnatti Red Stockings.

Of the two pitchers "Johnny" Ward is one of the most puzzling in the business, and has been with the Providence Club from their first season. Radbourn, who is also a capital man in the place, has just finished his second season with this team.

Nava won an enviable reputation on the Pacific coast as a catcher before he was invited, at the opening of the present season, to join this club. His alternate, Gilligan, has shown himself to be a good man by serving for two seasons in his present position.

In the field are three men who have maintained their respective positions since the formation of the club—John Ward, who acts as right fielder when not pitching, Thomas York, who is a Brooklyn man, and Paul A. Hines, who was one of the crack players of the Chicago nine from 1874 until 1878.

Joseph Start is another Brooklynite, and began playing in 1862 with the Atlantics. For twenty years he has been first-base man, and always of a crack club. He is known as "Old Reliable," and well deserves the sobriquet.

John Farrell, second-base man, is one of the best general players of the club, and has, during his comparatively short career of seven years, furnished some wonderful examples of fine play.

Jeremiah Denny, like Nava, is better known on the Pacific coast than in the East, but is rapidly gaining a fine reputation as a third-base man.

Thomas York. Paul A. Hines. Charles Reilly. Joseph Start. Jeremiah Denny. Vincent Nava. Manager Harry Wright. Charles Radbourn. Bernard Gilligan. George Wright. John Farrell. J. M. Ward.

THE PROVIDENCE BASE-BALL CLUB.—From a Photograph by the Photo-Mechanical Printing and Publishing Company, Chicago.—[See Page 619.]

The Providence Daily Journal.

VOLUME LXIX. NO. 256. PROVIDENCE, R. I., FRIDAY, OCTOBER 24, 1884. PRICE THREE CENTS.

PROVIDENCE JOURNAL.

PUBLISHED BY
KNOWLES, ANTHONY & DANIELSON.
Office No. 2 Weybosset street.

DAILY JOURNAL (Morning) $8 00 per annum.
MANUFACTURERS AND FARMERS JOURNAL (Mondays and Thursdays), $3 50 in advance, or $4 at the end of the year.
RHODE ISLAND COUNTRY JOURNAL (Fridays), $2 00 in advance, or $2 50 at the end of the year.
THE EVENING BULLETIN (every secular afternoon), $6 00 per annum.
☞ Postage free to all mail subscribers whose payment of subscription is made in advance.
☞ Advertisements of five lines or less in either paper, 50 cents for the first insertion and 15 cents for each subsequent insertion in each paper. One square, ten lines, $1 for the first insertion and 25 cents for each subsequent insertion in one paper; one-half additional if published in both papers. Transient advertisements are invariably payable in advance.

DAILY JOURNAL.

FRIDAY, OC

"THE OLD SOU

A Ringing Spe
at Terr

The South Befo
Vividly

Short Stops at Sull
tle, Crawfords

TERRE HAUTE,
Evansville at 8:30
stop was at Sullivan
there were about tw
bled. Mr. Blaine
was received in the
ner.
At Terre Haute
stration. As the tra
steam whistles in
locomotives sounde
reached the depot,
Blaine with wild che
by the reception c
Mayor and local a
procession through t
an hour.
Upon returning to
following speech: "
for years it has been
cipitated into this ca
and to neglect to no
look one of the most
factors in the nati
stand that question
membered that th
Souths, which we m
new South and the o
represents that awa
which is striking fo
ment of that natu
Union, which recog
protection, which c
of the civil conflict b
fully struggling in V
lina, in Tennessee a
late confederacy.
many men who se
armies. It naturall
publican party, and
ple away from the p
the contemplation
which wise and m
bring to the South in
The old South repre
lion and cherishes s
content; is perpetua
the rightfulness of t
bitter reproaches
umphed in the war
suffrage with abho
"white line," an
whatever amount
violence may becom
its own political and
South. It is unques
the old slave States,
party in the North
fourths of the effect
in the nation and in
triumph would be in
control of the gover
the Republicans is
provement and prog
as of the North,
everywhere and r
a determined an
Southern Democra
Democratic party,
said, is to conjoin th
York and Indiana
the sixteen Souther
York and Indiana to
means and where it
York has a greater a
of the Union in ma
of government, in
credit, in perpetua
which embodies the
past twenty years
policy. Indiana has
New York only, as h
are less. The citiz
fully comprehend
national credits, th
national pensioning
and the great
the control of th
to the old South w
reconciled temper,
its hostility to all N
stant longing to revi
absolute incapacity
magnitude of our gr
ing.] The North an
lican administration
ultimately come in
In the last ten years
made towards that,
may witness the effa
and the absolute
nanimous policies. [
all prospect of the
and destroyed by gi
sion of the national
of the baleful effects
be the crushing out
the South, and the p
that has been gain
laws which followed
ple of New York an
are now asked to aid
deplorable result, to
donment or reversal
industrial policies u
prospered so marvel
the war. [Cries of
don't, I cannot belie
cause such a course
stinct of patriotism,
sideration of en
[Cheers.]
At Brazil, in the I
trict, there was a
largely of miners.
speech on the tariff,
received, and when
that his auditors we
gested that those wh
trade ought to vote v
there were loud s
"never," "we are do
At Greencastle th
meeting, where Mr.
ally as he had spoke
At Crawfordsville
in the course which
character of Henry
there.
It was almost dark
at Lafayette. Here
by a large crowd.
stand, where he made a speech similar to the one at Terre Haute. He was then driven to the house of Gen. Geo. B. Williams, where he dined and will spend the night. In the evening he reviewed a large torchlight procession. To-morrow he goes to Springfield, Ill.

THE NATIONAL CAMPAIGN.

CIRCULAR LETTER FROM CHAIRMAN JONES.

FUNDS FOR LEGITIMATE EXPENSES ASKED FOR.

NEW YORK, Oct. 23.—The following circular letter has been issued from the headquarters of the Republican National Committee:

NEW YORK CITY, Oct. 22.

Dear Sir—The closing struggle for the continued ascendancy of those principles of government and policy of which the Republican party is the exponent, and under which this country has prospered so marvelously, is before us. It promises to be a severe one, demanding not only the most earnest and intelligent effort of all who believe that these principles are essential to our highest prosperity, but requiring, also, prompt and liberal contributions from all who desire

BATTLE OF THE GIANTS.

Providence vs. Metropolitans for the Championship of America.

Radbourn's Curves Enigmas to the New Yorkers.

The American Association Leaders Completely Shut Out.

Providence, 6; Metropolitan, 0.

NEW YORK, Oct. 23.—The Providence League champions and the Metropolitans, of this city, the champions of the American Association, played the first of a series of games for the championship of the United States, at the Polo grounds to-day. Great interest was felt in the contest, and over 2500 persons assembled to witness the game. The disagreeable weather was the means of keeping away probably three times the number present. A cold, raw wind blew across the grounds with considerable force, and made even the players shiver at times, and prevented any fine play. This was particularly the case with the home nine, who played far below the usual standard. Keefe pitched a miserable game, occasionally seeming to lose all command of the ball. Radbourn pitched in fine form, as usual. His curves were enigmas to those who faced him. Frequently the wind blew so that it was almost impossible to judge a high ball. In the first inning Providence took the lead, Hines and Farrell getting safe hits and scoring on wild pitches and passed balls. In the third inning Hines made a safe hit, went to second on a passed ball, and scored on two wild pitches. In the seventh inning Keefe was batted hard. Two base hits by Farrell and Gilligan, a three-bagger by Irwin, and a single by Denny gave the Providence nine, three earned runs. The full score was as follows:

PROVIDENCE.

	AB.	R.	1B.	TB.	PO.	A.	E.
Hines, c. f.	4	2	1	1	1	0	0
Carroll, l. f.	4	1	0	0	1	0	0
Radbourn p.	4	0	0	0	0	1	0
Start, 1b.	4	0	0	0	13	0	0
Farrell, 2b.	3	1	1	2	2	2	0
Irwin, s. s.	3	1	1	3	0	4	1
Gilligan, c.	3	1	1	2	8	2	0
Denny, 3b.	3	0	1	1	0	2	1
Radford, r. f.	3	0	0	0	2	0	1
Totals	31	6	5	9	27	11	3

METROPOLITAN.

	AB.	R.	1B.	TB.	PO.	A.	E.
Nelson, s. s.	4	0	0	0	2	2	0
Brady, r. f.	4	0	0	0	1	0	0
Esterbrook, 3b.	4	0	0	0	1	3	0
Roseman, c. f	3	0	0	0	0	0	0
Orr, 1b.	3	0	0	0	13	0	0
Troy, 2b.	3	0	1	1	0	5	0
Reipschlager, c.	3	0	0	0	7	2	1
Kennedy, l. f.	3	0	0	0	0	0	0
Keefe, p.	3	0	1	1	0	1	0
Total	30	0	2	2	24	13	1

Innings	1	2	3	4	5	6	7	8	9	
Providence	2	1	0	0	0	0	3	0	0	—6
Metropolitan	0	0	0	0	0	0	0	0	0	—0

Runs earned—Providence, 3. First base on errors—Metropolitan, 2. First base on balls—Providence, 2. Struck out—Providence, 8; Metropolitan, 9. Left on bases—Providence, 1; Metropolitan, 3. Three-base hit—Irwin. Two-base hit—Farrell and Gilligan. Total base hits—Providence, 9; Metropolitan, 2. Double play—Irwin, Farrell and Start. Wild pitches—Keefe, 4; Radbourn, 2. Passed balls—Reipschlager, 2; Gilligan, 2. Umpire—Kelly. Time—1 hour and 55 minutes.

BATTLE OF THE GIANTS.

Providence vs. Metropolitans for the Championship of America.

Radbourn's Curves Enigmas to the New Yorkers.

The American Association Leaders Completely Shut Out.

Providence, 6; Metropolitan, 0.
NEW YORK, Oct. 23.—The Providence League champions and the Metropolitans, of this city, of the American Association, f a series of games for the cham- Jnited States, at the Polo grounds terest was felt in the contest, and s assembled to witness the game. weather was the means of keep- y three times the number pre- w wind blew across the grounds le force, and made even the times, and prevented any fine s particularly the case with the played far below the usual stand- ched a miserable game, occasion- lese all command of the ball. d in fine form, as usual. His mas to those who faced him. vind blew so that it was almost lge a high ball. In the first in- took the lead, Hines and Farrell and scoring on wild pitches and the third inning Hines made a to second on a passed ball, and ld pitches. In the seventh in- atted hard. Two base hits by gan, a three-bagger by Irwin, and y gave the Providence nine, three e full score was as follows:

PROVIDENCE.

	AB.	R.	1B.	TB.	PO.	A.	E.
.....	4	2	1	1	1	0	0
.....	4	1	0	0	1	0	0
.....	4	0	0	0	0	1	0
.....	4	0	0	0	13	0	0
.....	3	1	1	2	2	2	0
.....	3	1	1	3	0	4	1
.....	3	1	1	2	8	2	0
.....	3	0	1	1	0	2	1
.....	3	0	0	0	2	0	1
...	31	6	5	9	27	11	3

METROPOLITAN.

	AB.	R.	1B.	TB.	PO.	A.	E.
.....	4	0	0	0	2	2	0
.....	4	0	0	0	1	0	0
.....	4	0	0	0	1	3	0
.....	3	0	0	0	0	0	0
.....	3	0	0	0	13	0	0
.....	3	0	1	1	0	5	0
.....	3	0	0	0	7	2	1
.....	3	0	0	0	0	0	0
.....	3	0	1	1	0	1	0
...	30	0	2	2	24	13	1

.....	1	2	3	4	5	6	7	8	9	
.....	2	1	0	0	0	0	3	0	0	—6
.....	0	0	0	0	0	0	0	0	0	—0

Providence, 3. First base on itan, 2. First base on balls—Pro uck out—Providence, 8; Metro- on bases—Providence, 1; Metro ree-base hit—Irwin. Two-base Gilligan. Total base hits—Pro- politan, 2. Double play—Irwin, rt. Wild pitches—Keefe, 4; Rad- balls—Reipschlager, 2; Gilligan, ly. Time—1 hour and 55 minutes.

AND SOUTH AMERICAN TRADE.

ring before the Congressmission in Philadelphia.

IA, Oct. 23.—Before the Cen- American Commission to-day, s, President of the Columbian ng American Consul, said the resented was anxious to im- ss relations with this country, to secure greater direct com- h the United States ports. ans want is some local agency, see full lines of samples and make payments with little t railroad freights as possible. verse, one of the proprie- Baldwin Locomotive Works, ness of the Baldwins had hed with Central and for about a quarter of s necessary for the countries heir railway material either r the United States, and the of material was generally pre- from his experience, Mr. hat was most needed to open was thorough information as nts of the country and the that can be maretked there. ting as agents, he could not system would be either prac- ble. Facility of transporta- er important condition. Un- laws all British steamers samples at nominal charges. case with American vessels. dwins frequently made ship- America by way of Europe. running direct to Valparaiso, eaching that country except Isthmus. He believed the overnment should do is to sub- lines, and therein, it seemed was the great problem. It portant to have enough ship- lines to afford competition possible rates. Merchants ers, he considered, must work ivation, and they could only represented in these coun- nts, but by native houses.

WART'S MILLIONS.

Alexander Stewart and hrown Out of Court.

Oct. 23.—Judge Wallace, in- s Circuit Court, to-day, dis- in the suit of Alex. Stewart inst Henry Hilton, on the ilure of the plaintiff to give sts. This suit is a contested tion of the A. T. Stewart es-

ster Thieves in Glen Cove.

Oct. 23.—This afternoon sev- s came over from Connecticut Harbor, Long Island, and the taking oysters from private Sheridan put out for the ned fire on him and compelled the shore. The constable red a tug boat and pursued rs." After a hot chase he nging one of the boats to and ire crew.

e and Telegraphic.

caused the death by suffoca- of Daniel Flynn and an un- ed "Pete" at the former's resi- herry street, New York city.

s, aged 24 years, pleaded zlement while a clerk in the fice yesterday. He was sen- year at hard labor in the

Grand Lodge of Ohio has ution declaring it to be the ody that the selling of intoxi- hould disqualify any one from r affiliation with any Masonic

, of the New York Supreme aside as excessive the ver- given to Miss Minnie Cum- ss in her suit against Miss De- a Murphy, the dressmaker, and Policeman Deeves.

A resolution was introduced in the Vermont House yesterday, by Representative Means, of Derby, providing that the Legislature shall refuse all appropriations in furtherance of the so-called Cotton Exposition at New Orleans, or refuse to aid in any way the Southern States, until such time as they shall change their most unjust and wicked course and give to all citizens within their borders, without distinction of race or color, their full rights under the constitution and laws of the United States. The bill was supported by Mr. Means alone and was dismissed.

Wm. H. Dempsey, of Washington, D. C., has been indicted by the United States Grand Jury, at Boston, on the charge of defrauding the Navy Department. He was a stationer, and supplied most of the stationery used in the different departments at the capital. His plan, as alleged, was to secure orders from the department and receive payment for goods without delivering them. Two clerks in the Department of Medicine and Surgery were, it is stated, confederates, filling out vouchers for goods that were never received. These practices have been going on about fourteen years, it is said, and over $75,000 has been lost to the government thereby. Dempsey is said to be under indictment in Washington upon similar charges.

Political Points.

The Prohibitionists of North Carolina have nominated a full electoral ticket.

Business Troubles.

Schedules in assignments have been filed in New York by Adolph Landis and Wm. J. Weinburg, merchants, of 48 Howard street, with liabilities of $54,026, and actual assets $10,418; by Philip Lust, manufacturers of feathers, at 128 Greene street, liabilities, $37,472, and actual assets $1692.

A meeting of the creditors of Fitz & Martin, bakers, of Boston and Lynn, was held Thursday. Liabilities, $20,000; assets, nominally about $5500.

Weld & Fay, manufacturers of overalls, etc., Boston, have failed. Liabilities unknown.

THE QUEBEC EXPLOSIONS.

What the Detectives Claim to Have Discovered.

MONTREAL, Oct. 23.—Information has to-day been communicated to the authorities in connection with the Quebec explosions, showing that the act was committed by the enemies of the contractor of the Parliament building. A detective here has obtained the evidence of an ex-partner of the parties implicated, who will swear that he was approached some time ago and asked to participate in the job, which he refused to do.

Gross Carelessness of a Female Physician.

BOSTON, Oct. 23.—Judge Burbank has returned his finding in the case of Isabella R. Hill, of Rockland, who died in South Boston, in August last. He says that the deceased came to her death from taking an overdose of "fluid extract of St. Ingatius bean," given her by Dr. Helen Cumming, of South Boston, the label on the bottle containing the directions, "one tablespoonful three times a day, before meals." The judge finds that the death was caused by the gross carelessness of Dr. Cumming, in pasting the above label upon the bottle.

Women's Christian Temperance Union.

ST. LOUIS, Mo., Oct. 23.—The Women's Christian Temperance Union resumed its sessions this morning. The report of work among foreigners was read. Thirty thousand pages of German literature have been put in circulation and distributed in various States, and new superintendents have been appointed in several States having large German, Scandinavian and Dutch populations. The report of the Treasurer showed the receipts for 1884 to be $7886, and the expenditures $6581.

chester Girl the 2:34 race in 2:33 and 2:33¼. The afternoon races included the 2:37 and free-to-all classes. Falka won the first race in three straight heats, and in the free-to-all Dan Smith took the first heat and Blue Bell the last three. Dan Smith was the favorite, and Blue Bell's victory in this class greatly surprised the betting fraternity. Following are the

SUMMARIES:

2:37 class, purse $300:

Falka, b. m., Z. E. Simons	1	1	1
Isloonen, b. m., J. H. Lewis	2	3	4
Regal, b. g., N. Dickinson	3	4	3
Sylvia M., g. m., T. W. Reynolds	5	2	2
Lizzie R., b. m., George Ryer	4	5	5

Time—2:38¼; 2:33¾; 2:35½.

Free-to-all, purse $400:

Blue Bell, c. m., W. R. Kendall	2	1	1	1
Dan Smith, b. g., Charles Dickerman	1	3	3	3
Boss H., b. g., Henry Pope	4	2	2	5
Kitty Ives, g. m., George Northrop	3	4	5	2
Huntress, b. m., W. H. Nelson	5	5	4	4

Time—2:31½; 2:30½; 2:30½; 2:31½.

A Pension Fraud Sentenced.

BOSTON, Oct. 23.—In the United States Court to-day Maria Goodall, colored, who was indicted for attempting to obtain a pension belonging to the estate of Thomas Levi Allston, late of Newton, in falsely representing she was his wife, pleaded guilty and was sentenced to one year at hard labor. The prisoner, in her statement to the Court, said that one Smith was the party who went with her to Providence, R. I., and represented himself as Mr. Allston in performing the bogus marriage ceremony with her. There being no evidence to hold Smith, he has been discharged.

The Allegheny Valley Railroad.

PITTSBURGH, Pa., Oct. 23.—In the United States Circuit Court to-day, John Armstrong, Examiner and Master in Equity, submitted a report in which he recommends the sale, by the receiver of the property, franchises, rights, interests and credits of the Allegheny Valley Railroad Company. The Master also finds that the debt of the company exceeds its assets by $4,077,000.

Havana Market.

HAVANA, Oct. 23.—Spanish gold, 226½. Exchange firm.

Burglars in a Post Office.

CONCORD, N. H., Oct. 23.—An attempt was made to burglarize the safe in the Post Office at Bayley's Bridge, Warner, some time last evening. The handles of the safe were found broken off, but could not be opened till the arrival of the locksmith from Concord. It is not known whether any of the contents were stolen. Besides stamps, it contained securities to a large amount, owned by Samuel W. Dowe, of Warner.

Institute of American Architects.

ALBANY, N. Y., Oct. 23.—Officers of the Institute of American Architects were elected to-day, as follows: President, Thomas W. Walter, of Philadelphia; Treasurer, P. P. Hatfield, of New York; Secretary, George C. Mason, Jr., of Newport, R. I.; Board of Trustees, H. M. Congdon, E. T. Littel, Napoleon Leebrun and A. J. Bion.

Virginia Drought Ended.

PETERSBURG, Va., Oct. 24.—The first rain in this section for more than eight weeks fell last night. It extended all along the Norfolk and Western Railroad as far as Lynchburg and along the Atlantic coast line as far south as Weldon. Rain is still badly needed throughout the southern districts.

The New York Dog Show.

NEW YORK, Oct. 23.—These prizes were awarded at the non-sporting dog show to-day: Special prize for best pair of mastiffs to Hero II. and Lorna Doone, Ashmont kennels, Boston. Extra prize for briudle dogs to S. L. Ford, Cromwell, Wm. H. Lee, of Boston.

The Ocean Steamers.

Passed Scilly, steamships Normandie, from New York for Havre; Leerdam, from New York.

At New York, steamships Lincoln City, from London; Sikh, from Chinese ports.

At Southampton, steamship Ems from New York.

CHARLES RADBOURN, Providence Club, Pitcher.
Photographed by Horton Brothers, Providence.

WILLIAM EWING,
New York Club, Catcher.

JOHN F. MORRILL,
Boston Club, First Base.

JOHN J. BURDOCK,
Boston Club, Second Base.

EDWARD N. WILLIAMSON,
Chicago Club, Third Base.

ARTHUR A. IRWIN, Providence Club, Short Stop.
Photographed by Horton Brothers, Providence.

JOSEPH HORNUNG,
Boston Club, Left Field.

GEORGE F. GORE,
Chicago Club, Centre Field.

MICHAEL J. KELLY,
Chicago Club, Right Field.

JOHN M. WARD, New York Club, "The Best Base Runner."
Photographed by Horton Brothers, Providence.

JAMES H. O'ROURKE, Champion Batsman of the National League for 1884, New York Club.

THOMAS J. ESTERBROOK, Champion Batsman of the American Association for 1884, New York Club.

CHAMPION BASE-BALL PLAYERS.—[See Page 311.]

ILLINOIS.—THE CHICAGO BASEBALL CLUB.
SEE PAGE 255.

THE CHICAGO BASEBALL CLUB.

THE present tour of the Chicago Baseball Club, in the Eastern cities of the National League, has excited an unusual degree of interest by reason of the active rivalry existing between the leading clubs for the honor of winning the League championship for 1885. In New York this interest was manifested by the attendance of great crowds of people to witness the important contests between the baseball giants of the New York and Chicago clubs. From the indications noted before the first month of the playing season is ended, it is evident that public interest in baseball is greater than ever before, and that the struggle for championship honors will attract the attention of a larger number of people than at any previous time. In Chicago, the portraits of whose representative team are given on another page, the most elaborate preparations have been made for the season's games. The new grounds of the Chicago Club have been fitted up at a cost of $30,000, a solid brick wall having been erected around the inclosure of 400 x 600 feet, at a cost of $10,000. This is the only athletic park in America that is inclosed by a brick wall, and in its general aspects it is said to be superior to anything of the kind this side the Atlantic. A quarter-mile bicycle track of improved construction is one of its features. The Chicago Baseball Club has a history co-extensive with that of the National League itself. During the tenure of the late President Hulbert, Chicago was the official headquarters of baseball in America. The President of the Chicago Club, Mr. A. G. Spaulding, now a wealthy and influential business man, will be remembered as the famous pitcher of the Forest City Club of Rockford, the Boston Red Stockings and the champion Chicagoes of 1876. The stockholders and directors of the Chicago Club are, without exception, gentlemen of wealth and high social standing, and in no city in the United States is baseball maintained upon a higher plane or more liberally patronized than in the wonderful Western metropolis. The players of the Chicago Club, like their city, are noted for their enterprise and spirit. This is peculiarly true of their batting, base-running and well-disciplined co-operation in fielding. Their captain and first baseman, Adrian C. Anson, is a conspicuous figure by reason of his physique, playing abilities, and thorough knowledge of the rules and laws of the game. In pitchers and catchers, the club has valuable material in Corcoran, Clarkson, Flint and Sutcliffe; an efficient in-field in Anson, Pfeffer, Burns and Williamson; and a famous trio of out-fielders in Dalrymple, Gore and Kelly.

1. Madison, the Father. 2. T. J. Cluverius, the Accused. 3. Counsel for Defense. 4 Counsel for Prosecution. 5, Jury. 6, Judge Atkins. 7, Sergeant.

VIRGINIA.—THE TRIAL, AT RICHMOND, OF T. J. CLUVERIUS FOR THE MURDER OF FANNIE LILLIAN MADISON.
FROM A SKETCH BY C. BERKELEY.—SEE PAGE 253.

MAZZANTINI, THE BULL-FIGHTER.

M. J. KELLY.

THE OLD DODGE DON'T WORK.

In Justice Tuttle's Court yesterday G. W. Young swore out a warrant for the arrest of Frank W. Lynch, a saloon-keeper, on a charge of larceny by bailee of $1,750, placed in his hands, as stakeholder of bets to be made on a foot-race, which took place Thursday, at City View Park, between E. S. Skinner and H. K. Struve. Geo. W. Millet swore out a similar complaint, charging Lynch with detaining $500, and H. K. Struve did the same thing for another $500, which he had put up as forfeit in the race. Lynch then had Skinner arrested, claiming that he had turned over the whole amunt to Skinner. In his testimony, Lynch acknowledged the receipt of the various sums of money, and also of an additional $1,250 that a Mr. Murphy had bet on the race, but claimed that Struve told him to give all the money up to Skinner, as it was "fixed" between the foot-racers and it would be all right, that they intended to "whack up;" Skinner to win the race. Lynch accordingly gave up all the money to Skinner as fast as it was placed in his hands, which, to say the least, was a queer way of doing things. After the race was run the referee decided that Struve had won it, and Young, Struve and Millett made demands on Lynch for the money, which he was unable to hand over. Skinner's testimony brought to light a "nice kettle of fish," which was nothing less than a deliberate swindle. It seems that all the money he and his friends had was $500, and that as fast as the money bet by the friends of Struve came in he took it and doubled up, thus virtually making Struve's backers bet against their own money. It is a plan of the most crooked kind, it no doubt being the plan for both Skinner and his trainer, a man named Friend, to "jump the city." Skinner says he gave the whole sum, which, as near as can be got at, is $4,000, to Friend, and now Friend cannot be found. Lynch was bound over in the sum of $3,000 ($1,000 on each count) to appear before the Grand Jury. Skinner was taken to the county jail in default of $3,000 bail. He was also bound to answer before the Grand Jury.—*Portland Oregonian.*

THE GYMNASTIC CHAMPIONSHIP—NEW YORK, Feb. 15, 1887—EDITOR OF THE CLIPPER—*Dear Sir*: Owing to the fact that no suitable hall (having a theatrical license) can be secured for the purpose of holding the annual gymnastic competition for the amateur championship of America, the American Athletic Club have decided to hold such competition at Prof. John Wood's Gymnasium, No. 6 East Twenty-eighth street, on Saturday evening, March 12, at 8 o'clock, Prof. Wood having kindly placed his gymnasium at the disposal of the club for that evening. Please notice that the date has been changed from Feb. 26 to March 12. Admission will be by invitation only. Respectfully, EXHIBITION COMMITTEE.

CURLING.—The final competition for the Ontario Tankard took place in Toronto, Can., Feb. 17. The Paris and St. Mary's Clubs were opposed, two rinks each, and the former won by the close score of 41 to 38......A four-rinks-a-side match was played in Brantford, Ont., Feb. 16, the Granites of Toronto defeating the Brantfords by 61 to 60......The annual point competition for gold and silver medals between members of the Thistle Club of Hamilton, Ont., came off 12, J. Crerar, R. L. Gunn and W. Vallance each scoring 14.

YALE'S JUMPERS.—The sixth trial in the high-jumping competition at Yale College was held Feb. 16, the competitors being: Shearman, '89, scratch; C. B. Berger, '88, 8. 1in.; Waite, '90, 2in.; Sherwood, '90, 2in.; Bayard, '90, 3in. The result of the trial was as follows: Bayard, 5ft. ¾in.; Waite, 5ft. ¾in.; Shearman, 5ft. 2¾in.; Sherwood, 4ft. 11¾in.; Berger, 4ft. 10¾in.

Now that H. M. Johnson has had the benefit of a lot of free advertising, and his vanity has been pleased by reading a sketch of his career, highly colored, in several papers, he, as upon former occasions, comes out with a flat denial of any intention to retire, but says he will come East and run in the Summer handicaps. So much for the grocery-clerk story.

IRELAND VS. ENGLAND.—The annual football match between the Association teams of Ireland and England was played at Sheffield, Eng., Feb. 5, before six thousand people. England won by seven goals to one. In the Rugby match, played at Dublin the same day, the Irishmen were victors by two goals to none.

POSTPONED.—On account of the serious illness of William R. Travers, president of the New York Athletic Club, the annual amateur boxing and wrestling championships, which were to have been held on Feb. 21, at the club house, have been indefinitely postponed.

THE reports read at the annual meeting of the London Athletic Club Feb. 2 showed that the working expenses of the past year gave a loss of about $2,000, while there had been a steady decrease in the gate-receipts—a fact due to opposition on the part of other clubs, wet weather, etc.

TOM CANNON won two successive falls from Prof. Miller in a Græco-Roman wrestling-match for $500 a side in her Majesty's Opera house, Melbourne, Aus., recently. The first round occupied 56m. and the second 6m. Miller is said to have had one of his ribs torn out of position, the cartilage giving way.

EUGENE WISWALL and J. A. Latham, the ball-player, wrestled in collar-and-elbow style for $50 a side at Cadet Hall, Lynn, Mass., Feb. 15. The former won three straight falls in 22m., 11m. 15s. and 1h. 15m., respectively.

THE new officers of the Owen Sound (Ont.) Gymnasium and Athletic Association are: President, Henry Durie; vice, John Parker; secretary-treasurer, H. C. Bellew.

A FOOTBALL MATCH between the Kearney Rangers and the Paterson Club was played in East Newark, N. J., Feb. 12, the former winning by 5 goals to 0.

THE Intercollegiate Athletic Association will hold their annual convention at the Fifth-avenue Hotel, this city, on Friday evening, Feb. 25.

J. A. SNOWDEN defeated Charles O. Walton in a five-mile race on rollers at the Casino Rink, in Poughkeepsie, N. Y., Feb. 18. Time, 16m. 36s.

BILLIARDS.

THE ALLEGED NEW POOL RULES.

The opening of the game is a slight change from the code of 1884, inasmuch as it requires that the striker shall drive at least two balls to a cushion, instead of three balls, in case he fails to hole one. As in 1884, all balls holed on the opening stroke count, none needing to be called until after that stroke. In view of the opposition this feature encountered in 1884, as making a call-game not a call-game, it requires great hardihood to adhere to it. A simple expedient would do the work effectually, without the need of having to send even one ball to a cushion, and at the same time permitting a call. This would also dispense with the nonsensical adjunct that the player who fails to pocket a ball or send at least two balls to a cushion shall be "scratched" three points and made to start again, three such "scratches" forfeiting the game. This regulation is made to appear additionally awkward, cumbersome and ludicrous by the fact that it would be wholly inoperative but for another of the modern rules of pool, viz., that the man who wins the lead can make his opponent take it. But for this, the aim of both, in view of the "scratch" law, might be to so "bank" as to lose the lead, thus presenting the spectacle of two men striving for something they don't want. The idea of banking for the lead at pool is itself hugely ridiculous, the more especially when, for that purpose, two white balls, as required by the new rules, have to be provided temporarily. The old and quick way of jerking marbles out of a jug was not good enough, it seems; and yet it has to be resorted to yet, because there isn't room for more than two or three men to "bank." As they couldn't have it their new way more once in a great while, why couldn't the modern law-makers let the old way play right straight through, alike for two-handed and for six handed games? Some night their extra ivory ball will be stolen, and they will be six dollars out.

As a supplement to the marked conflicts or incongruities pointed out last week, we now discuss three other rules. Although they are not calculated to be seriously harmful in their operations, yet, taken in connection with the rules that were analyzed in our last preceding issue, they indicate quite clearly that the code in its entirety does not deserve to be accepted as representing the intelligence of the pool-playing community.

Note to Rule 22.—As it is difficult to decide when a ball is in or out of the string when looking at it from a distance away from the table, or from the line of the string, it would not be just, under the circumstances, to punish the player [for having, when in hand, played on or with a ball inside the string, he not having been warned.—ED. CLIPPER.]; and further, if the opposing player or his umpire detect the striker so playing, it is better to check the striker by calling time, than to warn or prompt him by calling the attention of the referee to the matter.

The foregoing is unobjectionable enough, having been taken from an argument printed in THE CLIPPER in 1879 in support of Sec. 3 of Rule 6 of the then new Champion's Game of caroms; but we desire to call attention to the fact that Rule 22 prescribes the penalty, in case the striker does play after having had "Time!" called upon him, and pockets the ball, as simply that he shall not count it, and must, besides, lose his hand, both of which are proper. He does not lose three points, be it remembered. Now see this new rule:

Rule 23.—It is foul, and the striker forfeits three points, if, while in the act of striking, he has not at least one foot on the floor.

Why does he forfeit three points, and not the man who played after he was warned? It is as hard for the referee, without opponent or umpire secretly calling his attention to it, to see that the striker has not one foot on the floor as to see that he is beyond the string-line. The striker should simply lose his hand and not count the ball he may have pocketed.

Rule 25.—Should a ball that has come to a standstill move, without apparent cause, while the player is preparing to strike, it must be replaced. Should it move before he can stop his stroke, it and all the other balls set in motion by the stroke must be replaced, and the player shall repeat his stroke, inasmuch as, but for the moving of the ball, he might have counted where he missed, or missed where he counted.

It may puzzle some who read "it and all the other balls set in motion by the stroke" to understand what this can possibly mean at pool. It is Rule 10 of the code of the Champion's Game of caroms. It was a little strained even in that code; but it was designed to cover cases in which the first object-ball should shift slightly because of an inequality in the cloth or because of a jarring of the table, the moving of a ball the hundreth part of an inch often sufficing to make a man miss a carom by an inch, although his ball has had to go but three or four inches in passing from the first object-ball to the second. That movement would not appreciably affect the holing of a ball at pool unless the pocket openings were made very much smaller than they are, or unless the object-ball were far from the pocket; and consequently the only purpose of transferring this carom rule to pool is to pad out the latter code. The effect of such a rule in pool, where the number of players augment the chance of a vibration of the table, and where fifteen object balls, instead of two, increase by seven-fold the chance of one ball or another's moving owing simply to an inequality in the cloth, will be to encourage "kicks" on the part of those who, at critical moments, fail to "plug" successfully. The abject grotesqueness of this transfer of a rule from three-ball caroms to pool is evident in the fact that, whereas the moving of either of the two object-balls in ordinary billiards may help or mar a carom, at pool, as this rule rends, the striker can claim the right to try an unsuccessful stroke once more in case any one of the fifteen object-balls moves while he is trying to hole one only! That is what "a ball that has come to a standstill" means.

A LITTLE LIGHT.

In addition to the billiard-player who had volunteered us the information that he signed his name to the pool-code without having read it, we have come across another, who writes: "We never read the rules for pool, with the exception of that pertaining to the burst. We took Mr. ——'s word for the rest, which was that they were the same as usual. Our signing them was out of friendship for Mr. ——." This lets in a glimmer of light. Early in 1884, when it was proposed to make the opening striker send three balls to a cushion in case he failed to pocket none, it was manifest that no player could intelligently drive that number of balls. He whose name is in blank above held out for two balls, and our advice, when asked, was that, if the opening was to be regulated by balls to cushion, it would prevent any "burst" at all if fewer than three balls were stipulated, as two could be driven so that they would return into the pyramid. By patience and perseverance, and possibly by "sweet oil," the gentleman seems at last to have accomplished his purpose. At least his steadfastness is to be complimented. But as, in the case of any given shot from a fixed position, the third-rate player can, after a little experimenting, do about as much as the first-rate, in what respect does the latter gain anything by sending the two balls back into the bunch when his opponent is about as clever as himself at it? It is as we have said heretofore. The opening player must be coaxed into bursting the balls, instead of driven. There are several ways of bringing this about. The best way is for a congress of roomkeepers and experts to determine, at the same time that they formulate a code of pool rules that will last.

ON JAN. 24 in London, Eng., John Roberts Jr. began what the English papers term "a novelty and a new departure." Instead of giving D. Richards the usual odds, young Roberts barred himself from counting any ball that might enter the left-hand upper pocket. A critic remarks: "The idea was certainly a good one, as a change from the now rather wearisome succession of spot-barred matches; but to a great extent it spoils Roberts' game by stopping his magnificent breaks." The notion is not new in this country, and we do not think that it is new in England, either.

JAMES MURPHY, proprietor of a large pool-room in Chicago, was patronizing G. F. Slosson's bar one night last week, and then informed Slosson that he would back him to play Schaefer for $2,500 a side. The newspapers got hold of this, it was telegraphed to other cities, and the prediction was made not merely that there would be a match, but also that it would take place in Chicago. The next day, at his earliest leisure after reading the newspapers, Mr. Murphy called upon Slosson and informed him that during the interval he had become different.

JOHN NORTH, to whom young John Roberts gave 4,000 in 12,000, in London, Eng., was beaten 1,439. In the course of this match Roberts made an unusual number of consecutive caroms for an English game. Suppose we allow an English sporting journal to speak of it: "On the concluding day the champion laid himself out for nursery cannons, with the grand result that in one break of 184 he compiled a sequence of 74, equaling a similar performance of his own. This is probably a record, although Cook, at Bradford last November, against Peal, is said to have achieved 75 cannons. These records, however, simply rest on the authority of reporters, *who, except in London, are not very reliable.*"

THE tournament of the Billiard Association concluded in London, Eng., Jan. 29. Joseph Bennett, aided by the handicapper, won first prize. Peall and Richards tied for second prize. The other contestants were Mitchell, Cook, Collins, F. Bennett and the elder John Roberts. The tournament came off at the Albert Palace. Up to the last night but one the gate-money had amounted to but fifty dollars in the aggregate. This is why the tournay was called a "frost."

LAST WEEK we gave the result of the handicap pool tournament in South Framingham, Mass., so far as the first prize was concerned, it going to James Kedian of Ashland. The second prize has since been won by George Sumpter of Milford, and the third by Thomas Prescott of Natick. The games were played in Fred E. Lamb's room.

DOWN in South Framingham and Milford, Mass., they regard George Sumpter as "the best twelve-year-old pool-player in the world." Better let it go at that. Don't trot out all the possible twelve-year-old players in the country in expectation of matching Georgie. Let 'em keep on going to school.

PATSY FITZGERALD is jubilant over the activity that pool has shown at Keyser & Geraty's room, Nassau street, this Winter. This establishment is to be thoroughly overhauled in July next. Not only will it have new tables, but it is also to be newly frescoed.

THE experience of young Roberts in the game with D. Richards, elsewhere referred to, was such as to induce him to withdraw his challenge to play five pockets against the six of any man in England.

FRANK PARKER has withdrawn from the saloon business. He went into it on State street, Chicago, about six weeks ago. The establishment was sold last week. Parker is temporarily not busy.

RANDOLPH HEISER is inclined to be mysterious with regard to his practice-play for the benefit of Edward McLaughlin. Are we to look for another "dark horse?"

BASEBALL.

NOTABLE BITS OF BATTING IN 1886.

A marked improvement in batting, both collectively by clubs and individually, was noted last season. The largest number of safe hits was forty-four, which were equally divided between the Athletic and Brooklyn Clubs in a game of eight innings played May 2 in Brooklyn, N. Y. Six new balls were lost, being batted over the fence, and the supply becoming exhausted, the contest ended in a tie. The Brooklyns on June 24 made the largest number of safe hits to a game—twenty-nine—included in which were three triples and four doubles. The Pittsburg and Atlanta Clubs made a total of forty-two hits April 3 in Atlanta, Ga. Purcell and Stricker scored ten of the twenty-four hits credited to the home-team, while Glenn and Whitney got one-half of the hits made by the visitors. Remarkably heavy batting marked a seven-inning game played Aug. 12 in Louisville, Ky., the home-team then making no fewer than twenty-four safe hits with a total of forty bases, while the Brooklyns batted safely sixteen times and had a total of twenty-two bases. The thermometer was 96 degrees in the shade, and the players suffered greatly from the heat. In six successive championship contests in July the Louisvilles broke the batting record by making an average of seventeen hits to a game, and thus worked their way up from seventh to third place in the race for the pennant. Nearly every game was a tombstone to the memory of some pitcher. The Louisvilles were also credited with making twenty-four hits June 6, twenty-three hits Aug. 15, and twenty-one hits June 9. The St. Louis Browns batted fiercely in the six games played during the week ending April 29, making ninety-six hits for one hundred and forty-seven total bases. The Browns pounded Pechiney's pitching on April 27 for six triples, eight doubles and ten singles. The Cincinnatis also hit Hudson hard. The American Association champions also materially increased their batting averages on the morning of Decoration-day, when they got in twenty-five hits with a total of thirty-three bases, knocking Weaver out of the box in four innings. The Browns also batted safely twenty-one times Aug. 3 and nineteen times each on Aug. 7 and 11. The Detroits defeated the St. Louis Maroons June 12 by about the hardest hitting of the season. Sweeney was pounded very hard throughout, the Wolverines making twenty-one safe hits with a total of forty-four bases, included in which were seven home-runs, two each by Thompson and Rowe, and one each by Brouthers, Bennett and Crane. Other bits of big batting by clubs were twenty-eight hits by Leadville, July 9; twenty-six hits by Newark, June 19; twenty-five hits by Cincinnati, Aug. 12; twenty-four hits by Detroit, July 12; twenty-three hits by Chicago, July 20; twenty-two hits each by Newark (five innings), Oct. 1, and New York, July 26; and twenty-one hits by Chicago (eight innings), July 7. The Chicagos scored two home-runs, seven three-basers and six two-baggers in a game played April 26 in Leavenworth, Kas. The St. Louis Browns of the American Association and the Detroit Club of the National League led their respective associations in batting. In the concluding contest between the Newark and Hartford Clubs Oct. 1 in Newark, N. J., the home-team scored the highest number of runs made in an inning last season, sending twenty men to the bat in the second inning, seventeen of whom

scored, Trott, who went three times
the only man that failed to get in
Fourteen runs in an inning were m
ford Club June 19, Williamsport (
Manchester Club Aug. 27. The M:
their fourteen runs in the first
teen safe hits, eight of which we
The Williamsport team scored onl;
sending seventeen men to the ba
inning. A similar feat was accomp
Louis Browns Oct. 15, when they
their ten runs in the seventh inni
hits, including three two-baggers.
Club visited Lewiston, Pa., May 14
a game with the local club. The
score until the last half of the nin
they got in no fewer than nine ru
victory. The Kansas Citys scored t
runs in the eleventh inning of the
Detroits July 21, giving Getzein a p
safe hits, two of them doubles.
twice had a batting streak at the fi
that turned a seemingly sure defe
On June 4, the Brooklyns, after bei
times, batted out twelve runs in the
innings, off Mullane of the Cinci
these runs being earned. On Aug
lyns, after getting but two hits and
innings, batted Caruthers for nir
scored ten runs in their half of t
Hecker of the Louisville Club on A
against the Baltimores, beat all p
the American Association in three
runs, total bases and home-runs.
times to the bat and made seven
hits with a total of fifteen bases,
being home-runs and the other t
successive safe hits to a game wer
of the Savannah Club April 17, Hi
ington Club April 21, and Latham
Browns April 24. Brouthers of t
equaled Hecker's record of total
McCormick for three home-runs, a
single in a championship game p
Chicago, Ill. Douthett of the De
made on Sept. 15 a total of fourte
hits—a home-run, three three-bagg
Caruthers of the St. Louis Browns
two home-runs, a triple and a doubl
thirteen bases. Willard of the Har
twice made five hits and two hom
his total of bases being thirteen an
of the University of Pennsylvania
made two home-runs, a three-bagg
total of four hits and twelve base
Chicagos did not fail to make a
eighteen consecutive games, his b
two home-runs, a double and two
against the Bostons Aug. 24. Five s
were also made twice each by O'Nei
once each by Glenn, Caruthers, I
Denny, Zimmer, Dunlap, Ryan, F
Thompson, Hornung, Welch, Millig
Stovey, Werrick and Corkhill. In
more game, Aug. 26, Larkin did s
making two three-baggers and a ho
being a drive over the left field fe
inning, when the Athletics earned
scored in the contest. Harkins of t
batted for a home-run and two three
played May 14. Glenn of the Pitt
nine successive safe hits April 2 an
the Brooklyn scored eight safe hits
bat April 21 and 22. Glasscock of the
was credited with one triple, five
singles in three consecutive gam
Whitney of the Pittsburg Club on
of the St. Louis Maroons Aug. 27,
the Louisville Club Sept. 29 each
feat of making all of the three hits
respective clubs. Barkley of th
Kelly and Gore of the Chicagos e
the hits scored by their clubs in ga
7, May 29 and Oct. 19. Carroll s
three hits made by the Washingt
being home-runs. Rooks of the Osh
heavily June 16, getting three ho
Boston-Kansas City game Sept. 30,
three of the six runs scored were
left-field fence, by Morrill, Sutton and Myers, for home-runs. Richardson of the Detroits twice made two home-runs in a championship game. The feat of two home-runs in a professional game was also performed once each by O'Neil, Miller, Anson, Denny, Rowe and M. Mansell. No fewer than eighteen games were won by timely hits for home-runs, Farrar of the Philadelphias, Hines of the Washingtons, Peoples of the Brooklyns and Stovey of the Athletics each once batting for a home-run when three men were on the bases, and thus sending in four runs on one hit. Paul Hines twice, and Hecker, Corkhill, Stovey, Miller, McGarr, Bennett, Dunlap, McQuery, Glasscock, Sutton, Myers, Knowles and Rooks each once made a home-run that saved their club from being blanked. Roger Connor of the New York Club made one of the longest hits on record Sept. 11 at the Polo Grounds, this city. He drove the ball over the twenty-foot fence at right-field, fully four hundred feet away, it being the only time this feat has ever been accomplished. Stovey of the Athletics knocked the ball over the left-field fence on the Pittsburg grounds July 1. It was the third time the ball was ever hit over that fence, twice being by Stovey and once by Browning. On the same grounds, July 15, Schomberg of the Pittsburg Club made the longest hit of the local season. Myers of the Kansas City Club was the only one to bat the ball over the left-field fence of the League grounds in St. Louis, Mo., it being the second time this feat had ever been accomplished. Paul Hines was credited with the longest hits of the season on the League grounds in Philadelphia and Washington. Remarkably long hits were also made by W. Murphy July 19 in Boston, Mass.; Hillery Aug. 6 in Nashville, Tenn.; Visner Aug. 23 in Syracuse, N. Y.; Andrews Sept. 4 in Memphis, Tenn., and O'Neil Oct. 19 in Chicago, Ill.

The official averages of the leading professional associations show that Kelly, Anson, Brouthers, Con-

M. J. KELLY,

whose portrait we present to our readers this week, is the well-known professional, to secure whose release from Chicago the Boston Club claims to have paid $10,000. He was born Dec. 31, 1857, in Troy, N. Y., but his parents removed to Washington, D. C., when he was quite young, and his first experience in ball-playing was gained with a junior club of the latter city. His parents, in 1873, took up their residence in Paterson, N. J., where he caught for the Olympics, an amateur club. His initial engagement as a professional was with the Buckeyes of Columbus, O., during the latter part of the season of 1877, when he caught to the pitching of McCormick, now of the Chicago Club, alternating in that position with Barnie, who is the present proprietor and manager of the Baltimore team. His fine play with the Buckeyes led to his engagement by the Cincinnatis as their right fielder and change-catcher for the season of 1878, and he continued with that club during 1879. While playing with a combination team against the Chicagos in San Francisco, Cal., during the Winter of 1879–80, his excellent catching, batting and base-running attracted the attention of Anson, who at once secured his valuable services, and he has for the past seven seasons been connected with the Chicago Club, playing right-field and catcher, and occasionally short-stop and second-base. He excels in batting, having led the National League last season in that respect, and his average each year during his professional career has shown him to be in the front rank. A notable feat was the making of five safe hits, including three three-baggers, in a game with the New Yorks, Sept. 29, 1885. As a base-runner he is generally acknowledged to be the best that ever trod the diamond. What renders him superior to all others is his wonderful quickness in taking chances, no matter how desperate they may be. An instance of this may be cited in the Chicago-Boston game of May 28, 1885, when Kelly made an audacious but futile attempt to tie the score by running in from third-base while the ball was being pitched to the catcher, who was standing close up to the plate. Kelly was credited in 1885 with the remarkable record of scoring 124 runs off 126 hits in championship games, including the making, on June 16, in five times at the bat, of five out of the eight runs secured by the Chicagos against the Detroits. On Aug 24, 1886, he scored five runs in six times at the bat in a game with the Bostons. It must be said that his policy has always been the scoring of runs, whether honestly or not, and he has on more than one occasion ran from second-base to the home-plate without touching third-base, getting in the winning run in this manner in a game with the Boston Club in 1881. In addition to being able to field well in almost any position, Kelly is a clever coacher, earnest and hard worker for his club, and has a knowledge of all the tricks that help to win a closely-contested game. The official averages of the National League show that Kelly played in 675 championship games and scored 727 runs off 890 safe hits during the seven seasons he was connected with the Chicago Club.

seven seasons he was connected with the Chicago Club.

AT THE ELECTION Feb. 15 in Philadelphia, Pa., Charles Fulmer was chosen Police Magistrate, running far ahead of his ticket. Fulmer commenced playing professionally in 1869, when he pitched for the Athletic Club of his native city. He has played with the representative professional clubs of this city, Cleveland, Rockford, Louisville, Pittsburg, Buffalo, Cincinnati and St. Louis, and last year was an umpire of the National League staff. For several seasons Fulmer successfully managed a dramatic company playing "Uncle Tom's Cabin." At the Philadelphia election Dan Kleinfelder, formerly the catcher of the Athletics, was an unsuccessful candidate for the office of Common Councilman.

THE ANNUAL MEETING of the Amateur League was held Feb. 16 in this city. The pennant for last season's championship was officially presented to the Bergen Point Club. Officers for the ensuing year were chosen as follow: President, H. J. Tyndale, Staten Island Club; vice-president, Charles E. Annett, Bergen Point Club; secretary and treasurer, W. H. O'Flynn, Nassau Club.

THOMAS J. SMITH, who died of typhoid pneumonia Feb. 17 in Philadelphia, Pa., was the president of the Athletic Club in 1876, when it was a member of the National League. He was born May 17, 1837, in Philadelphia, and had served two terms as Receiver of Taxes of that city.

MANAGER BARNIE of the Baltimore Club is already gathering material for a team that he will take out to California in December next. So far he has signed Ramsey and Kerins of the Louisvilles for the trip.

THE PITTSBURG and Washington Clubs are bidding against each other for the release of Sutton by the Boston management.

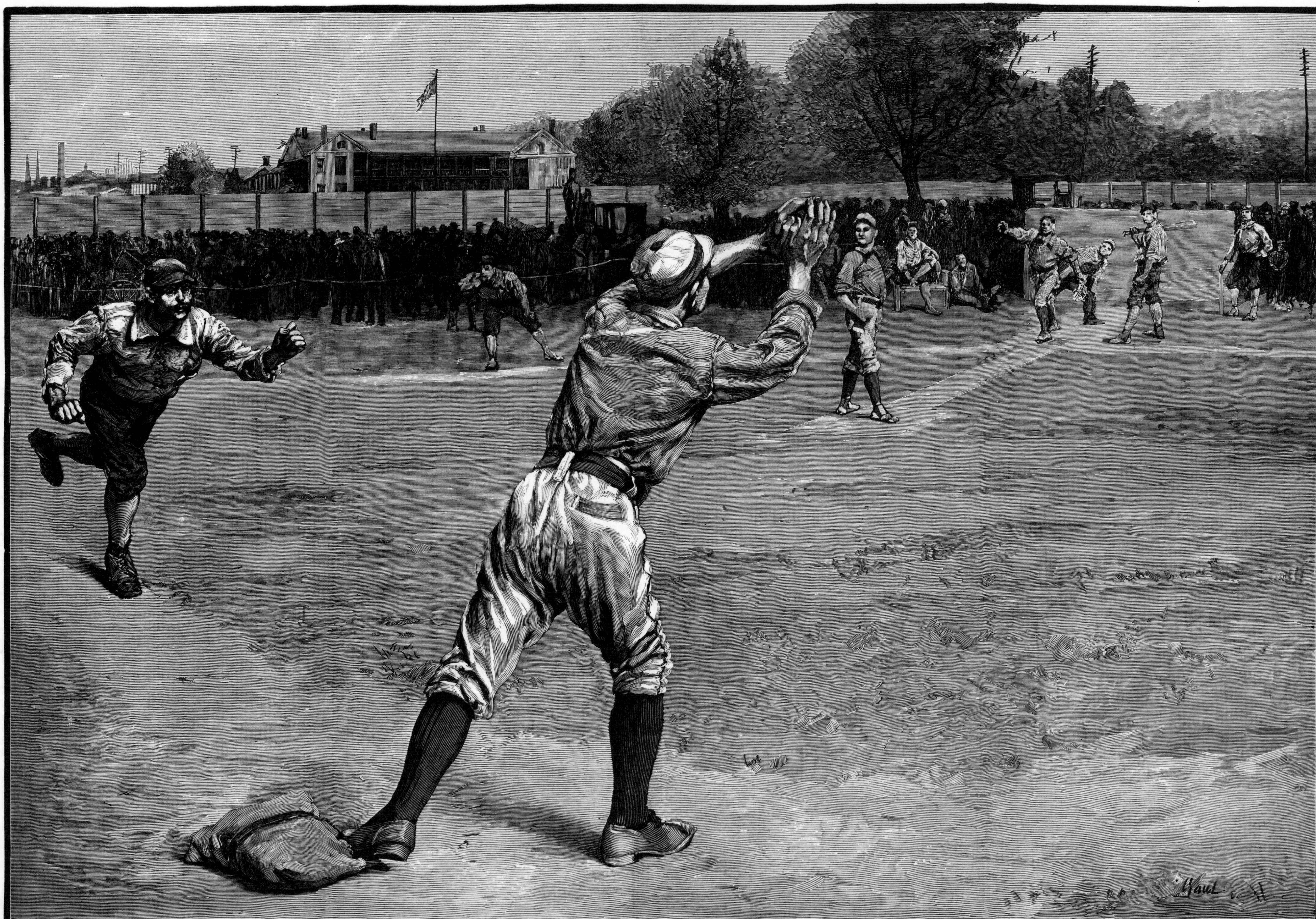

"THROWN OUT ON SECOND."—DRAWN BY GILBERT GAUL.—[SEE PAGE 647.]

MONMOUTH AND SARATOGA.

SUNSHINE AND ENJOYABLE RACING AT THE SEASIDE AND UP COUNTRY.

Mr. Haggin Wins the August Stakes for the Third Successive Year with Fresno, Mr. Cassatt Wins the Rahway Handicap with Eurus and Mr. Withers the West End Hotel Stakes with Cascade—Other Races.

Judges—R. W. Simmons, C. McDowell, J. Galway, D. D. Withers and A. J. Cassatt.
Timers—B. A. Haggin and W. R. Babcock.
Dismounting Judge—W. H. Barretto.
Secretary—J. H. Coster.
Starter—J. F. Caldwell.

A large crowd enjoyed seven excellent races at Monmouth Park yesterday, which were so promptly run that the trains all pulled out for home before 6 P. M., the "specials" running through on such excellent time that passengers were in New York by a little after 7 P. M. The weather was delightfully cool and pleasant, and as backers had a good day many are beginning to regret that the season at Monmouth will end in two weeks.

J. B. Haggin, who arrived Sunday by the Umbria from his month's trip to his family in Paris, was present and saw Fresno place, for the third successive year, the August Stakes to his credit, Santa Rita winning in 1886 and Fitz James in 1887. Fresno, who was bred at Woodburn and was bought a yearling for $2,100, confirmed his running for the Junior Champion Saturday to the letter. That race did him good. It put him on edge. Garrison did not hurry him at the start, but let him drop back last, but in the last quarter he came through and won, figuratively, in a walk. Diablo was second. He is an improving colt that will be apt to win one of the big fixtures before the end of the meeting. In the Rahway Handicap, for all ages, Eurus and Garrison proved irresistible, for the horse ran without swerving, thanks probably to the fact that Strideaway ran alongside of him in such a way that he never saw the inner rails until

COMEDIAN HOPPER'S BASE HITS.

The Ball-Tossers and Gen. Sherman Shed Tears of Laughter at Them.

The Giants and the Chicagos, who had faced each other on the Polo Grounds yesterday afternoon, sat opposite each other in the boxes at Wallack's last night and listened to the McCaull Opera Company in Prince Methusalem. No one would have thought, to see them dressed so quietly in black, that they were the athletes they are. At the game in the afternoon the entire opera company, Col. McCaull included, sat on their tally-ho coaches and witnessed the contest, and the two clubs had come in the evening to return the call. The house was packed to the doors, and when the two clubs came in they were given an ovation.

Just before the opera began Gen. Sherman, who is as fond of baseball as he used to be of forced marches, walked down the aisle to his seat in the middle of the house. He was instantly recognized by the ball-players in the boxes, as well as by the majority of the audience. Some one of Chicago's team began to applaud, and everybody took up the cue, and the old General bowed quietly to the impromptu reception.

As might be expected, Hopper let himself loose on the subject of baseball, and the men laughed heartily at the hits that the comedian threw at them. In the second act, when he sang the "Dotlet on the I," the house roared from the beginning to the end. One of the favorite verses is about the victory of the Giants, and before he sang the verse Hopper turned to the Chicagos and said: "You have had the pennant long enough to stand this." At the end the usher carried down an immense floral baseball from the Chicago Club with "C. B. B. C." on it. In honor of the occasion he recited with telling effect that humorous poem, "Casey's at the Bat." The audience literally went wild with enthusiasm, men got up on their seats and cheered, while old Gen. Sherman laughed until the tears ran down his cheeks. It was one of the wildest scenes ever seen in a theatre, and showed the popularity of Hopper and baseball. In the last act the roughs came in at the end of the march carrying the score of the game at the Polo Grounds yesterday, and on their second entrance carried the pennant and were followed by little Freddy D'Angelis as the mascot. The ball players were very enthusiastic over their reception, and said they would come again.

Third Race.—Purse $250; selling allowances; three-quarters of a mile.

	Lb.		Lb.
Macgregor	107	Sir Roderick	107
Marsh Redon	107	Walter T.	105
Relax	107	Kink	105
Little Tom	107	Carolina	105
Stripling	107	Ruse	104
Courtier	107	St. Albans	103
Valor	107	Jim Brennan	103
Bass Viol	107	Sweety	103
Lagardere	107	Editor	102
Frolic	107	Wanderment	102
Milton	107		

Fourth Race.—Purse $350; selling allowances; seven-eighths of a mile.

	Lb.		Lb.
Jim Clare	107	Saluda	92
Marion	107	Hermitage	91
Cornstarch	106	Boodle	91
Bertie W. colt	101	Crusader	90
Effie Hardy	96	Alveda	87
Miller	93	Gracie	84

Fifth Race.—Purse $550; Bushwick Handicap; one mile.

ANSON'S MEN VICTORIOUS.

THEY DOWN THE GIANTS IN A GAME MARKED BY LOOSE FIELDING.

Detroits Beaten by Boston—Senators Lose to the Pittsburgs—Hoosiers Whipped by the Phillies—Brooklyn Drops Another Game—Athletics Beat the Cowboys—Clevelands Shut Out by the Browns.

The League winners yesterday were Chicago, Philadelphia, Pittsburg and Boston. The winners in the Association were Louisville, Athletic, St. Louis and Cincinnati. The record to date is as follows:

League.	Won.	Lost.	Per cent.	Association.	Won.	Lost.	Per cent.
New York	57	30	.655	St. Louis	52	28	.650
Chicago	51	35	.593	Brooklyn	56	35	.615
Detroit	47	38	.553	Cincinnati	54	34	.614
Philadelphia	44	41	.518	Athletic	52	34	.605
Boston	42	45	.483	Baltimore	38	52	.422
Pittsburg	36	43	.456	Louisville	35	54	.393
Washington	33	53	.384	Cleveland	32	55	.368
Indianapolis	31	56	.356	Kansas City	27	60	.310

Anson's Men Down the Giants.

Jim Mutrie stood on the cinder path at the Polo Grounds last evening with his hands in his pockets and his heart in his mouth. As the last nerveless Giant fell beneath the prowess of the enemy a briny tear started from Jim's north eye, and, following the course of least resistance along his Grecian nose, fell with a dull thud upon his patent-leather shoe. Then Jim looked up into the grand stand where the members of Wallack's Theatre Company sat and muttered with a sigh the one word, "Jonahs."

That explained it all. The array of beauty in the upper tier had rattled the boys and they had been playing with one eye in the grand stand and the other on the ball. After the game De Wolf Hopper was seen trying to square himself with the heart-broken Mutrie, in the darkest and most secluded

Baseball, Polo Grounds, To-Day.

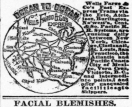

Grand League Championship Game—CHICAGO vs. NEW YORK. Game, 4 P. M. Admission, 50c. To-morrow, DETROIT.

WASHINGTON PARK, Brooklyn, to-day—Great game. Crack SAGAMORES vs. colored GORHAMS. Excellent coaching.

B'LYN A. C. GROUNDS to-day, Amateur Championship, STATEN ISLAND vs. BROOKLYN ATHLETICS, 4 P. M.

A New Rhode Island Newspaper.

WOONSOCKET, R. I., Aug. 14.—Rhode Island and Connecticut newspaper men and several capitalists have formed a joint stock company and will issue a new two-cent morning newspaper, to be called the *Record*, at Hartford early next week. It will be independent in politics, but will advocate Republican principles of protection.

SPORTING EXTRA.

The Evening Sun.

SPORTING EXTRA.

VOL. II.--NO. 172. NEW YORK, THURSDAY, OCTOBER 4, 1888. PRICE ONE CENT.

EXTRA

CHAMPIONS

Giants Nail the Pennant to Our Staff.

ANSON DOWNED AGAIN

And After Buck Gave Him a Show With a Pony Battery.

TO-DAY'S GAME SETTLES IT.

No Matter How or What We Lose Now, That Trophy is Ours.

ED CRANE PROVES HIMSELF A DAISY.

Tener Pitched for Chicago, but Our Boys Found Him.

NEW YORK - - - - - - - 1
CHICAGO - - - - - - - - 0

Since August last Baby Anson sat,
While the Giants were booming with ball and bat,
Tickling his own and his colts' ears, too,
With the cheering tune, to an old bazoo,
"Oh! we'll get there yet, and paint our town
Red, when the Giants come tumbling down."

But still our boys kept banging away,
As though the pennant must come to stay
With them for sure. And lo! it is here.
It's theirs to hoist, and it's ours to cheer,
While the Ansonites hobble off, weary and lame.
For the tumble they longed for never came.

POLO GROUNDS, Oct. 4.—It would have been hard to find a thoroughbred New Yorker to-day who did not feel gratified to see that the chilly blasts of yesterday had taken their departure to other climes and that the sun shone out bright and warm. It was a great day for Gotham. Its champion baseball club was to engage in a contest in which victory meant the floating of the champion flag beyond all doubt, and defeat, at the most, would probably only defer its possession for a few days. It was expected that the warm weather would bring out the Giants' great twirler, Sir Timothy Keefe.

There was a strong feeling of disappointment when the score cards showed that Crane and Brown were in the points, notwithstanding that they have recently done much clever work. The Chicagos had Tener and Farrell in the points, the same lanky, long-legged fellow who proved such a terror to the Giants during their last visit to Chicago. The fine weather brought out a much larger attendance than that of yesterday, and when play was called by Umpire Kelly, large accessions were being made to the 6,000 people already present. The two teams were placed as follows:

NEW YORK.		CHICAGO.	
Tiernan	right field	Ryan	centre field
Richardson	second base	Van Haltren	left field
Connor	first base	Duffy	right field
Ward	short stop	Anson	first base
Foster	left field	Pfeffer	second base
Gore	centre field	Williamson	short stop
Whitney	third base	Burns	third base
Brown	catcher	Tener	pitcher
Crane	pitcher	Farrell	catcher

FIRST INNING.—The home club again took the first turn at the bat. Tiernan was unable to get any fun out of Tener's drops and was disposed of at first on a bounder to Pfeffer. Richardson bunted the ball in front of the plate and was retired on Tener's line throw to Anson. Connor awakened an agreeable strain by planting one of Tener's good balls safely in centre field. Ward foul-tipped out. No runs.

For Chicago, Ryan lifted the ball to short left centre. Foster muffed it after a hard run. Van Haltren advanced Ryan to second on his out from Richardson to Connor. Ward's sharp fielding of Duffy's bounder prevented Ryan moving up. Big Chief Anson was received with a hearty round of applause. He was given his base on balls with two strikes called, the umpire's judgment on the last ball being greeted with strong expressions of disapproval. Ryan made a clean steal to third, and Anson went to second. Pfeffer struck out on three successive pitches, and the tin horns again made their their presence known. No runs.

SECOND INNING.—For New York Foster led off with a bounder to Pfeffer and was retired at first. Gore made the second out on Burns's assist to Anson. Whitney rapped a low fly right into Pfeffer's hands. No runs.

For the visitors Williamson had two strikes called and then rapped a whiskered liner into Connor's reliable hands. Burns failed to hit either of the three balls sent straight across the plate and resumed his seat on the players' bench. Tener could do no better, and sent his side to the field. No runs.

Prolonged applause greeted Crane's fine work.

THIRD INNING.—Brown was completely outwitted by Tener, and proved an easy victim on strikes. Crane did the same act after four balls were called. Tiernan broke the dreary monotony by slashing out a liner which Anson caught in fine style just as it was sailing over his head. No runs.

In the visitors' half Crane made a fine stop of Farrell's swift bounder and disposed of him at first. Ryan was sent to first on five successive bad balls. Van Haltren drove a bounder to Ward and the two Windy City players were doubled up with the assistance of Richardson and Connor, and the tooters sent out merry blasts on the keen air. No runs.

FOURTH INNING.—For New York Richardson sent the ball apparently safe over short, but Williamson jumped high in the air and made a splendid catch. Connor raised a commotion by lining the ball safely to centre, his second clean hit. Ward raised up a fly to Pfeffer. Connor won a round of applause by stealing second, Farrell throwing too high. He got no further, as Tener's curves proved too much for Foster to gauge. No runs.

For Chicago Duffy had two strikes called and then went out on a fly to Gore. Anson got to first on called balls. The big chief was advanced to second on Pfeffer's lively bounder, which Crane captured brilliantly on the jump and fielded to first in time. Anson stole third like a colt, Brown dropping the ball. But his energies were wasted, for Williamson struck out. No runs.

FIFTH INNING.—For the Giants, Gore aroused the tooters by leading off with a safe hit past second. Whitney increased the enthusiasm by advancing Gore to second with a pretty line drive to left. Brown's attempted sacrifice resulted in his going out on a foul tip.

Crane slashed out a scorching grounder, which Williamson was unable to handle, and the bases were full and the interest intense. Tiernan had two strikes called and the crowd became nervous. He then batted out a lively bounder which Williamson fielded in good style to the plate and Gore was forced out.

Before Richardson could do anything a wild pitch brought Whitney home with the first run of the game, and the tooters became hilarious. This seemed to rattle Tener, and he again filled the bases by sending Danny to first on balls. There was great jubilation as Connor came to the bat.

He tried to duplicate his two former good efforts by driving the ball toward the right centre field pickets. But little Duffy got in the way by jumping in the air and hauling down the stinger just as the tooters started to burst their lungs in a mighty effort. One run.

In the Chicagos' fifth Burns was unable to hit the ball, but reached first on Brown's muff of the third strike. Tener struck out and Burns got to second on Brown's wild throw to Richardson. Farrell also fanned the air, and there was great applause for Crane.

Burns stole third when Ryan had two strikes called, the batter interfering with Brown's throw. He missed the next good ball and Crane had won glory in striking four Chicago batters in succession. He received an ovation as he came in. No runs.

SIXTH INNING.—For the Giants, Ward led off with a hard hit to left, which Van Haltren captured. Foster was unable to hit the ball in three efforts, and as Farrell dropped the ball he started for first.

The catcher tried to run him down, but stumbled and fell and the sprinter reached the base amid great laughter. He immediately stole second, getting there by a great slide, which caused Pfeffer to drop the ball.

Williamson caused great amusement among the spectators by trying to catch Foster napping and finally got his hands hurt for his pains.

Tener at length made a wild throw to second, which Pfeffer got, while Williamson prevented Foster from reaching the base until he touched him.

Kelly declared him out and was rewarded with a vigorous round of hisses. Gore was given a life on Farrell's muff of a foul fly, and then went out on a fair fly to Burns. No runs.

For Chicago Van Haltren got his base on called balls. Duffy sent him to second on his out from Ward to Connor. Another close decision brought Kelly into disfavor.

Anson went out on a long fly to Tiernan, on which Van Haltren stole third easily. Pfeffer looked vicious and then ended the inning on Whitney's pretty assist of his slow bounder. No runs.

SEVENTH INNING.—Whitney struck out, Brown was retired on Burns's assist to first. Crane was received with loud applause and Tener graciously sent him to first on called balls.

The heavy weight pitcher stole second safely and tried to make third on Farrell's wild throw, but was put out on Ryan's timely assist to Burns. No runs.

For Chicago, Williamson struck out. Burns had two strikes called and was then retired on Richardson's assist to first. Tener struck out. No runs.

Crane became a great man. The air was filled with shouts of his name.

EIGHTH INNING.—In the Giants' eighth Tiernan's bounder was fielded in time to first by Pfeffer. Richardson went out on a similar assist by Williamson. Connor fouled out to Anson. No runs.

Ward made a great stop of Farrell's hot bounder and got it in time to first. Ryan hit safely to centre the first hit made by his side. Ryan stole second, Brown throwing wild. Van Haltren struck out.

Duffy went out on Ward's assist to first. No runs.

NINTH INNING.—For New York, Ward was retired at first on a low hit to Pfeffer.

Foster was hit on the arm by a pitched ball and took first.

He was caught napping at first on Tener's sharp throw to Anson.

Gore went out on a fly to Ryan. No runs.

For Chicagos, Anson got first on balls.

Pfeffer fouled out to Brown, a good catch.

Williamson went out on a fly to Tiernan.

Anson stole second.

Burns went out from Crane to Connor. No runs.

The score:

New York	0	0	0	0	1	0	0	0	0	—1
Chicago	0	0	0	0	0	0	0	0	0	—0

Base hits—New York, 4; Chicago, 1. Errors—New York, 5; Chicago, 6.

By winning to-day's game the Giants' percentage reaches .648 and the Chicagos have but .574. If the Giants lose all their scheduled games their percentage will be .604, and if Chicago wins all of theirs, they only get .601.

NEWARK VS. JERSEY CITY.

NEWARK 1
JERSEY CITY 0

NEWARK, Oct. 4.—The Jersey City club made its appearance on the grounds of the Newark club for the second time in the series for the State Championship. It was 3:30 when Umpire Terry called play. The Jersey City club had Landmann and O'Rourke as its battery, while Dooms and Duffy occupied the points for the home club.

The score:

Newark	0	0	0	0	0	0	0	0	1	—1
Jersey City	0	0	0	0	0	0	0	0	0	—0

Base hits—Newark, 7; Jersey City, 5. Errors—Newark, 2; Jersey City, 3.

BASEBALL GAMES ELSEWHERE.

AT BOSTON.

Boston	0	0	0	0	0	0	0	0	0	—0
Detroit	0	0	0	2	0	0	1	0	0	—3

Base hits—Boston, 2; Detroit, 4. Errors—Boston, 6; Detroit, 1.

Batteries—Sowders and Tate; Grubers and Wells. Umpire—Valentine.

AT PHILADELPHIA.

At the end of the 7th inning the score stood: Philadelphia, 7; Indianapolis, 4.

Batteries—Buffinton and Clements; Boyle and Myers. Umpire—Lynch.

AT PHILADELPHIA.

At the end of the 7th inning the score stood: Athletic, 4; Cleveland, 6.

Batteries—Weyhing and Townshend; O'Brien and McGuire. Umpire—Gaffney.

AT WASHINGTON.

At the end of the 7th inning the score stood: Washington, 2; Pittsburg, 0.

Batteries—O'Day and Mack; Morris and Carroll. Umpires—Powers and Daniels.

AT LOUISVILLE.

At the end of the 4th inning the score stood: Louisville, 2; Cincinnati, 2.

Batteries—Stratton and Cross; Viau and Baldwin. Umpire—McQuade.

AT ST. LOUIS.

At the end of the 4th inning the score stood: St. Louis, 2; Kansas City, 6.

Batteries—King and Doian; Sullivan and Daniels. Umpire—Doescher.

Weather Indications.

Fair, warmer, southwesterly winds.

CHAMPION GAMES.

Giants and Browns Arrange the World Series.

THEY'LL BEGIN IN NEW YORK.

President Day Frightens Von Der Ahe With a $100 to $5 Bet.

Two cheery-looking men accosted each other in the corridor of the Grand Central Hotel this morning, grasped each other warmly by the hand and exchanged congratulations. They were John B. Day, President of the New York Baseball Club, the new National League champions, and Chris Von der Ahe, President of the St. Louis Club, champions of the American Association. Mr. Day, who never bets, first broke the rapturous silence. He smilingly said:

"I'll bet you a hundred to five we best you."

The jolly little German baseball magnate grinned grimly, but said nothing. He consented, however, to smoke a fragrant Perfecto at John B.'s expense. They then retired to Mr. Von der Ahe's room, accompanied by Secretary Munson of the St. Louis Club, to arrange the great series of ball games which is to decide the championship of the world. After deliberating for an hour or more the meeting was adjourned without coming to any definite arrangement.

It was decided positively that the series would be opened in the East. Telegrams were sent to Boston, Philadelphia and Brooklyn regarding terms for the use of the grounds in the respective cities. No definite number of games were decided on, but the number will probably be nine. Until answers are received from the cities named the place of the opening game will not be definitely decided upon.

The two Presidents will meet again at 7:30 o'clock to-night, when the arrangements will be entirely concluded.

The games to be played between the two champion clubs promises to be the greatest series of baseball contests ever witnessed in this country. For years the supporters of the two clubs have vaunted the ability of their particular favorites to beat the other team, but the circumstances have always been of a character to prevent a meeting. Apart from the general interest that will attend the series there will be more money wagered on the games and on the ultimate result than has ever before been put up on baseball contests.

Naturally the Giants are the favorites in the betting circles in this city, but the lively, hustling game which the St. Louis "boys" play has many supporters among the betting people. It is said that a pool of $10,000 has been formed in the metropolis to be put up on the Giants, and if any of the denizens of the Mound City think their club can beat the Giants they will be given a chance to walk off with the small fortune by putting up the proper collateral to back their opinion.

IS THE WHEAT FLURRY OVER?

It Closes Inactive and Slightly Irregular—The Talent Think the Worst is Over.

The market closed dull at a fractional advance over the lowest prices of the day. The wild hurrah with which the market started cooled off, and during the last hour the trading was insignificant. The volume of business today was estimated at about one-quarter of what it was yesterday.

The range in prices for wheat is as follows: October opened at $1.12, its high price, was lowest at $1.09¾, closed at $1.10¾. November opened at $1.14½, its high point, lowest at $1.11¾, closed $1.12½. December opened at $1.16, was high at that price, lowest $1.13⅝, closed at $1.14¾. May opened at $1.19, was lowest at $1.16¾, closed $1.17⅞. October corn was highest at 52½c., lowest at 51⅞c., closed at 52⅛c. November opened at 53c., highest at 53¼c., lowest 52⅛c., closed 52⅝c. December opened and was highest at 53c., lowest at 52⅛c., closed 52⅝c.

Banker Henry Clews after the close, said: "The short interest in wheat was largely eliminated in the flurry of yesterday. The high price then reached was mainly due to the demoralization of the shorts and their anxiety to cover, and the fact that they did cover to so prodigious an extent is now the weak element in the situation, as a demand from such a quarter does not now exist, and no material demand is likely at present to come from the large operators at anything like present price for long account. Exporters as buyers are also entirely out of the market. If wheat is held up at present figures, Europe will draw upon the granaries of other countries, and will give American wheat the go-by, as was done during the season of the 'Keene corner.' It should be remembered that the present high price of wheat will force an economy in its consumption, and the immense corn crop will furnish a substitute in that direction. In regulating the price of wheat, the unprecedented corn crop should not be lost sight of, and it should be remembered that corn is food for both man and beast and the most wholesome and nutritious kind at that. My own experience in recently substituting corn food for wheat has resulted in great increase of animal spirits, and I recommend hereafter corn to be substituted for wheat until the latter recedes to its proper level. Forty cents a bushel for corn and $1.18 for wheat is entirely disproportionate."

A Chicago despatch after the close said: "The speculative fever has all died out of the wheat market. The volume of trading was not one-twentieth as large to-day as it was yesterday. Operators expect a dead market for some time."

GOOD GAMES BY AMATEURS.

The Boys Playing Much Better as the Season Closes.

The Atlantas scored their twelfth successive victory by defeating a strong picked nine at the Recreation Grounds. Score: Atlanta 26; Picked Nine, 3.

The Sylvans of Thirty-fourth street defeated the Unknowns. The batteries were Swortz and Murphy of the Sylvans and Stradler and Murry of the Unknowns. Score: Sylvans, 3; Unknowns, 2.

The New York Juniors defeated the Actives at Weehawken. The batteries were R. Carny and A. Smith of the New York Juniors and M. McCreery and C. Eyring of the Actives. Score: New York Juniors, 1; Actives, 0.

The Monitors of Lafayette avenue defeated the Osseos at Kippo Grounds, Brooklyn. The feature of the game was Mack's base running and coaching. The batteries were Willis and Ryder of the Monitors and Linton and Phelan of the Osseos. Score: Monitors, 9; Osseos, 6.

The Edgewoods defeated the Barnetts at South Broteer Island. The features of the game were the pitching of E. Brennan, and the catching of Hahn. The batteries were Brennan and Hahn of the Edgewoods and Sorahan and Clarke of the Barnetts. Score: Edgewoods, 8; Barnetts, 5.

The first and second class nines of Grammar School No. 15 crossed bats at Prospect Park for the championship of the same school. The latter nine won by the score of 13 to 11. The feature of the game was the batting of Herring and Weil of the First Class. The Batteries were Revile and Long for the Second Class and Henry and Temple for the First Class.

News of the Amateur Nines.

The Howards are anxious to play the Leos.

The I. A. L.s play their last game for this season on Sunday next with the Mount Cannons.

The Confidence Club would like to hear from any uniformed nine wishing a good game. Address James Honahan, New Rochelle, N. Y.

The John Polhemus B. B. C. having won nine out of ten games played this season, and after challenging all the leading printing trade nines, claim the championship and stand ready to defend their title.

The Star of Jersey City would like to hear from the following clubs: Emerald, Sagamore, Stapleton, Atlas, Senator, Commercial, Acme, Washington Market and Wilton for Saturday and Sunday games. Address John J. Holmes, 180 Sixth street, Jersey City.

Joe Lannon Coming to New York To-day.

BOSTON, Oct. 4.—Joe Lannon and his manager, Billy Mahoney, will start for New York at 9 this morning in the hope of learning that Joe is the unknown who is to be matched against Jake Kilrain. There were no new developments in the negotiations yesterday.

Broker Charles Allison Walsh Dead.

The death was announced on the Produce Exchange this afternoon of Charles Allison Walsh, the cotton and grain broker of 30 Broad street.

WELL DONE FIRENZI!

Garrison Rode the Gallant Filly to Victory.

SALVATOR WON A PRIZE, TOO.

Flitaway, Banner Bearer, Ovid and Fordham Came in First.

RACE TRACK, JEROME PARK, Oct. 4.—The weather was much pleasanter here to-day than it was yesterday, and the attendance was larger. The track was very fast, though dusty, albeit plentifully watered in front of the grand stand. The usual officers did duty.

A feature of to-day's betting was the winning of $6,000 by Sam Emery from Burton, the bookmader, on Flitaway, the winner of the first race.

FLITAWAY FIRST, MONTAGUE SECOND.

First Race.—Purse $800; entrance, $20 each, to second horse; for horses 3 years old, which have not won a sweepstakes for that age; non-winning and maiden allowances; one mile and a sixteenth.

Starters.	Jockeys.	W'hts.	Betting—Straight.	Place.
King Idle	McLaughlin	118	16 to 5	Even.
Montague	Hamilton	113	7 to 5	1 to 2
Pocatello	Martin	106	18 to 5	Even.
Geronimo	Winchell	106	50 to 1	15 to 1
Satisfaction	Littlefield	106	12 to 1	4 to 1
Flitaway	Williams	103	20 to 1	7 to 1

King Idle was indisposed to start, but after a little persuasion he joined the lot and away they went, with Pocatello in front, Satisfaction next, and Flitaway and Geronimo close up. King Idle was first out of sight around Picnic Hill, but Flitaway was the first to come into sight. King Idle went around the club house a head in front of Flitaway, but when again in sight the filly had the lead. She was never after headed and won by a head in 1:53¼. Montague, second, was a head before Satisfaction, third. Pocatello, King Idle, and Geronimo came in close behind.

The mutuals paid $80.50.

SALVATOR FIRST, MIMI FILLY SECOND.

Second Race.—The Tuckahoe Stakes; for 2-year-olds; non-winners of $1,000 at the time of closing; $50 entrance, $20 f., with $1,000 added, of which $200 to the second; the third to receive $100 out of the stakes; winning penalties. The Titan course, 1,400 yards.

Starters.	Jockeys.	W'hts.	Betting—Straight.	Place.
Salvator	Garrison	120	1 to 2	Out.
Sonoma	Hamilton	117	15 to 1	6 to 1
Mimi filly	Taylor	117	4 to 1	6 to 5
Limbo	Taral	108	15 to 1	4 to 1
Infanta	Martin	108	12 to 1	5 to 1
Daylight	Anderson	105	20 to 1	8 to 1
Rhono	Norvice	108	30 to 1	8 to 1
Philander	Littlefield	108	15 to 1	6 to 1

They were sent off in good shape at the first offer, with Salvator a trifle in front and Philander, Infanta and the Mimi filly next. The Mimi filly at once started out and, with Philander for runner up, made the pace until they were well straightened up on the homestretch, where Salvator came up out of the ruck and changed places with Philander. The filly made a game finish, and Salvator came away from her in the last few strides and won by half a length in 1:24. The Mimi filly, second, was two lengths before Daylight, third. Infanta, Limbo, Philander, Sonoma and Rhono finished as named.

The winner paid $7.45.

FIRENZI FIRST, TERRA COTTA SECOND.

Third Race.—The Manhattan Handicap, for 3-year-olds and upward, a sweepstakes of $50 each, h. f., with $1,500 added, of which $300 to second, the third to receive $150 out of the stakes; one mile and a quarter.

Starters.	Jockeys.	W'hts.	Betting—Straight.	Place.
Firenzi (4)	Garrison	126	Even.	1 to 2
Terra Cotta (4)	McLaughlin	119	10 to 1	3 to 1
Belvidere (4)	Hayward	115	15 to 1	5 to 1
Dunboyne (4)	Murphy	114	5 to 1	8 to 5
Frank Ward (5)	Taral	108	10 to 1	4 to 1
Connemara (4)	Anderson	105	5 to 1	8 to 5

Firenzi and Garrison were warmly applauded as they paraded past the stands, and so were Terra Cotta and McLaughlin. Connemara ran in blinders and behaved badly at the post.

After two false starts the flag fell and they started off with Terra Cotta first, Frank Ward, Dunboyne and Connemara next. Coming to the stands Connemara was in the lead, a length before Frank Ward, who was half a length in front of Terra Cotta, who was next the rail. As they passed just behind the timing stand Terra Cotta was crowded against the rail and McLaughlin yelled out: "Look out! look out!"

Connemara held the lead till they were passing the club house bluff when Firenzi, despite the fact that Garrison was holding her back with all his might, went to the front. McLaughlin on Terra Cotta stuck to her like wax and worked like a demon, but the gallant filly was as full of life as an egg is of meat, and won with ease by a length. Terra Cotta, second, was a length before Dunboyne. Belvidere, Connemara, and Frank Ward followed in order given.

The time by quarters was 0:27, 0:55, 1:20¾, 1:48 and 2:13¼. The mutuals paid $11.20.

BANNER BEARER FIRST, MIRABEAU SECOND.

Fourth Race.—A heavyweight free handicap sweepstakes, for 3-year-olds and upward; $20 each if not declared out, with $750 added, of which $200 to the second horse; three-quarters of a mile.

Starters.	Jockeys.	W'hts.	Betting—Straight.	Place.
Cambyses (4)	Fitzpatrick	136	7 to 1	2 to 1
Banner Bearer (5)	Williams	134	4 to 1	7 to 5
Oarsman (4)	Martin	128	8 to 1	2 to 1
Estrella (5)	Murphy	127	8 to 1	2 to 1
Kaloolah (4)	McLaughlin	126	8 to 1	3 to 1
Amos (3)	Taral	124	60 to 1	20 to 1
Mirabeau (3)	Garrison	121	2 to 1	4 to 5
Gen. Gordon (3)	Taylor	120	80 to 1	30 to 1

They scrapped at the post for several minutes before they could be got into line and motion. The flag fell on an excellent start. Jimmy at once took Kaloolah out, but Banner Bearer outpaced her and went out of sight around Club House Hill a head before Kaloolah, who had Mirabeau and Estrella immediately behind her. Kaloolah kept close to Banner Bearer to the last furlong post, where Mirabeau came up and pressed Banner Bearer very hard.

The finish was close and exciting, and it was anybody's race up to the last jump, but Banner Bearer ran truest, and won by a short head in 1:19. Mirabeau, second, was a length before Kaloolah, third. The others came in the following order: Cambyses, Oarsman, Gen. Gordon, Amos, and Estrella. The mutuals paid $30.15.

OVID FIRST, WILFRED SECOND.

Fifth Race.—Purse $700; entrance money, $20 each, to second horse; for 3-year-olds and upward; winning penalties, non-winning and maiden allowances; one mile.

Starters.	Jockeys.	W'hts.	Betting—Straight.	Place.
Ban Cloche (4)	Crittenden	113	15 to 1	4 to 1
Lelex (a)	Taral	110	2 to 1	4 to 5
Bess (3)	Anderson	110	7 to 2	Even
Ovid (4)	F. Littlefield	110	2 to 1	3 to 5
Royal Arch (a)	Church	110	30 to 1	8 to 1
Wilfred (4)	Hamilton	110	30 to 1	6 to 1
Osceola (4)	Palmer	105	20 to 1	4 to 1

They went away nicely bunched, with Wilfred, Bess, Lelex and Ovid heads apart. Going around Picnic Hill, Bess was a head in front of Ovid, who was two lengths before Wilfred, with Lelex next. Ovid was in the van as they came in sight a half length before Bess, who was a length in front of Wilfred.

Ovid was still a half length in front as they went out of sight around Club House hill, with Lelex, who had moved up to second, next. As they again reappeared Ovid was two lengths in front of Bess, with Wilfred, Osceola and Lelex heads apart. The field began to close on the leader at the head of the homestretch. Littlefield sat down to ride.

When they were well straightened out, both Wilfred and Osceola came with a rush, but it was without avail, as Ovid won by a short head in 1:45½. Wilfred, second, was a scant length before Osceola, third. Bess, Lelex, Ban Cloche and Royal Arch came in as named.

The mutuals paid $20.25.

FORDHAM FIRST, OCEAN SECOND.

Sixth Race.—Purse $600; entrance, $15 each, to second horse; for 3-year-olds and upward; the winner to be sold at auction; highest price, $3,000; selling allowances; beaten horses not liable to be claimed; Titan course, 1,400 yards.

Fordham won. Ocean was second and Drake third. Time, 1:23.

Inquest on the Latest Mutilated Body.

LONDON, Oct. 4.—An inquest was held to-day over the trunk of the body found on Tuesday in a recess on the Thames embankment. The surgeons who were present confirmed the belief that the arms which had previously been found floating in the river belonged to this body.

WALL STREET POSTSCRIPT.

Total Sales at the Stock Exchange To-day 227,430 Shares.

A Boston special to Dow, Jones & Co. states that the Bank of England rate has not been as high as 5 per cent. since February, 1887. The amount of reserve in the Bank of England Oct. 1 was £8,650,130 against £11,562,000 Aug. 1. For the same periods of 1887 the amounts were £9,009,724 against £11,121,000.

Reports come from Chicago that there is to be another advance in grain rates from all western points on the St. Paul road about the middle of October. St. Paul has already advanced rates to-day 1 cent. on all kinds of grain from Minnesota and Dakota, and it is not unlikely that other roads will follow with still further advances.

The New York office of Louisville & Nashville received a telegram this morning to the effect that 234,322 shares were voted at the annual meeting and that the old Board was re-elected.

The *Commercial Bulletin* figures that Reading's net earnings will fall about $1,000,000 short of all fixed and other charges ahead of the stock for the first nine months of 1888.

The Fitchburg Railroad Company has just contracted for 8,000 tons of heavy steel rails which it will use in the improvement of the track during the coming year.

Henry Villard of the Oregon & Transcontinental Company, accompanied by President T. F. Oakes of the Northern Pacific, arrived at Chicago to-day en route for their proposed tour of inspection over the Northern Pacific Railroad.

LATER REPORTS OF RAILROAD EARNINGS.

	1888.	1887.	Inc.	Dec.
K. C., Clin. & Springfield:				
3d week Sept.	$6,213	$4,997	$1,216	....
Kansas City, Fort Scott & Memphis:				
3d week Sept.	83,212	99,769	....	$16,557
Central Vermont:				
4th week Sept.	66,454	64,958	1,496	....
Ohio River:				
4th week Sept.	14,479	10,884	3,595	....
Jan. 1 to Sept. 30	330,759	255,043	75,716	....

GOOD RACING AT LATONIA.

The Attendance was Large and the Conditions were Favorable.

LATONIA, Oct. 4.—The meeting of the Latonia Jockey Club so far has been successful. The weather was clear, cool, and the track was in fine condition. The attendance was about the same as usual. The feature of the day was the Zoo Zoo stakes for 2-year-old fillies, at six furlongs.

The results were as follows:

EVERETT FIRST, LEONTINE SECOND.

First Race.—Purse $400, of which $100 to second; for maiden 3-year-olds and upward; six furlongs.

Everett won, with Leontine second, and Deer Lodge third. Time, 1:17¾.

LITBERT FIRST, HECTOR SECOND.

Second Race.—Selling; purse $400, of which $100 to second; for 3-year olds and upward; seven furlongs.

Litbert finished first, with Hector second, and Panama third. Time, 1:30¾.

HINDOOCRAFT FIRST, RIMINI SECOND.

Third Race.—Purse $400, of which $100 to second; for 2-year-olds; five furlongs.

Hindoocraft won in 1:03, with Rimini second and Tenny third.

LONGLIGHT FIRST, STRIDEAWAY SECOND.

Fourth Race.—A free handicap sweepstakes, for 3-year-olds and upward, of $10 each, with $500 added, of which $100 to second; one mile and seventy yards.

Longlight first, Strideaway second, and Lavinia Belle third. Time, 1:48½.

THE M'QUADE CASE.

The Ex-Alderman's Bail Will Be $20,000—He Is On His Way Home.

Clerk Toner of Lawyer Richard Newcombe's office appeared before Recorder Smyth in General Sessions to-day with an order for the remission back to General Sessions of ex-Alderman Arthur J. McQuade, whose conviction was recently reversed by the Court of Appeals. The Recorder signed the order and copies were made of the same for the District Attorney and the deputy Sheriffs who will go to Sing Sing to bring back McQuade.

About an hour later Richard S. Newcomb and Gen. B. F. Tracy went before the Recorder and made a motion for the reduction of the $25,000 bail asked for by District Attorney Fellows. They asked that it be fixed at $15,000. The Recorder stated that, in view of the fact that McQuade, during the first preparations of the trial did not evade the process of the law, &c., he would compromise the matter, making the amount of the bail $20,000.

Lawyer Newcombe's clerk, Mr. Toner, and two deputy sheriffs left for Sing Sing at 1 o'clock, bearing an order for the release and transfer of McQuade into their custody. The party will arrive in the city about 4 o'clock, when they will appear before Recorder Smyth.

HORNBACKER WANTS TO TRY AGAIN.

And Charlie McCarthy Says He is Very Willing to Give Him Another Go.

Charlie McCarthy, the bantam champion, having read the statement in a daily paper from Eugene Hornbacker, to the effect that he (Hornbacker) was starved and weakened by Turkish baths in order to get down to weight for his recent encounter with McCarthy, and that he would like to meet McCarthy again at catch weights, McCarthy to-day stated to an EVENING SUN representative that he would not meet him at catch weights, as the difference is too great, but that if Eugene desires to meet him again under the same conditions as the last match he will be only too glad to accommodate him.

DE CASTRO & DONNER'S REFINERIES.

They are Closed To-day as Predicted in Yesterday's Evening Sun.

As announced in THE EVENING SUN last night De Castro & Donner's North Third street refinery was closed last evening, and 700 men found this morning that they were thrown out of work indefinitely.

This action was in accordance with the order of Theodore A. Havemeyer, President of the Sugar Trust, and makes the second refinery belonging to this firm that the Sugar Trust has closed.

MAYOR CHAPIN INDORSES GOV. HILL.

Ringing Words of Commendation from Brooklyn's Great Democrat.

This morning Mayor Chapin of Brooklyn issued a letter indorsing the nomination of Gov. Hill.

The following are some extracts from it:

All Democratic supporters of President Cleveland should desire Gov. Hill's re-election. The defeat of Gov. Hill would be a distinct and serious injury to Democracy.

His official methods are careful and thorough. His mind is naturally vigorous. He has made his way step by step from most modest beginnings He is a skilful and well-equipped lawyer, and his writings are clear and obviously the result of study.

I do not hesitate to say that there are not twenty men in the country whose united efforts have done as much to hold the State in the Democratic column from 1885 to 1888 as has been done by Gov. Hill. In each State election he has been earnest and untiring.

A Democrat by instinct and training, and a keen politician as well, he has seen throughout that the Democratic cause has not reached the stage where it can endure defeat in its great Northern stronghold.

La Blanche Sent Up for Three Months.

BUFFALO, Oct. 4.—George La Blanche, John Leslie, William Baker and John Floss, convicted yesterday of aiding and abetting the prize-fight between Hattie Leslie and Alice Leary, were sentenced this morning. La Blanche and Floss were sentenced to three months, Leslie and Baker to six months at hard labor.

Hattie Leslie was discharged, and the indictment against Alice Leary was dismissed.

Massachusetts State Fair.

SPRINGFIELD, Mass., Oct. 4.—The big fair of the Bay State Agricultural Society opened here this morning under the most flattering auspices with magnificent weather. The entries in the various cattle classes are well filled with animals of the highest pedigree, and in some instances of great value.

De Baun to Be Surrendered.

SHERBROOKE, Que., Oct. 4.—Judge Rioux this morning, ordered that De Baun, the defaulting assistant cashier of the National Park Bank of New York, be surrendered to the United States authorities. The defense are applying for a writ of habeas corpus.

EXTRA

BROOKLYN LEADS.

Baltimores Will Probably Lose To-day.

A GREAT SLUGGING GAME.

The Score at the End of the 5th Inning Was:

BROOKLYN - - - - - - 10
BALTIMORE - - - - - - 6

WASHINGTON PARK, Oct. 4.—Cool but delightful baseball weather ruled here to-day. The baseball heart of Brooklyn, from Red Hook to Ridgewood, wagged with consequent joy. Foutz has on a red jersey and Darby O'Brien a blue one. Caruthers's white sweater completes the national colors. At Umpire Ferguson's bidding the nines came up as follows:

BROOKLYN.		BALTIMORE.	
Pinkney	third base	Griffin	centre field
Collins	second base	Tucker	first base
Burns	short stop	Farrell	short stop
Corkhill	centre field	Shindle	third base
Foutz	right field	Sommer	right field
O'Brien	left field	Goldsby	left field
Orr	first base	Greenwood	second base
Clark	catcher	Cantz	catcher
Caruthers	pitcher	Kilroy	pitcher

Umpire—Mr. Ferguson.

FIRST INNING.—A flash of the ash, a parabolic curve, and Mr. Foutz has killed Griffin. Tucker got on to the ball with his bat. His fly was muffed by Corkhill. Farrell's hit gave him one lap, and a passed ball by Orr gave him another.

Shindle's hit to left brought Tucker and Farrell home, and gave the batter third base. He also came home on a bad throw by Clark to Pinkney. Sommer struck out. Goldsby's three attempts added no lustre to his name. Three runs.

For Brooklyn Pinkney took his base without working for the privilege. Collins struck out. Burns took his base on balls. Pinkney came home on Corkhill's base hit, and Burns also crossed the plate on a poor throw home.

Corkhill scored on a poor throw of Foutz's hit to Farrell. O'Brien's three-baser brought Foutz home. Orr brought O'Brien over the plate with a clean hit over the second baseman's head. Clark's fumbled hit scored Orr. Caruthers was retired because he couldn't find the ball. Pinkney retired the side with six runs to Brooklyn's credit.

SECOND INNING.—Greenwood went to the cemetery from Clark to Orr. Cantz's fly was caught by Burns in fine style. Kilroy failed to get there before the ball. No runs.

For Brooklyn, Collins's red legs moved like the spokes of an ambulance wagon, but vainly. Imported Burns followed suit, the ball beating him to first.

One thousand yells greeted Corkhill's magnificent hit to far centre for three bases. Red Jersey Foutz made a similar hit and Corkhill came home, Foutz going to third. His long legs and a passed ball shoved the score up one. O'Brien got his base on a fumble. Orr's foul fly was caught by Tucker. Two runs.

THIRD INNING.—Griffin got to first with both feet. Tucker tucked a little one to short right which was fumbled. Griffin scored on a combination of errors.

Farrell's sacrifice brought Tucker home. Shindle went out to second base. Sommer did'nt get safely to second, and the nine sat down. Two runs.

A claim was made that Cantz had been injured on the hand, and Fulmer took his place after a long kick.

For Brooklyn, Clark fouled out. Caruthers missed three curves. Pinkney's foul tip was caught by Fulmer. No runs.

FOURTH INNING.—Goldsby got his base on Collins's fumble. Greenwood retired on a foul tip. Goldsby tried to steal second, but was caught. Fulmer failed to bring the ash and horsehide together. No runs.

For Brooklyn Imported Collins's foul tip took the back off a reporter's chair. He then struck out. Burns went to first on balls. Corkhill's base hit moved Burns up a base.

Foutz tried, but couldn't. Burns scored on a passed ball. O'Brien retired the nine from Farrell to Tucker. One run.

FIFTH INNING.—Kilroy's fly landed in Foutz's hands. Griffin's hit netted him two bases. He reached third and scored on Tucker's safe hit.

Farrell hit to the pitcher and went out at first.

Shindle's hit was captured by O'Brien. One run.

For Brooklyn, Orr got first on an error of first basemen.

Clark went out from Farrell to Tucker.

Caruthers struck out.

Pinkney's two-bagger scored Orr. Collins fouled to Shindle. One run.

Score at the end of 5th inning:

Brooklyn	6	2	0	1	1
Baltimore	3	0	2	0	1

TEEMER IS READY.

He Says He Wants to Row O'Connor, the Canadian Sculler.

John Teemer, the famous oarsman, who arrived in the city yesterday, seemed to be very much put out about the statement made by O'Connor, the Canadian sculler, to the effect that he would row Teemer at any time for $1,000 a side.

"I don't believe he wants to make a race with me," said Teemer. "I was ready to row him on the 29th of last month, according to agreement, and he flunked out of it on a technicality which existed only in his own mind. Now, I will put up $500 to bind a match in the hands of any responsible newspaper in New York city that he may name, with the understanding that we mutually agree on a referee. He wants the naming of both stakeholder and referee, but I do not think that is sporting procedure."

Teemer says he has not yet heard directly from Lanlan in regard to his having made a match with Peter Kemp, who now holds the championship of the world. He thinks the match has really been made and says he will go to Australia to row Kemp; but will first fill his present engagement with the rowing tricycle.

Harlem Bridge Roadbed to Be Relaid.

Harlem Bridge, which spans Harlem River at 130th street and Third avenue, is to have a new roadbed constructed on an entirely different plan from the old one. Instead of a solid layer of stringers, there will be only four stringers in each section, four by eight inches, on edge. The next layer will be three by six inch timbers, tarred and creosoted, and laid at right angle on the stringers, with sufficient space between them to allow the rain to run through easily. The top layer will consist of hard pine.

All the work will be done between the hours of 6 and 9 o'clock at night. The first section will be torn away and rebuilt to-night. It is thought that the work will be completed by Election day.

Pearson on the Franking Privilege.

Postmaster Pearson said to-day that he had not issued any orders to the Post Office employes concerning franked documents. The Postmaster, he says, has no authority to interfere with sealed matter sent through the mails, and has no way of determining whether the franking privilege is being violated. He considers it the duty of those to whom this franking privilege is extended to see that it is protected.

The World's Pacing Record Beaten.

NAPA, Cal., Oct. 4.—The World's pacing record of one mile for 3-year-olds, was beaten to-day by Gold Leaf. Time, 2:15.

Information for Fishermen.

HIGH WATER TO-MORROW.

Sandy Hook, 7:08 | Gov. Island, 7:33 | Hell Gate, 8:22

Professional Association Sharpers.

A short time ago a dapper looking young fellow giving the name of Anderson, who proved to be an excellent "stall," applied to liquor dealer Connors, of Duluth, Minn., for a situation, and was employed as a barkeeper. He showed up as a good sprinter, and his employer backed him against a number of local runners and won considerable money. Finally Connors backed his man against any comer, and a stranger, who subsequently proved to be Harry Bethune, the professional champion, appeared on the scene and made a match. The race was run, and Anderson, as might be expected, was beaten. Connors lost about $1.700, but he would not take his medicine quietly. He swore out a warrant against the two runners, and they were arrested by Detective Benson, of Duluth, Monday afternoon, in St. Paul. Anderson does not give his real name, but is believed to be Davis, the California sprinter. He secured the services of an attorney, and a writ of *habeas corpus* will be argued in the District Court next (this) week.—*Toronto Mail.*

HARVARD'S ATHLETES.—The Freshmen of Harvard College held their annual Fall sports on Holmes' Field, Cambridge, Mass., Oct. 29, the events resulting thus: Two mile bicycle race—W. B. Greenleaf (walk over), 6m. 23⅗s. Hundred yards dash—J. P. Lee, 10⅗s. Mile walk—C. T. R. Bates, 8m. 36s. Half mile run—G. L. Batchelder, 2m. 17⅘s. Running broad jump—J. P. Lee, 19ft. 3½in. Mile run—A. M. White (walk over). Four hundred and forty yards run—W. H. Wright, 2m. 54⅗s. High jump—J. P. Lee, 5ft. 5in. Pole vault—W. M. Duane (walk over). Two hundred and twenty yards run—J. P. Lee, 24s.

MILITARY ATHLETES.—The first annual Fall games of Company I, Twenty-third Regiment, will be held at the Armory, 171 Clermont avenue, Brooklyn, on Saturday evening, Nov. 24, at eight o'clock. Events: 50yd. dash, 220yd. dash, half mile dash, 1 mile walk, 1 mile run, 2 mile bicycle race (limit 100yd.), 1 mile bicycle race, 220yd. hurdle race (5 hurdles, 2ft. 6in. high), running high jump (limit 3in.), exhibition lacrosse, exhibition lawn tennis. Entrance fee, 50 cents for each event. W. G. Hegeman, official handicapper. Rules of A. A. U. govern all contests.

ADAMS ACADEMY.—The annual Fall games of the Adams Academy Athletic Association were held at Quincy, Mass., Oct. 30. Result: 100yd. dash—Won by W. S. Adams, 12s. Baseball throw—J. H. Osborne, 322ft. 2in. Three legged race—W. S. Adams and L. A. Frothingham, 16s. Quarter mile run—E. H. Johnson, 1m. 9¾s. Barrel roll—E. Y. Kittredge, 26s. Hurdle race—L. A. Frothingham, 16s. Half mile run—C. K. Carter, 3m. 4s. Tug of war, first class team. Long jump—L. A. Frothingham, 17ft. 11in.

A WRESTLING MATCH, Græco Roman style, between Tom Cannon and Antoine Pierre, took place at the Princess Rink, Cincinnati, O., on the evening of Oct. 29, the former winning two of the three falls and the match. The wrestling was rather tame.

TOFF LYNCH, on Oct. 23, attempted to walk four miles inside thirty minutes on the Cambridge road, at Newmarket, Eng., but loose going and a cold, boisterous wind were against the success of the undertaking, and he lost by three seconds.

THE TURF.

Runners at Clifton.

The crowd at the course of the Passaic County Agricultural Association, Clifton, N. J., on the afternoon of Oct. 31, was very large, while the weather was delightful, the track in capital condition and the sport enjoyable. Result: Purse $250, for two year olds, $50 to second, selling allowances, five furlongs—H. Bradley's Fiddlehead, by King Ernest, 111, Bender, first, in 1:05; Isis, 108, Barton, second, by two lengths; Singlestone, 115, Cullen the favorite, third, half a length behind......Purse $250, of which $50 to second, for three year olds, selling allowances, one mile—J. Meagher's Keystone, by Harry O'Fallon, 110, Whyburn, the favorite, first, in 1:46; Easterbrook, 105, Bergan, and Full Sail, [illegible] a dead heat, for second place...... Purse $250, of which $50 to second, selling allowances, a mile and a furlong—J. Delong's Pericles, by Strachino, aged, 108, Bergan, the favorite, first, in 1:59½; Lucy H., 5—105, Thompson, second, by a length and a half; Supervisor, 6—110, Camp, third, half a length behind......The Jersey City Handicap, purse $500, of which $50 to second, a mile and a furlong—P. H. Grill's Wilfred, by Wilful, 118, Bergan, the favorite, first, in 1:59; Brian Boru, 4—105, Cullen, second, by three lengths; Monmouth, 3—112, Camp, third, a head behind......Purse $500, for three year olds and upward, $50 to second, six furlongs—C. H. Desmond's Capulin, by Long John, 5—115, Hyslop, first, in 1:17¾; Armstrong, 5—115, Bergan, second, by two lengths; Herman, 5—115, Whyburn, third, by the same distance.

There was a big crowd at Clifton on Friday afternoon, and they would have enjoyed the fine weather and good racing much more had the favorites been more successful, all but one losing the "dust" placed on them by their confident backers. Result: Purse $250, for four year olds and upward, $50 to second, to carry 10lb above the scale, selling allowances, six furlongs—T. Carr's Alice, by Stonehenge, 4—125, Camp, first, in 1:19; Slasher, 5—119, Meagher, second, by ten lengtht; Richelieu, 4—122, Malone, third, a length behind......Purse $250, for two year olds, $50 to second, selling allowances, six furlongs—H. Bradley's Fiddlehead, by King Ernest, 111, Bender, the favorite, first, in 1:19; Zacataceas, 107, Ossler, second, by a length; Arizona, 108, Richardson, third, a neck away ....Purse $250, of which $50 to second, selling allowances, one mile—S. N. Stillwell's Souvenir, by Eolus, 5—102, Bergan, first, in 1:45; Lucy H., 5—108, Thompson, second, by two lengths; Lemon Blossom, 2—84, M. Lynch, third, six lengths away...... The Rutherford Handicap, purse $500, of which $50 to second, a mile and a furlong—H. C. Meyer's Bonnie S., by Scotlander, 106, Cullen, first, in 1:58½; Bright Eyes, 5—100, Ossler, second, by two lengths; Bill Bond, 5—116, G. Lynch, third, a head away..... Purse $500, for all ages, $50 to second, seven furlongs—C. McCaull's Malachi, by Iroquois, 2—87, J. Tribe, first, in 1:30; Wolfred, 115, Bergan, the favorite, second, by a head; Brian Boru, 4—118, Whyburn third, half a dozen lengths away.

Trotting in New England.

The Lawrence (Mass.) Riding Park Association held their Fall meeting last week, opening on Oct. 30. Result: Class 2:29, purse $300, for pacers and trotters—C. E. Mosher's Stubby S. first, Edgecliff (won the second heat) second. The first and third heats were won by Mike, but he was distanced in the fifth heat. Time, 2:34¼, 2:33, 2:31½, 2:32, 2:32½, 2:34. Class 2:34, purse $300—C. C. Mayberry's Chevalitta first, Jim Mack (won the second and third heats) second, Princess third and Kate R. fourth. Time, 2:32¼, 2:31¼, 2:32, 2:32¼, 2:32½. Class 2:22, for pacers and trotters, purse $200—F. M. Dodge's W. K. first, Rex (won the fourth heat) second, Alexander Box (won the third heat) third, Nellie O. fourth. Time, 2:29¼, 2:28¾, 2:23¼, 2:26¼, 2:27¼. Special race, purse $50—P. F. Brown's Robert F. first, Byronia (won the first and fourth heats) second, Daisy B. (won the second heat) third, and Tommy Thompson fourth. Class 2:37, purse $200—J. Shillington's Hattie W. first, Kate P. (won the first and third heats) second, and chunk third. Time, 2:37, 2:33½, 2:36½, 2:38½, 2:38½. Class 2:25, purse $200—A. J. Libbey's Nellie O. first, in 2:28¾, 2:28¾, 2:30; Billy T. second, Lexington Chief third and Columbus Girl fourth.

THE Great Tom Handicap, of $1,500, added to a sweepstakes of $75 each, for three year olds and upward, a mile, was run for at Lincoln, Eng., Nov. 1, and was won by W. Younger's Tyrone, by York, 5—111; Love in Idleness, 3—105, second; Greenwich, 6—96, third.

GUY made an attempt to beat the record at the track in Glenville, O., on Nov. 1, but, although the going was excellent, he failed, the mile being trotted in 2:12. He will be sent for it again in a few days.

THE new officers of the Ontario Jockey Club are as follow: President, W. Hendrie; vice presidents, F. Smith and T. C. Patterson.

The Guttenburg Runners.

Long delays at the post marked the racing at the track on the New Jersey heights on Tuesday afternoon, 30, and in consequence the good sized crowd in attendance left the grounds in no pleasant frame of mind, particularly as only two of the favorites managed to reach the winning post first. Result: Purse $200, of which $50 to second, for three year olds and upward, selling allowances, six furlongs—C. J. Donovan's Frank Mullins, by Macaroon, 6—102, Bergan, first, in 1:26½; Manhattan, 3—105, Ossler, second, by a length; Eugene Brodie, 6—97, Barton, the favorite, third, by the same distance......Purse $200, of which $50 to second, for three year olds and upward, selling allowances, six furlongs—J. F. Carmody's Dago, by St. Cyr, 5—112, Barton, the favorite, first, in 1:25½; Wayward, 5—112, Foster, second, by a neck; John Alexander, 6—112, Miller, third, by the same distance ..... Purse $200, for all ages, $50 to second, to carry 20lb above the scale, selling allowances, seven furlongs—C. Russell's Tunis, by Algerine, aged, 115, Miller, first, in 1:39¾; Don't Know, 2—96, Barton, the favorite, second, by a neck; Johnnie E., 4—124, M. J. Lynch, third three lengths away......Purse $200, of which $50 to second, selling allowances, six and a half furlongs—J. T. Carmody's Rebellion, by Luke Blackburn, 4—107, Barton, first, in 1:31½; Joe Mitchell, aged, 100, Bergan, the favorite, second, by a neck; Rebel Scout, aged, 105, Hueston, third, six lengths away......Purse $250, of which $50 to second, selling allowances, six furlongs—A. Wilkins' Servia, by Hindoo, 2—87, H. Penny, the favorite, first, in 1:23; Lemon, 3—104, Golliday, second, by two lengths; Relax, 4—105, Hyslop, third, three lengths away.

The opening of the rival meeting at Waverly affected the attendance on Thursday afternoon, yet there was a goodly crowd present, and the racing was first rate. Result: Purse $200, of which $50 to second, for two year olds, selling allowances, five furlongs—W. Bell & Co.'s Altitude, by Forester, 103, Sims, first, in 1:06; Consolation, 115, Crittenden, the favorite, second, by two lengths; King Alfonso-Fashionette colt, 103, Penny, third, four lengths away......Purse $200, for three year olds, $50 to second, six furlongs—P. Loughran's Boodle, by Bertram, 115, Miller, first, in 1:20; Joseph, 118, Bergan, the favorite, second, by a length; Manhattan, 118, Ossler, third, eight lengths away...... Purse $200, of which $50 to second, selling allowances, six and a half furlongs—F. M. Bray's Playfair, by Plenipo, 6—115, M. Barrett, first, in 1:27; Lizzie M., 103, Ossler, second, by four lengths; Havana, aged, 109, Foster, third, two lengths behind. ..... Purse $200, of which $50 to second, selling allowances, six and a half furlongs—C. A. Bader's Rednette, by Red Bluff, 5—106, Ossler, first, in 1:26; Tyrone, 5—109, Bergan, second, by two lengths; Bass Viol, 6—121, Miller, third, four lengths away. ......Purse $200, of which $50 to second, selling allowances, one mile—T. Crysler's Joe Mitchell, by Glengarry, aged, 103, Ossler, the favorite, first, in 1:46½; Frolic, aged, 110 Foster, second, by a
length; O'Fellus, 4—105, Bergan, t

A large crowd was in attendan
ternoon, and, although the v
threatening in the early portic
out fine, while the rain that fell
track materially. Result: Purse
$50 to second, six furlongs—M.
bor Lights, by Rayon d'Or, 3—10
1:20; California, 3—107, Ossler.
ond, by a length; Juggler, 3—
eight lengths away......Purse $
ances, $50 to second, seven fu
ney's Brynwood, by Woodlands
first, in 1:33; Silver Star, 4—112,
three lengths; Rednette, 5—102,
lengths away......Purse $250, o
ond, selling allowances, a mile
Rock City Stable's Fenelon, by R
field, the favorite, first, in 1
4—118, Barton, second, b
Top Sawyer, aged, 105, Gollida
behind......Purse $200, of whic
selling allowances, six furlongs—
by Stonehenge, aged, 109, Foster
in 1:19½; Una B., 107, aged, Lanc
lengths; Rebel Scout, aged, 10
neck behind......Purse $200, for
to second, five furlongs—W. Ga
by Jacobite, 112, Bergan, the
1:05¼; Millwood, 102, H. Pen
length and a half; King Alfons
102, Ossler, third, half a dozen l
......Purse $200, of which $50
allowances, seven furlongs—Sara
fred Jay, by Virgil, 3—95, Mulla
Saluda, 5—103, Miller, second, by
Donovan, 6—101, Golliday, third,

Union Jockey C

The gathering at Waverly Parl
day afternoon, Nov. 1, when the
this club was opened, was such
courage the management, whil
perfect, and the half mile track i
Result: Purse $250, for three year
$50 to second, five furlongs—W
by Kingfisher, 5—115, Dunn, the
1:04; Faster, 4—115, G. Lynch.
lengths; Chancellor, 3—113, San
behind......Purse $250, of whi
selling allowances, six furlongs—
stock, by Luke Blackburn, 3—96
1:18; Tony Pastor, 102, Coldier, th
by two lengths; Can't Tell, 3—9
head away......Purse $250, of
one, selling allowances, sev
Schulting & Co.'s Relax, by
Doane, first, in 1:31½; McLau
Lynch, second, by two lengt
4—112, third, a neck behind
for all ages, $50 to second, one
Raveller, by Reform, 4—115, Ber
first, in 1:43¾; Quincy, 5—115, C
two lengths; Leland, 4—115,
lengths away......Purse $250, f
second, to carry 10lb above weig
and seventy yards—Chapman &
sell, by Eolus, 6—125, Richardso
Orlando, aged, 125, Hogan, secon
Charley Arnold, 4—125, Meagher,
in the rear.

Saturday, 3, was the second da
and there was a fairly good cr
were compelled to endure tiresome waits between races, owing to the incompetency of the starter, the horses in the second race being over an hour at the post, and being finally sent away with the favorite standing still. This sort of work delayed matters so that the last event on the programme had to be declared off in consequence of darkness, and the people went home thoroughly disgusted. Result: Purse $250, of which $50 to second, for three year olds and upward, selling allowances, six furlongs—J. A. Batchelor's Chancellor, by Monday, 3—113, Dunn, the favorite, first, in 1:19; Mollie Thomas, aged, 115, Barber, second, by two lengths; Gounod, 3—110, Coldier, third, six lengths away. ......Purse $250, of which $50 to second, selling allowances, one mile—M. J. Kelly's Orlando, by Billet, 6—105, Doane, first, in 1:47. Can't Tell, 3—90, J. Tribe, second, by a neck; Count Luna, 4—105, Barber, third, six lengths in the rear..... Purse $250, for horses that had run and not won in 1888, seven furlongs—D. Nagle's Peter L., by Rebel, aged, 115, Coldier, the favorite, first, in 1:35; Mazie, 3—110, Horton, second, by a length; Judge Norton, 4—113, Avery, third, four lengths away......Purse $250, for all ages, of which $50 to second, a mile and seventy yards—F. Sassone's Pocomoke, by Reform, 5—118, Meagher, first, in 1:55; Orlando, 6—122, Hogan, second, by a length; Charley Russell, 6—122, Richardson, the favorite, third, a length and a half away.

SWEEPSTAKES TROT.—The great trotting sweepstakes, $1,000 each, for which were entered Bowerman Bros.' Hinda Wilkes, R. G. Stoner's Baron Wilkes, and B. J. Treacy's Bermuda, the winner to take all, was decided at the Fair Grounds, Lexington, Ky., on Nov. 1. All the conditions were highly favorable, and there was a large crowd to witness the contest. Baron Wilkes, the favorite, proved an easy winner in straight heats, with Bermuda second. Time, 2:20¾, 2:18¾, 2:18.

PATRON BEATEN.—The oft postponed trotting match between Prince Wilkes and Patron was decided at West Side Park, Nashville, Tenn., Oct. 31, before the running races took place. Patron was the favorite, but he was defeated in straight heats. Time, 2:15½, 2:20, 2:18½.

W. B. FASIG last week sold the grey trotting mare Mella G., by Dr. Herr, dam Lady Gist, to B. W. Curris for $2,000.

This week THE CLIPPER presents to its readers an excellent portrait of Adrian C. Anson. Probably no man has gained a greater reputation, or is better known in baseball circles, than the genial manager-captain of the Chicago team. Anson was born in Marshalltown, Ia., and has been a prominent figure on the ball field for many years. His baseball career began with amateur nines of his native city, in 1869. He remained an amateur until the end of the season of 1870. His first professional engagement was with the Forest Citys of Rockford, Ill., in 1871. Almost from the start Anson was a brilliant success as an all 'round player. He gained such a reputation while with the Forest Citys that he was engaged in 1872 by the Athletic Club, of Philadelphia, Pa., which was at that time the champion organization. Anson remained with the Athletics until the close of the season of 1875. In 1876, however, he went to the Chicago Club, where he has ever since been. As manager and captain, Anson has few if any equals, and certainly no superiors in the profession. His value as a player, captain and manager cannot be over estimated, as may readily be judged by the able way in which he has, during the past two years, brought his almost experimental teams to the front in the National League, and kept them there nearly the whole of the season, despite the great odds he had to contend against. Captain Anson handles his forces in a way not seen in any other professional team. His tact and ability while on the ball field deserve special commendation. As a batsman Anson ranks second to none, during the past seventeen years of his professional engagement, and his excellent work this year with the bat, in which he leads the National League, shows that he is still to be relied on in that respect. He can field exceedingly well in any position, always plays the game thoroughly, and never flags or loses heart. He is wonderfully agile for a man of his vast magnitude and muscle, standing, as he does, six feet two inches in height, and weighing about two hundred and twenty pounds. Few, if any, players in the profession are more widely known than Anson, his fame as a player and his long connection with the Chicago Club having made his name familiar to every patron of the game, juvenile or adult, and his ability as a team captain; his rarely erring judgment as to the requisite qualities of a ball player; his fidelity to all trusts imposed in him by his club's president, having made him an object of special prominence among ball players and ball club officials. He is very popular with his men, and always treats them courteously, although he, at the same time, exacts thorough discipline from them. Anson is not unreasonable, and therefore does not expect his men to accomplish impossibilities, and he is always ready to encourage a young player when he sees that the man is trying to do his best. Anson is known as a great "kicker," yet he seldoms enters a protest but he gains his point. He makes it a rule not to kick unless he has a good cause, and then he generally gains all he asks for. In conclusion we need only endorse that which John M. Ward, of the New York Club, recently printed concerning Anson: "Perhaps there is no player in the profession who goes on the field with a stronger determination to win. He shows his earnestness in every move, and his reputation as a 'kicker' is familiar, not only to all attendants at the games, but to many who have never seen him. He is not one of your senseless 'kickers,' who finds fault merely because he is being beaten, or to hear himself talk. He is of a most aggressive nature, and he cannot endure defeat. He is full of fight himself, and inspires his players with the same spirit. He is thoroughly versed in the rules of the game, and insists on every point that he can legally claim. I do him the credit to say that he never makes an objection without believing himself that he has some ground, either in right or rule, to support him. It is true, however, that he will go to the outside limit of the rule every time, and while his claims may be legitimate, so far as the rule is concerned, they are not always in accord with a sense of fair play. And, in his extreme eagerness to win, he will occasionally stoop to certain questionable tricks upon the field, and encourage them in his men. Not in reason of these faults, but in spite of them, he is the greatest baseball general on the ball field. In private life he is as pleasant a companion as one could wish to meet." Should Capt. Anson conclude to leave the Chicago Club, he could undoubtedly command the largest salary ever paid an exponent of the national game. His record as a team captain is the most brilliant in the history of the sport. "The old man" is bluff and direct in his methods of management, but his discipline has been healthy, and it has resulted in a career whose success has been the wonder and the envy of other great cities, which have struggled in vain for years to obtain the proud position so often gained by the Chicago Club.

they won the second game of the series, which caused general rejoicing among their friends, who were loud in praises of what the Browns had done, and who said the New Yorks were very fortunate in winning the first game. Those same friends predicted an easy walk over for the Western champions during the remainder of the games that were to be played. Now that the Browns have been beaten, and that by being out played at every point of the game, why set up the dismal howl of unfair treatment, or the thousand and one excuses for their defeats other than the true cause? Acknowledge the coin like a true sportsman, and not throw out slurs and innuendos that are apt to cause reflections to be cast upon one of the best and cleanest of out of door sports. Or, why harp on about what some other team might have done had it had the same chance? It cannot be denied that the Browns won the majority of the games from every other team in the American Association, except the Brooklyns, and they quit even with them. Therefore they were in every sense of the word the only team that had a right to defend the American Association in its struggle for the world's championship. The other teams had the same opportunities for winning first place that the Browns had, but they failed to accept them. Therefore, let them rest until any one of them does become champion of its organization and it will be given ample opportunity to show how well it can defend itself in the final struggle between the two big associations.

The representatives of the many newspapers thoughout the country put various estimates of the strength of the two teams before they met, but the real status was not gleaned until after the two teams had come together. It was then that the superiority of the New Yorks over the Browns was shown. Yet it was hard to convince the friends of the latter that this was the case, especially the ones who had been the loudest in their praises of what the Browns would do. THE CLIPPER took the ground, from the time it was known that these teams would meet for the final struggle, that no estimate could be formed as to the relative strength of the two teams until they met. This was done as a warning to writers not to go too far into the merits of their particular favorite, for in case of defeat they might have avoided just what was expected—

dent Day, Manager Mutrie and the players, each and all, were remembered, singly and collectively. It was an honor that they merited, for they had striven hard to accomplish a great task, and they succeeded most admirably. The strain on their nerves was severe, but they were equal to the emergency. Now that they have earned the proud title of world's champions let nothing be said or done that will in any way cast a reflection upon their good work. Let us hope the New Yorks will be able to meet some one of the other Association teams at the close of another season so as to satisfy the croakers, but if it is not to be their good fortune, then let them enjoy the honors they have already gained. If not next year, New York will surely play another world's series before many more seasons roll round.

Now that the work has been accomplished it will be well to talk about the men who took part in that great struggle. It required the united effort of all the men to land the club as champions of all champions. Every man did, or tried to do, all the work of his position, and in that he made a name for himself. New York now has a team that can hold its own in any baseball organization—a team that can hardly be improved upon. It is strong in every department, and will certainly make a very brilliant record for itself next season. There is little doubt that the same team, in every respect, will again appear on the ball field next season. Ewing, Brown and Murphy will do the catching, and it is needless to say that it will be well taken care of. Ewing has no superiors, and but few equals, in his position. No doubt Ewing will be found behind the bat in most of the games next season. That is, he will do about all the catching for Keefe and Welch. Ewing has done wonderful work during the past season and deserves all the praise that has been accorded him. He has proved beyond a doubt that he is a worker in every sense of the word, and, when the case demands it, that he will remain at his post, although he may be badly injured. In the deciding game at St. Louis, Oct. 25, Ewing had his hand injured very badly, and it caused him considerable pain, but he manfully remained throughout the game and the New Yorks won. It was this spirit throughout the series, on the part of the New Yorks, that helped them to win so easily.

There has been a great deal said already about John M. Ward and his retirement from the New Yorks with the close of the present season. But as most of this talk comes from outside sources little credence can be placed in the truthfulness of it. It is generally believed in this city, and by all persons who seem to know, that Ward will be found with the New York team next year. Just whether or not he will be on hand at the opening of the season is an unsettled question, but it is safe to predict that he will be found inside a New York uniform before the season is far advanced. Just before leaving St. Louis, to join the Australian party, the writer asked Johnny point blank if there was any truth in the report that he was going to play in any other city than New York next year, and his answer was: "I do not believe that Mr. Day will sell my release." The incredulous ones can draw whatever conclusions from those remarks they like, but the baseball enthusiasts of this city can rest assured that their favorite will be found with the New Yorks again next season. Without doubt Ward is a remarkable player. He is perfectly familiar with the rules of the game, and is quick to grasp upon any little technicality that would gain a point for his team. He is a thorough worker, and always plays hard to win. His work during the world's series was of the highest order, and was never surpassed by any other player in his position.

The world's championship was not attained without its mishaps, and some of the injuries proved quite serious. During the last game played in this city young Lyons of the St. Louis Browns was so badly injured in a collision with Robinson, while both were after the same ball, that it is quite likely he will never play ball again. While *en route* to St. Louis Superintendent Bell of the Polo Grounds was stricken down with apoplexy, and was confined to his bed all the time the club was away from home. Then at St. Louis Connor, Brown and Ewing were all injured. The former could not play in any of the last four games played in that city. It is nothing serious, however, and he may be all right again in a few weeks. Brown's injuries, which occured on Oct. 24, the same day as Connor's, are more serious. He had the bones in his thumb so badly shattered that it will require pretty nearly the whole Winter to put them in good shape again. Ewing's injury was described above. President Day was also on the sick list. He had an attack of pleurisy and came home feeling bad.

A sensational report was started while the two clubs were in Philadelphia, and before they had started for the West, to the effect that Tim Keefe would probably not pitch any more during the season. That his arm had given out, and that he had asked to go home, but that Manager Mutrie had refused his request. It was another one of the many fairy tales that are put in circulation during the playing season, and no one was more surprised than Keefe himself when he saw the item in print. He said that is about in keeping with many of the reports that are sent out over the country about ball players during the season. Keefe also exploded the silly report about his not being able
ig in cold weather by pitching in
Polo Grounds, Oct. 20. It was
hat day as one would wish to feel
izzardly" weather outright. Yet
id the Browns got only five safe
ry.

ouis Elmer Foster expressed a
a foot race with any man in the
o make it interesting, Elmer said
e stake any amount from $100 to
ct. he is ready and willing to run
rofession. He is looked upon as
st sprinters of the ball field, and
him and Sunday would be very

son certainly played the game of
rld's series. Some of his stops of
t balls and his backward running
aply wonderful, and caused the
re with amazement. Danny is
, and is filling his position at sec-
the very best men of that posi-
lso a good, reliable man at the

New York players did great work.
urke, Slattery, Whitney, Welch,
Gore, Brown, Murphy, George,
Hatfield, besides the ones already
id their share, and it is hard to say
e spared in case the club were
any of its men. The team for
about the same as the one pre-
e past season, notwithstanding
contrary.

me changes made in the Brooklyn
the old faces it is quite likely that
and Peeples will be among the
mer will have no trouble in get-
n, as there are few first class sec-
l he is among that number. Rad-
as signed with the Philadelphia
of the very best outfielders in the
an be used to good advantage on
e is one thing certain, that when
play in this city they can count
l delegation from Brooklyn to
games, friends of little Paul,
ar in Brooklyn. Manager Wright
ll by signing Jimmy Peeples. He
and can go in behind the bat for
nakes little difference to him who
Then Jimmy can be utilized in
n the nine in case of an emerg-
Billy Holbert, who will also greatly
ne in either of the old organiza-
e of the very best coaching catch-
sion. He can develop a young
than any other man in his line.
o make an excellent manager for
r league teams.

ise move on the part of the Brook-
gage Manager McGunnigle. He
vell during the past season, and
the management that if he could
n second place the first year he
etter with another trial. "Mac"
ly terms with all of the players,
ere anxious to have him manage
ar. Just what team McGunnigle
season, or how the men will be
own at present, nor can any in-
e subject be learned until the
hows up in the Spring. Charley
[illegible] of the Brooklyn grounds was asked about the team for next year, but he was about as communicative as a clam.

There may be one or two new men with the Brooklyn team when it appears before the public at the opening of the next championship season, but there is no certainty about that. The management have spoken about getting a man to play second base who can bat as well as he can field. Then it will be strong in every position. However, Collins may be found in that position when the team is again ready to play ball. The Brooklyns should make a big bid for the pennant next year. A series between them and the New Yorks would be very interesting, and would draw immense crowds of people every time the two teams would meet, either in this city or in Brooklyn.

The veteran ball player, "Lip" Pike, who is a great admirer of the Brooklyn team, last Spring offered to give to the player of the team who made the most runs during the season a complete outfit of furnishing goods. Pinkney was the lucky person to capture the prize, and before leaving for his home in Peoria, Ill., he called at Pike's establishment in Court Street, Brooklyn, and received a good supply of furnishing goods, enough to last him all Winter.

The Chicago and All American teams continued their work at Salt Lake City, Utah, Nov. 1, and, despite the wretched condition of the ground, played a fairly good game. The All Americans had little trouble in gauging Baldwin's delivery, and made thirteen clean hits, with a total of sixteen bases. Healy pitched for the All Americans, and proved a puzzler to the Chicagos. The players clothing was black with mud at the end of the game. Anson caught for the Chicagos, and did exceedingly well. The score was 10 to 3, in favor of the All Americans.

The annual meeting of the International Association will be held in Syracuse, N. Y., Nov. 21, and then the question whether Albany is to be represented next season, and by whom the team will be controlled, will probably be decided.

Vice President Botto, of the Louisville Club, was very anxious to sign Gil Hatfield, while the New Yorks were in St. Louis, but the young man preferred remaining with the local team for another season at the least.

LATEST NEWS.

The Evening Sun.

LATEST NEWS.

VOL. II.--NO. 212. NEW YORK, TUESDAY, NOVEMBER 20, 1888. PRICE ONE CENT.

EXTRA

GUTTENBURG RACES.

Lord Beaconsfield Beats Una B. by a Short Nose.

THE TRACK QUITE HEAVY.

Artless, Bishop, Bass Viol and Juggler Came in Victorious.

NORTH HUDSON DRIVING PARK, Nov. 20.—Something like 2,000 persons, nearly one-third of whom were ladies, were attracted here this afternoon by the excellent programme of six races which has become a fixture at this track. The going was quite heavy.

ARTLESS FIRST, HOLLOWOOD SECOND.

First Race.—Purse $200; maiden 2-year-olds; five furlongs.

The five starters acted in a very unruly manner and did not get the flag until half an hour had been put to waste. Ayalla, Artless and Ada Bell were first to show, but in the run to the stand Huntsman was next to Ayalla, who was still leading by half a length.

Coming to the quarter Bergen sent Artless, the favorite, to the front and kept him a length ahead until the homestretch, where he increased his lead, and coming away won easily by five lengths from Hollowood, who was twenty lengths from Huntsman. Ida Bell was a head behind and Ayalla away back. Time, 1:09.

Betting: Artless, even money and 1 to 2; Hollowood, 3 to 1. Mutuals paid $4.50, $3.60 and $3.50.

LORD BEACONSFIELD FIRST, UNA B. SECOND.

Second Race.—Purse $250; three-quarters of a mile.

Six started, with Armstrong, Una B. and Saluda first away. Lord Beaconsfield immediately took the lead, and at the stand was a length before Saluda. At the half Una B. was running third, half a length behind Saluda. In the homestretch Una B. moved up to second place and set sail for the leader.

Bergen, however, rode Lord Beaconsfield desperately, just winning by a short nose in 1.21¾. Una B., second, was two lengths in front of Saluda. Melodrama, Guess and Armstrong came in as named.

Betting: Beaconsfield, 9 to 5 and 3 to 5; Una B., 3 to 5. Mutuals paid $6.15, $2.70 and $2.65.

BISHOP FIRST, SILVER STAR SECOND.

Third Race.—Purse $250; selling allowances; seven furlongs.

Seven horses started. Silver Star ahead, Bishop and Pat Oakley leading the others. Silver star, Bishop, and Pat Oakley made the circuit in the order named, but going around the backstretch the second time Bishop passed Silver Star and Tunis forged into third place.

They finished in the same order, Bishop a winner by five lengths from Silver Star, who was half a length in front of Tunis. Time, [illegible]. Tenafly, Pat Oakley, Tiburon and Salvator followed.

Betting: Bishop, 7 to 10, and 1 to 3; Silver Star, 7 to 1. Mutuals paid, $4.25, $2.60 and $2.75.

BASS VIOL FIRST, ZERO SECOND.

Fourth Race.—Purse $200; selling allowances; three-quarters of a mile.

Of the ten starters Zero, Voucher and Bass Viol were in the front rank when they broke away, Joe Pierson and Frank Mullins being left at the post. Bass Viol led passing the stand, Nonsense second, Belmont next.

Ida West moved up to third place in the homestretch, but could not reach the leaders, who finished: Base Viol first by a length, Zero second, half a length before Ida West. Time, 1:31½.

Betting: Bass Viol, 3 to 1 and even money; Zero, 4 to 5. Mutuals paid $10.75, $4.75 and $3.10.

JUGGLER FIRST, REBELLION SECOND.

Fifth Race.—Purse $250, selling allowances; one mile.

Juggler won, Rebellion was second, and Brynwood third. Time, 1:50¾.

Betting: Juggler, 3½ to 1 and 7 to 10; Rebellion, 7 to 10. Mutuals paid $9.15, $5.75, and $5.30.

Entries for the Clifton Races.

RACE TRACK, CLIFTON, Nov. 20.—The entries and weights for to-morrow's races are as follows:

First Race.—Purse $250; maiden 2-year-olds; three-quarters of a mile; selling. Uintah, 111 pounds; Slippery Ike 105; Zacatacas, 105; Clarissa, 102; Spray colt, 100; Athalarie filly, 100; Arizona, 100; Futurity, 100; Polenta filly, 97; Gray Gown, 97.

Second Race.—Purse $250; one mile; selling. Courtier, 115 pounds; First Attempt, 115; Spring Eagle, 115; Slumber, 115; Little Mickey, 114; Satisfied, 114; Easterbok, 113; California, 110; Jack Cocks, 110; Fullsail, 110; Flush, 110; Charmer, 109.

Third Race.—Purse $250; one mile and a quarter; selling. Elgin, 113 pounds; Richelieu, 109; Jennie McFarland, 108; Argo, 107; Windsail, 105; Adrian, 105.

Fourth Race.—Purse $500; one mile and an eighth, handicap. Lancaster, 116 pounds; Bonnie S., 114; Amos, 113; Brian Boru, 111; Bill Bond, 110; Taxgatherer, 102; Mary T., 97.

Fifth Race.—Purse $500; one mile and a sixteenth. Wahoo, 120 pounds; Bonanza, 120; Eleve, 114; Leantaka, 88; Glory, 85.

All the Pool Rooms Closed.

All the pool rooms in the lower part of the city are closed to-day. Little knots of speculators gather about the entrances of the different rooms, asking each other "What's up now?" Even Peter De Lacy's place on Park row is deserted.

Notice was sent out from Headquarters to all police Captains this morning to see that the places were closed.

The bookmakers have been doing business openly for some time, and no later than yesterday it was possible for any one to gain admittance and make bets.

The Official Vote Announced.

The Board of County Canvassers met in the Council chamber of the Board of Aldermen this afternoon, and announced the official vote of the city of New York, cast two weeks ago to-day. All the Aldermen were present but Aldermen Cowie and Fitzsimons. Several of the officials-elect were present at the official announcement.

A Woman Shot.

At a late hour this afternoon an unknown man fired two shots at a woman on Second street, in front of No. 9, just off the Bowery. It is not known whether she was killed or not. An arrest was made.

Easton's Players Sold.

SCRANTON, Pa., Nov. 20.—The players reserved by the Easton club have been sold by the Central League, Easton forfeiting its franchise.

Colquitt Elected Senator.

ATLANTA, Ga., Nov. 20.—Alfred H. Colquitt was to-day elected United States Senator, receiving every vote cast in the Senate and House except two. Dugger of the House and Garen of the Senate voted for S. A. Daniell, Republican. Colquitt's total vote was 158 in the House and 38 in the Senate. Henry W. Grady was not nominated.

Distinguished Canadians in Town.

Mr. Hickson, the well-known Manager of the Grand Trunk Railroad of Canada, accompanied by his principal acolyte and rate-cutter, is in town on a visit to Mr. Sam Sloan, the President of the Delaware, Lackawanna & Western Railroad.

Keely Released on Bail.

PHILADELPHIA, Nov. 20.—Keely, the motor inventor, has been released from jail on bail.

A Brooklyn Store Burned.

Benjamin Rosenthall's clothing store, 203 Columbia street, Brooklyn, was burned last night. Damage to stock and building, $5,500. Insured for $5,000.

THE RACING AT WAVERLY.

Sir Roderick, Can't Tell, Arizona, Woodstock and Barnum Win.

RACE TRACK, WAVERLY, N. J., Nov. 20.—The weather was delightful here to-day although a trifle cool. The attendance was up to the usual average. The track was in fairly good condition.

SIR RODERICK FIRST, GOUNOD SECOND.

First Race.—Purse $100; for all ages; three-quarters of a mile.

Sir Roderick jumped away when the flag dropped, with Hysterics second and Gounod next. Sir Roderick cut out the pace, with Mabel and Gounod as the runners up until the head of the homestretch was reached. Then Sir Roderick drew away and won by a length in 1:22. Gounod, second, was a head before Mabel, third. Slasher, James A. II. and Hysterics followed as named.

Betting: Sir Roderick, 4 to 1 and even money; Gounod, 2 to 5.

CAN'T TELL FIRST, ADOLPH SECOND.

Second Race.—Purse $100; for all ages; selling allowances; seven furlongs.

Can't Tell was first away, with Adolph second and John J. S. and Hilda next. Adolph, accompanied by Can't Tell and Mazie, made the pace until the backstretch, where Mazie dropped back beaten.

Can't Tell took the lead on the upper turn, and won by half a length in 1:35. Adolph, second, was four lengths in front of John J. S., third. Hilda, Mazie and Pocomoke finished as named.

Betting: Can't Tell, 6 to 1, and 8 to 5; Adolph barred.

ARIZONA FIRST, DON'T KNOW SECOND.

Third Race.—Purse $100, for maiden 2-year-olds; three-quarters of a mile.

Don't Know took the lead when the flag dropped, with Arizona second and Goldie M. third. Don't Know and Arizona raced head and head together until the backstretch, where Arizona took the lead and was never troubled thereafter, winning by six lengths in 1:22.

Don't Know, second, was three lengths before Solona, third.

Betting: Arizona, 2 to 1 and 1 to 2; Don't Know, 4 to 5.

Murray rode the winner, making his third successive win of the day.

WOODSTOCK FIRST, PARKVILLE SECOND.

Fourth Race.—Purse $250; selling allowances for all ages; five-eighths of a mile.

Berlin got away in the lead with Woodstock, second, and Bridget Keating, third. Woodstock took the lead at the stand, and increasing his lead on the backstretch won by a good length in 1:07.

Parkville, second, was a length and a half before Major, third. Edward F., Bridget Keating, Electricity, Berlin and Sylla finished as named.

Betting: Woodstock, 7 to 5 and 3 to 5; Parkville, 7 to 5.

BARNUM FIRST, LONGITUDE SECOND.

Fifth Race.—Purse $100; for all ages; one mile.

Quincy was first away, with Barnum second and Longitude third. Barnum and Longitude immediately went out, and raced head and head until the homestretch, where Barnum came away, and won by two lengths in 1:49¾.

Longitude was second and Gray Cloud third.

Betting: Barnum, 7 to 10, barred for place; Longitude, even money.

YALE WILL BE ON HAND,

Though Capt. Corbin is Slightly Mystified by Princeton's Action.

NEW HAVEN, Conn., Nov. 20.—It is the opinion on the Yale campus to-day that the Yale football team will play with Princeton in New York Saturday, and Capt. Corbin is still at a loss to know why Princeton voted to play Saturday after having previously named Thanksgiving day as the most satisfactory date. It will be inconvenient for Yale to play Saturday, but she will not try to force Princeton to keep her first agreement. The Yale team is somewhat battered up after last Saturday's game with Wesleyan, but will be in good condition by the end of the week. The food which the eleven have been receiving at a private club having been proved unsatisfactory, all the men in training have gone to board at the New Haven House.

There is nothing new to-day in the Yale-Harvard negotiations, the mission to this city of Palmer, manager of last year's Harvard team, having come to naught. He talked the matter over with Capt. Corbin of the Yale team, and endeavored to arrange for a game at Cambridge for Saturday next. Corbin would not listen to such a proposition. The Yale boys are of the opinion that their eleven could defeat Harvard on Holmes's field as well as anywhere, but agree that Corbin must not back down now. Palmer returned to Cambridge without having accomplished anything.

PRINCETON, N. J., Nov. 20.—The question of the date of the Yale-Princeton game on the Polo Grounds has been decided. The Advisory Committee met yesterday and agreed that the game should be played on Saturday, as scheduled. A special train will be run from Princeton to New York on Saturday at 8:30, returning the same evening. Most of the college men will see the "Brass Monkey" at the Bijou after the game.

DUNCAN ROSS'S CHALLENGE.

Anxious to Hear from Tom Cannon, Who Claims to Be Champion.

BOSTON, Nov. 20.—The following card is published to-day:

To the Editor of the Herald:

I deposited $100 with the *Herald* and accepted the challence of Tom Cannon, the English wrestler, who is parading himself before the public as the champion mixed wrestler, notwithstanding the fact that H. M. Dufur of Marlboro was the champion until defeated by me recently. Cannon has no claim to the championship and has evaded a meeting with me for the past three months. I shall leave my money with the *Herald* for four more days for Cannon to cover. I will not pay any attention to the gate money challenge from Antonio Pierre of Scranton. I will only wrestle for a stake.

After my half mile race on Friday with the unknown I will be prepared to make a match with any wrestler in the world for $500 or $1,000. DUNCAN C. ROSS.

SACKVILLE'S IVORY POKER CHIPS.

They Brought More at Auction Than They Were Worth—Good Prices All Around.

WASHINGTON, Nov. 20.—The sale of the personal effects of Lord Sackville was continued to-day at the British Legation, and the crowd in attendance was if anything larger than that of yesterday. The big ball room of the Legation building was packed and the bidders had some difficulty in making their voices heard above the buzz of conversation and the running fire of comment brought out by each new article put up for sale. It was evident that Lord Sackville did not intend to take back many of his American possessions to Knole Park.

Among the articles sold were seven portable bath tubs, a work on etiquette, a set of ivory poker chips, a silk court dress, finely embroidered, worn during the time of Louis XVI., a silver shoe buttoner, a pair of opera glasses, and an envelope opener. All the articles brought more than they were worth. The chinaware was bought by hotel keepers, and most of the wine went the same road. Little trifles, German favors and other articles, more of the nature of souvenirs than of anything else, went off at prices probably greater than their original cost.

Lord Sackville has kept enough furniture to make life at the legation bearable during the short period that he will remain here. He and his daughters, the Misses West, took luncheon with friends to-day.

Great Bowling.

The bowling alleys of the Jersey City Athletic Club were filled last evening by a large and enthusiastic audience to witness the opening game of the bowling tournament. The game was between the Roseville Athletic Association and the home club, which carried off the pennant last year. The score was as follows:

JERSEY CITYS.	S.	S.	B.	ROSEVILLES.	S.	S.	B.
McLellan	2	5	3	Pearson	2	7	2
Curran	5	2	3	Eggers	2	4	5
Klein	0	6	4	Stewart	2	4	4
Brown	4	5	1	Titus	2	7	1
Davis	3	2	5	Dudley	3	4	4
Grant	2	3	5	Housel	4	3	4
Ryerson	2	3	5	Northrop	2	6	2
Vail	1	3	6	Tompson	1	4	5
Stewart	2	4	4	Griffith	0	4	6
Covalli	1	5	4	Westover	4	0	6
Totals	22	38	40	Totals	22	43	39

Total Rosevilles.......1,502 Total J. C. A. C.........1,467

The game was hotly contested, the J. C. A. C. being ahead up to the seventh frame.

The next game will take place this evening, between the Orange Athletic Club and the Palma Athletic Club, at the latter's alleys.

The Yeomen's Vocal Score.

On Thursday last Mr. Rudolph Aronson received the first instalment of the printed vocal score of "The Yeomen of the Guard." The book was issued simultaneously in London and New York. The first day's sale in London amounted to 30,000 copies.

THE DERBY MAY BE A CLEW.

IT WAS LEFT BY DUNNE'S ASSAILANT WHEN HE FLED.

The Unknown Took Driscoll's—In His Own Is the Stamp, "Westmore & Co."—The Police Searching for the Stranger.

Capt. Carpenter and Detectives Mullen and Clark of the Fourth precinct are continuing their search for the unknown assailant of Thomas F. Dunne. Up to noon to-day no trace of the mysterious individual had been discovered.

In the Oak street station house is a black derby hat which the police believe was the property of Dunne's assailant. It is an ordinary $2 hat, and has no mark by which the owner can be identified. On the inside lining Detective Clark found a K. of L. trade mark, upon which was stamped: "The United Hatters of North America." On the silk lining was stamped "Westmore & Co." This hat is the only clew the police have, and the stories told by the dead man's friends concerning it are conflicting.

David H. Driscoll, who was with Dunne at the time he was assaulted and who claims he grappled with his friend's assailant, says that the stranger, after being knocked down in the middle of Broadway, regained his feet, grabbed the first hat within his reach, and ran away. Driscoll picked up the other one, which he found was too small for him. He, however, wore it uptown, and yesterday morning purchased a new one on Fulton street, where he left the old one, which was this morning taken possession of by Detective Clark.

At the Oak street station, this morning, Capt. Carpenter and his detectives rigidly examined Driscoll, Michael T. Donovan, and James Reed. Strange as it may seem, not one of these men feel positive that they can identify the man whom they believe is responsible for the death of their friend.

When Driscoll and his associates first told their story to the police they said Dunne's assailant made some remark about being in a hurry to catch a train for Philadelphia. To-day they are not so sure that any such statement was made, but they still think he used the word Philadelphia.

Much has been said about the action of Policeman Collins of the Patrol Squad, who overhauled Dunne's assailant after a lively chase and brought him back for identification. Capt. McLaughlin of the Old Slip precinct and Capt. Carpenter of the Oak street precinct do not think that any of their patrolmen were negligent in their duties so far as Dunne's case is concerned.

A brother of the dead man was seen this morning, and in response to inquiries said that Thomas died nine months to a day after the death of his mother. The young man was not of a quarrelsome disposition by any means, and he could not account for the broil that occurred Sunday night. "Thomas," he said, "was not in good health. He has never fully recovered from a severe attack of pneumonia, and we thought he could not live at the time of his mother's death; but he pulled through, only to meet such an ending."

Mr. Dunne added that he was satisfied no murder was intended. It was simply a disagreement which terminated very disastrously.

Deputy Coroner W. F. Jenkins made an autopsy to-day on the body of Dunne.

The Doctor found a fracture of the base of the skull, probably the result of the fall he received after having been struck. In his opinion death resulted from the fracture.

"RAZZLE DAZZLE" ON BROADWAY.

"Dodgework" Wanted His Companion to Act His Part on the Street.

"The Brass Monkey" was loose in Broadway this morning. There was a lively little racket near Twenty-eighth street and in the Coleman House between two actors of the company who sing in the "Razzle Dazzle" song at the Bijou Theatre. One of them was Tom Murphy, a smooth faced, athletic young man, who is the central figure in this part and whose stage character is Dodgework. The name of the other was not known, as he disappeared.

Murphy, it seems, had been taking too much firewater, and it is supposed he tried to get his fellow actor to play his part in the street. There was a dispute between them, which resulted in the unknown member, who was a little man, fleeing from Dodgework.

This little man ran into the cafe of the Coleman House, closely pursued by Dodgework, who was hatless and who had blood in his eye. The chase was through the cafe out into the office, through the corridor and out of the Twenty-seventh street entrance and into Broadway again.

Just as the race was becoming exciting up town and with a large crowd following Officer Kelly of the Broadway squad appeared on the scene, and seized the belligerent star of "Razzle Dazzle." There was a short tussle between the officer and the actor, but the latter, finding himself in the hands of the law, quietly submitted to the arrest. The little actor was missing.

Murphy was taken to the Thirtieth street station house and locked up on a charge of intoxication. He gave his age as 27 years and said he resided at the Coleman House. He was arraigned in the Jefferson Market Police Court this afternoon.

FEATURES OF SPORTING LIFE.

Prize Ring and Athletic Notes of Interest to New Yorkers.

The winter racing meeting at New Orleans will begin to-day. Weather permitting, there will be running every Tuesday, Thursday, and Saturday. Mr. J. F. Caldwell will handle the starting flag, and Col. Simmons will be the presiding judge.

George Byers would like to play a game of hop scotch with any 14-year-old boy in New York for a medal.

"I may be an ass," said Jack Dempsey yesterday, alluding to the fact that Charlie Mitchell had so denominated him, "but no one ever thought me a cur, and that is what I think him to be. The darling wish of my life is to meet him in a ring in a finish fight. We can get a purse of $5,000 to fight for in San Francisco, and I'll bet him $5,000 or $10,000 on the outside that I whip him. Make it good and strong, for I want to get at him as I never wanted to get at any man in my life before." Jack is very much in earnest, and Mitchell cannot afford to ignore this challenge.

After the Heenan-Sayers international championship fight it was determined to give both men a fac simile of the English champion belt, to be retained by him forever. Money was subscribed for this purpose. Sayers got his belt, but poor Heenan never got his: in fact, none was ever made for him. The belt that Sayers owned is now for sale in England. The colors that Heenan wore when he met the gallant Sayers are now in the possession of old man Tullis, who keeps a saloon back of Union Hill, New Jersey.

A good many of the patrons of the Clifton track are complaining at the actions of the Erie Railroad people who run the first train returning from the track into an old milk shed, instead of the depot, and compel its passengers to wade ankle deep through mud and mire to reach the ferry. They believe that they pay enough for transportation to entitle them to better usage.

Tommy Kelly, the Harlem Spider, who lately made such a gallant draw with Eugene Hornbacker, has been matched to fight an unknown to a finish, at 105 pounds, within two weeks, for a stake of $250 a side. He will have to be a good one to do Tommy.

Johnnie Teemer feels that his future depends on his winning the race with O'Conner on the Potomac next Saturday, and he will pull as he never pulled before. Should O'Conner win there is a strong probability of his being sent to Australia to row for the championship of the world.

The next big event in California is the featherweight match between Johnny Havlin and Tommy Warren. They ought to make a rattling go, and there is do doubt but that the winner will know that he has had a fight.

The odds on the McAuliffe-Jackson fight are 10 to 6 on Joe. The El Doradoans feel sure that he will do the big darky.

Billy Bair, the man who developed Maud S. and drove her when she made all her records, has gone to pot, and is now in the vague "Out West."

Sale of Loubat's Team.

Two of the best-known road horses were sold at auction at the mart of Van Tassell & Kearney, on East Thirteenth street, to-day. They comprised the team of the late Shepard F. Knapp, and were latterly owned by J. F. Loubat, who is now in Europe. They were named Sweetness and Mate, and were sold peremptorily by Mr. Loubat's instructions. The price brought was $1,525, and the purchaser was Mr. O'Brien. The team is said to be worth $2,500.

Mechanics' Bank Building Brings $85,000.

The Mechanics and Traders' Bank Building, corner of the Bowery and Broome street, was sold at private sale yesterday to W. & J. Sloane, the carpet dealers, for $85,000.

The Obstructions at the Bridge Removed.

The Bureau of Encumbrances this morning blocked the Bridge entrances for half an hour while removing the fruit stands that have blocked the narrow walks approaching the Bridge for the past two years.

JAKE KILRAIN MOBBED.

ANGRY PHILADELPHIANS ATTACKED HIM AFTER A PERFORMANCE.

He Was With Charlie Mitchell, but the Crowd Was After Jake—The Police Got Him Away With Very Great Difficulty.

PHILADELPHIA, Nov. 20.—Jake Kilrain and Charlie Mitchell were mobbed last night in the rear of the Central Theatre. They arrived in this city yesterday in accordance with a contract made some time ago to appear as gladiators in the Rentz-Santley Burlesque Company. When Mitchell appeared on the stage last evening he was enthusiastically welcomed by an immense audience. He posed as Jack Dempsey and Mike Donovan, but the applause became a perfect hurricane when he appeared as "the celebrated modern athlete, John L. Sullivan."

As soon as he left the stage Manager Flemming stepped to the front and said:

"I take pleasure in introducing to you Jake Kilrain, the champion of the world."

A dead silence reigned for a few moments, but as soon as Kilrain appeared and made his bow he was greeted with a storm of hisses from the galleries which fairly drowned the applause in the pit. Then the crowd broke into one prolonged scream for:

"Sullivan! Sullivan! Sullivan!"

Kilrain bore it calmly for a moment; then flushed, bowed, and retired.

When the time arrived for the two pugilists to leave the theatre they were surrounded by a mob of 200 men and boys. It was at the rear entrance, and the gang made a rush for them. One policeman only was in sight, but he was plucky, and drawing his club charged on two of the ringleaders who had jammed Kilrain's hat down on his head in their efforts to strike him.

All the way along Sansom street the crowd kept hooting and hissing, endeavoring thereby to provoke Kilrain to raise his hand or speak, but he remained stolidly indifferent to their threats. Finally the two prize fighters jumped on a horse car, but it was only with the aid of the police that the trip to the Continental Hotel was successfully accomplished.

Speaking about the affair later in the evening, Kilrain said:

"I suppose the crowd was made up of the admirers of Sullivan, and they are slow to believe that he has had to take a back seat as champion."

THE DEADLY UMBRELLA TIP.

It Proves an Effective Weapon in an Angered Man's Hands.

Charles Martin, the cigar maker at 369 Fulton avenue, Brooklyn, who had his right eye badly gouged by the point of an umbrella in a scuffle last evening on the Park place platform of the elevated railroad is still at the Chambers Street Hospital. He is suffering from the effects of "a punch wound of eyelids, entering the orbit," and was unable to appear in court this morning.

Dr. Harris, the house surgeon, says the injury is not fatal from its present symptoms. There are most conflicting stories concerning the assault, although the police are inclined to believe that the man arrested for the deed is telling the truth.

The latter's name is Christian Scherfig, a Dane, 32 years old, a bookkeeper in the employ of L. Wertheimer & Co., general agents in this city for the Royal Porcelain Company of Copenhagen, Denmark. When arraigned before Justice Jacob M. Patterson in the Tombs Police Court this morning he told the following story:

"It was about 7:30 last night, as I was ascending the steps of the elevated station at Park place. There was quite a crowd, and Martin and his companion, Kelly, who were behind me, commenced pushing me ahead. I pushed back, and then they began punching me in the back. I remonstrated at their conduct, and they used bad language.

"When we reached the platform one got on one side of me and the other on the other side. Martin struck me in the face and Kelly began hitting me at the same time. I raised both hands and struck out. I had my umbrella in one hand as I let drive, the point of it struck Martin in the face.

"Policeman Murray of the Church street station, who was on the platform at the time, arrested the three of us and took us to the police station. I simply tried to defend myself and had no intention of using my umbrella as a weapon."

At the police station it was discovered that Martin, the injured man, was intoxicated and a charge to that effect was accordingly preferred against him. An ambulance was sent for, however, and he was at once removed to the hospital.

Kelly was allowed to go. He said last night that the row grew out of their having accidentally bumped into Scherfig and that the latter's assault was entirely uncalled for. He did not appear to testify in court this morning.

Scherfig was entirely sober at the time. He is a distinguished-looking man, with a heavy military mustache, and very gentlemanly in his manners.

He was for a time an officer in the Danish army. His left eye was badly bruised. Owing to the uncertainty of Martin's wounds, Justice Patterson decided to hold Scherfig in $1,000 pending the result of his injuries.

Scherfig's employer, Louis Wertheimer, went on his bail. Owing to the lateness of the hour at which he was arrested last evening Scherfig was unable to get bail, and passed the night in the station house. The blow must have been a heavy one, as the stick of the umbrella was broken off close to where the covering is attached to it.

MANY ATHLETES TO MEET.

Champions from Everywhere to Compete at Madison Square Garden.

The championship meeting of the Amateur Athletic Union, to be held at Madison Square Garden Wednesday evening, the 21st, promises to be the athletic event of the year. Eighteen events are on the programme, consisting of running, walking, jumping, hurdling and weight throwing. Two hundred and fifty entries have been received for this meeting, the largest number ever received for an indoor meet The athletes to compete represent most of the colleges that are prominent in athletic circles In the spurt runs Mr. G. E. Mesley of the Chicago club, who made the great race at Detroit last summer with W. C. Dohn, the champion, is entered. Among others on the entry list are J. S. King, the ex-Princeton College runner, who is now a member of the Columbia A. C. of Washington; W. C. White of the New York A. C.; T. Butcher of Pullman, Ill., and Walker of Detroit.

Entered for the long runs is the newly arrived English runner A. B. George. He will meet such men as Skillman, Gylbert, Collett and others. Otto Hassell, the champion walker of the Chicago Athletic Club, is entered in the three-quarter and four mile walks, where he will try to defeat such men as W. R. Burckhardt, the champion of America; W. E. Mixon, W. A. Berrian, W. Pallman and many others. C. A. J. Queckberner, who is now the holder of most of the world's records, will contest in the throwing of the shot and putting the heavy weights with G. R. Gray, W. L. Condon and O'Sullivan.

The hurdle races will be well contested by A. A. Jordan and E. Lentiehol of Yale. Over fifteen men have entered for the ball kick for accuracy, the most noted being Bull, Yale's famous player. Cartloads of earth have been carried in on the floor of the Garden to be used for the heavyweight throwing. Sam Crook, the champion jumper of Williams College, is entered in the jumping contest, and there is but little doubt that he will make a good showing.

J. R. Elder Will Referee the Race.

WASHINGTON, Nov. 20.—It has been practically settled that J. R. Elder of the Columbia Athletic Club will act as referee for the Teemer-O'Connor boat race next Saturday. Capt Gibson, the referee originally chosen, has declined to serve.

Reich's Death Watch Begun.

The death watch on the aged murderer, Adolph Reich, began this morning. Under Sheriff Sexton arrived at the Tombs early, accompanied by Deputy Sheriffs Delmour and Curraher. These he introduced to Reich, who greeted them cheerfully. Reich believes that Gov. Hill will commute his sentence, and consequently is in a comparatively cheerful frame of mind.

Condensed Telegrams.

A German gendarme has arrested a French employe of the Avricourt railway station while working in his own garden on German territory.

The police at Lille, France, have captured six thieves who some years ago stole bonds amounting to £20,000 from the cities of Brussels and Mons.

Weather Indications.

Colder; fair, northern winds.

Perry's Thermometer Record To-day.

6 A. M.	41	12 M.	42
9 A. M.	41	3:30 P. M.	44

Information for Fishermen.

HIGH WATER TO-MORROW.

Sandy Hook, 9:01 | Gov. Island..9:20 | Hell Gate...11:09

WALL STREET POSTSCRIPT.

An order for 45,000 tons of steel rails at $28 was placed yesterday by the Pennsylvania Railroad Company with the Cambria, Carnegie and Pennsylvania Steel Works.

The Niagara River Power Company of Buffalo, limited, has been incorporated to utilize the force of Niagara Rapids; capital, $225,000 in $50 shares. The company offers a prize of $100,000 to any inventor who will devise the method and machinery for effecting this object.

The bitter feeling against the New York Central people for their action in precipitating the trunk line war and endangering the earning capacity of hundreds of millions of dollars is daily growing apace.

The production of anthracite for the month of October was 4,187,526 tons, as against 3,185,298 last year, an increase of over 1,000,000 tons.

The following statement is official: Rates on Southwestern roads have not been advanced, but the freight agents of the different roads, including Atchison and Missouri Pacific, have been in session in St. Louis for several days arranging a schedule of advanced rates to be put in force on the approval of the general managers. These rates show an advance on the higher classes of 20 cents per hundred, and on the lower classes an advance of 20 per cent. That is, on the higher classes where the rate is $1 it will be $1.20. On the lower classes where the rate is $1.80 it will be $2.15, &c. The schedule will not be completed for two days. It will then be submitted to general the managers. If approved by them it will not be put in force before Jan. 1. The general plan for harmonizing differences in the Southwest by a system of clearings is not completed yet, and those who are working it out say there is nothing conclusive to be said about it yet.

The following from the annual report of President Stickney of the Chicago, St. Paul & Kansas City Railroad very fairly sums up the chaos resulting from the Inter-State Commerce law:

"It is customary to ascribe all the difficulties of maintaining equitable rates to the operation of the Inter-State Commerce act, which substitutes a new fundamental principle for the regulation of railways. The act is in conflict with the pre-existing body of law and custom, and the effort to conform to it by railroad managers whose staff is educated upon opposite principles has brought inevitable confusion. Tariffs have been in a state of chaos. This, perhaps, should not be surprising when we consider that within the district covered by the railways leading from Chicago westward there are over 200 junctions and competitive points, and that to make a rate between these junction points alone on a single class of freight requires more that 20,000 separate rates; further, as there are twelve different classes and commodities in the tariffs, these rates must be multiplied by twelve, making over 240,000 competitive rates; add to this the rates between non-competitive points and it will run up to possibly more than 100,000,000 separate rates to be worked out and adjusted upon an entirely new basis."

Mr. Midgley left Chicago for New York last night for the purpose of conferring with Mr. Gould and Mr. Huntington on the Southwestern rate question.

An ordinance was introduced last night in City Council at Chicago to repeal the Bell Telephone franchise.

Railroad Earnings.

	1888.	1887.	Inc.	Dec.
N. Y., Ont. & Western: 2d week Nov..	$29,152	$28,678	$474	....
Houston & Texas Central: 1st week Nov..	95,607	99,916	....	$4,308
Louisville, Evansville & St. Louis: 2d week Nov...	17,320	21,638	....	4,318
Chicago & East Illinois: 2d week Nov...	42,530	45,790	....	3,260
Annual statement Wagner Palace Car Company to Sept. 30:				
Gross receipts..	2,595,209	2,519,007	76,202	....
Expenses paid..	1,964,915	1,824,824	140,091	....
Milwaukee & Northern: 2d week Nov...	20,380	21,420	....	1,040

Albany special—Boston & Albany annual statement: Gross, $8,443,339; expenses, $5,883,640; net, $2,565,699; other income, $433,324; total charges, $1,329,215; surplus, $1,669,807; cash on hand, $732,280; profit and loss deficit, $547,383.

Denver and Rio Grande Western:	1888.	1887.	Inc.	Dec.
2d week Nov...	$33,175	$26,000	$7,175	....
Atlantic & Pacific: 2d week Nov...	$78,023	$51,994	$26,029	....
Fort Worth & Denver: 1st week Nov..	29,920	22,244	7,676	....
St. Louis, Arkansas & Texas: 2d week Nov...	82,800	75,752	7,048	....
Kingston & Pembroke: 2d week Nov...	2,824	2,725	99	....

WHEAT CLOSES WILDLY EXCITED.

Old Hutch and the Northwestern Millers Almost Create a Panic in Wheat.

The market to-day up to 1:45 P. M. was travelling along in a conservative way, when it suddenly dropped nearly out of sight, and the scenes in the wheat pit were of wild excitement. Stop orders were reached, and the great amount of liquidation going on sent the market off three points in as many minutes. Had the orders been large there would have been a good-sized panic, but fortunately the talent has been feeling its way of late.

To illustrate how the market acted, Henry Clews & Co. sent an order to sell 5,000 spot wheat in Chicago at the market 107½. The reply came that 106 was the best they could do and two minutes later it was selling at 104. The Northwestern millers were selling wheat right and left and Old Hutch was credited with being as big a bear as he was a bull three weeks ago. The close was at a slight recovery from the lowest prices on covering by shorts. The feeling was weak. The following despatch from Counselman & Day, Chicago, reviews the market there:

The wheat market has sustained another severe break to-day, accompanied by enormous offerings of long stuff. There was some buying by the large operators, which served to prevent the break for a time; but when they withdrew the feeling became heavy, and, with large offerings on stop orders, the decline was steady, with big sized reactions till the bottom was reached.

The opinion is gaining ground that quite a number of the bulls who have been long for some time past have thrown over their stuff and with only a moderate short interest outstanding there was but little resistance to the decline till all the stuff had been dumped. We look upon the market now as in a much more healthy condition, as we think with such free liquidation by the longs and a probable large increase in the short interest the market ought to do better.

Corn was a shade easier on pretty good receipts, though not as large as was expected, and the cool, dry weather, which is said to stimulate the movement in the interior and facilitate cribbing. The shipping demand was rather quiet. The weakness in wheat caused a dull feeling in the trade, and the easier feeling in the pork product did not help it.

Provisions were easier, with a fair volume of business Lard suffered the most decline. Pork was held by local buying mostly.

Short ribs were quiet. The foreign demand for lard continues fair, light stocks both at home and abroad being the cause.

The following is the range of prices for the day:

CHICAGO.

	Opening.	Highest.	Lowest.	Closing.
Wheat—				
November	....	....	....	$1.05¼
December	$1.09¾	$1.09¾	$1.04	1.05⅝
January	1.08¼	1.08¼	1.05¼	1.05⅝
May	1.12¼	1.12½	1.08¾	1.09⅝
Corn—				
November	.39¼	.39¼	.39¼	.39¼
December	.38	.38⅛	.37⅝	.37⅞
January	.37	.37	.36⅝	.36⅞
February	.38¾	.38¾	.38⅝	.38⅞
Oats—				
November	.25¾	.26⅛	.25¾	.26⅛
December	.26	.26¼	.26	.26¼
January	.29⅝	....	....	.29⅝
May	.29⅝	.30⅛	.29⅝	.30⅛
Pork—				
December	....	....	....	$14.65
January	$14.77	$14.80	$14.62	14.70
May	15.02	15.02	14.92	14.92
Lard—				
December	$8.37	$8.37	$8.30	$8.32
January	8.32	8.35	8.22	8.25
May	8.50	8.50	8.40	8.42
Short ribs—				
January	$7.52	$7.52	$7.45	$7.50
May	7.70	7.70	7.65	7.70

NEW YORK.

	Opening.	Highest.	Lowest.	Closing.
Wheat—				
November	....	....	....	1.04⅞
December	$1.07¼	$1.07¼	$1.04¾	$1.05¾
January	1.09	1.09	1.06⅜	1.07⅛
February	....	....	....	1.08⅜
May	1.14¼	1.14⅝	1.12⅛	1.12⅝
Corn—				
November	....	....	....	.48⅛
December	.48¼	.48⅛	.48¼	.48¼
January	.48⅜	.48⅜	.48⅜	.48⅝
February	....	....	....	.48
May	.47⅜	.47⅝	.47⅛	.47⅝
Oats—				
November	....	....	....	.31¼
December	.31⅛	.31⅛	.31⅛	.31⅛
January	.32¼	.32⅛	.32⅛	.32⅜
May	.35⅜	.35⅝	.35¼	.35¼

White Oats—December, 35¾c.; January, 36¼c.

Total sales on the New York Produce Exchange: Wheat, 11,520,000; corn, 312,000; oats, 395,000 bushels. Pork, 200 barrels; lard, 5,500 tierces. Flour, 13,000 barrels.

Mr. Hawk Made a Poor Grade of Whiskey.

HUTCHINSON, Kan., Nov. 20.—William Hawk was arrested here yesterday for moonshining within a stone's throw of the City Marshal's residence. Hawk had an old thrashing machine engine which he kept fired up all the time, and he was supposed to be making a chop mixture for feeding hogs. This he has kept up for nearly a year, and yesterday it was discovered that he was making a poor grade of whiskey. Hawk was sent to jail.

EXTRA

3 STRIKES; 4 BALLS

Next Year's Probable Baseball Rules.

SOME IMPORTANT CHANGES.

What the Committee on Rules Will Report to the National League.

The corridors of the Fifth Avenue Hotel presented an animated scene this morning. The great baseball men of the United States were present in force. They had gathered to attend the meeting of the National League of Baseball Clubs which is to be held to-morrow. The settling of last season's business and the making of new plans for the coming season will be attended to at this meeting. The delegates have been arriving ever since yesterday morning, and it was thought that they were about all here this morning with the exception of Harry Wright of Philadelphia, who was expected to arrive later in the day.

The various clubs are represented by the following men:

New York—J. B. Day and C. T. Dillingham. Pittsburg—W. A. Nimick, Horace Phillips, A. K. Scandart, J. P. O'Neill and H. B. Brown. Boston—A. H. Soden, W. H. Conant and J. B. Billings. Detroit—F. K. Stearns and W. J. Gray. Indianapolis—J. T. Brush and J. Martin. Washington—Walter Hewett and L. A. Burkett. Chicago—Walter Spalding. Cleveland—J. D. Robinson, George Howe and D. Hawley. Philadelphia—Col. John J. Rogers and A. J. Reach.

No business will be transacted by the League men until to-morrow morning. In the meantime high ball and low ball, the moving back of the pitcher and the chances of the Cleveland club taking the place of the moribund Detroit club in the League are being discussed in an informal way.

It is currently reported that the Boston men intend to secure John Ward as a short stop, if such a deal is possible, although they are reticent about the matter and refuse to make any definite statement. Ward comes high, and if the Bostonians are willing to pay the $15,000 asked, the New York management will undoubtedly part with him.

This morning the Joint Committee on Rules, consisting of three men from the League and three from the Association, met in Parlor F. With the assistance of the National Baseball Scorers' Association they will make some changes in the rules. The committee is composed of John J. Rogers of Philadelphia, John B. Day of New York and Walter Spalding of Chicago of the League, and President Byrne of Brooklyn, William Barnie of Baltimore and Manager Schmelz of Cincinnati of the Association.

Among the latest arrivals this morning were Harry Wright of Philadelphia and President N. E. Young of Washington.

This afternoon the Board of Directors of the League, consisting of W. A. Nimick, F. K. Stearns, A. H. Soden and W. Hewitt, will present the champion pennant to the winning New York club.

The meeting of the Committee on Rules is being held with closed doors. The suggestions as to changes in the rules are of the most varied character, each member taking his own ideas. Some want six strikes and two balls, others three strikes and three balls.

It was stated by a baseball expert this morning, that the three strikes and five balls rule which prevailed during the past season, had reduced the batting at least 25 per cent. from what it had been in former years. The prevailing desire, however, among the base ball men, seems to be that the ball should be hit oftener. The day for the battle between pitchers has evidently gone by.

Among the rumors circulated was one to the effect that the Cleveland Club would undoubtedly go into the vacancy made by the Detroit disbandment. Cincinnati is also ready to take the vacancy. It seems to be the general opinion that the Columbus Club will take the place made vacant in the Association in any event.

One of the members of the Committee on Rules has declared himself strongly in favor of putting the pitcher five feet further back from the batsman. In discussing this change he said that it was urged by opponents of the idea that the pitcher would thereby be enabled to get a more pronounced curve on the ball. This objection, however, he meets with the argument that the batter will have a better chance to estimate how the ball is going to cross the plate, because of the longer time which would elapse after the ball left the pitcher's hands.

The two points at issue are the high and low ball and moving back the pitcher. A majority of the Committee on Rules have declared themselves in favor of the high and low ball. Even if this plan proves to be the one chosen in committee it will need a two-thirds vote of both the Association and League men to carry it into effect.

The Committee on Rules was organized by the election of Mr. Byrne of Brooklyn as Chairman and Col. Rogers of Philadelphia as Secretary.

The Committee on Rules adjourned for lunch at 2:30 o'clock. The session so far had been quiet and harmonious. The first question which came up was the consideration of the high and low ball or moving the pitcher back five feet.

It was urged by some members of the committee that it would be impracticable to move the pitcher back because such action would put the pitcher almost opposite the first base and give him unlimited control of first base. As the positions are now the pitcher has to turn partially around in order to see the base, thus permitting the runner to base a chance for a life. It was unanimously resolved that three strikes and four balls would be the best way out of the difficulty, and the committee will so recommend to the Committees on Rules of the two organizations.

The second question was the discussion of the foul tip as distinguished from a foul ball knocked into the air. After a long and amicable discussion it was decided to do away with the foul tip altogether. During the coming season when a pitched ball grazes the bat and is caught by the catcher the batter will not be declared out. This decision of the committee was hailed with approbation when made known to baseball men in the corridors.

The third decision was in regard to the ball hitting the umpire. Games during the last season have largely been umpired from behind the pitcher. In many cases the ball struck the umpire and dropped to the ground, thus enabling the pitcher to quickly throw the ball to the first base, cutting off the runner. The rule as adopted by the committee to-day gives the runner a base and credits him with a base hit if the ball hits the umpire.

The next order of business was the passing of a resolution to codify the rules so that each rule shall appear under its appropriate heading. A good deal of annoyance has been caused by the lack of arrangement in the baseball manuals and the resolution is universally hailed as a decided step in the right direction.

During the luncheon hour Chairman Byrne discussed the changes in the rules. In reference to the proposed three strikes and four balls he said the new rule would have a tendency to keep the high-priced pitchers up to their work. It would have the effect, he said, of doing away with a good deal of the carelessness which has prevailed on the part of pitchers.

The decision of the committee in regard to the three strikes and four balls excited a good deal of animated discussion among the baseball men. Many expressed themselves as decidedly opposed to it, and prophesied that it would not be accepted by the League Committee on Rules. The argument is made that the batting instead of being increased will be lowered; that the new rule puts more strain on the pitcher and forces him to put nearly every ball over the plate.

The managers of the New York Club have invited the big guns of thebase ball profession visiting this city to attend the meeting of the Amateur Athletic Association of the United States which will be held at Madison Square Garden to-morrow night.

THE NEW BASE BALL PAVILION.

IT WILL BE THE LARGEST AND FINEST IN THE WORLD WHEN COMPLETED.

The monstrous and handsome pavilion on Gotham's new base ball park, which this afternoon will contain a select and enthusiastic crowd of admirers and supporters of the Giants, is a marvel in at least one respect: It is just two weeks ago since Architect John J. Deery drew his first line on it, and to-day it will accommodate in comfort 8,000 people.

Readers of THE GRAPHIC who will not have the pleasure of being present at the grand opening to day can form an accurate idea of the magnificent monument to Architect Deery's skill and the animated scenes on and in front of it by scanning the accompanying pictures made by THE GRAPHIC artist.

The pavilion—grand stand is obsolete now—is the largest of any of the bare ball pavilions in the country and, although designed and built in such a wonderfully short time, it is also the most complete in detail. It is not entirely finished yet. Only the first tier or deck will be occupied to-day, but work will be pushed until it is complete, the artisans stopping only for games. The dimensions and plan of the pavilion are interesting. It is 320 feet long on the field side, with the narrow depth at the ends of fifty feet and the wider depth in the centre, sixty feet. Its total length on the street or rear side is 410 feet. In shape it is the central part of a large segment of ninety feet radius, meeting slanting lines, each ending at eighty feet beyond first and third bases It is ninety feet from the home plate to the centre of the stand.

The first three rows of seats are entirely without obstruction In the fourth row is a line of supports, twenty-two in number, which is not great for the distance of 320 feet

The stand is supplied with tilting seats, with plenty of foot room in front. There are ten aisles 3 feet 6 inches wide There are two staircases 8 feet wide from the rear to the second tier, each having a projection terminating in a round tower, supporting flagstaffs. There are also spaces used for ladies' retiring rooms and dressing rooms for the players

The restaurant will be easy of access from both the pavilion and the open seats. At the corner of Eighth avenue and 155th street is a concourse thirty-two feet square where the people will assemble from the elevated railway platform as well as from the street. In the centre is a large ticket office with turn-stiles on either side to pass eight lines of people through simultaneously. They next go into another concourse, 30x32, from which a staircase eighteen feet wide leads down to the free seats. A small octagon ticket office is located there, where tickets to the pavilion are sold, and aisles lead to both the lower and upper tiers. There are stairways on both sides, so arranged as to distribute the crowds going in or coming out.

Between the pavilion and the free seats is a passage ten feet wide for carriages The free seats extend on each side of the pavilion at an angle of eight degrees in three courses of sixty feet each, making a continuous railing fronting the field of 690 feet.

The field is twenty feet wider than the Boston field and forty wider than the Chicago field. The centre field is not as long as that at Boston, but is just about the same as the Philadelphia centre field. Longer right field hits can be made on the Philadelphia, Boston or Chicago grounds than here

The grounds have been perfectly drained and the infield and centre field are in perfect condition to-day, but the left and right are a little soft, as the drains were only connected with a sewer on Saturday afternoon

The pavilion is portable The common idea is that this location is permanent, but it is not The managers expect to remain there only two or three seasons. They have better and larger grounds in view which cannot be obtained now, but will be eventually. Therefore the pavilion has been so constructed that it can be taken down, moved and rebuilt readily. It will be completed during the month

INSURING HAPPY DAYS.

[From To-day.]

Giggs—By the way, old man, I see your mother-in-law is cutting a great swell down in Narragansett. Has she got any means?

Figgs—Well, I should hope so! I pay her $10 a day, cash in advance, to keep away from the house.

THE GRAND STAND.

ENTRANCE AND REAR OF GRAND STAND.

[FROM DESIGNS BY J. J. DEERY, ARCHITECT.]

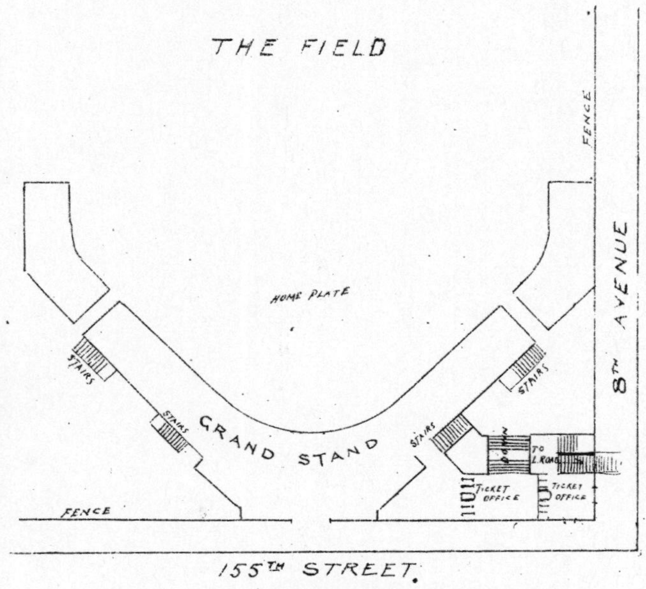

PLAN OF THE GROUNDS.

THE VIEW FROM THE GRAND STAND.

THE NEW POLO GROUNDS AT ONE HUNDRED AND FIFTY-FIFTH STREET AND EIGHTH AVENUE.

HARPER'S WEEKLY.
A JOURNAL OF CIVILIZATION.

VOL. XXXIII.—No. 1716. NEW YORK, SATURDAY, NOVEMBER 9, 1889. TEN CENTS A COPY, INCLUDING SUPPLEMENT.

WILLIAM EWING, CAPTAIN OF THE NEW YORK BASE-BALL CLUB.—DRAWN BY T. DE THULSTRUP.—[SEE PAGE 899.]

THE BASEBALL WAR.

The Situation of the League and Brotherhood Clubs.

BEST PLAYING WILL DRAW.

Battles on the Diamond Will Decide Which Is the Stronger.

The weather to-day indicates that the baseball season has begun.

All the leading clubs are home from their Southern trips and the battle will soon begin in earnest.

The rupture between the National League and the Brotherhood has given the national game a greater prominence than it has ever before had, and thousands will be interested in the sport for the first time.

The conflict between the two leading organizations promises to make the season the most exciting in the history of the game.

The views of THE EVENING SUN's correspondents from the different cities in which two clubs are located show that the fight is an even one at the start. In only two cities is there a strong preponderence of feeling: in Brooklyn for the League and in Chicago for the Brotherhood.

Our correspondent's views show one pertinent fact: The better ball playing will be

CAPT. EWING, NEW YORK (P. L.)

patronized. Sentiment for one side or another will not enter into it.

The people will pay their money and take their choice.

It will be a great year for young ball players.

The abbreviations "N. L." and "P. L." mean National Leage and Players' League.

IN THE METROPOLIS.

Both Sides Have Strong Teams, Good Grounds, and the Best Playing Will Win.

In endeavoring to obtain a fair and honest estimate of the patronage that will be accorded the two rival teams in this city, THE EVENING SUN has interviewed a large number of people who have heretofore been regular attendants at the ball games, and who are not associated by personal acquaintance or business with any of the ball players or managers.

Their main interest in the games is to see skilful exhibitions of ball playing and obtain the worth of their money. In nearly every instance, whether the individual was most kindly disposed toward the League or Brotherhood, the invariable summing up of each opinion was: "I will go to see the club that gives the best exhibition."

The intense feeling of rivalry that exists be-

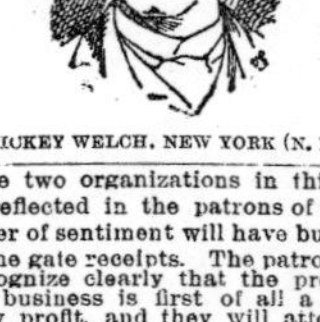

MICKEY WELCH, NEW YORK (N. L.)

tween the two organizations in this city will not be reflected in the patrons of the game. The matter of sentiment will have but little to do with the gate receipts. The patrons of the game recognize clearly that the professional baseball business is first of all a matter of pecuniary profit, and they will attend either one or the other of the games just as they would go to the theatre that offers them the most amusement.

The true and unadulterated condition of affairs to which the issue has been brought is this:

The courts have decided that the players had the legal right to leave their employers and go into business for themselves, but that

JESSE BURKITT, NEW YORK (N. L.)

they committed a breach of contract with the baseball directors for the season of 1890, which could not be legally enforced. They were under a moral obligation to first offer their services to the League for at least this season.

It is a battle on the ball field for the survival of the fittest.

The ball players having obtained their legal rights, their success now depends entirely upon themselves. If they govern themselves properly and play honest, winning ball, they will secure a good share of public support. Their failure to do so will be the ground on which they will split. Co-operative business organizations, however, are rarely successful, and there is no reason to suppose that the new scheme is likely to work a physical revolution among the players, as so many of them earnestly imagine. They are also likely to learn that in baseball, as in every other department of life, the principle holds that no man's services are so essential but what he can be satisfactorily replaced.

In the matter of conduct both on and off the diamond the members of the New York Players' club stand stronger than any of the other clubs in the new organization. During the two years in which they loomed up as the "World's Champions" they have earned a considerable measure of their popularity by their uniform good conduct and discipline. The local patrons of the game have never been disgusted with scandalous stories of riotousness and dissipation, such as were published of many of the clubs in other cities.

The old Giants consequently start out under very favorable circumstances. Their reputations are good, they have handsome new ball grounds, and they have only to repeat their former brilliant achievements to command success. Their team is one of the strongest in the Players' League, but without the services of Welch, Tiernan and Ward it is materially weaker than it was last year. Despite this, Ewing, Keefe and the other players express confidence in their ability to win the pennant again. Their present team could scarcely have won the League championship last year, and it is not quite clear how it is going to land on top in the Players' League in view of the Brotherhood boasts that their different teams are much stronger than were the Giants' opponents last year. The team's only serious weakness is at short, but Hatfield may possibly fill the position satisfactorily, now that he has a chance to play the position every day. With the same good discipline that characterized them during the past two years, the Giants are certain to make a good showing. They are well fixed in the matter of first-class batteries; they are accustomed to team work, and rank as high as any set of players in skill with the bat.

The team which the League club will place in the field is generally acknowledged a very strong one. In Glasscock and Denny it has pre-eminently the two best infielders in the country, who have this additional recommendation—they are heavy hitters. The batteries are particularly strong, and with the exception of Ewing they are as well trenched in this respect as the Giants. Smiling Mickey has few equals in the pitchers' box, and young Rusie, though only 18 years of age, showed himself last year quite the equal of Keefe or Clarkson, when he was pitted against them. Harry Boyle has always held a place among the star pitchers. In Buckley the League has a first-class backstop, only second to such players as Ewing and Tom Daly; he is

TIMOTHY J. KEEFE, NEW YORK (P. L.)

also a strong batter. Pat Murphy was acknowledged a superior catcher when he first joined the Giants, and played almost daily at a time when Ewing was disabled, and there is no doubt that with constant work to keep him in trim he will make a splendid record this year. In the outfield, with Hornung and Tiernan the League team will be much stronger than the Giants, though the latter's fielders as a trio may show up better at the bat.

In estimating the chances of the League club with the best players of the Indianapolis team, it has been held against the latter players that they never closed better than tail-enders in the National League. While this is true, it is very largely due to the lack of encouragement which was given them in the Hoosier capital. Ball players are very sensitive creatures, and severe or unjust criticism, from newspapers especially, is apt to be re-

JAMES A. M'PHEE, CINCINNATI (N. L.)

flected in poor ball playing. It takes very little to destroy their ambition and make them play in a "I-don't-give-a-cent" manner. All the old League players admit that Indianapolis was a very poor baseball town and that no team suffered more from unjust and incompetent criticism than the Hoosier team did. On the other hand, no team of ball players has ever been treated with greater consideration by both the public and the press than the New York Giants. Whether they were running in a losing or winning gait, they were constantly encouraged with generous support to do better.

The old Hoosiers achieved this distinction last year. It was the only club that away from home won the largest percentage and lost the smallest percentage of the games that made up its record. This is a rare thing in baseball, for almost every club is content to win half its games abroad. It is an evidence of the genuine grit of the Hoosiers, and their fine playing last year, under the inspiration of generous and impartial applause in this city and Boston, is, no doubt, still clearly remembered.

Averages, as a rule, cut a very unimportant figure in estimating the chances of a ball club, but it will no doubt be interesting to see how closely the rival teams in this city stand in this respect. We present two teams of only eight men each, for the reason that the League club's right fielder has not yet been permanently decided upon, while Slattery, for the Giants, had no record last year. The batteries selected are taken as the strongest in the New York and Indianapolis teams of last year.

The League team is: Boyle, p.; Buckley, c.; Hines, 1b.; Bassett, 2b.; Denny, 3b.; Glasscock, s. s.; Hornung, l. f., and Tiernan, r. f. The Players' team is: Keefe, p.; Ewing, c.; Connor, 1b.; Richardson, 2b.; Whitney, 3b.; Hatfield, s. s.; O'Rourke, l. f., and Gore, c. f. The National League team's average in batting is .258, the Players' .266. The fielding is .910 for the League, against .903. There is no material change with the averages of the other players included.

The metropolis will continue to be distinguished for its big, orderly gatherings and the ball grounds will continue to be a safe and attractive place to take ladies.

The two teams that will probably open the championship season are:

NATIONAL LEAGUE.	PLAYERS' LEAGUE.
P. Murphy..........catcher	Ewing..........catcher
Buckley..........catcher	Brown..........catcher
Clarke..........catcher	Vaughn..........catcher
Somers..........catcher	Keefe..........pitcher
Welch..........pitcher	E. Crane..........pitcher
Boyle..........pitcher	O'Day..........pitcher
Rusie..........pitcher	J. Ewing..........pitcher
Burkitt..........pitcher	Connor..........first base
Sherrott..........pitcher	Richardson..........second base
R. Murphy..........pitcher	Whitney..........third base
Scanlon or Hines..first base	Hatfield..........short stop
Bassett..........second base	O'Rourke..........left field
Denny..........third base	Gore..........centre field
Glasscock..........short stop	Slattery..........rightfield
Hornung..........left field	
Tiernan..........centre field	
Dooley..........right field	
S. Crane, Farrell and Siefke, extras.	

OVER IN BROOKLYN.

Byrne's Bridegrooms Have the Best of the Situation in Every Way.

It was a bold move on the part of the Brotherhood to place a team in Brooklyn. They have yet to prove that it was judicious and wise. The general sentiment is that they have made a mistake. With a weak force they expect to dislodge an enemy that is made up of champions on the ball field and that is strongly intrenched in the good estimation of the citizens.

That the Players' League already recognize their disadvantageous position is evident from the declaration of the voluble Ed Hanlon. In speaking of the necessity of avoiding conflicting dates he said: "As the schedules are at present, I am free to admit that John Ward has a very hard row to hoe. We cannot gainsay that fact. There is a champion club in that city, and it is an old one. Ward's team is a new one, and by changing the schedule he has everything to gain."

No baseball manager has been more liberal than President Byrne in getting a first-class team for his patrons, or more anxious to provide comfortable arrangements for them at the ball games.

It has taken him several years at a heavy expenditure to obtain a champion team, and he has one now that will compare favorably with the strongest in the country. Individually and collectively his players rank among the greatest "stars" in the baseball business. The names of Caruthers, Foutz, Terry, Bushong and others are as familiar and prominent as those of any ball players in the country. This year he has added Tom Daly to his team, who is generally recognized as one of the very greatest backstops in the country.

The Brooklyn Leaguers are not only strong on the ball field, but also off it. Their uniform manly behavior in private life has won great respect for them and has had much to do with their unusual popularity. Their familiar nickname, "The Bridegrooms," has carried with it a degree of interest that has helped to make them favorites, and also a degree of confidence that the players can always be relied upon to keep themselves in the best physical condition to play pennant-winning ball.

The opposing team of the Players' has a considerable number of strong players, and if they can be trained to good team work they may make a fair showing for a first year—and get considerable support if there are no conflicting dates. They have an exceedingly strong outfield and a fine infield, with the exception of third baseman Joyce, who is as yet an unknown quantity. In the matter of batteries they are behind the League team. Another player who may be signed by the Players' club is Pete Conway of the Pittsburgs. It is doubtful, however, whether he will help the club financially even if his arm is in pitching condition and can assist in winning games.

What Ward will accomplish as Captain of the new team will be watched with close interest. The old Giants' short stop is undoubtedly a great ball player, an exceedingly shrewd young man in counsel, and an able lieutenant on the ball field. As a Captain and manager he has not made any great achievements. He failed as Captain of the Giants for several seasons, but there is no doubt he had difficult obstacles to contend against which prevented perfect team work. Ewing, however, was able to overcome them, and that is what made him a great Captain.

As Captain of the All-Americas Ward was exceedingly ambitious and attained a certain degree of success. But after he left the baseball tourists in England Ed Hanlon took hold of the greatly weakened team and won more games than the stronger team had under Ward. After the return of the ball players to this country the All-Americas were again strengthened by Ward's addition to the team, and just managed to stand off the Chicagos in their tour of the American cities. Altogether there is not much reason to believe that Ward will bring out his Brooklyn team ahead, even though his individual excellence as a ball player is admitted.

The Players are making a bid for patronage by putting up a handsome grand stand on their ball ground. The comfort of the spectators will not, however, be any greater than at Washington Park. They will accomplish wonders if they can fix up their field this year to equal the League grounds. In the matter of location Byrnes has far the best of it. It is from ten to fifteen minutes nearer the big Bridge and the business centre by the elevated railroads.

One of the best baseball authorities in the country, who has for years devoted his particular attention to baseball affairs in Brooklyn, was asked what he thought of the situation in his city. He replied: "The presence of the Players' club will not make a difference of one

E. N. WILLIAMSON, CHICAGO (P. L.)

hundred a game at Washington Park from last year."

The presence of an American Association team is not apt to cut much of a figure in the League and Brotherhood fight. Under the present schedules they have comparatively few conflicting dates, and as the Brooklyn "Gladiators" are a strong team, they will doubtless draw big crowds when they have the field to themselves. On days when their dates conflict they will also draw well on account of their small price of admission—25 cents. Their grounds at Ridgewood are commodious and handsome, and are within easy reach of the big Bridge by the elevated railroad.

The two teams which will represent Brooklyn will be made up from the following talent:

NATIONAL LEAGUE.	PLAYERS' LEAGUE.
J. Newman..........catcher	P. Cook..........catcher
T. P. Daly..........catcher	E. W. Kinslow..........catcher
C. S. Reynolds..........catcher	C. F. Daily..........catcher
R. H. Clark..........catcher	J. Hayes..........catcher
A. J Bushong..........catcher	A. Weyhing..........pitcher
G. E. Stallings..........catcher	E. J. Sowders..........pitcher
W. F. Hughes..........pitcher	C. Murphy..........pitcher
W. H. Terry..........pitcher	G. E. Van Haltren..pitcher
R. L. Caruthers..........pitcher	P. Conway..........doubtful
D. L. Foutz..........first base	D. Orr..........first base
H. Collins..........second base	L. Bierbauer..second base
G. B. Pinkney..........third base	J. J. Joyce..........third base
G. J. Smith..........short stop	J. M. Ward..........short stop
W. D. O'Brien..........left field	J. E. Seery..........left field
J. S. Corkhill...centre field	G. E. Andrews.centre field
T. P. Burns..........right field	J. C. McGeachy..right field
	A. Sunday..........extra

AMONG THE BEANEATERS.

The Teams Are Evenly Matched, but Hubbites Are Angry Over Conflicting Dates.

BOSTON, April 2.—Boston's baseball cranks don't know whether to laugh or swear. They are doing a little of both just at present, and have not yet made up their minds whether to allow themselves to develop into chronic kickers, or to submit meekly to the inevitable and bestow their favors equally between the two clubs. This state of affairs is brought about by the war which was declared a week ago by the National League managers, when they revised their schedule so as to conflict as much as possible with that of the Brotherhood. This was anything but agreeable to the great army of baseball patrons in Boston. They had hoped for a continuous season of sport with the National

M. J. KELLY, BOSTON (P. L.)

and Brotherhood Leagues alternating, and they would have supported both with equal enthusiasm. Boston has earned the reputation of being the best baseball town in the country. Last season sixty-nine games were played on the home grounds, and the total attendance was 295,357, an average of 4,280 per game. Even when the club was playing a losing game there was a good crowd in attendance. They were interested in the game itself. Of course they wanted to see the home players win, and when they were leading the way to the pennant the attendance was enormous, especially when clubs like New York, Chicago or Philadelphia were the opponents.

Naturally, among this large aggregation of cranks, there are many—a few hundred, perhaps—who were drawn to the ground through personal prejudice. Some wanted to see the "Only Kel." Others went to see Billy Nash stop the red-hot bounders in his territory. Others went to see Dan Brouthers knock the cover off the ball. Others went to see Clarkson's wonderful pitching, and still others went to see the magnificent catching of Ganzel and Bennett. But the great mass of the lovers of the game went simply to see a good game of ball. They didn't care a rap whether the nine was managed by the Triumvirs, or whether they were playing for their own enrichment. These people, therefore, would have supported both leagues if the schedule had been arranged so as to have no conflicting dates. That is what they hoped for when the old players deserted from the League. But it is something they cannot have, owing to the physical impossibility of being in two places at the same time.

It is therefore a toss-up just now as to where the crowd will go when the championship season opens. The best ball-playing will draw the largest audiences, and it rests with the players of both sides to determine that problem. If they do their best it will result in the greatest season of first-class ball-playing ever known in the history of the game.

Both sides are well supported by strong players. The old League players have had more experience than their younger opponents in the present League team, but if the youngsters can keep up the pace which made them famous in the minor leagues from which they were culled, they will put up a game that would do credit to the old "stars."

There is this difference between the two clubs: Some of the old players have convivial habits, and, if they are to be judged by their past records, they will not go through the present season without yielding to their worst enemy. In that case the Brotherhood team will go to pieces just as surely under the new regime as they did under the old management. The youngsters on the present League team are, with one exception, teetotalers. They can be depended upon to do their best every time, and will not be forced to lay off in order to get rid of the "booze."

That knocked out "King Kel" last year and

DENNIS BROUTHERS, BOSTON (P. L.)

played the witches with Johnston, Radbourne, Madden and Dailey. That is a well-known fact. It is known among Boston's sporting men that it was the drinking of those five men that lost the championship to Boston last year. The knowing ones wink suggestively when they hear anything said about what Kelly will do with his men the coming season, and ask the question: "What guarantee is there that these men will behave themselves any better now that they are their own masters, than last year?"

If—and there is a great deal of significance to that little word—if these men can keep sober this year, they will be able to hold at least their half of the baseball patrons, and if they put up a strong winning game they will probably have the greater attendance at their grounds.

The prejudiced National League supporters are betting that these players haven't the "backbone" necessary to abstain for so long a time, and are looking for a break before the season is half over.

The National League youngsters are yet to be tried in a hard League championship battle, but those who know what they can do are confident that they will more than fill the vacancies left by the Brotherhood. The Brotherhood seems to have the strongest fielders. In batting, so far as records go, the League team excels, but these were made mostly in minor leagues, and it is not likely that they can beat the Brotherhood sluggers in their present ast company. The League batteries are by

JOHN CLARKSON, BOSTON (N. L.)

far the strongest, and the Brotherhood outfield seems to be stronger than that of the League. The infield players are pretty evenly matched.

In the matter of grounds, it is again a toss-up. The Brotherhood grounds are the larger, but as the outfield will be devoid of grass, it will not be as good for playing as the League grounds at the south end. The diamond will, of course, be sodded. The Brotherhood grounds are nearer the business district, but the facilities for reaching them are not good. A man must either walk a mile or ride in a barge in order to reach the grounds. There are not as yet any horse car lines running to the place, and it is doubtful if the West End Company goes to the expense of establishing such a line until the venture is an assured success. The grand stand and bleacheries at the new grounds will be completed in season for the opening games on Fast day.

The two teams are:

NATIONAL LEAGUE	PLAYERS' LEAGUE.
Bennett..........catcher	Mike Kelly..........catcher
Hardie..........catcher	M. Murphy..........catcher
Hodgman..........catcher	Swett..........catcher
Shelhane..........catcher	M. Kilroy..........pitcher
Clarkson..........pitcher	Radbourne..........pitcher
Nichols..........pitcher	Madden..........pitcher
Getzein..........pitcher	Dailey..........pitcher
Taber..........pitcher	Gumbert..........pitcher
Tucker..........first base	Brouthers..........first base
Smith..........second base	Quinn..........second base
Ganzel..........third base	Nash..........third base
Long..........short stop	A. Irwin..........short stop
McGarr..........left field	Richardson..........left field
Donovan..........centre field	Johnston..........centre field
Lowe..........right field	Stovey..........right field
Brodie..........extra	Brown..........extra

Computing the averages of all the men from last year's games, these grand averages are obtained: National League—Batting, .276; fielding, .879. Brotherhood—Batting, .272; fielding, .895. It will be seen by this that—on paper—the teams are very evenly matched.

IN THE QUAKER CITY.

Neither Team Is Very Strong, but the Brotherhood Has a Slight Call—The Best Ball Playing Will Win.

PHILADELPHIA, March 31.—The baseball feeling is somewhat divided. The favor of the baseball cranks who patronize the bleacheries is with the Players' League team as against the old League. The better class of patrons, or grand-standers, are generally inclined to the opinion that the Philadelphia League team is rather weak, and for that reason the Brotherhood team will draw the most money for a time, at least, and also because of the personal popularity of some of its players.

The popularity of Fogarty, and his selection as Captain of the local Brotherhood team, was wise from a box-office point of view. Cross, Milligan, Buffinton and Hallman are also popular, and each has a following among the admirers of the game. Mulvey's fast and loose methods have weakened his position, and he is not regarded with favor.

Comparing the two teams—National League and Players' League—the concensus of opinion of the people who pay their way seems to run as follows:

The League club is strong in catchers, with Clements, Shriver, Decker and Gray, three of whom are experienced, while the fourth, Gray, is regarded as very promising. In the box weakness prevails. Gleason is the best of the pitchers, but he has so often gone to pieces at critical stages that there are no great expectations regarding his work for the coming season. Day and Anderson, the young men who came from Cape May, have not yet developed great strength. Vickery, despite his having been an International Association star, is looked upon as wild, though he may, and probably will, improve in that respect. Smith is the exploded "phenom" whom everybody knows.

The infield is thought to be decidedly experimental. McCauley, who plays first, is said to be good both in the field and with the stick. Myers is all right at second, and Allen, who covers short, is spoken of as first-class, and certainly the best of all the new men. Mayer is untrained at third, and Mulvey's desertion has caused much uncertainty about the exact positions of the infielders. Hamilton, Burke and Thompson in the outfield are top notch players. Thompson is about the most popular of the Phillies, because of his habit of knocking the ball over the fence. Clements is another who has a strong hold on the baseball-going public. So far as batting is concerned, Thompson, Myers, Clements and Hamilton are the only members of the team who have faced first-class League pitchers and made reputations. The opinion prevails that the team needs two more good pitchers and an A1 third baseman.

The Brotherhood team is regarded here as the stronger. In battery work much is expected of such first-class players as Milligan, Cross and Hallman behind the bat, and Buffinton, Sanders and Cunningham in the box. Husted and Knell are experiments, although the former has done good work against the Brooklyn Players' team in the South.

The infield, so Brotherhood admirers declare, will be a stone wall, with Farrar at first, Pickett second, Shindle short and Mulvey third—that is, if the League does not restrain Mulvey and Pickett does not return to Kansas City. Shannon may play second if Pickett goes back. He is not regarded as first rate. Griffin, Fogarty and Wood could hardly be excelled as outfielders. Ruos, the substitute, is unknown here, but his work in the South is looked upon as pretty fair.

With the stick Milligan, Mulvey, Wood, Shindle, Sanders and Pickett are expected to do good work.

There is no advantage on either side in the location of grounds, but the League's field is a better playing ground than that of the Players, which is rough and uneven.

Both are within easy reaching distances by street car transit and the Reading and Pennsylvania Railroad lines, the League's being a trifle nearer to the latter station. The two grounds are just one block apart.

Some people think that the League has been badly treated by the Brotherhood, but the element of sympathy will work but little influence in the matter of gate receipts.

In the earlier part of the season the Players'

JACK GLASSCOCK, NEW YORK (N. L.)

team is likely to draw the larger crowds. If they show a tendency to come to the front the patronage will continue and increase. Philadelphia is a great town for winners.

If the League team should play better ball, comparatively, than the Brotherhood, the League will, as the season advances, capture a majority of the shekels.

The opinion is strong among many that the Athletic club will make a better showing against its fellow Association clubs than either the League or Players will in their respective organizations, and will make more money than either or perhaps both combined.

The two Philadelphia teams will be made up as follows:

NATIONAL LEAGUE.	PLAYERS' LEAGUE.
Clements..........catcher	Milligan..........catcher
Shriver..........catcher	Cross..........catcher
Decker..........catcher	Hallman..........catcher
Gray..........catcher	Buffinton..........pitcher
Gleason..........pitcher	Sanders..........pitcher
Day..........pitcher	Cunningham..........pitcher
Anderson..........pitcher	Husted..........pitcher
Vickery..........pitcher	Knell..........pitcher
Smith..........pitcher	Farrar..........first base
McCauley..........first base	Pickett (doubtful).....second base
Myers..........second base	
Allen..........short stop	Shindle..........short stop
Mayer..........third base	Mulvey..........third base
Hamilton..........left field	Wood..........left field
Burke..........centre field	Fogarty..........centre field
Thompson..........right field	Griffen..........right field
Ruos..........extra	Shannon..........extra

IN THE WINDY CITY.

The Brotherhood Team Is the Favorite with the Chicagoans.

CHICAGO, April 2.—A short time ago it seemed as if the Brotherhood's team of "stars" would have a walkover in this city. There has been a material change of sentiment, however, since "Old Anse" showed that he had some great baseball material among his "colts."

The famous old League Captain's personality, energy and enthusiasm will have much to do with holding up the League's end this season. He has so frequently taken a band of unknown players and made them prominent in a season that the evolution of his present raw recruits into possible pennant winners is bound to attract a large measure of public interest, whether individuals are ardent League or Brotherhood supporters. The uncertainty about the place that Anson's men will win in the League race will draw good attendances

THOMAS E. BURNS, CHICAGO (N. L.)

out of mere curiosity, if nothing more. Anson himself is still the most interesting figure on the ball field, and probably has more personal admirers than any player in the country. He has always been admired for his pluck and fighting qualities. Now the cranks praise him for his nerve in accepting the situation without a murmur, and immediately replacing his old players with new ones, and the confidence he shows in his young players turning out equally well. Their unexpectedly fine playing in the South has been the subject of favorable comment in baseball circles, and it is generally believed that they will open the championship season in much better playing form than any of the other League teams.

In Tom Burns, Anson has an able lieutenant. He is one of the most popular ball players in Chicago. His quiet, gentlemanly deportment, pronounced good habits, and marked ability have given him a place in public esteem that few players hold. The Brotherhood men have nothing to say against him; he made up his mind to stay in the League and stuck.

But when all this is said in favor of the League team, it is an evident fact that the Brotherhood team are the favorites here. They certainly have one of the greatest teams of baseball "stars" ever collected in one club. They are regarded as sure pennant winners, and that is what Chicago wants. The people here have for years been accustomed to a champion team, and have no use for anything else. The League Club managers made themselves very unpopular when they released Kelly and Clarkson to the Bostons, and have not yet been forgiven for it. The transactions will probably never be blotted out of the cranks' recollection until another champion team helps them to forget it.

The Brotherhood team is considered almost an ideal one in its playing strength, but doubt is frequently expressed about Capt. Comiskey's ability to harmonize its elements. The old St. Louis player has undoubtedly earned his great reputation as a baseball leader, but he will have to employ different methods here to bring his new stars into line. His severity accomplished wonders in St. Louis, but similar tactics will certainly cause disruption when applied to old League stars like Ryan, Pfeffer, Baldwin and Duffy. They are players of the highest rank and are blessed with temperaments that must be handled gingerly to keep them in the traces. At the outset the League players are not apt to feel overjoyed when they consider that they are not paid nearly as large salaries as the old Association "stars" in the team. Comiskey's team may prove that "the race is not always to the swiftest." Unless the most perfect team work is developed, the Brotherhood team will never finish on top.

The schedule arranging many conflicting dates shows that Spalding is in for a fight, and he will probably get the worst of it. But even admitting that his opponents will draw the biggest crowds, he is not likely to prove as big a loser as the Brotherhood. He can get along much better with a $30,000 team under adverse circumstances than the Players' League with a $60,000 team and larger gate receipts. He will, furthermore, not be so heavily burdened with the responsibility of "top notch" playing from the start. Comiskey's men will be expected to play pennant-winning ball from the jump, otherwise they may be voted "N. G." Anson's men will do well if they grow in strength with the season.

In the matter of suitable and convenient lo-

"OLD ANSE."

cation of baseball grounds the Brotherhood is at no disadvantage. Their new ground, which is almost completed, is situated at Thirty-fifth street and Wentworth avenue, about three miles from the centre of the city. Five lines of steam roads run to the grounds, carrying passengers in thirteen minutes from different depots, each within easy access to the heart of the city. A cable line runs within two short blocks of the park and two horse-car lines also carry passengers to it. The Chicago League grounds are reached by horse cars alone, and are nearly thirty minutes from down town. The Brotherhood grounds are 450x600 feet in size, and it will take a great drive to clear the fence. The grounds will have a seating capacity of 3,000 more than Spalding's Park. There can be no question that the Brotherhood has the best of the situation here, as it will have the strongest attraction.

The two teams will be made up as follows:

NATIONAL LEAGUE.	PLAYERS' LEAGUE.
Kittredge..........catcher	Boyle..........catcher
Nagle..........catcher	Farrell..........catcher
Lauer..........catcher	Darling..........catcher
Hutchinson..........pitcher	Baldwin..........pitcher
Sullivan..........pitcher	King..........pitcher
Coughlin..........pitcher	Dwyer..........pitcher
Inks..........pitcher	Barton..........pitcher
Anson..........first base	Comiskey..........first case
O'Brien..........second base	Pfeffer..........second base
Burns..........third base	Latham..........third base
Cooney..........short stop	Williamson..........short stop
Cliff Carroll..........left field	O'Neil..........left field
Wilmot..........centre field	Ryan..........centre field
Andrews..........right field	Duffy..........right field
Garvin and H. Earl..extras	Bastian..........extra

IN THE FOREST CITY.

Both Teams Regarded as Tail-enders—The League Has an Advantage in the Grounds.

CLEVELAND, April 2.—The men who will chase the nimble baseball over the grassy green in this city this summer, and who will be local kings or dismal failures, as the case may be, are:

LEAGUE.	BROTHERHOOD.
Zimmer..........catcher	Brennan..........catcher
Beatin..........pitcher	Sutcliffe..........catcher
Gilks..........pitcher	O'Brien..........pitcher
Parsons..........pitcher	Bakely..........pitcher
Lincoln..........pitcher	Hemming..........pitcher
McKean..........shortstop	Larkin..........first base
Veach..........first base	Stricker..........second base
Ardner..........second base	Tebeau..........third base
Smalley..........third base	Delehanty..........short stop
Davis..........centre field	Twitchell..........left field
Dailey..........right field	McAleer..........centre field
Stockwell..........left field	Browning..........right field

In addition to the above each club has several more unknown and untried players on its

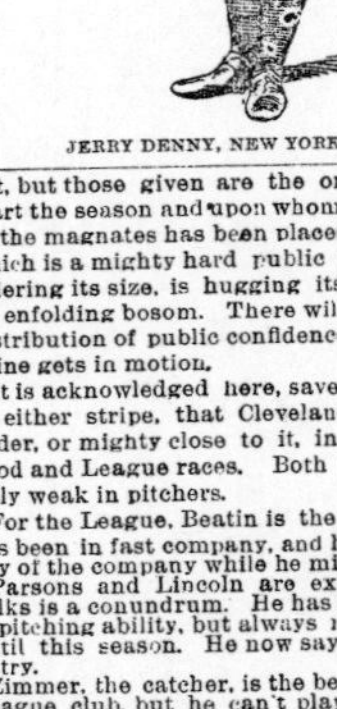

JERRY DENNY, NEW YORK (N. L.)

list, but those given are the ones who are to start the season and upon whom the confidence of the magnates has been placed. The public, which is a mighty hard public to please, considering its size, is hugging its confidence to an enfolding bosom. There will be no general distribution of public confidence until the machine gets in motion.

It is acknowledged here, save by the cranks of either stripe, that Cleveland will be a tail-ender, or mighty close to it, in both Brotherhood and League races. Both clubs are wofully weak in pitchers.

For the League, Beatin is the only one who has been in fast company, and he never scared any of the company while he mingled with it.

Parsons and Lincoln are experiments and Gilks is a conundrum. He has given evidence of pitching ability, but always refused to pitch until this season. He now says he is anxious to try.

Zimmer, the catcher, is the best man in the League club, but he can't play a game alone. The most promising of the new men is big Dailey, who has been swatting the ball all over Arkansas and running foot races before and after games. He weighs over 200 pounds and comes from California.

McKean, by his flopping, has killed all interest in himself. The balance of the club are not of the material calculated to work wonders or establish records. The spurt at the commencement of last season is not expected to be duplicated this spring.

The Brotherhood club is even worse off for pitchers than the League. O'Brien is a "killed" pitcher, and Bakely is too much of a follower of Pete Browning's habits to warrant the placing of any hopes in him. He was under tighter rein last year than he will be this season, and he couldn't keep himself in condition at all during '89. Hemming is a new man—another experiment.

The Brotherhood club is stronger on the bases than the League club. It is weaker behind the plate and weaker in the box.

Pete Browning is in the field. If the "old hoss" holds together and keeps the stocks of promises he has made the outfield of the Brotherhood club will be stronger than that of the League. But if "Old Pete" falls down the conditions will be reversed.

The Brotherhood club may get Pitcher Gruber. Al Johnson can sign him by assuring him that his salary will be paid. Gruber announces that he won't put his name down until he sees his pay in sight.

By the above it will be seen that advantages on either side are very slight. Both clubs are poor clubs and will play about the same grade of ball. The club which wins the most games at the outset will draw better for awhile than its opponent, but the League club will be ahead before the season is far advanced.

The League grounds are the largest in the country and as good as any. The stands are not as fine as they should be. The grounds are about twenty minutes' ride from the Square, where all the baseball crowds are picked up.

Johnson's Brotherhood grounds are further from the centre of town, but he announces that they will be reached in seventeen minutes. To do this he will run his electric cars at a rapid gait and in trains. It is safe to say, however, that Johnson can't make the run in seventeen minutes. It will be nearer twenty-five. His motor line is the only one passing the grounds. The grounds themselves are small, but the stands will be fine.

It is probable that baseball patrons in Cleveland will get better transportation service than any others in the country. Both Presidents are street railroad magnates, and their ball grounds are on the line of their respective roads. Robison of the League is putting in a cable line and expects to have it down soon. This will decrease the time to this ball park

BASEBALL STARS.

Biographical Sketches of Those Who Will Play To-day.

LEAGUERS AND PLAYERS.

How They Look and What Experts Think They Can Do.

With the umpire's cry of "Play ball!" this afternoon the greatest season in the history of the American national game will be begun. The conflict between the two principal Leagues will be exceedingly bitter and will form an interesting topic of public comment until the season closes.

With that THE EVENING SUN has nothing to do. Its only interest will be to publish the same full and correct accounts of baseball games that it has in other seasons. Of the merits of the teams the public will undoubtedly be able to decide to its entire satisfaction.

Upon one point, however, everybody in this great city is agreed, and that is that every club that bears the name "New York" on the shirt fronts of its players is expected to carry it to the front and hold it there until the champion ship is won.

It will be neither League nor Brotherhood that will hold popular favor, but "Champions."

The metropolis has two great clubs, from both of whom great things are expected. Both have the material to head the list in their respective races.

That they are a fine-looking body of men the subjoined cuts clearly indicate, and THE EVENING SUN publishes the ages, weights and heights of the two teams:

NEW YORK NATIONAL LEAGUE CLUB.

	Age.	Weight.	Height. Ft.	Height. In.
P. J. Murphy	29	170	5	10
R. D. Buckley	29	187	5	10½
J. A. Sommers	23	183	6	
T. O'Rourke	28	180	5	—
M. Welch	31	155	5	7
H. Boyle	29	190	5	11
A. Rusie	19	190	5	11
J. C. Burkett	21	155	5	8
R. Murphy	23	176	6	1
J. Sharrott	20	163	5	8½
S. Crane	30	190	6	—
M. Scanlon	25	190	6	1½
C. E. Bassett	26	170	5	10½
J. Denny	29	190	6	—
J. Glasscock	30	170	5	9
J. Hornung	32	158	5	8¾
M. Tiernan	23	160	5	8¾
A. F. Clarke	24	155	5	7½
C. L. Dooley	24	178	6	—
F. Siefke	20	165	5	11

NEW YORK PLAYERS' LEAGUE CLUB.

	Age.	Weight.	Height. Ft.	Height. In.
W. Ewing	30	180	5	10½
W. Brown	27	190	6	1
H. Vaughn	26	180	5	11
T. J. Keefe	31	185	5	10½
E. N. Crane	26	210	5	9
H. M. O'Day	27	190	5	11¾
J. Ewing	26	168	6	1
R. Connor	32	205	6	2
D. Richardson	27	165	5	8
A. W. Whitney	31	160	5	7
G. Hatfield	35	169	5	9½
J. O'Rourke	38	185	5	8
G. F. Gore	32	185	5	10½
M. J. Slattery	24	190	6	—

The average of the twenty League players is 26 years, 173¼ pounds, 5 feet 10¼ inches.

That of the fourteen Brotherhood players is 29 years, 183 pounds, 5 feet 10½ inches.

This places them very nearly on a par. The only decided differences are in the ages and weights, and the suppleness and enthusiasm of the younger players may fairly be considered an offset to the greater muscle and heaviness of the older ones.

THE PLAYERS' LEAGUE.

Sketches of Buck Ewing and the Members of the Brotherhood Club.

William Ewing, the manager and captain of the New York Players' League club, was born in Pendleton, O., thirty years ago. He stands 5 feet 10½ inches high and weighs 180 pounds. Buck's first experience as a baseball captain and manager occurred when he was about 14 years old, when he had charge of all the business affairs of a club in his native town, whose playing stock consisted of a ball and bat and a capital of 75 cents.

He first played professionally with the Mohawk Browns in Cincinnati in 1878 and 1879. He there attracted the attention of Manager Horace Phillips, who signed him with the Rochesters in 1880. After a short experience there he joined the Troy club. In company with Welch, Connor and other old Giants, he left the Laundry City club in 1883 and signed with the New York League club, with which club he remained until the recent baseball disruption.

Ewing is generally considered to be the best general baseball player in the country. As a backstop he stands in a class by himself. He is a pitcher of unusual excellence, and would doubtless rank with Welch and Keefe if he devoted his entire time to that kind of play. He excels also as an outfielder and on the bases. He is one of the safest hitters in the country, and possesses remarkably clever judgment in running bases.

Ewing drove a distillery wagon for a living when he first began to play ball, and is not ashamed of it now that he is a magnate as well as player and enjoys an enormous salary. Frequently on Western trips when the train was passing Cincinnati he would call attention to the little distillery, a couple of miles from the city, where he first began to earn his living.

William Brown, the big, good-natured Californian who so acceptably fills the place of backstop when Ewing does not play, is one of the best players in that position. There is no limit to his grit, and he is also a good, hard hitter. Bill's only drawback is a disposition to get rattled at exciting moments. With Ewing's coolness he would have no superior in the country.

Brown is a native of the Golden State, and is about 27 years old. He is 6 feet 1 inch in height, and weighs 190 pounds. His professional career has been brief. He had been playing but a year or two in California when he was signed by the New Yorks three years ago.

Harry Vaughn, the new catcher of the Players' club, is a native of Rural, O. He is 26 years old, is 26 years old, is 5 feet 11 inches tall and weighs 180 pounds. He rather a good-looking fellow and deserves an apology for the injustice of the cut. He has only played professionally since 1887 and has always been associated with long John Ewing as a battery. Their transfers from one club to another have always been made together. Vaughn's first professional experience was with the New Orleans club. In 1888 he played in Memphis, and last season he was with the lamented "Colonels" of Louisville. He is a very earnest player and has made a good impression here in his practise work.

Timothy J. Keefe, the star twirler of the local Brotherhood, is such a familiar figure to New Yorkers that any extended reference to his career is unnecessary. He is regarded by many baseball enthusiasts as the most skilful pitcher in the country. Two years ago he was admittedly so, but last year he fell off somewhat in his work and now his admirers are content to rank him with Clarkson at the head of the list. "Sir Timothy" has been a ball player since 1875, when he played at Lewiston, Me. In 1876 he played with "our boys" of Boston. For the next two years he was with the Westons. In '79 he joined the Uticas; in '80 he twirled in Albany and Troy. He became conspicuous in the baseball world in 1884 and 1885 with the Metropolitans. He signed with the New Yorks in 1885.

Keefe was one of the leaders in the Brotherhood movement, and won golden opinions by his manliness in expressing his judgment against the contract jumpers on both sides. Keefe is a fine looking man, with a coolness of judgment that no situation, however exciting, seems to disturb. He is 5 feet 10½ inches high, and weighs 185 pounds.

Edward N. Crane, the famous speedy pitcher, was born in South Boston 26 years ago. He is 5 feet 9 inches in height and weighs 210 pounds. Crane is not only a first-class twirler, but has had considerable experience as an outfielder. He was one of Spalding's round-the-world baseball tourists, and his massive physique attracted attention everywhere. In Italy and Paris he was termed "The Hercules." Crane is probably the best long-distance baseball thrower in the world. His exhibitions in Australia and England were regarded as little short of marvellous. Crane began his professional career with the Boston Unions in 1884. Since then he has played with the Providence, Buffalo, Washington and Toronto clubs. He joined the New Yorks two years ago. He is one of the heaviest batters among the well-known pitchers.

Henry M. O'Day made a great reputation for himself in the world's championship series between the New York and Brooklyn clubs. His fine work was largely instrumental in bringing the pennant to the metropolis. O'Day has played professionally since 1883, when he played with the Toledos. In 1885 and 1886 he was with the Pittsburgs and Detroits. Toward the close of the latter year he joined the Washingtons, and remained there until last August. President Day then purchased his release and gave him his first opportunity to distinguish himself. He was born in Chicago in 1863, stands 5 feet 11¾ inches high and weighs 190 pounds.

John Ewing, the new addition to the Players' club's pitching talent, is a brother of the celebrated Buck, but does not resemble him in any way. He is extremely tall and comparatively thin. His height is 6 feet 1 inch, and he weighs 168 pounds. He has been pitching to Vaughn since they first played professionally with the New Orleans club in 1887.

Long John, as he is termed, has good speed and command of the ball, and has shown good work in the exhibition games. If it is in him he is certain to develop into a great twirler under the instruction of his little brother Bill. He is 26 years old.

Roger Connor is one of the biggest and best first basemen in the country. He was born in Waterbury, Conn., in 1859. He was a sturdy youth, and grew to large proportions so rapidly, in fact, that when quite a young man he was called the Giant. He is over 6 feet 2 inches tall and weighs 205 pounds. His first professional baseball appearance was in 1888, when he joined the New Bedford team. He remained there two years, and in 1880 joined the Troys. His work on that team, mostly at third base, was of such a phenomenal character that in 1883 Jim Mutrie secured him for the New York team. Of his connection with the Giants it is almost unnecessary to speak. Everyone who ever visited the old Polo grounds or the new one at 155th street knows how admirably he has guarded first bag. Many a pitcher has come to dread him. The longest hit on the old Polo grounds was made by Rogers. It was over the right field fence in a game with the Bostons three years ago, and was a drive that aroused the wildest enthusiasm among the spectators. He afterwards duplicated the hit. He was also the first player to lift a ball over the centre field fence of the new Polo grounds.

Daniel Richardson, the great second baseman, has probably the shortest professional history of any prominent ball player in the country. Previous to joining the New Yorks in 1884 he had only played with the Elmira *Telegram* team of his native city. Danny is a great general player and is a twirler of no mean ability. He was originally taken on trial by the New Yorks. They were on the point of releasing him because there was no room for him when an accident to a fielder gave him a chance to show his skill. By the time the players had recovered another accident gave him an opportunity to display his ability in some other position. His merit was so positive that he was made a regular player. Danny is proud of the fact that he is a fellow townsmen of Gov. Hill. He is 27 years old, 5 feet 8 inches tall, and weighs 165 pounds.

Arthur W. Whitney, familiarly known as Artie, Whit, and the Count, has had a long baseball experience. He was born in Brockton, Mass., 31 years ago, is 5 feet 7 inches tall, and weighs 160 pounds. He first played professionally with the Fall River Club in 1877, in company with Gore and Mutrie. In 1878 and '79 he played with the Lowells, in 1880 with the Worcesters, '81 and '82 with the Detroits, '83 with the East Saginaws, and 84-87 with the Pittsburgs. In the latter year his release was purchased by the New York. Whitney is not only a great favorite on account of his skill as a ball player, but has won admiration by his modest, gentlemanly qualities, and the excellent care he takes to keep himself in condition.

There is no more earnest player in the profession than Gil Hatfield. He is a Hoboken boy, 35 years old, 5 feet 9½ inches tall, and weighs 169 pounds. He first learned the rudiments of the national game on the turf of the Elysian fields, but it was not until 1882 that he figured professionally. He was then a member of Jim Mutrie's Metropolitan reserves.

In 1883 he played in Hartford, Conn., '84 and '85 in Newark, '86 and '87 in Portland, Me., and in 1888 was signed by Mutrie to play with the Giants. His position is short stop, but heretofore he has not had much opportunity to distinguish himself. This year, however, as a member of the Brotherhood team, he will play that position regularly, and will probably give a good account of himself. It is the opportunity of his life, and if he will only remain cool at critical moments he is sure to succeed.

James O'Rourke is one of the oldest ball players. He and old Deacon White have ambled on the green diamond for so many years that they have become as sensitive about their ages as an old maid. O'Rourke is about 38 or 40 years old. He is 5 feet 8 inches tall, and weighs 185 pounds. He was at one time one of the best outfielders and general ball players in the country, but his present excellence is mainly as a batter. In this respect he has always held a very high position though it is marred somewhat by his inability to bat out a sacrifice when it is wanted.

George F. Gore was at one time considered the best centre fielder in the country, but, like his comrade O'Rourke, he has deteriorated in this respect, and is now more conspicuous for his safe, heavy batting qualities than his ability as a fielder. Gore began his professional career with the Fall River club in 1877, of which Jim Mutrie was manager. Mutrie had seen him play with the Resolutes at Portland, Me., the year previous, and took him on trial. Gore did not show up well at first, but Mutrie knew he was a ball player and took him along when he became manager of the New Bedfords in 1878. In that year Gore joined the Chicagos and remained with "old Anse" eight years. It was during this period that Gore shone as one of the star fielders of the country. Gore was born in Hartland, Me. He is 32 years old, stands 5 feet 10½ inches high, and weighs 185 pounds.

Michael J. Slattery is a South Boston boy, 24 years old. His native place has turned out more ball players than any other locality, and it is due to his early training that he occupies such a high place in the baseball world to-day. When 18 years old his playing attracted the attention of the organizers of the Boston Union Club, and he played with them through that memorable season. In '85 he played in Biddeford, Me., '86 with the Haverhills, '87 with the Torontos, and in '88 he made his debut before a New York crowd. He is a splendid fielder, a first-class base runner, hard hitter, and in general an A 1 ball player. He is 6 feet in height and weighs 190 pounds.

MUTRIE AND HIS MEN.

The Giants of To-day and What They Have Done.

James Mutrie, the handsome hustling manager of the New York National League club, is a native of Chelsea, Mass., and was ushered into the world of baseball strifes and struggles in 1870. "Smiling Jeemes" is a hard worker and enjoys the distinction of having managed more penant-winning clubs than any other man in the country. He numbers his championship flags at twelve and feels confident that fourteen will be the number when this season is over.

Mutrie began his baseball career as the catcher and shortstop of the Lewiston club of Maine. In 1876 he became captain and manager of the Fall River club. He afterward acted in the same capacity for the New Bedfords and Brocktons and piloted both to the New England championship. In 1880 he came to New York and helped to organize the famous Mets, and won several championships with them.

In 1885 he became manager of the New York National League club. His career with that famous organization is too well known to need more than a reference. Mutrie is one of the best judges of a baseball player in the country. Hanlon, Whitney, Gore and Latham were under him as youngsters. Jim is an exceedingly kind manager and nothing is too good for his "boys" if they will only play winning ball. He never gives up a fight, and his encouraging cry of "Have sand, have stomach!" is familiar all over the country.

Capt. John Glasscock, the short stop, also enjoys the Sullivan-Ewing distinction; he is considered in a class by himself. His name and that of Third Baseman Denny's has become almost inseparably linked in the baseball world. They are generally acknowledged to be pre-eminently the two best fielders in their positions in their country. Their exhibition, apart from the rest of their associates, is usually considered an art by itself.

Glasscock is a native of Wheeling, W. Va., and is 30 years old. He began his career as a ball player in 1876, as third baseman of the Standards of his native city. He first became well known when he joined the Buffalo club in the fall of 1877. In 1878 he played with the Alleghanys of Pittsburg, and, after it disbanded, joined the Cleveland club, with which he remained until 1882. He played at short in 1879, and soon came into prominence by the reason of his excellence. He afterward played with the St. Louis Unions, afterward changed to the St. Louis Maroons, and remained there until the club was transferred to Indianapolis, three years ago.

He is one of the heaviest and safest batters in the country, and is a first-class base runner. He stands 5 feet 9 inches high and weighs 190 pounds.

Jeremiah Denny is a New York boy, but his family removed to California when he was very young. He is a strapping specimen of a man. He is six feet tall and weighs 190 pounds. He is the third baseman par excellence of the country, and has no equal as a fielder in his position. He is a veritable stonewall at third, and leading pitchers have frequently said of him that he stops apparently easy balls that with other third basemen would be counted safe hits.

For several years past the New York club has been anxious to get him. Now that he is here he has already given evidence that the cranks will enjoy an exhibition of fielding for a whole season such as has never before been witnessed in this city.

Denny first became prominently known as a ball player in California in 1881. In 1882 he joined the famous old Providence team, and remained there until the club disbanded. He then joined the St. Louis League team, and was transferred from there with Glasscock, Boyle and others to the Indianapolis club in 1887.

Patrick J. Murphy, who will be one of the League club's principal backstops this year, was born at Auburn, Mass., 29 years ago. His professional career has been comparatively brief. He first played in the semi-professional team of Worcester, Mass. He joined the Newarks in 1885, but late in the season played with the Jersey City team. In the fall of 1887 he was signed by the New Yorks.

Murphy is a first-class catcher, an enthusiastic ball player, and a great coacher. He is as agile as a cat on his feet and stops the wildest of pitched balls. He works to win from start to finish, and without regular work this season he will show that he holds a place among the leading backstops of the country. He is 5 feet 10 inches tall and weighs 170 pounds.

Richard D. Buckley, the clever Hoosier catcher, was born in Troy in 1860. His professional career began in 1884 with the East Ends of Pittsburg. In 1885 he played with the Binghamtons; in 1886 and 1887 with the Syracuse club, and after that with the Indianapolis club until he came to New York. He is a quiet, hard-working player, and puts up a fine game at third. He is a hard hitter and is not afraid to sacrifice at the proper time. He is a heavily-built man, 5 feet 10½ inches high, and weighs 187 pounds.

J. A. Sommers is already quite well known in this vicinity as a backstop, having played with the Metropolitans at Staten Island in 1887. He has improved materially since then, and will give a good account of himself this season. He was born in Cleveland, O., 23 years ago. He is 6 feet tall, and weighs 186 pounds. His professional career began with the Cleveland Reserves in 1884. Since then he has played with the Geneva club, the Hamiltons of Ontario, Metropolitan, Boston and Chicago clubs.

Tom O'Rourke is a New York boy by birth.

MANAGER AND CAPTAIN WILLIAM EWING.

ROGER CONNOR, FIRST BASE.

M. J. SLATTERY, RIGHT FIELDER.

T. J. KEEFE, PITCHER.

JAMES O'ROURKE, LEFT FIELDER.

DANIEL RICHARDSON, SECOND BASE.

GILBERT HATFIELD, SHORT STOP.

J. EWING, PITCHER.

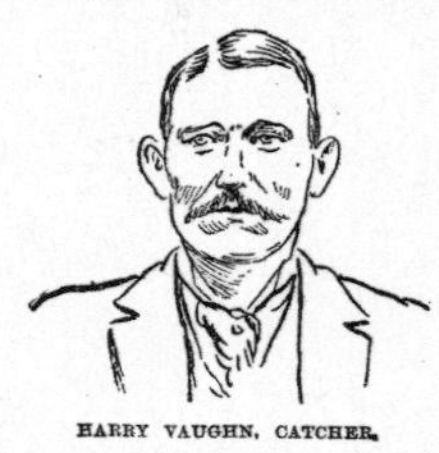

HARRY VAUGHN, CATCHER.

WILLIAM BROWN.

GEORGE GORE.

E. N. CRANE, PITCHER.

MANAGER JAMES MUTRIE.

MICHAEL WELCH, PITCHER.

MICHAEL TIERNAN, CENTRE FIELDER.

J. GLASSCOCK, SHORT STOP.

J. DENNY, THIRD BASE.

J. HORNUNG, LEFT FIELDER.

H. BOYLE, PITCHER.

C. E. BASSETT, SECOND BASE.

A. RUSIE, PITCHER.

J. A. SOMMERS, CATCHER.

J. C. BURKETT, PITCHER.

P. J. MURPHY, CATCHER.

Umpire McDermott gives his version of the trouble at the Boston-New York game, of April 24, in Boston, as follows: "Nobody regrets the outcome of that dispute more than I, but I must insist that I was right in my action. I do not claim to be infallible, and realize that I am liable to errors in judgment, but I always umpire a game and decide each point in accordance with my best judgment. It has been charged that I favored the Bostons right along previous to the trouble with Welch and Glasscock, but if any one will take the trouble to review the game they will see that it was not so. Tucker's hit over the right field fence I called a foul, thus preventing a home run for Boston, yet it was a very close decision, and if anybody was favored it was the New York Club. Again, when Hornung attempted to steal second I decided in his favor. But it was a very close decision, and if I had been desirous of favoring Boston I could have given that decision without being accused of unfairness. But, as it was so close, I gave the base runner the benefit of the doubt. In the seventh inning, when that trouble arose, the point at issue was misunderstood by the spectators. The kick was not over the decision at the plate, as some of the papers have declared. Long was undoubtedly safe. Neither Glasscock nor Welch dispute that fact. After play had been resumed Welch asked me what the last ball was. I replied: 'I called a ball.' Then he kicked, and I ordered him to pitch the ball. He refused to do so; then Glasscock started in, and I fined both him and Welch $10 each. Welch still refused to pitch the ball, and I told him he must either play ball or get out of the game. I did not order him out of the game. Welch made no answer, but threw the ball on the ground and started off. Then I took out my watch and told them I would give them one minute to get to their places, or I should declare the game forfeited to Boston, under the rules. As they still hesitated, I warned them, saying: 'Gentlemen, this minute is going very fast.' Then Glasscock called for Sharott, but the latter had not reached the box when the minute had expired, and so I called the game."

"Attendance at the National and Players' League games since the season began," said N. E. Young of the National League, "has been dwindling perceptibly, and it has clearly demonstrated the impossibility of two big baseball organizations making money. Divided attendance means dimished gate receipts, and somebody must go to the wall. In my opinion the National League is better fitted financially to stand the strain, and most undoubtedly it will play all the games scheduled for this season. Baseball patrons will go where the best game is being put up, as has been shown at Boston recently. Crowds flocked to the Brotherhood Park for a day or so, regardless of the League team on the other grounds, but now a reaction has set in, and simply because the Leaguers are playing better ball than their rivals. The increased attendance is a sufficient guarantee that the people are pleased. There is not the slightest intention upon the part of the backers of the National League to let down in their efforts to keep the game up at the proper pitch, and money will not be spared by which to further such a result and improve the national pastime as it should be. That brings me to a point in which I think the game can be improved, and that is the double umpire system. Undoubtedly the National League will have to take it up, and the only reason that it has not been done thus far this season has been the question of expense involved. It has been proposed to have a local substitute umpire in each National League city to help out the regular umpire, but such a plan would not be advisable. People demand that the umpires, who are sole judges of the game, shall be disinterested people as much as possible and entirely remove from any suspicion of bias or local prejudice."

President A. L. Johnson, of the Cleveland Club, of the Players' League, said: "I consider it an indication of a clear backdown which the National League is preparing to make. As everybody knows, at the last meeting of the Players' League I was in favor of changing our schedule to prevent conflicting dates as much as possible. My associates disagreed with me, and we did not change our schedule. When that step was taken I was satisfied and would have lost every cent I possess rather than back down. The National League people forced the fight, and now, rather than turn tail and run, they should take their medicine like men. I think that within the next few days an effort will be made to generally change the National League schedule. For a time this will save the National League, but finally people will not care to see its games at all, and the Players' League will have the field to itself. It is the most sensible thing that the National League people can do, however, but I don't know but that I would rather see the fight."

On account of the continued rain Manager Ward, of the Brooklyn Club, of the Players' League, decided to have the formal opening day, at Eastern Park, Brooklyn, on Wednesday, April 30, when the Brooklyns will have Capt. Ewing's New York Giants as opponents. Mayor Chapin has promised to be present and make the dedicatory address, and the occasion will be made a sort of a gala day. The stands will be decorated with flags and banners, and the Twenty-third Regiment Band will give a concert before and after the game. The Kings County Elevated Railroad Company will run express trains direct to the grounds from the Brooklyn entrance of the East River Bridge.

The injury sustained by Second Baseman Fitzgerald, of the Athletic Club, of the American Association, on April 18, in Philadelphia, is much more serious than was expected. Fitzgerald was hurt sliding in at the home plate, his left foot turning under him. The bones of his left leg, near the ankle, have been found to be badly fractured, and his limb had to be cast in plaster and boxed up. He will not be able to play for at least three months. George Shaffer's injury, received in the same game in sliding into third, is healing, and he will soon be able to play.

The Atlantic Association championship games, played April 22, were as follow: At Washington, the Hartfords, with Fagan in the box, defeated the home team by a score of 12 to 8. Malony and Mace did the pitching for the Washingtons. At Baltimore, the home team defeated the New Havens by a score of 5 to 3. Baker pitched for the Baltimores, and Horner for the visitors. At Wilmington, the Worcesters easily vanquished the home team by a score of 9 to 1. Stafford pitched for the former and Smith for the latter.

Peter Daly, who was for a number of years ground keeper at the Polo Grounds, died, April 20, at his home in this city. Daly had charge of the Polo Grounds when the Manhattan Polo Association played there, and when the old Metropolitan Club leased the property, Daly was retained by President Day, and he remained in his employ up to the time of his death.

In the fourth inning of the Rochester-Brooklyn game, played April 23, at Ridgewood Park, Simon, of the home team, tried to bunt the ball, and after several attempts succeeded in tapping one, but it flew up, and, striking his nose, broke it. He was taken in a carriage to a doctor, who repaired him.

The New York Club, of the National League, has signed Tommy Esterbrook, the well known player, who will be tried at first base. Few men know Esterbrook better than Manager Mutrie does, and he knows just how to handle him, and should get good work out of him if anyone can.

The Jersey Citys, of the Atlantic Association, had the Columbia College boys as opponents in a game played April 22, at Jersey City, and the latter were beaten by a score of 6 to 0. The collegians only made one safe hit off Pitcher Wheeler, of the Jersey Citys.

In the game between the Renovos and Lancasters, played April 26, at Renovo, Pa., Lynch, of the home team, retired the Lancasters in the seventh inning on three pitched balls. The Renovos won by a score of 11 to 8.

H. W. Tew, President of the New York and Pennsylvania League, resigned, and James A. Lindsey, of Bradford, Pa., was elected to fill the vacancy, with headquarters at Bradford. The league's championship season begins May 10.

The Evansville Club has released Catcher George McVey and Short Stop Harry Fuller and signed Pitcher Dave Sowders and Third Baseman John J. Kerby.

The Drummers of Erie have fine ground in prime order. Always good business for good visiting clubs having open dates. Communications should be addressed to P. E. McCully, manager.

In the game between the Cincinnatis and Chicagos, played April 24, at Cincinnati, McPhee made a safe hit each of the four times he was at bat, including a single, two doubles and a triple.

In the Boston-New York game, played April 24, in Boston, Clarkson, in sliding to the home plate in the seventh inning, wrenched his ankle, and had to be carried off the field.

Manager John M. Ward called at this office on April 26. He is the picture of health, and says his team is in good trim and will make an excellent showing this year.

W. H. Golby, formerly of the Baltimore Club, of the American Association, has signed with the Terre Hautes.

JOHN G. CLARKSON.

This week we present a portrait of John G. Clarkson. Probably no man has gained a greater reputation, in the few years of his professional career, than has the well known pitcher of the Boston Club, of the National League. Clarkson was born July 1, 1861, at Cambridge, Mass. Always fond of athletic sports, he naturally took to the national game, and learned to play ball while attending school. He was the catcher for the Webster School nine ten years ago, and from the inception it was seen that he was the making of a first class player. It was not long, however, until he conceived the idea that he might become a pitcher, and was therefore instructed in the arts of that department of the game, having no less a personage than the veteran George Wright as his tutor. It was in 1882, while pitching for the Beacon team, of Boston, that Clarkson attracted the attention of the management of the Worcester Club, of the National League, and he was at once engaged as an infielder and change pitcher. That was his first professional engagement, but, unfortunately for him, it did not prove a brilliant or lasting one. He was bothered with a bad shoulder, and, after six weeks, was laid off for the remainder of the season. In 1883 Clarkson was engaged for the Saginaw Club, of the Northwestern League. Arthur Whitney became acquainted with him in 1882, at Worcester, Mass., while visiting that city as a member of the Detroit team. Clarkson pitched for the Worcesters, against the visitors, and Whitney, seeing he would make a fine pitcher, engaged him for the Saginaw Club when he took charge of that team on the following year. Clarkson, therefore, owes his success, in a measure, to Whitney. Although Clarkson was engaged as a pitcher, he was not put in the box at the outset, because Nichols and McArthur, of the same club, were in fine form, and were both pitching excellent ball. Clarkson was used as a general utility man, and played everywhere, excepting behind the bat. He was not steady in the outfield, having a tendency to drop flies, and for a while was being weighed in the balance. The club was going to release him, but Whitney insisted on retaining him, and it was not long after that that the turning point in Clarkson's career as a pitcher came. The Saginaws and Peorias were having a desperate struggle for second place in their league. Three games were to be played between them, at Peoria, and the Saginaws needed them. In the first game, the Saginaws were shut out without scoring. The next day Clarkson faced them again, and they were blanked for the second time. In the third game, he was almost as successful as on the previous days. In the twenty-seven innings played, the Peorias were only able to score in one of them. It was while with this team that he established a reputation for skill and staying powers. Clarkson remained with the Saginaws until Aug. 14, 1884, when the club disbanded. Then he went to the Chicago Club, of the National League, and finished the season with it. He remained with the Chicagos until 1888, when he was released to the Boston Club, also of the National League, at his own request. From the beginning of the 1885 season, up to the time of his release, Clarkson was the mainstay of the Chicago Club in the pitching department. In 1885 he occupied the pitcher's box in no fewer than seventy championship games, and, although he did not head the pitchers' list in the official averages, he certainly deserved the title of the champion pitcher, as he filled that position in fifteen games more than the next highest man, Welch, of the New Yorks, who had fifty-five games to his credit. It was while with the Chicago Club that Clarkson gained renown on account of his remarkable success against the famous heavy hitting Detroit team. In a game against the Detroits, played Aug. 23, 1886, he accomplished the remarkable feat of shutting them out without a safe hit. It is not, however, simply the fact that he did accomplish such a feat, or that he may be able to do the same to any other team, that marks his ability as a pitcher. Being an intelligent man, he knows that every player has a weak point as a batsman, and he studies the man until he finds that weak point, and then he invariably has him at his mercy. He is always cool and steady, even under the most trying circumstances. He has on many occasions been known to retire the opposing side with two and sometimes three men on the bases. He has good command of the ball, and has all the curves, shoots and drop balls known to the art, and he uses them to the best advantage, and that is the chief cause of his success. During the past two seasons he has done the bulk of the pitching for the Boston Club, of the National League, and has never once weakened, as his temperate habits, and the excellent care he takes of himself, always keeps him in good condition. In no season has Clarkson pitched with more telling effect than he did last year, and it can safely be said that it was not Clarkson's fault that the Boston Club did not win the National League championship, for he pitched in more championship games than any other man, and, had he been properly supported, the chances are that Boston might have won the pennant last year. Clarkson is 5 feet 10 inches in height, and weighs about 160 pounds.

One of the evils of the reserve rule is shown in the following item: "Acting Manager Henry, of the Hartford Club, of the Atlantic Association, received a telegram on April 25, at Baltimore, from President Phelps, of the American Association, stating that Pitcher John Handiboe requested his release from reservation on the ground that no contract was tendered him by the Hartford Club up to April 1. The reply was that Handiboe would not be released unless he turned over a portion of the advance money given by the Hartfords last season. Henry says Handiboe lived and played in Columbus in 1888 and got $75 advance from the Hartfords. He pitched one game for the club and went home with a sore arm. He worked out $50 of the advance, and wrote the club that he wanted to get away. The reply was that if he gave back the balance he would be released. This he refused to do, and the club will not give him up." Yet they say it is the reserve rule that has elevated baseball and made it what it is. No doubt. Turkey for the clubs and buzzard for the players.

Manager Tom Loftus, of the Cincinnati Club, of the National League, is quoted as saying: "I have not a single sore armed pitcher, and I will be much surprised if you do not find we are very strong in the box this season. We should have won the first game with Chicago, but for an accident. Now, I want to tell you one thing, and you will find it is true. I mean to say Anson has got a great team of youngsters together. His outfield is better than it was last season when it comes to fielding, and they are no slouches on the hit. Why, there's old Cliff Carroll, who wasn't good enough for any club last season playing great ball this year. I do not understand why Al. Johnston's Cleveland combination, which I managed last year, is not playing better ball. The material is there, and the only way I can explain it is that the pitchers are out of condition."

The Boston Herald says: The Brooklyn Club, Players' League, which has just played a series of games in this city, has won golden praise from all who saw it play on account of its excellent organization, the fine exhibition of ball playing that it has given patrons, and, not least, for the exemplary conduct of its players. No nine ever visited this city in which the discipline was so excellent, and there was so much ambition to play good ball. The Club is sure to win its way into the hearts of the Brooklynites, and will undoubtedly receive a warm reception when it will open its new grounds against the Philadelphia Club. All wish Mr. Ward and his men the luck they deserve, and will be pleased to know that their next visit to this city will occur on June 17, for two games, for all are assured that the exhibitions on that day will be well worth witnessing.

Catcher Earle, formerly of the Cincinnatis, of the National League, has been signed by the St. Louis Club, of the American Association. President Von der Ahe is also negotiating with the Detroit Club, of the International League, for Higgins' release.

President McDermott has made the following assignments of umpires for the opening of the Tri-State League championship season April 30: Peeples at Wheeling, O'Brien at McKeesport, Hill at Youngstown and Green at Akron.

The game played April 23, at Cambridge, Mass., between the Harvard and Williams College teams, was won by the former by a score of 16 to 5.

The official score book of the Brooklyn Club, of the National League, is not only a novelty in its way, but is neat and handsome. The book contains thirty-two pages, over which are distributed beautifully engraved likenesses, with biographical sketches, of every member of the team. The two middle pages are devoted to the scoring of the game. The frontispiece is the design of Secretary Charley Ebbets, of the Brooklyn Club. The bat contains the name "Brooklyn." The homeplate beneath has the words "at home with," and then twenty-four balls, arranged in the form of a diamond, has the games to be played at home, and in chronological order. Upon each corner is a base with various inscriptions thereon. Nothing like this score book has ever been published before.

One thing that was lacking in the Louisville Club, of the American Association, last year was the absence of harmony. The players were poorly paid, and even then were compelled often to wait a week after pay day for their money. This season it is different. Every player signed was asked his price. There was no haggling, but each man signed at his own figures. In making Raymond captain the club has done wisely. He is a hard working, earnest player, has no bad habits, and has a faculty of impressing his men with the fact that they comprise the best ball team in the profession, and that they are never beaten until the third man is out in the last inning.

The directors of the Pittsburg Club, of the National League, decided April 25, to keep the admission to their games at 50 cents. Two of the club owners favored a reduction, but the majority was opposed. In the four Chicago-Pittsburg Players' League games, the total attendance was 11,706 people, while only 1,697 people attended the four games played by the Pittsburg-Cleveland teams, of the National League.

A benefit game will be played May 1, at Brotherhood Park, this city, between two nines from the Fourteenth Street Theatre and Bijou Opera House, for the benefit of John Sloan, stage hand, who recently lost his eyesight. A highly interesting game will be played on that occasion, as many prominent theatrical people will take part in it. The game will begin at 2.30 P. M.

The Kings County Elevated Railroad Company intends running express trains over its road this Summer, to accommodate the people who want to witness the games played at Eastern Park, Brooklyn. Trains will be run every eight minutes, and it will take sixteen minutes to go from the Brooklyn Bridge to the ball grounds.

Pitcher Widner, of the Columbus Club, of the American Association, is laid up with a split hand, and will not be able to play for some time. Al. Mays, formerly of the Brooklyn and Columbus Clubs, will be given a trial, as he claims that his arm is in good condition again.

The Boston Globe quotes Manager Ward as saying: "There have already been fines and squabbles in clubs connected with the National Agreement. If that had occurred with us, what a chorus of 'I told you so's' would have arisen."

The Strauss Athletic team, of Brooklyn, was defeated by the Staten Island Athletic nine, April 23, at Staten Island, by a score of 18 to 0. The visitors only made two safe hits off Pitcher Van Zandt, of the Staten Island Athletic Club.

In the St. Louis-Columbus game, played April 27, at St. Louis, Stivetts, of the home team, struck out the first seven men who faced him, and this so incensed Capt. Crooks, of the visiting team, that he walked up to Umpire Connell, as he stood back of the plate, and said: "You are rotten, and ought to be put off the grounds." The umpire made no reply. He was hooted and hissed by the Columbus men, and he finally ordered Manager Buckenberger ejected from the bench. "Buck" refused to go, and the policeman would not use force. Reilly was fined $25 for threatening to slug the umpire and calling him a "chump." Stivetts retired twelve of his opponents on strikes.

The attention of club officials has been called to the dangerous practice of pitchers exercising in front of the grand stand. Time and again has the ball passed into the stand and hit spectators, who are at the mercy of the ball, as they seldom see it until there is no time for avoiding it. Pitchers can practice just as well in front of the club house where their graceful movements can be admired without any dangerous results from wild pitching. It is to be hoped that the abominable practice will be stopped.

It is said that Pitcher Clarkson, of the Boston Club, of the National League, will not be able to accompany the Bostons when they leave home on their first trip. The injury to his foot sustained in the New York-Boston game April 24, in Boston, is more serious than was at first supposed. His doctor says it may be two weeks or more before he will be able to resume his position in the box.

Gardner & Co., of 276 and 278 Fulton Street, Brooklyn, have a fine assortment of cabinet pictures of the players of the Brooklyn Club, of the National League. The pictures are finished up in the highest state of the art, and in some cases rather flatter the men. Gardner & Co. have the exclusive right to photograph all teams playing at Washington Park, Brooklyn.

Charles L. Ward, a brother of Manager John M. Ward, has been appointed business manager of the Brooklyn Club, of the Players' League. The club has made an excellent selection, as it will find in Mr. Ward a man fully able to discharge the duties pertaining to that office.

THE PLAYERS' LEAGUE.

Interesting and Exciting Games Played by the New Organization.

One thousand three hundred and sixty-five people witnessed the New Yorks score their first championship victory by defeating the Philadelphias, April 22, at Brotherhood Park, this city. A prettier or more exciting game has not been played on those grounds this year. The visitors began with a rush, which, however, lasted only one inning. After that the New Yorks settled down to their work, and, by timely batting, clever base running and superior fielding, won. Crane made his first appearance in a championship game, and, although batted quite hard, did not fare so badly as Cunningham did. The runs were made as follow: Two bases on balls, a force hit, three singles, a double and an out gave the visitors five runs in the first. In the fifth Wood made a home run. In the seventh the Philadelphias scored two more on a two baser, two singles and an error. The New Yorks obtained their first runs in the second inning on a base on balls, a sacrifice and a single, and three more in the fourth on singles and a double. Two singles and a steal gave them one more in the sixth. Two singles and a passed ball added one more in the eighth. A base on balls, three singles, a double and an error netted four runs in the ninth. Wood did some phenomenal work in the outfield for the visitors. Two of his catches prevented at least five runs from being scored by the New Yorks. Richardson, Hatfield and Connor did the best work for the New Yorks.

NEW YORK.	T.	R.	B.	O.	A.	E.	PHILA.	T.	R.	B.	O.	A.	E.
Gore, rf	6	1	1	1	0	0	Griffin, lf	5	1	1	2	1	0
Rich'dson, 2b	6	2	2	5	6	0	Shindle, ss	5	0	1	2	1	1
Connor, 1b	6	2	3	11	1	0	Fogarty, cf	5	2	1	3	1	1
O'Rourke, lf	6	1	3	2	0	1	Wood, rf	5	3	3	3	1	0
Ewing, c	5	1	0	3	1	1	Pickett, 2b	5	1	2	0	2	0
Slattery, cf	5	2	4	2	0	0	Hallman, c	5	1	2	4	1	3
Whitney, 3b	5	1	1	1	1	1	Mulvey, 3b	5	0	1	5	3	0
Hatfield, ss	5	1	1	2	4	0	Farrar, 1b	4	0	0	7	1	0
Crane, p	5	2	3	0	1	0	Cun'ing'm, p	4	0	0	1	2	0
Totals	49	13	18	27	14	3	Totals	43	8	11	27	13	5

New York...... 0 3 1 3 0 1 0 1 4—13
Philadelphia... 5 0 0 0 0 2 0 0 0—8

Earned runs—New York, 5; Philadelphia, 6. Base on errors—N. Y., 1; P., 1. On balls—N. Y., 5; P., 4. Struck out—N. Y., 1; P., 2. Umpires, Ferguson and Holbert. Time, 1.58.

Hard hitting and clever fielding on the part of the New Yorks enabled them to defeat the visitors on April 23. O'Day was in fine trim and pitched in great form. The visitors only made three safe hits off him, and they were made after chances had been offered off his pitching to put the side out. In the second inning Slattery hit to far centre field for a home run, and gave the New Yorks their first tally. In the fourth inning they added another run on three singles. In the fifth inning an error by Pickett, a single by O'Rourke, and Ewing's long hit over the left field fence, let in three more runs. In the sixth two singles and two doubles netted three more runs. The visitors scored their only run in the eighth inning on Hatfield's muff of Farrar's fly and two singles.

NEW YORK.	T.	R.	B.	O.	A.	E.	PHILA.	T.	R.	B.	O.	A.	E.
Gore, rf	5	1	1	2	1	1	Griffin, lf	4	0	1	3	2	0
Rich'dson, 2b	5	1	2	3	4	0	Shindle, ss	4	0	1	3	2	0
Connor, 1b	5	1	0	6	0	0	Fogerty, cf	4	0	0	2	0	0
O'Rourke, lf	5	1	4	6	0	0	Wood, rf	4	0	0	2	0	0
Ewing, c	5	2	3	1	1	0	Pickett, 2b	4	0	0	2	4	3
Slattery, cf	5	1	2	3	0	0	Mulvey, 3b	4	0	0	1	4	1
Whitney, 3b	5	0	3	1	0	0	Farrar, 1b	3	1	1	10	0	1
Hatfield, ss	5	0	0	5	1	1	Cross, c	3	0	0	3	1	1
O'Day, p	4	1	1	0	1	0	Buffinton, p	3	0	0	1	1	0
Totals	44	8	16	27	8	2	Totals	33	1	3	27	14	6

New York....... 0 1 0 1 3 3 0 0 0—8
Philadelphia.... 0 0 0 0 0 0 0 1 0—1

Earned runs—New York, 7. Base on errors—N. Y., 4; Philadelphia, 2. On balls—P., 3. Struck out—N. Y., 1. Umpires, Ferguson and Holbert. Time, 1.27.

Boston vs. Brooklyn.

The Boston team was again outplayed by the Brooklyns, April 22, at Boston, and were easily beaten in a lively batting game, in which the visitors excelled. Manager Ward put in his little left handed pitcher, Sowders, and, although batted quite hard, he managed to keep the hits well scattered. Kilroy and Radbourn did the pitching for the home team, and both were batted hard, the Brooklyns managing to make many of their hits when most needed. Ward and Orr led the batting, the former making two home runs and a single, and Orr a home run and a two baser. Joyce's fielding was poor, he making three errors. Bauer's all 'round work was about the best ever seen on those grounds.

BOSTON.	T.	R.	B.	O.	A.	E.	BROOKLYN.	T.	R.	B.	O.	A.	E.
Brown, cf	6	2	1	1	0	0	Seery, lf	5	0	1	0	0	0
Rich'dson, lf	5	0	1	1	0	0	Bauer, 2b	5	3	2	2	5	0
Stovey, rf	5	1	2	0	0	0	Andrews, cf	4	1	1	1	0	0
Murphy, c	5	0	1	4	2	0	Ward, ss	4	3	3	1	4	0
Nash, 3b	5	1	1	2	2	0	Orr, 1b	4	1	2	10	0	0
Brouthers, 1b	5	0	1	14	0	0	M'Geachy, rf	4	1	1	4	0	0
Quinn, 2b	5	1	0	1	6	0	Joyce, 3b	4	1	1	3	5	3
Irwin, ss	5	1	1	0	1	0	Kinslow, c	4	0	0	6	4	2
Kilroy, p	2	0	0	0	4	0	Sowders, p	4	0	0	0	0	0
Radbourn, p	3	1	2	1	1	1							
Totals	46	7	10	24	16	1	Totals	38	10	11	27	18	5

Boston .... 1 1 1 1 1 0 0 1 2—8
Brooklyn........ 4 0 2 0 2 0 0 2 —10

Earned runs—Boston, 4; Brooklyn, 7. Base on errors—Bos., 2. On balls—Bos., 8; Brook., 2. Struck out—Bos., 5; Brook., 3. Umpires, Gaffney and Barnes. Time, 1.55.

The above result was reversed April 23, when the home team scored a victory in the presence of nearly 3,000 people. The Bostons outbatted the visitors, and took the lead in the sixth inning, when they secured six runs on five hits, a base on balls and a wild pitch. The visitors played an almost faultless game, but could not hit the ball when hits were most needed. Murphy's catching, and Nash on third, for the home team, and Bauer's second base play, were remarkably fine. Stovey made a home run. With two men out in the ninth inning, and three on the bases, Daley managed to strike out the batsman.

BOSTON.	T.	R.	B.	O.	A.	E.	BROOKLYN.	T.	R.	B.	O.	A.	E.
Brown, cf	5	2	3	2	0	0	Seery, lf	6	0	4	1	0	0
Rich'dson, lf	5	1	1	2	0	0	Bauer, 2b	5	0	1	2	5	0
Stovey, rf	5	3	3	2	0	1	Andrews, cf	5	0	0	1	0	0
Nash, 3b	5	2	2	4	1	0	Ward, ss	5	2	3	2	4	1
Brouthers, 1b	5	1	2	4	0	1	Orr, 1b	5	1	2	15	0	0
Quinn, 2b	5	0	1	1	0	2	McGeachy, rf	5	0	0	1	0	0
Irwin, ss	5	0	0	0	2	0	Joyce, 3b	5	1	0	0	1	0
Murphy, c	5	1	1	7	3	1	Daily, c	5	1	0	4	1	0
Daley, p	4	0	0	2	7	1	Van Halt'n, p	5	2	1	1	1	0
Totals	44	10	13	24	13	6	Totals	46	7	11	27	12	1

Boston.......... 2 0 0 0 2 6 0 0 0—10
Brooklyn........ 0 0 1 4 0 2 0 0 0—7

Earned runs—Boston, 8; Brooklyn, 3. Base on errors—Brook., 5. On balls—Bos., 4; Brook., 7. Struck out—Bos., 4; Brook., 8. Umpires, Gaffney and Barnes. Time, 2.23.

The game played April 14, was one bought forward, and, although the Bostons won with apparent ease, it does not indicate the real character of the game. It was a close and exciting contest, well fought at every point. The Brooklyns could not bat Radbourn's pitching with any effect, and the Bostons only made two hits off Conny Murphy during the first seven innings, but in the eighth they hit him for five singles and a sacrifice, which yielded five runs, and settled the game. Brilliant plays marked the contest from beginning to end. Ward made a wonderful stop, recovered the ball and threw the runner out at first. His work was of the highest order. Stovey made a great throw from his position to third base, and cut off the runner, who tried to reach that point on a hit to right field. Brouthers made a fine catch of a hot line ball from Orr's bat, as it was passing over his head.

BOSTON.	T.	R.	B.	O.	A.	E.	BROOKLYN.	T.	R.	B.	O.	A.	E.
Brown, cf	5	1	2	3	0	0	Seery, lf	5	0	1	2	0	0
Rich'dson, lf	5	1	0	1	0	0	Bauer, 2b	5	0	0	0	2	0
Stovey, rf	5	0	1	2	1	0	VanHalt'n, cf	4	0	0	2	0	0
Nash, 3b	4	1	1	1	3	1	Ward, ss	4	0	1	3	6	0
Brouthers, 1b	4	2	1	12	0	0	Orr, 1b	4	0	1	14	2	0
Quinn, 2b	4	0	1	4	4	0	McGeachy, rf	4	2	2	1	0	0
Irwin, ss	4	2	0	1	4	0	Joyce, 3b	4	1	0	2	2	0
Kelly, c	4	0	1	3	1	0	Cook, c	4	0	0	2	2	1
Radbourn, p	4	0	0	0	2	0	Murphy, p	4	0	2	1	6	1
Totals	39	7	7	27	15	1	Totals	38	3	7	27	20	2

Boston........... 0 0 1 0 0 0 1 5 —7
Brooklyn .... 0 0 0 0 0 0 1 0 2—3

Earned runs—Boston, 2. Base on errors—Bos., 1; Brooklyn, 1. On balls—Bos., 6; Brook., 5. Struck out—Bos., 3; Brook., 2. Umpires, Gaffney and Barnes. Time, 1.50.

Pittsburg vs. Chicago.

The Chicagos won their second victory over the Pittsburgs, April 22, at Pittsburg, by superior batting. Tener was very wild, and when he did get the ball over the plate he was batted hard by the Chicagos. King was hit safely only three times. He gave six men their base on balls, on which two of the three runs were made. The fine fielding of the home team prevented the Chicagos from scoring more runs than they did, as their batting was very heavy.

PITTSBURG.	T.	R.	B.	O.	A.	E.	CHICAGO.	T.	R.	B.	O.	A.	E.
Hanlon, cf	5	1	0	4	1	0	Latham, 3b	5	2	2	1	1	0
Visner, rf	5	0	0	1	0	0	Duffy, cf	4	0	2	0	0	0
Carroll, c	5	0	0	4	1	0	O'Neil, lf	4	0	0	3	0	0
Beckley, 1b	4	1	1	11	1	0	Comiskey, 1b	4	0	2	12	1	0
Fields, lf	4	0	0	0	1	0	Pfeffer, 2b	4	1	1	4	4	1
Kuehne, 3b	4	1	1	1	3	1	Farrell, rf	4	0	2	2	0	0
Tener, p	4	0	1	1	3	1	Boyle, c	4	1	2	2	0	1
Robinson, 2b	4	0	0	2	0	0	Bastian, ss	4	1	1	1	3	3
Corcoran, ss	4	0	0	0	4	0	King, p	4	0	0	2	5	0
Totals	39	3	3	24	14	2	Totals	37	5	12	27	14	5

Pittsburg........ 1 0 0 2 0 0 0 0 0—3
Chicago.......... 0 0 2 0 2 1 0 0 —5

Earned runs—Pittsburg, 1; Chicago, 3. Base on errors P., 2; C., 1. On balls—P., 6; C., 1. Struck out—P., 3; C., 1. Umpires, Gunning and Mathews. Time, 1.40.

The cloudy, threatening weather somewhat dampened the ardor of the enthusiasts and reduced the attendance at the game played April 23, at Pittsburg, between the home team and the Chicagos. Galvin was in fine form, and pitched one of his best games, and the visitors could do little with his delivery. Beckley and Bastian distinguished themselves by brilliant plays in the field. Beckley batted out a fine two bagger when the bases were full.

PITTSBURG.	T.	R.	B.	O.	A.	E.	CHICAGO.	T.	R.	B.	O.	A.	E.
Hanlon, cf	5	1	3	2	0	0	Latham, 3b	4	2	1	0	0	0
Visner, rf	5	2	1	3	1	0	Duffy, cf	4	0	0	2	0	0
Quinn, c	5	0	2	3	0	0	O'Neil, lf	4	0	1	2	0	0
Beckley, 1b	5	0	2	13	0	1	Comiskey, 1b	4	0	0	12	1	1
Fields, lf	4	0	0	1	0	0	Pfeffer, 2b	4	0	0	5	3	1
Kuehne, 3b	4	0	0	0	0	0	Farrell, rf	4	1	2	4	0	0
Robinson, 2b	4	0	0	2	3	0	Boyle, c	4	0	3	2	1	0
Corcoran, ss	4	1	2	2	2	1	Dwyer, p	3	0	0	0	1	0
Galvin, p	4	0	1	1	5	1	Bastian, ss	3	0	0	0	7	0
Totals	40	4	11	27	11	3	Totals	34	3	7	27	13	2

Pittsburg....... 0 0 2 1 1 0 0 0 0—4
Chicago......... 0 0 1 1 0 0 0 1 0—3

Earned runs—Pittsburg, 3; Chicago, 1. Base on errors—P., 2; C., 2. On balls—P., 3. Struck out—P., 2; C., 1. Umpires, Gunning and Mathews. Time, 1.50.

Buffalo vs. Cleveland.

The Clevelands received another crushing defeat at the hands of the home team, April 22, at Buffalo. Gruber was knocked out of the box at the end of the second inning. The two innings he was in the box he was touched up for eleven clean hits, including two double baggers and a triple baser. Bakely then went in, and the Buffalos made eight hits off him in seven innings. He gave eight men their base on balls, which, with timely batting, yielded nine runs. White made his first appearance in a championship game, and batted hard. Mack was hit on the knee by a pitched ball in the second inning, and gave way to Clark.

BUFFALO.	T.	R.	B.	O.	A.	E.	CLEVELAND.	T.	R.	B.	O.	A.	E.
Hoy, cf	7	3	4	4	0	0	Stricker, 2b	5	0	0	8	4	1
Rowe, ss	7	2	2	2	2	1	Deleh'nty, ss	5	3	2	1	7	0
Wise, 2b	7	2	3	2	2	0	Browning, lf	5	2	1	1	0	0
White, 1b	7	1	3	7	2	0	Twitchell, rf	5	0	0	1	1	0
Beecher, lf	6	1	3	0	0	0	Tebeau, 3b	5	0	1	3	2	1
Rainey, rf	6	3	3	3	1	1	Larkin, 1b	5	0	1	7	0	0
Mack, c	2	1	1	2	0	0	McAleer, cf	4	1	1	5	0	2
Keefe, p	6	3	1	0	2	0	Gruber, p	0	0	0	0	0	0
Clark, c	4	1	1	4	1	2	Brennan, c	4	1	0	1	1	0
Irwin, 3b	6	2	3	3	2	1	Bakely, p	4	0	0	0	0	0
Totals	54	19	24	27	12	5	Totals	42	7	6	27	15	4

Buffalo......... 6 2 0 2 0 0 1 4 4—19
Cleveland...... 2 0 1 1 0 3 0 0 0—7

Earned runs—Buffalo, 13; Cleveland, 1. Base on errors—B., 2; C., 1. On balls—B., 10; C., 9. Struck out—C., 6. Umpires, Jones and Knight. Time, 2.20.

The game scheduled for April 23, and prevented by rain, was played on 24, when the Buffalos scored their fourth victory over the visitors. Casey, an amateur pitcher from Cleveland, was given a trial by the Clevelands, but was removed from the box at the end of the fourth inning. Fourteen hits, including two doubles and a homer, coupled with six bases on balls, during these four innings, gave the Buffalos sixteen runs. Wise knocked the ball over the right field fence. Only once before has the feat been accomplished. Sunday, of the Brooklyns, of the Players' League, while with the Toledos did it last year. Hemming, who took Casey's place, did well, as only two hits were made off him during the remainder of the game. The Clevelands batted Haddock's pitching hard and came near winning the game in the last inning.

BUFFALO.	T.	R.	B.	O.	A.	E.	CLEVELAND.	T.	R.	B.	O.	A.	E.
Irwin, 3b	6	2	2	0	3	1	Stricker, 2b	7	2	2	4	6	0
Hoy, cf	6	2	0	1	0	0	Delehanty, ss	7	2	1	3	0	2
Rowe, ss	6	1	1	3	3	0	Browning, lf	6	2	3	1	0	0
Wise, 2b	6	3	2	2	4	3	Twitchell, rf	6	1	2	1	1	0
White, 1b	6	2	5	13	2	0	Tebeau, 3b	6	3	1	3	3	0
Beecher, lf	6	1	3	1	0	1	Larkin, 1b	6	2	2	10	0	0
Rainey, rf	6	3	1	1	0	0	McAleer, cf	6	3	3	3	0	0
Mack, c	5	2	0	6	2	0	Sutcliffe, c	6	0	3	1	2	1
Haddock, p	5	2	2	0	4	0	Casey, p	2	0	0	0	0	0
							Hemmings, p	4	0	0	0	2	0
Totals	52	18	16	27	18	5	Totals	56	15	17	*26	14	3

Buffalo......... 2 7 0 7 2 0 0 0 0—18
Cleveland...... 1 0 3 0 2 0 1 1 7—15

*Hoy out for not running.

Earned runs—Buffalo, 7; Cleveland, 6. Base on errors—B., 2; C., 2. On balls—B., 10; C., 8. Struck out—C., 6. Umpires, Jones and Knight. Time, 2.20.

Boston vs. New York.

The opening game between these teams, which was scheduled for April 25, at Boston, was delayed on account of rain until the following day, which was anything but a desirable one for the contest. The wind was raw and cold, yet the attendance, considering the weather, was a large one, numbering over 3,500 people. The game was marked by heavy batting, in which both teams took an active part. It was a fair sample of what the public may expect at any of the Players' League games this season. It is heavy batting the people want to see, and what the National League magnates have been trying to give them, but never fully accomplished it. At the beginning the Bostons commenced to bat the ball hard, and took what seemed to be a winning lead, but the visitors followed and administered to Kilroy one of the soundest drubbings he ever received. One inning was enough for Kilroy, who had been pounded for seven hits, including a home run and a two bagger, and he was replaced by Daley, who did much better against the visitors, and, aside from being a little wild, pitched a very clever game. The home team batted Crane's pitching in a way least expected. In the third inning, when Crane came to the bat, he was presented by Umpire Gaffney, on behalf of the Atlantic Boat Club, with a handsome ebony cane, with a heavily chased gold head. The batting honors were evenly divided, but superior base running and faultless fielding enabled the Bostons to win. The runs were made as follow: In the first inning Brown's single, H. Richardson's out, Stovey's single, a base on balls and errors by Hatfield and D. Richardson let in three runs for the Bostons. For the visitors, after two men were put out, Connor knocked the ball over the left field fence for a home run. Then followed singles by O'Rourke, Vaughn, Slattery, Whitney, Crane and a double by Hatfield, which netted six runs. A single, a wild throw, a base on balls, and another single gave the home team one more run in the second inning, and in the third it added two more runs on two bases on balls, a single and a wild pitch. The New Yorks also scored a run in their half of the inning on a base on balls, a single, a wild pitch and a sacrifice. In the fourth, the Bostons obtained another run on errors made by the visitors. The New Yorks also tallied one on Gore's single, a base on balls and O'Rouke's double. A base on balls and two singles gave the visitors one more run in the fifth inning. In the sixth inning, the Boston made three runs on Brown's single, H. Richardson's home run, an error by Hatfield and Brouther's two bagger. The New Yorks also scored another run most on balls, an error and a single. In the seventh, three doubles and a home run netted four runs and gave Boston the game.

BOSTON.	T.	R.	B.	O.	A.	E.	NEW YORK.	T.	R.	B.	O.	A.	E.
Brown, cf	5	3	2	1	2	0	Gore, rf	5	1	2	0	0	0
Rich'dson, lf	5	3	4	1	0	0	Rich'dson, 2b	5	0	2	2	2	1
Stovey, rf	5	2	2	0	0	0	Connor, 1b	5	1	2	8	0	0
Nash, 3b	5	3	2	1	3	0	O'Rourke, lf	5	2	2	3	0	0
Brouthers, 1b	5	1	3	9	0	0	Vaughn, c	5	2	1	5	1	2
Quinn, 2b	5	0	0	1	1	0	Slattery, cf	5	1	2	3	0	0
Irwin, ss	5	1	1	0	0	0	Whitney, 3b	5	1	1	0	0	0
Kelly, c	5	1	0	11	3	0	Hatfield, ss	5	2	2	2	2	2
Kilroy, p	0	0	0	0	0	0	Crane, p	5	0	1	1	2	0
Daley, p	5	0	1	0	2	0							
Totals	45	14	15	24	11	0	Totals	45	10	15	24	7	5

Boston............. 3 1 2 1 0 3 4 0—14
New York.......... 6 0 1 1 1 1 0 0—10

Earned runs—Boston, 4; New York, 6. Base on errors—B., 3. On balls—B., 4; N. Y., 8. Struck out—B., 4; N. Y., 8. Umpires, Gaffney and Barnes. Time, 2.15.

OPENING OF THE BASE-BALL SEASON OF 1890.

THE LEADING PLAYERS AND THEIR POSITIONS.

BY O. P. CAYLOR.

THE base-ball championship "season" opened on Saturday, April 19th, when two teams of players from Philadelphia appeared at the grounds of the National League and of the Brotherhood in this city. How there came to be two such rival organizations, and what are the prospects of the coming season, will be explained further on.

A. C. ANSON (LEAGUE).

Very recently a syndicate of capitalists made an offer, through the entirely responsible law firm of Tracy, Boardman, & Platt, to pay to the National League of Base-ball Clubs of America $1,000,000 for their franchises. The offer was read to the club owners at their meeting in Cleveland on the 4th of March, and without discussion was laid on the table by a unanimous vote.

Inasmuch as the National League of Base-ball Clubs is but one of a half-dozen or more prominent professional base-ball club organizations in the country, some idea may be had from the above-mentioned business transaction of the immense proportions which the great American sport has attained during the last ten years. The offer of $1,000,000 for the League franchises was considered to be absurdly small, the Boston club alone asserting that they would not sell out for less than that amount. The Boston club, however, own the block of ground upon which their team plays its games, and this plot, with the buildings upon it, is worth probably $250,000. The Philadelphia League club also own their own grounds, and have erected thereon costly permanent grand stands and club-houses. In the other six cities the clubs occupy grounds which are leased, and upon which they have put improvements which cost from $40,000 to $80,000 each.

During the winter which has just passed, a Brotherhood of Base-ball Players, most of whom withdrew from the service of the National League, organized an independent association of clubs, which they call the Players' League. They have rented grounds, and have fitted them up in National League cities, and propose during the season to conduct a competitive business against their former employers. They have secured in each city the moneyed backing of well-known business men, who are promised in return for their financial aid a certain share of the profits of the clubs to which they respectively give encouragement.

A bitter feeling exists between the two organizations. The Brotherhood of Players accuse the League "magnates" of forcing them into a revolt by reason of unfair and un-American modes of oppression in their club rules and regulations. On the other hand, the League officials allege that these rules were as much for the player's benefit as for the club's, and offer in proof thereof the fact that salaries under the workings of these rules more than doubled.

There was in every League player's contract for 1889 an option, called the reserve clause, which specified that if the club should "reserve" the player for 1890, it should be at a salary not less than that of the contract of 1889. The League claimed this to be an option. The Brotherhood players held that it was merely an option as to National Agreement clubs, and that they had a right to ignore it. Several law-suits grew out of the dispute. The New York club went into the courts and attempted to enjoin Ward and Ewing, two of their last season players, from playing with Brotherhood clubs, on the claim that they (the New York club) had a right under this reserve clause to the player's services. In both cases the courts decided against the club. Judge Wallace, in deciding the Ewing case, held that though the reserve clause was a contract morally binding Ewing to *negotiate* with the New York club for 1890, it was not such a contract that the club could enforce.

JOHN G. CLARKSON (LEAGUE).
FROM A PHOTOGRAPH BY CONLY, BOSTON.

It is admitted on both sides that the war between the two leagues will be a bitter one—a fight to the finish—and that the result will be the survival, possibly not of the fittest, but of the most enduring. The people who simply love the sport, and care nothing for the dispute between the old magnates and the new, will watch the games with considerable interest.

Besides the National League and the Players' or Brotherhood League there are three other combinations or circuits of clubs, including the principal cities in the eastern or central part of the country.

The National League holds franchises and has established clubs in Boston, New York, Brooklyn, Philadelphia, Pittsburgh, Cincinnati, Chicago, and Cleveland.

The Brotherhood clubs are located in Boston, New York, Brooklyn, Philadelphia, Chicago, Pittsburgh, Cleveland, and Buffalo. Thus it will appear that in only one National League city and one Brotherhood city the two organizations do not conflict.

Then there is the American Association of Base-ball Clubs, which is comprised of clubs in Brooklyn, Philadelphia, Rochester, Syracuse, Columbus, Toledo, Louisville, and St. Louis.

The Atlantic Association embraces a circuit composed of clubs in the cities of Baltimore, Wilmington (Delaware), Hartford, Newark, Jersey City, New Haven, Washington, and Worcester.

The Western Association has clubs in Minneapolis, St. Paul, Sioux City, Des Moines, Omaha, Kansas City, Denver, and St. Joseph.

There are also minor professional organizations, such as the Texas League of Clubs, in the larger cities of Texas, the California League, the Tri-State League, the International Association, and a number of others of lesser interest.

The reader will notice that, with the exception of the antagonism between the Brotherhood League and the National League, these various organizations do not conflict in territory except in the instances of Brooklyn and Philadelphia, where the National League and American Association occupy common territory by agreement.

It was this comity in business which of recent years made base-ball so profitable not only to clubs, but to professional players. The whole system is controlled and governed by a set of common base-ball laws, called the National Agreement, to which every professional base-ball organization of clubs in the country has subscribed, and is held bound except the Brotherhood League.

The supreme court to which all appeals are made in disputes between clubs of different organizations under the government of this National Agreement Confederation is a Board of Arbitration, consisting of three delegates from the National League and three from the American Association. The other leagues and associations enjoying the protection of this base-ball Magna Charta are qualified members, and while they are entitled to representation in the board, their representatives have no vote. The board has legislative as well as judicial powers. It has sole right to amend the National Agreement, repeal any part of it, and make changes or additions from time to time. The writer of this article had the honor of being a member of the original committee which formulated the tripartite agreement, and was secretary of the first Board of Arbitration. To Mr. A. G. Mills, of New York, base-ball owes the conception of that great instrument which has done so much for the game.

JOHN M. WARD (BROTHERHOOD).
FROM A PHOTOGRAPH BY J. HALL, BROOKLYN.

Before the National Agreement was formed for the confederation of leagues and associations, clubs preyed upon each other's players, and the least show of financial success made by a club in any city would at once call out rival or competitive clubs, until all were bankrupt, and the result would be a suspension of the game at that particular point for years. In this state of affairs there was no permanent value to a club's interests, and capital was very shy when asked to back up the game as a financial speculation.

Thus we see that the famous Red Stocking Club, of Cincinnati, in 1870 was completely thrown out of business and disrupted by the Boston and Washington clubs taking their favorite players for 1871. Instead of continuing to have the champion team of the United States, Cincinnati had no club at all in 1871, and no team. Neither was there another club organized in that city until late in 1875.

So, too, in Boston. When in 1875 the Chicago club took from the Boston club four of their famous players in the middle of the season, the pride was taken out of Boston patrons, and the club's business declined for several years, during which time instead of making money, it fell away to a total loss of nearly fifty thousand dollars.

Another evil from this unrestrained competition was the constant changing of players from team to team. And as it requires

DAN BROUTHERS (BROTHERHOOD).

TIMOTHY J. KEEFE (BROTHERHOOD).

WILLIAM B. EWING (BROTHERHOOD).

JEREMIAH DENNY (LEAGUE).

the working together of a set of ball-players for a whole season before they become familiar enough with each other's modes of play to bring about strong team-work, anything like perfection in base-ball playing in those days was almost an impossibility; and yet good team-work was acknowledged to be necessary to please patrons of the game, for without it that general excellence of play which is calculated to arouse enthusiasm was not to be expected.

It therefore became evident to the conservative leaders in the sport that some general law or set of rules must be formulated and adopted to govern all well-disposed organizations of clubs.

To this end was formed, in the autumn or winter of 1882, what was called the Tripartite Agreement, and which the next year was superseded by the National Agreement, an instrument which, it is claimed, has brought professional base-ball from its chaotic state of perpetual bankruptcy to a basis of well-founded business principles. It has stood the test of seven successive seasons, during which time a ball-player's salary has increased from an average of $1000 for seven months' service to an average of $3000, and clubs' franchises have in some instances been rated at half a million, whereas before the same sum could have bought up every ball club in the land in duplex.

EDWARD HANLON (BROTHERHOOD).

M. KILROY (BROTHERHOOD).

M. WELSH (LEAGUE).

What is this National Agreement? It is a common set of rules which does not govern clubs, but the various leagues and associations of clubs. First, it prevents ruinous competition by giving each club sole control of the patronage in the city where located, and allows no other league or association to give membership to any club which may organize to enter the city already occupied. Secondly, it allows every club, by a system of mutual notices, to "reserve" fourteen of its players for another season at a minimum salary. Thus reserved, no other club is permitted to negotiate with such players. In this way local favorites are retained from year to year, and the perfection of team-work is approached season after season. The effect of this rule or practice has been the mutual benefit of the players and clubs generally. It has not only increased the number of established professional clubs in the Union fourfold, and the number of players in the same proportion, but it has increased base-ball players' salaries from a maximum of $2500 to $6000 for seven months' service, and increased them *on an average* 200 per cent. As instances, note these cases: Ewing, the catcher, came to the New York club in 1883 for $3000, and last year received $5000, with a bonus of $1000 additional. Ward, the short-stop, played his first month in New York in 1882 for $75 a month, and last year drew $600 a month from the same club. Carpenter, the third-base-man, went to Cincinnati to play in 1882 at a salary of $800, and this year he was engaged for $2300. These men play no better now than they did in 1882, but the prosperity of their clubs in business has been their prosperity as well.

M. TIERNAN (LEAGUE).

W. D. O'BRIEN (LEAGUE).

Notwithstanding all this advancement in their salaried interests, many players of the National League began to chafe at some of the rules which the club officials made to control them. There was really no well-defined objection to the reserve rule, for the thinking players believed it benefited the profession generally for the reasons above given. But they objected to the practice of clubs selling their releases to other clubs; to the classification of the players into grades, to which certain set salaries attached; to the article in their contracts which permitted the club to discharge them after ten days' notice. A Brotherhood had been formed among the players, including all the National League players but about ten or twelve. Last summer, some time in June, when the championship season was at its height, the leaders of the Brotherhood drew up a bill of their grievances to be presented to the League. A committee of the Brotherhood called upon A. G. Spalding, of the Chicago Club, who was chairman of the League Standing Committee on Conference, and presenting their case, asked for an immediate answer, looking toward a correction of the aforesaid wrongs before the season of 1889 should close. Mr. Spalding, for the League, refused to break through that organization's established custom by "swapping horses while crossing a stream." He, however, assured the committee of players that as soon as the championship season was ended their request would be respectfully considered, equitably adjusted, and everything made satisfactory to the Brotherhood before contracts for 1890 were presented for signatures.

The leaders of the players, however, were not satisfied, and the most radical of them urged a general strike the day before July 4th—the big day of the year in base-ball financially. The cooler-headed men, however, prevented this proposed action. On July 14th a meeting of Brotherhood delegates was held at the Fifth Avenue Hotel, in New York city, and it was then and there resolved to cut loose from the League at the end of the season. Members from each chapter were delegated to secretly look up "financial backers" in the various cities, and report later on.

The consequence was that on the seventh day of September, and a few days about that period, the members of each chapter of the Brotherhood (or most of the members) signed an agreement to "strike" in November following, as soon as the championship season ended. Meanwhile financial backers in each League city were carefully selected, secured, and, together with the players, sworn to secrecy. The secret was so well guarded that though the plan was laid and perfected nearly three months before their contracts with the League terminated, there was no word of suspicion uttered to warn the club-owners until about October 1st. Even then the players, one and all, vehemently denied that there was an agreement to capture the business of the League.

The plan only partly succeeded. The belief of the leaders had been that they could take every player with them, and thus compel the dismantled League clubs to go out of business. But about one-third of the best players refused to desert their clubs, declaring that they understood, when they signed the agreement in September, that no revolt was to occur unless the clubs should refuse to grant certain requests, which they had been given no chance to consider.

This defection from the ranks of the Brotherhood players not only weakened their plan, but it left the National League clubs a nucleus around which to fortify and fight for the maintenance of their business interests. They proceeded to buy the releases of promising young players from contract with clubs of minor organizations under the National Agreement, and at the same time secured the membership of the American Association clubs in Brooklyn and Cincinnati, with their complement of fine players. The

W. HALLMAN (BROTHERHOOD).

A. WEYHING (BROTHERHOOD).

JOHN A. McPHEE (LEAGUE).

E. N. CRANE (BROTHERHOOD).

Indianapolis and Washington clubs, members of last year's League, were bought out, and the latter fine team transferred for the most part to New York city. Thus the old clubs will enter the season as well equipped with stellar attractions as the Brotherhood clubs, and better prepared financially for the fight. The Brotherhood in the start challenged the League to a fight to the finish. The latter accepted it, and there is no "possible, probable shadow

DAVID ORR (Brotherhood).

of doubt" but that one of the two organizations will in time have to surrender. Some of the cities occupied by both cannot possibly support two clubs, and an unbroken circuit of eight cities is always absolutely necessary in a financial sense.

It therefore follows that the season just opening will be the most exciting and the most important in the history of the national game.

Herewith is a full list of the players who constitute the teams of the various clubs of the League and the Brotherhood at the time this is written:

NATIONAL LEAGUE PLAYERS.

Boston (15 Men).

*John G. Clarkson,	Thomas J. Tucker,
*C. W. Ganzell,	Hermann Long,
*C. W. Bennett,	Louis W. Hardie,
*C. M. Smith,	A. Schellhouse,
C. A. Nichols,	John McGarr,
Robert A. Lowe,	J. P. Faber,
P. J. Donovan,	George E. Hodgman,

W. S. Brodie.

Philadelphia (15 Men).

*T. D. Vickery,	*William Day,
*S. L. Thompson,	Allen McCauley,
*John Clements,	R. G. Allen,
*Albert Meyers,	E. D. Burke,
*William Schriver,	Ed. Mayer,
*William Gleason,	W. R. Hamilton,
*E. H. Decker,	D. Anderson,

John F. Smith.

New York (18 Men).

*John W. Glasscock,	*A. W. Rusie,
*H. J. Boyle,	*R. D. Buckley,
*C. E. Bassett,	*Jesse Burkett,
*A. J. Somer,	*M. Tiernan,
M. J. Scanlon,	*P. J. Murphy,
*M. Welsh,	S. N. Crane,
Joseph Hornung,	Charles L. Dooley,
John H. Murphy,	A. F. Clarke,
*Jeremiah Denny,	M. Seifke.

Brooklyn (16 Men).

*George J. Smith,	*R. H. Clark,
*W. D. O'Brien,	*T. P. Daly,
*G. B. Pinkney,	*D. L. Foutz,
*W. H. Terry,	*T. P. Burns,
*R. L. Caruthers,	George T. Stallings,
*J. S. Corkhill,	*M. F. Hughes,
*H. Collins,	*J. Newman.
*Thomas Lovett,	*C. L. Reynolds.

W. A. LATHAM (Brotherhood).

C. A. COMISKEY (Brotherhood.)

Cleveland (15 Men).

*Edward Beatin,	L. C. Stockwell,
*E. J. McKean,	Joseph Sommer,
*Charles L. Zimmer,	John Wadsworth,
*R. J. Gilks,	W. D. Smalley,
George Davis,	Ezra P. Lincoln,
W. W. Veach,	Thomas J. Dowse,
Joseph Ardner,	C. J. Parsons,

Vincent Daily.

Cincinnati (16 Men).

*J. A. McPhee,	*James W. Keenan,
*C. G. Baldwin,	*J. W. Halliday,
*William M. Earle,	*T. J. Mullane,
*Hugh Nichol,	*James Duryea,
*O. P. Beard,	Jerry Harrington.
*L. Viau,	W. P. Rhines,
*Charles Marr,	Joseph W. Knight,
*John G Reilly,	F. J. Foreman.

Pittsburgh (19 Men).

P. J. Daniels,	Frederick Roat,
*William Sowders,	William Wilson,
*G. P. Miller,	John Kelty,
Guy Hecker,	Howard Brandenburg,
S. H. Laroque,	Frederick Schmitt,
Kirtley Baker,	Charles Gray,
Edward Mulhearn,	Philip Routcliff,
Henry Jones,	Henry Youngman,
W. H. Hemp,	John P. Berger.

*Fred Dunlap.

Chicago (16 Men).

*A. C. Anson,	J. J. Cooney,
*Thomas E. Burns,	J. C. Lauer,
*W. F. Hutchinson,	B. L. Garvin,
Cliff Carroll,	Matthew Schell,
*W. R. Wilmot,	M. J. Sullivan,
M. J. Kittridge,	Howard Earle,
Thomas Nagle,	W. E. Coughlin,
J. P. Andrews,	Peter J. O'Brien.

* Were League Players last year or members of the same clubs.

BROTHERHOOD PLAYERS.

Boston (16 Men).

M. J. Kelly,	C. A. Radbourne,
C. Swett,	Adison Gumbert,
M. E. Murphy,	M. Madden,
M. Kilroy,	W. Daley,
D. Brouthers,	J. Quinn,
Arthur Irwin,	William Nash,
H. Richardson,	R. F. Johnson,
H. Stovey,	Thomas Brown.

Buffalo (15 Men).

C. Mack,	W. Hallegan,
O. Clark,	A. Ferson,
G. Haddock,	G. W. Keefe,
G. H. Krock,	James L. White,
S. Wise,	J. C. Rowe,
John Irwin,	W. J. Rainey,
W. E. Hoy,	E. Beecher,

J. J. Carney.

Cleveland (15 Men).

C. N. Snyder,	E. E. Sutcliff,
John Brennan,	H. Gruber,
E. Bakeley,	J. F. O'Brien,
L. Hemmings,	H. Larkin,
John Stricker,	Paul Radford,
Oliver Tebeau,	J. McAleer,
L. P. Browning,	L. Twitchell,

E. J. Delehanty.

Chicago (15 Men).

John Boyle,	C. A. Farrell,
Del Darling,	M. E. Baldwin,
Charles King,	F. Dwyer,
Charles Bartson,	C. A. Comiskey,
F. N. Pfeffer,	E. N. Williamson,
•W. A. Latham,	H. Duffy,
J. Ryan,	J. O'Neil,

C. A. Bastian.

New York (14 Men).

William B. Ewing.	William Brown,
H. Vaughn,	H. O'Day,
T. J. Keefe,	E. N. Crane,
John Ewing,	Roger Conner,
Daniel Richardson,	Arthur Whitney,
G. Hatfield,	James O'Rourke,
M. J. Slattery.	George Gore.

M. J. KELLY (Brotherhood).

Brooklyn (16 Men).

David Orr,	L. Bierbauer,
John M. Ward,	W. Joyce,
A. Weyhing,	C. Murphy,
G. Van Haltern,	J. Sowders,
J. C. McGeachy,	G. E. Andrews,
C. Daily,	J. E. Seery,
Paul Cook,	John Hayes,
Arthur Sunday,	Thomas Kinslow.

Philadelphia (17 Men).

A. B. Sanders,	C. G. Buffinton,
J. Husted,	P. Knell,
Elmer Cunningham,	Lave Cross,
John Milligan,	W. Hallman,
M. Griffin,	J. G. Fogarty,
G. Wood,	S. D. Farrar,
D. Shannon,	William Shindle,
G. Rouse,	Joseph Mulvey,

C. M. Pickett.

Pittsburgh (15 Men).

Thomas Quinn,	J. Hurley,
F. W. Carroll,	J. J. Fields,
J. K. Tener,	J. F. Galvin,
Edward Morris,	H. E. Staley,
W. Robinson,	Thomas Corcoran,
William Kuehne,	J. P. Visner,
Edward Hanlon,	A. Maul,

J. P. Beckley.

A DIVE FOR SECOND BASE.

JOSEPH MULVEY (Brotherhood).

The desertion of so many of the old players from the National League teams has opened the way for the advancement of a considerable number of younger experts who have hitherto lacked the opportunities to advance themselves to the front in professional ball-playing. The season of 1890 will then be the more interesting because these new candidates for popular favor are to have a chance to win their laurels on the ball fields in the large cities.

THOMAS E. BURNS (League).

Among the new players are quite a number of college men. The New York club has three of them in its team—young men who respectively have been students of Harvard and Hamilton colleges, and Brown's University. Of the older players, Hutchinson and Bassett are the most notable as college graduates.

Probably no other player at this

S. L. THOMPSON (League).

time is so valuable in his professional capacity as Adrian C. Anson, of the Chicago club. Mr. Anson has played with the Chicagoes for fifteen years, and at no time during all those successive seasons could he have been spared by his club without serious loss. As a player, in fielding he has superiors; as a great batter he has peers; but as a captain—a general in his profession—he never had an equal. Captain Anson's judgment of a young player's abilities, after a short examination of his play, is seldom wrong. Thus his selection

CHARLES ZIMMER (League).

of new material for his team when it is needed has invariably been good; and after he has the material selected, he is unequalled in his ability to train it into the perfection of team-work. Thus he has on several occasions let discontented stars go to other clubs, filled their places with comparatively unheard-of new players, and continued the place of his club in the victorious front. This year, on account of the revolt of the Brotherhood, he has almost an entirely new team, only three of his last year's players remaining, and yet he promises to be able, with his "young blood" team to make a gallant and not unsuccessful fight for the National League championship. Captain Anson is a strict disciplinarian, unmovable in his commands, yet not unreasonably harsh or in anywise unjust. He leads, and asks his men to follow. There is no task which he imposes upon his players that he himself is not willing to assume.

The only rival Captain Anson ever had as a base-ball general is Charles A. Comiskey, of the Chicago Brotherhood club. For a number of years past Comiskey has been captain of the St. Louis American Association club, for which he and his team won the championship four successive years. Like Captain Anson, he is a hard worker, a strict master, an enthusiastic leader, and a splendid judge of rising young players.

At the head of the pitchers of the day stands, without doubt, John G. Clarkson, of the Boston League club, with which he has signed a three years' contract, calling for a cash equivalent of $30,000 for the three years. He is a young man of rare intelligence and good social standing. His magnificent work in his position last season for the Boston club won praise from the lips of every base-ball lover. He not only did the work with superior results, but he played in more championship games than any other professional pitcher.

Among the catchers, not one can be classed with William B. Ewing, of the New York Brotherhood club. His hard, sure batting, his peerless throwing to bases, his almost perfect judgment in making the right plays at the right time, give him his pre-eminent standing among the players of his position. Mr. Ewing is a fair sample of the possibilities which base-ball playing has for young men. Thirteen years ago he was a teamster in Cincinnati, working for $10 a week. Last summer he received over $6000 as his recompense for seven months' services. He now boldly announces that during the next five years he is absolutely sure of getting more each season than even that which he received in 1889.

Next to Ewing, and very nearly on his heels as a catcher, comes Charles W. Bennett, of the Boston League club. Mr. Bennett is a gentleman of excellent character and fair intelligence.

Perhaps no second-base-man in the profession has a right to call himself the superior of John A. McPhee, of the Cincinnati club, for which he has played the position eight seasons, and is now beginning the ninth. McPhee is as much a polished gentleman as he is a finished ball-player. His admirers who know him professionally are scarcely less numerous than his friends who know him socially. What Ross Barnes was to base-ball in 1876 John A. McPhee is to it to-day.

Jeremiah Denny, of the New York club, has no rival as a third-base-man. He is a Californian, but has lived so long in the East as a professional that the Pacific coast can hardly claim him. Denny, besides being able to play his base—the most difficult of all on the in-field—more skilfully than any of his rivals, is a heavy, sure batter, and a fair base-runner.

John W. Glasscock, of the same club, is acknowledged to be without a successful rival as a short-stop. His wonderful stops, "pick-ups," and quick throwing to bases are considered among the marvels of base-ball playing. By trade Mr. Glasscock is a ship-carpenter, and the fact that he receives twenty dollars a day for playing ball during the summer does not prevent him from earning a more moderate sum in wages during the winter by working at his trade.

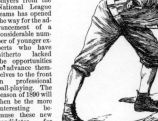

ROGER CONNER (Brotherhood).

JOHN G. REILLY (League).

D. L. FOUTZ (League).

Next in skill to Glasscock as a short-stop is John Montgomery Ward, leader of the Brotherhood, and captain of the Brooklyn Brotherhood club. Mr. Ward is called a brainy player, whose quick wit and ready judgment have served him well in play. He is besides a fine base-runner.

Among the out-fielders such men as Tiernan, Thompson, Corkhill, O'Brien, Wilmot, Kelly, Halliday, Hanlon, and O'Neil are notable players. All with the exception of Corkhill are also good batters.

The championship season of the National League began on the nineteenth day of April, and will close on the fourth day of October. In the Brotherhood the season opened also April 19th, and closes October 4th. The rules of the National Agreement prohibit any of its clubs from playing a game with the Brotherhood clubs, because the latter contain players who have become ineligible by reason of having signed National Agreement contracts, and repudiated their alleged obligations under them. There will consequently be no test of strength between the winners of the two championships. But next fall the champion club of the National League and the champion club of the American Association will play a series of games for the "championship of the world," as has been the practice for four years.

In concluding, it might not be amiss to note the tremendous strides professional base-ball has taken during the last fifteen years, until it has become an established business all over the United States. There are at this time about one hundred professional clubs banded together under the National Agreement. These one hundred clubs give employment to about fifteen hundred players, whose average salary is perhaps $1000 a season, making a total amount paid in salaries of $1,500,000. Besides the National Agreement clubs there are the eight Brotherhood clubs, embracing about one hundred and twenty players, whose salaries will aggregate $250,000, swelling the grand total to 1620 players and $1,750,000 in salaries.

These clubs during the season will travel about 450,000 miles by rail. Each club will carry from twelve to sixteen men in their journeying around, which means railroad tickets representing 6,300,000 miles. At an average of 2½ cents a mile, the cost of travel alone, not including sleeping-car accommodation, will be found to amount to something like $157,500—quite a neat drop in the earnings of the American railroads.

There is another class of business which profits from this base-ball playing—the hotels. During one-half of the playing season, about eighty days of each year, every club has its team on the circuit, and the players are for the most part quartered at the very best hotels. Not less than $200,000 is spent in this way among the various hotels in cities which support base-ball clubs. Probably $100,000 would be a small estimate of the rents paid by the clubs for their grounds, and certainly $200,000 would not more than pay the miscellaneous expenses, such as sleeping-car fares, carriage hire, advertising, salaries of ground employés, treasurers, and gate-keepers, and the purchase of supplies.

JOHN W. GLASSCOCK (League).

Add it all together, and you will have nearly two and a half-million of dollars paid out by professional base-ball clubs each year. It is not unlikely that these figures are too small to be correct, nor is it a hazardous guess to say that the profits of the whole season among all the clubs, over and above expenses, will reach a quarter of a million of dollars. Then we find the American people paying each season $2,750,000 for their amusement in base-ball. Three spectators, on an average, will represent a dollar. So that we have a total attendance during the season of about eight millions of people. Divide this up into one hundred and thirty playing days, and you will arrive at the conclusion that the average daily attendance in America on base-ball games where admission fees are charged is over fifty thousand. This season, I believe, it will exceed sixty thousand.

It is not an unreasonable estimate to say that every day during this summer five million Americans will examine the columns of their favorite newspapers to see the result of the professional base-ball games of the previous day.

A PICKED NINE.

THE NATIONAL GAME.

OPENING OF THE BASE-BALL SEASON.

BASE-BALL divides with poker the honor of being the national game. Among athletic sports it is supreme. It has no rival. It may be said without exaggeration that one-half of the adult male population of the United States are

KEEFE STRIKES OUT HIS THIRD VICTIM.

deeply interested in its welfare. They may not all play it themselves, but they have played it in their youth, and they still like to see it played, or to read about it. Their pulses beat with the old wild thrill when Brouthers makes a home-run or John Ward a double play. As the season approaches, the newspapers begin to fill with news, with reports of the condition of the various players, of the new accessions to the clubs, of the new rules, of the prospects of the game. Every one is on the *qui-vive*. At last the opening day comes, and for six months the nation becomes a nation of base-ball cranks. Sober business men, lawyers, doctors, heads of families, invent excuses to give their more serious avocations the slip and to appear among the howling, excited crowds at the home grounds. In hotel corridors, in bar-rooms, in the streets, in private houses, the one great topic of conversation seems to be the "features" of the day's game, or the respective chances of the clubs for the pennant. And then the season winds up in a blaze of glory. As the competitors near the home-stretch the enthusiasm runs riot, and culminates in a grand burst of excitement when they pass under the wires.

This year the base-ball season opens with new and complicated features. The Association is not exactly the Association of last year. Old clubs—as the Cincinnati, Baltimore—have disappeared; new clubs—as the Rochester, Syracuse, and Toledo—have made their appearance. Even the old clubs do not retain all the old favorites. The Brooklyn Club, for instance, is an entirely different organization from the last year's champions of the Association. The latter have been transferred almost bodily to the League, and are strongly backed for the League championship.

"BUCK'S" EYE ON THE BALL.

When you come to the League, however, you find a total disruption. There are changes in the localities and, consequently, in the names of several of the clubs; Washington disappears, and so does Indianapolis, and Brooklyn and Cincinnati take their place. But those clubs that retain their names are not the same clubs we knew and loved of yore. The Giants who won last year's pennant no longer make up the *personnel* of the New York Club. They have all gone, and their places are taken by new men—new not only to New York, but, with one or two exceptions, to the League diamond—men who have their reputations to make. And so with the other teams. You look down the list of players, and only here and there you recognize a name. Clarkson is still with the Bostons, but where is Mike Kelly, and where are Brown and Richardson and Brouthers and Nash, and all those great batters and fielders who gave the Giants so hard a tussle for the championship? Philadelphia has Clements and Gleason and Thompson, but where is Buffington, the great pitcher who was put forward whenever the club was on its mettle? where is Fogarty, the best all-round player in the nine? where "Sid" Farrar, Mulvey, and Hallman? Without these familiar names the Philadelphias are not the old nine whose name we delighted to abbreviate into "Phillies."

One answer covers all these queries. They have gone over to the Players' League.

It is hardly worth while here to retell the old story how, in 1885, John Ward and other enterprising ball-players organized themselves into what was known as the Brotherhood of Players, a sort of trade-union whose object was to protect the ball-player from the encroachments of the capitalists who hired him, and sought to own him; how they fought, with indifferent success, against the reserve rule—a rule that was never, indeed, enforced to its full extent, but which practically made the player a chattel who might be sold by one club to another without asking his consent or giving him any share in the purchase-money, a rule that offered the player only two alternatives, to become a slave or forfeit his means of livelihood;—how they also fought, and also with indifferent success, against the $2,000 salary-limit rule adopted by the National League; how the Brotherhood grew, until nearly all the players in the National League were members; how the National League, after having promised to repeal the salary-limit rule, and failed to do so, in the winter of 1888–89 passed the famous classification-law; how a meeting of the Brotherhood was called to protest against this action; how the president of the National League refused to treat with the Brotherhood Committee until fall; how a new meeting of the Brotherhood was called

DENNY (N. Y. N. L.) OUT AT FIRST.

on July 14th; and, finally, how it was decided in secret session that the players should see if they could not interest enough capitalists to start a new league which would respect the wishes and the rightful demands of the men, and in which the players might, if they chose, take a financial interest. Their success is now a matter of history. But the secret was well kept. Although rumors and counter-rumors had filled the air for weeks, it was a surprise to the base-ball magnates and to the entire world of base-ball lovers when, in November, 1889, the announcement was formally made that the members of the Brotherhood had seceded almost in a body from the National League, and would start a new league, to be known as the Players' League, which was backed by capitalists in eight of the principal cities of the Union.

The League magnates were aghast. They succeeded, indeed, in bribing back a few of the recalcitrant players. But the rest remained firm to their new allegiance. They abolished the obnoxious rules. But the time for concession and conciliation had passed. They appealed to the law. But the courts decided against them. They had to face the emergency, to provide new players to fill the vacancies of the old ones, to organize what was practically a new league. On the other hand, the men who had won their spurs in the National League grouped themselves into teams which, in many cases, retained the old names, and preserved the integrity of the old clubs. Thus the New Yorks, the Bostons, the Philadelphias of the Players' League, are substantially the "Giants" and "Phillies" and "Bean-eaters" of last year, and have carried over with them to the new organization much of the old prestige and popular following.

With all these complications, with all these new interests injected into the game, with these new rivalries and new incentives, the opening of the base-ball season has been looked forward to with the utmost interest and curiosity by the base-ball public; and nowhere was that interest more strongly manifested than in New York, where the grounds of the two rival associations are close neighbors, with only the width of a street to divide one from the other. Early on the afternoon of Saturday, April 19th, the cars of the Elevated Railroad began bearing the crowds to the scene of the coming conflicts; soon they became crowded almost to suffocation, and by the time game was called nearly 20,000 people—16,657, to be strictly accurate—had been landed at the gates. And how did they divide themselves? Not with any mathematical regularity, not without a show of

"BUCK" STOPS A WILD PITCH.

favoritism—12,013 squeezed themselves into the grounds of the Players' League, and 4,644 into the grounds of the National League. But the latter comforted themselves with the reflection that theirs was the more select audience of the two (for, until a better word is coined, we shall continue to use the word "audience," which purists have condemned without offering a substitute); and, indeed, the grand-stand of the National League looked like a gathering of the *élite*, so well dressed were the spectators, and especially the female portion thereof,—present in large numbers. But there were notable men and pretty women on the other grand-stand also, and the horny-handed sons of toil made a brave show upon the bleaching boards, where they were jammed and crowded without a seat to spare, so that they overflowed into the grounds and crowded in upon the players.

And the photographer was there, too. He was on both the grounds—he was lying in wait to bind upon paper the most striking scenes and incidents of the day's play for the benefit of the readers of THE ILLUSTRATED AMERICAN. He had a hard task before him. To take instantaneous photographs of pitchers, catchers, and batsmen while engaged in some feat occupying but a fraction of a second of time requires nerve, experience, skill. The movements of the players are not only lightning-like in speed, but the unexpected happens with startling persistence on a base-ball field, and the photographer has to strain every sense in order to keep pace with the game. Our artists are to be congratulated on the success with which they have triumphed over difficulties.

The opening games at both parks were between Philadelphia and New York, and in both cases Philadelphia won.

JUMPING FOR A HIGH ONE.

A LADIES' BASEBALL MATCH.

ANSON'S LATEST MASCOT.

UNCLE ADRIAN ENTERS THE GAME WEARING LONG WHISKERS.

They Evidently Prove Efficacious, for the Colts Win — A Pitchers' Battle Relieved by Many Good Plays—New York

ANSON'S LATEST MASCOT.

UNCLE ADRIAN ENTERS THE GAME WEARING LONG WHISKERS.

They Evidently Prove Efficacious, for the Colts Win — A Pitchers' Battle Relieved by Many Good Plays—New York Wins from Cleveland and Pittsburg Whitewashes Brooklyn—Rain Prevents the Cincinnati-Philadelphia Contest—Results in the Minor Associations.

	Games played.	Won.	Lost.	Per cent.
Chicago	111	70	41	.630
Boston	109	62	47	.568
New York	102	57	45	.558
Philadelphia	107	57	50	.532
Cleveland	112	51	61	.455
Brooklyn	106	47	59	.443
Pittsburg	109	45	64	.412
Cincinnati	110	44	66	.400

Am. Assn.	Won.	Lost.	P.C.	West. Assn.	Won.	Lost.	P.C.
Boston	79	33	.705	Sioux City	7	5	.583
St. Louis	72	46	.626	Denver	7	5	.583
Baltimore	61	49	.554	Kansas City	5	6	.454
Athletic	60	53	.530	Omaha	3	8	.272
Columbus	52	65	.444				
Milwaukee	47	64	.423				
Washington	38	68	.358				
Louisville	39	73	.348				

Games Scheduled for Today.

National League—Boston at Chicago, Brooklyn at Pittsburg, New York at Cleveland, Philadelphia at Cincinnati.

American Association—St. Louis at Boston, Milwaukee at Philadelphia, Louisville at Baltimore, Columbus at Washington.

Illinois-Iowa League—Quincy at Joliet, Rockford at Ottumwa.

Wisconsin League—Green Bay at Oconto, Marinette at Appleton, Fond du Lac at Oshkosh.

UNCLE ADRIAN WEARS WHISKERS.

He Treats the Crowd to a Surprise and Picks Up His Usual Victory.

When the Chicago players straggled on the field at the West Side Park yesterday afternoon the crowd was electrified to see in their midst a figure strangely familiar except as to its facial adornment and the snowy whiteness of its flowing locks. It was a commanding figure, with a beard of fulsome quantity that concealed even the lettering on the flannel shirt that covered an expansive chest. Hoary age clad in a baseball suit is an unknown quantity, and the crowd marveled in consequence. It recalled to the bleachers youthful visions of the revered Santa Claus, except that Santa Claus in white flannel knickerbockers and spiked shoes was rather contrary to the tradition. As the figure slowly approached the diamond some one with better powers of discernment than the others cried out: "O! it's only Anson." And so it was. The grand old man of baseball was hurling defiance into the teeth of age by aping its appearance. After the crowd had recovered from its surprise it grew superstitious and called loudly to the old man to "take 'em off," but Uncle Adrian was adamant. Those whiskers were on to stay, and stay they did during the nine innings of the game.

When their owner walked to the bat for the first time he notified Umpire Lynch that if a pitched ball so much as ruffled the serene flow of his beard he would claim a base by virtue of being hit. It might have been a fine point for Lynch to decide, but during the afternoon nothing disturbed the whiskers but Uncle's caresses and the nipping lake breeze that held high carnival during the game, causing the number of blue nose tips in the stand to grow with each inning as the contest progressed.

The game itself was a pretty contest that would have been thoroughly enjoyable to the 3,500 people present but for the unfavorable elements. It devolved into a pitchers' battle with Vickery and Nichols as the opposing factors, and to each is great credit due. While pitchers' battles are usually tiresome, the chances offered for scoring were frequent enough to keep the crowd interested from start to finish.

Nichols struck out eight men and Vickery six.

Schriver keeps up his batting. He picked up two singles yesterday.

Stovey played poorly in left. Besides two muffs he handled Ryan's two-bagger to left very clumsily.

Tucker's three-base hit would probably have been pulled down but for the blinding sun that prevented Ryan from judging the ball properly.

Today's game will be at the South Side. It will be the last with Boston here this season. The teams will be placed as follows:

Boston.	Position.	Chicago.
Staley	Pitcher	Gumbert.
Ganzel	Catcher	Kittridge.
Tucker	First base	Anson.
Quinn	Second base	Pfeffer.
Nash	Third base	Dahlen.
Long	Shortstop	Cooney.
Stovey	Left field	Wilmot.
Lowe	Center field	Ryan.
Brodie or Kelly	Right field	Carroll.

New York, 3; Cleveland, 2.

CLEVELAND, O., Sept. 4.—Inability to hit Ewing accounted for Cleveland's defeat today. Young pitched a good game, but was unfortunate in having one of his bases on balls score what proved to be the winning run. Score:

Cleveland	2	0	0	0	0	0	0	0	0	—2
New York	0	0	0	1	2	0	0	0	0	—3

Cleveland—Hits, 4; errors, 1. New York—Hits, 10; errors, 2. Earned runs—New York, 1. Two-base hits—Tebeau, Virtue, Gore. Stolen base—Childs. Left on bases—Cleveland, 6; New York, 5. Struck out—By Young, 2; Ewing, 2. Bases on balls—By Young, 8; Ewing, 4. Double plays—McKean, Virtue. First on errors—Cleveland, 1; New York, 1. Passed ball—Clark. Time—1:30. Umpire—Easlie. Batteries—Young and Zimmer; Ewing and Clark.

Pittsburg, 6; Brooklyn, 0.

PITTSBURG, Pa., Sept. 4.—The home team shut the Brooklyns out today by hard and timely hitting. The score:

Pittsburg	1	0	0	0	1	0	0	0	4	—6
Brooklyn	0	0	0	0	0	0	0	0	0	—0

Pittsburg—Hits, 11; errors, 2. Brooklyn—Hits, 8; errors, 2. Batteries—Calvin and Miller; Caruthers and Kinslow. Earned runs—Pittsburg, 4. Two-base

peg thus won by 168 runs.

Today will witness the last match of the Winnipeg tour, when the visitors will meet the redoubtable Pullman team on their own ground at 11 a. m. The form displayed by the visitors this week would indicate a close game. Their easy victories over the St. George and Wanderers teams prove them to be fine players. Though beaten by the Chicagos they ought to have made a better fight and on the true Pullman wicket they will no doubt be seen to advantage.

Their team will be about the same as has played through the week and Pullman will be strongly represented.

At Parkside today the St. George and Chicago first elevens will contest their last match in the Spalding cup competition, while their second elevens will play at Fullerton avenue.

In the evening the Chicago Cricket Association will hold a smoking concert at the Chicago club house at Parkside. The object is to raise funds to send the team that is to represent Chicago against Philadelphia in the latter city Friday and Saturday, Sept. 11 and 12. Among the singers will be Messrs. C. A. Knorr, F. Lawson, and John Morley. The Winnipeg team will attend in a body.

Men Who Travel.

An old railroad man named Lawton, now a sleeping-car superintendent at Indianapolis, has kept a record of his journeyings since 1863, and the total is 2,338,246 miles. Conductor S. G. Boone, late of the Reading, has covered 2,847,000 miles, and another Reading conductor has ridden something over 1,597,700 miles. Even these figures would be far surpassed by the record of some of the old Captains of the ocean steamships.

THIRTY TO ONE PRINCE.

VERGE D'OR AND A GOOD FIELD BEATEN BY A LONG SHOT.

The Columbian Stable Makes a Killing in the Principal Event of the Day at Garfield—Fitzpatrick's Riding of the Mulkey Crack Severely Criticised—Tom Roach the Only Winning Favorite, but a Number of Good Second Choices Win.

Verge d'Or made a bad second to Prince, a 30 to 1 shot, in the principal event at Garfield yesterday. His defeat was a body blow for the talent. It was even worse for some of the bookmakers, as the owners of Prince made a killing on the race. They are credited with having taken about $6,000 out of the ring—all on an investment of $200. One bookmaking firm, that of Barney Marks & Co., had to turn its board when Prince galloped in, having taken a single big bet on the horse. Other pencilers had also written cards on the Columbian Stable's entry.

This surprise came in the fourth race of the day, in which Verge d'Or had for his other company Brandolette, Ernest Race, Guido, and Ed Bell. Verge d'Or carried 125 pounds, giving twenty pounds to Prince and nearly as much to the others. "Daredevil" Fitzpatrick had the mount on Verge d'Or, and his riding was much criticised. His strong pull craned the colt's neck all the way to the last turn, where he was last. He succeeded in passing all but Prince, who could not be caught, although Fitzpatrick rode like a demon down the stretch.

After the race Fitzpatrick declared that Verge d'Or had no heart. The backers of the colt would not believe that and denounced Fitzpatrick's work in severe terms. Fitzpatrick says he rode according to instructions and expected to have no trouble in winning when he pleased. At the best he displayed poor judgment in holding Verge d'Or back so long. Of course Mulkey's colt was favorite at odds on of 7 to 10.

Erred in Judgment.

The judges said that while Fitzpatrick might have erred in judgment he rode an honest race. Verge d'Or has shown some queer performances but no one ever heard his courage question until yesterday. He has been campaigned all through the season and many think he has been overworked.

Prince, who furnished the surprise and played havoc with talent and bookmakers alike, is a 4-year-old colt by King Alfonso—Curlew and is owned in the Columbian Stable, of which Dr. Bergen is the chief owner. He has run in some good races during the season, but has not shown to advantage except at Washington Park once, when he finished second to Whitney. Aug. 21 he won his maiden victory as a 4-year-old at Garfield, beating Joe Woolman and Vattel. Wednesday last he finished fourth in a race with Alaho. His owners have apparently had him bottled up as a good thing.

Tom Roach was the only favorite that won during the day, but as the other winners were good second choices the bookmakers had but little the better of their financial battle with the public. The attendance was large, and the track was in good condition.

The free handicap brought out a good field, and the talent proceeded to light on Verge d'Or, who was considered the only sure thing on the board. Ed Bell, Guido, Ernest Race, and Brandolette were all to be had at from 5 to 10 to 1, while the bookies carelessly chalked up 20 and 30 and even 40 to 1 on Prince. A few pikes landed on Prince, but he was not played heavily enough in any one book to arouse suspicion.

Brandolette went away first, but Prince led by the wire after the first sixteenth, while Fitzpatrick was riding Verge d'Or in an exercise gait. At the quarter Prince went back and loafed along with Verge d'Or, both beginning to go up at the three-quarters. In turning to the stretch Griffin began to whip Prince, who entered the stretch well in advance of Verge d'Or still under persuasion. Fitzpatrick saw his danger and began riding for dear life. Prince was sent out at a great pace, and the "Daredevil" could not overtake him. Bound to reach the place, anyhow, and vainly hoping to come up with Prince, Fitzpatrick rode desperately all the way down, but Prince won easily by three lengths. Ed Bell was third, two lengths after Verge d'Or.

Zeke Hardy and Big Three.

Zeke Hardy won the first event without trouble. He was considered good, after the favorite Armiel. After the quarter Zeke went up to first place and was never headed. He won by two lengths, with Koko, a long-shot, in second, under great punishment.

Big Three carried 140 pounds in the free high-weight handicap, six others starting at from seventeen to twenty-two pounds lighter. Fitzpatrick let Burt Jordan, Gov. Ross, and Maud make the pace to the stretch, where he sent the Ruddys' strong horse up and won handily with plenty to spare.

Leh was a hot favorite in the next event, but there was a big play on Mary McGowan, although she had dumped the talent earlier in the week. Allen took Leh out early, and kept him in front nearly all the way to the stretch, only allowing Gov. Wheeler to show ahead at one or two points. Going to the stretch Hathaway let Mary McGowan out, and despite Allen's efforts on Leh, she won by a length.

Tom Roach, the favorite, got in first in the five furlong dash for 2-year-olds, only beating Cruickshank by a neck in an exciting finish. Unadilla started away well up with the others, but failed of his stride and did not show well in the beginning. After a gallant struggle she finished third. Angeree made the going to the stretch and then quit, allowing Roach to take the lead.

Another great finish marked the last race of the day. Louise M. was favorite. Tamerlane set the pace to the three-quarters, where Upman, Louise M., and Bob L. all came very fast and went away from the others. They were on very even terms coming home and all were well persuaded by whip and spur. Upman was first to the wire by a head, with Bob L. second, and the favorite third.

Summary of the Races.

The racing summary follows:

First race, purse $500, for 3-year-olds and upwards, selling, seven furlongs—Zeke Hardy, 110 pounds (Leary), 5 to 1, won; Koko, 114 (E. Jones), 8 to 1, second; Drake, 103 (Morris), 8 to 1, third. Time, 1:30¾. Modjeska, 105 (H. Smith), 10 to 1; Borealis, 105 (Fox), 6 to 1; Vattell, 110 (Jackson), 15 to 1; Nellie O., 105 (Griffin), 15 to 1; Aunt Cal, 107 (McDonald), 10 to 1; and Armeil, 107 (R. Jones), 4 to 1, finished in that order.

Second race, free high weight handicap, $600 added, for 3-year-olds and upwards, six furlongs—Big Three, 140 pounds (Fitzpatrick), 5 to 2, won; Gov. Ross, 123 (W. Harris), 4 to 1, second; Maud, 118 (Allen), 9 to 5, third. Time, 1:16. McGinty, 118 (Leary), 15 to 1; Burt Jordan, 118 (Jackson), 25 to 1; Lucille Manette, 118 (Griffin), 10 to 1; and Gaylord, 120 (Morgan), 40 to 1, finished in that order.

Third race, purse $600, for 3-year-olds and upwards, one mile—Mary McGowan, 109 pounds (Hathaway), 4 to 1, won; Leh, 112 (Allen), 7 to 5, second; Aristocrat, 102 (Burns), 20 to 1, third. Time, 1:45. Lewis Clark, 117 (Curry), 7 to 1; Sam Wood, 112 (A. McCarthy), 4 to 1; Langtry, 109 (R. Jones), 20 to 1; Romp, 109 (Hazlett), 20 to 1, and Gov. Wheeler, 112 (James), 75 to 1, finished in that order.

Fourth race, free handicap, $1,000 added, for 3-year-olds and upwards, one mile and a sixteenth—Prince, 105 pounds (Griffin), 30 to 1, won; Verge d'Or, 125 (Fitzpatrick), 7 to 10, second; Ed Bell, 108 (McDonald), 10 to 1, third. Time, 1:59. Ernest Race, 119 (Fox), 5 to 1; Brandolette, 108 (Goodale), 7 to 1; and Guido, 107 (H. Smith), 6 to 1, finished in that order.

Fifth race, purse $500, for 2-year-olds, five furlongs—Tom Roach, 103 pounds (Fink), 6 to 5, won; Cruickshank, 103 (Gemoets), 10 to 1, second; Unadilla, 105 (Goodale), 7 to 2, third. Time, 1:04. Freedom, 103 (Irving), 4 to 1; Angeree, 100 (Easley), 15 to 1; Niantic, 108 (Munson), 10 to 1; Sindbad, 103 (Elliott), 30 to 1; and Aggie B., 100 (McDonald), 6 to 1, finished in that order.

Sixth race, purse $600, for 3-year-olds and upwards, one mile—Upman, 102 pounds (McDonald), 4 to 1, won; Bob L., 107 (Goodale), 6 to 1, second; Louise M., 109 (Hazlitt), 3 to 2, third. Time, 1:44¼. New Castle, 112 (Griffin), 7 to 1; Lela May, 109 (J. Mooney), 7 to 1; Tamerlane, 112 (Fox), 8 to 1; Pickup, 109 (W. Harris), 5 to 1; and Anna Race, 109 (Richardson), 15 to 1, finished in that order.

Today's Race Card.

The Washington handicap, with $2,000 added, will bring out a fine field of 2-year-olds at Garfield today. Eighty horses are named for the six events on the card, for which the entries and weights are as follows:

First race, one mile, purse $500, for 3-year-olds and upward, selling, allowances—Joe Woolman, 90 pounds; Annie B., 97; Lord Lonsdale, 98; Mamie S., 99; Ora, 99; Pertuguese, 100; Vidette, 102; Steve Jerome, 102; Lucy Hitt, 103; Martin Russell, 104; Eolem, 106; Whittier, 112.

Second race, one mile and seventy yards, purse $600, for 2-year-olds, allowances—Sly Lisbon, 102 pounds; Little Annie, 102; Florence Slaughter, 102; Ormonde, 105; Zender, 105; Galbanum, 105; Bob L., 105; Joe Woolman, 105; Getaway, 115; Harry Weaver, 105; Gwendoline, 107; Mary McGowan, 112; Sidney, 115; Hagen, 115; Abby, 107.

Third race, seven furlongs, the Washington Handicap, $2,000 added, for 2-year-olds—Tom Elliott, 114 pounds; Farine, 117; Adalia, 115; Corinne, 100; Zantippa, 92; Gorman, 114; Goldstone, 108; Engarita, 90; Minnie Cee, 116; Jim Murphy, 105; Ray S., 111; Umatilla, 112; Yo Tambien, 118.

Fourth race, free handicap, $500 added, for 3-year-olds and up, seven furlongs—Jim Dunn, 98 pounds; Bonny Byrd, 105; Fred Taral, 114; Sis O'Lee, 107; Blue Maid, 103; Getaway, 103; Silverado, 102; Argenta, 103; Maud, 107; Somerset, 111; Lord Lonsdale, 90; Crab Cider, 105.

Fifth race, five furlongs, purse $500, for 2-year-olds, selling, allowances—Kangaroo, 90 pounds; Niantic, 90; Glencora, 92; Cruickshank, 92; First Day, 94; Actina, 94; Nancy Hakes, 96; Jack Richelieu, 96; Lord Clifton, 99; Ten to One, 102; Little Rock, 104; Harry Walker, 104; Bob Francis, 104; Miss Lulu, 104; Pendleton, 105; Big Casino, 110.

Sixth race, same conditions as first race—Ida Beeswing, 81 pounds; Odrey, 99; Hindoo Lass, 102; San Saba, 102; Hagen, 106; Ko Ko, 106; Miss Lou, 106; Jed, 106; Rosa, 106; Ira E. Bride, 106; Marie K., 109; Cadaverous, 109.

RACING IN THE RAIN AT LATONIA.

Uncle Bob, in Form, Makes a Show of His Field in the Handicap Event.

CINCINNATI, O., Sept. 4.—[Special.]—It rained today with but little intermission from morning till night, but as the club's program is to race rain or shine the sport went on. Strangely enough, too, there was only one scratch, and the attendance numbered at least 2,000, the regulars being out in force. Three of the five favorites won and the other two winners were well-backed second choices. B. J. Johnson broke his run of ill luck by winning with Uncle Bob. The son of Luke Blackburn was himself again, as he strung out the field a long way. Glockner used to be the champion mud horse, but today in a quagmire of slush, and with a light impost, he was beaten 100 yards by Uncle Bob. That obstinate brute, Billy Pinkerton, cut up all sorts of tantrums at the post in the third race, but he was finally got going and came in a close second to Royal Garter. Such a display of bespattered jockeys is seldom seen, and after each race it was impossible to distinguish the African from the Anglo-Saxon.

An ordinary lot of crabs started in the first race, and the talent selected Abilene (English) as the best mud animal among them, and made him a pronounced favorite, with J. T. (Sloan) second choice. The race was apparently between the pair until well on the homestretch, where Abilene began to tire, and Drift (Jordan) at 30 to 1 came with a rush and apparently made a dead heat with J. T. The latter, however, was awarded the purse. Time, 1:51¾.

Miss Hero (Freeman) was the favorite in the second race for 2-year-olds, but Paraloe (English), after getting away in the rear rushed to the front, and actually spread-eagled her field, winning in a big romp by four lengths, Miss Hero three lengths before Annie House. Time, 1:00.

Royal Garter (Freeman) was a pronounced favorite in the third race, and he led from start to finish and won after a terrific drive by nearly a length from Billy Pinkerton (Leaman), Tenacity (Porter) a close third. Time, 1:49½.

In the mile and seventy yards handicap, Uncle Bob (Leman), with the top weight, was at even money and heavily backed, Adrienne (Porter) was second choice, and in reality there was nothing in the race but the pair, for after Adrienne had piloted the lot to the head of the stretch Uncle Bob came very strong and half way to the string he was in front, and after that the race was over, as he won handily by two lengths, Adrienne ten lengths before Camilla. Time, 1:51¼.

A lot of maiden 2-year-olds started in the last race and Bob Toombs (English) had a slight call in the betting, Gayoso (Keith) second choice, and the finish was between the pair, Toombs winning by two lengths. Time, 1:08¼.

Entries and weights for Latonia races tomorrow:

First race, mile and seventy yards—Nellie Whittaker, 99 pounds; Joe Walton, 100; Outcry, 102; Jessie McFarland, 103; Tenacity, 103; John C., 106; Billy Pinkerton, 109.

Second race, mile and one-sixteenth—Drift, 95 pounds; First Lap, Hero, 102 each; Corinne Kinney, 104; Eli Kindig, 107; Royal Carter, Harry Weldon, Glockner, 109 each.

Third race, mile and 100 yards—Knoxville, 90 pounds; Faithful, 102; Lillian Lindsay, 105; Palisade, 105; Borka, 108; Prince Fortunatus, 120.

Fourth race, Avondale Stakes, one mile—Eugenia, 100 pounds; London Smoke and George K., 103 each; Fannie S., Pomfret, Mary C., 105 each; Douglas, 110; Sister Linda, 105.

Fifth race, four and a half furlongs—Lizzie English, 100 pounds; Puryear D., Old Pepper, 103 each; Jennie Wren, O'Sullivan, Nellie F., 105 each; Deceit, Ragner, Julia May, Roseola, 107 each; Sir Arthur, Hamline, 108 each; Boliver Buckner, 100.

Sixth race, four and a half furlongs—Greenwich, Helen N., 105 pounds each; Tillie S., Jean, Parolee, 107 each; Wautauga, Settle Up, Perblase, 108 each; Chief Justice, Falero, 110 each; Dore, 113; Matilda, 115.

Result at Gloucester.

PHILADELPHIA, Pa., Sept. 4.—[Special.]—The races at Gloucester today resulted as follows:

First race, seven furlongs—Little Ella (J. Bergen), won; Question (Merrick), second; Ceawood (J. Coffey), third. Time, 1:33. Betting, Little Ella, 3 to 1; Question, 8 to 1; Ceawood, 10 to 1.

Second race, five furlongs—Caution (Morris), won; Peerless colt (Griffin), second; Otero (J. Bergen), third. Time, 1:07¾. Betting, Caution, 6 to 1; Peerless colt, 10 to 1; Otero, even.

Third race, five furlongs—Hannibal (Doyle) won, Picket (McDermott) second; Oberlin (Coffey), third. Betting: Hannibal, 3 to 1; Picket, 4 to 5; Oberlin, 4 to 1.

Fourth race, six and one-half furlongs—Landseer (McDermott) won, Whitenose (Hollis) second, Wanderer II. (Larisey) third. Time, 1:27¼. Betting: Landseer, 10 to 1; Whitenose, 5 to 1; Wanderer II., 10 to 1.

Fifth race, one and one-quarter miles—Lotion (J. Bergen), won; Middlestone (Vint), second; Beantyre (McDermott), third. Time, 2:16¼. Betting: Lotion, 6 to 5; Middlestone, 6 to 5; Beantyre, 4 to 1.

Sixth race, four and one-half furlongs—Sunday (Davis), won; Valodia (Ross), second; Dirego (Morris), third. Time, :58¾. Betting: Sunday, 7 to 10; Valodia, 4 to 1; Dirego, 8 to 1.

Entries for Gloucester, N. J., races tomorrow follow:

First race, five furlongs—Harry Russell, 117 pounds; Cammack, 112; Foxhill, 112; John Atwood, 112; Prince Albert, 112; Adair, 106; Fleetwood, 106; Dunbarton, 106; Village Maid, 104; Cornelia, 104; Festus, 102; Kater Felto, 101; Little Dick, 98; Llewllyn, 96; Mamie S., 93.

Second race, six furlongs, 2-year-olds—Eddie M., 112 pounds; Monteila, 109; Uncle Sim, 107; Noble Duke, 105; Sister Ione, 104; Warpan, 102; Judge Toucey, 102; Vibrate filly, 102.

Third race, one and one-sixteenth miles, 3-year-olds—Pickett, 112 pounds; Baltimore II., 108; Duke John, 108; Ely, 106; Raleigh, 104; Flagrant, 102.

Fourth race, four and one-half furlongs, Flambeau, 112 pounds; Genevieve, 110; Faustina, 107; Prince Edward, 106; Uncertainty, 106; Repeater, 106; Express, 106; Vance, 106; Ecstacy, 103; Kirkina, 103; St. Omer, 100; Simon Pure, 100; Judge Mitchell, 100; Belshazzar, 80.

Fifth race, one mile handicap—Golden Rule, 112 pounds; Appomattox, 108; Lonely, 105; Martha, 102; Wenonah, 96; Ceawood, 95; Landseer, 95; Fannie Lewis colt, 95; Jack Murray, 93.

Sixth race, one mile, beaten horses—Clamor, 110 pounds; Character, 100; Spotwood, 100; Rapke, 100; Blue Grass, 100; Flemington, 100; Lordlike, 100; Rhoda, 100; Return, 100; Jim Worsen, 100; Ten Booker.

Racing in the Mud.

SALEM, Ind., Sept. 4.—[Special.]—Over 4,000 people were in attendance at the Washington County Fair yesterday and today. There would have been nearly double the attendance had it not rained. A large number came despite the rain. The races were partly run in the mud. The county purse was won by Windy Jim, owned by Walter Moore; time, 2:38. Free-for-all pace, Billy G., owned by Godfrey, was first; time, 2:27; Singer, T. E. Stewart owner, second. Three-minute pace, Bonnie C., Frank Cunningham owner, first; Col. Niger, S. M. Adair owner, second; Davy G., J. W. Henderson, owner, third; time, 2:40. In the 2:40 trot Bennett, James Pennypacker owner, was first; time, 2:40; Dan Voorhees, W. R. Holland owner, second; Free Nigger, C. Tucker owner, third. Running race, Joe Johnson, owned by M. R. Langdon, first. The fair will continue tomorrow, closing the meeting.

Results at Rockford.

ROCKFORD, Ill., Sept. 4.—[Special.]—The fall running and trotting meeting at the driving park closed today. The 2:30 trot, purse $500, was won by S. L. Caton's Murtha, six heats being trotted. The winner took the second, fourth, and sixth, and finishing eighth in the first and third. E. S. Jonnoth's Garnishee won second money and H. D. McKinney's Phaline third. The best time made was 2:25½. The 2:17 pacing race, purse $700, was won by A. D. Helm's Bawley in three straight heats, Lee H. second, and Simmie third. Best time, 2:19¾. William Arnott's Lena Lazel won the five-eighths of a mile running race heats, two in three, in two straight heats, Mollie V. second. Time, 1:03, 1:02½.

Won in Straight Heats.

LA CROSSE, Wis., Sept. 4.—[Special.]—At the Inter-State Circuit races today the attendance was 6,500. In the 2:32 trot, purse $700, nine starters, Pilot won in three straight, Hundallah second. Best time, 2:31. In the 2:22 trotting Pedro L. won in three straight, Moody second, Clara P. third. Best time, 2:26. The 3-year-old trot was won by Maggie Sherman in three straight, Lullaby second. Best time, 2:33½. Running mile and repeat Flora McDonald took both heats. Time, 1:57.

Monteg in Straight Heats.

TIPTON, Ia., Sept. 4.—[Special.]—In the 2:40 class Bromo, owned by Cottrell, took first money, getting the second, fourth, and fifth heats. Warfield Maud was a close contestant. George S., a Topeka horse, held up the rear. Best time, 2:42¼. The Novelty race for $200 was won easily by Monteg, owned by Milbourne of Mechanicsville, pacing in three staight heats. Best time, 2:36¾.

Ahead of the Game.

DECATUR, Ill., Sept. 4.—[Special.]—Secretary Reid closed the fall meeting of the Decatur Trotting club this afternoon with money ahead. Results: 2:30 trot—Martyr first; Twinebinder second; best time, 2:29¼. Free-for-all pace—Susie Brown first; Riley second; Walter Wilton third; Richball fourth; best time, 2:20¾. Running race won by Texas Girl.

Turf Notes.

O. J., City—The best records for a mile are: Straight course, Salvator, 1:35½; circular course, Racine, 1:39¼.

John Madden of Lexington has bought Zenobia, 2:22½, 4 years old, by King Almont, dam by Mambrino Boy, of Angus St. Clair, Toronto, for $4,750.

The Chicago pacing mare Maggie R., 2:16¼, by Kilbuck Tom—Topsy, is now owned by Monroe Salisbury of Margaret S.-Direct fame, who recently purchased her.

Guide, 2:20½, by Director—Imogene is one of the best trotters in California and said by such judges as Orrin Hickok to be better than Director was at the same age, 6.

The authorities say that the best 2-year-old in all England beyond cavil is Orme, by Ormonde, owned by the Duke of Westminster. He will be the winter favorite for the Derby.

C. W. Williams offers Budd Doble a bonus of $2,500 to trot Nancy Hanks against Allerton at Independence during the first week in November for a $5,000 purse. He is likely to get a game.

W. B. Rockford, Ill.—The Futurity course at Sheepshead Bay is some sixty yards less than six furlongs. It has been run in 1:12 on several occasions. The six-furlong record is Fides' 1:10¼, run at Morris Park.

So far of the Eastern stables leading the winning list for 1891 M. F. Dwyer is first, with $148,635. J. A. & A. H. Morris have won $138,025; David Gideon, $137,265, of which His Highness has landed $112,400; F. C. McLewee & Co., $66,180; P. J. Dwyer & Son, $59,395; W. C. Daly, $58,395.

WERE ENTITLED TO WIN.

FIVE RACES TAKEN BY THE BEST HORSES AT HAWTHORNE.

Only Two of These Warren Leland and Old Insolence, Were Favorites in the Books, However—The Other Winners Well Backed Second Choices—Good Day for the Intelligent Better, but the Ring Made Money.

There was a better crowd at Hawthorne yesterday to see some good racing come out of a very common card of three selling and two six furlong condition races. The track was fast and the weather fair.

Two favorites, Warren Leland, at 7 to 5, in the first race, and Insolence, at 4 to 5, in the last race, won. But all the other winners were well backed second choices. Barney, at 2 to 1, won the second race, as he should have won it. Silver Lake was an even money favorite and came fourth.

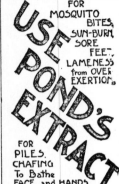

Buckhound, at 3 to 1, won the third race, Little Rock, the 6 to 5 choice, being third after a bad start and some poor jockeyship on him by Gardner. The odds against Buckhound were false.

Fan King, at 2 to 1, landed the fourth race, which was eminently proper, Jake Saunders, the even money favorite, with Overton up, never being in it and finishing fifth.

All around the best horses won and the intelligent better prospered. At that the comprehensive ring of two good and two poor bookmakers made money on the day. Betting intelligence was not predominant. Gardner, Thorpe, Curtis, Cooper, and Penny rode the winners. Penny had four mounts, and besides his win on Insolence was second twice and third once.

Warren Leland, Pearl Jennings, and Royal Flush were each well played for the first race at 6 furlongs. Corrigan's unreliable old mare opened favorite at 7 to 5, but Warren Leland soon displaced her and went to the post at that figure, Pearl at 2 to 1, and Royal Flush 3 to 1, a point above his opening price. The others were at long odds.

Won in the Stretch.

Annie Martin and the favorite were back of the bunch, with Tom Jones, Elzarra, and Pearl Jennings in front at the start. Elzarra took the lead after running fifty yards, and he, Clown, and Pearl Jennings were the order around the turns and into the stretch, where Warren Leland was last and on the outside, after a wide turn. But down the stretch Warren raced over the others and won, not particularly well ridden, by a length from Royal Flush, who beat Pearl Jennings a length for the place. The doggy Elzarra, who is as fast on his feet as ever common race-horse was, ran home at the tail of the field.

Jim Brown's mare, Silver Lake, was installed as an even-money favorite for the second race, a repetition in conditions and distance of the first. Barney, very good in these days, was second choice at 2 to 1, receding to 19 to 5 at the post. Lizzie Gwynne, for no good reason, was backed down from 7 to 5 to 1, principally by bookmaking money, Al Taylor leading a mild raid on "Cap" Widener's filly. Harry Kuhl was at 6 to 1, and Kismet, seeming outclassed and overweighted, at 15 to 1.

Kismet went away in the lead and ran down to and around the turn like a wild horse two lengths ahead of Lizzie Gwynne, who got off last and showed great speed in the first quarter. Barney and Silver Lake were together, third. So they showed at the head of the stretch, where Kismet began to come back and Lizzie Gwynne to tire. At the seven-furlong post Thorpe brought Barney up to Kismet and had beaten him when Harry Kuhl came through with a rush. But Thorpe, riding as hard as Penny, just managed to put Barney's head past the judicial eye before Harry Kuhl, Kismet third, a length away. Harry Kuhl's rejuvenation was remarkable, though Penny's riding may have caused it.

The third race was for 2-year-olds under selling conditions at five furlongs. The Harry O'Fallon colt, Little Rock, was a steady favorite at 6 to 5. Buckhound's stationary price was 3 to 1, Montclair's 6 to 1, and that improving colt, Arthur Davis, overlooked, was at 8 to 1, with Gen. Mitchell. The others were long shots. Volti, Arthur Davis, Gen. Mitchell, and Miss Bulwark were away in front and Start last to a good send-off. Buckhound was sixth away and Little Rock seventh. Arthur Davis and Miss Bulwark fought for the lead all around the turns, with Montclair two lengths back, leading the rest.

Buckhound by a Head.

So the leaders turned into the stretch lengths apart and Buckhound fifth, with a wide turn. Arthur Davis had beaten the rest and looked like a winner at the betting sheds, when Curtis brought Buckhound up and at the stand the pair were even under punishment. Buckhound lasted the best and won in the last ten strides by a head from Arthur Davis, Little Rock third, three lengths back.

The fourth race was another selling affair at seven furlongs, with some of the track's sprinters in. Ed Corrigan's Jake Saunders, back from none too glorious Eastern fields, with 120 pounds and "Monk" Overton up, was installed favorite, without good reason, at even money. He was at 6 to 5 when the horses came out. Fan King opened at evens, went to 2½ to 1, and closed at 2 to 1. Little Scissors was backed down from 4½ to 1 to 3 to 1. The other four were at long prices. Clown, Fan King, and Jake Saunders were the leaders in order when the flag dipped, and at the quarter Fan King led by three lengths, the Clown two before Col. Wheatley, with Mephisto a bad last. Fan King was four lengths in the lead at the half, three at the three-quarters, and nearly two into the stretch, with Col. Wheatley second, a neck before Climax, Little Scizzors fourth and closing. At the stand Penny got Scizzors up and closed on Fan King, who was in no danger, however, and won the race by a scant length from Scizzors, Col. Wheatley third, a length back.

Pat Dunne's recent acquisition, old Insolence, who has run very truly for his new owner, was the legitimate favorite for the last race, a selling event at nine furlongs, with six fair ones in. He ruled at 4 to 5 all through.

Carus was second choice at 2½ to 1, Rimini was at 5 to 1, and Falerna at 8 to 1. Justice and that aged dog, McMurtry, were long shots. The horses ran one-two-three on the betting. There was a weird stable plunge, with its attachments, on Falerna, and it only was irregular about the betting on the race. Rimini, Insolence, Carus was the starting order, Justice being last. Insolence was a head in front at the stand, with Rimini a length ahead of Justice. Insolence and Rimini fought it out all around, Rimini leading by a head into the stretch, with Carus third, two lengths back. Half way down Rimini cried enough, and Insolence, coming away, won by a length and a half from old Carus, who beat Rimini two lengths for the place, Falerna, a nose behind Rimini, fourth.

The racing summary follows:

The Racing Summary.

First race, purse $500, for non-winning starters since Aug. 1, allowances, six furlongs—Warren Leland, 99 pounds (Gardner) 7 to 5, won; Royal Flush, 96 (Perkinson), 3 to 1, second; Pearl Jennings, 102 (Penny), 2 to 1, third. Time, 1:18. Clown, 96 (Colby), 50 to 1; Tom Jones, 96 (Kennedy), 20 to 1; Annie Martin, 99 (Booker), 20 to 1; and Elzarra, 93 (Perkins), 8 to 1, ran unplaced.

Second race, purse $500, for performing non-winners since Aug. 1, six furlongs—Barney, 109 pounds (Thorpe), 9 to 5, won; Harry Kuhl, 106 (Penny), 6 to 1, second; Kismet, 109 (Regan), 15 to 1, third. Time, 1:17¾. Silver Lake, 109 (Hoggett) evens; and Lizzie Gwynne, 109 (Williams) 5 to 1, ran unplaced.

Third race, purse $500, for 2-year-olds, selling allowances—Buckhound, 112 pounds (Curtis), 3 to 1, won, Arthur Davis, 102 (Bullock), 8 to 1, second, Little Rock, 105 (Gardner), 6 to 5, third. Time, 1:05¼. Montclair, 102 (Penny), 6 to 1. Miss Bulwark, 99 (Williams), 10 to 1, Volte, 99 (Hoggett), 15 to 1, Highwayman, 96 (Regan), 15 to 1. Inez, 115 (O'Neil), 15 to 1, Gen. Mitchell, 105 (Thorpe), 8 to 1, and Start, 102 (Jackson), 20 to 1, ran unplaced.

Fourth race, purse $500, for 3-year-olds and upwards, selling allowances—Fan King, 115 pounds (Cooper), 2 to 1, won; Little Scizzors, 105 (Penny), 3 to 1, second; Col. Wheatley, 105 (Thorpe), 15 to 1, third. Time, 1:32. Climax II., 102 (Gardner), 12 to 1; Jake Saunders, 120 (Overton), 6 to 5; Clown, 96 (Colby), 50 to 1; and Mephisto, 108 (Regan), 15 to 1, ran unplaced.

Fifth race, purse $600, for all ages, selling allowances, one mile and one furlong—Insolence, 105 (Thorpe), 4 to 5, won; Carus, 102 (Penny), 2½ to 1, second; Rimini, 102 (Perkinson), 5 to 1, third; Falerna, 92 (Haggett), 8 to 1; Justice, 114 (Curtis), 10 to 1; and McMurtry, 97 (Gardner), 15 to 1, ran unplaced.

Today's Race Card.

Today's races, entries, and weights for Hawthorne are as follows. The card is a splendid one:

First race, purse $500, for 2-year-olds, allowances, five furlongs: Linita, 105 pounds; Jennie S., 115; Uncle Harry, 103; Jack Richelieu, 108; Harry Lyman, 103; Redina, 112; Mrs. Peck, 100.

Second race, purse $500, all ages, allowances, six furlongs—Helter Skelter, 114 pounds; Mary Mac, 99; Silverado, 111; Geraldine, 114; Tom Karl, 114; Prince Henry, 96; Roseland, 111; Mirabeau, 111; Fairy Queen, 99; Rival, 114.

Third race, handicap, $10 each, with $1,000 added, one mile and one-sixteenth—Rival, 104 pounds; Hotspur, 102; Joe Carter, 102; Miss Bowling, 85; Polemus, 100; Gilford, 96; Insolence, 103; Fred Taral, 109; Longlight, 95; Brookwood, 107.

Fourth race, purse $500, for 3-year-olds and upwards, selling allowances, six furlongs—Red Sign, 104 pounds; Atalanta, 95; Elzarra, 101; Sena A., 95; Rock, 107; Artistic, 96; Sanford, 89; Lela May, 107; Maud B., 104; Donovan, 95.

Fifth race, purse $500, for 3-year-olds and upwards, selling allowances, six furlongs—Queenie Trowbridge, 107 pounds; Rouser, 104; Red Fox, 107; Roley Boley, 107; Lizzie D., 104; Horace Leland, 104; Lew Carlile, 95; Lemon, 110.

Local Turf Notes.

Starter Chinn jotted down a fine against Fox for delaying a start at Garfield yesterday.

Ed Corrigan has nineteen yearlings of his own in the Hawthorne stables, among them some gems, one a son of Longfellow, out of that famous old race mare, Modesty.

An unusual thing in local racing was the appearance of Clown in both the first and fourth races at Hawthorne yesterday. He was fourth in the first race and sixth in the fourth.

The Latonia people wired Ed Corrigan yesterday offering to make a special event for Riley. The offer was declined and Riley will be seen in public no more this year. He has been turned out.

The McCaffertys had Fan King run up on them after winning the fourth race at Hawthorne. Joe Ullman, evidently acting for N. S. Hall & Co., bid the gelding up from $1,000, his entered price, in $100 steps to $1,900, Charles McCafferty raising him $10 each time. At $1,910 he was brought in. McCafferty laughed at the affair and acted as though at about $2,000 he would have let Ullman own a horse.

If the stories heard in down-town resorts last night were to be believed nearly everybody at Garfield played Prince yesterday. All the talk was of the surprising defeat of Verge d'Or. When the betting first opened on the race Prince was quoted as low as 5 to 1, but principally on boards where Verge d'Or was held out. As the game progressed the odds went up until, in some books, 50 to 1 could be found, and there were some small bets placed at those figures. But the average was 30 to 1. When the great fluctuations in the betting were reported to the Judges Col. Clark said that Prince had "no more chance in the race than a bob-tailed mule in fly-time." However he called Griffin, who enjoys the reputation of being an honest jockey, to the stand and ordered him to ride Prince out. And he did it.

ALLERTON BREAKS THE RECORD.

On the Kite Track at Independence He Puts the Stallion Mark Down to 2:10.

INDEPENDENCE, Ia., Sept. 4.—[Special.]—Records were again lowered on the kite today. In the 2:27 pace Reserve Fund, ch. s., by Nutwood, won, Longitude, b. s., by Osman, second. Best time, by Longitude, 2:19¾.

Ego, b. s., by Chief Justice A. L. Cable, Berwick, Ill., to beat 2:39¼, trotted in 2:27.

Narissa, b. m., by Pennant, to beat 2:29½, trotted in 2:29.

Nightengale, ch. m., by Alcantara, R. P. Brownlee, Little York, Ill., to beat 2:18¾, paced in 2:13¾.

Muscovite, b. s., by Nutwood, Fred Seacord, Galesburg, Ill., to beat 2:21¼, trotted in 2:21.

Crete, br. m., by Onmore, H. and J. D. Curran, Stevens Point, Wis., to beat 2:35, trotted in 2:29¾.

To beat 2:16 Pat Downing, b. s., by Abe Downing, H. and J. D. Curran, trotted the mile without a skip in 2:13½.

To beat 2:17 Incas, br. s., by Inca, A. G. Bast, Salt Lake City, trotted in 2:14½.

To beat 2:30¼ Elsie S., ch. m., by Superior, Dubois Bros., Denver, trotted in 2:29¼.

At 6:15, after the track had been scraped, dragged, and ironed down to the smoothness of a billiard table, Allerton was brought out to beat his record of 2:11. Horse and driver were never in better spirits, and the mile was made in 2:10 flat, breaking the stallion record of the world. He went without a break the entire mile. He was not urged until within the 100-yard distance, when whip and voice were brought into play and he covered the last quarter in 32 seconds. The quarters were made in 32¼, 1:05½, 1:38, 2:10, and Allerton has crowned himself king of stallions, honestly, too, for while two timers' watches marked the above an official timer and every other watch on the grounds credited him with 2:09¾.

Direct the little black pacing wonder, with a record of 2:09¼, had been warming up for a new mark, and the warming up was not in vain. The mile was another world record broken, and made without a skip in 2:06. Quarters, 32, 1:04, 1:35½, 2:06. It is safe to say that the three happiest men on the face of the earth tonight are Williams, Salisbury, and George Starr. Direct not only broke the stallion pacing record but the pacing record of the world.

At the Page County Fair.

CLARINDA, Ia., Sept. 4.—[Special.]—A large crowd attended the races of the last day of the Page County Fair. The feature of the day was the free-for-all pace. Following are the results: Free-for-all trot: Holden Davis won, J. M. B. second, Jack Fisher third. Best time, 2:29¼. Free-for-all pace: Lilly Banks won, Dan Tucker second, John L. third. Best time, 2:25½.

For the Championship of Michigan.

DETROIT, Mich., Sept. 4.—[Special.]—The fifteen-mile bicycle race for the amateur championship of Michigan and gold medal was run this morning on the Grosse Point road. The contestants were Will Rand of Detroit and Burt Hallett of Armada, Mich. George Lane acted as timer. The course was seven and one-half miles long, and was from the corner of McClellan street near the waterworks to the Sacred Heart Convent and return. The two riders started at 11:30. Both men worked with determination, and from the ribbon it seemed as though a close finish could be looked for. Exactly forty-three minutes and fifteen seconds after the start Rand reached the finish twenty feet ahead of his opponent.

City Officials Saw the Fight.

GALESBURG, Ill., Sept. 4.—[Special.]—Considerable excitement prevails here over a prize-fight that took place at midnight last night in a timber east of the city between Jackson and Tumbleson, two local bruisers. About one hundred witnessed the mill, including several city officials and professional men. Jackson was whipped in five rounds. This is the first prize-fight that was ever held here. The State's Attorney has determined to bring the offenders to justice.

General Sporting Notes.

Jack Keenan, whom Jack Dempsey whipped in two rounds in 1884, died Wednesday of consumption.

A telegram from Sydney states that Stansbury and Kemp will row Hanlan and O'Connor for $5,000 a side and single sculls for $2,500 a side.

The Occidental club, San Francisco, will match Danny Needham and Billy Maher for October. Maher will concede five pounds to Needham.

Johnson, the English bantam, seems to have weakened on his proposition to fight George Dixon, and is now after Cal McCarthy or Tommy Warren.

Bob Fitzsimmons and Jimmy Carroll have purchased a saloon in San Francisco. They leave for New Orleans soon and will show en route. When he arrives Carroll will go into training for his fight with Billy Myer.

Remedies for Mosquito Bites.

The unfortunate inhabitants of New Jersey, who have suffered more than most mortals from the mosquitoes, may be interested in the practical advice of a celebrated chemist. He says that of the various remedies recommended for mosquito bites, such as ammonia, oil of cloves, chloroform, and carbolized glycerine, none is better than ordinary soap. He is an ardent naturalist, and on his excursions in the country invariably carries a small piece of soap, with which, in case of a bite, he makes a lather over the affected part and allows it to dry. He declares that the relief is instantaneous, and that all pain soon ceases. There may be a fortune for some enterprising Yankee in "mosquito soap."

The Best.
ONE CENT
The Cheapest.

THE MORNING HERALD.

THE WEATHER PREDICTION
For Baltimore and Maryland.
FAIR,
SOUTHWEST WINDS,
WARMER.

ESTABLISHED 1875--WHOLE NUMBER 6148. BALTIMORE, WEDNESDAY, OCTOBER 3, 1894. PRICE ONE CENT.

AMID FIRES OF VICTORY.

Hanlon's Champions Welcomed by the Multitude.

THOUSANDS APPLAUD.

Orioles Wheeled in Triumph Through the City's Streets.

ROOTERS TAKE THE TOWN.

Nothing Like Their Demonstration Ever Seen Before.

Twenty Thousand People Gather About Camden Station to Greet the Victors—A Parade Two Miles Long, As Full of Life at the Tail As at the Head—Brilliant Banquet at the Rennert. Reception at the Fifth Maryland Armory—To-Day's Programme.

THE ovation given to a Roman conqueror returning home with his captives dragging at his chariot wheels wasn't a marker to the reception the Baltimore Base-ball Club got last night when they touched foot on Monumental City soil with the scalps of the eleven other National League teams dangling from their belts.

A scene like it had never been witnessed in this city and probably never will be again.

Rooters everywhere!

On the pavement, in the streets, on housetops, hanging from windows, straddling awning posts, hugging telegraph poles, on horseback and under horse's heels, in carriages and wagons and nondescript vehicles!

Fires of victory burned brightly throughout the town.

Bombs exploded from big mortars; Roman candles broke into myriads of fiery bits, many colored lanterns, torches and colored lights made the city blaze.

Music everywhere!

Bands from Washington and Cumberland and every town and hamlet that claims Baltimore as its big sister, all playing tunes that were meant to be songs of victory.

Police nowhere!

Vox Populi ruled, and with an iron hand that squelched all attempts at control.

Oh, it was glorious!

And, through it all the champion ball-tossers of the world, in whose honor the hubub was made, bore themselves modestly, but with a becoming sense of appreciation of the enthusiasm heaped upon them.

To adequately describe this great event in the history of Baltimore is a difficult task. First, it must be known—and last night it did seem to be pretty generally known—that Baltimore was base-ball crazy. Suffering from this affliction, the people were not responsible for what they did, and the antics they cut leads one to believe that they worked the irresponsibility-racket to a nicety.

In the first place, the whole city put on a gala dress. The orange and black of Maryland met the eye at every turn. It hid the fronts of big business houses, formed the main part of shop-window decorations and was worn by nearly every mother's son and father's daughter in the town. Even the horses were bedecked and seemed the prouder for it.

Then there were the rooters' badges thrust upon you at every corner, and pennant flags handled by enterprising fakirs. In all the state colors predominated.

Well along in the afternoon the crowds down town began to swell. Everybody was in a joyful mood, and used little tin horns to tell the rest of the rooters so. The result was a din that was deafening.

At rooters' headquarters, in the Carrollton Hotel parlors, the scene was animated. Chairman W. W. Johnson, the indefatigable, was dealing out badges and orders more liberally than he ever did postoffice appointments. Members of the reception committee buzzed about and marshals and their aides wanted to know what was expected of them.

The champions were scheduled to arrive at Camden Station at 6.35 o'clock. An hour before that time everybody in town it seemed, started for that point. The police got there ahead of them. Marshal Frey, Deputy Marshal Farnan and Captain Claiborne had control of things. Large squads from the Southern, Western and Southwestern districts were stationed in the vicinity of the depot. A squad of mounted officers were placed just ahead of the carriages for the players.

By this time the first of the paraders began to arrive. Little attention was paid to the official orders for the formation, although a few of the participants made some attempt to get to the position in line assigned to them.

The crowds kept up a perfect bedlam of horn-blows and cheers. All along the route of the parade people were packed like sardines. The street cars were forced to stop even before the line of march crossed them. People who were frozen out of a view of the parade for the time being shambled along, making the evening hideous with their noise. Nobody minded that. Everybody was in good humor, and gave and took much rough handling.

At 6.20 o'clock the carriages with the members of the reception committee drew up in front of Camdem Station. Fifteen minutes later two loud reports came from somewhere down in the depot yards. A loud huzza was heard in the distance and the people knew the champions were with them.

THE BALTIMORE BASE BALL CLUB.

THAT HOME RUN.

How the Champions Were Received As They Came Rolling in From the Great West.

In the words of the man who broke the bank at Monte Carlo the homeward trip of the Orioles was one grand triumphal march.

From the time the train struck the borders of West Virginia yesterday morning until it rolled into the depot at Washington, at every station great and small crowds were gathered to cheer the champions.

The championship lost for a time its local character. It was the North against the South again, and every man, woman and child south of Mason and Dixon's Line hailed the Orioles, not as the champions of Baltimore alone, but as the victorious representatives of all Maryland, Virginia and the great South.

When the train reached Grafton, W. Va., about 5 o'clock in the morning, a great mob was there gathered, and the boys were awakened by a mighty shout for "Jennings!" "Jennings!"

The populace woul d not be appeased until Hughey popped his sunburnt head out of the car window and gave the West Vir ginians a chance to gaze upon the gr eatest short stop on earth.

This same scene was re-enacted as the train passed along through Piedmont and Oakland. One after the other the players would be called for and made to show themselves.

At Cumberland a stop was made for breakfast, and here the boys met with a most beautifully enthusiastic reception. It seemed as if all Cumberland had turned out, and when the men alighted from the cars shout after shout arose and the crowd went wild.

The mob was so dense that it was with difficulty that a passage was forced to the hotel, just across the way from the station.

Everywhere could be seen the Oriole colors and everybody wore the Oriole badge. Banners were displayed bearing the following inspiriting legends:

"To the Orioles: Accept the thanks of Cumberland cranks."

"The last brick was put on Robbie's house at Cleveland, September 25."

"Your fight was game through thick and thin; you played good ball, and played to win. That's why we shout and raise this din, 'Maryland, My Maryland.'"

"Oh, no! We can't keep up our gait, but still we did win 18 straight."

"Well! Well! Well! Poor Old New York."

"It is Base Bal—timore with a vengeance."

Over the hotel porch was this inscription: "Cumberland Welcomes the Champions. Get at 'em!"

A band of 30 pieces was stationed in

A TYPICAL "ROOTER."

front of the hotel, and the first airs that greeted the Orioles was "Maryland, My Maryland." As the boys passed through the crowd to the hotel it seemed as if the people would go mad. They cheered until they were hoarse. They grasped the players by the hand. Staid citizens tore the badges from off their breasts and pinned them on the black sweaters of the Orioles.

When at last the players were seated at the tables the people were permitted to file in and out and feast their eyes on the boys who had brought the championship to Maryland. The crowd was largely made up of ladies and, en passant, it may be remarked that Cumberland can make as fine a showing in this line as any town in this land. The ladies were anxious to have the famous players pointed out, and whispers of which is Brouthers? is that Robinson? "What a handsome fellow McMahon is" could be heard everywhere.

The boys stood this battery of pretty eyes bravely, albeit some of the kids, like McGraw and Keeler, seemed to be a little affected.

As the team left the hotel one rather elderly dame rushed up to Dan Brouthers and shook his hand effusively. For a moment the color mounted into the cheeks of the old veteran, but he shook himself together and said with a courtly smile: "I am glad to have the privilege of shaking the hand of one of Cumberland's fair ladies." You can't phaze old Dan.

As Hanlon stepped out of the hotel loud shouts of "Hanlon!" "Hanlon!" were raised, and calls of "Speech!" "Speech!" were heard. The premier manager took off his hat, and, when the cheering died down, made the following "few remarks:"

"*Ladies and Gentlemen of Cumberland:* In behalf of the Baltimore Base-Ball Club I thank you for this hearty and unexpected greeting. When we have defeated the Giants in the Temple Cup series I promise you we will play a game in Cumberland."

When the train started the band again struck up "Maryland, My Maryland," and amid tumultuous shouts the boys left Cumberland behind. It was a magnificent reception, and gave the Orioles a foretaste of what they were to expect in Baltimore.

While in Cumberland Hanlon was presented with a mammoth glass bat by J. L. Heintz. This bat was a trophy won by the Frostburg team from Cumberland in '82. It was filled with 10-year-old whisky, and Hanlon says the whisky will be 10 years older before the cork is drawn.

The citizens of Cumberland having the affair in charge were: Captain Walker, J. J. McHenry, J. Loney, G. W. Snyder and J. L. Heintz. The banners were presented to the Orioles and came on with them to Baltimore.

At Martinsburg, W. Va., another glorious reception met the Orioles. The ladies of this pretty town were very much in evidence in this affair. They were drawn up en masse at the station and formed a perfect rainbow of beauty.

After the cheering was over State's Attorney U. S. G. Pitzger presented Manager Hanlon with a beautiful pennant framed in glass, the work of Martinsburg's fair maids. Hanlon, who by this time had got quite into the swim, made a neat speech of acceptance and in closing assured the ladies that their gift should be oriflamme to lead the Orioles to victory in '95.

The pennant was made in the Oriole colors and bore the following inscription: "Presented to the champion base-ball club of the United States by the ladies of Martinsburg, W. Va., October 2, 1894." The obverse side had this inscription: "Baltimore, 1894, Edward Hanlon, manager."

James F. Thompson, editor of the *World*, of Martinsburg, presented the team with a beautiful bank of flowers. J. W. Dodd, in behalf of the Martinsburg Band, gave the boys a handsome floral piece. The band was on the spot and discoursed sweet music.

Edw. B. Harner, Jr., first baseman, and Wilbur E. Evans, manager of the Martinsburg Base-Ball Club, presented Brouthers with a base ball decorated with the Oriole colors.

At both Cumberland and Martinsburg the team gave the Oriole yell: "Are We in It? Yes we are! Baltimore! Baltimore! Rah! Rah!" and sang the verse: "We'll Hang Johnny Ward to a Sour Apple Tree," much to the delight of the people.

When at last the train reached Washington, it found the committee of reception from Baltimore awaiting the champions. They took the boys across to the Hotel Emrich, where they had a general cleaning up, and donned the dress suits which had been furnished for the occasion by M. Dyrenforth & Co.

A collation was served at the hotel, in the course of which Mr. Poske, chairman of the reception committee, made an address of welcome to the Orioles. This was responded to by Manager Hanlon. The Mount Pleasant Fife and Drum Corps escorted the players to the station and accompanied them to Baltimore.

THEIR TRIUMPHAL ENTRY.

Fully Fifty Thousand People Greet the Champions at Camden Station—Scenes of Wild Enthusiasm.

Amid explosions like those of a bombardment, amid crowds the like of which were never seen in this city before, and agitated by the most intense feelings of enthusiasm, the members of the Baltimore Base-Ball Club arrived at Camden Station last evening at exactly 32 minutes after 6 o'clock, the train being three minutes ahead of time.

It is safe to say that nothing has ever happened in Baltimore to arouse, to such a wonderful extent, the feelings of the people. Everybody was wild. They yelled themselves hoarse while the train bearing the winners of the pennant was yet as far out of town as Relay station, but when the bright headlight of the locomotive beamed out at the far end of the train shed a mighty yell rang out and ascended to the skies.

As early as 4.30 o'clock the crowd began to manifest itself and to collect in front of the depot. It was a don't-care lot who thronged the streets and whose number increased every moment. Motormen rang their bells fiercely in the electric cars, and speed was reduced to a minimum so that no one would be hurt. But the crowd, which by 5.30 had grown into the thousands, was not to be kept back, and surged around with entire disregard of all conveyances and cars.

About this time a squad of policemen from the Southern district, commanded by Captain Claibourne and numbering 50, came up Camden street. When they reached Howard they separated and began to line the crowd up, keeping them as near the pavement as possible. Soon after this Marshal Frey, in his carriage, and Deputy Marshal Farnan arrived on the scene and took charge of the policemen, directing them here and there as they saw fit. Four mounted officers also rode up. From the Western Station Captain Cadwallader had over 30 men, who looked after the crowd on Pratt street.

As soon as everything was quieted comparatively an estimate of the crowd could be made. Persons accustomed to big crowds said that at 5 o'clock there were 5,000 people, at 5.30 o'clock 25,000, and when the train arrived bearing the players fully 50,000 people occupied the streets around the station.

Carriages lined up everywhere; floats of all descriptions with yelling crowds on board drove around trying to get to their respective points of formation in the parade. Old men, young men, middle-aged men, boys, girls, and it seemed to the observer everybody who was well enough to stand on his feet tried to get as near Camden Station as possible. The police kept the interior of the depot as clear as possible, but finally the crowd realizing this began to surge in, saying that they were going to buy railroad tickets. The majority of these did not do so, but many did, and tickets to Mount Winans, Lansdowne, St. Denis, Relay and other near-by points were sold in profusion. The buyers of these tickets found no trouble in getting on the platform where the players were to arrive. The crowd of these even became too big finally for the narrow walk and people, young and old, began to clamber on freight cars, passenger cars and locomotives trying to gain a point of vantage from which they could see the men as they dismounted from the train.

Much commotion was created by one of the trains starting with about 500 people clinging to the top and sides. When it was seen what a load of deadheads was on board the train was stopped, and the people waited till another lot of cars drew in and then rushed for seats. A number of boys and young men climbed up the poles supporting the roof to the cross-rafters, where they could get a good view, and, although faces at this height could scarcely be seen, owing to the vertical line of vision, they seemed to be happy.

Some of the people who got inside the platform railing thought they would be able to see it all. They were badly fooled, however, as the train drew out fully five minutes before the Champions' train hove in sight. Fifteen minutes before the train drew in with the players aboard standing room anywhere in the station was at a premium, and every available inch of space was fought for by the crowd. The baggage-rooms, the doors of which were locked, were at the time threatened seriously with invasion, so great was the desire on the part of the multitude to see the ovation.

Just as the hands of the clock in the northern end of Camden Station pointed to the hour of 6.30 a cry broke out 'way out on the platform:

"Here they come!"

A big headlight in the distance verified the truth of this shout, and a rush made at once for the stopping point. The big locomotive No. 1401, in charge of William H. Zepp, engineer, and William H. Franks, fireman, puffed slowly up and then, with what sounded like a grunt of satisfaction, stopped short.

Boom! Bang!! Biff!!!

The sounds of exploding mortars, crackers and fireworks were like pandemonium, to say nothing of the cheers and shouts of the crowd. As soon as those outside of the station heard the sounds

Continued on Second Page.

WEATHER OBSERVATIONS.

ALMANAC FOR BALTIMORE FOR THIS DAY.

Sun rises......5.58 A. M. | Sun sets.........5.40 P. M.
Moon rises...8.00 A. M. | Moon south....3.30 P. M.
High tide..................9.19 A. M. and 9.42 P. M.

LOCAL REPORT OCTOBER 2.

Time	Barom'ter reduced to Sea Level	Thermom.	Relative humidity	Direction of wind	Velocity of wind	Force	Rainfall	State of weather
8 A. M.	29.96	60	65	N	5	Fresh	.00	Clear.
8 P. M.	29.89	68	81	SE	2	Light	.00	Py Cy

Mean barometer..29.92 | Max. temperature......73
Mean temperature 62 | Min. temperature......51

Maximum velocity of wind, 12 miles per hour from the southeast.

Following are the maximum temperatures for the day and the character of the weather at 8 P. M. at the stations named:

New York, 74, clear; Philadelphia, 74, clear; Washington, 80, clear; Oswego, 54, raining; Erie, 76, cloudy; Cleveland, 78, raining; Buffalo, 70, raining; Toledo, 78, raining; Milwaukee, 72, clear; Albany, 66, cloudy; Sandusky, 89, cloudy; Rochester, 62, raining; Detroit, 74, cloudy; Eastport, 52, clear; Portland, 58, cloudy; Boston, 62, cloudy; Norfolk, 84, clear; Atlantic City, 68, clear; Wilmington, 82, clear; Charleston, 84, clear; Jacksonville, 90, clear; Savannah, 86, clear; St. Paul, 70, cloudy; Montgomery, 90, clear; Atlanta, 86, clear; Mobile, 84, clear; Knoxville, 86, clear; Lynchburg, 84, clear; Seattle, 52, cloudy; San Francisco, 66, clear; Los Angeles, 56, clear; Salt Lake City, 56, clear; Cincinnati, 84, partly cloudy; Pittsburg, 80, clear; St. Louis, 74, clear; Chicago, 74, clear; New Orleans, 88, clear; Galveston, 86, cloudy.

Indications.

Forecast for Wednesday—For Eastern New York, fair in southern, local showers in the morning, followed by fair in northern portion, south winds, warmer in northern portion.

For Eastern Pennsylvania, New Jersey, Delaware, the District of Columbia, Maryland and Virginia, fair, southwest winds, warmer in the interior.

For North Carolina, South Carolina and Georgia, fair, no change in the temperature, southwest winds.

For West Virginia, generally fair, warm southwest winds, followed at night by cooler, west winds.

For Western New York, light showers, followed by clearing weather, winds shifting to south, slightly warmer.

For Western Pennsylvania, generally fair, preceded in the early morning by local showers, warm, south winds, followed by cooler, fair weather on Wednesday night.

KING PINS OF THE BASEBALL ARENA AND CHAMPIONS OF '96.

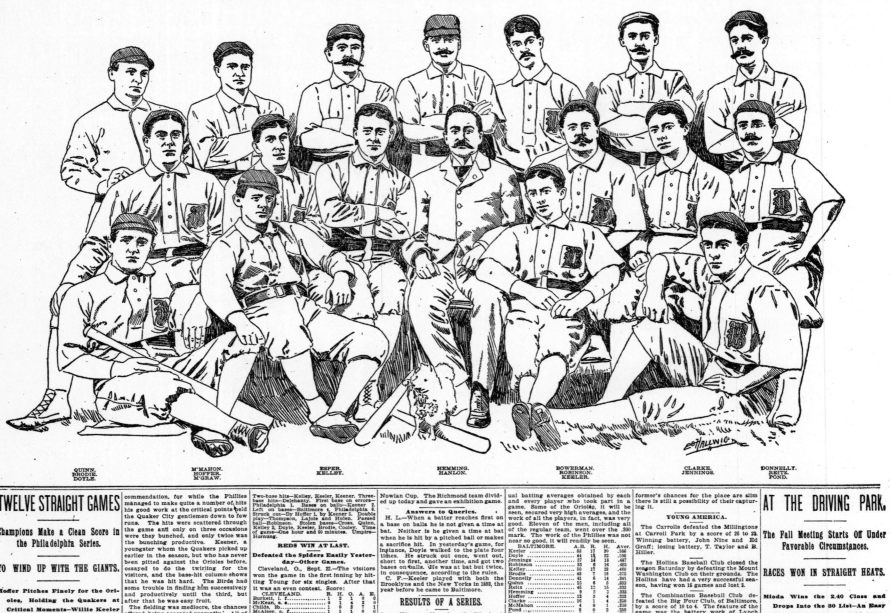

QUINN. BRODIE. DOYLE. — M'MAHON. HOFFER. M'GRAW. — ESPER. KELLEY. — HEMMING. HANLON. — BOWERMAN. ROBINSON. KEELER. — CLARKE. JENNINGS. — DONNELLY. REITZ. POND.

TWELVE STRAIGHT GAMES

Champions Make a Clean Score in the Philadelphia Series.

TO WIND UP WITH THE GIANTS.

Hoffer Pitches Finely for the Orioles, Holding the Quakers at Critical Moments—Willie Keeler Does a Great Stroke of Batting—Reitz Played Short—Scores of Other Games.

Standing of the Clubs.

CLUBS.	Won.	Lost.	Per Cent.
Baltimore	89	37	.706
Cleveland	78	46	.629
Cincinnati	77	50	.606
Boston	72	56	.563
Chicago	71	57	.555
Pittsburg	65	61	.516
New York	62	65	.488
Philadelphia	60	66	.476
Brooklyn	56	71	.441
Washington	56	71	.441
St. Louis	38	89	.299
Louisville	36	91	.283

Standing of the Clubs Sept. 23, 1895.

CLUBS.	Won.	Lost.	Per Cent.
Baltimore	81	42	.659
Cleveland	83	45	.648
Philadelphia	77	48	.616
Chicago	69	56	.552
Boston	68	56	.549
Brooklyn	67	58	.536
Pittsburg	66	60	.524
New York	64	60	.516
Cincinnati	61	60	.504
Washington	39	82	.322
St. Louis	37	86	.301
Louisville	33	92	.264

Attendance Figures.

Baltimore, 1,165.
Cleveland, 2,000.
Brooklyn, 1,000.
Washington, 3,786.

Today's Schedule.

Louisville at Cleveland.

The Orioles yesterday played the last scheduled game of the season at Union Park, and what is better, won it. They have still three more games to play with the Giants in New York, and then the season will be over.

Yesterday's game was with the Phillies, the twelfth and last game of the series between the Champs and Quakers. By capturing it the Orioles accomplished the truly remarkable feat of winning 12 straight games from the Phillies, and the result of the series is: Baltimore won 12, lost 0. This feat is seldom accomplished in these days.

The winning of the last game was accomplished more easily, perhaps, than the winning of any of the other 11. It was labeled "Baltimore's" from the very start, and the Champs had no difficulty in seeing that it went in the proper direction. It was a fast game, but was uninteresting. There were no features of especial interest to hold the attention of the crowd after Baltimore had taken its comfortable lead. The fielding was good as far as it went, but there was little in it out of the ordinary. The batting of the Orioles was good, and this furnished the only really interesting feature of the contest.

Little Willie Keeler's work with the stick was something to be proud of. He walked to the plate four times, and each time he made a hit. Two of the hits were clean singles to the outfield, another was a neat two-bagger, while the fourth was an infield hit, which Willie beat out by good base running. Donnelly hit safely three out of four times, while Kelley got a single and a double out of four times up. Reitz also hit safely twice, while Doyle managed to negotiate passes to first on two occasions, but failed to connect once with the ball for a safety.

Keener and Cross did the best stick work for the Phillies. Each got two hits, one of Keener's being a double. Delehanty's lone hit was for three bases, and was one of the longest hits made at Union Park for some days. It went over Brodie's head on the fly and hit the fence near the flagpole half way up.

Hoffer's work in the box is worthy of commendation, for while the Phillies managed to make quite a number of hits his good work at the critical points held the Quaker City gentlemen down to few runs. The hits were scattered through the game and only on three occasions were they bunched, and only twice was the bunching productive. Keener, a youngster whom the Quakers picked up earlier in the season, but who has never been pitted against the Orioles before, essayed to do the twirling for the visitors, and the base-hit column shows that he was hit hard. The Birds had some trouble in finding him successively and productively until the third, but after that he was easy fruit.

The fielding was mediocre, the chances offered being accepted promptly. All of them, with but one or two exceptions, were easy. Kelley's work in left was good, as was Donnelly's at third and Quinn's at second. Jennings went to Scranton on a little business trip yesterday and his place at short was taken by Henny Reitz, who fielded it well. Henny's work at short was excellent and Hallman was not far behind in the race for honors. Thompson played well in right and Grady's work behind the bat was above par.

The work of Umpire Hornung was execrable at times. On bases and balls and strikes he gave several rank decisions. Several objections were rendered, but nothing like a kick was made, probably because the players felt that there was no use to make too much of a fuss.

Philadelphia scored first in the third, which Cross opened with a beautiful single to centre, going to third on Keener's safe one to left. Keener took second on the throw in, and third on Cooley's out at first, on which Cross scored. Hulen's single to centre scored Keener. Hulen was thrown out trying to steal second, and Delehanty fouled to Robbie.

Baltimore took the lead in the same inning. Robbie fanned, and Hoffer was out at first on a bunt. Then Quinn singled, and Keeler followed suit. Donnelly sent a safe one for one base into right that bounded wrong on Thompson, and both Quinn and Keeler scored. Kelley sent a two-bagger to right, and Donnelly scored. Kelley stole third. Doyle was passed to first. While Keener stood at the plate with the ball discussing the matter with Grady Doyle leisurely trotted to second. Reitz banged a safe one to right, and Joe and Jack scored. Henny then tried to steal second, and was out a mile.

Baltimore made one in the fifth. After Quinn had died at first, Keeler put a two-bagger in left, stole second, and, on Cross' muff of Grady's throw to catch him, went home. Donnelly fanned, and Kelley died at first.

Quinn opened up the seventh with a fly to left. Keeler singled, and Donnelly followed suit. Kelley's single scored Keeler and put Donnelly on third. Kelley stole second, and Donnelly was thrown out trying to get home on the play to catch Joe at second. Doyle was passed to first, and took third on Reitz's single to centre, on which Kelley scored. Henny was out trying to steal second.

Philadelphia scored two in the last. After Lajoie had flied to Kelley, Hallman sent one to short, which Reitz fumbled. A passed ball advanced him to third, from where he scored on Grady's single. Cross flied to right. Keener put one over Kelley's head for two bases, scoring Grady. Cooley died at first.

The score:

BALTIMORE.	R.	H.	O.	A.	E.
Quinn, 2b	1	1	1	5	0
Keeler, r. f.	3	4	2	0	0
Donnelly, 3b	1	3	3	2	0
Kelley, l. f.	2	2	5	0	0
Doyle, 1b	1	0	10	0	0
Reitz, s. s.	0	2	1	4	1
Brodie, c. f.	0	1	2	0	0
Robinson, c.	0	1	3	1	0
Hoffer, p.	0	0	0	1	0
Totals	8	14	27	13	1

PHILADELPHIA.	R.	H.	O.	A.	E.
Cooley, c. f.	0	1	1	0	0
Hulen, s. s.	0	1	2	2	0
Delehanty, l. f.	0	1	1	0	0
Thompson, r. f.	0	0	2	1	0
Lajoie, 1b	0	1	8	1	0
Hallman, 2b	1	1	0	4	0
Grady, c.	1	1	7	3	0
Cross, 3b	1	2	2	0	1
Keener, p.	1	2	0	3	0
Mertes, l. f.	0	0	1	0	0
Totals	4	10	24	14	1

SCORE BY INNINGS.

Baltimore	0	0	5	0	1	0	2	0	x—8
Philadelphia	0	0	2	0	0	0	0	0	2—4

Earned runs—Baltimore 6, Philadelphia 2. Two-base hits—Kelley, Keeler, Keener. Three-base hits—Delehanty. First base on errors—Philadelphia 1. Bases on balls—Keener 2. Left on bases—Baltimore 4, Philadelphia 6. Struck out—By Hoffer 1, by Keener 5. Double play—Thompson, Lajoie and Hulen. Passed ball—Robinson. Stolen bases—Cross, Quinn, Kelley 2, Doyle, Keeler, Brodie, Cooley. Time of game—One hour and 50 minutes. Umpire—Hornung.

REDS WIN AT LAST.

Defeated the Spiders Easily Yesterday—Other Games.

Cleveland, O., Sept. 22.—The visitors won the game in the first inning by hitting Young for six singles. After that it was an even contest. Score:

CLEVELAND.	R.	H.	O.	A.	E.
Burkett, l. f.	1	2	1	0	0
McKean, s. s.	0	1	4	2	0
Childs, 2b	1	0	2	7	1
McAleer, c. f.	1	1	1	0	0
Zimmer, c.	0	2	4	0	0
McGarr, 3b	0	2	1	1	0
Tebeau, 1b	0	0	12	1	0
Blake, r. f.	0	2	1	0	0
Young, p.	0	0	1	2	1
Totals	3	10	27	13	2

CINCINNATI.	R.	H.	O.	A.	E.
Burke, l. f.	1	2	2	0	0
Hoy, c. f.	1	1	1	0	1
McPhee, 2b	0	1	6	5	0
Miller, r. f.	1	1	1	0	0
Vaughn, c.	1	1	1	0	0
Smith, s. s.	1	1	3	5	1
Irwin, 3b	1	0	3	2	1
Holliday, 1b	1	2	10	0	0
Foreman, p.	0	2	0	3	0
Totals	7	11	27	15	3

SCORE BY INNINGS.

Cleveland	0	0	1	0	0	1	0	1	0—3
Cincinnati	4	0	1	0	0	1	0	0	1—7

Earned runs—Cleveland 1, Cincinnati 4. First base by errors—Cleveland 1, Cincinnati 2. Left on bases—Cleveland 9, Cincinnati 6. First base on balls—Off Foreman 2. Struck out—By Young 1. Two-base hits—Zimmer, Hoy, Vaughn. Stolen bases—Burke, McPhee. Double plays—Irwin, McPhee, Holliday. Hit by pitcher—By Young 1. Wild pitch—Young 1. Time of game—One hour and 50 minutes. Umpire—Sheridan.

Joyceless Senators Won the Third.

Washington, Sept. 22.—The masterly pitching of McJames was the cause of New York's downfall today. The team ably supported him, Brown in centre-field making two phenomenal catches. Sullivan was batted hard. Game called at end of seventh inning on account of darkness. Score:

WASHINGTON.	R.	H.	O.	A.	E.
Lush, r. f.	1	0	1	0	0
De Mont, s. s.	0	2	3	1	0
Selbach, l. f.	3	2	1	0	0
Farrell, c.	0	4	5	0	0
Smith, 3b	0	1	4	1	1
O'Brien, 2b	0	0	0	1	0
Brown, c. f.	1	1	3	0	0
Cartwright, 1b	1	1	4	0	0
McJames, p.	1	0	0	1	0
Totals	7	11	21	4	1

NEW YORK.	R.	H.	O.	A.	E.
Van Haltren, c. f.	0	1	1	0	0
Tiernan, r. f.	0	1	1	0	0
Gleason, 2b	0	1	0	2	0
Joyce, 3b	0	0	1	1	0
Davis, s. s.	0	0	4	4	0
Beckley, 1b	0	0	10	1	0
Stafford, l. f.	0	0	1	0	0
Warner, c.	1	0	2	2	0
Sullivan, p.	0	0	1	3	1
Totals	1	3	21	13	1

SCORE BY INNINGS.

Washington	1	3	0	0	1	0	2—7
New York	0	0	0	0	0	0	1—1

Earned runs—Washington 4. Two-base hit—Farrell. Three-base hit—Selbach. Stolen bases—Selbach, Cartwright, McJames, Smith, Tiernan, Stafford. Double plays—Gleason, Davis and Beckley. First base on balls—Off McJames 6, off Sullivan 3. Struck out—By McJames 4, by Sullivan 1. Time of game—One hour and 49 minutes. Umpire—Lynch.

Brooklyn Falls Before Lewis.

Brooklyn, N. Y., Sept. 22.—The Brooklyn batsmen could do nothing against Lewis today. Only eight innings were played. The score:

BROOKLYN.	R.	H.	O.	A.	E.
Jones, r. f.	0	1	3	0	0
Anderson, 1b	1	0	8	2	0
Griffin, c. f.	0	2	1	1	0
Bonner, 2b	0	0	3	2	1
Corcoran, s. s.	0	1	3	5	1
Shindle, 3b	0	0	0	1	1
McCarthy, l. f.	0	0	2	0	0
Grim, c.	0	0	3	2	0
Kennedy, p.	0	0	1	0	0
Totals	1	4	24	13	3

BOSTON.	R.	H.	O.	A.	E.
Hamilton, c. f.	3	2	1	0	0
Tenney, r. f.	1	0	1	0	0
Duffy, l. f.	0	1	1	0	0
Long, s. s.	0	2	3	4	0
Tucker, 1b	0	1	8	2	0
McGann, 2b	1	1	1	3	0
Bergen, c.	0	0	7	0	0
Collins, 3b	1	3	1	0	0
Lewis, p.	0	0	1	1	0
Totals	6	10	24	10	0

SCORE BY INNINGS.

Brooklyn	1	0	0	0	0	0	0	0—1
Boston	1	1	0	0	1	0	2	1—6

Earned runs—Boston 3. First base by errors—Boston 2. Left on bases—Brooklyn 7, Boston 6. Base on balls—Off Kennedy 2, off Lewis 5. Struck out—By Kennedy 2, by Lewis 4. Home run—Collins. Sacrifice hits—Duffy, Shindle. Stolen bases—Long 2, McGann, Collins, Bonner, Corcoran. Double play—Long and Tucker. Passed balls—Grim 2. Wild pitches—Kennedy 1, Lewis 1. Time of game—One hour and 26 minutes. Umpire—Hurst.

Richmond Wins the Pennant.

Richmond, Va., Sept. 22.—The Norfolk team decided to forfeit today's game and end the championship series. Richmond therefore is winner of the pennant and Nowlan Cup. The Richmond team divided up today and gave an exhibition game.

Answers to Queries.

H. L.—When a batter reaches first on a base on balls he is not given a time at bat. Neither is he given a time at bat when he is hit by a pitched ball or makes a sacrifice hit. In yesterday's game, for instance, Doyle walked to the plate four times. He struck out once, went out, short to first, another time, and got two bases on balls. He was at bat but twice, in consequence, according to the rules.

C. F.—Keeler played with both the Brooklyns and the New Yorks in 1893, the year before he came to Baltimore.

RESULTS OF A SERIES.

Some Figures Showing the Work of the Orioles and Phillies in the Twelve Games They Played.

The series with the Quakers was ended yesterday, and resulted in an overwhelming success for the Orioles, who won every game played, or 12 in all. Baltimore has certainly proved a worse hoodoo to the Phillies than the Spiders are to the Orioles.

The Orioles did better against the Phillies than against any other club. They outplayed them in every department of the game—batting, base-running, fielding and pitching. In but one thing did the Philadelphia men make any sort of a showing, and that was in long-distance hitting. The Quakers made about as many long hits as did the local boys. Following are some figures showing the result of the series. The first set shows the work of each individual player, and is a combination of the tabulated scores of the 12 games and is itself arranged in the form of a tabulated score. It follows:

BALTIMORE.	A.B.	R.	H.	O.	A.	E.
Kelley, l. f.	50	17	23	20	1	0
Keeler, r. f.	53	17	30	27	0	0
Jennings, s. s.	37	14	18	43	34	6
Doyle, 1b	44	15	22	93	8	4
Reitz, 2b	45	12	15	23	41	2
Brodie, c. f.	48	7	18	26	1	0
Donnelly, 3b	41	6	14	14	15	2
Robinson, c.	33	6	16	34	4	2
Clarke, c.	16	1	4	13	4	1
Quinn, 2b. & 3b	15	6	5	4	11	0
McMahon, p.	4	0	1	0	3	0
Pond, p.	8	0	2	0	1	2
Hoffer, p.	12	3	4	2	6	1
Hemming, p.	9	2	3	1	5	0
Esper, p.	12	1	2	2	5	0
McGraw, 3b	0	1	0	0	0	0
Nops, p.	2	0	0	0	0	0
Bowerman, 1b	5	0	1	9	0	0
Totals	434	108	178	311	139	20

PHILA.	A.B.	R.	H.	O.	A.	E.
Hulen, s. s. & c. f.	43	7	11	24	12	5
Delehanty, l. f.	35	6	14	22	0	0
Thompson, r. f.	47	5	11	28	5	4
Brouthers, 1b	3	0	0	7	0	0
Boyle, c. & 1b	18	1	4	41	1	0
Hallman, 2b	41	6	17	30	35	6
Cross, s. s. & 3b	43	4	9	24	37	4
Grady, c.	29	3	8	16	13	2
Cooley, c. f.	32	6	9	10	0	0
Clements, c.	9	0	0	10	3	0
Nash, 3b	15	1	2	6	9	0
Orth, p.	4	0	2	0	3	0
Taylor, p.	17	0	5	1	10	0
Lucid, p.	6	0	1	2	1	1
Carsey, p.	4	1	1	0	1	0
Turner, l. f.	5	1	1	3	2	1
Sullivan, r. f.	4	0	0	0	0	1
Lajoie, 1b	28	2	5	57	4	0
Geier, r. f.	1	0	0	2	0	0
Gumbert, p.	5	1	0	0	2	0
Mertes, l. f. & s. s.	4	1	1	2	2	0
Wheeler, p.	2	0	0	1	2	0
Keener, p.	4	1	2	0	3	0
Totals	399	46	103	286	145	24

The next table shows the work of the pitchers. Hoffer made the best showing by a narrow margin, his work being just slightly better than that of Esper. The work of all the pitchers was good. For the Phillies, if any of their pitchers can be said to have done so, Wheeler made the best showing. Taylor undoubtedly did the worst. Each pitcher is credited in this table with the number of games won and lost by him, and the number of earned runs and base hits made off him by his opponents. Where two or more pitchers officiated in one game, the victory or defeat is credited to the one who pitched the largest number of innings, unless one of the others is directly responsible for the result. In this case the other men are credited only with the number of earned runs and base hits made off them.

BALTIMORE.	Won.	Lost.	Opp. B.H.	Opp. E.R.
McMahon	1	0	7	0
Pond	2	0	21	9
Hoffer	3	0	22	3
Hemming	2	0	23	8
Esper	3	0	24	4
Nops	1	0	6	1
Totals	12	0	103	25

PHILA.	Won.	Lost.	Opp. B.H.	Opp. E.R.
Orth	0	1	16	4
Taylor	0	5	68	30
Lucid	0	2	34	15
Carsey	0	1	13	7
Gumbert	0	1	23	9
Wheeler	0	1	10	3
Keener	0	1	14	6
Totals	0	12	178	74

The following table shows the individual batting averages obtained by each and every player who took part in a game. Some of the Orioles, it will be seen, secured very high averages, and the work of all the players, in fact, was very good. Eleven of the men, including all of the regular team, went over the .300 mark. The work of the Phillies was not near so good, it will readily be seen.

BALTIMORE.	A.B.	R.	H.	Aver.
Keeler	53	17	30	.566
Doyle	44	15	22	.500
Jennings	37	14	18	.487
Robinson	33	6	16	.485
Kelley	50	17	23	.460
Brodie	48	7	18	.375
Donnelly	41	6	14	.341
Quinn	15	6	5	.333
Reitz	45	12	15	.333
Hemming	9	2	3	.333
Hoffer	12	3	4	.333
Clarke	16	1	4	.250
McMahon	4	0	1	.250
Pond	8	0	2	.250
Bowerman	5	0	1	.200
Esper	12	1	2	.167
McGraw	0	1	0	.000
Nops	2	0	0	.000

PHILA.	A.B.	R.	H.	Aver.
Orth	4	0	2	.500
Keener	4	1	2	.500
Hallman	41	6	17	.415
Delehanty	35	6	14	.400
Taylor	17	0	5	.294
Cooley	32	6	9	.281
Grady	29	3	8	.278
Hulen	43	7	11	.256
Carsey	4	1	1	.250
Mertes	4	1	1	.250
Thompson	47	5	11	.234
Boyle	18	1	4	.222
Cross	43	4	9	.209
Turner	5	1	1	.200
Lajoie	28	2	5	.179
Lucid	6	0	1	.166
Nash	15	1	2	.133
Brouthers	3	0	0	.000
Clements	9	0	0	.000
Sullivan	4	0	0	.000
Geier	1	0	0	.000
Gumbert	5	1	0	.000
Wheeler	2	0	0	.000

The team averages show at a glance how it was that Baltimore won all the games. While the work in fielding was about even, the work at the bat shows a great difference in favor of Baltimore, and it was the difference, or rather, the batting, that won games.

TEAM BATTING.

	A.B.	R.	H.	Aver.
Baltimore	434	108	178	.410
Philadelphia	399	46	103	.258

TEAM FIELDING.

	P.O.	A.	E.	Aver.
Baltimore	311	139	20	.958
Philadelphia	286	145	24	.948

SCORE BY INNINGS.

Baltimore	9	9	16	3	17	7	17	18	12—108
Philadelphia	12	7	2	3	7	6	1	3	5—46

Earned runs—Baltimore 74, Philadelphia 25.

Two-base hits—Doyle 3, Keeler 2, Donnelly 2, Clarke 1, Jennings 1, Reitz 2, Brodie 3, Hemming 1, Robinson 1, Quinn 1, Kelley 2, Nash 1, Orth 1, Cross 2, Grady 1, Hallman 2, Thompson 1, Delehanty 3, Hulen 2, Cooley 1, Taylor 1, Mertes 1, Keener 1.

Three-base hits—Doyle 2, Kelley 2, Hoffer 1, Brodie 1, Keeler 1, Robinson 1, Esper 1, Hemming 1, Hulen 1, Grady 2, Cooley 1, Orth 1, Delehanty 2, Hallman 2.

Home runs—Keeler 1, Brodie 1, Thompson 1, Delehanty 2.

Bases on balls—Off McMahon 3, Pond 4, Hoffer 7, Hemming 11, Esper 10, Taylor 7, Lucid 6, Orth 2, Gumbert 4, Wheeler 4, Carsey 5, Keener 2.

Struck out—By McMahon 2, Pond 5, Hoffer 7, Hemming 5, Esper 2, Nops 2, Taylor 9, Orth 1, Gumbert 1, Wheeler 1, Carsey 1, Keener 5.

Hit by pitched ball—By Pond 2, Hoffer 2, Hemming 1, Esper 1, Lucid 2, Taylor 5, Orth 1, Gumbert 2, Wheeler 2.

Sacrifice hits—Doyle 1, Keeler 2, Donnelly 2, Kelley 2, Lucid 1, Nash 1, Delehanty 1, Clements 1, Cross 1.

Passed balls—Clarke 2, Robinson 1, Grady 4.

Wild pitches—Esper 1, Taylor 1, Gumbert 1, Wheeler 1, Carsey 1.

Double plays—Jennings and Doyle 2; Reitz and Doyle 1; Jennings, Reitz and Doyle 3; Hemming, Jennings and Doyle 1; Jennings and Reitz 1; Reitz, Jennings and Doyle 3; Donnelly, Jennings and Doyle 1; Doyle (unassisted) 1; Reitz, Jennings and Bowerman 1; Lucid, Hallman and Boyle 1; Hallman, Cross and Boyle 2; Cross, Hallman and Boyle 1; Thompson and Lajoie 1; Cross and Lajoie 1; Hulen, Hallman and Boyle 1; Mertes and Lajoie 1; Hulen, Hallman and Lajoie 1; Thompson, Lajoie and Hulen 1.

Stolen bases—Doyle 11, Keeler 8, Jennings 6, Reitz 5, Robinson 3, Brodie 4, Donnelly 2, Kelley 12, Hoffer 1, Quinn 4, Cross 2, Hulen 2, Turner 1, Nash 1, Delehanty 4, Lajoie 2, Boyle 1, Cooley 2.

Left on bases—Baltimore 89, Philadelphia 63.

Umpires—Hurst 8, Hornung 2, Conahan 1, Clarke and Carsey 1.

BASEBALL NOTES.

The Herald reproduces today a splendid group from a photograph of the Baltimore Baseball Club, three-time winners of the National League championship. The photograph is by John Betz, Jr., the well-known photographer of Northeast Baltimore, and is an excellent example of the picture-maker's art. All the Orioles with the exception of Corbett, Nops and the other youngsters recently signed are shown in the group.

Yesterday's was the last game on the home grounds with the exception of the Temple Cup contests.

Hughey Jennings went to Scranton yesterday to try and arrange for an exhibition game between the Scranton team and the Orioles to be played some time next week.

Final arrangements for the Temple Cup games cannot be made until it is definitely decided what team will win second place. The Reds and Spiders are still fighting it out and while the former's chances for the place are slim there is still a possibility of their capturing it.

YOUNG AMERICA.

The Carrolls defeated the Millingtons at Carroll Park by a score of 26 to 22. Winning battery, John Nine and Ed Graff; losing battery, T. Taylor and B. Hiller.

The Hollins Baseball Club closed the season Saturday by defeating the Mount Washington Club on their grounds. The Hollins have had a very successful season, having won 18 games and lost 2.

The Combination Baseball Club defeated the Big Four Club, of Baltimore, by a score of 10 to 4. The feature of the game was the battery work of Lynch and Nolan.

The Admirals have reorganized, with the following players, and would like to hear from teams averaging 16 to 18 years before the close of the season: J. Stallings, c. and l. f.; William Creamer, p.; William Cassiday, 1b.; F. Louck, 2b.; C. Doyle, s. s.; F. Appel, 3b.; H. Williams, l. f. and c.; G. Riebel, r. f.; G. Wilner, c. f.

CITY COLLEGE NOTES.

Subscriptions to Football Team Meeting With a Hearty Response.

The subscription for the benefit of the football team which was started Monday has thus far been met with a hearty response from the college students. Yesterday contributions were solicited by the football committee from the higher classmen and the remainder of the week will be spent among the first, second and third year classes. Last year's football eleven was poorly supported by the majority of the students and was neither financially nor otherwise a success.

Manager Rice yesterday received a letter from Gallaudet College, Washington, D. C., asking for a game on their grounds November 7. The challenge will probably be accepted. Thursday the candidates for the second eleven will meet on the lacrosse grounds, Druid Hill Park. Supplee, Sudler and R. Horner, of last season's reserves, are pushing the enterprise. The team played two games last year, winning one from Tome Institute, Port Deposit, and tieing for the other with the Polytechnic Institute. Supplee will manage the team.

At their meeting yesterday the Green Bag editors decided to offer four prizes for contributions from lower classmen. A '97 year-book will be given as a first prize to the one submitting the best original humorous pen sketch of college life. A '96 Green Bag will be presented to the next best contributor. Similar prizes will be awarded to the two students offering the best stories pertaining to the school life. Messrs. Rice and Reiley were appointed by the chief editor a committee to see to contributions from the under classmen and Messrs. Reese, Hayward and Singley will compile the statistics relative to the senior class. Today Business Manager Trippe will receive subscription blanks from the publishers of the book, and a canvass of the school will immediately be made. Books will be sold only by subscription.

Messrs. Cornelius, Fishhack and Byrne, of the junior class, are pushing forward the fall field day enterprise. If the Maryland Oval can be obtained the events will come off on the 31st of October.

Norman Boyer, president of the junior class entered the college today. The latter class will effect a reorganization next week and elect officers for the ensuing year.

Running at Patterson Park.

Charles Bristor defeated Edward P. Kirkness last night at Patterson Park in a 220-yard dash and quarter-mile run. Time, 28 seconds and 1 minute 7 seconds, respectively. Bristor ran an exhibition quarter mile in 1 minute 5 seconds, and one mile in 5 minutes 44 seconds unpaced. Male, of the Central Y. M. C. A., who is training for the outdoor pentathlon contest, did an unpaced mile in 5 minutes 47 seconds. He had never tried long distances. His running was as regular as clockwork, and at the finish he seemed very little exhausted.

Maryland Football Team.

The Maryland football team has organized with the following players: McCabe, Baily, Bland, Mullen, Humrichouse, Morgan, Bowen, Dulany, Glazes, Bear, Fisher and Fizzone. It would like to hear from teams whose average weight is from 140 to 145 pounds. Address all communication to G. Baily, manager, 1812 North Calvert street.

AT THE DRIVING PARK.

The Fall Meeting Starts Off Under Favorable Circumstances.

RACES WON IN STRAIGHT HEATS.

Mioda Wins the 2.40 Class and Drops Into the 30 List—An Easy Thing for Wyoming—Dick Hentschell Shows a Good One to Road Cart—The Summaries.

The fall meeting at the Gentlemen's Driving Park started off favorably yesterday. The attendance, despite the threatening weather, was good. The track was in fair condition and the races went off without a hitch.

The smiling countenance of Col. Patrick Martin, which has become such a feature of the Driving Park events, was missing, the colonel being now on the return trip from Europe. In the absence of Colonel Martin, the hospitalities of the occasion were administered and well administered by Mr. McAndrews.

Three races were scheduled and each was decided right off the reel in straight heats.

The first race was for 2.40 trotters. Before the first heat pools sold: Field, $10; Fannie K., $6. The winner of the race turned up in Miada, from Knoxville, Tenn., who won in straight heats without an effort and put herself into the 2.30 list. The Cottage Farm, Norfolk, showed up a good one in Jessie B., who took second money and looked as if she might have done better.

In the second heat of this race Clarence B., driven by Walter Snyder, was run into by Warren Boy, driven by Staton, and Snyder's sulky wheel was broken so that he was put out of the heat. He was allowed to start by the judges in the next heat. The same accident happened to Sprinter in the last heat.

Wyoming, a handsome son of that good horse Wilton, was picked as a favorite in the 2.24 class, and he rewarded the faith of his backers. The first two heats he won handily, but in the last heat he had a close call. Down the stretch he was pressed hard by Kinsale and Troth, and 20 feet from the wire he broke. Merrifield caught him quickly, however, and he just poked his nose in front as the wire was reached.

The last race was for 2.50 trotters and pacers to road carts and brought out a rather motley aggregation. William C. was the favorite before the start, pools selling: William C., $10; field, $5. William C., driven by Hentschell, turned out to be a very slick piece of goods, and the wonder is how his light has been kept concealed under a bushel, as it were, so many moons. The others were not in the same class with the bay, and halves in 1.14 were merely pie for him. The heats were simply processions; William C. led in each heat, and the rest were strung out at intervals for at least a quarter of a mile.

The racing was somewhat marred by incessant scoring, the starting judge, A. H. Merrill, of Danvers, Mass., seeming to have very little control over the drivers.

The summaries:

2.40 Class—Trotting; purse $500.

Miada, b. m., by Mimic, dam by Ada Wilkes (Cannon)	1	1	1
Jessie B., gr. m. (Hughes)	4	2	2
Warren Boy, sr. s. (Stolm)	2	3	4
Mike, b. g. (Merrifield)	9	5	3
Clarence B., bl. g. (Snyder)	3	8	6
Fannie K., b. m. (Myers)	6	4	7
Easter Lily, ch. m. (Hewitt)	5	7	5
Sprinter, b. s. (Dwyer)	7	6	8
Bellart, bl. s. (Barnes)	8	dis	
Miss Wilkes, b. m. (Kries)	dis		

Time—2.27¼, 2.24¼, 2.24½.

2.24 Class—Trotting; purse $500.

Wyoming, blk. s., by Wilton (Merrifield)	1	1	1
Kinsale, b. g. (Kilburn)	2	2	4
Troth, b. m. (Smith)	9	6	2
Mamie D., b. m. (Sinclair)	6	3	3
Fannie Agar, b. m. (Cannon)	3	8	9

Continued on Eighth Page.

PHILLIES BREAK BATTING RECORD.

Twenty-Seven Hits Score Seventeen Runs Against Cincinnati.

ALL HANDS GET IN THE GAME

While Donahue Was Keeping the Reds in Check the Phillies Were Hammering Dammann's Curves Almost at Will—Hot Fights for Positions.

The Phillies turned on Cincinnati yesterday and almost smothered the leaders. It was about as bad a defeat as the Reds or any other National League team has suffered this season. The Phillies made twenty-seven hits for a total of forty bases, which is the best batting record for '98. Every man, barring Pitcher Donahue, made from two to five hits. This makes Philadelphia's seventh victory out of nine games played on this trip.

The Eastern clubs came out on top in four out of the six contests. The fights for the various positions are now much closer. Boston is again right on the heels of Cincinnati and Chicago is pressing Cleveland and Baltimore hard. In the second division, Philadelphia is right on the heels of New York, only .001 per cent. separating the two teams in the race for seventh place. Washington and Brooklyn continue their battle for ninth position and Louisville yesterday tied St. Louis for the eleventh notch.

SCORES OF LEAGUE GAMES.

NATIONAL LEAGUE.
PHILADELPHIA 17, CINCINNATI 3.
BROOKLYN 8, PITSBURG 5.
CHICAGO 7, NEW YORK 5.
LOUSVILLE 9, BALTMORE 1.
WASHINGTON 13, ST. LOUIS 3.
BOSTON 10, CLEVELAND 5.

ATLANTIC LEAGUE.
READING, 6; LANCASTER, 4.
NEWARK, 11; RICHMOND, 8.
HARTFORD, 9; ALLENTOWN 7.
NORFOLK, 6; PATERSON, 4.

EASTERN LEAGUE.
SPRINGFIELD, 6; PROVIDENCE 5 (11 inn.).
SYRACUSE, 10; TORONTO, 5.
ROCHESTER, 9; BUFFALO, 2.
WILKES-BARRE, 1; MONTREAL, 0.

SCHEDULE FOR TO-DAY.

NATIONAL LEAGUE.
PHILADELPHIA AT CINCINNATI.
WASHINGTON AT ST. LOUIS.
NEW YORK AT CHICAGO.
BALTIMORE AT LOUISVILLE.
BOSTON AT CLEVELAND.
BROOKLYN AT PITTSBURG.

ATLANTIC LEAGUE.
HARTFORD AT ALLENTOWN.
NORFOLK AT PATERSON.
RICHMOND AT NEWARK.
READING AT LANCASTER.

EASTERN LEAGUE.
WILKES-BARRE AT MONTREAL (2 games).
ROCHESTER AT BUFFALO.
SYRACUSE AT TORONTO (2 games).
PROVIDENCE AT SPRINGFIELD.

RUNS MADE IN BUNCHES.

The Phillies Hammer Out 27 Hits at Dammann's Expense.

Special Despatch to "The Press."

Cincinnati, O., June 30.—"Wee Willie" Dammann was given a drubbing to-day that he will not forget for some years to come. The hard-hitting aggregation from Philadelphia broke the season's record at the bat at Willie's expense. They went at Willie with a determination, and sent out enough hits and scored enough runs in the opening inning to win the game. Dammann was hit for twenty-seven base hits, for a total of forty bases.

On Tuesday the little fellow shut out the St. Louis Browns, and was called upon again to-day after one day's rest. His physique is not of the kind that will stand too much work, and as a result, his delivery was the easiest thing the Quakers have struck this season. In the first two innings the Quakers scored six runs, just as they did in the game on Wednesday. They evidently feared that history might repeat itself, and that the Reds might give them another finish, so they just jumped in in the fourth and batted out six more runs, making it twelve. After that they helped themselves to five other tallies, just to make the thing sure. Donohue, on the other hand, was a puzzle to the Reds. He started out in a manner that invited all kinds of hitting, which, however, did not materialize. The Reds' outfield was kept very busy, McBride was particularly so. From the time game was called until the last man was retired Mac was kept busy chasing three-baggers. Lajoie was ill and had to give way after the fourth to Abbatticchio.

The Phillies started just as they did on Wednesday. Cooley hit a hot one at Dammann, which was knocked down, but Dick beat it to first. Douglass bunted and beat it out. Delahanty also beat out his bunt and the bases were full. Napoleon Lajoie then hit safely to center, scoring two runs. Flick and McFarland were retired, but hits by Lauder and Cross followed and four runs were scored. The Reds did nothing in their half, although McBride started with a base on balls. The Phillies were not through with Dammann. Five more hits were made off him in the second and two runs scored, making the score exactly what it was on Wednesday. Miller started the Reds' half of this inning with a single to right and stole second, but he died there.

Wise Mr. Cooley played in close behind second for Dammann in the third and "Wee Willie" showed him up by hitting to the center field fence for three bases. McBride's out scored him. Holliday walked and Corcoran flew out to Flick. Lajoie's error gave Beckley a life, but Miller died, from first to second. Corcoran's errors, two triples, a two-bagger and a wild throw by Corcoran gave the Phillies six runs in the fourth. There was no more run-getting until the sixth, when two doubles, a single and another error by Corcoran gave the Phillies two more tallies. Beckley's triple and a put out gave the Reds their second run in the last half of this inning.

Cooley hit a little pop fly in the seventh which both Holliday and Corcoran tried for. They collided and Cooley made a home run. A single and a double gave them another in the eighth. Beckley scored another run in the Reds' half of this inning on Abbatticchio's error and a single by Irwin. A base on balls and Delahanty's triple gave the Quakers their last run in the ninth. Score:—

CINCINNATI.

	A.b.	R.	H.	O.	A.	E.
McBride, cf	4	0	0	3	0	0
Holliday, lf	4	0	1	1	1	0
Corcoran, ss	5	0	0	3	4	3
Beckley, 1b	5	2	1	11	0	1
Miller, rf	4	0	1	0	0	0
Irwin, 3b	4	0	2	3	4	0
McPhee, 2b	3	0	1	3	4	0
Peitz, c	3	0	0	3	2	0
Dammann, p	4	1	1	0	3	0
Totals	36	3	7	27	18	4

PHILADELPHIA.

	A.b.	R.	H.	O.	A.	E.
Cooley, cf	6	4	5	5	0	0
Douglass, 1b	7	2	3	7	0	0
Delahanty, lf	6	3	3	1	0	0
Lajoie, 2b	3	2	2	2	3	1
Abbatticchio, 2b	3	0	1	1	1	2
Flick, rf	6	2	4	2	0	0
McFarland, c	6	1	4	2	0	1
Lauder, 3b	6	1	3	8	0	0
Cross, ss	5	1	2	3	5	0
Donahue, p	6	1	0	1	1	0
Totals	54	17	27	27	10	4

SCORE BY INNINGS.

Cincinnati	0	0	1	0	0	1	0	1	0	—3
Philadelphia	4	2	0	6	0	2	1	1	1	—17

Earned runs, Philadelphia 15, Cincinnati 2. Two-base hits, McFarland 2, Lauder, Cooley. Three-base hits, McFarland, Delahanty, Flick, Beckley, Dammann. Home run, Cooley. Stolen base, Miller. Double play, Dammann, Peitz and Beckley. First on balls, off Donahue 4, off Dammann 2. Struck out, by Donahue 2. Wild pitch, Dammann. Time, 1.50. Umpires, Emslie and Heydler.

Killen's Curves Pounded.

Pittsburg, June 30.—Killen was knocked out of the box in the fourth inning. Pittsburg could do nothing with Dunn until the seventh, when Padden made a home run on a long drive to left. In the eight, with the bases filled, Padden cleared them with a three-bagger. Attendance, 1200. Score:—

[illegible]

WATER TOO ROUGH FOR THE FRESHMEN

Race Between the First Year Crews Postponed Until 10.30 To-day.

THE 'VARSITY EVENT AT FIVE

Cornell Eights Are Favorites for Both Races With Penna. and Columbia Even for Second Choice—Quakers in Fine Condition.

By Telegraph from a Staff Correspondent.

Saratoga, N. Y., June 30.—Lake Saratoga had its turn this afternoon in being condemned as a place to row shell races. A southeast gale stirred up such a lot of whitecaps that the Freshman race between Cornell, Columbia and Pennsylvania had to be postponed until half-past 10 o'clock to-morrow morning.

The race was to have been rowed at 5 o'clock this afternoon, and Referee Gordon S. Carrigan, of the Schuylkill Navy, waited until 7 o'clock before he called it off. At that hour the whitecaps were still rolling.

While Boreas was ripping up the surface of the lake and painting things white, the spectators, a few bakers' dozen in number, were waiting patiently for the referee to yield the day to his superior. The crowd went to the lake early. It is a five-mile journey from the village of big hotels to the lake and a lame-backed trolley road runs a car down occasionally if the motormen are good-natured and the passengers are not in too much of a hurry. This afternoon the cars run on fire-alarm time, one going out about every forty-five minutes. Most of the spectators got there an hour and a half early. At 5 o'clock the white caps were thick as the rumors of Spanish victories. Long, graceful swells were rolling down the lake and the chances for a thunder storm seemed to be better than those for a boat race. Occasionally two or three Cornell men got together and attempted to give a cheer. Their efforts were so feeble that a crowd of Saratoga bicycle girls jumped up and drowned out the Ithacan basses. The Quakers tried to cheer once or twice, but there were not over two dozen Pennsylvanians present and eight of these were saving their wind for the race. One Columbia man gave an imitation of the yell of the New Yorkers, just to let the people know that Columbia had a cheer of her own. After a two-hour wait Referee Carrigan announced that there would be no race before to-morrow morning.

The 'Varsity race will also be rowed to-morrow at 5 o'clock in the afternoon. The hotel men who have been expecting [illegible]

[illegible] o'clock and rowed down over the course in good time. A better opportunity was given to judge of the stroke than yesterday, as in their long row up the lake they did not go above 27, and, being very tired, naturally showed up worse than usual. To-day, however, they picked up a good bit on their form, and while still very ragged from an Eastern standpoint, appeared to satisfy Coach O'Dea's expectations. The swing when rowed at 30, which will be their racing stroke, was not so far back as yesterday, but while their coach claims that it is less than that of Cornell's, yet it certainly seems to be considerably more. It is in the realms of probability that the Badgers may upset all calculations to-morrow, and under any circumstances it is to be deeply regretted that the Western crew has not had the same chance to rest and learn the course that the other crews have had, as the test of the stroke under the present circumstances is hardly a fair one. This much is certain, if Wisconsin under the [illegible] conditions can beat out any one of the three colleges opposed to her there must be enough in the stroke to warrant the attention of the Eastern coaches. O'Dea was undecided whether to send the boys out in the afternoon or not, as they have commenced to show the fatigue of their long journey, but the high wind decided things for him and the men remained in their quarters.

Alexander, the stroke of the '96 crew that defeated the Yale Freshmen, is here to assist in the coaching. Their shell is housed under a huge tent, as there is no boathouses to accommodate it. It is a cedar shell 61 feet long and possessing a much shorter fin keel than that of Columbia or Cornell. There has been no betting on Wisconsin as yet, and the crew themselves are hanging back for big odds, which they will doubtless be able to obtain as Wisconsin is considered out of the race.

MISS ARLINGTON'S TOUR.

The Girl Pitcher to Twirl Against Professional Teams.

Miss Lizzie Arlington, of this city, who has made such a sensation this season as a base ball player, is to make an extensive tour, when she will show the professional players that the woman that can throw straight has at last been discovered. On Saturday she will be a member

Miss Lizzie Arlington.

of the Philadelphia Reserves, a team composed of Nash, Abbatticchio, Elberfield, Fifield, etc., who will play the Richmonds at Philadelphia Park. Next week Miss Arlington will play up the State with Atlantic League teams, after which she will play in the New York State and Western Leagues.

Bloomsburg.	R.	H.	O.	A.	E.	Nescopeck.	R.	H.	O.	A.	E.
Miller, c	0	2	14	1	1	L.S'th, 1b	1	0	7	2	0
Sl's'r, p, 3b	0	1	1	8	0	Moore, cf	2	1	0	0	0
Bitt'r, 1b	0	2	8	1	0	Rough, rf	0	1	0	0	0
A.An's, ss	1	1	0	1	0	B.S'th, lf	0	0	0	0	1
W.An's, rf	2	1	2	0	0	Warntz, c	2	8	9	2	1
Nagle, 2b	1	1	1	4	2	Yohe, 3b	1	1	2	4	0
Hoff'n, cf	1	0	0	0	0	Sh'e, p, 3b	1	2	1	4	0
Ba'r, p, 3b	1	1	1	8	0	Taylor, 2b	1	2	8	2	0
Barn'y, lf	1	1	0	1	0	Mil'r, ss, p	0	0	5	8	0
Totals	7	10	27	24	3	Totals	8	10	27	22	2

Bloomsburg	0	0	1	1	1	0	2	1	1	—7
Nescopeck	1	0	0	1	1	0	2	2	1	—8

Struck out, by Shipe 2, by Miller 5, by Slusser 5, by Baker 6. Time, 1.50. Umpire, Bridle.

GOLF AT WISSAHICKON.

Semi-Finals for Philadelphia Cricket Club Championship.

The first match in the semi-finals for the championship of the Philadelphia Cricket Club was played on the Wissahickon links yesterday afternoon, J. Wilmer Biddle being pitted against Charles P. Lineaweaver.

The first round was hotly contested. Both started off well, halving the first hole in four; the second fell to Lineaweaver in six. The third was halved in three and Biddle evened matters up at the fourth, being down in five. Biddle also took the fifth, assuming the lead. The sixth was won by Lineaweaver in bogie figures; the seventh was halved, but the eighth went to Biddle by a fine put, being down in four. The last was halved, giving him the advantage of one up on the first round. Lineaweaver cut this down at the first hole on the second round, and also took the next, giving him a lead of one up. From this time on it was nip and tuck, the third going to Biddle in bogie figures. He also took the next, the fifth was halved and the sixth was won by Lineaweaver, making the score even up. Biddle again assumed the lead at the seventh, but immediately lost it at the eighth, and as they teed off for the last hole the match was once more even up. In driving off Biddle shied his ball and was forced to play from a bad lie, losing the hole by 5 to 6 and the match by one up. Both players were quite at their best and the match abounded in many brilliant shots. Lineaweaver will meet the winner of the Trotter-Biddle match in the finals. The cards were:—

Lineweaver	4	6	3	6	5	5	4	5	5—43	
Biddle	4	7	3	5	4	6	4	4	5—42	
Lineweaver	4	8	4	6	5	5	5	4	5—46	—89
Biddle	5	9	3	4	5	6	4	5	6—47	—89

THE SUMMER PRACTICE CUP.

The summary of the points scored in the contest for the Summer practice cup of the Philadelphia Cricket Club is as follows:—

		Points.
1	Joseph H. Patterson	19½
2	Charles A. Potter	18 1-3
3	Authur E. Newbold	9½
4	James I. Lineaweaver	5½
5	Henry L. Townsend	5½
6	Richard V. Buckley	5½
7	Charles P. Lineaweaver	5
8	Francis H. Bohlen	5
9	Dr. A. W. Biddle	5
10	J. Wilmer Biddle	4
11	William F. Brown	2⅓
12	C. T. Cowperthwait	2
13	J. E. D. Trask	2
14	Herbert M. Forrest	1 1-3
15	E. D. Toland	1
16	Isaac Starr, Jr	½
17	R. S. Benner	½
18	E. A. Ballard	1-3

AT HAVERFORD.

The tournament for the cup offered by Mrs. A. J. Cassatt was played on the Haverford links yesterday. The conditions were at eighteen holes, medal play, club handicap, open to the women golfers of the club. Miss Hannis proved the successful contestant, with the following card: 128—25—103.

A golf button was offered for the maker of the best gross score. Miss Elsie Cassatt and Miss Frances C. Griscom tied for it, both playing from scratch; their cards were:—

[illegible]

A BELMONT RECORD BROKEN.

Twilight and Kappolina Go the Mile in 2.20.

[illegible]

TRACK READY FOR NATIONAL MEET.

The Indianapolis Wheelmen Happy Over Completion of Oval for Big Races.

CYCLING CHAMPIONS HERE.

All the Crack Riders of the Country in Training at Willow Grove for Saturday's Meet — Other Cycling News.

After weeks of hard work the track and grand stand at the Newby Oval, where the races at the National Meet will occur, are finished and all hands have been turned to the completion of the bleachers. In consequence Indianapolis wheelmen are happy. The Newby Oval is situated just off Central Avenue, a few blocks north of Fall Creek, and is an attractive spot for the wheelmen. It is easily accessible both by wheel and street car. The work of constructing the track and the buildings at the park has been done under the direction of the Indianapolis Cycle Track Association, which was formed with a capital of $20,000.

The track is four laps to the mile, built under the supervision of Charles W. Ashinger, the old Philadelphia six-day rider, from designs furnished by Herbert W. Foltz, of the L. A. W. Racing Board. The home stretch is thirty feet wide, the back stretch and turns, twenty-five feet, the latter banked ten feet and built on the "whale-back" plan. This means that a section through the turns shows a curved line at the surface, the banking starting from the curves at the ratio of four feet in height for ten feet at the base and gradually curving outward until it reaches a plane almost horizontal at the extreme outside.

• • •

The victory of Church over Starbuck in the Australian pursuit race Wednesday evening will add additional interest to the former's fifteen-mile paced race with Henri Cissac, of France, which is the star attraction of the annual race meet of the Penn Wheelmen, which takes place at the Tioga track Saturday, July 9. Church is now at the top of the heap among the local riders, and the enthusiasts are anxious that he should occupy the same position among the racing men at large. His meeting with Cissac will be the first stepping stone in this direction, and should he win his way will be paved for match races with the best riders now performing in middle distance races. The riding of the local boy this season has been phenomenal, his record being a clean one to date.

• • •

The first entry for the two-mile tandem handicap professional to be run at the Castle Wheelmen's National Circuit meet at Tioga track on Saturday, July 16, was received on Tuesday from Johnny Zimmerman and B. B. Stevens, the midget tandem team who won the match race at Point Breeze track on Monday night last.

• • •

On account of the meeting night of the Castle Wheelmen falling on the Fourth of July, the president, A. J. Wallen, has called a meeting to be held this (Friday) evening at 8 o'clock. Members will please take notice.

• • •

The five-mile quadruplet pursuit race and the three-cornered one-mile match race, best two heats out of three, to be given at the Kenilworth Wheelmen's meet at Woodside, on July 4, have created no small amount of speculation among the racing men now in this city, as well as the general public, owing to the international element infused in each event. Of the quad race, the recent work of the Frenchmen has made them universal favorites—Bourotte for his plucky riding in five-mile events, the tandem riding of Boulay and Cavalley, and the victory of Cissac in Baltimore. Charley Church, who is to steer the American quad, said yesterday that he hoped to add this to his string of victories this season, a desire that was shared by McCurdy and the Turville brothers, all of whom are in the best possible condition.

• • •

There was no small amount of excitement out at Woodside on Wednesday over the final arrangements for the three-cornered race to be run between Johnson, of America; Robertson, of England, and Boulay, of France, at the Kenilworth meet on the Fourth, as to pace, etc. Each man had his own ideas on the subject. As definitely decided, the race for the big $300 purse will be run in three heats, the winners of the best two taking the money. The riders will line up on scratch and will catch their pacemakers as they ride past them in the stretch on the shot of the pistol. Each man is doing his best to secure the fastest possible teams in the way of pacemakers, and were yesterday hard at work out at Woodside in order to be in best possible condition for this important series of races, which will decide the relative merits of each man as to speed and holding pace, for the pacemakers will be as anxious to win as the principals.

• • •

The world's greatest cycle racing men are at present quartered in this city, and the far-famed track at Willow Grove has since Wednesday morning been the scene of some grand performances by the speed merchants of the bicycle track. The scenes which were witnessed in this city last August are outdone by the performances of to-day, for the reason that there are more genuine champions at the renowned board track than at any time since its erection.

Of course the attraction for the racing stars is the L. A. W. National Circuit meet of Saturday, when the two-mile championship of America will be run off under the auspices of the American Cycle Racing Association. This is one of the real big events of the year in American cycledom, and may well be classed as a derby, just as are the important races of Europe.

All the big guns of the racing business are entered, from the three-time victorious champion, Eddie Bald, the "Cannon Ball," of Buffalo, to our own local flyer, who prefers to earn a comfortable living by racing about the tracks of this city to the worry and hustling of traveling the country over as a "National Circuit chaser."

While National Circuit meets with the special sanction of the L. A. W. authorities are extraordinary events in the big cycle races of the year. Saturday's meet at Willow Grove is a greater event than any of the others. The two-mile championship race in itself, with its forty entries, comprising the fastest men of America and Europe, will beyond a doubt be one of the grandest, most exciting [illegible]

[illegible] oscillation when the wheel is raised from the ground is a sure indication of fine running qualities in the bearings. From repeated experiments it has been found that the best bearings, adjusted to produce the greatest efficiency under a load, will in no case afford the number of oscillations which may be obtained from the same bearings under a different adjustment. The driving wheel of a machine made of poor material and poorly constructed may be so adjusted as to spin and oscillate very freely and yet the bearings may prove entirely deficient when put to actual use under the rider.

• • •

When the limit was thought to have been reached by the great speed merchants of the present day, Jimmy Michael entered the field, with some rides in training that took the breath away from those who had so confidently predicted that no faster time would be made this season. When Michael averaged 1.44 for ten miles, last Monday, at Waltham, many said that would be as fast as men would ever travel this season. When, on the next day following, he did so much better that the time would not be made public, for fear of the cry of fake, people again wondered. When McDuffee followed Michael Tuesday and broke all his own best times and tied those of Michael, then people again wondered where the limit might be. There is no doubt that Jimmy Michael and Eddie McDuffee represent the fastest brigade of speed merchants of the country. It is these two riders that meet at Charles River Park, Boston, on Saturday. The record rides in practice having been made with but twenty to twenty-five pacemakers each, and thirty-two being the limit in their great fifteen-mile race, there is an excellent chance that the records of the world, both against time and in competition, will go by the board. Their contest Saturday will prove who is the best man, and should McDuffee win he will be an unbeaten man this season.

Nat Butler, A. C. Mertens, L. McFarland and O. L. Stevens, who will ride a five-mile team pursuit race as one of the star attractions of the annual race meet of the Penn Wheelmen, at the Tioga track, Saturday afternoon, July 9, are now in this city, the former at the Woodside Park track and the latter trio at Willow Grove. After the meet at the latter place, Monday, Mertens will transfer his quarters to Woodside, where he will train with his team mate, Butler. The principals in the star event of the meet—Henry Cissac, of France, and Charlie Church, of this city—who have been matched to ride a fifteen-mile paced race, are working out daily, back of pacing machines. The pacemaking outfit of the riders will be the best obtainable in this locality. This will be the first middle-distance race of any importance ever run on the Tioga track, and the riders engaged for the race are among the best in the country.

• • •

The following have been invited to act as officials of the Kenilworth Wheelmen's race meet at Woodside on the Fourth of July, Monday next: Referee, A. G. Powell; judges, Steven Rourke, E. A. Lally, Joseph Estoclet, A. Chancellor; timers, John Heishley, J. A. Mead, J. A. Heath, L. A. Hill; scorers, F. Smedley, C. McGee, A. J. Wallen; umpires, T. D. Haines, F. Boyd, F. McGrath; clerks of course, H. C. Alexander, G. Frankenfield; starter, W. Darrah; announcers, S. C. Boyer, P. C. Rosenberg.

• • •

There are over one hundred entries for the bicycle races at Tumbling Dam Park, near Bridgeton, N. J., on July 4, and it promises to be the biggest one day's meet ever held in South Jersey. There is much rivalry among Bridgeton wheelmen for a prize offered to the rider making the fastest mile upon the track in a sanctioned race this season. The track record is now 2.09 3-5, made by W. Le Roy Austin, of Tuckerton, last Fall.

A MILE IN 1.34 2.5.

McDuffee's Wonderful Performance at the Charles River Track.

Special Despatch to "The Press."

Boston, June 30.—Some limit may exist to the speed of the cycle riders of to-day, but the limit is unknown. Entirely unheralded and totally unexpected, Eddie McDuffie to-day rode one mile with a flying start in 1.34 2-5 at the Charles River track. This is three-fifths of a second under the world's record, held by J. Betts, of England. The great English rider took the world's record from McDuffee when the mark stood at 1.35 2-5, where it now stands as an American record. Of course the mile of McDuffie to-day cannot stand as an official record. It was not made under the conditions laid down by the L. A. W. The team paced McDuffee until 11 2-3 miles at an easy gait. He yelled for faster pace, and Manager Culver shouted to the team to give it to him. With a jerk the multicycle was under way. The team did the first third in 31 1-5, the second third in 32 15 and the third in 31.

CAPTURED $50,000 EVENT.

Rothschild's Filly Goletta Wins the Princess of Wales Stakes.

[illegible]

THE LATONIA RACES.

Cincinnati, June 30.—Pink Coat and Han D'Or, the two Derby winners, went down to defeat before the great 3-year old colt John Bright in the Himyar stakes at Latonia to-day. There were but three starters in the race, and John Bright was the outsider at 4 to 1. Han D'Or was always a favorite at 4 to 5, while 6 to 5 was the best price that could be had on Pink Coat. The race was at a mile and an eighth, and was run in the remarkable time of 1.53½. The summaries:—

[illegible]

SAILOR KING'S WINNING RUSH.

Best Out of a Good Field in the Spendthrift Stakes.

[illegible]

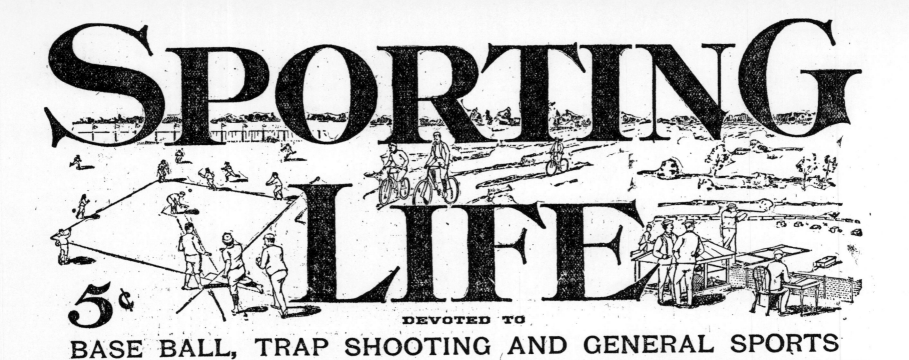

SPORTING LIFE

5¢

DEVOTED TO

BASE BALL, TRAP SHOOTING AND GENERAL SPORTS

VOLUME 33, NO. 8. PHILADELPHIA, MAY 13, 1899. PRICE, FIVE CENTS.

ONE MORE TRAMP?

WASHINGTON CLUB CONTEMPLATING TRANSFERS.

An Allegation That the Home Dates Will be Played on Foreign Grounds, a la Cleveland Last Season, Unless the Attendance Improves at Once.

Washington, D. C., May 9.—Editor "Sporting Life:"—The question of a wholesale transfer of championship games from Washington is the most important issue that now confronts the owners of [illegible] franchise. This has been [illegible] season at the capital, the lowest financially that the Wagners have experienced since they came into possession of the club. Affairs at National Park have reached such a dubious pass that it looks as if the only salvation for the owners is to repeat the policy inaugurated at Cleveland last season. Whether the Washington public would indorse a similar action on the part of the local owners is doubtful.

RESULT OF WAGNER'S POLICY.

But there are sound financial reasons for the removal of the team from Washington for the remainder of the season if the patronage does not increase on the return of the team to Washington after the engagement with Brooklyn and New York. That is the belief of President Wagner, who cannot see his way clear to carry on business at the home stand with the meagre receipts that passed the turnstile for the recent thirteen games played in Washington with Philadelphia, Boston, New York and Brooklyn.

WILL TELL THE TALE.

Mr. Wagner admits that some radical step must be taken in the matter of home games, unless the local patronage picks up. The financial exigencies of the club demand such a move, unless the public develops that interest that is inspired only by the sudden winning streak, which must come with the present series of games in New York and Brooklyn. Attendance at the games in Washington with Boston and Pittsburg next week depends on the result of the present series with New York and Brooklyn.

HANLON ADVISES MIGRATION.

Manager Hanlon, discussing the Washington situation, said: "I wanted Earl Wagner to transfer that Saturday game to Brooklyn, but he said he couldn't do it in justice to his patrons. It struck me that his patrons were so few that there were not enough of them to arouse a respectable kick. I would have paid him at least $1500 for his share of the receipts for that Saturday's game if we played in Brooklyn. If the Washingtons keep on losing he must, for his own financial salvation, transfer his games. Such a move might arouse the indignation of the Washington public, but what can Wagner do if the public do not turn out in sufficient numbers to give the team paying support?"

THE FINANCIAL VIEW.

Mr. Hanlon continued: "The Tebeau team last season drew paying multitudes to the games after their transfer. The present Senators, as a losing team, would scarcely be winners in a long stretch of games away from home now till the end of the season, for example. But even with the additional expense of railroad travel and hotel bills they would draw in at least five of the six cities of the first division. The Washington team is perhaps 50 per cent. cheaper than the Tebeau team of last year, and with such an economical outfit the local management could play to 40 per cent. less receipts, and still break more than even."

A Real Indian Team.

The Nebraska Indian Base Ball team, which is composed entirely of genuine red men, will begin their third annual tour on May 9. The Indians play their first came in Lincoln, Neb., with the University of Nebraska, and then tour East. They already have games booked through Iowa, Illinois and Indiana. They are anxious to secure games through Ohio and Pennsylvania for August and September. The manager is Guy W. Green, and he can be addressed at Lincoln, Neb.

HUGH DUFFY,
The Famous Captain and Outfielder of the Boston Team.

WHEELING WONDERING

Why Woodlock and Mazena Do Not Report as Ordered.

Wheeling, W. Va., May 7.—Editor "Sporting Life:"—A week's work on the home grounds gives us the record of two victories and three defeats. These figures would at the very least have been reversed had the team been made up as it was originally purchased from Springfield, but Whistler's treachery in stealing

WOODCOCK AND MAZENA

has made a weakness at short and second that has been the sole cause of our defeats. Those players have been awarded to us by the highest base ball tribunal, but they have not to date appeared on West Virginia soil, and we cannot understand the mystery. About half a dozen players have been tried at second, but only with varying success. As soon as we get the two players referred to on the team we believe it will strike a winning gait. All the other positions are well filled, and the batting of the team as a whole is good. The pitchers are doing first-class work, Crabill, Poole, Wells and Cummings being great favorites.

THE SUNDAY EXCURSIONS

given under the management of the Wheeling Club are proving very popular. Last Sunday a game was played at Canton, O., and to-day they are at Massillon. When a town sends big delegations to see games almost a hundred miles away it shows that the interest in the national game is at a high pitch. PICKWICK.

JIMMY CLINTON'S SON.

The Famous Father Sets the Young Future Great Right.

Brooklyn, May 7.—Editor "Sporting Life:"—In your last issue I see that you mention the fact of my son going to New Haven for his first professional engagement. He signed with T. L. Reilly the latter part of March, expecting to report early in May for preliminary work. You can imagine his surprise when he received a letter May 4 releasing him from his contract for the reason "that he had signed so many men in the last few days that he would have to cut down the list." This without ever giving him an oportunity of showing what he could do, and after his giving up a steady position so as to get in good shape by outdoor practice. If it had come two weeks earlier he could have gone to another club in the Connecticut League, which is now full.

I hope you will state the facts in the case in your next issue, so that managers will understand why he is at liberty to sign elsewhere, for they may think that New Haven has already tried and found him wanting, which will not be the case when once he has the oportunity of getting out professionally, and I ought to know a ball player when I see one. He has played second base and left field, the latter being his stronghold, and I say he is good enough for any minor league. Yours truly,

JAMES L. CLINTON.
370A Sixth avenue.

CINCINNATI CHEER.

THE REDS SHOWING IMPROVED FORM ALL 'ROUND.

Young Pitchers Put to the Test Successfully—Bancroft's Cuban Trip Scheme—Ewing to Give the No-Morning-Practice Idea a Trial.

Cincinnati, O., May 8.—Editor "Sporting Life:"—The Reds have shown considerable improvement in their all-round work during the past week. Particularly have they improved in batting. Steinfelt is now leading the team in this respect, and Quin is also now batting them out in his old familiar way. Jake Beckley, however, continues in hard luck. McPhee still suffers with his lame ankle, but McBride's injured knee is improving rapidly, and he expects to get into the game again within a few days. The Reds leave on their next trip on Monday evening of next week. They will visit Pittsburg, St. Louis and Cleveland in the order named.

TWO GOOD ONES.

It seems that in his new crop of pitchers for this season Captain Ewing has come upon two winners in the persons of Bill Phillips and "Noodles" Hahn. Phillips fairly earned his spurs in the game he pitched against Chicago. Hahn surprised even his most ardent admirers and put the doubting Thomases to rout by the splendid game he pitched against the St. Louis team on Friday. He pitched as masterly a game as one could wish to see, and beyond question earned himself a place on the regular team. Hahn shows improved form in every successive game. He has all the essentials of a star pitcher—speed, command, curves, a slow ball and nerve—and ought to be worked regularly in the box for Cincinnati.

A CUBAN TRIP.

Manager Bancroft is going to take a team of National League Stars to Cuba this fall. While in Chicago he was requested by Clark Griffin and Jimmy Calahan, of the Chicago team, to take charge of a base ball expedition to that country. Griffin and Callahan have a financial man who will furnish the money for the trip. Elmer Smith, of the Reds, has asked for a place on the team. Jake Beckley also wants to go. Manager Bancroft in 1879 took a team of professional players to Havana. Bannie was in charge of the celebrated Hop Bitters team that made the trip 20 years ago. It not only cleared expenses, but made a little money on the trip. If base ball would pay in Cuba 20 years ago it ought to be profitable now.

BOYLE'S STARTLING DISCOVERY.

Jack Boyle, the Phillies' old catcher and first baseman, underwent a surgical operation at Cincinnati on Thursday, for the purpose of endeavoring to regain the use of his arm. Dr. Walker, who performed the operation, found imbedded in Boyle's left shoulder, near the bone, the point of a knife blade. About six months ago Boyle was attacked by thugs and stabbed in the shoulder. The wound healed, but Jack lost the use of his left arm. He will soon be able to play ball again.

NO MORE MORNING PRACTICE.

Manager Ewing has decided to give the no-morning practice scheme a trial. Hereafter the players—that is, those who play every day—will not be asked to practice in the morning. They will warm up before the game, of course, but they will not be asked to waste the greater part of their strength making batting averages which count for naught, in the morning. If Ewing finds that the shelving of the continuous training scheme is a success there will be no more morning practice this season; but, on the other hand, if he finds that instead of having a good effect, it has a detrimental effect on the players, morning practice will be resumed.

Will Play For Pottstown.

Pottstown, May 4.—The Pottstown Base Ball Club will open the season May 13, and the following will probably comprise the team: Mock, first base; Gilbert, second base; H. Ritter, shortstop; Shellenberger, third base; S. Ritter, left field; Strong, centrefield; C. Shinehouse, right field; W. Fryer, catcher; pitchers, Rhoads, French, Reitnouer and J. Fryer.

THE DETROIT JOURNAL.

LAST EDITION. DETROIT, MICH., TUESDAY, JANUARY 29, 1901. TOMORROW--COLDER. PRICE TWO CENTS.

THE ORIGINAL CUBAN PATRIOT HAS ARRIVED.

REVIVALS TO BE HELD IN THE EMPIRE THEATER

Detroit Evangelical Ministers Unite in Conducting Them.

GENERAL CONFERENCE SO DECIDED TODAY

Some Objection Made to Use of an Opera House.

But the Final Decision Was Unanimous—Meetings Will Also Be Held in the Outside Districts.

There was a representative gathering of the ministers of the different denominations of the city in the Central M. E. church to attend the meeting called by the committee of the Pastors' union to consider projects for a great revival movement in Detroit.

The ministers spent an hour in prayer and at the conclusion, just as they were preparing to get to work, Dr. Boynton, seconded by Rev. W. B. Jennings, moved to exclude the press. The motion prevailed, Rev. W. F. Stewart, of the Mary Palmer church, and chairman of the M. E. preachers' meeting, being the only one to vote "no.", The reporters present left the room and the ministers settled down to work.

Recommendations from the committee were placed before them. These were to the effect that two weeks' evangelistic services should be held down town in some central place—the Empire theater was suggested—and that the city should be divided into districts in which contiguous churches should hold union meetings.

There appeared at first a rather decided feeling against the big central meeting.

"I think," said Rev. Marcus Scott, "that we want to do this thing quietly, without parade. Let's each rouse up our own churches so we can have them filled twice a day on Sunday."

Rev. F. C. O'Meara had suggested each church give up for the time being its own individual midweek services and join in with the union meetings, but this did not meet with favor either. Rev. W. F. Stewart contended that the prayer meeting was a most important service in the life of the church:

"What we must have," he said, "if this movement is ever to go through, is a spirit of greater consecration among the churches."

"We're getting a little wide of the point, I think, brethren," remarked Dr. Boynton. "Every preacher of the gospel is of course doing the very best he can in his own church, giving them the best that is in him. But we're not trying to get at the local churches. What we're trying to do is to get some plan for a federated movement whereby we shall reach non-church goers. We want to rouse the city. And what we want you to do now is to take the suggestions of the committee at par value, alter them if you please and fill them in in detail."

"I think the plan of having a meeting in the Empire theater is either too big or too little," said Rev. J. M. Barkley. "I don't know that what we want is a great popular meeting or meetings. I thought our idea last Thursday was to try to reach by personal work the merchants and manufacturers and rouse them to come to noon meetings or other church services. Perhaps the nights we are not busy in our own churches we might have evangelistic services somewhere, and during Lent or passion week we might have big down-town services."

Rev. W. H. Vincent thought the noon hour was too busy a one for the meetings to be successful and proposed 4 o'clock. He agreed with those who thought they should have some central point down town.

Rev. F. C. O'Meara contended that for the success of the plan meetings must be held at some place not known as a church.

"We want an impression to go all over this city like a thrill," he said. "We want to get people who don't go to church. Now if we advertise 'Meeting at the Empire theater tonight,' and just give the speaker's names, we'll get lots of people that never would go to a church. I tell you the sight of a united Christian ministry facing such an audience as we could gather there would be felt by the churches from end to end."

But the sound of the word theater was still a stumbling block for some.

"I want to ask you," said Rev. Marcus Scott to O'Meara, "how will it sound for us to be saying, 'meet me at the theater.'"

There was a general laugh and then the discussion switched on to whether the big meetings down town should be held before or after the district meetings and whether the Empire theater was not too large.

"I haven't been clear about any of the details of the plan," remarked Dr. George Elliott, "but one thing seems certain and that is the big meetings down town should be held first to create general interest. And I don't think the theater's a bit too large. We'll fill that all right and you know if once in a while there is a spare seat for a sinner, who comes late, it won't be a bad thing."

"There won't be any trouble about filling it," commented Dr. Curnick, "I'll have to hold my people back or you'll be having 500 of them down there. But it doesn't seem to me that it is quite worth all our while to do all this talking this morning to get after the bankers and merchants and manufacturers. The Y. M. C. A. does that sort of thing. There are other people we should reach."

Rev. J. M. Barkley told of the Chapman plan in 1893, and wanted to follow that now and get out in the districts to work first, finishing up with the coming down town part.

It was advanced several times that these meetings would interfere with local movements planned in the various churches, and it was always insisted by the committee that they intended every man should be free to do as he liked. Rev. John MacDowell thought that each church ought to be willing to give up something. That indeed it would be necessary for them to do so. But that whatever was done should be done now and done quickly.

Dr. MacLaurin advocated having meetings both afternoon and evenings. After a little more discussion Dr. Elliott moved the acceptance of the recommendations. Finally by a unanimous vote the recommendations were accepted and the committee instructed to arrange first for the two weeks' meeting in the Empire theater, if they found that place feasible, and then in the districts of the city. The committee was increased by adding one layman from each denomination. As it stands now it is: Revs. D. D. MacLaurin, N. Boynton, P. C. Curnick, J. MacDowell, W. H. Vincent, F. C. O'Meara, C. B. Newnan and Dr. James A. Post, Clarence A. Black, Aleander McVittie, C. W. Pickell, F. J. Webber and Frank Taylor. It was moved to allow any pastor absolutely prevented from attending to send a substitute.

COLDER TOMORROW.

Snow Tonight, With Clearing Weather and Brisk Winds Wednesday.

Temperatures today, as reported by the United States weather bureau in Detroit, were as follows:

6 a. m.	17°	11	19°
7	17°	12 noon	20°
8	18°	1 p. m.	21°
9	18°	2	21°
10	18°		

For Detroit and vicinity: Tonight, snow; Wednesday clearing, colder; winds brisk westerly Wednesday; min. tonight about 24 degrees and Wednesday night 6 degrees.

Barometer, 8 a. m., 29.867.

For lower Michigan: Snow tonight and probably Wednesday; colder Wednesday; brisk to high northwest winds Wednesday.

SUMMARY OF WEATHER CONDITIONS.

The temperature has risen slightly over the southwest and has fallen slightly elsewhere except over the Dakotas and the Canadian northwest and north of Lake Superior where it has fallen 8 degrees to 20 degrees. Much colder weather now appears to be developing over the northwest.

Light snow has fallen over the lake region, the upper Mississippi valley and over the northwest.

The conditions this morning are such that snow is expected to fall in this vicinity late this afternoon and tonight, clearing Wednesday, possibly 3 inches of snow will fall.

At 8 p. m. Monday snow covered the ground from Philadelphia north to Canada and northwestward to Minnesota in depth from 1 to 6 inches, except over upper Michigan where it is from 12 to 26 inches in depth. At the same time ice was from 3 to 14 inches thick throughout the lake region and from 14 to 22 inches thick over the northwest.

B. S. PAGUE,
Local Forecast Official.

DUE TO DANCE QUESTION.

BENTON HARBOR, Mich., Jan. 29.—Dancing has caused the downfall of Holy Trinity Episcopal church in this city. One faction wanted to dance and the other faction didn't. An eruption was the result and the pastor, Frederick Welham, left. The church is now closed on account of this dance war and it will probably not be reopened very soon.

STEWARDS ARE IN SESSION TODAY

D.J.Campau Protested Against a Suggestion to Place Detroit in Second Place.

CINCINNATI WANTS TO JOIN

But T. H. Griffin's Request May Not Be Granted.

The Grand Circuit Schedule Will Likely Be Settled This Afternoon—Twelve Horsemen Represent the Cities in the Circuit.

About a score of horsemen, stewards of the grand circuit, held their annual meeting in the Turkish room of the Cadillac today with D. J. Campau of this city in the chair. The following answered the roll call as representatives of the grand circuit associations mentioned: Detroit, J. H. Swart, D. J. Campau; Cleveland, W. G. Pollock, S. W. Giles; Columbus, Tom W. Garrett, C. Conrade; Buffalo, J. B. Sage, E. J. Trentor; Glens Falls, T. F. Cool; Readville and Hartford, C. M. Jewell; Providence, W. W. Dexter; Terra Haute, W. P. Ijams. New York was not represented, as there will be no circuit meting there this year, although there will be a running meet.

A representative of the New York State Fair association, with headquarters in Syracuse, made application for dates in the early part of September and vouched for the association's accepting any dates in this period the grand circuit might offer, holding the fair accordingly. The matter was referred to a committee. Syracuse will probably have dates offered her, but whether in the time limit suggested is not known.

T. H. Griffin, representing the directorate of the Oakley track in Cincinnati, made application for dates and admittance to the grand circuit. This matter was likewise referred to a committee. It seems that Mr. Griffin does not stand so well as he might with the powers of the grand circuit and the impression is that Cincinnati will be turned down.

When it came to arranging dates for the different associations constituting the circuit there was discord at once. In order to appease the cravings of Columbus and give the town a date to its liking it will be necessary for that city either to open the meeting or take a date away along in the season. The eastern tracks do not feel like waiving nything in Columbus' favor and D. J. Campau, as the head of the local association, protested about Detroit being second in the circuit. Detroit has always opened the grand circuit, the association here has done more for the circuit than any other and is the oldest in the combination, barring Cleveland. It was generally felt that Mr. Campau's objections to allowing Columbus to open the season were justified by these circumstances. As the stewards did not appear to be making any headway in the matter the whole question of dates was pushed aside until the gentlemen present had taken dinner with Mr.Swart, the meal being served at 2:30 o'clock.

BROCZKI IS STILL LIVING

But His Condition Is No Better and Death Is Only a Question of Time.

The condition of Charles E. Broczki, the man shot yesterday by Max Zientek, is reported no better and his death is just a question of time.

As yet the only charge against Zientek is assault with intent to kill, but after Broczki's death it will be changed to murder. The Pole takes his confinement stoically and seems to have not the slightest regret for the shooting.

Detectives Brooks and Lally, who have charge of the case, believe that Zientek will plead guilty when he comes to trial.

FUNERAL OF THE QUEEN IS REHEARSED

Osborne Pall Bearers Tug at a Dummy Coffin Containing Half a Ton of Sand.

PRINCES IMPERSONATED IN LONDON PARADE

Mounted Men Represent the King, Kaiser and Others.

The Eight Horses That Will Draw the Gun Carriage Bearing the Coffin, Drag a Truck of Equal Weight Through the Streets.

COWES, Jan. 29.—The outer coffin for the queen arrived last night. The non-commissioned officers detailed to carry the coffin rehearsed today with a dummy coffin filled with sand and weighing over half a ton.

LONDON, Jan. 29.—This morning there was a rehearsal along the route of the funeral procession. The eight Hanovarian horses which will draw the gun carriage took a heavily laden brake, estimated to be of the weight of the gun carriage and coffin, over the route. Numerous carriages followed and a number of mounted men, representing the foreign princes and others who will ride in the procession.

It has been arranged that the Eton boys will line the route from the Long Walk Gates to Windsor Castle, while the military Knights of Windsor will be on duty in the chapel during the funeral services.

It is now understood the funeral in London will be, approximately, as follows:

A sovereign's escort of 100 Life Guards, the massed bands of three regiments of Foot Guards; Field Marshal Earl Roberts and the headquarters staff; an army gun carriage with the body; the king, supported by the German emperor; the king of Portugal, and the other reigning sovereigns in the order of precedence; the dukes of Connaught and York, the equerries and aides-de-camp in attendance on royal personages; Queen Alexandra, the duchess of Saxe-Coburg and Gotha and other royal princesses, in four carriages, deeply draped, and in the rear of the procession, another sovereign's escort of 100 Life Guards.

It is estimated that 60 royal princes will participate in the procession.

As the funeral will be of a military character, there probably will be no pall-bearers, although possibly, at Windsor certain generals will act in this capacity while the coffin is being carried up the nave of St. George's chapel.

King Edward and the duke of Cambridge arrived in London at 3 o'clock this afternoon. A large crowd welcomed the king at Victoria station. His majesty will finally approve of the funeral arrangements during the course of the afternoon.

COWES, Jan. 29.—The king's order directing that the drapery of buildings be purple has created no little consternation. Many buildings here and in London and in other places are already covered with black. It will cause no end of expense to make the necessary alterations. In addition, the supply of purple is already getting short.

The main wing of Osborne house is expected to become the residence of Princess Beatrice in her capacity as governor of the Isle of Wight. The other part of the house will be reserved ior the king.

The duke of York is suffering from the strain of recent events and has been confined to his room since Thursuay. It is feared that he will be unable to take part in the ceremonies of Friday.

The only American wreath which has arrived at Osborne so far is one from Mrs. Syndey Everett of Boston, who is staying on the Isle of Wight. It is inscribed: "In token of lifelong veneration and reverence."

Gen. Sir Dighton Probyn, comptroller and treasurer of the household of the prince of Wales since 1877, is mentioned as likely to succeed Lord Edward Pelham-Clinton as master of the household. The office is in the personal gift of the king. Crown Prince Frederick of Denmark is expected to arrive in London tomorrow.

Prince Henry of Prussia sailed from Kiel yesterday on board the German battleship Baden, accompanied by the coast defense ship Hagen.

Prince George of Saxony is prevented by influenza from coming to the funeral. Prince John George will take his place.

Duke Albrecht will represent the king of Wurtemburg. The Crown Prince Ferdinand of Roumania is expected Thursday night in London.

The Orleans family will be represented by the duke of Chartres, younger brother of the late count of Paris; the duke of Alencon and the count of Eu, sons of the late duke of Nemours, between whom and the late queen in 1838, Louis Philippe, tried hard to arrange a marriage.

GEN. ALGER WAS OUT FOR A SHORT DRIVE

Gen. Russell A. Alger is slowly recovering from the effects of his late illness. He was out doors yesterday for the first time since he was taken ill. He was taken for a short ride and seemed to enjoy the crisp air. The general will be taken for a drive every pleasant day until he regains his strength.

PARLIAMENT MAY SOON BE DISSOLVED

Bad Drafting of the Act of 1867 May Make the Action Necessary

LONDON, Jan. 29.—The lawyers are still quibbling over technical points arising from the bad drafting of the act of 1867, by which Scotch, Irish and university members of parliament are excluded from the operation of that measure. Close constructionists—and L. V. Harcourt is one of them—assert that these members will be forced to seek re-election, and, since it is hardly credible that parliament can be partly dissolved, it follows that a general election will occur within six months. If this be true, the intent of the act of 1867 will be reversed, since the object aimed at was to prevent the dissolution of parliament in consequence of the death of a sovereign.

One point is in favor of the close constructionists. The faults in drafting the act were known, and the necessity for amending and rectifying it was recognized. It is reported that the ministers were intending ta do so this spring. Apparently it is not too late. The status of the Irish, Scotch and university members is good for six months in any event, and during that period the law can be amended.

POSSIBLE REVOLUTION IN FUEL PROBLEM

Important Experiments Are About to Be Made at Michigan Portland Cement Plant.

INVENTOR ASSERTS ONE TON OF COAL WILL DO WORK OF TEN

An Inexpensive Gas the Main Part of the Plan.

Holmes Brothers Own the Controlling Interest in the Device, and Are Taking No Chances Until the Scheme Shall Be Successfully Worked Out in Their Plant.

Preparations are being made at the plant of the Michigan Portland Cement company, Coldwater, for experiments which, it is hoped, will result in a revolution in the world's fuel problem.

It is asserted by the inventor that hereafter one ton of coal will be made to do the work which now requires 10 tons, thus conserving the world's coal supply to that extent. The reduction in fuel cost in any plant, under this process, it is asserted, will be at least one-half what it is at present.

The device which is relied upon to do this great work seems very simple, but it is one upon which the world's most noted scientists, it is said, have worked in vain for years. The tests about to be made represent the experiments and labors of 20 years on the part of the inventor.

Holmes Brothers of this city became aware some time ago of the existence of an experimental plant in Chicago by which, it was claimed, this wonderful saving in fuel could be effected. The inventor is a German named Engle, who took the precaution to patent his device in every country where there were patent laws. His Chicago plant seemed to work to perfection and was all right so far as anyone could detect. But Holmes Brothers had in mind other remarkable inventions which had turned out in time to be fakes, and, determined not to take any chances before investing, they insisted that Mr. Engle should set up an entirely new plant, in the big Coldwater factory, under direct supervision, and produce the same results as with the Chicago plant. To this Mr. Engle readily consented and he says he will soon successfully repeats the demonstration in the Michigan town.

As briefly described Mr. Engle's device is said ta be the combination, in just the right proportions, of oxygen and carbon to produce a gas which, fed into furnace over a small bed of coals, produces an intense heat.

There is a receiving and mixing chamber, into which ordinary air is received. By chemical action the oxygen is separated. From a very small stream of petroleum oil the carbon is obtained and the mixture perfected. The problem, it is claimed, has been to make this mixture in the right proportions and this is the secret of the process. From the mixing chamber the gas is conducted to the furnace.

The gas has been used, it is said, with great success in ore reduction by a process of evaporation. The heat applied to a retort, it is asserted by the inventor, causes all the metal parts of one to pass to another chember in gaseous vapors, there to be precipitated in a powder, and all within a couple of hours, while the present smelting process is a matter of days.

Enthusiasts who have witnessed the process say it will prove to be one of the world's greatest discoveries, one destined to be as important as the discovery of electricity and as far-reaching in its ultimate results. Holmes Bros. own a controlling interest in the device.

DUCHESS OF MARLBOROUGH MAY LIVE IN KING'S PALACE

Marlborough House, in Which the King Used to Live, May Be Sold to William K. Vanderbilt.

LONDON, Jan. 29.—There is a great deal of surmise as to what disposal will be made of the queen's late residence. Both the king and Queen Alexandra are devoted to Sandringham, so his majesty will probably retain that place; but it is thought Marlborough house will be given up. In the event of the duke and duchess of York not desiring to reside there it is considered likely that Wm. K. Vanderbilt will purchase the place for the duke and duchess of Marlborough, of which the duchess has long desired to gain possession.

REORGANIZATION OF AMERICAN BALL LEAGUE

Expansion Into a Major League is Completed at the Chicago Meeting.

SEASON WILL BE SAME AS LAST YEAR

New Plan Does Away With "Farming" of Players.

"Bunt" Hit May Be Abolished—President Johnson Says the League Will Go Ahead Regardless of Other Organizations.

CHICAGO, Jan. 29.—Reorganization of the American Baseball League, and its expansion from a minor to a major league, was completed at today's meeting of the magnates, and adjournment taken until some time in March.

At that meeting, which will be held in Philadelphia on a date to be announced later, the season's playing schedule will be given out by President Ban Johnson, and the committee on rules, consisting of Comiskey of Chicago, "Connie" Mack of Philadelphia, and McGraw of Baltimore, will make its report. The season will be of the same length as last year—140 days—although it is understood the opening date may be fixed a week later than last season.

The American League will submit contracts to its players on the plan advocated by the Players' Protective Association. This plan involves a graded system of contracts of three, four and five years—no player to be bound for a period longer than five years. At the end of that time he will be free to accept offers from any other club. The plan does away with the "farming" system, a clause in the contracts providing that "no player shall be traded ,farmed or sold to any other club, except with his consent."

So far as legislation on the playing rules is concerned no important change is looked for, although, possibly, action may be taken in the direction of abolishing the "bunt" hit. McGraw, however, has expressed strong opposition to any such action.

"The playing schedule will be given out at the March meeting," said President Johnson, at the close of today's meeting.

"The American League will go ahead regardless of any other organization, though, as far as that is concerned, we do not anticipate any serious conflict in the schedules."

Connie Mack, who was given the Philadelphia franchise, left this afternoon for the east, as did also most of the other eastern magnates. It was stated today that some Pittsburg capital is interested in the new Philadelphia team, but no confirmation of the report could be obtained.

Hugh Duffy, former Boston captain, has signed a formal contract to manage the Milwaukee American League team for the season.

From a Staff Correspondent.

CHICAGO, Jan. 29.—The American League adjourned sine die this afternoon. The schedule meeting will be held in Philadelphia March 1, and will adopt the schedule to be prepared by President Johnson. The schedule will be made up regardless of the National League schedule, the president saying he does not care if the two conflict. The demands of the Players' association were acceded to in every particular at the meeting today. A clause was inserted to the effect that no player shall be sold or traded unless he consents. A sliding three and five year reserve scale was adopted.

C. W. Somers was elected vice president. Somers delares that he will not leave Cleveland to make his home in Boston. He admits that the Boston grounds are far from being in condition as there is a lake on them at present and it will have to be filled up.

J. H. F.

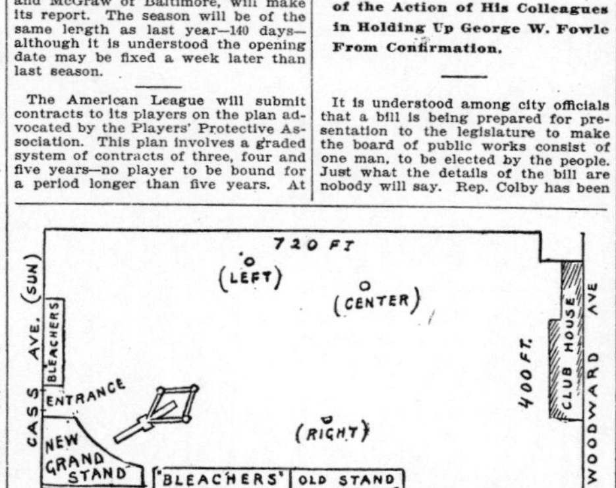

KOCH'S PLAN FOR D. A. C. BALL PARK.

KOCH'S PLAN FOR THE D. A. C. BASEBALL PARK

A. H. Koch, the prospective owner of the American Association franchise in this city, talked in an enthusiastic manner of his plans regarding this city, in interviews with Milwaukee reporters upon his return to that city Sunday. Mr. Koch confirmed the report that he had secured an option on the D. A. C. grounds, which he said would be the finest in the league. He says that the plans for the grand stand had already been prepared, and declared that it will be a credit to that portion of the city where it will be located. It will be of the most approved modern construction.

Mr. Koch also told the Milwaukee reporters that while Watkins was in Detroit he had laid out a plan for the stands and diamond.

A baseball man of this city, who is close to both Watkins and Koch, made the above rough sketch of the plans for the use of The Journal.

Railway Strike in Paris.

PARIS, Jan. 29.—A general strike of the employes of the underground railroads has been declared. The stations are occupied by troops. There is a general congestion of passenger traffic especially among shoppers and people traveling to and from business.

THEY WANT TO BUY THE MURPHY PROPERTY

Aldermen Magee and Houghton Are Working Up Scheme for Eighth Ward Park.

Ald. Magee and Houghton of the Eighth ward are working among the aldermen in behalf of their scheme for an Eighth ward park. There is not a park spot in the entire ward now, and the aldermen want the block bounded by Grand River, Commonwealth, Alexandrine and Avery avenues purhcased. It belonks to Simon J. Murphy and contains 26 lots. No figures have been obtained so far, because Mr. Murphy is out of the city.

TO ABOLISH THE PRESENT BOARD OF WORKS

A One Man Commission Proposed, to Be Elected By the People.

REP. COLBY IS LOOKING FOR INFORMATION

It Is Supposed He is Formulating a Bill For That Purpose.

Meanwhile Ald. Joy Complains of the Action of His Colleagues in Holding Up George W. Fowle From Confirmation.

It is understood among city officials that a bill is being prepared for presentation to the legislature to make the board of public works consist of one man, to be elected by the people. Just what the details of the bill are nobody will say. Rep. Colby has been asking the opinions of some of the city officials on such a bill.

Ald. Beamer, who is one of those who has been credited by some with a desire to see the board changed to a one-man board, says that he is opposed to the provisions of the proposed bill to make the one commissioner elective.

"My opinion is that the board, whether it consists of one man or three, should be appointed by the mayor, without confirmation by the council," declared Ald. Beamer today. "That would put the formation of the board into the mayor's hands absolutely and would make him responsible for what the board did."

Ald. Joy is one Republican alderman who has tired of the holding up of the mayor's nomination of George W. Fowle for the board of works. While he is hardly willing to say that he would bolt the Republican caucus, Mr. Joy has come to the conclusion that the opposition to Fowle is foolish.

"The only reason anybody has for opposing Fowle seems to be politics," said Mr. Joy this morning. "I can't see why they should act so. Fowle would make a good commissioner, I am sure, and I would like to see him confirmed."

A little later Mr. Joy stated that while he was not going to circulate a caucus call just yet, he did intend to get around and see the aldermen and sound them on the proposition of calling off the opposition to Fowle.

Some of the Republicans have made a "discovery," by which they profess to believe they can take the appointing power out of the hands of the mayor and name a board of works' commissioner themselves. The amendment to the charter passed by the legislature in 1895 provides that the mayor shall make appointments within 15 days after the expiration of terms or creating of vacancies. It goes on to say:

"Provided, that if the mayor shall make a nomination within said 15 days and the council reject the same, he may make another nomination or nominations, but not more than 15 days shall elapse between such rejection and new nomination."

The words "another" and "new" applying to nominations, some of the Republicans claim, preclude a renomination. They claim to have legal advice to that effect, and Ald. Beamer was around the city hall for some time this morning arguing that proposition to all-comers. He offered to bet that if the mayor did not send in a new name after Fowle's name is rejected tonight, the aldermen would make the appointment themselves.

Corporation Counsel Tarsney, who was consulted by the mayor when he heard what was on, emphatically declares that there is nothing in any such contention.

"The words 'new nomination,' mean another official act, that is all," he declared, "The aldermen have nothing to do with the name that is sent in."

Former Assistant Corporation Counsel C. D. Joslyn was even more emphatic in giving his opinion of the proposition from a legal standpoint.

"It's all nonsense," he declared, rather explosively. "That act was not meant to have anything to do with what nomination was sent in. It refers simply to other or new messages of nomination that the mayor is required to send to the council within the time limit prescribed."

The mayor himself is not inclined to pay any attention to the contention.

"I shall do just as I have said," he said this noon. "If the aldermen do not confirm Mr. Fowle tonight his name will be sent in again. There is no question of my right to send in his name as often as I please."

During the last century the center of population in the United States has moved from a point twenty miles east of Baltimore to western Indiana, a distance of 505 miles.

PATERSON MURDERERS GET THE LIMIT

McAlister, Death and Campbell to be Imprisoned 30 Years at Hard Labor.

KERR SENTENCED TO 15 YEARS' IMPRISONMENT

Judge Dixon Says the First Three Should Have Been Hanged.

The Judge Declares That if He Had Been on the Jury, He Would Have Voted to Convict Them of First Degree Murder.

PATERSON, N. J., Jan. 29.—Walter C. McAlister, William A. Death and Andrew J. Campbell, who were found guilty of murder in the second degree for the killing of Jennie Bosschieter, on October 18, 1900, by the administration of chloral and subsequent criminal assault, together with Geo. J. Kerr, who pleaded non vult contendre to a charge of criminal assault, were brought into the court of oyer and terminer here today for sentence by Judge Dixon.

McAlister, Campbell and Death were each sentenced to 30 years imprisonment at hard labor and Kerr to 15 years imprisonment at hard labor.

The sentence of all the men are the full terms of imprisonment which the law provides, but in the case of Kerr a fine of $1,000 might have been added.

In the court room were the father, step-mother and sister of Jennie Bosschieter who had been given seats where they could have a good view of all that transpired. A few minutes after court had been declared opened McAlister, Campbell and Death were brought in by deputy sheriffs and seated.

The proceedings began with a plea by Michael Dunn, one of the attorneys for the convicted men, for clemency for his clients. He urged that in the cases of Death and Campbell the question of their reformation was worthy of consideration by the court. Counsel also submitted, a petition signed by many citizens asking for mercy for Campbell, who had been known for many years to the petitioners as industrious, temperate and of good character. Ex-Judge Scott addressed the court in McAlister's behalf, urging good character and high family connections.

McAlister, Campbell and Death were then told to stand up. McAlister and Campbell looked extremely pale and Death had the appearance of suffering greatly under the strain.

Judge Dixon addressing the three prisoners said:

"You stand convicted of murder in the second degree. Had you been found guilty of murder in the first degree the punishment would have been death, but the leniency of the jury in the exercise of their lawful authority saved you from the gallows. We must administer laws as they are. It is true these sentences will destroy your lives, obliterating every prospect of an honorable existence among the people. The court cannot make any distinction but must sentence you for this crime.

"I trust the fearful consequences from this crime will help young men and young women of this community and point out to them that they cannot hope to secure happiness outside of virtue and honor. The sentence of the court is that each of you be imprisoned in the state prison at Trenton at hard labor for a term of thirty years."

The severity of the sentences was indicated by Judge Dixon yesterday after Kerr pleaded when he said that if he had been on the jury that tried them he would have found a verdict of murder in the first degree. Judge Dixon said that as far as Kerr was concerned the prosecutor had no evidence by which he could connect him with the drugging of Jennie Bosschieter. Consequently the charge of murder was eliminated from the indictment. The judge said that Sculthorpe, the hackman, was guilty with the others, but that he had come forward and told a true story of what had occurred on the night of the murder. On account of this action the prosecutor had very properly decided not to prosecute him.

STANDARD LIFE AND ACCIDENT PROMOTIONS

James S. Heaton Made Assistant Secretary and C. D. Harrington a Department Chief.

The largely increased business of the Standard Life & Accident Insurance Co. has made it necessary to create the office of assistant secretary. or this position the board of directors have seelcted James S. Heaton, for several years at the head of the company's claim department. Mr. Heaton is a graduate in law, having studied in the office of Wm. A. Moore and in the Detroit College of Law. He went south for a while after graduation and when he returned to Detroit took the position in the claim department, for which it was felt his legal education particularly fitted him. Mr. Heaton has a large circle of acquaintances.

Chas. D. Harrington, who came from Grand Rapids a year ago to take a position with the Standard as a home special agent, has also been promoted. He will hereafter be chief of the personal accident department. Mr. Harrintgon is well known throughout the state.

LATE LOCAL NOTES.

Most of the aldermen have signed a petition asking for the reappointment of Charles Hinkley as deputy oil inspector in Detroit.

Revival meetings are going on each night this week at the Simpson M. E. church. The pastor, Rev. Paul C. Curnick, will preach each night, and Rev. C. A. Heath, of Philadelphia, will sing Gospel hymns.

Rev. Robert Seymour, of the Bethel M. E. church, asks that no subscription for the benefit of that church be given to any one who does not bring a letter bearing the signature of Rev. W. F. Stewart and Rev. C. H. Perrin, president and secretary of the M. E. Preachers' meeting.

MANY INTERESTING BITS OF NEWS OF THE WORLD OF SPORTS

TENNIS EXPERTS GO TO MEADOW CLUB.

This Week's L. I. Tournament a Preliminary to "All Comers" at Newport.

ENGLISH CRACKS WILL AGAIN MEET YANKEES.

Doherty Brothers in the Doubles Are Scheduled to Engage the Fastest American Players.

With the completion of the international lawn-tennis matches last week, the experts begin to turn their attention to the National All-Comers tournament at the Casino courts, Newport.

This meeting is held a week later than usual this year, the opening play being scheduled for Tuesday, Aug. 19. This week's tournament is scheduled to the Meadow Club, of Southampton, L. I., for their annual invitation tourney. It is in the nature of a revival of the famous old-time Long Island championship.

It is on these courts that Sears, Slocum, Bob Wrenn and others whose names are woven into the history of American lawn tennis, won their first favors. And it is on the Meadow Club's faultlessly kept courts that the English trio—Dr. Joshua Pim and the Doherty brothers—will play to-morrow. They will be accompanied by nearly all of the top-class Americans, and the tournament will be in the nature of a preliminary to Newport.

Preparation for Newport.

The best American players have always looked upon the Long Island meeting as a tuning up for the national struggle. This is because the turf courts are always kept in excellent trim and afford opportunity for practice under the same conditions as prevail at Newport.

Judge Henry Howland has been more than successful this year in getting a large and representative list of men to compete for valuable prizes. The challenge cup and title was won by William A. Larned last year, and he will defend it against the winner of the tourney. He may have an opportunity of meeting William J. Clothier, the young Harvard man, who trimmed him so neatly at Longwood, and possibly Beals C. Wright, also of Harvard, who is a rival of Larned and has been only too anxious for a try with the national champion ever since they met in the finals at Newport last August.

Wrenn Brothers Entered.

Among the other men will be Bob Wrenn and George L. Wrenn, jr., Richard Stevens, Holcombe Ward, Edward P. Larned, Montgomery Ogden, Raymond D. Little, Frederick B. Alexander, Malcolm D. Whitman, the unbeaten national champion; Henry H. Whitman, his younger brother, and a host of men who closely approach the top class in point of skill.

The doubles matches in the Long Island meet should be productive of more than the usual round of clever sport. The Doherty brothers, former champions of England, and Ward and Davis, the international team, head the list. Then follow the Wrenn brothers, the two Larneds, who play extremely well together; Leo E. Ware and Beals C. Wright, or this pair may be changed to Wright and Clothier. Some of the veterans are expected to participate and the best-known of these men are Ford and Bob Huntington.

Teh tournament promises superb tennis.

Open Games of N. W. S. A. C. Next Saturday.

The New West Side A. C. will hold a set of games at the club grounds on Saturday, beginning at 2.30 P. M. The open events will be 70-yard run, 440-yard run, 600-yard novice, 1-mile run. With the exception of the novice race the events will be handicap.

PLAYERS WHO HAVE MADE RECENT BASEBALL HISTORY AND ESTABLISHED NEW RECORDS IN THE NATIONAL LEAGUE.

Capt. W Keeler

Capt. John J. McGraw

Victor G. Willis

P.J. Donovan

Capt. Jos. J. Kelly

Clarke

Hugh Jennings

Chesbro

Chesbro's Remarkable Pitching Astonishes the Oldest Fans, McGraw and His "Friends" the Umpires.

Much baseball history has been made during the present year, and, as is fit in the playing season at least, nearly all the important happenings have been engineered by players.

There is nothing the baseball enthusiasts take more interest in than the remarkable record being made by the Pittsburg Champions. Up to date they have done better than any team in the National League ever did in previous years. Now Pittsburg fans are calling on the Pirates to win at least one hundred and three games, and surpass the record of the Boston team, which won the pennant in the double season of 1902, with a record of 102 victories.

To Fred Clarke, manager-captain of the Pittsburg Club, much of the success of the Pirates is due. Clarke is known around the circuit as an aggressive player, who keeps his men on the jump at all times. Whether the Champions lead by ten runs, are even up with their opponents or are a few runs behind, it is all the same to Clarke, and he keeps the Pirates to their work.

The Pirates' leader has a sharp tongue and sharp spikes. He does not hesitate much to use either on opposing players. Within two years he has had personal encounters with Cupid Childs and Fred Tenney as the result of collisions on the bases.

Chesbro's New Pitching Record.

"Happy Jack" Chesbro, the star of the Pittsburg twirling staff, has unquestionably made a new record in the pitcher's box. He has pitched twenty games, of which but three were lost. His record of forty-eight consecutive innings without a run being scored off his delivery is the wonder of the season. Greminger, of Boston, broke Chesbro's streak in the forty-ninth inning. Since then "Happy Jack" has pitched in twenty-six innings without a run being scored by the opposing batsmen. Therefore, up to the last Pittsburg game at the Polo Grounds, Chesbro had pitched seventy-five innings with only one run scored against him. He has pitched three games against Brooklyn and shut them out by 5 to 0; 4 to 0 and 3 to 0.

Victor Willis, of the Boston Club, has taken part in more games than any National League twirler. His record of twenty-eight games has only been equalled by Cy Young, the Old War Horse, now pitching for the Boston-American League team.

No magnate, manager or player has been more in the public eye during the last month than John J. McGraw, the manager of the New York club. First of all, McGraw's signing with New York created a sensation. Then he and Joe Kelley pulled off the Baltimore deal, which hurt the American League much more than Ban Johnson and his supporters are willing to admit.

McGraw and the Umpires.

McGraw occupies the unique position of being the only ball player in this wide land who under any circumstances must not open his mouth in objection to an umpire's decision. McGraw has declared that the change from what he considers biased and incompetent umpires in the American League to men who understand their business has taught him a lesson, and he will not fight the judges of play, as he formerly did. Since this declaration the hammers on the American circuit have been poised ready to drop on McGraw's head. The delegates from Hammer Valley are chafing under the restraint. McGraw's friends hope he will not give them the opportunity they are so anxiously waiting for.

Joe Kelley, formerly of Baltimore and Brooklyn, now manager-captain of the Cincinnati team, has put new life into the Reds, and is likely to make them a formidable organization.

A Cincinnati writer has this to say of Kelley:

"That Joe Kelley will make a big difference in the Cincinnati team seems assured. He is a leader because he can set a pace which, if the other players can follow it, is bound to result in a winning combination. Furthermore, Kelley has been placed in charge of a fair ball team under all circumstances and a mighty good one in the present National League race, which really has but one first-class ball team in it and that is Pittsburg. Kelley classes with the stars of the profession. There is no way getting around that. He is a natural ballplayer, and as he was a member of five championship teams in the big league he must unquestionably have gathered enough ability to manage a team and keep it up to date in its methods."

Keeler a Popular Player.

Everybody knows Eddie Keeler and what he can do at the bat and on the field. It is his success as captain to the Brooklyn team that has gathered new laurels during the present season for the idol of the Brooklyn fans. Keeler's never-failing good-nature, coupled with his ability as a ball player, have made him one of the most popular players in the country with that portion of the public that attends ball games.

Hughey Jennings, leader of the Philadelphia team, has not had the success this season that attended him in 1901. The wholesale desertion of players of the ability of Delehanty, Cross, Flick, Donahue and Orth have left Jennings with a team that hardly possesses minor league ability. In Philadelphia those who work hard for the American League have taken advantage of the Phillies' slump to pound Jennings on every possible occasion.

The surprise of the National League season has been the splendid work done by the St. Louis Cardinals. Nobody begrudges Patsy Donovan the credit for having made the Cardinals the formidable aggregation they are to-day. Their recent two out of three victories from the Pirates, three out of five from New York and an even break with Boston shows how the Cardinals are working.

When Burkett, Heidrick, Wallace, Padden, Harper, McGann and others jumped the St. Louis Club last winter they left Donovan with just three players besides himself—Kruger, Ryan and Murphy—neither of whom is particularly strong. Nothing daunted, Donovan built up the team that is now playing as good ball as any club in the League.

WOMEN GOLFERS AT HARD PRACTICE.

All Looking Forward to the National Championship in October.

MISS HECKER AT WORK IN SCOTLAND.

With Miss Griscom She Is Studying Under the Best Professionals of That Country.

The women golfers of the country are active practising for the annual championship, which takes place in October upon the links of the Brookline Country Club, near Boston.

Since the first women's championship was played in this country, 1895, at the Meadow Brook Hunt Club links, the honor has been held by a metropolitan district woman with the exception of 1900, when it was won by Miss Francis Griscom, of the Merion Cricket Club of Philadelphia. Miss Griscom had spent the greater portion of the season on Scottish links under the best of foreign instruction, and she proved a complete surprise to the home talent.

Miss Griscom thoroughly absorbed the information she received abroad, and although she did not qualify last year, she is in Europe again this year under the instruction of the best of the famous professionals. In fact, Miss Genevieve Hecker, the present amateur woman champion, has become wise, and is now enjoying the wilds of Scotland, in company with her brother.

Miss Hecker Takes Warning.

Being beaten by Mrs. Edward A. Manice in the Women's Metropolitan Golf Association annual championship, played this season over the Essex County Country Club links, seems to have brought Miss Hecker to the belief that, although still the national champion, her form may be improved.

So many excellent women golfers came to the front last year from all parts of the country that the women from the metropolitan district were taken completely by surprise, and those who qualified each year were completely snowed under. Such experts as Miss Frances Griscom and Miss Ruth Underhill, the respective champions of 1900 and 1899, did not ever qualify in the first sixteen. Only three local women got within the charmed circle and Miss Hecker, who eventually won the championship, was the only one of them who survived the second round, while Mrs. N. Pendleton Rogers was the only other local player to get through the first round.

Mrs. Manice, of the Lenox Golf Club, who expects to win the championship this year, is training diligently for the event, and she is playing faultless golf this season.

There are others, however, with championship aspirations who dare not be overlooked. Chicago has two great players, Miss Bessie Anthony, Glenview Golf Club, and Miss J. Anna Carpenter, Chicago Golf Club. They are both brilliant players, and while Miss Carpenter just missed qualifying last year, she is considered one of the best women golfers in the West. Miss Anthony, who is the next greatest star of the West, and of whom much is expected, qualified last year and lasted until the second round, when she was put out by Miss Margaret Curtis, Essex County, Boston, who qualified at 97, tied with Miss Lucy Herron, Cincinnati; Mrs. E. A. Manice, Lenox, and Miss M. B. Adams, Wollaston.

Miss Curtis Is Boston's Hope.

Boston pins its faith on Miss Margaret Curtis. She was the runner up to Miss Griscom in 1900, after defeating Miss Beatrix Hoyt in a sensational match by 1 up in 20 holes in the semi-finals. Last year she beat Miss Pauline Mackay, Oakley Country Club, in the first round, and Miss Bessie Anthony, Chicago's star, in the second round by 1 up in 19 holes. She was beaten, however, by Miss Herron, Cincinnati, in the semi-finals.

With thirteen outside women qualifying in the last championship, it shows distinctly that the women in other parts of the country are making rapid progress in the game and that the championship is an open question. Miss Genevieve Hoyt is an excellent golfer, but she is not invincible, as was demonstrated by her defeat in the Metropolitan. She won the championship of that organization twice in succession and the national championship once, which is quite enough glory for anybody. Miss Beatrix Hoyt won the championship in 1896, 1897 and 1898, but she has scarcely been heard of since.

Arcanum Wheelmen Go to Coney Island To-Day.

The Royal Arcanum Wheelmen will hold a run to Coney Island. Members will be allowed the privilege of escorting their women friends. The start will be from the club-house at 10 A. M.

NEWS OF THE FUTURE GREAT BASEBALL PLAYERS.

Wanted, three good all-around players, sixteen years of age. Address Frank Bohne, No. 60 Clifton place.

* * *

An outfielder would like to join a uniformed team averaging from seventeen to nineteen years of age. Address Alex. Hesse, No. 150 Central avenue, Brooklyn.

* * *

An outfielder would like to join a team averaging fifteen to sixteen years of age, playing Sundays and holidays. Uniformed team preferred. Address James Hanley, No. 1238 Third avenue.

* * *

Aug. 3 the Clairmonts played the Orchard F. C. The score was a tie at the ninth inning, when the umpire called the game on account of darkness. We would like to hear from the Clark F. C., the Dexters and the Mascot A. C. for games. Address Sol. Finkelstein, No. 75 Forsyth street.

* * *

Carsons claim a game from the Monicas for non-appearance. They have all September dates open for team averaging from fourteen to fifteen years of age. Would like to hear from a manager not under nineteen years of age. Address Joseph Handler, No. 501 East Seventy-third street.

* * *

Florodoras will change their name to the Falcons. They would like to arrange games with teams averaging fifteen to sixteen years of age. Address W. Luken, No. 451 Hudson street.

* * *

Seneca Junior A. C. have given H. Hess his ten days' notice. They would like to hear from two players. Address Seneca Junior A. C., care of J. McGlone, No. 420 West Forty-fifth street.

* * *

Hustler A. C. would like to arrange games with teams averaging sixteen years of age, barring none. They line up as follows: J. Fitzpatrick, right field; J. Burke, centre field; J. Walker, third base; A. Semmon, second base; C. Johnson, shortstop; C. Euster, first base; T. Carey, catcher; J. Coleman, pitcher; J. Hefferan, left field. Address Hustler A. C., No. 535 West Thirty-second street.

* * *

St. Teresa Juniors would like to arrange Saturday and Sunday games with all teams averaging from thirteen to fifteen years of age. The Volunteers and St. Agnes Juniors preferred. Games to be played on our grounds or at Prospect Park. Address challenges to Peter Lavelle, No. 518 Park place, Brooklyn.

* * *

Pirate F. C. would like to arrange games with teams averaging thirteen to fourteen years of age. They would like to know if game with Council Juniors for Aug. 16 holds good. For games address R. Christensen, No. 823 Melrose avenue.

* * *

Pitkin Juniors would like to meet the Young Magnolias at our grounds. Average eleven to twelve years of age. Would like to hear from the Essex Juniors if game for Aug. 17 is O. K. Address David Leny, room 813, No. 116 Nassau street.

* * *

Young Monitors claim a game by 9 to 0 from the Orchard Juniors because of non-appearance. They would like to arrange games with teams averaging eleven to thirteen years of age, Young Monarchs preferred. Address Abe Cohen, No. 139 Division street.

* * *

Schulman Juniors would like to arrange games with teams averaging nine to eleven years of age. They line up as follows: S. Gans, shortstop; W. Aronson, left field; M. Cohen, centre field; J. Splain, second base; A. Holtz, third base; D. Dukoff, first base; A. Cohen, catcher; S. Morris, pitcher; H. Blumfeld, right field. Address S. Morris, No. 135 Canal street.

* * *

Riverside F. C., of Harlem, would like to arrange games on their grounds with teams averaging seventeen years of age for side bets. They have Aug. 17 and 24 open, A. M. and P. M. Address George Holston, No. 121 Twelfth avenue; telephone 318 Harlem.

* * *

Two good all-around players would like to join a team averaging from fifteen to seventeen years of age. Can play Saturdays, Sundays and all holidays. Address, or call between 7 and 8, Robert Ibe, No. 307 West Forty-third street.

* * *

Blue Bells would like to hear from a few players thirteen to fifteen years of age. They would also like to hear from the Vestry, Oronoke, Spalding A. C., Red Stars, Republics and other teams. Address J. Ryan, No. 203 West Sixty-seventh street.

* * *

White Clover Juniors would like to hear from a few all-around players. Would also like to book games with teams averaging from twelve to fourteen years. Address M. Lewis, No. 348 East Eighty-seventh street.

* * *

Tip Tops would like to hear from a good catcher and a fast outfielder. They must be good players. Address S. Caughey, No. 484 West Broadway.

* * *

Ivorys would like to arrange games with teams averaging fourteen to fifteen years of age. They line up as follows: J. Dundon, c.; H. Hildebrand, p.; F. Healy, 1b.; D. O'Brien, 2b.; J. Henry, 3b.; P. Jackson, ss.; J. Sullivan, lf.; P. Dunwoodie, cf.; H. Keleher, rf. For games address H. Keleher, No. 218 East Ninety-eighth street.

* * *

Ragtime Juniors would like to arrange a game with the Pierce B. B. C. for a side bet of $5. They have the following dates open: Aug. 24 and 31; also all Sundays in September. We are a uniformed team. Address Tom Korrbin, No. 421 East Twenty-fifth street.

* * *

Dooin Juniors defeated the crack Dayton team by 7 to 6. They claim championship. For games with teams averaging twelve to thirteen years of age address A. Buckley, No. 1319 Third avenue.

* * *

Lafayette A. C. will play the young Monitors on Aug. 17. They would like to arrange games with teams averaging ten to thirteen years of age. They would like to hear from the following teams: Black Diamonds, Columbia Juniors, Standard B. B., Orchard Juniors. Address all challenges to Young Feinberg and Young Esser, managers, No. 60 Essex street.

* * *

Bradford A. C., of South Brooklyn, would like to know if the games with the Claremont F. C. of Jersey City and the Kennedy A. C. of New York are good. Address F. Low, No. 204 Twenty-sixth street, Brooklyn.

* * *

Osceola Juniors defeated the Elnido Juniors by 18 to 15. The Osceola Juniors would like to arrange games with teams averaging twelve years of age. Would like to hear from the Young Powhatans. Address Wilfred Patterson, No. 112 East One Hundred and Fifteenth street.

* * *

Falcons would like to arrange games with teams averaging fourteen years of age. Brooklyn or Bronx teams preferred. Games to be played at Falcon grounds. Would like to hear from a good pitcher. Address W. Meyer, No. 354 East Eighty-seventh street.

* * *

Hustler A. C. would like to arrange games with uniformed teams averaging sixteen to seventeen years of age, Belmont Juniors of downtown, Romes, St. Pauls, Waltons and Orientals preferred; also Paulist Settlement. Address Thomas Burke, No. 535 West Thirty-second street.

* * *

Sumner A. C. has the following dates open: Aug. 16, 17, 24, 31, Sept. 4, 5, 12, 18, 19 and 26. They would like to arrange games with the Howards, Brightons, Empires, College Point A. C., Pearsalls, Star A. C., Marquettes, Little Falls and Peekskills. Address Charles Hickok, No. 13 Sumner avenue, Brooklyn.

* * *

Glenwoods have open dates. They would like to hear from the following teams: Cedars, Tenneys, Manhattan F. C., St. Alphonsus, Everett College, Laurel A. C., Skellys, Howards, Monarch A. C., Lenox A. C., Suburbans and Bronxes. Expenses paid for ten players. Address E. Gohrmann, No. 132 Steinler street, Astoria.

* * *

Parker Juniors would like to arrange games with a team averaging ten to twelve years of age. They line up as follows: Doyle, p.; White, c.; Shea, 1b.; McLoughlin, 2b.; McKenna, 3b.; Boundy, ss.; McCormack, lf.; C. Healy, rf.; R. Healy, cf. Address Robert White, No. 412 Greenwich street.

NOTES OF THE DIAMOND.

Pittsburg, Brooklyn, Boston, Chicago and Cincinnati are above their percentages of last season.

* * *

In 33 games Lajoie, playing for the Cleveland club, accepted 196 out of 199 chances—only three misplays. It is one of the most remarkable fielding records ever made.

* * *

It has been figured that the Pittsburg club was clear financially on the season by July 25, and that 400,000 spectators had seen the Pirates play up to that time.

* * *

Pittsburg fans are calling on the Pirates to win at least 103 games this season and excel all records. The record for won games in a season is now 102, made by the Bostons in the double season of 1892.

* * *

Joe Kelley says: "With the interests of the American League at heart Ban Johnson raised his own salary to $7,500 per year, and for a paltry couple of hundred dollars allowed Joe Cantillon, the best umpire in the business, to leave the American League."

* * *

Pitcher Wiley Piatt predicts that within a short time it will be necessary to put the pitcher's box several feet further back. He claims the twirlers are gradually gaining the ascendency in the endless duel between batter and pitcher. The frequency of small score games sustains Piatt's contention.

* * *

Long, Tenney and Carney are the only Boston Nationals signed for next season. Willis and Pittinger have refused to sign, and it is believed they have been captured by the American League.

* * *

In spite of the fact that the fans jolly "Orator" O'Rourke, he is still a first-class catcher, and few runners steal second on him. He has done much for the Connecticut League, and it is to be regretted that there are not more like him in the business.—Springfield Union.

* * *

That O'Neil battery, of St. Louis, has beaten the Pirates three times this season. This is a feat that no other battery in the country has accomplished. And Donovan was about to release both John and Mike.

* * *

"It won't cost you nothin' and we'll hand you something nice to come."

This is about the way Ban Johnson is putting his voice through a knothole in the fence between the two big leagues as he talks to President Barney Dreyfuss, of the Pittsburgs, trying to persuade him to leave his dollars and come over into the other yard, where a cake and lemonade layout is promised.—Pittsburg Dispatch.

LOCAL GOLFERS AT WORK FOR AUTUMN TOURNEYS.

A new record of 76 has been made for the Shinnecock Golf Club links by A. L. Ripley, Oakley Country Club, the left-handed player who defeated Walter J. Travis in the Shinnecock tournament of 1893.

* * *

R. C. Watson, jr., has set a lively pace for the men who will compete in the annual tournament of the Westbrook Golf Club, which is to be held this year Sept. 10, 11 and 12, as he has made a new amateur record for the course of 77.

* * *

William Holabird, jr., who was suddenly taken sick with typhoid fever the first day of the amateur championship at Glenview, is in a critical condition at present, and it is doubtful if he will recover. He is considered the most expert golfer in the West.

* * *

The Deal Beach Golf Club has arranged an attractive schedule of events for the month of August, and it is the intention to hold an invitation tournament Sept. 4, 5 and 6.

* * *

One of the most progressive golf clubs in the country is the Ekwanok Country Club, of Manchester, Vt., which is made up largely of metropolitan district players who are summering in the mountains. The club will hold four open tournaments within the next six weeks.

* * *

The Harbor Hill golfers felt like novices when they were beaten at Englewood by 39 to 1. The change of courses was too much for them.

* * *

A new record of 78 has been made for the Van Cortlandt Park links by Gilman P. Tiffany, the Powelton Golf Club expert, of Newburg. This clips five strokes off the professional record made by Harry Vardon.

* * *

The Innis Arden golfers feel greatly chagrined over their defeat at the hands of the Apawamis Club, at Rye, as 28 to 0 is more than they bargained for.

* * *

The Baltusrol Golf Club has closed its course for the month of August, as have the Richmond County Country Club and the Richmond Hill Golf Club. Morris County has compromised by playing no competitions and using temporary greens for practice.

* * *

While the Eastern Parkway Golf Club is a comparatively new organization, it is composed of some very enthusiastic golfers.

* * *

From all appearances, this is going to be one of the liveliest fall seasons the golfers have yet experienced.

* * *

The Long Isand Golf Association has proved a success, and next year there will be double the number of clubs in the organization.

* * *

Ardsley will join the Hudson River Golf Association next year, and possibly a point will be strained to make room for the St. Andrew's Golf Club, whose links are only a few miles back from the river.

* * *

The Crescent Athletic Club's eighteen-hole course was never in better condition than it is at present.

* * *

There is a movement on foot to organise a golf association among the exchanges of New York City. The Stock, Cotton and Produce Exchanges have well-formed organizations, and it is now up to the Coffee and Consolidated Exchanges to fall in line. There are many good golfers in both bodies.

ARCHERS TO COMPETE.

At Twenty-fourth Annual Meet of National Association.

Devotees of the old and manly sport of archery will have an opportunity to indulge in their favorite pastime at the twenty-fourth annual target meeting of the National Archery Association, to be held Aug. 13, 14 and 15 at Mountain Lake Park, Maryland.

The programme comprises five events for women archers and the same number for men. The chief competition will be the National team round, flight shooting, ninety-six arrows at fifty yards in both the women and men's classes. Medals and trophies will be awarded in all the competitions.

POLO PLAYERS MOVE TO NARRAGANSETT.

Narragansett Pier will be the scene this week of polo contests, following the sport which closed at Saratoga yesterday.

There are three cups at stake, the Narragansett, Rhode Island and Point Judith cups, the last named annually resulting in a fierce struggle. In 1899 it was won by Westchester, Myopia in 1900 and Bryn Mawr in 1901. This contest is without handicaps and several of the teams, including Bryn Mawr, Rockaway, Myopia, Dedham and Lakewood will have a look in.

From Narragansett the polo men go to Newport, where they will play from Aug. 21 to 30.

NEWS OF TENNIS EXPERTS IN SEVERAL FIELDS.

Another year will witness playing rules the same in every particular between the two great tennis-playing nations, England and America.

* * *

Spectators at the international competition claimed that two single matches at once in front of the grand stand was confusing. It was also a source of trouble to the umpires, who got scores mixed. This method is not to be tried in future events.

* * *

Society regretted that Miss Anna Sands could not be induced to enter a tournament with Miss Marion Jones and Miss Elizabeth Moore. She is very near their class in the handling of a tennis racket.

* * *

Larned's back-hand stroke is invincible when he is in form. Out of condition it is his worst play, and works his defeat.

* * *

Putting up cups for tennis contests is one of the philanthropic fads of Col. John Jacob Astor. Another trophy for the Nationals at Newport is rumored as contemplated by him.

Beals C. Wright has trained faithfully to beat William A. Larned the next time they meet. According to his friends, Wright will surely win, and is considered the safe end of a wager for the betting men.

* * *

Capt. W. H. Collins, of the English team, has expressed his satisfaction at the impartiality of the spectators during the matches so far played in this country. During the Longwood tournament this feature was particularly noticeable, and while patriotism continually asserted itself, the Britons got their full share of applause.

* * *

The defeat of Larned by W. J. Clothier, at Longwood, demonstrated the old story of an old and experienced player succumbing to a younger and fresher opponent.

* * *

It was estimated by some that nearly three thousand persons saw the English players contest on the Longwood courts during their first matches in this country.

* * *

Joshua Pim, the ex-champion of England, referred to as the "grand old man of tennis," is thirty years of age.

* * *

Sam Chase, Victor Elting, Everts Wrenn and J. A. Ryerson are included in the entries for the Onwentsia tournament, which starts on the Chicago courts to-morrow.

The Whole Country Congratulates Champions Through The Dispatch

TWENTY-SIX YEARS OF BASEBALL

By FRANK B. M'QUISTON.

PITTSBURG has had baseball in spots for 26 years. Beyond that limit the mind of the ball fan wandereth not. Four times have we taken second money in the race and now twice have we made them all look foolish by taking all the money. It was in the spring of 1876 that the game now acknowledged as the national sport first took a firm hold here. The Zanthers was a salaried team and a strong one. It made war on Wheeling and towns in Ohio. The success was marked and backers of the game the next season formed what was known as the Alleghenies and brought the late lamented Jimmy Galvin to this place. From this time on the rise of baseball was marked. The Alleghenies were in the Inter-State League and took second place, being beaten out under the wire by a Canadian team. In 1878 the Alleghenies entered the American Association, where they remained until 1888, when they entered the National League, where they have been ever since.

It was not until 1882, however, that the game was taken seriously here. Then it was that figures were kept on every move in the game. The contests became hard fights and interest was awakened and it has never been permitted to wane. In 1886, the last year spent in the American Association, we took second place.

Brotherhood Year Disastrous.

Baseball in Pittsburg received a heart blow in 1890—Brotherhood year. Many of the country's best players combined to run a league of their own and the attraction here was well patronized. It was demonstrated, however, that Pittsburg cannot support two clubs, for the National League club of this season was put a poor apology, while the Brotherhood team which located at Exposition Park was strong and had many popular players in the ranks.

The National League team was owned by J. Palmer O'Neil, who it is said lost $60,000 on the season. The club this year made at least two world's record marks which will stand for all time. They lost more games than did any club before or since and they played to the smallest crowd that ever saw a professional contest. The team lost 114 games and won 23, this season losing out on the race for last place in the last game of the season which they lost to Cincinnati. On one occasion but 21 people saw a game between Boston and Pittsburg here. It was a fast game, too. The Gumbert brothers of Pittsburg opposing each other. Ad pitching for Boston, Will for Pittsburg. Pittsburg won 1 to 0. It was after this game that J. Palmer O'Neil made his famous offer to pay the carfare of the entire audience. He loaded them all in one car and paid the conductor $1.10 for the 22, including himself.

George (Doggie) Miller had charge of the National League club this year and during the season he had more than 60 different players under contract. It was the custom of the club then to pick up young players in each city visited, play them during that particular series, then drop them until the show came that way again. This was permissable under a ruling of the league allowing a club manager to try a man five days before notifying the league. It was a good way to save carfare for a large team and in these days there was not much money coming into the treasury. So bad did things become as the season wore on the games scheduled for Pittsburg were transferred to other cities. For a time after the disasterous season of 1890 closed it seemed that baseball had received a blow from which it would scarcely recover but time, the great healer of many things, helped in this case too.

It was in 1893 that Pittsburg became delirious with baseball fever. There was a fearful battle for supremacy between Boston and Pittsburg, and the people from the East won out. Up until that year Pittsburg had never been suspected of having a look-in. The town was looked on by owners of other clubs as a good gate receipts village, but nothing to fear in the playing line. It remained for A. C. Buckinberger, now manager of the Boston National League team, to push Pittsburg up close to the king row. With Beckley, Bierbauer, Glasscock, Lyons, Smith, Van Haltren, Donovan, Stenzel, Ehret, Killen, Gumbert, Miller and Mack and others of less fame Pittsburg gave Boston a fearful race. Cleveland was as usual our Nemesis. The Ohio people seemed able to win from no one but Pittsburg, and we could beat her only with Ehret in the box. It remained for the despised Louisvilles to give Pittsburg the toss which worked our ruin. The Colonels had not won a game in weeks before coming here on their last trip of the season. We were closing rapidly on Boston, and as five games were scheduled with Louisville it looked certain that we would pass the Beaneaters in the stretch. That the lowly Louisvilles would do anything to us was not dreamed of, yet they took a brace and in three short, sad days beat us five straight games. This broke the hearts of Pittsburg fans, for three of the five games would, all things breaking even thereafter, have won the pennant for Pittsburg. Boston, with Charlie Nichols in the center, got away with us and took first place, Pittsburg second.

How the Championship Was Won.

In 1900 the fans got the fever bad. Again did the Pittsburg chase the leaders under the wire and but for some unfortunate breaks in luck might have won the flag. It was seen by the fans that there was something more to the Pittsburg team than had ever before been in uniform in Pittsburg. The Louisville contingent, which had played to poor houses when on Kentucky soil, braced up on seeing they were appreciated in Pittsburg, and the close of the season of 1900 saw fast ball. The winter months were put in by the cranks figuring out the race for the next season, and when Pittsburg lined up good and strong she was at once tipped as a good thing to play.

The season of 1901 was a remarkable one. Pittsburg took the lead early and was beaten out of first place but once, that on July 4, when Mathewson and the rest of the New Yorks beat Pittsburg at the opening game in Exposition Park. This beat us out of first place, but after eating dinner the Pittsburgs, now after the pennant, gave New York the foot, climbed back into the driver's seat and set the pace from that time until the end of the race.

The fierce playing of the Pittsburgs in that season was considered unusual because somewhat unexpected. It was thought early in the season that Clarke's youngsters were playing beyond their speed and that sooner or later they would trip up.

"Wait until they come East!" was the cry from over the mountains as the sound of the file grating on spikes was heard in New York, Brooklyn, Boston and Philadelphia. The whole baseball world looked on as Pittsburg slid over the hill and down into the camp of the enemy—the East—which has been the grave of many hopes of Western clubs. Never will that trip of the Pittsburgs be forgotten by the East. Like a band of demons the team after the championship crashed into the strong Eastern clubs mowing them down like wheat. Thirteen games won, one tied and one lost was the record which they brought back over the hills, and the baseball world gazing on the figures knew that the East, which had monopolized the pennant so long, had at last met a foe worthy of the weightiest consideration—Pittsburg. The pennant was won with ease.

Made a Runaway Race of It.

The race of 1902, which closed yesterday, was not a race in reality. Pittsburg was acknowledged as the strongest team in the history of baseball, and they set the pace from the fall of the flag. It was not a question of who would win the pennant (?), it was how bad Pittsburg would beat the other people. Only once in the entire distance were we out of first place, then but over night. Chicago on her first trip with Mal Eason up beat Pittsburg, and dropped us from the top perch. The next day we were back at the head of the procession, and from this time out there was nothing to the race save Pittsburg.

Has the runaway race made by Pittsburg done injury to baseball is the question to be answered later. Next year will tell. With the race close Pittsburg would probably have won many more games. Players have been out of the game on the slightest pretext where they would have been in and fighting hard were there but a chance of them being beaten. Not once in the last two and a half months of the season has Pittsburg had her team intact in the field.

RECORDS OF PITTSBURG TEAMS

The complete records of the Pittsburg Club for 20 years from 1882 to 1901, inclusive, is here shown. The record of this year's team will be found on the regular sporting page.

AMERICAN ASSOCIATION.

Year.	Games.	Won.	Lost.	Pct.	Rk.
1882	78	39	39	.500	4
1883	98	30	68	.306	7
1884	108	30	78	.277	10
1885	111	56	55	.504	3
1886	137	80	57	.584	2

NATIONAL LEAGUE.

Year.	Games.	Won.	Lost.	Pct.	Rk.
1887	124	55	69	.444	6
1888	134	66	68	.492	6
1889	132	61	71	.462	5
1890	137	23	114	.168	8
1891	135	55	80	.407	8
1892	153	80	73	.523	6
1893	129	81	48	.628	2
1894	130	65	65	.500	7
1895	132	71	61	.538	7
1896	129	66	63	.512	6
1897	131	60	71	.454	8
1898	148	72	76	.486	8
1899	147	75	72	.510	7
1900	139	79	60	.568	2
1901	139	90	49	.647	1

JIMMY GALVIN

Pitcher who first made Pittsburg famous as a ball town. He died during the past year.

HAS ADVERTISED PITTSBURG

J. Palmer O'Neil, Former Owner of the Pittsburg Club, Tells What the Game Has Done.

"Baseball has done more to advertise Pittsburg than has any other one given thing. Our ball games advertised the city when we had second rate or worse teams, but now, since we have a winner, it has advertised the city greatly."

So spoke J. Palmer O'Neil of Pittsburg, former owner of the Pittsburg ball club. "Twenty years ago when I went east to buy goods I found many people who did not know where Pittsburg was, and yet we were very strong with our mills, furnaces and big clearing house reports," continued Mr. O'Neil. "Really I have had people with whom I was dealing ask me where Pittsburg was. They have asked me if it were not near Altoona. Of course, some of them have been jesting, but the town was not so well known then as it got to be later when we got a ball team in the country's major league. Now there is not a paper of consequence in the country which does not publish the score of the Pittsburg games daily. Some may publish the score by innings, others may use but a paragraph, but all say something about Pittsburg daily, because here we have the champion of champion teams. There is not a man on the road who does not know just where Pittsburg is; not only this, but he must know the latest figures for Beaumont in batting. He will find someone along the line who wants to talk on the fine points of Pittsburg ball players, and he must be up to date. If any one should now ask if Pittsburg was not near Altoona, he would have the laugh turned against himself. Baseball has done a lot for Pittsburg. Pittsburg has done a lot for baseball, too.

"The team which has now won for the second time the pennant for Pittsburg is beyond doubt the fastest aggregation of ball players ever got together. The seven men constituting the infield and outfield of the twice champions are all fast men on the bases, good batters and good fielders, a combination but rarely found. I doubt if another such seven fast men was ever put together in one team.

"Much of the success of this team has been the result of playing together, and there is not one of them afraid to slide to a base, head foremost, if necessary. In the days of Mike Kelly we had an individual player. We have all heard the expression, "Slide Kelly, slide," but we hear it seldom now, for the infield and outfield of the Pittsburg team never hesitates to take this chance in getting a base. They each slide perhaps better than Kelly ever did. It was Mike, however, who first started this sort of heady baseball which is now seen in such a perfected form in the Pittsburg ball players."

MAL EASON,

Pitcher hailing from Brookville, Pa., who was responsible for Pittsburg dropping her hold on first place over night.

A BUSHEL OF CONGRATULATIONS

The Dispatch sporting editor has received the following telegrams of congratulation to the Pittsburgs winning the pennant again:

Will you kindly convey to President Dreyfuss my hearty congratulations on the brilliant success of his efforts to give the city of Pittsburg a champion baseball team. He has spared neither labor nor money in establishing this success, and to his plucky perseverance and his business tact and judgment is largely due the attainment of his object in placing a team in the field regardless of expense which has proved itself to be superior in playing strength of all the club's League adversaries during the past two seasons. To give eclat the winning of the League's pennant race of 1902 his team has "beat the record" of all previous championship campaigns in winning the pennant by an unprecedented score of victories.
HENRY CHADWICK,
Brooklyn, N. Y.

The Memphis club, best in the Southern League, congratulates the Pittsburg champions as the best on earth. CHARLES FRANK,
Manager Memphis Baseball Club.

On behalf of Hot Springs and Whittington Park I wish to congratulate the Pittsburg champions. With pleasure we await their coming for spring practice.
ROBERT E. PRICE,
Secretary Whittington Park Association.

Pittsburg's victory was a victory for square sportsmanship. With champions at both ends the old Keystone State looks pretty good to me.
FRANK HOUGH,
Philadelphia Inquirer.

I congratulate the city of Pittsburg, the players constituting the splendid team, the club and the management upon winning the pennant. FRANK G. SELEE,
Manager Chicago National League Club.

Congratulations to second-time champions. May their shadow never grow less. I consider them one of the best teams ever organized.
O. P. TEBEAU,
St. Louis.

Will Pittsburg and The Dispatch accept my congratulations of having a team that could win the pennant with so much ease? The National League champions of 1902 are surely a fine lot of boys. BAN B. JOHNSON,
President American League (per McRoy).

I think Pittsburg players deserve great credit for number of games won.
CLARKE C. GRIFFITH,
Chicago American League Club.

I congratulate Pittsburg upon its champion ball team, a team which perhaps has never had a superior and which has by so decisively winning the championship emphasized the fact that National League baseball is conducted honestly and in a sportsmanlike manner.
JAMES A. HART,
President Chicago National League Club.

Here's looking to a team that knew it had the championship won and yet played every game as if that alone decided the possession of the pennant. That's the kind of baseball that counts. JOHN B. FOSTER,
Baseball Editor New York Herald.

Pittsburg deserves great credit again for superior ball playing. Brooklyn is close enough to offer heartiest congratulations.
A. YAGER,
Baseball Editor Brooklyn Eagle.

Please convey my congratulations to the Pittsburg club and members of the team on the remarkable showing they have made in winning the championship of the National League.
H. F. KILFOYLE,
Cleveland Baseball Club.

Anything that adds to the honor of Pittsburg appeals to me, for it was in Pittsburg I received my first encouragement. The best club in the National League won the pennant, but I regret that the champions of the two leagues could not or cannot get together to determine the real championship. No matter who lost or who won the championship would remain in the old Keystone State.
CONNIE MACK,
Manager Champions American League.

Mr. Pulliam, Captain Clarke and the Pittsburg players have again demonstrated that they are a champion combination. I congratulate the above mentioned on their successful management and playing for the pennant of 1902. ANDREW FREEDMAN,
New York.

In the name of the fans of St. Joseph will you congratulate Fred Clarke and his Pirate band on their grand success during the season of 1902. Fred is an old St. Joseph boy and we are all proud of him. The Pirates are a great bunch. PERCY E. CHAMBERLAIN,
Sporting Editor the St. Joe (Mo.) Gazette.

Congratulations to Pittsburg should not be alone on her pennant team, but on having the only team that ever had the pennant won before the season started.
JOE S. JACKSON,
Detroit Free Press.

Everyone here is pleased that Pittsburg has again won the pennant. Congratulations and hope that you continue winning. Everyone awaits return of the boys here next spring to shake again. M. J. FINN,
Little Rock (Ark.) Baseball Club.

Cleveland fans have double cause for rejoicing in Pittsburg's second pennant. First, they regard Barney Dreyfuss as the best sport among the National League magnates; second, Wee Tommy Leach and Chief Zimmer are popular Clevelanders. H. H. EDWARDS,
Cleveland Plain Dealer.

New York didn't have a chance, so I must extend congratulations to Barney Dreyfuss, Harry Pulliam, etc., for the getting together of the greatest baseball team in the world. If New York cannot win the championship next year may Pittsburg float the third pennant is my sincere wish.
WALTER ST. DENIS,
Baseball Editor New York Evening World.

Hats off to the Pittsburg champions. They had the fight won early in the campaign, but they never rested on their oars.
J. ED. GRILLO,
Cincinnati Commercial-Tribune.

Please convey my complements to President Dreyfuss and Manager Clarke. The record of the Pirates this year is certainly a great one. SID MERCER,
St. Louis Republic.

I doubly congratulate Pittsburg. First on winning the League pennant twice consecutively. Second upon winning by the widest possible margin, although every consideration demanded a close race. In war and peace our national game is the one honest, incorruptible professional sport.
FRANCIS C. RICHTER,
Editor Sporting Life.

Pittsburg people should feel proud of the two-year champions. I congratulate you now, as I may not have a similar chance in the next 20 years.
FRANK DE HASS ROBISON,
St. Louis Baseball Club.

Hearty congratulations to the National League champions of 1902. An ideal ball team conducted on a high plane of sportsmanship.
Sporting News, St. Louis.

Congratulations to President Dreyfuss, Harry Pulliam, The Dispatch and everybody. Don't want to talk shop, but—watch Cincinnati next year. REN MULFORD,
Cincinnati Enquirer.

As an all round hustling baseball proposition from hustling Barney Druyfuss and elegant Colonel Pulliam to aggressive Fred Clarke and a string of fine individuals and team players the Pittsburg team is worthy of sincere congratulations from every lover of the national game for winning the National League championship for the second time. Let me add my sincere congratulations.
TIM H. MURNANE,
Boston Globe.

Anything that I can say in praise of Pittsburg's ball team would seem weak. I must congratulate the people of Pittsburg. They deserve just such a team as they now have. They worked hard and earnestly, spent their money freely and rooted desperately for years in order to get a good team. When they were beaten out of the race they took defeat with good grace and hoped for better days. Those days have come. I am glad. As manager of the champions in the Eastern League I join hands with the entire baseball world in congratulating Barney Dreyfuss, Harry Pulliam, Fred Clarke, all the other players and the people of Pittsburg. ED G. BARROW,
Manager, Toronto (Ont.) B. B. Club.

The baseball public of Cincinnati joins me in congratulating the Pittsburg club, but with the hope for a-like action from Pittsburg for Cincinnati next year.
AUGUST HERMAN,
President Cincinnati Baseball Club.

To the City of Pittsburg:

Greetings—Accept hearty congratulations on the justly won triumph of the Pirates.
P. J. DONOVAN,
Manager St. Louis N. L. Club.

CORNELIUS MACGILLICUDDY DESERVES GREATEST PRAISE

Almost twenty years ago there might be found any day in a certain Massachusetts shoe factory a young fellow who could make more shoes in a given time than any other man in the shop. He was then but 18 years of age. His body, like that of the fabled Darius, was long and lank and lean. There was but one thing in Massachusetts longer than his body—this was his name. He answered to the euphonius appellation of Cornelius Macgillicuddy. He had a middle name in his younger days, but the Humane Society made his parents cut it out.

By and bye someone discovered that he of long body and longer name could play ball. He was hired at a fair salary on condition that he would use a pruning knife on the name. After a week of careful thought the long one emerged from his cocoon under the non de plume of Connie Mack and he began to play ball.

This is a brief history of the early trials of one who to-day commands the admiration of the baseball world. As manager of the Athletics of Philadelphia in the American League this season he made a good start with such players as Lajoie, Bernhardt, Fraser and others, but at one fell swoop the National cut him down and took away all his stars. It looked like the funeral march for Connie Mack's hopes, but he did not despair. One day he walked into the office of President Ban Johnson and said:

"If you will agree to issue orders that no one is allowed on the coaching lines while he is pitching I will bring Rube Waddell from California and will win the pennant yet for Philadelphia and will make money for everybody."

"I will do it," said Johnson, ready to grasp at any straw to save the American from taking the count. He kept his word. So did Mack. In spite of his great handicap he pulled out winner in the pennant race with the aid of the eccentric but strong-armed Rube. Pittsburg people have a most friendly side for Mack. He was our star catcher for years and managed the club one season.

"PAPA NICK" IS VERY ILL AT HIS WASHINGTON HOME

While we rejoice that Pittsburg has attained the highest fame possible in baseball we must not forget that one who has done much to make the national game a success is stretched on a bed of pain and may not recover. We speak of Papa Nick Young, for years head of the National League and the highest authority in baseball. Some weeks ago Mr. Young fell over in his office in New York while talking with President Barney Dreyfuss of the Pittsburg champions. He was carried to a train and taken to his beautiful home on the outskirts of Washington. It is feared that he will not get well. His time of usefulness in baseball is past at least, but he has left with us a memory which will live long. N. E. Young is a son of the Empire State. He was born at Amsterdam, N. Y., September 12, 1840. He was what might be called sickly in his younger days and took to outdoor sports as a source of strength. At the age of 15 he was considered one of the best cricket players in America.

When the dark days in the history of our country came in the early 60s the young New York man was one of the first to rush to her aid. He shouldered his musket and went forth in the ranks of the Thirty-second New York Infantry, and later was transferred to the Signal Corps. It was between shots that Young first began his career as a ball player. He organized two teams in his regiment and played the game hard and often so long as he remained in the service. It was not until 1871, however, that he became famous as a ball player. He managed and played on the Olympics of Washington. In 1874 he managed the Chicagos for part of the season. Later in the year he was instrumental in organizing baseball into something from which has grown the present game. It was in 1884 that he was elected President of the national body, and he continued in office until the position of President was abolished at the meeting of last December in New York. He was then made Chairman of the Executive Committee.

THE OLD BREWERY NINE

"There has never been a gang of ball players worse maligned than the old Alleghenies of 1883—known throughtout the baseball world as the Brewery Nine," said A. G. Pratt yesterday afternoon. "These people did not follow in the footsteps of Francis Murphy, I will admit, but how they could play ball! I was manager of the team that year, and had my troubles. The Pittsburg team has won the pennant for the second time now, and are without doubt the greatest gang of players ever gathered together, but I want to add in passing that I would give a good bit to have seen a team as good as the present Pittsburgs stacked up against my old Brewery Nine. I am here to tell you that it would be no walkover and if this team of mine had one of their good spots there would have been nothing to it but the Brewery boys.

"I fear at this distance that the boys came by their nickname honestly. Some of them, at least, drank a little, but there was never such another gang of hitters in the world. When it comes to a show down there are but few Overbecks, Swartwoods, Peters or McLaughlins now. Those boys played the game from the first to the last.

"The story that one of my outfielders once stopped the game in the middle of an inning because it was too long, and he wanted to get a drink, and that he came in and got it from under the grandstand, is not true. Neither did I ever hear of or see a player have a bottle in his blouse pocket for comfort in field. I could tell some funny ones, though, were I disposed. I wish all teams now days would play ball as did the Brewery Nine. How we could kill the players leading the race, and how the bum teams would smash us," concluded Pratt, with a sigh.

THIS SPORTING PART DAILY WITH

The Inter Ocean.

VOLUME XXXII. CHICAGO, MONDAY MORNING, AUGUST 24, 1903. NUMBER 153.

WHITE SOX BREAK EVEN ON THE DAY

Comiskey's Young Men Win and Lose in a Double Header with the New Yorks.

D. GREEN MAKES BIG BATTING RECORD

Chicago Outfielder Puts in a Sensational Day Both at the Bat and in the Field—Dust from the Diamond.

STANDING OF THE CLUBS.

National League.

Clubs—	W.	L.	P.C.	Clubs—	W.	L.	P.C.
Pittsburg	70	37	.654	Brooklyn	52	54	.491
Chicago	**64**	**43**	**.598**	Boston	44	57	.436
New York	63	43	.594	Philadelphia	33	64	.340
Cincinnati	57	49	.538	St. Louis	37	73	.336

GAMES TODAY.

Chicago at New York.
Pittsburg at Philadelphia.
Cincinnati at Brooklyn.
St. Louis at Boston.

American League.

Clubs—	W.	L.	P.C.	Clubs—	W.	L.	P.C.
Boston	68	38	.642	New York	52	50	.510
Cleveland	59	46	.571	St. Louis	48	56	.461
Philadelphia	59	48	.551	**Chicago**	**48**	**59**	**.449**
Detroit	53	50	.515	Washington	32	72	.308

YESTERDAY'S RESULTS.

Boston, 5; St. Louis, 3 (first game).
Boston, 4; St. Louis, 2 (second game).
Detroit-Washington (postponed).
New York, 6; Chicago, 5 (first game).
Chicago, 3; New York, 1 (second game).

GAMES TODAY.

Philadelphia at Cleveland.
New York at Chicago.
Boston at St. Louis.
Washington at Detroit.

American Association.

Clubs—	W.	L.	P.C.	Clubs—	W.	L.	P.C.
St. Paul	74	36	.673	Kansas City	54	52	.509
Milwaukee	65	39	.625	Columbus	44	67	.396
Louisville	60	43	.583	Minneapolis	41	68	.376
Indian'polis	57	50	.532	Toledo	37	74	.333

YESTERDAY'S RESULTS.

Kansas City, 11; Toledo, 8 (first game).
Kansas City, 6; Toledo, 5 (second game).
Louisville, 10; Minneapolis, 3.
Columbus, 2; Milwaukee, 0.
Indianapolis, 10; St. Paul, 3.

"Three-I" League.

Clubs—	W.	L.	P.C.	Clubs—	W.	L.	P.C.
Blooming'n	61	40	.604	Rockford	51	48	.515
Decatur	55	41	.573	Ced. Rapids	45	50	.474
Davenport	52	42	.553	Dubuque	42	57	.424
Rock Island	49	46	.516	Springfield	35	64	.354

YESTERDAY'S RESULTS.

Rock Island, 7; Cedar Rapids, 6.
Dubuque, 15; Springfield, 4.
Rockford, 6; Bloomington, 3.
Davenport, 6; Decatur, 5.

Central League.

Clubs—	W.	L.	P.C.	Clubs—	W.	L.	P.C.
Ft. Wayne	76	37	.673	Dayton	50	62	.446
South Bend	73	41	.641	Wheeling	48	61	.440
Marion	58	53	.523	Terre Haute	48	63	.43?
Evansville	51	58	.468	Gd. Rapids	44	70	.386

YESTERDAY'S RESULTS.

Fort Wayne, 16; Marion, 2 (first game).
Fort Wayne, 9; Marion, 5 (second game).
Dayton, 6; Evansville, 5 (first game).
Dayton, 9; Evansville, 1 (second game).
South Bend, 7; Grand Rapids, 3 (first game).
South Bend, 2; Grand Rapids, 1 (second game).
Terre Haute, 8; Wheeling, 2.

Western League.

Clubs—	W.	L.	P.C.	Clubs—	W.	L.	P.C.
Milwaukee	64	35	.647	Denver	47	58	.448
Colo. Springs	62	40	.608	Des Moines	44	56	.440
Kan. City	53	47	.530	Peoria	44	59	.427
St. Joseph	49	49	.500	Omaha	39	58	.402

YESTERDAY'S RESULTS.

Kansas City, 9; Omaha, 7.
Colorado Springs, 10; Peoria, 1 (first game).
Colorado Springs, 8; Peoria, 6 (second game).
Milwaukee, 6; Denver, 0 (first game).
Denver, 6; Milwaukee, 0 (second game).
Des Moines, 10; St. Joseph, 8.

Although there were all kinds of ball playing on the South Side yesterday, and the White Sox and Highlanders split even on the day, it is the song of Daniel Green that must be sung.

Mr. Green came into prominence by reason of his batting eye. Pitchers who have faced the Chicago right fielder and who have permitted him to swat at the ball and hit it not were completely dumfounded over Daniel's performance. The first thing Daniel did to our old friend and former townsman, Clark Griffith, was to raise one of his curves over the score board. There was nobody on bases, worse luck, and Daniel trotted around in lonely glory while 10,000 people stood up and "hollered."

It was not expected that Daniel would repeat the performance, and he did not, but he had Mr. Griffith and his successor, Mr. Howell, so well fixed that during the course of the two games he knocked out a two-bagger and four singles. Griffith's shoot had no terrors for Daniel. The wily manager of the Highlanders had one of his days of long preparation, and did much dallying in the box, but he couldn't fool Daniel. And Mr. Howell was comparatively easy. So the fans shouted the glory of Daniel Green and counted the day well spent.

The first game yesterday was a heart-rending exhibition, lost to the White Sox after an uphill fight. Dr. White was in the box for Chicago, and our old comrade, Clark Griffith, did the pitching. White pitched "hard-luck" ball, but Griffith did clever work at the critical stages, and won out.

Roy Patterson's pitching, backed up by the hitting of Green and Jones, won the second game for the White Sox. The scores follow:

FIRST GAME.

New York.	R	H	P	A	E	Chicago.	R	H	P	A	E
Conroy, 3b	1	1	3	3	0	Holmes, lf	0	1	0	0	0
Keeler, rf	1	2	2	0	0	Isbell, 1b	0	0	13	1	1
Elb'rfeld, ss	2	1	2	3	2	Jones, cf	0	0	2	0	0
Ganzel, 1b	1	1	11	1	0	Green, rf	2	4	0	0	0
Willi'ms, 2b	0	0	1	4	1	Callah'n, 3b	1	2	3	4	0
Davis, lf	0	1	3	0	0	Magoon, 2b	2	1	5	2	1
M'Farl'd, cf	0	2	2	0	0	Tan'ehill, ss	0	1	3	8	0
Beville, c	1	0	8	0	0	Slattery, c	0	2	1	1	0
Griffith, p	0	0	0	2	0	White, p	0	0	0	2	1
Totals	6	8	27	13	3	Totals	5	11	27	18	3

New York ....3 1 0 0 1 0 0 1 0—6
Chicago ....0 0 0 2 0 0 3 0 0—5

Earned Runs—Chicago, 1; New York, 2. First Base on Balls—Off White, 3; off Griffith, 2. Struck Out—By White, 1; by Griffith, 1. Home Run—Green. Three-Base Hit—Conroy. Two-Base Hits—Magoon, Green, Callahan. Sacrifice Hits—Griffith, Ganzel, Davis. Stolen Base—White. Double Plays—Callahan (unassisted); Callahan, Tannehill, and Isbell; Tannehill, Magoon, and Isbell (2). Hit by Pitcher—By White, 2; by Griffith, 2. Umpire—Egan. Time of Game—2:10.

SECOND GAME.

Chicago.	R	H	P	A	E	New York.	R	H	P	A	E
D.H'mes, lf	0	3	3	0	0	Conroy, 3b	0	2	1	1	0
Isbell, 1b	1	0	13	0	0	Keeler, rf	0	1	2	0	1
Jones, cf	1	1	2	0	0	Elb'rfeld, ss	0	1	2	1	1
Green, rf	1	2	2	1	0	Ganzel, 1b	0	0	6	0	0
Callah'n, 3b	0	0	1	2	0	Willi'ms, 2b	1	0	0	3	0
Magoon, 2b	0	1	0	1	0	Davis, lf	0	1	4	0	0
L.T'hill, ss	0	1	2	1	1	M'Farl'd, cf	0	2	1	0	0
Slattery, c	0	0	4	0	0	Beville, c	0	1	2	3	0
Patterson, p	0	0	0	5	0	F.H'mes, 1b	0	0	6	0	1
						Howell, p	0	2	0	7	0
						*J. T'nehill	0	0	0	0	0
Totals	3	8	27	10	1	Totals	1	10	24	15	3

*Bated for Holmes in ninth inning.

Chicago ....0 1 0 0 0 0 0 2 *—3
New York ....0 0 0 1 0 0 0 0 0—1

Earned Run—Chicago, 1. First Base on Balls—Off Patterson, 4; off Howell, 3. Struck Out—By Patterson, 4; by Howell, 2. Three-Base Hits—Conroy, Jones. Sacrifice Hits—Howell, Jones, Callahan, Keeler. Stolen Base—Isbell. Double Play—Green and Isbell. Umpire—Egan. Time of Game—1:30.

JACK TANNER.

Boston, 5-4; St. Louis, 3-2.

ST. LOUIS, Mo., Aug. 23.—Boston won both games of a double-header here this afternoon, the first 5 to 3 and the second 4 to 2. Sudhoff and Young pitched in the second game, and Boston was lucky in winning, a triple play and a double being all that saved the visitors. Both games were full of sensational playing. Attendance, 21,300. Scores:

FIRST GAME.

Boston.	R	H	P	A	E	St. Louis.	R	H	P	A	E
D'gherty, lf	1	1	2	1	0	Burket, lf	0	1	1	0	1
Collins, 3b	1	1	0	1	0	Martin, rf	1	1	2	0	0
C.Stahl, cf	1	1	1	0	0	Hill, 3b	0	0	1	3	1
Freem'n, rf	0	1	1	1	0	Ander'n, 1b	1	1	10	0	0
Parent, ss	0	0	1	2	0	Wallace, ss	1	2	1	3	1
LaCh'ce, 1b	0	0	4	1	1	Heidrick, cf	0	0	4	0	0
Ferris, 2b	0	0	3	1	0	Friel, 2b	0	2	2	2	1
J. Stahl, c	1	1	13	1	0	Sugden, c	0	3	5	1	0
Hughes, p	1	2	2	0	0	Sievers, p	0	0	1	2	0
						*Hemphill	0	0	0	0	0
Totals	5	7	27	8	1	Totals	3	10	27	11	4

*Batted for Sievers in ninth inning.

Boston ....0 0 0 2 1 0 0 2 0—5
St. Louis ....3 0 0 0 0 0 0 0 0—3

Earned Runs—St. Louis, 2; Boston, 3. Two-Base Hits—Sugden, Wallace, Anderson, Hughes. Home Run—J. Stahl. Double Plays—Wallace and Anderson; Ferris and La Chance. Passed Ball—Stahl, 1. Stolen Bases—Heidrick, Ferris. Wild Pitch—By Sievers, 1. Bases on Balls—Off Hughes, 3. Struck Out—By Hughes, 10; by Sievers, 5. Left on Bases—St. Louis, 6; Boston, 3. Time—1:48. Umpire—Connolly.

SECOND GAME.

Boston.	R	H	P	A	E	St. Louis.	R	H	P	A	E
D'herty, lf	1	2	2	0	0	Burkett, lf	0	0	2	0	0
Collins, 3b	1	3	0	3	0	Martin, rf	0	1	2	0	0
C. Stahl, cf	0	1	1	0	0	Hill, 3b	0	2	3	0	0
Freem'n, rf	0	1	0	0	0	Ander'n, 1b	0	0	7	2	1
Parent, ss	1	2	2	3	0	Wallace, ss	0	0	0	7	0
LaCh'ce, 1b	0	1	13	0	0	Heidrick, cf	0	1	5	1	0
Ferris, 2b	1	2	4	5	0	Friel, 2b	0	1	3	3	0
Farrell, c	0	1	4	0	1	Sugden, c	0	0	3	1	0
Young, p	0	1	0	2	0	Sudhoff, p	1	0	0	0	0
Criger, c	0	0	1	0	0	He'phill, lf	1	1	1	0	0
Totals	4	14	27	13	1	Totals	2	7	27	15	1

Boston ....2 0 0 1 0 0 1 0 0—4
St. Louis ....0 0 0 0 0 2 0 0 0—2

Earned Runs—St. Louis, 1; Boston, 2. Two-Base Hits—Hill, Parent, Sudhoff. Sacrifice Hits—Freeman, Hill, La Chance. Double Plays—Hill (unassisted); Ferris and La Chance; Heidrick, Sugden, Anderson, Friel, Anderson, Friel, Wallace, and Heidrick. Triple Play—Ferris, Parent, and La Chance. Passed Balls—Farrell, 1. Stolen Bases—Heidrick, Dougherty (2). Hit by Pitched Ball—By Sudhoff, Farrell. Bases on Balls—Off Sudhoff, 3; off Young, 1. Struck Out—By Sudhoff, 2; by Young, 5. Left on Bases—St. Louis, 5; Boston, 13. Time—1:46. Umpire—Connolly.

AMERICAN ASSOCIATION.

Kansas City, 11-6; Toledo, 8-5.

KANSAS CITY, Mo., Aug. 23.—The locals won another double-header today, playing hard throughout both games, while Toledo played poorly. Score:

FIRST GAME.

Kan. City.	R	H	P	A	E	Toledo.	R	H	P	A	E
Hill, cf	2	3	5	0	0	Bernard, lf	1	2	5	0	0
Gear, rf	1	1	1	0	0	Owens, ss	1	3	3	4	0
Nance, 2b	1	1	1	3	1	Smith, rf	0	3	0	0	0
Grady, 3b	3	2	0	1	0	Bl'k'ship, c	1	1	3	2	0
Knoll, lf	0	1	1	0	0	Schaub, 3b	2	2	0	3	1
Butler, c	2	3	6	1	0	Turner, 1b	1	1	11	0	1
Rothfuss, 1b	1	1	9	0	0	Ball, cf	1	2	1	1	0
Leewe, ss	1	3	4	3	0	Childs, 2b	0	1	1	6	0
Alloway, p	0	0	0	0	0	Coughlin, p	1	1	0	3	0
Gibson, p	0	1	0	2	0						
Totals	11	16	27	10	1	Totals	8	16	24	19	2

Kansas City.............0 0 2 0 2 0 5 2 *—11
Toledo ....0 0 0 8 0 0 0 0 0— 8

Two-Base Hits—Hill, Gear, Butler, Leewee, Bernard (2). Home Runs—Grady, Turner, Ball. Sacrifice Hits—Nance, Bernard. Stolen Bases—Knoll, Leewe, Blankenship. Bases on Balls—Off Alloway, 1; off Gibson, 2; off Coughlin, 2. Struck Out—By Alloway, 1; by Gibson, 4. Hit by Pitched Ball—By Coughlin, 3. Innings Pitched—By Alloway, 3½; by Gibson, 5½. Hits—Off Alloway, 12; off Gibson, 4. Passed Ball—Blankenship. Left on Bases—Kansas City, 10; Toledo, 11. Time—2:00. Umpire—Cunningham. Attendance—5,500.

SECOND GAME.

Kan. City.	R	H	P	A	E	Toledo.	R	H	P	A	E
Hill, cf	2	2	1	0	1	Bernard, lf	0	0	1	0	0
Gear, 3b	1	1	0	0	1	Owens, ss	1	2	2	1	0
Nance, 2b	1	1	2	3	0	Smith, rf	0	0	0	0	0
Grady, c	1	1	2	0	0	Kleinow, c	0	0	2	0	0
Knoll, lf	0	1	2	0	0	Schaub, 3b	1	2	0	1	1
Durham, rf	0	1	0	1	0	Turner, 1b	1	2	5	0	0
Rothfuss, 1b	0	1	6	2	0	Ball, cf	0	1	0	0	0
Leewe, ss	1	0	1	4	0	Childs, 2b	1	1	2	2	0
Alloway, p	0	0	1	1	0	Cristall, p	1	2	0	1	0
Totals	6	8	15	11	2	Totals	5	10	12	5	1

Kansas City.............1 5 0 0 *—6
Toledo ....0 0 0 4 1—5

Game called to allow Toledo to catch train.

Two-Base Hits—Nance, Knoll, Turner (2), Cristall. Three-Base Hit—Owens. Stolen Base—Hill. Double Play—Rothfuss to Leewe to Rothfuss. Bases on Balls—Off Alloway, 1; off Cristall, 3. Struck Out—By Alloway, 2; by Cristall, 2. Hit by Pitcher—By Cristall, 1. Wild Pitch—Alloway. Left on Bases—Kansas City, 6; Toledo, 4. Time—1:05. Umpire—Cunningham. Attendance—5,500.

Indianapolis, 10; St. Paul, 3.

ST. PAUL, Minn., Aug. 23.—The locals were outplayed at all points by the visitors today, and Indianapolis took their first game of the present series. Attendance, 3,800. Score:

Indianap's.	R	H	P	A	E	St. Paul.	R	H	P	A	E
Kihm, 1b	1	1	7	0	0	Geier, 3b	0	0	0	5	1
Fox, 2b	2	2	1	3	0	Shannon, cf	0	1	3	1	0
Hog'ver, rf	0	3	3	0	0	Jackson, rf	0	0	2	0	0
Woodruff, lf	2	1	2	0	0	Schaefer, ss	2	2	3	1	1
Marcan, ss	1	0	0	1	0	Huggins, 2b	1	1	3	1	0
Heydon, c	1	0	6	0	0	Flournoy, lf	0	1	2	0	0
Coulter, cf	0	1	7	0	0	Wheeler, 1b	0	0	12	0	0
Tamsett, 3b	2	1	1	1	0	Sullivan, c	0	1	2	1	1
Kellum, p	1	1	0	1	0	Bailey, p	0	1	0	4	2
Totals	10	10	27	6	0	Totals	3	7	27	13	5

Indianapolis ....0 1 1 0 2 6 0 0 0—10
St. Paul ....0 2 0 1 0 0 0 0 0— 3

Earned Runs—St. Paul, 3; Indianapolis, 1. Two-Base Hit—Sullivan. Three-Base Hits—Schaefer, Shannon. Sacrifice Hits—Flournoy, Kellum, Heydon, Marcan (2). Stolen Bases—Fox (2), Hogriever. First Base on Balls—Off Kellum, 1; off Bailey, 1. Struck Out—By Kellum, Huggins (2), Wheeler, Geier, Shannon; by Bailey, Coulter. Passed Ball—Sullivan. Wild Pitch—Bailey. Hit by Pitched Ball—By Kellum, Schaefer. Left on Bases—St. Paul, 5; Indianapolis, 3. Time—1:55. Umpire—Haskell.

Columbus, 2; Milwaukee, 0.

MILWAUKEE, Wis., Aug. 23.—Columbus shut out Milwaukee today in the best and most closely played game seen here for some time. The field was muddy, but the fielding work was good and at times sensational. Gleason's one-handed catch of a foul over the bleachers' rail was the feature. Score:

Columbus.	R	H	P	A	E	Milwaukee.	R	H	P	A	E
Arndt, lf	1	2	3	0	0	Schla'y, 2b	0	1	3	2	0
Gleason, rf	1	1	3	1	0	Donahue, 1b	0	0	9	2	0
Clingman, ss	0	0	3	1	0	Wood, c	0	2	7	0	0
Raymer, 2b	0	1	1	7	0	Unglaub, 3b	0	0	1	1	0
Bannon, cf	0	1	1	0	0	Gamey, rf	0	1	2	0	0
Turner, 3b	0	0	1	0	0	Dunl'y, lf	0	0	1	0	0
Mellor, 1b	0	1	8	2	0	Hemphill, cf	0	1	1	0	0
Fox, c	0	0	5	0	0	Viox, ss	0	0	3	2	0
Dorner, p	0	0	2	2	1	Stimmel, p	0	0	0	3	0
Totals	2	6	27	13	1	Totals	0	5	27	10	0

Columbus ....0 0 0 0 0 0 0 2 0—2
Milwaukee ....0 0 0 0 0 0 0 0 0—0

Earned Run—Columbus. Sacrifice Hits—Wood, Clingman. Bases on Balls—Off Stimmel, 3; off Dorner, 2. Struck Out—By Stimmel, 6; by Dorner, 5. Double Play—Donahue to Viox. Left on Bases—Milwaukee, 7; Columbus, 7. Attendance—1,200. Umpire—Mullane. Time—1:35.

Louisville, 10; Minneapolis, 3.

MINNEAPOLIS, Minn., Aug. 23.—Louisville made it three straight from the locals today, batting McDonald terrifically in the eighth and ninth innings. Three doubles, a triple, and a single gave the visitors their five in the ninth. Score:

Louisville.	R	H	P	A	E	Min'apolis.	R	H	P	A	E
Kerwin, rf	2	2	1	0	0	D.Su'van, cf	1	2	2	0	0
Hart, lf	0	2	2	0	1	Maloney, 3b	0	1	0	1	0
Brash'r, 2b	0	2	2	2	0	Oyler, ss	0	1	3	4	2
Odwell, cf	1	1	3	0	0	McInt're, 1b	1	2	9	1	0
S.Su'van, 3b	1	1	2	1	0	Lally, lf	1	1	4	0	0
Schr'ver, 3b	2	2	11	0	1	Yeager, c	0	1	1	3	0
White, c	2	2	4	1	1	Spooner, rf	0	1	1	0	1
Quinlan, ss	0	2	1	4	0	Martin, 2b	0	1	5	3	0
Egan, p	2	2	1	4	0	McDon'ld, p	0	0	2	2	1
Totals	10	16	27	12	3	Totals	3	10	27	14	4

Louisville ....1 0 0 1 0 0 0 3 5—10
Minneapolis ....3 0 0 0 0 0 0 0 0— 3

Earned Runs—Minneapolis, 1; Louisville, 2. Two-Base Hits—McIntyre (2), Lally, Odwell, White, Egan. Three-Base Hit—Schreiver. Double Plays—Brashear to Quinlan to Schreiver; McIntyre (unassisted). First Base on Balls—Off McDonald, 2; off Egan, 1. Struck Out—By Egan, 3. Sacrifice Hits—Maloney, Odwell, Hart. Stolen Bases—Maloney, Martin, Quinlan. Left on Bases—Minneapolis, 7; Louisville, 7. Umpire—Foreman. Time—1:55. Attendance—1,500.

CENTRAL LEAGUE.

Fort Wayne, 16-9; Marion, 2-7.

MARION, Ind., Aug. 23.—Marion lost a double-header to Fort Wayne. The first was won by Fort Wayne's superior work, but the second was given them by the umpire. Score:

FIRST GAME.

Ft Wayne.	R	H	P	A	E	Marion.	R	H	P	A	E
Belden, rf	2	0	3	0	0	McGrew, ss	1	1	1	3	0
Hopke, 3b	2	3	2	1	2	Letcher, rf	0	0	5	0	1
Dennis, cf	3	2	4	0	0	Cooley, 2b	0	1	2	4	0
Myers, 1b	4	4	6	2	0	Grim, 1b	0	0	9	0	0
O'Con'l, 2b	1	2	2	3	0	Herbert, c	1	1	4	1	2
Ostick, c	1	0	6	1	1	Pickett, lf	0	0	1	0	0
Slear, lf	2	4	1	0	0	Law'nce, 3b	0	1	1	2	0
Lindsay, ss	0	1	0	3	1	Myers, cf	0	0	1	0	0
Alberts, p	1	0	2	1	0	McNeil, p	0	1	0	1	0
Totals	16	16	*26	11	4	Totals	2	5	24	11	3

*McGrew out, foul bunt.

Fort Wayne ....3 0 0 1 3 0 0 2 7—16
Marion ....0 1 0 0 1 0 0 0 0— 2

Stolen Bases—Slear, Ostick. Sacrifice Hits—Hopke, Lindsay. Two-Base Hits—McGrew, Cooley, Slear. Double Play—Hopke to O'Connell to Meyers. Home Runs—Myers, O'Connell, Hopke, Herbert. First Base on Balls—Off McNeil, 4; off Alberts, 5. Struck Out—By Alberts, 4. Hit by Pitched Ball—By McNeil, 1. Wild Pitch—McNeil. Passed Ball—Herbert. Earned Runs—Marion, 1; Fort Wayne, 8. Left on Bases—Marion, 10; Fort Wayne, 4. Time of Game—1:45. Umpire—McNamara.

SECOND GAME.

Ft. Wayne.	R	H	P	A	E	Marion.	R	H	P	A	E
Belden, rf	1	1	2	0	0	McGrew, ss	2	0	1	4	1
Hopke, 3b	0	1	3	3	0	Letcher, rf	1	2	3	0	0
Dennis, cf	0	0	0	0	0	Cooley, 2b	1	3	3	1	1
Myers, 1b	0	1	10	0	0	Grim, 1b	0	1	9	0	0
O'Con'l, 2b	2	0	1	3	0	Herbert, c	0	1	6	0	1
Ostick, c	1	1	8	3	0	Pickett, lf	0	0	1	0	0
Slear, lf	2	2	0	1	1	Law'nce, 3b	1	0	0	4	1
Lindsay, ss	2	2	2	2	0	Myers, cf	1	1	1	0	0
Carbiener, p	1	3	1	0	0	Frye, p	1	0	0	1	0
Totals	9	11	27	12	1	Totals	7	8	24	10	4

Fort Wayne ....0 0 0 3 0 2 0 4 *—9
Marion ....0 0 1 0 0 0 0 1 5—7

Sacrifice Hits—Herbert, Ostick, Dennis. Two-Base Hits—Carbiener, Letcher. Three-Base Hits—Slear, Carbiener. First Base on Balls—Off Frye, 2; off Carbiener, 5. Struck Out—By Frye, 6; by Carbiener, 8. Hit by Pitched Ball—By Carbiener, 1. Earned Runs—Fort Wayne, 5. Left on Bases—Marion, 7; Fort Wayne, 8. Time of Game—1:50. Umpire—McNamara. Attendance—2,142.

Terre Haute, 8; Wheeling, 4.

WHEELING, W. Va., Aug. 23.—Terre Haute bunched hits in the third and fourth off Smith and scored eight runs, winning the game. Pfister got his bumps in the fifth and was relieved by Terre Haute Smith. Miller, who relieved Smith of Wheeling, gave but one hit in four innings. Score:

Wheeling.	R	H	P	A	E	Ter. Haute.	R	H	P	A	E
Price, cf	0	1	2	1	0	Beecher, ss	1	1	3	3	0
Blakey, rf	1	1	0	0	0	Decker, cf	2	1	2	0	0
Curtis, lf	1	2	0	0	0	Th'pson, rf	2	2	0	0	0
Farrell, 1b	0	0	12	1	1	Dearm'd, 3b	1	3	3	2	0
Wentz, 2b	0	1	3	3	0	Rich'dson, c	0	1	4	0	0
Soxa'xis, ss	0	0	2	4	1	Conler, 1b	0	1	11	0	0
Deiters, 3b	0	1	3	4	0	Wilk'son, lf	0	2	3	0	0
Schriever, c	1	1	5	1	0	Kuhn, 2b	1	1	1	3	0
Smith, p	0	1	0	1	0	Pfister, p	1	0	0	2	0
Miller, p	1	2	0	1	0	Smith, p	0	0	0	2	0
Totals	4	10	27	16	2	Totals	8	12	27	12	0

Terre Haute ....0 0 4 4 0 0 0 0 0—8
Wheeling ....0 0 0 0 4 0 0 0 0—4

Stolen Bases—Blakey, Wilkerson. Two-Base Hits—Miller (2), Curtis, Richardson, Kuhn. Three-Base Hits—Schriever, Dearmond. Double Plays—Deiters to Wentz; Beecher to Conner. Sacrifice Hits—Blakey, Beecher. First Base on Balls—Off Smith of Wheeling, 1; off Miller, 1; off Pfister, 2. Hit Batsmen—By Smith of Wheeling, 1. Struck Out—By Smith of Wheeling, 1; by Miller, 3; by Pfister, 3. First Base on Errors—Terre Haute, 2. Left on Bases—Wheeling, 7; Terre Haute, 4. Base Hits—Off Smith of Wheeling, 11; off Miller, 1; off Pfister, 7; off Smith of Terre Haute, 3. Time—1:51. Paid Attendance—1,267. Umpire—Farrell.

Dayton, 6-9; Evansville, 5-1.

Special Dispatch to The Inter Ocean.

DAYTON, Ohio, Aug. 23.—Dayton won both games this afternoon. [illegible] the first game hits and errors were alike, [illegible] struck out ten men, and this had the [illegible]ing, [illegible] getting the extra run for Dayton.

In the second game the Evansville players appeared to be nervous, as they wanted to catch a train. Mullen held them down to three hits in seven innings. Willis was batted hard and was taken out in the second. Minor did little better. The game was called in the seventh. Score:

FIRST GAME.

Dayton.	R	H	P	A	E	Evansville.	R	H	P	A	E
Fay, cf	4	3	1	0	0	Quinn, cf	1	1	0	0	0
Tate, rf	2	3	1	0	0	Russell, rf	1	2	3	0	0
Miller, 2b	0	0	2	4	0	Bonner, 2b	0	0	1	3	0
McCon'l, 1b	0	1	10	0	0	News, 1b	1	2	10	2	0
Hitchc'ft, cf	0	1	1	1	0	O'Hara, cf	1	1	5	0	0
Havel, 3b	0	1	1	2	0	Lally, ss	0	0	0	4	0
Hoff, ss	0	0	1	3	1	McKinley, c	0	1	4	0	0
Fox, c	0	0	10	3	0	Bohanan, 3b	1	2	1	1	0
Hart, p	0	0	0	0	0	Minor, p	0	0	0	2	1
						*Ross	0	0	0	0	0
Totals	6	9	27	13	1	Totals	5	9	24	12	1

*Batted for Minor in ninth.

Dayton ....2 2 0 1 0 0 1 0 *—6
Evansville ....0 0 0 1 0 1 1 2 0—5

Sacrifice Hits—Miller, Quinn. Two-Base Hits—News, Bohanan. Stolen Bases—Bonnell, Bohanan, Foy (2). Home Run—Tate. Double Play—Hoff to Miller to McConnell. Base Hits—Off Hart, 2. Struck Out—By Hart, 10; by Minor, 3. Passed Ball—McKinley. Time of Game—1:35. Umpire—Kline.

SECOND GAME.

Dayton.	R	H	P	A	E	Evansville.	R	H	P	A	E
Foy, lf	2	1	0	1	0	Quinn, lf	0	0	2	0	0
Tate, c	0	0	3	2	0	Russell, rf	0	1	0	0	0
Miller, 2b	1	1	1	0	0	Bonner, 2b	1	1	2	2	1
McCon'l, 1b	4	3	12	1	0	News, 1b	0	0	8	0	1
Hitchc'ft, cf	2	2	0	0	0	O'Hara, cf	0	0	4	0	0
Havel, 3b	0	0	3	3	2	Lally, ss	0	0	2	3	0
Hoff, ss	2	1	1	5	1	McKinley, c	0	0	0	2	0
Withoft, rf	0	2	1	0	0	Bohanan, 3b	0	0	0	3	0
Mullen, p	0	1	0	0	0	Willis, p	0	0	0	0	0
						Minor, p	0	1	0	1	0
Totals	9	11	21	12		Totals	1	3	18	11	2

Dayton ....5 1 1 0 0 2 *—9
Evansville ....0 0 0 0 0 1 0—1

Stolen Bases—Minor, McConnell, Hitchcroft (2). Two-Base Hit—Foy. Innings Pitched—By Willis, 1; by Minor, 6. Base Hits—Off Willis, 3; off Minor, 8. Struck Out—By Mullen, 3. First Base on Balls—Off Mullen, 1; off Willis, 1; off Minor, 2. Wild Pitches—Willis, Minor. Passed Ball—McKinley. Time—1:00. Umpire—Kline.

Rock Island, 7; Cedar Rapids, 6.

CEDAR RAPIDS, Iowa, Aug. 23.—The visitors bunched hits on Beedles in the second, eighth, and ninth innings, and won, though Cedar Rapids made a big rally in the seventh inning, two singles, a triple, and three errors, yielding four scores. Dickey's triple and Hickey's single in the ninth, with one man hit by Beedles, did the business for the visitors. The score:

Ced. Rap.	R	H	P	A	E	Rock Isl'd.	R	H	P	A	E
K'n'dy, 2b	2	2	1	2	0	Crim, lf	1	1	5	0	0
Brown, 3b	1	3	3	2	0	Don'ley, cf	0	1	1	0	1
Fuller, 1b	0	0	12	0	0	V'ndine, 3b	0	0	0	3	1
Novacek, rf	2	2	1	1	0	Graham, rf	1	1	1	0	0
Himes, cf	0	2	0	0	0	Lister, 2b	3	2	0	1	0
Hausen, c	0	0	5	1	1	Lattimer, c	1	2	8	0	1
Roberts, lf	0	0	0	1	0	Dickey, 1b	1	1	10	0	0
Berte, ss	0	0	5	5	0	Hickey, ss	0	2	2	2	1
Beedles, p	1	0	0	3	0	Arthur, p	0	1	0	3	1
Totals	6	9	27	15	1	Totals	7	11	27	9	5

Cedar Rapids ....1 0 0 0 0 0 1 4 0—6
Rock Island ....0 3 0 0 0 0 0 1 1 2—7

Stolen Bases—Himes, Hickey. Two-Base Hits—Crim, Donnelley. Three-Base Hits—Novacek (2), Lister, Dickey. Base on Balls—Off Arthur, 1. Struck Out—By Beedles, 5; by Arthur, 7. Hit by Pitched Ball—By Beedles, 1. Time—1:40. Attendance—1,100. Umpire—Cusack.

Dubuque, 15; Springfield, 4.

DUBUQUE, Iowa, Aug. 23.—The locals hit Wenig to all parts of the grounds, and, with some weird playing on the part of the visitors, piled up a big score.

Dubuque.	R	H	P	A	E	Springfield.	R	H	P	A	E
Carr, 3b	1	3	1	1	0	Kinlock, cf	1	2	2	0	0
Hughes, ss	3	3	4	5	1	Eubright, 2b	2	1	2	0	1
Buelow, 1b	2	2	12	0	0	Caffryn, lf	0	2	3	0	0
Everett, cf	1	2	0	0	0	Hag'man, rf	1	1	0	0	0
Cahill, lf	3	1	3	0	0	Neal, ss	0	1	3	1	3
Eastman, 2b	0	1	1	4	2	Lyon, 2b, 3b	0	0	3	3	0
Burwell, rf	1	1	1	0	0	Reading, c	0	0	4	2	1
Lobeck, c	2	3	5	2	0	Belt, 1b, 3b	0	0	7	0	1
Eul, p	2	0	0	2	0	Wenig, p	0	1	0	3	0
Totals	15	16	27	14	3	Totals	4	8	24	9	6

Dubuque ....3 3 1 0 0 1 0 7 *—15
Springfield ....0 0 0 0 0 2 0 2 0— 4

Two-Base Hits—Carr, Lobeck. Three-Base Hits—Carr, Hughes. Stolen Bases—Hughes, Buelow (2), Everett, Cahill, Eul, Wenig. Sacrifice Hit—Eastman. Hit by Pitched Ball—Reading, Kinlock. Bases on Balls—Off Wenig, 3; off Eul, 1. Struck Out—By Wenig, 4; by Eul, 4. Umpire—Peters.

South Bend, 7-2; Grand Rapids, 3-1.

SOUTH BEND, Ind., Aug. 23.—The locals took a double header from Grand Rapids today. The second game was close and exciting throughout. The score:

FIRST GAME.

S. Bend.	R	H	P	A	E	G. Rapids.	R	H	P	A	E
Coffey, lf	2	2	4	0	0	Mack, 2b	1	2	1	1	1
Anders'n, cf	0	1	2	0	0	Maloney, cf	0	0	1	0	0
Sager, 3b	1	3	0	3	0	War'der, rf	1	0	2	0	0
Cogswell, rf	1	2	2	0	0	Geyer, lf	0	0	1	0	0
G'schow, ss	1	1	0	1	1	Hanford, 1b	0	1	11	1	0
Spangl'r, 1b	0	0	15	1	0	O'Neil, c	0	1	4	0	0
Grant, 2b	0	0	2	4	0	Barton, ss	1	2	4	2	2
Tieman, c	1	2	2	0	0	Burg, 3b	0	0	2	3	0
Ferguson, p	1	2	0	4	0	Farrell, p	0	1	1	7	0
Totals	7	13	27	13	1	Totals	3	7	27	14	3

South Bend ....0 0 1 0 0 2 0 4 0—7
Grand Rapids ....1 0 0 0 0 0 1 0 1—3

Summary: Two-Base Hit—Ferguson. Three-Base Hit—Geyer. Sacrifice Hits—Anderson (2), Groeschow, Spangler, Mack. Double Play—Barton to Hanford. Hit by Pitched Ball—Tieman. Struck Out—By Ferguson, 2; by Farrell, 3. Bases on Balls—Off Ferguson, 3; off Farrell, 2. Wild Pitch—Farrell. Time of Game—1:55. Umpire—Kiefer.

SECOND GAME.

S. Bend.	R	H	P	A	E	G. Rapids.	R	H	P	A	E
Coffey, lf	0	0	1	0	0	Mack, 2b	0	0	1	4	[illegible]
Ander'n, cf	1	1	1	0	0	Maloney, cf	0	[illegible]	3	[illegible]	[illegible]
Sager, 3b	0	0	1	1	1	War'der, rf	1	1	2	0	0
Cogswell, rf	0	2	1	0	0	Geyer, lf	0	2	2	1	0
G'schow, ss	0	0	3	6	2	Hanford, 1b	0	0	9	0	2
Spangl'r, 1b	0	0	8	3	0	O'Neil, c	0	2	7	1	0
Grant, 2b	1	1	4	3	0	Barton, ss	0	0	1	2	0
Andrews, c	0	1	5	[illegible]	0	Burg, 3b	0	0	2	1	0
Ream, p	0	1	3	[illegible]	0	Thomas, p	0	0	0	0	0
Totals	2	6	27	[illegible]	3	Totals	1	8	27	9	2

South Bend ....[illegible]1 0 0 0 0 0 1 0 0—2
Grand Rapids ....0 0 0 0 0 1 0 0 0—1

Summary: Two-[illegible] Base Hit—Maloney. Three-Base Hits—Cogsw[illegible] (2). Struck Out—By Ream, 5; by Thomas, 7. [illegible]ire—Steiner. Time of Game—1:50. Attendance [illegible],000.

THE NEW YORK "HIGHLANDERS."

New York American League Team—Reading from left to right: Top Line—Holmes, Chesbro, Bevel, Ganzel, Conroy, Tannehill, McFarland. Middle Line—Deering, Keeler, Griffith, Howell, Williams. Lower Line—Wolfe, mascot, Davis.

WHERE WILL THE SPORTS COME FROM?

Davies and Houseman Looking for a Play to Carry a Cast in Which Every Character Must Be a Star.

"Parson" Davies and Lou M. Houseman are working out a novel scheme which is none other than to go on the road next year with an all-star cast of "actor pugs" in some stirring drama. Just what the production will be is yet to be decided, but the cast, as figured out by Lou and the "Parson" at Rector's last night, is as follows:

Tim Hurst, "Parson" Davies, Billy Muldoon, Bat Masterson, Tom O'Rourke, George Siler, John L. Sullivan, Jake Kilrain, L. M. Houseman, Evan Lewis, James J. Corbett, Jack Root, Billy Delaney, Malachy Hogan, and Tom Jenkins for the main parts.

"Kid" Broad will be asked to take the rough soubrette's part, for it won't make any difference whether he can talk the part or not so long as he will look it.

The other women parts are to be filled by Joe Choynski, who played Miss Ophelia with Peter Jackson's "Uncle Tom" company; "Young" Corbett, Frank Erne, and Harry Harris, who will be the ingenue.

"Ten Nights in a Barroom" has been suggested as a very fitting production for this aggregation of fistic-histrionic talent. "The Road to Ruin" has also been suggested, but these are vetoed, as Houseman and the "Parson" say they want a brand-new play, and they are considering the advisability of asking "Big Bill" Naughton to write an appropriate scenario.

Davies and Houseman are very much in earnest regarding their latest scheme, and will take up the matter of securing the proposed cast immediately. They scout the idea of treating the venture as a joke, and consider the project perfectly feasible. The only objection advanced was by the "Parson," who said every member of the troupe would want 50 per cent of the gross receipts, which would not conduce to prosperity.

Davies has just arrived from the coast, where he incidentally witnessed the Jeffries-Corbett fight, although the real purport of his visit was to see a sister of his who is a sister of mercy in a convent near 'Frisco.

"While I was at the convent a Mrs. Gilmartin, who takes much interest in church affairs in 'Frisco, invited my sister and another nun and myself to take a drive in her brake through Golden Gate park," remarked the "Parson."

"We were talking of anything and everything but pugilism, when Jim Corbett and his wife passed us driving.

"Jim glanced our way, saw me, stiffened back, and then tipped his hat, and I heard this remark float back on the wind: 'Well, he's working the parson gag to the limit. How did he butt into a convent?' "

Davenport, 6; Decatur, 5.

DAVENPORT, Iowa, Aug. 23.—With two out in the eighth, Alperman and Williams batted in four runs, winning for Davenport. The greatest demonstration ever seen on the local grounds followed the hits. Score:

Davenport.	R	H	P	A	E	Decatur.	R	H	P	A	E
Ruby, lf	0	1	1	0	0	Harkey, 3b	1	2	0	2	1
Lyons, rf	0	0	0	0	0	Thorn'n, cf	1	2	1	0	0
Osteen, ss	1	1	0	4	0	McFar'd, rf	1	1	2	0	0
Crock't, 1b	1	2	13	0	0	Kuhn, 1b	0	1	13	0	0
Hines, 2b	2	1	4	1	1	Walters, lf	0	1	1	0	0
Alp'man, 3b	1	1	2	6	0	Andr'ws, 2b	1	1	2	1	1
Williams, c	1	3	6	3	0	Krebs, c	1	1	3	3	0
Sullivan, cf	0	1	1	0	1	Gruebn'r, ss	0	1	2	2	0
Jones, p	0	0	0	4	0	Balliett, p	0	0	0	3	0
Totals	6	10	27	18	2	Totals	5	10	24	11	2

Davenport ....0 1 0 0 1 0 0 4 *—6
Decatur ....1 0 0 0 1 0 0 2 1—5

Two-Base Hits—Hankey, Walters, Williams. Sacrifice Hits—Thornton, Krebs. Home Run—Williams. Stolen Bases—Hankey, McFarland, Andrews. Double Plays—Andrews to Krebs; Krebs to Kuhn; Alperman to Williams to Crockett. Bases on Balls—Off Balliett, 3; off Jones, 1. Hit by Pitched Ball—Ruby. Struck Out—By Jones, 4; by Balliett, 1. Time of Game—1:35. Umpire—Brown. Attendance—2,300.

Rockford, 6; Bloomington, 3.

ROCKFORD, Ill., Aug. 23.—The champions defeated Bloomington in a contest marked by spectacular fielding. Bishop was hit hard, especially in the eighth, when the locals landed on him for six singles. Score:

Rockford.	R	H	P	A	E	Bloom'ton.	R	H	P	A	E
Gifford, cf	2	2	2	0	0	Neuman, ss	0	1	3	2	0
Starke, 1b	2	2	14	0	0	Godwin, cf	0	1	1	0	1
Meek, c	1	2	4	0	0	Herbert, 3b	0	0	0	1	0
Mid'eton, rf	0	2	1	0	0	Mullaney, 1b	1	1	12	1	1
Hess, ss	0	1	1	4	1	Cassady, rf	1	2	0	0	0
Pattison, 3b	0	0	0	1	0	Connors, lf	0	1	1	0	0
O'Brien, 2b	0	2	2	2	1	Truby, 2b	1	1	3	4	0
Shour, lf	1	1	1	1	0	Donovan, c	0	1	4	2	0
Graham, p	0	0	2	6	0	Bishop, p	0	0	0	4	0
Totals	6	12	27	14	2	Totals	3	8	24	14	2

Two-Base Hit—Mullaney. Three-Base Hit—Donovan. Double Plays—Graham and St[illegible] O'Brien and Stark; Neuman and Mullaney; [illegible] Mullaney. Struck Out—By Graham, 2 [illegible] 5. Bases on Balls—Off Graham, 2; [illegible] Sacrifice Hits—Godwin, Starke, M[illegible] Umpire—Hart. Attendance—1,511.

INTERSTATE LEAGUE.

Standing of the Clubs.

Clubs—	W.	L.	P.C.	Clubs—	W.	L.	P.C.
Sycamore	16	5	.762	So. Chicago	9	9	.500
Racine	13	6	.685	Marquettes	9	10	.474
Aurora	12	6	.667	Kenosha	7	10	.412
Elgin	11	9	.550	Spaldings	4	12	.250
Gunthers	8	8	.500	Athletics	3	16	.158

South Chicago, 8; Elgin, 1.

ELGIN, Ill., Aug. 23.—The South Chicagos outplayed the Elgins at every stage of the game, defeating them by a score of 8 to 1. The features of the game were the brilliant fielding of Saxe, Babcock, and Fenton, and the stick work of the latter, and the pitching of Keeley. Elgin used up three pitchers in endeavoring to stave off defeat, but to no avail. Score:

S. Chicago.	R	H	P	A	E	Elgins.	R	H	P	A	E
McKee, 1b	1	1	5	0	0	Hanson, rf	0	0	0	0	0
Keeley, p	1	0	1	2	0	M.Don'e, 3b	0	1	0	3	2
Babcock, lf	0	1	5	1	0	McN'y, ss-cf	0	0	2	0	0
Donovan, c	1	0	5	1	0	Sears, c	0	0	7	1	1
Hill, ss	2	1	2	2	0	Cal'h'n, cf-p	0	2	3	0	0
Fenton, cf	1	2	0	0	0	T.Don'ue, 1b	0	2	8	0	1
Saxe, 3b	2	0	2	3	0	McP't'd, 2b	1	1	1	4	1
Andrews, 2b	1	2	2	1	1	Hutch'on, lf	0	1	1	0	0
Braden, rf	0	1	0	0	0	Egger, p	0	0	0	0	0
						Herten, cf	0	0	0	0	0
						Peeples, p	0	0	0	2	0
Totals	8	11	*26	7	2	Totals	1	7	27	12	5

*Donohue out, interfering with batted ball.

South Chicago ....0 2 0 3 0 0 0 3 0—8
Elgin ....0 1 0 0 0 0 0 0 0—1

Two-Base Hits—Braden, McPartland. Stolen Bases—McNerney, Donohue, Keeley (2), Andrews (2), Fenton. Double Plays—Keeley to McKee; Babcock to Saxe. Struck Out—By Keeley, 5; by Egger, 2; by Peeples, 3. First Base on Balls—Off Keeley, 2; off Egger, 1; off Callahan, 2. Umpire—McWaters. Attendance—900.

Aurora Shuts Out Gunthers.

Aurora shut out the Gunthers yesterday at Aurora, 5 to 0, without a hit. The features were the pitching of Munch and the phenomenal, all-around fielding of the Auroras.

Sycamore Team Forfeits.

The Athletics and Sycamores were scheduled to play at Hand's park, but the Sycamore team failed to put in an appearance, and Umpire Jack Pickett awarded the game to the Athletics by the score of 9 to 0.

Marquette-Kenosha Game Postponed.

The game between the Marquettes and the Kenoshas of the Interstate league that was scheduled for today was postponed, and will be played off on a double-header on Sept. 7.

WESTERN LEAGUE.

Denver, 0-6; Milwaukee, 6-0.

DENVER, Colo., Aug. 23.—Denver and Milwaukee broke even today, each being credited with a shut-out. The second game was stopped by rain. Attendance, 4,063. Score:

First game:
Milwaukee ......0 0 2 0 0 0 0 0 [illegible]—6 8 1
Denver ....0 0 0 0 0 0 0 0 0—0 6 1
Batteries—Kenna and Lucia; Eyler and Schiel.

Second game:
Denver ....0 1 0 1 0 2 2 0—6 9 0
Milwaukee ......0 0 0 0 0 0 0 0—0 [illegible]
Batteries—Lenike and Schiel; Vollendorf and Lucia.

Kansas City, 8; Omaha, 7.

OMAHA, Neb., Aug. 23.—Two hits and Mills' muff of Nichols' long fly in the twelfth inning gave the game to the visitors. Attendance, 3,200. Score:

Kansas City....0 4 2 1 0 0 0 0 0 0 0 1—8 11 3
Omaha ....0 0 1 0 3 3 0 0 0 0 0 0—7 10 6
Batteries—Nichols and Messitt; Sanders, Gonding, and Thomas.

Colorado Springs, 10-8; Peoria, 2-6.

COLORADO SPRINGS, Colo., Aug. 23.—Colorado Springs took a double header from Peoria today by good stick work. Both games were won on bunched hits. Score:

FIRST GAME.
Colo. Springs....0 0 4 2 3 0 0 1 *—10 15 2
Peoria ....[illegible]—2 9 3
Friend and Wilson; Villeman and Doran.

SECOND GAME.
Colo. Springs....[illegible]—8 12 2
Peoria ....[illegible]—6 12 1
Hart and Wilson; McNeely and Doran.

Des Moines, 10; St. Joseph, 8.

DES MOINES, Iowa, Aug. 23.—After apparently losing the game beyond redemption, Des Moines jumped on Chinn in the last half of the fourth for nine runs. In that inning Quinn got a triple and a home run. Score:

Des Moines.....0 0 0 9 1 0 0 0 *—10 14 2
St. Joseph......[illegible]—8 [illegible]
Miller and Fohl; Chinn, Diehl, and Garvin. Attendance—3,000.

Southern League.

Memphis, 2; Little Rock, 8.
Montgomery, 2; Nashville, 3 (twelve innings).
New Orleans, 2-0; Shreveport, 0-5.

LAST DAYS AT SARATOGA.

Season of Brilliant Racing at the "Spa" Closes This Week.

Special Dispatch to The Inter Ocean.

SARATOGA, N. Y., Aug. 23.—The racing at the Spa has entered on its last quartet of days. During the inclement weather the attendance daily is remarkable.

Taken as a whole, the racing has been brilliant throughout the meeting, and what may be called the sensation is the great form displayed by Hermis, and the greeting the high-priced horse received on each occasion that he has won shows he is still the idol he was just a year ago, when he was unbeatable.

The general impression here is that the West may not be looked to for a champion, as it is the opinion of many shrewd ones that Hermis can defeat the pride of the Haggin stable. Up to the present time the Westerners have shown up nothing of any importance of any age, with the exception of Flying Ship, a remarkably grand-looking 3-year-old filly, who has scored a brace of victories.

The great interest is now centered in the work of the Futurity candidates here. The youngster that has shown the best work is the colt Israelite, the property of the Messrs. Keene. He worked here seven furlongs in 1:27⅗, with the greatest ease.

NOTES OF THE AUTOS.

Dr. H. Nelson Jackson of Burlington, Vt., whose feat of crossing the United States from the Pacific to the Atlantic ocean in an automobile has been questioned, in a letter to the automobile editor of The Inter Ocean says in regard to the matter:

"There have been many exaggerated and false statements given out by the press and advertising agents as though they emanated from me. I did not use two machines, nor did I use the railroad; in fact, I did not touch Utah, as I went through Idaho, Wyoming, and Nebraska, and I passed through Oregon where there are no railroads. I left the railroad at Anderson, Cal., going to Alturas, then north to Lake View, Ore., and from there direct north to a little south of Prineville, then east to Burns and Vail, and saw the railroad at Ontario for the first time since leaving Anderson. With the exception of using the ferries to cross San Francisco bay and Snake river, and horses simply to pull us out of a deep stream once, and three times out of deep mud holes, my Winton No. 1,684 came all the way with her own power, and I am prepared to stake any sum on the above assertions."

• • •

The members of the Chicago Automobile club who made the run to Pistakee lake Sunday arrived home this morning, reporting an enjoyable trip.

• • •

A. C. Banker is awaiting the arrival of a thirty-five horse-power Peerless. As soon as he receives it he intends to set out on a tour to New York city.

PEWAUKEE REGATTA RESULTS.

Aspirant Wins the Waukesha Beach Trophy in a Close Finish.

Special Dispatch to The Inter Ocean.

PEWAUKEE, Wis., Aug. 23.—In the tenth regatta for the Waukesha Beach trophy the yacht Aspirant won out after a close race, defeating her next nearest competitor by one minute and one second. The northwest wind was fair, and good time was made. Start was at 3 o'clock.

All boats got over the line in close order, with Aspirant and Mercury leading. At the first turn the Dora led by a few seconds, and at the second mark the boats went around in the following order: Aspirant, Mercury, Dora. Summary:

Yacht and Owner—	Time.
Aspirant (F. Wolaeger)	3:50:34
Mercury (A. Pawling)	3:51:35
Argo (A. Pawling)	3:51:51
Allimac (Kopmeir Bros.)	3:52:59
[illegible]sclk (F. Luenzmann)	3:54:09

Judges—A. Nelson, A. C. Clark.
Timekeeper—C. F. White.

BEST ATHLETES OF EAST AND WEST

Championships of the Western and Eastern Divisions Decided Saturday.

WINNERS WILL RUN AT MILWAUKEE

Competition at Both Games Shows That the Quality of the Athletes of the Metropolitan and Western Clubs Is Fair.

With the passing of the Western and Metropolitan A. A. U. division championships, attention is now turned to the national championships to be held at Milwaukee Sept. 10 and 11.

The interest of every athlete in the middle West was drawn toward the games of these two divisions, for the best men in the Western association and that of the Metropolitan will be pitted against those of this district, the Central association, at the national championships.

Of the two districts, that of the Metropolitan interested the middle West boys more than any other, for the most formidable teams that Chicago, Milwaukee, and Detroit will meet are those of the New York A. C., Greater New York Irish A. C., Pastimes, New West Side A. C., and probably the Knickerbocker A. C., all members of the Metropolitan district.

In considering the work of the New York men, there are but a few instances where they surpass the middle West athletes, save in the weights, and their superiority here is granted. Flanagan and Sheridan of the Greater Irish A. C., and Feurbach, New York A. C., appear to have shown up better than the men of the Western association, while the performances of the Eastern athletes are better than the best of those of the middle West. However, Henneman and Plaw, if they compete, should be figured in one of the first three places in all of the weight events. Flanagan is not in the form that he displayed last year, and, consequently, is liable to suffer defeat. If Horgan of Ireland, Coe of Boston, and Dick Sheldon of Yale compete, the shot-put should go to them in one-two-three order.

By defeating Jim Mitchell in the fifty-six-pound weight event Flanagan seems to have clinched the right to meet Desmarteau of Montreal, last year's champion.

In the sprints the West seems to have a better chance than ever. Walsh captured the hundred Saturday in :10 1-5, while :10 3-5 was the best the St. Louis champion could do. Walsh again won the 220 in 23 3-5 seconds, poor time for a sprinter of his ability, while at St. Louis Heckwolf ran two-fifths of a second slower. Hahn, Blair, Eckersoll, and Hogenson of the Central association all beat these marks last spring by good margins.

The Quarter an Even Thing.

The quarter-mile run appears to be an even thing between the Central and Metropolitan districts, but unless the runners from these two districts improve by at least three seconds, the event should go to Reilly of Boston, who has been running close to 50 seconds all summer. Of the Central men, there is not one who can do 50 for the distance, but there are plenty who may be able to drop into second or third place.

John Wright of the New West Side Athletic club did not compete in the 880 Saturday and may not be present at Milwaukee next month. An equally fast man is the person of Valentine of the New York Athletic club who won that event in good time, with Bacon of the Greater Irish Athletic club a close second. The First regiment and Chicago university have some fast men for this event, but Alex Grant, if he should start, is liable to upset calculations of every one.

The only events which may reasonably be called open ones are the mile and two-mile. Kellogg, Grant, McEachron, Hall, and Joyce are about evenly matched, and these men will compete in either the one or two-mile runs. The Western games at St. Louis Saturday witnessed the return of Bernie Gallagher, the former intercollegiate mile champion, to the cinder path, and though he was defeated in 4:41, he clearly showed that he was rounding into his old form. Knox and Magee and the other Western men will have to put up gilt-edged performances in the pole vault to defeat Allias and Anderson of New York. Allias cleared 11 feet, 7 inches, while Anderson was but three inches back of the winner.

Excellent contests should be seen in the high and broad jumps. Prinstein has regained the form he was in at Paris, and Saturday won the championship with a jump of over 23 feet, while Green, the second man, was within half an inch of 23 feet. King, the winner of the Western championship, cleared but 21 feet 6 inches Saturday, so that he may be considered out of the running. Unless Kraenzlein competes first place should go to the East.

Baxter, Jones, Cotter, the Leahy brothers, and Freymark should present some high-class jumping in their event. The men are about equal, and with the reported form of the Leahys, they should be some where within the first three places.

GOTHAM'S TEAMS LOOK GOOD.

Both New York Clubs Will Probably Finish in the First Division.

Special Dispatch to The Inter Ocean.

NEW YORK, Aug. 23.—The waning baseball season finds the chance for both the New York American and the Nationals to finish in the first division. As between the two, the Nationals' chances of so finishing are the better. Indeed, there is little probability that they will not finish among the first four, and, after a campaign that for the most part has been attended by creditably consistent work, it will be a disappointment to their admirers if they do not land as good as second. That they will not do on their present clip, as they have lost six out of the last nine games. The biggest handicap from now on is that they finish in the West, but on past performances this need occasion no alarm, for the team has done admirably on the road, better, all the things considered, than on home grounds.

No team has created such a stir in New York in years as has McGraw's, and between it and the Chicagoes they have injected so much needed vitality into the National league constitution. All credit will be due McGraw and his players if they finish no worse than fourth.

A feature of the season in connection with them has been not only the big patronage they have had, but the fact that this patronage has been sustained. The end of the season is in sight, yet interest flags not at all. Such has not been the case here since 1899, when John Ward's New Yorks finished second.

The New York Americans are nearly through with their last Western trip, and play most of their games at home from now on, and, having been a better home team than a road aggregation, have abundant reason to expect to finish fourth or better. Fourth place is all that can be asked of a first-class team. Besides, on the face of it a team

NAPOLEON LAJOIE AND HANS WAGNER, GREATEST OF ALL BASEBALL PLAYERS.

Lajoie, the Giant Frenchman Who Plays Second Base for Cleveland American League Team, Is the Only Batsman Who Ever Broke a Baseball.

They Bat with the Strength of Dave Orr or Delehanty—They Field Like Herman Long or Bid McPhee—They Run Bases with the Speed of John Ward or Billy Hamilton.

Napoleon Lajoie and Hans Wagner, two of the greatest ball players that the National game has ever known, have been having a hard fight for the premier batting honors of the country all this season.

Lajoie leads the American League with .356 per cent. and Wagner has established the same figures against the National League twirlers.

Wagner is now out of the game for the season owing to an injury to one of his legs. Therefore Larry will either have to keep up the .356 clip or exceed it, or give up the honors to the sturdy Pirate.

In the opinion of experts both Lajoie and Wagner rank as batters with any of the great hitters of the past. Both would undoubtedly have better averages but for two reasons. One is that they are both impatient while at the bat and will hit at anything that comes within reach instead of working pitchers for bases on balls. Another reason is that the fielders play so much deeper for Larry and Hans than they do for most other batsmen that in almost every game they are robbed of hits on tremendous drives that would be safe with nearly any other man in the game.

Both are free hitters and can pick a ball from off their shoe tops or from behind their ears and poke it out for two bases. Both are fast in going to first base and can beat out short, slow hits with the speed of Willie Keeler and George Browne.

First Batter to Finish a Season with Batting Average of .400.

In past performances Lajoie has somewhat the better of Wagner. The Frenchman was the first major leaguer to go through an entire season with a batting average of .400 per cent. or more. He accomplished this remarkable feat in 1901, when he led the American League with a percentage of .422.

Both men began to attract attention in 1896, before which they found it difficult to make a living at baseball. Larry drove a hack in the winter in Woonsocket, R. I., and played semi-professional ball in summer. Wagner was a butcher boy in Carnegie, Pa., and played ball for a few dollars a game when his services were required.

Wagner's first professional engagement was with the Steubenville team, and his clubmates were Frank Bowerman, George Smith, last year with New York; Harry Smith and Claude Ritchey, both now Pirates, and Al Wagner, brother of Hans, now with the Toronto Eastern League team.

In 1896 Lajoie played with the Fall River team and Wagner with the Paterson club of the Atlantic League. Larry led the New England League with .429 per cent. Wagner batted .334 in the Atlantic.

In 1897 Lajoie joined the Philadelphia National League team and played there until 1900, when he jumped to the American League. Wagner played with Paterson and led the Atlantic League with .379 per cent. Behind him were such future greats as Elberfeld, Heidrick, Seybold, Keister and Dougherty.

Wagner Led the Big League in 1900 with an Average of .380.

Wagner finished the season of 1897 with the Louisville club and has been in the National League since. He led the league in 1900 with .380 per cent.

Beginning with 1896, and including last season, Lajoie has a grand average of .370 per cent. and Wagner .323.

In 1899 Lajoie made a record that proved him to be about the hardest hitter that ever played the game. On May 13 of that year, against Pitcher Colcolough, then with the New York club, Lajoie hit the ball so hard that he broke the rubber and made it unfit to play with. Later in the season he repeated the feat in Cincinnati. The Enquirer, of that city, described the incident as follows:

"Larry Lajoie, the terrific batter with the Philadelphia team, hit a ball so hard in Monday's game that he actually broke it. It was in the third inning. Lajoie straightened out on the first ball pitched. He met it squarely and pushed his weight against it. The ball went at a terrific rate of speed and struck the centre field fence near the top with a resounding whack. The ball caromed off the fence, and before Elmer Smith could field it Lajoie was on third. The ball was thrown to Umpire Burns for inspection. He examined it and threw the ball out of the game. The awful jolt that Lajoie gave it broke the rubber on the inside. It was knocked lopsided and was no longer fit for play."

Malachi Kittridge gives the following advice to the Washington pitchers:

"Place the ball at a medium rate of speed over the middle of the rubber, or cut the plate with a slow arched curve whenever Lajoie is facing you. The big Frenchman will write an obituary in the shape of a double, triple or homer on any ball that has steam behind it and veers over the outside or inside corners. I have seen him soak a high one in the inside on a level with his Adam's apple, and the next one he plucked off his socks knee high and on the inside. He's the most dangerous, eccentric and uncertain batsman the game has ever seen since Dave Orr quit."

Lajoie and the late Ed Delehanty were great chums. While on the Philadelphia team together, and later, they generally had about the same batting average. Last year Del just nosed out Larry for the American League batting honors with .376 per cent. to Larry's .369.

This year, when poor Del came to his untimely end, the figures showed them just even with .333 per cent.

Their Work at Shortstop Is as Brilliant as Their Batting.

Wagner and Lajoie are not only great batsmen, but brilliant fielders as well. Both glide over the ground so fast that impossible stops for other infielders look easy for them. Wagner's recent work at the Polo Grounds, when he shut off run after run by his great fielding, will be remembered. Lajoie at second is equally good on balls hit to either side of him. John McGraw says of Larry's fielding: "He is the only ball-player I ever saw that can handle a ball as well with one hand as with two. If he can get to a ball with either hand it is usually all up with the batter."

Both men are in the game all the time. There are some players who are not at all anxious to have the ball hit to them at critical stages of the game. At such times Larry and Hans just hanker for a chance to get hold of the ball. The more exciting the play the more they want to be in it.

Voting contests are now going on in several cities as to which is the best ball player in the country.

British Golfers Say Our Courses Are Not So Natural, and Therefore Not So Good as Theirs.

Will the golf courses in this country ever attain the high standard of excellence of those abroad? This is a question amateur golfers have been asking themselves quite frequently of late—in fact, ever since the Oxford-Cambridge cracks arrived on these shores. Every member of the British team has been repeatedly asked his opinion of the links in the United States as compared with the classic courses of Great Britain.

J. A. T. Bramston, the only member of the visiting delegation who continues to cling to the solid ball, when spoken to on the subject, probably hit the nail on the head when he remarked that the courses over here were not natural enough. There is more trouble on the average course in Scotland or England; neither does the rough stuff in front of the tees end so abruptly, and it frequently happens that drives of 180 yards are essential in order to avoid all difficulty.

In Great Britain they have more seaside links, with their natural sand traps, and these, according to Bramston, approach the ideal in golf courses. He likes the new course at Shinnecock Hills for that reason, but the Briton ranks the Myopia links near Boston ahead of any he has seen in this country. This opinion is pretty generally entertained by the other members of the visiting team.

While the foreign courses literally abound in trouble, the high, rank grass skirting the fair greens in America are practically unknown on the other side. In this country the Garden City course is by Americans considered ideal, but the Oxford-Cambridge men criticise the presence of the high grass so near the greens. They also class the course as monotonous.

Another criticism of our courses is that there is not enough difficulty in the average hazard. The Englishmen claim it is possible to slice or pull from the tees into shallow artificial sand traps, take out an iron and reach the green in 2. Much of the so-called trouble on the courses hereabouts would not be classed as such on the other side. The prevailing conditions in Great Britain make it necessary for the players to adapt themselves to more varied situations, which accounts largely for their ability to play so beautifully from indifferent lies.

Many American amateurs lose their nerve when confronted with a series of poor lies. The Britons think nothing of using their play clubs out of rough stuff. To be sure, one cannot score in low figures with everything going against him, but if he will keep his head long enough the ball will sooner or later begin to act kindly.

An observation concerning the general style of play over here, made by one of the Britons, is that nearly all the amateurs seem to bend their energies toward the development of an exceptionally long game, rather at the expense of their approaching and putting. It is a common thing in this lively ball age to see youngster after youngster get away drives of 200 yards or over, and as they leave the first tee one would be justified in classing them as likely champions.

The observing Bramston also remarks that the Americans are too prone to use their mashies when just off the edge of the green. The foreigners put wherever it is possible. None of the Englishmen agrees with the statement that putting is an inspiration. A deadly short game, they say, is the result of long and constant application.

The golfing of the Americans as a whole, considering the comparatively short length of time they have had to devote to the game, is in the opinion of the foreigners nothing short of extraordinary.

News and Gossip of the Diamond Stars That Twinkle in the American and National Leagues.

Chicago won the series from the Pittsburg Champions by twelve games to eight.

• • •

Catcher Billy Bergen, of Cincinnati, will not be able to play again this season.

• • •

Harry McCormick still leads the Eastern League in batting with .355 per cent. Matty McIntyre, of Buffalo, is second with .343.

• • •

Willie Keeler has not made an error in the last forty-five games He has made thirty-two hits in the last eighteen games.

• • •

Eddie Quick, the star pitcher of the Salt Lake Pacific team, will join the Greater New Yorks next week.

• • •

Four victories in twenty games played is the Cincinnati Reds record against the champion Pittsburgs.

• • •

According to a story from Cincinnati, Joe Kelley will play first base for the Reds next season and Jake Beckley will be let out.

• • •

Pitcher Bartley, of the South Texas League, has received an offer from Manager McGraw. They will meet in Cincinnati next week to talk it over.

• • •

In a series of games between the Nashville and Birmingham teams of the Southern League Nashville scored only five runs in three games, and all of them were homers.

• • •

Chicago appears to be the dumping ground of St. Louis cast-offs. Wicker, Williams and Currie, former Cardinals, are now helping the Cubs to win games.

• • •

Full returns from the Labor Day games do not indicate any falling off in the interest in the national game. Eight games in the National League drew 77,017 spectators, and 52,760 saw eight in the American.

• • •

A St. Louis critic says "Deerfoot" Barclay is playing left field for the Cardinals like "Shovel foot" Barclay.

• • •

"Jock" Menefee, the veteran pitcher, wants to bet $2,500 on Pittsburg against Boston. Menefee is in Chicago, and they are offering 10 to 9 on Collins's men in Boston.

• • •

Connie Mack's Athletics and the Phillies will play a post-season series beginning Sept. 30. In the series played before the season opened the Phillies won four out of five games.

• • •

Minor league umpires are likely to officiate in the post-season series between the National and American League teams. The big league umpires want $25 a day and expenses.

• • •

Charley Hickman and "Buck" Freeman are the champion long-distance sluggers. They lead the country in heavy hitting, each having made ten home runs.

• • •

Courtney, who began the season with the Highlanders and was traded to Detroit, has refused to be shifted to the Buffalo Eastern League team. For this he has been suspended by Detroit.

• • •

Willie Keeler fancies Boston for the post-season series. He thinks Collins's great infield and Creiger's accurate throwing will check the Pirates in bunting and base-running, and that Boston outclasses the National League champions in pitchers and catchers.

• • •

Pitcher Louis Bruce, the Indian, is much sought after by major league managers. The Toronto club wants $5,000 for his release.

• • •

Hughey Jennings says he will win the Eastern League championship with Baltimore next year and will then quit baseball and practice. Jennings will finish at the Cornell Law School next spring.

• • •

Rube Waddell, the stage-struck twirler, holds a marvellous record for strike outs. He played in thirty-seven games this season and fanned 301 men.

• • •

Patsy Donovan, who was ill with malarial fever, rejoined the St. Louis Club last week. He is still too weak to play with his team.

• • •

Considerable surprise has been expressed that John T. Brush accepted the courtesies of the Philadelphia National League club and allowed the New Yorks to play at Columbia Park.

• • •

It is not likely that any of the games between Collins's team and the Pirates will be played in this city. Henry Killilea, owner of the Boston Club, is opposed to playing them anywhere but in Pittsburg and Boston.

• • •

Barney Dreyfuss now says the Pirates shall play the Bostons only seven games in the championship series, instead of eleven as first arranged. "I have told the owners of the Boston team of my decision and they can do as they please—play or not." Perhaps Barney hopes it will be "not."

Wagner Is the Massive Shortstop of the Champion Pittsburg National League Team, Who Stands Alone Among Infielders as a Coverer of Ground.

…umble Stage Hand's Quick Wit Resulted in Salary Increase.

…lly Brady is a stickler for repartee in the plays …roduces, even as he was once a stickler for …s" in the fighters he was wont to manage. And …rtee off the stage hits him as happily as in the …en lines of the play. An instance of this occurred at a rehearsal recently, where an obliging …e hand did several little favors for Brady outside …egular line of work. Brady as he was leaving …heatre handed the man a cigar.

"This cigar's a bit heavy," he observed as the …e hand was thanking him, "you'd better wait and …e it after a good dinner."

"I'm sorry," said the other, "because that con…s me to wait till pay day till I smoke it."

When pay day arrived the stage hand found an in…ed salary and the scribbled line:

"You won't have to wait so long now before smoking."

…he Woodpile and the Wheat Field, Attel's Advice to a Boy.

A… Attel, the little Western fighter, deserves a … in some Hall of Fame if only for the advice he … a candidate for fistic honors who came to him … counsel. A Western youth sought an interview … Attel with a view to picking up some points on …ing. The boy went on to say he was the only … of a widow and that he and his mother had hith… worked the latter's little farm. Now, however … boy considered himself too good for farm work … had left his old mother to do all the work alone … he came to town to seek an opening as a pugilist. Attel heard him patiently. At the end of the life-story Abe asked:

"And you want me to prescribe the best course of training for you?"

"Yes, sir," cried the delighted youth.

"Well, I'll do it on one condition, and that is that you'll promise to follow my advice in every single detail."

"Oh, I promise, faithfully!"

"All right," said Attel, curtly. "The course of training I lay out for you is to get back to the farm on the next train and do a certain amount of farm work every day. You'll know when you're working hard enough by keeping it up until your mother has no more work to do. The physical culture apparatus I prescribe for you is the woodpile, with a course of ploughing, harvesting and chores on the side. That'll be all."

Chamber of Horrors and Not Bed Chamber, Said Delaney.

Billy Delaney was describing to some friends an experience he had while training Jeffries in California. He was belated, too far from the training quarters to return that night; so took refuge in a farm house until the following morning. The farmer, a shrewd New Englander who had recently emigrated West, charged Delaney $5 for a night's occupancy of the "spare bedroom." The mattress was stuffed with bulging cornhusks, the window was nailed shut, the room was full of mosquitoes, and a chorus of frogs in a near-by pond made night hideous. As Delaney emerged, haggard and hollow-eyed, next morning, his host greeted him with the remark:

"I bet I could let that bed chamber at $10 a day."

"You could," assented Delaney drearily, "but not as a bed chamber. You'd have to call it by its proper name—a chamber of horrors."

Schoolboys Preparing for Fall Season on the Track, Field and Gridiron.

Dr. Moore, of Columbia Grammar School, has been elected custodian of the New York Interscholastic Athletic Association. He is well versed in interscholastic sport, and has done much to put the association on the strong footing on which it stands to-day.

• • •

Young Lestrade, who so ably captained the Columbia Grammar School track team last year, has entered Columbia University. He will make a strong addition to the college track team. Trainer Hjertberg expects him to make a good showing in the 440 yard and half-mile runs.

• • •

Camp Rainbow, on Lower Saranac Lake, has practically closed for the season. All the youngsters are returning and in fit condition for a vigorous season on the gridiron. Athletic Director P. M. Seixas will come to the city to-morrow and will at once take up his work at the New York Military Academy, Cornwall-on-the-Hudson.

• • •

Schoolboy athletes throughout the country are praising the work of Charles J. Dieges, who designed the testimonial dedicated to the memory of the late William B. Curtis, father of American athletics. The work is a masterpiece, say the boys, and shows the true sportsmanship of Mr. Dieges, who has spared neither time nor expense in getting the testimonial up.

• • •

It has been said on good authority that several of the schools that resigned from the association last year will again apply for admission this year. It is almost an assured fact that they will be admitted, but they must all live up to the new rules.

• • •

Wrestling and boxing will be introduced in a majority of the school gymnasiums this season. The instructors believe in this sort of sport to build up the body. Prof. Whewell said last week that it is good preliminary work for football, as it hardens the boys to knocks and bumps.

• • •

Ever since 1887 there has been in one of the local savings banks $50 to the credit of the New York Interscholastic Athletic Association. No one seemed to know anything about it. Recently Mr. Rhoades, Chairman of the Advisory Committee, found out where the money was and had it transferred to the present association. The association has on hand now a balance of $80.

• • •

"The one-year clause will be as strictly enforced this fall as last spring," says ex-President Mahany. "The rumor to the contrary is all rot. The new law is now a permanent feature and it will so remain." Mahany further said that he is in favor of a permanent chairman to help conduct the meetings of the association.

• • •

Lester Klous, who left Dwight School last year to go the Pennsylvania Military Academy, will be back this year. The boy is a clever athlete and strong football player and should strengthen the various teams to a big extent. He was one of the best junior sprinters in 1902.

• • •

Howard Croker, youngest son of the ex-Tammany leader, will be back at Columbia Grammer School this fall. Last spring he made quite a showing in the pole vault, and as he will play football he is looked upon to follow in the footsteps of his brother Herbert, who did such good work for Dwight School at fullback and afterward making the all-interscholastic team.

Gus Ruhlin Tells Why Lipton Did Not Lift the Blooming Mug.

Gus Ruhlin the day after his fight with Kid Carter was returning to New York, when in the smoker he fell into a talk with an Englishman who had witnessed the fight. The Englishman had come to this country expressly for the yacht races and was disgusted with their result.

"What else could Lipton have expected," he growled disgustedly, "coming to a blooming country like this where people don't even speak real English? Why, the hotel people here actually speak of a 'lift' as an 'elevator.' How silly."

"Well," drawled Ruhlin slowly, "if Lipton learns enough of this American language, maybe next time he'll be able to 'elevate' the cup, even if he doesn't succeed in 'lifting' it."

Young "Terry" McGovern Thinks He's Improvement on Papa.

Terry McGovern is telling the following anecdote of his son, Terry, jr. (whose name, by the way, is not Terry at all, but Joe), who was sent to Sunday-school last week for the first time. On his return his father undertook to catechise him as to what religious truths he had gleaned at the first session.

"Well," said Terry, jr., at last, "they told me, for one thing, that God made everybody, and that He made me. Is that so?"

"Yes," replied Terry.

"Did He make you, too, papa?" queried the child.

"Yes, of course."

"Well," sighed Terry jr., after a moment's reflection, "He's turning out much better work nowadays than He used to in your time, isn't He, papa?"

Lou Dillon, Major Delmar and Billy Buck on Speedway.

Billy Buck, 2.07¾, the trotting champion of the year, has won $30,600 in stakes and purses, and if he retains his form his winnings will foot up over $50,000. Like Lou Dillon he is not fashionably bred, but he is a winner at that.

• • •

Ed Geers, the famous trainer and driver, is said to have picked up a "gold brick" in the horse Neddie Conners. This horse, it was claimed last fall, trotted three heats over a half-mile track in better than 2.12. However, Geers couldn't make him beat 2.12 once and has sent him South to be turned out. Next year he may do better.

• • •

Monroe Salisbury is now said to use an electric battery to arouse the latent energies of Monte Carlo. He once used a chain to belabor Directum. Suppose the next thing the California veteran will use will be a brass band.

• • •

Since Major Delmar has trotted a mile in 2.00¼ the horsemen know why he is so anxious for a match race with Lou Dillon.

• • •

E. E. Smathers, who paid $7,500 for Tom Keene at the Brighton Beach trotting meeting, only to see him beaten, won the horse out at Syracuse Thursday. Next year with careful handling Tom Keene will be fighting it out with the fastest pacers.

• • •

James Butler, of East View farm, seems to have in Direct one of the greatest sires in the world. Within two weeks the get of Direct have won races on four or five tracks in fast time.

• • •

There is talk of holding a trotting meeting in Chicago next July, when dash races will make up the daily programme.

Sporting Review AND GOSSIP

Pittsburg Baseball Club—Three Times Champions of the National League

Upper Row—Kennedy, Leever, Phillippe, Beaumont, Veil, Thompson, Ritchey, Carisch.
Middle Row—Phelps, Bransfield, Leach, Clarke, Weaver, Wagner, Smith.
Lower Row—Marshall, Kruger, Sebring, Pfeister.
*Note—Doheny was sick and Winham absent when this picture was taken.

CHAMPIONS ARE NOW IN LINE TO BE CONGRATULATED

They Won the Third Consecutive Pennant Against the Greatest Sort of Odds.

YOUNG TALENT FELL DOWN

Most of the Hard Work Fell on the Shoulders of the Old Guard.

BETTER CATCHING WAS NEEDED

By FRANK B. M'QUISTON.

Well, it's all over now. The pennant has been nailed by the boys for the third straight time. We cannot but feel proud of the record of the boys made under circumstances adverse. This time last year the American League had entered the Pittsburg camp and taken what was then thought to be the cream of baseball. They had taken Chesbro, Tannehill, O'Connor and others, rather they had made them offers which the Pittsburg club would not meet and they went. They had Leach also, but thanks to the peace conference at St. Louis he was saved from the wreck.

The eyes of the baseball world centered on Pittsburg as she started this season and as she progressed. The American League people openly boasted that they had robbed us of the best we had and that there would be nothing to the Pittsburg team. But the team struggled along and won the pennant just the same. They did it with Leever, Phillippe and Doheny. Each of these boys pitched better ball this year than did either Chesbro or Tannehill in their league. Not only better than did those boys this season, but better than ever did Chesbro and Tannehill. Only a little harder work was needed to bring out Phillippe and Leever to show the people what they could do. They have shown themselves to be the superior of the pair who went to the other league. Doheny, too, did some nice pitching during the season.

✤ ✤ ✤

The Young Talent Failed.

Looking over the situation now I cannot see just where they won it. Things did not break just as President Dreyfuss and Manager Fred Clarke had expected. There was a world of young talent in the team at the opening of the training season, but now none of them remain. Kane, Wilhelm and Falkenberg have gone. They were tried and found wanting. And when the team started out full of hope it was with the understanding that these youngsters were the best to be had for the money. Falkenburg was touted as a wonder; it was said that he would make the people forget that they had ever seen Chesbro pitch. He didn't. Falkenburg was a failure this year, but the chances are that he might have made good with another year in fast company. The Pittsburg club could take no chances though and such as Falkenburg had to make way.

So the bulk of the pitching fell on the shoulders of Leever and Phillippe and right royally did they bear the burden. The fine work of all the Pittsburg pitchers is more remarkable because of the rather poor article of backstop work put up by the catchers. Smith and Phelps did not catch the best ball in the world all season. There was a series of short spells when both were bad. Take the games of the last week for instance. They stole bases almost at will on Phelps and also on Smith. In Eddie Phelps, however, there is likely the making of the greatest catcher in the country. When he was good this season he was very good, and he was good more than half the time. Smith's catching was hardly up to the standard at any time. He does not hold his runners close enough to the base nor has he shown ability to play the game as it should be played. With first-class backstop work the Pittsburgs would have won perhaps 15 games more during the season.

We have now a good chance to guess at the make-up of the team for next season. That there will be some radical changes in the make-up I do not doubt. And those taking the places of others will not all be young talent either, though President Dreyfuss seems to have a world of it on hand. They will not all stick and make good. At best a youngster needs some time in the fast company. They do not become championship players in the National League at the first throw. They nearly all look good on paper, but when it comes to the real thing on a team like Pittsburg they seem slow and waterlogged. I expect to see some old heads tried and found fitting on the Pittsburg team by the time the season opens next spring. The owners of the club want to pull down the fourth straight pennant. The team will probably require some bolstering up in order to do this.

✤ ✤ ✤

That Post-Season Series.

The chances are now that the post-season series will be played. Doheny, who has been confined to his room for some time, will be out and around possibly tomorrow. Clarke says the left-hander will be at his best in a week's time. This being the case there need be but little to fear about that series. A man who has made a study of ball players, who knows what each team can do, said to me the other evening that Pittsburg could give Boston a lead of 25 per cent in pitching and yet beat them to death in the series. He also said that Pittsburg would not give Boston anything in the pitching line, that the Pittsburg boys were superior to the Boston American League players' pitchers. It is the common belief that Phillippe, Leever and Doheny, all being right, will pitch Boston off her feet, that Young, Dineen and Hughes will be unable to do much with our batters.

I must confess that the playing of the Pittsburgs since they came home for the finish has been disappointing. They have not at any time played their game. Perhaps, the fact that they were certain all the way that they would win may have had something to do with this. The Pittsburgs did not play the ball of which they are capable. They must get out and do their best in the Boston series, if one is played.

There have been some statements made about the Boston American League players holding up the club owners for a bit of the post-season gate money. This has done the players an injustice, I think. Be it known that with the end of this month the series with contracts of the American League players expire, while those in the National League run until October 15. The American League people, therefore, will not be under contract during the time these games were to be played, and they simply asked what would be done about paying them for their time. Surely there was nothing wrong about this. The owners of the American League team did not expect the boys to play the post-season series for nothing. Let us hope so, at least.

✤ ✤ ✤

The Question of Salaries.

It will be quite a surprise if there is not some sort of an explosion before long between certain players and club owners. There will be a big cut in salaries this fall and there will also be a big kick. That the magnates understand each other pretty well can be seen in the fact that no one seems tumbling over his own feet to sign up his players for next year. Many of the players had their inning last season, the club owners may take a little crack at being independent themselves now.

That the American League intends to make some changes was evidenced in the new contracts which they are submitting to their players. The contracts call for six months' service, as do those of the National League. This would make the player subject to his employers for some time before the season opens, as well as after it closes. Had the American people a longer contract with their players there would have been no trouble with the Boston players over the post-season series. It is likely that some changes in the methods of conducting business will be made this fall and winter.

WILL GIVE BASE DECISIONS

[Special Telegram to The Dispatch.]

NEW YORK, Sept. 17.—Following close on the invention of a pitching gun to supplant the star twirler of the diamond comes the news from Canada of an invention to aid the umpire in making correct decisions on plays at first base. This new device, which has been patented, consists of an electric plate attached to the initial bag and so arranged as to ring an electric bell if the first baseman touches the bag before the runner. On the other hand, if the batter reaches first base before it is touched by the baseman the plate is so adjusted that the bell will not ring.

Assuming that the device is always in working order, the umpire may, if he wishes, turn his back and be sure of giving an accurate decision at first. If the bell rings the runner is out; if it doesn't the runner's safe. Sounds simple.

Fandom and managers are now eagerly awaiting news of the invention of a batting machine which shall swell the average of every wielder of the wagon tongue to the .300 per cent mark.

GOOD TIMBER AT PRINCETON

Lots of Fine Material From Which to Build Up This Year's Eleven.

[Special Telegram to The Dispatch.]

PRINCETON, Sept. 18.—Football prospects at Princeton are brighter by far than they have been at the beginning of any season in recent years. Only two members of last year's team are missing this fall. They are Quarterback Pearson and Ross McClave. It is safe to say that Princeton has the team that will bear watching this fall. Last year the Tigers had to depend almost entirely upon a green eleven. Nearly all of the year was spent in developing material with the future in view. In the Yale game the Tigers had a team that averaged 190 pounds, heavier even than that of the Elis. This year all but two men are back. Let another season of training be given to the orange and black and they will finish in the front ranks without a doubt.

The Tigers' veteran captain, J. R. De Witt, with his strong and cunning toe, is almost a team by himself. His remarkable drop kicks of 45 and 50 yards for goals last fall stamp him as the greatest kicker the game has developed in recent years. The new rules, which put a premium on the kicking and running game, could not have been better adapted to Princeton's play. The Tigers will have the following veterans and substitutes from which to select a team: Ends, R. T. Davis, H. H. Henry, K. B. Crawford, N. B. Tooker, P. M. Brasher, F. Brown, J. A. Forney, H. C. Smith; tackles, R. R. Read, E. E. Brown, H. Short, N. Caruthers, C. S. Whelan, D. S. Pond, H. E. Newman, J. C. Semple, E. C. Hardy; guards, J. Bradley, E. L. Rafferty, J. R. De Witt, A. T. Baker, O. Dutcher, C. T. Titman, C. S. Whelen; centers, E. L. Barney, A. T. Baker, H. Short; quarterback, T. J. Burke, E. C. Chandle, R. Vetterlein, A. F. King; halfbacks, W. L. Foulke, S. E. Bush, H. R. Hart, J. D. Kafer, H. C. Smith, C. R. Simpson, A. H. Otis, E. S. Ward; fullbacks, R. McClave, J. C. Ames, J. D. Kafer, W. Delaney.

RAFFERTY PLAYS STRAIGHT BALL

Yale's Captain, a Pittsburger by the Way, Doesn't Worry Over the New Rules.

The young man who holds the center of the stage has always played the kind of football that has won championships for Yale, and that has something to do with his elevation to office. He pounds away until he drops in his tracks, and without any spectacular effects does his duty as he finds it and does not know enough to quit when he is hurt. There is lots of talk about the new rules and the wonderful "tricks" and strategies that will be sprung by cunning coaches. As a matter of fact, the magnificent elevens of Gordon Brown and George Chadwick battered their opponents to pieces, and put all fancy plays to confusion by the straight, hard football that will win as long as the game is worthy the name it bears.

And this is the sort that Rafferty plays, and he has the spirit that will keep his team up to this mark. He is not bothering his head about the new rules. That is for the coaches to heat their mental bearings over. His business is to make eleven men play the cleanest, hardest football that is in their strong bodies, their nerves and their brain cells, and when they are tired to make them remember that the other fellow is just as nearly ready to lie down and die and perhaps a little closer to the limit of endurance.

Captain Rafferty has the best quarterback in the country to build his team on. Of his other veterans there is Shevlin, one of the two best end rushes, if not the best, of last season, so that the ends are cared for. His two tackles, Hogan and Kinney, are the strongest and fastest in the country—on last year's record—and it is probable that Bloomer will be allowed to play. The big gap comes in the center, where Glass, Goss and Holt are missing. Chadwick is gone, but Metcalf, Rockwell and Bowman insure a formidable back field. Every man left is in the top flight, and the task cut out for Captain Rafferty is to hammer a center trio out of a most promising field of material. He has reason to hope, barring accidents, that his eleven will be as formidable as that of last year, though the fortunes of football war are often fickle.—Ralph D. Paine, in the Illustrated Sporting News.

WINNERS OF DIFFERENT PENNANTS DURING LIFE OF NATIONAL LEAGUE

Year.	Winners.	Won.	Lost.	Pct.	Managers.	Clubs.
1876	Chicago	52	14	.788	Spalding	8
1877	Boston	31	17	.646	H. Wright	6
1878	Boston	41	19	.680	H. Wright	6
1879	Providence	55	23	.705	George Wright	8
1880	Chicago	67	17	.798	Anson	8
1881	Chicago	56	28	.667	Anson	8
1882	Chicago	55	29	.655	Anson	8
1883	Boston	63	28	.750	Bancroft	8
1884	Providence	84	35	.643	Morrill	8
1885	Chicago	87	25	.776	Anson	8
1886	Chicago	90	34	.725	Anson	8
1887	Detroit	79	45	.637	Watkins	8
1888	New York	84	47	.641	Mutrie	8
1889	New York	83	43	.659	Mutrie	8
1890	Brooklyn	86	43	.667	McGunnigle	8
1891	Boston	87	51	.630	Selee	8
1892	Boston	102	48	.680	Selee	12
1893	Boston	86	43	.667	Selee	12
1894	Baltimore	89	39	.695	Hanlon	12
1895	Baltimore	87	43	.669	Hanlon	12
1896	Baltimore	90	39	.698	Hanlon	12
1897	Boston	93	39	.705	Selee	12
1898	Boston	102	47	.685	Selee	12
1899	Brooklyn	101	47	.682	Hanlon	12
1900	Brooklyn	82	54	.603	Hanlon	8
1901	Pittsburg	90	49	.647	Clarke	8
1902	Pittsburg	103	36	.741	Clarke	8
1903	Pittsburg	...	...	......	Clarke	8

THE AMATEUR SEASON IS DYING HARD

Many Good Nines Are Still in the Field—Waynesburg-Washington-Dravosburg Baseball Gossip.

By ARTHUR W. WILSON.

The cry of the quarterback as he gives the signals for his eleven in a football game is now heard throughout the land, but the baseball nines go merrily on. The wintry blasts that Old Boreas sent across this State on Thursday cooled the ardor of the baseball enthusiasts for a few hours, but Saturday's half holiday brought the boys back to the question of runs, base hits and the rights of an umpire.

The best semi-professional nines will not disband until October 10, so that exciting games may be looked for during the next three weeks. Homestead has games scheduled with P. A. C., Millvale and Waynesburg, while a series will probably be arranged with Rochester. Of the Ohio teams Warren, Niles, Ohio Works of Youngstown and East Liverpool will continue their season for several weeks. Bridgeville, Irwin, Manor, Electrics, Wilmerding, Johnstown and Sharon have games booked for the next two weeks. As none of the above cities will be represented by a football eleven it is well that the managers did not allow interest in baseball to die out with the closing of the season in the big leagues.

The winter season will see many a baseball league formed for the several counties, rivers and cities in these parts. There is already some talk of Waynesburg, Washington, Rochester, Bridgeville, Charleroi and several other towns coming into a Southwestern League. Such a league would serve to keep interest at the highest point and should be a paying venture as all of the above towns have made money and are represented by teams almost as good as Homestead; which was the pioneer semi-professional nine in this section.

Some Waynesburg-Washington Talk.

Washington went out of its way last Monday to beat Waynesburg by importing Winham and Weaver of the Pittsburg champions as a battery. Nothing daunted "Kid" Williams, and Frank Haller went into the points for Waynesburg, and when the Greene county lads threw the team representing the older college down 15 to 0 there was sadness and crepe in Washington, and now Manager Brownlee says he is sorry he imported Winham and Weaver. Let other managers take a lesson from Brownlee's experience and play their regular nine when they are engaged in battle.

Washington went to Waynesburg on Wednesday and dropped the final game of their eight-game series. Ike Collins held them down without a hit, while Waynesburg batted Ross Springer freely. J. E. Kobert, the Democratic nominee for Sheriff, Burgess Purman and the other backers of the Waynesburg team have asked Frank Haller of Allegheny to return and manage the team next year. Haller was given $1,000 with which to start the present team, which won two out of five games from Homestead, six out of eight from Washington, two out of three from Bridgeville, besides winning and tieing one at Wilmerding. Next year Haller will have $3,000 at his disposal, for the Waynesburg business men and attorneys want the championship of Western Pennsylvania and Ohio.

Dravosburg a Poor Ball Town.

Last season Southpaw Will Totten and several Iroquois players organized a ball team and secured grounds in Dravosburg. The town is small, but patronage from McKeesport was expected. Totten's men won one game from Homestead but lost the second one, Totten being the pitcher in both cases. The team made a very creditable record, and although the attendance had been light the East End boys went back to Dravosburg again. A new fence and stands were built. Totten's men won seven out of nine games, defeating such teams as Duquesne, West End A. C., Braddock A. C., Steel Works A. C. and Iroquois. The team lost to the Pittsburg Field Club by a score of 6 to 5, and one game to Duquesne.

Totten thought a benefit performance at the Alvin Theater might help pay the expenses, and after securing Mrs. Guy Bates Post (Sarah Truax) and a dozen Pittsburg entertainers he put on a literary show and musical entertainment. No one in Dravosburg came in for the performance, and, as little money was cleared after the performers were paid, the Dravosburg team was temporarily disbanded. McClaren and McDonough went to Waynesburg; Kinney and Soffell joined Bridgeville, Weisser went to Wheeling, while Totten was added to the P. A. C. pitching staff.

W. E. McBride of Homestead thought he would dabble in Dravosburg ball stock and he soon organized a team, with Spittal and Weisser of Totten's team as his battery. He played several games at home, but McKeesport was becoming excited over their Steel Works and Four A teams and that source of patronage soon dwindled away. McBride strengthened his team and went barnstorming. Games were lost at Waynesburg, Homestead, Washington, East Liverpool, Canonsburg and to P. A. C. Owing to the pitching of John Welsh and Spittal the Homestead games were the most exciting.

Two wekes ago Harry Holey's Homestead Greys went to Dravosburg, and the actual attendance was but 26 paid admissions to see a 7 to 6 game. This was too much for McBride, who then emulated Totten by paying his men and deciding to wait until next year, when Dame Fortune might have better things in store for them.

PROSPECTS GOOD AT GEORGETOWN

There Will Be a Good Football Team and the Candidates Are Now at Practice.

[Special Telegram to The Dispatch.]

WASHINGTON, Sept. 19.—The prospect for a strong team at Georgetown are bright. Forty candidates make up the squad now, which is fast getting into condition to uphold the blue and gray in the games with Princeton, Navel Cadets, Lehigh, Carlisle Indians, Columbia, and other teams.

C. M. Barry, captain of the 1901 team, is head coach with Frank Kerns, '03, S. L. Owen, '02, and Arthur Devlin, '01, as assistants. Phil King, the famous Princeton quarterback and late coach of the University of Wisconsin football and baseball teams, is advisory coach and supervisor of the work of the squad. Only three members of last season's team are missing. Seitz, left tackle, received his A. B. in June, while Edmonston, right end, has given up football and will devote his time to rowing. Russell, who played right tackle, rowed on the 'Varsity crew since 1900 and is debarred by the four-year rule. Given has played center for two years and has twice made that position on the All-Southern team, although he weighs 210 pounds when in condition and is one of the fastest men on the team. He is being tried at right tackle in the hope that he will be able to fill the position left vacant by the graduation of Seitz.

Rorke and Mahoney, last year's guards, are again candidates. Rorke has played on the team two years and did some of his best work in the Carolina game last November. Mahoney was a freshman last year, but played a consistent game throughout the season and this fall. With last season's experience to help him, he should be a most valuable member of the eleven.

Dean, a freshman from Boston High School, joined the squad during the week and he is looked upon as a promising candidate for tackle. He weighs 185 pounds and is very fast. With Given and Dean playing the positions Georgetown's tackles should be strong.

Preston Edmonston of last year's team, Graham and McGettigan of the scrubs and Kernan, a brother of the Captain of Harvard's team last fall, are the most prominent candidates for ends. Captain Hart and ex-Captain Reilly will probably retain the positions of halfbacks. Abbaticchio and Hardesty, quarterback and fullback, are out for the positions, but in Morgan, Captain of the baseball team, Hardesty has a dangerous rival for fullback. Schedule announced by Manager Beary follows:

September 26—Maryland Agricultural College at Washington.
September 30—Western Maryland College at Washington.
October 3—Princeton at Princeton.
October 17—Virginia Military Institute at Richmond.
October 24—North Carolina at Norfolk.
October 28—Naval Cadets at Annapolis.
October 31—Columbian at Washington.
November 7—Carlisle Indians at Washington
November 14—Probably University of Virginia at Washington.
November 21—Sullaudet College at Washington.
November 26—Lehigh at Washington.

Wagner on All-American Team.

Frank X. Finnegan of the Chicago American picks the following as the all-star team of 1903:

Pitcher..........McGinnity, New York Nationals
Catcher..........Kling, Chicago Nationals
First base........Davis, Philadelphia Americans
Second base.........Lajoie, Cleveland Americans
Shortstop...........Wagner, Pittsburg Nationals
Third base and capt..Collins, Boston Americans
Right field.........Donovan, St. Louis Nationals
Left field............Mertes, New York Nationals
Center field........F. Jones, Chicago Americans

THIS SPORTING PART DAILY WITH

The Inter Ocean.

VOLUME XXXII. CHICAGO, MONDAY MORNING, SEPTEMBER 21, 1903. NUMBER 181.

GREAT CROWD SEES THE CUBS LOSE

Umpire Emslie's Mistakes Cost the West Siders the Second Game of the New York Series.

POPULACE HISS AND GUY THE UMPIRE

Both Teams Are Overanxious and They Make Many Errors—Story of the Game—Dust from the Diamond and Baseball Gossip.

STANDING OF THE CLUBS.

National League.

Clubs—	W.	L.	P.C.	Clubs—	W.	L.	P.C.
Pittsburg	90	44	.672	Brooklyn	65	64	.508
New York	81	53	.605	Boston	57	77	.426
Chicago	**79**	**54**	**.594**	Philadelphia	44	84	.344
Cincinnati	71	60	.541	St. Louis	42	91	.316

YESTERDAY'S RESULTS.

Philadelphia, 8; Cincinnati, 4 (first game).
Cincinnati, 10; Philadelphia, 7 (second game).
New York, 6; Chicago, 2.
Boston, 7; St. Louis, 3 (first game).
Boston, 8; St. Louis, 3 (second game).

GAMES TODAY.

New York at Chicago.
Brooklyn at Pittsburg.

American League.

Clubs—	W.	L.	P.C.	Clubs—	W.	L.	P.C.
Boston	86	43	.667	St. Louis	62	66	.484
Cleveland	72	60	.545	Detroit	61	66	.480
Philadelphia	68	58	.540	**Chicago**	**55**	**71**	**.437**
New York	65	58	.528	Washington	41	88	.318

GAMES TODAY.

Detroit at Philadelphia.
Cleveland at New York.
Chicago at Boston.
St. Louis at Washington.

American Association.

Clubs—	W.	L.	P.C.	Clubs—	W.	L.	P.C.
St. Paul	88	45	.662	Kansas City	68	66	.507
Louisville	86	54	.614	Columbus	56	83	.403
Milwaukee	77	60	.562	Toledo	48	91	.345
Indianapolis	77	62	.554	Minneapolis	49	93	.345

YESTERDAY'S RESULTS.

Louisville, 4; Columbus, 0.
Kansas City, 7; St. Paul, 5 (first game).
Kansas City, 12; St. Paul, 5 (second game).
Indianapolis, 9; Toledo, 2.
Minneapolis, 4; Milwaukee, 0 (first game).
Milwaukee, 7; Minneapolis, 4 (second game).

By bunching a few timely hits and aided and abetted by the rank decisions of Umpire Robert Emslie, the New York "Giants" defeated the Chicago Cubs yesterday afternoon by a score of 6 to 2.

As a matter of fact, if Emslie had umpired a fairly decent game the score would have stood 3 to 2 in favor of Chicago.

Emslie's blunders were so frequent and inexcusable that the Cubs never had a chance to win out.

The writer is familiar with the fact that an umpire is always entitled to have a shade the best of it from the man who is reporting a ball game, but there are exceptions to all rules, and the "crime of yesterday" is a fair sample.

First of all, consider the conditions. Although the officials of the club did not give out the actual figures, and I am not a past master in estimating the size of crowds, I know for a fact that the biggest crowd of the season saw the game. It was a crowd that packed the stands and bleachers and overflowed into the field. It was a crowd that numbered at least 25,000 people, and in my humble opinion was the best behaved and most even tempered throng of men and women that ever gathered on a ball field. The crowd girdled the field and was alike excited and interested, and with the exception of two or three hundred Chicago rooters, the assembled populace wanted Chicago to win and made no secret of the fact.

And yet Umpire Emslie escaped with his life. After it was all over he walked off the field and through the grand stand to his dressing-room. He was hissed and hooted, but not a hand was laid on him. The chances are that his wretched decisions not only cost Chicago second place in the race for the National league pennant, but lost thousands of dollars which the followers of the West Side aggregation had wagered on the result. Knowing this, it is meet and proper to gloat over the fact that the crowd of thousands did nothing but hiss.

Game Proves Disappointing.

Considered as a ball game, pure and simple, the contest of the afternoon proved disappointing. Both teams were tuned up to concert pitch, and the result was that they mixed up good and bad ball with impressive rapidity. Errors were made that nine times out of ten would not have been made had the offenders been mixed up in an ordinary game of ball. But the strain was so tense, and the desire to win so strong, that the men on both sides were overanxious, and as a natural sequence did not play up to their true form.

As regards the pitching, Jack Taylor, although defeated, was a long way from being disgraced. He lacked his usual speed, but only in the fifth inning was he hit hard. Had Umpire Emslie not given him all the worst of it in the first inning, Taylor would have won his game with comparative ease. This first inning, by the way, was a fright. Brown led off for New York with a line hit to center field that Slagle failed to reach, and then made a bad return with the ball to the diamond, which yielded Brown a scratch two-bagger. The next two men up, Bresnahan and McGann, were quickly retired. Then Mertes drew a base on balls. Babb followed with a grounder to Evers, who fumbled the ball, and on his error Brown and Mertes scored. Lauder came up with a two-bagger and Gilbert followed with a single. This lucky hitting scored Babb and Lauder, and gave the visitors a long lead of four runs.

After that Taylor settled down and held the enemy safe until the fifth inning. In this inning the Giants sized them up for fair, bunching four two-baggers and a single. And yet this magnificent batting rally yielded but two runs.

The two runs scored by Chicago were made in the third inning on Slegel's two-bagger, Lauder's fumble, and Jones' infield hit, and singles by Tinker and Kling.

The score follows:

Chicago.	R	H	P	A	E	New York.	R	H	P	A	E
Slagle, cf.	1	2	1	0	0	Browne, rf.	1	1	2	0	0
McC'thy, lf.	0	0	1	1	0	Bresn'n, cf.	0	1	1	0	0
Chance, 1b.	0	0	13	0	0	McGann, 1b.	0	2	12	1	0
Jones, rf.	1	2	1	1	1	Mertes, lf.	2	1	2	0	0
Tinker, ss.	0	1	1	3	1	Babb, ss.	2	1	1	8	1
Kling, c.	0	1	8	1	0	Lauder, 3b.	1	2	3	3	3
Weir, 2b.	0	0	1	1	1	Gilbert, 2b.	0	2	4	2	0
Casey, 3b.	0	1	1	8	0	Warner, c.	0	0	1	1	0
Taylor, p.	0	0	0	5	1	McGinnity, p.	0	1	1	3	0
Totals	2	7	27	15	4	Totals	6	11	27	13	4

Chicago	0	0	2	0	0	0	0	0	0	—2
New York	4	0	0	0	2	0	0	0	0	—6

Earned Runs—New York, 2. First Base on Balls—Off Taylor, 1; Off McGinnity, 2. Struck Out—By Taylor, 5; by McGinnity, 1. Two-Base Hits—Browne, Lauder, Jones, Slagle, Mertes, McGann, Babb, Bresnahan. Sacrifice Hits—Bresnahan, Mertes. Stolen Bases—Mertes, Gilbert, Bresnahan. Double Play—Lauder and McGann. Passed Ball—Kling. Umpire—Emslie. Time of Game—1:35.

JACK TANNER.

Cincinnati, 4-10; Philadelphia, 8-7.

CINCINNATI, Ohio, Sept. 20.—Cincinnati again broke even with Philadelphia today. Cincinnati played a lose game in both contests, Corcoran being responsible for most of the runs of the visitors in the first game. It was agreed between the teams that the second game should be called in the seventh inning. Attendance, 13,578. The scores:

FIRST GAME.

Phila'phia.	R	H	P	A	E	Cincinnati.	R	H	P	A	E
Barry, lf.	0	3	3	0	0	Donlin, lf.	2	2	2	0	0
Gleason, cf.	1	1	4	0	0	Seymour, cf.	0	1	0	0	0
Wolve'n, 3b.	1	1	1	4	0	Dolan, rf.	0	2	0	0	0
Titus, rf.	2	3	1	0	0	Beckley, 1b.	0	0	8	2	0
Hallman, 2b.	1	2	1	4	0	D'rmond, 3b.	0	1	6	2	1
Douglas, 1b.	1	0	11	0	1	Daly, 2b.	1	1	3	3	2
Hulswitt, ss.	1	0	4	2	0	Corcoran, ss.	0	1	5	6	2
Dooin, c.	1	1	1	1	1	Fohl, c.	0	1	1	1	0
Mitchell, p.	0	1	1	1	0	Hahn, p.	1	1	1	3	0
						*Peitz	0	1	0	0	0
Totals	8	12	27	13	1	Totals	4	9	27	17	5

*Batted for Hahn in ninth.

Philadelphia	1	0	0	0	2	2	0	0	3	—8
Cincinnati	1	0	0	0	2	1	0	0	0	—4

Two-Base Hits—Gleason, Hallman. Three-Base Hit—Titus. Sacrifice Hits—Hallman, Dooin, Mitchell. Stolen Base—Beckley. Balk—Mitchell. Left on Bases—Cincinnati, 8; Philadelphia, 6. First Base on Balls—Off Hahn, 2; off Mitchell, 3. Hit by Pitched Ball—Hulswitt. Struck Out—By Hahn, 1; by Mitchell, 1. Passed Balls—Fohl, 2; Dooin, 2. Wild Pitches—Mitchell, 2; Hahn, 2. Time of Game—1:55. Umpires—O'Day and Hurst.

SECOND GAME.

Cincinnati.	R	H	P	A	E	Phila'phia.	R	H	P	A	E
Donlin, lf.	0	1	3	0	0	Barry, lf.	2	3	5	0	0
Seymour, cf.	0	1	0	0	0	Gleason, cf.	1	1	5	0	1
Dolan, rf.	1	2	2	0	0	Wolve'n, 3b.	0	1	1	1	0
Beckley, 1b.	2	0	5	1	1	Titus, rf.	1	1	2	0	0
D'rmond, 3b.	1	1	3	0	0	Hallman, 2b.	0	1	0	3	0
Daly, 2b.	1	1	1	3	0	Dougl's, 1b.	1	1	4	0	0
Corcoran, ss.	1	1	1	2	2	Hulswitt, ss.	1	0	1	2	2
Peitz, c.	2	1	5	0	0	Roth, c.	0	0	3	1	0
Ewing, p.	2	2	1	3	1	Fraser, p.	0	1	1	1	0
Totals	10	10	21	9	4	Totals	7	8	18	8	3

Cincinnati	0	2	0	5	0	3	*	—10
Philadelphia	1	0	0	0	0	6	0	—7

Earned Runs—Cincinnati, 7; Philadelphia, 2. Two-Base Hits—Dolan (2), Ewing, Barry. Sacrifice Hits—Daly, Gleason, Wolverton. Home Run—Corcoran. Stolen Bases—Barry, Seymour, Daly. Double Play—Corcoran, Daly, and Beckley. First Base on Balls—Off Ewing, 1; off Fraser, 1. Struck Out—By Ewing, 3; by Fraser, 2. Passed Balls—Peitz, 2; Roth, 1. Left on Bases—Cincinnati, 2; Philadelphia, 4. Time of Game—1:25. Umpires—Hurst and O'Day.

Boston, 7-8; St. Louis, 3-3.

ST. LOUIS, Mo., Sept. 20.—St. Louis lost both games of a double-header here today to Boston. Mike O'Neil, the Cardinal twirler, was hit hard throughout and was poorly supported in the field.

Moran, a Texas youth, essayed to pitch the second game, and he gave as raw an exhibition as was ever charged up to a major league recruit, giving ten free passes to first base. Attendance, 10,234. Scores:

FIRST GAME.

Boston.	R	H	P	A	E	St. Louis.	R	H	P	A	E
Dexter, rf.	1	2	0	0	0	Farrell, 2b.	0	2	2	3	0
McCreery, cf.	1	1	2	0	0	D'nl'avy, rf.	0	1	0	0	0
Ab'ch'io, 2b.	1	1	1	4	0	Smoot, cf.	2	3	1	0	0
Cooley, lf.	1	2	3	0	0	Brain, ss.	1	1	2	5	0
Gr'm'ger, 3b.	1	1	3	2	0	Burke, 3b.	0	2	0	2	0
Moran, c.	0	1	2	0	0	Barclay, lf.	0	0	4	0	1
Willis, 1b.	1	0	12	0	0	Ryan, 1b.	0	0	14	0	0
Aubrey, ss.	1	1	3	4	0	J. O'Neil, c.	0	1	3	3	0
Carney, p.	0	1	1	2	0	M. O'Neil, p.	0	1	1	3	0
						*Hackett	0	0	0	0	0
Totals	7	10	27	12	0	Totals	3	11	27	14	1

*Hackett batted for M. O'Neil in the ninth.

Boston	1	0	4	0	0	0	0	0	2	—7
St. Louis	1	0	0	0	0	2	0	0	0	—3

Earned Runs—St. Louis, 2; Boston, 4. Two-Base Hits—Dexter, Greminger, J. O'Neil. Three-Base Hits—Cooley, Dunleavy. Sacrifice Hit—Carney. Double Play—Brain, Farrell, and Ryan. Stolen Bases—Smoot, Brain, Burke. Bases on Balls—Off Carney, 1; off O'Neil, 3. Struck Out—By Carney, 2; by O'Neil, 2. Left on Bases—St. Louis, 8; Boston, 4. Umpires—Johnstone and Moran. Time—1:43.

SECOND GAME.

Boston.	R	H	P	A	E	St. Louis.	R	H	P	A	E
Dexter, rf.	2	1	0	0	0	Farrell, 2b.	0	1	4	0	0
McCreery, cf.	0	0	2	0	0	D'nl'avy, rf.	1	1	2	2	0
Ab'chio, 2b.	0	1	0	3	0	Smoot, cf.	0	1	2	0	1
Cooley, lf.	2	2	2	0	0	Brain, ss.	0	0	1	4	0
Gr'm'ger, 3b.	1	2	3	0	0	Burke, 3b.	0	0	1	1	1
P. Moran, c.	1	2	7	0	0	Barclay, lf.	0	2	4	0	0
Willis, 1b.	0	1	12	1	0	Ryan, 1b.	1	2	8	0	1
Aubrey, ss.	1	1	1	1	1	Coveney, c.	0	1	5	4	1
Malarkey, p.	1	0	1	3	0	C. Moran, p.	1	3	0	0	0
Totals	8	9	27	11	1	Totals	3	11	27	11	4

Boston	0	0	5	0	0	0	1	2	—8
St. Louis	0	0	2	1	0	0	0	0	—3

Earned Runs—St. Louis, 2; Boston, 2. Three-Base Hits—Smoot, Cooley. Sacrifice Hits—Dexter, P. Moran. Double Play—Dunleavy and Farrell. Passed Balls—P. Moran, 2. Stolen Bases—C. Moran, Dexter (2), Abbatiechio (2). Hit by Pitched Ball—By Moran, Malarkey. Wild Pitch—Moran. Bases on Balls—Off Moran, 10; off Malarkey, 1. Struck Out—By Malarkey, 5; by Moran, 5. Left on Bases—St. Louis, 7; Boston, 10. Umpires Moran and Johnstone. Time—2:09.

AMERICAN ASSOCIATION.

Kansas City, 7-12; St. Paul, 5-5.

KANSAS CITY, Mo., Sept. 20.—Kansas City won two games from St. Paul today by superior all-round playing. St. Paul's errors were costly in both games. Attendance, 5,500. Scores:

FIRST GAME.

K. City.	R	H	P	A	E	St. Paul.	R	H	P	A	E
Rothfuss, 1b.	0	1	7	0	0	Geier, 3b.	1	1	1	0	2
Hill, cf.	2	1	4	0	0	Shannon, cf.	1	0	2	0	0
Nance, 2b.	2	3	3	1	0	J'ks'n, rf-2b.	1	0	1	2	0
Butler, c.	1	2	6	3	1	Schaefer, ss.	0	3	2	2	2
Gear, rf.	0	1	1	0	0	Pierce, c.	0	1	8	1	0
Hall, 3b.	0	2	2	3	1	Flournoy, lf.	1	2	1	0	0
Knoll, lf.	0	1	1	0	0	Wh'l'r, 2b-1b.	0	2	6	1	0
Lewee, ss.	2	0	3	0	1	Sullivan, 1b.	0	0	1	0	0
Gibson, p.	0	1	0	1	0	Bartos, rf.	0	1	2	0	0
						Corbett, p.	1	0	0	2	0
Totals	7	12	27	8	3	Totals	5	10	24	8	4

Kansas City	0	0	0	0	1	0	3	3	*	—7
St. Paul	1	3	0	0	0	0	1	0	0	—5

SECOND GAME.

K. City.	R	H	P	A	E	St. Paul.	R	H	P	A	E
Rothfuss, 1b.	3	4	6	1	0	Geier, 3b.	1	1	0	0	0
Hill, cf.	2	1	1	1	0	Shannon, cf.	1	1	1	0	0
Nance, 2b.	4	0	0	2	0	Jackson, 2b.	1	2	1	2	0
Butler, c.	2	2	2	0	0	Schaefer, ss.	1	2	1	3	2
Gear, rf.	1	2	3	0	0	Pierce, rf.	0	0	0	0	0
Hall, 3b.	0	1	1	1	0	Flournoy, lf.	0	0	2	1	0
Knoll, lf.	0	1	1	0	0	Wheeler, 1b.	1	2	8	0	1
Lewee, ss.	0	0	0	2	0	Sullivan, c.	0	1	2	0	1
Alloway, p.	0	0	1	0	0	Bartos, p.	0	1	0	2	0
Totals	12	11	15	7	0	Totals	5	10	15	9	3

Game called at end of fifth inning; darkness.

Kansas City	4	3	0	2	3	—12
St. Paul	1	0	0	1	3	—5

Milwaukee, 0-7; Minneapolis, 4-4.

MILWAUKEE, Wis., Sept. 20.—Milwaukee was shut out in the first game with Minneapolis today, Williams pitching great ball until injured in the eighth inning.

FIRST GAME.

Minn'polis.	R	H	P	A	E	Milwaukee.	R	H	P	A	E
Sullivan, cf.	0	2	4	0	0	Ganley, rf.	0	0	0	0	0
Maloney, rf.	2	2	0	0	0	Donahue, 1b.	0	0	4	0	0
Oyler, ss.	0	1	1	6	1	Wood, c.	0	0	12	0	1
McIn're, 3b.	0	1	0	1	0	Unglaub, 3b.	0	1	0	0	1
Lally, lf.	0	0	3	0	0	Hemph'l, cf.	0	1	1	0	0
Yeager, c.	0	0	3	0	1	Dunle'vy, lf.	0	0	2	0	0
Spooner, 1b.	0	1	12	0	0	Viox, ss.	0	0	3	3	1
Martin, 2b.	1	1	4	5	1	Schlaf'y, 2b.	0	1	3	2	0
Williams, p.	0	0	0	4	0	Elliott, p.	0	1	0	4	0
McDon'ld, p.	1	1	0	0	0						
Totals	4	9	27	16	3	Totals	0	4	27	9	3

Minneapolis	0	0	0	1	0	0	0	0	3	—4
Milwaukee	0	0	0	0	0	0	0	0	0	—0

SECOND GAME.

Milwaukee.	R	H	P	A	E	Minn'polis.	R	H	P	A	E
Ganley, rf.	1	1	0	0	0	Sullivan, cf.	0	1	2	0	0
Donahue, 1b.	0	2	9	0	1	Maloney, rf.	1	1	1	0	0
Wood, c.	0	1	9	1	0	Oyler, ss.	2	2	3	2	1
Unglaub, 3b.	1	1	2	3	0	McIn're, 3b.	1	1	3	0	0
Hemph'l, cf.	3	2	2	0	0	Lally, lf.	0	3	2	0	0
Dunleavy, lf.	0	1	3	0	0	Yeager, c.	0	0	6	2	0
Viox, ss.	0	1	1	3	0	Spooner, 1b.	0	1	7	0	0
Schlaf'y, 2b.	1	2	1	1	0	Martin, 2b.	0	1	0	3	0
Stimmel, p.	0	0	0	0	0	McDon'ld, p.	0	1	0	4	0
Mueller, p.	1	1	0	3	1						
Totals	7	12	27	11	2	Totals	4	11	24	11	1

Milwaukee	0	1	0	1	0	3	2	0	*	—7
Minneapolis	2	0	2	0	0	0	0	0	0	—4

Louisville, 4; Columbus, 0.

COLUMBUS, Ohio, Sept. 20.—Louisville shut out Columbus today in the last game of the season. Akens, a new pitcher, was tried out by Louisville and he received splendid support, four fast double plays being made by the visitors. Attendance, 2,799. Score:

Louisville.	R	H	P	A	E	Columbus.	R	H	P	A	E
Kerwin, rf.	1	0	0	0	0	Arndt, lf.	0	1	2	0	0
Hart, 1b.	2	2	13	0	0	Turner, 3b.	0	0	3	1	0
Brash'r, 2b.	0	1	4	5	1	Bannon, cf.	0	0	4	0	0
Odwell, cf.	1	1	0	0	0	Clingm'n, ss.	0	1	1	1	1
Sul'v'n, 3b.	0	2	1	3	0	Mellor, 1b.	0	0	3	0	0
Clymer, lf.	0	0	3	0	0	Wagner, 2b.	0	0	1	1	1
Quinlan, ss.	0	0	0	4	0	Beach, rf.	0	1	3	0	1
White, c.	0	1	6	0	0	Fox, c.	0	1	7	3	0
Akers, p.	0	0	0	4	1	McMakin, p.	0	0	0	0	0
Totals	4	7	27	16	2	Totals	0	4	24	6	3

Louisville	1	0	2	0	0	0	0	1	*	—4
Columbus	0	0	0	0	0	0	0	0	0	—0

Indianapolis, 9; Toledo, 2.

TOLEDO, Ohio, Sept. 20.—The season was ended here today, the locals losing the game through poor field work and Cristall's wildness. Volz pitched well. The score:

Ind'polis.	R	H	P	A	E	Toledo.	R	H	P	A	E
Kihm, 1b.	3	3	10	0	0	Smith, lf.	0	0	3	0	0
Fox, 2b.	2	0	0	4	0	Owens, ss.	0	0	0	1	3
H'g'ver, rf.	1	0	4	0	0	Childs, 2b.	0	1	2	6	0
Woodr'f, lf.	0	1	0	0	0	Bern'rd, rf.	0	0	1	0	0
Coulter, cf.	0	1	3	1	2	Reisling, c.	1	1	8	0	0
Leslie, c.	0	2	6	0	0	Schaub, 3b.	1	2	1	3	1
Marcan, ss.	1	1	2	3	0	Turner, 1b.	0	1	11	0	0
Hess, 3b.	1	1	0	2	0	Hadding, cf.	0	1	1	0	0
Volz, p.	1	0	0	0	0	Cristall, p.	0	0	0	3	0
Totals	9	9	27	10	2	Totals	2	6	27	13	4

Indianapolis	2	0	3	0	0	0	0	4	0	—9
Toledo	0	2	0	0	0	0	0	0	0	—2

CHICAGO'S GROUP OF LIVELY CUBS.

Reading from left to right—Top row: Lundgren, Currie, Chance, McCarthy, Taylor, Jones, Kling, Graham, Weimer. Middle line: Harley, Evers, Wicker, Manager Selee, Williams, Menefee, Raub. Lower line: Slagle, Casey, Tinker.

DR. WHITE LEADS THE LOCAL PITCHERS

Star Left-Hander of the White Sox Heads the List, Despite Poor Support—The Figures.

Statistics showing, analytically and in detail, the work done by the pitchers of the two local ball teams, may be of much interest to the eager fans. These figures, when read and studied, tell a good deal of the year's story, so far as the local clubs are concerned. Only slabmen who have worked in fifteen games or more are considered.

The National league records show that Wicker has a slight margin in games won, but that Weimer is the hardest man of the lot to hit or to make runs against, Taylor ranking second in both particulars. Taylor is the steadiest pitcher, giving the fewest passes to the game, and Currie the wildest. Wicker is the best at fanning hostile batters. During the season Taylor has never been taken out of the box, while Weimer has been removed the oftenest—six times. Currie has been sent in nine times to save games if possible, and Lundgren six.

It will surprise anybody not a close critic of the game to know that Dr. White of the White Sox, in the face of discouragement and the fact that a weak team was behind him, has been really the most effective pitcher of the ten men under discussion. Fewer runs have been made off him per game, and fewer hits, than off even the successful Weimer. The work of Roy Patterson has also been superb, and that of Owen not a bit bad. Flaherty is the steadiest of the South Side pitchers, and Owen the best at compelling wind-jamming.

The figures:

National League.

Pitchers—	G	PC	H	R	BB	HB	SO
Wicker	27	.690	[illegible]	[illegible]	[illegible]	[illegible]	[illegible]
Weimer	30	.600	[illegible]	[illegible]	[illegible]	[illegible]	[illegible]
Taylor	30	.588	[illegible]	[illegible]	[illegible]	[illegible]	[illegible]
Lundgren	19	.579	[illegible]	[illegible]	[illegible]	[illegible]	[illegible]
Menefee	17	.412	[illegible]	[illegible]	[illegible]	[illegible]	[illegible]
Currie	20	.390	[illegible]	[illegible]	[illegible]	[illegible]	[illegible]

Summary: [illegible]

American League.

Pitchers—	G	PC	H	R	BB	HB	SO
White	34	.559	[illegible]	[illegible]	[illegible]	[illegible]	[illegible]
Patterson	26	.519	[illegible]	[illegible]	[illegible]	[illegible]	[illegible]
Owen	19	.421	78	165	42	8	65
Flaherty	32	.250	163	322	47	12	68

Summary:

Runs Per Game—White, 3.30; Patterson, 3.71; Owen, 4.11; Flaherty, 5.10.

Hits Per Game—White, 7.30; Patterson, 8; Owen, 8.68; Flaherty, 10.06.

Bases on Balls and Hit Batsmen Per Game—Flaherty, 1.84; Patterson, 2.11; White, 2.35; Owen, 2.63.

Struck Out Per Game—Owen, 3.42; White, 3.35; Patterson, 2.32; Flaherty, 2.13.

Times Taken Out of Game—Patterson, 4; Owen, 5; Flaherty, 6; White, 7.

Times Sent In to Finish Game—Owen, 6; Flaherty, 6; Patterson, 4; White, 1.

INTER-STATE LEAGUE.

Racine, 9; Marquette, 2.

RACINE, Wis., Sept. 20.—Racine defeated the Marquettes yesterday at Racine, by the score of 9 to 2. The Marquettes went all to pieces in the third inning, which the Racine boys took advantage of, along with a couple of hits which enabled them to score seven runs, after which time the Marquettes settled down to a good hard game, but it was then too late for them to do any damage. Score:

Racine.	R	H	P	A	E	Marquettes.	R	H	P	A	E
Duffy, lf.	2	1	2	0	0	C'vey, ss-lf.	0	1	3	2	2
O'Rourke, 2b.	1	2	4	4	0	F'ton, lf-ss.	0	0	3	2	0
Murphy, rf.	0	0	2	1	1	Kearney, rf.	0	1	0	0	0
Olle, 1b.	1	2	12	0	0	Post, cf.	0	1	0	0	0
Mahoney, 3b.	2	1	2	2	0	Riley, 1b.	1	1	6	0	1
Kloph, ss.	1	3	2	1	1	Koupalik, p.	1	1	3	1	1
Flavin, lf.	1	1	1	0	0	McG'non, 2b.	0	1	3	2	0
Herman, c.	1	2	2	1	1	Duffy, 3b.	0	1	1	0	1
Katole, p.	0	0	0	3	1	Rundle, c.	0	0	5	0	0
Totals	9	12	27	12	4	Totals	2	7	24	7	5

Racine	0	0	7	1	0	0	1	0	*	—9
Marquette	0	0	0	0	0	2	0	0	0	—2

Two-Base Hits—Duffy, Olle. Stolen Bases—O'Rourke, Duffy. Double Plays—Mahoney, O'Rourke, Olle; O'Rourke, Olle; Kaupalik, Riley. Struck Out—By Kaupalik, 2; by Katole, 1. Bases on Balls—Off Katole, 3; off Kaupalik, 3. Hit by Pitcher—By Kaupalik, 2; by Katole, 1. Umpire—McWaters. Attendance—650. Time—1:35.

Elgin, 9; Athletics, 2.

ELGIN, Ill., Sept. 20.—The Elgin team defeated the Athletics today in a fairly played game. Leitman pitched good ball, while the Elgins hits Kern hard with men on bases. The fielding of Gleason, Snelle, and Collins were features. Manager McGurn has suspended Third Baseman Thomas Cline for the balance of the season for failing to appear at the ground in the game last Sunday against Aurora. Score:

Aurora.	R	H	P	A	E	Athletics.	R	H	P	A	E
Collins, 3b.	0	1	2	3	1	Andrews, ss.	0	3	2	1	2
*Hickey, ss.	2	2	1	3	2	Hayes, 2b.	0	1	4	1	0
Asmussen, c.	1	0	7	0	0	J.Sh'b'ge, 1b.	0	0	8	0	1
Sears, rf.	1	1	1	0	0	Brown, c.	1	1	1	1	0
[illegible]						[illegible]					

Auroras, 2; Gunthers, 0.

[illegible]

WOMEN PRACTICE FOR CHAMPIONSHIP

Will Put In Week at the Chicago Golf Club Preparing for National Tourney.

Women golfers will take possession of the links of the Chicago Golf club this week to practice for the national championship which will be held over the course next week. Several Eastern women who have entered for the event are due within the next few days.

It is still a matter of conjecture whether Mrs. Stout, formerly Miss Genevieve Hecker, the present champion, will defend her title. In a letter to Miss Bessie Anthony, the Western champion, Mrs. Stout stated that she would not come West for the championship this season, as she had accepted the invitation of Mrs. Griscom of Philadelphia to meet Miss Rhona Adair, the British champion, over the links of the Huntingdon Valley Country club the week following the national event.

It was reported from the East last week, however, that Mrs. Stout would be here to compete. Western women are hopeful that she will come, as her absence might somewhat decrease interest in the event.

The Wheaton course was never in better shape for the championship. The Foulis brothers have given the course much attention within the past month, and it should be in prime condition next week.

This will be the first year the national championship has even been held in the West. A Western player has never won the event, and the number of Western contestants in the previous championships have been few. However, over a Chicago course, it is expected that the Western women will have a better chance against their Eastern sisters.

Miss Bessie Anthony, the Western champion, and Miss Mabel Higgins of Midlothian, her runner-up for the Western championship two weeks ago, are practicing hard for the event. Miss Anthony, in a match over the Glenview links last week with her tutor, "Larry" Auchterlonie, finished all even with him in eighteen holes, being allowed a stroke a hole. Miss Higgins has been practicing at Midlothian under the tutelage of George O'Neil, the Midlothian professional, who, it is said, will caddie for her in the national championship.

The college golfers who remained over for the Glenview open tournament will leave for the East today. Walter E. Egan and Chandler Egan return to Harvard, while Louis N. James, John D. Towne, and Phil Connell go back to Princeton. Bruce D. Smith will go to Yale.

Pairings for Westward Ho Tourney.

Members of the Westward Ho Golf club who qualified for the Butler Championship cup Saturday will compete in the first match round for the trophy next Saturday. The pairings are announced as follows:

Walter Kettlestrings vs. F. W. Morgan.
J. I. Cooper vs. Dr. L. W. Beebe.
R. M. Cutting vs. J. A. Martin.
Herbert Templeton vs. Perley Lowe.
C. H. Wells vs. Dr. J. E. Nyman.
J. H. Harper vs. H. E. Turner.
T. H. Gale vs. A. A. Strom.
F. A. Elliott vs. E. W. Chandler.

SECOND FLIGHT CUP.

Fred Hall vs. C. H. Burras.
A. T. Packard vs. Dr. A. Rea.
I. N. Conrad vs. C. S. Williard.
Frank Hall vs. F. W. Mehlop.
F. W. Lee vs. C. T. Rice.
W. G. Zoller vs. P. Blatchford.
C. L. Scroggs vs. Bruce Darling.
P. V. Castle vs. A. L. Goodman.

THIRD FLIGHT CUP.

F. W. Wilcox vs W. D. Hall.
W. Templeton vs. E. Johnson.
E. W. Heath vs. Dr. T. E. Roberts.
S. M. St. Clair vs. W. H. French.
C. E. Pickard vs. N. S. Patton.
J. B. Suydam vs. W. S. Holden.
J. W. Watson vs. E. H. Cheney.
G. Webster vs. E. F. Blatchford.

NOTES OF THE AUTOS.

F. E. Encell of Englewood has purchased a Ford car.

H. M. Ruby of Macon, Mo., was in Chicago on a visit last week and called on A. C. Banker of Wabash avenue, from whom he purchased a Ford car.

Dr. E. P. Dudley of Indiana avenue is driving a Knox car.

Robert Tarrant, secretary of the C. A. C., has been ill at Ann Arbor for several weeks. He returned to this city Friday.

Mr. and Mrs. A. Scott Ormsby of Emmettsburgh, Iowa, were visitors at the Chicago Automobile club late last week.

W. L. Hibbard of the Studebaker company spent last week at Milwaukee, delivering cars.

The members of the C. A. C. will leave Chicago Thursday night by boat for Grand Rapids, where they will be entertained by the G. R. club Friday afternoon, and Saturday they will be entertained with races, and on Sunday night will return to this city in time to participate in the centennial carnival.

IS WHITE A WELCHER?

Repudiates $1,200 Bet Taken by One of His Handbook Agents.

Bud White, the bookmaker, is being sought by Alexander Ryan, a railroad man, who wants to collect a bet of $1,200, and who threatens he will drive White out of the business in Chicago unless the bet is paid. An agent of White's named Joe Ford, operating in the saloon of Righeimer & O'Connor, at 73 Jackson street, took the bet from Ryan. The wager was on Don Domo, made on Sept. 10. The bet was taken and Ryan was told that "he was on."

After Don Domo had won Ford told Ryan that White had refused to honor it, alleging that the bet was made after post time.

M'GRAW'S BAND OF GOTHAM GIANTS.

Reading from left to right—Top line: Bresnahan, McGann, Van Haltren, Gilbert, Brown, Miller, Babb, Cronin, Warner. Lower line: Bowerman, McGinnity, McGraw, Mathewson, Taylor, Lander.

CHANGE DATES OF OLYMPIAN GAMES

Meeting Changed from June to August to Accommodate Schoolboys Who Expect to Compete.

MANY ENTRIES FROM CHICAGO

At Least Forty Youthful Athletes from the Schools in and Around Chicago Will Be Entered in the Preliminary Contests.

On account of the lateness of the season the dates for the Olympian games championships to be held at St. Louis next summer have been changed from Aug. 5 and 6 to June 29 and 30.

This change was made on account of many interscholastic athletes being away on their vacations at that time, and the inability of schools to keep their representatives together and to send a representative delegation to the most important interscholastic championships that will be held in America for many years. These games are open to schoolboys throughout the entire world, and the winners in each event will be awarded medals and wreaths emblematic of the Olympian world's championship.

The games are of especial interest to the West, on account of the prominent position that Western boys are expected to take, especially when it comes to a division of first prizes. Chicago boys should also figure well, for there is plenty of material her with which to combat the East successfully.

The meeting will last two days. Trial heats will be held on the first day, which will enable the boys who are to compete in the finals to rest up, and to do themselves justice. Several of the distance events will also be held on the first day, including the field events.

Many Entries from Chicago.

It is expected that there will be at least forty individual entries from the schools in and around Chicago. The matter of sending teams will be agitated shortly, and, as the railroad fares will be extremely low, owing to arrangements made by the exposition directors, it will be easy for school teams to meet expenses.

The events will include the regular interscholastic championship lists, besides a series of relay races. The latter will be made a feature. Relay teams are expected from the famous Taylor school of Philadelphia; Dwight school, New York; Louisville Manual Training high school; Louisville male high school; Worcester academy, Worcester, Mass; Andover academy, Andover, Mass.; Exeter academy, Exeter, N. H.; English high school, Boston, Mass.; Mooney high school, Murfreesboro, Tenn.; Walnut Hills high school, Cincinnati, Ohio, and many other high schools.

Several weeks ago negotiations were opened with the English schools for a dual meeting between the schools of New York and those of England, to take place on either this side of the water or in England, next summer. Since that time many have expressed a desire of paying the expenses of the English boys and have them compete at the World's Olympian interscholastic championships, which they will probably do. While they do not make a specialty of games among the English preparatory schools they have many good athletes, especially in the distace runs, for an English boy is never happy unless following the hounds afoot across fields and fences.

The South will also be strongly represented at the games, as New Orleans and Texas have almost promised to send up the best boys they have in the South. There will be plenty of entries from the Mississippi states, especially from Missouri. The crack Smith academy team will be entered in its entirety, and also the manual training and English high school of St. Louis.

California Will Compete.

California will have a team present from the famous Berkeley school at Berkeley, and preparations for the games next summer have already begun, for a big meeting will be held at San Francisco in October and another in December.

The Boston Athletic association, the guiding star of interscholastic games in the East, will look after the interests of the Massachusetts boys, and the winners in each event will probably be sent to St. Louis. The New England championships are always held on the first Saturday in June, which will give the New England representatives ample time to prepare for the big meeting. The Yale Athletic association will look after the New York schools, and entries are expected from Dwight school, Montclair (N. J.) high school, Princeton university preparatory school, New York high school, and many other private and public schools in and around New York.

The middle Atlantic states are also looked upon to furnish their quota, and University of Pennsylvania is expected to take care of the Philadelphia boys. The famous Taylor school of Philadelphia loses but one man from its relay team, so that its presence may be counted upon. Then the team has several good sprinters, including Mulligan, who will represent the Philadelphia school, if he does not go to Georgetown.

Washington will be represented by the East and West Division high schools and Georgetown university preparatory schools. There are some cracking good athletes at the university preparatory school, so that a strong team from that place may be looked for.

Kentucky will most likely be represented by the Louisville Manual Training high school team, champions of the South, and Louisville Male high school, champions of Indiana. The Manual Training school has won the Southern championship twice, and possesses some fine athletes. High school also has a number of good men, and both schools should be able to uphold the honor of their "old Kentucky home."

Tennessee has several good teams which may send one or two men. Branham and Hughes, at Spring Hill; Nashville high school and Bowen school of Nashville, and Mooney school at Murfreesboro are the best. The Southern championships are held the first Saturday in May, under the direction of Vanderbilt university, so that that university will look after its winners.

West of the Mississippi there should be many good boys. Iowa has always managed to turn out a record-breaker in some event, while the teams around Kansas City, though not as good as those of Chicago, have their usual star. In Colorado, Denver has some fast sprinters who should give a good account of themselves. Entry blanks for the games will be issued about Jan. 1, 1904, and mailed to every high school in the country.

Sycamore, 4; South Chicago, 3.

Sycamore defeated South Chicago for the fourth time this season yesterday in a featureless game, barring the pitching of Parker and Keeley.

Sycamore.	R	H	P	A	E	S. Chicago.	R	H	P	A	E
Ball, ss.	0	0	4	4	1	McKee, cf.	0	0	2	0	0
Uhler, lf.	1	1	5	0	0	Keeley, p.	0	2	1	4	0
Ryan, 3b.	0	0	0	0	3	Babcock, lf.	0	0	1	1	0
G't'nrich, cf.	0	1	3	0	0	Donovan, c.	0	1	6	1	0
J.C'mp'n, 2b.	1	1	1	2	1	Hill, rf.	1	1	1	0	0
J. Parker, p.	2	2	1	4	0	Holmes, 1b.	1	2	8	0	0
Black, rf.	0	0	0	0	0	And'ws, 2b.	0	0	2	0	1
Hughes, c.	0	0	4	1	1	Saxe, 3b.	1	1	3	2	2
H. P'ker, 1b.	0	1	9	0	0	Hoffm'n, ss.	0	0	3	0	0
Totals	4	6	27	11	6	Totals	3	7	27	8	3

Sycamore	1	0	1	0	2	0	0	0	0	—4
South Chicago	0	0	0	0	0	0	0	3	0	—3

SUSPICIONS THAT POST-SEASON SERIES WILL NOT BE PLAYED

POST SEASON GAMES MAY NOT BE PLAYED

Suspicions of Local Followers of the Game Aroused and Telegrams From Boston Help Some.

By FRANK B. M'QUISTON.

Have you heard of Grover Cleveland,
Who was done so brown by Bennie?
In November, just a year ago,
Grover says, "Keep up your courage;
I'll get there in '92, boys."
Will he do it? Well, I don't know.

Little Ko Ko, in "The Mascotte," made quite a hit here in the fall of 1889, by singing this verse in a topical song. Mr. Cleveland had Ko Ko guessing and the evidence is that Ko Ko's suspicions were aroused. Grover did "get there" again. This shows that Ko Ko didn't know all. We are for Ko Ko. We don't know whether the Boston series will be played or not. We hope, like Ko Ko on the Presidental gag, that we are wrong, but things now look dark and sad. Of course the word has been passed that the games go, but things in a baseball way have been known to slip a cog.

The yell has gone up here that Ritchey has a bad thumb, that he should be in a hospital. Leach has been away with a bad leg and Wagner has been going round with his right fin in a sling. To add something to this may it be recorded that Pitcher Doheny has left Pittsburg for his home in Andover, Mass., and will not again put on a Pittsburg uniform. This last is but rumor, but the first part is fact. Doheny left Pittsburg Monday evening.

Last, but not least, the story came last evening that Fred Clarke had hurt himself badly in making that home run in the ninth, and that he would probably be out of the game, not only for the rest of the season, but that he would also be out of the Boston-Pittsburg series. Clarke has a seance slated with Dr. Reese of Youngstown to-day at 4 p. m. Last night Mr. Clarke could not be found at his home, 1310 Allegheny avenue. He had come to Pittsburg to meet Secretary Locke. The chances are that Fred Clarke is not the worst injured man in the world. It was announced last evening that Pittsburg would play the series with Boston, even without Clarke, Ritchey and Kruger.

Will they do it; well, I don't know.

Like Ko Ko, we guess. And not this alone. Last evening the following telegram leaked in from Boston. Read it:

"It is said on good authority that certain members of Collins' team have struck, and that there is every prospect that the post-season series of games with Pittsburg arranged after so much difficulty will have to be abandoned. Members of the Plymouth Rocks whose contracts expire with the end of the American League playing season are determined, it is said, to ask for more than has been offered.

"It is said that the management of the club has refused to listen to the demands of the men, and for the present, at least, the series is practically off. In the agreement between Presidents Killilea and Dreyfuss the winning club is to receive 75 per cent of the net receipts of the nine games to be played. President Killilea has offered his men 50 per cent of the money received by the club, to be divided share and share alike between the players, regardless of the expiration of contracts."

WEIMER PITCHED GOOD BALL

CHICAGO, Sept. 22.—Weimer pitched another great game against New York to-day. Attendance, 5,100. Score:

CHICAGO	R.	H.	P.	A.	E.	N. YORK	R.	H.	P.	A.	E.
Slagle, m..	2	2	1	0	0	Browne, r..	0	1	0	0	0
M'Car'y, l.	1	3	3	0	0	Bres'an, m.	0	2	2	0	0
Will'ms, 1.	1	1	10	0	0	M'Gann, 1..	1	1	12	0	0
Jones, r.....	0	2	0	0	0	Mertes, l....	0	0	5	0	0
Tinker, s...	0	0	2	4	1	Babb, s......	0	0	1	6	0
Kling, c....	1	1	7	1	0	Lauder, 3...	0	1	0	2	0
Evers, 2....	0	1	1	1	0	Gilbert, 2...	0	0	0	2	0
Casey, 3....	1	1	1	2	0	Warner, c...	0	0	4	0	0
Weimer, p.	0	0	1	3	0	M'Gin'y, p..	0	1	0	4	1
Raub, c.....	0	0	1	0	0	*Dunn........	0	0	0	0	0
Totals....	6	11	27	11	1	Totals.....	1	6	24	14	1

*Batted for Babb in ninth.

Chicago ....0 0 3 2 0 0 1 0 *—6
New York..................0 0 0 0 0 0 0 0 1—1

Two-base hits—Slagle, McCarthy, Williams, Casey, McGann. Stolen bases—Jones, Slagle. Struck out—By Weimer, 6; by McGinnity, 2. Bases on balls—Off Weimer, 1; off McGinnity, 1. Hit with ball—McGann. Time—1:31. Umpire—O'Day.

EVEN BREAK IN REDTOWN

CINCINNATI, Sept. 22.—The feature of the games was Donlin's terrific batting, he getting six hits out of seven times at bat, four of them triples. Attendance 2,683. Scores.

CINCIN'I	R.	H.	P.	A.	E.	PHILA'IA	R.	H.	P.	A.	E.
Donlin, l...	1	3	0	1	1	Thomas, m.	2	3	8	0	0
Seym'r, m.	1	2	3	0	1	Gleason, 2..	2	2	1	0	2
Dolan, r....	0	0	2	0	0	Wolve'n, 3..	2	2	2	1	0
Beckley, 1.	1	3	5	2	0	Barry, l.....	2	2	1	0	0
DeArm'd,3.	2	2	2	1	1	Titus, r.....	1	3	3	1	0
Daly, 2.....	1	2	2	1	0	Douglass, 1.	2	2	7	0	0
Corcor'n, s.	0	1	4	0	0	Hulswitt, s.	0	1	1	5	0
Pohl, c.....	1	1	9	0	1	Dooin, c.....	0	2	4	0	0
Phillips, p.	0	0	0	5	1	Dug'eby, p.	1	2	0	2	0
Totals....	7	14	27	10	5	Totals....	12	19	27	9	2

Cincinnati.............. 0 0 0 2 1 2 2 0 0—7
Philadelphia............ 3 0 2 0 0 0 7 0 0—12

Two-base hits—Gleason, Titus, Daly, Hulswitt. Three-base hits—Barry, Corcoran, DeArmond, Wolverton, Douglass, Donlin, Seymour. Home run—Beckley. Bases on balls—Off Phillips, 2; off Duggleby, 1. Hit by pitched ball—Pohl, Hulswitt. Struck out—By Phillips, 5; by Duggleby, 2. Time—1:45. Umpires—Johnstone and Hurst.

SECOND GAME.

CINCIN'I	R.	H.	P.	A.	E.	PHILA'IA	R.	H.	P.	A.	E.
Donlin, l...	3	3	5	0	0	Thomas, m.	0	1	1	0	0
Seym'r, m.	1	2	0	0	0	Hallman, 2.	0	0	1	2	0
Dolan, r....	0	0	0	0	0	Wolve'n, 3..	0	1	2	1	0
Beckley, 1.	0	0	7	1	0	Barry, l.....	0	1	2	0	0
DeArm'd,3.	1	1	2	1	0	Titus, r.....	0	0	2	0	0
Daly, 2.....	0	0	1	3	0	Douglass, 1.	0	0	9	1	0
Corcor'n, s.	0	0	3	2	0	Hulswitt, s.	1	1	1	3	0
Peitz, c....	1	3	2	3	0	Dooin, c.....	0	2	2	0	0
Ewing, p...	2	1	1	2	0	Mitchell, p.	0	0	1	1	0
Totals....	8	10	21	12	0	Totals.....	1	6	21	8	0

Cincinnati...................... 1 0 3 4 0 0 0—8
Philadelphia.................... 0 0 0 0 0 0 1—1

Two-base hits—Peitz, Wolverton, Hulswitt. Three-base hits—Donlin (3), Seymour. Bases on balls—Off Ewing, 1; off Mitchell, 1. Time—1:15. Umpires—Johnstone and Hurst.

BETTS MADE POOR DEBUT

ST. LOUIS, Sept. 22.—Harry Betts, a local amateur, was given a trial in the box by St. Louis and was hit hard throughout. Attendance 1,200. Score:

ST. LOUIS	R.	H.	P.	A.	E.	BOSTON	R.	H.	P.	A.	E.
Farrell, 2..	0	1	5	3	0	Dexter, r....	0	0	1	0	0
Dunl'vy, r.	0	0	2	0	0	Tenney, 1...	2	4	8	0	0
Smoot, m..	1	1	3	0	0	Ab-chio, 2..	2	1	1	2	0
Burke, 3....	0	0	1	6	0	Cooley, l....	2	3	3	0	0
Barclay, l.	0	1	1	0	0	Gremin'r, 3.	1	0	3	5	0
Ryan, 1.....	0	1	10	1	0	M'Cre'y, m.	1	1	1	0	0
Bertes, s...	0	2	0	2	2	Moran, c....	1	2	8	0	0
Coveney, c.	0	0	4	3	0	Aubrey, s...	1	0	2	3	2
Betts, p....	0	0	1	1	0	Pittinger, p.	0	0	0	1	0
Totals....	1	6	27	15	2	Totals....	10	11	27	10	2

St. Louis................ 0 0 0 0 0 1 0 0 0—1
Boston................... 3 0 0 4 0 0 0 0 3—10

Two-base hit—McCreery. Three-base hit—Cooley. Stolen base—Tenney. Bases on balls—Off Betts, 5; off Pittinger, 1. Struck out—By Betts, 2; by Pittinger, 5. Left on bases—St. Louis, 7; Boston, 7. Time—1:35. Umpire—Moran.

NATIONAL LEAGUE

Yesterday's Results.

BROOKLYN.......	5	PITTSBURG.........	4
BOSTON............	10	ST. LOUIS...........	1
PHILADELPHIA..	12	CINCINNATI........	7
CINCINNATI......	8	PHILADELPHIA...	1
CHICAGO...........	6	NEW YORK.........	1

Standing of the Clubs.

	W.	L.	Pct.		W.	L.	Pct.
Pittsburg...	90	47	.657	Brooklyn....	68	64	.515
New York..	82	54	.603	Boston......	57	78	.422
Chicago.....	80	55	.593	Philadel'hia	47	84	.359
Cincinnati..	71	63	.530	St. Louis...	42	92	.313

Games To-Day.

New York at Pittsburg.

Official Scorer Banqueted.

John H. Gruber, one of the older and better known of Pittsburg newspapermen, and for 11 years official scorer of the Pittsburg Baseball Club, was tendered a banquet in honor of the fiftieth anniversary of his birth at the Lincoln Hotel last night. At the conclusion of yesterday's game between Pittsburg and Brooklyn Mr. Gruber was taken to the hotel under the impression that he was to meet a friend.

McGraw's New Yorkers, Who Will Appear Here To-Day

1. M'GANN.
2. GILBERT.
3. BABB.
4. LAUDER.
5. TAYLOR.
6. BOWERMAN.
7. CRONIN.
8. M'GINNITY.
9. M'GRAW.
10. BRESNAHAN.
11. MERTES.
12. VAN HALTREN.
13. WARNER.
14. BROWN.
15. DUNN.
16. MATTHEWSON.

TANNEHILL DROPS A CLOSE GAME

New York's Chances Were Blasted Yesterday by the Crowd From Cleveland.

NEW YORK, Sept. 22.—Cleveland again beat New York to-day and put an end to all hopes and aspirations of the locals. Attendance 8,372. Score:

N. YORK	R.	H.	P.	A.	E.	CLEVE'D	R.	H.	P.	A.	E.
Conroy, 3..	0	0	1	1	0	Flick, r.....	1	1	2	0	0
Fultz, m...	0	0	1	1	0	Bay, l.......	0	1	2	0	0
Keeler, r...	2	2	0	0	0	Bradley, 3..	0	1	1	7	0
Elberf'd, s.	0	1	5	2	1	Lajoie, 2...	0	1	2	2	1
Will'ms, 2.	1	2	4	5	0	Bemis, 1....	1	1	12	1	1
Ganzel, 1..	1	1	9	2	0	Thorney, m.	0	0	2	0	0
M'Far'd, l.	0	0	1	0	0	Abbott, c...	2	2	4	0	1
Beville, c..	0	1	5	4	0	Gochn'r, s..	1	2	1	5	0
Tan'hill, p.	0	1	1	0	0	Stovall, p...	0	1	1	2	0
Totals....	4	8	27	15	1	Totals.....	5	10	27	17	3

New York.................. 0 0 0 0 0 3 0 0 1—4
Cleveland................. 0 0 0 0 1 1 1 0 2—5

Two-base hit—Abbott. Three-base hit—Ganzel. Stolen bases—Keeler, McFarland. Double plays—Beville and Elberfeld; Williams, Elberfeld and Ganzel. Bases on balls—Off Stovall, 5; off Tannehill, 3. Struck out—By Stovall, 2; by Tannehill, 5. Wild pitches—Tannehill, 1; Stovall, 1. Time—1:50. Umpire—Sheridan.

SUDHOFF PITCHED NICE BALL

WASHINGTON, Sept. 22.—St. Louis won the final game of the series to-day. Score:

WASH'N	R.	H.	P.	A.	E.	ST. LOUIS	R.	H.	P.	A.	E.
Rob'on, m.	0	1	3	0	0	Burkett, l...	2	3	2	0	0
Hend'ks, r.	1	0	0	0	0	Swander, r.	0	1	1	0	0
Osteen, s...	0	1	4	5	1	Heid'ck, m.	0	1	2	0	0
Selbach, l..	0	1	3	0	0	And'rson, 1.	2	3	15	1	0
Clarke, 1...	0	0	13	0	0	Wallace, s..	2	1	2	4	2
Cough'n, 3.	1	1	0	3	1	Hill, 3......	0	1	0	3	0
M'Cor'k, 2.	0	0	2	5	0	Bowcock, 2.	0	1	0	4	0
Kit'dge, c..	0	1	2	0	0	Kahoe, c....	1	1	4	0	0
Patten, p...	0	0	0	2	0	Sudhoff, p...	1	0	1	4	0
Totals....	2	5	27	15	2	Totals.....	8	12	27	16	2

Washington ....0 0 0 0 0 0 0 1 1—2
St. Louis ....0 5 2 0 0 0 0 0 1—8

Two-base hits—Wallace, Bowcock. Three-base hits—Swander, Heidrick. Double plays—McCormick, Osteen and Clarke; Coughlin, Osteen and Clarke. First base on balls—Off Patten, 2. Struck out—By Patten, 1; by Sudhoff, 4. Left on bases—Washington, 3; St. Louis, 5. Time—1:25. Umpire—Connolly. Attendance—1,109.

CHICAGO CHECKS BOSTON

BOSTON, Sept. 22.—The home team's long string of successive wins was broken by Chicago to-day. Score:

BOSTON	R.	H.	P.	A.	E.	CHICAGO	R.	H.	P.	A.	E.
Dough'y, l.	0	1	1	0	0	Jones, m....	1	1	3	0	0
O'Brien, 3..	0	0	0	2	0	Callahan, l.	2	2	2	0	0
Stahl, m....	0	1	2	0	0	Clark, 3.....	1	1	0	3	0
Fre'man, r.	0	0	2	0	0	Green, r.....	1	1	2	0	1
Parent, s...	0	2	2	3	0	Tan'hill, s..	0	3	1	8	0
Lach'ce, 1.	0	0	9	0	0	Isbell, 1....	0	0	12	0	1
Ferris, 2....	0	0	5	2	1	Magoon, 2...	0	0	4	3	1
Farrell, c...	0	0	6	1	0	Sullivan, c..	1	0	3	0	0
Hughes, p...	0	0	0	3	0	Altrock, p...	1	2	0	2	0
Totals....	0	4	27	11	1	Totals.....	7	10	27	16	3

Boston ....0 0 0 0 0 0 0 0 0—0
Chicago ....3 0 1 0 1 2 0 0 0—7

Earned runs—Chicago, 6. Two-base hits—Jones, Dougherty. Three-base hit—Clark. Home run—Green. Stolen base—Tannehill. First base on balls—Off Hughes, 2; off Altrock, 1. Hit by pitched ball—By Hughes, Isbell. Struck out—By Hughes, 5; by Altrock, 2. Wild pitch—Hughes. Time—1:30. Umpire—O'Loughlin. Attendance—3,464.

HENLEY HAD A BAD INNING

PHILADELPHIA, Sept. 22.—Henley's bad inning and several costly errors by the locals gave Detroit to-day's game. Attendance, 3,056. Score:

DETROIT	R.	H.	P.	A.	E.	PHILA'IA	R.	H.	P.	A.	E.
Barrett, m.	0	2	1	0	0	Hartzel, l...	0	2	4	0	0
Lush, l.....	0	1	5	0	0	Pick'ng, m.	0	1	1	1	0
Crawf'd, r.	0	0	1	0	0	Davis, 1.....	1	2	6	2	2
Carr, 1.....	1	2	10	0	0	L. Cross, 3..	1	2	0	0	1
Yeager, 3...	2	1	0	1	0	Seybold, r...	1	2	3	0	0
Burns, 2....	1	1	3	6	0	D.Mur'y, 2..	1	2	2	1	0
J.Mur'y, s.	1	1	4	2	1	M. Cross, s.	0	0	3	3	1
Buelow, c..	1	2	3	0	0	Shreck, c....	1	4	7	3	0
Kitson, p...	1	0	0	2	0	Henley, p...	0	0	0	2	0
						Fairb'ks, p.	0	0	1	1	1
Totals....	7	10	27	11	1	Totals.....	4	15	27	13	5

Detroit ....0 1 0 5 0 0 0 0 1—7
Philadelphia ....0 0 0 0 0 1 1 2 0—4

Two-base hits—Carr, J. Murphy, Schreck (2), D. Murphy, Davis, L. Cross. Home run—Buelow. Stolen bases—Lush, Yeager, Kitson. Double plays—J. Murphy and Burns; Burns and Carr; Pickering and M. Cross; Fairbanks, Davis and Schreck. First base on balls—Off Henley, 4; off Fairbanks, 2. Struck out—By Kitson, 2; by Fairbanks, 4. Innings pitched—By Henley, 3½; by Fairbanks, 5½. Hits—Off Henley, 5; off Fairbanks, 5. Time—1:50. Umpire—Adams.

AMERICAN LEAGUE

Yesterday's Results.

DETROIT............	7	PHILADELPHIA...	4
ST. LOUIS...........	8	WASHINGTON......	2
CLEVELAND........	5	NEW YORK..........	4
CHICAGO............	7	BOSTON...............	0

Standing of the Clubs.

	W.	L.	Pct.		W.	L.	Pct.
Boston......	87	44	.664	New York..	65	70	.481
Cleveland...	74	50	.597	Detroit......	62	67	.481
Philadel'hia	69	59	.539	Chicago.....	57	73	.438
St. Louis....	63	67	.485	Washington	42	89	.321

Games To-Day.

Chicago at Philadelphia.
Cleveland at Washington.
New York at St. Louis.
Detroit at Boston.

Large Squad of Veterans.

PRINCETON, N. J., Sept. 22.—[Special.]—From the work of the Tiger football players in to-day's practice it seems that the coaches have selected the "quarterback kick" as one of the trick plays for this season. An unusually large list of old players will go to the 'varsity training table Wednesday. The 15 men are: Dewitt, Davis, Burke, Kafer, McClave, Foulke, Hart, Crawford, Tooker, Reed, Barney, Vetterline, Rafferty, Short and Bradley. Of the men at the table Burke and Kafer are two valuable players who were kept out of last year's Yale game by broken collarbones. Crawford and Tooker are ends who were substituted last season.

Geneva Badly Crippled.

BEAVER FALLS, Sept. 22.—[Special.]—Acting on the advice of Coach McFarland Manager John Barnes of the Geneva College football team has written to State College, canceling the game with that team scheduled for September 26. Geneva is in a badly crippled condition as a result of last Saturday's game with the alumni. Schmidt is on crutches, Martin walks with a cane and Owen Thompson, Finney and East are unable to don a uniform for practice.

Altoona Wins and Loses.

ALTOONA, Pa., Sept. 22.—[Special.]—The locals split even with their rivals from the capital city to-day. Bennett did great work for the home nine in the first game, but the second battle proved a cinch and easy walkover for Harrisburg, as Dan Miller was batted hard, losing 7 to 1.

WADDELL LIKED HIS NEW UNIFORM

Wore His First One All Saturday Night and All Sunday Up in Butler.

Up in Butler they are telling new stories daily about Rube Waddell, who is now a full-fledged actor. The latest one to come out has reached The Dispatch by mail through a friend from Sharon, Pa., who claims to be a close friend of the man who first played Waddell in a ball game at Butler.

Years ago when Rube was an awkward farmer boy he went to see a baseball game on the outskirts of Butler, and before the game opened he got on the field and began tossing the ball around. His arm was very strong even for a farmer lad and he could throw the ball hard and far. The manager of the little Butler team needed one with a good arm for middle field and he asked Rube to come and play with him the following Saturday.

"Will I get one of them suits?" said Rube, pointing to a player in uniform.

"Yes," said the manager.

"All right; I'll come," said Rube, and he did. The delight of Waddell when he got into that suit was amusing. He played the game out and did well, but when it came time to take the suit off Rube rebelled. No, sirree; that suit would stay where it was. He would not be buncombed. So, in spite of the pleadings and tears of the manager, Rube kept the uniform on, not only all that Saturday night, but all the following day, Sunday.

It was some time after that before the manager permitted Rube to put on his uniform again. He feared that he might never get it back.

Waynesburg Loses Again.

YOUNGSTOWN, O., Sept. 22.—[Special.]—Ohio Works took another fall out of Waynesburg to-day. The visitors' fielding was ragged and they could not hit Armstrong opportunely. Ohio Works made nine hits off Collins, while Waynesburg gathered in eight. The final score was 8 to 2.

A Post-Season Game.

MEMPHIS, Tenn., Sept. 22.—Memphis, 5; Little Rock, 4. Eleven innings.

MARKSMANSHIP BETTER IN ARMY THAN EVER BEFORE

WASHINGTON, Sept. 22.—Reports daily received by the War Department show that as a result of the new regulations for small arm firing the men are acquiring wonderful proficiency. These regulations require the men not only to hit the bullseye, but to estimate distances up to 10 per cent of 1,000 yards. In firing outside the target range at dummies the reports state that the results have been remarkable. The reports show excellent results in rapid pistol firing, it being a common thing for the men to put five shots in the bullseye at 25 yards in 10 seconds, although they are allowed 20 seconds in which to shoot. The War Department officials believe that the men are attaining a proficiency in marksmanship never before equaled in the history of the army.

EASTERN LEAGUE

Yesterday's Results.

JERSEY CITY......	11	BUFFALO...........	0
NEWARK...........	4	TORONTO...........	2
TORONTO...........	6	NEWARK............	0
PROVIDENCE.....	5	BALTIMORE........	3
PROVIDENCE.....	14	BALTIMORE........	4
MONTREAL.........	8	ROCHESTER........	4

Standing of the Clubs.

	W.	L.	Pct.		W.	L.	Pct.
Jersey City.	88	33	.727	Newark.....	74	59	.556
Buffalo......	76	41	.650	Providence.	43	84	.339
Toronto.....	77	45	.631	Montreal....	36	90	.286
Baltimore...	69	51	.578	Rochester...	33	93	.262

BROOKLYN DOWNS THE YOUNG ONES

Although Clarke Came to the Rescue With a Homer, Thompson Et Al. Were Beaten.

There was another seance of amateur baseball at Exposition Park yesterday, with Pittsburg on the short end of the scene. Thompson was in the points for Pittsburg and the Montana man put up a nice game outside of one inning, when he made a throw that cost us two runs. The new ones performed fairly well, and as the old guard, with the exception of Clarke, will be in line to-day there will be slight danger of Pittsburg losing.

Outside of the fact that Brooklyn took its fourth game here yesterday and that Schmidt, he of the pinwheel delivery, was the main factor in the Premiers' downfall there was another factor in yesterday's game. Fred Clarke is his name, and the 1,500 spectators present are still talking of how Freddy drove the ball far into middle field and against the fence, sending "Hans" Lobert in ahead of him, thus tieing the score. Bill Kennedy finished the game and Broooklyn won out.

Aided by the liberality of Thompson and a wild throw by the man from Helena Brooklyn copped three runs in the third. Dahlen and Flood walked and both men were safe on Marshall's attempt to catch Flood on Ritter's force out. Schmidt then bunted, Wild Bill Dahlen scoring. The Pittsburg pitcher secured the ball too late to catch his man, but made an awfully wild throw, the ball going to the right field bleachers. Flood and Ritter scored on the error.

The fifth opened auspiciously for Pittsburg, as Lobert, the Pittsburg Amateur Club third baseman, walked and stole second prettily. Carisch's hit sent him to third, but the Beltzhoover boy was caught at home, although he made a long slide to reach the home station. Carisch advanced on Beau's hit and counted on Sebring's out. Marshall fanned.

Brooklyn counted in the seventh on Dobbs' double and Dahlen's hit, which Marshall booted into right field.

Pittsburg came closer in the eighth, when Carisch doubled, his second hit and a timely one, and scored on Beau's single.

The ninth saw Pittsburg make a gallant finish, when John Lobert, the P. A. C. boy who is acceptably subbing for Pittsburg, sent a pretty double into right. The boy third baseman took third on Carisch's out, Flood to Doyle. Clarke then batted for Thompson and drove out one of the finest home runs of the year. The Pittsburg manager strained a tendon in running around and may be out of the game. Beaumont went out, while Sebring singled. Jimmy was caught trying to steal second.

Brooklyn won out in the tenth on Gessler's double, Kennedy's fumble of Flood's bunt and Strang's fly to Beau.

Marshall started well by singling in the tenth. Bransfield hit to Dahlen and both men were out. Claudius Ritchey again found Schmidt's benders for one, but Curtis forced the Emlenton boy and we all went home, vowing to return for the New York game to-day and Matthewson to-morrow. The score:

PITTSBURG.	AB.	R.	H.	P.	A.	E.
Beaumont, m..............	5	0	3	2	0	0
Sebring, r................	5	0	1	2	0	0
Marshall, s...............	5	0	1	3	2	0
Bransfield, 1.............	5	0	0	9	0	0
Ritchey, 2................	5	0	3	2	3	0
Curtis, l..................	5	0	0	3	0	0
Lobert, 3.................	3	1	1	3	2	1
Carisch, c................	4	2	2	6	2	0
Thompson, p..............	3	0	0	0	2	1
Kennedy, p................	0	0	0	0	0	1
*Clarke	1	1	1	0	0	0
Totals	41	4	12	30	11	3

BROOKLYN.	AB.	R.	H.	P.	A.	E.
Strang, 3.................	6	0	0	0	1	0
Sheckard, l...............	4	0	1	2	0	0
Dobbs, m..................	5	1	3	0	0	0
Doyle, 1...................	2	0	1	4	0	0
Jordan, 1.................	3	0	0	11	0	0
Dahlen, s.................	3	1	0	3	3	0
Gessler, r................	5	1	1	1	0	0
Flood, 2..................	3	1	0	3	6	0
Ritter, c.................	4	1	2	6	0	0
Schmidt, p................	4	0	1	0	4	0
Totals	39	5	9	30	14	0

*Batted for Thompson in ninth.

Brooklyn ....0 3 0 0 0 0 1 0 0 1—5
Pittsburg ....0 0 0 0 1 0 1 0 2 0—4

Home run—Clarke. Two-base hits—Lobert, Carisch, Doyle, Ritter, Dobbs, Gessler. Double play—Dahlen, Flood and Jordan. Stolen bases—Lobert, Sheckard, Dahlen, Ritter. Sacrifice hit—Flood. Struck out—By Thompson, 5 (Strang, Jordan, 2; Dahlen, Gessler); by Schmidt, 4 (Curtis, 2; Marshall, Bransfield. Base on balls—Off Thompson, 7 (Sheckard, 2; Dahlen, 2; Flood, Ritter, Schmidt; off Schmidt, 1 (Lobert). Time—2:15. Umpire—Emslie. Attendance—1,567.

NOTES OF THE GAME

Doyle was playing off second in the third when Thompson got the signal to throw to Marshall. The California boy blocked Doyle and Jack was caught by a slight margin. Doyle raised an awful howl and Emslie benched him, Jordan taking first.

Jimmy Sheckard received a liberal hand from the crowd when he gathered in Ritchey's short liner while on the dead run toward center.

Thompson contributed some pretty pitching in the third as he retired Strang, Jordan and Gessler on strikes. Sheckard had beaten out a bunt and Dobbs had worked in a scratch infield hit to Marshall, while Dahlen had walked. This did not phase Thompson, and when he fanned Gessler he received a hand all around.

Lobert walked in the fourth and stole second prettily. A hit sent him to third, but Hans was caught at home as Schmitt recovered after fumbling Thompson's hit.

Jimmy Sebring robbed Gessler of a sure double in the second by going into the air and getting Gessler's drive in his left hand as it neared the fence.

Curtis had a chance to show his home run ability in the fourth as Ritchey was on first, but the Wheeling man allowed two pretty ones to pass and missed the third one, which was also a good one.

Flood robbed Bransfield of a sure hit in the sixth as he caught Kitty's sizzler in his right hand and made a wonderfully quick and accurate throw to Jordan.

Reviews of Sports, Professional and Amateur—Football Gossip, Etc.

THE TROUBLE AT BOSTON MUCH TO BE DEPLORED

Foreign Ownership Policy of the American League Caused Friction—Pittsburg Boys Should Win the Coming Series.

By FRANK B. M'QUISTON.

The fuss over at Boston has been the absorbing topic in baseball during the week past and the end is not yet. No one is quite satisfied that the post-season series will be played. Most of the Pittsburg people feel with me that when we see the Boston fellows on the field then we will feel comfortably certain that they are about to play. Between this and next Thursday afternoon some of those American champions may discover that he has not yet got his winter coal in and insist on the club owners filling his cellar before he will go into the game.

The fuss between the club owners and the Boston players has given baseball a black eye, and the color will spread. Nothing in the national game for years could have a worse effect than this. And the players are not wholly to blame. The policy first adopted by the American League, that of syndicate ball and foreign owners, is surely most to blame for this most lamentable fuss. Baseball cannot be a success in any town where the club is owned by those residing in another city. Mr. Killilea, owner of the Boston champions, is a very busy Milwaukee attorney. Does any one suppose that had he but resided in the town where his money was invested in baseball and where he could be in daily touch with his players that they would have revolted and washed their soiled linen in public as Boston players did? No; there is not the right feeling, there cannot be the same feeling between magnate and player when one plays in a city so far distant from the other. The baseball fans who see the players perform daily are sure to side with them when it comes to a fuss with the club owners who reside far away. And I don't know but it is right. The Pittsburg Club was not a success as long as half of it was owned by a Chicago man. It would not be a success yet were the stock not owned and controlled by those who live, move and have their being, and also pay their taxes in Pittsburg. Mr. Killilea has had a severe lesson and he should now either move to Boston or sell his club to Boston people. Home capital makes baseball a success.

❖ ❖ ❖

The Trouble Discussed.

It is purely a matter of opinion as to who was right in the controversy and it is also a matter of opinion as to whether the series will yet occur. The Boston players, it is claimed, have taken a stand and have won out. They told Mr. Killilea that they would not accept his terms for playing the post-season series. Their contracts expire with the last day of this month, and he offered them by mail one-half of what the club made in the post-season series. They said they would not accept this but demanded all the money which should come the way of Boston. They claimed that they had won the pennant for Mr. Killilea and that they were entitled to any and all benefits which were to be derived from a post-season series inasmuch as they were not under salary. They offered to take Mr. Killilea in on an equal basis and give him the same as that falling to the lot of any player. This almost caused riot in Milwaukee, but it is now whispered that Mr. Killilea has agreed to give his players 75 per cent of what comes to Boston and he will take the remainder.

It is not ours to take sides with either in this case but to deplore the fact that such a squabble should have been precipitated. The players made the claim that they are the people. Mr. Killilea says that it was his money which put the team in Boston and it was he who paid the boys great salaries to play baseball and that, having played the game well and won, he offered them the chance to make a lot of money on the side by playing Pittsburg and at the same time clean up a little for himself. It shows a grasping after the dollar which might have been better left uncovered. Now every fan in Boston when he pays his 75 cents for a seat will do so figuring that so many cents of it will go to the players at home if they win the series and so many less if they lose. They will also figure how much of it goes to each Pittsburg player in case of winning or of losing, and when they get figuring this way it will not take long for the average Boston mathematician to get a result, and that will be that he is the common sucker that Killilea and the gang of Collins have been fighting over.

Magnates Will Remember It.

The players in either league will not profit in the least by what has occurred in Boston. The players have been allowed their head in this case and every magnate from Maine to California knows it. A certain degree of hard feeling has been engendered all round and it is to be supposed that when opportunity offers next to give the players a dig the magnates will seize it. There has been but little disposition on the part of the club owners anywhere to hurry signing players for next year and this portends a cut in salaries for those who have not long-term contracts. The club owners in either league will to a certain extent sympathize with Killilea and threy will not forget the Boston incident.

How much better is the situation in Pittsburg? Much better. The players are under contract until the middle of the present coming month and they are going into that series of games to earn their salaries. Of course they have been told through the newspapers that they will be well taken care of. They always have been in the past. I am satisfied that if each and all of the Pittsburg players were told by Mr. Dreyfuss that there would not be one cent of extra money in it for them, no matter if he cleared $50,000 on the series, that they would go into that series and play just as hard as they will beginning next Thursday (if Boston will play). The best of good feeling exists between the players here and the principal owner. It would not be so if he lived in some other city. I know that some days ago Leever and Phillippe went to President Dreyfuss and assured him that they were both in the best of shape and would alternate in the Boston series if he so desired. He thanked them and said he would probably call on them to pitch all the games. This is a proper feeling between club owner and player.

❖ ❖ ❖

Result of the Series.

The chances now favor the series to open Thursday. Pittsburg will be on hand to open no matter what happens in Boston between this and that time. The result of the series is the next thing to consider and dope out.

As readers already know, I am more than skeptical as to the truth of stories carried around that this and that player was in such fearful shape lately. I am more than satisfied that Pittsburg will beat Boston and badly, not only here, but I expect to see our boys take two of the three games in Boston. Yes, and at that we are handicapped. We go in with but two pitchers. Doheny is history and Winham is worse, so we have no left hander. But that is not where we are handicapped the worst. We have no extra outfielder or infielder to put in in case of accident. Little Kruger cannot go to Boston on account of his injury. Who then have we? We cannot take Curtis, the hard-hitting new outfielder because of the agreement not to play people who were put under contract after September 1. Curtis' batting might help some in a pinch, but his fielding is not up to the mark to which we have been accustomed and must have in Boston. In case of accident to any member of the regular team it would be necessary to put in one of the extra pitchers or one of the catchers. An injury to any one of the regular nine would leave us in bad shape.

But let us not think of that. Boston will get the beating of a lifetime. Of this I am satisfied. I know how the boys play ball when they have to. They feel that they will be called on to do a little ball playing down in Boston and they will do it. I have seen them play not a few games away from home and innumerable games at home. I have seen but few games at Exposition Park with the speed attending those away from home. It has always seemed necessary to get the foreign crowd with its jeers working right to start the Pittsburg people to playing baseball. I will be more than disappointed if Pittsburg does not play Boston off her feet right on her own grounds and before her own people, too. We hear much about our not being able to hit Young, Dineen and Hughes. Well, they must have improved. This Pittsburg gang can hit any pitcher that walks and hit him hard. (Well, 'er, I beg Mr. Matthewson's pardon. I had forgotten him. But at that they could have hit Matty if they had wanted to very bad.) Now we are going over to Boston with the eyes of the whole baseball world on us to play the champions of the American. Just watch us go. Let the boys go out quietly and rest assured that though we have but two pitchers we will do the town proud.

TRAINER MURPHY IS NOT SATISFIED

Says the Yale Eleven Will Have Rather a Hard Row to Hoe This Year.

[*Special Telegram to The Dispatch.*]

NEW HAVEN, Conn., Sept. 26.—"The Yale team will this year have the hardest row to hoe it has had since I have been here to win," said Mike Murphy, the Yale trainer and assistant coach, to-day. "This talk about a lot of fine, new, heavy material is bosh. There simply isn't anybody found yet in the freshman class who is heavy and good. What is more there isn't any good light material in sight. If there was we could, under the new rules, play first-class football with the light men. I think that better results could be secured with Glass and Bloomer and nine newsboys to fill out the eleven than with an eleven made up of the new material we have at hand. We had three first-class men who wanted to come here and tried to, but it was the old story. They slipped up in their examinations, and have gone to other colleges, two of them to Princeton."

Mr. Murphy's views are those of the other football officials, as far as a rebuke to the optimism which has been prevailing about Yale's rosy chances for this season are concerned. They have not found new material made to order, as they wish it, although some of last year's material is better and heavier than it was then. Headway in finding men for the three center positions just made vacant cannot be made. Smith, the freshman center of last season, has not shown up strong. Last year he was not hard for Princeton and Harvard, '06, to force back, and this year he is not any better. Roraback, who weighs 235, having come down from 250 in two weeks, is now given the preference for the place.

Morton, who snapped the ball back as first substitute last year, has been placed at guard, but he may be moved back. As he weighs 215 pounds, he looks an ideal candidate.

Tom Shevlin has gone to end, though he weighs 190 pounds. Kinney and Hogan are fixtures at tackle.

Captain Rafferty has been hurt as much as ever the past week, and has lived up to his reputation as the most unlucky man on the gridiron. He will probably play less than Yale captains usually do owing to his unfortunate fatality for severe accidents.

Ex-Captain Gates of the Andover eleven, Ogden Reid and Hare will play end much this fall as substitutes, although, barring accidents, Shevlin and Rafferty will hold the positions. Flanders and Bloomer have been alternating at guard on the opposite wing from Bloomer. Behind the line Rockwell has returned to his place with Donohue as his understudy, and with Walter Stillman tried for quarter, end and fullback alternately. Stillman has gained 10 pounds the past summer and is a fast dark horse candidate for the eleven. The back field has been weakened all week by the absence of players who have been away taking examinations in studies. Owsley and Bowman have been absent for this reason, and with Metcalf retired because of his knee the regular string of backs has been Mitchell, Farmer and Allen.

GREAT SWIMMER, EUGENE CURTIS

Made Good as an Outfielder When at Bethany, Aided by Buffalo Creek.

Eugene Curtis, who has made such a good reputation as a substitute outfielder on the Pittsburg team, first gained fame by reason of the fact that he could swim farther into Buffalo creek and save the ball than any other "kid" playing on the nine. Curtis is a native of Bethany, W. Va., and since his boyhood has been associated with college men. In other years Bethany had the best college team in the West. Men who are now high in business life were members of the team, but the "kids" had to play outside of the campus and across the creek in a field which belonged to a farmer, long since gone to his reward. Near the field Buffalo creek, about which amateur poets have been raving for the last half century, flowed.

The first time Curtis ever made good as an outfielder was about 15 years ago. The Middletown team had challenged the Bethany kids to play a game. The challenge was accepted and about 10 a. m. the Middletownites arrived, on foot. The game was set for 2 p. m., but owing to the fact that the club had arrived so early it was decided to play two games and the first was immediately started. The Middletown crowd were at the bat and the first fellow up—Ed Lane, who has since gained fame by reason of his daredevil work with Roosevelt's men in Cuba—cracked the ball into the creek. Curtis started for the ball and vaulted the rail fence at the edge of the field. The ball lit squarely in the middle of the creek. To lose it meant that there would be no game that afternoon. The ball was the only one the "kids" had.

Curtis ran to the edge of the creek. He wore a new uniform which his mother had just made for him. There was a hasty glance at the uniform and then it was decided to get the ball whether the uniform was ruined or not. He ran into the stream as far as possible and then swam to the ball. Back he came and the game was in progress in five minutes. That play fixed Curtis in left field and if ever the Allegheny gets into Exposition Park again Pittsburgers can look for a repetition of the performance.

The Team Which Will This Week Tackle the Pittsburgs

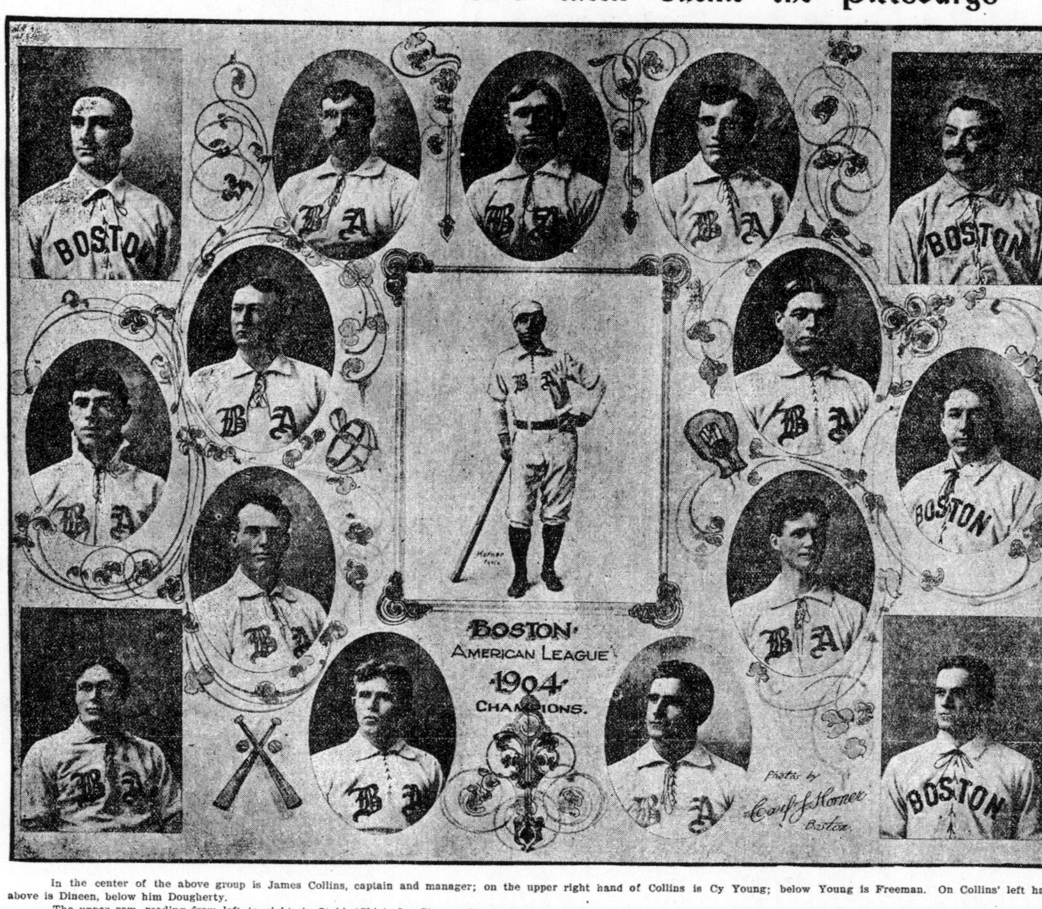

In the center of the above group is James Collins, captain and manager; on the upper right hand of Collins is Cy Young; below Young is Freeman. On Collins' left hand above is Dineen, below him Dougherty.

The upper row, reading from left to right, is Stahl (Chic), La Chance, Ferris, Parent and Farrell. The lower row in the same order—Strows, Winters, Criger, Stahl (Jake) and O'Brien. The player between Chic Stahl and Winters is Hughes; between Farrell and O'Brien is Gibson.

HOMESTEAD LEADS IN THE LOCAL RACE

P. A. C. and Millvale Are Behind Edmundson's Men, but Still Have a Chance.

By ARTHUR W. WILSON.

The three-cornered championship fight between Homestead, P. A. C. and Millvale and the remarkable winning streak of the Rochester nine have kept baseball interest at fever heat during the past week. The lovers of football cannot enthuse over a champion professional football eleven this fall, and for that reason they have continued to talk of the local teams. They not only discuss the games but they attend the contests and cheer their favorites. The champion Homesteads have had to fight to the finish to capture the three out of four games that they have won, and for that reason the followers of P. A. C. and Millvale have just cause to feel proud.

Before another week rolls by Mays Edmundson and his men will have again won the championship or a new nine will step into the seat of honor. As Homestead has to play a double-header at Friendship Park on Tuesday they will have to play much better than they did on Friday, or P. A. C. will oust them from the championship. On a previous appearance in the Bloomfield park the men from the steel town found Diebold for but one run, while Alexander Pearson was batted for four earned runs in one inning. The memory of that game and the fact that they outbatted Homestead on Friday should give Matthews' men confidence upon their final appearance.

❖ ❖ ❖

Homestead and P. A. C. Compared.

The games already played have demonstrated that the young pitchers on the P. A. C. can hold their own with Pearson and Brown, both of whom have shown resplendent in the fastest minor leagues.

Continue this comparison around the infield and throughout the outfield and who can pick a man who stands far above the others? Judging by the recent games "Hans" Lobert is a better player than Mays Edmundson. I dislike to make this statement, for I have long been an admirer of the ex-Westminster captain, but when a youngster breaks into prominence give him the credit. In the three games Lobert made five hits and stole two bases, while "Eddie" made two hits. Lobert had more chances than Eddie and accepted them all without a slip.

McLaughlin and McCloskey each made two hits in the three games, and the fact that he made one throw a bit wide doesn't show that the Aspinwall boy is not a star, when compared to the ex-Eastern leaguer.

At second Beuchner was a tower of strength to P. A. C. by his fielding, while Cosgrove fielded his position as faultlessly. Cosgrove outhit Beuchner by one bingle.

Mucker and Matthews each hit safely once during the series, while Torreyson was not so fortunate. The ex-Interstate leaguer had one error to his opponent's none.

Tate and Dick Taylor drew even in left with two hits each and several spectacular catches.

Harry McChesney shows a little stronger in middle for Homestead, as he made six hits, stole three bases and gathered in several remarkable catches, although Irve Cunningham had four, and Billy Campbell two hits during their career as middle fielders.

Charlie Nichol made one hit in two games, while Brown, Marshall and Coursey didn't hit safe during their games in right field against P. A. C.

Behind the bat there is little to place one man above another, when Lee Fohl is taken out. Fohl made two hits in the first game, and didn't allow a stolen base, while Coursey was not hitting safely and four P. A. C. men stole on him. Coursey and Mucker split even in hitting, with one bingle apiece in the second game, but Homestead stole three bases on Mucker. In the third game Marshall and Will Taylor were the opposing catchers. While Taylor hit safely to Marshall's walk the Des Moines catcher stole a base on his P. A. C. opponent.

Comparisons are not all of a baseball story, however, as dope never won games. While the players compare well together, amateurs against professionals, men who play one or two games a week versus men who play every day, it is known that Homestead distributed its six runs well enough to win two games, while P. A. C. could cull but one victory with its seven runs.

We thus see where the older team had a bit better team work. This was to be expected with Homestead playing its regular team every day, and P. A. C. using a catcher on first in some of the games.

A bunt toward first base with a runner on third, or a sacrifice, with a man on first and nobody out, would have turned the scale of defeat for P. A. C. in the last game at Homestead.

Collectively and individually either team is worthy of being the champions of Western Pennsylvania. Homestead has the best record so far this season, while the Amateurs—formerly known as the Junctions—will have another chance on Tuesday.

❖ ❖ ❖

Millvale and Rochester.

Not knowing at the time of writing the result of yesterday's Millvale-Homestead contest I cannot comment on the work of Ed Hickey's men. It is already known that Millvale, with Lew Moren on the rubber, beat P. A. C. 8 to 5. Johnny Yoedt being the P. A. C. slab artist. Millvale then visited Homestead, but Moren lost 5 to 0, as his teammates fielded and batted poorly. If Hickey won yesterday's game, and he should, considering that he was on his home grounds and that Moren is learning valuable baseball every day since Pittsburg gave him a trial, Millvale will go to Homestead to-morrow and with Cushman or Billy Campbell should put up a good fight, as both men have always troubled the steel workers.

There is a fourth team whose chances of winning the championship look good. Their mail is addressed to Rochester and A. A. Atterholt, Postmaster of the town, is the manager. The team is composed of local players, several of whom are employed in the mills. The team won 19 successive games, the Waynesburg, Bridgeville, Sharon, Niles and Warren (O.) teams being among the sufferers. This record was made during an extended stand at home. Homestead, Bridgeville and Waynesburg put forth good claims that Rochester liked its own field too well to play return games. Mr. Atterholt assured me on Friday that his team would play one game at Homestead and one with the steel workers upon a neutral field near Pittsburg.

Lovers of baseball will be glad to see such a series, for strong at-home teams look good when seen by outsiders.

Rochester's record justifies all Mr. Atterholt and the other business men of the town claim for their boys.

A few of the Rochester players are known to Pittsburgers. Eddie Miles is the former Wheeling Central League, Homestead and Johnstown second baseman. Lindsey formerly played with Wilmerding. Garvey and Simpson compose an ex-Homestead battery. The Rochester people consider Simpson a better pitcher than Alex. Pearson, who resides in that town. "Rube" Zeller is a husky youngster, who defeated Westminster College while pitching for Beaver College. Pitcher Pat Sweeney resides in McDonald, and did elegant work for Sistersville and Wheeling this season.

Finish of New York State League.

ALBANY, N. Y., Sept. 26.—Schenectady won the New York State League pennant, and strange to relate the Electric City organization is the only team in the league which has not made money this season. The managers and owners have lost several thousand dollars because of the poor attendance at the games. The State League finished in the following order:

	Won.	Lost.	Pct.
Schenectady	81	50	.619
Syracuse	80	53	.602
Troy	71	47	.602
Albany	64	62	.504
Utica	62	63	.496
Ilion	51	72	.415
Binghamton	50	72	.410
Johnstown	41	80	.339

GOOD FEELING AMONG TIGERS

Many Candidates for the Eleven and Most Are Doing Good Work.

[*Special Telegram to The Dispatch.*]

PRINCETON, N. J., Sept. 26.—The first week of the football season at the university here has been the means of inspiring confidence into the hearts of all the wearers of the Orange and the Black. There is no end of candidates from which to select the team, and what is most encouraging is the fact that the entire squad is showing a dash and enthusiasm which is seldom seen at the middle of the season. As a result of this the coaches have been able to get the men down to hard work earlier than they otherwise would, which is bound to count favorably in the team work.

Princeton is particularly fortunate in having lost but two of her last year's 'varsity. Pearson, the quarter back, and S. McClair, a half, are the only last year players who have graduated. Both of these places will be filled with seasoned players, who have had heaps of experience on scrub and as substitutes in 'varsity games.

This will make the lineup of the team composed of men who are practically veterans. In the center position, Short, who last year began the game at tackle, is the most likely candidate, while it is generally conceded in Princeton that Rafferty, the big 200-pound Pittsburg boy, a cousin of Yale's captain, and Bradley, another veteran of last year, will be the guards. Captain DeWitt, who was last year played at guard, principally to battle with Yale's giant, Glass, is now put back to his old place at tackle, where he is a power. Reed, also an old player, will be DeWitts's running mate on the other side of the center, and together they will make a pair of tackles that should care for all that will be coming to them. At least, that is the way the Tigers' coaches have reckoned it. The end positions on Nassau's team will as usual be strong. Ex-Captain Davis, Henry, Tooker and Crawford, another of Pittsburg's contributions to Princeton athletics, are all in excellent condition. Behind the line Burke, last year's star, who was injured just previous to the Yale game, and Vetterlein, the drop kicker from Penn Charter School, are both 'varsity material for the quarter back position, while Hart, Foulke, Kafer, Moore, R. McClair, Munn, King, and a host of others are all being played at half and full.

So far the freshman class has not brought forth any bright stars from preparatory schools, nor have there been unearthed any very heavy men, but for all this there are sufficient men from last year from which to select a first-class team. The season opens next Wednesday, and with but two exceptions all the games are scheduled to be played at Princeton.

DON'T WANT BY FORFEIT

Fans of Little Rock Seem to Favor Letting Memphis Have Pennant.

[*Special Telegram to The Dispatch.*]

LITTLE ROCK, Ark., Sept. 26.—The baseball fans of Little Rock are dead-game sports, and now that the unofficial standing at the close of the season has given the Southern League pennant to Memphis, there is a most decided opposition here to trying to get it for Little Rock on protested games. Little Rock was beaten out by but two points, holding the lead until the last minute. Early in the week the news was sent broadcast that Little Rock would make a strong fight for the pennant on protested games, but now it is doubtful. If the league meets October 10 they will try for the pennant; if it does not they will let it go to Memphis.

Last May, when Little Rock was playing in Nashville, Manager Fisher of that club played Hugh Hill, the outfielder and pitcher, in two games. Finn protested both games, and the protest is now on file in President Kavanaugh's office. It is strange that the only other protest is against Memphis, being made by Atlanta, because her man was called out when he tried to steal a base on a foul strike. Under the constitution, Little Rock has every right to the two games in which Hill played, or they should be thrown out, for Hill had been awarded to Kansas City by the national board, and Nashville had been instructed by President Kavanaugh not to play him. This was the ground on which Little Rock claimed the pennant, for if they were thrown out it would take two games off her lost column and throw her ahead of Memphis. The real truth is that Manager Finn would much prefer to finish second the third successive year than get the pennant, for the latter would cause the people to expect too much next year. James Delehanty of the Little Rock team, who has been drafted by Boston, leads the league in batting, with a percentage of .384.

COMING FISTIC BATTLES

Gus Ruhlin versus "Kid" Carter, Philadelphia, September 28.

Tom Wallace versus Jerry McCarthy, Salt Lake City, September 28.

Eddie Hanlon versus Benny Yanger, San Francisco, September 29.

Jack Johnson versus Hank Griffin, San Francisco, September 29.

Robert Fitzsimmons versus Con Coughlan, Philadelphia, September 30.

Jack Munroe versus Jack McCormack, Philadelphia, October 5.

"Kid" Carter versus Joe Walcott, Boston, October 7.

Terry McGovern versus Jimmy Briggs, Boston, October 6.

Terry McGovern versus Crockey Boyle, Philadelphia, October 12.

Jack Johnson versus Sandy Ferguson, San Francisco, October 16.

STRONG FIELD AT STATE COLLEGE

Whitworth, McIlveen, Forkum and Elder Are Veterans—Experienced Center Men Are Needed.

[*Special Telegram to The Dispatch.*]

STATE COLLEGE, Pa., Sept. 26.—No real test of the 'varsity's strength has yet been obtained, as the opening game with Dickinson Seminary proved too easy for any valuable observations to be made by Coaches Golden, Sweet and Junk. Only six of last year's 'varsity are back at school, but over 40 new candidates are trying for the team.

There are at present 32 men on the training table, but this number will be reduced this week to 25 or 26. All the candidates are comparatively new at the game. Coach Sweet played center last season with the Philadelphia professionals. Under his tuition Adams and Dunn, the center men, may develop excellently before the big games.

In Parry, Yeckley and Besicker a trio of fast end men is found. All are experienced and heavy, so that State is not worrying much about her ends. Parry played last season with the Steelton A. A., Yeckley was formerly with Indiana Normal and Besicker is from Bloomsburg Normal. The last two named performed well in the Yale game last year.

The positions which now worry the coaches are the guards and tackles. Arbuthnot is the only old man, out of six or seven after the tackle positions. Kiefer and Smith have shown up strong lately, also "Jack" Smiley, who played guard last year on the Franklin (Pa.) eleven. Woodward, White and Ray of Greensburg are fighting it out for guard.

There is an abundance of good material for quarter back. "Jack" Elder of Eldersridge, last year's heady little field general, is pushed by Saunders, Foose and Stayer, last season's quarter at Lafayette College. The last named is the heaviest man of the quartet, while Elder is the lightest, tipping the beam at 138.

The prospects for backs also look very bright, as old 'varsity men are available for all three. Captain Whitworth, a Pittsburg boy, will again be found at right half. As an end skirter "Whittie" has few equals, and his defensive play is also strong, while he captain's the team in fine shape. At the other half will probably be found another Pittsburg boy, Harry McIlveen, who made such a record this year for State in baseball. "Mac" is an aggressive player, always hard to get off his feet, and a great man for breaking interference. At full back will be found Forkum of New Castle, and a former W. & J. full back. He hits the line hard and low, and on the defensive backs up the line in grand style. This Western Pennsylvania back field will average about 180 pounds. The schedule for the season follows: October 1, Allegheny College, at State; October 10, University of Pennsylvania, at Philadelphia; October 17, Yale at New Haven; October 24, W. U. P., at Pittsburg; October 31, Annapolis, at Annapolis; November 7, University of West Virginia, at Pittsburg; November 14, Dickinson, at Williamsport; November 26, Steelton, at Steelton.

Answers to Correspondents.

Answer, McKees Rocks—Do you want a half mile, mile, five-mile or 24-hour bicycle champion?

Joe, Pittsburg, Pa.—Pittsburg beat the All-Americans. They won two, tied one and lost one.

A B C, New Castle, Pa.—The blow known as the solar plexus was that with which Fits put Corbett down at Carson City, Nevada. It is a sort of upper cut landed at the lower end of the ribs and is most easily landed when an opponent is leaning back or carrying his head out of way of a swing. Let some good fellow swing his left on that spot when you are standing straight and you'll know better.

7 O'CLOCK EDITION

The Pittsburg Dispatch.

BEST IN ALL WAYS AND ALL THE TIME...

58TH YEAR | WEDNESDAY MORNING, | GREATER PITTSBURG'S GREATEST NEWSPAPER | OCTOBER 7, 1903 | 16 PAGES—2 CENTS

A Big Crowd Sees Boston Team Downed by the Thrice Champion Pirates

AT EXPOSITION PARK YESTERDAY

DIVIDEND CUT CAUSES MUCH SATISFACTION

Action of Steel Corporation Is Pleasing in Conservative Business Circles.

STREET SURPRISED AT THE STATEMENT

One-Half Per Cent on Common Stock This Quarter.

ROCKEFELLER AND MORGAN IN ACCORD

Both Agree to Wisdom of Reduction, Although Earnings Justify Full Payment.

WHY THE CHANGE WAS MADE

[Special Telegram From The Dispatch Bureau.]

NEW YORK, Oct. 6.—The directors of the United States Steel Corporation met to-day at 71 Broadway and reduced the quarterly dividend on Steel common from 1 per cent to half of 1 per cent, thereby placing the stock on a 2 per cent basis for the year. The action of the directors was received with surprise in Wall street, but with general satisfaction in conservative business circles.

The earnings for the quarter would fully have justified the payment of the dividend. They were $32,302,821 net, as compared with $36,945,485 last year, and $28,663,843 in 1901. They are therefore nearly $4,000,000 more than they were the corresponding quarter of the first year, when the full 1 per cent dividend was paid.

Three months ago it was announced that Mr. Rockefeller was opposed to the payment of a full dividend on the common stock, and that it was only the personal influence of Mr. Morgan which secured the regular payment at that time.

When the steel trust was first organized and its stock placed on the market it was practically promised by Mr. Morgan that dividends on the common stock would be paid as long as the earnings of the trust footed up $100,000,000 a year. The earnings of the company so far have averaged $125,000,000 a year and on this account Mr. Morgan insisted that it was only justice to the stockholders that the dividend on the common stock be maintained at 4 per cent a year.

Morgan Favored Reduction.

Mr. Rockefeller, however, maintained, it is understood, that the trust could not expect, under present business conditions, to keep up the mammoth earnings for the next few years, and it would be only good business policy to cut the dividend on the common stock and increase the surplus of the trust until it reached at least $100,000,000. There is about $60,000,000 of surplus in the treasury of the corporation now. The steel trust was reported last month to have $508,492,200 of common stock outstanding. By the cut of 2 per cent a year in the dividend the yearly saving will be $10,169,904.

Your correspondent was informed by an authority high in the affairs of the company that the current stories that John D. Rockefeller compelled the Morgan interests to reduce the dividend is untrue. Morgan was thoroughly in accord with the other directors as to the wisdom of reducing the dividend and the decision of the directors was unanimous.

Judge Gary, as chairman of the board, presided at to-day's meeting. The other directors present were J. P. Morgan, George W. Perkins, Henry H. Rogers, H. C. Frick, Charles M. Schwab, E. C. Converse, James Gayley, D. G. Reid, W. E. Corey, Robert Bacon, Nathaniel Thayer, John F. Dryden, C. A. Griscom, Francis H. Peabody, Charles Steele, Norman H. Ream, P. A. B. Widener and William Edenborn.

Stock Opens Heavy.

Wall street waited for the news with as much eagerness as a nation seeks for first reports from the battlefield, for the effect on the stock market of decline in the United States Steel securities has been great and upon the decision of the directors and the showing of their company depends the immediate trend of the market.

The shares of the steel corporation could not be regarded as forecasters of what might take place at the meeting. They opened heavy, in accordance with the market for them abroad, rallied fractionally, went down again and then in the early afternoon suddenly became strong, with the preferred above 66, or nearly three points up from the low figure of the day, and the common close to 18. From that time on they were irregular. Toward the closing they became strong.

Up to the hour when the directors went into conference the betting on the dividend continued active, both on the Stock Exchange and on the curb. Some made wagers that the regular dividend would be paid; others that it would be cut, and a third group that it would be passed altogether. The largest amounts, however, were placed on the first proposition. Allen and McGraw bet $2,500 even that 1 per cent quarterly would be declared and a few minutes later placed the same amount on the prediction that it would not. Two similar bets were made in the sum of $5,000. Charlie Gates was betting on the exchange against the regular amount. Trading in the dividend was very brisk. It was offered down to 70 cents and then went up to 80. The dividends on 15,000 shares were sold at from 70 to 75.

Good Thing, Say Brokers.

After the announcement had been made that the common stock dividend had been cut to ½ per cent, many brokers expressed satisfaction. John Clews of the banking firm of Henry Clews & Co. said:

"We believe that the Street will take the Steel dividends favorably. It is a good thing for both the public and the

Continued on Second Page.

MORGAN'S NAME THE ONE USED IN STEEL DEAL

Arrangements for Sale of Bethlehem Plant Made in His Office.

SCHWAB SAYS NOTHING

[Special Telegram From The Dispatch Bureau.]

NEW YORK, Oct. 6.—Charles M. Schwab, former president of the steel trust, against whom charges are made in connection with the United States Shipbuilding Company, would make no reply to-day to the accusations that he got $30,000,000 worth of securities for the $10,000,000 Bethlehem steel plant by overstating its earnings and surplus, and that he wrecked the shipbuilding company so that he and his associates could get control of its assets.

From a friend of Mr. Schwab it was learned that the whole deal for the sale of the Bethlehem company, which is now being so bitterly attacked in the United States courts, was arranged in the offices of J. P. Morgan & Co. Mr. Morgan was abroad at the time, but his partner, George W. Perkins, conducted the matter.

Of the $10,000,000 preferred stock and the $10,000,000 of the common stock given to Mr. Schwab by the shipbuilding company as part payment for the Bethlehem plant $2,500,000 of each kind, or $5,000,000 in all, went to J. P. Morgan & Co.

The formal agreement for the sale of the Bethlehem steel plant was made in the name of J. P. Morgan & Co. and not in the name of Mr. Schwab. Why all of the blame for the transaction has been directed against Mr. Schwab is a mystery to those familiar with the real facts in the case. It is said that the firm of J. P. Morgan & Co. figured in the shipbuilding company's finances in other ways. The charge that the shipbuilding company paid a fabulous sum for the plant of the Bethlehem company is denied by friends of Mr. Schwab.

While he got $30,000,000 in securities—$10,000,000 in bonds, $10,000,000 in preferred and $10,000,000 in common stock—the market value of these, it is asserted, was only a fraction of their face value.

To-day the total value of these securities is very small. The bonds are selling at 14, which would make the block of $10,000,000 worth $1,400,000. Sales of the stock are very rare. The last made was $1 a share for the preferred and $1 a share for the common. On this basis the $10,000,000 of preferred stock would have an actual value of $100,000 and the $10,000,000 of common would have a like value. The total value of the $30,000,000 of securities is therefore $1,600,000.

Lewis Nixon, former President of the shipbuilding company, refused to-day to say anything in reply to the charges against Mr. Schwab.

All those interested in the shipbuilding litigation were in Philadelphia to-day, where argument was made in the United States Court of Appeals to have the receivership made by the United States Courts in New Jersey set aside.

To-morrow there will be a hearing before a special United States examiner in the law office of Samuel Untermeyer in the receivership proceedings. Among those summoned as witnesses are Charles M. Schwab, Lewis Nixon, Max Pam, E. LeRoy Dresser and others who took a leading part in the organization and financing of the company.

Contractor Badly Cut.

W. E. Walcott, a contractor of 40 Julius street, is confined to his home with serious knife wounds in his head and neck, said to have been inflicted by Thomas Jarrett, near the old East End stock yards, about 8 o'clock yesterday morning. Jarrett has not been apprehended.

SYMPATHY STRIKE OF IRONWORKERS IS COMING SOON

Bridge and Structural Men Will Endeavor to Aid New York.

SAY PARKS IS OUT OF IT

An international sympathy strike affecting the 60,000 organized bridge and structural ironworkers in the United States and Canada is scheduled to be called in a few weeks. Pittsburg will contribute 3,000 men, completely tieing up all bridge and structural work here and throwing out of employment thousands of men of other crafts in this city.

The strike is to be in sympathy with the fight of the New York members against the Cornell Construction Company, members of the big combine. Pittsburg men and members of the union in other large cities have been opposed to the strike because of Sam Parks' connection with the New York strike. Frank Buchanan, newly re-elected National President, is expected here to-day to assure the local people Parks will have nothing to do with the strike, whereupon it is predicted Pittsburg will vote to go out.

The national office and the various locals have been planning for this event for months. Pittsburg voted some months ago to begin a special strike assessment, and then, with other cities, instructed delegates to the last national convention to pledge the local's moral support to the New York strikers.

The Cornell Company is one of 12 companies in the Bridge Erectors' Association, the backbone of which is the American Bridge Company. It is the only one of the affiliated companies that declined to sign the present scale agreement of the men. The union has taken this as the first gun in a fight between the two associations, and which, if not checked now, will reach the point where all 12 will refuse to sign scale agreements of the future. Locals that are inclined to refrain from a sympathy strike will be impressed with the assertion that what is being done now in New York is what will be brought home to them, sooner or later, if they remain passive.

Local officials are reticent on the subject. Business Agent George Boyd refused to make a statement. It is admitted Buchanan is expected, if not to-day then before the regular meeting to-morrow night. He will address that meeting and ask a vote. Pittsburg is one of the strong unions. In the last few months 15 non-union jobs have been unionized, leaving only a scattering few outside the organization. The demand for structural men for the big bridge and structural contracts is greater than it has ever been.

ROYAL WEDDING

Prince Andrew of Greece Is Married to Princess Alice of Battenberg.

[By Associated Press Cable to The Dispatch.]

DARMSTADT, Oct. 6.—The civil marriage of Prince Andrew of Greece and Princess Alice of Battenberg was celebrated here at noon to-day. The King of Greece and Prince Louis of Battenberg, father of the bride, acted as witnesses at the wedding.

The ceremony took place at the old palace in the presence of a glittering assemblage of 200 sovereigns, Princes, diplomats and Cabinet Ministers. Dr. Glaessing, a state official, performed the ceremony.

CHAMPIONS OF THE AMERICAN PRESS OUR CHAMPIONS HARD

After a Fearful Ninth Inning Pittsburg Wins by the Narrow Margin of 5 to 4—Phillippe's Masterful Pitching Again Beats Boston's Pride and Dineen.

By FRANK B. M'QUISTON.

"Squeeze 'er, Ritch!"

Hans the Hitter has no college diploma, but he has a short way of getting across lots when he wants to say something. If he had studied for a million years he could not have better echoed the sentiments of almost 8,000 people last evening. He was using his every-day voice just as though he were asking Ritchey to pass the butter.

It was a pretty tough moment for us and ours. It was in the ninth inning, and those dratted Bostons had just waked to the fact that they could play ball. They had already dragged three across on this run of shad and needed but one more to tie up the game, two to win. Two hands were gone. Lachance and Ferris were thundering round the bases like mad, while O'Brien was tramping like a Trojan toward first. The ball was high in the air over second base. If it ever hit the ground it was all day with Pittsburg. Strong men who had applauded all through the argument now turned their faces away. They could not bear to see Pittsburg lose. Something akin to a sob ricochetted across the white plain of upturned faces. Quick and sharp came the call from Wagner, "Squeeze 'er, Ritch!"

And Ritchey "squz."

Rather a Close Call.

As the ball settled into the ready mitts of the little second baseman about 8,000 people went bughouse or called next door. It was over, but hard had been the way. As the thrice Champions fled under the wire with every sail set in this the fourth round for the championship of the world those Bostons were reaching for them at every jump. They came so near that the Pittsburgs could feel their breath as they flew. Coming? Why, they were hitting the ground so hard with their flippers that the mud was flying clear into the grandstand. Another finish like that and there will be a wholesale canceling of life insurance policies in Pittsburg. Heart disease got an awful boom in that ninth inning.

And they looked so easy, too. Phillippe, who handed them theirs twice in three days in Boston, went in to do the trick again. He did it. Yes, he got away with the game all right, but no one need mail him any post cards this morning to inform him that there was a game of baseball over at the park. He knows it. Just when we thought it was all over, when everyone was figuring out what he would order for supper when town was again reached, those pesky Bostons slipped up and before the police could be called they lit on Phil with clubs and came pretty near making him wish he was somewhere else.

There are a lot of people around town who think this Boston gang cannot play ball. It's a good bet to make that they don't know what they are talking about, even if one has to loan them the money to bet. On the last turn of the wheel yesterday they did some grand and lofty tumbling, which made people shiver. The gang filed out of the park last evening pretty well satisfied that the only time when it is a cinch that Boston is beat is when the other team is 1,000,000 runs ahead, and such people as Collins, Doherty, Stahl, Freeman, Dineen, Young, Criger and some others are locked up. Even then they are liable to turn in with the subs and do a whole lot of damage. Yesterday's score was 5 to 4. Thank goodness and the man who decreed that a baseball game shall be of only nine innings' duration.

Beautiful Was the Game.

If there was any kind of baseball not dished up (bum stuff excepted) those entering complaint can have their money back. It was Dineen against Phillippe. It seems like rubbing it in to ask a pitcher to go in against such a team of swatters as Boston three times in five days, but Phillippe was willing to take the risk and in he went. He came through with flying colors, and if any small boy from Maine to California were asked this morning to name the greatest pitcher in the world he would most likely say Phillippe, though he could not spell the name. It would have been all the same with us had Phillippe lost. The fans here would have loved him just the same, for he has thrown himself into the breach and nobly has he performed.

And he was up against some pitching, too. Pittsburg was batting viciously, with the confidence born of victory, and

Continued on Twelfth Page.

By GRIF ALEXANDER.

Despite Jupiter Pluvius, enough people went to the ball ground yesterday to pack the grandstand, the bleachers and the hastily improvised circus seats in front of the grandstand; but old Jupe got in his work in the back part of the ground, which was soggy and deserted by the populace.

Beans promote hilarity. This was evidenced by the conduct of the Boston rooters. They were chipper when they left the Monongahela House in carriages which bore a not inconspicuous part in the usual parade. There was a big bunch of them and from first to last they made their presence felt.

Whatever the regular sporting sharp may say to the contrary the fact remains that the Boston rooters were the feature of the game.

They wore red badges and red faces. Whenever occasion warranted and sometimes, when they rather sorter, kinder thought that kind of an occasion was about due, they got up on their hind legs and yelled. Ever so many of them had horns, which they tooted most zealously. On one occasion the band played "In the Good Old Summer Time," and every man Jack of them organized himself into a Herr Direktor and waved his horn as though it were a baton and sang and sang with all the vim his lungs would allow.

High Times in Grandstand.

On another occasion, when Boston scored its first run, they jumped up in the air and waved handkerchiefs and hats and screeched until their red faces became purple and their horns curled up in envy. One of the gang jumped on the roof of the shanty which covered the bench of the visiting players and danced a hornpipe and a jig and a breakdown and some other things to the great delight of those who saw and heard him.

But some of those who looked on and were silent during the clamor of the Bostonians would manifest malicious delight on the following and frequent occasions when it was up to the Pittsburg rooters to do some rooting. They would look at the beaneaters and grin the grin of derision, which was rude, but very human.

It has been mentioned that there was a band. It was a good band and knew all the really up-to-date and popular tunes. It played between innings and stopped the very minute the first ball was pitched, so that "The Good Old Summer Time" became the "The Good Old Sum—" and the audience was willing to become spectator and let it go at that. Which was as it should be.

The efforts of the crowd to rattle the pitcher, first one, then the other, had all their old-time vigor and din. But the din would be increased a hundred-fold when the crowd sought to show its approbation. At such times it drowned the music of the band and nobody noted the fact.

The Ubiquitous Rooter.

The individual rooter who had remarks to make was there in force. He complimented the player who pleased him, swiped the player who displeased him, gave sarcastic advice to all and sundry. To the batter who let the pitcher run up two or three "balls" he shouted "Good eye!" He cried "Go it, Tommy!" "It's all up to you, Honus!" and "A two-bagger! A two-bagger! That's what we want now!"—and sometimes got what he cried for and was happy when he got it; and he told the Boston players that they were not playing any American team this time and that they were up against it good and plenty, and let them never cease to remember the fact. Oh, yes, the individual rooter was a very lively individual and did much to promote the general hilarity of the occasion.

All through the game the excitement was intense and it grew instead of lessened. The report of the regular gentleman gives abundant reasons why this should be so. The fan was too busy every minute of his time to even eat peanuts or drink pop. The weather, too, had something to do with this.

Seated in one position on a bleacher seat cramps a man, and the old-time "Stretch!" was honored with the customary but ever-startling unanimity. To see a sea of faces rise as though on the crest of a wave and the dither of them all, which tells of legs well shaken, is a sight never to be forgotten.

When the game was over the same old crowd gathered on the field, paid homage to the players and scrambled and crushed through the all-too-narrow gates that led outside. And the same old street cars were jammed in the same old way.

PROMPT ACTION NOW PROMISED TO STEVENSON

Conferred Yesterday With Thomas S. Bigelow, Murry Verner and Mayor Hays.

PLEDGED TO REFORM

Prompt action upon all the legislation demanded by the "political orphans" was agreed upon at a conference in the office of Mayor Hays yesterday morning. The proclamation issued by the reform element, reiterating its demand for the passage of the franchise tax ordinance and other measures and the radical amendment of the Pennsylvania railroad's Duquesne way ordinance, was the immediate cause of the conference.

W. H. Stevenson was present to represent the independent element of the Citizens party, while Thomas S. Bigelow and County Chairman Verner represented the party organization and Mayor Hays held up the administration's end.

Mr. Stevenson yesterday refused to disclose what had occurred at the conference except to intimate that its decision had been perfectly satisfactory to him and referred his interrogators to County Chairman Verner for information. The latter said last night:

"The conference was perfectly satisfactory to all of us, including Mr. Stevenson. It was agreed that the general franchise tax ordinance shall be passed at the meeting of Select Council on Monday and promptly signed by Mayor Hays. As soon as this is accomplished we will meet again and decide on the next measure to be taken up and will concentrate our efforts to get that through Select Council. When the Duquesne way ordinances will be taken up I do not know. They were not specifically mentioned at the conference, and that point will be settled next week when we meet again after the passage of the franchise tax."

NEW COAL COMPANY ACQUIRES MUCH LAND

Pennsylvanians in Corporation Controlling 30,000 Acres in This and Other States.

[Special Telegram to The Dispatch.]

NEW YORK, Oct. 6.—Wall street and Pennsylvania interests to-day completed a deal whereby control was acquired of about 30,000 acres of coal lands in Pennsylvania, Ohio and West Virginia. The principal field is in Marshall county, W. Va., three miles from the Pennsylvania line on the Baltimore & Ohio and known to geologists as the "Pittsburg" seam, which Professor I. C. White, State Geologist of West Virginia, says contains 100,000,000 tons of coal.

The company, known as the Summit Coal Company, has a capital of $10,000,000. The output will be 4,000 tons a day. The organization was completed at a meeting at 170 Broadway to-day, when George H. Proctor, a California capitalist and mine operator, was elected president; I. C. Smitz of Connellsville, Pa., general manager; T. J. Yost, treasurer, and Henry B. Twombley, secretary.

E. E. Dilliner of Uniontown, Pa., and Charles C. Newman of Loundsville, W. Va., were elected in addition to the above as directors.

THE WEATHER (OFFICIAL)

For Western Pennsylvania, Ohio and West Virginia—Rain and cooler Wednesday. Colder Thursday.

(For detailed account see page 6).

CHINESE COURT BREAKS UP IN BLOODY RIOT

Trial of Chinese Six Companies Charges Is Rudely Interrupted.

POLICE RAID MEETING

Riot that threatened to end in murder prevailed in the Chinatown district of Second avenue yesterday afternoon. Thirty-five Celestials, members of the Yee and Lee factions of the Six Companies Society, a Chinese organization of San Francisco, engaged in a fierce fight during a session of a Chinese court, where two Mongolians disputed each other's right to occupy an Allegheny chop suey house.

Weapons of all descriptions were used and before the police arrived several of the participants were stretched on the blood-stained floor, apparently lifeless. The foreigners resented the interference of Detectives Cole and Eagan, but were finally driven back to the court room and 20 of the rioters arrested.

The fight occurred on the third floor of a building at 512 Second avenue, where a court session of business men and merchants was called to settle a dispute between Frank Lee and another Chinaman over a restaurant at 306 Federal street, Allegheny. Until lately the business there was conducted by E. J. Jackuay, an American. A few weeks ago, Jackuay sold out to Frank Lee.

According to the by-laws of the Six Companies organization, one member of the society cannot conduct business in a place unless the former occupant waives all claim. This Dick Wang, who had been in charge before Jackuay had possession, refused to do, and presented his case to the court.

Wang, it is alleged, secured the backing of the Yee family, and prepared to fight the case. When the court opened yesterday afternoon it was seen that the Lees were outnumbered. They explained the situation to Detectives Cole and Eagan, who repaired to the scene.

The detectives watched the proceedings from across the street. Things went along nicely until the counsel for Lee attempted to explain a technical point of the Six Companies law to the court. Fearing that something was wrong the Yees demanded an explanation. During the argument Frank Lee was struck on the jaw.

This was the signal for war. Chairs, cups, pipes and other weapons filled the air and bleeding Chinamen were piled high on the floor. The detectives hurried in. They were met by resistance at the door. Several of the rioters got past the officers. A riot call to Central station called out reinforcements. Two patrol wagons were filled with the prisoners.

Frank Lee, the Chinaman who was attacked, made information last night against seven of his alleged assailants before Alderman P. B. Rielley. The defendants, said to be members of the Yee Quetong faction, were committed to jail.

THE DISPATCH DIRECTORY

FIRST SECTION.

CHAMBERLAIN GIVES WARNING TO THE EMPIRE

Says Britain Is Doomed Unless Change in Present Policy Is Made.

EVENTUALLY BECOME FIFTH-RATE NATION

Draws Deadly Parallel Between Exports Now and Twenty Years Ago.

TARIFF BULWARK OF UNITED STATES

Colonies, Especially Canada, Are Following American Plan and Molding Fate of England.

SIGNS OF DECAY ARE EVIDENT

[By Associated Press Cable to The Dispatch.]

GLASGOW, Scotland, Oct. 6.—St. Andrew's Hall was packed to its capacity, 6,000, when Joseph Chamberlain rose at 8:10 this evening to deliver the first speech of his fiscal campaign. His appearance caused a tremendous outburst of enthusiasm, the ovation lasting for several minutes.

Mr. Chamberlain said that he was loyal to the party in which he had found a leader every member might be proud to follow, and warmly refuted the insinuation that under any conceivable circumstances would he come in competition with his friend and leader.

The former Colonial Secretary added that he desired to prepare the country for a struggle in which, if vanquished, it would lose its place among nations.

After the presentation of lengthy trade statistic, Mr. Chamberlain said that if the colonial trade did not increase with the population of the United Kingdom, with the decrease of foreign trade Great Britain would sink into a fifth-rate nation, and her fate would be the same as that of the empires of the past.

Tribute to Balfour.

Speaking of the consequence of the present policy to this country, Mr. Chamberalin pointed out the loss of the tinplate trade, which could have been retained. The result of the present policy, the speaker claimed, must be the entire loss of the colonial trade, while, on the contrary, with preferential treatment, the United Kingdom would capture the foreign trade with the colonies, and give employment to additional millions of workers.

The speaker paid the highest tribute to Mr. Balfour, with whose principles and policies he fully agreed, and said he admired the courage and resource with which the Premier had faced difficulties unsurpassed in political history. Mr. Chamberlain continued:

"I have invited discussion upon a question peculiarly within my province owing to my past life and the office I so recently held. Taking up the position of a pioneer, I go in front of the army. If the army is attacked I will return to it. It is possible that the nation may be prepared to go farther than the official programme. I now ask the question—is it so prepared? Great Britain in the past has played a great part in the world's history. I desire her to continue and see the realization of the great ideal of an empire such as the world has never seen. If that is to be attained, this matter should be treated on its merits without any personal feeling of bitterness and without entering on questions of purely party controversy."

Sees Signs of Decay.

The late Colonial Secretary alluded to the recent visit he paid to Venice, when he found the Campanile, which had stood for centuries and which when he previously visited Venice seemed as permanent as the city itself, now a mass of ruins. He continued:

"I do not say that I anticipate such a fate for the British Empire, but I do say that I see signs of decay, cracks and crevices showing that the foundations are not broad and deep enough to sustain it. Am I wrong to warn you? Is it not strange and inconsistent that the same people who indicted the Government for its unpreparedness in the South African war should now denounce me in language equally extravagant because I want to prepare you for a struggle so serious that if we are defeated the country will lose its place among the great nations; a struggle which we are invited to meet with antiquated methods and tactics."

Adducing statistics, Mr. Chamberlain contrasted the moderate increase of 7½ per cent in the export trade of Great Britain and the increase of 30 per cent in her population since 1872, with the enormous increase of trade in the United States and Germany, and asked how the country could expect to support its growing population with its trade practically stagnant for 30 years. He proceeded:

Shrinkage in Exports.

"On the other hand, the protected countries which you have been told—and myself one time believed—were going rapidly to wreck and ruin have progressed infinitely better in proportion than ourselves, and instead of, as Cobden believed, our remaining the workshop for the world, we are sending less and less of our manufactures abroad, while the protected countries are sending more and more of their manufactures here. Thus our manufactured exports, from £116,000,000 in 1872, have gradually dwindled to £73,500,000 in 1902, to the protected countries of Europe and the United States.

"In the same period our exports to non-manufacturing countries like Egypt, China and South America have practically remained unchanged. This loss of trade to the protected countries has not been noticed hitherto because during the same period our exports to the British colonies have increased in ratio to counterbalance this loss, and are now more valuable than our trade with the whole of Europe and the United States together. Our colonial trade, in fact, is the

Continued on Sixth Page.

MISS ADAIR WINNING

SHE DEFEATS MISS MACKAY

Oakley Club Player was Careful, but Irish Champion's Dashing Game was Irresistible.

Philadelphia, Oct. 7.—The first match play round of the invitation golf tourney given by Mrs. Clement A. Griscom, in honor of her guest, Miss Rhona K. Adair, the British champion, was concluded at the Merion cricket club links today at Haverford. Several surprises were in store and some unexpected victories were obtained, but the two best known players, Miss Adair and Mrs. C. T. Stout, formerly Miss Genevieve Hecker, still remain and will probably fight out the final on Saturday.

During the day arrangements were made for an international woman's team match to be played on Saturday. Nine Americans will play against nine Canadians and English women. Miss Adair will captain the English side, and Mrs. Stout will head the home team. The contest will be an individual one and in the event of any of either teams playing in the final result the present tourney their scores will count in the team match.

The match between Miss Adair and Miss Pauline Mackay was an interesting one throughout. The latter played a careful game, while the British champion played a bold, brilliant game. The pair squared their match at every other hole until the eighth was reached when Miss Adair took the lead and was never headed. From that point Miss Adair did not lose a hole. She won at the 15th by four up. The cards:

Miss Adair	6	5	*8	6	6	5	4	6	4—50	
Miss Mackay	5	7	5	7	5	7	3	7	6—52	
Miss Adair	6	6	5	5	4	5				
Miss Mackay	6	5	7	5	6	6				

* Approximated. Bye holes not played.

Mrs. Charles T. Stout had a good opponent in Mrs. T. W. Reath, of Riverton. The ex-champion could do nothing better than square her match at the ninth, the next four holes were halved, but by taking the next three Mrs. Stout won by three up and two to go.

The summaries of the first two cups:

First Cup.

Mrs. C. T. Stout, Essex Co., beat Mrs. T. W. Reath, Riverton, 3—2.

Miss K. Harley, Fall River, beat Mrs. C. F. Fox, H. V. C. C., 1 up.

Mrs. R. H. Parlow, Merion, beat Miss H. Curtis, Essex County, 3—2.

Miss A. McNeely, Merion, beat Miss E. A. Lockwood, Lexington, 1 up (19 holes).

Miss F. C. Osgood, Brookline, beat Mrs. E. A. Manice, Baltusrol, 5—4.

Miss M. Curtis, Essex Co., beat Miss Phepoe, Canada, 1 up.

Miss Rhona Adair, Portrush, beat Miss Pauline Mackay, Oakley, 4—3.

Miss G. Bishop, Brooklyn, beat Mrs. H. Fitzgerald, Aronomink, 1 up (19 holes).

Second Cup.

Miss Borden, Fall River, beat Miss A. E. Murray, Wilmington, 1 up (19 holes).

Miss Thompson, St. John, N. B., beat Mrs. Rogers, Baltusrol, 2—1.

Miss Oliver, Albany, beat Miss Greene, Montreal, 4—3.

Miss Gilbert, Huntington Valley, beat Miss M. B. Adams, Wollaston, 7—5.

Miss J. Spence, Merion, beat Miss K. Moulton, Minneapolis, 4—3.

Miss K. Harvey, Hamilton, beat Miss E. S. Porter, Oakley, 1 up.

Miss A. Phipps, Brookline, beat Mrs. Pierce, St. Davids, 6—4.

Mrs. Lefferts, Merion, beat Miss F. McNeeley, Merion, 1 up (19 holes).

Drawings for the Second Round.

First Cup—Mrs. C. T. Stout vs. Miss K. Harley; Mrs. R. H. Barlow vs. Miss A. P. McNeeley; Miss G. Bishop vs. Miss F. Osgood; Miss M. Curtis vs. Miss R. Adair.

Second Cup—Miss Borden vs. Miss Thompson; Miss Greene vs. Miss M. Adams; Miss Spence vs. Miss Harvey; Miss Phipps vs. Mrs. Lefferts.

MRS. WOOD ARLINGTON CHAMPION.

Arlington, Oct. 7.—The semi-finals and finals in the ladies' club championship, were finished, and resulted in Mrs. H. B. Wood winning the honor. Semi-finals: Mrs. H. B. Wood beat Mrs. W. G. Rice, 7—6; Miss F. A. Hill beat Miss A. Teel, 4—2. Finals: Mrs. Wood beat Miss Hill, 8—2.

SETTLED ON HOME GREEN.

Brookline, Oct. 7.—Two matches which were undecided up to the home green were played today in the first round of the match play at the Commonwealth Country Club for the fall cup, J. W. Kennedy defeating W. C. Cady by the score of 1 up, and L. A. Brown defeating H. O. Lamb by the score of 1 up. The winners of both matches played some brilliant golf and their medal scores were low. The remainder of the six matches will probably be played in the first round by the beginnng of next week.

WOODLAND G. C. CHAMPIONSHIP.

Newton, Oct. 7.—The first round at match play for the club championship of the Woodland G. C. resulted: A. Howard beat W. G. Bancroft, 5—4; W. W. Travis beat R. R. Perry, 3—2; E. W. Longley beat S. Smith, 1 up; E. N. Wright beat J. E. O'Connell, 3—2; A. J. Wellington beat F. J. Burrage, 7—6; E. E. Conover beat F. S. Ashenden, 1 up (19 holes); F. A. Pemberton beat P. D. Worcester, 7—6; W. L. Church beat P. Whiting, 5—4.

In a team match this afternoon on the links of the Newton Centre G. C., a team of the Woodland G. C. defeated the home team, 6—4, the scoring being by the Tuxedo system.

THREATENED TO KILL

Witness for Tillman Says Gonzales Was Going to "Kill the Rascal" if He Was Elected.

Lexington, S. C., Oct. 7.—The trial of J. H. Tillman was resumed today, the juror, Milton Sharpe, who has been sick, having improved sufficiently to permit him to be in court. The state rested without the introduction of further testimony, and the defence entered at once upon the presentation of its case.

The first witness called by the defence was T. B. Mitchell, who lived in Columbia in 1902. He testified that he had a conversation with Gonzales relative to J. H. Tillman, reciting what he stated Gonzales said concerning the defendant. The witness said among other things:—

"He said, 'I can slap his face and he would not resent it,' and he said, 'If he ever bats his eyes at me I'll fill him so full of lead that he will never tote it off.'"

A. J. Flowers, a street railway conductor, testified that he overheard a conversation on his street car in Columbia in 1902, in which Gonzales said that "If he did not succeed in defeating Tillman in the governor's office, he would never be seated, because he would kill the rascal."

JAIL FOR GENTLEMAN BURGLAR.

Hackensack, N. J., Oct. 7.—Geo. Howard, alias Kennard, known at the "Gentleman burglar," pleaded guilty today to burglary and was sentenced to 14 yrs. in state prison.

Hartford, Ct., Oct. 7.—C. F. Clements, '05, of Sunbury, Pa., was today elected captain of the Trinity College baseball team.

"CY" YOUNG HAD THE PIRATE BATSMEN AT HIS MERCY

Fusilade of Boston Hits Made Fifth Game of Series a Walkover

Pittsburg, Oct. 7.—A crowd that occupied every seat in the grandstand and bleachers and every available foot of standing room and then overflowed into the field three or four deep, turned out to witness the second game here of the championship series. Except for the high winds it was an ideal day for baseball. Ground rules were adopted, and

(Photo by Horner)
PITCHER "CY" YOUNG.

three bases allowed on a ball going into the crowd.

Young's pitching was too much for the Pittsburgs. He had the home players completely at his mercy, and it was only through an error by Parent in the 8th inning that prevented him scoring a shutout. On the other hand, Kennedy, for Pittsburg, was hit hard in the sixth and seventh innings, although errors were responsible for most of the runs scored. Thompson relieved Kennedy at the beginning of the eighth, and did well. Aside from Young's pitching, the batting of Dougherty and Collins were the only features.

Not a run was scored on either side until the sixth inning, when Boston succeeded in getting six men over the plate. A single, a base on balls, three errors and two three baggers tells the story.

In the seventh three singles, a base on balls and a three-base hit gave the visitors four more. Their last run came in the eighth. Stahl hit the first ball pitched into the crowd and came home on Lachance's fine single.

Pittsburg scored two runs in the eighth. After Phelps had struck out and Thompson had been retired at first on a hit to Parent, Beaumont singled and went to second on Parent's error of Clarke's hot grounder. Leach's three-base hit brought them both home. Attendance, 12,322. Score:—

BOSTON.

	a.b.	r.	b.h.	p.o.	a.	e.
Dougherty, lf	6	0	3	3	0	0
Collins, 3b	6	0	2	0	4	0
Stahl, cf	5	2	1	2	0	0
Freeman, rf	4	2	2	2	0	0
Parent, ss	5	1	2	1	4	1
Lachance, 1b	4	2	1	13	0	1
Ferris, 2b	5	2	1	1	3	0
Criger, c	3	1	0	5	0	0
Young, p	5	1	2	0	2	0
Totals	43	11	14	27	13	2

PITTSBURG.

	a.b.	r.	b.h.	p.o.	a.	e.
Beaumont, cf	4	1	1	0	0	0
Clarke, lf	4	1	0	3	0	1
Leach, 3b	4	0	2	2	1	1
Wagner, ss	4	0	0	1	3	2
Bransfield, 1b	4	0	0	9	1	0
Ritchey, 2b	4	0	1	1	4	0
Sebring, rf	4	0	1	2	0	0
Phelps, c	3	0	0	9	0	0
Kennedy, p	2	0	1	0	1	0
Thompson, p	1	0	0	0	1	0
Totals	34	2	6	27	11	4

Boston	0	0	0	0	0	6	4	1	0—11
Pittsburg	0	0	0	0	0	0	0	2	0—2

Earned runs—Boston, 4. Two-base hit—Kennedy. Three-base hits—Leach, Dougherty (2), Collins, Stahl, Young. Sacrifice hits—Phelps, Criger. Stolen bases—Collins, Stahl. First base on balls—Off Kennedy, 3. Struck out—By Kennedy, 3; by Thompson, 1; by Young, 4. Time—2:00. Umpires—Connolly and O'Day.

OTHER GAMES.

At Philadelphia—Nationals, 13; Americans, 3.

At Newark—Cleveland Americans, 11; Cincinnati Nationals, 5.

At Williamsport, Pa. (10 innings)—Williamsport, 6; Brooklyn (Nat.), 5.

MIXED DOUBLES ON LONGWOOD COURTS

The mixed doubles were begun yesterday in the tennis at Longwood, and, with all the events now in full swing, enhanced the interest and the attendance, despite the ominous weather.

Bets are already being placed, among the younger crowd of the stock exchange as to winners.

Mixed doubles, first round—Miss Evelyn Sears and B. S. Blake beat Miss J. G. Swift and W. L. OBrion, 6—3, 4—6, 6—1.

Miss J. Langmaid and H. J. Cochran beat Miss A. M. Swift and Robert Marcy, 6—1, 6—3.

Miss Pierce and H. D. Montgomery beat Miss E. T. Hunt and H. W. Horne, 6—2, 6—3.

Second round—Miss Margaret Nichols and W. E. Putnam, jr., beat Miss Marion Fenno and S. P. Ware, 7—5, 6—4.

Miss Eleanor Whitney and Kenneth Horton beat Miss Carter and E. F. Campbell, 6—4, 6—0.

Miss Eleanora Sears and Alfred Codman beat Miss Merrill and B. F. Merrill, 6—2, 6—0.

Miss Amy Putnam and R. C. Seaver beat Miss Webster and Chandler Hovey, 6—4, 6—3.

Miss Buffum and W. H. Parker beat Miss Margaret Whitman and A. N. Winslow, by default.

Miss E. E. Rotch and C. M. Rotch beat Miss Dorothy Lovering and G. A. Lyon, jr., 8—6, 4—6, 6—3.

Miss Pierce and H. D. Montgomery vs. Miss S. E. Russell and R. W. Coues, 6—1, 8—8 (unfinished).

The most interesting match in the singles involved the defeat of Miss Eleanora Sears by Miss Stevenson, after a prolonged battle.

Ladies' opening singles—Third round: Miss Evelyn Sears beat Miss Peabody, 6—1, 6—3.

Miss A. Stevenson beat Miss Eleanora Sears, 7—5, 3—6, 6—2. Miss Nichols beat Miss Whicher (no score).

Ladies' Doubles—First round: Miss Rogers and Miss Ritchie beat Mrs. Buffum and Mrs. Seaver, 8—10, 6—4, 6—2.

Miss Fenno and Miss Putnam beat Miss Shewell and Miss Chapman, 6—1, 6—0.

Miss Jones and Miss Hubbard beat Mrs. Wadsworth and Miss Winsor, 6—1, 6—3.

Miss Eleanora Sears and Miss Stevenson beat Miss Rotch and Miss Whitney, 6—4, 3—3.

The Misses Stockton beat Miss C. Williams and Miss H. Williams, 6—0, 6—2.

Second Round—Miss Evelyn Sears and Miss Nichols beat Miss Holmes and Miss Loring, 6—2, 6—4.

The Misses Stockton beat Miss Lewis and Miss Seaver, 6—0, 6—1.

Men's Doubles—Second round: Keyes and Smith beat Seaver and Foster, 6—2, 3—6, 6—4. Beals and Dockerman Abbot beat Miles and Eames, 6—5, 6—4.

Third Round—Beals and Bishop beat Dockerman and Abbot, 6—0, 6—4.

HARVARD UNPLACED IN SEMI-FINALS

Philadelphia, Oct. 7.—The second round of singles and doubles in the intercollegiate tennis tournament on the Merion Cricket grounds at Haverford was finished today and in both classes Harvard failed to get a place in the semi-finals. In the singles L. E. Mahan of Columbia easily defeated R. Bishop of Harvard in straight sets, and B. S. Prentice of Harvard was defeated by E. Clapp of Yale. Prentice and Larned of Harvard were defeated by Colket and Dewhurst of Penn. and Bishop and Cole, Harvard, were beaten by Clapp and Colstone, Yale.

The annual meeting of the intercollegiate tennis association was held here today, at which these officers were elected:—

President, B. S. Prentice, Harvard; vice-president, H. Behr, Yale; secretary and treasurer, B. Leroy, jr., Columbia; delegate to the national convention, I. C. Wright, Princeton.

Summary:—

Singles, Second Round.

Mahan, Columbia, beat Bishop, Harvard, 6—2, 6—4.

Thurber, Columbia, beat Cole, Yale, 6—4, 3—6, 6—2.

Clapp, Yale, beat Prentice, Harvard, 7—5, 6—2.

Dewhurst, Penn., beat Colket, Penn., 6—2, 6—4.

Doubles, Second Round.

Pittsman and Salisbury, Cornell, beat Swain and Buckwalter, Penn., 6—4, 6—1.

Colket and Dewhurst, Penn., beat Prentice and Larned, Harvard, 6—2, 4—6, 6—4.

Clapp and Coleston, Yale, beat Bishop and Cole, Harvard, 6—2, 6—2.

Mahan and McLaughlin, Columbia, beat Rendall and Thompson, Princeton, 7—5, 3—6, 6—4.

BABY FOUND IN A BARREL ON HISTORIC BEACON HILL

Abandoned on Beacon Hill, within a stone's throw of Boston's most historic homes, a baby girl was found about 7 p.m. yesterday by the residents of Mt. Vernon place. The child's cries attracted the occupants of 5 Mt. Vernon pl., and being repeated and continued with considerable vigor led to an investigation. Men and women rushed from their rooms, and, when opposite No. 14, were moved with pity and horror to discover that the author of the outcry was an infant doubled up in an ash barrel. The mite was about six weeks' old, as pretty as a picture, and well and beautifully dressed in white, with a costly lace cap on its little head.

One of the women took the little one from a well meaning, but unexperienced man, whose handling of the foundling terrified, instead of soothed her. But the tears soon ceased, when the baby found she was in the arms of the right sex again, smiles adorned the little mouth, and laughter danced in the dark blue eyes.

Officers of st. 3 responded to a telephone call, and there was a muttered imprecation or two for the heartless one (man or woman) who had left the infant to the mercies of unsmiling skies and a proverbially cold world.

Baby was taken to the Chardon st. home.

AUTOISTS IN DRIVING RAIN

But Most of the Machines on Test Run Make Good Time to Pine Hill, New York.

Pine Hill, N. Y., Oct. 7.—The automobiles which are making the endurance test of the National Assn. of automobile manufacturers from New York to Pittsburg, made the run from Weehawken to Pine Hill in exceptionally good time, considering the heavy roads encountered.

During the afternoon a drizzling rain made the highways, particularly in the Catskill, wet and sticky and there was some skidding on the heavy grades.

All the cars have so far escaped without serious accident and several have made a clean record. The innovation of spreading confetti on the curves of the road proved effective and only two operators reported losing their way. The first of the cars in the contest reached Pine Hill in a driving storm at 3 o'clock, and by 6 o'clock twenty-seven out of thirty-four competing cars had arrived.

BOSTON JEWS TO ACT.

Will Co-operate With Other Societies to Aid Friends in Russia.

Firm in the conviction that the Kishineff and other minor massacres which are now taking place in Russia are in the line of Russia's general policy to make her territory too warm for the Jews, the meeting held in the synagogue on Baldwin place last evening was well attended by prominent Jews of Boston and the vicinity, who came together to plan for the betterment of their suffering people in Russia.

Rabbi Margolies, Rabbi Silverman and ex-Rep. Borofsky addressed the gathering, and earnestly exhorted them to act in union with the principal Jewish societies.

Ex-Rep. Borofsky claimed that the plan to bring the Russian Jews to the United States was no longer feasible, on account of the immigration laws.

A meeting will be called on Sunday evening. The matter will be placed in the hands of the Argodes Harkeles Society, who are familiar with all the other organizations about Boston, for some decisive action.

HER SUICIDAL COURSE

ENGLAND'S WORKMEN MUST LOSE

Fearless Chamberlain Tells Scotts Protective Tariff is Britain's Only Remedy for Her Troubles.

London, Oct. 7.—Continuing his fiscal campaign Mr. Chamberlain tonight addressed a meeting of 4000 persons in the town hall of Greenock, Scotland. He dealt particularly with the questions of retaliation and reciprocity.

The late colonial secretary said that he was a free trader and wanted to live harmoniously with his neighbors, but he desired free exchange with all nations. If they would not exchange he was not a free trader at any price. He respected "our American cousins," had considerable respect for the Germans and great respect and greater friendship for the French.

The policy of these nations was to use tariffs to ease the home trade and exclude foreign trade, while under the present system in the United Kingdom trade was steadily decreasing.

Chamberlain asked why all protective nations prospered more than the United Kingdom.

Replying to the newspaper criticisms that he selected 1872, the greatest boom year of British trade, as the basis of his statistics, the speaker admitted that the first 25 years of Cobden's free trade was a flourishing period and free trade was then probably best for the country. But he was willing to take any period during the last 30 years to illustrate his arguments.

Asking why the foreign protective countries, even small nations like Sweden, had all prospered he said that he believed they were better strategists than the British.

Their policy as enunciated by the late Pres. McKinley and by the greatest of Americans long before, namely, Lincoln, by Bismarck, and other distinguished statesmen, had a great deal behind it.

He continued: "I say that you are inconsistent. You are adopting a suicidal course. If you persist in the present policy your workmen must either take lower wages or lose their work."

Chamberlain proceeded to refer to the enormous output of the U. S. Steel Corporation works and the diminishing home demand in the U. S. for steel, owing to the financial difficulties, the reduction in railway construction, etc. He quoted from an American paper an interview with a director of the steel corporation on the falling demand in which the director declared that they had no intention of diminishing the output and throwing out of employment thousands of American workmen. Instead, they would invade foreign markets.

Mr. Chamberlain contended that this steel would be sent to Great Britain, the only free market, and he said:—

"I warn you that within two or three years you will have dumped here 10,000,000 tons of American iron and thousands of British workmen will lose employment for the sole benefit of American workmen. I sympathize with American workmen but, after all, I belong to England.

Concluding his general restatement, the speaker said that agriculture in Great Britain was practically destroyed, the sugar trade was gone, the silk trade was gone, the iron and wool industries were threatened, and the same fate would come to the cotton trade.

London, Oct. 7.—While there is no evidence of a rush on the part of the exponents of public opinion or of the electorate to give Joseph Chamberlain's fiscal proposals immediate endorsement, there is ample proof of a desire to exhaustively examine his programme and accept or reject it on its merits, rather than on party lines.

The Evening Standard, a staunch government organ, commenting on Mr. Chamberlain's speech, says:—

"Altogether his speech strengthens the conclusion that the movement has been premature and that the facts, which are held to justify it, have been loosely collected and only half assimilated."

MYOPIA POLOISTS DEFEAT DEDHAM

Providence, R. I., Oct. 7.—The Myopia second polo team defeated Dedham second in the finals for the Rumford cups at the Rumford grounds, this afternoon, 10—5¾. The game was played in a drizzling rain, and in the last two periods the field was very soft, making fast play impossible.

The Myopia men started the game with a rush, and in the first two periods played all around their opponents. In the third period, however, the Dedham men got together, and for the remainder of the game had the advantage.

The Dedham team was decidedly lacking in team work, and the individual play of some of the members of the team was not as good as they have exhibited on previous occasions.

Norman was the individual star for the Myopia men, and the work of Fay at back was very creditable. For Dedham, Hamlin played the best game.

The game was witnessed by a considerable number of the local society people in spite of the threatening weather. The line-up and handicap of the teams:—

Myopia—No. 1, E. Dresel, 1; No. 2, M. Norman, 4; No. 3, J. F. Blake, 2; back, F. D. Fay, 3. Total, 10.

Dedham—No. 1, F. A. Street, 1; No. 2, C. W. Dabney, 1; No. 3, B. M. Hamlin, 4; back, M. Williams, 4. Total, 10.

ORDERED TO HALIFAX.

British Cruiser Retribution to Weigh Anchor Today.

Today, probably on the full tide just before noon, the British cruiser Retribution will leave Boston, returning direct to her station at Halifax.

The Retribution arrived in the harbor last Thursday as England's warship representation in honor of the visit and stay of the Honourable Artillery company of London.

The stay of the ship in the harbor has been very a pleasant one, all the officers and men agree. The captain and senior officers were guests at all the festivities in honor of the Honourables, the other officers were entertained fraternally by the officers of the other warships in the harbor and entertained in turn, while the men of the crew have all been granted shore leave and had a chance to see the city.

Quite a large number of visitors inspected the ship during her stay, and all expressed admiration for her arrangement, and the fine-looking men that made up her crew.

NO DIVORCE TO MRS. MOLINEUX.

St. Paul, Minn., Oct. 7.—Specials from the nine judicial districts of So. Dakota quote the circuit judges of each district as saying that they have not granted a degree of divorce to Mrs. R. B. Molineux of New York.

BATES TEAM ENTIRELY OUTCLASSED BY HARVARD

Score 23 to 0—Work of Crimson Team Shows Improvement Over a Week Ago

By the score of 23—0 Harvard defeated Bates on Soldiers Field yesterday afternoon in a good game of football.

Bates was not in the game at any stage, being completely outplayed except in the last minute of play, when she held the Crimson team for downs on the 8-yd. line, thus preventing a fifth touchdown.

The score was the same by which Bates was defeated last year, which should show that the Harvard team is in as good a state of development as it was a year ago at any rate.

While not entirely satisfactory to the coaches, the game showed a marked improvement over the affair with Maine last Saturday and the team to a man got into the plays with dash and spirit.

This was in a great measure due to the work of little Steve Noyes at quarter who ran the team in good style. He used good judgement in running the plays and also played well in the back field, cleverly running in a punt for 15 yds. with would-be tacklers all about him. Elkins succeeded him in the second half and also did good work, except for the last play when Harvard was held for downs. He sent Mills against centre where it seemed that another play would have been better.

Mills, who went into the game in the second half together with Nesmith and Schoelkopf, also put up a good game, plunging through the line for good consistent gains time after time and finally carrying the ball over for a touchdown three minutes after the half began.

Schoelkopf again showed up well, keeping his feet in good style and wriggling along for many yards when he looked to be down.

Hurley, however, at right half, was undoubtedly the star of the game during the one half he stayed in. He started the ball rolling in the first play of the game with a beautiful 40-yd. run around left end which would have certainly resulted in a touchdown had the little runner not stumbled.

Straight, hard line-bucking took the ball quickly to the 5-yd. line from where Hurley carried it over three minutes after the game had started. Noyes kicked goal making the score 6—0.

Bates elected to have Harvard receive the kickoff, which she did, and rushed the ball steadily down for a second touchdown which was made by Harrison on a line plunge of six yds.

Again Bates kicked off and again the Crimson advanced steadily down the field to a third touchdown, from which Noyes kicked goal, making the score 18—0.

After an exchange of kicks, in which Bowditch gained about 30 yds. by falling on a fumble, Bates had the ball on her own 15-yd. line for the first time of the day. A tandem formation similar to that of Maine was used and the first rush netted 3 yds. The second met with a repulse and it was third down with two yds. to gain when time was called for the half.

Several new men were put in on the Crimson team at the beginning of the second half, while Bates kept her original line-up throughout. The fresh Harvard backs ploughed through the line for many yards, securing a touchdown in three minutes from which Noyes failed to kick goal—score 23—0.

The rest of the game was all Harvard until, with only a few seconds to play, Bates braced on her own 8-yd. line and held for downs, having the ball in her own possession when time was called.

The line-up:—

Harvard.	Bates.
Burgess (Bartels), l.e.	r.e., Libbey
Parkinson, l.t.	r.t., Connor
Shea (Bleakie), l.g.	r.g., Turner
Carrick, c.	c., Cutten
Coburn, r.g.	l.g., Johnson
Knowlton, r.t.	l.t., Reed
Bowditch (Montgomery), r.e.	l.t., Cole
Noyes (Elkins), q.b.	q.b., Rounds
Randall (Nesmith), l.h.b.	r.h.b., White
Hurley (Schoelkopf), r.h.b.	l.h.b., Mahoney
Harrison (Mills), f.b.	f.b., Briggs

Score—Harvard, 23; Bates, 0. Touchdowns—Harrison, Hurley, Mills, Randall. Referee—Brown. Umpire—Holton of B. A. A. Linesmen—Sturgess, Bates and Hurd, Harvard. Time of halves—15 and 10 min. Attendance—3000.

OVESON HAS A RELAPSE.

Cambridge, Oct. 8.—Reports from Stillman Infirmary state that Oveson, the Harvard tackle who was taken there last Saturday with a slight concussion, has suffered a relapse which may necessitate his remaining out of college for some time to come.

It was thought at first that his injuries were slight, but developments have showed them to be serious.

BOWDOIN EASY FOR AMHERST.

Amherst, Oct. 7.—The Amherst football team in a game with Bowdoin this afternoon won an easy victory of 23 to 0, and showed continued improvement over last week's work. They had no difficulty in rushing the ball for touchdowns. On the other hand Bowdoin was weak and failed to carry the ball through the Amherst line. Shay, the freshman back, went in for the first time, and he had a part in the game from the start, making good gains. Lewis and Pierce also excelled for Amherst, and Finn, Fallanger and Bean did the best work for Bowdoin. Amherst made one touchdown in the first half and three in the second. The lineup:—

Amherst.	Bowdoin.
Chase, l.e.	l.e., Winslow (Fallanger)
Pierce, lt.t.	l.t., Finn
Palmer, l.g.	l.g., Davis
Behrends, c.	c., Sanborn
Howard, r.g.	r.g., Powers
Diehl (Joost), r.t.	r.t., Readman
Daniels, r.e.	r.e., Bean
Lewis, q.b.	q.b., Wiggin
Shay, lh.b.	l.h.b., Lowell
Hubbard, r.h.b.	r.h.b, Chapman
Coggeshall (Storke), f.b.	f.b., Selloon (Ryan)

The summary: Total score—Amherst, 23; Bowdoin, 0. Touchdowns—Coggeshall, Hubbard (2), Diehl (1). Goals—Lewis (3). Umpire—Pollard. Referee—McCurdy.

YALE'S IMPOSING SCORE.

New Haven, Conn., Oct. 7.—Yale ran up a big score in defeating Wesleyan at football today, making 33 points to the visitors' none. The game was marked by no sensational plays except that Yale smashed to pieces the only trick which the visitors had a chance to show the two or three times they got the ball on punts. The Yale offence was quick in forming and in expectation that it ripped to pieces the semblance of defence which the Wesleyan forwards tried to offer.

Capt. Rafferty thought it wise after the first half with 17 points scored to fill in many subs. and to keep adding them in place of regulars as the score rolled higher and there was no danger that the visitors would score on Yale.

The game started in typical Yale fashion, Bowman catching the kickoff and running the ball back to the 30 yd. line. At that point Metcalf and Mitchell carried the ball down the field without losing it once. Mitchell finally scored.

The second touchdown was made in the same manner of play, but Bowman was occasionally given the ball to carry. Metcalf scored on a fake tackles back play. The third touchdown was made as easily but Hogan was called upon inside the 25 yd. line. In the second half the halfbacks did almost equally well and the play was altered only in the point that Twitchell made two attempts to kick field goals and failed because the ball was heavy and wet.

McCoy's end running was the most interesting feature of the play toward the end of the game. Line-up:—

Yale.	Wesleyan.
Rafferty, Heare, Neal, l.e.	l.e., Eyster
Kinney, l.t.	l.t., North
Morton, l.g.	l.g., Taylor
Roraback, c.	c., Sneider
Bloomer, Flanders, r.g.	r.g., Gillespie
Hogan, Turner, r.t.	r.t., Forbes
Sherlin, Morehead, Spalding, r.e.	r.e., Packard
Rockwell, Twitchell, q.b.	q.b., Onthrop
Mitchell, McCoy, r.h.b.	r.h.b., Van Surden
Metcalf, Preston, Flynn, l.h.b.	l.h.b., Gildersleeve
Bowman, Farmer, Hoyt, f.b.	f.b., Rogers

Umpire—Dr. Samuel Hammond. Referee—T. B. Hull.

WILLIAMS BEATS "AGGIES."

Williamstown, Oct. 7.—By a score of 17 to 0, Williams defeated the Massachusetts "Aggies." All Williams' touchdowns were made on long runs. The Amherst team was much lighter, but put up a plucky game. Amherst blocked the line plunges well, and in the last half the team played very evenly.

EASY WIN FOR DARTMOUTH.

Burlington, Vt., Oct. 7.—Dartmouth easily won the game with the University of Vermont today, by a score of 36 to 0. The home team was outweighed by the visitors. In the first half U. of P. kicked off to Dartmouth's 40 yd. line. The ball was advanced mostly on line plays until Dartmouth had secured 18 points. In the second half Dartmouth added 18 more points on long gains by end runs and trick plays. The game ended with the ball in Dartmouth's possession on her 50 yd. line. Line-up and summary:—

Dartmouth.	U. of Vt.
Nullock (Lillard), l.e.	l.e., Patterson
Linsley, l.t.	l.t., Ranney
Gilman (Smith), l.g.	l.g., Bates
Pratt, c.	c., Gale
Gates, r.g.	r.g., Chamberlain
Turner (Pankert), r.t.	r.t., Page
Hurr and Glaze, r.e.	r.e., Campbell
Witham (Melville), q.b.	q.b., Bassett
Pattedson (Bancroft), l.h.b.	l.h.b., Williams
Vaughan (Mair), r.h.b.	r.h.b., Woodward
Connelly, f.b.	f.b., Newton

Score—Dartmouth, 36; University of Vermont, 0. Touchdowns—Vaughn (3), Patterson (2), Connelly (1). Goals—Vaghn (4), Manning (2). Referee—Pendleton.

OTHER RESULTS.

At Andover—Phillips-Andover, 60, Dorchester A.A. 0.

At Groton—Groton School 6, Somerville High 0.

At Williamstown—Williams freshmen 5, Drury Academy of No. Adams 0.

At Exeter, N. H.—Phillips-Exeter 17, Maplewood A. C. of Portsmouth, N. H., 0.

At Philadelphia — Pennsylvania 58, Haverford 0.

At New York—Columbia, 29; Hamilton, 0.

At Princeton—Princeton, 63; Gettysburg,0.

At Swarthmore, Pa.—Lehigh Univ, 10; Swarthmore College, 5.

At Southboro—Dean Academy, 23; St. Marks, 0.

TECHNOLOGY'S ANNUAL HANDICAP

Interest in the annual fall handicap meet at Tech, scheduled for Oct. 23 and 24, at the new oval on Irvington st., is already running high at the institute. Since the giving up of a varsity football eleven several years ago, Tech athletes have turned to track work with increasing interest, and this year's outlook for the track team is a good one. Regular training for the meet began at the oval Monday under direction of Coach Ma-

CAPT. CURTIS—M. I. T.

han. G. A. Curtis, '04, is again captain of Tech's track team. H. J. Mann, '06, is the manager.

The intercollegiate cross country run, to be held at New York Thanksgiving day, should this year include a strong entry from Technology. Training for this event began Monday as well, and Coach Mahan's system with the Tech boys last year was exceptionally successful.

The run with the Amherst team is arranged for Nov. 7 at Boston; Dartmouth will be taken on at a date now being arranged. The cross country team will be captained by Lorenz, '05.

HEALTH BOARD TO INVESTIGATE.

Cambridge, Oct. 7.—At the meeting of the board of health held tonight it was voted to investigate the existing conditions at Cider Mill pond, in the Mt. Auburn district, near the Payson park reservation.

Mayor McNamee and the water board will be invited by the board of health to accompany them to the pond Saturday morning next in view of abating the nuisance.

There has been a great deal of talk in regard to this for some time, as the pond is covered with a thick slime and is in a very unhealthy condition.

SHARK WAS UNCONTROLLABLE

New Sub-Marine Boat Nearly Sinks Torpedo Boat Dahlgren on Account of Strong Tide.

New York, Oct. 7.—The sub-marine torpedo boat Shark during a trial at Greenport, L. I., today rammed the torpedo boat Dahlgren, which barely escaped sinking with her crew of seven men. Lt. C. Nelson took the Shark out for a trial and steamed out into the middle of the bay making several quick dives.

When she reached the opposite shore she headed back for a long spin under water. The boat poked her nose under the surface and dived down 58 feet.

It was planned to run three and a half miles at the rate of six and one-half mi. an hour. Those on shore who figured when she would rise were becoming alarmed when she did not appear, when suddenly she rose less than 2 feet from the Dahlgren which was lying at the dock.

Lt. Nelson signalled to reverse her engines, but her headway was too strong and she crushed into the port side of the Dahlgren.

An examination showed that a hole four feet long had been torn through the plates just aft of the engine room. The only mark on the Shark was the tearing of the paint from her ram-like bow.

Lt. Nelson said afterward that the strong ebb tide made the Shark momentarily uncontrollable.

OBITUARY

BAKER, W. T. At Chicago, Oct. 7.

He was ex-president and for many years a member of the Chicago board of trade.

DALE—At North Andover, October 7th, Surgeon-General William Johnson Dale, M. D., in his 89th year.

Funeral at his residence, Friday, October 9th, at 12 noon, on arrival of train leaving Boston at 10:55 a.m., Boston & Maine, Eastern division, to Marble Ridge.

W. J. Dale, a distinguished physician of Boston, was born in Gloucester. His grandfather, William Johnson, fought at Bunker Hill; his paternal grandfather, Ebenezer, at Lexington; his father, Ebenezer, was a surgeon in the war of 1812. Dr. Dale was graduated at Harvard in 1837, at its medical school in 1840. In June, 1861, he was commissioned surgeon-general by Gov. Andrew, and in December of that year was appointed acting assistant surgeon of the U. S. A., which he retained till the close of the war.

He was on duty in Boston during the civil war, and had general supervision of all matters connected with the medical staff and the care of the sick and wounded that were sent home. His distribution of the state aid funds and his care of the soldiers after the war, are as remarkable as the wonderful ability he displayed in properly officering the Massachusetts regiments with medical officers.

In October, 1863, he was raised to the rank of brigadier-general. In recognition of his services, the U. S. authorities gave his name to a general hospital established at Worcester, Mass., opened in September, 1865.

Owing to his infirmity, deafness, he gave up public life in 1876, and settled on the farm of his ancestors, in N. Andover, a farm of some hundred acres, which came into the possession of the Johnson family by the original grant from the Indians in 1636. He was fond of pointing out to his friends the spot where one of his ancestors was scalped during an Indian raid.

He was married April, 1846, to Sarah Adams, daughter of Col. J. H. Adams of Boston. They had three children, two of whom died in infancy, and a son, W. J. Dale, jr., who died in 1896.

DENMAN, Herbert. In Idylwild, Cal., Oct. 3—50 yrs.

Mr. Denman, who was well-known in New York art circles, died from consumption, which had caused his removal two years ago from New York city to a milder climate. He was a bachelor, and a social favorite in the Players' and Century clubs. Born in Brooklyn Heights, of wealthy parents, his talent for painting was encouraged and he spent several years in Paris under Carolus Duran and other masters. He was a fellow-student of John Sargent and Carrol Beckwith. His principal work, called "The Trio," took a prize in the Paris Salon. Mr. Denman devoted himself to decorative work after returning to America in 1887, and panels by his brush decorated Frederick Vanderbilt's house at Dobbs Ferry, the Manhattan Hotel and the Waldorf-Astoria ballroom.

JOHNSON, Dr. J. B. At St. Louis, Mo., Oct. 7—86 yrs.

For over 60 yrs. he was a physician in St. Louis, and was the first vice-president of the National Medical Assn., founded in 1850. He was a native of Fairhaven.

LOUGHRAN, John. At Brooklyn, N. Y., Oct. 6—83 yrs.

He was president of the Manufacturers National bank, Brooklyn, and one of the best known financiers in that borough.

MOORE. At Providence, R. I., Oct. 5th, in the 66th year of her age, Emma Moore, wife of the late Dr. Joseph Moore of Amherst, N. S.

PEARSON, Col. B. N. At Chicago, Oct. 6—63 yrs.

He was assistant paymaster of Chicago. He entered the civil war as a private and came home with a brevet title of brigadier-general in command of the old regiment once commanded by J. A. Logan.

STAYMAN, Dr. Joseph. At Leavenworth, Kas., Oct. 7—86 yrs.

He was a noted horticulturist and originator of the Stayman apple and the Stayman strawberry. In 1860 he brought 500,000 fruit grafts to Kansas from Illinois, being the first man to start the apple industry in that state.

FUNERAL OF JUDGE PARMENTER.

Arlington, Oct. 7.—The funeral of ex-Chief Justice Parmenter took place this afternoon at the Unitarian church.

The service was conducted by Rev. Frederick Gill, and was largely attended. Among those present were many former professional associates of the deceased, including nearly all the judges and attaches of the Boston municipal courts.

The floral tributes were many and expressive of the esteem in which the deceased was held by a large circle of friends.

The service was simple, consisting only of an eulogy by Rev. Mr. Gill and singing by the Imperial Male Quartette.

The interment was at Cambridge cemetery.

MIDDLESEX HUNT'S HORSE SHOW.

The fourth annual horse show of the Middlesex Hunt Club will be held at the kennels, So. Lincoln, Oct. 17. Entries will positively close Oct. 10. Entrance fee will be $3 for single horses and $5 for tandems. Members are requested to remember that all the cash prizes for the farmer's classes come from these entries, and to make as many entries as possible. Entries should be made to Howard Snelling, So. Lincoln, and must be accompanied by cheque.

The judges are, for hunters, W. E. Bright, Dr. H. L. Morse, Robert Perkins; thoroughbreds, George Lee, Dr. H. L. Morse; saddle horses, W. E. Bright, Robert F. Perkins, Dr. H. L. Morse; driving classes, W. R. Warren, Tyler Morse, C. R. Dabny; farmers' classes, John F. Farrar, A. B. Sampson, L. P. Bent.

The horse show committee consists of Howard Snelling, A. H. Higginson and G. H. D. Lamson.

U. S. DAM BREAKS.

Seattle, Wash., Oct. 7.—The government dams at the head of Lake Union have given way, causing great damage.

THE HELEN BREWER MISSING.

London, Oct. 7.—The American ship Helen Brewer, Capt. Mahany, from Sourabaya, March 6, for Delaware Breakwater, has been posted at Lloyds as missing.

BOSTON DAILY ADVERTISER.

FORECAST FOR BOSTON: Fair Wednesday and Thursday; light variable winds.

VOL. 184, NO. 91. BOSTON, WEDNESDAY MORNING, OCTOBER 14, 1903. PRICE TWO CENTS.

ROCKEFELLER-MORGAN FEUD LED TO DRESSER'S EXPOSE

Members of J. P. Morgan's Firm Will Take Stand to Tell "Inside" Facts About the Sale of the Bethlehem Steel Plant

New York, Oct. 13.—The opinion is growing here that the "expose" of the shipbuilding trust and the attacks on J. P. Morgan especially, were engineered by parties friendly to the Rockefeller-Gould combination, which aims to dominate Wall st. The fight between these great interests now crops out in every move.

So serious has the matter become that Mr. Morgan will authorize his associates to go on the stand if necessary.

Whenever he is requested to appear as a witness, Mr. Perkins, of Mr. Morgan's firm, will take the chair, and has sent word that it will not even be necessary to subpoena him. Mr. Perkins' testimony, given under oath, will establish one fact, and that is that the firm of J. P. Morgan & Co. had absolutely nothing to do with the organization or the attempted financing of the United States Shipbuilding Corporation.

It was known here at the time Mr. Schwab first bought the Bethlehem property that some of those of authority in the Steel Corporation were not a little irritated at that transaction. The house of J. P. Morgan & Co. looked at Mr. Schwab's purchase with uneasy eyes. While they had no doubt of Mr. Schwab's ability as an expert manufacturer and marketer of steel, they had had comparatively trifling experience with or test of him as a financier.

In plain English, Mr. Schwab was, if not distrusted, at least not so well known as to make it certain to some of his associates that he would not regard his own interests as of a prior consideration to those of the United States Steel Corporation.

Therefore, if the question be pressed, there is little doubt that testimony will be given either by Mr. Perkins or some other competent to testify that it was deemed not merely advisable but imperative that the Bethlehem Steel property should be so held that it would not be a menace to the United States Steel. That testimony would explain how it happened that Mr. Morgan's firm, as managers of the Steel Underwriting Syndicate, took over the Bethlehem property. It would be interesting to know what argument or persuasion availed with Mr. Schwab so that he parted with it.

Now as to the contract to sell the Morgan holdings of shipbuilding shares first. That contract was, before it was signed, showed to the members of J. P. Morgan & Co.

They repudiated the contract in English which was vigorous if not euphonistic. They said that J. P. Morgan & Co. did not do business after the methods exploited in that contract; that these methods were not popular with reputable financiers of Wall st., whatever the ethics of the eminent counsel and financiers from other parts of the country who constructed that contract might be.

They almost literally threw the contract out of the door, but they forgot one thing and that was that, although they did not sign nor accept the contract they should also have demanded that no contract of that kind be executed with the name of J. P. Morgan & Co. left in it.

It was thus executed and it will be testified that this was done without the knowledge of J. P. Morgan & Co. and that not until after the failure of the underwriting syndicate did J. P. Morgan & Co. know that a contract that bandied their name in this humiliating way had been executed.

TREASURE SEEKERS DIG FOR THE "WADSWORTH TREASURE"

Hole is Hastily Sunk at Night and Then the Mysterious Strangers Vanish

Franklin, N. H., Oct. 13.—A man who claimed to be the nephew of the once famous eccentric and miser, Titus Wadsworth, approached the present owner of the Wadsworth estate in this place. He claimed to know where Wadsworth had buried the "treasure" which has now become historic.

Titus Wadsworth was known to be very thrifty and saving. When he died, two years ago, none of his wealth could be found. There were no bankbooks to any large amount. The walls of the house were sounded and showed no hiding place.

The present owner of the place, C. E. Currier, refused the professed nephew any right to dig for the treasure. Mr. Currier was skeptical of the story, and also felt that even if it were true, the man should not be allowed to take away the hoard without proving title.

The stranger took the refusal badly. He offered Currier a percentage of the buried gold. When that offer was refused he went away, leaving only a small hole where, he said, he had been digging for flagroot.

The following night a team with three men was seen in that neighborhood. The next morning it was found that a great hole, 30 ft. square and about 5 ft. deep had been dug on the spot where the stranger had first been at work.

Since that time the place has been watched, day and night. But the men have not reappeared.

Those who have visited the place have found small pieces of old wood in the dirt thrown out. It has been hinted that some sort of wooden chest must have been buried there.

If so, it has disappeared with the men and the wagon, and the lengendary "Titus Woodworth treasure" may have disappeared with them.

Woodworth was known to have been a college graduate, turned recluse and very saving. He spent almost nothing and had been saving his money for at least 50 yrs. His comments on investments showed him unusually well informed and the general impression was that he had amassed a fortune.

BOTH LOVED SAME WOMAN

BEAN IS SUSPECTED OF MURDER

Ephraim Root, Vermont Sawmill Hand, Dies From Effects of Frightful Clubbing—Jealousy the Cause.

Randolph, Vt., Oct. 13.—News reached here today that Ephraim Root, a sawmill employee, was beaten to death during last night at W. Rochester, and that Joe Bean, a fellow workman, is now under arrest charged with having committed the crime.

The homicide was in its nature one of unusual brutality. The victim was not only pounded into insensibility, but his body was atrociously maltreated and disfigured, as if the murderer's desire to kill would not be satisfied by the mere death of his victim.

According to the police, Root and Bean were in love with the same woman, and this murder, it will be claimed, was the outcome of Bean's jealousy.

Both Root and Bean were employed at Joseph Greene's saw mill at West Rochester. About 7 p.m. yesterday, Root visited Greene's barn to care for the horses. He did not return to the Greene house, where he made his home, at the usual time, and two hours were passed with no word from him.

Disturbed at the absence of the man, two of the Greene boys went out to the barn to look for him. He was found lying in an empty stall, unconscious and bleeding. The body was frightfully bruised and the face disfigured. The weapon used by the murderer could not be found.

Medical aid was summoned, but Root never regained his senses, and died at 3 a.m. today.

An investigation was started at once. The police authorities were told that Root and Joe Bean were reputed to be in love with a woman connected with Mr. Greene's household. A search for Bean showed that he was missing. Suspicion was then attached to the man and a close search was begun.

During the day Deputy Sheriff Tinkham located Bean at a farmhouse about four miles from the scene of the murder. Bean did not resist arrest.

State Atty. Blanchard arrived at Rochester tonight and took charge of the case

WEDNESDAY'S WEATHER

Washington, Oct. 13.—For New England: Fair Wednesday and Thursday; light, variable winds.

THE RECORD IN BOSTON.

	8 A.M.	8 P.M.
Barometer	29.94	29.93
Temperature	54	55
Dew point	48	46
Humidity	82%	71%
Wind	N	NE
Weather	Cloudy	Cloudy
Precipitation	.10	0

Max. temp., 57; min. temp., 51; max. wind, N, 18 mi. per hour.

IN OTHER CITIES AT 8 P.M.

Montreal, pt. cloudy, 56; New York, cloudy, 60; Washington, clear, 56; Jacksonville, clear, 70; New Orleans, clear, 76; St. Louis, clear, 68; Chicago, clear, 56; Bismarck, clear, 52; Denver, cloudy, 52.

BOSTON WINS THE BASEBALL CHAMPIONSHIP OF THE WORLD FROM PITTSBURG'S PIRATES

Final Score Was Three to Nothing—Dineen's Masterly Pitching Did It—Scenes of Remarkable Enthusiasm at the Huntington Ave. Grounds—What Victors and Vanquished Say

Photo by Staff Photographer.
THE BOSTON AMERICAN TEAM.
Standing row, reading from left—Winter, p.; O'Brien, utility; Farrell, c.; Dineen, p.; LaChance, 1b; Dougherty, lf.; Hughes, p.; Freeman, r.f.; Criger, c.
Seated—C. Stahl, c.f.; Parent, s.s.; Young, p.; Collins, 3b. (Capt.); Ferris, 2b.; Gibson, p.

JIMMIE COLLINS:—"What is there to say? We won; I believed all the way that we would win, even when things looked blackest for us. I want to thank press and public for their support and encouragement."

FRED CLARKE:—"I haven't a word to say except to congratulate Boston on having a magnificent ball team."

BARNEY DREYFUS:—"Boston won on her merits as the teams stood. I wish we had had our full string of pitchers. I say this, not to detract from the credit due Collins' boys, but in simple justice to my own. I am as proud of them as if they had won every game of the series."

The Boston Americans earned three runs and prevented Pittsburg from scoring in the eighth and consequently the final game of the series of nine for the world's championship on the Huntington ave. grounds yesterday.

It was Boston's, fifth and fourth successive, victory. Pittsburg won three games, the first, third and fourth of the series.

The score of the deciding game is appended:—

BOSTON.

	a.b.	r.	b.h.	p.o.	a.	e.
Dougherty, lf	4	0	0	3	0	0
Collins, 3b	4	0	1	0	2	0
Stahl, cf	4	0	0	2	0	0
Freeman, rf	4	1	1	2	0	0
Parent, ss	4	1	1	1	1	0
Lachance, 1b	4	1	1	11	0	0
Ferris, 2b	4	0	3	0	3	0
Criger, c	3	0	2	8	3	0
Dineen, p	3	0	1	0	3	0
Totals	34	3	10	27	12	0

PITTSBURG.

	a.b.	r.	b.h.	p.o.	a.	e.
Beaumont, cf	4	0	0	4	0	0
Clarke, lf	4	0	1	4	0	0
Leach, 3b	3	0	0	0	3	0
Wagner, ss	4	0	1	3	1	1
Bransfield, 1b	3	0	0	7	1	0
Ritchey, 2b	2	0	0	2	1	0
Sebring, rf	3	0	1	1	1	0
Phelps, c	3	0	0	3	0	0
Phillippe, p	3	0	1	0	2	0
Totals	29	0	4	24	9	1

Boston.................... 0 0 0 2 0 1 0 0 .—3

Three-base hits—Freeman, Lachance, Sebring. Stolen base—Wagner. Double play—Criger and Lachance. First on balls—Off Dineen, 2. Struck out—By Dineen, 7; by Phillippe, 2. Umpires—O'Day and Connolly. Attendance—7455. Time—1:35.

The game that made Boston once more the centre of the baseball universe was played rapidly. In spite of the heavy and slippery condition of the field the action was clean and fast.

A wide throw by Wagner was the only error scorable as such, and mistakes of judgment were few.

Both teams played as confidently as if some sage had spelled victory for them in advance, and the game was fought out to the end with the utmost determination.

The masterly pitching of Dineen, Criger's headwork at critical moments, and

Photo by Horner.
JAMES COLLINS,
Manager-Captain and star player of the Champions of the World.

the timely batting of Ferris were the three noteworthy and well-nigh decisive factors contributing to Boston's victory.

Dineen had terrific speed and superb command of sharply breaking curves. Only four hits were secured off his delivery. He gave two bases on balls, and thus out of a total of 31 men who faced him, only six reached first base.

In five out of the nine innings Pittsburg went out in order. In the other four innings the men on the bases, and as hits to the ropes went for three bases, absurdly enough, as it turned out there was no need for roping off the outfield, Pittsburg may be said to have had four chances of scoring.

Two of these chances were nipped in the bud by Criger. He threw sharply to first, catching Phillippe napping, in the sixth.

In the fourth, Pittsburg's fairest opportunity, Criger drew the clever Leach off third by a bluff throw to second, perfectly executed, and tagged the wee one for the third out.

Ferris' timely stickwork, the ultimate instance of baseball's unexpectedness to many of the fans, drove in all of Boston's runs.

Phillippe, the debonaire, whose masterly twirling contributed the larger part to each and every one of the victories Pittsburg had been able to achieve over Boston earlier in the series, but with memories of one subsequent defeat in mind, made desperate efforts to do more than can be expected of mortal twirler.

Had he won his game he could hardly have added to the glory his grand pitching in the post-season series has won for him, but no pitcher living can down Boston's hard-hitting team four games out of five in a straight series of nine.

Pittsburg did not win the National League pennant with Phillippe alone, but with Leever as well, and with Doheny besides. If Pittsburg echoes this remark in passing, let it be conceded that in this series there has been renown enough for all, and that the Pirates have been worthy opponents for Boston's champion team.

Boston batted Phillippe for 10 safe hits, two of which, by Freeman and Lachance, like Sebring's for Pittsburg, counting as three base hits under the ground rules. These extra-sackers were all fine drives, and might, in a free field, have counted, each of them, for a base more or less, according to the skill

CONTINUED ON PAGE EIGHT.

HANNA SAYS A PANIC WOULD FOLLOW HIS DEFEAT

Piqua, O., Oct. 13.—Sen. Hanna, in a bitter speech here, declared that his defeat would be followed by something like a panic in this country.

He threatened that a democratic victory would be the signal for the great financial houses to order reductions of working forces in the giant corporations of the country.

He went on:—

" 'I want to go on record on this proposition. 'If by your votes next month you serve notice upon the country that you favor casting aside the safe business principles that have brought the present prosperous conditions bye and bye—and it will not be very long—you will be eating at the soup houses again. And why?

" 'Within three weeks' time after such notice has been served the captains of industry will see that the vessels over which they preside lighten sail and hug the shore. Just now there is a lull in business and industries all over the land, due to the slight uncertainty as to the result of the election in Ohio and elsewhere. If this remote contingency has such a depressing effect upon the business of the country, think what a quietus would be put upon the industrial relations of the nation if on the morning of Nov. 4 it should be announced that Johnson had captured the Ohio legislature.' "

PROVINCETOWN WHALER LOST WITH ALL HANDS

Fayal, Azores, Oct. 13.—The American whaler, Joseph Manta, has been wrecked on the island of Pico, one of the Azores group. All on board were lost.

SHE WAS PROVINCETOWN'S CRACK SHIP

Provincetown, Oct. 13.—The Manta was called the best whaler that ever fitted from this port. She was commanded by Capt. J. C. Frates, whose home was in Fayal, where he leaves a widow. The crew of 14 were all Cape de Verde and Azore Islanders.

The Manta was built by Tarr & James at Essex, Mass., 1900, and left Provincetown in December of that year for a three years' cruise in the No. Atlantic. Since sailing she has landed about 1900 barrels of sperm oil at the Western Ids. for shipment to this country. She was at Fayal recently for the purpose of landing last season's catch and taking on a fresh supply of provisions and sailed on a cruise last Thursday. Pico, where the wreck is said to have taken place, is but an hour's sail from the Fayal Ids., and it is rather surprising that the Manta should not have gotten farther out into the Atlantic. There is no insurance on either the schooner or its contents.

The Manta, instead of being broad and bulky, as is the case in most whalers, was long, narrow and deep, with much the same lines as the Grand Bank fishermen.

GASTON RENEWS HIS ATTACK

Pittsfield, Oct. 13.—Col. Gaston, in a speech here tonight, continued his attacks upon the republican state administration. He said:—

The present tendency is to increase rather than to diminish; and when the expenditures of the present six months ending Dec. 31, 1903, are audited, the proof will be complete that the war with Spain, which a strong administration would have avoided, and the "criminal aggression" upon the Philippine Islanders, which a weak administration brought upon the country, will have cost the tax-payers $920,000,000, a sum slightly larger than the entire bonded debt of the United States, bearing interest, now outstanding.

The pretext of expansion of commerce in the east in justification of closing the door to trade in the Philippines to other nations, while strenuously urging the open door in China and other parts of Asia, has been exposed and it now excites derision only. In the computation of the cost of war and war fare to June 30, 1902, estimating that our Philippine expenses were to that time about $400,000,000, we found that we had been paying for five years about $1.05 per head of our population to secure an export which amounted to six and one-half cents (6½) per head, on which there might have been a profit to some one of one cent per head of the whole population.

The figures of the last year are even more grotesque. The cost of criminal aggression in the Philippine Islands during the fiscal year ending June 30, 1903, was not less than $1.25 per head, after making any allowance that any reasonable man could make for the alleged necessity of increasing the army and building battleships to meet every contingency. The exports from the United States to the Philippines have fallen off to less than five cents per head of our population.

We are still wasting the lives and health of American soldiers and bringing poverty and suffering upon the people of the Philippines under the pretence of benevolence. We cannot have the satisfaction of even claiming that it is justified by business reasons.

LONDON HONOURABLES BACK TO "AMERICA'S BEST CITY"

Great Throng Greets Military Companies on Arrival at N. Union Station—Lord Denbigh Says Boston is Best of All

THE PROGRAMME.

WEDNESDAY, OCT. 14.

11 a.m. to 5:30 p.m.—Guests of the Victorian Club at Country Club, Brookline.

6:30 p.m.—Return banquet given by the London Honourables to the Ancients at Hotel Somerset.

THURSDAY, OCT. 15.

4 p.m.—London Honourables leave for England on the Columbus.

Never was Lord Denbigh in better mood than last night when he stepped off the train which bore the Ancients and their English guests from Montreal to Boston.

"How does it seem to get back to Boston?" was the first question tossed at him, and his answer accorded with the general opinion of the entire Honourable company.

"It seems very good," he said. "I think I prefer Boston to any of the cities we've visited. The people of Boston are the most cordial, I think, that I've ever met.

"It seems a bit like home to get back here after our trip.

"I never saw so much enthusiasm and kindness as you show here in Boston."

It is not to be inferred from this that the Honourables' reception in other cities was by any means cold, for Lord Denbigh continued:

"Every place we visited gave a warm welcome, Fall River and New York, Montreal, Toronto, Washington and all. But none welcomed us so heartily as Boston has done. We came here first, and so I suppose Boston considers us as her special guests. I am glad to get back."

"How about your reception in Canada?" he was asked. "Was it as cold as the newspaper reports said?"

"Oh, no. It wasn't cold at all. We arrived in Montreal at a rather unseasonable time for reception, 8:30 a.m. So besides the garrison troops not many people met us. But we were given an excellent time there, and everywhere else."

"Did it seem quiet in Washington compared with the other cities?"

"Oh, no. We were well received there, though there was not much cheering. I understand they never cheer in Washington."

A vagrant smile stole across his ruddy countenance.

"Pres. Roosevelt received us very kindly. He is a kind, hearty, honest gentleman."

"Is there anything in this talk about your filling the late Sir Michael Herbert's place as ambassador to this country?" was one of the many questions aimed at Lord Denbigh by eager interviewers.

Lord Denbigh rather shied at the question.

"It's all rot, me dear boy," were his words. "All rot. Whoever made up such a story did not have the least idea what he was talking about."

"How about the story that Lady Denbigh refused all invitations sent her by the society leaders in New York?"

"Lady Denbigh did not have time to attend the social functions," was the answer. "How would she go about to them when we only stayed in New York one day. Lady Denbigh's time was taken up by receptions when her presence was required. She had a very pleasant trip.

"The trip itself was well planned and well carried out. It could not have been better."

After that it was Lord Denbigh's turn to ask questions:

"What paper are you from?" he said.

"The Advertiser," was the reply.

"Have you been in Boston long enough to know the different papers?"

"Oh, yes," he said, "they are very interesting. I like the American papers, though they carry their business much farther than the English ones do."

Lord Denbigh has learned of the one fault that newspapers here are said to have. "Now don't put in anything I haven't said, will you," he remarked at the end of the interview. "Some of the papers we've met do that."

BIG CROWD AT THE STATION

The two trains bearing the Honourables back to Boston from their trip about the country were late last night. They were due at 8 and 8:15 p.m.; they arrived at 10:15 p.m.

The North Union Station was filled with crowds of Bostonians waiting to greet their guests again. The crowd began to arrive early in the evening, as early as 7 o'clock. Every train that arrived was eagerly watched, as if the guests were liable to escape without being cheered.

By 9:30 the large train shed was jammed. The crowd was perfectly quiet. Everyone watched intently and those near the gates never once withdrew their gaze from the black wilderness of tracks outside the station. Many prominent men and women were among the watchers.

When several hundred years ago the British evacuated Boston, the faithful historian adds at the end of the chapter, "and they never returned again. Howe's fleet had left Boston for good."

On this later occasion, however, history repeated itself with a few additions. The British Honourables took Boston hearts by storm. They evacuated Boston for a trip about the country. And last night, contrary to precedent, they returned and were cheered and welcomed back by thousands of loyal natives.

"Here they are," would go up from the crowd, as each train appeared, and there would be a straining of necks and eyes, only to relapse again when the train turned out to be the wrong one.

At the very end of the long station where the pavement walks end and the myriad of tracks begins stood a group of newspaper men watching. Finally at about 10 p.m. a new light appeared among the thousand or more that were dancing about among the tracks. This one moved, it came nearer, and grew bigger and bigger with a sound of wheels and bell behind it, and the long Montreal express thundered into the station.

The sight when the train stopped was one of the kind pictured in historical war novels. A hundred red-jacketed, gold-laced soldiers swarmed out of the cars.

Instead of falling back in dismay, however, the waiting crowd gave a loud cheer, while the band struck up that appropriate old tune, "Auld Lang Sine." Many of the spectators took up the refrain, and signified by their looks and action that "auld acquaintances" should not be "forgot" so far as the London Honourables were concerned.

Lord and Lady Denbigh were in the last car. The latter was met by Mrs. Sidney Hedges and her two daughters, Mrs. Baylor and Mrs. Eastrick, who accompanied her to the hotel in a carriage. Col. Hedges, Lord Denbigh and the rest of the troop stood about till the second train arrived, bearing the remainder of the party.

The travelers were met by a squad of home guards from the Ancients. These drew up at the head of the procession, and with the Honourables in the rear, and two bands playing, marched out amid cheers. The line went up Canal st., Hanover, and stopped in Court sq. where the Ancients separated and marched to Faneuil Hall.

The Honourables were dismissed, and began a rush to Young's and the Parker House, where nearly everyone of the young soldiers had a letter or two waiting for him, after reading which they tumbled into bed, tired out.

The crowd, having followed the procession to Court sq., stayed about as long as an Honourable was in sight, and many lusty hurrahs were given before they dispersed.

RECEPTION OF VICTORIAN CLUB

—This Forenoon.

Today the Londoners' entertainment will recommence with an elaborate reception at the Country Club, Brookline, under the auspices of the Victorian Club.

The two companies will leave the Parker House at 11 a.m. in automobiles and carriages, and proceed to the Country Club along Tremont, Park, Beacon, Arlington sts., Commonwealth ave., Fenway, Riverway, Jamaicaway (Arnold Arboretum), May, Pond, Newton and Clyde sts.

One of the features of the dinner will be these toasts:

"The President of the United States," proposed by Capt. Talbot, H. B. M. consul at Boston; "King Edward, VII.," proposed by F. C. de Sumichrast, pres. of the Victorian Club; "The Commonwealth of Massachusetts," proposed by F. J. MacLeod, sec'y, and responded to by Lieut.-Gov. Guild; "The Honourable Artillery Company of London," proposed by Prof. de Sumichrast; responded to by Lord Denbigh; "The Ancient and Honorable Artillery Company of Massachusetts," proposed by C. H. Windeler, responded to by Col. Hedges; "Our American Kinsmen," proposed by A. F. Flint, responded to by F. C. Knauff, sec'y trans-Atlantic Society of America; "The Country Club," proposed by C. S. Skinner, responded to by Lawrence Curtis.

CONTINUED ON PAGE SEVEN.

Giants and Athletics Ready for the World's Championship.

THE NEW YORK NATIONALS, TWO TIMES PENNANT WINNERS, AND A VIEW OF THE POLO GROUNDS.

From Left to Right—Mertes, Clark, Browne, Wiltse, Devlin, Elliotte, McGann, Donlin, Gilbert, Taylor, Dahlen, Strang, McGinnity, "Mascot," Bresnahan, Ames, Manager McGraw.

Matthewson.

CHAMPION TEAMS READY FOR WORLD'S SERIES

Opening Game Between Giants and Athletics Scheduled at Philadelphia To-morrow.

BATTLE TO BE A GREAT ONE.

Clubs Evenly Matched, With Odds Slightly in Favor of New York.

When the Philadelphia Athletics and the New York Giants line up on the field at American League Park, in Philadelphia, to-morrow, there will be started a baseball duel the like of which has never before occurred in the annals of the national game. Each team has won the pennant of its respective league by superior play, and they are expected to display the acme of baseball in the series of seven games, which will decide the world's championship.

Which team will win is a question that only the culmination of the great battle will determine. The rival clubs are so evenly matched that even the report that one of the best pitchers of the Athletics is on the hospital list has influenced the betting only to the extent of making the Giants a 9 to 10 favorite. How much truth there is in the announcement that "Rube" Waddell, the famous, but erratic, twirler, is out of the game for the season, cannot be told. Suffice it to say that the rumor is ascribed to the well-known cunning of Manager Connie Mack, of the Athletics, who, it is said, hopes to steal a march on McGraw in this way. The general opinion is that Waddell will be a factor in the series, and a strong one at that.

There is no question that the many thousands of enthusiasts who attend the series will see every fine point of the national game brought out to the limit. They represent entirely different styles of play, the Giants hard hitting, aggressive, fighting for everything they can get; the Athletics, fast and perfect in fielding, average hitters and splendid inside workers. It will be hard all around ball playing, with a sprinkling of good generalship against thorough team work, aided by all the arts that make a perfect aggregation.

It will also be a battle of wits between the managers. Mack is up to all the tricks of the game, learned by years of experience at the head of a ball club; McGraw has learned his lessons in the highest school of baseball generalship. Both know their parts thoroughly, and the work of the managers will in itself be a feature of the series.

Experts have studied the methods of both and agree that it will be a brilliant contest between the two Macks. There are many who believe that Connie Mack will use his weak pitchers, so to speak, against the strong twirlers of the New Yorks, with the chances of winning a game, while he will reserve his best men for the weak men on the Giants, thereby cinching those particular battles.

This would be the proper thing to do in a long campaign, but in a short series of six games such a course is almost out of the question, as every victory counts. Beside, McGraw might be inclined to work the same way, which would bring the final decision down to the final game, and a battle royal at the end between the two best pitchers on both sides. Of course, the baseball world would like nothing better.

There is little to choose between the two teams, man for man. With Waddell in shape, the American Leaguers would have a better chance to win. The mighty Mathewson is the equal of the great southpaw at his best, while McGinnity offsets the clever Plank. Many American League supporters favor Plank on the ground that the "Iron Man" has shown a disposition to go back this year, but the National League rooters are of the opinion that McGinnity will be on the spot when the pinch comes. Coakley and Ames have fared about evenly in the campaign this season, but this is offset by the fact that Taylor has outpitched Bender on general results. Wilste easily outranks Henley.

It is certain, however, that the series will be a battle between pairs or trios at the most, Mathewson and McGinnity opposing Waddell and Plank or Coakley and Plank, provided Waddell is unavailable. Ames and Taylor and Bender and Henley will be kept in reserve .

On all-around playing, the Giants have better averages than their rivals, but this is ascribed to the fact that the New Yorks have been opposed by weaker teams than the Athletics. This may be true, but the National League winners shape up in every way the superior of anything in harness to-day, the Athletics, of course, excepted. What may favor the Giants in the series more than anything else is the fact that they have had an easy time all the way and are, therefore, in excellent shape to play so important a series. On the other hand, the Athletics have been compelled to play up to the highest notch from start to finish and are, therefore, inclined to relax, now that the regular season is over. Mack will have this to contend with, and it may prove a serious problem.

The games will alternate during the week, the teams playing at Philadelphia to-morrow, on the Polo Grounds Tuesday, at Philadelphia again Wednesday and Friday and in New York Thursday and Saturday. In the event of a tie, the date and place will be selected by the national commission, which will have full charge. The games are scheduled to begin at 3:30 o'clock, but it is likely that the time will be changed to 3.

Already a stampede is being made for tickets for the games in New York, and a similar report comes from Philadelphia. Speculators are rampant, and while the prices are 50 cents, $1, $1.50 and $2, according to location, the probabilities are that large sums will be paid for the privilege of witnessing the contests. The batting order for the first game to-morrow will probably be as follows:

New York.	Philadelphia.
Bresnahan, c.	Hartsel, l. f.
Browne, r. f.	Lord, c. f.
Donlin, c. f.	Davis, 1b.
McGann, 1b.	L. Cross, 3b.
Mertes, l. f.	Seybold, r. f.
Dahlen, s. s.	Murphy, 2b.
Devlin, 3b.	M. Cross, s. s.
Strang, 2b.	Schreck, c.
Mathewson, p.	Plank, p.

Umpires—Messrs. O'Day and Sheridan.

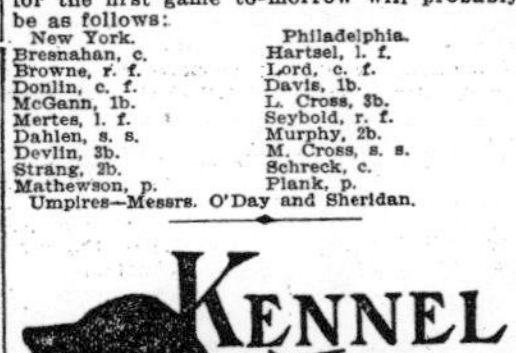

The New York, New Haven and Hartford Railroad Company has a rule that bird dogs shall not be transported on cars, so Connecticut hunters are to present a petition asking that during the open season the animals be transported on trolleys. The street cars in that state are mainly controlled by that corporation.

The American Kennel Club now has 99 clubs on its roll, the greatest number since it was organized. The treasury has a cash balance of more than $16,500. At its last meeting the following resolution was adopted:

Be it resolved, That a paid judge shall be defined as any one who shall have received or agrees to receive any monetary compensation for services as a judge at any dog show or field trial. Any judge receiving money for expenses shall be considered a paid judge; and be it further

Resolved, That the secretary or superintendent of all show-giving clubs shall, within ten days after the close of its show, forward to the secretary of the American Kennel Club a list of all judges who have or are to receive any monetary consideration for expenses or otherwise.

Dogs are to supersede chickens this year at the Utah state fair in Salt Lake City.

The New England Fox Hunting Club, organized to promote the native foxhound, will hold its first meet at Charlestown, N. H., November 6-11.

A certain new dog is loaded down with this name: "Roxane's Lady's Count Gladstone Jessie Rodfield's Galore."

A recent observer at the Westchester County fair show, writes:

Hitherto dog shows have been given that were not well conducted, and being judged by any who happened to award the prizes for cattle, hogs, potatoes and poultry, the awards were of no value, and the only advantage was that the country folk were kept somewhat in touch with the changes going on in kenneldom. They learned that the pug was no longer in favor with the better classes, what real Bostons were like, the difference between a Spitz and a Pomeranian, that a cocker spaniel was a small, black dog, and last year, when the judge turned out a beagle which had won under Mr. Rockefeller at Atlantic City, and awarded the prizes to cross-bred foxhounds, they were taught a lesson they might unlearn had they paid ten cents to visit the up-to-date show this year.

The Boston Terrier Club's specialty show will be held from November 15 to 18, and the exhibit of the Philadelphia Dog Show Association from November 28 to December 1.

A woman conducts at Pinner a week end fresh air resort for stylish canines whose delicate constitutions are not equal to the continuous strain of a London season.

The next tryout of the Connecticut Field Trial Club will be at Hampton, Conn., on October 31.

A meeting will be held November 1 at Robinson, Ill., to discuss uniformity in orders, a desirable change that is now being pushed by the American Field. The need of dog breakers adopting a uniform code of commands is to obvious to call for argument.

Dogs who travel alone on railroad trains no longer occasion surprise. The latest story is from Fairmont, Minn., where a black cocker spaniel named Rowdy frequently takes the Milwaukee Express and visits friends up and down the line for days at a time. There is a terrier that hops aboard the Long Island trains whenever he takes the notion and never has to show a pass or buy a ticket.

RECORDS OF THE TOURNAMENT BOWLERS.

Royal Arcanum Minor League.

Council.	W.	L.	T.P.	H.S.	Ave.
Alert	2	2	3,260	835	815
Algonquin	1	3	2,947	831	736
Amphion	1	3	3,029	773	754
Atlantic	2	2	3,306	874	826
Bedford	4	0	3,391	911	847
Bravura	4	0	3,517	934	879
Brevoort	1	1	1,511	759	755
Brooklyn	1	1	1,425	745	712
Burnside	0	2	1,435	746	717
Bushwick	0	4	3,026	813	756
Commonwealth	2	2	3,019	803	752
Dauntless	3	1	3,371	878	842
De Long	4	0	3,348	875	837
De Witt Clinton	1	3	2,775	737	693
East New York	1	1	1,648	841	824
Empire State	2	0	1,765	895	882
Fern	3	1	3,199	840	799
Fort Greene	3	1	3,340	861	835
Franklin	2	2	3,290	864	822
Fraternity	0	2	1,400	720	700
Fulton	3	1	3,262	930	815
General Putnam	0	4	2,918	770	729
General Slocum	3	1	2,922	817	730
Gilbert	1	3	3,028	826	757
Gramercy	2	0	1,541	775	770
Iolanthe	0	4	2,917	767	729
Lefferts	4	0	3,327	871	841
Long Island	4	0	3,215	908	803
Midwood	0	2	1,587	807	793
Osceola	0	4	2,641	715	660
Peerless	2	2	3,159	891	787
Philadelphos	0	2	1,696	856	848
Pro Patria	1	3	2,988	750	729
Ridgewood	1	3	2819	756	704
Undine	0	2	1,488	747	744
Williamsburg	1	1	1,656	838	828
Welcome	4	0	3,029	805	757

High team score—Bravura, 934.

INDIVIDUAL AVERAGES.

Name and council.	Games.	T.P.	H.S.	Ave.
Blue, Fulton	4	776	272	194
C. Fuchs, Philadelphos	2	386	204	193
A. Fuchs, Philadelphos	2	382	196	191
Moore, Fort Greene	4	761	232	190
Weingarth, Bedford	4	759	217	189
Kreyer, Empire State	2	379	197	189
Steininger, Dauntless	4	751	182	187
McNeil, Lefferts	4	747	203	186
Auer, Bravura	4	742	212	185
Redgate, Midwood	2	370	192	185
Hartcorn, Dauntless	4	731	206	182
A. Mowen, DeLong	2	364	188	182
Rathven, DeLong	4	720	191	180
L. Farr, Empire State	2	360	180	180
Hawkins, Franklin	4	717	188	179
Reibertanz, Welcome	4	716	193	179
Higgins, Empire State	2	358	199	179
Douglass, East New York	2	356	183	178
Graf, Williamsburg	2	356	189	178
Ruff, Fort Greene	4	711	205	177
Rose, DeLong	4	710	210	177
Hildebrand, Bravura	4	709	202	177

High individual score—Blue, Fulton, 272.

HIGHEST PERCENTAGE OF SPARES.

Name and council.	Games.	Sp's.	P.C
A. Mowen, DeLong	2	15	.750
Langfeld, East New York	2	13	.650
McNeil, Lefferts	4	23	.575
Wood, Alert	4	23	.575
Webber, Bravura	4	23	.575
Tooker, Fulton	4	23	.575

HIGHEST PERCENTAGE OF STRIKES.

Name of council.	Names.	St's.	PC.
Blue, Fulton	4	22	.550
Hartcorn, Dauntless	4	17	.425
Hildebrand, Bravura	4	16	.400
Reibertanz, Welcome	4	16	.400
Steininger, Dauntless	4	16	.400

LEAST PERCENTAGE OF BREAKS.

Name and council.	Games.	Br's.	P.C.
A. Mowen, DeLong	2	1	.050
McNeil, Lefferts	4	4	.100
A. Fuchs, Philadelphos	2	2	.100
Kreyer, Empire State	2	2	.100
Potts, Bravura	4	5	.125
Weingarth, Bedford	4	5	.125

Eastern League.

INDIVIDUAL.

Team.	W.	L.	T.P.	H.S.	Av.
New York	4	1	1,144	269	222
Philadelphia	3	2	917	200	183
Brooklyn	2	3	908	210	181
Newark	1	4	958	208	191

TWO MEN.

Team.	W.	L.	T.P.	H.S.	Av.
New York	2	1	1,101	372	367
Philadelphia	1	2	1,101	413	367
Brooklyn	2	1	1,133	438	377
Newark	1	2	1,128	409	376

THREE MEN.

Team.	W.	L.	T.P.	H.S.	Av.
New York	2	1	1,732	604	577
Philadelphia	2	1	1,691	611	563
Brooklyn	1	2	1,643	587	547
Newark	1	2	1,682	707	560

FIVE MEN.

Team.	W.	L.	T.P.	H.S.	Av.
Newark	3	0	2,852	1,010	950
Philadelphia	1	2	2,665	992	915
Brooklyn	1	2	2,665	927	888
New York	0	3	2,687	935	895

Universal National.

Team.	W.	L.	T.P.	H.S.	Ave.
Fern	4	0	3,484	894	871
Amphion	7	1	7,295	988	910
Borough Palace	3	1	3,536	964	884
Sylvan	4	2	5,539	977	923
Broadway	4	2	5,333	967	888
Circles	4	2	5,251	956	875
Invincible	3	3	5,197	935	866
Universal	2	2	3,666	965	916
Sioux	2	2	3,539	985	884
Palace	2	2	3,371	897	842
National	1	3	3,320	838	830
Varuna	0	2	1,692	860	846
Grand Central	0	4	3,497	861	874
Berkeley	0	4	3,149	825	787
Telephone	0	6	4,678	833	779

High team score—Amphion, 988.

INDIVIDUAL AVERAGES.

Name and team.	Games.	T.P.	H.S.	Ave.
Tuthill, Borough Palace	4	809	223	202
Nelson, Universal	4	788	231	197
Dickson, Sylvan	6	1,177	217	196
Staude, Amphion	8	1,567	214	195
Hulsberg, Invincible	6	1,170	222	195
Ketcham, Fern	4	779	200	194
Lake, Circles	9	1,160	226	193
Whitbeck, Berkeley	4	773	198	193
Brown, Sylvan	4	762	196	190
Smith, Sylvan	4	763	203	190

High individual score—Nelson, Universal, 231.

Greater New York.

Team.	W.	L.	T.P.	H.S.	Ave.
Williamsburg	3	0	2,775	931	925
Palace	5	1	5,275	910	879
Arlington	2	1	2,671	907	890
Universal	2	1	2,654	938	844
Metropolitan	2	1	2,564	888	854
Amphion	4	2	5076	883	849
Grand Central	1	2	2,620	902	873
Sylvan	1	2	2,599	888	866
Circle	1	2	2,549	892	849
Broadway	1	2	2,518	903	839
Invincible	2	4	5076	883	849
Pesby	0	3	2,556	894	852

INDIVIDUAL AVERAGES.

Name and team.	Games.	T.P.	H.S.	Ave.
Wichern, Arlington	3	610	226	203
Guggolz, Universal	3	588	214	196
Staude, Amphion	3	577	225	192
Totten, Grand Central	3	578	230	192
Dickson, Sylvan	3	575	213	191
Siemsen, Invincible	3	567	230	189
Williamson, Amphion	6	1138	202	188
Staude, Amphion	6	1104	224	186
Meincking, Arlington	3	558	213	186

High individual score—Totten, Grand Central, 230.

Grand Central.

Team.	W.	L.	T.P.	H.S.	Ave.
Sylvan	3	0	2,783	966	927
Metropolitan	2	0	1,997	1,054	998
Logan	2	0	1,953	1,055	976
Broadway	2	0	1,887	976	943
Amphion	2	0	17,17	890	858
Prosperity	3	1	3,643	992	910
Park Circle	1	1	1,667	888	833
Grand Central	2	2	2,792	1,034	948
Universal	2	2	3,619	938	904
Excelsior	2	2	3,558	968	889
Bay Ridge	1	3	3,513	902	878
Pesby	0	1	957	957	957
Palace	0	2	1,877	995	938
Nonpareil	0	4	3,451	904	862
Nassau	0	4	3,138	841	784

High team score—Logan, 1,055.

INDIVIDUAL AVERAGES.

Name and team.	Games.	T.P.	H.S.	Ave.
Tuthill, Logan	2	457	267	228
Sherwood, Metropolitan	2	457	244	228
Johnson Logan	2	435	246	217
Pringle, Broadway	2	430	225	215
DeMott, Grand Central	4	834	226	208
Guggolz, Universal	4	821	231	205
Cunningham, Palace	2	410	215	205
Helltas, Metropolitan	2	410	206	205

High individual score—Tuthill, Logan, 267.

Foresters League.

Court.	W.	L.	T.P.	H.S.	Ave.
Independent No. 1	2	0	1,931	1,001	965
Brooklyn	2	0	1,855	952	927
Utica	2	0	1,568	812	784
Fort Greene	1	1	1,736	911	868
Bushwick	1	1	1,732	877	866
Defender	1	1	1,592	897	796
Hopkinson	0	2	1,661	859	830
Atlantic	0	2	1,520	777	760
Acorn	0	2	1,450	756	725

High team score—Independent No. 1, 1,001.

INDIVIDUAL AVERAGES.

Name and court.	Games.	T.P.	H.S.	Ave.
G. Haller, Ind. No. 1	2	514	258	257
Jackson, Brooklyn	2	420	216	210
Baker, Bushwick	2	407	206	203
Woolney, Ind. No. 1	2	397	231	198
P. Haller, Ind. No. 1	2	380	191	190

High individual score—G. Haller, Independent No. 1, 258.

Gotham Palace.

Team.	W.	L.	T.P.	H.S.	Ave.
Sioux	6	0	5,468	959	911
Equal	3	0	2,491	846	880
Manhattan	5	1	5,086	890	847
East New York	4	2	5,280	942	880
Imperial	1	2	2,663	938	887
Atlantic	2	4	5,167	924	861
Exchange	0	3	2,397	817	799
Gotham Palace	0	6	5,121	911	853
Amphion	0	6	4,443	873	740

High team score—Sioux, 959.

INDIVIDUAL AVERAGES.

Name and team.	Games.	T.P.	H.S.	Ave.
Schraeter, Amphion	3	610	232	203
Hempstead, Sioux	6	1,181	231	196
Vascher, Imperial	3	588	225	196
Grau, East New York	6	1,174	255	195
Guggolz, Sioux	3	573	209	191
Doerzaph, Atlantic	6	1,128	207	188

High individual score—Grau, East New York, 255.

Germania.

Team.	W.	L.	T.P.	H.S.	Ave.
Pastime	4	0	3,319	864	829
Dobbins	2	0	1,572	804	786
Palace	2	2	3,321	877	830
Ivy Leaf	2	2	3,162	842	790
Corona	1	1	1,657	871	828
Bay Ridge	1	1	1,651	819	825
Lafayette	1	1	1,592	852	796
Acme	1	1	1,459	731	729
Corona	1	3	1,657	871	828
Borough Palace	0	2	1,627	818	813
Sunset	0	2	1,421	742	710

High team score—Palace, 877.

INDIVIDUAL AVERAGES.

Name and team.	Games.	T.P.	H.S.	Ave.
Knapp, Corona	2	388	197	194
Anderson, Pastime	4	739	224	184
Mitchell, Pastime	4	669	190	167

High individual score—Anderson, Pastime, 224.

Royal Arcanum Major League.

Council.	W.	L.	T.P.	H.S.	Ave.
Bushwick	2	0	1,765	886	882
Philadelphos	2	0	1,686	876	843
Gilbert	2	0	1,664	840	831
Gen. Slocum	2	0	1,610	816	805
Berkeley	1	1	1,739	877	869
De Long	1	1	1,632	861	816
Lefferts	1	1	1,541	772	770
Fort Green	1	1	1,521	777	760
Brooklyn	0	2	1,628	824	814
Welcome	0	2	1,622	828	811
Gramercy	0	2	1,503	776	751
Fulton	0	2	1,409	718	704

INDIVIDUAL AVERAGES.

Name and team.	Games.	T.P.	H.S.	Ave.
Ehler, Berkeley	2	399	213	199
Baker, Bushwick	2	387	194	193
Spencer, Fort Greene	2	384	199	192
White, Bushwick	2	380	211	190
Stoddard, Philadelphos	2	378	201	189
Bierds, Gilbert	2	366	187	183
Whitbeck, Berkeley	2	365	186	182
Halloran, Brooklyn	2	364	201	182
Kaiser, Bushwick	2	365	210	182
Blake, De Long	2	363	182	181

Custom House League.

Team.	W.	L.	T.P.	H.S.	Av.
H. B. and L.	3	0	2,553	803	784
Seventh Division	3	0	2,280	808	760
Second Division	3	0	2,272	791	757
Eleventh Division	3	0	2,179	884	726
Inspectors No. 2	2	1	2,515	879	838
R. F. Downing & Co.	2	1	2,388	830	796
Isaac Vought & Co.	2	1	2,282	808	760
Circle W.	2	1	2,278	789	759
Dinglestedt & Co.	1	2	2,299	788	766
Impost	1	2	2,158	768	719
Baese & Co.	1	2	2,113	720	707
Perry, Ryer & Co.	1	2	2,068	739	689
Appraisers No. 2	0	3	2,086	769	695
Thos. Meadows & Co.	0	3	2,047	726	682
Public stores	0	3	1,924	658	641
Naval office	0	3	1,639	595	546

High team score—Eleventh Division, 884.
High individual score—Kaley, Second Division, 234.

National Provident Union.

Council.	W.	L.	H.S.	Ave.
Concord No. 1	2	0	902	834
Washington No. 2	2	0	717	684
Logan No. 2	1	1	813	808
Unity No. 2	1	1	528	508
Washington No. 1	0	2	677	667
Garfield	0	2	370	365

High team score—Concord No. 1, 902.

INDIVIDUAL AVERAGES.

Name and team.	Ave.
Stone, Logan No. 2	195½
Schroeder, Concord No. 1	192½
Page, Concord No. 1	182½
Grinnelle, Logan No. 2	178
F. George, Concord No. 1	165½

Park Circle.

Team.	W.	L.	T.P.	H.S.	Ave
Park Circle	2	1	2,745	932	915
Amphion	2	1	2,597	874	865
Pesby	1	2	2,778	974	926
Grand Central	1	2	2,499	862	833

High team score—Pesby, 974.

INDIVIDUAL AVERAGES.

Name and team.	Games.	T.P	H.S.	Ave.
Erdman, Pesby	3	618	216	206
Spinelli, Pesby	3	590	204	196
Lake, Park Circle	3	571	193	190
Wendell, Park Circle	3	565	194	188
Hitchcock, Park Circle	3	560	202	186
Schroeder, Amphion	3	553	203	184
Conklin, Amphion	3	550	189	183
Volz, Park Circle	3	549	190	183
Smith, Pesby	3	551	202	183
Schroeder, Grand Central	3	525	189	175

High individual score—Erdman, Pesby, 216.

THE PHILADELPHIA ATHLETICS, AMERICAN LEAGUE CHAMPIONS

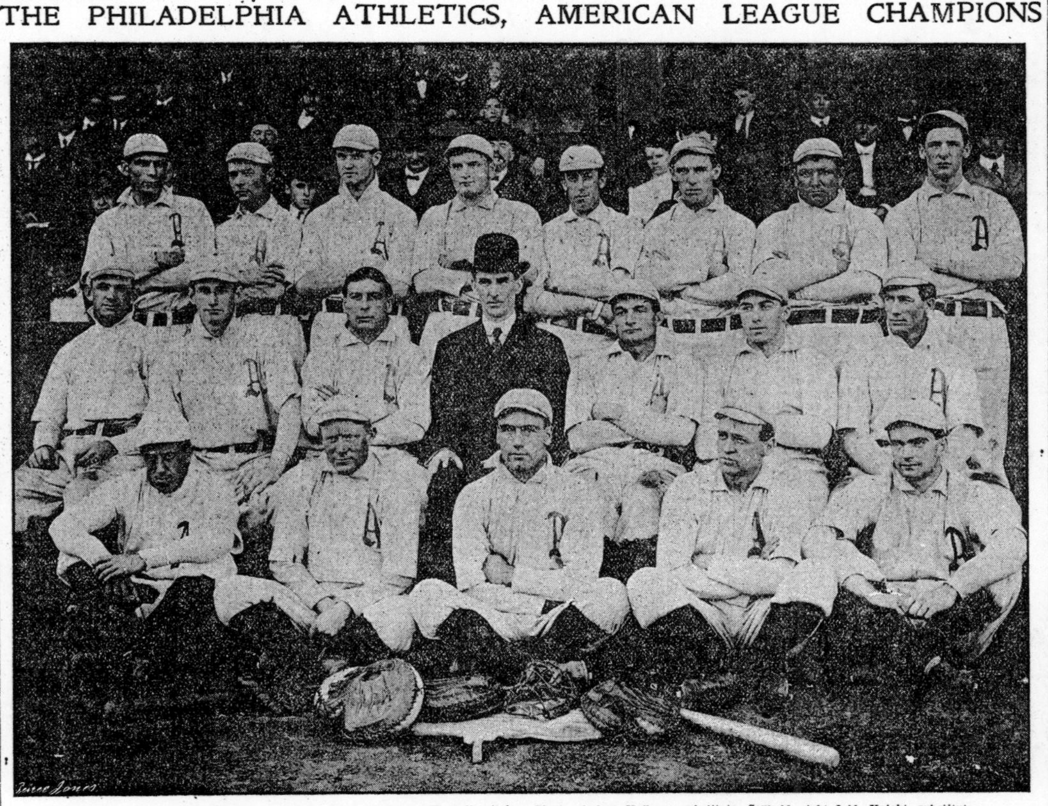

Top Row, from Left to Right—Bender, first base; Henley, pitcher; Waddell, pitcher; Plank, pitcher; Hoffman, substitute; Seybold, right field; Knight, substitute. Second Row—Murphy, second base; Coakley, pitcher; Shreck, catcher; Conny Mack, manager; Captain L. Cross, third base; Lord, center field; M. Cross, shortstop. Bottom Row—Myers, pitcher; Hartsel, left field; Powers, catcher; Barton, catcher; Dygert, pitcher.

Bowerman.

Jewelers League.

Team.	W.	L.	T.P.	H.S.	Ave.
Jos. Fahys & Co.	6	0	4,602	944	767
Cross & Beguelin	6	0	4,310	772	718
C. F. Wood & Co.	3	0	2,393	808	797
N. H. White & Co.	5	1	4,613	858	768
A. H. Smith & Co.	4	2	4,665	792	777
L. E. Waterman	4	2	4,457	794	744
Dennison Mfg. Co.	4	2	4,555	838	759
Avery & Brown & Co.	3	3	4,320	770	720
Tiffany & Co.	2	4	4,481	807	746
Udall & Ballou & Co.	2	4	41,23	750	687
Elgin National Watch Co	1	2	1,946	679	648
King Optical Co.	1	5	4,200	763	700
A. A. Webster & Co.	1	5	4,022	748	670
Aiken Lambert Co.	0	6	4,050	760	675
Gorham Mfg. Co.	0	6	3,853	690	642

High team score—Joseph Fahys & Co., 944.

INDIVIDUAL AVERAGES.

Name and team.	Games.	T.P.	H.S.	Ave.
Adams, Dennison Mfg. Co.	6	1,038	212	173
Roll, N. H. White & Co.	6	1,042	206	173
E. Wood, C. F. Wood & Co.	3	519	181	173
W. G. Wood, C. F. Wood & Co	3	510	191	170
Holker, King Opt. Co	5	858	192	171
Gruner, A. H. Smith & Co.	6	1,004	190	167
Haines, Jos. Fahys & Co.	5	838	224	167
Hutchinson, Smith & Co.	2	327	169	167
Ertel, Cross & Beguelin	6	977	201	162

High individual score—Haines, Jos. Fahys & Co., 224.

Broadway.

Team.	W.	L.	T.P.	H.S.	Ave.
East New York	2	0	1,786	898	893
Perry	2	0	1,746	930	878
Suydam	2	0	1,709	856	854
Broadway	3	1	3,563	939	890
Uncas	2	1	2,677	927	892
Grand Central	2	2	3,444	906	865
Palace	1	1	1,784	932	893
Buschwa	1	1	1,741	880	870
Gotham	1	1	1,681	850	840
Chauncey	1	1	1,675	881	837
Monarch	1	1	1,670	870	835
Clio	1	1	1,662	869	831
Universal	1	1	1,643	876	821
Melvina	1	1	1,585	826	792
Eldorado	1	1	1,578	797	789
Nonpareil	1	3	2,345	851	836
Linden Grove	1	3	3,212	811	803
Willoughby	1	3	3,120	874	780
Supreme	0	1	769	769	769
Adelphi	0	2	1,683	852	840

High team score—Broadway, 939.

INDIVIDUAL AVERAGES.

Name and team.	G.	T.P.	H.S.	Av.
Gates, Broadway	4	802	242	200
Kelly, Broadway	4	760	222	190
Gustafson, E. New York	2	401	222	200
Carey, Perry	2	377	209	188
Moore, East New York	2	374	192	187
Williamson, Perry	2	370	201	185
Hyet, Eldorado	2	368	192	184
Staude, Perry	2	363	211	181
Burchard, Willoughby	2	361	211	180
Gray, East New York	2	361	192	180

High individual score—Gates, Broadway, 242.

Ben Franklin League.

Team.	W.	L.	T.P.	H.S.	Ave.
Telegram	2	0	1,775	959	887
American Machinist	2	0	1,762	948	881
Journal	2	0	1,730	886	865
Mail	2	0	1,659	873	829
Kempster's	2	0	1,420	733	710
Globe	1	1	1,667	892	833
Evening Sun	1	1	1,622	833	811
Citizen	1	1	1,588	814	794
News	1	1	1,566	811	783
Trow	1	1	1,532	832	766
Redfield Bros.	1	1	1,529	773	764
Tribune	1	1	1,488	807	744
Greenwich Press	1	1	1,420	767	710
Burgoyne	0	2	1,617	809	808
Eagle	0	2	1,543	782	771
Standard Union	0	2	1,382	700	691
Kellogg	0	2	1,257	632	628
Cherouny	0	2	1,233	641	616

High team score—Telegram, 959.

INDIVIDUAL AVERAGES.

Name and team.	Games.	T.P.	H.S.	Ave.
Bearmore, Journal	2	417	222	208
Compton, Globe	2	413	225	206
Knecht, Telegram	2	404	214	202
Zehner, Evening Sun	2	399	218	199
Warren, Redfield Bros.	2	389	222	194
Tuttle, Trow	2	384	203	192
Langefeldt, Am. Machinist	2	366	187	183

High individual score—Compton, Globe, 225.

KNICKERBOCKER FIELD CLUB.

The Knickerbocker Field Club has completed preparations for an enjoyable bowling season. The committee having the matter in charge has made an effort to meet the demands of the large number of members who indulge in this sport. The formal opening will be next Tuesday evening. On October 20, and a later date, the women will be the guests of the club. On these two occasions there will be refreshments and suitable prizes.

A tournament has been arranged for five-men teams, on a handicap basis. As the contestants will number a large percentage of the club's membership this will be the event of the season. The contests will begin October 16 and will terminate in March.

The women have Friday evenings for their special meetings, and exceptionally good bowling is expected from their efforts to carry off the prizes each evening. There will be a series of individual contests on Monday evenings, in which the best bowlers of the club will take part. All of the four alleys will be open for the general use of the bowlers on Saturday evenings. Later in the season it is expected that arrangements will be made with many of the clubs in Brooklyn for a series of match games.

THE ONLY REPUBLICAN NEWSPAPER IN PHILADELPHIA

The Philadelphia Inquirer

VOL 153, NO 102 | TO DAY'S WEATHER—FAIR. | PHILADELPHIA, TUESDAY MORNING, OCTOBER 10, 1905 | ONE CENT

CHRISTY MATHEWSON'S CLEVER PITCHING GIVES NEW YORK THE FIRST GAME WITH ATHLETICS FOR WORLD'S CHAMPIONSHIP

THE COMMISSION LOOKING PLEASANT / MESSRS PULLIAM, HERRMANN & JOHNSON

MONTE CROSS

MATHEWSON

TALKING IT OVER - UMPIRES O'DAY & SHERIDAN, LAVE CROSS & MUGGSY McGRAW

ROOSEVELT WOULD OUST FOOTBALL'S BRUTAL FEATURES

President Holds Conference With College Authorities Looking to Modifications

BELIEVES REFORMS WAIT ON RADICAL CHANGES

Special to The Inquirer.

WASHINGTON, Oct. 9.—The modification of the rules of football in order to avoid the many brutal features which are now a part of the game was the subject of a long conference this afternoon between President Roosevelt, Walter Camp and Head Coach John Owsley, of Yale, Head Coach "Bill' Read and Dr. W. T. Nichols, of Harvard, and Head Coach Arthur Hildebrand and Professor John B. Fine, of Princeton.

These football authorities had been given a special invitation to lunch with the President this afternoon, and the conference followed, lasting more than an hour.

President in Deep Earnest

So far as could be learned to-night there was no definite action taken at the conference, but the President was very earnest in his desire to have as much as possible done to eliminate all unnecessary roughness.

He made many inquiries concerning the application of existing rules, and, it is said, declared his belief that there can be no satisfactory reform in the matter of roughness unless there is a radical change in the rules.

Open-Work Plays Favored

The president was particularly anxious that there be as little as possible of the heavy close formation plays, and was in favor of more open work.

The doing away with heavy mass plays, he believed, would avoid many of the serious injuries now incurred by members of the teams.

Another Conference Planned

The recent appearance of Theodore Roosevelt, Jr., as a candidate for the Harvard team, is believed to have stirred the President's interest in the game, and it is understood that there will be another similar conference here at the close of the season, or at least before the Football Rules Committee meets to consider changes in the rules for 1906.

All the conferees returned to their colleges to-night.

FRANCIS' LAWYER PUT UNDER ARREST WHILE COURT SITS

Counsel for Storey Cotton Man Accused of Approaching Witnesses

WOMAN SAID HE OFFERED POSITION

Charges of attempts to influence witnesses made against William J. Byron, a lawyer of Bradley Beach, N. J., furnished a climax to the first day of the trial of Stanley Francis yesterday.

Testimony was being given to show Francis' connection with the Storey Cotton Company, when Postoffice Inspectors Ryan and Cortelyou asked Byron to step out into the corridor of the United States District Court. He was then arrested, and at the conclusion of the court session was held under $1500 bail by Commissioner Craig.

Byron admitted that he had talked over the merits of the case with two of the government's most important witnesses, Gertrude Sundheim, of 3232 Monument street, who was head bookkeeper of the Storey Company, and Margaret Hope, of 1415 North Seventeenth street, who was one of the stenographers.

The two women declared that he had offered them fine positions if they would "eliminate local color from their testimony against Francis." The postal inspectors say they found a list of the names of five witnesses in the lawyer's pocket.

Says He Is Stone's Friend

Byron admitted that he was a friend of "Judge" Franklin Stone, alias Frank Marrin, and of Francis. Marrin, who fled this country at the time of the Storey Cotton crash, is anxious to return. Byron told the women witnesses that Marrin wanted to set up in business again.

It may be only a coincidence that Franklin Stone, alias Marrin, has engaged counsel recently and has begun a defense to a bankruptcy proceeding filed against him in this city, but the Postoffice Inspectors declare that Byron is only one of the factors in tampering with witnesses in the Francis case, and that an even more sensational arrest will be made in a few days.

Until the arrest of the Bradley Beach lawyer was made, the trial of Francis had been proceeding smoothly. Under the various aliases of Arthur S. Foster, Arthur S. Foster Francis and Stanley Francis, the defendant is charged with partial responsibility for the rise and fall of the Storey Cotton Company.

With Frank C. Marrin, alias "Judge" Stone, Sophia Beck, F. Ewart Storey, Walter B. Riggs, Thomas Quinlin, Patrick Kearns and A. O. Howard, he is alleged

Continued on Fifth Page— First Column

SERGEANT AT ROLL CALL LINES UP HIS POLICE

City Party Leaders Present When Orders Are Issued in the Tenderloin

"TURN IN FOR MAYOR OR LOSE YOUR JOBS"

"You must turn in for the City Party or lose your bread and butter."

This, in substance, was the order given over the desk at roll call last night to the policemen of the Tenth and Buttonwood streets station.

They were given by Acting Lieutenant Westcott in person, following several conferences with Superintendent of Police John Taylor. Moreover, two City Party leaders of the Fourteenth ward stood beside the sergeant's desk when he gave the orders.

The City Party can scarcely deny responsibility for this latest crack of the whip, for B. C. Garrison, City Party leader in the Fourteenth ward, is directly attached to the personal staff of Chairman Franklin S. Edmonds at City Party headquarters.

The Tenth and Buttonwood streets station covers two wards, the Thirteenth and Fourteenth. It is known as the Tenderloin station. For some reason only those policemen who live in the Fourteenth ward got their orders. The other half of the squad, those who live in Chairman Miles' ward, will probably get theirs to-night.

An Attempt at Secrecy

There was some attempt at secrecy about the matter. After the usual roll call was over Acting Lieutenant Westcott dismissed the Thirteenth ward end of the squad and asked the Fourteenth warders to remain. Then the doors were locked and the men brought up before the desk. With the City Party leaders by his side, nodding approval, Sergeant Westcott said:

"Men, we have always gone along with the Mayor and the administration. In the coming election it will be to your advantage to give your support to the City party ticket, because the Mayor and the Director are for the ticket. Remember you are working men, and unless you do it it means you bread and butter."

The Tenderloin is in a perturbed condition. Virtually every man in the district is under charges and can be discharged at a moment's notice. The way for this movement was paved during the Potter campaign against assessors. At that time Superintendent Taylor ordered almost every man in the district up for trial. The men were tried in turn and the verdicts handed in to Director Potter. Since then the men have never heard whether they were acquitted or convicted.

Continued on Third Page—First Column

MAN'S BONY NECK MAY AVERT ROPE

CHICAGO, Oct. 9.—Because of a peculiar freak of nature, Robert Gardiner, a prisoner in the county jail here, charged with the murder of Agnes Morrison, may escape the death penalty.

When he was arraigned in court to-day his attorney, William Buckner, startled the court by turning to Assistant State's Attorney Barbour and saying:

"This is a case where it won't do you any good to ask for the death penalty. They can't break this man's neck if they do try to hang him, and you may lose him altogether by hanging him and failing to execute the sentence in full."

It appears that the prisoner is suffering from ossification of the vertebrae and tissues of the neck.

According to Professor Steffenson, of Rush Medical College, only five cases similar have ever come to the notice of the medical profession.

Gardiner, who was formerly a cashier, carries his head tilted forward and slightly twisted to one side. He is unable to move his head or incline it except with great effort, and is hardly able to eat or speak, owing to the effect of the ossification on the sympathetic membranes of the throat and bronchial tubes.

Attorney Buckner declares that the hardening of bone and tissue has proceeded so far that it would be impossible to bring any strain upon the patient's neck that would be sufficiently severe to cause any discomfort other than a slight straining of the muscles.

HEARSE WAS STRUCK BY A TROLLEY CAR

Casket Not Damaged, But Funeral Was Delayed for About an Hour

A collision between a trolley car of the Philadelphia Rapid Transit Company and a hearse, in which the body of John Weimer, of 1038 Lawrence street, was being conveyed to Greenmount Cemetery yesterday afternoon, damaged the hearse and delayed the funeral for nearly an hour.

The hearse heading the funeral procession was moving up Fifth street, closely following a car of the Frankford division. The car was nearing the intersection of Germantown avenue when a patrol wagon, loaded with policemen, on their way to a fire at Second street and Montgomery avenue, came dashing down Montgomery avenue. The driver of the wagon shouted to the motorman to give way, and the motorman let his car go back.

The hearse, driven by Herman Pahler, of 312 Potts street, was following so close behind that it could not get out of the way.

ROUSING MEETING OF REPUBLICANS STARTS CAMPAIGN

Twentieth Ward's Loyal Citizens Greet Candidates at Girard Hall

DAVID H. LANE TELLS OF PARTY'S SUCCESSES

The opening gun of the Republican campaign was fired last night in the Twentieth ward with what was without doubt the largest gathering of voters that has ever taken place in the ward.

More than 4000 men crowded into Assembly Hall, Ninth street and Girard avenue, the largest hall in the ward. They filled the seats and aisles, overflowed the balconies and crowded the staircase.

It was a generous and spontaneous demonstration of the fealty of the voters of the Twentieth ward to the Republican party. They cheered the candidates of the Republican party who were there in person; they paid their tribute to the veteran leader, David H. Lane, with applause that seemed unceasing, and they greeted the remarks of the various speakers with an enthusiasm which was at once sincere and emphatic.

Every man in the crowded hall was there to pledge his support to the Republican ticket. Every voice that was raised in acclamation of the Republican principles enunciated came from a loyal Republican voter, for there had been no recourse to "fake reform" methods of packing the meeting with policemen and officeholders in plain clothes to cheer and applaud under orders from Gordon-Weaver officials at City Hall.

Flip-Flop Politics Flayed

The broadside of facts and argument which the Republican orators presented to the crowd carried conviction. The policy of "politics and procrastination," which the Gordon-Weaver outfit has been following for three months, was flayed in irrefutable logic. The Mayor's flip-flop actions on the grade crossings loan and other municipal matters was forcibly brought before the meeting.

George G. Pierie, president of the Twentieth Ward Republican Campaign Committee, presided. Upon the platform with him were the speakers, the Republican candidates, save William Emsley,

Continued on Second Page—Fifth Column

POLICE LIEUTENANT ORDERS MEN IN POLITICS

Even more brazen and high-handed than the methods of Superintendent of Police Taylor, in the Twenty-fourth ward, was the attempt of Acting Lieutenant Dever and most of the policemen of the Twentieth and Fitzwater streets station, last night, to coerce the officeholders in the Thirtieth ward into supporting the City Party-Democratic-Prohibition ticket.

"If you men cannot understand the orders of Mayor Weaver you must have thick skulls," shouted Acting Lieutenant Dever as he shook his fist in the faces of several officers who refused, as Republicans, to obey his mandate to turn out and work for the Gordon-Democratic-anti-Republican combination.

It was Dever who took the place of Lieutenant Steck when the latter was transferred recently to the Twentieth and Federal streets police station to take the place there of Lieutenant Black, who, after years of faithful service in the Police Department, was forced by Director of Public Safety Potter to resign.

Station Political Stronghold

Dever has transformed the station house since Potter made him acting lieutenant there into a Gordon-City Party stronghold and has sent policemen out from it to ring doorbells throughout the Thirtieth ward in the Gordon-City Party interests.

But although Dever has not hesitated to use the police under him to try to get votes for the Gordon-Democratic-Anti-Republican combination, it was not until last night that he had the effrontery, no doubt the result of assurances of support from Director Potter, to threaten city employes in the Thirtieth ward with Mayor Weaver's displeasure if they did not at once abandon the standard of the Republican party and turn in for the Gordon-Democratic-City Party-Anti-Republican outfit.

Dever first tried to fool the officeholders of the Thirtieth ward by issuing an invitation to attend a meeting at Croasdale's Hall, Twenty-second and Fitzwater streets, to "consider the best interests of the residents of the ward." A number of office-holders of the ward saw through Dever's game and failed to accept his invitation, whereupon Dever took forty-three of his men, thereby leaving but twenty-two to police the large district of which Director Potter has given him charge, and marched from the station house at Twentieth and Fitzwater streets to Croasdale's Hall, but two blocks distant. Leaving half the policemen at the hall, doubtless to see that the ctiy employes present did not return home, Dever issued forth and rounded up

Continued on Third Page—Fifth Column

Grand Crowd of 20,000 Witnesses Opening Battle Between Pennant Winners of Both Leagues

Connie Mack's Victorious Elephants Fail to Hit the Ball, While Giants Are Cheered by Thousands of Supporters

THE SCORE:

	Runs	Hits	Errors		Runs	Hits	Errors
New York	3	10	1	Athletics	0	4	0

Batteries—For New York, Mathewson, pitcher; Bresnahan, catcher. For Athletics, Plank, pitcher; Schreckengost, catcher.

	Won	Lost	P.C.		Won	Lost	P.C.
New York	1	0	1.000	Athletics	0	1	.000

Attendance 20,000

FIGHTING gamely till the sad finale to connect with Christy Mathewson's phenomenal twirling, those Athletics, champions of the American League, went down to defeat before the New York Giants, champions of the National League, yesterday at Columbia Park to the tune of 3 to 0 in the first of the world's championship series.

It was unquestionably the pitching of the Giants' premier boxman, backed up by great team work, that kept the White Elephants guessing and netted them nothing better than nine goose eggs.

Mathewson had been heralded as the chief one the Athletics might have to dread He had been touted as being in splendid form, and his deceptive drop ball yesterday did much to justify the claims of his backers. With the advantage of a fast and sure support, the Giants' star twirler proved a puzzle to those Athletics, and in their inability to hit him lies the story of the game. They got away with but four hits, while the Giants netted ten from Eddie Plank.

Nevertheless, Plank pitched good ball, and he fooled the Giants' best batsmen more than once. Altogether it was a great game, hotly contested from start to finish, and the grand crowd of Philadelphia and New York fans who witnessed it got the full worth of the championship prices that prevailed.

Crowd Was a Wonder

The crowd was a record-breaker in size and enthusiasm, and the management of Columbia Park, after deciding to limit the number of admissions, was forced to turn thousands away. Hundreds saw the game from the windows and roofs of houses overlooking the diamond, while others clung to telegraph poles or stood upon the tops of wagons ranged in long lines outside the grounds.

In a city already dippy for a month over base ball it was not surprising to find thousands of tongues wagging long before the game began as to the respective chances of the rival champions to win the series. In hotel lobbies and cafes, on the street and in trolley cars, almost everywhere, in fact, every phase of the championship series furnished food for discussion. The names of "Lave," "Socks," "Ossie," "Topsy," "Rube," "Eddie," "Danny" were in the mouths of the local fans, while the aggregation from Gotham rooted for Christy Mathewson. White Elephant rooters met backers of the Giants in friendly clashes which were often followed by bets being made in happy-go-lucky fashion. Everybody seemed to be talking base ball. Even the political situation took a back seat, and from the crowds that lingered in front of the bulletin boards one might have thought that nothing less than a Presidential election was on.

Giants Strike the Town

The fun really started when the Giants and a large following of New York rooters came to town in the morning. The aggregation had the Catholic Protectory Band, composed of boys with fifty-six pieces, with it and there was plenty of noise as the invaders proceeded to the Continental Hotel. There a big crowd of New York fans was awaiting the arrival of the National League champions, who received a great ovation. The crowd swarmed around the Giants and, sweeping them off their feet as they tumbled out of barouches and automobiles, literally carried them into the hotel. To impress local fans the New York bunch brought "Jim" Corbett, the pugilist-actor; Louis Mann, the comedian, and other stellar lights of Broadway with them. Many well-known New York sporting men were in the delegation and they began to wave thick wads of green stuff as soon as they struck town. Odds were 10 to 9 and 9 to 8 in New York's favor as a rule, although there was much even money in sight. Backers of the White Elephants were not at all unwilling to take a shy at New York money and betting became lively and frequent. More money probably

Continued on Tenth Page—Third Column

THE WEATHER

Forecasts from Washington—Delaware, New Jersey, Eastern Pennsylvania—Fair Tuesday, Wednesday, rain and colder; light to fresh south winds becoming variable.

Eastern New York—Fair Tuesday, Wednesday, rain and colder, fresh northeast to southeast winds becoming variable.

District of Columbia, Maryland—Fair Tuesday, Wednesday, rain and colder, light to fresh variable winds.

Western Pennsylvania—Partly cloudy Tuesday, rain and colder at night, and Wednesday, fresh east winds, becoming northwest by Wednesday and increasing.

New York Herald Forecast: In the Middle States and New England to-day, fair to partly overcast weather will prevail, with slight temperature changes, and light to fresh variable winds, mostly from southwesterly to southeasterly. On Wednesday, partly cloudy to overcast weather and nearly stationary temperature will prevail, with fresh easterly winds, followed in this section by rain; and on Thursday, overcast, slightly cooler weather, with occasional rain in the eastern districts.

European steamers now sailing will have mostly fair to partly overcast and hazy weather, with light and moderate variable winds, to the Banks.

For Detailed Weather Report See Second Page—Eighth Column

NIGHT EDITION

The Evening Sun.

NIGHT EDITION

TEMPERATURE.
Min., 51. Max., 70

Fair and slightly warmer to-night and to-morrow. Light to fresh S. winds.

VOL. XIX. NO. 182. NEW YORK, SATURDAY, OCTOBER 14, 1905—*Copyright, 1905, by The Sun Printing and Publishing Association.* PRICE ONE CEN

HEMERY WINS BIG AUTO RACE, DOING 283 MILES IN 276 MINUTES

A Close Finish with Heath, Who Is Only 3 Minutes Behind,

TRACY WAS THIRD

American Drives a Splendid Race.

LANCIA IN FOURTH

The Italian Had Done Magnificently When Christie Smashed Into Him.

THE FINISH.

Driver.	*Time.*	*Elapsed Time. H.M.S.*
HEMERY	10:52:08	4:36:08
HEATH	10:52:40	4:39:40
TRACY	11:04:26	4:58:26
LANCIA	11:03:31	5:00:31

MINEOLA, L. I., Oct. 14.—Hemery, of the French team, driving an 80 horse-power Darracq, won the second international race for the Vanderbilt Cup on Long Island to-day, covering the distance of 283 miles in the remarkably fast time of 4 hours 36 minutes and 8 seconds. Heath, in a 120 horse-power Panhard, was close behind him, making the distance in 4 hours 39 minutes and 40 seconds. Tracy was third in 4 hours 58 minutes and 20 seconds. Lancia was fourth in 5 hours and 31 seconds. As soon as Lancia and Tracy had finished the race was stopped. The average was about sixty-two miles an hour.

America has never seen such an automobile race as this. There were no controls, nineteen cars started and records for the course evaporated in the first round. No one was killed, which seemed remarkable in face of the fast time made. There were some mishaps, but actually no one was seriously hurt.

Nothing like to-day's crowd has ever witnessed an event of this kind in America. Society folks and others, from layer after layer of humanity to the lowest, lined deep along the roads, and as a final touch the weather might have been answer to the prayers of the most particular automobilist of them all. They have come from all over the world to meet on Long Island in the informal camaraderie of the motor car. Every seat in the comparatively small grand stand had been bespoken for days, and thousands of the overflow stretched, along the sides of the course around its entire length. To the east of the grand stand the spectators were packed fifty to sixty thick. Not only is it remarkable that some of the drivers or mechanics were not killed, but it is equally worthy of comment that none of the spectators suffered death. From midnight until the start of the race high-powered touring cars were dashing along all of the roads hereabouts, often at a speed exceeding the legal limit. These roads were thronged with pedestrians, and horses and carriages as well, but a kind providence watched over everything connected with the contest and saw it through smilingly.

FOXHALL KEENE'S ESCAPE.

Foxhall Keene, of the German team, in his 120 horse-power Mercedes, had perhaps the narrowest escape of all. At the curve, while trying to pass another car, he tore a great chunk of wood out of a telegraph pole and lost one of his tires. Both he and his mechanic were dashed from the car, the mechanic falling underneath. Mr. Keene was bruised and went to the grand stand, where he watched the completion of the race. He was on the sixth lap at the time and was driving well enough to justify many in picking him for a place. Lytle, in the 90 horse-power Pope-Toledo, lost his mechanic while going at a high rate of speed. The man was picked up dazed and bruised, but apparently whole.

THE LANCIA-CHRISTIE COLLISION.

The real tragedy of the race was the collision between Lancia's 120 horse-power Fiat and the 60 horse-power Christie. The Italian had won the sympathies of the crowd by his confident, dashing manner of driving, which clipped off mile after mile at a rate better than a mile a minute for seven laps, which left him way in the lead of Heath, Szisz and Hemery, his nearest competitors. He had stopped at the gasoline station at Lakeville and was just pulling out when Christie in his car crashed into him, damaging his car so that he was delayed for more than forty-five minutes. The Christie car did not finish in the elimination trials, but for some reason was chosen by the judges in place of one of the cars which did finish. To-day it had made only three rounds when it collided with Lancia, breaking two of its own wheels. Lancia worked like a slave, and laughing at those who had said his car was hurt beyond repair got back into the race and drove the last two rounds like a demon possessed.

TRACY'S SHOWING.

Tracy's driving was cautious and of the sort that shows results. When it was seen that he had won third place he was greatly cheered. The other American entries did not do so well, Christie making but three laps, Lytle four, Dingley four and White six. The driving of Szisz was reckless and fascinating to watch. Heath drove the same heady race which landed him in first place last year.

The policing of the course was excellent, and the absence of controls made it a snappy race. From start to finish everything went on the minute, and with the exception of some confusion at the grand stand before the start there was nothing to criticize and much to commend.

As soon as Tracy had finished the homeward marches began. All that had motor cars started cityward with them and the less fortunate walked to the nearest railroad stations. Mineola was the center, and many special trains had hard work getting the thousands to New York.

The winner's time was 4 hours, 36 minutes, 8 seconds. In other words he made the 283 miles in 276 minutes. This is an average of 61½ miles an hour, or at the rate of a mile in about 58 3-5 seconds.

The feature of the race up to 10 o'clock was the wonderful driving of Lancia, the Italian, in his Fiat.

He finished just half the race in 2 hours 2 minutes 5 seconds; in other words, he had traveled 142 miles in 122 minutes, an average of 69.8 miles an hour, or at a rate of one mile in 51½ seconds. Such driving was never before seen in America. He did the next round, the sixth, in 24 minutes 45 seconds.

When Heath won last year he did the 302 miles of that race in 326 minutes net time, with allowances deducted. His actual time was 6 hours 56 minutes 45 seconds.

In the preliminaries a few weeks ago Dingley did 113 miles in 121 minutes.

HOW THE RACE WAS RUN

Story in Detail of the 283-Mile Struggle.

MINEOLA, L. I., Oct. 14.—The second international race for the William K. Vanderbilt cup was run to-day over the twenty-eight mile course on Long Island before a crowd estimated to be the largest which has ever seen a similar contest in this country.

On account of its size and its curiosity the throng of spectators was handled with difficulty. Confusion reigned along the course from end to end during the two or three hours preceding the race. A hopeless tangle of cars, wagons and men and women filled the spaces between the stands at the start and finish line. There were many minor collisions and accidents in the dark of the early morning. There were 300 deputy sheriffs stationed along the course and thirty special deputies, sworn in from the Court of General Sessions, were placed at the stands. The officers and deputies had a herculean task before them when they started to clear the course.

It was semi-officially announced that the start would be made at 6:30 o'clock, but at the last minute it was decided to get the men off at 6 o'clock promptly.

THE START.

Jenatzy, of the German team, came to the line on time in his 120 horse-power Mercedes and made a good start amid a shout. Duray, in his 130 horse-power De Dietrich, was off a minute later. Dingley, of the American team, in his 60 horse-power Pope-Toledo, made a fast start, while the stands gave him a rousing cheer. Lancia, of the Italian team, in his 120 horse-power Fiat, and one of the favorites, made the best start so far, getting away with an air of confidence which won him the sympathy of the crowd.

Foxhall Keene, when he got away prettily in his Mercedes, received an ovation from the crowd. Wagner, of the French team, left at 6:05 o'clock in his 80 horse-power Darracq. Tracy, in his 90 horse-power Locomobile, was off next, with a rousing Godspeed. Nazzari, of the Italian team in his 120 horse-power Fiat, followed. Warden, of the German team, in his 120 horse-power Mercedes, the one doubtful starter, made a confident start. Szisz, in his 90 horse-power Renault, started nicely, gathering speed as he went down the hill.

BREESE'S CHRISTIE MISSING.

Car 12 was the next to the line. Nothing had been heard of No. 11, J. L. Breese's Christie. Cedrino, in his 90 horse-power Fiat, made an easy go-off. Word came that Jenatzy had passed the ten-mile post in the remarkable time of 6.08 3-5. Campbell, whose 120 horse-power Mercedes wore an "X" instead of the number "13," went away well. When Heath, the winner of last year's race, came up in his 120 horse-power Panhard, he got a cheer. Leaving, he raised his hat to the stand.

Lytle in the 90 horse-power Pope-Toledo got away with a cheer.

Word came that Jenatzy had passed the fifteen mile point at 6:12 o'clock. Chevrolet of the Italian team, in his 120 horse-power Fiat, left well. Hemery, of the French team, in his 80 horse-power Darracq, got off like a cyclone. White, of the American team, in his peculiar appearing White steamer, started with a big rush amid the laughter of the stand. Sartori, of the Italian team, in A. G. Vanderbilt's 90 horse-power Fiat, the last starter, went away with a cheer.

Reports from Wilton avenue at this time had Lancia ahead of Duray and Dingley. There were eighteen starters. Christie had been having trouble with his car and decided at the last moment not to compete. Word from Lancia had him making remarkable time over the course.

LANCIA DOES THE FIRST 28 MILES IN 23 MINUTES, 49 SECONDS.

The shout, "Car coming!" was heard for the first time during the race at 6:24 o'clock, and word passed along that Jenatzy was justifying his reputation by maintaining a remarkable speed on the first lap. Officers ran up and down waving flags and shouting to the crowd to get back. Jenatzy was no sooner seen than he was gone. His speed was fifty-five as he dropped between the stands. His official time for the first lap was 6:24:52.

Lancia was right behind him, having passed Duray and Dingley. His time was 6:26:49. Elapsed time, 23 minutes 49 seconds, which counted him a minute ahead of Jenatzy.

Duray followed at 6:27:26, elapsed time 26:20. Wagner in his Darracq got through at 6:29:50, elapsed time 24:50. Foxhall Keene went through the first lap at 6:31:21, elapsed time 27:21; he got a cheer. Dingley came through at 6:31:44, elapsed time 29:44. He was not going as well as the others. Nazzari floated past at 6:32:28, elapsed time 25:28.

Szisz, going like a comet, went by, having made the circuit in 24:55. Tracy finished the first lap in 28:14. Warden did it in 27:41. Cedrino got around in 25:36. Keene's time was 27:21. Christie left about 6:35, with a handicap of 28:25.

WHITE STEAMER STOPPED.

The White steamer had stopped at Bull's Head.

Campbell, in his Mercedes, went by at 6:40:21, elapsed time 28:21. Heath went by like a lightning flash at 6:41:02, elapsed time 28:02.

Up to this time there was no explanation of the delay to the Christie car. Lytle got past at 6:43:15, elapsed time 29:15. Chevrolet went by at 6:43:42, elapsed time 28:42. Hemery went through at 6:44:23, elapsed time 28:23. Sartori, the last to start, was going well. He completed the first lap at 6:45:04, elapsed time 27:41.

At 6:49 word came that Lancia had passed Hyde Park. Jenatzy completed the second lap at 6:49:25, elapsed time 49:25. Lancia was right behind him. Both were driving a reckless race.

Lancia's right hand left his wheel as he

(Continued on Second Page.)

TIME MADE BY THE AUTO RACERS AT EACH ROUND.

Driver.	*Start.*	*1st.*	*2d.*	*3d.*	*4th.*	*5th.*	*6th.*	*7th.*	*8th.*	*9th.*	*10th.*
JENATZY (1)	6:00	24:52	49:25	1:22:06	....	....	....	....	....	....	....
DURAY (2)	6:01	26:26	56:17	1:21:57	2:07:43	2:33:12	2:50:27	3:25:55	....	....	....
DINGLEY (3)	6:02	29:44	1:00:55	3:42:33	4:21:35	4:57:20	....	....	....	....	....
LANCIA (4)	6:03	23:49	47:20	1:10:45	1:34:03	2:02:05	2:25:50	2:49:52	4:01:09	4:25:09	5:00:31
KEENE (5)	6:04	27:21	54:24 2-5	1:23:05	1:54:10	2:20:33	....	....	....	....	....
WAGNER (6)	6:05	24:56	49:49	1:30:38	....	....	....	....	....	....	....
TRACY (7)	6:06	25:28	56:51	1:25:27	1:57:38	2:25:18	2:58:11	3:26:04	3:56:55	4:28:53	4:58:20
NAZZARI (8)	6:07	25:28	1:18:42	1:44:17	2:08:52	2:37:56	3:04:03	3:28:40	3:53:29	....	....
WARDEN (9)	6:08	27:41	55:07	1:22:30	1:49:45	2:25:46	3:05:19	4:11:18	4:51:23	....	....
SZISZ (10)	6:09	24:55	49:24 4-5	1:14:45	1:53:27	2:22:45	2:56:09	3:24:46	3:53:41	4:37:07	....
CHRISTIE (11)	6:10	58:08	1:28:29	2:44:13	....	....	....	....	....	....	....
CEDRINO (12)	6:11	25:36	53:54	....	....	....	....	....	....	....	....
CAMPBELL (13)	6:12	28:21	....	....	....	....	....	....	....	....	....
HEATH (14)	6:13	28:02	55:03	1:21:56	1:48:51	2:15:21	2:41:54	3:10:59	3:44:31	4:11:41	4:39:40
LYTLE (15)	6:14	29:15	2:00:17	2:35:49	3:15:52	....	....	....	....	....	....
CHEVROLET (16)	6:15	28:42	56:57	1:28:32	2:07:25	2:38:41	3:09:25	....	....	....	....
BASIL (17)	(Non-starter.)										
HEMERY (18)	6:16	28:23	54:24	1:20:20	1:58:58	2:23:27	2:48:55	3:14:20	3:39:15	4:08:33	4:36:08
WHITE (19)	6:17	51:31	1:36:23	2:18:54	3:09:14	....	....	....	....	....	....
SARTORI (20)	6:18	27:41	55:11	1:22:20	1:40:43	2:10:06	3:02:38	3:36:27	4:24:10	....	....

HYLAS WINS THE BIG STEEPLECHASE

White Plains Handicap Goes to Belmont Filly Tiptoe.

BELMONT PARK, Oct. 14.—One of the largest racing crowds of the season gathered at Belmont Park to-day for the closing session at the new course. The grand stand held more persons than on any previous day of the fall meeting, more than 30,000 persons being in the various enclosures at race time. The auto parking space was neraly swamped with machines coming from the Vanderbilt Cup race. It was a sleepy looking crowd who climbed out of the big touring cars, most of them having been up all night.

The program was first-class in every respect, but the Champion Steeplechase probably created the most interest. A fine field of jumpers had entered for the $10,000 event, which was at three and a half miles. The White Plains Handicap, for juveniles, had a big field of fine runners, and the Belmont Park Autumn Weight-for-Age, although only three starters were named, was well balanced and promised a close contest.

The scratches were: First race, Speedsmith, Midas, Commune and Flim Flam; second race, Pagan Bey; third race, King's Daughter, Klingsor and Battleaxe; sixth race, Louis H.

John A. Drake bought Penrhyn from H. M. Ziegler this morning, started him in the opening race, for 2-year-olds, and won him out very easily. Although the Planudes colt had been running in stake company, so much money was bet on Arklirta that he went to the post favorite at 9 to 5, with Penrhyn at 3s, backed from 9 to 2. It was only a gallop for Penrhyn. Sperling got him off in front and he stayed there, winning by five lengths. Arklirta was always in second place and easily beat Lancastrian which finished third.

The Champion Steeplechase was a beautiful exhibition of jumping, and the big crowd was kept in a frenzy of enthusiasm from start to finish. It resulted in a driving victory for Thomas Hitchcock's Hylas by a length and a half, from Ben Crockett with Jimmy Lane a fair third. Grandpa fell over the second jump and Coligny went down at the same obstacle the next time around.

Gansevoort led for a mile, only to tire, and then Ben Crockett took up the burden of leadership. He held on like a good one to the end of three miles and a quarter, where Hylas, handled in masterly fashion by Ray, got up and beat him out. Jimmy Lane was always well up. A remarkable feature in connection with the race was that Grandpa, although he fell before a quarter had been run, scrambled to his feet, and thereafter took jump for jump with the other horses, keeping inside the flags on every turn. He actually finished in third place and trotted back to the scales as if highly pleased at his performance. The race was easily the best cross-country of the year.

Third Race—White Plains Handicap; for 2-year-olds; $3,000 added; six furlongs.

Tiptoe won.

Snow was second.

Bridgeman was third.

August Belmont's entrants, Tiptoe and Bridgeman, ran first and third in the White Plains Handicap, Security, the heavily played favorite, and Bromdale Nymph, the second choice finishing out of the money. Security led in the stretch when he fell back.

IT WAS KING EDWARD.

He's Responsible for That Offer of Aid to France.

COLOGNE, Oct. 14.—The Frankfort *General Anzeiger* gives prominence to an interview with some one whom it calls "an exceptionally well-informed Britisher," who declares that Jean Jaurès, editor of the *Humanité*, is wrong on one point. It was not the British Government, but King Edward himself, who offered assistance to Delcassé.

When King Edward passed through Paris in April, he, through a confidential adviser, opened to Foreign Minister Delcassé the prospect of military aid. Consequently, Lord Lansdowne's declaration to the German Ambassador that the British Government had not offered France any help is literally correct.

DURHAM MUST APPEAR.

Dodges Conspiracy Hearing, but Has to Give Bail.

PHILADELPHIA, Oct. 14.—So that Israel W. Durham would not have to appear as a witness at the smallpox hospital conspiracy hearing before Magistrate Eisenbrown, at the Central Police station this afternoon, A. S. L. Shields, as attorney for the defendants, wanted a further hearing and each man was held in $5,000 bail for court.

Mr. Durham had failed to appear in answer to a subpœna and detectives were sent out to look for him. They found him at the office of Senator Penrose with State Senator James P. McNichol, who had also been supbœnaed. A conference was held and it was decided that the hearing should be discontinued and the defendants enter bail.

SUMMARIES OF BELMONT PARK RACES.

PENRHYN FIRST, ARKLIRTA SECOND.

FIRST RACE—For 2-year-olds, non-winners of two races; $900 added; six furlongs.

Horse.	*Wt.*	*St.*	¼	⅜	½	¾	*Fin.*	*Jockey.*	Betting *Op.*	*Cl.*	*Pl.*	*3d.*
Penrhyn	109	7	1^{1}	1^{4}	1^{2}	1^{4}	1^{11}	Sperling	7-2	3	6-5	7-10
Arklirta	109	2	2^{1}	$2^{1½}$	2^{2}	$2^{1½}$	2^{8}	Shaw	2	9-5	7-10	1-3
Lancastrian	109	3	$3^{½}$	$3^{½}$	3^{1}	$3^{½}$	3^{3}	Burns	8	8	3	3-5
Waterwing	109	5	7	7	7	5^{h}	$4^{1½}$	J. Jones	7	8	3	9-5
Brother Frank	109	4	5	$5^{½}$	4^{h}	4^{h}	5^{h}	Wiley	5	15	6	3
Pantoufle	106	1	6	8	8	$6^{½}$	6^{h}	Knapp	6	7	5-2	6-5
Old Guard	109	10	10	9	9	8	7^{h}	Heigesen	40	100	30	15
Tipping	99	11	11	11	11	11	8^{4}	Miller	12	20	8	4
Benevolent	109	9	8	6^{h}	6^{1}	7	9^{4}	O'Neil	10	15	5	5-2
Supreme	102	6	9	10	10	10	10	Dickson	50	60	20	12
Deviltree	106	8	$4^{½}$	4^{h}	5^{1}	9	11	Romanelli	10	20	8	4

Start good. Won easily. Time, 1:12 3-5. Winner, b. c., by Plaudes—Laurel. Owner, H. M. Ziegler.

HYLAS FIRST, BEN CROCKET SECOND.

SECOND RACE—The Seventh Champion Steeplechase; for 4-year-olds and upward $9,000 added; the National Steeplechase and Hunt Association to present to winner plate to the value of $500; about three miles and a half.

Horse.	*Wt.*	*St.*	1	2	2½	3	*Fin.*	*Jockey.*	Betting *Op.*	*Cl.*	*Pl.*	*3d.*
Hylas	151	2	5^{5}	4^{3}	2^{5}	1^{3}	$1^{1½}$	Ray	8-5	8-5	7-10	2-5
Ben Crocket	144	4	3^{15}	1^{1}	$1^{1½}$	2^{20}	2^{30}	Gallagher	4	5	2	4-5
Jimmy Lane	167	6	4^{2}	5^{5}	3^{10}	3^{30}	3^{100}	Owens	7-2	5	8-5	4-5
Gansevoort	152	3	1^{3}	2^{8}	4^{15}	4^{15}	4^{20}	Stone	7	10	3	8-5
Woolgatherer	133	3	5	6	6	5	5	E. Kelly	4	5	2	4-5
Grandpa	170	7	Fell					E. Heider	10	12	4	2
Coligny	167	1	3^{1}	$3^{½}$	Fell.			J. O'Brien	3-5	7-2	6-5	2-5

Start good. Won easily. Time, 6:57. Winner, b. g. by Meddler—Forget. Owner, T. Hitchcock, Jr.

GIANTS WIN THE SERIES

Fifth Game Decides World's Baseball Championship.

STAR PITCHERS' BATTLE

Mathewson and Bender, the Redskin, Do the Twirling.

POLO GROUNDS JAMMED

Crowd in Attendance Estimated at Nearly 30,000

SCORE BY INNINGS.

Athletics.. 0 0 0 0 0 0 0 0 0—0
New York. 0 0 0 0 1 0 0 1 x—2

POLO GROUNDS, Oct. 14.—A record breaking crowd filled the Polo Grounds until its very seams threatened to give way this afternoon to see the Athletics and Giants fight out the fifth game of the series for the championship of the world.

The Giants had already won three of the four games necessary to decide the series and the crowd expected to see the locals finish their post-season work to-day.

Half an hour before the game was called it was impossible to find even standing room in the stands, and there was an overflow crowd of 5,000 to 10,000 persons back of the outfields. On this account the ground rule that a hit into the crowd should be good for only two bases was again put in force.

Mathewson, the king of them all, and Bender, the Giants' only conqueror, were chosen to do the pitching, and the greatest of twirling battles was expected.

After a short but very snappy field practise, each good play receiving the crowd's loudest roar, Umpire Sheridan called the game.

The attendance was estimated at nearly 30,000.

NEW YORK.	PHILADELPHIA.
Bresnahan, c.	Hartsel, l. f.
Browne, r. f.	Lord, c. f.
Donlin, c. f.	Davis, 1 b.
McGann, 1 b.	L. Cross, 3 b.
Mertes, l. f.	Seybold, r. f.
Dahlen, ss.	Murphy, 2 b.
Devlin, 3 b.	M. Cross, s. s.
Gilbert, 2 b.	Powers, c.
Mathewson, p.	Bender, p.

Umpires—Sheridan and O'Day.

THE GAME.

FIRST INNING—The first ball pitched by Mathewson was a ball. The second Hartsel hit for a hard liner to short. Dahlen jumped for it but could not hold it, and it went for a hit. Lord's attempt to bunt was a foul, which Bresnahan caught. Davis forced Hartsel at second on a grounder to Devlin. Gilbert got Lave Cross's slow grounder to McGann in time to make three out. No runs.

Bresnahan sent a grounder to Monte Cross, whose quick throw to first caught him by inches. This was the first time in the series that Bresnahan had not reached first on his first time at bat. Monte Cross also threw Browne out at first. Bender threw out Donlin's bunt. No runs.

SECOND INNING—Seybold opened with a clean single to left. Murphy hit a grounder to Dahlen, who threw to Gilbert in time to catch Seybold. Gilbert got the ball to first ahead of Murphy. Monte Cross beat out a slow grounder to Devlin. Cross was out stealing on Bresnahan's quick throw to second. No runs.

Bender struck out McGann after giving him three balls. Mertes got the Giants' first hit, a clean single over short. He was out stealing second on Powers's perfect throw. Bender struck Dahlen out. No runs.

THIRD INNING—Mathewson fumbled Powers's easy grounder and he was safe. Bender's bunt to Mathewson forced Powers at second. Hartsel ripped a grounder to Devlin, who threw Bender out at second. Mathewson struck Lord out with slow drops. No runs.

Devlin sent up a high foul which Powers caught. Gilbert singled through short. Mathewson sacrificed to second on a nicely executed bunt to Lave Cross. Bresnahan lifted a high fly to Hartsel which retired the side. No runs.

FOURTH INNING—Davis sent an easy grounder which Gilbert handled. Mathewson struck Lave Cross out. Seybold was robbed of a base hit when Donlin caught his hard liner. No runs.

Browne lifted a short fly to Hartsel. Bender threw out Donlin's slow grounder. McGann broke his strike-out record by hitting a slow grounder, which Bender fielded. No runs.

Not a man on either side had reached second in the first four innings.

FIFTH INNING—Dahlen fielded Murphy's hard grounder to first. Monte Cross sent a fly to McGann. Powers hit into the left field crowd for two bases. The hit did no good, for Bender sent a grounder to Donlin and Powers was caught between second and third. No runs.

Mertes got his base on balls. The Indian was still wild and also gave Dahlen a base on balls. Devlin's out on a bunt along the third base line advanced both men. Gilbert sent a long fly to Hartsel and Mertes scored on the play, but Powers got the ball back to third in time to catch Dahlen stealing. The run counted, however, and the crowd went wild. One run.

SIXTH INNING—Hartsel beat out a bunt. Lord's grounder to Gilbert forced Hartsel at second. Mathewson struck out Davis and a quick throw from Bresnahan caught Lord off first. Davis singled. Lave Cross was the third man out, Devlin to McGann. No runs.

Lord made a nice running catch of Mathewson's long fly. Bresnahan beat out a bunt which would have rolled foul if Bender had let it go. Browne beat out another bunt, advancing Bresnahan to second. Donlin flied to Lord. McGann struck out again. No runs.

SEVENTH INNING—Mathewson struck Seybold out. Murphy was out on a grounder to Gilbert. Dahlen threw Monte Cross out. No runs.

Mertes grounded to Bender and Monte Cross threw Dahlen out.

Hartsel ran in and got Devlin's fly. No runs.

EIGHTH INNING—Powers lined to Mertes.

Bender fanned.

Hartsel was out, McGann to Mathewson. No runs.

Gilbert lined to Lord.

Mathewson walked.

Bresnahan hit into the left bleacher for two bases, sending Mathewson to third.

Browne's hit to Bender allowed Mathewson to score.

Browne was thrown out at first.

Bresnahan went to third.

Donlin fanned. One run.

NINTH INNING—The Athletics failed to score.

This was the fourth victory of the series for the Giants and gave them the world's championship.

BASEBALL TO-DAY.

At Boston.

First Game.

Boston (A. L.)	2	1	0	1	1	0	1	2	0	—8
Boston (N. L.)	0	0	1	0	0	0	0	1	0	—2

Hits, 13; errors, 2. Hits, 4; errors, 2.

Batteries—Gibson and Armbruster; Young and Needham. Umpires, Emslie and O'Loughlin.

Second Game.

Boston (N. L.)	2	1	0	—
Boston (A. L.)	1	0	0	—

Batteries—Fraser and Moran; Young and McGovern. Umpires, O'Loughlin and Emslie.

WILLIAMSON TO JAIL.

Oregon Congressman Sentenced to Serve Ten Months.

PORTLAND, Ore., Oct. 14.—J. N. Williamson, Congressman from the Second Oregon District, was to-day sentenced to pay $5 0 and serve ten months in prison. by Judge Hunt in the Federal Court. Williamson was convicted of complicity in Oregon land frauds.

RATIFYING TREATY.

WASHINGTON, Oct. 14.—Mr. Takahira, the Japanese Minister, called on the President this afternoon. The Minister said that the Russian and Japanese Governments would immediately inform each other officially of the ratification of the treaty of peace between the two countries.

FOOTBALL TO-DAY.

CAMBRIDGE, Mass., Oct. 14.—End of first half—Harvard, 6; Springfield Training School, 0.

JAMAICA ENTRIES.

JAMAICA RACETRACK, Oct. 14.—The conditions and entries for Monday's races are as follows:

First Race—For 2-year-olds; $700 added; five and a half furlongs.

Disobedient	112	Rust	110
Benevolent	115	Oak Duke	110
Clark Griffith	110	Father Cathem	115
Yalagal	107	Zienap	112
Jacobite	119	Lena J.	99
Brother Frank	115		

Second Race—For 4-year-olds and upward; selling; $700 added; one mile and a sixteenth.

Panique	98	*Pronta	101
*Lord Badge	103	*Embarrassment	100
Sals	100	Just So	98
Bronze Wing	103	The Huguenot	104
Oarsman	112	Columbia Girl	108
Knight of Rhodes	105	King Rose	108
Telephone	106	*Atwood	101
Hippocrates	105	Orthodox	106
Athlone	103	Martinmas	105

Third Race—For all ages; handicap; $1,000 added; six furlongs.

Israelite	126	Frontenac	120
Pretension	119	Rusk	116
Handzarra	115	Toscan	113
Mamie Worth	113	Bohemia	110
Graceful	111	Zeala	108
New Mown Hay	111	Preen	108
Consideration	107	Brother Frank	99
Lucy Young	93	Kittie Platt	93
Floralia	99	Monacodor	96
Royal Window	92	Mirthless	96

Fourth Race—The Pierrepont Handicap; for all ages; $2,500 added; one mile and a furlong.

Eugenia Burch	120	Dolly Spanker	119
Alma Dufour	117	Bad News	116
Merry Lark	115	Bedouin	115
Sidney C. Love	110	Tongorder	108
Coy Maid	107	Race King	104
Cederstrome	104	Oliver Cromwell	104
Santa Catalina	104	Von Tromp	103
True Wing	100	Miss Crawford	99
Sir Brillar	92		

Fifth Race—For 2-year-olds; selling; $700 added; six furlongs.

*Lone Hand	94	*Water Dog	90
*Programme	90	*Listless	90
Flavigny	95	Glenclare	98
Merrick	105	Turkey Foot	95
Delmore	98	Birmingham	98
Little Flea	98	Curly Jim	106
Ariston	95	*J. K. F.	97
Benevolent	104	Speed Smith	98

Sixth Race—For maidens 3 years old and upward; $600 added; one mile and a sixteenth.

Nom de Plume	107	Lindale	107
Salt and Pepper	107	Mdrica	107
Oliver Cromwell	1[illegible]1	Brilliant	107

*Apprentice allowance.

FIVE LOST OFF SHIF AT SE

Swept from th Campania in Mid-Ocean.

LINER IS HARD HI

Scoops Up an Enor mous Wave.

ONE DIES, MANY INJURED

Steerage Passengers Knocked About Helplessly.

PANIC SPREADS TERROR

Believed for a Time Big Vessel Is Sinking.

On the big Cunarder Campania, in to-day from Liverpool and Queenstown, comes the story of a sea disaster almost unparalleled in the annals of modern sea travel. Caught in a gale on Wednesday, Oct. 11, the big craft shipped a huge sea that swept the steerage deck on the port side from end to end, dashed the helpless passengers against the ironwork, crippling and maiming dozens, and finally burst the great steel doors in the vessel's rail and swept five passengers overboard.

The list of dead may grow when the steerage passengers are counted at Ellis Island. The dead are, John Graham, Mary Cosgrove, Annie Clary, unknown young woman, unknown man and Agnes Carleton, who died in the ship's hospital this morning after an operation.

The injured in the hospital are: Mary Hooligan, 25 years old, right leg broken; Annie Firaly, 23, compound fracture of left leg; Kate McAuliffe, severe bruises and broken ribs; Lizzie Roman, right knee fractured; Annie Roach, contusions of body; James Kane, possible fracture of skull; William Green, right arm broken and contusions; James Graham, contusions; Thomas Maher, right arm broken and contusions, and James Cunningham, sprained ankles and severe bruises.

Besides those seriously hurt dozens received injuries which were not of serious enough nature to confine them to the ship's hospital.

The utmost secrecy was preserved among the company's officers as to the real seriousness of the losses. Two of them stood guard over the captain and refused to allow him to be questioned. The boast of the Cunard company that it had never yet lost a passenger in an accident is a thing of the past.

The disaster came very suddenly and unexpectedly on Wednesday afternoon. The ship had had a run of bad weather for several days, and the wind had veered around to a nasty gale that threw up a bad quartering sea. By noon a gale was whipping the sea, so that the great vessel heaved and rolled badly. Down on the steerage deck promenade, perhaps ten feet wide by a couple of hundred feet long, sixty or eighty of the passengers were sitting, lounging or walking up and down the stretch.

The deck occupies the middle half of the ship. Its roof is the first cabin passengers' deck. Its rail is a cumbrous solid steel and oak bulwark, nearly five feet high, with heavy metal doors put in at regular intervals. Some of these doors are grated to permit air to enter and water to run out. Others are solid and are opened only when the gangplanks are thrown out.

It was just after the dinner hour and the steerage passengers had crept around to the lee side, out of the wind. A number of Swedes were singing up near the forward end and many of the women were sewing, knitting or gossiping idly as they clustered along the rail, sitting on odd foreign trunks and hampers or bunched up on the deck. A ship's officer strolled up and down, and a woman sitting on an upturned fruit crate was crooning to a baby.

The big ship was pitching a good deal in the heavy rollers, but not enough to drive her passengers inside. From the top of the solid rail to the deck above was stretched a heavy woven net, to keep any foolish steerage man, woman or child from falling or being washed overboard.

The ship began to run into heavier seas after a little and the steerage moved restlessly. Many of the passengers went inside. Suddenly the great craft shook at the attack of two huge rollers, then as she

(Continued on Second Page.)

MEMBERS OF THE CHICAGO WHITE STOCKINGS, PICKED TO WIN THE AMERICAN LEAGUE PENNANT FOR 1906

Roy Patterson, Pitcher

Frank Smith Pitcher

Nick Altrock, Pitcher

Walsh, Pitcher

Owen, Pitcher

"Doc" White, Pitcher

Geo. Davis, S.S.

J. Towne, Catcher

"Billie" Sullivan, Catcher

O'Neill, Sub. outfield

"Jiggs" Donohue, 1. b.

Rohe, Sub infielder

Photographs by Frank W. Smith, Leader Staff Photographer

Frank Isbel 2. b.

Pat Dougherty, left field

Fielder Jones C.F. (Manager)

Lee Tannehill - 3-b.

Hahn, right field.

SPORTS OF ALL SORTS

THE PICKED STAR TEAM OF BOTH LEAGUES.

Here are the pictures of a picked star team by the baseball expert of The Evening World—Bozeman Bulger. They are taken out of the various teams of the two leagues. The names are household words to lovers of the game, and it is easy to imagine what they would do to any other team picked to match them, not only in this country, but in any other part of the world.

KAUFMAN, HEAVYWEIGHT

"Al" Kaufman has been matched to fight "Jack" Johnson, the colored heavyweight, at the Colma Athletic Club, of Colma, Cal. The agreement is 60 per cent. of the gate receipts to the winner, with a side bet of $5,000. The date has not been determined upon, but it is agreed that they are to meet within the next six weeks. Johnson is the colored fighter who has been complaining all along that he could get no one to "go to." They are both Coast men and favorites out there. A lot of the Eastern sporting element will make the trip.

YALE'S FOOTBALL TEAM.

Here are two photos of Yale's football team at practice in the new-rule game. The top picture shows them at signal practice, and the bottom one depicts how the end play will look under the new rules. Coach Rockwell predicts a winning team this year. He has had an exceptional lot of well-developed men to pick from, and their experience has extended over two years of practice work as "subs."

BILLIARDIST HOPPE.

"WILLIE" HOPPE

"Willie" Hoppe is hard at practice for his championship match with "Jake" Schaefer on Oct. 17 for a bet of $500, the winner to take the gate receipts. It is to be 18.1 balk-line billiards.

Hoppe is the present champion of the world at 18.1 balk-line billiards, having won the title and the diamond medal given by the Brunswick-Balke-Collender Company from the French veteran, Maurice Vignaux.

The match takes place at Madison Square Billiard Hall, New York.

THROWER FLANAGAN.

John Flanagan, champion fifty-six pound weight and sixteen pound hammer thrower, of the Irish-American Athletic Club, comes out with the statement that he will stay one more year in the game in order to hang up a record that will last for all time. He is going after his own record, which is yet to be equalled, at the autumn games of the club.

PICTURE SECTION.

THE BROOKLYN DAILY EAGLE.

NEW YORK. TUESDAY. OCTOBER 9, 1906.—PAGES 1 TO 4.

SERIES FOR BASEBALL CHAMPIONSHIP OF WORLD BEGINS TO-DAY.

EVERY preparation for the world's championship baseball series that will start this afternoon in Chicago has been made. Accommodations have been prepared for 26,000 people and not a vacant place will be left from the present indications, for every box seat has been sold for over a week and a high premium is being paid for reserved seats by the eager fans. Five dollars a seat was the ruling price yesterday, where any seats could be found, and as high as $15 was paid during the day for choice sittings. "The Cubs are ready for the battle," said Manager Chance, "and we are in the best possible shape for it. If we are beaten, we will have no excuses at all to offer, for the team has not been in any better shape all year than they are now. We expect to win easy, for we took four out of five from the White Sox last fall and we are stronger this year by far than we were last fall. We will play ball all the time, however, for we realize that we cannot take things easy against Jones and his men." "The White Sox are in fine shape right now," said Manager Jones. "There will be no excuse for defeat this year. We did have trouble last season, as none of our pitchers were at their best, but now that we are in our best shape it will be a battle royal." The players of the two teams met with the members of the National Commission and the club owners at the Auditorium Annex yesterday and there listened to the reading of the rules that will govern the series. A few minor changes have been made in the rules since last year, but there is little variation from those that governed the Giants and Athletics last fall. One new rule provides the umpire with absolute power to punish any player that deserves it, and the commission will impose a fine on such player by keeping the amount out of his share of the receipts.

Top Row—Left to Right—Peister, Brown, Lundgren, Sheckard, Kling, Taylor. Middle Row—Schulte, Hoffman, Steinfeldt, Chance, Overall, Evers, Slagle. Bottom Row—Moran, Gessler, Reulbach, Walsh, McCormick, Tinker.

NEW MODELS FOR THE HISTORY EXHIBIT AT THE CHILDREN'S MUSEUM.

The Spanish Type.

"The Cavalier Comes to Call."

The Dutch Type.

Golden Eagle From Oxford County, Maine.

THREE new models have been added to the history exhibit at the Chidren's Museum. They are half of a series which is to show the six types of Europeans who left decided imprint on the early history of this country—the Spanish French, Dutch, and three sub-divisions of the English: the New England, formed of the blending of the Pilgrim and Puritan migration; the Friend or Quaker, which settled in Pennsylvania, with a group on Long Long Island, and the Cavalier, which colonized Maryland and southward. Spanish, Dutch and Cavalier types are finished. The models are each 11 inches high and of proportionate length and depth, the figure models being 7 inches. The Spanish group has a bit of the ambulatory of an old mission for background with some varieties of desert growth such as may be found in California disposed as in a garden in the foreground. The Cavalier model has for background one of the comfortable old red brick houses of the South with a rose hung porch, having Ionic pillars. For the Dutch type a frontier trading post scene has been chosen. It is a trader's cabin in the woods surrounded by the fence of logs. Careful study has been made of times and types in books, old prints and copies of famous pictures. This has been carried on at the Brooklyn Historical Library and in the library of the Children's Museum, which is rich in works on American history. In following out old books, it has been necessary to have constant recourse to the dictionary. For instance, it had to be found out that Cordovan leather is sheepskin dressed so as to look like morocco, generally black, etc. For the morion worn by the Spanish soldier, it was first necessary to look through pictures of that period in the book on the Madrid Gallery, then find a book on armor, decide on the proper form, translate from French or Spanish, and then magnify the picture until the design could be followed. For the Spanish soldier's dress the Racinet "History of Costume," and a German book on costumes, were consulted and translations made from the French and German. Old prints of Eastern Indians, Mohawks and Iroquois, were examined for the proper garbing and painting of the Indians. Elizabeth McClellan's and other books on costume, together with old pictures, furnished designs for the other models. These models were designed by Agnes E. Bowen and made by her with the exception of the desert growth, which was prepared by Miss Eleanor Horsfall, who does such work for the American Museum of Natural History, and the Spanish background and the porch for the cavalier group, which were made by John Bender, the Museum cabinetmaker.

WHITE SOX WIN WORLD'S SERIES BY ROUTING CUBS.

American League Players Earn Great and Decisive Victory by Thoroughly Outplaying Confident Favorites.

DOC WHITE OUTPITCHES BROWN AND OVERALL.

New Champions Get $1,400 Each and Cubs About $500 for Share of Receipts.

Final Standing of Teams.

	W.	L.	PC.		W.	L.	PC.
Americans.	4	2	.667	Nationals...	2	4	.333

By Charles Dryden.

CHICAGO, Oct. 14.—The world's championship was turned away from the Cubs to the White Sox to-day. Score 8 to 3.

To Dr. White is due a royal diadem of currycombs to top off the horse blankets—emblems of the world's greatest athletes. He had the Indian sign on the Cubs all the way. Brown, the last forlorn hope of the Cubs, went in to the mess with little more than his glove and a stock of Terre Haute sang froid. Mordecai took these assets with him when he left the hill a beaten athlete in the nightmare second round. Out came Mr. Overall in his great specialty of first aid to the bumped. No use. The Giant rescuer cleaned up the round and held the Sox until the eighth, but the damage was all in and assessed before Overall tackled a job already lost.

The Sox outbatted the enemy two to one. They combed Brown and his legatee fourteen times for long and short ones. Four of the five swats in the second were scratches, but they irritated the Cubs just the same. Isbell tore off three and is grieving some because none got into the double class.

Then turn to Mr. Hahn, the Spartan athlete, for a picture of vengeance in white. Is he hunk with the Cub pitchers for hitting him on the nose? Looks that way with four hits—two from each man. It was Mr. Pfiester who bruised the nose. To avoid further argument and dissipate hard feeling, Eddie raked Brown and Overall in equal quantities.

Cubs 2 to 1 Favorite.

To the victors belong the horse blankets, also about $1,400 each. The Cubs get less than $500 per athlete and the solace of knowing they tried their best and failed. In the eyes of the near-wise—the ones who bet and placed their money wrong—the race bore the earmarks of a selling-plater running away with a stake horse. Long before the battle opened the Sox were touted sure losers at 2 to 1 and sometimes 3 to 1.

Fielder Jones thinks that cuff-buttons bearing the pictures of Altrock and White would do nicely for presents. And on the manly bosom of each athlete he would hang a diamond sunburst or medallion displaying the pink resemblance of E. Walsh.

Before noon the gates were closed because a ticketless mob of thousands smashed the fence on the north. The cops were busy inside sifting the chaff from the wheat and clearing the yard of the waiting ticket brigade in front.

Athletes, managers, fanatics and all the rest are glad the riot is ended. Peace follows the war, and may there never be another like it.

In the first Hoffman singled to left and took second on Dougherty's fumble. Sheckard sacrificed. The run scored on Schulte's double to right. Chance bumped to White and Rohe tagged Schulte on the line. Steinfeldt walked and Tinker flied to centre.

Hahn beat a high bounder to Evers. Jones bunted in front of the plate and Kling nipped Hahn at second. Isbell pushed a safety to right. Schulte went after Davis's fly at the edge of the crowd, but claims he was pushed away from the ball. The drive went for two bases, scoring Jones. Rohe's grounder to short stopped Izzy on the way home. Rohe stole on the next pitch. Donohue sent a clean double to left, scoring Davis and Rohe. Dougherty grounded to Chance. Four hits and three runs off Premier Brown in the opener chased a chill down the spines of the Cubs.

Hahn the Hitting King.

After Sullivan and White went out in the second Hahn singled. Jones walked and Isbell scratched a hit that Evers knocked down back of the bag. With the bases full Davis drove a liner over short. Tinker popped up and batted the ball down. It dropped behind him. Hahn and Jones scored. Rohe hit safely past short and again the bags were loaded. Overall relieved Brown. Jiggs hit to Evers, who made the play to second for Rohe, but Tinker was slow in covering. A pass to Dougherty forced Davis home. Sullivan struck out.

The Cubs came to life in the fifth. King dumped a twister along the third base line and beat it. Overall doubled to right and Hoffman fanned. Sheckard's out, Isbell to first, scored King and Davis threw Schulte out. Jiggs, the human scoopnet, made a dandy play on both throws.

Chance started on a shoestring hope in the sixth. White soaked Husk on the instep and Steinfeldt skied to Rohe. Tinker singled. The big Cub leader made a desperate sneak for third, with Evers up and was flagged by Sullivan. Evers fouled to Sullivan.

Until the eighth Overall held the Sox safe at all points. Hahn singled to centre, making hit No. 4 and wiping away the sting of his broken nose. Jones sacrificed. Isbell smote to centre for one base and Hahn scored. Davis was thrown out by Tinker. Hoffman's great catch off Rohe ended it.

With one gone in the ninth Evers ...

LION TAKES SPIN IN AUTO THROUGH CROWDED STREETS.

LION TAKES AN AUTO RIDE.

King of Beasts Behaves Nobly While Touring Quaker Town at Head of Parade.

(Special to The World.)

JOHNSTOWN, Pa., Oct. 14.—Nothing since the flood here has stirred the populace of this smoky city along a curve of the Pennsylvania Railroad as much as the appearance of a king of beasts riding in an automobile. A sales agent of a Maxwell car either dreamed of another rush of waters and sought to emulate Noah or else he schemed to qualify as a Belasco press agent. At any rate, he mixed zoology with chemistry and physics in automobiling, and Leo had a ride.

The jungle king which caused the excitement was borrowed from a viciting menagerie and invited into the tonneau. He tok to his seat without hesitancy or any apparent as to the outcome of his first motor ride. In fact he was far less nervous than the chauffeur.

Leo's machine had barely felt the speed clutch when he became the leader in a parade of astonished citizens. It was notable, however, that all of his followers before getting in line assured themselves that he was not in danger of tumbling out.

AMERICA TRAILS ENGLAND IN TENNIS.

Westfall and Grant, Triumphant Yankees, Return with Praise for Britons' Management.

America's lawn tennis players, Herbert L. Westfall and Wylie C. Grant, arrived from their tour of the English courts aboard the Caledonia, of the Anchor Line yesterday and packed in their baggage were several cups that stood for titles and championships. Westfall, the young Kings County player, displayed the trophy of the Welsh covered court championship which the two Americans won at Llandudno, while Grant, of the New York Club, exhibited the valuable Gothic vase of silver emblematic of the West Sussex honors. The two Americans have played through a series of seven continuous weeks of the foremost tournaments in Ireland, Scotland and England, winning and reaching the finals in each against the ranking players of the courts on the other side of the Atlantic Ocean.

The trip was the first that the young expert Westfall had made to the foreign courts, and he was outspoken in declaring that the sport in this country was in its kindergarten stage. The meeting at Brighton, England, he said, opened his eyes, as there was a record entry list of 1,114 competitors, playing in a schedule of 21 events. This tournament was decided on a field of only fourteen available courts, and in the six days 732 matches were decided. Westfall has returned with new ideas as to the management of the sport, and he strongly advises the appointment of an official handicapper to hold the same position to the tournaments in this country as B. C. Evelegh does to the English meetings.

A. W. Gore, the English ex-champion, did not accompany the Americans, as was expected. Gore is coming to this country on business and will surely be here within three weeks, when he plans to get some play on indoor courts.

CARDINALS WIN FOR FIRST TIME IN SERIES.

ST. LOUIS, Oct. 14.—The St. Louis Nationals scored the first victory over the local Americans of the post-season series by winning the opening game of the final double header to-day, one to nothing. The second game was a five inning tie.

The record for the series stands Americans won 4; Nationals won 1; tied 3.

A feature was a match footrace between Niles, of the Americans, and Burch, of the Nationals, won by the former. Scores:

FIRST GAME.

										R.	H.	E.
Americans	0	0	0	0	0	0	0	0	0	0	5	0
Nationals	1	0	0	0	0	0	0	0	0	1	4	2

Batteries—Powell and O'Connor; McGlynn and Marshall.

SECOND GAME.

						R.	H.	E.
Americans	0	0	0	0	0	0	2	0
Nationals	0	0	0	0	0	0	3	2

Batteries—Pelty and Spencer; Hostetter and Marshall.

Highlanders Shut Out Hoboken.

With Joe Doyle doing the twirling, the Highlanders defeated the Hoboken team at Hoboken yesterday 3 to 0. Dugan allowed the Hilltopers only five hits, while Doyle was touched for eight.

Score by innings:

American	0	0	0	0	0	1	2	0	0	—3
Hoboken	0	0	0	0	0	0	0	0	0	—0

Batteries—Doyle and Thomas for New York; Dugan and O'Neil for Hoboken.

SHEPPARD MAKES OLD RECORD QUAKE.

Scratch Man in 600-Yard Run Nearly Equals Burke's Time-Honored Mark.

Melvin W. Sheppard, the famous Philadelphia runner, gave some of the speediest men in the East a handicap of from three to fifty yards in the 600-yard handicap at the fall games of the Irish-American Athletic Club yesterday at Celtic Park and beat them with apparent case. He covered the distance in 1 min. 11 3-5 sec., which is only a fraction of a second behind the world's record. As the track was heavy and slow this time was considered remarkably fast.

Following closely at the heels of Harry Hillman, the fleet runner of the N. Y. A. C., to whom he had given a start of three yards, Sheppard overhauled all the other contestants before half the distance had been run, and then shot past Hillman and finished first by several yards. Hillman was second, a similar distance ahead of Bart Freeman, of the Xavier A. C.

Ten thousand admirers of the Irish athletes were present and cheered the contestants lustily as they competed in the various events. Martin Sheridan, of Olympic games' fame, was loudly applauded when he made his appearance on the field, and he was vociferously cheered when he was proclaimed the winner of the discus handicap and the hop-step-and-jump event. In the latter he defeated the much-heralded Irish champion, Dennis Lanigan, by nearly four inches.

While running a close third in the 300-yard handicap O. C. Delmar, of the Mohawk A. C., was spiked by one of the runners and was painfully injured. He received a nasty gash an inch wide and several inches long just below the ankle. A physician attended him and he was taken home by friends.

There were twenty events decided, all of which were keenly contested.

The summaries:

600-Yard Handicap—Won by Melvin W. Sheppard, Irish-American A. C. (scratch); Harry Hillman, New York A. C. (8 yds.), second; L. Katzenstein, Mohawk A. C. (20 yds.), third. Time—1.11 3-5.

100-Yard Handicap—Won by G. B. Ford, unattached (9 yds.); William Slade, Pastime A. C. (7 yds.), second; L. B. Dorland, Elmwood A. C. (6½ yds.), third. Time—10s.

One-Mile Handicap—Won by B. Freeman, Xavier A. C. (35 yds.); M. Geis, Holy Cross A. C. (90 yds.), second; O. J. Devine, National A. C. (95 yds.), third. Time—4.29 2-5.

440-Yard Handicap (novice)—Won by C. B. Forest, Etna A. C.; W. R. Lynch, unattached, second; J. H. Hanlon, unattached, third. Time—55 3-5s.

100-Yard Handicap (3 feet limit)—Won by J. J. Archer, Irish-American A. C. (2½ yds.); W. M. Miller, Irish-American (3 yds.), second; Lawson Robertson, Irish-American (scratch), third. Time—10s.

Half-Mile Handicap—Won by C. Walters, Sterling A. C. (42 yds.); L. Katzenstein, Mohawk A. C. (24 yds.), second; J. Allord, Mohawk A. C. (42 yds.), third. Time—1.58.

One-Lap Obstacle Race—Won by H. C. de Lasselle, Lafayette College; John Eller, Irish-American A. C., second; John J. Healy, Annunciation Lyceum, third. Time—1 37 1-5.

300-Yard Handicap—Won by P. J. Murray, Xavier A. A. (21 yds.); A. Gennerich, Pastime A. C. (20 yds.), second; L. B. Dorland, Elmwood A. C. (16 yds.), third. Time—31 4-5s.

Two-mile steeplechase, handicap—Won by William Nelson, Pastime A. C. (15 sec.); Ben Mann, unattached (55 sec., second; Fred Lenz, Mohawk A. C. (45 sec.), third; time, 11m. 7 2-5s.

Throwing 16-pound hammer, handicap, from 9-foot circle—Won by John J. Flanagan, Irish-American A. C. (scratch), with throw of 166 ft. 8 in.; S. P. Gillies, New York A. C. (scratch), second, with throw of 158 ft. 5¼ in.; A. G. Williams, Xavier A. C. (15 ft.), third, with throw of 123 ft. 4½ in.

Throwing discus, handicap—Won by Martin ...

FEARFUL MAULING IN PRIVATE FIGHT.

Charley Lucas, in Ill Health, Stays 15 Rounds to Draw with Jeff O'Connell.

Fifteen rounds, all of them fast and exciting, were fought yesterday in this city by Jeff O'Connell, the English bantam, and Charley Lucas, brother of Fred Lucas, the welter-weight. The contest, which took place on a west side pier, ended in a draw. Both men were on their feet at the sound of the last gong.

The fight was for the gate receipts and a side bet of $200. About 300 persons, paying $2 each, witnessed the bout. The pugilists weighed in at 115 pounds at the ringside. Both fought a good fight, but Lucas got the bigger share of the punishment. He stood it gamely, despite the handicap of a heavy cold. Some of the blows landed by O'Connell fell upon the porous plasters which his antagonist was wearing by order of the doctor. But there were other blows that did not encounter these obstacles.

In the thirteenth round O'Connell drove the American hard, and it looked as if he would not be able to hold his own to the end of the round. Not only did he do so, however, but rallied so well in the fourteenth that bets on a draw found no-takers.

In the final round it was Lucas who did most of the punching, but the English lad could have stood a much fiercer onslaught evidently, as his condition at the end of the fight indicated.

The referee was Florrie Barnett and the timekeeper George Horn.

Old Rivals' Fight a Big Card.

With the fight between Terry McGovern and Young Corbett only three days off, the seats sold like hot cakes yesterday at the New Polo Athletic Club, and the indications are that a record-breaking crowd of New Yorkers will go to Philadelphia on Wednesday night by the special train and otherwise. Both McGovern and Corbett are training hard and each means to do battle from the start.

Kid Broad Back in the Ring.

Kid Broad has decided to re-enter the ring. He is now under the management of Frank Hurley and left last night to begin training at Webster, Mass. Broad expects to be matched soon to meet Matty Baldwin, of Boston, in a few weeks at catch weights before a Webster club.

Hendrick Won at Billiards.

In the amateur handicap 14.2-balk billiard tournament last night in progress at Oro Morningstar's Billiard Academy John A. Hendrick (300) easily defeated Hoe Iassic (200) by a score of 300 to 143. Hendrick averaged 11 14-26, with a high run of 47. Iassic's highest run was 57, and he averaged 5 11-26.

Xmas Dies After Workout.

After working six furlongs in 1.19, Xmas, a three-year-old filly trained by Frank Regan, dropped dead yesterday morning at the Gravesend track. The boy had just alighted and was leading her back to the stable when she toppled over. Death was due to spinal meningitis.

Belmont Park Entries.

First Race—For two-year olds; five and a half furlongs, straight.

Allofavor	109	Jennie Wells	109
Suada	109	Miss Spooner	109
Waterspeed	109	Reba Stone	109
Barbary Belle	109	Lady Ogden	109
Crimson Clover	109	Windfall	109
Pepper and Salt	109	Rain Queen	109
Sally K.	109	Spring Beauty	109
Rollicking Girl	109	Qualify	109
Vails	109	Safrana	109
Manana	109	Adelinette	109

RICH STAKES FOR RACING FAREWELL

Last Week of High-Class Sport at Belmont Ornamented by Splendid Programme.

TWO MINOR MEETINGS BOOKED TO FOLLOW.

Champion Stakes, Worth $7,000, Will Be Decided Wednesday, with Classy Starters.

Six days more of high-class racing!

This week ends the best class of the turf sport for the season. On Saturday Belmont Park closes its gates to race-goers for the year, and all the great thoroughbreds go into retirement. There are two other meetings, at Jamaica and Aqueduct, which round out the time allowed by law to race, but these meetings are much like cheap wine—fill a void, but not very palatable.

During the week twelve stakes will be decided at Belmont. Of this list the most important are the Champagne, the Harbor Hill Steeplechase, the Ramapo Handicap, the Champion Steeplechase, the White Plains Handicap and the Belmont Park Weight-for-Age.

The Champagne Stakes will be called on Wednesday. This is a stake worth $7,000, for two-year-olds. For many years it was the longest race of the season for youngsters, as its distance is seven furlongs. But several seasons ago the Coney Island Jockey Club offered the Flatbush at a similar distance, and in 1905 the Brighton Beach Racing Association inaugurated the Triumph Stakes at one mile.

The Belmont Stake is still an important event in spite of the new stakes, and yearly attracts good entries. This year Salvidere is eligible, also Peter Pan, Ballot, W. H. Daniel, Fountainblue and Kentucky Beau. As John E. Madden announced a month ago that Salvidere would not run again this season, the race will be contested for by the last named youngsters.

Rich Steeplechase Thursday.

The Harbor Hill Steeplechase, for three-year-olds, at two miles, will be decided on Thursday. This race was suggested by Clarence H. Mackey, who donates $3,000 and a silver cup to the winner. It was Mr. Mackay's idea to have a valuable race in the fall for horses of this age in order that owners would train good thoroughbreds for cross-country sport and not depend on broken-down cripples that had outlived their usefulness on the flat. "Mr. Cotton" won it last year with Delcanta, and he has two promising candidates for it now in St. Kevin and Sanctus. If either should win the cup that Mr. Mackay offers will become the property of Mr. Cotton. It is necessary to win this stake twice by an owner in order to secure the silver cup. Mr. Cotton's pair will find much opposition from T. S. Martin, Dulcian, Commodore Fontaine, Vendor and Mr. McCann, five of the most promising cross-country horses in America.

The Belmont Park Weight-for-Age race, at two and a quarter miles, is one of the features of the last day's racing. The fine steeplechaser, John M. P., is entered in this race, but as he is opposed by such fast-going horses as Running Water, Content, Entree and Angler, that like a distance of ground and are favored by the weights, his chance of winning is not very bright, great as he is over a long route.

Fine Prospects for Race.

The race should be well contested, as there are several candidates in it that fancy the long journey.

* * *

The news that "Boots" Durnell had been reinstated by the Pacific Coast Jockey Club stewards caused considerable surprise among turfmen at Sheepshead Bay yesterday. This action of the Western turf authorities was totally unexpected. It was known that John W. Gates had been busily engaged for months trying to effect this change of heart in the men who ruled Durnell off, but as he had failed so long turfmen had regarded the incident closed.

The Eastern Jockey Club has not acted on the Durnell-McCafferty case, and until they do so Durnell can neither visit the local tracks nor race horses. But as the Jockey Club rulings are reciprocal in cases of this kind it is only a matter of days before Durnell will be in good standing again.

It was the opinion of racegoers generally that the Pacific Coast officials should not stop with Durnell, but include John J. McCafferty in the rulings of clemency. The cases were similar and practically hinged on each other; if Durnell was worthy of pardon then McCafferty was entitled to the same kind of treatment, local turfmen declared. If this clemency is not shown to the latter then the much vaunted "All men are equal on and under the turf," is only a lie.

* * *

The publication of the prospectus of the new race track to be established on "Lucky" Baldwin's ranch, near Los Angeles, Cal., failed to disturb the serenity of Bookmaker George Rose's mind. Rose is the principal owner of the Ascot Park track, near the city of Los Angeles, and as such is more deeply interested in the new racing venture than any one in the East. When a reporter for the World referred to it yesterday Rose said:

"The proposed race track is a long ways off. It cannot be completed before next fall at least. When it is ready, I will welcome it because I think two tracks will serve to attract more horses to that part of California than one. I'm willing to meet the new officials and arrange for an equitable share of racing dates. There will be no race track warfare such as New Orleans experienced last year. There is room enough for two tracks."

* * *

Horsemen should not overlook the big list of valuable stakes that are offered by the Brighton Beach Racing Association, entries for which close to-day, ...

PENN'S CHANCES DROP WITH KICK.

Quarter-Back O'Brien's Field Goal Shows Quakers' Weak Point in New Game.

BIGGER OPPORTUNITIES NOW FOR LESSER TEAMS.

Princeton, Though hWeak, Has One Quality Favoring Her Under Present Rules.

By Charles Chadwick.

Quarterback O'Brien's drop kick at Philadelphia last Saturday, which won the game for Swarthmore (4-0), is the great play to date of the season, causing as it did, the first defeat under the new rules of a member of the traditional "Big Four." Pennsylvania seems seems to have gone under after a fierce struggle. ThTe Penn team has exhibited a weakness in open field work from the start, and an inability to keep in the same class with Yale, Harvard or Princeton. ThTeT weak Lehigh team has scored, not to mention others. Gettysburg has held Penn to a tie.

The victory of Swarthmore was due as much to O'Brien's low, well placed punts as to his drop kick, and the opportunity for the try at goal was due directly to the regaining of the ball by Swarthmore after outside kicks, which resulted in getting the ball into Pennsylvania territory.

After the usual attempts at the line, the drop kick was made necessary by a 15-yard penalty for holding. O'Brien stood on the 30-yard line, so close to his team that under ordinary conditions the ball would have been blocked. But Coble and the other heavy men in the Swarthmore line protected him so well and the pass was so accurate that O'Brien was able to get the ball off in time. It was a very pretty exhibition of cool headwork at an exciting and critical juncture.

Norton, the Navy quarter-back, had an almost odentical opportunity in the first half of the Princeton-Novy game (5-0) at Annapolis to accomplish an even more spectacular play, but the fortunes of war were against him.

Swarthmore has taken almost the same place secured once by Dartmouth and once by Amherst when they defeated Harvard

There is more of a chance this year than ever for teams of the second rank to rise in prominence. But it is still doubtful if in the long run a college like Swarthmore, with a smaller number of men to draw from than the larger universities possess, can keep the pace longer than one season.

Of the old "Big Four," Princeton is probably weaker now than Yale or Harvard, and Penn, though scored on, tied and defeated, is probably stronger in many points of the game than is generally supposed. The Quaker offense is fairly strong, as is shown by the way it took the ball through Swarthmore's line. Penn might have scored had it not been for the misfortune of several penalties.

Princeton, I have said, is probably a bit weaker than Yale or Harvard. But Princeton has one quality in a superb degree, that is bound to tell in her favor in playing the new game, as compared with Yale or Harvard. It may be summed up in a sentence. Yale and Harvard play the game, relying on their strength, Princeton expects and waits for a fumble or mistake of the adversary, and is ready to make more capital out of a loose ball than any other team in the history of the game. With forward passes and on side kicks, then, a Princeton team, inferior man to man, has an even better chance than hitherto of pulling a game out of the fire.

For another thing, Princeton's players are all in the pink of condition. After the gruellink contest with Annapolis, their appearance did not exhibit the slightest sign of fatigue or wear.

As to the Army and Navy, who meet in the annual dull in Dec. 1, the Navy seems to be having the best of it so far. The Army's tie game, 0-0, with Colgate, compares unfavorably with the 15 to 6 score of last year. But the Army's turn to be tried out comes later on, when on three successive Saturdays Harvard, Yale and Princeton will be faced.

FOOTBALL TEAM RECORDS.

YALE.		HARVARD.	
21 Wesleyan	0	7 Williams	0
51 Syracuse	0	10 Bowdoin	0
12 Springfield	0	10 Maine	0
17 Holy Cross	0	27 Bates	6
		21 Amherst Ag.	0
PRINCETON.		PENNSYLVANIA.	
24 Villa Nova	0	32 Lehigh	6
22 Stevens	0	6 Gettysburg	6
6 Wash. & Jeff.	0	11 North Carolina	0
52 Lehigh	0	47 Frank. & Mar.	6
5 Annapolis	0	0 Swarthmore	4
WEST POINT.		ANNAPOLIS.	
12 Tufts	0	0 Dickinson	0
24 Trinity	0	12 Maryland Ag.	0
0 Colgate	0	0 Princeton	5
CORNELL.		INDIANS.	
0 Colgate	0	6 Villa Nova	0
21 Hamilton	0	82 Albright	0
23 Oberlin	5	48 Susquehanna	0
23 Niagara	0	0 Penn. State	4
24 Bucknell	6		
DARTMOUTH.		BROWN.	
5 Norwich	0	12 N. Hampshire	0
8 Vermont	0	17 Wesleyan	0
16 Holy Cross	0	17 Amherst Ag.	0
4 Maine	0		
SWARTHMORE.		LAFAYETTE.	
4 Villa Nova	0	34 Wyoming Sem.	0
4 Pennsylvania	0	23 Ursinus	0
		24 Medico-Chi	0

Between the Five-Yard Lines.

Pennsylvania's defeat at the hands of Swarthmore was a remarkable example of faults and necessities under the new rules. There is no mistaking the fact that Swarthmore played better than Penn, but both elevens showed glaring weaknesses.

The greatest lesson of the game on Franklin Field was the cost of offside play and holding. Under the new rules penalties are severe, and referees like "Pa" Corbin will enforce them. They deprived Penn of two ...

NATHAN STRAUS'S TAD BEATEN ON SPEEDWAY.

Promise and Princess Pique Both Finish in Front of Millionaire's Horse.

All of the star performers were on the Speedway yesterday morning and exciting finishes were a feature of the day. The keenest contest of the morning was that in which Promise, driven by A. E. Perrin; Princess Pique, with Thomas Leahy up, and Nathan Straus's Ted, driven by the trainer, T. J. Sullivan, engaged. Ted maintained a slight advantage almost to the finish, but there both Promise and Princess Pique began to close on him. In the last few strides Ted showed signs of distress and his competitors reached the front so close together that no one present could name the winner. Ted finished a half length behind.

In an earlier start Ted and Promise made up the field, and the former finished in front. Promise turned the tables in the next brush, and with both horses strung out to the limit won the heat. Mr. Perrin then took the reins behind Alice Carr, and by a masterly drive managed to finish in front of Princess Pique.

Alice Carr had a keen tilt with Thos. Sharkey's bay pacer Midway, and again she was a winner. She concluded her unbroken list of victories by defeating Marcus Bruckheimer's Julia Varon.

The brown trotter Ila ranked among the best winners of the morning. S. E. Soteldo drove the daughter of Temple Bar, and his skill contributed in a large degree to her success. In her first start Ila finished in front of George Huber's Frankie Pandit, driven by the owner. Then Ila took the fast Lord Bromley, driven by Patrick Kennedy, into camp in clever fashion. She added another win to her credit by beating E. O. Burgen's Estrella, and ended the good work of the morning by defeating the big trotter Strangeleaf, driven by Louis Frank.

SHIPPING NEWS.

ALMANAC FOR MONDAY, OCT. 15.

Sun rises, 6.10 | Sun sets, 5.22 | Moon rises 3.1[illegible]

TIDES FOR TO-DAY.

	High Water A.M.	High Water P.M.	Low Water A.M.	Low Water P.M.
Sandy Hook	5.10	5.30	11.20	11.4[illegible]
Governor's Island	5.30	5.45	11.56	—
Hell Gate	7.23	7.38	1.28	—

Incoming Steamers.

DUE TO-DAY.

Principessa Laetitia	Gibraltar	Oct. 2
Dora	Gibraltar	Oct. 2
Delaware	Manchester	Oct. [illegible]

DUE TUESDAY, OCT. 16.

Carmania	Liverpool	Oct.
Oscar II.	Christiansand	Oct.
St. Cuthbert	Antwerp	Oct.
Chemnitz	Bremen	Oct.
Hudson	Havre	Oct.
Gorjistan	Gibraltar	Oct.
Siegmund	Barbados	Oct.
Phidias	New Orleans	Oct.
El Valle	New Orleans	Oct.
El Dorado	New Orleans	Oct.

DUE WEDNESDAY, OCT. 17.

WEATHER—FAIR.

Complete weather table on page 10.

YESTERDAY'S WEATHER.

Maximum temperature, degrees	80
Minimum temperature, degrees	49
Humidity, a. m., per cent	70
Humidity, p. m., per cent	58
Wind velocity, S., miles per hour	18
Precipitation	None

The Cleveland Leader.

VOL. 61.—NO. 276. THURSDAY, OCTOBER 3, 1907. ONE CENT In Greater Cleveland. Elsewhere, TWO CENTS.

REGISTER TO-DAY

BIG REGISTRATION IS URGED

ST. LOUIS, MO., October 2, '07.

Editor Cleveland Leader:

I sincerely hope that there may be a large registration to-morrow, and that the apparent interest in the election may be manifested by the number who indicate their intention to vote.

T. E. BURTON.

SLEEPER AFIRE ENDANGERS 15

Explosion Follows Big Four Coach Hitting Gas Pipes at Union Depot.

The lives of fifteen passengers in the sleeper Astol, of the Big Four's Twentieth Century Limited, derailed at the Union depot last night, were imperiled by a gas explosion, and Assistant Station Master W. L. Miller was baly burned. Miller's lantern, it is said, ignited the gas escaping at a hundred-pound pressure from the platform pipes, which were broken when the sleeper left the track.

In an instant the heavy Pullman was enveloped in flames. The report of the explosion and the flames caused consternation among the 400 people waiting on the depot platform. It was thought at first that none of the passengers in the car would escape.

Patrolman Tekler and John Kamerer, a depot usher, were the first to break into the car. Running past Miller, who was picking himself up from the platform and groping blindly about, the two rushed to the door of the sleeper and helped the passengers to a place of safety. There were women and children in the car, but, with the assistance of Tekler, Kamerer, Conductor W. J. Kearns, of Cincinnati, and others, all were removed to the platform. An alarm brought fire apparatus to the scene and the flames were easily extinguished after the gas was shut off.

Serious Wreck Averted.

Another and more serious accident was narowly averted by one of the railroad men, who, realizing that the Lake Shore's Twentieth Century train from Chicago was due to arrive within three minutes on the main track, flagged the fast train. Had this not been done there would have been a crash on the platform.

Miller was taken to the Cleveland General Hospital, where his hurts, which were not serious, were dressed. He returned to the depot within an hour and was able to go to his home in Lakewood unattended.

The Big Four section of the Twentieth Century train arrived on time at 8:40 o'clock. The sleeper, which was to be attached to the train going east, is cut off just as soon as the train comes in, so as to lose no time in attaching it to the east-bound coaches.

The Lake Shore train rolled in on time at 8:46 o'clock. Before the sleeper is moved from its place on the Big Four train the hose from the Pintsch gas pipe is attached and the reservoir tanks filled. The Lake Shore switch engine was coupled onto the dining car, the last coach on the Big Four train and next to the sleeper. This dining car was unoccupied except for the crew, as it was customary to close it before reaching the city.

Releases the Gas.

Conductor A. C. Fisk, of the switching crew, signaled his engineer to pull the two cars away, and they began to move. When the frog of a cross-over was reached the trucks of the dining car swerved to the switch while the trucks nearest the engine held the straight track. The wheels of the sleeper followed the cross-over, but left the rails a foot from the switch point and were buried deep in the depot platform.

The pipes of the Pintsch gas system lie directly under the planking of the platform. It is supposed that one of these pipes was broken by the wheels of the derailed sleeper and the gas gushed out. Miller, whose duty it was to see that no delay occurred in switching this sleeper, was standing near. He ran toward the switch engine, swinging his lamp and yelling at the engineer to stop.

Then came the explosion. The accident happened at the western end of the depot. The switch engine when it came to a standstill was just outside of the depot entrance. The heavy dining car rested against the pillar of the arch. Had it moved another foot a big section of the wall would have been pulled down.

The two Big Four cars formed a triangle, the apex of which came within three feet of the rails on which the Lake Shore express was due to arrive within three minutes. This train was brought to a standstill not more than a 100 yards without the depot.

The berths of the wrecked sleeper had been made up before reaching the depot, and the passengers were preparing to turn in. One or two were in bed. All were placed into another sleeper. The explosion shattered most of the windows of the sleeper and one end of the interior was scorched. In fighting the flames the firemen ruined the expensive interior with chemicals.

ELECTION BOOTHS ARE MOVED ABOUT

Registry Places Shifted and Voters Must Hunt Them.

MOST CHANGES ONLY A BLOCK

Haas Says Action Was Taken to Get Houses Out of Way.

If you don't find your voting booth when you go to register to-day HUNT FOR IT. Many have been moved, but you'll find them within a block of the former locations.

Voters in most of the wards of the city to-day may have some difficulty in finding the booths when they seek to register.

In the past three weeks the board of elections has authorized the removal of almost a hundred polling places.

For some reason no public announcement was made of these changes and people in all parts of the city to-day may have to do some scouting before they arrive at the booths.

No Mention Made.

A. J. Haas, secretary of the board of elections, says these changes have been going on for almost a month and that the board did not believe it was necessary to publish the fact. The list of changes, Mr. Haas says, is open to the inspection of anyone who cares to stop at the city hall and scrutinize it. As none of the booths is more than a block distant from its former location, the board thought the voters would have little or no trouble in getting to the proper registry places.

The trouble started with the booth at Prospect avenue S. E. and E. 40th street. This booth was in the street and was declared by Judge Lawrence to be a public nuisance. Furthermore, the booth was partially wrecked by an automobile one night. This brought it into public attention, and last Monday it was carried away to a vacant lot opposite No. 4709 Prospect avenue S. E.

Booths in the Way.

"We have been making similar changes in every ward in the city," said Mr. Haas last night.

"All these booths had been standing in the streets and were just as much in the way of traffic as the booth in Prospect avenue. So the board decided to move them all to vacant lots or to the strip of ground between the curb and the pavement. I don't think any of the voters will get lost in looking for the booths, for they are all close to where they were before."

REGISTER! REGISTER!

If you don't register you can't vote. First registration to-day. Booths open 8 a. m. to 2 p. m. and 4 p. m. to 9 p. m. Previous registration does not count.

HAS HUNCH, JUMPS, AND LIFE IS SAVED

Carpenter Owes Safety to Obedience to Sudden Impulse.

To his firm belief in some of the weird fancies of superstition and implicit obedience to the commands of premonitions, Charles Ross, thirty-five years old, of Orange avenue S. E., attributes the happy fact that he still is alive and active in swelling the fortunes of the butcher and baker.

Ross is a carpenter. Yesterday, while working on the scaffolding of a new building at Superior avenue S. E. and E. 18th street, suddenly, at the dictation of a premonition, he loaped from the point where he was working to the ground, thirty feet below, landing on a freshly-dumped sand-heap, badly frightened, but only slightly injured.

Scarcely had he leaped from the scaffolding before an immense timber crashed through the frail planks on which he had been standing, smashing them into splinters and tearing through the newly-laid first floor, ended its mad flight in the cellar.

BONDS ISSUED, MONEY WASTED

Debt of City Under Johnson Increases, Improvements Neglected.

BY JOHN T. BOURKE.

Mayor Tom L. Johnson again has taken his pen in hand to attempt a reply to the charges of extravagance brought against his administration.

He overlooks the right of the people to demand a detailed account of the steawardship of the servant, and meets the charges by admitting that more than $13,000,000 has been added to the city's indebtedness since he took office. He seeks, apparently, to square his administration with the people by telling for what general purposes the bonds were issued.

Mayor Says Specify.

And then he says if the money derived from the bond issues has not been wisely expended his critics should "specify." Apparently he doesn't think it is due the people that their mayor, who has the information at hand, owes it to the public to do the specifying himself, and prove that the money of the taxpayers has been judiciously expended.

Moreover, Mayor Johnson seems to beg the question when he confines his argument merely to the piling up of the bonded debt to the limit allowed by law. The people of Cleveland have never protested against the issuance of bonds when it is necessary to make needed improvements. The criticism which has been made is that bonds were issued for some things which should have been paid for out of the ordinary receipts of the municipality.

It has been charged that the operating expenses have increased more rapidly than the growth of the city warranted, and that the cost of running the government has been permitted to use up all the money raised by direct taxation, the tax on saloons, the tax on cigarettes, the interest on deposits and other sources of revenue.

Would Meet Expenses.

An economical administration, it is declared, would have been able to meet the operating cost of running the city out of the regular receipts, and also would have paid for some improvements which have been provided for through bond issues.

In the campaign prior to Mr. Johnson's first election as mayor in the spring of 1901, it was promised that if he were elected the lake front would be improved and lined with docks, at which passenger steamers would land, package boats discharge and take on freight, ore carriers unload their cargoes and coal carriers receive their loads of fuel for upper lake ports. The Democratic platform that year said on the same subject:

"We should be at liberty to supplement the expenditure of the national government in our harbor improve-

Continued on Second Page, 4th Column

PLAYS FOR LINERS IF WAVES PERMIT

Frohman Arranges to Operate Theaters on Ocean Steamers, but Fears Seasickness May Prevent Players Appearing.

[Special Dispatch to the Leader.]

NEW YORK, October 2.—Unless seasickness lays low all the players, Hamlet, ghost and all, the Maude-Fairy sisters, Tessie, McPoolen's Flats, "Il Trovatore" and others will appear on the boards in theaters built in the ocean greyhounds of the Cunard Line.

The ocean steamship company has accepted the offer of Charles Frohman to give theatrical performances on the big liners by regular players, who, for the time being, may be traveling to and from the United States and England.

Constructing Theaters.

Already specially constructed concert halls are being placed in three of the company's new liners. That part of it is comparatively easy. Also the play. But in this case the player's the thing.

How can a talented actress appear before the refined first cabin passengers at her best when the qualms of mal de mer have her at their mercy? That is one of the problems Mr. Frohman has yet to solve.

First Experiment.

The theater experiment will be tried on the Lucania first. In discussing the project, Alf Hayman, Mr. Frohman's manager, said to-day:

"Mr. Frohman is at present in London, co-operating with the Cunard Company. The scheme will probably be tried first on the Lucania. Light comedy will be given, and, if successful, other branches of theatricals will be put on the steamship boards. Frankly, the chief difficulty with the players would probably arise from seasickness, but I suppose the others would go on and fill the gaps. I cannot tell when the theater on high seas will be put into operation, as some of the details are not definitely settled."

TELEGRAPHERS MAY TIE UP LEASED WIRE LINES

Big Organizations Demand That Operators Now Getting Union Scale Quit Work in Sympathy With the Strikers.

Telegraph service in the United States, crippled as it is, will be worse if the big local unions in New York and Chicago prevail in their present purpose.

Their hope is to call out all the men working leased wires regardless of contracts.

Meetings were held simultaneously yesterday by these locals, the biggest in the United States, and the expression of each was that conditions demanded the immediate withdrawal of the leased wire operators from the ranks of the workers.

President Small is in Chicago, and last night declared against interfering with the leased wire men. The latter are under contract in most cases with brokers, packers and news service corporations. All are paid the scale demanded by the strikers or better. They have no complaint against conditions, and should they go out it would be simply a sympathetic move.

MAY INDICT OFFICIALS IN WAR ON GAMBLERS

State's Attorney Healy, of Chicago, in Whirlwind Finish of His Campaign Against Vice, Likely to Hit Men Higher Up.

(Leader-N. Y. Sun Leased Wire.)

CHICAGO, October 2.—Wholesale indictments of city and possibly county officers for bribery in having taken money as payment for police protection and non-interference with gamblers, are being sought by State's Attorney Healy in a whirlwind finish to his campaign against race track gambling, before the September grand jury.

The announcement of the broadened scope of his inquiry into gambling affairs was made in a petition filed by Mr. Healy to-day in Judge Chetlain's court to compel Horace Argo, right hand man of Monte Tennes, who controls the gambling situation in Chicago, to answer questions in the grand jury room and grant Argo immunity from prosecution.

WILL TRAIN PUPILS TO SPELL COMMON WORDS

Assistant Superintendent of Schools to Obtain From Business Men Lists of Terms Most Often Misspelled.

Warren Hicks, assistant superintendent of instruction, yesterday decided to ask Cleveland business men to submit to the school authorities lists of the words which they find most commonly misspelled.

"Thus spelling bees will become of practical value," said Mr. Hicks. "We wish to teach the scholars how to spell words used in every-day life. The first test this year will be early in December. We want lists two weeks earlier, if possible."

GIRL MISSING MONTH

Parents and Friends of Emma Peshik Report Disappearance, Fearing for Her Safety.

The disappearance of Miss Emma Peshik, a laundry employee, has caused her friends here and her parents in Bedford to fear for her safety..

Miss Peshik has not been heard from for a month. She is twenty-six years old and has many friends in Cleveland. For three years she was employed by Mrs. Seraphina Cannon, No. 5335 Broadway. Since she left there she has visited her frequently. Miss Peshik, her friends say, did not appear to be despondent before her disappearance. Prior to the time she was last seen she drew her money from the bank. Miss Pishek's parents have lived in Bedford several years.

Youth Dies in His Chair.

[Special Dispatch to the Leader.]

BELLEFONTAINE, O., October 2.—While sitting in his chair reading, John Merron, sixteen years old, of near Huntsville, expired. He had been an invalid for three years.

GIRL PITCHER AND HER BASEBALL TEAM

THE VERMILION TEAM

GIRL TOSSER WINS GAME, ALSO FANS

Chews Gum and Pitches All-Star Team to Standstill.

FORGETS, FIXES BOW AT NECK

Mixes Feminine Move With Her Joss-Like Delivery.

BY MARIETT M. BUGGIE.

Miss Alta Weiss, the girl wonder, pitched a winning game yesterday at League Park with the score 7 to 6. Her team, the Vermilions, defeated Vacha's All-Stars.

And the cheers which followed the girl pitcher's sensational playing echoed as far over the East End as those given to Larry.

She's graceful. And mighty pretty, too. But her arms look muscular and her legs, showing beneath the short blue plaited skirt, are built for speed and strength. Her hands are big and tough as a man's.

Is Strong and Active.

But the arms are strong, the legs swift and the hands sure in catching the speedy balls. The shapeless, spiked shoes she wears make her feet seem to cover the ground like seven-league boots. She's a hummer and the crowd was "for her" every moment.

The crowd was more enthusiastic when a big bouquet of flowers was given her. The crowd howled until her brother, who brought the flowers out to the plate where she was up at bat, opened the box and held up a huge bunch of asters.

Miss Weiss makes a hit with the men and women alike. When she first walked up to the pitcher's box she was cheered by 4,000 voices. She moves quietly and modestly along and pays no attention to anything except the game and the players. She yanks her cap down on her head with a pull at the visor and a pat at the back with the identical movement Addie Joss uses.

Makes Feminine Move.

But the eternal feminine crops out when she puts her fingers up and brushes the hair from her face or adjusts the bow at the back of her neck.

For an evident reason she chews gum. She's not a bit offensive about it. She makes a better delivery of the regular ball, although she keeps the men fooled by her variety.

Once after throwing a spit-ball she sent a slow one. The man had drawn three balls and two strikes. He struck at it and after the umpire yelled "He's out" she laughed till her cheeks were red and the crowd laughed with her. That settled it. Every bit of the cheering was for "Little Girl" from that moment.

Each inning the crowd liked her better and when the umpire ruled in favor of the All-Stars the mob howled and mocked him.

Wears Gymnasium Suit.

Miss Weiss wears a gymnasium suit of dark blue serge, with deep-plaited skirt reaching a bit below her knees. Her stockings are broken by wide white stripes like a barber pole. Around the cut-out neck two rows of white braid bind the edge and a similar treatment is given the bottoms of the short sleeves, which end above the elbow. Across her chest big, white letters spell "Vermilion."

After each inning her brother comes just out from under the players' bench and assists her into a brown sweater, while the crowd all the time is shouting and cheering.

Then she slips way back into the dark corner next to her father, who furnishes her with fresh handkerchiefs to wipe away the perspiration and gives her a glass of water. She's only eighteen, with light brown hair and blue eyes.

REGISTER! REGISTER!

If you don't register you can't vote. First registration to-day. Booths open 8 a. m. to 2 p. m. and 4 p. m. to 9 p. m. Previous registration does not count.

Summary of THE LEADER TO-DAY

Phones: Main and Erie 2.

City subscribers of the Leader will please make complaint direct to the Leader office whenever the delivery of the Leader is irregular or late.

WALLACE'S WIDOW DIES

Woman Who Aided Husband in "Ben Hur" and Other Literary Work is Dead in Indiana.

CRAWFORDSVILLE, IND., October 2.—Mrs. Susan E. Wallace, widow of General Lew Wallace, died last night. She had great literary ability and assisted her husband in his writings.

HORSE, MOTOR AND CAR MIX IN PANIC

Machine Frightens Beast, Which Runs and Bumps Into Trolley.

PASSENGERS, IN AFFRIGHT, JUMP

Cool Conductor Prevents Stampede and Police Stops Horse.

An unmanageable automobile, a runaway horse and a badly damaged street car were the central figures in a situation which resulted in a panic on an east-bound Detroit avenue car near the W. 83d street police station at 5 o'clock last evening.

Men and women jumped for their lives before the car could be brought to a stop by the motorman, when the horse, rushing at full speed, dashed into it and carried away the fender. The police say the fact that the street at this point is torn up for repaving and that those who fell landed on the soft dirt alone is responsible for the fact that no one was seriously injured.

Auto Starts Whole Trouble.

The trouble started at W. 89th street and Detroit avenue N. W. when a big automobile touring car, in which were two men, attempted to pass the delivery wagon of Wattson & Guest, of No. 5911 Euclid avenue N. E., which was in charge of Frank Davis. The car, it is alleged, became unmanageable and swerved suddenly to the left, forcing the horse into the gutter. The hood of the tonneau caught in the horse's bridle and tore it from him, and the animal, mad with fright, dashed up on the sidewalk and ran down Detroit avenue.

Swerving back into the street, the horse narrowly missed running into the car, crowded with people, as it passed W. 83d street, but the wagon caught the fender of the car, and carried it clear away. Three windows of the car were smashed when the wagon scraped along, and the crash of breaking glass and startled cries of frightened women added to the excitement.

Conductor is Cool.

The conductor of the car, whose name was not learned, did much to calm the frightened passengers. Calling to them that the danger was all over, and to keep quiet, he stationed himself in the door of the car, and prevented at least one elderly woman,

Continued on 3d Page, 5th Column.

MAYOR'S ZONE PLAN ASSAILED

Thrifty Suburbanites Condemn Idea of Low Fare in City Only.

HOWE'S STAND IS CRITICISED

Objected to Proposition Once Because of the Effect on Slum Districts.

Thrifty workers, owning their homes in the suburbs and holding positions in Cleveland, condemn Mayor Johnson's idea of having a three-cent rate within the city and an extra fare beyond the municipal boundaries.

Senator Fred C. Howe, while connected with the Chamber of Commerce, objected to the zone system because of its tendency to increase slum districts.

The publication of the transcript of testimony showing that Mayor Johnson never purposed extending the benefits of a three-cent fare to the territory outside of the city limits, created surprise among the suburbanites. In nearly every direction there are large settlements composed of men who come to Cleveland every day to work and return home at night.

Other Land Opened.

At the present time another subdivision is being built up along Coit avenue, in East Cleveland, and most of the men owning homes in this section draw their wages from Cleveland business concerns. H. Barrow lives at Coit avenue and Pitney street. In discussing the probability of the people of that section being made to pay two fares under Mayor Johnson's plan, Mr. Barrow said that he regretted the fact that this policy is supported by the mayor.

"I have always favored the three-cent idea," he said yesterday. "I have thought that Mayor Johnson was right and that he was trying to do the right thing by the people, but I do not like the idea of paying another fare to reach my home."

Several years ago, when lots in that neighborhood were cheap, Mr. Barrow bought a strip of land and later built a modest home. The grounds are tastefully arranged and the place bears evidence of the owner's care.

"Altogether my family uses the street cars twenty-five or thirty times a week and often more," he said. "My son Harry goes down town to business every day and my daughter also is a regular patron of the road. Just at present I have been unable to get around much on account of illness, but otherwise I use the line myself. If we are obliged to pay five-cent fare on the Euclid avenue line it will add quite a burden to almost everyone living out here. I had supposed that the low fare movement took in all these places outside of the city and I was willing to support the measure. I do not know what to say about the proposition now."

Surprised at Mayor.

H. T. Adams, formerly a clerk in a hardware store in Superior avenue and later a cigar manufacturer, owns a little home at No. 33 Pitney street. He always had favored a straight three-cent fare, he said, and was greatly surprised to read Mayor Johnson's testimony, in which the chief executive admitted under cross-examination that the low fare movement was designed to operate only within the city limits.

"When one is saving money for old age every penny counts, and I know many who would be affected under the mayor's plan," he said.

Several other people in the neighborhood declared that they had thought that three-cent fare in Cleveland meant three-cent fare as far as the lines extended.

"It is wrong to force people to remain in the crowded part of town by taxing them a high fare for the privilege of living out in the open country, where homes are cheap," said George Gardner, an electrical worker, living in the Frisbie addition.

"Mayor Johnson has never said a word about having three-cent fare exclusively for Clevelanders, and, if he had, I think the results might have been different. The workers are beginning to realize that the street car question has been exploited to make votes, and when it comes to a show-down we will have to pay the low fare concern just as much, if not more, than we would have to pay the other company. Seven tickets for a quarter suits me, and if the war is settled on that basis I shall not kick. Of course I should like to see Mayor Johnson get the credit of settling the matter, but it should be settled at once."

Comment Created.

The assertion of Mr. Howe that there is too much vacant territory in the city of Cleveland to cause congestion in the slums if a two-fare system is adopted created much comment in business circles yesterday. Before his connection with the low fare movement Mr. Howe was the chairman of the Chamber of Commerce committee on housing. This committee has jurisdiction over all questions brought before the ch

SPORTING SECTION

The World

NEW YORK, SUNDAY, SEPTEMBER 13, 1908.

TY COBB, HIS BASEBALL CAREER.

New Giants of the Sporting World--Told by Themselves. No. 12.

Greatest Batter in the American League Says He Learned to Play Ball by Throwing Cotton "Puffs" on His Grandfather's Plantation in Georgia. Declares the Detroit-Philadelphia Game Last Year Was the Greatest He Ever Played in. Tells of His Superstition and Dislike of Brooms, and How He Accounts for His Feelings.

BY E. G. BROWN.

Tyrus Raymond Cobb, star outfielder of the Detroit Americans, has had the most rapid rise in baseball circles of any of the great stars of the diamond. During his first full year in what professional ball players call "fast company" Cobb not only made good, but he surpassed the wildest prophecies of his most ardent admirers, for he led his league in batting and established an enviable record as a base-runner.

In less than four years he jumped from a fifty-dollar-a-month cub to one of the highest priced ball players in either league; and all this he has accomplished before reaching the age at which the ordinary American citizen can vote.

His great playing and wonderful batting for the Detroit Tigers last year was largely responsible for that team winning the American League championship, and he has been a great factor in keeping his team in the lead during the present season.

Last year Cobb was the baseball sensation; this year he has proven the baseball marvel.

Besides being the greatest batter in his league Cobb is probably the most nervous ball player that ever wore spiked shoes. When he first began his career as a real ball player it was next to impossible to keep him still. He generally began racing as soon as he was the "batter-up." He would run to the plate, smash the ball into the field and start on a mad chase to first If thrown out, he kept on running, turning around and continuing his gallop till he reached the players' bench.

"Ty," as every baseball fan in the country knows him, is a tall, well-knit Southerner, with hair as flaxen as pulled taffy, mild blue eyes, and a smile that reflects the Southern sun that bronzed his skin since he was a cotton picking tad on his grandfather's farm in Georgia. He is six feet and three-quarters of an inch in height, and weighs 178 pounds when stripped for action.

Cobb is proud of the fact that he is the youngest man who ever led either of the big leagues in batting, and his success on the diamond has gone far toward eliminating the juvenile tricks that were the bane of his fellow-players' existence when he first joined the Tigers.

In the following article Tyrus tells everything he can remember of his past life, both on and off the ball field:

By Tyrus Cobb.

You'd scarce expect one of my age to be writing a piece for the paper; but I am, as you can see for yourself. Maybe you'd also scarce expect one of my age to be "leadin' the league" in batting, but, &s. Four years ago I, too, would have been surprised, mayhap incredulous, if any one had told me that I would be doing both in Anno Domini 1908. But two years ago I would have believed anything about myself that any one prophesied, for just about that time I began to develop a great confidence in my ability to do things.

I was born at Royston, Ga., on Dec. 18, 1886. Royston is in Banks County, and on the day I arrived it was resting snugly under a snow bank, for they had a fair-sized fall of snow in Georgia that year. I get this information from hearsay. But I can readily believe that Royston was covered with snow, even if the fall wasn't a heavy one, for the whole town consisted of a farm or two. My grandfather owned a cotton plantation down there, and I was raised on his land.

Of course the news of my arrival spread about the countryside, and the ministers from the neighboring towns did a footrace to the farm so as to get the job of christening me. One patriarchial gentleman of the gospel was fleeter than his contemporaries, for he got there first, and by the time he came the family had already picked out a title for me. I don't know from what family archives they ever succeeded in digging the name of Tyrus, but they fell for it, and I was the goat. They separated Tyrus from Cobb by inserting Raymond, so you see I have one of those triangular names.

Was Cotton Picker.

The first thing that I can remember of my early life is that I picked cotton along with a lot of other kids. Most of the other kids were "shady" characters, and their mammies carried baskets filled with coton on their heads. Not on the kids' heads, but on their own, the mammies' heads.

Fooling with the cotton balls and fighting pitched battles with them got me into the habit of handling the sphere, and this early education stood me in good stead when, many years later, I broke into baseball. Contrary to the general belief, I began playing baseball twelve years ago. It was when I was a tot of eight years, and the position I held was shortstop on the Royston Midgets. I played with them for a season, at the end of which I retired with three 25-cent balls, a homemade bat and a catcher's mitt, spoils of a successful season on the diamond.

When I went out to try for the team next year I found that I had outgrown my midget's uniform, and was therefore campelled to "farm out" to the lankier team whom we had had as chief opponents the season before. We played one "league" game every week, and the contesting teams were always the same. The only difference in the line-up was the umpire, and when the latter official became keyed up to the proper pitch he would rule one of the players out of the game and take his place himself. A new umpire would be selected and the game continued.

When I grew older I played on a regularly organized amateur team known as the Roystons. Here I held down my old position of shortstop, and after a season with them and a fey flyers into what is called "semi-professional" ball, I signed up with the Augusta club of the South Atlantic League.

Batting Got Him Job.

The league was a new one, and I was among the first applicants for a job. "Con" Strouthers owned and managed the Augusta team, and he gave me a try-out. He had a speedy young fellow toss up a couple of aalls, but neither of them got past the plate. I didn't understand the science of batting then as well as I do now, and I just swung at each of the pitched balls for all I was worth. They sailed way out past any of the fielders, and then "Con" put in another pitcher.

He wasn't so speedy, but he had a tricky curve. First he put over an outcurve, and I stepped across the plate and whanged it. Then there came an inshoot, and it went the same way. After I had slammed out about seven flies Strouthers told me to report for duty right away. I was on the job about three hours earlier than anybody else. I was getting a salary of $50 a month, but I was so anxious to play that I believe I would have paid for the privilege.

I lacked experience, was young and unsophisticated, and I guess I was generally what is termed "punk" by the fans nowadays. At any rate, I did not make good, and and was farmed out to the Anniston club of Alabama, in the Tennesee-Alabama league. This was only a water-tank kind of a league, and here I made good. I knocked so many home runs that it got to be a common occurrence for me, my average with the stick being .370. The Anniston club paid me $75 a month, and it was not long before Strouthers recalled me to the Augusta club at a salary of $100 a month.

The main trouble with me while I was with the Augusta Club was that I was too "kiddish." I was always on the run, and try as I would, I could not break myself of the habit of chasing up and down the field and hopping about like a wild Indian. However, on my second trial with that team I came up to expectations, and after finishing the year at the head of the league in batting I heard things that led me to believe that the Detroit Club was after me.

I found out later that I was mistaken. The Detroit Club wasn't dying to get hold of me, but Manager William Armour had seen me at work and decided that I was good enough to travel with his team. I believe he even went so far as to pay the $750 out of his own pocket that the Augusta Club charged for my release. Later he was able to convince the Detroit Club that he had not made a mistake. You see after that I just had to make good. That was in 1905, and the next year I was an "extra" on the team until late in the season when they gave me a chance and I made the most of it.

Last year I came into my own. I am proud to say that I led the league in batting and base-stealing, and I hope to be able to say the same thing next year. Barring an accident, I don't see how I can help being in the lead in batting when the season ends, and from all indications I will have an excellent opportunity to show what I can do against the best pitchers in the other league.

Of course, I've got a little schooling. My folks always believed that school was good for a youngster, and they saw to it that I put in a good part of my time at readin' and 'ritin' and 'rithmetic. I've never regretted it. No one ever does. After finishing my elementary school education, I put in two years at a prep. school in Stone Mountain Park, and was just about ready to break into college when the death of my father prevented me from carrying out my plans.

Tells About Greatest Game.

I believe the greatest ball game that I ever played in was the one between Detroit and Philadelphia for the championship last season. Of course that game was not specifically for the pennant, but the winning of the rag depended on the outcome of the game. The Detroits were eight points ahead in the league race, and we had only two more games to play. We were scheduled to play a double header with Philadelphia, the last games with them for the season, and they were giving us a hard fight.

Let me see, this game took place at Philadelphia on Sept. 30 of last year.

The grounds were literally packed with people. The whole town was baseball mad, even worse than Chicago in the world's series. People climbed over centre field fence, trees outside of the field were festooned with fans and the housetops as far as one could see were suffused with enthusiasts who were unable to get any nearer the scene of action.

"Wild Bill" Donovan pitched the entire game for us. Dygert, the spit-ball artist, began the game for the Athletics. He lasted through the first inning and part of the second. Then we faced Rube Waddell and his wonderful left-hand shoots. He held us down for a while, but we got busy in the fourth inning and made four runs.

This didn't help much, for when we came to bat in the ninth the score stood 8 to 6 against us. Then we got to the Rube for fair. Sam Crawford singled, and I hit the ball over right field fence for a homer, thus tieing the score.

Say, if I live to be a hundred 'll never forget the joy that our boys felt, and showed that they felt, when they saw that ball go sailing over the fence. As I went around the bases Herman Schaefer went with me, step for step, pounding me on the back at every stride. The rest of the bunch stood dancing at the players' bench like a band of wild Indians.

We made another one in the eleventh, and the Athletics followed suit, again tieing up the score. The fourteenth inning was a squally one. Harry Davis lifted a high one to the edge of the crowd in centre. Crawford ran like a wild man to make the catch, and as he was about to grab the ball a cop pushed him and the ball went into the crowd.

If Umpire O'Loughlin had allowed the hit it would have been good for two bases under the ground rule, and Davis would have scored on Danny Murphy's single, which followed.

If you ever saw a scared cop, there was one at the game that afternoon. The excitement that followed his act of pushing Crawford was intense, and it looked for awhile as if there would be a riot. It seemed to me that every player on both teams was out on the field at once, arguing with Umpires O'Loughlin and Connolly.

While the argument was at its height Monte Cross, of the Athletics, and Claud Rossman, our first baseman, had a little mixup, and Claud was chased out of the game. The fans invaded the field and it took ten minutes to get them off. Rossman put on his street clothes and walked out among the crowd while they were uttering dire threats as to just how they were going to tear him to pieces when he appeared. They didn't recognize him, and he joined in the fracas, and was loudest in denunciation of himself. The crowd never tumbled.

Result Gave Detroit Pennant.

Well, the result of that game undoubtedly gave us the pennant. Neither side was able to score, and it was called a tie at the end of the seventeenth inning. I firmly believe that that was not only the greatest game I ever played in, but I am certain that in many respects it was the most sensational game in the history of baseball. Some folks have been kind enough to say that I saved the game. However that may be, I am certainly proud to have played in it.

Every baseball player that ever lived has some sort of hobby or superstition. I have one superstition that is silly, but I can't overcome it. It is this: I always like to have the umpire's broom on the right side of the plate when I go to bat. The umpires like to have it on the left side, and after dusting off the plate they invariably hurl it to the left. I always hoist it over to the right when I step up to the plate.

You see, I am a left-handed batter, and I hate to have that broom staring me in the face when I'm trying to solve the pitcher's delivery.

I never did take kindly to brooms, anyway. When I was quite a kid I used to have a burly negress for a nurse, and she used to scare me half to death by threatening to sweep me off the earth if I didn't behave myself. Then she used to tell me about a "passel o' witches" that rode about on dark nights on brooms, and I guess these things prejudiced me against brooms. Funny, isn't it?

BROKE STIFFY'S LEG AND BEAT JUNCTIONS.

Squirrel Killer Falls on Flingspeed's New "Directoire" Curve With Awful Force—Collegian Foiled.

By Bozeman Bulger.

Biographer's Note.—In bringing to light this heretofore untold incident in the career of the Peerless Big Tank Junctions and their long run of hard luck I am deeply indebted to "Doc" McDonough, a famous veteran of the Wire Grass League, who has written me a letter recalling the game in which the intrepid Stiffy Ashleg was compelled to play in the outfield for one inning, notwithstanding the impediment of his wooden limb. We are deeply thankful to all of the old timers who volunteered to aid in this historical research.

One beautiful spring morning Capt. Steve O'Hara and Fahrenheit Flingspeed, the great college pitcher of the Peerless Big Tank Junctions, were strolling through the woods. They had gone thither to talk over the prospects in the league, and if possible to arrive at some solution of the mysterious hard luck which had persistently pursued them. Beginning with the arrival of Stiffy Ashleg, the intrepid hitter with the wooden leg, early in the season, they had met with nothing but misfortune. With him and without him they would lose. If Stiffy played on an opposing club some particular feat of his would usually beat them. If he played on the Big Tank Junctions some ill luck would befall him that would cause them to lose again. From bad to worse it went.

"Well, Stiffy is back with us again," said Flingspeed, "and, notwithstanding his former desertion, I firmly believe he is on the level and trying to make amends."

"Whether we can win or not," interrupted O'Hara, "he is a great drawing card."

"Quite true," added Flingspeed. "But I have begun to believe that we can win anyway."

O'Hara looked up in surprise. "Out with it, Fahrenheit," he demanded. "Go on and tell me what is in the wind. I know you have something on your mind."

Then as they strode along through the rose-laden bushes the college pitcher began to tell of a new curve that he had discovered over night. Though he was a little mixed in his French, Flingspeed had decided to call his new curve the "Directoire." The word really had no bearing on the attainments of the invention, but because it sounded something like "direction" Flingspeed made up his mind to use it.

In brief, the Directoire curve was a ball so thrown that the batter could be made to hit it in any direction desired by the pitcher. To go into the geometrical intricacies of this ball would be a waste of space. Suffice it to say that the ball was set spinning so that when it came in contact with the round surface of a solid body—a bat, for instance—it would be hurled into the direction intended by the twirler who started it.

O'Hara was becoming deeply interested when sud-

Continued on Page Four, This Section

THE GREAT Breakfast Table Paper OF NEW ENGLAND

The Boston Post

14 PAGES TODAY

FOURTEEN PAGES—ONE CENT | Established 1831 | THURSDAY, SEPTEMBER 24, 1908*** | Copyright 1908 by Post Publishing Co. | ONE CENT

RIOT ENDS NEW YORK BALL GAME

Umpire Declares It No Contest After Fistic Battle on Field Over Decision

JOHN J. McGRAW MANAGER OF NEW YORKS

FRANK CHANCE CAPT. MANAGER OF CHICAGO "CUBS"

HARRY C PULLIAM PRESIDENT OF NATIONAL BASE BALL LEAGUE

BY PAUL H. SHANNON

POLO GROUNDS, NEW YORK, Sept. 23.—With the leadership in the most thrilling pennant race in history depending upon the result of this afternoon's battle, and a New York win virtually assured, a stupid play on the part of New York's substitute first baseman in the ninth inning snatched victory from the Giants' grasp, nearly nullified Al Bridwell's splendid hit to centre and precipitated a small sized riot, as well as robbing Mathewson of a well earned game.

The score should have been 2 to 1 in New York's favor, but tonight, while Umpire O'Day decides that the game was a tie and President Pulliam has ordered this tie to be played off tomorrow, President Murphy of Chicago insists that Chicago is now in first place, and claims a victory by a score of 9 to 0.

Following Merkle's neglect to touch second base, and the return of the ball from centre field, touching Merkle out, the players on both sides swarmed over the diamond, while the crowd rushed to assault the defenceless Chicago players.

In the mad scramble for the ball, Joe McGinnity rushed at Tinker and was

Continued on Page 10—First Column

ADMITS BIG NOTE ROBBERY

Messenger Boy Under Arrest for $44,000 Theft From Safe

The story of how a 16-year-old boy stole a small fortune in securities with a face value of $44,879.16 and lived undetected for over two months is revealed in the arrest yesterday afternoon by headquarters inspectors of Alfred J. McGuinness of 56 Yeomon street, Roxbury.

McGuinness was a messenger boy in the employ of the State street office of the Western Union Telegraph Company and he confessed to the police when arrested, they say, that it was he who on Aug. 20 entered the office of W. R. Chester & Co., lumber dealers, at 19 Doane street, and during the temporary inattention of the two women clerks, decamped with a leather wallet containing the securities.

ALFRED J. M'GUINNESS, Sixteen-year-old telegraph boy, who confessed yesterday to the stealing of securities worth nearly $45,000 two months ago.

In his confession young McGuinness implicated a confederate, who, he said, waited outside while he removed the wallet from the big office safe, then shared the booty.

Mr. Chester and his son had placed the securities in the wallet and put it in the safe, leaving the doors open. Then they temporarily left the office in the charge of the two women clerks.

A little later the wallet was missing and not the slightest clue to how it had disappeared was discovered. Fortunately the securities were all in the form of promissory notes and some quick work with the telephone and telegraph obviated any danger of the thief being able to negotiate them.

Continued on Page 8—Seventh Column

Cholera Invades Palace

ST. PETERSBURG, Sept. 23.—Not only has the number of cases of Asiatic cholera in this city increased today, but the disease has invaded the aristocratic precincts of St. Petersburg.

It has even reached the winter palace, one case having been discovered in the servants' quarters of the palace, in which extensive preparations are going on in the expectation that the Emperor and Empress will spend part of the coming season in the capital.

Other cases have been discovered in the palace of Grand Duke Nicholas Nicholaievitch, the Tauride Palace, the palace of Prince Alexander Oldenburg, a cousin of the Emperor, and the Imperial Opera House.

A number of diplomats and prominent society people have hurried their departure abroad, but the exodus has been checked to a considerable extent by the prospect of being held in quarantine at the frontier.

HASKELL CASE "SCANDAL AND DISGRACE," SAYS PRESIDENT

Roosevelt Makes a Violent Attack on Bryan in Demanding He Remove Oklahoma Governor From the Campaign---Says It Is Common Knowledge That Haskell Is Tied Up With Standard Oil

THE HON. J. B. FORAKER
Republican Senator from Ohio

GOVERNOR C. N. HASKELL
Treasurer of the Democratic campaign

THE TWO MEN AROUND WHOM THE PRESENT FIERCE POLITICAL CONTROVERSY RAGES

REFUSES TO AID HOWARD

Miss Sturtevant Says Murder Suspect Must Fight for Himself

NEW BEDFORD, Sept. 23.—Grace F. Sturtevant, the South Dartmouth young woman who stood by William C. Howard and secured his acquittal by her testimony supporting his own in a recent murder trial, will leave him to his own resources now that he has been arrested on the charge of killing his wife, Ida Howard.

The statement came from her own lips today—a prompt and emphatic denial of all claims made by the prisoner to the effect that she had been in his company last Saturday night at the time that his wife is supposed to have met her death in the river.

"He will have to fight for himself," she said. "I was not in his company, and he will get neither support of his false statements nor comforting words from me."

PLEADS NOT GUILTY

Today the prisoner, his very appearance suggesting his apparent misery of mind, was arraigned in the Third District Court, pleaded not guilty, and was held without bail till Oct. 3 on the charge of causing the death of his wife, whose body was found in three feet of water near the Padanaram bridge at South Dartmouth last Sunday.

After his arraignment came further disgrace and humiliation. He was served with a notice in his cell that he had been dishonorably discharged from membership in the 52d company of the United States Coast Artillery at Fort Rodman.

Continued on Page 14, First Column.

$80,000 PLEDGED TO ERIN

Redmond's Speech Thrills Irish Leaguers as Convention Closes

Subscription pledges totalling nearly $80,000, of a promise for $100,000, were a feature of the sessions which yesterday closed the fourth biennial convention of the United Irish League.

The unqualified assurance of continued support of the Irish party and an expression of the most implicit confidence in the leadership of Mr. Redmond came from the assemblage amid wild applause.

In return, Erin's envoys promised unceasing devotion and service to the betterment of Ireland.

Probably that which gave the league its greatest determination to continue the fight for the general uplifting of the people of Ireland, the fight for the right of local self-government, the acquisition of the land by the tenants, and the advancement of the cause of education, was the speech of John Redmond, who accompanied Messrs. Devlin and Fitzgibbon to this country.

ANSWER WITH CHEERS

His account of the achievements of the Irish party were listened to with rapt attention by the vast audience, and at the conclusion evidence of the heartiest approval of his leadership came in repeated volleys of cheers.

Joseph Devlin, who followed Mr. Redmond, told of the advance made all along the lines, as he said, laid down by Parnell and persistently followed by the Irish party under the leadership of Mr. Redmond.

Continued on Page 8—Third Column

FAIR

Forecast for Boston and vicinity—Fair Thursday; probably continued fair Friday; variable winds.

WASHINGTON, Sept. 23.—Forecast for New England: Generally fair Thursday and Friday, light south to southwest winds.

YESTERDAY'S TEMPERATURE

	1907.	1908.
3 a. m.	58	61
6 a. m.	58	60
9 a. m.	59	66
12 m.	60	74
3 p. m.	59	73
6 p. m.	59	73
9 p. m.	68	66
12 mid.	60	64

Roosevelt's Opinion of Haskell

"Utterly unfit for association with any man anxious to appeal to the American people on a moral issue."

"Intended for some reason of his own to protect the interests of a great corporation against the law."

"Disgraceful that he should be connected with the management of any national campaign."

"Unworthy of any position in our public life."

PRESIDENT ROOSEVELT'S ATTACK ON BRYAN

"I am not in charge of the campaign, but am greatly interested in it."

"It is up to you to say what shall be done with Governor Haskell."

"The facts concerning Haskell which I give you were available before he was chosen treasurer of your campaign committee."

"You may have advocated more radical measures against private monopolies than I have, but they will never work out in practice."

"Any measure you advocate would merely throw the entire business of the country into hopeless and utter confusion."

"I'll put Taft's deeds against your words and let the public judge which is the more lasting."

"It is entirely natural that the great law-defying corporations would wish to see you President rather than to see Taft elected."

"Your plans to stop corporation abuses are wholly chimerical."

WASHINGTON, Sept. 23.—President Roosevelt tonight, following upon a prolonged conference with members of the Cabinet at the White House, prepared and gave out his reply to W. J. Bryan, the Democratic candidate, relative to W. R. Hearst's charges that Governor Haskell, treasurer of the Democratic campaign committee, had represented Standard Oil interests both in Ohio and Oklahoma.

Mr. Bryan had demanded proof of the charges, promising that in the event of their substantiation Governor Haskell would be eliminated from the campaign.

Dismissing the Ohio case, which involved an allegation of attempted bribery, with the explanation that he had made no direct charge against Governor Haskell as regards that particular instance, President Roosevelt takes up the matter of the Prairie State Oil and Gas Company and argues that Governor Haskell's action in stopping legal proceedings begun by the Attorney-General of Oklahoma demonstrates conclusively that he was controlled by the great corporation to which the Oklahoma company was subsidiary.

Continued on Page 9—First Column

Falsehoods, Says Gov. Haskell

GUTHRIE, Okla., Sept. 23.—Governor Charles N. Haskell tonight issued a statement to the Associated Press in reply to President Roosevelt's letter to William J. Bryan.

The Prairie Gas & Oil Company Governor Haskell declared to be a joke on Roosevelt's stupidity, asserting that he had done nothing which would confer upon the Standard Oil subsidiary company more authority than it already possessed under a franchise granted it by Secretary Hitchcock.

The statement in part follows:

"To the Associated Press:

"President Roosevelt's letter is before me, and while this is the first time in my life that I have been made the subject of a cabinet meeting, I am thankful for the distinction and I wish to express my high regard for the office of the President and my profound respect for the wisdom of our fathers in making it possible to change the occupant of that high office every four years without the right granted to a crown prince to succeed the king.

"I assert that it is fair for me to assume that if my case was to be dignified by an all-day cabinet meeting, beyond question Mr. Hearst and his campaign associate, President Roosevelt, left no stone unturned to blacken my character. That being true, they certainly raked Ohio fore and aft concerning the Ohio Standard Oil commission of 1899, and found absolutely nothing reflecting on me. The President tried to waive his charge of last Monday aside by saying 'he will make no allusion to that.' He drops the subject because his original statement was untruthful, and he must know from what he knows and tried to find in Ohio, that I spoke the truth when I said that I never in all my life had any interest in or connection with, nor service for that company.

"I say the President knows now that my statement is true, and I regret that he tries to brush it aside without doing me candid justice. Were I to adopt the character of language so commonly used by the President, I would spell it in fewer letters than 'falsehood.'

"Mr. Roosevelt, I hope to speak in Ohio soon. May I hope to divide the time with some partisan of yours or Prince William, who will defend your action in this instance?

"President Roosevelt comes to Oklahoma and finds a substitute for his Ohio failure. Does he, in the case of the State against the Prairie Oil & Gas Company, which he complains I compelled to be dismissed?

"Yes, I did have it dismissed. We all know that the Prairie company is a Standard Oil off-spring, and don't forget the President claims to have known this also, and I charge that the political allies, Hearst and Roosevelt, both know that I acted properly.

"Now, Mr. President, why did your Secretary of the Interior grant what you knew to be a Standard Oil pipe line franchise in our then helpless territory and fasten it on our new State by a permanent statehood bill? Will Mr. Hearst or the President please answer?"

Merkle's Stupid Play Causes Riot

Blunder Turns New York's Victory Into Disputed Tie

Continued from First Page

only prevented from mixing it up by the actions of his fellow players, who grabbed and held him.

ASSAULTS CUBS' MANAGER

In the meantime, a certain police official, whose duty should have been to protect the visiting players, is accused of punching Chance and Del Howard, the latter refusing to leave Chance's side when the crowd rushed for the Cubs' manager. Chance had to leave the grounds under a tardy police protection, while Umpire O'Day, upon whose decision the Cubs claim victory, was also escorted to the grandstand by the police, who feared that the crowd would handle that official roughly when his verdict was made known.

As it was, O'Day did not make his ruling public until he was safely within the clubhouse. Then he declared that Merkle was out for not running to second base, and that the run supposed to have been scored by McCormick did not count. If th's run did not count, and the third out made it necessary to play an extra inning, then President Murphy claims that police protection should have been furnished and the players given an opportunity to continue. But as the 20,000 fans had already taken possession of the diamond this was impossible. This is why Murphy claims that the game is forfeited to Chicago.

The play on which the mix-up occurred was entirely the fault of Merkle, and shows that McGraw has had good reason for not playing the youngster on the first bag before. With the score one all, when New York came to bat in the ninth, Seymour was thrown out by Evers and then Devlin singled to centre. McCormick hit to Evers, who forced Devlin at second, and an instance of the strained relations between the two teams was furnished when the usually quiet Devlin showed an inclination to mix it up with Tinker. Then Merkle singled to right and McCormick went to third.

There were two out, and the dusk was fast gathering when Bridwell, looked upon as a forlorn hope in view of his recent light hitting, came to bat. The second ball pitched Bridwell caught squ[illegible]on the nose and drove it on a line over the second bag.

Never Touched Base

McCormick came rushing in, half the New York team rushed towards the clubhouse in the belief that it was all over, and it would have been all over had not Merkle, who had started for second base on Bridwell's hit, suddenly changed his mind when he saw Donlin and the others heading for the clubhouse, and decided to join them.

Joe Tinker yelled for Hoffman to throw the ball in; Hoffman returned it, the ball going over Evers' head, where Joe McGinnity, who had taken no part in the game, and had no right on the diamond, rushed forward and grasped it. In an instant half of the team were gathered about McGinnity, who refused to give the ball up to Tinker. Words were interchanged and McGinnity, who took umbrage at something Tinker said, threw the ball down, where Pfeister grasped it and threw it to Evers, who touched second base.

Then followed the assault upon Chance and Howard, and the furious demonstration of a thousand or so rooters, who wrestled with the police in an effort to get at the Chicago manager. The confusion was so great and the mix-up so general that half the spectators left the field rejoicing at a New York victory while the rest remained about the grounds, threatening to hand it to Umpire O'Day and the Chicago bunch.

In the fast gathering dusk it would have been impossible to play the game out, even had the Giants shown such a disposition, but the New York team had gone to the clubhouse and the crowd was in possession of the field. This unsatisfactory ending to a thrilling battle is greatly to be regretted inasmuch as it robs Mathewson of the credit of a wonderfully pitched game and deprives Al Bridwell of the credit of holding his team in the front of the race.

It even eclipses the memory of a series of sensational plays in which once more little Johnnie Evers and Joe Tinker shone as stars of the first magnitude and by giving Pfeister magnificent support had saved the latter repeatedly.

Puts Matty on Mound

In his eagerness to hold the Giants at the top McGraw had sent in Mathewson for the third time in six days, and although Joe Tinker connected with a straight one in the fifth and drove it to the clubhouse for a home run, this was the only time that the Chicago Cubs really threatened the plate.

Five hits, all scattered, was the sum total of the Cubs' batting, and Matty could seemingly have gone for nine more innings without losing a whit of his effectiveness but for the unfortunate ending of the game.

Pfeister, whose arm is in terribly bad shape, since he hurt it in the last Boston series, was persuaded to go in by Chance, and although every ball delivered by him caused untold agony, he stuck gamely to his task, though everyone could see that the southpaw was not right. He threw just five curve balls during the entire game, and every time that he twisted his wrist he nearly dropped to the slab, so great was h's agony. Tonight his arm is swollen to three times its normal size, and it is doubtful if he pitches any more this season.

That the Giants failed to score more than one run in eight innings is due entirely to the wonderful fielding of Tinker and Evers. Three times the Giants hit into double plays, phenomenal catches by Evers and Tinker doing the business. Had Mathewson been pitching for Chicago there would have been nothing to it but Chicago, and if Pfeister had been operating on the Giants' side it would have meant simply slaughter.

Tenney, who is suffering from varicose veins in his legs and a badly strained back, was unable to play today and an unlucky fate sent Merkle in his place. Those who cheered when the youngster took the veteran's place on the bag are tonight cursing at the chance that sent him into the game, while McGraw has handed the youngster a lecture that he will not soon forget.

Herzog got a pass in the first, and after Bresnahan went out on a fly to Tinker, took second when Hayden made a bad throw to first after catching Donlin's long fly. Herzog got no farther, however.

Chance made Chicago's first hit in the second, but got no farther than the middle sack.

Lose Fine Chance

In the second, with one down, McCormick was hit by a pitched ball and Merkle got a pass. Evers robbed Bridwell of a spanking hit by making a grand running stop over the second bag, cutting off Merkle. Then Mathewson forced Bridwell and a promising chance had been passed up.

Evers singled without result in the fourth, but in the fifth, with one out, Joe Tinker drove the ball on a line over second base. Donlin fielded the ball very slowly and Tinker had made the circuit before it came back. Chicago never looked dangerous after this.

NATIONAL LEAGUE FLAG RACE TOLD IN GAMES

New York leads Chicago by 6 points.
Chicago leads Pittsburg by 1 game.
Pittsburg leads Philadelphia by 12 1-2 games.
Philadelphia leads Cincinnati by 7 1-2 games.
Cincinnati leads Boston by 8 1-2 games.
Boston leads Brooklyn by 11 games.
Brooklyn leads St. Louis by 2 games.

TOLD IN A NUTSHELL

(NATIONAL.)

	R.	H.	E.	Att'ce.
(First Game.)				
BOSTON	7	7	2	1,891
ST. LOUIS	2	8	5	
(Second Game.)				
BOSTON	4	11	2	
ST. LOUIS	1	7	0	
PITTSBURG	2	8	0	
BROOKLYN	1	5	1	800
CINCINNATI	1	6	2	
PHILADELPHIA	0	6	2	1,426
NEW YORK	1	6	0	20,000
CHICAGO	1	5	3	
(No Game.)				

NATIONAL LEAGUE STANDING

	Won.	Lost.	P.C.
New York	87	50	.635
Chicago	90	53	.629
Pittsburg	89	54	.622
Philadelphia	74	64	.536
Cincinnati	68	73	.482
Boston	60	82	.423
Brooklyn	48	92	.343
St. Louis	47	95	.331

GAMES TODAY

(NATIONAL.)

Chicago at New York.
Pittsburg at Brooklyn.
Cincinnati at Philadelphia.

GAMES YET TO BE PLAYED IN THE NATIONAL LEAGUE

	New York	Chicago	Pittsburg	Philadel	Cincinnati	Boston	Brooklyn	St. Louis	Totals
New York	.	1	0	8	4	3	0	0	—16
Chicago	1	.	1	0	5	0	3	0	—10
Pittsburg	0	1	.	0	0	3	1	6	—11
Philadelphia	8	0	0	.	1	0	4	3	—16
Cincinnati	4	5	0	1	.	0	0	3	—13
Boston	3	0	3	0	0	.	6	0	—12
Brooklyn	0	3	1	4	0	6	.	0	—14
St. Louis	0	0	6	3	3	0	0	.	—12

Bridwell was robbed of another legitimate hit by a marvellous stop of Evers in the fifth. In the sixth the Giants tied it up. Herzog opened by driving a sharp grounder along the third base line. Steinfeldt made a wonderful stop, and with no chance of getting his man threw badly to first, Herzog taking second on the error. Bresnahan sacrificed and Donlin singled, tieing the score. Seymour followed with a hit, but Devlin popped to Tinker and Evers took care of McCormick's grounder.

The most thrilling play of the game had been pulled off in the fourth, when after Schulte had made a superb running catch off Seymour, Devlin singled to centre. McCormick smashed a ball that was labelled home run and was headed for centre field, but Evers jumped high in the air, the ball stuck in his left hand, and throwing to first he completed one of the greatest double plays ever made on the Polo grounds.

In the seventh wonderful work by Tinker alone retired the whole New York side. During this game Tinker accepted 14 out of 16 chances.

In the eighth Tinker fumbled Herzog's grounder and Bresnahan flied to Steinfeldt. Then Donlin lined to Tinker, and his fast throw to first doubled Herzog.

The story of the thrilling climax has already been told.

The score:

CHICAGO.

	AB.	R.	BH.	PO.	A.	E.
Hayden, r. f.	4	0	0	1	0	0
Evers, 2b	4	0	1	3	7	0
Schulte, l. f.	4	0	0	1	0	0
Chance, 1b	4	0	1	11	1	0
Steinfeldt, 3b	2	0	0	1	0	1
Hofman, c. f.	3	0	1	0	0	0
Tinker, s. s.	3	1	1	8	6	2
Kling, c.	3	0	1	0	1	0
Pfeister, p.	3	0	0	1	0	0
Totals	30	1	5	*26	15	3

NEW YORK.

	AB.	R.	BH.	PO.	A.	E.
Herzog, 2b	3	1	1	1	1	0
Bresnahan, c.	3	0	0	10	1	0
Donlin, r. f.	4	0	1	2	0	0
Seymour, c. f.	4	0	1	1	0	0
Devlin, 3b	4	0	2	0	2	0
McCormick, l. f.	3	0	0	1	0	0
Merkle, 1b	3	0	1	10	1	0
Bridwell, s. s.	4	0	0	2	3	0
Mathewson, p.	3	0	0	0	2	0
Totals	31	1	6	27	9	0

*Merkle out for not touching second.

Chicago ....0 0 0 0 1 0 0 0 0—1
New York ....0 0 0 0 0 1 0 0 0—1

Home run—Tinker. Sacrifice hits—Steinfeldt, Bresnahan. Double plays—Tinker and Chance (2); Evers and Chance; Mathewson, Bridwell and Merkle. Left on bases—New York, 7; Chicago, 3. Bases on balls—Off Pfeister, 2. First base on errors—New York, 2. Hit by pitcher—By Pfeister, 1. Struck out—By Mathewson, 9. Time—1h. 30m. Umpires—Emslie and O'Day.

CINCINNATI 1, PHILADELPHIA 0

(NATIONAL.)

PHILADELPHIA, Sept. 23.—In a pitchers' battle between two minor league recruits, Rowan for Cincinnati and Covaleski for Philadelphia, the former today won by 1 to 0. The only run of the game was scored in the ninth inning on a wild throw by Bransfield. Covaleski struck out 10 batsmen, at least one in every inning, except the ninth, and fanning three men in the sixth inning.

The score:

CINCINNATI.

	AB.	R.	BH.	PO.	A.	E.
Bayless, r. f	3	0	1	0	0	0
Kane, r. f	1	0	0	0	0	0
Egan, 2b	3	0	0	0	3	1
Lobert, ss	4	0	1	4	3	0
Rescher, l. f	3	1	1	2	0	0
Hoblitzel, 1b	3	0	1	13	1	0
Mowrey, 3b	3	0	1	3	4	1
Paskert, c. f	3	0	0	1	0	0
McLean, c	3	0	1	4	3	0
Rowan, p	2	0	0	0	3	0
Totals	29	1	6	27	17	2

PHILADELPHIA.

	AB.	R.	BH.	PO.	A.	E.
Grant, 3b	4	0	0	1	3	1
Knabe, 2b	4	0	0	1	1	0
Titus, r. f	4	0	1	0	1	0
Magee, l. f	4	0	0	0	0	0
Bransfield, 1b	4	0	0	10	1	1
Osborne, c. f	3	0	1	3	0	0
Shean, ss	3	0	1	1	3	0
Dooin, c	3	0	3	11	2	0
Covaleski, p	2	0	0	0	1	0
Totals	31	0	6	27	12	2

Cincinnati ....0 0 0 0 0 0 0 0 1—1

Two-base hits—Titus, Osborne, Dooin. Sacrifice hits—Egan, Hoblitzel, Covaleski. Double play—Shean and Bransfield. Left on bases—Cincinnati, 6; Philadelphia, 5. Bases on balls—Off Covaleski, 3. Bases on errors—Cincinnati, 1. Philadelphia, 2. Struck out—By Rowan, 4; by Covaleski, 10. Time—1h. 32m. Umpires—Owen and Rigler.

WE WON THE GAME DECLARES JOHN M'GRAW

NEW YORK, Sept. 23.—Tonight Manager McGraw, when informed that O'Day had refused to allow the run to count in the ninth and had called the game a tie, stated:

"I will not play two games tomorrow. We won that game fairly and squarely, for the winning run had crossed the plate, even before Bridwell had reached first on his hit. Right is right, and President Pulliam refused to allow a similar claim made by Chicago against Pittsburg some time since. Let's see what he says now."

Nevertheless, the impression is that if Pulliam declares this game a tie, Manager McGraw will have to double up tomorrow afternoon.

TWO DULL, SICKENING THUDS AND "FAREWELL" ST. LOUIS

NAPS LAND ON ANOTHER

Highlanders Act as First Aids 9-3

CLEVELAND, O., Sept. 23.—Cleveland won its tenth straight game today, defeating New York 9 to 3. Chesbro pitched great ball until the sixth, when Birmingham's triple drove in two runs.

In the seventh Cleveland scored five more by free hitting. Rhoades was a puzzle until the ninth. Manager Lajoie was hit three times, receiving a base on balls the other time up. The batting of Birmingham and Laporte and Ball's fielding featured the game.

The score:

CLEVELAND.

	AB.	R.	BH.	PO.	A.	E.
Goode, r. f.	4	1	1	2	0	0
Bradley, 3b	3	1	2	0	2	0
Hinchman, l. f.	5	1	2	1	0	0
Lajoie, 2b	0	2	0	3	4	0
Stovall, 1b	4	1	1	16	1	0
Bemis, c	4	2	2	1	1	0
Birmingham, c. f.	4	0	3	2	0	0
Perring, ss	4	0	0	1	2	1
Rhoades, p	4	1	1	0	3	0
Land, c	0	0	0	1	0	0
Totals	32	9	12	27	13	1

NEW YORK.

	AB.	R.	BH.	PO.	A.	E.
McIlveen, l. f.	4	1	1	4	0	0
Conroy, 3b	3	0	1	2	2	0
Cree, c. f.	3	1	0	0	0	0
Laporte, r. f.	4	1	2	0	0	0
Gardner, 2b	4	0	0	1	2	0
Moriarity, 1b	4	0	1	14	1	0
Ball, ss	4	0	1	1	4	0
Kleinow, c	3	0	0	1	1	0
Sweeny, c	1	0	0	1	1	0
Chesbro, p	2	0	1	0	3	0
Billiard, p	0	0	0	0	0	0
*O'Rourke	1	0	0	0	0	0
Totals	33	3	7	24	14	0

*Batted for Chesbro in eighth.

Cleveland ....1 0 0 0 0 2 6 0 .—9
New York ....1 0 0 0 0 0 0 0 2—3

Hits—Off Chesbro, 12 in 7 innings. Base on error—New York. Two-base hits—Hinchman, Bradley, Birmingham, Laporte, McIlveen. Three-base hit—Birmingham. Home run—Laporte. Sacrifice hits—Bradley, Conroy. Stolen bases—Goode, Lajoie, Birmingham, Bradley. Double plays—Perring, Lajoie and Stovall; Gardner, Moriarity and Sweeney. Bases on balls—Off Rhoades, 1; off Chesbro, 1; off Billiard, 1. Hit by pitched balls—By Billiard, 1; by Chesbro, 1. Left on bases—Cleveland, 8; New York, 5. Struck out—By Rhoades, 1; by Chesbro, 1. Time—1h. 28m. Umpires—Connolly and Egan.

SECOND GAME IN DETAIL

BOSTON

Innings	1	2	3	4	5	6	7	8
9 Becker	F7		bh bh7 bh7 bh8 *	fc			bh 2-5	
7 Kelley	B bh3		bh bh8 bh8 bh8 *		K		F3	
8 Browne	F2		3bh		bh 2-6		6-3	
3 Stem	bh		F9		K			bh bh2 bh4 bh4 *
5 Sweeney	5-3		F6			B bh4 bh6 bh6 *		F7
2 Bowerman		F2	F9			K		bh bh4
4 McGann		F4		5-3		bh 854		bh
6 Dahlen		B		F8		bh		F3
1 Flaherty		K		B 4-6		F8		F3
Runs	0	0	2	0	0	1	0	1
Hits	1	0	3	0	1	2	1	3

ST. LOUIS

Innings	1	2	3	4	5	6	7	8	9
8 Shaw	bh 6		F2		fc		fc		
4 Charles	6-3		fc			2bh		5-3	
5 Osteen	F6			6-3		F6			
5 Byrne								6-3	
Murray		F8		6-3		F9		F4	
3 Koney		bh		F8		B			F8
7 Delehanty		F5			B bh1 bh1	F8			4-3
2 Bliss		K			F6		2bh 5		bh E4 bh6 bh6 *
6 Morris			bh 4-6		F4		5-3		bh E8
1 Higgins			fc 5-4		bh 4-6		F9		
1 Murdock									K
Runs	0	0	0	0	0	0	0	0	1
Hits	1	1	1	0	1	1	1	0	1

KEY TO SCORE—Players are numbered: Pitcher, 1; catcher, 2; first baseman, 3; second baseman, 4; third baseman, 5; shortstop, 6; left fielder, 7; centre fielder, 8; right fielder, 9. Thus, a grounder fielded from short to first shows the batsman retired, 6-3. F9 means fly to right field, etc. As the players advance along the bases their progress is denoted in the squares, as bh, base hit; sb, stolen base; sh, sacrifice hit, etc. K means strikeout, B base on balls, fc fielder's choice, E error, x balk, pb passed ball, hp hit by pitcher, wp wild pitch, * run. Italic figures indicate "pinch hitters," o Bransfield out on infield fly.

BOSTONS TAKE A BRACE

Doves Take Bargain Day Games From St. Louis 7-2, 4-1

BY ARTHUR D. COOPER

Bargain day yesterday at the South End grounds furnished an afternoon's entertainment for a small audience, but those who attended had the pleasure of witnessing the Doves' double victory over the lowly Cardinals—7-2 and 4-1.

The first contest was somewhat like the one of the day previous, when the Kellyites cinched the game in the first few innings. "Buggs" Raymond was trotted out by McClosky in the first contest, and he had a very poor day, although the tallying was not due entirely to poor twirling, but rather to the wretched support accorded him. Charles Morris and Delehanty were the chief offenders, falling down on some very easy plays.

Lindaman pitched for Boston, and it was only due to the fact that he was given some good support that St. Louis did not make a better bid for the game. He was touched up for eight hits, while Boston got but seven from Raymond. Five of these were gathered in the first two innings. After the second Raymond put on the clamps, and two lone scattered bingles was all that could be made by the Doves.

Bill Sweeney was the star of the first contest, and his three-bagger with three on bases was one of the best hits seen on the grounds this year.

Billy Murray is satisfied at last, having put the ball over the left field fence, something which he has been trying to do all the season.

There was but one man on base when Murray stung the ball for a circuit, and these were the only tallies St. Louis made in the first contest. Bill Dahlen thought he would boost his average a mite, and got busy with the willow also. The story of the game might be told in the second inning. Graham was thrown out by Charles, McGann walked, Dahlen singled to left and took second as Delehanty rolled around the ball before picking it up; Lindaman walked, Becker singled, scoring McGann and Dahlen. Kelley was out at first, Bates walked, filling the bases, Stem was safe on Charles' muff, and Bill Sweeney tripled, clearing the sacks.

The score:

BOSTON.

	AB.	R.	BH.	TB.	PO.	A.	E.
Becker, r. f.	3	1	1	1	2	0	0
Kelley, l. f.	4	1	1	2	3	0	0
Bates, c. f.	2	1	0	0	3	0	1
Stem, 1b	4	1	1	1	9	0	0
Sweeney, 3b	3	0	2	4	2	0	1
Graham, c	4	0	0	0	5	0	0
McGann, 2b	3	1	2	2	2	2	0
Dahlen, ss	4	1	0	0	1	5	0
Lindaman, p	2	1	0	0	0	2	0
Totals	29	7	7	10	27	9	2

ST. LOUIS.

	AB.	R.	BH.	TB.	PO.	A.	E.
Shaw, c. f.	5	0	1	1	1	0	0
Charles, 2b	4	1	2	2	1	2	2
Osteen, 3b	5	0	1	1	0	2	0
Murray, r. f.	3	1	2	5	2	0	0
Koney, 1b	4	0	0	0	14	2	0
Delehanty, l. f.	4	0	0	0	1	0	1
Moran, c	4	0	1	1	2	3	1
Morris, ss	2	0	0	0	3	8	0
Raymond, p	1	0	1	1	0	4	1
*Lush	1	0	0	0	0	0	0
Totals	33	2	8	11	24	21	5

*Batted for Raymond in ninth.

Boston ....1 6 0 0 0 0 0 0 .—7
St. Lous ....0 0 2 0 0 0 0 0 0—2

Two-base hit—Kelley. Three-base hit—Sweeney. Home run—Murray. Stolen base—Stem. Bases on balls—Off Lindaman, 2; off Raymond, 5. Struck out—By Lindaman, 3; by Raymond, 2. Double play—McGann to Dahlen to Stem. Hit by pitched balls—Kelley, Murray. Time—2h. Umpire—Johnstone.

SECOND GAME

There was some interest taken in the second contest, as both teams played very good ball. Flaherty was accorded good support by the Doves and held the Cardinals runless until the final inning. Dahlen appeared in old-time form in the field and did all the work in the first inning. His catch off Byrne was as difficult a play as was witnessed on the South End grounds this year, while he showed his ability in the same inning by doubling Charles at first.

Browne replaced Bates in centre and Kelley again filled left field. Browne's triple in the third brought in the first two tallies of the game and one run was scored by the Doves in the sixth and eighth innings.

Becker and Stem shone in this contest and both played a good game in the field.

In the sixth inning the Doves scored another run, when Sweeney paved the way by drawing a pass. Bowerman struck out and Sweeney scored on singles by McGann and Dahlen.

The last tally was made in the eighth. Stem singled and was advanced by Bowerman's clout. He scored on a smashing single by McGann.

The only tally made by the Cardinals came in the last inning with two down. Bliss singled and took second on McGann's error. Morris singled, scoring Bliss.

The score:

BOSTON.

	AB.	R.	BH.	TB.	PO.	A.	E.
Becker, r. f.	4	1	2	2	2	0	0
Kelley, l. f.	3	1	1	1	0	0	0
Browne, c. f.	4	0	2	4	4	0	1
Stem, 1b	4	1	2	2	8	0	0
Sweeney, 3b	3	1	0	0	2	3	0
Bowerman, c	4	0	1	1	3	0	0
McGann, 2b	4	0	2	2	3	3	1
Dahlen, ss	3	0	1	1	5	5	0
Flaherty, p	2	0	0	0	0	0	0
Totals	31	4	11	13	27	11	2

ST. LOUIS.

	AB.	R.	BH.	TB.	PO.	A.	E.
Shaw, c. f.	4	0	1	1	2	1	0
Charles, 2b	4	0	1	2	2	1	0
Osteen, 3b	4	0	0	0	1	3	0
Murray, r. f.	4	0	0	0	2	0	0
Koney, 1b	3	0	1	1	6	0	0
Delehanty, l. f.	3	0	0	0	2	0	0
Bliss, c	4	1	1	2	6	2	0
Morris, ss	4	0	2	2	3	1	0
Higgins, p	3	0	1	1	0	0	0
aByrne	1	0	0	0	0	0	0
bMurdock	1	0	0	0	0	0	0
Totals	35	1	7	9	24	8	0

aBatted for Osteen in eighth. bBatted for Higgins in ninth.

Boston ....0 0 2 0 0 1 0 1 .—4
St. Louis ....0 0 0 0 0 0 0 0 1—1

Two-base hits—Charles, Bliss. Three-base hit—Browne. Sacrifice hit—Flaherty. Bases on balls—Off Flaherty, 1; off Higgins, 4. Struck out—By Flaherty, 2; by Higgins, 4. Double play—Dahlen to Stem. Time—1h. 35m. Umpire—Johnstone. Attendance—1891.

PITTSBURG 2, BROOKLYN 1

(NATIONAL.)

BROOKLYN, N. Y., Sept. 23.—Brooklyn was again defeated by Pittsburg today. As the score of 2 to 1 indicates, it was a pitchers' battle between Leifield and Wilhelm, the former having a slight advantage.

PITTSBURG.

	AB.	R.	BH.	PO.	A.	E.
Thomas, c. f.	3	0	0	3	0	0
Clarke, l. f.	4	0	1	5	0	0
Leach, 3b	4	1	1	0	3	0
Wagner, ss	4	0	2	3	3	0
Abbaticchio, 2b	3	1	0	2	1	0
Storke, 1b	4	0	2	10	2	0
Moeller, r. f	3	0	0	1	0	0
Gibson, c	4	0	2	2	3	0
Leifield, p	4	0	0	1	1	0
Totals	33	2	8	27	13	0

BROOKLYN.

	AB.	R.	BH.	PO.	A.	E.
Catterson, l. f	4	0	1	1	0	0
Lumley, r. f	4	0	1	4	0	0
Hummell, c. f	4	0	1	2	0	0
Jordan, 1b	4	0	0	12	0	0
Alperman, 2b	4	0	0	2	3	0
McMillan, ss	3	0	0	1	6	0
Sheehan, 3b	2	0	1	1	2	0
Dunn, c	3	1	1	4	3	1
Wilhelm, p	2	0	0	0	2	0
Totals	30	1	5	27	16	1

Pittsburg ....0 0 0 2 0 0 0 0 0—2
Brooklyn ....0 0 0 0 0 1 0 0 0—1

Three-base hits—Leach, Storke. Sacrifice hit—Wilhelm. Stolen bases—Wagner, Storke, Leifield. Left on bases—Pittsburg, 7; Brooklyn, 3. Bases on balls—Off Leifield, 1; off Wilhelm, 2. Hit by pitcher—By Wilhelm, 1. Struck out—By Leifield, 2; by Wilhelm, 4. Time—1h. 34m. Umpire—Klem.

Red Sox Drive Tigers Way Back

Loss of Third Straight Game 4-1 Puts Detroit in Third Place

DETROIT, Mich., Sept. 23.—The tattered Tigers drank to the dregs the cup of humiliation this afternoon when, for the third consecutive game, they fell victims to the scrappy Red Sox, after playing what is probably their worst game in the past two weeks, and that is going some.

With Donovan pitching the greatest sort of ball, striking out 10 men and allowing but a half-dozen hits, the only cluster coming on an inning in which the Red Sox should have been retired scoreless, the champions heaved and booted their opportunity away, and the Red Sox were right there, taking advantage of every slip.

Young twirled for the Red men of Mr. Taylor and was in far from his top form. In fact, he was found in the early stages with regularity up to the time of a scoring chance, when "Uncle" Cy, with the best of support at his back, would invariably brace and retire the side. Detroit's one run was secured in the sixth, when Cravath failed to get in front of Rossman's drive down the foul line, allowing it to go for a triple, Claude scoring a moment later on an infield out.

Won All the Way

As usual, the Red Sox won all the way. Young started the effective work in the third by a clean hit over second. McConnell's bounder was deflected from Buss by Donovan. Lord struck out and Speaker's unintentional bunt should have resulted in an easy out at first but Schmidt's throw to first was feet high and the ball rolled into right field, allowing the batsman to make third. Young and McConnell scoring. On Gessler's Texas leaguer over Schaefer, Speaker came home.

One out in the fourth and Stahl hit through Rossman for three bases. Schaefer had a fine chance to retire Jake at the plate on Criger's grounder, but booted it into centre field.

The Tigers kept pegging away at Young steadily in the opening half of the game.

McIntyre hit the first ball Cy pitched for a single, but Criger caught him napping off first, Stahl blocking till Hurst came clear across the field and viewed the Tiger firmly pinned several inches from the bag. Cobb and Bush worked in singles in the second, but Schmidt forced the former at third in a play in which the entire Boston team except Stahl either tried or succeeded in taking a part.

In the fourth the Tigers had the bases full and one out, but Coughlin was fanned and Lord threw out Donovan in sensational style, after fumbling Bill's hard drive which he knocked down with one hand.

Aside from the lamentable slips of the Tigers, the game was fielded sensationally by both teams. Lord and Speaker in particular pulled off dazzling plays and Stahl's first-basing was exceedingly high class. After trying for two years the Tigers at last pulled off one of the first-to-second and back double plays in the ninth, Bush being at the middle station and Stahl and Criger being the victims.

The score:

BOSTON.

	AB.	R.	BH.	PO.	A.	E.
McConnell, 2b	4	1	2	0	2	0
Lord, 3b	4	0	1	2	5	0
Speaker, c. f.	4	1	0	3	0	0
Gessler, r. f.	3	0	1	0	1	0
Cravath, l. f.	3	0	0	4	0	0
Wagner, ss	4	0	0	0	4	1
Stahl, 1b	4	1	2	11	0	0
Criger, c	4	0	0	7	1	0
Young, p	3	1	1	0	1	0
Totals	33	4	7	27	14	1

DETROIT.

	AB.	R.	BH.	PO.	A.	E.
McIntyre, l. f.	4	0	2	0	0	0
Schaefer, 2b	4	0	0	1	6	1
Crawford, c. f.	4	0	0	2	0	0
Cobb, r. f.	4	0	2	4	0	0
Rossman, 1b	4	1	1	6	1	1
Schmidt, c	4	0	0	10	1	1
Bush, ss	4	0	2	4	2	0
Coughlin, 3b	3	0	1	0	0	0
Donovan, p	3	0	0	0	0	0
aThomas	1	0	0	0	0	0
bMullin	1	0	0	0	0	0
Totals	36	1	8	27	10	3

aBatted for Coughlin in ninth. bBatted for Donovan in ninth.

Boston ....0 0 3 1 0 0 0 0 0—4
Detroit ....0 0 0 0 0 1 0 0 0—1

Three-base hits—Rossman, Stahl. Stolen base—Cobb. Double plays—Schaefer and Bush; Rossman, Bush and Rossman. Left on bases—Detroit, 7; Boston, 4. Bases on balls—Off Donovan, 2; off Young, 1. Bases on errors—Boston, 2. Struck out—By Donovan, 10; by Young, 5. Time—1h. 40m. Umpires—Evans and Hurst.

ST. LOUIS 5, WASHINGTON 4

(AMERICAN.)

ST. LOUIS, Sept. 23.—A batting rally in the ninth inning, netting four runs, gave St. Louis the third game of the Washington series by the score of 5 to 4.

The score:

ST. LOUIS.

	AB.	R.	BH.	PO.	A.	E.
Stone, l. f	5	2	0	2	0	0
T. Jones, 1b	4	1	2	12	1	0
Hofman, c. f.	5	1	2	1	0	0
Schweitzer, r. f	1	0	0	0	0	0
Hartzell, r. f	4	0	1	2	0	0
Ferris, 3b	5	0	2	1	0	0
Williams, 2b	4	0	0	0	1	0
Wallace, ss	4	0	0	3	5	1
Spencer, c	4	1	1	4	2	0
Howell, p	3	0	1	1	2	0
Yeager, 2b	2	0	1	1	5	0
Pelty, p	0	0	0	0	0	0
aCriss	1	0	0	0	0	0
Totals	38	5	9	27	16	1

WASHINGTON.

	AB.	R.	BH.	PO.	A.	E.
Milan, c. f.	3	0	1	2	0	0
Ganley, l. f	4	0	0	1	0	1
Unglaub, 3b	4	1	1	1	2	0
Delehanty, ss., 2b	4	0	0	2	6	0
Pickering, r. f	4	1	1	0	0	0
Freeman, 1b	3	1	2	13	0	0
McBride, ss	2	1	0	2	3	1
Street, c	3	0	0	3	0	1
Witherup, p	4	0	2	0	4	0
Cates, 2b	1	0	0	1	0	1
Totals	32	4	7	b25	15	4

aBatted for Pelty in the ninth.
bOne out when winning run scored.

St. Louis ....1 0 0 0 0 0 0 0 4—5
Washington ....0 0 0 0 0 0 4 0 0—4

Two-base hit—Spencer. Hits—Off Howell, 6 in 6 1-3 innings; off Pelty, 1 in 1 2-3 innings. Sacrifice hits—T. Jones, Yeager, Milan. Double play—Delehanty, McBride and Freeman. Left on bases—St. Louis, 11; Washington, 5. Bases on balls—Off Howell, 1; off Witherup, 1. Hit by pitcher—By Howell, 2. Struck out—By Howell, 1; by Pelty, 2; by Witherup, 3. Time—1h. 56m. Umpires—Kerin and Sheridan.

AMERICAN LEAGUE FLAG RACE TOLD IN GAMES

Cleveland leads Chicago by 1 1-2 games.
Chicago leads Detroit by 1 game.
Detroit leads St. Louis by 1 game.
St. Louis leads Boston by 10 games.
Boston leads Philadelphia by 2 games.
Philadelphia leads Washington by 5 games.
Washington leads New York by 14 1-2 games.

TOLD IN A NUTSHELL

(AMERICAN.)

	R.	H.	E.	Att'ce.
BOSTON	4	7	1	
DETROIT	1	8	3	2,710
CLEVELAND	9	12	1	7,161
NEW YORK	3	7	0	
CHICAGO	3	8	1	4,700
PHILADELPHIA	2	5	0	
(10 innings.)				
ST. LOUIS	5	9	1	3,000
WASHINGTON	4	7	4	

AMERICAN LEAGUE STANDING

	Won.	Lost.	P.C.
Cleveland	83	60	.580
Chicago	81	61	.570
Detroit	79	61	.564
St. Louis	78	62	.557
Boston	68	72	.486
Philadelphia	65	73	.471
Washington	59	77	.434
New York	46	93	.331

GAMES TODAY

(AMERICAN.)

Boston at St. Louis.
New York at Chicago.
Philadelphia at Detroit.
Washington at Cleveland.

GAMES YET TO BE PLAYED IN THE AMERICAN LEAGUE

	Cleveland	Chicago	Detroit	St. Louis	Boston	Philadel	Washington	New York	Totals
Cleveland	.	2	0	3	0	3	3	0	—11
Chicago	2	.	3	1	3	0	1	2	—12
Detroit	0	3	.	2	0	4	5	0	—14
St. Louis	3	1	2	.	3	1	0	4	—14
Boston	0	3	0	3	.	6	0	2	—14
Philadelphia	3	0	4	1	6	.	2	0	—16
Washington	3	1	5	0	0	2	.	7	—18
New York	0	2	0	4	2	0	7	.	—15

WHITE SOX IN SECOND PLACE

CHICAGO, Sept. 23.—Chicago defeated Philadelphia here today 3 to 2 in a hard-fought 10-inning game. The visitors tied the score by opportune hitting in the sixth and eighth, and Chicago won out in the extra inning on a double, a passed ball and a single.

CHICAGO.

	AB.	R.	BH.	PO.	A.	E.
Hahn, r. f.	5	0	1	1	0	0
Jones, c. f.	2	0	0	2	0	0
Isbell, 1b	5	1	2	12	0	0
Anderson, l. f.	3	0	0	1	0	0
G. Davis, 2b	4	0	1	1	3	0
Parent, s. s.	3	0	0	2	1	0
aDougherty	1	0	0	0	0	0
Atz, s. s.	1	0	1	0	0	0
Sullivan, c.	4	1	1	7	0	0
Shaw, c.	0	0	0	2	0	0
Tannehill, 3b	3	1	1	2	3	0
Smith, p.	2	0	1	0	5	1
Totals	33	3	8	30	12	1

PHILADELPHIA.

	AB.	R.	BH.	PO.	A.	E.
Nichols, s. s.	5	1	1	2	2	0
Oldring, l f.	4	0	0	2	0	0
Baker, 3b	4	1	2	0	3	0
Coombs, c. f.	4	0	1	1	0	0
Sibold, r. f.	4	0	0	2	0	0
H. Davis, 1b	3	0	0	18	2	0
Barr, 2b	4	0	1	0	2	0
Lapp, c.	3	0	0	2	2	0
Flater, p.	3	0	0	2	5	0
Totals	34	2	5	b29	16	0

aBatted for Parent in eighth. bTwo out when winning run scored.

Chicago ....0 0 1 0 1 0 0 0 0 1—3
Philadelphia ....0 0 0 0 0 1 0 1 0 0—2

Two-base hits—Barr, Coombs, Baker (2), Smith, Isbell. Three-base hit—Hahn. Sacrifice hits—Flater, Smith (2), Tannehill. Stolen bases—Jones, Tannehill. Double plays—Smith, Tannehill and Isbell; Tannehill, Davis and Isbell. Left on bases—Chicago, 10; Philadelphia, 5. Bases on balls—Off Flater, 6; off Smith, 1. Hit by pitched ball—H. Davis. Struck out—By Smith, 9; by Flater, 2. Passed balls—Lapp (2). Wild pitches—Flater, Smith. Time—2h. 10m. Umpire—O'Loughlin.

The Boston Post

14 PAGES TODAY

FOURTEEN PAGES—ONE CENT | Established 1831 | FRIDAY, SEPTEMBER 25, 1908** | Copyright 1908 by Post Publishing Co. | ONE CENT

The Old Time Professionals and Amateurs Lined Up Before the Game

(Photo by Horner.)

Top row, reading from left to right—George Wood, Tommy Bond, James O'Rourke, Walter Barnes, John Manning, Dr. S. A. Hopkins, Samuel H. Hooper, Robert Wheelock, Jere Hurley, George Rich, Mertie Hackett, Tommy McCarthy, Clarence Smith, Alan Hubbard, Rufus S. Woodward, Harry Burt, John Nunn, George Richardson, George Foster, William Fulsom, James A. Gallivan, L. A. Frothingham, Colonel Samuel E. Winslow, William H. Coolidge, Walter I. Badger, Colonel Everett C. Benton and W. F. Garcelon. Bottom row—"Tim" Murnane, Frank Barrows, Harry Schaefer, John Morrill, F. H. Whitney, A. G. Spalding, Dr. Thomas Gunning, George A. Sawyer, J. W. Rollins, John Kent, Webster Thayer, Ivers W. Adams, John A. Lowell, George A. Flagg, John Foster, Fred Thayer, Frank W. Blair, Samuel J. Elder, A. H. Latham, James Tyng, the Rev. C. F. Carter, Harry Beaman, Arthur Crocker, Billy Nash, Charles H. Burt and Frank Whitney

OLD TIME PROS WIN GAME 7-5

Have Merry Baseball Contest With Ex-Collegiate Diamond Stars

BY EDWARD M'GRATH

They came, they played, they conquered. Conquered a goodly portion of Old Dad Time's influences and showed us baseball as it was in the making.

The Old Timers, those who made money at the diamond sport and the sons of many colleges, stars all, gambolled on the green of the Huntington avenue grounds so spryly and, eke, skilfully, that the big gathering many a time was forced to goggle, applaud and turn to one another and murmur, "What d'ye know about that?"

To begin with there were no errors made on either side, nary a bobble. Any scorer caught with such an ornery, low-down disposition as to put a black mark agin the day's record of any of the grand old boys is excommunicated from the order of scribes for lese majeste.

What few small, insignificant slipups as were apparent at times don't go as official.

NOTABLES ALL THERE

As for the list of baseball notables who showed up to a man and did their extra finest, the only remark to be made is that the whole b'ilin' o' them were there. From the time "Al" Spalding, portly and impressive, tossed the bat with Walter Badger, the old Yale star, to see which of the teams was going to get the first lick at the ball up to the last put out in the seventh, when the supper hour had been overdue several and many minutes, there was always something doing.

Overwhelming Talent

The wealth of talent available was so great that every inning saw a shift. Consequently, a box score of the game would be merely a tangle-brain tale with nothing to commend it. In mercy, it is withheld.

Harvard uniforms prevailed in the team that opened up the fray, for the ex-collegians Hooper of the '75 Harvard team serving the teasers as they were doled out in the days of old.

Thunders of applause cleft the welkin as A. G. Spalding strode to the platter and poised his willow wand just like you've seen him in those old pictures. The megaphone artists, two in number, vociferated that "Al" was thirsting for a high ball from the pitcher. They came in bunches, and after many moments "Al" spanked one to Mr. Munn of Harvard '79 at shortstop, who tossed him out at first.

With the tilt thus pried open, all went as merry as a tinker's chorus. Jimmy O'Rourke, who still keeps up with the youngsters in the minors, tore off a sassy single, as did Tim Murnane, but there was nothing doing for the Professionals in the way of tallies for the first inning.

Continued on Page 10—Second Column

TEN EYCK HELD FOR OFFICERS

Syracuse Stroke Charged With Swindling Bank Clerk Gauss

SALEM, Sept. 24.—Young James Ten Eyck, the famous oarsman and stroke of the victorious Syracuse varsity crew this year, has been arrested at Syracuse for the Salem police, and will be brought here tomorrow to answer a charge of grand larceny.

It is alleged that last August Ten Eyck, working with several others, swindled Stephen S. Gauss, aged 21, a clerk in the Salem Savings Bank, out of $1500. Gauss, to make up the loss, confessed to taking $1500 of the bank's money.

Gauss, in his complaint to the Salem police, claimed he did not know the names of his erstwhile friends, but described to the officers what they know as the "sucker" pool game. The descriptions of the swindlers led the police to swear out a warrant for Ten Eyck and two others, whose names were not known.

The game in which Gauss lost his money was played in Boston last month. Ten Eyck was traced to Worcester, thence to New York, and, with the opening of the school year at Syracuse, the police learned that he had returned to his studies. When placed under arrest he denied his guilt, and claimed that he had no connection with any swindling gang.

Ten Eyck is the son of James Ten Eyck, famous in the sporting world a few years ago. Young Ten Eyck was brought up to the rowing game from a boy, and, under his father's training, became without doubt the best oarsman of his age in the world. The exhibitions he made in both this country and England will long be remembered by those who are followers of the sport. His splendid work as stroke of the varsity crew of Syracuse aided in securing the victory for his college in the intercollegiate regatta on the Hudson.

GRAFTING SKIN TO HIDE BURNS

MALDEN, Sept. 24.—Mrs. Annie Pearlswig, who was nearly burned to death in a fire at her home on Cross street, July 30, is having skin grafted to the seared portions of her face. The operations which, it is believed, will be entirely successful, are expected to restore the beauty for which she was noted before her accident.

Bernard McGovern of Middlesex street, a friend of Mrs. Pearlswig, was the first to give up pieces of his skin. The operation was performed this week, several strips being taken from his body. McGovern suffered no ill effects.

Tomorrow Joseph Pearlswig, husband of the injured woman, will submit to the operator's knife, and will probably a little later do so again. Dr. Fritz W. Gay is in charge of the skin grafting, assisted by Drs. Victor Shapiro and William J. McBain.

The operation is being watched with great interest by the medical profession here, as it is the first of its kind to be performed in Malden. Mrs. Pearlswig is at the Malden Hospital.

MYSTERY SHROUDS SHOOTING

Clinton E. Childs Refuses to Tell How He Received Wound

Clinton E. Childs, who was taken to the City Hospital in a dying condition yesterday from the room he occupied with his son at 613 Massachusetts avenue and who has since resolutely refused to tell who fired a 38-calibre bullet through his body, was a passenger on the car that left Waverley at 5:31 a. m.

This fact was established last night by the investigations of Officer John Argy of the Belmont police and a Post reporter.

A REMARKABLE FEAT

How the desperately wounded man managed to walk to the end of the car line to catch the Boston car from Waverley and then get home and up into his room is a mystery to the City Hospital doctors. Who shot him and why an attempt was made to kill him, apparently, is still more of a mystery to the Boston and Belmont police.

Childs has been employed as the manager of Yatter's pool room at 578 Washington street. Wednesday evening is his "night off."

When Harold Childs was awakened by his father throwing himself down on the bed and groaning he was so terrified he did not stop to investigate but hastily put on some clothing and ran to summon Dr. George H. Bowles at the corner of Massachusetts avenue and Washington street.

Continued on Page 5—Third Column

KILLED DURING HEAVY STORM

SALISBURY, Sept. 24.—During a terrific thunder shower here this evening the electric power transfer station for the Haverhill, Danvers & Amesbury Street Railway Company and the Citizens' Street Railway Company of Newburyport was struck by a bolt of lightning.

Chester Parker, who was in charge of the station at night, was killed, and a friend, Robert Dale, narrowly escaped death.

When the building caught fire Parker called up the police station and asked that Chief Electrician Atkinson of the road be notified.

After Parker telephoned to Captain Wells he went with Dale to get some sand to put on the fire. Their idea was to carry the sand in buckets or pails. There were rows of buckets hanging on both walls of the long room. Parker went to the side of the building where the high tension wires come in. Dale went to the other side of the room. He reached up to grab a bucket, and received a bad shock.

Realizing that everything in the room must be charged with electricity, he yelled to Parker: "Don't touch those buckets!" But he was too late. Parker had already touched the edge of a bucket. And there he hung, a corpse, clinging to the bucket edge. Later it was found that 13,200 volts of electricity had passed through his body.

STANDARD GAVE UP $100,000

Roosevelt Ordered Money Returned, but Cortelyou Refused

NEW YORK, Sept. 24.—The full story of the Standard Oil's connection with the Republican campaign in 1904 was made public tonight.

The source of the information cannot be divulged, but on absolute authority this is the story:

ROGERS REFUSED AT FIRST

Early in the 1904 campaign the Standard Oil Company, as well as other trusts, railroads, banks and large corporations, received a request to contribute to the Republican national campaign fund.

This request was ignored, Henry H. Rogers being responsible for its refusal. Later, when the second call for campaign funds was made, Mr. Cortelyou, chairman of the Republican national committee, sent word to Mr. Rogers asking for an appointment at which the existing conditions could be explained and the financial support of Standard Oil secured.

Continued on Page 4—Fifth Column

YESTERDAY'S DEVELOPMENTS IN THE NATIONAL CAMPAIGN

Bryan preparing to demand the resignation of Haskell as treasurer of the Democratic campaign committee.

Chairman Mack of the Democratic national committee says that the story of a $300,000 contribution to the fund was told simply to stimulate interest in collections.

Kern assails Roosevelt, declaring his attack on Haskell premature and uncalled for.

Taft, in his speech at Milwaukee, promises, if elected, to call a special session of Congress to revise the tariff.

Tremendous enthusiasm greets Bryan in his speeches at Cincinnati. He calls on Roosevelt to live up to his "square deal" declarations.

BRYAN TO PUT HASKELL OUT

CINCINNATI, O., Sept. 24.—Upon authority second only to that of Mr. Bryan himself the statement can be made that probably before the beginning of next week formal announcement will be made of the resignation by Governor Charles N. Haskell of Oklahoma of the office of treasurer of the Democratic national committee.

It is known that Mr. Bryan today virtually decided definitely to request Governor Haskell's resignation if the Governor should not within the next 48 hours tender it voluntarily.

STREAM OF TELEGRAMS

A stream of telegrams has been pouring in upon Mr. Bryan all day about the Haskell case. They have come from all parts of the country.

Governor Haskell has made frequent efforts today to get in communication with Mr. Bryan for the purpose of arranging a personal interview with the nominee tomorrow at Terre Haute or some other point in Indiana, in which State Mr. Bryan will be campaigning tomorrow.

But it is stated that Mr. Bryan irrevocably has made up his mind that Governor Haskell must be separated from all further official connection with the Democratic campaign.

Senators Wanted Standard's Cash

Senator McLaurin Asked Archbold for "Proper Support"—Republican Asked for $1000 in Letters Read by Hearst

THE HON. JOSEPH C. SIBLEY

Republican Congressman from Pennsylvania, the author of the "Confidential Letters" to John D. Archbold of the Standard Oil Trust

What Sibley Wrote to Standard Oil Head

"Personal and confidential.

"House of Representatives,
"Washington, Nov. 23, 1903.

"My Dear Mr. A.—A Rep. United States Senator came to me today to make a loan of $1000. I told him I did not have it, but would try and get it for him and would let him know in a day or two.

"Do you want to make the investment? He is one who will do anything in the world that is right for his friends if ever needed. Please telegraph me Yes or No. I will give you name when I see you.

"I don't know but what I ought to come over and see you. Events are crowding and I am on the inside of them, and think I am playing no small hand and want to know whether to go ahead. The nomination of a Republican President is not yet settled. No man can safely predict the nominee and guess I have got hold of the real situation as closely as anyone here.

"If you need me for any purpose, telegraph me and I will come over.

"Sincerely yours, JOSEPH C. SIBLEY."

How Standard Oil Trust Offered Political "Aid"

"Personal.

"November 30, 1898.

"Mr. N. F. Clark, Pittsburg, Penn.:

"Dear Mr. Clark—As West Virginia seems to have gone Democratic, which will give her a Democratic United States Senator to succeed Faulkner, I write to ask whether Governor Fleming has made any intimation of his intentions in respect to a candidacy for this place.

"There is probably no man in West Virginia better qualified or who would make a more capable and honorable Senator than he. If he has said nothing to you, won't you please raise the question with him and tell him that we all here would be greatly interested in having him make an effort for the place, and would be only too happy to extend any aid that may be in our power. I would like to hear from you just as promptly as possible on this subject. If it is possible for you to confer with him either personally or by telephone at once, will be glad to have you do so, and please telegraph me in cipher the result. Yours very truly, JOHN D. ARCHBOLD."

Sibley Shows How the Senators Were Lined Up by Him

REPUBLICAN CONGRESSMAN SAID HE WAS ON INSIDE

Hearst Says Haskell Was Ally of the Steel Trust

NEW YORK, Sept. 24.—William Randolph Hearst continued to throw bombs into the camps of both old parties tonight.

The occasion was nominally the opening of the Independence party's State convention in Cooper Union, but actually it was another club swinging display by the party's founder.

First, he hit Governor Haskell and produced letters tending to show that the financial head of the Democratic national campaign was one of the originators of the steel trust.

Then he read other letters that implicated Senator McLaurin of South Carolina and Congressman Sibley of Pennsylvania in deals with the Standard Oil Company.

Incidentally, Mr. Hearst intimated that Mr. Kern, the Democratic nominee for Vice-President, might appropriately be looking about for somebody to defend him. This would seem to indicate still another attack to come.

HUGHES AS TOWN MARSHAL

Mr. Hearst said in part:

"You Independence Party men of New York have every reason for patriotic effort in this campaign. One of the old parties has nominated Mr. Hughes, who throughout his term has served the great privileged interests with the consummate skill of a trained corporation lawyer.

"He has created public service commissions whose only service has been to protect corrupt corporations in the pillage of the people.

"His opposition to race track gambling is creditable, and would amply justify his election as town marshal; but his abject subservience to privileged interests is not creditable, and does not justify his reelection as Governor.

Continued on Page 2—Fifth Column

HIGH TIDE TODAY

A. M. 11:15 | P. M. 11:30

FAIR

Forecast for Boston and vicinity—Friday, fair; Saturday, fair, probably followed by showers in the afternoon or night; variable winds.

WASHINGTON, Sept. 24.—Forecast:
For New England—Fair Friday and Saturday; light, variable winds.
For eastern New York—Fair Friday and probably Saturday; light, variable winds.

YESTERDAY'S TEMPERATURE

The thermometer at Thompson's Spa, 219 Washington street, recorded the temperature yesterday as follows:

	1907.	1908.
3 a. m.	60	60
6 a. m.	63	59
9 a. m.	67	63
12 m.	75	75
3 p. m.	78	78
6 p. m.	74	73
9 p. m.	69	75
12 mid.	69	67

Average temperature yesterday, 68 9-24.
Average temperature one year ago yesterday 69 7-24.

The Boston Post

EXTRA

TWELVE PAGES—ONE CENT | Established 1831 | SATURDAY, OCTOBER 3, 1908** | Copyright 1908 by Post Publishing Co. | TWELVE PAGES—ONE CENT

Oct 3, 1908
172627

FIRE SWEEPS WINTHROP BEACH---3 HOTELS GONE

EXPLOSION IN CREST HALL---TWO DEAD IN RUINS

TWO FLASHLIGHT PHOTOS OF CREST HALL AS IT WAS BU... A FRONT VIEW

Bitter Row in Camp of Republicans

Rum and Democrats Aiding Frothingham, Says Cole—Hot Time in Convention Promised

MOTHER TRIED TO KILL TOTS

MEDFORD, Oct. 2.—Driven to desperation over a quarrel last night with her husband, Mrs. Annie Hickey, wife of John J. Hickey, of 12 Harvard avenue, tried to commit suicide today and take the lives of her three small children, John, 4 months; Annie, 3 years, and Margaret, 5 years, by gas.

FOUND UNCONSCIOUS ON BED

When Patrolman Fred Lewis and Thomas Hutchinson broke down the door of the house the gas fumes almost overpowered them. Mrs. Hickey lay unconscious upon the bed, a rubber tube beside her. Little Margaret lay across her feet and Annie was found under the bed, also unconscious.

John, the baby, when found, was conscious, lustily crying for his mother, whose almost lifeless body lay across him in such a manner that the deadly fumes were unable to reach him.

The family owe their lives to the fact that the gas was supplied from a quarter-in-the-slot meter.

The woman had to all appearances waited until the children had gone to sleep and then lay down herself.

The children were removed to Mrs. Hayes' apartments, and after treatment by Dr. J. W. Bean were finally restored to consciousness. Dr. Robinson attended Mrs. Hickey. Unceasing efforts succeeded in bringing back faint signs of life. At a late hour all the patients were reported comfortable.

THE COLE STATEMENT

"We are pleased beyond expression at the reception tendered us by our friends tonight, and at the evident opposition to the attempt of so-called leaders to create band wagon sentiment for our opponents.

"It is clear that Mr. Frothingham's friends are desperately trying to make a showing on the first ballot, and they have failed. The Hibbard machine did notable work for Mr. Frothingham with a numerous Democratic delegation, but we would remind the delegates that the lining up of men in the hotel corridors and the display of red badges at the bar do not count in the deliberations of a Republican convention.

"The turbulent and riotous crowd that shouted 'Frothingham, that's he,' in the ear of Speaker Cole, and but for his friends would have crowded him from his reception room, was another unfortunate incident, and one of Mr. Frothingham's managers expressed annoyance at the demonstration."

The wildest night before that the Republicans ever had at the American House wound up with the promise today at Symphony Hall of the most rancorous struggle that ever convulsed a Republican State convention.

With harmony thrown to the winds it is to be a smashing, tearing fight from start to finish.

Continued on Page 3—First Column

HARVARD MAN EI...

Elie Edson Runs ... Widow of Arthur ... Died a Sui...

PROVIDENCE, Oct. 2.—Elie Charlier Edson, Harvard first year law student and member of a fashionable New York family, secured a license here today to wed Mrs. Eleanor May Mann, widow of Arthur Mann of Boston and Windsor, Vt., who committed suicide at Nantasket last year, after financial reverses.

The affair was an elopement. The friends of Mrs. Mann in Boston and her parents in Pawtucket, R. I., were unaware of the intended marriage, and the most intimate acquaintances of young Edson were surprised.

GROOM'S PARENTS ABROAD

The father of the Harvard man is Tracey Edson, United States naval officer, and he, with Mrs. Edson, who was once a famous beauty of Paris, is touring in France.

After getting the necessary papers the couple quickly left the office of the city clerk, presumably to have the ceremony performed as soon as possible. Tonight they cannot be located, but it is thought that they went to New York on their honeymoon.

In securing the license Edson gave his age as 26 years and his home as New York. Mrs. Mann said she was 30 and came from Boston.

The Mann Suicide

The marriage of Mrs. Mann recalls the sensational suicide of her husband, Arthur Mann, at Anchor cottage, Nantasket, in December last. For years Mr. Mann had been one of the foremost manufacturers of Vermont and had an office on Lincoln street, Boston. Mr. and Mrs. Mann and their one child lived in elaborate style on Commonwealth avenue.

On account of the panic in the money market Mr. Mann suffered severe business reverses, and shortly before he took his life his place was assigned. Up to three years ago he was reputed to be worth several millions, but it was found that the bulk of this had been lost in the stock market. His business had been the handling of prison shoes, the labor being done in the State prison at Windsor.

Mr. and Mrs. Mann were at Windsor together the day before the suicide for a week's stay. The husband pleaded business in Boston and left, and the following day his wife learned that he had gone to the Mann cottage at Nantasket and shot himself.

Mr. Edson is one of the most popular young men at Harvard. He is prominent socially, and in 1905 he was a foremost member in the Cercle Francais. He was born in Paris, and his early education was in the schools of that city. Later he attended school at Tunis. He has visited all parts of the world, and returned only a week ago from France.

Edson occupied sumptous rooms at Holyoke House at Harvard, and yesterday morning he informed the janitor that he was going to Pride's Crossing to attend a shoot.

His chums at Harvard and those with whom he was associated at the Holyoke House were greatly surprised to learn of the Providence trip.

EI...

Long... velt

ROCK... Roosevel... years fr... today o... Congress... speech h... Tri-State... that che... again.

DE...

Mr. L... during t... fence of... He first... leader fo... Howard... speaker... would be... fice for a...

Follow... ously de... Roosevel... for the... then sha... ical polic... of Roose... fabled a... lion's sk...

Mr. L... would be... the polls... the stat... House b...

He urg... aid in d... and save... ly radica... gated by...

MO... $20...

NEW... doubt wh... national... when th... check to... has been... hope is e... ager tha... soon be...

PITCHES RECORD CONTEST

Not a Chicagoan Gets Past Addie Joss to First Base

PRINCIPAL POINTS IN THE GREAT GAME

Joss pitched a no-hit, no-run game.

Joss did not allow a man to reach first base.

Walsh struck out 15 men in eight innings.

Walsh struck out Goode four times and Lajoie and Clarke twice each.

Manager Lajoie made several phenomenal pickups, accepting 10 chances without an error.

Cleveland got but four balls past the infield.

Only five Cleveland men reached first base.

Birmingham scores only run of game through Chicago mixup of signals.

CLEVELAND, Oct. 2.—Adrian Joss leaped into exclusive society in the family of American pitchers when he defeated the White Sox today. One to nothing, without permitting a single Chicago batsman to reach first base.

Incidentally Eddie Walsh, Chicago's remarkable flinger, shattered some pitching records of 1908, fanning 15 men, the greatest number of strike-outs registered this year in any game other than an extra inning contest. Waddell fanned 17 in a 10-inning affray. Walsh pitched only eight innings.

Only three times has the performance of Joss been equalled in the major leagues, once by John M. Ward in 1880, pitching for Providence against Buffalo; once by Lee Richmond, pitching for Worcester against Cleveland, in 1880, and the third time by "Cy" Young, pitching for the Boston Americans against the Athletics, Aug. 5, 1904.

...NANY GUESTS NOW MISSING---HUNDREDS FLED IN WILD PANIC

Winthrop's boulevard section was swept by a conflagration last night, which caused the loss of two lives and a property loss estimated at over $300,000.

That Mrs. Henry Dumont was overcome by the flames and perished is certain, for two firemen participating in an effort to rescue her from her apartment on the third floor of Crest Hall saw her throw up her hands and disappear when an explosion thwarted them in their gallant efforts.

A man was reported to have lost his life, but if this is so, the identity of the victim is yet to be learned.

The flames swept the section of hotels and summer cottages on the boulevard. Beginning at a point east of Ocean View avenue, the fire crossed that thoroughfare and completely wiped out the buildings along the boulevard to Irwin street and other structures behind the buildings facing the sea.

GALLANT ATTEMPT AT RESCUE

Crest Hall was where the fire started and that great structure of wood soon went down. Then followed the destruction of the Ocean View House, the Crest Hall Annex, the Milbank Villa, a new cement building recently erected to take the place of one destroyed by fire a year ago; the Crest Hall stables, the home of George Knowles at 33 Ocean View avenue and several other cottages on Irwin street.

Hundreds witnessed the gallant attempt of two fire fighters to rescue Mrs. Henry Dumont.

They saw her standing in a frame of fire made by the flames. They saw the brave fire fighters rushing up the ladders. They beheld her hands held out to them in supplication and saw her sink back into the glow just as succor seemed to be at hand.

The heroes who tried to save her were two sturdy fire fighters of the Winthrop department, "Jack" McCarthy and William Taylor.

Mrs. Dumont had occupied Room 57, Crest Hall, with her husband, and when the cry of fire resounded through the hotel at 11:15 o'clock, Mr. Dumont stepped into the hall, for others had seen him as they passed down the stairs, and called upon him to hasten, for the carpetings under their feet were beginning to smoke. He went back, but when he reached the door of the room his wife had disappeared from sight, and thinking that she had passed out by some other and more safe route, he lost no time in getting out himself.

What was his horror, after getting down to the boulevard, when he saw his wife standing at the window. The lower stories of the hotel were a mass of seething flames at that time. The husband tried to rush into the hotel, but men gathered about and held him back. "The firemen will save her," they cried.

Mounted the Ladder

Then the ladder went up against the blazing wall of the hostelry. McCarthy went up first. Behind him came the sturdy form of Taylor. Both paid no attention to the showers of sparks that swept down upon them and threatened to encompass them.

She saw them coming and leaned out over the sill as though she would reach down to the brave men. At one time those below thought that she was about to jump, and uged her with shouts of encouragement to refrain.

Up to the top of the ladder the brave fire fighters made their way. They had almost reached her. Then in an instant came the roar of an explosion. The ladder swayed, yet they did not mind.

The hot air blew out of the glass and the frame itself, and sheets of flame followed in their wake. No human form could withstand it. Those in the streets knew that death was at hand. The woman held up her hands and fell backward into the flames.

McCarthy and Taylor went up to the window, despite the flames that raged over their heads. Then they saw that it would be death to them to pass into that raging furnace.

Continued on Page 2—Third Column

VICTIMS OF FIRE

MRS. HENRY DUMONT, 40, guest at Crest Hall.

Unknown man, body in ruins of Crest Hall.

Unconfirmed rumor that several other guests are missing.

INJURED IN FIRE

WALTER G. YEAGER, fell while making way to ground by way of rope; both legs fractured.

FIREMAN POFFIN of Winthrop department; severe bruises.

HUGH FRASIER, Hose 3, Revere; face and hands cut; Metcalf Hospital.

MRS. IDE, Boston; fractured legs.

NELLIE FOLEY, 20, domestic, top floor Ocean View; overcome by smoke, rescued by Metropolitan Officer J. A. Philbrick; in precarious condition at Dr. Gage's home.

BUILDINGS DESTROYED IN WINTHROP FIRE

Crest Hall, 3-story, wooden, owned by Fred Hall.

Crest Hall annex, 3-story, wooden.

Ocean View House, 5-story, wooden, owned by Mrs. I. B. O'Bri...

Milbank Villa, 2 1-2-story, wooden, owned by Frank Bass.

Milfred Cottage, 2 1-2-story, wooden, owned and occupied by ...er Haynes and Walter Morrison.

Cottage of Harry Blanchard, corner of Irving street, 2 1... wooden.

Cottage of Philip Nelligan, on Irving street, 2 1-2-story.

Cottage of George B. Knowles, 3... Ocean View avenue.

Chicago Nationals Win the Pennant

Johnny Evers, the star second sacker of the three-times champion Chicago Cubs

Continued from First Page

FAILS IN SUPREME TEST

Given as good support as the New York team has accorded any one of its pitchers this year, with his own team hitting both Pfeister and Brown and at a time when hits meant runs, Mathewson failed to show the speed expected of him and after that third inning the result was hardly in doubt to those who were familiar with the capabilities of both teams.

For the Cubs, playing the game as a unit, fielding and backing up in perfect style and showing a smoothness and team work that was utterly lacking in the Giants' makeup, looked by far the better team, and before the game was half finished, even the Giants' warmest supporters were willing to acknowledge this.

The victory of the Cubs is all the more creditable in view of the fact that from start to finish they were handicapped all the way, first by the antagonism shown them by the immense crowd, secondly by the ugly tactics of the New York team, again by the one-sided umpiring, all in favor of the home team, and lastly, by the actions of certain rowdies who did their best to interfere with the work of the Cubs.

Attack Chicago Players

McGinnity had started the trouble even before the game began by forcing his way onto the diamond while the Cubs were in practice and shoving Chance out of the way. The bad blood evidenced then found its vent at various stages during the progress of the game and finally made its appearance among the spectators at the close of the game, when they chased various members of the Chicago team to the dressing-rooms, roughly handling some of them without the police making the slightest attempt to interfere.

Manager Chance and Pitcher Pfeister were severely pounded by unknown toughs and Hoffman was hit by a flying bottle, while the rest of the team were chased to their quarters in full view of thousands of people who looked calmly on.

It was an unfortunate ending to such a grand game as that of today, and it is more unfortunate from the fact that New York has thereby stamped itself as a town of very hard losers. The Chicago players tonight are exceedingly bitter about the treatment meted out to them and stated that they hoped it would never be their lot to play with such a prize at stake in a town like New York again.

Police Charge Crowd

Fights innumerable occurred in the bleachers and the mounted police were forced to charge the crowd on the Eighth avenue repeatedly in order to prevent the outside gates being battered down. Several small accidents occurred and one middle-aged man, who climbed the elevated structure in the absence of the police guard in the hope of obtaining a view of the game, fell to the pavement beneath and was instantly killed.

Scores of people who had purchased boxes in the grandstand at advanced prices were utterly unable to get anywhere near the gate, and while thousands more could have been accommodated in the big field the club people were afraid to take the risk of letting more inside.

Win on Merits

The Chicago team won to-day's game clearly on its merits. The fielding of Tinker, Chance, Steinfeldt and Evers was of the cleanest possible description, while Schulte and Sheckard made some great catches in the outfield. The catching of Johnnie Kling as usual was of the finest order, and Brown was never more himself than when men were on bases and scoring seemed imminent.

For just two innings it looked like New York, as Pfeister's wildness in the first and the adverse rulings of Umpires Klem and Johnstone had given the Giants a lead of one run. But with the advent of Mordecai Brown and the opening of the fourth the game took on a different aspect and from then on it was only a question of whether New York could possibly tie.

In the last Chicago game Mr. Merkle made a boneheaded play that cost his team a pennant, and today another stupid piece of work, on the part of another favorite, Charlie Herzog, had a lot to do with altering New York's chances. This occurred in the first inning, when he ran off first on a passed third strike and thereby caused a double play. Had he held his base New York might have had two and perhaps three runs in the opening inning instead of the lonely one.

Gates Closed Early

As early as 11 o'clock the gates were opened, but by 1 o'clock the crowd had become so dense that the gates were closed. Travel on the "L" was congested, the surface cars were packed to suffocation and for blocks around the Polo Grounds the throng had become so vast by 1 o'clock that it required the aid of the mounted police to force a passage through.

The writer and Manager Kelley of the Boston Nationals were forced to make their entrance by a side gate, and only for the recognition on Joe's part of a friendly police sergeant the Post's correspondent might have been forced to view the game from the bridge.

The appearance of the Chicago team on the field was the signal for a wild outburst of hooting and hisses, groans and curses in many instances marking the appearance of Frank Chance. Throughout the game Chance was called every kind of a name, that of "Yellow dog" being the most popular.

Evers, Pfeister and one or two others shared Chance's unpopularity and it quickly became apparent that the Cubs were in for a hard row. The reception given to the Giants when they issued from the club house was of course vastly different, and Mathewson, Donlin, Herzog and others were made to feel that New York expected them to down the Cubs in the final test.

Strange to say the Chicago team showed up very poorly in practice, Chance, Evers and Tinker muffed and Steinfedt fumbled repeatedly. The crowd yelled with joy at each of these miscues.

At 2:30 o'clock the New York team ran out on the diamond for their practice, and Moran, who had been batting out grounders to his teammates, still stayed at the plate. McGinnity came over to eject him, Chance came running in and in a second the players of both teams were grouped about the plate in a belligerent attitude.

The police were quickly on hand, the umpires ran out to help matters and finally, without any of the threatened blows being struck, Moran left the plate, while the crowd once more paid due respect to the Cubs.

During the Cubs' practice every ball that a Chicago player fouled into the grandstand or bleachers was retained by the crowd. The attitude of the fans, bleachers and grandstand alike, was decidedly hostile.

Giants Take Field

At just 3 o'clock the Giants took the field and Mathewson was given a tremendous reception when he entered the box. Umpire Johnstone went behind the plate while Klem officiated on the bases. The din was terrific as Sheckard struck out.

Evers was thrown out on a beautiful play by Herzog, and then, just to show that he still possesses some of his old-time cunning. Schulte was fanned by Mathewson. The crowd went wild. Then the Giants came in to get the run that gave them their short-lived lead and caused the fans to think for two short innings that the championship was to be theirs.

The very first ball that Pfeister threw hit Tenney and the veteran ambled to first amidst a terrible din. Herzog proved a patient waiter and worked the Cubs' big southpaw for a pass. Then Bresnahan played stupidly. Instead of bunting and advancing both men he swung wildly three times, amidst great dismay.

The third strike Kling muffed and Herzog, forgetting that the batsman was out, ran off his base. Like a shot Kling lined the ball to Chance and a double play was the result. This was a costly slip up on the part of Bresnahan and Herzog, for the next batsman was Mike Donlin, and after getting in the hole for two strikes Mike drove the ball on a line to right field.

The hit was a pretty close one, hugging the line all the way, and Chance and his men protested bitterly when Johnstone called it fair. But the umpire's decision went, of course, and Tenney scored. It would have made a big difference had Bresnahan advanced his men a peg.

Seymour was passed, and then Brown, who had been warming up all the time, was called in. He ended the inning by fanning Devlin, and the latter looked for an instant as though he intended to hand Johnstone a punch. McGraw sent him out to the field, however.

Chance opened Chicago's second with a clean hit to right and a moment later was thrown out by Mathewson, who shot the ball suddenly to Tenney.

Chance was not out by right and he showed his rage too openly, for which he came near leaving the game at once. In the heated argument that resulted Moran was put off the coaching line. Hoffman, for hinting that the decision "smelled," was put out of the game.

Then Steinfeldt and Howard fanned in succession and the crowd yelled itself hoarse. "Matty's going to get the strike-out record," yelled some enthusiast. It came near to being a knockout in the third.

Two star catches by Schulte and a quick play by Tinker retired New York in their half of the second and then Chicago went in for the third inning and the pennant.

Tinker, who has always been a terror to Mathewson, opened by driving the ball to centre field for a triple. The ground rule robbed him of a home run. Kling slammed the ball safely to left, scoring Tinker.

Brown laid down a fine sacrifice hit, advancing Kling to second. Sheckard flied to centre, but Evers was the next man up and Matt was afraid to take a chance, and instead of letting Johnny hit it he passed him up, and then Schulte followed with a double, scoring Kling and sending Evers to third.

Chance faced Matty for the second time and lined out his second hit, a beautiful double to right field. The hit scored two runs, and as it showed ultimately, won the game. Steinfeldt closed the inning with a strikeout, but there was little jubilation when Matty came to the New York bench this time.

Tenney was the first man to face Brown in the third, and Fred started a good-looking rally by lining a beauty to centre. Herzog, however, momentarily killed the chances by popping up to Kling.

Bresnahan followed with a nice hit, but Donlin forced him at second, Tenney taking third. Then Seymour did the expected and "popped up" to Schulte.

In the fourth and the fifth the Cubs went out in order, and in the sixth, although Chance and Steinfeldt singled, there was nothing doing in the way of runs. In the seventh they went down in order, and in the eighth, although Evers connected for a two-bagger with Wiltse, who had taken Matty's place, and Tenney erred on Schulte's fast grounder, a quick double play on McCormick's fine return of Chance's fly killed off a promising chance.

Giants Fill Bases

After the third inning, when Herzog's fly nipped the Giants' chance, and Kling was nearly hit by the bottles thrown at him while he was catching it, the Giants did not see first again until the seventh, when Devlin led off with a fine hit to left field.

McCormick followed with another safe drive, and Brown seemed to go bad momentarily, for he passed Bridwell, the next batsman, filling the bases with none down.

At this stage Doyle was sent in to bat for Mathewson, but his effort was an easy fly to Kling. Tenney drove out a long fly to right, on which Devlin scored. But Herzog could not get the ball past Tinker, and the Giants' last score for the season of 1908 had been made.

In the eighth and ninth the Giants went down in order and the pennant had passed from the waiting grasp of the "near champions" of Gotham.

The score:

CHICAGO.

	AB.	R.	BH.	PO.	A.	E.
Sheckard, l. f	4	0	0	4	0	0
Evers, 2b	3	1	1	0	3	0
Schulte, r. f	4	1	1	4	0	0
Chance, 1b	4	0	3	13	0	0
Steinfeldt, 3b	4	0	1	0	3	0
Hofman, c. f	0	0	0	0	0	0
Howard, c. f	4	0	0	1	0	0
Tinker, ss	4	1	1	1	4	0
Kling, c	3	1	1	4	1	0
Pfeister, p	0	0	0	0	0	0
Brown, p	2	0	0	0	1	0
Totals	32	4	8	27	12	0

NEW YORK.

	AB.	R.	BH.	PO.	A.	E.
Tenney, 1b	2	1	1	9	0	1
Herzog, 2b	3	0	0	1	2	0
Bresnahan, c	4	0	1	10	2	0
Donlin, r. f	4	0	1	0	0	0
Seymour, c. f	3	0	0	2	0	0
Devlin, 3b	4	1	1	2	0	0
McCormick, l. f	4	0	1	3	1	0
Bridwell, ss	3	0	0	0	1	0
Mathewson, p	2	0	0	0	3	0
*Doyle	1	0	0	0	0	0
Wiltse, p	0	0	0	0	0	0
Totals	30	2	5	27	9	1

*Batted for Mathewson in seventh.

Chicago	0	0	4	0	0	0	0	0	0	—4
New York	1	0	0	0	0	0	1	0	0	—2

Two-base hits—Donlin, Schulte, Chance, Evers. Three-base hit—Tinker. Hits—Off Pfeister, 1 in 2-3 inning; off Brown, 4 in 8 1-3 innings; off Mathewson, 7 in 7 innings; off Wiltse, 1 in 2 innings. Sacrifice hits—Tenney, Brown. Double plays—Kling and Chance; McCormick and Bresnahan. Left on bases—Chicago, 3; New York, 6. Bases on balls—Off Pfeister, 2; off Brown, 1; off Mathewson, 1. Bases on errors—Chicago, 1. Hit by pitcher—By Pfeister, 1. Struck out—By Mathewson, 7; by Wiltse, 2; by Pfeister, 1; by Brown, 1. Time—1h. 40m. Umpires—Johnstone and Klem.

Bright Stars in Yesterday's Game

MORDECAI BROWN. MANAGER FRANK CHANCE.

The great pitcher of the Chicago Cubs who jumped into the breach yesterday and held the Giants in the deciding game of the season, and the captain-manager of the thrice champion aggregation

ELIS START SECRET WORK

Are Preparing Plays for West Point Game

NEW HAVEN, Conn., Oct. 8.—Wheaton was again star at the Yale football practice. Three dashing runs by him through the Scrubs' line of from 20 to 40 yards netted the regulars two touchdowns, and Hobbs' two goals rounded the varsity score to 12 points. Wheaton's work in a broken field has been the cleverest feature of the Yale daily practice.

Logan, Murphy and Philbin are still laid up with injuries received in the Syracuse game. Mersereau was tried at left end today and displayed brilliancy.

The best distance kicking of the season was done by Henry Holt, second eleven fullback. He twice booted the oval 65 yards. Haines and Warren, the players injured last week, reported.

It was learned today that the varsity went early to the field yesterday and took a short secret signal practice behind closed gates. All the drill today was open, but secret practice will be held at times before the West Point game.

The lineup: Left end, Mersereau; left tackle, Hobbs; left guard, Andrus; centre, Biddle; right guard, Cooney; right tackle, Goebel; right end, Burch; quarterback, Hopkins; left halfback, Wheaton; right halfback, Lynn; fullback, Coy.

NAME YOUR CHOICE FOR ALL-AMERICAN BALL TEAM

Now is the time for all good fans to take their pens in hand and help pick out the All-America baseball team.

The Post will be glad to hear from its readers on this important matter.

Send in your selections to the Baseball Editor. Write on one side of the paper only. Pick but one player for each position.

As many of the selections as possible will be printed in the Post from day to day.

BITS OF BASEBALL FROM GOTHAM GAME

NEW YORK, Oct. 8.—A big Boston delegation, including Nuff Ced McGreevey, John Keenan, Larry Hanrahan and others, were on hand.

Andy Freedman was there rooting for the Giants, but his appearance did not call for a very enthusiastic outburst.

The Cubs met certain members of the Boston team in the Hotel Somerset corridor, but did not give them a very enthusiastic reception.

The proposed trip to Cuba by Mathewson, Tenney and other members of the New York team will now probably be abandoned.

"I don't care if Detroit wins so long as we beat these fellows," said Johnny Evers before the game. The feeling between the two teams has certainly been most bitter.

Brother John and Mrs. Dovey, Dick Gilmore and a good many of the Boston brigade waited over in New York to see the last game. But tonight everyone is getting ready to go West.

WASHINGTON SCORES FINAL WIN OVER NEW YORK 7—5

WASHINGTON, Oct. 8.—Washington closed the American league series here today with a victory, defeating New York 7 to 5. Both sides took things easy and errors were frequent.

WASHINGTON.

	AB.	R.	BH.	PO.	A.	E.
Milan, c. f	5	1	2	0	0	1
Edmondson, l. f	3	1	1	4	0	2
Unglaub, 2b	4	0	1	4	4	0
Pickering, r. f	4	0	0	1	0	0
Freeman, 1b	4	3	2	11	1	1
McBride, ss	4	1	2	2	2	0
Street, c	4	0	1	4	2	0
Shipke, 3b	4	1	1	0	1	0
Keeley, p	4	0	1	1	4	0
Totals	36	7	11	27	14	4

NEW YORK.

	AB.	R.	BH.	PO.	A.	E.
Cree, c. f	5	0	2	0	0	0
Gardiner, 2b	5	1	4	6	1	1
Laporte, l. f	5	0	1	1	0	1
Moriarity, 1b	4	1	1	9	0	1
O'Rourke, ss	4	2	1	0	4	1
Blair, c	3	0	0	6	2	1
Donovan, 3b	4	1	2	2	5	0
Sweeney, r. f	3	0	0	0	0	1
Lake, p	4	0	0	0	1	0
Totals	37	5	11	24	13	6

Washington	3	0	1	0	1	0	0	2	.	—7
New York	0	1	0	3	1	0	0	0	0	—5

Two-base hits—McBride, Donovan. Sacrifice hit—Blair. Stolen bases—Milan, Pickering, Freeman. Left on bases—Washington, 6; New York, 4. Bases on balls—Off Keeley, 1; off Lake, 1. Bases on errors—Washington, 4; New York, 2. Struck out—By Keeley, 3; by Lake, 3. Time—1h. 30m. Umpire—Evans.

MURPHY EXPECTS CUBS WILL BEAT DETROIT

NEW YORK, Oct. 8.—"The winning of the third successive National league pennant by the Cubs we can claim with pardonable pride is the most remarkable achievement ever accomplished in organized professional baseball," said President Murphy of the Chicago team, after the great victory at the polo grounds.

"Manager Chance deserves a world of credit for his generalship, individual play and incessant earnestness. Every member of the team is also deserving of unstinted praise. No gamer ball club has ever trod the diamond. During the season just passed we have had between 70 and 80 serious accidents, and in a very few games indeed have we been able to put our full lineup on the field.

"The New York Giants have put up a great fight and Manager McGraw and his men deserve the commendation, good will and support of all New Yorkers. They fought us to a finish, but in my judgment the better team won.

"I am glad our victory today was a decisive one, so that it cannot be charged to anything of a technical nature. We will go into the world's series in good condition and confident of success, and if we should be defeated we will have no excuses to offer.

"We leave New York at 8 o'clock tonight for the West and expect instructions en route from the National Commission, which has supervision of the world's championship series, as to whether our destination shall be Chicago or Detroit.

"There has been some talk that the first game will be in Detroit on Saturday, and if that proves true we will have to eat up space about as rapidly as we did when we boarded the Twentieth Century flyer on a few hours' notice, hustled into New York and won the flag in the time-honored National league in the presence of a hostile audience, nearly all of whom were rooting with might and main for the gallant Giants.

"Notwithstanding that we won decisively from Detroit a year ago, we feel that that team has been greatly strengthened and that they will give us a hard battle for the highest honors in professional baseball. We expect to win, but realize we will have to extend ourselves to the limit in order to once more secure the highest honor in the national game."

WORLD'S SERIES BEGINS SATURDAY AT DETROIT

CINCINNATI, O., Oct. 8.—Beginning at 2 o'clock in the afternoon of Saturday, Oct. 10, the baseball teams of Chicago and Detroit, which have just won the closest recorded contest for the championship of the National and American leagues, will meet at Detroit to enter on a series of games for the baseball championship of the world.

But one game will be played in Detroit before the scene shifts.

The Sunday and Monday contests go to Chicago, while the Tuesday and Wednesday games are to be played at Detroit and the sixth game, if one is necessary, will then be transferred to Chicago.

Control of the games is given to two umpires from each league. From the National league Umpires O'Day and Klem were designated by President Pulliam, while President Johnson of the American league named Sheridan and Connolly to represent his organization.

According to the rules to govern the contests neither of the contesting clubs shall be permitted to pay a bonus or prize to any or all of its players who may take part in the series.

The admission to the games at Chicago will be: General admission $1, grand stand (unreserved) $1.50, grand stand (reserved) $2, box seats $2.50.

At Detroit: General admission $1, pavilion $1.50, grand stand $2, box seats $2.50.

The schedule as adopted was determined by lot, as is provided for by the rules. If any of the games scheduled at any park is postponed on account of rain or any other cause the teams will be required to play such postponed game on the first day available after such postponement and at the same park, provided, however, that the game scheduled for the Chicago park on Sunday, Oct. 11, shall be played at that park.

In case it becomes necessary to play the seventh game, the city in which it is to be played will be determined by the national commission.

The Players

The following players will be eligible to participate in the games, and none others

Chicago National League club—Brown, Chance, Durbin, Evers, Fraser, Howard, Hofman, Kling, Kroh, Lundgren, Marshall, Moran, Overall, Pfeister, Reulbach, Sheckard, Slagle, Schulte, Steinfeldt, Tinker, Zimmerman.

Detroit American League club—Coughlin, Cobb, Crawford, Downs, Donovan, Jones, Jennings, Killian, Killifer, Mullin, O'Leary, Rossman, Schmidt, Summers, Suggs, Schaefer, Thomas, Willets, Winter, McIntyre.

The games shall be called in both cities at 2 p. m.

Rain checks shall be issued each day, regardless of the weather conditions. Should a game be postponed on account of the weather the checks issued shall be good only for the next game in the same city.

The entire commission and its secretary will be represented at the game.

The official scorers selected by the commission are A. J. Flanner and Francis C. Richter.

FAMED TRANSYLVANIA GOES TO SPANISH QUEEN

LEXINGTON, Ky., Oct. 8.—The Transylvania, the most prized stake for light harness horses, was easily won today by the overwhelming favorite. Spanish Queen, owned by G. H. Estabrook and driven by Gus Macey.

The pacing division of the Futurity was unfinished and goes over until tomorrow. Catherine Direct, the favorite, won the first and fourth heats; Colonel Forest the second and third heats.

ST. ALPHONSUS WANTS GAMES

The St. Alphonsus Association team, owing to a cancellation of dates, would like to play some strong team Saturday, Oct. 10; also Oct. 17. They wish to meet the strongest teams in the State and have a few open dates. John J. Riley, manager, 214 Milk street. Phone Main 3907.

NEW YORK, SUNDAY, OCTOBER 11, 1908.

LAW HIS LIFE WORK; BASEBALL HIS LOVE

Manager Hugh Jennings of Detroits Tells Story of His Career.

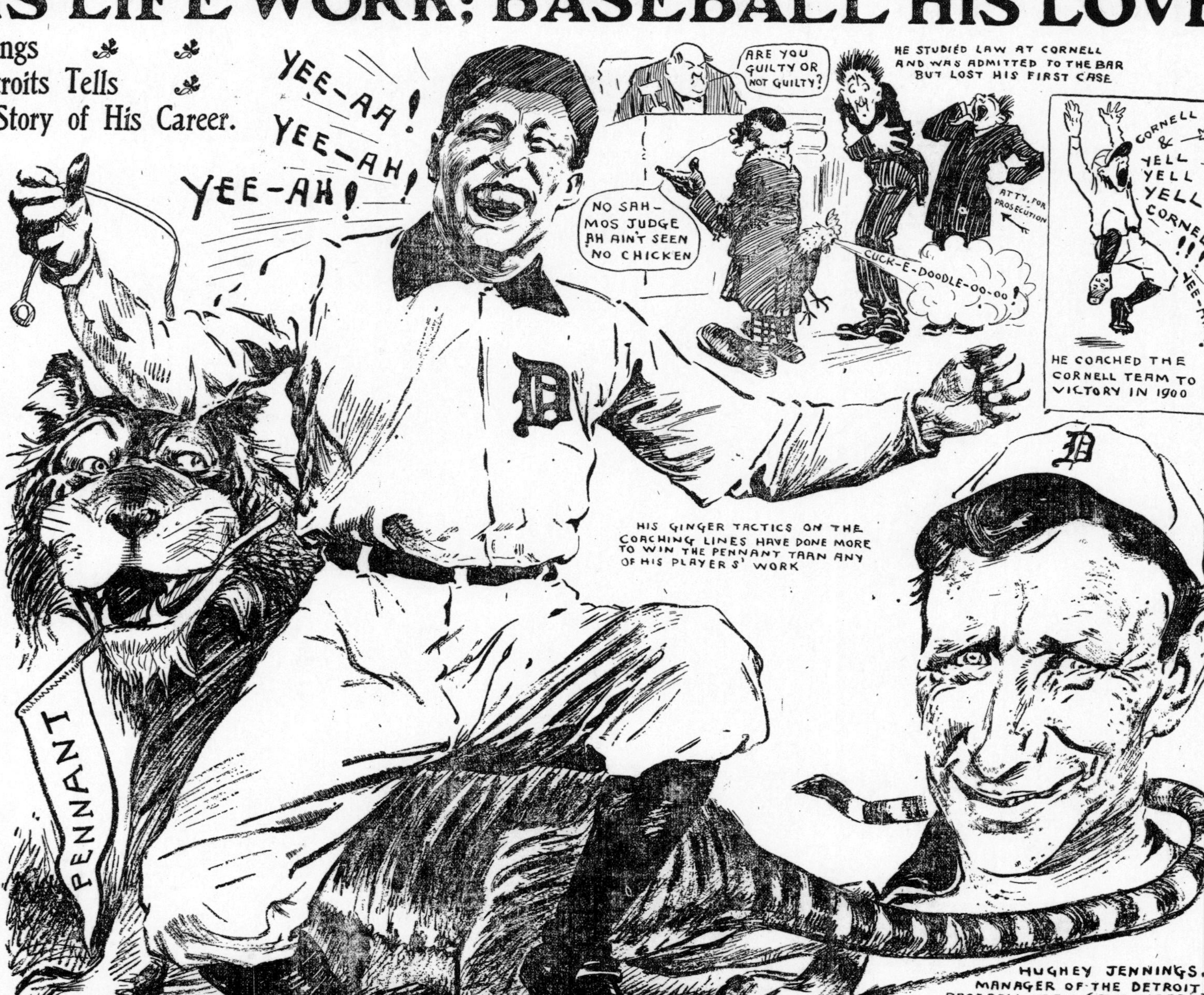

Versatile Manager Who Has Twice Piloted the Detroit Americans Straight to the Pennant Tells of His Early Life—Discusses His First Law Case and Explains How He Lost It—Unlike Others Who Play the Game, He Has Wrung an Education From It.

By E. G. Brown.

Hughey "E-e-e-yah" Jennings, the sorrel-topped, gingery gentleman who has twice in succession brought the championship of the American Baseball League to Detroit with his team of Tigers, is one of the very few baseball players who have wrung an education from the great national game. While he was a member of the famous "Big Four" of the Baltimore Orioles, Jennings and John McGraw, between whom there existed a warm friendship, went to St. Bonaventure's College. Here Jennings applied himself with great diligence, and after being graduated he continued his studies at Cornell Law School. Now Hughey is a real lawyer, and he dispenses legal wisdom with all the sagacity that he exhibits on the ball field.

Jennings is recognized as one of the brainiest ball players of his time. He was never known to allow "record" to stand in the way of his playing. The fact that he was not afraid of being charged with errors made him take chances that no other shortstop ever dreamed of taking, and when Jennings finally ended his career at that position he was dubbed the "greatest shortstop that ever lived." This despite the fact that Herman Long, of Boston, played the same position so brilliantly.

But Hughey's strenuous playing finally told on him, and in his later years as an active player his arm gave out and he was forced to play easier positions. Once, in 1896, Jennings finished second in rank among the batters, his per cent. for the season being .307.

Jennings is a freckle-faced, auburn-haired, good-natured fellow, always merry and enthusiastic. He is 5 feet 9 inches in height, and weighs about 160 pounds. He has a masterful personality; he showed this by the manner in which he harmonized the Detroit team and practically brought "order out of chaos" when he first took charge of that then internally divided aggregation of ball players. He has held and still holds responsible positions in baseball circles.

In the following article Hughey tells for the first time the real "story of his life:"

By Hugh A. Jennings,

Manager of the Detroit Baseball Team.

Did you ever see anything like it? I guess you never did, nor did anybody else. And now that the dust has settled we've got to beat our old rivals, the Cubs, if we want to gain the title of world's champion baseball players. Undoubtedly this has been the greatest year for the national game that ever was, and, so far as I am concerned, I had no sooner begun to relax from the nervous tension that the close race worked me into when the world's [series] now playing tightened me up again. And [right] here I want to say that I am exceedingly [sorry] that the Giants did not annex the pennant. [They] made a grand struggle for the flag—but what's [the] use? I'd better cut out the baseball talk and [begin] writing my little piece, or I'll never finish.

[C]ontrary to the general belief, I was born in [Pi]ttston, Pa., on April 2, 1871. Too many other men [who] have been fortunate enough to claim the early [da]ys in April for their birthdays have made humorous allusions to the narrow escapes they have had, and how they fooled their confiding parents and prophetic family physicians by not appearing on April 1, for me to go over the ground already well worn. Let it suffice that I was durned glad to be born at all, and have never ceased to be grateful.

At the top of this article you will see in black type the legend "Hugh A. Jennings." That means me. I wasn't born with it, but I accumulated it soon after my birth. The A stands for Ambrose, and there are those who have declared that my middle name is responsible for the ambrosial color of my hair and my disposition. Personally, I am not aware that I have any disposition, but my friends all say I have, so I let it go at that.

Was Precocious Youngster.

I can't remember much about my very early childhood, aside from the fact that I was one of those precocious youngsters that occur in every American family, and that I was passionately fond of athletics in any way, shape or form. When you come right down to it, the only legal form of athletics that a kid can indulge in is baseball; so it was not at all wonderful that I, like all the rest of the boys in the town, should turn to it for recreation and exercise. I suppose every one knows how little boys have to prevaricate and evade when their mothers ask them if they have been "in swimming," but baseball covers a multitude of juvenile sins, and it always covered mine.

I remember that I was always the catcher in those corner-lot competitions, and years later, when I finally entered the professional game, that was the position at which I began playing.

I went to elementary school, and before I had gained any scholastic degree my father moved his whole family and household goods to Moosic, Pa. This latter town has often been credited as my birthplace from the fact that I first began to stir things in the baseball way there. I went to grammar school, played on the school team, and then began playing semi-professional ball. I was about eighteen or nineteen years of age when I played with the Lehighton (Pa.) team.

Of course pretty nearly every town in that vicinity is or was a coal mining town, and my father was a miner. I tried my hand at mining, too, in a modest sort of way. It was my duty to pick slate and other foreign substances out of the coal. My teammates generally delayed their games till I was through with my work down in the coal mines, so that I could do the back-stop work for the nine. But I found it too gloomy underneath the ground, and when the chance offered I was only too glad to give up mining for baseball.

I was playing with the Lehighton team in 1890, I believe it was, when one day I received a wire from John C. Chapman, then manager of the Louisville club, offering me $175 a month to play with his team. I accepted the offer immediately and received instructions to meet the team in Louisville. I got there on time. In fact, I was ahead of time, and the hours couldn't pass quickly enough for me while I was waiting to meet Chapman. He had been in Philadelphia with his team when he read an account of a game in which I had made fifteen put-outs and four hits, one of them being a home run.

When he saw me I was as green as I was red-headed, but he signed me to catch for his team. When I began playing his first baseman, Harry Taylor, got hurt, and Chapman put me at first base to take his place. It was my first experience at first, but I believe I made good. At any rate, my employer was well satisfied with my work, and when Cahill, who was playing shortstop, was injured I was put in his place. This seemed to be my natural position, and at the end of the season Mr. Chapman asked me what salary I wanted to continue my playing through the next season. I left the price of my services to him, and, after offering me $1,400, he filled in the contract for $1,750. I made up my mind to deserve his generosity, and I worked like everything to make good.

I played on the Louisvule team for three years, and then was "thrown in" with Harry Taylor when the Louisville team traded him to Ned Hanlon, then manager of the Baltimores, for "Silent Tim" O'Rourke. I warmed the bench for a long time before I got a chance with the old Orioles, but when it finally did come I took advantage of it. Keeler, McGraw, Kelly and myself became known as the "Big Four" while on this team of pennant winners, and I believe that it was there that I got my first real start in baseball.

"Foxey" Ned Hanlon thought he saw a god ball player in me, and he did everything he could to develop me. He told me things about the game that I had never dreamed of, and my batting and fielding averages improved rapidly. It was while with Hanlon that I developed the trick of getting hit by the ball, just as John McGraw grew into the habit of getting to first base by fouling off all of the good strikes and letting only the "balls" go past. Of my ability to get hit by the pitcher, more anon. And I might add, never again.

It was while with the Baltimore Orioles that I conceived the idea that a little more education would not seriously hamper me, and, with McGraw, I began attending St. Bonaventure's College in Allegheny, N. Y., during the winters. I tsuck to it until I was graduated, and in 1900 I entered Cornell Law School. A history of my life as a college student would be irrelevant, but I must admit that I had some pretty hot times while in college. I worked just as hard in school as I did on the diamond, and when I received my degree and was admitted to the bar I was so proud that I could feel myself expanding. Now I'm a full-fledged knight of the diary, and when my baseball days are over I'll give all my attention to my law practice. My brother and I have offices in Scranton, Pa. He takes care of the practice while I'm plaing ball.

His First Law Case.

This reminds me of my first case. It happened in Baltimore, and my client was an old negro who was accused of having stolen something, probably a chicken. There were about fifty people who had seen him commit the crime, and he hadn't a witness nor an alibi. All of my friends advised me not to take the case, but I was obdurate, and, of course, when the case was called we didn't have a leg to stand on. In court my client took the stand and, after being sworn, said in answer to the first question:

"'Deed, boss, I do' know nothin' 'bout dis yere case. I done all de work up till now; let my lawyer prove an alibi. Whatever he says will be all right."

Then he tried to tell the Court that he was in Oklahoma or some such place as that when the thievery occurred, despite th efact that he was arrested an hour after the chicken was stolen. Naturally I lost the case. But you can't expect to win all the time, as the old negro said when he was being led away to serve his time.

When the Baltimores consolidated with Brooklyn in 1899 I went with them. I played two years on the Brooklyns, and then spent two years with the Philadelphia Club. In 1903 I was made manager of the Baltimore team of the Eastern League. From there I came to De'rtoit, and I'm anchored there yet.

I think the greatest play, undoubtedly the most spectacular one I ever made, happened in Washington in the old days, so long ago that I don't remember exactly what year it was. The field seats were low, and were protected in front by a triple row of barbed wires. One of the Washington players knocked a high foul in that direction, and I went after the ball. I let out a yell and made a flying leap for it as it descended. I caught the ball with one hand, but I didn't land on the ground. Instead, when I came down, I found myself stuck in the fence, and I hung suspended there, kicking and struggling until some of my teammates released me. But I got the fly, and was lucky enough to escape with a few scratches.

I've been banged on the head and bunged up so much that I'm beginning to think my skull is solid. Once at Cornell I dived into an empty swimming tank, landing on my head and spraining my wrists. But the worst rap I ever got was at the Polo Grounds, when one of Rusie's inshoots hit me on the head.

WEATHER FORECAST
FOR MILWAUKEE AND VICINITY: Fair and continued warm tonight and Thursday.

Milwaukee Daily News

THE DAILY NEWS does not make wild and extravagant circulation claims—but it can SHOW WHERE THE PAPERS GO.

TWENTYSECOND YEAR. | WEDNESDAY, OCTOBER 14, 1908. | FIVE O'CLOCK—ONE CENT.

FORM A SOCIETY TO OPPOSE SUBWAYS

CITIZENS OF NORTHWEST SIDE INSIST ON DEPRESSION OF RAILWAY TRACKS

EFFECT PERMANENT ORGANIZATION IN ITS SUPPORT

Large and Enthusiastic Meeting Held and Subject Discussed—Repudiate Ald. Braun's Ordinance to Provide for Subways—Insist That Tracks Must Be Lowered From Menomonee Valley to City Limits.

Track depression from the Menomonee valley to the northern city limits is wanted by the citizens of the Northwest side. By unanimous vote the mass meeting last night in Nineteenth district school No. 1 declined to endorse the ordinance of Ald. August E. Braun, providing for subways at Clark and Center streets.

After rejecting resolutions calling for the endorsement of the Braun ordinance in its entirety, the association inserted in its articles of organization a provision calling for the depression of the northern division of tracks of the Chicago, Milwaukee & St. Paul Railway company through to the limits of the city.

May Amend His Ordinance

With the citizens of the Northwest standing solidly for consistent depression, Ald. Braun probably will amend his ordinance pending before the council. The ordinance provides for elevation north of North avenue and subways at Clark and Center street.

The Daily News from the first has advocated track depression from the Menomonee valley to the city limits. It is the only correct solution of the problem. The citizens repudiated the plan urged by a certain afternoon sheet designed to relieve the Milwaukee road of the cost of depressing its dangerous tracks north of North avenue and building overhead bridges.

With plans for annexing much of the territory north of the present city limits well under way it would be the height of folly for the city deliberately to go ahead and permit the construction of subways that would have to be torn out before the passing of the present generation.

It was the sentiment of the mass meeting last night that the putting in of the subway at Fond du Lac avenue was a mistake, that it ought not be permitted to prevent the proper solution of the grade crossing problem, and that if necessary the city should pay the cost of taking out the subway.

Permanent Organization Effected

A permanent organization, to be known as Northwest Side Track Depression association, was formed to force the proper solution of the grade crossing problem. An executive committee to raise funds to fight for track depression throughout the length of the northern division within the city limits was appointed by the president of the permanent organization.

Ald. Joseph P. Carney led the argument for track depression all the way through. His first statement for track depression was greeted with cheers. It was plain to be seen that the 400 persons who attended the meeting and became charter members of the association were opposed to the Braun compromise plan.

Ald. Braun Explains

Before the meeting had progressed very far Ald. Braun himself announced that he favored track depression all of the way through but had taken up the hybrid proposition because maps and grades for subways at Clark and Center streets already had been prepared by the city engineer.

Ald. Carney then stated that but a short time ago City Engineer Charles J. Poetsch had told him that the only solution of the problem before the Northwest side was track depression from the Menomonee valley to the northern city limits.

With Ald. Braun ready, apparently to amend his ordinance to make a good job through not only the Fifteenth and Nineteenth wards but the Twenty-second ward as well, the citizens of the Northwest side back of the project, and many of the aldermen already in favor of track depression, it would appear that the demands made last night will be met by the council without delay.

Aldermen Join Association

Ald. Oscar Atlpeter, Jacob Rummel and John Hassmann attended the meeting last night and became charter members of the permanent organization, so they stand already pledged for complete track depression.

That track depression throughout will not be opposed by the manufacturers is believed by those who attended the organization of the track depression association last night. Louis G. Bohmrich, attorney for the association of industries in that district, said no one could stem the demand for track depression, that the manufacturers knew it, and that they were willing to meet their share of the temporary inconvenience and expense in making the change.

He fought for the addition of a phrase that would pledge the association to have due regard for sidetrack facilities. All who spoke at the meeting urged that nothing be done to harm the manufacturers, but it was practically the unanimous decision of the meeting not to accept the amendment offered by Mr. Bohmrich, for fear it would hinder the carrying out of the depression plans.

Protests Against Subways

The articles of organization were presented by a committee composed of Ernest A. Kehr, George Reinhardt and George F. Moss. In defining the purposes of the organization the articles generally endorsed the Braun ordinance. Ald. Carney urged that action on the articles be deferred until the intent of the ordinance could be stated.

As soon as it was understood the Braun ordinance provided for track elevation north of North avenue to the city limits, with subways at Clark and Center streets immediately, and subways at all other crossings in the future, protests were made from all parts of the hall. Mr. Kehr, chairman of the committee, said the committee would not have included endorsement of the Braun ordinance had it known subways were called for at any point. Mr. Reinhardt of the committee made a similar statement.

"The Fond du Lac avenue subway never should have gone in," said R. J. Grant. "Beyond that point are high banks on either side of the track. The city is going to grow in that direction. In deciding this question we must look at least five or ten years ahead. While we are doing away with the grade crossing we might as well take the correct solution.

Ald. Carney Cheered

"We should put no more money into subways when they will have to be torn out later. If it cost the city $50,000 to

(Continued on Page 6)

NELSON EXPLAINS WHY SPEAKER IS "CZAR"

HOT SHOT FROM REPUBLICAN FOR EXISTING RULES IN LOWER HOUSE

SECOND DISTRICT CONGRESSMAN URGES REFORM

Speech Delivered as Guest of City Club of Chicago Attracts International Attention—Senate, He Declares, Is Much More Liberally Governed Than House of Representatives—Speaker More Powerful Than the President—Will Continue Fight for Reform.

Chicago, Ill., Oct. 14.—Asserting that the much abused United States senate is a more liberally governed body than is the house of representatives, Congressman John M. Nelson of the Second district of Wisconsin, speaking as the guest of the City club of Chicago, this afternoon gave an exhaustive historical exposition of how the rules and rulings of the house have gradually centered authority in the hands of the speaker until that official has practically become the whole house and has more power for good or evil to the country than has the president himself.

Mr. Nelson's subject was "Necessity for Parliamentary Reform in the House of Representatives," and after pointing out such necessity he proposed several ways to obtain the needed remedy and invited further suggestions from his colleagues in the house providing for the appointment of a committee to investigate and report on a revision of the rules and followed it up with a vigorous speech in defense of it. This resolution is still pending, and Mr. Nelson will labor at the next session to obtain favorable action upon it.

Calling attention to the fact that the procedure of the house is to be found in the rulings of speakers rather than in the rules, Mr. Nelson discussed the proposition from six points of view, that of the individual representative or district, the relation of the house and senate, the dispatch of business, the relation of the executive to congress, the social and political conditions, and parliamentary reform as fundamental to all reforms.

At the last session of congress Mr. Nelson introduced a resolution in the or others.

Greater Power Than President

Discussing the relations of the speaker and the president, Mr. Nelson said:

"What a tragedy it is on representative government! The people of the United States are about to elect a president. But the people do not realize that there is one member of congress, responsible to only a single district, who may have far greater power than the president. The president will have appointments to make. He is supposed to carry out the laws, but as a matter of fact these laws are executed by departments now organized from bottom to top. He will only change the

(Continued on Page 5)

SLAIN BY INSANE PATIENT

Green Bay, Wis., Oct. 14.—Sneaking up behind him as he was working at the Brown County Insane asylum, Ernest Neuman struck William McDougal over the head and fractured his skull, causing death in a few hours.

The tragedy occurred some time yesterday morning, but McDougal was not found until evening between two piles of wood, after a search for him had been made.

Neuman slashed the throat of another inmate of the institution some five years ago and is one of the most desperate men the authorities have ever had to deal with.

He says he killed McDougal because he wanted to send him to heaven and so he wouldn't have to work so hard.

FEAR FERDINAND'S CROWN WILL BE COSTLY

Sofia, Oct. 14.—Diplomatists in Sofia are of the opinion that the troubles and embarrassments of Bulgaria have only begun. They anticipate the government will be obliged to breast a strong reaction on the part of the public when payment of the heavy expenses incurred in securing a crown and the title of emperor for Prince Ferdinand is put up to the tight-fisted Bulgarian peasantry. It is costing a good deal of money to keep the reserves with the colors and among the compensations due Turkey is the funded Rumelian debt, upon which Bulgaria in the past has paid $600,000 a year. It is estimated that Bulgaria will need a foreign loan of not less than $24,000,000 to meet these demands.

TAFT'S TRAIN IS AGAIN IN A WRECK

Cadiz, O., Oct. 14.—Judge Taft's special train was derailed again today. The accident this time occurred on a spur running from the Pennsylvania railroad at Cadiz Junction to this place.

Two engines were attached to the train and the front trucks of one of the tenders left the track.

The train was climbing a steep grade at the time, but the tender went bumping along the track for two car lengths before the train was brought to a stop.

On one side of the track there was an embankment about twenty feet high.

DROP SUIT AGAINST MOON AND BARBER

Eau Claire, Wis., Oct. 14.—The case of the United States against Barber and Moon, based on Idaho land transactions, was on today, before United States Commissioner McBain, dismissed without prejudice to the government on telephone instructions to the commissioner from United States District Atty. Wheeler of Janesville. It is not known whether or not the government will begin over again.

"DIGNIFIED" PAGES FROM "STRENUOUS LIFE"

YOU'RE CANNED
GENERAL MILES GOT A TASTE OF PRESIDENTIAL "DIGNITY"
LIAR!
THOSE WHO DISAGREE WITH HIM ARE TREATED WITH "DIGNITY"
'TAINT ENOUGH'
MR. FAMILYMAN IS TOLD THAT HE LACKS ABOUT 14 OF THE "DIGNIFIED"
SKIDOO
MRS MORRIS LEARNED ABOUT "DIGNITY" AT THE WHITE HOUSE
WHO OWNS THIS RIVER ANYHOW?
A MISSISSIPPI RIVER CAPTAIN LOST HIS LICEN E ON ACCOUNT OF "DIGNITY"
AT THE FRONT DOOR
HARRIMAN AT THE BACK DOOR
CAMPAIGN FUND
A DIPLOMATIC SITUATION IS HANDLED WITH "DIGNITY"
HE'S A FOUR FLUSHER
W.J.B
"DIGNITY" EXPLAINED
ME TOO'
'DIGNITY' ON THE RAMPAGE

BOMB IS HURLED BY ANTI-STRIKERS IN NEW YORK

New York, Oct. 14.—The bomb made its first appearance today in the struggle between the New York taxicab company and its striking chauffeurs which has been in progress for more than a week.

The company declares that a deliberate attempt was made by the strikers to destroy the property of the company and the strikers maintain that the missile was hurled in an attempt to turn public sympathy against them or by some misguided sympathizers.

The bomb was thrown early today into the big enclosure in Eighth avenue between Fiftysixth and Fiftyseventh streets, where 250 taxicabs belonging to the New York Taxicab company were stored for the night. The explosion shook the buildings for blocks and hundreds of persons in the neighborhood were thrown into wild excitement. Police details from many stations were rushed to the scene and for a time all their efforts were required to control the great crowd which had gathered in the vicinity. The explosion tore a great hole in the ground. One of the special policemen on guard declares that he saw the bomb thrown over a high fence around the enclosure. It struck near a big tank of gasoline.

Some of the strike leaders expressed a belief that it was not a bomb at all but an explosion of gasoline due to the inexperience of some of the men who had taken the places of the strikers.

WOMEN IN A RAID ON PARLIAMENT HALED INTO POLICE COURT

London, Oct. 14.—A great crowd surrounded the Bow street police court this morning when the women suffragists and the men without work who were arrested yesterday during the disorders in front of the houses of parliament were arraigned.

In the throng were many women wearing badges with the words "Votes for women." The three leaders of the militant suffragists, Mrs. Drummond, Mrs. Pankhurst and Miss Cristabel Pankhurst, demanded a trial by jury. Their cases were postponed until Oct. 21.

Police Supt. Wells testified that traffic had been disorganized for four hours and that eight policemen had been injured by the demonstrators. Miss Pankhurst acted as attorney for Mrs. Drummond and Mrs. Pankhurst and her cross examination of Supt. Wells furnished much amusement for the spectators. Most of the other prisoners were ordered to give bonds for their good behavior, with the alternative of imprisonment from one to two months. As on previous occasions the women elected to go to jail. When one of them was offered her freedom on her personal recognizance she said to the presiding magistrate:

"You wont get any of my money. I will go to prison. Down with Asquith." Another declared that she had not obstructed the police, far from it, it was the police who had obstructed her.

NOTED SINGERS FEAR THE "13TH;" REFUSE TO LAND THAT DATE

New York, Oct. 14.—Despite the strenuous efforts of Capt. Pollak of the North German Lloyd Steamship Kaiser Wilhelm der Grosse to land his load of opera singers, conductors, pianists and actresses last night, he failed because the superstition regarding the fatal "13th" proved too strong and not one of the celebrities he had on board his ship would leave it until today.

On the Kaiser Wilhelm were Signor Campanini, musical director of the Manhattan Opera company; Mme Johanna Gadski, one of the leading sopranos of the Metropolitan opera company; Daddi, baritone in Oscar Hammerstein's company; Mlle. Matja von Neissen-Stone, a new contralto for the Metropolitan; Josef Thevinne, the noted pianist, and Nellie Roland, who is to appear with Marion Terry in "Divorce." Not one of them could be persuaded to set foot on land last night.

In vain Oscar Hammerstein who was on the dock to get Campanini implored him to come ashore in order that they might talk over the impending operatic season that is so soon to open. It was no use.

100 MEN ARE NEAR TO DEATH IN A BURNING MINE

Koenigshuette, Oct. 14.—Fire broke out this morning in one of the galleries of the Koenigsbrube coal mine. One hundred men at the time were in one of the deep galleries, and it was thought for a while that they would be lost. They managed, however, to make their escape through an adjoining shaft. Twentythree men in another gallery were brought out unconscious from suffocation. Twenty of these were revived but three succumbed.

BRITISH FLEET AT RHODES

Smyrna, Asiatic Turkey, Oct. 14.—Six British warships from Malta arrived this morning off the island of Rhodes, a Turkish island in the Mediterranean off the southwest coast of Asia-Minor.

MANN'S PAPER TRUST QUEST REACHES MINNESOTA

Minneapolis, Minn., Oct. 14.—Congressman Mann, who is at the head of the congressional committee investigating the workings of the alleged paper trust, arrived here this morning to continue the taking of testimony in relation to forestry conditions, what the supply of pulp wood will be for the future and as to the conditions of the spruce forests in Northern Minnesota.

TUCKER TOO ILL TO TRAVEL

St. Louis, Mo., Oct. 14.—No attempt to renew his journey to Hot Springs, Ark., was made today by Col. William F. Tucker, assistant paymaster general of the United States army whose arrest on charges of wife abandonment was reported from Decatur, Ill., yesterday. Dr. Louis H. Behrens, the house physician, stated that an attempt to move him might result fatally.

CITY CAN BUILD PUBLIC LIGHT PLANT

NO CERTIFICATE OF NECESSITY REQUIRED UNDER PUBLIC UTILITIES ACT

CITY ATTY. KELLY GIVES AN OPINION

Ald. Bogk Changes Front and Declares Municipal Plant Would Put Present Lighting Company Out of Business—Has Written a Letter to Rate Commission to Ascertain the Rights of the Municipality.

That the city has power to build a municipal light plant to furnish current for its own uses is the opinion of City Atty. John T. Kelly. No certificate of necessity under the public utilities act need be asked by the city from the railroad commission.

Ald. Frederick C. Bogk, who voted for the adoption of the resolution of Ald. Henry Smith, directing the board of public works to build a plant on the Fifth ward site capable of producing current for 1,000 lamps of 2,000 candle power each, has written a letter on his own responsibility to the commission relative to the situation.

Put Present Plant Out of Business

"The building of a municipal light plant would put the plant of the street railway out of business," Ald. Bogk said today, when asked why he had raised the contention that the city has no power under the public utilities act to build a municipal plant. "The company has all of its conduits in and would suffer great loss if the street lighting were done by the city."

When comment was made over the solicitation manifested by Ald. Bogk for the street railway company, he declared that he had the interests of the city at heart in raising the point: that if the question were an important one it should be raised and answered before work had been begun on the municipal plant, and that he felt it his duty to write to the commission and ascertain where the city stands.

An Indeterminate Contract

"The street railway has an indeterminate contract with the city for street lighting and I don't feel sure that the city, under the public utilities act, can compete with the private corporation," said Ald. Bogk. The attention of the aldermen was directed to the fact that the city's contract with the Milwaukee Electric Railway & Light company is for a definite period.

"Well, the franchise of the company is indeterminate," said Mr. Bogk. "That is what I meant. I think we ought to find out whether we have power to build a municipal light plant before we expend any money for the construction of a plant." Ald. Bogk was informed that City Atty Kelly had stated but a few minutes before that in his opinion the city has power to build.

"I am glad to hear it," Ald. Bogk replied. "I'll go and see Mr. Kelly."

Mr. Kelly said he did not believe it was the intention of the legislature to limit the power of a municipality to furnish its own light, notwithstanding that the statute is broad in its terms.

Not at Mercy of Corporation

"It would seem to be that it was not the intention of the legislature, in passing the enactment, to hamper any of the governmental departments to place it at the mercy of a private corporation," Mr. Kelly declared. "That would be in conflict with the sover-

(Continued on Page 7)

EXTRA!

CUBS AGAIN CHAMPIONS OF THE WORLD

DEFEAT THE TIGERS IN THE DECIDING GAME OF THE SERIES

INTEREST IN CONTEST DECREASES AT DETROIT AS RESULT OF PREVIOUS GAMES—OVERALL AND DONOVAN SELECTED TO DO THE PITCHING—BOTH TEAMS CONFIDENT OF VICTORY BEFORE THE GAME BEGAN

BATTING ORDER OF THE TEAMS

DETROIT—	CHICAGO—
McIntyre, lf.	Sheckard, lf.
O'Leary, ss.	Evers, 2b.
Crawford, cf.	Schulte, rf.
Cobb, rf.	Chance, 1b.
Rossman, 1b.	Steinfeldt, 3b.
Coughlin, 3b.	Hoffman, cf.
Schaefer, 2b.	Tinker, ss.
Schmidt, c.	Kling, c.
Donovan, p.	Overall, p.

Umpires, Sheridan, American; O'Day, National.

SCORE BY INNINGS

Chicago	1	0	0	0	1	0	0	0	0	—2
Detroit	0	0	0	0	0	0	0	0	0	—0

Detroit, Mich., Oct. 14.—The Chicago Cubs are still the champions of the baseball world.

They won that title when they today took the fifth game of the championship series from the Detroit American league team, and by this victory won four of the five games played.

The attendance today was not over 7,000—indicating that Detroit fans had arrived at the decision that Jennings' team was outclassed by the crack Chicago National league champions.

That the conclusion was correct was evidenced today when the Cubs played rings around the Tigers.

Overall was in the box for Chicago and he pitched a wonderful game. His strikeouts were the wonder of the fans and even the Detroit crowd was forced to applaud his wonderful control.

In one inning, with two men on bases, Overall struck out three men. And this is only a sample of his work throughout. In the first six innings of the game he had retired nine men on strikes.

Donovan was selected to do the throwing for the Tigers. He pitched a steady game the greater part of the time, but it showed only ordinary form, and he was hit frequently by the Cubs.

The story of the game by innings shows how Detroit lost:

FIRST INNING.

Chicago—Three singles gave Chicago one run in the first. After Sheckard flew out to Schaefer. Evers, Schulte and Chance hit safely, and Evers scored. Steinfield sent a high one to center and Schulte was put out at third on Hofman's liner. One run.

Detroit—Overall struck out three Tigers in their half of the first. McIntyre was given a pass, after which O'Leary fanned. Crawford singled and then the mighty Cobb struck out. Rossman hit at a third strike wild pitch and reached first. Then "Germany" Schaefer fanned. No runs.

SECOND INNING

Chicago—Joe Tinker was thrown out at first by Coughlin. Kling sent a high foul to Schmidt. Overall grounded out on an infield liner. No runs.

Detroit—Schmidt fanned. Coughlin was thrown out, Tinker to Rossman. Donovan got free transportation to first and then stole second. McIntyre flied out to center. No runs.

THIRD INNING

Chicago—Three flies put three Cubs out of business. Sheckard sent a high one to Rossman, Evers' skyscraper was caught by O'Leary and Schulte's fly went to McIntyre. No runs.

Detroit—O'Leary went out, Steinfeldt to Chance. Evers and Chance retired Crawford. Cobb's fly was caught by Sheckard. No runs.

FOURTH INNING.

Chicago—Chance sent a long one to Cobb. Steinfeldt walked but was caught trying to steal. Hofman hit the atmosphere three times. No runs.

Detroit—Rossman fanned. Schaefer got a pass. Schmidt struck out. Schaefer was caught trying to steal. No runs.

FIFTH INNING.

Chicago—Tinker out to O'Leary. Kling walked. Overall sacrificed, Schmidt to Rossman, Sheckard walked. Evers hit out a two-bagger, Kling scoring. Sheckard went out to Coughlin, Schulte out to first. One run.

Detroit—Coughlin singled and Donovan fanned. McIntyre hit out a double and O'Leary followed with a fly to center. Crawford struck out. No runs.

SIXTH INNING.

Chicago—Chance beat out a bunt. Steinfeldt sacrificed to Rossman unassisted. Hofman's fly was caught by McIntyre. Tinker sent a high one to Crawford. No runs.

Detroit—Cobb got a pass. Rossman forced Cobb at second. Schaefer struck out. Schmidt flew out to Evers. No runs.

SEVENTH INNING.

Chicago—Kling flied Crawford. Overall singled but was later called out because he was hit by a batted ball. Sheckard singled but was caught asleep at first. No runs.

Detroit—Coughlin out, Steinfeldt to Chance. Donovan's liner put him out of business, Tinker to Chance. McIntyre flied to Sheckard. No runs.

EIGHTH INNING.

Chicago—Evers singled and Schulte sacrificed, Kling to Rossman. Chance laced out a safe one after which Steinfeldt fanned. Evers and Chance tried to work the double steal act and Evers was nabbed. No runs.

Detroit—O'Leary popped to Chance. Crawford out, Evers to Chance. Cobb out, Tinker to Chance. No runs.

Neither team scored in the ninth.

MORSE, THE PROMOTER, PUT ON TRIAL IN NEW YORK

New York, Oct. 14.—Charles W. Morse, organizer and promoter of the American Ice company and the Consolidated Steamship company, and who until the panic of a year ago controlled several banks in this city, will face a jury in the criminal branch of the United States circuit court today. With Alfred H. Curtis, former president of the National Bank of North America, Morse was indicted by the federal grand jury last March.

The indictments followed an investigation into the conduct of the National Bank of North America after that institution had been forced to close its doors at the time of the panic. Violation of the National banking laws and conspiracy are alleged in the indictments. Should the trial result in conviction and the judgment subsequently be affirmed by the higher courts, there would be no alterative from a jail sentence, the penalty for violation of the national banking law being from five to ten years' imprisonment.

As was to be expected every step of the proceedings following the indictments has been contested by counsel for the respondents. The alleged violation of the banking law as charged in the indictments are three in number—over certification, misapplication of funds, and the making of false entries in reports or books of account. On the misapplication charge it is alleged that Morse was allowed to overdraw his account more than $200,000.

Morse and Curtis have been at liberty on bail.

MRS. LANGTRY WINS RACE

Newmarket, Eng., Oct. 14.—Mrs. Langtry's Yentoi won the Czarewitch stakes, 2¼ miles for the 3-year-olds and upwards, on the Newmarket track today. This is the first classic event Mrs. Langtry has won since the heyday of her racing career, a dozen or more years ago.

The Road to Success

Kermit Roosevelt was talking to a reporter about his forthcoming trip to Africa.

"I hope in the African wilds," said the young man, "to have many exciting and novel adventures. But I trust that I will engage in no such startling feat as was once undertaken by a New Yorker.

"This New Yorker, a big game hunter of many years' experience, was lion shooting in Uganda. He had excellent luck. Nearly every day he posed in a complacent attitude beside a freshly killed lion, and his photographer snapped him for the magazines.

"One afternoon the photographer, who was taking a nap in the hut, was awakened by a loud noise. He rose and looked out. Sprinting toward him from the jungle, hat gone and coattails flying, came his chief, and, with terrible roars and growls, a huge lion bounded at his heels.

"The photographer gazed spellbound at the strange and exciting picture. His chief, perceiving him, shouted:

" 'Quick, quick! Open the door, George! I'm bringing him home alive.' "—Exchange.

A Real Genius

Blyson—Rhymer is quite a genius, isn't he?

Plunket—Yes, indeed. His wife now takes in washing to support him.

BATTLE FOR THE WORLD'S TITLE

THREE NATIONAL LEAGUE TEAMS WIN THEIR GAMES

ATTENDANCE AND RECEIPTS

Paid attendance	29,577
Gross receipts	$40,271.50
Players' share	21,746.61
Each club owner	7,248.87
National commission .	4,027.15

The attendance at the first game of the world's series in Detroit last year was 10,812, and the gross receipts, $16,473.

Each of the three National league teams contesting for various championships with American league teams were victorious in the opening struggles Friday. One would, therefore, say the Nationals are the stronger, but it will take a few more games in each series to prove that.

Four runs were scored by each of the winning teams. None of the losing teams made more than two runs.

It is estimated that 60,000 persons witnessed the three important contests Friday.

In Pittsburg, where the first of the world's series was played, 30,000 people were on hand and saw the Pirates beat Detroit by a score of 4 to 1. In Chicago about 18,000 watched the Cubs win the first for the Chicago championship by a 4-to-0 score. Down in New York McGraw's Giants tackled the Boston Americans for the Eastern championship and the Giants won by a score of 4 to 2.

The Pirates won because they outfielded their western foes and because they solved George Mullin just at the right times.

Charley Adams, a busher in actual experience, was intrusted by Manager Clarke with the task of downing the hard hitting Detroiters and to him should go most of the credit for the victory. He was as cool as Etah when coolness was demanded of him and he didn't seem to care whether it was Ty Cobb or Tom Jones facing him in the crisis.

To be sure Adams had great support and the chances are he was saved from a tie or worse by Tommy Leach, Pittsburg's miniature center fielder. Leach robbed Ty Cobb of at least a triple in the seventh inning, when two men were on the bases and two were out. If the drive had gone safe it is almost a cinch Ty would have tried for a home run on it, and any one who knows the Georgian knows he would have made it a close play at the plate. Tommy's grab spoiled Detroit's one chance to win, for Adams never was in trouble except this once after the Pirates had taken the lead in the fifth. Detroit's errors came at bad times but even perfect play by the Tigers would not have won for them.

Outgeneraled, outpitched and blinded by the merciless attack of the mighty Cub machine, Sullivan's gallant White Sox, faltering in the pinches yesterday, fell in defeat, dropping battle No. 1 of the city championship, 4 to 0, before 16,762 frenzied and semi-maudlin students of the national pastime.

Jeff Overall, the ponderous Californian, hero of the world's championships of 1907 and 1908, literally toyed with the Sox, doling out only four hits, all widely scattered, while the Cub veterans, playing like well oiled machines, repulsed every effort of the Sox to push a runner by third base.

It was a grueling combat between two of the best molded ball clubs in the world. From start to finish the rivals, cheered on by blue-blooded constituents, struggling desperately, the Sox ever striving after the initial round to cut down the Cubs' advantage and their foes putting up a determined fight to retain the margin.

The New York Nationals, though outbatted, won the first game of their post season series with the Boston Americans by a score of 4 to 2. Wood outpitched Mathewson, except in the matter of strike outs, but his own error and misplays by Carrigan and Lord in the fourth inning enabled New York to win the game.

Speaker was the star of the contest, making the record hit of the year to right field and halting a runner at the plate by a magnificent throw.

The paid attendance was 4,573 and the receipts $2,956.25. Of these the national commission receives $295.62, the players $1,596.37, and the clubs $1,064.26.

FOOTBALL TEAMS TO SEE PLAY AT SHUBERT

The Shubert theater will be invaded by football players tonight when members of the football teams of Marquette and Monmouth, Mich., universities will be guests of Manager Arthur S. Friend at "The Man From Mexico." The players, accompanied by their respective team managers, will assemble at Marquette and march to the theater in a body, accompanied by several of the Marquette faculty.

FAST HORSES ARE ENTERED IN RACING MATINEE

C. W. Hunter will be the starter for the races at Washington park Sunday afternoon. A good list of entries has been secured as follows:

Class 1 pace—Copper Belles (Fredman), Warren G. (Starr), Lady Hontas (Sterneman).

Class 1 trot—Capitola (Hubinger), St. Paul (Ziegler), Butcher Girl (Klib), Deil Boy (Becker), Lady Hake (Hake), Clara B. (Barr).

Class 4 pace—Lady (Heppes), Maurine (Demerath), Dolly E. (Erickson), Handsome Harry (Manger).

Free for all pace—Oakley D. (Sterneman), Billy Sunday (Ziegelbauer).

Class 2 pace—Daisy D. (Deuster), Joe Schaeffer (Nelson), Michael Ney (Miller).

Class 3 pace—Lord Zetland (Geiger), Octo (Schroeder), Lady Dide (Higgs).

Class 5 pace—Douglas (Ziegelbauer), Silver City Boy (Hake), Glaucus (Haensel).

Class 2 trot—Jake (Conahan), Jim P. (Peterson), Yerxia (Guttknecht).

Judges—G. Dwinnell, Waukesha; Geo. Brew, A. Manger.

AMERICAN SKAT CLUB IS PLANNING TOURNEY

The first skat tournament of the American Skat club will be held on Sunday, Oct. 24, at 2 o'clock in the afternoon at the Hippodrome. The club will give $500 in cash prizes. This is one of the seven tournaments to be given this winter by the club. Dates scheduled for the other tournaments are Nov. 28, Dec. 26, Jan. 23, Feb. 27 and 10, March 27 and April 24.

FIRST FOR EASTERN TITLE TO THE GIANTS

Boston—	AB	H	P	A	E
McConnell, 2b	4	1	2	3	0
Lord, 3b	4	1	1	1	1
Speaker, cf	4	3	5	1	0
Stahl, 1b	4	2	6	0	0
Carrigan, c	4	0	4	1	1
Niles, lf	4	2	1	0	0
French, ss	3	0	2	3	1
xDonohue	1	0	0	0	0
Hooper, rf	3	1	3	0	0
Wood, p	3	0	0	0	1
Totals	34	10	24	9	4

New York—	AB	H	P	A	E
Doyle, 2b	4	0	1	4	0
Seymour, cf	4	0	0	1	0
McCormick	4	1	0	0	0
Murray, rf	4	0	2	0	0
Devlin, 3b	4	1	2	0	0
Bridwell, ss	2	1	2	5	1
Tenney, 1b	3	1	5	1	0
Myers, c	3	1	11	1	1
Schlei, c	0	0	4	0	0
Mathewson, p	3	1	0	3	0
Totals	31	6	27	15	2

xBatted for French in ninth inning.

SCORE BY INNINGS.

Boston	1	0	0	0	0	0	1	0	0	—2
New York	1	0	0	3	0	0	0	0	x	—4

SUMMARY.

Runs—Lord, Speaker, Doyle, Devlin, Bridwell, Tenney. Two-base hit—Lord. Three-base hits—Myers, Stahl. Home run—Speaker. Stolen bases—Lord, Speaker 2, Doyle 2, Niles, French, Devlin, Stahl. Double play—Speaker to Carrigan. Struck out—By Mathewson 11, by Wood 3. Base no balls—Off Wood 1. Umpires—Rigler and Connolly.

HUGH JENNINGS

I am not ready to admit by any means that the better team won Friday. The result of the game but shows the luck which enters into baseball. Things broke a trifle bad for us all the way. Pittsburg played wonderful ball.

A good looking man nearly always thinks he is also smart, and these two notions take up most of his time.

HURRAH FOR THE PIRATES!

THE GAME IN FIGURES

Detroit—	AB	R	H	TB	SH	SB	PO	A	E
D. Jones, lf	3	0	2	2	0	0	5	0	1
Bush, ss	2	0	0	0	1	0	1	0	1
Cobb, rf	3	1	0	0	0	1	2	0	1
Crawford, cf.	4	0	1	1	0	0	1	0	0
Delehanty, 2b.	4	0	1	1	0	0	0	4	1
Moriarity 3b	4	0	1	1	0	0	0	1	0
T. Jones, 1b	3	0	0	0	0	0	10	0	0
xMcIntyre	1	0	0	0	0	0	0	0	0
Schmidt, c	3	0	0	0	0	0	5	0	1
Mullin, p	3	0	1	1	0	0	0	5	0
Totals	30	1	6	6	1	1	24	10	5

Pittsburg—	AB	R	H	TB	SH	SB	PO	A	E
Byrne, 3b	3	0	0	0	0	0	2	3	0
Leach, cf	3	0	0	0	1	0	4	0	0
Clarke, lf	4	1	1	4	0	0	2	0	0
Wagner, ss	3	1	1	2	0	0	0	6	0
Miller, 2b	4	0	1	1	0	1	6	0	0
Abstein, 1b	3	1	0	0	0	0	8	1	0
Wilson, rf	3	0	1	1	0	1	0	0	0
Gibson, c	3	1	1	2	0	0	4	0	0
Adams, p	3	0	0	0	0	0	0	0	0
Totals	29	4	5	10	1	2	*26	12	0

xMcIntyre batted for T. Jones in ninth.
*Delehanty out; hit by batted ball.

SCORE BY INNINGS.

Detroit	1	0	0	0	0	0	0	0	0	—1
Pittsburg	0	0	0	1	2	1	0	0	x	—4

SUMMARY.

Two Base Hits—Gibson, Wagner.
Home Run—Clarke.
Struck Out—By Mullin, 4 (Leach, Wilson, Byrne, Abstein); by Adams, 2 (Delehanty, Mullin).
Bases on Balls—Off Adams, 4; off Mullin, 1.
Hit by Pitcher—Wagner, Byrne.

HOW THE CUBS BEAT CHICAGO WHITE SOX

Cubs—	AB	H	P	A	E
Evers, 2b	4	3	1	3	0
Sheckard, lf	4	0	0	0	0
Schulte, rf	2	0	1	0	0
Chance, 1b	3	1	7	0	0
Steinfeldt, 3b	2	1	1	1	1
Hofman, cf	3	1	9	0	0
Tinker, ss	3	0	2	1	1
Archer, c	2	0	6	3	0
Overall, p	3	0	0	1	0
Totals	26	6	27	9	2

Sox—	AB	H	P	A	E
Altizer, rf	4	1	0	0	0
Isbell, 1b	3	1	7	0	0
Cole, cf	4	0	1	1	0
Dougherty, lf	4	0	0	0	0
Purtell, 2b	4	1	3	6	2
Parent, ss	3	1	3	3	0
Tannehill, 3b	3	0	2	0	1
Sullivan, c	3	0	8	3	0
Walsh, p	3	0	0	4	1
Totals	31	4	24	19	4

SCORE BY INNINGS.

Cubs	2	0	0	1	0	0	0	1	x	—4
Sox	0	0	0	0	0	0	0	0	0	—0

SUMMARY.

Runs—Evers, 2; Schulte, Chance. Two base hits—Isbell, Evers. Sacrifice hit—Steinfeldt. Stolen bases—Schulte, 2; Isbell, Evers. Double play—Purtell to Parent to Isbell. Left on bases—Sox, 6; Cubs 2. Base on balls—Off Walsh, 2; off Overall, 1. Struck out—By Walsh, 7; by Overall, 5. Wild pitches—Overall, Walsh. Time—1:40. Umpires—O'Day and Sheridan.

FRED CLARKE

The better team won the game. There was nothing left to desire in our play save that we might have done some more hitting. I knew Adams was one of the best pitchers in any league.

The Sisson & Sewell Juniors will play the Tigers Juniors Sunday morning at the haymarket. Would like to hear of out-of-town games, averaging 75 to 85 pounds. Address Louis Kaufman, 517 Vliet street.

FOOTBALL GAMES TODAY

WEST.

Chicago vs. Indiana at Marshall field.
Purdue vs. Northwestern at Lafayette.
Illinois vs. Kentucky at Urbana.
Minnesota vs. Ames at Minneapolis.
Wisconsin vs. Lawrence at Madison.
Marquette vs. Monmouth at Milwaukee.
Michigan vs. Case at Ann Arbor.
Ohio State vs. Wooster at Columbus.
Nebraska vs. Knox at Lincoln.

EAST.

Harvard vs. Williams at Cambridge.
Yale vs. Springfield at New Haven.
Princeton vs. Fordham at Princeton.
Cornell vs. Oberlin at Ithaca.
Dartmouth vs. Bowdoin at Hanover.
Carlisle vs. Penn State at Wilkesbarre.
Syracuse vs. Rochester at Syracuse.
Pennsylvania vs. West Virginia at Philadelphia.

MILWAUKEE HIGH SCHOOLS.

South Division vs. Wauwatosa at Wauwatosa.
West Division vs. Racine at Racine.
East Division vs. Lake Forest at Lake Forest.

RACINE TO KEEP ITS TEAM IN STATE LEAGUE

The Racine Baseball association has decided to remain with the Wisconsin-Illinois league. At a meeting held last night this decision was made final. Manager William Armstrong has been asked to remain and secure a team for the season. On account of the cost of a new grand stand and $1,200 paid for a franchise, the treasurer's report shows no money on hand at present.

MATCH THREE GOOD PACERS AT LEXINGTON

Through a match arranged yesterday three great pacers, Lady Maud C. and Dan S., owned by Miss Lotta Crabtree of Boston, and Hedgewood Boy, owned by George Estabrook of Denver, will meet at Lexington next week under saddle. Reamy May will ride Dan S., and H. K. Devereaux of Cleveland Hedgewood Boy, while the other rider has not been selected.

WILL ENTERTAIN MICHIGAN ROOTERS

The coming Michigan-Marquette game has thoroughly aroused the interest of the alumni and the "old grads" are looking forward to the game with enthusiasm and determination to appreciate it to the fullest.

Starting from Gimbel's store a parade of the Michigan rooters, led by the University band, will proceed through the downtown streets Saturday morning. After the parade the Michigan rooters will be taken in hand and entertained by Col. Pabst.

The game will be held at Marquette field. Arrangements for handling the large crowd expected have been completed. It is a curious fact that the initial letters, or "varsity letter" of both Michigan and Marquette are the same, as are the Michigan Athletic and Marquette colors. Owing to this situation the Michigan rooters will use their varsity colors, maize and light blue, and the Michigan section will, therefore, be a mass of light blue and chrysanthemum.

In expectation of the great crowd that will attend the game, the Marquette athletic council is erecting stands which, with those already built, will comfortably care for 12,000 people. Even with these arrangements and seating capacity the crowd is expected to tax the field to its limit.

The Michigan section will be the center of the west stand between the thirtyfive-yard lines and directly in the center of the playing field.

BOWLING

BUSINESS MEN'S LEAGUE.

	(1)	(2)	(3)
Polachecks	852	877	839
Blik's Togs	919	902	859
Huebschs	896	838	905
Noxalls	843	849	924
Hardwares	805	940	907
Sentinels	921	886	976

TELEPHONE LEAGUE.

	(1)	(2)	(3)
Engineers	670	766	732
Treasurers	805	700	781

FEDERAL RUBBER LEAGUE.

	(1)	(2)	(3)
Vehicles	725	734	746
Press	622	665	734
Autos	687	714	680
Office	625	678	711

NORTH SIDE BUSINESS MEN'S LEAGUE.

	(1)	(2)	(3)
Beckers	757	837	828
S. H. Ryes	738	800	836
Sissons	898	746	779
Strauss	891	965	739

NORTH SIDE BOWLING LEAGUE.

	(1)	(2)	(3)
Grosskopfs	711	778	840
T. B. H.'s	679	727	770
Leaders	739	868	779
Rheinfranks	878	809	842

BADGER LEAGUE.

	(1)	(2)	(3)
Globes	871	849	823
Cremos	905	948	832

KILBOURN LEAGUE.

	(1)	(2)	(3)
Straws	878	865	896
W. & B.'s	867	877	875

FULLER-WARREN LEAGUE.

	(1)	(2)	(3)
Regals	646	716	790
Splendids	773	745	770

REGULATION LEAGUE.

	(1)	(2)	(3)
Vick's Colts	721	839	779
F. E. D.	811	898	877

MILWAUKEE TENPIN LEAGUE.

	(1)	(2)	(3)
Pluggers	924	1047	1019
Repeaters	943	764	1014

VIBRATION FROM MACHINE CAUSES "SEASICKNESS"

Racine, Wis., Oct. 9.—An investigation by the board of education because of "seasickness" among the students of the domestic science classes resulted in the discovery that changes must be made in the building where domestir science is taught. For a month the girl students of domestic science have daily become ill and the reason could not be ascertained, but when school commissioners visited the building they found that the floors where the domestic science classes were at work seemed to roll like a steamer in a heavy sea and the cause was soon discovered. On the first floor of the building the manual training classes were instructed and machinery, shafts, etc., had been installed. The operating of the machinery caused a vibration throughout the second floor of the building and caused seasickness among the girls of the domestic science classes.

CHAMPION PITTSBURG TEAM

BIG DEAL IN TIMBER LAND CONSUMMATED

Ashland, Wis., Oct. 9.—A deal has been consummated whereby the Mellen Lumber company has taken up all of the interests of the Glidden Veneer company and the Shanagolden Lumber company, according to reports from Glidden. All of the vast tracts of timber owned by these two companies, together with logging railroads and the sawmill of the Glidden Veneer company, are included in the deal, and under the arrangements that have been made this means the closing down of the Shanagolden works and the Glidden Veneer company.

The Mellen Lumber company is a new corporation formed last winter by Messrs. John Joyce, C. F. Latimer and L. K. Baker of this city, H. I. Latimer and George E. Foster of Mellen and others from Wausau, Grand Rapids, Chicago and Michigan. The capital stock of the Mellen Lumber company was first fixed at $450,000, but with this new deal the capital stock is to be increased from this amount to $1,000,000, and a large number of prominent lumbermen in the Northwest have gone into the new company.

The land owned by the Glidden Veneer company and the Shanagolden Lumber company amounts to 70,000 acres, so that this deal is one of the largest ever consummated in this county and it will give the Mellen Lumber company the ownership of upward of 100,000 acres of land.

OFFICIAL NOTICE—L—57

Office of City Clerk, Milwaukee, Oct. 7, 1909.

Notice is hereby given, pursuant to Chapter 190 of the Laws of 1909, that the following applications for licenses to sell intoxicating liquors in the city of Milwaukee have been filed in this office, the granting of which is now pending:

FIRST WARD.

Name of Applicant—
ALOIS ENGELHARDT,
Location where business is to be conducted—777 North Water street.
Bondsmen—LOUIS KEEPNER and JOHN W. WIESNER.

FIFTH WARD.

Name of Applicant—
NIKOLAS SARAC
Location where business is to be conducted—76 First avenue.
Bondsmen—UNITED SURETY CO.

EIGHTEENTH WARD.

Name of Applicant—
FELIX KUSKOWSKI,
Location where business is to be conducted—880 Pulaski street.
Bondsmen—AMERICAN FIDELITY CO.

EDWIN HINKEL, City Clerk.

ALL THE LATEST SPORTING NEWS

LEWIS IS EASY MARK FOR THE THUNDERBOLT

Billy Papke and Willie Lewis of New York went six rounds at Pittsburg last night. At the conclusion of the half dozen rounds Papke easily was given the public's favorable verdict.

Lewis, holding on and half unrecognizable, after his fifteen minute beating weakly signified his intention to ask for a return match.

Papke, unmarked and smiling, said he believed he had proven his supremacy over Lewis, and would not agree to a match at any early date.

As the gong sounded for the opening round Lewis rushed in with a rapid succession of rights and lefts to Papke's body, none of the blows hurting Papke. After careful sparring Papke led with a vicious right jolt to Lewis' stomach. In the clinches Papke was warned three times to break clean, the crowd hooting the Illinois lad's slowness in breaking away from Lewis.

As the men came up for the second round Papke turned loose a right swing to the jaw. Lewis fell to the floor and rested until the count of nine had been tolled off by the referee. The third round was a repetition of the second, with Lewis receiving blows on the jaw which forced him on two occasions to rest for the full allowance of time. Papke came out from the round without a mark, while Lewis had a badly split lip and his right eye was closed.

With Papke practically holding his man on his feet, the fourth round ended amid the hoots of the crowd, who were of the opinion that Papke could have put his man away. Lewis came back after the minute rest in the fifth round, seemingly greatly rested, and before Papke could cover, had sprung a series of left and right swings that plainly staggered the Illinois wonder. Papke caught himself and before the fifth period had ended Lewis was hanging on.

In the sixth and last round Papke easily led the New York lad. Lewis with a broken nose, which had been half torn off by Papke's ripping uppercuts in the in fighting, was helpless in the hands of Papke, but managed to last until the gong sounded.

DECIDE TITLE OF THE S. D. LEAGUE SUNDAY

Tomorrow will be a big day at the Social Democratic ball park, Schiller and Howell avenues. At 3:30 the Coming Nations and the Twentieth warders will clash for the championship game in the race. Deuter, the old standby of the Nations, will be seen in the box for the Nations, while either Rades or Jeske will hand out the benders for the Twentieth warders. In the first game the Twentyfirst warders and the Heralds will play. This game will be called promptly at 2 p. m., in order to give the other teams an opportunity to start promptly. Both teams are evenly matched and the winners of tomorrow's game will climb into third place. Sunday will also be county central committee day and Social Democrats from all parts of the city have promised to attend.

The Seventeenth ward S. D., will leave at 1 o'clock tomorrow afternoon for South Milwaukee where they will cross bats with the strong team of that place. R. Couts will umpire the game at South Milwaukee while Mr. Kuhn will handle the indicator at the double-header in the park.

The batteries: Coming Nations, Deuter and Bunde; Twentyfirst ward, Hiller and Styles; Twentieth ward, Rades, Jeske and Knipple; Heralds, Johnson, Hilgendorf, Barber or Jones; Seventeenth ward, Dostal and Schoemann; South Milwaukee, Anderson and McCarrier.

CITY LEAGUE POST SEASON GAME OF INTEREST

Everything is in readiness for Sunday afternoon's big post-season game, when the Calkins of Waukesha, champions of the City league, clash with the Kosciuskos at 2:30 o'clock at the South Side park for a $200 purse.

Three times the past season did these two clubs meet and each time a great battle took place. It is a matter of record that every one of these combats with the exception of one, went the extra inning route, while the third was won by a single run, so fiercely were they fought. Of these the Waukeshas were victorious twice, while the Kosciuskos were returned the winners once.

The two star twirlers of the league, George Cleary and Jim Jach, who were the principals in these sensational battles and who are both slated for faster company next year, are down to face each other on the mound again. Both are in fine trim for this game and another splendid duel is sure to be the result. Jack Luell will umpire the game.

WRESTLING AT THE STAR

A finish wrestling match between Giovanni Raicevitch, the Italian champion, and Tony Franks, the heavyweight champion of Chicago, will be held at the New Star theater tonight. A purse of $100 will be awarded to the winner of the match, best two out of three falls.

JOHNSON DOPES SYSTEM KETCHEL MAY USE

Jack Johnson and Willus Britt, manager of Stanley Ketchel, had an impromptu meeting in the private offices of Promoter Coffroth. It gave an insight into the manner of fight that Johnson expects Ketchel to make, and also shows Ketchel's plan. The meeting was altogether unarranged. After a short discussion of general topics, Britt suggested that Ketchel's plan would be to make Johnson come after him when they entered the ring.

"Nothing to that," retorted Johnson. "Ketchel is coming in at me this way," and he illustrated by whirling his arms in windmill fashion, "and I'll get him like this," and his right uppercut went digging its way through the atmosphere.

CHAMPION ATTELL BEATS PATSY KLINE

Without any apparent exertion, Abe Attell, the champion featherweight, won from Patsy Kline at Philadelphia last night. Attell handed Kline a fierce walloping and came within an ace of finishing the Jersey boy in the second round. Abe sent Patsy down with a hard right, and in the same round opened a cut on Kline's nose. The count of eight was run up on Patsy while he was trying to get together on the ropes. From then to the finish it was all Attell. The little champion landed whenever he pleased. In the last round Kline was in such bad shape that Attell loked over to the referee, thinking he would stop the bout. Kline was game enough to take the beating and went the limit.

HARD LUCK?

ANSWER TO QUERY

Sporting Editor Daily News: To settle a wager, who did Manske of Milwaukee play with before he came to the Brewers? A FAN.

Des Moines and Minneapolis.

FIGHT PICTURES GIVE LINE ON JOHNSON

The presentation of the moving pictures of the Tommy Burns-Jack Johnson fight is timely for local fight fans. Critical observers of the game will be able to find a clew to the winner of the battle scheduled for next Saturday at Frisco, especially those who witness the reproduction of the Papke-Ketchel fight, which concludes tonight. The style of Ketchel and the style of Johnson is of the utmost importance to local fight fans just now.

The pictures of the Burns-Johnson go show them in every round of the battle, which was staged by Hugh McIntosh.

Johnson is meeting much the same game that he had in Burns in the coming fight with Ketchel and those who have seen the pictures of both fights will be able to form an opinion of the outcome of the pending battle at Colma.

CHAMPION'S TRAINING STUNTS DISPLEASE FANS

ATHLETIC MANAGER CHOSEN FOR RIPON

Roy H. Cameron of Oshkosh, has been elected to the general managership of all athletics at Ripon college. The office is a new one filling the positions formerly occupied by the various team managers. Harold Murphy White of Oshkosh was elected president of the athletic board, and Ira Parker of Tomahawk, vice president and secretary.

Repeated warnings and good advices does not seem to be acceptable to Champion Jack Johnson but if the big colored fellow continues to ignore the words of those closest to him he may have to let go of the title. Stanley Ketchel will force the big fellow to take a back seat unless Johnson takes a notion immediately to settle down to business.

Reports from the coast are to the effect that Johnson is loafing; that he is giving little attention to training stunts, and that he believes the Michigan boy is so easy that active training and proper conditioning are not necessary. But he will find out his mistake. Ketchel will let him know that it is no runaway. Of course on the face of it all Johnson looks a little bit better than others who seek his scalp but to stack up against a proposition like Ketchel—unless in first class condition—looks like suicide from here.

Ketchel and Johnson are booked to clash a week from today. Johnson therefore has only about a week to get in shape. Ketchel has been training for three weeks. It was not necessary for him to work unusually hard because he was in shape before he went to the coast, having put himself in condition for his bout with Sam Langford which was prevented by the authorities. Therefore one can bank that when Stanley Ketchel enters the ring he will be in shape to give Mr. Johnson a tryout never to be forgotten. Don't imagine that Ketchel has no chance to win! He hits pretty hard and fights all the time and if he can get the champion out of condition, it will be an awful lacing that the Texan will get.

Johnson is confident of winning. He says he is bigger, stronger and a harder hitter than his opponent. That is true, but it must be remembered that Johnson can't take as much body punishment as Ketchel. It looks from here that Ketchel will work for the body especially if he knows that Johnson has not trained faithfully. Ketchel knows what it is to get into the squared circle after a vacation with wine, women and song. He knows that several close calls have been put up to him because he was not in the best possible shape.

It's a bit peculiar that Johnson does not settle down to business and do more training that he is. No matter how "easy" an opponent looks, a fellow like Ketchel is always dangerous. Johnson's friends have tried hard to make him get down to hard work so that he would not be winded after fighting eight or ten rounds. But the big fellow just smiles and remarks that the fight will not go eight or nine rounds. That kind of "dope" never brings home the money. Few pugilists not in excellent shape have won fights and should Ketchel slip one over on the boy from Galveston, Johnson will have himself to blame.

Betting on the fight is slow although small sums are being taken at Tom Corbett's place and other sporting resorts on the coast. Johnson is the favorite but unless he shifts and does some good work, Ketchel money will flow in. It would be a big boost for Ketchel to put Johnson away and that he will try mighty hard to accomplish that is not to be doubted. Fitzsimmons held the middle and heavyweight titles at one time and unless Johnson gets busy in a hurry, it wouldn't be surprising to see Ketchel hold two titles within a week. It's up to Johnson. He has been in the game long enough to know that a fellow of Ketchel's caliber is hard to beat. If he fails to profit by the experience of others, it is his own fault.

With Johnson beaten, no one would ever hear of him again and he would have a mighty hard time trying to get a match with a top notcher. It's a cinch Ketchel wouldn't give him another chance.

AMERICAN LEAGUE LEADERS

WEST PARK WILL PLAY CITY LEAGUE TEAM

White City park will be the scene of a battle Sunday when the West Parks, champions of the semi-pros, meet the fast McGreals team of the City league. Both teams have been strengthened, the McGreals being reinforced by E. Lee and Addis, while Tony Schiefer will cover first base for the Parks. Southpaw Lewis, with a season's record average of four hits and ten strike outs per game, will oppose the crafty Monk Lee on the slab.

ALLEGED FAKE WRESTLERS ARE ARRESTED

Jack Carroll, for a time Gotch's manager; Bert Warner of Minneapolis, and Winn Sharris of Spokane were arrested at Curfew, Wash., as members of the Maybray gang of wrestling and footrace swindlers recently indicted at Omaha and Council Bluffs.

The Arlingtons are rounding into first-class condition and have open dates on Oct. 17, 24 and 31, for the strongest 120-pound team in the city of state. Kenosha and Racine teams preferred. Would like a practice game for Oct. 10. Address Frank Ruehl, 667 Tenth street.

TONNAGE TAX ISSUE WILL BE PROMINENT

LAKE SUPERIOR COPPER AND IRON MINING MEN PREPARING FOR FIGHT

SOUTHERN MICHIGAN SENTIMENT FAVORS PLAN

But Persons Acquainted With Situation Claim Tax Would Be Unjust and a Blow to Many Industries—Chase S. Osborn May Lead Fight Against a Tax—News of Lake Superior Mining Districts.

Calumet, Mich., Oct. 9.—Lake Superior copper and iron mining men believe that the tonnage tax issue will play an important part in the next gubernatorial campaign in Michigan. The proposition was first brought up during the last session of the legislature, a bill to place a tax on the copper and iron produced in the upper peninsula being introduced by one of the two Democratic members. This measure was defeated, principally because it was fathered by a Democrat, but there was undeniably considerable sentiment in favor of something of the sort, and plenty of intimations were made that the issue would come up later at a more opportune time and that the grangers of lower Michigan would take it in hand. There is now plenty of evidence that the issue will be prominent in the next campaign for the governorship.

Farmers Favor Plan

The farmers of the lower part of the state are much in favor of a tonnage tax and it is believed they will support the candidate who will come out squarely in favor of it. Just who this candidate will be is a question. Several lower peninsula men have already announced they will be in the field for the Republican nomination at the primaries, but as yet not one of them has made known his attitude toward a tonnage tax. Chase S. Osborn of Sault Ste. Marie is prominently mentioned as a probable candidate for the Republican nomination, and it is believed if he consents to make the run that he will have the support of all upper peninsula interests, as it is known Mr. Osborn is opposed to a tonnage tax and would come out fearlessly against it.

Blow to Mining Companies

A tax on copper and iron in Michigan would be a serious blow to the mining companies, and indirectly to the business and laboring men of the upper peninsula, whose degree of prosperity and success is almost entirely dependent on the mining operations. That such a tax would be unjust to the interests of the upper peninsula is claimed to all acquainted with the situation, and it is safe to assert that every effort would be made by mining men and others in this region to combat the Southern Michigan sentiment in favor of it. Under existing taxation conditions, it is believed, the copper and iron mines are paying more than their just share of the state taxation burden, and it is realized that an additional tax would put a damper on further development of mineral resources, and handicap operating mines. In fact, it is declared that a tonnage tax would undoubtedly result in the closing down of some mines, which are now operating on a small margin of profit, throwing thousands of men out of employment and injuring business generally.

Lake

The biggest event of the week in Lake Superior copper mining circles was the cutting of the rich lode at the fifth level by the Lake Copper company. This was an outcome eagerly awaited for some time as it establishes the continuity of the ore body down to a depth of 750 feet. For about a month a cross-cut has been driven from the shaft to cut the vein, and the encountering of the lode has greatly strengthened the belief of the company that the Lake will make a big mine. The formation averages about 80 feet in width, about 60 of which is well mineralized, and extends across the property about 3,500 feet. There is little apprehension that the vein will not prove consistent at the lowest depth that can be reached within the property. The development of the ground owned by the company has been spectacular, and as far as operations have progressed it is one of the most notable successes in the history of the district.

Like Taxing Farm Products

Taxing the products of the mines, it is argued, would be as unjust as taxing the products of the farm. The late Gov. Johnson of Minnesota realized this when he vetoed a similar proposition in that state last spring. He did not believe such a law would be a square deal, and after the legislature had passed the bill, and in the face of a wave of sentiment in favor of it, he denounced the measure and thereby saved the mining companies of Minnesota many hardships and paved the way for a greater development and advancement of the mineral industry of that commonwealth.

Keweenaw

It is reported that the Keweenaw Copper company, which is conducting diamond drill operations on its lands in Keweenaw county in the hope of encountering copper in commercial quantities, has cut the Osceola lode, the vein showing a width of 18 feet and carrying good values. The rumor lacks verification.

Wolverine

The Wolverine Copper Mining company, known in local circles as the "Little Calumet & Hecla," paid a semi-annual dividend of $5 per share on Oct. 1, making the total amount of dividends paid to date, $6,000,000. The Wolverine is fortunate in that its ground is so rich that it can produce copper at a low cost. It also is favored with a first-class management. Underground the mine is looking fine and with very little money required for construction expenses its future is full of promise for the shareholders.

Calumet & Hecla

Calumet & Hecla is shipping considerable copper by rail to Chicago and other lower points. The company's local stocks of metal are kept well below the normal.

Victoria

The management of the Victoria Copper company has discontinued diamond drill and other exploratory work until there is a decided advance in the price of copper so that this work may be paid from the earnings. Stoping ground has been blocked out to supply the stamp mill with 500 tons of rock per day for several years.

September Products

September mine products were: Mohawk, 1,207,200 pounds of mineral, an increase of 129,700 pounds compared with the output for the same month last year; Wolverine, 1,017,700 pounds of mineral, an increase of 7,000 pounds from the output of the same month last year; Champion, 2,496,000, increase of 47,000; Baltic, 2,542,000, increase of 338,000; Trimountain, 728,000, increase 4,000; Franklin, 228,000; Quincy, 1,550.

MAROONS VS. RIPPLE & MEYERS

The Maroons will play a practice game Sunday morning with the Ripple & Meyers. All players report on Fourteenth and Burleigh streets. Players not reporting are out of the teams. The Maroons have open dates Nov. 7, 14, 21 and 28. All teams from 105 to 110 pounds wishing games, city or state, address Joseph Milbauer, room 40, New Insurance building.

PROFESSIONAL and AMATEUR BASEBALL.

LATEST SPORTING NEWS

Address All Communications to Sporting Editor.
JAMES C. WEBSTER.

YACHTING, RACING, and OTHER ATHLETICS.

CAPT. COY SHOWS KICKING ABILITY IN FIRST WORK-OUT

APPEARS TO BE ABLE TO KICK AS WELL AS LAST YEAR.

Drop Kicks Pretty Goal From The 50-Yard Line.

Takes Part in Scrimmage—Shifted Line-up Seems Stronger Than Old One—Messinger and Deming Still Being Used on the Varsity.

By James C. Webster.

That captain "Ted" Coy of the Yale football team will be able to kick as well this season as he did last is the firm belief today of those who saw him practising at the field yesterday afternoon for the first time this season. During part of the time that the backs were catching punts and the ends were running down under them, Coy practised punting and drop kicking. On one occasion he sent the ball high over the goal post and directly in the center from the 50 yard line. The ball went so high over the bar that there is no question but that it would have been a goal had he been standing in the center of the field—the 55-yard line—at the time he kicked. In punting he did not let out, preferring to take things easy for the time being.

Coy went through signal practice yesterday, lining up at fullback. He worked at this but a short time, devoting considerable of the afternoon to coaching the eleven with Howard Jones and Captain Biglow of the 1907 eleven. He did not line up in the scrimmage except for two plays. He dropped back on one occasion and made an onside kick which resulted in a touchdown and attempted a field goal which fell short. He practised forward passing the ball to Kilpatrick and show accuracy as well as ability to throw a long distance. He will work out with the team every afternoon, but will not play before the Colgate game, Oct. 23.

The changes in the line-up, as announced in The Leader yesterday—Andrus at tackle, Lilley at guard and Cooney at center—was an improvement. In the scrimmage with the freshmen, this line appeared to be stronger than any Yale has put on the field up to the present. Holes through which the backs made long gains were made constantly by the linemen, and when the ball was in the possession of the freshmen, the line held like a stone wall. Yale's line this year is one of the best the university has had in recent years. The men are heavy, but every one is fast.

Messinger and Deming, New Haven boys, were again used at right halfback and fullback respectively on the 'varsity eleven. Both are showing up well. Messinger is eradicating his worst fault—slowness—in a most promising manner. Deming was called upon to punt several times.

Special attention was given to the linemen yesterday. Two sets were pitted against each other. Howard Bird stood where one of the backfield candicates could take signals from him, and without a quarterback this man received the ball on the pass from Conety at center, and tried to make gains wherever Bird signalled with his hand for him to go. In this manner no one but the man rushing the ball knew where the play was to go, and the 'varsity line men were made to make openings on every play in case the ball was supposed to be taken through their position.

Head Coach Biglow, Backfield Coach Wheaton and L. H. Biglow, captain of the Yale 1907 team, were the only coaches at the field.

The first and second teams lined up as follows:

Kilpatrick	Left end.	Brooks
Hobbs	Left tackle.	Brown
Lilley	Left guard.	Bronson
Cooney	Center.	Hyde
Goebel	Right guard.	Greenough
Paul	Right tackle.	Francis
Logan	Right end.	Naedele
Howe	Quarterback.	Johnson
Daly	Left halfback.	French
Messinger	Right halfback.	Kistler
Deming	Fullback.	Holt

Jack Johnson Downed

"Gunboat" Smith, a seaman from one of the United States cruisers anchored in the San Fransico harbor, scored a knock-down in a four round bout last night with Jack Johnson, the negro heavyweight. Coming out of a clinch in the last round, the sailor swung a right over hand chop which took Johnson flush on the chin. The champion went down flat on his back and when he recovered his feet he was so dazed that his manager cut the round short.

CEDAR HILLS WIN 10-3

DEFEAT INDEPENDENTS IN FINAL GAME OF THE SEASON.

Score Seven Runs in Seventh off Billy Mulligan

At End of Sixth Inning Independents Lead, 5 to 3—Pitts Gets a Home Run—Gaffe, Foley, Harrigan and Donnegan Credited With Three-Baggers.

The fast Cedar Hill baseball team has another victory to its credit today. In a seventh inning batting rally they scored seven runs and beat out the Independents on the Cedar Hill park grounds, 10 to 8. Mulligan was hit hard in this inning. Pitts connected for a home run, while Gaffe, Foley and Harrigan of the Cedar Hills each made a three-bagger. Jimmy Donegan of the Independents also hit for three bases.

The score:

INDEPENDENTS.

	ab.	r.	1b.	po.	a.	e.
O'Neil, lf.	4	1	1	1	0	0
Lawlor, 2b	2	0	0	0	2	1
McNerney, ss.	5	2	3	2	4	1
Miller, 3b	4	1	2	1	3	0
Donnegan, rf.	3	1	1	2	0	0
Loveday, cf.	3	1	1	1	0	0
Barry, 1b	4	1	2	10	0	1
Fowler, c.	4	1	2	7	0	0
Mulligan, p.	3	0	1	1	3	0
Totals	32	8	13	25	12	3

CEDAR HILLS.

	ab.	r.	1b.	po.	a.	e.
Gaffe, 2b	5	1	2	0	2	1
Harrigan, lf.	5	2	2	2	0	0
Pitts, 3b	5	2	2	1	3	0
W. Forslund, cf.	4	2	2	2	0	0
F. Forslund, 1b	4	0	1	10	0	1
Byrnes, rf.	4	0	1	2	1	0
J. Foley, ss.	3	2	2	0	4	1
Livigney, c.	3	1	1	12	1	0
Miller, p.	2	0	1	0	3	0
Totals	35	10	14	29	14	3

Score by Innings:

Cedar Hills	1 0 0 2 0 0 7 0 *	—10
Independents	0 3 0 1 1 0 1 2 0	— 8

Summary — Bases on balls, Miller 2, Mulligan 4; two-base hits, W. Forslund, Foley, Barry, McNerney; three-base hits, Gaffe, Foley, Harrigan, Donnegan; struck out, by Miller 10, by Mulligan 7; home run, Pitts; time of game, 2:10; umpire, Sheridan; attendance, 2,000.

JENNINGS STILL SURE

IS CONFIDENT TIGERS WILL TAKE SERIES FROM PIRATES.

Declares Detroit Will Win To-day and Tomorrow.

Mullin and Donovan Look Better Than Pittsburg Pitchers—Players Will Participate in Biggest Financial Split of Any World's Series.

Detroit, Oct. 12.—"Clarke's team was lucky to win yesterday. We are going to beat the Pirates today and tomorrow and I am confident we will take the concluding game of the series," said Hughey Jennings, leader of the scrappy Detroit Tigers today.

Jennings' men have a splendid chance to make good, too, for Mullin and Wild Bill Donovan look superior to anything Manager Clarke can offer in the pitching line and the Tiger batters are hittin gthe ball just as hard as the Pirates. Today's game will be played on a heavy field as it rained hard until late yesterday. The weather man predicts showers for today but the game will be played if there is any possible chance. The day dawned clear and cool with the sun shining brightly and a stiff chilly wind blowing.

The players engaged in the series will participate in the biggest financial split up of any world's series. The receipts of 1907 and 1908 have been passed and the totals of 1906, when the Cubs and Sox battled ftor the championship, will be no longer a record. The gross receipts in 1906 were $106,550 and so far this year $102,832 have poured into the treasury.

The 1906 totals were for six games and this mark will be broken with the receipts of today's game which is the fourth.

The players pool will easily reach the $66,000 mark. The club owners will also come in for a big rake off, as the players do not share in the receipts of any games after the fourth.

Secretary Will Locke of the Pittsburg club, announced today that he had received word from Pittsburg carrying the assurance that the largest crowd of the series will be on hand to greet the Pirates after their two-day trip.

Clarke's Pirates deserve more credit for Monday's victory than the Detroit fans are willing to give. The Pirates' leader showed that he was a shrewd and able manager by playing just exactly the kind of ball they were not expected to place on exhibition.

The Detroit papers stated that the Tigers would be at a disadvantage because of the heavy field. They argued that bunting would be dangerous because of the heavy goin, and that Jennings' men would not be able to show their usual speed on the bases, while Clarke's heavier and slower men would not be bothered.

Clarke took the bull by the horns at the very start. Byrne commenced the game with a bunt, and this started Summers' balloon. Dashing work on the bases and the bungling work of the Tigers helped some and in a twinkling the Pittsburg club had the game practically cinched.

Clarke hardly knows which way to turn for hurlers. Camnitz seems to be out of the running and he will have to depend on Adams and Willis in his next two games. Jennings said today that he expected to send Mullin in for today's game, Wild Bill Donovon in at Pittsburg Wednesday and Mullin again Thursday.

Clarke is confident his men will win the championship notwithstanding his pitching situation. He thinks that Maddox would have made a better showing in yesterday's game if the weather had been dry. It rained hard during the last three innings and Maddox partially lost control of the wet ball.

Lefty Leifield is begging for a chance to show what a real southpaw can do against the Tigers.

It was reported late yesterday that Hughey Jennings had purchased Billy Murray's stock in the Philadelphia National league club and would succeed Murray as manager of the Quakers. Murray denied that he had disposed of his holdings and Jennings stated that he did not care to discuss the matter.

HANS WAGNER,

Pittsburg shortstop who made four hits and stole four bases in game with Detroit yesterday afternoon.

BOWLING

INDUSTRIAL LEAGUE

Academy Alleys:

HOMESTEADS.

Hooker	167	169	158	494
Boland	149	143	189	481
Murphy	159	139	119	417
Scheiffele	219	201	142	562
Phillips	184	175	217	576
Totals	878	827	825	2530

GIANTS.

Minnehan	173	173	173	619
Sommers	199	224	139	562
Stanford	191	138	146	475
Dunn	140	135	162	437
C. Finnegan	211	179	179	569
Totals	914	849	799	2562

In a match between R. Rausch and H. Buchter vs. J. and C. Rausch last night the former won by the following scores:

H. Rausch	156	157	160	473
Bucher	157	195	170	522
Totals	313	352	330	995
J. Rausch	171	203	147	521
C. Rausch	124	221	122	368
Totals	295	424	269	889

The New Haven State league bowlers meet Stamford here tonight. The local team will be composed of Phillips, Scheiffele, Upson, Rompf and Johnson.

Other games are Meriden at Waterbury, Middletown at Bridgeport and Wallingford at Hartford.

Interleague Series

FOURTH DAY'S GAME.

In Detroit—Ptitsburg Nationals, 8; Detroit Americans, 6.

In Boston—The New York-Boston game was postponed on account of wet grounds.

In Chicago—The National-American game was postponed on accounts of wet grounds.

STANDING OF THE CLUBS.

WORLD'S SERIES.

	W.	L.	P.C.
Pittsburg Nationals	2	1	.667
Detroit Americans	1	2	.333

NEW YOR-BOSTON SERIES.

	W.	L.	P.C.
New York Nationals	1	1	.500
Boston Americans	1	1	.500

CHICAGO SERIES.

	W.	L.	P.C.
Chicago Nationals	2	1	.667
Chicago Americans	1	2	.333

GAMES SCHEDULED FOR TODAY.

Pittsburg in Detroit.
New York in Boston.
Chicago teams n Chicago.

FOOTBALL NOTES

Capt. Coy did more work yesterday than spectators really expected to see him do.

With Cooney at center, Lilley at guard, and Andrus at tackle, the Yale team is stronger than with any other combination in those three places.

Coaches were few in number at the field yesterday but great in knowledge. Captain Biglow of the 1907 eleven worked hard all afternoon assisting Head Coach Jones.

Smith, Brown's right guard, will be unable to play any more this season, as a result of the injury to his leg in the Amherst game. Corp will take his place.

West Point intends to put in a hard week of strenuous practice for the Yale game. Coach Nelly was dissatisfied with the showing of his men against Trinity Saturday.

There is talk of a shake-up in the Princeton lineup as a résult of the poor showing in the past two games. Cunningham may be used at quarterback. Dawson going to one of the halves.

The Carlisle Indians are sore because of the alleged rough playing of Pennsylvania state Saturday, and may refuse to play the Quakers again. The Indians will meet Syracuse in New York Saturday.

Of course it is easy to say that the Williams score against Harvard was a fluke, but for that matter the crimson's safety originated in a poor pass. Fluke football is a dangerous thing to reputations.—Boston Globe.

Bell, one of the two veteran linemen, has been declared ineligible by the Cornell faculty, owing to troubles in studies. Cornell loses a fine guard in Bell. Leventry, the big tackle, who has been ill since the start of the season, will join the squad this week.

Princeton and Dartmouth will meet again this fall, but at Princeton instead of New York. The Tiger faculty would not allow the Jersey men to play away from home, as they have other games at Annapolis and New Haven. Princeton's share of the 1908 Dartmouth game on the Polo grounds was about $8,000.

Harry Kersberg saw Yale and Springfield play and his report to the Harvard coaches is that the Blue is going to have "some team' 'this fall.

This is "Hurry Up" Yost's last year under his contract with Michigan. Keene Fitzpatrick, the trainer, may be seen in the east another year.

The Pennsylvanias expect to score four touchdowns on Brown Saturday.

The Carlisle Indians will play their Syracuse game in New York Saturday on the polo grounds, but most of the enthusiasts will go to West Point for the Yale-Army game.

Williams held Dartmouth to a 0 to 0 score last fall, and has an even chance to win with a beter team than 1908's at Hanover Saturday.

From now out the Harvard second team will use plays against the 'varsity which the coaches have seen used by the team to play on Soldiers' field.

Minot, Corbett and Smith are not an impossible first string combination for the back field.

Oberlin, in scoring a touchdown against Cornell was put across on a 80-yard run-in of a kick by Capt. Orep, who in two previous games fooled the Ithacans.

Capt. Miller of U. of P. did a graceful thing Saturday in the West Virginia game. Wiley, one of Coach Lueder's men, was taken out, but the man substituted was hurt and Wiley was allowed to return to the game, the visitors being shy on substitutes.

Fordham has two sterling ends in McCarthy and McCaffrey.

No more midweek games for any of the big eastern college elevens except at Princeton.

Capt. Reginer of Brown has two younger brothers who are promising first-year candidates for Dorchester high.

Harry McDeavitt, the former Dartmouth star, now coaching Colby, has built his attack around Ralph Good, the quarterback, who is a remarkably fast player. Good was the center of interest in the Tufts-Colby game.

Geary, the quarteback of the Fordham team, attended Holy Cross formerly, and last February he won the 40-yard das invitation at the B. A. A. games. Two eastern Massachusetts players are on the Fordham team, Thomas Scanlon of South Boston and Harry "Dad" White of Waltham.

WHEN SHOPPING.

Before going shopping, try to decide exactly what you want and what you can afford to pay for it.

But never try and carry colors in your mind's eye. Practically no one can do this successfully, and it is impossible, too, to match shades by artificial light.

PIRATES GETTING A RUNNING START, AGAIN BEAT TIGERS

DETROIT LOSES THIRD GAME OF THE SERIES, 8 TO 6.

Batting desperately against great odds, the Detroit Tigers were vanquished by the Pittsburg Pirates in the third game for the World's Championship in Detroit yesterday afternoon. The schore of the sensational struggle was 8 to 6, the Corsairs collecting half a dozen runs before the Jungleites were able to get a man across the plate. Poor pitching by "Kickapoo" Summers, Detroit's pioneer boxman, who was blown from the slab before the first inning was finished, and the failure of Sam Crawford to do anything with the willow, were the causes of the American leaguers' reverse. Pittsburg's play was anything but brilliant, the big lead the Pirates got in the first two innings, however, enabling the visitors to win their second game of the set.

The Tigers, apparently hopelessly in the rear at the end of the first inning, fought to the last ditch and might have earned a draw if Ralph Works had been able to handle the wet sphere in the ninth frame, for it was in the terminal that the Pirate procured the runs that enabled them to pull out winners. Victory surely would have been the portion of Jenning's men had Crawford been able to do any hitting. Five times the barber from Wahoo, Neb., faced Nick Maddox, and on every occasion the Pittsburg pitcher got the verdict over the batter.

Crawford's show with the willow was pitiable. He forced Bush at second in the first inning and did the same thing to Cobb five periods later. In the seventh Sam halted a Detroit rally by popping in the air to Abstein, and in the ninth, with one man on the paths, he grounded to short, his out pushing the runner up a peg. The nearest approach Crawford came to a hit was when he made a long drive in the fourth inning, which Fred Clarke pulled down.

Everything broke against the Royal Bengals. Jennings, who is no seer, could not foretell that Eddie Summers was going to prove a distinct disappointment as a baffler, nor that Crawford would let so many chances slip by to break up the game. Neither could Jennings foresee that Matty McIntyre and George Mullin, who constituted his pinch-hitting brigade, would each strike out.

It would have been a great day for Mullin to pitch, as the afternoon was dark, and Jennings undoubtedly would have sent the portly twirler in against the Pirates had it not been for a bit of superstition. While Big George was warming up, together with Summers and Willetts, he was called to the plate and a purse containing $120 in new one-dollar bills, made up by Detroit rooters in recognition of his briliant work during the season, was presented to him. Jennings though Mullin would be nervous after the gift, and so picked Summers to make the Pirate craft turn turtle. Instead, the Corsairs stood "Kickapoo" on his head and drove him to shelter in the first inning, one man being out and four athletes being over the plate when the Medicine Man withdrew by request from the contest. Before Edgar Willetts could get his balloon ball working right, the Pirates scored two runs.

Willetts handed out ciphers for five straight innings, retiring from the fray in the seventh so that Maty McIntyre could strike out for him. Works started out finely, but when rain began falling in the ninth he experienced difficulty in controlling the sphere and thé Pirates got to him for a pair of runs, sufficient to give them the decision.

The Tigers made one more hit off Maddox than the Pirates gleaned off the deliveries of Summers, Willetts and Works, but for the third time the National Leaguers had the edge on their adversaries in fielding.

Hans Wagner made a brilliant debut before a Detroit crowd and lived up to his reputation of being the greatest baseball player in the world. The Teuton Terror made four singles and stole a quartet of sacks. It is hardly necessary to say that Charley Schmidt was Detroit's backstop, Jennings, for some reason, still imagining that the coal miner is a good pegger and a better man to have behind the bat that Stanage.

Tiny Owen Bush, who only celebrated his twenty-first birthday on the afternoon the World's Series started, divided the batting honors of the conflict with Wagner. The dimnutive Tiger, like Honus, bingled safely four times and was among those present in the two rallies made by the Jungleites. Jim Delahanty did some spirited slugging in the early part of the controversy and led the attack on Maddox in the seventh inning that resulted in Detroit scoring four times. The former Senator, however, ended the game by skying to Clarke, Cobb being left on third.

Ty Cobb made the star fielding play of the game when he caught Jack Miller's low fly in the ninth innings. The Georgian had to turn a somersault to make the capture, but he came up with the ball in his hand. Other good catches were made by Clarke on Crawford in the fourth inning and by Crawford on Leach in the same session.

For the first time a world's championship game was umpired by three men. The extra official was Billy Klem, who did patrol duty in right field on account of the crowd to judge the value of hits out that way. Klem's duties were nil, as not once was he called upon to make a decision.

Though the Pirates have won two games to the Tigers' one, the Jungleites showed in the last three innings yesterday that they are far from out of the series and that if Mullin and Donovan repeat their excellent box tricks of last Friday and Saturday the world's honors may fall to the Detroits.

Score of yesterday's game:

DETROIT.

	a.b.	h.	p.o	a.	e.
D. Jones, l. f.	2	2	0	0	0
Bush, ss.	1	4	4	3	1
Cobb, r. f.	0	2	3	0	0
Crawford, c. f.	0	0	5	0	1
Delehanty, 2b	1	3	3	0	0
Moriarity, 3b	1	0	0	3	0
T. Jones, 1b	1	1	7	0	0
Schmidt, c.	0	0	3	2	1
Summers, p.	0	0	0	1	0
Willett, p.	0	0	2	3	0
*McIntyre	0	0	0	0	0
Works, p.	0	[illegible]	[illegible]	[illegible]	[illegible]
**Mullin	0	0	0	0	0
	6	12	27	13	3

PITTS BURG.

	a.b.	h.	p.o	a.	e.
Byrne, 3b	1	2	2	2	0
Leach, c. f.	3	2	1	0	0
Clarke, l. f.	1	0	5	0	0
Wagner, ss.	1	4	3	4	0
Miller, 2b	1	0	3	5	1
Abstein, 1b	1	2	8	0	1
Wilson, r. f.	0	1	0	0	0
Gibson, c.	0	0	5	1	0
Maddox, p.	0	0	0	1	0
	[illegible]	11	27	13	2

*Batted for Willett in the seventh inning.

**Batted for Works in the ninth nning.

Score by innngs:

Detroit	0 0 0 0 0 0 4 0 2	—6
Pitsburg	5 1 0 0 0 0 0 0 2	—8

Base hits, off Summers 4 in on-ethrd of an inning, off Willett 3 in six and two-thirds innngs, off Works 4 in two innings; first base on balls, off Summers 1, off Maddox 2; left on bases, Detroit 8, Pitsburg 6; struck out, by Works 3, by Maddox 2; two base hits, Delehanty 2, Cobb, Abstein, Leach; stolen bases, Wawner 4, Leach; wild pitch, Summers; hit by pitched ball, by Willett 2; time of game, 2:05; umpires, Messrs. O'Loughlin and Johnstone.

YALE BASEBALL AVE.

OFFICIAL PERCENTAGES OF UNIVERSITY BALL PLAYERS.

Van Vlect Leads Murphy in Batting by Six Points.

Star Pitcher Hits For .311, While Captain's Average is .305—Seven Members of Last Season's Nine Have Perfect Fielding Averages.

D. L. Reynolds, official scorer of the Yale baseball team, today announces the averages of the Yale men for the season as follows:

BATTING.

Name.	G.	A.B.	R.	H.	Av.
Corey	3	5	2	3	.600
Hartwell	1	3	0	1	.333
Van Vleck	20	61	11	19	.311
Murphy	30	121	16	37	.305
Philbin	26	88	14	25	.284
Sweeney	12	24	2	6	.250
Wheaton	13	46	4	11	.239
Jefferson	29	108	12	24	.222
Logan	28	88	6	18	.204
Rose	10	20	4	4	.200
Fels	24	76	11	14	.183
Badger	26	101	14	18	.178
Mallory	28	97	6	17	.175
Parsons	3	6	1	1	.166
Lippitt	4	6	1	1	.166
Cushman	14	47	3	5	.106
McIntyre	3	10	0	1	.100
Merritt	21	37	3	3	.081
McKee	1	3	0	0	.000
Daly	1	1	0	0	.000
Rend	2	3	0	0	.000
Coy	1	1	1	0	.000
Mosser	4	6	0	0	.000

EXTRA BASE HITS.

Two-baggers—Philbin 4, Murphy 2, Fels 2, Mallory, Jefferson, Sweeney and Van Vleck.

Three-baggers—Murphy 3, Jefferson 3, Mallory 2, Logan, Wheaton, Van Vleck.

Home run—Van Vleck.

SACRIFICE HITS.

Fels 9, Logan 5, Jefferson 4, Mallory 4, Badger 2, Van Vleck 2, Philbin, Merritt.

STOLEN BASES.

Logan 18, Murphy 14, Philbin 11, Van Vleck 7, Badger 6, Mallory 6, Wheaton 4, Jefferson 4, Rend 2, Corey, Hartwell, Sweeney, Cushman and Coy.

FIELDING AVERAGES.

	p.o.	a.	e.	av.
Corey	1	0	0	1.000
Rend	8	0	0	1.000
Merritt	6	29	0	1.000
Hartwell	0	5	0	1.000
Coy	0	1	0	1.000
Mosser	3	1	0	1.000
Daly	2	0	0	1.000
Philbin	182	37	7	.969
Jefferson	293	29	11	.966
Murphy	52	3	2	.964
Rose	2	20	1	.956
Van Vleck	13	55	4	.944
Sweeney	38	7	3	.937
Fels	45	54	10	.908
Logan	45	63	11	.907
Parsons	0	9	1	.900
Mallory	39	4	5	.895
Badger	43	49	12	.884
Cushman	18	24	7	.851
Wheaton	8	1	2	.818
McKee	0	0	0	.500
McIntyre	3	5	0	.000
Lippitt	0	0	0	.000

PITCHER'S RECORDS.

Merritt—21 games; 108 1-3 innings pitched; 61 hits off; 3 two baggers; 3 three baggers; 1 home run; 17 bases on balls; 96 strike out; 4 wild pitches; no balks; 19 runs scored; 13 men hit.

Van Vleck—14 games; 77 2-3 innings pitched; 62 hits off; 5 two baggers; 3 three baggers; 2 home runs; 29 bases on balls; 52 strike outs; 2 wild pitches; no balks; 30 runs scored; 4 men hit.

Rose—10 games; 63 innings pitched; 35 hits; 2 two baggers; 1 three bagger; no home runs; 17 bases on balls; 56 strike outs; 2 wild pitches; no balks; 15 runs; 6 men hit.

New Haven Sunday Leader.

VOL. XVIII, NO. 192 — NEW HAVEN, CONN., SUNDAY, OCTOBER 17 1909 — WITH COLOR SUPPLEMENT—28 PAGES—FIVE CENTS

PIRATES WIN FINAL GAME FROM TIGERS BY SCORE OF 8 TO 0

Pittsburg Nationals Now Champions of the World.

"BABE" ADAMS ALLOWS DETROIT BUT EIGHT HITS

Clarke's Young Twirler Wins His Third Game of Series—"Wild Bill" Donovan and George Mullin Pitch Poorly for American Leaguers.

PIRATES WIN FINAL.

Total figures for the world's series:

Total attendance, seven games, 145,807.

Total receipts, $188,302.50.

Pittsburg players divide $40,-154.94.

Detroit players divide $26,-769.96.

Each Pittsburg player gets $1,-825.22.

Each Detroit player gets $1,274.76.

Each club receives $51,272.67.

National Commission's share, $18,302.50.

Gross receipts, $19,677.

Detroit, Mich., Oct. 16.—Pittsburg Pirates, Champions of the World.

That is what they call Fred Clarke's plucky crew for at least one year. They won this title by defeating Jennings' game bunch of Tigers in a one-sided game this afternoon in the most spectacular world's championship series ever played. Score: Pittsburg, 8; Detroit, 0.

"Babe" Adams is the hero of the series. This youngster, who won his spurs with the Pittsburg club only this season, pitched three games for Clarke's squad and won them all. He began the clash by winning the first game played and ended it fittingly by shutting the Tigers out in the final contest.

No pitcher ever displayed better form than Adams did in today's game. He was never in trouble. He kept the Tigers' six hits so well scattered that Jennings' men were greatly discouraged, and although they fought gamely to the end they were unable to accomplish anything.

Manager Jennings set aside all precedent when he sent in "Wild Bill" Donovan to pitch the final game. Donovan is a hot weather pitcher. He thrives when the sun blazes down on

(Continued on Page Eight.)

SPAIN IN UPROAR

WILD SCENES OF RIOT, PILLAGE AND CRIME.

Queen of the Seas Tottering Into Decay.

Execution of Ferrer Was Oil on Fire That is Now Bursting Into Flames—Mobs Incessantly Demand Attention, But Defy Police Control.

Hendays, France, Oct. 16.—Through the wall of government censorship that hems in Spain, there seeps tonight news that indicates that the old time "Queen of the Seas" is in dire straits and that the throne and government are tottering. From Madrid comes news of wild scenes in the senate and an administrative climax practically beyond control. From the provinces stragglers bring in tales of rioting, pillage and courts martial.

Messages from Madrid declare that the populace is learning but slowly of the world-wide protests that followed the execution of Francisco Ferrer, the Barcelona leader, and of the wave of opposition to Spain that is sweeping Europe.

Every foreign newspaper is being confiscated by the frontier guards and the telegraphic censorship has been extended to cover messages entering Spain.

In the Senate today, under most vigorous interpellations, the foreign secretary admitted that the government was in receipt of detailed accounts of the anti-Spanish demonstrations from embassies all over the world. In making the admission, however, the secretary indignantly declared that the government will brook no intererence with its actions in this crisis, and that no change in its policy need be expected.

Amid the wild disorder that followed this declaration Senators Diaz Moreu and Dairla, with others of the opposition, shouted their condemnation of the government, and loosed a flood of invective at the cabinet, declaring that the government is the real anarchist, and demanding that the cabinet resign immediately. The senate adjourned with the members all on their feet shouting wildly.

News from the provinces is almost unobtainable directly, but stragglers from the province of Catalont, arriving

(Continued on Page Three.)

FAIRFIELD SITE FOR SANATORIUM IS DECIDED UPON

Commission Cannot Accept Meriden's Undercliff Proposition.

CONDITIONS PROVIDED MAKE IT IMPOSSIBLE

Tuberculosis Commissioners Have No Power to Impose on State Conditions That Meriden Has Tacked on to Proposed Gift to State.

A meeting of the state tuberculosis commission was held in Hartford yesterday afternoon. When interviewed, last evening, Commissioner Hall stated that the deeds have been passed for a sanatorium location site in Fairfield county. The property acquired is a farm of seventy acres on the southern end of Coram Hill in the town of Huntington and the site overlooks the Housatonc valley, also affording a view of Long Island sound on a clear day.

The farm cost $7,500 and there ore two houses on it in a well preserved condition that are reasonably worth in the neighborhood of $6,000. The location is also reasonably accessible being about a five minute walk from the trolley and it occupies a retired and quiet position.

It is expected that a city water supply can be arranged for and if not there are two or three good springs on the property. There is also facilities for gas and electric lighting. The property was purchased from Dwight E. Blakeslee and Alfred Shaw.

Of the two buildings on the location, the larger will be used as a sort of administration building for the doctors' office and a reception room, etc. The smaller house will be used for the nurses and other employes. A man is to be put to work tomorrow morning putting the two buildings in shape and considerable repair work is to be done.

Several shacks are to be erected, each one to hold twenty patients. The central portions of these shacks are to be used for bath rooms, lockers and dressing rooms. There are to be wings on the shacks in the shape of piazzas each large enough to accommodate ten beds. The piazzas will extend all around the shacks except on the north, where there will be protections from the winds coming from that direction. Thefront of each shack will be open.

It is estimated that the three county houses will accommodate a total of about three hundred patients and about ninety of these are to be accommodated at the Fairfield sanitarium. It is expected that it will soon be opened so that it can accommodate fifty patients.

A small wooden building which used to be located in the Wooster school yard in this city has been purchased from the board of education for $75 and is to be used as one of the shacks.

The location of the New Haven county sanitarium has not yet been decided upon as the commission canot accept the Meriden offer.

This offer was for the giving of nine acres of land with an understanding that the state must expend $40,000 on buildings in two years, and that the entire property must revert to the city if the state ever gave it up as a tuberculosis sanitarium.

The next meeting of the commission is to be held in this city next Saturday.

POLITICAL POT BOILING MADLY IN WEST HAVEN

ALLINGTOWN AROUSED OVER PROPOSED RESCINDING OF HYDRANT VOTE.

Rumor That Selectmen Are to Be Asked for Another Town Meeting.

So That Recent Vote May Be Changed—Efficient School Committee in Allingtown—Has Been Making Extensive Improvements Without Cost to Town—Over a Million Dollars' Worth of Taxable Property in Allingtown.

Just now things are sizzling in West Haven-Allingtown politics, and there is likely to be some fun before matters are finally adjusted. It is thought that the condition of local Allingtown matters just at present may cut a considerable figure in future elections

(Continued on Page Nine.)

PITTSBURG NATIONALS, CHAMPIONS OF THE WORLD.

The Pittsburg players as numbered in the accompanying group and their positions are as follows:
(1) Miller, second base; (2) Hyatt, utility; (3) Liefield, pitcher; (4) Phillippi, pitcher; (5) Sitton, pitcher; (6) Camnitz, pitcher; (7) Byrne, third base; (8) Frock, pitcher; (9) Clarke, left field and manager; (10) Leever, pitcher; (11) Willis, pitcher; (12) Leach, center field; (13) Adams, pitcher; (14) Maddox, pitcher; (15) Abstein, first base; (16) Schriver, catcher; (17) Gibson, catcher; (18) Wilson, right field; (19) Wagner, shortstop; (20) O'Connor, catcher.

OLEO MAKERS ARE GETTING VERY BUSY IN THIS STATE

CREAMERY BUTTER TO GO UP TO 50 CENTS A POUND.

Farmers Prefer to Sell Cow's Milk as Milk.

Demand For Signs Comes in Frequently to the State Dairy Commissioner—Food Laws Are Hunting the Farmers to Some Extent.

Hubert F. Potter, state dairy commissioner, was in New Haven yesterday looking into some alleged violations regarding the pure food laws. It is understood that there may be some interesting developments in regard to the operations of Mr. Potter's office within a few days, as to those who deal in food products.

But what is now most interesting is his statement in regard to the price of eggs and butter.

He says that pure creamery butter will probably go up to 50 CENTS A POUND WITHIN A SHORT TIME.

"The cause of this high price," said Mr. Potter, "is that the demand for fresh milk is increasing and that farmers find that they can do better selling their milk direct than by turning it into the dairies for butter making.

"We are," said Commissioner Potter, "receiving a great many applications for oleomargarine signs from the men who run restaurants, hotels, bakeries, etc. It goes to show that the high price of butter has increased the demand for the oleo product.

"The oleo men have been getting very busy in the New England states recently. Our office receives several applications every day for signs to be displayed under the law, which show that oleo is sold or used in the establishment," said Mr. Potter.

Another feature of the pure food laws that Mr. Potter referred to as being harmful to the farmers is the law regarding the sale of vinegar.

The law says that vinegar shall have four per cent of acidity and four per cent of solids.

The grocers know about this law and are afraid of buying from farmers on account of it. They prefer to buy from the large wholesalers, where they get a guarantee as to the percentage of acidity and solids.

The farmer makes a certain amount of cider each year and drinks some of it and the rest he lets get hard. But the product he has for vinegar he does not know how to guage exactly, although it is a good product. The grocer who deals in cider knows this and is afraid to buy from the farmer on account of the pure food law.

This is a state law and it is likely an effort will be made to repeal it in the next legislature.

Mr. Potter said that two new federal pure food laws have given his department considerable more work to do.

In regard to the price of commodities it was learned yesterday that fresh eggs were going up to 55 cents a dozen and western eggs will soon sell for 35 cents.

JAPANESE TO RECIEVE ROYAL WELCOME HERE

FINANCIAL AND INDUSTRIAL LEADERS OF EMPIRE ARRIVE OCTOBER 22.

Something About Men And Their Mission.

Eight of the Delegates Have Their Wives Traveling With Them and Local Chamber of Commerce Will See That the Party is Well Cared For.

A party of the leading bankers, merchants and men of affairs, several statesmen and a few newspaper editors of the leading journals of Japan will visit New Haven under the auspices of the Chamber of Commerce for a few hours next Friday morning. They are traveling through the United States as the Royal Japanese Commercial commissioners, and in a sense represent both the Japanese government and the Japanese Chambers of Commerce. They are intent on seeing what they can of the commerce of this country with the avowed purpose of increasing trade relations between Japan and this country. Already they have traveled about six weeks by special train, visiting the leading cities between Seattle and New York.

New Haven is the only city in Connecticut that they will visit. They will go from here to Providence. Unfortunately they have cut their schedule down, now that they are beginning to feel the fatigue of continuous journeying, so that New Haven will have them only in the morning and Providence in the afternoon.

(Continued on Page Seven.)

General Montgomery Dines Farmers' Club

The Farmers' club of the Union League were splendidly entertained by General Phelps Montgomery at his summer home, Mountain Glen Farm, Mt. Carmel, yesterday afternoon.

The club left the Union League to the number of about thirty, early in the afternoon, going to the general's farm in automobiles.

The handsome farm grounds were thoroughly inspected after the party's arrival, and then a sumptuous repast was enjoyed. Amusements such as baseball, etc., was enjoyed after the dinner and at an early hour last evening the return was made to this city, after a unanimous vote of thanks had been afforded General Montgomery for his royal entertainment.

COOK PREPARES DATA.

Brooklyn, N. Y., Oct. 16.—Dr. Frederick A. Cook, the Arctic explorer, made the announcement late tonight that he would cancel all his engagements so far as possible and devote his time to gathering data to forward to the University of Copenhagen and then to the other geographical societies of the world

FULL LICENSES ARE TAKEN OUT NOW AT SHORE RESORTS

PECULIAR OPERATION OF THE NEW EXCISE LAW.

East Haven Can Give But Two on the Littoraj.

Quite a Hustle to Get the Prize—New Haven Men Not So Much Alarmed, But Must Look Out for Dropping of Number on Account of Convictions at Law.

The new law regarding the issuance of licenses which provides that one shall be issued to each 500 inhabitants, and no more, has changed the whole order of things as these relate to the shore licenses.

The fact is that licensees at the shore have gotten busy this week and put in their applications.

They cannot wait under the new law, as they must take out a full year's license now.

In the old days they could take out a half year's license, a short term, but the new bill makes it almost imperative that a full year shall be taken out.

Take East Haven, for instance, there can be but two licenses granted there for the next license year. The fellow who waits is lost.

The license grant is based on the census of 1900. East Haven then had short of 1,500 population. It no doubt now has twice this population, but the estimate does not count under the new state law of one license to each 500 of population.

So that East Haven is entitled to only two licenses. One is to be at Mansfield Grove and the other at the Momauguin.

The commissioners will not think of an application for the village.

The same sort of fear, if you may call it so, applies as to the town of West Haven. The men down there, or the most of them, have been taking out half year licenses in the past. They are all taking out full year licenses this year.

They are not going to allow somebody else to step in ahead of them and pre-empt the number as allowed by law.

So far as New Haven is concerned there will be many transfers throughout the year, but no new licenses will be granted. The number as a total will remain at 450 until convictions brings down the number in the long run.

An interesting part of the applications as regards the shore is that Charles Zapp has applied for a license for Mansfield's Grove, in East Haven. It is understood that Charles Mansfield has leased the grove to Mr. Zapp.

PASSENGERS SAFE.

New Orleans, Oct. 16.—A wireless message from the steamer Comus, which set out Wednesday to rescue the passengers and crew of the steamer Antilles, wrecked on a reef off the Bahama Islands, was received tonight, announcing that the transfer was safely made and that it was expected the Antilles would be floated within a few hours. Among the Antilles' passengers is Governor Sanders of Louisiana. The Comus will take the passengers to New York.

TAFT REPLIES TO STRIKING TOAST BY PRES. DIAZ

Graceful Tributes and Reiterating of National Amity.

EPOCH MAKING BANQUET BRILLIANT AFFAIR

Famous Maximillian China Used and Heirlooms Decorated Room While Distinguished Men Dined to Cement Friendship of Nations.

El Paso, Texas, Oct. 16.—W. H. Taft, first president of the United States to leave the country, was a guest tonight at a banquet tendered to him by President Porfirio Diaz of the Republic of Mexico.

In a brilliant banquet hall, especially built for the occasion in the patio of the old custom house at Siudad Juarez, the two presidents toasted each other and the nations which they repsented while gorgeously uniformed officials and statesmen in civilian dress applauded the sentiments of friendship between the nations.

Distinguished soldiers, statesmen and diplomats were gathered for the occasion. The banquet hall was brilliantly decorated, and the famous Maximillian china, one of the heirlooms of the old Mexican kingdom, was used.

When President Diaz rose to propose his toast to President Taft, the hum of conversation through the hall ceased, and when he ceased speaking a burst of applause followed his declaration of friendship.

President Diaz proposed the following toast:

"Mr. President, Gentlemen: The visit of his Excellency, President Taft today to the Mexican territory will make an epoch in the history of Mexico. We have had in our midst very illustrious visitors, such as General U. S. Grant and the Hon. Messrs. Seward and Root, but never before have we seen in our land the chief magistrate of the great American union. This striking trait of international courtesy, which Mexico acknowledges and appreciates to its full value and significance, will henceforth stand as a precedent for other Latin-American republics to cultivate unbroken relations among themselves, with us and with every other nation of the continent.

"Actuated by the sentiments which are also those of my co-patriots, I raise my glass to the everlasting enjoyment by the country of the immortal Washington, of all the happiness and prosperity which justly belongs to the intelligent industry and eminent civicism that are the characteristics of the manly and cultured American peo-

(Continued on Page Nine).

JOHN LILLEY AND YALE MEN ARRESTED

New York, Oct. 16.—John L. Lilley, 'varsity tackle, son of the late Governor Lilley of Connecticut, was arrested today for speeding his car on Pelham Parkway, going to the Yale-West Point football game. Taken to a magistrate's court headmitted he was traveling about 25 miles an hour. The law allows 15. Bail was furnished and Lilley continued on his way. Half a dozen other Yale men were arrested with Lilley.

REPUBLICAN CLUB ANNIVERSARY PLANS

CELEBRATION TO BE CONDUCTED ON A GENEROUS SCALE.

This Unique Political Body Has Had Intensely Interesting Career and Committee is Composed of Leading Republicans in City.

Plans for the observance in a special manner of the twenty-fifth anniversary of the organization of the Young Men's Republican club began to take doefinite shape last night when the sub-committee of the general committee named by President Seymour M. Judd to take charge, met to arrange for the entertainment of the club members on the evening of November 13th which is the date of the actual formatioin of this unique political body. To those who have not given the matter of the club's career much thought the mere fact of a twenty-fifth milestone being reached has not seemed to be worth a little study. Hundreds, and it might be said thousands of the members who have been enrolled in the past dozen years or so have not been in touch with the trials of the small band of men, then very young in years and swayed more by political enthusiasm than practical experience, who in 1884 came together to form a "Young Republican

(Continued on Page Three.)

WEST POINT LOSES GREAT GAME TO YALE BY SCORE OF 17-0

Bulldog Fails to Score in First Half of Contest.

SPECTACULAR OPEN FIELD WORK OF PHILBIN, FEATURE

Johnson Does Unusually Well at Punting—Coy Plays Fullback Part of Time—Yale Displays Championship Possibilities.

West Point, N. Y., Oct. 16.—The Yale bull dog and the Army mule chewed and kicked each other on West Point plains this afternoon in their annual football tussle, with neither having the advantage in the first half.

The Yale coaches gave the bull dog some raw meat in the intermission, and when he again trotted onto the field he snarled the mule from shoulder to withers and piled up three touchdowns, closing the day handsomely with a score of 17 to 0.

It was a decisive triumph for modern football, a style that Yale only adopted after she saw that the old-fashioned game of line boring and attempts at end running were of no avail. Then, by means of some cleverly executed forward passes, in which Captain Coy, Quarterback Howe and End Vaugh played the principal part, Yale scored two touchdowns, the other coming through the spectacular open field work of Philbin, who with Captain Pullen of the Army carried off the individual honors of the day.

Yale gave every evidence of having a team of championship possibilities, though at times her defense was woefully loose, allowing Hyatt, Dean and Browne to make big gains. In the second half, however, the defense stuck together beautifully and West Point was snagged on almost every play.

West Point tried the forward pass repeatedly, her first effort, a pass from Hyatt to Byrne, being the prettiest play of the day. The combination of Howe and Vaughn, who were freshman stars at Yale last year, was the most effective in Yale's repertory, the big rangy end seeming to know instinctively just where to place himself for the quarter's passes.

A prominent feature of the game was the penalization of West Point three times for delaying the game, once by changing signals, again by Hyatt's fail-

(Continued on Page Eight.)

BRIDGEPORT FORGE CO. PLANT GUTTED

LOSS $100,000 IN FIRE LATE LAST NIGHT.

Two Firemen Dying, Hurt by Falling Walls.

Bridgeport, Oct. 16.—A sudden and disastrous fire almost completely destroyed the big plant of the Bridgeport Fore Co. late tonight, and the total damage is estimated at fully $50,000, a part of which is covered by insurance.

Two firemen, John J. King and Ste-

(Continued on Page Three).

TROLLIES CRASH AT CHESTNUT RIDGE

The New Haven-Derby express on the Connecticut company's line, shortly after 7 o'clock last night crashed into the rear end of a traction car from New Haven bound for Waterbury via Derby, injuring two persons who were standing on the rear platform of the Waterbury car. The Waterbury car was standing on the tracks at Chestnut Ridge, changing crews with a car from Derby, bound for New Haven, when the accident happened. It is stated that the car from New Haven was running at a high speed when the crash occurred.

An effort was made to learn the cause of the accident at the division office in Derby tonight but there it was stated that the blame had not yet been placed.

WEATHER REPORT

Washington, Oct. 16.—Forecast for Sunday and Monday:

New England—Generally fair and continued cool Sunday and Monday; brisk westerly winds.

Eastern New York—Fair and continued cool Sunday and probably Monday; moderate westerly winds, becoming variable.

APPROXIMATELY TWELVE MILLION DOLLARS ARE ALREADY INVESTED IN THE GROUNDS AND BUILDINGS OF THE PROFESSIONAL BASEBALL LEAGUES, AND THE GAME'S POPULARITY IS STILL GROWING.

SHIBE PARK, THE HOME OF THE AMERICAN LEAGUE TEAM IN PHILADELPHIA.
Externally one would hardly think of this inclosure as the home of a baseball club. The structures are absolutely fireproof and will accommodate 23,000 persons. It represents an investment of $750,000.

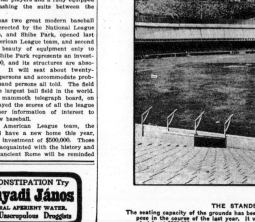

NEW AMERICAN LEAGUE BASEBALL PARK AT CLEVELAND.
It is fireproof and seats approximately 20,000 persons. There are facilities for drying the grounds rapidly on rainy days by means of an elaborate drainage system.

"FANS" STIR IN SLUMBER.

Will Emerge from Hibernation at Umpires' Shout, "Play Ball."

In eight great cities of the United States, including New York, on next Thursday afternoon, league umpires will stand in their places and shout: "Play ball!" With that shout the professional baseball season of 1910 will be formally opened. Probably never before was there so much interest in its opening. Every year sees a greater attendance at the games and greater profits from presentation of the efforts of skilful players. Last year, for instance, the attendance at the games of the two major leagues was 7,978,108, while that at the games of the minor leagues has been put roughly at more than 250,000,000. This meant receipts estimated at $5,983,581 by the sixteen teams of the two big leagues and of $8,750,000 by teams of the minor leagues, or a total of $14,733,581 for organized baseball in one year. The games were played in 267 cities.

If any one is looking for additional facts to support the claim of baseball to being the national game, he may find one in the statement that the number of paid admissions to see the games of the two major leagues from 1901 to 1909, inclusive, was 50,134,235, or well over half the estimated population of the United States. So strong is the hold of the game on the American public that it has become a great business in which men strive for franchises and give bonuses of thousands of dollars for star players. It is so profitable an enterprise that men are willing to spend hundreds of thousands of dollars for the provision of comfortable and safe accommodations for the entertainment of the great armies of spectators who daily, in the season, throng through the gates of their fields. And a man's ability to coach runners, steal bases and hit a ball with a stick has become worth sums of money that, looked at from a financial point of view, put baseball playing in a class ahead of the professions of the ministry and of teaching. Few legislators receive the salaries paid the average player on a major league team.

It is only within recent years that the game has become so characteristically American as to have a real financial value; yet since the possibility of substantial financial returns has become apparent the game has grown like an infant industry. It has taken on "features" like a completely appointed modern hotel, and some of these features, incidentally, are kept as secret as the combination on the hotel safe. For one thing, the matter of a player's salary is kept a state secret, for if the well paid man tells his salary it may mean that another will find fault because his is not so large. Again, the small salaried man wants to have himself considered as big a person as his superior, and so if he talks at all it is to put the figure in the realm of "stage money." The managers don't tell, because it is poor business policy to do so, and so if one desires to get anywhere near the "almost" figures he must do some careful calculating with what figures he can obtain.

The fields or parks in the different cities where the major league games are played have been valued at $3,000,000 for each of the leagues, or $6,000,000 for the two. This is probably an underestimate, for the ground value of the home of the Yankees, at 168th street and Broadway, alone has recently been placed at $1,700,000. The valuation of the Polo Grounds, the home of the Giants, is probably in excess of $525,000. It is said that the owners of this famous ground have received more than $400,000 in rentals since 1890.

THE NEW HOME OF THE CHICAGO AMERICAN LEAGUE TEAM.
This baseball field, with its structure modelled after the Roman Coliseum, is fireproof, accommodates 32,000 spectators with seats and represents an expenditure of $500,000.

Shibe Park, the home of the Philadelphia American League team, represents an investment of $750,000 to be carried by the profits of baseball, while Forbes Field, in Pittsburg, the home of the Pirates, is valued at $900,000. In addition, the value of the grounds used by the minor leagues has been placed at $6,000,000. This makes a total investment to be carried in the name of professional baseball of approximately $12,000,000.

The profitable nature of the game in the last two or three years has led to great expenditures for improved ball parks. Advantage has been taken of this necessity for enlargement of the space for spectators in a number of cities to create new parks with everything of more expensive construction. The buildings in new parks opened last year and to be opened this year are of fireproof construction and provided with clubrooms, with baths for the players and elevators for the ease of the spectators. Parlors with maids have been included for the benefit of the women patrons of the soprt. Systems of drainage have been laid in the grounds, so that a shower need not make them "unplayable."

Forbes Field, in Pittsburg, is an illustration of the length to which baseball investment will go. The inclosure, which is so roomy and free from flaws that there are no ground rules, has been styled the million-dollar baseball park. The ground is valued at $500,000 and the fireproof stands, of concrete and steel construction, are said to have cost $400,000 in addition, making a total cost, as mentioned above, of $900,000. Even the bleachers are concrete, with metal seat supports. The field will accommodate more than thirty thousand persons seated, and eventually will have provision for fifty thousand spectators. There are private rooms with baths for star players and a fully equipped laundry for washing the suits between the games.

Philadelphia has two great modern baseball parks, the one erected by the National League three years ago, and Shibe Park, opened last year by the American League team, and second in luxury and beauty of equipment only to Forbes Field. Shibe Park represents an investment of $750,000, and its structures are absolutely fireproof. It will seat about twenty-three thousand persons and accommodate probably forty thousand persons all told. The field is said to be the largest ball field in the world. A feature is a mammoth telegraph board, on which are displayed the scores of all the league games and other information of interest to those who follow baseball.

The Chicago American League team, the White Sox, will have a new home this year, representing an investment of $500,000. Those "fans" who are acquainted with the history and architecture of ancient Rome will be reminded of the city sitting on the seven hills when they approach the entrance to the arena upon which the sport of a modern republic is presented to the gaze of the populace. The façade is patterned after the Roman Coliseum. The seating capacity is thirty-two thousand persons. There are elevators for their use.

The Chicago National League team has a remodelled home, costing $600,000 and built of granite, steel and concrete. The St. Louis American League team also has new quarters of concrete and iron, opened a year ago.

What has been described as one of the "most complete" baseball structures in the world is to be opened this year as the home of the Cleveland American League team. It will seat about twenty thousand persons and accommodate ten thousand more on a pinch. It also is of fireproof construction and equipped with all the conveniences of a modern theatre, including a ladies' parlor with negro maids in attendance.

The manager of the Giants does not intend to be obliged to turn away 150,000 "fans," as he is said to have been obliged to do two years ago because of lack of accommodations. The stands have been increased in size and will now seat 37,000 persons. There will be standing space for 3,000 more. Overhanging bay window boxes to the number of 166 have been placed in the upper part of the grandstand, and the slope of the ground behind the infield has been altered by the deposit of 7,000 cartloads of earth. The improvements cost approximately $150,000.

Next year the Washington and Detroit American League teams will probably have remodelled homes. Both have purchased property for this purpose. Other clubs also are thinking of making improvements in their quarters.

While the dividends of the Giants are said to be 30 per cent a year, and those of some of the other clubs approximate this rate, the cost of baseball is tremendous. The salary list of the players in the major and minor leagues has been affirmed recently by an authority to be $5,000,000 a year. By a little calculation a fair estimate of the salary list of the major leagues has been made. The sixteen teams in these leagues are limited to twenty-five men each. The salaries range from $1,500 to $6,000. The average salary is $3,000. Ergo, twenty-five players times sixteen clubs times $3,000, if calculated with mathematical precision, equals $1,200,000 in salaries alone for the two major leagues. This sum, doubtless, is exceeded, for there are some officials and players who receive salaries that seem regal for such a democratic game.

Byron Bancroft Johnson, styled "Ban" Johnson for short, was recently re-elected president, secretary and treasurer of the National American League with a salary of $25,000 a year to continue for twenty years. In view of the fact that he holds three offices, at a salary half of that which ex-President Roosevelt received for running the country, he might almost be styled a baseball king. Mathewson, the crack pitcher of the New York Giants, has a contract for $10,000 a year, but it is believed that he receives nearer $15,000. John P. Wagner, more familiarly known as Hans or Honus, is supposed to receive $10,000 for his six months' work as a shortstop on the Pittsburg National League team, while Lajoie, the second baseman on the Cleveland American League team, is a sufficiently able player to command for his six months' services as much as a United States Senator receives from the United States Treasury for his part in deciding the destines of the great Republic.

The salaries of the 6,960 players in the minor leagues amounted last season to $3,800,-

Continued on eighth page.

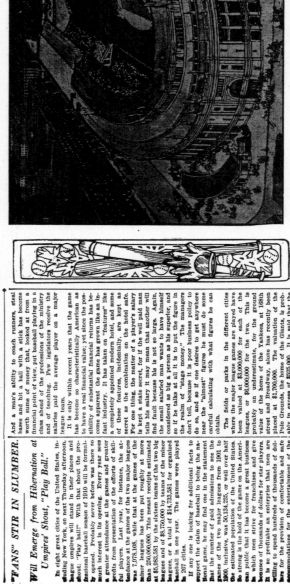

THE MOST RICHLY EQUIPPED BASEBALL FIELD IN AMERICA.
Forbes Field, Pittsburg, the home of the National League team of that city. The grounds cost $500,000 and the grading and structures $400,000. Its fireproof stands will accommodate 30,000 persons. Ultimately it will have a seating capacity of 50,000.
(Copyright, 1909, by the Pittsburg Athletic Company.)

THE STANDS AT THE POLO GROUNDS, HOME OF THE NEW YORK GIANTS.
The seating capacity of the grounds has been increased to 32,000 by the addition of wings to the stand, $150,000 having been spent for this purpose in the course of the last year. It will now be possible for 40,000 to get inside the grounds. The field and structures have a valuation of at least $525,000.

SCENES AT THE OPENING OF THE AMERICAN LEAGUE BASE BALL SEASON IN THIS CITY.

PANORAMA OF THE BALL GROUNDS, MADE AFTER THE GAME WAS UNDER WAY.

WORLD OF SPORTS

(Continued from Eighteenth Page.)

sacks by dropping a short fly behind Barry. With only one out and the bases full, Lelivelt struck out, and Elberfeld skied to Oldring.

The eighth was the only inning of the game in which the Nationals expired without a struggle.

Following is the official score:

WASHINGTON.	A.B.	R.	H.	O.	A.	E.
Milan, cf	3	1	2	1	0	0
Schaefer, 2b	4	1	3	2	3	0
Lelivelt, lf	3	0	2	2	0	0
Elberfeld, 3b	4	0	1	1	2	0
Gessler, rf	4	0	0	0	0	0
Unglaub, 1b	4	0	3	10	0	0
McBride, ss	4	0	0	2	3	1
Street, c	3	0	1	9	0	0
Johnson, p	3	1	1	0	2	0
Totals	32	3	13	27	10	1

PHILADELPHIA.	A.B.	R.	H.	O.	A.	E.
Hartsel, lf	3	0	0	0	0	0
Oldring, cf	4	0	0	1	0	0
Collins, 2b	4	0	0	2	6	0
Baker, 3b	3	0	1	3	3	0
Davis, 1b	4	0	0	8	0	0
Murphy, rf	3	0	0	1	1	0
Barry, ss	3	0	0	3	1	0
Thomas, c	2	0	0	6	2	0
Plank, p	3	0	0	0	3	0
Totals	29	0	1	24	16	0

Washington	1	0	0	0	2	0	0	0	x	—3
Philadelphia	0	0	0	0	0	0	0	0	0	—0

Two-base hits—Schaefer (2), Lelivelt (2), Milan, Johnson, Baker. Sacrifice hit—Lelivelt. Stolen bases—Unglaub, Plank. Double plays—Murphy and Baker; Barry, Collins and Davis. Left on bases—Washington, 7; Philadelphia, 5. Bases on balls—Off Johnson, 3. First base on errors—Philadelphia, 1. Hit by pitcher—Plank, 1. Struck out—By Johnson, 9; by Plank, 6. Wild pitch—Johnson, 1. Umpires—Evans and Egan. Time of game—1 hour and 55 minutes. utes.

COMMENT ON THE GAME.

Walter Johnson was a proud boy last night, although he tried in his usual modest way to conceal his joy. He was proud of the fact that he had won, but that he had the honor of pitching before the President of the United States added great satisfaction to him, especially as he acquitted himself so well. When the President tossed out the first ball, the first in the history of base ball in this country, Umpire Bill Evans turned it over to Johnson. Walter started for the box, but Evans called him back and exchanged balls, the one the President had thrown being tossed over to Manager McAleer to keep for the young pitcher as a souvenir of the occasion. Today the ball was taken to the White House by one of Johnson's friends and the President wrote his name thereon.

At the Dewey last night Water Johnson said:

"I am pretty short of cash just now, as the club doesn't start paying salaries until the first of the month, but one hundred dollars wouldn't buy that ball from me."

Johnson was asked about his condition during the game and said:

"I never felt better in my life, nor stronger at the finish. When I went into the box I made up my mind to win that game or throw my arm off trying. I recognized the honor the President was doing the Washington club and base ball in general in coming out to the game, and I knew I could never return to California if I didn't win.

"I am glad the first game is out of the way, as everybody felt a bit nervous. It was a nice victory, and you can take it from me, the Nationals will win many more just like it."

Just before the game started President Taft expressed a wish to be introduced to Manager McAleer of the Nationals, and Connie Mack of the Athletics. Walking arm in arm the rival managers were escorted to the box and paid their respects to the chief executive, after being introduced by President Noyes of the Washington club.

"It would not be courteous of me in the presence of Mr. Mack to wish that Washington would win," said Mr. Taft to McAleer, "but I am out here as a fan and will applaud all the good plays."

He did, too.

Many of the spectators were worked up

THE PRESIDENT THROWING OUT THE BALL THAT OPENED THE 1910 SEASON.

(Copyright by Clinedinst.)

over the fact that but one hit was made off Johnson, and that could have been prevented but for the fact that Right Fielder Gessler fell over one of the onlookers in trying to catch the ball. Baker hit the ball on the nose and Gessler was within about six inches of grasping the sphere, when down he went in a heap. The man he fell over was as much perturbed as the "fans," but the poor fellow is a cripple and simply couldn't get out of the way. He made an effort to roll away, but had only moved a foot or two when "Doc" struck him.

Outside of McBride's pesky little fumble the game was played in the most artistic fashion, several stops and throws being of the hair-raising order. Walter Johnson is entitled to the most praise on account of his great pitching, but Eddie Collins was there with the fielding stunts that made the spectators cheer time after time. In the second inning Street drove a wicked grounder into right. Collins had started to cover second, but came back and while fully extended gathered in the ball and tossed "Gabby" out at first. It was a clear case of robbery. In the third Collins made another pretty stop on Elberfeld. In the sixth Gessler drove a hot one at Plank and it rolled off toward the right. Collins came over on the run and swished the ball to Davis, using his hands as a broom, and beat Gessler by an eyelash.

Milan and Schaefer had a mix-up over their private signals and a run was probably thrown away. "Zeb" had started with a double and was on second when "Dutch" inadvertently signaled him to go to third on the next pitched ball. At first Milan thought the play was wrong, but he finally concluded Schaefer saw an opening and wanted to hit and run. He started for third and was an easy out, Schaefer missing the ball. The players agreed that Milan was right, and said it was a good thing it came up without disastrous results, as it will make everybody more careful in the matter of signs.

Danny Murphy remarked to McBride as he passed him at the end of the eighth inning, "I fooled them that time. I got a piece of the ball anyway." Murphy had popped to McBride and on two former occasions had struck out. "I think we are lucky to touch that ball let alone get it safe," concluded Murphy.

The hitting of the Nationals was very pleasing to the well wishers of the club, especially as it was done against a "hoodoo" twirler like Eddie Plank. Thirteen hits for a total of nineteen bases seldom came Washington's way last season and here's hoping it will be repeated time and time again by the Nationals this year.

The big bunch of American beauty roses sent out to Manager McAleer came from the "fans" around the Dewey Hotel. The satchel for Lelivelt, the flowers for Milan and the bats given Unglaub and Street came from personal friends.

Manager McAleer was proud of his boys, as he calls them, and after the game made a pleasant speech to the crowd in the clubhouse. Mac is some talker when in his class, although big banquets are too much for him. He thanked everybody for doing their best and said he expected the team to play like they had throughout the season. "Don't mind the base hits or errors. I know your worth and ability. Get the games. You all look good to me, and I don't think there is any team in the country has anything on us."

Mac tried loafing around the Dewey, but so many "fans" flocked in that he retreated to the theater for the evening.

It will be either Walker or Reisling this afternoon, the selection depending upon the one who warms up and looks the best to McAleer just previous to the game.

Manager Mack said he would probably work "Big Chief" Bender, so there is trouble ahead for the local boys, as the Indian is very good this spring.

If both twirlers are right it should be a battle worth going miles to see.

The batting of Schaefer and Unglaub was of the juicy sort, the former getting two doubles and a single, while the latter had three singles. The Dutchman's first double would have been a home run in a regular game, as it carried inside the clubhouse. Unglaub was particularly pleased over his three hits, as his father had come over from Baltimore to see the Nationals perform.

Manager Connie Mack was bitterly disappointed. He was interviewed at his hotel last night and said:

"I wanted this game mighty bad. It always encourages a team to win the opener. Eddie Plank seemed to be in such

CONNIE MACK,
Manager of the Athletics.

grand shape that I felt sure he could stop the Washington hitters. I did not figure on Walter Johnson. He surprised me by his work. The Athletics simply could not connect, and you know a team looks awfully bad when it isn't hitting. I believe that Johnson is in better form than he ever was in his life before."

Police Capt. Doyle handled the crowd in a masterful manner and was frequently cheered by it for keeping the rash spectators within bounds. Left to themselves, many would have roosted right in the box with the pitchers.

Charles Bennett, the secretary of the Senate, had a narrow escape from serious injury in the fourth inning, when a line foul struck him on the side of the head. The ball came on a line from Baker's bat and was one of Johnson's speediest shoots. It went directly at Vice President Sherman, but he ducked in time to save himself, and Bennett, being back of him, got the smash.

The Philadelphia team has arranged a box party for the Gayety this evening and many of the Nationals will be with it.

In the opinion of those who are supposed to know, never has a major league base ball championship season begun with so great a wave of excitement as spread throughout the great cities of the continent yesterday. Estimates gathered from various sources show that even at a minimum 200,000 persons saw the eight games which started the sixteen teams in the American and National leagues on their rapid march toward the pennant.

Among Those at the Game.

President Taft, who arrived at the park about half an hour before the game started, occupied a box on the right side of the grandstand, and a short distance from the Nationals' bench. The box had previously been draped in American flags, while a comfortable armchair was also put at the President's disposal. Accompanying the President were Mrs. Taft, Capt. Archibald Butt, military aid to the President; Mrs. Eckstein of Cincinnati and Brig. Gen. Clarence Edwards.

Vice President Sherman occupied a box on the left side of the grandstand. Accompanying him were Charles G. Bennett, secretary of the United States Senate; Representative Joseph Gaines of West Virginia, Representative Nicholas Longworth of Ohio Clarence Moore, George Howard, Larz Anderson, Spoff Pearsall, Assistant Secretary of State Chandler Hale, Viscount de Sibour and Commander Davis.

Among the members of the Metropolitan Club in boxes were Oden Horstmann, Capt. Sowerby of the British embassy, Montgomery Blair, W. B. Hibbs, John M. Biddle, Samuel G. Blythe, Philip McMillan and Col. Charles McCauley.

In the box adjoining the President's were Col. Robert N. Harper, Robert Dove, A. G. Plant, Thomas P. Morgan jr., John Summerville, Evans Browne, J. Miller Kenyon, E. F. Connoly, Alexander Britton, Harry Reid and Lloyd Smoot.

Mr. and Mrs. Harry Wardman occupied a box near the center of the grandstand. They had as their guests Mr. and Mrs. Hilton and Miss Glasscock.

Senator Simon Guggenheim of Colorado arrived at the grounds a little late and occupied a seat in the grandstand.

Misses L. M. and C. P. Finlet had as their guests Miss Alice Whiting and Messrs. H. Hickey and J. C. Crawford.

Representative Cooper of Washington occupied a seat in the grandstand with a party of friends, while Representative Fairchilds of New York and friends were also seated in the stand.

Others who witnessed the defeat of the Athletics were Representative Loudenslager of New Jersey, H. C. Pearson, Capt. Harry Coope, C. J. Huey, Anthony W. Smith, Ralph Johnston, Charles A. Jaquette, E. J. Stellwagen, Gen. M. E. Urell, D. C. N. G., retired; Dr. and Mrs. L. H. Guthry, Dr. M. Dahre, Mr. and Mrs. M. J. Colbert, S. W. Woodward, John B. Sieman, jr.; Misses Katherine, Helen and Margaret Woodward, Gen. George H. Harries, Robert Wilkins, Sidney Bieber, T. C. Thompson, Miss Espey Leigh, Matthew W. Trimble, jr.; Commander Cleland Davis, Huntington Mills, Col. W. D. Denny, Clarence F. Norment, Col. George C. Rankin, Frank Walker, David Moore, F. S. Anderson, Wade Powers, L. N. Stevenson, Al Muhlheisen, T. F. Snyder Mr. and Mrs. H. C.

ARRIVAL OF THE PRESIDENT AND PARTY.

From left to right—Mrs. Taft, Thomas C. Noyes, president of the Washington club; Archibald Butt, the President and Mrs. Eckstein of Cincinnati.

(Copyright by Clinedinst.)

Wilson, Senor de la Barra, Mexican ambassador to the United States; Romolo Algere, second secretary of the Mexican embassy; M. Ricoy, first secretary of the Mexican embassy; Mr. and Mrs. de Peretti de la Rocca, Judge Ashley M. Gould, W. F. Hitt, Capt. Fortesque, U. S. A.; William Corcoran Eustis and Miss Katherine Elkins.

YANKEES AND REDS TIE.

Darkness Ends Fourteen-Inning Game, Score 4 to 4.

NEW YORK, April 15.—The Highlanders and Red Sox opened here yesterday to a crowd of 22,000, the biggest opening attendance at American League Park. There was no room for more. The game went fourteen innings and ended in a tie. It was full of fast and exciting plays. Big Jim Vaughn pitched superbly for the locals, and with good support would have won. Cicotte was knocked out in the eighth, but Wood, who succeeded him, was very effective. The score:

Boston.	R.	H.	O.	A.	E.	N. Y.	R.	H.	O.	A.	E.
M'C'n'll,2b	0	0	2	2	0	H'mphill,cf	1	3	0	0	0
Lord,3b	2	3	4	3	0	Wolter,rf	1	1	3	1	0
Speaker,cf	0	2	4	0	1	Chase,1b	1	2	21	1	0
Stahl,1b	0	0	17	1	0	Engle,lf	0	0	0	0	0
Wagner,ss	0	2	3	5	0	Gardner,2b	0	1	5	2	0
Neiles,rf	0	0	2	0	0	Foster,ss	0	1	3	9	2
Hooper,lf	0	1	1	0	0	Austin,3b	0	1	2	3	1
Carrigan,c	0	1	8	1	0	Sweeney,c	1	1	8	4	1
Cicotte,p	2	1	0	7	0	Vaughn,p	0	0	0	7	0
Wood,p	0	0	1	0	0						
Totals	4	10	42	19	1	Totals	4	10	42	27	4

Boston	1	0	2	0	1	0	0	0	0	0	0	0	0	0—4
New York	0	0	1	0	0	1	0	2	0	0	0	0	0	0—4

Left on bases—Boston, 6; New York, 6. Bases on balls—Off Cicotte, 1; off Vaughn, 2. Struck out—By Cicotte, 1; by Wood, 6; by Vaughn, 7. Three-base hit—Lord. Two-base hits—Speaker, Hemphill, Chase, Sweeney. Sacrifice hits—McConnell, Wolter, Austin. Sacrifice fly—Chase. Stolen bases—Hooper, Wolter. Double play—Foster to Gardner to Chase. Passed balls—Carrigan, Sweeney. Umpires—Messrs. Connolly and Dineen. Time of game—2 hours and 45 minutes.

CLEVELAND WINS.

Mullin and Joss Both Hit Hard. Score, 9 to 7.

DETROIT, April 15.—Neither Joss nor Mullin was in condition yesterday. Mullin was fine at the start and for four innings looked as though he would pitch a shutout, then he became wild and easy. Joss reversed this form. From the beginning the game was featureless.

Perfect weather brought out a crowd of over 14,000 people to see the opening of the season. Mayor Breitmeyer pitched the first ball, it being caught by Charlie Bennett, famous in base ball circles years ago. Score:

Detroit.	R.	H.	O.	A.	E.	Clevel'd.	R.	H.	O.	A.	E.
M'Int're,lf	0	0	3	0	0	Kruger,lf	0	2	1	1	0
Bush,ss	2	2	1	4	0	Bradley,3b	0	1	1	1	0
Cobb,rf	3	2	1	0	0	Turner,2b	2	2	2	3	0
Crawf'd,cf	1	4	1	1	0	Lajoie,1b	1	1	12	2	1
D'l'h'ty,2b	0	0	1	0	0	Lord,rf	1	2	1	0	0
Mor'ity,3b	0	1	3	4	0	Clark,c	2	1	6	1	0
Jones,1b	1	1	12	2	0	B'm'b'm,cf	2	1	3	0	0
Stanage,c	0	0	6	2	0	Ball,ss	0	1	2	0	1
Mullin,p	0	0	2	5	1	Joss,p	1	2	2	5	0
Totals	7	10	30	18	1	Totals	9	13	30	13	2

Detroit	2	0	1	1	0	0	0	0	1	2—7
Cleveland	0	0	0	0	2	2	1	0	0	4—9

Two-base hits—Cobb (2), Crawford, Moriarity, Lajoie, Kruger, Joss, Turner, Clark. Sacrifice hits—Bradley, Turner, Jones. Stolen bases—Cobb, Lajoie. Bases on balls—Off Joss, 1; off Mullin, 2. Hit by pitcher—By Mullin, 1; by Joss, 1. Left on bases—Cleveland, 6; Detroit, 4. Struck out—By Joss, 5; by Mullin, 5. Wild pitches—Mullin, 2. Umpires—Messrs. Sheridan and Kerin. Time of game—2 hours and 22 minutes.

SMITH A PUZZLE.

Chicago White Sox Blank St. Louis Browns, 3 to 0.

CHICAGO, April 15.—The White Sox opened the season here yesterday afternoon with a victory over the St. Louis Browns by the score of 3 to 0. The White Sox played in excellent form and the Browns were also speedy. Smith, pitching for the Sox, allowed but one hit.

The opening game drew a crowd close to 20,000, which is one of the largest that ever attended an opening game in Chicago. Score:

Chicago.	R.	H.	O.	A.	E.	St. Louis.	R.	H.	O.	A.	E.
Hahn,rf	1	0	3	0	0	Stone,lf	0	0	0	0	0
Zeider,2b	0	1	0	3	0	W'lace,3b	0	0	0	3	0
Parent,cf	0	0	4	0	0	H'fman,cf	0	0	0	0	0
D'gh'ty,lf	2	1	0	0	0	Griggs,2b	0	0	3	4	0
Gandil,1b	0	1	10	3	0	Hartz'l,ss	0	0	2	3	0
Purtell,3b	0	1	0	3	0	Abstein,1b	0	0	14	0	1
B'kburn,ss	0	0	3	2	0	Dem'tt,rf	0	1	3	0	0
Payne,c	0	1	5	1	0	Stephens,c	0	0	2	2	0
Smith,p	0	0	2	2	0	Graham,p	0	0	0	1	1
						Lake,p	0	0	0	0	0
						*Criss	0	0	0	0	0
Totals	3	5	27	14	0	Totals	0	1	24	13	2

*Batted for Lake in the ninth inning.

St. Louis	0	0	0	0	0	0	0	0	0	0—0
Chicago	0	0	0	0	1	1	0	1	x	—3

Two-base hit—Dougherty. Sacrifice hits—Spencer, Parent. Struck out—By Smith, 5; by Graham, 1; by Lake, 1. Bases on balls—Off Smith, 2; off Graham, 3; off Lake, 1. Left on bases—Chicago, 7; St. Louis, 1. Hit by pitcher—By Graham, 1. Umpires—Messrs. O'Loughlin and Perrin. Time of game—1 hour and 40 minutes.

JIM BARRY KNOCKED OUT BY LANGFORD

Big Negro Drops His Opponent in Sixteenth Round at Los Angeles.

LOS ANGELES, April 15.—For the ninth time in their ring careers Sam Langford and Jim Barry faced each other yesterday afternoon in what was scheduled to be a twenty-five-round fight. It lasted but sixteen rounds, and then Langford, grown tired of the prolonged affair, landed a right swing on the jaw that put Barry away so hard that his seconds had to carry him to his corner and work over him for some time to revive him.

In the second round Barry sent a stiff right to the mouth that brought blood, but the bell interrupted further hostilities. Toward the end of the third round Langford pretended to be groggy and reeled toward the ropes, but Barry, who had been very cautious throughout the session, refused to be inveigled even into leading, and the gong sounded with neither making an attempt to fight. At the end of the fifth round Barry landed lefts and rights that made Langford's mouth bleed freely.

The tenth round marked the beginning of the end for Barry. The negro landed on his body and jaw with both lefts and rights and Barry tried to hang on. A straight right on the jaw sent the white man down for the count of eight, and when he got up Langford went for him and landed three hard rights on the jaw, forcing Barry to take the count of seven.

In the middle of the eleventh round Barry electrified the spectators by knocking Langford through the ropes and on top of the spectators with a hard right swing, but the negro clambered back unhurt just as the round ended. The thirteenth round was a bloody one, with Barry's nose and mouth contributing their full portions.

The fifteenth round saw Langford pepper Barry's face so that when the sixteenth round began the white man's left eye was closed and he could do little but hold on. As they broke from one of their many wrestling fits Langford caught Barry flush on the jaw with a right swing and Barry went out.

CLOSE GAME EXPECTED.

Georgetown and Virginia Teams to Meet in Charlottesville.

With both schools represented by nines far weaker than any of past years, the annual base ball series between Georgetown and Virginia will open at Charlottesville tomorrow afternoon. The second game will be played on Georgetown Field May 2. Last season the battles resulted in Virginia winning the first and Georgetown the second, each victory going to the team playing on the home grounds.

Because of this, and also the fact that both aggregations have so far shown that they stand about equal, from comparison of scores, tomorrow's contest promises to be a close one and hard fought. Virginia has won very few games this season, although lately the team has begun to display signs of strength. Especially is this so in the box, where Culberson, Brown and Witmer have been holding forth. Although it has not been definitely announced, it is more than likely that Brown will be used against Georgetown. He has played at Andover for two years, and at present seems to be one of the best of the young twirlers among the southern colleges.

Roan will be on the receiving end for the Southerners, with Lile, Hitch and Douglas covering first, second and third, respectively. Fitchett will hold down the

(Continued on Twentieth Page.)

CLEVELAND PLAIN DEALER.

SIXTY-NINTH YEAR. SIXTEEN PAGES. CLEVELAND, FRIDAY MORNING, APRIL 22, 1910. PRICE—One Cent in Greater Cleveland. Two Cents Outside Greater Cleveland. NO. 112.

MARK TWAIN DIES VICTIM OF SORROW

Nation's Greatest Humorist, Grieving for Departed Ones, Gives Up Fight.

Last Words Written to Daughter Are Request for His Glasses.

END COMES PEACEFULLY

Death Follows Lapse Into Unconciousness While Small Group Surrounds Bed—Recent Loss of Daughter and Literary Friends Prove Too Much for Man Who Made World Laugh—Argues With Nurses of Futility in Attempting to Prolong Life Which Had Been Darkened

MARK TWAIN'S CAREER.

Born—In Florida, Mo., Nov. 30, 1835. Full name, Samuel Langhorne Clemens.

Died—Redding, Ct., April 21, 1910. Age, seventy-four years, five months.

Educated in common schools, became printer's apprentice, then cub to a Mississippi river pilot, later a full fledged pilot.

In the '60s he was a silver miner in Nevada, a gold miner in California, a reporter in San Francisco, and from this entry into the newspaper field became general correspondent, writer and lecturer.

Married in 1870 to Miss Olivia L. Langdon of Elmira, N. Y. Four children were born, but only one child survives him.

Entered publishing firm in 1885, and its failure some years later left him a poor man and debt of many thousands that he considered himself bound to pay. And he paid it by a lecture trip around the world and some late books.

Best known works: "Huckleberry Finn," Innocents Abroad," "Tom Sawyer," "A Tramp Abroad" and his latest work, "Eve's Diary." Left an autobiography partly written.

BY PLAIN DEALER'S LEASED WIRE.

REDDING, Ct., April 21.—Samuel Langhorne Clemens ("Mark Twain"), beloved the world over because he made it laugh, is dead. He passed away without pain at 6:22 o'clock this evening of angina pectoris in his country home, Stormfield, back in the wild Camarack hills. For five hours he had been unconscious and the end was almost unnoticeable. It was simply a cessation of pulse and respiration.

At his bedside were his only living child, Clara, who is the wife of Ossip Gabrilowitsch, the Russian pianist; Albert Bigelow Paine, his secretary and literary executor, who was almost a son to him; Drs. Edward Quintard and Robert Halsey, the heart specialists, who had kept him alive by stimulants for nearly twenty-four hours, and his servants, headed by "Old Katie," who for thirty years had been his housekeeper. His last words were spoken to his daughter. What they were she only heard, for they were faint and almost inarticulate. Unable then to speak, he grasped a book pad and pencil—the instant to write something—even in the face of approaching senselessness.

He traced the words "Give me my glasses." With the spectacles adjusted he gazed at the paper, placed his pencil to it as though to put down some farewell message, then his strength waned and the writing materials slipped from his grip. He smiled wearily at his daughter; then his head sank back to the pillow and he lapsed into the coma.

Yesterday was a bad day for the little knot of anxious watchers at the bedside. For long hours the gray, aquiline features lay molded in the inertia of death, while the pulse sank lower and lower, but late at night Mark Twain passed from stupor into the first natural sleep he had known since he returned from Bermuda and this morning he woke refreshed, even faintly cheerful and in full possession of all his faculties.

Seizes Favorite Book.

Mr. Paine said tonight that the book Mark Twain took up from the coverlet beside him when he asked for his glasses was Carlyle's "History of the French Revolution," his inseparable companion, and greatest favorite.

There was no thought at the time, however, that the end was so near. At 5 o'clock, Dr. Robert Halsey, who had been continuously in attendance said: "Mr. Clemens is not so strong at this hour as he was at the corresponding hour yesterday, but he had wonderful vitality and he may rally again."

A tank of oxygen still stands uncalled for at Redding station. Oxygen was tried yesterday and the physicians explained that it was of no value because the valvular action of the heart was not disordered. There was only an extreme and increasing debility, accompanied by labored respiration.

Mark Twain did not die in anguish. Sedatives soothed his pain, but in the moments of consciousness the men-

Continued on 7th Page, 3d Column.

SCENES AT THE DEDICATION OF CLEVELAND'S NEW BASEBALL PARK

Players and officials parading to the flag staff to hoist the club flag.

A portion of the floral tributes to the Cleveland club. Those shown in the foreground are Ban Johnson, president of the American league; "Garry" Herrmann, chairman of the National commission; C. W. Somers, vice president of the American league, and J. F. Kilfoyl, president of the Cleveland club.

President Ban Johnson pitches first ball.

HARDING DECLARES FOR TAFT AT TIPPS

Candidate for Governor Boldly Defends President and Tariff Policy.

Urges Party to Retain Natural Poise and Not Become Stampeded.

Boldly proclaiming the doctrine of Republicanism as advocated by President Taft, defending the Payne-Aldrich tariff law as the "best that was possible under existing conditions," condemning the clamor about tariff-made high prices as tommyrot, applauding prosecution of graft in the state, but resenting any attempt to discredit years of honorable Republican administration, Warren G. Harding, candidate for governor, delivered one of the strongest political speeches Cleveland Republicans have heard in years at the Tippecanoe club last night.

Harding's speech was a distinct demand to the party not to become stampeded, to maintain its normal poise and to go forward under the banner of William H. Taft to the victory that he promised as certain.

Harding's speech was much in the nature of a campaign opening address. It was strong, virile, to the point and emphatic. The Marion man did not straddle. He didn't try to carry water on both shoulders. He was emphatic on every point upon which he undertook to speak. He carried words of cheer and comfort to Republicans everywhere.

Overshadows Other Speeches.

Harding's speech completely overshadowed talks by W. H. Phipps, state oil inspector, who wants to be secretary of state, and Brigham Young of Ada, O., who would like to be state dairy and food commissioner. Phipps defended party organizations and urged the necessity of the organization of every city, village, township and school district in the state.

The state oil inspector referred to Gov. Harmon as a dodger and charged that in legislative affairs, re-

Continued on 6th Page, 1st Column.

Today's News.

LOCAL WEATHER.

Fair and warmer; east to southwest winds.

TEMPERATURE COMPARISONS.

April 21, 1909.		April 21, 1910.	
Max. 68	Min. 42	Max. 45	Min. 38

Vincennes Man Killed by Auto.

VINCENNES, Ind., April 21.—Solomon Davis, sixty years old, was killed tonight when an automobile plunged over a ten-foot embankment. Florice J. Tougaw, who piloted the machine, sustained severe injuries. Three other occupants of the machine were hurt.

Kill "Safe and Sane" Fourth.

SPECIAL TO THE PLAIN DEALER.

PAINESVILLE, O., April 21.—At a meeting of the city council, it was voted not to have a "sane and safe" Fourth.

VETOES BALL BILL, HEARS OF THREATS

Governor Calls Sunday Sport Measure Illegal in Explaining Action.

Harmon's Opponents Say Course Means Republican Executive.

Plain Dealer Bureau,
44 E. Broad-st.,
COLUMBUS, O., April 21.

Gov. Harmon today vetoed the Anderson Sunday baseball bill on constitutional grounds and communicated his disapproval to both branches of the general assembly. The reading of the governor's message was accompanied by excitement in both senate and house. Further consideration of the bill was postponed until next Tuesday. In the meantime friends of the bill will canvass the situation to see if there is a chance to pass it over the veto.

To pass the bill over the governor's head will require a two-thirds vote in both branches. In view of the fact that the bill secured but fifty-nine votes in the house, a bare constitutional majority, the task of securing seventy-eight votes, necessary to override the objections of the governor, appears insurmountable.

In his message Gov. Harmon said the assembly, to make the bill constitutional, should first repeal the law making Sunday baseball an offense and then add the referendum feature giving local communities an opportunity to bar Sunday ball if they desired to do so. Although it is late in the session, an effort may be made to follow this course.

It was not done in the first place, however, because friends of the bill did not believe enough votes could be mustered in the house for a straight repeal of the Sunday baseball law.

Make Political Threats.

Angry over the veto of the bill its friends filled the halls of the legislature with political threats. For the most part they were similar to the public statement of Representative Brenner of Springfield, who said: "Gov. Harmon's veto means a Republican governor."

Gov. Harmon, himself an ardent baseball fan, avoided discussion of any moral issue that might be involved in the passage of the bill and confined explanation of his action entirely to the constitutional questions.

Continued on 2d Page, 5th Column.

PEACE OUTLOOK DARKENS.

Efforts to Settle Peru-Ecuador Trouble Futile When Former Country Hesitates.

WASHINGTON, April 21.—United States Minister Fox has telegraphed the state department from Quito, Ecuador, that great uneasiness is felt throughout that country on account of the growing danger of a war with Peru.

It is pointed out here that the action of Ecuador in naming three representatives to come to Washington, expecting that Peru would do the same, with a view to settling their differences, seems to have been precipitate.

So far as can be learned, Peru still maintains her position to abide by the findings of the King of Spain, to whom the matters in dispute were submitted.

ADVANCE FOR THOUSANDS

Wage Increase Affecting 60,000 Granted to Sheet and Tin Plate Men.

SPECIAL TO THE PLAIN DEALER.

SHARON, Pa., April 21.—Beginning May 1 the 2,000 local employes and all workmen in the employ of the American Sheet & Tin Plate Co. will receive a voluntary increase. All the plants of the corporation located in probably a dozen cities have been operated open shop since the inception of the strike declared against them July 1 last by the Amalgamated Association of Iron, Sheet and Tin Workers.

The nonunion workmen will receive more per gross ton after May 1 than was ever paid in industrial history for tin working.

A summary of the increase of the hot mill employes is: Rollers, from 1 to 16 cents per ton; doublers, from 1 to 11 cents per ton; heaters, from 1 to 40 cents per ton; catchers, from 1 to 5 cents per ton; screw boys, from 1 to 2 cents per ton, and shear men, from 1 to 2 cents per ton, the varying increases being based on the gauge of tin being made. Over 60,000 men are affected.

PREFERS HELL TO HOUSE.

Witness Before Committee Asserts He Would Rather be in Hades Than in Congress.

WASHINGTON, April 21.—"I'd prefer to be in hell with my back broken rather than be a congressman," declared President W. F. Schilling of the Minnesota Dairymen's association, before the house committee on agriculture today.

The committee was hearing the exponents of the butter interests opposed to the proposed oleomargarine legislation.

Schilling said the farmers did not know "what all this is about" and that after listening to the statements he had heard during the hearing he had come to believe that if congressmen never earned their salaries before, they do after they come to Washington.

EXCORIATES LEVINE IN BITTER LETTER

Kohler, Replying to Judge, Says Latter's Rulings Demoralize Police.

Court, in Answer, Declares Chief is Stooping to Conspiracy.

"In my judgment, the rulings of Judge Levine have done more to encourage crime and criminals in Cleveland, than those of any man who ever occupied the bench."—Chief of Police Fred Kohler, in a letter to Mayor Baehr.

With this statement, Kohler summed up his side of the case yesterday in the war of words between him and Police Judge Levine. Starting three days ago over the question of convicting automobile speeders, the argument between the two men reached a climax yesterday, when Kohler, in reply to Levine's report to Mayor Baehr, set forth his side of the case in an open letter.

"I accuse the chief of stooping to a conspiracy," was the reply of Levine when shown the contents of the letter. "For a long time he has been trying his best to put my court in a bad light before the public. The court must work in the open where its acts can be known by all, but the chief works through a system where the responsibility can be shifted, and he can escape blame. He has done every thing possible to further his ends to saddle the blame for non-conviction upon my court. He has held back evidence until I discharged the prisoner for lack of it, and has then placed the evidence in the hands of the grand jury."

"I make my statements bold and plain," said Kohler, "and I have the proof to back them with."

"The chief is guilty of misrepresentation and falsehood," replied Levine. "He has dragged my name into this, in order to make his escape from the condemnation that is his. He wants to divert attention from the main issue so he can escape explaining why he does not enforce the law."

Mayor Baehr, in answer to Levine's open letter of Wednesday, was on hand early in police court yesterday. He listened intently, while eleven men charged with committing various offenses with their automobiles, appeared before Police Judges Levine and McGannon and answered the charges against them. Then the mayor retired to Levine's private of-

Continued on 6th Page, 5th Column.

NEW BALL PARK DEDICATED BEFORE IMMENSE THRONG

Record Crowd Sees Cleveland's Opening Game and Wildly Cheers.

Baseball Magnates, City Officials and Fans of All Kinds Are on Hand.

NEW MARK FOR CROWD

Eighteen Thousand, Eight Hundred and Thirty-Two Persons Find Seats Within the Capacious Stands—New Flag is Raised by President Ban Johnson and "Garry" Herrmann—Visiting Officials Declare the Plant to be the Best in the American League.

A shouting, holiday crowd of 18,832 Clevelanders yesterday afternoon initiated into service the world's best ball plant—saw the people from across the lake leave their imprint on the score board—looked for rain that didn't come—and gave vent to brotherly sympathy for what the Naps earnestly tried to do.

After all the affair was everything that could be wished. The grounds and grand stand were up to expectation—so was the attendance, 4,000 larger than on any opening day in the city's history—so was the weather.

Chief Kohler was there with sixty policemen, ten detectives, two patrol wagons and a reserve of twenty-six men in the E. 55th-st. station. Harry Thomas, Mike Goldsmith, Tom Farrell and eighty more labor leaders and workers were present, a few with cameras, some with notebooks. There was no friction. The boycotters maintain they saw hundreds of persons of whom they made note, and that union men who went through the turnstiles were few and far between.

In the magnificent grand stand there were some empty seats, not more than 2,000. The great "lower pavilion" and the great "upper pavilion" that overhangs it were solid with men and women and children. The bleachers were densely packed. In the standing room adjacent to the bleachers no room was left.

Variety of Tickets New to Fans.

People did have something of a time finding their seats. There was a rich variety of color in tickets and each variety led to a gangway that belonged to it alone. Over doorways were signs, "white and blue tickets this way," "red and green tickets this way," "lilac and pink tickets this way." People matched colors to find the straight and proper path. The doorways are narrow, but by and by verybody got through. There was many a woman's hat that hesitated.

At a few minutes before 3 Ciricillo's band marched into the diamond to the home plate and formed a square. The Tigers quit practicing and lined up single file behind it. The Naps made their first appearance under a heavy fire of cheers, and fell into single file behind the band, elbow to elbow with the Detroiters. Ban Johnson, president of the American league; "Garry" Herrmann, chairman of the national baseball commission, Charlie Somers and Jack Kilfoyl wedged themselves in behind the musicians.

"Hail the Conquering Hero Comes" struck up the impartial band and the procession moved out through the pitcher's box and center field to the flagstaff. There President Johnson hoisted the white "League park" banner.

As the parade turned back toward home a squad of photographers confronted the players, who obligingly broke rank and reformed in one long line across the field. Then they modestly faced the lenses and let the photographers indulge riotously.

Gigantic Baseball of Carnations.

At the home plate the teams found a baseball two feet in diameter, of white carnations, awaiting them. It was a gift. So were four broad baskets of flowers, one as big as a wash basket, brimming with American Beauties—also three bouquets and an armful of roses dangling from a bat.

Then a rooters' club, which calls itself the Horse Thief association and is composed of advertising men, poured on to the diamond. The members' faces were hid in black masks, as in initiation exercises. With brief ritual they announced that both teams and the umpires had been made full fledged club members, and left.

From the pitchers' box Ban Johnson sent a grounder to "Garry" Herrmann, who stood in the catcher's place. Herrmann fumbled, but retrieved, and the Cleveland baseball season was on.

From then on for that solid mass of spectators it was an hour of hope and waiting, with a cheer interspersed when a run for the Naps seemed imminent. Several times a score seemed near, but each time the heroic work of the Tigers averted it. When Larry Lajoie picked up the whiffletree the spectators cheered again and leaned forward, eager, expectant. He drew his line in the sand, coughed, swung and fouled.

In the seventh the Tigers, after scoring four runs, got three men on bases, but they brought in only one

Continued on 11th Page, 3d Column.

Inaugural is Inauspicious, as the Naps Are Unable to Score a Run.

Clevelanders Powerless Before the Masterly Pitching of Willett.

YOUNG HIT HARD IN SPOTS

Shadow Cast by the New Stand Produces a Misjudged Fly, Which Starts Detroit on the Way to Its First Two Runs, the Total Being Increased to Five by Means of a Seventh-Inning Batting Rally—Only One Error and That Costs a Run.

Eighteen thousand eight hundred and thirty-two Clevelanders paid their way into League park yesterday to see the finest baseball plant in the American league and to be present when the Naps put a third twist in the Tiger's tail. They saw the new stand all right, but there was a hitch in the other part of the program, as Detroit won the game by the score of 5 to 0.

Miles of copy have been written about the uncertainties and integrity of the national game and yesterday's game was but another illustration of the honesty of baseball. Manager McGuire and his thirty white clad warriors would have given a good deal to have celebrated the dedication of the new park with a victory, but the fates, through their personal representative, Edgar Willett of Wichita, Ks., decreed otherwise.

The Naps would have liked to have won just for the sake of Cy Young the grand old man of the game. Cy was making his twenty-first annual debut as a big league pitcher and a victory would have been sweeter than nectar to him but it was not to be. Cy pitched his first game at League park when the seating capacity was not half what it is now. He has seen the city grow in a baseball way until now it can boast of having the best park in the circuit. He would have willingly parted with an acre or two off his Peoli farm to have won that game but the Detroiters ruled otherwise.

The famous old pitcher never worked harder in his life. He had terriffic speed and his control was all that could be desired except in two innings. He fanned six of the champions, twice striking out Ty Cobb, the best batter in the league, but he could not win. Had the Detroit club been entirely composed of Cobbs, Cy might have got away with a victory, but unfortunately for him there was a man named Sam Crawford, another by the name of Tom Jones in the Tiger line up which also included such evil-doers as Stanage, Willett and McIntyre. These were the men who had no respect for age and persisted in poking out safe hits just when hits were not appreciated by the 18,000 Clevelanders present.

When Edgar Willett has control there is no pitcher in the American league who can excel him in ability to puzzle the opposing batters. When he can locate that plate, there are some clubs who consider themselves lucky to get a few fouls off his delivery. And, unfortunately for Cleveland, yesterday was one of the days when Edgar Willett was feeling just right. He did not strike out any of the Naps, but he persisted in feeding them slants and shoots which they persisted in hitting to sections of the field occupied by Detroiters. Except in five instances, the Cleveland batters gave splendid exhibitions of hitting the ball "where they are."

Willett Keeps Hits Scattered.

During the first six rounds the Naps managed to collect one hit, a single by Clarke in the second inning. It was a beauty skimmer close to second base. But from then on until the seventh there was not the semblance of a hit that went to the credit of Cleveland. To start the seventh, Lajoie drew a lucky bounding hit. In the eighth Cy Young slammed one to center that netted the veteran two bases. Had he not been carrying weight for age, he might have made the hit good for three sacks. Bradley singled in this same round, but Young is not as nimble on his feet as he was once, and was content to stop at third. That is why the Naps failed to escape a shut out. The Naps' fifth hit was made in the final round, when Clarke doubled to the right field fence. But there were two out at the time and the game ended without him advancing.

Old Cy was good and bad in spots, but the damage done during his soluble moments resulted in Detroit making five runs. The first two can be blamed on to the new stand for it cast such a shade that Krueger in left field was not able to judge Stanage's line drive until too late. That mistake cost two runs, and Cy himself was responsible for three that the champions added in the seventh inning.

Rarely has a more impatient crowd

Continued on 11th Page, 1st Column.

$100---For Identifying These Baseball Players---$100

HERE ARE PICTURES OF 108 NATIONAL LEAGUE PLAYERS. CAN YOU IDENTIFY THEM?

For the Most Correct Identification Lists Received up to Six O'Clock P. M. Friday, Aug. 12, the Following Prizes Will Be Awarded: First Prize $25.00; Second Prize $15.00; Third Prize $10.00; Fifty Prizes of $1.00 Each.

Address identification lists to Baseball Editor, Boston Sunday Post. In case of ties the lists earliest received will be given preference.

THE SPORTING WORLD

HOW CUBS AND ATHLETICS WILL LINE UP IN WORLD'S BASEBALL SERIES.

NAPOLEON LAJOIE MAKES EIGHT HITS OUT OF EIGHT TIMES AT BAT

MERE BASEBALL LOSES INTEREST IN FACE OF LAJOIE'S STICKWORK

Efforts of Frenchman Are More Enthralling Than Nap-Brown Double-Header—McGuire and O'Connor Act as Catchers.

SPECIAL TO THE PLAIN DEALER.

ST. LOUIS, Oct. 9.—The efforts of Nap Lajoie at the bat were the big features of today's double header between Cleveland and St. Louis. Neither the players nor the spectators seemed to care much who won. All interest centered in the big Frenchman's batting prowess and whenever he made a hit the local populace went wild.

There was considerable wildness, considering the fact that Lajoie made eight bingles in the two games, enough to win him the auto, according to unofficial figures.

The Browns, thanks to some uphill work and a batfest in the ninth inning, took the opening game, 5 to 4.

Naps Lose the First.

The second went to the Naps, 3-0, this contest being featured by the presence of Managers Jim McGuire and Jack O'Connor, both famous veteran catchers, behind the bat. O'Connor caught only one inning, but the "Deacon" went the route and helped Falkenberg to his shut-out.

It was Nelson against Blanding in the opener. Bronkie's single, Jackson's double, Lajoie's triple and Stovall's single gave the Naps three runs in the first inning. Doubles by Corriden and Griggs netted the Browns a tally in their opening round. The Naps raised their total to four in the second on a double by Graney and Jackson's single. Hartsel's single, Stephen's double and Nelson's demise gave the Browns their second score in round 2. The third run resulted in the third when Corriden and Stone singled, Wallace walked and Northen forced Wallace, Corriden tallying in the sixth. Hartsell's single, Stephen's sacrifice and Nelson's single tied it up for the Browns. It remained 4-4 until the ninth. Then Griggs hit a triple to the flag pole in right center and Wallace scored him with a single over second.

Texas Leaguer Pitches.

Malloy, a young right-hander from the Houston (Texas league) club, was Falkenberg's opponent in the wind-up. Birmingham, who succeeded Bronkie on third, started with a single. Graney forced him but went to third when Malloy heayed wide to first. Lajoie scored him with a scratch single to Corriden. Two more were added by the Naps in the third.

Birmingham opened with a double to left while Truesdale fumbled Graney's roller. Jackson put a single in left and Birmingham paid off. Lajoie laid down a bunt to Corriden that was scored a sacrifice and was safe while Graney scored on Corriden's poor heave. Scores:

FIRST GAME.

ST. LOUIS.	A.B.	R.	H.	O.	A.	E.
Truesdale, 2b	5	0	0	1	3	1
Corridon, 3b	5	2	3	1	1	0
Stone, l f	5	0	2	1	0	0
Griggs, 1b	5	1	3	13	1	0
Wallace, ss	3	0	1	3	6	1
Northen, c f	4	0	0	2	0	0
Hartzell, r f	3	2	1	1	0	0
Stephens, c	3	0	2	4	4	0
Nelson, p	3	0	1	1	6	0
Totals	36	5	13	27	21	2

CLEVELAND.	A.B.	R.	H.	O.	A.	E.
Bronkie, 3b	3	1	1	1	1	1
Braney, l f	4	1	1	4	0	0
Jackson, c f	4	1	2	1	0	0
Lajoie, 2b	4	1	4	4	1	0
Easterly, r f	4	0	0	1	0	0
Stoval, 1b	4	0	2	7	0	0
Smith, c	4	0	0	4	1	0
Peckinpaugh, ss	4	0	0	2	6	0
Blanding, p	4	0	0	0	1	0
Totals	35	4	10	*24	10	1

*None out when winning run scored.

St. Louis .... 1 1 1 0 0 1 0 0 1—5
Cleveland .... 3 1 0 0 0 0 0 0 0—4

Two-base hits—Jackson, Corridon, Graney, Stephens. Three-base hit — Lajoie. Sacrifice hit—Stephens. Stolen bases—Bronkie, Stovall, Griggs. Wild pitch—Blanding. First base on balls—Off Nelson 1, off Blanding 4. Struck out—By Nelson 4, by Blanding 4. Left on bases—St. Louis 12, Cleveland 5. Time—1:42. Umpire—Evans.

SECOND GAME.

ST. LOUIS.	A.B.	R.	H.	O.	A.	E.
Truesdale, 2b	4	0	0	2	0	1
Corridon, 3b	4	0	2	3	1	1
Stone, l f	4	0	1	0	0	0
Griggs, 1b	4	0	0	10	0	0
Wallace, ss	3	0	1	1	4	0
Northern, c f	3	0	0	2	0	0
Hartzell, r f	3	0	0	2	0	0
O'Connor, c	0	0	0	1	0	0
Malloy, p	3	0	0	0	5	1
Killifer, c	3	0	0	6	2	0
Totals	31	0	5	27	12	3

CLEVELAND.	A.B.	R.	H.	O.	A.	E.
Birmingham, 3b	4	1	2	1	5	0
Graney, l f	5	2	0	1	0	2
Jackson, c f	4	0	2	1	0	0
Lajoie, 2b	4	0	4	0	4	0
Easterly, r f	4	0	0	2	0	0
Hohnhorst, 1b	3	0	1	18	0	0
McGuire, c	3	0	0	2	1	0
Peckinpaugh, ss	4	0	1	2	4	0
Falkenberg, p	3	0	0	0	5	0
Totals	34	3	10	27	19	2

Cleveland .... 1 0 2 0 0 0 0 0 0—3

Two-base hits—Birmingham, Corridon. Sacrifice hit—Lajoie. Double plays—Malloy, Truesdale and Griggs; Lajoie, Peckinpaugh and Hohnhorst. Passed balls—McGuire, Killifer. Stolen base—Stone. Hit by pitched ball—By Malloy (McGuire). Wild pitch—Malloy. First base on balls—Off Malloy 4. Struck out—By Malloy 6, by Falkenberg 1. Left on bases—St. Louis 4, Cleveland 10. Time—1:15. Umpire—Evans.

NOTES OF THE GAME

About 10,000 people saw the final baseball show of the season. It was the largest crowd at Sportsman's park in months. Lajoie was responsible for the majority of the fans' presence. It is believed that Grover Land cracked his collarbone as the result of a tumble in gathering in a foul from Stephen's bat Saturday.

Manager McGuire showed Bronkie at third and Peckinpaugh at short in the opener. Hohnhorst went to first, vice Stovall in the second.

O'Connor had no intention of catching until Billy Evans anounced McGuire as the Cleveland receiver. Then Jack donned the mask and pad. A crack on the bare hand by a foul tip convinced him he had enough in one round. The crowd swarmed on the field after the game and almost carried Lajoie out on his way.

Cleveland fans could hardly have given Larry a better reception.

BATTING KING OF MAJOR LEAGUES

Napoleon Lajoie, famous Cleveland batsman who is probable winner of the automobile which is to be awarded to America's leading hitter.

LAJOIE WINS AUTO IN FINAL STRETCH

CONTINUED FROM FIRST PAGE.

were tallied and 10,000 throats cheered Lajoie as the king of American batsmen.

But Larry's triumph is tinged with a charge of illegitimacy. St. Louis sporting writers assert that Lajoie was favored by opposing fielders. They say that the St. Louis pitchers placed the ball where Larry could hit it to best advantage.

They maintain that Corridon, the Brown third baseman, did not field to the best of his ability when the Cleveland champion drove the ball into Corridon's territory. They insist that other fielders abetted him and aided Lajoie in his race for highest honors. Among others who wrote in similar strain, the baseball editor of the St. Louis Globe Democrat gave the following description of the St. Louis infield's work:

"Every time Lajoie stepped up to the plate Corridon walked out to the very edge of the grass almost. The Browns' third sacker was virtually playing a short left field for Larry. This always resulted in the same old thing happening, that of Lajoie bunting down the third base line, Corridon rushing in to field the ball and then not throwing because a throw to first would have been useless.

"In the third inning of the second game a boy who carried bats for the teams, was sen all the way up to the second deck of the grand stand to find out whether Lajoie had been credited with a hit on his roller to Corridon, which the latter fumbled. A man was on base at the time, and as Lajoie bunted he was credited with a sacrifice and Corridon, who fumbled, with an error.

"At this stage Lajoie had piled up only five hits. He needed seven to tie Cobb's mark and eight to win. Therefore Larry would have to be at bat three more times to get the same number of hits. And he did. In the fifth Larry beat out a bunt to Corridon. In the seventh Malloy failed to get the ball over for Falkenberg. Birmingham also drew a pass. Malloy, after passing two batters, settled down and shot the ball squarely over the plate, forcing Graney and Jackson to strike out. Lajoie stepped up to the plate and cracked out his seventh bunt, a little roller to Corridon. Easterly fanned. In the eighth Hohnhorst walked, McGuire was hit by a pitched ball, Peckinpaugh fanned, Falkenberg forced Hohnhorst. Birmingham was out, Killifer to Griggs. This left just three men to come up in the ninth, and Lajoie was the third man to step up to the plate. Graney fanned, Jackson was out on a tap. Lajoie bunted to Corridon an. was safe, getting his eighth hit."

Official figures of the rival batsmen will not be given out until the first game of the world's series at Philadelphia, Oct. 17. Until then the persistent followers of the great hitters in this contest for the first prize ever offered to spur on players effective with the bat will have to be content with figures that have not undergone the sanction of Ban Johnson.

In these unofficial figures there is a slight variance. Of the Cleveland papers, the Plain Dealer, the Leader and the Press award the palm to Lajoie. The News alone disputes the Frenchman's claim. The News places Cobb in the lead by .06 of one so-called point.

With the preponderance of these unofficial figures favoring Lajoie, and with the supposed assurance that the eight hits made in eight times at bat yesterday will stand the official test, the claim of the Clevelander to the batting championship apparently will be upheld by the announcement to be made by the president of the league. But at all events, the race between Lajoie and Cobb will stand as the feature of the American league for the season which ended yesterday.

Lajoie started his wonderful batting early in the season. Even in training he met the ball with considerable success. In May he led both leagues. In June he was overtaken by Snodgrass, who held top position for a long time. Then Cobb wrested the honor away from him and held it for a short time, Lajoie overtaking and passing him.

As the season neared the end, it was stated that errors in computation had been discovered which placed Cobb in the van when Lajoie was supposed to be leading. This statement was made shortly after the Detroit outfielder had been suffering from trouble with his eyes, which ailment was supposed to have caused his falling off in hitting, allowing Lajoie to jump into the lead.

From then on, the contest narrowed until victory or defeat for the Cleveland Frenchman hinged on his batting in the final double header. To achieve success, he must make a perfect record and hit safely at least seven times. Lajoie entered the first contest in second place among the "auto chasers." He began the second game with victory in sight and when it ended his name led all the rest.

BARNARD DOESN'T THINK PROTEST WILL AVAIL MUCH

E. S. Barnard, vice president of the Cleveland baseball club, was jubilant last night when he heard of Lajoie's feat at St. Louis. He was asked if there was any fear of a protest.

"I don't see how anyone can protest with good grace," he said. "Lajoie played right up to the minute and Cobb quit when he thought his average was heavy enough to insure his winning the auto."

CUBS WIN DESPITE COLE'S WILDNESS

Champions Down Bresnahan's Club When Kane Drives in Deciding Run.

White Fails to Locate Plate and Cincy Defeats Pittsburg.

CHICAGO, Oct. 9.—Chicago won the first game of the series from St. Louis today 4 to 3 in a ninth-inning rally. Kane starred for the new champions, getting three singles and driving home the deciding count. Cole was wild, giving ten bases on balls, but was lucky in the pinches. The score:

Chicago.	A	R	H	O	A	St. Louis.	A	R	H	O	A
Beaumont,l	3	1	1	0	0	Huggins,2	2	1	0	2	3
Schulte,r	5	0	1	1	0	Ellis,l	5	1	0	2	0
Hofm'n,m-1	4	1	1	14	0	Mowrey,3	3	0	0	2	1
Chance,1	0	1	0	1	0	Konetchy,1	3	0	0	14	0
Kane,m	4	0	3	2	0	Evans,r	4	0	2	1	1
Zim'rman,2	3	0	2	1	2	Phelps,c	4	0	1	3	1
Steinfeldt,3	3	0	1	0	4	Abbott,m	2	0	0	2	0
Tinker,s	2	0	1	5	6	Betcher,s	3	1	0	0	7
Needham,c	4	0	1	3	2	Steele,p	4	0	1	0	4
Cole,p	4	1	0	0	2						
Totals	32	4	11	27	16	Totals	30	3	4	*26	17

*Two out when winning run scored.

Chicago .... 3 0 0 0 0 0 0 0 1—4
St. Louis .... 2 1 0 0 0 0 0 0 0—3

Errors—Tinker 2.

Two-base hits—Zimmerman, Steele, Tinker, Schulte, Evans. Sacrifice hits—Tinker 2, Zimmerman. Double plays—Tinker and Hofman; Zimmerman, Tinker and Hofman. Left on bases—Chicago 9, St. Louis 11. First base on balls—Off Cole 10, off Steele 5. First on errors—St. Louis 2. Hit by pitcher—By Cole (Evans). Struck out—By Cole 2, by Steele 1. Wild pitch—Cole. Time—1:55. Umpires—Rigler and O'Day.

Cincy Easily Beats Pirates.

CINCINNATI, Oct. 9.—Cincinnati today defeated Pittsburg, 7 to 1, in the final game of the National league season on the home grounds. White was hit opportunely. His wildness also accounted for several runs. Wilson's home run in the seventh inning was the feature. Directly following the game the Cincinnati and Pittsburg teams contested in a field day exhibition. Score:

Cin'nati.	A	R	H	O	A	Pittsb'g.	A	R	H	O	A
Miller,m	5	0	0	2	0	McCarthy,s	4	0	0	0	4
Altizer,s	4	2	3	2	0	Leach,m	4	0	1	3	0
Hoblitzel,1	3	3	1	9	0	Campbell,l	3	0	2	3	0
Mitchell,r	2	0	1	1	1	Wagner,1	4	0	0	8	0
Paskert,l	3	0	1	4	0	Miller,2	4	0	0	4	3
Lobert,3	3	1	0	2	2	Wilson,r	4	1	2	3	0
Clarke,c	4	1	2	2	0	Simon,c	4	0	0	2	2
Roth,c	0	0	0	1	0	M'Kechnie,3	3	0	0	1	0
Corcoran,2	3	0	1	4	5	White,p	3	0	2	0	3
Beebe,p	4	0	0	0	3						
Totals	31	7	9	27	11	Totals	33	1	7	24	12

Cincinnati .... 1 0 2 0 0 0 4 0 *—7
Pittsburg .... 0 0 0 0 0 0 1 0 0—1

Errors—Altizer, McCarthy, Campbell, Miller.

Two-base hits—Hoblitzel, Campbell. Three-base hit—Clarke. Home run—Wilson. Sacrifice hits—Mitchell, Corcoran, Campbell. Stolen bases—Hoblitzel, Lobert. Double play—McCarthy, Miller to Wagner. Left on bases—Pittsburg 6, Cincinnati 9. First base on balls—Off White 7. Struck out—By White 1, by Beebe 2. Passed ball—Clarke. Time—1:50. Umpires—Brennan and Emslie.

Euclid Beach Parks Win.

SPECIAL TO THE PLAIN DEALER.

SANDUSKY, O., Oct. 9.—The Euclid Beach Parks defeated Sandusky today in a pitchers' battle. Upp for the locals allowed but two hits, but errors lost the game. Score:

		R.	H.	E.
Euclids	0 1 0 0 0 0 0 0 0	1	2	2
Sandusky	0 0 0 0 0 0 0 0 0	0	5	4

Batteries—Smith and Schwabe; Upp and McConville.

Two Games Not Played.

Two of the games scheduled for the closing day of the Wildey league season were not played yesterday. Anchors did not put in an appearance and Glenn got the game by forfeit. Neither the Mayflowers, the pennant winners, nor the Phenix teams had a full nine on the field so the contest was called off by Umpire Killeen.

DETROIT WINS FINAL

Tigers Slam Chicago Indian Twirler in the Sixth Inning.

CHICAGO, Oct. 9.—Detroit won the final game of the season from Chicago here today, 2 to 1, pounding Chouneau, an Indian recruit, for four hits and two runs in the sixth inning. Score:

Chicago.	A	R	H	O	A	Detroit.	A	R	H	O	A
Messenger,l	3	0	0	1	0	Bush,3	3	0	0	0	2
Zeider,3	1	0	0	1	5	O'Leary,s	4	0	0	2	5
Meloan,r	4	0	0	2	1	Crawford,m	4	1	2	2	0
Chouin'rd,2	4	0	1	2	3	Kirke,2	4	1	1	3	5
Parent,s	3	0	1	1	5	T. Jones,1	4	0	1	10	2
C. Mullen,1	4	0	1	13	0	G.Mullin,1	4	0	2	1	0
Zwilling,m	3	1	0	2	0	Willett,r	4	0	1	0	0
Payne,c	4	0	2	5	1	Stanage,c	4	0	0	7	3
Chouneau,p	1	0	0	0	0	Donovan,p	3	0	0	2	2
Lange,p	2	0	0	0	0						
Totals	29	1	5	27	15	Totals	34	2	7	27	19

Detroit .... 0 0 0 0 0 2 0 0 0—2
Chicago .... 0 0 1 0 0 0 0 0 0—1

Errors—Zeider, Chouneau, T. Jones, G. Mullin.

Two-base hit—C. Mullen. Three-base hits—Willett, Crawford. Hits—Off Chouneau, 6 in 5 1-3 innings; off Lange, 1 in 3 2-3 innings. Sacrifice hit—Zeider. Double play—Meloan to Mullen. Left on bases—Chicago 8, Detroit 6. Bases on balls—Off Donovan 5, off Lange 1. First base on errors—Chicago 1, Detroit 2. Hit by pitcher—By Donovan 1 (Chouneau). Struck out—By Chouneau 1, by Lange 2, by Donovan 6. Time—1:30. Umpires—Perrine and Sheridan.

Play Tie Game.

The Meyers Prospects and Mahon-Kings, second place winners of the City and Cleveland leagues respectively, engaged in an 8 to 8 tie game yesterday. The former team came from behind and tied the score in the eighth and the contest was called at the end of the ninth on account of darkness. Heavy hitting featured. The play-off will come next week. Score:

M. Prospects .... 2 1 0 0 0 3 0 2 0—8
Mahon-Kings .... 3 4 0 0 0 1 0 0 0—8

All-Pros Win Again.

Births All Professionals beat the Cleveland and City league Stars by the score of 5 to 2. It was the sixteenth straight game for the All Pros. The features were the battery work of Leber and Powers and the running one-handed catch of Kallal. Score:

Births All Pros........ 1 0 0 1 0 3—5
City League Stars........ 1 0 1 0 0 0—2

Football Results.

The Giddings defeated the Lakeview Tigers 5 to 2 in a fast game.

The Centurys won from the Echo Jrs 16 to 2.

The Denisons played a tie game with the Smith Superiors in a cracking good contest yesterday, the score standing 0 to 0.

The Cincinnati club will arrive here Wednesday evening and will establish headquarters at the Hotel Euclid.

LEJEUNE BREAKS THROWING RECORD THAT HAS STOOD FOR THIRTY-SIX YEARS

Evansville Central League Player Hurls Baseball 426 Feet 6 1-4 Inches in Field Day Event at Cincinnati.

CINCINNATI, Oct. 9.—The world's record for the long distance throwing of a baseball, that had stood for thirty-six years, was broken at the field day between the Cincinnati and Pittsburg National league teams here today when Sheldon Lejeune of the Evansville club of the Central league threw the sphere 426 feet 6 1-4 inches, 25 feet 10 3-4 inches over the old record.

This long distance throwing event was in a special match between Lejuene and Escar Fandree of Springfield. The record that has stood for more than a third of a century was made by Tom Hatfield, and was 400 feet 7 1-2 inches.

In the other field events that followed Pittsburg was unable to carry off any honors. In two events the visitors succeeded in getting ties, but were outdone in the finals. The following are the summaries:

Beating out a bunt—John Lobert and Ward Miller, both of Cincinnati, tied at 3 2-5 seconds, and divided the prize money.

Fungo hitting—Won by Rowan of Cincinnati. Distance 398 feet 6 1-2 inches.

Circling the bases—Campbell of Pittsburg and Lobert of Cincinnati tied. Time 14 seconds. In the run-off Lobert won by repeating the circuit in 14 seconds.

Catchers' accurate throwing—Won by McLean, Cincinnati, by making two bullseyes out of three throws.

Pitchers' control contest—Won by Harry Gaspar, Cincinnati. Record, eight strikes out of eleven balls thrown.

Outfielders' accurate throwing—Paskert, Cincinnati, and Wilson, Pittsburg, tied on two throws, Paskert winning on the third.

100 yard dash—Won by Lobert, Cincinnati; Campbell, Pittsburg, second; and W. Miller, Cincinnati, third. J. Miller, Pittsburg, also started.

LOCAL COLLEGES SHOW GOOD FORM

Saturday's Games Make Case and Reserve Look Like Possible Champs.

State is One Good Bet While Oberlin's Tie Tells Nothing.

The local college football elevens agreeably surprised their supporters in Saturday's games. Nobody ever imagined that Case would play a tie with Michigan, while few expected to see Reserve make the score it did. The results made the stock of the neighboring football teams go away up to the places of the high and mighty in state pigskin circles.

Fogg and his crowd went up to Ann Arbor hoping to hold the Wolverines to as low a score as possible. However, those same hopes were not sanguine. As a matter of fact it was confidently predicted, even by the Case supporters, that the team was in for one of the worst drubbings handed out in the annual game between the two institutions in years. A tie was not even at the end of the most fanciful predictions.

However, a tie it was and it came as a gladsome change from the years of beatings that Case has had at the hands of the "hurry up" squad. Besides, it upset the dope on both Case and Michigan. The former must have been developing greatly by some absent treatment method for at no time in the practice to date have the team or the men showed signs of first-class form, either on the offense or the defense.

Of course the stories that have emanated from the Michigan camp that Yost has the best team in years cannot be taken seriously in the light of Saturday's game. Such reports, however, help to demoralize a team and may have had muct to do with the result, as Case was generally believed to be much weaker than usual. It might have been overconfidence matched against man's inherent strife for self-preservation, Case playing in the latter role. Case must henceforth be considered more seriously than the work prior to Saturday would justify.

Reserve's great game and victory on Saturday brings to the red and white laurels that were well deserved. A good development has been going on for the past two weeks, and a closer contest was generally expected. No one in the local camp predicted a victory for Reserve, but it was believed that the red and white aggregation would be heard from before the game passed into history. There is a fine working spirit among the men, and those that closely follow the practice each day expected it to show just as it did.

On the other hand it was conceded that Wesleyan had not had a real tryout. The two teams that had been defeated by large scores will hardly compare favorably with the local high school teams, so that the big scores made by the Methodists really meant nothing. As a matter of fact, they hurt the down state team more in the Reserve game than they benefited as practice at the time they were played.

The victory was well earned. According to the admission of Coach St. John after the game, Reserve was outweighed just an even dozen pounds to the man. The weights of the red and white men are known and as a whole the team is the lightest since the advent of Budget Seaman. That Reserve won is in itself a great thing, but the team cannot make much capital of that. It is not what has been done but what will be done at this stage of the season. Those things that have been accomplished serve now only as a guide post to the greater things that remain to be done. With Ohio State next on the horizon it will be up to Reserve.

Oberlin's showing at Cornell can hardly be classed in the same list of great deeds. Cornell's football is demoralized. Practice was at a standstill last week for several days and the coaches threw up their hands in disgust. In fact, they were on the point of leaving all together. The faculty fails to see the game just now and the men are kept on the hill when they ought to be plugging away on Percy field.

Of course, Oberlin was in better shape than the week before in the Buchtel contest. Development is expected and before the end of the season the other teams in the state can expect the same old contests with Oberlin. The real strength of the team cannot now be determined.

State looks mighty formidable. Just what Columbus can do is always an unknown quantity in this section, but they came up to a guess in the Saturday game. Jones' men are going in fine shape and Reserve will have to go some next Saturday. The game is too early for the meeting of the two teams for much will depend on the outcome. State looks like a real championship team.

Kenyon's victory was not unexpected. Pierce is getting his men into line late, but they seem to be working pretty well. Kenyon is not to be feared as much as a year ago, however. Denison can be regarded as the usual Denison from all appearances. Wooster again got its bumps, Buchtel keeping right on the job as in the week before. The Akron college will have cause to be proud of its 1910 team. Heidelberg is also out of the race, but the boys are plugging hard and the team will round into better shape as the season advances.

There is much endeavor on the part of the coaches just now to delve into the depths of the possibilities of the new rules. To do this they are overlooking much that was a couple of years deemed important. This tends to make the teams more even in strength, or rather to tie the scores where teams of something like the same strength got together. However, there is no chance of doping out the game under the newest rules and relative scores tell absolutely nothing.

LEAGUE STANDINGS

AMERICAN.

Clubs.	Pl'y'd.	W.	L.	Pct.
Philadelphia	150	102	48	680
New York	150	87	63	580
Detroit	154	86	68	558
Boston	152	81	71	533
Cleveland	152	71	81	467
Chicago	153	68	85	444
Washington	151	66	85	437
St. Louis	154	47	107	305

NATIONAL.

Clubs.	Pl'y'd.	W.	L.	Pct.
Chicago	149	101	48	678
New York	151	90	61	596
Pittsburg	153	86	67	562
Philadelphia	151	77	74	510
Cincinnati	154	75	79	487
Brooklyn	152	64	88	421
St. Louis	148	61	87	412
Boston	152	51	101	336

YESTERDAY'S RESULTS.

American League.

St. Louis 5, Cleveland 4.
Cleveland 3, St. Louis 0.
Detroit 2, Chicago 1.

National League.

Chicago 4, St. Louis 3.
Cincinnati 7, Pittsburg 1.

TODAY'S GAMES.

National League.

St. Louis at Chicago.
Philadelphia at New York.
Boston at Brooklyn.

TO ACCEPT COM.'S RULING

Auto Firm Will Award Car According to National Commission's Action.

DETROIT, Oct. 9.—President Hugh Chalmers of the Chalmers Motor Co. was asked tonight whether he would demand official investigation of the final game in St. Louis before presenting the automobile which he offered for the champion batter of the world.

"Under the terms of our deed of gift," said Mr. Chalmers, "we are required to accept the ruling of the national commission as to the winner of the automobile, and it will be ready for the man whom the commission names. Our company probably will not ask that the alleged quitting of the St. Louis club be investigated, relying on the commission to take any such action that it may deem necessary or expedient."

Kramers Draw a Blank.

The Kramers were blanked 3 to 0 yesterday in a fast game by the McIntyres. Mace fanned thirteen, and allowed but one hit. Score:

McIntyres	A	R	H	O	A	Kramers.	A	R	H	O	A
Sutton,r	3	1	2	1	1	Yost,3	3	0	0	1	3
McCarthy,l	4	0	0	0	0	Bedhune,2	3	0	0	2	3
Hobart,2	4	0	1	1	2	Butler,l	3	0	1	0	1
Welch,s	2	0	0	0	1	Whearty,1	2	0	0	8	0
Kosler,1	4	0	0	8	0	Burton,s	2	0	0	2	2
McDonald,3	2	1	0	2	2	Elben,r	3	0	0	1	0
Dehaney,m	3	1	1	0	0	Jones,m	3	0	0	0	0
Hopkins,c	3	0	1	12	4	Meyers,c	1	0	0	7	2
Mace,p	3	0	1	0	0	Shenning,p	1	0	0	0	2
Totals	28	3	6	24	10	Totals	21	0	1	21	13

McIntyres .... 1 2 0 0 0 0 0 *—3

Errors—Yost, Burton.

Two-base hit—Sutton. Three-base hits—Hobart, Dehaney. Sacrifice hit—Schenning. Stolen bases—Sutton, Welch 2, McDonald, Butler. First base on balls—Off Mace 3, off Schenning 3. Hit by pitcher—Sutton. Struck out—By Mace 13, by Schenning 6. Umpire—Smith.

GREAT ALL STAR BASEBALL CLUB WILL GIVE ATHLETICS WORK-OUT

Speaker, Cobb, Harry Lord and Milan Are Among Luminaries Who Will Play Against the Mackmen This Week.

SPECIAL TO THE PLAIN DEALER.

PHILADELPHIA, Oct. 9.—Connie Mack's regulars and an augmented reserve team clash tomorrow afternoon in an exhibition game while commencing Tuesday the great all star combination of the American league starts a series that will last until Saturday.

Philadelphian's will have the opportunity of seeing one of the best players in the country on one team. Ty Cobb, whose batting and fielding prevented the Athletic's from winning pennants in 1907 and 1909, comes to Shibe park to do his best toward keeping the Mackmen on their top form in order that they may be successful in the world's series. Cobb will cover right field in the games. In center the All-stars have another luminary in Tris Speaker, the brilliant Boston player. Clyde Milan, whom Mack rates as the best young outfielder in the country, will be in left. Milan was induced to enter the games by his manager, Jimmy McAleer of Washington, who will also act as the leader for the All-stars.

There are also some big names in the infield. Harry Lord of the White Sox, than whom there is no better hitting and fielding third baseman in the country, will cover his familiar position. The able Mr. McBride of Washington, will be at short and Elberfeld of the same team at second. Jake Stahl, the big first-sacker of the Boston team, will be at the first corner.

Every member of the pitching staff and the catching corps is a brilliant performer. Ed Walsh and Doc. White of the White Sox, and Walter Johnson of Washington, will do the pitching, while Billy Sullivan of the Sox, and Charley Street and Ainsmith of Washington will catch.

Manager McAleer has informed Mack that the All-star team wil play as swift baseball in the post-season series as it does in the championship race.

Connie Mack has not a word to say in regard to his plans for the battles with the Cubs. "It has always been my practice," said Mack, "to announce my battery for the next game to the morning papers, but I am not going to do this in the series with Chicago. Too much hinges on the result of the games and no person will know the identity of my pitchers and catchers as well as the rest of the line-up until the teams are sent into action by the umpires."

The Athletics leader also steadfastly declines to make any prediction about the outcome.

Among the fans there is much speculation about two points, the outfield and catching departments. It is an assured fact that barring injuries, Davis, Collins, Barry and Baker will cover the infield positions in every game in the series.

It is possible that Mack may make a shift in the outfield. Murphy, in right, and Oldring in center, are fixtures, but there is an element of doubt about left field. Bris Lord is first choice and is likely to be the man used in the first game. The result of the opening game and the performance of Lord in it will have much to do with his chances of playing in the remaining games. Should Mack bench Lord, Strunk or Hartzell will get a chance.

There is much uncertainty about the name of the man who will catch the opening game. Many believe that it lies between Ira Thomas and Jack Lapp.

SILK MAY UMPIRE GAME.

It is Possible American Leagu Arbiter May Act in Hinkel-Telling Contest.

The game that will attract a good deal of attention will be the second game between the Hinkels and Tellings at League park next Wednesday, Columbus day, Oct. 12, at 2:30 o'clock.

A good deal has been said pro and con in regard to the first game that was won by the Hinkels and a battle royal can be looked for.

Both teams have appealed to Vice President Barnard of the Cleveland club to secure the services as umpire of Silk O'Loughlin, who will be here to umpire the series between the Cincinanti National league team and the Naps on Thursday. Providing it does not rain in Cincinnati on Tuesday both teams will be here Wednesday and the Cincinnati team will practice at the park on Wednesday morning.

Both teams will be allowed only such players that were eligible to play in the first game.

GRAYS HOLD FIRST PLACE IN POLO RACE

Five Victories and One Defeat Record for Past Week.

WILLIAMS BEST GOAL GETTER

Brockton Man Leads National League with 34 Counts.—Duggan Holds First Honors in Rush Taking with 94. Pence Advances to First Place Among Goaltends.

THE WEEK'S SCHEDULE.

MONDAY.
Worcester at Fall River.
New Haven at New Bedford.
Hartford at Brockton.

TUESDAY.
Brockton at Fall River.
New Haven at Worcester.
Providence at New Bedford.
Hartford at Taunton.

WEDNESDAY.
Taunton at Brockton.
Fall River at Hartford.
Providence at Worcester.
New Bedford at New Haven.

THURSDAY.
Worcester at Brockton.
New Bedford at Hartford.
Providence at Taunton.
Fall River at New Haven.

FRIDAY.
Worcester at Providence.
New Haven at Fall River.
Hartford at New Bedford.
Brockton at Taunton.

SATURDAY.
Fall River at Providence.
New Bedford at Worcester.
Taunton at New Haven.
Brockton at Hartford.

By a great winning streak the Providence polo team jumped to the top of the column of the National League standing last week, seven games being won in a string, of which five were corralled last week and two the week before. Of the six games played last week but one was lost, and that, curiously enough, was the worst defeat of the season and the first setback on the home floor. New Haven was the team to stop the onward rush of the Grays and enjoys the distinction of being the only aggregation to date to beat McGilvray's men, the other defeat being adminstered at New Haven.

Taunton and New Haven share the honors of making the second best showing of the week, with four wins and but two defeats each. Taunton begins the third week of the season in third place, a higher position than the Emeralds held during all of last season. But if Manager McCarthy's boys continue to put up the game they have shown so far this season they will have to be reckoned with when the final winner is hung up.

New Bedford shook off Brockton during the week and closed the six days with an even break, with three won and the same number lost, and, withal, in second place. Fall River found the going rough and could capture but two games of the six played. Hartford won its second game of the season, but dropped the other three played, while Worcester played three and lost them all, not a single victory being credited to the team from the heart of the Bay State to date. Manager Phelan has had his troubles in all directions. Several players whom he expected to report have refused to join the team and he has been forced to get along the best he could with the few stars he has. The new ring in Worcester was dedicated Saturday night, and before an immense crowd the home team succumbed to Fall River by a one-sided score.

It is probable that Manager Phelan will land a good player or two in a day or two, and better things may be expected of the team.

There will be no game at Infantry Hall to-night, as the hall has been let for another purpose, and the game scheduled for to-night will be played later, probably on a Saturday afternoon. The Grays will take a rest, as will the Worcesters, who were originally scheduled to play the game.

Williams of the Brocktons leads in goal-making with 34 and has a considerable advantage over Lincoln, the second man, who has scored 28 times. Lewis and Hart are tied for third place with 26 each, and Curtis and Harkins are tied for fourth with 23 apiece.

Duggan has a long lead in taking rushes and has beaten his opponent to the spot 94 times. Hart holds second place with 59 and Lewis is close behind with 58. Taylor has got there first an even 50 times. Holderness is the champion foul maker and has been penalized 12 times so far this season, while Saunders is a close second with nine.

Pence, by some grand work in the goal circle last week, advanced to first place among the goaltends with an average of .908. Sutherland holds second place with .902, this pair being the only ones over the .900 mark. The averages:

RUSHES TAKEN.

Duggan	94	Loxon	20
Hart	59	Fahrner	16
Lewis	58	Curtis	15
Long	58	Harkins	12
Taylor	50	Williams	7
Quigley	34	Cunningham, Sr.	3
Lincoln	31	Mercer	1
McCarthy	27		

GOALS SCORED.

Williams	34	Lyons	9
Lincoln	28	Mercer	9
Lewis	26	Hardy	8
Hart	26	Fahrner	6
Harkins	23	Cunningham, Sr.	6
Curtis	23	Harrold	6
Duggan	21	Fahey	[illegible]
Quigley	21	Welch	4
Pierce	18	Menard	4
Jean	17	Miller	4
Taylor	15	Hickey	2
McGilvray	13	Cunningham, Jr.	2
McCarthy	12	Holderness	1
Roberts	11	Doherty	1
Long	11	Griffith	1
Bone	11	Cameron	1
Loxon	11	Whatmough	1
Mansfield	10	Shaughnessy	1
Thompson	10		

FOULS MADE.

Holderness	12	Fahey	2
Saunders	9	Mullen	1
Hardy	7	Hickey	1
Griffith	6	Harrold	1
O'Brien	4	Duggan	1
Gardner	4	Roberts	1
Doherty	3	Jean	1
Menard	3	Long	1
Lincoln	2	Lyons	1
Carrigan	2	Mercer	1
Foley	2	Miller	1
Dufresne	2	Hart	1
Cameron	2	Bone	1
Taylor	2	Loxon	1

GOALTENDS' AVERAGES.

	Stopped.	Missed.	P.C.
Pence	496	50	.908
Sutherland	461	50	.902
Rannon	466	52	.899
Mullen	405	46	.898
Sutton	436	55	.888
Cusick	338	44	.885
Harper	515	72	.877
Mallory	414	62	.870

CITY POLO LEAGUE AVERAGES.

Covill and Oldham Divide Honors in Goal Making.

The averages for the second week of the City Polo League show a slight change in the standing of the players. Davis, the speedy rusher of the Rogan team, has a lead of four points over Covill in taking rushes, with Rabbitt a close third.

Covill and Oldham are tied for first place in scoring goals, both rushers having caged the opposing goal guardians five times. Tom Carroll has first place in making fouls, the lanky halfback having been penalized four times for getting strangle holds on opponents.

The race for the high honors in guarding the cages promises to be a close one this season, as the players are showing better form in driving the pill at the coops. Flynn holds first place with a fine percentage of .901, while Blount is close after him with .881. Friday evening the Gilland and Puritan teams will play and on Saturday evening Alco will clash with St. Teresas. The averages:

RUSHES TAKEN.

Davis	16	Clancy	5
Covill	12	Wallace	3
Rabbitt	10	Connolly	2

GOALS MADE.

Covill	5	Pierce	2
Oldham	5	Rabbitt	2
Davis	4	Alexander	2
Kehoe	3	Clancy	1
Connolly	3	H. Carroll	1
Wallace	2	Brown	1

FOULS.

T. Carroll	4	Allard	1
Connolly	1	H. Carroll	1
Oldham	1		

GOALTENDS' AVERAGES.

	Stopped.	Missed.	P.C.
Flynn	64	7	.901
Blount	37	5	.881
Allard	32	6	.842
Anderson	35	8	.814
W. Carroll	19	6	.760

HARVARD WON HORSESHOE GAME.

So Declares M. E. Webb of Saturday's Contest at Cambridge.

Melville E. Webb, Jr., the football expert of the Boston Globe, has this to say of Saturday's Brown game at Harvard: "The Harvard football team, which has had things pretty much its own way this season, ran up against a snag yesterday in the eleven that Ed Robinson brought up to Soldiers Field from Brown University.

"Harvard won the game, 12 to 0, but was mighty lucky to get away with the victory at all. Almost at the end of the first half, in which Harvard once was held for downs on Brown's five-yard mark, the Crimson players recovered the ball on Brown's 11-yard line on a muffed kick, and then pushed across for a touchdown.

"Later, in the second half, after Brown had made a wonderful journey down the field for 88 yards on 16 plays, three of which were successful forward passes, Graustein, a Harvard halfback, intercepted a forward pass on the Crimson's six-yard line and then ran the entire length of the field for another score.

"In a way, it was horseshoe football for Harvard.

"There were times in the game when Brown's sense of following the ball, which is so important in the new game, was much keener than Harvard's, but the Crimson players took advantage of Brown's mistakes just at the right moments, and profited by them.

"At the same time, however, there was not 12 points, or two touchdowns, difference in the strength of the teams as they played yesterday, and the Brown team rightfully returned to Providence feeling that it had lost another opportunity to hold the Cambridge team to a tie score.

"Until the last period Brown was on the defensive all the time. The play was continually on its side of the field, Harvard, although several times within striking distance, was unable to reach the goal line. All this time Brown used straight line plays in its attack, and it was not until it began its long journey down the field that the strength and variety of its rushing game was exposed.

"It was a great game for the rushlines. The Brown line men were the strongest and the best coached that the Crimson forwards have met this year. The Brown right wing and centre really outplayed the Harvard left wing all the afternoon, and after Capt. Withington had retired from the Harvard right flank the Providence left wing was more than on a par with its opposites.

"Harvard had some plays than went with all the fire, speed and effectiveness shown in the earlier games, but Brown was quick to analyze the play and presented a rushline defence that at times was overpowering."

No Trades with Cincinnati.

Philadelphia, Oct. 23.—Horace Fogel is at home, while Dooin is in Chicago, but the President of the Phillies says his manager would not trade Grant or Doolan to Cincinnati for Lobert without first consulting him. Looks like no deal.

The Sporting World

BOXING BASEBALL CYCLING YACHTING

PHILADELPHIA ATHLETICS WINNERS OF WORLD'S BASEBALL CHAMPIONSHIP

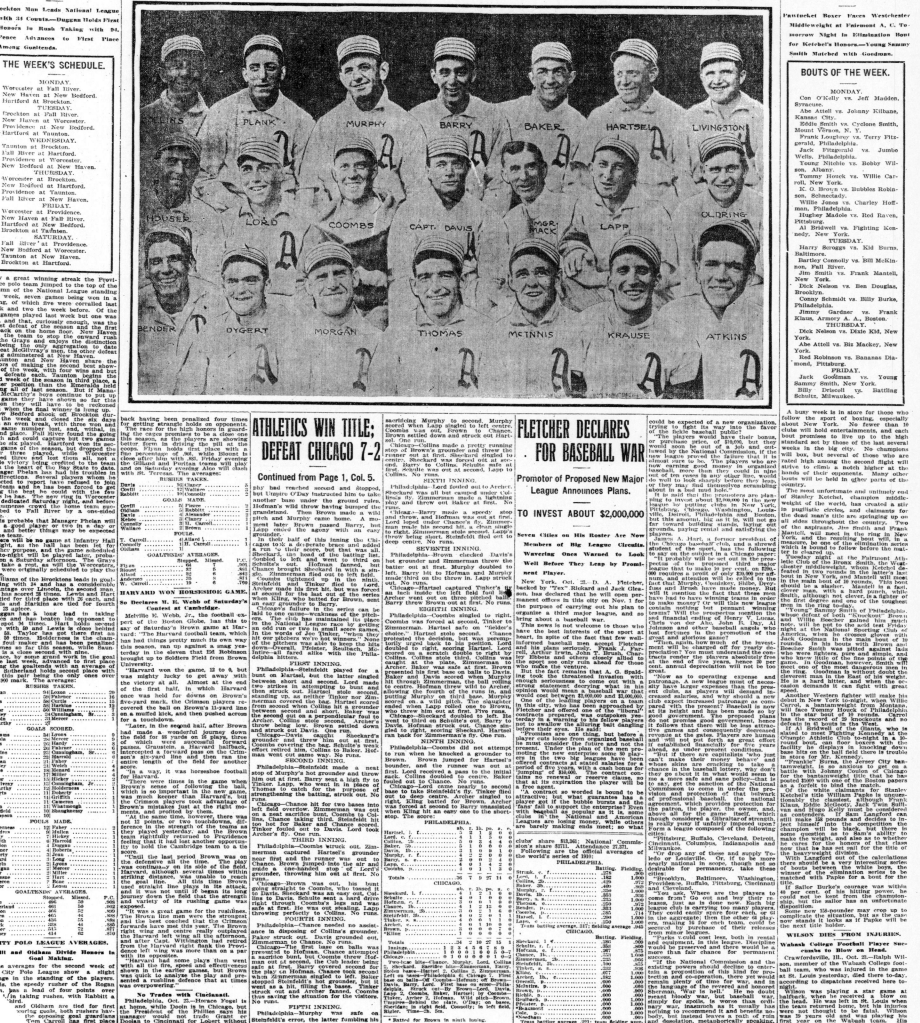

ATHLETICS WIN TITLE; DEFEAT CHICAGO 7-2

Continued from Page 1, Col. 5.

phy had reached second and stopped, but Umpire O'Day instructed him to take another base under the ground rules. Hofman's wild throw having bumped the grandstand. Then Brown made a wild pitch and Murphy came home. A moment later Brown passed Barry, but Lapp ended the agony with an easy grounder.

In their half of this inning the Chicagos took a desperate brace and added a run to their score, but that was all. Sheckard, the head of the batting list, doubled to left and went to third on Schulte's out. Hofman fanned, but Chance brought Sheckard in with a single. Zimmerman flied out to left field.

Coombs tightened up in the ninth. Steinfeldt and Tinker flied to Lord. Archer made his first hit, but was forced at second for the last out of the series when Kling, who batted for Brown, sent an easy grounder to Barry.

Chicago's failure in the series can be laid to one cause—weakness of the pitchers. The club has maintained its place in the National League race by getting an odd run or two in small score games. In the words of Joe Tinker, "when they hit our pitchers we're not winners." None of the pitchers was able to keep the hits down—Overall, Pfeister, Reulbach, McIntire—all fared alike with the Philadelphia hitters.

FIRST INNING.

Philadelphia—Steinfeldt played for a bunt on Hartsel, but the latter singled between short and second. Lord made two strikes in attempting to bunt and then struck out. Hartsel stole second, standing up, as neither Tinker nor Zimmerman covered the bag. Hartsel scored from second when Collins hit a grounder between second and short. Baker was the second out on a perpendicular foul to Archer. Collins stole second, Archer's throw being low. Brown settled down and struck out Davis. One run.

Chicago—Davis caught Sheckard's grounder and threw him out at first, Coombs covering the bag. Schulte's weak effort retired him, Collins to Baker. Hofman went out same way. No runs.

SECOND INNING.

Philadelphia—Steinfeldt made a neat stop of Murphy's hot grounder and threw him out at first. Barry sent a high fly to Tinker. Lapp, who went in in place of Thomas to catch for the purpose of strengthening the batting, struck out. No runs.

Chicago—Chance hit for two bases into left field overflow. Zimmerman was out on a neat sacrifice bunt, Coombs to Collins, Chance taking third. Steinfeldt hit too hot for Baker and Chance scored. Tinker fouled out to Davis. Lord took Archer's fly. One run.

THIRD INNING.

Philadelphia—Coombs struck out. Zimmerman captured Hartsel's grounder near first and the runner was out to Chance. Brown jumped into the air and made a one-handed stop of Lord's grounder, throwing him out at first. No runs.

Chicago—Brown was out, his bunt going straight to Coombs, who tossed it to Davis. Sheckard was an easy out, Collins to Davis. Schulte sent a hard drive right through Coombs's legs and was safe at first. He was out stealing, Lapp throwing perfectly to Collins. No runs.

FOURTH INNING.

Philadelphia—Chance needed no assistance in disposing of Collins's grounder. Baker struck out. Davis grounded out, Zimmerman to Chance. No runs.

Chicago—The first base on balls was presented to Hofman. Chance attempted a sacrifice bunt, but Coombs threw Hofman out at second, the Cub leader being safe at first. Barry covered second for the play on Hofman. Chance took second when Zimmerman singled to left. Baker stopped Steinfeldt's hot grounder, but it went as a hit, filling the bases. Tinker struck out and Archer fanned, Coombs thus saving the situation for the visitors. No runs.

FIFTH INNING.

Philadelphia—Murphy was safe on Steinfeldt's error, the latter fumbling his grounder. Barry was out to Chance, sacrificing Murphy to second. Murphy scored when Lapp singled to left centre. Coombs was out, Brown to Chance. Brown settled down and struck out Hartsel. One run.

Chicago—Collins made a pretty running stop of Brown's grounder and threw the runner out at first. Sheckard singled to centre. Sheckard was forced out at second, Barry to Collins. Schulte safe at first. Schulte was out at second, Lapp to Collins. No runs.

SIXTH INNING.

Philadelphia—Lord fouled out to Archer. Sheckard was all but camped under Collins's fly. Zimmerman made a lightning play and threw out Baker at first. No runs.

Chicago—Barry made a speedy stop and throw, and Hofman was out at first. Lord loped under Chance's fly. Zimmerman made his second hit, a clean single to right. Zimmerman stole second. Lapp's throw being short. Steinfeldt flied out to deep centre. No runs.

SEVENTH INNING.

Philadelphia—Brown checked Davis's hot grounder and Zimmerman threw the batter out at first. Murphy doubled to left. Barry hit to Hofman and Murphy made third on the throw in. Lapp struck out. No runs.

Chicago—Hartsel captured Tinker's fly an inch inside the left field foul line. Archer went out on three pitched balls. Barry threw Brown out at first. No runs.

EIGHTH INNING.

Philadelphia—Coombs singled to right. Coombs was forced at second, Tinker to Zimmerman. Hartsel safe on "fielder's choice." Hartsel stole second. Chance protested the decision, but was peremptorily urged back to his position. Lord doubled to right, scoring Hartsel. Lord scored on a scratch double to right by Collins. Collins stole third. Collins was caught at the plate, Zimmerman to Archer. Baker was safe at first. Brown presented his first base on balls to Davis. Baker and Davis scored when Murphy hit through Zimmerman, the ball rolling to centre. Hofman threw wild to Archer, allowing the fourth of the runs in, and putting Murphy on third base. Murphy scored on a wild pitch. The slaughter ended when Lapp rolled one to Brown, who threw him out at first. Five runs.

Chicago—Sheckard doubled to left. He went to third on Schulte's out. Barry to Davis. Hofman struck out. Chance singled to right, scoring Sheckard. Hartsel ran back for Zimmerman's fly. One run.

NINTH INNING.

Philadelphia—Coombs did not attempt to run when he knocked a grounder to Brown. Brown jumped for Hartsel's bounder, and the runner was out at first. Lord received a pass to the initial sack. Collins doubled to centre. Baker fouled out to Chance. No runs.

Chicago—Lord came nearly to second base to take Steinfeldt's fly. Tinker flied out to deep centre. Archer singled to right. Kling batted for Brown. Archer was forced at second to Barry unassisted when Kling hit an easy one to the shortstop. The score:

PHILADELPHIA.

	ab.	r.	1b.	po.	a.	e.
Hartsel, l. f.	5	2	1	2	0	0
Lord, c. f.	4	1	1	5	0	0
Collins, 2b	5	0	3	4	4	0
Baker, 3b	5	1	0	0	0	0
Davis, 1b	3	1	0	9	1	0
Murphy, r. f.	4	2	2	0	0	0
Barry, s. s.	2	0	0	2	4	0
Lapp, c.	4	0	1	4	2	0
Coombs, p.	4	0	1	1	3	0
Totals	36	7	9	27	14	0

CHICAGO.

	ab.	r.	1b.	po.	a.	e.
Sheckard, l. f.	4	1	2	1	0	0
Schulte	4	0	1	0	0	0
Hofman, c. f.	3	0	0	1	0	0
Chance, 1b.	4	1	2	13	0	0
Zimmerman, 2b	3	0	2	1	6	0
Steinfeldt, 3b	4	0	2	0	1	1
Tinker, s. s.	4	0	0	1	1	0
Archer, c.	4	0	1	10	0	0
Brown, p.	3	0	0	0	7	0
*Kling	1	0	0	0	0	0
Totals	34	2	10	27	15	1

Innings	1	2	3	4	5	6	7	8	9	
Philadelphia	1	0	0	0	1	0	0	5	0	—7
Chicago	0	1	0	0	0	0	0	1	0	—2

Two-base hits—Chance, Murphy, Lord, Collins 2, Sheckard. Sacrifice hits—Zimmerman, Barry. Stolen bases—Hartsel 2, Collins 2, Zimmerman. Left on bases—Philadelphia 6; Chicago 7. First base on balls—Off Coombs—Hofman; off Brown—Davis, Barry, Lord. First base on error—Philadelphia. Struck out—By Brown—Lord, Davis, Lapp 2, Coombs, Baker, Hartsel; by Coombs—Tinker, Archer 2, Hofman. Wild pitch—Brown. Umpires—Behind the plate, O'Day; on bases, Sheridan; in right field, Connolly; in left field, Rigler. Time—2h. 5m.

* Batted for Brown in ninth inning.

Receipts, $37,116; players' share $20,042; clubs' share $13,361; National Commission's share $3711. Attendance 27,371.

Following are the official averages of the world's series of 1910:

PHILADELPHIA.

	Batting.	Fielding.
Strunk, c. f.	.278	.900
Lord, l. f.	.182	1.000
Collins, 2b	.429	.972
Baker, 3b	.409	.869
Murphy, r. f.	.350	1.000
Davis, 1b	.353	.936
Barry, s. s.	.235	1.000
Thomas, c.	.250	.972
Bender, p.	.333	1.000
Coombs, p.	.385	.714
Harsel, l. f.	.200	1.000
Lapp, c.	.250	1.000

Team batting average .317; fielding average .945

CHICAGO.

	Batting.	Fielding.
Sheckard, l. f.	.286	.909
Schulte, r. f.	.353	.800
Hofman, c. f.	.267	.875
Chance, 1b.	.353	1.000
Zimmerman, 2b.	.235	.966
Steinfeldt, 3b.	.100	.875
Tinker, s. s.	.333	.926
Kling, c.	.077	1.000
Archer, 1b., c.	.182	1.000
Overall, p.	.000	.000
McIntire, p.	.000	.666
Brown, p.	.000	.909
Richie, p.	.000	.000
Reulbach, p.	.000	1.000
Pfeister, p.	.000	1.000
*Beaumont	.000	.000
Cole, p.	.000	1.000
*Needham	.000	.000

Team batting average .221; team fielding average .954.

FLETCHER DECLARES FOR BASEBALL WAR

Promotor of Proposed New Major League Announces Plans.

TO INVEST ABOUT $2,000,000

Seven Cities on His Roster Are Now Members of Big League Circuits. Wavering Ones Warned to Look Well Before They Leap by Prominent Player.

New York, Oct. 23.—D. A. Fletcher, backed by "Tex" Rickard and Jack Gleason, has declared that he will open permanent offices in this city on Nov. 1 for the purpose of carrying out his plan to organize a third major league, and so bring about a baseball war.

This news is not welcome to those who have the best interests of the sport at heart, in spite of the fact that few well-informed baseball men accept Fletcher and his plans seriously. Frank J. Farrell, Arthur Irwin, John T. Brush, Charley Ebbets and others closely allied to the sport see only ruin ahead for those who make the venture.

But the fact remains that A. G. Spalding took the threatened invasion with enough seriousness to come out with a strong statement decrying what in his opinion would mean a baseball war that would cost between $2,000,000 and $3,000,000.

One of the leading players on a team in this city, who has been approached by Fletcher and offered one of the "liberal" contracts prepared, was outspoken yesterday in a warning to his fellow players not to swallow the alluring bait dangling before their eyes. He said:

"Promises are one thing, but before a player cuts loose from organized baseball he must consider the future and not the present. Under the plan of the men promoting the new enterprise some 80 players in the two big leagues have been offered contracts at stated salaries for a period of five years, with a cash bonus for 'jumping' of $10,000. The contract contains no renewal or reserve clause, so that at its expiration the player will be a free agent.

"A contract so worded is bound to be attractive; but what guarantee has a player got if the bubble bursts and the 'fans' fail to support the enterprise? Even with baseball as popular as it is, some clubs in the National and American Leagues are losing money, while others are barely making ends meet; so what could be expected of a new organization, trying to fight its way into the favor of the fickle baseball public?

"The players would have their bonus, or purchase price, of $10,000, but they would soon be out of a job and outlawed by the National Commission, if the new league proved the failure that it is almost sure to be. The players who are now earning good money in organized baseball, more than they could in nine out of ten cases in any other line, would do well to look sharply before they leap, or they may find themselves scrambling about in a bad mud hole."

It is said that the promoters are planning to invest about $2,000,000 in the new league by putting clubs in New York, Pittsburg, Chicago, Washington, Louisville, Detroit, Philadelphia and Boston, but this amount, big as it is, will not go far toward building stands, laying out grounds, paying rental and satisfying the players.

James A. Hart, a former president of the Chicago baseball club, and a shrewd student of the sport, has the following to say on the subject in a Chicago paper:

"It probably will be set out in the prospectus of the proposed third major league that to make 10 per cent. on $200,000 requires a profit of only $20,000 per annum, and attention will be called to the fact that Murphy, Comiskey, Shibe, Dreyfuss and Brush have made money. But will it mention the fact that these men have had to have winning teams in order to make money? Or will this new league contain nothing but pennant winning teams? Will the prospectus mention the sad financial ending of Henry V. Lucas, Chris von der Ahe, John B. Day, Al Johnson and other baseball angels who lost fortunes in the promotion of the great and glorious game?

"Then, again, how much of the investment will be charged off for yearly depreciation? You must understand the contracts render the players absolutely free at the end of five years, hence 20 per cent. annual depreciation will not be too great.

"Now as to operating expense and patronage. A new league must of necessity have larger expenses than the present clubs, as players will demand increased salaries, and why should a new club expect increased patronage as compared with the present? Baseball is now at its height and has been made so by good government. The proposed plans do not promise good government, hence it follows that there will be less attractive games and consequently decreased revenue at the gates. Players are human and will not put forth as great effort if established financially for five years ahead, as under present conditions.

"But if there are capitalists 'who just can't make their money behave' and whose skins are cracking to take a chance in the baseball lottery, why don't they go about it in what would seem to me a more safe and sane policy—that is to say, get the sanction of the National Commission to come in under the provision and protection of that bulwark of professional baseball, the national agreement, which provides protection for the patron, the player, the owner, and, above all for the game itself, which though considered a Gibraltar of strength, is really puny if unfairly imposed upon? Form a league composed of the following cities:

"Pittsburg, Buffalo, Cleveland, Detroit, Cincinnati, Columbus, Indianapolis and Milwaukee.

"Or drop any of these and supply Toledo or Louisville. Or, if to be more nearly national in scope, though not so desirable for permanency, take these cities:

"Brooklyn, Baltimore, Washington, Providence, Buffalo, Pittsburg, Cincinnati and Cleveland.

"You ask, Where are the players to come from? Go out and buy their releases, just as is done now. Each big league club is carrying too many players. They could easily spare four each, or 64 in the aggregate; then the other 64 players, making 16 for each team, could be secured by purchase of their releases from minor leagues.

"Parks would cost less, both in rental and equipment, in this league. Discipline would be preserved and there would be a more than fair chance for permanent success.

"If the National Commission and the existing powers should decline to entertain a proposition of this kind for protection and co-operation, there yet would remain plenty of time for war, and in the language of the revered and honored Sherman, 'War is hell.' He no doubt meant bloody war, but baseball war, simply for spoils, is worse than ordinary war, inasmuch as it usually has nothing to recommend it and benefits nobody, but instead leaves a path of ruin and desolation, metaphorically speaking, which takes years to repair."

BUSY WEEK PROMISED FOR RING FOLLOWERS

Clubs All Over Country Have Matches Carded for Next 6 Days.

MANTELL MEETS JIM SMITH

Pawtucket Boxer Faces Westchester Middleweight at Fairmont A. C. To-morrow Night in Elimination Bout for Ketchel's Honors.—Young Sammy Smith Matched with Goodman.

BOUTS OF THE WEEK.

MONDAY.
Con O'Kelly vs. Jeff Madden, Syracuse.
Abe Attell vs. Johnny Kilbane, Kansas City.
Eddie Smith vs. Cyclone Smith, Mount Vernon, N. Y.
Frank Loughrey vs. Terry Fitzgerald, Philadelphia.
Jack Fitzgerald vs. Jumbo Wells, Philadelphia.
Young Nitchie vs. Bobby Wilson, Albany.
Tommy Houck vs. Willie Carroll, New York.
K. O. Brown vs. Bubbles Robinson, Schnectady.
Willie Jones vs. Charley Hoffman, Philadelphia.
Hughey Madole vs. Red Raven, Pittsburg.
Al Bridwell vs. Fighting Kennedy, New York.

TUESDAY.
Harry Scroggs vs. Kid Burns, Baltimore.
Bartley Connolly vs. Bill McKinnon, Fall River.
Jim Smith vs. Frank Mantell, New York.
Dick Nelson vs. Ben Douglas, Brooklyn.
Conny Schmidt vs. Billy Burke, Philadelphia.
Jimmy Gardner vs. Frank Klaus, Armory A. A., Boston.

THURSDAY.
Dick Nelson vs. Dixie Kid, New York.
Abe Attell vs. Biz Mackey, New York.
Red Robinson vs. Bananas Diamond, Pittsburg.

FRIDAY.
Jack Goodman vs. Young Sammy Smith, New York.
Billy Driscoll vs. Battling Schultz, Milwaukee.

A busy week is in store for those who follow the sport of boxing, especially about New York. No fewer than 10 clubs will hold entertainments, and each bout promises to live up to the high standard set by those of the last several weeks in the big city. No champions will box, but several of those who are rated high among the second flight will strive to climb a notch higher at the hands of their opponents. Many other bouts will be held in other parts of the country.

The most unfortunate and untimely end of Stanley Ketchel, champion middleweight of the world, has created a stir in pugilistic circles, and claimants for the dead man's title are springing up on all sides throughout the country. Two of the aspirants, Jim Smith and Frank Mantell, will meet in the ring in New York, and the resulting bout will, in a measure, be one of the elimination series which is bound to follow before the matter is cleared up.

Tuesday night at the Fairmont Athletic Club of the Bronx Smith, the Westchester middleweight, whom Ketchel defeated in two rounds in the latter's last bout in New York, and Mantell will meet in the main bout of 10 rounds. This bout should be a slasher. Mantell is a fast, clever man, with a hard punch, while Smith, although not clever, is a fighter of the first degree and one of the toughest men in the ring to-day.

"Young" Sammy Smith of Philadelphia, whose defeat of both "Knockout" Brown and Willie Beecher gained him much note, will be put to the acid test Friday night at the National Sporting Club of America, when he crosses gloves with Jack Goodman in the main bout of 10 rounds. In his bouts with Brown and Beecher Smith was pitted against lads who were fighters, pure and simple, and who knew little of the fine points of the game. In Goodman, however, Smith will meet one of the most dangerous men in the ring. Goodman is without doubt the cleverest man in the East of his weight. He is a hard hitter, and when the occasion demands it can fight with great speed.

Another Western fighter will make his debut in New York to-night, when Willie Carrol, a bantamweight from Montana, will face Tommy Houck of Philadelphia in the star bout of 10 rounds. Carrol has the record of 29 knockouts and no defeats in 41 bouts in the West.

If Al Bridwell of the Giants, who is slated to meet Fighting Kennedy at the Olympic Athletic Club to-night in a 10-round bout, can floor boxers with the facility he displays in knocking down base hits on the ball field there is trouble in store for Mr. Kennedy.

"Frankie" Burns, the Jersey City bantamweight, is so anxious to get on a battle with Johnny Coulon of Chicago for the bantamweight title that he has posted $1000 with one of the Boston papers as a forfeit to bind the match.

Of the white claimants for Stanley Ketchel's title William Papke is unquestionably the classiest, although Frank Klaus, Eddie McGooty, Jack Twin Sullivan and Hugo Kelly must be considered as contenders. If Sam Langford can still make 158 pounds and decides to inject himself into the competition the champion will be black, but there is some question as to Sam's ability to make the weight, and also as to whether he cares for the honors of that class now that he has set sail for the title of the heavyweight division.

With Langford out of the calculations there should be a very interesting series of bouts between the white boys, the winner of the elimination series to be matched with Papke for a bout for the title.

If Sailor Burke's courage was within 40 per cent. of his hitting power, he could not be kept from the championship, but the sailor has an unfortunate disposition.

Some new 158-pounder may crop up to complicate the situation, but as the case now stands it looks as if Papke will be the next title holder.

WILSON DIES FROM INJURIES.

Wabash College Football Player Succumbs to Blow on Head.

Crawfordsville, Ill., Oct. 23.—Ralph Wilson, member of the Wabash College football team, who was injured in the game at St. Louis yesterday, died there to-day, according to dispatches received here to-night.

Wilson was playing a star game at halfback, when he received a blow on the head. He was left in St. Louis when the team returned home, but his injuries were not thought to be fatal. Wilson was 19 years old and was playing his first year on the Wabash team. His home was in this city.

The Detroit Free Press
SPORTING SECTION

TIGES SLAY ELEPHANTS

Athletics Are Beaten Back Under Volley of Hits of All Classifications—Coombs Lasts Less Than Two Innings.

COBB LEADS IN THE TERRIFIC BATFEST

Leaders Secure Seventeen Hits for a Total of Thirty-one Bases—Three Hurlers Buried in the Wreck.

BY E. A. BATCHELOR.

Philadelphia, Pa., August 1.—Connie Mack's system of selecting pitchers at last has been discovered. The lean leader of the waning world's champions picks the deceivers like a woman picks winners at the race track—by jabbing a hatpin in the score card. Connie's hand must have slipped when he chose Jack Coombs today, for the Colby man gave about as bad an exhibition as the Tigers have been able to enjoy this season. The only unpleasant thing about the whole afternoon's merriment was that Connie wouldn't let Jack stay on view longer. At the most hilarious moment of a screaming second inning the hero of the world's series was dethroned and a mere stripling, Martin by name, was substituted.

Martin didn't exactly stop the Tigers, but he toned them down so that runs instead of coming in bevies filtered across the plate one at a time. Martin was making his debut on the home grounds though he is not a stranger to the Tigers, having faced them in one of the games of that big series last month after somebody else had been peppered. In the last inning Connie sent another of the fraternity brothers to the slab, this one being Danforth, who comes from a small Texas college. There was no particular reason for his appearing at this time except that Connie figured nothing could be lost and the game might end a little quicker with a change of cannoneers.

All Fared Alike.

From the trio of boxmen the Tigers took just 13 runs, while the Athletics total harvest amounted to but six, three of which were practically gifts, while the others were the result of a collection of much hammering in the third inning, the only period in the day that Summers looked anything but strong. As Eddie was some 10 runs to the good at this point there was really no cause for alarm over the earnest efforts of the Macks to give their friends a little action.

By consulting the summary the gentle reader will find that all of the Tigers' blows were not of the spare type of singles. Two doubles, three triples and a pair of home runs added to ten of the smaller denomination, brought the total of bases up to 31, which really isn't so bad for a club that is fighting on hostile shores. There were a few bases on balls and some errors to help out, beside the hitting. The Tigers scored in each of the first five innings and hit safely up to the eighth.

Everything but the second chapter might have been omitted without altering the result, for the Tigers got more in this inning than the Mackmen could accumulate altogether. This was one of those innings—Bennett park regulars know the kind—when outfielders drop from exhaustion and infielders refuse to risk their lives in front of cannon ball liners. The judicious mixture of two bases on balls, two triples, a home run and three singles acounted for seven tallies. There might have been more but for the retirement of Coombs in the midst of the entertainment, only one run being scored after Martin went to the front to save the remnants of his club's honor.

Typical Batting Orgie.

This was a period of hitting that even the Tigers, known for their frightful orgies with the flail, seldom have duplicated. Every one of the hits was clean, and in most cases the batsman jumped on the first ball handed him. It was a thing of joy to those few in the stands who were pulling for the visitors, and must have impressed, even if it didn't delight, the Mackmen's partisans.

Connie's people themselves had one inning in which they raised some rumpus, four doubles and a single—giving them three well-earned runs. But for a great one-hand catch by Bush, who speared a triple in its infancy and started a double play, at least six and possibly more runs would have been scored. The hit butchery occurred after the third double, and it cut off one man who would have registered instanter and another who would have been in a position to profit by subsequent whalings. Aside from this round, Summers had the home push groping around like moles trying to locate his knuckle ball. Two of the other three runs were a present from Captain Moriarty, who happened to cut loose a throw that was a corker for distance but that needed some corrections in the altitude and windage.

Several times the Mackmen opened innings by getting men on first or second, only to see them perish without denting the last base. When the "chief" really extended himself, he looked as strong as on Friday, though there never was the inspiration for the sort of efforts that marked his unfortunate opening here.

Cobb's Work Marvelous.

Ty Cobb has been promising to show the Philadelphia fans some of the Georgia special brand of offensive play ever since he came here and today he made good his promises. The Peach faced Coombs twice and Martin twice. First time up he cracked out a triple. Then came a homer, with two men on. A modest single was all that he cared for the third time. Then he walked so that he could have the pleasure of stealing the next two pillows. It looked as though the Peach intended to advance on the plate by the same method, but Delahanty forestalled this enterprise by combing a double to left.

Ty showed himself a sportsman by retiring after the fifth inning, so that the Athletics might have a

Continued on Page Ten.

TY COBB POSES EXCLUSIVELY FOR THE DETROIT FREE PRESS.

—Copyright, 1911, by C. M. Hayes & Co.

The Georgian's wonderful work at bat and in the field has earned for him an undying reputation as the greatest baseball player who ever lived. His feats on the diamond are unparalleled and his name is a household word where the game still is in its infancy.

GEE! AINT THIS GREAT?

DETROIT.

	AB	R	H	TB	BB	SH	SB	PO	A	E
Jones, l. f.	4	2	1	1	2	0	2	3	0	0
Bush, s. s.	5	2	2	3	1	0	0	4	6	0
Cobb, c. f.	3	3	3	8	1	0	2	1	0	0
Schaller, c. f.	2	0	0	0	0	0	0	3	0	0
Crawford, r. f.	6	1	2	5	0	0	0	1	0	0
Delahanty, 1b.	5	2	3	6	0	0	0	11	0	0
Moriarty, 3b.	5	1	2	4	0	0	0	0	2	2
O'Leary, 2b.	3	1	1	1	1	0	0	4	5	0
Stanage, c.	5	0	1	1	0	0	0	0	1	0
Summers, p.	4	1	2	2	0	1	0	0	2	0
Totals	42	13	17	31	5	1	4	27	16	2

PHILADELPHIA.

	AB	R	H	TB	BB	SH	SB	PO	A	E
Lord, l. f.	5	0	2	5	0	0	0	2	0	0
Oldring, c. f.	5	1	2	2	0	0	0	3	0	0
Collins, 2b.	4	1	2	3	0	1	0	2	1	0
Baker, 3b.	4	0	1	1	0	0	0	1	2	1
Barry, s. s.	4	0	1	2	0	0	0	1	3	1
Murphy, r. f.	3	0	1	1	1	0	0	1	0	0
McInnes, 1b.	4	0	0	0	0	0	0	10	0	0
Lapp, c.	2	1	1	2	0	0	0	5	0	0
Livingstone, c.	1	1	0	0	0	0	0	2	0	0
Coombs, p.	0	0	0	0	0	0	0	0	0	0
Martin, p.	3	2	1	2	0	0	0	0	3	0
Danforth, p.	0	0	0	0	0	0	0	0	0	0
*Strunk	1	0	0	0	0	0	0	0	0	0
Totals	36	6	11	18	1	1	0	27	9	2

*Batted for Danforth in the ninth.

Innings	1	2	3	4	5	6	7	8	9
Detroit	2	7	1	1	1	0	1	0	0—13
Philadelphia	0	0	3	0	0	0	3	0	0— 6

Hits—Off Coombs, 9 in 1 2-3 innings; off Martin, 8 in 6 1-3 innings. Two-base hits—Bush, Delahanty, Lord, Collins, Lapp, Barry, Martin. Three-base hits—Cobb, Delahanty, Moriarty, Lord. Home runs—Cobb, Crawford. Struck out—By Martin 4; by Danforth 1. Bases on balls—Off Summers 1; off Coombs 1; off Martin 3; off Danforth 1. Double plays—Bush, O'Leary and Delahanty; Bush and O'Leary. Left on bases—Detroit 9; Philadelphia 6. Hit by pitched ball—By Martin (O'Leary); by Summers (Livingstone). Time, 1:50. Umpires, Egan and Connolly.

PIRATES' STREAK STILL UNBROKEN

Pittsburg Makes It Thirteen Straight Victories by Beating Boston in Last of Series.

Pittsburg, August 1.—In a featureless game today Pittsburg won from Boston, 10 to 2. It was the local team's thirteenth straight victory. Score:

PITTSBURG.	AB	H	O	A	E	BOSTON.	AB	H	O	A	E
Byrne,3..	5	1	0	3	1	Swee'y,2.	4	0	2	2	0
Leach,m.	4	2	5	0	0	Tenney,1.	4	0	5	0	1
Carey,l..	4	3	4	0	0	Pfeffer,1.	1	0	0	0	0
Wagner,s	4	1	0	4	2	Kaiser,l..	3	1	5	0	0
J.Miller,2	2	2	6	3	0	Ing'ton,3.	4	0	0	2	0
McKe'e,1	4	1	10	0	0	Spratt,s..	3	1	2	2	2
Wilson,r.	4	1	0	0	0	RMil'r,m	3	1	2	0	0
Simon,c..	4	0	2	1	0	Flah'ty,r	4	1	2	0	0
Ferry,p..	3	2	0	0	0	Kling,c..	3	1	6	2	1
						Matt'n,p.	3	1	0	1	0
Totals..	34	13	27	11	3	Totals..	32	6	24	9	4

Innings	1	2	3	4	5	6	7	8	9
Pittsburg	1	0	5	0	1	3	0	0	*—10
Boston	0	0	1	0	0	0	0	1	0— 2

Runs—Byrne 2, Leach 3, Carey 2, J. Miller, McKechnie, Ferry—10; Tenney, Kling—2. Two-base hits—Wilson, R. Miller, Kling. Three-base hits—Byrne, Carey, McKechnie. Home run—Carey. Sacrifice hit—Mattern. Sacrifice flies—Carey, J. Miller, R. Miller. Stolen bases—Leach 2, Spratt. Double play—Miller and McKechnie. First base on balls—Off Ferry 2, off Mattern 3. Wild pitch—Ferry. Left on bases—Pittsburg 6, Boston 9. First base on errors—Pittsburg 1, Boston 3. Time—1:50. Umpires—O'Day and Emslie.

REGATTA SURE TO BE SUCCESS

Entries Already Include Some of the Fastest Speedboats of the Great Lakes.

With the Van Bierk II., LaTrunda II., Disturber II., Leow Victor, Sand Burr II., Intruder II. and other speed boats entered in the events, the second annual regatta of the Great Lakes Power Boat league is assuming proportions beyond the fondest hopes of those who have the affair in charge. Some of the best speed and sport of its kind ever seen on the great lakes in all probability will be dished up Thursday, Friday and Saturday.

The raising of the Van Bierk II., which was accomplished yesterday, and the fact that her motor, which is an 80-horsepower Van Bierk model, is all right and will be ready to run as soon as it can be cleaned, which will take less than a day, means that there will be some very keen competition from the local end, as this boat is a speed marvel.

There are 11 organizations affiliated with the G. L. P. L., including Cleveland, Buffalo and Toledo, and it is expected that all of these clubs will be well represented in the events by their power boats. They also will send cruisers to compete in the event for that class of boats.

The Detroit Motor Boat club course is recognized as one of the best on the lakes and with the proper weather conditions some of the existing records are due to go by the boards.

Jeannette and Ross Draw.

New York, August 1.—Joe Jeannette, of Boston, and Tony Ross, of Pittsburg, fought ten fast rounds to a draw here tonight. Jeannette drew blood in the second round, but as the contest progressed Ross improved and forced the fighting in the later rounds.

Fight Still is on Over Stanley Robinson Estate

St. Louis, Mo., August 1.—F. N. Abercrombie filed a mandamus suit in the circuit court today against Probate Judge Holtcamp asking that he be compelled to appoint Abercrombie executor of the estate of M. Stanley Robinson, who was the owner of the St. Louis National baseball club. The suit follows an unsuccessful attempt of Abercrombie to have Judge Holtcamp appoint him executor.

MAGEE'S FATE IS STILL UNSETTLED

National Commission Deliberates Through Two Sessions Without Reaching Verdict.

Chicago, August 1.—Directors of the National Baseball league, after spending the day considering the appeal of Outfielder Sherwood Magee, of Philadelphia, who was suspended for an attack on Umpire Finneran, consumed a considerable portion of the night without deciding Magee's fate. After hearing numerous witnesses during the day, the board resumed its investigation tonight, and after several hours' discussion seemed no nearer an agreement than at the dinner adjournment.

The air of mystery and secrecy which accompanied the day session was maintained at night and members of the board declined to discuss the case. President Lynch, however, denied a rumor which gained ground that Magee was to be reinstated after an elaborate apology to Finneran.

Magee's teammates on the Philadelphia team, who had tarried here expecting to be called as witnesses, but who had cooled their heels all day in the hotel lobbies without being sent for, departed for Cincinnati at 9 o'clock. Soon afterwards Finneran and Umpire Rigler, who had officiated with Finneran on July 10, when the disturbance in the field took place, left for St. Louis, where they will officiate tomorrow.

FORT ERIE ENTRIES.

First race, 2-year-olds, maiden fillies, selling, 5 furlongs—Onrico, 105; Wood Dove, 105; Diamond Buckle, 105; Dorothy T., 105; Lady Eastman, 110; Yankee Lotus, 110; Long Ago, 110; Betsy Banks, 110.

Second race, 2-year-olds, colts and geldings, selling, 6 furlongs—Nottingham, 96; Eltoro, 102; Thirty Forty, 103; Mad River, 104; McCreary, 105; Tactics, 106; Slay Lad, 96.

Third race, 3-year-olds and up, handicap, Canadian owned, 1 1-16 miles—Caper Sauce, 102; Chief Kee, 112; Galatine, 130; Ta Nun Da, 121.

Fourth race, 3-year-olds and up, handicap, 1 3-16 miles—Aylmer, 97; Bob R., 101; Bourbon Beau, 105; Superstition, 105; Governor Gray, 112; Olambala, 120.

Fifth race, 3-year-olds and up, selling, 6 furlongs—Joe Galtens, 100; Towton Field, 100; Apple Prince, 101; Hand Running, 101; Lady Irma, 105; Little Father, 108; Rose Queen, 112; Cohort, 112; Beau Coup, 115; Campion, 115.

Sixth race, 4-year-olds and up, selling, 1 3-16 miles—Cheek, 99; Roman Wing, 101; Hang, 103; Third Rail, 104; Long Hand, 108; Topland, 108.

Seventh race, 3-year-olds, conditions, mile and 70 yards—Edda, 100; *Night Fall, 100; *Amalfi, 105; Red Wine, 105; Kormak, 105; Martin W. Littleton, 105; Rogon, 105. *Wilson" entry.

O'TOOLE STAYS WITH ST. PAUL

Report That He is to Join Pirates Friday is Unfounded, Says Kelly.

St. Paul, Minn., August 1.—"There's no chance of O'Toole's reporting to Pittsburg on Friday," said Manager Kelly of the St. Paul baseball club tonight, when told of a report that O'Toole would start shortly for Pittsburg.

"We refuse to contradict our previous statement that O'Toole will not leave us until the end of the season, or at least until St. Paul is completely out of the association running. O'Toole will pitch for St. Paul on Friday."

ADDITIONAL SPORTING NEWS ON PAGES 10 and 12

SEMI PRO BALL GETS A JOLTING

National Commission Slaps Fine on Brooklyn for Permitting Talent to Play Independently.

Cincinnati, O., August 1.—Because officers of the Brooklyn National league baseball club gave Pitcher Ragon permission to play in an exhibition game at Long Branch, N. J., on July 16, the club was fined $50 by the National Baseball commission today.

The rule under which this action was taken was made in the first place at the instance of President Ebbets of Brooklyn. It provides that National agreement players may appear only with the clubs holding their contracts, and was promulgated to prevent independent teams from obtaining major leaguers as attractions in opposition to regularly scheduled games.

Good Lucks Want Contest.

Good Lucks want a game for next Sunday with any strong city or state teams. For games call Ackerman's cafe.

$103.17 is All That's Left of Ketchel's Fortune

San Francisco, August 1.—All that is left of the fortune made in the prize ring by Stanley Ketchel, once middleweight champion, came to $103.17 when his estate was settled today in the probate court. The money will be forwarded to Kent county, Michigan.

AMERICAN ASS'N WILL PETITION

Magnates Draw Up Document Said to Have Bearing on Proposed Classification Clause.

Chicago, August 1.—Seven members of the American Association of Baseball Clubs and President T. M. Chivington of the organization, after several hours' wrangling in secret, reached a decision which resulted in the drawing up of a petition to be presented to Garry Herrmann, chairman of the National commission.

Members of the league refused to discuss the petition, but it is reported on good authority that it is based on a proposed classification clause which makes the price of a ball player not more than $5,000 when sale is contemplated to the major leagues.

Further information is that the American association is handicapped in purchasing a player from the minor leagues because of the present classification clause. It is said that this feature of the petition, if acted on favorably by the national body in baseball, will greatly assist the association team owners in drafting players.

The members of the organization who attended the secret session included President W. H. Watkins of Indianapolis; William Grayson, Louisvill!; E. M. Schoenborn, Columbus; Charles S. Havenor, Milwaukee; George Tebeau, Kansas City; George E. Lennon, St. Paul, and a proxy who represented M. E. Cantillon of Minneapolis. Mr. Armour of Toledo was not represented.

Reports were current that the association club owners were to take preliminary action looking toward the possible placing of an American association team in Chicago, but President Chivington and the team owners state that such action was not even considered at today's meeting.

White Hopes Again Will Engage in Elimination Bouts

New York, August 1.—Another round-up of "white hopes" is planned with a view to picking a challenger of World Champion Jack Johnson. The National Sporting Club of America here issued an invitation to heavyweights today to attend a tournament on August 10. The winner will be matched with Al Palzer, who won the first "white hope" elimination tourney here recently.

Japs Sail for Home.

Seattle, Wash., August 1.—The 16 members of the Waseda baseball team sailed for Japan today, after completing a tour of the United States.

Toronto Millionaire Adds to Stable.

Lexington, Ky., August 1.—Robert Davies, the millionaire Toronto brewer and turfman, bought from Harry Stanhope the yearling colt by Marta Santa-Baltimore Belle and from Dr. J. D. Neet the yearling colt by Cesarion-Glass Slipper, paying $2,500 for the two. Twenty-one thoroughbred yearlings, the property of John E. Madden, August Belmont, Fred Presgrave and R. T. Wilson, were shipped from here to Saratoga today

EAST VS. SOUTH IN FINAL ROUND

Touchard and Little Will Be Pitted Against Doyle Bros. in Lake Forest Tourney.

Lake Forest, Ill., August 1.—Gustave Touchard and Raymond D. Little of New York defeated Maurice E. McLoughlin of San Francisco and Thomas C. Bundy of Los Angeles in the first round of the National tennis doubles prelimaries today, at the Onwentsia club, 6-4, 6-4, 7-9, 3-6, 10-8. Little had one of his brilliant days, and his net work was flawless. He outguessed McLoughlin, against whom he was placed, time after time, and it was only the wonderful rallying of the young San Francisco man that prevented a more crushing defeat. Touchard also displayed remarkable cleverness. His cross-court drives were of the highest order, and the combination of Little's steadiness and Touchard's brilliant driving proved to be a winning one.

It will be east against the south in the final round of the National doubles preliminaries tomorrow, Touchard and Little playing H. E. Doyle and Conrad B. Doyle of Washington, brothers, who defeated C. M. Bull, Jr., and Harry Martin of New York, Western champions, 6-4, 8-6, 6-1.

RAIN KNOCKS RACING CARD

Deluge at Fair Grounds Forces Postponement of Blue Ribbon Events to Today, Program Going Back One Day.

GREAT INTEREST IN RICH COLT EVENT

Justice Brooke is the Choice, but Miss Stokes, Lady Jay, Margaret Parrish and Mainleaf Are Not Friendless.

BY FRANK S. COOKE.

Instead of what was expected to be one of the greatest races among 3-year-old trotters the Blue Ribbon crowd gazed at a sea of mud in the home stretch yesterday afternoon, which moved the program back a day and oinsures sport on Saturday afternoon. The weather man had said showers, but trotting folks are optimistic, and upwards of 3,000 of them journeyed to the fair grounds in spite of the clouds which began to gather from all points at about noon. There was a lively wind, which kept the bags of moisture in motion until intensely black recruits came up from the west, and soon after 1:30 o'clock there was a regular cloudburst. Water came down in such volumes that the track could not shed it, and there were puddles along the rail and mud on the outside.

In the announcement of the postponement Mr. Walker made plain that all tickets bought for Tuesday will be honored any day of the week, and if the weather permits the program will be carried on just as planned, only a day later. This means a start at 2 o'clock as usual today, and the condition of the track will depend upon the morning. The soil dries quickly when there is wind and sunshine and last night the devotees of racing were eagerly looking at the sky.

Colt Race is the Hit.

Some time ago it was said in these columns that the colt race would be the feature of this year's meeting, and the men who are interested to the greatest extent are bearing this out. For two weeks they have talked more about the three-year-old trot than any of the events on the blue ribbon card. On the eve of the race they are keeping it up and anywhere you go somebody is certain to ask you if you think Justice Brooke can win.

This particular race is the three-year-old division of The Horseman futurity and has a guaranteed value of $10,000. It is to be raced on the three heat plan and the division of the money is as follows: For each heat, $2,500 to the winner, $400 to the second and $200 to the third. Then there is the handsome $500 cup to go to the owner of the colt which stands first in the summary and $200 to the nominator of its dam.

This is the richest of the newspaper futurities and it is the first engagement of these young trotters. The custom was to race the futurities in September and October, but last year The Horseman event at Detroit proved so satisfactory that it is to be tried again, but this time with a far better field.

Field of Great Speed.

Of the eight colts and fillies that are to start in the big stake today no less than five are regarded as having a royal chance to win. Two of them now are champions, Justice Brooke, 2:09 1-2, being the best two-year-old stallion and Miss Stokes, the champion yearling with a mark of 2:14 1-4, which she reduced just ten seconds last year.

Both of these have trained well this year and Justice Brooke has been a mile in 2:10 1-4 while Miss Stokes went in 2:09, some say 2:08 3-4, at Kalamazoo. Lady Jay has been a mile in 2:10 1-2, a half in 1:01 1-2 and a quarter in 29 seconds. Margaret Parrish has not beaten 2:13 for the mile but she trotted a half in 1:00 1-2, and a quarter in 30 seconds. Mainleaf

Continued on Page Ten.

BERKLEY WARD NEWS

BERKLEY BRIEFS

Miss Mattie R. Etheridge, after a delightful visit to relatives and friends in Norfolk and Princess Anne counties, has returned to her home in South Norfolk.

Misses Helen and Allie Johnson, of Windsor, Va., and Mrs. Ely, of Brambleton, are visiting Mrs. M. L. Johnson, 302 Chestnut street.

Charles Mercer and family, of Georgetown, South Carolina, are visiting the former's sisters, Miss Mamie Mercer and Mrs. Annie Smith, on Wellington avenue, South Norfolk.

The condition of C. C. Ferebee, who was operated on at St. Christopher's Hospital last Sunday, is now very favorable.

Mrs. J. B. Warren and sister, Miss Carrie M. Rhea, left Friday for Raleigh and Windsor, N. C., to spend some time with relatives and friends.

Miss Marie Frick, of Richmond, who has been the guest of her aunt, Mrs. Beck, and Miss Carrie Rhea have returned home.

Mrs. H. L. Newberry and Miss Gladys Hanbury, of South Norfolk, left via the Norfolk Southern Thursday night for Raleigh and Durham, N. C.

Mrs. S. E. West, who has been visiting her son, James F. West, in New Brunswick, N. J., has returned to her home, 17 Clifton street.

George Dashiell and sisters left last evening via Old Dominion Line for New York, where they will visit the former's daughter, Mrs. Herbert Foster, in Staten Island.

J. C. Daniel, of Waistonburg, N. C., was in Berkley Thursday calling on friends.

Former Alderman George W. Jones, formerly of the ward, now of New York, was in Berkley Thursday on business.

Miss Lee Burns, of Charleston, S. C., who has been visiting Miss Mamie Mercer, on Wellington avenue, South Norfolk, left for her home yesterday morning.

The pastor of South Norfolk Christian church, Rev. Daniel A. Keys, will leave Monday morning for Surry county, Va., to conduct a series of evangelistic services for New Lebanon Christian church, Rev. C. C. Jones, pastor.

Rev. M. L. Bryant, pastor of First Christian church, returned from Berea Christian church, Nansemond county, where he assisted Rev. I. W. Johnson, in a series of revival meetings. They had a very successful meeting.

Miss Helen C. Mann, daughter of Captain and Mrs. T. J. Mann, No. 121 Walnut Street, has returned after a very pleasant sojourn of several weeks in eastern North Carolina.

Mrs. M. E. Winborne, Miss Annie Winborne and Mrs. S. E. Eley left yesterday morning for Willoughby Beach, to spend several days.

Mrs. R. J. Johnston of Holland, Va., was the guest of her aunt, Mrs. M. E. Winborne, and family, yesterday.

Mrs. A. R. Evett and children have returned from Washington, N. C., to their home, Berkley avenue and Stafford street.

Felton Allingood, 203 Mulberry street, leaves today to spend his vacation at Morehead City, N. C.

The Misses Sykes gave a delightful hayride in honor of their guest, Mrs. Nettie Speight. Among those enjoying the occasion were: Mises Myrna, Ruth and Vertie Harrell and Julia Sykes, Messrs. George and Kenneth Sykes. The party was chaperoned by Mrs. Walter Harrell and Mrs. Nettie Speight.

Mrs. G. W. Sykes, Mrs. Nettie Speight, Misses Bettie and Gracie Sykes, Russell, Johnnie and Kennie Sykes were guests of friends at Virginia Beach yesterday.

Mrs. George Stafford and children of Raleigh, N. C., are the guests of her sister, Mrs. E. C. White, in Chestnut street.

William Z. Harrell is slowly improving at the Lawford hospital.

Mrs. D. H. Speight, Mrs. G. W. Sykes and Mrs. Nettie Speight were guests of Mrs. E. C. White Thursday.

Arthur E. Rice, U. S. A., stationed at Charleston, S. C., is visiting his family at the residence of her parents, Mr. and Mrs. T. W. Hackett, 146 Seaboard Avenue, South Norfolk.

Mr. and Mrs. George H. Frey, have gone to the Blue Ridge Summitt, where they will spend three weeks.

Grady Hill returned last evening from New York, Philadelphia and Eastern Shore, Va., where he spent his vacation.

The little son of Mr. and Mrs. George G. Martin, was operated on this week at one of the hospitals. The little fellow is doing well.

Harry Gibson and mother, Mrs. Gibson of Rosemont, have returned from New York City and other northern points, where they spent ten days.

Mr. and Mrs. J. Mebza Saunders and son, Merrion of Elon College, N. C., after a visit to his aunt, Mrs. M. E. Winborne in Popular Avenue, left yesterday to visit Mr. Saunders's sister, Mrs. Susie Bane in Suffolk, and from there will visit his father, John Saunders at Carrsville.

IN BERKLEY CHURCHES

South Norfolk Christian church, Rev. Daniel A. Keys, pastor. Services Sunday, 9:30 a. m. Sunday school, R. W. Spruill, superintendent. 11 a. m., preaching by pastor. subject, "The Gracious Design of Christ's Coming." 8 p. m., preaching by pastor, subject, "The Church, The Garden of the Lord." A special invitation is extended to all.

IN THE HOSPITAL.

The following are receiving treatment at the Lawford Hospital:

Minnie Levy, little daughter of Mr. and Mrs. Moses Levy, Liberty street, is a medical patient.

W. Z. Harroll is undergoing treatment.

Miss Mary Cobb is convalescent.

Mrs. J. W. Perry, Compostella, is undergoing treetment.

THIRTY DAYS FOR NEGRO

Thirty days on a charge of contempt of court in removing goods from his home, Berkley avenue, Norfolk county, which had been levied on by Constable Rogers, South Norfolk, is the penalty received by William Hill, negro, at the hands of Justice P. L. Poindexter yesterday.

RESIDENCE DAMAGED BY FIRE

The residence of W. D. Bigbie was damaged by fire to the extent of about $25.

The blaze, which caught from a spark in the shingle roof, was quickly extinguished with chemicals.

American League

	Won.	Lost.	Pc.
Athletics	71	39	.645
Detroit	68	44	.607
Boston	58	53	.528
New York	57	55	.509
Cleveland	56	56	.500
Chicago	55	56	.495
Washington	47	65	.420
St. Louis	33	77	.300

YESTERDAY'S SCORES

St. Louis, 2; Washington, 3.
Cleveland, 5; New York, 4.
Detroit, 3; Boston, 9.
Chicago, 7; Philadelphia, 5.

TODAY'S SCHEDULE

Athletics at Chicago.
Boston at Detroit.
Washington at St. Louis.
New York at Cleveland.

WASHINGTON DEFEATS ST LOUIS, SCORE 3 TO 2

St. Louis, Aug. 18.—Tom Hughes had the better of Barney Pelty in a pitchers' battle, and Washington won from St. Louis again today, 3 to 2.

Score:		R.	H.	E.
Washington	000 001 020—3		7	2
St. Louis	000 000 020—2		5	2

Pelty and Stephens; Hughes and Street. Time, 2 hours. Umpires, Perrine and Dineen.

CLEVELAND TURNED TABLES ON YANKEES

Cleveland, O., Aug. 18.—Cleveland turned the tables on New York today, and won, 5 to 4. Fisher was hit hard throughout, but Cleveland failed to score until the sixth. Jackson's batting was again a feature. New York all but tied the score in the ninth, but Turner's catch of Knight's line drive saved the game.

Score:		R.	H.	E.
Cleveland	000 001 22*—5		13	1
New York	000 000 013—4		8	2

Krapp and G. Fisher; R. Fisher, Quinn and Sweeney. Time, 2:15. Umpires, Mullin and O'Loughlin.

TIGERS WERE EASY FOR BOSTON, 9 TO 3

Detroit, Mich., Aug. 18.—Willett and Works were both easy for Boston today, and this, coupled with poor fielding, gave Donovan's men the second victory of the series, 9 to 3. Del Gainer made his first appearance on first base since May 20, when his right forearm was broken by a ball pitched by Coombs, of Philadelphia.

Score:		R.	H.	E.
Boston	003 031 002—9		16	3
Detroit	100 001 100—3		11	4

Killalay, Nagle and Carrigan; Willett, Works and Stanage. Time, 2:11. Umpires, Evans and Egan.

CHICAGO DEFEATED ATHLETICS, 7 TO 5

Chicago, Aug. 18.—A triple, a double and two singles by the locals, broke a tie game, which Chicago won, 7 to 5, from Philadelphia today. Morgan's wildness, coupled with two hits and an error, gave the locals five runs in the opening inning. Timely hitting by the visitors in the second and fourth innings, coupled with bases on balls and two errors, enabled them to tie the score. Payne was hit in the mouth by a ball thrown to him by the "Ball Boy." He was removing his mask and did not see the ball.

Score:		R.	H.	E.
Chicago	500 000 20*—7		12	3
Philadelphia	030 200 000—5		10	1

Scott, Mogridge, Walsh and Sullivan, Payne and Block; Morgan, Krause, Danforth and Thomas and Lapp. Time, 2:20. Umpires, Parker and Sheridan.

She Is Good Baseball Player

Miss Carrie Kilbourne, sixteen-year-old girl of Brooklyn, who is declared to be the best woman baseball player in the world. Miss Kilbourne is shown in these photographs at bat and pitching for the Internes team of the German Hospital, of Brooklyn, against the internes of the St. Catherine Hospital. She was the only member of the fair sex in the game, and her pitching and batting were the deciding factors in the victory of her team. Not a man reached first base off her delivery, which comprised an intermingling of every sort of curve known to baseball. At bat in the ninth inning she slammed out a clean two-bagger, driving the winning run across the plate.

TARS DROPPED SECOND GAME TO THE COLTS

Richmond Came Up From The Rear And By Hitting Poole Won In The Tenth

VIRGINIA LEAGUE.

	Won.	Lost.	Pc.
Petersburg	57	44	.564
Norfolk	56	47	.544
Roanoke	53	50	.515
Lynchburg	51	53	.490
Richmond	47	56	.456
Danville	44	58	.431

YESTERDAY'S SCORES:

Petersburg, 2; Roanoke, 1.
Lynchburg, 8; Danville, 3.
Richmond, 5; Norfolk, 4.

TODAY'S SCHEDULE

Roanoke at Petersburg.
Danville at Lynchburg.
Norfolk at Richmond.

Richmond, Va., Aug. 18.—After losing many chances to score earlier by poor base-running, Richmond started a rally in the eighth this afternoon. A double and three singles brough the runs across. Wallace, who had already secured four hits, came up in the ninth and hit over left field fence, tieing the score. Babb's triple and an out gave Norfolk their first run; a pass and three singles adding three in the sixth. In the tenth, Priest singled and stole second, third and home, with the winning run. The batting of Wallace and Priest featured the game.

RICHMOND.	AB	R.	H.	PO.	A.	E.
Priest, 1b.	6	1	4	14	0	0
Griffin, 2b.	4	0	1	2	1	0
Mattis, lf.	5	0	0	2	0	0
Wallace, cf.	5	2	5	4	2	0
Martin, ss.	4	1	2	2	4	0
Charles, rf.	4	1	1	1	0	0
Baker, 3b.	5	0	2	2	4	1
Cowan, c.	3	0	0	3	1	0
Hanks, p.	5	0	2	0	3	0
Totals	41	5	17	30	15	1

NORFOLK.	AB.	R.	H.	PO.	A.	E.
Babb, ss.	4	2	2	2	3	0
Dodge, 2b.	4	0	1	5	0	0
Kirscher, cf.	3	1	2	2	0	0
Block, c.	4	1	1	6	1	1
Staub, lf.	4	0	0	2	0	0
Curtis, 3b.	4	0	1	1	0	0
Walsh, rf.	4	0	0	6	1	0
Foiles, 1b.	4	0	1	4	1	0
Poole, p.	4	0	0	1	3	0
Totals	35	4	8	*29	9	1

*Two out when winning run was made.

Score by innings:

Richmond	000 000 031 1—5
Norfolk	100 003 000 0—4

Summary: Two-base hit, Wallace. Three base hit, Babb. Home run, Wallace. Stolen bases Martin 1; Priest 4. Double play, Wallace to Priest. Sacrifice hits, Martin, Dodge, Kirscher. Base on balls, off Hanks 1; off Poole 2. Left on bases, Richmond 10; Norfolk 4. Hit by pitched ball, Charles. Struck out, by Hanks 2; by Poole 4. Time of game, 2:10. Umpire, Henderson. Attendance, 1,200.

EASTERN LEAGUE.

Baltimore 1; Rochester 5.
Jersey City-Buffalo, postponed; rain.
Newark 4; Montreal 3.
Second game, postponed; rain.
Only three games scheduled.

AMERICAN ASSOCIATION

Louisville 0; Toledo 4.
Kansas City-St. Paul. postponed; rain.
Milwaukee 2; Minneapolis 6.
Indianapolis 2; Columbus 0.
Secod game, Columbus 10; Indianapolis 2—called end eighth; darknee.

TWIN CITY SCHEDULE

TWIN-CITY LEAGUE.

	Won.	Lost.	Pct.
Franklin	6	2	.750
Rosemont	5	3	.625
Naval Hospital	4	3	.571
Redmen	4	3	.571
Y. M. A.	4	4	.500
Scottville	3	4	.429
Prentis Place	2	5	.280
Trinity	2	6	.250

Today's Schedule.

Y. M. A. at Trinity.
Red Men at Rosemont.
Naval Hospital at Franklin.
Scottsville at Prentis Place.

Ot a meeting of the league directors last night at which the contested games of last Saturdey were considered it was decided that the Red Men-Scottsville game must be played over in the Rosemont-Prentis Place game the directors held that Rosemont's contest was unjustified.

The canoe raffled off for the benefit of the Y. M. A. club has been won by Miss Nora Lawler, 1000 Colonial avenue.

National League

	Won.	Lost.	Pc.
Chicago	63	39	.618
New York	64	41	.610
Pittsburg	65	42	.607
Philadelphia	59	47	.557
St. Louis	58	48	.547
Cincinnati	46	59	.438
Brooklyn	40	65	.381
Boston	27	81	.250

YESTERDAY'S SCORES

Boston, 5; Chicago, 2.
(Rain in other cities.)

TODAY'S SCHEDULE

St. Louis at Philadelphia.
Cincinnati at New York.
Pittsburg at Brooklyn.
Chicago at Boston.

BOSTON AGAIN DEFEATS CHICAGO, SCORE 5 TO 2

Boston, Aug. 18.—The wildness of Reulbach and Toney gave Boston five runs today, and the locals were ahead of the Cubs, 5 to 2, when the game was called after the sixth inning, because of darkness and rain. Manager Chance and Pitcher Richie, of the Cubs, were put off the field, and Catcher Archer was ruled out of the game, following arguments with Umpire Johnstone.

Score:		R.	H.	E.
Boston	302 000—5		2	0
Chicago	011 000—2		3	1

Tyler and Rariden; Reulbach, Toney and Archer and Graham. Time, 1:35. Umpires, Johnstone and Eason.

CAROLINA ASSOCIATION.

Charlotte 8; Greensboro 6.
Winston-Salem 5; Grenville 2.
Anderson 5; Spartanburg 3.

SOUTH ATLANTIC LEAGUE

Savannah-Macon, postponed; rain.
Jacksonville 1; S. A. L. 5.
Columbus 8; Charleston .3
Albany 2; Columbus 3.

SOUTHERN LEAGUE.

Chattanooga 7; New Orleans 0.
Nashville 4; Montgomery 2.
Atlanta 1; Mobile 5.
Birmingham-Memphis not scheduled.

DANVILLE 3; LYNCHBURG 8

Pitcher Jobson Was Easy Plucking For Shoemakers, Bruck In Fine Form

Lynchburg, Va., Aug 18.—Jobson, the ex-outlaw and erstwile Colt, proved easy plucking for Lynchburg today for he was hit hard and the locals won 8 to 3. Bruck was in fine form and he eased down after the third. Both teams played good ball in the field but the game with that was listless and uninteresting. One of the fatures was a homer by Hudgins who hit over center.

The score:

Lynchburg—	AB.	R.	H.	PO.	A.	E
Keating, ss	4	0	1	2	1	0
Woolums, 1b	5	3	3	8	1	0
Morrison, 3b	4	1	1	0	2	0
Krebs, cf	4	1	3	2	0	(
Hooker, lf	3	1	2	2	0	(
Brooks, rf	3	1	0	4	0	(
McDonnell, 2b	4	0	1	1	1	0
Bien, c	4	0	1	7	0	(
Bruck, p	4	1	2	1	6	(
Totals	35	8	14	27	11	0

Danville—	AB.	R.	H.	PO.	A.	E.
Bowen, ss	4	0	0	2	6	1
Kaufman, lf	4	0	0	1	0	0
Schrader, 1b	3	1	1	11	1	0
Jackson, cf	3	0	0	2	0	0
Cooper, 3b	3	0	2	2	4	0
Mayberry, 2b	3	0	0	4	4	0
Mace, c	0	0	0	0	1	0
Hudgins, c	4	1	2	2	0	0
Boyne, rf	4	0	0	0	0	0
Jobson, p	4	1	1	0	1	0
Totals	32	3	6	24	17	1

Score by innings—	R.
Lynchburg	430 100 00*—8
Danville	000 111 000—3

Summary: Two base hits, Krebs and Schrader. Three base hits, McDonnell and Morrison. Home run, Hudgins. Stolen bases, Woolums, McDonnell. Double plays, Cooper, Schrader and Hudgins, Mayberry, Bowen and Schrader. Sacrifice hits, Keating and Mayberry. Base on balls, off Bruck, 1; off Johnson, 2. Left on bases, Lynchburg, 6; Danville, 6. Hit by pitched balls, Cooper and Schrader. Struck out, by Bruck, 5; by Jobson, 1. Wild pitches, Jobson, 1. Time of game, 1:41. Umpire, Wilson.

APPALACHIAN LEAGUE.

Knoxville 2; Morristown 1.
Johnson City 4; Bristol 2.
Cleveland 3; Asheville 2.

COMPENSATED.

That failing sight has its compensation is evidenced by a man who took the matter optimistically. On speaking to a friend about the matter he said:

"Yes, sir! Things look good to me that I hear other people criticising like the mischief. Every girl has a flawless complexion; everybody's hair looks as if it grew there and didn't have to be pinned on; all my friends are handsome; the streets seem clean and my clothes look new.

"Then when I put on my spectacles —! But I've learned not to, except when I want to read. When my straw hat gets too spotty my good wife punches me up and says it's time to buy a new one, and when she needs a frock she just quietly hauls my specs out of my pocket, hands them to me pointedly, and stands before me in a good light. Rose-colored spectacles are all right, she tells me, when I'm looking at her face, but she prefers me to inspect her last summer's gown with my strongest, cleanest lenses."

The dead letter mail in the United States last year amounted to 13,000,000 peices, of which 7,000,000 were opened and returned to their owners.

PETERSBURG WINS AGAIN

Hamilton in Great Shape And Easily Outpitched Roanoke's Twirler, Gardin

Petersburg, Va., Aug. 18.—Pitching magnificent ball and backed by great support, Hamilton won his second game in three days today and for the second time letting his opponents down with three hits, Roanoke forcing across one run in the ninth after Petersburg had tallied twice in the fourth. Of three hits off Hamilton one was an infield scratch in the seventh and two were clean singles in the ninth. All scores were made after two were out, the Hustlers getting two in the fourth on three successive singles and the Tigers one in the ninth on two singles and an error. Gardin pitched a good game, but his teammates did not bat behind him and he could not win.

The score:

PETERSBURG.	Ab.	R.	H.	Po.	A.	E.
Anthony, cf	3	0	0	1	0	0
Booe, lf.	4	0	0	4	0	0
Busch, ss.	4	0	1	1	1	2
Keliher, 1b.	4	1	2	12	0	0
Laughlin, c.	2	1	2	3	1	0
Spencer, rf.	2	0	0	2	0	0
Howedell, 3b.	4	0	2	3	0	0
Guiheen, 2b.	3	0	0	1	4	1
Hamilton, p.	3	0	0	0	2	0
Totals	29	2	7	27	8	3

ROANOKE.	Ab.	R.	H.	Po.	A.	E.
Ginn, cf.	4	1	1	0	0	1
Shaughnessy, c.	3	0	0	4	0	0
Pressly, 1b.	4	0	1	13	0	1
McAuley, 3b.	4	0	0	1	0	0
Draper, rf.	4	0	0	2	0	0
Titman, lf.	3	0	0	0	0	0
Shields, 2b.	2	0	0	1	4	0
Cefalu, ss.	3	0	0	3	1	0
Gardin, p.	3	0	0	0	5	0
Totals	30	1	2	24	10	2

Score by innings:

Roanoke	000 000 001—1
Petersburg	000 200 00*—2

Summary: Two-base hit, Busch. Double plays, Shields, Cefalu, Pressly. Bases on balls, off Hamilton 1, off Gardin 3. Left on bases, Petersburg 7, Roanoke 5. Struck out, by Hamilton 3, by Gardin 3. Time of game, 2 hours. Umpires, Pender and Flynn. Attendance, 1,000.

THE FARM IS NOT A REFUGE.

City Folks Should be on Their Guard Against Land Agitators.

"The present back-to-the land agitation," says Dean L. N. Bailey, of Cornell, an authority on country life, "is primarily a city or town impulse, expressing the desire of townspeople to escape, or of cities to find relief, or of real estate dealers to sell land; and in part it is the result of the doubtful propaganda to decrease the cost of living by sending more persons to the land, on the mostly mistaken assumption that more products will thereby be secured for the world's markets.

"The back-to-the land agitation is not to be discouraged, yet we are not to expect more of it than it can accomplish; but whatever the outward movement to the land may be, the effect to effectualize rural society, for the people who now comprise this society, is one of the fundamental problems now before the people.

"The open country needs good farmers, whether they are country bred or city bred; but it cannot utilize or assimilate to any great extent the typical urban-minded man, and the farm is not a refuge.

"It seems to me that what is really needed is a back-to-the-village movement. This should be more than a mere suburban movement. The suburban dedevelopment enlarges the boundaries of the city. It is perfectly feasible, however, to establish manufacturing and other concentrated enterprises in villages in many parts of the country. Persons connected with these enterprises could own small pieces of land, and by working these areas could add something to their means of support, and also satisfy their desire for a nature-connection.

"City people must be on their guard against attractive land schemes. Now and then it is possible to pay for the land and make a living out of it at the same time, but these cases are so few that the intending purchaser would better not make his calculations on them. Farming is no longer a poor man's business. It requires capital to equip and run a farm as well as to buy it, the same as in other businesses. It is a common fault of land schemes to magnify the income, and to minimize both the risks and the amount of needed capital. Plans that read well may be wholly unsound or even impossible when transacted into plain business practice. The exploiting of exceptional results in reporter's English and with charming pictures is having a dangerous effect on the public mind."

September Circulation
AVERAGES
Sunday Post 292,520
Gain Over 1910, 27,856
Daily Post 363,606
Gain Over 1910, 15,087

The Boston Post

BASEBALL EXTRA

SIXTEEN PAGES—ONE CENT | Established 1831. | TUESDAY, OCTOBER 17, 1911 *** | Copyright, 1911, by Post Publishing Co. | SIXTEEN PAGES—ONE CENT

BAKER DEFEATS NEW YORKERS WITH A HOME RUN IN THE SIXTH

AN ACTUAL PHOTOGRAPH TAKEN BY POST PHOTOGRAPHER THOMAS A. LUKE AT SHIBE PARK, PHILADELPHIA, DURING YESTERDAY'S GREAT GAME AND RUSHED THROUGH TO THE POST IN TIME TO BREAK ALL RECORDS FOR QUICK TRANSPORTATION OF NEWS PHOTOGRAPHS. THIS PICTURE WAS TAKEN DURING THE FIRST INNING, AFTER LORD HAD SCORED ON MARQUARD'S WILD PITCH. BAKER IS AT THE BAT AND EDDIE COLLINS IS ON FIRST BASE, WHICH HE REACHED ON A SINGLE. MARQUARD IS SHOWN IN THE PITCHER'S BOX, JUST WINDING UP TO DELIVER A BALL TO BAKER. MEYERS IS CATCHING AND THE UMPIRE BEHIND MEYERS IS CONNELLY. THE BIG CROWD IS SEEN ON THE FIRST BASE BLEACHERS AND ON THE END OF THE GRAND STAND.

MINISTER FIANCE MUST FACE CHURCH

Immanuel Officials Will Demand That Rev. Richeson Explain His Relations With Miss Linnell Who Died a Suicide

MISS AVIS LINNELL, WHO ENDED HER LIFE WHEN SHE LEARNED THAT THE MINISTER WHOM SHE WAS ENGAGED TO MARRY HAD ANNOUNCED HIS ENGAGEMENT TO ANOTHER.

The congregation of the Immanuel Church of Cambridge is in a frenzy of excitement over the prominent position of their pastor, the Rev. Clarence V. T. Richeson, in the tragedy of 19-year-old Avis Linnell's death.

Already prominent members of the church have stirred the ordinance committee to action, and Chairman Perry and Clerk Campbell have called a meeting of the ordinance committee for the coming week.

Continued On Page 7—First Column

BOOING AT IRISH PLAYERS

Several of Audience Ejected From Plymouth Theatre

Mingled hisses and clapping, expressions of enthusiastic approval and even more vehement condemnation, last night greeted the first production in America of J. S. Synge's "The Playboy of the Western World," by the Irish players at the Plymouth Theatre.

Dr. T. J. Dillon of Roxbury and several other prominent citizens of Boston were requested to leave the theatre when their expression of indignation was loud enough for others to hear.

Continued On Page 5—Third Column

HIGH TIDE TO-DAY

7:06 A. M. — 7:30 P. M.

SUN Rises 5:59. Sets 5:01. MOON 25 days old. Rises 12:38.

Day 11 hrs. 2 min. long; 290th day of year. Day's decrease 4 hours 15 minutes. Twenty-fifth day of autumn.

Light auto lamps at 5:31.

TODAY'S ANNIVERSARIES

Burgoyne surrendered to Americans at Saratoga, 1777.
Delaware and Chesapeake canal opened, 1829.
Eric Pape, artist, born, 1870.

FAIR

Forecast for Boston and vicinity: Fair Tuesday, followed by rain during the night or Wednesday; light easterly winds, increasing Tuesday night.

WASHINGTON, Oct. 16.—Forecast for New England: Increasing cloudiness Tuesday, probably followed by showers Tuesday night; Wednesday showers; moderate to brisk east and southeast winds.

YESTERDAY'S TEMPERATURE

Reported by Thompson's Spa.

	'10	'11		'10	'11
3 a. m.	55	54	3 p. m.	72	61
6 a. m.	57	52	6 p. m.	65	59
9 a. m.	62	54	9 p. m.	60	57
12 m.	71	58	12 mid.	56	54

Average temperature yesterday, 56 9-24.
Average one year ago yesterday, 62 2-24.
The weather Tuesday, a year ago, was clear.

DYNAMITE IN FRONT OF TAFT TRAIN

Watchman Has Battle With Would-Be Wreckers

SAN FRANCISCO, Cal., Oct. 16.—A report received here today by officials of the Southern Pacific Railway Company from C. B. Brown, section foreman for the road at Naples, Cal., described the discovery of 36 sticks of dynamite under the Cairtan viaduct, 20 miles north of Santa Barbara, several hours before President Taft's special train passed over the bridge en route to Los Angeles this morning.

The dynamite was found after the

Continued On Page 5—Sixth Column

THE OFFICIAL SCORE

PHILADELPHIA.

	AB.	R.	BH.	TB.	PO.	A.	E.
Lord, l f	4	1	1	1	2	1	0
Oldring, c f	3	0	0	0	1	0	0
Collins, 2b	3	1	2	3	2	4	0
Baker, 3b	3	1	1	4	1	1	0
Murphy, r f	3	0	0	0	0	0	0
Davis, 1b	3	0	0	0	10	0	0
Barry, ss	3	0	0	0	2	2	0
Thomas, c	3	0	0	0	9	0	0
Plank, p	3	0	0	0	0	2	0
Totals	28	3	4	8	27	10	0

NEW YORK.

	AB.	R.	BH.	TB.	PO.	A.	E.
Devore, l f	4	0	0	0	5	0	1
Doyle, 2b	4	0	0	0	1	2	0
Snodgrass, c f	3	0	2	2	1	0	0
Murray, r f	4	0	0	0	0	0	1
Merkle, 1b	3	0	1	1	7	0	1
Herzog, 3b	3	1	1	2	1	1	0
Fletcher, ss	3	0	0	0	1	1	0
Meyers, c	3	0	1	1	8	1	0
Marquard, p	2	0	0	0	0	2	0
Crandall, p	1	0	0	0	0	0	0
Totals	30	1	5	6	24	7	3

Philadelphia	1	0	0	0	0	2	0	0		—3
New York	0	1	0	0	0	0	0	0	0	—1

Two-base hits—Herzog, Collins. Home run—Baker. Hits—Off Marquard 4 in 25 times at bat in 7 innings. Sacrifice hit—Oldring. Left on bases—New York 3, Philadelphia 2. Hit by pitcher—By Plank, Snodgrass. Struck out—By Marquard 4, by Crandall 2, by Plank 8. Wild pitch—Marquard. Time—1h. 52m. Umpires—At the plate, Connolly; on the bases, Brennan; left field, Klem; right field, Dineen.

World's Series to Date

FIRST GAME.

	R.	H.	E.	Att'ce.
Giants	2	5	0	—32,281
Athletics	1	6	2	

SECOND GAME.

	R.	H.	E.	Att'ce.
Athletics	3	4	0	—26,286
Giants	1	5	3	

Post's Baseball Photos Today Break All Records

The Boston Post this morning, with its usual enterprise, is able to give its readers photographs of the second game in the great world's series, played yesterday in Philadelphia. This is the first time in the history of New England newspaper printing that photographs of an event taking place in Philadelphia in the afternoon have ever been reproduced in the issue of a New England newspaper the next morning. This clean beat is only another example of the now familiar saying, "Look to the Post first for the big news."

BY PAUL H. SHANNON

PHILADELPHIA, Oct. 16.—On beautiful Shibe park, where two glorious pennants have been won and the emblem of a world's championship still proudly flutters, Connie Mack's all conquering Athletics today blotted out the sins of Saturday.

Three to one was the score by which the Mackmen turned the trick, and Fortune, fickle in her favors on Saturday, today assigned to the hard hitting John Franklin Baker the happy opportunity

Continued On Page 12—First Column

September Circulation
AVERAGES
Sunday Post **292,520**
Gain Over 1910, 27,856
Daily Post **363,606**
Gain Over 1910, 15,087

The Boston Post

EXTRA

SIXTEEN PAGES—ONE CENT | *Established 1831.* | WEDNESDAY, OCTOBER 18, 1911 ** * | *Copyright, 1911, by Post Publishing Co.* | SIXTEEN PAGES—ONE CENT

BAKER HITS HOMER AND ATHLETICS WIN 3 TO 2

Murphy run down between third and home in the fifth inning of yesterday's game at the Polo Grounds, New York, between the Giants and the Athletics. Herzog making the put-out and Mathewson guarding the plate. This play was made on Lapp's slow bounder to Matty. Jack Coombs, in his sweater, is seen waiting his turn at the plate.

(Photo by Thomas A. Luke, Post Staff Photographer.)

For other action pictures of yesterday's game see page 14.

DARTMOUTH STAR HURT

Hogsett Out of Game for Season

HANOVER, N. H., Oct. 17.—The most serious accident of the season to the Dartmouth football team happened in this afternoon's practice when "Bobby" Hogsett, the Green's star halfback and drop-kicker, received a painful injury to his shoulder. Although the injury will not prevent him from attending classes he will probably be out of the game for the rest of the season. As a consequence of Hogsett's injury, Dana, the first string right end, will be shifted to half and Barends and Elcock will be tried out at end.

GOODWIN SAYS TRUST ILLEGAL

LOS ANGELES, Cal., Oct. 17.—Nat Goodwin could not get personal service on his former wife, Edna Goodrich Goodwin, now the Baroness Keane, and had to have the summons published to have set aside a deed of trust as illegal in which he conveyed nearly $200,000 to T. H. Dudley in trust for his wife. A demurrer to the actor's complaint to have the deed set aside was submitted to Judge Wood on briefs. Goodwin alleges the deed was made on the former Miss Goodrich's promise of marriage and that at that time he was the husband of Jessie Dermott Goodwin (Maxine Elliott) and for that reason the transaction was illegal. He says T. E. Adler recorded the transaction without his knowledge.

EASY FOR BROCKTON

Brockton High whitewashed the Hyde Park High team yesterday afternoon in a game played on the Stony Brook reservation, Hyde Park, 20 to 0.

MAN CONVICTED BY BOY OF SIX

Knew Nature of Oath in Counterfeiting Case

On the testimony of a 6-year-old boy, who said that if he did not tell the truth he would go to hell, Thomasso Mantata, a non-English speaking mill-mechanic of Palmer, was convicted by a jury in the United States District Court yesterday of passing a counterfeit quarter on June 1 last.

The youthful witness was Joseph Ruckley of Palmer, a manly little fellow with light hair and handsome blue eyes, who referred to Mantata, 40 years old, as "Tommy."

The child, who is of Polish descent but speaks and understands English well, was not big enough to look over the witness stand and for that reason Judge Dodge, who presided at the trial, had him stand up on the judge's platform beside the bench.

While standing there he was placed under oath. After he had taken the oath to tell the truth, Assistant United States District Attorney Mark Sullivan asked him what would happen to him if he did not tell the truth. He replied very earnestly that he would go to hell.

His mother, who sat back in the courtroom, smiled with the rest of the auditors at the simple faith of the child. There was nothing precocious about him, but the charm of his point of view in his testimony seemed to please everyone and the venerable judge guarded him like a father.

He testified that Mantata gave him a quarter while he was playing on the back piazza of his home in Palmer and that some Polish people who were present said that the quarter was no good. He went to a neighboring store, however, and asked to have it changed as he wanted to buy some ice cream with it. The storekeeper refused the coin as counterfeit and Joseph hastened back to Mantata and told him about it.

After the jury had reported its verdict, Judge Dodge placed the case on file as Mantata had already served three months in jail unable to secure $500 bail.

Mathewson and Coombs Pitch Third Great Duel of Series—Athletics Get to "Big Six" in Ninth

Attendance for Three Games Reaches 101,000

NEW YORK, Oct. 16.—The National Commission tonight announced that the total paid attendance at today's game was 37,216. The total receipts were $75,593, which is divided as follows: To the National Commission, $7,559.30; to the players, $40,820.22; to the clubs, $27,213.48.

The total figures of attendance and receipts for the three games played are as follows:

	1st 2 Games	Tuesday	Total
Paid attendance	64,567	37,216	101,783
Receipts	$120,321.50	$75,593.00	$195,914.50
National Commission's share	12,032.15	7,559.30	19,591.45
Players' share	64,973.61	40,820.22	105,793.83
Clubs' share	43,315.74	27,213.48	70,529.22

BY PAUL H. SHANNON

NEW YORK, Oct. 17.—Swept from his tottering pedestal as the idol of New York fandom, Christy Mathewson, hitherto invincible to the Mackmen, received his first bitter taste of defeat at the hands of the Athletics in the world's series this afternoon, when, after 11 innings of a bitterly waged contest, he was forced to take the count by the score of 3 to 2.

With the flying sphere wafted by the destructive war club of Frank Baker, vanished Matty's supremacy over the tribe of Mack. When the horsehide, driven by another of those terrific swats of the Philadelphia third baseman, cleared the cement wall for a home run, the peerless pitcher of the Giants recognized that his day had come.

"Won in the Ninth" is the title of the book written by the pitcher-author,

Continued On Page 10—First Column

HIGH TIDE TO-DAY

8:10 A. M. — 8:33 P. M.

SUN Rises at 6:00. Sets 4:59. **MOON** 26 days old. Rises 1:52.
Day 10h. 59m. long; 291st day of year.
Day's decrease, 4h. 18m.
Twenty-sixth day of autumn.

Light auto lamps at 5:29.

TODAY'S ANNIVERSARIES

Roger Williams was tried for heresy, 1635.
Hosea Ballou, Universalist clergyman, first president of Tufts College, born, 1796.
United States took formal possession of Porto Rico, 1898.

RAIN

Forecast for Boston and vicinity: Wednesday rain; moderate southeast winds. Thursday fair.

WASHINGTON, Oct. 17.—Forecast for New England: Rain Wednesday; brisk to high east winds. Thursday fair.

YESTERDAY'S TEMPERATURE
Reported by Thompson's Spa.

	'10	'11		'10	'11
3 a. m.	51	53	3 p. m.	70	54
6 a. m.	52	53	6 p. m.	68	54
9 a. m.	55	55	9 p. m.	63	54
12 m.	68	53	12 mid.	59	53

The weather Wednesday, a year ago, was fair.

AVIS LINNELL NOT A SUICIDE

Either Took Drug by Accident or Deadly Poison Was Sent Her by Design—Medical Examiner's Report Causes Police to Suspect Possible Murder

MISS AVIS LINNELL.

Tremendous surprise was caused last night by the statement of Medical Examiner Leary that Avis Linnell, who was found dead in her room, was not a suicide, but that she was killed, either by accident or design.

He is certain that the young girl did not know the deadly nature of the poison she was taking. He is convinced from his investigations that she took the most deadly poison known, under the impression that it was a harmless drug.

Continued On Page 3—First Column

BURST TIRE COST LIVES OF WOMEN

Two of Four Occupants Killed When Auto Turns Turtle

WAREHOUSE POINT, Conn., Oct. 17.—Mrs. Rose Richards of Henrysburg, Quebec, 49 years old, was instantly killed and Mrs. Julian Richards, 72, of North Adams only breathed a few moments this afternoon when the touring

Continued on Page 5—Third Column

CAR RUSHES DOWN HILL INTO ROLLER

Man's Arm Torn Off and Five Others Injured

WORCESTER, Oct. 17.—Six people were injured and 25 thrown in a panic when a car speeding down a hill crashed into a steam roller and was demolished on Lincoln street this afternoon.

Robert A. Stickney of Melrose was the worst injured. His arm was torn from his shoulder, four ribs were broken and he was paralyzed on one side, when he was extricated from beneath the wreckage. He was rushed to a private hospital in Springfield, his life in the balance.

Mrs. George Rogers of Clinton was cut about the neck by glass. Every window in the car was broken and the

Continued On Page 5—Second Column

ONE CENT EVERYWHERE

LOS ANGELES EVENING HERALD

AN INDEPENDENT NEWSPAPER

LAST EDITION

COMPLETE MARKET REPORTS

VOL. XXXVIII. WEATHER—FAIR SATURDAY, MAY 18, 1912. WEATHER—FAIR NO. 202.

COBB TEAM QUITS FIELD BIG BASEBALL WAR IS ON

Ty Cobb, the Cause of It All. This Excellent Likeness of Famous Ball Player in Characteristic Pose Lent to Evening Herald by Howland and Dewey of 510 S. Bdwy.

Detroit Americans Refuse to Play Because Star Is Not Reinstated

TYRUS COBB

I am sorry I struck the man, but he called me names and a baseball player must have protection.

BAN JOHNSON

I suspended Cobb and refuse to reinstate him. The Detroit team's threats will be disregarded.

DETROIT TEAM

We won't play unless Cobb is reinstated. We'll go barnstorming and take a trip to Japan.

THE UMPIRE

"Play ball!"—And Hugh Jennings' scrub team takes the strikers' places in the league.

WASHINGTON, D. C., May 18.—The Georgia delegation to congress today sent this telegram to Cobb:

"As Georgians we commend your actions in resenting an uncalled for insult. We hope for your exoneration and restoration to your place in that clean sport, baseball. We are proud of your record as a leader in your profession."

PHILADELPHIA, May 18.—"Put the Detroit team in the field today if it costs ten thousand dollars," is the order of Manager Hugh Jennings of the American league's striking Tigers, received today from President Navin, who telegraphed from the train on which he is rushing here.

President Ban Johnson of the American league positively refused today to reinstate Ty Cobb, the suspended star of the Detroit club, and the remainder of the Tiger team reiterated the announcement that they were battling for their rights and would not resume play until Cobb was reinstated.

OTHERS MAY STRIKE

At 3 o'clock the game started between the Athletics and a team composed of Detroit veterans and members of the St. Joseph baseball club of this city.

There is fear that other American league clubs may become disaffected and the strike may become general. The Detroit players, such notable baseball figures as "Wild Bill" Donovan, Sam Crawford, Ownie Bush and George Mullin are striving to extend the scope of the strike and prevent any American league games until Cobb is allowed to play.

It is recognized that if the American league is not able to maintain the stand taken by its president the whole power of organized baseball will be nullified.

COBB PRAISES MATES

Manager Jennings said this afternoon:

"The men are right in a way, but they should have waited until Johnson had a chance to consider the matter. They will not play. I wish Johnson would come to Philadelphia and straighten the tangle."

Cobb said: "This is the most loyal team in the world. The fellows will stick. I know if they do not let me play today it means eighteen men will walk away from the grounds. You can bet your soul on that."

President Navin of the Detroit team wired to Jennings he is on his way to Philadelphia and said Jennings should

(CONTINUED ON PAGE TWO)

SLAYER SUSPECT HAD DIFFERENT DISGUISES, BELIEF

Detectives Say Several People Saw Man, Each Time with Changed Dress

VICTIM'S TRUNK NOW SOUGHT

Officers Believe Perpetrator of Crime Is Hiding in Vicinity of City

That the slayer of the woman found in the vacant house on Arlington avenue is an adept at "makeup" and has appeared to the different persons with whom he came in contact as entirely different men is the conclusion the police reached this afternoon.

A new clew which has made the search for C. or T. Dillon far more complex than at first imagined was uncovered by the police this afternoon and the police now feel more at sea than before.

The clew, which finally turned out to be worthless and very confusing, was the finding in a Chicago railroad office of a railroad ticket sold to "T. Dillon" from Chicago to Los Angeles, but a glance at the date of the ticket shows that it was sold May 11 and that T. Dillon, who is now on his way here, is not in this case and knows no more about it than what he may have read in newspapers while en route.

This T. Dillon, the police were informed, is on his way to Los Angeles to join his wife, who has been here several weeks. He is employed by a big Chicago transfer company.

The police believe the slayer is still in Southern California and within 200 miles of Los Angeles.

It is believed that he departed from the city on an electric car and that no ticket to the east has yet been purchased by him.

A careful examination of the records in all ticket offices of the city has shown that no ticket for any very long trip has been purchased by a man answering the description of the alleged slayer and no return ticket purchased in the east has been validated.

The hope of the police that the trunks of the couple will eventually be secured was greatly increased this morning, when after an examination of all the transfer companies and warehouses in the city it was definitely announced that no man answering the description has taken his baggage from any place or had it transferred since the day of the crime.

If the postal cards which were found near the house of mystery have any connection with the crime, they will show that more than one visit was made to the house, for the cards are believed to have been dropped about May 1.

POLICE ELIMINATING RAILROAD MAN OF CHICAGO FROM SEARCH

After a careful comparison of the descriptions of the Chicago railroad man whom the police say has been sought for as C. or T. Dillon the detectives are inclined to drop him from the case. The principal portions of their descriptions are compared as follows:

Height: Chicago man, five eight; Dillon, five eight.

Weight: Chicago man, 200; Dillon, 185.

Eyes: Chicago man, blue; Dillon, bluish-gray.

Complexion: Chicago man, very light; Dillon, dark.

Hair: Chicago man, light; Dillon, dark.

Nose: Chicago man, prominent; Dillon, prominent.

Habits: Chicago man, drinks heavily; Dillon, drinks heavily.

Chicago man, in Chicago year ago;

(CONTINUED ON PAGE TWO)

Say, You, Fire Chief Eley, Can You or Any One Else Do This?

Nine Lines Must Run from 3 Plugs to 3 Houses Without Crossing

PHILADELPHIA, May 18.—Rivaling the famous "fifteen" game of a few years ago in popularity, and simpler by reason of the fact that it requires no more apparatus than a lead pencil and a piece of paper to work it, is a puzzle that has Philadelphia by the ears.

Nobody seems to know where it originated, but "everybody's doing it" on the streets, in the trolley and subway cars and in stores and offices. The problem is this: There are three detached houses on fire on one side of a street and three fire plugs on the other. The firemen must run one line of hose from each plug to each house, nine lines in all, without crossing any of the lines.

Simple as it seems, it still awaits solution. When a man first sees it he thinks he can solve it in the first attempt, but the more he tries it the more mystified he gets and the more anxious is he to end the mystery.

Locates Mother After 16 Years

After having been separated for sixteen years, Miss Ellen Rich, 260 West Forty-second street, New York, and her mother, Mrs. Agnes J. Rich, who lives at 847½ Hawthorne street, Los Angeles, are to be reunited. The mother was found through the bureau of investigations recently established by Chief Sebastian.

Miss Rich wrote to invoke the aid of the department and her mother was found very easily despite the fact that she had repeatedly written to former friends to get trace of her mother and had been unsuccessful.

Miss Rich said in her letter that she had four brothers, whose names were Charles, Fred, Oliver and Theodore, and that she had a half-sister named Bixbey. She remembered very little else because she said she was taken east while very young.

A list of all the Rich families living in the city was taken from the directory and Mrs. A. S. Wells was instructed to interview them. She found, fortunately, that Mrs. Agnes Rich, the first one she called upon, was the mother. The daughter has been informed and it is expected she will come to see her mother.

CUSTOM HOUSE REVENUE FOR APRIL $54,378.65

The official report of the Los Angeles custom house shows that during the month of April imports through this port amounted to $222,160 valuation, from which a revenue amounting to $54,378.65 was collected.

The largest single item was the importation of tobacco, amounting to $27,514. Nitrate of soda came next, totaling $21,163.

The heaviest importing country was England, from which the imports amounted to $32,470. The smallest importation came from Sweden, amounting to $7. Exports from this port are estimated at $12,703.

MAN HUNTERS ARE HOT ON TRAIL OF ROBBERS

ST. LOUIS, Mo., May 18.—A special train carrying Pinkerton, railroad and St. Louis detectives left East St. Louis this morning for Booneville, Ark., where two men, said to be the bandits who held up the train at Hattiesburg, Miss., escaping with $140,000, alighted from a Mobile-Ohio tarin this morning.

The sheriff of Booneville has been telegraphed to pursue the men.

Both men answered the description of the robbers and caried two suitcases.

HOUSE MAKES COMMITTEE ON BANKS ALL POWERFUL

WASHINGTON, D. C., May 18.—By viva voce vote the house today passed the Pujo amendment to the United States statutes extending the powers of the banking and currency committee of the house so it can call for statements from national banks. This makes the power of the committee almost unlimited.

BANK CLEARINGS MONTH TO BE $100,000,000

If the present daily rate of clearings through the Los Angeles banks is maintained until the end of this month it is very probable that the grand total of $100,000,000 will be attained, thereby establishing a record for this city. Regardless of the fact that there has already been one holiday and another half holiday, the average daily clearings posted by the Los Angeles Clearing House association have exceeded those marked during any previous year for the corresponding month.

Clearings to the amount of $21,491,970.15 were recorded during the week ending May 16, including six working days. This is regarded as the best in the history of this city by the officials of the local clearing house.

During the last four days, from May 15 to May 18, inclusive, the remarkable total of $20,832,880.20 has been posted through the clearing house as indicative of the enormous volume of business transacted through the local banking institutions. These figures as compared to any corresponding period in recent years show in a very plain and concise manner the rate at which Los Angeles is expanding and the no less remarkable manner in which business of all lines is keeping pace with her growth.

There have been only fifteen days so far this month during which clearings could be made and in this period a total of $63,584,542.98 has been recorded. The daily average has been far above that at first predicted through banking circles, inasmuch as last month was an exceptional period and one hard to beat and it was also argued that during the festive carnival of Shriners business would naturally show a slight tendency to fall off, but all these predictions have come to naught and from all appearances a total monthly report will be issued that will eclipse all previous records.

INVITES CHARITY DELEGATES

Mayor Newton D. Baker of Cleveland, O., in a letter to Mayor Alexander today invited Los Angeles' executive to send delegates to the national conference of charities and correction board in Cleveland June 12 to 19.

TERMINAL RATES TO TORRANCE GRANTED

Commerce Commission Orders 50 Cents Per Ton Cut from Charges June 11

After a battle of eighteen months, the interstate commerce commission has granted terminal rates between eastern points and the new industrial city, Torrance, on the line of both the Southern Pacific and the Pacific Electric roads to the harbor. The rate will be effective June 11. This means a saving to shippers of 50 cents per ton excess charges between this city and Torrance. But the effect of the order extends the same terminal rates to other cities and towns in the industrial district between this city and the harbor.

At present, for instance, a shipment is made from Chicago to Torrance. Under the present system this shipment would come—say—over the Southern Pacific and be delivered by that company at its terminals here to the Pacific Electric for transfer to Torrance, with 50 cents a ton excess charge. Now the shipments will go through to Torrance without extra charge.

The same rates will be available for shipments out of Torrance to points in the east and north. This means much to the development of Torrance and also to the other towns along the lines of the Southern Pacific and Pacific Electric in the industrial districts between here and the harbor. The Southern Pacific was today notified of the decision of the interstate commerce commission, and the schedules will be changed by June 11.

SHOUP OBJECTS TO 'SPLIT-NICKEL' FARES

Tells City Club Members That the Public Does Not Demand It; Prefers Good Service

Paul Shoup, vice president and managing director of the Pacific Electric Railway company, and City Councilman Haines W. Reed discussed the proposed electric railway rate regulation ordinance at the weekly luncheon of the City club at the Westminster hotel shortly after noon today.

Mr. Shoup handled his subject along broad lines, outlining the policy of the Pacific Electric as liberal and willing to co-operate with the city in the regulation of the rates and the control of the operation of the roads in the system.

"The attitude of the railway companies," said Mr. Shoup, "should not be misunderstood. They do not deny the public right of public utilities and indeed the city already exercises a very considerable power over these electric railways. It prescribes the nature of the roadbed they may construct, the type of rail, requires them to pave between and two feet outside the tracks, regulates the nature of the overhead construction and indeed at this time is suggesting a change in the poles that support trolley wires.

"The Pacific Electric has not the slightest objection to the city inspecting its books or to the city requiring it to furnish reports of the nature now demanded by the inter-state commerce commission."

Referring to "splitting the nickel" fares Mr. Shoup said:

"The first protest from the electric railway companies arises from the fact that in granting the franchises the city has in almost every instance exercised its power of regulation with reference to fares by exacting that the fares shall not be higher than 5 cents; that transfers shall be granted between this and other lines under the same ownership; that special rates be made for children and for a great many of the different department employes of the city, and son on."

JUNE VENIRE OF 80 DRAWN

A venire of eighty jurors was drawn in extra session No. 1 of the superior court today for duty in that department during the month of June. The venire will report on June 3.

TEN IN BOX TO HEAR DARROW EVIDENCE TUESDAY

F. E. Golding's Statement Is Surprise to Both Defense and Prosecution

TWO MORE JURORS NEEDED TO BEGIN TESTIMONY

Prosecutor Fears Oratory of the Accused Lawyer, Is Hint in Questions

PANEL TO BE COMPLETE MONDAY, IS NOW BELIEF

Seven Men Already Sworn to Try Indicted Chicago Labor Attorney

The following ten men have been sworn as permanent jurors to hear the evidence in the Darrow case:

W. R. Williams, L. T. Lammers, A. J. Snyder, E. K. Pierce, P. C. Paul Ritter, O. S. Cravath, L. A. Leavitt, Q. M. Dunbar, Edgar A. Moore and F. E. Golding.

J. J. Lower, 259 North Fair Oaks avenue, Pasadena, and Elijah B. Lefler, 1249 West Third street, Los Angeles, were called into the jury box for examination just prior to the noon adjournment.

With ten permanent jurors in the box and two talesmen giving every promise under examination of satisfying both the state and the defense as to their absolute qualifications and lack of all bias and prejudice, there is every indication at present that the introduction of evidence in the trial of Clarence S. Darrow, Chicago labor attorney, philosopher and writer, charged with the bribery of jurors in the McNamara case, will commence not later than next Tuesday morning.

When court concluded yesterday there were seven permanent jurors fully sworn to hear the evidence against Darrow. This morning when court reconvened District Attorney John D. Fredericks stated that he desired to re-examine Juror M. A. Cravath of Pasadena. Permission was granted by the court and the district attorney proceeded to show that Mr. Cravath possessed a marked prejudice against the state and a too friendly sentiment for the defense and the men allied with it.

NO CHALLENGES

Immediately upon Mr. Cravath's departure from the box Venireman F. W. Taylor, residing at 1639 West Twentieth street, was called to fill his place. Mr. Taylor was passed for cause by both Chief Counsel Rogers and District Attorney Fredericks.

When the following talesmen, O. M. Dunbar, Fred E. Cole, F. E. Golding, Edgar A. Moore and L. A. Leavitt and F. W. Taylor rose to be sworn, Chief Counsel Rogers announced that he wished to peremptorily challenge Messrs. Taylor and Cole. The district attorney stated that no challenges would be used. Messrs. Dunbar, Moore, Leavitt and Golding then were sworn, while Messrs. Cole and Taylor left the courtroom.

Immediately after this proceeding was over Clerk Smith summoned Messrs. J. J. Lowers, residing at 259 North Fair Oaks avenue, Pasadena, and Elijah B. Lefler, residing at 1249 West Third street, into the box for examination. Their examination had not been finished up to the noon adjournment. The matter will be resumed on Tuesday afternoon at 2 o'clock.

To date the defense has expended

(CONTINUED ON PAGE TWO)

CLEAN But Not Dull

New-York Tribune

PROGRESSIVE But Not Radical

[Copyright, 1912, by The Tribune Association.]

VOL. LXXII....No 23,926. To-day, fair; cooler to-night. To-morrow, fair; moderate winds. NEW-YORK, SUNDAY, MAY 19, 1912.—FIVE PARTS—SIXTY PAGES. PRICE FIVE CENTS.

MOVES TO SMASH THE COFFEE 'TRUST'

Wise Incidentally Seeks to S...

ROSALSKY BROUGHT INTO COURT PROBE

Judge Who Gave Brandt Long ...

STRIKE IN BASEBALL NOW A STERN REALITY

Detroit Tikers Fulfil Threat and Refuse to Play Without "Ty" Cobb.

AMATEURS IN THEIR PLACES

Makeshift Team Disgusts 'Fans,' Who Demand Money Back—Sympathy of Other Teams Enlisted.

[By Telegraph to The Tribune.]

Philadelphia, May 18.—After a few minutes of practice at Shibe Park this afternoon the entire Detroit team, numbering eighteen men, walked off the field, and the first strike in the history of organized baseball began. When the players were informed that the suspension of "Ty" Cobb by President Johnson stood and that the star outfielder would not be allowed to play in the game to-day, the Tigers were not long in coming to a decision. Sweaters and gloves were gather up and the team left the field.

Hugh Jennings, manager of the team, had some amateur and semi-professional players in waiting, as he had been informed by his men this noon that if the suspension stood they would not play. They agreed to go to the grounds, however, and when they arrived there fifteen thousand "fans" were assembled to see what would be done.

As the Tigers marched on to the field, at 2:30 o'clock, and the spectators saw that Cobb was among them, they were cheered loudly and long. They took the usual practice, and Cobb went to centre-field. As soon as the umpires saw "Ty" they went up to him and told him to leave the field, as he was under suspension.

As soon as Cobb was seen leaving the grounds the other players picked up their gloves and sweaters and followed. Silently they filed out of the exit under the grandstand. "Bill" Burns, the former Phillies' pitcher, being the last to depart. They returned to their hotel, where they spent the rest of the afternoon laying plans for the secret meeting of representatives of all the American League teams that will be held in this city soon, probably to-morrow.

At this meeting an organization will be formed among the players for the purpose of protecting themselves in the future against quick judgment of their cases by the head of the league without giving them a hearing. The National League teams have been invited to attend the meeting, and it is probable that several of the teams in the older organization will be represented.

A few minutes after the Tigers had left Shibe Park Jennings trotted out his recruited organization, amid the jibes of the spectators. "Jim" McGuire, the Detroit scout, and "Joe" Sugden, the Tigers' trainer, were in the line-up, but they were the only ones who were not amateurs or semi-professionals.

The young Tigers, who were defeated by a score of 24 to 2, made a miserable showing, and the "fans" grew disgusted. In the fifth inning three thousand Phila-

THE PARADE OF NEW YORK'S POLICEMEN GOING UP FIFTH AVENUE; MOUNTED MEN NEAR 42D STREET.

MAYOR GAYNOR AND COMMISSIONER WALDO PINNING MEDALS ON THE HONOR MEN.

GENIUS FOLLOWS LEFT HAND

Orange Pastor Plans Association of "Southpaws."

Orange, N. J., May 18.—Any left-handed folk who have been inclined to regard their structural peculiarity as something to be ashamed of as putting them in the class with "queer" ones, are invited to attend the services to-morrow night in the Orange Methodist Church and hear from the lips of the Rev. Dr. William A. Frye, the pastor, who is himself left-handed, that all "southpaws" are geniuses.

Dr. Frye has set out to form an association of left-handed people, and the sermon to-morrow night is to be the first step in that movement. He has sent out invitations to all the left-handed people he knows, and followed it up with a general call to people who attack their problems from the wrong side to come and hear him.

He will preach on the text: "But when the children of Israel cried unto the Lord the Lord raised them up a deliverer, Ehud, the son of Gera, a Benjamite, a man left-handed."

"Most great geniuses, though not all," says the pastor in his invitation, "are left-handed, though perhaps I should say left-handed people are geniuses. There is a real reason for it. The reason people are right-handed is that the left lobe of the brain is more developed. There is a distinct advantage in having the right lobe of the brain more developed. If that side is the more developed you are left-handed."

IS LYNCHING "ACCIDENT"?

Louisiana Courts Asked to Decide This Novel Question.

Baton Rouge, La., May 18.—Whether to be lynched is the same thing as being the victim of an accident is an interesting question which the courts of Louisiana have been called on to decide.

The point came up here to-day, when the widow of Frank Miles, a negro, who was hanged by a mob in Shreveport for writing an insulting note to a white woman, filed proceedings against an insurance company to obtain the payment of a $400 accident policy carried by the mob's victim.

The petition does not specify that Miles was the victim of an accident, but recites that he was found "hanging from the limb of a tree in the rear of the baseball park, with a rope tied about his neck."

PHŒBUS SNOW ON JOB, OHO!

Spotless White, Day and Night, Makes Subway Glow.

Did you ever know that pretty, dainty Phœbe Snow, has brothers, thousands, in a row; that the spotless girl in white has brothers, just as spotless, quite, who open gates and bow so low, in the subway—well, it's so!

Summer must be here, all right, for the subway boys in white, appeared yesterday to show they can be neat as Phœbe Snow. And on every train which ran through the subway every man shone as bright as any pin. Passengers getting out and in marvelled at the brave array, and the darkness of the tubes was lighted up like break o' day.

Every gateman's name was Phœbus, Phœbus Snow, of Spotless Town, as he smiled in cheery fashion, worked his "chopper" up and down. Now that summer's come to stay, and the boys in white are here, the tube becomes the "great white way" till the leaves begin to sere.

If you don't believe this story, go see the boys in all their glory. Be it guard or "chopper" man, each is spotless, spick and span. They will serve you, day and night, those cleanly boys in spotless white.

FIVE INDIANS DIE IN FIRE.

Crowder, Okla., May 18.—Five students were burned to death to-day when fire destroyed the main building of the Creek and Seminole Indian College at Doley. None of the victims was more than nineteen years old.

STRIKE IN BASEBALL NOW A STERN REALITY

Detroit Tikers Fulfil Threat and Refuse to Play Without "Ty" Cobb.

AMATEURS IN THEIR PLACES

Makeshift Team Disgusts 'Fans,' Who Demand Money Back—Sympathy of Other Teams Enlisted.

[By Telegraph to The Tribune.]

Philadelphia, May 18.—After a few minutes of practice at Shibe Park this afternoon the entire Detroit team, numbering eighteen men, walked off the field, and the first strike in the history of organized baseball began. When the players were informed that the suspension of "Ty" Cobb by President Johnson stood and that the star outfielder would not be allowed to play in the game to-day, the Tigers were not long in coming to a decision. Sweaters and gloves were gather up and the team left the field.

Hugh Jennings, manager of the team, had some amateur and semi-professional players in waiting, as he had been informed by his men this noon that if the suspension stood they would not play. They agreed to go to the grounds, however, and when they arrived there fifteen thousand "fans" were assembled to see what would be done.

As the Tigers marched on to the field, at 2:30 o'clock, and the spectators saw that Cobb was among them, they were cheered loudly and long. They took the usual practice, and Cobb went to centre-field. As soon as the umpires saw "Ty" they went up to him and told him to leave the field, as he was under suspension.

As soon as Cobb was seen leaving the grounds the other players picked up their gloves and sweaters and followed. Silently they filed out of the exit under the grandstand. "Bill" Burns, the former Phillies' pitcher, being the last to depart. They returned to their hotel, where they spent the rest of the afternoon laying plans for the secret meeting of representatives of all the American League teams that will be held in this city soon, probably to-morrow.

At this meeting an organization will be formed among the players for the purpose of protecting themselves in the future against quick judgment of their cases by the head of the league without giving them a hearing. The National League teams have been invited to attend the meeting, and it is probable that several of the teams in the older organization will be represented.

A few minutes after the Tigers had left Shibe Park Jennings trotted out his recruited organization, amid the jibes of the spectators. "Jim" McGuire, the Detroit scout, and "Joe" Sugden, the Tigers' trainer, were in the line-up, but they were the only ones who were not amateurs or semi-professionals.

The young Tigers, who were defeated by a score of 24 to 2, made a miserable showing, and the "fans" grew disgusted. In the fifth inning three thousand Phila-

Continued on fourteenth page, fifth column.

CROWDS WATCH POLICE IN BIGGEST PARADE

City's "Finest" Cheered Continuously All Along Four Miles of March.

MEN OF ALL GRADES, 7,784

Seven Members of Department Receive Medals from Mayor at Reviewing Stand at Public Library.

More policemen than New York ever saw gathered together before marched up the backbone of Manhattan yesterday to 57th street. Almost a million citizens, adorning either curb for the four miles of the line of march, cheered them on their annual pilgrimage into the hearts of the taxpayers. The "finest" reached their goal long before they reached 57th street.

The marchers numbered 7,784 blue coated guardians of the peace, officers and men, or, rather, all officers of varying degree, though uniformly big and upstanding. And yet this army, great as any in the field in Mexico, left about 3,000 of the entire force behind to garrison the precincts in its absence. For, though nearly a million of New York's flora and fauna fringed the parade, several other millions, including the birds of prey, pursued their daily vocations unemotionally indifferent to the city's greatest annual spectacle of potential valor and brass buttons.

No finer day for the show could have blessed the town. A cloudless sky, a benignant but not too familiar sun and a breeze that arrived in little puffs when most needed, provided the best assortment of light, air and temperature possible. It was a day to cheer on the straw hat trade by an appeal to the intellect rather than to the emotions.

The parade route led from Chambers street and Broadway, abreast of City Hall Park, up Broadway to 23d street and thence up Fifth avenue to 57th street. The reviewing stand stood in front of the Public Library, at 41st street, and there Mayor Gaynor, Commissioner Waldo and a distinguished body of men, military and civil, domestic and foreign, reviewed the troops of peace as the latter legged it by to the strains of one band after another. It was there also that the honor company halted while the Mayor pinned medals on its seven recruits for 1912.

Long Delay Tests Patience.

But before the vanguard had attained the reviewing stand a delay ensued that sorely tried the patience of the thousands gathered thereabout on the sidewalks, in the stand and on the generous terraces and steps of the Public Library. One o'clock came, then two, and still the only amusement afforded was that of watching the police "fans" at the street corners struggling with one another and with the officers on duty for advantageous posts.

The absence of the Mayor and Police Commissioner Waldo from the reviewing

Continued on seventh page, fourth column.

PANAMA ALMOST DUG OUT

Remaining Excavation Should Be Done Within Eleven Months.

Panama, May 18.—The total amount of excavation on the Panama Canal during the year ending May 1 was 30,736,364 cubic yards, which leaves only 26,836,494 cubic yards to be excavated.

The Gatun locks are 93 per cent finished, Pedro Miguel 92 per cent and Miraflores 61 per cent.

The total amount spent on the canal so far is $251,376,491; for fortifications, $669,156.

CRUISER MAKES 30 KNOTS

Germany's Fastest Big Ship Is Now the Goeben.

Cuxhaven, May 18.—The German turbine cruiser Goeben in a trial trip today developed a speed of 30 knots over a measured course. This makes her the speediest ship in the German navy.

The armored cruiser battleship Moltke last September developed a speed of 29½ knots. The Moltke is the flagship of the German squadron that will visit America next month.

STUDENTS BLOW UP HEARSE

Union Boys Rush It to Campus Ahead of the Police.

[By Telegraph to The Tribune.]

Schenectady, N. Y., May 18.—In celebration of the arrival of "moving up day" fifty or more students of Union College started a frolic last night which promises to end in trouble for some of them.

The college boys got possession of a $2,000 hearse belonging to Mrs. E. C. Smith, of No. 26 Yates avenue, and started to take it to the campus. A policeman who saw them on the march whistled for help, and when other officers joined him started in pursuit.

The students rushed the hearse to the campus, set it on fire and disappeared in the dormitories as the police dashed through the old "Blue Gate." Just as the officers reached the campus there was a loud explosion, and the hearse was scattered over the grounds. It is believed the students put a can of gasolene in the vehicle before setting it afire.

"John Doe" warrants were issued today, and the police declare they will arrest every student concerned in the affair, charging them with larceny and various other offences.

Had it not been for a faculty edict against the scheme the college boys would have marked "moving up day" by flying a Union pennant from the tower of the wireless station.

ELOPED FROM OKLAHOMA

Fleeing Ranchman and Fiancee Wed in Wilmington.

[By Telegraph to The Tribune.]

Wilmington, Del., May 18.—Wilmington is becoming nationally conspicuous as a Gretna Green. Bernard Givalthley, a wealthy ranch owner of Oklahoma City, Okla., eloped to this city with Miss Gertrude Carter, of Lawton, Okla. They were wedded here by the Rev. George L. Wolfe, the preacher who married Edith Gaynor and Harry K. Vingut when they eloped to Wilmington from New York.

The father of Miss Carter objected to his daughter becoming the bride of the ranch owner. The couple thereupon went to Philadelphia. They had trouble in getting a marriage license in the Quaker City, and decided to come to Wilmington.

MUST VOTE FAR APART

Precinct Line Divides Husband and Wife in Los Angeles.

[By Telegraph to The Tribune.]

Los Angeles, May 18.—The result of a unique election question, just decided by the District Attorney, is a house standing alone, yet divided against itself. It is the residence of Dr. and Mrs. H. R. Goodwin, in Glendale.

A precinct line runs through the house. Dr. Goodwin has apartments on one side of this line and Mrs. Goodwin on the other, and the point was raised whether they could vote in the same precinct. Mrs. Goodwin was turned away when she asked for a ballot because her apartments were on the other side of the precinct line.

"The District Attorney held that the Goodwins must vote on opposite sides of the boundary and many blocks apart.

TAFT SURE OHIO WILL SUPPORT HIM

He Closes a Week's Campaign Confident His Appeals to His Home State Have Been Successful.

FIGHT REGARDED AS VITAL

Managers of Each of the Candidates in Each of the Parties Predict a Victory in the Primaries on Tuesday.

Springfield, Ohio, May 18.—Confident that his appeals to the pride of Ohio in an Ohio President have been of some avail and that his chance of capturing this state's delegation to the Republican National Convention has improved greatly since he crossed the Ohio River last Monday, President Taft closed the week's campaign to-night with a speech here.

Only one more day, Monday, will be devoted by the President to this campaign. When he makes his last speech in Dayton on Monday night he will have travelled almost three thousand miles in Ohio, will have spoken in every Congress district in the state and will have visited seventy-three of its eighty-eight counties.

Theodore Roosevelt, who began his Ohio speechmaking on Tuesday, wound up his week's work to-night at Cleveland, having closely followed the President through the state.

At the end of the most strenuous week's campaign Ohio has ever known the managers of each of the candidates for the Republican Presidential nomination claim certain victory at the primaries on Tuesday.

State the Deciding Point.

The state is conceded by most politicians to be the deciding point in the battle for the Presidential nominations, and especially in the fights of the two native sons, President Taft and Governor Harmon.

President Taft declared in Cleveland that he considered Ohio the pivotal point in the pre-convention campaign. Colonel Roosevelt, while insisting that he will carry the state, declared he could win the nomination even should he be defeated at the Ohio primaries.

President Taft, Colonel Roosevelt, Senator La Follette, among the Republicans, and a score of lesser lights have spent the greater part of the week on trains, and no section of the state has been neglected. Candidates even spent one day in West Union, Adams County, unmindful of the fact that the great majority of men in the county had been disfranchised for frauds in former elections and had no vote.

Competition in the Democratic ranks is hardly less keen than among the Republicans. William J. Bryan, backed by Harvey C. Garber, national committeeman, urged voters to support Governor Woodrow Wilson of New Jersey and to defeat Governor Harmon in a trip through the state just ahead of the Ohio executive.

Lewis C. Laylin, who has managed President Taft's state campaign, made the following prediction:

The primary election next Tuesday will be a complete vindication of President Taft by his native state and an emphatic indorsement of his administration.

The trend of sentiment constantly has been for the President—marvellously so in the last week. I now have reliable information from every section of the state, and I am confident Taft will have the state convention and the six delegates-at-large, and if the Taft voters go to the polls on primary day, he will have the district delegates.

No Roosevelt Prediction.

Walter F. Brown, Roosevelt's Ohio manager, refused to make predictions on the outcome of Tuesday's primaries, although the press bureau of the Roosevelt committee declared the colonel would carry the state by a big majority.

Lieutenant Governor H. L. Nichols, Governor Harmon's manager, said:

The result of the primaries next Tuesday will show to the country that Judson Harmon is still beloved by the Democracy of Ohio, which could not be swayed by the pernicious activity of the few persons calling themselves his enemies.

The demonstrations accorded the Governor served to emphasize the feeling that he would be rewarded by such a decisive vote as to bring him clearly to the forefront as the most formidable candidate for the nomination at Baltimore.

Harvey C. Garber predicted the defeat of Governor Harmon in practically every one of the twenty-one Ohio districts, saying:

Progressive Democrats will sweep Ohio next Tuesday. The six delegates-at-large will be Progressives. The Bryan, Clark, Kern, James, Ross, Marshall vote will be against Harmon and for Wilson, so that the six delegates named under the rules for Wilson will go to Baltimore pledged to vote first, last and all the time for a Progressive and against any reactionary.

Senator La Follette, who spoke to-night in Toledo, will close his fight in Cleveland on Monday. His national manager, Walter L. Houser, would make no prediction, but added to the day's interest by making public a partial list of Senator La Follette's campaign contributions. Chief of these were:

Charles R. Crane, Chicago, $20,000; Gifford Pinchot, Washington, $10,000; Amos R. Pinchot, New York, $10,000; William Kent, California, $10,000; Alfred R. Baker, Chicago, $2,000; Rudolph Spreckels, San Francisco, $2,500, and William Flinn, Pittsburgh, $1,000.

Ohio politicians who have been with Mr. Taft say that never in the state's history has there been such a campaign. In his talks to-day to the farmers in the counties along the western border of the state, from Lake Erie southward, the President's feeling of confidence in the outcome was reflected in his manner.

Although he used plain language about Colonel Theodore Roosevelt and the "Ohio bosses," at times, his old smile, that had appeared seldom of late, was again in evidence, and he talked optimistically of the coming election with friends on board his private car.

Yesterday's Circulation: 455,882 POSTS

The Boston Post

20 Pages Today

TWENTY PAGES—ONE CENT | Established 1831 | THURSDAY, OCTOBER 10, 1912 *** | Copyright, 1912, by Post Publishing Co. | TWENTY PAGES—ONE CENT

"The Greatest Game of Baseball Ever Played"—Ty Cobb

MIGHTY STRUGGLE ENDS IN TIE IN THE ELEVENTH INNING 6 TO 6

Fans in Frenzy as Battle See-Saws Back and Forth—First Red Sox Lead Then Giants—Speaker Ties Game Up After It Had Been Lost by a Terrific Drive to Centre Field Seats—Collins and Hall Knocked Out of Box—Mathewson Hit Hard—Greatest Struggle in World Series History Seen by 30,148

LEWIS SCORING THE TYING RUN IN THE EIGHTH INNING OF YESTERDAY'S WORLD'S SERIES BATTLE AT FENWAY PARK, WHEN GARDNER'S WICKED DRIVE THROUGH FLETCHER SENT HIM HOME ALL THE WAY FROM SECOND.

SAY GIRL ROBBED TO SAVE HOME

Claim She Took $1000 from General Electric

The theft of $1000—ten packages of $100 in bills—from the paymaster's office of the General Electric Company at Lynn on Aug. 23 was cleared up yesterday, according to the police, by the arrest of Miss Louise M. Lawless, 26, who is alleged to have stolen the money to pay off a $400 mortgage on her father's home at Clinton.

The girl, a trusted clerk in the office, has been employed by the firm for eight years, four of which were spent in the Lynn office. Her most intimate friend, Francis Turner, 26, of 13 Park street, Lynn, was also arrested, charged with receiving stolen property, the police having information that $400 of the stolen money was on deposit at a Boston bank in his name.

SAY BOTH CONFESSED

Both are alleged to have confessed, the girl to stealing the money and Turner to having taken the money from the girl but with no knowledge that it was stolen.

Turner was bailed out yesterday, shortly after being held under $400 bonds by Judge Lummus and Miss Lawless was bailed last night by her father, who went surety to the amount of $600. Both pleaded not guilty and their cases were continued until Oct. 19. John O'Brien of Worcester, a schoolmate of the girl, appeared as attorney for her.

They were both arrested at the home of Jesse M. Turner, 76 1-2 Washington street, a brother of the arrested man, where they were playing whist when Inspector Stacey Burckes walked into the house. Although under suspicion for the past four days and constantly being grilled by the police, Miss Lawless did not break down and confess until confronted by the inspector, who had just returned from a trip to Clinton, where he had been making an investigation.

Smuggled in Apron

The police say the girl admitted taking the money from the office, by smuggling it beneath an apron. She says $400 of it she gave to Turner, who deposited it in Boston. This sum was recovered today and the other $400, which was sent to her home to pay on the mortgage, the police say will be recovered.

The other $200 is still missing and the girl says she does not know where it has gone. She says she did not spend it and nothing except a new $18 suit was found among her effects.

The girl's father, Michael Lawless, and her sister, Katherine, took her home with them from the police station last night after she had been held there about 20 hours. Her sister who was present at her arrest received permission to stay with Miss Lawless at the station and did her best to cheer the girl who has failed noticeably in health during the past week.

BOY KIDNAPPED FROM SCHOOLROOM

Mother Says That Father Whom She Is Suing for Non-Support Took Child Away

MRS. JAMES DEBELLE AND HER SON FREDERICK, WHO WAS KIDNAPPED YESTERDAY.
(Photo by J. E. Purdy & Co.)

Armed with legal documents, which are alleged to have been issued without due investigation, James Debelle stalked into the Perkins school on St. Botolph street yesterday afternoon during class hours and demanded his son, Frederick, 8 years old, from the boy's teacher, Miss Anna C. Cousens.

CHILDREN EXCITED

The children were much excited and the teacher did not know exactly what course to pursue, but on account of the attitude of the man and the fact that the boy said that the man was his father, she allowed him to take the boy away. The youngster has not been seen since by his mother, Mrs. Sarah J. Debelle of 27 Berwick park. She admits that the kidnapper was the boy's father but that he had no right to take the child as he now is being sued for non-support.

Shortly after Frederick was born, it is claimed, James Debelle gave up his work and made no attempt to support his wife and child. The wife says she finally left her husband and went to live on Berwick park.

The husband took rooms near the house occupied by his wife and child and frequently saw them. However, he gave them no money, Mrs. Debelle asserts.

Last March the boy was run over by an automobile and seriously injured. It was thought he could not recover. According to Mrs. Debelle, her husband brought claims for damages, but instead of paying for his son's medical attendance he left the city with the money.

Mrs. Debelle immediately instituted proceedings for non-support.

The case is to come up very soon, and it is Mrs. Debelle's belief that the notice of the suit being served on her husband may have induced him to kidnap the child.

The mother is frantic and spent last evening visiting the various places where she knew her husband had roomed in the hope that he had brought the boy there with him. Up to a late hour she had not been successful in seeing her son, but she had located a place in Winthrop, where she believes he is being held.

TODAY'S ANNIVERSARIES, ETC.

Colonel Robert Gould Shaw, commander of the first colored regiment from the North in the Civil War, born 1837.

Battle of Blue Springs, Tenn., 1863.

Score killed in Paris by explosion of bomb intended for Bonaparte, 1800.

MONTENEGRO STARTS WAR

PODGORITZA, Montenegro, Oct. 9.—The Montenegrin army opened the war against Turkey this morning by attacking a strong Turkish position opposite Podgoritza. Prince Peter, the youngest son of King Nicholas, fired the first shot.

This was the signal for firing all along the line, and an artillery duel ensued. Within 21 minutes five Turkish guns were silenced, and the Turks retreated from their first position on Mt. Planinitza.

By noon the Turks had evacuated the mountain.

KING PRESENT

Podgoritza is the headquarters of the Montenegrin forces and amid the enthusiastic cheering of the people King Nicholas with Prince Mirko, his second son, and staff, rode early to the mountains to survey positions. The Montene-

Continued on, Page 18—Sixth Col.

M'GRAW CALLS IT POOR GAME

Says Matty Would Have Scored Shut-Out With Good Support—Praises Red Sox

BY JOHN J. McGRAW
Manager of the Giants

(Copyright, 1912, by the Boston Post and the New York Times.)

Well, we stand just about where we did yesterday morning. If anything we are in a better strategic position, for we are constantly

Continued on Page 11—7th Column

SHOWERS

The weather man does not hold out any promise of a good baseball day today. Unsettled, with showers, is the prediction. Should rain interfere today, the game will be played in Boston tomorrow.

HIGH TIDE TODAY

A. M. 10:44 | P. M. 11:13

Portland 12m., Gloucester 30m., Newport 3h. 44m. earlier.

SUN Rises 5:51 Sets 5:11 **MOON** New today

Total eclipse of the sun today, invisible in New England.

284th day of year; 18th day of autumn.

Day 11h. 20m. long; day's decrease 3h. 57m.

Venus sets 6:14 p. m., Jupiter sets 7:49 p. m., Saturn rises 7:18 p. m.

Light auto lamps tonight at 5:41.

SHOWERS

Forecast for Boston and vicinity—Unsettled, with occasional showers Thursday; Friday, fair and cooler,

WASHINGTON, Oct. 9.—Forecast for New England: Local rains Thursday; Friday, fair, somewhat colder; moderate south winds, becoming northwest Friday.

YESTERDAY'S TEMPERATURE
Reported by Thompson's Spa.

	'11	'12		'11	'12
3 a. m.	47	46	3 p. m.	70	66
6 a. m.	47	50	6 p. m.	66	60
9 a. m.	55	56	9 p. m.	60	58
12 m.	67	65	12 mid.	56	58

Average temperature yesterday 57 5-24.
Average one year ago yesterday 58 2-24.

Today's Game to Be Played Here "Second Game" Coupons Are Good

Today's game between the Red Sox and Giants will be played at Fenway Park. This was officially announced last night by the National Commission, the ruling being made because of the fact that yesterday's game was not a decisive contest. Should it rain today, preventing a game, the teams will play here Friday. A decisive game must be played in Boston before the rivals move back to the Polo Grounds, New York.

Holders of three-game reserved seat tickets will be admitted today, of course. Today's game counts as the second game in Boston and tickets will be good the same as if they were to be used Friday, which day was originally scheduled for the second game here. Should rain not intervene, the third game in Boston will be played Saturday. If it should be necessary to play a fourth contest here, the original three-game tickets will be of no value, but a special reserved sale will be held for the extra contest.

Admission tickets to unreserved seats for today's game will be on sale this morning starting at 10:30 o'clock.

BY PAUL H. SHANNON
Baseball Editor of the Post

Two great teams—two valiant foes, striving with every ounce of energy for mastery in an ever-memorable struggle on Fenway Park yesterday, alike met defeat from an unexpected source when darkness, unwelcome and unsought, sheathed the weapons of the rival factions and rendered the disappointing verdict of a draw.

For 11 innings the crash of bat and the plaudits of a frenzied multitude had transformed Fenway Park into a veritable bedlam. For 11 innings the wiles of Mathewson, the craft of McGraw, and the onslaught of the Giants' batsmen had met their match in the strategy of Stahl and Wagner or the destructive clubs of Speaker, Hooper and Gardner.

Again and again victory and then defeat flirted with the fears and hopes of the contending claimants for supremacy in baseball. Again and again the roar of jubilation attending the achievement of a Red Sox hero gave place to the frightened murmur that signalized some menacing attack by one of McGraw's dangerous clan.

Continued on Page 8—1st Column

FINAL EDITION
INCLUDING FULL TRANSACTIONS
TEMPERATURE.
Min. 44. Max. 59.

The Evening Sun.

FINAL EDITION
INCLUDING FULL TRANSACTIONS
Fair and cool, with frost to-night; moderate variable winds, becoming S.

VOL. XXVI. NO. 182. NEW YORK, WEDNESDAY, OCTOBER 16, 1912.—Copyright, 1912, by The Sun Printing and Publishing Association. PRICE ONE CENT.

THE RED SOX WIN THE WORLD'S CHAMPIONSHIP

EVERYTHING IN ROOSEVELT'S FAVOR AND CONDITION EXCELLENT, SAY SURGEONS; END OF DANGER PERIOD ON FRIDAY

Colonel Passes a Good Night and His Pulse and Temperature To-day Show Improvement.

WIFE IS WITH HIM

Mrs. Roosevelt Takes Quarters in Hospital Where Husband Lies.

EATS HEARTY BREAKFAST

"Feeling Fine," Were His First Words When He Awoke This Morning.

CHICAGO, Oct. 16.—At 1:30 o'clock this this afternoon the following bulletin was issued regarding Col. Roosevelt's condition:

"Pulse, 90; temperature, 98.6 throughout the morning. Breathing little easier. General condition excellent."

The physicians issued the following bulletin at 9:20 o'clock:

"The records show that Col. Roosevelt had a very good night; that his temperature and pulse are normal; that his highest pulse since 9 o'clock last night was 80, temperature 98.8; that his pulse at 6 o'clock this morning was 74, temperature 98.6 and respiration 20; that he is having less irration of his pleura from the injured rib than he did yesterday; that he did not have to have an anodyne for the pain. General condition excellent.

"JOHN B. MURPHY,
"ARTHUR DEAN BEVAN,
"S. L. TERRELL."

Soon after the bulletin was issued Dr. Murphy said: "Unless the bullet strikes a nerve or infection is evident from the very first it is not customary immediately to operate in cases of this kind. The body will incapsulate the missile in a dry tissue and do more than any surgeon to prevent infection. Should infection come symptoms will show probably by the fourth day. If by the sixth no symptoms have become evident the patient may be decided out of danger.

"There was no sign to-day of tetanus or other complications and we are hopeful none will develop. The Colonel's condition is excellent. His temperature and respiration are normal and he is in a cheerful frame of mind. All things taken into consideration he could not be better."

"It is a mighty good thing to have Mrs. Roosevelt here," said Dr. John B. Murphy with a smile to a reporter of THE EVENING SUN. "She is able to keep the Colonel's mind off the campaign and will be able also to keep him in bed as long as he ought to stay."

Col. Theodore Roosevelt passed an exceptionally good night in the Mercy Hospital in Chicago, sleeping almost the entire time. The physicians said that his condition was most encouraging.

The Colonel's pulse at 7 o'clock this morning was 74, his temperature 98.6 and his respiration 20. This was a marked improvement over his condition at 10 o'clock last night.

There were no signs that the bullet in the right side of his chest had set up any infection.

Dr. Scurry L. Terrell, Col. Roosevelt's personal physician, said to-day: "If there is any danger to the Colonel from bloodpoisoning or lockjaw it will be indicated by Friday by the presence of pus about the wound."

A mild dose of anti-tetanus serum was injected late yesterday as a preventive to lockjaw.

The result of the chemical analysis of the bullets remaining in the revolver used by Schrank to wound Col. Roosevelt showed that there was no poison on them.

Mrs. Roosevelt, accompanied by Miss Ethel, Theodore, Jr., and Dr. Albert Lambert, reached the hospital this morning and went at once to the Col-

(Continued on Second Page.)

Copyright American Press Association.
JOHN SCHRANK.
Photograph of Col. Roosevelt's Assailant Taken in Milwaukee Yesterday When He Was Arraigned in Court.

ENVOYS LEAVE BALKANS.

Studied Affront in Withdrawal of Sultan's Ministers To-day.

CONSTANTINOPLE, Oct. 16.—The Porte received telegrams to-day announcing that the Turkish Ministers have left Greece, Bulgaria and Servia without asking for their passports.

It was not denied that the informal style of their departure was intended as an affront to the Balkan allies.

NO POISON ON BULLETS.

Result of Chemical Test of Missiles Schrank Carried.

MILWAUKEE, Oct. 16.—The result of the chemical analysis of the bullets remaining in the revolver used by Schrank to wound Col. Roosevelt showed that there was no poison on them.

HAVE SCHRANK'S VALISE.

One Found by Police in Charleston Contained Cartridges.

CHARLESTON, S. C., Oct. 16.—The police are holding at headquarters the valise left in this city by John Schrank. It contained many letters couched in incoherent phrases, chief of which was "Down with Roosevelt; we want no king in America."

The grip also contained naturalization papers issued to John Scrank, a box of .38-calibre cartridges, a box which had contained a pistol of the same calibre and a razor, as well as a well worn outfit of clothing.

Schrank came here by steamship and stopped at the Moseley House. The police here to-day wired the Milwaukee authorities asking them whether they wanted the grip.

BULKY DYNAMITE EXHIBITS.

Government to Identify Documents and Read Them to Jury.

INDIANAPOLIS, Ind., Oct. 16.—It was apparent to-day that the plan of the Government in the dynamite conspiracy case was first to identify all of the thousand or more documentary exhibits and then to read them to the jury to make the evidence more effective.

WEATHER REPORT.

Fair and cool, with frost to-night; increasing cloudiness and slightly warmer to-morrow; moderate variable winds, becoming southerly.

WASHINGTON, Oct. 16.—Eastern New York—Fair to-night with frost, heavy in the interior; slightly warmer.

Western Pennsylvania, Ohio and western New York—Fair to-night and Thursday; slowly rising temperature.

TO-DAY'S RECORD IN THIS CITY.

Temperature.

8 A. M.	44	12 A. M.	51
9 A. M.	45	1 A. M.	53
10 A. M.	47	2 P. M.	59
11 A. M.	51		

Humidity.

8 A. M.	55	12 A. M.	40
9 A. M.	60	1 P. M.	39
10 A. M.	65	2 P. M.	42
11 A. M.	60		

Barometer.

8 A. M.	30.39	12 A. M.	30.36
9 A. M.	30.39	1 P. M.	30.34
10 A. M.	30.39	2 P. M.	30.32
11 A. M.	30.39		

Miniature Almanac.
Wednesday, Oct. 16.

A.M.	P.M.	P.M.
Sun rises....6:09	Moon sets....9:24	Sun sets....5:1

Tide Table.

	Low water.	High water
Sandy Hook	5:04 A. M.	11:28 A. M.
Governors Island	6:10 A. M.	12:08 P. M.
Hell Gate	7:45 A. M.	1:58 P. M.

STATE'S BECKER CASE NEARLY IN

Prosecution Will Finish Evidence To-day.

MRS. ROSENTHAL ON STAND

Harry Pollok Corroborates Rose in Part.

The State will close its case against Lieut. Charles Becker to-day. Announcement to that effect was made in court at the end of the morning session, when Assistant District Attorney Frank Moss said to Justice Goff, before whom the case is being tried:

"Your Honor, if you will consent to an adjournment now (1 o'clock) we will close our case this afternoon. We have been trying to expedite the trial as much as possible."

District Attorney Whitman will concentrate his efforts during the remainder of the day on the attempt to get before the jury the bank accounts of Lieut. Becker. If he succeeds in introducing them a score of witnesses will be called to testify as to the sources of the suddenly accumulated wealth of the lieutenant accused of the murder of Herman Rosenthal. During the period of eight months prior to the murder the District Attorney has discovered Becker deposited approximately $100,000.

HART TO OPEN FOR DEFENCE.

John W. Hart, attorney of record for Becker, will deliver the opening address for the defence. It is probable, however, that this will not take place until to-morrow morning. It will depend, of course, on the length of time required by the State to complete its direct case.

Thomas Coupe, the former night clerk at the Elks Club, who fled to England because he claimed his life was threatened after he had testified before the Grand Jury, will be used in rebuttal by the prosecution, District Attorney Whitman said. Coupe is expected to arrive here in company with Assistant Dis-

(Continued on Eighth Page.)

BULGARIA DECLARES WAR.

Joins With Montenegro to Lead Balkan Allies Against Turks.

SOFIA, Bulgaria, Oct. 16.—Bulgaria's declaration of war against Turkey was published here this afternoon.

It was expected that the Servian and Greek declarations of war would follow.

Several days ago Bulgaria submitted an ultimatum to Turkey demanding certain reforms. At the same time the Sofia Government sent a note to the Powers notifying them of its demands.

BRITISH LANDING IN CRETE.

Protectorate to Be Upheld in Event of Islanders' Revolt.

LONDON, Oct. 16.—A landing by British bluejackets at Suda Bay, in Crete, was momentarily expected to-day.

The Christian Cretans, long restive under Turkish rule, have given new signs of open revolt in order to join Greece.

England, among other Powers exercising a protectorate over the island, it is stated, considers itself under obligation o safeguard Turkish interests there.

RUSSO-CHINESE BANK THEFT MADE GOOD

About $400,000 of Value of Securities Wider Stole Recovered.

About $400,000 of the value of the gilt-edged securities stolen from the Russo-Chinese Bank at 50 Pine street, in this city, last year by Erwin J. Wider, one of the clerks, have been recovered. It was learned to-day from the bank's headquarters in St. Petersburg. The amount recovered represents 80 per cent. of the securities stolen. The financial representative of the bank here would not discuss the settlement.

A visit to the bank this afternoon gave the impression of moving day. Boxes littered the hallway of the second floor. According to one of the clerks these boxes contained books, records, &c., of the branch here and they are to be shipped to St. Petersburg.

"We are winding up here," said the clerk. "M. Etienne de Markowski, our agent, will probably be recalled to London. When the office is closed here it is expected that the American business will be handled by the National City Bank and Ladenburg, Thalmann & Co., who have been retained as our correspondents."

Julius Goldman, counsel for the bank, said that the amount secured in settlement was enough to satisfy the directors. The lawyer declined to reveal the terms of the settlement.

FIRE IN GOVERNOR'S MANSION.

Gov. Dix Slept Soundly While Firemen Put Out Basement Blaze.

ALBANY, Oct. 16.—Gov. Dix and the members of his family slept soundly early this morning while the fire department responded to a "still" alarm and put out a fire in the basement of the Executive Mansion.

The floor timbers under the kitchen range caught fire, and although smoke filled the basement for some time it was nearly an hour and a half before the night watchman located the blaze.

Gov. Dix did not know of the fire until he awoke several hours later.

AMERICAN HORSES WIN.

Whitney and Keene Entries Capture Premier Honors.

NEWMARKET, England, Oct. 16.—American owned horses were prominent in the races at the second October meeting here to-day. H. P. Whitney's filly by Watercress—Hamburg Belle won the Two Year Old Plate of 100 sovereigns added to a sweepstakes of 5 sovereigns each for starters. The distance was five furlongs, and a dozen horses ran.

The second horse to finish was the Duke of Devonshire's colt by Spearmint—Claque, and Surcingel, owned by Leopold de Rothschild, was third.

J. R. Keene's Castleton beat two other horses for premier honors in the Kennett Plate of 200 sovereigns, distance five furlongs. Only three-year-olds were eligible. J. B. Joel's Absurd secured second place and Sol Joel's Lady Flo was last.

Mr. Whitney's Whisk Broom was second in the Select Stakes of 10 sovereigns each for starters, with 300 sovereigns added. The distance was one mile and four ran. Long Set, owned by Sol Joel, was the winner, and J. B. Joel's The Story was third.

His Majesty's Dorando won the Autumn Plate of 200 sovereigns for three-year-olds. Ten other horses went the distance of seven furlongs. E. Hulton's Ambush was second and Leopold de Rothschild's Ormus was third.

MOTORMAN KILLS BANDIT.

Disguised Gunman Tried to Rob Conductor on Oakland Car.

OAKLAND, Cal., Oct. 16.—An unidentified bandit, wearing a false mustache and wig, was shot and instantly killed here late last night by Motorman H. J. Hegwer, after the bandit had attempted to rob the conductor of a Grant avenue car.

V. E. Meeker, the conductor, fought with the bandit and suffered the loss of the middle finger of his right hand, which was shot off. The motorman came from the front of the car and shot the robber dead.

MATTY ON MOUND FOR GIANTS

Stahl Sends Bedient to Box in the Final Game.

A SMALL CROWD

Only 12,000 Fans Turn Out for the Deciding Contest.

ROYAL ROOTERS ABSENT

Resent Snub of Management by Staying Away.

FENWAY PARK, BOSTON, Oct. 16.—The Giants and Red Sox met here this afternoon in the deciding game of the world's baseball championship series of 1912. With the two teams tied at three victories each and another eleven inning game tied, it would naturally be expected that enthusiasm and interest in the contest would be at concert pitch. Such, however, was not the case. A most unwonted state of affairs existed. Apparently the Red Sox rooters had lost all hope of the championship coming to the Hub and preferred to stay at home rather than witness the final humiliating of their baseball pets.

Thirty minutes before the contest was scheduled to begin long rows of empty seats in both bleachers and grand stands stared the players of both teams in the face as they practised on the diamond. This was not due to any lack of opportunity to secure seats, for the box offices had been open almost continuously since 8 o'clock last night. It appeared that Boston fans conceded the series to the New York club after their gallant uphill fight in which they drew up on even terms with the Red Sox and forced them to make a last stand on their home grounds. Neither could the weather man be blamed for the absence of the cheering thousands that had heretofore encouraged the Red Sox in their battles with the Giants.

Aside from the fact that there was the snap of autumn in the air and a rather stiff wind blowing out from the northwest conditions were most satisfactory for the deciding game. There was not the slightest fleck of white cloud to be seen in the blue vault of the sky above and the afternoon sun illuminated every section of Fenway Park. The diamond and base lines were dry and fast and the players sprinted about during the practice session without fear of slips or trip. There was not a single stand surrounding the playing field that bore its full quota of spectators aside from the bleachers back of left field. The huge grand stands, including the $2 sections back of first and third bases, were not even half filled. And there was not the slightest congestion or indication of an eleventh hour rush, which has heretofore filled vacant stretches at the last moment. What this lack of support will mean to the Red Sox it was hard to determine before the game. The psychology of baseball is an important factor in the national game, and the row after row of empty benches which faced the Red Sox was a clear indication of hope abandoned so far as the fans were concerned. From the press box it appeared as though the Boston players failed to put the same snap and ginger in their practice.

Manager Jake Stahl warmed up both Wood and Bedient, while McGraw had both Marquard and Mathewson out for preliminary exercise. All four of the twirlers appeared to have plenty of speed and curves at their command. It was estimated that just before the game began not more than 12,000 spectators were quartered within the walls of Fenway Park, and in place of the long lines of late comers who usually swell the attendance the faint hearted fans dribbled in two and three at a time, apparently making little or no impression on the yawning stretches of yellow benches and seats. The Royal Rooters Club, which had trouble with the management over their seat reservations, were conspicuous by their absence. While undoubtedly many of the club members were present as individuals, there was no band parade or other features which have made the preceding games so spectacular. The club manager in a last desperate effort to create enthusiasm and support for the Red Sox had a number of men and boys throughout grand stands and bleachers distributing club pennants for the fans to use in this, the closing game of the series.

THE SCORE BY INNINGS.

GIANTS.................. 0 0 1 0 0 0 0 0 0 1 2
BOSTON.................. 0 0 0 0 0 0 1 [illegible] 0 [illegible] 2

BATTING ORDER, EIGHTH GAME.

GIANTS.	RED SOX.
Devore, r. f.	Hooper, r. f.
Doyle, 2b.	Yerkes, 2b.
Snodgrass, c. f.	Speaker, c. f.
Murray, l. f.	Lewis, l. f.
Merkle, 1b.	Gardner, 3b.
Herzog, 3b.	Stahl, 1b.
Meyers, c.	Wagner, ss.
Fletcher, ss.	Cady, c.
Mathewson, p.	Bedient, p.

FIRST INNING.

Promptly at 2 o'clock Josh Devore came to the plate bat in hand for the Giants. Bedient faced him steadily and his first offering was a ball. With two and three on him he hit a slow roller to Wagner and was out at Stahl's station. Larry Doyle took his time and had three balls and two strikes before he followed Devore out over the Wagner-Stahl route. Apparently McGraw had given orders to wait Bedient out and it worked in Snodgrass's case, for he walked on the fifth pitched ball. Snodgrass was safe at second when Wagner muffed Cady's perfect throw, which reached the bag ten feet ahead of the runner. Murray raised two fouls into the stands before he hit to Gardner and was out at first after making a slide that upset Jake Stahl in a heap. No runs, no hits, one error.

Hooper was first to face Mathewson. He attempted to bunt, with the result that he bounced the ball directly into Merkle's hand for the initial out at first. Yerkes struck out on four pitched balls. Speaker made a single to right and took second when Doyle dropped Devore's perfect throw. The error had no effect, for Lewis struck out. No runs, one hit, one error.

SECOND INNING.

Merkle tried to wait out Bedient, but was fooled by a straight third strike on the outside corner of the plate. Herzog flied out to Speaker in deep centre. The game was stopped while Umpire O'Loughlin drove several Giants and Red Sox away from the foul lines in the deep outfield. The crowds became impatient and yelled "Play ball!" and a great uproar of wooden clappers accompanied the players to the bench. Meyers was safe at first when Gardner made an inexcusable error of his easy roller toward third. Fletcher hit the first ball pitched to centre for a single, putting Meyers on second. The Chief took a big lead of second and Cady threw down to catch him. Meyers raced on to third, and when Gardner muffed Yerkes's perfect throw the Indian was safe and Fletcher moved to second. Matty ended the inning by flying to Speaker in deep centre. No runs, one hit, two errors.

Gardner refused to hit at any of Matty's curves, and so he got a pass to first. It was Mathewson's first pass on balls during the series. Manager Stahl forced Gardner, Doyle to Fletcher. The ball was hard hit and Doyle made a poor toss to Fletcher, who grabbed the ball lying at full length with one foot on the bag. On the hit and run play Wagner singled to left, sending Stahl to second. McGraw had Tesreau, Crandall and Marquard warming up. Cady flied out to Merkle. Bedient went out, Doyle to Merkle. No runs, one hit, no errors.

THIRD INNING.

Bedient threw three straight balls, and Stahl, Cady and Gardner all came in to the box to steady Bedient. It did not help, for he walked Devore on four balls. Doyle went down, Gardner to Stahl, while Devore moved on to second. Snodgrass grounded out to Stahl and Devore reached third on the play. The Giants' first run came in when Murray doubled to left centre, sending Devore home. Speaker made a great try for the ball, but could just get his finger tips on it. Wagner threw Merkle out at first. One run, one hit, no errors.

Doyle and Merkle accounted for Hooper. Yerkes was out, Matty to Merkle, on an easy one. Matty fanned Speaker with a high ball outside the plate. No runs, no hits, no errors.

FOURTH INNING.

Herzog opened with a long, clean hit, which followed the left field foul line clear down into the bleachers. He reached third easily, but under the ground rules the hit was good for but two bases and he had to go back to the midway. Meyers crossed the Red Sox with a sacrifice, Gardner to Stahl, Herzog going to third. Fletcher flied out to Gardner. Mathewson flied out to Hooper. No runs, one hit, no errors.

Fletcher threw Lewis out to Merkle. Gardner drove a liner at Snodgrass in deep centre. Snodgrass muffed the ball but raced back and got it on the roll, and Gardner tried to reach third on the misplay and was out, Snodgrass to Doyle to Herzog. Stahl fanned. No runs, no hits, one error.

FIFTH INNING.

Devore bounced a hit off Bedient's left shin and was safe at first. Devore was out stealing second, Cady to Wagner, who blocked him four feet off the bag. Hooper made a great catch of Doyle's long smash. The ball was clearing the right field bleacher fence when Hooper shot into the air and pulled it down amid terrific chering. Snodgrass smashed a long single between Gardner and Wagner. Murray fouled out to Cady. No runs, two hits, no errors.

Murray raced way back to the bleacher wall and caught Wagner's high lift. Cady almost duplicated Wagner's fly, making the second out. Bedient flied out to Devore. Matty retired the side on three pitched balls. No runs, no hits, no errors.

$100,000 UP IN WALL STREET.

Prevailing Odds for To-day's Game Were 10 to 8 on the Giants.

It was estimated that about $100,000 would change hands in the Wall Street district this afternoon on the outcome of the world's baseball championship series. About $10,000 of this was put up this morning, the most of it at odds of 10 to 8 on the Giants. The majority of the bets were made on this basis, but it was reported at noon that one member of the Stock Exchange had put up $30,000 at odds of 10 to 8 on the Red Sox.

The small bets were innumerable. A crowd of messenger boys, reversing the prevalent odds, pooled their savings to the amount of $40 and bet it on the Giants against $50 put up by Eck Lane, a cigar dealer. Incidentally Lane will pay out about $25,000 in bets placed with him when to-day's game is over. Another Wall street cigar dealer has held stakes to the amount of about $15,000.

The brokers generally were expressing gratification this morning that there was to be "only one more afternoon of it." Ever since the start of the series help has been at a premium in the Street. Messenger boys and clerks have elbowed each other around the tickers and left business to take care of itself. Now that the series is about at an end the brokers say they expect to resume work.

Wall Street, where interest has been exceptionally keen ever since the first game, has contributed between $50,000 and $70,000 to the gate receipts of the series.

THE PRESIDENT LEAVES TO SPEAK AT WORCESTER

Will Address Antiquarian Society There To-night.

The President and Mrs. Taft left New York at 9:15 o'clock this morning over the New Haven road for Worcester, Mass., where Mr. Taft will deliver a speech this evening before the American Antiquarian Society. The President and his party will reach Worcester at 2:15 this afternoon. Mrs. Taft will continue on to Boston and Beverly.

Mr. Taft will be the guest of Mr. Waldo Lincoln in Worcester. After attending a public meeting of the American Antiquarian Society in the afternoon the President will go to Mr. Lincoln's home, where he will pass the night. To-morrow the President will motor to Beverly.

Mr. and Mrs. Taft stayed last night at the Holland House in this city, the guests of Charles P. Taft of Cincinnati, the President's brother.

Senator W. Murray Crane of Massachusetts called to see the President a short time before Mr. Taft went down to breakfast at 8:45. It could not be learned what was talked about at the brief interview.

The President and Mrs. Taft breakfasted with Charles P. Taft and the latter's wife and daughter. During the meal a uniformed policeman and an employee of the hotel kept a careful watch at the door, while a dozen or more secret service men walked about the lobby and the sidewalk in front of the hotel.

A fair sized crowd greeted the Presidential party cordially when they entered the machines waiting at the door to convey them to the Grand Central station. Mr. Taft appeared more cheerful to-day than yesterday and wore his customary smile.

SPECIAL COTTON REPORT.

September Consumption of Staple in Census Bureau Figures.

WASHINGTON, Oct. 16.—A special report by the Census Bureau to-day gave the total amount of cotton consumed during September as 437,322 bales and the total of active spindles in operation during the same month as 29,795,792.

Cotton on hand Sept. 30 was: manufacturers' hands, 722,781 bales; independent warehouses, 1,387,897 bal

Total imports in September w 10,510 bales and exports 729,859.

BASEBALL :: BOXING :: RACING

ALL THE LATEST SPORTING NEWS

LAURENCE H. WOLTZ
Sporting Editor

BOSTON WINS WORLD'S CHAMPIONSHIP FROM THE MOST EXCITING BATTLE OF THE

IN TENTH-INNING RALLY BOSTON DOWNED GIANTS AND WON GAME

BOTH AGGREGATIONS PLAYED GREAT BALL THROUGHOUT THE ENTIRE TEN INNINGS OF GRUELLING BATTLE FOR TITLE

THE MIGHTY "SMOKY" JOE RELIEVED BEDIENT IN SEVENTH INNING AND PITCHED MASTERFUL BALL FOR RED SOX—BEDIENT ALSO PITCHED GREAT BALL FOR THE FIRST SEVEN ROUNDS.

LUCK AGAINST GREAT MATHEWSON

SNODGRASS' ERROR IN TENTH INNING PAVED THE WAY TO VITCORY FOR J. GARLAND STAHL'S ATHLETES — MEYERS ALLOWING SPEAKER'S FOUL TO DROP HELPED CONSIDERABLY IN LOSING GAME FOR GIANTS.

By Laurence H. Woltz.

FENWAY PARK, Boston, Oct. 16 (Special).—Today's baseball game which went to the Boston Red Sox in the tenth inning after two were out, by the score of 3 to 2, brought to an end the greatest series of baseball games ever played for the world's championship. However today's exhibition was more of a tragedy of the diamond than it was an exhibition of the great pastime, and in saying this I am not forgetting that the game was replete with the brilliant plays that are possible in baseball. But, the tragedy part came in the Boston's part of the tenth when the game was literally handed to the American Leaguers, and the great and grand Christy Mathewson had seen another world series game lost for him within the twinkling of an eye.

Crime to Lose the Game.

It was nothing short of a crime, a heinous crime, for Matty to lose that game, but this must be said of him, he is not bemoaning the defeat tonight, and is not censuring the work of Fred Snodgrass and Chief Meyers, both of whom contributed in serving the game and the world championship to the American Leaguers on the proverbial silver platter. Snodgrass has been the "goat" of the Giant camp ever since the series opened, and he brought his season's work to a close with the most glaring error that has ever been made on a baseball diamond, and an error that will long be remembered by the fans who witnessed the game. Matty went the entire route for the Giants, while Bedient worked the first seven innings against the Giants, followed by Joe Wood, who pitched the remaining innings. Bedient was removed in the seventh to allow Hendrikson to bat for him.

Boston Fans Quitters.

The Boston crowd, the fans, not players, proved themselves quitters of the rankest kind, and today's struggle brought out the smallest crowd that has yet attended one of the 1912 games. There were several thousond of empty seats when the umpires got the game under way; there was no brass band present to play Tessie, the battle song of the Sox, and there was no organized rooting. The game, had it been played in New York, would have drawn at least forty thousand fans, and thousands would have had to have been refused admission at the gates.

But once before under the modern system had two ball clubs ever gone to seven games to end a big series. Today two clubs had not only whirled, lashed, reeled and fought their way to seven games, but having tied a record in this respect they were no closer to solving the solution as to the 1912 world championship than they were at the start. It appeared a certainty that one of the clubs must lose today's game, thereby losing the great championship by the narrow margin of one game. All of this considered it was astonishing to look over the stands when the game was under way and note the number of empty seats, both in bleachers and grandstand.

Rumors Afloat.

"The fans" quit with the playing of Tuesday's game when the Sox were snowed under by the Giants. Then, those of the narrow-minded variety, started hollering that the series was a "frame-up" for the purpose of making money and all that sort of rot. Then again the saddest blow was the treatment accorded the Boston royal rooters Tuesday afternoon by the Boston management, who refused to give them the same reserved section in the bleachrs that they had occupied ever since the series started. This band of rooters had been game to the core; they had followed the team to and from New York, and they gave Boston a whole lot of advertising in the big city of New York. They came out in the morning papers today with a severe roast for the Boston management, and announced to the public that they were through for the 1912 season. All these things considered it can be seen why the attendance dropped off so, at that it shows a mighty poor spirit on the part of the Bostonians to think that the deciding game of the series should have been attended by the smallest crowd of the entire series. This is an item that will give baseball writers something to argue about all winter, when the "hot stove league" has

oCntinued on Page Seven.

"RED" JOHN MURRAY

Who secured two two-base hits in yesterday's game and also scored one of the two runs made by the Giants.

The Box Score

NEW YORK.	AB	R	H	PO	A	E
Devore, rf	3	1	1	3	1	0
Doyle, 2b	5	0	0	1	3	1
Snodgrass, cf	4	0	1	4	1	1
Murray, lf	5	1	2	3	0	0
Merkle, 1b	5	0	1	10	0	0
Herzog, 3b	5	0	2	2	1	0
Meyers, c	3	0	0	4	1	0
Fletcher, ss	3	0	1	2	3	0
**McCormick	1	0	0	0	0	0
Shafer, ss	0	0	0	0	0	0
Mathewson, p	4	0	1	0	3	0
Totals	38	2	9	z29	15	2

zTwo out when winning run scored.

BOSTON.	AB	R	H	PO	A	E
Hooper, rf	5	0	0	3	0	0
Yerkes, 2b	4	1	1	0	3	0
Speaker, cf	4	0	2	2	0	1
Lewis, lf	4	0	0	1	0	0
Gardner, 3b	3	0	1	1	4	2
Stahl, 1b	4	1	2	15	0	1
Wagner, ss	3	0	1	3	5	1
Cady, c	4	0	0	5	3	0
Bedient, p	2	0	0	0	1	0
*Henricksen	1	0	1	0	0	0
Wood, p	0	0	0	2	0	0
***Engle	1	1	0	0	0	0
Totals	35	3	8	30	18	5

*Batted for Bedient in seventh.
**Batted for Fletcher in ninth.
***Batted for Wood in tenth.

Score by innings—

New York	0	0	1	0	0	0	0	0	0	1—2
Boston	0	0	0	0	0	0	1	0	0	2—3

Summary—Two-base hits, Murray 2, Herzog, Gardner, Henriksen, Stahl; pitching record, off Bedient, 1 run and 6 hits in 26 times at bat in 7 innings, off Wood 1 run and 3 hits in 12 times at bat in 3 innings; sacrifice hit, Meyers; sacrifice fly, Gardner; stolen base, Devore; left on bases, New York 11, Boston 9; first base on balls, off Bedient 3, off Mathewson 5, off Wood 1; first base on errors, New York 1, Boston 1; struck out, by Mathewson 4, by Bedient 2, by Wood 2. Time, 2:37. Umpires at plate, O'Loughlin; on bases, Rigler; left field, Klem; right field, Evans.

SANFORD HIGH SCHOOL WILL PLAY D. H. S. FOOTBALL TEAM AT BARRS FIELD ON SATURDAY

On next Saturday afternoon at Barrs field, on Durkee avenue, the Duval high school football eleven will tackle the Sanford high school. The athletes on the local club have been out daily working and at the present each pigskin performer is said to be in thte very best of condition.

A great deal of improvement is manifesting itself as a result of the hard work. Prof. Wilbur and Mr. Bird are trying hard to remedy the weak spots which appeared in the Columbia game last week and when the next game is played, the friends of Duval's pigskin warriors will see a team which will be truly worthy of their heartiest support. The whole team is being given a hard drill in tackling and signal practice and good results are already apparent.

The line composed of Albertson, Lasker, Schwartz, Dowling, and Capt. Upchurch are showing more speed and aggressiveness each day and their opponents will have hard work getting through.

The ends are given daily drills in getting down under punts and in handling forward passed and are showing great improvement. A merry fight is on for these positions, with Maull Houston, Lovell and Jackson as the leading candidates.

Sinclair at quarterback is handling the team well and bids fair to make a first class quarter. The other members of the backfield (Stockton, Toomer, Tracy and Bryan) are rapidly gaining speed in running plays and will make other teams sit up and take notice. A great deal of time is being spent on the formation of interference and a wonderful improvement is already noted in this department of the game.

Dowling is doing fine work in getting off punts and Sinclair is beginning to show class in the drop kicking line. With other members of the team also coming strong in this line it seems an assured fact that Duval will be well taken care of in the kicking department.

Remember the first home game of the season will be played at Barrs field next Saturday afternoon, when Duval will line up against Sanford high school. A great game is expected and present indications point to a large crowd. Let everybody come out and encourage the local team. The game will be called at 3 o'clock. Admission 25 cents.

Foster Rockwell, the former Eli star, is expected at New Haven soon to help coach the Eli quarterbacks.

GATE RECEIPTS.

Boston, Oct. 16.—The attendance and receipts at today's game was announced by the National Commission as follows:
Total paid attendance, 17,034.
Total receipts, $30,500.
National Commission's share, $3,050.
Each club's share, $13,725.

CHRISTY MATHEWSON PITCHED WONDERFUL BALL THROUGHOUT THE ENTIRE GAME—COSTLY ERRORS LOST BATTLE FOR NEW YORK'S STAR TWIRLER — BEDIENT AND WOOD WERE AS STEADY AS AN EIGHT-DAY CLOCK.

ATTENDANCE WAS POOR

RED SOX WINNING YESTERDAY'S GAME GIVES THEM CHAMPIONSHIP TITLE—EACH HUB CITY PLAYER RECEIVES $4,024 AND THE LOSERS ONLY RECEIVE $2,566 — TOTAL RECEIPTS FOR EIGHT GAMES $490,833.

Boston, Oct. 16.—The Boston Red Sox, pennant winners of the American League, are the world's baseball champions of 1912. Defeating the New York Nationals today by a score of 3 to 2 in ten innings of a bitterly fought struggle, they captured their fourth victory of the world's series and carried off the premier honors in baseball.

The Giants won three games of the series that was played before more than a quarter of a million people and one contest was a tie. The total receipts for the eight games was $490,833 and each Red Sox player received $4,024 while the Giant players each came in for $2,566.

Today's was a game of excitement and changing emotions for the 17,000 spectators who went to Fenway park to see the teams which had struggled valiantly for seven games with honors even meet in the deciding contest. Never was a ball game more hard fought, for it was not until twilight had fallen upon the tenth inning that the red stockinged Yerkes flashed over the plate with the winning run.

Giants Scored.

The Giants broke into the run column in the third inning. Devore received a base on balls. Doyle went out, Gardner to Stahl, Devore taking second. Snodgrass grounded out to Stahl, unassisted, and Devore slid into third. Play was suspended a moment until Manager McGraw had finished a little tailoring, patching up a hole in Devore's trousers with a safety pin. The operation ended, up came "Red" Murray, who smashed a terrific drive to left center. The speedy Speaker was off immediately after the ball hit the bat, but was just able to touch the ball with his fingers. Devore had trotted home with the first run and Murray rested on second when the ball was returned to the infield. New York rooters were beside themselves with joy for they figured with Mathewson pitching Boston could not get two runs to beat their one. Merkle ended the inning by grounding out, Wagner to Stahl.

Score Was Tied.

The Red Sox opened the seventh, in which they tied the score, by Gardner flying to Snodgrass. Stahl dropped a single in left, Murray, Snodgrass and Fletcher balking each other in trying to get the fly.

The Red manager moved down to second when Wagner was given a base on balls. It was up to Cady to do something but the home rooters groaned when he popped a fly into the waiting hands of Fletcher. Henriksen, batting for Bedient, let a couple of balls go by him and then he opened on the next pitch and slammed the ball down the left field base line for two bases and Stahl came home with the tying run amid great excitement. Wagner took third on the play. Hooper tried hard to bring Wagner home, but he flew out to Snodgrass. "Smoky Joe" Wood was given a royal reception when he went into the pitching box for the Red Sox in the eighth.

Neither team pushed any additional runs over the plate in the eighth and ninth innings, and into the tenth inning the contest went. The Giants chilled the hopes of the Boston crowd by scoring a run on a double into the bleachers by Murray and a hit by Merkle to center, which Speaker juggled. Hundreds of fans tore up their score cards, jammed their hats down over their heads and disconsolately left the grounds, for Mathewson was pitching a game which was baffling Boston's batsmen.

Engle Starts Fireworks.

Engle led off for the Red Sox in the last half of the tenth. He had gone to the bat for Joe Wood. The Red Sox pinch hitter sent up a towering fly to left-center. Snodgrass moved over toward the bleacher seats and waited for the ball to drop. He muffed it, and before the ball was recovered Engle was on second base. No one was out, and the crowd was in a frenzy of joy.

Hooper tried to sacrifice but Mathewson foiled him and the best the Red Sox gardener could do was a fly to Snodgrass. The Giant pitcher tried to work the corners of the plate for Yerkes, but Yerkes waited him out and walked on four balls. With Engle on second and Yerkes on first, Tris Speaker came up. The crowd to a man was now yelling.

Speaker swung his big bat, The first ball was a curve and inside, and Speaker popped up a high foul. Meyers, Merkle and Mathewson went after it, but it fell safe among them. New York's last chance to stop the Bostons passed with the failure to get that foul ball. Mathewson started a high fast one and Speaker met it fairly. On a line over Doyle's head the ball was driven and Engle rushed over the plate with the tieing run. On the throw in, Yerkes went to third and Speaker dashed on to second.

The New York infield drew in and Lewis was purposely passed so that a runner could be forced at the plate on an infield grounder. Then came the finish. Gardner, with three balls and one strike on him smashed a long fly to Devore. Yerkes set himself at third and dashed for home when the ball dropped into Devore's hands.

The Indian Meyers crouched at the plate to take the throw he expected from Devore. The instant he had caught it Devore whipped the ball homeyard On came the flying Yerkes; on came the ball. Mathewson, who saw the throw would be wide, threw up his hands and Meyers turned away without trying for the ball. Yerkes did not know the throw was wild, however, and he plunged head foremost and slid over the plate in a cloud of dust with the run that won the championship for the Red Sox.

Crowd Cheered.

The crowd fairly screamed in a delirium of joy. Men threw their hats in the air and cheered until they could cheer no more. Hundreds rushed upon the field and gathering about the Red Sox bench, applauded the winning players. Mathewson buried himself in his great coat and walked from the field. Scores of persons followed the pitcher and patted him on the back, congratulating him upon his fine work in the box. Manager McGraw elbowed his way through the throng to the Red Sox clubhouse beneath the stand, where he congratulated Manager Stahl and the Red Sox players. He exchanged blows with a spectator on the way on account of an insulting remark made by the spectator.

SNODGRASS

Who dropped Engle's line drive in the tenth round, which allowed the Boston hitter to make second base safely and this greatly helped the Stahlmen win the contest.

THE GAME BY INNINGS.

FIRST INNING.

New York—The first ball pitched was a ball. Devore out, Wagner to Stahl. It was a beautiful stop and throw. Doyle out, Wagner to Stahl. The crowd was on tension and cheered every play. The Giants were waiting Bedient out to the last ball and strike, fifteen balls being thrown to the plate before the first two men were retired. Snodgras walked. Snodgrass stole second. Wagner dropped the ball

Continued on Page Seven.

BASEBALL BOXING :: RACING

ALL THE LATEST SPORTING NEWS

LAURENCE H. WOLTZ
Sporting Editor

M'GRAW'S NEW YORK GIANTS IN EIGHT GAMES WHICH WERE PLAYED FOR TITLE

BOSTON WINS CHAMPIONSHIP FROM NEW YORK GIANTS

Continued from Page Six.

her opening, which is now ready for opening up here.

Tenth Inning.

But before I proceed further, I must get that disgusting third inning out of my system, if not, it may make me ill. Now, mind you, after the Giants had taken their tenth inning, the score was 2 to 1 in favor of New York, this due to the grand, healthy two-base wallop by Red Murray, and a most timely single by Fred Merkle in the tenth. It was these two hits that gave the Giants their one-run lead and what looked to be a sure victory.

Snodgrass' Rank Error.

Well, here the little tragedy goes. It was Mr. Joe Wood's turn to lead off in the tenth for the Sox, but instead of sending this fellow up to the plate, Manager Stahl called upon Clyde Engle, a person whom we all know well. Clyde did not look dangerous this afternoon, in fact such a grand game of ball was Matty pitching that none of the Sox looked troublesome. After getting Engle two and two, Mathewson served up a "floater," and Engle hooked it. However, it was only a high fly to center field, and it was a 100 to 1 shot that Snodgrass would catch it. Did he catch it? Well, certainly not. After camping under the ball, all set for the innocent and inoffensive looking little pill, he allowed it to hit in his glove and then bound away, and while all of this bunk was going on Engle was safely camped on second base. Hooper was the next batter, and he flew out to center field, Snodgrass managing to squeeze this one. Next, we have the mighty Tris Speaker, the boy who has made Texas a muchly talked of state up this way this summer. Well, Speaker fouled one into the stands, then he took one, it being called a strike. He next hit a little pop foul fly that Fred Merkle could have caught after running only about ten feet. However, instead of letting Merkle have the ball, Chief Meyers darted down the foul line like a steam locomotive and Merkle had nothing to do but stop, else he and Meyers would have come together and somebody would have been seriously injured. As the result of this decidedly rank piece of work on the part of Meyers, the ball fell a few feet in front of both Merkle and Meyers, hitting the ground without molestation. I am just a little ahead of my story. Just before Speaker took his place at bat, Steve Yerkes succeeded in working Matty for a base on balls, and he was on first and Engle on second when Speaker stepped up.

But back to Speaker's turn at bat. After he was given new life by the boneheadedness of Meyers, who went after a foul fly far out of his territory, he singled to right field, Engle scoring and Yerkes taking third. Speaker himself took second on the throw to third, which was made in attempting to nail Yerkes. Lewis was the next batter, and he walked. Gardner ended the game, and placed the stamp "1912 world champions" on the Boston field, when he sent a long fly to Josh Devore, Yerkes scoring after the catch. Now, good folks, you can carefully look over the tenth inning and see why Christy Mathewson and the New York Giants lost the final game of the greatest series ever staged for the big prize.

Giants Confident.

The Giants were quite confident that they would land today's game, and they really started off like winners. McGraw told me just before he went to the ball yard that he was strong in the belief that he could beat any club that he could tie. Mac hobnobbed with a few of us last night, and he was just about as confident a little rooster as I have ever seen. With Jake Stahl things were quite different as many were predicting that Stahl had thrown up the sponge; this, however, was anything but the truth. At the same time there was not the same confidence and fighting spirit in the camp of the Red Sox that there was in the Giant quarters.

Bedient Selected.

Bedient, the 22-year-old youngster, was selected to oppose the peerless Matty, and the game started according to schedule at 2 o'clock. The Giants scored first, they making one in the third as the result of a base on balls and a slashing double to center field by Hero Jack Murray.

The lone score looked like it was to be the big one until the seventh, when the Bostons drove one across the pan. Prior to this time the Red Sox had had several opportunities to score, but Matty was crafty and steady in the pinches. With men on bases, he took things as easily as he would spending an evening with his wife, and rocking along in a big Morris chair. He simply smiled,

HUGH BEDIENT

Who pitched fine ball for the Boston Red Sox in yesterday's deciding game. Bedient is one of the youngest athletes on the Boston club.

pawed a little in the dirt and pitched some sure enough ball. In the second Boston had runners on first and second and only one out, yet no score. In the sixth they had men on first and second and only one out. Again there was no score. It was a case of Matty having the goods in the right spots. To be sure, the big blonde was twirling a masterful game, and no one dreamed that it later was to be tossed to the winds for him by a couple of his teammates.

Boston Tied the Score.

In the seventh, the Beantown brigade tied the score. One was out when Stahl's little pop fly fell safe for a hit as the result of a mixing of the signals between Fletcher and Snodgrass and Murray. Another piece of tough luck for Matty, for after Wagner walked and Cady died on a pop to Fletcher Manager Stahl put Hendrickson in to bat for Bedient, and the "pinch hitter" made good by smashing out a clean double down the left field line, Stahl scoring.

Tied Until Tenth.

The game rocked along one and one until the tenth, when the Giants uncorked what they certainly thought to be the winning run. Witih one out Red Murray, again I say hero, put a line drive into the center field bleachers, the blow counting for two bases, this per ground rule agreement, then Merkle nucorked a timely single and Murray scored and Merkle took second when Speaker let the ball get through his pins. Herzog and Meyers were the next two batters, and went out easily. The Bostons' tenth and how Christy Mathewson was robbed of a baseball game, the biggest game of the 1912 season, I have told before.

Matty Lost.

In the fifth inning Mathewson pitched only three balls, the first three batters hitting the first ball pitched straight at some waiting fielder. In the Giants' fith Larry Doyle was robbed of a sure home run by Hooper, who made a remarkable catch in right field.

Well, it's all over now, and the players, newspaper men and fans are all glad of it. Buck Herzog told me this morning the strain of the series was enough to put one in the bug house. Hughey Jennings says he has almost gone "nutty" over watching the series and reporting it for a New York daily. It has been a grand series but now that it is all over I am ready to say that the series was won by a good ball club, but certainly no better than the Giants. When the official figures are compiled, and the figures don't lie, you will see where the Giants rank as the better team.

McGraw Cheerful.

Tonight McGraw was the most cheerful member of the New York club. I was talking with him just before he left for New York on the late afternoon train, and he smilingly remarked: "Well, those are the breaks of baseball." He was evidently not all broken up and downcast over the defeat, for he invited me to have lunch with him in New York tomorrow, after which he expects to run down to Laurel for a few days to see his old friend, Curley Brown.

Training Camp Wanted.

Here's a tip for the owners of the Jacksonville baseball park: Jack Ryder of the Cincinnati Inquirer informed me tonight that he thought the Reds would be glad to secure Jacksonville as a training camp. As Murphy of the Cubs is yet undecided as to what section of Florida he intends selecting for his training camp, it would be a good idea for the Jackksonville folks to write to Harry Herrman of the Reds immediately. Ryder informs me that all of the scribes are daffy to have the club train in Jacksonville, and it is at this request that I make this suggestion to the Jacksonville club owners through the Times-Union.

IN TENTH-INNING RALLY BOSTON DOWNED GIANTS

Continued from Page Six.

when thrown by Cady. The throw was perfect. Snodgrass over-played the base, but scrambled back before Wagner could recover the ball. Murray out, Gardner to Stahl.

No runs; no hits; no errors.

Boston—There was a perfect storm of applause for the Boston players as they went to the bench. Hooper went out to Merkle, unassisted., bunting the first bal pitched almost into Merkle's hands. Yerkes struck out Speaker made a two-bagger to right by daring base running. The umpire at first declared him out, but reversed himself after he saw that Doyle had dropped the ball. Devore threw to Doyle. Lewis struck out.

The official scorer decided that Speaker's hit was a single.

No runs; one hit; one error.

SECOND INNING.

New York—Merkle struck out. Herzog flew out to Speaker. Meyers was safe when Gardner let the ball, which was a slow roller, go between his legs. Fletcher singled to center, Meyers going to second. On a throw from Cady to Wagner to catch Meyers napping the New York catcher turned and ran to third and was safe when Gardner dropped Wagner's throw. Fletcher took second on the play. Mathewson flew out to Speaker.

No runs; one hit; two errors.

Boston—Gardner walked. It was Mathewson's first base on balls in twenty-one innings. Gardner was forced at second when Doyle took Stahl's grounder and tossed to Fletcher. Wagner singled to left, Stahl taking second. Cady sent up a high fly to Merkle. Bedient out, Doyle to Merkle.

No runs; one hit; no errors.

THIRD INNING.

New York—Devore walked. Bedient was unsteady and unable to locate the plate. Doyle out, Gardner to Stahl. Devore safe on second. Snodgrass out, Stahl, unassisted. Devore went to third. scored on Murray's two-bagger to left. Speaker made a great try for the ball Merkle out, Wagner to Stahl.

One run; one hit; no errors.

Boston—Hooper out, Doyle to Merkle. Yerkes was out, Mathewson to Merkle. Speaker struck out. Mathewson's drop ball was going nicely. He continually worked the inside corner of the plate.

No runs; no hits; no errors.

FOURTH INNING.

New York—Herzog got a long hit to left field for two bases. Meyers sacrificed, Gardner to Stahl; Herzog going to third. Fletcher flew out to Gardner, Mathewson flied out to Hooper.

No runs; one hit; no errors.

Boston—Lewis out on a fly to Merkle. Snodgrass dropped Gardner's long fly, and he was out at third. The official scorer has credited Gardner with a two-base hit. Stahl struck out.

No runs; one hit; no errors.

FIFTH INNING.

New York—Devore got an infield hit. Devore was out stealing, Cady to Wagner, being blocked ten feet off the base. Doyle flew out to Hooper. It was the most remarkable catch of the world's series; running with the ball, he caught it just as it was about to pass into the crowd in right field. The catch prevented a home run. Snodgras singled to left. Murray fouled out to Cady.

No runs; two hits; no errors.

Boston—Wagner flew out to Murray. Cady also flew out to Murray. Bedient flew out to Devore. Mathewson retired the Red Sox in this inning on three pitched balls.

No runs; no hits; no errors.

SIXTH INNING.

New York—Merkle sent a high fly to Hooper. Herzog out, Gardner to Stahl, who picked the shortstop's low throw out of the dirt. Meyers walked. Fletcher struck out.

No runs; no hits; no errors.

Boston—Hooper popped out to Merkle. Yerkes got a single to right. He tried to pull away from the plate, and the ball struck his bat and flew out beyond Doyle's reach. Speaker walked, Yerkes going to second. Speaker was forced at second when Fletcher took Lewis' grounder and tossed to Doyle. Yerkes went to third on the play. On an attempted double steal, Yerkes was out at third on throws from Meyers to Mathewson to Herzog.

No runs; one hit; no errors.

SEVENTH INNING.

New York—Mathewson sent up a high foul, which Stahl dropped. Mathewson singled to center. Mathewson was forced at second when Bedient took Devore's bunt and threw to Wagner. Doyle flied out to Wagner. Devore stole second. Snodgrass out, Wagner to Stahl.

No runs; one hit; one error.

Boston—Gardner flew out to Snodgrass. Stahl got a single to left when Murray and Fletcher let the ball fall between them. Wagner walked, Stahl going to second. Cady flew out to Fletcher. Hendrickson batting for Bedient. Stahl scored on Henriksen's two-base hit; Wagner took third. Hooper flied out to Snodgrass.

One run; two hits; no errors.

EIGHTH INNING.

New York—Wood went in to pitch for Boston. Murray out to Stahl, unassisted. Merkle out, Yerkes to Stahl. Herzog singled to right. Meyers out, Yerkes to Stahl.

No runs; one hit; no errors.

Boston—Yerkes was out at first when his grounder bounded from Mathewson's hand to Herzog, who threw the runner out at first. Speaker out, Doyle to Merkle. Fletcher threw out Lewis at first.

No runs; no hits; no errors.

NINTH INNING.

New York—McCormick went in to bat for Fletcher. McCormick flew out to Lewis. Mathewson struck out. Devore walked. Doyle out, Yerkes to Stahl.

No runs; no hits; no errors.

Boston—Shafer was now playing shortstop for New York. Gardner flied out to Snodgrass. Stahl doubled to left. Wagner flew out to Devore. Cady flew out to Murray.

No runs; one hit; no errors.

TENTH INNING.

New York—Snodgrass out, Wood to Stahl. Murray got a double into the left field crowd. Murray scored on Merkle's hit; Merkle took second when Speaker fumbled the ball. Herzog struck out. Meyers out, Wood to Stahl.

One run; two hits; one error.

Boston—Engle went in to bat for Wood. Snodgrass dropped Engle's fly, and the batter reached second. Hooper flied to Snodgrass. Yerkes walked, Merkle and Meyers let Speaker's foul ball fall between them. Engle scored on Speaker's hit to right, and on the throw in Yerkes went to third. Speaker took second. Yerkes went to third. Lewis walked and the bases were now filled. Yerkes scored on Gardner's sacrifice fly to Devore.

Two runs; one hit; one error.

Two brothers, Tom and Jim Drohan, of the Kewanee team, are the leading pitchers of the season in the Central Association.

MIAMI FANS EXPECTING TO SEE MANY BIG LEAGUE GAMES

Times-Union Bureau, Miami, Oct. 16.—There is a prospect that the lovers of baseball will have an opportunity to see the Giants and the Philadelphia Athletics play on the Royal Palm diamond about the 1st of November. Arrangements were made for a game between Miami's local team and the Philadelphia Athletics, on November 1 and 2. Since it has been learned that the Giants will be in this city, the guests of William Hull, for a two weeks' stay, spending the most of their time hunting and fishing. Efforts are being made by Manager Hill to bring the teams together for two or more games. At this writing everything looks favorable for the event, and should Mr. Hill be successful it is probable that an effort will be made to secure a special train from both the North and South. If it is impossible to secure special trains, a low excursion rate on the regular trains would bring thousands of people to see the games.

CHICAGO AMERICANS DOWNED NATIONALS IN POOR CONTEST

Chicago, Oct. 16.—The Chicago National League club went to pieces in the eighth inning of today's game for the Chicago championship with the Chicago Americans. Both Reulbach and Cheney were batted out of the box and the "Sox" clinched the game by scoring four runs. The series now stands 3 to 2 in favor of the National League.

White was wild and gave way to Benz in the fourth inning. Benz was equally wild but held the National Leaguers to two Hits.

Score:

		R	H	E
Nationals	..1 2 0 0 0 1 0 0 1	5	5	2
Americans	.0 0 1 0 0 2 0 4 *	7	9	1

Batteries: Reulbach, Cheney, Smith and Archer; White, Benz and Schalk.

WARLINGHAM WON.

New Market, Eng., Oct. 16.—The Cesrewitch stake was won today by the three-year-old Warlingham, an outsider, against whom odds of 33 to 1 were laid. Tottles was second and Winthrop third. There were eighteen runners.

The race was a weight for age handicap, the distance being two miles and a quarter.

Pitcher Pickett, of the Bloomington team in the Three-I League, pitched two no-hit, no-run games this season.

"Red" Murray didn't get a hit in the world's series last year, but came across with the hit, in the big series this year, that scored the Giants' first run.

GLARING MUFF BY SNODGRASS BRINGS ON GIANTS' DEFEAT

BOSTONESE GO MAD WHEN SOX WIN

Gardner's Long Sacrifice Fly Scores Yerkes With Winning Run in the Tenth.

BOSTON, October 16.—The Boston Red Sox, pennant winners of the American League, are the world's champions of 1912. Defeating the New York Nationals to-day 3 to 2 in ten innings they captured their fourth victory of the world's series and carried off the premier honors in baseball.

The Giants won three games of the series that were played before more than a quarter of a million people and one contest was a tie.

To-day's was a game of excitement and changing emotions for the 17,000 spectators who went to Fenway Park to see the teams meet in the deciding contest. Not until twilight had fallen on the tenth inning did Red Stocking's Ed Yerkes flash over the plate with the winning run.

Nine Innings of Dueling.

Nine innings of a pitching duel between the master boxman of the Giants, Christy Mathewson, and the stripling Bedient and "Smokq" Joe Wood for the Red Sox found the two contenders for championship honors with a tally each.

Into the tenth inning the contest went, and the Giants chilled the hopes of the Boston crowd by scoring a run on a double into the bleachers by Murray and a hit by Merkle to center which Speaker juggled.

Engle led off for the Red Sox in the last half of the tenth. He had gone to bat for Joe Wood and there was a groan when the Red Sox pinch hitter sent up a towering fly to left center. Snodgrass moved over toward the bleacher seats and waited for the ball to drop. He muffed it, and before the ball was recovered Engle was on second base. No one out and the crowd was in a frenzy of joy.

Hooper tried to sarifice but Mathewson foiled him and the best the Red Sox right gardener could do was a fly to Snodgrass. The Giant pitcher tried to work corners of the plate for Yerkes but Yerkes waited him out and walked on four balls.

Disastrous Misjudge.

With Engle on second and Yerkes on first, Tris Speaker came up. The first ball pitched was a curve and inside and Speaker popped up a high foul. Myers, Merkle and Mathewson went after it, but it fell safe between them. New York's last chance to stop the Bostons passed with the failure to get that foul ball. Mathewson started a high fast one and Speaker met it fairly. On a line over Doyle's head the ball was driven and Engle rushed over the plate with the tying run. On the throw in, Yerkes went to third and Speaker dashed on to second.

The New York infield drew in and Lewis purposely was passed so that a runner could be forced at the plate on an infield grounder. Then came the finish. Gardner with three balls and one strike on him, smashed a long fly to Devore. Yerkes set himself at third and dashed for home when the ball dropped in Devore's hands.

Meyers crouched at the plate to take the throw he expected from Devore. Instantly he had caught it Devore whipped the ball homeward. On came the flying Yerkes—on came the ball.

Matty Throws Up His Hands.

Mathewson, who saw that the throw of the little left fielder would be wide, threw up his hands and Meyers turned away without trying for the ball. Yerkes did not know the throw was wide, however, and he plunged head foremost and slid over the plate in a cloud of dust with the run that won the world's championship for th. Red Sox.

Manager McGraw elbowed his way through the throng to the Red Sox clubhouse beneath the stand, where he congratulated Manager Stahl and the Red Sox players.

"I can't say that I am glad, Jake, but one of the teams had to win; it was to be the Red Sox, and congratulations are in order," said Manager McGraw, addressing Stahl.

A spectator addressed an insulting remark to McGraw as he walked across the diamond and blows were passed, but no damage was done.

Giants Score in Third.

The Giants broke into the run column in the third inning. Devore waited and received a base on balls. Doyle went out, Gardner to Stahl, and Devore sprinted to third. "Red" Murray smashed a terrific drive to left center field. The speedy Speaker was off immediately the ball hit the bat, but, after a hard sprint, he was just able to touch the ball with his fingers. Devore trotted home with the first run and Murray rested on second base when the ball was returned to the infield. Merkle ended the inning by grounding out, Wagner to Stahl.

The American League champions went out in order in their half of the third. Hooper died on a weak grounder, Doyle to Merkle, Mathewson relayed Yerkes' grounder to first and Speaker struck out.

Mathewson, the Giants' first batter up in the seventh, sent up a high foul and Stahl muffed it, costing him an error. Mathewson then singled to center, but was forced at second when Devore tried to sacrifice, Bedient to Wagner. Doyle filed to Wagner and Snodgrass grounded out, Gardner to Stahl.

Sox Tie It Up in Seventh.

The Red Sox opened the seventh, in which they tied the score, by Gardner flying to Snodgrass. Stahl dropped a single in left, Murray, Snodgrass and Fletcher balking each other in trying to get the fly. The Red Sox manager moved down to second when Wagner was given a base on balls. Cady popped a fly into the waiting hands of Fletcher. Henriksen, batting for Bedient, let a couple of balls go by him, and then he opened on the next pitched and slammed the ball down the left field base line for two bases, and Stahl came home with the tying run amid great excitement. Wagner took third on the play. Hooper tried hard to bring Wagner home, but he flew out to Snodgrass.

"Smoky Joe" Wood was given a royal reception when he went into the pitching box for the Red Sox in the eighth. Murray rolled out to Stahl unassisted, and Merkle was out, Yerkes to Stahl. Herzog got the first hit off Wood when he shot a single to right, but Meyers ended the inning by grounding out, Yerkes to Stahl.

Then came the tenth and final inning.

Bosstown, the Hub of the Baseball Universe :-: :-: By Chopin

'MY KNOCK TO WOOD WON TITLE FOR STAHL'S MEN'

"Injury to Great Pitcher Put Him Out of Game and Opened Way for Engle."

By John ("Chief") Meyers.
Giant's Catcher.

BOSTON, October 16.—We met defeat at the hands of the Boston Red Sox to-day in the deciding game of the world's championship series. We lost to Boston and have reason to hold up our heads and look our supporters squarely in the face. We gave Boston the very best we had and I think the victors will not begrudge us a share of the honor.

Not until Yerkes pattered over the plate with the winning run did I despair of the championship. Some of the sting was taken from the defeat in the realization that we were never whipped until the last play failed.

Anybody Else but Matty.

I wouldn't have minded it half so much if it had been any pitcher but Matty. He is the greatest pitcher that the world has ever known or will ever know, I am firmly convinced. In each of his three starts against the Red Sox he pitched as fine ball as any one ever delivered anywhere. It was not his fault that he failed to win a game.

I have every admiration for Joe Wood, who foiled us in our aspirations. He should feel grateful to me for I think I made him a world's idol to-day.

Helped Boost Wood.

I literally knocked Wood into fame, a game and a world's championship when I drove one of his fast shoots straight for his head in the tenth. Wood threw out his bare hand for protection. The ball hit him on the palm, dropped in front and gave him the opportunity to retire me and our side.

That ball put Wood out of commission. He was in great pain as he walked to the bench. His hand was injured so badly that he could not take his turn at bat. Engle hit for him and got two bases on an error. But for the injury Stahl would never have dared lift his only remaining good pitcher, for Wood is a very good hitter. Had that ball got past the box, nothing could have prevented Merkle from scoring.

Falling of Speaker's Foul Helps Red Sox

(Continued from Page 11, Column 4.)

third and Speaker reaching second on Devore's throw to the plate. Lewis walked, filling the bases, and Mathewson seemed tired. He gave Duffy four balls in succession. He motioned to his outfield to move over toward right for Larry Gardner and pitched a couple of called balls to Larry. On the next ball Gardner raised a long fly to Josh Devore and Yerkes scored with ease after the catch. The game was over.

Perhaps no team ever won a world's championship at such cost as the Boston Red Sox, or rather the Boston Red Sox management. The smallest crowd of the series saw the game to-day, there being great splotches of vacancy in the bleachers and the stands. The treatment of the Royal Rooters by the local management, which failed to reserve seats yesterday for the body of fans who have been following the Sox throughout the fight, caused a general boycott on the game and lost the management most of the fat gate it had anticipated.

The failure of Stahl in New York on Monday to start Wood in New York and make a desperate try to end it then and there has done inestimable damage to the game here. For, in addition to placing the championship in jeopardy it has given rise to criticism of the cupidity of the management.

McGraw Congratulates Stahl.

As soon as the game was over to-day Manager McGraw trotted over to Manager Stahl and extended his congratulations.

The Giants left for New York late this afternoon and most of them will leave New York immediately for their homes in the Middle West. They were bewailing their luck, but least cast down was Mathewson, veteran of good, bad and indifferent luck on the diamond. "Big Six" is now eagerly anticipating a hunting trip as soon as he gets back to New York.

"Silk" O'Loughlin was behind the bat to-day, while Billy Rigler of the National League was on the bases. Klem was in left and Bill Evans in right. Both O'Loughlin and Rigler had some close ones.

Bedient got away rather poorly today, while Mathewson seemed to be in perfect form as the game started. Bedient walked Snodgrass in the first inning after Devore and Doyle had been retired, and Snodgrass stole second, but Murray could not help.

With two out in the Red Sox' side of the first, Speaker hit the first ball Matty pitched him for a single to right. He tried to take second on the blow, and Devore made a perfect throw which had the Texan off, but Doyle dropped the ball. Rigler had to reverse his decision on this play, having first called Speaker out. Mathewson fanned Duffy Lewis on three pitched balls.

Minnesota Is Reorganized.

MINNEAPOLIS, October 16.—With Solemn, left tackle, out of the game for at least two weeks with an injured arm, sustained in practice, and with the game with Nebraska scheduled for next Saturday, Coach Williams practically has begun a reorganization of the University of Minnesota football team.

Stirring Battle All Told in Minute Detail

Eventful Innings Are Described by Plays

Mathewson, the Mighty, Holds Victory in Grasp, but His Support Wavers.

Boston—	AB.	R.	BH.	SH.	SB.	BB.	PO.	A.	E.
Hooper, rf.	5	0	0	0	0	0	3	0	0
Yerkes, 2b.	4	1	1	0	0	1	0	3	0
Speaker, cf.	4	0	2	0	0	1	2	0	1
Lewis, lf.	4	0	0	0	0	1	1	0	0
Gardner, 3b.	3	0	0	1	0	1	1	4	2
Stahl, 1b.	4	1	2	0	0	0	14	0	0
Wagner, ss.	3	0	1	0	0	1	3	4	0
Cady, c.	4	0	0	0	0	0	6	2	0
Bedient, p.	2	0	0	0	0	0	0	1	0
*Hendriksen	1	0	1	0	0	0	0	0	0
Wood, p.	0	0	0	0	0	0	0	2	0
**Engle	1	1	0	0	0	0	0	0	0
Totals	35	3	7	1	0	5	30	16	3

*Hendriksen batted for Bedient in seventh.
**Engle batted for Wood in tenth.

New York—	AB.	R.	BH.	SH.	SB.	BB.	PO.	A.	E.
Devore, rf.	3	1	1	0	1	2	3	0	0
Doyle, 2b.	5	0	0	0	0	0	1	5	0
Snodgrass, cf.	4	0	1	0	1	1	4	1	2
Murray, lf.	5	1	2	0	0	0	3	0	0
Merkle, 1b.	5	0	1	0	0	0	10	0	0
Herzog, 3b.	5	0	2	0	0	0	2	1	0
Meyers, c.	3	0	0	1	0	1	4	1	1
Fletcher, ss.	3	0	1	0	0	0	2	3	0
***McCormick	1	0	0	0	0	0	0	0	0
Shafer, ss.	0	0	0	0	0	0	0	0	0
Mathewson, p.	4	0	1	0	0	0	0	3	0
Totals	38	2	9	1	2	4	*29	14	3

***McCormick batted for Fletcher in ninth.
*Two out when winning run score.

Score by innings:	1	2	3	4	5	6	7	8	9	10	
New York	0	0	1	0	0	0	0	0	0	1	—2
Base hits	0	1	1	1	2	0	1	1	0	2	—9
Boston	0	0	0	0	0	0	1	0	0	2	—3
Base hits	1	1	0	0	0	1	2	0	1	1	—7

Hits—Off Bedient, 6 in 7 innings. Two-base hits—Speaker, Murray (2), Herzog, Henriksen, Stahl. Bases on balls—Off Bedient, 3; off Mathewson, 5; off Wood, 1. Struck out—By Mathewson, 4 (Yerkes, Lewis, Speaker, Stahl); by Bedient, 1 (Merkle); by Wood, 2 (Mathewson, Herzog). Umpires—O'Loughlin, Rigler, Evans and Klem. Time of game—2:30.

FIRST INNING.

New York—Devore out, Wagner to Stahl. It was a nice stop and throw. Doyle out, Wagner to Stahl. The crowd is excited and cheered every play. Snodgrass walked. Snodgrass stole second, Wagner dropping Cady's perfect throw. Snodgrass overstepped the bag, but scrambled back before Wagner recovered the ball. Murray out, Gardner to Stahl. No runs. No hits. No errors.

Boston—The Boston players were greeted with a storm of applause. Hooper bunted the first ball pitched and went out to Merkle, unassisted. Yerkes fanned. Speaker made a two-base hit by daring base running. The umpire first declared him out, but later reversed the decision when Doyle dropped Devore's throw. Lewis fanned. No runs. One hit. One error.

The official scorer has credited Speaker with a single.

SECOND INNING.

New York—Merkle fanned. Herzog flew to Speaker. Meyers was safe when Gardner let the ball go between his lgs. Fletcher singled, Meyers taking second. On a throw from Cady to Wagner to catch Meyers napping, the New York catcher turned and ran to third, and was safe when Gardner dropped Wagner's throw. Fletcher took second on the play. Mathewson flew to Speaker. No runs. One hit. Two errors.

Boston—Gardner walked. It was Mathewson's first base on balls in twenty-one innings. Gardner was forced at second when Doyle took Stahl's grounder and tossed to Fletcher. Wagner singled to left, Stahl taking second. Cady sent a high fly to Merkle. Bedient out, Doyle to Merkle. No runs. One hit. No errors.

THIRD INNING.

New York—Devore walked, Bedient being unsteady and unable to locate the plate. Doyle was out, Gardner to Stahl, Devore taking second. Snodgrass was out to Stahl, unassisted. Devore moved to third. Devore scored on Murray's two-base hit to left. Speaker made a great try for the ball. Merkle out, Wagner to Stahl. One run. One hit. No errors.

Boston—Hooper out, Doyle to Merkle. Yerkes out, Mathewson to Merkle. Speaker fanned. No runs. No hits. No errors.

Mathewson's big drop was going nicely and he continually worked the inside corners of the plate.

FOURTH INNING.

New York—Herzog got a long hit to left for two bases. Meyers sacrificed, Gardner to Stahl. Herzog took third. Fletcher flew to Gardner. Mathewson flew to Hooper. No runs. One hit. No errors.

Boston—Lewis out, Fletcher to Merkle. Snodgrass dropped Gardner's long fly, but he was out at third on the relay from Snodgrass to Doyle to Herzog. The official scorer, however, has credited Gardner with a two-base hit. Stahl fanned. No runs. One hit. No errors.

FIFTH INNING.

New York—Devore got an infield hit, the ball bounding off Bedient's shin to the home plate. Devore was out stealing, Cady to Wagner. He was blocked ten feet off the bag. Doyle flew to Hooper. It was the most remarkable catch of the whole world's series. Running with the ball, he caught it just as it was about to land in the crowd in right field. The play prevented a home run. Snodgrass singled to left. Murray fouled out to Cady. No runs. Two hits. No errors.

Boston—Wagner flew to Murray. Cady also flew to Murray. Bedient flew to Devore. Mathewson retired the Sox on three pitched balls. No runs. No hits. No errors.

SIXTH INNING.

New York—Merkle sent a high fly to Hooper. Herzog out, Wagner to Stahl. The latter picked the shortstop's throw out of the dirt. Meyers walked. Fletcher fanned. No runs. No hits. No errors.

Boston—Hooper popped out to Merkle. Yerkes singled to right. He tried to pull away from the plate, but the ball struck his bat and flew out beyond Doyle's reach. Speaker walked, Yerkes taking second. Speaker was forced at second when Fletcher took Lewis' grounder and tossed to Doyle. Yerkes took third on the play. On an attempted double steal, Yerkes was out at third on a throw from Meyers to Mathewson to Herzog. No runs. One hit. No errors.

SEVENTH INNING.

New York—Mathewson sent up a high foul, which Stahl muffed. Mathewson singled to center. Mathewson was forced at second when Bedient took Devore's bunt and threw to Wagner. Doyle flew to Wagner. Devore stole second. Snodgrass out, Gardner to Stahl. No runs. One hit. One error.

Boston—Gardner flew to Snodgrass. Stahl singled when Murray and Fletcher let the ball fall between them. Wagner walked, Stahl going to second. Cady flew to Fletcher. Henrickson batted for Bedient. Stahl scored on Henrickson's two-bagger. Wagner went to third. Hooper flew to Snodgrass. One run. Two hits. No errors.

EIGHTH INNING.

New York—Murray out to Stahl, unassisted. Merkle out, Yerkes to Stahl. Herzog singled to right. Meyers out, Yerkes to Stahl. No runs. One hit. No errors.

Wood replaced Bedient in the box for Boston.

Boston—Yerkes was out when his grounder went through Mathewson's hands to Herzog, who tossed to first. Speaker out, Doyle to Merkle. Fletcher threw Lewis out. No runs. No hits. No errors.

NINTH INNING.

New York—McCormick batted for Fletcher and flew out to Lewis. Mathewson fanned. Devore walked. Doyle out, Yerkes to Stahl. No runs. No hits. No errors.

Schaefer went to shortstop for New York.

Boston—Gardner flew to Snodgrass. Stahl doubled to left. Wagner flew out to Devore. Cady flew to Murray. No runs. One hit. No errors.

TENTH INNING.

New York—Snodgrass out, Wood to Stahl. Murray doubled to the left field crowd. Murray scored on Merkle's hit. Merkle took second when Speaker fumbled the ball. Herzog fanned. Meyers out, Wood to Stahl. One run. Two hits. No errors.

Boston—Engle batted for Wood, and went to second when Snodgrass dropped his fly. Hooper flew to Snodgrass. Yerkes walked. Merkle and Meyers let Speaker's foul fly fall between them. Engle scored on Speaker's drive to right, and on the throw in Speaker took second, Yerkes going to third. Lewis walked. The bases are now filled. Yerkes scored on Gardner's sacrifice fly to Devore. Two runs. One hit. One error.

To-day was almost bitter cold, the weather chilling the spectators and bothering the players. It began with a temperature of less than 40 degrees, and, although it warmed up a little as the day advanced and the sun shone brightly, conditions still remained more suitable for football than for baseball.

New York was favored in the betting at odds of 10 to 8.

'SOX ARE LUCKIEST CHAMPIONS IN HISTORY'

So Says Marquard Who Thinks Stahl's Band Outlucked His Team for Title.

By Rube Marquard.

BOSTON, October 16.—I don't like to take glory away from a victor, but the Red Sox are the luckiest world's champions that ever lived. They won the deciding battle to-day, but if they had not secured every break there was in the game they would never have scored a run, let alone win.

Poor Matty was beaten out of a victory that should never have been. I would willingly give up my share of the receipts to have seen him win.

And I feel sorry for Snodgrass. I suppose he will be blamed for our loss. He dropped that long fly of Engle's and it paved the way to a Boston victory. But I don't have any hard feeling toward him.

Was Not a Bone Play.

It was not a bone play, simply an error. And there is no perfect man. Fate was against him and you can't down fate. It was an error that beat us. Not an error that shows in the official records, but an error that counted a thousand times as much—an error of judgment. It was on a foul pop that Speaker raised between the plate and first base in the tenth inning. Merkle thought Meyers had it and Meyers thought Merkle had it, and it fell safe. It was not a bone play, but again it was simply a case where fate ruled and fate anchored on the Red Sox' bench all afternoon.

Should Never Have Had Life.

That was the play that cost us the game, for on the next ball Speaker, who by all rights should have been out, drove a line single to right. This scored Engle and left Boston runners on third and second. Matty tried hard to fan Gardner, but Larry was not to be denied and he slammed a long sacrifice fly to Devore in deep left and Yerkes had no trouble in cashing the winning run.

I must say that the Boston boys, despite the awful strain they were under, played clean ball. They are a fine lot of fellows, and I will be pulling for them to win the American League pennant again next year.

RALLY GIVES WHITE SOX FIFTH GAME AT CHICAGO

CHICAGO, October 16.—A great rally by the White Sox in the eighth inning gave them to-day's game in the Chicago championship series. The series now stands: Cubs, 3 games; Sox, 2 games. The Nationals need one victory to win the title; the American Leaguers two.

In the Sox' eighth Benz singled to center and Rath waked, whereupon Cheney relieved Reulbach. Lord singled, scoring Benz and Rath. Mattick grounded out, but Collins' single scored Lord. Borton singled to right, Collins going to second. Smith replaced Cheney. Johnson walked, filling the bases. Zeider flied to Leach, Collins scoring after the catch. Schalk forced Johnson, Downs to Tinker.

Two-base hits—Archer, Rath. Base on balls—Off White, 2; off Reulbach, 1; off Smith, 1; off Benz, 6. Struck out—By White, 1; by Reulbach, 6; by Benz, 2. Umpires—Dineen, Eason, Connolly, Owens.

Clubs—	R.	H.	E.
Americans	9	9	1
Nationals	5	5	2

Batteries—White, Benz and Schalk; Reulbach, Cheney, Smith and Archer.

CARDINALS WIN TITLE BY DEFEATING BROWNS

ST. LOUIS, October 16.—The local National League club retained the baseball championship in St. Louis by winning from the St. Louis Americans in the seventh game of the interleague series. To-day's victory made it four wins for the champions, three for the Americans and one game a tie.

The National Leaguers hit Hamilton when hits counted for runs, while Steele held the Americans to four scattered hits and was backed up by some great fielding.

Clubs—	R.	H.	E.
Nationals	6	1	7
Americans	1	4	2

Batteries—White, Benz and Schalk; Reulbach, and Alexander, Stephens.

YOUNGSTER IS HERO OF THE FINAL GAME

Olaf Hendriksen Ties Score in Seventh Inning With Two-Base Drive.

By Bill Carrigan.
Red Sox Catcher.

BOSTON, October 16.—I consider that Olaf Henriksen is the hero of the final battle in the world's series. It was his two-base drive in the seventh inning that brought in the tying run and put us in the game at a time when we were finding the man Mathewson a hard nut to crack.

Next I give credit to Speaker, whose line drive to the right in the tenth scored the second tying run and put Yerkes on third, Speaker taking second on the throw-in. This placed us in the proper position to win if we were to do so. There was only one out, Hooper having retired after a hard drive to Snodgrass. It was up to Duffy Lewis. Matty would not give him a good one and he walked to first, filling the bases.

Gardner Comes Through.

That put it up to Gardner, and Larry was equal to the occasion. His long fly to Devore enabled Yerkes to score the winning run and the greatest world's series in history then ended.

Bedient pitched a great game of call, considering what was at stake. He handled himself with that same self-possession he had when he defeated the Giants a few days ago. It was not on account of fear of him that Stahl took him out and sent Wood in to pitch the last few innings. It was only to allow a pinch hitter to bat for him. The move saved us from defeat. Wood finished up in grand style.

Stahl Great General.

Stahl made his moves with great judgment throughout the series. He pitched the right man at the right time. Once or twice things happened to upset his figures, but, take the series as a whole, you will find that he hardly made a mistake in judgment.

The Giants are a great team and they played great ball, but I believe if they were in our league we would beat them the same way we did the other teams in our league. We had the better team. I am preud to be a member of it.

Fans Boycott Game; Poor Crowd Attends

(Continued from Page 11, Col. 7.)

ball, for it was his duty to try for a peg to the plate, but he fumbled in his haste and Merkle ran on to second. One of the most surprising things in the series followed. Charley Herzog, who had played ball all the way as if he were superhuman, struck out. There was no question about it. He just naturally whiffed and went back to the bench without audible comment. The next occurence was lucky for Wood in two respects. Chief Meyers' blow might have gone through to center and scored Merkle. Furthermore, it might have killed "Smoky Joe." As it was, it hit him in the right side and dropped lifeless in front of him. He had sense enough left to pick it up and toss to Stahl in plenty of time to get the Chief for the last out. Wood was badly hurt by this clout and he had to be assisted to the bench. Fortunately there was no more work for him to do.

Down in the right field corner Ray Collins had been warming up constantly and it would have been up to Ray to get busy if the Sox had tallied only one run instead of two.

Wood in Helpless Shape.

Wood is a pretty fair hitter, but in his helpless condition there was no chance to send him up to bat. So Clyde Engle was the party chosen. It will be remembered that Clyde, in one of the other battles, had delivered a double in a pinch. This time, he hit as hard as he could, but he struck slightly under the ball. Snodgrass raced over toward left, waved Murray away and camped under the falling pil. It struck his hands squarely and kept right on to the ground, moved by the law of gravity.

Engle had not run as fast as he could from the plate, but he speeded up enough to get to second before Fred could recover the sphere and hurl it to the infield. The Sox were now playing for one run, so Hooper was sent up to sacrifice. His two attempts went foul. When he had to hit, he sent a long fly to center and it must be confessed that Snodgrass made a good catch of it.

At this juncture, Matty made his only mistake of the inning. He passed Yerkes. We are not saying that the cool youngster wouldn't have hit safely, but it was bad business to walk him and Mathewson didn't mean to. Then came Merkle's contribution to the cause. Speaker lifted the first pitch for a foul and it struck bottom, although it ought to have been caught easily. As was mentioned before, Merkle, Meyers and Matty started for it, and all of them stopped.

No Trifling With Speaker.

It isn't safe to trifle this way with the Speaker person. He picked up his bat which he had thrown in disgust toward the bench. The next thing Matty served him, he cracked on the nose. It traveled to right field a mile a minute and Engle sped home with the tieing run. Yerkes hustled to third. Tris waited to see what became of Devore's throw and when he observed that Meyers fumbled it, he chased to second. Duffy Lewis, who had been anything but a hero, came up with the chance of a lifetime staring him in the face. Matty tried to make him swing at two bad ones. He refused. Then Meyers and Mathewson consulted and decided it was better to walk Duff and try for a double play rather than put one over. So Lewis strolled and choked the bases. Matty pitched all the knew to Gardner and was rewarded by getting two strikes on the Boston third sacker. Two balls followed and then Larry pulled a long fly to right, a fly that Devore had to go back after. He caught it all right and aimed a throw towards Meyers, for that was his duty. But the throw reached the Indian long after Yerkes had touched the plate.

The game would have belonged to New York in the regular nine innings but for the greatest play of the series—catch by Harry Hooper that robbed Doyle of an apparently sure home run.

New-York Tribune

VOL. LXXII..No. 24,180. To-day, fair; to-morrow, rain or snow; variable winds. NEW-YORK, TUESDAY, JANUARY 28, 1913.—16 PAGES. PRICE ONE CENT In City of New York, Jersey City and Hoboken. ELSEWHERE TWO CENTS.

2,000 WAITERS IN RIOTOUS MARCH

Eleven Arrested During Parade After Meeting for Hurling Missiles Through Leading Hotel Windows.

STIRRED BY GIRL'S SPEECH

Further Incensed by Message That Only Those Who Tear Up Union Cards and Renounce Leaders Will Be Taken Back.

Eleven arrests were made by the police yesterday from the ranks of the striking hotel waiters, when two thousand of them paraded up and down Broadway, Mourth, Fifth and Sixth avenues in riotous fashion after an enthusiastic mass meeting in Bryant Hall.

In only one or two small hotels were the strikers taken back, while in all the larger hostleries their demands met with a flat refusal, and they were told that the hotels were doing very nicely with the men who had taken their places.

Then, as if to further incense them, came messages from one or two of the more prominent hotels, saying that some of the men might be taken back if they would first tear up their union cards and renounce their leaders.

This came while the men were being addressed by Miss Elizabeth Gurley Flynn, the popular young woman leader, who told them in ringing tones that she would stick by them until their hair turned gray and their beards trailed the ground. With roars of approval, the meeting broke up and the march of the riotous two thousand began.

Down Sixth avenue to the McAlpin they went, where they yelled "scab!" in the windows. Then they continued on to the Martinique and to the Imperial, where they threw stones, and five were arrested. The rest marched to the Hoffbrau Haus and then to Shanley's where there was more violence and where four more were arrested. Then they went to the Victoria and up Fifth avenue to the Waldorf, where they again rioted and hooted until two more were placed under arrest. They then divided, some going up Fifth avenue and some up Sixth. They held similar demonstrations outside the new Vanderbilt, the Park Avenue, the Belmont and the Knickerbocker, where the police dispersed them.

Proprietors Ignore Demands.

Most of the hotel proprietors got no further in reading the typewritten demands of the strikers than the first line, which said: "All workers who have been on strike shall be re-instated in their former positions." The only large restaurant that took back any strikers yesterday was Rector's. In the past two days that restaurant has re-engaged about ninety strikers. The strikers believe that Louis Martin will follow Rector's to-day.

The first part of the afternoon mass meeting in Bryant Hall was devoted to an attack upon the newspapers printing that the backbone of the strike was broken. One of the speakers, an Industrial Workers of the World man, became violent in his denunciation. Miss Flynn, however, devoted her time to assuring the strikers that their fight was far from being lost.

"At the very onset I wish to say," she told them, "that as far as the strikers are concerned, they don't care if they never get their jobs back. Their jobs are not sufficiently luxurious. The general strike stands to-day as it did yesterday and the day before. As long as you boys stand together, I and every Industrial Worker of the World man will stand with you. You know

Continued on second page, sixth column.

This Morning's News

TO BE WILSON'S NEWSBOY

"Sammie" April Doesn't Worry Over Coming Change.

Washington, Jan. 27.—Among a score of persons who draw their pay checks from the White House executive offices and face a change of administration with some apprehension, there is one quite serene with confidence that his income is not to be disturbed. He is "Sammie" April, an eleven-year-old lad, who delivers the afternoon papers to President Taft and the executive offices, and each month proudly bears off a United States Treasury warrant for $2 50.

"Sammie" forced a monopoly for himself on the White House newspaper trade by virtue of a pair of fleet young legs which got him there first. "Sammie" has assurances from somewhere that he is to be Mr. Wilson's official newsboy, and he is quite happy.

SEARCH HIGH AND LOW FOR ARIZONA'S VOTES

Baby State's Messenger Missing and Her Choice for President May Not Be Recorded.

LOST—The electoral vote of Arizona and its bearer. Finder please send at once to the office of the Vice-President of the United States.

Washington, Jan. 27.—Senators and representatives of the baby state of Arizona sent broadcast to-night the foregoing notice when, at 8 o'clock, the time limit had expired for receiving returns from the national election last November and Wilfred T. Webb, custodian of three votes for Woodrow Wilson and Thomas R. Marshall, had failed to appear in the Capitol.

For twenty-four hours before the Vice-President's office was closed for the night, with every electoral vote except Arizona's on file, a systematic search of Washington hotels and clubs had been conducted in vain for Webb, who left Phoenix more than ten days ago and was due here on Saturday.

Webb was last heard from in St. Louis four or five days ago, but his friends could get no word of him from there to-night.

If the penalty for failure should be enforced Arizona would lose its vote in the Electoral College and the official messenger would lose his mileage. The duplicate set of Arizona's ballots, sent by mail, are on hand, and it is probable that no penalty will be enforced if Webb arrives to-morrow.

BACK TO SEA HE LOVED

Ashes of Captain Riebman To Be Scattered in Ocean.

[By Telegraph to The Tribune.]

Philadelphia, Jan. 27.—When the North German Lloyd liner Chemnitz reaches this port in a day or so, the ashes of Captain Adolph Riebman, formerly master of the steamship, will be placed on board, and on her outward trip they will be scattered to the winds in the middle of the Atlantic.

Captain Riebman died early in the winter in Cincinnati, and his body was cremated. His widow and the company have complied with his wishes to have his ashes thus disposed of.

While he was commander of the Chemnitz, Captain Riebman never met with an accident. After he had retired from the service he spent many months of suffering, and, according to the widow, he blamed his ill fortune on the fact that he had been compelled to give up the sea.

CHILD'S LIFE HELD AT $150

Parents' Grief Doesn't Count, Says Pennsylvania Court.

[By Telegraph to The Tribune.]

Pottsville, Penn., Jan. 27.—A child's life is worth in damages to the parents just the medical and funeral cost, according to the case of Charles Kost against the Borough of Ashland.

Annie Kost, eight years old, was killed when an electric light pole fell on her. A jury a year ago gave the parents $3,000 damages, but the Supreme Court reversed this decision to-day, declaring that no damages can be awarded for the grief of parents and that positive testimony must be submitted to prove loss of money before damages can be decreed.

As no direct testimony can be produced concerning the probable earnings of a girl when she gets old enough to work, this limited the jury to a verdict of $150, the cost of the funeral and doctor's bill, according to direction of the local court.

TAFT MEETS A PROGRESSIVE

Sir Horace Plunkett Really One, Says President.

Washington, Jan 27.—"In our workaday politics one gets just a little bit tired of the use of the term progressive by gentlemen who work no progress except for platform purposes, and so when we meet a man who has made progress for the people such as we are all seeking he is entitled to our respect."

That was President Taft's tribute to Sir Horace Plunkett, member of the English Parliament and originator of the scheme of agricultural co-operative finance in Ireland, at a banquet here to-night of the Southern Commercial Congress. The President continued:

> We once thought in this country that we couldn't learn anything about agriculture from countries on the other side. Now we have reached a point where we can calculate that unless we do something to improve agriculture we will have to import what we eat and be dependent on other countries.
>
> We have a great deal to learn and I have no doubt that from such men as Sir Horace we can learn a great deal. He has shown by what he's done and not by what he's said that he is a real progressive.

Sir Horace and Senator Fletcher, of Florida, discussed the proposed system of low credits for farmers of the United States.

OLYMPIC HERO TO BE STRIPPED OF HIS HONORS

Jim Thorpe, the All Around Champion, Admits That He Played on Professional Baseball Teams.

APOLOGY TO ALL NATIONS

Viking Ship and Bust of King of Sweden, Won in Decathlon and Pentathlon at Olympic Games, Must Be Returned.

ATHLETIC MARVEL PENITENT

Sac and Fox Indian Who Startled the World on Track, Field and Gridiron Last Year Says He Did Not Realize the Mistake He Made.

James Thorpe, hero of the Olympic games, national all around champion and football player extraordinary, is a self-confessed professional. The man who helped pil up the points for the United States at the Olympic games in Stockholm, Sweden, last july by winning the decathlon and pentathlon, admitted yesterday in a letter to James E. Sullivan, secretary of the Amateur Athletic Union, that he had played professional baseball in the Eastern Carolina League in 1909 and 1910.

This puts an end to the doubt and uncertainty concerning his standing, since charges were made a few days ago, and also to the necessity for a hearing or a trial, while a public apology to all nations was made by the American Olympic committee.

Thorpe will now be called upon to return all the prizes he has won in competing as a registered athlete in the Amateur Athletic Union, and methetorically speaking, the laurel wreath placed on his head by the King of Sweden with the words: "You, sir, are the greatest athlete in the world," will be stripped from his brow.

Must Return Olympic Trophies.

Those much coveted trophies, the Viking ship offered by the Czar of Russia to the winner of the cathlon at the Olympic games, and the bronze bust of the King of Sweden, offered by himself, to the winner of the pentathlon, both of which were all around competitions, will be lost to this country and must be shipped as soon as possible to their owners. H. Weislander, of Sweden, who finished second to Thorpe in the decathlon, will now be the proud possessor of the Viking ship, while F. R. Bie, of Norway, who finished second in the pentathlon, will ge the bust of the King of Sweden.

John Bredemus, of Princeton, also will profit through the stripping of honors from the great athlete of the Carlisle Indian School, as he finished second to Thorpe in the all around championship at Celtic Park last September. On that occasion Thorpe established a world's record by piling up a total of 7,476 points. This mark, too, must be wiped off the books and the record will revert to the previous holder, Martin Sheridan, with 7,385 points.

Thorpe's admission will rock the athletic world to its foundation and the shock will be none the less severe even though its force was partly broken by the developments of the last few days. The effect will be farreaching and through the Olympic games will involve every country where track and field athletics thrive. It may lead to criticisms which will amount to slurs and may be responsible for investigations in other directions which will stir up much muddy water.

Thorpe's Letter of Admission.

Thorpe wrote a straightforward letter, throughout which one may easily detect a note of sadness. He made a clean breast of the whole case and spared himself nothing in writing as follows from Carlisle, Penn., under date of January 26:

> When the interview with Mr. Clancy stating that I had played baseball on the Winston-Salem team was shown me, I told Mr. Warner that it was not true and, in fact, I did not play on that team. But so much has been said in the papers since then that I went to the school authorities this morning and told them just what there was in the stories.
>
> I played baseball at Rocky Mount and at Fayetteville, N. C., in the summer of 1909 and 1910 under my own name. On the same teams I played with were several college men from the North who were earning money by ball playing during their vacations and who were regarded as amateurs at home.
>
> I did not play for the money there was in it because my property brings me in enough money to live on, but because I liked to play ball. I was not very wise to the ways of the world and did not realize that this was wrong, and it would make me a professional in track sports, although I learned from the other players that it would be better for me not to let any one know that I was playing, and for that reason I never told any one at the school about it until to-day.
>
> In the fall of 1911 I applied for re-admission to this school, and came back to continue my studies and take part in the school sports, and of course I wanted to get on the Olympic team and take the trip to Stockholm. I had Mr. Warner send in my application for registering in the Amateur Athletic Union, after I had answered the questions and signed it, and I received my card allowing me to compete in the winter meets and other track sports.
>
> I never realized until now what a big mistake I made by keeping it a secret about my ball playing, and I am sorry I did so. I hope I will be partly excused by the fact that I was simply an Indian schoolboy, and did not know all about such things. In fact, I did not know that I was doing wrong, because I was doing what I knew several other college men

Continued on tenth page, first column.

JIM THORPE, THE SELF-CONFESSED PROFESSIONAL, AND THE OLYMPIC TROPHIES HE MUST RETURN.

SICKLES ARRESTED, BUT ESCAPES JAIL

General Gets Bail Bond for $30,000, Then Turns His Faithful Wife and Son from Door.

HOUSEKEEPER STILL THERE

Widow of General Longstreet and Other Friends of Veteran Offer to Aid Him to Repay Money Due to New York State.

General Daniel E. Sickles was arrested yesterday afternoon at his Fifth avenue house by Sheriff Harburger. The aged commander was saved from going to Ludlow Street jail by the sheriff, who had put off serving the Attorney General's warrant until Daniel P. Hays, counsel for General Sickles produced the necessary bail bond for $30,000, which insures the appearance of the general at his trial in a civil suit for the recovery of a $23,476 shortage in his accountings with the state Monument Fund Commission, of which he was chairman.

The "arrest" was made and the bond furnished while General Sickles's faithful wife and his son were preparing to go to his home for a conference which, it was expected, would have resulted in Mrs. Sickles again extricating the general from his financial troubles. Her assistance was predicated upon her husband dismissing at once his housekeeper, Miss Eleanor Earle Wilmerding, whose presence in the Sickles home was a cause of the estrangement of husband and wife.

General Sickles had before their arrival obtained the bond from a surety company. When Mrs. Sickles and her son arrived at the house they were refused admission.

General Sickles and Sheriff Harburger both saw to it that the formal "arrest" was properly "set" and attended by all the dramatic accessories the situation demanded from their points of view. The Sheriff went to the house at No. 23 Fifth avenue accompanied by General Sickles's attorney, the Sheriff's counsel, bond clerk and the customary Harburger retinue of reporters and photographers. The Sheriff made a dramatic pause on the doorstep and after the customary demur, yielded to the "entreaties" of the photographers and posed for a picture.

General Amid His Relics.

This indispensable portion of the programme disposed of, Sheriff Harburger tapped on the front door just as a policeman began "shooing" a crowd of morbidly curious persons on its way. The door opened and General Sickles's negro servant admitted the Sheriff, his counsel, bond clerk and one reporter. They found General Sickles in his library.

The general, clad in a shiny black suit, sat between his crutches with his wooden leg resting on a hassock. Across the back of a chair near by lay his tattered and bloodstained uniform, smelly with preservatives, and propped up in another chair was a large paint-

Continued on second page, third column.

WELLESLEY FACES STRIKE

Girls Threaten Open Rebellion Against Chaperones.

[By Telegraph to The Tribune.]

Boston, Jan. 27.—Wellesley College seethed and sizzled to-day with the news that an equal rights strike is impending in which all the girls—"freshies," "sophs," juniors and seniors—are threatening to take part.

Already many Wellesley girls are in revolt, and their leaders say that the flames of rbellion will break forth unless the faculty gives them the right to entertain young men visitors the same as other girls do. They say "equal representation or a revolution." The girls declare they are protesting against "old fogyism."

"We want the right to entertain our men friends when and where we like, and we don't want any chaperones butting in," the girls say.

A. H. WOODS PREDICTS A THEATRICAL PANIC

Says N. Y. Has 68 Theatres and Only Four Successes—Disaster Within 6 Months.

[By Cable to The Tribune.]

London, Jan. 27.—A. H. Woods, the New York theatrical manager, who is now in London and who sails for home on Saturday next, predicts within six months one of the greatest theatrical panics America has ever known. He added:

"It wouldn't surprise me if before long half the theatres on Broadway were turned into automobile garages, where people will store their cars while enjoying the evening at the picture palaces. The whole trouble is that there are too many theatres in New York and no plays to put in them—that is, no successes. At the present time there are only four real successes in New York and there are sixty-eight theatres.

"I have had to go to Paris to arrange with Pierre Veber and a French colleague of his to writet a play. I had to go there because there did not seem to be any good material in America. The average American playwright will deal with the conventional. They all want to tell the same old triangular love story of which the publit is now soh eartily tired."

FIND RANGE DANGEROUS

Committee Favors Shields Around Blauvelt Targets.

[By Telegraph to The Tribune.]

Albany, Jan. 27.—A report will be made to Governor Sulzer this week which will determine the fate of the Blauvelt rifle range of the national guard in Rockland County. It was inspected to-day by a committee composed of Major General O'Ryan, Coloned Thurston, of the Ordnance Department, Senator Blauvelt, of Rockland County, and Senator Herrick and Assemblyman Cuvillier, chairman of the Senate and Assembly committees on military affairs, respectively.

The inspection was made as the result of complaints that rifle practice on the range was dangerous to persons living in surrounding farm houses. The committee believes that these complaints were well founded. The farmhouse of George Broadbent, of Grand View, is about a thousand yards back of the rifle range targets, and it is reported that while members of his family were sitting on the porch a short time ago bullets struck the pillars and side of the house. No one was injured, but on many occasions cattle and chickens have been killed by stray bullets.

Many other residents in the vicinity have held that the range should be removed, but the inspecting committee believes that it can be made safe by shields about the targets. This probably will be one of the recommendations in the committee's report.

The Blauvelt range was purchased and equipped three years ago, at a cost of more than $200,000, to replace the Creedmoor, Long Island, range, which was abandoned largely because of protests from property owners.

SYLVIA PANKHURST IS UNDER ARREST

Militant Suffragette Caught Trying to Throw Stone Through Painting in the Commons Building.

WILD ACTS THREATENED

British Government Drops the Franchise Bill, and Call-to Arms of Forward Woman Faction Is Result.

[By Cable to The Tribune.]

London, Jan. 28.—The first shot in the suffragette campaign was fired last night just after 11 o'clock, when St. Stephen's Hall, adjoining the House of Commons, was almost deserted. A young woman who had been within the Parliament building all the evening attempted to throw a stone wrapped in a handkerchief through the glass which covers a large painting on the west side hall, but she was too excited to aim correctly and no damage was done. She was at once detained and proved to be Miss Sylvia Pankhurst.

Simultaneously with the withdrawal of the franchise bill yesterday the suffragettes declared war. There is to be more destruction of property and a militant campaign that will stop short only of taking human life. This was announced by Mrs. Emmeline Pankhurst amid the delighted cheers of her followers at a meeting of the Women's Social and Political Union last night.

After referring to the withdrawal of the franchise bill and expressing the opinion that the Parliamentary farce was played out, she said she was going to be militant and that they could help her by helping to make militancy successful. Volunteers were invited to give in their names and addresses. This militancy was guerilla warfare and must be carried out, she said, with discretion. They must replace force with women's wit and take the enemy unawares.

Regard for Human Life.

There was just one thing they would regard, and that was human life; short of that they were warranted in using all the methods used in war. As to the destruction of property, what did men do in time of war? If it were necessary so to act to win the vote they were going to do as much damage to other people's property as they could. As soon as the people had had enough of it they would clamor to the government to give women the vote. Militancy would go on until they had a government measure.

It is clear that there is now a much greater question involved by the amazing course of events of the last few days than the troubles of a government, and that is the safety of the public. How critical the situation is may be judged from the fact that the police have received instructions to be on their guard against vitriol and revolvers.

By a secret ruse the leaders of the Women's Freedom League have managed to address crowds from different points in Trafalgar Square. Last night, before the police descended upon them

Continued on third page, third column.

SULZER URGES STATE CONTROL OF EXCHANGES

Governor Tells Legislature Time Is Ripe to Step In and End "Flagrant Abuses" and Schemes.

CALLS FOR DRASTIC LAWS

If Commonwealth Fails to Devise Remedies for Conditions, He Says, It Can't Find Fault if Federal Government Acts.

WOULD STOP "WASH SALES"

Executive Recommends Prohibiting Manipulation of Prices Without Regard to Prices and False Statements in Advertisements of Securities.

Albany, Jan. 27.—State supervision and regulation of the New York Stock Exchange and other stock exchanges are advocated by Governor Sulzer in a message sent by him to the Legislature to-night.

The time is ripe, in the Governor's opinion, for the state to step in and end "flagrant abuses, shifty schemes and clever combinations to catch the unwary and to mislead the public." To effect this he recommends the enactment of a group of laws, at least one of which shall provide imprisonment as a penalty for its violation. These laws, the Governor says, should apply to certain practices which have been shown to exist by the Pujo committee of the House of Representatives and other investigators.

"The testimony of some of the governors of the exchanges," Governor Sulzer says, "leaves no doubt in the minds of men of judgment that the exchanges have been either incapable or unwilling to devise measures that will effectively eradicate the evils. It is now the obvious duty of the state, it seems to me, to devise the remedies. If the state neglects to do its plain duty the state should find no fault if the federal government acts in the premises."

New Laws Asked For.

Among the measures which Governor Sulzer would have enacted are:

A law to distinguish clearly proper transactions of purchase and sale from those that are the result of combinations to raise or depress artificially the price of securities without regard to their true value or legitimate supply and demand.

A law to prohibit brokers from sending backward and forward among themselves blocks of a particular stock with intent to deceive or mislead outsiders.

A law to prohibit brokers from selling for their own account the same stocks they have been ordered to buy for their customers at the time customers' orders are executed.

A law clearly prohibiting insolvent brokers from continuing to buy and sell after they become insolvent.

A law making it a criminal offense "to issue any statement or publish any advertisement as to the value of any stock or other security, or as to the financial condition of any corporation or company issuing or about to issue stock or securities, where any promise or prediction contained in such statement or advertisement is known to be false or to be not fairly justified by existing conditions."

Governor Sulzer also recommends, but leaves to the Legislature for decision, changes in existing laws and the enactment of new laws governing short sales, the hypothecation of securities, bucket shops, usury (under which head he also classes the raising of call money rates to more than 6 per cent), the relations between exchanges and the consolidation of exchanges. In his message the Governor says, in part:

Can't Destroy Exchanges.

> These stock exchanges are an inevitable necessity. They cannot be destroyed without doing irreparable injury to business. When properly conducted they constitute an efficient agency for promoting industrial and commercial prosperity. As at present constituted, however, they are beyond the regulative powers of any administrative department of the state.
>
> That evils requiring immediate remedy exist is beyond dispute. These evils are easily discovered and readily stated, but the remedies to be applied require deliberate consideration and the most delicate adjustment to meet the situation, so as to benefit the public at large and at the same time not disturb economic and industrial conditions.
>
> It is demonstrated that the members of the exchanges are aware of these occurrences, but ignore them, manifesting a surprising indifference to the public interest and to the reputation of the exchanges, which is often besmirched by these vicious operations.
>
> It is now conceded by some of the officials that a gambling taint is present in some of the transactions—a concession that confirms the general opinion.
>
> It has been established that transactions in their nature essentially fictitious which make manipulations possible are carried on without serious attempts at restraint, on the pretence that they are in form in compliance with the regulations.
>
> Abuses of the mechanisms and violations of just and equitable principles of trading are treated leniently instead of being vigorously condemned and followed by condign punishment.
>
> The testimony before a committee of the House of Representatives further shows that in cases where members have been punished for extreme violations of the rules it also indicates quite clearly that there are habitual evasions, undisclosed because not investigated.

Governors Lax.

Governor Sulzer points out that many of the evil practices are not disclosed until the books of members who fail are examined, but this, he declares, has

THE BROOKLYN DAILY EAGLE

PICTURE AND SPORTING SECTION NEW YORK CITY, WEDNESDAY, APRIL 9, 1913. PICTURE AND SPORTING SECTION

BROOKLYN TEAM STARTS 1913 PENNANT RACE

Today is the day of days in Brooklyn baseball. By special dispensation of the high Moguls of the National League the season opens in Brooklyn a day ahead of the regular opening on the big circuit. This privilege was accorded to provide an unrivald opening for our new Ebbets Filed, one of the finest baseball parks in the country.

So here we are, all ready for the big show—an opening game against the Philadelphias that's bound to prove a real thriller.

President Charles Ebbets and his side partner, Edward J. McKeever, take pleasure in presenting for your consideration the aggregation of Brooklyn ball-tossers who have aspirations of taking a climb up the ladder of fame this year.

If you don't know the young men in the picture, here's the architect's plans and specifications to help you out:

Back row, left to right: Wheat, Stengel, Kirkpatrick, Curtis, Cutshaw, Wagner, Smith, Yingling, Rucker, Ragan. Middle row: Hummel, Daubert, Hall, Callahan, Dahlen, Miller, Meyer, Moran, Phelps. Front row: Fisher, Erwin, Mascot, Allen, Fischer.

If you're not on deck when Borough President Steers throws the ball out for the opening of festivities this afternoon you're missing one grand big, glorious occasion.

THE BROOKLYN DAILY EAGLE

PICTURE AND SPORTING SECTION · NEW YORK CITY, WEDNESDAY, JULY 16, 1913. · PICTURE AND SPORTING SECTION

SCENES AT THE OFFICIAL DEDICATION OF EBBETS FIELD

BASEBALL NOTABLES PRESENT AT FORMAL CEREMONIES YESTERDAY THAT MARKED THE COMPLETION OF BROOKLYN'S FINE BALL FIELD

Members of the Brooklyn and Chicago Baseball Teams Parading Across Ebbets Field to Raise the Flag Presented by the National League to the Brooklyn Club

A Party of Prominent Women at the Ceremonies. Left to Right—Miss Esta E. Murphy, Mrs. J. Dalton, Miss Catherin Conklin and Mrs. E. J. McKeever.

Johnny Evers, Manager of the Cubs, and Bill Dahlen, Raising the National League Gonfalon Over Ebbets Field.

Ban Johnson, President of the American League, and "Steve" McKeever at Ebbets Field Yesterday.

OUT OF THE PAST — BETWEEN THE LINES.

THE PASSING OF AN OLD STAGE FAVORITE.

THE headlines in the morning newspapers of yesterday: "Clara Morris' Home Is Sold," will cause sensations of regret in the breasts of many gray-haired people all over the United States. It is the end of a long struggle and a submission to the inevitable. Clara Morris is 64 years old, and has been totally blind these three years. And for more years than can be recalled now, she has been a pitiable sufferer from a spinal trouble which finally reached the point when it took her from the stage. Indeed, it would have been far better for her fame had she left the stage years before she did. She was still playing her old plays when she was a wreck of her former self, giving little evidence of the power with which she had, in former days, swept audiences from their self-control. Those who saw her in these days when the anodynes with which she suppressed the pain by which she was racked, were placed where she could frequently reach them in the course of her acting, could hardly be made to believe that she had been an artist on whose utterances large, and indeed, most intelligent audiences, hung breathless. It was only yesterday that a man of middle age said: "I never saw Clara Morris but once, and that was in 'Miss Multon.' I was drawn to the theater where she was playing by her great reputation. And as I sat before that stage and watched her, one of a small audience, I wondered how it was that she had gained her reputation. It seemer to me that I knew fifty minor actresses who could have done much better. but when I was least expecting it there was, in her great scene of the play, a flash of her old power, and I realized that I was looking upon the wreck of a once great woman."

It is forty-three years ago since she made her appearance in New York City under the management of Augustin Daly. She had been playing in Cleveland for a number of years, her genius having been discovered when she was in the ballet, by the manager of the house at which she was employed. John Ellsler, an old-time manager and in his day a great trainer of raw material. And under his molding influence she had become his leading lady in the stock company he maintained. It was in Cleveland that she was seen by Augustin Daly, who quickly appreciating her power, engaged her. At that time Daly was the manager of the famous little house in Twenty-fourth street, his first Fifth Avenue Theater. She was unknown in New York and so when she was announced as a new aspirant for favor in the part of Anne Sylvester, in Daly's dramatization of Wilkie Collins' "Man and Wife," in 1870, it meant little. But Daly already had a reputation for high-class productions and there were a number of artists in the cast well-known to New York—"Jimmie" Lewis, William Davidge, Fanny Davenport, Linda Dietz, Ida Vernon, etc., so the house was crowded at the first performance, and all the first nighters were asking who the new woman was that Daly had picked up. Before the evening was over they knew. She indeed made an impression on her first entrance. But there were some who were inclined to be critical because of her raw enunciation and some crudities to which they were not accustomed on that stage. But she grew in favor as the play progressed. When, however, that scene was reached wherein Anne Sylvester denounces Geoffrey Delomayne, and she loosed that power which was within her, that fashionable and self-contained audience got up on its legs and howled and voted her the greatest emotional actress that had been seen in years in New York, outdoing Matilda Heron who had set the high water mark. The next day she was the talk of the town.

Augustin Daly had stolen out from the stage to watch her rendering of the scene and its effect on the audience. The writer who was on that night one of the audience, will never forget the expression of his face as he watched its progress—surprise, horror passing into triumphant delight. The explanation was that Clara had abandoned the instructions of the rehearsals which were keyed to a suppressed scene of distress. She had cut loose and obeyed the promptings of inspiration and swung it up to the heights of intensity. "Dan" Harkins, who played the part of Delomayne, put it on record that the outburst was so unexpected and so strong and so intense that he was swept from his feet, losing his bearing and was able to bear his part only in the fact that her speech was a long one, and time was given him to gather himself. Old man Davidge was in the wings as she came off the scene, and to him with cool indifference, she said: "I played that scene just as Daly did not want me to. But it was in me and had to come out. I suppose now that I shall get my walking papers." But she did not. She went on to other successes, holding the town for successive seasons. When she left Daly's management it was to enter upon a career as a star.

Some thirty-six years ago, when Clara Morris was at the height of her popularity, she purchased four acres of land overlooking the Hudson River on Riverdale avenue, in the Bronx. And there she has dwelt since. This property, in the wonderful increase of its value, should have made her rich, but it seems to have been burdened with mortgages, which doubtless were placed on the property to sustain the losses incurred when the tide of affairs turned in her stage relation. Some two years ago a fund was raised by her old admirers to lift the mortgage of $80,000 which burdened the property. What has occurred to necessitate the sale of the property has not been made public. Miss Morris was in the full sweep of her career when she married Frederick C. Harriott who was of the well-known Havemeyer family. Harriott was a theorist, largely interested in the stage, but purely from an artistic point of view. Thereafter he devoted himself wholly to the interests of his famous wife. It used to be said that he exercised much influence over the art life of his wife, but the current idea was that it was a misfortune for Miss Morris that she took herself out of the influence of Augustin Daly when she did. After Miss Morris retired from the stage she devoted herself to writing, and discovered in this branch of endeavor the same dramatic quality that had marked her stage work. The end of her career is in sad contrast with the days of her brilliant work in the theater. She was a Canadian and her name was Morrison.

Have You A Pretty Girl?

If so, take her photograph and send it in before Saturday, July 19. The prize amateur photographs in this Eagle Beauty Contest will be published Friday, July 25. An award of $5 will be made for the best picture and four prizes of $1 each for the next in order. Get into the contest! Send in pictures of your pretty girl friends, at home, in the country, on the seashore. And—

WATCH THE PICTURE SECTION [illegible] FOR CONTEST [illegible].

Write your name and address on the back of each picture submitted, and enclose postage for return. Address Picture Editor, Brooklyn Daily Eagle.

JULY 16 IN HISTORY.

1429—The town of Rheims, in France, was taken from the English by Joan or Arc.

1717—Battle under the walls of Belgrade; the Austrians defeated the Turks.

1760—Battle of Exdorf; the Prince of Brunswick defeated the Prussians.

1794—Battle of Wigoya; the Poles defeated the Russians.

1833—Cornerstone of New York University laid.

1857—Battle of Maharajpur (Indian Mutiny).

1912—Herman Rosenthal, a confessed gambler, was assassinated in the streets of New York by men who escaped in an automobile.

TODAY'S BIRTHDAY HONORS.

Congressman James C. McLaughlin, Republican, of Michigan, was born in Illinois, 50 years ago; 1864, moved to Muskegon, Mich., where he has since resided; was educated in the public schools of Muskegon and in the literary and law departments of the University of Michigan, graduating from the latter in 1883; has been prosecuting attorney of his county; in 1901 he was appointed by the Governor of the State a member of the Board of State Tax Commissioners and State Board of Assessors; was elected to the Sixtieth, Sixty-first and Sixty-second Congresses, and re-elected to the Sixty-third Congress.

A SMILE A SECOND

The Auto Bug.

He always goes up hill on "high"
  And never has to stop;
He's going twenty when he starts
  And fifty o'er the top.

His lighting tank ne'er bothers him.
  One tank lasts him a year;
And so, you see, he hasn't got
  This one expense to fear.

He doesn't use much gasoline,
  He makes a gallon do
To carry him for twenty miles
  And maybe twenty-two.

He is an expert driver and
  Just cannot lose his poise.
He never worries when he hears
  An unaccustomed noise.

In all the years he owned his car,
  He's never bought a tire.
But he's no genius, is this man—
  He's just a common liar.

The Diary of a Bonehead.

The good wife had a grand surprise for me this morning. She appeared in a weird creation, which she was pleased to style a hat. It looked to me like the fag end of a misspent life topped off with a rooster's tail that had been dyed pink.

"How do you like it?" she asked, beamingly. "I made it all myself out of some leavings that I found around the house. The frame is an old 'Gates Ajar' which we had left from uncle's funeral five years ago and the trimming didn't cost a cent."

Then I told her how I liked it. My guardian angel must have been taking a much needed nap at that moment.

"It looks to me," said I, "like an Oklahoma corner that has been struck by a cyclone. It makes more noise than a German band after an all-night session following a Schwabenfest picnic. It jars on the nerves worse than a tin peddler's squeaky wagon while the horses are running away. It offends the temperament of an artistic soul like mine to the point of incipient insanity. Hogarth in his wildest dreams never turned out a pictured creation like that hat, if it is a hat. Maybe I am mistaken. Maybe it is only some horrible nightmare that has come over me on account of that lobster a la Newburg last evening. You don't expect to wear that thing out-of-doors, do you?"

"I did expect to," said she with a sort of a grin and determined look, "but seeing that you don't like it, I won't."

I went down town very well satisfied with myself. I had certainly put one freak hat out of business. When I got home, the awakening came. My wife was wearing a bird of paradise creation which had enough expensive trimming to furnish hats for all of Solomon's wives. It had all of the breadth and reach of a grocery wagon umbrella and it towered into the air like the Woolworth building.

"You didn't like the one I made," said she, "so I do hope you will like this noe."

The bill she handed me made a noise exactly like $97.50.

On Hot Weather.

Yes, it is hot. It is always hot in the summer. If you don't like it why don't you move to Spitzbergen instead of sticking around here and kicking to the rest of us about it. We are just as hot as you are.

If we didn't have hot weather in the summer we wouldn't have anything to eat in the winter. Ever stop to think of that? There wouldn't be a buckwheat pancake in this country.

Just try and think how you are going to enjoy those buckwheat cakes and that maple syrup and pork gravy next winter.

While it is hot take the muffler off your oatmobile. Why allow the poor thing to suffer?

How would you like to be a wax beauty in a store window just about now?

How would you like to be putting on a tin roof or painting a steeple?

How would you like to be stoking a battleship—

Or working in a nice cool foundry?

What are you kicking about?

Signs of the Times.

When a Mexican is not beating his sword into a plowshare he is beating his plowshare into a sword.

Advices from London are to the effect that the tailors are busy turning out a new play for John Drew.

If the President keeps on appointing Pages to Ambassadorships he will soon have a whole book.

The Wilson administration certainly believes in boosting the business of the grape growers.

The heels of women's shoes may be lower this year, but the price is not.

Another things for parents to worry about is that their little daughters may some day marry Nat Goodwin or De Wolf Hopper.

Nobody seems to be lying awake nights planning to get Tom Marshall's place on the ticket in 1916.

Perhaps that Missouri jury was right after all. Perhaps 50 cents is all a Missouri kiss is worth.

Massachusetts man has made a fortune out of a fountain pen, but not by writing poetry.

Japan is also in favor of peace, not having money enough to be in favor of anything else.

June is the month that makes the old bachelor feel like a piker.

It costs Uncle Sam only one-tenth of a cent to wash and iron a greenback, and he doesn't leave any saw edges or tear out the buttonholes, either.

Detectives arrested a dealer for selling over-ripe cheese. There are some clews so strong that even detectives cannot miss them.

At any rate the people are not able to forget the Wilson administration for any length of time.

If the umpires ever form a union there will be some real trouble in store for the magnates.

According to Uncle Abner.

By the time Hank Tumms and his wife finally decide where to go on their vacation it is time to begin buyin' coal again and they postpone their trip until the next year.

A feller will haggle for an hour in a grocery store over the price of a pound of cheese, but will go to a garage and pay three prices for gasoline without a murmur and be glad to get it.

When the average minister gits through settlin' the differences in his church choir he hasn't much strength left to spread the truth among the members of his congregation.

BY ROY K. MOULTON.

The New York Press

PART IV. NEW YORK, SUNDAY MORNING, SEPTEMBER 7, 1913. PART IV.

M'GRAW WHEN HE WON HIS FIRST PENNANT.

JOHN J. McGRAW, THE "Little Napoleon" of BASE-BALL

M'GRAW TEACHING A "ROOKIE" HOW TO SLIDE.

New York Giants' Pennant Winner Unlike Great Corsican in That He Has Never Yet Been in a Waterloo

Man Who Put New York On the Baseball Map Started at a Salary of $60 a Month

By FREDERICK G. LIEB.

TWOSCORE years ago—on the morn of April 7, 1873, to be more precise—old Mr. Stork went visiting in and around Truxton, N. Y., and left a little bundle with an honest Irish family. Leaving bundles with honest Erin families is one of the stork's pet habits, or, perhaps, we should say eccentricities.

The bundle dropped in Truxton contained a chubby little baby of the masculine gender, with wonderfully well developed lungs. No sooner did he open his peepers and take a glance at his surroundings than he clenched his tiny fists and proceeded to exercise said lungs at regular intervals. These lung exercises were accompanied by sundry calisthenics of his tiny larynx the result being a combination of unearthly yowls which made the neighbors within a radius of 500 rods wear earmuffs.

Baseball Stopped the Squall.

Various attempts were made to silence the new arrival (Maxim silencers were not yet in vogue) when the pa of the flock got a sudden inspiration to exhibit a baseball within sight of his offspring. It was a happy thought, for no sooner did the newcomer lamp the leather-coated globule than his jaws closed like a trap, and thereafter peace reigned in that household. The magic charm had been discovered.

The daddy of this youngster was a pretty shrewd gink—most Irishmen are—and contrary to what baseball historians may say, he was the real father of inside base-bawl. The family monaker of this tribe was McGraw, and when it came time to fasten a handle on the newcomer they voted in favor of John Joseph. Later the fans voted in favor of Mugsy, but this title has been dropped as being unrefined, and now exists only in the provinces. His pals and hirelings on the New York Giants call him "Mac," and the critics of the national pastime have a fondness for speaking of him as the Little Napoleon.

Licked, but Never Out.

Little Napoleon is about nine-tenths right, too. The only thing that is wrong about this high-sounding handle is that John J. McGraw has never been in a Waterloo. They have licked him, that is true, but nobody has ever succeeded in sentencing him to St. Helena. At times Judge Lynch of the National League has found it necessary to sentence him to five days in the cooler, but John J. has been such a model Christian since the Giants went on their latest pennant spree in 1911 that President Lynch has congratulated McGraw on bossing the best behaved team in his circuit.

That chatter about the Giants being a rowdy club is all tommy-rot, and small-town talk. Why, Crab Evers, the midget leader of the Cubs, has been chased to the bastile oftener this season than the whole New York team combined. McGraw may have been an umpire baiter in his early days in Baltimore, but, to-day he is one of the best little friends the National League arbitrators can boast of.

"Mac" actually fines players for getting into a rumpus with an Ump, and has even been known to smile at one of the species when he met him on Broadway. The indicator holder in question was not Hanky Panky O'Day, however. Though McGraw has let up on the umpires, it would do no harm to quote his favorite philosophy on the umpire question. He put this plank into his platform when he first broke into baseball twenty-three years ago, and it still stands. The plank reads: "All umpires are fatheads."

But we are skipping ahead of our story and must back up forty years again, to the time when little Jawn Joseph lost out in the bawling debate with his proud pa back in old Truxton. Truxton, which gave McGraw to the world, cannot be found on the ordinary map, but they say it is on a railroad folder. According to McGraw, his birthplace is near Troy, and you have to take his word for it.

If the crafty little manager of the Giants was in France and had Paris way up in the race, the frog-eating bugs would look Truxton up and build him a monument. No person in France can call himself important unless somebody has built him a monument in his birthplace. Perhaps if John J. wins the world's championship for New York next month the fans will catch onto the idea.

M'GRAW ON THE COACHING LINE.

Never Was Teacher's Pet.

The McGraws were not handicapped with large quantities of wealth, and Johnny Joe had neither nurse, chauffeur nor coachman to hinder his actions. His nurse was old Dame Nature, one of the greatest little nurses you can get to take care of kiddies, and her charges are very reasonable.

McGraw went to the village school and was never the teacher's pet, neither did any one ever call him Claude, Percival or Clarence for short. McGraw never said so, but we think it is safe to say that he could lick any kid in his school, whether they were heavyweight, middleweight, lightweight or featherweight. Furthermore, he could play rings around any other boy at baseball, which was still more important.

M'GRAW WATCHING A CRITICAL PLAY.

Like the famous Little Corporal of Corsica, who caused such commotion in the European League before they caged him between the bases, the Napoleon of the national pastime started on his chosen career at a very tender age. Before "Mac" reached the age which entitled him to cast a vote he had seen much of Uncle Sam's domains and had already won undying fame as a baseball star.

McGraw broke into his first professional box score shortly after he discarded his short trousers. He made such a reputation around his home town as a hard hitter and demon fielder that he was recommended to the manager of the Olean team, which club was then in the New York State League.

First Contract at 17.

In the spring of 1890 John McGraw, then only 17 years old, affixed his signature to his first baseball contract. "Mac" says he will never forget the first game he played with Olean. There was no 40,000 mob watching the battle, but the few hundred bugs scattered in the bleachers and grand stand looked to McGraw like all the people in the world. It would have been very strange if a kid of 17 years old would not have been a little nervous making his professional debut, and McGraw frankly admits he was.

The Olean club had a giant on first base who was almost seven feet tall, and McGraw says the first baseman looked bigger to him than the Woolworth building. John Joseph made a mental note it would be hard to throw the ball over the first baseman's knob, but on the first chance he got at third base he succeeded in turning the trick.

"Mac" made a nice stop of a hard hit grounder, but his throw to first base could hardly be termed a work of art. The ball kept rising like a fly to the outfield, and by the time it reached the neighborhood of first base it was eight feet above the first baseman's sky piece and still ascending. That peg might have broken many a rookie, but not John J. McGraw.

On his next chance he decided not to put so much steam behind his chuck to first, and the change in tactics promptly bore fruit. Instead of pegging the ball into the next county, the horse-hide nested softly in the big first baseman's mitt. McGraw made a pair of hits in his first game, and his debut was very satisfactory in spite of his mighty throw on his first chance.

M'GRAW AT PRACTICE.

JOHN M'GRAW AT HOME.

Tried Luck in Iowa.

John J. drew a check of sixty bones per month for guarding third base for Olean—a rather meek sum when compared to the princely stipend he now draws for managing the New York Giants, but nevertheless a pretty fair salary for a 17-year-old kid.

McGraw stuck it out with Olean one year, but in 1891 he left New York State flat and moved his base of supplies to Cedar Rapids, Iowa. The Little Napoleon was destined not to return to his native State for eleven years, when he came to little old New York to take care of the Giants. In Cedar Rapids the remuneration was slightly better than it was in Olean, and McGraw's rise in the Iowa city was rapid. His playing at shortstop soon attracted the attention of a big league scout, and in August, 1891, McGraw reported to the Baltimore National League team, which was a tail-ender in a twelve-club circuit.

McGraw's start as an Oriole may best be described by a prominent sporting writer, a native of Baltimore, who was present at the Baltimore grounds when John J. made his first appearance in big league toggery. "McGraw looked as though he did not weigh ninety pounds soaking wet, and though he was 18 he did not look more than 15. They wished a uniform on him about ten sizes too big, and his head was almost lost in the collar.

"He was not quite as big as little Tommy McMillan, formerly of the Brooklyns and the Yankees, and most fans took him for a new bat boy. However, as soon as he got out on the field it was easy to see he was a ball player. His aggressiveness and the manner in which he went about his work during the preliminary practice made a big hit with everybody who saw him."

Hanlon Saw His Worth.

Billy Barney was manager of the Orioles when McGraw broke into the fast set, and Bill paid little attention to the midget rookie. Our hero finished the 1891 season as a bench warmer, with an occasional infield assignment. In May, 1892, that wonderful baseball genius, Ned Hanlon, succeeded Billy Barney as manager of the Orioles and Hanlon took an early fancy to little McGraw.

Perhaps no manager in the history of the game, unless it is McGraw himself or Connie Mack, ever showed more ability to see a diamond in a rough, uncut stone than Hanlon. Hanlon saw McGraw was a wonderful prospect in spite

(Continued on Third Page.)

Johnny McGraw's Stars Who Will Strive to Bring the World's Title to Manhattan

Connie Mack's Band of Athletes Who Will Battle Giants for Championship of Universe

FINAL EXTRA

THE BOSTON TRAVELER
AND EVENING HERALD

FINAL EXTRA

89TH YEAR. | THE WEATHER—Unsettled, probably with rain tonight and Thursday; increasing easterly winds. | BOSTON, WEDNESDAY, OCTOBER 8, 1913. | 16 PAGES. | ONE CENT.

MATTY AND PLANK IN PITCHING DUEL

SCORE BY INNINGS		1	2	3	4	5	6	7	8	9	10	11	12	13	14	15	Total
GIANTS	Mathewson, p.; McLean, c.	0	0	0	0												
ATHLETICS	Plank, p.; Lapp, c.	0	0	0	0												

3 BURNED IN RUBBER SHOP BLAZE

Flames Flash Into Faces of Employe and Two Firemen

Three men were seriously burned in a fire in the Ellis Rubber Company's plant in the rear of the Malden knitting mills on Franklin street, Malden, shortly before noon today.

More than 100 girl operatives in the knitting mills were thrown into a panic and fled from their benches.

The injured men are Herbert C. Ellis, an employe of the rubber company, living at 64 Clark street, Malden; Frederick MacDonald, electrician of the Malden fire department, and Hoseman Walter A. Dunham of the fire department.

Though the fire raged fiercely in the rubber plant, and frequent explosions of gasoline and naphtha occurred, the building, which is of brick and concrete, was but little damaged except for the roof, which was nearly destroyed. The quick work of the fire department prevented the spread of the flames to the knitting mill, which is only a few yards distant.

The fire originated in the main building of the rubber works. Ellis was pouring hot cement into buckets when one of them blazed up. Immediately the other buckets caught, sending a flash of flame many feet into the air. Ellis's clothing caught fire and before he could rush out the back door into a field he was nearly strangled by the flames and smoke.

When the department arrived MacDonald and Dunham went inside the main building to the room where the fire originated. A 400-gallon tank of gasoline, exploding, sent sheets of flame toward them, terribly burning them about the face, hands, arms and body. MacDonald became unconscious but was taken out to safety by fellow-firemen.

Dunham, who had entered by a door from another part of the factory, which closed behind him and could not be

(Continued on Page Four, Column 1.)

PRISON DOPE THIEVES ALL RECOVERING

Man Who Stole Atropine for Morphine Sent to Cell

All the atropine victims at the Deer island house of correction are on the road to recovery and out of danger, according to reports from the institution today.

The officials also announced that they had sent Thomas Bolaski, the young Pole who distributed the drug to the prisoners, back to his cell and he will no longer be allowed freedom of the institution as a "trusty." It is the intention of the officers to put Bolaski before the court for furnishing the prisoners with drugs at the expiration of his present sentence. His sentence expires in November.

Bolaski was sent to the island Aug. 13 from the South Boston court on the charge of having morphine in his possession for the purpose of distributing it. He was given three months.

Penal Institutions Commissioner Gore has started an investigation to determine how Bolaski had access to that part of the dispensary where the drugs are kept.

THE WEATHER

FORECAST—Unsettled, probably with rain tonight and Thursday; increasing easterly winds.

I BET SEVEN CENTS IT'D RAIN,——
BUT—
— — ?

Sun rose 5:49, sets 5:15. Thursday, rises 5:50, sets 5:13. High tide, 6 A. M., 6:15 P. M. Thursday, 7 A. M., 7:15 P. M.

Light auto lamps before 5:45.

Boston observations, 8 A. M.—Barometer, 30.27 temperature, 60; highest yesterday, 63; lowest last night, 58; humidity, 97%; wind, northeast, 3 miles, misting; precipitation, trace.

Other temperatures—New York, 58; Washington, 64; Jacksonville, 66; New Orleans, 72; St. Louis, 66; Chicago, 62; St. Paul, 4; Des Moines, 32; Kansas City, 58; Denver, 42; Bismarck, 34; Salt Lake City, 50; San Francisco, 56; Portland, Ore., 50.

Morning reports from Atlantic and European stations—London, 54, rain; Paris, 54, cloudy; Cuxhaven, 52, partly cloudy; Bermuda, 78, partly cloudy; Havana 70, clear.

Highland Light—Wind, east, 5 miles, dense fog.

Hull—Wind, northeast, 6 miles, dense fog.

STAKED LIFE ON GIANTS, TAKES GAS

New Yorker Bet All He Could Raise on McGraw's Team

NEW YORK, Oct. 8—One life was staked on the Giants winning the opening game yesterday. The man who laid the bet with death was George M. Still, who kept a restaurant at 195 Third avenue, and had an oyster business at the foot of Pike street. His body, self-slain, was found in his home over the Third avenue restaurant at 5 o'clock this morning.

The story of the tragic wager was told to the police by the dead man's son, George M. Still Jr., who was associated in the management of the restaurant.

"Father," said he, "was a Giant fan. I am, too. I knew he was deeply interested in the opening game and I knew he had no doubt about the home team winning. He could not get away from business to see the big contest, but asked me to go and tell him all about it when I got home.

"I had a story to tell that I knew he would take hard, but I had no idea it meant as much to him as I know now. He owed $5000, due in a few days. He was worried over the debt and told me some days ago he didn't see how he could raise the money.

"When I got back to the restaurant he had heard the news from the game and was very blue. Then he confided to me that he had bet all the money he could get hold of on the Giants. It was the only way he could think of to raise the $5000 and save the oyster business, he said.

"He asked me about the details of the game, particularly about Baker's home run. Then he shook his head disconsolately and went out to a saloon. He got a couple of drinks and came back. The rest of the evening he was very quiet, and I could see he was taking things hard. About 10:30 o'clock he went to bed, still downcast."

The police learned that Still had two children, George and a daughter, Almina, who is away at school. The present Mrs. Still is George's stepmtoher. She lives at the Third avenue address, where the housework is done by Eliza McDowell.

The sleeping apartments are on the top floor of the three-story building. The kitchen, dining room and parlor are on the second floor. Miss McDowell was awakened by the odor of gas and aroused her employer's son. They traced the gas to the kitchen, and found the door locked. George broke it in and saw his father lying in the middle of the floor dead.

Two gas jets were open and from a third in the range extended a rubber tube, which had been in Still's mouth but had fallen to the floor when he lost consciousness. The dead man was partly dressed. He left no note.

"He did not tell me what he intended to do," said George, "but I know from what he said last night that this is a direct result of the Giants losing yesterday."

$100,000 LOSS IN ROCKPORT BLAZE

ROCKPORT, Oct. 8—The plant of the Cape Ann Tool Company on Granite street, Pigeon Cove, was destroyed by fire early today with a loss of $100,000. It was the biggest fire in Rockport for 30 years. The fire started at 1:20 A. M. in the annealing room, where furnaces are used in tempering tools. Inside of 10 minutes the whole wooden building, measuring 140 by 70 feet, was ablaze. The fire was discovered by Night Watchman Alfred Saunders, who summoned the fire department, but it spread with such rapidity that the apparatus could do practically nothing. It was 6 A. M. before the blaze burned itself out. Sixty men were thrown out of work by the destruction of the plant.

Christy Mathewson, Giants' Veteran, Who Started in Box

FEDERAL GENERAL AND 125 EXECUTED

Reprisals by Rebels at Torreon After Four-Day Battle.

LAREDO, Tex., Oct. 8—Federal Gen. Alvarez, his staff and 125 federal soldiers were executed yesterday in Torreon, Mexico, under orders of Gen. Francisco Villa of the Constitutionalist forces, according to information from reliable sources brought here today.

With the city of Torreon, the rebels captured practically all of the federals' arms and artillery. The battle lasted four days with heavy losses to both sides.

FOSS NOMINATION PAPERS ARE READY

Necessary Signatures Secured and Governor Will Be Asked to Sign.

The "Foss For Fourth Term" committee met today.

This can be positively stated on the authority of former Mayor James M. W. Hall of Cambridge, who took out the independent nomination papers for the Governor. It can also be stated that the necessary 1000 signatures to nominate the Governor as an independent have been gathered, with a few to spare.

Who is this committee in addition to Mr. Hall, where the committee met, and what it did, Mr. Hall refused to tell.

The "committee" will report on the size of the "call of the people" for the Governor to accept another term. With its report will be handed to the Governor the nomination papers, which he must sign before they san be filed, and a petition signed by men who want him to run again.

INJURIES KEEP THREE GIANT STARS OUT

By GRANTLAND RICE

SHIBE PARK, Philadelphia, Oct. 8—Philadelphia fans were baseball mad as they packed Shibe Park to its capacity for the second contest of the world's series between the New York Giants, National League pennant holders, and the Philadelphia Athletics, champions of the American League. With one victory wrested from the Giants, the Athletics set about to capture the second contest of the series on the home ball yard and establish a good lead in the effort to win four out of the seven contests. All of 20,000 persons had passed through the turnstiles before play began.

The National leaguers were not a whit crestfallen over their defeat in New York yesterday and every Giant was ready to declare that Bender would be beaten the next time the Indian went to the pitching mound. A Scotch mist as thick as a Newfoundland fog kept the thousands in fear that a heavy downpour would stop the game. An industrious brass band helped to keep the minds of the fans from threatening weather. The entire infield and far into the outer gardens was completely covered with canvas to keep off the dampness. Later the covers were peeled off, leaving the diamond in fine playing condition.

McLean Replaces Meyers.

In the batting practice, this afternoon, Chief Meyers of the Giants, again hurt his hand, thereby adding another to the long list of the Giants' cripples. That the injury was of a serious nature was indicated by the fact that Meyers was not in the line-up this afternoon, and Larry McLean—Lucky Larry, as he is known these days—found himself in the first world's series games.

It was a good-natured crowd that filled the big double-decked grandstand and outfield stands. One victory was a fine tonic to the spirits of the Athletic fans, and they vigorously cheered the home folks at fielding and batting practice. Massed in solid phalanx behind the Giants' playing bench were several hundred New Yorkers, enthusiastic, hopeful, and ready to encourage the National leaguers.

FIRST INNING

GIANTS—Herzog flied to Collins. Doyle flied to Strunk in short centre. Fletcher fanned.—NO RUNS, NO HITS, NO ERRORS.

Plank's sizzling cross-fire worked in the opening inning and mowed the first three batters in order. He took plenty of time and was quite willing to meet the Giants' determination to wait him out. His wind-up on Fletcher was a fast drop, which the shortstop swung high above.

ATHLETICS—Murphy was safe on Doyle's fumble of an easy grounder. It was the Giants' first error of the series. Oldring singled to left, and the stands aroused from the gloom. Collins came up during a conference between McLean and Matty, and got a hand. Collins sacrificed, Snodgrass to Doyle, and there was an Athletic player on second and third, one out and Baker up. Baker fanned. Matty kept everything outside the pan and worked a pair of fadeaways on Baker for two fouls. Baker's swing at the last one was a very hard one. McInnis flied out to Burns.—NO RUNS, ONE HIT, ONE ERROR.

Matty got off in the first inning to a bit of his usual world's series bad luck when Doyle made an inexcusable fumble of an easy tap of Murphy. Oldring followed with a single. Matty responded in his world series style, and after fanning Baker pulled himself out of a hole. He showed the heart that has made his name famous everywhere he is known.

SECOND INNING

GIANTS—Burns fanned. Plank was using an inside curve with a fast break to splendid advantage. Shafer flied to Murphy. Murray fanned.—NO RUNS, NO HITS, NO ERRORS.

The one-two-three order again prevailed in the Giants' half of the second, Plank disposing of the three men with 10 pitched balls. An in curve alternating with a high one did the business.

ATHLETICS—Strunk out, Doyle to Snodgrass, on an easy chance. Barry got a hand as Matty called Herzog over for a consultation on the batter. He responded with a long fly to Burns. Lapp fanned on three pitched balls.—NO RUNS, NO HITS, NO ERRORS.

Matty disposed of the Athletics in this session with seven pitched balls. His easiest effort being on Lapp, who made three lunges without getting near any of them. Matty's fadeaway appeared to be working in gilt-edge style.

THIRD INNING

GIANTS—McLean popped to Barry in deep short. Snodgrass singled down the left foul line and hobbled down to first. It was the first hit off Plank. Matty got a warm hand as he came to the plate. Matty singled to left centre, and took second on the throw to third to catch Snodgrass, both players being safe. It would have been an easy double but for Matty's fear of overrunning the limping Snodgrass. Wiltse was put in to run for Snodgrass. Herzog bounded one to Plank, who threw to Lapp. Lapp ran Wiltse down between the plate and third, Herzog taking second and Matty third. Plank got an assist and Lapp a put-out on Wiltse. Doyle drew three balls and then Plank cut the plate with the next two. Doyle flied to Oldring.—NO RUNS, TWO HITS, NO ERRORS.

The Giants' crippled condition told heavily against them in their half of the third, that would have been an easy scoring bee on a single by Snodgrass and a safe slam by Matty, flashed in the pan as a result of Snodgrass's inability to score on Matty's safe rap. Matty's punch was to deep left centre, and would have been an easy double and an easy scoring ticket for Snodgrass had the latter been in his usual form.

ATHLETICS—Wiltse relieved Snodgrass at first. Plank out, Doyle to Wiltse. Murphy out on an attempted bunt, Matty to Wiltse. Oldring out, Herzog to Wiltse.—NO RUNS, NO HITS, NO ERRORS.

Matty made short work of the Athletics in their half of the third, disposing of the first three men up with five pitched balls. Three of these were weak taps to the infield, one was a ball and one a strike.

THE LINE-UP

ATHLETICS.

MURPHY	Right Field
OLDRING	Left Field
COLLINS	Second Base
BAKER	Third Base
McINNES	First Base
STRUNK	Centre Field
BARRY	Shortstop
LAPP	Catcher
PLANK	Pitcher

GIANTS.

HERZOG	Third Base
DOYLE	Second Base
FLETCHER	Shortstop
BURNS	Left Field
SHAFER	Centre Field
MURRAY	Right Field
McLEAN	Catcher
SNODGRASS, WILTSE	1st Base
MATHEWSON	Pitcher

FOURTH INNING

GIANTS—Fletcher out, Barry to McInnis, on a play which tested the speed of the Athletic infield and the throwing arm of Barry. Burns fanned on four pitched balls. Shafer was safe on Baker's low throw to McInnis, which chalks an error for the gentleman from Trappe. Shafer out, Lapp to Collins, on an attempted steal.—NO RUNS, NO HITS, ONE ERROR.

Lapp's throwing arm nipped a Giant chance in the fourth, when it nailed Shafer by a yard on an attempted steal. Tilly had gotten a life on Baker's error, but it was a very short one.

ATHLETICS—Collins died at first, when Matty leaped up and pulled down a high bounder. Baker came up amidst a dead calm. Matty cut the plate with the first one, threw two wild ones, and when he put the next one over Baker slammed it for a safe drive past Doyle, who deflected, but could not stop it. McInnis out, Doyle to Wiltse. This was not a sacrifice, as McInnis slammed the ball hard. Strunk drew three and two, and then drew the fourth and a pass, the first issued off Matty. With men on first and second, Barry came up and forced Strunk at second, Doyle unassisted.—NO RUNS, ONE HIT, NO ERRORS.

Up to the end of the fourth inning but four of Matty's offerings had been hit outside the infield. Two were fly balls and two were singles. Big Six appeared to be working easily and mixing things in a highly entertaining style.

TWO OF SPENCER'S "VICTIMS" LIVING

CHICAGO, Oct. 8—Capt. John J. Halpin, chief of the detective bureau, will not allow Harry Spencer, confessed slayer of Mrs. Mildred Allison Rexroat, to be removed to Dupage county until he has completed investigation of Spencer's other "confessions."

"Spencer seems to have taken it for granted that he killed everybody he hit with a hammer," said Capt. Halpin. "In at least two of these cases we have found that the victims recovered, but he was guilty of robbery in both of them."

FATHER OF 28 IS PUT ON PROBATION

Frank D'Meallo, the 70-year-old father of 28 children, who was arrested yesterday for not sending his 12-year-old daughter, Olympia, to school, was placed on probation in the municipal court today by Judge Bennett. The 12 children who are still living of the original 28 range in age from 4 years to 45.

D'Meallo says he will take his family back to Italy after Christmas. Despite the size of the family, the daughter Olympia is the only one who speaks English. His excuse for not sending his daughter to school was that he did not think it would do her much good to go for the few months before Christmas.

SIDELIGHTS OF GAME IN SHIBE PARK TODAY

By WALTER E. HAPGOOD.

SHIBE PARK, Philadelphia, Oct. 8—Playing conditions this afternoon were almost identical with those at the Polo grounds yesterday. The sky was overcast and the afternoon was cold. At times there was a rift in the clouds and it would lighten up. Then it would grow dark again and it would seem as if it would rain at any minute.

Here at Shibe Park an entirely different ticket arrangement prevails than at the Polo Grounds. Here there was an advance sale of everything except the unreserved bleacher section. The result was the crowds did not gather so early, being provided with tickets in advance and so knowing seats were reserved for them.

While there were 30,000 at the Polo grounds at 12 o'clock yesterday, not more than 10,000 arrived here at the same hour. Most of those were the bleacherites occupying the seats that back up left field. Outside the grounds the long row of buildings furnished a cheap and improvised grandstand for hundreds of fans who sat out more or less on crates and packing boxes, enjoying almost as good view of the game as those who paid higher prices.

The players of the opposing teams entered the grounds with none of the theatrical fringes that characterized their initial appearance at the Polo groundse yesterday. The Athletics slipped out of their dugouts singly and in pairs, and of course there was no trace of Connie Mack, whose inherent modesty kept him as usual in the background.

The Giants did come upon the field in a body, and it may not have been intentional but the band stationed at the home plate was playing some sort of a funeral selection on the order of the "Dead March" from "Saul" when the McGraw men took their bats.

The Athletics even to their malformed mascot, the little hunchback of doubtful age, were attired in their home uniforms of white, while the Giants wore their customary uniforms of lavender in place of the canary yellow creation in which they were attired for the opening game.

In the practice before the game it was evident that it was small chance of Merkle covering first base. Two doctors, so the story went, spent most of the night over his ailing ankle. He came upon the field limping but made no effort to warm up in the practice.

The players complained that the field was not in as good condition for playing as were the Polo grounds yesterday. There had been rain enough during the morning to create a slippery surface along the base lines, and in parts it was really muddy. The outfield was likewise as treacherous.

Being the visitors, the Giants took their batting practice first this afternoon with Schupp and Schauer doing most of the twirling. They hit the ball with more confidence than yesterday, lining out a lot of long drives that kept the large delegation of Philadelphia's finest arrayed in the outfield, dodging a lot of the high and hard-hit ones.

Shortly after 1 o'clock both clubs completed their batting practice, and the catching cage, which to the uninitiated looked much like a Beachey aeroplane, was tumbled off the ground, and the fielding practice was started.

When the Athletics started out for fielding practice, 20 minutes or so before the game, the sky lighted up perceptibly. Both Strunk and Walsh were out in centrefield for fielding practice.

The crowd was as much interested in the warming-up practice as in the practice fielding of the rival team. On the Athletics' side Plank and Brown warmed up, but Plank worked the longer, and it was purely evident that Mack intended using him as per his previous arrangements.

On the Giants' side Mathewson and Tesreau both worked out whatever kinks there were in their arms. All the time Mathewson was warming up McGraw stood in earnest conversation with him. Tesreau, after throwing not over 50 balls, went back to the dugout, leaving Mathewson by himself.

Walter Johnson, who, like Lajoie, has yet to be a principal in a world's series game, motored up to the home plate before the game in a Chalmers, the machine that he won as the most useful player in the American league this year. Walter accepted the automobile and is now in line to open a garage, having one car in Coffeyville, Kan., another in Washington, and now this new six-seater.

Lewiston Journal Sporting Section

CHRISTY MATHEWSON HERO OF THE GAME

PHILADELPHIA, Oct. 9.—Christy Mathewson, master manipulator of the baseball, led the New York Giants to a victory at Shibe Park. Wednesday when he shut out the Philadelphia Athletics in a ten-inning battle by a 3 to 0 score in the second game of the world's series. Hero of a decade of league and world's championship play the famous veteran rose to the highest pinnacle of his diamond career by an exhibition of all-round play that wrung volleys of applause from the 20,000 Athletic supporters, who were massed in the stands and bleachers expecting to witness a second triumph from the standard bearers of the American League.

Box score experts will point to their figures to prove that 11 other Giants were instrumental in winning the second contest of series, but the Philadelphia fans, who filed sadly out of the Athletics' ball park, spoke only of Mathewson.

For a trifle over two hours and twenty minutes the man whose requiem was sung by thousands of fans after the final game against the Boston Red Sox in the world's series of 1912, turned back the hard-hitting Athletics without a semblance of a break. Then when he saw that his team mates could not wrest victory from Plank, he took his bat and drove in the run that won the game. Spurred on by his example the other Giants added two more to clinch the contest, but they were not needed. Mathewson was the master to the end, Oldring, Collins and Baker being unable to drive the ball outside the diamond in the tenth and final inning, altho 20,000 adherents pleaded for a hit that might start a winning rally.

Regardless of the disappointment over the outcome of the game, as viewed from a Philadelphia standpoin,t not a single one of the thousands of spectators who witnessed the play regretted the hours spent in stands or bleachers. As an exhibition of high class baseball and sensational play the game was all that an ideal world's championship contest should be in fiction or in reality.

For nine innings the rival clubs battled without advantage, brilliant fielding and thrilling coups shutting out runs that appeared assured. In the tenth with the shades of darkness settling over the park the hero of the game terminated the contest just as the dramatist would have staged the final scene. The Athletics had a chance to win in the ninth and many thought poor generalship on the bench and coaching lines threw away the one opportunity that the fortunes of baseball cast their way.

Wonderful Pitching.

Both Mathewson and Plank had twirled a game that was little short of wonderful up to this point and Plank was beginning to falter under the strain. Their teamates, too, were a-tremble with the responsibilities that each inning was heaping on their shoulders. With the Athletics at bat in the last half of the ninth and but a solitary run needed to close the contest, Strunk opened with a single past second. Barry bunted toward Larry Doyle, who ran in and scooped the ball up, whirled and threw wildly past Wiltse at first in an attempt to catch the Athletics' shortstop. The ball sailed clear to the right field grandstand while Strunk and Barry raced around the bases. Strunk was held at third when he had ample time to score. It was the Athletics' lone chance for Wiltse and Mathewson cut down three Athletics in a row immediately after by a brilliant exhibition of infielding, and then came the Giants' rush to victory.

Larry McLean, who substituted for Meyers, when the Indian split his finger in practice, singled to right field in the tenth inning. Grant ran for him and reached second on Wiltse's sacrifice. Mathewson then clinched the game with his clean smash to center on which Grant scored. Right here the Athletics cracked. Herzog hit to Collins, who threw to Barry to catch Mathewson at second. Apparently Barry was unable to see the ball except to dodge it, as it flashed by him on the way to left field.

Mathewson and Herzog gained an additional base on the misplay. Plank hit Doyle, filling the bases. Fletcher followed with a bounder over Baker's head, scoring Mathewson and Herzog and the Giants had two more runs than were needed, as it ultimately proved, to win the game.

Aside from the brilliancy of Mathewson, the two teams were evenly matched. Plank was not quite so steady as his rival in the box, giving two bases on balls and hitting one batter to Mathewson's solitary pass. The Giants secured seven hits off Plank to the Athletics' eight from Matty, who struck out five batters to Plank's six. New York had eight men left on bases to Philadelphia's ten. Fletcher, McLean and Mathewson secured two hits each, a total of six out of the seven recorded by the Giants. Baker was the only Athletic player to get to Mathewson for more than one hit, the home run batsman being credited with two.

Had it not been for Mathewson's remarkable exhibition in the box and at bat, George Wiltse would have been hailed as the star of the game. As it was his play was such that it brought him congratulations from both players and fans.

Substituted for Snodgrass, first as runner and then at first base in the third inning, he played a game that equalled anything that Merkle, the Giants' regular, has shown this season. As if to test his courage and stamina, ball after ball was flashed his way during the next seven innings. Not an error or a flaw marred his work and the climax came in the ninth when he cut two Athletics down at the plate and took Mathewson's throw at first for the third out.

According to the figures of the National Commission, 20,563 persons paid admission to witness the game. The receipts amounted to $49,640. Compared with the records of the first game here in 1911, the attendance was approximately 5,000 less, but the receipts $6,000 greater, due to the increase in the prices for the seats this season. Probably 4,000 more saw the game from points of vantage outside the park. The two rows of brick houses that overlook Shibe Park on two sides were literally swarming with spectators. On roofs and porches temporary stands had been erected and these were black with men and boys who climbed thru windows and roof scuttles to the tiers of pine benches, paying the thrifty householders 50 cents to a dollar for the privilege.

In other respects the scenes attendant on the gathering of the fans were much the same as at the opening game in New York, except upon a smaller scale. Lines of men and boys stood all night in the drizzle awaiting the opening of the gates to the bleachers and long before noon this section of the stands was crowded to its utmost capacity. The grandstand seats being all reserved, the holders of these coupons gathered slowly and it was not until the second inning that the vacancies were filled.

Outside the park thousands stood thruout the game, echoing the cheers of those within, while automobiles lined the streets for several squares around the baseball arena. The spectators were noticeably fair in their treatment of the players of the two clubs, applauding every good play regardless of whether made by Athletic or Giant. Naturally they rooted hardest for an Athletic victory but when it was seen that Mathewson was invulnerable, the thousands rose up and cheered the old master in a way that could not have been surpassed even at the Polo grounds.

Opposing Pitchers in Wednesday's Battle

CHRISTOPHER MATHEWSON.

EDWARD S. PLANK.

Game Play by Play.

After the conferences between umpires and managers McGraw and Captain Dan Murphy were over, the Athletics took the field and Herzog led off for New York. After having two balls and a strike Herzog sent a high fly to Collins and was out amid the cheers of the crowd. Captain Doyle drove a fly out to Strunk in center field and Fletcher ended the inning by falling a victim to strikes.

The home rooters cheered Eddie Murphy as he faced the old reliable Mathewson. His first pitch was a ball, unusual for him in a world's series game, but the second was a strike and then Murphy sent a slow grounder to Doyle. The New York captain in his anxiety to make a quick throw to head off the fleet runner, let the ball go between his legs and Murphy was safe. Reuben Oldring waited for what he wanted and slashed a single to left field, sending Murphy down to second base. Then Collins did what everybody expected him to do, sacrificed, Snodgrass to Doyle, advancing both teammates.

"Hit 'er out, Bake," shouted the Athletic rooters as the home run hero stepped to the plate, picked up some dirt and rubbed it on his hands. Mathewson, unperturbed, pitched a wide outshoot for Baker to bite at, but the slugger let it go by for a ball. The crowd shouted, but the "old master" quickly had two strikes on him by Baker fouling the ball. On the next pitch the hard-hitting third baseman was out on strikes.

"You didn't do it that time," shouted some one from the stand from behind the Giants' bench. McInnis flied to Burns, leaving Murphy and Oldring stranded on the bases.

Burns, first up for New York in the second inning, struck out on Plank's cross-fire balls. Shafer hit up a long fly that fell into Murphy's hands, and Murray was quickly disposed of by Plank, who struck him out. Plank was going very good and it looked as if the game would settle down to a pitchers' battle.

The Athletics did not trouble Mathewson in the second inning as much as they did in the first. Strunk shot a grounder to Doyle, who got the ball cleanly this time and tossed the fast center fielder out by inches. Burns took care of Barry's high fly and Lapp went out by the strikeout route.

The best that Larry McLean could do when he came to bat in the third inning for New York was to pop up a fly to Barry. Snodgrass shot a single into left field and the crowd got its first good idea of the New Yorker's "charley horse," for he hobbled slowly to first. With Mathewson at the bat, Plank had little fear of Snodgrass trying to steal even tho he took a long lead off the base. The Philadelphia battery noticed this and Plank sent up a very wide outshoot, which Lapp shot to McInnis, but Snodgrass was easily under the throw and safe at the bag. Mathewson drove a long single to center field and Snodgrass ran as fast as he could and just beat the throw-in to third, the Giants' pitcher going to second on the throw. Wiltse here replaced the crippled Snodgrass. Herzog bounded a grounder to Plank, who caught Wiltse between third and home and he was run down by Lapp, who raced almost to third to get him. Mathewson moved up to third on the play and Herzog took second. The Athletics' infield played in to get the nearest runner but they did not have to do this, for Doyle flied out to Oldring after having three balls and two strikes.

The American League champions were quickly disposed of in their half of the third. Plank was thrown out, Doyle to Wiltse, who replaced Snodgrass at first base. Eddie Murphy, changing his style of play, tried to get away with a safe bunt, but Mathewson fielded the ball in fine style and got the runner at first. Oldring shot a fast grounder to Herzog, who made a pretty throw to Wiltse, retiring the side.

Fletcher Started Hitting.

New York rooters shouted for Fletcher to "start something" when he went to bat in the fourth inning and he responded by slashing the ball to Barry, who made a fine stop and throw to first, getting the ball there ahead of the runner. Burns, still unable to solve the puzzling cross-fire balls of Plank, struck out for the second time amid much cheering on the part of the home crowd. Shafer hit a grounder to Baker, who had lots of time to get the ball to first, but threw low and Shafer was safe on the error. McGraw, who was coaching at first base, said something to Shafer and a moment later he darted for second in an attempted steal,but Lapp's throw to Collins beat him and he was out.

In the Athletics' half of the fourth Collins hit to Mathewson and was out at first. Baker brought the fans to their feet by driving a hot single to right field. Doyle got his fingers on it as it shot past him on the left side, but only deflected the ball. Baker went to second on McInnis' out, Doyle to Wiltse. Mathewson had two strikes on Strunk when he lost his sense of location for a moment, and the Athletic batter got the first base on balls of the game. With two smart runners on the bases and a brainy man at the bat, the crowd shouted for a run. The runners were off with the pitch and Barry hit the ball, but it bounded slowly to second where Doyle scooped it and touched second, retiring the side. This was the second time in four innings that the Athletics had two men left on the bases.

New York managed to get two men on the bases in the fifth inning after which Plank tightened up. Murray drove a fly to left which Oldring easily held and McLean got his first hit of the game by smashing a single close along the third base foul line. Wiltse failed to advance him by striking out. Mathewson worked Plank for a base on balls. It was then up to Herzog but the third baseman drove at Collins and he was out at first.

Catcher Lapp was an easy out at first in Philadelphia's fifth. Plank rammed a single between first and second. He was left there, however, as Murphy drove a long fly to Burns, who backed almost to the bleacher seats in left field to make the catch and Oldring was thrown out at first by Fletcher.

The sixth inning was quickly over. Both pitchers were going in magnificent style. Doyle sent a weak bounder to Plank and was tossed out. Fletcher sent up a high foul that McInnis got under and he was out. Murphy took care of Burns' long fly.

In the Athletics' half Umpire Connolly was hooted when he called Collins' grounder a foul. The ball was bounding along the third base foul line when Herzog got it and dropped it, the ball falling on foul territory. It was the second strike on Collins and he was called out on strikes as Mathewson shot the next ball across the plate. Baker drove a wicked grounder that looked as if it would go to center field, but Fletched managed to get up to it as the ball shot over second and made a fine throw to first while on the run. This was one of the best fielding plays of the game and brought forth much cheering. McInnis struck out.

In the seventh inning Shafer for New York flied to Strunk. Murray put up a fly that Barry took in without any trouble. McLean drove a long fly to Oldring.

One of the best catches of the day was made by Burns, who ran in and got Strunk's short fly almost off the ground. Barry hit to Herzog, who made a pretty throw to first ahead of the runner. Lapp shot a single past Wiltse but was left on first when Plank sent up a pop fly to Fletcher.

With the eighth inning beginning and both pitchers going as well as when the started, it looked like extra innings. A light mist spread over the ball park, giving the two pitchers a little more advantage over the batters. Wiltse opened New York's half by going out, Collins to McInnis. Mathewson, who seemed to have no trouble in hitting Plank, smashed a hard drive to right field. Murphy barely got up to the ball, picked it off his shoetops and turned a somersault. He held the ball, however, and Umpire Egan, who was in right field, signalled that Murphy had made the out.

Herzog hit a high fly to center field for which Strunk had to do some sprinting to get.

Matty In Trouble.

Mathewson's first real trouble came in the eighth inning with the top of the Athletics' batting order up. Murphy grounded out to Wiltse, who was playing a fine game around first base. Oldring was the second out, Fletcher to Wiltse. Collins brought the crowd to its feet by shooting a single into left field. Again the cry came for Baker to hit a home run and he responded with a sharp single to left field, Collins being held on second. McInnis ended the inning by forcing Collins at third, Herzog making the out unassisted.

The ninth inning opened with Doyle flying out to Strunk. Fletcher brought cheers from the Giants' supporters by hitting to center field for a base. Burns received a base on balls and Fletcher moved to second. There was some excitement on the Giants' bench at the prospect of scoring but the New York players were doomed to disappointment. Shafer flied to Oldring and Murray amid tremendous cheering, sent up a fly to Murphy.

Then came the Athletics' ninth, in which they had golden opportunities to win the game. The crowd rose to its feet as Strunk singled to center. Barry in attempting to sacrifice him, hit a slow bounder toward second and Doyle running in picked up the ball and tossed it to first as Barry flashed over the bag. The throw was bad and Barry raced to second and Strunk went on to third. There was a chance for Strunk to score but he was held at third. It looked like a sure victory for the Athletics. All the New York infield surrounded Mathewson and after a short conference the big pitcher again went into the box. Lapp hit weakly to Wiltse and the latter shot the ball to McLean as Strunk rushed to the plate. McLean easily put the ball on the runner and he was out, Strunk not touching the plate as he slid past it. Barry moved up to third on the out. The excitement was great among the crowd. It was expected that Manager Mack would send in a pinch hitter for Plank. Plank after reaching the plate was called away but Mack decided to let the pitcher bat. Plank hit to Wiltse, who shot the ball to McLean, catching Barry coming home. Barry darted back toward third and McLean threw the ball to Herzog, who then returned it to Mathewson down the line, and Barry was touched out. Lapp reached third and Plank second. Murphy ended the inning by sending an easy grounder to Mathewson, who threw him out. It was great pitching on the part of Mathewson and he received generous applause as he walked to the plate.

The memorable tenth inning saw victory go to the Giants. McLean opened it with a single to right center. Grant was ordered to run for McLean and went down to second on Wiltse's sacrifice hit, Plank putting the ball on Wiltse as he ran toward first base. Mathewson then came to time and won his own game on a single to center field on which Grant came home. Grant, thinking the play at the plate would be close, slid in but he made the home base easily. Herzog shot a grounder at Collins and the latter threw the ball to Barry to force Mathewson. Barry appeared to lose sight of the ball and it went over his head as Mathewson reached second and he kept on to third as the ball rolled into center field, Herzog reaching second. Plank hit Doyle with a pitched ball and the bases were full. Fletcher caught one of Plank's fast inshoots on the end of his bat and drove it down the third base line. The ball took an unexpected bounce and shot far over Baker's head for a single on which Mathewson and Herzog crossed the plate. Burns struck out for the third time and Shafer flied to Murphy.

Mathewson held Philadelphia safe in the latter's half of the inning. Oldring went out, Herzog to Wiltse. Collins struck out and Doyle picked up Baker's grounder and tossed him out at first.

The paid attendance at today's game was 20,563. Total receipts amounted to $49,640, of which the National commission received $4,964. Each club's share was $8,935.20 and the players received $26,805.60.

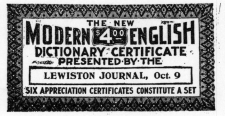

The official box score:—

New York.

	AB	R	BH	PO	A	E
Herzog, 3b.	5	1	0	1	4	0
Doyle, 2b.	4	0	0	3	5	2
Fletcher, ss.	5	0	2	1	3	0
Burns, l.f.	4	0	0	4	0	0
Shafer, c.f.	5	0	0	0	0	0
Murray, r.f.	4	0	0	0	0	0
McLean, c.	4	0	2	5	1	0
Grant**	0	1	0	0	0	0
Wilson, c.	0	0	0	1	0	0
Snodgrass, 1b.	1	0	1	1	1	0
Wiltse, 1b.*	2	0	0	13	3	0
Mathewson, p.	3	1	2	1	3	0
Totals	37	3	7	30	20	2

*Ran for Snodgrass in second.
**Ran for McLean in tenth.

Philadelphia.

	AB	R	BH	PO	A	E
E. Murphy, r.f.	5	0	0	5	0	0
Oldring, l.f.	5	0	1	4	0	0
Collins, 2b.	4	0	1	2	2	1
Baker, 3b.	5	0	2	0	0	1
McInnis, 1b.	4	0	0	5	0	0
Strunk, c.f.	3	0	1	4	0	0
Barry, ss.	4	0	1	2	1	0
Lapp, c.	4	0	1	7	1	0
Plank, p.	4	0	1	1	2	0
Totals	38	0	8	30	6	2

New York	0	0	0	0	0	0	0	0	0	3—3
Philadelphia	0	0	0	0	0	0	0	0	0	0—0

Sacrifice hits, Collins, Wiltse. Left on bases, New York 8, Philadelphia 10. First base on balls, off Mathewson 1, off Plank 2. First on errors, New York 1, Philadelphia 2. Hit by pitcher, by Plank, Doyle. Struck out, by Mathewson 5, by Plank 6. Time, 2.22. Umpires: Plate, Connolly; bases, Rigler; left field, Klem; right field, Egan.

Matty's Father a Fan.

TUNKHANNOCK, Pa., Oct. 9.—There was a gray-haired man watching the scoreboard here Wednesday during the progress of the world's series game in Philadelphia, to whom the success of Christy Mathewson meant more sentimentally than to anyone else, except perhaps the Giant star pitcher himself. It was Mathewson's father, G. B. Mathewson, of Factoryville. He had been summoned here as a witness in a court proceeding, but when his name was called to take the stand he could not be found. Officers were sent in search of him and the elder Mathewson was discovered in front of the scoreboard, applauding and smiling broadly as every succeeding report told of his son's wonderful pitching.

"I used to play amateur baseball myself in Chicago," said the old man, with a disappointed expression on his face, as he accompanied the officers back to court.

"I've never even dream tho, that my boy would achieve fame as Christy has in the baseball world."

Dropped Dead When Matty Singled In Tenth.

NEW YORK, Oct. 9.—A middle aged man who had been leading the cheering in front of a Park Row bulletin board Wednesday dropped dead of heart disease as the news was flashed that Mathewson had made a hit in the tenth inning. The victim of over-excitement carried a Bowery mission membership card in his pocket and letters addressed to Edward O'Brien.

Dropped Dead In Philadelphia.

PHILADELPHIA, Oct. 9.—While watching an electric scoreboard during Wednesday's game between the Giants and Athletics, John Sherrick collapsed on the sidewalk and died a few minutes later. It was during the first inning of the contest and eyewitnesses declare that Sherrick had just yelled "Give us another homer, Baker."

When the play reproduced on the scoreboard showed that the Athletics star batsman had struck out the excitedfan dropped to the pavement. Heart failure is believed to have caused his death.

BROWN OF BOWDOIN INJURES HIS LEG

BRUNSWICK, Oct. 9.—A five-mile hare and hound race and the second in the series of the freshmen-sophomore baseball game, together with the football practice, gave the majority of the athletes at Bowdoin college an opportunity to take part Wednesday afternoon.

Over 300 men took part in the hare and hound race in which the hares, Lawrence W. Irving, '16, of West Roxbury, Mass., and Frank H. L. Hargrave, '16, of West Buxton, won by 15 minutes.

The baseball game went only five and a half innings when it was called on account of darkness. The sophomores won 4 to 1. Score by innings:—

Sophomores	1	0	0	0	2	1—4	2	2
Freshmen	0	1	0	0	0	x—1	3	8

Batteries, Knight and Churchill; Bradford and Carll.

At the football practice it became known that Lew Brown of Portland, quarterback, would probably be unable to take part in the game against Trinity to be played here Saturday, owing to an injury to his leg. Woodbury P. Brigham, the Roxbury, Mass., freshman, who played a fine game at halfback against Wesleyan last week, was called home to-day by the critical illness of his mother, and may not be able to play again this fall. The varsity is now lining up with Coolbroth, freshman from Dexter, at fullback, Foster and LaCasce, halfbacks, Capt. Weatherill and Leadbetter, ends, and Fitzgerald, quarterback, a radical change from the lineup of the last two weeks.

Brown, showing decided improvement in football since the Colby game, defeated Rhode Island State College Wednesday afternoon 19 to 0.

J. N. Camden's Bringhurst, a two-year-old gelding, established a new world's running record for 5½ furlongs at the Churchill Downs track, Louisville, Ky., Wednesday afternoon, going the distance in 1.04 3-5. This reduced by one-fifth of a second the record established by Lady Irma at San Anita Park, Calif., in December, 1908.

[Continued on eleventh page.]

COMPLETE BASEBALL With Box Score

THE BOSTON TRAVELER
AND EVENING HERALD

COMPLETE BASEBALL With Box Score

89TH YEAR. | THE WEATHER—Unsettled tonight; Sunday probably rain; easterly to southerly winds. | BOSTON, SATURDAY, OCTOBER 11, 1913. | 14 PAGES | ONE CENT.

ATHLETICS TAKE WORLD'S SERIES

SCORE BY INNINGS		1	2	3	4	5	6	7	8	9	10	11	12	13	14	15	Total
ATHLETICS	Plank, p.; Schang, c.	1	0	2	0	0	0	0	0	0							3
GIANTS	Mathewson, p.; McLean, c.	0	0	0	0	1	0	0	0	0							1

136 PERISH IN FIRE ABOARD LINER AT SEA

Ten Ships, Summoned by S O S Call, Rescue 521 Aboard Volturno of Uranium Line

SCORES OF IMMIGRANTS TRAPPED IN THEIR BUNKS

LIVERPOOL, Oct. 11—One hundred and thirty-six men, women and children, mostly Russian, Dalmatian, Polish and German immigrants. bound for Canada, lost their lives when the Uranium line steamship Volturno caught fire in mid-Atlantic Thursday and burned to the water's edge on Friday.

Ten big liners, led by the Cunarder Carmania, Capt. Barr, stood by the stricken ship and battled for many hours in a fierce gale to rescue the passengers and crew, and were able to take off and pick up 521 persons. While hundreds of passengers aboard the rescue fleet crowded the rails and looked on spellbound with horror, the captains manoeuvred in desperate attempts to get alongside the Volturno, but were unable to do so until daybreak Friday.

CARMANIA RESCUES FIRST ELEVEN.

Capt. Barr then ran a lifeboat under the stern of the Volturno and took off 11 passengers. Other captains followed and the survivors taken from the Volturno, as well as those picked up in the two Volturno lifeboats that got away during the fire, were distributed among the rescuing liners.

From Thursday noon the Carmania stood by, helpless on account of the terrific storm and mountainous waves, until early Friday. The last of the surviving passengers and crew were taken off at 9:30 Friday morning. The Carmania was alone with the burning liner until the Grosser Kurfurst and the Seidlitz came up about 4 o'clock Thursday afternoon. The other seven rescue ships arrived shortly afterward.

FOUR LIFEBOATS ARE SMASHED.

While the Carmania's passengers looked on, frantic and helpless, four lifeboats lowered from the Volturno were smashed against the side of the heavily-rolling ship, and their passengers, including women and children, were drowned. The broken propeller of the Volturno had fouled the tackle of the lifeboats so that only six could be lowered and only two got away.

As darkness fell, the Carmania kept her powerful searchlights playing on the waters around the burning boat. Capt. Barr also threw out burning buoys all night, to light the scene.

Their ghostly light played on the poop of the Volturno and showed plainly the hopeless women, children and men huddled there throughout the night.

At midnight, some hope was aroused when the fire appeared to be dying down. Capt. Barr made another attempt to get a boat to the ship, and when this failed, he ran the Carmania head on within 100 feet of the Volturno's stern. It was impossible, however, to get a line aboard her.

VOLTURNO SINKING AT DAYBREAK.

The fire broke out again fiercely in the after engine room before dawn and when daylight came it was seen that the Volturno was sinking by the head.

The gale had abated by then and lifeboats from the rescue fleet were run alongside the burning liner, taking off the last of the survivors.

About 9 o'clock Thursday night a burst of flame lighted the sky and the surging waves for miles around. It was followed by a terrific explosion, which sent clouds of sparks and burning fragments high in the air. Several steerage passengers with life belts jumped into the water and were picked up by the Carmania's boats.

The Volturno was abandoned at 9:20 A M. Friday, and sank a few min-

(Continued on Page Five, Column 5.)

TODAY'S SNAPSHOT DIAGRAM

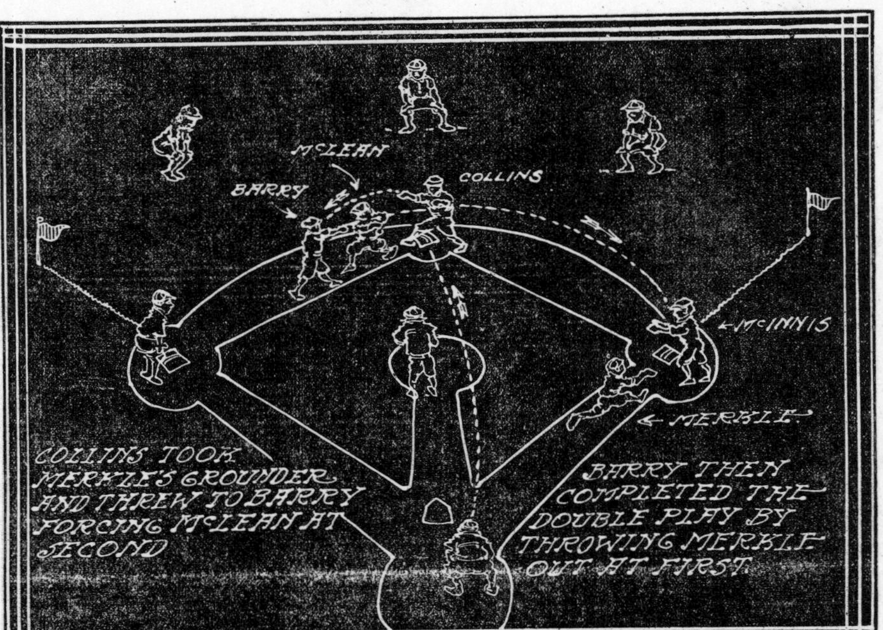
McLEAN
COLLINS
BARRY
McINNIS
MERKLE
COLLINS TOOK MERKLE'S GROUNDER AND THREW TO BARRY FORCING McLEAN AT SECOND
BARRY THEN COMPLETED THE DOUBLE PLAY BY THROWING MERKLE OUT AT FIRST

WHEN THE GIANTS BEGAN TO HOPE

Giant rooters took hope in the fifth inning. After Burns went out Shafer was given the first walk of the game. Plank dropped Murray's pop fly. McLean followed with his customary single, scoring Shafer. Right then the Athletics' infield came through with its famous doubl play, Collins to Barry to McInnis.

WILLIAMS-HARVARD TIED IN 4TH PERIOD

HARVARD STADIUM, Oct. 11—Williams matched its fast and experienced eleven against Harvard's powerful football machine on the Stadium turf this afternon. Before the game started there were but few who were willing to say that Harvard would not be forced to show all the football it had. A year ago a Williams team that was not a bit better than the one Coach Fred Daly brought down from Williamstown this fall played Harvard a good game, and though defeated, 26-3, was the first eleven to score on the crimson.

It was evident when the teams lined up for the opening kick-off that Harvard was putting its full strength into the game. Trumbull was at centre, Pennock was at one of the guards, and the backfield trio was made up of Brickley, Hardwick and Mahan, considered by many to be one of the best combinations ever gathered in a Harvard backfield. Harvard men were instructed to keep their eyes on several of the good Williams players, notably Half-back Toolan, Full-back Turner and Quarterback Hunnewell, the last named a Winchester boy. The heavy, fine mist that started falling early in the afternoon of necessity slowed up the game and was distasteful to both Coach Daly and Coach Haughton, who wanted to have the game played under good football conditions, particularly as regards the footing.

THE LINE-UP.

HARVARD.	WILLIAMS.
O'Brien, l.e.	r.e., Walker
Storer, l.t.	r.t., Driscoll
Mills, l.g.	r.g., Furness
Trumbull, c.	c., Tompkins
Pennock, r.g.	l.g., Eells
Hitchcock, r.t.	l.t., Walker
Coolidge, r.e.	l.e., Vinal
Bradlee, q.b.	q.b., Hunnewell
Mahan, l.h.b.	r.h.b., Payson
Hardwick, r.h.b.	l.h.b., Toolan
Brickley, f.b.	f.b., Turner

Official: Referee—W. R. Okeson, Lehigh. Umpire—E. G. Hapgood, Brown. Head Linesman—H. R. Bankart, Dartmouth. Twelve-minute periods.

FIRST QUARTER

The first quarter was a series of fumbles, due largely to the wet ball and the slippery field. Harvard kicked off and Toolan was tackled by Mahan on Williams's 15-yard line. Williams tried two forward passes which failed and then punted outside at the Crimson 45-yard line.

Brickley plowed through right tackle for 20 yards. Harvard carried the ball to Williams's 15-yard line and fumbled. Williams failed to gain in two downs, fumbled on the third and Harvard had the ball on its enemy's 20-yard line. In two rushes Harvard made first down on Williams's 10-yard line. Harvard fumbled, Williams getting the ball.

The Purple could not gain and punted outside at their own 25-yard line. Harvard quickly brought the ball back to Williams's eight-yard line, but Brickley, who tried to make a touchdonw with a yard to go on the fourth down, was stopped by Williams's left wing, and it was Williams's ball again.

Hunnewell punted to Williams's 30-yard line, and the period ended with the ball in Williams's possession on its 13-yar line. Score—Harvard 0, Williams 0.

SECOND PERIOD

Hunnewell was forced to punt. There was itnerference with a fair catch and Harvard had the ball on Williams's 40-yard line, first down, a 15-yard penalty. Harvard ploughed through the right wing to the 25-yard line. Here Williams braced and Quarterback Bradlee finally ordered Charley Brickley to drop back. He kicked a goal from the field from the 20-yard line. Logan replaced Bradlee at quarterback. Score—Harvard 3, Williams 0.

Williams received the kick-off again but could not gain and punted to Harvard's 43-yard line, where Hardwick fumbled, recovered and was downed. After one line play Harvard punted and the ball rolled over Williams's lien for a

(Continued on Page 5, Column 4.)

BOX SCORE OF TODAY'S GAME

ATHLETICS

	ab.	r.	bh.	tb.	po.	a.	e.
E. Murphy, r.f.	3	1	2	2	3	0	0
Oldring, l.f.	4	2	0	0	3	0	0
Collins, 2b	3	0	1	1	2	3	0
Baker, 3b.	3	0	2	2	0	2	0
McInnis, 1b	2	0	0	0	14	0	0
Strunk, c.f.	4	0	0	0	2	0	0
Barry, s.s.	4	0	0	0	2	7	0
Schang, c.	4	0	1	1	1	0	0
Plank, p.	3	0	0	0	0	1	1
Totals	30	3	6	6	27	13	1

GIANTS

	ab.	r.	bh.	tb.	po.	a.	e.
Herzog, 3b.	4	0	0	0	1	2	0
Doyle, 2b.	4	0	0	0	1	7	1
Fletcher, s.s.	3	0	0	0	2	3	0
Burns, l.f.	3	0	0	0	2	0	1
Shafer, c.f.	2	1	0	0	2	0	0
Murray, r.f.	3	0	0	0	2	0	0
McLean, c.	3	0	1	1	3	1	0
Merkle, 1b.	3	0	0	0	14	0	0
Mathewson, p.	2	0	1	1	0	2	0
*Crandall	1	0	0	0	0	0	0
Totals	28	1	2	2	27	15	2

Left on bases—Philadelphia 4. First base on errors—Philadelphia 1. Sacrifice hits—Collins, McInnis. Sacrifice flies—Baker, McInnis. Struck out—By Mathewson, Schang 2; by Plank, Herzog. Bases on balls—Off Mathewson, Murphy; off Plank, Shafer. Double plays—Collins to Barry to McInnis 3; Barry to Collins to McInnis. Umpires—Klem at plate, Egan on bases, Connolly and Rigler on foul lines. Time—1:39. Attendance—36,000.

*Batted for Mathewson in 9th inning.

THE WEATHER

FORECAST — Unsettled tonight; Sunday, probably rain, followed by clearing and cooler; easterly to southerly winds.

Sun rose 5:52, sets 5:10; Sunday, rises 5:53, sets 5:08. High tide, 8:45 A. M., 9 P. M.; Sunday, 9:30 A. M., 5:45 P. M.

Light auto lamps before 5:40 P. M.

Boston observations, 8 A. M. Barometer, 30.13; temperature, 60; highest yesterday, 66; lowest last night, 59; humidity, 97%; wind, east, 7 miles; misting; precipitation past 24 hours, .04 of an inch.

FRANKLIN PARK AVIARY OPENS MONDAY AFTERNOON

The new Franklin Park aviary, which has been under construction during the past two years and which cost $150,000, will be opened officially Monday afternoon at 3 o'clock by Mayor Fitzgerald, who will deliver an address. The park commissioners will also be present. The aviary will contain 100 bird cages, in which will be birds from all ove rthe world.

PLANK WINS FROM MATTY

Giants Able to Register but Two Lone Hits off Mack's Veteran Twirler

By GRANTLAND RICE.

POLO GROUNDS, NEW YORK, Oct. 11—Eddie Plank won the world's baseball championship for Connie Mack's Athletics here this afternoon, when, in the fifth game of the series the Athletics annexed their fourth victory by a score of 3 to 1.

Two lone singles was the gross hitting effort of the Giants. Plank duplicated Matty's effort of the second game when, like his veteran contemporary, he weathered every storm and by a superb demonstration of all those things which make for pitching excellence he stood the Giants on their beam end. If anything, the greater glory must go to Matty, for, while the Mackmen won, he was forced to make up with brains what was lacking in his good right arm. Plank's famous southpaw was there forty ways today, and to the very last flicker had the stuff to make puny the efforts of the Giant batters.

Carry Plank Out on Shoulders.

No kid pitcher could have displayed greater stuff in a fresh young arm than was unrolled by the Gettysburg gattler. At the conclusion of the game his team mates displayed their sentiments in the matter by bearing the veteran twirler from the field on their shoulders as their team mates worked a revolving wedge through the throng of admiration-wrapped rooters.

Just so certainly as Plank was there, just so certainly were the Giant batters not there, and while the veteran Mathewson pitched the full nine innings without an earned run being registered off his delivery.

Two fatal errors behind him were sufficient, with the scratch hits he yielded, to give the Athletics the run needed to cinch the game and the championship. In a like manner the one lone run registered by the Giants was only made possible by an addition to the error column, but in this case the error was charged to Plank himself.

Plank Pitched His Greatest Game.

Following their usual tactics, the Mackmen made a vicious assault in the early innings and stacked up a lead which the brilliant Matty could not stop. Murphy, the first man up, laced out a single and was forced by Oldring. Collins singled, putting Oldring on third. Baker flied to Burns and Oldring scored when Burns threw high to McLean. The throw was in plenty of time to have nailed the runner, and only Burns's bad peg made the tally possible.

In the third inning Doyle's fumble and Merkle's delay in running down Murphy caught off third on Baker's easy grounder cost two more runs. From this point on Matty took the game away from his support and gave his fielders no hard chances to handle. He worked a faultless game in the six closing rounds, but his batting support was too pitifully weak against Plank's great pitching, but 29 Giants facing him. Plank says this may be the last ball game that he will ever pitch, as he is 40 years old. If it is, he can always remember it as his greatest game.

Connie Mack's Third Championship.

At the finish the crowd was all there with the ovation for Plank. For inning after inning it was obvious that the veteran had his opponents curled up and withered. The only question in any mind was whether his wonderful work could be stretched across the full nine frames. When Doyle's final flicker dropped in Murphy's mitt, 35,000 pair of eyes were focuesd on the veteran hero of the day and most of the 35,000 tried to get into the swirling mob which swarmed onto the field to cheer him on his exit.

Today's victory gives Connie Mack three world's series in four years and adds considerably to the dimensions of his present niche in the baseball Hall of fame. For the series the Athletics hit safely 46 times for 23 runs. The Giants connected with 33 hits for 15 runs.

FIRST INNING

ATHLETICS—Murphy singled, hitting the first ball pitched. Oldring forced Murphy, Matty to Fletcher, on an attempted sacrifice bunt. Collins singled to right, putting Oldring on third. Baker flied to Burns, Oldring scoring on the throw-in and Collins taking second when Burns threw too high to McLean. Collins out, Herzog to Doyle, when McInnis bounded one to the third baseman.—ONE RUN, TWO HITS, ONE ERROR.

Mathewson promised to be an easy victim of the Mackian sluggers, but rallied, and some sharp fielding saved him with but a single run getting over.

GIANTS—Herzog flied to Murphy. Doyle out, Barry to McInnis. Fletcher flied to Oldring, who backed up against the bleacher fence.—NO RUNS, NO HITS, NO ERRORS.

Plank worked a sizzling cross-fire on the Giants with fatal effect. The ball fairly smoked, and it was obvious that Eddie was putting everything possible on it. The Giant batters crowded the plate in an effort to get the veteran's goat, but without avail.

SECOND INNING

ATHLETICS—Strunk out, Doyle to Merkle. Barry flied to Murray. Schang singled, the ball hitting Matty's glove. Plank popped to Herzog.—NO RUNS, ONE HIT, NO ERRORS.

Matty had the plate located to a T in his second session, and was warping over a splendid curve which fooled the Athletic batters. They swung hard, but none of their connections produced sound or crack that reverberated through the first inning. Matty was working good.

GIANTS—Burns out, Baker to McInnis. Shafer fouled to McInnis in front of the boxes. Murray out, Plank to McInnis.—NO RUNS, NO HITS, NO ERRORS.

Plank did fine work and got grand support. Baker's assist on Burns's hot smash and McInnis's catch of a fast foul by Shafer being spectacular.

THIRD INNING

ATHLETICS—Murphy singled through short. Oldring safe on Doyle's muff of a hot grounder. Collins sacrificed, Merkle unassisted. Baker was safe and Murphy scored when Merkle attempted to tag Baker on the line. Baker got credit for a hit. McInnis flied out to Burns, Oldring scoring on the throw in. Strunk out, Doyle to Merkle.—TWO RUNS, TWO HITS, ONE ERROR.

A couple of hits off Matty, one a very scratchy affair, and a crack in the Giants' support gave the Athletics a pair of tallies in the third. Merkle's bad judgment in not throwing out Murphy at the plate was undoubtedly the chief factor in the Giants' difficulty.

GIANTS—McLean flied to Oldring. Merkle lined to Collins. The "Old Marster" received an ovation. Plank gave him a grin and got the outfield in position. Matty out, Barry to McInnis.—NO RUNS, NO HITS, NO ERRORS.

It was very much Plank, the veteran winding up the third round without having allowed a single Giant to reach the first bag.

FOURTH INNING

ATHLETICS—Barry out, Fletcher to Merkle. Schang flied out to Murray. Plank flied out to Fletcher, who made a pretty catch while running backward.—NO RUNS, NO HITS, NO ERRORS.

This was Matty's best inning, and the first in which he disposed of the first three men up.

GIANTS—Herzog fanned. It was Plank's first strike-out. Doyle out, McInnis unassisted. Fletcher flied to Strunk.—NO RUNS, NO HITS, NO ERRORS.

Plank got a warm hand as he came in after finishing his fourth hitless inning. The old veteran had eased up considerably and appeared to be running much smoother than at the start. He had everything.

FIFTH INNING

ATHLETICS—Murphy out, Doyle to Merkle. Oldring out, Doyle to Merkle, on the first ball pitched. Collins flied to Shafer.—NO RUNS, NO HITS, NO ERRORS.

Matty wound up the festivities in this

(Continued on Page Five, Column 1)

Part 2

The New York Times

Oct 12 1913

Baseball Section

THE NAPOLEONS OF BASEBALL

JOHN J. McGRAW.

McGraw, the Giant's manager, was born at Truxton, N. Y., in 1873. He began to play baseball when he was but seventeen years of age, and in 1891 Manager Barnie engaged him for the then tail-end Baltimore club. In 1900, along with Catcher Robinson, McGraw was sold to the St. Louis National League club, and he played all that season in the Mound City. In 1901 he and Robinson organized a new Baltimore club, and in 1902 he was transferred with several other players to New York. Under McGraw's management the Giants won the National League championship in 1904-05 and the world's championship in 1905, lost the league pennant only by a technicality in 1908, finished third in 1909, a good second in 1910, and first in 1911-12.

CONNIE MACK.

Cornelius McGillicuddy, better known as Connie Mack, is one of the cleverest of managers. He was born at Brookfield, Mass., in 1862. For six seasons he caught for Pittsburgh, and he was manager from 1894 to 1896. Then he assumed the management of the Milwaukee (Western League) club. In 1901 he transferred his Milwaukee franchise to Philadelphia and organized the Athletic Club, one of the mainstays of the American League. In 1902 he molded a championship team from material that would have defied any other manager. In 1903 the Athletics finished second, in 1904 fifth, in 1905 first, in 1906 fourth, in 1907 second, in 1908 sixth, in 1909 second, in 1910 and 1911 first, in 1912 second, and this year again in first place.

(Photo (C) by Underwood & Underwood.)

Big Interest Centers About Gunboat Smith-Pelkey Mill

LITTLE TO JUDGE THE SKILL OF PELKEY BY

Aside From His Bout With McCarty, and He Didn't Have Chance to Show There, Not Much Is Known of Canadian's Prowess With His Fists—Will Outweigh Smith Many Pounds.

BY GEORGE T. PARDY.

NEW YORK, December 27.—In many sections of the country where worshipers of the muscular cult abound, the glad New Year will be duly celebrated to the melodious sound of the five-ounce soaker bestowing swats and slaps on the jowls of the slugger.

Chief interest is centered in the 20-round tussle between Gunboat Smith and Arthur Pelky, scheduled for Jim Coffroth's 'Frisco arena, and up to date the ex-navy man reigns a decided favorite in betting circles. This is as it ought to be, for on straight listed performances Gunboat holds a decided lead over all his heavyweight contemporaries. His record now contains victories over Moran, Willard, Wells, Rodel, Morris, Sam Langford and many lesser lights of the ring.

There are those who dispute the correctness of the verdict which named Smith winner over Willard, his defeat of Morris was registered on a foul in a very unsatisfactory struggle; and the Boston engagement with Langford came in for a good deal of adverse criticism, because of a strong suspicion that there was something fishy about the affair.

Carries Weight.

But the action of the referee in the bout with Morris carries due weight, as does that of the third man in the arena who pronounced him conquerer of Willard; and the decision of the Boston umpire also stands. There is no appeal from a referee's decree, and Smith must be considered as fully entitled to his laurels. Nobody can dispute Gunboat's willingness to tackle anybody Manager Tom Buckley selects as an opponent for him, and this trait has tended to greatly enhance his popularity with the rank and file of fight patrons.

Pelky is expected to enter the ring weighing around the 205 mark, which would give him an advantage of some 25 pounds over Buckley's battler. But Smith is accustomed to face even heavier weight odds than this, as witness his encounters with those twin mammoths of pugilism—Willard and Morris; so that Pelky's superiority in poundage isn't at all likely to feaze him.

If one were disposed to rely implicitly on the predictions made by ex-Heavyweight Champion Tommy Burns, manager and trainer of Pelky, the latter has a genuine copper-riveted cinch on the decision, outclassing Smith in punching power, cleverness, and every other angle in the fistic category. But Burns, although something of a scrapper himself in the past and therefore supposedly a good judge of fighting material, is apt to wax a trifle too enthusiastic over his discoveries in the boxing line.

Made Memsic Then.

It was Burns who at one time boosted George Memsic's claims to recognition as a star lightweight, and pointed out the Chicago Bohemian as a sure future champion of that class. But Memsic slumped disastrously and never came within several miles of the goal. Also it was Tommy who made himself responsible for the debut of Jack Lester as a "formidable white hope," and aided in the shipping of the said young man to Australia, where Burns confidently predicted his protege would clean up everything in sight. Instead of cleaning up, Lester was sent to the cleaners, being whipped in turn by Johnny Thompson, Bill Turner, Jack Howard and Langford, and going over the knockout route in each instance.

When Burns was booming Lester he was every whit as eloquent in his praises of Jack's wonderful abilities as he has been in his recent outbursts of Pelkyism.

It isn't very long ago since Burns and Pelky were abusing each other through the press, Arthur making accusations of fake work in connection with that little six-round go between them up Calgary way, and Burns stigmatizing Pelky as a "beastly ingrate," or words to that effect. Then came a reconciliation, and the present partnership between the pair, a sort of mutual admiration party with Burns as chief spouter, and Pelky playing chorus. The ex-heavyweight champion doesn't hesitate to declare that by dint of long and steady practice with him Pelky has developed the best left hand ever possessed by a pug, not even excepting that of the dusky gent who robbed Tommy of first chop honors. Also, Burns says he is willing to pin his faith on the superiority of Pelky's right hand wallop as opposed to that hurled by Gunboat Smith.

Always Boosting.

Was there ever, we wonder, a white hope pilot since the Reno episode who didn't indulge in just such fulsome praise of his entry for championship stakes? There is a possibility that Burns may have shaped and polished Pelky into a pugilistic gem of the first water, but you can't make the eastern sporting contingent believe it. Pelky's eastern debut was made here May 27, 1911, when he appeared in the heavyweight tournament promoted by O'Rourke. He made a good showing among the other novices, and was said to have had much the better of Palzer to whom first honors were awarded. But on being offered a second chance with Palzer he refused to accept for reasons best known to himself. New York expert opinion classed Pelky as a big, strong chap who could punch hard and wasn't lacking in gameness, but with everything to learn from a scientific standpoint.

Between his appearance in the Gotham tourney and the tragic bout with Luther McCarty which resulted in the latter's death last summer Pelky accomplished nothing of consequence in his profession, for the bout with Burns had too much of a "business arrangement" air to be taken seriously, and a couple of other contests with mediocre performers brought him no fame. The McCarty battle didn't last long enough to furnish a line on Pelky as he is today, and wasn't even a proof of his ability to hit hard, for there was no conclusive evidence that Luther's demise was due to the effects of a blow administered by his opponent. Therefore it follows that we have absolutely nothing to go on when doping out Pelky's chances of defeating the Gunner, except Burns's assertion that a few months of his tutelage has transformed Arthur into a sort of amalgamated Fitz-Jeffries-Corbett fighting machine of abnormal strength and skill.

May Be Good at That.

However, making allowance for 90 per cent literary flub-dub in the press proclamations issued by Burns anent his fighter, Pelky ought to be a much improved boxer if he was capable of profiting by Tommy's instructions. There are some glove-wielders who are absolutely incapable of learning anything new. Al Palzer was a chunk-headed specimen of the breed and there have been many others. With such persons the attempt to smooth off their rough angles frequently results in spoiling them altogether as sluggers and turning them into machine-made puppets unable to think for themselves.

If Pelky is one-half as good as Burns maintains, his battle with Smith ought to be a hummer. A victory over Smith would put Pelky in the front rank of the heavies at a single jump and utterly confound the prophecies of the "wise ones" who aver that Tommy is talking like a tin pan. There is certainly strong reason for believing that Burns is perfectly sincere in his avowal of faith in his man, if the report be true that he is willing to bet to the last ditch on Pelky at better than even money.

87 PLAYERS IN HOLIDAY GOLF

Stagg, of Chicago, Loses Special Gold Medal Match at Pinehurst.

Pinehurst, N. C., December 27.—Eighty-seven players drove off today in the qualification round of the annual holiday golf tournament.

Those who qualified for the first division and still continue match play through Wednesday were the following: H. V. Seggerman, Englewood; A. A. Stagg, Chicago; W. A. Barber, Jr., Princeton; W. E. Truesdell, Fox Hills; William Souther, Dyker Meadows; B. P. Merriman, Waterbury; C. B. Hudson, North Fork; C. L. Becker, Woodland; W. G. Clark, Wollaston; W. V. Booth, Jr., Onwentsia; George H. Crocker, Brookline; S. Leroy, Newport; T. B. Boyd, Bellerieve; H. G. White, Ridgewood; Robert Hunter, Weeburn, and W. L. Otis, New York.

In a special gold medal match H. V. Seggerman, of Englewood, defeated A. A. Stagg, of Chicago, 81 to 83.

JERSEY SOCCERITES WIN

St. Louis, December 27.—True Blues of Paterson, N. J., today defeated the Columbian Athletic club team of St. Louis in soccer football, 5 to 0.

In the first half the play was almost entirely in the territory of the local team.

Weinman's After Games.

Weinman A. C. has organized for the season and will have a strong basketball team in the field. Business meeting will be held January 8. Following players are requested to be present: F. Keenan, W. Look, R. Gardella, P. Keenan, Charles Donnley, T. Oliver, Red Hill, W. Short and G. Cole. The Weinmans would like to book games with any 16-year-old team in the city. For games call Cherry 142-R Thursday evening after 7:30 and ask for Frank.

Shamrocks Want Game.

Brennan's Shamrocks are without a game for Tuesday night and would like to hear from some fast 17-year-old teams having gyms. Call Cherry 2627-J between 5 and 7 Monday night and ask for Warren.

RECORDS MADE BY LEADING BOXERS DURING YEAR 1913

JACK BRITTON.

Jan. 10—Joe Thomas, New Orleans....W. 10
Jan. 27—Jimmy Evans, Memphis...K. O. 7
Mar. 7—Packey McFarland, N. York..L. 10
May 20—Eddie Murphy, Kenosha......D. 10
July 4—Charley White, N. Orleans.K. O. 18
Nov. 27—Mike Glover, New York......D. 10
Dec. 8—Packey McFarland, Milwau..L. 10

JIMMY CLABBY.

Feb. 3—K. O. Brown, Milwaukee.....W. 10
May 2—Eddie McGoorty, Denver.....D. 10
July 4—Sailor Petrosky, Frisco......W. 20
Nov. 27—Frank Logan, Frisco.........W. 20

JOHNNY COULON.

Apr. 30—Johnny Kudran, Windsor..K. O. 5
May 12—Frankie Bradley, Phila........D. 6
June 23—Frankie Burns, Kenosha.....D. 10

LEACH CROSS.

Jan. 14—Joe Rivers, New York.....No D. 10
Jan. 21—Jimmy Duffy, Buffalo..........D. 10
Jan. 29—Young Shugrue, N. York..No D. 10
Mar. 10—Joe Mandot, N. Orleans......K. 10
Apr. 8—Joe Rivers, New York..........L. 10
July 4—Bud Anderson, Los Angeles..K. 12
Oct. 10—Willie Ritchie, New York.....L. 10
Nov. 27—Joe Rivers, Vernon............L. 20

JACK DILLON.

Jan. 9—Frank Mantell, Providence..W. 15
Jan. 18—Al Rogers, Pittsburgh........W. 6
Jan. 22—Leo Houck, Philadelphia.....W. 6
May 29—Frank Klaus, Indianapolis...W. 10
July 3—Bill McKinnon, Indianap's...K. 10
Nov. 3—Gus Christie, Milwaukee.....W. 10
Nov. 27—Sailor Petrosky, Butte........W. 10

JOHNNY DUNDEE.

Jan. 27—Special Hirsch, New York....W. 10
Apr. 29—Johnny Kilbane, Vernon.......D. 10
June 17—Jack White, Vernon............W. 20
July 4—Tommy Dixon, Los Angeles..W. 10
Aug. 12—Jack White, Vernon........K. O. 9
Nov. 27—Charley White, N. Orleans..W. 10
Dec. 15—Johnny Griffith, Canton.......D. 10

MIKE GIBBONS.

Oct. 9—Spike Kelly, Kenosha.........W. 10
May 29—Jimmy Perry, Pittsburgh..K. O. 2
Dec. 10—Wildcat Ferns, N. Orleans.K. O. 2

SPIKE KELLY.

Jan. 13—Ray Bronson, Memphis........W. 8
Feb. 7—Tommy Howell, K. City......D. 10
Apr. 11—Billy Walters, Kenosha.......W. 10
Oct. 9—Mike Gibbons, Kenosha........L. 10
Oct. 23—Billy Walters, Superior.......W. 10
Nov. 29—Lee Barrett, Milwaukee......D. 10
Dec. 15—Billy Walters, St. Joe........W. 15

STEVE KETCHELL.

Jan. 1—Pat Drouillard, G. Rapids....K. 6
Jan. 6—George Myers, Stockton, Ill..W. 10
Jan. 30—Art Stewart, Hammond.......D. 10
Sept. 1—Danny Goodman, Superior....W. 10

JOHNNY KILBANE.

Jan. 1—Abbie Kirk, St. Louis..........K. 2
Feb. 18—George Kirkwood, N. York.K.O. 6
Apr. 29—Johnny Dundee, Vernon.......D. 20
June 10—Jimmy Fox, Oakland......K. O. 6
Sept. 6—Jimmy Walsh, Boston.........W. 12
Oct. 8—Kid Julian, New York.........W. 10
Oct. 17—Eddie O'Keefe, New York..K.O. 1
Oct. 30—Knockout Mars, Cincinnati.K.O. 7
Sep. 16—Jimmy Walsh, Boston..........W. 12

FRANK KLAUS.

Mar. 5—Billy Papke, Paris.............W. 15
May 24—Ed. McGoorty, Pittsburgh....D. 6
May 29—Jack Dillon, Indianapolis......L. 10
Sep. 29—Eddie McGoorty, Milwaukee..L. 10
Oct. 11—George Chipp, Pittsburgh.K.O. by 6

JOE MANDOT.

Feb. 10—Mickey Sheridan, Memphis...W. 8
Mar. 10—Leach Cross, N. Orleans.K.O. by 10
Mar. 24—Johnny Lore, N Orleans.....W. 10
May 10—Bud Anderson, Los Angeles.. K. O. by 12
Dec. 10—Patsy Drouillard, Windsor..W. 8

MATTY M'CUE.

May 15—Jeff O'Connell, Racine.....K. O. 1
May 26—Patsy Brannigan, Milwau....L. 10
Sept. 1—Tommy Dougherty, Racine.K.O. 7
Oct. 28—Cal Delaney, Racine...........L. 10
Dec. 10—Tommy Bresnahan, Racine...D. 10

LUTHER M'CARTY.

Jan. 1—Al Palzer, Vernon..............K. 15
Apr. 16—Jim Flynn, Philadelphia......W. 6
May 24—Arthur Pelkey, Calgary...Killed 1

PACKEY M'FARLAND.

Mar. 7—Jack Britton, New York.....W. 10
Oct. 17—Tommy Murphy, New York..W. 10
Nov. 20—Kid Alberts, New York.......W. 10
Nov. 26—Harry Brewer, Windsor......W. 10
Dec. 4—Harry Trendall, St. Louis...W. 18
Dec. 8—Jack Britton, Milwaukee.....L. 10

EDDIE M'GOORTY.

Jan. 22—Fred Hicks, New York.......W. 10
Feb. 27—Gus Christie, Fond du Lac..W. 10
May 2—Jimmy Clabby, Denver.......D. 10
Sep. 10—Battling Levonsky, N. York.W. 10
Sep. 20—Frank Klaus, Milwaukee.....W. 10

CARL MORRIS.

July 3—Jack Geyer, Denver...........D. 10
Dec. 2—Jess Willard, New York......L. 10

"HARLEM" TOMMY MURPHY.

Jan. 1—Frankie Burns, Frisco........K. 17
Feb. 22—Ad Wolgast, Frisco...........D. 20
Apr. 19—Ad Wolgast, Frisco...........W. 20
Oct. 17—Packey McFarland, N. York.L. 10

WILLIE RITCHIE.

July 4—Joe Rivers, Fresno............K. 11
Oct. 10—Leach Cross ....W. 10

JOE RIVERS.

Jan. 14—Leach Cross, New York..No D. 10
Feb. 22—K. O. Brown, Vernon......K. O. 10
Mar. 8—Leach Cross, New York......W. 10
July 4—Willie Ritchie, Fresno..K.O. by 11
Oct. 28—Frankie Russell, N. Orleans.W. 10
Nov. 27—Leach Cross, Vernon.........W. 20

GUNBOAT SMITH.

Mar. 14—Bombadier Wells, N. York.K.O. 12
Apr. 11—Harry West, Cincinnati...K.O. 2
Apr. 11—Boer Rodel, New York.....K.O. 3
Apr. 27—Fred McKay, New York...K.O. 2
May 20—Jess Willard, Fresno.........W. 20
July 3—Carl Morris, New York..W. F. 5
Aug. 8—Jim Flynn, New York......K.O. 5
Oct. 21—Tony Ross, Philadelphia...K.O. 10
Oct. 31—Charley Miller, New York.K.O. 3
Nov. 17—Sam Langford, Boston.......W. 10

CHARLEY WHITE.

Jan. 10—Tommy Bresnahan, Omaha..W. 10
Mar. 10—Pal Moore, Kenosha..........W. 10
Apr. 21—Joe Thomas, N. Orleans...K.O. 8
May 9—George Meyers, Aurora....K.O. 2
July 4—Jack Britton, N. Orleans.....L. 18
July 18—Jake Abel, Atlanta.........K.O. 2
Aug. 16—Frank Whitney, Atlanta....W. 10
Sept. 1—Johnny Griffith, Canton......W. 12
Sep. 16—Mickey Sheridan, Racine...K.O. 2

JESS WILLARD.

Jan. 22—Frank Bauer, Ft. Wayne.....K. 5
Mar. 5—Jack Leon, Ft. Wayne.....K.O. 4
May 20—Gunboat Smith, Fresno.......L. 20
July 4—Al Williams, Reno.............K. 8
Aug. 22—Bull Young, Vernon..........Killed
Nov. 17—George Rodel, Milwaukee....D. 10
Nov. 17—Kid Kansas, Canton........K.O. 5
Nov. 24—Jack Reid, Fort Wayne......K. 2
Nov. 27—Johnny Dundee, N. Orleans..L. 10
Dec. 2—Carl Morris, New York.......W. 10
Dec. 12—One Round Davis, Buffalo.K.O. 2
Dec. 19—Ad Wolgast, Milwaukee......W. 10

KID WILLIAMS.

Feb. 12—Eddie Campi, Los Angeles...W. 20
Nov. 24—Battling Reddick, Phila........ 6
Nov. 27—Dick Lodeman, Milwaukee..W. 10

AD WOLGAST.

Feb. 22—Tommy Murphy, Frisco.......D. 20
April 19—Tommy Murphy, Frisco......L. 20
May 10—Azevedo, Oakland ....L. 10
Oct. 13—Battling Nelson, Milwaukee..W. 10
Dec. 19—Charley White, Milwaukee...L. 10

PAL BROWN.

Jan. 27—Jack Redmond, Milwaukee.K.O. 7
Jan. 29—Patsy Drouillard, Windsor...W. 10
Oct. 5—Hughie Mehegan, Sidney, N. S. W. ....W. 10

VALENTINE K. O. BROWN.

Jan. 20—Frankie Russell, N. Orleans.W. 10
Feb. 22—Joe Rivers, Vernon......K.O. by 10
Feb. 3—Jimmy Clabby ,Milwaukee....L. 10

FRANKIE BURNS.

Mar. 29—Eddie Campi, Vernon.........L. 20
June 23—Johnny Coulon, Kenosha......D. 10
Sep. 12—Carl Denning, Denver......K.O. 2
Mar. 29—Frankie Burns, Vernon......W. 20
Oct. 10—Frankie Burns, Denver.........D. 10

GEORGE CARPENTER.

May 31—Bombardier Wells, Ghent..K.O. 4
Dec. 8—Bombardier Wells, London.K.O. 1

GEORGE CHIP.

Oct. 11—Frank Klaus, Pittsburgh...K.O. 6
Nov. 25—Tim O'Neil, Racine...........W. 10

ARTHUR PELKY.

May 24—Luther McCarty, Calgary.K. O. 1

MICKEY SHERIDAN.

Feb. 3—Joe Mandot, Memphis..........L. 8
Feb. 13—Patsy Drouillard, Gr. Rapids.D. 6
May 9—Danny Goodman, T Haute...D. 10
Sept. 10—Patsy Drouillard, Peoria....D. 10

BILLY WALTERS.

Feb. 22—Wildcat Ferns, St. Joseph....D. 15
Sep. 1—Eddie Clabby, Hammond......W. 10
Sep. 12—Young Denny, N. Orleans.....D. 10
Sep. 26—Wildcat Ferns, Kenosha.......L. 10
Oct. 23—Spike Kelly, Superior..........D. 10
Dec. 16—Spike Kelly, St. Joseph......D. 15

JACK WHITE.

June 17—Johnny Dundee, Vernon.......L. 20
Aug. 12—Johnny Dundee, Vernon......K. 9
Nov. 1—Joe Bayley, Vancouver..K.O. by 9
Dec. 15—Cleve Bridges, Memphis....K.O. 7

CLAIMS COLORED CHAMPIONSHIP OF THE STATE

STORY AND CLARK BASEBALL TEAM.

Left to right, top row—Thornton, 2 b.; Henderson, c.; Manager White, p.; Turner, p.; McJohnson, 3 b.; Swans, r. f.; Gray, 1 b.; Holloway, umpire.

Sitting, left to right—Davis, c. f.; Jenkins, l. f.; Peet, mascot; Kelly, s. s.; Franklin, c.

This team won 35 games and lost 11 in 1913. "Cannon-ball" Johnson, the star pitcher, is missing from the picture.

PLAYERS OF OTHER DAYS

JAMES E. WHITNEY.

BY JOHN H. GRUBER.

Pitcher James E. Whitney, "Grasshopper Jim," was a native of California, who came east in 1881, and was a success with the Boston team, from the jump. In that year he assisted Tommy Bond, doing the bulk of the work, however, and the following year succeeded Bond, and had Bobby Mathews as a side partner. In the first year of Whitney's connection with the Beaneaters, the team ended in sixth place. In 1882 it went two points higher, finishing in fourth place, and in 1883, it won the National league championship. This advance in position until finally the goal was reached, was mainly due to the splendid efforts of the Grasshopper, who was not only a good pitcher, but an excellent batsman.

By the time the season of 1883 came along, Bond and Mathews were no longer with the Boston team. The club secured Charles Buffinton to help Whitney. The new man made rapid strides in his profession and the pair soon were regarded as among the best in the country. They remained together for three years, 1883-84-85. In 1883, as noted, Boston won the championship; in 1884 it landed in second place, and in 1885 in sixth. In 1881 Buffinton became the premier boxman, pitching nearly twice as many games as did Whitney.

In 1886 the Boston club engaged Charley Radbourne, the veteran Providence pitcher (the Rhode Island town having quit the National league), and William Stemmyer, who had shown exceptional skill in minor circles, Whitney was therefore released.

Buffinton Is Sold.

Buffinton lasted only one year longer. After the close of the season of 1886, the Boston club created somewhat of a sensation by disposing of the services of Buffinton to the Philadelphia club. It is a singular fact that the last game pitched by Buffinton for Boston was against the Philadelphia team. It was played at Boston on September 17, 1886, and Buffinton lost 10 to 4, the Phillies getting 16 hits off him and Radbourne, who relieved him after the sixth inning. The Philadelphia pitcher in that game was the famous Charley Ferguson, one of the best all-round players the game ever knew. He died on April 29, 1888, his death being universally regretted.

Buffinton remained three years with the Philadelphia team, 1887-88-89, and in 1890 jumped to the Philadelphia Players' league team. In 1891 he was with the Boston team of the then "outlawed" American association. In 1892 he was with the Baltimore team of the National league, the league that year expanding into a 12-club circuit. This was Buffinton's last year in baseball. The club asked him to agree to a cut in salary, but Buffinton declined, and was released on the last day of June. The last game he pitched was against Washington at Baltimore on June 28. The Baltimores lost by a score of 12 to 8, the Senators getting 13 singles, one double, one triple and one home run, a total of 22 bases.

From Ocean to Ocean.

The Washington pitcher was Phil Knell, who was released a little later and went to Philadelphia. There he was also let go, and then signed with the San Francisco club, which handed him the blue envelope after a few weeks, and he then finished the season with the Los Angeles team. Here is the spectacle of a player getting four jobs in one season and crossing the continent from ocean to ocean to fill them. This is certainly a record.

Baltimore in that year, 1892, being its first in the National league, finished absolutely last, that is, in twelfth place. However, it had the nucleus of a championship team. Hanlon, coming from Pittsburgh early in May, succeeded George Van Haltren as manager. He already had John McMahon and Wilbert Robinson as a battery, John McGraw at third base and later Joe Kelley (who came from Pittsburgh in exchange for Van Haltren), in the outfield. In a couple of years, in 1894 in fact, the famous Oriole lineup was complete, with Dan Brouthers, Henry Reitz, John McGraw and Hugh Jennings, infielders; Joe Kelley, Walter Brodie and Willie Keeler, outfielders; John McMahon, Charles Esper, Kid Gleason, George Hemming and later William Hoffer, Arlington Pond, Arthur Clarkson and Joe Corbett, pitchers; Wilbert Robinson, William J. Clarke and later Frank Bowerman, catchers. This combination won the championship three times in succession, in 1894-95-96. Buffinton was not the only old pitcher to retire from the Oriole bunch before it landed the pennant. Egyptian John Healy, Adonis Bill Terry and Frank Foreman were also among those dropped.

Goes to Kansas City.

After Whitney was let go by the Boston club he joined the Kansas City team, which remained in the National league only one year, 1886. However, the Cowboys did not finish in last place, but managed to keep ahead of the Washington Senators, who finished last in the procession. At Kansas City Whitney's companion in the pitcher's box was George Weidwan, who had done hard work for the Detroit team the previous four years and who ended his big league career that year. He died at New York in 1905.

In the following year, 1887, Whitney was engaged by the Washington club, and his catcher was Connie Mack, the present successful manager of the Philadelphia Athletics. Mack, the year before, had been secured by Washington from the Hartford club of the Eastern league along with William Krieg and George Q. Shock. The pitching staff of the Senators when Whitney joined consisted of Hank O'Day, Frand Gilmore and Fred Dupee Shaw, but in 1888 Whitney and O'Day did all the work. Gilmore that year was with Syracuse, and Shaw, before the season of 1887 ended was playing in Portland, Ore. O'Day is the noted National league umpire.

Whitney was a steady pitcher with good control. He gave comparatively few bases on balls, and never distinguished himself by striking out more than the ordinary number of batsmen in a game. One of the best games he pitched for the Senators was played at Washington on September 30, 1887, when he defeated the New York Giants, who had Tim Keefe in the box, by a score of 1 to 0. That year it took four strikes to retire a batsman and in the game Whitney struck out 10 men, and Keefe struck out the same number, making 20 strikeouts in all. This alone gave prominence to the contest, the interest in which was hightened by the fact that the Giants were shut out.

Arrival of Amos Rusie.

In 1889 Whitney signed with the Indianapolis club, which then was in its last year in the National league. There Whitney saw the arrival of Amos Rusie, destined to become a famous pitcher. Early in the season Jim was released and joined the Buffalo team of the International league. At Buffalo he worked side by side with Pitcher Will White, brother of Deacon Jim White. Will was probably the only pitcher who wore spectacles. He made a great success while a member of the Cincinnati team for which he pitched first in the National league and then in the American association. With the peak of his cap pulled close over his eyes his appearance must have been uncanny and sinister to the batter. At any rate, he was looked upon as one of the most effective pitchers of his time. His work with Buffalo was the last he did on the diamond.

The year 1890 was the last for Whitney in baseball. He joined the Athletics of Philadelphia, then members of the American association, in June, but a month later was released. He was a sick man who could not do himself or his team justice. He sought his bed, and on May 19 of the following year, 1891, he died at Binghamton, N. Y., of consumption.

EBONY-HUED BOXER GETS IN BAD SPOT

France Finally is Disgusted With Negro Gladiator Since Johnson's Rotten Showing in Paris Last Week.

BLACK RACE OF BOXERS RAPIDLY DYING OUT

Not So Many Years Ago We Had Some of the Best in the World—Three of Them Held Titles.

Fistic followers in France have none but themselves to blame for the turn pugilistic affairs have taken in Paris.

They were warned that the thing was impending, yet they went ahead and tempted fate, the fruits of which were forced down their throats in abundance twice in less than a week.

Negro boxers have been chased out of America, dispelled in Australia and forced to remain inactive in England. But in face of it all France threw open its doors, welcomed the black and apparently gloried in their presence.

Now wails of anguish emanate from gay Paree because Jack Johnson failed miserably in an effort to dispose of a fourth-rater and the rottenness of the Langford-Jeannette encore.

It appears that the exits for ebony-hued fighters is clear and that the doors to oblivion are yawning to receive them. When America doesn't want them, England won't have them and Australia refuses to tolerate them, all that is necessary to effectively put the screws on is action on the part of France's boxing commission to prohibit that crowd from further participation in bouts in the country.

Is Becoming Extinct.

The time is near when the Ethiopian race—pugilistically speaking—will become extinct. The black fighter is dying out. There remain three of any account now, but they are rapidly approaching that stage of all fighters' careers when they must quit. Sentiments are so strong against the black that rarely is one developed. A boy of the color may display wonderful ability but can't get encouragement, and, finding attempts to start useless, gives it up.

Time has wrought great changes in pugilism. It wasn't a great many years ago when the black fighter was a magnate at box offices and among them were some of the greatest masters of boxing the world produced. There were Peter Jackson, Joe Wolcott, Joe Gans, George Dixon, Jerry Marshall, Jack Blackburn, Dave Holly, Bobby Dobbs, Larry Temple, "Kentucky Rosebud" and scores of others.

Three Held Titles.

Three of them held world's championships—george Dixon, Joe Gans, and Joe Wolcott, while Peter Jackson was acknowledged to be the premier fistic exponent ever sent out of the Antipodes, not barring Bob. Fitzsimmons. They were drawing cards, every one of them and either died or retired respected despite their color.

Boxers of the Ethiopian race might have continued in the public's esteem had there not come a dark cloud over their lives in the person of Jack Johnson, disgraced in his private and professional life.

ST. LOUIS JUNIORS STRONG

Team Has Three New Stars for 1913 Season.

St. Louis Juniors, after holding several practice sessions under the tutelage of Coach O'Driscoll, is now ready to start its regular schedule.

This team should be considered as one of the topnotchers in the 16 and 17-year-old class, as it is composed of several stars in Quinn, Partlin and Grace, formerly of the U. of D. Minims. Quinn plays a stellar game at forward, while the two latter excel as guards. This trio, in addition to Kain, Kelly and Lagrou, completes the roster. The latter trio plays at forward, guard and center, respectively, and were the mainstays of last season's St. Louis Juniors team.

Any 16 or 17-year-old teams, with or without gyms, desirous of booking games call "Jim" at Grand 3793-J, or write James Grace, 493 Wabash avenue.

PASTIME CRIBBAGE CLUB

STANDING.

	W	L	Pct.		W	L	Pct.
Hempel....	52	29	.684	Napiontek.	39	52	.481
Koehler...	49	32	.605	Ihde.......	38	43	.469
Zarnowski.	49	32	.605	Sudds.......	38	43	.469
Kullos.....	48	33	.593	Beveridge.	37	44	.457
Falk.......	45	36	.556	Robson....	26	55	.321
Dominik...	45	36	.556	Liety......	21	60	.259

Woodwards to Meet.

Woodwards will hold a special meeting Monday evening, December 29, at the residence of J. Gorham, 318 Bellevue avenue.

All football and former baseball members are urgently requested to be on hand, as further arrangements for the obtaining of sweater-coats will be discussed. The Woodwards have decided to enter a basketball team on the courts this season, and as the discussion regarding the completion of their schedule and other business matters will be up, the attendance of all candidates is hoped for.

Senecas Seek Opposition.

Senecas would like a game for either Monday or Tuesday evening with any good 15-year-old team. For games call West 1117 after 10 o'clock a. m. and ask for Ray.

WEATHER TOMORROW
Fair And Warmer

THE BALTIMORE NEWS.

FINANCIAL
LAST EDITION
COMPLETE STOCKS

VOL. LXXXIV—NO. 159. CIRCULATION—{ Saturday, 72,300. Sunday, 57,060. MONDAY EVENING, APRIL 13, 1914. SIXTEEN PAGES PRICE ONE CENT

GUNMEN TOTTER TO CHAIR; MAY BE CONFESSION

"Whitey Lewis' " Statement Interrupted By Electric Current.

GHASTLY SCENE AT SING SING PRISON

Each Of Men Condemned For Rosenthal's Murder Went To Death Praying.

Albany, N. Y., April 13.—Some of the gunmen are believed to have confessed before they died. Superintendent John B. Riley of the State Prison Department said today that a statement would arrive here from Ossining today which would show that "no injustice had been done by the executions." He knew nothing of the nature of the statement.

The statement is declared to implicate no one but the men who died today.

Governor Glynn refused to discuss the statement, although it is known that the contents of it have been made known to him. The Governor is declared to be satisfied that the four men executed this morning were guilty.

No word was forthcoming as to whether the "confession" was made by all or one of the condemned men.

Gave Warden Statement.

It was given to Warden Clancy this morning about 4 o'clock. No promises were held out to the writer, it is said, but in the last hours on earth there was a voluntary change in the attitude of some of the condemned.

The report persists that the statement came from "Dago Frank." For days there has been a constant rumor that he would tell all before he died. A remark made by Mr. Riley strengthened the belief that "Dago Frank" confessed.

"The men had the same opportunity to make this statement when I was down to Sing Sing last week," he said, "but they did not choose to avail themselves of it."

Expected Final Confession.

Mr. Riley went to the prison under the impression that "Dago Frank" wanted to make a final confession. But the prisoner would not talk. Had he broken silence, it was generally understood the death penalty would not have been inflicted today. No reprieve would have been granted, it is declared, but the executions would not have taken place until next Saturday. Hope that such a delay might give time for new court action was held out to the gunmen by their relatives.

Mr. Riley said today that he would issue a formal statement as soon as the messenger arrives.

"Dago Frank" Accused Others.

Ossining, N. Y., April 13.—It was reported here this afternoon that Frank Cirofici, before being put to death this morning, made a confession to Warden Clancy and Father Cashin, in which he admitted that justice had been done. "Dago Frank" is said to have stated that while he was not present at the murder of

Continued On Page 5, Column 1.

WEATHER

For Baltimore till 8 P. M. Tuesday: Fair tonight. Tuesday, fair and warmer; gentle northerly to northeasterly breezes.

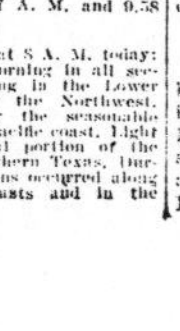

The News is the ONLY Baltimore evening paper with the Associated Press dispatches.

Anyone wishing standard time for setting watch or clock at any hour of the day can get it by calling up The News—C. & P., St. Paul 100.

For the Mariner: Steamers departing today for European ports will have gentle to moderate northwesterly to northerly breezes, with fair weather, to the Grand Banks.

Hourly Record Of Temperature.

6 A. M.	42	11 A. M.	48
7 A. M.	42	12 M.	49
8 A. M.	43	1 P. M.	51
9 A. M.	44	2 P. M.	52
10 A. M.	46	3 P. M.	52

Humidity at 8 A. M. today was 44 per cent.
Sun sets today at 6.40 P. M.
Sun rises tomorrow at 5.31 A. M.
High tide today at 9.05 P. M.
High tide tomorrow at 9.47 A. M. and 9.58 P. M.

General weather conditions at 8 A. M. today: The weather is fair this morning in all sections of the country excepting in the Lower Mississippi valley and over the Northwest. The temperatures are below the seasonable average excepting along the Pacific coast. Light frosts occurred in the central portion of the Mississippi valley and in Northern Texas. During the last 24 hours light rains occurred along the South Atlantic Gulf coasts and in the Northwest.

MEXICAN GUNS MUST FIRE THAT SALUTE TO FLAG

President Insists On Usual Apology For Arrest Of U. S. Marines.

JOHN LIND ARRIVES TO SUBMIT REPORT

Will Have Conference With Wilson And Bryan Before Going West To Rest.

Washington, April 13.—President Wilson told callers today that a salute would be fired to the American flag by Mexican Federals at Tampico as an apology for the recent arrest of American marines.

The President spoke with such confidence that his hearers took it to imply that the point would be insisted upon. The President has already approved Rear Admiral Mayo's demand for the salute as an apology.

Time Not Important.

Secretary Daniels also had notified Admiral Mayo that his action is approved. "The salute will be fired" was his positive announcement today. He added that he did not consider the element of time an important one because of the difficulties of communication between Washington and Tampico.

Secretary Bryan was reticent about the Tampico incident. He said he was in close correspondence with Charge O'Shaughnessy over Huerta's promised investigation. He declined to reveal any dispatches between the State Department and the Charge, and would neither affirm nor deny reports that General Huerta had forbidden the salute. In some official circles the suggestion that Huerta would refuse to permit the salute was received with surprise. In their opinion the refusal might compel drastic action on the part of the United States.

Lind In Washington.

John Lind, President Wilson's personal representative in Mexico, arrived here early today on board the Presidential yacht Mayflower.

A Government automobile waited for the President's envoy as he came ashore to set foot on American soil for the first time in many months. Mr. Lind went at once to an uptown hotel near the White House. President Wilson said that he hoped to confer with Mr. Lind later today. Secretary Bryan had arranged his trip to Miami, Fla., so he could have a conference with Mr. Lind before leaving.

On the Mayflower with Mr. Lind were Mrs. F. F. Fletcher, wife of Rear Admiral Fletcher, and her two daughters, and Mr. Lind's daughter, Miss Jenny. Mrs. Lind was expected here from Minnesota today to join her husband.

Going West To Rest.

So far as was known early today, Mr. Lind's plan was to go West for a rest, probably to French Lick, Ind. There was no plan today about his returning to Mexico.

Mr. Lind remained at his hotel only a few minutes and then disappered before inquirers could reach him. It was said he was expected at the White House during the day. Secretary Bryan said he had planned a conference with the President's envoy but did not know whether it would be at the White House with the President ort he State Department.

When President Wilson recently announced that Mr. Lind was returning to the United States, he stated that it was for a short vacation, made necessary by a long stay in a tropical climate and specifically pointed out that it would be a mistake to interpret his return as indicating any other development in the situation.

Lunches With Bryan.

Mr. Lind brought much information for conferences with the President and Secretary Bryan. The first of these took place at a luncheon with Mr. Bryan.

Mr. Lind greeted inquirirers by asking if it were true that Rear Admiral Mayo had been ordered to revoke his demand for the firing of a salute to the American colors at Tampico and when he was informed that President Wilson had insisted that the salute be fired he smiled approvingly. He was uncommunicative about conditions in Mexico.

"It is odd," said the former Governor, "that a man has to go abroad to get a reputation. When I was in public life in this country some people said I was talkative, but I seem to have gotten a reputation for silence."

Mr. Lind said his plans were not definite and depended largely on his talks with President Wilson and Secretary Bryan. He left Mexico at his own request, he said, because he needed rest and change. He intimated that he was ready to go back should a contingency arise requiring his return.

It is understood that Mr. Lind brings the President a good deal of information descriptive of general conditions and in no way affecting the diplomatic status of affairs.

News Suppressed.

The rigorous censorship that has been established in Mexico and the inability of the people in Southern Mexico to learn definitely about Constitutionalist victories in the north are phases of the situation which Lind probably will tell officials here.

Federal League Parade Starting From The Emerson

GOVERNOR CAN HELP IN PRISON REFORMS

By Signing Bills Now Before Him Can Start Movement.

Whether Maryland is to take a step forward in the management of its prisons Governor Goldsborough is expected to decide in the next few days. He now has before him the two bills passed by the Legislature, which constitute a transformation of the scheme of prison management, and unless he signs them all the work that has been done in the interest of prison reform will have to be done over again two years hence, with results extremely problematical. Indeed, it is very doubtful whether in two years the situation in regard to penal legislation will be as favorable as it was at the session just closed.

Examination of the two bills now before the Governor shows that, while the Democratic majority could not resist the temptation to name the members of the new Board of Control, which is to take the place of the boards of the House of Correction and the Penitentiary, it has still left in the bills the essentials of a sweeping reorganization of the penal system.

Open Way To Reform.

If the members of the Board picked by the Democrats do not measure up to their opportunities it will be for the next Goevrnor, who has the appointing power, to make such a change as will bring the desired results.

The sweeping out of the separate boards and the substituting of a central board of three is a great step forward. It means a centralization of responsibility that was not possible under the old board system, with one prison being managed without any reference to the other. It means that any good methods found in use in one institution will be promptly adopted in the other. It is held by persons in close touch with the whole question of prison reform that it will be much easier two years hence to obtain legislation strengthening the pending bills than successfully to go over the whole ground and secure new legislation.

Basis Of A Sound System.

Of course, it is not to be denied that the Democrats in passing the bills followed the lines of political expediency. Had there been a Democratic Governor it is not likely that any penal reform legislation would have succeeded. But as there was practical certainty that by letting the bills die the Democrats might lose some of the places they now hold and by passing them they might save some, they passed them. But the basis of a new system is left and friends of Governor Goldsborough believe that he will sign them unless he becomes convinced that the men named for the Board of Prison Control intend to set their faces against modern methods.

Former Maryland Slave Observes 114th Birthday

Philadelphia, April 13. — "Aunt" Mahala Ayer yesterday celebrated her one hundred and fourteenth birthday at the Home for Aged Colored persons in this city. She dressed herself unaided and attended Easter services in the Chapel of the Institution, afterward receiving congratulations of scores of visitors who called to wish her well.

The officials of the home had prepared a huge cake for the aged woman and she placed 114 candles on it herself, remarking as she did so:

"I guess I'll put a lot more candles on my birthday cakes before I'm called home, for I never felt better in my life."

"Aunt" Mahala was born a slave on the plantation of John Fossitt in Maryland, April 12, 1800. She attributes her great age to never having allowed anything to worry her or cause discontent.

TODAY IN CONGRESS

Washington, April 13.

SENATE—(Met at noon.)

Canals Committee resumed public hearings on the repeal of the Panama tolls exemption.

Senator Lewis introduced three bills for a new Federal commission to regulate industry and finance.

HOUSE—(Met at noon.)

Took up District of Columbia legislation.

ROBBED MAILS TO PAY ALIMONY, SAYS M'COY

Letter-Carrier Arrested With Six Marked $1 Bills In His Pocket.

Claiming that his wife, from whom he is separated, hounded him until he was driven to desperation, John H. McCoy, formerly of 3734 East Lombard street, a letter-carrier in the local postoffice, charged his spouse with being the cause of his arrest on the charge of robbing the mails when taken into custody today by Government authorities.

McCoy was found with marked money on his person and confessed.

The arrest of McCoy was the result of a trap laid by Maj. Samuel T. Hooton and Postoffice Inspectors Jas. B. Robertson and Hal B. Mosby. Seven letters were addressed to Graham & Co. in the Phoenix Building, each of which contained a one-dollar bill bearing a mark by which to identify it. When McCoy took them to deliver the officers trailed him. Later they ascertained that the letters had not been delivered and found six of the marked bills in his pockets.

"My wife and I are not living together," said he, "and she is now preparing to get a divorce. I have to pay alimony and other expenses and was pushed for money. The way my wife treated me made me take the chance, and I felt so bad that I didn't care what happened to me.'

DEPOPULATES CITY HALL

Department Heads And Employees Seek Relief From "Baseballitis" At Terrapin Park.

"Baseballitis" broke out in the City Hall this morning, and before 12 o'clock the epidemic had practically "cleaned out" the administration building. The Health Department was no exception to the "disease," the germs having spread to the Gay street annex to such an extent that Health Commissioner Gorter and his assistant, Dr. C. Hampson Jones, gave up in despair and watched their force one by one succumb to the epidemic and seek relief at Terrapin Park, on the York road.

Whether it will be necessary to establish a "quarantine" to fight the "malady" among City Hall employees will depend largely on the success of Otto Knabe's team today in the opening event at Baltimore's new baseball park. If the home team wins a "quarantine" probably will be necessary.

Incidentally, there was very little going on at the City Hall this morning except preparations to be on hand when Mayor Preston throws the ball that will start the game between the Terrapins and the Buffalo team.

A half-day holiday was declared by the Mayor in conformity with the provisions of a bill passed at the recent sesson of the Legislature.

Employes of all the departments secured their tickets long in advance of the opening game, and those who were not so fortunate took their chances on standing-room.

Many of the heads of departments bought box seats and made preparations to take their families.

PARADE STARTS TO ONLOOKERS' CHEERS

Players And Magnates Ride Majestically Through Streets.

With the way cleared through the cheering thousands by a double platoon of mounted police and headed by Farson's Band, the Terrapins and Buffaloes started their procession to the York road grounds at 12.25 o'clock from Baltimore and Calvert streets.

The local and visiting magnates traveled majestically in carriages and bowed happily to the applause that greeted them almost continuously throughout the downtown section. The route was changed slightly at the last moment, and as actually followed out was down Baltimore to Holliday, to Lexington, to St. Paul, and down the latter street to Baltimore street, and out to Charles street, and thence north to North avenue, east to Greenmount, and out the York road to the grounds.

Big Ones Bow Happily.

The first carriage contained the president of the Federal League, J. A. Gilmore of Chicago; President Carroll Rasin of the Terrapins, Gustave Stewart, vice-president of the local and "Ned" Hanlon. The second carriage took President William Robertson of the Buffalo team, Treasurer J. S. Wilson of the locals, S. S. Janney, the attorney of the Terrapins, and George S. Ward, the Brooklyn Federal magnate.

In the third were W. S. and R. B. Ward, directors of the Brooklyn Federals, with Treasurer Oliver Cabana of the Buffalo squad and Director A. Schleunes of the local team. The fourth carriage contained Director Harry Busick, "Phil" Poe, Walter Katzenstein and C. W. Smith of the Terrapins.

Getaway Noisy One.

The getaway of the parading ballplayers was a noisy one and attended by considerable difficulty in placing the right man in the right carriage, due to the fact that several thousand people had gathered to get a close view of the local and visiting baseball celebrities.

The mounted police, however, worked wonders and with a preliminary flourish from the band the column was headed down Baltimore street, after which the paraders had nothing to do but smile happily and bow gracefully in acknowledging the cheers that greeted them on every side.

He Waited Too Long To Sue For His Whiskers

Washington, April 13.—E. A. O'Sullivan, a New Orleans lawyer, wanted to sue Paul Felix and William W. Stiles for $60,000 because they cut off his whiskers in 1908, in an election prank, but the Supreme Court today decided he had waited too long and threw out his case.

Killed At Fire

Culpeper, Va., April 13.—Carter Parr, 19, was killed, several men were seriously hurt and damage of about $50,000 was done by a fire that destroyed four business buildings here today.

The News Baseball Extra

Immediately after the close of the game at Terrapin Park this afternoon, The News will issue an extra, giving a full account of the contest, including a play-by-play story of each inning.

The 5.30 o'clock edition of The News will be discontinued and Baseball Extras will be issued.

NEW FEDERAL LEAGUE OPENS SEASON AT TERRAPIN PARK; GREAT OUTPOURING OF "FANS"

Every Seat In Large Pavilions Filled Long Before 3 O'Clock.

WEATHER IS IDEAL FOR DEBUT OF TEAM

Hundreds Of Spectators Overflow Into Field—Scene One Of Great Expectancy.

Line-Up Today At Terrapin Park

BALTIMORE.	BUFFALO.
Meyer, r. f.	Hanford, c. f.
Knabe, 2b.	Downey, 2b.
Zinn, c. f.	Louden, s. s.
Simmons, l. f.	Bonnin, r. f.
Swacina, 1b.	Delenhanty, l. f.
Walsh, 3b.	Smith, 3b.
Doolan, s. s.	Agler, 1b.
Jacklitsch, c.	Blair, c.
Quinn, p.	Moore, p.
Wilheim, p.	Ford, p.
Suggs, p.	Krapp, p.

Umpires—Bush and Mannassau.

Players Get Rousing Reception As They Trot Out To Diamond.

PERSONS EARLY ON HAND FOR TICKETS

Two Boys Take Stand Outside Gate At 6 A. M.—High Officials Here For Combat.

At 3 o'clock this afternoon, as The News goes to press, the largest crowd ever gathered at a local ball game waited with bated breath for the umpire to call "Play ball!" as Knabe's Terrapins and the Buffalo Federals lined up for the opening game of the new 'big league" season.

Amid the plaudits of the many thousands who filled every available space in the stands and overflowed onto the field, the players of the Baltimore and Buffalo teams trotted out on the diamond, and as 3 o'clock approached the umpires put in their appearance, preparatory to starting the initial contest in the history of the organization that has promised a new era in the national game.

The city seemed baseball wild. Downtown this morning everybody appeared to be filled with the spirit of the day's game. The crowds that watched the ball players' parade adjourned en mass to the grounds, and all the trolley lines leading to the York road field were taxed to accommodate the swarms that were anxious to witness the opening game.

In order to provide transportation for as many as possible the Railways Company shifted a large number of cars to the lines that run to Federal League Park and the uptown routes of several other lines were temporarily diverted in order to carry the fans to their destination with as little inconvenience as possible.

Crowds Pack Cars.

By 1 o'clock all northeast-bound cars were filled inside and out long before they reached North avenue, and at 2 o'clock the conveyances were packed before they left the center of the city. Determined fans clung to the platforms and steps of the cars and even stood on the buffers outside the rear vestibules.

The automobile string that went to the grounds was a long and continuous one and there was difficulty in finding standing room for the big array of themselves in the neighborhood of the amusement park.

The employees of many big concerns hired private omnibuses to haul them out to the game. Most of these were labeled with big streamers telling who the occupants of the vehicle were. All were crowded as full as they could be and the merry funseekers took preliminary trips about the business section, blowing horns and ringing bells to give vent to some extent to the enthusiasm that they could not repress.

Every Seat Taken.

Practically every seat in the great pavilions was filled long before 3 o'clock, and the bleachers, after becoming overtaxed, turned hundreds into the field.

From early morning the enthusiastic fans had been gathering, and the crush at the gates when they were finally opened at noon was so great as to require the services of a big contingent of policemen to keep them in order and prevent fans hurting one another.

Ideal weather blessed the opening, and the trolley cars dumped myriads of passengers out on York road, from where they made their way to the gates, generally on the run.

Seats Bring Big Offers.

The demand for tickets was so great that many persons who were unable to get near the ticket sellers offered to purchase the lucky pasteboards from the more fortunate who had possessed themselves of them. The prospective buyers were liberal in their offers of premiums over and above the face value of the tickets. But there were apparently few persons who were willing to sacrifice their chance to see the game in exchange for the proffered fees.

Men of every walk of life were in the line of ticket buyers, bankers and staid lawyers elbowing with clerks and representatives of humbler callings.

There was a goodly number of women in the throng that filled the grounds, and their gay dresses added life and spirit to the scene. Enthusiasm was rampant. The crowd began to cheer when the gates were opened and every opportunity that offered for a display of enthusiasm was quickly seized upon and heralded with loud acclaim.

Ovation For Players.

The advent of the ball players on the grounds was the signal for the first real big demonstration. The men had been parading about town in carriages. The band that had accompanied them took a position on the field early in the afternoon and soon afterward the players themselves strolled out for preliminary practice. Each man got the glad hand and a lusty cheer, and some of the better known were honored with particularly vociferous outbursts.

The bleacher entrance gate was swung open shortly after 11 A. M., and a minute afterward the first admission ticket was purchased.

The opening of the gate was greeted with a cheer that could be heard for blocks, and simultaneously a smile appeared on the face of each person in line, some of whom had been standing in line since 7 o'clock.

At the same time, a score of "scalpers," who had armed their "dummies" with a bank roll with which to purchase tickets, assumed a disappointed appearance when they discovered their game had been knocked in the head by the officials with the rule that each person who purchased a ticket had to pass immediately into the park.

Protests made by them were of no avail, for a large delegation, representing the strong arm of the law, was on hand to see that the rule was enforced.

Boy First Ticket Buyer.

The first two "fans" who bought tickets over the counter at the park were Walter Feldpush, 15 years old, of 2417 Maryland avenue, and Charles P. Ohler of the same address, both of whom arrived at the park shortly after 6 o'clock this morning and took their stand directly in front of the gate.

The oldest "fan" in the long line that stood for over five hours was Thomas J. Kelly, 66 years old, of 1804 Potomac street, Canton. Kelly, who is a stevedore and a dyed-in-the-wool fan, was at the park shortly after 7 o'clock. With a newspaper he closely studied the line-up, and forcast a victory for the Terrapins this afternoon.

Three female fans had a long wait to obtain tickets. They were Mrs. Fannie Mance, 522 Rossiter avenue, Govans; Mrs. Edward S. Potts and Miss Anna Long of 823 Bond street. Mrs. Mance, munching a sandwich and drinking a bottle of soda water, was discussing the merits of the "Feds" with other "fans" of the sterner sex.

"I waited in New York six hours to see a world's championship game, and I'm going to see the game this afternoon if I have to crawl through a knothole in the fence," she said in explaining just how desirous she was of seeing the combat.

Every inch of the stands are bedecked with red, white and blue streamers, while thousands of American flags made the spectacle one of brilliance. Here President Carroll Rasin and Secretary Goldman were out early hustling to leave nothing undone.

Buffalo Delegation Confident.

The Buffalo delegation wore confident smiles and gorgeous jewelry. They were marshaled by Secretary John L. Kelly and headed by President William Robertson, flanked by Treasurer Oliver Cabana, Jr. Among them were such well-known "fans" as George C. Riley, H. J. McDonald, Stuart Berrill, George Obernauer and Harry Gilchrist.

Towering over the bulk of the ball "fans" in the Emerson lobby this morning was the smiling countenance of the "Feds'" chief umpire, Big Bill Brennan, who is charged with keeping the "Fed" umpire corps in good order.

Brennan will make the procession and the game today, and, moreover, he thinks the local organization stands up well on paper.

Brennan Lauds Terrapins.

"Baltimore has a fine team," said "Big Bill," "and they ought to be close in on the top when the fight this season for the championship begins to close down."

For his part, President Gilmore—the one big chief of the League—brought a broad smile away from his breakfast at the Emerson this morning.

Gimore Enthusiastic.

"Baltimore is the town in the whole baseball world," declared the League's president, "and the weather is just what we had all hoped for. and the town is evidently going to do all and more than we had counted on to make the beginning of the real battle a success for the Federal League. Baltimore was chosen as one of the main stragetic points, and, therefore, the best place to open up the real struggle."

Bayliss of Chicago was one of the nationally known ball "fans" at the Emerson this morning along with President Gilmore and George S., R. B. and William S. Ward of Brooklyn. The three Wards are millionaires who have taken care of the Federal end in Brooklyn, and who will watch the opening game this afternoon.

"Abe" Marks, who was formerly official score card seller at Dunnie's park, but who jumped to the "Feds," was on hand early.

Waiting For Fouls.

With the hope that the first man up knocks a foul over the fence, Sheridan Smith, 15 years old, and Harry Dutton, 11 years old, are patiently waiting on the outside of the park, with over a thousand other boys, to get in on a foul. Both boys declare they saw most of the Saturday games last year by chasing fouls. and expect to have the same luck this year.

Acting Marshal Manning had the parade route policed by 250 uniformed men, while headquarters detectives and policemen in plain clothes were scattered all the way from Calvert and Baltimore streets to York road and Twenty-ninth street. The mounted policemen were under command of Sergeant Clancy. At every corner along the parade route there was a policeman detailed, and these were kept on duty until the rush of crowds going to the parks had practically ceased. Then they were drawn into the neighborhood of the parks.

Police Handle Crowds.

In addition to the regular uniformed policemen a squad of 26 traffic policemen under command of Sergeant Zimmerman were on hand to handle the vehicular traffic. All vehicles were ordered to enter Twenty-ninth street from York road and go on through to Guilford avenue or Calvert street. In the vicinity of the two parks the police were under the personal supervision of Acting Marshal Manning and were divided into details commanded by Captain Moxley of the Northern district, Captain Zellers of the Central district, Captain Morheiser of the Northeastern district, Captain Santry of the Southern district and Acting Captain Strott of the Southwestern district.

Managers Exchange Greetings.

Otto Knabe, leader of the Baltimore Terrapins, and Larry Schlafly, boss of the Buffalo Feds said "Good morning" to each other today in the Emerson Hotel at 8.30 o'clock, but it was much in the nature you would expect a pair of gamecocks to greet each other. It was a good morning with a "wait - until - this-afternoon" look attached to it, and, after all, this afternoon is what the fans are interested in. Baseball talk that speaks of magnates, schedules and trades interests the fans, but the rooters after all are vitally concerned in the game on the field. The other doings only concern them in a small way, but when the battle is being waged on the field they can go there and yelp their merry heads off.

Columns and columns have been written about the Terrapins and how well they size up, and this afternoon it will be up to them to show. Manager Knabe says his boys are in good condition, and the only unpleasant feature that comes to mind is the serious accident to Kirkpatrick. Manager Knabe says the infielder was showing better form than at any time, and he will undoubtedly be missed from the line-up.

The all-important subject of the pitcher was the one that took up much thought on the part of both managers. The chilly winds of this morning made the Terrapin boss rather uncertain, but the choice lies between Kaiser Wilhelm and "Jack" Quinn. This pair of flingers is advanced more than any other of the hurling corps, and it was a toss-up this morning which one would be called on to serve up his benders.

There is a number of other Buffalo Feds who will get a big welcome this afternoon. "Kid" Agler, who will cover first, was the initial sack guardian for Newark at one time. "Billy" Louden went from Newark to Detroit, and "Tom" Downey, who is playing second, was an Oriole for a short while last year.

Schlafly's team has shown good form in its preliminary games, althought it has been somewhat hampered by bad weather at the training camp.

Will Sue Killifer.

President James A. Gilmore was one of the early arrivals this morning, coming down from New York in company with the Wards of Brooklyn and "Bill" Brennan, umpire-in-chief of the independent organization. While eating breakfast at the Emerson the president of the League took time to say that reports that the League would sue Catcher Killifer of the Philadelphia Nationals for $25,000 was no idle dream. Instructions have been given to the counsel of the organization to enter suit against Killifer as soon as the necessary arrangements can be made.

Mr. Gilmore said, he was too interested in the big opening today to be worrying about suits and was not anxious to discuss the matter. He did say, however, that the recent decision in the Killifer case was an absolute victory for the Feds despite the fact that the verdict leaves Killifer still with the Philadelphia Nationals.

Mr. Gilmore and the magnates who were here several weeks ago and are back in town today are thoroughly aroused over the local enthusiasm. and nothing but success forms the subject of their conversation. Gilmore made one prediction on which Baltimoreans will have to be shown, and that was that Chicago will have a bigger opening than this city.

Dunnie's Team Looks To Have Good Chance For Landing International Top Honors

DUNN STARTS OUT WITH DANDY OUTFIT

Orioles And Buffalos Loom Up As Contenders For League Pennant.

BIRDS STRONG IN FIELD AND AT BAT

Pitching Staff May Prove Strongest Asset, As Men Are Both Young And Capable.

By DANNY

With Jack Dunn's boys starting out the season this afternoon, it is not amiss to discuss his squad's chances, and the whys thereof. Without qualification, it can be said that the Oriole leader is starting out his season better fortified than at the beginning of any year since he assumed the management of the Baltimore team in 1907. There have been years when possibly the local International team was stronger during the season than the present aggregation, but even that may be considered in the nature of a mooted matter.

If there is one department upon which hinges some doubt, it is the hurling staff, and yet Dunnie's flingers may prove his strongest asset, without creating a big surprise. He has an exceptionally good quartet of left-handers in Danforth, Cottrell, Ruth and Caporal. Danforth has shown better early form than for several years, and if this is any indication he should prove a most valuable man. Cottrell is also looked upon to prove a regular. Babe Ruth, whom Dunnie signed from St. Mary's Industrial School, looks like a real find. The youngster has still considerable to learn about the art of pitching, but apparently has all the natural ability that could be desired. If he continues the sort of work he has shown, he will be nothing short of a sensation. Caporal may prove the real thing. He is one of the pitchers whose coming to hand or otherwise will prove so much to Dunn. Dunnie's stock of right-handers includes Russell, Morrisette, Davidson and Jarman. Russell is looked upon as a regular, but it is up to the others to work out their own salvation. Morrisette has had considerable experience and should be a big improvement over his form of last year. If Davidson can master control he should make a good man. Dunnie is particularly sweet on him. Jarman showed great form against Scranton and may furnish the wiseacres a surprise.

Ben Egan will do the bulk of the catching and Ben is pegging them out in great style. Lidgate should make a good helper, but Dunnie will try and get another backstop in addition to his present pair.

The Oriole infield looks particularly good. Gleichmann at first base is a bang-up man as far as his fielding is concerned, and it is thought he will improve with the willow. When Midkiff gets back in harness Ball probably will go back to the keystone sack. The ability of Ball, Derrick, Midkiff and Parent is well known, and fans figure out that Dunnie will have no difficulty as far as his infield is concerned.

In Daniels, Cree and Twombly Dunnie apparently has a trio of tip-top men. Twombly should show improvement over his previous seasons, and Daniels should be able to toe the mark. In Cree Dunn undoubtedly has as good an outfielder as is in the league. A number of American League players who have been here for exhibition contests have expressed great surprise at the fact that the necessary waivers were obtained on him. Cree is hitting in grand style, covers heap of ground and plays the game hard all the time. It is expected that he will prove a consistent .300 hitter throughout the season. Capron and Dunn, Jr., are slated for utility outfield duty.

—✦—

While Manager Dunn is not claiming the pennant or anything of that sort, he is, nevertheless, sanguine that he will be among the first three at the close. Rochester and Newark, which were considered the clubs that would furnish contention, both suffered from Fed raids. Just how well they fill the gaps will mean much in the final show-down. International clubs will not find it so easy to get men from the National and American Leagues, due to the opportunity the Reds offer, and strengthening the squads will consequently become a more serious matter than in previous seasons.

From this stage of the proceedings it is almost a toss-up between all of the clubs excepting Baltimore and Buffalo, which undoubtedly loom up as the rel pennant contenders of the Barrow circuit.

Edgecombes Organize

The Edgecombe Athletic Club of the Interurban League has reorganized for the coming season. The membership of this club has made quite an increase over last season, and judging from its roster will give a good account of itself on the diamond. Manager George Atkinson will make his selection from the following: William R. German, the star pitcher and manager of Loyola College; James Richmond, George N. Zellinger, E. McGee, W. S. Lucas, Arthur Gerlach, H. A. Feldman, C. McCormick, R. K. Peacock, F. Heckinger, John Conn, L. Strauss, J. J. McCabe, J. Timmons, J. Hitchens, J. Shallenberger and J. F. McDermott, Jr., captain.

It will open the season on its home grounds at Pimlico, Saturday, May 2, with the Preston Athletic Club.

In Checker League

A special meeting of the Interclub Checker League has been called for 8 o'clock tomorrow night in the Elmwood Athletic Club's rooms, Lafayette and Greenmount avenues. The purpose of this meeting is to settle the games protested by the Harlem and Eagle Clubs, and all members are requested to attend.

Elmwoods To Meet

A special meeting of the Elmwood Athletic Club will be held at 8 o'clock tonight in its clubrooms, Lafayette and Greenmount avenues. All members are urged to attend, as matters of importance will be discussed.

Knights Play C. C. C.

The baseball team of the Knights of the Holy Grail will play the Cross Country Club nine Saturday afternoon on the Knights' grounds on Arlington avenue, Waverly.

THESE PLAYERS WILL REPRESENT BALTIMORE IN THE INTERNATIONAL CIRCUIT

M'GOVERN AND M'COY TO CLASH IN ARENA

Setto Tonight, Booked For 15 Rounds, Should Furnish Good Sport.

Philly McGovern of Brooklyn, brother of the famous Terry, and Young McCoy of this city will figure in the main bout tonight at the boxing entertainment under the auspices of the American Athletic Club. The stto is booked to go 15 rounds, and the articles of agreement call for the boys weighing in at 120 pounds ringside.

McGovern has been here for about 10 days and is said to be in good shape. He has been training diligently at a private gymnasium in East Baltimore, and it is said he will have no difficulty in making the weight. McCoy has worked at Joe Tipman's gymnasium and will easily meet the weight stipulation, for he recently weighed in at 116 pounds for a bout.

McGovern carries a good wallop, and one with which McCoy will not be able to take any liberties. The local lad is probably a bit more clever than the visitor, and it will be up to McCoy to carry the fighting to McGovern if he expects to gain the verdict. Both boys are able to stand a good bit of punishment.

McGovern has a number of staunch rooters among the racetrack followers, and they will probably make him a favorite tonight.

In addition to a number of bouts between boys who will be making their debut, there will be three six-rounders between boys well known here. In the semi-windup Oliver Barrett of this city and Tommy O'Dare of Philadelphia will clash. Battling Webb and Johnny Stone and Battling Stokes and Battling Morgan will figure in the others.

Abe Ullman will referee the events.

AWAITS BALL TEAMS

South America Greatly Interested In Proposed Tour To Be Made Next Year.

The sporting clubs in South American cities have already become interested in the proposed invasion of the major league baseball clubs which has been suggested for the fall of 1915. Word has been received that the project is expected to be a success and that the enthusiasm for baseball in South America runs high. Manager McGraw said that it was the idea of the promoters of the proposed trip to end the tour on the Pacific coast before the closing of the Panama Exposition in 1915.

The latest suggestion for the tour is to have the two clubs, made up of the star players of both leagues, play a few exhibition games in the East and South after the world's series and then go to Cuba. The itinerary would then call for a brief visit to Panama, and from there to South America, playing in the leading cities on both sides of the continent. The plan is to travel down the east side and come north on the west side of South America.

Then a longer stay could be made at Panama, playing in all the principal places in the canal zone, where the numerous Americans would welcome the baseball teams.

It is planned to go to the Pacific coast and play in several cities in California before the close of the big fair. As the trip is now proposed, the baseball party would be sure to meet favorable weather conditions throughout the trip.

SEVENTEENTH ROUND IN HARLEM LEAGUE

Checker Contestants Are To Meet At Club Rooms Friday Night.

The seventeenth round in the Harlem Athletic Club Checker League will be played Friday at 8 P. M. at the clubrooms, 1103 McCulloh street. The league is rapidly drawing to a close, only one more round remaining after this one.

Important games are scheduled for this round, second place being at stake when B. Goodman and Pickering meet Mauck and H. Goodman, respectively. Roberts will oppose Furman in three games, while DeBarry and Heyman will meet. The last contest will be between Needle and Scrivner.

In the games played last round Needle strengthened his position by taking two out of three from DeBarry, while B. Goodman won three from Heyman. Pickering defeated Furman three games, the tie for second place remaining unbroken. Mauck broke H. Goodman's record of 45 straight by defeating him in one out of three games. The Scrivner-Roberts match was postponed. The schedule for the next round is as follows: DeBarry vs. Heyman, Mauck vs. B. Goodman, Needle vs. Scrivner, Roberts vs. Furman and H. Goodman vs. Pickering.

Postponed Contest—Scrivner vs. Roberts.

The official standing to date follows:

	Won.	Lost.	Pct.
H. Goodman	47	1	.979
Mauck	42	6	.875
Pickering	33	15	.688
B. Goodman	33	15	.688
Needle	25	23	.521
Furman	15	30	.333
Roberts	14	31	.311
DeBarry	9	30	.231
Heyman	5	34	.128
Scrivner	0	36	.000

Matches are desired with strong local clubs. Address Harlem Athletic Club, 1103 McCulloh street.

Church's Ball Team

Christ Lutheran Church will have a representative baseball team on the diamond this year and would like to arrange contests with the tip-top nines of the city. Address James G. McCallister, 221 West Baltimore street.

Junior League Meets

A meeting of the members of the Baltimore Junior and the American Junior Baseball Leagues will be held at 221 West Baltimore street at 8 o'clock tonight.

Kaisers Beat Molars

The Kaisers showed surprising form and won three games from the Molars in Joe Tipman's Duckpin League. Smith of the Molars had high individual score one game, 132. The results follow:

MOLARS.				KAISERS.			
Askins	87	84	100	Marriott	111	101	90
Samuel	101	99	95	Zeller	90	100	104
Cook	91	87	82	Yellott	112	108	111
Smith	132	112	95	Lindsay	93	84	104
Hoy	102	98	93	Bair	126	106	116
Totals	513	470	465	Totals	532	499	525

Baseball At A Glance

FEDERAL LEAGUE

Games Tomorrow.

Brooklyn at Baltimore.
Chicago at St. Louis.
Buffalo at Pittsburgh.
Indianapolis at Kansas City.

Yesterday's Results.

Indianapolis, 7; Kansas City, 2.
St. Louis, 3; Chicago, 1.
Brooklyn-Baltimore, rain.
Buffalo-Pittsburgh, rain.

Standing Of The Clubs.

	W.	L.	Pct.		W.	L.	Pct.
Brooklyn	2	0	1.000	Chicago	2	3	.400
St. Louis	4	1	.800	Ind'apolis	2	3	.400
Buffalo	2	1	.667	Baltimore	1	2	.333
Kan. City	2	3	.400	Pittsb'gh	0	2	.000

INTERNATIONAL LEAGUE

Games Tomorrow.

Buffalo at Baltimore.
Montreal at Jersey City.
Toronto at Providence.
Rochester at Newark.

NATIONAL LEAGUE

Games Tomorrow.

Boston at Philadelphia.
New York at Brooklyn.
Cincinnati at Chicago.

Yesterday's Results.

St. Louis, 2; Chicago, 0.
New York-Brooklyn, rain.
Pittsburgh-Cincinnati, rain.
Boston-Philadelphia rain.

Standing Of The Clubs.

	W.	L.	Pct.		W.	L.	Pct.
Phila	3	0	1.000	Chicago	2	3	.400
Brooklyn	3	0	1.000	Cincinnati	1	3	.250
Pittsb'rgh	5	1	.833	Boston	0	3	.000
St. Louis	3	4	.429	New York	0	3	.000

AMERICAN LEAGUE

Games Tomorrow.

Chicago at Cleveland.
Detroit at St. Louis.
Athletics at Boston.
Washington at New York.

Yesterday's Results.

Athletics, 8; Boston, 2.
Athletics, 6; Boston, 0.
Cleveland-Detroit, rain.
St. Louis-Chicago, rain.
Washington-New York, rain.

Standing Of The Clubs.

	W.	L.	Pct.		W.	L.	Pct.
Chicago	5	1	.833	Detroit	3	2	.600
Wash'ton	3	1	.750	Athletics	2	3	.400
New York	2	1	.667	Boston	2	4	.333
St. Louis	3	2	.600	Cleveland	0	6	.000

Arcade's New Officers

The Arcade Athletic Club held a reelection of officers last night in its clubrooms, Barclay street, near Twentieth. Raymond Hoyle was elected president, while Lawrence Nolan and Herbert Brown will fill the treasurer and secretary's chairs, respectively. The following were elected to the board of governors: Walter James, Frank Lemmon, Leroy Moran and Joseph Lynch.

DUNDEE TOO CLEVER FOR GEORGE CHANEY

Philadelphia Scribes Unanimously Give Verdict To The New Yorker.

Philadelphia scribes were unanimous this morning in giving Johnny Dundee the verdict over George Chaney last night in their six-round bout before the Olympia Club. As both boys weighed close on to 130 pounds, it can be seen that neither will ever have an easy time making the legitimate bantam-weight limit of 122 pounds. The following are excerpts from the various Philadelphia papers of this morning:

Record: "Johnny Dundee, the aggressive little New York lightweight, proved entirely too fast, and too clever for Chaney in the wind-up at the Olympia. This pair have been doing good work in this city during the last winter, and there was a great desire to see them together, and as a result their encounter last night drew a big crowd. There was never an idle moment in the entire bout, and the spectators saw one of the fastest bouts ever witnessed in this city. Dundee was the aggressor from the time they shook hands till the end of the contest. But he always found Chaney willing, and always dangerous, and only the wonderful ducking and blocking of the New Yorker enabled him to escape the vicious swings which Chaney sent to his head, missing him many times by inches, as Dundee would dodge under them."

—✦—

Press: "Johnny Dundee of New York had his straight left jab working to perfection last night in the Olympia ring and at the end of six rounds he emerged a winner over George Chaney of Baltimore. Repeatedly and straight to the mark went Dundee's left and it beat Chaney's face into a pulp. Chaney, on the other hand, was depending almost entirely upon his southpaw to produce the knockout wallop, but the New Yorker was too shifty and too experienced to let Chaney's dangerous blow land cleanly. Chaney's face was badly cut at the end of the fracas, while Dundee did not bear a mark."

—✦—

Inquirer: "The fight itself was a hummer from the start and Dundee was forced to extend himself, as Chaney was right there with his short-arm wallops and landed a bunch of them. But Dundee's wonderful jab and his all-around cleverness easily gave him the advantage. As early as the second round he had Chaney's nose bleeding, and repeated landings on the probosis kept the claret flowing. Chaney, however, kept right after Dundee, and getting in close would let go short swings. Quite a few missed their mark owing to Johnny's cleverness, but some others landed. That they had a sting in them was shown by Dundee's furious onslaughts that followed."

North American: "Dundee's victory was by no means easy. The Baltimorean with his deadly left-hand knockout wallop was always dangerous, but Dundee was a ring general. He kept shooting a straight left jab to George's face that very seldom failed to find its mark. Dundee also kept his right poised for use, and when George shifted his guard to try and block the lightning left, Johnny would send over the right to the head or body that hurt Chaney. Chaney did some terrific punching. Many times he landed his terrific left on Dundee's jaw, and on each occasion it shook Johnny up; but Dundee, whenever hurt, came back strong and pounded George hard."

JACK CARROLL'S Sporting Gossip and Comment

Let's Get Together

Conflict No. 1 today. Only 17 more.

—✦—

It's pretty tough on a fellow to walk up Twenty-ninth street with a game on either side of him. Gee, if he could only cut himself in two and see both.

—✦—

Those Athletics woke up yesterday and celebrated Bunker Hill Day by taking two from the Red Sox. Now watch the champs trot along. Isn't it funny what a difference one day makes?

—✦—

George Chaney was up against the real thing in Johnny Dundee last night and the dispatches show that George put up a rattling fast mill even if the verdict did go to the other boy. In a longer fight George's wallop might produce.

—✦—

Seeing a man named McGovern participate in a boxing match is of interest in itself. Philly and Young McCoy should make a fast setto tonight.

—✦—

Marlboro changes hands.

—✦—

The National and American League say they will hold on to all of their surplus material to beat the Feds. That sounds all right, but where are the Class AA and Class A organizations going to get any strength if their best are taken yearly and none returned? It can't be done, that's all.

—✦—

Buck Herzog is learning the woes of a manager quickly. Having his crack Indian pitcher Johnson jump is a blow of no small proportions for the Red leader.

—✦—

There is a letter at this office for the manager of the Marshall Athletic Club baseball team.

—✦—

Athletics hit their stride.

—✦—

The eyes of the athletic world will be focused on Franklin Field, Philadelphia, next Saturday, when the annual relay carnival of the University of Pennsylvania will be held. A storm of protest is brewing against the new baton-passing rule. Many college-athletic authorities agree that the events this year will prove failures because of the lack of proper passing of the stick in the relays. The Oxford team's objection to the use of the baton in the coming four-mile relay appears to be well grounded. If it is to be a contest of dexterity instead of speed, they might as well change the event to a potato race. That six-ounce baton is going to feel like a six-pound one for the milers on their last lap.

—✦—

The young and untried genuine chip of the old block, Young Jake Schaefer, lived up to all the good things that have been said about him by decisively defeating the veteran George Slosson in one of the 14.1 balkline billiard matches in New York last night. Four hundred points to 254 was the result. The son of Wizard Jake, Sr., went through the frames like an expert.

—✦—

Penn relay games next.

HARVARD TWELVE TO PLAY MT. WASHINGTON

Crimson Team Will Give The Hillmen Tough Battle This Afternoon.

Harvard University's crack lacrosse team will engage the Mount Washington Club twelve at Mount Washington at 5 o'clock this afternoon. The Crimson representatives have been going like a house afire and the Mountaineers are sure to experience rough going.

The Harvard team is on its annual tour and so far has made a fine record.

HOPPE MAKES RECORD

In Balkline Title Play He Makes Run Of 125 Points And Wins Game.

New York, April 21.—The first two games of the 14.1 world's championship billiard tournament were played in the grand ballroom at the Hotel Astor last night. Willie Hoppe defeated Harry Kline, and young Jacob Schaeffer was the victor over George Slosson. This is the first tournament of the kind ever held.

In his match with Kline Hoppe made a new world's mark with a run of 125. This game was played in 18 innings, and the score was Hoppe 400, Kline 234. Hoppe's average was 22, 2-9, while Kline made a high run of 54 and averaged 13.

Schaeffer, who is but 17 years of age, and is a son of the former famous billiard player, defeated Slsson by a score of 400 to 254. This game was played in 31 innings. Schaeffer's high run was 51 and his average 12 28-31. Slosson was credited with a high run of 41 and averaged 8 6-31.

CINCINNATI REDS TO PLAY HERE JUNE 14

With Buck Herzog There Will Be Three Baltimore Boys.

CHIEF JOHNSON OF REDS FLOPS TO K. C.

Mike Mowrey Gets Praise For His Work At Third With Pittsburgh Pirates.

Buck Herzog's Cincinnati Reds will meet Jack Dunn's Orioles on Sunday, June 14, at Back River. Secretary Frank Bancroft of the Cincinnati team wired that he has completed all arrangements to have the Reds appear here on that date. It will be the first appearance of Buck Herzog, the Ridgely (Md.) farmer in this city as a team leader, and a record crowd is sure to turn out for the game. With Herzog will be Maurice Uhler, Bill Kellogg and Lew Deal, all Baltimore boys, and the Back River grounds will no doubt be taxed to the limit.

—✦—

A dispatch received from Cincinnati this morning states that Dutch Mellon, the former St. John's College star catcher, had been released by Manager Herzog to the Dayton (Central League) Club. Mellon has all the earmarks of a good man.

Manager Herzog is having his trials these days. George (Chief) Johnson, his big Indian pitcher, last night jumped the team and signed a three-year contract to play with the Kansas City (Federal League) Club. It is also rumored that Marsans, the Cuban outfielder of the Reds, will go to the independents if enough money is offered him.

—✦—

One player has been added to the roster of the Rochester Hustlers as a result of the Western trip of Manager Ganzel. That player is W. L. McAllester, late of the St. Louis Americans. The Hustler chief blew into Rochester early yesterday morning and left late last night for New York, where he will join the Hustler squad.

—✦—

Ed Donnelly, the former Oriole, is now a free agent. Harry Smith announced that Ed had purchased his release from the Newark Club. The Tigers had too many pitchers and Ed is the third twirler to feel the axe.

—✦—

A Pittsburgh scribe has the following to say as regards Mike Mowrey, the Baltimore boy, who is guarding the hot corner for the Pirates: "Mowrey is filling the third-base job in a manner which has won him words of praise from all who have seen him. Without going back to compare him with Byrne, he is certainly a vast improvement over the man who preceded him—Dolan. Mike has been hitting the ball very hard in the games played to date. He is a big, strong, husky individual, who ought to be able to stand an entire season of grueling infield work without crumbling. Mike has fitted well into the Pirate machine, and the change from St. Louis seems to have done him a lot of good. There is no better third baseman in the business when he is at the top of his form, and he is a dangerous man at the bat."

—✦—

With Hamilton back in the fold and Bill James coming through with a fairly good game in his first trial in the big league against the Detroit Tigers, Manager Ricky of St. Louis has three left-handers and four right-handers who can be counted upon as regulars for the coming campaign.

The southpaws—Hamilton, Wellman and Leverenz—were with the club during the 1913 campaign. Also two of the right-handers, Mitchell and Baumgardner. Wylie Taylor, who should be a regular this year, was with the team the latter part of the 1913 campaign and hurled several good games. James is the other regular.

Oxford Men Get First Practice On U. Of P. Field

Philadelphia, April 21.—The Oxford University four-mile relay team held its first practice yesterday on Franklin Field. After indulging in a short workout, the visitors declared that they were all in good condition for next Saturday's race.

Captain Jackson said the only effect the change in climate had had on himself and the other athletes was that they seemed to require more drinking water.

Norman Taber, the former Brown student, who is a member of the English team, said he felt sure that the climate will not affect the athletes, and that they will be on edge when the four-mile race is called.

JAMES AND DEVORE HITTING .317; CARRIGAN, YERKES, SCOTT, EVERS GAIN

Carrigan's New Southpaw

Pitcher George (Babe) Ruth, Formerly of Baltimore Orioles, But Now with Lannin's Red Sox.

New Red Sox Here for Start vs. Naps

Ex-Orioles Arrive This Morning Eager to Work —Confer with Owner Lannin.

Those Cleveland Naps have been fairly easy picking for these Red Sox so far this season, but the series which starts this afternoon at Fenway Park at 3 o'clock, may be an altogether different proposition. When the Red Sox took their last swing through the West they took four straight from Birmingham's men, but when the Naps were here in May they managed to take all but one of the four games from the Lannins. So the season's count to date between these two teams is five wins for Boston and only three for the Naps.

But the Naps as they came into Boston on the 7 o'clock express this morning showed plenty of ambition and confidence in their carriage. They feel that they are just now getting their feet down on terra firma again, with Jay Kirke, our old Braves friend, doing so well at first base and with Ray Chapman playing back there at short with his old-time brilliancy.

Three Ex-Orioles in Town and Confer with Owner Lannin

President Lannin's three latest acquisitions, Pitchers George Ruth and Eddie Shore and Catcher Ben Egan, bought from Manager Jack Dunn of the Baltimore Orioles, arrived in Boston this morning on the Federal express at 10 o'clock. They were met at the Back Bay station by Owner Lannin and immediately went to the downtown offices of the club, where they were closeted for a brief time with their new boss.

It is taken for granted that Ruth, Shore and Egan signed new contracts with Boston during their conferences with President Lannin. They will all be out in uniform this afternoon, and the chances are slightly better than even that one of the pitchers will be asked to go in and work. In that event it will be interesting to see whether Carrigan sends in Ben Egan to hold up the hurler whose eccentricities he knows very well, or whether Boss Bill will go in himself to do his well known stunt of coaching a kid pitcher to a victory.

All three of the ex-Orioles expressed themselves as very pleased to play ball in Boston. The two pitchers are newcomers to major league company, but Egan, an old-time follower of Connie Mack, knows from experience that Boston Red Sox players are envied their lot by the men on the other teams in the circuit.

Naps Never Did Shy at Left-Handed Pitching

The Cleveland Naps are ball players who apparently have little fear of left-handed pitching, even when it is as effective as that of Leonard's has been all year. Lajoie, Jackson, Kirke and Turner are all free and easy hitters who are liable to connect with any sort of pitching, even wild pitches. Unlike the Tigers and the Athletics, the Naps have little fear of southpaws.

Leonard worked Wednesday for nearly a whole game against those lucky White Sox and there is the chance that Carrigan will not feel justified in starting him this afternoon. Joe Wood's sore arm is better and possibly Boss Bill will feel that Woodie will be able to stand up under the stress of starting this afternoon's game. But of course that all depends upon how Smoky Joe feels just prior to the start of hostilities.

But for Orioles Bill's Hurlers Would Be Much Shot to Pieces

If it wasn't for the fact that President Lannin bought Ruth and Shore from the Baltimore Orioles, the Red Sox pitching corps would be in a very much shot-to-pieces condition just now. There is no telling just how Rankin Johnson's elbow will pan out. Joe Wood's arm is too valuable an asset to the club to be forced to do work it is unfit to undertake. George Foster's knee is in such delicate condition that there is no telling when he'll be able to come back and take up his turn in the box.

Hugh Bedient showed yesterday that it will only be a short time before he can be relied upon to do his old-time brilliant little bit of pitching, but still can't be counted in as a regular dependable like Leonard and Collins. And as for Fred Coumbe, his rough treatment Wednesday makes it uncertain whether or not he can be relied upon to repeat his three-hit stunt which he worked against the Athletics over in Philadelphia. Ruth and Shore surely are welcome, and the sooner they work the better. And there's a chance that either one of them may be asked to work this afternoon.

LEADING TEN SLUGGERS.

	2-b. hits.	3-b. hits.	Home runs.	Total base on hits.	Extra bases.	Grand ave
Walker, St. L.	17	12	3	140	50	.528
Crawford, Det.	12	14	4	143	52	.505
Cobb, Det.	14	2	1	74	21	.487
Jackson, Clev.	12	6	2	92	30	.487
Baker, Ath.	11	1	7	129	34	.459
Milan, Wash.	14	8	1	118	33	.420
Speaker, Boston	15	7	1	112	32	.412
E. Collins, Ath.	11	6	1	114	26	.412
Shanks, Wash.	13	6	4	104	37	.382
Kavanagh, Det.	14	4	3	99	31	.369

LEADING TEN RUN GETTERS.

Player. Club.	g.	r.	avg.
E. Collins, Ath.	76	59	.78
Speaker, Boston	77	48	.62
Bush, Det.	77	48	.62
E. Murphy, Ath.	74	46	.62
Shotten, St. L.	77	46	.60
Baker, Ath.	74	43	.58
Hooper, Boston	77	43	.56
Kavanaugh, Det.	74	40	.54
Foster, Wash.	74	40	.54
Pratt, St. L.	78	40	.51

LEADING TEN BASE STEALERS.

Player. Club.	g.	sb.	avg.
Maisel, N. Y.	65	29	.45
Milan, Wash.	73	27	.37
E. Collins, Ath.	76	28	.36
Pratt, St. L.	78	21	.27
Peckinpaugh, N. Y.	70	19	.27
G. Williams, St. L.	70	19	.27
Blackburn, Chi.	67	18	.27
Speaker, Boston	77	19	.25
Moriarty, Det.	63	16	.25
Shotten, St. L.	77	18	.23

TRIPLE PLAYS.

Washington 1, vs. Athletics—Gandil, Foster and McBride.

Washington 1, vs. Athletics—Gandil, Henry and Gandil.

New York 1, vs. Washington—Maisel, Sweeney, Williams and Maisel.

Cleveland 1, vs. St. Louis—Turner, Lajoie, Johnston and Carisch.

DOUBLE PLAYS.

Cleveland	55	Detroit	58
St. Louis	58	Chicago	47
Washington	51	New York	31
Athletics	57	**Boston**	47

PASSED BALLS.

Cleveland	18	Washington	13
Athletics	10	St. Louis	20
Chicago	11	New York	9
Detroit	10	**Boston**	7

Big League Batting and Fielding Records

These records are compiled from the official scores printed in the various cities in the two major leagues. These figures, which will be a weekly feature of The Traveler, are complete up to Thursday's games.

AMERICAN LEAGUE

BATTING AVERAGES.

Players. Clubs.	G.	AB.	R.	H.	2B.	3B.	HR.	SB.	SH.	TB.	EB.	AVE.
Cobb, Det.	43	152	28	53	14	2	1	13	4	74	21	.349
C. Walker, St. L.	78	265	40	90	17	12	3	15	9	140	50	.340
Baker, Ath.	74	281	43	95	11	1	7	6	5	129	34	.338
Jackson, Clev.	52	189	26	62	12	6	2	11	6	92	30	.328
Lelivelt, Clev.	33	64	5	21	5	1	0	2	1	28	7	.328
Crawford, Det.	77	283	34	91	12	14	4	13	9	143	52	.322
E. Collins, Ath.	76	277	59	88	11	6	1	28	13	114	26	.318
Covaleskie, Det.	21	44	1	14	2	0	0	0	5	16	2	.318
Milan, Wash.	78	281	36	85	14	8	1	27	5	118	33	.302
Speaker, Bos.	77	272	48	80	15	7	1	19	4	112	32	.294
Wood, Clev.	44	141	17	41	3	2	1	5	0	51	10	.291
A. Williams, Wash.	34	62	10	18	2	3	1	0	2	29	11	.290
Schalk, Chi.	62	183	12	53	8	1	0	12	10	63	10	.290
Shotten, St. L.	77	292	46	84	8	1	0	12	10	63	10	.290
Gandil, Wash.	67	240	22	68	8	7	0	18	5	106	22	.288
McInnis, Ath.	76	287	34	81	8	5	0	14	11	86	18	.283
J. Bush, Ath.	18	32	3	9	3	0	1	1	1	15	6	.281
Oldring, Ath.	64	260	37	72	10	2	2	11	5	92	20	.277
Leary, St. L.	78	282	19	78	16	7	0	2	5	108	30	.277
E. Walker, St. L.	28	40	5	11	2	0	1	2	0	16	5	.275
E. Foster, Wash.	74	287	40	79	10	2	1	16	4	96	17	.275
Fournier, Chi.	27	80	11	22	2	2	0	1	3	28	6	.275
Cook, N. Y.	47	143	14	39	3	1	1	8	2	47	8	.273
Lewis, Bos.	69	249	20	67	18	2	1	15	11	92	25	.269
Strunk, Ath.	63	210	26	56	6	3	2	10	11	74	18	.267
Demmitt, Chi.	67	236	30	63	5	7	1	3	5	85	22	.267
Leibold, Clev.	58	207	24	55	8	3	0	4	1	69	14	.266
Burns, Det.	77	268	27	71	10	1	3	16	13	92	21	.265
D. Johnston, Clev.	56	197	27	52	7	1	0	12	6	61	9	.264
Hooper, Boston	77	271	48	71	11	7	1	9	4	99	28	.262
G. Williams, St. L.	70	233	27	61	11	2	3	19	5	85	24	.262
J. Collins, Chi.	74	279	29	73	18	2	2	15	10	101	28	.262
Cady, Boston	32	84	7	22	3	1	0	2	0	27	5	.262
Hellman, Det.	22	54	8	14	3	0	1	0	4	20	6	.259
O. Bush, Det.	77	283	48	73	8	2	0	16	5	85	12	.258
Barry, Ath.	63	206	23	53	6	0	0	9	13	59	6	.257
Moeller, Wash.	70	270	39	69	10	4	0	14	6	87	18	.256
[illegible]												
Benz, Chi.	22	46	2	5	2	0	0	0	2	10	3	.111
Bisland, Clev.	19	57	9	6	1	0	0	1	1	7	1	.105
Cicotte, Chi.	21	50	2	5	0	0	0	0	2	5	0	.100
Warhop, N. Y.	22	32	3	3	1	0	0	0	1	4	1	.094
Collamore, Clev.	16	24	0	2	1	0	0	0	1	3	1	.083
Engel, Wash.	15	12	3	1	0	0	0	0	0	1	0	.083
R. Collins, Boston	20	38	2	3	0	0	0	0	4	3	0	.079
Leonard, Boston	20	44	1	3	1	0	0	0	6	4	1	.068
W. James, St. L.	21	46	0	3	1	0	0	0	2	4	1	.065
Bedient, Boston	22	31	3	2	0	0	0	0	0	2	0	.065
Mains, Det.	21	31	1	2	0	0	0	0	0	2	0	.065
W. Mitchell, Clev.	23	39	2	2	1	0	0	0	3	3	1	.051
M. Hall, Det.	19	23	0	1	0	0	0	0	0	1	0	.043
Hagerman, Clev.	17	38	0	0	0	0	0	0	1	0	0	.000
James, Clev.	17	12	1	0	0	0	0	0	1	0	0	.000
Blanding, Clev.	18	21	0	0	0	0	0	0	0	0	0	.000
Brown, N. Y.	15	20	0	0	0	0	0	0	1	0	0	.000

PITCHERS' RECORDS.

Pitchers and clubs.	g.	w.	l.	Shut-outs w.	Shut-outs l.	te.	so.	bb.	hts.	Five Hits or Less 0 h.	1 h.	2 h.	3 h.	4 h.	5 h.	ave.
Walsh, Chi.	2	1	0	0	0	0	6	3	5	0	0	0	0	0	0	1.000
Wolfgang, Chi.	5	1	0	0	0	0	4	6	10	0	0	0	0	0	0	1.000
Cooper, Boston	7	1	0	0	0	0	3	9	18	0	0	0	0	0	0	1.000
Reynolds, Det.	10	1	0	0	0	0	11	18	11	0	0	0	0	0	0	1.000
V. Gregg, Clev.	12	7	1	1	1	0	38	31	55	0	0	0	0	0	1	.875
Plank, Ath.	19	9	2	4	0	0	55	21	74	0	0	0	1	0	1	.818
Shawkey, Ath.	17	8	2	2	2	2	42	39	106	0	0	0	1	0	0	.800
Wood, Boston	8	4	1	1	0	0	24	10	33	0	0	0	1	0	2	.800
Leonard, Boston	20	11	3	4	2	1	101	38	91	0	0	0	2	2	2	.786
Bender, Ath.	12	6	2	3	0	0	44	32	68	0	0	0	0	3	1	.750
Faber, Chi.	20	6	2	2	0	0	44	34	53	0	1	0	2	1	1	.750
Weilman, St. L.	21	10	4	3	1	1	60	35	101	0	0	0	0	0	1	.714
Coveleskie, Det.	21	12	6	5	3	0	62	45	97	0	1	1	0	4	0	.667
Pennnock, Ath.	13	4	2	1	1	1	41	31	61	0	0	0	0	1	0	.667
Boehler, Det.	8	2	1	1	0	0	17	29	24	0	0	0	0	0	0	.667
Bressler, Ath.	12	2	1	0	0	0	17	18	25	0	0	0	0	0	0	.667
W. Johnson, Wash.	23	14	8	6	4	0	97	33	127	0	0	0	2	3	2	.636
Wyckoff, Ath.	19	8	5	0	0	1	54	73	91	0	0	0	2	3	2	.615
Caldwell, N. Y.	22	11	7	3	3	0	60	33	104	0	0	0	2	1	0	.611
Mains, Det.	21	6	4	1	3	0	42	46	91	0	0	0	2	1	0	.600
Dauss, Det.	24	10	7	3	2	0	73	39	135	0	0	0	0	0	1	.588
Benz, Chi.	22	10	7	3	3	1	67	28	100	1	1	0	0	1	1	.588
G. Foster, Boston	18	7	5	5	1	0	55	28	82	0	0	1	1	2	2	.583
W. James, St. L.	21	7	5	1	2	0	44	51	119	0	0	0	0	0	2	.583
Boehling, Wash.	10	8	6	2	0	0	64	55	125	0	0	1	1	1	0	.571
Ayers, Wash.	25	9	7	2	1	0	74	23	100	0	0	0	1	1	0	.563
[illegible]																
McHale, N. Y.	15	4	8	0	3	0	24	15	101	0	0	0	0	1	0	.333
Hagerman, Clev.	17	4	8	2	3	0	56	54	101	0	0	0	0	2	0	.333
Taylor, St. L.	12	2	4	1	1	0	17	20	29	0	1	0	0	0	0	.333
R. Mitchell, St. L.	15	2	4	0	1	0	20	17	71	0	0	0	0	0	0	.333
Coumbe, Boston	13	1	2	0	0	1	9	10	37	0	0	0	1	0	0	.333
Bedient, Boston	22	4	9	1	1	0	45	30	115	0	0	0	1	0	1	.308
R. Johnson, Boston	14	3	9	2	5	0	20	28	83	0	0	0	0	0	1	.250
Collamore, Clev.	16	2	6	0	1	0	20	39	73	0	0	0	0	0	0	.250
Bowman, Clev.	12	1	4	1	1	0	14	26	85	0	0	0	0	0	0	.200
Warhop, N. Y.	19	2	9	0	3	1	32	20	79	0	0	0	0	0	2	.182
Brown, N. Y.	15	1	6	0	3	0	19	26	65	0	0	0	0	0	0	.143
Keating, N. Y.	16	1	7	0	2	0	59	47	105	0	0	0	0	0	1	.125
Blanding, Clev.	17	1	8	0	3	0	15	27	75	0	0	0	0	1	0	.111
J. Williams, Det.	2	0	1	0	0	0	1	5	6	0	0	0	0	0	0	.000
Pieh, N. Y.	4	0	1	0	1	0	3	7	14	0	0	0	0	0	0	.000
Morton, Clev.	6	0	1	0	0	0	8	6	7	0	0	0	0	0	0	.000
Hoch, St. L.	6	0	1	0	0	0	4	10	18	0	0	0	0	0	0	.000
Bentley, Wash.	11	0	2	0	0	0	15	10	31	0	0	0	0	0	0	.000
Leverenz, St. L.	7	0	3	0	2	0	7	19	23	0	0	1	0	0	0	.000
W. James, Clev.	17	0	3	0	0	1	16	31	43	0	0	0	0	0	0	.000
Cavett, Det.	10	0	4	0	1	0	15	12	27	0	0	0	0	0	0	.000
Lathrop, Chi.	2	—	—	0	0	0	1	1	3	0	0	0	0	0	0	.000
Harper, Wash.	5	—	—	0	0	0	6	6	5	0	0	0	0	0	0	.000
Jasper, Chi.	11	—	—	0	0	0	13	13	13	0	0	0	0	0	0	.000

CLUB BATTING. RECORDS.

Clubs.	G.	Times atbat.	r.	b.h.	s.b.	s.h.	ave.
Athletics	76	2494	338	647	107	104	.259
Detroit	77	2479	270	614	106	100	.248
Washington	74	2383	277	579	109	67	.243
Boston	78	2393	262	581	86	87	.243
St. Louis	78	2420	252	570	105	82	.236
Chicago	74	2341	232	552	93	100	.236
Cleveland	73	2380	256	560	86	73	.235
New York	70	2182	204	462	112	48	.212

LONG HITS BY CLUBS.

Clubs.	2-b. hits.	3-b. hits.	Home runs.	Total base on hits.	Extra bases.	Grand ave.
Athletics	77	32	18	842	195	.338
Detroit	96	37	12	820	206	.331
St. Louis	93	45	9	776	206	.321
Washington	91	36	9	765	186	.321
Boston	103	31	5	761	180	.318
Chicago	83	26	8	731	179	.312
Cleveland	86	30	4	718	158	.302
New York	59	18	6	575	113	.261

CLUB FIELDING RECORDS.

Clubs.	g.	po.	a.	e.	tc.	a.
Washington	74	1983	968	104	3055	.966
Boston	78	2088	956	109	3153	.965
Athletics	76	2041	955	115	3111	.963
New York	70	1822	890	111	2823	.961
Detroit	77	2085	1167	137	3389	.960
Cleveland	73	1925	929	131	2985	.956
Chicago	74	1978	1018	139	3185	.956
St. Louis	78	2090	1004	152	3246	.953

NATIONAL LEAGUE

BATTING AVERAGES.

Players. Clubs.	G.	AB.	R.	H.	2B.	3B.	HR.	SB.	SH.	TB.	EB.	AVE.
[illegible]												

PITCHERS' RECORDS.

Pitchers and clubs.	g.	w.	l.	Shut-outs w.	Shut-outs l.	te.	so.	bb.	hts.	Five Hits or Less 0 h.	1 h.	2 h.	3 h.	4 h.	5 h.	ave.
[illegible]																
Hess, Boston	5	2	3	1	0	0	9	15	31	0	0	0	0	1	1	.400
Zabel, Chi.	12	2	3	0	0	0	26	24	46	0	0	0	0	0	1	.400
Jacobs, Phila.	12	2	3	0	1	0	14	16	60	0	0	0	0	0	0	.400
Perdue, St. L.	9	3	5	0	1	0	13	11	62	0	0	0	0	0	0	.375
Harmon, Pitts.	15	4	7	0	3	0	19	25	91	0	0	0	0	0	1	.364
Pierce, Chi.	18	4	7	0	1	0	47	43	73	0	0	0	0	0	3	.364
Douglass, Cin.	21	4	7	0	0	1	46	43	68	0	0	0	0	2	1	.364
Rixey, Phila.	4	1	2	0	0	0	7	7	27	0	0	0	0	0	0	.333
Strand, Boston	6	1	2	0	0	0	16	10	25	0	0	0	0	0	0	.333
C. Smith, Chi.	8	1	2	0	0	0	5	9	18	0	0	0	0	0	0	.333
Cocreham, Boston	9	1	2	0	0	0	8	17	27	0	0	0	0	0	0	.333
Ragon, Bkl.	15	3	7	0	2	0	31	38	74	0	0	0	0	0	0	.300
Reulbach, Bkl.	23	5	12	1	4	0	60	42	114	0	0	0	1	1	0	.294
Crutcher, Boston	18	2	5	1	1	0	25	35	98	0	0	0	0	0	0	.286
Rowan, Cin.	10	1	3	0	0	0	13	9	35	0	0	0	0	0	0	.250
Oeschger, Phila.	18	2	7	0	0	0	27	32	88	0	0	0	0	0	1	.222
O'Toole, Pitts.	11	1	4	0	1	0	22	25	46	0	0	0	0	1	0	.200
Hagerman, Chi.	12	1	4	0	0	0	21	21	50	0	0	0	0	0	1	.200
Davis, Boston	1	0	1	0	0	0	2	4	10	0	0	0	0	0	0	.000
Luque, Boston	2	0	1	0	0	0	1	4	5	0	0	0	0	0	0	.000
Mattison, Phila.	4	0	1	0	0	0	16	7	25	0	0	0	0	0	0	.000
Baumgartner, Phila.	1	—	—	0	0	0	1	0	2	0	0	0	0	0	0	.000
Mamaux, Pitts.	3	—	—	0	0	0	7	4	2	0	0	0	0	0	0	.000
Schupp, N. Y.	3	—	—	0	0	0	5	4	6	0	0	0	0	0	0	.000
Neihaus, St. L.	3	—	—	0	0	0	0	4	7	0	0	0	0	0	0	.000
Schauer, N. Y.	4	—	—	0	0	0	3	4	10	0	0	0	0	0	0	.000
Schmutz, Bkl.	5	—	—	0	0	0	7	3	7	0	0	0	0	0	0	.000
Stack, Chi.	5	—	—	0	0	0	7	8	7	0	0	0	0	0	0	.000
Lear, Cin.	7	—	—	0	0	0	6	10	13	0	0	0	0	0	0	.000
Koerster, Cin.	9	—	—	0	0	0	11	17	23	0	0	0	0	0	0	.000

CLUB BATTING RECORDS.

Clubs.	G.	Times atbat.	r.	b.h.	s.b.	s.h.	ave.
Philadelphia	67	2274	305	607	67	69	.267
New York	68	2232	318	595	118	69	.267
Brooklyn	67	2228	262	591	86	74	.265
Boston	70	2309	240	564	47	78	.244
Chicago	73	2473	319	598	89	95	.242
St. Louis	76	2468	278	593	107	89	.240
Pittsburgh	70	2257	232	541	76	72	.240
Cincinnati	73	2282	279	546	114	84	.239

LONG HITS BY CLUBS.

Clubs.	2-b. hits.	3-b. hits.	Home runs.	Total base on hits.	Extra bases.	Grand ave.
Philadelphia	96	23	31	842	235	.370
Brooklyn	71	40	18	796	205	.357
New York	92	29	11	778	183	.349
Chicago	105	37	22	843	245	.341
St. Louis	110	28	17	810	217	.328
Boston	87	23	18	751	187	.325
Pittsburgh	76	33	3	717	176	.318
Cincinnati	68	39	11	725	179	.318

Another Sox Ex-Oriole

Eddie Shore, the Tall Right-Handed Pitcher the Sox Got in the Big Buy.

Braves Want 3 Out of 4 from Chicago

Tribesmen Want Get-Away Game from Cubs Before Going After the Fighting Cardinals.

CHICAGO, July 11—It's going to be a fight for an even break for the Cubs this afternoon on the West Side, the while these peppery and strenuous Boston Braves are trying for a three out of four break for the series. After this afternoon's game the Bostonians march on to St. Louis, where they play Miller Huggins's fighters tomorrow afternoon and the three succeeding days.

And the Windy City fans will be glad to see the last of these dynamic Tribesmen. When the Cubs were within striking distance of first place, with the Boston tail-enders next on the list as opponents, things really did look promising for Hank O'Day to drag his men up into first place. But the cellar men proved capable of playing first-place ball, and that's the reason the Cubs haven't profited by the Braves' stay in Chicago, though the New York pace setters have been playing very inferior ball at St. Louis, the while the Braves were standing off Hank's men.

Something Rather Strange About Zimm's Unexpected Return

Chief Stallings isn't altogether satisfied over yesterday's game. He simply wonders how Heine Zimmerman managed to exert strong enough influence to be allowed back in the game before his three-day suspension period had elapsed. Without any question the return of the Great Zimm was largely responsible for the win of the Cubs yesterday. With the Bronx freshet back on the hot corner, the entire Cub machine took heart and played better ball than it showed the day before when Zimm was kicking his heels in a grand stand seat.

Yet Stallings has always been an advocate of not putting the stars out of the game, maintaining that a fine to come out of the pocket of the player would do more real good in keeping discipline. But all the same this changed decision on Zimm is perplexing.

Otto Hess wasn't ready to start yesterday. But he felt good. His wrist didn't bother him and he told the Chief that he was willing to go in and try. Now Stallings wishes that he had clung to his morning plan and had started Little Fordham Dick Rudolph. The Braves are only two and one half games away from the Pittsburgh Pirates, who are in seventh place, and the Chief hates to realize that anything he has done cost a chance to lessen the distance between his trailers and the field.

Dick Rudolph will probably work this afternoon, though both Paul Strand and George Davis, kid southpaw and right-hander, respectively, are trying to convince Stallings that it will be a good thing to give them a chance to start this getaway game against the Cubs.

Maranville continues to be the idol of the West side fans. Funny about the game this midget plays in Chicago. He has been the sensation of the games here every time Boston has hooked up with the Cubs this year. Yesterday he started one of his lightning double plays, with Johnny Evers taking his usually lightning part. The Rabbit got a single and a triple at the bat, and accepted nine chances in the field without the trace of an error, a wonderful bit of defensive work.

Busted Finger May Keep Gowdy Out for Fortnight.

As Cather performs in each succeeding game a little better than in the preceding game, Stallings has quite made up his mind that he has a gem of the first water in the light-haired boy from St. Louis. Yesterday Cather made a single and a double and also made a great running back jumping-up catch in right field.

The hard luck of yesterday's game was that Hank Gowdy should get a broken finger. It happened in the fifth and a foul tip did the dirty work. Hank, in other years, was very prone to injury; but this is the first time the jinx happened to catch up with him this year. He will be out of the game for a couple of weeks, unless, perchance, the doctor made a mistake and called a bad sprain a busted finger.

Standings in Four Leagues

AMERICAN

	Won.	Lost.	P.C.
Philadelphia	44	31	.587
Detroit	44	35	.557
Chicago	41	34	.547
Washington	41	35	.539
St. Louis	41	37	.526
BOSTON	40	38	.513
New York	27	45	.375
Cleveland	26	49	.347

GAMES TODAY.

Cleveland at Boston.
St. Louis at Philadelphia (2 games).
Detroit at Washington.
Chicago at New York.

NEW ENGLAND

	Won.	Lost.	P.C.
Worcester	35	22	.614
Lawrence	36	23	.610
Portland	32	25	.561
Lynn	30	28	.517
Lowell	30	30	.500
Lewiston	27	31	.466
Haverhill	26	31	.456
Fitchburg	18	44	.290

GAMES TODAY.

Lawrence at Lynn.
Lowell at Haverhill.
Worcester at Portland.
Fitchburg at Lewiston.

NATIONAL

	Won.	Lost.	P.C.
New York	41	29	.586
Chicago	41	34	.547
St. Louis	40	36	.526
Philadelphia	34	35	.493
Cincinnati	36	38	.486
Brooklyn	33	36	.478
Pittsburgh	32	38	.457
BOSTON	30	41	.423

GAMES TODAY.

Boston at Chicago.
New York at St. Louis.
Philadelphia at Pittsburgh.
Brooklyn at Cincinnati.

FEDERAL

	Won.	Lost.	P.C.
Chicago	43	28	.606
Indianapolis	38	31	.551
Buffalo	36	31	.537
Baltimore	36	34	.514
Brooklyn	33	34	.493
Kansas City	34	41	.453
Pittsburgh	30	39	.435
St. Louis	31	43	.419

GAMES TODAY.

Pittsburgh at Brooklyn.
Buffalo at Baltimore.
Kansas City at St. Louis.
Indianapolis at Chicago.

LEADING TEN SLUGGERS.

	2-b. hits.	3-b. hits.	Home runs.	Total base on hits.	Extra bases.	Grand ave.
Connolly, Boston	12	4	5	84	35	.491
Cravath, Phi.	11	6	8	119	47	.490
Saier, Chi.	13	6	9	117	52	.455
S. Magee, Phi.	19	2	5	107	38	.451
Burns, N. Y.	20	5	0	109	30	.440
Wheat, Bkn.	6	6	6	101	36	.437
Clark, Cin.	11	6	2	87	29	.437
Luderus, Phi.	7	5	10	108	46	.434
Leach, Chi.	14	6	3	117	35	.411
Zimmerman, Chi.	16	5	2	107	32	.405

CLUB FIELDING RECORDS.

Clubs.	Games.	Putouts.	Assists.	Errors.	T'tl chances.	Ave.
Boston	70	1872	950	93	2915	.968
St. Louis	76	2106	1035	105	3246	.968
Pittsburgh	70	1845	882	98	2825	.965
Brooklyn	67	1803	858	113	2774	.959
Cincinnati	73	1933	956	137	3026	.955
New York	68	1779	880	117	2776	.953
Chicago	75	2048	941	159	3148	.949
Philadelphia	67	1811	851	159	2821	.944

LEADING TEN BASE STEALERS.

Player. Club.	g.	sb.	avg.
Herzog, Cin.	68	29	.43
Burns, N. Y.	68	28	.41
Bescher, N. Y.	68	24	.35
Dolan, St. L.	61	19	.31
Lobert, Phi.	67	19	.28
L. Magee, St. L.	73	19	.26
Carey, Pitts.	70	18	.26
Moran, Cin.	71	18	.25
Good, Chi.	75	17	.23
Huggins, St. L.	75	16	.21

LEADING TEN RUN GETTERS.

Player. Club.	g.	r.	avg.
Burns, N. Y.	68	53	.78
Daubert, Brk.	56	38	.68
Doyle, N. Y.	59	39	.66
Saier, Chi.	72	46	.64
Lobert, Phi.	67	42	.63
S. Magee, Phi.	63	39	.62
Bescher, N. Y.	68	42	.61
Cravath, Phi.	67	40	.60
Zimmerman, Chi.	69	40	.58
Huggins, St. L.	75	40	.53

DOUBLE PLAYS.

Brooklyn	52	Chicago	47
New York	55	Cincinnati	50
Philadelphia	42	Pittsburgh	43
St. Louis	54	**Boston**	63

TRIPLE PLAYS.

New York 1, vs. Philadelphia—Doyle, Merkle, Fletcher and McLean.

Chicago 1, vs. St. Louis—Johnson, Leach, Zimmerman and Bresnahan.

But 65 Points Separate First and Sixth American League Teams

AMERICAN WINS LONG AIR FLIGHT

Hendon to Paris and Back in Seven Hours

LONDON, July 11.—An American, Walter L. Brock, today captured first honors in the aeroplane race from Hendon to Paris and return. Brock outdistanced his nearest rival, Raoul Garros, a French aviator, by more than an hour. His flying time for the distance—502 miles in a direct line—was 7h. 3m. 6s.

FALLS INTO CHANNEL

A thrilling incident of the race was a plunge into the English Channel which Baron Carbery suffered when his aeroplane fell from a considerable height when half way across on the return trip.

Lord Carbery kept afloat with the aid of a life belt until picked up by a passing steamer. He was transferred to the battleship St. Vincent, which sent a wireless message to Dover requesting that a destroyer be sent to assist in bringing the aeroplane ashore.

One of the conditions of the race required that competitors should carry life belts, and the wisdom of this precaution was demonstrated by Lord Carbery's experience.

Eugene Renaux met with misfortune in losing his way several times on his way to Paris, more than seven hours being required to make the trip to the French capital. After his arrival there Renaux said he would start on the return journey, but would descend at Calais and withdraw from the race. He carried a woman passenger.

Garros finished in 8 hours 28 minutes 47 seconds, actual flying time. He had some trouble with his propellers and steering planes on the outward flight.

Two other British entrants, Reginald H. Carr and Louis Noel, descended before reaching the coast on the flight to Paris.

BROWNS DIVIDE WITH ATHLETICS

Clarence Walker's Homers Win First—Macks Take Second

PHILADELPHIA, July 11.—Two home run hits by C. Walker, one of which decided the game, featured a 12-inning battle between Philadelphia and St. Louis in the first contest of a double-header here today, St. Louis winning by 4 to 3.

The score:

ST. LOUIS.	AB.	R.	BH.	TB.	PO.	A.	E.
Shotten, c f	5	1	2	2	0	0	0
Pratt, 2b	5	1	3	4	5	6	0
Williams, r f	5	0	2	2	0	0	0
C. Walker, l f	6	2	3	9	2	1	0
Leary, 1b	6	0	4	4	11	1	0
Austin, 3b	6	0	1	1	4	0	0
Lavan, ss	2	0	0	0	2	2	0
Wares, ss	2	0	0	0	3	5	1
Crossin, c	4	0	0	0	9	1	0
Weilman, p	3	0	1	1	0	1	0
Baumgardner, p	2	0	0	0	0	1	0
aE. Walker	1	0	0	0	0	0	0
Totals	47	4	16	23	36	18	1

PHILA.	AB.	R.	BH.	TB.	PO.	A.	E.
Walsh, r f	5	1	1	2	3	0	0
Oldring, l f	6	0	2	3	3	0	1
Collins, 2b	3	1	0	0	5	2	0
Baker, 3b	4	0	1	1	3	0	0
McInnis, 1b	5	0	3	3	8	0	0
Strunk, c f	3	0	1	1	3	0	0
Barry, ss	5	0	0	0	1	4	0
Schang, c	4	0	1	1	10	4	0
Shawkey, p	4	1	0	0	0	3	0
bKopf	0	0	0	0	0	0	0
Totals	39	3	9	11	36	13	1

aBatted for Lavan in 5th. bBatted for Shawkey in 12th.

St. Louis ...... 2 0 0 0 1 0 0 0 0 0 0 1—4
Philadelphia... 0 0 0 1 2 0 0 0 0 0 0 0—3

Two-base hits—Pratt, Walsh, Oldring. Home runs—C. Walker 2. Hits—Off Weilman 6 in 5 innings, off Baumgardner 8 in 7. Sacrifice hits—Pratt, Collins. Stolen bases—Collins, Strunk. Double plays—Pratt to Lavan to Leary, Lavan to Leary, Crossin (unassisted), Wares to Pratt to Leary. Bases on balls—Off Weilman 4, off Baumgardner 4, off Shawkey 3. Struck out—By Weilman 2, by Baumgardner 2, by Shawkey 8. Time—3h. 8m. Umpires—Chill and Sheridan.

(SECOND GAME.)

Philadelphia captured the second game, 6 to 4. Collins scored the tieing run in the eighth inning by getting under a throw by Austin on McInnis' grounder. St. Louis protested hard and James and Agnew were benched by Umpire Chill.

Weilman and Crossin became St. Louis' battery, and the former handed out three passes, which with a triple steal by Strunk, Barry and Davies scored two more runs.

Davies, formerly of Amherst College, who twirled a fine game for Philadelphia, made his major league debut.

The scores:

PHILADELPHIA.	AB.	R.	BH.	TB.	PO.	A.	E.
Walsh, r f	3	1	1	1	1	0	0
Oldring, l f	4	1	0	0	1	0	0
Collins, 2b	2	1	1	1	2	8	0
Baker, 3b	4	0	3	4	1	4	0
McInnis, 1b	4	1	0	0	11	0	0
Strunk, c f	2	2	0	0	3	0	0
Barry, ss	4	0	2	2	1	2	2
Lapp, c	3	0	0	0	6	4	0
Schang, c	1	0	0	0	1	0	0
Davies, p	3	0	2	3	0	3	1
Totals	30	6	9	11	27	16	3

ST. LOUIS.	AB.	R.	BH.	TB.	PO.	A.	E.
Shotten, c f	4	1	1	1	3	0	0
Pratt, 2b	4	0	3	4	3	0	0
Williams, r f	2	0	1	1	1	1	0
Rumler, r f	2	0	1	1	1	0	0
C. Walker, l f	3	0	0	0	1	0	0
E. Walker, l f	0	0	0	0	0	0	0
Leary, 1b	4	1	0	0	6	1	0
Austin, 3b	3	0	0	0	0	1	1
Lavan, ss	3	1	1	1	2	5	1
Agnew, c	3	0	0	0	4	3	0
Crossin, c	1	0	0	0	3	0	0
James, p	1	1	1	1	0	1	0
Weilman, p	0	0	0	0	0	1	0
*Jenkins	1	0	0	0	0	0	0
Totals	31	4	8	9	24	13	2

*Batted for Lavan in the 9th.

Philadelphia ...... 0 0 2 1 0 0 0 3 .—6
St. Louis .... 1 0 0 0 0 1 2 0 0—4

Two-base hits—Pratt, Baker, Davies. Hits—Off James 9 in 7 innings. Sacrifice hit—C. Walker. Stolen bases—Leary, Strunk, Barry, Davies. Double plays—Agnew to Lavan, Leary to Lavan, Davies to Baker to Lapp, Baker to Collins to McInnis. Bases on balls—Off James 4, off Weilman 3, off Davies 3. Struck out—By James 2, by Weilman 1, by Davies 4. Passed balls—Agnew, Lapp. Time—2h. 25m. Umpires—Chill and Sheridan.

JINX BEATS INX AT CARTER FIELD DAY

Two hundred office and factory employees of the Carter's Ink Company of East Cambridge held their annual field day at the Riverside recreation grounds yesterday. A baseball game between the Inx and the Jinx was won by the Jinx. President Robert Carter played right field on the winning team.

STILL THEY COME

The Cincinnati Reds have still another outfield candidate. He is McLaughlin, who hails from Colgate University, and he is sent on by Scout Tom O'Hara, though just why has not yet appeared.

THE THREE NEW RED SOX PLAYERS PURCHASED FROM BALTIMORE

Catcher Egan. Pitcher Ruth. Pitcher Shore.

Stop White Sox Cry of Mackmen

Belief That Team That Beats Chicago Will Win American League Flag

Three weeks ago throughout the American league circuit swept the hurry call to beware the Red Sox and stop the Boston American league outfit from getting too close to the head of the procession.

In the fear inspired by the Boston team's great start on the recent Western trip, anxious managers, foreseeing a possible repetition of the triumphal swath cut by the Hub clan two seasons ago, urged each other to brace and repel the advance of the aggregation that Bill Carrigan leads.

SWEEPING ALL BEFORE

But the scene has change somewhat, and while the Red Sox are by no means out of it, the Sox team of a different hue has charged in to the limelight with an insistence that cannot be denied. Coming from the West with an impetus that has swept the Tigers, Naps and even Browns, the Chicago White Sox, headed by one of the greatest pitching staffs of recent years, has mounted the ladder with a speed that has diverted the anxious eyes of Connie Mack and his champions from the Fenway Park heroes. "Stop the White Sox" is now the cry.

Up to yesterday the Chicago team had won 17 of the last 20 games played. Less than a month ago, securely berthed, it would seem, in sixth place, the White Sox began a winning streak that has made them regarded as the most likely contenders with the Mackmen.

Detroit may be playing fine ball and the formerly despised Browns show a speed unkown to the Hedges tribe for years, but those who have seen Callahan's club perform this past week at Fenway Park are quite prepared to believe that the team that beats the White Sox out will surely grab the flag.

Began Against Red Sox

The winning streak of the White Sox began with the arrival of the Boston team in the Windy City on their last Western trip. Previous to this event the Chicago club, nearly disrupted by internal trouble and tormented by the Federal league and its agents, had suffered a slump which made it look like a certain second division finisher. When Boston reached the camp of the Comiskeyites the former had won 10 and lost but three games on the trip and a spirit of confidence permeated the entire Boston outfit. It was here that the Red Sox were temporarily halted and the White Sox began to climb.

After winning the first game from Chicago Boston reckoned on four victories out of the five games to be played, but at this juncture Chase conferred an everlasting favor on the club by jumping to the Federals. As a consequence the White Sox started to win, took the remaining four games from Boston, cleaned up pretty nearly with Detroit, St. Louis and Cleveland, and then headed East to resume its easy conquest of the Red Sox.

There is strong reason for making the White Sox favorites in the race just now. While outside of the pitching staff the baseball fan would hesitate to single out any of the team as real stars, it can be set down as positive that this aggregation is even now one of the best balanced and most aggressive teams in the American league.

Faber a Big Factor

It has the best pitching staff in its history and perhaps the greatest of all Callahan's twirlers is Red Faber, practically unknown to baseball till this year, yet now ranking as one of the greatest in the game. Some few weeks ago Faber accomplished the noteworthy feat of holding the Athletics to one scratch hit in nine innings. Since that time he has come with a rush and he promises to be the sensation of the year. At the present time he is doing the stunt previously enacted by Big Ed Walsh and Walter Johnson.

At the critical moment when his team ties the score or gets that one run edge he is jumped in by Callahan and he never fails to hold his opponents safe.

Next in effectiveness comes "Butcher" Benz, who has pitched one no-hit game this season and a couple of one-hit games. Also this great hurling staff reckons Jim Scott, Eddie Cicotte, Lefty Russell, Big Ed. Walsh and a couple of youngsters who can be sent in to work in a pinch.

But with Benz, Faber, Cicotte, Scott, Russell and Walsh ready to work in turn there is little chance for the youngsters getting into a game except at very remote periods.

Schalk a Wonder

Behind the bat the finest young catcher in the land performs. Ray Schalk, great last year but even greater this season, a splendid receiver, a brainy youngster, an accurate thrower and a fine batsman, eclipses anybody else in this position. So clever is Schalk that another first rate performer—Red Kuhn—gets little chance to work.

With Fournier improving in his work every day the Sox possess a better than average infield. Blackburne has at last come into his own and his batting, base running and fielding have cut a big figure in the team's recent remarkable showing. Weaver, the captain, is even excelling Blackburne, and a clever substitute in Berger can jump in and take either man's place.

At third is young Breton, a civil engineer and recent graduate of the University of Illinois. So well does Callahan think of him that he jumped him into Alcock's place before he had attained his diploma, and even when the team was starting to win Breton was grinding away at his final examinations.

Alcock is another substitute that can give a fine account of himself on the left-hand side of the diamond.

Strong in Outfield

In the outfield the present trio are performing admirably. There are few better ball players in the country than John Collins the right fielder. He is a consistently hard hitter, a fair base runner and fine ground coverer. He throws well also, and his all round work has been a big factor in the team success. Ping Bodie, not the fleetest of foot but a clever fielder and at times an exceptionally hard hitter is holding his job down regularly. In Ray Demmitt the White Sox have a very efficient left fielder and a hard hitter.

Furthermore within a fortnight or so young Chappelle the high-priced ball player purchased from the association last summer is expected to report. Misfortune has attended this player's career in the major league and a severe case of blood poisoning nearly cost him a leg this spring. He has now recovered from the ill effects of that malady and is now slowly getting into shape. When he does get into a uniform and into the game the Callahan tribe will look more formidable than ever.

OSTEGREN RELEASED TO FITCHBURG CLUB

One of the Red Sox tryouts was let go to the minors yesterday, as Ostegren, the former Holy Cross player and first baseman, has been sent to the Fitchburg club of the New England league to go through his baptism of fire. Ostegren is husky, quick, a good fielder and may develop as a hitter. If he does, he will be recalled in good time, but there is little chance of his displacing Janvrin and Gainer.

Fans Greet Duffy Lewis Enthusiastically

When Duffy Lewis, after making that all-important hit in the seventh, was sent out to displace Olaf Henriksen in left field, the fans welcomed him with a cheer that might be heard for blocks away. The team has sadly missed the hard-throwing and hard-hitting left fielder during these past 10 days. With Hooper back in the lineup on Monday, the Sox may be depended upon to play true to form.

BASEBALL IN BRIEF FORM

TOLD IN A NUTSHELL

(AMERICAN LEAGUE.)

	R.	H.	E.	Att'ce.
BOSTON	4	8	1	11,087
CLEVELAND	3	8	4	
NEW YORK	9	12	1	12,500
CHICAGO	4	8	4	
ST. LOUIS	4	16	1	
PHILADELPHIA	3	9	1	7,000
(First game, 12 innings.)				
PHILADELPHIA	6	9	3	
ST. LOUIS	4	8	2	
(Second game.)				
WASHINGTON	4	10	0	7,118
DETROIT	2	7	6	

(NATIONAL LEAGUE.)

	R.	H.	E.	Att'ce.
BOSTON	5	10	0	
CHICAGO	2	6	4	5,500
CINCINNATI	6	9	4	3,500
BROOKLYN	5	11	2	
NEW YORK	13	18	2	
ST. LOUIS	9	16	4	12,000
PITTSBURG	3	7	1	5,000
PHILADELPHIA	1	3	2	

(FEDERAL.)

	R.	H.	E.
INDIANAPOLIS	3	8	0
CHICAGO	2	3	3
BROOKLYN	1	5	0
PITTSBURG	0	3	2
(First game.)			
BROOKLYN	8	14	0
PITTSBURG	2	7	4
(Second game.)			
BALTIMORE	2	7	1
BUFFALO	1	8	0
(First game.)			
BUFFALO	3	12	1
BALTIMORE	3	8	5
(Second game, 13 innings.)			
ST. LOUIS	6	11	2
KANSAS CITY	3	7	3

(NEW ENGLAND.)

	R.	H.	E.
First game:			
LYNN	5	9	1
LAWRENCE	1	5	0
Second game, 7 innings:			
LAWRENCE	7	5	0
LYNN	3	6	4
First game:			
HAVERHILL	3	7	2
LOWELL	2	6	1
Second game, 7 innings:			
HAVERHILL	4	9	2
LOWELL	3	8	0
PORTLAND	10	14	3
WORCESTER	9	13	2
LEWISTON	5	12	4
FITCHBURG	4	12	3
(11 innings.)			

(COLONIAL.)

	R.	H.	E.
NEW BEDFORD	3	7	1
TAUNTON	1	3	4
(First game.)			
TAUNTON	5	4	0
NEW BEDFORD	1	4	2
(Second game.)			
FALL RIVER	12	13	4
WOONSOCKET	7	14	2
PAWTUCKET	5	8	3
BROCKTON	2	7	1
(First game.)			
PAWTUCKET	5	4	2
BROCKTON	4	8	1
(Second game.)			

GAMES TODAY

FEDERAL LEAGUE.

Kansas City at St. Louis.
Indianapolis at Chicago.

AMERICAN ASSOCIATION

At Louisville—Louisville 9, St. Paul 3.
At Indianapolis—Indianapolis 11, Milwaukee 5.
At Cleveland—Kansas City 15, Cleveland 9.
At Columbus—Columbus 14, Minneapolis 2.

SOUTHERN ASSOCIATION

Atlanta 4, Montgomery 8 (first game), Atlanta 3, Montgomery 3 (second game, 13 innings, darkness).
New Orleans 8, Memphis 4.
Mobile 11, Nashville 0.
Chattanooga 3, Birmingham 0 (first game), Birmingham 7, Chattanooga 5 (second game).

AMERICAN LEAGUE STANDING

	W.	L.	P.C.
Philadelphia	45	32	.584
Detroit	44	36	.550
Washington	42	35	.545
Chicago	41	35	.539
St. Louis	42	38	.525
Boston	41	38	.519
New York	28	45	.384
Cleveland	26	50	.342

Standing a Year Ago

	Won.	Lost.	Per Ct.
Philadelphia	56	20	.737
Cleveland	49	31	.613
Washington	44	36	.550
Chicago	43	38	.531
Boston	38	37	.493
St. Louis	33	52	.388
Detroit	32	52	.381
New York	23	52	.307

NATIONAL LEAGUE STANDING

	W.	L.	P.C.
New York	42	29	.592
Chicago	41	35	.539
St. Louis	40	37	.519
Cincinnati	37	38	.493
Philadelphia	34	36	.486
Brooklyn	33	37	.471
Pittsburg	33	38	.465
Boston	31	41	.431

Standing a Year Ago

	Won.	Lost.	Per Ct.
New York	50	24	.676
Philadelphia	41	30	.577
Chicago	41	37	.526
Pittsburg	38	39	.494
Brooklyn	35	37	.486
Boston	33	42	.440
St. Louis	33	45	.423
Cincinnati	31	48	.392

FEDERAL LEAGUE STANDING

	W.	L.	P.C.
Chicago	43	29	.597
Indianapolis	39	31	.557
Buffalo	37	31	.544
Brooklyn	35	34	.507
Baltimore	36	35	.507
Kansas City	34	42	.447
St. Louis	32	43	.427
Pittsburg	30	41	.423

N. E. LEAGUE STANDING

	Won.	Lost.	P.C.
Lawrence	37	24	.607
Worcester	35	23	.603
Portland	33	25	.569
Lynn	31	29	.517
Lowell	30	32	.484
Lewiston	28	31	.475
Haverhill	28	31	.475
Fitchburg	18	45	.286

COLONIAL LEAGUE STANDING

	Won.	Lost.	P.C.
Fall River	31	18	.633
New Bedford	28	21	.571
Pawtucket	26	23	.531
Woonsocket	25	23	.521
Taunton	18	29	.383
Brockton	18	32	.360

GAMES TODAY

NATIONAL LEAGUE.

Boston at St. Louis.
New York at Chicago.
Philadelphia at Cincinnati.

GIANTS WIN WEIRD SLUGGING CONTEST

Cards and New Yorkers Hit for Total of 60 Bases

ST. LOUIS, July 11.—New York won today from St. Louis, 13 to 9, in a weird contest, in which 25 players took part. Thirty-four hits, for a total of 60 bases, were made. Wilson, Dolan, Doyle and Cruise, the latter a pinch hitter, each hit for home runs.

The score:

NEW YORK	AB.	R.	BH.	TB.	PO.	A.	E.
Bescher, c f	5	1	1	1	1	0	0
Doyle, 2b	5	1	2	5	2	2	1
Burns, l f	5	3	3	4	4	0	0
Snodgrass, r f, 1b	5	2	2	3	9	1	0
Fletcher, ss	5	1	2	3	1	4	0
Merkle, 1b	2	0	1	2	5	0	0
Murray, r f	3	3	2	4	2	0	0
Meyers, c	4	1	3	3	2	1	0
Stock, 3b	4	0	1	2	0	5	0
Mathewson, p	4	1	1	1	1	3	1
Totals	42	13	18	28	27	16	2

ST. LOUIS.	AB.	R.	BH.	TB.	PO.	A.	E.
Huggins, 2b	4	1	0	0	4	1	1
Magee, c f	5	2	4	6	3	1	0
Dolan, l f	5	1	2	5	1	0	0
J. Miller, 1b	5	0	1	3	9	0	0
Wilson, r f	4	1	1	4	3	0	0
Beck, 3b	4	1	2	4	4	2	0
Wingo, c	4	0	2	2	3	4	1
Butler, ss	4	1	2	3	0	2	1
Sallee, p	1	1	1	1	0	1	0
Griner, p	0	0	0	0	0	0	0
aC. Miller	1	0	0	0	0	0	0
Steele, p	1	0	0	0	0	0	0
Niehaus, p	0	0	0	0	0	0	1
bCruise	1	1	1	4	0	0	0
cDressen	1	0	0	0	0	0	0
Totals	40	9	16	32	27	11	4

aBatted for Sallee in 5th. bBatted for Niehaus in 9th. cBatted for Huggins in 9th.

New York ...... 0 0 0 0 4 2 4 0 3—13
St. Louis ...... 0 1 3 0 1 1 2 0 1— 9

Two-base hits—Butler, Fletcher, Merkle, Burns, Stock, Snodgrass. Three-base hits—Beck, J. Miller, Murray, Magee. Home runs—Wilson, Dolan, Doyle, Cruise. Sacrifice fly—Stock. Stolen bases—Magee, Bescher, Murray, Burns, Snodgrass. Double plays—Doyle to Merkle, Mathewson to Snodgrass. Base on balls—Off Niehaus 1. Struck out—By Sallee 1, by Steele 1, by Mathewson 11. Hits—Off Sallee 7 in 5 innings, off Griner 3 in 2-3 inning, off Steele 7 in 2 1-3 innings, off Niehaus 1 in 1 inning. Time—2h. 25m. Umpires—Quigley and Eason.

GOOD SHIP MEOW WINS RACE AT GLOUCESTER

GLOUCESTER, July 11.—Priscilla Smith, captain of the good ship Meow, put it all over the members of the Annisquam Yacht Club in this afternoon's race and handily defeated her old rival, Gertrude Wiggin. Priscilla came across the finish line a winner by almost three minutes and away down at the end, the very end, was Gertrude Wiggin, disappointed but with a smile on her face.

The race between the Princess and the Snipe in the 15-foot class was particularly exciting, the Princess coming across with the bowsprit of the Snipe poking over her stern.

CLASS T—15-FOOTERS.

Name and owner.	El. time.
Nisan II., D. H. Woodbury	1:26:00
Princess, J. P. Prince	1:30:41
Snipe, Sherburne Wiggin	1:30:42

15-FOOT CATS.

Meow, Priscilla Smith	1:05:50
Scat, Windsor Gale	1:07:46
Katzenjammer, Jack Hooper	1:10:20
Katchmie, W. O. Adams	1:11:58
Catalan, Harry Duane	1:12:42
Cataline, James Guiler	1:13:10
Paws, Mary Damon	1:13:25
Kittiewake, C. L. Hight	1:14:20
Catspaw, Gertrude Wiggin	1:14:30
Katrina, H. D. Williams	Withdrew

13-FOOT DOGS.

Tyke, Sam Gordon	1:50:20
Bowwow, Sumner Andrew	Withdrew
Growler, Donald Simmons	Withdrew

Portland Downs League Leaders

Wins in Ninth With Two Out—Hickman Makes Deciding Hit

PORTLAND, Me., July 11.—Portland won from Worcester this afternoon, 10 to 9, in a game that abounded in sensations. With the score 8 to 1 against them, the Worcester players fell on Mayberry in the seventh and batted in four runs. In the ninth, with one run scored, the bases full and none out, Watkins displaced Mayberry and struck out the first two men. A hit by Roes followed, sending in two runs, and two bases on balls forced in another. This gave the visitors a lead of one. In Portland's half, with two out, Dowell, Whitehouse and McClesky, who batted in place of Lonergan, singled in succession. With the bases full, Hickman drove the ball to right, scoring two runs. Whitehouse just reached the plate ahead of the ball.

The score:

PORTLAND.	BH.	PO.	A.	E.	WORCESTER.	BH.	PO.	A.	E.
Burns, cf	2	1	0	0	Carroll, c	1	3	0	0
Clemens, lf	0	2	0	0	Shorten, rf	2	1	0	0
Bowcock, 2b	2	2	4	1	Strands, 3b	2	1	0	0
Dowell, 1b	2	13	0	0	Potteiger, cf	3	3	0	0
Whiteh'e, rf	2	0	0	0	McCune, 1b	0	6	1	0
Lonergan, ss	0	1	3	2	Roes, lf	1	1	0	0
Hickm'n, 3b	4	0	1	0	Dowd, 2b	2	6	2	1
Hayden, c	0	8	0	0	Cooney, ss	1	5	2	1
Mayberry, p	1	0	7	0	Van Dyke, p	0	0	2	0
Watkins, p	0	0	0	0	Gaw, p	1	0	3	0
aMcCleskey	1	0	0	0					
Totals	14	27	15	3	Totals	13	b26	9	2

aBatted for Lonergan in ninth. bTwo out when winning run made.

Portland ...... 1 4 1 0 0 2 0 0 2—10
Worcester ...... 0 0 1 0 0 0 4 0 4— 9

Runs—Burns, Clemens, Bowcock, Dowell, Whitehouse, Lonergan 2, Hickman 2, Hayden, Carroll 2, Shorten 2, Strands, Dowd 2, Gaw 2. Two-base hits—Bowcock, Hickman, Shorten, Dowd 2. Three-base hit—Potteiger. Hits—Off Mayberry 12 in 8 innings (none out in ninth), off Watkins 1 in 1 inning, off Van Dyke 5 in 1 2-3 innings, off Gaw 9 in 7 innings (one out in ninth when winning run was made). Sacrifice hits—Hayden, Mayberry, Carroll. Stolen bases—Burns, Hayden, Dowd. Double plays—Lonergan to Bowcock to Dowell, Cooney to Dowd to McCune. Bases on balls—Off Mayberry 1, off Watkins 2, off Van Dyke 1, off Gaw 2. Struck out—By Mayberry 3, by Watkins 3, by Gaw 2. Time—2h. 10m. Umpire—Bannon.

LYNN AND LAWRENCE EACH GET A GAME

LYNN, July 11.—Durning and Pearson both pitched fine ball today, the former winning the first game of a double-header for Lynn by a score of 5 to 1, while Pearson gave Lawrence an even break by holding the home team in the second, the visitors winning 7 to 3 in seven innings.

The scores:

LYNN.	BH.	PO.	A.	E.	LAWRENCE.	BH.	PO.	A.	E.
Porter, rf	2	2	0	0	O'Connell, cf	0	1	0	0
Merrill, lf	1	2	0	0	Lynch, ss	2	2	3	0
Moulton, 2b	0	2	2	0	Luyster, rf	0	1	0	0
Murphy, c	1	3	1	0	Bruggy, c	1	3	2	0
Orcutt, cf	2	4	0	0	Mahoney, 2b	0	2	3	0
Courtney, 1b	1	10	0	0	Conley, 3b	1	1	4	0
Sheehan, 3b	1	1	2	0	Peploski, lf	0	0	0	0
Fahey, ss	1	2	3	1	Aubrey, 1b	0	14	0	0
Durning, p	0	1	3	0	Fullerton, p	1	0	2	0
					*Pearson	0	0	0	0
Totals	9	27	9	1	Totals	5	24	14	0

*Batted for Fullerton in 9th.

Lynn ...... 0 1 0 2 2 0 0 0 .—5
Lawrence ...... 0 1 0 0 0 0 0 0 0—1

Runs—Porter, Murphy, Orcutt 2, Durning, Peploski. Two-base hit—Orcutt. Three-base hits—Murphy, Porter. Sacrifice hits—Luyster, Aubrey. Stolen bases—Orcutt 2. Bases on balls—Off Durning 4. Struck out—By Durning 3, by Fullerton 8. Time—1h. 50m. Umpire—Keeler.

SECOND GAME.

LAWRENCE.	BH.	PO.	A.	E.	LYNN.	BH.	PO.	A.	E.
Peploski, lf	0	0	0	0	Porter, rf	1	2	0	0
Lynch, ss	0	3	2	0	Merrill, lf	1	1	0	1
Luyster, rf	0	1	0	0	Moulton, 2b	0	0	1	1
Bruggy, c	0	8	0	0	Murphy, c	3	3	2	1
Mahoney, 2b	1	2	1	0	Orcutt, cf	0	2	0	0
Conley, 3b	1	0	1	0	Courtney, 1b	0	12	0	0
O'Connell, cf	1	1	0	0	Sheehan, 3b	0	0	3	1
Aubrey, 1b	1	8	0	0	Fahey, ss	0	1	6	0
Pearson, p	0	0	3	0	Dedrich, p	0	0	3	0
Totals	5	21	7	0	Totals	6	21	15	4

Lawrence ...... 0 2 0 2 0 1 2—7
Lynn ...... 0 0 2 0 0 1 0—3

Runs—Lynch, Luyster, Bruggy, Mahoney, O'Connell 2, Aubrey, Porter, Murphy, Fahey. Two-base hits—Porter, Conley, Luyster, Murphy. Sacrifice hit—Dedrich. Stolen bases—Bruggy, Aubrey, Conley. Double play—Lynch to Aubrey. Bases on balls—Off Dedrich 5, off Pearson 1. Struck out—By Dedrich 2, by Pearson 8. Passed ball—Murphy. Time—1h. 30m. Umpire—Keeler.

HAVERHILL WINS TWO

HAVERHILL, July 11.—Haverhill came from behind in both games of a double-header with Lowell today, winning both contests in the final inning. The scores were 3 to 1 and 4 to 3. McMahon's double and Wilson's fine bunt defeated Lowell in the first game, while in the second, a seven-inning affair, three doubles after one man was out gave Haverhill the game.

Umpire Doherty was overcome by the heat after the first game and players gave the decisions in the final contest.

The scores:

HAVERHILL.	BH.	PO.	A.	E.	LOWELL.	BH.	PO.	A.	E.
Campb'll, 2b	1	1	0	0	Dee, ss	2	2	5	0
Gaston, c	0	4	1	0	DeGroff, rf	1	2	0	0
Howard, cf	1	3	0	0	Mathews, cf	0	0	0	0
Duggan, lf	1	2	0	0	Stimpson, lf	2	0	0	0
Smith, 1b	0	7	0	0	Burke, 3b	0	0	3	1
Yelle, 3b	2	1	5	0	Cargo, 2b	0	4	3	0
M'Mahon, ss	1	4	2	0	Kelly, 1b	1	10	0	0
Wil'n, rf, 2b	1	4	0	1	Wacob, c	0	6	0	0
Flah'y, c, 2b	0	0	0	0	Maybohm, p	0	0	2	0
Southern, p	0	0	2	1	Shenk, p	0	0	1	0
Totals	7	27	10	2	Totals	6	*24	14	1

*None out when winning run was scored.

Haverhill ...... 0 0 0 0 0 0 2 0 1—3
Lowell ...... 1 0 0 0 0 0 0 1 0—2

Runs—Duggan, Smith, McMahon, Dee, Stimpson. Two-base hits—Campbell, McMahon. Home runs—Dee, Stimpson. Hits—Off Maybohm 5 in 5 2-3 innings, off Shenk 2 in 3 1-3 innings. Stolen base—DeGroff. Double plays—Dee to Cargo to Kelly 2, Shenk to Dee to Kelly. Bases on balls—Off Southern 1, off Maybohm 5. Struck out—By Southern 4, by Maybohm 5, by Shenk 1. Wild pitch—Southern. Time—2h. Umpire—Doherty.

(SECOND GAME.)

HAVERHILL.	BH.	PO.	A.	E.	LOWELL.	BH.	PO.	A.	E.
Wilson, 2b	2	0	2	2	Dee, ss	2	4	3	0
Howard, cf	1	5	0	0	DeGroff, rf	2	0	0	0
Duggan, lf	3	1	0	0	Mathews, cf	1	2	1	0
Smith, 1b	0	7	0	0	Stimpson, lf	0	0	0	0
Yelle, 3b	0	0	2	0	Burke, 3b	1	1	0	0
M'Mahon, ss	1	2	2	0	Cargo, 2b	0	0	3	0
Flaherty, rf	0	0	0	0	Kelly, 1b	1	10	0	0
Gaston, c	2	6	4	0	Greenbalge, c	0	2	2	0
Reiger, p	0	0	3	0	Cook, p	1	0	3	0
Totals	9	21	13	2	Totals	8	*19	12	0

*One out when winning run scored.

Haverhill ...... 0 0 1 0 1 0 2—4
Lowell ...... 0 0 1 0 1 1 0—3

Runs—Wilson 2, Howard, Gaston, Dee, Burke, Cook. Two-base hits—Gaston, Wilson, Howard, Mathews. Home run—Burke. Sacrifice hit—Mathews. Stolen bases—Duggan 2, Howard 2. Bases on balls—Off Reiger 3, off Cook 4. Struck out—By Reiger 4, by Cook 2. Passed ball—Gaston. Time—1h. 50m. Umpires—Southern and Wacob.

LEWISTON 5, FITCHBURG 4

LEWISTON, Me., July 11.—Lewiston's batting rally in the 11th defeated Fitchburg here today 5 to 4. A hit by Thomas, a three-bagger by Brignolia and a hit by Mundy, with no one out, was responsible for the scoring. Fitchburg tied the score in the eighth.

The score:

LEWISTON.	BH.	PO.	A.	E.	FITCHBURG.	BH.	PO.	A.	E.
Mundy, rf	1	0	0	0	Kane, cf	0	3	0	1
Judge, 1b	1	9	0	0	Spires, 3b	0	2	0	0
Maloney, lf	0	7	0	0	Reed, rf	2	2	0	0
Casey, c	5	7	2	0	Sweatt, 2b	1	1	1	0
Phoenix, 2b	0	2	2	2	Kilhullen, c	2	8	0	0
Shea, cf	1	4	0	1	*Torphy, 1b	1	9	0	0
O'Co'nell, 3b	0	2	3	0	King, lf	1	4	0	0
Thomas, ss	2	1	4	1	Cooney, ss	2	1	6	2
Brignolia, p	2	1	8	0	Condon, p	1	0	1	0
					Scanlon, p	2	0	1	0
Totals	12	33	14	4	Totals	12	30	9	3

Lewiston ...0 2 0 1 0 0 0 0 0 0 2—5
Fitchburg ...0 2 0 0 0 0 0 1 0 0 1—4

Runs—Casey, Shea, O'Connell, Thomas, Brignolia, Sweatt, King, Cooney, Scanlon. Two-base hits—Kilhullen, Sweatt. Three-base hits—Condon, Reed, Brignolia. Hits—Off Condon 2, off Scanlon 10. Sacrifice hits—Torphy, Mundy, Phoenix. Stolen bases—Casey, Thomas. Double play—Thomas to Phoenix to Judge. Bases on balls—Off Condon 1, off Scanlon 1. Struck out—By Scanlon 3, by Brignolia 5. Time—2h. Umpire—Black.

FITCHBURG MAN SHOOT WINNER

S. W. Putnam Now Holds N. E. Trap Title

PORTLAND, Me., July 11.—S. W. Putnam of Fitchburg, Mass., won the New England amateur championship at trap shooting at today's tournament, breaking 98 targets in 100. E. A. Randall of Portland was high gun for the day with a score of 193 out of 200.

The cup for highest average for the two days of the tournament was won by C. H. Randall with a total of 384 targets out of 400. W. G. Hill of Portland won in competition with the professionals, his score being 385 out of 400.

FINAL TEST FOR DAVIS CUP MEN

26 Players to Begin Matches on Monday

SEABRIGHT, N. J., July 11.—The draw for the singles matches which will afford final practice for the tennis stars before the selection of the United States Davis cup team was made here today by B. S. Prentice, who will act as referee of the tournament, along with R. D. Wrenn, G. T. Adee and H. W. Slocum, the Davis cup committee.

26 TO START

Twenty-six players are drawn to begin play Monday. Maurice E. McLaughlin, national champion, is not in the list, as he appears only in the doubles with T. C. Bundy.

The draw follows:

Seabright singles (second round—first round byes)—Dean Mathey vs. G. F. Touchard.

First round—G. L. Wrenn vs. G. P. Gardner, Jr.; W. M. Johnston vs. Robert Leroy, Leonard Beekman vs. A. S. Dabney, G. M. Church vs. N. W. Niles, Hugh Tallant vs. H. L. Hackett, W. J. Clothier vs. W. M. Hall, R. L. Murray vs. R. Harte, W. F. Johnson vs. S. S. Marden, W. M. Washburn vs. F. C. Inman, R. Norris Williams, 2d, vs. L. E. Mahan.

Second round—first round byes—K. H. Behr vs. W. A. Larned, B. S. Prentice vs. T. C. Bundy.

TRADE DERRICK FOR MOLLWITZ

Cincinnati-Chicago Deal Finally Completed

CINCINNATI, July 11.—President August Herrmann of the Cincinnati National league baseball club announced today that the deal for an exchange of players between the Cincinnati and Chicago National league clubs had been satisfactorily arranged.

By the agreement reached between Herrmann and Charles P. Taft, owners of the Chicago team, the latter club is to get Shortstop Claude Derrick in exchange for First Baseman Mollwitz. Cincinnati is also to get a money consideration, but Outfielder Williams is not included in the deal.

CONFIRMS DEAL

CHICAGO, July 11.—President Thomas of the Chicago National league baseball club this afternoon confirmed the announcement of the Derrick-Mollwitz trade, and added that Derrick would be in Chicago tomorrow and would play in the Chicago-New York series. He added that Mollwitz would start for Cincinnati tonight.

SENATORS DEFEAT TIGERS IN OPENER

Give Boehling Errorless Support and Hit Well

WASHINGTON, July 11.—Hits combined with errors in the first and fourth innings gave Washington a 4-to-2 victory over Detroit today. Two singles and two errors gave Washington a run in the first inning. Milan's double, a single and two bases on balls added three more runs in the fourth. Boehling pitched a good game, striking out four men and giving but one pass. He was aided by errorless support.

WASHINGTON.	AB.	R.	BH.	TB.	PO.	A.	E.
Moeller, r f	3	1	2	2	3	0	0
Foster, 3b	4	1	0	0	1	2	0
Milan, c f	4	1	3	3	1	0	0
Williams, 1b	4	1	2	2	9	1	0
Shanks, l f	2	0	1	1	1	0	0
Morgan, 2b	3	0	0	0	2	4	0
McBride, ss	2	0	0	0	4	6	0
Henry, c	3	0	1	1	5	1	0
Boehling, p	2	0	1	1	1	2	0
Totals	25	4	10	10	27	16	0

DETROIT.	AB.	R.	BH.	TB.	PO.	A.	E.
Bush, ss	4	0	0	0	3	1	3
Purtell, 3b	4	0	1	1	4	2	1
Hellman, c f	3	0	1	1	0	0	0
Crawford, r f	4	0	2	2	0	0	0
Veach, l f	4	1	2	4	1	0	0
Kavanaugh, 2b	4	0	1	1	1	3	0
Burns, 1b	3	0	0	0	11	1	2
Stanage, c	2	0	0	0	3	4	0
Baker, c	1	0	0	0	1	1	0
Dauss, p	2	0	0	0	0	1	0
Hall, p	0	0	0	0	0	1	0
Reynolds, p	0	0	0	0	0	0	0
aDubuc	1	0	0	0	0	0	0
bHigh	0	1	0	0	0	0	0
Totals	32	2	7	9	24	14	6

aBatted for Hall in the 8th. bRan for Hellman in the 9th.

Washington ...... 1 0 0 3 0 0 0 0 .—4
Detroit ...... 0 1 0 0 0 0 0 0 1—2

Two-base hits—Veach 2, Milan. Hits—Off Dauss 5 in 4 innings, off Hall 4 in 3 innings, off Reynolds 1 in 1 inning. Sacrifice hits—Shanks 2, Morgan, Boehling, Moeller. Stolen bases—Foster. Double plays—Purtell to Burns to Purtell, McBride to Morgan to Williams. Bases on balls—Off Dauss 2, off Hall 1, off Boehling 1. Struck out—By Dauss 3, by Hall 1, by Boehling 4. Time—1h. 45m. Umpires—Egan and Evans.

RUTH CREDITED WITH WIN IN HIS DEBUT IN THE HUB

(Continued from Page One S.)

ly jogged home. Janvrin filed to Chapman.

Ruth in the second and third had the Naps under his thumb, retiring them in order, with the Red Sox doing not much better off Mitchell in their half of these same innings.

Speaker Drops Graney's Fly.

The fourth saw both sides engaged in the run-getting game. Cleveland started it when Speaker dropped Graney's fly after a hard run, Graney bringing up on second base, with Turner neatly sacrificing him to third. Then Jackson singled and Graney was a run-getter. Speaker got under Lajoie's fly ball. With two down, Kirke's single sent Jackson to third, but Chapman was an easy out, Yerkes to Janvrin.

The score was now tied, but it didn't remain so long. Gardner, first up on the Sox side, singled. Janvrin sacrificed the third baseman to second. Rehg was out, Turner to Kirke, Gardner taking third. Yerkes walked and then started to steal. O'Neill, after holding Gardner at third, whipped to second, but the throw was wild and Gardner tore home in safety. Carrigan had his catching togs all on, not thinking he would get a time at bat, but he ripped them off in an instant, and the next had the ball in left field for a single, Yerkes scoring from second. Ruth flied to Jackson, who made a grand catch.

Tie Score in Seventh.

The score was now 3 to 1 in Boston's favor, and there it remained through the fifth and sixth innings, although in the sixth Gardner and Janvrin, leading off, both got singles and were moved to third on Rehg's out. Yerkes and Carrigan failed to bring in the pair.

The seventh threatened to be disastrous for the Red Sox, with the Naps tieing up the score before Boston could get a chance at bat. 'Twas in this inning that the Naps began hitting Ruth. Kirke and Chapman both singled. Leibold bunted to Gardner, whose nice throw resulted in the retirement of the batsman, but put both base-runners in a position to score on O'Neill's hit to left. Mitchell hit into a Yerkes-to-Janvrin double play, ending the visitors' half.

At this stage Duffy Lewis was sent in to bat for Ruth, and after the inning was over Lewis trotted out in left field, finishing the game in his old position.

Speaker's Timely Single.

Lewis's hit was a hot liner toward Kirke, who made a lunge for it and got the ball, but fell down in the attempt. Mitchell ran to cover the bag, but by the time Kirke had recovered himself sufficiently to make the throw Lewis was already there. Kirke nevertheless whipped the ball to first. The throw was wide and wild and Duffy ran to second base, from which position he watched Henriksen pop to Graney. Scott hit to Mitchell and Lewis was eventually run down between second and third, Scott getting to second on the run-down. At this stage Speaker scored his timely tap, a single to left, and Scott chased home with the winning run. Speaker was thrown out stealing.

Then Leonard went into the box and retired the Cleveland club in short order in the eighth and ninth innings, but in no shorter order than did Mitchell the Red Sox in the last of the eighth. In one hour and 35 minutes from the time play had started hostilities were over with the Red Sox a winner.

AMERICAN LEAGUE

YESTERDAY'S RESULTS.

At Boston—Boston 4, Cleveland 3.
At Philadelphia—First game, St. Louis 4, Philadelphia 3 (12 innings); second game, Philadelphia 6, St. Louis 4.
At Washington—Washington 4, Detroit 2.
At New York—New York 9, Chicago 4.

STANDING OF THE CLUBS.

	Won.	Lost.	P.C.
Philadelphia	45	32	.584
Detroit	44	36	.550
Washington	42	35	.545
Chicago	41	35	.539
St. Louis	42	38	.525
BOSTON	41	38	.519
New York	28	45	.384
Cleveland	26	50	.342

BOSTON.	ab.	r.	bh.	tb.	po.	a.	e.
Henriksen, lf	4	0	0	0	0	0	0
Leonard, p	0	0	0	0	0	0	0
Scott, ss	4	1	1	1	2	3	0
Speaker, cf	4	1	1	1	3	1	1
Gardner, 3b	4	1	3	5	1	4	0
Janvrin, 1b	3	0	1	1	15	2	0
Rehg, rf	4	0	0	0	0	0	0
Yerkes, 2b	2	1	0	0	0	6	0
Carrigan, c	2	0	1	1	6	0	0
Ruth, p	2	0	0	0	0	4	0
Lewis, lf	0	0	1	1	0	0	0
Totals	29	4	8	10	27	21	1
CLEVELAND.							
Graney, lf	4	1	2	2	4	0	0
Turner, 3	3	0	0	0	2	4	0
Jackson, rf	4	0	2	2	1	0	0
Lajoie, 2b	4	0	0	0	0	0	0
Kirke, 1b	4	1	2	2	5	2	1
Chapman, s	4	1	1	1	3	1	0
Leibold, cf	2	0	0	0	2	0	0
O'Neill, c	3	0	1	1	6	2	2
Mitchell, p	3	0	0	0	1	1	1
Totals	31	3	8	8	24	10	4

Innings	1	2	3	4	5	6	7	8	9	
Boston	1	0	0	2	0	0	1	0	..	—4
Cleveland	0	0	0	1	0	0	2	0	0	—3

Three-base hit—Gardner. Sacrifice hits—Turner, Leibold, Janvrin. Stolen bases—Yerkes, Speaker. First base on balls—Yerkes, Carrigan. First base on error—Cleveland. Left on bases—Boston 5, Cleveland 3. Struck out—Henriksen, Scott, Janvrin, Carrigan, Ruth; by Ruth, Mitchell; by Leonard, Graney, Turner, Kirke, Chapman. Double plays—Scott to Janvrin. Time—1h. 35m. Umpires—Connolly and O'Loughlin. Attendance—11,087.

Red Sox $27,500 Trio of Players Arriving Yesterday

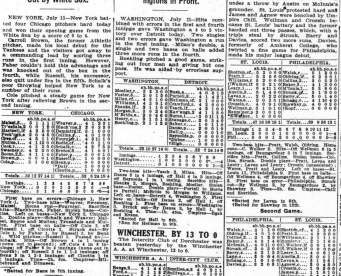

From Left to Right—Pitcher Babe Ruth, Regarded the Most Sensational Twirler Uncovered This Season; Catcher Ben Egan, Formerly with Athletics; Pitcher Shore, a Right-hander Who Is Counted a Comer.

YANKS BAT FOUR PITCHERS FOR GAME

At That They Are Lucky, for Their Own Man Is Knocked Out by White Sox.

NEW YORK, July 11—New York batted four Chicago pitchers hard today and won their opening game from the White Sox by a score of 9 to 4.

Carroll Brown, the former Athletic pitcher, made his local debut for the Yankees and the visitors got away to a commanding lead by scoring three runs in the first inning. However, Faber couldn't hold this advantage and was knocked out of the box in the fourth, while Russell, his successor, also quit under fire in the fifth. Schalk's poor throwing helped New York to a number of their runs.

Cole pitched a steady game for New York after relieving Brown in the second inning.

NEW YORK.	ab.	bh.	po.	a.	e.	CHICAGO.	ab.	bh.	po.	a.	e.
Maisel,3	3	1	1	1	1	Weaver,s	4	1	2	3	1
Tr'esdale,2	0	0	1	2	0	Black'rne,2	2	0	2	5	0
Hartzell,lf	4	2	8	0	0	Demmitt,lf	3	1	0	0	0
Peck'ugh,s	2	0	4	5	0	Collins,r	4	0	1	0	0
Cree,cf	4	3	1	1	0	Fournier,1	4	3	11	1	0
Mullen,1	4	1	12	0	0	Bodie,cf	4	0	1	1	0
Cook,r	4	1	2	0	0	Schalk,c	4	2	7	5	2
Sweeney,c	4	2	2	0	0	Breton,3	4	1	0	0	1
Boone,2,3	4	1	1	4	0	Faber,p	0	0	0	1	0
Brown,p	0	0	0	1	0	Russell,p	1	0	0	0	0
Cole,p	3	1	0	0	0	Benz,p	0	0	0	0	0
						*Daly	1	0	0	0	0
						Cicotte,p	1	0	0	3	0
Totals	32	12	27	14	1	Totals	32	8	24	19	4

Innings	1	2	3	4	5	6	7	8	9	
New York	0	3	0	2	2	0	2	0	.	—9
Chicago	3	1	0	0	0	0	0	0	0	—4

First base on errors—Chicago 1, New York 1. Two-base hits—Weaver, Sweeney, Maisel. Home run—Fournier. Sacrifice hits—Blackburne, Faber. Stolen base—Collins. Left on bases—New York 2, Chicago 5. Double plays—Schalk and Weaver; Maisel, Boone and Mullen; Truesdale and Mullen. First base on balls—Off Cole 2, off Russell 1, off Cicotte 2. Struck out—By Cole 1, by Faber 1, by Russell 2, by Benz 1. Wild pitches—Russell 2. Passed ball—Schalk. Hits—Off Brown 4 in 1 inning (none out in second); off Cole 4 in 8 innings; off Faber 6 in 3 innings (none out in fourth); off Russell 3 in 1 1-3 innings; off Benz 3 in 1 2-3 innings; off Cicotte 1 in 2 innings. Time—2h. 6m. Umpires—Hildebrand and Dinneen.

*Batted for Benz in 7th inning.

SENATORS SCORE OVER THE TIGERS

Hits Combined with Errors in Early Innings Put Washingtons in Front.

WASHINGTON, July 11—Hits combined with errors in the first and fourth innings gave Washington a 4 to 2 victory over Detroit today. Two singles and two errors gave Washington a run in the first inning. Milan's double, a single and two bases on balls added three more runs in the fourth.

Boehling pitched a good game, striking out four men and giving but one pass. He was aided by errorless support.

WASHINGTON.	ab.	bh.	po.	a.	e.	DETROIT.	ab.	bh.	po.	a.	e.
Moeller,r	3	2	3	0	0	Bush,s	4	0	3	1	3
Foster,3	2	0	1	2	0	Purtell,3	4	1	4	2	1
Milan,cf	4	3	1	0	0	Heilman,cf	3	1	0	0	0
Williams,1	4	2	9	1	0	Crawford,r	4	2	0	0	0
Shanks,lf	2	1	1	0	0	Veach,lf	4	2	1	0	0
Morgan,2	3	0	2	4	0	Kav'augh,2	4	1	1	3	0
M'Bride,s	2	0	4	6	0	Burns,1	3	0	11	1	2
Henry,c	3	1	5	1	0	Stanage,c	2	0	3	4	0
Boehling,p	2	1	1	2	0	Baker,c	1	0	1	1	0
						Dauss,p	2	0	0	1	0
						Hall,p	0	0	0	1	0
						Reynolds,p	0	0	0	0	0
						*Dubuc	1	0	0	0	0
						†High	0	0	0	0	0
Totals	25	10	27	16	0	Totals	32	7	24	14	6

Innings	1	2	3	4	5	6	7	8	9	
Washington	1	0	0	3	0	0	0	0	..	—4
Detroit	0	1	0	0	0	0	0	0	1	—2

Two-base hits—Veach 2, Milan. Hits—Off Dauss 5 in 4 innings, off Hall 4 in 3 innings, off Reynolds 1 in 1 inning. Sacrifice hits—Shanks 2, Morgan, Boehling, Moeller. Stolen base—Foster. Double plays—Purtell to Burns to Purtell; McBride to Morgan to Williams. Left on bases—Detroit 4, Washington 5. First base on balls—Off Dauss 2, off Hall 1, off Boehling 1. First base on errors—Washington 3. Struck out—By Dauss 3, by Hall 1, by Boehling 4. Time—1h. 45m. Umpires—Egan and Evans.

*Batted for Hall in 8th.
†Ran for Heilman in 9th.

MAYNARD BLANKS S. ACTON

MAYNARD, July 11—Everett Hardy, the old Harvard pitcher, had the South Acton team eating out of his hand this afternoon and Maynard won, 4 to 0. Hardy allowed but two hits, while Bond after being banged for eight safeties and four runs in the first two innings tightened up and didn't allow a hit thereafter. Wilder, formerly with the Haverhill club of the New England League, played a fine game for the home club.

MAYNARD.	ab.	bh.	po.	a.	e.	SOUTH ACTON.	ab.	bh.	po.	a.	e.
Ryan,lf	4	1	2	0	0	Hayes,r	4	0	0	0	0
Lent,3	4	1	1	1	1	Bixby,1	4	0	9	0	2
Wilder,c	4	2	9	1	0	Blues,s	3	0	0	1	1
Flaherty,r	4	2	2	0	0	Jamieson,c	3	0	12	2	0
Woods,1	4	1	6	0	1	Patterson,3	4	2	2	1	0
Murray,s	4	1	0	4	0	M'Carthy,2	3	0	0	4	0
Rain'lle,cf	3	0	1	0	0	Foley,cf	1	0	0	1	0
Brayden,2	3	0	5	1	0	Schultz,lf	3	0	0	0	0
Hardy,p	3	0	0	2	0	Bond,p	3	0	1	2	0
Totals	33	8	27	9	2	Totals	28	2	24	11	3

Innings	1	2	3	4	5	6	7	8	9	
Maynard	2	2	0	0	0	0	0	0	..	—4

Runs—Ryan, Lent, Wilder, Flaherty. Two-base hits—Ryan, Patterson. Stolen bases—Flaherty, Murray. First base on balls—Off Hardy 3. Struck out—By Bond 11, by Hardy 6. Time—1h. 40m. Umpire—Sebastian.

EVERETT TEAM WINS

The Everett baseball team defeated East Boston rather easily on Everett High school field, yesterday afternoon, 8 to 4.

EVERETT B. B.	ab.	bh.	po.	a.	e.	EAST BOSTON.	ab.	bh.	po.	a.	e.
Bennett,2	4	0	2	1	1	Flaherty,s	5	1	0	1	2
Mansur,s	4	2	0	3	1	Powers,2	4	0	0	1	0
O'Neil,lf	2	1	2	1	0	Rice,1	4	2	12	0	1
Cossette,1	3	0	9	1	0	Pettine,r	4	2	1	0	0
Drummy,cf	4	2	3	0	0	Murphy,cf	3	0	1	0	0
Devere,2	3	0	6	2	1	WPowers,lf	3	0	2	1	1
Gilbert,p	4	2	2	2	0	Masuchi,3	4	0	1	1	1
Driscoll,3	3	1	3	1	1	TFlaherty,c	4	2	7	1	0
Cahill,r	4	0	0	0	0	Buzzy,p	3	0	0	6	0
Totals	31	8	27	11	4	Totals	34	7	24	11	5

Innings	1	2	3	4	5	6	7	8	9	
Everett B. B. C.	0	1	0	0	0	2	0	5	..	—8
East Boston	0	0	0	0	2	0	1	1	0	—4

Sacrifice hits—Mansur, Cossette, O'Neil 2. First base on balls—Off Gilbert 2, off Buzzy 3. Struck out—By Gilbert 5, by Buzzy 5. Time—1h. 45m. Umpire—Mansur.

WINCHESTER, BY 13 TO 0

The Intercity Club of Dorchester was beaten yesterday by the Winchester A. A. at Winchester, 13 to 0.

WINCHESTER A. A.	ab.	bh.	po.	a.	e.	INTER-CITY CLUB.	ab.	bh.	po.	a.	e.
Bangs,2	4	1	4	4	0	Smullen,s,3	4	0	2	1	1
Ford,s	5	1	1	3	2	Sullivan,c	2	0	1	0	0
Kenney,1	5	1	7	0	1	Connolly,r	2	0	0	0	0
Don'llen,cf	5	1	2	0	0	Shuttle,cf,s	4	2	3	0	1
Leland,r	3	1	3	0	0	Stock,1	3	1	7	2	1
Ho'gan,lf,3	5	1	2	0	0	Carolan,lf	3	0	3	0	0
Murray,3,lf	3	1	0	0	0	Hoefling,3,c	4	0	6	2	1
M'Queen,c	4	1	8	0	0	Wholley,2	4	0	1	2	0
Tift,p	4	1	0	2	0	M'Vey,p	3	0	0	2	2
						M'Isaac,r	1	0	0	0	2
						Curran,cf	2	0	1	0	0
Totals	38	9	27	9	3	Totals	32	3	24	9	8

Innings	1	2	3	4	5	6	7	8	9	
Winchester A. A.	0	0	9	1	0	0	3	0	..	—13

Runs—Bangs 3, Ford, Kenney, Donnellen, Leland, Halligan, Murray 3, McQueen, Tift. Two-base hit—Donnellen. Stolen bases—Lift, Stack, Haefling. First base on balls—Off Tift 1, off McVey 2. Struck out—By Tift 8, by McVey 3. Double plays—Bangs and Ford; Stack and Haefling. Passed balls—Haefling 2. Wild pitch—McVey. Hit by pitched ball—Leland, Murray, Stack. Time—1h. 45m. Umpire—Coady.

FIRST DEFEAT IN 13 GAMES

MANCHESTER-BY-THE-SEA, July 11—The Imperials of Danvers found Grover, lefthanded twirler of the Manchester, invincible today and met their first defeat in 13 games. Grover struck out 16 men, Manchester winning the game, 16 to 1.

Innings	1	2	3	4	5	6	7	8	9	r.	h.	e.
Manchester	1	0	2	4	1	5	0	3	.	—16	9	3
Danvers	0	0	0	0	0	0	0	1	0	—1	4	8

Batteries—Redding and Kenney; Grover and Collins.

INTERNATIONAL LEAGUE

At Rochester—Rochester 8-9-5, Toronto 5-8-2. Hoff and Williams; Hearne, Herbert, Palermo and Kritchell.

At Buffalo—First game, Montreal 3-7-0, Buffalo 1-10-2. Dale and Howley; Fullenweider and Lalonge. Second game, Montreal 2-5-0, Buffalo 0-5-1. Miller and Madden; McConnell and Stephens.

At Jersey City—

Innings	1	2	3	4	5	6	7	8	9	10	r.	h.	e.
Jersey City	0	0	0	0	0	0	0	0	0	1	—1	8	0
Providence	0	0	0	0	0	0	0	0	0	0	—0	6	1

Williams and Tyler; Bentley and Kercher.

At Baltimore—Baltimore 2-8-0, Newark 0-3-2. Collett and McAvoy; Mattern and Wheat.

AMERICAN ASSOCIATION

At Louisville—Louisville 9, St. Paul 3.
At Indianapolis—Indianapolis 11, Milwaukee 5.
At Cleveland—Kansas City 15, Cleveland 9.
At Columbus—Columbus 14, Minneapolis 2.

WALKER'S HOMERS HELP BROWNS IN

One of the Clouts Decides Game in 12th Round Over the Macks.

PHILADELPHIA, July 11—Two home run hits by C. Walker, one of which decided the game, featured a 12-inning battle between Philadelphia and St. Louis in the first contest of a double-header here today, St. Louis winning by 4 to 3.

Philadelphia captured the second game, 6 to 4. Collins scored the tieing run in the eighth inning by getting under a throw by Austin on McInnis's grounder. St. Louis protested hard and James and Agnew were benched by Umpire Chill. Weilman and Crossin became St. Louis' battery and the former handed out three passes, which, with a triple steal by Strunk, Barry and Davies, scored two more runs. Davies, formerly of Amherst College, who twirled a fine game for Philadelphia, made his major league debut.

ST. LOUIS.	ab.	bh.	po.	a.	e.	PHILADELPHIA.	ab.	bh.	po.	a.	e.
Shotton,cf	5	2	0	0	0	Walsh,r	5	1	8	0	0
Pratt,2	5	3	5	6	0	Oldring,lf	6	2	3	0	1
Williams,r	5	2	0	0	0	Collins,2	3	0	5	2	0
CWalker,lf	6	3	2	1	0	Baker,3	4	1	3	0	0
Leary,1	6	4	11	1	0	M'Innis,1	5	3	8	0	0
Austin,3	6	1	4	0	0	Strunk,cf	3	1	3	0	0
Lavan,s	2	0	2	2	0	Barry,s	5	0	1	4	0
Wares,s	2	0	3	5	1	Schang,c	4	1	10	4	0
Crossin,c	4	0	9	1	0	Shawkey,p	4	0	0	3	0
Weilman,p	3	1	0	1	0	†Kopf	0	0	0	0	0
Baum'ner,p	2	0	0	1	0						
*EWalker	1	0	0	0	0						
Totals	47	16	36	18	1	Totals	39	9	36	13	1

Innings	1	2	3	4	5	6	7	8	9	10	11	12	
St. Louis	2	0	0	0	1	0	0	0	0	0	0	1	—4
Phil	0	0	0	1	2	0	0	0	0	0	0	0	—3

Two-base hits—Pratt, Walsh, Oldring. Home runs—C. Walker 2. Hits—Off Weilman 6 in 5 innings, off Baumgardner 3 in 7 innings. Sacrifice hits—Pratt, Collins. Stolen bases—Collins, Strunk. Double plays—Pratt, Lavan and Leary; Lavan and Leary; Crossin (unassisted); Wares, Pratt and Leary. Left on bases—St. Louis 11, Philadelphia 9. First base on balls—Off Weilman 4, off Baumgardner 4, off Shawkey 3. First base on error—Philadelphia. Struck out—By Weilman 2, by Baumgardner 2, by Shawkey 8. Time—3h. 8m. Umpires—Chill and Sheridan.

*Batted for Lavan in 5th.
†Batted for Shawkey in 12th.

Second Game.

PHILADELPHIA.	ab.	bh.	po.	a.	e.	ST. LOUIS.	ab.	bh.	po.	a.	e.
Walsh,r	3	1	1	0	0	Shotton,cf	4	1	3	0	0
Oldring,lf	4	0	1	0	0	Pratt,2	4	3	3	0	0
Collins,2	2	1	2	3	0	Williams,r	2	1	1	1	0
Baker,3	4	3	1	4	0	Rumler,r	2	1	1	0	0
McInnis,1	4	0	11	0	0	C.Walker,lf	3	0	1	0	0
Strunk,cf	2	0	3	0	0	E.Walker,lf	0	0	0	0	0
Barry,s	4	2	1	2	2	Leary,1	4	0	6	1	0
Lapp,c	3	0	6	4	0	Austin,3	3	0	0	1	1
Schang,c	1	0	1	0	0	Lavan,s	3	1	2	5	1
Davies,p	3	2	0	8	1	Agnew,c	3	0	4	8	0
						Crossin,c	1	0	3	0	0
						James,p	1	1	0	1	0
						Weilman,p	0	0	0	1	0
						*Jenkins	1	0	0	0	0
Totals	30	9	27	16	3	Totals	31	8	24	18	2

Innings	1	2	3	4	5	6	7	8	9	
Philadelphia	0	0	2	1	0	0	0	3	..	—6
St. Louis	1	0	0	0	0	1	2	0	0	—4

Two-base hits—Pratt, Baker, Davies. Hits—Off James 9 in 7 innings, none out in eighth; off Weilman none in 1 inning. Sacrifice hit—C. Walker. Stolen bases—Leary, Strunk, Barry, Davies. Double plays—Agnew and Lavan; Leary and Lavan; Davies, Baker and Lapp; Baker, Collins and McInnis. Left on bases—St. Louis 4, Philadelphia 7. First base on balls—Off James 4, off Weilman 3, off Davies 3. First base on errors—St. Louis 3. Struck out—By James 2, by Weilman 1, by Davies 4. Passed balls—Agnew, Lapp. Time—2h. 25m. Umpires—Chill and Sheridan.

*Batted for Lavan in 9th.

TWILIGHT LEAGUE GAMES

The Twilight League baseball series was continued at the old American League Park yesterday with the Boston Y. M. C. A. team and the Cubs furnishing the excitement. The former team took the Cubs into camp by a score of 13 to 9.

Green, the one-armed right fielder of the Cubs, featured with two fine catches. He also got a hit at three times at the bat.

Innings	1	2	3	4	5	6	7	8	9	r.	h.	e.
Bos. Y.M.C.A.	2	0	2	5	0	0	3	1	0	—13	16	3
Cubs	1	2	4	1	0	0	0	0	1	—9	10	6

Batteries—Albert and Bickford; Gotsoe and Garrity.

The Valley A. C. baseball team defeated the South End Federals, 16 to 0, in the Twilight League series. Hallet struck-out 20.

Innings	1	2	3	4	5	6	7	8	9	r.	h.	e.
Val. A. C.	5	0	3	0	1	2	1	3	1	—16	14	1
S. E. Feds	0	0	0	0	0	0	0	0	0	—0	3	3

Batteries—Valley A. C., Hallett and Fownes; S. E. Federals, Saunders and Sinnett.

COLONIAL LEAGUE

At New Bedford—First game, New Bedford 3, Taunton 1; second game, Taunton 5, New Bedford 1.
At Woonsocket—Fall River 12, Woonsocket 7.
At Pawtucket—First game, Pawtucket 5, Brockton 2; second game, Pawtucket 5, Brockton 4.

LYNN AND LAWRENCE SPLIT HONORS IN DOUBLE HEADER

Durning's Pitching Clinches First Game, Pearson Taking Second Clash.

Durning and Pearson both pitched fine ball at Lynn yesterday, the former winning the first game of a double-header for Lynn by a score of 5 to 1, while Pearson gave Lawrence an even break by holding the home team in the second, the visitors winning, 7 to 3, in seven innings. Fahey, the Lynn shortstop, fielded sensationally in both contests.

LYNN.	ab.	bh.	po.	a.	e.	LAWRENCE.	ab.	bh.	po.	a.	e.
Porter,r	4	2	2	0	0	O'Con'ell,cf	3	0	1	0	0
Merrill,lf	4	1	2	0	0	Lynch,s	4	2	2	3	0
Moulton,2	4	0	2	0	0	Luyster,r	3	0	1	0	0
Murphy,c	4	1	3	1	0	Bruggy,c	4	1	3	2	0
Orcutt,cf	4	2	4	0	0	Mahoney,2	3	0	2	3	0
Courtney,1	3	1	10	0	0	Conley,3	3	1	1	4	0
Sheehan,3	3	1	1	2	0	Peploski,lf	3	0	0	0	0
Fahey,s	3	1	2	3	1	Aubrey,1	2	0	14	0	0
Durning,p	3	0	1	3	0	Fullerton,p	3	1	0	2	0
						*Pearson	1	0	0	0	0
Totals	32	9	27	9	1	Totals	29	5	24	14	0

Innings	1	2	3	4	5	6	7	8	9	
Lynn	0	1	0	2	2	0	0	0	.	—5
Lawrence	0	1	0	0	0	0	0	0	0	—1

Two-base hit—Orcutt. Three-base hits—Murphy, Porter. Sacrifice hits—Luyster, Aubrey. Stolen bases—Orcutt 2. Left on bases—Lynn 4, Lawrence 6. First base on balls—Off Durning 4. First base on errors—Lawrence 1. Struck out—By Durning 3, by Fullerton 3. Time—1h. 50m. Umpire—Keeler.

*Batted for Fullerton in 9th inning.

Second Game.

LAWRENCE.	ab.	bh.	po.	a.	e.	LYNN.	ab.	bh.	po.	a.	e.
Peploski,lf	3	0	0	0	0	Porter,r	3	1	2	0	0
Lynch,s	3	0	3	2	0	Merrill,lf	3	1	1	0	1
Luyster,r	4	1	0	1	0	Moulton,2	3	0	0	1	1
Bruggy,c	3	0	8	0	0	Murphy,c	3	3	3	2	1
Mahoney,2	3	1	0	0	0	Orcutt,cf	3	1	2	0	0
Conley,3	4	1	1	1	0	Courtney,1	3	0	12	0	0
O'C'nell,cf	3	1	1	0	0	Sheehan,3	3	0	0	3	1
Aubrey,1	3	1	8	0	0	Fahey,s	1	0	1	6	0
Pearson,p	2	0	0	3	0	Dedrich,p	1	0	0	3	0
Totals	28	5	21	7	0	Totals	23	6	21	15	4

Innings	1	2	3	4	5	6	7	
Lawrence	0	2	0	2	0	1	2	—7
Lynn	0	0	2	0	0	0	1	—3

Two-base hits—Porter, Conley, Luyster, Murphy. Sacrifice hit—Dedrich. Stolen bases—Bruggy, Aubrey, Conley. Double play—Lynch and Aubrey. Left on bases—Lynn 2, Lawrence 5. First base on balls—Off Dedrich 5, off Pearson 1. First base on errors—Lawrence 2. Struck out—By Dedrich 2, by Pearson 8. Passed ball—Murphy. Time—1h. 30m. Umpire—Keeler.

TWO FOR HAVERHILL

HAVERHILL, July 11 — Haverhill came from behind in both games of a double-header with Lowell today, winning both contests in the final inning. The scores were 3 to 1 and 4 to 3. McMahon's double and Wilson's fine bunt defeated Lowell in the first game, while in the second, a seven inning affair, three doubles after one man was out gave Haverhill the game.

Umpire Doherty was overcome by the heat after the first game and players gave the decisions in the final contest.

First Game.

HAVERHILL.	ab.	bh.	po.	a.	e.	LOWELL.	ab.	bh.	po.	a.	e.
Campbell,2	2	1	1	0	0	Dee,s	4	2	2	5	0
Gaston,c	2	0	4	1	0	DeGroff,r	4	1	2	0	0
Howard,cf	4	1	3	0	0	Mathews,cf	4	0	0	0	0
Duggan,lf	3	1	2	0	0	Stimpson,lf	3	2	0	0	0
Smith,1	1	0	7	0	0	Burke,3	4	0	0	3	1
Yelle,3	4	2	1	5	0	Cargo,2	4	0	4	3	0
M'Mahon,s	3	1	4	2	0	Kelly,1	4	1	10	0	0
Wilson,r,2	3	1	4	0	1	Wacob,c	4	0	6	0	0
Flah'ty,c,2	3	0	1	0	0	Maybohm,p	2	0	0	2	0
Southern,p	3	0	0	2	1	Shenk,p	1	0	0	1	0
Totals	28	7	27	10	2	Totals	34	6	*24	14	1

Innings	1	2	3	4	5	6	7	8	9	
Haverhill	0	0	0	0	0	2	0	0	1	—3
Lowell	1	0	0	0	0	0	1	0	0	—2

Two-base hits—Campbell, McMahon. Home runs—Dee, Stimpson. Hits—Off Maybohm, 5 in 5 2-3; Shenk, 2 in 3 1-3 innings. Stolen base—DeGroff. Double plays—Dee, Cargo and Kelly 2; Shenk; Dee and Kelly. Left on bases—Haverhill 7, Lowell 6. First base on balls—Off Southern 1, off Maybohm 5. First base on errors—Lowell 2. Hit by pitcher—(By Shenk) Smith. Struck out—By Southern 4, by Maybohm 5, by Shenk 1. Wild pitch—Southern. Time—2h. Umpire—Doherty.

*None out when winning run scored.

Second Game.

HAVERHILL.	ab.	bh.	po.	a.	e.	LOWELL.	ab.	bh.	po.	a.	e.
Wilson,2	4	2	0	2	2	Dee,s	4	2	4	3	0
Howard,cf	2	1	5	0	0	DeGroff,r	4	2	0	0	0
Duggan,lf	3	3	1	0	0	Mathews,cf	3	1	2	1	0
Smith,1	2	0	7	0	0	Stimpson,lf	4	0	0	0	0
Yelle,3	3	0	0	2	0	Burke,3	3	1	1	0	0
McMahon,s	3	1	2	2	0	Cargo,2	2	0	0	3	0
Flaherty,r	2	0	0	0	0	Kelly,1	2	1	10	0	0
Gaston,c	3	2	6	4	0	Gr'nhalge,c	2	0	2	2	0
Reiger,p	3	0	0	3	0	Cook,p	3	1	0	3	0
Totals	25	9	21	13	2	Totals	27	8	*19	12	0

Innings	1	2	3	4	5	6	7	
Haverhill	0	0	1	0	1	0	2	—4
Lowell	0	0	1	0	1	1	0	—3

Two-base hits — Gaston, Wilson, Howard, Mathews. Home run—Burke. Sacrifice hit—Mathews. Stolen bases—Duggan 2, Howard 2. Left on bases—Haverhill 6, Lowell 7. First base on balls—Off Reiger 3, off Cook 4. First base on errors—Lawrence 1. Struck out—By Reiger 4, by Cook 2. Passed ball—Gaston. Time—1h. 50m. Umpires—Southern and Wacob.

*One out when winning run was scored.

NEW ENGLAND LEAGUE

YESTERDAY'S RESULTS.

At Lynn—First game, Lynn 5, Lawrence 1; second game, Lawrence 7, Lynn 3 (7 innings).
At Portland—Portland 10, Worcester 9.
At Lewiston—Lewiston 5, Fitchburg 4 (11 innings).
At Haverhill—First game, Haverhill 3, Lowell 2; second game, Haverhill 4, Lowell 3 (7 innings).

STANDING OF THE CLUBS.

	Won.	Lost.	P.C.
Lawrence	37	24	.607
Worcester	35	23	.603
Portland	33	25	.569
Lynn	31	20	.517
Lowell	30	32	.484
Lewiston	28	31	.475
Haverhill	28	31	.475
Fitchburg	18	45	.286

PORTLAND 10, WORCESTER 9

PORTLAND, Me., July 11—Portland won from Worcester this afternoon, 10 to 9, in a game that abounded in sensations. With the score 8 to 1 against them, the Worcester players fell on Mayberry in the seventh and batted in four runs. In the ninth with one run scored, the bases full and none out, Watkins displaced Mayberry and struck out the first two men. A hit by Roes followed, sending in two runs and two bases on balls forced in another. This gave the visitors a lead of one. In Portland's half, with two out, Dowell, Whitehouse and McCleskey, who batted in place of Lonergan, singled in succession. With the bases filled Hickman drove the ball to right, scoring two runs. Whitehouse just reached the plate ahead of the ball.

PORTLAND.	ab.	bh.	po.	a.	e.	WORCESTER.	ab.	bh.	po.	a.	e.
Burns,cf	5	2	1	0	0	Carroll,c	3	1	3	0	0
Clemens,lf	5	0	2	0	0	Shorten,r	5	2	1	0	0
Bowcock,2	5	2	2	4	1	Strands,3	5	2	1	0	0
Dowell,1	5	2	18	0	0	Potteiger,cf	5	3	3	0	0
Whit'use,r	5	2	0	0	0	M'Cune,1	5	0	6	1	0
Lonergan,s	3	0	1	3	2	Roes,lf	5	1	1	0	0
Hickman,3	5	4	0	1	0	Dowd,2	4	2	6	2	1
Hayden,c	2	0	8	0	0	Cooney,s	4	1	5	2	1
Mayberry,p	2	1	0	7	0	VanDyke,p	0	0	0	1	0
Watkins,p	0	0	0	0	0	Gaw,p	5	1	0	3	0
*M'Cleskey	1	1	0	0	0						
Totals	38	14	27	15	3	Totals	41	13	†26	9	2

Innings	1	2	3	4	5	6	7	8	9	
Portland	1	4	1	0	0	2	0	0	2	—10
Worcester	0	0	1	0	0	0	4	0	4	—9

Two-base hits—Bowcock, Hickman, Shorten, Dowd 2. Three-base hit—Potteiger. Hits—Off Mayberry 12 in 8 innings (none out in 9th); off Watkins 1 in 1 inning; off Van Dyke 5 in 1 2-3 innings; off Gaw 9 in 7 innings (1 out in 9th when winning run was made). Sacrifice hits—Hayden, Mayberry, Carroll. Stolen bases—Burns, Hayden, Dowd. Double plays—Lonergan to Bowcock to Dowell; Cooney to Dowd to McCune. Left on bases—Portland 7, Worcester 9. First base on balls—Off Mayberry 1, off Watkins 2, off Van Dyke 1, off Gaw 2. First base on errors—Portland 2, Worcester 3. Struck out—By Mayberry 3, by Watkins 3, by Gaw 2. Time—2h. 10m. Umpire—Bannon.

*Batted for Lonergan in 9th inning.
†Two out when winning run was scored.

LEWISTON IN THE 11TH

LEWISTON, Me., July 11—Lewiston's batting rally in the 11th defeated Fitchburg here today 5 to 4. A hit by Thomas, a three-bagger by Brignolia and a hit by Mundy with no one out was responsible for the scoring. Fitchburg tied the score in the eighth.

LEWISTON.	ab.	bh.	po.	a.	e.	FITCHBURG.	ab.	bh.	po.	a.	e.
Mundy,r	5	1	0	0	0	Kane,cf	5	0	3	0	1
Judge,1	5	1	9	0	0	Spires,3	5	0	2	0	0
Maloney,lf	5	0	7	0	0	Reed,r	5	2	2	0	0
Casey,c	5	5	7	2	0	Sweatt,2	5	1	1	1	0
Phoenix,2	4	0	2	2	2	Kilhullen,c	5	2	8	0	0
Shea,cf	5	1	4	0	1	Torphy,1	4	1	9	0	0
O'Connell,3	4	0	2	3	0	King,lf	5	1	4	0	0
Thomas,s	4	2	1	4	1	Cooney,s	5	2	1	6	2
Brignolia,p	5	2	1	3	0	Condon,p	1	1	0	1	0
						Scanlon,p	3	2	0	1	0
Totals	42	12	33	14	4	Totals	43	12	*30	9	3

Innings	1	2	3	4	5	6	7	8	9	10	11	
Lewiston	0	2	0	1	0	0	0	0	0	0	2	—5
Fitchburg	0	2	0	0	0	0	0	1	0	0	1	—4

Two-base hits—Kilhullen, Sweatt. Three-base hits—Condon, Reed, Brignolia. Hits—Off Condon 2, off Scanlon 10. Sacrifice hits—Torphy, Mundy, Phoenix. Stolen bases—Casey, Thomas. Double play—Thomas to Phoenix to Judge. Left on bases—Lewiston 11, Fitchburg 7. First base on balls—Off Condon 1, off Scanlon 1. First base on errors—Lewiston 2, Fitchburg 2. Struck out—By Scanlon 3, by Brignolia 5. Time—2h. Umpire—Black.

*None out when winning run scored.

HATHERLY CLUB THERE

The Hatherly Club of North Scituate defeated the Samet A. C. of Dorchester 11 to 2 in the game played at North Scituate yesterday. Brennan and Sullivan were the battery for the winning team and Gibson and Husband were in the points for the Dorchester nine.

Innings	1	2	3	4	5	6	7	8	9	
Hatherly Club	0	0	3	0	0	3	3	2	.	—11
Samet A. C.	0	0	0	1	0	0	0	0	1	—2

SOUTHERN ASSOCIATION

At Atlanta—First game, Atlanta 4, Montgomery 3; second game, Atlanta 3, Montgomery 3 (13 innings; darkness).
At Memphis—New Orleans 8, Memphis 4.
At Nashville—Mobile 11, Nashville 9.
At Chattanooga—First game, Chattanooga 3, Birmingham 0; second game, Birmingham 7, Chattanooga 5.

TIP TOPS SCORE DOUBLE VICTORY

Defeat Pittsburghs in Both Ends, Seaton Pitching a Grand Contest.

FEDERAL LEAGUE

YESTERDAY'S RESULTS.

At Brooklyn—First game, Brooklyn 1, Pittsburgh 0; second game, Brooklyn 8, Pittsburgh 2.
At Chicago—Indianapolis 3, Chicago 2.
At Baltimore—First game, Baltimore 2, Buffalo 1; second game, Buffalo 3, Baltimore 3 (13 innings).
At St. Louis—St. Louis 6, Kansas City 3.

STANDING OF THE CLUBS.

	Won.	Lost.	P.C.
Chicago	43	29	.597
Indianapolis	39	31	.557
Buffalo	36	32	.529
Baltimore	37	34	.521
Brooklyn	35	34	.507
Kansas City	34	42	.447
St. Louis	32	43	.427
Pittsburgh	30	41	.423

GAMES TODAY.

Kansas City at St. Louis.
Indianapolis at Chicago.

BROOKLYN, July 11—Brooklyn defeated Pittsburgh in both games of a double-header today, 1 to 0 and 8 to 2.

Seaton had the better of Barger in a pitchers' battle in the first game, the Brooklyn twirler striking out eight men. Walker was hammered for 14 hits, including a home run and two triples, in the second game and received poor support.

BROOKLYN.	ab.	bh.	po.	a.	e.	PITTSBURGH.	ab.	bh.	po.	a.	e.
Cooper,lf	3	2	2	0	0	Savage,r	3	0	3	0	0
Myers,1	4	0	9	1	0	Jones,lf	3	0	1	0	0
Shaw,cf	3	0	3	0	0	Oakes,cf	4	0	3	0	1
Evans,lf	3	0	2	0	0	Lennox,3	4	0	0	4	0
Hofman,2	3	0	1	3	0	M'Donald,2	4	2	1	2	0
Westerzil,3	2	0	1	0	0	Bradley,1	2	0	0	0	0
Holt,s	3	1	1	1	0	Holly,s	3	0	3	2	0
Land,c	3	1	8	0	0	Berry,c	3	0	4	2	0
Seaton,p	3	1	0	2	0	Barger,p	3	1	1	1	0
Totals	27	5	27	7	0	Totals	29	3	24	11	1

Innings	1	2	3	4	5	6	7	8	9	
Brooklyn	0	1	0	0	0	0	0	0	.	—1

Two-base hits—McDonald, Barger. Sacrifice hit—Bradley. Stolen base—Seaton. Left on bases—Brooklyn 5, Pittsburgh 5. Struck out—By Seaton 7, by Barger 3. First base on balls—Off Seaton 2, off Barger 3. Umpires—Goeckel and Cross. Time—1h. 45m.

Second Game.

BROOKLYN.	ab.	bh.	po.	a.	e.	PITTSBURGH.	ab.	bh.	po.	a.	e.
Cooper,lf	4	1	1	0	0	Savage,r	2	0	0	1	0
Myers,1	4	1	11	0	0	Jones,lf	4	0	1	0	0
Shaw,cf	5	4	2	0	0	Oakes,cf	4	0	1	0	0
Evans,r	3	0	4	0	0	Lennox,3	3	1	0	4	0
Hofman,2	4	2	5	4	0	Rheam,3	2	1	0	0	0
Westerzil,3	4	1	0	0	0	M'Donald,2	4	1	1	4	2
Holt,s	4	2	2	5	0	Bradley,1	3	1	11	1	0
Owens,c	3	2	2	1	0	Holly,s	4	2	1	2	0
Lafitte,p	4	1	0	2	0	Roberts,c	4	1	7	1	1
						Walker,p	3	0	2	0	0
						*Berry	1	1	0	0	0
Totals	35	14	27	12	0	Totals	34	8	24	13	3

Innings	1	2	3	4	5	6	7	8	9	
Brooklyn	2	1	2	2	0	0	0	1	.	—8
Pittsburgh	0	1	0	1	0	0	0	0	0	—2

Two-base hits—Owens, Bradley, Roberts. Three-base hit—Hofman. Home run—Cooper. Sacrifice hits—Evans, Cooper. Stolen bases—Shaw, Roberts. First base on errors—Brooklyn 1. Left on bases—Brooklyn 7, Pittsburgh 7. Double plays—McDonald, Holly and Bradley; Holt, Hofman and Myers. Struck out—By Lafitte 1, by Walker 4. First base on balls—Off Lafitte 4, off Walker 1. Umpires—Goeckel and Cross. Time—1h. 50m.

*Batted for Walker in 9th inning.

INDIANS 3, CHIFEDS 2

CHICAGO, July 11—Falkenberg held Chicago to three hits, Indianapolis winning through timely hitting off Lange, 3 to 2. Zwilling's home run following a pass to Wilson was responsible for the home scores.

INDIANAPOLIS.	ab.	bh.	po.	a.	e.	CHICAGO.	ab.	bh.	po.	a.	e.
C'mpb'll,cf	4	0	1	0	0	Zeider,3	3	1	1	2	0
M'K'hnie,3	4	2	2	3	0	Fritz,3	1	0	0	1	1
Kauff,r	4	0	1	0	0	Farrell,2	4	0	1	0	0
Laporte,2	4	1	0	5	0	Tinker,s	4	0	0	2	0
Carr,1	4	1	15	3	0	Wilson,c	2	1	7	2	0
Esmond,s	4	3	0	1	0	Zwilling,cf	3	1	2	0	0
Rousch,lf	4	2	1	0	0	Wickland,r	3	0	0	0	0
Rariden,c	3	0	4	2	0	Beck,1	3	0	11	0	0
Falk'erg,p	4	0	3	3	0	Flack,lf	3	0	2	0	0
						Lange,p	3	0	3	1	1
Totals	35	9	27	17	0	Totals	29	3	27	8	2

Innings	1	2	3	4	5	6	7	8	9	
Indianapolis	0	2	0	0	0	0	0	1	0	—3
Chicago	0	2	0	0	0	0	0	0	0	—2

Three-base hit—Rousch. Home run—Zwilling. Double play—Lange to Beck. Stolen bases—McKechnie, Wilson, Zeider, Rousch. Struck out—By Lange 4, by Falkenberg 4. Umpires—Van Sickle and Anderson. Time—1h. 37m.

WINTHROP ATHLETICS IN

Only three hits were made off Benson, the twirler of the Winthrop Athletics, in their game with the Milton Town team at Winthrop ytsterday afternoon. The local boys won 10 to 3. The visitors made their hits in the first inning, each hit bringing in a run.

Innings..... 1 2 3 4 5 6 7 8 9 r. h. e.
Winthrop.... 1 0 3 5 0 0 0 0 1 0—10 15 1
Milton....... 3 0 0 0 0 0 0 0 0 0— 3 3 1

Batteries—Winthrop, Benson and McDonald; Milton, Riser and Norris.

BRAVES TAKE ANOTHER FROM THE CLIMBING CUBS

(Continued from Page One S.)

opened with a good bunt. Rudolph was safe on Corriden's fumble. Devore singled to left, scoring Whaling.

BOSTON.	ab.	r.	bh.	tb.	po.	a.	e.
Devore, cf	5	2	2	2	2	0	0
Evers, 2b	4	2	2	2	2	1	0
Connolly, lf	4	0	2	2	4	0	0
Maranville, ss	3	0	0	0	2	6	0
Schmidt, 1b	4	0	2	3	13	1	0
Deal, 3b	4	0	1	1	2	6	0
Cather, rf	4	0	0	0	1	0	0
Whaling, c	4	1	1	1	1	1	0
Rudolph, p	4	0	0	0	0	3	0
Totals	36	5	10	11	27	18	0
CHICAGO.							
Leach, cf	4	0	1	3	0	0	1
Good, rf	4	0	0	0	3	0	1
Saier, 1b	4	1	3	7	9	1	0
Zimmerman, 3b	4	0	0	0	0	4	0
Schulte, lf	3	1	1	3	4	0	0
Sweeney, 2b	3	0	1	1	3	2	0
Corriden, ss	3	0	0	0	1	0	2
Bresnahan, c	2	0	0	0	5	1	0
*Williams	1	0	0	0	0	0	0
Hargrave, c	0	0	0	0	1	0	0
Humphries, p	1	0	0	0	0	0	0
Hageman, p	1	0	0	0	0	0	0
†Bates	1	0	0	0	0	0	0
Smith, p	0	0	0	0	0	0	0
Totals	31	2	6	14	‡26	8	4

Innings	1	2	3	4	5	6	7	8	9	
Boston	0	0	2	0	2	0	0	0	1	—5
Chicago	1	1	0	0	0	0	0	0	0	—2

Two-base hits—Schmidt, Saier. Three-base hits—Schulte, Leach. Home run—Saier. Hits—Off Humphries 7 in 4 1-3 innings, off Hageman 1 in 3 2-3 innings, off Smith 2 in 1 inning. Sacrifice hit—Evers. Stolen base—Connolly. Double plays—Deal to Whaling to Deal to Evers; Zimmerman to Sweeney to Saier. Left on bases—Boston 8, Chicago 3. First base on balls—Off Humphries 1, off Hageman 2. Struck out—By Humphries 3, by Hageman 1, by Smith 1. Time—2h. 10m. Umpires—Byron and Johnson.

*Batted for Bresnahan in eighth.
†Batted for Hageman in eighth.
‡Deal out, hit by batted ball.

NATIONAL LEAGUE

YESTERDAY'S RESULTS.

At Chicago—Boston 5, Chicago 2.
At Pittsburgh—Pittsburgh 3, Philadelphia 1.
At Concinnati—Cincinnati 6, Brooklyn 5.
At St. Louis—New York 13, St. Louis 9.

STANDING OF THE CLUBS.

	Won.	Lost.	P.C.
New York	42	29	.592
Chicago	41	35	.539
St. Louis	40	37	.519
Cincinnati	37	38	.493
Philadelphia	34	36	.486
Brooklyn	33	37	.471
Pittsburgh	33	38	.465
BOSTON	31	41	.431

GAMES TODAY.

Boston at St. Louis.
New York at Chicago.
Philadelphia at Cincinnati

JUST 34 HITS, TOTAL OF 60 BASES, IN GIANTS AND CARDINALS HITTING BEE

ST. LOUIS, July 11—New York won today from St. Louis, 13 to 9, in a wierd contest in which 25 players took part. Thirty-four hits for a total of 60 bases were made. Wilson, Dolan, Doyle and Cruise, the latter a pinch hitter, each hit for home runs.

NEW YORK.	ab.	bh.	po.	a.	e.	ST. LOUIS.	ab.	bh.	po.	a.	e.
Bescher,cf	5	1	1	0	0	Huggins,2	4	0	4	1	1
Doyle,2	5	2	2	2	1	Magee,cf	5	4	3	1	0
Burns,lf	5	3	4	0	0	Dolan,lf	5	2	1	0	0
S'dgr'ss,r,1	5	2	9	1	0	JMiller,1	5	1	9	0	0
Fletcher,s	5	2	1	4	0	Wilson,r	4	1	3	0	0
Merkle,1	2	1	5	0	0	Beck,3	4	2	4	2	0
Murray,r	3	2	2	0	0	Wingo,c	4	2	3	4	1
Meyers,c	4	3	2	1	0	Butler,s	4	2	0	2	1
Stock,3	4	1	0	5	0	Sallee,p	1	1	0	1	0
M'thw'on,p	4	1	1	3	1	Griner,p	0	0	0	0	0
						*CMiller	1	0	0	0	0
						Steele,p	1	0	0	0	0
						Niehaus,p	0	0	0	0	1
						†Cruise	1	1	0	0	0
						‡Dressen	1	0	0	0	0
Totals	42	18	27	16	2	Totals	40	16	27	11	4

Innings	1	2	3	4	5	6	7	8	9	
New York	0	0	0	0	4	2	4	0	3	—13
St. Louis	0	1	3	0	1	1	2	0	1	—9

Two-base hits—Butler, Fletcher, Merkle, Burns, Stock, Snodgrass. Three-base hits—Beck, J. Miller, Murray, Magee. Home runs—Wilson, Dolan, Doyle, Cruise. Sacrifice fly—Stock. Stolen bases—Magee, Bescher, Murray, Burns, Snodgrass. Double plays—Doyle to Merkle, Mathewson to Snodgrass. First base on balls—Off Niehaus 1. Struck out—By Sallee 1, by Steele 1, by Mathewson 11. Hits—Off Sallee 7 in 5 innings, off Griner 3 in 2-3 innings, off Steele 7 in 2 1-3 innings, off Niehaus 1 in 11 innings. Left on bases—St. Louis 4, New York 4. Time—2h. 25m. Umpires—Quigley and Eason.

*Batted for Salle in 5th.
†Batted for Niehaus in 9th.
‡Batted for Huggins in 9th.

CLARKE'S ROOKIES TURN THE TRICK

Pittsburgh Breaks Losing Streak When Regulars Are Put on Bench.

PITTSBURGH, July 11—Pittsburgh defeated Philadelphia today, 3 to 1, in the last game of the series. Manager Clarke, hoping to break his team's losing streak, sent four regulars, Mitchell, Carey, Mowrey and Gibson to the bench, and replaced them with substitutes. He also called in Mamaux, his youngest pitcher, who allowed only three scattered hits.

Philadelphia scored its only run in the first inning on Byrne's double and two-infield outs.

PITTSBURGH.	ab.	bh.	po.	a.	e.	PHILADELPHIA.	ab.	bh.	po.	a.	e.
Mensor,lf	4	1	3	0	0	Byrne,2	4	2	2	2	1
Leonard,3	4	1	1	2	0	Paskert,cf	3	0	2	0	0
Wagner,s	3	1	2	6	1	Becker,r	3	1	1	0	0
Viox,2	4	1	1	2	0	Lobert,3	2	0	2	4	0
Konetchy,1	4	1	13	1	0	Magee,lf	4	0	1	0	0
JasKelly,r	4	0	2	0	0	Luderus,1	4	0	11	0	0
JosKelly,cf	3	0	2	0	0	Martin,s	3	0	1	3	1
Coleman,c	4	1	2	1	0	Killifer,c	3	0	4	0	0
Mamaux,p	3	1	1	3	0	Rixey,p	2	0	0	2	0
						*Cravath	1	0	0	0	0
						Oeschger,p	0	0	0	0	0
Totals	33	7	27	15	1	Totals	29	3	24	11	2

Innings	1	2	3	4	5	6	7	8	9	
Pittsburgh	0	0	0	1	1	1	0	0	..	—3
Philadelphia	1	0	0	0	0	0	0	0	0	—1

Two-base hit—Byrne. Hits—Off Rixey 7 in 7 innings, off Oeschger none in one inning. Stolen bases—Becker, Wagner, Konetchy. First base on balls—Off Rixey 2, off Mamaux 3. Wild pitch—Rixey. First base on errors—Philadelphia 1, Pittsburgh 2. Sacrifice hit—Lobert. Left on bases—Philadelphia 5, Pittsburgh 8. Struck out—By Rixey 3, by Mamaux 1. Time—1h. 38m. Umpires—Klem and Emslie.

*Batted for Rixey in 8th.

TERRAPINS WIN AND DRAW

BALTIMORE, Md., July 11—Baltimore won the first game from Buffalo today by the score of 2 to 1. It was a pitchers' duel, with the local man getting a shade the better of the battle.

The second game was called at the end of the 13th inning, because of darkness. The pitching of Anderson of Buffalo featured.

BALTIMORE.	ab.	bh.	po.	a.	e.	BUFFALO.	ab.	bh.	po.	a.	e.
Meyer,r	4	1	0	0	0	D'l'hanty,lf	4	2	0	0	0
Duncan,cf	4	3	3	0	0	Agler,1	3	1	12	0	0
Zinn,lf	4	0	1	0	0	Louden,s	4	0	3	2	0
Swacina,1	4	2	10	1	0	Hanford,cf	4	1	1	0	0
Walsh,3	4	0	2	2	0	Booe,r	3	1	2	0	0
Doolan,s	4	0	5	7	0	Downey,2	3	0	4	7	0
Knabe,2	1	1	3	2	1	Smith,3	3	1	0	2	0
Russell,c	3	0	3	2	0	Blair,c	2	0	2	2	0
Quinn,p	2	0	0	1	0	*Young	1	0	0	0	0
						Krapp,p	2	0	0	3	0
						Lavigne,c	1	0	0	0	0
						Moran,p	0	0	0	0	0
Totals	30	7	27	15	1	Totals	30	6	24	16	0

Innings	1	2	3	4	5	6	7	8	9	
Baltimore	1	0	1	0	0	0	0	0	..	—2
Buffalo	1	0	0	0	0	0	0	0	0	—1

Two-base hits—Swacina, Duncan 2, Knabe. Three-base hits—Duncan, Delehanty. Double play—Knabe to Swacina. First base on balls—Off Quinn 1, off Krapp 3. Struck out—By Quinn 3, by Krapp 1. Left on bases—Baltimore 7, Buffalo 3. First base on errors—Buffalo 1. Umpires—McCormick and Cusack. Time—1h. 45m.

*Batted for Blair in 8th.

Second Game.

BALTIMORE.	ab.	bh.	po.	a.	e.	BUFFALO.	ab.	bh.	po.	a.	e.
Meyer,r	5	0	4	0	1	Del'hanty,lf	5	0	1	1	0
Duncan,cf	4	1	3	0	0	Agler,1	5	1	23	0	0
Zinn,lf	5	3	3	0	0	Louden,s	5	2	2	4	0
Swacina,1	5	0	10	1	1	Hanford,cf	6	4	2	0	0
Walsh,3	5	0	1	1	0	Booe,r	5	2	0	1	0
Doolan,s	5	0	2	2	2	Downey,2	6	0	2	7	1
Knabe,2	4	2	5	4	0	FredSmith,3	3	1	2	6	0
J'klitsch,c	5	1	10	4	1	Lavigne,c	4	1	5	4	0
F.Smith,p	2	0	1	1	0	Blair,c	0	0	2	0	0
Conley,p	2	0	0	3	0	Anderson,p	6	0	0	3	0
*Simons	1	1	0	0	0	†Schlafly	1	1	0	0	0
Totals	48	8	39	16	5	Totals	46	12	39	26	1

In'gs	1	2	3	4	5	6	7	8	9	10	11	12	13	
Balt.	0	1	0	2	0	0	0	0	0	0	0	0	0	—3
Buffalo	0	1	1	0	0	0	1	0	0	0	0	0	0	—3

Two-base hits—Jacklitsch, Schlafly. Three-base hit—Zinn. Home runs—Knabe, Louden. Sacrifice hits—Duncan, Louden, Booe. Stolen bases—Knabe, Hanford, Booe 2, Fred Smith. Double plays—Knabe to Swacina; Fred Smith to Downey to Agler. First base on balls—Off Smith 3, off Conley 3, off Anderson 3. Struck out—By Smith 5, by Conley 5, by Anderson 7. Left on bases—Baltimore 4, Buffalo 9. Umpires—Cusack and McCormick. Time—3h.

*Batted for Smith in 7th.
†Batted for Lavigne in 13th.

K. O. K. A. 3, RANGER 2

[Special Dispatch to The Herald.]

GLOUCESTER, July 11—The Knights of King Arthur, with Lothrop in the box, defeated the Massachusetts Training Ship Ranger boys, 3 to 2, this afternoon.

Innings	1	2	3	4	5	6	7	8	9	r.	h.	e.
K. of K. A.	1	1	0	0	0	0	0	1	0	—3	7	2
Ranger	0	2	0	0	0	0	0	0	0	—2	6	1

DODGERS FALL SHORT IN NINTH

Make Great Rally but Just Fail to Catch Cincis—Score Is 6 to 5.

CINCINNATI, O., July 11—Brooklyn rallied in the ninth inning of today's game and came within one run of tying the score which was 6 to 5 in favor of Cincinnati when the contest ended. A daring attempt by Egan, who had tripled in the ninth, to stretch the drive into a home run ended the hostilities, as there were two men out when he went to bat.

Both Derrick, who was traded to the Chicago Nationals for First Baseman Mollwitz, and Catcher Erwin, whom Cincinnati purchased from Brooklyn today, fielded their positions well and were factors in the batting.

CINCINNATI.	ab.	bh.	po.	a.	e.	BROOKLYN.	ab.	bh.	po.	a.	e.
Moran,r	4	1	0	0	0	O'Mara,s	4	2	2	1	[illegible]
Herzog,1	4	1	11	0	0	Hummel,1	4	0	9	0	[illegible]
Tw'mb'y,lf	3	0	2	1	0	Myers,cf	4	2	2	1	[illegible]
Niehoff,3	4	3	1	0	0	Wheat,lf	4	3	3	0	[illegible]
Groh,2	2	1	2	6	0	Cutshaw,2	3	2	2	5	[illegible]
Derrick,s	4	1	4	4	1	Stengel,r	4	0	1	0	[illegible]
Miller,cf	4	1	3	0	2	Smith,3	4	0	1	3	[illegible]
Erwin,c	3	1	4	3	0	Fischer,c	4	1	4	2	[illegible]
Ames,p	3	0	0	3	1	Pfeffer,p	2	0	0	2	[illegible]
						Aitchison,p	0	0	0	1	[illegible]
						*Dalton	1	0	0	0	[illegible]
						†Egan	1	1	0	0	[illegible]
Totals	31	9	27	17	4	Totals	35	11	24	15	2

Innings	1	2	3	4	5	6	7	8	9	
Cincinnati	0	1	0	3	2	0	0	0	..	—6
Brooklyn	0	0	0	1	0	1	0	0	3	—5

Two-base hits—Miller, O'Mara, Derrick. Three-base hit—Egan. Home runs—Erwin, Niehoff. Hits—Off Pfeffer 8 in 6 innings, off Aitchison 1 in 2 innings. Sacrifice hits—Groh 2. Sacrifice fly—Cutshaw. Stolen bases—Derrick, Twombley. Double plays—Groh to Herzog; Groh, Derrick to Herzog. Left on bases—Brooklyn 4, Cincinnati 4. Balk—Pfeffer. First base on balls—Off Pfeffer 1. Struck out—By Pfeffer 3, by Ames 3. Passed ball—Erwin. Wild pitch—Ames. Time—2h. Umpires—Rigler and Hart.

*Batted for Pfeffer in 7th.
†Batted for Aitchison in 9th.

RAIN CHECKS TITULAR GAME AT BEVERLY

The city of Beverly baseball championship was not decided yesterday as rain cut in on the Beverly Farms-Progressive game in the 12th inning, with the teams having five runs each. The Progressives had previously won a game and was leading yesterday until the eighth inning, when the Progressives made three runs. Goldsmith of the Progressives featured with a home run and a three bagger. Trayers, Progressive's pitcher, fanned 16.

BEVERLY FARMS.	ab.	bh.	po.	a.	e.	PROGRESSIVES.	ab.	bh.	po.	a.	e.
Hillery,2	5	0	8	1	0	Donahue,r	3	1	0	0	0
Hopkins,s	4	2	2	3	0	Goldsimth,3	5	2	0	2	0
Hastell,r	5	2	1	0	0	Toomey,2	5	2	0	2	0
Welch,lf	5	1	2	0	0	Murch,1	5	0	9	0	0
M'P'son,cf	5	1	3	0	0	Low,s	5	2	2	2	0
Conroy,3	4	1	1	2	1	Lovett,r	3	0	1	0	0
Sudbay,1	5	0	12	0	0	Murphy,cf	4	0	3	0	0
Perkins,c	4	2	8	1	0	Baker,c	4	0	16	0	1
M'Nair,p	4	0	1	2	0	Trayers,p	4	3	2	4	1
Totals	41	9	33	9	1	Totals	38	10	33	11	2

Innings	1	2	3	4	5	6	7	8	9	10	11	
Beverly Farms	3	0	1	1	0	0	0	0	0	0	0	—5
Progressives	0	0	0	1	1	0	0	3	0	0	0	—5

Runs—Hopkins 2, McPherson 2, Welch, Goldsmith 2, Donahue, Low, Trayers. Two-base hits—Trayers 2, Perkins. Three-base hits—Goldsmith, Dow. Home runs—Goldsmith, McPherson. Sacrifice hits—Donahue, Lovett. Stolen base—McPherson. First base on balls—McNair 1, Trayers 1. Struck out—McNair 7, Trayers 16. Passed ball—Baker. Hit by pitched ball—Conroy. Time—2h. Umpire—Waters.

ST. LOUIS FINDS HARRIS

ST. LOUIS, July 11—Going to the relief of Adams in the seventh inning when the game was tied, 3 to 3, Harris gave St. Louis four hits, which, combined with a double steal, netted the local team three runs and the victory.

ST. LOUIS.	ab.	bh.	po.	a.	e.	KANSAS CITY.	ab.	bh.	po.	a.	e.
Tobin,r	3	1	1	0	0	Chadb'ne,lf	4	2	1	0	1
W.Miller,lf	4	0	1	0	0	Gilmore,r	3	1	1	0	0
Drake,cf	4	1	2	0	0	Stovall,1	3	0	9	1	0
H.Miller,1	3	1	18	0	0	Easterly,c	4	1	2	2	0
Boucher,3	4	4	0	3	1	Perring,3	3	0	2	2	0
Bridwell,s	4	1	2	3	0	Kruger,cf	4	0	2	0	0
Misse,2	4	0	1	6	1	Goodwin,s	4	1	2	4	2
Chapman,c	4	1	2	2	0	Derringer,2	3	1	4	3	0
Brown,p	1	1	0	0	0	Adams,p	2	0	1	2	0
Crandall,p	1	1	0	2	0	Harris,p	0	0	0	1	0
						*Coles	1	1	0	0	0
						†Weuworthy	1	0	0	0	0
Totals	32	11	27	16	2	Totals	32	7	24	16	8

Innings	1	2	3	4	5	6	7	8	9	
St. Louis	0	1	2	0	0	0	3	0	..	—6
Kansas City	0	0	0	0	0	2	1	0	0	—3

Two-base hits — Derringer, Brown, Chadbourne. Sacrifice hits—Gilmore, Derringer, Tobin. Double play—Derringer, Goodwin and Stovall. Stolen bases—Chadbourne, Gilmore, Drake, W. Miller, Derringer. Struck out—By Brown 1, by Adams 1, by Crandall 1. First base on balls—Off Brown 2, off Adams 2, off Crandall 1. Umpires—Brennan and Shannon. Time—1h. 33m.

*Batted for Adams in 7th.
†Batted for Harris in 9th.

Tigers Drive Ruth From Box in Fourth Inning and Beat Red Sox 5-2

Cady Fails to Hit Red Sox Lose Out

Tigers, Incidentally, Remind Ruth the American League Is Not the International

BY PAUL H. SHANNON

If Forrest Cady had come through with a badly needed hit in yesterday's seventh inning, when the bases were filled and Dauss of the Tigers was on the verge of a big ascension, the initial conflict of this most important series with the Detroit team might have ended in a rout for Jennings' team and pushed the Sox a couple of notches higher in the standing.

But for once big Cady was unequal to the emergency, and the belated rally, ending almost as suddenly as it began, did little better than to give the locals two runs against the visitors' five. In short, this was the score by which the Jungaleers annexed the first of the big four-game series.

DAUSS BESTS RUTH

Against George Dauss, always Boston's Nemesis and one of the cleverest twirlers in the American league, the locals sent a recruit to try conclusions yesterday and the result was not exactly to the Boston twirler's credit. "Babe" Ruth, who made such a successful major league debut against the forlorn Naps on Saturday last, found in the Tigers a team of another stripe, and although a misjudged ball opened the way for that onslaught in the fourth it is doubtful if he could have held his own against a slabster of Dauss' calibre. Three innings and a fraction had hardly elapsed before the S. O. S. signal was sounded by Manager Carrigan and Rankin Johnson was hurried to the rescue. While Johnson, aided by Scott's clever stop, pulled his team out of a bad hole in the fourth his wildness and two clean hits allowed the Tigers three runs in the following session, the exact margin by which they won.

It was old Sam Crawford and his copartner in savagery, one Veach, who blighted the hopes of the ex-Baltimorean. Up to the fourth Ruth had been doing a mighty good job on the rubber, but when he opened this session with a pass and then saw Sam Crawford line a double into right, a hit by the way that Hooper would have corralled, he let down visibly and a three-bagger by Veach saw his finish. In spite of the enforced absence of the great Ty Cobb and the apparent weakness occasioned by Heilman and Billie Purtell in the lineup, the Tigers played splendid ball and nearly 9000 fans witnessed a rejuvenation that tells pretty plainly why the Tigers are once again on the pennant trail. Fighting like the Tigers of old and fielding superbly, the Jennings tribe played splendid ball and the substitutes, Purtell and Heilman, gave just as classy an exhibition as any of their mates.

In only one inning did Dauss show any signs of weakening. This was in the seventh when four of Boston's seven hits came together and a base on balls, included in the combination, threatened to cut away a formidable lead. Had Dutch Leonard, Ray Collins, Foster or any of the men who usually prevail against the Jungaleers been on the slab yesterday Dauss would surely have had the most stubborn kind of a battle on his hands, and regardless of his unfailing effectiveness against this Boston team the outcome might well have hung in the balance. But give any first class twirler a five-run lead and it takes something like an earthquake to unsettle him.

After going runless for three innings Ruth made the mistake of walking Heilman in the fourth as a starter and then came the knockout blow from old Wahoo Sam's bat. It came in the shape of a long high fly to the uttermost limits of right field, and although Walter Rehg was playing away back to the fences and almost in the next county he arrived in time to corral the ball, but, nevertheless, seemed overcome by the heat or something, as he missed it altogether. The hit went for a double and would have counted for three sacks had not Heilman held up near second through fear that the fly would be caught. Then Veach tripled and sent in two runs while Ruth sought the friendly ministrations of Doc Green and Johnson cantered to the mound. Rankin did good work here for he disposed of the next three men without allowing Veach to tally.

But all of Johnson's good work was undone by the sorry showing he made in the following inning. Here he started badly by walking the pitcher first, and then Bush singled. On an attempt to field Purtell's bunt to third for a force-out the sacks were filled with none down. A hit and an infield out thereafter let Detroit's three runs score. After this Johnson pitched two effective innings, as did Coumbe, who worked in the two last sessions.

Boston's one big inning was the seventh. Speaker led off here with a hit, but Lewis flied to left. Gardner's single sent Speaker to third, and an infield single by Janvrin let him score. Yerkes' long two-bagger struck near the top of the left field fence, Gardner running home. Thomas drew a pass and the sacks were filled. Here Cady was sent in cold to hit for Johnson and fanned, while Rehg's best effort produced a force-out. The Sox failed to hit safely either in the eighth or ninth.

The score:

DETROIT.	AB.	R.	BH.	TB.	PO.	A.	E.
Bush, ss	4	1	1	1	2	5	0
Purtell, 3b	4	1	0	0	0	3	0
Heelmar, c f	3	1	1	1	2	0	0
Crawford, r f	2	1	1	2	3	1	0
Veach, l f	3	0	2	4	4	0	0
Kavanagh, 2b	4	0	0	0	2	0	0
Burns, 1b	4	0	1	2	10	0	0
Stanage, c	3	0	0	0	4	2	0
Dauss, p	3	1	0	0	0	1	0
Totals	30	5	6	10	27	12	0

BOSTON.	AB.	R.	BH.	TB.	PO.	A.	E.
Rehg, r f	4	0	2	2	1	0	0
Scott, ss	4	0	0	0	5	4	2
Speaker, c f	4	1	2	2	5	1	0
Lewis, l f	3	0	0	0	3	0	0
Gardner, 3b	4	1	1	1	1	2	0
Janvrin, 1b	4	0	1	1	6	1	0
Yerkes, 2b	2	0	1	2	1	2	0
Carrigan, c	1	0	0	0	2	0	0
Thomas, c	0	0	0	0	2	1	0
Ruth, p	1	0	0	0	0	1	0
Johnson, p	1	0	0	0	0	2	0
Coumbe, p	0	0	0	0	1	0	0
aHenriksen	1	0	0	0	0	0	0
bCady	1	0	0	0	0	0	0
Totals	30	2	7	8	27	14	2

aHit for Carrigan in 5th. bHit for Johnson in 7th.

Detroit ....0 0 0 2 3 0 0 0 0—5
Boston ....0 0 0 0 0 0 2 0 0—2

Hits by innings:
Boston ....1 0 0 1 0 1 4 0 0—7
Detroit ....1 0 0 2 2 0 0 1 0—6

Two base hits—Crawford, Yerkes, Burns. Three-base hit—Veach. Sacrifice hits—Purtell, Veach, Stanage. Stolen base—Bush. Bases on balls—Off Ruth 1, off Johnson 5, off Dauss 3. Struck out—By Johnson 2, by Dauss 3. Double plays—Crawford to Burns, Speaker to Johnson to Gardner to Scott to Thomas, Yerkes to Janvrin to Thomas. Hits—Off Ruth 3 in 3 innings (none out in the fourth), off Johnson 2 in 4 innings, off Coumbe 1 in 2 innings. Time—1h. 58m. Attendance—8936. Umpires—Dineen and Sheridan.

ROBINS WIN BOTH GAMES FROM PIRATES

PITTSBURG, July 16.—Brooklyn won both parts of a double-header here today, the scores being 4 to 3 and 5 to 2.

The scores:

BROOKLYN.	AB.	R.	BH.	TB.	PO.	A.	E.
O'Mara, ss	3	1	2	3	6	2	1
Daubert, 1b	3	1	1	2	8	1	0
Myers, c f	4	0	0	0	1	0	0
Wheat, l f	4	0	2	3	2	0	0
Cutshaw, 2b	3	0	0	0	2	0	1
Stengel, r f	1	0	0	0	0	0	0
Hummell, r f	3	0	0	0	0	1	0
Smith, 3b	4	0	0	0	2	5	0
Miller, c	4	0	1	1	6	1	0
Rucker, p	2	1	1	1	0	3	0
aEgan	0	1	0	0	0	0	0
Ragan, p	1	0	0	0	0	1	0
Totals	32	4	7	10	27	14	2

PITTSBURG.	AB.	R.	BH.	TB.	PO.	A.	E.
Mensor, l f	2	0	1	1	2	0	0
Mowrey, 3b	4	0	1	1	1	0	0
Wagner, ss	4	0	1	1	1	3	0
Viox, 2b	3	0	0	0	3	2	0
Konetchy, 1b	4	0	1	3	10	0	0
Mitchell, r f	4	0	0	0	3	0	0
J Kelly, c f	3	0	0	0	4	0	0
bCarey	1	0	1	1	0	0	0
Coleman, c	3	0	1	1	1	1	0
cJas. Kelly	0	1	0	0	0	0	0
Gibson, c	0	0	0	0	2	0	0
dLeonard	0	0	0	0	0	0	0
O'Toole, p	3	2	2	4	0	2	0
Mamaux, p	0	0	0	0	0	2	0
eHyatt	1	0	0	0	0	0	0
Totals	32	3	8	12	27	10	0

aBatted for Rucker in the eighth. bBatted for Jos. Kelly in the ninth. cRan for Coleman in the seventh. dBatted for Gibson in the ninth. eBatted for Mamaux in the ninth.

Brooklyn ....0 0 0 0 0 1 0 3 0—4
Pittsburg ....0 0 1 0 0 0 2 0 0—3

Two-base hits—O'Mara, Daubert, Wheat. Three-base hits—Konetchy, O'Toole. Hits—Off O'Toole 5 in 7 innings (none out in eighth), off Mamaux 2 in 2 innings, off Rucker 7 in 7 innings, off Ragan 1 in 2 innings. Bases on balls—Off Rucker 2, off Ragan 1, off O'Toole 2, off Mamaux 1. Sacrifice hits—O'Mara, Mowrey, Mensor, Leonard. Struck out—By Rucker 3, by Ragan 2, by O'Toole 1, by Mamoux 1. Time—1h. 45m. Umpires—Lincoln and Byron.

SECOND GAME.

BROOKLYN.	AB.	R.	BH.	TB.	PO.	A.	E.
O'Mara, ss	4	1	1	3	1	2	0
Daubert, 1b	3	2	1	1	5	0	0
Meyers, c f	5	0	2	2	4	0	0
Wheat, l f	2	1	1	1	1	0	0
Cutshaw, 2b	3	1	2	2	5	2	0
Hummel, r f	3	0	0	0	2	0	0
Smith, 2b	2	0	1	2	3	1	1
McCarthy, c	4	0	2	2	6	0	0
Pfeffer, p	4	0	1	1	0	3	0
Totals	31	5	11	14	27	8	1

PITTSBURG.	AB.	R.	BH.	TB.	PO.	A.	E.
Mensor, c f	3	0	0	0	1	0	0
Leonard, 3b	4	0	0	0	2	1	1
J. Wagner, ss	4	2	2	3	2	4	0
Viox, 2b	4	0	1	1	1	4	0
Konetchy, 1b	3	0	1	1	11	0	0
Jas. Kelly, r f	4	0	1	2	1	1	0
Carey, l f	4	0	1	1	3	0	0
Gibson, c	1	0	0	0	1	0	0
Coleman, c	1	0	0	0	4	1	0
aFalsey	1	0	0	0	0	0	0
W. Wagner, c	1	0	0	0	1	1	0
Kantlehner, p	0	0	0	0	0	0	0
McQuillan, p	2	0	1	1	0	1	0
bHyatt	1	0	0	0	0	0	0
Conzelman, p	0	0	0	0	0	2	0
cMowrey	1	0	0	0	0	0	0
Totals	34	2	7	9	27	15	1

aBatted for Coleman in the 7th. bBatted for McQuillan in the 7th. cBatted for Conzelman in the 8th.

Brooklyn ....4 0 0 0 1 0 0 0 0—5
Pittsburg ....0 0 0 0 0 1 0 1 0—2

Two-base hits—Smith, Jas. Kelly, J. Wagner. Three-base hit—O'Mara. Hits—Off Kantlehner 4 in 1-3 inning, off McQuillan 5 in 6 2-3 innings, off Conzelman 2 in 2 innings. Stolen base—J. Wagner. Bases on balls—Off Pfeffer 1, off Kantlehner 3, off McQuillan 3. Sacrifice hits—Cutshaw, O'Mara, Daubert. Sacrifice flies—Smith, Konetchy. Struck out—By Pfeffer 5, by McQuillan 3, by Conzelman 1. Time—1h. 57m. Umpires—Byron and Johnson.

HIGHLANDERS BEAT BROWNS IN OPENER

NEW YORK, July 16.—New York won the first game of the St. Louis series by a score of 6 to 4.

NEW YORK.	AB.	R.	BH.	TB.	PO.	A.	E.
Truesdale, 2b	3	0	0	0	2	4	2
Hartzell, l f	3	0	0	0	1	0	0
Peckinpaugh, ss	3	0	0	0	0	1	0
Cree, c f	4	2	1	1	2	0	0
Mullen, 1b	3	0	0	0	11	0	0
Cook, r f	1	2	1	1	2	0	0
Sweeney, c	2	1	0	0	8	3	0
Maisel, 3b	4	1	1	1	1	1	1
Pieh, p	0	0	0	0	0	3	0
aCaldwell	1	0	1	1	0	0	0
Brown, p	2	0	1	1	0	1	0
Totals	26	6	5	5	27	13	3

ST. LOUIS.	AB.	R.	BH.	TB.	PO.	A.	E.
Shotten, c f	3	1	0	0	2	0	0
Pratt, 2b	4	1	1	1	3	1	1
Williams, r f	4	0	1	1	2	0	0
C. Walker, l f	4	0	1	1	2	0	0
Leary, 1b	3	1	0	0	7	0	0
Austin, 3b	4	1	2	2	0	2	1
Lavan, ss	3	0	0	0	3	2	0
bRumler	1	0	0	0	0	0	0
Agnew, c	3	0	0	0	5	2	0
cHoward	1	0	1	2	0	0	0
Baumgardner, p	1	0	0	0	0	1	0
James, p	1	0	0	0	0	1	0
dE. Walker	0	0	0	0	0	0	0
Weilman, p	0	0	0	0	0	0	0
eRickey	1	0	0	0	0	0	0
Totals	33	4	6	7	24	9	2

aBatted for Pieh in 4th. bBatted for Lavan in 9th. cBatted for Agnew in 9th. dBatted for James in 7th. Batted for Weilman in 9th.

New York ....0 0 0 4 1 0 0 1 .—6
St. Louis ....0 1 2 0 0 0 0 0 1—4

Two-base hit—Howard. Sacrifice hits—Sweeney 2, Mullen. Stolen bases—Peckinpaugh, Leary, Lavan. Bases on balls—Off Pieh 2, off Brown 2, off Baumgardner 4, off James 2. Struck out—By Pieh 2, by Brown 7, by Baumgardner 3, by James 1, by Weilman 1. Hit by pitcher—Cook by Baumgardner, Cook by Weilman. Wild pitch—James. Hits—Off Baumgardner 1 in 3 1-3 innings, off James 3 in 2 2-3 innings, off Weilman 1 in 2 innings, off Pieh 4 in 4 innings, off Brown 2 in 5 innings. Time—2h. 50m. Umpires—Connolly and Chill.

PHILLIES BUY M'AVOY

MUSKOGEE, Okla., July 16.—G. R. McAvoy, manager and second baseman of the Muskogee, Western Association club, yesterday, was sold to the Philadelphia National league club. He left last night to join the Philadelphia team in St. Louis.

"The most dangerous thing in the theatre is novelty," says George M. Cohan and George Jean Nathan, in an article in the next Sunday Magazine.

Hoblitzel Bought by Pres. Lannin

Former Cincinnati First Baseman to Come Monday

RICHARD HOBLITZEL, FIRST BASEMAN OF THE CINCINNATI REDS, WHO HAS BEEN PURCHASED BY THE RED SOX.

Richard Hoblitzel, first baseman of the Cincinnati Reds, one of the stars in his position, a grand batsman, good base-runner and a splendid fielder, has been purchased by the Boston Red Sox.

PRICE PAID WAS LARGE

Closely following the purchase of three Baltimore players last week came the announcement yesterday by President Lannin that the Cincinnati star was now his property and that the deal was closed by wire yesterday forenoon. The purchase price is said to have been well in excess of $5000 and the expenditure of this sum on top of the $27,000 paid last week to Baltimore emphasizes the fact that the Red Sox magnate does not intend to stop until he has gathered a real pennant winner for Carrigan to manage.

Just what the securing of Hoblitzell means to the team at this time is perhaps better understood by the Detroit and White Sox players who have all along figured the Boston team as the most dangerous contender in the race. Yesterday morning Ty Cobb stated he dreaded the Red Sox above all the rest. With Hoblitzel in a Boston uniform and his batting strength included in the regular lineup, the Sox look far more formidable than they did 24 hours ago.

In the internal trouble that developed among the Reds, Hoblitzell, it is said, was lined up in opposition to Herzog, perhaps, as many believe, because Herzog was made manager when he himself figured he should be considered. Waivers were asked on Hoblitzell finally and then as quickly recalled when it was found that certain clubs were after him. As Cincinnati could not afford to strengthen other National league clubs and it became literally impossible to allow a National league club to become the purchaser, the Red Sox bid was ultimately considered, President Ban Johnson using his influence to save Hoblitzell from the Federal league and fittingly reward President Lannin for his liberality and loyalty towards organized ball.

Hoblitzell will report Monday. This does not mean that either Gainer or Janvrin is to be disposed of. It simply means that Lannin is bound to get the very best there is in baseball, and Janvrin, particularly, may be shifted to some other position, as he is a mighty good all-round infielder. Perhaps the Red Sox magnate intends to gather a second team of nearly equal strength with his first.

NAPS SHUT OUT SENATORS 2 TO 0

WASHINGTON, July 16.—Washington got only two hits off Hagerman today and Cleveland won a shut-out, 2 to 0.

The score:

CLEVELAND.	AB.	R.	BH.	TB.	PO.	A.	E.
Graney, l f	3	1	1	4	1	0	0
Turner, 3b	3	0	0	0	1	2	0
Jackson, c f	4	0	2	2	2	0	0
Kirke, r f	4	0	0	0	3	0	0
Chapman, ss	3	0	0	0	1	6	0
Johnston, 1b	2	0	0	0	12	0	0
Olson, 2b	4	0	1	1	2	1	0
O'Neill, c	3	1	0	0	5	2	0
Hagerman, p	3	0	0	0	0	0	0
Totals	29	2	4	7	27	11	0

WASHINGTON.	AB.	R.	BH.	TB.	PO.	A.	E.
Moeller, r f	3	0	0	0	1	0	0
Foster, 3b	4	0	0	0	1	1	0
Milan, c f	3	0	0	0	3	0	0
Gandil, 1b	4	0	0	0	7	1	0
Williams, c	4	0	1	1	9	1	0
Shanks, l f	3	0	0	0	1	0	0
Morgan, 2b	2	0	0	0	0	3	0
McBride, ss	2	0	1	1	4	4	0
Shaw, p	0	0	0	0	0	1	0
Boehling, p	2	0	0	0	0	1	0
aSchaefer	1	0	0	0	0	0	0
Totals	28	0	2	2	b26	12	0

aBatted for Shaw in the third. bHagerman out on third bunted strike.

Cleveland ....1 0 1 0 0 0 0 0 0—2

Home run—Graney. Hits—Off Shaw 2 in 3 innings, off Boehling 2 in 6 innings. Stolen bases—O'Neill, Olson. Double play—O'Neill to Turner. Bases on balls—Off Hagerman 1, off Shaw 3, off Boehling 2. Hit by pitched ball—Johnston. Struck out—By Hagerman 5, by Shaw 2, by Boehling 4. Time—2h. Umpires—O'Loughlin and Hildebrand.

WATCH FOR OIL LEAKS

A point deserving attention at the hands of many automobile designers is that of making cars oil tight. This is a fault found justly with many modern cars and is especially in evidence at points in housings carrying loads of heavy grease which often oozes out, damaging finish and collecting dust.

How the Zotwots surprised the Jay-foul, told by Bob Dean, in story and pictures, is an amusing feature in colors in the next Sunday Post.

PHILLIES DEFEAT CARDINALS IN 10TH

ST. LOUIS, July 16.—St. Louis tied the score in the seventh inning by bunching hits off Tincup and Alexander, but Philadelphia won 6 to 3 in the tenth inning.

The score:

PHILADELPHIA.	AB.	R.	BH.	TB.	PO.	A.	E.
Byrne, 2b	4	2	2	2	2	3	0
Paskert, c f	3	1	1	1	1	0	0
Cravath, r f	1	1	1	2	1	0	0
Becker, r f, l f	5	1	3	4	2	0	0
Lobert, 3b	4	0	1	1	0	2	0
S. Magee, l f, c f	4	0	2	4	6	0	0
Luderus, 1b	4	0	1	2	8	2	0
Martin, ss	4	0	0	0	3	1	1
Killifer, c	4	0	0	0	6	0	0
Tincup, p	2	0	0	0	0	3	0
Alexander, p	2	1	0	0	1	1	0
Totals	37	6	11	16	30	12	1

ST. LOUIS.	AB.	R.	BH.	TB.	PO.	A.	E.
Huggins, 2b	3	0	2	2	1	1	1
L. Magee, 1b	2	0	0	0	6	0	0
Dressen, 1b	2	0	1	1	4	0	1
Dolan, l f	4	0	1	1	2	0	0
J. Miller, ss	5	0	1	1	4	5	0
Wilson, r f	4	1	1	1	0	0	0
Beck, 3b	5	1	2	2	0	1	0
Wingo, c	4	1	2	2	10	2	1
Riggert, c f	4	0	0	0	1	1	0
Doak, p	2	0	0	0	2	3	0
*Cruise	0	0	0	0	0	0	0
Perritt, p	1	0	0	0	0	1	1
Totals	36	3	10	10	30	15	4

*Batted for Doak in 7th.

Philadelphia ...2 0 1 0 0 0 0 0 0 3—6
St. Louis.......0 0 0 0 0 0 3 0 0 0—3

Two-base hits—Becker, Luderus, Cravath. Three-base hits—S. Magee, Wingo. Hits—Off Tincup 4 in 6 innings (none out in 7th), off Alexander 6 in 4 innings, off Doak 6 in 7 innings, off Perritt 5 in 3 innings. Sacrifice hits—Martin, Paskert. Sacrifice fly—Cruise. Stolen bases—L. Magee, Paskert. Double play—Doak (unassisted). Left on bases—Philadelphia 4, St. Louis 8. Bases on balls—Off Tincup 4, off Doak 1. Struck out—By Tincup 2, by Alexander 1, by Doak 5, by Perritt 3. Time—2h. 15m. Umpires—Hart and Rigler.

ATHLETICS OUTBAT WHITE SOX AND WIN

PHILADELPHIA, July 16.—Hard hitting featured today's game, which was won by Philadelphia from Chicago by 10 to 6.

The score:

PHILA.	AB.	R.	BH.	TB.	PO.	A.	E.
Murphy, r f	3	1	2	3	1	0	0
Oldring, l f	5	1	3	4	1	0	0
E. Collins, 2b	4	2	2	2	2	4	0
Baker, 3b	4	2	3	4	0	5	0
McInnis, 1b	3	1	0	0	14	0	0
Walsh, c f	5	1	3	6	1	0	0
Barry, ss	4	0	0	0	4	2	0
Schang, c	5	1	2	3	3	3	0
Bender, p	1	0	1	1	1	1	0
Bush, p	0	0	0	0	0	0	0
Bressler, p	1	0	0	0	0	0	0
*Davis	1	1	1	1	0	0	0
Totals	36	10	17	24	27	15	0

CHICAGO.	AB.	R.	BH.	TB.	PO.	A.	E.
Weaver, ss	4	0	2	3	2	3	0
Berger, ss	1	0	0	0	1	1	0
Blackburn, 2b	3	1	0	0	1	3	1
Demmitt, l f	3	0	2	2	0	0	0
Daly, l f	1	0	0	0	0	0	0
J. Collins, r f	4	1	1	2	0	0	0
Fournier, 1b	5	1	4	8	10	0	0
Bodie, c f	5	2	2	5	1	0	0
Schalk, c	4	0	1	1	5	7	0
Breton, 3b	3	0	0	0	3	6	0
Russell, p	2	1	1	1	0	1	0
Faber, p	1	0	0	0	1	0	0
Totals	36	6	13	22	24	21	1

*Batted for Bush in sixth.

Philadelphia ..... 2 0 3 0 0 2 0 3 .—10
Chicago .... 0 1 0 4 0 1 0 0 0— 6

Two-base hits—Weaver, J. Collins, Fournier, Murphy, Oldring, Baker, Schang. Home runs—Fournier, Bodie, Walsh. Hits—Off Russell 7 in 3 innings, off Faber 10 in 5, off Bender 9 in 3 2-3, off Bush 3 in 2 1-3, off Bressler 1 in 3. Sacrifice hits—J. Collins, Murphy, McInnis. Double play—Breton to Schalk to Fournier. Bases on balls—Off Russell 2, off Faber 4, off Bush 4, off Bressler 1. Hit by pitcher—Breton by Bush. Struck out—By Russell 1, by Faber 2, by Bush 1, by Bressler 2. Time—2h. 15m. Umpires—Egan and Evans.

Darkness Stops the Braves-Reds Game

Cloudburst Which Followed Kept Crowd in Grandstand for More Than an Hour

CINCINNATI, July 16.—The opening game between the Braves and Reds at Redland Field today was called on account of darkness in the last half of the fourth inning, with the score a tie at 1 to 1.

Low lying clouds hung over the park from the start of the battle, and the gloom finally became so intense that Umpire Mal Eason called it off with one Red Sox out in the last half of the fourth. Five minutes after play was stopped a terrific cloudburst occurred, flooding the field and keeping the crowd in the grand stand for an hour.

Ames and Crutcher were the opposing pitchers and both were in good form. Moran scored for the Reds in the first inning on a pass, two passed balls by Hank Gowdy and a sacrifice fly by Herzog.

Moran singled in the third, but was left, and he was the only Red to get on base. The Braves tied it up in the third on an error by Lohr, who muffed Gowdy's easy fly, and then Ames threw wild on Crutcher's bunt. These wobbles were followed by a pass which filled the bases and a sacrifice fly scoring the tying run. The Braves got three hits off Ames in four innings, while the Reds got only one off Crutcher.

The game will not be played off until Aug. 17, during the last visit of the Bostons to this city. It is probable that the same pitchers will be used tomorrow as started today.

Herzog and Evers got into quite an altercation on the field as play was stopped, but it ended in argument only, and the men did not come together. Evers played today in spite of a badly spiked shin and he will be in the remaining games of the series.

Dick Hoblitzell, who has played first base for the Reds for the past six years, was sold for a cash consideration to the Boston Americans this morning, and was on the field in a Red uniform for the last time today. He will leave for Boston tomorrow and may arrive in time for the Saturday game at Fenway Park.

Hobby, always considered a good hitter, fell down badly this year and could not get going. He played in the first 75 games of this season, but hit around .200, and when Mollwitz was secured from the Cubs and made good, waivers were at once asked on Hobby. All the National league clubs waived, but the Red Sox claimed him, and he was sold for something in advance of the waiver price. He has been with the Reds since the fall of 1908, but is only 26 years old, and may start hitting again with his shift to different company.

Los Angeles Examiner

SATURDAY — LOS ANGELES, JULY 18, 1914 — SATURDAY

'RUBE' MARQUARD BEATS PIRATES IN 21 INNNGS, 3 TO 1

Angels Lose Fourth Straight Battle to Portland Beavers and Drop Into Second Place by Fraction of Point

KLEPFER LOSES TO LEIFIELD IN GREAT BATTLE; SCORE IS 2 TO 1

Friend Happy Hogan Declares He Hasn't Any Luck at All These Days; Seals Make It Three Victories in Four Games Played

Slight Mistake in Ninth Allows S. F. to Put Over Winning Run; Ed Erred in Allowing O'Leary to Double, Driving in Tally

Coast League Standing

	Won	Lost	Pct.
Portland	52	3	.5473
Los Angeles	58	48	.5471
Venice	54	48	.529
San Francisco	55	51	.519
Sacramento	48	56	.462
Oakland	41	62	.398

Yesterday's Results

San Francisco, 2; Venice, 1.
Portland, 6; Los Angeles, 1.
Oakland, 4; Sacramento, 1.

Games Today

Venice and San Francisco at Washington Park. Two games. First game called at 1:45 o'clock.
Sacramento and Oakland at San Francisco.
Los Angeles and Portland at Portland.

How They'll Stand Tonight

	Win	Lose
Los Angeles	.551	.542
Portland	.552	.542
Venice	.534	.524
San Francisco	.523	.514
Sacramento	.467	.457
Oakland	.404	.394

By H. F. Weller

WANTED—The left hind foot of a mangy, one-eyed jack-rabbit, caught in a cemetery at the dark of the moon by a hunch-backed colored person. Call at "Hap" Hogan's and receive suitable reward.

"Hap" has lost so many games in the last three weeks that he has become desperate. He and Trainer "Shine" Scott are accustomed to carrying a rabbit's foot, a four-leaved clover and sundry other articles of furniture around with them, but the whole works has been lost—hence the worried look on Hogan's noble brow.

Perhaps it would be well to state before we go any farther that "Lefty" Leifield outlucked "Big Ed" Klepfer yesterday afternoon, and the Seals made it three out of four for the series by winning two to one.

Mistake Costs Klepfer Game

A slight mistake of "Big Ed's" in the ninth cost him his game. With Justin Fitzgerald on first, one out and the score a tie, Elliott signed for a pitchout, and Ed didn't get it quite far enough out. O'Leary caught the ball on the end of his bat and drove it down the first-base line just inside the bag for a double. "Fitz" only got to third on the hit, but a moment later Roy Schaller beat out a hit to the infield and the winning run was over.

With certain reservations it was a pitchers' battle all the way. A little luck helped "Fitz" to score in the first. He singled to left on the first ball pitched. Then Klepfer caught him flat-footed off the bag and "Babe" Borton had to toss the game away by hurling the ball in the general direction of Rivera.

Wild Pitch Scores "Fitz"

"Fitz" took third on the error and then walked over the pan when Ed let loose a wild heave which Elliott was unable to corral with his leather cushion. Klepfer did not give O'Leary or Schaller a chance. He stood both of them on their ears for strike-outs and then Jerry Downs popped up a dinky foul to Elliott. One—two—three, but it was too late.

The Seals got just two more bingles off "Big Ed" in the next seven innings while the Tigers reached "Lefty" for five in the same space of time, tying up the count in the fifth on Borton's double, McArdle's sacrifice and Elliott's single.

Del Howard's boys looked more like a ball club yesterday than at any time this week. Roy Corhan had Hogan shouting "They can't keep that up forever," but just the same Roy pulled one in the final inning that

(Continued on Page 2, Column 6.)

Fog Jinx Camping on Trail of Cup Defense Sloops

Trial Race Between Resolute, Vanitie and Defiance Is Again Postponed

(By Associated Press)

NEWPORT, R. I., July 17.—Too much fog today again prevented the race of the cup defenders, Defiance, Resolute and Vanitie. An effort will be made to give the yachts a try-out tomorrow, when the series will end. Clearing weather is promised for this last race.

Never before have the cup class yachts met with such adverse conditions on their trial races as have prevailed here for more than a week.

The cup candidates came here on July 6 for a series of ten races, from which the America's cup committee expected to obtain considerable information as to the relative abilities of the boats on all points of sailing, to be used with other matter gathered in fifteen more races to be sailed next month.

After tomorrow the three boats will return to their ship yards for cleaning, alterations and repairs. Their next meeting will be in the first run of the New York Yacht Club cruise on July 31, from Glencove to Smithtown. There will be five of these runs on the cruise. There are fifteen more races for the cup defenders.

Californians Lead in Oregon Tourney

(By Associated Press)

PORTLAND, July 17.—In an exciting semi-final contest for the Oregon State tennis championship here today, L. K. Richardson of Portland defeated R. J. Breck of San Francisco. This leaves the final match tomorrow to be contested between Richardson and H. Van Dyke Johns of San Francisco. The score was 6-2, 1-6, 5-7, 6-2, 6-2.

One of the hardest fought and most exciting matches was between H. Van Dyke Johns of San Francisco, coast junior champion, and Brandt Wickersham, the Portland expert, which was won by Johns, 6-4, 6-1, 7-5.

Walcott Is Barred From Boxing Bout

(By Associated Press)

NEW YORK, July 17.—Joe Walcott of Boston, the Barbados negro who was for years the recognized welterweight champion pugilist, was to have taken part in a bout here tonight, but the New York State Athletic Commission would not allow him to enter the ring, on the grounds that he had passed the age when, in the opinion of the commission, it would be safe to permit him to risk another fistic battle.

Walcott was born April 7, 1872, and thus is more than 42 years old.

International Canoe Race Is Postponed

NEW YORK, July 17.—The first of the international sailing canoe races between Leo Friede, defender, and Ralph Britton, challenger of Canada, was a little more than three-fourths completed in a light south wind on Gravsend Bay today when the breeze died away altogether. The match was called off until tomorrow morning.

Coffman President of Motorcycle Body

(By Associated Press)

ST. LOUIS, July 17.—Albert B. Coffman of Toledo, Ohio, was chosen president of the Federation of American Motorcyclists in annual convention here today. The site of the 1915 convention will be settled at the final meeting of the convention tomorrow. The races, being held in conjunction with the annual business meeting will continue through Sunday.

Milan Out of Game for at Least Month

WASHINGTON, July 17.—Clyde Milan, centerfielder of the Washington Americans, will be out of the game for at least a month as the result of his collision with Moeller when both went after a fly in today's game with Cleveland. Milan got a double fracture of the right lower jaw and a wrenched shoulder.

Brashear Released by Portland Club

(By Associated Press)

PORTLAND, Ore., July 17.—Roy Brashear, utility infielder, was unconditionally released by the Portland Pacific Coast League team on the score of economy. He formerly played with Venice.

BEAVERS FIGHT WAY TO FIRST PLACE, 6 TO 1

Larry Pape Holds Angels Safe While His Teammates Bat In Victory

'LONG TOM' HUGHES VICTIM

Extra Base Blcws Bring About Downfall of Ancient One; Lober Stars at Bat

(By Leased Wire to the "Examiner")

PORTLAND, July 17.—Larry Pape, who has been warming the Portland bench for the past two months, debuted today with a regular blare. It was quite a fashionable affair, with all the lady fans on hand. Larry held Los Angeles to six hits and one run, while his mates batted the club into the leadership of the Coast League for the first time this season. Of course the lead is not much to brag about, but it shows that the Mackmen are on their way.

After putting up their fourth straight victory, the Angels and Beavers were aligned like this in their fight for the top rung:

Club	Won	Lost	Pct.
Portland	52	43	.547368
Los Angeles	58	48	.547170

Long Tom Hughes was Dillon's selection and the attenuated one was the medium for a flock of triples and doubles for the Beaver larder, not to speak of a long homer, over the right center field fence, by Ty Lober. It is said on a good deal of authority that when Ty's homer cleared the fence, "Scotty" had to pack ice on Pop's wrinkled dome.

Pape in Great Shape

Pape has been in shape to work for several days, but the other Beaver hurlers have been going in such fine shape that there wasn't much of a chance for him to break in until he demanded to show Boss McCredie what he had hidden away in his right arm.

It looked for a moment as if the Angels were going to get away with Larry. McCreedie took no chances throughout the game and kept Reiger warming up. Wolter got a single to left and Gedeon bunted, Pape throwing low to second. Maggart hit into a double play and Wolter scored on Kore's boot of Abstein's ground ball.

The Angels were out in front but a moment. With one out in the second, Kores singled to center. Then Lober biffed the ball over the right center field fence and the locals were never headed. That seemed to take all the cunning out of Long Tom's wing, for Fisher followed with a double to right and Bancroft got a scratch double to center.

Rodgers Is Real Peeved

At the start of the sixth inning Hughes whistled one a little too close to Rodgers' dome to suit the raw beef eater. Bill had already felt a jab in the back from one of Hughes' fast ones, and it made him a bit peeved. He dropped his bat, walked out to the pitcher's box and laid down the law to Hughes. It was almost ludicrous to see the Angel tower over the pugnacious Beaver. It was a regular Niagara Falls affair and there was no outward display of belligerency. It must have gotten the Hughes goat, for Rodgers was passed when the game was resumed, but he was out stealing.

Then Doane doubled to the right field fence and scored on Kores' three-bagger to center field, the latter coming in on a bad relay from Maggart to Metzger. Boles was playing short because Moore has a sore hand. Then Lober walked and scored from first on Fisher's double to center.

Bancroft opened the seventh with a triple to right, but was caught in a beautiful double at the plate on Rodgers' fly to Ellis.

Manager McCredie tonight released Roy Brashear, utility man. Now that the team has struck its stride he did not feel that he needed Brashear.

LOS ANGELES	AB	R	H	O	A
Wolter,rf	3	1	1	0	0
Gedeon,2b	4	0	1	2	2
Maggert,cf	3	0	0	2	0
Astein,1b	4	0	0	9	2
Ellis,lf	3	0	1	2	0
Boles,ss	4	0	1	1	3
Metzer,3b	3	0	1	0	0
Brooks,c	2	0	0	4	3
Hughes,p	3	0	1	2	3
Meek,c	1	0	0	2	0
Totals	30	1	6	24	14

PORTLAND	AB	R	H	O	A
Banc'ft,ss	4	0	2	6	3
Derrick,1b	4	0	1	6	0
Rod'rs,2b	2	0	1	1	4
Doane,rf	4	1	1	3	0
Ryan,cf	3	0	0	0	0
Kores,3b	4	2	2	1	1
Lober,lf	2	2	1	3	0
Fisher,c	3	1	2	5	3
Pape,p	3	0	0	1	1
Speas,cf	1	0	0	1	0
Total	30	6	10	27	12

SCORE BY INNINGS

Los Angeles	1	0	0	0	0	0	0	0	0	—1
Hits	1	2	0	0	0	0	1	1	1	—6
Portland	0	3	0	0	0	3	0	0	*	—6
Hits	0	4	1	0	1	3	1	0	*	—10

SUMMARY

Errors—Boles, Kores, Pape. Struck out—By Hughes, 3; Pape, 4. Bases on balls—Off Pape, 3; Hughes, 2. Two-base hits—Fisher, 2; Bancroft, Doane, Kores. Three-base hit—Bancroft. Home run—Lober. Double plays—Rodgers to Bancroft to Derrick, 2; Ellis to Meek. Stolen bases—Rodgers, 2; Maggert. Hit by pitched ball—By Hughes (Rodgers). Runs responsible for—Hughes, 4; Pape, 0. Time—1:55. Umpires—McCarthy and Held.

RICHARD ('Rube') Marquard, Wonderful Giant Southpaw Who Held Pirates Runless for Twenty-Innings at Pittsburg Yesterday.

PICATO DEFEATS FREDDIE ANDREWS

'Babe' Given Decision When Jones Tosses Sponge Into Ring in Eleventh Round

In rather a slow battle that was featured by a great amount of clinching Babe Picato of this city was given a knockout decision over Freddie Andrews of Milwaukee in the eleventh round of a scheduled twenty rounds at the Vernon arena last night.

Andrews was on his feet at the time, but was leaning back against the ropes with his arms crossed before his face, seeking to ward off the blows that Picato was swinging to his face and body. Freddie stood and took his medicine without flinching or trying to run, and after half a minute of this slugging Manager Tom Jones threw a sponge into the ring to save Andrews from a possible knockout and Referee Eyton gave the decision to Picato.

A small house greeted the boxers, for it was an off-day card that appealed only to the regulars, but as popular prices were in effect the enthusiasts probably got all they paid for.

Main Event Is Slow

The main event was rather slow, with the gallery gods yelling continually for Picato to fight. He was practically on the defensive for seven rounds and really did no leading, making Andrews bring the fight to him.

He had Andrews bleeding from the nose in the fifth and later on opened a cut over Freddie's right eye, while the only damage noted on Picato was on his upper lip, from which a drop of blood trickled occasionally.

Andrews had the better of the first round and Picato got the second. The next three were even, with Andrews forcing matters and Picato holding his own in the exchanges. Freddie led in the sixth and seventh, for Picato would not fight, although Andrews' blows did not sting him.

Picato Takes Lead

In the eighth Picato made his first bid for the lead and met Freddie's advances with right and left swings that slowed Andrews a trifle. Picato was easily the best in the ninth and raised a welt over Andrews' right eye. The tenth was another slow one, with honors even.

The eleventh opened up as the others had, with Andrews forcing things, but Picato met him more than half way and slammed him hard with right and left swings to the head. Finally he backed him against the ropes on the east side of the ring and as Freddie held his arms in front of his face to protect, Picato stepped back and landed right and left swings on him at will. It was only a question of time until Andrews would have been knocked down and out, and probably to prevent this Jones threw a sponge into the ring.

In the first prelim of six rounds, Steve Dalton earned a knockout over Jack Gillis in the second round, and in the semi-final of ten rounds Earl Puryear easily beat Walter Williams to a decision.

Inman Arrives for Match With Hoppe

(By Associated Press)

NEW YORK, July 17.—Melbourne Inman, the English professional billiard champion, arrived today from London on the Aquitania. He was met by Willie Hoppe, whom he is to meet in matches at American and English billiards. The first of eleven sessions will be played in New York on September 28. The men will also play in Chicago and Montreal.

Lloyds Lays Odds Against Shamrock

(By Associated Press)

LONDON, July 17.—A policy has been issued at Lloyds to pay the total loss if the Shamrock IV wins back the America's cup from the United States, the premium paid being 35 guineas per cent. The yacht is insured in the London market in the value of £18,000. This is equivalent to odds of 27 to 10 against Sir Thomas Lipton's yacht.

$50,000 Race Won by Hapsburg Colt

(By Associated Press)

LONDON, July 17.—The Eclipse stakes of $50,000 at Sandown Park races was won today by H. Cholmondeley's three-year-old Hapsburg. Sol Joel's Honeywood was second, and Sir John Thursby's Kennymore third. Thirteen ran. The distance was a mile and a quarter.

Ouimet Takes 75 on Braeburn Links

(By Associated Press)

NEWTON, Mass., July 17.—Francis Ouimet, national open golf champion, made a remarkably low medal score in the third round of the Massachusetts amateur golf championship at Braeburn today. In defeating G. H. Pushee of Braeburn he was around the course in 75, winning by a score of five up and three to play.

McMahon Will Box Gilbert in August

Tom McMahon, heavyweight, has been signed up to fight Dick Gilbert fifteen rounds either August 10 or 15 at Great Falls, Mont. Jimmy Dime, McMahon's manager, closed the match yesterday.

Jimmy Dime stated yesterday that he would not think of sending McMahon against Jess Willard unless he was given a big guarantee.

Pitches No-Hit, No-Run Game

(By Associated Press)

DULUTH, Minn., July 17.—James Withers, who played with the Kansas City American Association and Sioux City Western League teams earlier in the season, pitched a no-hit, no-run game for Duluth against Virginia today. This is the third hitless game of the season in the Northern League.

Club Standings and Results of Baseball Games

American League

	W.	L.	Pct.		W.	L.	Pct.
Philadelphia	46	32	.590	Washington	43	38	.531
Detroit	46	38	.548	St. Louis	42	39	.519
Boston	45	39	.536	New York	31	46	.403
Chicago	43	38	.531	Cleveland	28	53	.346

YESTERDAY'S RESULTS

St. Louis-New York—Rain.
Philadelphia-Chicago—Rain.
Cleveland, 3; Washington, 1.
Boston, 8; Detroit, 2.

GAMES TODAY

St. Louis at New York.
Chicago at Philadelphia.
Cleveland at Washington.
Detroit at Boston.

Federal League

	W.	L.	Pct.		W.	L.	Pct.
Chicago	46	33	.582	Buffalo	39	37	.513
Indianapolis	43	34	.558	Kansas City	37	45	.451
Baltimore	42	37	.532	St. Louis	35	46	.432
Brooklyn	39	35	.527	Pittsburg	35	48	.422

YESTERDAY'S RESULTS

Indianapolis, 8; St. Louis, 2.
Baltimore, 4; Buffalo, 3.
Pittsburg, 6; Brooklyn, 4.
Kansas City, 3; Chicago, 2.

GAMES TODAY

Chicago at Kansas City.
Baltimore at Buffalo.
Brooklyn at Pittsburg.
Indianapolis at St. Louis.

International League

	W	L	Pct.		W	L	Pct.
Baltimore	50	26	.658	Toronto	36	38	.486
Rochester	48	30	.615	Newark	34	40	.459
Buffalo	46	30	.605	Jersey City	24	50	.324
Providence	40	33	.548	Montreal	24	51	.320

YESTERDAY'S RESULTS.

Rochester 4, Montreal 0.
Buffalo 6, Toronto 2.
Jersey City 8, Providence 3.
Newark 1, Baltimore 0.

American Association

	W	L	Pct.		W	L	Pct.
Milwaukee	48	37	.565	Minneapolis	44	43	.506
Louisville	48	42	.533	Columbus	43	46	.483
Kansas City	49	44	.527	Cleveland	37	41	.474
Indianapolis	48	44	.522	St. Paul	32	57	.360

YESTERDAY'S RESULTS.

Columbus 2, Milwaukee 1.
St. Paul 4, Cleveland 2. (first game.)
Cleveland 8, St. Paul 3. (second game.)
Minneapolis 4, Indianapolis 2.
Louisville 5, Kansas City 4.

Western League

	W.	L.	Pct.		W.	L.	Pct.
Sioux City	51	36	.586	Lincoln	45	41	.523
Denver	49	36	.576	Omaha	40	45	.471
St. Joseph	49	37	.570	Wichita	35	54	.393
Des Moines	46	42	.523	Topeka	31	56	.356

YESTERDAY'S RESULTS

Omaha, 13; Topeka, 3.
Sioux City, 6; Wichita, 0.
Lincoln, 8; St. Joseph, 1.
Denver, 13; Des Moines, 5 (called end eighth on account of rain).

Northwestern League

	W.	L.	Pct.		W.	L.	Pct.
Spokane	57	36	.613	Portland	37	57	.394
Seattle	60	38	.612	Victoria	38	59	.392
Vancouver	60	38	.612	Tacoma	37	61	.377

YESTERDAY'S RESULTS

Portland	0	6	1
Tacoma	4	7	0

Hansen and Murray; McGinnity and Brottem.

Spokane	1	11	0
Seattle	2	5	1

Arlett and Shea; Dell, Bonner and Cadman.

Victoria	1	5	1
Vancouver	5	15	1

Driscoll, McKenry and Hoffman; Hunt and Cheek.

NEW YORK AND PITTSBURG SET NEW MARK IN OLDER LEAGUE

Longest Previous Game in National Was That Between Cubs and Phillies in 1905, Won by Chicago, 2-1, After 20 Innings

Bescher's Single and Doyle's Homer in Twenty-first Frame Bring in Runs That Beat Adams, Who Travels Entire Distance

National League Standing

	W.	L.	Pct.
New York	45	31	.592
Chicago	44	37	.543
St. Louis	43	40	.518
Cincinnati	39	41	.488
Philadelphia	37	39	.487
Brooklyn	35	39	.473
Pittsburg	34	41	.453
Boston	34	43	.442

Yesterday's Results

St. Louis, 18; Philadelphia, 4.
Chicago, 3; Brooklyn, 2.
Boston, 1; Cincinnati, 0.
New York, 3; Pittsburg, 1 (21 innings).

Games Today

Boston at Cincinnati.
Brooklyn at Chicago.
New York at Pittsburg.
Philadelphia at St. Louis.

(By Leased Wire to the "Examiner")

PITTSBURG, July 17. — "Rube" Marquard, after allowing a single tally in the first inning of today's battle with the Pirates, pitched twenty innings of shut-out ball and the Giants won the longest game in the history of the National League and the next to the longest in the history of major league baseball. The final count was 3 to 1.

Marquard for the Giants and "Babe" Adams for the Pirates went the full twenty-one-inning route without relief, and darkness had almost fallen when Bescher singled and scored ahead of Larry Doyle, who hit to deep center for a home run.

The Giants had tied the score in the third when Bescher scored from third on Burns' sacrifice fly.

The Pirates counted in the first inning when Marquard hit Mensor. Mensor took second on Mowrey's sacrifice and scored when Wagner sent out a long triple. From that time on the "Rube" was invincible.

The Philadelphia and Boston American League clubs hold the major league record for the longest game, which was played at Boston on September 1, 1906. The game went twenty-four innings and was won by the Athletics, 4 to 1. The Cubs and Philadelphia went twenty innings on August 24, 1905, Chicago winning, 2 to 1. The minor league record for long games is held by Decatur and Bloomington, who battled for twenty-six innings last year, Decatur winning, 2 to 1.

NEW YORK	AB	R	H	O	A
Bescher,cf	9	2	3	7	1
Doyle, 2b	9	1	2	3	6
Burns,lf	8	0	2	11	0
Robrtsn,rf	8	0	0	3	0
Fletcher,ss	8	0	2	2	11
Merkle,1b	8	0	0	25	0
Meyers,c	6	0	2	3	1
*Murray	0	0	0	0	0
McLean,c	2	0	0	1	1
Stock,3b	5	0	0	3	4
‡Snodgrass	1	0	0	0	0
Grant,3b	1	0	0	0	2
Mrquard,p	8	0	1	0	5
Totals	73	3	12	63	31

PITTSBURG	AB	R	H	O	A
Mensor,lf	7	1	1	8	0
Mowrey,3b	7	0	1	2	9
Wagner,ss	9	0	3	5	6
Viox,2b	7	0	2	2	7
Knetchy,1b	8	0	2	23	0
Mitchell,rf	9	0	1	3	0
Kelly,cf	9	0	2	10	0
Gibson,c	4	0	1	9	0
*‡Carey	0	0	0	0	0
Coleman,c	4	0	1	1	2
Adams,p	7	0	1	0	3
Totals	71	1	15	63	27

*Ran for Gibson in tenth.
‡Ran for Meyers in fifteenth.
*‡Batted for Stock in eighteenth.

N. Y. ..001000000000000000002—3
Pittsbrg 100000000000000000000—1

Errors—Robertson, Fletcher, Wagner, 2, Viox. Three-base hits—Burns, Wagner. Home run—Doyle. Stolen bases—Burns, 2, Fletcher, Bescher, 2. Double plays—Viox, Wagner to Konetchy, Fletcher, Doyle to Merkle, 2. Bases on balls—Marquard, 2. Hit by pitched ball—By Marquard, Mensor. First on errors—New York, 2; Pittsburg, 2. Sacrifice hits—Mowrey, Adams, Viox, Mensor, Stock. Sacrifice fly—Burns. Left on bases—New York, 9; Pittsburg, 15. Struck out—Marquard, 2; Adams, 6. Time—3:42. Umpires—Byron and Johnson.

Cubs Whip Brooklyn, 3-2

CHICAGO, July 17.—The Cubs won from Brooklyn, 3 to 2, getting but one hit off Allen. Three Dodger errors and a base on balls gave the locals two in the fourth. In the sixth Goode doubled, the only Chicago hit, Allen's wild throw, and Schulte's sacrifice scored the winning run. Vaughn was wild in the first two innings, fours hits scoring two Brooklyn runs.

BROOKLYN	AB	R	H	O	A
O'Mara,ss	5	0	0	0	0
Daubert,1b	3	1	0	11	0
Myers,cf	4	0	2	2	0
Wheat,lf	4	0	1	3	0
Cutshw,2b	4	0	0	2	5
Hummel,rf	4	0	1	4	0
Smith,3b	4	1	1	0	2
Miller,c	4	0	1	2	0
Allen,p	2	0	0	0	3
*Egan	1	0	0	0	0
Totals	35	2	6	24	10

CHICAGO	AB	R	H	O	A
Leach,cf	4	0	0	1	0
Good,rf	3	1	1	2	0
Saier,1b	3	1	0	10	0
Zimmrmn,3b	4	0	0	0	2
Schulte,rf	2	0	0	2	0
Sweeny,2b	2	0	0	1	3
Derrick,ss	3	0	0	3	3
Brsnahan,c	3	0	0	8	2
Vaughn,p	3	0	0	0	3
Totals	26	3	1	27	13

*Batted for Allen in the ninth.

Brooklyn	1	1	0	0	0	0	0	0	0	—2
Chicago	0	0	0	2	0	1	0	0	*	—3

Errors—Myers, Cutshaw, Miller (2), Allen.

THE BEST PHOTO TAKEN OF THE BRAVES

Every Fan Will Prize This Souvenir of the Great Boston National League Team That Has Made 1914 a Memorable Baseball Year

REMARKABLE GROUP PICTURE OF THE BRAVES. SNAPPED BY MAURICE FEINBERG OF THE POST STAFF.

Back row, left to right—Bill James, Cathers, Deal, Davis, Cottrell, Cochreham, Hess, Mann, Gowdy, Schmidt, Whaling. Middle row, left to right—Whitted, Dugey, Tyler, Strand, Devore, Gilbert, Smith, Moran. Bottom row, left to right—Connolly, Mitchell, Willie Connors (mascot), Rudolph, Maranville, Crutcher, Martin, Captain Evers.

"Expensive Luxury," Nat Goodwin Said When Wife No. 4 Divorced Him

Nat Goodwin's Story

BY HIMSELF

CHAPTER XXXVI.
TOURING WITH EDNA GOODRICH

WE went along, producing "When We Were Twenty-One," "An American Citizen," one act of "The Merchant of Venice" (thank Heaven it was only one act!) and an original play written by George Broadhurst, which made a tremendous hit in the South but was a failure in the East.

My star-wife complained of being ill at the end of the season and I sent her to a famous specialist in Minnesota for a series of treatments. Her recovery was almost instantaneous! In five days from the day she left me she wired me in California that she was in New York about to start for Europe! She asked that I follow her.

I replied I had just reached Los Angeles and had business that would keep me there—at least over night.

This was the beginning of the end indeed.

My wife remained abroad that summer, but the Jeffries-Johnson fight-disappointment almost offset that benediction.

Preparatory to my going back into my profession I bought a play from George Broadhurst. Present in a box at the opening performance of the play was my quondam "young and handsome star" who returned to New York just in time to grace the occasion.. Later she descended on our little organization while we were playing in Toronto and this time she hurled accusations of all kinds at my head—any one of which would have enabled her to divorce me even in England! When the trial of her divorce action came along all these charges were disproven—but that one session in Toronto was not conducted along Parliamentary lines, so far as she was concerned.

That she had instituted the proceedings didn't bother me at all. Having done all the affirmative work in two other divorce actions I thought I might as well take it easy this time and let her do it!

I can say, however, that it is a most expensive luxury —being divorced. It's much cheaper to use the active tense of that verb!

CHAPTER XXXVII.
WITH AUTHOR CARLTON

TO drop my matrimonial career for a while and turn to recollections of my professional enterprises, I wish to write in this chapter of Author Carlton.

After "A Gilded Fool" was launched I at once made a contract with Carlton for another play, and in a few weeks he submitted a scenario to me which I accepted. This play was to follow "In Mizzoura." During the interim between "The Gilded Fool" and "In Mizzoura," Carlton wholly evolved the plot of "Ambition." In time he submitted two acts.

I was more than pleased, as the character of Senator Beck appealed to me. It had a fine story and all the parts were unique and full of character. After receiving the two acts I looked about for adequate people for the roles and was fortunate enough to secure the services of Annie Russell, Henry Bergman and Clarence Montaine, and with the other members of my company, I considered it a perfect cast. Later I was fortunate enough to be surrounded by such players as George Fawcett, Louis Payne, John Saville, Estelle Mortimer and Jean Claire Walters.

I arranged to open my season early in September at Miner's Fifth Avenue Theatre, New York, and called my company for rehearsals of "David Garrick." I was anxious to appear in that role in New York, having previously performed it on the road with some degree of success. My idea was to put on Garrick for one week and follow with "Ambition." I still had only two acts of the Carlton play. I had been trying for weeks to get possession of the last act, having some anxiety as to how Carlton intended ending the play, but it was impossible to locate him.

He turned up on the first night of "David Garrick," promising me my last act of "Ambition" on the following day, assuring me it was finished. I waited until Wednesday, but he failed to keep his word. I knew he was unreliable, but never thought him ungrateful. Through his negligence we were forced to announce "David Garrick" for a second week. This was asking the public to accept a pretty tall order, but there was no alternative.

On Friday, too late for rehearsal, I took the new play home with me and read it most carefully and was very much disappointed. It plainly showed the earmarks of hasty composition. However, there was no choice, and I produced it as quickly as possible.

On the first night we were all extremely nervous, and up to the ending of the second act I thought we had a failure. That ending, however, gave me a splendid moment and I received several curtain calls. The papers were very kind on the following morning, more so, I considered, than we deserved. I played it two weeks to gradually decreasing business, the last week being simply ghastly!

I honestly believe I could have drawn more money alone with a desk and glass of water.

I had no faith in the play, and after the first performance began rehearsals of another, called "A House of Cards," by Sydney Rosenfeld. Previously I had sent it into the discard after three rehearsals. It proved worthy of its title and tumbled down shortly after at the Garden Theatre.

The manager of a Philadelphia theatre, where I was to open after the engagement at the Fifth Avenue, came over and saw our performance of "Ambition" (to a $90 house) and entered a most violent objection to my appearing at his theatre in that play. I informed him that I had nothing which I could substitute and that it would take me at least two weeks to prepare any of the plays in my repertoire, with the exception of "David Garrick." There was no alternative; he must accept "Ambition" or close the theatre. He concluded to take a chance, and one of those psychological events which shapes the destinies of players took place.

We opened to nearly $1200—and that was the lightest house of the engagement! We played to capacity business there and everywhere all through that season. It proved to be one of my greatest successes.

I never understood Carlton's failure to furnish the play as he had agreed, until a few days after I opened in Philadelphia I read the announcement of the production of a new play of his by a manager who had previously refused to give him a hearing. He forgot (!) I had lifted him from the streets of Boston, clothed him, loaned him money and taken him to my mother's home. He forgot (!) that when he became suddenly ill it was my mother who nursed him back to health as if he were one of her own children!

The last time that I saw this gifted but ungrateful man was a few years ago at Atlantic City. He was a physical wreck, but mentally a giant still. He had invented some new electrical appliance and his mind scintillated as I had never known it to scintillate before. I knew he was doomed, and felt grieved. I left his chamber with a heavy heart.

Since writing this, poor Carlton has joined the vast majority.

CHAPTER XXXVIII.
I FIND THE VERY BEST PHYLLIS

IT WAS George Broadhurst, as Fate, who brought onto my horizon a young woman that presently was to save my life—and that is the least of countless benefits she has bestowed upon me!

Broadhurst spent most of his time in Southern California from 1907 to 1909 and not a little of it at my beach home. After my long run of failures I hoped I had landed a winner in his new play "The Captain," which I took to New York for production there. He accompanied me and undertook to select the cast.

It was he who engaged as my leading woman Miss Margaret Moreland.

The play was a fizzle, as complete as any of the others.

To round out my season I revived several of my tried and trusted old plays and did fairly good business on the road.

If I accomplished nothing else, that season could be set down by me as a success, inasmuch as I discovered in Miss Moreland's acting of Phyllis in "When We Were Twenty-One," the finest performance that role ever received and I knew that in her lay the ability to become a really great emotional actress—a distinct discovery in these days.

I recruited a company in Los Angeles following this engagement, engaging Miss Moreland as my leading woman, and opened in Phenix, Arizona, playing my way across the country and arriving in New York in the holiday season of 1911. It was during this cross-country tour that I received a telegram from George C. Tyler which resulted in my proving to not a few doubting Thomases that I could "come back."

Next week Mr. Goodwin will give his personal impressions of famous men he met on and off the stage.

How an English Cabby Beat Nat Goodwin in Repartee

I WAS returning from the Newmarket races in England after a very poor day, having failed to back a winner. Arriving at Waterloo station I found it was raining in torrents. Not fancying hansom cabs in that kind of weather I permitted the crowd to rush along the platform in a frantic endeavor to secure a cab, having made up my mind to content myself with a four-wheeler. It is not a particular attractive vehicle (four-wheelers are generally in use all night and retain a stuffy and most uncomfortable aroma therefore), but it is safe!

At the station there is an opening of about 50 feet from one platform to another, unsheltered and roofless. I looked across and discovered a solitary cab with an old man holding the ribbons listlessly. The downpour fell about his narrow shoulders, which were meagrely protected by the thinnest of rubber covering. After I had shouted several times for him to come over and get me he slowly turned and replied:

"You come over here; my beast is a bit weary."

I dug my head into my coat and waded across the street, drenching myself to the skin in that short interval. I quickly opened the cab door, fell upon the damp cushions and gasped, "Carleton Hotel."

"Righto, Governor," came the response from the all but drowned cabby and the vehicle began its weary journey, fairly crawling down Waterloo Hill. Having a very important dinner party on hand and realizing it was late, I became somewhat anxious. Leaning out of the window I shouted:

"My good man, send your horse along. I am in great haste."

"He's doing his level, Governor," he replied. "I can't shove him. He's human as we are, and besides he's been out all night."

I sank back onto the cushions, biting my nails in sheer desperation as the cab moved even more slowly. Again indulging myself in a shower bath from the open window, I looked out and pleaded:

"For heaven's sake, driver, send that horse along; he's simply crawling."

"He's striving 'ard, Governor," came back the reply, "but he's no sprinter at his best. I'll get you to the Carleton, never fear."

By this time I was frantic. I opened the door and stood on the step, disregarding the rain, and shouted:

"You fool, I'm not going to a funeral."

"Nor me to no bloomin' fire neither," replied the cabby, cheerfully.

Lewiston Journal Sporting Section

BENDER AND JAMES WILL PROBABLY START GAME

Altho Neither Manager Has Given Any Indication of His Choice.

PHILADELPHIA, Oct. 7—The Boston Braves, champions of the National league, are in this city preparing for the opening of the world's series here on Friday when they meet the Philadelphia Athletics, winners of the American league race. The Bostonians, who ended their National league's schedule in Brooklyn yesterday, planned a light practice this morning on the National league grounds, while the present world's champions expect to work out at Shibe park, where the first two games of the series will be staged. The National league players will all get a line on their opponents when they view the contest between the Athletics and New York in the farewell game of the American league schedule here to-day.

Neither of the opposing managers has indicated who will be his pitching selection for the opening game, but a majority of the critics believe that Bender, the veteran Indian twirler, will be Connie Mack's selection, and that he will be opposed by James, who, they figure, is the best fitted of the Boston moundsmen to repeat during the short series if necessary. Manager Stallings says that he has not yet made up his mind whether James, Taylor, Rudolph or one of the other Boston pitchers will be given the honor of opening the

[Continued on eleventh page.]

Chief Bender, Athletics' Mainstay in Box.

[Photo by Underwood & Underwood, New York.

THIRD BASEMAN SMITH, OF BRAVES, BREAKS LEG

Photo by Underwood & Underwood.

J. CARLISLE SMITH.

NEW YORK, Oct. 7—James C. Smith, third baseman of the Boston National League club, broke his right leg just above the ankle in sliding to second base in the ninth inning of the first game of Tuesday's double header with Brooklyn. Smith will be unable to play in the world's series and his place will be taken by Charles Deal, utility infielder.

Manager Stallings and Captain Evers, questioned as to what effect the loss of Smith would have on the work of the Braves in the championship series both declared that his absence would not be a serious handicap to the team's effectiveness, as Deal could fill the place satisfactorily. Other members of the team expressed the same opinion. All the players declared themselves confident of winning against the Athletics in the big series.

"I am extremely sorry that such an unfortunate accident should deprive us of Smith's services at such a critical stage," said Manager Stallings. "But we are singularly fortunate in having a reliable substitute in Deal for third base. Early in the season Deal suffered from charley horse, and throat trouble, but he is fully recovered and I have no fear but that he will play the position in fine shape. Smith's loss is a big one to our infield, but I cannot say that his enforced absence will weaken it. Deal will fill the bill perfectly and the only difference will be that Smith was a better hitter.

"We are well prepared for just such a contingency. I am glad to be in a position to say there is not a place on the team into which we could not put a substitute at a moment's notice. Every substitute we have is well fitted to play the position he was chosen for and let me tell you we are going to give the Athletics the hardest run they ever got when we meet them in the coming series.

"Poor Smith is badly injured but the boys will acquit themselves in the championship series with redoubled efforts and we will see that Smith will receive cheering news during the games. This will make up, in part, for his inability to be even an onlooker."

Captain Evers endorsed everything that Manager Stallings had said, and added:

"Don't think for a moment that the loss of Smith will weaken our infield. The work of our men in the games to come will bear out my contention that Deal will prove to be a first class man at third. No one knows better than I what Deal is made of and take it from me, barring his lesser batting power, 'Charlie' will fill 'Red's' place to the entire satisfaction of everyone interested in the welfare and success of our team."

The Braves left here for Philadelphia tonight. There they will tune up for the championship series, which will begin on Friday.

Rube Oldring of Athletic Advisory Board.

Photo. by Underwood & Underwood

"RABBIT" MARANVILLE DESERVING OF NICKNAME WHICH HE BEARS

In the World's Series Baseball Magazine, "Rabbit" Maranville of the Braves, is briefly classified as follows:—

Walter J. Maranville, shortstop. Born at Springfield, Mass. Resides in Springfield. First professional engagement at New Bedford. Bats right and throws right-handed. Height, 5 feet 4 inches. Weight, 142. Age, 22.

The backbone of a club, the story continues, is at second base. The brunt of the fielding chances center there, and upon the combined strength of its guardians depends, in a great measure, the repelling of the sluggers' assaults with the bat. Moreover, it is at second base that the fleet-footed base stealers die, and it is this same deadly corner that acts as a pivot for those crushing double plays which so take the life out of the opposing club. An impregnable second base position requires a nicety of balance and a perfection of co-operation between those two players who fill the infield gap at second and short. Now and again, in a baseball generation, two players are found who fulfill all the requirements of this difficult role. And where they occur is the foundation of a formidable club.

When John Evers left Chicago, he found another Tinker at his right hand. And in this fact the good people who are unable to account for the astonishing success of the Braves may find their explanation. Of Evers we have nothing to say. His exploits have been told often and well. But the career of Maranville must be written as the story of the most sensational shortstop in the National league.

The "Rabbit" well deserves his name. Those spectators who have seen him skim along the ground, scoop up a zipping grounder, a few inches from the dusty surface, and line it with the speed and precision of a rifle bullet to first, will appreciate the aptness of the nick-name. Probably the most diminutive player in the big leagues, one of the fleetest and surest judges of a ball close to the ground, he is a marvel, in action a living realization of all that becomes the natural ball player.

"Rabbit" Maranville, otherwise christened Walter J., on the nineteenth of November, 1892. The name suggests French ancestry, but as both his parents were unmistakably Irish, it is safe to assume that the various rumors of French or Spanish origin, claimed for the youthful prodigy, are rumors only.

Maranville played on the local grammar school team as a pitcher. He also played on the local high school club, and eventually, with a strong, semi-professional aggregation known as the Blue Labels. His work was stellar, and it generally conceded that he had a big league berth reserve, even at that early age. A large step towards that goal was taken when he was signed up for the New Bedford club of the New England League. The city of whale oil, Portuguese immigrants, and cotton looms, was duly and visibly impressed with the antics of the new addition to their club, And as New Bedford is no great distance from Boston the latter city, in due time heard of his exploits, and, in the fall of 1912 the National club of that city signed Maranville to a contract, and installed him at short.

It was not, however, until 1913, that Maranville began to burn up the circuits and remind the admiring public that Hans Wagner did not possess an unlimited mortgage on all those talents requisite to a shortstop in good standing. His hitting still remained rather fitful, but his fielding was grand. The indulgent public, remembering that the shortstop is the most valuable, for his ability to knock down twisting grounders and line them to first base, welcomed Maranville like a long lost brother, and his career was fairly commenced.

In many respects, Maranville's work on the diamond duplicates that of Owen Bush, of the Tigers. Bush also is a midget on stature, one of the hardest men in the world to pitch to, a marvel of fielding effectiveness, and a fast man on the bases. Incidentally, there are many people who consider Bush the greatest shortstop in the American League, just as there are many who make the same claim for Maranville in the National.

Maranville is not yet twenty-two years old. Coming up from obscurity, to a dizzy height at the very pinnacle of his profession, and linked for the first time in his career with a winning club, there is much to turn a youngster's head. Some people have claimed as much for Maranville in his circus stunts and grand stand plays on the field. There is no evidence, however, of such a serious defect, for no defect in a ball player is more serious than this same chestiness, or more apt to annihilate brilliant prospects. Quiet, likeable, by no means boastful, Maranville's future exploits will be watched with interest by a whole army of earnest wellwishers.

Maranville has no settled occupation outside baseball, the profession into which he entered at so early an age. Last winter he was on the stage for a time, and professed a great fondness for the footlights. He is still too young to have any great proclivity for other occupations. There is a bright career as a player before the National League's most sensational shortstop.

VETERAN BACKSTOPS TO DO BULK OF WORK IN THE COMING SERIES

NEW YORK, Oct. 7—In all likelihood only four men will be called upon to work at the receiving ends of the batteries during the coming World's Championship Series between the Philadelphia Athletics and Boston Nationals. Each club will undoubtedly depend upon the two catchers who have given such a good account of themselves all thru the playing season. They will take an important part in the struggle for as soon as a catcher dons the mitt and mask of his calling in a contest he assumes an immense amount of responsibility. In fact there is no telling how many of the games are directed from behind the plate. In addition to exchanging signals with the pitcher as to the weakness or strength of the batters, he has to be a quick thinker, keen sighted, always alert and invariably accurate in throwing to head of the base pilferers.

In this department Connie Mack is probably the more fortunate in having Lapp and Schang, both of whom have had previous experience in World's Championship games. Lapp played in the 1910, 1911 and 1913 games, each time on the winning side and this will be the fourth time his services will be needed for the retention of the flag in Philadelphia. Altho only thirty years old Lapp has had a lot of experience during the nine years he has been identified with professional baseball. He stands five feet, ten and one-half inches and weighs about 170 pounds. Last year he took part in only one of the five games played for the championship.

Schang, on whom most of the work behind the bat devolved in the Athletic's-Grant's series a year ago, bore the brunt of the work thruout this year's American League season. Last year he caught in four of the five games played in the World's Series and may do the larger share again in the coming contests. He is 24 years old is five feet, nine inches tall and weighs about 180 pounds. His experience in major league baseball dates back just four years. Ira Thomas, the veteran catcher, is another on whom Manager Mack could call in case of accident to either of the two mentioned, but he has not been in the game much during the past season and it is not likely that his services will be needed. The Athletics also have a fourth catcher in McAvoy, late of the Baltimore International League team, but it is not at all probable that he will be called upon to go behind the bat against the Braves.

Manager Stallings has two very reliable receivers in Gowdy and Whaling, both of whom have been wonderfully successful this past season. Both are young men and each has been identified with professional baseball for five years. The success of the team, phenomenal as it was, in landing the National League pennant, this year speaks volumes for the work of the batteries and the catchers naturally are not to be overlooked for the parts they played so well in bringing about the unlooked for victory.

Gowdy, who did the lion's share of catching for the Braves during the season, stands one inch over six feet and weighs 197 pounds. Whaling, who is 25 years old, just one year older than Gowdy, also is a six-footer and weighs 188 pounds.

The season's record of the Athletics' and Braves' catchers, as compiled from unofficial figures, is as follows:

Philadelphia Athletics

Name	G.	P.O.	A.	E.	P.C	B't'g
Schang	95	470	156	29	.956	.268
Lapp	59	283	82	10	.973	.234

Boston Braves

Name	G.	P.O.	A.	E.	P.C.	B't'g
Gowdy	94	435	155	12	.979	.238
Whaling	56	249	86	6	.982	.215

SPORTING TIPS

To the younger set of sport lovers the announcement of the death of William R. Pitman at Brooklyn, N. Y., the other day does not mean anything but to the old-timer the sad news brings back a flood of memories. Pitman, always known as "Happy Days" was a native of Maine and the first rider in the State of any note, appearing in Bangor way back in the high wheel days. Mr. Pitman began his cycling days in November, 1877. He always was an amateur rider and was the holder of the 100-mile tricycle that weighed 106 pounds and was the only one of four competitors to finish. Until ten years ago Mr. Pitman made it a custom on his birthday, April 12, to celebrate the event by making a century run on a bicycle.. In later years he rode a motorcycle.

The Boston mail today was anxiously awaited by many Lewiston and Auburn men who had sent in their orders for tickets to the world's series. A good-sized delegation will go to Boston from here, many planning to make the trip by automobile.

The cool weather this week was welcomed by the football men. Hard practice with the mercury around seventy degrees isn't any fun.

Colby's eleven is practicing behind closed gates in preparation for the game with Tufts next Saturday. Captain Fraser is back with the squad but will not take part in any hard work for a couple of weeks owing to his injuries.

The annual Colby freshman-sophomore track meet takes place this afternoon.

The Lawrence high school football team has organized at Fairfield with Louis Ryan, '13, as captain. The boys hope to secure Jack Lowney of Dorchester, Mass., Colby '16 as coach.

Judson E. Langen, Brunswick, has offered a handsome loving cup to the Bowdoin College athletic association if the football team wins the Maine championship. If the football team should fail to win the championship Mr. Langen announces his intention of repeating the offer for the baseball championship next spring.

Leach Cross of New York outfought Walter Mohr of Brooklyn in a ten round contest in Brooklyn, Tuesday night.

Captain Collins of the Athletics.

Photograph, Underwood & Underwood, New York.]

BASEBALL FOR BUSY FANS

AMERICAN.

Boston 8; Washington 4.
Philadelphia 1; New York 2.
No other games scheduled.

Standing.

	Won	Lost	Per ct. Won
Philadelphia	99	52	.656
Boston	91	61	.599
Washington	80	73	.523
Detroit	80	73	.523
St. Louis	70	82	.461
Chicago	70	83	.458
New York	67	85	.411
Cleveland	51	102	.333

Games To-day.

Washington at Boston.
New York at Philadelphia.

NATIONAL.

First Game, Brooklyn 3; Boston 2. Second game, Brooklyn 3; Boston 7. (7 innings by agreement).

First game, New York 5; Philadelphia 1. Second game, New York 0; Philadelphia 8. (7 innings; darkness).

No other games scheduled.

Standing.

	Won	Lost	Per ct. Won
Boston	94	59	.614
New York	84	70	.546
St. Louis	81	72	.530
Chicago	78	76	.507
Brooklyn	75	79	.487
Philadelphia	74	80	.481
Pittsburgh	69	85	.448
Cincinnati	60	94	.390

(League closed).

FEDERAL.

First game, Baltimore 11; Pittsburgh 1. Second game, Baltimore 1; Pittsburgh 1 (10 innings; darkness).

Buffalo 3; Brooklyn 1.

Indianapolis 7; St. Louis 4.

First game, Chicago 0; Kansas City 1. Second game, Kansas City 5; Chicago 3. (7 innings; darkness).

Standing.

	Won	Lost	Per ct. Won
Indianapolis	87	65	.572
Chicago	86	67	.56.
Baltimore	80	68	.541
Buffalo	78	68	.534
Brooklyn	74	75	.497
Kansas City	67	83	.44[illegible]
Pittsburgh	62	82	.431
St. Louis	62	87	.416

Games To-day.

Kansas City at Chicago.
St. Louis at Indianapolis.
Pittsburgh at Baltimore.
Brooklyn at Buffalo.

18 Pages Today

The Boston Post

EXTRA

EIGHTEEN PAGES—ONE CENT | Established 1831. | TUESDAY, OCTOBER 13, 1914 | Copyrighted, 1914, by Post Publishing Co. | EIGHTEEN PAGES—ONE CENT

AIRMEN TRY TO BLOW UP NOTRE DAME

Aviators Deliberately Aimed at Paris Cathedral

Special Cable to the London Daily Mail and Boston Post.

PARIS, Oct. 12.—Edmund Haracourt, commissioner of historic monuments, is positive that the German aviators in their raid of yesterday tried to destroy the Cathedral of Notre Dame.

CAREFULLY AIMED

He says he saw four bombs dropped from a Taube machine which were aimed carefully at the cathedral. M. Haracourt made an investigation today of the damage caused by the bombs. He says the first bomb fell a short distance from the Rue de la Broise. The second dropped in the Seine beside the house of Cardinal Amette, archbishop of Paris.

The third fell in the square in front of the cathedral a few yards from the doors of that edifice and threw flames in the air to a height above the trees around the square. The fourth bomb struck the roof of the cathedral and smashed off six small wooden beams of the north transepts of the roof where a hole was broken as large as a man's body.

One of the principal supporting beams of the roof was torn to pieces while the heat melted the lead in the stained glass surrounding the clock-like window of the north transept, which was riddled by fragments of the bomb.

N. E. SUFFRAGE LEAGUE OPENS CONVENTION

WORCESTER, Oct. 12.—The New England Suffrage League opened its 11th annual convention in this city today at the Belmont Avenue Church. The organization is composed of colored citizens of New England who are agitating for the restoration of ballot rights in the Southern States.

GERMANS MOVING ON FRENCH COAST CITIES

Troops Released From Antwerp Sweeping Down Belgian Coast to Channel Ports—Sharp Fighting Near Lille, Threaten Allied Left Wing—Allies Will Defend Ostend to Save Belgian Army

A GROUP OF BELGIAN PRIESTS AND NUNS TAKEN AMID THE RUINS OF THE CHURCH AT TERMONDE.

The city changed hands no less than four times, and it was finally reduced to ruins by the Germans. This photo was taken by Edwin F. Weigle, war photographer for the Boston Post and Chicago Tribune.

WAR NEWS IN BRIEF FORM

An official Berlin statement makes the claim that the British blew up 10 of the Antwerp forts and that the Belgians lost 20,000 men as prisoners.—OFFICIAL.

The allies drove back several attacks of the Germans between Lassigny and Roye. Cavalry engagements continue in the regions of La Bassee, Estaires and Hazebrouck.—OFFICIAL.

The French brigade of marine fusileers in an action against the Germans on the latter's left wing, repulsed the enemy, the German losses being 200 killed and 50 prisoners. The French losses were 9 killed, 39 wounded, 1 missing.—OFFICIAL.

Despatches from both Vienna and Petrograd indicate that the Austrian army at Przemysl, by the aid of reinforcements, has turned on the Russians and forced them to retreat from before the besieged city.—OFFICIAL.

Six more bombs were hurled into the streets of Paris from a German areoplane, but no damage was done. French aviators started in pursuit.—OFFICIAL.

The Russian armored cruiser Pallada was torpedoed by a German submarine in the Baltic Sea on Sunday and sank with all her crew.—OFFICIAL.

LONDON, Oct. 12.—Once more, as in the early days of the war, the cavalry are sweeping westward to cut off communications between England and the northern coast of France.

Continued on Page 8—First Column

HIGH TIDE TO-DAY
A. M. 5:40 | P. M. 6:03
Portland 24m., Gloucester 26m., Newport 3h. 38m. earlier.

SUN Rises 5:53, Sets 5:07. MOON Rises 12:03 a. m. tonight.

Moon's changes—Last quarter Oct. 12, new moon Oct. 19, first quarter Oct. 25, full moon Nov. 2.
286th day of year; 21st day of autumn.
Day 11h. 14m. long; day's decrease 4h. 5m.
Evening stars—Venus very brilliant in west in early evening; Jupiter in the south.

Light auto lamps tonight at 5:37; other vehicles at 6:07.

TODAY'S ANNIVERSARIES, ETC.
Molly Pitcher, heroine of the battle of Monmouth, born, 1744.
Parnell arrested under the coercion act, 1881.
One year ago today: Episcopal general convention voted against change in name of church.

FAIR—COOLER

Forecast for Boston and vicinity—Tuesday, fair and cooler; Wednesday, fair; moderate north to east winds.

WASHINGTON, Oct. 12.—Forecast for New England: Fair Tuesday; Wednesday, unsettled.

YOUNG CHEMIST SHOOTS HIMSELF

A shot echoing through the house at 14 Rutland square at 11 o'clock last night led Miss Ella J. Barden, a lodger, to run to the room on the fourth floor from which the sound seemed to come. There she found the occupant, Raymond L. Bacon, lying in the closet with a bullet hole in his head and a .38-calibre revolver near his hand.

He was taken to the City Hospital in the East Dedham street ambulance, but died a few minutes after reaching there. Bacon was a chemist, 30 years old, and unmarried. He had roomed at the Rutland square address for two years. Recently, the police learned, he had been out of work and despondent.

PNEUMONIA KILLS SON, FATHER STRICKEN ALSO

Eugene L. McCarthy of 22 Deering street, Mattapan, auditor for the Hugh Nawn Construction Company, died suddenly of pneumonia at the City Hospital last evening. His father, Eugene McCarthy of Eden street, Charlestown, is also stricken with pneumonia, and may not live.

The son was taken to the hospital Friday, and placed on the dangerous list Saturday. He is survived by a wife, whom he married about a year ago.

BRAVES WIN IN 12TH BY DESPERATE FINISH 5 TO 4

Wonderful Display of Gameness Gives Boston Third Victory—Apparently Soundly Beaten, Get Two Runs in Ninth and Tie Score—Gowdy's Two-Bagger and Bush's Error Win Game in 12th—Wonderful Batting by Gowdy Features Contest—Record Crowd Sees Most Spectacular Game

Maranville out at third in the fourth inning of yesterday's game at Fenway Park. The Rabbit, when he came to bat, sent a single to centre and then stole second. As Schang's poor throw to Collins to cut him off got away from the Athletics' second baseman, Maranville kept on to third. Gowdy was then walked. On an attempted double steal Maranville was thrown out at third on a quick throw from Collins to Baker.

BY ED McGRATH

Steadfast the Braves, undying their rock-ribbed courage. Locked in bitter embrace with their desperate rivals of the clan of Mack for 12 tense innings of a world's series struggle, that will go down in baseball history as a masterpiece of masterpieces, the henchmen of Stallings finally burst through the bonds that had held them in restraint so long and with the climax of a miscue to aid swept through to victory.

Engraved in letters of gold is the score, Boston 5, Philadelphia 4. To the dying monarchs of the American league the score and result spells the gloom of the passing of the great crown of supremacy as leaders of the world of baseball.

PASSING OF TITLE AWAITED

Thus is it written. That vast army of fans that swarmed and struggled and fought to enter the gates of Fenway Park yesterday afternoon were fated to witness the twilight of the baseball gods.

For if ever the passing of the long-time rulers of the destiny of baseball's greatest honor, the world's title, was awaiting its call, it was there on the greensward of Fenway Park yesterday.

Thrice have the Braves now pitted their all against the full powers possessed by their antagonists. Thrice have the men of Boston found that their all, a compound of everything that goes to make them the worthy mastermen of the American diamond, is of the stuff to render the Athletics their vassals.

There on the home park of the Braves, surrounded by all the enormous host of enthusiasts, numbered in excess of 35,000, with every incentive to make the stand that would prove them to have the qualities of genuine defenders of their proud title, the Athletics fell.

LAST STAND OF GREAT TEAM

It was the last stand, if there was ever the last stand of a great team, desperate in the conviction that victory now was absolutely to turn on the full command of all that they possessed of courage, playing ability and brains. And the men of Mack with loins girded up, with grim determination written in every move, fought and fought and fought. They fought with every nerve strained.

Not once did they surrender until in that fatal 12th there came the little rift within the armor. Alas for Joe Bush. Joe, the hero of past world's series, the wild peg that shot from his hand past the waiting Baker at third base sounded the knell.

Continued on Page 10—Third Col.

Fair skies will arch Fenway Park for today's world's series game, but there will be more of a real October zip in the air, according to the weatherman's predictions.

THIS IS THE OFFICIAL SCORE

BOSTON.	AB.	R.	BH.	TB.	PO.	A.	E.
Moran, r. f	4	1	0	0	2	0	0
Evers, 2b	5	0	3	3	3	5	0
Connolly, l. f	4	0	0	0	1	0	1
Whitted c. f	5	0	0	0	2	0	0
Schmidt, 1b	5	1	1	1	17	1	0
Deal, 3b	5	0	1	2	2	3	0
Maranville, s. s	4	1	1	1	2	3	0
Gowdy, c	4	1	3	8	6	0	0
aMann	0	1	0	0	0	0	0
Tyler, p	3	0	0	0	1	5	0
bDevore	1	0	0	0	0	0	0
James, p	0	0	0	0	0	2	0
cGilbert	1	0	0	0	0	0	0
Totals	41	5	9	15	36	19	1
PHILADELPHIA.	**AB.**	**R.**	**BH.**	**TB.**	**PO.**	**A.**	**E.**
Murphy, r. f	5	2	2	4	2	0	0
Oldring, l. f	5	0	0	0	1	0	0
Collins, 2b	4	0	1	1	1	4	0
Baker, 3b	5	0	2	3	4	4	0
McInnis, 1b	5	1	1	2	18	0	0
Walsh, c. f	4	0	1	1	1	0	0
Barry, s. s	5	0	0	0	0	7	0
Schang, c	4	1	1	1	6	1	1
Bush, p	5	0	0	0	0	5	1
Totals	42	4	8	12	d33	21	2

aRan for Gowdy in 12th.
bBatted for Tyler in 10th.
cBatted for James in 12th.
dNone out in 12th when winning run was scored.

Boston	0	1	0	1	0	0	0	0	0	2	0	1	—5
Philadelphia	1	0	0	1	0	0	0	0	0	2	0	0	—4

Two-base hits — Murphy 2, Gowdy 2, McInnis, Deal, Baker. Home run—Gowdy. Hits—Off Tyler, 8 in 10 innings; off James, none in two innings. Sacrifice hit—Oldring. Sacrifice flies—Collins, Moran, Connolly. Stolen bases—Collins, Evers, Maranville 2. Double play—Evers, Maranville and Schmidt. First base on balls — Bush 4, Tyler 3, James 3. Struck out—Bush 4, Tyler 4, James 1. Time—3h. 6m. Umpires—At plate, Klem; on bases, Dineen; left field, Byron; right field, Hildebrand.

EVERETT HIGH WINS FROM RINDGE TECH

Everett won from Rindge Technical at the Everett High field yesterday morning, the Cambridge lads never having a ghost of a show to win, being trimmed 21 to 0.

NIGHT FINAL EDITION
TEMPERATURE.
Min. 58. Max. 61.

The Evening Sun.

NIGHT FINAL EDITION
Local Forecast—Unsettled and cool to-night; probably rain to-morrow.
(Detailed Weather Report on Page 2.)

VOL. XXVIII.—NO. 181. NEW YORK, TUESDAY, OCTOBER 13, 1914.—Copyright, 1914, by the Sun Printing and Publishing Association. PRICE ONE CENT.

BRAVES NOW CHAMPIONS, TAKING FOUR STRAIGHT

MANY GAINS CLAIMED BY ALLIES; GERMAN ARMY CORPS IN LILLE

New Offensive Move Started on Germany's Right Wing---They Occupy Ghent---Belgian Government May Go to France.

PARIS, Oct. 13.—The official communique issued by the War Office at 3 o'clock this afternoon told of the renewal of the offensive by the Allies against the armies of Von Kluck and Von Boehn on the German right. It also contained the admission that the Germans had occupied Lille.

The communique follows:

"First—On our left wing our forces have once more taken the offensive in the regions of Hazebrouck and Bethune against the enemy's forces, composed for the most part of cavalry drawn from the battlefront at Bailleul, Estaires and La Bassee.

"The town of Lille, which has been held by one of our territorial detachments, was attacked and occupied by a German corps d'armee. Between Arras and Albert we have made considerable progress.

"Second—In the centre we have also made progress in the region of Berry-au-Bac and advanced slightly toward Souain, to the west of Argonne and to the north of Malancourt, between Argonne and the Meuse.

"On the right bank of the Meuse our troops who hold the heights of the Meuse to the east of Verdun have advanced to the south of the road leading from Verdun to Metz. In the Apremont region we have gained a little ground on our right and driven back a German attack on our left.

"Third—On our right wing (Vosges and Alsace) there has been no change.

"On the whole yesterday was marked by sensible progress made by our forces along the many points of the battlefield.

"Fourth—In Galicia the Austrian forces who had been beaten are trying to reform their lines about twenty-five miles west of Przemysl."

Gen. d'Amande, commanding the French forces on the extreme left, has received reenforcements in the belief that the next big general conflict of the war will be staged on Belgian soil. The allied forces in this theatre of the war are said to be well situated. Cavalry encounters continue without cessation.

The rehabilitated French aeronautical division is showing unusual activity in aerial patrol work in guarding against repetitions of the German bomb dropping over Paris during the past two days.

Belgian Government Will Seek Haven in France

BORDEAUX, Oct. 13.—Temporary offices have been provided at Havre by the French Government for several Belgian officials and ministers who have reached that city from Ostend, and it is definitely stated that the Belgian Government will be transferred to France.

OSTEND, Oct. 13.—It is believed that raids by German airships are largely responsible for the removal of the Belgian Government to France. Three German aviators flew over the city late Monday afternoon and two of them dropped bombs. Neither of them exploded, but the raids caused a panic that is driving the people to England.

LONDON, Oct. 13.—There is no doubt that the lines are being drawn for a big battle in northwest France and Belgium. The German troops released by the capture of Antwerp are advancing rapidly to join the other forces in the move toward Ostend.

Ghent has been occupied and the big German guns are now reported bombarding Bruges, but twenty-three miles from Ostend.

The occupation of Ghent has not been officially confirmed, but despatches from several points to-day assert that the city is now in the hands of the Germans, who have pushed on in the direction of Bruges.

Movements of large forces from the direction of Lille to Courtrai in Belgium indicate that the Germans expect to have to fight a big battle.

Meanwhile on the left wing of the Allies severe fighting is reported. The Allies are said to be making a desperate attempt to win a decisive victory in the flanking movement against Von Kluck before the German troops from Antwerp can come to his assistance.

More Troops to Defend Ostend.

It is reported that the Allies have already sent forward strong forces of troops to check the Geman advance and defend Ostend. The Geman movement from Antwerp is undoubtedly aimed at the seacoast towns, with Ostend as the first objective, and the Allies are sure to make their best efforts to prevent success for such a dangerous movement.

A despatch from Calais to-day reported that the Germans were evidently making unusual preparations for a bat-

(Continued on Second Page.)

RUSSIANS SWEPT BACK TO VISTULA

Germans Hold Country as Far as Warsaw, Says Berlin.

LONDON, Oct. 13.—Advices from Berlin by way of Amsterdam say that the following German communication as to events in the Eastern theatre of war has been issued:

"After their expulsion from East Prussia the Russian armies were pursued across the frontier. The centre of the German military operations is now in Poland. The whole of Poland west of the Vistula is now in German possession, the Russians occupying only Warsaw.

"The few kilometres lost by the Germans in Russia's territory near the East Prussian frontier were of little importance, as it was never intended definitely to occupy or govern Suwalki.

"It is not true that the siege of Ossowetz has been abandoned, as the fortress has never been besieged. During our retreat to the East Prussian frontier our troops nowhere were defeated, but on the contrary repulsed many attacks of the Russians."

[If Poland, west of the Vistula, has been cleared of Russian troops the indications are that the portion of the Czar's army which has been proceeding

(Continued on Second Page.)

FACES TASK OF SUBDUING SOUTH AFRICAN REBELLION.

Gen. Louis Botha, Premier and Leader of Boer Loyalists.

M'KIM TORN WILL CASE UP IN COURT AGAIN

Jury to Decide if Nieces Get Fortune.

Nassau county's famous torn will case, which sprang into public notice following the death, in 1912, of Joseph McKim, wealthy builder of Far Rockaway, came up in the Special Term of the Nassau County Supreme Court to-day and was put over until November for trial before a jury. Justice Clarke's order was on the motion of Daniel Whitlock, attorney for the widow and two daughters of McKim.

Joseph McKim was 91 years old when he died in the River Crest Sanitarium, Astoria, L. I., on July 9, 1912. He had been adjudged insane prior to his commitment. William Willett, Jr., who has since been convicted in the Kings County Supreme Court nomination scandal, was appointed as a committee of person and estate.

In January, 1912, Mrs. Wilhelmina Collins, a niece of McKim, began an action before County Judge Humphrey to have McKim declared competent and Willett removed. The action was opposed by Mrs. McKim and the two daughters, Anna and Frances. Judge Humphrey decided against Mrs. Collins.

At the time Mrs. Collins began her fight she knew that McKim prior to being taken to the sanitarium had written a will in his own handwriting, disinheriting his wife and daughters and distributing his fortune among various nieces and nephews. This document was in the custody of Lewis L. Fosdick. It was drawn up on June 4, 1909.

Mrs. McKim persuaded her husband to write a letter to Fosdick asking him to destroy the will. The document was torn up in the presence of Anna McKim, but Fosdick preserved the pieces in an envelope. McKim died intestate. The present action is backed by the nieces and nephews in an effort to have the torn will admitted to probate.

McKim was at one time reputed to be worth nearly $1,000,000, but his fortune dwindled until the amount now in contention will run only between $25,000 and $50,000.

PAPAL SECRETARY OF STATE.

Pope Benedict Offers the Place to Cardinal Gasparri.

ROME, Oct. 13.—Pope Benedict to-day offered the Papal Secretaryship of State to Cardinal Pietro Gasparri, titular Bishop of Cesari di Palestine. The Cardinal is loath to accept the high honor and has not yet returned his answer. Cardinal Ferrata's recent death from appendicitis left the office of Papal Secretary of State vacant.

Cardinal Gasparri is one of the youngest of the members of the Sacred College, being 52 years of age. He was elevated to the Cardinalate on Dec. 16, 1907.

$100,000 Gold Bars to Canada.

There was withdrawn to-day from the Assay Office $100,000 in gold bars for shipment to Canada.

MARTIAL LAW IN SOUTH AFRICA AS BOERS REVOLT

Rebellion Led by Col. Maritz Aims to Set Up Republic in Colony.

ANTI-BRITISH PARTY BACKED BY GERMAN

Loyal Troops in Northwest Cape Province Disarmed by Their Comrades.

LONDON, Oct. 13.—Martial law has been proclaimed throughout South Africa, following discovery of a plot by Col. Maritz's command looking toward establishment of a republic in the Northwest Cape provinces.

The admission that open rebellion has been encountered and that a force of Anti-British Boers, armed with German guns and aided by German troops, is now in that territory, was made by the official press bureau to-day.

No attempt was made to-day to disguise the seriousness of the situation. The bureau claimed to have no definite word as to the number of men concerned in the revolt or of the location of the hostile force.

While the press bureau is silent as to Gen. Botha's action in this crisis, it is understood here that the former Boer leader, now Premier of the Union, will take immediate steps to suppress the revolt.

Gen. Botha is in command of the Union expedition into German Southwest Africa.

Governor's Proclamation.

The proclamation imposing martial law is as follows:

Whereas, The Government of the protectorate of German Southwest Africa has through a widespread secret propaganda persistently endeavored to seduce citizens of the Union and officers and members of the defence forces of the Union from their allegiance; and

Whereas, These efforts have so far succeeded that Lieut. Col. Solomon Gerhardus Maritz, together with a number of his officers and a portion of the forces under his command, has shamefully and traitorously gone over to the enemy and is now in open rebellion against the Government and the people of the Union, and is, in conjunction with forces of the enemy, invading the northern portion of the Cape province; and

Whereas, There is grave reason to think the Government of German Southwest Africa has, through its numerous spies and agents, communicated with and corrupted also other citizens of the Union under the false and treacherous pretext of favoring the establishment of a republic in South Africa; and,

Whereas, The Government of the Union considers it necessary to take effective measures to protect and defend the interests of the Union and its loyal and law abiding citizens against these inseditious and treacherous attacks from within and without, and to that end to declare martial law.

Continuing, the proclamation declares the whole Union of South Africa is under martial law as understood and administered in time of war, and dating as from to-day.

The proclamation is signed by Lord Buxton, Governor-General of the Union, and countersigned by Gen. Smuts, Minister of Defence.

There are regularly only 7,000 British troops in the South African Union, and it is believed that in many cases the officers have been recalled to aid in the European war. The permanent force for defence is the South African Mounted Riflemen.

How Disaffection Grew.

The bureau's statement recounts that there has been a certain amount of disaffection since the resignation of Commandant-General Beyers and that the South African Government finally determined to supersede Col. Maritz, commanding in the Northwest Cape provinces. Col. Maritz defied the order removing him and forwarded an ultimatum to the Cape Town authorities

(Continued on Second Page.)

STALLINGS USES RUDOLPH AGAIN; MACK GIVES SHAWKEY A CHANCE

Fenway Park Is Packed Despite Cold Wind.

ROOTERS RIOT

Late Comers Are Bombarded With Paper Missiles by Joyous Fans.

By JOE VILA.

FENWAY PARK, BOSTON, OCT. 13.—Although a cold wind chilled the fans that packed the stands to capacity to-day for the fourth game of the World's Series it did not chill their enthusiasm. The game started at 2:04 amid wild cheers.

Rudolph and Shawkey were opposed on the mound.

FIRST INNING.

Rudolph's first pitch cut the plate and was called a strike. On the second Murphy rapped to Evers, who threw him out at first. Rube Oldring was next and fouled the first ball to Gowdy. Collins had the first one called, and then singled to centre on the next pitch, a clean hit.

Rudolph made numerous vain attempts to catch Collins off first. Two balls went by on Baker, but the third was called a strike by Byron. Rudolph made another attempt to nail Collins, but it was fruitless. Then Baker raised a lofty fly which Whitted caught after a short run, gauging the ball cleverly in spite of the high wind. No runs, one hit, no errors, one left.

Shawkey, a right hander, wore a red undershirt under his uniform, thereby resembling a human danger signal. The first two were balls, the third was a strike and the fourth was a slashing liner to Baker. Baker also picked up Evers's bounder near the bag and easily threw him out at first with a fast peg to McInnis.

The first one Shawkey delivered to Connolly was a strike, the second was a ball and Connolly fouled the third into the grand stand. On the next pitch, Connolly was out on a curving fly to Oldring about ten yards from the left field bleachers. No runs, no hits, no errors, none left.

SECOND INNING.

Rudolph burned over a first strike on McInnis, the second was fouled off, putting McInnis in the hole. On the next pitch Deal made a left handed stop of McInnis's sharp grounder and with a pretty throw to Schmidt he got Stuffy by a step. Walsh hit the second ball over Connolly's head, which was poorly handled and went for a two-bagger. Maranville retired Barry at first, Walsh remaining at second.

Schang let the first go by, the second was too far away from the corner and the third was also outside. Schang missed the next by a foot as the ball dropped down past his knees. Rudolph pitched the fifth ball wide of the plate, and the count was three and two. Then Schang swung with all his might and was out. Rudolph was cheered as he walked to the bench. No runs, one hit, no errors, one left.

Klem called the first one to Whitted a ball and the second a strike. Whitted hit the third ball on a deal line to Oldring, who grabbed it without moving a step. Shawkey knocked down a hard hit from Schmidt and threw him out. Gowdy was loudly applauded when he stepped to the plate. The first two were wide and the next was a strike. The next was wide and Stallings signalled Gowdy to wait. The next was called a strike, though it looked to be outside.

Gowdy hammered a long foul into the left field stand, the fans fighting for possession of the ball. Shawkey failed to get over the fourth and Gowdy walked. Maranville was greeted with more applause and let the first go over for a strike. Then Maranville hit to Barry, who forced Gowdy easily at second and the side was out. No runs, no hits, no errors, one left.

THIRD INNING.

Shawkey missed the first ball. The second was called a strike by Byron and he missed the third also by two feet. Murphy hit a hard smash straight on the third base line, Deal making a fine stop and perfect throw to Schmidt, getting the runner.

Oldring hit the first ball for a single to left centre, Maranville making a desperate effort to get one hand on the ball. Oldring tried to steal second, but Rudolph pitched out and Gowdy's magnificent throw nailed the runner at second. No runs, one hit, no errors, none left.

Deal hit the first ball for a high fly to Oldring and was out. Rudolph got a great hand as he walked to the plate. The first ball was called a strike.

The second was a strike and the next a ball. Rudolph hit an easy grounder to Barry, who threw him out at first. Moran was also out the same way on a hopper, Barry to McInnis. No runs, no hits, no errors, none left.

FOURTH INNING.

On the first ball Collins hit sharply to Evers, who handled the ball nicely on a sharp bound and threw him out at first. Baker let the first go by for a ball. Umpire Byron warned the Braves to keep quiet on the bench. Baker had two and one and Rudolph did not seem anxious to put them over. Then Baker hit one too hot for Schmidt and it was a base hit, striking Big Schmidt in the cheek. Evers tried to field the ball to Rudolph at first, but Baker was at first ahead of it. Time was called while Schmidt nursed his bruise, but he resumed play.

McInnis followed with a single to left, Connolly throwing to third too late to get Baker, but Deal whipped the pill to Evers at second and McInnis was called out by Hiludebrand Rudolph pitched over a first strike to Walsh, who also fanned at the second a wide curve. Rudolph tried to get one over the corner but Byron called it a ball. The fourth also was too far outside. Rudolph tride still another wide curve and Walsh fell for it and mossed it by a foot. The crowd burst into awild cheer. No runs, two hits.

When Evers came up Shawkey had a no hit record to that point. He was going great guns, and the crowd began to worry. Evers had two strikes and a ball, and the young Mack pitcher decided to play with him. He pitched a wide one, but Johnny refused to bite.

The next was good and was fouled over the grand stand. Shawkey hurled the fifth far above the Boston captain's bean and the next was wide and Evers trotted to first.

Up came Slugger Joe Connolly, and the crowd howled. Schang saved a wild pitch by making a diving stop of a ball that hit the ground. Collins momentarily juggled Connolly's hard grounder and had to throw to first, getting the batter, but Evers reached second in safety.

Shawkey pitched two strikes in succession to Whitted and then wasted one. Whitted hit one too hard for Collins, the ball hitting Eddie in the shin, Whitted being safe at first and Evers at third. Time was called while Collins nursed his hurt.

The official scorer gave it as an error for Collins despite his crack in the leg. Collins was limping when play was resumed. Again playing the hit and run game, Evers scored when Barry had no chance to get whitted at second and therefore threw Schmidt out at first, while the crowd went wild.

Shawkey pulled down a solid smash from Gowdy's bat and tossed it to McInnis for the third out. One run, no hits, one error, one left.

THE SCORE BY INNINGS

AT BOSTON.

ATHLETICS	0	0	0	0	1	0	0	0	0	1
BOSTON..	0	0	0	1	2	0	0	0		3

BATTING ORDER---FOURTH GAME.

ATHLETICS.		BRAVES.	
Murphy	Right Field	Moran	Right Field
Oldring	Left Field	Evers	Second Base
Collins	Second Base	Connolly	Left Field
Baker	Third Base	Whitted	Centre Field
McInnis	First Base	Schmidt	First Base
Walsh	Centre Field	Gowdy	Catcher
Barry	Shortstop	Maranville	Shortstop
Schang	Catcher	Deal	Third Base
Shawkey	Pitcher	Rudolph	Pitcher

Umpires—American League, Dineen and Hildebrand; National League, Klem and Byron.

WOOD'S ACCOUNTS STRAIGHT.

Louis G. Stevenson Succeeds Him as Secretary of State.

SPRINGFIELD, Ill., Oct. 13.—State Auditor Brady, investigating the accounts of Secretary of State Harry Wood, who killed himself yesterday, declared to-day that the accounts were perfectly straight.

Gov. Dunne to-day appointed Louis G. Stevenson of Bloomington, son of Adlai E. Stevenson, to succeed Wood.

GIANTS NEED BUT ONE MORE GAME

Demaree and Warhop on the Firing Line.

SCORE BY INNINGS.

YANKEES.....	0	1	0	0	—
GIANTS.......	0	0	0		—

POLO GROUNDS, Oct. 13.—Jack Warhop, who scored the only victory for the Yanks in the present series, was sent back against the Giants by Manager Peckinpaugh this afternoon. Al Demaree was the choice of Mike Donlin, who was again in charge of the Giants.

Umpire Rigler was behind the bat, Evans on the bases, Hart in right and Connolly in left.

The crowd was the smallest of the series; hardly a thousand were in the stands when play was called.

The batting order:

Giants.	Yankees.
Bescher, l. f.	Maisel, 3b.
Doyle, 2b.	Hartzell, l. f.
Burns, r. f.	Cook, r. f.
Fletcher, ss.	Cree, c. f.
Snodgrass, c. f.	Mullen, 1b.
Grant, 3b.	Peckinpaugh, ss.
Merkle, 1b.	Nunamaker, c.
Meyers, c.	Boone, 2b.
Demaree, p.	Warhop, p.

Umpires—Rigler, Evans, Hart and Connolly.

FIRST INNING.

Maisel was called out on strikes. Demaree threw out Hartzell. Cook flied to Fletcher. No runs, no hits, no errors, none left.

Boone threw out Bescher. Doyle singled to centre. Burns flied to Cook. Fletcher fouled to Nunamaker. No runs, one hit, no errors, one left.

SECOND INNING.

Cree doubled over third. When Meyers attempted to catch Cree off second, he threw the ball to centre field and Cree scored. Mullen was hit by a pitched ball. Peckinpaugh hit into a double play, Doyle to Fletcher to Merkle. Nunamaker hit the left field fence for a double. Boone grounded to Merkle. One run, two hits, one error, one left.

Boone threw out Snodgrass. Grant singled past Maisel. Merkle flied to Hratzell. Grant out stealing, Nunamaker to Boone. No runs, one hit, no errors, none left.

GUGGENHEIM DIVORCE STANDS.

Appellate Division Affirms Decision of Lower Court.

CHICAGO, Oct. 13.—The Appellate Court to-day handed down two opinions affirming the decision of the Circuit Court in refusing to annul the divorce granted Grace Guggenheim-Wahl from William Guggenheim, the smelter magnate.

Mr. Guggenheim brought suit to annul the decree onthe ground that it was granted by fraud.

RUSH PLEA FOR THAW'S RETURN.

New York Lawyers Want Case Advanced.

WASHINGTON, Oct. 13.—Application for the advancement of the litigation over the extradition of Harry K. Thaw from New Hampshire to New York was made before the Supreme Court this afternoon by attorneys representing New York State. William Travers Jerome had made a statement of the reason for a speedy decision of the case, alleging that the stay of Thaw in New Hampshire was a scandal to the State of New York.

July Circulation Averages:
Daily Post 513,925 Gain 67,503 per day over July, 1914. Daily Post's Greatest July!
Sunday Post 341,396 Gain 27,499 per Sunday over July, 1914 Sunday Post's Greatest July!

The Boston Post

EXTRA

SIXTEEN PAGES—ONE CENT | Established 1831. | THURSDAY, AUGUST 19, 1915 ** | Copyrighted, 1915, by Post Publishing Co. | SIXTEEN PAGES—ONE CENT

47,000 STORM NEW BRAVES PARK; 10,000 TURNED AWAY

Greatest Crowd in Baseball History at Opening of New Field at Allston—Braves Dedicate New Grounds by Victory Over St. Louis 3 to 1—Many Notables Present

HERE IS GIVEN AN IDEA OF THE MASS OF HUMANITY THAT PACKED THE BLEACHER SECTIONS OF FIRST BASE AND RIGHT FIELD. IN THE FOREGROUND ARE THE FIRST BASE BLEACHERS, JAMMED TO THE LIMIT, WHILE BEYOND IS THE 25-CENT SECTION, LIKEWISE SO COMPLETELY FILLED THAT IT WAS IMPOSSIBLE TO GET ANOTHER FAN INTO IT.

New Park Is Largest Baseball Field in World

Ticket Office Swamped by Rush of Eager Fans

Many Presentations to Mark the Opener

SOME FIRSTS NOTED AT OPENING GAME

The first hit was made by Arthur Butler of the Cardinals, a single.

Hank Gowdy got the first putout, and Dick Rudolph the credit of causing the first strikeout, when Miller Huggins, the first batter up in the first inning, went down on strikes.

Sherwood Magee caught the first fly.

Arthur Butler of the Cardinals made the first assist, the same being on Johnny Evers in the first inning.

Butler also made the first error on the new park.

Charley Schmidt of the Braves made the first sacrifice hit.

Evers was the first to get a base on balls.

Tommy Long of the Cardinals was the first man to get an extra base hit, getting a double in the fourth inning.

Sherwood Magee scored the first run.

Rabbit Maranville drove in the first run with a single.

BY CHARLES E. PARKER

Forty-seven thousand persons, forming the greatest baseball crowd in the long history of the game, paid homage to the national pastime—to the Braves as a team and to President James E. Caffney as a clubowner and the sponsor of the greatest baseball park in the world—yesterday afternoon at the formal opening of Braves Field, the new Boston National league grounds.

Continued on Page 3—Second Col.

Yesterday's Baseball Results

NATIONAL LEAGUE
Boston 3, St. Louis 1.
Pittsburg 8, Philadelphia 4.
Chicago 9, Brooklyn 0.
Cincinnati 7, New York 4.

AMERICAN LEAGUE
Chicago 5, Boston 3.
Detroit 4, Philadelphia 1.
Cleveland 3, Washington 0.
New York-St. Louis, rain.

NEW ENGLAND LEAGUE
Lowell 4, Lewiston 3.
Lynn 4, Manchester 0.
Fitchburg 3, Lawrence 0; Lawrence 4, Fitchburg 0.
Worcester 4, Portland 3; Portland 16, Worcester 10.

FEDERAL LEAGUE
Baltimore 6, Chicago 0.
Pittsburg 12, Brooklyn 5.
Buffalo 3, Kansas City 2; Buffalo 3, Kansas City 2.

COLONIAL LEAGUE
Hartford 9, Pawtucket 6.
Brockton 3, New Bedford 1; New Bedford 3, Brockton 1.
Springfield 7, New Haven 6.

HIGH TIDE TODAY

A. M. 5:36 | P. M. 6:01

Portland 24m., Gloucester 26m., Newport 3h. 38m. earlier.

SUN Rises 4:54 Sets 6:41. **MOON** 9 days old. Sets 11:31 p.m.

Moon's changes—Full moon Aug. 24, last quarter Sept. 1, new moon Sept. 9, first quarter Sept. 16.

Full moons for year—Sept. 23, Oct. 22, Nov. 21, Dec. 21.

231st day of year; only 34 more days of summer; 384th day of war.

Day 13h. 47m. long; day's decrease 1h. 32m. since June 22.

Morning stars—Saturn, Venus, Jupiter.

Light auto lamps tonight at 7:11; other vehicles at 7:41.

TODAY'S ANNIVERSARIES, ETC.

Naval battle between the Constitution and the Guerriere, 1812.

One year ago today—Germans take Liege forts and sweep all upper Belgium.

FAIR

Forecast for Boston and vicinity—Fair Thursday and Friday; continued cool; moderate northwest to north winds.

WASHINGTON, Aug. 18.—Forecast for New England and eastern New York—Fair Thursday and Friday.

YESTERDAY'S TEMPERATURE
Recorded at Thompson's Spa.

	'14	'15		'14	'15
3 a. m.	67	59	3 p. m.	77	70
6 a. m.	66	58	6 p. m.	77	70
9 a. m.	75	63	9 p. m.	74	66
12 m.	79	68	12 mid.	71	63

Average temperature yesterday 64 12-24.
Average one year ago yesterday 73 5-24.

GALVESTON STORM COST $30,000,000

Other Coast Cities Report Heavy Damage

ONE HUNDRED LIVES LOST IN HURRICANE

Gigantic Sea Wall Saves Galveston Greater Loss

Direct word from the storm-swept communities of the southeast Texas coast is bringing details of the tropical hurricane which put Galveston, Houston, Texas City and scores of other towns in dire peril.

With large sections of the district yet unheard from the death list was more than 100, the heaviest reported loss being from Virginia Point, opposite Galveston. The property damage may exceed $30,000,000, with Galveston contributing half that amount.

According to information available last night the deaths were recorded as follows:

Virginia Point, 30; Texas City, 18; Galveston, 14; Morgan's Point, 11; Hitchcock, 7; Laporte, 7; Port Arthur, 4; Lynchburg, 3; Sylvan Beach, 3; Seabrook, 3; Houston, 2.

Continued on Page 9—Third Column

WOMAN DRAWS PISTOL IN CAR

Two Men Grapple With Her as Other Fans Flee

Except for two men, who grappled with her, the passengers on a "baseball special" quickly fled about 3 o'clock yesterday afternoon, when a woman pulled a 32-calibre loaded revolver from her corsage and pointed it at a man whom she declared had annoyed her.

The car was at Commonwealth avenue and St. Mary street when the incident occurred. Thoughts of passengers immediately turned from baseball to a place of safety.

The two men who remained in the car were John J. Hartigan of 115 Bowdoin street, Dorchester, and John C. Harty of 6 Shepard avenue. They grabbed the woman, and were in the act of taking the revolver from her grasp when Patrolman McGillivray of the Back Bay station came along.

The officer quickly disarmed the woman, who seemed to be laboring under a hallucination, and took her to the station house. Up to the time that she had brandished the revolver she had attracted no attention.

After the woman was taken to the Back Bay police station, Dr. Sherwood said that she was suffering from a mental depression and later she was taken to the Psychopathic Hospital. Late last evening her son visited the hospital. The authorities refused to give out her name. She is past middle life.

125 MORE MEN JOIN STRIKERS

Leaders Claim 875 Machinists Now Out

PAWTUCKET, Aug. 18.—One hundred of the 125 men employed on the night shift of the Potter & Johnson machine works tonight joined the ranks of the employees who struck today to enforce their demands for a new time and wage schedule. Machinists' leaders claim tonight that 875 of 1025 employees of the company were on strike.

Joseph H. Gilmore, organizer for the union, said that unless the demands for a 48-hour week and five cents an hour wage increase were acceded to, a strike would be called also at the Sellew Machine works this week, and that similar demands would be made upon the Narragansett Machine Company within a few days.

CHOLERA SPREADING IN AUSTRIA-HUNGARY

PARIS, Aug. 18, 9:40 a. m.—A Havas despatch from Zurich says that the latest report regarding cholera made by the Austro-Hungarian minister of interior states that the disease is spreading in that kingdom. Six hundred and seventy new cases have been officially reported, the majority in Galicia.

LYNCHERS TO BE PROTECTED

County Will Take No Action Against Frank's Slayers Unless Forced To

THOMAS E. WATSON,
Former Congressman from Georgia and once Populist candidate for President, who is directly charged with instigating, by his violent propaganda, the lynching of Leo Frank. Watson spread broadcast over the State weekly denunciations of Frank, coupled with threatening anti-Jewish agitation.

BY JOHN J. LEARY, JR.
Staff Correspondent of Boston Post and Chicago Tribune

MARIETTA, Ga., Aug. 18.—This is alibi day in Marietta. Not a leading citizen but has one of those useful legal devices ready for use, yet there is not a shadow of doubt that substantially every man and woman in Marietta knows who lynched Frank, any more than there is doubt in my mind that I talked with members of the mob this afternoon.

Plainly outsiders are not wanted in Marietta just now, unless they show early in their visit that they are not private detectives or secret service operators. When one establishes his identity, however, information minus names, and always prefaced with "I heard on good authority," or "I understand," is forthcoming. This boiled down leaves these conclusions clear:

PLANNED WEEKS AGO

That the lynching of Frank was carefully planned weeks ago. That on several occasions after the date was actually set the lynchers quit for one reason or another. That there were two groups, one of about 15 men working in Milledgeville paving the way for another group of 25 from this place. That the local mob was made up of men prominent in the affairs of the town and county. That at a postponed meeting of the Progressive League, a sort of chamber of commerce, many well known faces were mising Monday night. That Cobb county will take no action unless forced to do so by outside forces. That a movement is now under foot in Atlanta to uncover the murderers of Frank by means of offering a large reward—this because leading citizens there fear the mob spirit is becoming too rampant in this part of the State; that Georgia has ex-Judge Newton A. Morris to thank for it that Frank's body was not burned by a mob led by Bob Howell, ex-convict and local bad man, and that at bottom Frank was a victim of politics.

Decided After Commutation

To an extent also latent race prejudice figured, but, next to politics in importance is the exaggerated idea of chivalry, that causes a certain type of Southerners to insist upon his devotion to his women folk, and his insistence upon protecting their honor.

It was first decided to lynch Frank just after his sentence was commuted. From the start it was the plan to bring him to this place where Mary Phagan was born and here lynch him. After the convict Green attempted to murder him, the plan was left in abey-

Continued on Page 8—Third Column

FIRES UPON YOUNG GIRL IN THEATRE

Suitor, Angered by Quarrel, Tries to Slay Her

NEW BEDFORD, Aug. 18.—Leon E. Either tried to shoot Miss Mary Holland in a crowded moving picture theatre on Acushnet avenue late this afternoon, as the result of a quarrel the two had earlier in the day.

As the lights flashed on at the end of a picture drama, Either rose from his seat in the front row of the balcony, located the Holland girl, who was sitting in an orchestra seat, pulled out a revolver, aimed carefully and fired.

CAPTURED BY USHERS

In an instant there was an uproar in the place. Men and women jumped in fright from their seats, and two ushers rushed at Either, who made no attempt to avoid them, and offered no resistance.

Ushers went through the lower floor to discover if anyone was wounded, but a search showed that the bullet had gone between the seats two rows ahead of where Miss Holland was sitting, without touching a person.

Either, who lives on North Front street, and has worked in the mills at the North End, where Miss Holland had also been employed in the past, was arrested and held on the charge of assault with a dangerous weapon and attempt to kill.

According to the police, Either has been attentive to Miss Holland. Early today they are believed to have had a quarrel, during which it is alleged Miss Holland slapped Either's face, whereupon he left her and went to his home, and secured a revolver.

About mid-afternoon he saw the young woman enter a moving picture theatre on Acushnet avenue, and followed her. Miss Holland took a seat on the orchestra floor, while Either went to the balcony. He waited until the picture which was being shown was ended and the theatre lights turned on, and then did the shooting.

LODGE PRAISES WILSON

Reply to Austria Right, Says Senior Senator

BY ROBERT L. NORTON

Senator Lodge strongly supports President Wilson in the attitude the administration has taken in the note to Austria refusing to declare an embargo on the sale of arms and ammunition to the allies.

Last Saturday at Worcester the Senator said that he would support the President in his foreign policy when he believed him to be right, and criticise him when he thought him wrong. In his speech before the fourth Middlesex senatorial district outing at Suntaug Inn last night Mr. Lodge said that the reply to the Austrian note "Was able and unanswerable."

RAPS MEXICAN POLICY

But Senator Lodge's indorsement of the postion taken by the administration on the Austria note was negative somewhat by his biting criticism of the policy in Mexico and what he described as the belated awakening to the demand for armed preparedness "when votes were fluttering in its face."

The reception given to the senior Senator deserves more than passing attention. It was voluminous, enthusiastic and sincere. As at Worcester, the candidates on the State ticket were sidetracked. Mr. Lodge did not refer to the State fight except as it might effect the result in 1916. In his series of speeches, of which this is the second, he proposes to lay down the issues for

Continued on Page 5—Fifth Column

RUSSIAN LINE IS CRUMBLING

With Kovno Taken and Brest-Litovsk Threatened Further Retreat Seems Necessary

LONDON, Aug. 18.—The capture of the fortress of Kovno, announced in the official report from Berlin this afternoon, is considered one of the worst blows of the war to Russia.

The amazingly short time in which the fortress was taken is looked upon as conclusive proof that the Russians have no ammunition for the heavy artillery, and without such equipment the military experts cannot see how they can make a stand anywhere.

The retreat from the Warsaw line was considered comparatively unimportant as long as the Russian commander-in-chief was able to keep his armies intact. It was then generally hoped, and confidently expected in some quarters, that the Russians would be able to permanently check the German advance on the Kovno-Grodno-Brest-Litovsk line. And now that one of the main fortresses of that line is gone there seems to be little hope for the rest of the line holding.

In fact the capture of Kovno leaves the road open to Vilna and the Warsaw Petrograd railway. It further permits of a flank movement on the Russian forces operating further down on the line.

Continued on Page 5—First Column

1-DAY STRIKE OF ALL WOMEN

N. Y. Suffragists to Show "Their Place Not in Home"

NEW YORK, Aug. 18.—A one-day strike of women in an effort to combat the relevancy, in modern day conditions, of the contention made by politicians and others that "woman's place is in the home" is proposed by the Empire State campaign committee of the Woman's Suffrage Association.

Mrs. Norman De R. Whitehouse, who initiated the plan and has the matter in charge, has sent a letter to members of the Women's Trade Union League, to leaders of women's local clubs, suffragists and social and settlement workers, in which she says:

"My idea is not to strike in order to win our suffrage campaign on Nov. 2, but merely in order to awaken the opponents of woman suffrage who use the phrase 'Woman's place' is in the home' to its meaninglessness as applied to modern conditions.

"All women will be asked to stay at home for one day. Home women will be asked to refrain from any of those activities outside the home that go with their work as purchasing and distributing agents or as careful mothers. Women employed outside the home will be asked to make the sacrifice and take the risks of staying 'in the home.'"

The date tentatively set for the unique strike is late September or early October.

CUT LOAN TO ENGLAND TO 150 MILLION

Feared Half Billion Loan Could Not Be Placed

NEW YORK, Aug. 18.—A reduction in the proposed foreign loan to be floated here from the half billion dollars first suggested to $100,000,000 or $150,000,000, seemed probable tonight as the result of all-day conferences of international financiers here, and by cable between this city and London.

While it was generally thought that this amount would be utterly inadequate to meet the volume of bills which are coming due rapidly against foreign buyers of American supplies, it was felt that the sum would be sufficient to right the foreign exchange markets temporarily, at least, and restore to normal value the foreign moneys now at low levels of depreciation.

DIFFCULTY IN PLACING

The chief reason for the contemplated reduction in the size of the loan, however, was understood to be the belief that a large loan, such as was first projected, could not be readily placed here.

Continued on Page 7—Sixth Column

SENATORS BUY SAWYER

DES MOINES, Iowa, Aug. 18.—Carl Sawyer, second baseman of the Des Moines Western league club, has been sold to the Washington American league club it was announced today by Manager Isbell.

Pirates Here for Series — Braves Blank Cards — Red Sox Beat White Sox

CRUCIAL SERIES IN OUR MIDST

For Today the Pirates Come Here and Flag May Be Won or Lost.

The day of the "crucial series" has arrived in the land.

Heretofore series came and series went, but with the days of the brown and sere fast approaching, every clash has a special import to the teams still fighting for pennants.

Wherefore, today should be another big day at the new Braves Field. For the Pirates, tied with the champions for the last hole in the first division of the National league, are in our midst.

The first double-header of the new home will be played this afternoon with the same Pirates. If the Braves can slam the Clarkes down a few times in the coming series, they will be putting one of their dangerous opponents out of the running, while benefiting themselves otherwise. If they can't—but why speculate on the sad side of life?

Out in Pittsburgh recently the Braves cleaned up said Pirates, with a whole lot of fireworks on the side, such as a near row between Fred Clarke and Johnny Evers, the banishment of the same Johnny by ol' Bob Emslie, a preferment of a lot of charges against the same Johnny by Barney Dreyfuss and a consequent investigation of the Trojan. At that time the Pirates were right up next to the top, and the Brave blow was an awful shock. They have recovered, however, and a ɔ apparently going as well as ever.

The Braves by this time are used to their new field, and in addition have the winning spirit again, the same no doubt being fostered by the sight of the enormous stands and the consideration of what big checks a world series would mean.

Wherefore, the present series should be a hot one, from start to finish. Both outfit are only 4½ games back of the leaders and both are cocksure of ultimately making it up.

For today's double battle, Manager Stallings has Lefty George Tyler, one of the her es of the Pittsburgh encounter, and Li tle Dick Rudolph, who signalized the pening day. For the Corsairs, Harmon and Southpaw Kantlehner appear the likely candidates, though if the efficient Monsiur Mamaux has recovered from his recent slight indisposition, chances are he will be worked.

SOUTHERN ASSOCIATION

At Atlanta—(First game) Atlanta 5, Little Rock 0 (seven innings by agreement); (second game) Little Rock 3, Atlanta 2 (seven innings by agreement).
At Birmingham—(First game) Chattanooga 1, Birmingham 0; (second game) Birmingham 0, Chattanooga 0 (called in 8th inning; darkness).
At Mobile—Nashville 7, Mobile 5.

AMERICAN ASSOCIATION

At Milwaukee—Milwaukee 13, Indianapolis 0.
At Minneapolis—Minneapolis 3, Columbus 2.
At Kansas City—Louisville 4, Kansas City 3.
At St. Paul—Cleveland 4, St. Paul 3 (13 innings).

NATIONAL LEAGUE

YESTERDAY'S RESULTS

At Boston—Boston 1, St. Louis 0.
At Brooklyn—Brooklyn 6, Chicago 5 (10 innings).
At Philadelphia—Philadelphia 4, Pittsburgh 3 (11 innings).
At New York—New York 7, Cincinnati 0.

STANDING OF THE CLUBS

	Won.	Lost.	P. C.
Philadelphia	57	48	.543
Brooklyn	60	51	.541
Chicago	55	54	.505
BOSTON	54	54	.500
Pittsburgh	56	56	.500
New York	51	54	.486
St. Louis	52	60	.464
Cincinnati	51	59	.464

GAMES TODAY

Pittsburgh at Boston (2 games).
Chicago at Philadelphia.
St. Louis at New York.
Cincinnati at Brooklyn (2 games).

INTERNATIONAL LEAGUE

YESTERDAY'S RESULTS

At Richmond—Providence 10, Richmond 9.
At Rochester—Rochester 4, Montreal 1.
At Buffalo—Toronto 1, Buffalo 0.
At Jersey City—Jersey City 10, Harrisburg 3.

STANDING OF THE CLUBS

	Won.	Lost.	P. C.
Providence	70	37	.654
Buffalo	61	40	.604
Montreal	56	51	.523
Harrisburg	51	53	.490
Toronto	49	57	.462
Rochester	46	57	.447
Richmond	46	60	.434
Jersey City	39	63	.382

GAMES TODAY

Providence at Richmond.
Montreal at Rochester.
Jersey City at Harrisburg.
Toronto at Buffalo (2 games).

NEW ENGLAND LEAGUE

YESTERDAY'S RESULTS

At Lynn—(First game) Lynn 2, Lowell 1. (Second game) Lowel 14, Lynn 2.
At Fitchburg—Fitchburg 3, Worcester 1.
At Lewiston—Lewiston 6, Lawrence 5 (10 innings).
At Portland—Portland 4, Manchester 1.

STANDING OF THE CLUBS

	Won.	Lost.	P. C.
Portland	63	37	.630
Lawrence	57	39	.593
Worcester	54	44	.551
Lynn	51	49	.510
Lowell	42	51	.452
Lewiston	41	52	.441
Manchester	41	56	.423
Fitchburg	38	60	.388

GAMES TODAY

Lynn at Worcester.
Fitchburg at Lowell.
Lawrence at Lewiston (2 games).
Manchester at Portland (2 games).

ONE OF THOSE PIRATES WITH US TODAY

Hans Wagner.

RED SOX COP AND STILL HOLD ONTO FIRST PLACE

Vicious Assault on Joe Benz in Opening Round Gives Them Victory Over Chicagos.

[Special Dispatch to The Herald.]

CHICAGO, Ill., Aug. 20—The Red Sox are still in first place. They won the final game of their series here by a count of 4 to 1 and saved themselves from dropping into second place, because the Tigers also won. Today's game was won in the very first inning, for the leaders made such a vicious attack on Joe Benz in that round that they drove three runs over the plate and sent Joe to the coop after five men had faced him ɩ ɩ only one man had been retired.

Ernes Shore was opposed to the butcher boy and he went through the whole game without any runs being scored on him until the last round, when he let up for just a minute and the locals got in their work and saved themselves a shutout. Reb Russell had to be rushed to the rescue of Benz in the opening round and stood his ground for the remainder of the game without letting the leaders get more than one run off him.

The game was just another of those hard-fought contests that the fans have watched in the three-game series. Thrilling plays were the usual thing instead of the unusual. The White Sox could get only six hits up to the ninth inning, when they made three more after two men were out. The Boston infield was like a stonewall when it came to poking the wallops through it. The Chicago infield was almost as tight.

Red Sox Feeling Better.

The Red Sox were in a very much happier frame of mind when they left here tonight for St. Louis, than they have been at any time since they arrived. They still have the lead and are going to a place where they expect to be able to hold their own against the fast coming Tigers. The White Sox are far enough out of the way for the present so that Manager Carrigan is not worrying at all about them.

The acquisition of Joe Jackson, which was announced tonight by President Comiskey of the White Sox, will greatly strengthen the locals so that they are likely to cause considerably trouble yet before the race is over.

The hitting honors for the Red Sox were fairly well scattered for the day. Scott, Speaker, Lewis and Gardner all had two hits apiece. Hooper, Hoblitzel and Cady had the other three hits. Shore won his game here on the former visit of the team and his work today was just as good as it was on that occasion.

The crowd today was the largest of the series. It was the weekly free gate for the ladies and they turn out in large droves. Fully five of the 15,000 that went through the turnstiles during the afternoon were ladies.

The game started off with a furious attack on Joe Benz. Hooper waited after getting two strikes on him and was rewarded with a base on balls. A passed ball let him go to second. Scott singled to left and Hooper stopped at third. Speaker then poled one of his usual drives through the left side of the infield and scored Hooper and put Scott on second. Hoblitzel flied to Felsch in short centre and Lewis then singled to centre, filling the bases. At this point Manager Rowland decided that Benz would not do and motioned for Russell to hurry from the bullpen.

Gardner Drives In Two.

Before Reb could get his whip working just right Gardner landed on him for a two-bagger to right field that scored Scott and Speaker and put Lewis on third. Barry fouled out to the catcher and Cady walked, again filling up the bases. The round ended with Shore's roller to Russell.

The White Sox came back in a furious attack on Shore in their opener, but the attempt was unsuccessful. Murphy led off with a single to centre, and Weaver went out on a long drive to Hooper. Eddie Collins sent a hot drive right at Gardner and was retired without any trouble, but John Collins was safe when Shore fumbled his hot grounder and Murphy took third on the play. John Collins then stole second and Liebold walked, filling up the bases. Felsch could not deliver, but went out on a drive to Hooper in right field.

There was very little to the game after that first round in the way of a battle. Russell and Shore got down to working order and made short work of the batters.

In the fourth inning it looked as if the Red Sox were going to score, for Hooper and Scott had singled, with one down, and Speaker was at bat, when he tried to lay down a bunt and popped into Russell's mitt and forced Hooper at second. Two hits were made by the White Sox in the fifth, but two men were out when the second hit was made and Shore was not worried at all.

Hoblitzel scored the fourth run of the game in the seventh, when he landed on a three-bagger, after two were out. He rode home on a wild pitch just before Lewis struck out.

The White Sox rallied for just a minute in the ninth, and it looked as if they were going to cause a little trouble. After two men were retired, Murphy landed his second single of the game in centre field and Weaver came through with another hit, putting Murphy on second. Eddie then drove a two-bagger into left field and scored Murphy and put Weaver on third. With John Collins at bat, it looked just a little like trouble, but "Shono" popped out on a nice easy one to Hoblitzel and ended the game.

BOSTON.	ab.	r.	bh.	tb.	po.	a.	e.
Hooper, r.f.	4	1	1	1	2	0	0
Scott, s.s.	5	1	2	2	2	4	0
Speaker, c.f.	5	1	2	4	2	0	0
Hoblitzel, 1b	4	1	1	3	16	0	0
Lewis, l.f.	4	0	2	2	0	0	0
Gardner, 3b	4	0	2	3	0	4	0
Barry, 2b	3	0	0	0	2	3	0
Cady, c.	3	0	1	1	3	1	0
Shore, p.	4	0	0	0	0	6	1
Totals	36	4	11	16	27	18	1
CHICAGO.							
Murphy, r.f.	5	1	2	2	2	0	0
Weaver, s.s.	5	0	2	3	1	1	0
E. Collins, 2b	5	0	2	3	3	5	0
J. Collins, 1b	4	0	0	0	11	0	0
Liebold, l.f.	2	0	0	0	1	0	0
Felsch, c.f.	4	0	1	1	4	0	0
Schalk, c.	4	0	1	1	4	0	0
Blackburne, 3b	3	0	0	0	0	1	0
Benz, p.	0	0	0	0	0	0	0
Russell, p.	4	0	1	1	1	2	0
*Jackson	1	0	0	0	0	0	0
Totals	37	1	9	11	27	9	0

Innings	1	2	3	4	5	6	7	8	9	
Boston	3	0	0	0	0	0	1	0	0	—4
Chicago	0	0	0	0	0	0	0	0	1	—1

Two-base hits—Gardner, Weaver, E. Collins. Three-base hits—Speaker, Hoblitzel. Stolen base—J. Collins. Earned runs—Boston 4, Chicago 1. Sacrifice hit—Barry. Double play—Russell, Weaver and E. Collins. Left on bases—Chicago 12, Boston 8. First base on errors—Chicago 1. First base on balls—Off Benz 1, off Russell 1, off Shore 3. Hits—Off Benz 3 in 1-3 inning, off Russell 8 in 8 2-3 innings. Struck out—By Russell 3, by Shore 3. Wild pitch—Russell. Passed ball—Schalk. Umpires—Chill and Evans. Time—1h. 58m.

*Batted for Blackburne in 9th inning.

NOTES OF THE RED SOX

The Red Sox left for St. Louis late tonight and will have a strenuous three days of it with the Browns.

The ladies' day jinx was blamed for the defeat by the White Sox. Rowland's men have never been able to overcome the hoodoo of a ladies day, they claim.

Joe Kelley, the Yankee's scout, watched the game from the press box. His team will follow the Red Sox here and play two games tomorrow.

The purchase of Joe Jackson by the Chicago club will strengthen the locals in their batting department very much. Rowland expected to use him in the outfield and not on first base.

John Collins robbed Scott of a hit in the fifth inning by grabbing his hot bounder in his glove way back of first, after racing to his left just along the foul line.

Speaker thought he would catch the White Sox infield asleep in the fourth when he tried to lay down a bunt and beat it to first. The ball popped into the air, though, and fell into Russell's mit without much trouble, so that Hooper was doubled off second and a triple play would have been possible if it had been necessary, as Scott was within a few feet of second base.

Benz did not seem to have anything that fooled the speed boys today. His speed was gone and his curves were breaking over the plate just right for the Red Sox to meet easily.

Carrigan expects to play a double-header tomorrow when he gets to St. Louis but is not sure whether the two games will be staged tomorrow or Sunday.

SENATORS 8, INDIANS 0

CLEVELAND, Aug. 20—The only Cleveland player to reach second base today was O'Neill, who doubled in the fifth inning. With Harper pitching such great ball, Washington had no trouble winning 8 to 0, as Brenton was hit hard in the sixth and seventh innings after his support had missed chances to retire the side.

WASHINGTON	ab.	bh.	po.	a.	e.	CLEVELAND	ab.	bh.	po.	a.	e.
Moeller, lf.	4	0	2	0	0	Willie, cf.	2	0	3	0	1
Foster, 2	5	1	2	2	0	Graney, cf.	0	0	0	0	0
Milan, cf.	4	2	8	0	0	Turner, 3	4	1	0	2	0
Shanks, 3	5	3	0	2	0	Chapman, s.	4	2	1	6	1
Gandil, 1	5	2	9	0	0	Jackson, r.	4	0	2	0	0
Acosta, r.	3	1	1	0	0	Kirke, 1	2	0	8	2	0
Williams, c.	3	2	4	2	0	Smith, lf.	3	0	4	0	0
M'Bride, s.	3	0	1	2	0	Wamb'nss, 2	3	0	3	3	1
Harper, p.	4	0	0	1	0	O'Neill, c.	3	1	4	0	0
						Brenton, p.	2	0	1	3	0
						Collamore, p	1	0	1	0	0
						*Evans	1	0	0	0	0
Totals	36	11	27	9	0	Totals	29	4	27	16	3

Innings	1	2	3	4	5	6	7	8	9	
Washington	0	0	0	0	1	2	5	0	0	—8

Runs—Moeller, Foster, Milan, Shanks, Gandil, Acosta, Harper. Earned runs—Washington 1. Two-base hit—O'Neill. Sacrifice hit—McBride. Stolen base—Gandil, Shanks. Double play—Turner, Wambsganns and Kirke; McBride, Foster and Gandil. Hits—Off Brenton, 9 in 6 2-3 innings; off Collamore, 2 in 2 1-3 innings. First base on balls—Off Brenton 4; off Harper 2. Hit by pitcher—By Brenton (Williams). Struck out—By Brenton 2; by Harper 5. First base on errors—Washington 1. Left on bases—Cleveland 4; Washington 7. Time—1h. 35m. Umpires—O'Loughlin and Hildebrand.

*Batted for Willie in 8th inning.

RESCUE TOM HUGHES SHUTS OUT THE CARDS

Magee Comes Home with Only Run of Game When Schmidt Makes a Timely Safety.

By N. J. FLATLEY.

It looked like the millennium.

Rescue Tom Hughes started a game, finished it and won it.

Johnny Evers pulled a real old-fashioned bone.

Sherwood Magee was knocked off the bases when the Braves needed a run.

If you need anything more than that to convince you that yesterday's game was a topsy-turvy affair, you sure must be some skeptic.

To begin at the beginning, Rescue Tom shut out the Cardinals and after ages and ages added a victory to his record, though as a matter of fact the same Tom has helped to win more games for the Braves lately than any other pitcher on the squad.

The score of the affair was 1 to 0, the lone tally being marked up when, as we have hinted, Sherwood Magee crossed the platter in the fourth inning. Sherwood had paved the way by whaling a lusty triple to the left field fence, and Charlie Schmidt shattered recent tradition by shooting a hot oneshot between first and second.

Troyjohn—to steal Burt Whitman's stuff—pulled his boner in the fifth. Troyjohn was on first in that particular stanza, with only one out. Connolly, who replaced Compton for the day, wafted a soft fly to right field. Just as though the ball was soaring into the bleachers, Troyjohn went tearing around the bases. Consequently a double play was a very simple matter after Chief Wilson had grabbed the ball. Thereafter John rapped his head at frequent intervals and made more fun of himself than the crowd made of him, and as the ivory performance didn't hurt, it furnished a lot of amusement and added to the gaiety of a rather tame occasion.

The day was tame because there was so much good pitching that there wasn't must hitting, and there weren't many men on. Neither were there many good plays, most of the balls hit going directly at somebody or other. The banner play of the afternoon was the final performance of the day.

Some Double Play.

It was a double killing, executed at the expense of Cosey Dolan, who had done most of the hitting during the afternoon. With the speedy Bescher on first as the result of a single, Cosey slapped one at third. Red Smith snared it and hurled to Evers. Jawn grabbed it, touched second and, with Bescher right on top of him, pegged to first. And his throw beat Cosey a full step, though he made it while twisting around.

So far as the pitching went, Rescue Tom didn't allow enough Cards to reach to fill a Ford. Just four swats were made off his assortment of shoots in the afternoon, one in the second and one in each of the last three chapters. Rescue Tom fanned eight of the visitors and put across the stunt generally when matters looked threatening and all in all deserved all the cheers that he got during the pastime. It sure looks as if Thomas had derricked himself out of the rescue role and would henceforth and hereafter be destined to join the regulars once again.

Speaking of pitching, you gotta hand it to the begoggled Lee Meadows, also. Lee hurled for the Cardinals and Lee didn't let the Braves do an awful lot to him. Matter of fact, if it wasn't for the swell way Rescue Tom went along Lee probably would have won. He permitted but four safe bumps, but was unfortunate enough to have two of them come in the fourth frame. Other than that he was what the experts call invincible. Lee was removed after the seventh for a pinch-hitter and the port-sided Rube Robinson went through the final Brave round unscathed.

And Then the Run.

Unlike the day before there was little trouble with the umpires. A Card kick on a decision when Charlie Schmidt was almost caught off second, and another Card kick when Rube Robinson balked in the eighth summing up the afternoon's bickerings.

The first inning of the battle was tame, but the second was somewhat exciting. To begin with Cose Dolan opened for the Cards with a two-base shot through Smith, but never managed to score. Then the Braves got the corners jammed. After Magee has flied, Schmidt walked and Smith singled, just out of Huggins's reach. Maranville's grounder moved them along. Whereupon Hammering Hennery Gowdy was passed and the strategy was vindicated, as Hughes rolled to the box.

Nobody arrived in the third, but the Braves won the game in the fourth. Magee hit the fence for the first time, reached third and counted on Schmidt's safety. Smith hit hard, but right at Wilson and Maranville forced Big Charlie. Gowdy was popped by a pitched ball, but Hughes fouled out.

Troy Johnny let his mental cogs slip in the fifth, but until the seventh there were no sign of an outbreak. In that stanza Dolan whaled a tremendous double to deep left, and took third while Maranville was booting Wilson's rap. All this with only one out, but Hughes, remembering his rescue days, fanned Miller and forced Betzel to fly.

It looked as if the Braves were going to add to their score in the eighth when Evers worked a pass out of Robinson, but Connolly rapped into a forceout and both Magee and Schmidt skided to right. That double play we have mentioned snuffed out the Cardinals in the ninth, gave the Braves two out of three for the series, brought them into a tie with the Pirates—who come here today—for fourth place and held the margin beneath the Phillies safe.

BRAVES.	ab.	r.	bh.	tb.	po.	a.	e.
Moran, r.f.	4	0	0	0	0	0	0
Evers, 2b	2	0	0	0	2	1	0
Connolly, c.f.	4	0	0	0	3	0	0
Magee, r.f.	4	1	1	3	4	0	0
Schmidt, 1b	3	0	1	1	6	1	0
Smith, 3b	2	0	1	1	1	1	0
Maranville, ss	3	0	0	0	2	3	1
Gowdy, c.	1	0	0	0	9	2	0
Hughes, p.	3	0	1	2	0	2	0
Totals	26	1	4	7	27	10	1
ST. LOUIS.							
Huggins, 2b	4	0	0	0	0	3	0
Hyatt, 1b	1	0	0	0	0	0	0
Butler, ss	4	0	0	0	3	1	0
Bescher, l.f.	3	0	1	1	3	0	0
Dolan, c.f.	3	0	2	4	1	0	0
Wilson, r.f.	2	0	0	0	4	1	0
Miller, 1b, 2b	3	0	0	0	8	1	0
Betzel, 3b	3	0	0	0	0	0	0
Snyder, c.	3	0	0	0	4	1	0
Meadows, p.	2	0	0	0	1	2	0
Robinson, p.	0	0	0	0	0	1	0
*Long	1	0	1	1	0	0	0
Totals	29	0	4	6	24	10	0

Innings	1	2	3	4	5	6	7	8	9	
Braves	0	0	0	1	0	0	0	0	..	—1

Two-base hits—Dolan 2, Hughes. Three-base hit—Magee. Sacrifice hit—Wilson. Left on bases—Braves 7, St. Louis 4. First base on balls—Off Hughes 1, off Meadows 4, off Robinson 1. Struck out—By Hughes 8, by Meadows 2. Hit by pitched ball—By Hughes (Dolan), by Meadows (Gowdy). Balk—Robinson. Hits—Off Meadows 4 in 7 innings, off Robinson 0 in 1 inning. Double plays—Wilson to Miller to Meadows; Smith to Evers to Schmidt. Umpires—Klem and Emslie. Time—1h. 50m. Attendance—1500.

*Batted for Meadows in 7th inning.

NOTES OF THE BRAVES

Hennery Gowdy gave the crowd something to giggle at in the opening round, as he did a concentric circle stunt under Butler's high foul. Hank finally pirouetted under the ball and held it.

After Dolan had led off in the second with a double through Smith and had been sacrificed to third, Hughes got busy, made Miller pop to the Rabbit and fanned Betzel. At that it looked as if Smith might at least have halted Cosy's bang.

Firsts being popular anent the new park, it is worthy of mention that Ed McGrath was the first writer to set 'em up for the experts and the rest of us in the p. b. It was pop, of course.

Miller Huggins made a great try to get to Smith's hit in the second, but couldn't get back quite far enough. It was something like the bump Mann made over Collins's roof in the W. S.

Sherwood Magee pulled down the honor of first bumping the fence, his triple in the fourth going the length of the park along the left line. When the Brave slid into third he pulled the mattress from its anchors and the game had to be held up.

Capt. Johnny Evers was caught asleep in the fifth. Connolly hoisted an easy fly to right with one out and the Trojan on first. The latter went around the bases full tilt and consequently was easily doubled.

Miller Huggins was fanned the first two trips he made to the saucer, whereas the day before he walked twice, which probably explains why the Braves led yesterday and trailed Thursday.

Red Smith made a great catch of a Huggins foul in the sixth, galloping over to the boxes beyond the Brave bench for the hoist.

A big cheer went up when the first inning Red Sox score was posted. Fans here are beginning to get het up for a local world's series.

Maranville's boot in the seventh was due to his haste to get the ball to third ahead of Dolan. He tried to throw before he made the scoop.

Robinson's balk in the eighth caused a wild Cardinal bowl, though offense was apparent. Huggins was ejected for too much kicking.

The Braves will play an exhibition game at New Haven on the Sunday before Labor day, while en route for New York and the final swing around the circuit. Their opponents will be the New Haven Colonials, a bunch of college stars.

Two games, 1:30 today.

GIANTS 7, REDS 0

NEW YORK, Aug. 20—New York rallied behind Tesreau's fine pitching today and easily defeated Cincinnati in the last game of the series by a score of 7 to 0. Tesreau allowed only five scattered hits and only one visitor reached third. The entire Giant team batted around in the first inning, when New York made four runs on Lear.

NEW YORK	ab.	bh.	po.	a.	e.	CINCINNATI	ab.	bh.	po.	a.	e.
Burns, lf.	2	1	3	0	0	Groh, 3	4	1	0	1	0
Robertson, r	4	2	1	0	0	Herzog, s.	4	2	1	4	0
Doyle, 2	4	2	0	1	0	Williams, lf.	4	1	4	1	0
Fletcher, s.	3	1	1	5	0	Killifer, cf.	4	0	0	0	0
Merkle, cf.	2	1	4	0	0	Griffiths, r.	4	0	2	0	0
Kelly, 1	3	0	10	0	0	Wingo, c.	3	0	5	2	0
Lobert, 3	4	2	2	0	0	Wagner, 2	3	0	2	4	1
Dooin, c.	3	1	5	0	1	Mollwitz, 1	3	1	10	0	0
Wendell, c.	1	0	1	0	0	Lear, p.	2	0	0	2	0
Tesreau, p.	4	0	0	3	0	*Rodgers	1	0	0	0	0
						M'Cluskey, p	0	0	0	0	0
Totals	30	10	27	9	1	Totals	32	5	24	14	1

Innings	1	2	3	4	5	6	7	8	9	
New York	4	0	0	1	0	0	2	0	.	—7

Runs—Burns, Robertson 2, Doyle 2, Fletcher, Lobert. Two-base hits—Fletcher, Mollwitz. Stolen bases—Lobert, Burns. Earned runs—New York 5. Sacrifice flys—Merkle, Kelly. Double plays—Wingo and Herzog; Herzog, Wagner and Mollwitz. Left on bases—New York 3, Cincinnati 5. First base on errors—New York 1. First base on balls—Off Lear 3. Hits—Off Lear 10 in 7 innings, off McCluskey none in one inning. Hit by pitcher—Lear 1 (Fletcher). Struck out—By Tesreau 4, by McCluskey 2. Umpires—Byron and Eason. Time—1h. 22m.

*Batted for Lear in 8th inning.

PHILLIES WIN THE 11TH

PHILADELPHIA, Aug. 20—A home run drive by Bancroft with one out in the eleventh inning gave Philadelphia a 4 to 3 victory over Pittsburgh today. Rixey, who started the game for the home team, was hit much harder than Cooper, the former being taken out in the eighth inning after Pittsburgh tied the score. Alexander did grand work as a rescue twirler. Bancroft and Viox starred at the bat, each making three hits and receiving a pass in five trips to the plate.

PHILADELPHIA	ab.	bh.	po.	a.	e.	PITTSBURGH	ab.	bh.	po.	a.	e.
Byrne, 3	5	0	0	2	0	Costello, lf.	5	2	3	0	0
Bancroft, s.	4	3	3	3	0	Collins, cf.	5	0	4	0	0
Paskert, cf.	3	0	2	0	0	Johnston, 1	5	2	10	0	0
Cravath, r.	4	1	3	0	0	Hinchman, r.	4	1	3	0	0
Luderus, 1	4	1	14	2	0	Wagner, s.	4	2	2	3	0
Whitted, lf.	4	0	2	0	0	Viox, 2	4	3	2	3	0
Niehoff, 2	4	1	4	10	0	Baird, 3	5	0	1	2	0
Killifer, c.	4	2	4	0	0	Gibson, c.	5	2	5	1	1
Rixey, p.	2	0	1	1	0	Cooper, p.	5	0	1	1	0
Alex'nder, p	1	0	0	1	0						
Totals	35	8	33	19	0	Totals	42	12	*31	10	1

Innings	1	2	3	4	5	6	7	8	9	10	11	
Philadelphia	0	0	1	2	0	0	0	0	0	0	1	—4
Pittsburgh	1	0	0	0	0	1	0	1	0	0	0	—3

Runs—Bancroft 2, Cravath, Niehoff, Johnston, Hinchman, Wagner. Two-base hits—Johnston, Gibson, Luderus, Niehoff. Home runs—Wagner, Bancroft, Cravath. Stolen bases, Niehoff. Earned runs—Pittsburgh 3, Philadelphia 3. Sacrifice hits—Wagner, Paskert, Rixey. Double plays—Wagner, Viox and Johnston; Byrne, Niehoff and Luderus; Bancroft, Niehoff and Luderus. Left on bases—Pittsburgh 9, Philadelphia 3. Bases on balls—Off Cooper 1, off Rixey 2. Hits—Off Rixey 10 in 7 1-3 innings, off Alexander, 2 in 3 2-3 innings. Struck out—By Cooper 2, by Rixey 2, by Alexander 1. Umpires—O'Day and Stockdale. Time—1h. 52m.

*One out when winning run scored.

DODGERS BEAT CUBS 10TH

BROOKLYN, Aug. 20—Brooklyn beat Chicago, 6 to 5, in a sensational 10-inning game today, five pitchers being used. The Dodgers got a two-run lead in the first two innings but the Cubs eventually tied the score and got a one-run lead in their half of the tenth.

Lavender, who had relieved Zabel in the seventh, opened Brooklyn's half of the tenth by hitting Myers. Olson sacrificed and Daubert beat out an infield hit. Lavender started to walk Wheat but changed his mind and put them over the plate. Wheat hit the second ball for a drive to deep left centre, Myers and Daubert coming home with the tying and winning runs.

O'Mara was taken sick in the second inning and Olson, who made his first appearance in a regular position for Brooklyn, made a timely triple on his first time up.

BROOKLYN	ab.	bh.	po.	a.	e.	CHICAGO	ab.	bh.	po.	a.	e.
Myers, cf.	4	2	0	0	0	Good, r.	5	2	2	0	0
O'Mara, s.	0	0	0	0	0	Fisher, s.	5	2	1	4	0
Olson, s.	2	1	3	2	1	Schulte, lf.	4	1	2	0	0
Daubert, 1	3	1	10	0	0	Zim'rman, 2	5	2	2	3	0
Wheat, lf.	4	2	2	0	0	Saier, 1	5	1	11	1	0
Cutshaw, 2	4	1	6	5	0	Murray, cf.	3	1	5	0	0
Stengel, r.	4	0	1	1	0	Phelan, 3	3	0	2	1	0
Getz, 3	4	0	1	3	0	B'esnahan, c	3	2	2	1	0
M'Carty, c.	4	0	7	2	0	Zabel, p.	2	0	0	1	1
Douglas, p.	2	0	0	0	0	*Williams	1	1	0	0	0
Dell, p.	0	0	0	0	0	Lavender, p.	1	0	1	2	0
‡Schultz	1	0	0	0	0						
Smith, p.	1	0	0	2	0						
Totals	33	7	30	15	1	Totals	37	12	†28	13	1

Innings	1	2	3	4	5	6	7	8	9	10	
Brooklyn	3	1	0	0	0	0	0	0	0	2	—6
Chicago	1	1	0	0	1	0	1	0	0	1	—5

Runs—Myers 2, O'Mara, Daubert 2, Wheat, Good 2, Fisher, Murray, Phelan. Two-base hits—Fisher, Williams. Three-base hits—Zimmerman, Olson, Wheat. Stolen bases—Good 3; Zimmerman, Murray, Cutshaw. Earned runs—Chicago, 4; Brooklyn, 5. Sacrifice hits—Olson, Daubert. Double plays—Cutshaw and Daubert 2. Left on bases—Chicago 6, Brooklyn 6. First base on errors—Chicago 1. Bases on balls—Off Douglas, 1; off Zabel, 2; off Smith, 3; off Lavender, 2. Hits—Off Douglas, 8 in 4 2-3 innings; off Dell, 2 in 2 1-3 innings; off Smith, 2 in 3 innings; off Zabel, 4 in 6 innings; off Lavender, 3 in 3 1-3 innings. Hit by pitcher—By Lavender (Myers). Struck out—By Douglas 2; by Zabel 2; by Smith 4. Wild pitch—Dell. Umpires—Rigler and Cockill. Time—2h. 20m.

*Batted for Zabel in 7th inning.
†One out when winning run scored.
‡Batted for Dell in 7th.

GANZEL MAKES TRADE

[Special Dispatch to The Herald.]

NEW YORK, Aug. 20—The first official act of John Ganzel, the new manager of the Brookfeds, was completed today when he traded Tom Seaton of the Brooklyn pitching staff for Cy Falkenberg, one of Newark's pitchers. Tom Seaton has not been showing any surprising form in the box this year, and especially since the emery ball has been barred his work has fallen off.

INDIAN WHO BECOMES WHITE SOX PLAYER

Joe Jackson.

MARSANS, BACK IN FOLD, PLAYS LIKE CHAMPION

Cuban Stars for Sloofeds, but They Are Beaten 8 to 1 by the Brooklyn Tip Tops.

BROOKLYN, Aug. 20—Brooklyn defeated St. Louis today, 8 to 1. The game marked the first appearance in a long time of Armando Marsans, the Cuban, who was yesterday permitted to play by a court decision. Marsans made one hit and two sensational catches. Marion pitched great ball for Brooklyn.

BROOKLYN	ab.	bh.	po.	a.	e.	ST. LOUIS	ab.	bh.	po.	a.	e.
Anderson, r	5	2	1	0	0	Tobin, r.	4	1	1	1	1
Helfrich, 2	4	3	0	2	0	Vaughn, 2	3	0	2	2	1
Cooper, lf.	3	1	3	1	0	Miller, lf.	4	1	1	1	0
Kauff, cf.	4	3	2	0	0	Marsans, cf.	4	1	3	2	0
Myers, 1	3	1	12	1	0	Borton, 1	3	0	11	0	0
Halt, 3	3	2	2	2	0	Kores, 3	4	1	1	5	0
FdSmith, s.	4	2	2	4	2	Hartley, c.	3	2	2	3	2
Land, c.	4	1	4	1	0	Johnson, s.	3	0	3	3	0
Marion, p.	4	1	1	3	0	Watson, p.	0	0	0	0	0
						Crandall, p.	1	1	0	0	0
						Willett, p.	1	0	0	4	0
						*Bridwell	1	0	0	0	0
Totals	34	16	27	14	2	Totals	31	7	24	20	4

Innings	1	2	3	4	5	6	7	8	9	
Brooklyn	0	4	1	2	0	1	0	0	.	—8
St. Louis	0	0	1	0	0	0	0	0	0	—1

First base on balls—Off Marion, 2; off Crandall, 2. Struck out—By Marion, 2; by Willett 2. Hit by pitched ball—Crandall, Halt. Hits—Off Watson, 3 in 1 2-3 innings; off Crandall, 5 in 2 1-3; off Willett, 3 in 5. Two-base hits—Tobin, Kores, Kauff. Three-base hit—Anderson. Sacrifice hits—Vaughn, Myers. Stolen bases—Helfrich, Kauff, Myers, Halt, Fred Smith. Double plays—Helfrich, Land, Halt to Myers; Marsans to Johnson; Johnson to Borton. Umpires—Mullin and Johnstone. Time—1h. 36m.

*Batted for Willet in ninth.

PACKERS 8, TERRAPINS 4

BALTIMORE, Md., Aug. 20—Kansas City had no trouble making it two in a row by taking today's game, 8 to 4. Bailey lasted less than an inning for Baltimore, and Suggs was driven from the box later on. Packard was never forced to extend himself.

KANSAS CITY	ab.	bh.	po.	a.	e.	BALTIMORE	ab.	bh.	po.	a.	e.
Chad'rne, cf	3	1	1	0	0	K'patrick, 3	5	2	1	2	0
K'worthy, 2	5	2	2	5	1	Duncan, lf.	5	2	5	0	0
Kruger, lf.	4	1	0	0	0	Zinn, cf.	4	1	1	0	1
Perring, 3	5	2	1	2	0	Evans, r.	3	0	4	1	0
Stovall, 1	5	2	14	3	0	Swacina, 1	4	1	8	0	0
Gilmore, r.	4	1	0	0	0	J'cklitsch, c	3	0	4	1	0
Rawlings, s.	4	1	2	3	0	Eakle, 2	4	1	0	2	1
Brown, c.	3	2	4	0	0	Doolan, s.	3	0	3	3	0
Packard, p.	4	0	3	5	0	Gallagher, s.	1	0	0	0	0
						Bailey, p.	0	0	1	0	0
						Suggs, p.	2	0	0	1	0
						Leclair, p.	0	0	0	0	0
						*M'Candless	1	0	0	0	0
						†Quinn	1	0	0	0	0
Totals	37	12	27	18	1	Totals	36	7	27	10	2

Innings	1	2	3	4	5	6	7	8	9	
Kansas City	3	2	0	0	0	0	3	0	0	—8
Baltimore	0	0	2	0	0	1	0	1	0	—4

Two-base hits—Kenworthy 2, Quinn, Perring, Eakle, Stovall, Gilmore, Brown, Swacina. Three-base hit—Chadbourne. Sacrifice hit—Kruger. Stolen bases—Kirkpatrick, 3; Kenworthy. Double play—Evans to Swacina. Bases on balls—Off Bailey, 2; off Suggs, 1. Hit by pitched balls—By Bailey (Brown); by Packard, (Evans). Struck out—By Suggs, 1; Leclair, 2; Packard, 4. Umpires—McCormack and Wilhelm. Time—1h. 55m.

*Batted for Suggs in the 7th.
†Batted for Leclair in the 9th.

BUFFEDS 7, WHALES 3

BUFFALO, Aug. 20—Buffalo took the second game of the series from Chicago today, 7 to 3. The locals were not puzzled by McConnell's delivery, while Schulz put in only one bad inning. Meyer broke the tie in the fifth inning with a homer into the right field bleachers.

BUFFALO	ab.	bh.	po.	a.	e.	CHICAGO	ab.	bh.	po.	a.	e.
Meyer, lf.	5	3	2	0	0	Tinker, 2	1	0	2	2	0
Lord, 3	3	2	2	0	0	Fritz, 2	2	1	2	2	0
Dalton, r.	3	1	0	0	0	Zwilling, 1	1	0	2	0	0
Chase, 1	1	1	5	0	0	Beck, 1	3	0	2	2	0
Hofman, 1	3	0	4	0	0	Flack, r.	3	0	1	0	0
Louden, 2	2	0	4	2	0	Fischer, c.	4	1	1	2	0
Engle, cf.	3	2	5	0	0	Westerzil, 3	3	1	1	1	0
Roach, s.	4	1	0	4	0	Hanford, cf.	4	0	0	0	0
Allen, c.	4	2	5	1	0	Mann, lf.	3	0	3	1	0
Schulz, p.	4	0	0	2	0	Smith, s.	3	1	4	3	2
						M'Connell, p	3	1	0	4	0
						Black, p.	0	0	0	2	0
						*Hendrix	1	0	0	0	0
Totals	32	12	27	9	0	Totals	31	5	24	19	2

Innings	1	2	3	4	5	6	7	8	9	
Buffalo	2	0	0	1	3	1	0	0	.	—7
Chicago	0	0	0	0	3	0	0	0	0	—3

Hits—Off McConnell 12. First base on balls—Off Schulz 5, off McConnell 3. Struck out—By Schulz 6, by McConnell 1. Home run—Meyer. Two-base hit—Meyer. Sacrifice hits—Engle, Lord. Stolen bases—Dalton, Chase, Louden. Double plays—Louden and Chase; Beck, Smith and Beck. Wild pitch—Schulz. Umpires—O'Brien and Brennan. Time—1h. 40m.

*Batted for Black in ninth.

SLOOFEDS GET MARSANS

ST. LOUIS, Aug. 20—An application of the Cincinnati Nationa s' for a writ setting aside the federal court decree modifying the injunction against Armando Marsans, the Cuban ball player, was denied by Judge Dyer in the United States district court here today, and Marsans will be permitted to play with the St. Louis Federals for the present. The judge granted an appeal to the circuit court of appeals.

LYNN AND LOWELL SPLIT

Lynn and Lowell shared honors in yesterday's double-header at Lynn. The locals won the first game, 2 to 1, when Holmes drove a homer over the fence with a man on base. In the second game Lowell batted freely and ran the bases with daring for a total of 14 runs, Lynn scoring only two.

Innings	1	2	3	4	5	6	7	8	9		r.	h.	e.
Lynn	0	0	0	0	0	0	0	2	0	.	—2	3	3
Lowell	0	0	0	0	0	0	1	0	0		—1	7	0

Batteries—McCabe and Haight; Lohman and Ahearn.

Second Game.

Innings	1	2	3	4	5	6	7		r.	h.	e.
Lowell	3	1	4	0	5	1	0		—14	16	0
Lynn	1	0	1	0	0	0	0		—2	9	5

Batteries—Green and Ahearn; Dedrich, Jewett and Haight.

FITCHBURG 3, WORCESTER 1

FITCHBURG, Aug 20—Fitchburg defeated Worcester in a well played game today, 3 to 1. The locals scored the two runs necessary to win in the second inning on an error, a single, a sacrifice and Gaston's double.

Innings	1	2	3	4	5	6	7	8	9		r.	h.	e.
Fitchburg	0	2	0	0	0	0	0	0	1	.	—3	6	0
Worcester	0	0	0	0	0	1	0	0	0		—1	11	3

Batteries—Tuckey and Gaston; Van Dyke and Hand.

PORTLAND, 4 TO 1

PORTLAND, Me., Aug. 20—Portland defeated Manchester today, 4 to 1. The two teams earned a run apiece and the visitors' errors helped Portland to three others. Fast work by the Portland infield contributed to holding down the run-making of their opponents.

Innings	1	2	3	4	5	6	7	8	9		r.	h.	e.
Portland	0	0	2	0	1	0	0	1	.		—4	7	1
Manchester	0	0	0	0	0	0	0	1	0		—1	9	3

Batteries—More and Hayden; McGinley and Kilhullen.

LEWISTON 6, LAWRENCE 5

LEWISTON, Me., Aug. 20—Thompson of Lawrence outpitched two Lewiston twirlers today, but errors behind him enabled Lewiston to tie the score in the eighth and win, 6 to 5, in the tenth when Becker doubled and scored on two sacrifice hits. Stops by Mahoney, McCarthy and Prysock were features.

Innings	1	2	3	4	5	6	7	8	9	10		r.	h.	e.
Lewiston	0	0	3	0	0	0	0	2	0	1		—6	7	3
Lawrence	0	0	1	2	1	1	0	0	0	0		—5	8	6

Batteries—Tuero, Whittaker and Foster; Thompson and Flaherty.

TIGERS MAKE IT 9 IN ROW

DETROIT, Aug. 20—Detroit continued its unbroken string of victories today, making it nine straight with a 11 to 1 defeat of Philadelphia. Bressler went to pieces in the third inning, giving five bases on balls and allowing two hits. Three of the passes and one of the hits came with the bases filled, netting the Tigers five runs.

Bill James, recently purchased from St. Louis, pitched a fine game for the Tigers.

Cobb and Crawford attempted a double steal in the seventh. McAvoy's throw retired Crawford at second and Kopf's lightning relay to the plate caught Cobb, who attempted to score from second.

DETROIT	ab.	bh.	po.	a.	e.	PHILADELPHIA	ab.	bh.	po.	a.	e.
Vitt, 3	5	2	0	3	0	Kopf, s.	5	2	2	4	2
Bush, s.	4	0	0	5	0	L.Davies, cf.	4	1	2	0	0
Cobb, cf.	3	2	1	0	0	Strunk, 1	3	2	9	0	0
Crawford, r.	5	2	2	0	0	Lajoie, 2	3	1	2	2	0
Veach, lf.	4	1	2	0	0	Walsh, r.	4	0	0	1	0
Burns, 1	5	3	16	0	1	Oldring, lf.	4	1	2	0	0
Young, 2	3	1	1	2	0	Malone, 3	4	1	1	1	0
K'vanagh, 2	1	1	1	1	0	M'Avoy, c.	4	0	6	3	1
Stanage, c.	3	0	4	0	0	Bressler, p.	1	0	0	1	0
James, p.	2	1	0	6	0	Pillion, p.	1	0	0	1	0
						Fillingim, p.	1	0	0	0	0
Totals	35	13	27	17	1	Totals	34	8	24	13	3

Innings	1	2	3	4	5	6	7	8	9	
Detroit	0	0	5	1	0	5	0	0	.	—11
Philadelphia	0	0	0	0	0	0	0	1	0	—1

Runs—Vitt, Bush, Cobb 2, Crawford, Veach, Burns, Kavanagh, Stanage 2, James, Kopf. Three-base hit—Kavanagh. Stolen bases—Kopf, Cobb, Strunk. Earned runs—Philadelphia, 1; Detroit, 10. Sacrifice hit—James. Sacrifice fly—Lajoie. Double play—McAvoy to Lajoie to Kopf to McAvoy. Left on bases—Philadelphia, 9; Detroit, 10. First base on errors—Philadelphia, 1; Detroit, 2. Bases on balls—Off Bressler, 5; Pillion, 1; Fillingim, 2; off James, 2. Hits—Off Bressler, 2 in 3 innings; off Pillion, 9 in 2 1-3 innings; off Fillingim, 2 in 2 2-3 innings. Hit by pitcher—By Pillion, (James). Struck out—By Bressler, 1; by James, 3; by Fillingim, 1. Wild pitches—Fillingim, James. Umpires—Wallace and Connolly. Time—1h. 54m.

INTERNATIONAL LEAGUE

At Buffalo—

	r.	h.	e.
Toronto	1	5	4
Buffalo	0	8	0

Batteries—Luque and Kocher; Bader and Onslow.

At Rochester—

	r.	h.	e.
Rochester	4	9	3
Montreal	1	7	1

Batteries—Herche and Williams; Fullerton and Howley.

At Richmond—

Innings	1	2	3	4	5	6	7	8	9		r.	h.	e.
Providence	1	5	1	0	0	0	3	0	0		—10	19	2
Richmond	2	3	1	0	0	1	2	0	0		—9	14	4

Batteries—Cooper, Schultz and Casey; Cottrell, Morrissette and Sweeney.

At York, Pa.—

	r.	h.	e.
Jersey City	10	11	0
Harrisburg	2	12	3

Batteries—Bruck and Tragessor; Chabek and Regan.

WHITE SOX GET JOE JACKSON

Comiskey Pays $25,000 and Three Players to Cleveland for Slugging Outfielder.

CHICAGO, Aug. 20—Joe Jackson, for five years one of the leading batsmen of the American league, was purchased today by President Comiskey of the White Sox from the Cleveland club, and left the Ohio metropolis to join the Rowlands in time to play in tomorrow's double-header against the New York Yankees, weather permitting.

The price paid for the services of the outfielder is announced to be $25,000 in cash and three players. Owner Somers of the Indians left for Chicago to meet Comiskey and decide on the identity of three players who will go to Cleveland in the deal.

Comiskey obtained the Cleveland slugger only after outbidding three other American League club owners, who opened negotiations for the player as soon as the wires spread the information his services were on the market.

Boston, Washington and New York was reported to be the three teams eager to add Jackson to their rosters. The Washington club owners offered $20,000 cash and two players, according to authentic information, and was confident of getting him at that figure. The deal was announced as practically closed early yesterday.

Comiskey did not do business by wire, but sent Secretary Harry Grabiner to Cleveland to watch the bidding and delay all offers until the others dropped out. Shortly after today's ball game his secretary telephoned Comiskey from Cleveland that he had been successful in closing the deal, and that he would bring the outfielder back with him on the first available train.

Manager Rowland announced he would play Jackson in the outfield, but had not decided tonight in which field. He probably will replace Leibold, but whether or not Jackson will be placed in right field or left was uncertain.

Jackson is the fourth American league player purchased by Comiskey in his efforts to build up a championship team.

DOUBLE BILLS ANNOUNCED

NEW YORK, Aug. 20—Secretary John A. Heydler of the National league today announced the official list of dates fixed for the playing off the postponed and tie games:

At Boston—With Pittsburgh Aug. 21 (two), with New York Oct. 4 (two).
At Brooklyn—With Cincinnati Aug. 21 (two), with St. Louis Aug. 25 (two), with Pittsburgh Aug. 28 (two), with Boston Sept. 8 (two).
At New York—With St. Louis Aug. 23 (two), with Pittsburgh Aug. 25 (two), with Philadelphia Sept. 2 (two).
At Philadelphia—With Chicago Aug. 23 (two), with Cincinnati Aug. 25 (two), with St. Louis Aug. 30 (two), with New York Sept. 9 (two).
At Pittsburgh—With St. Louis Sept. 1 (two), with Boston Sept 10 (two), with New York Sept. 17 (two) and Sept. 18 (two).
At Cincinnati—With New York Sept. 12 (two), with Philadelphia Sept. 17 (open), with Brooklyn Sept. 24 (open).
At Chicago—With Boston Sept. 15 (open), with New York Sept. 22 (open), with Philadelphia Sept. 23 (two) and Sept. 24 (two), with Cincinnati Sept 27 (two), Sept. 28 (two) and Sept. 30 (open).
At St. Louis—With Boston Sept. 16 (two).

SUNDAY GAME SCHEDULED

The Montreal-Providence game of the International league, scheduled at Providence Aug. 25, has been brought forward to tomorrow, and will be played at Rocky Point.

N. BEDFORD 6, BROCKTON 4

BROCKTON, Aug. 20—New Bedford beat Brockton today in an exciting game, 6 to 4. The home team rallied in the ninth, but poor base running resulted in the scoring of only 3 runs. Jacobson's muff of an easy fly in the seventh let in 3 runs.

Innings	1	2	3	4	5	6	7	8	9	
New Bedford	2	1	0	0	0	0	3	0	0	—6
Brockton	0	0	0	1	0	0	0	0	3	—4

Batteries—Tillman and Phillips; Warwick and Dempsey.

SPRINGFIELD, 13 TO 7

HARTFORD, Aug. 20—In a loose and ragged game today Springfield defeated Hartford, 13 to 7. Whitehouse was the only aggressive player for Hartford, his five hits out of five times up for eight bases figuring in every one of Hartford's runs.

Innings	1	2	3	4	5	6	7	8	9		r.	h.	e.
Springfield	2	4	0	0	0	2	1	4	0		—13	11	3
Hartford	1	0	0	1	0	1	2	0	2		—7	11	7

Batteries—Manser and Lavigne; Leonard and Texter.

GAME ENDS TIE IN 12TH

NEW HAVEN, Aug. 20—New Haven and Pawtucket battled for 12 innings to a 3 to 3 tie today, when darkness ended the contest.

In'gs	1	2	3	4	5	6	7	8	9	10	11	12		r.	h.	e.
New Haven—	1	0	0	1	0	0	0	1	0	0	0	0		—3	8	1
Pawtucket—	3	0	0	0	0	0	0	0	0	0	0	0		—3	10	1

Batteries—Eaton and Soper; Watling, Houck and Murphy.

AMERICAN LEAGUE

YESTERDAY'S RESULTS

At Chicago—Boston 4, Chicago 1.
At Detroit—Detroit 11, Philadelphia 1.
At Cleveland—Washington 8, Cleveland 0.

STANDING OF THE CLUBS

	Won.	Lost.	P. C.
BOSTON	70	37	.654
Detroit	73	39	.652
Chicago	66	43	.606
Washington	56	53	.514
New York	51	51	.500
Cleveland	42	68	.382
St. Louis	41	68	.376
Philadelphia	34	74	.315

GAMES TODAY

Boston at St. Louis.
Philadelphia at Cleveland.
New York at Chicago.
Washington at Detroit.

FEDERAL LEAGUE

YESTERDAY'S RESULTS

At Baltimore—Kansas City 8, Baltimore 4.
At Brooklyn—Brooklyn 8, St. Louis 1.
At Buffalo—Buffalo 7, Chicago 3.

STANDING OF THE CLUBS

	Won.	Lost.	P. C.
Newark	61	48	.560
Kansas City	63	50	.558
Pittsburgh	60	48	.556
Chicago	62	50	.554
St. Louis	59	52	.532
Buffalo	54	64	.458
Brooklyn	51	64	.443
Baltimore	39	73	.348

GAMES TODAY

Kansas City at Baltimore.
St. Louis at Brooklyn.
Chicago at Buffalo.
Pittsburgh at Newark.

COLONIAL LEAGUE

YESTERDAY'S RESULTS

At Hartford—Springfield 13, Hartford 7.
At New Haven—New Haven 3, Pawtucket 3 (game called in 12th, darkness).
At Brockton—New Bedford 6, Brockton 4.

STANDING OF THE CLUBS

	Won.	Lost.	P. C.
Hartford	45	31	.570
New Bedford	45	38	.542
Brockton	44	38	.537
New Haven	43	41	.512
Springfield	38	41	.481
Pawtucket	34	41	.453

GAMES TODAY

Springfield at Hartford (2 games).
Pawtucket at New Haven (2 games).
New Bedford at Brockton (2 games).

"Alexander the Great" and "Ty" Cobb Are World's Series Reporters for the PUBLIC LEDGER

The Ledger has commissioned the "Greatest Pitcher of All Time" and the "Finest All-round Baseball Player in the World" to write for you the inside story of the World's Series.

Grover Cleveland Alexander, the biggest playing factor of the Phillies, will give you every move of the players on both teams, just as it happens. Right from the thick of it, the idol of the Philadelphia fans will give his impressions to Ledger Readers.

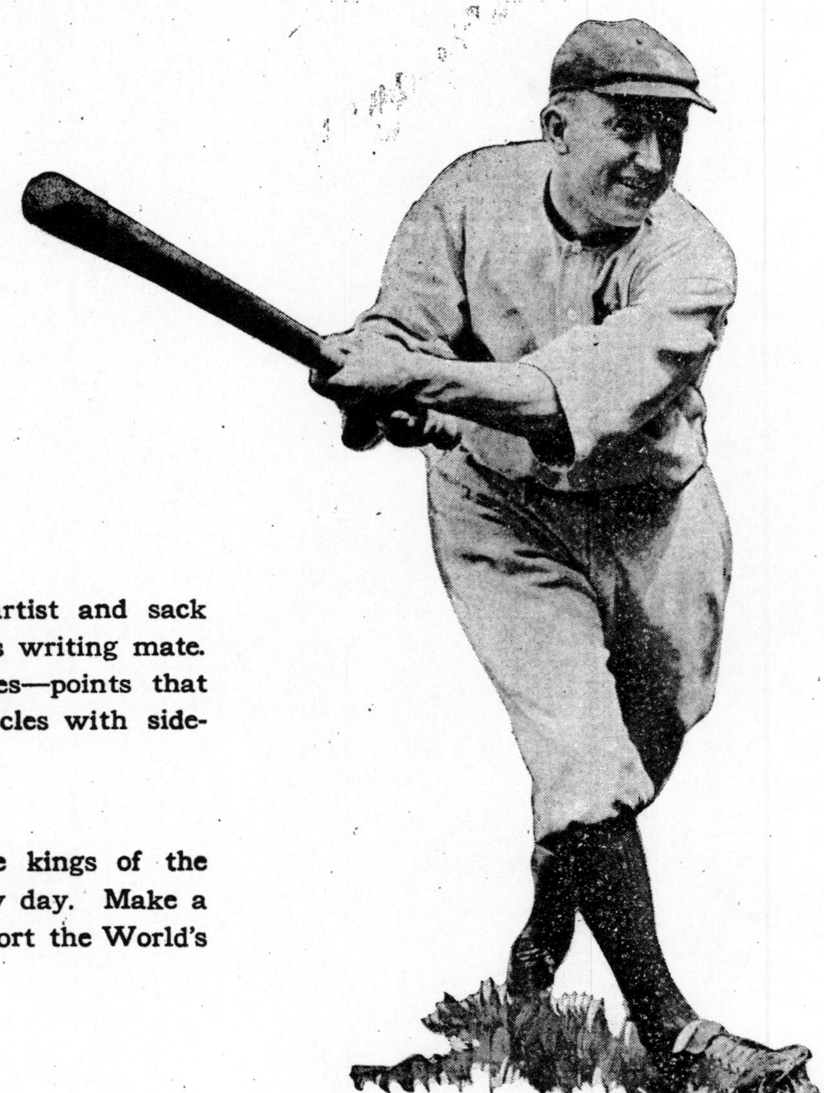

Tyrus Raymond Cobb, the most wonderful stick artist and sack robber the game has ever known, will be Alexander's writing mate. He will give you the microscopic things of the series—points that even good players overlook, and will season his articles with sidelights from his wonderful knowledge of the game.

Fans! Here's REAL baseball news, collected by the kings of the diamond! Don't miss these articles—read them every day. Make a mental note now that Alexander and Cobb are to report the World's Series for the

PUBLIC LEDGER

BOSTON'S AMERICAN LEAGUE CHAMPIONS

THE RED SOX CLAN.

Front row, left to right—Lewis, Wagner, Speaker, Hooper, Foster, Scott. Second row—Leonard, Henriksen, Gardner, Manager Carrigan, Cady, Janvrin, Thomas. Third row—Collins, Wood, Gainor, Shore, Gregg, Ruth, Mays, Hoblitzell, Barry, Trainer Green. Back row—President Joseph J. Lannin, Paul Lannin.

Royal Rooters Get Turn Down

President Baker Starts War by Barring Them Phillie Bleachers for Series

Continued From First Page

clared that the only seats he would reserve for Boston fans would be the $5 chairs in the new temporary grand stand boxes.

NO TESSIE IN PHILLIE

Such a ruling, if supported by the national commission, will mean that concerted cheering and singing will be impossible, and the long made plans of Boston fans will have been for naught. President Baker's reason for such a stand is not known. The Boston fans, and particularly the Royal Rooters, are known the country over for the cheering and singing support they give the Boston teams in world's series contests. The strains of "Tessie," the baseball battle hymn of the Red Sox and the Braves, in past world's series have played prominent parts in adding color and "getting goats," and many believe that it is an effort to prevent such showing of loyalty and its possible effect on the Phillies players, that the ultimatum was issued.

In past world's series the opponents of Boston clubs always set aside a section of 300 or 400 seats for the visiting fans and fully two months ago the Royal Rooters and many other fans began making plans for the coming world's series. Bands were engaged; "Tessie" was rehearsed; mechanical apparatus for creating noise purchased, and those intending to make the Philadelphia trip have been setting aside expense money, all with the end in view of accompanying and supporting the Red Sox team, and the ultimatum of President Baker has aroused the keenest disappointment and even anger.

With the intent of learning what section of the Philadelphia park had been reserved for the Boston fans, President Lannin called upon President Baker late yesterday afternoon.

"I think we will need about 400 seats," he remarked to President Baker, according to the report of their conversation.

Nothing Doing for Royals

Considerable surprise at his remark was evidenced by President Baker, who replied that he would be unable to reserve any bleacher section for Boston fans.

Considerable more surprise was evidenced by President Lannin at President Baker's remark.

"Why, Mr. Baker," said President Lannin, "you must know that Boston is a real baseball city, and if you were in Philadelphia last year you must know how the Royal Rooters and other fans supported the Boston team. Every owner whose team has engaged a Boston agregation in such a series allots an entire section to Boston fans. The fans themselves count on it, and I am asking only the customary courtesies."

"I can't help it," the Phillies' owner is said to have replied. "Our park is small and Philadelphia rooters are our first consideration. The only reserved seats I can grant Boston fans are the chairs in the temporary grandstand boxes. They sell at $5 a chair, and I will be pleased to reserve them for Boston people."

"I think that is a very unsatisfactory and a very unwise stand to take," then asserted President Lannin. "And furthermore," he continued, "I know the National Commission rulings allow me better consideration. I shall want 400 seats and I propose to secure them, and if you cannot assist me I certainly shall go before the commission with my demand."

And so the conversation ended.

President Lannin was considerably wrought up about the affair when he left the room, and officers of the Royal Rooters shared that feeling when the Red Sox president communicated the stand taken by the Phillies' owner.

"Afraid of Tessie"

"He's afraid of 'Tessie,'" remarked one of the rooters, and many others evidently shared this view.

"What chance would we have of getting together when our seats were scattered through the temporary boxes?" remarked another fan. "The price of those seats would prevent many loyal fans from making the trip, and those that did would be so widely scattered that there could not be any concerted cheering or singing, and there would be no place for our bands."

"Mr. Baker wants to remember that his club is coming here for 11 games next year and the year after and, in fact, as long as there is a National league and Boston and Philadelphia have teams in that league. If he treats Boston fans in the manner he evidently intends, he will find his journeys to Boston in the future very unprofitable."

"If his park is so small, why didn't he make a bid for the Athletics' park?" questioned another rooter. "Surely if Philadelphia fans are his first consideration, he should have enough space to accommodate them and a lot more besides. I guess he's afraid we'll get the Phillies goats."

Several voiced their opinions in other and stronger language, and to a man the Royal Rooters and the fans of Boston will be behind President Lannin when he places his case before the National Commission. Until it has been decided, however, there will be much uncertainty and considerable ill feeling toward the Phillies' management.

You'll find pictures from all over the world in the Pictorial Section of the next Sunday Post.

HARVARD TEAMS IN DEADLOCK

Varsity Plays 6-6 Tie in Scrimmage With Seconds

Scrimmaging for the Harvard varsity came to an end yesterday with a good stiff hour of fierce offensive and defensive line plugging by both teams.

The second and third varsity were the first to scrimmage against Teams B and C of the second squad.

Then Team A of the varsity, minus Mahan and King, faced Team A of the second eleven, and, fight as they would, they could only tie up 6 to 6 with the second eleven in 20 minutes of scrimmage.

BEST PRACTICE YET

Fumbling played far too important a part with the substitutes of the varsity and the second's subs profited so much by this that they were able to force Willcox back of his own goal line for a safety. One of his backs had dropped the ball.

The varsity and the second eleven played the best football that has been turned out yet on Soldiers Field. Fortunately, the second team had Murray Taylor at quarterback and Henry Minot in the backfield. This combination of head work and speed made the plays go well, for the second's line were charging together, hard and successfully.

In the varsity line Soucy and Harte again appeared as the varsity ends, Dadmun was playing a guard position and for the first time Jose Harris, sub varsity centre last year, returned to real scrimmage. His appendicitis operation of a month ago seems to have left no traces on this sturdy centre.

The scrimmage brought out many important things. First, Westmore Willcox promises to be invaluable for his speed and quickness in the backfield. Yesterday he intercepted a forward pass at top speed and ran 60 yards for a touchdown.

Appreciate Brickley

Charles Brickley's advent was welcomed by coaches and players alike. He took all the drop kickers, including Whitney, Rollins, Boles, Gardner, Doherty, Wilcox, Murray, Horween, Roninson and Horne. This is the first drop-kicking drill the men have had at Harvard, and they all came away from the lesson knowing a lot more about how it was done. Brickley will be here for another two days, and will leave Saturday night for his team at Johns Hopkins.

D. C. Watson, '16, the varsity quarterback, has had a day off and did not appear yesterday. Mahan and King watched the game and did not scrimmage. Cowen is still out of the play with an injured ankle. Today's practice will be light in view of the hard game on Saturday.

JACKSON SOPHS ELECT OFFICERS

At the first class meeting of the year Miss Jane Davies of Somerville, daughter of Dean Caroline S. Davies of Jackson College, was elected the president of the sophomore class. The honor of being vice-president fell to Miss Muriel Nickerson of Chelsea, while Miss Helen Sibley of Bristol, N. H., was chosen secretary, and Miss Lucile Morse of Arlington treasurer. After a second ballot, owing to a tie, the honor of being chosen marshal of the class fell to Miss Dorothy Danvers of Glenbrook, Conn.

BOOK HOPPE FOR TOURNEY

NEW YORK, Sept. 30.—Announcement was made today that a handicap billiard tournament at the 18-inch balk line game, two shots in balk and two in anchor, will be held at the Music Hall of the New York Theatre from Monday, Nov. 15, to Tuesday, Nov. 23, inclusive. The number of participants will be limited to six. Games will be on a basis of 500 points and William F. Hoppe, the champion, will be at scratch. Entries will close Oct. 20.

WOOD VS. JOHNSON IN WASHINGTON TODAY

Joe Wood, the smoky person on the Red Sox twirling staff, and Walter Johnson, the Kansas cyclone of Clarke Griffith's outfit of Washington Senators, are booked to clash today in the opening game of the final series between the two clubs, and all Washington is agog with the expectation of witnessing a twirlers' battle of the calibre that Boston fans saw when the pair met here in 1912.

PIRATES WHIP ST. LOUIS 6-5

Victory Boosts Pittsburg Into First Division at Expense of Chicago

ST. LOUIS, Sept. 30.—Pittsburg went into the first division by defeating St. Louis in a 10-inning game here today, 6 to 5. Errors by the home team gave the visitors their first four runs.

A triple by Roche with two out in the ninth tied the score for the locals. Pittsburg won in the 10th on a single by Viox and Gibson's double.

The score:

PITTSBURG.	AB.	R.	BH.	TB.	PO.	A.	E.
Carey, l f	5	0	1	2	2	0	0
Johnson, 1b	4	0	0	0	16	0	0
Barney, c f	5	0	0	0	1	0	0
Hinchman, r f	5	1	0	0	0	0	0
Wagner, ss	5	0	1	1	3	6	2
Viox, 2b	4	3	3	3	1	3	1
Baird, 3b	3	1	1	1	1	4	0
Gibson, c	3	1	2	3	6	0	0
Adams, p	1	0	0	0	0	2	0
aCostello	1	0	1	1	0	0	0
Kantlehner, p	3	0	2	2	0	0	0
Harmon, p	0	0	0	0	0	1	0
Totals	39	6	11	13	30	16	3

ST. LOUIS.	AB.	R.	BH.	TB.	PO.	A.	E.
Huggins, 2b	4	0	0	0	1	2	1
bRoche	1	0	1	3	0	0	0
Perdue, p	0	0	0	0	0	0	0
Smith, l f	4	0	1	1	1	0	0
cBeck, r f	1	0	0	0	0	0	0
Dolan, c f	4	0	2	4	3	0	1
Miller, 1b, 2b	5	1	0	0	12	1	0
Long, r f, l f	5	1	1	3	4	1	0
Betzel, 3b	4	1	1	1	2	2	0
dHyatt	1	0	0	0	0	0	0
Snyder, c	4	0	2	3	4	1	0
Hornsby, ss	3	1	1	1	2	4	2
Meadows, p	1	0	0	0	0	2	0
Robinson, p	1	0	0	0	0	1	0
Sallee, p	1	0	0	0	0	1	0
eGonzales, 1b	0	1	0	0	1	0	0
Totals	39	5	9	16	30	15	4

aBatted for Adams in the 4th. bBatted for Huggins in the 9th. cBatted for Smith in the 9th. dBatted for Betzel in the 10th. eBatted for Sallee in the 9th.

Pittsburg	0	1	0	3	1	0	0	0	0	1	—6
St. Louis	0	3	0	0	0	0	0	0	2	0	—5

Two-base hits—Snyder, Carey, Gibson. Three-base hits—Long, Dolan, Roche. Earned runs—Pittsburg 2, St. Louis 4. Sacrifice hits—Dolan, Hornsby, Viox, Johnson, Baird. Double play—Hornsby to Miller. Bases on balls—Off Kantlehner 1, off Meadows 2, off Robinson 2. Hits—Off Adams 4 in 3 innings, off Kantlehner 4 in 6 innings, off Harmon 1 in 1 inning, off Meadows 4 in 8 1-3 innings, off Robinson 2 in 1 1-3 innings, off Sallee 3 in 4 1-3 innings, off Perdue 2 in 1 inning. Struck out—By Kantlehner 1, by Meadows 3. Umpires—Quigley and Eason. Time—2h. 8m.

HERZOG SUSPENDS CLARK

CHICAGO, Sept. 30.—Manager Herzog of the Cincinnati baseball club announced today the suspension for the balance of the season of Tom Clark, catcher, for breaking training rules.

TUFTS WORKS LINE PASSES

Work on the forward pass marked the Tufts football practice on the Oval yesterday afternoon. For more than an hour Coach Whelan ran the men through a snappy signal practice, in which the perfection of the forward passing game played an important part.

The pass over the line has always been one of the strong points of the Brown and Blue elevens since it came into prominence, and Coach Whelan is working hard with the squad this season in order to bring it up to the standard of past teams.

L. A. Sanborn, the veteran end of last season, who reported to the coaches for the first time Wednesday and replaced Nellis at end during the practice yesterday, showed his old-time form at the position.

The first setback to the squad occurred yesterday during the scrimmage, "Ollie" Wescott, the star halfback, injuring his ankle. Wescott will remain out of the practice for a few days, but the coach is hopeful of getting him in a part of the Norwich contest Saturday.

DETROIT QUITS THE LIMELIGHT

DETROIT, Mich., Sept. 30.—Boston became the American league champion today, although not playing, through Detroit's loss of the final game with St. Louis 8 to 2.

Wellman won his eighth game of the year from the Tigers, and would not have been scored on but for three errors, bunched in one inning. With a single exception, every game won from the local team by St. Louis this season has been pitched by Wellman. He has been beaten by the Tigers but once.

The result was determined in the fifth, when five hits, including a double and triple, were bunched with a pass, for five tallies.

The score:

ST. LOUIS.	AB.	R.	BH.	TB.	PO.	A.	E.
Shotton, l f	4	1	1	3	2	0	0
Howard, 1b	3	0	0	0	10	0	0
Sisler, r f	5	1	2	5	1	0	0
Pratt, 2b	5	2	3	4	7	2	1
Walker, c f	5	1	3	6	2	0	0
Austin, 3b	4	1	2	2	3	2	0
Lavan, ss	5	0	0	0	1	7	1
Agnew, c	3	1	1	1	1	1	2
Wellman, p	4	1	2	2	0	3	0
Totals	38	8	14	23	27	15	4

DETROIT.	AB.	R.	BH.	TB.	PO.	A.	E.
Bush, ss	4	1	1	1	2	1	1
Vitt, 3b	5	0	0	0	4	1	0
Cobb, c f	4	1	2	2	4	1	0
Veach, l f	4	0	0	0	2	0	0
Crawford, r f	4	0	0	0	2	0	0
Burns, 1b	3	0	1	1	5	1	1
Young, 2b	2	0	0	0	4	1	1
Baker, c	3	0	1	1	4	3	0
Dauss, p	3	0	0	0	0	1	0
aDubuc	1	0	1	1	0	0	0
bBoland	0	0	0	0	0	0	0
Totals	33	2	6	6	27	9	3

aBatted for Dauss in 9th. bRan for Dubuc in 9th.

St. Louis	0	0	0	5	0	0	0	0	3	—8
Detroit	0	0	2	0	0	0	0	0	0	—2

Two-base hits—Pratt, Walker. Three-base hits—Shotton, Walker. Home run—Sisler. Stolen bases—Vitt, Cobb 2, Howard. Earned runs—St. Louis 5. Double play—Baker to Vitt. Sacrifice hit—Howard. Bases on balls—Off Wellman 7, off Dauss 2. Struck out—By Wellman 1, by Dauss 3. Umpires—Wallace and Evans. Time—1h. 55m.

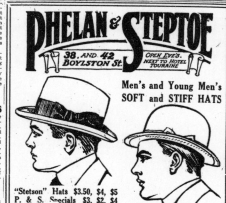

M'GRAW TIPS SERIES BETTORS

All those who are inclined to play a hunch on the result of the coming world's series now have an inside line, as Johnny McGraw has come forth with his advance dope and picked the Phils to run away with the championship. As a picker of winners John is reported to have nothing on Jim Corbett.

BRICKLEY ALWAYS WELCOME

Charley Brickley's presence at Cambridge ought to make itse[illegible] next few days. Brickley is coming to town just to give some of the Crimson kickers the once over, and then will beat it back to his charges at Johns Hopkins. By the way, it is a cinch that Harvard would give a good deal to have another Brickley toe in the lineup this season.

IN THE FIELD OF SPORTS

The Los Angeles Times

XXXIVTH YEAR. MONDAY MORNING, OCTOBER 4, 1915.—4 PAGES. PART III.

ONE POINT DECIDES PENNANT WINNER OF FEDS.

Closest Ever.

WHALES TAKE FED PENNANT.

Deciding Game was a Race Against Darkness.

Flack's Double in the Night Tells Tale.

Crowds Turned Away from Ball Park.

BY G. W. ALEXSON.

[BY DIRECT WIRE—EXCLUSIVE DISPATCH.]

CHICAGO, Oct. 3.—Before a raving mob of 34,000 fans the Whales today landed a pennant for Chicago by beating the Pittsburgh Federal Leaguers at Weegham Park in the second game of a double-header after having suffered a wild eleven-inning defeat in the first. The initial combat went the Rebels' way, 5 to 4, while the second was sawed off in the seventh inning, 3 to 0.

It was a race with the charioteer of the sun for the bunting. Shadows were growing longer every moment, with the rays of the setting orb silhouetting the surging human fringe against the outfield walls.

DEATH GRIPS.

For five innings the rivals had been at death grips without either side able to come within hailing distance of the plate. Bailey was pitching pennant ball for Chicago, while Knetzer was making a last ditch stand for the Rebels. The team that could squeeze over a solitary run would most likely be in possession of the bunting, as the game might be called any minute. It was already too dark for the spectators to follow the gyrations of the ball as it played hide and seek between the pitcher and the catcher or gamboled off the shinbones of some groping infielder.

The Rebs had been retired in their half of the sixth and it was up to Mike Doolan, first up for the Whales, to stir the dying embers of a fading season. Mike made good and shot the ball between short and third for a single. He was neatly sacrificed by Bailey, and Zeider's infield out relayed him to third. Here it was where fortune cast Maximillian Flack for the hero role. Could he deliver? If he could not the Whales would probably never get another chance.

Two balls and two strikes had been called on Max. The roars from stand, bleachers and field had died down to a whisper, as a blurred, round object started on a journey for the fence in right center. Mack had collided with the ball and the noise of the blow carried around the Federal League circuit, as the wallop put Pittsburgh and St. Louis out of the pennant race. Oakes finally dug the sphere from out among the latest trouser patterns, but there was no profit in the digging as Doolan had crossed the plate and Max had been given the credit for a two-bagger.

It matters not that Zwilling followed him with another double scoring Flack or that Wilson's single sent Aleck home for the third and last run. That tally by Doolan looked as big as a house in the gloaming and it was ample and sufficient, for the game was called in the next inning after Pittsburgh had failed to reach first.

No master baseball scene shifter could have staged a better setting for the windup pennant race. The perfect October day shunted a good slice of the north side, and the south and west side as well, to the ball park. As early as noon long lines of fans began to find their way through the turnstiles. At 1 o'clock it was a mob, with the ticket sellers swamped. At 2 o'clock it became necessary to shut the gates, as it seemed as if every available inch of room inside the park had been pre-empted.

With the closing of the gates a roaring mob of some 10,000 were voicing protests on the outside.

JESS WILLARD TO FIGHT IN MARCH.

[BY A. P. NIGHT WIRE.]

OKLAHOMA CITY (Okla.) Oct. 3.—Jess Willard announced tonight that his first fight to defend the title of world's champion heavyweight pugilist probably would take place in New Orleans, the challenger to be "the logical contender" for the title, selected by the sporting writers of the country. He said he would accept the offer of New Orleans promoters for a twenty-round match during Mardi Gras, in March.

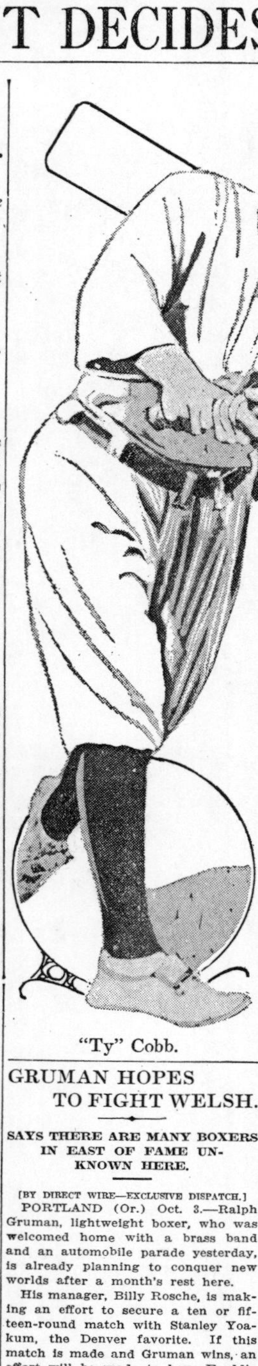

"Ty" Cobb.

GRUMAN HOPES TO FIGHT WELSH.

SAYS THERE ARE MANY BOXERS IN EAST OF FAME UNKNOWN HERE.

[BY DIRECT WIRE—EXCLUSIVE DISPATCH.]

PORTLAND (Or.) Oct. 3.—Ralph Gruman, lightweight boxer, who was welcomed home with a brass band and an automobile parade yesterday, is already planning to conquer new worlds after a month's rest here.

His manager, Billy Rosche, is making an effort to secure a ten or fifteen-round match with Stanley Yoakum, the Denver favorite. If this match is made and Gruman wins, an effort will be made to have Freddie Welsh appear against Gruman in a twenty-round bout in Denver.

Gruman may fight in Nevada on his way East in case he does not secure a bout with Yoakum.

Reviewing his string of victories in New York, Gruman said:

"The first bout I had with Jimmy Duffy, a tough Brooklyn boy, and, by the way, I want to tell you that they have some tough boys in New York that the western fight fans never heard about. I beat Duffy in ten rounds and then met Buddy Ryan, a Bronx kid. Buddy lasted four rounds. Jene Moriarity of Syracuse was my next victim in a ten-round bout and I nearly knocked him out, as I did Paul Bloom, whom I met a couple of weeks later.

"My last bout was with Joe Azevedo, the Sacramento boy, who is as tough as they make 'em. I secured the decision over Azevedo, but from the seventh round on the California boy did not know what he was doing.

"I had him all but out and in a longer battle he would have been sent down for the count."

HINKEY STYLE OF OPEN PLAY DOOMED AT YALE.

[BY DIRECT WIRE—EXCLUSIVE DISPATCH.]

NEW HAVEN (Ct.) Oct. 3.—Saturday's defeat has thrown a gloom over Yale. There are now eight teams that have defeated the Blue—Harvard, Princeton, West Point, Columbia, Lehigh, Brown, Washington and Jefferson and Virginia.

Many who have watched the development of Yale football for years believe the Virginia game has sounded the death knell of the Hinkey style of open play. It was a wet day, but Virginia seemed to have solved the problem of working out a defense for the lateral and forward passes and it is doubtful whether Yale could have done any better on a dry field.

There will probably be a shake-up in the Yale back field and a period of the hardest practice the Blue squad has had this season, as a result of the defeat by the University of Virginia yesterday.

Guernsey whose work slowed up the interference Saturday will probably be replaced by Scovil or Charlie Taft, while Thompson will give way to Bentley or Lowry. In the line, Roberts will probably be replaced by Kent, who took his place yesterday after Coolman had broken through the Yale line several times.

Capt. Wilson's poor kicking lost the Blue many yards yesterday and his fumbling was one of the weakest spots in the play of the Elis.

Friends Again.

LAST TILT FOR TIGERS-ANGELS.

BAYLESS AND WILHOIT WIN FINAL GAME.

Local Clubs Divide Final Series of Season—Morning Game Sees the Downfall of Fairbanks—Decanniere and Love Work in Afternoon Affair and Dec Shuts Out Scraphs.

BY HARRY A. WILLIAMS.

The affairs of the Angels and Tigers, as among themselves, were wound up for the year yesterday. They split a double-header, and in so doing executed a double split, as the splitting of the double-header resulted in the splitting of the series, four games to four. They also split the gate receipts, sixty and forty. Vernon, being the home team, got the 60 per cent. or hog end of the financial returns.

As splitters our ball teams are in a class by themselves. They played six series this season. Of these, two were tied. The Tigers won two and Los Angeles an equal number. Only in total number of games played was there any difference, and that was so small as to be hardly visible to the naked eye. Of the forty-three combats between them, Los Angeles won twenty-two and Vernon twenty-one, giving the Angels a margin of one game. This means that Earl Houck, the singing undertaker who bet a hat on the Angels, wins his wager. He will select a Peaceful Valley dicer. There was a time when the Angels couldn't win a majority of games from the Tigers. This merely goes to show what constant practice will do for a ball team.

ALL OVER.

It is all over so far as the Tigers and Angels are individually concerned. They will not meet again this year. The athletes, now that it is over, do not entertain any hard feelings for each other. If they bit one another or shoved their spikes into one another, nothing personal was intended. Their actions were purely of a professional nature, and not actuated by malice or a desire to kill. A month from now many of them will be found partaking of the same free lunch just as though nothing had ever happened. As the poet once said, "One free lunch makes the whole world kin."

Doc's athletes will beat it for San Francisco today to find what it looks like up there in the fall of the year. Pa's players remain here for the express purpose of meeting the great Oakland team, starting Wednesday. The Oaklets, being in sixth place, and therefore not used to traveling very fast, can't get here in time to open Tuesday. The scores were:

THUS.

Morning—Los Angeles, 7; Vernon, 4.

Afternoon—Vernon, 1; Los Angeles, 0.

Strange what a difference of one or two hours will make in the behavior of a couple of ball teams.

In the opening combat, White tried out Fred Fairbanks, the young and tender right-hander who has been making a loud noise in the sugar beet belt adjacent to Oxnard. Fairbanks should not be weighed on the scales of public opinion through his showing yesterday. He displayed a lot of stuff at times, and fielded his position nicely. It is very trying for a busher to make his initial appearance in a park which is so small that almost any kind of a healthy fly goes for a home run. Coming from a town where a large sugar factory is located he should be a sweet pitcher. But until he is allowed to play ball in a regular park nobody will know whether he is any good or not.

HIGH-MINDED.

The afternoon game was a high-minded combat between Frank Decanniere and Slim Love. Each showed wonderful deftness with his southpaw. It is really remarkable that anybody can throw a ball at all with his or her left hand, let alone pitching a game like these guys did. It has become a common saying that the only way to beat Slim is to shut out his team, and that is what Decanniere did. It was an even thing until the eighth, with neither side getting in speaking distance of the plate. In that round, Bayless cut loose with a double. He took third on a sacrifice and Joe Wilhoit smashed a vicious grounder against Johnny Butler's defenseless shin for the winning punch.

Prior to this there were some tense situations, and some especially fine fielding by Kane, McMullen and Zeb and Koerner. In the third, Beef speared a hot grounder over first by Spencer, and tossed to Slim for a put-out. Had not Koerner made this splendid stop Tub could have been

(Continued on Second Page.)

Peerless.

TY COBB'S RECORD IS GREATEST EVER MADE.

Complete Story of Famous Player Told in Figures for Season — Hits Right-handers as Hard as Southpaws. Steals More Bases than Any Modern Player and Proves Best in More Departments of Game.

TABULATED BY AL MUNRO ELIAS.

EVER since Ty Cobb broke into the Big League, he has been climbing, and, at the conclusion of each season, the experts have pronounced him at the pinnacle. Then he generally went higher the next year. But in the season just drawing to a close he has gone further than ever. It looks like the pinnacle this time sure. Perhaps it isn't. No one knows what Cobb will do.

Appended is the absolute record of what Cobb has done since the first game of this season up until midnight of September 25. It covers the complete season except for a few days. The table shows just how many hits Cobb has made off the different pitchers. The fan can find out which twirlers Ty hits hardest and which are the biggest problem to him. From scanning the figures it is evident that no pitcher has Cobb stopped. He is not "soft" for any of them.

The table shows his daily average over the period included and by studying the figures it is easy to see that Ty hits right handers as hard as he does southpaws. It shows the number of consecutive games in which he made a hit. You can discover the period of the season when he did his hardest batting and when he slumped. His runs of continuous games in which he made hits are remarkable.

Cobb has accomplished something else in the past season. He has broken the modern record for stolen bases held previously by Milan, which was eighty-eight bases for one season. Ty is now well over ninety and probably will touch the century mark.

It is the greatest season ever had by a Big Leaguer. Cobb has shown more all-'round ability this year than was ever before displayed by a ball player. It is generally acknowledged that almost through his efforts alone the Detroit Tigers were kept in the race right up to the last week.

Cobb played in every game from the opening day of the season through the battle of Saturday, September 25th. He played all through each contest with the exception of two innings on July 14th when he retired with Detroit leading by the score of 12 to 0. It is a wonderful record for a ball player. The table below shows everything he has done every day except when he changed his chewing gum and fixed his cap. Here, then, is Ty Cobb's box score for the season:

Date.	A.B.	R.	1B.	2B.	3B.	HR.	Total bases on hits.	Off pitcher.		Off catcher.	
April 14......	4	1	1	0	0	0	1	Mitchell	0	O'Neill	.250
April 15......	4	1	1	0	0	1	5	Steen	1	O'Neill	.500
April 16......	3	2	1	0	0	0	1	Hagerman	2	Egan	.333
April 17......	3	2	2	0	0	0	2	Morton	1	Egan	.667
April 18......	3	3	0	1	1	0	5	Scott	0	Schalk	.667
April 19......	3	0	1	0	0	0	1	Faber	0	Schalk	.333
April 20......	3	3	1	0	1	0	4	Cicotte	0	Schalk	.667
April 21......	2	1	0	1	0	0	2	Russell	0	Schalk	.500
April 22......	4	2	2	0	0	0	2	Mitchell	1	O'Neill	.500
April 23......	3	1	1	0	0	0	1	Coumbe	1	Egan	.333
April 24......	4	0	0	0	0	0	0	Steen	2	O'Neill	.000
April 25......	4	0	1	0	0	0	1	Morton	1	Egan	.250
April 26......	3	0	1	0	0	0	1	Weilman	1	Leary	.333
April 27......	3	1	0	0	1	0	3	Lowdermilk	0	Leary	.333
April 28......	4	4	2	0	1	0	5	James	1	Agnew	.750
April 29......	2	0	0	0	0	0	0	Hamilton	0	Agnew	.000
April 30......	2	1	0	0	0	0	0	Faber	0	Schalk	.000
May 1......	2	0	0	0	0	0	0	Russell	0	Schalk	.000
May 2......	4	1	2	0	0	0	2	Cicotte	0	Schalk	.500
May 4......	2	1	0	0	0	0	0	Hamilton	0	Agnew	.000
May 5......	4	0	3	0	0	0	3	Lowdermilk	0	Agnew	.750
May 7......	4	3	3	0	0	0	3	Hamilton	2	Agnew	.750
May 8......	4	1	1	0	0	0	1	Weilman	0	Agnew	.250
May 9......	4	0	1	0	0	0	1	Johnson	1	Ainsmith	.250
May 11......	3	1	2	0	0	0	2	Ruth	0	Thomas	.667
May 12......	4	0	1	0	0	0	1	Shore	0	Cady	.250
May 13......	1	2	0	0	0	0	0	Leonard	2	Thomas	.000
May 15......	4	0	1	0	0	0	1	Foster	0	Thomas	.250
May 16......	4	1	0	2	0	0	4	McHale	0	Sweeney	.500
May 19......	1	1	1	0	0	0	1	Keating	4	Nunamaker	1.000
May 21......	3	2	2	0	0	0	2	Shawkey	0	Schang	.667
May 22......	4	0	1	0	0	0	1	Wyckoff	0	Schang	.250
May 23......	5	2	3	0	0	0	3	Pennock	0	Schang	.600
May 24......	3	1	1	0	0	0	1	Boehling	0	Ainsmith	.333
May 25......	5	1	2	0	1	0	5	Gallia	0	Ainsmith	.600
May 26......	2	2	2	0	0	0	2	Shaw	1	Ainsmith	1.000
May 27......	4	0	3	0	0	0	3	Johnson	0	Henry	.750
May 29......	2	2	0	1	0	0	2	Weilman	0	Agnew	.500
May 29......	3	0	1	1	0	0	3	Lowdermilk	2	Agnew	.667
May 30......	4	0	0	0	0	0	0	Weilman	0	Agnew	.000
May 30......	3	0	1	0	0	0	1	Hamilton	0	Agnew	.333
May 31......	4	2	1	0	0	0	1	Russell	1	Schalk	.250
May 31......	4	0	1	0	0	0	1	Russell	0	Schalk	.250
June 1......	3	0	0	0	0	0	0	Faber	1	Schalk	.000
June 2......	5	2	2	0	0	0	2	Benz	2	Schalk	.400
June 4......	4	2	1	0	1	0	4	Caldwell	2	Sweeney	.500
June 5......	5	2	2	0	0	1	6	Fisher	1	Sweeney	.600
June 6......	4	1	0	1	0	0	2	Donovan	0	Nunamaker	.250
June 7......	3	2	0	1	0	0	2	Keating	0	Nunamaker	.333
June 8......	3	0	1	0	0	0	1	Caldwell	0	Sweeney	.333
June 9......	5	2	3	0	0	0	3	Collins	3	Carrigan	.600
June 10......	5	2	3	0	0	0	3	Shore	2	Cady	.600
June 11......	3	1	0	0	0	0	0	Foster	0	Thomas	.000
June 12......	5	1	2	0	0	0	2	Shawkey	4	Schang	.400
June 14......	3	0	0	0	0	0	0	Bush	1	Schang	.000
June 16......	3	1	0	0	0	0	0	Wyckoff	0	Lapp	.000
June 17......	4	0	1	0	0	0	1	Ayres	1	Henry	.250
June 18......	3	2	2	0	0	0	2	Boehling	3	Henry	.667
June 19......	3	0	1	0	0	0	1	Johnson	0	Ainsmith	.333
June 20......	3	0	1	0	0	0	1	Weilman	1	Agnew	.333
June 22......	6	1	1	1	0	0	3	Hamilton	0	Agnew	.333
June 23......	3	1	0	1	0	0	2	James	1	Severeid	.333
June 24......	5	2	1	1	1	0	6	Hamilton	3	Severeid	.600
June 26......	2	0	0	0	0	0	0	Weilman	1	Agnew	.000
June 27......	2	3	1	0	1	0	4	Coumbe	2	O'Neill	1.000
June 28......	3	1	1	0	0	0	1	Hagerman	1	Egan	.333
June 30......	3	1	0	0	0	0	0	Mitchell	0	O'Neill	.000
July 1......	3	0	1	0	0	0	1	Scott	0	Schalk	.333
July 2......	3	0	1	0	0	0	1	Faber	0	Schalk	.333
July 3......	3	2	1	1	0	0	3	Russell	0	Schalk	.667
July 4......	5	2	3	0	0	0	3	Scott	0	Schalk	.600
July 5......	4	1	2	0	0	0	2	Coumbe	0	O'Neill	.500
July 5......	5	1	1	1	0	0	3	Hagerman	0	O'Neill	.400
July 6......	3	1	0	1	0	0	2	Walker	0	O'Neill	.333
July 9......	2	3	1	0	0	0	1	Ruth	2	Cady	.500
July 10......	3	0	1	0	0	0	1	Foster	0	Thomas	.333
July 11......	4	3	2	0	0	0	2	Shore	1	Cady	.500
July 12......	5	2	1	0	1	0	4	Leonard	0	Thomas	.400
July 13......	4	1	1	2	0	0	5	Warhop	0	Nunamaker	.750
July 13......	4	0	2	0	0	0	2	Cole	1	Sweeney	.500
July 14......	2	2	0	0	0	0	0	Caldwell	1	Sweeney	.000
July 17......	4	0	1	0	0	0	1	Bush	0	Lapp	.250
July 18......	4	1	3	0	0	0	3	Bressler	1	Lapp	.750
July 19......	4	1	1	1	0	0	3	Wyckoff	2	Lapp	.500
July 20......	4	0	1	0	0	0	1	Knowlson	0	Lapp	.250
July 21......	4	1	1	0	0	0	1	Sheehan	1	Lapp	.250
July 23......	2	0	1	0	0	0	1	Gallia	1	Henry	.500
July 24......	3	1	1	0	0	0	1	Johnson	1	Ainsmith	.333
July 24......	2	0	0	0	0	0	0	Boehling	0	Henry	.000
July 25......	2	1	0	0	0	0	0	Ayres	0	Henry	.000
July 27......	4	0	2	0	0	0	2	Fisher	0	Nunamaker	.500
July 28......	4	0	0	2	0	0	4	Caldwell	0	Sweeney	.500
July 29......	4	2	1	0	1	0	4	Warhop	0	Nunamaker	.500
July 30......	4	0	0	0	0	0	0	Leonard	0	Thomas	.000
July 31......	3	1	1	0	0	0	1	Foster	0	Cady	.333
Aug. 2......	4	0	1	0	1	0	4	Collins	0	Carrigan	.500
Aug. 3......	4	0	2	0	0	0	2	Shore	0	Cady	.500
Aug. 4......	4	0	1	0	0	0	1	Wyckoff	0	Lapp	.250
Aug. 5......	6	0	0	0	0	0	0	Bressler	0	Lapp	.000
Aug. 5......	5	1	2	0	0	0	2	Sheehan	0	Lapp	.400
Aug. 7......	3	1	1	0	0	0	1	Fillingim	1	Lapp	.33
Aug. 7......	5	1	3	0	0	0	3	Wyckoff	2	Lapp	.600
Aug. 7......	5	1	3	0	0	0	3	Boehling	0	Henry	.167
Aug. 9......	6	1	0	0	1	0	3	Johnson	0	Ainsmith	.400
Aug. 10......	5	2	2	0	0	0	2	Gallia	0	Henry	.000
Aug. 11......	4	0	0	0	0	0	0	Scott	0	Schalk	.750
Aug. 14......	4	3	2	0	1	0	5	Faber	0	Schalk	.333
Aug. 15......	3	1	1	0	0	0	1	Walker	3	Egan	.600
Aug. 16......	4	1	2	0	0	0	2	Hagerman	0	Egan	.500
Aug. 16......	2	0	1	0	0	0	1	Harstad	3	Egan	.800
Aug. 17......	5	3	2	2	0	0	6	Jones	0	Haworth	.200
Aug. 17......	5	1	1	0	0	0	3	Sheehan	0	Lapp	.500
Aug. 18......	4	0	1	1	0	0	3	Wyckoff	1	McAvoy	.333
Aug. 19......	3	1	1	0	0	0	1	Bressler	1	McAvoy	.667
Aug. 20......	3	2	2	0	0	0	2	Johnson	0	Williams	.250
Aug. 22......	4	0	1	0	0	0	2	Gallia	0	Henry	.000
Aug. 22......	4	0	0	0	0	0	0	Shore	6	Cady	.250
Aug. 24......	4	0	0	0	1	0	3	Ruth	0	Thomas	.200
Aug. 25......	5	0	0	1	0	0	2	Foster	1	Thomas	.500
Aug. 26......	4	2	2	0	0	0	2	Cole	1	Nunamaker	.667
Aug. 27......	5	0	0	0	0	0	0	Pieh	0	Alexander	.000
Aug. 28......	3	0	0	0	0	0	0	Caldwell	0	Nunamaker	.000
Aug. 28......	4	0	0	0	0	0	0	Fisher	0	Kruger	.000
Aug. 29......	2	0	0	0	0	0	0	Shawkey	0	Nunamaker	.000
Aug. 31......	5	0	1	0	0	1	0	Russell	3	Schalk	.200
Sept. 1......	2	1	0	0	0	0	0	Scott	0	Schalk	.000
Sept. 2......	4	1	3	0	0	0	3	Russell	0	Mayer	.750
Sept. 3......	2	0	1	0	0	0	1	Hamilton	1	Severeid	.500
Sept. 4......	2	0	0	0	0	0	0	Weilman	0	Agnew	.000
Sept. 4......	3	1	0	0	0	0	0	Koob	1	Severeid	.000
Sept. 5......	5	2	0	0	0	0	0	Sisler	0	Severeid	.000
Sept. 5......	4	2	1	0	0	0	1	Hoff	1	Agnew	.250
Sept. 7......	5	2	2	0	0	0	2	Russell	0	Schalk	.400
Sept. 8......	5	2	1	1	0	0	3	Faber	0	Schalk	.400
Sept. 9......	3	1	2	1	0	0	4	Hagerman	1	O'Neill	1.000
Sept. 10......	4	0	2	0	0	0	2	Klepfer	1	O'Neill	.500
Sept. 11......	3	2	1	1	0	0	3	Caldwell	0	Nunamaker	.667
Sept. 13......	5	0	1	0	0	0	1	Fisher	0	Nunamaker	.200
Sept. 14......	3	0	1	0	0	0	1	Mogridge	1	Alexander	.333
Sept. 15......	3	0	2	0	0	0	2	Caldwell	0	Nunamaker	.667
Sept. 16......	3	2	1	0	0	0	1	Foster	1	Thomas	.333
Sept. 17......	4	1	0	0	0	1	4	Leonard	0	Carrigan	.250
Sept. 18......	4	0	0	1	0	0	2	Shore	0	Cady	.250
Sept. 20......	3	0	1	0	0	0	1	Ruth	0	Carrigan	.333
Sept. 21......	5	1	3	0	0	0	3	Bush	2	McAvoy	.600
Sept. 22......	5	2	2	0	0	0	2	Wyckoff	1	McAvoy	.400
Sept. 23......	5	1	1	0	0	0	1	Sheehan	1	McAvoy	.200
Sept. 24......	4	0	2	0	0	0	2	Johnson	1	Williams	.500
Sept. 25......	3	1	0	0	0	0	0	Dumont	1	Henry	.000
Sept. 25......	5	0	1	0	0	0	1	Gallia	1	Williams	.200
Totals	543	141	159	27	14	3	267		91		.374

Total games, 150.

Includes games played September 25.

World's Series Number

PUBLIC LEDGER

Pictorial Section

PHILADELPHIA, SUNDAY, OCTOBER 10, 1915

THE MODERN ALEXANDER THE GREAT WHO HAS A WORLD'S SERIES TO CONQUER

PENNANTS ARE NOT NEW TO THE BOSTON RED SOX, WHICH CLUB HAS CAPTURED THE TITLE FOUR TIMES IN FIFTEEN SEASONS

HOOPER, Outfielder

MAYS, Pitcher

JANVRIN, Infielder

SPEAKER, Outfielder

SCOTT, Shortstop

HENRIKSEN Outfielder

WAGNER Infielder

BILL CARRIGAN Manager and Catcher

GAINOR First Baseman

SHORE Pitcher

CADY, Catcher

WOOD, Pitcher

THOMAS Catcher

LEONARD, Pitcher

BARRY, Second Baseman

HOBLITZELL First Baseman

GARDNER, Third Baseman

GREGG, Pitcher

LEWIS, Outfielder

RUTH, Pitcher

FOSTER, Pitcher

COLLINS, Pitcher

IN THE THIRTY-THIRD YEAR OF THEIR CONTINUED EXISTENCE, THE PHILLIES FOR THE FIRST TIME WON THE PENNANT

STOCK, Third Baseman

RIXEY, Pitcher

LUDERUS, First Baseman and Captain

BECKER, Outfielder

BANCROFT, Shortstop

BURNS, Catcher

NIEHOFF, Second Baseman

TINCUP, Pitcher

DEMAREE, Pitcher

PAT MORAN
Manager

BAUMGARTNER, Pitcher

PASKERT, Outfielder

KILLEFER, Catcher

McQUILLAN, Pitcher

DUGEY, Infielder

WHITTED, Outfielder

CRAVATH, Outfielder

BYRNE, Third Baseman

ALEXANDER, Pitcher

CHALMERS, Pitcher

WEISER, Outfielder

ADAMS, Catcher

MAYER, Pitcher

SPORTING SECTION

LOS ANGELES IS THE LARGEST CITY WEST OF ST. LOUIS, MO.

LOS ANGELES EXPRESS

ONLY EVENING PAPER IN LOS ANGELES WITH THE ASSOCIATED PRESS NEWS SERVICE

SPORTING SECTION

VOLUME 45 NO. 169 | Fair tonight, Sunday | SATURDAY OCTOBER 9 1915 | Forty-fifth Year | ONE CENT In Los Angeles City and County | Elsewhere Two Cents | Hotels, Trains Five Cents | By Carrier 50 Cts. Month

TY COBB 8-TIME BATTING CHAMPION

OLD TIGER HAS 'PEP' ENOUGH TO LEAD ALL IN RUNS AND BASES

[By Associated Press]

CHICAGO, Oct. 9.—For the eighth time in his career, Ty Cobb is champion batter of the American league, according to averages published here today.

Beginning in 1907 the Detroit player has led the hitters in every season except in 1908, when the official scorers gave Criss of St. Louis the palm, he having batted .341 in 64 games to Cobb's .324 in 150 games.

Today Cobb's average for the season just ended is .369.

In stolen bases the Georgian has set a new league record at 97 for the season. The old mark for the American league was 88, credited to Milan of Washington in 1912. In runs scored, Cobb is ahead of all with 144 and leads in total bases with 271.

Collins Close Up

Those following Cobb in batting, who have played in at least half the games are: E. Collins, Chicago, .333; Fournier, Chicago, .325; Speaker, Boston, .319; McInnis, Philadelphia, .314; Jackson, Chicago, .309; Veach, Detroit, .308; Kirke, Cleveland, .303; Crawford, Detroit, 297.

Bobbie Roth, Cleveland, led the league in circuit drives with seven.

Detroit leads in club batting with .265.

Pitchers who finished in the .600 class were: Wood, Boston, won 15, lost 5; Shore, Boston, 20 and 7; Ruth, Boston, 18 and 7; Foster, Boston, 20 and 8; Boland, Detroit, 13 and 6; Johnson, Washington, 27 and 13; Scott, Chicago, 24 and 12; Leonard, Boston, 14 and 7; Dauss, Detroit, 23 and 12; Faber, Chicago, 24 and 13; Covaleskie, Detroit, 23 and 13; Gallia, 17 and 10; Ayers, Washington, 15 and 9; Fisher, New York, 18 and 11; Benz, Chicago, 15 and 10.

Larry Doyle of New York is the National's champion batter, with an average of .315; Cravath of Philadelphia led in runs scored, with 88, in total bases with 268, and in home runs with 24—one below the big league record set by Buck Freeman of Washington, in 1899. Manager Herzog was the leading base stealer with 34.

Following Doyle, the leading batters were: Luderus, Philadelphia, .313; Griffith, Cincinnati, .307; Daubert, Brooklyn, .304; Hinchman, Pittsburg, .304; Snyder, St. Louis, .301; Merkle, New York, .296.

Cincinnati led in club batting, with .254. The following pitchers finished in the 600 class: Toney, Cincinnati, won 16, lost 4; Alexander, Philadelphia, 31 and 9; Mamaux, Pittsburg, 21 and 8; Standridge, Chicago, 4 and 2; Pierce, Chicago, 13 and 7; Coombs, Brooklyn, 15 and 9; Ragan, Boston, 18 and 11; S. Smith, Brooklyn, 13 and 8; Vaughn, Chicago, 20 and 13.

Bennie Kauf Leads

Bennie Kauff won the Federal league championship, with .340, though Watson of Buffalo in 29 games batted .396. Kauff led in stolen bases, with 54, and in total bases with 247. Berton of St. Louis led in runs scored, with 99, and Hal Chase of Buffalo in home runs, with 17. The leading batters who followed Kauff were: Magee, Brooklyn, .328; Fischer, Chicago, .326; Campbell, Newark, .314; Flack, Chicago, .313; Konetchy, Pittsburg, .310; A. Wilson, Chicago, .307; Evans, Baltimore, .307; W. Miller, St. Louis, .307; Mann, Chicago, .306; Rousch, Newark, .302; Tobin, St. Louis, .299.

Brooklyn finished first in club batting, with .265. The .600 pitchers were: McConnell, Chicago, won 24, lost 10; M. Brown, Chicago, 17 and 8; Crandall, St. Louis, 21 and 10; Reulbach, Newark, 21 and 10; Allen, Pittsburg, 23 and 12; Cullop, Kansas City, 22 and 12; Plank, St. Louis, 21 and 12; F. Smith, Baltimore-Brooklyn, 10 and 6; Packard, Kansas City, 19 and 12; F. Anderson, Buffalo, 19 and 12; Rogge, Pittsburg, 17 and 11; Schulz, Buffalo, 21 and 14.

BOYS OF STANFORD HAPPY AT RUGBY VICTORY

[By Associated Press]

SAN FRANCISCO, Oct. 9.—Stanford university's decisive victory over the Olympic club rugby team last Saturday has heartened the student body. The first game between the two teams resulted in a scoreless tie, the showing of the varsity fifteen being anything but encouraging.

During the last week, however, the Cardinal players have regained much of their last year's form and swing and from now on the coaches are looking for steady improvement.

Santa Clara, which supersedes the University of California as Stanford's rival in the "big game," is said to have one of the strongest combinations in its history and is being seriously considered as a factor when the two teams line up.

Boom for Rugby

News from Los Angeles that a number of club rugby fifteens have been organized with a view to playing a series of games in this vicinity against Stanford, Santa Clara and the Olympic club has added stimulus to the rugby outlook. The members of these teams are drawn largely from the high school players, former collegians and the Los Angeles Athletic club.

The showing of California against the Olympic club's eleven last Saturday was not particularly encouraging to Coach Schaeffer. The clubmen led for the first three periods and it was not until the last few minutes of the game that the collegians were able to pull out a victory. Their playing was ragged and their defensive work away below par.

Today Schaeffer's men had a game scheduled against the Originals, a team made up largely of men who played with the Oakland Commercial club, which gave the collegians a drubbing two weeks ago. The encounter was expected to show whether the varsity had stiffened up its defense during the past week.

Pomona vs. L. A. A. C.

The Stanford varsity game against the Barbarian fifteen of San Francisco also was counted on as a stiff try-out.

In the North, the University of Washington faced its first encounter of the season with the Washington Park team, which will include Pike and Wagner in the line-up. The University of Oregon faced Washington State college at Pullman, Wash.; the Aggies took on Whitman at Corvallis and Gonzaga and Montana School of Mines met to exchange kicks at Spokane.

The principal game for the South was Pomona and the Los Angeles Athletic club, at Claremont. The Olympic club's American team went to Reno to take on the University of Nevada.

BARRY GOING GOOD

Alexander Barry is playing a good game of handball at the Los Angeles Athletic club. Barry is developing rapidly and is at the present time one of the best performers in Class C.

HANEY STAR AT POLY

Fred Haney is the star of the Polytechnic high eleven. Haney is being used in the backfield by Coach Roy Haslett and is carrying the ball through all opponents in great style

I Told You So

By M. B. Cook

There is a meanest man somewhere—a meanest woman, too;
A fool is born most every day—some experts say " a few."
But they are in the background in this Boston day of woe
And on the stage there stands the pest who shouts: "I told you so!"

This same old sport insisted that the Sox would surely get
Beneath the hide of Grover, Philadelphia's angel pet;
But when the Phillies took the first and beat the Red Sox foe
The pest stood up and shouted out: "Aha, I told you so!"

Say, fans, let's get together now and gather up some stone—
And bats, and bricks, and knives and things that can and will break bones—
And jump upon the dratted frame of him who has a fit
And shouts each day: "I told you so!" Come on, let's murder "it."

Burns Will Marry Girl of Monterey

SAN FRANCISCO, Oct. 9.—Eddie Burns, catcher for the Philadelphia team of the National Baseball league in the world's series, is to marry Miss Viola Laporte of Monterey, Cal., immediately after the close of the series, it became known here today.

Miss Laporte is a descendant of the early Spanish founders of Monterey. Burns learned his baseball on the sandlots of San Francisco.

Yale Gridiron Squad Meets Lehigh Team At New Haven Today

NEW YORK, Oct. 9.—How far Yale has been able to improve its football team since its defeat by the University of Virginia is expected to be shown today in the Yale-Lehigh game at New Haven. Lehigh has not been defeated this year.

The Carlisle Indians are regarded as likely to give Harvard a hard fight at Cambridge. Syracuse is not considered a formidable opponent for Princeton at Princeton.

Among other games on the schedule are:

Pennsylvania vs. Penn State, at Philadelphia.

Army vs. Gettysburg, at West Point.

Navy vs. Pittsburg, at Annapolis.

Williams vs. Cornell at Ithaca.

Brown vs. Amherst, at Amherst.

Championship Honors At Stake in Chicago, Northwestern Game

CHICAGO, Oct. 9.—Championship honors of the University of Chicago and Northwestern University were at stake today in the only important football game among the "Big Nine" colleges.

Defeat for either eleven means elimination from the "Big Nine" championship race.

It was Chicago's first game of the season and its strength was uncertain, while Northwestern was considered by critics to have the best team developed there in the last decade.

Next in importance to the Chicago-Northwestern contest was the game between Illinois and the Missouri School of Mines at Champaign.

Minnesota, which is regarded as championship timber in the "Big Nine," had Ames as its opponent today.

P. Schneider Brings Bride to Los Angeles

Pete Schneider, pitcher of the Cincinnati Reds, and his bride of two months, arrived in Los Angeles today from Cincinnati. Pete is a product of Southern California and has been one of the mainstays of the Reds' pitching department this season.

He does not intend to play winter ball, as he injured his salary wing last winter pitching in the Imperial Valley Winter league.

FOOTBALL TODAY

SOUTHERN CALIFORNIA

Occidental college vs. Sherman Indians at old Oxy field.

Oxy freshmen vs. Hollywood at old Oxy field.

Pomona college vs. L. A. A. C. at Claremont.

Manual Arts vs. Throop college at Manual Arts.

Santa Barbara vs. Whittier State school at Manual Arts.

U. S. C. seconds vs. U. S. C. thirds at Long Beach.

U. S. C. frosh vs. Long Beach at Long Beach.

Harvard Military academy vs. Lincoln at Downey playgrounds.

Polytechnic vs. Pasadena at Pasadena.

Venice and Gardena at Venice (league game).

Redlands university vs. Redlands high school at Redlands.

Normal school vs. Santa Ana at Santa Ana.

• • •

NORTHERN CALIFORNIA

California vs. Originals at Berkeley.

California frosh vs. Sacramento A. C. at Berkeley.

Stanford vs. Barbarians (rugby).

Stanford vs. U. S. Marines at Stanford (soccer).

U. of C. vs. Allies at Berkeley (soccer).

• • •

EAST

Yale vs. Lehigh at New Haven.

Harvard vs. Carlisle at Cambridge.

Princeton vs. Syracuse at Princeton.

Dartmouth vs. Tufts at Hanover.

Pennsylvania vs. Penn State at Philadelphia.

Cornell vs. Williams at Ithaca.

Army vs. Gettysburg at West Point.

Navy vs. Pittsburg at Annapolis.

• • •

WEST

Chicago vs. Northwestern at Evanston.

Illinois vs. Rolla Miners at Urbana.

Minnesota vs. Ames at Minneapolis.

Wisconsin vs. Marquette at Madison.

Iowa vs. Morningside at Iowa City.

Purdue vs. Beloit at Lafayette.

Indiana vs. Miami at Bloomington.

Ohio vs. Case at Columbus.

Notre Dame vs. Haskell at South Bend.

Michigan vs. Mount Union at Ann Arbor.

Nebraska vs. Kansas Ag[illegible]

SPEED, CRY FOOTBALL COACHES

Gridiron Games Declared to Be Won Largely by Solving Attack of Foes; Brains Wanted by Mentors

By Harry R. Brand

Avoirdupois has been displaced as a main essential of gridiron machines. Instead the coaches now cry for speed and fellows who can think and not work mechanically. They care not for the husky 200-pounder, who weighs ninety pounds from the neck up, because present-day football battles are not won by the superior weight of one eleven, but by the brain power of those who form the personnel of the tanbark elevens.

Football has changed. Those who played the game a decade ago can hardly recognize it. The line bucking methods have passed away and the forward and lateral pass and open game has taken its place. A coach nowadays would rather have a light man with a little gray matter on the team than many lumberous gents who could qualify for the "Concrete league."

Scientific Sport

Present-day football tussles are won largely by solving the attack of the opposing aggregation. Any eleven capable of doing this will come out victorious in the end, while the troupe that depends on weight and straight football will be forced to "bite the dust."

Football has switched from a battering line game to a scientific sport. The coach would like to put heavy men on the team, but he must not for fear of being defeated by a large score. He now looks for the man who has something other than weight. In days of yore a man who tipped the beam around 250 pounds was sure of a place on his college or high school team, but this is not so in this present age. Give the coach a speedy man with something other than bone above the shoulders and he will turn out a winner.

The football mentor of the twentieth century would like to have heavy men on his team, but he is afraid. He knows that should his proteges meet an eleven built for speed his men will be lost. It is not an unusual sight in Southern California to see several huskies decorating the sidelines, while the lighter men are on the field wearing the school colors in battle against all foes.

Speed Wanted

And it is this very thing that has made football the most popular of all rah-rah sports. The sight of a forward pass hurled many yards through the atmosphere is thrilling, while the rugby pass never fails to bring the spectators to their feet.

The open game has displaced the line battering sport and the brainier and more shifty men have become the football stars, while the lad who boasts of weight is relegated to the sidelines, where, with the other huskies, he watches the lighter men represent the school on the football field.

L. A. A. C. FOOTBALLERS AT POMONA COLLEGE

POMONA, Oct. 9.—Los Angeles Athletic club footballers arrived here from Los Angeles at noon today and the men were extremely confident of winning the game with the Pomona college eleven at Claremont.

Coach Sid Neighbors said before the game that his men were in good shape for the game, while the Sage Hens are not in condition for a hard battle.

BRAVES WILL MEET SCOTT NINE SUNDAY

The Sterling Braves will meet the E. E. Scott team Sunday at Doyle's. Manager Pirrone of the Braves has signed Irish Muesel of the Elmira club of the New York State league to play first base.

George Duncan, late of the Hayden (Ariz.) team, will do the receiving for the Braves.

LOS ANGELES HIGH TO START FALL PRACTICE

Los Angeles high school baseball candidates will start fall practice at Echo park Tuesday afternoon. More than 30 are expected to report for work.

Coach Clendennin and Leo Skepner, former Blue and White baseball star, will be in charge of the newcomers. Skepner is not eligible for the team and will help the coach with the men.

U. OF C. DEFEATS WASEDA

TOKIO, Oct. 9.—The University of Chicago baseball team touring Japan defeated Waseda university today. Score:

	R	H	E
University of Chicago	2	5	2
Waseda	0	3	1

PAT MORAN, LEADER OF HEAVY-HITTING PHILADELPHIA CLUB

PHILLIES' SCOUT SAYS HARMONY WON SUCCESS

PHILADELPHIA, Oct. 9.—Scout Billy Neal of the Phillies, winners of the first world series tilt, in an interview today gave the reason as he sees them for the wonderful success of the Philadelphia club.

"You're going to read a lot this winter," said Neal, in that quizzical manner of his, "about the luck the Phillies have had. Of course there is always some luck, but other things have counted.

"First of all, there is harmony. When we reorganized the club last winter, we decided that we could get along with fewer stars and a better balanced club. We didn't want any bad actors or any hard feeling.

We traded right and left, and what a world of criticism came at us for what was called 'wrecking' a ball team.

The result is that all this year not one mean word has been said by one ball player to another. I know, because I have traveled with the team. We have had games booted away, and yet there has been no criticism, such as a lot of stars are apt to make.

"Stars spell factions, and we decided to do away with factions and get the team pulling together. I rather imagine that results have proved the correctness of our theory.

"For another thing, there's Pat Moran, our manager. I consider he is one of the smartest men in baseball, and I'm not saying this because he is a winner.

Moran is credited by a lot of people with having been the brains behind Frank Chance and the famous Cub machine. At all events, he knows inside baseball, and although a strict disciplinarian, he is liked by every ball player who knows him personally.

In fact lots of Philadelphia players who have always been hard to handle in the past have beeen like children with Moran."

VERNON MARKSMEN TO SHOOT FOR BRUNER CUP

The Stanton A. Bruner challenge trophy will again be contested for tomorrow at the Vernon Gun club, at 50 targets, from the 16-yard range.

In addition to the cup, four watch fobs will be up, representing classes A, B, C and D.

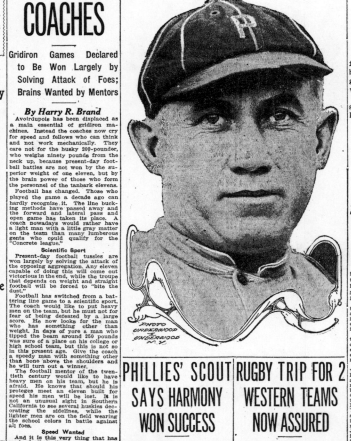

RUGBY TRIP FOR 2 WESTERN TEAMS NOW ASSURED

STANFORD UNIVERSITY, Oct. 9.—That plans for the trip of two American rugby teams to the Antipodes are now actively under way and that it is merely a question of getting teams to oppose two American squads, once they are sent to Australia, is the substance of a letter just received by the Daily Palo Alto, the student paper here.

According to Rev. M. Mullineaux, who writes the letter, the Oxford scholar who wishes to pay the expenses of 40 American players to the Antipodes, will do so in 1916 if the present war makes the trip impossible this season.

ENCINA CLUB TAKES FRATERNITY TOURNEY

STANFORD UNIVERSITY, Oct. 9. Encina club captured the interfraternity and club tennis tournament here, when Herb Hahn, a senior and captain of last year's tennis team, defeated Allyn Barber of Los Angeles, representing the Zeta Psi fraternity.

Hahn and Barber's sets resulted as follows:

6-3, 2-6, 6-3, 6-3.

JEVNE, CUE ARTIST, HERE

Lloyd Jevne, former three-cushion billiard titleholder, arrived in Los Angeles today to pass the winter. He is the first of the many billiard players to come West to winter in sunny California.

INDIANS AND TIGERS READY

Sherman Indian football players and Occidental are ready for their game on Baer field today. A good-sized crowd was on hand for the battle. A preliminary contest was scheduled between the Oxy frosh and Hollywood high elevens.

LEAVITT LEAVES TONIGHT

Owner Leavitt of the Oakland baseball team will leave tonight for Oakland. The Oak boss intended to leave last night, but business interfered with his departure.

DOMINGUEZ CLUB SHOOT

The opening shoot of the Dominguez Gun club will be held next Friday at the club's grounds. This is the first of the twice-weekly shoots to be held by the club during the duck season.

BILL BURNS PICKED TO FACE ANGELS IN SERIES STANDING TIE

Manager Rowdy Elliott of the Oaks picked Bill Burns to face the Angels in the fifth game of the series today. The trans-bay leader felt confident the big southpaw would be able to give the Oaklets a three-to-two lead over the Seraphs for the week. The series now stands at two games all.

Manager Dillon announced that Lefty Scoggins was his selection for mound duty, though he said he might decide at the last minute to start Grover Brant.

The line-ups:

OAKLAND—	LOS ANGELES—
Stow, 2b	Maggert, cf
Hosp, ss	McMullin, 2b
Middleton, cf	Ellis, lf
Johnston, cf	Koerner, 1b
Ness, 1b	Harper, rf
Gardner, rf	Terry, ss
Kuhn, c	Boles, c
Litschi, 3b	Butler, 3b
Burns, p	Scoggins, p

TRAPSHOOTERS READY TO SEEK TARGETS AFIELD

With three hunting seasons opening next month, when rifles will have to be put aside and the shotguns hauled out, oiled and cleaned and petted, shooters will drop trapshooting for a time.

This game, which enables shooters to get a bird on the wing better, has added greatly in preparing sportsmen for the three seasons—the reopening of the rabbit season and the opening of the duck and quail season.

Once these seasons have opened, the gun clubs will undoubtedly be deserted for a while. Then the novelty of shooting in the field will wear off and the "sport alluring" will once more claim its own.

That trap shooting has elements which attract men who breathe and live sport is evident by its naming among it enthusiastic followers such men as Honus Wagner of the Pittsburg National league team; "Big Chief" Bender, the Indian twirler of the world's championship Athletics; Lester German, who forsook the New York Nationals to become a professional "player" of the "sport alluring," and many other baseball celebrities. On the other hand we see John Philip Sousa finding invigorating recreation in making dust of the furtive "clay pigeon."

Pleasure Without Regret

To the man or woman possessed of a tender heart, who has no pleasure in the destruction of living creatures, trap shooting affords pleasure without regret.

No other sport can show as large a number of participants in its annual meets as does trap shooting. Among the big evens, in each of which the number of shooters runs up into the hundreds, are the Eastern handicap, the Western handicap, the Southern handicap, the Pacific Coast handicap, the Post Season handicap, and the Grand American handicap. In the latter event the number of shooters is usually around 400.

In general, trap shooting consists of shooting with a shotgun at targets thrown from traps. The targets or pigeons are composed of river silt and tar, moulded into a shape similar to that of a saucer. This is impelled by the releasing of a strong spring when the word "pull" is called to the trap boy.

Shoot in Fives

The shooters, in squads, usually of five, take their places 16 or more yards in the rear of the traps and shoot in rotation.

Your skilled trap shooter is a fellow with steel nerves. Locally we have such nervy men as Bob Bungay, the champion of Los Angeles with a 20-gauge, and Frank Mellus and Heine Pfirrmann, jr., both of whom are world's champions at night shooting with 20 gauges.

The skilled trap shooter possesses quick and unerring judgment, and unfaltering action. In the majority of cases these positive, manly qualities were as latent in the trap shooter as they are in the average man, until the devotee of the trap and gun took up this most fascinating of recreations.

TROJAN FOOTBALL TEAM ON EDGE FOR FIRST FRAY

U. S. C. football followers are looking forward to a successful campaign for their varsity in the next few weeks. Next Saturday afternoon the Trojans are slated to meet the St. Mary's college eleven on Bovard field.

Reports from the North have it that the Catholics have a strong combination. They will have to be high class to show up the Wesleyans, and, unless the Methodists are sadly mistaken, the Northerners will journey home holding the short end of the score.

October 23 is the date of the University of Southern California-University of California game at Berkeley. Many are the students, dopesters, officials and otherwise at the Trojan school who believe that the red jersey athletes will hand the Blue and Gold a sound beating.

Glaze's men look strong now and figure to be stronger before they journey North for their first real tussle. Open football, judging from the L. A. A. C. game last Saturday, will be the chief U. S. C. offensive factor.

By the time of the Trojan-Bear fray on Bovard field Thanksgiving day, Coach Ralph Glaze figures to present to the public's gaze a finished varsity.

The Wesleyans ought to be able to show strength in open plays, forward passes, and they are sure to be able to gain yards on bucks through most any lines that face them this season, unless the Bears spring an awful surprise.

Glaze made a very creditable showing in 1914, considering the scarcity of material, numerous injuries and the change from the rugby to the American game.

The greenest kind of material greeted Glaze on his initial attempt at coaching in Southern California. He fought a discouraging battle.

This fall the outlook is different. Experienced material is plentiful out U. S. C. way. If serious injuries befall some U. S. C. stars, other men will be on hand who are almost as good, to jump into the vacant places.

Los Angeles Gun Club Of Venice Gets Trophy

Fred H. Teeple, secretary of the Los Angeles Gun club of Venice, announces that the DuPont company has awarded the club a beginners' day trophy of bronze and silver for a high attendance. The cup will be up for competition tomorrow in a special contest of 50 blue rocks at 16 yards.

The contenders will be segregated into four classes, A, B, C and D, with added bird handicaps, assuring all contestants of a fair chance of winning. The shoot is open to all amateurs and will start at 10 o'clock.

20 Pages Today

The Boston Post

EXTRA

TWENTY PAGES—ONE CENT | Established 1831. | THURSDAY, OCTOBER 14, 1915 ** | Copyrighted, 1915, by Post Publishing Co. | TWENTY PAGES—ONE CENT

ZEPPELIN BOMBS KILL 8 IN LONDON, 34 HURT

Fires Started at Many Points in British Metropolis—Serbians Report Field Strewn With German Dead After Semandria Battle

Mystery in Russia's Plan to Invade Bulgaria

DELCASSE RESIGNS IN FRENCH CRISIS

Deputies Vote Confidence in Government After Fight

LONDON, Oct. 13.—Another Zeppelin raid over London tonight has resulted in the killing of eight persons, of whom two were women, and the injuring of 34 others.

The censorship prohibits the sending of details, and it is officially stated that the property damage was small, but from the bulletin given out by the home office at midnight it is apparent that the raid was one of the most serious London has yet experienced.

Continued on Page 6—First Column

THEOPHILE DELCASSE.

Who has resigned his position in the French cabinet as foreign minister, owing, it is declared in Paris, to his dissatisfaction with the government's diplomacy in the Balkans.

HIGH TIDE TODAY

A. M. 3:06 — P. M. 3:26

Portland 24m., Gloucester 26m., Newport 3h. 38m. earlier.

SUN Rises 5:54. Sets 5:06. **MOON** Six days old. Sets 9:35 p. m.

Moon's changes—New Moon Oct. 8, full Oct. 22, last quarter Oct. 30, new moon Nov. ., first quarter Nov. 13, full Nov. 21.

287th day of year; 22d day of autumn; 420th day of war.

Day 11h. 12m. long; day's decrease since June 22 4h. 7m.

Light auto lamps tonight at 5:36; other vehicles at 6:06.

TODAY'S ANNIVERSARIES, ETC.

William Penn, founder of Pennsylvania, born, 1644.

CLOUDY

Forecast for Boston and vicinity—Increasing cloudiness Thursday, followed by showers late Thursday or Friday; moderate temperatures, moderate southerly winds.

WASHINGTON, Oct. 13.—Forecast for New England: Partly cloudy Thursday, showers at night or Friday.

YESTERDAY'S TEMPERATURE

	'14	'15		'14	'15
3 a. m.	54	56	3 p. m.	53	77
6 a. m.	50	55	6 p. m.	53	72
9 a. m.	51	67	9 p. m.	51	62
12 m.	52	77	12 mid.	47	61

Average temperature yesterday 65 1-24.

Autoist Caught After Chase

WORCESTER, Oct. 13.—A sensational automobile chase from this city to Marlboro came tonight when a motorist, driving a zigzag course down Shrewsbury street, crashed into another machine in which W. H. Bartlett, a teller in the Worcester Trust Company, was riding with his wife.

AFTER THE AUTOIST

Apparently believing that he had left the Bartlett car disabled, the lone motorist threw his own machine into high speed and made off in the direction of Marlboro. But the damage to the Bartlett car proved to be only a broken mudguard, and within three minutes of the crash the bank teller was off in pursuit.

With his wife beside him, Bartlett drove his car at a 60-mile an hour clip to the outskirts of the city. There he picked up Officer James Dolan and again the chase was on. The fleeing motorist still sped away zig-zagging down the roadways, every moment barely escaping disaster.

The wild race continued for full 16 miles and into Marlboro. There, on West Main street, the Bartlett machine overtook the other, and Dolan called out to the fleeing driver to stop, threatening to shoot if he did not. The machine came to a stop, and with Marlboro officers, Dolan arrested the driver.

At the Marlboro police station he gave his name as Louis Deplessis of 24 Paris street, Marlboro. He was charged with operating a machine while under the influence of liquor, and admitted to bail in the sum of $100. He will be arraigned tomorrow in the District Court before Judge McDonald.

WATCHING WOOING OF MRS. GALT

Neighbors Peek as President Pays Call

KEEP VIGIL UP FOR OVER THREE HOURS

"He's Heels Over Head in Love," Declares One

BY PAUL WAITT
Staff Correspondent of the Boston Post

WASHINGTON, Oct. 13.—President Wilson called upon his bride-to-be this afternoon, just like a hero in a book, and it begins to look as if that little affair between one lady named Priscilla and a gentleman named John Alden will be relegated to second place in the history of American romances.

A charming lady, who lives in the vicinity of 1308 Twentieth street, the home of Mrs. Galt, who during the past week has spent a greater part of her time peeking through some gauzy curtains at the imposing front door of the Galt home, remarked this afternoon to the Post reporter:

"Why, the President is like a schoolboy; he is just head over heels in love."

It was 4 o'clock this afternoon when the President's car swept around Dupont Circle into Twentieth street and up to the Galt home. A car following came to a stop at the junction of New Hampshire avenue and Twentieth street.

Already a colored footman was holding open the door of the President's car.

Continued on Page 12—Fourth Col.

FOOT AND MOUTH QUARANTINE ON

WASHINGTON, Oct. 13.—Because of an outbreak of foot and mouth disease in Worcester county, Mass., which was reported today to the Department of Agriculture, the department has placed the county under closed quarantine, effective tomorrow.

The outbreak is the first discovered east of Indiana in many months, and is the only known infection at present outside of Illinois.

DR. DUMBA REACHES ENGLAND; DOESN'T LAND

FALMOUTH, Oct. 14, 2:15 a. m.—Dr. Constantin T. Dumba, the former ambassador of Austria-Hungary to the United States, whose recall was requested by President Wilson, has arrived at this port on board the steamer Nieuw Amsterdam.

He did not come ashore.

TWO HOME RUNS WIN SERIES FOR RED SOX

New World's Champions Defeat Philadelphia 5 to 4 in Final Game—Home Run by Lewis With One on Base Ties Up Game and Hooper Wins It by Terrific Homer in the Ninth, Closing Spectacular Contest

CHILDREN TO GET MILLIONS

Estate of Grandfather Left to Son and Daughters of Baroness Von Schroeder of Brookline

BARON AND BARONESS ALBRECHT VON SCHROEDER,
Recently of Brookline. Baroness von Schroeder's children by a former marriage are to inherit millions by the terms of their grandfather's will.

DENVER, Col., Oct. 13.—The three young children of Baroness Albrecht von Schroeder of Brookline, Mass., are heirs to a fortune of $4,500,000 through the will of their grandfather, Dennis Sullivan, pioneer mining man and Denver banker, it became known here today. Mr. Sullivan died in this city a few days ago.

Baroness von Schroeder, who was the widow of Barry Sullivan, the son of the deceased banker, is at the present time in Germany serving with the German Red Cross. Her present husband is a lieutenant in the German army at the front and was formerly manager of the Hamburg-American line in New England.

GIVEN TO CHILDREN

The will is to be probated this week, it was learned, and the estate, which includes especially valuable Denver property, stock in a number of this city's leading mercantile institutions, as well as several mining properties and sugar manufactories, will be turned over to a trustee for the children, it is believed, as soon as the von Schroeders can be located in Germany. The only

Continued on Page 2—Fifth Column

Hooper Gets Two Home Runs—Great Batting Features Game

SCORE OF FINAL GAME OF WORLD'S SERIES

BOSTON

	AB.	R.	BH.	TB.	PO.	A.	E.
Hooper, r. f	4	2	3	9	2	0	1
Scott, s. s	5	0	0	0	2	2	0
Speaker, c. f	5	0	1	1	3	0	0
Hoblitzell, 1b	1	0	0	0	1	0	0
Gainer, 1b	3	1	1	1	9	0	0
Lewis, l. f	4	1	1	4	0	0	0
Gardner, 3b	3	1	1	3	2	3	0
Barry, 2b	4	0	1	1	1	0	0
Thomas, c	2	0	1	1	4	3	0
Cady, c	1	0	0	0	2	1	0
Foster, p	4	0	1	1	1	3	0
Totals	36	5	10	21	27	12	1

PHILADELPHIA

	AB.	R.	BH.	TB.	PO.	A.	E.
Stock, 3b	3	0	0	0	0	1	0
Bancroft, s. s	4	1	2	2	3	6	1
Paskert, c. f	4	1	2	2	3	0	0
Cravath, r. f	1	0	0	0	1	0	0
*Dugey	0	0	0	0	0	0	0
Becker, r. f	0	0	0	0	0	0	0
Luderus, 1b	2	1	2	6	13	2	0
Whitted, l. f	4	0	0	0	2	0	0
Niehoff, 2b	4	1	1	1	2	2	0
Burns, c	4	0	1	1	2	2	0
Mayer, p	1	0	0	0	1	0	0
Rixey, p	2	0	1	1	0	1	0
**Killifer	1	0	0	0	0	0	0
Totals	32	4	9	13	27	14	1

*Ran for Cravath in eighth inning.
**Killifer batted for Rixey in ninth.

Boston	0	1	1	0	0	0	0	2	1	—5
Philadelphia	2	0	0	2	0	0	0	0	0	—4

Two-base hit—Luderus. Three-base hit—Gardner. Home runs—Hooper 2, Lewis, Luderus. Earned runs—Boston 5, Philadelphia 3. Double plays—Foster to Thomas to Hoblitzell; Bancroft to Luderus. Left on bases—Boston 7, Philadelphia 5. First base on errors—Boston 1. Bases on balls—Off Rixey 2, off Foster 2. Hits—Off Mayer, 6 in 2 1-3 innings; off Rixey, 4 in 6 2-3 innings. Hit by pitcher—By Foster (Stock, Luderus); by Rixey (Hooper). Struck out—By Foster 5, by Rixey 2. Umpires—At plate, Klem; on bases, O'Loughlin; left field, Evans; right field, Rigler. Time of game—2h. 15m.

BY PAUL H. SHANNON

PHILADELPHIA, Oct. 13.—Carrigan and his Red Sox are champions of the world again tonight. They won the deciding game of the series with Philadelphia today, 5 to 4.

For the second time within four years, and for the third time since the American league was organized, the supreme title in baseball has passed into the possession of the Boston team and the hopes of the National league adherents have been shattered. In downing the Quakers, defeating them for the fourth successive game and bringing the big contests to an end in five thrilling battles, the Red Sox maintained Boston's reputation of never having been beaten out in the struggle for a world's championship.

Continued on Page 15—First Col.

BARNSTORMING TRIP TO COAST CALLED OFF

PHILADELPHIA, Oct. 13.—The proposed Western trip of the world's champion Red Sox and the Phillies, champions of the National league, has been called off.

The New York Nationals---The Giants---1916 Team

(C) Int. Film.

Back Row, from Left to Right—Kocher, Hunter, Stroud, Kelly, Mathewson, Perrit, Schaurer, Tesreau, Kauff, Merkle. Middle Row—Fletcher, McKetchie, Rariden, Palmero, Benton, McGraw, Raush, Robertson, Burns. Lower Row—Anderson, George Conroy (Bat Boy), Wendell, Schupp, Cornelius, Lynch, (Bat Boys) Doyle, Dooin.

Billie Burke

FORTY FAMOUS FILM FOLK

A series of beautiful new portraits in gravure of the most popular motion picture players—suitable for framing or preserving in an album—Cut out each week and keep.

31—BILLIE BURKE, They Say Is Getting $4,500 a Week for Her Work in "Gloria's Romance," a New Film Serial by Mr. and Mrs. Rupert Hughes, and the Costumes She Wears Cost Another Small Fortune—*George Kleine*.

32—LILA CHESTER Was a Principal in "The Million Dollar Mystery," Played With Robert Warwick in "The Sins of Society," and Was Holbrook Blinn's Leading Woman in "The Unpardonable Sin."—*Equitable*.

Lila Chester

A CLEAN NEWSPAPER FOR THE HOME, WITH CLEAN NEWS AND CLEAN ADVERTISEMENTS

Second Section
Local—Editorial
Society—Magazine

MORNING TRIBUNE

INDEPENDENT · PROGRESSIVE · LOS ANGELES · PIONEER PENNY · MORNING DAILY

Pages 9 to 16
Local—Editorial
Society—Magazine

VOLUME VI NO. 99 SIXTEEN PAGES

TUESDAY MORNING OCTOBER 10 1916

ONE CENT In Los Angeles and Suburbs · 5 Cents Elsewhere · By Carrier 45 Cts. Per Month

GAINER'S HIT GIVES RED SOX VICTORY, 2 TO 1

HUGHES DEFIES BLACKLISTING OF AMERICANS BY BRITISH

Republican Candidate, in Stirring Speech in Philadelphia, Denounces Attitude of Wilson Toward Europe

[By Tribune Leased Wire]

PHILADELPHIA, Oct. 9.—Charles E. Hughes in a speech at the Metropolitan opera house here tonight vigorously assailed the administration for its foreign and Mexican policies and outlined the Republican party program in two respects, as follows:

"We do not propose to tolerate any improper interference with American property, with American mails or with legitimate commercial intercourse.

"No American who is exercising only American rights shall be put on any blacklist by any foreign nation."

Mr. Hughes' attack on the administration's foreign and Mexican policies was couched in more vigorous terms than any he has heretofore employed.

"Asks Confidence Vote"

"The administration asks for a vote of confidence," he said, "but its defenders certainly protest when its record is critically examined. When its humiliating failure to safeguard American rights is held up to deserved condemnation, it seeks to escape by asserting that its conduct had no alternative but war; that to disapprove its conduct is to favor war."

Mr. Hughes today opened the third trip of his presidential campaign with an address in Newark, N. J., in which he scored the administration for the enactment of the Adamson law.

Mr. Hughes quoted Senator Underwood, Democrat, to uphold his contention that the law was not properly an eight-hour, but was a wage measure instead. The nominee declared that "it was sought to give an impression that what was done was to fix an eight-hour work day and this was already approved by the judgment of society."

This was a "shameless perversion," Mr. Hughes declared.

His heaviest battery of assault on

[CONTINUED ON PAGE 12, COLUMN 3[

NORTON OPPOSES $10,000 MORE FOR CAPLAN SECRET FUND

District Attorney Threatens to Halt Dynamiting Charge Trial Unless Supervisors Grant Additional Money

Whether the board of supervisors shall vote $10,000 into a revolving fund to defray secret expenses of the second trial of David Caplan, jointly charged with Matthew A. Schmidt with murder in connection with the dynamiting of a Los Angeles newspaper plant October 1, 1910, or the trial shall be halted, will be determined by the board this morning. The district attorney was instructed to appear before the board yesterday afternoon with vouchers showing how he expended a secret service fund of $10,000 last year in the Caplan trial. Then the board became involved in other matters and action was postponed until this morning.

Emissaries of the district attorney asserted the trial, scheduled to be begun next Monday, cannot proceed unless the district attorney is liberally supplied with money to pay witnesses brought here from all over the United States, and meet other expenses.

Secret Service Payments

This threat to halt the trial, however, did not cause Supervisor R. H. Norton to forsake the stand he had taken—that he, as a member of the board, would not authorize payment of secret service funds for purposes he knew nothing of.

Supervisor J. J. Hamilton reiterated his statement that he would not secretly review accounts of this character.

The district attorney was represented before the board, while his demand for $10,455.89 was under discussion, by Asa Keyes and William C. Doran, deputies, and Bonner Richardson, his secretary. The latter had several verbal passages with Supervisor Norton, the two standing on their feet and hurling charges at one another across the smooth mahogany table.

$10,000 Payment Sought

The district attorney has expended the $10,000 granted him last year to defray the expenses of the Caplan trial and now asks that he be reimbursed. The supervisors put the construction on it that he wants a second revolving fund of $10,000. Whatever construction is placed upon it the fact remains that the money has been expended and that the second trial cannot proceed, according to the district attorney, unless he shall be authorized to expend $10,000 more.

Sensational southpaw effective in second fray with N. L. champions; Ruth is Boston idol

Babe Ruth holds Robin club in hand during entire game; may hurl another fray

SAFE BLOW IN 14TH BY PINCH SWATTER COSTS ROBINS GAME

American League Title Holders Take 2nd Title Game From Superbas; Sherrod Smith in Rare Form; Cutshaw's Bobble Disastrous; Babe Ruth Proves Winner

By Damon Runyon

BOSTON, Oct. 9.—His name is Del Gainer and tonight he is a hero. Batting for Larry Gardner, in the fourteenth inning of the second game of the current world's series, he poled out a pinch hit which enabled the Boston Red Sox to beat the Brooklyn Dodgers by a score of 2 to 1.

For thirteen innings the teams had battled through the longest game in the history of world's series competition, and then, when it seemed that darkness would intervene and put a stop to the game, Del Gainer stepped into the breach and broke up the pastime.

Yet Brooklyn should have won. They should have won by the score of 1 to 0. Yet they lost. An unfortunate fumble —not an error—by George Cutshaw, the Brooklyn second baseman, in the third inning, paved the way for the run which brought the Sox on even terms with the Dodgers.

Myers Hits Homer

In the first inning Hy Myers slammed out a terrific home run. Off to an early advantage, the Dodgers should have won. They have the reputation of winning when out in the lead. But they lost, though in losing again flashed a fight which thrilled over 41,000 baseball insects.

For more than two hours the teams fought stubbornly and tenaciously and whole-heartedly. From the third inning to the fourteenth they battled on even terms.

Then, with the stage set for a dramatic climax, with darkness coming on, Mr. Gainer, the villain, appeared upon the stage. Mr. Gainer is quite an actor. He looked over one strike, and then swung upon the ball and sent it to left field.

Zack Wheat scurried for the ball, picked it up and threw to the plate. But McNally, who had been put in to run for Dick Hoblitzel, scampered across the plate with the winning run.

Much could be said of this person Gainer, the villain. His first name is Delos, and it is said that his habits are exemplary, though it is hard to believe this of a person who would deliberately ruin a perfectly good pastime which to all intents and purposes belonged to the Dodgers. He has a middle name, has this Gainer, but a diligent search has failed to reveal it. The initial, however, is C, just what the name itself is we do not know, but we suspect that it is Clouter, or some such thing as that.

Dodgers Looked Like Winners

Hy Myers, who has acted like a perfectly respectable hero in the two games which have been played thus far, drove a home run in the opening frame and with Sherrod Smith pitching wonderful ball, it seemed that the Dodgers were going to return to Brooklyn with a game to their credit.

Babe Ruth and Sherrod Smith were the opposing pitchers. Until today's game neither had ever taken part in a world's series contest. Yet upon the occasion of their joint debut they did much to make baseball history. For never in the history of professional baseball had a world's series game gone to fourteen innings.

That one run should have been enough to hold the Red Sox safe, but they tied the score in the third. The first man up, Everett Scott, tripled to left. Thomas hit to Cutshaw and Cutshaw made a very good play in holding Scott to third, and then tossing out Thomas at first. Ruth, who is a notable long distance hitter, also smashed at the first ball pitched to him, and hit a roller to Cutshaw. The Dodger second baseman got the ball all right but then dropped it. Had he held it, he could easily have retired Scott at the home plate..

As it was he lost his chance of getting Scott so he tossed out Ruth at first while Scott scored.

Smith Forgets Self

Before all this had occurred, however, Sherrod Smith had mussed up an opportunity for a run which would have enabled the Dodgers to retain a margin even against that Sox tally in the third. In the Dodgers' side of the same inning after Otto Miller had been thrown out by Scott, Smith hit a terrific drive to right. It was an easy two bagger but when he reached second Smith decided to keep on going. Down at third base Jack Coombs, wrapped up in a dingy old sweater, was waving his hands, and yelling as he tried to make Smith stop at second, but Smith was on his way. He slid into third only to find the ball in the hands of Gardner. The next minute Johnston

[CONTINUED ON PAGE 14, COLUMNS 2-3]

Bought Oil Locations for $50, Burge States

[Special to the Tribune]

SAN FRANCISCO, Oct. 9.—How E. D. Burge, Kern county oil man, bought out in 1907 a number of fellow locators on oil lands now valued at $2,000,000 for $50 apiece, now and then riding into the thousands when the bargaining was harder, was an interesting story told by him in the government's suit to oust various claimants to three-quarters of a section in the west side oil fields of Kern county.

It is the contention of the government that the lands in question were originally acquired by Burge through dummy locators and there was no diligent prosecution of work or discovery of oil prior to President Taft's withdrawal order.

WILL IMPROVE TERMINAL

Harbor Commission Promises Dock Betterments for Steamship Co.

Following an informal conference with the Los Angeles harbor commissioners, H. F. Alexander, president of the newly organized Pacific Steamship company, announced last night that the commissioners had intimated they would be willing to favor extensions and improvements to the new municipal dock at the harbor sufficient to accommodate the improved service contemplated by the company.

The Pacific Steamship company is a consolidation of the former Pacific Coast Steamship company and the Pacific Alaska Navigation company.

Mr. Alexander was accompanied by R. J. Ringwood, vice president, and Fred M. Barry, assistant manager. On Sunday the officials of the company inspected the municipal docks.

ATHLETE BREAKS LEG IN GRIDIRON TACKLE

Buford Doyle, one of the best-known athletes of the city, sustained a compound fracture of the right leg in a night football practice held at Twelfth and Grand avenue last night. The injury was inflicted in a scrimmage and was the result of a tackle by the victim's brother, L. O. Doyle. The injured man was rushed to the receiving hospital, where the fracture was reduced. He was then taken to the Sisters' hospital.

$20,000 SUIT ON PESTHOUSE WILL

Relatives of C. W. Groger Declare He Had Fortune in Michigan

Trust funds valued at $20,000 are said to be involved in a sensational will suit filed yesterday in the superior court.

The will purports to be that of Charles W. Groger, thirty-eight years old, who died last April at the Los Angeles pesthouse.

In the contest petition, filed by Michael F. Shannon in behalf of two half-brothers, a half-sister and five second cousins, the charge is made that the will was forged.

Charles Chrysler is named in the document as sole beneficiary and executor.

In a petition for probate the estate was valued at not to exceed $100. It is declared, however, that he had a large interest in trust funds in Grand Rapids, Mich.

STREET CAR MAN DIES

J. G. Knapp of Alhambra, Well Known in Traction Circles, Succumbs

Following a long illness J. G. Knapp, well known in street railway circles, died yesterday at the Sisters' hospital. He leaves a widow and three daughters, two of whom are living at their Alhambra home, the third being a resident of Washington.

Mr. Knapp for a number of years has been foreman of division four of the Los Angeles railway system. He had been a resident of this city for twenty-one years, coming here with the interests which started the old Los Angeles Traction company, since absorbed.

The funeral will be held at 10 o'clock tomorrow morning from the undertaking parlors of W. A. Brown, 1335 South Flower street. The services will be under direction of the Rev. Clifford, former pastor of the First Baptist church of Alhambra.

Spain claims to be furnishing more than three-quarters of the world's supply of olive oil.

THE WEATHER

United States Department of Agriculture
Weather Bureau

LOS ANGELES FORECAST

Forecast until 5 o'clock tonight:

For Los Angeles and vicinity: Unsettled, probably showers.

High temperature yesterday......... 67 degrees
Low temperature yesterday.......... 56 degrees

PACIFIC COAST FORECAST

Southern California: Weather unsettled Tuesday, probably showers; light westerly wind.

Sacramento, Santa Clara and San Joaquin valleys: Unsettled weather Tuesday, probably showers; light variable winds.

San Francisco and vicinity: Unsettled weather Tuesday, probably showers; light variable wind.

TABLE OF TEMPERATURES

Maximum and minimum temperatures in cities in the United States and Canada yesterday were as follows:

Stations—	H.	L.	Stations—	H.	L.
Los Angeles	67	56	Pasadena	..	49
Abilene	74	62	Phoenix	86	56
Boise	60	42	Pittsburg	70	68
Bonita	..	49	Pomona	..	50
Boston	80	66	Portland, Ore.	70	46
Buffalo	54	54	Rapid City	44	34
Calgary	68	24	Red Bluff	74	58
Chicago	52	50	Redlands	..	53
Corona	..	50	Reno	56	38
Denver	38	38	Riverside	69	50
Des Moines	56	44	Roseburg	74	34
Dodge City	50	42	Roswell	62	50
Duluth	42	30	St. Louis	52	60
Durango	64	46	St. Paul	50	34
Escondido	..	48	Sacramento	70	50
Eureka	62	46	Salt Lake	66	42
Flagstaff	60	34	Santa Barbara	..	45
Fresno	68	50	S. Bernardino	..	52
Galveston	82	76	San Diego	66	54
Havre	50	22	S. Fernando	..	42
Helena	44	18	S. Francisco	64	54
Huron	52	30	S. L. Obispo	62	50
Independence	82	38	Seattle	68	46
Jacksonville	84	72	Sheridan	46	32
Kamloops	60	32	Spokane	64	34
Kansas City	54	48	Swift Current	48	22
Knoxville	78	[illegible]	Tampa	88	74
Memphis	86	70	Tonopah	52	40
Modena	62	34	Tucson	100	..
Montreal	42	40	Tustin	..	52
Moorhead	48	28	Washington	86	64
New Orleans	88	72	Williston	48	20
New York	64	64	Winnemucca	62	36
North Head	60	54	Winnipeg	48	22
North Platte	50	36	Yuma	84	52
Oklahoma	70	54	Mt. Wilson	..	37
Omaha	56	..			

LOS ANGELES DATA

Time.	Bar.	Tem.	Hum.	Wind.	Vel.	Weather.
5 a. m.	29.99	57	90	NE	4	Cloudy
5 p. m.	29.97	62	67	SW	10	Pt. Cldy

THE TIDES

For October 10, 1916.)

High.		Low.	
8:21 a. m.	6.4 ft.	2:04 a. m.	0.3 ft.
8:54 p. m.	5.4 ft.	2:43 p. m.	—0.4 ft.

RAINFALL DATA

	Last 24 hours.	Seasonal to date.
Red Bluff	.00	3.35
Sacramento	.00	1.00
San Francisco	.19	1.99
San Jose	.14	1.53
Fresno	.00	1.50

EXTRA **THE BOSTON HERALD** EXTRA

VOL. CXL, NO. 105. FRIDAY MORNING, OCTOBER 13, 1916—SIXTEEN PAGES. ONE CENT.

Red Sox Again World's Baseball Champions

ITALIANS GAIN NEW GROUND IN TRIESTE DRIVE

Add 1771 to Toll of Prisoners, Which Is 30,881, in Fighting in Julian Alps Since Aug. 6—Berlin Says Roumanians Still Fall Back — Bucharest Reports Rallies.

BRITISH TROOPS REACH OUTSKIRTS OF SERES

Important Town in Greek Macedonia Strongly Held — Allies Push Forward on Somme, Where Artillery Duels Grow More Intense—Hand-to-Hand Fighting in South.

LONDON, Oct. 12—Another step forward in their quest of Trieste has been made by the Italians in the region south of Gorizia, additional points of vantage to their progress having been captured and 1771 men made prisoner.

In this region, which is about 16 miles northwest of Trieste and in the Julian Alps, to the east, the Italians from Aug. 6 to the present, report they have captured 30,881 Austrians. On the Carso plateau, heavy Austrian attacks against the positions recently taken by the Italians have been repulsed.

Retreat of Roumanians.

Along the entire eastern Transylvanian front the Roumanians are still in retreat, and in the north also are beginning to fall back before the troops of the Teutonic allies, according to Berlin. Bucharest says, however, that attacks at various points on their northern and northwestern fronts have been repelled.

The British troops have reached the outskirts of the important town of Seres, in Greek Macedonia, north of Lake Tahinos, having driven their opponents from the outlying districts. London reports that the town is strongly held by the Teutonic allies. Both Berlin and Sofia report the repulse of attacks along the Cerna river and on both sides of the Vardar.

On the Somme Front.

That the British have gained some additional ground north of Thiepval, south of the Ancre river, in France, and on the Le Sars-Gueudecourt line, is indicated in the Berlin official communication, which says British attacks here failed, "for the most part," before the German curtain of fire. West of Sailly-Saillisel the French have made a farther advance.

South of the Somme violent artillery duels are in progress, especially between Genermont and Chaulnes. In the town of Ablaincourt the Germans and French are engaged in hand-to-hand fighting.

ROUMANIANS FALL BACK TO AVOID ENVELOPMENT

Berlin Reports Pursuit of the Enemy on Wide Front.

BERLIN, Oct. 12 (via London)—Teuton troops are pursuing the Roumanian forces on the whole eastern Transylvanian front, says the official statement issued today by German army headquarters staff. The second Roumanian army, the announcement adds, has been driven back into the frontier positions.

The announcement follows:

"In the Maros valley the enemy was unable to resist an encircling attack. Farther north, also, he is beginning to retreat. He is being pursued on the whole eastern Transylvania front.

"The second Roumanian army has been driven back to the frontier positions. In mountain battles during the last two days we have captured 18 officers, 639 men, one four-inch cannon, five machine guns, much ammunition and many rifles. Enemy advances on both sides of Vulcan pass were repulsed."

BUCHAREST, Oct. 12 (via London)—Roumanian troops yesterday repulsed attacks of Gen. von Falkenhayn's army

(Continued on Page Two, Column 4.)

The King Is Dead; Long Live the King

GUARD KILLS FRAMINGHAM MAN AT EL PASO

Leo Graham, Member of Michigan Regiment, Told Massachusetts Surgeons He Was Shot After Argument Over Cards—Officers Assert Shooting Was Accidental

[Special Dispatch to the Herald.]

EL PASO, Oct. 12—Leo Graham of Framingham, Mass., was fatally wounded under suspicious circumstances at Camp Cotton this afternoon while a prisoner in the camp of the 31st Michigan regiment, of which he was a member. He died an hour and a half later in the division hospital at Camp Cotton.

Graham was 22 years old. He enlisted in the 31st Michigan this summer while working as a bell boy in a Detroit hotel. His parents live at Eames and Pratt streets, Framingham.

He was confined in the regimental guardhouse for some trifling offence committed while on the hike with his regiment last week. The cause of his shooting was given out at the headquarters of the Michigan regiment tonight as accidental. It was said that Albert C. Sauer, guard over the regiment's prisoners, had been examining the mechanism of his rifle and believing it unloaded had pulled the trigger, the bullet hitting Graham in the right shoulder and passing through his body as he stood in the doorway of the guardhouse.

Graham was attended by Maj. Jones,

(Continued on Page Two, Column 5.)

JOCKEY KILLED; 2 MAY DIE IN RACING MISHAP

Rider Comes a Cropper and Is Kicked to Death by Horse in Steeplechase.

[Special Dispatch to the Herald.]

NEW YORK, Oct. 12—One jockey is dead and two more are probably dying as the result of accidents in the running of the Harbor Hill steeplechase this afternoon under the auspices of the Piping Rock Racing Association at Locust Valley, which was won by W. R. Coe's King James's filly, Bet.

W. Murphy, a professional rider, mounted on J. E. Davis's Brooks, came a cropper at one of the jumps on the far side of the course and was kicked several times in the head while prostrate on the ground, and died tonight. W. Hogan and Ernest Heider, who met with similar accidents, were reported tonight of having fair chances of recovery.

AVIATOR ELOPES BUT PAIR MISS GRETNA GREEN

Porter Adams of Boston and Miss Irene Gourlay of Toronto Are Married at Springfield, Vt., When His Chauffeur Fails to Make Bend in Road to Bellows Falls.

Porter Adams, wealthy aviator, of this city, yesterday eloped with Miss Irene Gourlay, a Toronto girl, and was married to her in the rectory of a Congregational church in Springfield, Vt.

Seated last night in a private drawing room at the Copley-Plaza, with his bride standing at his side, Mr. Adams told a Herald reporter how, in the afternoon, he had taken Miss Gourlay in his racing car at White River Junction, Vt., sped away from his mother and later rejoined her, bringing news of his marriage.

Saw Name in Register.

The fact of the elopement first became known when one of Mr. Adams' friends, glancing on the register at the hotel last night, saw written there "Mr. and Mrs. Porter Adams."

When the Herald reporter knocked on the door of the Adams suite, Mr. Adams answered the call, and seeing that it was impossible to "kill" the story, introduced the caller to his wife and then, laughingly, permitted himself to be questioned.

"You see, it was this way," he said. "Miss Gourlay and I have been engaged for several years, but we have never announced it. Last week she came to Boston to visit some friends, and then I took her Monday in my car to Bretton Woods, where my mother has been staying for several weeks at the Mt. Washington.

"Yesterday mother, some of her friends, Mrs. Adams and I started to drive back to Boston. We had two cars, and at White River Junction I asked Mrs. Adams—Irene, that is—to get in my racing car and we would drive to Bellows Falls—you call it Gretna Green, don't you?—and be married there.

Surprised Mother.

"Had my mother any objections to the marriage? Of course not. I might say the result was expected, but the means unexpected.

"But Irene and I both hate fuss and bother and as we knew mother would drive down by way of Bellows Falls, we thought we would be standing in front of a drugstore, perhaps eating peanuts, when she drove by.

"Well, to make a long story short, we got in the car and drove about 45 miles in—well, only a few minutes. I felt one of the rear tires go flat, but the chauffeur said he had received so many jolts he missed that one."

Here Mr. Adams became enthusiastic and digressed for an instant to mention the merits of his car.

"It's a special model, you know," he said, "and it can go."

Then he resumed his story.

"When we came to the sharp turn in the road that leads to Bellows Falls, my chauffeur couldn't take the bend and keep the road, so we drove on to Springfield. There we got a minister—what was his name, dear?"

"Beardslee," answered Mrs. Adams. "The Rev. J. R., I think."

"Well," resumed Mr. Adams, "he

(Continued on Page Three, Column 4.)

SEE DEFIANCE TO HUGHES IN TALK BY PRESIDENT

Indianapolis Crowd Interprets Wilson's Descent to Vernacular as Challenge to Opponent to "Put Up or Shut Up"—Executive Had Said He Would Avoid Politics.

RECEPTION APPEARS TO LACK REAL ENTHUSIASM

Says Wilson Objected to Preparedness Parade

[Special Dispatch to the Herald.]

NEW YORK, Oct. 12—President Wilson was anxious to have the big preparedness parade held in this city last May stopped, on the ground that it might "irritate" the German-Americans, according to a signed statement by Charles H. Sherrill, former United States minister to Argentina, which was made public tonight by Chairman William R. Willcox of the Republican national committee. Mr. Sherrill was the originator, moving spirit and organizer of the big preparedness demonstration.

He says he was summoned by telephone to the mayor's office, where he was told that a telephone message had been received from the "administration in Washington" urging that the parade be abandoned.

Mr. Sherrill said that after the meeting with the mayor he consulted Carl L. Schurz, son of the late Carl Schurz, and that, as a result of conferences Mr. Schurz had with Bernard H. Ridder of the Staats Zeitung and other prominent German-Americans, Mr. Ridder assured Mayor Mitchel that there would be no feeling against the parade, but that, on the contrary, it would receive the cordial support of the German-American newspapers in this city.

By JAMES C. WHITE.

INDIANAPOLIS, Oct. 12—On board Wilson special, Oct. 12—Despite advance announcements that his speeches on this tour would be educational and not political, President Wilson, at the Indianapolis Fair Grounds this afternoon, managed to break over the bounds he had set in a manner most satisfactory to the Democratic leaders and campaign managers who were in attendance on him.

Speaking of "good roads," under the chairmanship of Gov. Ralston, he managed in the course of his remarks to decry the raising of a sectional issue in the country, which he stamped as an evidence of ignorance, and also to pay to himself a very pretty, if somewhat involved, compliment for his skill as the "counsel of the country," in bringing about a settlement of the railroad strike.

Drops Into Vernacular.

What attracted the most attention and also applause, if it must be said, was his demand, which the audience at least construed as being directed at Gov. Hughes, to either "put up or shut up."

It was noted that while his speech in the main was distinguished by the exquisite phrasing that has made his note-writing a feature instead of an incident in the handling of foreign affairs, he dropped bluntly into the vernacular in driving this thought home on his audience.

"Speeches," he said, "are not interesting because of the man who makes them or the words he uses. They are interesting only in proportion as the people who hear him believe what he says.

"If I didn't think speeches contributed to the common thought, that they had nothing to do with selfish purpose, I wouldn't make any. I remember once at a meeting a great, hard-fisted fellow told me he did not agree with a word I said, but thought I meant it. Then he explained that he thought the men at this particular meeting had talked through their hats.

"Now, talking through the hat," the President said, "ought to be a dead industry. It ought to be discouraged by silence and empty halls, and every man ought to have as a motto over the stage those simple and familiar words: 'Put up or shut up.' "

The storm of applause that greeted his remarks fairly took the President aback. He had been looking for evidence of sympathy from the crowd, but this was more than he expected. The men who had interestedly but quietly listened to his fine eulogies of good roads as articles of human intercourse, stood up cheering for what they interpreted as a drive at Gov. Hughes.

Ready for Own Medicine.

Even his following remark, that he was ready to take his own medicine, that if he didn't "put up" he was willing to "shut up," did not dull the commotion.

The audience, anxious for scrapping talk, also construed a reference to the recent railroad settlement in his words

(Continued on Page Fourteen, Column 5.)

HUGHES WOULD HAVE BROKEN WITH GERMANY

Tells Democratic Heckler He Would Have Notified Berlin When Warning as to Lusitania Was Issued, and Acted After the Sinking—His Reply Starts Wild Applause.

KENTUCKIANS THRONG TO LISTEN TO CANDIDATE

[Special Dispatch to the Herald.]

LOUISVILLE, Oct. 12—Charles E. Hughes, tonight before a great audience here, declared unequivocally that he would have broken off diplomatic relations with Germany when the Lusitania was sunk if he had been President.

He made this declaration in impassioned tones in answer to a Democratic heckler who had been planted in the crowd.

The declaration caused a tumult in the hall, and it was several minutes before Mr. Hughes could again make himself heard. He shouted he would have it made clear that when he said "strict accountability," he meant what he said. He said further that when the notice was published by the German embassy warning passengers off the Lusitania, he would have made it known that to sink the Lusitania would mean a break in friendly relations, and that with the sinking of the ship he would have made good his word.

The crowd was on its feet demanding that the heckler be put out. There was a din of cheering for Mr. Hughes and shouts of "You're right" and "that's what we would have done." Mr. Hughes waved his hands high above his head to quiet the crowd, but it was some time before he could continue. It was evident that the candidate was thoroughly stirred.

Candidate Interrupted.

Mr. Hughes was in the midst of his discussion on the maintenance of American rights when he was interrupted by the question.

"The path of peace is the path of self-respect, which maintains the dignity of our citizenship and cements the friendship of all nations," he said. A man from the audience interrupted him.

"Justice Hughes, just a moment. Please permit a respectful interruption," shouted the man. "What would you have done ."

The heckler got no further for the moment. His voice was drowned in cries, hoots and catcalls.

"Please permit the question to be asked," requested Mr. Hughes. "I do not want anyone shut off from a courteous question. Go on, sir," the nominee added, turning to the questioner. "Please ask your question?"

"I ask you, with all respect that I know, what you would have done when the Lusitania was sunk—see if you can answer that."

Mr. Hughes paused for a moment.

"I will answer this," the nominee said. There was considerable confusion in the hall, and he continued, "now permit me to answer.

"Sir, I would have had the state department at the very beginning of the administration so equipped as to command the respect of the world, and next, I would have so conducted affairs in Mexico as to show that our words meant peace and good-will and the protection at all events of the lives and property of American citizens.

"And next when I said strict accountability, every nation would have known that that was meant; and further, when notice was published with respect to the action threatened, I would have made it known in terms unequivocable and unmistakable that we should not tolerate a continuance of friendly relations through the ordinary diplomatic channels if that action were taken.

"And the Lusitania, sir, would never have been sunk."

The audience applauded long and lustily.

Mr. Hughes spoke in six towns today to audiences that had come, for the most part, for miles to hear him. They came down from the mountains, men and women, on foot, on horseback and on muleback. Some of the mounts had saddles, some had none, and many of the women that came to hear him came wearing their faded sun bonnets and smoked their clay pipes as he talked. At Pikeville, first stop of the day, hundreds had journeyed since sun-up. A special train from Marrowbone, crowded to capacity, swelled the crowd.

Audiences in Open Fields.

At several stops the nominee's special train was backed down a spur track and he spoke to audiences in open fields. They sat on horses and mules and in the farm wagons to listen. Some brought their families along and there were several hundred children, including babies in their mother's arms, in each of these crowds.

In his speech in Phoenix Hall tonight, Mr. Hughes devoted much of his attention to the protective tariff and to what he termed "the new slavery."

"We have heard much of the new freedom," he said. "It seems to have a surprising and deplorable range. It has meant freedom to sacrifice the principles of the merit system which our opponents pledged themselves to enforce. Thousands of offices have been created with the provision that they might be filled without reference to the requirements of the civil service act.

"It means freedom to subvert the principles of government by yielding its authority to the demands of force. In this last phase, instead of the new freedom, we have the new slavery. What are the characteristics of this new slavery? It is the use of the forms of free institutions to tyrannize over the public, to impose demands without inquiry as to their justice.

SHORE, IN WINNING HIS SECOND GAME OF SERIES, YIELDS BUT THREE HITS

Boston Americans, Before the Largest Crowd That Ever Saw a Ball Game, 42,620 Persons, Prove Right to Be Called Best Team in World—Brooklyns Disappointing.

ONLY TALLY OF ENEMY IS THE GIFT OF CADY

Long Ernie Shore Has His "Down Ball" Working Perfectly and Three Hits Are All the Hard-Hitting (Before the Series) National League Champions Are Able to Make.

By JOHN J. HALLAHAN.

Any doubt as to the Boston Red Sox being the champions of the baseball world was settled once and for all yesterday afternoon at Braves Field, when, before the greatest crowd—42,620—that ever saw a world series game, they trampled on the Brooklyn Dodgers. The National leaguers were beaten 4 to 1 in the final game, just as the series went, and Ernie Shore, who pitched such swell ball for eight innings last Saturday and then wobbled, showed such wobbling was only a happening in his young life, and not a regular thing.

Three measly hits and a run, which was charitable on the part of big Forest Cady, the catcher, when he let a ball get away from him in the second inning, was all the so-called hard-hitting Dodgers could do in the shortest game of the series.

When all is said and done, the Red Sox, led by Bill Carrigan for the last time, for Bill retired from the game when Everett Scott clutched Mowrey's lift for the final out, was far classier than the pennant winners of the National league.

Boss Bill, who must be recognized as the greatest of all managers, gave the large throng little chance to see him on the field. He went out for instructions before the battle opened and then hid away in the dugout all afternoon.

There were several things that stood out in the final clash.

First, the wonderful way that long Ernie Shore throttled the Dodgers. He had his famous "down ball" working like a charm and it was not until the fourth round that Brooklyn players were able to hit a ball out of the infield. This was a fly to Shorten, and it was not until the fifth that a hit was scratched off Shore's glove and Meyers did it. The others made in the seventh and ninth had the only true ring of hits. He gave but one base on balls.

Carrigan had nothing but praise for his men after the game yesterday. "The men played the kind of ball that makes champions," he said. "They defeated the Brooklyn club just as they had the Tigers and the White Sox, when they faced them in the crucial series. It was my last appearance as manager and while I don't care to say anything about the big series, I want to admit the Dodgers were better than I thought they were."

First Inning.

Long Ernie Shore warmed up with Cady as Gardner stood alongside and inspired him with words of how the world series money would be spent. Umpires Connolly and O'Day held a conference with Manager Robinson and Capt. Daubert near the plate. After Connolly wiped off the plate, Robinson went over and watched Pfeffer warm up with Meyers in front of the Dodgers' bench.

The first ball whizzed over on Myers for a called strike, and then Connolly ordered Pfeffer to stop warming up, as the game was on. The next was another called strike, and Shore stepped back on the grass behind the box. He dug his toe in the turf and picked up some dirt. The Guilford collegian shot over a curve and it was another called strike and the crowd cheered madly. Myers did not like the decision.

As Jake Daubert walked to the plate Shore again went back on the grass and picked up some dirt. Daubert asked to be allowed to look at the ball. The first ball was low and outside, and the next was fouled against the screen. Again Shore stepped back on the grass and picked up some dirt. The next pitch was wide of the plate. Daubert fouled the next, Cady picking the ball up and tossing it to Hobby. The Dodger field general topped the next and Shore carefully tossed to Hobby ahead of the sprinting Robin.

Stengel saw two balls go by that were low. He then hit a grounder to Scott and the star shortstop sent a shiver down the spines of the crowd by uncorking a wild heave. The ball went high over Hobby's head. Dick jumped

(Continued on Page Six, Column 1.)

In the World's Series Baseball Hall of Fame

ERNEST SHORE

—and—

all other members of the Red Sox team.

The world's championship is theirs, without a flaw in the title.

They earned it by superior skill, true sportsmanship, manly conduct.

Good will and congratulations.

Official Box Score of Deciding Game of Series

BOSTON (A)	ab.	r.	bh.	tb.	po.	a.	e.
Hooper, r.f.	3	2	1	1	1	0	0
Janvrin, 2b.	4	0	2	3	0	1	0
Shorten, c.f.	3	0	1	1	3	0	0
Hoblitzell, 1b.	3	0	0	0	11	1	0
Lewis, l.f.	3	1	2	4	1	0	0
Gardner, 3b.	2	0	0	0	0	5	0
Scott, s.s.	3	0	0	0	2	3	2
Cady, c.	3	1	1	1	5	1	0
Shore, p.	3	0	0	0	1	3	0
Totals	27	4	7	10	27	14	2

BROOKLYN (N).	ab.	r.	bh.	tb.	po.	a.	e.
Myers, c.f.	4	0	0	0	0	0	0
Daubert, 1b.	4	0	0	0	10	1	0
Stengel, r.f.	4	0	1	1	0	0	0
Wheat, l.f.	4	0	0	0	5	0	0
Cutshaw, 2b.	3	1	0	0	2	3	0
Mowrey, 3b.	3	0	1	1	1	3	1
Olson, ss.	3	0	0	0	2	3	2
Meyers, c.	3	0	1	1	4	2	0
Pfeffer, p.	2	0	0	0	0	1	0
Dell, p.	0	0	0	0	0	0	0
*Merkle	1	0	0	0	0	0	0
Totals	31	1	3	3	24	13	3

Innings	1	2	3	4	5	6	7	8	9	
Boston (A)	0	1	2	0	1	0	0	0	.	—4
Brooklyn (N)	0	1	0	0	0	0	0	0	0	—1

Two-base hit—Janvrin. Three-base hit—Lewis. Sacrifice hits—Mowrey, Shorten. Sacrifice fly—Gardner. First base on balls—Off Shore 1, off Pfeffer 2. Hits—Off Pfeffer, 6 in 7 innings; off Dell, 1 in 1 inning. Left on bases—Boston 3, Brooklyn 5. Struck out—By Shore 4, by Pfeffer 2. Passed ball—Cady. Wild pitches—Pfeffer 2. Time—1h. 43m. Umpires—Connolly at plate; O'Day on bases; Dinneen in right field; Quigley in left field. Attendance—42,620.

*Batted for Pfeffer in 8th inning.

Comparison of Receipts In World Series Games

FIFTH GAME IN 1916.

Official Attendance	42,620
Total Receipts	$83,873.00
National Commission	8,387.30
Clubs' Share	75,485.70
Each Club's Share	37,742.85

TOTAL FIVE GAMES IN 1916.

Official Attendance	162,359
Total Receipts	$385,590.50
National Commission	38,559.05
Players' Share	162,927.45
Red Sox, Winning Share, 60 per cent	97,756.47
Brooklyn, Losing Share, 40 per cent	65,170.98
Each Red Sox Share (22 players qualifying for full shares and six for half shares)	3,910.26
Each Brooklyn share (23 players qualifying)	2,834.82

FIFTH GAME IN 1915.

Official Attendance	20,306
Total Receipts	$52,029.00
National Commission	5,202.90
Each Club's Share	23,413.05

TOTAL FIVE GAMES IN 1915.

Official Attendance	143,351
Total Receipts	$320,361.50
National Commission	32,036.15
Each Club's Share	23,413.05

Record Crowd Takes Victory Calmly, for Game Brings Out No Wild Enthusiasm Such as Has Marked Other Final Struggles Here — Shore the Idol of the Spectators.

DAY IS GREAT ONE FOR MANAGER CARRIGAN

Leader of Team Quits National Sport and Retires to Civil Life—Sizing up of Work Gives Boston Players the Best of It in Every Department—Brooklyn Hitters Fail.

By N. J. FLATLEY.

Visitors out of Boston can still lord the lowly rest of the universe. The Red Sox yesterday won once more the baseball title of the well known world. The Carrigans defeated Brooklyn, before the greatest crowd that ever watched a ball game, 4 to 1. Led by tall, serious-looking Ernest Shore, pitcher and professor of mathematics, the champions of the American league downed the champions of the National league with consummate ease and dispatch. Some 42,620 fans watched the series of 1916 come to a close, several hundred more than saw the Carrigans open up against the Phillies last fall.

The great crowd packed the massive pavilion, filled the bleacher stands to overflowing and spread out behind the fence in centrefield; jammed the long aisles of the great concrete horseshoe and overflowed into the back of the grandstand. While the game was in progress an army clogged the streets about the park, a disappointed army, because the gates had been closed and the field was filled up.

While a big band was playing "This Is the End of a Perfect Day" and hero Everett Scott was catching Mike Mowrey's pop fly, thereby ending the game and the series, a mighty cheer rocked the very foundations of the massive ball yard. A yelling crowd scrambled down onto the field and marched around back of the red-clad Royal Rooters' band. President Lannin was hauled to the front of the parade, hats were thrown in the air, and the familiar-to-Boston three cheers and tiger were given for all the players and the manager and the Brooklyns and Charlie Ebbets and everybody.

And Boston Is Happy.

The Red Sox had won the pennant again and Boston was happy. After the cheering and the marching, the gathered thousands wended out of the vast en-

(Continued on Page Seven, Column 3.)

THE WEATHER

Increasing Cloudiness

FOR BOSTON AND VICINITY—Friday increasing cloudiness, probably rain at night and Saturday; warmer Friday; moderate southerly wind.

FOR SOUTHERN NEW ENGLAND—Partly cloudy and warmer Friday, rain at night and probably Saturday.

FOR NORTHERN NEW ENGLAND—Partly cloudy and warmer Friday, probably rain in western portion; Saturday, rain.

WINDS—For Friday and Saturday, north and middle Atlantic coast, moderate south. South Atlantic coast, moderate northeast. J. W. SMITH, Meteorologist.

Observations in Boston.

For 24 hours ending at 8 P. M.

Mean barometer	30.32
Mean temperature	50.0
Mean dew point	43.0
Mean relative humidity	78.0
Maximum temperature	55.0
Minimum temperature	44.0

Summary of Conditions.

The disturbances that were over the extreme central west and the Canadian northwest Wednesday night appear to have consolidated into a single disturbance that tonight extends from the lower Missouri valley northeastward to James Bay. It has been attended by general rains in the Missouri and upper Mississippi valleys and the upper lake region and is preceded to the eatsward by a general rise in temperature to above normal conditions.

There will be rain Friday night or Saturday in New England and the middle Atlantic states. It will be warmer Friday in the Atlantic states.

Yesterday's Temperatures.

	8 P.M.	Max		8 P.M.	Max
Albany	54	64	Los Angeles	60	68
Atlantic City	42	66	Montreal	48	50
Bismarck	52	62	Nantucket	48	62
Boston	51	55	New Orleans	72	82
Buffalo	56	58	New York	58	64
Charleston	64	74	Philadelphia	60	70
Chicago	56	68	Pittsburgh	62	68
Denver	56	58	Portland, Me.	44	50
Des Moines	66	72	Portland, Ore.	60	60
Eastport	40	50	San Francisco	54	60
Galveston	75	82	St. Louis	72	78
Hatteras	42	68	St. Paul	56	62
Helena	52	62	Seattle	48	50
Jacksonville	68	72	Washington	58	70
Kansas City	66	72			

All vehicles must be lighted at 5:36 P. M.

ALMANAC. . . . . OCTOBER 13

STANDARD TIME.

Sun Rises	5:54	Length of Day	11:12
Sun Sets	5:06	Moon Rises	6:06 PM
High Water	12:12 AM		12:27 PM
Height of Tide	9ft 9in AM		10ft 6in PM
Moon's last qr., Oct. 18	8h. 9m., evening, E		
New Moon, Oct. 26	3h. 37m., evening, W		
Moon's 1st qr., Nov. 2	0h. 51m., evening, E		
Full Moon, Nov. 9	3h. 18m., evening, E		

ROTOGRAVURE SECTION

THE SUNDAY HERALD

BOSTON, SUNDAY, OCT. 22, 1916

The Best Ball Team in the World—the "Also Rans"—and the Fans Who Cheered the Boston Men

(Photographs by International Film Service, Central News Service and Underwood & Underwood.)

The Winners, Left to Right,—Top Row: Sam Jones, P.; Heine Wagner, S. S.; Dufty Lewis, L. F.; Dell Gainer, 1 B.; Vean Gregg, P.; Sam Agnew, C.; Jack Barry, 2 B.; Olaf Henricksen, C. F.; Phil Wyckoff, P.; Doc Charlie Green, Trainer. Middle Row: Jimmy Walsh, C. F.; Harry Hooper, R. F.; George Goose Egg Foster, P.; Chet Thomas, C.; Bill Carrigan, Manager; Tilly Walker, C. F.; Childe Harold Janvrin, 2 B.; Forest Cady, C.; Larry Gardner, 3 B. Lower Row: Dr. Dick Hoblitzell, 1 B.; Herb Pennock, P.; Ernie Shore, P.; Red Glennon, Mascot; Carl Mays, P.; Chick Shorten, C. F.; Dutch Leonard, P.; Mike McNally, U. I.

The Royal Rooters Marching on to the Field at Brooklyn; You Might Know That the Band Played "Tessie."

The Way the Field Looked Just as Daubert Banged a Fast Drive to Left Field in the Third Game. The Crowd Went Wild, but Alas! He Was Thrown Out at the Plate.

The Rival Managers, Robinson of the Dodgers (Left), and Carrigan, Who Faced the Camera Without Trepidation.

These Are the Brooklyn Dodgers; They Won the Pennant of the National League, but They Found Certain Obstacles in the Way When They Undertook to Capture the World's Flag.

CUBS AND REDS PLAY NINE HITLESS, RUNLESS INNINGS; REDS VICTORS

KOPF GETS WINNING RUN AND FIRST HIT

Scores on Williams' Error and Thorpe's Infield Grounder Beating Vaughn.

ROBINS AND GIANTS IN TIE

Teams Play Fourteen Innings Without Victory; Phillies Defeat Braves.

CHICAGO, May 2.—A world's record was established here today in the game between Chicago and Cincinnati, each club going nine innings without a hit or run. The game was a fine pitching duel between Vaughn and Toney.

The game was won by Cincinnati, 1 to 0, in the tenth inning, when Kopf singled to right field, went to third when Williams dropped Chase's fly, and scored on Thorpe's grounder. Prior to this inning the visitors had three men reach first, two on walks and one on an error, but two double plays kept them from second base. Chicago managed to get Williams to second on a base on balls and an infield out.

Vaughn outpitched Toney in the duel, striking out ten of his opponents to Toney's three, but Toney's support was perfect, Cueto on one play backing into the left field fence for Merkle's long fly.

Groh was banished from the game by Umpire Orth in the seventh for arguing a decision.

Cin'ati—	AB.	H.	O.	A.	Chgo.—	AB.	H.	O.	A.
Groh 3b.	1	0	2	2	Zelder ss.	4	0	1	0
aGets 3b.	1	0	2	1	Wolter rf.	4	0	0	0
Kopf ss.	4	1	1	4	Doyle 2b.	4	0	5	4
Neal cf.	4	0	1	0	Merkle 1b.	4	0	7	1
Chase 1b.	4	0	12	0	Williams cf	2	0	2	0
Thorpe rf	4	1	1	0	Mann lf.	3	0	0	0
Shean 2b.	3	0	3	2	Wilson c.	3	0	14	1
Cueto lf.	3	0	3	2	Deal 3b.	3	0	1	0
Huhn c.	3	0	3	0	Vaughn p.	3	0	0	3
Toney p.	3	0	0	1					
Totals	30	2	30	10	Totals	30	0	30	9

aBatted for Groh in the seventh.
Score by innings:
Cincinnati ....0 0 0 0 0 0 0 0 0 1—1
Chicago ....0 0 0 0 0 0 0 0 0 0—0
Summary—Errors, Zeider, Williams; stolen base, Chase; double plays, Doyle to Merkle to Zeider, Vaughn to Doyle to Merkle; bases on balls off Tony 2, off Vaughn 3; struck out, by Vaughn 10, by Toney 3. Umpires, Orth and Rigler.

Robins 2—Giants 2.

NEW YORK, May 2.—New York and Brooklyn played a 14 inning tie here today, the score being, 2 to 2. Both Schupp and Cheney pitched splendid ball, the Brooklyn pitcher being especially efficient in the closing innings.

Burns opened the tenth inning for New York with a double and the twelfth with a triple, but the succeeding batsmen could not score him.

Schupp was hit hard early in the game, permitting eight hits in the first six innings and only two in the last eight.

Brook.—	AB.	H.	O.	A.	N.York.—	AB.	H.	O.	A.
Johnston rf	6	1	2	0	Burns lf.	5	2	3	0
Daub'rt 1b	5	1	11	1	Kauff cf.	6	2	3	0
Myers cf.	6	1	2	0	Rob'son rf	5	0	3	1
Wheat lf.	4	0	2	0	Zimm'n 3b	5	0	0	3
Hickm'n lf	2	0	2	1	Fletcher ss	4	1	6	4
Fab'que ss	4	2	5	2	Kilduff 2b	4	0	1	5
C'tshaw 2b	6	1	5	0	Holke 1b.	4	0	15	3
Mowrey 3b	6	2	4	4	McCarty c.	5	2	10	1
Miller c.	3	1	9	3	aMurray	0	0	0	0
Cheney p.	5	1	0	2	Schupp p.	6	1	1	6
Totals	49	10	42	13	Totals	44	8	42	23

aRan for McCarty in fourteenth.
Score by innings:
Brooklyn ..0 0 0 1 0 1 0 0 0 0 0 0 0 0—2
New York..1 0 0 0 0 0 0 1 0 0 0 0 0 0—2
Summary—Errors, Johnston, Miller 2, Fletcher 2, McCarty; two base hits, Myers, Mowrey, Burns; three base hit, Burns; home run, Fabrique; stolen bases, Robertson, Zimmerman, Kilduff; double plays, Schupp to Fletcher to Holke, Fabrique to Cutshaw, Mowrey to Cutshaw; bases on balls, off Schupp 4, off Cheney 9; struck out, by Schupp 8, by Cheney 7. Umpires, O'Day and Bransfield.

Cardinals 4—Pirates 0.

PITTSBUDGH, May 2.—Good pitching by Ames helped St. Louis shut out Pittsburgh 4 to 0 today. Grimes also pitched well but received poor support.

St. Lou.—	AB.	H.	O.	A.	Pitts.—	AB.	H.	O.	A.
Bescher lf	3	0	1	0	All'berg rf	4	1	2	0
Betzel 2b	4	0	3	4	Bigbee lf.	4	1	2	0
J. S'th rf	4	2	2	0	Carey cf.	3	0	1	0
Miller 1b.	4	1	14	0	H'ch'n 1b	3	0	11	0
H'rnsby ss	4	1	1	5	Baird 3b.	3	0	0	1
Cruise cf	2	1	3	0	Ward ss.	2	0	2	6
F. S'th 3b	4	0	1	3	Fischer c.	3	0	7	1
Snyder c	4	0	2	1	Gleason 2b	3	0	2	2
Ames p.	4	0	0	3	Grimes p.	2	0	0	4
					aKing	1	0	0	0
Totals	33	5	27	16	Totals	28	2	27	14

aBatted for Grimes in ninth.
Score by innings:
St. Louis ....1 0 0 0 0 2 0 1 0—4
Pittsburgh ....0 0 0 0 0 0 0 0 0—0
Summary—Errors, Baird, Ward 2; three base hit, J. Smith; stolen bases, Cruise, Bigbee; double play, Gleason to Ward to Hinchman; bases on balls, off Ames 2, off Grimes 3; struck out, by Ames 2, by Grimes 7. Umpires, Klem and Emslie.

Phillies 2—Braves 1.

PHILADELPHIA, May 2.—An error by Smith gave Philadelphia the run which decided today's game with Boston, 2 to 1. Stock was caught between second and third. Gowdy threw to Smith who held the ball and then threw over Konetchy's head trying to catch Cravath going back to first base.

Boston—	AB.	H.	O.	A.	P'phia—	AB.	H.	O.	A.
M'ville ss.	4	1	3	4	Paskert cf	3	0	0	0
Massey 2b	2	0	1	4	Bancroft ss	4	0	1	6
Collins rf.	4	0	2	0	Stock 3b	4	3	2	0
Magee lf	4	1	2	0	Cravath rf	3	1	0	0
K'etchy 1b	3	0	8	2	Whitted lf	3	0	3	0
Smith 3b.	3	1	0	0	Luderus 1b	3	0	12	0
Wilhoit cf	3	3	2	1	Niehoff 2b	3	1	4	3
Gowdy c.	3	0	5	3	Killifer c.	3	2	5	0
Barnes p.	3	0	1	2	Oeschger p	3	0	0	0
Totals	29	6	24	16	Totals	29	7	27	13

Score by innings:
Boston ....0 1 0 0 0 0 0 0 0—1
Philadelphia ....0 0 0 0 0 2 0 0 *—2
Summary—Errors, Massey, Smith; two base hits, Stock 3, Cravath; double plays, Massey to Maranville to Konetchy, Stock (unassisted), Stock to Niehoff to Luderus, Bancroft to Niehoff to Luderus; bases on balls, off Barnes 2, off Oeschger 1; struck out, by Barnes 3, by Oeschger 4. Umpires, Byron and Quigley.

TO RACE IN WARTIME

Wisconsin State Fair Announces Two $5,000 Stakes.

MILWAUKEE, May 2.—Business men of Milwaukee have made it possible for the state fair this year to announce two $5,000 stakes, the richest harness racing events to be decided outside the grand circuit.

Fifty members of the Chamber of Commerce have guaranteed a $5,000 stake for 2:12 trotters and a leading hotel man has guaranteed a $5,000 stake for 2:12 pacers. The Chamber of Commerce event will be raced on "Milwaukee day," Thursday, Sept. 13, and the other event has been planned for "State and Governor's day," Sept. 12.

TENNIS NOT MAN'S GAME

KANSAS CITY, Mo., May 2.—That tennis is no longer a man's game is the decision of the Kansas City Tennis association.

President Paul Pinkerton has notified the five largest clubs that the association will not even sanction interclub matches. He declares that more serious work than tennis playing confronts the players.

AIN'T IT A GRAND AND GLORIOUS FEELIN'? - (Copyright by The Tribune Association.) - By BRIGGS

C. A. WILL START ITS SEASON TODAY

President Ford Says League Will Operate Unless Havner Prevents It.

MUST HAVE SUNDAY GAMES

Declares Circuit Cannot Survive Without Sabbath Receipts.

FORT DODGE, Ia., May 2.—John F. Ford, president of the Central association, which opens its season tomorrow, in a statement given out late today in answer to a query as to whether the clubs of the league would disband on account of Attorney General Havener's decision to inforce the "blue laws" within the next ten days, said that it was likely the various clubs would proceed with the season's schedule as arranged.

None of the teams, however, he said, could pull through the season without large financial loss, as the chief revenue comes from the Sunday games. Howe long they would be willing to continue depends on how fast the deficit piles up and how long the stockholders would be willing to stand the additional assessemtns.

Much Money Spent.

"The various clubs have expended huge sums o money already in putting their teams into shape for the opening of the season, and they will be likely to proceed with the season's schedule as arranged," President Ford said. "How long they can run depends on how fast the deficit piles up and how willing the stockholders are to stand the additional assessments.

Half of Receipts on Sundays.

"However," he continued, "the club owners will have to decide for themselves as there are eight teams in the league. From 40 to 50 per cent of the receipts come from Sunday games, and it would be impossible to pay expenses if Sunday games are not played.

"There are nine Sunday games in each city and they each bring fro $600 to $14,000 dollars or something like $8,000 for the season, averaging it for each town," he said.

TO AVOID DOUBLEHEADERS

DETROIT, May 2.—In order to avoid the strain of doubleheaders, Manager Jennings is strongly in favor of opening the baseball season two weeks earlier and playing a little later in the fall.

As usual mid-April has been responsible for postponements, which mean doubleheaders in mid-season.

FOOTBALL DRIVE IS ON

LAFAYETTE, Ind., May 2.—With forty men in the moleskins, Purdue opened the football drive for next fall.

While most of the work so far has been of a preliminary nature, Coach O'Donnell has given the squad a number of plays and has lined the men up for scrimmage.

ONLY A FEW LEFT

Connie Mack's Athletics won their last American league pennant in 1914, but were beaten by the Boston Braves in the world's series. Mack went through that season with twenty-four men. Of that number the tall manager still retains Leslie Bush, pitcher; Wally Schang, catcher; Stuffy McInnis, first base, and Amos Strunk, outfield. The other members of the 1914 champions were Bender, Bressler, Coombs, Davies, Plank, Pennock, Brown, Shawkey, Wyckoff, Lapp, McAvoy, E. Collins, Baker, Barry, Kopf. Oldring, Murphy, Walsh, Daley and Thompson. In the American league today are Plank, Pennock, Shawkey, Wyckoff, E. Collins, Baker, Barry, Murphy and Walsh, while the National league has provided berths for Coombs and Kopf.

BEARS BUNCH THEIR HITS

Take Loosely Played Contest From Sioux City.

Denver Makes Seven Errors and Indians Two.

SIOUX CITY, May 2.—Bunched hits in the second and fifth enabled Denver to defeat Sioux City this afternoon, 7 to 5. The game was loosely played, nine errors being made by the two teams.

					Soo City—	AB.	H.	O.	A.
Wuffli 3b	3	0	1	0	Gilmore lf.	4	1	0	0
K'leher ss	5	1	1	4	aLecro	1	[illegible]	0	0
Oakes cf.	4	1	0	1	Cooney 2b.	3	0	7	4
Butcher lf	3	1	2	0	Connolly cf	4	2	1	1
Mills 1b.	5	1	13	0	Watson rf.	4	0	1	1
Hart'n rf	4	2	2	1	Metx 1b.	4	0	8	0
Shanley 2b	4	2	2	5	Rider ss.	3	1	3	0
Shestak c	4	3	5	2	Hungo 3b.	3	0	0	3
S'thson p	3	2	0	3	Crosby c.	3	2	7	4
Totals	35	13	27	16	Adams p.	2	0	0	1
					Grover p.	1	0	0	0
					aaMueller	1	0	0	0
					Totals	33	7	27	16

aBatted for Gilmore in ninth.
aaBatted for Griver in ninth.
Score by innings:
Denver ....0 2 0 0 3 1 0 1 0 0—7
Sioux City ....0 2 1 1 0 0 0 0 0 1—5
Summary—Errors, Mills, Shanley, Shestak 2, Smithson, Hungo 2; two base hits, Shanley, Gilmore, Connolly, Kelleher, Mills, Shestak; sacrifice hits, Hungo, Crosby, Smithson; stolen bases, Watson 2, Rader, Butcher 2, Hartman; double plays, Watson to Metz, Crosby to Cooney, Kelleher to Shanley to Mills; hits and earned runs, off Adams 2 runs 7 hits in 4 2-3 innings, off Grover 2 runs 6 hits in 4 1-3 innings; bases on balls, off Smithson 3, off Adams 4, off Grover 1; struck out, by Smithson 5, by Adams 3, by Grover 3; wild pitch, Smithson; passed ball, Shestak. Time, 2:15. Umpire, McGilvray.

Star Refuses Huge Sum to Play Prof. Baseball

ST. LOUIS, May 2.—Not for $50,000 a year would Harry Legore, Yale football and baseball star, play professional baseball, he informs Phil Ball, president of the St. Louis Americans.

Legore made the statement in refusing a contract offered him at the close of the present college year.

His Crime.

Captain—What's he charged with, Mr. Casey?

Officer—I don't know the regular name fer it, captain; but I caught him a-flirtin' in the park.

Captain—Ah, that's impersonatin' an officer.—Judge.

M. CUETO, REDS' SPEEDY CUBAN, ONE OF NATIONAL LEAGUE'S UTILITY STARS

MANUEL CUETO.

CINCINNATI, April 13.—Manuel Cueto, the Reds' small Cuban outfielder, may not play a regular outfield game this season and perhaps will be used largely as a utility man, but he has won a warm spot in the hearts of local fans. Cueto set out early in the training season determined to win a regular job in the lineup. And the high class ball he has been playing from the first has been the favorite topic of local fans.

When Eddie Roush, the Reds' outfield star, showed a reluctance to appear for spring training it was thought that Eddie had holdout ideas and that perhaps he planned to stay away for keeps unless his salary was fattened. Cueto saw his chance to get a place in the regular lineup and it must be admitted that he hit a faster clip in his efforts to land it than anyone would have thought him capable of. Cueto not only fielded in a thoroughly faultless way and showed the most delightful speed on the bases, but he hit the ball at a fiendish clip all through the training season, and in the barnstorming games. It began to appear to Red fans that Eddie Roush might stay away forever if he chose so long as there was such class to Cueto to replace him.

Roush returned, however, to report that he had no holdout demands to make, but had only stayed away as he needed the time to look after a mine or two he is interested in and a few other things that required his attention. Eddie had reached the best sort of shape with his own home training and the suspicion was current that he simply wanted to escape the drudgery of the spring training trip.

If Roush was not one of the brightest stars among the game's younger outfielders, his truancy might have caused him some little grief, not to say the loss of a good job. Roush shared the starring honors of the Reds with Bennie Kauff at the time that organization was disbanded and there are plenty who will tell you that Roush is even a better man than Kauff. At least it is certain that Eddie is one of the best, and though Cueto's performing had been of the highest class throughout he could hardly expect to nose Roush out of the job.

The Reds are pleased to see that they have in Cueto one of the star utility players of the league. If Cueto continues to pound the ball as he has so far he will close the season with a hot record even though he isn't in the lineup every day.

GIANT KANSAN TO TACKLE CADDOCK

Allan Eustace Signs to Grapple With World's Champion Here Monday.

SHOULD MAKE GOOD MATCH

Heavyweights Will Wrestle in Auditorium; Full House Expected.

Oscar Thorson, who is promoting the Earl Caddock wrestling match at the Auditorium next Monday night, yesterday matched Allan Eustace, the giant Kansan, with the Anita grappler, for the contest in which the world's heavyweight championship will be involved.

Eustace was signed after Thorson had negotiated with several of the best wrestlers in the country and had eliminated them one by one for the reason that he did not believe they would put up a strong enough battle with Caddock.

Challenge Lost Match.

Eustace is the grappler who challenged the winner of the Stecher-Caddock match through The Register-Tribune late in March. Thorson, after much dickering, finally secured Caddock's consent to meet the big Jayhawker, and immediately closed the contract of the bout.

Eustace is a young doctor, who has delayed practicing at his profession, because he and his friends believe he has the ability to become heavyweight wrestling champion.

Eustace a Physician.

There is more money in wrestling if, you are a top-notcher, than there is in building up a doctor's practice.

The young grappler will have the opportunity here Monday of demonstrating his ability. Among those who vouch for his strength and speed is Jess Westergaard, the local heavyweight, who has seen Eustace in action. Westergaard says the Kansan will make any wrestler in the game hustle to throw him.

Staged at Auditorium.

Thorson announced yesterday that the Auditorium has been rented for the match. He expects to fill it to capacity, as the interest in Caddock all over Iowa is intense, and Des Moines is not behind the remainder of the state in its admiration of the popular Anita boy. Wrestling is due for a boom such as has not been seen in Iowa since Frank Gotch was at his best.

DANGER IN PIGSKIN, SAYS INDIAN STAR

DETROIT, May 2.—Declaring that football is too dangerous, Jim Thorpe, although offered tempting salaries from semiprofessional football promoters, has refused to don the moleskins next fall.

Since Thorpe was sold to Cincinnati by the Giants, his batting has shown marked improvement. He is determined not to ruin his baseball career by football injuries.

MUFFS FOUL, GETS ERROR

Jones Only Center Fielder to Get Error on Such a Play.

DETROIT, May. 2.—Fielder Jones, manager of the St. Louis Americans, believes he is the only major league center fielder that ever received an error for muffing a foul ball.

Years ago Jones was playing the middle garden for Brooklyn. Joe Kelley was in left and Willie Keeler in right field. A left field hitter of the McInnis type came to bat, and the outfielders shifted so sharply that Jones was really playing left field.

The batter sent up a long fly, which threatened to drop close to the left field foul line. Kelley and Jones raced after the ball, and the latter got his hands on it, but the sphere fell from his grasp on foul territory.

JOE BERGER HURLS LOCALS TO VICTORY

Wichita Forces Des Moines to Go Ten Innings to Grab Contest.

DAVIS' THROW IS COSTLY

Cass Gets Two Doubles and a Single and Scores Tying Run in Fifth.

Des Moines defeated Wichita, 2 to 1, today in a ten inning pitchers' battle between Berger and Lyons. An infield hit by Ewoldt, Davis' error of Spencer's sacrifice, a base on balls and a late throw to the plate on an infield grounded, gave the locals the winning run.

Berger was wild at the start and as a result gave four of the five hits made off him in the first four innings. Beginning with the fifth he was almost invincible, and never was in danger.

Lyons, a former Chicago White Sox recruit, had a lot of stuff and puzzled the local batsmen most of the time. However, Cass hit him for a single and two doubles, one of the latter being followed by a two-bagger off Ewoldt's bat in the fifth inning, the combination netting the winning run.

Wichita's run was made in the first frame on a pass to to Goodwin, a hit batsman and Coy's single.

The score:

Wichita—	AB.	R.	H.	TB.	SH.	SB.	PO.	A.	E.
Goodwin, 2b	4	1	0	0	0	0	2	3	0
Davis, 3b	5	0	0	0	0	0	1	3	1
Jones, 1b	4	0	0	0	0	0	9	0	0
Coy, rf	4	0	1	1	0	0	2	0	0
Yaryan, c	4	0	1	1	0	0	8	1	0
Payton, ss	3	0	1	1	0	1	3	2	0
Washburn, cf	4	0	1	1	0	0	1	0	0
Harvey, lf	4	0	1	1	0	0	1	0	0
Lyons, p	4	0	0	0	0	0	0	1	0
Totals	36	1	5	5	0	1	a27	10	1
Des Moines—	AB.	R.	H.	TB.	SH.	SB.	PO.	A.	E.
Cass, lf	4	1	3	5	0	0	1	0	0
Ewoldt, 3b	4	1	2	3	0	0	3	3	1
Spencer, cf	3	0	1	1	2	0	1	1	0
Hunter, rf	3	0	1	2	0	0	2	1	0
Hartford, ss	5	0	0	0	0	0	0	5	0
Coffey, 2b	3	0	0	0	0	0	4	1	1
Sweeney, 1b	4	0	0	0	0	0	11	0	1
Spahr, c	4	0	1	1	0	0	8	1	0
Berger, p	4	0	0	0	0	0	0	5	0
Totals	35	2	8	12	2	0	30	17	4

aNone out when winning run scored.
Score by innings:
Wichita ....1 0 0 0 0 0 0 0 0 0—1
Des Moines ....0 0 0 0 1 0 0 0 0 1—2
Summary—Two base hits, Cass, 2, Ewoldt Hunter; left on bases, Wichita 8, Des Moines 12; struck out, by Berger 7, by Lyons 7; first on balls, off Lyons 2, off Berger 2; hit by pitcher, by Berger (Jones); by Lyons (Coffey, Hunter.) Umpire, Jacobs. Time 1:57.

BOGUS MONEY NEAR PERFECT

Counterfeit Coins Hard to Detect Flooding Rochester.

ROCHESTER, N. Y., May 3.—This city is being flooded with spurious currency of all denominations, from a dime to a half dollar. The counterfeits are excellent and are only detected after having been handled a few times. The usual smooth surfaces and generally oily conditions that appear on most bogus coins are absent in the new counterfeits.

Mrs. Annie Junda, an elderly woman, who lives in No. 34 Niagara street, was arrested in a department store where she had given a clerk a bogus half dollar for some goods. Lieutenant Ellis turned her over to the federal authorities, who say the coin is a replica of the others picked up about the city. At the office of United States Marshal Lynn it was said that coins representing several hundred dollars had been accumulated in Rochester by federal authorities.

One day last week a stranger gave the son of Patrolman Joseph Courneen a bad dime in payment for a newspaper The piece was of copper, and had not been silvered.

BOYS FIND MAN'S HEAD

No Murder—Used for Experiments, M. D. Explains.

BROOKLYN, N. Y., May 3.—For a time the other night the police thought they had another Guldensuppe case on their hands, when some boys, playing on the roof of an extension at 58 Flatbush avenue, found a human head in a pail, a hammer alongside it. The boys are still running.

"Murder!" exclaimed the police.

"Rot!" replied Dr. George C. Ferguson, a dentist, who has an office there. "I use the head for experimental purposes. I wished to find out something about a disease of the jaw which killed the man who originally owned the head."

DUBUQUE IS READY NOW

Manager Hughes Pronounces His Team Ready to Start.

DUBUQUE, Ia., May 2.—In anticipation of landing well up in the face for the Central association rag, Manager Hughes of the Dubuque team has whipped his men into shape for the opening game with Waterloo, at Waterloo, Thursday. When he gets them running, Hughes says he will have one of the best teams in the league.

Scott Dye, an outfielder, has been released to Dubuque by Jack Tighe, Rock Island Three I manager. He is the fifth man sent to Dubuque by Tighe.

VITT IS REINSTATED

Detroit Infielder Again in Good Standing.

CINCINNATI, May 2.—The national baseball commission today reinstated Player Oscar Vitt of the Detroit Americans. In making its decision the commission says:

"Insubordination of this kind will not be condoned in future.

Vitt did not report to the Detroit club until late in April owing to differences over salary.

VERNON GETS SNODGRASS

Major League Veteran to Play in Coast League.

LOS ANGELES, May 1.—Fred Snodgrass, former New York National league outfielder, who refused to report to the Boston National league club this year and was unconditionally released, was signed today by Vernon in the Pacific Coast league.

Decoration.

"Gladys Maud spent weeks and weeks toiling on her graduation essay."

"The mental strain must have been fearful."

"Yes, indeed. It took her ten days to select a ribbon."—Brooklyn Citizen.

LEAGUE GAME RESULTS AND STANDING OF CLUBS

WESTERN LEAGUE.

	W.	L.	Pct.		W.	L.	Pct.
Denver	6	3	.667	Sioux City	5	5	.500
Des Moines	7	4	.636	Joplin	4	5	.444
Lincoln	6	4	.600	Omaha	4	5	.444
St. Joseph	5	4	.556	Wichita	3	10	.231

YESTERDAY'S RESULTS.
Des Moines ....2; Wichita 1
Denver ....7; Sioux City 5
Other games postponed........Wet grounds

GAMES TODAY.
W'hita at D. Moines. | Denver at Soo City.
Joplin at Omaha. | St. Joe at Lincoln.

AMERICAN LEAGUE.

	W.	L.	Pct.		W.	L.	Pct.
Boston	9	4	.692	Clevel'd	8	10	.444
Chicago	11	6	.647	Phila	6	8	.429
New York	8	6	.571	Detroit	6	9	.400
St. Louis	8	8	.500	Wash'gton	5	10	.333

YESTERDAY'S RESULTS.
Chicago ....8; Cleveland 3
Detroit ....2; St. Louis 0
New York ....2; Washington 0
Philadelphia at Boston........Cold

GAMES TODAY.
Detroit at St. Lo's. | Chicago at Cleveland
N. York at Wash. | Philadelphia at Bos.

NATIONAL LEAGUE.

	W.	L.	Pct.		W.	L.	Pct.
New York	8	4	.667	Cinc'n'ti.	10	10	.500
St. Louis	10	7	.588	Boston	5	6	.453
Chicago	10	8	.556	Pittsburgh	7	12	.368
Phila.	7	6	.538	Brooklyn.	3	7	.300

YESTERDAY'S RESULTS.
Philadelphia ....2; Boston 1
St. Louis ....4; Pittsburgh 0
Cincinnati ....1; Chicago 0
Brooklyn ....2; New York 2

GAMES TODAY.
Brooklyn at N. Y. | Boston at Phila.
St. Louis at Pitts. | Cincin'ti at Chicago.

AMERICAN ASSOCIATION.

	W.	L.	Pct.		W.	L.	Pct.
Indianap.	14	5	.737	Columbus.	8	9	.471
Kan. City.	8	5	.615	Minneap.	5	7	.417
Louisville	11	8	.579	St. Paul	3	9	.257
Milwaukee	7	7	.500	Toledo	4	12	.250

YESTERDAY'S RESULTS.
Indianapolis ....10; Milwaukee 1
Minneapolis ....3; Columbus 1
St. Paul ....6; Louisville 3
Kansas City at Toledo........Wet grounds

PACIFIC COAST LEAGUE.
Oakland ....4; Portland 3
Los Angeles ....7; San Francisco 1
Vernon ....3; Salt Lake City 1

SOUTHERN ASSOCIATION.
Nashville ....1; Chattanooga 0
Little Rock ....7; Memphis 6
New Orleans ....7; Atlanta 2
Birmingham ....10; Mobile 3

DRAKE TEAM LOSES ATHLETES TO WAR

Mainstays in Blue and White Squad Unable to Meet Grinnell Scarlet and Black.

GRINNELL FIRST IN 1916

Three Enlist in Coast Artillery and Eight Apply for Fort Snelling.

All hopes for a winning Drake team against Grinnell Saturday in their annual dual meet were shattered yesterday when it was announced that several of the mainstays of the Blue and White squad will leave for Fort Logan, Colo.

Carson, Lennen and Smith, all reliable point winners, have enlisted in the coast artillery service and will leave some time today. Captain Lucy, Allbaugh, Powers, Jordan, Crail, Price Blackburn and Ervin have applied for entrance to Fort Snelling.

Last year Grinnell won by a narrow margin of four points. Drake failed to take a first in the dashes, but came back strong in the field events. Barden of Grinnell is said to have done :53 2-5 this year in the quarter. With Smith of Drake out of the race this should be comparatively easy for the Grinnell speedsters.

Both the short dashes are conceded to Hoyt without a struggle, Captain Lucy of Drake should place in this event if he is in the contest.

Drake's relay teams have both been shot to pieces by the war, and no prediction can be made as to the probable outcome of these races.

The jumps will undoubtedly go to the Scarlet athletes. Ervin, with a sprained ankle, will be useless in the broad jump, and Carson will have left school by Saturday. Stock of Grinnell in the high jump is reported to have done 5 feet 8 inches this year, while the best Drake can offer is the winner of third place last year at 5 feet 2 inches.

The Bulldogs have placed faith in Ervin and Lucy to bring back points in the lows, and Kiner, a first year man, is doped to tally in the high sticks.

Warnock in the shot and discus is doped to take premier honors. His showing of 115 feet in the discus and 36 feet in the shot this year is better than anything the Grinnell weight men have produced. The pole vault, in which Drake counted three places last year, is conceded to Ervin, the Blue and White winner of this event in the state meet last year.

WHITE SOX DEFEAT CLEVELAND 8 TO 3

Chicago Americans Bat Ball Hard and Easily Trounce the Indians.

YANKEES BEAT W. JOHNSON

Hit Washington Star Hard; With Dauss Pitching Detroit Blanks St. Louis.

CLEVELAND, May 2.—Chicago defeated Cleveland, 8 to 3, today. Chicago hit Coumbe, Smith and Gould hard in the fifth and sixth. Williams kept Cleveland's few hits well scattered.

Chicago—	AB.	H.	O.	A.	Cl'eland—	AB.	H.	O.	A.
J.Cols rf lf	5	4	7	0	Allison cf	2	1	2	0
Weaver 3b	5	1	0	3	Kav'agh rf	3	0	2	1
E. Cols 2b	3	2	4	0	Chapm'n ss	3	0	3	3
Jackson lf	2	0	1	0	Graney lf.	4	0	0	0
Murphy rf	3	0	0	0	Guisto 1b.	3	1	11	1
Felsch cf.	4	1	4	0	Roth rf cf	4	1	2	0
Gandil 1b.	3	1	6	0	Wamby 2b	3	1	4	2
Risberg ss	4	1	0	2	Turner 3b.	4	2	1	5
Schalk c.	4	1	5	0	O'Neill c.	2	0	2	0
Williams p	1	0	0	4	Coumbe p.	1	0	0	1
					Smith p.	0	0	0	0
					Gould p.	1	1	0	1
					aWood	1	0	0	0
					bBillings	1	0	0	0
Totals	34	11	27	10	Totals	32	7	27	14

aBatted for Allison in the fifth.
bBatted for Gould in the ninth.
Score by innings:
Chicago ....1 0 0 0 3 4 0 0 0—8
Cleveland ....0 0 0 1 0 0 2 0 0—3
Summary—Errors, Murphy, Felsch, Wambganss 2; two base hits, E. Collins, Felsch, Schalk; three base hits, J. Collins, Weaver, Risberg; stolen base, J. Collins; double plays, Turner to Wambsganss to Guisto, Weaver to E. Collins to Gandil, Kavanagh to Guisto; bases on balls, off Williams 2, off Coumbe 2, off Gould 1; hits, off Coumbe 4 in 5 innings, off Smith 3 in no innings; struck out, by Williams 5, by Coumbe 1, by Gould 1. Umpires, Hildebrand and O'Laughlin.

Yankees 2—Senators 0.

WASHINGTON, D. C., May 2.—Fisher outpitched Walter Johnson today, allowing four scattered hits and no runs while his teammates were getting nine hits and scoring twice.

N. Y'k—	AB.	H.	O.	A.	Wash.—	AB.	H.	O.	A.
Gilh'l'y rf	3	1	2	0	Judge 1b.	3	1	9	0
High lf.	3	2	2	0	Foster 3b	3	0	3	2
Maisel 2b	3	0	3	2	Milan cf.	4	1	2	0
Pipp 1b.	3	2	8	1	Rice rf.	4	0	1	0
Baker 3b.	4	2	1	2	Men'ky lf.	4	1	4	0
Magee cf	4	0	1	0	Morgan 2b	4	0	1	2
P'k'p'h ss	4	1	4	4	MBride ss	4	1	2	4
N'm'k'r c	4	0	5	1	Ainsm'h c	2	0	5	3
Fisher p.	4	1	1	0	Johns'n p	2	0	0	1
Totals	32	9	27	10	Totals	30	4	27	12

Score by innings:
New York ....0 1 0 0 0 0 1 0 0—2
Washington ....0 0 0 0 0 0 0 0 0—0
Summary—Errors, Peckinpaugh, Milan; two base hits, Fisher, Gilhooley; three base hit, High; stolen bases, Foster, Johnson; double plays, McBride to Morgan to Judge, Peckinpaugh to Pipp; bases on balls, off Fisher 4, off Johnson 4; struck out by Johnson 5, by Fisher 2. Umpires, Owen and Dinneen.
NAT

Tigers 2—Browns 0.

ST. LOUIS, May 2.—Detroit's timely hitting behind Dauss' good twirling beat St. Louis, 2 to 0, today. After the first inning St. Louis got but one man as far as third.

Two double plays by the home team cut off several runs.

Detroit—	AB.	H.	O.	A.	S.Louis—	AB.	H.	O.	A.
Bush ss.	5	1	0	5	Shotton lf.	3	2	2	0
Young 2b.	5	2	2	1	Austin 3b.	3	0	0	1
Cobb rf.	4	1	3	0	aRumler	1	0	0	0
Veach lf.	3	1	2	0	Paulette 3b	0	0	0	0
Heilm'n cf	4	2	3	0	Sisler 1b.	4	3	11	0
Burns 1b.	3	0	11	0	K'wrt'y 2b	2	0	0	2
Vitt 3b.	3	2	1	1	Pratt 2b.	2	0	1	2
Stanage c	3	0	5	3	J'cbson rf	4	0	1	0
Dauss p.	4	0	0	5	Marsans cf	4	0	3	0
					Severeid c	3	0	4	0
Totals	34	9	27	15	Lavan ss.	2	0	3	4
					bS'oan	0	0	0	0
					cJohnson	0	0	1	0
					Weilman p	0	0	0	2
					Groom p.	2	0	0	2
					dMiller	1	1	0	0
					Hamilton p	0	0	0	0
					Totals	31	6	*26	13

aBatted for Austin in eighth.
bBatted for Lavan in eighth.
cRan for Sloan in eighth.
dBatted for Groom in eighth.
*Bush hit by own batted ball.
Score by innings:
Detroit ....1 0 0 0 0 0 0 1 0—2
St. Louis ....0 0 0 0 0 0 0 0 0—0
Summary—Errors, Shotton, Paulette, Sisler, Groom; two base hits, Heilman, Sisler; stolen bases, Shotton, Veach; double plays, Kenworthy to Lavan to Sisler, Lavan to Pratt to Sisler; bases on balls, off Dauss 2, off Weilman 1; hits, off Weilman 6 in 2 innings (none out in third), off Groom 3 in 6 innings; struck out, by Dauss 4, by Groom 2. Umpires, Evans and Nallin.

TY COBB SWINGS AGAIN

"Silk" O'Loughlin Kids Detroit Outfielder.

CLEVELAND, O., May 2.—Ty Cobb, the Detroit star, is through questioning the decisions of "Silk" O'Laughlin, the veteran American league umpire. O'Laughlin called a strike in a recent game here that Ty throught was too high. He protested.

"Never missed a strike in my life, Tyrus," "Silk" said.

"Well, that one was too high," said Cobb.

"Trouble with you, Ty, is that you took too long a stride," retorted O'Laughlin.

"What do you mean?" flashed back Ty. "Are you trying to tell me how to bat?"

"Well, aren't you trying to tell me how to umpire?" was "Silk's" quick comeback.

Ty took another swing.

Confesses to Murder of Ruth Cruger

THE BOSTON TRAVELER

93D YEAR. BOSTON, SATURDAY, JUNE 23, 1917—TWELVE PAGES. ONE CENT.

WAR EXTRA

RUTH ATTACKS UMPIRE

COCCHI SAYS JEALOUS RAGE CAUSED ACT

Declares He Killed the Girl Because He Couldn't Win Her Love.

BREAKS DOWN WHILE MAKING HIS CONFESSION

(By the Associated Press.)

BOLOGNA, Italy, June 23—Alfredo Cocchi, the fugitive New York motorcycle dealer, abandoned today his pretense of innocence of the murder of Ruth Cruger and confessed his guilt. Jealousy was his motive. He was unable, he declared, to win her love, and became furious when she rebuffed his persistent attentions.

The young Italian, whose escape the New York police failed to prevent, wept as he made the admissions after searching interrogation by Judge Zucconi broke down his reserve. Prior to this examination, Cocchi had coolly and insistently maintained he had known Miss Cruger only two days before her disappearance in February, when she went to his shop to have her skates sharpened, and had declared his conduct toward her was entirely correct.

Cocchi Gives Details.

Under Judge Zucconi's searching questions today, however, Cocchi finally burst into tears. He became so agitated as his confession fell haltingly from his lips that the persons surrounding him believed he was about to have an epileptic fit. He was granted time to recover and then resumed the story of how the 18-year-old girl met death at his hands in the building from the cellar of which her body was recently unearthed.

Cocchi has been reported to be growing more restless in the close confinement under which he was kept by the Italian authorities. This morning he declared he was ill with a fever and asked to be sent to a hospital. The prison doctor could find no symptom of sickness, and his request was refused.

Cocchi shows great interest in what the newspapers are saying about him and has begged to be allowed to read the papers. This also was refused as against the prison rules. The prisoner is not allowed to see any one but his jailer.

After making up his mind to tell the truth, Cocchi talked freely and without reserve gave full details of his crime, including the burial of Miss Cruger's body.

After the confession had been completed the judge directed the clerk to read to Cocchi the written report of his deposition. The prisoner said it was correct, and later signed it.

On returning to his cell Cocchi said to the prison attendants: "At last I feel relieved. I have freed myself from a nightmare which tortured my conscience. Now I have told everything, and I am ready to suffer any penalty."

Judge Zucconi questioned an American woman, a relative of Miss Cruger, who came here for the purpose of giving testimony concerning the motive for the crime and the circumstances under which it was committed. The name and address of this woman have not been ascertained.

Fled to Italy Soon After Girl Disappeared.

Alfredo Cocchi went to Bologna from New York in February after the disappearance of Ruth Cruger, a girl 18 years old. When the girl's body was discovered in the basement of Cocchi's motorcycle shop in New York Police

(Continued on Page Three, Column 6.)

MISS ELEANOR PUTZKI, a Washington Girl Scout, Who is the Recipient of a Gold Eaglet Given Her by Mrs. Woodrow Wilson.

Take Step to Impeach Pro-German Mayor

Chicago City Council Will Begin Proceedings Next Monday.

CHICAGO, June 23—A meeting of the judiciary committee of the city council to consider proceedings against Mayor Thompson, asked in a resolution referred to the committee in yesterday's council meeting, was called for Monday by Chairman Otto Kerner today.

The City Hall and the Tribune building were practically under martial law today. Scores of policemen were guarding the school board offices in both places to prevent forcible ousting of Mayor Thompson's appointees, the latest of whom were repidiated by the city council late yesterday.

Thompson faces two proceedings that may cost him his job—impeachment by the council, or malfeasance in office—charges threatened by State Attorney Hoyne.

The mayor had not returned to the City Hall since his hurried exit late yesterday, just after a book hurled at him by an unidentified alderman missed his head by inches. The book throwing was the climax of a riot which resulted when the Thompson faction in the council attempted to force an adjournment.

The present trouble is the result of a factional war in the school board which had its inception last week when Thomp-

(Continued on Page Three, Column 1.)

NAMES BAY STATE BOARD ON EXEMPTION

President Wilson Selects Candidates Suggested by Gov. McCall.

APPOINTED UNDER SELECTIVE DRAFT LAW

President Wilson has appointed the men for the Massachusetts exemption boards which will operate under the selective conscription act. The President appointed the men nominated to him by the Governor, and the lists were made public today.

The exemption boards for Boston are as follows:

District 1, ward 1—Edward G. Graves, Thomas F. Rice, Dr. William A. Morrison.

District 2, ward 2—William G. Maguire, George H. Shields, Dr. James H. Strong.

District 3, wards 3 and 4—Augustus A. Fales, Luke Mullen, Dr. John F. O'Brien.

District 4, precincts 1 to 4, ward 5—Peter P. Porter, Felix Marcella, Dr. Domizio A. Costa.

District 5, precincts 5 to 11, ward 5—Francis Clare, Adolphus Burroughs, Dr. Charles F. Wilinski.

District 6, ward 6—Michael J. O'Leary, Charles E. Stone, Dr. John Cotting.

District 7, ward 7—Freeman O. Emerson, William J. Conlon, Dr. Walter R. Mansfield.

District 8, ward 8—Abraham Cohen, Benjamin F. Powell, Dr. Jacob B. Bruce.

District 9, ward 9—George F. Lawley, Patrick H. Jennings, Dr. George O. Jenkins.

District 10, ward 10—John A. Hanson, Michael A. Murphy, Dr. John L. Mayers.

District 11, ward 11—James G. Gillespie, William B. Rand, Dr. Charlton B. Allard.

District 12, ward 12—John F. Stevens, William M. Pillar, Dr. John Toomey.

District 13, ward 13—Thomas J. Fay, Martin Milmore, Dr. Samuel Courtney.

District 14, ward 14—John C. Crossen, James P. Fox, Dr. Thomas V. Toohey.

District 15, ward 15—Stephen Liddy, Albert E. Langlois, Dr. Frank McDonald.

District 16, ward 16—Shirley P. Graves, Harry P. Nawn, Dr. William D. Keeler.

District 17, ward 17—Miles O'Brien, Elias Saklad, Dr. Thomas J. Coyle.

District 18, ward 18—J. Walter Mullen, John F. Doherty, Dr. Edward H. Ferguson.

District 19, ward 19—Michael H. Sullivan, William J. Hill, Dr. Joseph E. Ingoldsby.

District 20, ward 20—Walter B. Grant, Stephen R. Casey, Dr. Frederick V. Hardwick.

District 21, ward 21—Harry P. Craig, James E. Clinton, Dr. Nathaniel R. Perkins.

District 22, ward 22—Michael J. Murray, Frank Leveroni, Dr. Edwin T. Rollins.

District 23, ward 23—Arthur W. Joslin, Louis Epple, Dr. F. C. Jillson.

District 24, ward 24—Dennis W. Mahoney, Llewellyn S. Evans, Dr. Ralph O. Dodge.

District 25, ward 25—Fred E. J. Dowling, Thomas H. Connolly, Dr. Harold G. Giddings.

Division 1—George P. Lawrence, North Adams; Michael L. Monohan, Wiliamstown; Dr. R. Delos Canedy, North Adams.

Division 2—Fred R. Shaw, Adams; Francis U. Stearns, Adams; Dr. Harry B. Holmes, Adams.

Division 3—Bart Bossidy, Lee; Walter B. Sanford, Great Barrington; Dr. Clifford S. Chapin, Great Barrington .

(Continued on Page Two, Column One.)

U-BOAT SUNK BY YANKEE GUN CREW

Navy Department Receives Confirmation of Destruction of Submarine.

SHOTS FROM FREIGHTER GO TRUE TO THE MARK

WASHINGTON, June 23—Confirmation of the sinking of a German submarine by the navy gun crew of an armed American merchantman mentioned in dispatches was received today by the navy department. Apparently the submarine was sunk as nothing further was seen of it.

AN ATLANTIC PORT, June 23—A fight between an American freight steamship and a German submarine which took place June 6, one day out from Genoa, Italy, and resulted in the navy gunners on the American vessel scoring at least one hit, was reported by the captain of the steamer on his arrival today.

The captain said the U-boat appeared at a distance of about 500 yards, and launched a torpedo. The torpedo's wake was clearly discernible and it was possible so to manoeuvre the vessel that it missed the ship by about 20 feet. Fire was immediately opened on the U-boat from a stern gun and four shots were discharged in rapid succession as the submarine submerged. The second shot, the captain said, cut off the periscope.

THE WEATHER

I'M THE ORIGINAL JUNE BUG!

FORECAST—Showers and local storms late tonight and Sunday; moderate variable winds.

OBSERVATIONS.

The trough of low pressure that extends from Lake Superior southwest to Texas and New Mexico, is attended by showery conditions trat reach eastward to the upper Ohio valley and Lake Erie. The pressure is near the average, with fair weather in the rest of the country. Temperatures are somewhat higher in the West, the Southwest and the lower Ohio valley, but slight changes otherwise.

Boston observations at 8 A. M.—Barometer, 29.97 inches; temperature, 74; highest yesterday, 87; lowest last night, 68; humidity, 43%; clear; wind, northwest, 7 miles per hour.

Highland Light, 8 A. M.—Very hazy; southwest, 5 miles per hour.

Hull—Very smoky; west, 6 miles per hour.

TEMPERATURES, 8 A. M.

Albany	68	Cleveland	66
Eastport, Me.	48	Detroit	58
Greenville, Me.	60	Duluth	44
Hartord	70	Cincinnati	72
Jacksonville	76	Kansas City, Mo.	76
Nantucket	64	Memphis	78
New York	74	St. Louis	76
Norfolk, Va.	72	New Orleans	76
Northfield, Vt.	64	Omaha	68
Philadelphia	78	St. Paul	54
Portland, Me.	70	Denver	58
Washington, D C.	74	Los Angeles	62
Buffalo	60	Portland, Or.	54
Chicago	60	San Francisco	50

ALMANAC.............JUNE 23

Sun Rises	4:08	Length of Day	15:17
Sun Sets	7:25	Moon Sets	9:51 PM
High Water	1:29 AM		2:01 PM
Height of Tide	19ft 7in AM		8ft 6in PM

Moon's 1st qr., June 27...11h. 8m., morning, E
Full Moon, July 4........4h. 40m., evening, E
Moon's last qr., July 11..7h. 12m., morning, W
New Moon, July 18.....10h. 20m., evening, W

All vehicles must be lighted at 7:55 P. M.

Gigantic Plan to Undermine Selective Draft

Department of Justice nvestigating Latest Move of Pacifists.

By WEBB MILLER
[United Press Staff Correspondent]

WASHINGTON, June 23—Two "pacifist" organizations have launched a huge campaign that, if carried out, officials said today, would greatly undermine the selective draft law.

These organizations, it was stated, are attempting to open up a channel for escape from military service. More than 10,000 have enrolled in the propaganda.

Agents of the department of justice are fixing their attention upon the activities of representatives of the organizations.

So far efforts of the "pacifists" are confined to attempts to have inserted in the exemption regulations which will be published probably Monday a clause that would specifically permit persons professing "conscientious objections" to war to escape selective draft and enrollment of members with the implied promise that their membership constitutes them "objectors."

The most active organization is the American Union Against Militarism. Its headquarters is in New York. One of the officials of the organization declared to the United Press that not less than 10,000 persons had enrolled since June 5, registration day. The other organization had headquarters at Northfield, Minn.

In their activities the pacifists appealed to President Wilson and Secretary Baker to provide for exemption of "conscientious objectors" and members of pacifist unions. This would furnish their big membership with exemption.

Thwarted in this, they are suggesting that objectors be allowed to enlist in industries to avoid bearing arms.

After an appeal to the war department, Roger N. Baldwin, field secretary of the Union Against Militarism, received a letter from Secretary Baker pointing out that the draft law fails to provide for "conscientious objectors" and stating that the department cannot "go behind the law" in administering it.

With two of their avenues shut off, the organizations are seeking to obtain a liberal interpretation of a clause in the law that permits the exemption of recognized religious sects or organizations.

PICKETS' SURPRISE ATTACK A FAILURE

WASHINGTON, June 23—Escaping a line of police outside of suffrage headquarters today, two militant pickets bore a banner to the White House gates and were promptly arrested by two policewomen. The police characterized the affair as a "surprise attack," but the policewomen were on hand a few minutes after the pickets arrived.

The two women arrested were Mrs. Lawrence Lewis of Philadelphia, who was previously attacked during the anti-suffrage demonstrations this week, and Miss Gladys Greiner of Baltimore.

The banner they bore said:

"Mr. President, you say we in the United States are interested only in human liberty"—an extract from Wilson's address on the "New Freedom."

EXPLOSION ON ME. CENTRAL R. R.

WATERVILLE, Me., June 23—A stick of dynamite exploded early today on the tracks of the Lewiston branch of the Maine Central railroad near the North Street bridge here, tore up one of the rails, shattered windows in houses nearby and caused considerable excitement among the residents.

An east-bound freight train had passed the spot a few minutes before the explosion and another freight train, also east-bound, was approaching. The breaking of the rail set the signals in the block and halted the second train.

The police said they were of the opinion the dynamite was placed there. They are investigating a report, they said, that threats against railroad property had been made yesterday when reports were received by several hundred striking railroad repair and shopmen that strike-breakers were expected before another day.

ORDERED TO SWITZERLAND

BERNE, Switzerland, June 23—The federal council has ordered the Swiss minister at Petrograd to come to Berne and make an oral report on recent incidents, including the expulsion of Robert Crimm from Russia and his relations with Dr. Hoffmann, former Swiss foreign minister.

By helping the army the American Red Cross helps to protect your home. Give to the fund.

EXPLOSION KILLS 136 IN AUSTRIA

Munitions Plant at Bloeweg Blows up—Total Casualties Over 1000 .

CARELESSNESS, SAYS MINISTER OF DEFENCE

AMSTERDAM, June 23—More than 1000 persons were killed or injured or are missing in consequence of an explosion in munitions factories at Bloeweg. Announcement was made in the lower House of the Austrian Parliament by the minister of defence and forwarded today in a dispatch from Vienna.

Due to Carelessness.

The casualties were given by the minister as follows:

Dead, 136; missing, 170; wounded, 625. Of the wounded 520 received only slight injuries.

The minster said the explosion probably was due to carelessness on the part of the men employed in a trench mortar workshop.

The plant is said to have been ruined.

FIND CLUB BROKE THE EXCISE LAWS

A verdict of guilty was announced today by the license commissioners after a week's investigation of charges against the Tennis and Racquet Club that liquor was served by the club to a member at a place other than the club premises. The charge was placed on file.

Not guilty was the finding of another charge, that the club had "delivered intoxicating liquor to be transported for hire or reward to a railroad corporation in a vessel or package not plainly marked as to contents."

ITALIAN MISSION CLOSING N. Y. VISIT

NEW YORK, June 23—A public reception at the City College stadium and a private luncheon at the home of Dr. Nicholas Murray Butler, president of Columbia University, will end the program of entertainment in New York today for the Italian commission.

Members of the commission will be in the city until tomorrow evening, but their time will be their own. They are expected to accept several unofficial invitations to attend functions. A performance at Carnegie Hall tonight for the benefit of Italian and Russian Red Cross probably will be attended by most of the visitors.

POPE ISSUES GUIDE ON SERMONS

ROME, June 23—The Osservatore Romano publishes an encyclical letter from the Pope on preaching in churches. The pontiff traces general lines for the preachers to follow, indicates subjects, and adds:

"Sermons should be exclusively religious, and seek to please God and not man."

N. Y. BUYS THREE ROOKIES

CHARLESTON, S. C., June 23—Players Ward, shortstop, and Camp, centerfielder of the Charleston club have been sold to the New York American league club, delivery to be made after the South Atlantic league season closes.

DECISIONS ANGER RED SOX PITCHER; PUNCHES OWENS

FENWAY PARK, June 23.

AFTER pitching four balls to Morgan of the Washington club in the first game of today's double-header, "Babe" Ruth, pitcher of the Red Sox, became peever at Umpire Owens's decisions and, walking from the pitchers' box, punched the umpire on the jaw.

Thomas, who was catching Ruth, tried to prevent the big pitcher from having more trouble with the umpire, but was brushed aside.

The police, and Boston and Washington players rushed onto the field and managed to stop the trouble.

Ruth was put out of the game and will probably draw an indefinite suspension. Shore was sent in to pitch.

Ruth had been ordered out of the game before he struck Owens.

FIRST INNING.

Doc Ayers was picked by Griff to oppose the Sox. Barry's men have won seven of the eight games played with Washington this season. The umpires are Owens at the plate and McCormick and Dinneen in the field.

SENATORS—After Ruth passed Morgan, Shore went in to pitch, and Agnew to catch, Sam at once caught Morgan stealing, Scott handling the ball. Scott threw out Foster, and Barry went into right field for Milan's fly.—NO RUNS.

RED SOX—Hooper fouled to Henry. Barry died Shanks to Judge. Hobby flied to Milan.—NO RUNS.

SECOND INNNIG.

SENATORS—Both Rice and Judge bounced to the box and were thrown out. Jameison rolled to Hobby and was thrown out, Shore covering first—NO RUNS.

Red Sox—Gardner punched a safety to right, Lewis bunted and when the ball badly for Judge, he beat it out. Walker socrificed the pair along, Ayers to Morgan, who covered first. Scott popped gently to Shanks. Thomas scratched a hit through Foster, scoring Gardner, putting Lewis on third. Ayers tossed Shore out.—ONE RUN.

THIRD INNING.

SENATORS—Scott took Shanks' nasty bounder and got him at first. Henry struck out. Ayers was out, Scott to Hobby—NO RUNS.

RED SOX—Morgan went back and captured Hooper's fly. Foster made a fast play and nipped Barry at first. Hobby sent a long fly to right.—NO RUNS.

FOURTH INNING.

SENATORS—Scott's long throw beat Morgan to first. Gardner picked Foster's foul off the rail of the Senators' dugout. Milan grounded for the box.—NO RUNS.

BABE RUTH
Red Sox Pitcher Who Struck Umpire Owens in Today's Game.

SENATORS.	RED SOX.
Morgan, 2b.	Hooper, r.f.
Foster, 3b.	Barry, 2b.
Milan, c.f.	Hoblitzell, 1b.
Rice, r.f	Gardner, 3b.
Judge, 1b.	Lewis, l.f.
Jamieson, l.f.	Walker, c.f.
Shanks, s.s.	Scott, s.s.
Henry, c.	Thomas, c.
Ayers, p.	Shore, p.

Umpires—Owens at plate, McCromcik and Dineen on bases.

BRAVES GAME

LINE-UP

BOSTON.	BROOKLYN.
Kelly, c.f.	Olson, s.s.
Evers, 2b.	Daubert, 1b.
Wilhoit, r.f.	Hickman, c.f.
Magee, l.f.	Stengel, r.f.
Konetchy, 1b.	Wheat, l.f.
Smith, 3b.	Cutshaw, 2b.
Gowdy, c.	Mowrey, 3b.
Maranville, s.s.	Miller, c.
Barnes, p.	Cadore, p.

Umpires—Rigler and Orth.

BROOKLYN, June 23—The Braves and Dodgers clashed here today in a double-header before a big crowd. Barnes was selected to pitch for Boston and Cadore for Brooklyn, in the first game.

FIRST INNING.

BOSTON—Kelly singled to centre, Evers to pitcher, Kelly going to second, Wilhoit forced Evers, Cutshaw to Olson, Kelly taking third, Magee fanned. On the third strike a double steal was tried but Wilhoit was out, Miller to Cutshaw to Daubert, before Kelly could score.—NO RUNS.

BROOKLYN—Olson flied to Kelly, Daubert singled to right. Hickman beat out a hit to short. Stengel tripled to centre, scoring Daubert and Hickman. Wheat doubled to centre, scoring Stengel. Cutshaw flied to Kelly, so did Mowrey.—3 RUNS.

SECOND INNING.

BOSTON—Cutshaw threw out Konetchy. Olson threw out Smith. Mowrey threw out Gowdy.—NO RUNS.

BROOKLYN—Miler singled to left, Cadore faned. Olson singled to Konetchy, Miller taking second; Daubert hit into a double play. Maranville to Evers to Konetchy.—NO RUNS.

THIRD INNING.

BOSTON—Olson tossed out Maranville. Barnes singled to left. Kelly flied to Wheat. Evers lofted to Daubert.—NO RUNS.

BROOKLYN—Maranville tossed out Hickman. Stengel flied to Kelly. Maranville tossed out Wheat.—NO RUNS.

FOURTH INNING.

BOSTON—Wilhoit popped to Daubert. Magee flied to Stengel, Konetchy walked and took third on a wild pitch, Smith flied out to Wheat—NO RUNS.

BROOKLYN—Cutshaw lined out to Kelly. Mowrey struck out. Miller popped to Maranville.—NO RUNS.

FIFTH INNING.

BOSTON—Cutshaw tossed out Gowdy. Olson threw out Maranville. Barnes popped to Olson.—NO RUNS.

BROOKLY—Cadore lined out to Kelly. Olson popped to Gowdy, Daubert singled to centre, and was out stealing, Gowdy to Maranville—NO RUNS.

HOUSE CHEERS BAKHMETIEFF

WASHINGTON, June 23—A storm of cheers that echoed and reverberated throughout the Capitol greeted Prof. Boris Bakhmetieff, head of the Russian mission and new ambassador to the United States when he told the House today that "Russia rejects any idea of a separate peace."

"The statement that Russia has wanted a separate peace is without foundation of any kind," Bakhmetieff said. "Russia is for the establishment of a firm and lasting peace between Democratic nations.

"German autocracy renders such a peace impossible. It is always a menace to Russian freedom.

"The new Russia is organizing its armies for action in common with its allies. Russia will not fail to be a worthy partner in the league of honor."

AWARD CAMP CONTRACTS

WASHINGTON, June 23—The war department today awarded the three remaining contracts for cantonment camps.

The Annapolis junction cantonment went to Smith, Hauser and M. F. McIsaac, New York city; Little Rock, Ark., to James Stewart & Co., Chicago; Yaphank, L. I., to Thompson Starrett Company, New York.

FORESTER MADE MAJOR

PARIS, June 23—Among the latest re-enforcements to the American military mission is Maj. Harry Solon Graves, chief forester of the United States, who was commissioned a major in the reserves when he volunteered to investigate forestry conditions in France. He will consider the feasibility of bringing over a regiment of American woodsmen to aid in the conservation of French forests.

Red Sox Defeat All-Stars — Braves Finally Bow to Reds

Red Sox and Stars Make Murnane Day Success

Brilliant Baseball and Many Special Events Are Provided for 17,000 Fans—Barrys Win, 2 to 0, from the Wonders.

ALL-STARS WHO PLAYED BALL ON MURNANE MEMORIAL DAY AT FENWAY PARK

Reds Raid Hughes in One Round and Win Game

Five-Run Rally in Second Round Enough, but Another Tally Is Added for Luck—Eller Is Good in the Pinches

ALL-STARS WHO PLAYED BALL ON MURNANE MEMORIAL DAY AT FENWAY PARK

Back Row (Left to Right)—H. Jennings, Detroit; W. Johnson, Washington; J. McInnis, Athletics; S. O'Neill, Cleveland; J. Jackson, Chicago; Connie Mack, Athletics; R. Chapman, Cleveland; T. Cobb, Detroit; S. Weaver, Chicago; Willie O'Connor, Mascot. Front Row—H. Ehmke, Detroit; Walter Maranville, Braves; W. Schang, Athletics; T. Speaker, Cleveland; U. Shocker, New York Yankees; Tom Raftery.

the distance in 14 seconds, which is a remarkable performance, all the more solid because he started from a right handed batting position, with high grade time keepers on the job.

The funniest happening was the throwing for accuracy. Agnew, O'Neill, Schang, Maranville, Thomas, Cobb, Jackson, Walker, Mayer, Hooper, Lewis Johnson and Speaker all took three shots at the barrel rigged up cannon wise on an empty tonic case over second base. None even hit the barrel on the fly. Then up stepped happy Dutch Leonard, southpaw artist. His very first peg, an easy, half side-arm sweep, pushed the ball through the geometrical centre of the bottom of the barrel, clean as a whistle. The prize was his forthwith, minus any more throws. All the winners were given handsome loving cups, the gifts of special admirers of Murnane.

Game Itself Sparkled.

The game itself was a gem. The best play was in the sixth at the expense of the Red Sox. Hoblitzell tried to score from second base on Walker's single to centre field. At that particular time Joe Jackson was patrolling the centre field stretch—Ty, Tris and Joe alternated in all three fields—and he picked up the ball and threw on a line to Catcher Schang. The latter caught the ball a few feet down the first base line and then dove for the insliding Hobby, just managing to touch out the latter by less than a foot, a beautiful, daring play, which will live forever with those who saw it unfold.

In the fourth Weaver hit into a fast double play which Gardner started but on which Barry pivoted perfectly. The very last putout of the game was a foul catch by the intrepid Thomas, who held the ball off McInnis's bat after

Hobby's bounding single over second. Then Lewis tripled, two balls and one strike, to distant right centre and the two runs were over, the game as well.

Summary of Special Events.

Throwing baseball for distance—Won by Joe Jackson, Chicago (A.), distance, 296ft. 8in.; second, George Lewis, Boston (A.), distance, 384ft. ½in.; third, Clarence Walker, Boston (A.), distance, 383ft. ½in.

Fungo batting for distance—Won by George Ruth, Boston (A.), distance, 402ft. 8in.; second Carl Mays, Boston (A.), distance, 373ft.; third, Walter Johnson, Washington (A.), distance, 360ft.

Running to first after bunt, from left-handed position—Won by Michael McNally, Boston (A.), time 3 1-5s., equalling record; second, Ty Cobb, Detroit, Walter Maranville, Boston (N.), Harold Janvrin, Boston (A.), Harry Hooper, Boston (A.). Time—5 2-5s.

Circling bases after bunt—Won by Ray Chapman, Cleveland, time 14s.; second, Harry Hooper, Boston (A.), time 14 2-5s.; third, Michael McNally, Boston (A.), time 14 3-5s.

Throwing from home to second for accuracy—Won by Hubert Leonard, Boston (A.).

NOTES OF MURNANE DAY

A lot of fun, a lot of arguments settled forever and a lot of good enough baseball crowded into nine innings.

If good Tim were only alive to enjoy such an afternoon of great sport.

Where do the Red Sox stand in the baseball world? They've beaten one of the best teams that could be gathered together and yet they are only runners-up in their league.

Will Rogers of the Follies won the lariat contest without much effort, although Tris Speaker did swing the rope with the cleverness of a full-fledged cowboy.

The spirit of the All-Stars was immense. They seemed to get more fun out of the occasion than the fans. Yet the ball game was a serious affair, with both teams giving their best efforts.

Cobb, Speaker and Jackson crossed up the crowd. It looked for a time as though the question of the leading centrefielder would be settled, but the three outfielders changed positions every inning.

The warm applause that Buck Weaver received on his first trip to the plate must have made the Chicago boy feel happy. Local fans appreciate a good ball player and Buck's trip over to help out yesterday's occasion put him in solid with the crowd.

Willie Connor, the Braves mascot, slung bats for the All-Stars.

When Rabbit Maranville went to the bat to start the game a fan remarked that the local city series was about to begin.

Will Rogers, togged out in a Red Sox sweater and straw hat, took care of first base coaching for the Sox. Will urged the Sox to go after the bush leaguers and beat them up.

Hugh Jennings was in rare form on third base. Hugh had to stand a lot of joshing from the crowd. "How would you like to manage a team like that, Hughie?" was a popular query to sorrel top.

While Jackson grabbed the long distance throwing honors, the pegs of Walker, Speaker and Lewis were the most accurate to the plate.

Before the announcer gave out Cobb's time going down to first one fan suggested that the time was 1 1-5 seconds.

The girls from the Follies show were right on the job. They did a hustling business with score cards.

The dash Will Rogers made around the field on his black mare with a lariat twirling in a big noose was picturesque. Rogers finished at home plate and gathering all the players around his horse dropped the noose and lassoed about 25 ball players.

Ty Cobb mounted the horse and did a few dashes up and down the field.

Lewis cheated in the dash to first stunt when he ran 15 feet before he hit the ball. The crowd appreciated the joke.

John L. Sullivan and the Rabbit furnished a laugh when the little fellow squared off to the old gladiator after the latter had declared him out at first.

Dr. Kelly, now of Buenos Ayres, who umpired his first game in 1866 and is still umpiring in his home city, was among those present. Dr. Kelly was an old friend of the late Tim.

The Buffalo groundkeeper sent $1 to the fund and regretted he could not send more.

The baseball events were conducted in clever style, which emphasized the value of experienced men on the job.

The prizes were gifts of Charles H. Taylor.

The advance choice for the second game looks to be Poll Perritt vs. Tex Russell.

Poll hails from Louisiana. Russell is a Mississippi product. The Louisiana Lath from down among the bayous got a slow start, hit his stride late in June, and ever since has been tearing the trail wide open. He has won about nine-tenths of his starts since June. With a fast, rib-ripping sweep, Perritt should be one of the most effective pitchers of the series. No lath is easy to hit at 60 feet. And Perritt makes a lath look bulky.

Russell is back upon one of his best years. He has won about 80 per cent. of his games and has been highly effective. In the last stages of the campaign he hasn't been quite as effective as Perritt, and if these two meet, the Giants' right hander will have none the worse of the advance dope. Both men have been under fire long enough to hold their balance. The gap separating their effectiveness isn't very wide. Perritt is a bit more pointed toward a low-hit game.

The Third Game

Schupp and Perritt will work Saturday and Sunday for New York. Cicotte and Russell will work the first two games for Chicago. The third game, the New York opener, will not be played until Tuesday. This means that McGraw and Rowland, if they care to, can easily start Cicotte and Schupp again with a three-day rest.

They may adopt these tactics. But if they switch, McGraw will very possibly send Slim Sallee against the Sox, while Rowland counters with Red Faber against the Giants.

Sallee is a veteran of extended standing—a wise, cool left hander who has been pitching for over 12 years.

A clash between these two would be a clash of opposites, for Faber is a big, young right hander, with fine speed, whereas Sallee relies very little on a fast ball which is none too fast.

American leaguers believe that Faber will be effective against the Giants and a hard man for them to beat. He isn't as steady nor yet as experienced as Sallee, but a fast ball under control covers up a multitude of deficits.

In the way of a season's effectiveness, these two are closely upon a par.

The Fourth Choice

The fourth choice in each camp probably will be Rube Benton for the Giants and Williams for the Sox—both left handers who have completed good years.

It is a matter of more than hazy doubt as to whether Benton or Williams will start a game where two or three pitchers can easily do the bulk of the work. Williams has won more games than Benton and has had a somewhat better season from the start.

The Two Staffs

Chicago looks to have a somewhat stronger staff, but the belief in many quarters that New York's pitching contingent is weak and uncertain is out of line with the facts.

Schupp and Perritt will be hard to hit, and Schupp and Perritt can easily pitch four or five of the first six games.

Cicotte, Russell and Faber should be just a whit more effective, but the difference, so far as standard season values go, isn't very thick. There is no such preponderance on one side as the Red Sox had with Ruth, Leonard and Shore. If pitching alone is to decide the issue, it should go to seven games. But the pitching on neither side is decisive enough to give either club any undue advantage.

(Tomorrow—The Catching.)

Innings	1	2	3	4	5	6	7	8	9	
Chicago	2	1	3	0	0	0	0	0	0	—6
Washington	0	1	0	0	0	0	0	0	0	—1

Runs—McMullin, E. Collins, Felsch, Murphy, Gandil, Lynn, Gharrity. Two-base hit—Risberg. Stolen bases—E. Collins, Milan. Sacrifice hit—Benz. Sacrifice fly—Lynn. Double play—Hasbrook to Risberg to Jourdan. Left on bases—Chicago 10, Washington 5. First base on errors—Chicago 1. First base on balls—Off Shaw 2, off Benz 1, off Gallia 2. Hits and earned runs—Off Shaw, 5 and 3 in 2 innings; off Gallia, 5 and 3 in 6 innings; off Craft, 2 and 0 in 1 inning; off Benz, 6 and 1 in 9 innings. Struck out—By Benz 2, by Shaw 1, by Gallia 4, by Craft 1. Umpires—O'Loughlin and Moriarity. Time—1h. 40m.

*Batted for Gallia in 8th.

Scott, who pitched brilliantly in the tie game on Tuesday, worked the last two rounds for the Braves. In the seventh he was stung for singles by Kopf, Neale and Magee, earning a final tally for the Reds.

NOTES OF THE BRAVES

The Braves left tonight for Chicago where they have a short two-game series with the Cubs. They lay off tomorrow, playing single games at Weeghman Park on Saturday and Sunday, which will close the championship season in Chicago. The Braves play one game at Pittsburgh on Monday, closing the season for the Pirates

INDIANAPOLIS IN LEAD

TORONTO, Sept. 27—Indianapolis won the third game of the inter-league series from Toronto today, 9 to 3, making the American Association champions the victors in two of the three games played here. Both teams left tonight for Indianapolis.

Innings	1	2	3	4	5	6	7	8	9	r.	h.	e.
Indianapolis	0	0	0	1	0	1	0	5	2	—9	11	0
Toronto	0	0	0	0	0	0	0	3	0	—3	7	3

Batteries—Northrop and Gossett; Leake and LaLonge.

WEATHER
Fair; Warmer.

The Detroit Free Press

MICHIGAN'S GREATEST NEWSPAPER

LAST EDITION

VOL. 83, NO. 10. DETROIT, MICHIGAN, SUNDAY, OCTOBER 7, 1917.—NINETY-FOUR PAGES. PRICE: In Detroit......6c Elsewhere......7c

PAVING MERGER HIT IN JUDGE'S SECOND BLAST

Charges by Connolly Say "Illegality is Patent and Indefensible."

COMPETITION CUT; PRICES ADVANCED

Dissolution of Combine Urged; City Divided Into Four Parts.

Charging that the Detroit Asphalt Paving company is a merger whose "illegality is so patent as to be indefensible," Judge William F. Connolly, in his second grand jury presentment, issued Saturday, urges that prompt steps should be taken to dissolve the corporation, "for whose existence there can be no legal excuse or warrant."

Laying bare a small part of the detailed evidence, in what he says is "designedly a conservative statement of the facts in testimony," Judge Connolly shows how paving competition in Detroit has been stifled for the last three years; how paving prices have gone steadily upward under the manipulation of the combine, and how the city has been divided into four parts by the members of the combine, which has worked on the basis of "all for one and one for all."

Wm. E. Currie Devised Combine.

William E. Currie, master mind of the combine, who frankly admitted being the father of the organization, according to the presentment, is president of the Detroit Asphalt Paving company and is also the head of Thomas E. Currie company, one of the four units of the paving trust.

The other members are John A. Mercier, who occasionally appears as an individual bidder on paving contracts, though President Currie says the Detroit Asphalt Paving company does all the work; Richard Porath, Julius Porath and Thomas E. Currie, the latter being the nominal head of the William E. Currie interests.

Up to 1915 there was some competition in city paving, when reinforced concrete was permitted in city streets, but at that time, Detroit paving specifications were shaped to eliminate the reinforced concrete for street paving. It is used on a few small alley jobs, but that is all.

Incorporated in 1914.

And in connection with the shaping of the specifications, it is interesting to note that the Detroit Asphalt Paving company, which deals in "asphaltic concrete," the specified pavement, was incorporated in 1914.

Referring to that part of the program, Judge Connolly says:

"The allegations with reference to this action are of such a serious and blasting nature that I hesitate to give them publicity without further substantiation of their accuracy."

How City Was Divided.

Pointing out how the Curries took the southeastern part of the city for "their territory;" how Mercier took the northeastern part, Julius Porath the northwestern part, and Ferdinand Porath and son the southwestern part, and how the Cleveland Trinidad Paving company was "allowed" to do all the work north of the boulevard, Judge Connolly raps the city government when he says, "It is obvious that the facts disclosed lay close to the surface, and this is but an indication of what might

Continued on Page Twelve, Column Two.

MICHIGAN GOAL IS $124,000,000

Detroit and Wayne County Organization Perfected for Second Loan Drive.

MONDAY MASS MEETING CAMPAIGN'S BIG EVENT

Dr. Newell Dwight Hillis Will Be Principal Speaker at Armory Assembly.

With its Detroit and Wayne county organization perfected and including fully 10,000 people from every branch of industry, and with chairmen in its other 82 counties completing the final details for their campaigns, Michigan is set and ready for the great drive starting Monday morning for the $124,000,000 that is its apportionment of the second Liberty loan of $3,000,000,000.

Every one of Wayne county's 10,000 workers, among which are 100 organized teams that begin their work early Monday, received his final instructions Saturday afternoon at the headquarters of the executive committee in the Detroit Board of Commerce building.

Pastors to Present Plea.

Sunday is Liberty loan day. Pastors of every denomination in Detroit will tell their congregations the investment opportunities afforded by government bonds, and also will lay stress on the importance of backing up the country financially and equipping the men who have been selected for service abroad.

Many activities are planned for Monday. First of all there will be a noon-day meeting in the Board of Commerce auditorium, at which all team captains and their co-workers are expected to be present. These will be held daily during the intensive drive, and announcements will be received from the captains of the amount of the subscriptions received.

The mass meeting in the Detroit armory at 8 o'clock Monday night will be the big event of the campaign. Dr. Newell Dwight Hillis, pastor of Plymouth church, Brooklyn, a speaker of international reputation, and several Detroit men will speak. Dr. Hillis recently returned from the front and will recount many of his experiences, relating some of the terrible atrocities of the Germans. For the bond salesmen tickets to the mass meeting will be given out at the Monday noon meeting. The 500 Detroit business men who volunteered to sponsor the mass assemblage also will receive tickets at the Board of Commerce.

Special Musical Program.

Racicot's choir, of SS. Peter and Paul's cathedral, will sing the "Marseillaise" in French. A big military band will play several patriotic numbers, and the meeting will be preceded by a parade in which the men who have volunteered to serve as bond salesmen will march to the armory. Abner E. Larned, chairman of the bond sales committee, will preside.

Mayor Marx will issue a proclamation Monday calling the attention of the citizens to the urgent necessity of subscribing to the government bonds. At the same time the

Continued on Page Four, Column Five.

THEIR DEFENSIVE PLAY AIDED GREATLY IN DEFEAT OF GIANTS

EDDIE COLLINS.

JOE JACKSON.

These clever fielders delivered the fielding features of the first game of the world's series at Chicago Saturday. Jackson cut off a certain run by a spectacular catch, after which he turned a summersault, while Collins was a rock on which the New York Nationals split at second base.

WHITE SOX BEAT GIANTS IN FIRST GAME FOR TITLE

Eddie Cicotte Wins Over Sallee By Score of 2 to 1.

FELSCH'S HOME RUN DECIDING FACTOR

Huge Crowd Sees Teams Clash for Highest Baseball Honors.

BY E. A. BATCHELOR.

Chicago, Oct. 6.—These Germans aren't so bad after all, if you catch them young enough and remove them from the baneful influence of the Kaiser and his pals.

Take this fellow "Hap" Felsch, for example. He is a German right from Milwaukee, but he made a lot of Americans very joyous this afternoon, when he stepped up and prodded one of Sallee's curves clear out of the park and gave Chicago what proved to be the winning run of the first game of the world's series. The Sox by bunching two singles and a double had previously acquired one marker and Felsch's lick finished their scoring for the day. New York made just one run, a triple by McCarthy and an unexpected but none the less welcome single from Sallee producing it in the fifth inning.

It was a typical world's series game, featured by good pitching on both sides and by a few brilliant fielding plays but for the most part rather prosy. There wasn't much chance for either club to start one of those soul-stirring rallies in which everybody but the groundkeeper bats. It was hard to get even one hit an inning and next to impossible to make more. Once the Giants got a couple together and another time the Sox combined three but these were the only things approaching concerted attack.

Cicotte At His Best.

Of course Eddie Cicotte pitched for the Sox. Manager Rowland made the wise move in leading his ace. Every Detroiter has reason to throw out his chest over the performance of our fellow citizens, too. He not only lived up to his reputation as the best pitcher in the American league this year, but was even better in this crisis than he usually is. Cool, crafty and possessed of an array of stuff that served completely to execute the Giants, he was master of the situation at all times, getting better and better as the game progressed.

New York made seven hits off Eddie, including a double and the triple that averted a shutout. Six of these came in the first five innings and one of them was the veriest scratch, made possible by Gandil's bad judgment in leaving his bag to try for a ground ball that Collins fielded only to have no place to chuck it. In the last four rounds, Cicotte faced only 13 men, one of these hitting and another receiving a life on Weaver's bad throw, the only Chicago error. The little Frenchman had almost perfect control, once throwing 13 balls in a row straight over the plate. He had the Giants chasing bad balls and groping around for his "shiner" and "knuckler" like myopic old maids.

Used Good Judgment.

One of the most impressive things about Cicotte was his splendid judgment. He knew just what to pitch at all times and was able to get the ball right where he wanted it. He didn't really get all his numerous kinds of bafflers going until the middle of the game, but when he once unlimbered his broadside batteries, the Giants folded up like an accordion. All the reputed murderous tendencies of the National leaguers were held in abeyance and in the latter part of the contest. McGraw's people seemed to be showing very little spirit.

"Slim" Sallee pitched a splendid game himself and, omitting the German uprising in the fourth, would have had an even break with Cicotte. He, like his opponent, was tapped for seven safeties, three of them extra basers, but the Sox hit him harder than the Giants did Cicotte, several safeties being stolen from them by bad luck or good

Continued on Page 19, Column 7

FORD TRIP PART OF BERLIN PLOT

Detroiter Innocent Victim of Mme. Schwimmer, Aid to Von Bernstorff.

RUSSIAN COMMISSION IN TRAITOR CLIQUE

Bernstein Expose Shows That Nicholas Led Ring to Betray Slavs.

BY HERMAN BERNSTEIN.

New York, Oct, 6.—Russia was betrayed in this war by Czarina Alexandra, now exiled with the Czar in Siberia.

Russia was betrayed by Permier Stuermer, who died a prisoner on the eve of his trial for high treason.

Russia was betrayed by Minister of the Interior Protopopoff, a creature of Rasputin, and he is now awaiting his fate in the fortress of Peter and Paul.

Russia was betrayed by War Minister Soukhomlinoff, now condemned to imprisonment for life at hard labor.

Russia was betrayed by Colonel Myasoyedov, who was killed by the old regime in great haste for fear lest he might name his fellow conspirators and traitors in the highest places.

German spies and agents, provocateurs, have worked in Russia uninterruptedly and brazenly throughout the war. They were active in the palaces of the Czar, in the cabinet, in the police department and at headquarters of the general staff.

Generals in Conspiracy.

Russian generals, sympathizing with Germany for many reasons and knowing the spirit and will of their masters, betrayed Russia to Germany. The old regime betrayed the people of Russia and thus also betrayed Russia's allies.

Hundreds of thousands of lives, the flower of Russia, were sacrificed on the battlefields, victims of this conspiracy.

The revolution came in a large measure as a protest against this stupendous betrayal.

Germany's system of espionage in Russia was built long before the outbreak of the war. During the war the German government worked unhindered within the Russian empire and not a single Russian military secret remained a secret to the German military staff.

Mr. Spann, brother of a member of the Kaiser's cabinet, was director of the Putiloff works, the largest munitions factory in Russia. There were mysterious explosions in the Putiloff works in the course of the war. There were repeated labor disorders among the tens of thousands of laborers in the Putiloff works, and large supplies of munitions were stored at the weakest points at the front, which fell into the hands of the Germans.

During the old regime Spann was charged with treason. As he was

Continued on Page Three, Column One.

COAL PROMISED CITY 'AT ONCE'

Detroit Relief Committee's Plea Stirs Action at Washington.

More Than Quarter Million Tons Less Here Now Than Year Ago.

From the Washington Bureau of The Detroit Free Press, 401 Metropolitan Bldg.

Washington, Oct. 6.—City Controller George Engel, Engineering Inspector John C. McCabe and Chairman A. T. Waterfall, of the traffic committee of the Board of Commerce, who spent most of Friday and the morning of Saturday urging upon Fuel Administrator Garfield and other government officials the seriousness of the coal situation at Detroit, were much encouraged when they boarded the train for home today.

Controller Engel made this statement for the committee to the Free Press:

"We have telegraphed Mayor Marx that Fuel Administrator Garfield promised immediate relief. Dr. Garfield told us that the people who supply the dealers in Detroit will be instructed to ship immediately more coal than they have been shipping within the past three weeks. This applies to anthracite as well as to bituminous.

"We were instructed to make a careful survey of Detroit's future requirements of coal based upon absolute facts, and were assured by Dr. Garfield that everything will be done. No hoarding of coal will be permitted.

"Conditions in the country at large warrant only such supply as is necessary to take care of actual needs. It will be the administrative duty and function of each municipality to make an accurate survey to show just what is the extent of these needs."

Detroit's Coal Supply Far Behind This Time Last Year

Detroit and Wayne county have now on hand 252,000 tons less of hard coal than they had at this time last year, according to statistics made public in Washington Saturday by the national fuel administration.

The soft coal shortage is placed at 236,000 tons, but it is explained that this figure is not as nearly accurate as that for hard coal, as purchases of large industrial firms, direct from producers, are not included.

If Michigan should not receive its full quota of fuel, the coal committee stated, the 30 per cent of coal dealers of the state, who refused to give the committee the data requested, must be held to blame.

Otherwise there is little change in the situation. City Fuel Expert Charles A. Wertz believes he will be able to obtain sufficient coal to meet the requirements of the public schools, public lighting plant and all other municipal departments. From 20,000 to 25,000 tons are needed to complete the schools' stock for the winter.

The 7,000 tons of coal recently received by Van Antwerp & Co., with which the Burroughs Adding Machine company is being supplied, was contracted for last June before the government fixed prices, not lately, as was stated. Six dollars a ton was paid for this supply by Van Antwerp & Co.

OFFICIAL SCORE

CHICAGO AMERICANS.

	AB	R	H	TB	SH	SB	O	A	E
J. Collins, rf	4	1	3	4	0	0	1	0	0
McMullin, 3b	3	0	1	2	1	0	0	3	0
E. Collins, 2b	3	0	0	0	0	0	2	1	0
Jackson, lf	3	0	0	0	0	0	5	0	0
Felsch, cf	3	1	1	4	0	0	4	0	0
Gandil, 1b	3	0	1	1	0	1	10	1	0
Weaver, ss	3	0	0	0	0	0	2	1	1
Schalk, c	3	0	0	0	0	0	3	0	0
Cicotte, p	3	0	1	1	0	0	0	4	0
Totals	28	2	7	12	1	1	27	10	1

NEW YORK NATIONALS.

	AB	R	H	TB	SH	SB	O	A	E
Burns, lf	3	0	1	1	0	1	2	0	0
Herzog, 2b	4	0	1	1	0	0	3	1	0
Kauff, cf	4	0	0	0	0	0	0	0	0
Zimmerman, 3b	4	0	0	0	0	0	1	3	0
Fletcher, ss	4	0	0	0	0	0	2	3	0
Robertson, rf	4	0	1	2	0	0	0	1	0
Holke, 1b	3	0	2	2	0	0	14	0	0
McCarty, c	3	1	1	3	0	0	2	1	1
Sallee, p	3	0	1	1	0	0	0	6	0
Totals	32	1	7	10	0	1	24	15	1

Innings	1	2	3	4	5	6	7	8	9—R
New York Nationals	0	0	0	0	1	0	0	0	0—1
Chicago Americans	0	0	1	1	0	0	0	0	x—2

Three-base hit—McCarty.
Two-base hits—McMullin, Robertson, J. Collins.
Home run—Felsch.
Double plays—Weaver to E. Collins to Gandil.
Left on bases—New York Nationals 5; Chicago Americans 3.
First base on errors—New York Nationals 1.
Bases on balls—Off Cicotte 1.
Hits and earned runs—Off Sallee, 2 runs in 8 innings; off Cicotte, 1 run in 9.
Struck out—By Cicotte 2; Sallee 2.
Umpires—O'Loughlin behind the plate; Klem at first base; Rigler at second base; Evans at third base.
Time—1:48.

DETROIT GAINS 94,118 IN YEAR

1917 City Directory, Just Out, Indicates Population of City is 914,896.

Remarkable Expansion of Industries and Activities is Recorded.

"Dynamic Detroit" is shown to have a population of 914,896 by R. L. Polk & Co.'s 1917 city directory, just issued from the press. The volume contains 407,402 individual names, an increase of 40,921 over the number of names in the 1916 issue.

Formerly it was customary to compute the total population by multiplying the number of names by 2.3 to allow for women and children not included. This multiple 2.3 has been found conservative and were it applied this year the estimated population for Greater Detroit would be 937,024.

Gain in Year is 94,118.

However, the publishers followed the plan adopted in 1911. The multiple 2.3 has been applied only to the increased number of names appearing in Detroit since 1910 and the result added to the figures of the United States census of this year. The increase in population figured on this basis from 1911 to 1914, inclusive, was 328,083. Add to these figures 94,118, the estimated increase in population during the past year based on the increase of 40,921 names in this issue of the directory, and we have a net increase in population of 422,201 since 1910, which, added to the United States census of that year, 492,695, gives Greater Detroit an estimated population July 1, 1917, of 914,896.

The volume contains in the introductory a mass of statistics touching almost every phase of the city's activities furnished from official sources. The offer convincing evidence of Detroit's continued prosperity and show the growth of the city in population, manufacturing and investment. A chronology gives important items concerning the city from 1697 to 1917.

Work Larger Than Ever.

The work contains 2,642 pages and is made up in different form from previous issues. To provide for the enormous increase in information contained in the directory without making it unwieldly and without eliminating any of the information given heretofore, the pages have been lengthened to permit more names to the column and widened to allow for three in place of two columns in the list of names as in the former editions and five columns in the street and householders' directory. The pages are

Continued on Page Four, Column Four.

9 BROUGHT HERE AS AUTO THIEVES

Two Groups of Prisoners Face Trial in Detroit.

Nine alleged automobile thieves, who were arrested in Nashville, Tenn., and Dayton, O., were brought back to Detroit Saturday night. John Casper, Edward Leonard, Ernest Harrison and Frank Sepler are charged with stealing a car from the Hudson Motor company last January.

The car was abandoned in Bowling Green, Ky., and, police say, the four men stole another auto in that city. For attempting to steal an auto in Nashville, they were arrested, and sentenced to serve six months in prison. When their time was up a few days ago, they were rearrested by Detectives Potter and Wright, and brought to Detroit.

Harry A. Lewis, Lewis Pomerchiek, Norman Bushey, Robert Trombley and Max Glet are charged with stealing a car owned by the Leonard B. Orloss company. They were captured by Dayton police and brought back here by Detectives Hogan and Graus.

All are charged with grand larceny.

BLOODY STRIKE GRIPS NORTHERN ARGENTINA

Special to The Free Press.

Buenos Ayres, Oct. 6.—Strike riots broke out in northern sections of Argentina tonight. All negotiations for a settlement of the strike have been fruitless. Details of the riots in the north are lacking, but reports state there was considerable bloodshed.

MILITANT WOMEN SEIZED BY POLICE

Alice Paul, Chief, Taken With 10 White House Pickets.

Special to The Free Press.

Washington, Oct. 6.—Prompt arrest greeted 11 suffragists who attempted to revive White House picketing today.

They were later released on $25 bail each, which was left in their behalf by Mrs. John Branham, of Baltimore.

Those arrested were Alice Paul, Moorestown, N. J., leader of the party; Frances Kahl, Buffalo, N. Y.; Maud Jameson, Washington; Kate Heffelfinger, Shamokin, Pa.; Vivian Pearce, San Diego, Cal.; Lou Daniels, Washington, D. C.; Minnie Honesy, Hartford, Ct.; Joy Young, New York city; Matilda Young, Washington; Rose Winslow, New York, and Elizabeth Spencer, Colorado Springs.

BRIDES JILT TWO, FEARING 'OFF TO WAR'

Grooms Find Their Licenses Useless; Return Them to Marriage Bureau.

There are many slips 'twixt a marriage license and a wedding ceremony. William H. Duthie and Frank Jakubiak found so, much to their displeasure and returned unused licenses to Joseph Pilarski, marriage license clerk, Saturday.

The young men are very much in the prime of life, 27 years old, and subject to draft. That is the reason the brides balked at taking a chance.

Mrs. Elva Duffy, 24 years old, was to have been married to Jakubiak, but feared losing a second husband when she learned he was subject to military duty.

William H. Duthie, 28 years old, who is a student in the aviation camp at Mt. Clemens, took out a license to marry Agnes A. Flanagan, who recently arrived from London. Agnes said she was going to marry him only on condition he brought back the Kaiser's head.

NEGRO SHOTS KILL 3 IN WHITE POSSE

But One of Seven Unscathed in Alabama Fight.

Montgomery, Ala., Oct. 6.—In a battle over a Negro, three white men are dead and three wounded at La Pine, 35 miles south of here.

The shooting was done when a posse with a warrant went to Oliver Enger's home to demand he give up the Negro, wanted for holding up a white man. Their summons was met with a hail of shot from the Negro's house.

Enzer, W. L. Griffith and Hub Cannon were shot dead. Hugh Enzer was so badly wounded he will die; Professor L. H. Hudson and Justin Enzer also were wounded, but less seriously. The sheriff and more men immediately went to La Pine.

Only one man of seven engaged in the fight escaped death or injury.

WARM DAYS, THEN COOL, WEEK'S WEATHER MENU

Washington, Oct. 6.—Weather predictions for the Great Lakes region for the week beginning Sunday, issued by the weather bureau today are: Frequent alternations from warm to cool and probably showers about Wednesday and again at end of week; warmer Sunday followed by cooler Monday or Tuesday.

'DRY' HEADS NEW NATIONAL PARTY

Tennessee Prohibitionist is Chosen as Chairman.

Chicago, Oct. 6.—The new National party, which was formed here by an amalgamation of Prohibitionists, Progressives, Independents, Social-Democrats and Single Taxers, has selected Dr. Ira Landrith, of Tennessee, Prohibitionist candidate for vice-president in 1916, as permanent chairman. His headquarters will be in Chicago.

Fred H. Chase, of New York, a Progressive, has been selected as secretary. A Social-Democrat is to be named assistant secretary and W. F. Cochran, of Baltimore, an Independent, is to serve as treasurer.

Plans of the new party call for the publication of a propaganda pamphlet of which John Spargo, of Vermont, is to be the author. A national convention is to be held next spring.

PARIS EDITOR EXPLAINS CHARGES OF SEDITION

Paris, Oct. 6.—Captain Bouchardon, of the Paris military court, investigator into various charges made recently of traitorous or seditious conduct, began today to take the deposition of Leon Daudet, newspaper editor.

In a letter to President Poincare Daudet recently accused Louis J. Malvy, formerly minister of the interior, of traitorous conduct in betraying military secrets.

L'Action Francaise, M. Daudet's newspaper, again was seized today on account of an article it contained signed by M. Daudet.

GERARD'S EXPOSE TODAY

Printed on Page One, Metropolitan Section, Describes the First Meeting with the Emperor.

To impress the new ambassador, Emperor Wilhelm donned the uniform of the Death's Head Hussars, of which he is high commander. He condescended to unbend after formalities. There followed a life close to the imperial court for Gerard, which that democratic American reveals in all its ramifications. Read the story in the former ambassador's revelations on Page One, Metropolitan Section, of today's Detroit Free Press.

TURMEL ARRESTED AS FRENCH TRAITOR

Deputy Is Accused of Taking Bribe From Germany.

Paris, Oct. 6.—Louis Turmel, representing Cotes-De-Nord in the chamber of deputies, was arrested today, accused of commerce with the enemy. The warrant was issued by an examining magistrate.

An official statement issued by the chamber of deputies September 17 s[illegible] envelope containing $5,000 in Swiss bank bills had been found in Deputy Turmel's locker in the building.

Later a news dispatch from Paris stated that M. Turmel refused to explain how he came into possession of the money.

EDSEL FORD LOSES EXEMPTION CLAIM

Board Ruling Leaves an Appeal to Wilson Only Chance.

Edsel B. Ford, vice-president, secretary and director of the Ford Motor company, was denied his claim of exemption from the draft army on the industrial clause, by the Detroit exemption board Saturday.

Unless Mr. Ford appeals to the president of the United States—the only course left to follow, he will be called to service in the second draft.

In his affidavit to the exemption board, Mr. Ford declared he is engaged in the manufacture of farm tractors and army field ambulances and trucks, air craft engines and parts used in signal corps work of the United States army.

According to members of the board, Mr. Ford's claim is denied because his relations with the Ford Motor company are not such as to entitle him to exemption under section 44, part 3, of the rules and regulations prescribed by the president of the United States for local and district boards. The board cited the case of James Couzens, who resigned from the company.

POLES IN AMERICA TO JOIN OWN ARMY

Paderewski Backs Plan; Training Camp to Be Near Niagara.

Washington, Oct. 6.—A campaign to recruit Poles in the United States for a Polish army, now training in France, was indorsed today by the war department.

It will start tomorrow under the direction of the national department of the Polish Central Relief committee of Chicago, whose chairman, I. J. Paderewski, the pianist, issued an appeal today to unnaturalized Poles to enlist.

Recruits will be trained at a camp already established by Polish interests near Niagara-on-the-Lake, Ontario. Polish-American subject to draft and men with dependents will not be accepted.

WORLD'S SERIES — San Francisco Examiner — SPORT PAGES

T TUESDAY SAN FRANCISCO, OCTOBER 16, 1917 TUESDAY C

WHITE SOX WIN THE WORLD'S CHAMPIONSHIP

New York Giants Go Down to Defeat in Final Game of Great Baseball Series by Score of 4 to 2

A VIEW OF THE POLO GROUNDS IN NEW YORK AND TWO OF THE WINNING PITCHERS

Harry (Slim) Sallee of the Giants is in the panel at the left and Eddie Cicotte of the Sox at the right. Photo by the International Film Service.

33,000 FANS LIE BACK AND GASP AS HEINE JOINS THE GOAT CLUB

Scenario of the Fatal Fourth Provides a Close-Up of the Pride of the Bronx, Surrounded by a Spectacle of Horrid Silence

BY DAMON RUNYON

NEW YORK, October 15.—**Scenario:**

The "Fatal Fourth."

Dedication:

Heine, this is AW-ALL for you!

Now a close up of Heine Zimmerman, the pride of the Bronx.

Let the film flicker!

The plot moves this way:

Heine Zimmerman thought he could outrun Eddie Collins.

Now a close up of the figures 4 to 2, the score by which the New York Giants lost the championship of the baseball world to the Chicago White Sox, pennant-winners in the American League.

Now a panoramic view entitled Horrid Silence, depicting that sector of the Polo Grounds back of third base, where all this season the loyal citizens of the Bronx have congregated, booming their baseball battle cry for the favorite son of the region beyond the Harlem;

"Heine, this is ALL for you."

Finally, an interior scene:

The living-room of the goatery of baseball, showing a number of gentlemen of familiar aspect—all members of this club. Here cut in close ups of John Anderson and Fred Merkle and Fred Snodgrass watching the door in attitudes of expectancy; a committee on reception—

"Heine, this is ALL for you!"

A TOUGH TEUTONIC ERA.

Well, it has been a tough era for Teutonic thought, one way and another.

Von Kluck thought he was going to eat a dinner in Paris. The Kaiser thought he could lick the world. Heine Zim thought he could outrun Eddie Collins. It has certainly been tough!

Heine's thought bubbled in his brain to-day until he had chased Eddie Collins across the plate with what proved to be one of the winning runs in the sixth and last game of the world's series of 1917 while 33,000 fans lay back in their seats and gasped, like landed trout, in astonishment.

The balloting for chief goat of the series ended right there.

Poor Heine Zim was unanimously elected.

"Heine," called one voice from the silence back of third as the inning ended, "this is AW-ALL for you."

But even the brave Bronx onions were too stunned to give the old answering whoop.

The "Heine Zimmerman Boosting and Bawling-out Bund," as the congregation of rooters for the redoubtable Zim came to

(Continued on Page 4, Column 1.)

World·Series Box Score

CHICAGO AMERICANS.	AB.	R.	BH.	PO.	A.	E.
J. Collins, rf	3	0	0	1	0	0
Leibold, rf	2	0	1	1	0	0
McMullin, 3b	5	0	0	0	1	0
E. Collins, 2b	4	1	1	1	8	0
Jackson, lf	4	1	1	1	0	0
Felsch, cf	3	1	0	3	0	0
Gandil, 1b	4	0	2	14	0	0
Weaver, ss	4	1	1	2	2	0
Schalk, c	3	0	1	4	1	1
Faber, p	2	0	0	0	0	0
Totals	34	4	7	27	12	1

NEW YORK NATIONALS.	AB.	R.	BH.	PO.	A.	E.
Burns, lf	4	1	0	2	0	0
Herzog, 2b	4	0	2	2	5	0
Kauff, cf	4	0	0	2	0	1
Zimmerman, 3b	4	0	0	1	2	1
Fletcher, ss	4	0	1	1	2	0
Robertson, rf	3	0	1	0	1	1
Holke, 1b	4	0	1	12	0	0
Rariden, c	3	1	0	7	1	0
Benton, p	1	0	0	0	0	0
Wilhoit, *	0	0	0	0	0	0
Perritt, p	1	0	1	0	1	0
McCarty, **	1	0	0	0	0	0
Totals	33	2	6	27	12	3

*—Batted for Benton in fifth.

**—Batted for Perritt in ninth.

Score by innings—	1	2	3	4	5	6	7	8	9	
Chicago	0	0	0	3	0	0	0	0	1	4
New York	0	0	0	0	2	0	0	0	0	2

Two-base hit—Holke. Three-base hit—Herzog. Sacrifice hit—Faber. Left on bases—Chicago, 7; New York, 7. First base on errors—Chicago, 2. Bases on balls—Off Faber, 2; off Benton, 1; off Perritt, 2. Hits and earned runs—Off Faber, hits 6, runs 2 in 9 innings; off Benton, hits 4, runs none in 5 innings; off Perritt, hits 3, runs nine in 4 innings. Hit by pitcher—By Faber (Robertson). Struck out—By Faber, 4; by Benton, 3; by Perritt, 3. Passed ball—Schalk. Umpires—At plate, Klem; first base, O'Loughlin; second base, Evans; third base, Rigler. Time of game—2:18.

The Fatal Fourth

—BY ARTHUR STRUWE—

NEW YORK, October 15.—The "fatal fourth" inning to-day knocked the Giants out of the world's championship and gave the premier honors to the White Sox. It was "fatal" in all that the word implies. The Giants went to pieces in that inning. Two errors and a "bone" play by Zimmerman gave the Sox three runs. It was enough.

The "fatal fourth" has figured in all the games played between the White Sox and the Giants. Here's how the inning figured:

First game—Felsch knocked a home run. It won the game for the Sox.

Second game—The Sox made five runs and won the game.

Third game—Robertson's triple started the Giants on their first victory.

Fourth game—Kouff hit a home run. His hit was enough to win, although the Giants scored five runs.

Fifth game—The Giants made two runs and apparently had the game sewed up, but the Sox won out by tying the score in the seventh and batting out a victory in the eighth.

Sixth and final game—Sox made three runs.

The prize bonehead play of the series fell to Zimmerman's lot. He pulled it in the "fatal" inning. It followed an error he had previously made — and he made them both on Eddie Collins, captain of the victorious team. The team began with Collins' hit to Zim. Heine must have been disconcerted by the Bronx contingent that was on hand to root for the "home boy." He threw wild. Eddie got to second. Then Robertson came into the fracas with a muff of Jackson's high fly. Eddie got to third. This brought "Happy' Felsch up. "Happy" tapped weakly to Benton. Eddie Collins was trapped between third and home. Benton chased him back almost to third, when he threw the ball to Zim. Heine then pulled his bone. He chased Collins, although Rariden was near

(Continued on Page 3, Column 3.)

The Play by Innings

FIRST INNING.

The umpires conferred with the managers at the plate before the game to discuss rules for field discipline.

Judge Hylan, Democratic candidate for mayor threw out the ball.

Chicago—John Collins up. Strike 1. Foul, strike 2. Fletcher came in beind Benton and took Collins' hopper and threw him out.

McMullin up. Ball 1. McMullin sent up a weak foul to Rariden.

Eddie Collins up. The stands booed Eddie Collins to the echo. Strike 1. E. Collins singled sharply over second.

Jackson up. Strike 1. Herzog took Jackson's slow roller and tossed him out.

No runs, one hit, no errors.

New York—Burns up. Eddie Collins threw out Burns at first. Burns hitting the first ball pitched.

Herzog up. Strike 1. Ball 1. Herzog shot a single over McMullin's head, the stands breaking into a cheer.

Kauff up. Foul, strike 1. Strike 2. Ball 1. Kauff struck out, Faber's wide curves being too much for him.

Zimmerman up. Ball 1. Zimmerman sent a long drive right into Jackson's hands.

No runs, one hit, no errors.

SECOND INNING.

Chicago—Felsch up. Strike 1. Ball 1. Ball 2. Strike 2. Ball 3. Felsch struck out, failing to offer at the third strike.

Gandil up. Gandil punched a single over the middle bag.

Weaver up. Herzog threw out Weaver. Gandil moving to second.

Schalk up. Strike 1. Zimmerman threw out Schalk, making a nice play on the Chicago catcher's grounder.

No no runs, one hit, no errors.

New York—Fletcher up. Strike 1. Schalk ran down the line and took Fletcher's roller and threw him out.

Robertson up. Foul, strike 1. Eddie Collins took Robertson's smash and got his man at first.

Holke up. Ball 1. Holke got a double against the left field fence. A little higher it would have gone into the stands for a home run.

Rariden up. Eddie Collins threw out Rariden, who hit the first ball pitched.

No runs, one hit, no errors.

THIRD INNING.

Chicago—Faber up. Ball 1. Strike 2. Foul, strike 2. Foul. Faber struck out.

John Collins up. Foul, strike 1.

(Continued on Page 3, Column 3.)

Dave Robertson Leads World Series Hitters

CHICAGO.	G.	AB.	R.	H.	2B.	3B.	HR.	TB.	SH.	SB.	BB.	SO.	Avg.
Risberg, ut.	2	2	0	1	0	0	0	1	0	0	0	0	.500
E. Collins, 2b	6	22	4	9	1	0	0	10	0	3	2	3	.409
Leibold, rf.	2	5	1	2	0	0	0	2	0	0	1	1	.400
Weaver, ss.	6	21	3	7	1	0	0	8	0	0	0	2	.333
Jackson, lf.	6	23	4	7	0	0	0	7	0	1	1	0	.304
J. Collins, rf.	6	21	2	6	1	0	0	7	0	0	0	2	.286
Gandil, 1b	6	23	1	6	1	0	0	7	0	1	0	2	.273
Felsch, cf.	6	22	4	6	1	0	1	10	0	0	1	5	.273
Schalk, c.	6	19	1	5	0	0	0	5	0	1	2	1	.263
Faber, p.	4	7	0	1	0	0	0	1	1	0	2	3	.143
Cicotte, p.	3	7	0	1	0	0	0	1	0	0	1	2	.143
McMullin, 3b	6	24	1	3	1	0	0	4	2	0	1	6	.125
Lynn, ut.	1	1	0	0	0	0	0	0	0	0	0	1	---
Williams, p.	1	0	0	0	0	0	0	0	0	0	0	0	---
Danforth, p.	1	0	0	0	0	0	0	0	0	0	0	0	---
Russell, p.	1	0	0	0	0	0	0	0	0	0	0	0	---
Grand total		197	21	54	6	0	1	63	3	6	11	28	.274

New York.	G.	AB.	R.	H.	2B.	3B.	HR.	TB.	SH.	SB.	BB.	SO.	Aver.
Perritt, p.	3	2	0	2	0	0	0	2	0	0	0	0	1.000
Robertson, rf.	6	22	3	11	1	1	0	14	0	2	0	0	.500
McCarty, c.	3	5	1	2	0	1	0	4	0	0	0	0	.400
Rariden, c.	5	13	2	5	0	0	0	5	1	0	2	1	.385
Holke, 1b.	6	21	1	6	2	0	0	8	0	0	0	6	.286
Herzog, 2b.	6	24	1	6	0	1	0	8	1	0	0	4	.250
Burns, lf.	6	22	3	5	0	0	0	5	0	1	3	6	.227
Fletcher, ss.	6	25	2	5	1	0	0	6	0	0	0	2	.200
Schupp, p.	2	4	0	1	0	0	0	1	0	0	0	1	.200
Sallee, p.	2	6	0	1	0	0	0	1	1	0	0	2	.167
Kauff, cf.	6	25	2	4	1	0	2	11	0	1	0	2	.160
Zimmerman, 3b	6	25	1	3	0	1	0	5	0	0	0	0	.120
Benton, p.	2	4	0	0	0	0	0	0	0	0	0	3	---
Wilhoit, ut.	2	1	0	0	0	0	0	0	0	0	1	0	---
Anderson, p.	1	0	0	0	0	0	0	0	0	0	0	0	---
Tesreau, p.	1	0	0	0	0	0	0	0	0	0	0	0	---
Thorpe, rf.	1	0	0	0	0	0	0	0	0	0	0	0	---
Grand total		199	16	51	5	4	2	70	3	4	6	27	.256

Bill Lange Buys 'Gold Brick' From Chicago Slicker

BILL LANGE, who is always spoken of in Chicago as "the famous outfielder of Cap Anson's old Colts," saw the world series.

He also saw Lincoln Park, which is one of Chicago's municipal institutions, and he has the distinction of being the only person who ever bought tickets to go through it. This story has come back from Chicago, and in consequence there is a movement afoot in club circles where Bill is prominent to have a committee of ordinary bunko sharks take him out on his return home and sell him the water rights of the Golden Gate.

Bill was out motoring with R. G. Sherman, more familiarly known as Bob, with whom he stopped during his visit to Chicago. As they approached the entrance to the park Sherman remarked that he'd have to get tickets to go through.

"Let me get 'em," said Bill. "Gee whiz! Can't I buy anything on this trip at all?"

"All right," agreed Sherman, and at the same time passed a wink to a park cop. The cop "wised up" immediately and gave Bill two tickets in exchange for $2 of perfectly good imported-from-California money.

Later on Bill glanced at his tickets. They read:

"Seventh Annual Reception and Dance Given by Lincoln Park Police Social and Benevolent Association, Wednesday Evening, November 21. Admit One Couple."

'HEINE' CHASES SOX INTO THE CHAMPIONSHIP

Giants' Third-Sacker Runs a Footrace With Eddie Collins —and Loses.

BY JAMES J. CORBETT

NEW YOIK, October 15.—Heine Zimmerman elected to run a foot race with Eddie Collins this afternoon and chased the White Sox into the baseball championship of the world.

The blue ribbon diamond struggle of 1917 is over, and the white hose warriors from Chicago are the victors. They deserved to win, they were the better team. In mechanical powers they didn't outclass their Giant rivals but in brains and gameness—the deciding factor in every contest—they rose up supreme.

In all world series history no team has shown more gameness or fighting spirit than the Sox. In two games they came from behind and battered their way to triumph.

They foozled afield at different times, played poorly in two games, but whenever they were backed against the wall they played the game in a sensational fashion. And, so they won.

The hero of the series is Urban ("Red") Faber, the sorrel topped right hander who figured in four out of six battles and won three. It was his splendid box work to-day that halted the Giants in their frenzied efforts to smash out a victory after the outlook became well nigh hopeless after the fourth inning. And it was Faber who foiled the Giants in the second game and checked them in the fifth. Before the big fight began he wasn't figured among the valuable assets of the Chicagoans. But it was "Red" who hurled the Sox to the pinnacle of the baseball world.

The game practically ended in the "fatal fourth" when Zimmerman, who had played a great game in all the other games of the series, executed two errors—one of hand and the other of head. Rarely has "boner" been made that was as weird as "Heine's": never was a worse one "pulled" in so critical a combat.

As Eddie Collins walked to the plate in the "fatal fourth" the crow wondered:

Will there be some scoring in this inning as there has been in the fourth of every other game?

The answer came quickly.

Collins shot an easy bounder at Zimmerman, who fielded it beautifully. Heinie had plenty of time to make the throw, and he took it. Then he let loose as he saw Eddie whizzing like an express train to first. The heave was low—very low, and bounded past Holke while Eddie ambled on to second amid the groans of the crowd. Joe Jackson then lifted a fly in short right. Robertson trotted in for it, set himself for the catch and then executed a "Snodgrass." The ball trickled through his finger while Collins hiked to third and Jackson anchored on first.

THE BONE PLAY.

"Happy" Felsch followed with an easy bounder to "Rube" Benton. The southpaw, seeing that Collins had started for home, chased him back with a bluff throw. Then "Rube" threw quickly to Zimmerman when he saw that Collins apparently was trapped.

As Heinie made the catch, Eddie,

Sport | Taylor Cleans Cubans--Lose To Rube | Sport

A. B. C's. VERSUS AMERICAN GIANTS

TITANS OF THE BUSINESS IN HUGE WARFARE — CHICAGO WINS IN THE INITIAL CONTEST —WHITWORTH SHADES DISMAKES IN A FIERCE PITCHERS' BATTLE.

By Dave Wyatt.

CHICAGO, Ill.—The American Giants walked off with the lion's share of the big contest, which, by the way, is the opening wedge to a long series of games between the two big guns of the hit, run and slide game, amongst folks of color. The score of 3-2 perhaps would best serve as a camouflage to a game that could be considered good, bad or indifferent. Both teams were worked down to a wire edge, and their play did not glide as smoothly as many had looked for; in fact, some of our best and most consistent performers had a day off, and their behavior at the pastiming stuff setled to such a low level that we fear there is going to be a mighty host of strained tendons, hurt feelings and cracked nerves before the long series, starting here, going through Ciney, onward to Pittsburgh, extending to Washington, and climaxing at "Chi," ends.

Perhaps the most important feature of the initial contest was the tiger-like attitude assumed by the Hoosiers. Those boys are really going to become ferocious; that is certainly good news, especially for the fans who will witness the play for the next few weeks. The A.'s have a sort of creeping idea that they have a better pitching staff, just as good an infield and a faster outfield; the question of catchers produces a stunner for the figure fiends, many of whom sway towards Foster's gang; but at any rate, C. I. Taylor tells us that whatever advantage, if there be any, that age, experience or prestige have bestowed upon the Windy City clan, he is going to out-game them, and thereby cause the chilly-hoofed baseball bugs of the Hoosier capital to fully realize that they have all along been barking up the wrong tree. The most important mention of the big game we take to be the masterful pitching of Whitworth for the Giants; but "Dizzy" was but a step short of the same grand form. However, Whitworth struck out three A's regular and often; he fanned the first and only three who faced him in the seventh, fanned two in quick succession upon different occasions, and was extremely stingy at holding back hits. Dismukes pitched one of those good, old consistent games that are good enough to bring home the bacon, but somehow "Dizzy" just can't shake off the jinx that "Rube" has planted near his dugout.

Twilight Baseball.

Uncle Sam has given us an hour or so more of daylight. He also threw an awful shock into us when his agents swooped down upon the A.'s and Americans' game and snared a prize bunch of would-be and actual slackers. Expectation of such a move kept the crowd down some. **The slogan is, Carry your white classification card.** The remainder of the series of games will be played starting at 6 o'clock in the evening; such arrangements are not new, generally speaking, but will be out for first trial in Chicago, where it is thought it will meet with favorable consideration by the many workers here, the majority of whom are at leasure by 5:30 p. m. C. I. Taylor will cart his team from here to Richmond, Ind., where he will try an innovation that is quite new, and one that none other but an energetic one would try. He will play at 6 o'clock Friday evening at Richmond, Ind.; he plays the same town Saturday at 3 o'clock; then he jumps over to Anderson, Ind., and plays the same day Saturday) at 6 o'clock. His club plays at Indianapolis Sunday, and then will play a three-game series at Cincinnati with the American Giants. Andrew "Rube" Foster has a month's schedule that will seriously test the merits of his champions. After he shakes off the A.'s, he takes on some big leaguers from Camp Grant for Saturday, July 20; Sunday the champion Beloit, Wis., team comes for a double bill; the team pulls out Sunday night for "Cincy," and from right now up until August 11 they are up against nothing else but tough sledging upon foreign territory. The breezy baseball babble of this column will be forwarded from the front; that is, if I don't lose my fingers dishing out the pasteboards from the box office; in such a case, Mr. Foster, who is some writer, will see that the goodies reach you. We go to press a little early, so the twilight stuff just about misses us; at any rate, whatever Mr. "String Beans" Williams and Jefferies does, if it's good, you'll get; also keep Foster's rookies, Key and Fields, upon your mind.

Mendez, one time known as king of pitchers, joined the Americans. He has developed into a classy infielder and will take Bobby Williams' place, in case the little shortstop is suddenly called for national service. In the meantime, fans, line up all along the route; a rare baseball treat awaits you. It's a case of toss up the coin and take heads or tails; take it from me, they are certainly a most evenly matched pair of ball teams; both have blood in their eyes and vengeance within their hearts. Don't miss it.

The score:

Giants.	R.	H.	P.	A.
Barber, rf.	0	3	0	0
DeMoss, 2b.	1	1	3	2
Hill, cf.	1	0	2	0
Gans, lf.	0	0	2	1
Duncan, lf.	0	0	0	0
Francis, 3b.	0	0	1	1
Grant, 1b.	0	2	5	2
Petway, c.	0	0	9	2
Williams, ss.	1	1	2	3
Whitworth, p.	0	1	2	2
Totals	3	8	*27	13

A. B. C.	R.	H.	P.	A.
Shively, lf.	0	1	0	0
Warfield, 2b.	0	1	1	3
Lyons, rf.	0	1	2	0
B. Taylor, 1b.	1	0	12	0
Clark, ss.	0	1	0	1
Charleston, cf.	1	1	2	1
Malacher, 3b.	0	1	4	4
Powell, c.	0	0	3	3
Dismukes, p.	0	1	0	2
Totals	2	7	24	14

*Malacher out for interference.

Giants ....1 0 0 0 1 1 0 0 *—3
A. B. C.........0 1 0 0 0 1 0 0 0—2

Errors—De Moss, Whitworth, Dismukes. Two-base hits—Charleston, De Moss. Bases on balls—Off Whitworth, 5; off Dismukes, 4. Struck out—By Whitworth, 9; by Dismukes, 3.

MIKE O'NEILL GETTING AN EXHIBITION TEAM

WATERTOWN, N. Y., July 12.—Mike O'Neill, former manager of the Syracuse Stars, in the New York State League, last year, and pilot of the Shreveport team of the Texas League, which suspended last week, will bring a team to this city to appear in exhibition games with Pop Watkins' Havana Red Sox. Both clubs will go on a barnstorming trip through Northwestern New York. His team will be picked stars of the Texas League.

C. I. SPEAKS

REVIEWS BASEBALL SITUATION; TELLS WHY HE CONTEMPLATED MOVING.

Much comment, pro and con has been indulged in during the last fortnight, since it was first announced that the A. B. C.'s would be transferred to another city, and many anxious fans have requested that I not only retract the statement, but state the facts as to why such an announcement should be made.

In the very outset, I want to say that the announcement was not made without its qualifying clauses, and neither was it made without serious consideration.

There is little need at this time to go back over the past history of the A. B. C.'s and how we have worked to build up an institution that the citizens of this city would feel a special pride in. Almost the entire population is familiar with the A. B. C.'s of former years and the many disgraceful scenes that could be seen on the ball field and in the stands at the old Northwestern grounds. In fact, very few of the fair sex could even think of attending a ball game. And I have heard many men say that they wouldn't be caught at a ball game at Northwestern Park as far back as six years ago. Those conditions have changed, men, women and children attend the games without compunction. There is no single institution in the city of Indianapolis that was as much abased and abused as baseball, yet in a few short seasons it has been elevated to a very lofty plane. The club was scarcely known outside of Indianapolis. Today, the A. B. C.'s have an international reputation. One can scarcely pick up a newspaper in any section of this country except he sees something on its sport page about the Indianapolis A. B. C.'s. That, in itself, ought to make every citizen take a special pride in the club; because of the wonderful amount of advertsing the club gives to the city in which you live. There is no ball club in the entire country more talked of than the A. B. C.'s, except the American Giants. There is no club in the country that has made a more enviable reputation for clean sport and good conduct on and off the ball field. These and many other things can be truthfully said relative to the A. B. C.'s and the sterling worth the club is to the city, but let this suffice.

Now, don't forget the financial burden we carry in maintaining this wonderful ball club. Here are a few of the things we have to contend with: One of the questions we have to answer at least one hundred times per week is, "When are you going to play the American Giants?" and, "When are the Cubans coming?" We usually tell the inquirer the American Giants will be here the latter part of July or some time during the month of August and that the Cubans will be here at some stated time. They usually reply, "All right, I'm coming out to see you play them and you must win." Now, fans, do you get the point? Those people ask those questions in good faith. But listen—we can only play the Cubans here three Sundays during one season and the American Giants one Sunday—four Sundays all told. We have about twelve Sundays at home during a season. There are eight Sundays that we must play clubs that the Indianapolis fans have little interest in and, as a result, we are compelled to play to small attendance. In other words, you expect me to maintain a high-class ball club so you can have the privilege of coming out to see about four games during the ball season. There are many good clubs over the State and unless you are willing to come out to see them perform, you will have little possibility of seeing the big colored clubs in action on the home lot. The reason is obvious—we will have disbanded before the time arrives for the American Giants to come.

Then there is another feature. The people of Chicago will go out in appreciable numbers to watch the American Giants play any club booked, for they fully realize that unless they do, it would be impossible to maintain a high-class club.

Then again, there is no city that I ever played in where the fans show such open demonstrations in favor of the visiting ball clubs. I have, on numerous occasions, had visitors come to me after the game and inquire why the fans rooted so intensely for the visiting club. I have also had people come to me and say that they had some guests at the game and the guests were compelled on numerous occasions to seek information as to the reasons for the fans pulling so hard for the visitors. They have asked be to explain and my answer is, "It's a repudiation of the home club and the work that I am trying to do." I have known the fans of Indianapolis to root so hard for the Cubans that I have crawled out of the dugout to take a peep up in the stands to see what it was all about.

There is little doubt but that the fans have made the Cubans the unruly, unsportsmanlike and wrangling set they are. They make it a specialty to kick on every decision rendered by the umpire and the Indianapolis fans sustain them in such unsportsmanlike tactics. The Cubans, who by their wrangling tactics have diminished greatly in popularity in all parts of the country, have long since learned that the fans of Indianapolis believe that every time they kick on decisions rendered that they are in reality being cheated and the fans will get on the umpire and in turn the umpire will give them all the best of the close decisions.

When it comes to my club kicking and wrangling, even the Indianapolis fans will say that my club does no useless kicking and never delays the game. We continue playing whether we are behind or in front, it matters not if it looks as though a rain will halt the game or if the 6 o'clock Sunday closing law will stop the game. On many occasions we could have warded off defeat by stalling and delaying the game until the bell had rung announcing 6 o'clock, but I haven't learned those kind of tactics. The people paid their money and the players ought to be forced to continue playing with reasonable haste until the game has been legally terminated. And unless much of the unnecessary, unsportsmanlike wrangling and delaying of the game is stopped, the game is destined to come into disrepute and the attendance greatly lowered. That the umpires make some bad decisions goes without saying, but the people and players make them doubly worse. Of course, we understand that a few "dime gamblers" raise a howl on everything close unless that be the way he has laid his money. He screams out at the top of his voice: "Robber, robber." "C. I., why don't you get an umpire?" etc. Then, when this continual howling is indulged in from the stands, many well-meaning fans get convinced that these fellows attend practically all the games and therefore regard them as an authority on the game and become convinced that the umpire is robbing the visiting club and a general howl is raised from the stands and I am made the goat. It was just this kind of thing that so peeved me a few Sundays ago that I announced that unless the fans wanted the A. B. C.'s in their midst we certainly won't stay.

You ought to have the privilege of watching an American ball club play a game at Havana, Cuba. I have seen as high as one hundred policemen on duty at the big Sunday games there and a couple of patrol wagons. The American players do about as much wrangling in twenty games there as the Cubans do in one game here.

Certainly, I would rather remain in Indianapolis than to move away, but there are several cities with more than twice the population of Indianapolis standing with open arms for the club. The people of Indianapolis can best answer the question, "Will the A. B. C.'s be transferred to another city?"

C. I. TAYLOR.

AUBURN STARS

DEFEAT HAVANA REDS IN FINAL GAME OF SERIES.

AUBURN, N. Y., July 13.—The Auburn Stars won the first game of the series today from the Havana Red Sox, by the count of 4 to 2, before the largest crowd of the season. The Stars got two ni the second on a double and single by Smith and an error by Forest at shortstop, when he made a wild peg to first. The Stars came back in the seventh and put two more runs across the plate. The Red Sox got two in the eighth inning, when Wassam singled and Lander worked Demsey for a free pass to first. McDonald tripled to the scoreboard, scoring Wassam and Lander. Fuller completed the inning by fanning.

Summary: Two-base hits—Tobin, Massam. Three-base hit—McDonald. Stolen bases—Harris, Forest, Davis. Struck out—By L. Archer, 5; by Demsey, 7. Bases on balls—Off L. Archer, 2; off Demsey, 2. Time—1:35. Umpires—Kerwin and Herlan.

TAYLOR REDEEMING

Takes Three Straights From the Islanders.

A. B. C.'s take three straights from Cubans. Games played up state at Muncie, July 10 and 11; at Anderson, July 12. This was rather refreshing news for the Indianapolis fans who had began to suspect that the Cubans outclassed the A.'s.

The three straight victories straighten up the line of Taylor's men as it concerns the Cubans and then some, being ahead one game. Before the up-state games were played the standing was 7 to 5 games in favor of the Cubans. The result is now 8 to 7 in favor of the A.'s.

MUNCIE, July 10.—With a real hit, a four-base play over the long left field fence, Powell, A. B. C. catcher, sent in the winning run ahead of him, and it came in the last half of the ninth, after the Cubans had tied the score at one all in their half of the final frame.

Score by innings:

Cubans ....0 0 0 0 0 0 0 0 1—1
Taylors ....1 0 0 0 0 0 0 0 2—3

Summary: Stolen bases—Torrente, Guerra. Sacrifice hits—Jeminez, Pedrose (2). Villa, Warfield, Clark, Charleston, Malarcher (2). Two-base hits—Shively, Charleston, Guerra. Home run Powell. Struck out—By Dismukes, 3; by Baro, 2. Bases on balls—Off Dismukes, 2; off Baro, 2. Hit by pitcher—By Dismukes, Jeminez. Left on bases—Taylors 7; Umpire—Freddie Long. Time of game—One hour, 40 minutes.

MUNCE, July 11.—Torrente started the big squabble when he jerked Junco in the second inning and went in himself. C. I. Taylor kept it up when the Cubans refused to play in the fifth and Umps Long helped it along in the seventh when he started to leave. But it was all over when Umps Long called the game because of darkness at the finish of the eighth with the count 8 to 2 in favor of the Taylors.

Taylors .... 0 6 0 1 0 1 0 0—8
Cubans .... 0 0 0 0 0 0 0 2—2

Summary: Sacrifice hits—Warfield, Clark, Baro, Campos. Sacrifice fly—Taylor. Stolen bases—Shively, B. Taylor. Three-base hit—B. Taylor. Two-base hits—Powell, Torrente, Portuondo. Double plays—Portuondo to Pedroso. Passed balls—Rodriquez (2). Innings pitched—By Williams, 8; by Junco, 1 2-3; by Torrente, 6; by Campos 1-3. Hits—Off Williams 3 in 8 innings; off Junco, 7 in 1 2-3 innings; off Torrento, 4 in 6 innings. Base on balls—Off Williams, 6 in 8 innings; off Junco, 1 in 1 2-3 innings; off Torrente, 4 in 6 innings. Struck out—By Williams, 2; by Torrente, 1. Hit by pitcher—Williams. Losing pitcher—Junco. Time of game—2 hours. Umpires—Freddie Long and Paddy King.

Anderson, July 12.—Taylor's A. B. C.'s annexed their third straight game from the Cuban All-Stars in as many days yesterday at Athletic park in a big slugging match, 16 to 6.

Pitching airtight ball for four innings Campus and Jeffries loosened up in the final frames to permit both clubs to chase merrily around the sacks, especially the Indianapolis team. The big blowup came in the eighth when the A. B. C.'s sent nine tallies across the rubber on the same amount of stinging blows. Charleston, centerfielder connected for two homers in this inning, both over the right center wall. He also collided for a triple.

Score by innings: R. H. E.

Cuban All-Stars 000 003 030— 6 4 1
A. B. C.'s .... 000 014 29x—16 20 2

Batteries—Campus and Rodiquez; Jeffries and Powell.

COLORED MAN GIVES UP RECORD NAG FOR AUTO

MARION, Ind., July 11.—Margaret Margrave, the roan mare which won the 2:12 pacing event in the Grand Circuit races Tuesday and established a record of 2:06¼, was bred and owned until a few weeks ago by Silas Jones, a colored man of Grant county. Jones campaigned the mare three years ago and had received offers for her by horsemen, but had declined all offers until this spring, when he traded her to Eikenberry Bros., of Russiaville, for an automobile.

ALLIES WIN

Defeat Excelsior Spring Cubs 7 to 0.

KANSAS CITY, Mo., July 12.—The K. C. Allies defeated the Excelsior Springs Cubs at Excelsior Springs, 7 to 0.

Two base hits—Turner, Boyd, Jones. Three base hits—Gordon, McNair. Stolen bases—McNair, Staples. Sacrifice hit—Boyd. Sacrifice fly—Hicks, Double plays—Tyree to Hicks to Turner; Johnson to Jones to Washington. Left on bases, Cubs, 7; Allies, 7. Bases on balls—Off Tyrell, 1; Richard, 2. Hits off Richard—13 in 8; off of Walters, 1 in 1. Hit by pitcher—Richard, 1. Struck out—By Tyrel, 1; by Hichard, 1. Losing pitcher—Richard.

K. C. All Stars forfeited their game to the Allies on the 4th of July, 9 to 0. Art Smith, who started to pitch for the All Stars had been sold to Indianapolis by the K. C. Blues and failed to report and disbarred from all league grounds, the All Stars refusing to use any other pitcher, forfeited the game.

Sunday, July 7, the Allies defeated the soldiers in both games of a double header at Association Park, 8 to 1 and 9 to 3. The Allies will play at Wichita, Kans., on the 14; Topeka, 21. On the 28th the Allies will play Topeka at Kansas City. On the 3, 4 and 5 of August the Allies will play the St. Louis Giants under the leadership of Gatewood. After the series with the Giants the Allies will leave for a trip through Ohio, meeting Chappie Johnson's team, the Dayton Maco's, Covington Tigers and Roger's Areselbes of Cleveland.

ANSWERING KID FIELDS

THE CHAMP OF THE WORLD

BUFFALO, N. Y., July 1, 1918.
Sporting Editor The Freeman.

Dear Sir:

I am answering Kid Fields' challenge, the Indianapolis featherweight. I will fight him before any club that will stage the bout. I know that Fields is a good fighter, but I am almost sure that I can beat him, as he will not beat me.

Yours in sport,
SAM JOHNSON,
Colored Featherweight Champion of the World, 393 Michigan avenue, Buffalo, N. Y.

P. S.—It's hard for me to get a fight with a boy of my weight, but come on, featherweights, I will give you no more than a K. O. But you boys may have an easy time, for I am an old man, 3 years old. But I can go some yet.

Additional Stage News

DOUBLE BIRTHDAY PARTY CELEBRATED ON SILAS GREEN SHOW.

On Thursday, the glorious Fourth of July, at Chattanooga, Tenn., there was celebrated at the home of Mrs. Marie Williams, 309 E. 9th St., a double birthday celebration, it being the birthdays of Mr. R. C. Puggsley, general manager of Prof. Eph. Williams' Silas Green Co., and Mr. Frank Smedlay, our genial basso profundo, he being 63 years old and hale and hearty as a young lad. There was an abundance of ice cream and cake and cigars and other delicacies served by the Misses Alma Saulsby, Anna Ruffin and Mrs. Ada Lockhart Booker. There were several nice selections rendered by the Silas Greene orchestra, under the leadership of Mr. Jesse Reeves, who has filled the position of orchestra leader over here for a number of years. Speeches were in order of the event, after which the orchestra rendered "Home, Sweet Home," to which we all repaired, declaring a pleasant, well spent evening.

Those present were Mrs. Marie Williams, Mrs. Ada L. Booker, the Misses Anna Ruffin, Alma Saulsby and Mrs. Edna Mae Davenport; the Messrs. Norman Mason, band leader of Silas Green Band; Lawrence Booker, Oscar Lowe, John McKinney, Walter Hoyt, Robert Everleigh, Brent Sparks, Jesse Reeves, Elmer Moore, Harry Tinsley, Chas. Collier, John Pamplin, James Lewis (Silas Green), Everette Butler, Willard Davenport, Chicken Jones, Gus Drew, Mr. John E. Williams and Mrs. Vivian L. Davis, respectively son and daughter of Prof. Eph. Williams.

GEORGIA SMART SET MINSTRELS.

The Georgia Smart Set has been playing to a very nice business, Kentucky, Indiana, and Illinois, for the past five weeks. The show has been retaining its past reputation by giving a clean first-class performance. Mr. A. J. McFarland, our genial stage manager, is a strenuous worker, for he strives daily to introduce something new and novel to entertain and please our patrons, who leave the tent nightly seemingly very well satisfied. We have lost one musician to the draft, and one on business transactions, but some have left presumably under the impression that the show would stop upon their retirement. Such never happened, as we are going to continue until the end of the season, or the war conditions force us to close. Every one on the show is in the finest of health and extends best wishes to all friends. The band of twelve certainly pleases the public daily, and the natives applaud the concert numbers as they are rendered, and there appears to be nothing missing from the parade.

Mrs. S. C. Elliott joined the show at Henderson, Ky., and is quite an addition, receiving great applause nightly, singing and dancing. Mr. Edward Walker is also another joiner as tuba player, B. and O. The show runs very smoothly and has played in opera houses on several occasions, and the natives claim the company should play houses all the time. The Georgia Smart Set Company shows its patriotism very freely, as they have organized Red Cross, Thrift Stamp and Liberty Bond clubs. Capt. Dick Anderson has put thirty-seven years in the show business, and is certainly a goer for an old man of nearly fifty-two years of age. Capt. Dick invites correspondence from all friends. The public simply goes wild at the appearance of Uncle Sam, and Uncle Mose during the first part finale. Read the best there is and be wise—The Freeman.

STAGE NOTES.

Clark and Kinky at Louisville this week. Will jump to New York later on to take up Eastern time. At the Washington, Indianapolis, last week.

Alberta Perkins ,after a big week at the Washington, Indianapolis, is at the Lincoln, Cincinnati. Nelson and Taylor in Cincinnati this week.

Crosby and Jones at the Lyric, Indianapolis, this week. Jones is known as "Spareribs" and not "String Beans."

Johnny Woods in Cincinnati next week. He sends best regards to Edwells and Edwells, now playing at Chattanooga. Johnny would like a line from his son Tommy.

THE FREEMAN IN ST. LOUIS.
Get the Freeman in St. Louis, Mo., at Harry Bowman's news stand, 2319 Market St.

The sacrifices we make and the loyalty we show today will bring us the richest of rewards. Not alone will our own hearts rejoice in the doing of good, but generations to come will remember how much they owe to us. We are not living our own little span today, for we shall be immortal. In ages to come Americans of the future will realize that their happiness is a gift from us, their freedom was purchased with the blood of our bravest sons and their country—splendid and eternal—a monument to our day. What one of us could ask more?

20 Pages Today

The Boston Post

EXTRA

TWENTY PAGES—ONE CENT | Established 1831 | FRIDAY, SEPTEMBER 6 1918 ** | Copyright, 1918, by Post Publishing Co. | TWENTY PAGES—ONE CENT

GERMANS IN HEADLONG RETREAT ACROSS AISNE

Driven Back Eight Miles in a Day by the French and American Forces—Mangin Driving Forward in Direction of Laon Threatens to Cut in Back of Chemin des Dames and Trap Germans Fleeing From the Aisne—French Take 30 Villages East of Noyon

RUTH'S GREAT PITCHING GIVES RED SOX FIRST

Batting of Whiteman and McInnis Scores Boston's Lone Tally, Whitewashing Cubs

Less Than 20,000 See Game—Weather Poor—Bush and Tyler Today

BY PAUL H. SHANNON

CHICAGO, Sept. 5.—Striking the first, and usually the most effective blow in the annual struggle for a world's championship, the Boston Red Sox this afternoon won the opening decision from Fred Mitchell's Cubs by a 1 to 0 score, and after one of the cleanest and most bitterly-fought battles ever chronicled in the post-season clash for baseball's sweepstakes. Superb pitching by Big Babe Ruth, and twirling hardly less effec-

Continued on Page 14—First Col.

"STUFFY" M'INNIS.

Whose hit in fourth inning scored Shean from second with the only run of the game and won the contest for the Red Sox.

PROOFS OF SINKING OF 150 U-BOATS

British Government Publishes Names of Commanders

MAN WHO SANK THE LUSITANIA ON LIST

Authors of Atrocious Crimes Have Paid Penalty

LONDON, Sept. 5.—Although the British government does not intend to adopt the practice of giving proof of official utterances made by its ministers, it has been thought desirable to print in tomorrow's newspapers the names of the commanding officers of 150 German submarines which have been disposed of, in order to substantiate the statement of Premier Lloyd George in the House of Commons, that "at least 150 of these ocean pests have been destroyed."

MOST OF OFFICERS DEAD

The statement to be published tomorrow does not include the names of officers commanding Austrian submarines put out of action.

A majority of the 150 officers mentioned are dead. Some of them are

Continued on Page 6—Seventh Col.

RAISE FOR LOW PAID FIREMEN

All to Get $1100—Mayor Refuses Increases Above That Class—Soldiers Ready

A flat refusal to increase the maximum pay of Boston firemen from $1400 to $1700, and an announcement of better wages for the $900 probationers and the $1000 men will be Mayor Peters' formal answer this morning to the delegation that will call on him concerning the threatened strike in the Boston fire department, scheduled to take place Monday morning.

In stating last night that there will be no concessions at this time to the firemen in the classes above the $1000 grade, the Mayor declared that those men who are unwilling to abide by his ruling "may, of course, resign their positions and seek higher paid employment elsewhere."

WILL CALL ON STATE GUARD

Furthermore, the Mayor announced his determination, if the emergency arose, of manning the apparatus with members of the State Guard. He will, should exigencies require such action, call upon Governor McCall for the impressing of the guardsmen into service, not only as fire fighters, but also to do guard duty as an aid to the police in quelling any outbreaks.

Assurance has reached the Mayor that the officers of the fire department will remain at their posts, should a strike be called. The information conveyed to the Mayor was that the members of the Officers' Club, at a recent meeting, voted against joining in a strike.

Continued on Page 9—Third Column

REPORT HERTLING RESIGNS

Bad Health Given as Chancellor's Reason

LONDON, Sept. 5—Count George F. von Hertling, the imperial German chancellor, has resigned, giving bad health as the cause for his retirement, according to the Geneva correspondent of the Daily Express, quoting a despatch received in Geneva from Munich, Bavaria.

It may be that Hertling's retirement was caused by his statement on Wednesday that the Kaiser's dynasty was in danger through the failure to secure needed franchise reforms.

YESTERDAY'S TEMPERATURE

	'17	'18		'17	'18
3 a. m.	55	66	3 p. m.	64	69
6 a. m.	52	65	6 p. m.	63	79
9 a. m.	60	64	9 p. m.	60	74
12 m.	64	67	12 m.	58	70

YEOWOMAN AND SAILOR LOSE LIVES

Killed in Auto Upset, Second Yeowoman Dying

RUN INTO PILE OF EARTH ON ROADWAY

Pinned Under Car at Hampton Falls, N. H.

MARIE GEORGE,

HAMPTON FALLS, N. H., Sept. 5.—Mary Monahan of Allston, Mass., a yeowoman, and Seaman P. J.

Continued on Page 10—Fourth Col.

Only East of Rheims Is the German Line Still Holding

British Gain in Flanders and Are Drawing Nearer Cambrai

BY ASSOCIATED PRESS

The French and Americans are fast driving the Germans out of their positions in southern Picardy and in the sector between the Vesle and Aisne rivers.

So rapid has been the progress of the allies—the French in Picardy and the Americans and French from Soissons eastward toward Rheims—that the retirement of the enemy has almost the appearance at present of the beginning of a rout.

Meanwhile Field Marshal Haig in the north, from Peronne to Ypres, has been almost as busily engaged with his troops in carrying out successful maneuvres which are only in a slightly less degree of rapidity forcing the Germans everywhere to give ground. Haig's men again have made the Germans taste bitter defeat on

Continued on Page 10—Sixth Col.

HIGH TIDE TODAY (AT NAVY YARD)
A. M. 12:48 — P. M. 1:08

SUN Rises 6:13, Sets 7:12 **MOON** Sets at 7:19 p. m.
Light all vehicles tonight at 7:42.

TODAY'S ANNIVERSARIES, ETC.

The Mayflower sailed from England for America, 1620.—President McKinley shot at Pan-American Exposition, 1901.—Kaiser took command of German army at Nancy, 1914.—Street railway strike declared on in New York, 1916.

One year ago today—The House passes a bill authorizing bond issues totalling $11,538,945,460.

FAIR—COOLER

Forecast for Boston and vicinity: Showers early Friday morning, followed by fair and cooler; Saturday fair, moderate temperature, moderate northwest winds.

WASHINGTON, Sept. 5.—Forecast for southern New England, east New York: Showers early Friday morning, followed by fair; Saturday fair.

Northern New England: Showers Friday, cooler New Hampshire and Vermont; Saturday fair.

ASKS FULL REPORT ON ROUND-UP

President Seeks Facts of Raid on Slackers in New York

WASHINGTON, Sept. 5.—President Wilson has asked Attorney-General Gregory for a complete report of the circumstances surrounding the "slacker round-up" in New York city this week, in which upwards of 40,000 men were taken into custody by agents.

Continued on Page 7—Third Column

Ludendorff Says U. S. Will Not Win the War

AMSTERDAM, Sept. 5.—That American assistance will be a decisive factor in the war is a vain hope on the part of the entente, according to General Ludendorff, the first quartermaster-genera[l] of the German army, in a statement t[o] the Vienna newspapers.

General Ludendorff, however, admitte[d] that the Americans were rendering n[o] inconsiderable assistance to the allie[s] both in men and material.

"The French have always lived upon hopes," said Ludendorff. "First it was hopes of Russia; now it is hopes of America. We settled with the Russian steam roller; we shall settle with the Americans.

"Our will to victory remains unbroken; we shall break the enemy's will to annihilate."

Today will be a proud memory in the lives of millions of men. America offers them the proud privilege reserved only for the elect of the world, of participating in the wondrous crusade for liberty. They go to join the pioneers at the frontiers of freedom, to share their glory and their sacrifice, and to be part of that army of happy warriors who will some day return with all the honors that mankind can bestow.

—The Great— Breakfast Table Paper —of New England—

The Boston Post

EXTRA

EIGHTEEN PAGES—ONE CENT · Established 1831 · THURSDAY SEPTEMBER 12 1918 ** · Copyrighted, 1918, by Post Publishing Co. · EIGHTEEN PAGES—ONE CENT

13,000,000 TO ANSWER FREEDOM'S CALL TODAY

Nation to Honor Great Army of Patriots Who Will Offer Themselves to the Country to Serve Until Victory Crowns America's Cause—Massachusetts Will Register 450,000 Men and Will Make the Day Memorable by Patriotic Exercises in Many Towns

ALLIED DRIVE IS SLOWING UP AT ALL POINTS

German Defence Is Stronger and Bad Weather Handicaps Allies —Huns Begin Counter Attacks

After an offensive which has lasted continuously for eight weeks—by far the longest sustained offensive of the war—the forces of the allies are drawn up in front of the Hindenburg line along practically its entire length.

Reports by allied aviators are to the effect that the German high command has been rushing up fresh troops to man the Hindenburg defences and the next few days may witness a titanic struggle for mastery along the entire Hindenburg system from Ypres to the Chemin des Dames.

This battle will practically decide whether the allies are to settle down to a period of trench warfare or the Germans be compelled to give up the greater part of France and Belgium and make a retreat to the Meuse line.

Some reports say that the German high command has been rushing fresh

Continued on Page 18—Second Col.

AMERICAN TROOPS AT ARCHANGEL

Number Not Giv n Out by Gen. March in Announcement

WASHINGTON, Sept. 11.—American troops have landed at Archangel to assist the other allied forces there in their campaign to the re-establishment of order in northern Russia. This announcement wasauthorized tonight by General March, chief of staff.

NUMBER NOT REVEALED

For military reasons the number of soldiers landing was not revealed, nor was it made clear from whence they had embarked. It was assumed, however, that the soldiers had been sent from English camps, where Americans are training.

General March's announcement was made public through the committee on public information, which issued this statement:

"By order of General March, the safe arrival of American troops at Archangel is announced."

After the allied forces landed on the shores of the White Sea, several months ago, there were reports that American troops were co-operating with them, but it subsequently developed that the forcesm were marines from American warships. The troops, the arrival of which is now announced, are the first from the United States to be sent into northern Russia.

Who Will Be Included in the First Calls

Besides the 19 and 20-year-old classes, 60,000 men who have reached 21 since Aug. 24, as 3000 youths of 18 reach their 19th birthday each day, the date Sept. 12 fixes a dividing line for them. Men now between 21 and 31 who by circumstances of location or condition on previous registration days are included.

Claims Czarina and Four Daughters Killed

LONDON, Sept. 12.—The Daily Express claims to have unquestionable information that the former Empress of Russia and her four daughters have been murdered by Bolsheviki.

U-BOAT SENT TO BOTTOM

Made Attack on Ship Carrying 2800 U. S. Troops

SHOWS OUR CONVOYS ARE NEAR PERFECT

Washington Gives Out First News of Recent Fight

WASHINGTON, Sept. 11.—News of the torpedoing of the British liner Persic, with 2800 American troops on board in the war zone on Sept. 6 was given to the American people today first through the British admiralty and then later through the Navy Department. All the soldiers were rescued by accompanying destroyers, the steamer itself was beached and the enemy submarine is believed to have been accounted for.

CONVOYING PERFECT

Officials here viewed the result of the attack more as an allied success than a disaster. The fact that the steamer was torpedoed when she ws endeavoring to overtake the convoyed fleet of transports after overcoming engine trouble which had forced her to lag, convinced officials that submarine commanders still are fearful of attacking troopships in convoy. And the immediate and the successful assistance rendered by the destroyers was taken as additional evidence that the convoying system now in vogue is practically perfect.

First word of the attack on the Persic, it was learned, officially reached the Navy Department on the night of Sept. 6 in a brief despatch from Vice Admiral Sims; although navy officials have emphatically denied in the interim that any important news of submarine activities was being withheld. It was understood that the British Admiralty expressed the request that they be permitted to announce the news of the attack.

Rumors that a troopship had been sunk, probably with heavy loss of life, have been current in Washington since the publication of what evidently was

Continued on Page 13—Fourth Col.

RED SOX ARE AGAIN WORLD'S CHAMPIONS

Mays Holds Cubs in Check While Tyler Fails to Work Sox—Whiteman's Wonderful Work Mainly Responsible for 2 to 1 Victory

GEORGE WHITEMAN OUT AT THIRD.

Whiteman reached first in safety in the third inning of yesterday's game at Fenway Park when Right Fielder Flack muffed his curving line drive and allowed Mays and Shean to score. A few seconds later McInnis shot a roller toward Hollocher, who threw to first too late to get Stuffy. Whitey was off with the crack of McInnis' rap and kept on to third on the play. Merkle, after taking Hollocher's throw, pegged to Deal, who is seen in the picture putting the ball on the clever veteran. However, Whitey's hit did the damage.

BY PAUL H. SHANNON

Again are the Boston Red Sox baseball champions of the world.

At exactly five minutes past three o'clock yesterday afternoon, even before the wires began to tell the country that Barrow's men had delivered the punch that was to win the deciding contest in this great struggle for the supreme title, a carrier pigeon, released from the press stand by exultant soldiers started on its long flight to Camp Devens with the news of the fatal third inning and the downfall of the Chicago Cubs.

Continued on Page 12—First Col.

MRS. EATON WINS RIGHT TO CONTEST

Mrs. Ella F. Bartlett Eaton, the second wife, and now the widow of the late Charles S. Eaton, proprietor of Thompson's Spa, has won the right to contest for a larger portion of the well known restaurateur's estate than that given her by the ante-nuptial agreement which she signed.

Judge Braley finds, after long deliberation of the evidence, brought out at many hearings before him in the court house in Boston, that the agreements of partnership between Mr. Eaton and his three sons were entered into for the purpose of avoiding this ante-nuptial agreement and rendering its terms nugatory. Nor were they less fraudulent, to use the language of Judge Braley's findings, because consummated openly.

Continued on Page 5—First Column

Register as Early as Possible and Be Prepared With Your Answers

Everything Is in Readiness to Deal With Great Army of Registrants

With flags flying, bells ringing and bands playing 450,000 male residents of Massachusetts will today register for service in the armies of the United States subject to the call of the government—another stern and formidable protest to autocracy that a free and democratic nation stands ready to sacrifice everything for the principles upon which it was founded.

Today every male resident of this State, and every other State in the Union, between the ages of 18 and 46 will register. This means that more than 13,000,000 men will attest their willingness to serve Uncle Sam as he needs them.

GREATEST ONE-DAY JOB

The greatest one-day civilian undertaking ever attempted by any nation will be the work of registering these millions, including boys nearing majority and men fast reaching the second last stage of life.

Continued on Page 6—First Column

Every Bar in State Will Be Closed Today

The whole of Massachusetts will be bone dry today. Every saloon, cafe and club will refuse to sell any form of liquor and thus abide by the request of Governor McCall, who asked the dispensers of liquor to close their places of business while registration is being carried out.

HIGH TIDE TODAY (AT NAVY YARD)

A. M. 4.35 · P. M. 4:50

SUN Rises 6:20. Sets 7:01. · MOON Sets at 10:36 p. m.

Light all vehicles tonight at 7:31.

TODAY'S ANNIVERSARIES, ETC.

One year ago today—Argentina orders German minister to leave country. The Senate adopts a resolution for the drafting for military service of all friendly aliens in the country. The American steamer Wilmore is sunk by a German submarine off the French coast.

RAIN—WARMER

Forecast for Boston and vicinity: Rain Thursday and Thursday night; slightly warmer. Friday probably fair; moderate south and southwest winds.

WASHINGTON, Sept. 11.—Forecast for southern New England: Rain Thursday west, Thursday and Thursday night east portion; slightly warmer. Friday probably fair.

Northern New England: Rain Thursday or Thursday night and probably Friday; warmer Thursday.

WOMAN SPY KEPT HUNS INFORMED

Postal Operator Told of Munition Ship Movements

NEW YORK, Sept. 11.—Information has been obtained that Miss Wanda Kreutingzer, a Postal Telegraph Company operator who was taken into custody here today, has transmitted directly to the German government important information regarding munition ships, obtained from cablegrams and telegrams which passed through her hands, according to a statement tonight by federal officials.

DID IT FOR LOVE OF GERMANY

These transmissions, the statement said, were made in 1914 and 1915. But within the last six weeks, it is asserted, Miss Kreutingzer has furnished similar information "to persons she believed to represent the imperial German government." The operator has been under surveillance for some time.

Miss Kreutingzer, who is a registered enemy alien, told her examiners she was born in Posen, Germany, 42 years ago. She has been employed by the Postal Company for 16 years, and she has been in the United States 20 years. She has been employed as an operator in the Chicago office until the outbreak of the war, when she obtained a transfer to the New York office.

According to the statement, Miss Kruetingzer received no money for her services doing the work, because of her love of the "homeland."

A presidential warrant for her internment as a dangerous enemy alien has been requested, it was announced.

Now Everybody Can Make a Home Run as Babe Shows How to Do It

FOLLOWING BIG BABE RUTH, THE HOME RUN KING, THROUGH, ON ONE OF HIS LONG DRIVES, BY THE AID OF THE CAMERA

Here is the way Babe Ruth, the king of home run getters, swings at a ball when he knocks out one of his famous long drives that has made him the slugging wonder of baseball. Starting from right to left the pictures show just how he does it from the time he starts to meet the ball with his bat, until he completes the action and has sent the ball to the far corner of the ball park or over the fence. Babe posed himself for these photographs, which were taken by George Murray of the Boston Post staff. George tried to tell Babe how he wanted to catch him in action to show how he does the trick, but Babe wouldn't stand for it. "Your game is taking pictures, mine is poling home runs," says Babe. "I'll take the different poses myself as if it was for a movie. Then they'll be right. All you have got to do is shoot the camera." And George did.

Busting Babe and His Diadem

Clouting Hercules Is One of Celebrities of Country

By NEAL R. O'HARA

Boston's pretty proud of your 26th, Babe. As proud as it was of its own 26th last spring, when it came back from war. Honestly, we don't know but that our 26th Y. D. and your 26th H. R. are on the same level,

The way you've been whaling the ball all season has given you title to the Prince of Whales. But today you're the Home Run King. That ball you crowned yesterday certainly gives you the rank and throne.

HERE'S HOPING BABE DOES IT AGAIN.

Buck Freeman held the home run record long enough. And, believe us, we're all glad to see you passing the Buck. Not that Freeman wasn't a sweet hitter—they don't pack bonbons sweeter than that boy. But you've been clubbing the ball so hard this season you couldn't be denied. And we expect you to be the H. R. king for a long, long time—till next year, at least, when you'll probably make a whole lot more.

You are the mastodon of hitters, Babe—the dinosaur of slam artists. If you lived in the Stone Age, you'd doubtless be swinging an elm tree at every boulder they pitched to you.

But this is another age. Today you swing a mean club and get the same results. If the club that's surrounding you were only as good as the one you swing, they'd have a silk pennant for the Red Sox, instead of the lisle trophy, or whatever they give a second-division outfit.

However, we can't have everything. And although they may say we are sucking sour grapes, we don't know but that we'd rather have the world's champion slugger in Boston than the world's champion ball team.

We've got so used to winning pennants, it's a relief to have some other club win. Anyway, it's only fair to let the West have the best ball team once in a while. Besides, a world's champion ball club is made each season, but they don't produce champion sluggers that often.

IT WAS HARDER ON THE PITCHERS, WE'LL SAY.

You've had a hard and a soft time this season, Babe. Hard, because all the pitchers were working against you, and working hard. And soft, because you didn't do much running.

As we look back on the season, you haven't done much else than walk. For, as we recall it, you always got either a home run or a base on balls. If you got four balls, you walked to first; and, if you slammed the ball over the fence, you walked all the way around to home. Bryan has done more running than you.

You are the only 20th Century Express in Baseball, Babe. You never make local stops at second or third. The only place you stop for water is the dugout, after you've gone all the way around. You either make the whole trip on a single ticket, or else you go to first on the ticket some pitcher gives you.

Yea, bo—and you've put the ball over the top more times than any general. Many a day, when the Sox were having a zero at the bat, you stepped to the plate and put it over the top for at least one tally.

You've covered more ground going home than Ludendorff ever covered. You've given the ball more rides in the air than Eddie Rickenbacker ever took. And you've done more for the league than Henry Cabot Lodge —a lot more!

Hence, Babe, we take off our fall fedora to you. We'd have a medal struck out for you, but we know you wouldn't care for anything that's been struck out. We'd give you the freedom of the city, only there's been more bevo than freedom in Boston since last July. But, kid, we'll give you anything you ask for—anything at all. And all we ask in return is that you try for that 27th today.

Sure you've got the makings of another home run.

Mightiest hitter in baseball's history, more powerful than any of the great sluggers of the past, the undisputed home run king of all time, Big Babe Ruth, Boston battering ram, stands supreme among the big batters of the day.

HONORS ALL HIS OWN

No longer does he share honors with Buck Freeman, the home run champion of another generation. Today all baseballdom bows to Babe, with his world's record mark of 26 home runs.

Realizing his dream of years, eclipsing the mark at which he had aimed ever since Joe Lannin, the former Red Sox magnate, brought him to Boston from Baltimore, Big Babe Ruth yesterday shattered the record which has stood for two long decades when he caught hold of one of Thormahlen's fast ones and drove it into the right field pavilion at the Polo Grounds for his 26th home run of the year.

This terrific wallop, made in the eighth inning, when Boston led by the meagre margin of one run, settled the fate of battle apparently, just as most of his long distance drives this year have determined the result in the Red Sox' favor.

Surprised All Critics

In creating a new home run record and collecting most of his circuit drives on foreign fields, Ruth has accomplished the apparently impossible and excelled a mark which the wisest critics of the game firmly believed would stand for all time. And small wonder that the big crowd that packed the Polo Grounds yesterday in the hope that Ruth might realize his ambition went fairly frantic as the sphere disappeared from view and the mark that had stood unassailed for 20 long years was erased from world's record chronicles.

And long before Big Babe had finished shaking hands with his mates, even while the police were driving back from the Boston dugout the hundreds of fans who swarmed around in the hope of shaking the hand of Boston's burly Batterer, the fans began to appreciate the tremendous achievement that Babe had accomplished.

For, in wiping the mark of Buck Freeman from the official slate it must be understood that Ruth had to overcome the disadvantage of far larger parks, even more effective pitchers and pitching policies than ever existed in the days when Buck Freeman startled the baseball world by clouting out his 25 circuit wallops.

Harder to Make 'Em Now

In almost every instance the big league parks of today are nearly twice as large as those of 20 years ago. Were the same small parks that saw Freeman make his record standing today Ruth, without a doubt, would have eclipsed the official figures long since. Then, too, Ruth has been batting against some of the greatest twirlers that ever stood upon the rubber and in addition to this in nearly every game opposing pitchers have figured discretion as the better part of valor and walked him intentionally in the pinch.

Although Big Babe has been after the home-run record for many a long day no player in the American league, no well versed fan even, had the slightest idea that he had a chance of reaching the title of home run king until that memorable day in Chicago last month when he drove the ball into the right field bleachers at Comiskey Park—scored his 17th homer and wiped out Seybold's American League record of 16 home runs.

This was at that time supposed to be glory enough, but Babe didn't stop there. He kept right on hammering out the deadly four-baggers, bunched the circuit clouts at St. Louis and Detroit and with 23 to his credit came back to Fenway Park, two weeks ago, ready to wipe Freeman's figures off the slate.

Great Week's Work

On Labor Day afternoon, in the presence of nearly 30,000 people, he drove the ball far into the right field bleachers for his 24th. Last Friday afternoon, before an admiring crowd at Philadelphia, he evened the mark set 20 years ago. Yesterday's great achievement was the consummation of an entire season's battering.

And in no case was any home run that Ruth knocked out a gift. The greatest twirlers in the American league had to stand and watch the sphere driven by Babe's bat sink out of sight. Covaleskie, Ehmke, Dauss, Davenport, Shocker, Morton, Leonard, Shawkey, Johnson, Harper, Shaw, Thormahlen and Mogridge, right handers and southpaws, impartially, have been compelled to see their choicest offerings sent flying beyond the pale.

And in eclipsing the mark yesterday afternoon at the Polo Grounds Babe was compelled to face Thormahlen, one of the greatest southpaws in the business.

Today, against the St. Louis Browns on Fenway Park, Babe will make an effort to shatter his own record. It is nearly as good as an even bet that he will score 30 home runs before the season is brought to an end.

DAVE SHEAN IS COACHING TEAM

The Arlington Council, Knights of Columbus, baseball club, is to practice every evening this week to get in trim for the second of the series of games with the Winchester town team for the championship of the Mystic Valley. The contest is to be staged next Saturday afternoon on the Spy Pond Athletic Field, Arlington. Dave Shean, the former Red Sox second baseman, will coach the boys again this week. The Arlington outfit won the first game of the series, 2 to 0, in 11 innings at Winchester last Saturday, and another Arlington victory will give the series to the Spy Pond nine.

As a Mob Smasher, That Bunch Coach Fisher Is Training Would Do

Big Three Have New Coaches

Harvard Sticks to Old System—Tigers and Yale to Change

New coaching talent all around the Big Three circuit this fall make the early season predictions less stable than usual. Haughton of Harvard, Tad Jones of Yale and Speedy Rush of Princeton, who were head coaches during the last season when intercollegiate football was played, are all displaced this year.

NO CHANGE AT HARVARD

The Harvard policy of development is less likely to be changed than that of Princeton or Yale. Haughton's former line coach, Bob Fisher, is in control at Cambridge, and P. D.'s system for moulding a big league team will not be altered by the new head coach. At Yale, however, Dr. Al Sharpe has taken up the head coachship after some years of conspicuous success at Cornell, and the system bequeathed by Tad Jones stands a good chance of being altered when Sharpe starts training the Eli squad next Monday.

Princeton is slated for a drastic shift in coaching work. Speedy Rush has been succeeded by Bill Roper, and a great deal of the old Rush system will be scrapped as soon as the Tiger team gets under way. Rush, in his several years' tenure at Princeton, just fell short of doing a satisfactory job. With heart-breaking regularity he sent very good elevens against Harvard and Yale, only to have them nosed out at every meeting.

They still have confidence that Speedy is a good coach, however, for Cornell has signed him to teach varsity football at Ithaca this fall, in the place of Dr. Sharpe, who has gone to Yale. Rush is out of the Big Three, but with Cornell this year he will still have a chance to show his class in games against Dartmouth and Pennsylvania.

Is a Bull for Kicking

Sharpe will have Dr. Billy Bull for his right-hand man this year, and between them Yale will have a couple of M. D.'s that should give the Elis a fast pace, once the season gets under way. Dr. Bull will work with the backfield candidates and punters, and still another M. D., Dr. Arthur Brides, will have charge of the line from tackle to tackle. Johnny Cates will direct the ends.

Eddie Mahan is looked for at Harvard before the season gets well under way. He has been in Rumania as an officer of the Marine Corps, but the last report was that he was proceeding home. Mahan will be discharged from the U. S. M. C. on reaching this side, and he will coach the backfield men and punters at Harvard when he is once more free to get into a gridiron suit.

Mahan was originally slated to be head coach at Boston College, but his delay in getting away from the Rumanian assignment and the uncertainty as to when he would reach the United States caused the B. C. athletic committee to decide on Frank Cavanaugh for head coach.

Princeton's head coach, Bill Roper, is not precisely a newcomer in Big Three circles. In 1917, when Princeton was playing informal varsity football along with other big Eastern colleges, Roper was in charge, having succeeded Speedy Rush that fall. But he never was able to send a Tiger varsity outfit against Harvard or Yale, and this will be his first season of regular football. Previously Roper had done coaching at Princeton, his most notable team being the one that trimmed both Harvard and Yale in 1911, when Sam White gained his glory.

Outside of the Big Three there are other teams that will have new coaching systems to test this autumn. Colonel Charlie Daly will be in charge of the Army at West Point. Daly will have a hard time moulding his team, for the war shattered the lineup of material that was formerly at the military academy. The Navy is in quite as bad shape, however, so the break is even, so far as the Army's main game goes. The Army-Navy game to be held on Nov. 29 at New York will be the first service clash since 1916.

TO HOLD BIKE RACES SATURDAY NIGHT

Rain again forced Nat Butler to call off the bike races scheduled for last night at his Revere cycle track. It was the sixth postponement in three weeks, and rather than buck the weatherman Nat has decided not to hold another race meet until Saturday night.

For this meet he carries over the one-hour Brassard paced race with the same list of starters, George Wiley, Clarence Carman, Frank Corry and the premier rider of the season, Vincent Madonna. The postponement will help rather than hinder these riders, as they need rest after their strenuous races of the last few weeks on other tracks.

In addition to the Brassard race, Manager Butler has secured Alfred Goulett, the rider who performed so brilliantly in a special match race at the Revere oval earlier in the season, and Oscar Egg, the Swiss champion. They will meet in a series of races, the first to be a sprint and the second a pursuit race, with the riders starting on opposite sides of the track. The third race, if necessary, will be decided by a drop of a coin. The bike fans have never seen Egg in action at Revere, but he has a wonderful reputation in Newark and on European tracks. He has never lost a championship race on the pursuit plan.

TO HEAD HOCKEY TEAM

Miss Marion Wing, who last year was captain of the Arlington High School girls' field hockey eleven, has been chosen as leader of the team again this fall. Miss Lorraine Cooledge is manager of the team this year. The team will start practice next week.

And Now It's the New League

There was a time when the National league held the spite championship. In those days the American league was held up as a model of virtue, concord and harmony. But we notice no National league club had the meanness to protest the Giants and Cubs transferring an unplayed New York date to Chicago. Detroit papers please copy.

TWO NEW TROTTING RECORDS

Four-Year-Olds Shatter Marks in Grand Circuit

SYRACUSE, N. Y., Sept. 10.—Two new world's records were written into trotting history at the New York State Fair Grand Circuit meeting this afternoon when in the 2:07 trot, Echo Direct and Easton shattered existing marks for four-year-old geldings. Echo Direct trotted the third heat in 2:05 1-4.

In the fourth heat Ben White piloted Easton to a mark when he drove the big roan around the course in 2:06 3-4.

INTEREST IN BIG STAKE

Chief interest in the day's events appeared to centre in the three-cornered pacing duel in the 2:10 pace for the Syracuse stake of $3000 in which Goldie Todd vanquished Senardo and Frank Dewey after three sensational heats. Senardo took the first heat in 2:03 1-4, with Goldie Todd challenging gamely. The next two heats fell to Goldie Todd, with Frank Dewey outpacing Senardo to take second honors.

The Ka-Noo-No 3-year-old trot for a purse of $2012.50 went to Brother Peter. The winner took the first heat in 2:09 1-4, but finished third in the second, which was won by Little Lee. In the third heat Brother Peter literally ran away from the field.

Irish Voter won the 2:12 pace in straight heats in hard stretch drives, coming from behind each time.

2:07 trot, purse $1000; 3-heat plan:

Easton, ro. g., by The Tramp (White)	1	2	2	1
Echo Direct, b. g. (Brusie)	5	3	1	2
Peter June, ch. g. (Jones)	3	1	4	3
Busy's Lassie, b. m. (Cox)	2	4	3	ro
Charley Penn, b. g. (Dickerson)	4	5	5	ro

Time—2:07½, 2:07¼, 2:05¼, 2:06¾.

2:12 pace, purse $1000; 3-heat plan:

Irish Voter, b. g., by John A. McErron (Noble)	1	1	1
Prince Pepper, blk. g. (Hyde)	2	2	3
Fred Hal, b. g. (McPherson)	3	3	2
Florence Peters, ch. m. (Cox)	4	4	dr

Time—2:08¼, 2:06½, 2:08½.

3-year-old trot, "The Ka-Noo-No," purse $2012.50:

Brother Peter, b. c., by Peter the Great (Thomas)	1	3	1
Little Lee, b. g. (McDonald)	2	1	4
Grace Drake, blk. f. (White)	6	2	2
King Stout, ch. h. (Stout)	3	4	3
Wiki Waki, b. g. (Jones)	4	6	dr

Eliza Dillon, Peter Worth, Liberty Todd and Bourbon Watts also started.

Time—2:09¼, 2:08¼, 2:09½.

2:10 pace, The Syracuse, purse $3000; 3-heat plan:

Goldie Todd, b. m., by Todd Mac (Jones)	2	1	1
Senardo, b. g. (Murphy)	1	3	3
Frank Dewey, br. h. (Cox)	3	2	2

Time—2:03¼, 2:05¼, 2:08¼.

To beat 2:14 trotting:

Electro Dillon, b. h., by Dillon Axworthy (Crossman) ..... Won

Time—2:07½.

"CALAMITY" IS GOOD FOR AMES

Hard Luck Pitcher Goes to Phils

ST. LOUIS, Sept. 10.—Leon Ames, big red-headed right-hander, who has been pitching ball for the Cardinals since 1915, was released to Philadelphia in the National league yesterday. President Rickey of the local club had asked for waivers on Ames and the Phillies averred that they could find a place for Leon on their roster.

During his 16 years in major league service Ames has proven himself one of the greatest pitchers in the game's recent history. Not only is he living thrice the life of the average major leaguer, but he has to his credit some brilliant individual pitching accomplishments, among them a nine inning no hit game for the New York Giants in 1909. A peculiar feature of this game, the opening one of the season, is the fact that New York lost in the 13th inning. Ames lost so many of the so-called hard luck affairs that he has been nicknamed "Calamity."

The Cardinals also purchased the release of Harold Janvrin, the former Red Sox and Washington player, from the Buffalo club of the International league.

MITCHELL SCHOOL TO BE STRONG ON GRID

BILLERICA, Sept. 10.—The Mitchell Military Boys' School of this town is looking forward to a big year in athletics. The school opens for the new term on Wednesday, Sept. 24, and soon after the boys have all returned and the school has been fully organized a call will be issued for candidates for the school eleven.

The school has been represented on the gridiron for many seasons with a strong team, and this year should prove no exception. Although a number of the members of last year's eleven have completed their course, still some of the veteran pigskin chasers will be on hand to form a nucleus for the 1919 eleven. Frank H. Leighton of the faculty will coach the football team, as he has done for many years. A hard schedule of games with the high schools in this section is now being arranged, and the season will probably open early in October and close the latter part of November.

WINS ST. LEGER STAKE

DONCASTER, England, Sept. 10.—The Earl of Derby's Keysoe today won the St. Leger stakes, 6500 sovereigns. Dominion was second and Major Waldorf Astor's Buchan third.

Today's running of the St. Leger was the first since 1914. The race is for three-year-old entire colts and fillies, one mile, six furlongs, 132 yards.

MAKER AND BREAKER OF WORLD'S HOME RUN RECORD

Here are the home run kings of the past and present. On the left is Buck Freeman, who formerly wore a Boston American uniform when Jimmy Collins piloted them to a world's championship in 1903. This picture of Buck was taken in Toledo, Ohio, the day that "Babe" made his 26th home run. He is now an umpire in the American Association. Freeman was a member of the Washington National League Club in 1899 when he made his mark of 25 home runs. He says pitchers and batters are both much better now than in his time and ball parks much larger. On the right is big "Babe" Ruth, the Red Sox heavy slugger. No more comment is needed in his case.

BOXING GOSSIP

By Doc Almy

Jimmy Hill, the Australian featherweight champion, accompanied by Tim O'Sullivan, his manager, and former representative of Les Darcy, was in town yesterday in search of bouts. The pair plan to remain here about a week, during which time they will challenge every lightweight of class that there is the slightest chance of meeting in a Boston ring. Benny Valger, Charley Parker and Johnny Dundee lead the list of opponents that Hill is anxious to meet. Harry Carlson, Frankie Britt and Kloby will not be overlooked. It will be interesting to note the excuses that will be made by these folks to avoid meeting Hill in a decision battle. Yet Hill is a full fledged champion, and worthy of the attention of any boxer of class in the country.

* * * *

It is a curious thing that some of those who had been boosting Johnny Donovan of South Boston for a week to beat Charley Parker are the first to the front with the report that there was something wrong with the bout at the Mechanics building, and that Donovan "dove" for the South End lightweight. It is possible they have it correct, but from my seat, one yard from the ropes, I saw Parker whip one or two beauts into Donovan's ribs, and then clout him left and right to the jaw, and the clouts were genuine ones all right. If Donovan "dove," as has been intimated in some quarters, he took some reminders of the fight to the mat with him.

* * * *

Some time during Tuesday night a drug store at the corner of West Newton street and Huntington avenue was more or less damaged and looted by vandals, who took advantage of the police strike to get busy. Unhappily the store is located across the avenue from where the Armory A. A. conducted its boxing tournament, all of which has led some to the supposition that it must have been fight fans who did the damage. As the boxing show was over by 10:30, and the looting is thought not to have occurred until about 3 o'clock yesterday morning, while some vandals who horn into fights may have had a hand in the business, that any real followers of boxing or any other major sport had a part in the mischief, is stretching it rather fine. And again, if it were followers of boxing who were mixed up in the looting, how can the looting in South Boston be accounted for, seeing that much of the trouble in that section took place while the bouts in Boston were in progress?

* * * *

The Casino A. C. of Lynn presents a rugged welterweight contest tonight which takes on the aspect of an elimination contest that should go a long way toward determining who should be the next opponent of Young Kloby of Lawrence. Chick West of Holyoke meets Paul Doyle, Tony Palazola's champion, for 12 rounds. In the other bouts, both of which are eight-rounders, Sydney Green of Memphis meets Jack Noyes of Chicago. Noyes made a wonderful showing against Battling Bagley at the Commercial Club last Friday night, and Bunch O'Neil of Lynn meets Sankie Anderson of Revere.

* * * *

From the way Shaver O'Brien laid up in his bout with Sailor Joe Gibbs at the A. A. A. show the other night, he evidently has a very high opinion of the Joe Gibbs who hails from Woonsocket, R. I., whom he is scheduled to meet at the Commercial A. C. tomorrow night, in one of the three 10-rounders there. And he has reason to, for it will be recalled that J. G. of Woonsocket dropped Shaver cold one evening at the Grand Opera House.

Over in England they cannot understand how Gerald Paterson, the Australian tennis crack, was ever beaten in the American tennis championship tournament after winning the British title.

UNIONS ORDERED TO GET READY FOR STRIKE

Continued from First Page

ment, highly significant in phraseology, placing the responsibility for the police strike on the Governor, Mayor and police commissioner and begging, as a "last word," the people to preserve law and order during the days to come.

WARNED THE GOVERNOR

The statement is as follows:

"Mr. Jennings, the business agent of the Boston Central Labor Union, and myself both pictured to Governor Coolidge and Mayor Peters repeatedly the situation we thought was going to exist if the police went on strike and we practically begged them to have the police commissioner restdained from going through with his order suspending the officers of the union.

"Also we begged the Governor repeatedly to call a conference in which he and the Mayor and police commissioner and all parties concerned in the controversy could sit down and see if something could not be done to avert such a situation as now exists.

Implored Him to Act

"Governor Coolidge attended the morning session Tuesday of the State Branch of the American Federation of Labor at Greenfield, and Mr. Jennings again begged him and implored him to take some action.

"Now the responsibility of the present crisis is squarely on the shoulders of the parties who would not act to save the situation, and who would not listen to the advice of the officers of the Central Labor Union, the Governor, the Mayor and police commissioner.

"I advise the people to preserve order regardless of the doings of others. As the last word we are going to say we instruct and implore the people to preserve law and order in our city. We will be in Boston tomorrow morning."

Central Union Meets Tonight

The executive board of the Boston Central Labor Union meets in a special session at Wells Memorial Hall at 1 o'clock this afternoon. All past presidents of the organization will assist in the deliberations.

The Central Labor Union meets tonight at the same hall. In the event that martial law is declared during the day the meeting will be held outside Boston.

The local labor officials are attending the sessions of the State branch at Greenfield. They left hurriedly for Boston early this morning.

Have Unions Ready to Act

The heads of all Greater Boston locals have been instructed from Greenfield by telegram to have their organizations ready for instant action.

William S. O'Connor, secretary of the Boston Central Labor Union, and the ranking labor official in the city, received the following telegram from President O'Donnell and Business Agent Jennings last night:

"Announce a special meeting of the central body Thursday night. Have asked all Boston leaders here to ask their locals to be ready for instant action. Will arrive in Boston before noon tomorrow."

The street carmen and the telephone workers will be among the first asked to go out in sympathy with the police, it was believed in labor circles last night.

Both organizations have voted full support to the Boston Policemen's Union.

BUYS ARMY BLANKETS

Two thousand army blankets have been purchased in Baltimore by City Manager Bingham of Waltham, to be placed on sale the latter part of next week at $4.65 each.

CONVENTION ENDS

Action to Allow Boston Delegates to Go Home to Handle Situation—Moral and Financial Support to Policemen—Officers Elected

GREENFIELD, Sept. 10.—The 34th annual convention of the State branch of the American Federation of Labor, in session here, came to a sudden end tonight to enable Greater Boston labor leaders to get back to their locals and assume control during the crisis in Boston.

Sentiment of the convention was strong to support the police to the limit. General strike talk was prevalent. It was felt that organized labor would fight the matter out to the bitter end.

Pledge Full Support

The convention passed resolutions pledging full moral and financial support to the Boston Policemen's Union.

The resolutions, introduced and signed by President Michael J. O'Donnell of the Boston Central Labor Union and P. Harry Jennings, business agent of the organization, were as follows:

"Whereas, the labor movement of Boston has been grossly insulted by the police commissioner and the Mayor of Boston in their determination to stamp out trade unionism among the policemen of Boston, and

"Whereas, the time for conversations and ordinary conciliations has now passed, because of these facts, and it is necessary for the labor movement of Boston to make known the fact that trade unionism and the right of collective bargaining is here to stay, despite the Hunnish attitude of Police Commissioner Edwin U. Curtis, therefore be it

"Resolved, that the State Federation of Labor hereby gives its moral and financial support to the Boston Central Labor Union, and the Boston Policemen's Union and its affiliated bodies in the battle now on to maintain the right of collective bargaining in this State."

Passed Unanimously

The resolutions were passed unanimously and amid great enthusiasm. They were hailed as the precursor of a general sympathetic strike of organized labor in Greater Boston to support the police.

Elections concluded the business of the convention. William A. Nealey of Lynn was re-elected president, and Martin T. Joyce secretary-treasurer. Charles J. Hodsdon of Boston was elected legislative agent. Lynn was named as the city for the next convention. Seven vice-presidents were chosen, as follows: Edward F. McGrady, past president of the Boston Central Labor Union; Jeremiah F. Driscoll of Boston, business agent of the Milk Driver's Union; Mabel Gillespie, president of the Bookkeepers, Stenographers and Accountants' Union of Boston; Thomas Garrity, business agent of the Bartender's Union; Frank Warnock, president of the Lowell Central Labor Union; Michael Cohan, president of the Brockton Central Labor Union, and Michael J. Hines, business agent of the Bottlers' and Drivers' Union. Michael J. O'Donnell was named as delegate to the American Federation of Labor.

Miss Gillespie Re-elected

Miss Gillespie is the first woman delegate to be elected to high office in labor councils. She served last year and was re-elected today.

Among the important resolutions endorsed at the morning business session was one approving the bill granting equal pay to men and women teachers for equal work. Resolutions of sympathy were passed on the deaths of John Mitchell and Solomon Gompers, father of the president of the American Federation of Labor. The convention stood in silent meditation for one minute as a tribute to John Mitchell.

Most of the Boston labor men left on the late afternoon trains. Others will leave on the first trains in the morning.

DAN MORGAN HANDS BELL 3000 BUCKS

Calls Tommy Kloby "The Lawrence Nightmare"

BY DOC ALMY

"Dumb" Dan Morgan of New York wants the fight fans of New England in general, and those of Lawrence in particular, to know that he is not a "swanker."

He called up the writer on the long-distance phone from New York, last evening, to say so.

HAS $3000 WAGER

Also he said that he has $3000 to wager on Eddie Fitzsimmons of New York, will bring the "kale" with him to Boston, and will post it to the effect that Fitz can stop Tommy "Kloby" Corcoran of Lawrence inside 12 rounds.

It was Billy Bell's fling at Morgan in behalf of Kloby, which appeared in yesterday's Post which got "Dumb" Dan's goat. And it got him on the pocketbook, too.

"You can tell the fans of New England," said Morgan, "that if Kloby will agree to box at 140 or under, ringside, Fitz will meet him any time or any place, and I will wager $3000 in cash that my man stops the chap who in New York has been dubbed 'The Lawrence Nightmare.'

Coming to Hub

"I will come to Boston on Friday night with the money and deposit it, providing, of course, Bell will let his man box Fitz and will post that hunk of money he loves to rave about that Kloby won't run out of the match. I won't sign a paper unless Bell posts at least $1000 that Kloby will appear when wanted. Now let's hear who does the squaking."

So much for so much. Incidental to the talk of a Fitzsimmons-Kloby battle Morgan imparted the information that Benny Leonard had just refused an offer of $10,000 to meet Fitzsimmons in an eight-round, no decision bout before a Newark club, all of which should make Bell and his prize feel very cheerful with reverse English.

PLAY PORTLAND TEAM SUNDAY

The usual service games will be held at Braves Field next Sunday, the principal game being one between the Northeastern Headquarters team and the Fort Williams team from Portland, Me. All the men on both the teams are enlisted men actually in the service at the present time.

The Fort Williams men won the championship in Maine this season and won their last game from the Northeastern Headquarters team on a close decision, with a score of 4 to 3.

The headquarters team is looking forward to winning the decision next Sunday, but expects a close battle all the way. If it is possible to so arrange it, the U. S. Shipping Board team will be one of the contestants in the other game.

Yale's Captain Watches Harvard

Tim Callahan Lamps the Crimson Players in Muddy Practics

The Harvard football players worked out for two hours in the mud yesterday under the watchful eyes of Tim Callahan, captain-elect of the Yale gridiron team which will oppose the Crimson eleven Nov. 22. The big Eli centre is in fine condition and looks fit to jump right into the Blue moleskins.

SHOULD MAKE GOOD POLICE

Fred W. Moore, graduate treasurer of the Harvard Athletic Association, gave the Crimson squad a talk in the locker building before the start of practice regarding the police strike. He said that any player who wished to offer his services to the Commonwealth should not hesitate because of football. It was up to each individual to decide for himself, and his chances of making the team would not be decreased by the fact that he quit practice to volunteer.

Few of the regular gridiron stars seemed to think that it would be needful for them to sign up now with the four regiments of State Guards on duty. George Batchelder, the "H" man, who played end against Yale in 1916, signed up earlier in the day. Morris Phinney, who played on the other end of the line in the Yale game that season, went in to the Chamber of Commerce building to talk it over, but he has not yet decided to enroll. Both the players are the most experienced candidates for the wing positions that Head Coach Bob Fisher now has in Cambridge.

Fiske Brown, who played guard on the service eleven last fall, enrolled in the volunteer police early, and is waiting to be called. He is a big, husky lad, tipping the scales at 210 pounds, a good aspirant for the regular guard position on the Crimson eleven.

Redington Fiske, who came out for centre a few days, joined the emergency police force and is on the same beat with George Soper, a Crimson candidate track manager.

Players Suffer From Gas

Poisonous gas, inhaled in the trenches of France, is now causing a little trouble among the Harvard candidates. Mose Hadley, the most prospective candidate for tackle at the start of the season, has been obliged to let up in his work, and Dr. Nichols has asked all the gassed players to report for treatment. Hadley was an officer with the 101st Infantry in France during a large part of the war. He believed the effects of a gas attack had passed over until a rugged gridiron drill Monday affected his playing. The doctor declared that the gas affects the heart and he has not yet decided whether the big Crimson ace will be able to complete the season.

"Tubby" Clark, the 235-pound guard of the 1916 team, was out for a light drill yesterday on Soldiers Field. "Tubby" is going to see the doctor Monday. His back, injured some weeks ago at golf, seems to be coming along all right, but the Cambridge Colossus is not going to take any big chances until the doctor gives the word.

Henry Sprague, who played on Percy Haughton's first victorious team that won from Yale by a margin of a field goal, was out to help Sam Felton develop the kickers yesterday. He was impressed with the punting of Ralph Horween and some of the other Crimson booters who have been showing unusual form lately.

Centres Improve

Paul Withington, newly appointed coach of the freshman team, who recently returned from France, where he piloted the 89th Division team to the gridiron championship of the A. E. F., took charge of the centres yesterday. He drilled the pivot men for a couple of hours and they seemed to gain considerably in a short time.

Only one new candidate, Austin Blair, varsity catcher, reported yesterday. He was a candidate for the backfield of the 1921 freshman eleven, but he may try for end on the varsity this season.

Workmen were busy erecting the score board and putting the finishing touches on the Stadium, so that everything will be in readiness for the team. Practice yesterday consisted of the regular Harvard conditioning work. Bill Snow, the guard coach, advanced his class of candidates along a peg yesterday with stanching, charging and wrestling drills.

"Pooch" Donovan put the entire squad through a session of sprinting before practice started and then sent them around the Stadium on the run after the coaches had finished their work.

MACKS GET PITCHER

PHILADELPHIA, Sept. 10.—The Philadelphia Americans have purchased Pat Martin, a left-handed pitcher, from the Binghamton club of the International league for $6000.

STRIKERS WILL STICK TO A. F. OF L.

Anxious to Restore Order in City They Say

It was reported by members of the Policemen's Union last night that representatives of the Mayor's Citizen Committee of 34 were seeking James H. Vahey or John F. Feeney, attorneys for the union. The report stated that the committee was ready to offer to accede to all demands of the policemen even to their unionizing, with the one exception that the men should not be affiliated with the American Federation of Labor.

Union leaders stated last night that they would not leave the fold of the federation. The report has made them confident of victory. "It shows," they said, "that they are on the run." Another man said, "It will be a great victory. Thank God. And I hope the matter will be settled speedily."

NEW MEMBERS JOIN

Last night's meeting was fully as largely attended as Tuesday night's meeting. Many new members came into the union yesterday and were present at the meeting last night. Reports were current at the meeting of support from other police departments throughout the State and it is believed there will be difficulty in obtaining men from the police of other cities to come to Boston on special duty, if attempts along this line are made.

It was stated that 155 out of 190 Metropolitan policemen had quit, when ordered to duty in Boston. It was also reported that the Chelsea police had refused to do police duty in Boston if called upon as a unite to perform such duty.

Park Police Attend Meeting

It was also reported from the headquarters that the marine engineers on the police boat, queried the union as to whether they would support them if they quit work without sanction. The engineers will go out this morning.

Most of the Metropolitan policemen, who had been ordered to Boston for duty last night, and refused to perform this duty, went to the union headquarters of the Boston police last night and sat in at their meeting. They assured the Boston men of their support. The men were minus the numbers on their helmets.

Sorry for Disorders

The police expressed themselves as sorry for the display of rampage which is sweeping the city, and are anxious to get back to work so that the city may be placed in a normal condition again. They still persist, however, that their union is the only relief for them from what they term the shackles of bondage, which have held them, while members of the Boston police force.

The headquarters were open all day yesterday, and union men were present throughout the day.

Expect Firemen to Join

At one time during the day the fire apparatus clattered by the headquarters. It is expected that these men may go out in sympathetic strike. As the apparatus passed, the police went to the windows and cheered. The firemen in return smiled and waved up at the policemen.

James H. Vahey, attorney for the Policemen's Union, stated last night that ho had heard nothing from the Mayor's committee, or nothing of the rumor that representatives of the citizens' committee were ready to accede to all demands of the police, even to their having a union, with the exception of the fact they they should be affiliated with the American Federation of Labor.

EXTRA!

A LOYAL PAPER FOR LOYAL PEOPLE
PRICE 3 CENTS

The Bulletin

5 P.M. EDITION

VOL. 129. 64TH YEAR. TWENTY-FOUR PAGES. SAN FRANCISCO, THURSDAY, OCTOBER 9, 1919. 50c per month by mail or carrier. Trains and Boats, 5c per copy. NUMBER 3.

REDS WIN SERIES

THE GAME BY INNINGS

The score by innings follows:

FIRST INNING.

Cincinnati—Rath popped to Risberg, who went on the grass back of third base to make the catch. Daubert singled. Groh singled, sending Daubert to second. James went out to warm up. Rousch doubled to right, scoring Daubert, Groh taking third. Duncan doubled to left, scoring Groh and Rousch. James now pitching for Chicago. Williams took a terrific punishment during his short stay in the box. Two doubles and two singles netted the Reds three runs before he was withdrawn. Kopf walked. Wilkinson warming up for Chicago. Neale fanned. Rariden singled, scoring Duncan and sending Kopf to third. Rariden stole second. Eller flied to Felsch. Four runs, five hits, no errors.

Chicago—Leibold singled. Ring went out to warm up for the Reds. E. Collins doubled to left, sending Leibold to third. Weaver fanned. Jackson popped to Kopf. Felsch fanned. No runs, two hits, no errors.

SECOND INNING.

Cincinnati—Rath fanned. Daubert flied to Jackson. Groh singled to Gandil, who threw to James, who covered first, but was too late. Groh slid into first base and hurt his leg. Groh returned to first base and the crowd gave him warm applause. Rousch doubled, scoring Groh, but Rousch was caught when he overran second, Jackson to Schalk to Weaver to E. Collins. One run, two hits, no errors.

Chicago—Gandil lined to Daubert. Risberg walked. Rariden dropped Schalk's easy pop foul and an error. Schalk singled, sending Risberg to second. James fouled to Groh. Leibold fanned. No runs, one hit, one error.

THIRD INNING.

Cincinnati—Duncan out, Weaver to Gandil. Kopf out, Weaver to Gandil. Neale walked. Neale out stealing, Schalk to E. Collins. No runs, no hits, no errors.

Chicago—E. Collins lined to Duncan. Weaver popped to Rath. Jackson drove the ball into the right field bleachers for the first home run of the series. Felsch out, Kopf to Daubert. One run, one hit, no error.

FOURTH INNING.

Cincinnati—Rariden lined to Gandil. Eller was hit by pitched ball. Rath singled. Eller went to second. Daubert singled. Eller was caught at the plate on Leibold's throw to the plate. Rath went to third on the hit and Daubert took second on the throw-in. Groh popped to E. Collins. No runs, two hits, no errors.

Chicago—Gandil flied to Neale. Risberg fanned. Schalk out, Groh to Daubert. No runs, no hits, no errors.

FIFTH INNING.

Cincinnati—Rousch out, E. Collins to Gandil. Duncan lined to E. Collins, Kopf tripled to right. Neale singled, scoring Kopf. Neale stole second. Rariden out, Risberg to Gandil. One run, two hits, no errors.

Chicago—James fanned. Leibold out, Kopf to Daubert. E. Collins out, Kopf to Daubert. No runs, no hits, no errors.

SIXTH INNING.

Cincinnati—Eller singled. Rath walked. Wilkinson now pitching for Chicago. Daubert bunted. Schalk made a bad throw to Weaver and all were safe. Lowdermilk warming up now for Chicago. Groh fanned. Rousch singled, scoring Eller and Rath, sending Daubert to third. Duncan singled, scoring Daubert and sending Rousch to third, Duncan going to second on Leibold's throw to Weaver to catch Rousch. Kopf walked, filling the bases. Neale hit to Weaver, who threw to Schalk, forcing Rousch at the plate. Schalk caught Kopf off second with a snap throw to Risberg. Three runs, three hits, one error.

(Continued In Red.)

Reds Knock Williams from Pitcher's Box

CHICAGO, Oct. 9.—"Lefty" Williams, twice loser to the Cincinnati Reds, started today's game for "Kid" Gleason, but he didn't finish it. In fact, the big southpaw lasted less than an inning.

With Rath down, the Reds started a swatfest that ended only when Williams surrendered the mound to James. Daubert was the first to get a safety. Groh landed for another single, and along came Rousch to claim a double that scored Daubert. Duncan likewise doubled, scoring Groh and Rousch, whereupon Claudie departed for the showers.

James took up the Sox's burden with Duncan on second. When he walked Kopf, Wilkinson started warming up. Rariden's single scored Duncan and the Reds were retired with but four runs and five hits for their half of the inning.

CINCINNATI WINS WORLD'S SERIES. SCORE, 10-5.

LAST HALF SIXTH: Chicago—Weaver singled. Jackson flied to Ruosch. Rousch also took care of Felsch's high fly. Neale caught Gandil's fly. No runs, one hit, n eorrors.

SEVENTH. Cincinnati—Rariden flied to Felsch. Eller fanned. Rath walked and stole second. Daubert also walked. Groh hoisted to Leibold. No runs, no hits, no errors.

Chicago—Risberg flied to Rath. Schalk lifted a high foul to Rariden. Wilkinson struck out. No runs, no hits, no errors.

EIGHTH: Cincinnati—Rousch hit by pitched ball. Duncan sacrificed, Wilkinson to Gandil. Kopf fouled to Weaver. Neale walked. Rariden singled, Rousch scoring, Neale reaching third and Rariden second on Jackson's throw to plate. Risberg threw out Eller at first. One run, one hit, no errors.

Chicago—Leibold flied to Neale. Ed Collins singled. Weaver doubled, putting Ed. Collins on third. Jackson doubled, scoring Ed. Collins and Weaver. Felsch popped to Daubert. Gandil tripled, Jackson scoring. Rousch fumbled Risberg's fly, Gandil trotting home. Rath tossed out Schalk. Four runs, four hits.

NINTH: Cincinnati—Rath singled. Daubert sacrificed, Wilkinson to Gandil, Rath taking second. Groh hoisted to Leibold. Weaver threw out Rousch. No runs, one hit, no errors.

Chicago—Murphy, batting for Wilkinson, hit by pitcher. Leibold flied to Rousch. Ed. Collins singled, Murphy going to second. Weaver flied to Neale, Murphy going to third. Ed. Collins stole second. Jackson thrown out by Rath. No runs, one hit.

INDUSTRY TRUCE ASKED

'Sky Pilot' Leads Derby

TERMINATION OF STRIKE IS NOT LIKELY

OAKLAND, Oct. 9.—W. R. Alberger, vice-president and general manager of the San Francisco and Oakland Terminal Railways Company, announced today that he had telegraphed Governor William D. Stephens that a state of mob violence existed here as a result of the strike of platform men and that the local authorities were unable to maintain order.

Alberger said he had not asked the Governor to send troops.

OAKLAND, Oct. 9.—All hope for a peaceful termination of the car strike was sent adrift today when in reply to the City Council's ultimatum that the company and the car men reach an adjustment of their differences both declared themselves unalterably opposed to arbitration.

The carmen declared that they offered arbitration on every point yesterday and that this was refused. They now state that they are willing to arbitrate on all points except the eight-hour day. On this they will stand. The company, however, flatly refuses union recognition and declares itself unwilling to arbitrate at all.

Matters were further complicated when at a meeting of Electrical Workers' Union No. 283, last night, it was decided to call out all electrical workers, pilots and engineers in sympathy with the carmen's strike. This will preclude the possibility of operating the cars with non-union crews. The decision will also have the effect of plunging Oakland, Alameda, Berkeley and all Alameda and Contra Costa towns that are supplied by the Great Western Power Company and Pacific Gas and Electric Company into darkness.

W. R. Alberger, vice president of the company, notified the Berkeley council today that he would accede to the council's rulings and submit all non-union employees to the chief of police for a test as to their sanity and ability to operate the cars.

CITY TO SUPPLY BUSSES.

Commissioner Soderberg announced in council this morning that $300,000 is available to establish automobile

(Continued on Next Page, Column 2.)

GREAT STRAIN ON BIRDMEN CROSSING RANGE

By MAJOR CARL SPATZ
(Assistant Air Officer, Western Department, and pilot of De Haviland Bluebird in transcontinental race, writing daily story of flight for The Bulletin.)

SALT LAKE, Oct. 8.—Every flier in the transcontinental race who left San Francisco this morning was hanging to his life only by his motor. We crossed mountains at an elevation of 12,000 feet in the East Humboldt range in Nevada, and three-fourths of the distance we were all on compass course, with no landing fields in sight. Nursing one's motor was the chief occupation—that and speed, speed and more speed.

The strain was terrific, but there is not one of us that would abandon the race for any prize the world has to offer. We all grieve for Crissy and condole with his widow.

I was third into Salt Lake. Captain Lowell H. Smith and Lieutenant E. C. Kiel preceding me in the order named by 34 minutes and 15 minutes, respectively. The trick of the race, I am convinced, is going to be to beat those fellows. They are in splendid shape, with ships in good conditions and we three could have reached Cheyenne today but for the fact that the field at Green River was not in proper shape. This is lamentable, for it destroys all chance of reaching New York Friday.

120 MILES AN HOUR.

Our flying rate has been 120 miles

(Continued on Next Page, Column 1.)

Captain Smith, S. F. Air Racer, Is at Cheyenne

(By United Press)

CHEYENNE, Wyo., Oct. 9.—Catain J. H. Smith in a De Haviland 4, leader of the San Francisco starters in the air race, landed here this afternoon.

RAWLINS, Wyo., Oct. 9.—Four of the Pacific Coast starters in the transcontinental aerial derby arrived here this morning without stopping at Green River control station, on account of in ability to make out the landing field.

The aviators reported weather conditions dangerous for flying.

(By Associated Press)

SALT LAKE CITY, Oct. 9.—Army airplanes Nos. 58, 61 and 62, piloted by Captain Lowell H. Smith, Major Carl Spatz and Lieutenant E. C. Kiel, respectively, left Buena Vista Field on the second lap of their transcontinental derby at 7:55 this morning.

They "hopped off" in the order named, the same order as their arrival yesterday from San Francisco. Rawlins, Wyo., was to be the first stop.

RACER LEAVES SACRAMENTO.

SACRAMENTO, Oct. 9.—Lieutenant G. E. Rice, piloting a Sopwith, last of the eastbound transcontinental racers to reach Sacramento yesterday, took the air at Mather Field for the flight across the Sierras at 8:09 this morning.

RAWLINS NEXT STOP.

SALT LAKE CITY, Oct. 9.—Green River, Wyo., has been eliminated as a stop for eastbound fliers in the transcontinental airplane derby. The commander of the control stop at Rawlins, Wyo., was notified from here to prepare for the reception of six aviators who had left here up to 8:50 o'clock a. m.

The landing field at Green River had been found in bad condition. Machines 48, 62, 61, 63, 55 and 59 had departed up to 8:59 o'clock this morning in the order named.

SALT LAKE CITY, Oct. 9.—Major J. C. P. Barthoff, flying a Sopwith, who was stalled last night at Salduro, Utah, 100 miles west of here, arrived at Buena Vista field, near here, at 10:03 o'clock this morning. Lieutenant H. E. Queen, No. 52, and Lieutenant R. S. Worthington, No. 60, left for Rawlins at 10:10.

Lieutenant Robert Kauch and Observer Maxwell were forced to descend at Coalville, Utah, about forty miles east of here, on account of cold weather. They are said to be out of the race. All of the aviators report extremely cold weather over the mountains.

PLANE LEAVES CANADA FOR N. Y.

HALIFAX, N. S., Oct. 9.—The bombing plane "Atlantic" left Harrisboro, N. S., for New York at 11:40 a. m. today. Weather conditions were favorable, and Commander Kerr expected to complete the flight before sundown.

MAYNARD AT ST PAUL BIG AIR DERBY

(By Associated Press)

ELMYRA, N. Y., Oct. 9.—Plane No. 20, Captain John Marquette, is reported 18 miles from this city, near Waverly, with nose stuck in mud.

ASHTABULA, Ohio, Oct. 9.—Airplane No. 45, in the transcontinental aerial derby, fell into Lake Erie, three miles east of Ashtabula harbor, this morning. The two occupants were rescued by a steamer.

The plane was piloted by Second Lieutenant T. Hynes. Second Lieutenant T. K. Matthews was carried as a passenger.

MAYNARD IN LEAD.

ST. PAUL, Neb., Oct. 9.—Lieutenant B. W. Maynard, a Baptist minister, who was in the overseas flying service, driving a De Haviland 4,4 arrived here at 2:45 p. m. from Chicago. He made the 132 miles from Omaha in 98 minutes.

OMAHA, Neb., Oct. 9.—Lieutenant B. W. Maynard, a Baptist minister, who was in the overseas flying service, driving a De Haviland 4, arrived at Ak-San-Ben flying field at 12:48 p. m. today from Chicago. He was the first cross-country flier to reach this point.

WEATHER CLEAR.

CHICAGO, Oct. 9.—At 9:45 a. m. Captain Hoag, commander at Ashland Field, sent a message to Bryan Field, Ohio, to start all westbound airplanes from that point as soon as they were ready, as weather conditions in Chicago had sufficiently improved to make flying safe.

LANDS IN RAIN.

CLEVELAND, Oct. 9.—Lieutenant Alex Pearson Jr., driving machine No. 8, was the first flyer to reach Glenn Martin Field here from Buffalo this morning, landing at 9:07 a. m. during a heavy downpour of rain.

At that time the four machines that had been waiting to start west since daylight, were still here.

The second flyer to land here this morning was Captain J. O. Donaldson machine No. 50, who landed in

(Continued on Next Page, Column 4.)

Ratify Treaty, Demand Made In Resolutions

(By Associated Press)

DETROIT, Oct. 9.—Resolutions appealing to the United State Senate to ratify the peace treaty with Germany and the covenant of the League of Nations were introduced today in the house of deputies of the Triennial general convention of the Protestant Episcopal Church, in session here and given a place on the calendar.

ATLANTA, Ga., Oct. 9.—Prior to the annual "memorial service" with nearly 8000 persons assembled, the resolutions committee of the Confederate Veterans in session here, presented today its report including a memorial to the United States Senate urging speedy ratification of the peace treaty without amendment or reservations.

Arms Seized in Gary by Officers

(By Associated Press)

CHICAGO, Oct. 9.—Federal agents today made another series of raids on the homes of radical leaders at Gary, Ind., and seized a quantity of firearms, red flags and revolutionary literature.

Claims of officials of the steel mills that strikers were returning to work in increasing numbers were denied by union labor leaders.

ARBITRATION IS URGED TO END STEEL STRIKE

(By Associated Press)

WASHINGTON, Oct. 9.—An immediate industrial truce to continue three months, creation of an arbitration board by the President and Congress, and immediate arbitration of the nationwide steel strike, were among proposals made today to the industrial conference here. The first two were presented by representatives of the public and the last by the labor group.

Bernard M. Baruch, chairman of the public group, made the proposal for the industrial truce, while Samuel Gompers, president of the American Federation of Labor and chairman of the labor group, proposed arbitration of the steel strike. Gompers' plan contemplated immediate return of the steel strikers to work pending the outcome of efforts to arbitrate the dispute.

Gavin McNab, of San Francisco,

(Continued on Next Page, Column 5.)

CINCINNATI vs. CHICAGO AT CHICAGO.

Cincinnati—	AB	R	BH	PO	A	E
Rath, 2b.	4	1	2	2	2	0
Daubert, 1b.	4	2	2	8	0	0
Groh, 3b.	6	2	2	1	1	0
Rousch, cf.	5	2	3	3	0	1
Duncan, lf.	4	1	2	1	0	0
Kopf, ss.	4	1	1	1	3	0
Neale, rf.	3	0	1	4	0	0
Rariden, c.	5	0	2	7	0	1
Eller, p.	4	1	1	0	0	0
	0	0	0	0	0	0
	0	0	0	0	0	0
	0	0	0	0	0	0
	0	0	0	0	0	0
	0	0	0	0	0	0
	0	0	0	0	0	0
	0	0	0	0	0	0
Totals	[illegible]	10	16	27		2

Chicago—	AB	R	BH	PO	A	E
Liebold, cf.	4	0	1	2	2	0
E Collins, 2b	5	1	8	4	1	0
Weaver, 3b	5	1	2	1	5	0
Jackson, lf	4	2	2	1	0	0
Felsch, rf.	4	[illegible]	0	[illegible]	[illegible]	[illegible]
Gandil, 1b	4	1	[illegible]	[illegible]	[illegible]	[illegible]
Risberg, ss	3	0	0	2	[illegible]	[illegible]
Schalk, c.	4	0	1	6	3	1
Williams, p.	0	0	0	0	0	0
James, p.	2	0	0	0	0	0
Wilkinson, p.	1	0	0	0	*2	0
Murphy, lf.	0	0	0	0	0	0
	0	0	0	0	0	0
	0	0	0	0	0	0
	0	0	0	0	0	0
	0	0	0	0	0	0
Totals	37	5	10	27	16	1

"It matters not how long you live, but how well"—*Publius Syrus*

Cardinal Mercier's Own Story On Page 8

The Boston Post

THE GREAT Breakfast Table Paper OF NEW ENGLAND

TWENTY-TWO PAGES—TWO CENTS | Established 1831 | TUESDAY, JANUARY 6, 1920 ** | Copyright, 1920, by Post Publishing Co. | TWENTY-TWO PAGES—TWO CENTS

BABE RUTH SOLD TO THE YANKEES

Frazee Disposes of Mighty Slugger for Cash—Price Is Said to Be $125,000—Greatest Sum Ever Paid for a Baseball Player in the Game's History

Ruth Termed a Handicap and Not an Asset by the Red Sox President

Purchase Price Is Pledged to Secure New Stars for the Boston Club

HUGGINS ANNOUNCES THAT RUTH HAS SIGNED

LOS ANGELES, Cal., Jan. 5.—Miller Huggins, manager of the New York Americans, tonight announced he had signed "Babe" Ruth, champion home run hitter, to play with the Yankees next season. Papers were exchanged here late today, Huggins said. He refused to state what salary Ruth was to receive.

BY PAUL H. SHANNON

George (Babe) Ruth, greatest home run swatter of all time, will drive out home runs for the Boston Red Sox no more. Yesterday afternoon the home run record king passed into the possession of the New York Yankees, the deal being closed over the telephone by Colonel Huston of the New York club and President Harry Frazee, the Red Sox magnate.

Continued on Page 15—First Col.

REDS WILL BATTLE TO STAY HERE

Many Have Retained Counsel to Fight Deportation

PRISONERS TO GET SPEEDY HEARINGS

City Appropriates $15,000 to Stay Radicals

RAID ON "REDS" IS RESUMED IN GOTHAM

NEW YORK, Jan. 5.—The sweeping raids against "Reds" by federal agents, which netted nearly 700 prisoners last Friday night, were resumed at 7:30 tonight when 10 large automobiles and two army transport wagons left the local headquarters of the Department of Justice to round up Communists and other sedition mongers, who escaped the first dragnet. Twenty-five houses had been raided and about 75 persons arrested up to midnight.

More than half of the 413 men and women radicals now at Deer Island as a result of the nation-wide Red raid of last Friday have engaged counsel and are going to make a desperate legal fight to remain in this country. Their battle against deportation will be carried to the Supreme Court if necessary.

It became known yesterday that those arrested on deportation warrants will be charged with various offences, each of which is often regard-

Continued on Page 11—Fourth Col.

WOMAN SAVED FROM DEATH

Mrs. Conroy Burned and Ankle Broken

Mrs. Ellen Conroy, 72-year-old invalid of 4 Pleasant street, Dorchester, was saved from burning to death in her home early last night by Mrs. Margaret Hyland, a tenant in the same house, who rushed to the woman's assistance after she had been enveloped in flames while sitting in her kitchen. The woman's shawl caught fire while she was lighting a gas jet.

Mrs. Hyland extinguished the flames on the woman's clothes as well as on the table at which she was sitting.

Leaving Mrs. Conroy alone in the house while she went to the street, Mrs. Hyland again heard groans, and found that the woman had toppled down the stairs in trying to leave the house, breaking her ankle. An ambulance removed her to the City Hospital, where her name was placed on the danger list.

"WETS" LOSE, BUT TO START NEW BATTLE

Supreme Court, 5 to 4 Against 2.75 War-Time Beer—New Fight to Be Under the Constitutional Amendment

THE WAGON'S LATEST RECRUIT.

WASHINGTON, Jan. 5.—By a margin of one vote the Supreme Court today upheld the right of Congress to define intoxicating liquors, insofar as applied to war-time prohibition. The "wets" will now make their fight for 2.75 per cent beer under the constitutional amendment, and they are hopeful of better success.

In a five to four opinion rendered by Associate Justice Brandeis, the court today sustained the constitutionality of provisions in the Volstead prohibition enforcement act prohibiting the manufacture and sale of beverages containing one-half of 1 per cent or more of alcohol. Associate Justices Day, Vandevanter, McReynolds and Clarke dissented.

DECISION IS SWEEPING

Validity of the federal prohibition constitutional amendment and of portions of the Volstead act affecting its enforcement was not involved in the proceedings, but the opinion was regarded as so sweeping as to leave little hope among "wet" adherents.

Wayne B. Wheeler, general counsel for the Anti-Saloon League of America, hailed it as "a sweeping victory," and in a statement tonight said the

Continued on Page 22—Second Col.

COOLIDGE NOT TO SEEK PRESIDENCY

Says Office Must Seek the Man—Runs Strong in Poll of the Roosevelt Club

BY ROBERT T. BRADY

A poll participated in by a little more than half of the members of the Roosevelt Club, announced by Vice-President Robert M. Washburn last night, showed Leonard Wood a favorite for the Republican nomination for President, with Governor

Continued on Page 11—Second Col.

PLANS FLIGHT OVER PACIFIC

VANCOUVER, B. C., Jan. 5.—Major D. A. Yarnold, British Royal Flying Corps ace, who is credited with 83 German airplanes, announced today that he intends to leave tomorrow for England to make arrangements for an attempted flight across the Pacific from Australia to San Francisco.

A special Vickers-Viking machine will be built at Waybridge, England, for the flight, he said. He must secure permission to make the flight, he said, from the British war office.

GALLI-CURCI WINS HER DIVORCE SUIT

Case Goes Practically by Default—Husband Withdraws Spicy Answer to Suit

CHICAGO, Jan. 5.—Mme. Amelita Galli-Curci today won a divorce from Luigi Curci, artist. Judge Charles A. McDonald in the Superior Court indicated he would sign a decree.

The hearing, which ended a year of brief drawing, deposition taking and detailed evidence seeking, was a disappointment to several hundred court fans, who had expected a bitter legal battle extending over several days. The case went practically by default, the spicy answer to Mme. Galli-Curci's bill being withdrawn at the last moment.

HUSBAND NOT IN COURT

Nevertheless, the diva was there, and she offered a bit of bright testimony and told tales of Luigi Curci's "other loves." Two pictures of those loves were introduced.

Luigi Curci was not in court. His attorney, Roy D. Keehn, declined to cross-examine the witnesses. When Mme. Galli-Curci heard Judge McDonald say "that's all," she sighed and smiled and declared that her thoughts in the future would be far from matrimony.

The charge against Luigi Curci was infidelity. The girl named was one Melissa Brown of Flischman's. In a deposition Miss Brown admitted that Curci had made love to her in a motor car on a lonely moonlit road.

On Girl's Admission

It is upon that deposition, Attorney Joseph B. Fleming said, that the divorce will be granted. Mr. Fleming represented Mme. Galli-Curci.

Continued on Page 4—Second Col.

MME. AMELITA GALLI-CURCI, Noted opera singer, who yesterday secured a divorce.

MORE SHOTS IN PHOENIX PARK

Mysterious Affair at Irish Viceroy's Lodge

LONDON, Jan. 5.—"There was another mysterious affair in Phoenix Park shortly after Sunday midnight," says a Central News despatch from Dublin. "A volley of shots was heard in the park. Then all was quiet for 25 minutes, when a fusillade started and lasted for several minutes. It apparently came from the direction of the magazine of the fort near the viceregal lodge.

"It is also stated that from then until dawn the park was scoured by armored cars with bright searchlights. No official explanation has yet been made."

DIES OF BURNS

Mrs. John Cooper of 16 Burridge place, Malden, died at the Malden Hospital last night as the result of burns received when her dress caught fire from a gas stove.

WILSON WILL GREET LEADERS

To Send 'Important Word' to Jackson Banquet

WASHINGTON, Jan. 5.—Announcement from the White House that President Wilson plans to send "an important word of greeting" to the Democratic dinner here on Jackson Day, Jan. 8, aroused great interest among Democratic leaders arriving today to attend the love feast and the quadrennial meeting of the party's national committee, both of which are to be held Thursday.

Prominent Democrats said they had no information as to the message of the President beyond the brief announcement from the White House, and there was wide speculation as to whether the "word of greeting" would take up the question of a third term or would outline the President's views on party policies.

HIGH TIDE TODAY

A. M. 11:21 | P. M. 11:56

SUN Rises 7:13. Sets 4:27. MOON Rises at 5:51 p. m.

Light all vehicles tonight at 4:57.

TODAY'S ANNIVERSARIES, ETC.

Twelfth Day or twelfth tide.

Russia annihilated Turkish army corps at Sarryramysh, 1915.

Fire in New York subway killed one and affected 200 others, 1915.

One year ago today—Theodore Roosevelt died.—President Wilson returned to Paris.

FAIR—WARMER

Forecast for Boston and vicinity: Fair and warmer Tuesday and Wednesday; moderate shifting winds, becoming southerly.

WASHINGTON, Jan. 5.—Forecast for New England: Fair and warmer Tuesday; Wednesday partly cloudy and warmer.

Winds off Atlantic coast—North of Sandy Hook, moderate to fresh, shifting, becoming south, fair; Sandy Hook to Hatteras, fresh northeast, except variable, becoming south, off New Jersey coast, fair.

In the middle Atlantic States and New England fair weather will prevail Tuesday and Wednesday.

Temperatures will rise slowly.

YESTERDAY'S TEMPERATURE

Reported by Thompson's Spa.

	'19	'20		'19	'20
3 a. m.	18	9	3 p. m.	25	27
6 a. m.	17	9	6 p. m.	25	27
9 a. m.	18	18	9 p. m.	21	19
12 m.	23	23	12 mid.	21	18

Average temperature yesterday, 17 18-24.
Average temperature one year ago, 20 22-24.

TEACHERS' PAY RAISE IN EFFECT

Three-Fourths of the Force Get $384 Increase

The salary schedule for teachers, members of the supervisory force and other employees of the Boston school department—all of which embody the recent increases authorized by the Legislature—were passed by the school committee last night.

An order was passed also making the salaries of the assistant superintendents $6000. This was opposed by Michael H. Corcoran, but he was outvoted four to one. The same order authorized the pay of the business agent and the secretary at $5496, and that of the schoolhouse custodian at $3300. All the increases take effect on Jan. 1 of this year.

GREATEST TO MISS ABORN

Practically three-fourths of the teachers get the benefit of the $384 increase which was embodied in the committee's bill passed by the Legislature.

The one person in the entire school department getting the biggest increase, according to the schedule, is Miss Caroline D. Aborn, the present director of kindergartens. She receives a $480 minimum increase. Under the old schedule her minimum salary was $1620. It is now $2100.

The next highest increases go to three assistant directors of the Mechanic Arts High School. They get a raise of $408 as a maximum.

The smallest increase goes to the masters. They will draw a $72 raise.

According to a statement submitted by Secretary Apollonio, the number of pupils in the schools who were savings bank depositors on Oct. 31, 1919, was 5520, with deposits of $15,916. This shows a decrease from a year ago. Then 6564 pupils had on deposit $21,143.

PERSHING AIDS TO FIGHT FIRE

Directs Battle With Flames at Camp Grant

ROCKFORD, Ill., Jan. 5.—Fire broke out in one of the buildings at Camp Grant soon after the arrival of General Pershing today and he directed the work of the camp firemen in fighting the flames, which were quickly extinguished. General Pershing inspected the camp this morning and was the guest of Rockford this afternoon. Ten thousand school children paraded for him.

BRITONS WIN TWO MILE RELAY AND SET WORLD'S RECORD

20,000 Track and Field Fans See Oxford-Cambridge Set Record

Britons Cover Two Mile Relay in Fast Time of Seven Minutes, 50 2-5 Seconds —Illnois in Second Place

By JACK VEDOCK

Franklin Field, Phila., May 1.

Two new sectional and one word's record fell here today in the Penn relays, while a crowd of 20,000 cheering spectators looked on. The weather was perfect and performances of the athletes were altogether brilliant.

Perhaps the happiest quartette of athletes in the world tonight are W. G. Latham, H. B. Stallard, W. R. Mulligan and B. G. Rudd, of the Oxford-Cambridge, two mile relay team. Running in the order named these athletes captured the two mile collegiate relay championships of America and broke the world's record for the distance, running the race in 7 minutes, 50 2-5 seconds better than the record. Each of the quartette ran a brilliant half mile and Rudd, finished a good 20 yards ahead of his field. Illinois was second and Pennsylvania third.

The sectional records were broken by John Hopkins in the one mile. South Atlantic A. A. championships also at one mile. John Hopkins team ran its winning race in 3:27 4-5. The old record was 3:32 1-5 made by John Hopkins last year. Rutgers won its first in 3:26 4-5. The former mark was 3:30.

F. Scholz of Missouri University won the special 100 yard dash in 10 1-5 seconds. His victory was rather expected and he looks like Olympic material. Five heats were necessary prior to the final in this event and Scholz ran against Lever, of Pennsylvania; Brown, Princeton; Laurie, Princeton Leconey, Lafayette and Messengile, Missouri, winning his race by a good margin.

Nabor, of Wabash, put H. P. Jenne of Oxford out of the 120 yard high hurdle race finals by winning his heat in fine form. Nabor did not finish in the money in the final heat however, which grought out Earl Tompson of Dartmouth as a brilliant victor.

The performance of Shields and his mates Morrell, Newcomer and Orr of Penn State in winning the national four mile relay championship was altogether brilliant. Shields was clocked by some of his railbirds in the last mile in 4:20.

Penn had to be content with one track victory of importance. Eby, Davis, Maxim and Rogers cleaned up the one mile relay championship with ease. Eby ran away from his field in the last quarter.

Walsh Refuses to Play on Open Field

(Special to The Union.)

The Bridgeport game, scheduled for this afternoon, was postponed. Manager Edward Walsh, of Bridgeport, refused to play on the Common because it is not an enclosed park, and after a big crowd had assembled at Wahconah park, he refused to play there because the outfield was soggy. The Pittsfield management wanted to go ahead with the contest, but Umpire Brown would not force the Bridgeport club to play against the will of Walsh. The head of the Pittsfield club will protest to the owners of the Bridgeport club about Walsh's actions which meant a loss of $1,000 or more to Pittsfield and nearly $700 to Bridgeport. It is figured over $3,000 fans would have attended the way they were pouring onto the field when the game was called off.

VETERAN STARS OF NEW HAVEN CLUB.

Captain Neal Ball, Walter Torphy, Everett Nutter, Earl Stimpson.

Braves and Dodgers Battle 26 Innings to Draw Game

Boston, May 1.—One of the greatest pitching duels ever staged in the major leagues went to a 1 and 1 tie here this afternoon after 26 innings. The game was called on account of darkness. The game set a new record.

Leon Cadore, hurling for the Brooklyn Dodgers, and Joe Oeschger, on the mound for the Braves, went the full 26 innings. Cadore only allowed nine hits, while Oeschger was touched up for 15. But in the pinches, when a hit would have meant a run and victory for the other team, both twirlers were invincible.

Olsen saved the game for the Dodgers in the ninth when, with the bases full and only one out, he stabbed a hard hit ball from Pick, tagged Powell and doubled Pick at first.

Brooklyn filled up the bases in the 17th with one down, but the Braves engineered a double play and cut them off. The score:

B'klyn 0 0 0 0 1 0 0 0 0 0 0 0 0 0 0 0 0 0 0 0 0 0 0 0 0 0—1 9 2
Boston 0 0 0 0 0 1 0 0 0 0 0 0 0 0 0 0 0 0 0 0 0 0 0 0 0 0—1 15 2

Batteries—Cadore and Krueger, Elliott; Oeschger and O'Neill, Gowdy. Umpires—Hart and McCormick.

Blue Smears Green Team in Loose Contest at Yale Field, 10 to 4

Kelley Twirls Strong Baseball in Pinches and Is Cleverly Supported — Sawyer Stars Afield and at Bat

Capt. Rabbit Sawyer helped his team considerably in defeating Dartmouth yesterday by a score of 10 to 4. The Yale leader had a great day, fielding his chances without an error, while he connected for four hits in six trips to the plate.

The visitors flashed strong in the first inning by scoring three runs on a quartet of good hits, but they were unable to hold their lead due to loose fielding and poor throwing behind Capt. Merritt, while the Yale stickers also found his slants with telling effect pounding out 12 hits.

E. B. Kelley twirled for the Blue and although a trifle unsteady at times, he proved strong in the pinches and aside from the first frame and the final, had complete control of the situation. Excellent support was also accorded him by his teammates, the playing of Crane in the left garden as well as the fine work of Diamond, Holmes and Capt. Sawyer, in the infield, being chock full of features.

A brilliant piece of Sawyer's work occurred in the fifth inning with three men on the bases. Rabbit socked a pretty hit to right field, scoring Diamond, and made for second on the short throw-in bringing Sawyer into a hot box. While the Dartmouth players were trying to run down Sawyer, Holmes and Crane both worked their way across the plate, while Sawyer zig-zagged back and forth, finally landing safe on second when Kopw dropped the ball after tagging him.

Bruce, Kopf and Maynard featured for Dartmouth, Bruce making a brilliant stop of Parson's drive in the third inning, while the latter two also picked them up in good style. Catcher Ross experienced some difficulty in pegging to the sacks as well as holding the ball on one occasion at home when he could have shut off a run, with the result that Yale tallied at least a quartet of runs on his loose work.

Dartmouth cut the platter with thre runs in the opening frame. Reese leading off with a single and scoring on Kopf's three-base clout. Maynard came through with a single sending in Maynard. Yale got a run in the same inning, Capt. Sawyer tallying on Faherty's steal of second. Yale knotted up the score in its half of the third. Sawyer and Parsons both scoring when Catcher Ross in trying to throw Aldrich out at first, hit the latter with the ball, same rolling into right field. Peters scored Kelley in the fourth with a pretty single to left. Three runs more were scored in the fifth by Yale on Eawyer's nice bit of work, while the Blue wound up the eighth by registering three more runs on some timely hitting by Aldrich and Pitcher Kelley and an error vy Ross.

Dartmouth earned a run in the ninthwhen Grundman led off with a single and Ross drove him in with a neat hit to right field.

The score:

DARTMOUTH.

	A.B.	R.	H.	O.	A.	E.
Reese, lf	3	1	1	1	0	0
Kopf, 2b-ss	4	1	2	2	5	1
Mawnard, ss-2b	5	1	1	3	2	1
Merritt, p	3	0	2	0	4	0
Robertson, 1b	4	0	0	11	1	0
Bruce, 3b	3	0	1	0	3	1
Grundman, cf	2	1	1	2	0	0
Browne, rf	3	0	0	1	0	0
Ross, c	3	0	1	4	1	4
Totals	30	4	9	24	16	7

YALE.

	A.B.	R.	H.	O.	A.	E.
Crane, lf	3	1	0	4	1	0
Sawyer, 2b	6	2	4	4	2	0
Peters, c	4	0	1	4	4	1
Faherty, cf	4	7	1	0	0	0
Parsons, rf	4	1	2	8	1	0
Aldrich, ss	4	1	1	1	1	0
Diamond, 1b	4	2	0	8	1	0
Holmes, 3b	4	1	2	3	0	0
Kelley, p	4	1	1	0	1	0
Totals	37	10	12	27	11	1

Dartmouth ....3 0 0 0 0 0 0 0 1— 4
Yale ....1 0 2 1 3 0 0 3 *—10

Left on bases, Dartmouth 6; Yale 12; three-base hit, Kouf; sacrifice hits, Grundman, Peters, Parsons; Stolen bases, Faherty, Parsons; first base on balls, off Merrit 5, Kelley 7; struck out, by Merritt 2, Kelley 2; hit by pitcher, Bruce, Faherty, Crane; wild pitches, Merritt; time of game, 2:10; umpire, Johnstone.

Quinnipiac Club to Hold Monthly Meeting

The regular monthly meeting of the Quinnipiac Rifle and Revolver club will be held tomorrow evening, at 8 o'clock at the club.

On Saturday evening, May 8, there will be an entertainment and social followed by refreshments, in honor of the winners of the National Rifle association matches, complete announcements of which will be announced later. The Remington Rifle club and the Bridgeport Rifle club will be the guests of the evening.

The following committee will have charge of arrangements. Morris Asher, Harry Shepard, Frank Rogers and Edward Murphy.

As They Fade-Away

By BOB WILSON

DUGAN SHOWS AT HIS BEST

Home pride compels us to take especial notice of Josephus Dugan, the New Havener, who is rounding out his fourth season as a member of Connie Mack's Athletics. Despite the fact that Mack is having all sorts of engine trouble again, the work of Dugan has been one of the scintillating features of the early season play. During the past week we had the good fortune to see the Athletics perform. The team as a whole, didn't look any too good, but Dugan stood out like a carnation above a bunch of horse radish. His fielding was phenomenal while his stickwork showed considerable improvement over that of other years. Aside from Tillie Walker and George Burns the New Haven boy is the most dangerous hitter in the squad. He is apt to prod the ball out of the orchard at any old time. This fact was proven during the past week when he negotiated two home run slams. The latest batch of unofficial averages show the brilliant Joe pounding the ball for a .328 average.

DEAD BALL CAUSES TROUBLE

Eastern League managers claim that the new rule making the ball dead if it hits the bat when a batsman is dodging a wild pitch is already causing trouble. The umpire's judgement as to whether the batter tried to dodge decides and of course that judgement is disputed according to the advantage gained by the teams playing. Every time some batters hit a foul now or an easy grounder to the infield they claim they were trying to dodge a wild pitch.

* * * *

Burlesque presentations to ballplayers will no longer be permitted in either major league. The rule is made that umpires must be satisfied the presentation is no joke. The action is taken by both major presidents as a result of the stunt of Philadelphia fans presenting Babe Ruth with an old brown derby hat. As everybody knows who keeps up with the joke column, a "brown derby" is equivalent to a boob's cap.

* * * *

Although Chic Brown has seen better days as an exponent of the art of hit and get away, he continues to increase his delapidated bank-roll by boxing from time to time. For swapping punches for six rounds with Collie Pleines before the Winchester Athletic Association at the Arena a few nights ago Brown drew down a straight guarantee of $300. Brown, surprised also a majority of the fans by winning the popular verdict.

* * * * *

Our old friend, Jim Braden, the man who accounted for all of the tallies chalked up by Yale in the championship games with Harvard and Princeton on the gridiron last fall, has bobbed up in Pittsburgh. Jim is employed in the steel mills but finds enough time to dabble in politics. He is furthering the candidacy of General Wood for president. "Every citizen should interest himself in politics", writes the former plunging fullback and drop-kicking star. "I am working hard for General Wood in this section of the country when not listening to the roar of the steel furnaces. I look to see Wood nominated on the second or third ballot."

* * * * *

It developed during the past week that President Weiss of the New Haven baseball club has been burning the wires in an effort to snare Emmons Bowen, property of the Giants, from the Rochester club of the International League. While the acquisition of Bowen would be accepted as an excellent move among local fans, the prospects of him coming here are not bright. First of all, Bowen is well satisfied with his present berth, and secondly, he would bid professional baseball a fond farewell before playing under Weiss. Bowen is also authority for the statement that he will quit baseball at the close of the present season unless he shows suitable proficiency in his work to go back to the Giants. He is a firm believer in the theory that a man need not spend four years in college to round out a baseball career.

* * * * *

After casting their eyes over the first lot of major league box-scores, minor league managers are wondering why the big fellows have clung so long to their new talent and what they propose doing with it. So far as the scores indicate mighty few of the newcomers are being used, and the subject is being brought up, of course, by the fact that the minors could make active use of the youngsters who are decorating major league benches. Without going into the old discussion of whether or not it is better for a young player's development that he sit on the major league team's bench and absorb knowledge or go to a minor team and get the actual playing experience, and, letting the facts as to the number there may be on the major benches speak for themselves, the question might be asked: What encouragement do the minors offer the majors for sending out young players who show such possibilities that they may be desired again by the majors? There is, as is well known, an official ban on a minor league club granting a major league club the privilege of sending a player out under an option of recall, and the major club's privilege of drafting a player owned outright by the minor club is denied. Under the circumstances isn't it natural that a major club might hesitate to release a young player who shows possibilities?

* * * * *

My how times have changed! Only a few years ago no metropolitan bowling tournament was a success unless a New Haven team finished well up in the money. Today, however, local bowlers are fortunate if they win enough dough to cover their traveling expenses.

* * * * *

Our side-kick, Grantland Rice, announces that "on paper" the Yankees have the class of the whole American League when it comes to pitching in Mays, Shawkey, Quinn, Mogridge, Shore and Thormahlen. Well, on paper they look pretty good, but not on paper on which box-scores are being printed.

* * * * *

Nutter's experience as a barber during the past winter seems to have brightened his batting lamps. So far Nutter is going great guns.

* * * * *

Here's one for the Ouija Board. While Pete Trivoulidas was out winning the Boston Marathon race, who was home tending the peanut stand?

NEW HAVEN BUNCHES HITS FOR 8 TO 4 WIN

Chief Bender Mounts Slab in Late Innings and Holds Ponies at Arm's Length—Becker Hits Homer

(Special to The Union.)

Springfield, Mass., May 1.

By bunching hits in the third and sixth innings, New Haven defeated Springfield here today in the opening home game of the season by a score of 8 to 4. All of New Haven's runs were earned, and although Springfield got a fine start in the first two innings by some heavy hitting, in which Becker drove the ball over the right field fence for a home run, the Indians came from behind and pulled the game out of the fire. It was the fourth time in the history of League park that a ball has been driven out to the right field fence.

Bender used good judgment in handling his pitchers, yanking Watson out in the first inning and Manilla the moment the Ponies began to get dangerous. Springfield could not touch Bender in the final innings of the game, so good was his control. A crowd of about 1,600 braved the chilly blasts that swept over the field. The score:

NEW HAVEN.

	AB.	R.	H	O.	A.	E.
Nutter, cf.	5	2	4	3	0	0
Burke, rf	2	0	0	1	0	0
Stimpson, lf.	4	1	2	1	0	0
Ball, 2b.	4	2	2	5	2	0
Torphy, 1b.	5	1	2	10	1	0
Joseph, 3b.	4	1	1	1	1	1
Murray, ss.	2	1	1	0	3	0
Wilson, c.	4	0	1	5	2	0
Watson, p.	0	0	0	0	0	0
Manilla, p.	1	0	0	0	2	0
Bender, p.	0	0	0	1	1	0
Totals	31	8	13	27	12	1

SPRINGFIELD.

	AB.	R.	H.	O.	A.	E.
Becker, 2b.	3	1	1	3	4	0
Gonzeles, ss.	3	1	2	2	1	1
Goebel, cf.	3	0	1	2	0	0
Lennox, 1b.	4	0	0	12	1	1
Burnett, rf.	4	1	1	1	0	0
Duffy, lf.	4	0	0	2	0	0
Rice, 3b.	4	1	3	0	1	1
Rudolph, c.	3	0	0	4	4	0
Sewall, p.	4	0	0	1	7	1
*Wilder	1	0	0	0	0	0
Totals	33	4	8	27	18	4

*Batted for Sewall in ninth.

New Haven. 0 0 3 0 0 3 1 1 0—8
Springfield . 2 1 0 0 0 1 0 0 0—4

Two-base hits, Stimpson 2, Ball, Torphy; home run, Becker; sacrifice hits, Burke 3, Murray, Bender, Rudolph; sacrifice flies, Murray, [illegible] 2, [illegible] Joseph, [illegible] plays, [illegible] Lennox [illegible] hits [illegible] and [illegible] first); off [illegible] innings [illegible] Bender 1 [illegible] off Sewall [illegible] earned runs; left on bases New Haven 6, Springfield 4; first base on errors, New Haven 3. Springfield [illegible] bases on balls, off Manilla 2, off Sewall 3; struck out, by Manilla 3, by Bender 2, by Sewall 1; wild pitch, Sewall; passed balls, Wilson [illegible] Rudolph 1; umpire, Ennis; time, two hours.

Bowling Champs Hold Dinner at Tabard Inn

The Gamble-Desmond company bowling team gathered around the festive boards at Tabard Inn last night to celebrate its feast in capturing the championship in the Mercantile league. The dinner and speeches were enjoyed by all. Following is the final and official standing of the league:

Gamble-Desmond Co.	17	4
J. Johnson & Sons	17	7
Edw. Malley & Co.	13	11
Shartenberg's	3	13
Bessey-Richey	2	13

FORMER NEW HAVENERS STARRING IN MAJORS

ROGER PECKINPAUGH
Yankees

MICKEY DEVINE
Red Sox

WHITE SOX OUTBATTED BUT DEFEAT BROWNS

St. Louis, May 1.

Although outhit by the Browns, the champion White Sox won a loosely played game here today by the score of 9 to 5. Chicago "sewed" up the game in the second inning, when they scored six runs. The score:

R.H.E.
Chicago ... 1 6 0 0 0 0 0 1 1—9 9 1
St. Louis... 1 1 0 0 1 1 0 0 1—5 12 4

Batteries — Faber, Kerr and Schalk; Vangilder, Dauss, Burrell and Billings. Umpires—Chill and Owens.

TWELFTH DEFEAT IN ROW FOR COBB'S CROWD

Detroit, May 1.

Hughey Jennings' Tigers suffered their 12th straight defeat today, when they lost to Cleveland by a score of 9 to 3. Coveleskie continued his winning streak, and although he allowed 10 hits, managed to keep them well scattered. The score.

Cleveland .. 4 0 0 0 2 0 0 3 0—9 5 0
Detroit .... 0 0 0 1 1 0 0 0 1—3 10 2

Batteries—Coveleskie and O'Neill; Ehmke, Okey, Alten and Ainsmith. Umpires—Hildebrand and Evans.

WORLD'S CHAMPIONS TROUNCE PIRATES, 7-1

Pittsburgh, May 1.

The world's champions simply walked awad with today's game, beating the Pirates 7 to 1. Reuter scattered the eight hits he allowed Babe Adams was hit hard.

The score.

Cincinnati ..0 1 0 0 2 1 3 0 0—7 11 1
Pittsburgh ..1 0 0 0 0 0 0 0 0—1 8 3

Reuter and Wingo-Adams, Mead-er and Hafner. Umpires—Klem and Emslie.

At Baltimore, first game:

	R.	H.	E.
Rochester	[illegible]	[illegible]	3
Baltimore	7	11	[illegible]

At Baltimore, second game:

	R.	H.	E.
Rochester	3	7	3
Baltimore	[illegible]	[illegible]	[illegible]

BABE RUTH POUNDS PILL FOR HOME RUN

New York, May 1.

Babe Ruth finally came into his own, when he slammed one of Pennock's offerings for a home run in the sixth inning of the Boston-New York game here today. It was the longest hit ever seen on the Polo grounds, clearing the right field stand. The Yankees had no trouble in defeating Boston. The score:

Boston .... 0 0 0 0 0 0 0 0 0—0 4 1
New York.. 1 0 0 1 0 2 2 0 *—6 10 0

Batteries—Pennock, Fortune and Walters, Devine; Shawkey and Ruel. Umpires—Dineen and Nallin.

CARDS POUND THREE CUB PITCHERS HARD

Chicago, May 1.

The Cardinals had no trouble in beating the Cubs today, hitting the three Chicago pitchers hard. The secore was 12 to 4. Haine replaced Jacobs for St. Louis when the Cubs started on a batting rally.

The score:

St. Louis 4 0 2 0 1 1 0 1 3—12 18 4
Chicago ... 0 0 0 0 0 3 1 0 0— 4 5 4

Jacobs, Haines and Dilhoefer; Carter, Martin Bailey and Killifer, O'Farrell. Umpires—Rigler and Moran.

MACKMEN SCORE SIX TIMES IN ONE ROUND

Washington, May 1.

Connie Mack's Athletics beat Washington here today, when they pounced on Shaw in the fifth inning and succeeded in scoring six runs. The score:

R.H.E.
Philadelphia 0 2 0 0 6 0 0 1 0—9 13 4
Washington 0 0 0 1 0 0 1 1 1—4 8 5

Batteries—Kinney and Perkins; Shaw and Gharrity. Umpires—Moriarity and Connelly.

The National Board has awarded rights to Outfielder George Orme to the Brantford Club. Brantford claimed to have bought Orme last fall from Flint, making the deal with the president of the club. In the meantime Manager Pearce of Flint, sold him to Milwaukee.

BRIDGEPORT CROSSED OFF CARPENTIER TOUR

Georges Carpentier, French and European light heavyweight and heavyweight boxing champion and contender for the world's heavyweight championship now held by Jack Dempsey, will not appear in exhibition in either Bridgeport or Hartford on May 15. The contracts on which Joseph Mulvihill, promoter, had been planning to bring Carpentier to Connecticut were called in by Jack Curley, Carpentier's touring manager, yesterday morning.

Mulvihill made the following statement last night:

"The Carpentier exhibitions in Bridgeport and Hartford have been called off. Jack Curley called our contract in this morning on the ground that so much adverse criticism of the fight and malicious misrepresentations and lies concerning the exhibition and the promoters had been published in Bridgeport that he was disgusted with the whole thing. Hartford was linked with Bridgeport in the contracts is lost to Hartford also.

"Curley said there were a hundred cities clamoring for a booking. He showed me a sheaf of telegrams two inches high imploring bookings, some of them even asking if dates already given out couldn't be cancelled. Considering the big demand for the world war hero, Curley refused to be bothered with a city where so much malicious antagonism has been shown.

"More than that—the gentlemen who were associated with me in the enterprise were quite ready to drop the affair. They declared they had no desire to become the bone of contntion for the police and boxing commissions.

"The loss of this exhibition is one that I feel keenly, and I have no doubt that the Bridgeport public will regret it. The exhibition would have meant a big thing for the city in more ways than one."

HARTFORD SENATORS PLAY INDIANS TODAY

Chief Bender Slated to Toe Mound in Sabbath Day Baseball Contest at the East Shore

The Hartford ball club of the Eastern league will open its season at the Lighthouse park this afternoon when it hooks up with the victorious New Haven cub, victors in its two starts against the Springfield club and running on even terms with the Worcester club for the league lead.

The lineup of the New Haven team will be the same as that which handed Springfield its second defeat of the season in Springfield yesterday.

Ralph Head will undoubtedly be the pitching selection of Manager Howley of the visiting team. He is one of two veterans of Hartford's teams of former years. Mike Damm, the big boy from the Brooklyn shipyards, is down to do the receiving.

Martie Murphy of the Michigan-Antario league, wil head the batting order. Fred Bailey, formerly of the Braves, comes next. Mal Barry star first sacker, will bat third. "Brick" Kane is the clean-up hitter. Al Harber, Phil Neher and the battery follows in order.

Opposed to Hartford on the firing line will be the famed chief Bender, who got into action in Springfield yesterday. All the chief wants is a warm afternoon to limber up his pitching wing. Watson will also be on the firing line if necessary. Nutter is looked for to feature again after his sensational performances of the last two days.

The game will start at 3:30 and "Kitty" Bransfield will umpire.

NUTTER AND WILSON LOOK GOOD TO FANS

Opening Day Performancec of Local Stars Augers Well for Successful Season — Chief Bender Pleased

(By BOB WILSON)

For a team that was picked by many fans for the second division, the New Haven Indians have started off nobly. As a result of their victory over Springfield here in Opening day the locals are feeling rather chesty—not too confident, but with just enough to make the proverbial hope spring in the breast of every fan in New Haven.

Except for a weak spot here and there Manager Bender is confident that he will be able to place a team in the field that will be in a position to hold its own with any other club in the league. The pitching, which was so uncertain last year, has improved to an appreciable extent while the return of the veteran Neal Ball has served to steady the inner works.

Nutter and Wilson according to Bender are two of the best players now performing in the minor leagues Bender was pleasently surprised with the form flashed by Nutter while he believes the acquisition of Wilson will go a long ways toward improving the stamp of approval on Red Torphy at first base while he is positive in his assertion that there can be no improvement over Stimpson.

Whether or not Murray, former Trinity star, will be able to fill the bill at shortstop remains a question. Murray didn't look any too good in his opening performance but he will be afforded ample opportunity to make good. The same applies to Joseprs, third baseman, who appears to be a better hitter than he is a fielder.

Hartford is scheduled to oppose the locals on the Lighthouse lawn this afternoon and there is a possibility of Chief Bender serving them up for the home crow. Play will start at 3:30 o'clock.

BLUE SECONDS WIN OVER HOTCHKISS, 7-0

Chittenden Yields But Four Scattered Hits and Fans Six in Ball Contest at Lakeville

While the Yale 'varsity were trouncing Dartmouth yesterday, the Eli second team found little difficulty in administering defeat to the Hotchkiss Prep nine in Lakeville, the 'varsity understudies winning by a score of 7 to 0.

Chittendon twirled the entire game for the Blue, allowing but four scattered hits and fanning six men. Pond, who pitched for Hotchkiss, fanned 10 men, but loose fielding, coupled with opportune hitting by the winners spelt his downfall.

Larner led Eli in hitting, getting two hits composed of a two-bagger and a single. Pitcher Pond gathered two of the four hits made by the losers.

Batteries—Chittendon and Cannon; Pond and Smith.

INTERNATIONAL LEAGUE.

At Jersey City, first game:

	R.	H.	E.
Toronto	4	11	1
Jersey City	5	10	1

At Jersey City, second game:

	R.	H.	E.
Toronto	5	13	2
Jersey City	6	13	2

NEVER BEATEN BY KACEYS, SAYS MAHER

Manager Maher of the Gamblle-Desmond bowling team, takes exception to an article appearing in an afternoon newspaper last week to the effect that his team had been beaten by the Knights of Columbus. The letter follows:

Sporting Editor Union:

Dear Sir—In a recent issue of an afternoon paper an item stating that the K. of C. bowling team had defeated the winners in the Mercantile league is absolutely untrue. The Gamble-Desmond Co. team, winners in the Mercantile league, have never played the K. of C. team, much less to be beaten by them, but have sought a series a month or so ago, but in vain. This is surely no fault of ours.

If you will kindly rectify this misstatement and add that the Gamble-Desmond Co team winners in the Mercantile league, now stand ready to bowl the winners of the present series between the K. of C. team and the Seamless Rubber Co. for the city title.

Manager Gamble-Desmond Bowling Team.

At Syracuse:

	R.	H.	E.
Syracuse	7	10	5
Buffalo	9	8	2

Phillies Chalk Up Victory Over Giants

Philadelphia, May 1.

The Giants continued on their losing way today the Phils, trimming them, 5 to 2. Rixey held the Giants sluggers helpless until the ninth when he left down long enough to get two runs. The Phils drove Barnes to cover in three innings and hit Douglas, who succeeded him, hard. The score:

New York ...0 0 0 0 0 0 0 0 2—2 5 1
Philadelphia 1 0 1 0 1 1 1 0 x—5 12 0

Barnes, Douglas, Winters and McCarthy; Rixey and Wheat. Umpires—O'Day and Harrison.

Managers of Major League Baseball Teams in the Thick of the Fight for the 1920 Championship Pennant

HUGHIE JENNINGS
Manager of the Detroit American League team, who have lost their first nine games.

MILLER HUGGINS
Leader of the New York Americans and former star of St. Louis Cardinals.

WILBERT ROBINSON
Manager of Brooklyn National Leaguers, whom he has once before piloted to a pennant.

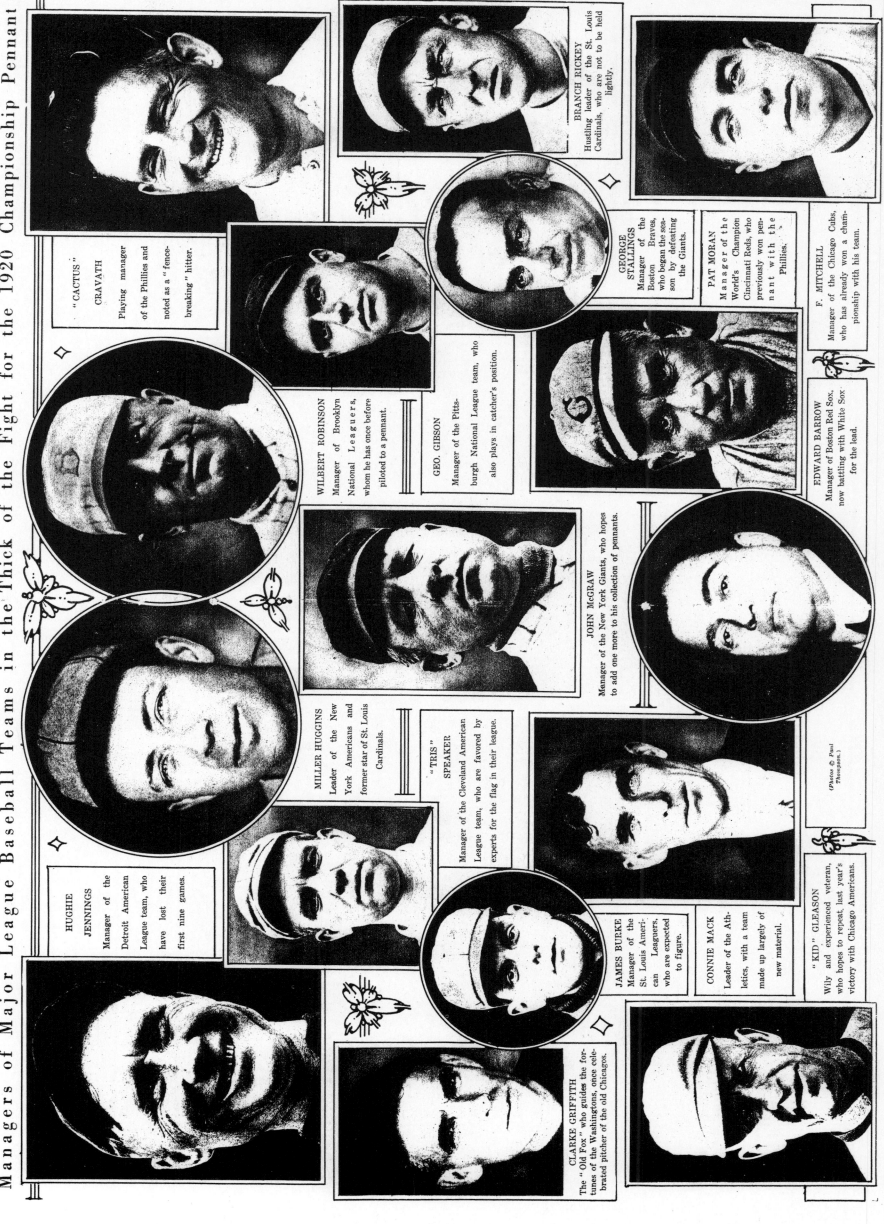

"CACTUS" CRAVATH
Playing manager of the Phillies and noted as a "fence-breaking" hitter.

"TRIS" SPEAKER
Manager of the Cleveland American League team, who are favored by experts for the flag in their league.

GEO. GIBSON
Manager of the Pittsburgh National League team, who also plays in catcher's position.

CLARKE GRIFFITH
The "Old Fox" who guides the fortunes of the Washingtons, once celebrated pitcher of the old Chicagos.

JAMES BURKE
Manager of the St. Louis American Leaguers, who are expected to figure.

JOHN McGRAW
Manager of the New York Giants, who hopes to add one more to his collection of pennants.

BRANCH RICKEY
Hustling leader of the St. Louis Cardinals, who are not to be held lightly.

GEORGE STALLINGS
Manager of the Boston Braves, who began the season by defeating the Giants.

"KID" GLEASON
Wily and experienced veteran, who hopes to repeat last year's victory with Chicago Americans.

CONNIE MACK
Leader of the Athletics, with a team made up largely of new material.

EDWARD BARROW
Manager of Boston Red Sox, now battling with White Sox for the lead.

PAT MORAN
Manager of the World's Champion Cincinnati Reds, who previously won pennant with the Phillies.

F. MITCHELL
Manager of the Chicago Cubs, who has already won a championship with his team.

(Photos © Paul Thompson.)

JESS SWEETSER IS COLLEGE CHAMPION; DEFEATS WARD, 4-3

Yale Breaks Tie With Harvard When Its Star Wins Golf Final at Nassau.

(Special to The Eagle.)

Glen Cove, L. I., June 26—Using a varied collection of instruments, chief of which was perhaps the driver, Jess W. Sweetser of Ardsley and Yale, inscribed his name on the list of intercollegiate golf champions today at the Nassau Country Club by defeating James C. Ward of the Mission Hills Club, Kansas City and Williams College, in the final by 4 and 3 in 36 holes.

Ward was 4 down at lunch and when he lost the first three afternoon holes it was thought the match would soon be over, but the Missourian displayed true Western grit so well that Sweetser had to go to the 15th or 33d hole of the day to clinch the match. The cards and table analysis:

MORNING.

Par, out	4	5	5	3	5	5	4	3	4—38	
Sweetser, out	4	5	5	3	6	6	4	3	4—40	
Ward, out	5	6	5	3	4	6	5	3	5—42	
Par, in	5	4	4	3	5	3	5	4	4—37	75
Sweetser, in	5	4	6	4	3	3	5	4	4—38	78
Ward, in	5	4	5	3	4	4	5	5	4—39	81

AFTERNOON.

Sweetser, out	4	5	5	4	4	5	4	3	4—38
Ward, out	5	6	6	3	5	4	4	3	3—39
Sweetser, in	5	4	5	4	4	3			
Ward, in	5	5	5	3	3	3			

TABLE ANALYSIS—33 HOLES.

	A.M. 18 Holes. Sweeser	Ward	P.M. 15 Holes. Sweeser	Ward	Total. Sweeser	Ward
Played odd after tee-shot, long holes	6	8	2	9	8	17
Played odd after tee-shot, short holes	2	2	1	3	3	5
Played odd after tee-shot, all holes	8	10	3	12	11	22
In trouble from tee, long holes	2	4	0	5	2	9
Sliced to trouble from tee	0	1	0	2	0	3
Pulled to trouble from tee	2	2	0	3	2	5
Topped drives	0	1	0	0	0	1
In trouble from tee, short holes	0	1	2	1	2	2
Sliced, short holes	0	1	0	0	0	1
Pulled, short holes	0	0	1	0	1	0
Brassies misplayed	4	1	0	1	4	2
Irons misplayed through green	3	2	0	0	3	2
In traps and hazards, all kinds	3	3	1	0	4	3
Total trouble, tee shots	2	5	2	6	4	11
Total trouble, through green	6	6	0	2	6	8
Greens reached in fewer strokes	6	2	5	1	11	3
Played odd on putting green lying alike, long holes	3	3	2	3	5	6
Putts	35*	33	30	27	65	60
Single-putt greens	4	5	1	4	5	9
Three-putt greens	3*	2	1	1	4	3
Holes won with putt	4	2	1	3	5	5
Halves saved with putts	1	4	0	1	1	5
Stymies laid by	0	1	0	0	0	1
Holed from off green	0	0	0	0	0	0
Out of bounds	0	0	0	0	0	0

*Includes stymie.

The victory of Sweetser of Yale breaks the tie between Yale and Harvard at eight individual championships. Yale's last annexing of the title was in 1915, when F. R. Blossom won at Greenwich. Harvard won last in 1916 at Oakmont.

The afternoon round yesterday proved longer than was expected after Ward had lost the first three holes. Though 7 down going to the 22d, Ward refused to crack and won three of the remaining out holes to stand only 5 down at the turn.

His opponent was dormie 6 when the 12th was halved, but the Missourian came back with two holes, the 13th and 14th. To keep a player like Sweetser as he was going yesterday from getting a half in six holes calls for something like super golf, which even Hagen or Ouimet might fight shy of essaying, and the short 15th or 33d hole of the day gave Sweetser a half in par 3 for the match.

Sweetser Always in Front.

Sweetser won the first two holes in the morning and never allowed Ward to square. The nearest the latter came to evens was on the 5th and 13th in the morning, when he was only 1 down. But beginning with the 14th in the first round Sweetser got a safe lead by winning three of the last five holes and halving the other two.

At the end of the first half in the morning Sweetser was 3 up, the first 18 saw him 4 up and the first half of the afternoon put him 5 up.

Ward was beaten by an erratic long game. Usually a straight driver, he was "all over the lot" yesterday with wood, perhaps due to the fact that he was teeing up the ball in front of the left foot. But for his steady putting he would not have kept the match going far in the afternoon.

The table analysis shows Sweetser was not in trouble once from the long hole tees, but Ward had five such "troubles." Three of these were on the first three opening holes and cost him each of the holes.

Play by Holes.

Three putts accounted for Ward's loss of the first morning hole. Both pulled to rough on the second. Ward tried for distance out and found a bunker. Sweetser played safely short. Both were just off the green in 3. Sweetser's chip was 3 feet from the cup, Ward 20 feet, and it was the former's hole, 5—6.

When Ward sliced his drive to a trap on the third it looked like a win for Jess, but he topped his brassie, and a half resulted. Trapped on a sliced iron and taking 2 to get out, Sweetser lost the fifth. Ward gave a lesson in sticking to one's game, though apparently "out" of a hole, by getting a half on the sixth.

He topped his drive to long grass near the tee, was out still in rough and eventually was short of the green on his fourth. On his second Sweetser was just off the fairway in rough almost green high. Did Ward despair? He did not. He played his fifth with great care, and got close enough for a putt and a 6. Sweetser was on poorly, and took three putts for a half.

Sweetser's Luck on Ninth.

Failing to get the green of the seventh by a few inches on his second cost Ward the seventh, and after a half in 3 of the pond eighth Sweetser came to his "luck hole," the ninth. Friday in the semi-final, after hooking to rough he put his out close up for a bird 3, and yesterday, after doing the same with his drive, he was out to the green in 2, and Ward kindly took three putts to hand him the hole. This gave Sweetser a lead of 3 at the turn.

Ward's hooked drive on the tenth was lost for a minute in long grass, and when the gallery stood off, not aiding in the search, J. B. Coles Tappan, former president of the Metropolitan Golf Association, suggested helping, and started for the spot, in cheerful and sportsmanlike opposition to the gallery at Arcola, in the Jersey championship, where the players were compelled to do the looking by themselves. Mr. Tappan was surprised when told that such a sentiment against helping existed in the sister State.

Sweetser's sliced brassie to a trap enabled Ward to get a half after the poor drive. Jess hooked his iron second on the eleventh to the woods flag high, but was out for a single putt and a half. A stymie cost Sweetser the twelfth. It was such a puzzling stymie that Jess laid down half a dozen clubs by the ball before selecting a niblick to try a jump.

Three putts lost Sweetser the short thirteenth, but he picked up the fourteenth wih a bird 3 by getting the green in 2, Ward being just off at the right on the like. Trapped on his tee shot, Ward lost the short fifteneth, and the seventeenth went against him when his iron second was hooked to rough at the green. Sweetser pulled his drive wildly, but got a good lie on the second fairway. His second shot was just off the green at the left, and he was on for a winning single putt. The home hole was a half, Ward failing to get down a four-footer for a bird 3 after a fine iron.

The Afternoon Round.

To be 4 down at noon and then lose the first three holes of the second round was the depressing start of Ward in the afternoon. The opener went against him when he was off the line a little to the right on a long ball and stopped in rough. His out was in a mound and his third short of green. When his chip failed to drop he conceded the hole to Sweetser, who was on in two perfect shots.

A hooked drive to rough and an iron sliced off near the third tee lost Ward the second and another tee hook to rough with 3 putts lost him the third. He was now 7 down.

The Wisconsonian came to life on the short 4th, where both were over the green an inch or two into thick grass, but Ward was "on" for a winning lone putt. Sweetser offset this by taking the 5th where his second was on while Ward was short.

Both on the 6th green in 3, Ward was up close for a winning solitary putt. Halves without incident on the next two were followed by Ward's winning of the 9th, where after equal drives he got his chip up for a single putt and a winning 3. At the turn Ward was 5 down, one worse than at noon.

The 10th he should have lost as he sliced his drive to rough in the bowl of the old 10th green, but Sweetser obligingly sliced his brassie to short of the green to give a half.

Missing a three-foot putt for a half, Ward lost the 11th, but got a half on the 12th after a hooked drive to rough when Sweetser took three putts.

Then Ward made a gallant effort to save the match. He won the short 13th when Sweetser was trapped from the tee and the 14th by laying his approach up dead for a bird 3. But by getting down a six-foot putt on the short 15th Sweetser got a half for the match.

Winner's Fine Debut in 1919.

Sweetser was unknown as a golfer until last year when he entered the Westchester County championship at Aapawamis, playing from the Ardsley Club. He astonished the field by lowering the course record from 72 to 69. Then a few weeks later he carried Ned Sawyer to the 38th green in the final of the Victory Cup tournament at Siwanoy. His steadiness then under trying circumstances showed he had an ideal temperament for match play. Still further along in the season he received a setback at the Arcola, (N. J.) tournament where in the final he was beaten by E. M. Wild by something like 9 and 7.

This year he had done no competitive playing till this college championship, but in his matches more than in the medal competition for the team title he showed he had regained the form that marked his early play last year. On his way to final he defeated T. J. E. Pulling 3 and 2, A. P. Boyd 4 and 2, A. T. Buffington 9 and 7 and J. Simpson Dean, the medalist, 2 and 1.

The defeated finalist, Ward, as already told in The Eagle, has won the Missouri title three consecutive years though only 19 years old now. He defeated these players in his half of the Nassau bracket: E. M. Bacon, 1 up; D. H. Ankeny 5 and 4; Martin W. Littleton Jr., 7 and 6, and J. A. Moss 2 up. Both Sweetser and Ward are just starting their college careers and they ought to be much in the spotlight in the collegiate championships for several years.

Pirates Beat Cubs By a Late Rally

Pittsburg, Pa., June 26—Pittsburg won from Chicago here today, 9 to 4, in a game featured by heavy hitting. The visitors scored one run off Hamilton in the first inning and three in the second. Meador and Ponder held Chicago scoreless for seven innings. In the eighth the Pirates came from behind, scoring six runs on six hits and two walks. Score:

Chicago.

Name.	ab	r	1b	po	a
Flack,rf	4	1	1	1	1
H'locher,ss	4	0	1	3	1
Terry 2b	4	0	0	0	2
Merkle,1b	5	0	2	6	0
Barber,lf	4	0	0	2	0
O'Farrell,c	3	1	2	6	1
Herzog,3b	3	1	0	3	3
Paskert,cf	4	1	3	3	1
Vaughn,p	4	0	1	0	1
Totals	35	4	10	24	10

Pittsburg.

Name.	ab	r	1b	po	a
Bigbee,lf	5	1	1	2	0
Carey,cf	5	1	1	3	0
S'hworth,rf	5	2	5	2	0
Whitted,3b	4	1	1	0	0
Cutshaw,2b	0	0	0	0	1
Meador,p	2	0	0	0	1
Grimm,1b	5	0	1	13	0
Caton,ss	3	2	1	1	6
Schm'dt,c	2	0	1	1	0
Lee,c	1	1	1	1	0
Hamilton p	0	0	0	0	3
Barbare,2b	4	1	4	3	3
*Nicholson	1	0	0	0	0
Ponder,p	1	0	1	1	0
†Mckechnie	1	0	0	0	0
Hoeffner,c	0	0	0	0	0
Totals	39	9	17	27	14

*Batted for Meador in seventh inning.
†Batted for Lee in eighth inning.

Chicago	1	3	0	0	0	0	0	0	0	—4
Pittsburg	0	0	1	0	0	2	0	6	..	—9

Errors—Flack, Terry, Whitted. Two-base hits—Lee, Merkle. Three-base hits—O'Farrell, Paskert, Southworth. Stolen bases—Bigbee, O'Farrell, Southworth, Hollocher. Sacrifices—Flack, Hollocher. Double plays—Caton, Barbare and Grimm; Herzog and Merkle. Left on bases—Chicago, 9; Pittsburg, 10. Base on balls—Off Vaughn, 4; off Hamilton, 1; off Ponder, 2. Hits—Off Vaughn, 17 in 8 innings; off Hamilton, 3 in 2 innings; off Ponder, 3 in 2 innings; off Meador, 4 in 5 innings. Struck out—By Vaughn, 4; by Ponder, 1. Wild pitch—Ponder. Winning pitcher—Ponder. Losing pitcher—Vaughn. Umpires—Rigler and Moran. Time—2 hours 7 minutes.

Ruth Smith Stars In Fancy Diving

The second of a series of swimming meets for women was held yesterday in the pool of the Betsy Head Memorial. Miss Ruth Smith, swimming star of the Morningside A. C., duplicated the feat of her sister, who won the fancy diving last Saturday, by winning the fancy diving contest. Miss Smith garnered 48 points with her superb diving. She was closely seconded by Miss Gene O'Connell, who scored 40.2 points. The summaries:

50-Yard Novice, Qualifying Round—W. E. Wainright, Hazel Jennings, Violet Rogers, Dorothy Murtagh, May Deyscher and Jeannette Kilppel. Best time, 37 4-5 seconds.

100-Yard Novice, Qualifying Round—Marion Himmelstein, Elizabeth Ferguson, Yvonne Caradi, Gene O'Connell, W. E. Wainright and Anna Surda. Best time, 1 minute 33 seconds.

300-Yard Handicap—Lucy Freeman, Martha Wilcock, Marion Kerner. Best time, 5:46 3-5.

100-Yard Handicap, Qualifying Round—Louise M. Bole, Martha Wilcock, Jennie Tugwell. Best time, 1:29 1-5.

Diving Contest—Won by Ruth Smith with 48.1 points; Gene O'Connell, second with 40.2 points; Edna Sweeney, third with 36.6 points.

Santa Barbara Four Beats Philadelphia C. C. at Polo

(Special to The Eagle.)

Hempstead, L. I., June 26—The Santa Barbara four won an easy polo victory on Cochran Field, Meadowbrook, today over the Philadelphia C. C. team. The score was 11 to 7.

A feature of the game was the goal scored by B. McFadden, the Philadelphia back, in the fifth period. After carrying the ball from the center of the field, McFadden drove it through the goal posts from a distance of over sixty yards, and at a hard angle.

G. Moore, playing forward for the Pacific Coast players, scored five of the 11 goals made by his team. W. S. Stokes made three of the seven goals scored by the Philadelphians. The lineup and summary:

Santa Barbara (11).		Philadelphia C. C. (7)	
No. 1—G. Moore	1	T. Stokes	4
No. 2—H.B.Black'll	4	W. S. Stokes	4
No. 3—W. Tevis Jr	4	E. L. Stokes	4
		—McFadden	3
Total	16		
Back—Col.N.B.N'ng.	6	Total	15

Goals—First period, Moore, Santa Barbara; Blackwell, Santa Barbara. Second period, Nutting, Santa Barbara, 2; W. S. Stokes, Philadelphia. Third period, Moore, Santa Barbara; Tevis, Santa Barbara; W. S. Stokes, Philadelphia. Fourth period, Moore, Santa Barbara; W. S. Stokes, Philadelphia. Fifth period, McFadden, Philadelphia. Sixth period, Tevis, Santa Barbara; Moore, Santa Barbara; T. Stokes, Philadelphia. Seventh period, McFadden, Philadelphia; Blackwell, Santa Barbara; Moore, Santa Barbara. Eighth period, T. Stokes, Philadelphia. Referee—O. T. Holt.

Claims Catholic Schools Championship

Top row—(left to right)—Bob Cahill, Jack Kilgallen, manager; Brother Francis, coach; Jack Gallagher.
Middle row—Charley Beers, Jack Kenny, Dan Gillespie and Jack Flynn.
Bottom row—Billy Sullivan, Eddie Keating, Jack Wilkinson, Myles McPartland and Jack Tracey, mascot.

THE St. Francis Prep baseball team, which claims the Catholic High School championship of Brooklyn and the Boro High School title as well, has completed one of the most successful seasons in the history of the institution. The team chalked up 13 victories, suffered four defeats, and played a scoreless tie. Among its list of victims are Brooklyn Prep, Manual, Bushwick, Newtown, Freeport, Bryant, Adelphi, Manhattan Prep and Cathedral Prep. The manner in which the Butler st. boys outclassed their opponents can be seen by the fact that they scored 157 runs to their opponents' 50, registered 190 hits for a grand batting average of .358, including 20 doubles, 8 triples and 4 home runs, and stole 172 bases.

Two of the pitchers, Eddie Keating and Dan Gillespie, entered the Hall of Fame by twirling no-hit, no-run, no-walk games. Incidently, these were the only two perfect games turned in in scholastic circles this year. Besides his no-hit game, Gillespie also twirled a one-hit, two-hit, and a three-hit game, and issuesd only one pass during the entire season. Keating turned in victories over Cathedral, Manual, Freeport, Bushwick and St. Francis College. Bill Sullivan graced the mound on several occasions and triumphed over Newtown and Manhattan Prep. "Rody" Cooney also took a turn in the box and turned back Brooklyn Prep, after Sullivan had spotted them five runs.

Charley Beers, who was elected captain of next year's team, was a tower of strength behind the plate. He was master of his pitchers at all times, and held them in check when they seemed on the verge of blowing. His mighty arm was respected by opposing base runners. Charley was also a ponderous hitter, his average for the season being well over .400. Jack Gallagher, first base, batted near .400 and fielded par excellence; Bob Cahill, second base, batted .300 and fielded very well; Rody Cooney, shortstop, batted .379; Jack Kenny, third base, batted .378; Bill Sullivan, all-scholastic selection, batted .420 and fielded all season without an error; Jim Bartley batted .310 and made some sensational plays; Myles McPartland batted .360, including two home runs and fielded faultlessly; John (Lefty) Flynn, pinch hitter par excellence and utility man, batted .500. Other substitutes, Jake Kipp, Jack Costello, Jack Wilkenson and Jack McCauley, all did well when called upon.

Credit for the team's success is due to Brother Francis, who has a wide knowledge of the game and can handle players.

Jack Kenny, Eddie Keating and John Flynn and Jack Costello are lost by graduation, but there is a nucleus for another strong team next year. This year's record follows:

St. Francis Prep	0	St. Peter's Prep	0
St. Francis Prep	16	Adelphi Academy	0
St. Francis Prep	6	Newton H. S.	0
St. Francis Prep	1	Erasmus	7
St. Francis Prep	0	De LaSalle	2
St. Francis Prep	8	Brooklyn Prep	7
St. Francis Prep	10	Cathedral Prep	5
St. Francis Prep	7	Brownes B. C.	0
St. Francis Prep	17	Manual T. S.	3
St. Francis Prep	9	*New Utchecht	0
St. Francis Prep	2	Clason M. A.	4
St. Francis Prep	16	Manhattan Prep	8
St. Francis Prep	13	Bryant	0
St. Francis Prep	5	Cathedral Prep	12
St. Francis Prep	10	Freeport High	0
St. Francis Prep	11	Bushwick	0
St. Francis Prep	23	Xavier Alumni	1
St. Francis Prep	3	St. Francis College	1
Total	157	Total	50

*Forfeit.
Won—13. Lost—4.

NEW RECORD IN 3,000 METER WALK MADE BY PLANT

Detsch Equals World's Mark at Olympic Tryouts—Pat Ryan a Winner.

Franklin Field, Philadelphia, June 26—The 3,000-meter walk was the only event in which a new record was made in the Eastern track and field tryouts here today. William Plant of the Morningside A. A. covered the distance in 12 minutes, 56 2-5 seconds, a new record for the event. A. G. Detsch, running unattached from the Metropolitan District, equalled the world's record in the 440-yard hurdles when he covered the distance in 54 3-5 seconds, over 3-foot hurdles. The record will not stand, however, as he toppled the ninth hurdle.

In the final of the 880-yard run, only the third men in the trial heats competed, the first and second place winners saving themselves for the final tryouts at Boston in July.

Earl W. Eby, captain of the University of Pennsylvania track team and champion of the American Expeditionary Forces in the 400-meter, won his heat today in the 880-yard race in 1 minute and 54 2-5 seconds. Edward J. Meehan, Western Conference champion, was second in this heat, while Homer Baker of Glencoe was shut out, taking fourth place. A. B. Helffrich, New York A. C., won the other trial heat in 1 minute and 57 seconds. Robert Crawford, Millrose A. A., was second, Lawrence A. Brown of the University of Pennsylvania getting fourth place.

George A. Bronder Jr., the inter-Allied javelin thrower, was on the field, but did not compete, while F. H. Prem, inter-Allied title holder, finished third in the hop, skip and jump. Patrick J. Ryan, another inter-Allied champion, representing Loughlin Lyceum of Brooklyn, was an easy winner in the hammer throw.

The Metropolitan District of New York took first places in 12 of the 19 events on the program, Boston taking 2, the Allegheny District 1, the Middle Atlantic District 1. Two firsts went to the Chicago A. A. athletes, Myers and Landers, who competed under their college registrations. John M. Watt of Cornell, winner of the 120-yard high hurdles, competed from the Niagara District.

Summaries.

100-Yard Dash—First, L. Murchison, New York A. C.; second, Harold B. Lever, Meadowbrook Club; third, William D. Hayes, Boston A. C. Time, 10 seconds.

One-mile Run—First, H. C. Cutbill, Boston A. C.; second, M. L. Shields, Meadowbrook; third, L. G. Watson, Meadowbrook. Time, 4 minutes 22 seconds.

Hammer Throw—First, Patrick Ryan, Loughlin Lyceum, Brooklyn, 171 feet 6 inches; second, O. F. Dahdrow, Boston A. C., 154 feet ¾ inches; third, William S. McCormick, unattached, 136 feet 6¼ inches.

Shot Put—First, P. J. McDonald, New York A. C., 46 feet 1½ inches; second, M. G. Cann, New York A. C., 44 feet 7 inches; third, W. C. Beers, N. Y. A. C., 43 feet 4¼ inches.

5,000-Meter Run—First, John Simmons, New York A. C.; second, I. C. Dresser, New York A. C.; third, Max Boland, Paulist A. C. Time, 15 minutes 30 4-5 seconds.

120-Yard High Hurdles—First, John M. Watt, unattached; second, Harold E. Barron, Meadowbrook; third, Tevis Huhn, Princeton University. Time, 15 1-5 seconds.

440-Yard Run—First, J. W. Driscoll, Boston A. C.; second, James J. O'Brien, Loughlin Lyceum, Brooklyn; third, J. C. Robbins, New York A. C. Time, 49 4-5 seconds.

56-Pound Weight—First, P. J. McDonald, New York A. C., 36 feet 4½ inches; second, Patrick Ryan, Loughlin Lyceum, Brooklyn, 32 feet 2 inches; third, Thomas Anderson, St. Christopher A. C., 31 feet ½ inch.

High Jump—First, R. W. Landon, New York A. C., 6 feet 4 inches; second, Louis Watson, Alpha A. C., 6 feet 3 inches; third, Walter L. Whalen, Boston A. C., 6 feet 1¼ inches.

Broad Jump—First, Hugo Politzer, Mohawk A. C., 23 feet ½ inch; second, Paul Courtois, Mohawk A. C., 23 feet; third, Ira D. Bertolett, Germantown B. C., 22 feet 9 inches.

3,000-Metre Walk—First, William Plant, Morningside A. A.; second, Richard F. Reamer, American Walkers' Association; third, J. B. Pearman, New York A. C. Time, 12 minutes 56 2-5 seconds.

Javelin Throw—First, J. C. Lincoln, New York A. C., 184 feet 9½ inches; second, F. S. Emery, Meadowbrook Club, 169 feet; third, W. Helbig, Central High School, Newark, 158 feet 3¾ inches.

Hop-Step-and-Jump—First, Sherman Landers, University of Pennsylvania, 47 feet 4½ inches; second, William Rosenberg, Glencoe A. C., 45 feet 8 1-8 inches; third, H. Prem, New York A. C., 45 feet.

220 Yard Dash—First, Allen Woodring, Meadowbrook; second, A. B. Kelly, New York A. C.; third, D. H. DeWitt, New York A. C. Time, 21 4-5 seconds.

880 Yards Run—First, Sandy Evans, Salem Crescent Club; second, Joseph T. Higgins, Fordham University. Time, 2:03.

440 Yards Hurdle—First, A. G. Delsch, unattached; second, Frank F. Loomis, Chicago A. A.; third, William H. Meanix, Boston A. A. Time, 54 3-5 seconds.

10,000 Meter Run—First, Earl Johnson, Morgan Community Club; second, George Cornetta, New York A. C.; third, P. Plynn, Paulist A C. Time, 32:38 4-5.

Chicago A. A. Athletes Best in Mid-West Trials

Stagg Field, Chicago, June 26—Athletic stars running under the colors of the Chicago Athletic Association carried off the lion's share of honors in the mid-West trials for the American Olympic team at Stagg Field today, scoring 68 points in the nineteen events. The Illinois Athletic Club team of Chicago was second, with 30 points.

Although no records were shattered several noteworthy performances were made. Joie Ray of the Illinois A. C., American champion distance runner, won the mile run in the remarkable fast time of 4:16. Jackson Scholz of the University of Missouri, Western conference champion, took the measure of Howard Drew of Drake University, joint holder of the world's record in the 100-yard event, breaking the tape in 0:10. Scholz, however, was defeated in the 220-yard event, which went to Hassengale, a teammate. Drew was second.

The Chicago A. A. qualified 22 men, who will compete in the finals at Cambridge, Mass., July 17. The C. A. A. stars scored in every event except one.

Summaries.

440-Yard Run—First, R. S. Emory, Chicago A. A.; second, L. Butler, University of Michigan; third, G. S. Bretnall, Cornell (Iowa) College. Time, 49 1-5 seconds.

100-Yard Dash—First, Jackson Scholz, University of Missouri; second, H. P. Drew, Drake University; third, Jo Loomis, Chicago A. A. Time, 10 seconds.

Hammer Throw—First, B. Bennett, Chicago A. A., 155 feet; second, J. Shanahan, Illinois A. C., 138 feet 10 inches; third, K. L. Wilson, Chicago A. A., 137 feet 6 inches.

Mile Run—First, Joie Ray, Illinois A. C.; second, A. A. Schardt, Chicago A. A.; third, D. C. Stone, Illinois A. C. Time, 4:16.

5,000-Metre Run—First, Ray B. Watson, Kansas Aggies; second, C. C. Furnas, Purdue University; third, W. T. Foreman, Chicago A. A. Time, 15:40.

Pole Vault—First, F. K. Foss, Chicago A. A., 13 feet; second, T. P. Gardner, Yale University, 12 feet 9 inches; third, E. Knourek, Illinois A. C., 12 feet 6 inches.

120-Yard Hurdles—First, Walker Smith, Chicago A. C.; second, Waldo Ames, Chicago A. A.; third, A. I. Andrews, Chicago. Time, 15 1-5 seconds.

High Jump—First, J. Murphy, Notre Dame, 6 feet 3 inches; tied for second and third, George Krogness, Chicago A. A., and S. M. Osborn, University of Illinois, 6 feet.

Shot Put—First, Arlie Mucks, Chicago A. A., 43 feet; second, J. L. Baker, University of Michigan, 42 feet 4½ inches; third, E. A. Sandfur, University of Kansas, 40 feet 9½ inches.

3,000-Metre Walk—First, Alex. Zeeler, Chicago A. A.; second, E. L. Malone, Cleveland A. C.; third, A. Parker, Logan Square A. C., Chicago. Time, 14:44 1-5.

440-Yard Hurdles—First, Floyd Smart, Chicago A. C.; second, M. K. Paterson, Drake University; third, M. Burke, Illinois A. C. Time, 55 3-5 seconds.

Broad Jump—First, Sol Butler, Dubuque College, 23 feet 9 inches; second, Robert Strawn, Northwestern University, 21 feet 8 inches; third, C. E. Jaquith, Chicago A. A., 21 feet 7 inches.

880-Yard Run—First, Tom Campbell, Yale University; second, P. M. Spink, Chicago A. A.; third, R. E. Johnson, Des Moines (Iowa) College. Time, 1:55 3-5.

56-Pound Weight—First, J. Shanahan, Illinois A. C., 31 feet 4½ inches; second, P. McIntyre, Illinois A. C., 30 feet 1½ inches; third, O. R. Benson, Chicago A. A., 29 feet 11 inches.

Discus Throw—First, M. R. Husted, Chicago A. A., 135 feet 6¾ inches; second, E. Gilfillan, Illinois A. C., 132 feet 10½ inches; third, Arlie Mucks, Chicago A. A., 130 feet 10½ inches.

Running Hop-Step-Jump—First, D. F. Ahearn, Illinois A. C., 47 feet 8¾ inches; second, C. E. Jaquith, Chicago A. A., 46 feet ¼ inch; third, W. B. Overbee, University of Illinois, 45 feet 7 1-8 inches.

220-Yard Dash—First, G. P. Massengale, University of Missouri; second, H. P. Drew, Drake University; third, Jackson, University of Missouri. Time, 21 4-5 seconds.

10,000-Metre Run—First, A. Patasoni, Haskell Institute; second, S. Christenson, Logan Square A. C., Chicago; third, G. S. Gobler, Chicago A. A. Time, 33 minutes 36 3-5 seconds.

Javelin Throw—First, K. L. Wilson, Chicago A. A., 182 feet; second, M. Angler, Illinois A. C., 179 feet 4 inches; third, R. F. Miller, Purdue University, 174 feet 5 inches.

PLATT TAKES GOLF FINAL.

Philadelphia, June 26—J. Wood Platt, national semi-finalist last year, won the golf championship of Philadelphia today by defeating Horace H. Francine, a former title holder, in the deciding 36 hole match by 8 and 6 in 36 holes. Francine, who was 4 down at the end of the first 18 holes, went to pieces in the final round. The play was at the Huntingdon Valley links.

GHERRIG'S HOMER WITH BASES FULL WINS FOR COMMERCE

Manhattan Boys Capture Scholastic World's Series Battle at Chicago.

(Special to The Eagle.)

Chicago, Ill., June 26—Hank Gherrig, the Babe Ruth of the high schools, lived up to his reputation today in the world's series game between Lane Tech High and the New York High School of Commerce for the high school championship. He uncorked a homer which cleared the right field wall at Cubs Field when the bases were full in the ninth inning and the Easterners took the title by a 12 to 6 score.

The game was a hard fought affair, the boys never letting up for a minute. The Easterners outplayed the local lads in all departments. They played steadier and were on their toes from the first gong until the last man was out.

Walsh got away to a poor start and when Ryrholm took the mound he was unable to stop the visitors, who had overcome their early stage fright and began to hit. Little Jacobs, who did the twirling for the New York champions, pitched a very creditable game. Only once were the local boys able to solve his delivery, and in this round, the third, they counted three times after two men were out. Jacobs's pitching, however, was not solely responsible for the runs, as Strohm helped the Lane boys with a pair of errors.

Jacobs got in hot water at another stage of the game when Johnson fumbled Christman's grounder in the fourth. He finally settled down, and as his teammates began crossing the plate his courage returned and he performed like a veteran.

McLoughlin hurt his ankle in running out a hit to first base early in the game, but after the leg had been bandaged he resumed his place behind the bat. Score:

Lane.

Name.	ab	r	h	po	a
P'sq'li,2b,ss	5	0	2	3	2
Pfleg'r,lf,3b	5	0	0	2	0
C'man,3b,cf	5	2	3	1	4
R'rholm,c,p	4	2	1	6	3
Graham,rf	4	0	1	0	0
Stev'son,1b	5	0	3	6	1
Hanson,ss	2	0	0	3	0
Schick,2b	0	0	0	0	0
Budach,lf	2	0	0	1	1
Empey,lf	3	0	0	0	1
Walsh,p	2	1	1	0	2
Marq'rds,c	3	1	2	4	1
*Heim	1	0	0	0	0
Totals	41	6	13	27	14

Commerce.

Name.	ab	r	h	po	a
†Bunora,ss	5	2	1	2	5
Johnson,3b	3	2	2	0	4
Gherrig,1b	4	4	1	3	0
M'L'ghlin,c	3	2	1	7	1
Strohm,cf	4	1	2	1	0
Ro'm'da,2b	4	0	0	2	3
Starke,rf	3	0	2	0	0
Troy,lf	5	0	2	2	0
Jacobs,p	4	1	0	0	2
Totals	36	12	11	27	15

*Batted for Hanson in seventh.
†Ran for McLoughlin in sixth.

Commerce	3	0	0	1	2	2	0	0	4	—12
Lane	0	0	3	0	2	0	0	1	0	—6

Errors—Pasquinelli, Pfleger, Chrisman (2), Hanson, Johnson, Strohm (2), Troy (2). Two-base hits—Chrisman, Stevenson, Marquardt, Bunora. Home run—Gherrig. Struck out—By Walsh, 4; by Ryrholm, 4; by Jacobs, 7. Bases on balls—Off Walsh, 2; off Ryrholm, 4. Double play—Johnson to Bunora to Gherrig. Hits—Off Walsh, 7 in 5 innings. Hit by pitcher—By Jacobs (Ryrholm, Hanson, Schick); by Walsh (McLoughlin); by Ryrholm (Johnson). Wild pitch—Ryrholm, 2. Time—2, hours and 46 minutes. Umpires—Cusack and Driscoll.

Howard High Gunner At Bergen Beach Traps

J. A. Howard was the high scratch gunner in the weekly shoot of the Bergen Beach Gun Club yesterday. He took the event with a card of 96 out of a possible 100 targets. He also was tied for the high handicap trophy along with E. B. Magnus and I. J. Kauder. The trio all had 100 targets. As Howard was not eligible for both cups, the other two only shot off for the handicap trophy. It was won by Magnus, Kauder taking third prize. The scores:

Name.	Hit.	Hp.	Tl.
J. A. Howard	96	6	100
E. B. Magnus	88	14	100
I. J. Kauder	84	18	100
W. Schroeder	91	6	97
F. A. J. Hering	91	6	97
J. F. Simonson	91	4	95
D. I. Bothas	74	25	95
E. W. Voorhies	74	12	86
S. C. Fowler	81	4	85
B. Moran	53	25	78
W. J. Doyle	75	0	75
F. W. Hertel	50	22	72
J. A. Moran	33	25	58

Small Yachts Sail Fast Race on Sound

The smaller classes enrolled in the Yacht Racing Association of Long Island Sound held an interesting regatta under the burgee of the Orienta Yacht Club of Mamaroneck yesterday. Although only eleven yachts came to the starting line, the craft had the best scrap of the summer. The wind was northeast and had enough body to send the yachts over a six-mile course in splendid time.

The start was made off Delancy Point, the committee, made up of J. Bister, R. Halsey, L. C. Herkenroph and W. A. Russel, using Commodore E. J. Lascari's yacht Avallon as the starting boat. As the wind came, the yachts had a close reach from the starting line to Scotch Caps, then a run to Execution Rock, followed by a beat home.

The winner in the Star Class was Gordon Curry's Aquilla. In the Sailing Canoe Class Leo Friede again came home first in his Mermaid. Pal-o-Mine, the property of H. A. Cole, was the only other canoe to sail. Off Scotch Caps the canoe capsized. Her skipper righted the canoe only to capsize again later in the race. He then gave up the race. In the Orienta One-design Class the winner was A. K. Griffen's Alice. The summary:

STAR CLASS—START [illegible]—COURSE 6 MILES.

HARVARD RALLIES AND BEATS YALE, WINNING SERIES

Five Runs in Sixth Turns Tide When the Blue is Leading 2 to 0.

(Special to The Eagle.)

Fenway Park, Boston, Mass., June 26—Harvard's 'varsity baseball nine came through with a rush in the sixth inning of its playoff ball game with Yale today, hammering home five runs against the New Haven southpaw Frank Coxe, who won at Cambridge a few days ago. Yale was leading 2 to 0 at the time, Felton having been poorly supported by his catcher, whose error and a passed ball accounted for both of Yale's runs.

The final score was 6 to 3, giving Harvard the series by two games to one. As Yale beat Princeton and

GHERRIG'S HOMER WITH BASES FULL WINS FOR COMMERCE

Manhattan Boys Capture Scholastic World's Series Battle at Chicago.

(Special to The Eagle.)

Chicago, Ill., June 26—Hank Gherrig, the Babe Ruth of the high schools, lived up to his reputation today in the world's series game between Lane Tech High and the New York High School of Commerce for the high school championship. He uncorked a homer which cleared the right field wall at Cubs Field when the bases were full in the ninth inning and the Easterners took the title by a 12 to 6 score.

The game was a hard fought affair, the boys never letting up for a minute. The Easterners outplayed the local lads in all departments. They played steadier and were on their toes from the first gong until the last man was out.

Walsh got away to a poor start and when Ryrholm took the mound he was unable to stop the visitors, who had overcome their early stage fright and began to hit. Little Jacobs, who did the twirling for the New York champions, pitched a very creditable game. Only once were the local boys able to solve his delivery, and in this round, the third, they counted three times after two men were out. Jacobs's pitching, however, was not solely responsible for the runs, as Strohm helped the Lane boys with a pair of errors.

Jacobs got in hot water at another stage of the game when Johnson fumbled Christman's grounder in the fourth. He finally settled down, and as his teammates began crossing the plate his courage returned and he performed like a veteran.

McLoughlin hurt his ankle in running out a hit to first base early in the game, but after the leg had been bandaged he resumed his place behind the bat. Score:

Lane.

Name.	ab	r	h	po	a
P'sq'li,2b,ss	5	0	2	3	2
Pfleg'r,lf,3b	5	0	0	2	0
C'man,3b,cf	5	2	3	1	4
R'rholm,c,p	4	2	1	6	3
Graham,rf	4	0	1	0	0
Stev'son,1b	5	0	3	6	1
Hanson,ss	2	0	0	3	0
Schick,2b	0	0	0	0	0
Budach,lf	2	0	0	1	1
Empey,lf	3	0	0	0	1
Walsh,p	2	1	1	0	2
Marq'rds,c	3	1	2	4	1
*Heim	1	0	0	0	0
Totals	41	6	13	27	14

Commerce.

Name.	ab	r	h	po	a
†Bunora,ss	5	2	1	2	5
Johnson,3b	3	2	2	0	4
Gherrig,1b	4	4	1	3	0
M'L'ghlin,c	3	2	1	7	1
Strohm,cf	4	1	2	1	0
Ro'm'da,2b	4	0	0	2	3
Starke,rf	3	0	2	0	0
Troy,lf	5	0	2	2	0
Jacobs,p	4	1	0	0	2
Totals	36	12	11	27	15

*Batted for Hanson in seventh.
†Ran for McLoughlin in sixth.

Commerce	3	0	0	1	2	2	0	0	4	—12
Lane	0	0	3	0	2	0	0	1	0	—6

Errors—Pasquinelli, Pfleger, Chrisman (2), Hanson, Johnson, Strohm (2), Troy (2). Two-base hits—Chrisman, Stevenson, Marquardt, Bunora. Home run—Gherrig. Struck out—By Walsh, 4; by Ryrholm, 4; by Jacobs, 7. Bases on balls—Off Walsh, 2; off Ryrholm, 4. Double play—Johnson to Bunora to Gherrig. Hits—Off Walsh, 7 in 5 innings. Hit by pitcher—By Jacobs (Ryrholm, Hanson, Schick); by Walsh (McLoughlin); by Ryrholm (Johnson). Wild pitch—Ryrholm, 2. Time—2, hours and 46 minutes. Umpires—Cusack and Driscoll.

Y. M. C. A. League.

											R.	H.	E.
Prospect Park	0	0	0	0	0	0	0	0	1	—	1	1	4
Eastern Dist	1	2	0	1	1	1	2	7	..	—	15	8	3

Batteries—Doyle and Pickinish; E. Vallor and Petor.

								R.	H.	E.
Carlton	3	0	2	1	2	0	—	8	7	2
Central Strollers	1	0	1	0	2	1	—	5	8	5

Batteries—Robinson and Seamon; Memmott and Isakson.

											R.	H.	E.
Central Colts	0	3	1	0	3	0	0	0	0	—	7	10	7
Bedford	0	1	0	0	0	0	0	4	3	—	8	10	9

Batteries—Bischoff and Van Bogen; Peterson and Bolk.

HOVEY IS NUTMEG CHAMPION.

Bridgeport, Conn., June 26—Roger H. Hovey, of Shuttle Meadow, won the Connecticut golf amateur championship for the third time this afternoon, when he defeated Reginald M. Lewis, of Greenwich, 5 and 4. Hovey was never hard pressed, finishing the morning play 5 up.

F. M. Hancock, of Meiacomet, won the Rhode Island golf championship yesterday by defeating J. A. Cammons, of Wannamoisett, in the 36-hole final over the latter course.

Ruth Hits Two More Home Runs, Increasing His Total to Thirty-one and Setting a New High Record

YANKS LOSE ONE AFTER BEATING SOX

Win First Game, 8 to 2; Drop Second, 8 to 5—Costly Errors.

By WILLIAM B. HANNA.

Babe Ruth broke the home run record at the Polo Grounds yesterday afternoon and the White Sox broke a long string of defeats sustained in Baberuthville, also known as New York. The White Sox won the second of the two games after losing five in succession here, and in that one Colossus Babe rocketed one home run into the right field bleachers and exploded another in the lower tier of the grandstand. The Yanks took the first game, 8 to 2; the Sox beat them, 8 to 5, in the second.

The hit with which Ruth broke his home run record of last year—twenty-nine—was delivered in the fourth inning of the second game, and was the mightier of the two. It was a drive worthy the creation of a new record and of the longest and hardest hitter since time was.

He poled it far up into the right field bleachers. It was made off Dick Kerr, as was his second. He didn't stop with the new figures of thirty homers, but sent them kiting up to thirty-one. The Yanks made three home runs in this game, but still Kerr beat them. The small southpaw received better support than Thormahlen of the Yanks did. His backing varied from steady and sure to brilliant and sure, Thormahlen's varied from brilliant to poor.

The opposing troops were late going into action. A water laden cloud burst all over the greenery about 1 o'clock and made such a quagmire of the field that Huggins decided to play but one game, and that at 3:30. He got to thinking it over, however, and decided to start in at 2 o'clock on a double header. That made a knockout hit with the crowd, which went to 27,000 before the day was over, and there was an ovation for Hug when he came sloshing through the mire to the dugout.

Bob Shawkey, out for nearly a month, pitched his first game since he ripped a rib muscle loose from its moorings one rare June day in darkest St. Louis. He made a success of his reappearance and, moreover, wasn't in the least annoyed at the spirit of camaraderie shown by his fellows in giving him a big lead early.

The Yanks rattled the hits off Wilkinson at a furious rate in the first two innings and utilized them to stow away six runs. Peck, Pipp, Pratt, Bodie, Ruel and Shawkey carried on the assault. Bodie sent a homer plunging into the left field gallery in the fifth inning after l'Enfant had hit for two bases. Rain shelved the game for half an hour just after the Sox, who dawdled and stalled over it, finished their half of the fifth inning.

Meusel Climbs the Wall.

The fielding feat of this game was contributed by Meusel. He backed into the wall, jumped and came down with a liner from Weaver's willow. The Sox, aided by a smattering of hits and a fumble by Peck, took unto themselves two runs, which gave the Yankees no concern whatsoever.

Herbert Thormahlen was removed in the thick of a batting spell in the second game, which the Yankees frittered away through errors by Hannah and slow fielding in other places. Hits were bunched on Thormahlen, who weakened after going six innings at top speed, but nevertheless misplays turned the tide and with clean support he probably would have gone through to success.

Hannah's misplays were costly, but he was doing his best after having been on the sick list, and the groans and panning visited on him by the crowd, or a certain rough neck element of it, were unmanly, ungenerous and undeserved. "Rough neck" is used advisedly. It's only the rough neck element that would do that sort of thing. The point arose, why catch Hannah if he wasn't fit and with Ruel going well, and then again it must be remembered that slow fielding by Ward and Meusel helped in the downfall.

Ward was slow on bunts, though the wet grass didn't help him any, but also he was great on hard hit balls to his position. He handled hot shot splendidly. Weaver, Eddie Collins and Jackson made whirlwind plays for the Sox, plays which saved the game for them. Jackson scaled the left field woodwork and clutched a rip roarer from Meusel, and Collins, paragon of all second basemen, dived for a searing slash from Bodie's mallet and converted it into a double play. In no previous game had the Sox shown such class.

Jackson hit to right for a home run in the second. Ruth hit into the bleachers in the fourth. His home run followed a single by Pipp. Pratt tripled in the sixth after a two bagger by Peck, and the lead looked succulent.

A Pass Starts Mischief.

The seventh and eighth innings went all awry. A pass to Felsch in the seventh started mischief. J. Collins singled and Risberg poked a single into right, on which Felsch scored. Schalk fouled out, and when Kerr hit to Ward the latter had a cinch play at the plate. John Collins was a goner until Hannah dropped the throw, then he put on full speed and tallied.

Leibold beat an infield hit to Ward, and Eddie Collins batted in Schalk. Ward lined into a double play in the seventh after Bodie had opened with a single. The Sox filled the bases in the eighth before anybody was out. Jackson whacked to centre. Ward wasn't spry enough on Felsch's bunt to get anybody, and John Collins's lazy hit to right was played in a lazy manner by Meusel. Fast footwork would have made an out of it.

Thormahlen was excused and Shore summoned. The first thing Shore did was to loose a wild pitch, which was no fault of Hannah's, though he was blamed by soreheads. The wild pitch let Jackson tread the plate. Peck threw out Risberg, and in trying to field Schalk's squeeze bunt Shore slipped. Felsch would have scored whether he had or not, but Schalk would have been the second out. As it was Kerr sacrificed. Leibold stabbed right with a single and J. Collins ambled home. Hannah inserted a bad throw to make matters worse in this inning.

Peck dropped a home run into the left field seats in the eighth. Ruth, first up, fired one into the lower grand stand in the ninth. With two out Wardie tripled past Felsch. Allowing him to turn third and keep on for the plate with Eddie Collins having the relay at the time was sheer bone on the part of the coach. Yet that was what O'Leary allowed him to do.

With that piece of scintillating granite headwork the last chance for victory went glimmering. Under the circumstances there was no justification whatever for taking the home run chance. A home run at that particular moment was not worth the corrugated rim of a lead quarter. The scores:

Babe Ruth's Record of 31 Home Runs

BABE RUTH yesterday got two home runs off Dick Kerr, the left hander of the White Sox, and set a new record for hitting home runs in any one season. The Ruth mark now is 31. The complete record is as follows:

MAY.

Date. Pitcher and Club.		Men on Base.	Place.
1—Pennock, Boston	(L)	0	N. Y.
2—Jones, Boston	(R)	1	N. Y.
11—Wilkinson, Chicago	(R)	1	N. Y.
11—Kerr, Chicago	(L)	0	N. Y.
12—Williams, Chicago	(L)	0	N. Y.
23—Wellman, St. Louis	(L)	1	N. Y.
25—Leonard, Detroit	(L)	1	N. Y.
26—Dauss, Detroit	(R)	0	N. Y.
27—Harper, Boston	(L)	0	Boston
27—Karr, Boston	(R)	0	Boston
29—Bush, Boston	(R)	1	Boston
31—Johnson, Washington	(R)	1	N. Y.

JUNE.

2—Zachary, Washington	(L)	1	N. Y.
2—Carlson, Washington	(R)	0	N. Y.
2—Snyder, Washington	(R)	0	N. Y.
10—Okrie, Detroit	(L)	1	Det.
13—Myers, Cleveland	(R)	0	Cleve.
16—Faber, Chicago	(R)	1	Chi.
17—Williams, Chicago	(L)	2	Chi.
23—Shocker, St. Louis	(R)	0	St. L.
25—Pennock, Boston	(L)	0	N. Y.
25—Pennock, Boston	(L)	0	N. Y.
30—Bigbee, Athletics	(R)	0	Phila.
30—Perry, Athletics	(R)	1	Phila.

JULY.

9—Oldham, Detroit	(L)	0	N. Y.
10—Dauss, Detroit	(R)	0	N. Y.
11—Ehmke, Detroit	(R)	0	N. Y.
14—Davis, St. Louis	(R)	0	N. Y.
15—Burwell, St. Louis	(R)	2	N. Y.
19—Kerr, Chicago	(L)	1	N. Y.
19—Kerr, Chicago	(L)	0	N. Y.

FIRST GAME.

CHICAGO (A.)

	ab	r	h	o	a	e
Leib'ld,rf	5	0	1	1	0	0
E.Co's,2b	4	0	0	7	2	0
Wea'r,3b	4	0	2	1	2	0
Jack'n,lf	3	1	2	2	0	1
Felsch,cf	4	0	1	3	2	0
J.Col's,1b	4	0	1	6	0	0
Risb'rg,ss	2	0	1	2	5	0
Schalk,c	4	1	1	2	1	0
Wilki'n,p	3	0	0	0	1	0
*Jourdan	1	0	0	0	0	0
Totals	34	2	9	24	13	1

NEW YORK (A.)

	ab	r	h	o	a	e
Peck,ss	5	2	2	2	4	1
Pipp,1b	5	1	3	6	2	0
Pratt,2b	4	1	1	2	3	0
Ruth,lf	2	1	1	1	0	0
Meusel,rf	4	0	1	1	0	0
Bodie,cf	4	1	2	6	0	0
Ward,3b	3	0	1	1	0	0
Ruel,c	4	1	1	6	0	0
Shawk'y,p	3	1	1	2	1	0
Totals	34	8	13	27	10	1

*Batted for Wilkinson in the ninth inning and grounded out.

Chicago .... 0 0 0 0 0 1 0 0 1—2
New York .... 2 4 0 0 2 0 0 0 x—8

Runs batted in—By Leibold, 1; by Risberg, 1; by Pipp, 1; by Pratt, 1; by Bodie, 3; by Shawkey, 1; by Meusel, 1. Two base hits—Felsch, Ruth. Three base hit—Pipp. Home run—Bodie. Sacrifice fly—Risberg. Stolen bases—Pratt, Bodie. First base on error—Chicago. Left on bases—Chicago, 9; New York, 7. Double plays—Risberg, E. Collins and J. Collins; Pratt, Peck and Pipp, 2. Bases on balls—Off Wilkinson, 5; off Shawkey, 2. Struck out—By Wilkinson, 2; by Shawkey, 4. Earned runs—Off Wilkinson, 8; off Shawkey, 1. Umpires—Chill and Moriarty. Time of game—1 hour and 50 minutes.

SECOND GAME.

CHICAGO (A.)

	ab	r	h	o	a	e
Leib'ld,rf	5	0	2	2	0	0
E.Col's,2b	5	0	1	1	4	0
W'ver,3b	5	0	0	1	5	0
J'ckson,lf	5	2	2	2	0	0
Felsch,cf	4	2	2	1	1	0
J.Col's,1b	4	2	3	14	0	0
Risb'g,ss	5	0	1	1	3	0
Schalk,c	4	1	2	4	0	0
Kerr,p	3	1	0	1	4	0
Totals	40	8	13	27	17	0

NEW YORK (A.)

	ab	r	h	o	a	e
Peck,ss	4	2	2	0	2	1
Pipp,1b	3	1	1	12	1	0
Pratt,2b	4	0	1	1	3	0
Ruth,lf	3	2	2	3	0	0
Meusel,rf	4	0	1	2	0	0
Bodie,cf	4	0	2	2	0	0
Ward,3b	4	0	1	2	3	0
Hannah,c	3	0	0	4	1	2
Thorm'n,p	2	0	0	0	1	0
Shore,p	0	0	0	0	1	0
*Lewis	1	0	0	0	0	0
McGraw,p	0	0	0	1	0	0
Totals	32	5	10	27	14	3

*Batted for Shore in the eighth inning and grounded out.

Chicago .... 0 1 0 0 0 0 3 4 0—8
New York .... 0 0 0 2 0 1 0 1 1—5

Runs batted in—By Jackson, 1; by Leibold, 1; by E. Collins, 1; by Risberg, 1; by Schalk, 1; by Peckinpaugh, 1; by Pratt, 1; by Ruth, 3. Two base hit—Peckinpaugh. Three base hits—Pratt, Ward. Home runs—Jackson, Peckinpaugh, Ruth, 2. Sacrifice hits—Kerr, Pipp. First base on error—Chicago. Left on bases—Chicago, 7; New York, 2. Double plays—Risberg, E. Collins and J. Collins; E. Collins, Risberg and J. Collins; Weaver and J. Collins. Bases on balls—Off Thormahlen, 2; off Kerr, 1. Struck out—By Thormahlen, 1; by Kerr, 3. Wild pitch—Shore. Hits—Off Thormahlen, 9 in 7 innings (nobody out in eighth when relieved); off Shore, 2 in 1 inning; off McGraw, 2 in 1 inning. Losing pitcher—Thormahlen. Earned runs—Off Kerr, 5; off Thormahlen, 5; off Shore, 1. Umpires—Moriarty and Chill. Time of game—1 hour and 50 minutes.

VAUGHN HITS HOMER AND BLANKS BRAVES

Cub Twirler Outshines Rudolph—Score Is 5 to 0.

CHICAGO, July 19 (National).—Vaughn outpitched Rudolph to-day and Chicago shut out Boston, 5 to 0. Vaughn's home run drive in the third inning was enough to win, but the locals bunched a single by Merkle and a double by Robertson after Herzog had been hit by a pitched ball and scored two more in that inning. Score:

BOSTON (N.)

	ab	r	h	o	a	e
Powell,cf	4	0	0	4	0	0
Pick,2b	4	0	3	5	5	0
Mann,lf	4	0	1	1	0	0
Eayrs,rf	4	0	1	0	0	1
Sul'vn,1b	4	0	0	12	0	0
Bo'ckl,3b	3	0	0	0	1	0
M'rnvl,ss	4	0	0	1	7	1
Gowdy,c	3	0	0	1	1	0
R'dlph,p	3	0	1	0	2	0
*Ford	0	0	0	0	0	0
Totals	33	0	6	24	16	2

CHICAGO (N.)

	ab	r	h	o	a	e
Flack,rf	3	1	1	1	0	0
Herzog,2b	3	1	0	2	1	1
Terry,ss	4	0	0	1	2	0
Merkle,1b	3	2	1	9	1	1
R'brtsn,lf	3	0	2	1	0	0
Tw'mby,cf	4	0	0	2	0	0
Deal,3b	3	0	1	3	4	0
Daly,c	3	0	0	7	0	0
Vaughn,p	3	1	1	1	2	1
Totals	29	5	6	27	10	3

*Batted for Rudolph in the ninth inning.

Boston .... 0 0 0 0 0 0 0 0 0—0
Chicago .... 0 0 3 0 0 1 1 0 x—5

Two base hits—Robertson, Pick. Home run—Vaughn. Sacrifices—Robertson, Daly. Double plays—Maranville, Pick and Sullivan; Deal and Merkle, 2. Left on bases—Boston, 9; Chicago, 6. Bases on balls—Off Vaughn, 2; off Rudolph, 2. Hit by pitcher—By Rudolph, 2 (Deal, Herzog); by Vaughn (Gowdy). Struck out—By Vaughn, 5; by Rudolph, 1. Umpires—O'Day and McCormick. Time of game—1 hour and 38 minutes.

EASTERN LEAGUE.

	R.	H.	E.
Bridgeport	3	6	3
Hartford	0	4	0

Batteries—Stuffer and Skiff; Pennington and Dammo.

At Albany—

	R.	H.	E.
Waterbury	4	10	0
Albany	1	2	4

Batteries—Stubing and Shinault; Marquis and Sweatt.

At Pittsfield—

	R.	H.	E.
Pittsfield	7	14	3
Worcester	6	11	2

Batteries—McQuade, Snover and Smith; Keifer, McClelland, Colley and Redman.

At New Haven—

	R.	H.	E.
Springfield	5	11	1
New Haven	6	11	3

Batteries—Mayberry and Wilder; James, Rikard and Nagle. Ten innings.

AT TARRYTOWN.

											R.	H.	E.
Atlantic City	0	2	0	0	4	0	0	2	0	—8	14	2
Chevrolet	1	0	0	3	0	0	0	0	0	—4	7	3

Batteries—McAreny, Dehm and Tobin; Tecarr and Ruddy.

MAMAUX'S WILD PEG BEATS THE DODGERS

Allows Daubert to Score for Reds in Ninth.

Special to THE SUN AND NEW YORK HERALD.

CINCINNATI, July 19.—The champion Reds evened their series with the league leading Dodgers this afternoon when they took the fourth game of the series by a score of 5 to 4. The Dodgers now are only two games in the lead. Mamaux's wild throw over Koney's head in the ninth inning scored Daubert with the tally that gave the Reds a victory.

Pfeffer started for the Dodgers but the Reds hit him hard and he was chased off the slab in the fourth inning. Mamaux relieved him and had only two bad innings, the sixth and ninth.

Ruether, the Reds' twirler, was hit freely in the first six chapters, but finished strong. Not a hit was made off him in the last three stanzas. Ruether's worst sessions were his fifth and sixth when the Dodgers did all their scoring. The leaders bunched four hits off his left handed slants in the sixth inning for three runs and forged to the front, but the Reds came back in their half of the same inning and evened the count.

Groh greeted Pfeffer in the first session with a long triple. Daubert and Roush failed to bring him home. Duncan, however, bounced a single to left and Groh scored.

In the third round the champions made another run when Daubert doubled and crossed the plate on Kopf's single. In the next inning Wingo started the Reds on the road to another tally with a single. Ruether tried to sacrifice and rolled to Johnston, who threw to second. Olson muffed the peg and both were safe. Groh followed with a single to left and Wingo scored. The hit ended Pfeffer's stay and Mamaux took his place. Daubert sacrificed. Roush flied to Wheat. Ruether left third before Zach caught the ball, and when Olson called for the pellet and stepped on third Umpire Moran called Ruether out.

The Dodgers pushed their first tally over the plate on successive singles by Johnston, Neis and Wheat in the fifth and in the next session threatened to chase Ruether off the mound. Kilduff led off with a double to left, but was out at third when he tried for three bases. His ambition cost a run as Krueger followed with a long single on which he would easily have scored from second. Mamaux walked and Olson sacrificed. Johnston's single to Sicking scored Krueger. Neis chased Mamaux and Johnston home with a triple. Sicking then made a good stop of Wheat's smash and threw him out.

The Reds tied the score in the same session when Wingo singled, stole second and scored on Daubert's single. Jake was the first Red to face Mamaux in the ninth, and after fouling off a couple he doubled to centre. The ball bounded over Myers's head but was recovered by Wheat. Roush then bunted to Mamaux and had the throw beat. Mamaux hurled the ball over Koney's head and the former Dodger crossed the plate with the winning run. The score:

BROOKLYN (N.)

	ab	r	h	o	a	e
Olson,ss	4	0	1	6	2	1
J'hnsn,3b	5	2	2	0	2	0
Neis,rf	5	0	2	2	0	0
Wheat,lf	5	0	2	3	1	0
Myers,cf	2	0	0	3	0	0
K'ntey,1b	4	0	1	7	1	0
K'ldff,2b	2	0	1	1	3	0
El'lott,c	1	0	0	0	1	0
Kru'gr,c	2	0	1	0	1	0
*McCabe	0	1	0	0	0	0
Miller,c	1	0	0	2	0	0
Pfeffer,p	1	0	0	0	0	0
Mam'x,p	1	1	0	0	1	1
Totals	33	4	10	†24	12	2

CINCINNATI (N.)

	ab	r	h	o	a	e
Groh,3b	4	1	2	2	3	0
D'ubrt,1b	4	2	3	12	0	0
Roush,cf	5	0	1	2	0	0
Duncan,lf	3	0	1	2	1	0
Kopf,ss	3	0	1	0	1	0
Neale,rf	3	0	0	2	0	0
Sicking,2b	4	0	1	5	6	0
Wingo,c	4	2	3	2	0	0
Ruether,p	4	0	0	0	3	0
Totals	34	5	12	27	14	0

*Ran for Krueger in the sixth inning.
†None out when winning run was scored.

Brooklyn .... 0 0 0 0 1 3 0 0 0—4
Cincinnati .... 1 0 1 1 0 1 0 0 1—5

Two base hits—Daubert, 2; Kilduff. Three base hits—Groh, Neis. Stolen bases—Daubert, Kopf, Wingo. Sacrifice hits—Daubert, Olson, Myers. Double plays—Groh, Sicking and Daubert; Wheat, Krueger and Olsen. Left on bases—Brooklyn, 9; Cincinnati, 10. Bases on balls—Off Ruether, 5; off Pfeffer, 3; off Mamaux, 1. Hits—Off Pfeffer, 7 in 3 1-3 innings; off Mamaux, 5 in 4 2-3 innings. Struck out—By Ruether, 2; by Mamaux, 1. Wild pitch—Mamaux. Losing pitcher—Mamaux. Umpires—Moran and Rigler. Time of game—2 hours and 5 minutes.

CARDS WIN IN TWELFTH.

With Double Sherdel Paves Way to Defeat of Phillies.

ST. LOUIS, July 19 (National).—St. Louis won from Philadelphia, 3 to 2, in twelve innings to-day, getting an even break on the series.

Sherdel was steady throughout and paved the way toward winning his own game in the twelfth when he doubled to centre. Smith sacrificed and Fournier's line single put Sherdel across the plate.

Cravath, batting for Wrightstone, tied the score in the ninth after two were down when he doubled to left, driving in two runs. The score:

PHILADELPHIA (N.)

	ab	r	h	o	a	e
LeB'au,lf	5	0	0	5	1	0
JMr,2b,3b	5	1	1	3	3	0
St'ngel,rf	5	0	0	2	1	0
Wil'ms,cf	5	1	2	2	1	0
Meusel,1b	5	0	1	11	1	0
W's'ne,3b	3	0	2	2	2	0
R'w'gs,2b	1	0	0	2	2	0
RMil'r,ss	5	0	0	2	4	0
Wheat,c	5	0	1	2	1	0
Hubbell,p	5	0	1	0	2	0
*Cravath	1	0	1	0	0	0
†Causey	0	0	0	0	0	0
Totals	45	2	9	‡34	18	0

ST. LOUIS (N.)

	ab	r	h	o	a	e
Smith,lf	5	1	0	3	0	0
F'rnier,1b	5	0	2	13	1	0
Stock,3b	5	0	1	0	3	0
H'nsby,2b	3	0	0	0	1	0
Lavan,ss	5	0	1	3	2	0
Clemons,c	5	0	1	0	0	0
H'hcote,rf	5	0	3	2	0	0
McHe'y,cf	5	1	3	5	0	0
Sherdel,p	4	1	1	1	1	1
Totals	42	3	12	36	8	1

*Batted for Wrightstone in ninth inning.
†Ran for Cravath in ninth inning.
‡One out when winning run was scored.

Philadelphia ..... 0 0 0 0 0 0 0 0 2 0 0 0—2
St. Louis .... 0 0 0 0 0 0 0 2 0 0 0 1—3

Two base hits—Cravath, Stock, 2; McHenry, Heathcote, Sherdel. Three base hit—Meusel. Sacrifices—Sherdel, Fournier, Smith. Double plays—Wheat, Meusel and Wheat; Meusel and Wheat. Left on bases—Philadelphia, 7; St. Louis, 10. Bases on balls—Off Hubbell, 2. Struck out—By Hubbell, 1; by Sherdel, 5. Umpires—Klem nad Emslie. Time of game—2 hours and 5 minutes.

DODGERS' MASCOT DROWNED.

The body of Benjamin W. Lewis, 16 year old mascot of the Brooklyn National League baseball team, was sent from Columbus, Ohio, to Brooklyn yesterday. Benny lived at 385 Greene avenue, Brooklyn, with his parents, Mr. and Mrs. Benjamin Lewis. He was drowned in the pool in Indianola Park at Columbus on Sunday while on a visit to his aunt and uncle, Mr. and Mrs. Arthur Miller. He idolized Zack Wheat and was a favorite with all the Brooklyn players. He recently passed an examination for machinist at the Brooklyn Navy Yard.

Maranville and Holke Headed for New York

IT was learned yesterday that a deal between the Giants and the Braves is near consummation. It is likely to be completed and the players transferred before the Giants return to the Polo Grounds next week. According to the best of information Rabbit Maranville and Walter Holke are to become Giants, and George Kelly, Jess Winters and another pitcher as well as an infielder are to go to the Bostons. Maranville will play shortstop and Dave Bancroft will move over to second base.

A third club may be involved in the deal, which has been brewing for the last three weeks, but struck a snag last week. It is said that this snag has been removed. Holke, it will be remembered, was with the Giants for many seasons and was released to the Reds in the deal which made Chase a Giant. The Reds sent Holke to the Braves.

INDIANS DIVIDE WITH RED SOX

Cleveland Loses Second Game in Ten Innings.

BOSTON, July 19 (American).—Boston and Cleveland divided a double header to-day, Cleveland winning the first, 10 to 6, and Boston the second, 5 to 4, in ten innings. Both teams batted hard. The scores:

FIRST GAME.

CLEVELAND (A.)

	ab	r	h	o	a	e
Jame'n,lf	6	1	2	3	0	0
Chap'n,ss	5	2	3	1	5	0
Spea'r,cf	5	2	3	4	0	0
Wood,cf	0	0	0	1	0	0
Smith,rf	5	0	1	2	0	0
Gard'r,3b	5	0	1	1	1	0
Wam's,2b	4	1	2	2	3	0
John'n,1b	4	1	1	12	0	0
O'Neill,c	4	2	3	1	0	1
Covel'ie,p	3	1	1	0	2	0
Bagby,p	1	0	0	0	1	0
Tot'ls	42	10	17	27	12	1

BOSTON (A.)

	ab	r	h	o	a	e
Hooper,rf	5	0	1	2	1	2
Foster,3b	3	2	0	2	0	0
Menos'y,lf	5	0	2	2	0	0
Schang,c	4	2	2	6	0	1
McIn'is,1b	4	0	1	11	1	1
McNa'y,2b	4	0	1	1	6	2
Scott,ss	4	0	0	1	2	0
Bailey,cf	4	1	3	2	0	0
Bush,p	4	1	1	0	3	0
Totals	37	6	11	27	13	6

Cleveland .... 1 0 0 1 3 1 0 0 4—10
Boston .... 2 0 0 0 0 1 3 0 0— 6

Two base hits—Coveleskie, Wambsganss, O'Neill, Menoskey. Three base hit—Speaker. Sacrifice—Coveleskie. Stolen base—Schang. Double plays—Chapman and Johnson; McNally and McInnis; Scott and McInnis. Left on bases—Cleveland, 12; Boston, 6. Bases on balls—Off Coveleskie, 1; off Bush, 6. Hits—Off Coveleskie, 10 in 6 1-3 innings; off Bagby, 1 in 2 2-3 innings. Hit by pitcher—By Coveleskie (Foster). Struck out—By Coveleskie, 1; by Bush, 3. Winning pitcher—Bagby. Umpires—Connolly and Nally. Time of game—2 hours and 1 minute.

SECOND GAME.

CLEVELAND (A.)

	ab	r	h	o	a	e
Jami'n,lf	5	1	2	1	0	0
Chap'n,ss	5	1	2	1	6	0
Spea'r,cf	3	1	1	7	0	0
Wood,rf	5	0	1	3	0	0
Gard'r,3b	3	1	1	1	2	0
Wam's,2b	5	0	0	3	2	0
John'n,1b	5	0	4	8	0	0
O'Neill,c	3	0	0	5	2	0
Bagby,p	4	0	1	0	1	0
Uhle,p	1	0	0	0	0	0
Tot'ls	39	4	12	*29	13	0

BOSTON (A.)

	ab	r	h	o	a	e
Bailey,cf	3	0	0	2	0	0
Schang,cf	1	1	0	0	0	0
Fo'ter,3b	6	0	2	1	5	1
Menos'y,lf	5	3	4	2	0	0
Hooper,rf	4	0	2	2	0	0
McIn'is,1b	5	0	1	13	1	0
McNa'y,2b	4	1	3	2	3	0
†Karr	1	0	0	0	0	0
‡Jones	0	0	0	0	0	0
Vitt,2b	0	0	0	1	0	0
Scott,ss	5	0	1	2	5	1
Walters,c	4	0	1	4	2	0
Pennock,p	5	0	1	1	3	0
Totals	43	5	15	30	19	2

*Two out when winning run was scored.
†Batted for McNally in the ninth inning.
‡Ran for Karr in the ninth innings.

Cleveland ...... 0 0 0 3 0 0 1 0 0 0—4
Boston .... 1 0 0 0 1 0 0 1 1 1—5

Two base hits—Johnston, Chapman, McInnis. Three base hit—Johnston. Stolen base—Schang. Sacrifices—O'Neill, Speaker, Gardner. Double play—Foster, McNally and McInnis. Left on bases—Cleveland, 10; Boston, 13. Bases on balls—Off Bagby, 3; off Pennock, 4. Hits—Off Bagby, 14 in 8 innings (none out in ninth); off Uhle, 1 in 1 2-3 innings. Hit by pitcher—By Uhle (Schang) Struck out—By Bagby, 2; by Pennock, 1. Losing pitcher—Uhle. Umpires—Nallin and Connolly. Time of game—2 hours and 1 minutes.

WELCH'S HOMER DECIDES GAME.

PHILADELPHIA, July 19 (American).—Welch's home run with two on base, culminating a bombardment of Weilman in the fifth inning, won to-day's game from St. Louis, 9 to 4. Keefe was batted from the box in the first inning, but Rommel held the visitors safe. Griffin made his first hit since July 1 and Severeid his first error in his last thirty-six games. The score:

ST. LOUIS (A.)

	ab	r	h	o	a	e
Tobin,rf	4	1	2	2	0	0
G'deon,2b	2	0	0	2	3	0
Sisler,1b	4	1	1	6	0	0
J'hson,cf	4	0	0	7	0	0
Wil'ms,lf	4	1	2	4	0	0
Smith,3b	4	0	0	1	0	0
Gerber,ss	4	0	0	0	2	0
S'v'reid,c	4	1	2	2	0	1
W'lman,p	1	0	0	0	1	0
Sot'ron,p	1	0	0	0	0	1
*Billings	1	0	0	0	0	0
Totals	33	4	7	24	6	2

PHILADELPHIA (A.)

	ab	r	h	o	a	e
Witt,rf	4	0	2	1	0	0
Dykes,3b	4	1	1	4	2	0
Walker,lf	5	1	3	1	0	0
Welch,cf	4	1	2	3	0	0
Dugan,2b	4	0	0	1	3	0
Perkins,c	4	0	1	2	0	0
Griffin,1b	4	2	2	13	1	0
Th'mas,ss	4	2	1	2	5	1
Keefe,p	0	0	0	0	1	1
Rommel,p	3	2	2	0	3	0
Totals	36	9	14	27	15	2

*Batted for Sothoron in ninth inning.

St. Louis .... 3 0 0 0 1 0 0 0 0—4
Philadelphia ..... 0 0 0 1 5 3 0 0 x—9

Home run—Welch. Stolen bases—Sisler, Williams. Sacrifices—Gedeon, 2; Rommel, Dykes. Double play—Gedeon and Sisler. Left on bases—St. Louis, 5; Philadelphia, 6. Hits—Off Weilman, 8 in 5 innings; off Sothoron, 6 in 3 innings; off Keefe, 3 in 1 inning; off Rommel, 4 in 8 innings. Hit by pitched ball—By Rommel (Weilman). Struck out—By Weilman, 1; by Rommel, 1. Winning pitcher—Rommel. Losing pitcher—Weilman. Umpires—Evans and Hildebrand. Time of game—1 hour and 29 minutes.

INTERNATIONAL LEAGUE.

RESULTS OF YESTERDAY'S GAMES.

Jersey City, 2; Rochester, 1.
Baltimore, 3; Toronto, 0.
Other games were postponed on account of rain.

STANDING OF THE CLUBS.

	W.	L.	PC.		W.	L.	PC.
Buffalo	57	28	.671	Reading	43	43	.500
Baltimore	56	30	.651	Jersey City	32	54	.372
Toronto	57	32	.640	Rochester	28	57	.329
Akron	52	34	.605	Syracuse	18	65	.217

GAMES SCHEDULED FOR TO-DAY.

Jersey City in Rochester.
Syracuse in Buffalo.
Baltimore in Toronto.
Reading in Akron.

AT ROCHESTER.

											R.	H.	E.
Jersey City	0	0	0	2	0	0	0	0	0	—2	5	2
Rochester	0	0	0	0	0	0	1	0	0	—1	7	3

Batteries—Biemiller and Freitag; Clifford and Ross.

AT TORONTO.

											R.	H.	E.
Baltimore	0	0	0	0	3	0	0	0	0	—3	4	1
Toronto	0	0	0	0	0	0	0	0	0	—0	3	0

Batteries—Bentley and Casey; Shea, Heck and Devine, Sandberg.

The Syracuse-Buffalo and Reading-Akron games were postponed on account of rain.

AMERICAN ASSOCIATION.

At Minneapolis—

	R.	H.	E.
Indianapolis	10	17	1
Minneapolis	9	12	0

Batteries—Rogge and Gossett; Craft, Hovlick and Mayer.

At Milwaukee—

	R.	H.	E.
Columbus	4	10	5
Milwaukee	6	7	1

Batteries—Lyons and Hartley; Gearing and Gaston.

At St. Paul—

	R.	H.	E.
Louisville	3	11	0
St. Paul	6	15	0

Batteries—Graham and Meyer; Hall and Hargrave.

At Kansas City—

	R.	H.	E.
Toledo	4	6	1
Kansas City	6	12	0

Batteries—Middleton and Murphy; Alexander and Sheney.

SOUTHERN ASSOCIATION.

At New Orleans—

	R.	H.	E.
New Orleans	2	6	2
Atlanta	3	10	0

Batteries—Walker and De Berry; Markle and Mills. Eleven innings.

At Memphis—

	R.	H.	E.
Memphis	4	5	0
Little Rock	2	7	0

Batteries—Goodbred and Bischoff; Hengeveld, Carlson and Kohlbecker.

At Chattanooga—

	R.	H.	E.
Chattanooga	6	10	1
Nashville	1	4	3

Batteries—Cunningham and Neiderkorn; Perdue and Jonnard.

The Mobile-Birmingham game was postponed on account of wet grounds.

American and National League Records.

RESULTS OF YESTERDAY'S GAMES.

AMERICAN LEAGUE.

New York, 8; Chicago, 2 (first game).
Chicago, 8; New York, 5 (second game).
Cleveland, 10; Boston, 6 (first game).
Boston, 5; Cleveland, 4 (10 innings, second game).
Philadelphia, 9; St. Louis, 4.
The Detroit-Washington game was postponed on account of rain.

NATIONAL LEAGUE.

The New York-Pittsburg game was postponed on account of rain.
Cincinnati, 5; Brooklyn, 4.
Chicago, 5; Boston, 0.
St. Louis, 3; Philadelphia, 2 (12 innings).

STANDING OF THE CLUBS.

	Played.	Won.	Lost.	P. C.		Played.	Won.	Lost.	P. C.
Cleveland	85	57	28	.671	Brooklyn	86	51	35	.593
New York	88	57	31	.648	Cincinnati	80	46	34	.575
Chicago	84	51	33	.607	Pittsburg	78	40	38	.513
Washington	79	39	40	.494	St. Louis	85	42	43	.494
St. Louis	84	41	43	.488	Chicago	87	42	45	.483
Boston	81	38	43	.469	New York	81	39	42	.481
Detroit	80	27	53	.337	Boston	74	33	41	.446
Philadelphia	87	24	63	.276	Philadelphia	81	33	48	.407

GAMES SCHEDULED FOR TO-DAY.

Chicago in New York (two games).
Cleveland in Boston.
St. Louis in Philadelphia.
Detroit in Washington.

New York in Pittsburg.
Brooklyn in Cincinnati.

WEST POINT PLAYS FAST POLO GAME

Fine Team Work Beats Rumson Flycatchers, 15 to 3.

Special to THE SUN AND NEW YORK HERALD.

RED BANK, N. J., July 19.—Showing superior team work and all round play the fast West Point polo team defeated the Rumson Fly Catchers in the second match played to-day in the Rumson Country Club polo tournament by the score of 15 goals to 3.

West Point was conceded one goal handicap and was held to a 3—2 score in the first half. The visitors started in with a rush in the second half and held the Rumson Fly Catchers scoreless except in the fifth period, when Harry East, who did all the scoring for his team, made a pretty goal from a difficult angle by hitting the ball as it bounced off a pony.

In the fifth chukker G. Jason Waters's pony scored a goal for West Point, Capt. Brown scored a free hit after a safety and Capt. Anderson added one more. In the sixth period Capt. Anderson made another goal on a free hit following a safety by Harry East. Capt. Anderson added two more in the seventh, one of which was a free hit on G. Jason Waters's foul. Capt. Brown also tallied two goals in this period.

West Point scored four more goals in the final chukker with pretty shots by Capt. Anderson, Capt. Wilson and Capt. Brown and a free hit by Capt. Brown on a foul hook called on Peter Hauck, Jr.

West Point will meet on Thursday the winner of to-morrow's game between Eatontown's and Rumson's first team. Fred Gilman will replace N. J. Stern at No. 1 for Eatontown, the latter having suffered a slight concussion when two ponies collided in a game played Saturday on the Eatontown club field at Camp Vail. The final match for the Rumson Country Club cup will be played Saturday.

The lineup and summary:

WEST POINT. Pos.	Hcp.	RUMSON FLYC'ERS. Pos.	Hcp.
1—Capt.A.H.Wilson	3	1—T. S. Field	1
2—Capt.R.E.And'on.	2	2—Harry East	7
3—Capt.J.L.Devers	1	3—Peter Hauck, Jr.	1
Back—Capt.L.Brown	3	Back—G. J. Waters	1
Total	9	Total	10

Goals—West Point: By Capt. Anderson, 5; by Capt. Brown, 6; by Capt. Wilson, 2; by pony, 1; by handicap, 1. Total, 15. Rumson Flycatchers: By East, 3. Referees—J. Ford Johnson, Jr., and J. Berens Waters. Timer—B. W. Brown.

BLOOMER FULLY RECOVERED.

Amateur Fencing Champion Returns From Chicago.

Millard J. Bloomer, Jr., national junior foils and epee champion of America and twice intercollegiate foils champion, who was wounded in an exhibition fencing contest with James Knox, former foils champion of the Illinois Athletic Club, returned to this city Saturday, fully recovered and in excellent form. After qualifying as a member of the American Olympic fencing team, of which he is a member, he was given his order for a passport to Antwerp, sailing on July 26 with the rest of the United States members to defend the American titles to the world championships.

Examination of the scars from Bloomer's wound proved that his life was only spared. One triangle mark of the blade under the right arm showed where his body was pierced, and the other scar, in the midde of his back, nine inches below the collar bone, gave evidence that the steel had entered the flesh for the distance of a foot.

SYRACUSE CREW CONQUERS.

Defeats Duluth Boat Club Eight by Two Feet.

DULUTH, July 19.—Syracuse University's senior eight defeated the Duluth Boat Club senior eight on St. Louis Bay here this afternoon by a margin of two feet in a mile and a quarter race. The time was: Syracuse, 6 minutes 17 seconds; Duluth, 6 minutes 17½ seconds.

The race was a desperate struggle to the finish. At the half way mark Duluth nosed slightly ahead; then a supreme effort by the Syracuse crew cut down the lead and the varsity shell flashed across the line, winner by a half second.

Both crews leave to-night for Worcester, Mass., where they are entered in the National Regatta, and will again compete for the privilege of representing this country in the Olympic meet. Dad Ten Eyck coaches the Syracuse crew and his son the Duluthians.

HULSEBOSCH TO MAKE TRIP.

Paulist A. C. Cross Country Runner to Compete in Olympics.

Albert J. Hulsebosch, the cross-country and steeplechase runner of the Paulist Athletic Club, has been chosen to compete in those events for this country in the Olympic games at Antwerp next month. Hulsebosch's name was omitted in the original selections yesterday because of an error on the part of the Olympic committee.

The committee got the Paulist athlete's name confused with A. L. Huelsenbeck of the New York A. C., and the Mercury Footer was selected instead of the "Winged P" man. The New York A. C. representative will not make the trip.

Notes of the Diamond.

The Rev. Dr. Daniel Mannix, Archbishop of Melbourne, will attend the double header today, the guest of Col. Ruppert. He will throw out the new ball.

W. J. Miles and A. Ahrens—A is right.

Constant Reader, Paterson, N. J.—They did not play on July 3.

Frank J. Hotaling—The Yankees play at the Polo Grounds July 24, 25 and 26, then go West.

Herman Sachs—A wins the bet, as the first game of a double header is the regularly scheduled game for that day.

I. Whitford—The best way to tell you is by illustrating. Say the Yanks have won 54 games to Cleveland's 55, and the Yanks have lost 30 games to Cleveland's 27. Subtract 54 from 55, which leaves one. Subtract 27 from 30, which leaves three. Add one and three, which makes four, and divide by two, which makes two. The Yanks, therefore, would be two games behind. If the Yanks had won 55 games to Cleveland's 54 the difference, one, must be subtracted from the difference in games lost, which would give two instead of four. Two divided by two gives one; that is, the Clevelands would be one game ahead. When it is said that a team is one game behind it means that team to catch up must win one while the other is losing one.

LAST WORK FOR NAVY CREWS.

Special to THE SUN AND NEW YORK HERALD.

ANNAPOLIS, Md., July 19.—The Naval Academy crews had their last practice this morning before leaving for Worcester, Mass., where they will compete on Friday and Saturday for the honor of representing the United States in the Olympic games at Antwerp. An eight and a four will compete in the intermediate races on Saturday, and the varsity eight in the senior event Saturday. The Naval eight regards Syracuse as its special rival, each having won one of the two previous races this season.

ENGINEERS' GAMES NEXT SUNDAY.

More than 200 entries are in for the athletic carnival under the auspices of the Local 20 International Union of Steam and Operating Engineers at Celtic Park next Sunday afternoon. Practically all the stars of the Metropolitan Association will be seen in the four A. A. U. events.

Leading Hitters in Major Leagues

AMERICAN LEAGUE.

Player and Club.	G.	A.B.	R.	H.	P.C.
Speaker, Cleveland	85	330	81	136	.412
Sisler, St. Louis	84	340	65	137	.403
Jackson, Chicago	80	319	59	128	.401
Ruth, New York	82	274	92	108	.394
Rice, Washington	79	317	47	117	.369

NATIONAL LEAGUE.

Player and Club.	G.	A.B.	R.	H.	P.C.
Hornsby, St. Louis	85	335	52	119	.355
E. Smith, New York	49	145	10	49	.338
Roush, Cincinnati	77	289	35	96	.332
J. Smith, St. Louis	56	180	38	59	.328
Konetchy, Brooklyn	72	281	33	91	.324

MARSHALL RETAINS LEAD AT CHESS

Only One More Round to Be Played in Masters' Tourney.

ATLANTIC CITY, N. J., July 19.—With one more round left to be played in the masters' tournament of the Atlantic City Chess Congress on the Million Dollar Pier, Frank J. Marshall, United States champion, retained the lead to-day by winning his game in the ninth and semi-final round from C. T. Sharp, the Philadelphia city champion, who put up a capital fight, but resigned after forty-three moves. Marshall had the white side of a queen's pawn opening, which Sharp treated with a counter gambit.

In a rook and pawn ending, the American champion obtained the upper hand by means of two connected passed pawns. This victory gave Marshall 6½ victories and 2½ defeats, still half a point better than the record of Jaffe of New York, who wrested second place from Mlotkowski of Los Angeles by defeating the Westerner in forty-one moves. Jaffe played the queen's pawn opening and won the "exchange" on the twenty-sixth move, after which he had the game well in hand.

Players.	Won.	Lost.	Players.	Won.	Lost.
Marshall	6½	2½	Jackson	4	5
Jaffe	6	3	Sharp	3½	5½
Mlotkowski	5	4	Neidich	2	7

GOTHAM SENDS BEST TO WORCESTER RACES

Harlem River Clubs Well Represented at Big Gathering

Out of the dozen cities to take part in the forty-sixth national amateur regatta at Worcester, Mass., on Friday and Saturday New York is second to Philadelphia in the number of clubs represented. The Lone Star Boat Club, the most active on the Harlem River this season, heads the list with entries in the senior and intermediate double shells. The winners of the former event are to be the American Olympic candidates. The seniors, David S. Mainin and Henry Frolisch, distinguished themselves July 5 by taking third place at the people's regatta at Philadelphia, and on the same day the intermediate crew finished second in their race. Wilfrid L. Schwab and Samuel Siegel of the intermediate shell are 35 years of age and their weights average 136 pounds.

Louis Zoha, the captain of the First Bohemian Boat Club and metropolitan title holder in the senior single shell, is to compete against his old rival Henry R. Hiller of the Atalantas in the association singles, the winner of which will hold the national championship. In a race held here some weeks ago Hiller finished three feet behind Zoha, and since then both men have been in hard training.

The second New York entry in the senior double shell comes from the Metropolitan Rowing Club and consists of Stanford Wells and John Shultz. Wells is an excellent oarsman and Shultz has for some years been head coach of the Metropolitans.

The New York Athletic Club is sending a crack crew to compete in one of the four Olympic championship races, the senior quadruple scull shells, or centipede. Stroke Krouche has been a prominent figure in American rowing for some years and lately distinguished himself at Philadelphia.

The course at Worcester extends for one and a quarter miles straightaway on Lake Quinsigamond, and several thousand spectators are expected to be present. The New York crews are to leave Thursday morning and intend to put in a stiff afternoon's practice before the races begin.

The local entries are:

Lone Star Boat Club:
Senior Double Shell—David S. Mainin, stroke; Henry Frolisch, bow.
Intermediate Double Shell—Wilfrid L. Schwab, stroke; Samuel Siegel, bow.
Metropolitan Rowing Club:
Senior Double Shell—Stanford Wells, stroke; John Shultz, bow.
Atalanta Boat Club:
Association Single Shell—Henry R. Heller.
First Bohemian Boat Club:
Association Single Shell—Louis Zoha.
New York Athletic Club:
Senior Quadruple Scull Shells, Centipede—C. Krouche, stroke; P. O. Smith, H. C. Schopp, Dewitt C. Baker; positions undecided.

STOCKS
PAGES 18 AND 19

THE CLEVELAND NEWS

FINAL NEWS EDITION

VOL. 79.—NO. 230. Published on six days of the week by the Cleveland Company, Cleveland, O. Entered as second class matter at Cleveland postoffice under the act of March 3, 1879. CLEVELAND, TUESDAY, AUGUST 17, 1920. PRICE THREE CENTS

CHAPMAN DEAD, STRUCK BY BALL

PLAYERS TO DEMAND MAYS GO

TWO CLUBS TO ASK OUSTER

Tiger, Red Sox Teams Frame Resolutions.

BOSTON, Aug. 17.—Players of the Detroit and Boston clubs of the American League today prepared to draw up a petition asking for the banishment from organized baseball of Carl Mays, of the New York Americans, who pitched the ball that fractured the skull of Ray Chapman, Cleveland shortstop, in yesterday's game.

Probability that members of both teams would refuse to play in any game in which Mays was the pitcher was expressed by some of the players.

Hold Protest Meeting.

The Red Sox team held a meeting in the clubhouse yesterday when word was received of Chapman's injury. It was agreed, according to Outfielder Menoskey, that all would sign a petition to President Johnson of the league to have Mays ruled out of the game if Chapman should die, and that the players would not go to bat against his uitching again. With News of his death this morning the players expressed their sorrow and then discussed the carrying out of the plan for a petition.

"Stuffy" McInnis, Red Sox first baseman, hurried from his seaside home at Manchester to be at the clubhouse

Continued on 2d Page, 3d Column

BOY CRUSHED TO DEATH BY TRUCK; DRIVER JAILED

An unidentified boy of ten was instantly killed shortly before noon Tuesday, when a motor truck ran him down as he crossed E. 9th st. at Superior ave.

Police held the driver, John Garvin, 10605 Arthur ave., on a charge of manslaughter.

The boy had waited until the signal of the traffic officer cleared the street of east and west-bound traffic. He did not see the truck, which turned out of Superior ave., until it was almost on him, witnesses said.

The boy's body was taken to county morgue. He wore a dark coat, a blue and white blouse, corduroy knickerbockers and black tennis slippers.

SUFFRAGISTS ELATED BY COMMITTEE O. K.

BULLETINS

NASHVILLE, Tenn., Aug. 17.—Debate on adoption of a resolution proposing ratification of the federal suffrage amendment was opened today in the lower house of the Tennessee legislature with prospects of a vote within a few hours. The Senate already has adopted the ratification resolution.

NASHVILLE, Tenn., Aug. 17.—Suffrage hopes are high for ratification of the nineteenth amendment by the Tennessee House of Representatives today.

When the House met at 10:30 o'clock this morning the committee on constitutional amendments submitted a favorable report on ratification. This will force the antis to move the adoption of a minority report. Upon the motion to table this the first test vote will come.

An almost complete attendance of members is assured. Monday afternoon ninety-eight of the ninety-nine were on hand. Both sides left no stone unturned to have their full strength on hand.

Shuns Auto; Buggy Proves Hoodoo, Too

DOVER, O., Aug. 17.—When Mrs. Isaac Haver, of Newcomerstown, was injured a short time ago in an automobile accident she forswore all automobile rides in the future. Last week she made her first trip since the accident in a buggy, but the horse ran away and she was thrown to the ground and again injured.

Rose "Feeling" 'n Odor Fade, Alas!

DOVER, O., Aug. 17.—When New Philadelphia police arrested George Akers, of Dubois, Pa., for intoxication they looked in vain for the bunch of roses they thought he must be carrying. Then they discovered that he had been drinking an expensive brand of rose toilet water. "Last night I felt as good as I smelled, but today I feel exactly as I look," said Akers in court.

Cool Air and Damp Streets Predicted by Weather Prophet

It's going to stay cool for a couple of days now with continued cloudiness and probably occasional rain.

At least that's what Weather Forecaster Emery predicts.

At midnight the mercury started to slide downward from the 69-degree mark. At 5 a. m. it reached 64 and by noon it had been pushed up to 68. The hourly readings follow:

12 midnight	69	8 a. m.	66
1 a. m.	68	9 a. m.	67
2 a. m.	68	10 a. m.	67
3 a. m.	67	11 a. m.	67
4 a. m.	65	12 noon	68
5 a. m.	64	1 p. m.	69
6 a. m.	64	2 p. m.	69
7 a. m.	65	3 p. m.	68

U. S. PROBE IS ORDERED INTO MILK PRICES

"Agents" Are Blamed for Recent Boost Here.

A federal investigation of the milk situation in Cleveland and three other Ohio cities was ordered Tuesday by the state fair price commission. Special experts of the department of justice are to be assigned to the points of investigation immediately.

The milk probe follows an investigation of prices charged in Cleveland, Columbus, East Liverpool and Akron and the application from dealers in numerous sections for price increases.

According to Maurice Langan, secretary of the state fair price commission at Columbus, who is in charge of the probe, paid agents of the producers' association and not the producers themselves are responsible for the agitation for higher prices.

The Farmers' Co-operative Milk Company, the membership of which includes the majority of producers that supply Cleveland with milk, has been granted an increase totaling 5 cents per gallon in less than two months.

During the same period retail prices were boosted 4 cents per gallon. The present wholesale price is 35½ cents. At the last conference betgeen retailrs and producers at which the August price was fixed the latter held out for 36 cents per gallon. They were offered 35, but declared they would discontinue shipments unless granted more.

Dr. R. C. Roueche, head of the local fair price commission, declared there is little need of an investigation of the milk situation here. He said from the best figures available both retailers and producers were making only a fair margin of profit.

Household Suggestions appear daily in The News.

The News sport page is the best in the city.

A FLOWER FROM A FAN

A flower from a fan!

That's the best tribute that can be paid to Ray Chapman, Cleveland shortstop, who died in New York early Tuesday morning, the result of having his skull fractured by being hit by a pitched ball.

The News suggests that each fan—man, woman and kiddie—buy one flower for Ray Chapman, that is, contribute ten cents to pay for one flower to go into an immense floral offering for Chappie's funeral.

Arrangements have been made with H. O. Van Hart, of the First National Bank, to receive contributions to "A Flower From a Fan" fund. Take your dime to the First National Bank and by so doing you will be paying tribute to the memory of the greatest shortstop and mose gentlemanly player Cleveland has ever had.

Let's make "A Flower From a Fan" the biggest tribute ever paid to any ball player. We believe there are thousands of lovers of baseball in Cleveland who gladly will wend their way to the First National Bank and turn in their contribution to Mr. Van Hart.

Chappie never was one for showiness in any manner, shape or form. He was just a plain every day sort of a fellow, and we believe that if he could have his own way about it "A Flower From a Fan" tribute would please him more than anything else.

Don't wait, fans. Take in your dime at once to Mr. Van Hart. We want all the contributions in by Wednesday afternoon at the very latest. Each dime will be used to purchase one flower, a silent tribute to the memory of Chappie, a sort of "Shower of Sorrow" in flowers from the fans who really admired, respected and loved Ray Chapman.

LATE NEWS BULLETINS

HEAR 26 DIE IN CRASH

CHICAGO, Aug. 17.—Railroad offices here have a report that a Chicago, Gary and South Bend interurban jumped the tracks at Portage Crossing, four miles west of South Bend, killing twenty-six passengers.

Gets 99-Year Sentence.

LEAVENWORTH, Kan., Aug. 17.—John Mosher, credited with being the most dangerous prisoner in the American overseas army, today was brought here from Coblenz, Germany, where he was convicted of murdering Sergt. Lester Call. He was sentenced to ninety-nine years at hard labor.

Harding Remains on Porch.

MARION, Aug. 17.—Senator Harding today vetoed all proposals that he speak elsewhere than from his front porch on Labor day, September 6. The first stage of a conference between the Senator and other Republican leaders here resulted in an announcement by Republican Chairman Hays the nominee "had expressed a decided preference" for his original plan to deliver a Labor day address in Marion.

McGraw Seeks Indictment.

NEW YORK, Aug. 17.—John J. McGraw, manager of the New York Giants, today demanded he be indicted in order that he might establish his innocence of any participation in bringing about injuries to John C. Slavin, who was found unconscious in front of the McGraw home.

One Killed in Search of Irish Residence

DUBLIN, Aug. 17.—One civilian was killed and another wounded during the search of a house by British soldiers at Derrygallon, county Cork, according to a message from that place today.

"Chappie," Idol of Indian Fans, Killed in Game; Widowed Bride

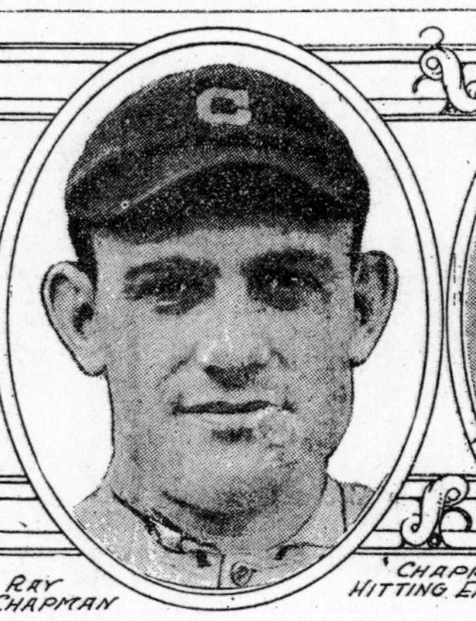

RAY CHAPMAN

'CHAPPIE' HITTING EM OUT.

MRS. RAY CHAPMAN.

Sugar, at 21 Cents, Is Season's "Low"

Sugar was quoted on the retail market at 21 cents Tuesday. This is a new low level for the summer and a drop of 9 cents from the market's high point, reached several weeks ago. Although the market retail price was quoted at 21 cents some dealers in the city were selling at 20 cents.

Buying was light and, it is predicted, sugar prices will continue to drop.

Potatoes have declined 21 cents since the new crop came into the market. Potatoes were quoted at 4 cents per pound, retail, when the market opened.

The News is the only afternoon paper in the city carrying Associated Press dispatches.

Ray Chapman, a Tribute

BY ED BANG

Ray Chapman is dead!

The dots and dashes spelling out this doleful and heartrending message came over the wire from New York shortly before 6 o'clock Tuesday morning. Although the news was somewhat anticipated, as it was known that the fracture to Ray's skull might prove fatal, still it came like a thunderbolt from a clear sky.

The greatest shortstop, that is, considering all-around ability, batting, throwing, base running, bunting, fielding and ground covering ability, to say nothing of fight, spirit and conscientiousness, ever to wear a Cleveland uniform, will never again be seen covering two-thirds of the ground between second and third. Never again will we hear the fans yell: "Atta boy, Chappie!" "Speed up, Ray, old boy," "Show 'em where you live, Chappie." Never again will we see the speeder among the fastest men in baseball score all the way from first on a short hit, or scoot from first to third on a bunt. Chappie has lived his baseball career and a wonderful one it was, and his life, which was the sort that every mother would have her son live.

The writer has known Ray Chapman ever since the first day he came to Cleveland and donned the regalia of the then Naps back in the fag end of the 1912 season. And we have rejoiced in the success that he attained year after year, for we formed a liking for him that first day. With all the fight and determination at his command he never admitted defeat until the last man was out.

And Ray lived his life the same way. He was clean cut, high-minded, honest and straightforward. He had a personality that was contagious, for once you met Ray Chapman you were glad to list him among your friends. Chappie was just as much at home in the ballroom in the highest society as he was among his diamond associates on the field, on the bench or in the clubhouse. He was his 100 per cent self all the time, no frills or furbelows, and it was this trait that won him fast friends among the heads of manufacturing, industrial and mercantile concerns as well as among the newsies on the street corners. All of them will mourn the passing not only of Chappie the great shortstop, but Ray Chapman the man and their friend.

I was proud to list Chappie among my closest friends and on more than one occasion he flattered me by making me his confidant. Ray had his little troubles now and then but nothing could long cast a cloud over that wonderful sunny and cheery disposition. It was his smile and words of cheer that ofttimes brought his teammates out of their "case of dumps" after losing a hard-fought game. And it was this same disposition that brought joy to hundreds in the everyday walks of life.

Chappie did not live to realize his life ambition, that of playing on a pennant-winning and possibly a world's championship team, and that when it seemed almost within his grasp. There was some talk about Ray's retiring from baseball following his marriage to Miss Kathleen Daly last fall, but Ray said that he would not quit the game until he had helped his best friend, Tris Speaker, win a pennant and world's championship.

"Then, well, I guess I'll be a real business man, but gee! it'll be hard to pull away from my pal Spoke and the rest of the boys," said Chappie.

But if the Indians should win the pennant and world's championship—and there is not one of the players who would not willingly pass up the honor if it would only bring Chappie back—everybody will realize that the achievement could not have been accomplished without the aid given by the great little shortstop in the past, who has been called to his reward.

75 DETROIT NURSES TO ATTEND LEGION MEET

Seventy-five members of the nurses' post of the American Legion of Detroit will attend the convention here September 27, 28 and 29. They will be in uniform and will take part in the parade the opening day.

Open-air movie shows will be held in front of the clubrooms of the legion, E. 21st st. and Euclid ave., on August 27 as a means of stimulating interest. This will mark the first appearance of the local legion band, which will lead the parade on September 27.

Legion posts in the city and county will put on entertanments of their own during the three days. Victory post has already leased Dreamland hall for a dance on the opening night. Other posts are planning like amusements.

The News sport page is the best in in the city

THE WEATHER

THE NEWS BAROMETER

STORMY · RAIN · CHANGE · FAIR · VERY DRY

(Sea level)
11 a. m. 30.18

Partly cloudy and cool Tuesday night. Wednesday partly cloudy; slightly warmer in afternoon. Moderate northeast and east winds.

OPERATION TO SAVE INDIAN'S LIFE FAILS

Mays, Whose Pitch Hit Star, Exonerated; Bring Body to Cleveland Wednesday; National League Flags at Half-Mast.

BY FRANK F. O'NEILL
Special Correspondent for THE NEWS

NEW YORK, Aug. 17.—Raymond Chapman, shortstop of the Cleveland Indians, died at 4:50 this morning in St. Lawrence hospital of a fractured skull, as the result of being hit on the head by a pitched ball thrown by Carl Mays, a pitcher of the New York Yankees, in yesterday's game on the Polo grounds.

Col. Jacob Ruppert, president of the Yankee club, upon learning of Chapman's death, immediately announced there would be no game today between the Cleveland and Yankee clubs.

As the result of the death of Chapman, Tris Speaker, manager of the Indians and roommate of the shortstop is ill.

The district attorney's office indicated today it was not planning to investigate yesterday's accident. A formal police investigation, however, was started when a detective was sent to interview Pitcher Mays.

Police Exonerate Mays.

Mays later voluntarily appeared at the homicide bureau of the district attorney's office in company with the detective sent to interview him, where he was examined by Assistant District Attorney Joyce. After the interview Joyce declared Chapman's death was due to accident purely, and indicated no further investigation by the district attorney or the police would follow.

Mays returned to his lodgings unescorted.

President Heydler, of the National League, announced this afternoon that all flags of the league's club fields would be fflown at half mast this week in tribute to Ray Chapman. All the league's players also will wear insignia of mourning, he said.

Chapman's body will be taken to Cleveland tomorrow, where funeral services will be observed.

To Father Connors, of Philadelphia, who married the Chapmans, fell the duty today of breaking the news of her husband's death to Mrs. Chapman on her arrival here. She was so overcome by grief she had to postpone a visit to the undertaking rooms, where the body was taken.

Teammates, however, viewed the body. Jack Graney, a particular friend of Chapman, broke down and sobbed.

Chapman was operated on at 12:30 o'clock this morning, after a conference of several surgeons, Manager Speaker and Secretary McNichols of the Indians. Chapman had been growing worse steadily during the evening and it was agreed it would be unwise to delay the operation.

An X-ray photograph of the injury earlier in the evening had disclosed the fact Chapman had sustained a depressed fracture on the left side of the skull.

Piece of Skull Removed.

The surgical work was in charge of Drs. Joseph Cascie, A. A. White and of the St. Lawrence hospital staff. Drs. Poseph Cascie, A. A. White and J. E. Quinn were the attendants. The operation required one hour. The surgeons made an incision three and a half inches long through the base of the skull on the left side. They found a rupture of the lateral sinus and a quantity of clotted blood. A small piece of the skull was removed.

There is no disposition on the part of Manager Speaker or any of his players to regard the accident as due to the so-called "bean ball" because Mays was the pitcher. The Yankee hurler, in his version of the accident, said the ball was a "sailer."

Chapman was the first batter in the fifth inning and he was hit with the first ball pitched. He seemed to have been looking for a curve and did not make any effort to move before he was hit. Then he collapsed.

All Baseball Mourns.

The loss, terrible as it is to the Cleveland players, is not theirs alone. Chapman was one of the representative players of the game. He was popular with baseball fans all over the circuit and enjoyed the love and esteem of his fellow players.

Eliminating the human side of the tragedy, if this be possible, baseball fans realize a terrific smash has been dealt to the pennant hopes and chances of the Indians. Unless Speaker, the great gray leader of the Tribe, can perform the task of Atlas, we may say the chances of the Injuns fell with Chapman.

The case of the dead player was almost analagous with that of "Chick" Fewster, the dashing youngster of the Yankees. "Chick's" skull was fractured in a game at Jacksonville last spring. After a delicate operation, performed in Johns-Hopkins hospital this spring, he is up and doing. The period of recuperation with Fewster was long and weary, the operation pre-

Continued on 2d Page, 1st Column

Alliance Gets New Plant.

ALLIANCE, O., Aug. 17.—The H. K. Ferguson Company, of Cleveland, yesterday broke ground for the erection of an addition to the Transue-Williams Company plant. The building is to be brick and will be 100 feet wide and 200 feet long. The work is to be pushed forward and completed as soon as possible.

COX RENDS PAST TO BARE HARDING AS 'REACTIONARY'

COLUMBUS, Aug. 17.—Senator Harding was again attacked as "reactionary" by Gov. Cox, his Democratic opponent, today.

Addressing the Ohio Democratic convention and laying down his state leadership, Cox reviewed the contest he had in 1912 when he supported and Senator Harding opposed the new Ohio constitution.

"It has, in considerable degree," said Gov. Cox, "made the bast upon which the presidential contest is being fought this year, for the reason that the issue now, as in the past, is between progress and reaction."

Cox cited a statement by Harding, after adoption of the new state constitution, that it meant "Socialism and revolution."

Refers to Lobbyists.

The opponents, Gov. Cox said, also were aided by "paid lobbyists" and moneyed interests.

"To his credit," the governor continued, "it must be stated that he believed that he was right.

"He mistook the spirit of the whole movement. It was an orderly process of evolution. He designated it as socialism.

"The point, however," Governor Cox declared, "is that he still believes in reaction and I still believe in progress."

Governor Cox detailed numerous reforms which he said had resulted, such as the workman's compensation law, reduction of lawsuits, protection of the ballot, rural school progress, mothers' pensions and prison reform.

"In every contest between progress and reaction," Cox continued, "whether state, national or international, you will find the elements very much the same. The forward step is always surrounded by articulated misgivings, sincere in some instances, but ordinarily the evidenceof selfish desire, or political design.

"It required governmental intervention to allay unrest within this state. The reactionary regard it as revolution."

Platform Lauds Cox.

The tentative draft of the platform presented to the convention for adoption lauds the record of Governor Cox, thanks the national democracy for nominating him for the presidency, urges the election to the governorship of A. V. Donahey on his business record as state auditor, and pledges economy in state government and a more equal distribution of taxes.

Referring to taxes, the platform pledges the Democratic party to enact a debt limitation "as strong as iron bands that will limit the amount of debt that can be created by public officials." The platform charges the Republican majority in the eighty-third General Assembly "cowardly refused to obey the pledge of their own platform adopted in 1918 to reform the methods of taxation in our state."

The platform strongly urges home rule in taxation, and says:

"People residing in a taxing district should not be limited in the creation of public debt provided a majority of the electors residing in such district shall authorize the same."

Mayor Runs Away, Woods Is in Charge—But Just for 10 Days

Cleveland is to have a new mayor for the next ten days.

Law Director Woods will serve as acting mayor while Mayor FitzGerald takes his vacation. FitzGerald is to leave Tuesday night for Atlantic City. He may also visit several other eastern points.

Youthful Role of "Ma" Brings Bullets

NEW YORK, Aug. 17.—Emil Coudry, who was arrested for shooting and wounding his wife and daughter, told the police he was angered because his wife dressed like a girl and posed as the sister of the daughter.

EIGHT WHITE SOX INDICTED FOR FRAUD

FIVE YEARS AND $10,000 FINE IS PENALTY IF FOUND GUILTY

HARDING GETS BIG OVATION IN W. VIRGINIA

Nominee Declares Administration Has Drawn Lifeblood from Business Channels to Keep Itself Alive.

By Associated Press.

WHEELING, W. VA., September 28—Speaking to a crowd which packed the Wheeling Auditorium, Senator Warren G. Harding laid down here tonight a policy of government economy and strict business administration.

So dense was the crowd along the line from the Senator's hotel to the Auditorium that both his car and that which carried Mrs. Harding were lost for a time in traffic jams.

When the nominee arrived the crowd rose and cheered for more than a minute.

Senator Harding told his Auditorium audience here why he had preferred the front-porch campaign.

"It wasn't because I didn't desire to come to you and preach the gospel of Americanism from the Republican standpoint," he said. "But I chose to speak from the front porch over at Marion for the very reason that I have encountered here in Wheeling today. I didn't like to disappoint anyone. When I come to your city I find the tide Republicanism running high and there are 30,000 people in Wheeling who want to hear the gospel of Republicanism as I delight to preach it; but only about 5000 of us can crowd in here.

"One thing I could do in Marion was that I could talk to virtually all of the American people through the medium of the great American press.

Must Put House in Order.

"I think the American people have heard—I know they have heard up in Maine, and I think they have heard everywhere—and have resolved we ought to do two things, first, to put our own house in order and then let the world know that we can manage our own affairs.

The Republican nominee quoted Treasury Department figures to support his charge of unwarranted expenditures and asserted that the administration's proposal for a new issue of Treasury certificates would be to further handicap the money market and to increase the cost of living. He scored President Wilson for his veto of the budget bill passed by the last Republican Congress and promised that a budget system would be one of the first policies inaugurated by a new Republican administration.

"Unless we check the existing system of waste and extravagance," he continued, "we shall run head-on into disaster."

Makes Six Addresses.

The Republican nominee's speech here was the sixth he had delivered during the day in West Virginia. He made short rear-platform talks to crowds at Grafton, Fairmont, Mannington, Cameron and Moundsville, assailing the labor provisions of the peace treaty and declaring that the Democratic administration might greatly ease the coal situation if it chose by invoking the car allotment provisions of the Cummins-Esch railway bill.

In his night speech here Senator Harding said that the deficit for the last year would have been nearer $3,000,000,000 than $1,000,000,000, had not the Republican Congress cut down administration requests for appropriations.

Referring to the proposal for a new treasury certificate issue, the Senator declared it was time the people inquired into the administration's method of financing if the nation was to be saved from serious consequences.

Says Collapse Is Imminent.

"Industrial reports from one end of the country to the other indicate a falling off in business, a stringency in the money market," Senator Harding said. "These conditions are due to the gigantic failure of the Democratic administration to function as a business organization. It has drawn the very lifeblood from the channels of business to keep itself alive—a process which, if continued, will inevitably produce a collapse of our financial system."

The Republican budget bill, said the nominee, would have co-ordinated the expenditures of the various federal departments and bureaus and would have made it necessary for the President to call his Cabinet members into conference, agree on a financial policy and then adhere to that policy. President Wilson's veto of the bill, he said, "did not relate to its great constructive features, but to a small detail of par-

Continued on Page 2, Column 2.

Hecklers Bombard Cox in South Dakota

Nominee Says Germany Should Be Admitted to League of Nations and Stands by Volstead Act as Construed by Supreme Court.

By Associated Press.

SIOUX FALLS, S. D., September 28.—A statement regarding the Volstead prohibition enforcement law—that he would oppose "any measure that is in conflict with the constitution and the eighteenth amendment as interpreted by the Supreme Court," and bombardments of questions regarding the League of Nations from persons of German blood, marked a lively tour of South Dakota today by Gov. Cox. The Democratic presidential candidate also launched new criticism of Senator Harding, his Republican opponent, assailing bitterly the Senator's Baltimore speech of yesterday and again dubbing him a "brewer."

Gov. Cox's statement upon the Volstead act was in response to a question from a man at Mitchell late today.

"My attitude with reference to that whole question is," Gov. Cox replied, "I shall oppose any measure that is in conflict with the constitution of the United States and the eighteenth amendment as interpreted by the Supreme Court."

That Germany should be welcomed into the League of Nations and "treated as well as any other nation" was stated by Gov. Cox in reply to persons of German blood or descent, forming a large part of communities the candidate reached today.

Assails Senator Harding.

Gov. Cox assailed Senator Harding, denouncing the Senator's demur yesterday at Baltimore to a question upon the league, and the Republican nominee's statement that he was "without a single program constructive about an association of nations," Gov. Cox declared the situation "deplorable and pitiable."

"The candidate of the senatorial oligarchy, by his statement," the Governor declared in addressing a large audience here tonight at the Auditorium closing his South Dakota tour, "pleads guilty on behalf of himself and his associates for the most stupendous conspiracy the world has ever seen."

The League of Nations, progress and agricultural topics were preached by the Governor to all of his fifteen South Dakota audiences.

Several persons, mostly with pronounced German accents, questioned the Governor at different places. Some appeared friendly and caused the Governor to give his views on questions interesting his audiences.

Cox Criticises Harding.

YANKTON, S. D., September 28.—Gov. Cox, Democratic presidential candidate, issued a statement here today rebuking Senator Harding for the Republican nominee's objection to questioning during the Senator's speech in Baltimore last night.

The Governor declared that the Senator was asking the American people to follow him on the league issue when the Senator himself does not know his own policy. The statement was, in part:

"The candidate should welcome inquiries. I can understand how a member of a senatorial oligarchy which has defied public wishes and the public interest would develop as a habit the thought that the senatorial mind should not be questioned.

"Senator Harding would have the American people follow him and ignore the intensive labors of eminent men. His message to America is: 'I know not where I am going, but I ask you to follow me.' Never before in the history of presidential campaigns has there developed a situation more deplorable and pitiable."

Cox Replies to Auditor.

MITCHELL, S. D., September 28.—Touring South Dakota today, Gov. Cox of Ohio discussed the League of Nations and farming problems and criticised freely Senator Harding's objection to questioning during his Baltimore speech.

"America first" and the German slogan, "Deutschland uber alles" were debated by the Governor at Tripp with a

Continued on Page 5, Column 5.

FAIR, COOLER WEATHER FORECAST FOR TODAY

Forecast for St. Louis and Vicinity—Fair and cooler Wednesday, Thursday fair and continued cool.

Temperature readings follow:

6 a. m.	61	3 p. m.	81
9 a. m.	71	5 p. m.	78
11 a. m.	77	7 p. m.	73
1 p. m.	79	9 p. m.	68

Temperature—Maximum, 81 degrees at 3 p. m.; minimum, 61 degrees at 7 a. m. Wind—Direction at 7 p. m., north; velocity at 7 p. m., thirteen miles an hour. Relative humidity at 7 p. m., 45 per cent. River stage at 7 a. m., 4.4 feet.

Forecast by States.

Illinois and Missouri—Fair and cooler Wednesday; Thursday fair and continued cool.

MICHAEL W. CADLE DIES AT HOME HERE

Had Been Assistant Chief of Locomotive Engineers Since 1904.

Michael W. Cadle, 62 years old, assistant grand chief of the Brotherhood of Locomotive Engineers, died last night at his home, 4474 Washington avenue. He had been ill for two weeks of a complication of diseases.

Cadle had been assistant chief in the organization since 1904, and had held important offices with the brotherhood previous to that time. With W. S. Stone, grand chief of the brotherhood, Cadle conferred in Washington with government officials in the recent wage settlements, and national legislation conferences.

His office was in Cleveland, Ohio, but his duties required him to travel throughout the country. He was taken ill in Pensacola, Fla., Septehmber 19 and brought to his home here.

He is survived by his wife, a son, Robert Cadle, a student in St. Mary's College, St. Mary's, Kan., and two daughters, Miss Catherine Cadle and Miss Helen Cadle.

The funeral will be held in Sedalia, Mo., Cadle's former home. The family will accompany the body to Sedalia tomorrow morning, and burial will probably be on Friday morning.

REED ASKED TO STUMP STATE FOR DEMOCRATS

Ousted Senator Has Not Replied to State Committee's Invitation.

Senator James A. Reed of Missouri, a bitter opponent of the League of Nations, who was ousted as a delegate from the Fifth Missouri District by the Democratic National Convention, has been invited by officers of the Democratic State Committee to take the stump in Missouri for the Democratic state and national tickets, it was learned yesterday.

Reed's invitation is said to have been extended personally by State Chairman C. E. Yancey Monday night as Reed passed through St. Louis on his way from Washington to Kansas City. Chairman Yancey said yesterday he saw Reed for a few minutes Monday. He said that was all he cared to say about the proposition at this time.

Lieut. Gov. Wallace Crossley is reported to have been responsible for the invitation to Reed to make speeches on behalf of the Democratic ticket in Missouri. Crossley is director of publicity for the Democratic State Committee.

Reed, it is said, gave no definite answer to the request to campaign for the ticket.

TORCH-LIGHT PARADE PROPOSED FOR HARDING

Republican City Club Appoints Committee to Prepare for Candidate's Reception.

The Republican City Committee at a meeting last night appointed a subcommittee to make preliminary arrangements for the Harding meeting at the Coliseum on October 16.

Upon the subcommittee were appointed Committeemen E. E. Butler, A. H. Meyer, Walter Bischof, Anton Schuler and Gabe Roth to plan the arrangements for the Harding meeting and reception, subject to the approval of the City Committee. It will meet next Tuesday to discuss the plans of the subcommittee, of which Butler is chairman.

Butler said the committee will meet tomorrow at 12 o'clock at the headquarters of the City Committee to take up its work. The committee will recommend a torchlight parade, it is expected, although some of the members of the committee last night apparently were opposed to the suggestion. Committeeman Herman Bader created a laugh in the committee by declaring that he did not want a parade because the cobblestones hurt his feet.

A Reception Committee, composed of upstate Republicans, appointed by Chairman J. G. Hughes, and of city Republicans, selected by Chairman Strodtman, will be announced later.

Wilson Pardons Banker.

WASHINGTON, September 28.—Howard Showalter, a banker of Fairmont, W. Va., who was sentenced to five years in Federal Prison in 1917 for misapplication of national bank funds, was granted a pardon today by President Wilson.

Mother of Millionaire Draft Evaders Found Guilty of Conspiracy

Mrs. Bergdoll and Four Others Convicted of Aiding Sons.

By Associated Press.

PHILADELPHIA, PA., September 28.—Mrs. Emma C. Bergdoll and her four co-defendants were found guilty tonight of conspiracy to aid two of her sons, Grover and Erwin, to evade the draft.

The verdict was returned before Judge Dickinson in the United States District Court.

The case was given to the jurymen before noon today, but it was after 8 o'clock tonight before they reached a verdict.

Mrs. Bergdoll, her son, Charles A. Braun, and former Magistrate James E. Romig were found guilty on every count under which they had been indicted.

Albert S. Mitchell and Henry Schuh were acquitted on the indictments in which they were defendants but found guilty, with a recommendation for mercy, on the joint bills.

On application of their counsel the defendants were released on $10,000 bail each pending a motion for a new trial.

Trial Lasted Five Days.

The trial started last Monday and testimony was completed Friday. There were seven indictments, including fifty-six counts. In two of the indictments all five defendants were charged with conspiring with Grover and Erwin Bergdoll to assist them in evading the draft. The other five indictments charged each defendant separately with conspiring with the Bergdoll brothers to evade the draft.

Braun, who changed his name because of his brothers' escapades, was accused of harboring Erwin at his home. Mitchell, an automobile salesman, and Schuh, formerly proprietor of a cafe in this city, were implicated in the furnishing of an automobile for Erwin's use.

In his charge today, Judge Dickinson said:

"It is too much to expect any mother to surrender her own son," then he added:

"Pity and sympathy for a deserter are no excuse for harboring a deserter or aiding his escape."

The question that faced the jury, he said, was whether the defendants conspired to block the recruiting of an American Army by keeping Grover and Erwin out of a uniform.

SENATORIAL RACE COST CHIPERFIELD $9600

None of Other Candidates Has Filed Second Part of Report.

WASHINGTON, September 28.—In his race for the Republican senatorial nomination in Illinois, Burnett M. Chiperfield of Canton, former member of the House of Representatves, spent $9600, according to his statement filed here today. Candidates for the United States Senate are liable to prosecution for a campaign expenditure of more than $10,000.

Although only a day or two remains, none of the Republican or Democratic senatorial candidates in Illinois has filed the second statement installment required by law, except Chiperfield.

His first statement contained expenditures of $9100. His second statement, received here today, notes additional expenditures of $500 for advertising his meetings, providing music for them, etc.

First statements thus far filed include: W. B. McKinley, Republican, $6490; Frank L. Smith, Republican, $2673.46; Peter A. Waller, Democrat, $2099.18; Robert Emmett Burke, Democrat, $599. Burke is the only man acknowledging any contributions. He says he received contributions of $970.

Eight Famous White Sox Players Indicted and Suspended for Throwing World Series Games

By Associated Press.

CHICAGO, ILL., September 28.—Following are the playing records of the eight players indicted by the grand jury:

Edward V. Cicotte—Pitcher. Born in Detroit in 1884. Played his first professional baseball when 20 years old with Sault Ste. Marie. Sent to the Southern League, bought by Detroit and sent back to the minors. Bought by Boston Americans and sold to Chicago in 1912. Married. Lives in Detroit.

Claude Williams—Pitcher. Born in 1893 in Aurora, Mo. Broke into professional baseball in 1912 with Nashville (Southern League) team. Given tryout by Detroit and sent to Salt Lake. Purchased by Chicago in 1916. Married. Lives in Atlanta, Ga.

Charles A. Risberg—Shortstop. Born in San Francisco in 1894. Played first professional baseball with Vernon (Coast League) club. Bought by the White Sox in 1916. Married. Home in San Francisco.

George A. Weaver—Third baseman. Born at Stowe, Pa. Twenty-nine years old. Started his baseball career at Northampton, Mass., in 1910. Played with York in Pennsylvania League. Purchased by Chicago in 1911. Was farmed to San Francisco and recalled in 1912. Married and lives in Chicago.

Fred McMullin—Utility infielder. Twenty-nine years old. Born in Scammon, Kan. Played with Seattle in Coast League and later with Los Angeles, from which club he was obtained by the White Sox in 1912. Married and lives in Los Angeles.

Joseph Jackson—Outfielder. Born in Greenville, S. C. in 1887. Started playing ball there and made his major-league debut with Cleveland. After starring there for several years he was obtained by Chicago in 1915 for Pitcher Klepfer, Outfielder Roth and a cash bonus. Married. Lives in Savannah, Ga.

Oscar Felsch—Outfielder. Born in Milwaukee in 1891. Began playing ball professionally at Fond du Lac, Wis., in 1913. Then went to Milwaukee in the American Association and was bought by Chicago in 1914. Home in Milwaukee. Married.

Arnold Gandil—First baseman. Born in St. Paul in 1889. Broke into professional baseball in Shreveport, La., in 1908. Played with Sacramento, Coast League, until bought by Chicago in 1912. Released to Montreal in 1913. Bought by Washington in 1914, sold by Washington to Cleveland in 1916 and then sold to Chicago in 1917. Did not report this season. Married. Lives in Los Angeles.

United Drug Company Head Explains Plans

President Liggett Tells Business Men St. Louis Is Ideal City and Promises $15,000,000 Yearly Production.

A comprehensive idea of what the establishment of the new plant of the United Drug Company, on King's Highway, near Natural Bridge avenue, will mean to the City of St. Louis and how the commercial development of the city will be affected by the successful operation of this tremendous industry, capable of producing $15,000,000 worth of goods per annum, was outlined at a joint meeting of the Chamber of Commerce and the St. Louis Advertising Club at noon yesterday by Louis K. Liggett of Boston, president of the United Drug Company, who is here to attend the national convention of the Rexall Druggists.

There were approximately 250 business and professional men who heard Liggett's address and among them there was none who was not impressed by the forceful and clear manner in which this man, who looks much more like a jovial and good-natured country gentleman than like the head of the biggest industrial concern of its kind in the world, discussed problems vitally affecting the future growth of St. Louis and also questions of national interest.

Liggett predicted a brilliant commercial future for this city, which, he said, had most excellent railroad facilities and almost ideal labor conditions for manufacturing purposes. He assailed the present system of national taxation and in particular directed his attacks against the excess profit tax, which, he said, could not be but destructive to commercial development in America. He also took a few forceful punches at the income tax as it is now, and urged that all those with incomes of less than $10,000 per year, should be exempted entirely from income taxation, and for others the tax rate should be greatly reduced. There was much applause and evidence of genuine appreciation among those who heard these discussions.

Makes Hit at Start.

The first outburst of applause came when Liggett, after having been introduced by Frank O. Watts, president of the First National Bank, turned to the crowd and addressed them as "Fellow-St. Louisans." From that moment up to the time the meeting was declared closed there was almost continuous cheering and applauding.

"We have come here to do business," Liggett said, "and for this purpose we have built here a plant which already has cost $6,000,000 and which before long probably will cost $7,000,000. That is a large thing for a group of druggists to undertake. We have now approximately 50,000 shareholders in our organization, and they are distributed over all English-speaking countries of the earth. But the business is not controlled by these shareholders. Those who are managing it do not control it by shares. It was built up from a small beginning and it has grown big, and I can truthfully say that it has never taken a step back, nor has it ever changed its policy since those forty men who were the organizers met in a room at the Brunswick Hotel in Boston.

"And our policies are simple. We allow but one shareholder in a community. He has the exclusive right to sell and handle the products turned out by our plants. He has this right as long as he lives up to the charter of the corporation; and the charter, too, is simple. It is rather a mutual benefit

Continued on Page 4, Column 3.

TWO KILLED IN CLASH OF TROOPS AND CROWD

Several Persons Hurt When Soldiers Shoot in Fight.

BULLETIN.

BELFAST, September 28.—Two civilians were shot dead and a number of persons were wounded during a clash between soldiers and a crowd on the Falls road late today.

Soldier Slain.

MALLOW, COUNTY CORK, IRELAND, September 28.—The military barracks here were raided this morning, the raiders succeeding in escaping with arms. One soldier was shot dead.

More Rioting in Belfast.

BELFAST, September 28.—There was a recurrence last night of the rioting and shooting which have been in progress here at intervals since the week-end. The outbreak occurred in the old Lodge road district, where shipyard workers were attacked by armed men. Seven persons were wounded by the revolver firing. The military dispersed the rioters by bayonet charges. There were seventeen arrests for violations of the curfew law.

M. E. CONFERENCE OPENS AT POPLAR BLUFF, MO.

Rev. E. C. Webb of St. Louis Replies to Address of Welcome.

POPLAR BLUFF, MO., September 28.—The St. Louis conference of the Southern Methodist Church convened here today for a six-day session. Scores of clergymen arrived on all trains.

Rev. R. L. Russell of Nashville, Tenn., presided at the opening session tonight.

Mayor John W. Berrymann delivered an address of welcome while the response was given by Rev. E. C. Webb, pastor of the Grand Avenue Church of St. Louis.

Dr. H. C. Morrison of Louisville, Ky., preached the sermon, which was directed specifically to the undergraduates of the conference.

The business session will open Wednesday morning with Bishop W. B. Murray of Memphis presiding.

CICOTTE GOT $10,000 AND JOE JACKSON $5000

Williams Also Said to Have Received $10,000—Felsch, Risberg Weaver, McMullin, Gandil Are Others Indicted.

'This Is Just the Start, We Will Purge Game,' Prosecutor Says

CHICAGO, ILL., September 28.—Assistant State's Attorney Hartley Replogle, in charge of the case, said tonight that indictments to be drawn up tomorrow on today's true bills may contain several counts. The true bills themselves specified but one offense—"conspiracy to commit an illegal act." The penalty provided upon conviction on this count would be one to five years in the Penitentiary and a fine of not more than $10,000.

"This is just the beginning," Replogle said tonight. "We will have more indictments within a few days, and before we get through we will have purged organized baseball of everything that is crooked and dishonest.

"We are going after the gamblers now. There will be indictments within a few days against men in Philadelphia, Indianapolis, St. Louis, Des Moines, Pittsburgh, Cincinnati and other cities. More baseball players also will be indicted. We've got the goods on these men, and we are going the limit."

BY ASSOCIATED PRESS.

CHICAGO, ILL., September 29.—Indictments were voted against eight baseball stars today and confessions obtained from two of them, when the Old Roman, Charles A. Comiskey, owner of the oft-time champion Chicago White Sox, smashed his pennant-chasing machine to clean up baseball. The confessions told how the Sox threw last year's world's championship to Cincinnati for money paid by gamblers.

Seven Sox regulars and one former player had true bills voted against them by the Cook County grand jury, and the seven were immediately suspended by Comiskey. With his team only half a game behind the league-leading Cleveland Indians, the White Sox owner served notice on his seven stars that if they were found guilty he would drive them out of organized baseball for the remainder of their lives.

Jackson Just Tapped Ball.

Officials of Chief Justice Charles McDonald's court lifted the curtain on the grand jury proceedings sufficiently to show a great hitter, Joe Jackson, declaring that he deliberately just tapped the ball; a picture of one of the world's most famous pitchers, Cicotte, in tears, and glimpses of alleged bribes of $5000 or $10,000 discovered under pillows, or on beds by famous athletes about to retire.

Around the courtroom were some of baseball's greatest leaders, among them John J. McGraw, manager of the New York Giants, awaiting a call to testify tomorrow, and John Heydler, president of the National League, who went before the grand jurors this afternoon.

The exact nature of the information Comiskey put before the grand jury was not disclosed. The men whom the jury involved as a result of testimony uncovered by their owner, were:

Eddie Cicotte, star pitcher, who waived immunity and confessed, according to court attaches, that he took a $10,000 bribe.

Arnold ("Chick") Gandil, former first baseman.

"Shoeless Joe" Jackson, heavy-hitting left fielder.

Oscar ("Happy") Felsch, center fielder.

Charles ("Swede") Risberg, shortstop.

Claude Williams, pitcher.

Continued on Page 3, Column 1.

THE WEATHER.
Western Pennsylvania, Ohio and West Virginia—FAIR AND COOL Monday. Sun rises, 6:27; sets, 5:46.

The Pittsburgh Post

GOOD MORNING!
If Cleveland wins the game today,
Ebbets is going to see,
Just how Harding's going to feel
On the morning of November three.

79TH YEAR—NO 31. MONDAY MORNING, OCTOBER 11, 1920. **** TWO CENTS A COPY.

CLEVELAND 8, BROOKLYN 1

UNASSISTED TRIPLE PLAY AND HOME RUN WITH BASES FULL MARK THRILLING GAME

PATRIOTISM AS DUTY IS STRESSED AT HOLY NAME SOCIETY RALLY

Many Distinguished Visitors Attend Meeting.

BOLSHEVISM ARRAIGNED

With a eulogy to those of Catholic faith who fought for the liberation and in defense of America from Bunker Hill to the Marne, Judge Thomas H. Dowd of Salamanca, N. Y., yesterday afternoon told 10,000 members of the Pittsburgh Diocesan Union Holy Name Society that the greatest duty of the American Catholic layman was to return, in exchange for the liberty and protection of the Nation, utmost love and devotion for the greatest democracy in the history of the world.

"There is your duty," asserted Judge Dowd. "It is the duty of every Catholic layman of America to bring about that love and devotion for this great country which has given you so much. It there was anything ever worth living for, anything worth fighting for, anything worth dying for—it is the American flag."

The occasion was that of the annual rally day of the society, when Catholics from all over the Pittsburgh district, coming in steady streams, converged at the Exposition auditorium. This manner of coming to the meeting independently superceded the processions through the city streets of former years.

DISTINGUISHED VISITORS.

Among the distinguished visitors, besides Judge Dowd, were Rt. Rev. Regis Canevin, biship of Pittsburgh; Rev. John Belford of Brooklyn, N. Y., and Rt. Rev. Father Aurelius, arch-abbot of St. Vincents.

At 3 o'clock, when the great hall was filled with members of the society and their guests, the meeting was opened with a prayer by the spiritual director, Rev. Francis J. McCabe. Following this, the "Star Spangled Banner" was sung. Henry Fitzpatrick, president of the organization, delivered a brief address of introduction, explaining the purpose of the rally. He introduced the chairman of the meeting, Joseph A. Beck, of this city.

WARNS AGAINST ATHEISM.

Mr. Beck spoke on the work of the society and told of its history and growth. He also uttered a warning

(Continued on Page Two, Col. Five.)

BRITISH VESSELS READY TO ATTACK RED SUBMARINES

AMERICA'S TAX BILL FOR YEAR APPROXIMATELY $5,408,075,468, REPORT SHOWS

Sum Paid Into U. S. Treasury Shows Big Increase.

'MISCELLANEOUS' REVENUE GROWS

BY THE ASSOCIATED PRESS.

WASHINGTON, Oct. 10—America's tax bill for the fiscal year ending June 30 amounted to $5,408,075,468, approximately a billion and a half dollars more than was paid into the Federal treasury in previous 12 months.

Final figures for the year were contained in the preliminary report of the commissioner of internal revenue, made public tonight. It shows that from income and profits taxes the Government received approximately three-fourths of all its revenue. In these two items there was an increase of $1,356,000,000 over the fiscal year of 1919, receipts for the two years being: 1920, $3,957,701,000; 1919, $2,600,000,000.

DRY LAW CUTS.

From multifarious sources of "miscellaneous" taxation. The levy produced $1,450,374,000, an increase over the previous year of $201,000,000.

In the first full year of the prohibition era, there was a net reduction of $343,000,000 in taxes on distilled and fermented liquors, the report shows. From distilled spirits the Government received $97,907,000 in the last fiscal year, while taxes from the same source in 1919 were $365,211,000. Taxes on fermented liquors for the last fiscal year aggregated $41,965,000 and for the fiscal year of 1919, $117,839,000.

The report also shows comparative revenues for the fiscal years of 1909 and 1920. The former date was the last full year in which the Government derived its principal revenues from three sources — distilled spirits, fermented

(Continued on Page Two, Col. Three.)

Soviet Is Warned by Curzon in Tart Note.

ANTI-ENGLISH MOVE IS SEEN

BY THE ASSOCIATED PRESS.

LONDON, Oct. 10.—Any Russian submarines encountered on the high seas will be attacked on sight by British naval forces, according to a note sent by Earl Curzon, British foreign secretary, to M. Tchitcherin, Russian Bolshevik foreign minister, October 2, published along with other correspondence recently exchanged between Great Britain and Soviet Russia.

Earl Curzon points out he previously sent a communication regarding a submarine launched in the Black sea, in which he said that, in view of repeated declarations of leading members of the Soviet government that that government considered itself in a state of war with Great Britain, and in view of the impossibility in these circumstances of waiting to ascertain whether the intentions of the submarine controlled by the Soviet government were hostile or not, there was no alternative but to issue orders to British ships to attack the submarine should it be encountered on the high seas.

Upon hearing rumors that submarines of the Bolshevik fleet had put to sea in the Baltic, Earl Curzon sent his note. Tchitcherin replied that Leonid Krassin, soviet representative in London, would receive instructions in the matter.

DEMANDS COMPENSATION.

Earl Curzon also demanded compensation for the widow and son of Charles Frederick Davison, alleged to have been "murdered in cold blood with no charge preferred against him" by the soviet authorities in January last.

Yesterday Earl Curzon sent a lengthy reply to Krassin's note of October 6, in which the British foreign secretary says some of Krassin's points are trivial and far-fetched, based on erroneous information or widely removed from the facts. He points out that Great Britain, more than any other power, has sought to bring about peace between Sovet Russia and Poland and "has only been called upon to stand by its treaty engagements to its allies by the bad faith which characterized both military and diplomatic movements of the soviet authorities."

Concerning the use of Danzig for the transmission of munitions, Curzon asserts this was an obligation imposed upon the allies by the treaty of Ver-

(Continued on Page Two, Col. Three.)

NATIONS LEAGUE WITH CHANGES IS SEEN BY TAFT IF HARDING WINS

VANCOUVER, B. C., Oct. 10.—Election of Senator Warren G. Harding to the presidency of the United States will mean the ultimate ratification of the League of Nations with reservations and "the elimination of all further dispute," William Howard Taft, former President of the United States, declared here on his arrival last night, at the head of the arbitration board of the Grand Trunk Pacific Railway.

"Governor Cox has asked me how I can support Senator Harding when the senator has denounced the League of Nations," said Taft. "Cox is not quite right if he says Harding is opposed to the League of Nations idea. Harding wants a league that will be constituted more like a court. Harding wants a league, but not Mr. Wilson's league.

"Obviously there will have to be some compromise and it may very well be that the kind of league Senator Harding supports will form the basis of the compromise."

Taft said while personally he was in favor of the League of Nations and was willing to accept it as presented by President Wilson with Article X, he added he "was bitterly disappointed when the President did not accept the reservations voted by the Republicans who, with a few Democrats, constituted a majority in the Senate." He said recent statements of Lord Grey in a letter to the "Times," at the time the reservations were under discussion, indicated there "was no doubt the United States could have entered the league with the consent of the other nations."

Held for Shooting

Negress Alleged to Have Wounded Two.

Mrs. Lena Mercher, a Negress, of 2706 Penn avenue, was held over at a hearing yesterday morning before Magistrate P. J. Sullivan in the Penn avenue police station, where she was placed late Saturday night in connection with the shooting of Mr. and Mrs. Ernest Jacques, Negroes, of 1728 Spring way.

Police allege that Mrs. Jacques objected to Mrs. Mercher speaking to Jacques on the street, and that the two women quarreled. Mrs. Mercher, it is said, fired a shot through the open door of Jacques' home, and when Jacques and his wife fled into their home, fired seven more shots through the door. Mrs. Jacques was shot twice, one bullet entering each leg, and another bullet lodged in Jacques' right leg. Both were taken to the West Penn Hospital.

Murders Decrease

Chicago Records Show Drop; Hangings Prove Benefit.

CHICAGO, Oct. 10.—During eight months there have been 112 murders here—crimes about which there can be no question. Several other cases of murder are listed as "suicide." This compares with 243 murders during the same period in 1919, showing a decrease of 136. These figures lose some of their significance from the fact that the race riots took place in 1919, during whoch 39 persons were murdered.

Records show a marked diminution in murders directly after there has been a hanging or two.

SERIES INNOVATIONS MADE BY WAMBSGANSS AND SMITH

WORLD SERIES BOX SCORE

BROOKLYN.	AB.	R.	H.	P.	A.	E.
Olson, ss.	4	0	2	3	5	0
Sheehan, 3b.	3	0	1	1	1	1
Griffith, rf.	4	0	0	0	0	0
Wheat, lf.	4	1	2	3	0	0
Myers, m.	4	0	2	0	0	0
Konetchy, 1b.	4	0	2	9	2	0
Kilduff, 2b.	4	0	1	5	6	0
Miller, c.	2	0	2	0	1	0
Krueger, c.	2	0	1	2	1	0
Grimes, p.	1	0	0	0	1	0
Mitchell, p.	2	0	0	1	0	0
Totals	34	1	13	24	17	1

CLEVELAND.	AB.	R.	H.	P.	A.	E.
Jamieson, lf.	4	1	2	2	1	0
Graney, lf.	1	0	0	0	0	0
Wambsganss, 2b.	5	1	1	7	2	0
Speaker, m.	3	2	1	1	0	0
E. Smith, rf.	4	1	3	0	0	0
Gardner, 3b.	4	0	1	2	2	1
W. Johnston, 1b.	3	1	2	9	1	0
Sewell, ss.	3	0	0	2	4	0
O'Neill, c.	2	1	0	3	1	1
Thomas, c.	0	0	0	1	0	0
Bagby, p.	4	1	2	0	2	0
Totals	33	8	12	27	13	2

Brooklyn	0 0 0	0 0 0	0 0 1—1
Cleveland	4 0 0	3 1 0	0 0 *—8

Three-base hits—Konetchy, E. Smith.
Home runs—E. Smith, Bagby.
Sacrifices—Sheehan, W. Johnston.
Double plays—Olson to Kilduff to Konetchy; Jamieson to O'Neill; Gardner to Wambsganss to Johnston; Johnston to Sewell to Johnston.
Triple play—Wambsganss (unassisted).
Left on bases—Brooklyn, 7; Cleveland, 6.
Base on balls—Off Grimes, 1; off Mitchell, 3.
Hits—Off Grimes, 9 in 3 1-3 innings; off Mitchell, 3 in 4 2-3 innings.
Struck out—By Bagby, 3; by Mitchell, 1.
Wild pitch—Bagby.
Passed ball—Miller.
Losing pitcher—Grimes.
Umpires—Klem, at plate; Connolly, at first; O'Day, at second; Dineen, at third.
Time of game—1:49.

Scenario Writer Never Could Imagine a Game Like This; Unique Plays Overshadow Other Sensational Feats; Grimes Knocked Out.

CLEVELANDERS ALREADY REGARD PENNANT AS WON

BY THE ASSOCIATED PRESS.

CLEVELAND, Oct. 10.—In a baseball game erupting sensational, unique and thrilling plays far beyond the wildest dreams on an imaginative fiction or scenario writer, the Cleveland Americans defeated the Brooklyn Nationals, 8 to 1, in the fifth contest of the world's series here this afternoon. An unassisted triple play by Wambsganss, a native born son of Cleveland, and home runs by Elmer Smith and Jim Bagby were a trio of individual features which formed flashlight photographs on the brains of the fans which no future diamond battle can erase.

The victory broke the tie existing between the pennant winners of the two major leagues and tonight Cleveland is confident that the glory of the first major league pennant ever won by this city will be overshadowed by the great glory of the world's series banner flung to the breeze next spring.

The Robins, crushed by the two terrible catastrophes of Saturday and today, are clinging desperately to the hope that Sherrod Smith may be able to check the savage batting onslaught of the Indians, but the home team and fans declare that nothing can stop the rush of the Clevelanders, now that they have solved the mysteries of the Flatbush hurling staff.

TWO WORLD RECORDS.

The calibre of the play may be gathered from the fact that two world's records were established during the hectic hour and 49 minutes in which the tribe of Speaker tore great handfuls of plumage from the stunned and helpless Robins. Never before in the history of the world's series had a triple play been made by one player and so seldom has this baseball feat been accomplished in the history of either major or minor leagues that each and every such play is familiar to thousands of fans.

A home run with the bases full is also an innovation in the modern history of the super-series. Yet both these records were made at League Park here this afternoon, with a second home run, four double plays and a score of other fielding and batting features which would have been acclaimed just as thrilling in a normal world's series conflict.

There was something uncannily local about Wambsganss' triple. The Indians' second baseman was born in Cleveland in 1894, and after learning some fundamentals of the National game at Concordia College, entered the professional baseball ranks. After a comparatively short period of minor league experience with the Cedar Rapids club of the Central Association, he came to the local team in 1914 and has since been a fixture with the Indians. That a native-born ball player of Cleveland should have made such an unusual and infrequent play is a coincidence, but that a previous similar play should have been made in the same park 11 years ago savors of something beyond coincidence.

HISTORY REPEATED.

But 11 times in the records of the American pastime has an unassisted triple play been accomplished, if the annals of baseball can be relied on. Of these feats, but two were previously scored in the major leagues.

It was Neal Ball of the Cleveland club of 1909 who swept three opposing players out on a similar handling of the ball. In that year, during the game between the Boston Redsox and the Indians, played on July 19, Stahl was on first and Wagner on second, with McConnel at bat, when Ball accomplished the play which is the dream of every fielder in the game.

Today the stage setting was much the same. Both Kilduff and Miller had singled to center in turn at the beginning of the fifth inning and were perched on second and first respectively, when Pitcher Mitchell came to bat.

The Brooklyn hurler who had previously relieved Grimes in the box, drove a hot liner high and to the left of second base. Wamsganss leaped into the air and came down with the ball clutched in the gloved hand. For the fraction of a second he appeared to hesitate and it looked as though the play would take the usual course of a force out.

Then Wamsby realized the golden fielding opportunity that confronted him and before the startled spectators could grasp the play, he had sprinted to second and stepping on the canvas bag, eliminated Kilduff who was well on his way to third. Miller was tearing down to the midway sack under the belief that it was an absolutely safe one and it was a comparatively easy matter for Wambsganss to run up the base line and, touching the oncoming runner, completed the first triple play ever made

(Continued on Page Nine.)

Professor Quits For Beauty Parlor

Says Women Care About Outside of Heads Only.

CHICAGO, Oct. 10.—Laboring under the misapprehension that what women have inside their heads makes some difference, Oscar M. Heath, former professor of English in the Englewood High school, wasted 30 years of his life dispensing knowledge. He admits it in announcing that his Culture Review school will cease to exist after January 1.

"I struggled along with the idea that teaching was a noble art," said the professor. "There are about 3,000 teachers in Chicago today whom I have instructed. But I saw nothing ahead of me in my old age but the poorhouse. So I started a beauty parlor and I found out that it is the outside of their heads, not the inside, that women wish to have fixed; and I paid income tax this year for the first time.

"It takes brains to teach. It doesn't take any to run a beauty parlor. So I'm going to devote the rest of my life to the latter.

"Girls working in restaurants, who cannot utter a grammatical sentence, are making $50 a week in salary and tips. Why waste money and time in being educated, they reason."

You are a shareholder in the greatest corporation in the world. Vote your stock! No proxies accepted.

The Citizenship Committee of the Civic Club of Allegheny County.

Veteran Is Buried

Vincent McCarriher, of company I, Three Hundred Nineteenth infantry, who died in France of wounds suffered while in action, was buried with full military honors yesterday in the Glenwillard cemetery. McCarriher was wounded October 9, 1918, while fighting in the Argonne and died in a base hospital December 22, 1918.

The funeral was in charge of Sewickley Valley Post, No. 4, American Legion, under the direction of J. C. Mansfield, post commander. McCarriher was a resident of Glenwillard. A plot of ground has been set aside by residents of that town upon which they intend to build a monument in honor of the dead soldier. Dr. A. C. Howell, the post chaplain, conducted the services at the cemetery.

HOW CAN TAFT DENY "HIS OWN CHILD," HAVING DRAFTED TERMS OF PROTECTION FOR MONROE DOCTRINE IN PEACE PACT?

Wilson's Memorandum Gives Exact Wording of Cables Written by Ex-President to President in Paris.

ADVICE TAKEN "LITERALLY"

BY THE ASSOCIATED PRESS.

SPRINGFIELD, Ill., Oct. 10.—Cable correspondence between President Wilson and former President Taft in 1919, during drafting of the League of Nations covenant at Paris, was made public here tonight by Governor Cox of Ohio, Democratic presidential candidate, together with a statement by the candidate criticizing severely Senator Lodge of Massachusetts, and other league opponents.

Taft, the correspondence detailed, sought and had cable communication with President Wilson, submitting numerous suggestions for changes in the tentative league draft and advising the President regarding its presentation to the Senate.

Governor Cox, who is scheduled to make addresses here and in East St. Louis and St. Louis, Mo., tomorrow, issued the statement, he said, because of the equivocal position of ex-President Taft and other friends of the league now occupy in their support of the candidate of the league destructionists." The correspondence, Cox said, was "initiated by him (Taft) as a result of his study of the draft agreement" and quoted Taft's "own words when sincerity of mind and intelligence were not beclouded by the partisan prejudice of a political campaign."

TAFT'S ADVICE TAKEN.

The White House memorandum, containing some of the cables exchanged by the President and Taft, stated that in "every instance" the President followed Taft's suggestions, and Cox's statement declared that "every suggestion of Taft was followed literally." The correspondence indicated that Taft's suggestions dealt principally with protecting the Monroe Doctrine and dealing with American domestic questions, withdrawal from the league, unanimous league decisions and disarmament. The correspondence made public contained two telegrams from the President to Taft and several from Taft to the executive, including one in which A. Lawrence Lowell, former president of Harvard University, joined.

The White House memorandum quoted at length league amendments to show adoption of Taft's suggestions.

The final cablegram Taft sent to Secretary Tumulty and forwarded to the President, as given in the published correspondence, was dated June 28, 1919, just before the President returned to present the treaty to the Senate. It read:

I would like to send a return message and that is that the President argue to the league and its necessity, the impossibility to secure peace without it, the dreadful unrest in Europe, the pressure of our allies to ratify and secure peace at once, and the need of the league with the United States to stabilize and to resist Bolshevism, the necessity for renewal of negotiation if an important amendment like striking out Article X is made, the absurdity of a congressional declaration of peace on one side, the giving up of all objects of the war in such a peace if Germany were to make a similar declaration. I hope sincerely he will not attack the Republican senators. His appeal will be much more influential if he pleads his cause and does not attack the opposition.

On March 16, 1919, the correspondence showed, Tumulty sent the President a message stating that Taft desired to cable the President direct with suggestions not looking to change "of the structure of the league, the plan of action or its real character, but simply removing objections in minds of conscientious Americans which its language does not justify and whose fears could be removed without any considerable change of language."

The reply given by President Wilson said he would "appreciate Taft's offer of suggestions and welcome them.

"The sooner they are sent, the better," the President's reply added. "You need give yourself no uneasiness about my yielding anything with regard to the embodiment of the proposed convention in the treaty."

On March 16, the correspondence showed, Taft cabled a reservation for the Monroe Doctrine, stating that it "alone would probably carry tthe treaty, but others would make it certain." Taft's detailed suggestions were:

If you bring back the treaty with the League of Nations in it, make more specific reservations of the Monroe Doctrine, fix a term for duration of the league and the limit of armament, require expressly unanimity of action in executive council and body of delegates, and add to Article XV a provision that where the executive council of the body of delegates finds the difference to grow out of an exclusively domestic policy, it shall recommend no settlement, the ground will be completely out from under the opponents of the league in the Senate.

The latter, Taft said, would cover tariff, Japanese immigration and similar domestic questions.

Submitting drafts of proposed amendments and detailed arguments in their behalf, one of Taft's messages stated:

"The Republican senators are trying to stir up anxiety among Republicans lest this be a limitation upon our tariff. It would help much to meet and remove objections and cut the ground under senatorial obstruction."

Regarding the Monroe Doctrine's protection, Taft was quoted as follows:

"My impression is that if the one article already sent, on the Monroe Doctrine, be inserted in the treaty, sufficient Republicans who signed the round robin would probably retreat from their position and vote for ratification so that it would carry. If the other suggestions were adopted, I feel confident that all but a few who oppose any league at all but a few who oppose any league at all would be driven to accept them and to stand for the league."

Another message by Taft on March 28, 1919, on the same subjeict, said:

"Venture to suggest to President that failure to reserve Monroe Doctrine more specifically in face of opposition in conference will give great weight to objection that league as first reported endangers doctrine. It will seriously embarrass advocates of league, it will certainly lead to Senate amendments embodying doctrine and other provisions in form less likely to secure subsequent acquiescence of other nations than proper reservation now. Deem some kind of Monroe Doctrine amendment now to Article X vital to acceptance of league in this country. I say this with full realization that complications in conference are many and not clearly understood here. A strong and successful stand now will carry the league."

Another, on April 13, signed by Taft and A. Lawrence Lowell, read:

"Friends of the covenant are seriously alarmed over report that no amendment will be made more specifically safeguarding Monroe Doctrine. At full meeting of executive committee of league to enforce peace, with 30 members from 18 states present, unanimous opinion that without such amendments Republican senators will certainly defeat ratification of treaty because publication will sustain them. With such amendment, the treaty will be promp ly ratified."

The White House memorandum made public by Cox said the league's reservation of domestic questions was made "as suggested by Taft and almost in his own words." All of the other suggestions from Taft, it stated, were followed, as shown by quotations from the league covenant.

In making public the correspondence, Cox's statement said that time had ar-

(Continued on Page Three, Col. Five.)

Many Messages From League to Enforce Peace Head on How Senate Would Object To Parts Of Pact.

TEXT WORDED TO COMPLY

"Wilson Was Right!" Stenographic Notes Show No Armed Aid Pledge to Balkans

WASHINGTON, Oct. 10.—President Wilson today came into possession of a transcript of the stenographic report of his remarks at the secret session of the Paris peace conference held on May 31, 1919. The transcript was furnished by an American stenographer who, in a letter to Secretary Tumulty, says he is willing to make affidavit to the correctness of his report.

Officials who have seen the letter from the stenographer and the transcript of President Wilson's speech at the plenary session indicate that they are elated over this testimony. They claim that it will refute the statements of Senator Spencer of Missouri, that the President, replying to complaints of Premier Bratiano of Rumania, at the secret session, said that "if the world is again troubled the United States will again send to this side of the water their army and their fleet." President Wilson, in a telegram to Spencer, denounced the senator's accusation as "false," and in a subsequent telegram to Spencer, said: "I am perfectly content to leave it to the voters of Missouri to determine which of us is telling the truth."

The transcript of the speech was furnished to the White House by Fred M. Carlson, who was the chief stenographer of the American peace commission at Paris. Carlson's letter is understood to have been sent voluntarily. In it he says that he was present at the plenary session of May 31, 1919, and reported the proceedings stenographically. He made a stenographic report of President Wilson's remarks, he says, and retained his notes.

Carlson says he had seen Spencer's allegation that the President had promised American military and naval aid to the Rumanians and that, believing that the remarks of the President had been misrepresented, he felt impelled to do what was necessary to correct any wrong impression drawn from what was said by the President. As the session was secret, Carlson felt that he was bound to observe confidence as to what transpired there, but if the public interest makes it essential that the President's remarks should be published he would be glad to make affidavit to the correctness of his stenographic notes and his transcript of them which he enclosed with his letter.

"Failure is often that early morning hour of darkness, which precedes the dawning of Success"—*L. M. Hodges*

The Boston Post

28 Pages Today

TWENTY-EIGHT PAGES—TWO CENTS   *Established 1831*   WEDNESDAY OCTOBER 13 1920   *Copyright, 1920, by Post Publishing Co.*   TWENTY-EIGHT PAGES—TWO CENTS

CLEVELAND TAKES SUPREME HONORS

Indians Win Seventh Game of Series 3 to 0 and Are Now Champions of the World—Coveleskie Pitches His Third Successive Victory and Holds Brooklyn Helpless—Grimes Unable to Keep Cleveland in Check

BOSTON'S POLICE SHOW FINE FORM IN PARADE

Many World War Veterans in Line With Honor Decorations—Thousands Cheer Marchers—Riot Gun Squad Wins Much Applause

THE SHOTGUN COMPANY OF BOSTON POLICE FORCE IN PARADE.
The men, in command of Lieutenant Joseph F. Hurley, received much applause for their businesslike appearance. Their guns and cartridge belts made a hit with the spectators all along the route. Croix de Guerres and Distinguished Service crosses flapped from more than one uniform coat in this outfit. All are ex-service men and all dead shots.

Boston's new police force received the plaudits of thousands yesterday when it made its first formal bow in a parade through the city's streets.

Continued on Page 25—First Column

MAN CHASE HAS PLENTY OF THRILLS

Theatre-Goers Duck Lone Fugitive With Drawn Gun

Thousands of theatre-bound pedestrians on Tremont, School and connecting streets witnessed more hair-raising action from real life in 10 minutes last night than was their

Continued on Page 15—6th Column

JURY SEES LOVE NOTE BOX FOUND

Mrs. Brown Will Bare Story of Her Life Today

BY ROY ATKINSON
Post Staff Correspondent

OSSIPEE, N. H., Oct. 12.—A little tin box, which may later be known as the "Clandestine Post Office," was discovered late this afternoon under a boulder near the scene of the

Continued on Page 15—3d Column

MAN O' WAR'S WINNINGS MORE THAN $250,000

WINDSOR, Ont., Oct. 12.—In Man o' War's two years on the tracks he has piled up for his owner a fortune that far surpasses the total won by any other American horse. With today's purse and cup his winnings total more than $250,000, as compared to the $199,550 won by Domino in three years. Man o' War was purchased by Mr. Riddle from Major August Belmont as a yearling for $5000.

He has been beaten only once, Harry Payne Whitney's Upset taking the Sanford Memorial from him at Saratoga last year.

TWO KILLED ON CROSSING THREE DYING

Train Throws Auto Fifty Feet at Shirley

FATHER AND MOTHER INSTANTLY KILLED

Two Daughters and Son-in-Law Dangerously Injured

FITCHBURG, Oct. 12.—Two persons were killed and three others were probably fatally hurt in a collision between an automobile and a locomotive on the Fitchburg division of the Boston & Maine railroad, a mile east of Shirley station, this afternoon. The dead are:

Fred Mador, 47 years old, of East Templeton and his wife, Mrs. Mary R. Mador, 45 years old.

Their daughter Goldie, 16 years old, and her sister, Mrs. Moses Jodoin and Mr. and Mrs. Mador's son-in-law, Moses Jodoin, are at Burbank Hospital tonight and all three are on the danger list.

CAR THROWN 50 FEET

Their car was smashed to bits. Mr. and Mrs. Mador were instantly

Continued on Page 8—1st Column

MRS. EVANS IN CUSTODY

Arrested in Norwich for Refusing to Obey Officer

NORWICH, Conn., Oct. 12.—Mrs. Glendower Evans of Brookline, Mass., was arrested here this evening on a charge of refusing to obey an officer.

She was addressing a big crowd of men in Ferry street, on the right of free speech and free assembly when a patrolman notified Albert Boardman, owner of the automobile from which she was speaking that he would have to move on as he was obstructing the street. Mrs. Evans, who was also notified that she must stop speaking, adjorned the meeting, but Boardman declined to move on and the patrolman took both to the police station followed by a big crowd. They were both released on $100 bail and continued the meeting indoors.

The meeting which Mrs. Evans attempted to address was held under the auspices of the American Civil Liberties Union as a protest against the recent arrest of Boardman, who is a Socialist agitator. Mayor Lerou in conjunction with the Mayors of a number of other Connecticut cities has refused to allow Socialist agitators to speak in the open air.

Tris Speaker, manager of the world's champion Cleveland team. No wonder he is smiling and looks happy.

MAN O'WAR WINS BY EIGHT LENGTHS

Time 2:03 Record for Canada--Has Lead From Start--Tons of Money Bet on Race

BY C. B. CARBERRY

WINDSOR, Ont., Oct. 12.—Man o' War, the golden chestnut colt, made turf history today.

For long years to come men will remember his name and tell of his triumph. His lone rival, Sir Barton, went down to defeat in the greatest of turf classics, a race for a purse of $75,000 and a $5000 gold cup.

Continued on Page 19—First Col.

ARMENIA DECLARES WAR UPON TURKEY

LONDON, Oct. 12 (United News).—Armenia has declared war on Turkey and the Turkish Nationalists have ordered a general mobilization, according to a despatch from Reuter's Constantinople correspondent.

HIGH TIDE TODAY AT NAVY YARD
A. M. 12:42 P. M. 12:58

SUN Rises 6:54. Sets 6:06. **MOON** Sets at 7:01 p. m.
Light all vehicles tonight at 6:36.
(By Daylight Saving time.)

TODAY'S ANNIVERSARIES, ETC.

Belgian government removed from Ostend to Havre, France, 1914.

Greek government refuses to support Serbia against invaders, 1915.

Americans capture Grand Pre after four days' fighting, 1918.

One year ago today—Allied cruisers aid in defence of Riga against German attack.—President Poincare signs French douments ratifying German peace treaty.—Reds call on Gary strikers to rise against soldiers.

FAIR

Forecast for Boston and vicinity: Fair Wednesday and probably Thursday; warmer Thursday; moderate northeast winds Wednesday, becoming southerly Thursday.

WASHINGTON, Oct. 12.—Forecast for New England: Fair Wednesday and probably Thursday, somewhat warmer Thursday.

The outlook is for generally fair weather Wednesday and Thursday in New England, with little temperature changes. It is probable that the weather will become unsettled with showers in the North Atlantic States by Friday, followed by colder weather.

The Old Farmer's Prediction

I expect the weather will be fairly good, but just a mite cool today and tonight.

Speaker Shares Triumph With His Star Pitcher by Poling Out a Long Triple

Brooklyn Is Clearly Outclassed—Cleveland Goes Wild Over Victory of Its Team

SPEAKER EMBRACES MOTHER AFTER GAME

CLEVELAND, Oct. 12. — Tris Speaker, directly after the game, made a dash from centre field toward the grandstand, where his mother and other relatives occupied a lower tier box. His progress was slow, but once he reached the rail he vaulted over the iron front and into his mother's arms like a small schoolboy. The scene was so unusual that for a moment there was a complete cessation of the cheering, which, however, broke out with treble vigor when Mrs. Speaker hugged, patted and kissed her gray-haired son, and the latter responded in a manner which indicated that he regarded his mother's approval and caresses far above any other rewards that might come to him as a result of the victory of his team in winning the greatest honor that can come to a professional baseball player.

BY PAUL H. SHANNON

CLEVELAND, Oct. 12.—Tris Speaker and his Cleveland Indians are today the new champions of the world.

After waiting fully half a century for laurels that twice before had been nearly attained, the new title holders came into their own at 3:55 o'clock this afternoon when Konetchy's weak grounder to young Joe Sewell forced a runner at second, closed the conflict and put an end to a struggle whose finish had been foreshadowed ever since the Brooklyn Dodgers began their pitiful stand here on Saturday last.

Continued on Page 18—First Col.

Cox Here Next Tuesday

Governor Cox of Ohio, Democratic candidate for President, will speak on Boston Common next Tuesday evening, Oct. 19, at 8:30 o'clock, according to an announcement made last night by Michael J. O'Leary, chairman of the State Democratic committee.

The Governor will enter the State from the West on his special train next Tuesday morning. He will speak at Worcester at 9:30 o'clock, and will be met there, according to present plans, by members of the State committee and other prominent Democrats. He will speak at Lynn at 6:30 o'clock, and from Lynn he will come to Boston. Two speeches are planned for him here—the address on the Common and a brief talk before the Harvard Union just preceding it.

CARPENTIER KNOCKS OUT LEVINSKY

French Champion Puts Rival Away in the Fourth Round

JERSEY CITY, N. J., Oct. 12.—Under the white flare of five great arc lights that shut out the stars, Georges Carpentier, heavyweight champion of Europe, knocked out Battling Levinsky tonight in the first few seconds of the fourth round. A right hook to the jaw was the winning smash. 35,000 fight fans from the highest to the lowest brows in the Metropolitan circuit paid out more than $350,000 to see the fast Frenchman baffle and bewilder the shrinking Levinsky, who made no effort to fight back at any stage.

VERY EASY FOR FRENCHMAN

Carpentier, pale and wan looking with a half smile and wide extended

Continued on Page 6—1st Column

19TH WARD WOMAN SLAYER GIVES UP

THE CHICAGO EVENING POST

THIRTY-SECOND YEAR — MONDAY, JULY 25, 1921. — PRICE THREE CENTS

FINAL SPORTING EXTRA

Turn page for *The Post's* "Home" Front Page

CICOTTE AND JACKSON'S CONFESSIONS ADMITTED

SHIPS WATCHED FOR ABSCONDING CHICAGO BANKER

Canadian Ports Searched After Finding Spurgin Auto in Detroit.

Outgoing steamers from Canadian and American ports and the eastern points of entrance along the Dominion border were watched carefully today for Warren C. Spurgin, missing bank president, who left a deficit of over $1,000,000 in the Michigan Avenue Trust company in the wake of his flight a week ago.

The international search followed the finding of Mrs. Spurgin's automobile in a garage in Detroit yesterday.

Locally, interest centered on the announcement that First Assistant State's Attorney Ernest S. Hodges had been placed in charge of the work of investigating the causes for the failure, and that Chief Investigator Ben Newmark would go before the grand jury tomorrow and ask that the books and records of the bank be brought in.

Plans for Indictment.

Mr. Newmark spent the morning in conference with the examiners who were auditing the books of the closed institution. He was told there was sufficient evidence in the accounts to warrant grand jury action, but refused to give the names of the person or persons who might be named in the indictments.

A bill for a money decree was filed in the Superior court against all present and former stockholders and the missing president this afternoon by six of the bank's creditors, who say that about $5,000 is due them.

From the outstanding obligations of the institution, amounting to $3,500,000, there can be collected about $150,000 from the stockholders, who are responsible only to the extent of their holdings. The bill also asks that the court order the stockholders to pay to the court as trustee such moneys as they are liable for and that it be distributed only on the order of the court.

The firms filing the bill are H. P. Springs company, Leonard Leonard of Barker & Jackson, the I. C. Auto Top company, Charles Alcock Jr. of the Alcock Plumbing company and the Charles N. Lentz Dairy company.

Meanwhile a committee of depositors headed by Rev. Johnston Myers, 2320 South Michigan avenue, sought to salvage as much of their savings as possible out of the wreckage left by the fugitive.

This committee, meeting today, urged depositors to defer action until a report has been made by the bank examiners.

"I consider it highly important that all concerned act together in this matter," said Thomas J. Hay, president of the Chicago Automobile Trade association and a spokesman for the committee. "If conflicting factions and separate comimttees are formed, it will tend to create confusion and delay in settlement of the bank's affairs.

Other members of the committee are H. V. Keane of the American Bank Note company and S. H. Adams.

Fiance Reveals Flight.

Direction of the search toward Detroit followed a statement made to Chief Investigator Ben Newmark of the state's attorney's office by Herman Byler, fiance of 21-year-old Vivian Spurgin.

Byler said Mrs. Spurgin and her daughter decided Saturday to close the apartment at 5758 Kenwood avenue and send the furniture to a storage house. The two and Byler left Chicago very early Monday morning, Byler returning from Gary, Ind.

Then followed a series of letters from the girl dated at Niles City, New Buffalo, Grand Rapids, Jackson and Detroit.

Operatives discovered that two women answering the description of Mrs. Spurgin and her daughter, called at the Detroit Y. W. C. A. Thursday and asked to be directed to a private home, where they might obtain rooms. They spent the night in a Second boulevard residence and left the next day.

"In her last letter," Newmark said, "the daughter spoke of the nearness of the Canadian line. She used in that connection one significant phrase, 'You know what that means.'

"I think Spurgin fled ahead of them thru Detroit into Canada and then to the east coast. I think so much of it that I am having every steamer now en route to Europe paged by wireless for him."

Because there is a possibility that Mrs. Spurgin fled merely to avoid the impending notoriety and does not intend to join the missing banker at some agreed rendezvous, detectives were sent ... ndiana to investigate reports that ... in had been seen there in com... with a brunette, who is said to be ... cagoan.

French Lick Has Clue.

...ry Pollard, porter at the French ... Springs hotel, said a couple tally ... ith the descriptions of the banker ... he young woman arrived Saturday ... in a dust-covered Illinois automo... The man inquired the way to West ... n, according to another witness, and ... a few hours later.

...e depositors' meeting yesterday ... h resulted in the selection of the ... mittee, proved to be a stormy one. ... ns were made both for a warrant ... Spurgin and for a demand of a... ediate detailed accounting, which ... show the degree of insolvency for ... institution. The committee was ... full power to act in any way seen

...k officials asserted that if deposits ... withdrawn, the institution will ... ance to pull thru and pay 100 ... dollar.

Whisky Truck Wins Race with Bandits, Then Loses Cargo

A daring race thru town between a truckload of liquor and two pursuing cars of bandits, the temporary escape of the truck when its driver eluded his pursuers and sought refuge in the P. & L. garage, then the holdup of two garage employes and the looting of the truck were the features in a venture in whisky running this morning.

The driver of the truck, a big blond who gave his name as A. B. Rowe of South Bend, Ind., drove his truck into the P. & L. garage at 48 East 51st street late last night and asked if he might leave it overnight.

A short time later five armed bandits forced their way thru the office, pushed guns into the sides of Thomas Entrickes, night watchman, and Dave Crockett, porter, and demanded the whisky.

Entrickes told them there was no liquor in the garage, but the bandits said they had been trailing it and knew better.

They searched the garage and presently one of them shouted:

"I've got her, boys; a nice load of hootch."

The truck was stripped of its contents, which were removed to two cars waiting outside. As soon as the bandits drove away Entrickes notified the police. They are searching today for the big blonde, believed to be the leader of one of the most powerful of the whisky running gang.

Alliing's Sloop Is Winning Yacht in Mackinac Race

MACKINAC ISLAND, Mich., July 25.—Virginia, Carlos Allings' class Q sloop, won the Mackinac race today by two minutes and seven seconrs from its nearest competitor. Its time was 38:57:59.

J. G. Glaver's Mavourneen finished at 12:19 p. m., its corrected time for the race being 40 hours 59 minutes and 54 seconds. Dorello was the first boat to cross the line thirty-four minutes ahead of Mavourneen. Intrepid finished a few minutes behind Mavourneen. No other boats were in sight.

A heavy squall blew up out of the west and helped the sailboats materially on their way, leaving them off Little Traverse bay this morning. The wind flattened out at daybreak, but later on freshened and gave signs of holding.

The first motor-boat to finish here was Dick Davis' P. D. Q., which started from Chicago Saturday night at 6 o'clock and crossed the line here at 2:06:14 yesterday afternoon, making the run of 331 miles in 20 hours 6 minutes 14 seconds, which constitutes a record for the motor-boat race. Roberts' Maurence, which put in here this morning, had to go into Frankfort yesterday afternoon at 4 o'clock for gas and lost three hours. It made the run in 38 hours and 30 minutes, having crossed here at 6:30 this morning.

IT'S SURE DRY! EVEN SIGNS OF STEINS MUST GO

"—And you will notify all saloon-keepers to take down all signs advertising drinks with more than the legal per cent of alcohol."—Extract from an Order.

Thus is written the end of the time-old tavern advertisements, in an order from Prohibition Director Kjellander to his men to warn dramshop keepers to pull down all signs that attract the dusty larnyx. Good-by old goat of Bock beer fame!

Not only are the probihition men massed for a drive against the liquor signs, but the district attorney is co-operating with them. Adieu, Pere Duffy, we knew you well.

And if saloon-keepers do not heed the first warning received, officials announced today they will be arrested and prosecuted under the federal statutes. Farewell, you "Beer That Made Milwaukee Famous."

NORMA ADVISES GIRLS BEST WAY TO WIN THE MEN

Boys, Norma was in town today.

Yeah, little Norma Talmadge. And she's got a whole lot of advice to give away free.

It's the girl without the make-up, Norma says, who drags in the derby.

"Be natural," advises Miss Talmadge. "It's the only safe way. I know very well I'd hate to act a part and then have the man I was interested in find me out."

Miss Talmadge only graced Chicago for a little while today. She stopped here while waiting the departure of a train for New York.

Grange Chief Suspended for Radical Utterances

FREDONIA, N. Y., July 25.—S. J. Lowell, master of the National Grange, announced today that he had written to William Bouck, master of the Washington State Grange, suspending him from office forthwith for alleged radical utterances at the June meeting of the Washington Grange.

ALDERMEN ASK CITY TO SUE FOR FEES OF EXPERTS

Vote to Ask Courts to Get Records of Men Who Received $2,741,000.

After being blocked at every turn by Mayor Thompson's leaders, the aldermanic subcommittee of the finance committee which has been investigating the payment of "expert's" fees by the city for three weeks, this afternoon threw down a gauntlet before the city hall clique when it recommended that the city sue for the recovery of $2,741,000 paid the experts.

When Eugene H. Dupee, counsel for the board of local improvements, defied the subcommittee and refused to appear to be questioned this afternoon the investigators voted their recommendation to sue. If the council accepts this recommendation the administration must start court action against its staunchest supporers.

The committee charged that the administration had sought to halt the investigation by refusing to produce documentary evidence and give testimony If court action is taken this testimony can be forced.

Here's the List.

Those "experts" the committee seeks to sue and the amounts they received are:

Austin J. Lynch	$544,000
Frank H. Mesce	460,000
Edward C. Waller Jr.	580,000
Ernest H. Lyons	580,000
Arthur S. Merigold	577,000

While the finance subcommittee acted other aldermen were proposing to seek the co-operation of Mayor Thompson in the proposed investigation or survey of all departments in the city government. This plan was broached by Ald. Eaton of the 6th ward to Ald. Lyle of the 32d.

Proposition Is Surprise.

Ald. Eaton is chairman of the special commission named by the city council to conduct the investigation. Ald. Lyle introduced the order calling for the creation of the commission.

The knowledge that the mayor is bitterly opposed to the Municipal Voters' league, the Chicago Bureau of Public Efficiency and the City club, whose representatives are to serve on the commission, made the suggestion of Ald. Lyle of more than ordinary interest. Ald. Eaton would not say whether such an invitation would be extended to the mayor. He indicated it was a matter the entire commission should pass on.

"I intend to confer with Ald. John Richert, chairman of the finance committee, tomorrow," said Ald. Eaton. "I believe the commission should get together as quickly as possible and that the investigation should be pushed thruout the summer so a report will be ready for the council when it reconvenes next October. As to inviting the mayor to co-operate with the commission, that is a matter for the investigating body to decide."

"Why should not Mayor Thompson be asked to aid the commission?" said Ald. Lyle. "When I introduced the order I had no intention of opening up the way whereby enemies of the mayor would be put in a position to attack him personally. I believe the different civic organizations understood this. My whole idea is to bring about reorganization of the city government, eliminate waste and useless expenses, and put each and every department on a sound working basis.

Sees Mayor Willing.

"I believe if Mayor Thompson can be convinced that nothing is intended against him personally he would be glad to give his whole support and co-operation."

Ask Public to Help Find "Tax Bill Fixers"

An appeal for aid in finding individuals who represent themselves as in a position to "fix" your tax bill with the board of assessors and the board of review, is made today by Stephen D. Griffin, chief clerk for the board of review. "We have received half a dozen telephone calls in the last few days," Mr. Griffin said, "in which people tell us that two men, giving the names of Adams and Courtney, entered their places of business, said they were members of the Cook County Employes' Benevolent association and claim they are in position to fix taxes for the complainant.

Report Benson, Brother of Whipped Man, Shot Dead

HOUSTON, Texas, July 25.—Reports from sources believed reliable were to the effect that M. C. Benson was shot to death this morning at League City. Benson was the brother of the G. C. Benson of Dickinson, whipped a week ago, according to reports received.

300 Great Lakes Sailors Leave for Pacific Fleet

Three hundred sailors from the Great Lakes station left Chicago today over the Wabash railroad for San Francisco, whence they will be distributed to the Pacific fleet.

Fire on Mauretania; Fear It Will Spread

LONDON, July 25.—Fire, which, it was feared, would prove of a serious nature, broke out on the Cunard liner Mauretania as she was lying at her dock in Southampton this afternoon.

BITTER CLASH SEEN TOMORROW IN SMALL CASE

Governor's Troops Expected to Block Sheriff if Arrest Is Ordered.

(Special to The Post.)

SPRINGFIELD, Ill., July 25.—Belief that tomorrow will see trouble in this city between the civil and military authorities is growing as the time approaches for Circuit Court Judge Smith to announce his decision on the issue of whether Gov. Small can be brought into court to answer the indictments brought in against him.

If the court rules that the criminal code is not to be suspended in the case of the governor, what then? The way the matter will be brought to a head is for the governor to pay no attention to the sheriff's writ.

There is no issue before Judge Smith until this is done, the present hearings being preliminary arrangements made in behalf of the governor because of courtesy to his high office. If the court decides that the occupant of this office is no less amenable to criminal statutes than any other citizen of the state, he will order the clerk of his court to release the writs, which the latter has been holding, and turn them over to the sheriff. Upon hs being done, the sheriff probably will telephone the governor, personally, that his presence is desired in court on the writs.

Problem for Sheriff.

Then will the issue arise. Up to that moment there will be no need of arrests or of calling out the state militia. If the governor goes to court and gives bond, there will be no civil trouble. If on the other hand he declines the end is not in sight.

Sheriff Mester then will have two courses before him. Either then and there to attempt to gain physical possession of the governor and bring him into court, or to return and notify the court that the defendant refuses to recognize the writs, and ask for court instructions. In such case, the court will then have the issue before it of whether or not to use force to bring in the governor, as would be done in the case of any other defendant.

All the outward signs of Gov. Small's movements indicate resistance, but in spite of this his close downstate friends not affiliated with the Thompson-Lundin machine say they cannot imagine his resisting a court summons and calling out the militia. Still the governor's conduct would indicate such a course was in mind.

Fink a Diplomat.

However, downstate friends point to the retention by the governor of Attorney Albert Fink, who was chief counsel for William Lorimer. Attorney Fink, by characteristics, leans toward diplomacy, and is not regarded as an attorney who would get a client in over his head urging needless fighting.

Politically, he is not the enemy of Gov. Small's Springfield foes, as is Attorney George B. Gillespie, his chief counsel in urging fight. Attorney Fink, to the contrary, is rather on intimate speaking terms with Richard Sullivan, anti-Small leader of Sangamon county, and is a well-known friend of State's Attorney Mortimer, whereas Attorney Gillespie was always in opposition to these rivals.

Soldiers Kept Ready.

Some downstaters profess to see in the retention of Attorney Fink an indication by Gov. Small not to go the full route of fighting marked out by Attorney Gillespie.

The governor still maintains today the close guard around him to prevent a surprise arrest. Officers and prominent members of the state militia are present in Springfield ready to answer a summons for military aid should the governor decide upon such a course.

Hoover Urges Power to War Finance Board

WASHINGTON, July 25.—Legislation to broaden powers of the war finance corporation, enabling it to handle the triple financial problems of the railroads, farm credits and export financing, was suggested today by Secretary Hoover to effect economic readjustment thruout the country. Mr. Hoover said he had recommended such a step with the approval of Secretary Mellon and Eugene Meyer Jr., managing director of the war finance corporation. It was believed in administration circles that President Harding in his note to congress tomorrow on the railroad finanical situation would present a proposal of this nature.

Wages of 1,000 Iron Miners Cut at Duluth

DULUTH, July 25.—Additional reduction of 10 per cent in the wages of its 10,000 miners and further curtailment of operations in the Lake Superior district was announced today by the Oliver Iron Mining company, a subsidiary of the United States Steel corporation. The wage cut becomes effective Aug. 1.

3 Members of Family Killed in Auto Crash

FELTON, Del., July 25.—Three members of one family were killed and a fourth seriously injured today when their automobile was struck by a Pennsylvania railroad train at Masten's Corner, near here. The dead are Mr. and Mrs. Herman Scott and their 12-year-old son.

16 Held Up by Masked Men and Robbed of $7,000

Four daring robberies were staged by as many groups of bandits within two hours this afternoon, the visits netting the robbers $8,000. None of the men were captured.

The most profitable haul was at the Borden Farm Products company at 2800 North Talman avenue, where sixteen employes were held up by five masked men who escaped after robbing the concern of between $5,000 and $7,000.

Girls Are Held Up.

The bandits entered the office of the company just after a number of drivers had made their departure.

"Put 'em up where they can't do any harm," one of the quintet ordered.

George Anderson, the manager; Clifford Bartel, cashier, and fourteen others, including Catherine Snell and Kate Neilsen, stenographers, complied. The same robber then commanded the group to line up facing the wall. Again they complied.

Then two bandits vaulted a counter in front of the cashier's cage and robbed the till.

Not more than three minutes elapsed from the time the bandits appeared until they had dashed out to an automobile parked across the street.

Steal $2,000 Gems.

A trio of bandits drove up in a high-powered car to the jewelry store of Tenerelli & La Manna, 531 Milwaukee avenue, and after holding up Philip Tenerelli departed with $2,000 in jewelry and a few trifles from the display shelves in the window.

A drug store came next. George Dewey, 7150 South Robey street, left the store of W. A. Jungk, 100 West 79th street, with $450 in cash and $80 in checks, destined for the store's account with the Mutual Trust and Savings bank.

A lone bandit intercepted Mr. Dewey a few blocks from the store, and the checks and currency never reached their destination.

The fourth robbery? You've guessed it. A. & P., 4310 Wentworth avenue, two bandits, loss $40.

Greeks Repel Turks at Eski-Shehr and Capture Division

SMYRNA, Asia, July 25.—(By the Associated Press, Greece-Turk.)—An attempt by the Turks to recapture Eski-shehr and Ineunu has failed. Severe losses were inflicted on the Turks by the Greeks. One entire division of Turks was captured.

Greeks Advance 25 Miles.

ATHENS, Greece, July 25.—(Greek Official Agency.)—The Greeks in Asia Minor have been following up energetically the victory they gained over the Turkish nationalists in the fighting brought on by the attempt of the Kemalites to recapture the keypoint of Eski-Shehr, on the Bagdad railway, according to official advices from the fighting front received here. The Greeks captured forty guns and took a great number of prisoners, the announcement states. Within a short time after the close of the battle and the definite repulse of the Turkish effort the Greeks had advanced more than twenty-five miles to the east of Eski-Shehr, and were continuing their pursuit of the enemy toward the interior.

Revolt at Konieh.

LONDON, July 25.—Dispatches from Athens to the Exchange Telegraph company say that Sunday newspapers there publish reports from Smyrna telling of a revolution in the city of Konieh, a railway center about 350 miles south of Angora. The reports declare Turkish nationalist government authorities have been overthrown by the population of Konieh.

U. S. and Britain Parley on New Immigration Law

LONDON, July 25.—(By the Associated Press.)—Negotiations are in progress between the governments of Great Britain and the United States for a settlement of the difficulties incidental to the first application of the new American immigration law, Cecil B. Harmsworth, under secretary for foreign affairs, announced in the house of commons today. Mr. Harmsworth's announcement was in response to a question as to "what steps are being taken by the British authorities to protect British subjects arriving in New York."

Refuses Sanity Test for Woman in T. R. Note Case

NEW YORK, July 25.—Judge Talley today refused to appoint a commission to test the sanity of Mrs. Emma Richardson Burkett of Hillsdale, Ind., who is awaiting trial on charge of forging the indorsement of the late Theodore Roosevelt to a note for $69,900.

Remarried After Being Divorced for 30 Years

DIXON, Ill., July 25.—Walden Atwood, aged 75, and Mrs. Lina Atwood, aged 56, both of Oregon, who were divorced thirty years ago, were remarried here today.

Ship Breaks Feed Pump.

NEW YORK, July 25.—The new United States shipping board steamship American Legion, which left here Saturday for Rio Janeiro on her maiden trip, has put into Bermuda because of a broken feed pump, the Munson line operator of the vessel, was advised today.

COURT DECIDES IMMUNITY OFFER WAS NOT MADE

McDonald on Stand Says Waivers Were Signed; Plea for Williams.

By Peter D. Vroom.

The confessions of "Eddie" Cicotte, "Joe" Jackson and Claude Williams relative to the alleged conspiracy to "throw" the world series of 1919, are admissible as evidence and they were related to the jury.

Judge McDonald took the stand and related the confessions of the three players as given first to him and later to the grand jury, being careful in each instance to mention no names other than those who confessed.

This ruling was made late today by Judge Friend and constitute a distinct victory for the prosecution, since the court's action was predicated on his belief that the confessions were not obtained by means of promises of immunity. Altho beaten at this point, the nine attorneys for the defense started a renewed argument that the state had not proved a conspiracy.

The three players, Cicotte, Jackson and Williams, earlier had positively testified to conversations with Alfred S. Austrian, attorney for Charles A. Comiskey, owner of the White Sox; Hartley L. Replogle, former assistant state's attorney, and Chief Justice McDonald of the Criminal courts, and claimed immunity had been promised them by one or more of this trio, altho admitting they might have signed waivers of immunity.

But all their statements were shattered when Judge McDonald took the stand at the opening of the afternoon session, which, like most of the morning, was held with the jury absent. He denied having told either of the men that he would promise them anything but a fair trial before a court, with the exception that in the case of Williams, who said he fell because of his small salary.

Judge McDonald said he told the pitcher that he "believed the trial court probably would take into consideration" these phases of the affair.

Conflicts with Judge's Story.

Curiously enough, altho Judge McDonald said he talked with Williams for fifteen minutes, the player had said he did not talk at all with the judge.

Judge McDonald testified:

"When Cicotte was brought into my chambers he was crying. He told me a good deal about his life, his wife and his babies and then about the world's series.

"I told Cicotte he could expect nothing, that he would be indicted, and that he would have to give bond the same as any one. When Cicotte would not name the gamblers in the deal I told him he was not telling all of the truth.

No Promises to Cicotte.

"Mr. Replogle made no promises to Cicotte in my presence. I went to the grand-jury room with Cicotte and Replogle and nothing was said about immunity on the way. Nothing was said about any promise anyone else may have made Cicotte.

In the jury-room I heard Mr. Replogle read the immunity waiver to Cicotte. I heard Replogle ask him to sign it, and I saw Cicotte sign it.

"Nothing was said in my presence to Joe Jackson about immunity, either. I told him he would have to sign an immunity waiver and give bond. After he came out of the jury-room Jackson came to me and said: 'Swede Risberg said he would bump me off if I confessed to the jury. Can't you send some officers out with me to protect me.' I sent two bailiffs with Jackson.

Touched by Williams' Story.

"Williams told me he only got $2,800 or $3,000 a year. He appealed to my sympathy and I will admit that his story made me feel that he deserved some consideration, altho I promised him none.

"I did tell him, however, that if he would make a clean breast of this affair and help to clean up the rotten situation a trial court might and probably would take that into consideration."

Johnson Accuses Rothstein.

Ban Johnson, president of the American league, today injected a new angle of an old phase of the scandal—the theft of the immunity waivers and a transcript of the grand jury testimony of Cicotte, Jackson and Williams—when he charged specifically that Arnold Rothstein, New York gambler, paid $10,000 for these papers to an attache of State's Attorney Hoyne's office.

After Rothstein found the confessions did not implicate him to the extent of criminal liability he gave them to a friend, who is managing editor of a New York newspaper. This editor, Mr. Johnson asserts, offered copies of the confessions for sale all over the country.

An added feature of the early session was that Mr. Austrian, the first witness while the jury was present, emphatically denied he ever had called Harry G. Redmon of East St. Louis, Friday's star witness, a "blackmailer, blackguard," or anything of the kind. He had heard that Redmon said that if he "got back the $5,500 he had lost on the 1919 world's series through 'crossing' he would tell how it had been thrown."

Cross-examination failed to shake this testimony. During the Cicotte questioning Assistant State's Attorney Gorman observed to Attorney Henry A. Berger "that after the Redmon incident you and Mr. Frumberg (who said Austrian had told him the quoted opinions of Redmon) had better hold your peace." Mr. Frumberg jumped to his feet, shouting that he would have witnesses to prove Austrian was correctly quoted. Mr. Berger added to the uproar.

With Hartley L. Replogle, former assistant state's attorney, concluding his testimony as to the presentation of Cicotte, Jackson and Claude Williams to the grand jury last fall, the players took the stand.

Awed by Judge.

"This is going to be a long and hard trial," Cicotte quoted Austrian as saying to him "and you don't want your wife and babies here and you want to keep out of the penitentiary." Then Mr. Replogle took me before Judge McDonald, who said, "You know that you know more than you've told.' I didn't answer for a moment, and the judge turned to Replogle and said, 'Go ahead, indict him.' I said to Replogle on my way to the grand-jury room, 'Don't this go about what you and Austrian promised me?' and he said, 'Sure it does.' Then I went before the grand jury."

Cicotte said he was taken to Attorney Austrian's office by Harry M. Garbiner,

(Continued on Next Page.)

WOMAN GIVES UP IN ESPOSITO KILLING CASE

Mother instinct is believed by the police to have resulted in the surrender late today of Mrs. Emilia Pancio, who yesterday, it is charged, stabbed to death Mrs. Virginia Esposito, a rival for the affections of the former's husband. Mrs. Pancio gave her self up to avoid having her six children removed to the juvenile home.

NEW YORK-PITTSBURG BOX SCORE

	1	2	3	4	5	6	7	8	9	R
New York (at Pittsburg)	0	0	0	1	0	0	2	0	0	3
Pittsburg	2	0	0	0	1	1	2	0	X	6

New York—	R	H	P	A	E	Pittsburg—	R	H	P	A	E
Burns, lf	0	0	3	0	0	Bigbee, lf	1	1	1	0	0
Bancroft, ss	0	1	1	2	0	Carey, cf	3	3	11	0	0
Frisch, 3b	1	2	1	2	0	Mar'ville, ss	1	1	3	3	2
Young, rf	0	2	4	0	0	Cutshaw, 2b	0	2	3	1	0
Kelly, 1b	0	0	9	0	0	Whitted, rf	0	1	1	0	0
Cun'ham, cf	1	0	2	0	0	Barnhart, 3b	1	2	1	1	0
Rawlings, 2b	1	2	1	4	0	Grimm, 1b	0	1	5	0	0
Snyder, c	0	2	2	0	0	Schmidt, c	0	1	2	1	0
Douglas, p	0	0	0	1	0	Adams, p	0	1	0	2	0
Sallee, p	0	0	0	1	0						
Smith, c	0	0	0	0	0						
Total	3	9	24	8	0	Total	6	13	27	8	2

Smith batted for Douglas in 7th. Causey ran for Snyder in 7th. Brown batted for Sallee in 9th.
Sacrifice Hits—Maranville, Burns, Cutshaw.
Two-base Hits—Carey (2), Snyder.
Three-base Hits—Barnhart (2), Adams.
Stolen Bases—Frisch, Young, Carey.

BABE RUTH GETS TWO HOME RUNS AT CINCINNATI

CINCINNATI, July 25.—Babe Ruth knocked the ball over the centerfield fence with the bases full in the fifth inning of an exhibition game here this afternoon between the Cincinnati Reds and the New York Yankees. He made another in the seventh inning with one man on.

BOOTLEGGER WINS INTERNATIONAL SLOOP RACE

MONTREAL, July 25.—The sloop Bootlegger of St. Paul, Minn., won the trophy defended by boats entered by the Royal St. Lawrence Yacht club, taking first place for a second time in the international races at Lake St. Louis.

HEAD OF WASHINGTON AND JEFFERSON UNIVERSITY DIES

DENVER, July 25.—Samuel C. Black, president of Washington and Jefferson university, Washington, Pa., died at a local hospital early today after a two-week illness growing out of complications resulting from an attack of influenza last April. He was on a honeymoon trip to National parks.

SEES TARIFF KEEP PRICES UP

WASHINGTON, July 25.—Application of the American valuation plan of assessing duties on foreign goods would increase prices of similar merchandise in this country, Thomas Walker Page, chairman of the tariff commission, told the senate finance committee today in the first senate hearing on the permanent tariff bill. Mr. Page declared that, with a higher value forced on imported goods by the Fordney home value plan, American manufacturers naturally would not reduce their prices.

RACE RESULTS (EMPIRE CITY)

First—Beverly Belle, 5-2; Fifty Fifty, even; Lady Delhi, even
Second—Apple Jack, 4-5; Fort Churchill, 8-5; Blue Belle, 3-5.
Third—Restraint, 2-1; Margaret White, even; Plurality, 2-1.
Fourth—Purchase, 1-8; Dry Moon, 7-10; Dimmesdale, 1-3.
Fifth—Tan II., 10-1; Knight of the Heather, 6-1; Salute, 3-2.
Sixth—Simple Simon, even; Kirtle, 3-5; Wreckless, even.

RACE RESULTS (WINDSOR)

First—Momentum, 31.50; Peace Pal, 4.35; Forestall, 3.50.
Second—Gilt Fringe, 13.40; Tuanorea, 5.85; Nonskid, 4.00.
Third—Merrimac, 8.40; All Right, 25.05; Be Sure, 8.45.
Fourth—Dodge, 5.40; King Thrush, 3.15; Best Hoff, 2.50.

Ben H. Atwell Sues Chicago Opera Company

Ben H. Atwell, formerly eastern depresentative in New York of the Chicago Opera association, has brought suit there against the organization in the Supreef court for $6,000. Mr. Atwell alleges this amoun tis due him because ... defendant, on March 1, 1920, "w... fully discharged him." He states ... until that date he received a salr... the rate of $12,000 a year.

Tex Admits He Caused Films to Come Over Line

NEW YORK, July 25.—Tex Rickard, promoter of the Dempsey-Carpentier bout, and F. C. Quimby, motion-picture producer, today admitted to United States Attorney Hayward that they had caused a film of the fight to be brought across the state line from New Jersey.

Mr. Hayward, who sumouned the pair for examination in connection with an advertised attempt to show the movie in New York, said after a conference with them that they had asserted they believed transportation of the film was no violation of the federal law and that any offense there might be would consist in public exhibition of it.

Mr. Hayward announced that the frankness of the two men would not make it necessary for him to place the matter before the federal grand jury. He said that he would proceed against them by means of an information charging them with a misdemeanor.

The federal attorney also said that he would not proceed against the truckmen who had transported the film, for Mr. Rickard and Mr. Qiumby had declared he probably was ignorant of what he was handling. Neither will action be taken against anyone concerned in exhibiting the film to wounded soldiers at the Fox Hills hospital here.

Mr. Hayward asserted that the pair had intimated they would plead guilty to violating the interstate commerce law if such a charge were formally brought against them. The maximum punishment on conviction would be a year's imprisonment or a $1,000 fine.

JOHNNY EVERS IS OUT AS CUB PILO

THE CHICAGO EVENING POST

THIRTY-SECOND YEAR WEDNESDAY, AUGUST 3, 1921. PRICE THREE CENTS

XXX LAST EDITIO

Turn page for *The Post's* "Home" Front Pag

LANDIS BARS ACQUITTED SOX FROM LEAGUE BALL

ACCUSED BROKER REVEALS RECORD OF WORTHINGTON

Clinnin to Rush Stout to Grand Jury; Link "Big Tim" Murphy to the "Trust."

What the federal authorities believe to be a crushing blow at any defense which John W. Worthington, Chicago "Wallingford" and alleged head of a ation-wide band of mail robbers, may fer against the charges on which he s indicted came this afternoon when seph W. Stout, Lasalle street broker, de a detailed statement of Worthing-'s opperations to Assistant United tes District Attorney Clinnin.

important was the statement that Clinnin intimated Stout would be n before the grand jury immediately a witness, instead of being held for secution. Stout was released on $10,- bond.

Stout Loses $30,000.

out's story dates back to 1902, when vas associated with Worthington in operation of a life insurance com- Worthington, according to the ent, wrecked this, and Stout lost which he had invested, he said. the object of recovering this loss, asserted, he remained as partner Vorthington in the manipulations sulted in the creation and wreck- the Federal National bank of and of several small banks in The business relations contin- l Worthington's recent arrest. innin refused to make public fur- tails of the statement, beyond hat it was of the utmost im- He would not state how far nent dealt with the alleged mail- perations which brought Worth- to his latest contact with the ithorities.

Link Up "Big Tim."

less vital was the discovery the day of a link between the Securities company, of which ngton is president, and "Big Tim" , who is accused of engineering arborn street mail raid. rtment of justice agents said und a letter addressed to Mur- Worthington's office. The letter t s et. Yesterday they found and three paper wrapped ning, among other securi- stolen at the Dearborn

ging into the affairs of Securities, which, it is ality was only a "blind," rs of a highly organized eves, were active in sev- today. Clinnin, first assistant said he would go be- ury and obtain "double its against the twenty- with Worthington. the government's case . Clinnin said, "we these men on some

vere busy in tele- five men sought on ts who are believed icago. Wires were dozen cities along

ere under arrest, Park, and Arthur West 69th street, aid to have dis- le paper stolen Goldsmith is al- rthington's chief

Clue.

found on much n the offices of ompany at 105 ere agents also om looted mail l in suitcases. l intelligence offi- ns caused Worth- to bring Gold-

ere in the hands oday. Five men C. Ellington, J. J. Epps and ps, a Chicago rticipation in the obbery, and was Harschmann won 1919, as alleged dle trust" con- rench, a broker lue sky" finan-

ch.

wen T. Evans, curities com- while their t bonds for the surety $50,000, or estate val-

in the sent to t also is conspira- the Dear-

au
air
ga-
ev-

Report Evers Out and Killefer In as Cub Manager

Indications this afternoon were that Johnny Evers had quit as manager of the Cubs and that Bill Killefer, the catcher, was to be named his successor.

No announcement could be obtained from Cub officials. Evers was not at the park when the first game of the double-header with Boston started and it was explained that he is sick. But the rumor spread—and it was neither affirmed nor denied—that the Cub stockholders held a meeting yesterday and decided that a change in management is necessary.

Killefer has not been doing much catching lately. He went behind the bat in the first game and backstopped for Alexander.

Spurgin Safe with Friends in Mexico, Is El Paso Report

BULLETIN.

SAN ANTONIO, Texas, Aug. 3.—A man believed to have been Warren C. Spurgin, missing president of the Michigan Avenue Trust company of Chicago, attempted to hire a Kelly aviator to take him from Marfa last Sunday across the Mexican border, it was learned here this morning when flyers returned from the border.

EL PASO, Texas, Aug. 3.—Immigration officers along the border today believed Warren C. Spurgin, missing Chicago banker, is somewhere in Mexico, probably with friends he is known to have been associated with, who used to make El Paso their headquarters.

From authentic sources it was learned today that prior to leaving Chicago he had communicated with two former residents of this city who are now in the interior of Mexico.

Poses as Mining Man.

Posing as a mining man, a person who answers the description of the missing banker got off the train at Marfa, Texas, July 19, hired an automobile, drove to Presidio, and on July 20 crossed the river into Mexico. This was further confirmed today when local immigration authorities announced that they had received a report from immigration men at Presidio and Marfa.

The report received here said that the stranger who answers Spurgin's description presented a passport made out in the name of "Scott." He said he was a mining man. His only baggage was a large suitcase, resembling one, the immigration men reported, which is said to have been carried by Spurgin.

Left in Automobile.

The report also said that after he had passed inspection he hired a Mexican in a rowboat to take him across the river. Persons coming from the Mexican side to the American reported that the stranger left Ojinaga, Chihuahua, the border town across from Presidio, in an automobile, presumably for Chihuahua City.

4 NEW BILLS IN NATURALIZATION FRAUD QUIZ

Further indictments against four men charged with participation in the recent "naturalization shakedown" were returned yesterday, it became known today following the raising of the men's bonds by Judge Landis.

Those named in the new bills are:

Martin P. McNichols, 2822 South Loomis street, former clerk in the naturalization bureau, bonds increased from $5,000 to $25,000 on charges of impersonating a government officer.

Herman Bartels, former clerk in the Circuit court, bonds increased from $10,000 to $25,000 on charges of defrauding the government.

Edward J. Zappan, former clerk in the records department of the county clerk's office, bonds increased from $10,000 to $25,000 on charges of defrauding the government.

Alvin Addison, alleged go-between, bonds increased from $10,000 to $40,000, after federal officials said he was suspected in connection with several Canadian bank robberies.

It was said that for several years a system of extortion was carried on by which applicants for citizenship were intimidated and threatened with refusal of their applications and then told to go from the federal naturalization bureau to see Bartels in the county building to have the case "fixed."

Fined Auto in River; Search for Lost Driver

OGDEN, Utah, Aug. 3.—With the headlights burning and the emergency brake set, an automobile, bearing an Idaho license number, was found late last night partially submerged in the river off a thirty-foot embankment where the Lincoln highway passes thru Weber canyon five miles east of here. From a few effects found in the car the sheriff's office said a search was being made in the river for the body of Roland R. Mason of Idaho Falls, Idaho.

Burlington Train Robbery Frustrated by Porter

HAMBURG, Iowa, Aug. 3.—By lock- a would-be bandit in a vestibule be- on the cars a porter on the south- Chicago, Burlington and Quincy ger yesterday frustrated a train The bandit, a negro who lled

DAWES TELLS OF YANKS' DEEDS IN BOOK ON WAR

Intimate Diary Sings Praise of Pershing; Silent on Own Achievements.

Anything said or written these days by Brig. Gen. Charles Gates Dawes, chairman of the directorate of the Central Trust company of Illinois, comptroller of the currency under President McKinley and brigadier general of engineers in France with the American expeditionary forces, is of interest to the people.

Hence, his book, "A Journal of the Great War," published in two volumes by Houghton Mifflin company, will find many readers.

The man who cursed congressmen of his own party for detractions against America's part in the war, is little seen in this book, which is an intimate diary, obviously written in the methodical and careful way Mr. Dawes goes about things, but still with a feeling that some day it might be worth publishing, not for personal glory, but for the education of America as to their country's deeds in the world war. This impression is strengthened as the story of his difficulties in maintaining the American supplies at par is developed.

Thru it all runs a vein of deep admiration and a David and Jonathan sort of affection for Gen. John J. Pershing, his friend of many decades. He never tires of singing Pershing's praises, of recounting his ability, of narrating his humanness.

Like the immortal diarist of old England, Samuel Pepys, for whom Dawes has the liveliest admiration, incidentally, the Chicago banker bares his soul curiously sometimes; at other times he is discreet and chary of recording violent impressions, greatly unlike the hero of "Hell and Maria."

War Is Forgotten.

By way of explanation, or possible apology, since he is a modest man as regards himself, Gen. Dawes speaks of the lassitude of America today toward the war of yesteryear, saying:

"Among our people the awr is largely forgotten, or remmebered because of some personal consequence or some prospetcive personal consequence. Yet an elemental convulsion of humanity has occurred, so profound in its effects upon life on the earth that it will be studied and described for thousands of years."

Foch, in his opinion, "will be regarded in history as the greatest of all soldier," and Mr. Dawes speaks of the difficulties that arose before central control of armies was agreed to and the noted Frenchman placed in supreme charge of the allied cause. There was, however, "one great commander who offered to surrender power for the common good befoe an emergency became acute—John J. Pershing—and whatever condemnation history will visit upon others in this respect, his fame will only shine the brighter."

Mr. Dawes tells of his advocacy of an application of "caupling up the rear of the three allied armies in France . . . to be an extension over the allied of his (Foch's) plan "of the American supply procurement. Foch favored it since he could get no co-operation as to supplies in the rear of his lines, and four months later had the plan adopted with Gen. Payot of his staff as chairman of the military board of allied supply.

Pershing as Prophet.

In starting his journal proper, dated at St. Nazaire, France, Aug. 21, 1917, the first he had kept since the death from drowning of his son, Rufus Fearing, in 1912, the author skips rapidly over his military preliminaries and gets into intimacies in Washington enroute to France. At the Metropolitan club, for instance, an old friend remarks to their mutual friend, Pershing, that he would become the great hero of the war, to which the general replied:

"Tell me one man who started in this war in supreme command who lasted. What I am going to do is sim-

(Continued on Next Page.)

Truck and Meat Worth $2,000 Taken by Thieves

Laurence Cannon, driver of a truck for Fred Oppenheimer, commission merchant at 322 South Water street, was deprived of his truckload of meat today by thieves. The load was worth more than $2,000. He entered the Booth fisheries, at State and Lake streets, about noon, and when he came out the truck and meat were gone. Nobody knew how it happened, tho the streets were crowded with people at the time.

Arrest Man Accused of Murdering Auto Dealer

EAST LIVERPOOL, Ohio, Aug. 3.—Harry Mitchell, alias Carmen, wanted on a first degree murder charge, in connection with the death of Harry D. Cummins, Steubenville automobile dealer, was arrested last night by authorities at Salem, Ohio. He was removed to the county jail at Lisbon, where he will be held pending arrival of the Steubenville officials.

Farmers Elect Ben Marsh.

WASHINGTON, Aug. 3.—Election of Benjamin C. Marsh as managing director of the Farmers' National council was announced today by Herbert F. Baker, president of

MAYOR VETOES ORDER TO FIX PAY OF EXPERTS

City Employes Also Barred as Witnesses in "Last-Minute" Action.

Mayor Thompson today vetoed two orders passed July 22 by the council, one fixing the number of real estate experts at nine and their pay at $50 a day when working and the other, introduced by Ald. John Lyle, providing for investigation of city department by a commission of members of civic and official organizations.

Except for the good memory of one of the faithful, the mayor might have forgotten all about rejecting the Lyle order. It was after the debate over his veto of the experts' fee ordinance, which was sent back to the finance committee.

"How about the veto on that investigation order?" it was whispered in the mayor's ear.

Forthwith there was action. James Breen, assistant corporation counsel, and Ald. Anderson delved briskly into records. Today, it was found, was the last on which the order could be vetoed.

Ettelson Swings into Action.

Then Corporation Counsel Ettelson swung into action and presently there came forth a neatly typewritten statement of the mayor's attitude toward investigating his administration.

He objected because various agencies nominated for representation on the inquiry commission are hostile to him. The president of the Municipal Voters' league is a traction official. The mayor took the opportunity to repeat his charge that the traction companies are robbing the people of Chicago of $50,000 a day.

It is well known that traction officials are bitter enemies of his, the mayor said. Furthermore, he said, the M. V. L. has accepted money from other of his foes.

No Inquiry by Foes.

"I am not opposed to any honest investigation at any time or any place," he said, "but I am against an inquiry conducted by the agencies named in this resolution."

Ald. James Bowler of the 19th ward moved that the council's action in adopting the resolution be reconsidered and the motion was carried almost unanimously.

In vetoing the order fixing the number of experts and their pay, the mayor found two questions presented. They are, he said:

Whether the council can control appropriations after passage of the annual budget?

How far, if at all, the council may exercise control of the board of local improvements, which employs the experts?

Claims Usurpation of Functions.

After the budget has passed and the five-day period for amendment has expired, "disbursement of the moneys appropriated is vested in the executive branch of the municipal government," the message read. By tying strings to its appropriations, the council is "usurping functions not vested in it by law," the mayor argued.

The question of how much control the council may exercise over the board of local improvements, "which is created by statute and not by ordinance," is involved in litigation now pending over the payment of experts and, the mayor thinks, "should be there settled."

Interested in Fees.

In his message the mayor indicated he was most concerned with the part of the council order fixing the experts' pay, and the influence which, if not vetoed, it might have in extending the council's authority in disposing of the budget and control of the local improvements board.

"This order cannot be separated into parts, one of which I can approve and another of which I can disapprove," the message read. "Therefore, it must stand or fall as an entirety."

The mayor recommended that the order be reconsidered and placed on file.

Some brisk debating followed reading of the mayor's message:

"This investigation was started at the instigation of the president of the board of local improvements," said Ald. Schwartz. "I can charge here and now that money had been paid to these experts unlawfully. Their bills were incorrectly and wrongfully charged and presented.

Based on "Reconstruction" Value.

"It is my knowledge that the fees were not based on the original value of the buildings they appraised, minus the depreciation, but on the reconstruction value.

"The president was asked how these fees were arrived at and he refused to answer—so there is only one conclusion to draw and that is that the city was charged wrongfully."

Ald Lyle entered the argument and brought it to such a heat that the mayor had to rap repeatedly for order.

"Why the members of this council should argue and investigate a thing that may sway the minds of the jurors (referring to lawsuits over the experts' fees) is beyond me," said Ald. Lyle.

"I don't believe Ald Schwartz is on the square in t tter," said Ald. John Tor there (pol sible to th to punish

Car Kills Couple; Aged Husband in Futile Hero Role

Injuries received last night when they were struck by an automobile while crossing the street hand-in-hand caused the deaths early today of Mr. and Mrs. Bror Gustafson, 57 and 56 years old, of 2743 Best avenue.

They were returning from a picture show. At Ashland avenue and Nelson street, where automobile travel is brisk, Mr. Gustafson took his wife's hand as they stepped from the curb.

Tries to Save His Wife.

Half-way across an approaching automobile swung sharply at them. Mrs. Gustafson screamed in fright and attracted the attention of persons on the sidewalk.

Gustafson could have saved himself with two or three quick steps, the witnesses said, but he embraced his wife and tried to lift her to safety.

The automobile struck them squarely. Gustafson died of a broken neck soon after. Mrs. Gustafson died two hours later.

Autoist in Jail.

"I had to swing out quickly to avoid hitting another car," said the motorist who hit them, James Mesart of 1934 Maud avenue. "The shade of the trees along the street made it so dark I couldn't see the crossing."

Mesart was held by the Sheffield avenue police and a companion, David Forsberg of 4824 Gunnison avenue, was pledged to attend the inquest.

Mrs. Marie McCurdy, 1335 Sedgwick street, and Mrs. Casey Trascy, 1442 North Park avenue, were cut and bruised and suffered possible internal injuries when they were struck by a taxicab driven by Arthur Harmder, 3931 North Robey street. The accident occurred at Wilson avenue and Sheridan road. Harmder was released by the police after questioning.

AUTO THIEF SHOT IN CHASE IS NEAR DEATH

Show Girl and Companion Are Held by Police.

An automobile thief who chose to shoot it out with a motorcycle policeman at racing speed along Sheridan road was near death today, and his two companions, one of them a girl, were under arrest.

Motorcycle Policeman Frank Schaefer hailed the speeding car near Calvary cemetery. He was answered by a shot and he started in pursuit. Half a hundred shots cracked back and forth until at Greenleaf avenue and Sheridan road one of the policeman's bullets smashed the automobile windshield, and it swung head on into a tree.

Pinned Under Car.

The car rocked on its side and pinned the three passengers fast. Schaefer was attempting to rescue them when the driver, Edward Clark of 711 Cass street, pointed his revolver at the bluecoated back.

Policemen George Schwennson, Martin O'Malley and George Trauster of the Rogers Park detail arrived at the fortunate second. Schwennson fired twice at Clark, shooting him thru both lungs

In the excitement of attending to Clark, his companions, Arden Babcock and Peggy Evers, a show girl, both living at 749 Cass street, fled toward a vacant house. Schaefer pursued and caught them.

Confesses Stealing Auto.

The wrecked automobile was stolen last evening from the Paige Motor Sales company at 4820 Broadway. Babcock confessed, the police said, a number of recent robberies, and they believe the trio was returning from some foray along the north shore when Schaefer interrupted their flight.

MALLOY REFUSES TO STAND TRIAL BY POLICE BOARD

Capt. Dennis Malloy today failed to obtain a hearing on his charges that the trial board was prejudiced against him and left the room with his attorney, Thomas Lantry, declaring it was useless to stand trial.

Malloy declared that Deputy Alcock was prejudiced against his case, had openly showed his hostility and was not a fit person to sit on his trial.

When the board refused to hear the petition Attorney Lantry insisted that he be heard.

"If you don't keep quiet," Commissioner Geary shouted, "I'll have you thrown out of here."

Lantry and his client declared they would go voluntarily, and left. Capt. Malloy's case was immediately called and the commission ordered the record to show he had not responded.

The charges grew out of the theft of a truckload of beer in Malloy's district. He is charged with neglect of duty, disobedience of orders, inattention to duty and three minor counts.

Witnesses who were called before the board after the captain departed included Lieut. Fitzgerald of the Stockyards station, Operator Thomas J. Morgan and Police Sergeants Bingham and Burns.

Call Virgin Island Judge.

AN JUAN, Porto Malmin of

COMISKEY AND BAN STAND PAT ON "BLACKLIST"

Judge Asserts the Organization Has No Place for "Crooked Players."

"They can't play with the White Sox."—Charles A. Comiskey.

"No player who throws a ball game or sits in a conference with a bunch of crooked players and gamblers will ever play professional baseball."—Judge Kenesaw Mountain Landis.

"The fact that the outfit was freed by a Cook county jury does not alter the conditions one iota or minimize the magnitude of the offense."—B. B. Johnson, President American League.

By Peter D. Vroom.

The verdict of acquittal rendered by a "jury of their peers" does not mean that the eight "Black Sox" accused of "throwing" the world's series of 1919 have been deloused and become White Sox potentialities once more. And it does not mean they can play again in organized baseball. Not if Judge Landis, high commissioner of the American national sport, has anything to say about it. He said plenty today, too. So did Charles A. Comiskey, owner of the White Sox.

It is possible that some or all of the players will attempt by legal means to be reinstated, and some delicate legal problems are involved if such action is taken. Ror the time being, however, George ("Buck") Weaver will continue to take half the profits of a drug store on South Halsted and West 69th streets and "Eddie" Cicotte, "Joe" Jackson, "Chick" Gandil, "Swede" Risberg, "Lefty" Williams and "Happy" Felsch will tour the country with enough others to make up a ball club.

Landis Gives Statement.

Judge Landis would not discuss the cases of the former White Sox directly, but gave out the following statement, as his view of the situation, resulting from the "not guilty" verdicts returned last night by the jury which heard the accused men tried in Judge Friend's Criminal court:

"Regardless of the verdict of the jury, no player that throws a ball game, no player that undertakes or promises to throw a ball game, no player that sits in a conference with a bunch of crooked players and gamblers where the ways and means of throwing games are planned and discussed and does not promptly tell his club about it, will ever play professional baseball.

"Of ocurse, I don't know that any of these men will apply for reinstatement, but if they do, above are at least a few of the rules that will be enforced.

"Just keep it in mind that regardless of the verdicts of juries, baseball is entirely competent to protect itself against the crooks, both inside and outside the game."

"Cicotte confessed to me that he and seven other players conspired to throw the world's series of 1919," said the "Old Roman." "Until this confession can be explained away not one of these men can play on the White Sox."

Ban Johnson Disappointed.

President Byron Bancroft Johnson of the American league, who was assailed vigorously during the trial by attorneys for the defense, was disappointed at the acquittal.

"The trial of the indicted players and gamblers uncovered the greatest crime it was possible to commit in baseball," said he. "The fact that the outfit was freed by a Cook county jury does not alter the conditions one iota or minimize the magnitude of the offense. The players are as odious to a clean and right-thinking public as the crooks and thieves they dealt with.

"The energetic prosecution of the state clearly indicates that crimes of this character will not be permitted to go unchallenged."

"William ("Kid") Gleason, manager of the White Sox, today and during the 1919 series, expressed himself vigorously at Boston, where the Sox open a series today. He asserted none of the "washed" "Black Sox" ever would play with their old team, or any other he was manager of, and he denied he had fraternized with the accused in the Chicago courtroom.

Can't Play Again—Gleason.

"Wish them well," exclaimed Gleason with baseball expletives. "Not much. I don't think they'll ever play in organized baseball again. I know they'll never play with any team I manage."

The White Sox players named "Eddie" Collins as spokesman and the captain said there would be nothing to say unless unexpected action was taken by the baseball authorities.

"I am very much pleased that Judge Landis will not permit the former White Sox to play again in professional baseball," said Thomas J. Hickey, president of the American association, whose headquarters are in Chicago. "I am greatly disappointed at the verdict. I feel that the state should have had some kind of conviction as those men should have been punished."

Weaver Wants to Get Back.

ted a few days ago in The P

CUBS—BOX SCORE

Boston (at Chicago) — 0 2 0 0 1 0 0 0 2 — 5
Cubs (first game) — 1 1 0 0 1 0 0 0 0 — 3

Cubs—	R	H	P	A	E	Boston—	R	H	P	A	E
Flack, rf	1	1	1	1	0	Powell, cf	2	4	1	0	0
Hollocher, ss	0	1	2	1	0	Barbare, ss	0	1	3	4	0
Kelleher, 2b	0	2	4	2	0	South'h, rf	0	3	0	0	0
Grimes, 1b	0	0	8	2	0	Cruise, lf	1	1	4	0	0
Sullivan, lf	0	0	5	1	0	Boeckel, 3b	1	1	2	3	1
Twombly, cf	0	1	1	1	0	Holke, 1b	0	2	11	2	0
Deal, 3b	1	0	1	3	0	Ford, 2b	0	0	2	5	0
Killefer, c	1	1	5	1	0	O'Neill, c	0	1	3	1	0
Alexander, p	0	0	0	5	0	Oeschger, p	1	0	1	0	0
Total	3	6	27	17	0	Total	5	13	27	15	1

Sacrifice Hits—Ford, Barbare, Alexander.
Two-base Hit—Southworth. Home Run—Flack.
Bases on Balls—Off Alexander, 3; off Oeschger, 1.
Stolen Base—Deal.
Double Plays—Flack to Killefer; Barbare to Ford to Holke.
Struck Out—By Alexander, 4; by Oeschger, 1.
Hit by Pitched Ball—By Oeschger (Kelleher, Killefer).

SOX—BOX SCORE

Sox (at Boston) — 0 0 1 1 0 0 0 0 0 — 2
Boston — 1 0 2 0 0 0 0 0 X — 3

Sox—	R	H	P	A	E	Boston—	R	H	P	A	E
Johnson, ss	0	0	2	3	0	Leibold, cf	1	2	0	0	0
Mulligan, 3b	0	2	3	4	0	Foster, 2b	0	1	1	2	0
Collins, 2b	0	2	4	3	0	Menosky, lf	1	3	3	0	0
Strunk, cf	1	0	0	0	0	Pratt, 2b	0	1	1	2	0
Falk, lf	0	1	0	0	0	McInnis, 1b	0	0	13	1	0
Sheely, 1b	0	1	11	1	0	J. Collins, rf	0	0	2	0	0
McClellan, rg	0	1	0	0	0	Scott, ss	0	0	3	7	0
Schalk, c	1	3	4	1	0	Ruel, c	0	0	3	1	0
Faber, p	0	0	0	2	0	Myers, p	1	1	1	4	0
Total	2	10	24	14	0	Total	3	8	27	16	0

Sacrifice Hits—Pratt, Faber (2), Foster.
Two-base Hit—Menosky. Three-base Hit—E. Collins.
Bases on Balls—Off Faber, 1; off Myers, 1.
Double Play—Johnson to E. Collins to Sheely.
Struck Out—By Faber, 2; by Myers, 2.

NATIONAL LEAGUE

Boston (at Chicago) — 0 0 1 0 1
Cubs (second game) — 0 0 0 0 0
Scott-Gibson, Boston; Martin-O'Farrell, Cubs.

Philadelphia (at Pittsburg) — 0 3 2 0 0 0 0
Pittsburg — 0 0 1 0 2 3 0
Hubbell-Bruggy, Philadelphia; Cooper-Schmidt, Pittsburg.
Brooklyn-Cincinnati game postponed; wet grounds.

AMERICAN LEAGUE

Cleveland-Washington game postponed; rain.
Detroit-New York game postponed; wet grounds.
St. Louis-Philadelphia game postponed; rain.

RACE RESULTS (SARATOGA)

First—Perigourdine, 15-1; Pahaska, 1-2; Fluff, 5-1.
Second—Oilman, 5-2; Big Heart, 8-5; Pegasus, even.
Third—Sennings Park, 3-5; Thunderclap, 6-5; P. Jones, even.
Fourth—Tody, 4-1; Ararat, 3-5; Billy McLaughlin, 1-4.

RACE RESULTS (HAMILTON)

First—Champlain, 5.95; Buster, 7.90; Humorist, 3.00.
Second—Transpero, 4.80; Monus, 3.85; McCoburn, out.
Third—Wessie B., 7.50; Petie, 4.90; Capt. Scott, out.

RACE RESULTS (WINDSOR)

First—Blarney Boy, 4.80; Tatim, 3.80; Carry On, 3.60.
Second—Hysteria, 5.35; Bumpety Bumps, 3.20; Gahinta, 3.65.

GREECE WARNED AGAINST MOVE ON CONSTANTINOPLE

LONDON, Aug. 3.—(By the Associated Press.)—The allies have warned Greece that an advance on Constantinople by her troops, which now are engaged in war with the Turkish nationalists, will not be tolerated, it was authoritatively stated here today.

No ground exists, however, it is added, for believing that Greece contemplates any such advance, which would bring her into conflict with the allied army of occupation.

Reports from Athens that Great Britain favors a Greek advance on Constantinople were absurd—the exact reverse of the truth. Great Britain, it was declared, is maintaining strict neutrality between Turkey and Greece.

Gets $1,450 Mortgages; Withholds Land; Arrested

Failure to turn over a deed for five acres of land after he had received two real estate mortgages totaling $1,150 and $300 in cash in payment caused A. C. Tisdelle to be held to the grand jury in $3,000 bonds today by Judge Cook on complaint of Leo Weber, 4118 West Monroe street. Tisdelle acknowledged payments, but said the title to the land had not been cleared.

Revolution Breaks Out in Portugal, Says Madrid Report

LONDON, Aug. 3.—A Reuters' dispatch, filed in Madrid yesterday, states that following rumors from Vigo that a revolution had broken out in Lisbon, a telegram received direct from the Portuguese capital said extensive precautionary measures had been taken in that city.

Troops had been brought in from the provinces, the dispatch added, but all was quiet in Lisbon and thruout the country. The troops in Lisbon are said to be confined to their barracks.

British official circles and the Portuguese legation in this city were not able today to throw any light on the reports of disorder in Portugal.

Supreme Court Reverses Sentence of Fled Cashier

LINCOLN, Neb., Aug. 3.—State Sh iff Gus Hyers has started a search Ray A. Lower, former cashier of failed alparaiso (Neb.) State bar whose sentence to the Nebraska pe tentiary on a conviction of loaned n ey to himse'

Mar

San Francisco Chronicle
LEADING NEWSPAPER of the PACIFIC COAST
REG. U. S. PAT. OFF.

WEATHER
SAN FRANCISCO, OAKLAND AND VICINITY
Wednesday foggy, becoming fair; moderate westerly winds.
G. H. WILLSON, Forecaster.
Complete Weather Report on Page 11.

FOUNDED 1865—VOL. CXIX, NO. 19 CCC SAN FRANCISCO, CAL., WEDNESDAY, AUGUST 3, 1921—TWENTY-SIX PAGES DAILY 5 CENTS, SUNDAY 10 CENTS: DAILY AND SUNDAY PER MONTH, $1.15

CHICAGO 'BLACK SOX' ACQUITTED

World Joins in Mourning Death of Enrico Caruso

One Dead, Nine Rescued In $250,000 Mill Fire

FREED PLAYERS JUBILANT OVER JURY'S VERDICT

Seven Diamond Stars Are Cheered Wildly When Decision Is Read

CICOTTE THANKS FOREMAN

Court Officials Take Part in "Love Feast" After End of Trial

Special by Leased Wire to The Chronicle

CHICAGO, August 2.—They acquitted the Black Sox tonight.

Amidst scenes of the wildest enthusiasm, in which the ball players pounded each other on the back and fought to be the first to shake hands with the jurors, the seven ball players and two gamblers charged with conspiracy to throw the 1919 world's series games were acquitted on all charges tonight.

The courtroom, which had been a babel of tongues as the spectators speculated on the verdict, hushed when the jury entered. [illegible]

[illegible] Not Guilty Verdict

Announcement of the verdict was greeted by cheers. Bailiffs pounded for order. For a moment the crowd quieted as the clerk read the verdicts acquitting the others and then they broke forth again.

Bailiffs, noticing Judge Friend's smiles, joined in the whistling and shouting as the judge started for his chambers.

Eddie Cicotte leaped to his feet and pounded Joe Jackson on the back. "Lefty" Williams, his hands hot and moist from worry, shook hands wildly with every person he met.

Cicotte was the first player to the jury box. He grasped the hand of William Barry, the foreman.

"Thanks!" he shouted, "I knew you'd do it!"

Lawyers and Bailiffs Take Part in Display

For the next few minutes the court room was like a love feast as

(Continued on Page 2, Column 6)

Last Portrait of Caruso Greatest Tenor, Dead in Italy

This photograph of Enrico Caruso, taken only a short time before his death, is the last portrait taken before the voice of the world's greatest tenor was stilled. It is the first to arrive in America since Caruso left for Italy.

GREAT TENOR'S VOICE STILLED WHEN AT BEST

Career Comes to Sudden End With Famous Singer's Powers Unimpaired

RELATIVES AT BEDSIDE

Operation Followed Reports to American Friends That He Was Recovering

NAPLES (Italy), August 2 (by the Associated Press).—Enrico Caruso died today.

The great singer, whose ultimate recovery had been hoped for under the benign influences of his own Italy, passed away at 9 a. m. at the Hotel Vesuvius. He had been brought here hurriedly from Sorrento, on the Bay of Naples, where less than a week ago he avowed his returning strength and expressed the conviction that he would sing as before.

He had been able to visit the [illegible] sanctuary of Our Lady of [illegible]

Attends Luncheon Given in His Honor

He went also to the Island of Capri, where he attended a luncheon in his honor. But soon afterward unfavorable symptoms, in the form of a high fever, manifested themselves and his wife telegraphed to a Rome specialist to come to Sorrento; it was then discovered a new internal abscess had developed.

Caruso's removal to Rome for an operation was advised, but he showed such weakness that it was impossible to transfer him further than Naples, where he arrived Sunday evening. Four physicians were called, and their examination showed the presence of a subphrenic abscess, accompanied by severe peritonitis.

Operation Performed In Naples at Noon

An operation to be performed at noon today was decided on, but the patient's condition became suddenly worse at 4:30 a. m. Heart stimulation had been resorted to hourly.

In order that Caruso should not tire himself, the physicians ordered him not to speak, so during his last night he uttered no word. Of the members of his family present at the death bed, the most pathetic was his old mother, who had always clung obstinately to her little home, despite her son's efforts to accustom her to the material comforts of life.

Present also at the bedside were his wife, who was Dorothy, daughter of Park Benjamin of New York; Caruso's little daughter, Gloria, and his son, Rodolfo; his brother; Giovanni;

(Continued on Page 8, Column 2.)

Women Hold Up S. F. Auto Party In Roseburg, Or.

Three Heavily Armed Bandits Drive Up to Car of Orchestra Leader

Three young women, masked and heavily armed, held up and robbed William Prior, leader of the Portola Theater orchestra; his sister, Mrs. George Henshaw, and her husband, early yesterday morning, just outside of Roseburg, Or., and then escaped.

The women bandits drove up alongside of the machine driven by Prior, pointed revolvers at those in Prior's machine and compelled him to stop.

When Prior shut off the gas of his motor, the three women bandits jumped from their black roadster, which was described as of high horse-power, and ordered them to get out on the roadway.

Warn Victims to Do As Told or Suffer Death

"Just do as you are told or we will shoot and kill you," one of the women highway robbers said.

Prior was searched and $40 taken from him. The women robbers decided that his travelers' checks were of no value and they also disdained to [illegible]. They also refused to take his valuable violin.

Mrs. Henshaw was stripped of her jewelry and her purse was taken from her.

Henshaw was also robbed of his money, but his watch was not taken.

All the while the victims were standing in the roadway they were covered by revolvers in the hands of two of the women bandits. Only one was searched at a time, two of the women with the revolvers stood guard, while the third did the searching.

Instead of being allowed to continue on their way toward the California line, in which direction Prior had been going, the women bandits, after taking money and jewelry from the two men and the woman, commanded Prior to turn his machine about and drive in the opposite direction.

The speedster, containing the women robbers, waited until Prior had driven north from Roseburg and then they drove off, coming south and disappeared.

Prior telephoned the police from a farmhouse near Roseburg and a Sheriff's posse was organized to hunt for the three women.

The women, Prior told the police, were heavily armed and their faces

(Continued on Page 2, Column 8)

SHIP ON ROCKS IN GOLDEN GATE AT FORT POINT

Ottillie Fjord From Pago-Pago Loses Way in Dense Fog Entering Harbor

CREW OF 13 ON BOARD

Life-Saving Crew Fails to Reach Craft, but Stand By for Daybreak

The three-masted schooner Ottillie Fjord went on the rocks 500 yards below the old fort at Fort Point at 11 o'clock last night during a heavy fog. The vessel at an early hour this morning was fast on the treacherous rocks and efforts of several tugs to move her were futile.

Captain Hans Olsen with his crew of twelve men were preparing to leave the ship should her seams open. The first distress signals were picked up shortly after the Fjord struck by the Fort Point Coast Guard station.

Coast Guard Crew Go to Distressed Ship

Headed by Captain Clark, the crew of the station went to the scene, but owing to the rough sea, were forced to turn back for a larger boat. At 2 o'clock this morning they again set out for the stranded ship.

The Ottillie Fjord struck the rocks during a heavy fog which settled around the heads shortly before dusk. The point where the ship struck is near the Golden Gate, and for miles the shore line is rocky.

Should the sea become rough, it is feared that the vessel will pound to pieces.

Vessel Left Pago-Pago For This Port May 12

The Ottillie Fjord left Pago-Pago for San Francisco May 12 with a cargo of copra. She is operated by the Pacific States Trading Company and is of 261 tons. She was built in Fairhaven in 1892.

Canary's Autopsy Uncovers Diamond In Crop of Bird

Man Strikes Wife on Jaw for Snoring; Bear Slain After Killing Seventeen Sheep

WILLOWS, August 2.—Mrs. George Simpson, wife of the superintendent of the Furman ranch, yesterday reported finding a one-fourth carat diamond in a digestive organ of a pet canary on which she performed an autopsy. Mrs. Simpson purchased the bird several months ago in San Francisco. Recently it became ill, refused food and would not sing. After the canary died Mrs. Simpson held the post-mortem. The bird's gizzard was found diseased and in an abscess inside the organ she found the diamond. The dealer who sold the bird declared it was imported and Mrs. Simpson is ahead one diamond.

Husband Knocks Wife Out of Bed When She Snores

Because Mrs. Norma Skinner, 1939 Golden Gate avenue, did not cease snoring immediately when her husband, John Skinner, driver of an ice wagon, told her to do so, he is alleged to have struck her in the jaw and knocked her out of bed. Mrs. Skinner, who is soon to become a mother, appeared before Police [illegible] yesterday and secured BY FALL her husband's arrest. Mrs. Skinner asserted that she had caused her husband's arrest once before in Seattle, when he accorded her the same treatment because she snored.

Trapper Kills 500-Pound Bear With Sheep Appetite

PORTLAND (Or.), August 2.—A 500-pound black bear with an exceptional appetite for mutton was trapped and killed in the Santiam national forest Monday night by A. G. Ames, government trapper, according to a report reaching here today. The bear had a record of killing and eating portions of seventeen fat sheep in one night and nine the next. Sheepherders whose flocks were growing smaller as the bear's visits continued sent for Ames, who set two traps and caught bruin the night after his arrival.

Big Snake Hunt Begun In Bone-Dry Burlingame

Special Dispatch to The Chronicle.

BURLINGAME, August 2.—A big snake that loves the bathtub and is fond of the wash bowl of "my lady's boudoir" has been worrying Mrs. A. Stedem, 312 Lincoln avenue.

Mrs. Stedem has often seen the snake coiled up in her bathtub, she declares, and at other times it has been seen in the wash basin. Each time she has carefully locked the bathroom door and summoned City Clerk J. R. Murphy and Frank Marshall, superintendent of the city water works, to the rescue.

But each time the serpent has mysteriously disappeared. Burlingame is a dry town and there is no doubt about it being a real snake, police declare.

3-ALARM BLAZE AT NORTH BEACH FULL OF THRILLS

Children Carried Out of Adjacent Dwellings Endangered by Flames

EXCITEMENT KILLS MAN

High Wind at One Time Threatens to Carry Fire to Other Property

One man dropped dead, nine children were rescued, and the plant of the International Milling Company, 781 Beach street, was destroyed by a fire last night which caused a loss estimated at close to $250,000. Joe Partineco, 56 years old, and living at 860 North Point street, died from excitement as he watched a baby being carried from a house adjoining the burning structure. Three alarms were sounded, and with the arrival of the first piece of apparatus, the four-story building housing the milling company was a mass of flames.

Break Into Houses [illegible]

[illegible] Corporal Aloysius O'Brien of North End Station, Dr. F. R. Carfagni, 2287 Green street, and Eugene Fappiano, 2013 North Point street, when more than a dozen small houses adjoining the burning mill were threatened, the three men rushed into the places returning with the terror stricken children. In the home of Antonio Alberto, 3016 Larkin street, Mrs. Alberto and her three children were rescued with difficulty. Mrs. Alberto at first refused to leave the house. Two of her children were ill while an 18-months-old baby was found in a rear room which was filled with smoke.

Two children, four and six years old, were brought out of the home of Peter Connas, 3008 Larkin street. Breaking through a window in the place occupied by Peter Imperiala, which adjoined, two children, were brought to safety.

Attracted by cries in the home of Manuel Foppioni, O'Brien, assisted by Carfagni and Foppiano, carried two children, three and four years old to the street.

Policemen and Doctor Rescue Children

The fire was discovered by P. J. Ward, special officer. When the flames were at their height, a strong west wind began sweeping over the scene, endangering the private dwell-

(Continued on Page 2, Column 7)

Modesto Fugitive Captured by Ruse

Alleged Criminal Suddenly "Covered" With Gun

MODESTO, August 2.—Frank Hurlburt, who was being sought by a posse under Sheriff R. L. Dallas for an alleged attack on Mrs. Carl Konow, wife of a rancher near here, was captured by H. R. Drake, rancher and member of the posse, and a companion, after he had left his hiding place in the bed of the Stanislaus river, a few miles from here, and sought a ride in Drake's wagon.

After riding with Hurlburt for a short distance Drake suddenly whipped out his revolver and covered Hurlburt, while Drake's companion took two revolvers from the hunted man's pockets.

Hurlburt was brought to the county jail here, where it was reported by the Sheriff that he had admitted the attack on Mrs. Konow.

After leaving his hiding place Hurlburt struck out along the highway toward Escalon, apparently unaware that the posse members were so close to him. He had a camping outfit strapped to his back.

Reputed Relative Of Harding Drowns

SALT LAKE CITY, August 2.—Lewis H. Harding, secretary of the Salt Lake Rotary Club, prominent in Masonic circles, and reported to be a distant relative of President Harding, was drowned while on a fishing trip at Jackson's lake, near Moran, Wyo., today, according to a telegram received by his business partner.

GASOLINE PRICE CUT TWO CENTS

Gasoline in San Francisco costs 23 cents a gallon today, as the result of a cut of two cents a gallon in the price of the fuel announced last night by officials of the Standard Oil Company. The reduction in price announced last night, takes effect immediately, and is the result of telegraphic orders received by the local officials yesterday after-

Continued on Page 2, Column 3)

Coal Men Indicted For Price Fixing

Baltimore Coal Exchange Members in Trouble

BALTIMORE, August 2.—The officers, directors and individual members of the Baltimore Coal Exchange were indicted by the grand jury on charges of making a monoply through a combine to manipulate and fix the price of anthracite coal.

The evidence placed before the grand jury by State's Attorney Leach indicates that the alleged combine was formed the fifteenth of last August.

The indictment avers that 90 per cent of the coal dealers in Baltimore are members of the coal exchange and are parties to a combine or trust for the manipulation of prices. Twenty-six men, including Hugh C. Hill, president of the exchange, were named by the grand jury as parties to the alleged monopoly.

OAKLAND VOTES AGAINST STRIKE

The Alameda county Building Trades Council voted against joining in the general strike proposed by the San Francisco Building Trades Council at a joint meeting of the two councils in Oakland last night.

Following the vote, which was the subject of protest by San Francisco representatives present, members of the Alameda council stated that while they believed the vote was representative of union opinion in Oakland, and the county in general, the council did not wish to dictate to the rank and file.

For this reason the council de-

(Continued on Page 2, Column 5)

U. S. Investigating Chilean Incident

SANTIAGO (Chile), August 2.—The Chilean foreign ministry today received cable advices from the Chilean ambassador at Washington, saying reports of the address of Albert Douglas, head of the United States delegation to the Peruvian centennial celebration last week in Lima, had caused a great impression in the American capital and that immediate measures had been taken by the American State Department to investigate the real facts.

WASHINGTON, August 2.—Unofficial reports that remarks of Albert Douglas, chief of the American mission representing the United States at the Peruvian independence centennial, had offended Chile, caused the State Department to cable today to the American embassy for a copy of the commissioner's speech.

Bystander Risks Life to Save Girl

Mechanic Swims to Rescue of Drowning Bather

Jack Meehan, a mechanic employed in the machine shops of Crane & Company, is a hero today as a result of a thrilling rescue from drowning of twenty-year-old Eva Collins, a San Francisco girl, at Guerneville last Thursday.

Swimming in the Russian river with a girl companion Miss Collins waded out of her depth. Meehan, who was standing on the beach, heard her screams for help and plunged into the water. He had reached her side and the girl gripped him with a drowning person's strength. Joseph Moynahan, of 97 Stillman street, who was in a canoe close by, hurried to their aid and succeeded in bringing the couple ashore.

Meehan is a typical blushing hero and refused to make a statement other than the rescue was a fact.

Aviator Rescues Man From Drowning

SAN DIEGO, August 2.—Lieutenant Robert H. Harrell of the Pacific air force, flying a powerful seaplane, today rescued Private J. H. Higgins of the marine corps from drowning in San Diego harbor.

Higgins, in a small skiff, capsized and he lay over in the water, one hand grasping the skiff. Lieutenant Harrell, flying overhead, saw his predicament and brought his plane down to the water and taxied to the skiff. Higgins was floating face down when he was reached. The pilot dragged the marine into the cockpit of the seaplane and flew to the North island naval air station. There Higgins was resuscitated.

Warrants Issued in Chicago Liquor Case

Special by Leased Wire to The Chronicle

CHICAGO, August 2.—Judge Landis issued bench warrants today for Mr. and Mrs. James W. Walsh, alleged leaders of the "de luxe liquor ring," which is said to have peddled between $75,000 and $100,000 worth of booze to prominent Chicagoans. An additional warrant was signed for John E. McGrath, who was indicted with the others.

Today Assistant District Attorney Roy J. Egan will leave for Detroit where the trio are now at liberty on bonds. A removal hearing will be held tomorrow.

Film Stars Named By Whisky Runner

Ex-Mayor of S. F. Is Also Mentioned in Case

Special Dispatch to The Chronicle.

LOS ANGELES, August 2.—A former mayor of San Francisco and a dozen or more stars of movieland were mentioned in connection with an alleged liquor smuggling plot unfolded to Government officers by Fred McCoy, following his arrest near Tia Juana with a large quantity of contraband liquor in his possession. Assistant United States District Attorney Thomas Green is investigating McCoy's story, and if it turns out to be true a liquor scandal eclipsing any that has been uncovered since the Nation went dry will result, according to that official. McCoy's tale mentioned a well organized smuggling ring with nightly meetings at the U. S. Grant Hotel in San Diego.

According to the Federal Prosecutor McCoy was arrested by customs agents last Friday and a seven-passenger touring car with three concealed tanks containing high grade whisky seized. He became nervous, the officers reported, and threatened to spill the beans in full detail unless friends immediately put up bonds for his release. He got into telegraphic communication with Ben Cohen, well known in the moving picture world here, and his bond of $100 was furnished. A fashionably dressed woman appeared with Cohen at the jail. According to statements attributed to McCoy San Diego was the headquarters of the booze running syndicate. Names mentioned by McCoy in connection with the plot may furnish the basis for a number of federal warrants against well known persons within a few days, Green stated.

Combine on Sea, Says La Follette

Declares American and British Interests Allied

WASHINGTON, August 2.—An "alliance" between American and British financiers to aid British shipping interests, was charged in the Senate today by Senator La Follette, of Wisconsin. J. P. Morgan & Co. and associates, he said, had "combined" with British financiers, the Morgan company controlling, through directorates, railroads which transported American products for shipment on British ships. The British shipping interests, he said, were represented through the International Mercantile Marine Company, which was thoroughly British, although supposed to be an American corporation.

Senator La Follette spoke in behalf of his resolution for Congressional inquiry. The shipping board's recent attempt to dispossess the United States Mail Company of a fleet of ships was said by Senator La Follette apparently to have behind it employes of the board "with old-time British shipping affiliations."

GIANTS AND YANKS MEET IN 1921 WORLD'S SERIES

BABE RUTH, OUTFIELD. YANKEES

BOB MEUSEL, OUTFIELD. YANKEES

FRED TONEY, PITCHER, GIANTS.

WAITE HOYT. PITCHER • YANKEES

ELMER MILLER OUTFIELD • YANKEES

RIP COLLINS, PITCHER • YANKEES

CARL MAYS. PITCHER, YANKEES

CECIL CAUSEY, PITCHER, GIANTS.

PHIL DOUGLAS PITCHER GIANTS

DAVE BANCROFT, S.STOP • GIANTS

WALLIE PIPP, 1ST BASE • YANKEES

ART NEHF, PITCHER, GIANTS

JESS BARNES, PITCHER • GIANTS

BOB SHAWKEY, PITCHER, YANKEES

WALLIE SCHANG, CATCHER YANKEES

JOHN J. McGRAW, MANAGER GIANTS

FRANK FRISCH THIRD BASE GIANTS

GEORGE KELLY FIRST BASE GIANTS

ROSS YOUNG OUTFIELD GIANTS

MILLER HUGGINS MANAGER YANKEES

American League Has Far Better Record in Championship Play; McGraw Has Well Balanced Club; Huggins' Stars Inconsistent.

By FREDERICK G. LIEB,
Official Scorer at Polo Grounds for Both Major Leagues.

What chance has the National league to score a victory in the 1921 world's series, which begins Wednesday? That is the question of the hour. And there is no gainsaying that the National league has been a bear for taking world's series punishment. The parent major league has won only two series since 1909, and one of those was the crooked series thrown by the White Sox in 1919.

In sizing up the Giants, we want to go on record as saying that McGraw's club probably is the best club entered into the world's series by the National league since the Braves scored their notable victory of 1914. Some call it McGraw's best ball club, but that is an exaggeration. The present club has no Mathewson nor McGinnity, not even a Marquard or a Tesreau. Burns and Young both are flyhawks, and, though Meusel is not as nimble an outfielder as his two running mates, Emil is a fairly able defensive player.

In Smith and Snyder the Giants have perhaps the best balanced catching staff in the major leagues. There are better catchers than either Earl or Frank, but no club is equipped with two catchers of such high grade. By using Smith, a left-handed batsman, against right-handers, and Snyder, a right-handed hitter, against southpaws, McGraw is able to throw his full batting strength into each game without interfering with the catching efficiency of his team.

The Giants have a dangerous, versatile attack, a sort of combination of the old base-running tactics of McGraw's National league champions of 1911, 1912 and 1913, and the slam-bang system of the modern Yankees. The Giants can play the hit-and-run game, and play it well, and they also can produce their share of slugging. They don't hit them quite as far as their New York American league brethren, but McGraw has quite an able colony of home-run hitters.

Giants Have Some Busters.

No National league pitcher will deny that George Kelly can smack 'em. George had twenty-two homers up to Labor day, while the catching department, Snyder and Smith, boasted of seventeen four-baggers between them. All told, the Giants had rapped eighty-one home-runs, a healthy collection, we will say.

The New York Nationals were hitting .303 when we closed our figures, the first time the National league ever put a team hitting .300 into a world's series.

The Giants rank far above the Yanks in base-running. Frankie Frisch, who has shown the way along the base paths to all major rivals this year, had forty-nine stolen bases to his credit when we closed our books.

The Giants again will be in charge of John McGraw, a veteran of four Temple Cup series and five modern world's series clashes between the pennant winners of the National and American leagues. It is true that heretofore world's series managerial experience has not helped McGraw much in contests with American league adversaries; but the manager of the bench cannot catch flies in the outfield, nor strike out a Frank Baker in the pinch.

Though admiring the "brute strength" of the Huggins band, the writer does not consider the Yankees a great club, though it is a team which might slug its way through to a victory in a world's series, as it has slugged its way through the American league.

The Yanks, however, are erratic and inconsistent—a club which will rise to the heights one day only to descend to the lowest depths of mediocrity the next. New York's splendid record for two years against the strong Cleveland team and its miserable record against the seventh-place White Sox, who beat them in thirteen out of twenty-two games this year, is an example of Yankee inconsistency.

The New York Americans also are a team which must win by a big margin or they will not win at all. It is not a one-run club—a team which can nose out an adversary by scores of 3 to 2, 4 to 3 and 2 to 1. They are at their best in slamming out victories by scores of 12 to 5, 14 to 4 or such lopsided figures. Usually the Yanks drop the close ones.

Good Pitching Stops 'Em.

Good pitching stops the Yanks. Faber, Kerr, Rommel, Uhle, Shocker and a few others have caused the Yankees trouble all year, but when they get just an ordinary pitcher they surely murder him. It is just a club which falls for so-called "jinx" pitchers. Kerr has taken the Yanks six times this season. Faber, Shocker and Rommel four times and Uhle licked them three games.

Ruth overtowers the entire club, and he can well make opposing hurlers tremble. No player in the long history of baseball equals him as an individual scoring machine.

Bob Meusel, Frank Baker, Roger Peckinpaugh, Wallie Schang, Walter Pipp and Aaron Ward are other noted extra-base sluggers. Once this club gets going against a faltering pitcher it is not long before it will score a knockout.

As a club, the Yankees hit .303, the same batting figure the Giants boast, but the big strength is ability to hit them to and over the fences.

The Yankee pitching is as inconsistent as the rest of the team. As the season draws near to a close Waite Hoyt, former Brooklyn scholastic star, is the most dependable hurler on Huggins's staff. The club has the faculty of always scoring big for Mays, and hard hitting has helped Carl to many victories.

Shawkey's expected slump late in the season has worked a hardship on the rest of the staff. At the time of writing Bob had been knocked out of the box in his last four games and was experiencing one of his worst slumps since coming into the American league.

(Copyright, 1921, by Al Munro Elias.)

THE GIANTS.

BATTING RECORDS.									FIELDING RECORDS.				
Player and pos.	Gs.	AB.	R.	H.	2B.	3B.	HR.	TB.	SB.	PC.	PO.	A.	E.	P.C.
Sallee, p	35	22	2	8	1	0	0	9	0	.364	3	18	0	1.000
Young, rf	122	426	74	142	21	15	3	202	21	.333	213	15	7	.970
Berry, util.	9	6	0	2	0	1	0	4	0	.333	6	0	0	1.000
Frisch, 3b	133	538	103	178	27	15	9	259	49	.331	212	387	24	.961
Smith, c	79	200	29	66	7	4	9	108	3	.330	168	55	6	.974
Meusel, lf	128	506	82	165	27	11	14	256	12	.326	240	24	11	.960
Bancroft, ss	133	526	107	167	23	10	6	228	14	.317	348	460	31	.963
Snyder, c	93	264	30	83	11	1	8	120	2	.314	256	89	6	.983
Gaston, util	9	16	1	5	1	1	0	8	0	.312	4	0	0	1.000
Gonzales, util	10	16	1	5	0	0	0	5	0	.312	40	1	1	.976
Kelly, 1b	130	508	81	155	40	7	22	275	4	.305	1334	94	16	.989
Burns, cf	130	541	104	164	24	9	4	218	19	.303	320	16	11	.968
Brown, util	67	124	16	36	5	2	0	45	1	.290	62	2	3	.955
Rawlings, 2b	127	487	50	137	20	3	2	169	8	.281	300	428	24	.968
Cunningham, util	33	65	10	17	2	1	1	24	0	.262	33	1	0	1.000
Stengel, util	38	74	9	19	2	1	0	23	1	.257	31	5	1	.973
Nehf, p	35	78	9	18	2	0	0	20	0	.231	14	65	5	.936
Ryan, p	35	44	2	9	1	0	0	10	0	.205	5	31	0	1.000
Douglas, p	36	69	5	14	2	0	1	19	1	.203	5	52	2	.966
Toney, p	37	81	10	16	1	0	3	26	1	.197	4	58	2	.969
Barnes, p	39	89	9	17	0	1	0	19	1	.191	20	60	0	1.000
Causey, p	13	21	2	4	2	0	0	6	0	.190	2	13	2	.941
Shea, p	6	8	0	1	0	0	0	1	0	.125	2	5	0	1.000
Grand totals		4709	737	1428	219	82	81	2054	137	.303	3622	1879	152	.973

Sacrifice hits—Frisch 21, Young 18, Bancroft 18, Kelly 15, Rawlings 14, Nehf 8, Burns 7, Douglas 5, Sallee 4, Smith 4, Meusel 3, Brown 3, Cunningham 3, Ryan 3, Barnes 3, Snyder 2, Gonzales 1 and Toney 1. Total, 133 sacrifice hits.

Smith had 4 passed balls and Snyder 2.

The following Giants bat right-handed—Sallee, Berry, Meusel, Snyder, Gaston, Gonzales, Kelly, Burns, Brown, Rawlings, Cunningham, Ryan, Douglas, Toney, Causey and Shea.

These Giants bat left-handed—Young, Smith, Stengel, Nehf and Barnes.

Frisch and Bancroft are turn-over batters.

THE YANKEES.

BATTING RECORDS.									FIELDING RECORDS.				
Player and pos.	Gs.	AB.	R.	H.	2B.	3B.	HR.	TB.	SB.	PC.	PO.	A.	E.	P.C.
Ruth, lf	127	449	150	173	38	12	51	388	14	.385	305	16	9	.973
DeVormer, c	15	32	4	12	2	0	0	14	1	.375	24	6	2	.937
Meusel, rf	124	498	83	165	35	14	18	285	13	.331	214	28	17	.934
Ward, 2b	127	470	63	151	26	7	4	203	6	.321	242	402	27	.960
Mays, p	44	128	14	41	4	1	2	53	0	.320	10	93	2	.981
Baker, 3b	85	320	46	97	16	2	9	144	8	.303	91	170	11	.960
Schang, c	111	364	58	109	24	3	4	151	6	.299	422	86	11	.979
Roth, util	38	142	27	42	3	2	2	55	1	.296	65	6	3	.959
Pipp, 1b	127	492	77	144	31	8	6	209	12	.293	1344	75	10	.993
Shawkey, p	82	82	13	24	2	1	1	31	0	.293	13	31	3	.936
Peckinpaugh, ss	124	477	111	139	24	6	7	196	2	.291	202	348	37	.943
Fewster, cf	30	197	38	55	15	0	0	70	3	.279	70	4	2	.974
Hawks, util	39	69	15	19	2	3	2	33	0	.275	30	0	1	.968
Miller, cf	30	128	23	35	4	3	2	51	1	.274	64	5	5	.932
Mitchell, util	12	36	4	9	0	0	0	9	1	.250	12	23	6	.854
McNally, 3b	45	125	19	31	1	1	0	34	2	.248	47	87	7	.950
Piercy, p	11	27	2	6	2	0	0	8	0	.222	3	19	3	.880
Hoyt, p	37	88	7	19	1	1	0	22	0	.207	11	56	4	.944
Collins, p	27	54	4	11	0	1	0	13	0	.204	2	28	2	.937
Ferguson, p	17	20	1	4	0	0	0	4	0	.200	2	13	0	1.000
Quinn, p	28	36	1	7	1	0	0	8	0	.194	1	31	0	1.000
Hofmann, c	22	60	7	11	2	0	1	16	0	.167	69	11	5	.941
Harper, p	15	10	1	1	0	0	0	1	0	.100	0	3	0	1.000
Grand totals		4304	768	1305	236	65	100	1908	70	.303	3303	1541	167	.967

Sacrifice hits—Pipp 30, Peckinpaugh 28, Ward 19, Baker 9, McNally 8, Hoyt 8, Miller 7, Meusel 7, Shawkey 7, Schang 6, Mays 5, Roth 3, Quinn 3, Ruth 2, Fewster 2, DeVormer 2, Collins 2, Hawks 1 and Mitchell 1.

The following Yankees bat right-handed—Devormer, Meusel, Ward, Roth, Shawkey, Peckinpaugh, Fewster, Miller, McNally, Piercy, Hoyt, Ferguson, Quinn and Hofmann.

These Yankees bat left-handed—Ruth, Mays, Baker, Pipp, Hawks and Harper.

Schang, Collins and Mitchell are turn-over batters.

Woodchuck Hole Gives Player Circuit Clout

If the big league outfielders had to do their fly stabbing under conditions faced by outer gardeners in the Adirondack league their fielding averages would not look so well in the annual baseball guides.

In a recent game between Malone and Loon Lake, at the latter resort, one of the Malone players busted one on the trade-mark for a humming bird into short right field. The outfielder came in fast, trying hard for a pickup, but as he stopped to scoop the ball it faded from the scene.

A frantic search revealed that the old apple had shot cleanly into a woodchuck hole, down which it sailed so far that a new ball had to be put in play. It was probably the shortest home-run on record.

Fans Pay Huge Sums for World Series

More than 178,700 persons paid their way to see the world series games last year between the Brooklyn Nationals and the Cleveland Americans, in which the latter team won five games to two. The official gross receipts were $564,800.

The receipts were distributed as follows:

Contesting players' share	$161,162.06
Purse for Cleveland (twenty-seven men)	96,697.24
Purse for Brooklyn (twenty-nine men)	64,464.82
Each Cleveland player	4,168.00
Each Brooklyn player	2,419.00
Purse for second place teams (about fifty-two men)	27,431.00
Purse for third place teams (about fifty-five men)	21,488.28
Each second place player (about)	685.80
Each third place player (about)	400.00
Cleveland club's share	73,359.32
Brooklyn club's share	73,359.31
American league treasury	73,359.32
National league treasury	73,359.31
National commission's shares	56,480.00

World's series attendance and receipts by years, since 1905:

Year	Games	Attendance	Receipts	Players' Pool
1905	5	91,033	$ 68,405	$ 27,391
1906	6	99,864	106,550	33,401
1907	5	78,068	101,728	54,933
1908	5	62,232	94,975	46,173
1909	7	145,807	188,862	66,925
1910	5	124,222	179,980	79,072
1911	6	179,851	342,364	127,910
1912	8	252,237	490,833	147,572
1913	5	150,992	325,979	135,164
1914	4	110,009	225,739	121,899
1915	5	143,351	320,361	144,899
1916	5	162,359	385,590	162,927
1917	5	185,691	425,878	152,888
1918	6	128,483	179,619	69,527
1919	8	236,928	722,414	195,262

Coane Reported as Previous Stockholder

According to information from a reliable source, Robert Coane, reported as having bought the Chandler interests in the Philadelphia National league baseball club, has been a stockholder in the company for some time.

The informant refused to say how much stock Mr. Coane formerly held and when he secured it, but did say that the wealthy clubman had stock previous to securing the Chandler interests last week.

It is reported that Mr. Coane is now a majority stockholders, as the Chandler interests are said to have been one-fourth of the entire stock. In addition to Mr. Coane, William F. Baker, president of the club; Colonel Edward T. Murphy and L. C. Ruch, the latter a lifelong friend of Baker and a New Yorker, are the stockholders of the club.

The report that Mr. Coane has secured at least a fourth interest in the club sets at rest rumors that Pittsburg men have been after the club and had secured an option on the stock.

NORTH ENDERS NEGLECT VOTE

Curley Censures Residents for Low Registration

The North End was severely censured yesterday afternoon for its low percentage of voters, by ex-Mayor James M. Curley, who, at a mass meeting held by the Pathfinders' Club at the North Bennett Street Industrial School, declared that "until the residents of such districts cease to neglect their citizenship privileges, no legislation can possibly be passed relieving their economic situation."

"Only one woman in 10 in this ward," Mr. Curley asserted, "has registered herself as a voter. The percentage of registered men is almost as low. It has been demonstrated that no American party or governing body at present will or can make laws relieving the pressure brought on working people by our intensive system. To pass the laws that are needed, laws assuring the prohibition of child labor, laws providing for the support of the aged, and laws defending and protecting maternity, the people whom those laws will aid must learn the need of them, and the means of getting them."

TEN CAUGHT IN RAID ON ROXBURY GAME

Ten men were arrested yesterday afternoon in a gambling raid conducted by the police of the Dudley street station at 171 Hampden street, Roxbury. Seven men were booked on the charge of gambling and three on the charge of being present where gaming implements were found.

CHANGES IN 'TECH' FACULTY

11 Promotions; Three New Members On Staff

Seventeen changes in the faculty of the Institute of Technology are announced by the Tech corporation for the ensuing college year which begins today at the Cambridge institution. Of these, eleven are promotions, three additions of new members, while the remaining three are resignations.

TO FULL PROFESSORS

Harold K. Barrows of the civil engineering department; George E. Russell, also of the civil engineering department, and Frederick G. Keyes of the chemistry department have been raised from the grade of associate professor to that of full professor. Professor Keyes is also director of the research laboratory of physical chemistry.

Assistant Professors Theodore N. Taft of the mechanical engineering department, C. R. Hayward of the mining engineering department, H. B. Phillips of the mathematical department and D. A. MacInnes of the chemistry department have been promoted to the rank of associate professor. I. H. Cowdry of the mechanical engineering department and F. S. Dellenbaugh of the electrical engineering department have been raised from instructors to assistant professors. L. W. Parsons and C. S. Venable, both research associates of applied chemistry, are also made assistant professors.

Professors Henry W. Keith, formerly of the department of naval architecture and marine engineering, has again joined the institute after several years' absence. Other additions to the Tech faculty staff are Captain William B. Wright, who will be a member of the military science and tactics division, and J. W. Bunker, who joins the biology department as assistant professor.

Professor Edward F. Miller, head of the mechanical engineering department, was elected chairman of the Tech faculty to succeed Dr. H. P. Talbot, who is now acting dean. Professor Miller has been connected with Tech ever since his graduation in 1886. In 1912 he succeeded Gaetano Lanza as head of the mechanical engineering department, while also holding the post of director of the engineering laboratories. He has been a prominent member of many State commissions on boiler regulation and during the war was appointed by the government to conduct the work of intensively training marine engineers for the emergency fleet. Professor Miller is also a member of the administrative committee, which has been conducting the affairs of the Institute ever since the late Dr. Maclaurin's death.

The only resignations from the faculty this year are those of former Dean Burton, who left to go to California; of Professor Dwight Porter, who retired to private life after serving Tech for 39 years, and of Professor P. G. Woodward of the department of chemistry.

COURSES BY STATE WILL OPEN TODAY

Classes to Include Spanish, Italian and French

Enrolments for eight university classes to be organized in Boston in the month of October will be accepted at the State House. Five of these are language classes, including courses in conversational French, Italian, Spanish, and two courses in oral English.

CLASS TONIGHT

The class in conversational Spanish opens tonight at 8 p. m. at the Lecture Hall, Boston Public Library. Senor Charles A. Monge will again conduct the course. The first regular meeting of the class in conversational French will be held on Tuesday, Oct. 4, at the Lecture Hall of the library, the elementary sections of the class meeting at 4:45 and 8 p. m. and the advanced section meeting at 7 p. m.

Captain Andre Morize, professor of French literature, Harvard University, is giving instruction in French. Students of conversational French will meet in the Continuation School, Brimmer building, Common street, at 5 p. m., Thursday, Oct. 13, for their first regular class session. Mr. Paul V. Donovan is in charge of instruction in Italian.

Automobile Courses

At the Massachusetts Normal Art School, corner Exeter and Newbury streets, classes in oral English story-telling, public speaking, and gasolene automobiles will be organized. The gasolene automobile course will be opened to operators of cars on Thursday, Oct. 13, at 7:30 p. m. This 10-lesson course is offered to the public under the instruction of Arthur Ashworth. The course in oral English story-telling will begin Tuesday, Oct. 18, at 7:30 p. m. and the class in public speaking will begin Friday, Oct. 21, at 7:30 p. m. Mrs. Margaret Shipman Jamison will give instruction in story-telling and William Hoffman of the Boston University faculty will instruct students of public speaking.

Harvard Co-operating

Harvard University is again co-operating with the division in its arrangements to give accountancy classes in the college buildings. Sever Hall will be used by the State to accommodate elementary accounting classes and classes in principles of accounting. Principles of accounting is open to those who have completed the elementary course. Over 1000 students were enrolled in this course last year and of this number it is expected that 600 students will take the advanced course this year. This record-breaking enrolment indicated the increased demand for accountancy courses in Massachusetts, especially in large centres. The class in elementary accounting opens Wednesday, Oct. 25, at 7 p. m., and the class in principles of accounting begins Friday, Oct. 28, at 7 p. m. Enrolment for these two and all State classes may be made at the first class meeting, as well as by written or personal application made through the office of the Division of University Extension at the State House, Room 217.

PREMIER IN LONDON SOON

Expected to Call Cabinet Meeting Thursday

LONDON, Oct. 2 (United News).—Returning to London, according to his present plans, on Wednesday, Premier Lloyd George will call a Cabinet meeting Thursday at which the British representatives to the Irish peace conference probably will be elected.

Undoubtedly Mr. Lloyd George himself will act as chief of the delegation, although it is probable that he will not attend every session of the conference himself.

SECOND NANTASKET BOAT BREAKS DOWN

Two hundred or more Sunday pleasure seekers on board the Nantasket Steamboat Line Steamer Old Colony were furnished with un-looked for excitement yesterday afternoon when the boat became disabled off Bumkin Island on its 2:15 o'clock trip from Boston. The steering apparatus went wrong and for nearly a half hour the craft was jockeyed back and forth until, after it had turned circles many times, the crew finally worked it to the pier at Pemberton.

The passengers were disembarked and a special train of the New Haven took them to Nantasket over the electric branch. The Old Colony was sent to the Supply Pier at Hull for repairs. She tied up beside the Steamer Betty Alden which had an almost similar mishap a short distance from the same place just 24 hours previously.

HAIL OIL GIVES MIKE TOO SMOOTH TONGUE

With pocket bulging from a pint of alcohol mixed with highly perfumed hair oil, Michael Mulkern, six feet one, of Kerry, Ireland, and South End, undertook to deliver a lecture on the Common to a crowd of 100 toward Saturday midnight, and got himself incarcerated for intoxication.

It received special notice yesterday morning becaue Mr. Mulkearn upon leaving the Lagrange street cellroom claimed that his tongue was hanging out and they had no right to deprive him of the "hair of the dog." In fact he might get mad and go to court about it. If he does it may make a better story.

WINDOW DEDICATED

Dedicatory services were held yesterday in the First Baptist Church, Melrose, when a memorial window installed on the Main street side of the church auditorium, and donated by Thomas D. Lockwood, a former treasurer of the church, was unveiled and accepted by the trustees. A window opposite on the other side, was a gift from Mr. Lockwood, and dedicated in 1915.

$100,000 FOR CANCER REMEDY

Prize for Medicinal Relief by Anonymous Donor

NEW YORK, Oct. 2.—A prize of $100,000 for the discovery of a medicinal remedy to relieve cancer has been offered by an anonymous donor through the Cosmopolitan Cancer Research Society of Brooklyn, it was announced today.

The reward will be known as the Cosmopolitan cancer prize and was made in anticipation of the observance of National Cancer Week, Oct. 30 to Nov. 5, when physicians, surgeons, chemists and scientists will hold nation-wide clinics and conferences dealing with the disease. Requirements of the award call for mothod of treatment and full information, with therapeutic proof in at least 50 cases.

NEWTON BOY INJURED

John Brennan, 7-year-old son of Mr. and Mrs. James Brennan of 11 Church street, Newton, was struck and knocked down by an automobile last night near his home. He was not seriously injured, and after being treated at the office of Dr. Emerson of Church street the lad was taken to his home.

TELLER DENIES TAKING FUNDS

Hill Says He Didn't Know Money Was Missing

Clarence O. Hill, the Belmont bank teller who was arrested on Saturday charged with larcency of $2500 from the Waverley Trust Company where he was employed, denies the theft and charges that someone else must have taken the money he is accused of removing from the bank's deposits.

"I don't know what happened to the money. I never took it. I never spent a cent of anyone's money but my own. I didn't know there was any money missing until the detectives sent for me to visit their office," he declared yesterday when seen at his home, 40 Pleasant street.

COMPLETE BOX SCORE OF THE GAME

5:30 P. M.

SPORTING EXTRA

The Evening Bulletin.

5:30 P. M.

VOLUME LIX. NO. 241. FRIDAY—Fair PROVIDENCE, R. I., THURSDAY, OCTOBER 13, 1921. 40 PAGES TWO CENTS. 14 Cents Per Week Delivered by Carrier.

GIANTS WIN WORLD'S SERIES CHAMPIONSHIP

ROGER PECKINPAUGH

Yankee Captain Whose Error in First Inning Allowed Giants to Score With Run That Meant World Title

COMPLETE BOX SCORE OF EIGHTH WORLD SERIES GAME

GIANTS

	AB	R	H	PO	A	E
Burns, m.....	4	0	1	3	0	0
Bancroft, s...	3	1	0	0	4	0
Frisch, 3......	4	0	0	2	3	0
Young, r.....	2	0	1	0	0	0
Kelly, 1b.....	4	0	0	13	1	0
E. Meusel, l...	4	0	1	1	0	0
Rawlings, 2...	4	0	3	4	4	0
Snyder, c.....	2	0	0	4	0	0
Nehf, p.......	4	0	0	0	0	0
Totals.....	31	1	6	27	12	0

YANKEES

	AB	R	H	PO	A	E
Fewster, l....	3	0	0	2	0	0
Peck'p'gh, s..	2	0	0	2	2	1
Miller, m.....	4	0	1	1	0	0
R. Meusel, r...	4	0	0	2	0	0
Pipp, 1b......	3	0	1	11	0	0
Ward, 2......	3	0	1	0	2	0
Baker, 3......	3	0	0	1	3	0
Schang, c.....	3	0	0	8	1	0
Hoyt, p.......	3	0	1	0	3	0
†Ruth	1	0	0	0	0	0
Totals.....	29	0	4	27	11	1

INNINGS	1	2	3	4	5	6	7	8	9	R	H	E
GIANTS	1	0	0	0	0	0	0	0	0	1	6	0
YANKEES	0	0	0	0	0	0	0	0	0	0	4	1

Struck out—By Hoyt 7; by Nehf 3.
Base on balls—Off Hoyt 4; off Nehf 5.
Wild pitch—Nehf.
First base on errors—Giants 1.
Left on bases—Giants 9; Qankees 7.
Stolen base—Young.
Two-base hits—Rawlings 2.
Sacrifice hits—Snyder 2.
Double play—Bancroft to Rawlings to Kelly.

†Batted for Pipp in ninth.

DAVE BANCROFT

Field Leader of Giants Who Scored for Giants in First Inning That Meant World Title for His Team

DEATH OF SENATOR KNOX MOURNED BY OFFICIAL WASHINGTON

Expressions of Sorrow Voiced at Passing of Notable Figure.—Services To-morrow to be Followed by Funeral at Valley Forge Saturday.

By the Associated Press

Washington, Oct. 13.—Official Washington mourned to-day the death of Philander C. Knox, Senator from Pennsylvania, who died last night suddenly from a stroke of paralysis. From all quarters, executive, legislative, judicial and diplomatic, came expressions of regret at the passing of a notable figure in domestic and world affairs.

Funeral arrangements, completed to-day, provided for services here and at the late Senator's home at Valley Forge, Pa. Services will be held here at 11 o'clock to-morrow at St. John's Episcopal Church, with President Harding, Cabinet members, Senators and Representatives, members of the Diplomatic Corps and others prominent in political, professional and social life, in attendance.

Members of the Senate foreign relations committee, on which Senator Knox had a leading place, are to be the honorary pall bearers. The active bearers, all personal friends of the family, will be Maj. Charles Wilson, Maj. J. Reuben Clark, Jr., William Watson Smith of Pittsburgh, Frederick D. Faust, Walter E. Clark, formerly Governor of Alaska, and W. F. Martin, the Senator's secretary.

After to-morrow's services the body will be taken to Valley Forge to rest Friday night in the book room of the Senator's country home there. Services will be held in Valley Forge Memorial Chapel Saturday at 2:30 p. m. The body will be interred in the chapel, where President Harding spoke last summer during a week-end visit at the Knox home.

Flags at Half-Mast

As a mark of respect, Capitol flags were at half-mast to-day, to remain for 30 days, the official mourning period.

Senator Knox was stricken suddenly last evening as he was about to enter the dining room of his residence on K street for dinner. He suffered a paralytic stroke and died within 15 minutes without regaining consciousness. Mrs.

Continued on Page 4, Col. 1.

Series Results

FIRST GAME
Yankees 3, Giants 0

SECOND GAME
Yankees 3, Giants 0

THIRD GAME
Giants 13, Yankees 5

FOURTH GAME
Giants 4, Yankees 2

FIFTH GAME
Yankees 3, Giants 1

SIXTH GAME
Giants 8, Yankees 5

SEVENTH GAME
Giants 2, Yankees 1

EIGHTH GAME
Giants 1, Yankees 0

McGRAW OUTFIT TAKES FINAL CONTEST, 1 TO 0

Bobble by Peckinpaugh Responsible for Giant Victory

(Special to the Evening Bulletin)

Polo Grounds, New York, Oct. 13.—The New York Giants to-day won the world's baseball championship.

By copping to-day the Giants chased the jinx that has been following them in this great Fall event since 1905. That year for the first time under the present system, the Giants grabbed off the National League pennant and in the post-season series defeated the Athletics. Up to this year they have since been in four series, losing them all. To-day's result:

Giants 1, Yankees 0

The Giants won to-day's game and the world title in the first inning. Cracking of the Yankee defence cost the American Leaguers this crucial battle as did the same thing yesterday when the Giants went into the lead. Heart-breaking as were the bobbles that robbed Mays of a win yesterday, they had nothing on the one turned in by the Yankee captain in this final clash. With two gone and two on in this opening inning, Kelly drove one straight at Peckinpaugh. With any base to play for, except home, Yankee fans were just settling back with a sigh of relief. Lo and behold, Peck let the ball go through him, and before he could recover himself Bancroft had scored with the tally that meant the long end of the purse.

Continuing their driving attack to-day the Giants came through with flying colors. The Yankees, however, put up a game, but losing fight and died hard.

While the series might have gone one more game, it proved as it was predicted it would be—historic. Never before has this great Fall event proved such a ding-dong affair. Winning the first two games almost hands down, the Yankees were picked to clean up in short order. Then came the blowout, and before Huggins knew it he was travelling on two flat shoes, with no lead at all. Patches were put on and once more the Yankees found themselves out in front with a one-game margin, only to be tied the next day and to be headed yesterday. Yesterday's blow was the one that broke the camel's back.

In their half of the first the Yankees had a chance, but could not connect with the hit that meant runs. With one out Peck walked

MAGAZINE
TRIBUNE INSTITUTE
BOOK SECTION

New York Tribune

MAGAZINE
TRIBUNE INSTITUTE
BOOK SECTION

PART V FOURTEEN PAGES SUNDAY, APRIL 2, 1922 FOURTEEN PAGES PART V

THE HIGH COST OF BASEBALL

Times May Be Hard and Taxes Burdensome, but the Public Still Has Money Enough to Make a $2,500,000 Payroll Possible in the Two Big Leagues

By ARTHUR CHAPMAN

Tim Keefe, who used to pitch his head off for old Jim Mutrie for $3,200

John M. Ward, a predecessor of that other John, M'Graw, who captained and managed for $7,500, and who never got more than $3,500 as a player

The pay of these four, Ruth, Hornsby, Cobb and Speaker, will total this year about $125,000

Buck Ewing, famous for having refused $10,000 to come back

Roger Connor, whose $3,500 salary made him one of the nabobs of Jim Mutrie's old Giants

THIS will be in excess of a $2,000,000 year in big league baseball, so far as salaries are concerned.

Baseball officials are inclined to believe that the salaries in the National and American leagues will run closer to a total of $2,500,000 than to $2,000,000. Salaries in the National League, it is estimated, will reach $1,200,000 and the American League total probably will be over that figure. When a George Herman Ruth extracts an estimated $75,000 a year from the coffers of the New York American League Club, exclusive of any bonuses which may or may not be paid for home runs, and when a Rogers Hornsby sets back the St. Louis National League team for $25,000, with more in sight in the event of certain successes, it is no wonder the directors of the baseball machine say things are reaching a pass where something will have to break.

There are pictures of Ruth and Hornsby in the offices of the magnates, but such portraits inspire mixed feelings in the men who may be exhuming the necessary cash to keep the stars satisfied. Below Ruth and Hornsby there come lesser figures—but all are getting overpaid as any club treasurer will tell you with a tremor in his voice. If "movie" men want to get some affecting close-ups, with real tears instead of the glycerine substitutes, they should turn the film guns on a baseball treasurer this spring and get him to talking shop.

It is figured that the big league pay rolls will be 25 per cent larger than last year. There is no team in the sixteen under $100,000. From that the club pay roll goes up to $225,000. Hold-ups don't haggle about mere differences of $500 or $1,000 any more. Sometimes differences between players and managers amount to more than a star player's entire salary in an earlier and less favored era. This difference may be $2,500 or $3,000.

The player sometimes gets it in its entirety, or perhaps it is compromised and he gets $1,500. But he gets something, for, with the baseball competition so keen, the managers are not running the risk of defeat by failure to sign any star players.

In this way baseball is a proposition entirely unique. It is a co-operative business, as evidenced by the sharing of gate receipts to bolster the weak clubs. The visiting team gets 50 per cent of the general gate admission. The home team gets its 50 per cent of the gate and in addition gets all the grandstand receipts. Thus teams like the New York clubs that have a large grandstand patronage make more money than the clubs in other towns where the bleacherite still survives in bulk.

But this division of the gate is as far as baseball co-operation goes—in theory, at least. When it comes to signing players, each club is "on its own." Salaries are at the discretion of the management, in contrast with the days when salary limits were in effect.

It was not always so in baseball. Before the Brotherhood revolt matters were reversed. There was a salary limit of $2,400—which was not being observed to the letter—and there was no division of the gate receipts with the visiting teams. As John M. Ward pointed out to the writer of this article, the failure to look after the weaker teams led to the formation of the Players' League.

"They were going to establish a salary limit of $2,000 in the National League," said Mr. Ward, who is now a lawyer with an office at 277 Broadway and who was shortstop of the New York Giants when the break came. "We tried to convince the club owners that they should let the visiting teams have half the gate receipts. This would have insured good financial returns to such a team as Indianapolis, where a $2,000 salary limit otherwise would have been all the team could stand. But the team owners would not listen to this proposition and the players organized their own league. But now the leagues adopt the gate sharing system, which is a direct outcome of the Brotherhood movement. Most people look on the Players' League as the outcome of a strike on the part of the players. It was not. It was forced upon the players, and it has been proved to be justified. If the leagues had not adopted the gate sharing plan which the players wanted them to adopt at the time of the Brotherhood such teams as the present-day Athletics would not be able to exist, because their receipts at home are not sufficient to support them."

The baseball magnates freely admit that the Brotherhood was the first big means of raising salaries. In fact, salary raises in the realm of professional baseball are divided into three eras, succeeding the pre-Brotherhood days, when $3,500 was top hole. The first real boost came when the Brotherhood was organized and the stars got the taste of real salaries. Then the American League made five-

George Gore, whose first venture in professional baseball netted him $10 a week and his board

figure salaries anything but novelties, owing to the keen competition it created for star players; and, third, the Federal League piled on the agony just a little more by creating more competition, more bidding and more luxury for the stars.

James Mutrie, manager of the New York National League team from 1883 to 1891 and of the old Metropolitans before that, knows a lot about the salaries paid to players in the days before any of the upward tendencies became noticeable. Mr. Mutrie, on behalf of John B. Day, whom he interested financially in the team, gathered up from various sources the players who were later to become immortalized by the name of Giants—a name applied by the manager himself.

Mr. Mutrie now lives at New Brighton, S. I., and on fair days gets down to the ferry at St. George, where he talks baseball affairs. Not only does he know about salaries paid to oldtime National League stars, but Mr. Mutrie recalls the days at the very beginning of baseball, when players were paid by the game. He played professionally in 1862. Before that he had played as an amateur. The distinction was marked in those days.

"I remember knocking a home run that won a game," said Mr. Mutrie, "and some enthusiastic spectators ran out on the field and began stuffing dollar bills into my pocket. I had to give them all back, as if I had taken money I would have lost my amateur rating."

Mr. Mutrie played with the Chelsea, New Bedford, Brockton and Fall River teams. He was well known as a shortstop and catcher. In those days catching was something to test a man's nerve, as there was no baseball armor.

"I got my collarbone broken in a game," said Mr. Mutrie, looking reminiscently at his gnarled fingers, "and I could only run around in circles. I've had to take catchers out of the game with their hands split. Shortstop was a dangerous position on account of the rough grounds. Once, when I was fielding a hot grounder, the ball struck a stone and the

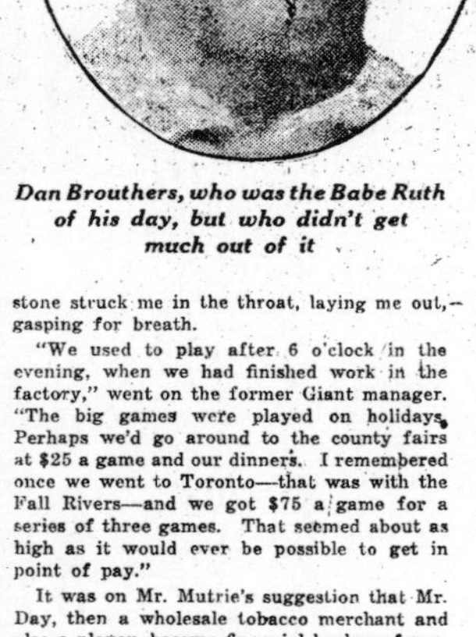

Dan Brouthers, who was the Babe Ruth of his day, but who didn't get much out of it

stone struck me in the throat, laying me out,—gasping for breath.

"We used to play after 6 o'clock in the evening, when we had finished work in the factory," went on the former Giant manager. "The big games were played on holidays. Perhaps we'd go around to the county fairs at $25 a game and our dinners. I remembered once we went to Toronto—that was with the Fall Rivers—and we got $75 a game for a series of three games. That seemed about as high as it would ever be possible to get in point of pay."

It was on Mr. Mutrie's suggestion that Mr. Day, then a wholesale tobacco merchant and also a player, became financial backer of professional baseball in New York. For years Day and Mutrie ran the baseball show in New York, with the "Mets" and later the Giants, but both lost out when the Brotherhood formed a rival organization and left the National League with few of its stars.

"I can recall the names of a hundred players who started professionally at from $40 to $50 a month," said Mr. Mutrie. "Take George Gore, one of the greatest fielders that ever lived. I was with the Fall Rivers, and we had a game scheduled with the Portland, Me., team. There was a fellow on the Port-

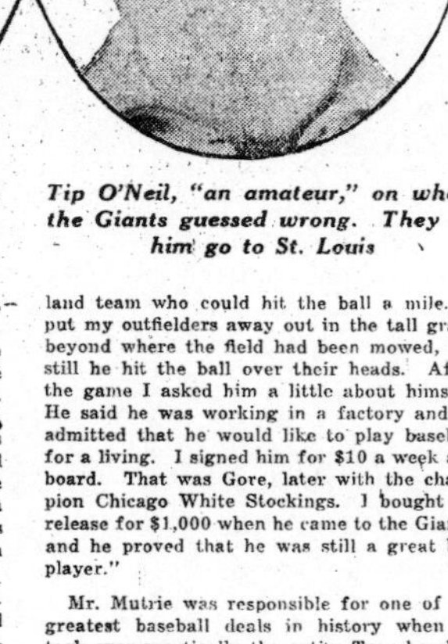

Tip O'Neil, "an amateur," on whom the Giants guessed wrong. They let him go to St. Louis

land team who could hit the ball a mile. I put my outfielders away out in the tall grass, beyond where the field had been mowed, but still he hit the ball over their heads. After the game I asked him a little about himself. He said he was working in a factory and he admitted that he would like to play baseball for a living. I signed him for $10 a week and board. That was Gore, later with the champion Chicago White Stockings. I bought his release for $1,000 when he came to the Giants, and he proved that he was still a great ball player."

Mr. Mutrie was responsible for one of the greatest baseball deals in history when he took over practically the entire Troy baseball team for the New York club. Troy and Worcester dropped out of the National League circuit in 1882 and New York and Philadelphia were admitted in their stead. Mutrie and Day had been running the Metropolitan team in New York, a member of the American Association. Mutrie was the first manager on the ground when it was known that the Troy team was to disband. He came back with a bag of players that would delight the heart of any manager to-day—Buck Ewing, catcher; Mickey Welch, pitcher; Roger Connor, first base; Ed Caskins, shortstop, and Pat Gilles-

Danny Richardson, who never let his salary of $1,800 take his mind off his work around second base

pie, outfielder. Ewing is rated as one of the greatest catchers of all time. Welch was a wonderful pitcher, as his record shows, and Connor ranks as one of the great first basemen of the game. These men became the nucleus of the Giants. John Montgomery Ward was secured from the Providence team. "Tip" O'Neill was picked up as an amateur, but was later let go, only to win fame at St. Louis with Comiskey's pennant-winning Browns. Dorgan, who had been with the "Mets," was an outfielder, and Danny Richardson, the smallest man on the team but one of the most valuable, was second baseman and all-round utility player. With Tim Keefe, a "Met" star, and Mickey Welch to do the pitching, the Giants became the talk of the baseball world.

Ewing was not only a marvelous catcher and swift on the bases, but he could play almost any other position on the team. In fact, he did play third base and actually went into the pitcher's box and won a few games. Yet Buck Ewing never got over $3,500 salary.

"After Ewing retired I offered him $10,000 salary to come back," said Mr. Mutrie. "That was probably the biggest salary ever offered up to that time. But Ewing felt that he was through on account of his leg, which always had given him trouble. Ewing was a marvelous player, largely because he seemed to have the gift of thinking out each play before the play was actually made.

"Roger Connor received $3,500, Keefe $3,200 and Danny Richardson $1,500. Dorgan we got from Syracuse. He got no more than Richardson. Jim O'Rourke was the highest salaried man on the old Giants. He got a little better than $3,500.

"Umpires didn't get so much money in those days as they do now. Five dollars a game was the average pay. Also they got rough treatment. I remember one game I umpired in Lowell, Mass., when the crowd took after me. I was getting kicked and clawed and hit with stones when a woman in a buggy came up. She called the crowd cowards, and laid about her right and left with her buggy whip, forcing them back. Then she told me to jump in the buggy, which I did, and she drove me to safety."

John Ward came to the New York team as a pitcher at a salary of $3,000, which was large in those days. Later it was advanced to $3,500, which was as far as the ambitious players of that time figured on going. When a man had attained to the $3,500 class he was a headliner and could have nothing more to expect. Yet to-day a man in Ward's position probably would be drawing from $20,000 to $25,000 a year and his managerial ability would get him something extra.

Ward had won fame as a pitcher with the Providence team, and he upheld his reputation in the box when he joined the New Yorks. He shut out the Buffalo team without a hit or run and was counted as one of the greatest boxmen of his day. But the strain on his arm proved too severe, and at his own request he was given an infield position, being moved to shortstop in 1885, where he performed brilliantly. When he went to the Brooklyn club as captain and manager in the Brotherhood movement Ward received $7,500.

"Later, when I went back to the New Yorks," said Mr. Ward recently, "I was told that I was down for $3,500 salary. I said that was less than half what I had been getting with the Brooklyns. Mr. Talcott, however, told me that he had lost much money the year before and that he hoped I would help him out. In case the club made money it was agreed that I was to get more. It so happened that the club made $35,000 profit that year, and I received a percentage of that, bringing my pay up to what it had been with the Brooklyns."

When he secured Ward for the New York team Mr. Mutrie went to Boston to put the deal through. Somebody with a turn for practical joking and who knew that the New York manager was always scouting about for talent said to one of the Boston players:

"Jim Mutrie, of the New York team, is in town and he is after you."

The Boston player was excited. He had visions of being signed up at what was then a large salary. He went to Mutrie and said:

"Mr. Mutrie, I hear you are after my services. I don't like to leave Boston, but I'll go to New York on one condition—a $2,000 advance, so I can raise the mortgage on my house."

Mutrie listened in surprise, and finally had to tell the player that some one had been playing a practical joke—that he was not in Boston to sign up any player from the team representing that city.

Although the players didn't get such big salaries, money went further in those days and they managed to have a good time.

"One night I met another manager in a hotel," said Mr. Mutrie. "He boasted to me that all his players were in. I happened to know that he was mistaken. Some of my players were not in, and I knew they were out with his players. I did not like to shake his supreme confidence in his team, but I advised him to watch the back door of the hotel. He did so and caught six of his players as they came in long after the hour when they were supposed to have been in bed. He put a $200 fine on each man, and in those days $200 meant something."

The records of baseball do not indicate that many athletes retired with fortunes. The stars of the very early period of the game apparently played more for the love of the spor than for any financial reward. "Old Hoss Radbourne, a marvelous pitcher, never go more than $1,500 a year. Mike Kelly, one of the greatest of catchers, who, with his pitching partner, Clarkson, was sold to Boston, did not receive much salary. The term "Ten Thousand Dollar Kelly" referred to his sale price and not to the salary he drew.

Some players who received good salaries an who were in harness a long time saved u enough to enable them to retire without ar financial cares to harass them. Cy Young w such a player, but his gift of saving was rare in his profession as his pitching gif Most of the players figure they have a f years still coming, and it will be time enou to save later. Then they find suddenly th they are through. Tendons don't weaken gr ually as a rule—they go all of a sudden. P haps the player makes application as an pire and is given a position, or is taken c of by some team as coach or scout. Or haps he joins the big army that disapp Then somebody says of him: "Remembe Bill So-and-So? He's on the police force

(Continued on page six)

DAILY PAGE OF NEWS ST. LOUIS POST-DISPATCH PHOTOGRAPHS FROM THE WORLD OF SPORT

22 FRIDAY EVENING, SEPTEMBER 22, 1922.

George Sisler, Named "Most Valuable Player" by American League Trophy Committee

Hooking the bag with his right toes, as he slides away from a baseman. Sisler leads the world in stolen bases.

At bat Sisler leads the world with an average well over .400 and with the largest number of base hits.

In action at first. He is unquestionably the greatest first-sacker in the game.

The start of a hook slide falling away to the right of the bag

Closeup of Sisler, whose name will be first on the monument at Washington

After the Yanks Had Beat It With the Bacon the Red Sox Sent Pennock to Lock the Smokehouse Door

Hornsby Finishes Season With .401 Batting Mark; Cardinals Tie for Third

Cardinals' Second Sacker Is First National League Player to Accomplish Swat Feat in 23 Years — Pfeffer Keeps 12 Hits Well Scattered.

CHICAGO, Oct. 2.—Rogers Hornsby, the Cardinals' slugging second sacker, by getting three hits in five trips to the plate in the final game of the season with the Cubs yesterday, batted himself into the hall of fame, among the select .400 hitters. Hornsby is the first National League clubber to accomplish the feat since 1899, when Ed Delahanty of the Phillies won the title with .408. Hornsby's unofficial average was .401. The Cardinal star has now won the batting title three successive years.

The Cardinals won yesterday's contest, 7-1, and thereby went to a tie for third place with the Pirates, who dropped a double bill to the Reds. The two victories enabled Moran's team to finish second. Jeff Pfeffer hurled for the Rickeymen. He was belted for 12 safeties, but kept them well scattered.

Hitting for a .400 average for the season was not the only honor snared by Hornsby during 1922. He is the new major league home run king, with a total of 42, three better than the figure for Kenneth Williams of the Browns. "Babe" Ruth, who created a record of 59 four baggers a year ago, finished with 35. Hornsby also topped the National League in hits with 250 to his credit. He also beat his 1921 record for driving in runs.

Feat Performed 10 Times.

Hornsby's feat of hitting .400, has been performed only 10 times in the National League. R. Barnes of Chicago, was the first to accomplish it in 1876 when he hit .403. Others to turn the trick are: Capt. A. C. Anson, Chicago .407 in 1879 and .421 in 1887; J. Stenzel, Pittsburg, .409 in 1893; Hugh Duffy, Boston, .433 in 1894; Jess Burkett, .423 in 1895 and .410 in 1896; Willie Keeler, .432 in 1897; Delahanty, .408 in 1899 and Hornsby, .401 in 1922. That shows that 23 years passed without a .400 clubber in the senior circuit.

A year ago, Hornsby topped the hitters with an average of .397, missing the .400 goal, when he slumped at the fag end of the campaign. In 1920, he showed the way for the swatters in the N. L. with .370.

Hornsby started on the way to his record breaking feat in the first inning, when he singled against Kaufman. He repeated in the third, while his final safety came in the eighth, when he beat out a perfect bunt down the third base line.

In capturing the home run championship, July and September were the best months for Hornsby. He hit 10 in each of these two months. He had nine in May; five in August and four each in April and June.

Pfeffer Tight in Pinches.

Although the Bruins made a dozen safeties against Pfeffer yesterday, the big right hander was tight in the pinches. The lone run off him came in the first inning. Thereafter the Cubs threatened repeatedly, but could not come through with a hit when needed.

Jack Smith's homer gave the Cardinals one in the first. In the third, the Rickeymen added four, Jim Bottomly hitting a homer with Hornsby on the paths in this frame. The Cardinals' final two-markers came in the eighth.

Mitchell Defeats Diegel and Wins Southern Honors

British Golf Star Captures Title After 39 Holes of Play Over Nashville Course.

By the Associated Press.

NASHVILLE, Tenn., Oct. 2.—The Southern Golf Association crown, carrying with it the title of open golf champion of the South, was placed upon the head of Abe Mitchell of England here yesterday, after he had won the play-off to break the tie with Leo Diegel of New Orleans, when both players finished 72 holes in the association's fourth annual tournament in 280 strokes, four under par for the four rounds over the Belle Meade Country Club course.

Repeating his performance of Saturday, Diegel again tied Mitchell's score of 146 for 36 holes on the home green by shooting a "birdie" 4 after going to the afternoon round four strokes down to the Englishman, and at one time—on the third hole of the outward nine—being six strokes behind.

In an effort to break the knot, it was decided to play three more holes, and the struggle virtually ended on the thirty-eighth green, where Diegel for the third time during the day hooked his ball into the rough. But, unlike the other occasions, the game New Orleans player had a lie that was practically unplayable, his ball lying in a difficult position close to a tree at the edge of the green.

Diegel Gets Poor Drive.

Two attempts at an out found him in a sand trap and the fourth left him 15 feet from the cup. Two putts gave Diegel a six against Mitchell's par three. Having halved the first, Diegel was three strokes behind and the next was played perfunctorily, both clipping off birdie 4s.

The thousand who followed the players throughout the day sent up a cheer for Mitchell, as Diegel grasped his hand. In addition to the title of Southern open champion, Mitchell was given a cash prize of $1500 and Diegel received $1000 cash for finishing in second place.

Cards for the morning round follow:

Mitchell—
Out ..4 4 4 4 4 3 5 2 4—34
In ...4 5 4 4 3 4 2 6 4—36—70
Diegel—
Out ..4 4 5 5 4 4 4 3 4—37
In ...3 4 5 5 4 3 3 5 5—37—74

Afternoon Cards.

Mitchell—
Out 544 454 434—37
In .555 443 355—39—76—70—146
Diegel—
Out 555 344 444—38
In ..443 453 325—34—72—74—146

Score for the three extra holes:
Mitchell ......4 3 4—11—146—157
Diegel ....4 6 4—14—146—160

Local Net Stars Again Win From Memphis Players

St. Louis Municipal Racquet Wielders Capture Three Intercity Matches.

By Davison Obear.

The St. Louis municipal tennis team defeated the Memphis players in an intercity contest on the Forest Park courts yesterday afternoon. Three matches were played, while Saturday two contests were held. Local players captured all five matches, defeating Memphis, 5 to 0.

Yesterday the program consisted of two singles and one doubles encounter. Five players represented St. Louis, while the Memphis Associated Amateurs sent two players.

Ted Heuerman opened the play yesterday. In a singles contest he defeated Jimmie Elmore of Memphis in straight sets, 6—1, 6—1. Elmore was the runnerup in the recent municipal tournament in Memphis. The Memphis player put forth his best efforts against Heuerman, but did not have the necessary speed to win. Elmore made a number of excellent returns in the match, but could not cope with the placement drives of his opponent.

Kammann Defeats Yerger.

In a second singles match Karl Kammann, local municipal champion, defeated George S. Yerger, the Memphis star. The first set was easy for the St. Louis player, but the second found Yerger improved in his play. Kammann won this match by a 6—0, 6—3 score. Yerger is the ranking player of Memphis and the State of Tennessee. He won the municipal championship of Memphis this season.

Yerger has an excellent fast service and seems to execute his strokes with ease and grace. His ground strokes lack the speed of Kammann's and this was one reason for his defeat yesterday. Yerger was apparently off form when at the net position in yesterday's match in both singles and doubles.

Charles Barnes and Kammann won the doubles encounter from Elmore and Yerger. Play was very close in both sets, which the local municipal champions win by a 6—4, 6—3 score. Barnes and Kammann kept the lead in the first set, but in the serond set the Memphis team threatened to win. They won the first two games, but the victors soon tied the score and won the set.

The complete summary of the five matches played in the two days follows:

St. Louis 5, Memphis 0.

Singles.

Elmer Schwarz, St. Louis, defeated Jimmie Elmore, Memphis, 8—6, 6—4; Karl Kammann, St. Louis, defeated George S. Yerger, Memphis, 6—0, 6—3; Ted Heuerman, St. Louis, defeated Jimmie Elmore, Memphis, 6—1, 6—1.

Doubles.

Schwarz and Schwarz, St. Louis, defeated Elmore and Yerger, Memphis, 6—3, 6—2; Barnes and Kammann, St. Louis, defeated Elmore and Yerger, Memphis, 6—4, 6—3.

MOBILE BEATS TULSA IN THIRD GAME, 9-3

By the Associated Press.

TULSA, Ok., Oct. 2.—Lefty Fuhr was in fine form yesterday and the Mobile, Dixie series champions, defeated the Tulsa Western League champions, 9 to 3. It was a fast game on a muddy field. Of the three games of the class A championship series, Tulsa has won two and Mobile one.

Tulsa's skipper sent McLaughlin to the rubber to oppose Fuhr, but he proved to be very little opposition. Russell, Haugland and Black were all given a trial on the mound, but they all looked alike to the Southerners.

ENGLISH WOMAN SOCCER TEAM DEFEATED, 7 TO 5

By the Associated Press.

NEW YORK, Oct. 2.—Fully 7000 soccer fans, comprising one of the largest crowds that ever filled New York Oval, greeted the British women soccer players, representing the Newcastle United Women's Football Club, yesterday and witnessed a thrilling contest of 90 minutes and, incidentally, the second defeat administered to the fair invaders since their arrival in this country. The Centro-Hispano eleven, runners-up in the Metropolitan Football League, which had been selected to oppose the visitors, won by a score of 7 goals to 5, after cutting down a 3—2 lead established by the women in the first period of play.

MOUNT VERNON OUTFIT WINS TROLLEY TITLE

The Mount Vernon club won the championship in the Missouri-Illinois Trolley League defeating the White Roses of Belleville, 12—4, in the second and deciding game of the series. Vaughn and Groh pitched for the winners, and Gockel, a Cardinal recruit, for the losers.

Jonnard May Prove Real Star Of Giants in World's Series

Young Right-Hander Has Great Fast Ball, Good Control and Plenty of Courage—Howe Expects Scott to Baffle Yankee Sluggers.

By Irwin M. Howe,
Official Statistician of the American League.

According to the judgment of managers, players and umpires, manager McGraw faces the most serious problem that has ever confronted a leader of a world's series contender as he undertakes to fashion a reasonably strong hurling staff out of the material at his command.

The Giants' leader has several classy pitchers on his pay roll, but during the last six weeks not one of them has hurled a really good game. McGraw's only two dependable pitchers, Nehf and Ryan, have both shown signs of wear. The purchase of McQuillan helped the Giants land the National flag, but this curve-ball artist, apparently, is unable to regain his 1921 form, and the Yankees will face him with a world of confidence. Jess Barnes is an in and outer, while his younger brother has been used but little, mostly to finish games. Another remaining possibility is Claude Jonnard, whom we will discuss later on. Big Jack Scott, who signed as a free agent after his release by Cincinnati, because his pitching days were supposed to be over, is likely to pitch a creditable game or possibly two, but it is doubtful if he can hold the Yankee sluggers to a low score.

Pitchers Are Easy to Hit.

We learn that the National League composite team has amassed a grand average of .309 against the Giants' five regulars.

It should be remembered, too, that the comparisons are all in favor of the Giant twirlers. The manner in which the Cardinals' batting order was shifted made it impossible to use any of the St. Louis sluggers against the Giants' pitchers.

Considering the Giant staff in detail, it is conceded that Nehf probably is the best left-hander in the league, except Cooper. Rixey has had a great year, but most managers would choose Nehf, when in form, in preference to Rixey. Nehf pitched magnificently against the Yankees last fall and if he goes into the game this week as fit as he was last year, the Yankees are sure of a tough game. For some time, however, Artie has been away off form and he would have small hope of checking the Yankee sluggers in the condition he has shown for two months. What he has been able to do in the last 10 days toward regaining his true form the public does not know and there is no way of finding out until he starts a game.

Scott Has Done Good Work.

Jack Scott has shown the best of any of McGraw's regulars ever since he joined the Giants. I think he will be likely to give his opponents a hard battle, at least for five or six innings, when, if the Giants have an even break or a lead of a run or so, McGraw will shift to one of his second string men and thus try to save Scott for another start. Scott is a smart curve ball pitcher, which he alternates with a fast overhand and a slow ball.

Jesse Barnes was poison to the Yankees a year ago, but he, like all the rest of the Giants' twirlers, has been very inconsistent for three months. Barnes' best asset is a mighty hook, sandwiched in with an occasional fast one and a typical old-fashioned slow ball that just carries to the plate. A pitcher with Barnes' kind of deliveries must have control and that has been Jess' trouble most of the time this season.

Hugh McQuillan is another curve ball hurler, who has had to "slow up" often during the past two months to get the ball over the plate, while Bill Ryan depends upon a mixture of a little of everything. Ryan has been more effective all season than any of the regulars and he has saved many a game in the last 60 days by his ability to step in on short notice and throw the ball over the plate.

Manager McGraw has a hurler on his staff that few people have paid any attention to, but who, I think, may cut considerable ice in this series and that individual is Claude Jonnard. Jonnard has been much used to finsh games and he has done that specialty so well that at this writing he is credited with six victories for the season and only one defeat. He has a wonderful fast ball, good control and plenty of courage. I will be surprised if he does not start a game. If he does he will make a good showing. Virgil Barnes has been worked but little and one can only judge that the Giants' leader does not consider him National League caliber at this time.

If Nehf, McQuillan, Ryan, Scott and Jess Barnes were all in top form it is fair to say that even then the Giants would have the worst of the argument so far as pitchers are concerned, but they would be close enough to the Yankees to make the outcome of a short series uncertain.

Season's Records Of Giant Hurlers

Following are the season's record of the Giants' pitchers for the season:

NAME.	W.	L.	Inn.	R.
Nehf	17	10	243	113
Ryan	13	7	152	57
J. Barnes	12	8	177	79
Jonnard	6	1	41	13
Scott	4	2	37	21
McQuillan	9	10	168	82

Wittenberg Wins Title.

The tennis tournament for the championship of the Federal Reserve Bank came to a close when the final round of the singles event was played. Louis Wittenberg retained his title as champion by defeating Lathrop Bailey in straight sets. The score was 6—0, 6—1. Witttenberg won the first tournament in 1920. The event was not completed last season. Every season the tournament draws an entry of nearly 50 players and some close matches take place. No doubles were played this season.

Martin Will Not Meet Harry Greb

Soldier Boxer to Oppose Floyd Johnson of California in East Friday Night.

By Bert Igoe,

NEW YORK, Oct. 2.—Harry Greb will not meet Bob Martin at the Garden on Friday night. Instead the soldier boy will face Floyd Johnson, the hard-hitting Californian. A far better match, we would say off hand, with all due respect to the plunging Greb. Greb can just about outpoint any man in the country over a short distance and that might even include the solid man of the world, Dempsey.

A better fight because, in our opinion it will be a matter of downright hitting between Martin and Johnson.

After all it is hitting and not powder puffing that the pop-eyed customers want.

Johnson, a pupil of the resourceful Alex Greggains of Frisco, is a deep chested, round shouldered natural hitter. Twenty-two and full of pluck and ambition. The same can be said of Martin. Johnson has had five fights in the East and each and every time he has accounted for a bruised and belittled bloke. He is a sweet hitter. He has the Greggains left, as artful a southpaw poke as you have seen in many a day.

If Martin had the Johnson left he might some day be the heavyweight champion of the world.

Muldoon Steps In.

William Muldoon, chairman of the State Athletic Commission, informed Frank Flournoy that Greb could not be trotted out in any arena unless he first met Johnny Wilson. Strange, the commission, if we remember correctly, set Greb down for refusing to fight one Rosenberg. Therefore it would seem quite fair to us to have take on this Rosenberg,

EXTRA

LONG BRANCH DAILY RECORD

EXTRA

VOL. 21—NUMBER 233* | LONG BRANCH, N. J., THURSDAY, OCTOBER 5, 1922—12 PAGES | Weather—Fair tonight and Friday. | PRICE THREE CENT

DARKNESS ENDS SECOND WORLD STRUGGLE ON 3 TO 3 TIE

McGraw's Men Score Three Runs in Opening Inning, Partly Thanks to Meusel's Homer —Yanks Also Score in First

Giants Goose-egged, After Initial Spurt, Until Finish

Wild Enthusiasm When Ruth in Eighth Scores on Meusel's Double, Evening Score—Yankee Fielders Too Much for Giants' Husky Sluggers

Polo Grounds, N. Y., Oct. 25 (By The Associated Press).—The Giants and the Yankees battled for 10 innings to a tie score when darkness called a halt. The Giants might have been able to play their half of another inning, but the light was fading fast, and Umpire Hilderbrand, realizing that the Yankees would have to go to bat in near-darkness, called the

Thirty-six thousand persons or more saw a pitcher's battle in which Barnes and Shawkey fought it down to the last period.

The Giants made their three runs in the first inning on singles by Groh and Frisch and a home run smash by Meusel. They did little with Shawkey thereafter. Barnes used a slow ball throughout the contest. The Yankees scored their first run in the opening frame when Bancroft made a bad error and Pipp came through with a single.

Ward made a home run in the fourth and the Yanks scored their third run on doubles by Ruth and Meusel in the eighth.

Robert Shawkey—yclept "Bob the Gob," and curve-ball-flinger extraordinary of the New York Yankees—faced the Giants this afternoon in the second joust of the world's series tournament. The National Leaguers having won the initial tilt, Manager Huggins sent Shawkey to the pitching mound to try to baffle the Giants in their course with his mystifying hooks and fast ball. Jesse Barnes took up the Giants' burden in the box.

Huggins brought his players on the field early and put them through a long batting practice. The mite manager said his club would probably start to hitting on all cylinders at once and there would be a batting orgy of unrestrained violence.

Some thirty-odd thousand folk came out to see the sport, but the early rush for the unreserved sections was missing and the crowd filtered into the upper stands and bleachers as slowly as on some late September day when the cellar champions are playing the home folks in football weather.

The reserve stands, sold out to capacity for the series, did not fill up until the players took their fielding workout. October had resurrected a day from July's hot wave and another sultry afternoon gave the pitchers an incentive to turn on their speed.

Nick Altrock and Al. Schacht, buffoons of baseball, came out to amuse the early comers with their antics, while a brass band whiled away the minutes that dragged until "Babe" Ruth and company, garbed in home uniforms of white, broke into the picture through the wooden gate that leads from the clubhouse to the playing field. Blume, a pitcher from Colgate, a right-hander, fed the Giants his curves during the technical visitors' batting practice. Then Carmen Hill, who wears spectacles and pitches a mean curve, shot up a few for the Giants to hit. Jess Barnes appeared in the batting practice, as he was Manager McGraw's choice for pitching duty.

The Giants were the first to take fielding practice and executed some lightning fast double plays with fancy stops and throws.

The Yankees also gave a brilliant exhibition in fielding practice, both Dugan and Scott making pretty one-hand stabs and quick throws.

The four umpires lined up at the plate and were duly photographed in the most approved fashion.

Captain Bancroft went over the ground rules with Umpire-in-Chief Hildebrand, while the Yankees prepared to take the field.

FIRST INNING

Giants: Sam Jones and Carl Mays went down into the bull pen to get into condition in case they should be called upon. Bancroft up: Strike one, ball one, foul strike two, foul, foul. Ward tossed out Bancroft, going far to his left to get a mean bounder. Groh up: Strike one, foul strike two, ball one, ball two, Groh singled over second. This was his fourth hit in the series. Frisch up: Foul strike one, foul strike two. Frisch got a Texas Leaguer into left field which Scott could not quite reach. Groh went to second. Meusel up: Foul strike one, strike two, ball one. Meusel hit a home run into the left field stand, scoring Groh and Frisch ahead of him.

Young up: Foul strike one, ball one, ball two, strike two. Young flied out to Witt. Kelly up: Kelly fouled out to Schang.

Three runs, three hits, no errors.

Yankees: Witt up: Ball one, foul strike one, ball two, foul strike two. Witt bunted, but the ball rolled foul. Groh made a nice play on Witt's roller and got him at first. Dugan up: Foul strike one, ball one, ball two. Dugan going to second. Ruth up: Banroft took Dugan's grounder and threw to the grand stand, Dugan going to second. Ruth up: Ruth went out to first, Kelly unassisted, Dugan going to third. Pipp up: Ball one. Dugan scored when Popp got a single off Kelly's glove. Meusel up: Ball one, ball two, strike one, strike two. Meusel flied out to Young.

One run, one hit, one error.

SECOND INNING.

Giants: Stengel up: Ball one, ball two, strike one, foul, strike two. Stengel beat out an infield hit. Snyder up: Ball one. Snyder got a single over Pipp's head. Stengel went to second. Stengel hurt his leg in going to second and Cuningham ran for him. Barnes up: Ball one, ball two, foul, strike one, strike two. Barnes hit into a double play Scott, to Ward, to Pipp, Cunningham going to third. Bancroft up: Strike one, foul, strike two, ball one. Bancroft flied out to Ruth, who took the ball near the right field stand.

No runs, two hits, no errors.

Yankees: Cunningham went into centre field for the Giants. Schang up: Strike one, ball one. Frisch tossed out Schang, who hit at a slow curve. Ward up: Groh got Ward at first. Scott up: Ball one, ball two, strike one, ball three, strike two, foul. Frisch robbed Scott of a hit by making a diving catch of his grounder and getting his man at first.

No runs, no hits, no errors.

THIRD INNING.

Giants: Groh up: Strike one, ball one, strike two, ball two, ball three, foul, foul. Groh walked. Frisch up: Ball one. Frisch lined out to Ruth. Meusel up: Strike one, foul, strike two. Meusel flies out to Ruth. Young up: Ball one, ball two, foul, strike one, and the Giants were trying the hit and run play, foul, strike two, ball three. Younk walked. Kelly up: Foul strike one, strike two, ball one. Kelly churned the air for the third out.

No runs, no hits, no errors.

Yankees. Shawkey up: Ball one, strike one, strike two, ball two, ball three, foul, foul, foul; fou. Groh threw out Shawkey. Witt up: Ball one strike one, strike two, ball two. Witt fouled out to Groh. Dugan up: Ball one, ball two. Dugan got a two-base hit to left. Ruth up: ball one, ball two, strike one. Barnes pitched nothing but slow balls to Ruth, ball three. Ruth walked. Pipp up: Barnes threw out Pipp at first.

No runs, one hit, no errors.

FOURTH INNING

Giants: Cunningham up: Ball one, ball two, strike one, foul strike two. Cunningham struck out. Snyder up; Strike one. Snyder fouled out to Dugan. Barnes up: The crowd booed Barnes because he had passed Babe Ruth. Strike one, strike two, ball one. Barnes struck out.

No runs, no hits, no errors.

Yankees: Meusel up: Strike one, strike two, ball one. Meusel fouled out to Snyder. Schang up: Ball one, strike one, ball two, strike two, foul. Schang struck out. Snyder dropping the third strike and throwing him out at first. Ward up: Ball one. Ward got a home run over the left field fence. Scott up: Foul strike one, ball one. Frisch went into center field for Scotts Texas Leaguer, robbing the Yankee shortstop of a hit for the second time in the game.

One run, one hit, and no errors.

FIFTH INNING.

Giants. Bancroft up: Ball one, foul, strike one, foul, strike two, ball two, ball three. Bancroft lined out to Pipp. Groh up: Strike one. Scott threw out Groh at first. Frisch up: Frisch beat out a bunt. Meusel up: Ball one, foul, strike one. Meusel got a blow into the grandstand that was foul by inches, ball two. It was a wild pitch for Shawkey and a steal for Frisch. Frisch went to third on a wild pitch, ball three. Scott threw out Meusel at first.

No runs, one hit, no errors.

Yankees. Shawkey up: Strike one. Shawkey flied out to Cunningham. Witt up: Ball one. Barnes took Witt's hopper and tossed him out. Dugan up: Ball one, strike one, foul, strike two, ball two, foul, ball three. Dugan got a single to left. Ruth up: Ball one, ball two, strike one, foul, strike two, foul. Frisch threw out Ruth at first.

No runs, no hits, no errors.

SIXTH INNING

Giants: Young up: Ball one. Young beat out a slow roller to Scott. Kelly up: Strike one, ball one. Kelly forced Young, Shawkey to Ward. Cunningham up. Ball one, foul strike one, ball two. Cunningham flied to Ruth. Snyder up: Snyder flied out to Ruth.

No runs, one hit, no errors.

Yankees: Dugan up: Strike one, Barnes tossed out Dugan. Ruth up: Strike one. Ruth got along hit into left field for two bases. Pipp up: Ball one. Pipp up: Ball one. Pipp flied out to Cunningham and Ruth raced to third on the catch. Meusel up: Foul strike one, foul strike two, Ruth was stealing home when Meusel fouled off the pitcher, ball one, ball two, ball three. Ruth scored on Meusel's double to left which he made by fast base running. Schang up: Kelly took Schangs grounder and touched first.

One run, two hits, no errors.

SEVENTH INNING.

Giants. Barnes up: Ball one, strike one. Ward took Barnes hot shot and threw him out at first. Bancroft up: Ball one, ball two. Shawkey complained bitterly to Umpire Hildebrand on his calling of balls and strikes. Bancroft went out ot Pipp, unassisted. Groh up: Ball one. Groh popped to Ward.

No runs, no hits, no errors.

Yankees. Scott up: Kelly took Scott's roller and touched first. Shawkey up: Strike one, strike two. Shawkey fanned on three pitched balls. Witt up: Ball one, foul, strike one, foul, strike two. Witt fanned.

No runs, no hits, no errors.

EIGHTH INNING.

Giants. Frisch up: Ball one, foul, strike one, foul, strike two, foul, foul, ball two, foul. Frisch fouled out to Dugan. Meusel up: Meusel sent up a high foul which Pipp took. Young up: Ball one, ball two, strike one, strike two, foul. Young flied out to Meusel.

No runs, no hits, no errors.

Yankees. Pipp up: Ball one, ball two, ball three, strike one, strike two. Pipp fouled out to Snyder. Meusel up: Ball one, ball two, foul, strike one, ball three. Meusel got a base on balls. Schang up: Frisch threw out Schang at first, Meusel going to second. Ward up: Ball one, ball two, strike one, ball three, strike two. Ward fanned.

No runs, no hits, no errors.

NINTH INNING.

Giants. Kelly up: Strike one, ball one, ball two, strike two. Kelly sent up a high one which Dugan took. Smith batted for Cunningham. Smith up: Foul, strike one, ball one, strike two, foul. Smith fanned. Snyder up: Strike one, ball one. Ward threw out Snyder at first.

No runs, no hits, no errors.

Yankees. King went into center field for the Giants. Ward up: Ball one, ball two, strike one, strike two, ball three. Ward struck out. Scott up: Strike one. Scott got a single inso center. Shawkey up: Strike one. Shawkey forced Scott, Barnes to Bancroft. Witt up: Strike one, ball one. Witt got a single into left sending Shawkey to second. Dugan up: Ball one, ball two, foul, strike one, strike two. Dugan fanned.

No runs, two hits, no errors.

TENTH INNING.

Giants. Barnes up: Strike one. Shawkey threw out Barnes. Bancroft up: Ball one, foul, strike one, ball two, strike two. Bancroft singled sharply into second field, and was out trying to stretch his hit, Witt to Ward. Groh up: Strike one, strike two, foul. Ward threw out Groh.

No runs, one hit, no errors.

Yankees: Ruth up: Ball one, Ball two, Ruth fouled out to Snyder. Pipp up: Ball one. Kelly took Pipp's roller and touched him on the leg. Meusel up: Meusel fouled out to Snyder.

No runs, no hits, no errors.

Flash game called darkness. Tie score of three-three.

The following official box score tellsits own story:

GIANTS

	A.B.	R	H	P.O.	A	E
Bancroft, ss	5	0	1	1	0	1
Groh, 3b	4	1	1	1	3	0
Frisch, 2b	4	1	2	1	4	0
E. Meusel, lf	4	1	1	0	0	0
Young, rf	3	0	1	2	0	0
Kelly, 1b	4	0	0	15	0	0
Stengel, cf	1	0	1	0	0	0
Cunningham, zcf.	2	0	0	1	0	0
King, cf	0	0	0	0	0	0
Snyder, c	4	0	1	9	1	0
J. Barnes, p	4	0	0	0	4	0
Earl Smith, zz ...	1	0	0	0	0	0
Totals	36	3	8	30	12	1

YANKEES

	A.B.	R	H	P.O.	A	E
Witt, cf	5	0	1	1	1	0
Dugan, 3b	5	1	2	3	0	0
Ruth, rf	4	1	1	5	0	0
Pipp, 1b	5	0	1	11	0	0
R. Meusel, lf	4	0	1	1	0	0
Schang, c	4	0	0	5	0	0
Ward, 2b	4	1	1	4	5	0
Scott, ss	4	0	1	0	3	0
Shawkey, p	4	0	0	0	2	0
	30	3	8	30	11	0

z—Ran for Stengel in 2nd.

zz—Batted for Cunningham in 9th

Giants	3	0	0	0	0	0	0	0	0	0	—3
Yankees ..	1	0	0	1	0	0	0	1	0	0	—3

(Called at end of 10th—Darkness).

Two base hits Dugan, Ruth and R. Meusel. Home runs—E. Meusel and Ward. Stolen base—Frisch. Double play—Scott, Ward and Pipp.

Left on bases—Yankees 8, Giants 5. Bases on balls off—Shawkey 2, (Groh, Young) off J. Barnes 2 (Ruth, R. Meusel). Struck out by Shawkey 4, (Kelly, cunningham, J. Barnes and Smith), By J. Barnes 6, (Schang, Ward 2, Shawkey, Witt and Dugan). Wild pitches—Schawkey 2. Umpires—Hildebrand (Amn), umpire in chief, at plate. McCormick (Nat.) first base: Owens (Amn) second base: Klem (Nat.) third base. Time of game 2:41.

RUMSON POLICE OFFICER IS DISMISSED FROM FORCE FOR ACCEPTING BRIBES

Peter Conk Loses Position, But Officer John McLaughlin Jointly Accused, Is Exonerated After Hearing Before Mayor and Council—Automobilists Were Victims—Son of Well-known Long Branch Citizen Brought Into Case.

The son of a well-known Long Branch citizen whose name was not divulged, was brought into the Rumson police scandal last night at the special meeting of the Mayor and Council of the Borough of Rumson in the town hall. Peter Conk was found guilty and dismissed from the police force, and John McLaughlin was exonerated of the specific charge brought against him.

The hall was crowded to overflowing, many persons being shut out from the meeting, and no women were present. The hearing began promptly at 8:30 o'clock, when Mayor W. H. Mahoney called for order and the first witness for the prosecution was called. Joseph McVey, of Atlantic Highlands, and New York City, was summoned to corroborate Joseph Dender, who testified against the two police officers on Sept. 28. McVey made a good appearance on the stand and made his statements in straightforward manner. He seemed to make a better impression upon the Council than the previous witnesses. His testimony corroborated that of Dender and the severe cross-examination of John J. Quinn for the defense did not shake him. McVey is a bank clerk employed in New York City and has lived in Atlantic Highlands for about 10 years. The testimony was to the effect that on the evening of July 30, Dender, accompanied by McVey and two girls, were on their way from the Highlands to Red Bank in a roadster and had parked on the Ridge Road after having inadvertently switched off the car lights. Officer Conk approached them and received $5 from Dender to let them off.

Both Conk and McLaughlin appeared in their own defense, McLaughlin, making a good witness for himself but being of little use to Conk. Both officers denied that they had received any money and both stated that, if they had done so, they would admit it. Conk said on the stand that if it had been a larger sum he might have been tempted, but not by a mere $3 or $5.

Lawyer Quinn summed up for the defense in a scathing denunciation of Earl Whittley, who had previously testified against Conk and McLaughlin, and in praise of the two police officers.

Senator William A. Stevens, counsel for the Borough of Rumson, summed up for the other side. He declared that the sole object of the hearing was to see justice done. The Senator stated that a son of a wealthy and well-known resident of the City of Long Branch had been held up in a similar manner and had likewise paid money to Conk; and that there were several others who had the same complaints, but it was not thought necessary to bring any more witnesses.

Senator Stevens finished speaking at 10:30 o'clock, and the hall was cleared of everybody but the Mayor and members of the Council. They deliberated for nearly an hour and a half before the Mayor announced that they had reached a decision. It was exactly 12 o'clock when the decision was announced to the crowd who had again entered the hall.

ONE MAN FORMS CROWD—EIGHT POLICE GUARD HIM

New York, Oct. 5.—There was great interest among the "cash" or bleacher customers at the Polo Grounds for the second game of the world series last night and today. The crowd gathered early—at midnight last night—and he was still there at 7 o'clock this morning waiting for the gates to open.

About 5 o'clock he had company. Eight big patrolmen arrived and with customary vigor saw to it that the line kept strict order.

The lone man waiting when the sun came up today—yes, there was only one man in all the city who got there early, and he doesn't live here—was Raymond Degeer, of Stamford, Conn., and he formed his own line, held his own place and did his own resting as best he could while the eight policemen watched him to see that he did not get unruly.

SCOUT COUNCIL TO HAVE MEETING

Several Matters Of Importance To Be Discussed At Session.

A special meeting of the Long Branch District Council of the Boy Scouts of America will be held tonight at 8 o'clock in Bartley J. Wright's office in the Brent Good Building. Several matters of importance will be discussed, it is said, and all the members of the council are urged to attend.

Activities in Scout work are on the increase at the present time. Friday night an over-night hike will be staged, the Scouts leaving the Scout office in Red Bank and going to Old Camp Monmouth, on the Shark River. Long Branch Scouts wishing to attend this hike will meet the party at camp. The program on the trip will include camp instruction, Scout tests, a "lion hunt," sturgeon-spearing contests between troops, a rifle match and other sports.

The Scouts will return to their homes Saturday afternoon. Those who have stated their desire to attend have been told to bring their blankets, food and cooking utensils.

DISCOVER RECTOR POSSESSED $40,000

Take Body To Morgue For Autopsy—Results Are Awaited.

New Brunswick, Oct. 5.—Authorities who are seeking to unravel the mystery surrounding the murders of the Rev. Edward Wheeler Hall and Mrs. Eleanor Reinhardt Mills, choir singer in his church, learned today that the minister had $40,000 in securities in a safe-deposit box on the day he died. These securities, it was learned, could have been changed into cash in ten minutes in any broker's office either here or in New York.

Continued on Third Page

REPORT NEUTRAL ZONE AROUND CONSTANTINOPLE VIOLATED BY KEMALISTS

Turkish Nationalist Cavalry Said to Have Appeared at Kandra—Agreement Reached Provides no Fortifications Shall be Built on Either Side of Straits, and That British Operations in Turkey Shall Cease Immediately.

Constantinople, Oct. 5 (By The Associated Press.)—The Mudania conference was reconvened at 10 o'clock this morning with Thrace the chief subject for consideration. The attitude of the Greek delegates on the question was declared to be giving the conference considerable concern.

Constantinople, Oct. 5 (By The Associated Press.)—British General headquarters reports the appearance of Turkish Nationalist cavalry at Kandra, in the Constantinople neutral zone.

Kandra is approximately 65 miles east of Constantinople, near the Black Sea coast of the Ismid peninsula.

This is the first reported violation by the Kemalists of the Constantinople neutral zone, although Turkish cavalry has repeatedly violated the neutral zone around Chanak, on the southern shore of the Dardanelles. The Ismid Peninsula offers the only direct approach on Constantinople for land forces.

According to telegrams from Turkish sources in Mudania, the agreement regarding the neutral zones reached by the Allied and Turkish representatives provides that no fortifications shall be constructed on either side of the Straits of Dardanelles, and that the military operations of the British in Turkey shall cease immediately.

A purported outline of the agreement published by the Figaro, Paris newspaper, says the British are to withdraw from the southern shore of the Dardanelles to Gallipoli and that the Turks are to retire behind the line formed by the Granicus and Skamander Rivers.

Lines of Agreement Announced

Paris, Oct. 5 (By The Associated Press).—An agreement has been reached by the conference of Allied and Turkish military leaders at Mudania, and will be signed some time today, according to private dispatches received here.

The main lines of the agreement, says the Figaro, are:

First, the British and Turks both

(Continued on Third Page.)

MAYOR HOUSMAN TO STAY AT HOSPITAL

New York Surgeon Will Not Set Leg Until Swelling Subsides.

Mayor Clarence J. Housman, who is nursing a broken left leg, spent a fairly good night at the Monmouth Memorial Hospital, although suffering considerable pain as a result of his injury, which was caused by a fall when he tripped while gathering dahlias at "The Homestead" on Wednesday.

Dr. John W. Moorehead, of New York, summoned by the Mayor's own physician, Dr. Harry B. Slocum to set the broken limb, did not reach Long Branch until after 8 o'clock last night. He found the Mayor's leg much swollen and he decided that it would not be wise to attempt to put it in a plaster cast until the swelling subsided, which is expected to keep the Mayor at the hospital for the next four or five days. It had been hoped yesterday that the plaster cast could be put on last night and the Mayor taken home today.

Mayor Housman is quite cheerful and takes his accident with much philosophy. He sees all visitors and welcomes the break they make in the monotony of being bed-ridden. Dr. Moorehead spoke most encouragingly of the prospects of early comple recovery.

MAN'S TORSO FOUND IN BRONX GARDEN

Believed To Be That Of Man Whose Severed Head Was Found.

New York, Oct. 5.—A man's torso, believed to be that of the man whose severed head was found in the Bronx zoological garden near New York on Sunday, was found today in the Bronx botanical garden by policemen.

The torso was found by two women who were seeking mushrooms. Without stopping to open the package in which it was covered they rushed for aid. The torso was covered with oil cloth, and the bundle was drapped with twine such as plumbers often use.

SPECTACULAR GUN FIGHT TAKES PLACE

One Man Dead And Another Injured As Result Of Battle.

Peoria, Ill., Oct. 5.—The bullet-riddled body of Henry Miller, river front habitue, lay in a morgue here today and Frank L. Boswell, railroad detective, was in a hospital with a bullet in his leg, casualties of a spectacular gun fight on the banks of the Illinois River last night.

Miller, routed by a gas bomb hurled by the police into his shack where he barricaded himself after shooting Boswell, fell amid the rattle of riot guns when he staggered into view, choking from the gas fumes, but still showing fight. He was shot down as he leveled his pistol at his besiegers.

Gas bombs were used when the police failed in their attempt to rout Miller by setting fire to the shack. The barricaded man succeeded in extinguishing the flames while hidden inside the rude building.

Boswell, in making his rounds, passed Miller's shack last night. The detective said today that Miller fired two shots after telling Boswell to mind his own business. Boswell ran for the shelter of a railroad car, but dropped with one of Miller's bullets in his left leg.

William Reise and McKinley Hill, neighbors of Miller, braved the fire of Miller's gun and carried Boswell to safety while railroad detectives and police rushed to the scene.

This Issue Carries the Most Complete Report in Connecticut on the World Series Baseball Game

Average Circulation For Week Ending Oct. 7 32,602

The Hartford Courant

Local Rains, Cooler Today; Fair Tomorrow.

Established 1764, VOL. (DAILY EDITION) LXXXVI. HARTFORD, CONN., MONDAY MORNING, OCTOBER 9, 1922—18 PAGES. Member of the ASSOCIATED PRESS. PRICE 3 CENTS.

GIANTS WIN GAME, 5-3, AND WORLD CHAMPIONSHIP
CYCLONIC RALLY IN EIGHTH INNING DEFEATS YANKS;
GOVERNOR LAKE RESCINDS BAN ON HUNTING SEASON

HUNTERS IN CONN. ARE FREE TODAY TO ENJOY SPORT

Fish and Game Superintendent Announces Proclamation by Lake Nullifying Former Edict.

DANGER OF FOREST FIRES IS ALLAYED

County Wardens Told to Inform Their Deputies—Inquiries From Sportsmen Deluge "Courant."

Superintendent John W. Titcomb of the state board of fisheries and game gave to the press last night a proclamation by Governor Lake, issued on his advice, whereby the governor's proclamation, issued Friday, suspending the hunting season throughout Connecticut for two weeks, was rescinded. The season will open this morning.

"The danger of forest fires having been allayed, I proclaim that the suspension of the open season delayed by proclamation and order on October 6 will not be put into effect," the proclamation read. "I urge that the fullest publicity be given by the press to the rescinding proclamation in order that the public, game wardens and other officials may be advised that the open season for hunting is effective tomorrow, October 9."

County Wardens Informed.

Superintendent Titcomb was in telephone communication last night with Governor Lake, who was in New York City. County Wardens were told by telephone to inform deputy wardens to be ready for the beginning of the open season this morning, and to see that all hunters had licenses.

"Courant" Deluged With Inquiries.

Wardens throughout the state were deluged with telephone inquiries yesterday by hunters, who wanted to know of the season would continue to be suspended, or whether the rain of the last two days would change the situation. The number of inquiries at "The Courant" almost equalled those of baseball enthusiasts, who were keen to know the result of the Giants-Yankee game.

GREEK GOVERNMENT YIELDS TO ALLIES

Athens, Oct. 8.—(By The Associated Press.)—The Greek government has instructed its delegates at the Mudania Conference to accept decisions which may be unanimously agreed upon by the Allied representatives. This action was taken following the receipt of advices from former Premier Venizelos that Eastern Thrace must be considered as lost to Greece.

Greece will endeavor to secure two months time to permit of the evacuation of her army and the Greek civilian population, which is estimated to aggregate 250,000. It is probable that another 300,000 Greeks and Armenians will leave Constantinople for Greece, which will make more crushing the problem of the country, which is already burdened with refugees.

Constantinople, Oct. 8.—(By The Associated Press.)—A despatch from Athens to the local newspaper "Kirix" says the Greek government has instructed General Mazarakis to sign the Mudania Armistice Convention, thereby agreeing to the evacuation of Eastern Thrace.

DRIVER LOSES EAR IN AUTO ACCIDENT

(Special to The Courant).

Meriden, October 8.

A public service car bearing the license number 0-1657, listed as owned by Edward Beckman of New Britain, knocked over a telephone pole early this morning on the North Colony road near the Carey farm and, after the driver lost control climbed over a stone wall beside the road. The police were at the scene of the accident shortly after it happened and, although it was said that there were several people in the car, everyone had disappeared. It was said that the driver lost an ear and that several others of the party were injured. The police are investigating.

Ex-Warden Bridges Dead.

Greenfield, Mass., Oct. 8.—General Benjamin F. Bridges, warden of the Charlestown state prison for twenty years until his retirement in 1914, died at his home here today. He was 8? years old.

Baby Is Drowned as Car Crashes Down Into Pond

(Special to The Courant).

Thompsonville, Oct. 8.

A roadster heavily loaded with wearing apparel and other articles, besides containing Mr. and Mrs. T. S. Walsh and their two children of Savannah, Ga., en route to Worcester, Mass., crushed through an iron fence on Freshwater bridge here shortly after 1 o'clock this morning, and a 7-month-old baby was drowned in the pond below when the machine overturned in three feet of water. Mrs. Walsh was internally injured and was taken to the Springfield Hospital as was her daughter, Irene, 4 years old. Her recovery was not expected tonight. They were attended by Dr. F. F. Simonton and Dr. Thomas A. Alcorn. Mr. Walsh was unharmed.

The Walshes had been on the road about two weeks and hoped to reach Worcester this morning. John F. Connor and Howard Lavine, local men, were on their way home when they saw the accident. They immediately jumped into the water and recovered the body of the baby, with the aid of others who were passing in an automobile. The party lost all their possessions.

BOYS LURE CHICKS WITH BAITED HOOKS

(Special to The Courant.)

New Britain, Oct. 8.

John Chika of No. 86 Gold street has at last discovered by what fell route his chickens have been disappearing.

Apprised by a steady squawking outside his house today, he looked out the window, and saw a fat capon being hauled off at the end of a fish line.

In short, the rude boys of the neighborhood have been baiting hooks with choice morsels of meat, luring away his fowls. Somehow, they were never returned.

Chika complained to the police.

WORLD WAR "VETS" TO BACK M'LEAN

Ex-Service Men Will Organize at Republican Club Tonight.

Many Hartford service men will gather at the Republican Club at 8 o'clock tonight to form an organization to aid in the re-election of Senator George P. McLean. The meeting has been called by Captain Clarence W. Seymour, former state commander of the American Legion. Senator McLean's record in Washington has appealed to all veterans of the Warld War, irrespective of political affiliations, and the organization which will be formed tonight will be one in which the former soldiers will express their appreciation of Senator McLean's efforts in their behalf. All ex-service men are invited to tonight's meeting

BRISTOL MAN HURT IN AUTO ACCIDENT

(Special to The Courant).

Plainville, October 8.

James Blodgett of Bristol is at the New Britain General Hospital suffering from a fractured right leg as a result of being struck by an automobile on East Main street tonight as he was crossing from the right side of the street to the home of his mother on the corner of Crown and Main streets.

Mr. Blodgett had returned from a fishing trip and, when on the way to Bristol, stopped here to see his mother. The car was driven by James Pompeii of this place. He summoned medical aid and took the injured man to the hospital.

ELETRIAL STORM VISITS SPRINGFIELD

Springfield, Mass., Oct. 8.—Streets were flooded and trolley car service impaired in towns and cities throughout this section today during a heavy rain and electrical storm.

Grand Opera Season.

New York, Oct. 8.—The Metropolitan opera Company announced tonight the opening of its fifteenth season of grand opera under the direction of Giulio Gatti-Casazza. The season will open November 13 and last twentythreee weeks.

Two novelties, six revivals and a standard repertoire of fifty-five operas are listed for the season. More than a score of new singers are in the company and there have been noteworthy additions to other departments into which the organization is divided.

Sarazen Operated On.

Yonkers, N. Y. Oct. 8.—Within twenty-four hours after he had defeated Walter Hagen, British Open Golf champion, Gene Sarazen, American National Open champion, was on the operating table at St. John's Hospital, where he was brought this morning from the Westchester-Biltmore Country Club, suffering from appendicitis. The operation took place this afternoon and the champion is reported to be resting comfortably.

GOVERNMENT BOND ISSUE ANNOUNCED

$500,000,000 at 4 1-4 Per Cent. Will Be First Offered Since War.

Washington, Oct. 8.—The first government bond issue since the war was announced tonight by the treasury.

Secretary Mellon offered for subscription an issue of about $500,000,000, of 4¼ per cent. thirty year treasury bonds as part of the program for refunding short term debt.

The new issue will be dated October 16, 1922, bearing interest at 4¼ per cent. annually, payable April 15, and October 15 on a semi-annual basis. The bonds will mature October 15, 1952, but may be redeemed at the option of the United States after October 15, 1947.

Bearer bonds of the new issue with interest coupons attached will be issued in denominations of $100, $500, $1,000, $5,000 and $10,000, while bonds registered as to principal and interest will be issued in denominations of $100, $500, $1,000, $5,000, $10,000, $50,000 and $100,000. All will carry the usual tax exemption provisions. Secretary Mellon reserved the right to allot additional bonds above the $500,000,000 amount fixed for subscriptions to the extent that 4¼ per cent. Victory notes or treasury certificates of the series maturing December 15, 1922, are tendered in payment. Applications for new bonds not exceeding $10,000 from any one subscriber will be allotted in full but applications for an amount in excess of $10,000 will be received subject to allotment.

PLANE AVERAGES OVER 220 MILES AN HOUR

Detroit, Mich., Oct. 8.—Details of the test flight of one of the Army's new airplanes, the Army-Curtiss racer No. 2, held at Curtiss Field, Garden City, last Monday, reveal that Lieutenant R. L. Maughan, piloted the plane over a straightaway kilometer course at the rate of 220.458 miles an hour, faster than any human being ever traveled. The official report of the test was given out upon the arrival at Selfridge Field of Lieutenant Maughan and the record breaking racer, which will be one of the twenty-three contenders for the Pulitzer trophy next Saturday.

The electrically timed kilometer was placed in a ten-mile straightaway. The first dash was made in 10.4 seconds, or at the rate of 215.1 miles an hour; the second was made in 10 seconds flat or at the rate of 223.704 miles an hour.

HINTON IN SEAPLANE REACHES SAN JUAN

San Juan, Porto Rico, Oct. 8.—(By the Associated Press.)—Lieutenant Walter Hinton, piloting the hydroairplane Sampaio Correia II, on a flight from Florida to Rio Jeniero, arrived here at 2 o'clock this afternoon from San Domingo.

Coke Secured by Curley.

Boston, Oct. 8.—The collier E. C. Pope made port here last night with 2,000 tons of coke from Alabama, the first fruits of Mayor Curley's trip to points South recently in an effort to obtain fuel for Boston. It was said that the coke would be distributed at $14 or less a ton.

TWO TO ONE ODDS ON REPUBLICAN TICKET TO CARRY THE STATE

Odds of two to one on the republican ticket to carry the state are the prevailing figures in Hartford, according to those who are given to speculating on elections. Little money has been offered thus far, it is said, chiefly because of the demand of those willing to back the democrats for odds ranging from two to one to four to one.

BRITISH INSIST TURKS WITHDRAW ALL TROOPS FROM NEUTRAL ZONES

Harington Threatens Demonstration on Turkish Flanks — Stops Ferry Service on Bosphorus and Sea of Marmora.

HITCH OVER TURKISH GENDARMES IN THRACE

Constantinople, Oct. 8.—(By The Associated Press)—General Harington today demanded of Ismet Pasha that the Turks withdraw their forces from the neutral zone near Ismid. Unless this was done, he declared, he might be obliged to make a demonstration on both flanks of the Turkish forces.

Immediate suspension of the ferryboats on the Bosphorus and the Sea of Marmora has been ordered by the British.

A Diplomat in close touch with the Mudania conference expressed the belief tonight that the next twenty-four hours would spell either peace or war.

The Turks at Mudania today refused to specify the number of gendarmes they desired to send to Thrace. The British delegation had instructions to insist on limitation of the number permitted.

Allies Present United Front.

Mudania, Oct. 8.—(By The Associated Press.)—The Allies presented a united front on their return to Mudania at 10 o'clock tonight, and the feeling of all three delegations was that Ismet Pasha would be forced to yield.

The delegation expressed optimism regarding the outcome, contending there was little doubt that the Turks would accept the Allied demands, leaving the question of the limitation of the Turkish Gendarmes only as a possibility of friction.

New Hitch in Parley.

A new hitch arose in the negotiations this morning, when it was announced that the new instructions to the French and Italian delegation had not been received. The British delegation received final instructions from London, and Generals Charpy and Mombelli decided to return to Constantinople for a consultation with the high commissioners there.

(Concluded on Page 2.)

FIND BURIAL PLACE OF ANTIOCHUS, COUSIN OF HEROD THE GREAT

Philadelphia, Oct. 9.—The nearest approach to unearthing contemporary records of Christ today was announced by Dr. George Byron Gordon, director of the Museum of the University of Pennsylvania. The discovery was made by Dr. Clarence Stanley Fisher, director of excavations at Beth Shan, in Palestine.

The discovery was the burial place of Antiochus, the first cousin of Herod the Great. Antiochus in all probability, Dr. Gordon asserted, was one of the men charged by Herod with directing the slaughter of the children in Bethlehem as narrated by Matthew in a vain effort to kill the Christ child who had been described by the wise men as the "King of the Jews."

Dr. Gordon also announced that Dr. Fisher has found, in deeper levels of occupation, the first known sarcophagi of the Philistines. Readers of the Bible will recall that they defeated King Saul on Mount Gilboa, which overshadows the ancient fortress city, and cutting off his head hauled his body to the city walls.

Levels of six cities so far have been found at Beth Shan, Dr. Gordon declared, while more are known to be below. The site is said to have been occupied for a longer continuous period than any other place of human habitation. It is also the most fought over spot in the world, since it serves as the gateway between Mesopotamia and Egypt and was necessary to the conquest of Parestine.

FOOTBALL TICKETS

For Army and Iowa Games — Watch "Courant."

"The Courant" will have a number of tickets for sale for the Yale-Iowa game of next Saturday, October 14th, and for the Yale-West Point game of Saturday, October 28th. The details of the sale will be announced in "The Courant" tomorrow, Tuesday morning.

HARDING ISSUES NATION-WIDE CALL FOR NEAR EAST AID

Red Cross and Other Agencies Will Work Together Under Special Committee Headed by W. H. Hays.

PRESIDENT TAKES PERSONAL INTEREST

Hopes People Will Respond Generously in Efforts to Provide For Thousands of Refugees.

Washington, Oct. 8.—A nation-wide appeal for funds for the relief of the thousands of refugees in the Near East was authorized today by President Harding. The money will be distributed through the American Red Cross and the Near East relief, working jointly, and will be raised by a special committee headed by ex-Postmaster General Hays.

This statement was issued by the President:

"A recognized and most appealing emergency exists in the Near East. After full conference it is unanimously agreed that the American Red Cross and the Near East Relief, two governmentally recognized agencies, are the logical instrumentalities through which this relief may be extended and it is a manifest duty that they should take care of the situation. It has been decided that these two organizations will take care of the situation jointly. In a campaign of most cordial cooperation they will command the facilities for most efficient ministration.

"In order to meet the situation there is created a special fund to be known as 'Near East emergency fund.' The special fund is to be raised by a nation-wide appeal, which appeal is endorsed and will be engaged in by the American Red Cross, the Near East Relief, the Y. M. C. A., Y. W. C. A., the federal council of churches, the Relief Administration, the Jewish American Administration, the Jewish Joint Distribution Committee, and other organizations having interests in the Near East.

"Money may be sent to Eliot Wadsworth, treasurer of the American Red Cross, Washington, D. C., Cleveland H. Dodge, treasurer of Near East Relief, 151 Fifth avenue, New York, or the 'Literary Digest,' 354 Fourth avenue, New York. A special emphasis and appeal for funds will be made during the roll call of the American

(Concluded on Page 2.)

Man Missing Two Days Found Dead in Woods

(Special to The Courant.)

East Hampton, Oct. 8.

Jeremiah House, 83 years old, of East Hampton, who disappeared from his home Friday about noon, was found dead today in a stretch of woodland about an eighth of a mile from the state highway. The fully clothed body was found by Alec Sherman, 13 years old, who was on his way to bring a herd of cows from pasture.

Mr. House lived with his son, Samuel House, a carpenter, and was a character about the countryside. Almost daily he walked to the home of his daughter, Mrs. Frank Taylor, in Middle Haddam. Friday morning he had made this trip, returned home and after dinner set out again. There being no marks on the body, it is thought Mr. House become confused and collapsed in exhaustion. Death was probably due to exhaustion and exposure, although a statement from the medical examiner could not be secured last night.

Searching parties have been hunting for Mr. House since Friday afternoon. He had been traced by the marks of his cane and boots as far as Marlborough.

'Beaten by Our Own Faults', says Huggins; 'Had Breaks'-McGraw

Manager of Champions Tells of Best Piece of Strategy in Series—"I Followed My Judgment and Lost," Says Yank Pilot.

MILLER HUGGINS, YANKS.

JOHN McGRAW, GIANTS.

New York, Oct. 8.—(By the Associated Press.)—Ill luck for the Yankees, following one of the smartest pieces of baseball strategy employed during the present world series, lost the fifth and deciding game of the 1922 world baseball championship for the New York Americans, in the opinion of John McGraw, manager of the Giants.

The strategic move, referred to occurred in the eighth inning, when with men on second and third and two out, Huggins ordered Bush to pass "Pep" Young, the Giant rightfielder, a left-handed batter. The Yankees at that time were one run ahead of the Nationals who needed a hit to tie or take the lead.

"Young", said McGraw, "is rated as a sure hitter to right field. By pitching to Young the Yankee infielders would be forced to play back, making it difficult to cut off a run at the plate should he hit one in the infield. On the other hand, should he have driven to right, it would have been hard for Ruth's throw to beat the runner on third to the plate.

"Kelly has been a weak hitter. He had not batted effectively against any of the Yankee hurlers. Huggins figured all these things and ordered Young passed. That, in my opinion, was the best piece of strategy in the series.

"But Kelly broke the law of baseball averages and hit. That was bad luck for the Yankees and a great bit of work by our first baseman.

Made Most of Breaks.

"The Giants have fought their best throughout the series, and fighting has won for them. We have had good pitching; so have the Yankees, but we had the breaks and we took advantage to them."

Huggin's View.

"There isn't any use quibbling about it," said Miller Huggins. "We were whipped soundly and well and mostly through our own faults. John McGraw has a great ball team. His men had lots of good luck, but they didn't miss one opportunity to score during the series. They didn't throw a chance away.

"In today's game, when Bush was in trouble in the eighth, I ordered him to pass Young because Young is a dangerous hitter. Kelly had been the weakest batter of the Nationals; he is a right-handed batter and it was sound judgment, I think, to pass Young and work on the first baseman. The tying and winning runs were on the bases anyway, so the passing of Young couldn't hurt much.

"Bush kicked on my order to pass Young, but that was natural. I followed the dictates of my judgment, and lost."

The Yankee players praised Huggins for his leadership throughout the series. They declared that the mistakes that had been made were their own.

NEITHER CLUB WILL GET ENOUGH FROM SERIES TO PAY OVERHEAD

New York, Oct. 8.—(By The Associated Press.)—Some of the 40,000 persons who trudged out of the Polo Grounds after the last game of the world's series today had a vision before them as they walked—a picture of the two sets of club owners sitting snugly in the counting room, snickering to themselves and calling a moving van to cart away their profits.

They were in the counting room and no doubt they were sitting down, puffing on big, fat cigars, and listening to the music of adding machines—but it was about as pleasant to them as a Turkish melody is in a Greek restaurant. It is stated unofficially that neither club company will get enough sheckels to pay its expenses out of the series, one of the few times that it has happened.

And this despite the fact that on each of the five days that a game was played the record for total receipts of previous series was broken.

Each New York club will receive approximately $41,218—which is generally believed to be less than it cost either club to meet its world series overhead. Compared to the $108,027 that each operating combination took to its coffers last year it looks like a bankrupt sale.

Greatest paid attendance was at today's game, when 38,551 trickled past the turnstiles. The total attendance for the five games was 185,947.

The total receipts were $605,475, of which $120,554, the receipts of the second game, went to charity. Of the remaining $484,921, the players share, including those members of the two teams in each league to finish second and third in the pennant races, was $247,309.71. Seventy-five per cent of this, about $185,482, is to be divided among the members of the two world's series teams, and the other $61,827 to the runners-up in the league scrambles.

The champion Giants get $111,289 to split among themselves, but since the division is rarely equal to all who are eligible—one or two generally getting a small cut—it is impossible to tell accurately what the average slice will be. The prospect, however, is about $4,470, which is far from being a record breaker—though the shortness of the series makes it pretty high for five days' work.

The losing Yankees get the balance of $74,193, which, figured on a basis of conjecture similar to that used in estimating the individual Giants' share, would be about $3,225.

Each club actually gets $82,436.57, but both of them must pay half of that to its respective league treasury.

The remainder of the gate receipts, $72,591.11, goes to the advisory council, presided over by Commissioner Landis. It probably will be enough to pay his salary and for the maintenance of his office.

MRS. FLETCHER PROMOTED IN PROBATE COURT

Mrs. Maude R. Fletcher of No. 50 Hungerford street was appointed head clerk in the record department of the probate court by Judge Walter H. Clark to succeed Miss Martha K. Bahruth, who resigned recently. Mrs. Fletcher has been employed in the probate court for several years, having been first appointed by Judge L. P. Waldo Marvin. Mrs. Fletcher is a member of Trinity Church and has been active in the work of the Girl's Friendly Society.

LOCAL BOY, RUNAWAY, IS HELD IN DENVER

Louis Lettieri, 15 years old, son of Mr. and Mrs. Ralph Letteiri of No. 49 South street, is being held by the Denver, Colo., police pending the arrival of his parents.

The boy ran away from home September 27 and an alarm was sent out in the hope that he would be located in neighboring towns, but no information was obtained until a telegram was received from Chief of Police Smith of Denver.

FURIOUS RUSH WINS WORLD TITLE SECOND CONSECUTIVE YEAR

Only Third Time in History That Victory Has Been So Decisive and Losers So Thoroughly Outclassed

YOUNG IS PASSED THEN KELLY DELIVERS

Huggins Orders Bush to Walk Giant Outfielder Only to Have First Baseman Upset Strategy.

New York, Oct. 8.—(By The Associated Press). — The New York Giants once more are baseball champions of the world. They reached that pinnacle of success for the second consecutive year in a furious uphill rush this afternoon that flung the Yankees to defeat, 5 to 3, and crushed a disgusted pitcher, "Bullet Joe" Bush.

It was the second successive time that the Yanks have bucked the Giants in a world's series and failed. This year they went down ingloriously, without the solace of having captured even one of the five games that comprised the battle for the title. The best the Yankees could do was to tie the second game of the series. The Giants won the other four.

Third Decisive Championship.

In all the annals of the game only two clubs ever triumphed in a world's series in such a decisive fashion. In 1907 the Chicago Nationals won four straight victories over the Detroit Americans after fighting a twelve inning first game tie at 3-3. Seven years later the Boston Braves surprised the fans of the entire nation by wrecking Connie Mack's superb Athletics four times in a row.

Huggins' Strategy Fails.

The final downfall of the Yanks was that of a house momentarily divided. Miller Huggins, the head of the household which was then enjoying a 3 to 2 lead over the Giants, differed with his pitcher, Joe Bush, in his strategic program for blocking the onslaught of the champions in the eighth inning. Bush became angry and before he could calm himself, long George Kelly had smacked one of his curves so hard and so far that one Giant raced across the plate with the run that tied the Yankees and another Giant trotted in with the score that beat them.

A Glimpse of Victory.

The Yanks enjoyed the prospect of a victory for only fifteen minutes. When they came to bat in the seventh the score was deadlocked at 2-all. They made a run on Meusel's scratch hit, Schang's sacrifice bunt, a wild pitch by Art Nehf, the Giant southpaw, and a short sacrifice fly to center field from the bat of Everett Scott. The throw-in of this fly almost caught Meusel as he slid for home. It seemed the Yanks barely had squeezed out a vitcory.

The Giants Rally.

And then in the eighth, the courageous Giants flung out their challenge. Pipp, the Yanks' first baseman, halted them for a moment by stopping Bancroft's hard blow back of first base and leaping to the bag just in time to beat the runner. But the fighting Giants would not be denied a victory quick and sure. Groh cut the diamond squarely in half with a single that ripped through the turf into center field. Frisch hit a liner that bounded to McMillan in center field, who juggled it, and the batter was credited with a two bagger, while Groh went on to third. Irish Meusel shot a roller to short, Scott hurling the ball home so fast that Groh could not safely reach the plate. He started to return to third, but was run down by Schang.

When the ball was thrown back to the box, Bush found himself in trouble. Frisch, the fastest runner on either team, stood perched on third base and Irish Meusel was on second.

Indecision Costly.

At the plate, swinging his bat left-handed, stood Pep Young, who usual

Baseball, Golf, Tennis, Turf, Track, Boxing, Wrestling—all expertly reported by expert reporters, Best in the West.

CHARACTER · QUALITY · AMERICA FIRST · ACCURACY · ENTERPRISE

Los Angeles Examiner Sports

AN AMERICAN PAPER FOR THE AMERICAN PEOPLE · THE GREAT NEWSPAPER OF THE GREAT SOUTHWEST

The Examiner carries the most complete Sporting Section of any newspaper West of Chicago.

THURSDAY, APRIL 19, 1923 · SECTION III—PAGE 1

74,200 SEE RUTH SMASH FIRST HOMER

Yanks Beat Red Sox; Dodgers Cop in Ninth

Greatest Ball Crowd in History Sees Chance Lose, 4-1

By Thomas L. Cummiskey
Universal Service Sports Editor

NEW YORK, April 18.—Seventy - four thousand, two hundred persons saw Babe Ruth hit a home run that won the opening game for the Yankees from the Boston Red Sox today at the dedication of the gigantic new Yankee Stadium.

The score was 4 to 1. Babe's homer came with two on base in the fourth inning, and went like a shot from a rifle into the right field bleachers.

The sensation of that hit, working on the emotions of far and away the biggest crowd baseball has ever known, was something well nigh indescribable. The game's greatest figure came into his own at the psychological moment. A genius in drama could not have thought of anything more thrilling. It was stupendous, tremendous, moved past compare, that homer, and the spectacle it cast into being.

A fat book of colorful adjectives, used with little or no discretion, could be rapped out on typewriters and still fail to portray in any comprehensive degree the wonder of it all. Baseball reached its zenith of thrills when the Babe got that wallop. In unison the 74,000 arose to cheer, to shout, to give a demonstration hysterical in its aspects.

DRAMATIC DEDICATION

Truly, the Yankee Stadium, $3,000,000 edifice in baseball in the greatest city in the world, was dedicated in a manner beyond the fondest dreams of Colonels Ruppert and Huston, the owners, the "gambling colonels." Some sages have said: "Baseball is in its infancy," but today they must have been wrong. Today baseball came into a glorious manhood.

The fourth inning:

Aaron Ward, first up, got the Yankees' first hit in the Stadium, and Everett Scott sacrificed him to second. Bob Shawkey, honored in pitching the opening game, hit to Pitcher Ehmke of the Sox, and Ward was trapped between second and third, but delayed his demise long enough for Shawkey to reach second.

"Whitey" Witt got a pass. Joe Dugan dropped a short fly safe in center and Shawkey scored, while Witt scurried to third. Then, up came Babe Ruth, the Sultan of Swat, the Bambino, the Monarch of Maul.

LIKE RIFLE BULLET

It was his second appearance at the plate. The first time, in the opening inning, he had flied to right, with no one on. Now was his chance, the crowd told him, long and loud, as if the Babe didn't know it. He fouled one. He fouled another, strike two. Two balls came over, the Babe looking them over. Then he socked it, viciously, vengefully, with a herculean follow-through swing. On the line the pellet shot, not more than thirty feet from the ground, into the right field bleachers.

Witt, Dugan and the Babe paraded the bases, while the crowd was lost to sanity in its enthusiasm. Babe jogged around, his homely face in smiles, until he reached the plate. There he took off his cap, uplifted his face to the towering stands and bowed. He lifted his cap, he smiled from ear to ear.

TICKLED TO DEATH

The Babe had made his homer, the earliest he has ever made in a big league season, and there was none more thrilled, more joyoue than he. As he tarried briefly at the plate, he was the greatest hero baseball has known, with the most tremendous adulitation a player has known. It was a demonstration deserved, and whole-heartedly given.

Except for this inning, the game was rather listless. That fourth inning was largely to blame. Nothing thereafter could have at all approached it. The poor Red Sox, fighting valiently under a fighting leader, Frank Chance, got a run in the seventh. It came on a pass to Harris and a triple by McMillan, ex-Yankee. Otherwise, he had the Sox at his mercy, got brilliant fielding and Ehmke performed strongly for the visitors.

CROWD BREAKS RECORDS

The biggest crowd before today was in Boston, in 1917, in a world's series game between the great Red Sox of that day.
Sox of that day. It was approximately 42,000.

The 90,000 that saw Jack Dempsey knock out Georges Carpentier and the 77,000 that attended a Yale-Harvard football game are the only sport crowds that have surpassed today's vast throng in this country.

Today's crowds in colorful aspects and demonstration can only be likened to the throngs we read about in ancient history—the throngs of the Coliseum of Rome. They say it was of 350,000 capacity. They must have made some noise. Yet it is hard to think they rivaled the 75,000 of today.

Judge Landis, Gov. Smith, Col.

(Continued on Page 3, Column 3)

Williams and Heilman Also Get 1st Homers

ST. LOUIS, April 18.

KEN WILLIAMS of the Browns hit a circuit drive in the seventh inning of today's opening game with Detroit. Francis was pitching for the Tigers. No one was on base. Williams lead the American League in homers last year.

Ken Williams

ST. LOUIS, April 18.—Rightfielder Heilman of Detroit knocked a homer in the sixth inning of today's game with the Browns, driving in Cobb ahead of him. Danforth was pitching for the locals.

Wilshire Golf Team Humbles Los Angeles, 3-2

CAPT. GEORGE CLINE of the Wilshire Country Club golf team yesterday led his followers out to the Los Angeles Country Club and defeated Major Karnes and the Los Angeles golfers, 3 to 2, in one of the best contested interclub matches of the season. This was the first match of the year in which Cline played and he celebrated his return to tournament ranks by shooting the last nine of the North Course in 34. He and Frank Deleot defeated Harley Moore and E. K. Brown, 3 and 1.

The feature match of the day at Los Angeles was that in which Norman Macbeth and Elmer Ralphs defeated A. D. S. Johnston and Everett Seaver, 2 and 1. In accomplishing this Macbeth turned in a card of 69 for the eighteen holes.

Annandale defeated Midwick, 3 to 2, at Midwick in an interclub match that was replete with thrills. Scotty Armstrong and Les Gordon of Midwick won a marathon match from Dr. Paul Hunter and H. B. Ingalls of Annandale, defeating that distinguished duo 1 up on the twentieth hole.

Annandale, 3; Midwick, 2.
E. S. Armstrong and L. S. Gordon (M.) defeated Dr. Paul Hunter and H. B. Ingalls, 1 up, 20 holes.
W. P. Herbert and J. L. Mothershead (M.) defeated C. M. Ransome and C. P. Erdman, 4 and 3.
Nate Mears and Frank Chaffee (A.) defeated W. B. Tait and C. G. Lathrop (M.), 6 and 5.
Bob Finkbine and W. J. Bowman (A.) defeated S. C. Fertig and A. F. Halstead (M.), 4 and 3.
R. M. Modisette and L. Barnes (A.) defeated J. S. Cravens and H. Coppell (M.), 3 and 2.
Wilshire, 3; Los Angeles, 2.
Norman Macbeth and E. Ralphs (W.) defeated A. D. S. Johnston and E. H. Seaver (L. A.), 2 and 1.
W. D. Whelan and M. E. McLoughlin (W.), defeated C. H. Palmer and Frank Tatum (L. A.), 2 up.
George Thomas and H. T. Major (L. A.) defeated Pat Higgins and Dr. H. C. Humes (W.), 2 and 1.
J. T. Gilmer and W. H. Spinks (L. A.) defeated W. G. Nevin and J. C. Hodge (W.), 6 and 5.
George Cline and Frank Deleot (W.) defeated E. K. Brown and H. A. Moore (L. A.), 3 and 1.

Gastine Draws With Don Davis

SAN DIEGO, April 18.—Henry Gastine of Los Angeles and Don Davis of San Diego drew in the main event at Dreamland tonight after four hard-fought rounds.

Frisco Lewis knocked out Joe Chaney of Los Angeles in the third

Al Shapiro won from Kid Sweeney.

Sammy Sandos, Navy, drew with Packy McMullin of Los Angeles.

Billy Wilson, Navy, knocked out Charley Gall of San Diego in the third round.

Murphy, 2-Miler, Lost to Cards in Bears' Meet

STANFORD UNIVERSITY, Cal., April 18.

PAUL MURPHY, Stanford's crack two-miler, was ruled ineligible here today to participate in next Saturday's track and field meet with the University of California.

The decision, under the conference rules, is based on the fact that Murphy has not put in a sufficient number of hours in study according to the announcement of the scholarship committee.

Murphy has covered the eight laps in 10:7, but it was figured that he would come close to Hayes' time of 9:53. in competition next Saturday.

Stanford had figured on him for sure place points.

Cubs Even Series With Pirates; Score, 7 to 2

BROOKLYN, April 18. — The Brooklyn Dodgers staged a riotous ninth inning today to beat out the Phillies, 6 to 5. The visitors apparently had sewed up the game in the ninth when Sand boosted a homer over the wall, driving in Walker to make the score 5 to 1. Wheat greeted Ralph Head, who had held the Dodgers to three hits in eight innings, with a circuit swat over the right field wall. Schleibner singled and Barber walked. Hubbell relieved Head and after passing Reuther and allowing DeBerry a hit, was sent to the showers. Meadows then passed Grimes and Olson's single won the game without a Dodger being retired in the inning.

Giants Win Again

BOSTON, April 18.—Long hits off Watson and Oeschger enabled the world champion Giants to beat Boston, 7 to 4, today. Scott was given brilliant support and his home run to right center in the fourth also scored Snyder. When Scott walked Gowdy in the last of the ninth, Barnes relieved him. Bagwell hit the left field wall on the fly, getting only a double for this unprecedented feat.

Cubs Square Series

CHICAGO, April 18.—Boehler weakened in the eighth inning and Chicago pounded out six hits, including two doubles and a triple, broke a tie score and defeated Pittsburg 7 to 2 in the second game of the series. Johnny Kelleher of Chicago knocked the ball into the newly erected left bleachers for a home run, the first in the new park. Grimm of Pittsburg duplicated the feat a little later. Alexander pitched in fine form.

Toney Beats Reds

CINCINNATI, O., April 18.—Fred Toney outpitched Rixey in the second game of the season here today and St. Louis evened up the series by beating Cincinnati, 4 to 2. Rixey was wild and was hit safely in every inning, but one. Mann made the first home run of the local season on a long drive to right center inside the grounds in the third inning. Score:

Buick Sets Up 108-Mile Record

OVER the bed of Roger's dry lake, a remarkable natural race course in the Mojave desert, one mile from Murock, Joe Nikrent, veteran race driver on Tuesday made a straightaway record of better than 108 miles an hour with a Buick Special Six from the Howard Automobile Company, over a measured mile.

The speed test was made under the sanction of the A. A. A. and was supervised by officials of that body. Fred J. Wagner handled the flags and Val Haresnape and Hal Weller did the timing with the official electric timing device.

Three trials were made to a flying start. The first resulted in a score of 33.49 seconds, an average of 107.48 miles per hour. The second dash with the motor well warmed up was done in 33.26 seconds making the remarkable record for a car said to be 90 per cent stock of 108.24 miles per hour. The last trial developed a speed of 33.31 for the mile, an average of 108 per hour.

Plan Veteran Golfers Union

CHICAGO, April 18.—(By The Associated Press.)—Tentative plans were made today for the formation of a National golf association of players more than fifty years old, and recommendations were made for a meeting, to be held in Chicago within a couple weeks, to formulate plans for the organization.

It was suggested that the body be known as Seniors' Golf Association and that State bodies be created, so that there eventually would be forty-eight regional associations, which would hold annual tournaments. The champions of these State organizations would then meet in a National championship for men past the half century milestone.

It was recommended that the senior golfers be divided by periods of five years in age, so that all those between 50 and 55 years old would constitute one class and the succeeding classes would range in age from 55 to 60 and so on to the Octogenarians.

Veteran New York Fight Manager Reported Dying

CHICAGO, April 18. — Charley Harvey of New York, pioneer manager of boxers, was reported to be dying in a hospital here tonight as the result of an automobile accident today in which three others were injured. He suffered a triangular fracture of the skull over the left eye and has not gained consciousness.

Babe's No. 1

Babe Ruth

BASEBALL RESULTS STANDINGS SCHEDULES

Coast League Standing

	W.	L.	Pct.	If Win	If Lose
San Francisco..	9	5	.643	.667	.600
Sacramento	8	5	.615	.643	.578
VERNON	7	5	.583	.615	.538
Salt Lake City	7	5	.583	.615	.538
Portland	6	8	.429	.467	.400
LOS ANGELES.	5	7	.417	.462	.385
Seattle	5	7	.417	.462	.385
Oakland	4	9	.308	.357	.286

YESTERDAY'S RESULTS

Sacramento, 6; Oakland 4.
San Francisco, 4; Portland 1.
Seattle, 1; LOS ANGELES, 0.
VERNON and Salt Lake, rain.

GAMES TODAY

Salt Lake at VERNON.
Sacramento at Oakland.
LOS ANGELES at Seattle.
San Francisco at Portland.

American Legaue

	W.	L.	Pct.		W.	L.	Pct.
New York	1	0	1.000	Boston..	0	1	.000
Philadl..	1	0	1.000	Wash'ngtn	0	1	.000
Clv'land.	1	0	1.000	Chicago..	0	1	.000
Detroit..	1	0	1.000	St. Louis	0	1	.000

YESTERDAY'S RESULTS

New York, 4; Boston, 1.
Philadelphia, 3; Washington, 1.
Cleveland, 6; Chicago, 5.
Detroit, 9; St. Louis, 6.

TODAY'S GAMES

Chicago at Cleveland.
Detroit at St. Louis.
Washington at Philadelphia.
Boston at New York.

National League

	W	L	Pct.		W	L	Pct.
New York	2	0	1.000	St. Louis	1	1	.500
Brooklyn.	1	0	1.000	Chicago..	1	1	.500
Cincinnati	1	1	.500	Philadel..	0	1	.000
Pittsburg.	1	1	.500	Boston...	0	2	.000

YESTERDAY'S RESULTS

Brooklyn, 6; Philadelphia, 5.
New York, 7; Boston, 4.
Chicago, 7; Pittsburg, 2.
St. Louis, 4; Cincinnati, 2.

TODAY'S GAMES

New York at Boston (2 games).
Philadelphia at Broklyn.
Pittsburg at Chicago.

Western League

	W.	L.	Pct.		W.	L.	Pct.
Wichita..	6	0	1.000	Sioux City	2	4	.333
Okl. City.	5	1	.833	Omaha...	2	5	.286
Tulsa.....	5	2	.714	D. Moines	1	5	.167
St. Joe...	4	2	.667	Denver...	0	6	.000

YESTERDAY'S RESULTS

Wichita, 9; Omaha, 3.
Sioux City, 8; Oklahoma City, 5.
St. Joseph, 11; Denver, 2.
Tulsa, 17; Des Moines, 7.

Minnesota House Kills Small Town Boxing Bill

ST. PAUL, April 18.—The Minnesota House tonight killed the Senate bill which would have permitted boxing in cities of the second, third and fourth class when ten members objected to its consideration. Boxing is permitted in Minneapolis, St. Paul and Duluth.

American Ass'n Opens Up Today

By Associated Press
CHICAGO, April 18.

FACING the brightest prospects in its twenty-one years of unbroken campaigning, the American Association will open its season tomorrow with Columbus playing at Toledo, Louisville at Indianapolis, Minneapolis at Milwaukee and St. Paul at Kansas City.

Southern Golfers Win; Angels Shut Out, 1-0

Miss Cameron and Miss Kavanagh Take Matches

SAN FRANCISCO, April 18.—The women golfers claim to have fixed the "weather man" and Old Sol was on the job, smiling his brightest. So that's that.

Mrs. Brent Potter shocked the "talent" by defeating Mrs. Robert A. Roos in the second round of the State championship on the Ingleside links by a margin of two and one.

Despite her impressive victory over Mrs. Albert B. Swinerton on Tuesday, the San Jose and Lincoln Park player was conceded little chance to defeat the Beresford golfer, who has always made such a good showing in representative events. But a golfer who can win a match on the long eighteenth with a five as Mrs. Potter did against Mrs. Swinerton must not be overlooked.

It was a thrilling match from the start and there was never more than two holes margin separating the two players. Both of them played daring and sporty golf, taking chances when necessary despite the high wind that prevailed. And Mrs. Roos is no "wind player" as has been demonstrated on several occasions.

WEARIES OPPONENT

They were all square at the turn, but the local player gradually wore down her opponent to the dormy stage and all Mrs. Roos could do on the seventeenth was to earn a half. The approaches to the sixteenth green would have done justice to any man golfer.

Miss Doreen Kavanagh, title holder, and Miss Margaret Cameron, challenger, the representatives from Southern California, emerged successfully in the semi-final round, but the State champion looked to have quite a battle on her hands in the early stages of the match.

As a matter of fact, Mrs. Charles F. Ford of Claremont held her to an even basis to the turn and a crowd gather to witness a close finish. But the end was surprisingly near, as Miss Doreen commenced one of her streaks of putting and took the next five holes in succession. The twelfth was surely stolen by the Los Angeles player after it looked as though Mrs. Ford had the edge.

MISS HANCHETT LOSES

Mrs. W. C. Van Antwerp had a walkover from Miss Alice Hanchett, who was expected to give her a much closer argument. But there was no denyin the Burlingame player today, and six and five just about represents the difference between the two golfers on the day's play.

Mrs. Van Antwerp was sinking her putts persistently. She averaged two less than par on the greens played.

Miss Margaret Cameron was not caught napping by Mrs. H. A. Prole today and was in excellent form, winning in easy fashion.

Miss Mildred Landreth defeated Mrs. Herbert Schmidt in the second flight.

CHAMPIONSHIP FLIGHT

Miss Doreen Kavanagh defeated Mrs. C. Ford, 5 and 4.
Mrs. W. C. Van Antwerp defeated Miss Alice Hanchett, 6 and 5.
Mrs. Brent Potter defeated Mrs. Robert A. Roos, 2 and 1.
Miss Margaret Caramon defeated Mrs. H. A. Prole, 7 and 6.

English Fight Title to Yank

LONDON, April 18.—(By the Associated Press.)—Edward P. Eagan, the American student at Oxford, who holds the Olympic light heavyweight boxing championship, tonight defeated F. J. Hulks of St. Pancras, in the third round at Alexander Palace, thus winning the boxing association heavyweight championship.

Eagan trained for the bout in Dublin, acting as sparring partner for Mike McTigue, Tonight was the thirty-ninth time the championship had been contested and Eagan is the first American to win it.

Eagan competed also in the light heavyweight class, but was beaten on points in this event by H. J. Mitchell, holder of the title.

Man Falls, Badly Hurt, at Seals-Beavers Game

PORTLAND, Ore., April 18.—Falling in some unexplained manner from the grandstand of Recreation Park, where a game was in progress this afternoon between the Portland and San Francisco clubs of the Pacific Coast Baseball League, Louis E. Geer, a Portland postal clerk, struck upon his head on a cement approach outside the gate and suffered injuries which a doctor summoned from the crowd feared might prove fatal.

Geer was hastened to a hospital. The game was not interrupted.

ASTORIA REGATTA AGAIN

ASTORIA, Ore., April 18.—The rejuvenation of the old Astoria regatta, which for many years was among the leading water carnivals on the Pacific Coast, is being planned and committees have been named to arrange for the feature next August.

Chance Gets Excited When Season Opens

NEW YORK, April 18.

FRANK CHANCE, once peerless leader of the old Chicago Cubs, sat among his Red Sox in the visitors' dugout at the Yankee stadium today trembling like an oak leaf in the late fall.

"What's the matter, boss, cold?" asked "Chick" Fewster, the Red Sox shortstop.

Frank Chance

"Cold, nothing," smiled Chance. "Excited, like a fish that's been hauled out on a river bank, then thrown back into the stream."

Tennessee Nine Nosed Out by New Mexico, 4-3

THE U. S. S. NEW MEXICO ball team downed the Tennessee nine, 4 to 3, in the feature attraction of Pacific Fleet baseball yesterday afternoon at San Pedro. The hitting of Peckerick for the winners and the hurling of Jacoby for the Rebel Ship featured the day.

In the second game of the afternoon the U. S. S. California nosed out the U. S. S. Idaho, 4 to 2. Sailor Arrow Smith, the Prune Barge's new backstop, showed up in great style, both behind the plate and at bat. The fielding of Pat Phelan of the winners also featured.

The Pennsylvania walloped the U. S. S. Arizona, 13 to 6, in the third game at the Athletic Field. The contest was slowed up by poor fielding on the part of the losers.

The Lone Star State ship, Texas, defeated the Oklahoma, 6 to 1. Hinson pitched excellent ball for the losers, striking our 14 opposing batsmen, but was given poor support by his teammates.

The scores:

New Mexico	4	9	2
Tennessee	3	7	1

Langley and Davis; Jacoby and Morganroth.

California	4	5	2
Idaho	2	6	3

Hanlon and Arrowsmith; Smith and Corrella.

Pennsylvania	13	7	1
Arizona	6	6	2

Colburn and Kingsley; Fletcher and Lewis.

Texas	6	10	2
Oklahoma	1	5	6

Miller and Kelly; Hinson and Sullick.

Ad Wolgast, or Double, Is Dead

PEORIA, Ill., April 18.—While Ad Wolgast is claimed to be alive in Los Angeles, death last night of "Ed" Wolgast at the State Insane Asylum brings to light one of the greatest cases of similarity on record.

Frances Wolgast, a sister of Ad, telephoned from Cadillac, Mich., tonight inquiring about the dead man and furnished a complete description of her brother. This had a broken nose, a scar on one of his legs, and had a broken arm. So had this man. Ad had a scar from an operation for appendicitis and so had this man. Both are the same age, same weight and same height. Ad never had "cauliflower ears" neither has this man. The dead man was taken into the asylum about three months ago. Little is known of him. He has the appearance of having been a prize fighter. The body is being held.

Anzacs Out of Davis Cup Play; Net Minus 2 Stars

By Associated Press
MELBOURNE, Australia, April 18.

AUSTRALIA will not participate in the Davis cup lawn tennis competition ths year, it has been decided, owing to the inability of Gerald L. Patterson and Pat O'Hara Wood, members of last year's team, to go to Honolulu for the initial test with Hawaii.

HONOLULU, April 18.—(By Associated Press.)—A. L. Castle, president of the Hawaii Tennis Association, today said that in the event Australia defaults with Hawaii in the Davis cup match play, the Hawaiian team would go to the mainland to play the winner of the Canada-Japan match.

Yaryan Smashes Out Home Run for Victory

By Mark Kelly

SEATTLE, April 18.—Smack! It sounded like that, did Yama Yaryan's home run into the water-soaked bleachers. It came about in the ninth inning of an air-tight game of ball, and it brought to a spectacular close the interesting opener between Seattle and Los Angeles. It gave a rosy finish to what started out as a duel, drab afternoon, and it gave Seattle victory in the first opening day engagement that this city has won since it advent into the Coast League.

It wasn't much of an opening, if you consider the crowd and the weather. The crowd was about seven thousand—about half of the throng that would have checked through the turnstiles had it been fair. And the weather was awful. But the ball game was the neatest opening day contest the Queen City has ever ben privileged to gaze upon. And the swet part of it is, the tribe won.

Today when Harry Gardner and Tom Hughes, the rival slabsters squared away for their duel it was raining hard. For three and one half scoreless innings the clubs played. Umpire Jimmy Toman finally called a halt to wipe the rain drops from his red neck and change his dripping socks. After a fifteen minute wait, Old Sol, just three hours late, came out in all his glory and the clubs knuckled down to an exhibition of very fancy baseball.

As has ben stated, Yam Yaryan won it; won it in such a sudden and unexpected manner that it was a full five seconds before the fans realized the meaning of Yam's wallop. The score was nothing-all, as the broad shouldered catcher ankled to the plate in the ninth.

A young right hander named Hanna and Harry Gardner were treating the crowd to a neat exhibition of pitching. Well nigh perfect defense work by the opposing forces had blocked what few chances there were for scores. That's how things stood when Yaryan cleaned the mud from his cleaks, pounded his bat on the log and faced the pitcher.

Smack! The first ball pitched was met squarely by Yam's club and it whistled straight and fair halfway up in the left fiend bleachers. It was a real home run. It broke up the party right there and it sen tthe customers home to their cold suppers quite contented and satisfied with their ball club.

Two bits of fielding by Red Baldwin, Wolverton's sensational young third sacker, and by Golvin, the Los Angeles first baseman, ranked as exceptional plays. Both were turned into double plays and Golvin's in particular was as pretty a bit of fielding as one would see in a long spell. The Angel infielder dashed headlong, scooping Billy Orr's bunt as it was about to settle onto the grass and doubled Eldred at first. A truly great play it was.

GARDNER WEAKENS

Gardner had easy sailing until the sixth, when he began to weaken a trifle. McAuley and Daly both singled in the seventh, after two were down and Harry threw one wild to Hanna, McAuley and Daly advancing. But the crafty Gardner struck out the pitcher and saved himself much trouble.

The Tribe was in position to score in the same inning. Gardner walked. Lane hit the first ball. Johnson drove a single past third base. Rohwer waited until there was three and two on him, and then lifted one to center.

More trouble for Harry in the eighth, some poor base running on the part of Twombly robbing the Angels of a golden opportunity.

The eighth inning saw Golvin's great play. Eldred, first up, had singled and Orr's sacrifice attempt looked like a success until Golvin pulled a "Houdini" and converted it into a double play. Janvrin beat out a scratchy hit in the same inning, but Baldwin's hard bounder was flagged by Charley Deal at third, who forced the runner at second.

And the next incident worth mentioning was Mr. Yaryan.

LOS ANGELES	AB	H	O	A	E	SEATTLE	AB	H	O	A	E
Twmby,rf	4	2	0	0	0	Lane,lf..	3	0	1	0	1
McCabe,lf	3	1	4	0	0	Jhnton,1b	4	2	13	0	0
Deal,3b..	4	1	1	1	0	Rohwer,rf	4	1	0	0	0
Griggs,1b	1	0	2	0	0	Eldred,cf	4	2	2	0	0
Hood,cf..	4	0	2	0	0	Orr,ss...	4	0	1	6	0
Krug,2b.	3	0	3	1	0	Jnvrin,2b.	4	1	4	6	0
McAly,ss.	3	1	1	1	0	Bldwin,3b	4	1	2	3	0
Daly,c...	4	2	8	1	0	Yaryan,c.	4	2	3	1	0
Hughes,p	1	0	0	0	0	Gardner,p	2	1	1	1	0
Hanna,p..	3	0	0	1	0						
Golvin,1b	2	0	3	1	0						
Totals	32	7	*24	6	0	Totals	33	11	27	17	1

*None out when winning run scored.

Los Angeles ...	0	0	0	0	0	0	0	0	0	—0
Hits	0	0	0	0	0	1	2	3	1	—7
Seattle	0	0	0	0	0	0	0	0	1	—1
Hits	2	3	0	0	2	0	1	2	1	—11

Innings pitched—By Hughes, 2. Home run—Yaryan. Bases on balls—Off Hughes, 1; Hanna, 1; Gardner, 4. Struck out—By Hughes, 3; Hanna, 4; Gardner, 4. Double plays—Baldwin to Johnston; Golvin to Krug. Runs responsible for—Hanna, 1. Charge defeat to Hanna. Wild pitches—Gardner, Hanna. Time—2:05. Umpires—Toman and Becker.

INDOOR BALL GAMES START

REDLANDS, April 18. — Teams representing Notchers' clubs of the Methodist, Baptist, Christian, Presbyterian and Yucaipa churches will compete in an indoor baseball league, games starting this week and continuing to May 24. The games will be at the Y. M. C. A. gymnasium.

Willie Kamm

This Coast League youngster, for whom the Chicago White Sox paid $100,000, made his major league debut yesterday fielding, cleaning two balls for assists and smashing out a two-base hit. Below we have an International Newsreel actiongraph of this stellar third-sacker.

Sudden Returns to Card Track

STANFORD UNIVERSITY, Cal., April 18.—Eddie Sudden, star track man and winner for Stanford of the 100 and 220-yard dashes in the California Stanford University track meet last year, registered at the University today. His registration fee has not yet been paid, but it is anticipated the fee will be paid tomorrow.

JAIL MAN AS CRASH KILLS GIRL

THREE CENTS CITY AND COUNTY

LOS ANGELES EVENING HERALD AN INDEPENDENT NEWSPAPER

EVENING NEWS EDITION

Reg. U. S. Patent Office. Copyright, 1923, by Evening Herald Publishing Company

The Evening Herald Grows Just Like Los Angeles

VOL. XLVIII THREE CENTS Hotels and Trains, Five Cents WEDNESDAY, OCTOBER 10, 1923 THREE CENTS Hotels and Trains, Five Cents NO. 294

WORLD SERIES OPENED IN N. Y.

Nab 'Badge' Bandit Suspect

Babe Ruth, Home Run Slugger, and One of New York Yankees' Mainstays in Today's Game with Giants Opened World Series

The Bambino, Batting Hero, in His Characteristic Pose. The Yanks Pin a Great Amount of Their Confidence on Ruth's Ability to Slam the Pill for Circuit Runs.

70,000 PACK STADIUM TO WATCH FIRST CLASH OF YANKS AND GIANTS

YANKEE STADIUM, NEW YORK, Oct. 10.—A crowd estimated at 70,000 packed the stadium today when the Giants, representing the National league, and the Yankees, flag winners in the American league, trotted on the field for the first game of the world's series. It was the third successive time the series has been entirely a New York affair.

More than 36,000 fans filed through the general admission gates which were thrown open at 10 o'clock. Many of the fans had waited in line throughout the night in order to be among the first to enter the unreserved sections. The reserved spaces filled more slowly, but there was scarcely a vacant seat an hour before game time.

Both teams received an ovation when they came onto the field. The Yankees, being the home club, were last to go through their preliminary workout.

PIPP AT FIRST

Babe Ruth, the greatest slugger of them all, was in his accustomed place in right field and Bobby Meusel, his slugging teammate, was in center. Walter Pipp, limping slightly because of a weak ankle, was at first base, but handled himself in a way that assured the fans he is in shape to go through the series in good form.

Although the Yankees entered the game slight favorites, the Giants got the biggest reception when they took the field. Ross Young, who has been on the hospital list, showed a lot of speed in right field and Cunningham, former Coast league star, worked out in center.

PITCHERS WORK OUT

The pitchers for both clubs worked out easily. Pennock and Hoyt started tossing the ball over to warm up for the Yanks and Ryan and Nehf warmed up for McGraw. Snyder and Gowdy handled the offerings of the Giants' pitchers, while Schang and Hoffman were the receiving stars in the Yankee bull pen.

Babe Ruth, voted by a committee of baseball critics the most valuable player to his club in the American league, was the center of all eyes when the clubs took the field.

After the greatest year of his

(CONTINUED ON PAGE THIRTEEN)

Nehf and Hoyt to Pitch Opener

NEW YORK, Oct. 10.—Arthur Nehf, Giants' star southpaw, and Waite Hoyt, youthful righthander of the Yankees, were tentatively picked today to start the world's series. The probable batting order of the team follows:

GIANTS—Bancroft, ss.; Groh, 3b.; Frisch, 2b.; Young, rf.; Meusel, lf.; Cunningham, cf.; Kelly. 1b.; Snyder, c.; Nehf, p.

YANKEES—Witt, cf.; Dugan, 3b.; Ruth, lf.; Pipp, 1b.; Meusel, rf.; Ward, 2b.; Schang, c.; Scott, ss.; Hoyt, p.

N. Y. Showgirl in Court on Charge Of Stabbing Man

NEW YORK, Oct. 10.—Pretty Moravia Balfour, showgirl who is alleged to have stabbed Andre Sherri, producer, in the arm in front of the Victoria theater, was to appear in the Washington Heights police court today on a charge of assault with a deadly weapon.

Miss Balfour said Sherri threatened to kill her when she demanded two months' pay she declared is due her; that he struck her with a cane and that she defended herself with a nail file. Sherri alleges she stabbed him with a pair of scissors. Miss Balfour further alleges that Sherri is "Tony" Macalus, notorious underworld character, who was involved in the Carl Fischer Hanson extortion and bribery case of 15 years ago.

Hold L. A. Youth in Street Fight Death

Charged with manslaughter for the death of Roy W. Root, age 27 years, who died of injuries received in a street fight, R. W. Rousey, age 19 years, 217 East Forty-second street, was held by the police today. Rousey is said to have attempted to become peacemaker in the fight and was struck by Root. He retaliated, knocking Root down and inflicting fatal injuries.

WARM IN THE YUKON

DAWSON, Yukon Territory, Oct. 10. — The oldest settlers here cannot remember another year when the city was not icebound in October. The last steamer of the summer sailed for the south today and no trace of the freeze has yet appeared.

JAIL MAN AS GIRL KILLED IN CRASH

Tragedy today brought an abrupt close to what the police describe as a thrilling early morning joyride by two young Los Angeles couples in an automobile when the heavy car, careening down a narrow, little-used road in Beverly glen, near Sawtelle, skidded and turned over, the accident resulting in the death of pretty Miss Florence Duncan, 24, of the Hoffman apartments, 1241 Ingraham street, Los Angeles.

The three other persons, George Robinson of 719 Whittier boulevard, Lillie Viral of 840 South Flower Xstreet and Louis J. Vaughn of 2222 West Eighth street, were slightly injured when the car hurtled from the road and pinned Miss Duncan beneath it.

MAN ARRESTED

The victim of the accident died without regaining consciousness and before an ambulance could reach the scene from Sawtelle.

Robinson, companion of Miss Duncan, was alleged to have been driving the automobile when he lost control of it. He was arrested by Police Officers A. L. Peterson and R. C. Rasmusses of Sawtelle and placed in the city jail on a charge of suspicion of manslaughter.

According to the arresting officers, Robinson apparently had been drinking before the accident occurred. They said they were greeted with a scene of desolation when they reached the place where the accident occurred.

The body of the dead woman was pinned beneath the heavy au-

(CONTINUED ON PAGE TWELVE)

Tigers, Angels Open Last Series of Year

Frank Shellenback and Jakie May, two of the pitchers left at home by the Tigers, were told to warm up for the opening game of the series against the Angels at Washington park today.

Marty Krug ordered Ote Crandall and Roy Hannah to warm up for his squad.

Today's game marked the opening of the final series of the season. The line-up:

TIGERS—	ANGELS—
H. High, lf	McCabe, lf
Schneider, rf	Jacobs, ss
Gillespie, cf	Twombly, rf
Burke, 1b	Hood, cf
Zanic, c	Smith, 3b
Rader, 2b	Golvin, 1b
Warner, 3b	Lindimore, 2b
Slade, ss	Rego, c
May, p	Crandall, p

$77,000 Shortage Found in Bank; Doors Are Closed

ERIE, Pa., Oct. 10.—The Citizens Bank of Alban, Erie county, was closed today by state bank examiners. A shortage of $77,000 has been found.

Ralph J. Griswold, cashier, has been taken into custody on complaint of State Bank Examiner Beckman, charged with being responsible for the shortage.

Woman Slayer of Boy, 13, Hanged

By International News Service

GLASGOW, Oct. 10.—Mrs. John Newell, convicted of the murder of 13-year-old John Johnstone, was hanged here today.

PRISONER CONFESSES HIGHWAY HOLDUP

Check Story in Attempt to Solve Forty Other Robberies

The notorious "badge bandit," who has operated in Los Angeles county for months with more than two score of holdups, and 12 attacks on women at the point of a pistol, is believed by the police to have been captured.

His description said to conform closely to that of the "badge bandit," a man giving the name of C. S. Hammock, was taken into custody at dawn today near Redondo Beach, following the wrecking of an automobile he is alleged to have used in the holdup and robbery of the Burton oil station, Market street and Redondo boulevard.

SIGNS CONFESSION

Boastful of his career of crime, and proud that he "always works alone," the suspected "badge bandit" made a signed and written confession of his night of banditry to Chief of Police Henry of Redondo Beach, the chief reported. In an effort to verify his suspicion that Hammock is the "badge bandit," Chief Henry planned to bring him to the sheriff's office for a close examination.

Hammock was captured when a Redondo Beach motorcycle officer and the constable of Gardena hurried to Riverside and Western avenue where an automobile was reported to have been wrecked against a telegraph pole. Hammock and a man giving the name of Shirley Shephard were taken into custody.

BREAKS UNDER GRILLING

For more than an hour Hammock refused to talk to Redondo Beach police, Chief Henry said. Attracted by the close resemblance of his pris-

(CONTINUED ON PAGE TWELVE)

FRENCH REJECT BERLIN RUHR PARLEY PLAN

By International News Service

PARIS, Oct. 10.—Premier Poincare today flatly rejected the German proposal for a French, Belgian and German commission to settle the Ruhr problem through direct negotiations. It had previously been rejected by Belgium.

By International News Service

BERLIN, Oct. 10.—Communist charges of disloyalty against Hugo Stinnes, Germany's foremost industrial magnate, were exploded today by Stinnes' official explanation of his visit to Dusseldorf to confer on Ruhr affairs with General deGoutee, commander of the French army in the Ruhr. It was stated that the Stresemann cabinet did not object to Stinners' visit.

Stinnes did not see Chancellor Stresemann before his departure, but he has an alibi. He tried to see the chancellor, but the latter was too busy with the ministerial crisis to grant an audience.

Stinnes knew that no Socialist minister could accede to his demands, but he evidently hoped to create dissention in the cabinet.

The industrial magnate had been

(CONTINUED ON PAGE TWELVE)

SEVERE EARTH TREMORS IN MALAY ARE RECORDED

SYDNEY Australia, Oct. 10.—An earthquake disturbance, believed to center in the north Malay archipelago, was recorded by the observatory seismograph today.

LONDON, Oct. 10.—Earth tremors were recorded by the West Bromwich observatory seismograph this morning.

DUBLIN, Oct. 10.—The seismograph at Rathfarnham Castle observatory registered severe earthquake shocks this morning. The

(CONTINUED ON PAGE TWELVE)

Baseball, Football, Golf, Tennis, Track, Boxing, Turf and Amateur Sports expertly reported by the best sporting writers in the West

CHARACTER QUALITY AMERICA FIRST ENTERPRISE ACCURACY

Los Angeles Examiner Sports

AN AMERICAN PAPER FOR THE AMERICAN PEOPLE — THE GREAT NEWSPAPER OF THE GREAT SOUTHWEST

The Examiner carries the most complete Daily Sports Section of any newspaper west of New York

THURSDAY, OCTOBER 11, 1923 — SECTION III—PAGE 1

GIANTS WIN; STENGEL HERO

WHATNOTS More What Than Not

Negro vs. Indian Some Ancient History Old Time Stars White Race, Beware!

—By Mark Kelly—

Maurice Webb, a student of football, has the floor for the day. What the young man has to say is interesting:

* * *

HOW'D you like to see a game between an All Star Indian team and the eleven greatest Negroes? Who do you think would win? Naturally your mind would leap to the great teams put out by Pop Warner at Carlisle and you would say the Indians. But just wait till you hear this array of dusky-hued warriors.

Starting at the ends we'd have Robeson, unanimously chosen All American in 1917 and 1918. Standing six feet three, shoeless and scaling two hundred and thirty pounds on the hoof, this Rutgers blackbird was the terror of every team he faced and the plays that gained around his end could be counted on the fingers of the left hand of a right-handed blind butcher. At the other terminal we station one Mistah Williams, End Extraordinary. A place had to be reserved for him on the All Eastern and frequently the All A during the years he cavorted on the gridiron for Brown University.

* * *

AT tackle, Duke Slater, Iowa, the sensation of Middle Western football for three years. Picked by Camp regularly. As his running mate, G. E. Smith from the Michigan Aggies probably not so well known, but one of the greatest all round linemen in the history of the game. Can you imagine a tackle being pulled out of the line to run back punts? That was one of this tarbaby's regular jobs. Walt Gordon, now assistant coach at California. His ability is well known to Pacific Coast football fans.

Johnson, Columbia guard, who was also one of the finest basketball players ever turned out in the East. Turner, who centered for a Chicago High School and later played tackle for Northwestern is another wonder. Charley West, W. and J.'s quarter this year, is a running fool. Took Eastern Pentathlon honors in last year's track season. Try and find somebody who hasn't heard of Fred Pollard, that wonderful little Brown halfback. Sol Butler, Olympic games satellite, more famous for his deeds on the cinder path than at half, but only because he hails from a comparatively obscure college, Dubuque.

* * *

SHELBURNE at full is probably the best man who has played that position for the Green of Dartmouth in recent years. Some lineup. Six All American and the rest picked for their respective sectional teams. Even with such an imposing muster roll of names the Indians would probably bring home the kinky scalps.

Perform a little tuning, get the old radio all set and listen in on this bunch of Redskins. Ends: Pete Calac, All-A fullback at Carlisle and later end at West Virginia Wesleyan. If there ever was a man who hit the line any harder or tacked a runner more viciously than this wild man, he's still in Borneo. Evans, a little papoose from Haskell, who, barring Weaver of Center, is the topnotch converter of goals from touchdowns for all time, and the kind of fellow who took passes off his left ear. Missed one goal from touchdown in four years and was so broken up about it he quit the team and joined the army.

* * *

PLAYING one of the tackles we would have Joe Guyon, Jim Thorpe's twin brother. Why amplify that statement? Cooper, Louisiana State tackle for many moons and one of the finest linemen ever put out in the Sunny South where football players bloom like apple blossoms in Normandy.

Elmer Busch, another of Warner's wonder men and receiving the selection in '12 and '13. Busch was generally conceded to be the greatest guard at leading interference since the year one and was the man responsible for many of Thorpe, Guyon, et al's long runs. Bergie, a marvelous center, is switched to guard on account of the presence of Pete Garlow, who could not be ousted from the pivot position save by a precious few centers of recent years.

* * *

NOW for the backfield. Gustave Welch, absolutely the trickiest quarter that ever callled a signal. The only time opponents ever knew where the ball was when this gentleman was playing was when they saw it planted behind the goal posts for another touchdown. Welch's pet individual specialty was eighty and ninety-yard runs from scrimmage. Jim Thorpe. Plenty spoken. We will not talk foolish. A worthy comrade for this superman was Arcasa. As a runner pure and simple the great "Jeems" himself had little on him.

Finally, we come to Murdock, Haskell famous fullback. 'Tis said this guy could hit a dime at fifty yards with a football. Probably a slight exaggeration, but unquestionably some passer. A runaway mallet would do but little more damage to an opposing line. Well, there they are. A couple of teams like that would pack the coliseum and leave a mob standing outside.

* * *

IN case there wasn't enough color in this battle to suit everybody, we might inject Sammie Kai Kee, California's Chinese halfback of several seasons back; and "Sneeze" Achiu, yellow flash now playing at the University of Dayton. To even things up we'd give the other side Brash, one of the greatest players ever attending the University of Hawaii. Hawaii left a dark brown taste in Pomona's mouth last year, you know. Old timers will recall "Sonny" Cunha, the smiling Hawaiian lineman, who was such a sensation at Yale years ago.

The white footballers had better watch their step, or the boys of color will be stealing their thunder.

Yankees Display Genius; Giant Win Proves It

—By Ring W. Lardner—

YANKEE STADIUM, N. Y., Oct. 10.—Well, boys, they have started again and it looks maybe we would be out of the trenches by Saturday night. At the conclusion of this battle the general consensus of opinion among us half-witted newspaper men that it was a game that could of been lost by only one team in the world, namely, the Yankees.

It takes real genius to get beat in a ball game like this one, and it don't seem hardly possible that the Giants can lose any of the rest of them, no matter how hard they try.

The only thing might save the American League champs would be to have last year's umpires re-engaged, so that some game might be called while it was still a tie.

However, it might help a little if Manager Huggins would change his tactics and every time one of his boys gets on base, send in somebody to run for him. The Yanks made a whole lot of runs this season, and in order to make runs they must of visited different bases, but today they acted like it was their first trip away from home. This ain't knocking the Giants, who played their regular worlds' serious baseball and deserved to win. And personly I am glad it was Casey, mighty Casey, that busted it up, though I don't suppose he care whether I like him or not. Well, to begin at the beginning. On the way from the subway to the press gate the writer must of passed at least 50 policemens but was neither recognized nor hit over the head. Outside the gate I run into the high commissioner of baseball, who asked the newspaper boys the other day to kindly keep his name out of the paper on the grounds that the people was not interested. The Judge helped me get away with a couple of Harry Stevens' hot roast beef sandwiches which was so good that I took some of the juice home on my coat to show the wife and kiddies.

At 1 o'clock Judge L——s went out on the field and decided it was light enough to play. The clients was then entertained by a novelty in the way of batting and fielding practice, which is usually held in secret before a big game. Messrs. Altrock and Schacht staged their imitation of the misunderstanding between our champion and the Wild Bull and it was voted the best baseball's star comics has ever put on. Personly I would of enjoyed it and the ball game more if the boys had not given me a press seat that was not only made for Jackie Coogan, but was bounded on the front by the largest steel pillar in The Bronx. If the serious goes over 3 games it will be called on acct. of cramps as far as I am conserned.

The gent that announced the batteries in the press box said that Hurt would pitch for the Yankees. This is what they call him in Brooklyn. Amongst the prominent experts present was Jack Hendricks and Clarence Rowland. Jack is covering the serious for Jim Jam Jems and Clarence for the Encyclopedia. When Mr. Watson was named as the Giant pitcher, Nick, lately of Boston, said that McGraw was probably sending him in as punishment for not obeying the training rules. He was released on parole after two nervous innings. Mr. Hurt got bumped off in the next innings and I practically decided to nick name the game a air-tight pitchers' battle. It took one hour and 5 minutes to get the first three innings over and Judge L——s gave the gathering gloom a couple of dirty looks.

During the long and tedious progress of the third inning I sought an interview with Mrs. Caroline Dorsey of Travers City, Mich. Mrs. Dorsey is the lady who stood in line in front of the general admission ticket window since May 14, hoping against hope that she would get a ticket.

At 10 o'clock this morning she received the coveted pasteboard and picked out a choice seat under the score board.

"Mrs. Dorsey," I said to her, "what do you think of the game?"

She did not hear me the first time, on account of being so far away, so I had to put the query once more.

"Mrs. Dorsey," I said, "what do you think of the game?"

She did not hear me this time either, and when the game was over I asked some of the people who had sat near her if they had heard her say what she had thought of the game, but I could get no information that sounded reliable.

The pastime speeded up after Bush and Ryan took what is called the helm. With the sun under cover, the Giants was unable to see Mr. Bush's fast ball until he got in the hole to Mr. Stengel in the ninth, when Casey ran an exhibition circuit of the bases. He had been scheduled to run this race against Papyrus before the game, but the horse failed to leave his stall. Plenty of Yanks got on base, but once there they seemed to be overcome by nausea.

The disease was contagious and Yankee fans all had it leaving the park.

"BUGS" BAER SAYS

Yanks Curl Up Like Bed Spring. Take Flop After Getting Three-Run Jump on the Giants.

THE Giants pasted their usual label on the Yanks in New York's annual baseball convention. he series has been here so often it starts to look like an old-home week for Casey Stengel. Casey looked up his contract in the ninth and decided that his bonus clause called for no overtime.

SO he broadcast one of Bush's wave lengths and came home while the Yanks' outfield buckle brigade was passing the ball to one another.

BY THE time Witt got the ball to Meusel it wasn't a ball any more. It was a souvenir. For Casey was back in the covered wagon by that time.

THE Yanks got a three-run jump on the Giants, but curled up like a bedspring when the Giants started to ask Hoyt questions with their bats.

JUDGE LANDIS was there to see that everything was on the up and up. He started the series wrong by faking a throw for the photographers.

M'GRAW crossed everybody and himself by starting Mule Watson.

HOYT lasted long enough to tell his folks he was in the series.

THE Yanks were hitting everything that came across until Watson started to fool them with wild pitches.

EVANS, O'Day, Hart and Nallin were the four umpires of the Apocalppse.

EACH one of the first three innings was a world series in itself. The Yanks' three run lead looked like Turkey in the oven. But it never reached the dining room.

THE Giants came back in the third and started to figure out the population of the United States in base runners. They scored four times and the bell boy showed Mr. Hoyt to his room.

BABE RUTH knocked himself for a foul when he bumped into Frank Snyder at the plate in the fifth. Babah hit a three-bagger but was out at the platei n a right-of-way collision with Snyder.

RYAN and Bush took charge of the shooting gallery when Watson and Hoyt were paged by their managers. The Yanks tied it up in the seventh with a three-bagger that Joe Dugan had been asving ever since he left Philadelphia.

RYAN pitched golf style. Always trying to get himself into a hole.

KELLY'S throw on Dugan in the fifth was like a beard at a House of David banquet. Right over the plate.

* * *

CASEY STENGEL kept on gishing until he laid the lumber against Bush in the ninth. Casey whacked one loose to the fence and ran like he was going to meet Papyrus next week.

* * *

IT was the longest hit of the game, and Casey could have crawled around on all fours. The old boy stalls all summer, but he certainly takes charge of the series.

RENAULT WINS AGAIN.

MONTREAL, Oct. 10. — Jack Renault, heavyweight champion of Canada, was awarded the decision over Soldier Jones of Toronto tonight at the end of their ten-round match.

Casey at the Bat!

Oh! Somewhere in this favored land the sun is shining bright,
The band is playing somewhere, and somewhere hearts are light;
And somewhere men are laughing, and somewhere children shout,
But there is no joy in Yankville — after mighty Casey's clout!

—With apologies to Thayer.

CASEY STENGEL

Photo by American Staff Photographer

HOME RUN IN NINTH BREAKS UP 4 TO 4 TIE

Hoyt Batted Out in Third; Ryan Relieves Watson and Pitches Effectively

By DAMON RUNYON

Staff Correspondent Universal Service

YANKEE STADIUM, NEW YORK, Oct. 10.—This is the way old "Casey" Stengel ran this afternoon, running his home-run home.

This is the way old "Casey" Stengel ran, running his home-run home to a Giant victory over the Yankees by a score of 5 to 4 in the first game of the World's Series of 1923.

This is the way old "Casey" Stengel ran, running his home-run home, when two were out in the ninth inning and the score was tied, and the ball was still bounding inside the Yankee yard.

This is the way:

His mouth wide open—

His warped-out legs bending beneath him at every stride—

His arms flying back and forth, like those of a man swimming with a crawl stroke—

His flanks heaving, his breath whistling, his head far back.

Yankee infielders, passed by old "Casey" Stengel as he was running his home-run home, say "Casey" was muttering to himself, adjuring himself to greater speed, as a jockey mutters to his horse in a race, that he was saying:

"Go on, Casey."

People generally laugh when they see old "Casey" Stengel run, but they were not laughing while he was running his home-run home this afternoon. People—sixty thousand of 'em—men and women, were standing in the Yankee stands and bleachers up there in the Bronx roaring sympathetically, whether they were for or against the the Giants:

"Come on, Casey."

The warped old legs, twisted and bent by many a year of baseball campaigning, just barely held out until "Casey" Stengel reached the plate, running his home-run home.

Then they collapsed.

They gave not inwardly, as legs often do, but outwardly, so that old 'Casey" Stengel fell sprawling, all spread out over the plate, with Schang, the catcher of the Yankees, futilely reaching for him with the ball.

He suggested a huge crab spread out down there, his arms and legs wiggling in all directions, with Billy Evans, the American League umpire, poised over him in a set pose, his right thumb jerked backwards to indicate that old "Casey" was safe.

Half a dozen Giants rushed forward to help old "Casey" to his feet, to hammer him on his feet, to bawl congratulations in his ear as he limped unsteadily, still panting furiously, to the bench, where John J. McGraw, chief of the Giants, relaxed his stern features in a smile for the man who had won the game.

"Casey" Stengel's warped old legs, one of them broken not so long ago, wouldn't carry him out for the next inning, when the Yankees made a dying effort to undo the damage done by "Casey." His place in centerfield was taken by young Bill Cunningham, whose legs are still unwarped, and "Casey" sat on the bench with John J. McGraw.

Not Much Expected

No one expected much of "Casey" Stengel when he appeared at the plate in the Giants' side of the ninth inning, the score a tie at 4 to 4.

Ross Young and "Irish" Meusel, stout, dependable hitters, had been quickly disposed of by the superb pitching of "Bullet Joe" Bush.

No one expected Stengel to accomplish anything where they had failed. Bush, pitching as only Bush can pitch in an emergency, soon had two strikes and three balls on "Casey." He was at the plate so long that many fans were fidgeting nervously, wondering why he didn't hurry up and get put out, so the game could go on.

"Casey" Stengel is not an imposing figure at bat, not an imposing figure under any circumstances. Those warped old legs have something to do with it. A man with

(Continued on Page 2, Column 1)

Papyrus' Jockey Given Ovation as He Leaves

LONDON, Oct. 10.

STEVE DONAGHUE, England's champion jockey, who will ride Papyrus in his race against Zev at Belmont Park, October 20, had an enthusiastic send off at Waterloo station today when he left for Southampton to embark on the liner Olympic for New York. Crowds on their way to business assembled outside the platform barrier and shouted the familiar race course slogan, "Come on Steve," as the little jockey made his way to the train.

"Papyrus is a generous, game horse, as I well know and I hope I shall win," he said.

Jockey Dillon Boxes Tonight

Jockey Joe Dillon, holder of the New York boxing commission's junior flyweight champi nship belt, makes his bow to Southern California glove patrons in the main event of the C. P. O. club's weekly boxing show at San Pedro this Thursday night.

Matchmaker Luke Lucas of the harbor club has dug up the toughest sort of opposition for Jockey Joe. Art Springer, one of the busiest and best bantams in this section, will do the glove flinging for the other side. If Dillon can best Springer he will be in demand.

Lucas has Larry Murphy and Georgie Siddon boxing the semi-windup at 126 pounds. Dean Hood of the Union Tool Company and Bert Meyers, a San Francisco boy, will appear in the special event at 155 pounds.

World's Series Box

GIANTS

	AB	R	H	PO	A	E
Bancroft, ss	4	1	1	2	0	0
Groh, 3b	4	1	2	1	3	0
Frisch, 2b	4	0	1	3	2	0
Young, rf	3	0	0	1	0	0
E. Meusel, lf	4	0	0	6	0	0
Stengel, cf	3	1	2	2	0	0
Kelly, 1b	3	1	1	5	2	0
Gowdy, c	0	0	0	1	0	0
Snyder, c	2	0	0	4	1	0
Watson, p	0	0	0	0	1	0
Ryan, p	2	0	0	1	2	0
Bentley	1	0	1	0	0	0
Maguire	0	1	0	0	0	0
Gearin	0	0	0	0	0	0
Cunningham, cf	0	0	0	1	0	0
Totals	30	5	8	27	11	0

Bentley batted for Watson in third.
Maguire ran for Gowdy in third.
Gearin ran for Bentley in third.

YANKEES

	AB	R	H	PO	A	E
Witt, cf	5	0	1	5	0	0
Dugan, 3b	4	0	1	0	3	0
Ruth, rf	4	1	1	3	0	0
R. Meusel, lf	4	0	1	0	0	0
Pipp, 1b	4	0	2	10	0	0
Ward, 2b	4	1	2	5	3	0
Schang, c	3	1	2	2	3	1
Scott, ss	2	0	0	2	6	0
Hoyt, p	1	0	0	0	0	0
Bush, p	3	1	2	0	1	0
Hendrick	1	0	0	0	0	0
Johnson, ss	0	0	0	0	0	0
Totals	35	4	12	27	16	1

Hendrick batted for Scott in eighth.

Giants	0	0	4	0	0	0	0	0	1	—5
Yankees	1	2	0	0	0	0	1	0	0	—4

Earned runs—Giants, 5; Yankees, 4. Two-base hits—R. Meusel, Bush, Schang. Three-base hits—Groh, Dugan, Ruth. Home run—Stengel. Bases on balls—Off Bush, 2; Ryan, 1; Watson, 1. Struck out—By Watson, 1 (Hoyt); by Ryan, 1 (Scott); by Bush, 2 (Ryan and Snyder). Left on bases—Giants, 2; Yankees, 6. Double plays—Scott to Ward to Pipp, 2; Frisch to Snyder. Stolen base—Bancroft. Sacrifice hit—Scott. Wild pitch—Ryan. Three runs, 4 hits off Watson in two innings; 4 runs, 4 hits off Hoyt in 2 1-3 innings. Losing pitcher—Bush. Winning pitcher—Ryan. Time—2:05.

Records Fall As Fans File Into Stadium

NEW YORK, Oct. 10.

ATTENDANCE and receipts for the first world series game today broke all previous records. Total attendance was 55,307; total receipts $181,912. Of the total sum, the players will get $92,775.12; each club will get $30,925.05; the baseball commission will get $27,286.80.

Sherman Battles Layman to Draw

GEORGE SHERMAN and Joe Layman battled to a hard fought draw last night in the main event at the San Fernando arena. In the semi-windup "Pewee Nolan, substituting for Benny Diaz, won the decision over Frankie Layman in a fast affair. Following are the remaining bouts and results:

"Peanuts" Jensen won over Riff Howard.
Billy Blake was knocked out by Young Lotti.
Young Richie won over Joe Carroll.
Mike Downey won over Walter Williams.

Cubs Defeat White Sox in Opening Game

CHICAGO, Oct. 10.—The National League drew first blood in the Chicago city series today when the Cubs defeated the American League White Sox, 8 to 4. Charley Robertson, the Sox starting pitcher, paved the way to the Cub victory with a bad throw to the plate in the fourth inning, which allowed two of the four Cubs' runs of the inning to score.

Score:

WHITE SOX	AB	H	O	A	E	CUBS	AB	H	O	A	E
Mostil,cf.	5	1	1	0	0	Statz,cf..	3	3	2	0	0
Hooper,rf	5	1	1	0	0	Adams,ss	4	4	3	7	0
Colins,2b	3	2	2	1	0	Grntm,2b	5	0	4	8	3
Sheely,1b	4	0	12	1	0	Grimes,1b	3	1	12	1	1
Falk,lf...	4	0	0	0	0	Fribrg,3b	2	1	0	2	0
Kamm,3b	4	1	1	2	0	Miller,lf.	4	1	0	0	0
M'Clan,ss	4	3	2	2	0	Hethte,rf	4	0	1	0	0
Schalk,c.	4	1	4	2	0	Hartnet,c	2	1	5	1	0
Robtson,p	2	1	1	1	1	Alexndr,p	3	0	0	0	0
Lyons,p..	1	0	0	4	0						
Strunk...	1	1	0	0	0						
Totals..	37	11	24	13	1	Totals..	30	11	27	19	4

White Sox.....	0	0	1	0	2	1	0	0	0	—4
Cubs..........	0	0	2	4	0	1	0	1	*	—8

Cubs Strunk batted for Lyons in ninth.

Two base hits—Statz, Adams (2), McClellan. Three base hit—Adams. Home run—Collins. Stolen bases—Collins, Adams. Bases on balls—Off Robertson, 2; Alexander, 3; Lyons, 2. Struck out—By Alexander, 4; Robertson, 1; Lyons, 1. Losing pitcher—Robertson. Umpires—Klem, Holmes, Quigley and Ormsby.

22,000 Tickets to Bear-Trojan Battle on Sale

THE public sale of tickets for the California-U. S. C. game, to be played November 10 at the Los Angeles Coliseum, will start today. Graduate Manager Gwynne Wilson of the Trojan institution yesterday sent 22,000 choice seats to the five sporting goods stores. These will be sold to the public and represent the best of the remaining seats. There are no box seats for sale, as the allotment is oversubscribed. San Francisco has requested 15,000 seats.

Hope Wins Over Adams at Venice

WILLIE HOPE won the decision over Johnny Adams, San Bernardino lightweight, last night at the Venice boxing show. In the semi-windup Marty Burman scored a knockout over Red Burke in the first round.

CHARACTER QUALITY AMERICA FIRST ACCURACY ENTERPRISE

Seattle Post-Intelligencer Sports

ANY AMERICAN PAPER FOR THE AMERICAN PEOPLE

RUTH'S TWO HOME RUNS DEFEAT GIANTS, 4 TO 2

We're Not Worried Now, Says Bambino

Babe Hopes To Get Hold Of Another

Bambino Declares if Giants Will Only Give Him Chance He Will Repeat

By BABE RUTH

POLO GROUNDS, New York, Oct. 11.—The world's champions saw a lot of things today on their home grounds that must have given them a pretty jolt.

Babe Ruth

In the first place, and above everything else, they saw a left-handed pitcher for the first time in the three years our two clubs have been battling for the highest honors in baseball.

It was the first win in our last ten starts against the Giants, and maybe it took a left-hander to turn the trick, but believe me, the frail, game boy also made the old worm turn.

Inning after inning their batters, good batters all of them, according to averages the best in the entire National League, nibbled away at Pennock's snaky slow curves and all they got was two lonesome tallies. Sure they touched him up for eight or nine safe swats, but if it hadn't been for that terrible wild pitch that landed in his kidneys, I'll tell you he would have pitched a three-hit game.

RUTH EXPLAINS GAME

The game itself, the home runs, the lambasting of Giant pitchers, the courage and cunning of Pennock and all the other thrills, were the smallest part of the afternoon's work so far as our ball club is concerned.

The victory, which has been so long coming, was like a "shot in the arm," as the saying goes. The feeling of happiness that came over us as Jackson's fly settled in Bob Meusel's glove was something that cannot show in any box score, but, say, what it means to every last one of us could only be explained by one of these experts who write deep stuff about the effect of mind over matter.

If we lost that tough game Wednesday through the "mind over matter route," then I want to know what's the inside explanation on the Giant collapse on Thursday. We have outslugged the Giants in both games, we have driven left handers and right handers to the showers, and we have given them all the breaks and still hold them to an even split. I guess they call that mind over matter. And if this idea of "pitching to Ruth" is another specimen of mind over matter, all I got to say is that this Yankee ball club doesn't object to losing its mind completely.

YANKS AFTER RUNS

Let us have some more of the dope stuff. Let's have some more of the trick stuff. Let's have some more pitching working on the manikin basis—you know, the string and make 'em swing the arms. Let's have all that kind of baseball for the rest of the week, but listen, in the meantime we'll be out there getting runs for Huggins.

I have carefully avoided any predictions for this world series, especially on the question of home runs. But I hope I'll be excused for referring to the fact that I came across at the Polo Grounds. Of course, I'll admit I only got two, but then the series is just getting started. Maybe if they keep pitching to me and only walk me twice a game I might get hold of another one.

From what we've seen of Watson, Ryan, McQuillan and Bentley, it does not look to me like the Yankees have much to worry over when we go up against Nehf or Scott. I'm speaking for the entire chance.

Friday's game is just like starting the series all over again and as we have already had the best of the hitting and the best of the pitching, the Yankees are not bordering on any breakdown worrying about "mind over matter."

40,482 Fans See Yankees Win Contest

NEW YORK, Oct. 11.—Fans, 40,482 strong, paid $158,498 to see the second game of the world's series.

TODAY'S FIGURES	
Paid attendance...	40,482
Receipts	$158,480.00
Advisory board....	23,774.70
Each club's share.	26,944.66
Players' share.....	80,833.98

TOTAL TWO GAMES	
Paid attendance...$	95,789.00
Receipts	340,410.00
Advisory board....	51,661.50
Each club's share.	57,869.70
Players' share.....	173,609.10

Ruth to Go Down In Ball History For Great Work

Bambino's Name to Stand on Records Because of Sensational Feat

NEW YORK, Oct. 11.—(By Associated Press.)—When the last baseball is tossed and the tarpaulin is pulled over the diamond to cover it for all time, and when the records of the game are compiled with finality, in all probability one mark will stand out unequaled at the top of the list. Alongside the record will be the name of George Herman Ruth. And, if the compiler is human, he'll add, in parenthesis, "Babe."

RECORD IS KNOWN

Ruth's diamond history is too well known to be detailed again. Everyone knows that he first gained fame as a pitcher when he went to the Boston American League Club from the Baltimore Orioles, and that he first became celebrated as a world's series pitcher. Notable as were his achievements on the mound they did not compare with the prodigious batting that he accomplished when he came to the New York Yankees as a centerfielder and slugger extraordinary.

He holds the record for homerun hitting. But though he had participated in numerous world's series—this is his third since joining the Yankees—he always failed miserably to hit in the October classic. A wheel slipped; something went wrong; Ruth couldn't do much damage to world's series pitchers, until today. And today he came into his own, his two home runs being the margin by which his team triumphed over the Giants and evened the series.

IN SAME STYLE

Manager McGraw of the Giants has been quoted as saying that his pitchers would deliver to Ruth just as they did to any ordinary batter, whether in the belief that his men had mastered the bambino's weaknesses or because he thought the fans desired to see Ruth smack the ball is unknown.

Cruikshank Takes Qualifying Honor In Western Open

Hutchinson, Hagen, Reid and Oakes Tie for Second Place in Opening Play

MEMPHIS, Tenn., Oct. 11.—"Wee Bobby" Cruikshank of Westfield, N. J., small of stature but mighty of wrist, literally ironed his way to premier qualifying honors today in the Western open golf tournament with a score of 140 for the two days of qualifying play, topping a field of 110 entrants in the battle for the Western classic. Cruikshank and sixty-five other players will battle through a thirty-six final tomorrow for the title.

"Jock" Hutchison equaled the course record of 67, four under par, in today's eighteen holes, and tied with Wilbur Oakes, Chattanooga; Wilfred Reid, Detroit, and Walter Hagen, New York, as runner-up to Cruikshank for low qualifying score.

Yanks Are Not Getting The Breaks

Despite Win Yesterday, Americans Are Failing to Receive Any Luck

By WAITE HOYT

(Copyright, 1923, by Universal Service.)

NEW YORK, Oct. 11.—The Yanks are still getting the worst of it on the "breaks," but in spite of it all, the team rose up like one man today and smote the Giants the telling blow that spelled victory.

Waite Hoyt

But I knew it had to be. It was a Yank day. Ten hits, three of them home runs, coupled with Herb Pennock's masterly pitching, sent the clan McGraw full on their backs. The Yankees now pack a wallop like Firpo, but they have with it the skill of a Tommy Gibbons, so "us boys" are feeling rather pretty this balmy autumn evening.

DISPLAY ABILITY

Ruth, Pennock and Dugan displayed enough ability today to win any game without any outside help. Not that they didn't get it, for the Yanks' machine played a wonderful game and not a single error was chalked against them.

If the Giants begin to pass Ruth that means the rest of the Yanks will rise up and do their darndest to send the Babe around to the plate. It makes them mad to have Babe passed, and when Ruth is on, passed or by a slap of the baseball to where they ain't, then the Yanks are dangerous.

A word of praise for Dugan. Dugan to me has always seemed to possess more animation and spirit than any of the Yankees. He goes about it unobserved, but he is fighting for every point.

Pretty swinging bunts were thrust in his direction today. Coming in with the grace and ease of Devlin or Zimmerman, he scooped the ball with his bare hand and nipped the runners by a fraction of a second. He is without a peer in baseball and stands alone in his position.

PENNOCH PERFECT

As expected Pennock is the pitcher who will bother the Giants most. His work today so far as I could see was well nigh perfect.

I will point out one of his few slips, which was in feeding Meusel a slow ball. Meusel drove that one into the stands for a homer. But that was all. Once but not twice as Mr. Opper says. But to laud Pennock for this particular game would be only to tell of what he did all during the Yankee season. He was the most consistent pitcher on our staff, and surely deserves the glory of today's win.

The Yanks have the spirit that wins. They want the Giants to fight them. That was one of the best things Ty Cobb's Tigers did last season and when the Tigers fought us we always won.

YOUNG LOOKS BAD

Young pulled a play at second that was entirely uncalled for. Meusel hit a ball to Scott, who relayed it to Ward. Young deliberately run out of line to block Ward's play for a double. He did it to perfection by sliding and knocking Ward off his feet. Hart didn't see the play.

Young went at least four feet out of line to execute a supposedly smart play, but in a dirty way. The Yanks are trying to play this series as sportsmen, but the Giants had better not push us very far with that sort of playing.

Well, tomorrow is another one. I look for a pitchers' battle between Sam Jones and Jack Scott. Be out to see it.

BIG GRID GAME

The University of Washington will meet the University of Southern California's football team here, Oct. 20.

ZAM! ZIP! TWO FOR THE BAMBINO!

AND along came Ruth—twice in succession—and two times did the Babe blast home runs into the stands. Ruth brought in three of the four runs, winning the game almost single-handed, for the Yankees yesterday afternoon. The King of Swat has assumed the position of the mightiest player in the series.

Two Thundering Circuit Drives Into Stand Give Americans First Victory

Bambino Crosses Threshold of World Series Glory When He Breaks Defense of McGraw—Pennock Twirls Nationals Into Subjection

NEW YORK, Oct. 11.—(By Associated Press.)—Babe Ruth crossed with mighty tread today the threshold of world's series glory that has been barred to him for two years.

Driving out two thundering home-run thrusts in successive innings, a feat unparalleled in championship baseball history, Ruth was the dynamo in the powerful attack that enabled the New York Yankees to turn the tables on the Giants, capture the second game of the series by a score of 4 to 2 and square the count with the world's titleholders in the 1923 struggle for diamond supremacy.

Official Score

YANKS—	AB.	R.	H.	PO.	A.	E.
Witt, cf..........	5	0	0	1	0	0
Dugan, 3b.... ..	4	0	1	2	3	0
Ruth, rf.........	3	2	2	3	0	0
R. Meusel, lf.....	4	0	1	4	0	0
Pipp, 1b.........	3	1	1	13	0	0
Ward, 2b........	4	1	2	3	4	0
Schang, c........	4	0	1	1	0	0
Scott, ss	4	0	2	0	6	0
Pennock, p......	3	0	0	0	1	0
Totals.......	34	4	10	27	14	0

GIANTS—	AB.	R.	H.	PO.	A.	E.
Bancroft, ss......	4	0	0	0	6	0
Groh, 3b.........	3	1	1	0	1	0
Frisch, 2b.......	4	0	2	2	6	0
Young, rf........	4	0	2	0	0	2
E. Meusel, lf.....	4	1	2	4	0	0
Cunningham, cf..	3	0	0	1	0	0
Kelly, 1b.........	4	0	1	16	1	0
Snyder, c	4	0	0	3	1	0
McQuillan, p.....	1	0	0	0	0	0
Bentley, p........	2	0	1	0	2	0
*Gowdy	1	0	0	0	0	0
Stengel, cf	0	0	0	1	0	0
†Jackson	1	0	0	0	0	0
Totals.......	35	2	9	27	17	2

*Batted for Cunningham in eighth.

†Batted for Bentley in ninth.

Yankees	0	1	0	2	1	0	0	0	0	—4
Giants	0	1	0	0	0	1	0	0	0	—2

Two-base hits—Bentley, Dugan. Home runs—Ward, E. Meusel, Ruth (2). Double plays—Bancroft to Frisch to Kelly (2), Scott to Ward to Pipp. Left on bases—Yankees 8, Giants 8. Base on balls—McQuillan 2, Pennock 1, Bentley 2. Struck out—McQuillan 1 (R. Meusel), Pennock 1 (Kelly). Hits—McQuillan 5 in 3 2-3 innings, Bentley five in 3 1-3 innings, Pennock 9 in 9. Hit by pitcher—Bentley (Pennock). Winning pitcher—Pennock. Losing pitcher—McQuillan. Umpires—O'Day at plate; Nallin at first base; Hart at second base; Evans at third base. Time of game—2:07.

First up in the fourth inning, with the score tied at one-all, the great slugger put the Yankees in the lead with a terrific, towering blow that landed atop the second tier of the right-field grandstand and started the downfall of Hugh McQuillan, Giant ace. Another run was scored in that hectic inning, but on his next turn at bat, in the fifth, the Babe crashed one of Jack Bentley's southpaw slants into the lower right-field stands. That blow was the climax of the game; Yankee victory was clinched then and thereafter it proved merely a formality to carry on to the finish.

SPECTACULAR TRIUMPH

It was a spectacular triumph for the Yankees, whose punch mastered John McGraw's strategy and gave them the first world's series victory they have known since the fifth game of the 1921 championship— a span over which eight defeats and one tie have been the disastrous portion of the American League champions. It was a brilliant day for Herb Pennock, fragile left-hander, who twirled the Giants into subjection in masterful fashion, and Joe Dugan, fleet-footed third sacker, whose marvelous defensive play brought him repeatedly into the limelight.

But, over and above the mere outcome of the game, the brilliant cogs that fitted into the winning Yankee machine, it was the day of days for Ruth, baseball's star of stars, who had come into his own and found the end of the rainbow of world's series fame for which he had sought before in vain. True, Ruth earned his spurs as a pitcher, hanging up a record of twenty-nine scoreless innings in championship play that still stands, but it was batting laurels that the greatest home run hitter of all time was seeking and he gained them today. No matter what he does the rest of the series, his place among series immortals is secure.

BRUTE FORCE WINS

Thus it was a triumph even greater for Ruth than for the Yankees; the ascendancy of brute force, the power of the wallop, over the tactical genius of John McGraw, baseball's "master mind." For behind the struggle for premier diamond honors from the start has been the greatest drama of all, the matching of Ruth's dynamic individuality against the strategy of the gray-haired, silent leader of the Giants.

Two years ago Ruth was handicapped in the series by injuries; last year he was a "bust," outguessed, baffled by the tactics of the "Little Napoleon." But tonight he is a triumphant figure, a vital force that upset with sheer might the best laid calculations of his opponent. And, knowing the confidence that his great achievement today has inspired, he may prove the deciding factor in the outcome of the third straight battle between Gotham's rival clubs and spoil McGraw's hopes of a third successive championship.

RUTH'S DRIVES RECORD

Ruth's feat of two home runs in a single world's series game has been done thrice in two decades of championship history, but in none of these instances were the circuit blows made in successive innings and successive times at bat. P. H. Dougherty of the Boston Americans was the first to accomplish the trick, in 1903. It was duplicated in 1915, by Harry Hooper, also of the Boston Americans, who drove out home runs in the third and ninth innings of the fifth game of the series with the Philadelphia Nationals; and again in 1917 by Benny Kauff of the Giants, who hit for the circuit in the fourth and eighth innings of the fourth game of the series with the Chicago White Sox.

Yesterday the story of victory

(Continued on Page 2, Column 2.)

Earlington-Tacoma Golf Match Delayed

Match play between the Earlington Golf and Country Club and Tacoma, scheduled for Sunday, has been indefinitely postponed, according to officials of the Earlington Club.

Ring Lardner, Damon Runyon, Babe Ruth, Johnny Evers, Waite Hoyt and Other Writers Are Covering World Series for Readers of This Newspaper

5:30 P. M.

SPORTING EXTRA

The Evening Bulletin.

5:30 P. M.

VOLUME LXI. NO. 242. TUESDAY: Fair. PROVIDENCE, MONDAY, OCTOBER 15, 1923 32 PAGES TWO CENTS 14 Cents Per Week Delivered by Carrier.

YANKS WIN WORLD'S BASEBALL CHAMPIONSHIP

"BOB" MEUSEL

Yankee Outfielder Who Won World Series for His Team To-day When He Drove Tieing and Winning Runs Across in the Eighth

COMPLETE BOX SCORE OF SIXTH WORLD SERIES GAME

YANKEES

	AB	R	H	PO	A	E
Witt, m......	3	0	0	3	1	0
Haines, m....	0	1	0	0	0	0
Dugan, 3......	3	1	0	2	1	0
Ruth, r.......	3	1	1	1	0	0
R. Meusel, l ...	4	0	1	1	0	0
Pipp, 1b......	4	0	0	12	0	0
Ward, 2......	4	0	1	0	7	0
Schang, c	4	1	1	7	0	0
Scott, s......	4	1	1	1	2	0
Pennock, p ...	2	0	0	0	1	0
*Hofman, ...	0	0	0	0	0	0
‡Bush, ...	0	0	0	0	0	0
xJohnson, ...	0	1	0	0	0	0
Jones, p......	0	0	0	0	1	0
Totals.....	31	6	5	27	13	0

GIANTS

	AB	R	H	PO	A	E
Bancroft, s ...	4	0	0	1	7	0
Groh, 3	4	1	1	1	2	0
Frisch, 2.....	4	2	3	0	6	0
Young, r	4	0	2	0	0	0
E. Meusel, l...	4	0	1	1	0	0
Cun'gham, m .	3	0	1	0	0	1
Stengel, m....	1	0	0	0	0	0
Kelly, 1b.....	4	0	0	20	0	0
Snyder, c.....	4	1	2	4	0	0
Nehf, p	3	0	0	0	5	0
Ryan, p	0	0	0	0	0	0
†Bentley ...	1	0	0	0	0	0
Totals.....	36	4	10	27	29	1

INNINGS	1	2	3	4	5	6	7	8	9	R	H	E
YANKEES	1	0	0	0	0	0	0	5	0	6	5	0
GIANTS	1	0	0	1	1	0	1	0	0	4	10	1

Hits—Off Nehf 4 in 7 1-3 innings; off Pennock 9 in 7 innings.
Three base hit—Frisch.
Home runs—Ruth, Snyder.
Double plays—Nehf to Bancroft to Kelly.
Struck Out—By Nehf 3, by Pennock 5, by Ryan 1.
Bases on Balls—Off Nehf 3, off Ryan 1.
Left on bases—Yankees 2, Giants 4.
Time of game—2h. 8m.
Umpires — Evans, Nallin, Hart, O'Day.

*Hofmann batted for Pennock in seventh.
†Bentley batted for Ryan in ninth.
‡Bush batted for Witt in seventh.
xJohnson ran for Bush in seventh.

GEORGE "BABE" RUTH

The Mighty Bambino, Who Created New World Series Record To-day When He Got a Home Run in the First Inning, Making Three Circuit Clouts for the Series.

TWELVE INDICTED HERE ON GAMBLING CHARGES

Nearly Score of Secret Bills Are Also Returned as Grand Jury Reports in Superior Court

The crusade against gamblers which has been conducted in different sections of the State hit Providence County to-day when the September grand jury, which has been in session the past few weeks in the Superior Court building, returned indictments against the following:

George B. Briggs of Warwick, charged with being a common gambler in Cranston and Pawtuxet Valley.

Joseph Payan, alleged manager of the Pilgrim Club in Cranston, charged with being a common gambler and with maintaining a nuisance.

John F. Hennessey of East Providence, charged with being a common gambler and with maintaining a nuisance.

James Cianci, alleged proprietor of the Silver Lake Hotel in Cranston, which recently burned, charged with being a common gambler and with maintaining a nuisance.

William Riley of North Providence, charged with being a common gambler.

Joseph Lizard of North Providence, alleged to be in the employ of William Riley, charged with being a common gambler.

Bessie Cook, alias Ramsey, alleged proprietor of the Admiral Inn, Cumberland, which was raided Friday night by Sheriff Jonathan Andrews and Deputy Thomas, charged with being a common gambler and with maintaining a nuisance.

Briggs, Riley and Lizard are alleged to be the owners or operators of slot machines.

Bertha Koch of Foster, two indictments, alleging maintaining gambling nuisances.

Jacob Kulze, alleged proprietor of the Sunnyside Hotel, Johnston, maintaining common gambling nuisance.

James P. Cahill, Foster, alleged proprietor of the Hartford Pike House, two indictments, alleging common gambler and maintaining gambling unisance.

Joseph George, alias Blind Joe. Woonsocket, maintaining common nuisance.

Cornelius Keating, alleged proprietor of the St. Cloud Hotel, Johnston, maintaining nuisance.

Nineteen secret indictments were also returned, a large number of which were said to be the result of the crusade of the Attorney General's office against gambling.

The report of the grand jury shows that thus far 26 gambling indictments have been filed against 12 different persons, in addition to the secret indictments.

No indictments were found against the following: James E. Spelman, charged

Continued on Page 2, Col. 5.

SIX, TRAPPED IN ATTIC, BURN TO DEATH IN BROOKLYN

Firemen Find Charred Bodies in Ruins Two Hours After Blaze is Discovered.—Investigation of Cause Ordered.

[By the Associated Press]

New York, Oct. 15.—Six persons were trapped in an attic and burned to death, and a seventh, a woman, suffered grave injuries in leaping from the flames in a fire which early to-day destroyed a frame three-story dwelling in the Bensonhurst section of Brooklyn.

The dead are:

Mrs. Lillian Andrews, her nephew, Charles, and niece, Margaret.

George Kyne, playwright.

Francis Poncho Fowler.

Miss Roberta Wigert.

Mrs. Anna Andrews, who was trapped with the others in the attic of the building, leaped through a window, sustaining internal injuries which may prove fatal.

Neighbors, seeing smoke rolling from the basement of the dwelling house, rushed to the spot just in time to see Mrs. Anna Andrews leap from a window of the attic apartment. Two hours later firemen found the charred bodies of the six victims. They apparently had been overcome after escape had been cut off by the flames.

The body of Charles Andrews, 19-year-old athlete and student at Polytechnic Institute, Brooklyn, lay just inside of a rear window. Near him lay his aunt, Mrs. Lillian Andrews. The body of 12-year-old Margaret was found clasped in the arms of Miss Wigert, a maid, in an adjoining room.

The ruins of a third bedroom disclosed the body of Fowler. Kyne had been trapped in the bathroom in an attempt to reach a window. They were roomers in the Andrews home.

A dozen occupants of the first and second floor apartments of the burned building were awakened and led through the flames to safety by Dr. Thomas McNickle, a dentist, and his brother, whose four nieces were among the rescued.

Heads of the fire department have ordered an investigation to determine the origin of the fire.

TWO CIVILIANS KILLED IN MEININGEN, GERMANY

Troops Aid Police in Clearing Streets of Rioters.

[By the Associated Press]

Berlin, Oct. 15.—Two civilians are reported to have been killed and several others injured at Meiningen Saturday night when the Reichswehr was called upon to help the police clear the streets of rioters.

Three persons were injured in a food riot at Frankfort-on-Main on Saturday.

NO IDLENESS IN FRANCE, LABOR STATISTICS SHOW

Only 66 in All Paris Out of Work; 1275 in Whole Country.

[By the Associated Press]

Paris, Oct. 15.—The French Government has no unemployment problem on its hands. Statistics compiled by the Ministry of Labor show that only 1275 persons are out of work in all France, of whom 66 are in Paris, whereas in March, 1921, the number of unemployed was 91,225. Of this number 45,100 were in Paris.

Series Results

FIRST GAME
GIANTS 5—YANKEES 4

SECOND GAME
YANKEES 4—GIANTS 2

THIRD GAME
GIANTS 1—YANKEES 0

FOURTH GAME
YANKEES 8—GIANTS 4

FIFTH GAME
YANKEES 8—GIANTS 1

SIXTH GAME
YANKEES 6—GIANTS 4

4 MEN SEIZED WITH LIQUOR-LADEN CARS FAIL TO RAISE BAIL

Quartet Apprehended Early Yesterday Morning in East Providence is Jailed.—464 Bottles of Whiskey Found in Two Machines Are Valued at $5000.

Four alleged rum runners, piloting two liquor-laden touring cars, fell victims to the vigilance of Patrolmen Frederick Hancock and John Estes of the East Providence police after an exciting chase at 3 o'clock yesterday morning. The haul aggregated 464 bottles of Scotch whiskey, valued at $5000, and the prisoners, W. B. Bradley and Bertram M. Armstrong of Albany, King Johnson of Riverside and Alex Carron, formerly of East Providence, arraigned before Judge Malcolm D. Champlin in the Seventh District Court, East Providence, yesterday forenoon, were jailed in default of bail. Trial was set for next Saturday.

All entered not guilty pleas. Bradley was charged with carrying a concealed weapon and transporting liquor. Bail was set at $500 on the first charge and $1000 on the second.

Armstrong's case was similarly disposed of. Johnson and Carron were charged with transporting liquor only. Their bail was $1000 each.

Signal Unheeded

Hancock, on duty in Riverside, signalled a touring car to stop when he saw it speeding into Turner avenue. The big automobile hurtled on, unheeding, how-

Continued on Page 3, Col. 4.

NEW PRESIDENT OF CHINA IS TENDERED RECEPTION

Pekin, Oct. 15.—(By the Associated Press.))—The entire diplomatic body attended the reception this morning to Marshal Tsao Kun, the new President of China.

BABE RUTH GETS THIRD HOME RUN, NEW RECORD

Mighty Swatsmith Sets Mark That May Stand for All Time

Special to the Evening Bulletin.

Polo Grounds, New York, Oct. 15.—All hail the Yankees, new baseball champions of the world. After two years of dismal failure the American League crew under Miller Huggins came into its own to-day. The result of to-day's final set-to of the 1923 struggle was:

Yankees 6, Giants 4

Starters in the blue ribbon classic of baseball the past three years, each year against "Jawn" McGraw and his Giants, the Yankees landed the bacon this year for the first time. Two years ago the Yankees obtained an early lead and it looked as though there was nothing to it but the American Leaguers. Then, in one of the most sensational rallies ever witnessed in the fall classic, the Giants took three straight and the series, making monkey's out of Babe Ruth and the other big sticks of the Yankee crew.

Last year the Yanks made their punkiest showing, falling down miserably in five games, the best they could do being to tie the Giants in one of the games and losing the other four. But this year it was a different story. Losing the first game, the Yankees came back in the second and evened the series. Casey Stengel gave the Giants a 2 to 1 lead in the third game when his home run was the only run scored in the set-to.

But in the fourth battle the Yankees unlimbered their heavy artillery and when the smoke of battle had cleared away they were out on the long end of an 8 to 4 score, the clan of Huggins having crushed to a pulp the Giant firing squad. Hit after hit of every description rolled off the bats of the American Leaguers. Yesterday it was almost a repetition of the day before, Babe Ruth et al., taking kindly to everything

He Is as Guilty Who Holds the Bag as He That Puts in

WISCONSIN ★ NEWS ★ SPORTS

WHIPCORD MUSCLES OF SHOULDERS AND ARMS

Here Is How Rogers Hornsby, Champion Batter of the National League, Lines 'Em Out. Study His Style and LearnHow to Wallop the Pill a Mile

At the Plate Ready to Start His Swing

With Eye on Ball Hornsby Starts Bat to Meet It

Mickey Walker, World's Welterweight Champion, Will Be Fea

SENATORS WIN

THE SAN FRANCISCO CALL AND POST
AN INDEPENDENT NEWSPAPER

CALL AND POST, VOL. 116, NO. 80
SAN FRANCISCO CALL, VOL. 136, NO. 80
36 PAGES—SAN FRANCISCO, FRIDAY, OCTOBER 10, 1924 3c

'OTHER MAN' SOLVES S. F. TRUNK MURDER

Game in Detail

FIRST INNING

Giants—In Washington batting order Taylor will bat seventh and Ruel eighth. Lindstrom up. Ball 1. Strike 1. Strike 2. Lindstrom fanned, missing a wide curve. Frisch up. Ball 1. Ball 2. Ball 3. Strike 1. Frisch got a ticket to first. Young up. Manager Harris went to the pitcher's box and talked to Ogden and then conferred with Umpire Dineen. Ogden left the box and was replaced by Mogridge, the left-hander. Ball 1. Foul, strike 1. Strike 2. Foul. Young struck out fishing for a wide curve. Kelly up. Foul, strike 1. Taylor threw out Kelly. No runs, no hits, no errors.

Senators—McNeely up. Lindstrom took McNeely's hopper and got him at first. Harris up. Strike 1. Strike 2. Ball 1. Ball 2. Harris went out on strikes. Rice up. Ball 1. Ball 2. Strike 1. Strike 2. Foul. Barnes tossed out Rice, who hit a weak roller to the box. No runs, no hits, no errors.

SECOND INNING

Giants—Terry up. Terry hit a hot grounder to Harris, who threw him out. Wilson up. Bluege robbed Wilson of a hit back of second base and nailed the batter with a fast throw. Jackson up. Ball 1. Taylor took Jackson's grounder and made a wild throw to first. Gowdy up. Ball 1. Gowdy singled into left, Jackson halting at second. Barnes up. Strike 1. Foul, strike 2. Ball 1. Ball 2. Ball 3. Foul. Barnes struck out. No runs, one hit, one error.

Senators — Goslin up. Strike 1. Ball 1. Strike 2. Goslin struck out, being fed nothing but wide curves. Judge up. Strike 1. Ball 1. Strike 2. Frisch made a leaping catch of Judge's hot liner. Bluege up. Ball 1. Ball 2. Bluege went out, Jackson to Terry. No runs, no hits, no errors.

THIRD INNIN3

Giants — Lindstrom up. Ball 1. Taylor threw out Lindstrom at first. Frisch up. Strike 1. Frisch bunted and was safe at first. Young up. Strike 1. Ball 1. Foul, strike 2. Foul. Young popped to Judge. Kelly up. Kelly forced Frisch, Bluege to Harris. No runs, one hit, no errors.

Senators—Taylor up. Ball 1. Foul, strike 1. Strike 2. Taylor took three healthy swings and sat down. Ruel up. Ball 1. Ball 2. Strike 1. Ball 3. Strike 2. Foul. Ruel went out, Barnes to Terry. Mogridge up. Foul, strike 1. Strike 2. Mogridge went out on strikes. It was his fifth straight strikeout in the series. No runs, no hits, no errors.

FOURTH INNING

Giants—Terry up. Strike 1. Strike 2. Ball 1. Ball 2. Terry fanned. Wilson up Strike 1. Ball 1. Ball 2. Ball 3. Bluege threw out Wilson, making a pretty play on his puzzling drive. Jackson up. Ball 1. Bluege also got Jackson at first. No runs, no hits, no errors.

Senators—Mrs. Coolidge applauded Mogridge as he walked to the bench. McNeely up. Ball 1. Strike 1. Ball 2. Foul, strike 2. Foul. McNeely fanned, biting on a drop curve for his last strike. Harris up. Strike 1. Ball 1. Ball 2. Strike 2. Ball 3. Harris got a home run in the left field stands. President Coolidge and the whole crowd arose and cheered. The President continued to applaud for a minute or more after Harris had circled the bases. Rice up. Wilson came in and made a shoestring catch of Rice's seeming hit. Goslin up. Strike 1. Ball 1. Foul, strike 2. Terry took Goslin's grounder and beat him to the bag. One run, one hit, no errors.

FIFTH INNING

Giants—Gowdy up. Harris raced into center and took Gowdy's pop. Barnes up. Strike 1. Bluege threw out Barnes. He went over behind second to take Barnes' grounder. Lindstrom up. Ball 1. Lindstrom hit into left for two bases. Frisch up. Ball 1. Foul, strike 1. Strike 2. Goslin took Frisch's drive. No runs, one hit, no errors.

Senators—Judge up. Foul, strike 1. Strike 2. Judge went out, Terry to Barnes. Bluege up. Strike 1. Strike 2. Foul. Ball 1. Ball 2. Ball 3. Foul. Johnson threw out Bluege at first. Jackson made a neat stop. Taylor up. Strike 1. Strike 2. Ball 1. Foul. Ball 2. Foul. Ball 3. Taylor went out on strikes. Barnes threw curve after curve to the Senators and in five innings had only made one hit. No runs, no hits, no errors.

SIXTH INNING

Giants—The crowd cheered when Walter Johnson went out into right field to talk to Marberry. Young up. Strike 1. Ball 1. Ball 2. Ball 3 Young got a base on balls. Kelly up. Ball 1. Strike 1. Ball 2. Ball 3. Kelly singled into centerfield, Young going to third. Meusel batted for Terry. Meusel up. As soon as Meusel came to the bat, Manager Harris replaced Mogridge with Marberry. The Senatohs' infield played back. Meusel flied to Rice, Young scoring on the catch. Kelly held first. Wilson up. Ball 1. Wilson singled to center, Kelly going to third. Jackson up. Kelly scored when Judge juggled Jackson's grounder, Wilson went to second and Jackson being safe at first. Gowdy up. Fou, strike 1. Strike 2. Ball 1. Foul. Ball 2. Ball 3. Wilson scored when Gowdy's grounder went through Bluege. Jackson went to third o nthe error. Barnes up. Barnes lined out to Rice, Jackson holding third. Lindstrom up. Strike 1. Strike 2. Lindstrom struck out.

Three rnns, two hits, two errors.

Senators—Kelly went to first, Wilson went to center and Meusel went to left field. Ruel up. Ball 1. Lindstrom threw out Ruel. Marberry up. Ball 1. Lindstror also threw out Marberry. McNeely up. Foul, strike 1. Ball 1. McNeely flied out to Young. No runs, no hits, no errors.

Continued in Red, Cols. 7 and 8

PRESIDENT IS EARLY ARRIVAL AT GAME

GRIFFITH STADIUM, WASHINGTON, Oct. 10 (By the Associated Press).—The climax to one of baseball's most sensational championship battles came today when the New York Giants, four time National League champions, and the Washington Senators, American League title holders for the first time, drew up their lines for the seventh and deciding game for the 1924 series.

For pitching duty in the deciding game the rival managers called upon youngsters, Ogden being the choice for the Senators and Barnes for the Giants. Ruel and Gowdy completed the batteries. Ogden was relieved after pitching to two men and Mogridge took his place.

The Senators, victorious but crippled yesterday in the courageous stand that put them back on even

Con. on Page Sixteen, Col. One

Justice McKenna's Wife Thought Dying

WASHINGTON, Oct. 10 (International News Service).—Mrs. Amanda E. McKenna, wife of Justice Joseph E. McKenna of the United States Supreme Court, is gravely ill and hope for her recovery has virtually been abandoned by physicians, it became known here today.

Justice and Mrs. McKenna celebrated their golden wedding anniversary several years ago. They were married in San Francisco in 1865.

SHENANDOAH NEAR DISASTER ON PEAK

PHOENIX, Ariz., Oct. 10 (By Associated Press).—The giant airship Shenandoah narrowly missed disaster early today when she sailed within fifteen feet of the top of Picacho peak between Tucson and Casa Grande, Ariz., according to a radio message picked up here.

TUCSON, Ariz., Oct. 10 (By International News Service).—Sailing majestically over this city just after daybreak the big dirigible Shenandoah, en route to San Diego, was given a rousing welcome.

The giant airship was sighted over the city at 6:35 a. m. (mountain time), her great body glinting in the rising sun.

The entire population of the city was out, thousands having waited for her appearance the greater part of the night. Every available noise-making apparatus was called into

Cont'd. on Page Sixteen, Col. Five

STOCKTON GIRLS VIE FOR HONOR OF RULING FETE AS QUEEN WITH 'KING POTATO'

The race is on in the delta lands of San Joaquin Valley to wear the crown on "Potato Day." The four contestants pictured are: Left to right, upper, Miss Alice Knudsen, Miss Emma H. Alford, and, below, Miss Maris Proudfit and Miss Anita Ohm.

COLLEGE OUSTS DARWIN TEACHER

By Associated Press.

MACON, Ga., Oct. 10.—Dr. Henry Fox, professor of biology at Mercer University, has been asked by the board of trustees of the university to resign. The teachings of Dr. Fox on evolution and his religious beliefs are said to be out of harmony with the fundamental beliefs of the Baptists of Georgia.

Growers Hope to Wrest Title Now Held by Great Britain

Special Dispatch to The Call.

STOCKTON, Oct. 10.—If Helen of Troy had hailed from Stockton instead of Greece, Paris would never have awarded her an apple for being the most beautiful woman in the world. He would have given her a potato; thus scoring one for the pride of the delta lands of San Joaquin County.

Of course, what Paris really gave

Continued on Page Sixteen, Col. Two

PLANS TO SAVE GIRL BARRED BY SLAYING

The motive that prompted Howard A. Davies to slay his wife, Fern; the man whom she loved and with whom she intended to flee, and the knife with which it is presumed she was killed and then butchered, were uncovered today by Constable S. A. Landini of Colma in an effort to clear up the unsolved and important features of the case.

At the same time it was revealed that while the body of Fern Davies lay mutilated and hidden in a trunk at 1651 Market street, where she was murdered, two uniformed police called at the house to question her on a minor complaint.

Fred Brookes, an employe of the Montague Steel and Pipe Works, 1000 Third street, and living at 1751 Eighth avenue, is "the man in the case."

ADMITS LOVING GIRL

He admitted to Landini that he loved the girl, that she had planned to leave her husband and go with him and that Davies had warned him to keep away, and also had threatened him.

All this, he said, he had told to a fortune teller, who, when interviewed by Landini, corroborated Brookes' story.

"I loved this girl better than any other woman in the world," Brookes said today. "She was planning to leave Davies for me. Davies knew this. He did not want to lose her. On the night she was murdered I phoned her to ask her to accompany me to a spiritualistic medium.

"Davies answered the phone. He said she had gone out and he did not know when she would be in, and I went to the medium and told her the story of my love for Fern."

Landini found this medium today in the person of Mme. Alma D[illegible]ore, 1689 Geary street, who substantiated the statement of Brookes that he had been to her and confessed his love for Fern.

HEARD SCREAM FOR HELP

Following this came the revelation, from Mrs. Marie Pappens, landlady

Continued on Page Three, Col. Two

BASEBALL

Giants	0	0	0	0	0	3	0	0	0	0	0	0—	3
Senators	0	0	0	1	0	0	0	2	0	0	0	1—	4

Giants...	ab	r	h	po	a	e	Senators.	ab	r	h	po	a	e
Lindstrom 3b	5	0	1	0	3	0	McNeely cf.	6	0	1	0	0	0
Frisch 2b..	5	0	2	3	4	0	Harris 2b..	5	1	3	4	1	0
Young rf ..	3	0	1	2	0	0	Rice rf.....	5	0	0	2	0	0
Kelly cf 1b	5	1	1	8	1	0	Goslin lf...	5	0	2	3	0	0
Terry 1b...	2	1	0	6	1	0	Judge 1b...	4	0	1	11	1	1
Wilson lf cf	5	1	1	4	0	0	Bluege ss..	5	0	0	1	7	2
Jackson ss.	6	0	0	1	4	2	Taylor 3b..	3	0	0	0	3	1
Gowdy c...	6	0	1	7	0	1	Ruel c......	5	2	2	13	0	0
V.Barnes p.	4	0	0	1	2	0	Mogridge p.	1	0	0	0	0	0
Nehf p.....	0	0	0	0	0	0	Marberry p.	1	0	0	1	0	0
Meusel lf..	2	0	1	1	0	0	Johnson p..	3	0	0	0	1	0
Bentley p..	0	0	0	0	0	0	Miller 3b	1	0	0	1	1	0
Groh	1	0	1	0	0	0	Liebold	1	1	1	0	0	0
Totals...	44	3	9	34	15	3	Totals...	43	4	10	36	14	4

GIANTS-SENATORS GAME—Cont. From Col. 2
(Abbreviations—S, Strike; B, Ball; F, Foul.)

7TH INN.: Giants—Frisch up. S1. F,S2. B1. B2. Fouled out to Ruel. Young up. B1. S1. B2. B3. S2. Walked. Kelly up. F,S1. F,S2. B1. B2. Out, Taylor to Judge; Young went to 3rd. Meusel up. S1. F,S2. B1. Out, Marberry unassisted. 0r, 0h, 0e.

Senators—Harris up. B1. Singled infield. Rice up. Hit into a double play, Kelly to Jackson. Goslin up. S1. B1. F,S2. B2. B3. Singled to right. Judge up. Flied out to Wilson. 0r, 2h, 0e.

8TH INN.: Giants—Wilson up. S1. S2. Struck out. Jackson up. Bluege juggled Jackson's grounder and the batter was safe. Gowdy up. B1. Flied out to Goslin. Barnes up. S1. S2. Fanned. 0r, 0h, 1e.

Senators—Bluege up. S1. F,S2. Fouled out to Gowdy. Liebold batting for Taylor. B1. S1. Doubled to left. Ruel up. B1. Singled infield; Liebold to 3rd. Tate batting for Marberry. B1. F,S1. S2. B2. B3. Walked. Shirley running for Tate. McNeely up. B1. Flied to Meusel; Liebold holding 3rd. Harris up. Liebold and Ruel scored on Harris' single into left. The crowd was frantic. Shirley on 2nd. Rice up. Barnes taken from the box and replaced by Nehf. Rice up. F,S1. B1. F,S2. F. B2. Out, Kelly unassisted. 2r, 3h, 0e.

9TH INN: Giants—Walter Johnson pitching for the Senators. Miller went to 3rd. Lindstrom up. B1. Popped to Miller. Frisch up. B1. S1. Frisch got a long hit into center. Young up. B1. B2. B3. Walked. Young was purposely passed. Kelly up. S1. S2. Kelly fanned. Meusel up. F,S1. B1. Young stole 2nd. B2. Miller threw out Meusel. 0r, 1h, 0e.

Senators—Goslin up. S1. Out, Frisch to Kelly. Judge up. B1. Singled. Bluege up. S1. B1. S2. Bluege safe on Jackson's error. Judge to 3rd. Nehf taken from box replaced by McQuillan. Miller up. B1. Hit int oa double, Jackson to Frisch to Kelly. 0r, 0h, 1e.

10TH INN.: Giants—Wilson up. B1. B2. B3. S1. Walked. Jackson up. F,S1. B1. S2. Fanned. Gowdy up F,S1. Hit into a double play, Johnson to Bluege to Judge 0r 0h, 0e.

Senators—Ruel up. S1. F,S2. B1. Out, Frisch to Kelly. Johnson up. S1. S2. B1. Flied to Wilson. McNeely up. F,S1. F,S2. B1. Fanned. 0r, 0h, 0e.

11TH INN.: Giants—Groh batting for McQuillan.. S1. B1. Singled. Southworth running for Groh. Lindstrom up. Sacrificed, Judge to Harris. Frisch up. B1. F,S1. B2. F,S2. Fanned. Young up. B1. B2. B3. Walked. Kelly up. S1. F,S2. B1. Fanedn. 0r, 1h, 0e.

Senators—Bentley pitching. Harris up. B1. Flied to Young. Rice up. Flied to Wilson. Goslin up. S1. B1. Doubled. Judge up. Walked. Bluege up. Forced Judge, Jackson to Frisch. 0r, 0h, 0e.

12TH INN.: Giants—Meusel singled. Wilson up. B1. B2. S1. F,S2. Fanned. Jackson forced Meusel. Gowdy up. S1. Flied to Goslin. 0r, 1h, 0e. Senators—Miller up. B1. Out, Frisch to Kelly. Ruel up. F,S1. F,S2. F. B1. Doubled. Johnson up. Safe on Jackson's error. McNeely up. F,S1. Ruel scored on McNeely's double.

STORM IN SAN PEDRO HARBOR

SAN PEDRO, Oct. 10.—Anchors were torn loose by a thrty-six mile gale and the four-masted barkentine Lackawanna drifted among the battleships in "Man o' War Row" in the outer harbor shortly before noon today.

Picture Section
in 2 Parts
PART 1

Chicago Sunday Tribune.
THE WORLD'S GREATEST NEWSPAPER

October 19, 1924

AMID SCENES OF THE WILDEST EXCITEMENT, the Senators, who haven't been much in baseball hitherto, won a world championship in Washington the other day. You may have read about it. Here are two of the spectators—Calvin Coolidge, President of the United States, and Mrs. Coolidge—registering the wildest excitement. A home run by Stanley Harris, boy manager of the Senators, was the immediate occasion of the quite unrestrained handclapping and the pleased presidential grin, both of which phenomena are, as you might say, rare.
(Photograph from Pacific & Atlantic.)

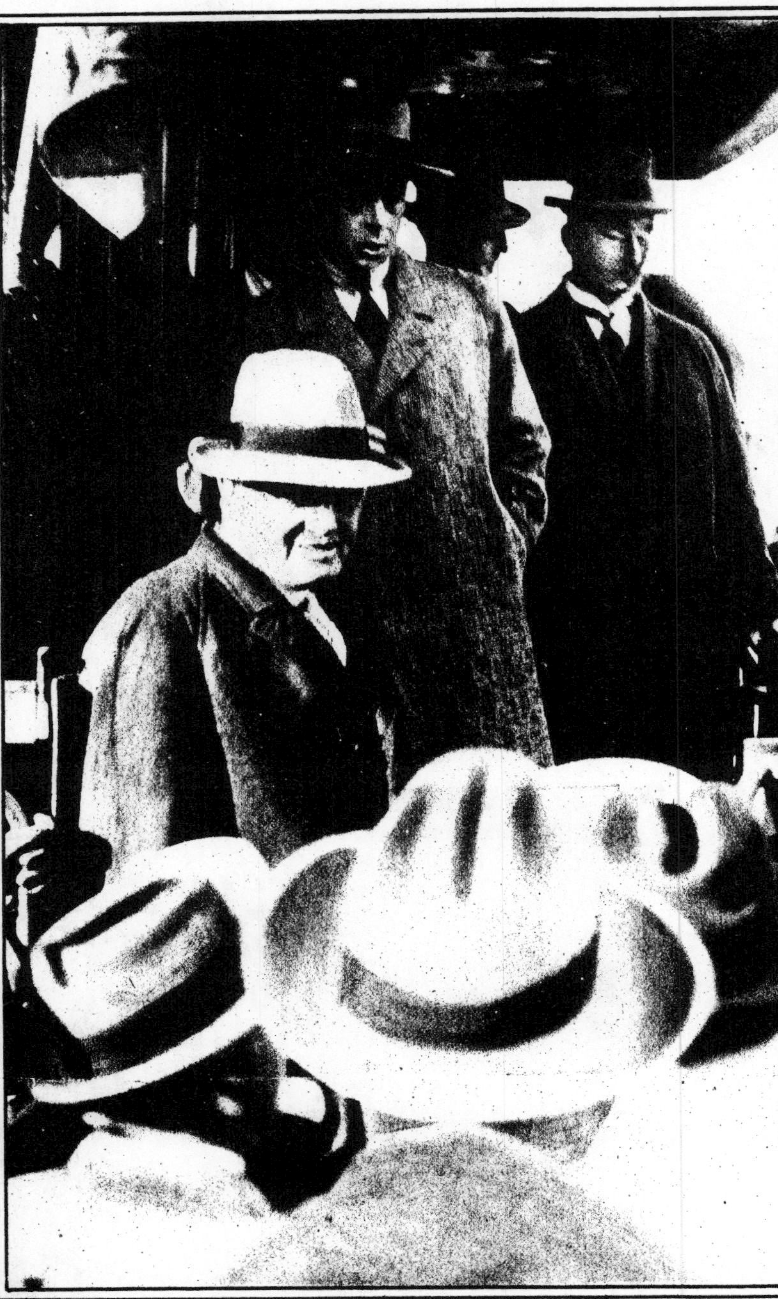

MR. WINDSOR ARRIVES—Chicago's first glimpse of the Prince of Wales Monday was vouchsafed the waiting citizenry not in Chicago proper, but in Lake Forest. Here is the royal visitor leaving his train in the north shore suburb, ready for a day of seemly excitements. The man in the foreground, with the lightish hat, is Louis F. Swift, the prince's host in Chicago.
(Photograph from Pacific & Atlantic.)

WHEN THE FINAL GAME WAS OVER, with the Senators victorious and the Giants beaten, 35,000 crazy, jubilant fans surged onto the field and staged the maddest demonstration ever seen in the history of baseball. The camera here has caught only a little section of the mob, but it shows what the crowd was like.
(Photograph from Pacific & Atlantic.)

THE WINNING RUN—Darkness was approaching and nerves were near the breaking point when McNeely of the Senators hit what looked like a harmless grounder toward third. Something happened to the ball; it bounded over the Giants' third baseman's head, and "Muddy" Ruel, who had been biding his time on the bases, charged over the plate. His score brought the Senators their first world title. 'Twas a dramatic moment.
(Photograph from Pacific & Atlantic.)

AT THE TURN OF THE TIDE—"Nemo" Leibold sliding to second—and making it—in the crucial eighth inning, when the Senators' ebbing fortunes began to rise. The Giants had been ahead, and the case, for the Senators, seemed hopeless. Then Leibold smashed his double down the third base line, the "break" of the game arrived, and, with the score tied at the end of the inning, the struggle became an even one.
(Photograph from Pacific & Atlantic.)

COBB, AS A YOUTH, WORE HIS SIDES RAW LEARNING TO SLIDE

Given Less Instruction Than Any Other Player

Leidy, Sensing That Ty Preferred His Own Counsel, Allowed Him to Think for Himself.

Chapter VIII.

By H. G. SALSINGER.

TY COBB had less actual instruction in base ball than any man that ever became a star in the major leagues. Cobb always preferred his own counsel. George Leidy decided this soon after he came to know Cobb. He felt certain that the best way to develop Cobb would be to fire his imagination and if that was fired sufficiently Cobb would develop himself. Trying to superintend that development would mean only retarding his progress, as he would not take kindly to advice.

Leidy let Cobb figure things out for himself. He told him how various great batters of the past worked at the plate. He gave him various suggestions while narrating yarns, knowing that Cobb would perceive the base ball wisdom contained in his stories and adopt what was best suited to his needs.

Start this life story of Ty Cobb anywhere. It is so written that each chapter forms a distinct feature of Cobb's life and career, and is complete in itself.

LEARNING IN EARNEST.

The manager soon noticed that Cobb was spending a great deal more time at the ball park than other players. Cobb would be at the park when the others arrived for morning practice and he would linger after they departed.

Leidy had told Cobb a story about Christy Mathewson, then reaching his top form as a pitcher. "This Mathewson used to have poor control and so he'd come out to the park early and get a catcher to come along. He'd have the catcher hold his glove in one certain position and keep on pitching, trying to hit the hollow of the glove. And in the winter he cut a hole twice as big as a base ball and about the height of the average man's waist line in the side of his barn and he'd pitch for hours trying to throw the ball through the hole. That's how he learned control. You got to keep pluggin' at one certain thing till you get it down pat."

Another time he spoke of Hans Wagner. The great Wagner at that time was becoming recognized as the best player of his time.

WAGNER HELD UP.

"You know this Wagner used to be a poor fielder," Leidy would tell Cobb. "He was first an outfielder and he wanted to play the infield. They had him playing the outfield. They didn't think he could play the infield. Wagner used to get up early in the morning and go to the park. He'd get a couple of kids in the neighborhood to hit grounders to him. But he found he was slow getting started. He couldn't get the jump in going after a ball. So Wagner took off his shoes and would play in his stocking feet. He would dig little trenches around the shortfield and he would set himself in these trenches in his stocking feet. You see that gave him a chance to start quicker. He couldn't slip while he was standing in them little trenches. He kept this up for weeks and they couldn't figure out what made the infield so rough around short until one day one of the players happened to come to the park early and there he saw Wagner digging holes. But, he learned to start quick.

"All of them fellows that made big reputations in base ball got their start that way. They practiced for hours and hours till they got the thing down pat."

Cobb decided to do likewise. He, too, practiced for hours and hours.

There was sliding. Cobb could not slide. He borrowed an old and torn base sack from the groundkeeper. In one corner of the field he spaded up the ground. At one end of this spaded plot he set the bag. Then he practiced sliding. He would slide for an hour at a time. He practiced early in the morning and late in the afternoon, after the game. Sometimes his hips were raw. Often he came into the clubhouse with his uniform soaked with blood. He learned to slide. He did not stop at the conventional slide. As soon as he mastered that he developed other slides. After a few years in the majors Cobb was sliding in eight different ways.

LEARNING TO FIELD.

He had started as a shortstop. He was now playing the outfield. Judging fly balls was difficult for him. He missed many. He started to learn. He had players bat fly balls to him by the hour. Leidy did it often, gladly. Cobb asked for short flies and long flies, flies to the the right of him and the left of him. He learned to go to the left and the right much sooner than he got the knack of coming in and going out on a direct center line. This is the most difficult chance an outfielder encounters. A ball hit in the air directly at him is extremely hard to judge. Those to the left and right are easy in comparison. They look by far the hardest. Most outfielders miss the chances that to a spectators seem the easiest. Ball players understand why, the spectator never seems to realize it.

Cobb played for Leidy during the remainder of the season of 1904. He participated in 37 games and batted for an average of .237, the lowest he ever hit during his professional base ball career. Leidy was not disappointed. "You've made a fine start," he told Cobb. "You'll set the league on fire next year." Leidy was still working on the boy's imagination.

(Tomorrow: Chapter IX—"The Nut.")

Ty Cobb's Perfect Sliding Form

HARD work, hours of practice at the park in after hours, raw and bleeding sides, made Ty Cobb supreme in the art of sliding into bases. This photograph was made when Cobb was at the top of his fame.

THREE MAY TIE FOR TOP RUNG

Y. M. O. Must Defeat Hughes Brothers to Make This Possible, However.

Today's Schedule.

Hughes Brothers vs. Y. M. O., Nykiel Field. Officials—Ritter, referee; Horning, umpire; Maloney, head linesman.

Lincoln Park vs. Wayne at Wayne. Officials—Owens, referee; Preshaw, umpire; Mason, head linesman.

Kenyons vs. Jerry McCarthys, Mack Park. Officials—Lawton, referee; Duncan, umpire; Kennedy, head linesman.

Nationals vs. Deno Drugs, River Rouge. Officials—Van Tassell, referee; Remington, umpire; Brown, head linesman.

Woodlands vs. Daniel Sales, Daniel Sales Field. Officials—Blied, referee; Anderson, umpire; Huber, head linesman.

TUESDAY'S GAMES.

Hughes Brothers vs. Daniel Sales, Nykiel Field. Officials—Lawton, referee; Horning, umpire; Kennedy, head linesman.

KENYONS vs. Woodlands, Mack Park. Officials—Remington, referee; Van Tassell, umpire; Huber, head linesman.

By H. H. BARCUS.

Three teams may be tied for first place in the Detroit Foot Ball League as a result of today's championship games. Should Young Men's Order, one of three teams tied for second place, win from Hughes Brothers, 1923 champions and undefeated leaders this year, while Kenyons win from McCarthys and Nationals beat Reno Drugs, the three runnersup will go into a tie for the top position in the league while the leaders will be relegated to second place.

There is a possibility that Y. M. O. will win from Hughes Brothers, but it is only a slight one. Throughout the present season the 1923 champions have played a top notch brand of foot ball scoring a total of 157 points in four games, while their opponents have failed to register a single point.

The four victories have given Hughes Brothers a total of eight place points, the league having decided to use the point system to award the championship this year, two points being awarded for a victory, one for a tie and none for a defeat.

LOSE ONE, TIE ONE.

While Hughes Brothers have won all their games the Y. M. O. has scored three victories, tied one game and lost another, losing to the Kenyons by a 7 to 6 score last week. Kenyons have won three games and tied one while Nationals have made a similar performance.

The Order eleven will go into the game with Hughes Brothers with a determination to win realizing that another defeat will eliminate it from further championship consideration. A victory, on the other hand, will make the Y. M. O. a serious contender for the league crown, despite the setback at the hands of the Kenyons. The Y. M. O. will be strengthened for its game with the champions having been given permission by the league to add two players to its roster to take the place of injured men.

KENYONS MEET McCARTHYS.

Kenyons, the surprise member of the league, hooks up with Jerry McCarthys at Mack Park. The Kenyons pulled the unexpected last week winning from the Y. M. O. when the latter eleven was picked as a sure winner. The Kenyons pulled a similar feat last year when they came through with a victory over Hughes Brothers, then known as the St. Johns. Brandau, star backfield man, will be back in the Kenyon lineup after having been on the injured list for several weeks.

The McCarthys undoubtedly will give the Kenyons a hard battle. The Jerry Macs started weakly but have been going strong winning their last starts and looking better in each succeeding game. They have a chance to climb up among the leaders by winning today's game.

NATIONALS SHOULD WIN.

Nationals are favored to come through over Reno Drugs who suffered a severe setback at the hands of Hughes Brothers last week. Daniel Sales are picked to win from Woodlands who have not scored a victory this season. Wayne is doped to whip Lincoln Park, another club which has yet to break into the win column.

Two games will be played on Tuesday, Armistice Day. Hughes Brothers will hook up with Daniel Sales at Nykiel Field while Kenyons hook up with the Woodlands at Mack Park. Both of the leaders should win these encounters.

DETROITER IS STAR IN DAYTON VICTORY

DAYTON, Ohio, Nov. 8.—The University of Dayton defeated Toledo University this afternoon, 52 to 6. Joe Cogley, a Detroit boy, played a great game at guard for Dayton. He was given a great ovation after having intercepted two passes. The University of Dayton plays John Carroll University, conqueror of Detroit, at Dayton in two weeks.

Deaf Mute Captains High School Eleven

MILFORD, Ill., Nov. 8.—The Milford Township High School foot ball team has a deaf mute for captain. Harold Pruitt has been elected to the position, despite his affliction. The signals are given to him by finger numbers and his inability to hear appears no handicap. Capt. Pruitt also is a star basket ball player and a javelin thrower. His home is in Wellington. The Milford foot ball squad has lost but one game so far this season.

Plays 7 Years Without Miss

Mr. "Dutch" Lodewyck, Married and Everything, Is a Star at End.

SPEAKING of veterans, consider "Dutch" Lodewyck, end on Central Michigan Normal's eleven, who in seven consecutive years of foot ball has never missed starting a game.

In every game that his high school and Normal School teams have played during that time, "Dutch" has always been on an end. "Dutch's" real name is Bourke W. Lodewyck. He acquired the "Dutch" at Cadillac High School. After three years of foot ball at Cadillace, he brought his nickname and his foot ball ability to Mt. Pleasant, where he made the varsity at Central Michigan Normal for the first game. He's now in his fourth year at Central.

"Dutch" has proved to be one of Normal's cogs this year. The new coach, Lester Barnard, from Western Tennessee, brought with him a sackful of Eastern end plays, and Lodweyck has executed them.

Lodewyck is a four-letter man. In basket ball, he is a regular at guard, in base ball he stars in right field, and in field events he hurls the javelin.

Mrs "Dutch" Lodewyck, nee Marion Davies, is a co-ed at Central Normal.

Scoring Mark To Michigan

MICHIGAN leads all foot ball teams in scoring points. Wolverine teams, during 1901, 1902, 1903, 1904, 1905, scored 2,679 points in 57 games, an average of 534 points a season or, 46.8 points a game. Minnesota teams of the same years scored 2,444 points in 59 games, 488 points a season, or an average of 41.4 points a game. Centre College, in 1919, 1920, 1921, 1922, 1923, put over 1,930 points in 49 games, an average of 386 a season or, 39.4 a game. California, Vanderbilt, Georgia Tech., University of Texas, Notre Dame, Henry Kendall College, now the University of Tulsa, are other colleges that have turned in unusual records in running up big scores. All have marks of 1,000 or more for five consecutive seasons.

BRITISH SOCCER

LONDON, Nov. 8.—Results of league soccer foot ball games, played today were as follows:

ENGLISH LEAGUE—FIRST DIVISION.

Arsenal 0, Notts County 1; Astonvilla 2, Bolton W. 2; Blackburn R. 1, Westbrom A. 0; Bury 3, Sunderland 0; Huddersfield T. 1, Tottenham H. 2; Liverpool 3, Preston N. E. 1; Manchester City 2, Everton 2; Newcastle United 3, Burnley 0; Nottingham F. 2, Cardiff City 1; Sheffield U. 1, Leeds United 1; Westham U. 0, Birmingham 1.

SECOND DIVISION.

Barnsley 3, Coventry City 1; Blackpool 1, Chelsea 2; Bradford C. 0, Clapton 0; Derby C. 3, Southampton 0; Fulham 2, Leicester City 2; Hull City 3, Stockport C. 0; Middlesbrough 0, Oldham C. A. 0; Portsmouth 1, Manchester U. 1; Portvale 1, The Wednesday 0; South Shields 1, Crystal Palace 1; Wolverhampton W. 1, Stoke 0.

SCOTTISH LEAGUE—FIRST DIVISION.

Ayr United 1, Dundee 0; Celtic 6, Kilmarnock 0; Cowdenheath 2, Aierdrionians 1; Falkirk 7, Queens Park 0; Hamilton A. 0, Hibernians 2; Hearts 1, Aberdeen 1; Patrick 2, Motherwell 2; St. Johnstone 1, Merton 3; St. Mirren 3, Raith Rovers 0; Third Lanark 1, Rangers 1.

Boxing

STEVE DEMPSEY, Detroit lightweight, has been matched to meet Jack Pinney, of Toledo, in the eight-round main event of the Fairview A. C. weekly show, Tuesday night. Ralph Carmona and Donald Burchard, Detroit featherweights, are to clash in the six-round semifinal. Jimmy Robe, of Kalamazoo, is scheduled to go six rounds with Georgie Enos, of Los Angeles. They also are featherweights. Three other bouts are to be arranged.

BURNS A FINGER TO HELP SPORT

But Osmun Doesn't Care About That as Long as Ice Skating Prospers.

Mr. Walter Osmun, salted peanut king, trout expert and leading skating impresario of the Sovereign State of Michigan, has filed his annual report. It deals with what transpired during the skating season of 1923-24, and the possibilities of the season of 1924-25.

The forefinger of Mr. Walter Osmun's right hand forms the most interesting feature of the report. It is presented as proof of the success attending the season of 1923-24. Mr. Osmun introduces the finger as Exhibit A.

Mr. Osmun is a bit foggy on the subject of ice races. That is, Mr. Osmun is unable to testify as to the exact number of races held. "But I can say," he writes, "that the events took from 1 to 5 o'clock every day to skate off the different events, and the gun was going all the time. I was starter in all events mentioned. I purchased 650 blanks, and I believe I had about 25 cartridges left. That would indicate about 300 races all told. I know I nursed a sore finger from powder burns for about three weeks after the season was over."

ALTAR OF SACRIFICE.

There is no regret over the powder burns. Knowing Mr. Osmun as we do, he would gladly sacrifice a finger to see skating made even more popular in this section. He is just that kind of man. He does not give a single salted peanut kernel's worth of consideration to a sore finger as long as he can pull the trigger and start the races and add to the enthusiasm of skating. He simply mentions the sore finger to show how many races were held.

This season will see a number of big skating events here. There will be the usual Winter Carnival at Belle Isle, conducted by the Recreation Commission; other carnivals at Orion Lake and Green Lake, a Silver Skates Derby and a speed Derby, besides a few more now under consideration.

DEPENDS ON FINGER.

The Michigan Skating Association now has a membership of 298. Last season 1,000 competed in races. Membership in the association is not compulsory for participation in speed events.

If Mr. Walter Osmun's trigger finger can withstand the powder burns during the approaching winter, there probably will be no end to ice skating. It all depends on the durability of the forefinger of Mr. Walter Osmun's right hand.

BOSTON COLLEGE SMEARS MARQUETTE TEAM, 34 TO 7

BOSTON, Nov. 8.—Boston College took ample revenge for last year's defeat by Marquette today when it buried the "Golden Avalanche," 34 to 7. Chuck Darling, Boston fullback, was the star, scoring four of his team's five touchdowns. Darling intercepted a pass in the first few minutes of play and raced 55 yards for a touchdown. Marquette's only score came in the third period when Curtin crossed the Boston College line.

VANDERBILT WINS

NASHVILLE, Tenn., Nov. 8.—Mississippi A. and M. Aggies went down in defeat here today before the Vanderbilt Commodores on a soggy field, 18 to 0. Vanderbilt scored a touchdown in the first, second and third quarters, but failed to kick goal each time. Reese raced 54 yards in the first for the Aggie's goal, while in the next periods Ryan carried the pigskin goalward for Vandy, the Commodore fullback never failed to gain when given the ball. His line plunging was pronounced excellent.

PICK POLOISTS MONDAY NIGHT

Grennan and Ide To Name Those Who Will Represent Detroit.

By HARRY LEDUC.

A polo team made up the best indoor players in Detroit and Grosse Pointe will represent the city in the Midwest Indoor tournament to be held in the Chicago Riding Academy the second week of January. Selection of the squad which will try for the three positions of indoor polo will be announced tomorrow night at the Detroit Riding and Hunt Club.

This announcement, marking the official start of the indoor polo season, was made by Phil H. Grennan, following an indoor scrimmage Friday night. Grennan and Maj. C. E. Ide, of Grosse Pointe, will select the squad.

EXPENSES OF FOUR.

Those in charge of the Chicago tournament are defraying the expenses of a team of three and one substitute and eight ponies. The tournament, originally scheduled for the second week in December, was deferred until January to permit completion of the Chicago Riding Academy, a new polo outlay not far from the heart of the city. The tournament is to last a week and, if plans carry, will attract the outstanding polo teams of the Middle West and possibly some of the East. Besides Detroit, Cleveland, Dayton, Toledo and Buffalo are certain to enter teams.

The number of polo players in Detroit is not so great as to make it difficult to name those who will be on the squad selected Monday night. This number is further reduced by the fact that many who play summer polo do not go in for the indoor game.

OUTSTANDING PLAYERS.

Players generally accepted as outstanding are Grennan, Fred Colin, Capt. Fleming, a former Army player, who is a recent arrival here; Jerry McCarthy, Gerald Christopher and Maj. Ide. Only four can be selected. Grennan, Fleming and Colin have the greater experience, but McCarthy and Christopher have made particular progress within the year. Christopher was in several of the Gold Hats' matches as early as last spring. McCarthy played in all the Gold Hats' fall matches with Grosse Pointe.

BIG RAPIDS HAS A STAR

BIG RAPIDS, Mich., Nov. 8.—Big Rapids High School has a halfback in Tonkin, who is believed here to be one of the best in Michigan high school circles. Tonkin has starred in every game this season and has always been good for big gains, although not well supported. In the game at Muskegon Heights last week it was Tonkin more than any other player, who brought victory. The halfback succeeded in making long gains against the Heights eleven and finally placed his team in position to score the only touchdown of the game.

CENTRE'S STARS SOUTH'S FIRST ON ALL-AMERICAN

"Bo" McMillin and Weaver, of Centre College, Danville, Ky., were the selections from the south for W. Camp's big team in 1919. They were the first from southern colleges to receive the honor. Fincher, of Georgia Tech., in 1920, was placed on the first team of Walter Camp's All-American eleven.

Ty Blames Him

Refusal to Report Cost Detroit Pennant, Cobb Says.

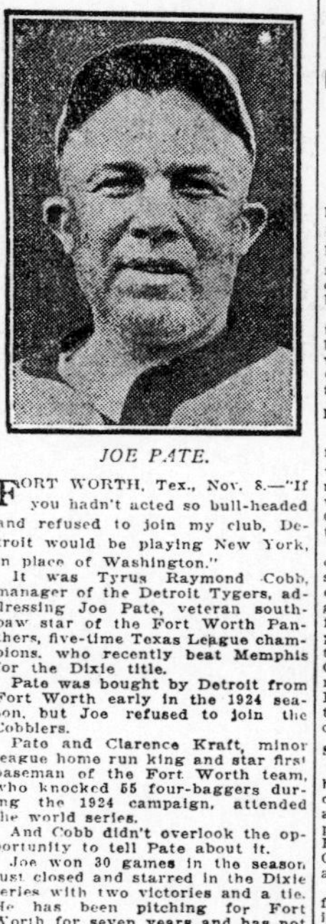

JOE PATE.

FORT WORTH, Tex., Nov. 8.—"If you hadn't acted so bull-headed and refused to join my club, Detroit would be playing New York, in place of Washington."

It was Tyrus Raymond Cobb, manager of the Detroit Tygers, addressing Joe Pate, veteran southpaw star of the Fort Worth Panthers, five-time Texas League champions, who recently beat Memphis for the Dixie title.

Pate was bought by Detroit from Fort Worth early in the 1924 season, but Joe refused to join the Cobblers.

Pato and Clarence Kraft, minor league home run king and star first baseman of the Fort Worth team, who knocked 55 four-baggers during the 1924 campaign, attended the world series.

And Cobb didn't overlook the opportunity to tell Pate about it.

Joe won 30 games in the season just closed and starred in the Dixie series with two victories and a tie. He has been pitching for Fort Worth for seven years and has not won less than 25 games in any one season.

Harriers, Too, At Marquette

THE fame of Marquette is not confined entirely to the gridiron.

In Melvin Shimek, of Kenosha, Wis., a sophomore, Marquette has a cross-country runner who bids fair to show his heels to the rest of the intercollegiate athletes.

Coached by Conrad Jennings, formerly of Michigan, Shimek broke the Western Conference record at a recent meet against University of Wisconsin at Madison. The record was formerly held by Isbel, of Michigan.

Really—Too Bad.

Walter Hagen draws $30,000 a year from a golf club in St. Petersburg, Fla.

COURT PRACTICE OPENS AT 'CITY'

Basket Ball Outlook Is Bright at Municipal College; 40 Players Out.

With the foot ball season still having two weeks to go City College has already started basket ball practice and is looking for a much more successful season on the courts than it has had on the foot ball gridiron.

Until Coach David Holmes is through with foot ball the basket ball squad will be under the supervision of Meyer Blatt, former City College basket ball captain and three-sport letter man at the school.

FORTY CANDIDATES REPORT.

The first workout of the season for the court squad was held last week, 40 candidates for the team reporting to Coach Blatt. Practice will be held twice each week until Coach Holmes can devote his entire time to basket ball.

With four letter men as a neucleus City College should have a strong basket ball outfit. The veterans back are Miller and Ertell, guards, and Townsend and Weldon, forwards. A flock of high school players are also out for positions on the team. In Moore, Northwestern; Gunn, Cass Tech; Baker and Jerome, Eastern; Griffin, U. of D., and Kaufmann, who played with Central in 1921, the Munies have plenty of good material.

SOME PLAY FOOT BALL.

From the foot ball squad the basket ball team should get Masasceck, Stemmelen, Grimaldi, Zuber and one or two others. Masasceck played basket ball with Northern High, Stemmelen with U. of D High, Grimaldi with Assumption College and Zuber with Petoskey High.

Besides the 'varsity quintet a freshmen team also is being organized which will be drilled by Coach Blatt, now handling the first team. A schedule of games will be arranged for the first year men with city and state high schools and junior colleges. The games will be played as preliminaries to the 'varsity contests.

City College has always been quite successful in basket ball. With the material it has now the municipal school should have its most successful season on the courts.

SOME POOR TEAMS

There are records chronicled in collegiate foot ball history which tell of teams that never scored a point during an entire season. George Washington University, in 1907, failed to score while the opposition scored 87 points. Next season this same team won nine out of 11 games, blanking its opponents in eight of them. Hamilton College failed to score in a game in 1907. Worcester Polytechnic Institute didn't cross its opponents' goal in seven games which constitutes its schedule in 1908. The enemy rolled up 153 points.

COBB'S HITS NET SIXTEEN BASES; NEW RECORD ESTABLISHED

Three Homers, Brace of Singles, A Double, Shatters Old Mark

New York, May 6.—(A. P.)—The triple tie for first place honors in the American league persists today with Washington, Philadelphia and Cleveland all smarting under defeats.

While the New York Yankees backed out of their slump of five consecutive defeats and handed the aspiring Philadelphia Athletics an 8 to 4 trimming yesterday, the Boston Americans were busily engaged in humbling the world champions in Washington to the tune of 9 to 4. Meantime, the Chicago White Sox nipped in the bud any prospects of the Cleveland Indians forging to the front by trimming them, 7 to 2, thus maintaining the three cornered scramble for leadership, ever another day.

Ty Cobb opened a batting assault on the St. Louis Browns by driving out three home runs, a double and a brace of singles for a total of 16 bases, a new record for modern major league baseball, with his Tigers winning in a walk, 14 to 8. The previous mark shattered by Cobb was held by Eddie Gharrity, Washington catcher, who ran his total of bases for one game to 13 in June, 1919.

Before the origin of the American league, the old record was held jointly by Bobby Lowe of the Boston Nationals, who in 1894 gathered four homers and a single, and by Ed Delehanty of the Philadelphia Nationals, who duplicated the feat in 1896.

The only other major leaguers who have equalled Cobb's three home runs in a single game in the present baseball era are George Kelly of the New York Giants, Ken Williams of the St. Louis Browns, Cy Williams and Walter Henline, both of the Phillies.

Cobb is now the leading batsman of both American and National leagues with an average of .531.

The Phillies had a field day at the expense of three Giant pitchers and weakened the hold of the National league leaders on first place by registering a 13 to 5 victory. Cy Williams and Russell Wrightstone collected a pair of home runs apiece.

In Boston, Burleigh Grimes steadied the uncertain Brooklyn Dodgers by allowing the Braves but six scattered hits and the Robins won, 6 to 1.

Rain prevented the two other scheduled games in the National.

The Yankees yesterday acquired Outfielder Bob Veach and Pitcher Alex Ferguson of the Boston Red Sox in return for Ray Francis, southpaw pitcher, and $8,000 in cash. Veach may take the outfield vacancy caused by the illness of Babe Ruth.

Sid Terris Outpoints Dundee In the Garden's Last Battle

New York, May 6 — Madison Square Garden, for three decades the scene of big sporting events and public assemblage, has sung its swan song. A turbulent throng of 13,000 last night watched Sid Terris, youthful New York lightweight outpoint the veteran Johnny Dundee in the building's faerwell athletic event.

The statue of Diana atop the Garden tower will be lowered today as wreckers begin to tear down the structure to make way for an office building. A new Madison Square Garden will be built by Tex Rickard several score blocks from Madison Square.

There was a roar of disapproval against the decision for Terris, as Dundee's plucky stand won him the favor of the audience. Fight fans left the famous old building as a parting "taps" was played by a veteran army sergeant.

"BABE" DENIES HE IS THROUGH

New York, May 6—"Babe" Ruth yesterday went to bat verbally against a report that he is "through" as a major league baseball star.

Propped up by pillows in his bed at the hospital, where for more than three weeks he has been recovering from indigestion and influenza, Ruth declared the statement was "bunk, pure and simple, because I am still at my best."

The home run champion said he felt that he was facing the most trying experience of his life. Being obliged to remain in a bed while the Yankees were losing ball games inflicted on him a greater hardship, he said, than any other misfortune he could visualize.

Ruth declared he had no intention of going to his farm in Sudbury, Mass., to recuperate after leaving the hospital. He admitted losing 35 pounds since his removal to the institution.

"As soon as I can work out in the sunshine with the Yankees, I'll get back the weight I've lost, and you can look for me to hit plenty of homers during the remainder of the season,' he concluded.

BALTIMORE HAS KIND

Baltimore in the International League has picked up a great prospect in Johnny Roser, outfielder. Roser has been hitting the ball at a terrific clip, getting nine homerun wallops in the first ten days of play.

Answer to Yesterday's Puzzle.

S. H. S. DEFEATED BY WOODLAWNS

The Woodlawn A. C. baseball team took its fourth straight game of the season yesterday afternoon when it defeated the Saratoga high school team in a practice game, by a score of 3 to 2. "Heap" Wilsey, hurling for the Woodlawns, alowed only four hits and struck out ten men.

Nichols, Christopher and Smith twirled for the high school team and were touched for ten hits and struck out only one man.

The Woodlawns would like to book games with other high school teams in this vicinity, for other teams averaging 16 to 18 years. William Calahan, 67 VanDam street is the manager.

The lineups: High school — Bloom, c; Nichols, p; Foy, 1b; Hays, 2b; Yeackel, ss; Smith, 3b and p; Stiles, lf; Pierce, cf; Pfreunder, rf; Ritchie, lf; Biffer, cf.

Woodlawns—H. Wilsey, p; C. Ford, c; T. Van Wagner, 1b; Dunnigan, 2b; C. Wilsey, ss; Curren, cf; Callahan, r; M. Foley, lf.

SPORTING GOSSIP

BY THE ASSOCIATED PRESS

Eddie Kane, manager of Tom Gibbons, has announced that he expects the St. Paul heavyweight in New York Monday to begin training for his battle with Gene Tunney at the Polo Grounds, June 5. Kane has selected an Atlantic City site for the Gibbons training camp.

The Ruth family enjoyed a family reunion yesterday at the New York hospital in which the home run champion and Mrs. Ruth are recovering from breakdowns. Babe made the visit to Mrs. Ruth's room, two flights above, via wheel chair.

Boxing promoter Tex Rickard and his staff bade adieu to old Madison Square Garden today to occupy offices on an old car barn site at Fiftieth street and Eighth avenue, New York, pending the opening of the new Madison Square Garden in November.

The Referee

When did Benny Leonard beat Freddy Welsh for the lightweight title and how many rounds did the fight go?—F. G. H.

Leonard defeated Welsh in 1917, winning on a kayo in the ninth session.

Did George Mullin of the old Detroit Tygers ever pitch a no-hit game, and if so, when?—C. V. S.

Mullin hurled a no-hit contest against St. Louis in the afternoon game of July 4, 1912.

Has Glenna Collett ever competed for the British women's golf title in the past?—F. R. T.

No, this will be her first foreign invasion.

BASEBALL CHART

YESTERDAY'S RESULTS

National League.

Philadelphia, 13; New York, 5.
Brooklyn, 6; Boston, 1.
Cincinnati at Chicago (cold weather.)
St. Louis at Pittsburgh (rain).

American League.

New York, 8; Philadelphia, 4.
Boston, 9; Washington, 4.
Chicago, 7; Cleveland, 2.
Chicago, 7; Cleveland, 2.
Detroit, 14; St. Louis, 8.

International League.

Baltimore 1; Rochester, 0.
Toronto, 5; Reading, 3.
Buffalo, 14; Newark, 1.
Jersey City at Syracuse (wet grounds).

Eastern League.

Waterbury, 6; Albany, 5.
New Haven, 8; Bridgeport, 4.
Springfield, 9; Worcester, 5.
Pittsfield, 8; Hartford, 4.

STANDING OF THE CLUBS.

National League.

	W.	L.	P.C.
New York	11	5	.688
Cincinnati	10	6	.625
Chicago	10	7	.588
Philadelphia	9	9	.500
Brooklyn	7	9	.438
Pittsburgh	6	9	.400
Boston	6	10	.375
St. Louis	6	10	.275

American League.

	W	L.	P.C.
Philadelphia	11	5	.688
Cleveland	11	5	.688
Washington	11	5	.688
Chicago	12	7	.632
St. Louis	9	11	.450
Boston	5	11	.313
New York	5	11	.313
Detroit	5	14	.263

International League.

	W.	L.	P.C.
Baltimore	14	4	.775
Jersey City	13	7	.632
Toronto	10	9	.526
Buffalo	10	11	.476
Newark	8	10	.444
Reading	7	10	.412
Rochester	7	10	.412
Syracuse	5	13	.313

Eastern League.

	W.	L.	P.C.
Waterbury	7	4	.636
Ne Haven	6	4	.600
Bridgeport	5	5	.500
Hartford	6	6	.500
Albany	6	7	.462
Worcester	5	6	.455
Springfield	5	6	.455
Pittsfield	4	6	.400

RUNS FOR THE WEEK.

National League.

	M.	T.	W.	T.	F.	S.	To
New York	12	5	..	..	..	..	17
Cincinnati	..	..	..	..	..	..	0
Chicago	..	..	..	..	..	..	0
Philadelphia	2	13	..	..	..	..	15
Brooklyn	5	6	..	..	..	..	11
Pittsburgh	..	..	..	..	..	..	0
St. Louis	..	..	..	..	..	..	0
Boston	6	1	..	..	..	..	7

American League.

	M.	T.	W.	T.	F.	S.	To.
New York	7	8	..	..	..	..	15
Cleveland	..	2	..	..	..	..	2
Washington	..	4	..	..	..	..	4
Philadelphia	8	4	..	..	..	..	12
Chicago	..	7	..	..	..	..	7
St. Louis	5	8	..	..	..	..	13
Boston	..	9	..	..	..	..	9
Detroit	4	14	..	..	..	..	18

SPORTING GOSSIP

Negotiations have been practically closed for a world's featherweight championship bout between Louis (Kid) Kaplan of Meriden, Conn.; and Red Chapman, Boston boxer to be held as the main attraction in Long Island City, June 9, under the auspices of the Long Island City Elks. This match intended to replace a postponed match between Charley (Phil) Rosenberg, world bantamweight champion, and Frankie Genario, American flyweight titleholder.

BRIEF SKETCHES OF BIG STARS

By ART CARLSON

JAMES J. DYKES
Athletics
Third Baseman

Born—Philadelphia, Pa., Nov. 10, 1896.

Major League Career—Joined Athletics in 1917. Optional to Gettysburg, Blue Ridge League, same season. Recalled in 1918. Optional to Atlanta, Southern Association, in 1919. Recalled later same campaign. (Also used at second base and shortstop.)

Outstanding Feats—Batted .312 in 1924, showing a gain of 60 points over previous season. While playing second base in game played Aug. 28, 1921, accepted 17 chances —9 putouts and 8 assists—for an American League record. Fielded .964 as second baseman in 1923.

EIGHT OF FIRST 11 SAFETIES ARE FOR EXTRA BASES

Chicago, May 6.—Leo Hartnett, star catcher for the Chicago Cubs, hung up a rather odd record during the first 10 days of the 1925 season.

Hartnett, in that period, not only crashed out six home runs but he also garnered a pair of doubles out of 11 safe blows. Quite a display of extra-base hitting for so early in the season.

Moreover, he topped the National League in run-getting with the same number as he made hits—11. It's a bit unusual for a backstop to lead the pack in the run column. But then Hartnett seems to be bent on doing a lot of out-of-the-ordinary things this campaign.

Hartnett, by the way, has been with the Cubs three seasons. And each year his hitting has improved. Last season he clouted for a mark of .299. But the way he has started this jamboree he should better that performance considerably.

So sensational has Hartnett's work at the plate been, that Manager Killefer has placed him in the cleanup position, a rather unusual post for a catcher.

Around The CAMP FIRE

With Will H. Oilg

OVER THE PORTAGE

In spite of the fact that automobile roads have penetrated almost all of our wildernesses and frontiers, it is still impossible to get into the real forests, to enjoy the quiet, the solitude, the hushed beauty of the wilderness, without getting out and working for it.

In the west pack trail leads on from the roads, in the east and south the foot paths reach out beyond the highways, in the north the portages take the canoe voyageur off the beaten lanes of travel. Of these, the portage is the most interesting. The freight routes of the early trappers and traders through the north, always by water, were dependent on the backs of men in part; and the vacationist of today who penetrates those regions must, in exactly the same manner, carry his equipment of life on his shoulders when the portages, those barriers that keep the wilderness wild, are met.

The most primitive pack harness, and one that is even now commonly used in the canoe country, consists of a single strap called a "tump line," by means of which the load is suspended from the packer's head. After the neck muscles become hardened to this form of exercise, surprisingly heavy burdens can be portaged in this manner.

The well known sash of the coureur de bois is utilized as a combination head and breast strap when packing and is worn around the waist like a girdle at other times. This strong, brightly colored and picturesque sash is still sold at all frontier posts of the Hudson's Bay Company.

A carrying harness that allowed the packer to shift a portion of the strain from the head to the shoulders, and vice versa, was used by the early timber cruisers of Michigan Packstrap and consisted of a head strap and two padded shoulder straps. These were riveted to another set of straps and buckles that bound the load into a compact bundle. This device was very popular during the Klondike gold rush and is still favored by many old woodsmen.

Seeking an improvement on these arrangements, a leather worker of Duluth devised and patented a Packsack that made his name famous among the pioneers of every timbered and mineral region on earth. It was literally a sack to be packed and its great popularity was chiefly due to the scientific accuracy with which the carrying harness was placed. Although it has been on the market for more than forty years, it remains today the favorite of the white men who travel the wilds.

All of these things are necessary for wilderness travel. You cannot enter a wilderness by automobile, for the automobile and the road it travels on can never be parts of a wilderness. The wilderness lies only in the realm of unassisted human endeavor.

Additional Sports Page 12

CROSSWORD PUZZLE

If the horizontal words stump you, the vertical words crossing them should help you out. And vice versa.

HORIZONTAL

1. Paleness.
6. To rove.
11. Blackbird (cuckoo family).
12. Steel block containing pattern for forging.
14. To cut timber.
15. Rock containing metal.
16. Redeems from captivity.
17. Shiverings.
18. To soak flax.
19. Carmine.
20. Nights.
23. Settees.
25. Medicine in small ball.
27. Eats according to prescribed rules.
29. Common poultry disease.
30. Principle.
31. Sanctuaries.
33. Treatment.
34. Frozen dessert.
35. Wing part of a seed.
36. To sow.
40. To construct.
44. Twisted (as clothes).
45. Value of bond at time of issue.
47. To clean with a broom.
49. Piece of iron in a millstone.
50. Equipped for war.
52. Sea eagle.
53. Beer.
54. Skill.
56. Bears witness.
58. Body.
60. Digit of the foot.
61. Aurora.
62. To hasten.
63. Constellation sometimes called Lion.
64. Thermometers with compound bulb (unkeyed letter r)
65. To be diminished.

VERTICAL

1. Separated.
2. Collection of facts.
3. Flaxseed.
4. Smell.
5. Makes verses.
6. Articles of merchandise.
7. Feared.
8. Condemning.
9. To sin.
10. Conclusion.
13. To impede.
14. Leather strip.
21. By way of.
22. Inflamed boil on eye.
24. Part of fish used in swimming
25. Vegetable growing in pod.
26. Sheltered.
28. Prick of a bee.
30. Emperors.
32. To perform.
33. Rubber tree.
36. To open by leverage.
37. Crescent shaped.
38. Common conjunction.
39. Thigh of a hog.
41. Female sheep.
42. Grain used for food (pl.).
43. Seven plus three.
44. A garland.
45. To iron.
46. To stretch.
48. A human being.
50. Contraltos.
51. Hook used in trolling.
53. Towards sea.
55. Largest plant.
57. Plaything.
59. To observe.

UNION WINS MATCH

The Union College golf team defeated Syracuse University, New York State intercollegiate golf champions, 4 to 2, on the links of the Mohawk Golf club, Schenectady, yesterday.

Billy Evans Says—

Pitching is perhaps the most precarious position on the ball field.

Incidentally, pitching is most vital to a club's success. The power of a team can largely be measured by the strength of its pitching staff.

When I was in Orlando, Fla., this spring, I had a chat with Carl Mays, former star pitcher of the American League. Last season with the Cincinnati Reds he was one of the most effective hurlers in the National League.

Mays never looked in better shape and was cutting loose with the ball in mid-season form.

"He was the most useful man on the staff last season," remarked Manager Jack Hendricks." He was a great starter and an equally good relief pitcher."

It was apparent that Hendricks was banking strongly on Mays for another big year.

Just prior to the opening of the season something went wrong with Mays' arm. He has been unable to throw a ball for several weeks. It is feared he is through.

Infielders and outfielders, and in some cases catchers, have continued to star after suffering arm injuries, but pitchers seldom survive the ordeal with any degree of success.

One snap of the arm, one pitched ball, put Mays out of the running as a big leaguer, temporarily, at least, if not for good.

That is what a manager is constantly up against relative to the most important asset of his ball club, pitching.

"If I get the pitching and I should get it, I will be up there," remarked Manager Robinson of the Brooklyn club when I met him in the south.

Pitcher Burleigh Grimes held out until the last moment and didn't get much spring work. As a result he was not ready at the opening of the season.

The great Dazzy Vance, while he has been able to win, has not pitched the ball of which he is capable.

So far Robinson hasn't got the pitching he expected, as a result his club has got away to a slow start.

Pitching is the thing. However, a club that has the batting punch as supplied by Wheat, Fournier and Brown must be reckoned with. When the Brooklyn pitching arrives the club will be most troublesome.

Losing a ball game through a club making nine runs in the eighth and seven runs in the ninth was an experience the Cleveland and Detroit clubs recently underwent.

Cleveland had only a one run lead when Chicago broke loose in the eighth to a 12-4 victory, so the rout was not so discouraging.

Detroit, however, went into the ninth inning leading, 8 to 3, only to be beaten, 10 to 8. That was a terrible blow.

In those two games, two pinch-hitters had an unusual experience, Elsh, batting for Chicago against Cleveland, walked twice on eight straight balls. Rice of St. Louis in the Detroit game, hit safely twice.

Hank Severeid, the other pinch-hitter used by St. Louis, connected for a home run with two on the bases.

A seven-run rally in the ninth, defeating a club leading by five runs, will rank as one of the toughest breaks of the year for the Tygers.

It certainly is the unusual for a pinch hitter to get two singles in the same inning and the other pinch-swinger to connect for a home run.

Collins and White Sox Early Spring Sensation

BY BILLY EVANS.

The spring sensation of the American League is unquestionably Eddie Collins and his Chicago White Sox.

The showing of the White Sox in the first few weeks of play has been as much of a surprise as that of the Detroit Tygers has been disappoing.

No one figured Chicago, a poor tailender last season, while Detroit was highly regarded by all the experts. Yet in the first 15 games played, Chicago won nine, while Detroit captured only three of its first 14 starts.

It is possible that the Chicago White Sox are playing over their head, but I doubt it. And, while no one picks Collins and Co., to win the pennant, the club is going to prove troublesome.

Why should a club that finished last in 1924 show such a complete reversal of form in the spring of the following season?

Six letters—Morale—tell the whole story.

The Chicago White Sox of this year are a happy family, every player giving his best efforts. They are out to win every ball game possible.

Have Respect for Leader.

The players have the highest regard for their manager, Eddie Collins. His remarkable record as a player commands respect. His methods as a manager meet with the hearty approval of his charges.

In other words, they are for their manager strong. That explains the changed morale of the club.

However, it takes other assets aside from the proper morale to win ball games. Having umpired with the Sox during the first few weeks of play and carefully dissected their play, it is apparent to me that smart baseball has been the greatest contributing factor to the club's early success.

Here are some of the ways the White Sox have put over the necessary run or runs to win ball games:

Worked a double steal of second and third with one out, putting the men in position to score on a long fly to the outfield.

The runner from third scored easily and the runner on second, seeing the throw was wide, continued on to the plate and made it on a close play.

Those two runs were just enough to win by a one-run margin.

On three other occasions a steal of second had placed the runner in position to score the winning run on a base hit and the batsman delivered in each instance.

Smartness in Winning Games.

In one game the ancient squeeze play was revived to put over the winning marker.

In two games baserunners have tried to score from second on long flies to the outfield. Ty Cobb was one of the last players to pull such a stunt and he hasn't performed it for years. The play failed, but only by a scant margin each time.

In another game with runners on first and second and no one out, everyone expecting a bunt, Pitcher Robertson pushed the ball past the third baseman, proving the turning point in the game.

As an illustration of the improved morale, Johnny Mostil, who stole about seven bases last season, pilfered that many in a week this year.

Chicago is winning because it is playing smart baseball under a smart manager. It is going to be an interesting ball club no matter where it finishes.

COLLEGE BASEBALL

Columbia, 11; Syracuse, 6.
N. Y. U. and Colgate, (rain).
Bowdoin, 8; Harvard, 5.
New Hampshire, 5; Boston Univesitry, 4.
Amherst, 2; Massachusetts Aggies, 1.
Providence College, 3; Villanova, 1.
Temple, 5; Gettysburg, 1.
Juanita, 6; Mt. St. Mary's, 5.
Yale Junior Varsity, 6; Princeton Junior Varsity, 5.
Mercersburg, 15; Princeton Freshmen, 1.
Pratt Institute, 10; Delaware, 0.

GUESSWORD LIMERICK

If I fail to say "yessum" or "thanky"
I'll explain why I seem to be —— (1)
My poor nose is so —— (2)
It just hurts more and —— (3)
Our new girl used cold starch on my —— (4).

(1) Peevishly unreasonable.
(2) Irritated.
(3) In exceeding quantity.
(4) Flirtation flag.

THE GUMPS—HE KNEW A GOOD LOT

Senators and Pirates Ready for Opening Tilt of World Series

THE SPORTING WORLD IN GENERAL and Pittsburgh and Washington in particular are all agog this morning as representatives of the rival cities await the umpire's "Play ball" in the first clash of baseball's annual classic. Walter Johnson (central figure) and Lee Meadows (upper left) have been selected as the probable starting pitchers. Manager Bucky Harris (upper right), Goose Goslin (lower left) and Max Carey are others who are expected to play prominent parts in deciding the winner

The Examiner Circulates More Than 1,350,000 Copies Every Week

CALIFORNIA FORECAST
Los Angeles and vicinity—Fair Thursday warmer in the interior.
San Francisco and vicinity—Fair and mild Thursday.
COAST TEMPERATURES (MEAN)
Los Angeles .....63 Portland 61
Sacramento .....63 San Diego 62
San Francisco...64 Seattle 58
Spokane ....43 Tacoma (max)..68
Vancouver (min).48 Salt Lake........49

Los Angeles Examiner

CHARACTER QUALITY AMERICA FIRST! ENTERPRISE ACCURACY
AN AMERICAN PAPER FOR THE AMERICAN PEOPLE THE GREAT NEWSPAPER OF THE GREAT SOUTHWEST

LATEST NEWS EXTRA

VOL. XXII—NO. 301 Official Forecast--Fair For complete weather report See Page 6, Part II. LOS ANGELES, THURSDAY, OCTOBER 8, 1925 S PRICE FIVE CENTS

CHRISTY MATHEWSON, BASEBALL STAR, DIES

11,617 Convicts Paroled in State

Today

Ponca City Without Taxes.
"Battling" Bonfils, Editor.
Pious Coolidge Wish.
Prices on the Hoof.

By Arthur Brisbane

—Copyright, 1925, by Star Company—

AS YOU travel across the country, from one ocean to the other, reading newspapers, lighthouses of information and warning, along the way, you keep in touch with the world.

The *Pueblo Chieftain*, published in Colorado, 4690 feet above sea level, and read by healthy people, gives information annoying to corporation owners, convinced that the people haven't enough brains to do anything for themselves.

Ponca City, in Oklahoma, with 15,000 population, is free from taxes. Buy your house and that's the end of it. No tax gatherer comes around. And it's simple, as O. P. Callahan, Ponca's mayor, will tell you. The people of Ponca City own their light and power departments, managed with the municipal water works. Profit on the city's light, water and power plant is sufficient to pay all taxes.

How does that impress you? And please note that rates charged for water, light and power in tax-free Ponca City are lower than in other places where citizens pay taxes and also enrich public service corporations, privately owned.

THE Denver Post, property of "Battling" Bonfils, seems to spread over Western America like a fog over London, from Kansas City to Albuquerque, and tells you everything, with an emphasis that jars effete easterners.

Bonfils, under his slogan, "IT'S A PRIVILEGE TO LIVE IN COLORADO," gives you the full text of President Coolidge's speech before the American Legion convention. He tells of admirers giving the President a "two gallon" cowboy hat, size 7⅛. Called "two gallon" because the crown is big enough to hold two gallons. In the President's case, it would be two gallons of water. McMullen, Governor of Nebraska, got a hat one-eighth size bigger than the President's, but the President's excellent speech proves that it is the quality of the head, not the quantity, that counts.

THE President hopes that much money now spent on war, preparation and materials, "to hire men to build fleets and carry muskets," will be used in "the making of good roads, building better homes, promotion of education, and all the other arts of peace."

One hundred and fifteen million amens greet that pious wish and the President will work through his term and through his second term beginning in 1929 to make the wish reality. He knows, however, that as we build a better country we must always be prepared for anybody that would take it from us.

THE President can save money on the standing army, on battleships that cost $60,000,000 each to start with, and gigantic coast defense guns that are obsolete jokes.

A great fleet of fighting airships, a sufficient fleet of submarines to welcome any troop carriers or plane carriers from abroad, a small Navy with light, fast cruisers, is all this country needs, and wouldn't cost much.

Within ten years, thanks to Ford and others, the air will be full of flying machines, as the ground is now covered with automobiles, and every Ford flying machine is arranged so that, if necessary to defend the country, it can carry a bomb and a quick-firing gun in place of passengers or freight.

Fifty thousand of the Ford commercial flying machines will soon be part of our defense equipment to take care of any invaders, as the rifles of the early Americans, used ordinarily for bears and Indians, took care of King George once.

AS YOU see men eagerly reading stock market quotations in the East, so you see them here reading the livestock market quotations. Cows sell for $4.50 a hundred pounds "on the hoof." "Canners and cutters," old animals that have done their duty for years, from $2.60 to $3.50. Bulls bring $2.75 to $4.00. "Wyoming feeder steers" averaging 1033

(Continued on Page 2, Columns 5-6)

AIR INQUIRY MUZZLED BY SECRETARY

Moffett Withdraws Testimony; Marines Back Mitchell's Plea for Unified Service

WASHINGTON, Oct. 7.—That Secretary of the Navy Wilbur, by appointing a general naval board to study aviation problems, subsequent to the creation of the President's inquiry board, has puzzled high naval officers whose testimony on the aircraft question the President's board desired, was demonstrated today, when Rear Admiral Moffett, chief of the Bureau of Aeronautics, was recalled before the board for further testimony.

Rear Admiral Moffett

Moffett told the board that inasmuch as the Navy board has taken up the question of aircraft in its relation to the Navy, he was prevented from giving testimony upon some of the things regarding which he was questioned.

TESTIMONY CHANGED

Moffett also made marked changes in his tetimony, expressing views which were entirely out of harmony with views he previously put in the record.

For example, Mofett in his first appearance before the board declared he stood for separate recognition of the Navy aviators in order to give them a definite status in the service.

In today testimony, Moffett came out flatly in opposition to a separate corps and declared that the present system, against which a great majority of the flyers have protested, is all right and should be left unchanged.

Members of the board were amazed at the change in Moffett's attitude. Senator Bingham inquired:

> **"If the operation of the Navy board if going to prevent officers of the Navy from telling us their views, how is the President's board to get the information desired?"**

AWAITS DECISIONS

Moffett told the board that he wanted to await the decisions of the Navy Board before presenting any recommendation for changes in the present system.

"Then you now withdraw your previous testimony on that point?" Representative Vinson inquired.

"I do," was the reply.

"Is that because you believe the

(Continued on Page 4, Column 4)

In His Prime

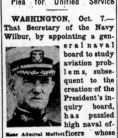

CHRISTY MATHEWSON, called the greatest pitcher of them all. Picture shows the "Big Six" in his prime.

GERMAN PRINCE WINS AMERICAN

BY ROBERT J. PREW

Staff Correspondent Universal Service
Special Cable to Universal Service
(Copyright, 1925, by Universal Service).

LONDON, Oct. 7.—A royal romance, in which one of the parties is an American girl, will culminate in the formal engagement later this month of Prince Johannes de Liechtenstein and Alice Elizabeth Volck. The girl is a grand-daughter and the heiress of Madame Da Gama, wife of Domicio Da Gama, who until last summer was the Brazilian ambassador to London.

The Prince is a scion of the third branch of the famous sovereign house of Liechtenstein. He is 25, while the bride-elect is only 17. She was sent to Paris to continue her education at a private school and met her future husband at a party last spring.

This will not be the first early marriage in her family, for Madame Da Gama was not 15 when, as Elizabeth Bates, she married Doctor Volck of New York. After the death of her first husband she married James Hearn, New York dry goods king, who in his will bequeathed her between seven and eight million dollars.

The father of Alice Delamar, who was a great friend of Hearn's, doubled the bequest.

Madame Da Gama disinherited Alice's father, Adalbert Volck, and willed his share of her fortune to her granddaughter. The marriage settlement is not completed, but her friends believe the future princess will inherit at least $7,000,000.

IDOL OF FANS LOSES LONG HEALTH FIGHT

Just Twenty Years Ago That 'Big Six' Made Greatest Record in Series Against Athletics

SARANAC LAKE, N. Y., Oct. 7.—(By Associated Press.)—Christy Mathewson is dead.

Baseball's "Big Six" lost his fight against tuberculosis tonight, just as the game's great climax, the world's series, in which he played an all-important part in 1905, had got under way at Pittsburgh.

More than five years ago, the great pitcher, loved and honored wherever the game is played, began what was to be a losing struggle. Gassed in the world war in France, where he served with distinction, Mathewson returned from overseas to coach with the Giants, the club with which he won his fame, but the illness which was finally to take his life forced him to retire for recuperation in 1920.

For three years Mathewson fought the fight and it was believed he had won. He returned to baseball as president and part owner of the Boston club of the National League and it was in the line of duty with that club that he suffered a setback which compelled his return here, once more to wage a plucky but losing fight through the summer and early fall.

On the training trip South last spring with the Braves, Mathewson took cold and he never fully recovered. He had been in bed at his home ever since, Mrs. Mathewson being in constant attendance.

Funeral services will be held in Lewiston, Pa., Saturday morning, it was announced. The body will be taken from the home here tomorrow night.

Series Crowd Shocked By Old Hero's Death

PITTSBURGH, Pa., Oct. 7.—(By Associated Press.)—The passing of Christy Mathewson brought a heavy touch of gloom late tonight to baseball men gathered here for the world's series, and expressions of sympathy were given by Commissioner Landis and Presidents Heydler and Johnson as well as the players who first knew Matty as a fellow player, then a manager and the president of the Boston Braves.

There will be no postponement of the World's Series game tomorrow, but Commissioner Landis directed that appropriate action be taken to honor the man and ball player whose name ranks with the leading pitchers of all time.

Baseball men quickly recalled that just twenty years ago Mathewson hung up a record as a World's Series pitcher that has yet to be equaled—shutting out the opposing club three times. Not a run was scored by the Philadelphia Athletics against Mathewson, who was pitching for the Giants.

His record for that series shows three successive wins. Each was a shutout. He pitched the Giants to a 3-to-0 victory in the first game. He won the third game by a lopsided score of 9 to 0, and then came right back in the fifth game with a 2-to-0 shutout.

Mathewson had a brilliant career of seventeen years with the New York Giants. "Matty" started his major league career in 1900, coming to McGraw and New York from Norfolk in the Virginia League.

U. S. Cardinal Decorated by Italian King

By Universal Service

CHICAGO, Oct. 7.

THE star and cross of the Royal Italian Order of the Crown of Italy was bestowed on Cardinal Mundelein today. The award was made by Premier Mussolini with the unanimous approval of the cabinet, the first time an American has so been honored by the Italian government.

Cardinal Mundelein

The massive insignia were brought to the prelate today by Dr. Leopold Zunini, Italian consul-general, who was specially delegated by Premier Mussolini to be king's messenger.

"My government recognizes in his eminence not only a great American and a churchman, but one of the outstanding great men of the world," Dr. Zunini said.

GLORIA GOULD SAILS ALONE

BY CHOLLY KNICKERBOCKER

Universal Service Society Editor.

NEW YORK, Oct. 7. — Gloria Gould Bishop has embarked quietly, almost secretly, for Europe.

Henry A. Bishop Jr. has gone to a retreat in the Maine woods.

Those who are not polite are saying the youngest of the late Mrs. George J. Gould's daughters is anxious to obtain legal sanction in the matter of resuming her maiden name.

Gloria has a positive passion for keeping in the public eye. No temperamental prima donna obtains a greater thrill than Gloria when her name is put up in electric lights and her photographic likeness appears in the public prints.

In her campaign for publicity Gloria has almost lost sight of friend husband, Henry. She prefers to be known as Gloria and rarely uses the Bishop cognomen she annexed at the altar.

Much secrecy surrounds Gloria's departure on Saturday last on the Majestic. She has arranged to sublet her apartment in town and her friends say she will establish a residence in the French capital.

Hubert Piatt Main, Hymn Composer, Dies

NEWARK, N. J., Oct. 7.—(By Associated Press).—Hubert Piatt Main, 87, widely known composer of hymns and Gospel songs, died at his home here today. Hehad written nearly 1000 religious songs among them "Hold Thou My Hand," "Shall We Meet Beyond the River?" "The Bright Forever," "In The Fadelesss Springtime" and "Christ My All." Mr. Main had collected a library of hymn books estimated at 7000 volumes. More than half of that collection is in the Chicago library.

Addresses of Examiner offices are listed every day in the upper left corner of Page 1, Section 2.

NEW AIR MAIL SERVICE OPENS JAN. 1

7 Planes Will Cover Route to Salt Lake; Others Handle San Francisco Transportation

Seven Douglas pursuit planes designed for transportation of mail and express between Los Angeles and Salt Lake, by way of Las Vegas, Nev., are to be in operation by January 1, 1926.

Four all-metal Ford planes designed for combination passenger and freight service between Los Angeles and San Francisco, will be in operation by February 1, 1926.

Nine additional all-metal Ford planes, each capable of carrying eight passengers, will be in operation between Los Angeles and San Francisco, by October 1, 1926.

Daily mail service both ways, on a 7-hour and 15-minute schedule, between Los Angeles and Salt Lake, with a 15-minute stop at Las Vegas, before the first of the year.

PROGRAM ANNOUNCED

This was the ambitious air program announced here yesterday by Harris M. Hanshue, president and general manager of the recently formed Western Air Express Company of Los Angeles, upon receipt of advices from Washington that the local company had been awarded the air mail contract between this city and Salt Lake.

"The Western Air Express Company," Hanshue said yesterday, "was formed in July, this year, in the firm conviction and belief that the time is ripe on the Pacific Coast for further development of commercial aviation. In addition to B. L. Graves, William May Garland, Major C. C. Moseley and other prominent local men, we have associated with us such nationally-known men as Col. E. J. Hall of Berkeley, one of the designers of the Liberty motor, and George M. Holley of Detroit, president of the Holley Carburetor Company.

ORDER PLANES AT ONCE

> **"Awarding of the air mail contract to our company means that we will at once order the planes and necessary equipment to carry out the terms of our contract. Planes are not yet actually available, inasmuch as we contemplate using the Douglas pursuit planes, manufactured at the Santa Monica plant of Donald Douglas.**
>
> **"These planes are capable of maintaining a speed of 145 miles an hour. We expect to get into operation just as soon as possible and shall have the full seven planes flying by January 1."**

Commenting on the proposed

(Continued on Page 4, Column 2)

Romance Gone

Anna Q. Nilsson springs surprise when she asks decree from rich shoe merchant, and "happy marriage" goes on rocks.—Seely photo.

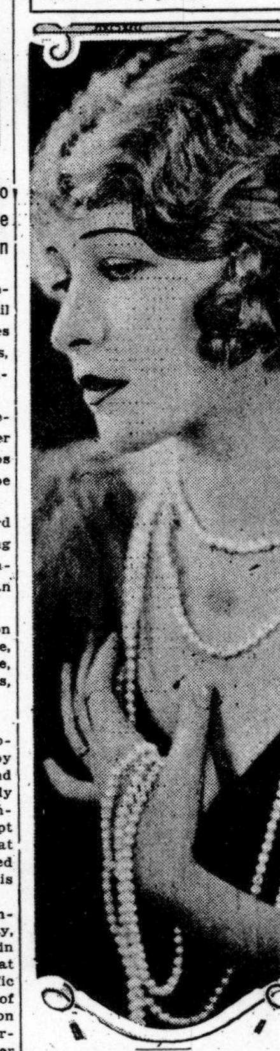

ANNA NILSSON SEEKS DIVORCE

Another one of Hollywood's "perfect romances" has foundered upon the matrimonial shoals.

This time the wrecked marital craft was captained by John M. Gunnerson, wealthy shoe manufacturer, with Anna Q. Nilsson as his mate.

Suit for divorce was filed by the screen star in Superior Court yesterday.

"Anna Gunnerson vs. J. Marshall Gunnerson" was the title of the document in which finis was written to the romance of the couple who for more than two years have been regarded as one of the film capital's happiest wedded pairs.

Charges of failure to provide and cruel and inhuman treatment constitute the grounds upon which Miss Nilsson seeks to gain her freedom from her husband.

PRISON LAW EVILS BARED BY EXAMINER

'Life Sentences' Average Only 12 Years Under Plan Whose Working Is Widely Condemned

Because of the storm of protest which the parole of E. A. ("Big Hutch") Hutchings occasioned, The Examiner caused an investigation to be made of the system for the purpose of giving its readers information as to how it functions.

The facts presented in the following article, the first of a series on the subject, were obtained from the records of San Quentin and Folsom prisons, from the Los Angeles police department and other sources.

Every precaution has been taken to maintain accuracy throughout. It is designed to be wholly informative on a subject concerning which neither jurists nor the public are generally familiar.

By Leslie Dowell

California's Board of Prison Directors, generally known as the Prison Parole Board, including those past and present, have turned out of the gates of San Quentin and Folsom since the passage of the law in 1893, 11,617 convicts.

The total number paroled for the fiscal year ended June 30, 1925, was 783, or an average of 65 a month.

San Quentin contributes more

ENERALLY FAIR TONIGHT AND FRIDAY;
MODERATE TEMPERATURE.
emperature today, 12 M. (Eagle Sta.)...66
Year ago (clear)...62
Average for 10 years (same date)...63
Complete Report on Page 18.

BROOKLYN DAILY EAGLE

WORLD SERIES EXTRA ★★★

POSTSCRIPT EDITION M 2 Volume 85 No. 286 ★ NEW YORK CITY, THURSDAY, OCTOBER 15, 1925. ★ 34 PAGES. THREE CENTS

PIRATES WIN WORLD CHAMPIONSHIP; TAKE FINAL GAME FROM SENATORS, 9-7

LAST INNINGS OF GAME PLAYED IN DRIVING RAIN

Peckinpaugh Hits Homer In Eighth—Pirates Then Stage Rally.

Forbes Field, Oct. 15—Hazen Cuyler's two-base hit, with two on in the eighth inning, gave Pittsburg the deciding game in the World's Series over the Washington Senators here today.

FIRST INNING.

Washington—Vic Aldridge drew a great hand when he stepped into the pitcher's box. Sam Rice lined the first pitch into left field foul territory. He swung into the next and bounced a single over second base. Stan Harris lifted a fly to Barnhart. Goslin let one high and inside pass for ball one. He laso ignored the second ball, which was on the outside. Aldridge tried a slow ball, but it was wild and into the dirt for ball three. Rice scooted down to second on the wild pitch. Goslin walked. Aldridge's first pitch to Joe Harris was outside and his second high. The next was another wild pitch, Rice going to third and Goslin taking second. Joe Harris walked, filling the bases.

Joe Judge looked over one too far outside then took a called strike. Ball two was high and ball three low. After a called strike two, Judge fouled off three good ones, then walked. The pass to Judge forced Rice across the plate and left the bases full. Bluege took a called strike, then let a wide one drift by. After fouling the next, Bluege singled savagely into left field, Goslin scoring, Harris going to third and Judge to second. Bluege's hit was amolst a home run, hitting near the top of the screen and bounding back on the playing field. By this time, Manager McKechnie came to the conclusion that this was not Aldridge's day. The stocky curve ball pitcher replaced by "Jughandle" Johnny Morrison, another exponent of the curve. Roger Peckinpaugh took one ball on the inside then slammed one down at Glenn Wright, who threw to Eddie Moore at second for an apparent force play on Bluege. But the umpires ruled that Earl Smith had interfered with Peckinpaugh at the plate and declared all runners safe. Joe Harris scoring. Ruel let one on the outside pass for a ball, then swung futilely at strike one. After another ball passed on the outside of the plate, strike two was called.

Then Ruel hit one down to Moore, who fumbled it, Judge scoring and the bases remaining filled. Johnson fanned on three pitched balls, fouling off the first two, then missing a wide curve entirely. Rice, up for the second time in the inning, took a count of two and three, then ended the hectic inning witih a fly to Barnhart. Four runs, two hits, one error.

Pittsburg—Moore, with an idea to take advantage of Johnson's alleged lameness, started right off bunting. His first bunt rolled foul. The next was fair, but Johnson hustled over and threw him out at first. Carey let a low one pass for a ball, then took two called strikes. Johnson was taking his time. Ball two was low and ball three outside. Carey fouled one off, then gave the Pittsburg bugs their first chance to yell with a slashing two-base hit into right field. Cuyler came up, swung at three pitched balls, missed them all and sat right down again. Barnhart also fanned on three pitched balls. He missed the first, fouled the second, then missed a wide curve for the third strike. No runs, one hit, no errors.

SECOND INNING.

Washington—Stan Harris absolutely ignored the first three pitches, which were either too close or too far out. The "boy" manager then let two "cripples" go for called strikes. He hit the big one hard, but Cuyler galloped over and caught the ball as it was about to sail into the right-field stands. Goslin stood still while an outside ball drifted by, took two called strikes, then hit a fly to Carey in short center. Joe Harris permitted two wide ones to sail past. He swung at the next and missed for strike one. Another ball, then Joe grounded out to right. Morrison used his "jughandle" curve throughout the inning. No runs, no hits, no errors.

Pittsburg—Johnson's first to Pie Traynor was low and inside for ball one. The next was a called strike. Traynor fouled one off, took another ball, then hit a hopper to Johnson. "Barney" took the ball and threw wide to first, but Joe Judge nailed the bad throw and beat Traynor to the bag. Glenn Wright took a called strike, fouled off another, then singled solidly to center field. As McInnis came up it starter to rain again. McInnis let an outside ball go by, then also singled to center, Wright taking second. Earl Smith missed strike one. The next was ball one. Smith swung at the third pitch and grounded to Stan Harris, who converted the hopper into a double play by touching McInnis on the base path, then throwing Smith out at first. No runs, no hits, no errors.

THIRD INNING.

Washington—Judge took a ball that was low and inside. He drove the next into right center for a clean single. Bluege fouled off the first one trying to lay down a sacrifice bunt. He then popped a high fly to Moore. Peck ignored a perfectly good strike and fouled off strike two. After letting two weste balls go by, Peck hit to right field. Cuyler made a sensational catch, but then threw wildly past first in an effort to double up Judge who took second. Ruel waited until the count of two and two, then hit a long one to center. Carey raced out and snared the drive. No runs, one hit, one error.

Pittsburg—Morrison banged a single to center field. Moore took a ball, then crashed a fast one to left for a double and Morrison galloped all the way over the plate. Stan Harris became worried at this stage and walked over to pat Johnson on the back. Carey slashed into the first ball and hit a sharp single past Stan Harris, Moore scoring. Cuyler swung at and missed the first strike, then took ball. Then Carey and Cuyler attempted the hit-and-run play. Carey reached second, while Cuyler was out at first, Peck to Judge. Johnson had trouble getting the ball over for Barnhart. His first was low and his next inside and high. On the next, which was also a ball, Carey caught Ruel napping and stole third. "Muddy" did not even throw to stop him. Barnhart then took a called strike. On the next Barnhart dropped one of those tantalizing Texas League singles to right field, Carey scoring. Traynor let two on the inside pass for balls. After taking a called strike, "Pie" forced Barnhart, Peckinpaugh to Stan Harris. Wright hit at the first ball, and popped up to Stan Harris. Three runs, four hits, no errors.

FOURTH INNING.

Washington—It was raining, but not very hard. The darkness made it hard to follow the ball on the field. Johnson flied out to Carey in left center. Rice fouled one off, let one ball pass, then drove a single past McInnis. Stan Harris fouled one, took a ball, then fouled off another. The next was a called third strike. The first to Goslin was a ball and the next two were strikes. Then Goslin singled to left, Rice sprinting to third. When Barnhart threw to third base, Goslin went for second and made it. Joe Harris slammed one into right for two bases, Rice and Goslin scoring. Judge let the first two go by for balls. The next was a called strike, but the next was high and ball three. After taking a called second strike and fouling another one off, Judge lifted a fly to Cuyler. Two runs, three hits, no errors.

Pittsburg—"Stuffy" McInnis rapped a single to left on the first pitched ball. Smith also swung at the first ball but Sam Rice made a shoestring catch of his low liner to center. McInnis had to race back to first at top speed to avoid being doubled. George Grantham was sent in to bat for Morrison. He let an inside ball go by, also a called first strike. Grantham fouled the next three, then was retired on a long fly to Joe Harris. Moore hit a high one which Goslin gobbled. No runs, one hit, no errors.

FIFTH INNING.

Washington—Ray Kremer, who pitched and won Tuesday's game, went to the mound for Pittsburg. Bluege whaled away at the first ball, but Traynor leaped high in the air to nail his grounder and threw him out at first. Peck also swung at the first one and grounded out, Wright to McInnis. Ruel let a high one pass for ball one. The second was called a strike. The next was low and ball two. Ruel fouled off the next two, then cracked a low fly to center. Carey made a neat catch. No runs, no hits, no errors.

Pittsburg—Carey made his third hit and second twobagger of the game on the first pitched ball. It was a hard drive to center. Cuyler swung at the first one and hit a spectator in the back with a foul liner. Then Cuyler banked another double to deep left, scoring Carey. It was raining steadily at this stage. Barnhart let a high ball pass and took two called strikes. Johnson whipped the next one over and Barnhart fanned. Traynor swung at the first one and fouled out to Ruel. Wright let two balls sail by, then missed the next for strike one. After fouling off strike two, Wright let an outside one go for ball three. Wright fouled two more off, then lifted a pop to Stan Harris. One run, two hits, no errors.

SIXTH INNING.

Washington—Johnson fouled off two, then popped to Wright. Rice swung at the first ball and was thrown out on a slow bounder to Wright. The first to Stan Harris was called a strike. The next was high and inside and ball one. He fanned the air vainly at the next two. It was his second strikeout of the game. No runs, no hits, no errors.

Pittsburg—McInnis flied to Goslin. Smith slammed a long fly to Rice on the first pitched ball. Kremer swung at and missed the first two, then succeeded in fouling one off. Johnson threw two waste balls on the outside, then forced the Pirate to pop a foul to Ruel. No runs, no hits, no errors.

SEVENTH INNING.

Washington—It began to rain hard at this stage and the bleacherites began to cover themselves with umbrellas and newspapers. Goslin hit an easy splash to Kremer and was tossed out at first. Joe Harris popped a foul toward the third base bases and Traynor caught it. Judge hit a long one to right field. Cuyler misjudged the ball but caught it after a hard run. No runs, no hits, no errors.

Pittsburg—Moore let one on the inside pass for ball one. Strike one was called, then Moore hit an easy pop fly to Peckinpaugh, who proceeded to drop the ball. Moore was safe at first on Peckinpaugh's seventh error of the series. Carey swung into the first ball and hit his third double of the game to left field, Moore scoring from first. It was also Carey's fourth hit of the game. The ball landed close to the foul line and the Senators claimed it to be a foul. Cuyler sacrificed on the first pitch, Johnson throwing the batter out at first, while Carey, who represented the tying run, reached third. Barnhart grounded to Stan Harris, who threw him out at first. It was so dark at this stage that the fielders hardly could see the ball. "Pie" Traynor pushed Carey across with a long clout to right for three bases, but "Pie," attempting to stretch it into a home run, was out at the plate, Joe Harris to Stan Harris to Ruel. Two runs, two hits, one error.

EIGHTH INNING.

Washington—Bluege swung at the first ball and grounded out to Traynor. Peck proceeded to make up for his costly error by smashing a home run into the left field stands on the first ball, the drive clearing the barrier in front of the scoreboard. Ruel waited through two balls and a strike, then was robbed of a hit by Traynor, who made a remarkable stop of his sharp grounder and threw him out at first. Johnson swung at the first one and fouled out to Smith. One run, one hit, no errors.

Pittsburg — Wright fouled to Judge.

It was so wet out on the field that Johnson, first obtaining the conset of the umpire, took a capful of sawdust to scatter around the mound.

McInnis flied to Rice.

Smith doubled to right.

Yde ran for Smith and Bigbee batted for Kremer.

Bigbee doubled to left, scoring Yde with the tying run.

Moore walked.

Carey grounded to Peck, who tossed to Stan Harris at second, but the umpire ruled that Moore was safe and the bases were filled. Peck was given his eighth error of the series.

Bigbee and Moore scored on Cuyler's double to deep right field.

Then the umpires ruled that Cuyler's drive was a two-base hit under the ground rules. Carey went back to third and Cuyler back to second.

Barnhart flied to Stan Harris. Three runs, three hits, one error.

NINTH INNING.

Washington—The Pittsburg bugs were jubilant at the world's championship vision before them. Red Oldham, a left-hander, went in to pitch for the Pirates and Johnny Gooch took Smith's place behind the bat.

Bigbee went to left field. Rice was called out on strikes.

Moore took Stan Harris' pop fly.

Goslin fanned. No runs, no hits, no errors.

The Senators failed to score in their half of the ninth.

SCORE BY INNINGS

SENATORS	4	0	0	2	0	0	0	1	0	— 7
PIRATES	0	0	3	0	1	0	2	3	x	— 9

The Box Score

WASHINGTON

	AB.	R.	H.	O.	A.	E.
Rice, c. f.	5	2	2	3	0	0
S. Harris, 2b.	5	0	0	3	2	0
Goslin, l. f.	4	2	1	2	0	0
J. Harris, r. f.	3	1	1	4	2	0
Judge, 1b.	3	1	1	6	0	0
Bluege, 3b.	4	0	1	0	0	0
Peckinpaugh, s. s.	3	1	1	0	2	2
Ruel, c.	4	0	0	6	0	0
Johnson, p.	4	0	0	0	3	0
Totals	35	7	7	27	9	2

PITTSBURG

	AB.	R.	H.	O.	A.	E.
Moore, 2b.	4	3	1	2	0	1
Carey, c. f.	5	4	4	4	0	0
Cuyler r. f.	4	0	2	4	0	1
Barnhart, l. f.	5	0	1	2	0	0
Traynor, 3b.	4	0	1	1	3	0
Wright, s. s.	4	0	1	1	3	0
McInnis, 1b.	4	0	2	7	0	0
Smith, c.	4	0	1	4	0	0
Yde,	0	1	0	0	0	0
Aldridge, p.	0	0	0	0	0	0
Morrison, p.	1	1	1	0	0	0
Grantham	1	0	0	0	0	0
Kremer, p.	1	0	0	0	1	0
Bigbee	1	0	1	0	0	0
Gooch, c.	0	0	0	2	0	0
Oldham, p.	0	0	0	0	0	0
Totals	38	9	15	27	7	2

Two-base hits—Carey 3, Moore, J. Harris, Cuyler 2, Smith, Bigbee. Three-base hit—Traynor. Home run—Peckinpaugh. Sacrifice hit—Cuyler. Stolen base—Carey. Double play—S. Harris and Judge. Bases on balls—Off Johnson, 1; off Aldridge, 3. Struck out—By Johnson, 3; by Morrison, 2; by Kremer, 1. Wild pitches—Aldridge, 2. Hits—Off Aldridge, 2 in 1-3 inning; off Morrison, 4 in 3 2-3 innings. Umpires—McCormick, Moriarty, Rigler and Owens.

LAUREL ENTRIES

FOR FRIDAY.

First race, all ages, 6 furlongs—Kosciusko, 105; Vulgate, 102; Merry, 102; Alice Joyce, 102; †Basalt, 102; Stone, 105; Bar Light, 105; Muriel S. 102; *Marco Belle, 97; *Espanol, 100; †Dignify, 102; Columbia II, 102; Half Ballot, 105; Casus Belli, 105. †S. Ross entry.

Second race, all ages, 6 furlongs—*You Know, 113; *Belle of Boyce, 110; Ormeolus, 118; Pikros, 118; Shining Light, 118; Clean, 118; Hubar, 118; Hanky Rice, 118; *Eye Lash, 113; *Liason, 113; *Lady Allumeur, 115.

Third race—3-year-olds up, 6 furlongs—*Delusive, 103; *Exalted Ruler, 102; *BerniceHarrar, 104; Hazy, 112; Bill O'Flynn, 116; *Sonny, 113; *Who Knows Me, 107; Mint Stick, 114; Oakwood, 108; *Erica, 109.

Fourth race, 3-year-olds up, mile and 1-16—Normana, 105; Brown Stout, 105; Ebb Tide, 110; Margaret St. L., 105; *Just, 107; *Rose Cloud, 100.

Fifth race, all ages, 6 furlongs—Son Ami, 92; Taps, 109; Lieutenant II, 114; Digit, 115; †Courageous, 110; Laddie Buck, 112; Scotch Broom, 109; Franconia, *10; *Candy Kid, 120. †H. P. Whitney entry.

Sixth race, 2-year-olds, 6 furlongs—Majuba, 108; Compromise, 106; Be Yourself, 111; *Toyland, 114; *Wormwold, 103; Ferrash, 113; †Marengo, 111; Forestar, 107; Green Blazes, 110; *Cobra, 106 The Engineer, 115; †*Cinderetta, 107. †Musante entry.

Seventh race, 3-year-olds up, mile and a quarter—*Ed Pendelton, 102; Bounce, 109; Seaman, 101; Asa Jewell, 109; *Fornovo, 104; Pilgrim, 113; Noel, 105.

Four Racing Results at Jamaica

3 Men Killed in Subway Accident

Scores Winning Run

GERMANY ACCEPTS SECURITY COMPACT TO OUTLAW WARS

Agreement Reached at Locarno to Be Signed by Germany, France and Belgium, With Great Britain and Italy as Guarantors. France Gains Right to Protect Her Eastern Allies, Poland and Czechoslovakia, if Attacked.

Locarno, Switzerland, Oct. 15 (AP)—Germany today officially announced her adhesion to the Rhine pact of mutual guarantees, framed at the security conference here with the object of outlawing war.

The pact will be signed by Germany, France and Belgium as the principal parties, and by Great Britain and Italy as guarantors.

After the announcement of Germany's adhesion, the conference at its eighth plenary meeting adopted the text of the draft security pact.

Polish-German Problem Virtually Solved.

A solution of the problem of the Polish-German arbitration treaty has practically been reached by enlarging the scope of the treaty to make it virtually the same as the treaties between Germany and France and Germany and Belgium. This means that all possible disputes, even those arising out of frontier questions, would be submitted to arbitration.

The official communique issued after the meeting said:

"At today's plenary session, the conference accepted the complete text of the draft security pact, and then the question of arbitration treaties was taken up. Poland and Czechoslovakia were invited to attend."

The Polish and Czechoslovakian representatives were invited to join the meeting, it was explained, to hear a statement outlining the work of the jurists on the draft treaties of arbitration between Germany and France and Germany and Belgium, the text of which have been adopted by the delegations concerned.

They, on their part, gave the conference an account of the advanced state of the negotiations for the drafting of arbitration treaties between Poland and Germany and Czechoslovakia and Germany.

It was decided to defer to a later meeting discussion of the date for publication of all the agreements submitted to the conference for final adoption.

Mussolini Arrives.

Premier Mussolini of Italy arrived at Locarno this afternoon to take part in the closing labors of the Security Conference. The Italian leader, who is Foreign Minister as well as Premier, came from Milan by motorcar.

Austen Chamberlain, British Foreign Secretary, called upon him soon after his arrival.

Present indications are that the ceremony of signing the Rhine security pact will take place on Saturday.

Austen Chamberlain, addressing a luncheon of correspondents today, said that the conference is reaching an end which is marked by a plenitude of results which hardly any one at its start could have predicted. This auspicious outcome, he asserted, was due to the fact that all the delegations had shown the same goodwill and determination to triumph over all difficulties.

Chamberlain Sees Peace of Consent.

"We ourselves were surprised to see how difficulties disappeared," Mr. Chamberlain said, "and how the clouds of last night were dissipated by the beautiful sunshine of today. The destiny of the entire world depended upon the success of our work. Relations have been established here which will have their repercussion and repetition in the near future in the relations between other nations, and there will emerge for Europe not a peace imposed, but a peace consented to by all, which will give to all our peoples that appeasement for which they have need after so many years of sacrifice and suffering."

French Desire Acceded To.

The French desire for a guarantee for France's Eastern allies, Poland and Czechoslovakia, has been acceded to through an arrangement for special additional direct treaties between them under which France will have the right to protect the teritorial integrity of her allies and defend them against flagrant aggression. Germany is willing to adhere to this.

One of the last points in the discussions—that regarding a formula for Germany's arbitration treaties with Poland and Czechoslovakia—has been bridged and now requires only the sanction of all the delegates.

LATE NEWS

FATAL CRASH IN INTERBORO TUBE AT 110TH ST. AND LEXINGTON AVE.

Police Headquarters has been notified that three persons are known to be dead in a subway accident at 110th st. and Lexington ave., Manhattan, about 3:30 o'clock this afternoon. The three men killed are said to have been track walkers employed by the I. R. T.

Green Re-elected President of A. F. of L.

Atlantic City, N. J., Oct. 15 (AP)—William Green of Coshocton, Ohio, this afternoon was unanimously re-elected president of the American Federation of Labor.

Miner Arrested in $85,000 Insurance Fraud

William H. Turner of McCarr, Ky., a coal mining foreman, who was thought to have been killed in an explosion in a mine shaft at McCarr in January, 1924, and whose family collected, it is alleged, $85,000 in insurance, was arrested this afternoon when he arrived here on the steamship Resolute.

Two Found Slain Near Bloody Auto

Kenosha, Wis., Oct. 15 (AP)—A blood-bespattered automobile found along a highway six miles north of Kenosha today led to the finding of the bodies of a man and a woman nearby, both believed to have been murdered.

RACING RESULTS

At Jamaica

FIRST RACE

1—Buck Pond, 120 (Coltiletti)	3-1	4-5	1-3
2—Thunderbolt, 113 (Harvey)	10-1	3-1	6-5
3—Gene Austin, 127 (M. Fator)	6-1	8-5	3-5

Time, 1:15. Alliance, Invictus and Zero Hour also ran.

SECOND RACE

1—Priscilla Ruley, 115 (Maiben)	4-1	8-5	4-5
2—Catalan, 118 (Buxton)	3-1	7-5	3-5
3—Julie, 107 (Richards)	15-1	5-1	5-2

Time, 1:13. Volante, Gnome Girl, Forecaster and Avisack also ran.

THIRD RACE

1—Hayward, 115 (Catrone)	3-1	6-5	1-2
2—Escapader, 111 (Peternell)	6-5	1-2	1-5
3—Devastation, 111 (Maiben)	7-1	5-2	1-1

Time, 1:45 2-5. Rowland's Request and Viburnum also ran.

FOURTH RACE

1—Sarmaticus, 122 (Richards)	4-5	1-5	Out
2—Cross Fire, 106 (L. Fator)	15-1	3-1	4-5
3—Espino, 106 (Maiben)	5-1	6-5	1-4

Time, 1:12 3-5. Timmara also ran.

DEMAND ARREST, PUNISHMENT OF DONAHUE THIEF

Grand Jury Action to Clear Gem Robbery Mystery Is Likely.

The increasing public demand for capture and punishment of the thief who stole and returned Mrs. Jessie Woolworth Donahue's $683,000 jewels, regardless whether or not influential persons are involved, may lead to a Grand Jury investigation.

The case with which the jewels were recovered, the complete mystery surrounding their return and the embarrassed reticence of all officials connected with the case all point to powerful forces at work to suppress the real story.

If the Donahue gem robbery remains a mystery, as seems more than probable at present, it will mark one more case involving persons of wealth and power in which the efforts of the police have been strangely futile. Notable among these are the murder of Joseph B. Elwell, the murder of "Dot" King and the theft and recovery of the Cosden jewels, a case which bore striking similarities to the Donahue affair.

Not the least interesting feature of the Donahue case is the rivalry between high police officials. Chief Inspector John D. Coughlin took immediate charge of the investigation, but his men hardly had begun to work before Police Commissioner Enright apepared on the scene and took personal charge of the case. It was the first case in many months in which the Commissioner had shown so keen an interest.

A "Man of Mystery."

The Commissioner and the Chief Inspector long have been at swords' points, according to common gossip at Police Headquarters. Coughlin immediately redoubled his efforts. The Commissioner, after the first day or two, appeared to drop the case, at least so far as any personal direction was concerned.

So far as appeared on the surface the efforts of neither the Chief Inspector nor the Commissioner accomplished anything. The man who engineered the return of the jewels is Noel C. Scaffa, insurance company detective and something of a man of mystery who has figured in other stolen gem recoveries.

Scaffa kept his own counsel, so far as the public was concerned, but

Continued on Page 2.

North American Makes Offer to Miss. Electric

Boston, Oct. 15—The North American Company is offering 1 2-3 shares of common for each common share of Central Mississippi Valley electric properties under Stone & Webster management. The offer is similar to that recently made for common stock of Mississippi River Power Company.

B. L. GERRY'S SARMATICUS WINS OCEANUS STAKES

By W. C. VREELAND.
(Staff Correspondent of The Eagle.)

Jamaica Race Track, Oct. 15—B. L. Gerry's brown colt Sarmaticus was the winner of the Oceanus Handicap, valued at $2,500 in the feature event of the day. He was a 4 to 5 favorite whem they went to the post. Cross Fire, at 15 to 1, was second, with Espino, taking third money.

Zero Hour, backed from 2 to 1 to 6 to 5, failed to show any of his old time liking for mud and was badly beaten for the first race. Buck Pond and Thunderbolt, head and head, raced well out in front and in the drive home Buck Pond won by half a length. Gene Austin, outrun in the early stages, closed fast at the end but was beaten a length by Thunderbolt.

The Belair Stable's Priscilla Ruley obtained a step at the barrier in the start for the second race and because of it she gained such a big early lead that she never was caught. She sprinted away from a fast field and, with her head in the air, made all the running and easily landed the money by three lengths. Catalan, slow to break at the start, closed a big gap and finished second, two lengths in front of Julie. Gnome Girl was second for three furlongs and then stopped. Avisack and Forecaster were unable to untrack themselves.

Hayward was the tip for the third and he was backed from 5 to 1 down to 3 to 1. For seven furlongs he dogged the steps of Escapader, which easily showed the way, under a pull, to the stretch where he ran wide. This gave Hayward a chance to close on the inside, and catching the leader a sixteenth from the finish beat him out by a length and a half. Escapader was eight lengths in front of Devastation.

LATONIA RESULTS

First race—Miss Mischief, 102 (A. Mortensen), $8.70, $3.10 and $2.70, first; Miss Rosedale, 107 (M. Garner), $3.40 and $2.70, second; Winding Thru, 103 (S. Griffin), $4.00, third. Time, 1:16 4-5. Elsass, Silent Lillian and Ethel K also ran.

Second race—Pangold, 108 (H. Long), $13.70, $7.50 and $3.70, first; Poison, 100 (G. Johnson), $5.50 and $3.20, second; Lady Allen, 100 (A. Mortensen), $3.30, third. Time, 1:12. Oak, Elsie Louise, M'Lisa and Passenger also ran.

Third race—Waponoca, 98 (G. Johnson), $5.70, $3.20 and $2.40, first; Lighter, 114 (R. Harrington), $3 and $2.40, second; Nivlag, 114 (D. Connelly), $3.20, third. Time, 1:49. Escarpolette, Stump Jr. also ran.

LAUREL RESULTS

First race—Gun Boat, 136 (B. Haynes), $31.70, $8.80, $5.30, first; Kangaroo, 142 (L. Veitch), $13.40, $6.40, second; Bridge, 132 (Neander), $12, third. Time, 4:31. Jolly Roger, Broomwrack, Greek Friar, Regal Toy, Sea Soldier and Casette also ran.

Second race—Pay Girl, 110 (C. Lang), $10.80, $5 and $4.40, first; fBilly Mann, 108 (C. McCrossen), $7.80 and $9.90, second; fBar Light, 110 (Wallace), $9.90, third. Time, 1:17 3-5. Columbia II, fJimmy Brown, Saramaletta, Queen Navarre, Lucky Pick, Foreman, Tarnhelm, Yami, Princess Apple also ran. Couple, Pay Girl and Princess Apple, Carter entry. fMutual field.

Third race—Paavo, 108 (P. Walls), $6.70, $4.70, $3.30, first; Nat Evens, 108 (Barnes), $8.30, $5.50, second; Fly Leaf, 106 (McAtee), $4.30, third. Time, 1:08 4-5. Garden Rose, Revelry, Chocolate Soldier, Adria, and Beneficent also ran.

Fourth race—Maxie, 110 (Barnes), $10.10, $5.10 and $3.60, first Demi John, 110 (E. Fator), $4.80 and $4, second; Who Cares, 110 (Hudgins), $5.10, third. Time, 1:51. Tony Griffith, Trajanus, Crosswise and Black Art also ran.

Golden Rule, 107 (P. Walls), $17.60, $7.70 and $4.90, first; Backbone, 106 (McAtee), $16.10 and $7, second; Maid at Arms 112 (Barnes), $3.60, third. Time, 1:48 1-5. Rockminster, Pepp and Florence Nightingale also ran.

FAIRMOUNT PARK RESULTS

First race—Kendall, 113 (Herbert), $17.70, $6.50, $3.90, first; Belle K, 107 (V. Wallis), $3.40, $2.70, second; Dalton, 113 (R. Costello), $3.00, third. Time, 1:16. Colfin, Sir Ralph, Orphelin, Chestnut Girl, Harry Maxim and Dr. F. T. Adams also ran.

Second race—Mr. Biltmore, 104 (F. Mormile), $15, $6.60 and $5, first; Power, 110 (J. Dillea), $4 and $3.50, second; Phil's Sister, 99 (W. Charles), $25.60, third. Time, 1:16 2-5. Viennese, Protectress, Douglass H. Johnston, Peter Pom, Chief Tierney and Trafalgar also ran.

Third race—Sandalwood, 111 (L. Montgomery), $4.20, $2.80 and $2.80, first; Miss Emmert, 105 (J. Colen), $3.90 and $3.20, second; Mulciber, 116 (A. Vuillemot), $5.30, third. Time, 1:09. Ellen Jane, Hardman, Candorosa, Hole Card and Sam Mengel also ran.

SPECIAL BASEBALL PHOTOGRAVURE SECTION

THE CHICAGO DAILY NEWS.

SPECIAL BASEBALL PHOTOGRAVURE SECTION

51ST YEAR—88. TUESDAY, APRIL 13, 1926. A PART OF TO-DAY'S ISSUE

PLAY BALL!

Closeup Studies of Some of the White Sox Players Who Are Scheduled to Open the Season at Comiskey Park This Afternoon, Where They Meet the St. Louis Browns.

Cub Players Who Are Scheduled to Start the Season Against the Reds at Cincinnati Are Pictured on Page 3. The Cubs Will Open Their Chicago Year One Week from To-Morrow, April 21, with the Cincinnati Reds.

Above—A Hot Single. Scene in the White Sox Training Camp at Shreveport, La., Showing Tom Gulley of the Rookie Squad at Bat. The Catcher is George Smith and Behind Him Is Umpire Weber of the Texas League.

Left—Willie Kamm, Third Baseman, Who Came from San Francisco as Charles A. Comiskey's "$100,000 Beauty" and Has Continued to Make Good.

Right—"Whispering Bill" Barrett, One of the Most Agile Outfielders on the White Sox Team.

Right — Showing Young Shreveport How It's Done. Ted Lyons, Pitcher, Seen at the Southern Training Camp as He Demonstrated the Correct Grip for Throwing the "Knuckle Ball."

Batting Them Out. Texas Has Produced Few Sturdier Sons than Outfielder Bib Falk. He's a Right-Hander and Southpaw, Too, and Can Play Almost Any Position in an Emergency. He Has Been Pointing Himself for a Hard Season at Left Field.

Signaling the Pitcher. Ray Schalk Is the Clever Illinois Lad Who Put Litchfield on the Map by His Artistic Backstopping. He Has Caught 1,625 Games for the Chicago American League Team.

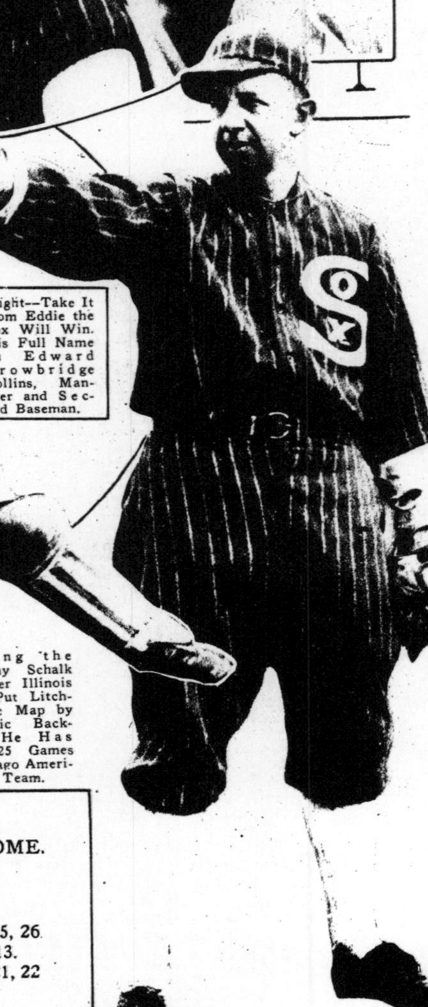

Right—Take It from Eddie the Sox Will Win. His Full Name Is Edward Trowbridge Collins, Manager and Second Baseman.

With Eye Undimmed and Right Arm Strong and Sure, Urban ("Red") Faber, Veteran Pitcher, Is Ready for the Opening of the Big League Season of 1926. "Red" Is the Only Pitcher with the White Sox Team Who Has a World Series Record. He Was a National Diamond Hero in 1917 When He Won Three Games of the Four He Pitched Against the New York Giants.

THE SEASON'S SCHEDULE OF WHITE SOX GAMES AT HOME.

With Browns—April 13, 14, 15, 16; June 25, 26, 27, 28; Sept. 8, 9, 10.
With Detroit—May 3, 4, 5; May 27, 28, 29, 30; Aug. 14, 15, Sept. 6.
With Cleveland—April 17, 18, 19, 20; June 21, 22, 23, 24; July 5, 6.
With Washington—June 12, 13, 14, 15; July 27, 28, 29, 30; Sept. 24, 25, 26
With Philadelphia—June 8, 9, 10, 11; Aug. 7, 8, 9, 10; Sept. 11, 12, 13.
With New York—June 17, 18, 19, 20; July 31, Aug. 1, 2, 3; Sept. 20, 21, 22
With Boston—June 5, 6, 7; Aug. 4, 5, 6; Sept. 15, 16, 17, 18, 19.

YANKS TROUNCED, 12-6; GIANTS BEAT ROBINS, 8-2

New York American Sports
CHARACTER QUALITY AMERICA FIRST ACCURACY ENTERPRISE
AN AMERICAN PAPER FOR ... PEOPLE

★ ★ ★ Editorial Telephone, Beekman 2000 — TUESDAY, AUGUST 31, 1926 — Business Telephone, Columbus 7000

Pinchot Backs Wiener in Clash Over Tickets for Big Title Fight

Governor of Pennsylvania Announces He'll Stand by Boxing Head in Controversy with Rickard—Aronson Quits as Co-Promoter

PHILADELPHIA, Aug. 30.—After Governor Pinchot came out strong here today, backing Chairman Frank L. Wiener in his ticket controversy with Tex Rickard, promotor of the Dempsey-Tunney battle in the Sesqui Stadium September 23, Rickard said he was misunderstood in his argument with the head of the Pennsylvania State Athletic Commission.

"I never told Mr. Wiener I'd have him put off the boxing commission. He threatened that he would revoke my license and have the fight taken out of the State. I said, 'If you do that you'll be apt to lose your job.' The public must remember that the 6,000 tickets is a personal allotment to Mr. Wiener. I do not know what he is going to do with them. I have orders for 2,000 tickets from Pennsylvanians. Most of these applications have been in my hands for a long time. It will mean that many of those people will have to take seats further back."

At the Bellevue Stratford, Rickard today showed a list of the names of 12,910 persons throughout the United States who have written for reservations. The list contains many of the leading men of the country. Rickard complained that as a result of Wiener's action in taking the 4,000 seats, he would be unable to fulfill the orders he has received, inasmuch as the Stadium will contain only 14,714 ringside seats on the night of the fight.

"Mr. Rickard seems to have forgotten it is the Governor of Pennsylvania who decides who shall be on the State Athletic Commission," said Governor Pinchot here today. "Mr. Rickard is not Governor of Pennsylvania, I am.

"I am behind Mr. Wiener. I shall be behind him all the way in his efforts to protect the rights of our people. We are less impressed in this State by New York promoters than—judging from Mr. Rickard's remarks—

Continued on Page 20.

DEMPSEY BANGS BOXING MATES IN FIVE ROUNDS

Herman Is Badly Battered by Champ; None Escapes Heavy Bombardment of His Fists

By Sam Hall.

ATLANTIC CITY, N. J., Aug. 30.—Jack Dempsey looked good enough today to swim the English Channel, now that Hans Vierkotter has proved that the men still can display athletic prowess.

The champion boxed in a bathing suit before fifteen hundred people and showed obvious signs of being capable of tackling any body of water for a few hours or any body of men for a few rounds.

Jack did tackle a body of five men, one at a time, and all of them left with respect for the fistic ability of the man who is to risk his world's heavyweight boxing championship in a fight with Gene Tunney, of Greenwich Village, at Philadelphia the night of September 23.

Jack Dempsey.

When he came into the ring he said facetiously to assembled visitors from far and wide:

"Good afternoon; have you swum the English Channel yet? Tiger Flowers says he can do it. Two weeks more of this excellent work and I may try it myself."

5 ROUNDS OF BOXING.

Dempsey worked nine rounds in all but only five at boxing. His sparring partners were Charlie Anderson, the tall Chicago colored man; huge Will Ttate, who has boxed with the champion for eight years and does not know yet what to do when Jack unlimbers; Tillie Kid Herman, of El Paso; Frankie

Continued on Page 20.

BLACK BILL WINS ON FOUL

Referee Gives Cuban Flyweight Decision Over Benny Marks in the Seventh Round

By JOSEPH GORDON.

Black Bill, Cuban flyweight, won over Benny Marks, of Brownsville, on a foul in the seventh round of a scheduled ten-rounder. Up until the time of the accident the bout was pretty even.

Marks hit Bill low several times in the sixth round and was cautioned by Referee Joe Bernstein. Exactly twenty-one seconds of the seventh round had elapsed when Marks again struck the Cuban low, and, although he was not hurt, the referee immediately intervened and ordered Marks to his corner and awarded the contest to Bill.

The decision was well received by the large attendance, which numbered about 7,000.

Ernie Jarvis, England's representative in the flyweight division, won a clean-cut victory over Lou Goldberg, of Brownsville, in the ten-round semi-final.

The Englishman administered a two-handed body attack to his rugged antagonist throughout the contest, and was impressive in victory.

Harry Traube, 116 pounds, won a spirited six-rounder over Billy Kelly, 112½ pounds.

Billy Humphries, 123½ pounds, won the decision over Frankie McKenna, 123 pounds, in a six-round contest.

Lou Lambert, 120 pounds, defeated Charley Indelicato, 120 pounds in four rounds.

Meadowbrook '4' Win from Rumson

With the score 10 to 6 against them at the end of the sixth period, the Meadowbrook-Army four, captained by Deveraux Milburn at back, staged a brilliant rally in the last two chuckkers when the fast U. S. Army player, Captain C. H. Gerhardt tallied six consecutive goals, clinching victory over the hard-fighting Rumson team at Rumson yesterday by the score of 12 to 10.

Rumson, conceded a handicap of six goals, showed unexpected strength in the offensive as well as defensive play. J. Watson Webb was unmounted in the final chukker when his pony turned short, but he escaped uninjured. Milburn's team proved a powerful and well balanced combination. The spectacular Argentines, who scored their first American triumph on Herbert Field, will make their tournament debut today when they face the powerful Hurricane team Stephen Sanford brought with him from England. The South Americans total 33 goals now, and the Hurricane four. The summaries:

Meadowbrook-Army (12).	Pos.	Rumson. (10).
Capt. C. H. Gerhardt	No. 1	H. E. Talbot, Jr.
J. Watson Webb	No. 2	Gerald Balding
Capt. P. P. Rodes	No. 3	M. Stevenson
Devereaux Milburn	Back	B. K. Gatins

Goals—Meadowbrook-Army: Gerhardt, 6; Webb, 3; Rodes, 3. Total, 12. Rumson: Talbott, 2; Balding, 1; Gatins, 1; allowed by handicap, 6. Total, 10. Referee—Edwin Steward 3d. Timer—B. W. Brown.

Here's Melvin Ott, the seventeen-year-old recruit of the Giants who will develop into one of the greatest hitters in the game, according to Manager McGraw. The latter thinks so well of this youngster that he has placed him at the top of the batting order whenever Ott is pressed into service. Ott was a catcher when he reported last Spring. Since then McGraw has converted him into an outfielder.

Trenton Beats A's in 10 Innings, 6-5

TRENTON, N. J., Aug. 30 (AP).—The Trenton A. A. baseball team nosed out the Philadelphia Athletics by a 6 to 5 score in a ten-inning exhibition contest here today.

Two walks followed by three singles off Ike Powers allowed Trenton to tie the score in the seventh inning and Powers was replaced by Rube Walberg. An error by Bishop and two singles brought in the winning run.

Welch and Hauser each made a home run for the Athletics.

Fights with Cop, Says He's Tunney

ATLANTIC CITY, N. J., Aug. 30.—"Gene Tunney" was lodged in jail here to day on the charge of being drunk and diorderly. Under grilling of the judge he admitted his real name was Carl Vogt, of Philadelphia, and that he had given his name as "Gene Tunney" because of pride over the "great fight" he had put up against a policeman.

Vogt when accosted by the officer started an immediate brawl and when it was all over Vogt was in a subdued condition.

Dreyfuss Supports Clarke and Son

Returning from a visit to Europe today, Barney Dreyfuss, president of the world champion Pittsburgh Pirates, said that he gave full support to Fred Clarke, his assistant, and Sam Dreyfuss, his son, in a recent shakeup or the Pirates.

The change in personnel of the Pittsburgh team involved the release of Adams and Bigbee and transfer of Carey to Booklyn. Dreyfuss said that he knew nothing of the affair, other than news printed, but that he left Clarke and Sam Dreyfuss in charge of the club's affairs, with full authority to act.

M'QUILLAN AND MUELLER PAIR TO STOP LONG LOSING STREAK

Astoria Hurler Holds Brooklyn Batters to Five Hits, While Mates Make Fifteen

Heinie Aids in Rout of Dodgers with Brace of Homers; Big Moose Clabaugh in Debut

HUGHIE McQUILLAN and Heinie Mueller teamed to pull the Giants out of their losing streak over at Ebbets Field yesterday afternoon. Astoria Hughie did the pitching and Heinie most of the batting as the Clan McGraw slammed the Robins for an 8 to 2 loss.

Heinie's contributions to the cause were a pair of home runs and they accounted for half the Manhattan runs. As the thing turned out the homers weren't altogether necessary, but as game clinchers they served the purpose admirably. The first four-bagger in the fifth, with two mates aboard, took the game completely beond the reach of the Flatbush gang.

Hugh McQuillan.

All four of the pitchers Uncle Robbie trotted out onto the greensward found favor with the New York stickers. Only one of the Giants, Paul Florence, went hitless, and that he was so fortunate was due only to the fact that he neglected to touch first base while running out a seeming double to left in the ninth.

PARADE OF PITCHERS.

Mueller's homer made a casualty of Bob McGraw. Doug. McWeeny, Jess Barnes and Lefty Williams were the others who tried their luck with ill success. In all the New Yorkers collected fifteen blows good for twenty-five bases.

McQuillan meanwhile limited the Robins to five. He set them down in order during the first four frames and did almost as well in the last four.

The fifth produced two of the hits, Cox's single and a double by Marriott, and one of the Flatbush runs, and in the ninth the Robins added a charity tally. Hughie's fast one was really fast. It was his best effort in quite a spell.

The Giants had the game safely stowed away before they ever took the field. A couple of slow hopping grounders, a solid base hit to center and a successful double steal gave them three runs. McQuillan needed no more.

Mueller's first homer doubled the count in the fifth, as Terry and Tyson were on the runways at the moment. McWeeny was tapped for

Continued on Page 19.

RUNYON SAYS

Time for Training Guff.
Boys Are in Good Health.
Mr. Tunney's Language.
He Knows How to Talk.
Has Drawing Room Style.

—By DAMON RUNYON—

I SHALL have my peek at the champion, Mr. Dempsey, and his challenger, Mr. Tunney, within the next fortnight and will advise my anxious readers as to how the boys appear to me.

However, I have already warned you of my incompetency in the matter of judging the physical condition of fighters from viewing them at their training, so you are not to expect too much.

I gather from the training camp reports of those better versed in these affairs than myself that I shall find both men in good health, anyway, both confident and both eager for the gong. I would be eager myself if the gong meant that I was to get $450,000, as in Mr. Dempsey's case, or $125,000, as in Mr. Tunney's case.

I shall view the lads at their daily maltreatment of their sparring mates, including welters and middleweights. I shall take note of the eyes of Mr. Dempsey and Mr. Tunney with special reference to the clarity thereof, and to the color and texture of their respective hides, or skins, and will endeavor to judge of their wind by whether their breath comes in long or short pants.

I imagine Mr. Tunney will breathe in short pants. He has been breathing in short pants for some little time, judging from the snap-shots of him in those bicycle breeches. I shall observe as carefully as possible each and every little thing that goes on in the training work of the two boys, and in the end I expect to have a vast fund of misinformation.

IF you want my personal opinion, rendered in a moment of calmness, all this training for a ten-round gallop is strictly the old asparagus, especially if Mr. Dempsey and Mr. Tunney "always keep themselves in good condition," as we have frequently been informed. I mean to say, I think it is largely

Continued on Page 20.

Leroy Beats Conway in Bout at Newark

Russell Leroy, Fargo, N. D., lightweight, outpointed Al Conway, of Philadelphia, by a wide margin in a ten-round bout at Newark last night, according to the Associated Press. Leroy weighed 137 pounds and Conway 138. Earl Blue, also of Fargo, knocked out high hat McCullough, colored middleweight of this city, in the fifth round of a scheduled ten-round bout. Blue weighed 164 pounds and McCullough 160.

Not Neighborly

NEW YORK.

	AB	R	H	TB	SO	BB	SB	O	A	E
Ott, lf	5	0	2	2	0	0	0	2	0	0
Lindstrom, 3b	4	1	1	1	0	0	0	0	3	0
Jackson, ss	5	1	2	4	0	0	0	2	6	0
Kelly, 2b	4	1	2	2	0	1	1	1	2	0
Terry, 1b	4	2	2	3	1	1	1	14	2	0
Tyson, cf	5	1	2	3	1	0	0	1	0	0
Mueller, rf	5	2	3	9	0	0	0	3	0	0
Florence, c	5	0	0	0	0	0	0	3	0	0
McQuillan, p	5	0	1	1	2	0	0	1	3	1
Totals	42	8	15	25	4	2	2	27	16	1

BROOKLYN.

	AB	R	H	TB	SO	BB	SB	O	A	E
Fewster, 2b	3	0	0	0	0	0	0	4	1	0
Jacobson, cf	4	0	0	0	0	0	0	2	0	0
Felix, lf	4	1	1	1	1	0	0	1	1	0
Herman, 1b	4	0	1	1	0	0	0	8	0	0
Cox, rf	4	1	1	1	0	0	0	1	0	0
Marriott, 3b	3	0	1	2	0	0	0	0	4	1
Butler, ss	2	0	1	1	0	0	0	6	2	2
Deberry, c	2	0	0	0	0	0	0	4	2	0
O'Neil, c	0	0	0	0	0	0	0	1	0	0
McGraw, p	1	0	0	0	1	0	0	0	0	0
McWeeny, p	0	0	0	0	0	0	0	0	0	0
Barnes, p	0	0	0	0	0	0	0	0	0	0
Williams, p	0	0	0	0	0	0	0	0	1	0
a Standaert	1	0	0	0	0	0	0	0	0	0
b Fournier	1	0	0	0	0	0	0	0	0	0
c Clabaugh	1	0	0	0	0	0	0	0	0	0
d Wheat	1	0	0	0	0	0	0	0	0	0
e Bohne	0	0	0	0	0	0	0	0	0	0
Totals	31	2	5	6	2	0	0	27	11	3

a Batted for McWeeny in sixth inning.
b Batted for Deberry in eighth inning.
c Batted for Barnes in eighth inning.
d Batted for Fewster in ninth inning.
e Ran for Wheat in ninth inning.

New York	3	0	0	0	3	1	1	0	0	—8
Brooklyn	0	0	0	0	1	0	0	0	1	—2

Three-base hit—Jackson. Home run—Mueller. Sacrifice hits—Lindstrom, Butler. Stolen bases—Kelly, Terry. Double plays—Terry, unassisted. Bases on balls—Off McGraw, 1; McQuillan, 1. Struck out—By McGraw, 2; McQuillan, 3; Barnes, 1; Williams, 1. Balk—Williams. Hits—Off McGraw, 11 in 4 innings, none out in fifth inning; McWeeny, 2 in 2 innings; Barnes, 1 in 2 innings. Umpires—Moran, McLaughlin and Wilson. Time of game—One hour and forty-nine minutes.

SENATORS PILE UP NINE RUNS BEFORE YANKS KNOCK OFF ONE

Hugmen Gather Plenty of Hits Off Big Barney, but Errors Offset Heavy Slamming

Three Twirlers Called Upon to Try and Save Situation; Five Passes Prove Costly

By John Kieran.

THE Senators made their final appearance of the season at the Stadium yesterday, and if that's the way they play it's just as well that they won't be back again. They paddled a flock of Yankee pitchers to a fare-thee-well by way of saying good-bye. The score was 12 to 6, with the Hugmen clinging desperately to the short end.

The Hugmen did some paddling on their own account, and against the pitching of none other than Sir Walter Johnson. The battering of Big Barney extended as far as eleven hits for eighteen bases, and included doubles by Ruth and Meusel, a triple by Combs, and Signor Antonio Lazzeri's seventeenth homer of the fast fading season.

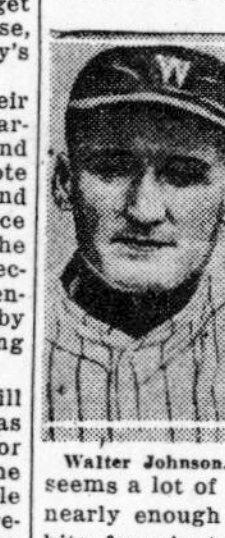
Walter Johnson.

ERRORS HELP VICTORS.

Viewed from any direction, this seems a lot of hitting, but it wasn't nearly enough to offset the twelve hits for nineteen bases which the Senators got off Sam Jones, E. Garlick Braxton, Walter Beall and Herb McQuaid. Five bases on balls and four Yankee errors helped to put the Senators far out in front.

It wasn't until the Senators had scored nine runs that the Yanks could get to Johnson for a tally of two. Big Barney eased off under a big lead and let the boys amuse themselves a bit with their bats. He struck out eight just to keep up the habit.

Sam Jones was the first victim of the day. A couple of hits and an error filled up the bases in the first inning and Joseph Ignatius Judge emptied them with considerable rapidity by hoisting a homer into the right field bleachers.

The third inning was just as bad. Koenig fumbled a grounder, Jones himself hit one batter, and made a two-base wild throw to first, and Goslin got a hit.

Two runs were over and there were shrill cries of "Help" from all corners of the Stadium. Jones crawled to safety on his hands and knees, and E. Garlick Braxton made a short and not too successful appearance. A couple of hits

Continued on Page 19.

The Old Master!

WASHINGTON.

	AB	R	H	TB	SO	BB	SB	O	A	E
McNeely, lf	5	1	1	2	0	0	0	3	0	0
Rice, rf	4	3	3	4	0	1	1	3	0	0
Goslin, cf	5	2	1	1	0	0	0	1	0	1
Myer, ss	3	3	2	3	0	2	0	3	2	0
Judge, 1b	4	3	1	4	0	0	0	6	3	1
S. Harris, 2b	5	0	2	2	2	0	0	1	1	0
Ruel, c	4	0	1	1	0	1	0	8	0	0
Reeves, 3b	4	0	2	2	1	1	0	1	2	0
Johnson, p	5	0	0	0	2	0	0	1	2	0
Totals	39	12	12	19	5	5	1	27	10	2

NEW YORK.

	AB	R	H	TB	SO	BB	SB	O	A	E
Koenig, ss	4	1	2	2	0	1	0	1	1	1
Combs, cf	4	1	1	3	0	1	0	1	0	0
Gehrig, 1b	4	1	1	1	0	0	0	11	1	1
Ruth, rf	4	1	1	2	1	1	0	1	0	1
Meusel, lf	5	1	2	3	2	0	1	1	0	0
Lazzeri, 2b	5	1	2	5	1	0	0	3	2	0
Dugan, 3b	1	0	0	0	1	0	0	0	1	0
Gazella, 3b	4	0	0	0	0	0	0	1	2	0
Bengough, c	3	0	1	1	1	1	0	8	2	0
Jones, p	0	0	0	0	0	0	0	0	0	1
Braxton, p	1	0	1	1	0	0	0	0	0	0
Beall, p	2	0	0	0	2	0	0	0	2	0
McQuaid, p	0	0	0	0	0	0	0	0	2	0
a Carlyle	1	0	0	0	0	0	0	0	0	0
Totals	38	6	11	18	8	4	1	27	13	4

a Batted for Beall in eighth inning.

Washington	4	0	4	1	0	0	0	1	2	—12
New York	0	0	0	1	0	0	0	2	3	—6

Home runs—Judge, Lazzeri. Three-base hits—Rice, Combs. Two-base hits—McNeeley, Myer, Ruth, Meusel. Sacrifice hit—Gehrig. Double Plays—Dugan to Gehrig to Koenig; Judge to Myer to Judge; Gazzella to Lazzeri to Gehrig. Hits—Off Jones, 5 in 2 innings, none out in third; Braxton, 2 in 1 inning, Beall, 3 in 5 innings; McQuaid, 2 in 1 inning. Struck out—By Jones, 1; Braxton, 3; Beall, 3; Johnson, 8. Bases on balls—Off Jones, 1; Beall, 4; Johnson, 4. Hit by pitched ball—By Jones (Judge). Wild pitch—Beall. Left on bases—Washington, 6; New York, 10. Losing pitcher—Jones. Umpires—Moriarity, McGowan and Dineen. Time of game—Two hours and fifteen minutes.

It is great to have a good reputation—providing that it is your own.—G. H. Riley.

PAGE INDEX TO FEATURES

The Boston Post

TWENTY-EIGHT PAGES—TWO CENTS Established 1831 THURSDAY OCTOBER 7 1926 Copyright, 1926, by Post Publishing Co. TWENTY-EIGHT PAGES—TWO CENTS

BABE'S THREE HOMERS LAM SPOTS OFF CARDS

Mighty Slugger Leads Yanks in Vicious Attack on Five St. Louis Pitchers—Slams Ball Out of Lot Every Chance He Has to Hit It—Walked Twice to Prevent Further Damage—Rabid Missouri Fans Cheer Great Batter

Score 10 to 5—Each Team Has 14 Hits, but Cardinals Fail in Pinches

St. Louis Pitchers Very Bad —Hoyt Goes Full Route for New York

BY PAUL H. SHANNON

ST. LOUIS, Oct. 6—Yankee guns, spiked since the opening of the series, last Friday, resumed firing today and the carnage amongst the Cardinal pitchers was awful. Led by Battering Babe Ruth, whose record-breaking work only served to confirm his sole right to the title of Sultan of Swat, the New York bombardieres riddled the St. Louis moundsmen with shot and shell, jogged through to an easy victory by the score of 10 to 5, and Yanks and Cardinals, as a result, are once more upon even terms.

Continued on Page 20—First Col.

This is a remarkable picture of Babe Ruth in action. It shows the Big Bam posed for his deadly swing at the on-coming ball. Note how far back Ruth has set his bat before he swings. Also the position of his right foot. The ball you see here figured in its last play in this picture. It landed over in the next county. (Photo by A. L. Belcher.)

Babe Sure Now That Yankees Will Win Out

BY BABE RUTH

ST. LOUIS, Mo., Oct. 6—At last we've come out of our hitting slump.

And now we'll win the World's Series. That's as sure as fate. The handwriting is on the wall.

I'm not taking anything away from the Cardinals. They have a great ball club, a fighting ball club. But I don't believe there's a club in the country can beat us when we're pounding the ball.

The cause that looked hopeless 24 hours ago looks entirely different now. From here on out the burden of the job rests on the Cardinals. We've come from behind, we've shown our teeth, we've taught them to respect our hitting ability. Now it's up to them.

Continued on Page 19—First Col.

BUD STILLMAN TO MARRY MAID IN HOUSEHOLD

Parents Highly Pleased With Boy's Choice of Lena Wilson, Child From the Woods

Born and Brought Up in Poverty--- Will Soon Enter Portals of High Society

GRANDE MERE, Que., Oct. 6—Into the golden circle of New York's millionaire society there stepped, figuratively, today a timid girl who had been a servant in the house of Mr. and Mrs. James A. Stillman. She walked into the charmed circle where she had been a domestic as the affianced bride-to-be of young James Stillman, son of the couple whose love affairs had held New York's interest for years.

Continued on Page 16—Seventh Col.

TRUCK KILLS WOMAN OF 70

While on her way to church, Mrs. Catherine McGuire, 70, of 63 Forest street, Roxbury, was knocked down and killed by an automobile truck at Dunmore and Dudley streets, Roxbury, shortly after 7 o'clock last night.

The truck, a light moving van, is owned by the Chelsea Moving & Trucking Company and was operated by Morris Levine of 90 Ash street, Chelsea. It was headed north along Dudley street. Mrs. McGuire was crossing the thoroughfare to attend the evening devotions at St. Patrick's Catholic Church.

GREEN NOT TO ADDRESS CHURCHMEN

F. of L. Head Refuses Federal Council's Invitation

DETROIT, Oct. 6 (AP)—Following vigorous denunciation in the American Federation of Labor convention of the action of Detroit ministers and Y. M. C. A. officials in closing their pulpits to labor speakers, President Green of the Federation tonight declined an invitation from the Federal Council of Churches of Christ in America, to speak Sunday afternoon at a mass meeting under the auspices of the council at the First Congregational Church of Detroit.

Continued on Page 16—Eighth Col.

FIFTY COSTUMES FOR QUEEN MARIE

Beautiful Dresses and Gowns for All Occasions Selected for Rumanian Ruler's U. S. Tour

BY ELIZABETH H. WHARTON

PARIS, Oct. 6—Queen Marie of Rumania has already chosen 50 costumes for her American tour. They are all models especially adapted for her from big collections, notably those of Patou and Redfern. Winter models in tones of chestnut, copper, dark brown and petunia red have been created to suit the Queen's luxurious but restrained taste and her graceful and mature dignity.

Continued on Page 16—First Col.

PEACHES AND MA BUILT MUCH ALIKE

Mother Can Wear Daughter's Fine Clothes---Peaches Out for the Real Money Now

NEW YORK, Oct. 6 (United News)—Waiting with his slipper for his Cinderella Girl, who fled, Edward West Browning, whose gift of gold brought worldly luxury to his youthful wife, has let it be known that mothers-in-law even enter and destroy fairy stories.

Through a statement by his attorney, Francis C. Dale, the man who wielded the magic wand for "Peaches" Heenan, has told something of his troubles. Meantime, the girl and her mother, Mrs. Catherine Heenan, remain separated from their benefactor, and shopkeepers are seeking to collect clothing bills which "Peaches" charged to her "Daddy" before the flight.

Continued on Page 16—Fourth Col.

HIGH TIDE TODAY

A.M. AT NAVY YARD P.M.
11:22 11:41

SUN Rises 5:47 Sets 5:17 MOON Sets at 6:03 p. m.

Light all vehicles tonight at 5:47

Partly Cloudy: Cooler

Forecast for Boston and vicinity—Thursday partly cloudy, somewhat cooler, Friday fair. Moderate to fresh west and northwest winds.

For Full Weather Report See Page 2

The Old Farmer's Prediction

I guess folks can bank on today's weather being fairly good and a little cooler than yesterday.

SCHOONER IS SAFE IN PORT

Had Rammed the Rocks Off Horton's Point

NEW LONDON, Oct. 6 (AP)—Kept afloat with great difficulty after she had rammed against rocks of Horton's Point in Long Island Sound today, the 75-foot fishing schooner John and Mary of New Bedford, Mass., was safe in port here tonight.

The vessel as towed in by the coast guard patrol boat 236, sent from the base when the John and Mary was reported to be sinking in the Sound 14 miles southwest of Bartlett's Reeff off Greenpoint. The schooner was damaged by the crash.

FERRYBOAT RUNS AWAY, 1 DROWNED

WILKSBARRE, Pa., Oct. 6 (AP)—A ferryboat slipped its cable and floated beyond control in a swift current in the Susquehanna River at Retreat today and struck an obstruction 100 yards down stream, hurling 16 passengers and three automobiles into more than 10 feet of water. All were rescued except Mrs. Andrew Kryzienski of Korn Crest, Hanover Township. It is believed she was drowned and her body carried down the river, which is swollen by last night's heavy rain.

GETTING A BATH

FITCHBURG, Oct. 6—For the first time in 50 years the Fitchburg station of the Boston & Maine is getting bath. The oldest inhabitant remembers that the station was cleaned up in 1877. The officials decided to do it again, and have turned the nozzles of the sand-blast guns against the begrimed walls. About 1976 or 1977 it is due for another cleaning.

BRIDES—DON'T BE TOO NEAT

Lecturer at School for New Wives So Advises

The first course ever given for brides, married and prospective, opened last night at Boston University, when Mrs. Elizabeth Macdonald, authority on homemaking, gave the first lecture of a series instructing young women how to charm their husbands.

"Don't be neat. Men dislike neat women," was the first dictum.

"Just be orderly. There is a great distinction between 'neat' and 'orderly.'"

Continued on Page 16—First Col.

The Post Sells a Total Number of Copies Each Week Day Morning More Than the Combined Sales of the Other Boston Morning Papers, Globe, Herald, Advertiser All Put Together!

"Courteousness is the deadliest poison."—*Buddha*

The Boston Post

TWENTY PAGES—TWO CENTS | Established 1831 | MONDAY OCTOBER 11 1926 ** | TWENTY PAGES—TWO CENTS

ST. LOUIS WINS SERIES TAKES FINAL GAME 3-2

Alexander Rushes to Rescue With Three Yankees On Bases in Seventh Inning and Strikes Out Lazzeri—Then Holds Yanks Runless for Rest of Game—Babe Ruth Poles Out Home Run But Great Work by Thevenow Cuts Off at Least Three Runs

WOMEN TRY TO MOB "BANKER"

Secretary of Eagle Investment Company Has Narrow Escape at Meeting of Irate Investors

ONE OF THE ANXIOUS WOMEN INVESTORS
Miss May Stearn, a music student, who sent Samuel Gordon a check for $1000 just before he was arrested. She is shown with her brother-in-law, J. J. Crossinan.

One of the officers of the Eagle Investment Company was mobbed by excited women yesterday afternoon when he walked into the Scenic Temple, where a turbulent meeting of the irate investors was in progress. He was escorted out of the hall by police officers, with the women storming behind and guarded from the angry investors who surrounded him in the street until he was safely loaded into a taxi.

POLICE CLEAR HALL

The meeting of these investors, many of whom claim to have lost their life savings through President Samuel J. Gordon's alleged shortage of $200,000, continued to grow in excitement until it was finally stopped late in the day with a detail of police clearing the hall.

During the afternoon at least six different chairmen tried to handle the meeting. Parliamentary law went by the board as a dozen different speakers tried to be heard at once. Sergeant John J. Gale took the platform at one time when the crowd was getting out of control and succeeded in calming them for a time with a threat of immediate adjournment. A short time later when about half of the audience was crowded on the platform he ordered the hall cleared.

Continued on Page 6—Fifth Col.

DENY LOWELL WILL RESIGN

Rumor Appears Without Foundation

Country-wide rumors that President Abbott Lawrence Lowell of Harvard University had resigned or is about to resign caused quite a furore last night. The story, which originated in Cambridge, travelled like wildfire and had reached the Middle West early in the evening.

Members of the Harvard Corporation told the Post last night they had heard the report and believed it to be unfounded. The official spokesman for the university made a positive denial.

Francis Welles Hunnewell of Wellesley, secretary to the Harvard College Corporation, said: "I have not heard even a hint that President Lowell has any thought of resigning. I am sure the story is untrue. I think I would be one of the first to know about it if it were true."

President Lowell himself could not be reached.

Efforts to trace the rumors indicated they originated in a private news bureau in Cambridge.

PASSING OFFICER LEADS TO ARREST

Raymond F. Chase, 30, of Springvale street, Everett, drove his automobile past Traffic Officer John J. Lavan at Morton street and Blue Hill avenue, Mattapan, early last night, despite an order from the officer to halt. The officer pursued him for a mile and overtaking him placed him under arrest on charges of drunkenness and operating while under the influence of liquor.

COLUMBIA PICKED TO WIN TODAY

First of Gloucester Fishermen's Races This Morning

FORD FASTER BOAT, BUT HUNCH HINDERS

Winner to Challenge Champ of Nova Scotian Trials

FOR ONLOOKERS AT FISHERMEN'S RACE

Start and finish of race off the whistling buoy at Eastern Point, Gloucester Harbor.

Excellent points of observation for the race are Eastern Point, Bass Rocks, Brier Neck, Long Beach and the "Back Shore."

Race starts at 10 a. m.

For purposes of identification the Columbia will bear the number 3 on its sails and the Ford number 5.

GLOUCESTER, Oct. 10—This world-famous fishing port is seething with excitement tonight on the eve of the Fishermen's Championship Races, which start off the whistling buoy at Eastern Point tomorrow morning at 10 o'clock with the two crack fishing schooners, Columbia and Henry Ford, as the contenders.

Continued on Page 6—Fourth Col.

FIRST SNOWFALL IN BERKSHIRES

LENOX, Oct. 10—Snow fell over the Berkshires twice overnight, laying a white mantle over the changing foliage and covering the State roads with a thin, slushy layer that made motoring extremely dangerous for week-end traffic. The first fall came shortly after midnight and after a long letup came a second flurry at 8 o'clock this morning.

BABE'S FINAL HOMER OF 1926 SEASON
Babe Ruth did his best to keep the Yankees in yesterday's final battle with St. Louis. This picture shows Babe crossing the plate after his home run drive into the right field bleachers in the third. Mascot Bennett is shaking Ruth's hand. Bob Meusel is waiting his turn at bat, and Bob O'Farrell, the Cardinal catcher, is standing behind the plate.

TWO KILLED WHEN AUTO HITS FENCE

Harvard Student and Brother Victims at Marblehead

MARBLEHEAD, Oct. 10—Robert Doble, a first year student at Harvard, and his younger brother, Philip, a Beverly High School pupil, sons of Mr. and Mrs. Leon C. Doble of 75 Lovett street, Beverly, were killed here early tonight, and three others had a narrow escape from death, when an automobile in which they were riding crashed into an iron fence along the Causeway, ripped off about 30 feet of the fence and then turned over, pinning all five underneath.

Continued on Page 6—Sixth Col.

The Old Farmer's Prediction

Today's weather is apt to continue unsettled and somewhat warmer. There is a chance of showers during today or tonight.

DAUGHERTY JUROR CHARGES DURESS

Tells of Vile Language Used to Sway Him—Illness of Juror Delays Deliberations

NEW YORK, Oct. 10—Owing to the illness of a juror, the jury in the Daugherty-Miller conspiracy trial was excused at 9:55 o'clock tonight until 10 o'clock tomorrow. It had not reached a verdict at that time.

NEW YORK, Oct. 10 (AP)—A verdict reached only under duress of the majority is the sole alternative to immediate discharge of the jury in the Daugherty Miller conspiracy trial, one juror asserted from the jury box tonight.

COMPLAINS TO JUDGE

The juror, Henry van Ost, is generally believed to be the pivot of an acquittal group in the jury, although in his complaints of "duress" to Judge Julian W. Mack, he described a hypothetical juror who had "made up his

Continued on Page 6—Seventh Col.

QUEEN MARIE NOW PACKING

Royal Suite Overflows With Trunks

PARIS, Oct. 10—Members of Queen Marie's party today began packing in preparation for her departure for the United States Tuesday. Tonight the rooms of the royal suite in the Hotel Ritz proved to be too small to hold all of the luggage which was necessary to accommodate all of the Paris purchases of the Queen, and dozens of trunks of all sizes were placed in the corridors.

Whether this was due to the size of the new wardrobe purchased in Paris was not known, but on the trip from Paris to Cherbourg Monday three cars will be required to accommodate the royal party, whereas two sufficed to bring them from Bucharest to Paris.

New York Fielding Errors Make Hoyt's Good Work in Box All in Vain

Cold Weather and Threatened Rain Keep Crowd Down to 38,000

Hornsby Goes Home to Bury His Mother

NEW YORK, Oct. 10 (AP)—Manager Hornsby left immediately after the game for Texas to bury his mother. He was to stop at St. Louis only an hour to change trains and then continue his journey to Austin. His mother died Sept. 29, leaving a dying request that Rogers stay with his team and give his efforts to winning the world's baseball championship for St. Louis. The young Cardinal manager carried out her last wishes to the letter. The body was not interred pending his return to Austin for the burial services. And now he is going home.

BY PAUL H. SHANNON

YANKEE STADIUM, New York, Oct. 10—Baseball's sceptre, a heritage from the Pittsburg Pirates, remains in possession of the National league forces, for tonight the St. Louis Cardinals are champions of the world. The final chapter in a struggle which went the full seven games and was finished on a sodden field was written this afternoon at the Stadium when Rogers Hornsby and his clan repelled every attempt of the American leaguers to retrieve the ghastly mistakes of a tragic fourth inning and won both the game and the title by the score of 3 to 2.

Continued on Page 13—First Col.

HIGH TIDE TODAY AT NAVY YARD
A. M. 1:33 — P. M. 1:43
SUN Rises 5:51 Sets 5:10 — MOON Sets at 8:07 p. m.
Light all vehicles tonight at 5:40.

UNSETTLED

Forecast for Boston and vicinity—Unsettled: probably showers Monday. Tuesday partly cloudy. Not much change in temperature. Moderate west winds shifting to north.

YESTERDAY'S TEMPERATURE
(Recorded at Thompson's Spa)

	'25	'26		'25	'26
3 a. m.	46	44	3 p. m.	38	53
6 a. m.	41	43	6 p. m.	39	50
9 a. m.	37	46	9 p. m.	39	50
12 m.	36	53	12 mid.	40	47

Average temperature yesterday, 48.
Average temperature year ago, 40 2-24.

For Full Weather Report See Page 2

ASKS POLICE TO 'PHONE FOLKS

But Gasoleneless Motorist Gets Arrested

Bernard J. McLaughlin of 252 Western avenue, Lynn, ran out of gasolene while motoring through Saugus yesterday morning at 2 o'clock, and went to Lincoln and Morton avenues, forced open a police signal box and telephoned headquarters at Saugus to notify his folks of his predicament. Instead Officer Roland Mansfield was sent to the scene and placed McLaughlin under arrest on a charge of destroying property.

SHERIFF'S CASE FOR GOVERNOR

MONTPELIER, Vt., Oct. 10—Speculation was rife here today as to what action Governor Billings might take here tomorrow when he will take under official review the charges that have been made against High Sheriff Wallace L. Fairbanks of Windsor county.

The sheriff, who is 57 years old, is at present out on bail after pleading not guilty to a grand jury indictment charging him with undue familiarities with Miss Irma Stoodley, a 20-year-old Chester girl now held in jail here awaiting sentence after a plea of guilty to an offence with the sheriff.

BEST BET TODAY: WILD ASTER

LATEST SPORTS EXTRA

Baltimore American

CHARACTER QUALITY AMERICA FIRST ENTERPRISE ACCURACY

AN AMERICAN PAPER FOR THE AMERICAN PEOPLE

Est. 1773—Vol. CCXLI. Copyright, 1927, by Baltimore Publishing Co. Registered in U. S. Patent Office. M MONDAY, APRIL 4, 1927 PLaza 8600 Entered as second-class matter at the Baltimore Postoffice. 2 Cents in Baltimore and Within 30-Mile Radius. ELSEWHERE Three Cents.

COBB HITS HOMER; MACKS WIN

Boley, Lamar Athletics Regulars

HALE, BRANOM ALSO FAVORED BY CONNIE TO START SEASON

By STARR MATTHEWS.

With his feet propped upon a couple of dry boards, made into a temporary bridge to keep his feet out of a pool of water, I found Connie Mack yesterday afternoon on the visitors' bench at Oriole Park taking as much interest in the exhibition game as some managers do in a championship contest.

"Are you going to win the pennant this year?" I fired as an opening shot.

"I wouldn't like to say just that," replied the courteous leader of the Philadelphia Athletics, seriously. "It's something to say that you are going to beat seven other teams in such a race. And some of the clubs are very strong, also very smart. But I'll say we are much stronger."

"Where are you stronger?" was the next query, that being the natural question to ask.

"Joe Boley and Ty Cobb are giving us that extra strength," came the reply without an instant's hesitation.

GENERAL EXPLANATION.

Then Connie Mack settled into a general explanation, which was about as follows:

"Ty is fast rounding into shape. By the time the season is a couple of weeks old he'll be going at his best pace. He looks good now and is almost on edge.

"Boley is making splendid plays. That adds defensive strength and he'll hit as well as Galloway, maybe better. I never knew how good Boley was or, at least, how well he was regarded by other players until I bought him. Since then I have met so many players who played with him and their reports have been wonderful. Yes, Boley and Cobb will add a lot of strength to our team."

"Who'll start at second?" I asked.

"Well, I suppose Eddie Collins will start, but Max Bishop is just wonderful this spring. He took on some weight and it has done him a world of good. Some men are handicapped by weight, but Max is the exception to that rule. He's going to play a lot of baseball for us this season.

"Collins, of course, is a great man at the bat. Also he's smart in the field, but Bishop looks better than at any time in his career."

LAMAR GOING GREAT.

Having concluded long ago that Cobb and Al Simmons were fixtures in the garden, I inquired about the left field position. It is there that Zach Wheat, former captain of the Brooklyn Robins and for years one of the truly

Continued on Page 10, Column 8.

TONIGHT'S CARD OF BOXING AT 104TH ARMORY

Main bout, twelve rounds to decision, Buster Brown vs. Benny Schwartz.

Three six-rounders: Sylvan Bass vs. Sailor Jack Denley, Joey Britton vs. Joe Piscatelli, Ernie Brooks vs. Sammy Marino.

First contest, 8.30 o'clock.

Ty Cobb Swings, Then Watches the Ball Soar Into the Bleacher

BEHIND THE PLATE you see Lake catching and Byers umpiring. —American Staff Photo.

12,000 SHIVERING FANS SEE ORIOLES BLANKED IN STIRRING CONTEST

Scott's Wild Throw, Texas Leaguers By Simmons and Hale and Branom's Double Net Majors 3 of Their 4 Runs

By CHICK FOREMAN

Twelve thousand shivering, baseball-hungry fans braved wintry winds yesterday afternoon to fill Oriole Park and get their first taste of the national pastime this year. They saw the Philadelphia Athletics blank Jack Dunn's Orioles by a 4-to-0 score.

The fans were amply rewarded for the pains their noses, toes and fingers bore and gamely stuck through to the end of the contest, so, to make their stay for the late innings a pleasant one, Tyrus Raymond Cobb drove a home run into the right-field bleacher in his final trip to the plate in the ninth inning and then concluded his performance in the field during the Orioles' time at bat by making two stirring running catches, the last one ending the game, with 100 small boys endeavoring to relieve the Georgia Peach of the ball in a mad scramble.

True to his word, Manager Connie Mack of the Athletics had several Baltimore favorites in his line-up. Joe Boley, for eight years the Oriole shortstop, was at that position for the Macks, and Lefty Grove, another Oriole product, twirled the first five innings.

Lefty Grove Had No Mercy

Joe and Lefty never played better ball than they did yesterday. Joe scooped them up around his old stamping ground in his customary manner and Lefty simply breezed them past the Oriole batters. He had no mercy on his old teammates. Lefty pitched four hitless innings and then eased up in the fifth and permitted two safeties. He fanned five batsmen and in the second inning struck out the side.

Continued on Page 10, Column 5.

The American's Bowie Selections For Today

By CLARENCE L. SMITH.

FIRST RACE—H. P. Whitney-L. S. Thompson entry (Shylight and Tum On), Dancing, Ral Freeman entry (Apple Pie and High Hope).
SECOND—Wild Aster, Marcellus, Opperman.
THIRD—Suky, Red Spider, Beau Gallant.
FOURTH—Golden Rule, Resourceful, Forecaster.
FIFTH—Harlan, Spugs, Kosciusko.
SIXTH—Compromise, Muskallonge, Jacques.
SEVENTH—North Breeze, Macbeth, Tod Renesor.

Brown and Schwartz On Edge For Battle

Buster Brown, promising local featherweight, will get his second shot as a star-bout performer tonight when he faces Benny Schwartz, another Baltimore product of the roped arena, in the main combat of the Olympia Athletic Club at the One Hundred and Fourth Medical Regiment Armory. The contest will be over the usual twelve-round route, and the meeting of the boys has created quite a bit of interest in fistic circles throughout the city. Opinion as to the probable outcome of the encounter seems to be divided, but the closer followers of the game are inclined to give the edge to

Continued on Page 10, Column 4.

WINFREY ENTRY PICKED TO WIN

By CLARENCE L. SMITH.

Bowie's race program today is minus an outstanding feature, but it's a well balanced one and should be productive of an afternoon of interesting sport. Thoroughbreds of the cheaper variety will be seen under colors.

What looms as the best contest on the card is the fourth number, a gallop of a mile and a sixteenth for four-year-olds and upward. This has attracted a field of eight, and it promises to be a keen contest from the drop of the flag until they dash past the judges. Those entered are C. Bild's Golden Rule, F. M. Kelly's Resourceful, T. W. O'Brien's Forecaster, W. C. Trover's Warman, F. Serio's Flagship, W. J. Owens' Canister, D. L. Rice's Dancing Fool and Tom Francis' Delusive.

GOLDEN RULE FAVORED.

Golden Rule, winner of two races at New Orleans, is given the call here, though the former carrier of the silks of Commander J. K. L. Ross is not pitted against easy opposition. The soft going should be just to the liking of the big bay

Continued on Page 10, Column 1.

Box Score of Battle Of Macks and Birds

ORIOLES	AB.	R.	H.	O.	A.	E.
Maisel, 3b	4	0	2	1	2	0
Slayback, 2b	3	0	0	1	0	0
Brunier, 2b	1	0	0	0	0	0
Porter, cf	4	0	0	3	0	0
Brower, rf	3	0	0	4	0	0
Sheedy, 1b	3	0	0	7	0	0
Hohman, lf	3	0	1	1	1	0
Scott, ss	3	0	2	3	2	1
Lake, c	3	0	0	7	2	0
Earnshaw, p	1	0	0	0	1	0
Ogden, p	2	0	0	0	0	0
Total	30	0	5	27	8	1

ATHLETICS	AB.	R.	H.	O.	A.	E.
French, lf	4	0	0	0	0	0
Collins, 2b	3	1	0	0	1	0
Cobb, rf	3	1	1	3	0	0
Simmons, cf	4	1	1	0	0	0
Metzler, cf	0	0	0	0	0	0
Hale, 3b	4	1	2	2	3	1
Branom, 1b	4	0	2	11	1	0
Boley, ss	4	0	1	2	5	0
Fox, c	3	0	0	9	0	0
Grove, p	2	0	0	0	0	0
Walberg, p	1	0	0	0	1	0
Total	32	4	7	27	11	1

SCORE BY INNINGS

Athletics	0	0	0	3	0	0	0	0	1	—4
Orioles	0	0	0	0	0	0	0	0	0	—0

Two-base hits—Branom, Maisel. Home run—Cobb. Stolen base—Cobb. Bases on balls—Off Ogden, 2. Struck out—By Grove, 5; by Earnshaw, 3; by Ogden, 3; by Walberg, 2. Hits—Off Grove, 2 in 5 innings; off Walberg, 3 in 4; off Earnshaw, 4 in 4; off Ogden, 3 in 5. Double plays—Walberg, Boley and Branom; Lake and Scott; Hale, Boley and Branom. Winning pitcher—Grove. Losing pitcher—Earnshaw. Umpires—Byers and Ward. Time—1.45.

ST. CLEMENT'S LISTING

St. Clement's Rosedale has reorganized for the coming season, with James L. Wilkie as manager and Butts Karl as captain. Season opening Sunday, May 1. Teams playing unlimited baseball, communicate with James L. Wilkie, Essex, or Chesaco avenue, Raspburg, Md.

TWO TWIRLERS WANTED

The Bluebird Athletic Club would like to sign two good pitchers playing in the sixteen-year-old class. Address A. Heck, 900 Patterson Park avenue, or phone Wolfe 2137.

How Athletics Defeated Birds in Opening Game

FIRST INNING — Athletics — Maisel threw out French. Collins flied to Porter. Cobb popped to Sheedy. No run, no hit, no error.

Orioles — Maisel grounded to Branom. Slayback fanned. Boley went back of third for Porter's foul twister. No run, no hit, no error.

SECOND INNING — Athletics — Simmons skied to Brower. Hale singled to left and was out at second trying to stretch it. Hohman to Slayback. Branom flied to Scott. No run, one hit, no error.

Orioles — Brower and Sheedy fanned. Hohman was called out on strikes. No run, no hit, no error.

THIRD INNING — Athletics — Boley was called out on strikes. Fox and Grove fanned. No run, no hit, no error.

Orioles—Boley threw out Scott. Hale threw out Lake. Earnshaw fanned. No run, no hit, no error.

FOURTH INNING.—Athletics — Earnshaw threw out French. Scott fielded Collins' grounder but threw it past Sheedy to the stand, Collins taking second. Cobb lofted to Brower. Simmons dropped a Texas leaguer back of second, scoring Collins. Hale sunk a Texas leaguer in the water-soaked grass back of second, Simmons advancing to second. Branom doubled to deep center, scoring Simmons and Hale

Continued on Page 10, Column 3.

HARVARD'S CREW BEATS YALE ON THAMES

CHARACTER · QUALITY · AMERICA FIRST · ACCURACY · ENTERPRISE
New York American Sports
AN AMERICAN PAPER FOR THE AMERICAN PEOPLE

☆☆☆ SATURDAY, JUNE 25, 1927 7

Terry's Boot Gives Phils Even Break With McGraw Clan

Quakers Tie Count in Ninth and Win in Tenth Inning of Second Game.

PHILADELPHIA, Pa., June 24.—Our renovated Giants almost won a double-header from the Phils today. They got away with the first game, 7 to 3, without any undue agony, and had the second battle apparently won, but kicked it away.

BILL TERRY
Makes Costly Error.

The home athletes tied the score in the ninth through some inept Giant fielding and knocked in the winning run in the tenth, 6 to 5, when Thompson's single scored Williams, who had Bill Terry's error was fairly responsible for the Giant debacle in walked.

Bill Terry's fatal error was fairly responsible for the Giant debacle [illegible] the second contest. With a man on first, one out and our boys two runs to the good, Bill dropped Friberg's foul pop. The said Friberg retaliated by whanging a two-bagger to l[illegible], scoring one run.

Nixon, a pinch hitter, was tossed out and the game would have ended right there if it had not been for Bill's boot. Then Mokan smote a double and the score was tied.

In the tenth Williams walked, Wrightstone sacrificed, Thompson singled and the crowd went home. All these hits and runs were made while Don Songer was on the mound. He had relieved Burliegh Grimes in the seventh and was doing well until the fatal episode in the ninth.

WHAT RAJAH DID

FIRST GAME.

First Inning—Hit a home run over the rightfield wall.
Third Inning—Doubled to left, stole third and scored on Terry's infield hit.
Fourth Inning—Was thrown out by Kaufmann.
Sixth Inning—Grounded out to Thompson.
Eighth Inning—Walked.

SECOND GAME.

First Inning—Walked.
Third Inning—Lined to left.
Sixth Inning—Lined to center.
Eighth Inning—Was hit by a pitched ball.
Ninth Inning—Singled to center.

The second game opened with a lot of loose work on both sides. Our athletes got a run in the first on Reese's single, two walks and a force play. Reese scored while Terry was forcing Hornsby at second.

GRIMES FALTERS.

The Phillies were practically presented wtih a pair of tallies in the home half. One run was the result of Jackson's error, a single by Wrightstone and double by Leach; then Grimes walked the next two men and forced in a run.

Our boys were bereft of at least one run by Leach's slick catch in the fourth. With Jackson on first, Ott drove a potential three-bagger toward the scoreboard. Leach speared it after a hard run and doubled up Jackson, who was half way home.

Again, in the sixth, Leach's uncanny fielding kept the Giants from scoring. He streaked across the field and caught Hornsby's line drive on a dead run. This unfortunate in-

Continued on Page 8.

Jack Turns 32; Dempseys Hold Brithday Party

ANOTHER milestone in the colorful career of Jack Dempsey was passed yesterday. The former heavyweight champion celebrated his thirty-second birthday.

Newspaper men and camp attaches attended a party given in honor of the occasion at Tom Luther's camp at White Sulphur Springs last night. Mrs. Dempsey provided a birthday cake with thirty-two candles.

HEENEY SCORES CLASSY VICTORY OVER DE MAVE

FIGHTING his third bout in America, Tom Heeney, New Zealand heavyweight, scored an artistic victory over Jack De Mave, of Hoboken, in the main event of ten rounds last night at the Coney Island Stadium.

De Mave, outweighed by nine pounds, put up a game resistance to the onslaughts of the man from "down under," but he ran a poor second all the way. Heeney employed a left hook to splendid advantage, shaking his light opponent with volleys of lefts to the head and occasional shots to the stomach. His right was not as good a weapon, although he uppercut with it nicely and jarred De Mave badly at times with straight shots to the heart.

Yale Okun, 170, jabbed his way to a decision over Tony Marullo, 171, in the semi-final. This was Yale's first start here since his return from London, where he lost to Phil Scott, British heavyweight champion, on a foul.

Okun rained left jabs on the New Orleans veteran for ten rounds, and by keeping Tony's face full of gloves broke up many of Marullo's attacks. Tony took his lacing nonchalantly and in the last few rounds managed to land not a few rights on Okun's pan. Tony gashed Yale's lips with some rights in the seventh and had the New Yorker tired and holding in the last three rounds. Okun never forgot to use his left, however, and came home first.

Sandy Siefert, 181½, a Pittsburgh entry, was too cagy for the younger George La Rocco, 179, in the second heat, and grabbed off a decision on experience plus a steady fire of short jolts to the body.

Johnny Urban, Pittsburgh heavyweight, added Tom Roper to his list of victims in the opening bout. Urban clouted Thomas with a short right hander and deposited him on the canvas in the sixth. Roper got up balmy and Urban nailed him with another right. Tom folded up for the evening. Roper weighed 189½, Urban 185.

RICKARD BESTS COMMISSION IN BARGAIN CLASH

Solons Fail to Get Tex' Promise of Title Fight Here in Return for High Ticket Scale

By Ed Frayné.

MEMBERS of the New York Boxing Commission attempted to drive a sharp bargain with Promoter George Tex Rickard yesterday, but they came out second best.

TEX RICKARD
Beats Commission.

In return for their approval of a championship ticket price for the Jack Dempsey-Jack Sharkey match, the commissioners requested Rickard to give his pledge that Gene Tunney would defend his heavyweight title in New York.

When the smoke cleared away, it was learned that Rickard held a legal permit to charge from $3 to $27.50 for Sharkey and Dempsey. He also held a license for Dempsey. The Commission is holding the bag, as the boys would say.

DIALOGUE TELLS STORY.

The dialogue that took place between Commissioner William Muldoon and Rickard, as told by Rickard, tells the story.

MULDOON—"If we allow you to charge $27.50 for this match, will you be satisfied with the same maximum for the heavyweight championship bout in the Fall?"

RICKARD—"I would have to be."

MULDOON—"Then we could be assured that you will hold the championship match in New York?"

RICKARD—"I hope to."

Whereupon the interview wa[s] ended, and the Commission gave th[e] promoter what amounts to a tax o[f] $1,000,000 on New York pocketbooks In exchange the Commission feel[s] that Rickard is obligated to stag[e] the big bout in this city.

SAID NO SUCH THING.

Rickard quoted his own replie[s] after the meeting to show that h[e] said "no such thing." From hi[s] evasive answers, it can be seen tha[t] the promoter intends to go elsewher[e] with his September event.

Rickard registered exasperatio[n] when he learned that his conversa[tion] tion with Muldoon had been inte[r]preted as a promise that he woul[d] stage his September bout in Ne[w] York. He quoted what Muldoon ha[d] said, and what he had said in a

Continued on Page 9

History of the Crew Classic

Date.	Won by	Time—Winner.	Time—Loser.
1855	Harvard		
a1859	Harvard	19:18	20:18
1859	Yale	19:14	19:16
1860	Harvard	18:53	19:05
1864	Yale	19:01	19:43⅛
1865	Yale	18:42½	19:09
1866	Harvard	18:43½	19:10
1867	Harvard	18:13	19:25½
1868	Harvard	17:48½	18:38½
1869	Harvard	18:02	18:11
1870	Harvard	Foul	Disq.
1876	Yale	22:02	22:33
1877	Harvard	24:36	24:44
1878	Harvard	20:44⅜	21:29
1879	Harvard	24:15	24:58
1880	Yale	24:25	25:09
1881	Yale	22:13	22:19
1882	Harvard	20:47½	20:50½
1883	Harvard	25:46	25:59
1884	Yale	20:31	20:46
1885	Harvard	25:15½	26:30
1886	Yale	20:41¼	21:05
1887	Yale	22:56	23:10½
1888	Yale	20:10	21:24½
1889	Yale	21:39	21:55
1890	Yale	21:29	21:40
1891	Harvard	21:23	21:57
1892	Yale	20:48	21:42¼
1893	Yale	25:01½	25:15
1894	Yale	23:47	24:40
1895	Yale	21:45	22:15
1899	Harvard	20:52½	21:13
1900	Yale	21:12	21:37
1901	Yale	23:37	23:45
1902	Yale	20:20	20:38
1903	Yale	20:19⅘	20:29⅜
1904	Yale	21:40½	22:10
1905	Yale	22:33½	22:36
1906	Harvard	23:02	23:11
1907	Yale	21:10	21:13
1908	Harvard	20:10	24:45
1909	Harvard	21:50	22:10
1910	Harvard	20:46½	21:04
1911	Harvard	22:44	23:40
1912	Harvard	21:43½	22:04
1913	Harvard	21:42½	22:20
1914	Yale	21:16	21:16
1915	Yale	20:52	21:13
1916	Harvard	b20:02	20:17
c1917	—	—	—
d1918	Harvard	10:58	11:04
1919	Yale	21:42⅛	21:47
1920	Harvard	23:11	23:46
1921	Yale	20:41	20:44
1922	Yale	21:53	22:06
1923	Yale	22:10	22:35
1924	Yale	21:583/5	22:11
1925	Yale	20:26	20:32
1926	Yale	20:14⅗	20:21
1927	Harvard	22:25⅕	22:29

aCitiens' Regatta.
bRecord for Thames River course.
cNo race on account of war.
dThe 1918 race was a two-mile informal contest at Derby, Conn.

He's Up There to Stay

The two Biggest Things in New York, Lou Gehrig and the Woolworth Building. Gehrig is the sensation of the majors.
Standing on top of the world. Only three homers behind Ruth.
21 HOME RUNS.

Lou "Buster" Gehrig of Ya[nks]

U. S. NET STARS VICTORS AGAIN AT WIMBLEDON

Helen Wills Wins from Miss Bennett and Tilden and Hunter Come Through

WIMBLEDON, England, June 24 (AP).—American players had a field day here on the fifth day of the Wimbledon tennis championships. They won "four and a half' victories today with no defeats, not including the success of an American-Japanese doubles team.

Each member of the America's "Big Four"—Helen Wills, Elizabeth **Ryan, William T. Tilden and Francis T. Hunter—won a victory in the singles. Each of them reached the quarter-finals, with the exception of Helen Wills, who is a round behind her teammates in the play.**

Watson M. Washburn, paired with Takeichi Harada, Japan, won over the Hon. C. Campbell and St. James Mahony, Ireland, in the second round of the men's doubles, 6—0, 6—4, 2—6, 6—2. The "half victory" for the Americans came when L. A. Godfree and D. M. Greig retired in the third set of their match against Tilden and Hunter in the second round of the men's doubles. The Americans were leading, 6—0, 10—8, and the third set was tied at two-all when the English pair withdrew on accoount of an injury to Greig's knee.

HARD PRESSED.

Hunter was the only one of the "Biig Four" to have a real battle in the singles today. The others all won in straight sets.

Hunter's entry into the quarter-finals was disputed by J. C. Gregory, who ranks amonk England's first five players. Their meeting was a battle royal, with Hunter finally emerging the victor by scores of 4—6, 7—5, 6—2, 4—6, 6—3. It was only by a wonderful finish that Hunter saved the match after trailing 1—3 in the final set.

Hunter faces another tremendous task in the quarter-finals, for Henri Cochet, one of France's "Three Musketeers" stands between him and the semi-finals.

EASY FOR BIG BILL.

Tilden had little difficulty in disposing of Christian Boussus, young French player, whom he defeated 6—1, 7—5, 6—2, to become the first player to reach the quarter finals. In the second set Boussus, by brilliant returns, held the match even up to five-all.

Helen Wills eliminated Miss Eileen Bennett, of England, 7—5, 6—3. Miss Wills trailed 1—4 in the first set, and Miss Bennett maintained her lead up to 5—3. The ninth game was love-forty on Miss Wills service, but "Little Poker Face" staved off defeat and took the game after deuce had been called four times.

That was the turning point of the match. The California girl gave a particularly sparkling exhibition in the last three games.

Elizabeth Ryan reached the quarter-finals by defeating Miss E. H. Harvey, of England, 7—5, 6—1. Like Miss Wills, she started poorly. Her drives would not behave in the first set and kept dropping a few inches over the baseline, so she re-

Continued on Page 9

Mandell Signs To Defend His Title July 15

DETROIT, June 24 (INS).—Sammy Mandell, light weight champion of the world, and Phil McGraw, Detroit's slashing contender, will engage in a title bout at the University of Detroit Stadium on the night of July 15. The boys signed articles for the fight this afternoon.

Mandell will receive $50,000 for placing his crown in jeopardy, while McGraw is guaranteed $7,500 and will get a bonus of $5,000 if the gate tops the $125,000 mark.

The fight will be over a ten-round route.

Blue Crosses Finish Line Three-Quarters Of Length Behind

Momentary Disaster as Eli Oarsman Catches a "Crab" with Mile to Go Kills Possibility of Seventh Successive Victory.

NEW LONDON, Conn., June 24 (AP).—Leading from start to finish of a thriling four-mile race, Harvard's varsity swept out of the shadows of defeat this evening to conquer Yale for the first time in seven years in the climax event of America's most historic college regatta.

The Crimson's stalwart, fighting eight won by fully three-quarters of a length in the long drive down the Thames River, but most, if not all, of this margin was gained when momentary disaster—the catching of a "crab"—hit the Eli shell and virtually put it out of the race with a mile to go just when it seemed to be overhauling the Cambridge crew.

F. F. ROBINSON.
Bows in Defeat.

It was a brilliant triumph for Harvard's sturdy sons, the first they have known in this classic event since 1920. And it was also a heart-breaking defeat for a Yale boat that entered the race a slight favorite, and might have won for the seventh successive year but for the upset that threw it out of gear for a few precious seconds.

RECORDS CRACKED.

This sudden and dramatic break in the heralded Eli machine—the product of the same "system" that had sent two crews, the freshman and unior varsity, to sensational and record-smashing triumphs over Harvard in the preliminary races earlier in the day—came at a moment when the Elis, coming from behind, seemed to be cutting down Harvard's lead with the swift sureness of a "grim reaper."

To observers along the banks and in the observation trains, it seemed that the Eli No. 6, Dana Baratholomew, of Ansonia, Conn., lost his stroke—failing to get his oar out of the water as he caught what oarsmen figuratively call a "crab." Instantly, the whole Yale shell lost the beautiful precision, the rhythm that had been sending it along in space-devouring strides.

CUT AWAY LENGTH.

Yale had cut down nearly a length of Harvard's earlier margin and was within a uarter-length of being on even terms when it appeared to come almost to a standstill. Oars flashed, a tense silence gripped the thousands of spectatirs on shore and boats then a groan from the Yale followers as the Crimson shot ahead again. It all took probably less than three seconds until the Elis pulled themselves together again and dug in their blades, but it was enough to give the Crimson back its lost advantage, with another mile in which to defend it.

Yale's prospects unquestionably were blasted then and there, but the Elis displayed their grit by coming back to stage a whirlwind, fighting finish. They did succeed in cutting down about a quarter of a length—some fifteen feet—of Harvard's margin in the last dish to the railroad bridge, through lanes of colorful, tooting craft. But this spurt was not enough to seriously menace Harvard's lead.

SHOW THEIR METTLE.

The Crimson had been waiting a long time for this triumph. Oppor-

Continued on Page 9

Sharpshooters Are Not All in Marine Corps

THE latest golf shot for the well-known book was delivered today by P. Miller-Jones, of Richmond County, playing against Leonard Martin in the beaten sixteen of the metropolitan amateur championship.

From the fifteenth tee at Nassau, Jones drove a ball out of bounds, and incurring a penalty of loss of distance drove another. Then, while Martin looked on in amazement—that young man having already won the hole in his own mind—Jones took out a spoon and laid it accurately against the ball. It covered a bit more than 200 yards via air, but rolled on the green and disappeared into the cup for an extraordinary bird 3. Martin lost the hole.

TAYLOR GIVEN VERDICT OVER BROOKLYN BOY

CHICAGO, June 24.—Bud Taylor, generally recognized as the bantamweight champion of the world, clinched his claim to the title by defeating Tony Canzoneri, of Brooklyn, here tonight.

The Terre Haute Terror was awarded the decision at the close of a viciously contested ten-round bout.

Taylor opened up with a furious attack, driving Canzoneri to the ropes at the start of the first round and proceeded to carry the fight to the challenger. He nailed Tony with two or three hard rights, drawing blood from Tony's mouth and Taylor was bleeding from the mouth, too, before the round was over.

Taylor centered his attack on the body in the second round, while Canzoneri attempted to box Bud at long range. Their heads were bobbing from an exchange of rights that kept the crowd in an uproar.

Canzoneri traded punch for punch in the third, forcing Taylor to break ground for the first time. Tony inflicted the greater punishment, planting half a dozen rights on Taylor's chin and dropping left hooks to the body.

Canzoneri danced around Taylor in the fourth, spearing him with lefts to the face and frequently landed two or three times without a return. He nailed Bud with three hard rights but near the close of the round Taylor ripped into him, trading rights in a wild exchange in the middle of the ring. Canzoneri had the round by a wide margin.

Canzoneri employed his left hook effectively in the fifth, shooting it to the body and jaw, with Taylor puzzled and retreating.

TAYLOR SPEEDS UP.

Taylor took the play away from Tony in the sixth, chasing Canzoneri

Continued on Page 9

Texas Freshie Wins His Way to Tennis Final

WILMINGTON, Del., June 24.—Berkley Bell, University of Texas freshman, entered the final of the Delaware State men's singles tennis championships today against Manuel Alonso when he disposed of Ben Gorchakoff, the Pacific Coast star from Occidental College, in eighteen minutes of actual play. Bell won, 6—0, 6—1, over the Los Angeles player, who had previously brushed aside Fritz Mercur and Wallace F. Johnson.

Alonso, former Spanish Davis Cup star, forced out Wilmer Allison, University of Texas, in the other semi-final, 6—0, 6—4.

Mrs. Marion Zinderstein Jessup, formerly of Boston, went into the final of the women's singles, when she easily defeated Miss Penelope Anderson, of Richmond, Va., in straight sets, 6—2, 6—3. Mrs. Jessup will play Miss Margaret Blake, of Boston, for the title tomorrow.

Miss Eleanor Goss, of New York, paired with Miss Isabelle Lee Mumford, of Boston, was eliminated in the semi-final of women's doubles by Miss Blake and Mrs. Anna Fuller Hubbard, of Belair, Md., 6—4, 6—2.

Earl Smith Fined $500 and Suspended 30 Days

AS a penalty for his assault on Manager Daave Bancroft, of the Boston Braves, on June 18 last, Earl Smith, of the Pittsburgh Club, was yesterday fined $500 and suspended from all privileges of the field for a period of thirty days by President John A. Heydler of the National League.

The assault took place at Forbes Field, Pittsburgh, in a game between the home team and Boston. Up to the time of Bancroft's third turn at bat in the seventh inning, the game had proceeded with little or no friction, and with the score at that time 4 to 0 in favor of Pittsburgh.

During this particular turn at bat Smith, in undertone, made personal remarks to Bancroft, and there also was some dispute between the two on a called ball. Bancroft was given a base on balls.

On reaching first he called to Umpire McCormick: "Did you hear what he (Smith) called me?" Then he turned to Umpire Klem at first base and said. "This fellow is abusing me something awful. What am I going to do about it?"

Only fragments of what Smith said were heard by the umpires, but nothing serious enough to have justified them in ejecting Smith from the game. Both officials were positive in their testimony that they did not hear Bancroft use bad language to Smith.

Bancroft and Moome scored on a hit, there being no play at the plate. After touching the plate Bancroft stopped and complained to Umpire McCormick, repeating the vile language he alleged Smith had used to him, and again asked the umpire if he had not heard it.

Without warning Smith, a big man of exceptional strength and power, then str[uck] Bancroft in the face with such force that the latter fell in a helpless heap and was carried, unconscious and bleeding, from the field.

According to President Heydler, there was no way to determine Smith's real state of mind except by his actions, and by these, both at the time of the assault and afterward, in the former's opinion Smitn convicted himself. The evidence of the umpires showed that with practically no provocation he roused himself to such a rage that his act might have resulted seriously or even fatally.

TY COBB MAKES 4,000TH HIT OF HIS MAJOR LEAGUE CAREER

Double Places Him 570 Ahead of Nearest Rival

Only Hans Wagner, With Lifetime Total of 3,430, Approaches Cobb's Astounding Batting Record.

By H. G. SALSINGER

TYRUS RAYMOND COBB, superman of base ball, made the four thousandth hit of his major league career in the first inning of yesterday's game. It was a two-bagger.

In August of 1905 Cobb made the first hit of his big league career on the same field. It, also, was a two-bagger and he made the hit off Jack Chesbro of the New York Highlanders.

It required Cobb more than two decades to acquire 4,000 hits, but he has 570 more hits than his nearest rival was able to accumulate in a lifetime. His nearest rival is John P. (Hans) Wagner, who used to play for Pittsburgh. Wagner, in 21 seasons of competition along the Big Line, managed to gather 3,430 hits.

Cobb's record is remarkable considering that he has made 570 more hits than his nearest rival and that his career is by no means at an end. When he retires he will have a record that no one should ever come near in the future. He leads in nearly every department of individual offensive effort and there is no player on the horizon who even promises to someday challenge him. Rogers Hornsby did, for awhile, but Rogers dropped last season and his work this year indicates that there is no chance for him to approach Cobb's lifetime batting percentage of .369. His season's average is .358.

ONE OUT OF FOUR.

Cobb's four thousandth hit, in the first inning yesterday, was by no means as clean as his first two-bagger off Chesbro in 1905. He sent a line drive into right field and Heilmann, trying for a one-handed catch, got his gloved hand on the ball, but it bounded out and gave Cobb a scratch two-bagger. In the third inning Cobb hit another line drive to right. The ball struck Heilmann's gloved hand and bounded into the air. Heilmann caught the ball as it descended and registered the putout. Cobb was at bat twice after that and grounded to Gehringer each time. His record was one hit in four times at bat.

The third game of the Detroit-Philadelphia series, which Detroit won by a 5 to 3 score, was a pitchers' battle between Sam Gibson and Bob Grove. Gibson pitched good ball, but so did Grove. Gibson won because he had better fielding support.

GIFT RUNS.

Bad fielding by the Athletics enabled Detroit to score three runs. In the first inning Gehringer singled with one out. Manush hit to Bishop and Bishop had an easy double play ahead of him, but he missed the bag in trying to touch second and he got only Manush. Fothergill then sent a grounder into right. Cobb tore in after the ball, intending to cut it off and throw out Gehringer at the plate. But he missed the ball and it rolled to right field fence, a scratch home run on which two men scored. Heilmann then doubled and Blue singled him home.

Philadelphia had scored two runs in the opening half of the first on Bishop's single, Cobb's scratch double and Cochrane's single.

Both pitchers were tough after the first. Detroit got another run in the third as the result of some more bad fielding. Gehringer slashed a two-bagger to left field corner and took third when Fothergill's sharp bounder glanced off Hale's chest for a fluke single. Boley and Bishop let the ball roll between them and since neither seemed inclined to pick it up, Gehringer ran home.

Heilmann hit the ball into the bleachers in center in the fifth and that was Detroit's last run.

Philadelphia got one after the first. It came in the sixth. McManus fumbled Simmons' grounder with one out and Cochrane singled him to third. He scored on Lamar's sacrifice fly to Heilmann.

BOX SCORE

DETROIT.	AB	H	O	A	PHILADELPHIA.	AB	H	O	A
Warner,3	4	0	0	1	Bishop,2.	4	2	0	5
Gehr'ger,2	4	2	1	6	Hale,3...	4	1	2	2
Man'sh,m	4	0	1	0	Cobb,r....	4	1	2	0
Foth'g'l,lf	4	2	0	0	Sim'ons,m	4	0	2	0
Heilm'n,r	4	4	6	0	Cochr'ne,c	4	2	4	0
Blue,1...	4	1	10	0	Lamar,lf..	2	0	2	0
'Manus,s.	4	0	2	1	Dykes,1..	4	1	10	0
Woodall,c.	2	0	7	1	Boley,s...	3	0	2	3
Gibson,p.	2	0	0	1	Grove,p..	2	0	0	2
					*Collins..	1	0	0	0
					†Wheat..	1	0	0	0
Totals	38	9	27	10	Totals.	33	7	24	12

*Batted for Boley in ninth inning.
†Batted for Grove in ninth inning.

Detroit	3	0	1	0	1	0	0	0	x	—5
Philadelphia	2	0	0	0	0	1	0	0	0	—3

Runs—Gehringer 2, Fothergill, Heilmann 2, Bishop, Cobb, Simmons. Errors—McManus. Sacrifice hits—Gibson, Lamar. Two-base hits—Cobb, Heilmann 2, Gehringer. Home runs—Fothergill, Heilmann. Struck out—By Gibson 6; by Grove, 4. Bases on balls—Off Gibson, 2; Grove, 1. Left on bases—Detroit, 5; Philadelphia, 6. Time—1:44. Umpires—Van Graflan Connolly and Rowland.

HELEN JACOBS TAKES MATCH IN LOVE SETS

EAST HAMPTON, N. Y, July 19.—Miss Helen Jacobs, California's 18-year-old tennis champion, playing in her first eastern tournament Monday, defeated Mrs. D. L. Hopkins, of Baltimore, 6-0, 6-0. Two other matches were completed before rain interfered. Miss Penelope Anderson, of Richmond, Va., defeated Mrs. Frederick Schmitz, of New York, 6-2, 6-0, and Miss Josephine Crookshank, of California, won from Miss Gertrude Dwyer, 6-2, 6-4.

TIGER NOTES

HARRY HEILMANN got four for four yesterday. The four included two doubles, a single and a homerun. Heilmann, who was in a long slump at the start of the season and for the first two months of the pennant race, has caught his stride and anyone who believes that he is out of the race for the batting championship is mistaken. His average is better than .350 and going at his present pace he will soon be numbered among the first five. If precedent holds true then Heilmann will win the batting title this season. It is an odd year and he has always won in odd years—1921, 1923 and 1925.

• • •

Bob Grove is the strikeout leader of major league pitchers. He struck out four yesterday but Sam Gibson went him two better. Three of Grove's four strikeouts were scored over Lu Blue while Gibson struck out six different batters.

• • •

The series concludes this afternoon. Philadelphia must win today to break even. The Tigers must win to capture the series.

• • •

Heilmann was the only Tiger to get on base after the fourth inning. He got on twice, hitting a homerun and a two-bagger.

• • •

Al. Simmons had a tough time at bat yesterday. Up four times he failed to get a hit and struck out once.

• • •

Three scattered singles is all the hitting the Athletics did in the last eight innings.

• • •

Manush's running catch of Lamar's short fly in the ninth and Blue's dash to the grandstand for Boley's foul fly in the fifth, were the fielding features of the game.

• • •

Having watched THE Van Graflan umpire behind the plate another afternoon we won't have to see "Abie's Irish Rose" again for another year. Van Graflan would have been a great addition to the Cherry Sisters' act.

• • •

Eddie Collins and Zack Wheat both pinch-batted in the ninth and both lined to Heilmann. They ended an inglorious afternoon for the Athletics.

• • •

Woodall had a part in retiring each batter who was retired in the first inning. He was credited with two putouts and an assist.

• • •

When Umpire Rowland called Manush out at first in the opening inning nearly everybody on the Detroit team offered a protest. The kicking continued for five minutes, or more. Umpire Rowland probably felt that he was wrong but like the eminent Thomas Connolly he knew that he was official and he took advantage of it.

Hauser's Triple Starts It:

KANSAS CITY, July 19.—A triple by Hauser started an eighth-inning rally which netted Kansas City three runs and brought the team from behind to defeat Indianapolis 7 to 5 yesterday. It was Sheehan's thirteenth victory of the season.

INQUIRY STARTED INTO FIGHT TICKETS

Two Garden Treasurers Ordered To Appear.

NEW YORK, July 19.—(AP)—Two box office treasurers of Madison Square Garden, who have had sole charge of the sale and apportionment of tickets to the Dempsey-Sharkey fight for Thursday night, were ordered to appear today before United States Commissioner Cotter to tell what they know of ticket speculation.

Subpenas were issued for Benjamin Bennett and Joseph Doynton, because of reports that exorbitant prices were being charged by Broadway ticket agencies, and that the general public had been unable to purchase tickets for the better seats.

Charles H. Tuttle, United States attorney, who has been conducting an investigation into the manner in which New York theater treasurers and ticket agencies have been selling tickets, said that he had summoned the Madison Square Garden treasurers to learn, if possible, why the public had been unable to buy choice seats, and also, what means, if any, the Garden management had undertaken to protect the public from the "scalpers."

Boxing

CHICAGO—(AP)—The winner of the ten-round bout between Eddie Shea, the west-side Italian, and Joey Sangor of Milwaukee here Thursday night will be matched to meet Ray Chapman, the eastern featherweight.

Fights Last Night.

(By the Associated Press.)

NEW YORK—Paul Berlenbach defeated Bill Conley of Lewiston, Me., (10). Louis Gonzales, Tampa, Fla., beat Al Irving, New York (6). Marco Polo won from Jimmy Griffith (4).

JERSEY CITY, N. J.—Dickie Dixson, Fort Worth, knocked out Giovanni Salerno, Italy (4).

HOLYOKE, Mass.—Bobby Garcia, Baltimore, defeated Sammy Offerman, New York (10).

NEW YORK—Louis Gonzales, Tampa, Fla., lightweight, won a six-round decision over Al Irving, of New York. Marco Polo, Pittsburgh, won in four rounds from Jim Griffith, New York heavyweight.

TROY, N. Y.—Mickey Cangro, Staten Island welterweight, and Joey Silvers, of New York, went 12 rounds to a draw.

LYNN, Mass.—Ed Keeley, Boston heavyweight, was knocked out in the eighth round of a scheduled 10-round bout by Jack Gagnon, of New Bedford, Mass.

PHILADELPHIA—Joey Hatfield, 135, of Conshocken, Pa., won a decision over Al Winkler, 132, of Philadelphia—10 rounds.

HOLYOKE, Mass.—Bobby Garcia, Baltimore, defeated Sammy Osserman, New York, 10 rounds.

SCRANTON, Pa.—Billy Pollock, Scranton, advanced into the final round of the regional lightweight boxing tournament by defeating Pep O'Brien, of Old Forge, Pa., 10 rounds.

NEW YORK—Tommy Loughran, light-heavyweight challenger, of Philadelphia, will meet Tony Marullo at the Queensboro Stadium tonight. Loughran expects to use Marullo as a stepping stone to a bout with Jack Delaney.

TAKE DOUBLES TITLE

Helen Holtz and Loraine Walton defeated Mrs. Hall and Mrs. Andrews for the Municipal doubles tennis championship at Northwestern Field courts yesterday, 6-2, 6-0.

The Umpire

By H. G. Salsinger

THE LIGHTWEIGHT division of boxing has fallen into the same low and dull state as the welterweight division.

When a Sammy Mandell can parade as champion of the lightweights and when a Joe Dundee can pose as king of the welterweights, then the lightweight and welterweight classes must be in a bad way.

There is something to be said in favor of Mandell over Dundee: he is a fast and energetic boxer. Dundee is neither a boxer nor a slugger.

Mandell's weakness is the absolute lack of punch. He is the first claimant of the lightweight title who ever lacked a punch, unless you want to advance the name of Freddy Welsh. However, Welsh was a better boxer than Mandell and while Welsh was a light hitter he still carried more kick to his blows than Mandell.

• • •

THE PRESENT state of decay of these two divisions is regrettable. They have, in the past, delivered some of the greatest of ring entertainers.

Among the welters have been such boxing immortals as Tommy Ryan, Mysterious Billy Smith, Kid McCoy and Joe Wolcott. There were others, ranking not far below these four masters. Rube Ferns, Matty Mathews, Jack Britton, Ted Kid Lewis and certain contenders were performers of unusual skill and any of them several times as good as Dundee.

The lightweights have given such men as Jack McAuliffe, Kid Lavigne, Joe Gans and Benny Leonard, four of the best ringsters of all time and the best four lightweights in history. Ad. Wolgast, Bat Nelson, Willie Ritchie, Packey McFarland, Joe Rivers, Willie Jackson, Lew Tendler, Freddy Welsh, Charlie White and others were all considerably better than Mandell.

• • •

BENNY LEONARD retired from the ring because there were no more lightweights who could give him a match. There have been no worth-while lightweights since.

Leonard took the title with him. And, when he retired, he was still at the top of his fighting form.

Leonard, in that form, could fight a Mandell every night of the week, including Sundays, and put on two matinees besides. He could win every bout and win as he pleased. Mandell, with Leonard intent on finishing the bout as quickly as possible, would not be in the ring long enough to get used to the overhead lights.

• • •

A BOUT, advertised as a world's lightweight championship battle, was held in Detroit last Saturday night and caused no ripple of excitement.

Nobody became enthusiastic about the Mandell-McGraw match for the same reason that no one became enthusiastic over the Dundee-Latzo bout

No match in the welterweight or lightweight division can get anybody steamed up. These classes present a field of second and third-class performers with Mandell the best in either division because he is a fast boxer but while the best in either division he is still a few miles removed from the masterful Leonard, who not alone was a better boxer than Mandell but also a hard hitter and a much better ring general. There is no comparison between Leonard and Mandell.

• • •

THE ARGUMENT may be advanced that Johnny Dundee was a leading lightweight who fought Leonard more than a dozen times and managed to stay each time.

Dundee was not a knocker out. He was a boxer, not a fighter. The same thing can be said of Mandell but Dundee was a much better boxer than Mandell and a more intelligent one. He was a flashy boxer and Mandell lacks that flash. He is not a showman. Dundee was distinctly a showman. He could provide a clever and interesting show, when opposed to a man who showed as little skill as McGraw did against Mandell. He would have satisfied the crowd to some extent while winning; Mandell made the bout a dull and displeasing spectacle.

Mandell, unlike Dundee, "boxes over his head," as one expert expressed it. He keeps on slapping without any definite purpose behind the taps. His apparent object is to hit his opponent as many times as possible. He produces a monotonous routine.

• • •

AS FAR AS the several Leonard-Dundee meetings are concerned, they form chapters in the Leonard boxing career that may as well be overlooked. It would have been a shame had Leonard disposed of Dundee. He always managed to make an excellent foil for Leonard. They gave a fine show every time they met and it was profitable to have as many meetings as possible. They always drew well. They looked good. The crowd liked the act but there came a time when the act had run long enough. What is known as "wise" money was bet in abundance that Dundee would not come up for the eighth round in the proposed Dundee-Leonard fight in New Haven, Conn. The New Haven authorities prevented the bout and Leonard and Dundee never met again.

• • •

THE DINAN STADIUM program last Saturday night did nothing to make boxing more popular in Detroit. It was dull and boresome stuff. It left nearly everybody sore and disgruntled. The next attempt to stage a championship bout will be a financial failure if such an attempt is made this summer or in the autumn. Maybe, after the memory of last Saturday's fiasco dims, another attempt will draw but for the remainder of the outdoor season those who have any idea of giving another show, had better abandon the plan.

FINN SETS RECORD WINNING DECATHLON

Yrjola Breaks Mark Made by Osborn in Olympics.

HELSINGFORS, Finland, July 19.—(AP)—Paavo Yrjola, Finland's greatest all-round athlete, shattered the world's record for the decathlon yesterday in the Finnish track and field championships. He scored a total of 8,018.99 points for the 10-event test. Wrjola's performance is more than 300 points better than the present registered world's decathlon record of 7,710.775, made by Harold Osborn, of the Illinois Athletic Club, in winning the event for America in the 1924 Olympics at Paris.

The Finn also beat this mark last year with a point total of 7,831.03, but it has not yet been passed on by international authorities.

MACFARLANE ISSUES CHALLENGE TO HAGEN

Foreign-Born Golfers Want To Play Home-Breds.

NEW YORK, July 19. — (AP) — A special golf tournament of 72 holes, including singles and foursomes, between American professionals and foreign-born golfers living in the United States was in the making today.

Willie Macfarlane, professional at the Oak Ridge Club, Tuckahoe, N. Y., and national open champion in 1925, transmitted a challenge to Walter Hagen, captain of America's Ryder Cup team of home-breds.

Hagen's acceptance of the challenge in the name of the American-born professionals is believed assured.

Tiger Batting

	G	AB	R	H	HR	Pct.
Smith	11	6	2	3	1	.500
Neun	47	109	24	40	0	.367
Heilmann..	74	256	55	91	5	.355
Fothergill..	81	307	62	106	5	.345
Bassler....	45	124	14	42	0	.341
Gehringer..	64	231	54	78	3	.337
Woodall ..	48	125	13	39	0	.322
Manush ..	86	346	61	104	0	.300
Gibson ...	18	32	3	9	0	.281
Tavener ..	84	309	32	81	4	.281
Warner ...	62	312	33	58	0	.274
McManus..	86	353	48	96	1	.271
Wingo ...	42	149	25	38	0	.259
Collins ...	17	32	7	8	0	.250
Carroll ...	45	94	14	24	0	.248
Whitehill..	23	43	2	9	0	.209
Stoner ...	19	40	2	7	0	.175
Ruble	19	27	6	4	0	.148
Hankins ..	16	7	0	1	0	.143
Shea	15	37	2	5	0	.135

Western League.

Lincoln 9, Des Moines 5.
Omaha 19, Denver 7.
Tulsa 2, Wichita 1.
Oklahoma City 8, Amarillo 6.

The MINORS

American Association.

	W	L	Pct		W	L	Pct
Toledo...	54	34	.614	St. Paul..	48	43	.527
Milwauke	51	38	.573	Indianapls	38	52	.422
Kan. City	50	38	.568	Columbus.	36	54	.400
Minnaplis	49	44	.527	Louisville	36	59	.379

Louisville 12, Milwaukee 10.
Kansas City 7, Indianapolis 5.
St. Paul 6, Toledo 5.
Minneapolis 12, Columbus 6.

International League.

	W	L	Pct		W	L	Pct
Buffalo..	60	33	.645	Toronto..	48	46	.511
Syracuse.	60	38	.612	Rochester	45	48	.484
Baltimore	53	41	.564	Jersey City	42	52	.447
Newark..	52	45	.536	Reading...	20	77	.206

Buffalo 14, Newark 4.
Syracuse 6, Baltimore 5.
Rochester 11, Reading 2.
Jersey City 3, Toronto 0.

Southern Association.

Mobile 12, Little Rock 8.
Chattanooga 10, Memphis 0.
Only games played.

Texas League.

Wichita Falls 12, San Antonio 3.
Beaumont 2, Shreveport 0.
Houston 6, Fort Worth 0.
Only three games.

WIN IN ELEVENTH INNING

MILWAUKEE, Wis., July 19.—Riffe's triple scoring Caffney and Holley's single bringing in Riffe broke up a struggle between Milwaukee and Louisville in the eleventh inning yesterday and gave the Colonels a 12-10 victory. Riconda hit a home run for the Brewers.

WITH Starr Matthews

Oriental Hope Wins at Timonium

CHARACTER QUALITY AMERICA FIRST ENTERPRISE ACCURACY

Baltimore American Sports

AN AMERICAN PAPER FOR THE AMERICAN PEOPLE

THURSDAY, SEPTEMBER 8, 1927

RUTH'S 5 HOMERS IN 3 GAMES EQUAL MARK

Giants Half a Game From Top As Pirates Lose

THERE are many persons in these United States who believe that Babe Ruth will break his 1921 record for home runs. I hope so.

The Bambino, who came off the lots of Baltimore, has made forty-nine circuit smashes so far and has twenty games to go. If he can wallop eleven over the fence before the curtain falls a new chapter will be written in baseball's history about the greatness of this lad from St. Mary's Industrial School.

Experts, students of the game and fans differ as to the brightest star of baseball. Some say Honus Wagner, some say Ty Cobb, but I believe Babe Ruth has won more games for his team since he struck his real stride with the Boston Red Sox than any man ever did. And, after all, results stand for something. A batting record, thrilling slides, an unexpected theft, a great fielding stunt, marvelous pitching all count for much but it is an old saying that "As Babe Ruth goes, so go the Yanks."

That expression never would have become so popular, so often used, if it were not true that Babe Ruth continually turned the tide for the Highlanders. To me, it is an admmission that Babe Ruth is the most valuable man in baseball to his team. That being so, I cannot help thinking he deserves to be rated the greatest player of all time, not only as a box office attraction, which is conceded, but as a man who wins games.

* * *

Honus Wagner won many a game by his play in all departments, and so has Ty Cobb, but I doubt if either had such a depressing effect upon the opposing team as Ruth has. With one blow Ruth has turned defeat into victory so often that even wise men of the mound like Grover Cleveland Alexander prefer to pass him in a pinch. Wise old Alex did that very thing in the last World's Series and I've a notion that he used his bean.

* * *

With forty-nine home runs, Babe Ruth has come back. There's no doubt about it now. A year and a half ago many experts were relegating him to the rear ranks. He seemed to them a "hollow shell," even as Jack Dempsey did to those who witnessed his defeat by Gene Tunney, but last year the Bambino returned to show he had some of his old clouting powers left. This season he rises once again to the throne as Sultan of Swat, whether or not he establishes a new record.

Babe Ruth is a great ballplayer. He may not read the sort of literature selected by Gene Tunney, Eddie Collins and others, but, like Jack Dempsey, he has the punch. In addition, he has a keen knowledge of baseball. He may not be a mental giant off the field, but he's far above most of the college men in baseball brains.

* * *

Some time ago I picked the Giants to win the National League pennant. A friend of mine hastened to me recently with the information that New York has eight double-headers, all from home. When I made the prediction last February, I didn't have that in mind, of course, but I can see no reason at this writing to change. I prefer to stand on the original prediction.

My friend pointed out that the Giants' pitchers are weak, but I felt a couple of weeks ago that the Cubs' twirlers would crack under the strain. That Chicago now is in fourth place is not surprising. That really is about where the Cubs belong. It also may be remembered that I served notice that the Cards were dangerous. Their pitchers are capable veterans, so if they fight it out with the Giants or the Pirates, do not be amazed.

* * *

As a matter of fact the Pirates may blow at any minute. Their pitchers, too, have been called upon to do a lot of extra work. If it were not for the wonderful hurling of Carman Hill I imagine the Bucs would have been out of the hunt a long while ago. So, when everything is considered, the pitchers of all four clubs probably are feeling the strain of this sensational race.

Ravens' Stars Return to Grid

COLLEGE PARK, Md., Sept. 7.—Gus Crothers, regrlar guard, and Charlie Pugh, speedy halfback and clever drop-kicker, have joined the University of Maryland football squad, leaving only John Leatherman of last year's varsity aggregation to get into uniform.

Ed Tenney, quarterback, who was out of the game last season on account of an appendicitis operation, and Bill Heintz, tackle, will report Friday.

WANTS TO BOOK GAME

The Lyon Club of the J. E. A. would like to book a game with a fourteen year old team, address Dave Greenburg, 2029 East Pratt street.

Costly Boots By Bucs Give Reds Victory In Last Game

Harris, Barnhart and Smith Make Errors; Wright's Home Run Is Wasted.

PITTSBURGH, Sept. 7—(A. P.). Cincinnati gave the pennant aspirations of the Pittsburgh Pirates another jolt today by taking the odd game of a five-game series, six to five. With the second place Giants idle, the defeat narrowed the Pirates' hold on first place to a half game.

Hill, who started for Pittsburgh was wild and was relieved by Dawson in the eighth. Costly fielding fumbles also figured largely in the Cincinnati scoring.

MUFF STARTS IT.

The Reds scored three runs in the third inning on two walks, a double by Dressen, a sacrifice fly and Harris' muff of Wright's throw on Bressler's grounder.

Cincinnati put two more runs across in the next inning on a single, another walk and a second two-base hit by Dressen ,the second run going in on Barnhart's low return to Traynor of Dressen's hit.

The visitors' sixth run was scored in the sixth on a single by Sukeforth, a stolen base, Smith's wild throw and Dressen's sacrifice fly.

WRIGHT HITS HOMER.

The Pirates were held scoreless until the third, when two runs were counted on a walk, singles by the Waner brothers, and a double steal on which Lloyd Waner scored. Wright's double and Traynor's single added another in the sixth. Wright hit for the circuit in the eighth with the bases empty.

Pittsburgh attempted a comeback in the last inning when Harris tripled with one out and scored on Smith's sacrifice fly. Brickell was sent in to pinch hit for Dawson, but lined out to Pittenger.

Lloyd Waner returned to middle field after having been out of the game since Monday with a split finger.

CINCINNATI.	AB.	R.	H.	O.	A.
Dres'n,3.	3	1	2	2	2
Purdy,m.	5	1	1	5	0
Pipp,1...	4	0	1	10	0
Bress'r,l	4	0	0	2	0
Allen,r..	5	0	1	1	0
Ford,s..	3	0	0	4	4
Pitt'er,2.	4	1	2	2	3
Suke'th,c	2	3	1	1	0
Lucas,p..	2	0	0	0	1
Totals.	32	6	8	27	10

PITTSBURGH.	AB.	R.	H.	O.	A.
LWa'r,m	4	1	1	6	0
Barnh't,l	4	0	0	3	0
PWa'r,r.	4	0	2	0	0
Wright,s	4	2	2	2	6
Tray'r,3.	4	0	1	2	3
Gra'm,2.	4	0	0	1	4
Harris,1.	4	1	1	9	0
Smith,c.	3	0	1	3	1
Hill,p...	1	1	0	1	1
1 Como'y	1	0	0	0	0
Daw'n,p.	0	0	0	0	0
2 Bric'll.	1	0	0	0	0
Totals.	34	5	8	27	15

1 Batted for Hill in seventh.
2 Batted for Dawson in ninth.

SCORE BY INNINGS.

Cincinnati........ 0 0 3 2 0 1 0 0 0—6
Pittsburgh........ 0 0 2 0 0 1 0 1 1—5

Errors—Barnhart, Harris, Smith. Two-base hits—Dressen (2), Allen, Wright, Pittenger. Three-base hit—Harris. Home run — Wright. Stolen bases — L. Waner, P. Waner, Pittenger, Sukeforth. Sacrifices—Pipp, Dressen, Bressler, Smith. Double play—Grantham, Wright to Harris. Left on bases — Cincinnati, 8; Pittsburgh, 4. Bases on balls—Off Hill, 5; off Lucas 1; off Dawson, 1. Struck out—By Hill, 2. Hits—Off Hill, 7 in 7 innings; off Dawson, 1 in 2. Losing pitcher—Hill. Umpires—Wilson, Quigley and Pfirman.

BETTY NUTHALL IS TENDERED BIG CIVIC RECEPTION

By Universal Service.
(Special Cable Dispatch.)

RICHMOND, England, Sept. 7.

BETTY NUTHALL, pretty British tennis prodigy, was tendered a civic reception upon her arrival home today by the Mayor of Richmond, civil officials and other notables.

Throngs flocked to the Town Hall, where Mayor Hewitt presented the comely girl athlete with a silver ros ebowl. Betty acknowledged the gift with a smile and a pretty little speech. "I thank you ever so much for the lovely reception you have given me tonight. I think it is awfully nice. I enjoyed my trip to America, but I am glad to be back.

Among the notables to greet Betty were Counsellor Arthur of Richmond; the Mayor and Mayoress of Kingston, the town were Betty was born, and Sir Newton Moore, memmer of Pallament.

THE AMERICAN'S SELECTIONS FOR TIMONIUM TODAY

By CLARENCE L. SMITH.

FIRST RACE—Double Tip, Church Bramton, Cassette.
SECOND—El 'Oudiane, Rigel, Pichonne.
THIRD — Appellate, Evelyn Sawyer, Courser.
FOURTH — Little Papoose, May Roma, Toiler.
FIFTH—Oblique, Rock Light, Lieutenant Farrell.
SIXTH—Lisab. Castilla, Dr. Charles Wells.
SEVENTH—Who Knows Me, King Albert, Bluemont.
BEST BET—Appellate.

Cards Split, But Gain On Loop Leader

By Associated Press.

ST. LOUIS, Mo., Sept. 7.—The third-place St. Louis Cardinals and the fourth-place Chicago Cubs divided a double-header here today, the Cardinals taking the first, 6 to 2, and the Cubs copping the second, 8 to 4.

The world's champions gained ground on Pittsburgh, in first place, as the Pirates lost to Cincinnati. The Cardinals are now two games behind first place and one and one-half games behind New York, in second place.

The Cardinals swatted Carlson and Nehf for thirteen safeties in the first game, including a home run by Bell with two on in the sixth. Orsatti, recently obtained from Houston, got four hits. Frankhouse pitched well until the eighth, when he was relieved by Haines after walking two men.

The Cubs batted Rhem out in the fourth inning of the second game after he had allowed three runs. Wilson, Chicago centerfielder, hit his twenty-fourth and twenty-fifth homers of the season in the seventh and ninth innings. No one was on base either time.

CHICAGO.	AB.	R.	H.	O.	A.
Ada's,3,s	5	0	0	0	5
Engli'h,s	3	0	1	1	1
Yoter,3..	1	0	0	0	2
Heat'e,r.	4	0	0	2	0
Steph'n,l	3	0	1	2	0
Wils'n,m	3	1	2	4	0
Grimm,1	4	0	1	12	0
Hart't,c.	3	0	0	3	0
Beck,2...	4	1	1	0	3
Carls'n,p	2	0	0	0	0
Nehf,p...	0	0	0	0	1
1 Webb..	1	0	1	0	0
2 Scott...	1	0	1	0	0
Totals.	34	2	8	24	12

ST. LOUIS.	AB.	R.	H.	O.	A.
Ors'ti,m.	5	0	4	3	0
Bot'ley,1	4	0	0	10	1
Frisch,2.	4	1	0	2	5
Clark,r..	3	1	1	4	0
Holm,r..	0	0	0	0	0
Hafey,l..	3	2	2	3	0
LBell,3..	4	1	2	1	0
O'Far'l,c	4	0	1	1	0
Schu'le,s	4	0	1	2	5
Fran'e,p.	3	0	2	1	2
Haines,p.	1	0	0	0	0
3 Blades.	1	1	0	0	0
Totals.	36	6	13	27	13

1 Batted for Carlson in seventh.
2 Batted for Nehf in ninth.
3 Batted for Clark in seventh.

SCORE BY INNINGS.

Chicago........ 0 0 0 1 0 0 1 0 0—2
St. Louis........ 0 0 0 0 0 3 3 0 x—6

Errors—Yoter; Frisch, Frankhouse. Two-base hits—Schuble, Scott. Three-base hits—Beck. Home run—Bell. Sacrifice—Bottomley. Double plays—Beck, English and Grimm; Frisch, Schuble and Bottomley; Schuble, Frisch and Bottomley. Left on bases—Chicago, 9; St. Louis, 8. Bases on balls—Off Carlson, 1; off Frankhouse 4. Struck out—By Carlson, 1; by Nehf, 1; by Frankhouse, 1. Hits—Off Carlson, 9 in 6 innings; off Nehf, 4 in 2; off Frankhouse, 7 in 7; off Haines, 1 in 2. Winning pitcher — Frankhouse. Losing pitcher — Carlson. Umpires—Klem, Reardon and McCormick.

SECOND GAME.

CHICAGO.	AB.	R.	H.	O.	A.
Adams,s	5	0	1	0	2
Pick,3...	5	1	1	1	2
Heat'e,r.	4	0	2	2	0
Steph'n,l	4	0	0	3	0
Wil'n,m.	2	3	2	2	0
Grimm,1.	4	1	1	14	0
Gonz's,c	2	1	1	4	1
Beck,2..	3	2	1	1	7
Blake,p.	4	0	1	0	0
Totals.	33	8	10	27	12

ST. LOUIS.	AB.	R.	H.	O.	A.
Orsa'i,m	4	0	2	2	0
Bot'ley,1	3	0	0	15	0
Frisch,2.	3	0	1	5	5
Clark,r..	3	0	0	3	0
Hafey,l.	3	1	1	0	0
LBell,3..	4	0	0	0	2
O'Far'l,c	2	0	1	2	0
Torpo'r,s	1	1	0	0	0
Schu'le,s	2	0	0	0	5
Schulte,c	2	1	1	0	0
Rhem,p..	1	0	0	0	1
Ring,p..	0	0	0	0	1
Reinh't,p	2	1	1	0	0
1 Sout'th	1	0	0	0	0
Totals.	31	4	7	27	14

1 Batted for Ring in fifth.

SCORE BY INNINGS.

Chicago........ 1 0 0 3 2 0 1 0 1—8
St. Louis........ 0 1 0 0 0 0 3 0 0—4

Errors—Clark, Schuble. Home runs—Beck ,Wilson (2). Sacrifices—Wilson, Bottomley, Frisch, Gonzales. Double plays—Schuble to Frisch, to Bottomley (3); Adams to Beck, to Grimm. Left on bases—Chicago, 7; St. Louis, 6. Bases on balls—Off Blake, 4; off Rhem, 2; off Ring, 3; off Reinhart, 1. Struck out—By Blake, 4; by Rhem, 1; by Ring, 1. Hits—Off Rhem, 7 in 3⅓ innings; off Ring, 1 in 1⅔; off Reinhart, 2 in 4. Hit by pitcher—By Rhem (Stephenson). Losing pitcher—Rhem. Umpires—Reardon, McCormick and Klem.

Ty Cobb On Mound In Exhibition Game

ALLENTOWN, Pa., Sept. 7—(A. P.). — Ty Cobb pitched the last three innings of an exhibition game here today in which the Philadelphia Athletics defeated Allentown, 7 to 4. Cobb allowed only two hits in three innings, but one of these was a home run by Billy Klucharich, an eighteen-year-old youngster, in the final round.

										R.	H.	E.
Athletics...	0	5	0	0	1	0	0	1	0	7	12	1
Allentown...	1	0	0	0	2	0	0	0	1	4	9	0

Batteries—Powers, Cobb and Perkins; Weiser, Stauffer, Hendrix and Slemmer.

Hitting in His Best Stride

BABE RUTH.

Oriental Hope Wins Feature at Timonium

TIMONIUM RACE TRACK, Md., Sept. 7.—Oriental Hope, five-year-old daughter of Bard of Hope-Oriental Star, belonging to Mrs. C. C. Smithson of Washington, accounted for the mile and one-sixteenth of the fourth race, looked upon as the star event of a card made up of claiming events. It was Oriental Hope's second victory of the meeting.

The victory enabled form players to register their fourth consecutive victory of the afternoon, so it was not a bit surprising that Jockey Albert Hunt was given a rousing reception when he galloped Oriental Hope back to the winner's circle.

ON TOP ALL WAY.

Hunt took Oriental Hope right to the front as soon as Starter James Milton dispatched the field of seven. However, Hunt had to hand ride his mount for three-quarters of a mile, as King Albert and Bellfont both tried to wrest the lead from the Washington-owned mare.

Turning for home, Hunt let Oriental Hope do her best and she raced past the judges' stand an easy winner over F. J. Boyle's Bell font, an outsider in the wagering. M. J. Cremen's Zeod slipped into the show money.

BEA NABS FIRST.

Form players started out on the right foot when they backed W. McNair's Bea into favoritism, and the two-year-old daughter of Sporting Blood-Satire just lasted to whip J. Booker's Rout Step.

The last named was on the outside of the winner all the way and this cost her the race by half a length. Third money went to Irish Lord, belonging to J. P. McGovern of Baltimore, who was the medium of a big play right at post time, but who broke slowly.

A million dollar stretch ride by Danny Mergler is all that enabled H. Hoffman's Lemnos, the favorite, to win the six furlong sprint of the second event.

RUSHED INTO LEAD.

Rushed into the lead at the break, Lemnos was kept going at a fast clip by Ima Vamp, and then when Somerset challenged from the head of the stretch home, he caught a tiring pacemaker. However, Mergler booted and whipped with all his old-time ability to have Lemnos home a short head in front of F. Laux's gelding Somerset, who was an easy winner of the place over Janon Fisher's Ima Vamp, who ran an improved race under her light impost.

SUBTLE WINS THIRD.

Players of form horses registered their third consecutive victory of the afternoon when J. B. Key's Subtle, five-year-old daughter of Huon-Niobe, was a handy winner of the six and one-half furlong sprint, offered as the third race.

D. Emery, leading winning rider at this meeting, took pace for half a mile from Button Bright and Dream Maker, but going down the back stretch, Emery sent Subtle on top, and the mare was home by three lengths in advance of C. L. Whiting's Dream Maker. The latter was driving at the end to stall off J. C. Bennett's Button Bright.

INTERNATIONAL LEAGUE

STANDING OF CLUBS.

	Won	Lost	Pct.
Buffalo	105	51	.673
Syracuse	95	58	.621
Newark	83	71	.540
Toronto	80	72	.527
BALTIMORE	76	75	.503
Rochester	77	78	.497
Jersey City	62	93	.400
Reading	35	117	.230

RESULTS YESTERDAY.

BALTIMORE, 9-3; Reading, 6-6.
Toronto, 7; Syracuse, 6.
Buffalo, 12-8; Rochester, 1-0.
Newark, 6-4; Jersey City, 1-0.

GAMES TODAY.

Jersey City at BALTIMORE.
Reading at Newark.
Syracuse at Toronto.
Other clubs not scheduled.

AMERICAN ASSOCIATION

Indianapolis, 6; Columbus, 3.
Toledo, 14; Louisville, 1.
Milwaukee-Minneapolis; rain.
Kansas City-St. Paul; rain.

SOUTH ATLANTIC LEAGUE

Augusta, 5-5; Macon, 4-1.
Columbia, 8; Charlotte, 6.
Knoxville, 10; Asheville, 0.
Greenville, 7; Spartanburg, 2.

NATIONAL LEAGUE

STANDING OF CLUBS.

	Won	Lost	Pct.
Pittsburgh	76	53	.589
New York	75	53	.586
St. Louis	73	54	.575
Chicago	75	57	.568
Cincinnati	60	68	.469
Boston	55	75	.430
Brooklyn	56	76	.424
Philadelphia	48	84	.364

RESULTS YESTERDAY.

Cincinnati, 6; Pittsburgh, 5.
St. Louis, 6-4; Chicago, 2-8.
Phila., 3-1; Brooklyn, 2-9.
Other clubs not scheduled.

GAMES TODAY.

No games scheduled.

VIRGINIA LEAGUE

Norfolk, 12; Portsmouth, 10.
Petersburg, 12; Richmond, 2.
Kinston, 5; Wilson, 4.

SOUTHERN ASSOCIATION

Atlanta, 5; Birmingham, 2.
Little Rock, 8; Chattanooga, 3.
Only games scheduled.

Gene Nurses Sore Eye and Finds Climate Big Handicap

TUNNEY CAMP, LAKE VILLA, Ill., Sept. 7—(A. P.).—Nursing a cracked eye lid, inflicted by Chuck Wiggins' head in a sparring bout, Gene Tunney declared a holiday today and visited with friends across the Lake Villa. The vacation will continue through tomorrow, with boxing workouts probable for both Friday and Saturday.

Gene exposed the cut over his right eye, before leaving camp for the day and assured newspaper men it would heal completely by the end of the week.

SIMILAR ACCIDENT.

Just a year ago this time while training for the first battle with Jack Dempsey, Gene said he suffered a similar accident without harmful results. No stitches were necessary to close the wound.

The oppressive heat bothered the heavyweight champion today and brought him back from his early morning road work in a lather of perspiration. The title-holder is finding difficulty adjusting himself to the change in climate from the cool, thin air of Speculator , N. Y., where Tunney trained for five months in the foothills of the Adirondack mountains before settling down here to the final stage of preparation for his return match with Dempsey at Soldier Field, September 22.

OVER 192 POUNDS

With the bout but two weeks away, Gene scaled slightly over 192 pounds today, almost six more than he weighed for the battle at Philadelphia last fall. The champion's fine condition and lack of excess poundage have convinced observers that Tunney cannot pull himself below the 190-pound notch within the next two weeks.

Dempsey To Put On Togs Again For Active Work

LINCOLN FIELDS, Crete, Ill., Sept. 7—(A. P.).—After a forty-eight-hour lay off, Jack Dempsey will put on his ring togs tomorrow to resume training for his world's heavyweight championship with Gene Tunney.

The boxing tomorrow and Friday will be private, except to newspaper correspondents, but the former title-holder may appear before the public on Saturday, because the Kickapoo Indians are going to make Dempsey a chief on that day. Tom Gibbons was made a chief by the Blackfeet at Shelby before he fought Dempsey, and the latter wants to catch up on the St. Paul veterans.

Dempsey, as a result of his loafing for two days, was peppy and cheerful and no doubt will be full of fight when he goes against his sparring mates tomorrow. Manager Flynn said the boxing will be of a more serious nature from now on, with light, fast opponents alternating with the heavyweights.

There was no activity around Dempseys' camp today. He loafed around all morning, giving up his road work.

Navy Gridders Again Scrimmage

ANNAPOLIS, Md., Sept. 7.—For the second time during the present season the Naval Academy varsity eleven engaged in a scrimmage this afternoon, lining up against squad B for a session, devoted almost entirely to offensive work.

Lloyd, Clifton Welchel and Schuber were in the backfield most of the time. While the first backfield combination is by no means settled, the continued use of this quartet indicates that the coaches have their eyes on them as strong candidates for regular berths.

Prior to the scrimmage, the backs were given a lot of coaching in kicking and handling the ball. Tom Hamilton, last year's back, directed the kickers, while Harry Caldwell, another back, took charge of the receiving end. Some of the kickers are Lloyd, Miller, Clifton, Nieman and Woerner.

SEAT DIAGRAM FOR ARENA TO BE DISPLAYED

By GENE FOWLER,
Universal Service Staff Correspondent.

CHICAGO, Sept. 7.

TEX RICKARD'S mysterious committee on seats for the battle of the bird's-eye view tonight promised to produce a diagram of Soldiers' Field. The plat of the Stadium of magnificent distances, it was announced, would be ready for publication on September 18. The fight, if any, is scheduled for the evening of September 22.

In all the shuddering situation, wherein 60,000 ringside seats out of a total of 161,000 parking spaces for the hips are to be dispensed at $40 a toss, the diagram phase stood out like a discord in Walter Damrosch's ear. No matter how much the public clamored for a look at a diagram before buying one of the distant fortified ringside seats, Rickard's committee was firm.

Birds Share Double Bill With Reading

READING, Pa., Sept. 7.—The Orioles and Reading split a double bill this afternoon, the Birds winning the opener, 9 to 6, and the Aces capturing the seven-inning night cap, 6 to 3.

The Birds were ahead up to the sixth inning of the night cap, but the Aces landed on Fred Vincent and crashed out five runs to win easily.

Woodgie hurled for the Aces. The Birds left after the game for Baltimore. They will be idle at home tomorrow and Friday, but will oppose Jersey City in double bills on Saturday and Sunday.

BALTIMORE.	AB.	R.	H.	O.	A.
Arch'n,m	5	1	3	2	0
Gaud'te,r	6	0	0	3	1
Few'er,2	5	1	2	1	5
Porter,l.	5	2	3	2	0
Maisel,3.	4	2	2	1	1
Urb'ski,s	2	1	1	2	5
Brunier,1	5	1	3	10	1
Freitag,c	4	1	1	5	0
Ch'ers,p.	5	0	0	1	0
Earn'w,p	0	0	0	0	0
Totals.	41	9	15	27	13

READING.	AB.	R.	H.	O.	A.
Sewell,3.	5	2	3	0	4
Crane,s.	4	0	1	1	4
Doug'y,l.	5	1	2	5	0
Ferrell,r	5	0	1	1	0
Hawks,1	4	0	1	11	0
Jar'tt,m	4	0	0	4	0
Wilkie,2.	4	2	2	4	3
Davis,c.	4	1	2	1	1
Roup'h,p	3	0	1	0	1
1 Oesch'r	1	0	0	0	0
Totals.	39	6	13	27	13

1 Batted for Rouprich in ninth.

SCORE BY INNINGS.

BALTIMORE..... 0 0 5 0 1 0 2 1 0—9
Reading......... 2 0 0 1 0 0 0 0 3—6

Errors—Chambers; Wilkie (2). Two base hits—Brunier (2), Freitag, Maisel, Archdeacon, Davis, Sewell, Crane, Porter. Three-base hit—Wilkie. Home run—Porter. Sacrifices—Urbanski (2). Left on bases—Baltimore, 11; Reading, 7. Bases on balls—Off Rouprich, 5; off Chambers, 1. Struck out—By Chambers, 4. Umpires—Meyers and Gaston.

SECOND GAME.

BALTIMORE.	AB.	R.	H.	O.	A.
Arc'n,m.	3	0	1	2	0
Gaud'e,r	3	0	0	4	0
Fews'r,2	2	0	2	2	1
Porter,l.	4	0	1	1	0
Maisel,3.	4	0	0	0	2
Urb'ki,s	3	2	3	1	0
Bruni'r,1	3	1	2	6	0
Lake,c..	3	0	1	1	1
Vinc't,p.	2	0	0	1	0
Ear'w,p.	0	0	0	0	0
Totals.	27	3	10	18	4

READING.	AB.	R.	H.	O.	A.
Sewell,3.	3	0	0	0	1
Crane,s.	4	0	2	2	3
Doug'y,l.	4	1	2	1	0
Ferrell,r	3	1	1	0	0
Hawks,1.	2	1	1	11	0
Jar'tt,m.	2	0	0	3	1
Wilke,2.	2	1	0	3	5
Seng'k,c.	1	1	0	1	1
Davis,c..	1	1	1	0	0
Wood'e,p	1	0	1	0	2
Totals.	23	6	8	21	13

SCORE BY INNINGS.

BALTIMORE......... 0 0 0 2 0 1 0—3
Reading......... 0 0 1 0 0 5 x—6

Errors—Sewell, Woodgie. Two-base hits—Fewster (2), Hawks. Three-base hits—Brunier, Woodgie, Urbanski. Stolen bases—Porter, Davis. Sacrifices—Woodgie (2), Fewster, Vincent, Jarrett. Double plays—Wilke to Hawks; Crane to Wilke, to Hawks. Left on bases — Baltimore, 8; Reading, 6. Bases on balls—Off Woodgie, 3; off Vincent, 2; off Earnshaw, 2. Hits—Off Vincent, 6 in 5 innings; off Earnshaw, 2 in 1. Losing pitcher—Vincent. Umpires—Haston and Meyers.

FAIRFIELD DAIRYMEN WANT SUNDAY GAMES

The Fairfield Farms Dairy baseball team is without games for Sunday and would like to schedule a strong club having grounds. Call Milton C. Greer, Liberty 3404.

AMERICANS WIN IN INTERNATIONAL ATHLETIC GAMES

By Associated Press.

DRESDEN, Germany, Sept. 7.

RAY CONGER, Illinois Athletic Club, captured the 1500-meter run in 4 minutes 12.9 seconds here today at the international track meet.

Henry H. Cummings, Newark Athletic Club (America), won the 100-meter sprint in 10.6 seconds; Jackson V. Scholz, New York Athletic Club, was third. Cummings also won the 200-meter in 21.7 seconds, with Scholz second.

Ruth Must Make 11 More In 20 Games To Beat 1921

Swat King Now Four Ahead of Gehrig; His Bat Trims Red Sox.

AMERICAN LEAGUE

STANDING OF CLUBS.

	Won	Lost	Pct.
New York	93	40	.699
Philadelphia	76	56	.576
Detroit	70	61	.534
Washington	69	61	.531
Chicago	62	68	.477
Cleveland	59	73	.447
St. Louis	54	77	.412
Boston	42	89	.320

RESULTS YESTERDAY.

New York, 12; Boston, 10.
Other clubs not scheduled.

GAMES TODAY.

Cleveland at Boston.
Chicago at Washington.
Detroit at Philadelphia.
St. Louis at New York.

BOSTON, Sept. 7.—Babe Ruth, the Baltimore Bambino who earns $70,000 a year, batted the Yankees to a 12 to 10 victory today over the Red Sox and drew closer to his famous home run record of fifty-nine in 1921, when he clouted two balls out of the lot. This pair, added to the three he made yesterday in the double-header, gave five in two days and placed his total at forty-nine. If he continues at this pace, he will break his old mark, for he has twenty more games to play and eleven more homers to make to set a new record. At this same stage of the 1921 race Ruth had made fifty-four homer so he now is five behind in that respect.

TIES FIRST RECORD.

By making five homers in three consecutive games, Ruth tied a record first made in 1882 by Mike Mildoon, of Cleveland. Babe also equalled this performance in 1921. Old Mike (King) Kelly turned the trick for Chicago in 1885 and Ken Williams duplicated it in 1922.

PLEASES 12,000 FANS.

More interesting, at this particular time, however, is the fact that Ruth now has a lead of four circuit clouts over Lou Gehrig, his "busting twin," who has given him such a hectic race this season.

The 12,000 fans, attracted to the

Continued on Page 12, Column 1.

CHARACTER QUALITY AMERICA FIRST ENTERPRISE ACCURACY

Los Angeles Examiner Sports

AN AMERICAN PAPER FOR THE AMERICAN PEOPLE THE GREAT NEWSPAPER OF THE GREAT SOUTHWEST

FRIDAY, SEPTEMBER 30, 1927 CC SECTION I—PAGE

RUTH EQUALS RECORD

Wham! Wham! The Bam's a Wow

TWO LUSCIOUS HOME RUNS and his record of 1921 was tied by that great swat Sultan Babe Ruth yesterday when he pickled the pill for his fifty-eighth and fifty-ninth homers of the season. He still has two days to get another and break the mark.—International Newsreel photo.

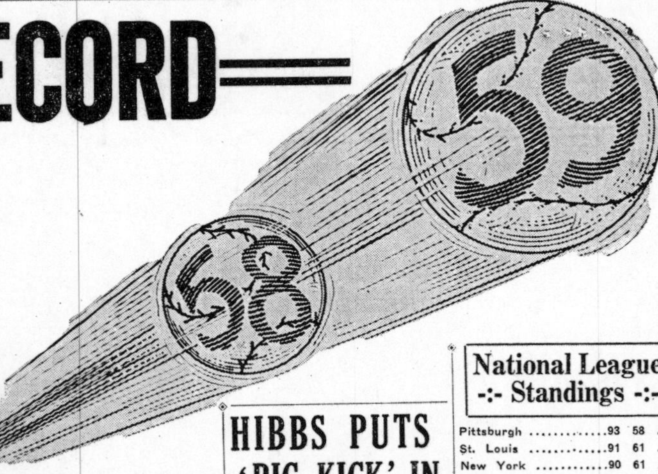

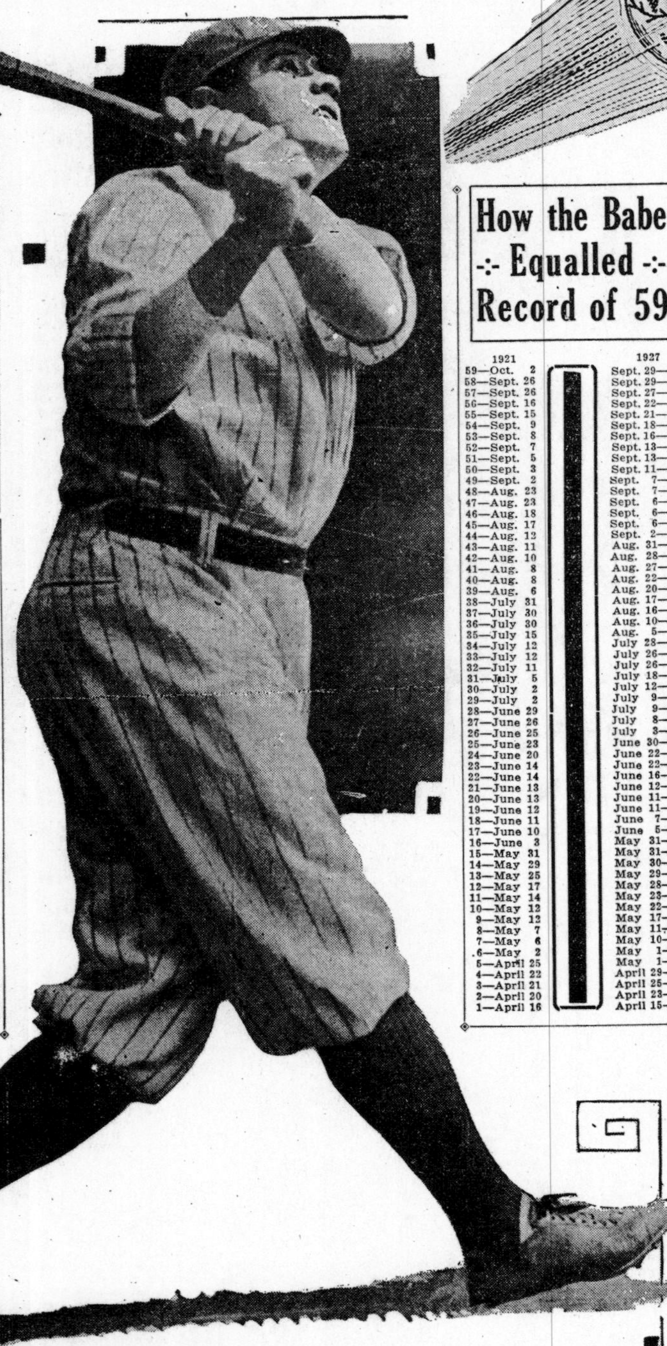

WHAT NOTS

by Mark Kelly

REMEMBER Johnny Mack Brown, that good-looking halfback of Alabama's Crimson Tide who two years ago against Washington ran the Huskies' ends bow-legged and played a big part in Washington's downfall?

The boy had the speed of an antelope and the fight of a tiger. He took more rough handling than a house-mover can give a baby grand and kept bouncing back for more. Once, I recall, George Wilson stood Mr. Brown on his head near the side-lines, twisted his leg and gave him quite a tackle. Two plays later Mr.

Johnny Mack Brown Back in Limelight

George Wilson was present but not voting.

Johnny Mack Brown made the All-Southern twice and that he failed of All-American rating is due to the fact that the boys selecting that mythical organization know little of their geography and believe that the South is just a place to sing mammy songs about.

* * *

When he finished his collegiate term Johnny Mack Brown was taken in hand by Champ Pickens, the granddaddy of Dixie football.

"With that classic pan of yours, my boy, we'll go to Hollywood and bust into those pictures. I'm your manager," says Mr. Champ Pickens, who forthwith made the grade.

Metro-Goldwyn-Mayer accepted Johnny Mack Brown at one-fifth of Champ Pickens' rating, and even that percentage was unusually high.

* * *

JOHNNY MACK BROWN made good.

As a cinema player he bids fair to equal his football brilliance. It is rarely that a "green pea" ascends with the speed that Johnny Mack Brown has generated. He was cast in the leading male role opposite Miss Marion Davies in her starring picture, "The Fair Co-ed," a college picture which is said to be one of Miss Davies' very best cinema attainments. The picture is on exhibition next week at the Metropolitan.

And Johnny Made Good in Pictures

Of a modest, likeable demeanor Johnny Mack Brown was given every opportunity to "make" himself.

* * *

Recently Al Green was casting for a new picture and somebody told him that Johnny Mack Brown would make a good leading man for the cast.

Mr. Green yowled, "No experience," but reluctantly

consented to look at some of Mr. Brown's work in rushes of "The Fair Co-ed."

"Quit cranking," he yelled when they were halfway through. "I've seen enough —get me that baby at any cost."

And when the Fox folks tried to borrow Johnny Mack Brown from Metro-Goldwyn-Mayer they were politely given the bird. Mr. Brown's services were not for hire.

* * *

I BELIEVE that it was "The Fair Co-ed" which gave several other football players a lot of summer work and winter spending money. I know that Capt. Morley Drury of U. S. C. was given a minor role at fat pay and Jess Hibbs and other U. S. C. stars are in the cast. If you want to get a closeup of your favorite football player such as you cannot get on the football field where the boys wear gas masks, get a load of that picture next week. They say it really has college atmosphere and is faithful to detail in every regard. Most of the campus scenes were taken at Pomona College in Claremont.

Other Stars Appear in 'Fair Co-ed'

* * *

But to get back to Mr. Champ Pickens and Dixie football.

Mr. Pickens has a new idea which constant polishing has made fairly brilliant. It is Mr. Pickens' idea that an all-southern eleven, picked from the entire Southland and

(Continued on Page 17)

PRO NET STARS CLASH IN TITLE MATCHES HERE

Richards and Kinsey to Oppose Wesbrook, Snodgrass at Palomar Club

STEALING a march on the tennis tournament which will be staged next week by the Los Angeles Tennis Club, four well-known professionals—Vincent Richards, Howard Kinsey, Harvey Snodgrass and Walter Wesbrook—will meet this afternoon in two singles matches and one double canto on the courts of Palomar Country Club. The singles match between Richards and Snodgrass is billed as a championship of the world affair.

Vincent Richards

Both Richards and Kinsey were former members of the Davis cup teams, but have been out of the amateur class since they made the world tennis tour under the banner of C. C. Pyle. Richards, who hails from New York, and Kinsey, who is a San Francisco boy, will oppose Snodgrass, who has charge of the tennis activities of the Palomar Club, and Wesbrook who is employed at the Midwick Country Club.

In the first singles match of the day, which gets under way at 1 o'clock, Snodgrass will match his powerful driving strokes against the flashy court work and accurate place shots of Richards.

Following the matches today, Vincent Richards will spend a little time in Southern California before leaving for Japan. His trip to Japan is taken for the purpose of playing several exhibition games while in the land of the rising sun.

Carson Bigbee of Ducks in Hospital

SAN FRANCISCO, Sept. 29.—(AP) Carson Bigbee, outfielder of the Portland club, is in a hospital here suffering from a blood clot in the right leg, the result of being struck by a pitched ball recently. His condition is said to be not serious.

How the Babe -:- Equalled -:- Record of 59

1921	1927
59—Oct. 2	Sept. 29—59
58—Sept. 26	Sept. 29—58
57—Sept. 26	Sept. 27—57
56—Sept. 16	Sept. 22—56
55—Sept. 15	Sept. 21—55
54—Sept. 9	Sept. 18—54
53—Sept. 8	Sept. 16—53
52—Sept. 7	Sept. 13—52
51—Sept. 5	Sept. 13—51
50—Sept. 3	Sept. 11—50
49—Sept. 2	Sept. 7—49
48—Aug. 23	Sept. 7—48
47—Aug. 23	Sept. 6—47
46—Aug. 18	Sept. 6—46
45—Aug. 17	Sept. 6—45
44—Aug. 12	Sept. 2—44
43—Aug. 11	Aug. 31—43
42—Aug. 10	Aug. 28—42
41—Aug. 8	Aug. 27—41
40—Aug. 8	Aug. 22—40
39—Aug. 6	Aug. 20—39
38—July 31	Aug. 17—38
37—July 30	Aug. 16—37
36—July 30	Aug. 10—36
35—July 15	Aug. 5—35
34—July 12	July 28—34
33—July 12	July 26—33
32—July 11	July 26—32
31—July 5	July 18—31
30—July 2	July 12—30
29—July 2	July 9—29
28—June 29	July 9—28
27—June 26	July 8—27
26—June 25	July 3—26
25—June 23	June 30—25
24—June 20	June 22—24
23—June 14	June 22—23
22—June 14	June 16—22
21—June 13	June 12—21
20—June 13	June 11—20
19—June 12	June 11—19
18—June 11	June 7—18
17—June 10	June 5—17
16—June 3	May 31—16
15—May 31	May 31—15
14—May 29	May 30—14
13—May 25	May 29—13
12—May 17	May 28—12
11—May 14	May 23—11
10—May 12	May 22—10
9—May 12	May 17—9
8—May 7	May 11—8
7—May 6	May 10—7
6—May 2	May 1—6
5—April 25	May 1—5
4—April 22	April 29—4
3—April 21	April 25—3
2—April 20	April 23—2
1—April 16	April 15—1

HIBBS PUTS 'BIG KICK' IN U. S. C. DRILL

Jesse Shows Skill in Punting and Mentors Are Astounded; Broncos Reach City Today

By Martin Burke

A REAL kick was added to the Southern California football team yesterday. It was a 100 per cent kick to pep up a squad that has been floundering along on less than the legal one-half of 1 per cent.

Jesse Hibbs

Jesse Hibbs furnished the kick. Handsome Hibbs they call him at U. S. C. because he is good-looking enough to grab off junior leads in some of our very best Hollywood pictures.

Kicking in the face of a charging line, Hibbs got off some of the finest punts ever delivered at Bovard Field. Long, wriggling spirals with a skid at the finish that handcuffed the waiting safety man. Forty, fifty, fifty-five, sixty yards and better that ball traveled.

Coach Howard Jones has been moaning the absence of a real kicker to put the kick in his team. He found one yesterday in his versatile, vigorous tackle—Jesse Hibbs.

MENTORS ASTOUNDED

When Hibbs got off his first long drive after Drury, Elliott and Williams had taken their turn, the Trojan mentors were a bit astounded. Cliff Herd, who attends to the booting department and who has been bringing Hibbs along, told him to try again.

Zowie! And off there floated a sky-scraper, high enough for any end to cover and long enough to keep the best team in its own territory. Another was tried. The tackles slipped through in a concentrated effort to block the drive. Right off their outstretched hands it shot and well-placed in the corner of the field.

Still another and another until the truth finally dawned on every one. U. S. C. had finally found a punter after years without one.

Hibbs is not a fast kicker. But with practice he's getting quicker and is bound to improve. He is as steady as a rock and has the leg drive and strength that is essential to a first-class punt producer.

DRURY SHIFTS

When Hibbs dropped back to the rear position Captain Drury shifted to tackle to plug the gap. Having once played in the line, Drury can take care of the job in fancy style.

The varsity worked on defense against Notre Dame plays for an hour and then polished up on the booting and covering of kicks. To offset the uncovering of Hibbs was an unfortunate and possibly serious injury to Johnny Fox, the leading light in the race for the center position.

In blocking a line charge Fox rapped his right arm on Ward's head with such telling effect that he couldn't use his arm afterwards. An X-ray will be taken today to determine whether or not any bones have been broken. Ward reported no damage to his head, which is something of a pointer on how hard his head really is. All kidding aside, Ward is coming as fast as any of the green men on the squad and may win himself a steady berth at center or tackle.

Santa Clara arrives here today and will work out this afternoon at the Coliseum in preparation for the contest Saturday.

Cochran Trails German, 500-332

CHICAGO, Sept. 29.—(AP)—Eric Hagenlacher of Germany tonight took the first block of 500 points from the defending champion, Welker Cochrane, Hollywood, Cal., in their match for the 18.2 Balkline billiard crown. The former titleholder ran out his score in the sixteenth inning while Cochrane totaled but 332. Cochrane won the title in Washington last March when Hagenlacher was runner up.

National League -:- Standings -:-

Pittsburgh	93	58	.616
St. Louis	91	61	.599
New York	90	61	.596
Chicago	85	67	.559
Cincinnati	73	77	.487
Brooklyn	63	87	.420
Boston	57	93	.380
Philadelphia	51	99	.340

YESTERDAY'S RESULTS

Cincinnati, 3; St. Louis, 2.
Philadelphia, 7; Boston, 1.
Only games scheduled.

GAMES TODAY

Philadelphia at Boston.
Pittsburgh at Cincinnati.
Only games scheduled.

Reds Blast Cards' Flag Hopes, 3-2

CINCINNATI, Sept. 29.—(AP)—The Cincinnati Reds dealt the Cardinals a crushing blow in their pennant pursuit today by hanging up a 3 to 2 victory in the final of a three-game series. As the Pirates were not scheduled, the St. Louis club fell back to 2½ games behind Pittsburgh.

As the Cardinals now have only two games left to play, the best they can do is to force the Corsairs to a tie, granting they win both contests while Pittsburgh drops three. St. Louis held on to second place by a half game over the idle Giants.

But a scant crowd of 340 witnessed the contest on a soggy field drenched by two days of rain.

Frankhouse, Card hurler, had one bad inning, the fourth, when he contributed a wild throw which, with three hits and a sacrifice, brought in three runs.

Jakie May came through as the winning pitcher, allowing eight hits, one of which was a homer by Frisch. The Reds made only five safeties.

St. Louis	AB	H	O	A	Cincinnati	AB	H	O	A
Douthit,cf.	4	1	6	0	Dressen,3b.	4	0	1	1
Frisch,2b.	4	2	3	2	Walker,rf.	4	0	0	0
Hafey,rf.	4	1	1	0	Pipp,1b.	3	1	10	0
Botomley,1b	3	0	8	0	Bressler,lf.	2	0	2	0
Blades,lf.	2	1	2	0	Allen,cf.	4	2	5	0
Holm,2b.	3	0	1	1	Ford,ss.	4	1	3	5
Snyder,c.	4	1	2	0	Critz,2b.	2	0	3	4
Maranvil,ss	3	1	1	4	Picinich,c.	3	1	3	2
L.Bell	1	0	0	0	May,p.	3	0	0	1
Frankhse,p.	3	1	0	1					
Totals	31	8	24	8	Totals	29	5	27	13

L. Bell batted for Maranville in ninth.

St. Louis	0	0	0	0	1	1	0	0	0	—2
Cincinnati	0	0	0	3	0	0	0	0	x	—3

Errors—Maranville, Frankhouse. Two-base hits—Douthit, Pipp, Picinich, Allen. Home run—Frisch. Sacrifices—Bressler, Critz, Holm. Double plays—Critz to Ford to Pipp (2); Picinich to Ford. Left on bases—St. Louis, 6; Cincinnati, 6. Bases on balls—Off Frankhouse, 2; off May, 2. Struck out—By Frankhouse, 2; by May, 4. Hit by pitcher—Bottomley by May. Umpires—McCormick, O'Day and Reardon. Time—1:27.

Davies Wins in Culver Final

WILLIE DAVIES won a ten-round decision over Freddie Imperial in the main event at Culver City last night. It was a close, hard-fought battle throughout. William Kasababian scored a knockout over Ted Lopez in the second round of the scheduled six-round semi-windup. Oscar Baker scored a knockout over Al Dresden in the first 30 seconds of the first round of the special event. Victor Bertley won the nod over Earl Caustian and Neil Bruce won the decision over Lew Sauber in the four-round preliminaries.

BABE SPANKS TWO TO KNOT MARK OF 59

2 Washington Pitchers Victims of Outburst; Second Knock Comes With Sacks Full

NEW YORK, Sept. 29.—(AP)—Carrying on in a furious September finish, Babe Ruth today knocked out two mammoth home runs to tie his great record of 59, accomplished in 1921. The mighty slugger of the New York Yankees stands on the brink of establishing a new mark, since he has two more days left in the campaign.

Miller Huggins

The king of the swat is one home run in advance of his output in 1921, for at that time No. 59 fell during the Yanks' 153d game, while today was New York's 152d.

Horace Lisenbee of the Senators was the victim of Babe's first rap today. It came in the first inning with the sacks empty. In the fifth, Paul Hopkins, a young pitcher, who just joined the Washington Club, received a baptism of fire when Ruth drove out No. 59, with the bases full. That gave Ruth three homers in the last two games, two of which dropped with the sacks loaded.

GETS RECEPTION

Some 5000 fans rejoiced with Ruth and gave him a great ovation when he equalled his former standard. Lou Gehrig, his teammate and rival for home run honors, this season, was the first to congratulate Ruth with a handshake at the plate. At the Yanks' dugout a warm reception awaited him from his co-players and Manager Miller Huggins.

This has been the greatest month in Ruth's home run career. With fifteen thus far, his best previous maonthly assortment was thirteen in June, 1921.

Ruth started the month still battling with Lou Gehrig and well behind the 1921 record. Gehrig had led him during the greater part of the season and the speculation was about even that the young Columbia product would beat Ruth out.

LOU FALLS BACK

The first three months of the current season found Ruth and Gehrig deadlocked, with twenty-five apiece. Early in the present month, they were running neck and neck again, when Gehrig clipped a homer in Boston. That was on Labor Day, and tied the sluggers at 45. Then Ruth started stepping out and Ruth has hit 14 while Gehrig made but one. The Yanks won today's game by a score of 15 to 4.

Washington	AB	H	O	A	New York	AB	H	O	A
Rice,rf.	3	0	0	0	Combs,cf.	5	1	4	0
Hopkins,p.	1	0	0	2	Koenig,ss.	5	3	0	2
Harris,2b.	4	2	1	3	Ruth,rf.	5	3	3	0
Stewart,2b.	1	0	0	1	Paschal,rf.	0	0	1	0
Ganzel,cf.	4	2	2	0	Gehrig,1b.	3	1	9	0
Goslin,lf.	5	1	3	2	Durst,1b.	0	0	0	1
Judge,1b.	4	2	7	1	Meusel,lf.	5	3	3	0
Speaker,1b.	0	0	2	0	Lazzeri,2b.	1	1	0	0
Tate,c.	4	2	5	0	Dugan,3b.	3	1	1	3
Bluege,3b.	4	0	0	0	Gazella,3b.	2	0	0	1
Reeves,ss.	4	1	2	4	Collins,c.	2	2	5	0
Lisenbee,p.	1	0	0	0	Shocker,p.	1	0	0	0
Marberry,p.	0	0	0	0	Ruether,p.	2	1	0	0
Barnes,rf.	3	0	2	1	Shawkey,p.	1	0	1	0
Totals	38	10	24	14	Totals	38	19	27	8

Washington	0	2	0	0	2	0	0	0	0	—4
New York	1	7	0	3	4	0	0	0	*	—15

Errors—Koenig, Reeves, Stewart. Home runs—Ruth, 2; Reeves, Ganzel. Three-base hits—Ruth, Meusel. Two-base hits—Collins, Meusel, 2. Stolen bases—Lazzeri. Double plays—Judge to Harris; Reeves to Judge; Barnes to Judge. Bases on balls—Off Lisenbee, 3; Marberry, 1; Hopkins, 1; Shocker, 1; Ruether, 1. Struck out—By Lisenbee, 1; Marberry, 1; Hopkins, 1; Ruether, 1; Shawkey, 3. Wild pitch—Lisenbee. Winning pitcher—Shocker. Losing pitcher—Lisenbee. Umpires—Dineen, Connolly and Owens.

Lamar Awarded Nod Over Diez

JOHNNY LAMAR won a close ten-round decision over Joe Diez in the ten-round main event at Pasadena last night. In the six-round semi-windup Joe Bailey won the nod over Jack O'Brien. Marcellino Lomeli was given the nod over Harry Cerrera in the six-round special event. In the two four-round preliminaries Young Firpo won the decision over Cliff Martinez and John Hayward knocked out Cliff Figueroa in the third round.

AUTO RACER INJURED

FRESNO, Sept. 29.—(AP)—In the first few minutes of automobile racing car tryouts on the half-mile dirt track at the Fresno district fair, Bill Paige of Reno was seriously injured this afternoon when his car crashed through the fence on the south turn of the dirt track.

Terris Handed Pummeling by Spanish Star

NEW YORK, Sept. 29.—(AP)—Hilario Martinez, hard-punching Spanish lightweight, scored a sensational ten-round victory over Sid Terris, crack New York title contender, in the feature match at the Queensboro Stadium tonight. Terris was knocked down for three counts of nine in the second round and barely kept his feet under Martinez' merciless attack in several others.

Davy Arad, Panama bantamweight, lost to Milton Cohen of New York on a foul in the first round of a ten-round semi-final.

HACKLEY SCORES K. O.

DAYTON, Ky., Sept. 29.—(AP)—Jimmy Hackley, Los Angeles junior lightweight, knocked out Carl Schmadel, Indianapolis, in the first round of a scheduled ten-round bout here tonight.

Capacity Attendances Forecast for Net Meet

CAPACITY attendance every day of the big tournament to be held next week at the Los Angeles Tennis Club under the auspices of the Tennis Patrons' Association of Southern California was forecast yesterday by officials of the latter organization as a result of the first four days' sale of season tickets.

Arrival here this week of Big Bill Tilden, famous American net star; Miss Kea Bouman, champion of Holland, and plans to greet Molla Mallory, Francis T. Hunter, Jean Washer, champion of Belgium; Alonso, Spanish champion, and others tomorrow and Sunday has greatly stimulated interest in the matches, which will begin at 2 o'clock Monday afternoon.

Plans have been completed for the dinner-dance to be given Saturday night at the Tennis Club in honor of the visiting and local players to participate in the tourney, according to Harold H. Braley, president of the patrons' organization; Clif Herd, president of the L. A. Tennis Club, and E. Avery McCarthy, chairman of the entertainment committee.

Society women of the city are arranging a series of dinners and other receptions for the noted players for the next week. Patronesses of the tourney include some of the most socially prominent women of Southern California. Radio talks will be made from 9 to 10 o'clock Monday night by Tilden and other courts.

Pittsburgh Can Cinch Rag With Victory Today

NEW YORK, Sept. 29.—(AP)—The Pirates were shoved virtually into the National League championship today without a struggle, as the Cardinals were cut down by the Reds to diminish the St. Louis' flag possibility to the event of a tie. The Corsairs stand a chance of definitely capturing the bunting tomorrow by a victory over the Reds. All Pittsburgh needs to take the banner is one triumph in three remaining starts. However, if the Buccaneers drop the three games and the Cards and Giants sweep all their encounters, the clubs will be tangled in a triple tie with the standing as follows:

	W.	L.	Ave.
Pittsburgh	93	61	.604
St. Louis	03	61	.604
New York	93	61	.604

1926 Officials Handle Stanford, U. S. C. Game

THE same quartet of officials that functioned in last year's Trojan-Stanford game will again handle the contest, it was officially announced yesterday at the University of Southern California offices. The officials are:

Evans, former Stanford coach, referee.
Ralph McCord, Illinois, umpire.
Badenoch, Chicago, head lineman.
Dud Clark, Oregon, field judge.

The list of officials for the U. S. C.-California game to be played in the Los Angeles Coliseum on October 29 is as follows:

George Varnell, Chicago, referee.
McCord, umpire.
Fitzpatrick, head lineman.
Badenoch, field judge.

WOMAN SHOOTS U. S. JUDGE ON BENCH

91 St. Louis Tornado Dead

NIGHT EDITION

AMERICAN LEAGUE

At New York—

		R.	H.	E.
Washington	0 0 0 2 0 0 0 0 0	2	5	0
New York	0 0 0 1 0 1 0 2 x	4	9	1

Batteries—Zachary and Ruel; Pipgras, Pennock and Bengough.

At Chicago (first game, 13 innings)—

		R.	H.	E.
Detroit	0 0 0 0 1 2 0 1 0 0 0 0 0	4	9	2
Chicago	0 0 0 0 3 1 0 0 0 0 0 0 1	5	9	0

Batteries—Gibson and Bassler; Thomas and McCurdy.

At Chicago (2nd game, called, darkness)—

		R.	H.	E.
Detroit	0 0 0 1 0 0	1	6	0
Chicago	0 0 3 0 1 x	4	7	0

Batteries—Stoner and Woodall; Faber and Crouse.

At St. Louis (first game)—

		R.	H.	E.
Cleveland	0 0 0 0 0 3 1 0 1	5	8	1
St. Louis	1 0 0 1 0 0 2 0 0	4	10	0

Batteries—Hudlin and Sewell; Blaeholder and Schang.

At St. Louis (second game)—

		R.	H.	E.
Cleveland	4 0 0 0 0 0 0 0 0	4	5	1
St. Louis	2 2 0 4 0 0 1 0 x	9	13	2

Batteries—Underhill, McKain and Myatt; Wright and Dixon.

NATIONAL LEAGUE

At Cincinnati—

		R.	H.	E.
Pittsburg	0 0 0 0 0 0 0 1 0	1	5	0
Cincinnati	0 0 0 0 0 1 1 0 x	2	8	0

Batteries—Aldridge, Miljus and Gooch, Spencer; Lucas and Picinich, Hargrave.

At Brookklyn—

		R.	H.	E.
New York	2 1 0 0 0 0 1 0 1	5	6	1
Brooklyn	0 0 0 0 4 0 6 0 x	10	9	5

Batteries—Henry, Barnes, Fitzsimmons and Cummings, Taylor; Vance and Deberry.

At Boston—

		R.	H.	E.
Philadelphia	1 0 0 0 1 0 0 0 0	2	6	0
Boston	3 4 0 1 0 3 1 0 x	12	18	0

Batteries—Taber, Scott and Jonnard, O'Donnell; Genewich and Hogan.

LITTLE WORLD SERIES

At Toledo—

		R.	H.	E.
Buffalo	0 0 0 1 0 0 0 1 0	2	5	2
Toledo	0 2 3 0 0 0 0 0 x	5	7	1

Batteries—Mangum, Stryker and Devins; Barnes and O'Neill.

EASTERN BALL SCORES

THREE CENTS

LOS ANGELES EVENING HERALD
AN INDEPENDENT NEWSPAPER

Reg. U. S. Patent Office. Copyright, 1927, by Evening Herald Publishing Company

The Evening Herald Grows Just Like Los Angeles

VOL. LII THREE CENTS Hotels and Trains Five Cents FRIDAY, SEPTEMBER 30, 1927 Hotels and Trains Five Cents THREE CENTS NO. 286

RUTH HITS 60TH HOME RUN

WIDOW FIRES FOUR SHOTS AT JURIST IN COURT

SALT LAKE CITY, Sept. 30.—After brooding over a decision against her in a damage suit, Mrs. Eliza Simmons, a widow, shot and wounded Judge Tilman F. Johnson in the federal district court here today.

Mrs. Simmons walked into the courtroom with other spectators before the opening of the morning session and took a seat in the front row next to the bailiff.

FIRES FOUR SHOTS

When Judge Johnson entered and mounted the bench Mrs. Simmons stepped quickly forward and fired four times at him before court attendants could reach her.

A bailiff finally wrested the gun from her and she was placed under arrest. She made no attempt to escape and gave no reason for her act.

Court records showed Judge Johnson had rendered a decision against Mrs. Simmons in 1925 in her suit to collect $10,000 damages from the Utah Copper Co. for the death of her husband.

BROODED OVER SUIT

Following affirmation of this decision by the circuit court of appeals, court costs were collected from Mrs. Simmons a short time ago.

Since then, acquaintances said she had brooded over the case and been extremely despondent. She has four children.

Judge Johnson, 65 years of age, was appointed to the federal bench in 1912 by President Wilson. He made his home in Ogden and had been a prominent member of the Utah bar for many years.

Big Boulder Keeps Ship From Sinking As It Runs Aground

SAN DIEGO, Sept. 30.—A huge boulder that stuck in the hull of the freight Circinus when it grounded 17 miles south of the border was all that kept the ship from sinking, a diver discovered here yesterday.

The ship was floated Wednesday and brought here for temporary repairs. The diver found that the rock had punctured both bottoms of the ship and was embedded firmly. Mattresses were placed around the boulder from the inside of the ship and last night the ship left under tow for Los Angeles harbor, where it will go into dry dock.

GIRLS BODIES FOUND; OVER 1000 HURT IN STORM

ST. LOUIS, Sept. 30.—The death toll of the tornado which wrecked buildings over an area of six square miles here yesterday, reached 91 this afternoon with recovery of three more bodies of girl students from the ruins of Central high school.

Two other bodies of girls were taken out yesterday from the school building debris, where three floors caved in from pressure of the 80-mile-an-hour wind. Two of the three bodies brought out this afternoon were identified as those of Alice Berner, 15, and Bois Shaw, 14.

INJURED TOLL GROWS

The toll of injured also grew through the day, totaling somewhere between 1000 and 1500, many seriously hurt.

More than 25,000 were homeless.

Thirteen were known missing and unaccounted for.

Property damage could not be accurately estimated, but was variously placed by officials at between $50,000,000 and $100,000,000.

With relatives of the missing wandering hysterically among the ruins searching for their loved ones, city officials acted promptly to halt any possible outbreak of disorders. Every available city and county officer was on continuous duty in the stricken areas and the entire Missouri National guard was called out to reinforce them under orders to shoot to kill anyone caught looting.

Despite the widespread destruction, Mayor Victor Miller today announced St. Louis would not need outside help.

APPEAL IS MET

He declared his appeal for funds had been met so bountifully by St. Louis citizens that adequate money was available for relief work. He stated the local Red Cross and other relief agencies were meeting the situation heroically and fully.

Mayor Miller received word today that the 1000 regular army soldiers at Jefferson barracks would be dispatched to the city by the federal government to aid in guard work.

Food stations using war department supplies were today sent into the wrecked areas, and food was dispensed to the homeless from rolling army canteens.

Fully six square miles of buildings and streets on the west side were devastated by the tornado, which hurtled into the city shortly after 1 o'clck yesterday afternoon.

The storm gained in intensity as it tore through Manchester and

(CONTINUED ON PAGE TWENTY)

Awards in Quake At Santa Barbara Upheld by Court

By Pacific Coast News Service

SAN FRANCISCO, Sept. 30.—Rumblings of the earthquake in Santa Barbara two years ago were heard again in the state supreme court here today when the higher tribunal upheld two industrial commission awards growing out of the disaster.

The first award was to Louisa Mosteiro, whose husband, Segismondo, was killed during the quake while employed in a building as a janitor. Mrs. Mosteiro was awarded $5000.

The second award was to William D. Wilson, dairyman, who was injured during the quake when bricks from a building fell on his head.

Zasu Pitts' Mate Flies from L. A. to Mother's Bedside

By International News Service

CHICAGO, Sept. 30.—Tom Gallery, motion picture actor and husband of Zasu Pitts, is winging across the continent from his home in Beverly Hills, Cal., to the bedside of his mother here. Mrs. Gallery is critically ill and has not yet been told that her son is expected to be here tomorrow morning.

The husky 6-foot young actor is known to Chicagoans as the son of Police Captain Mike Gallery.

"Tom left Los Angeles in a plane that had been used in an aviation picture," the captain said this afternoon. "He and the pilot took off as soon as the last scene was shot and they're due here early tomorrow."

Weather Bureau Forecasts Clear Skies for So. Cal.

Clear skies were promised for tonight and tomorrow throughout Southern California by Col. H. B. Hersey today in the official weather bureau forecast.

Moderate temperature will continue, Colonel Hersey said. The thermometer stood at 58 early today, rising to 68 just before noon.

3 PARTIALLY IDENTIFY SUSPECT

Three employes of the Los Angeles department of water and power today partially identified a picture of Joseph C. Senellan, 33, held in the county jail at Ventura, as one of the two men who bound them and gagged them with rubber balls during the $73,600 payroll robbery at the bureau last Monday, according to police.

Detective Lieutenants Evans and Tomasen, who brought the picture of Senellan to Los Angeles, immediately returned to Ventura to bring Senellan back to Los Angeles. Police said he would be confronted by the three bureau employes, S. F. Arthurs, Glenn Brockway and George Pessill.

CAUGHT IN CHASE

A too desperate attempt to escape arrest on a speeding charge and a scar on his face led to the examination of Senellan as a suspect in connection with the payroll holdup.

Senellan bears a scar on his nose and cheek. One of the bandits wore a piece of tape, as if to conceal a scar, in the same place.

Senellan first came to the attention of police when he shot an auto through Santa Barbara at a high rate of speed. State Motorcycle Police Inspector J. Blackwell started after him, sounding his siren as he went.

CAR TURNS OVER

Down the coast highway the pair raced. As they passed through hamlets motorcycle policemen and police cars joined the chase. A stream of shots was directed at the fleeing car and although lead pierced the body and windshield, the driver kept ahead of his pursuers.

Turns at high speed and wild careening to avoid tourist cars added thrills to the chase. One state officer was thrown from his motorcycle and the machine burst into flames.

One mile north of Malibu junc-

(CONTINUED ON PAGE EIGHTEEN)

Top photo shows the globe-girdling plane Pride of Detroit landing at Vail field, Los Angeles, today, after a flight from San Francisco. Below, the world flight companions in adventure, Edward F. Schlee, left, and William S. Brock, are pictured just as they stepped from the plane. Brock asked for a light for his cigaret and somebody gave him a carton of matches.

BERLENBACH TO FIGHT MICKEY WALKER HERE

By United Press

NEW YORK, Sept. 30.—Mickey Walker, middleweight champion of the world, and Paul Berlenbach, who is attempting a "come-back," were signed this afternoon to fight 10 rounds in Los Angeles for the middleweight title.

Dick Donald, promoter, signed the two fighters.

The fight will take place this fall, the exact date to be announced later.

MILK POISONS IOWANS

OSAGE, Ia., Sept. 30.—Mrs. Elmer Morris, McIntire, near here, and several other persons were poisoned by milk from a cow that had been bitten by a rattlesnake. All are recovering.

WORLD FLIERS HERE, PLAN TO TRY AGAIN

That they probably will start out again on a 'round-the-world flight, completing their flight next time by flying from Japan to Hawaii and then to California, was the declaration here today of William S. Brock and Edward F. Schlee, 'round-the-world fliers.

This was the word of the two fearless aviators when they alighted at Vail field at 12:19 p. m. from San Francisco on their return flight to Detroit, their home city, in the monoplane Pride of Detroit.

Brock and Schlee made a perfect landing at the Western Air Express field on Telegraph road and were met by a small crowd of persons who knew approximately when the fliers were expected. It was not

(CONTINUED ON PAGE EIGHTEEN)

Stars 8, Indians 7

INDIANS—	Ab	R	H	Po	A	E
Callaghan, cf	5	0	0	5	0	0
Ellsworth, 2b	5	3	2	5	2	1
Easterling, lf	3	1	3	3	1	0
Huft, rf	4	1	1	2	0	0
Hudgens, 1b	5	0	1	3	0	0
Sherlock, ss	4	0	0	2	1	1
Kimmick, 3b	4	1	1	2	2	0
Borreani, c	4	1	1	3	1	0
Nance, p	3	0	0	1	0	1
Guilland, p	1	0	1	0	0	0
Totals	38	7	10	26	7	3

STARS—	Ab	R	H	Po	A	E
Lee, ss	3	1	1	0	2	1
Bouton, 3b	2	2	0	2	0	0
Twombly, lf	3	0	0	6	0	0
McNulty, cf	4	1	2	3	0	0
Lowell, 1b	4	2	1	7	0	0
Frederick, rf	4	1	1	3	0	0
Kerr, 2b	3	1	2	2	1	0
Cook, c	3	0	1	6	1	1
Agnew, c	1	0	1	0	0	0
McCabe, p	3	0	0	0	0	0
Teachout, p	0	0	0	0	0	0
Heath	1	0	0	0	0	0
Totals	31	8	9	27	4	2

Seattle	102 010 021	7
Hollywood	400 100 021	8

Ninth Inning Rally Wins For Stars

At Sacramento— R. H. E.

ANGELS	0 1 0 2
SOLONS	0 0 0 7

Batteries—Cunningham and Hannah; Keefe and Severeid.

At Oakland— R. H. E.

SEALS	0 0 2 0 0
OAKS	1 0 2 0 3

Batteries—Ferguson and Jolley; Delaney and Read.

At San Francisco— R. H. E.

BEAVERS	3 0 0 0
BELLS	0 0 1 0

Batteries—Hughes and Yelle; Pillette and Baldwin.

Scoring one run in the last half of the ninth inning gave Hollywiod a 8 to 7 victory over Seattle in the fourth game of the local series at Wrigley field this afternoon.

FIRST INNING

INDIANS—Callaghan flied to Frederick. Ellsworth popped to Lowell and was safe

(CONTIN'D ON PAGE TWENTY-TWO)

SWAT KING SETS NEW WORLD'S RECORD

YANKEE STADIUM, NEW YORK, Sept. 30.—Babe Ruth, baseball's master slugger, today broke the record of 59 home runs in a single season that he set six years ago.

In the eighth inning of the next to last game of the regular schedule Ruth's bat met squarely a ball thrown by Pitcher Tom Zachary of the Washington Senators and propelled it into the right-field bleachers.

It was the sixtieth homer Ruth has hit since the season's first game in mid-April and the four hundred and sixteenth he has hit since he first came to the major leagues with the Boston Red Sox in 1915.

SCORES KOENIG

Koenig, who had tripled, scored ahead of Ruth.

Ruth had been up three times before. Once he walked and twice he singled. The Yankees and the Senators were tied at two-all in the eighth when Ruth came to the plate.

One ball.

One strike.

Then the southpaw let fly with one just to Ruth's liking.

The climax of the king of clout's greatest season came after a brilliant performance yesterday, when he knocked two homers, tying his previous best performance for a season.

New York won the game, 4 to 2. Pipgras and Pennock hurled for the Yankees, allowing only five hits. Zachary for the Senators yielded nine safeties.

BAN JOHNSON HITS AT JUDGE LANDIS IN FIERY STATEMENT

CHICAGO, Sept. 30.—Byron Bancroft Johnson, founder of the American league and pilot of that organization through a stormy quarter century, today fired a parting shot at his two most bitter enemies, Baseball Commissioner K. M. Landis and Charles Comiskey, owner of the Chicago White Sox.

Johnson, who resigned under pressure in July with the provision that he be given time to "set his house in order," is expected to retire from baseball within a few days, although he refused today to set a definite date.

Judge Landis laughed when he

(CONTINUED ON PAGE TWENTY-TWO)

FILIPINO FLYWEIGHT SHOWS FANS REAL CLASS

Madigan Puts Team Through Secret Drills

St. Mary's Squad May Spring Big Surprise on the Bears in Berl ley Mix.

St. Mary's team may be dangerous when its meets the California grid varsity at Memorial Stadium Saturday. Coach "Slip" Madiis reported to be working on an offensive combination and the Saints' practice has been secret.

Although there is a great deal of gloom at the Broadway college because Larry Bettencourt is out of the fray, camp followers believe that the six remaining star Saint linemen are enough to hold the Bears at bay.

These six huskies, Scarlett and Frankian, ends; Hicks and Tobin, tackles; Illia and Mulcahy, guards, are all powerful football players.

Illia and Mulcahy, with the green sophomore, Seghetti, between them, will form a pretty strong mid-line combination. The fact that Bettencourt is out indirectly aids the California passing game. Few players here or on any gridiron rush the passer with such speed and effectiveness as Bettencourt. Bettencourt, hurrying the passer, was the chief reason why Pop Warner's men did not get over with their passing attack.

It is doubtful that the Saints will play the same type of waiting game against the Bears they displayed in trouncing the Cardinals. The Saints simply lay entrenched, awaited the attack, and then acted accordingly.

Madigan used but few plays last Saturday, so California scouts saw little variety of offense. Madigan did not need the plays, and the line was winning his ball game for him.

California has a number of fast backs. Can they match Hill, Wilton and Hyland? Is there a power back in Berkeley to match Hoffman? At least California has no power attack, or has as yet displayed none. St. Mary's famed running attack, the famous play which Andy Smith, Price and a number of coaches have all failed to stop heretofore, will be much in evidence.

Can the St. Mary's line hold the Bears as well as they did Stanford?

With Gus O'Gorman and Toots Kasper in the hospital, too, St. Mary's sophomores will bear the brunt of the backfield work. Simas will probably be the only regular to start in the backfield, and he is a sophomore. Cal Pitchford, Pat Bogan and Dick Scarlett, as well as Joe Rooney and Scotty McIntyre are all almost sure to see action. Jack Merrick is only a possibility, and unless his injury shows rapid movement he will not be at his best.

California is out to win. The Bears have a lot to gain by victory and the Saints everything to lose.

MURDER, MANSLAUGHTER AND LITTLE OOM PAUL WANER

Above on the left you will find the smiling face of LOU GEHRIG, otherwise Mister Manslaughter. He crashed a triple in the first inning of the opening game of the world series yesterday and brought Ruth home with the first run of the game. On the right is Mister Murder, otherwise known as BABE RUTH, who got three out of four.

These affectionate terms were wished on the Yankee stars by opposing pitchers. Below is little "OOM PAUL" WANER, late of Ada and San Francisco. Paul lived up to the expectations of thousands of admiring fans and came through with three hits for the Pirates yesterday.

Dado Easily Beats Murray At Auditorium

Billy Taylor Loses First Fight When Stopped by Frankie Stetson.

By BOB SHAND

Speedy Dado, Filipino flyweight, romped to an easy 10-round decision over Frankie Murray at the Auditorium last night. Had not Murray been smart he would have been knocked out, but the Philadelphia mite has been in the racket for a long, long time and he knows how to take care of himself. Dado sprayed him with all kinds of punches, but always favoring a right hook. Had he straightened out the right occasionally he might have won more decisively, but as it was he was master of the situation at all times and won as he pleased.

Under the guidance of Dolph Thomas, Dado will learn much, but he probably will not do so well under the management of Frank Churchill, who is said to hold a contract on the youngster's services. Thomas has taught Dado many of the finer points of the game since the youth arrived here and he will give him many more valuable tips if Dado remains here instead of going to New York as he plans to do. The little stranger is about the fastest boy in the flyweight class. He has a remarkable eye and his timing is about perfect. Against a less experienced boy he would have shown to better advantage last night, but Murray made him do all the fighting while the Filipino's long suit is countering. Murray was accidentally butted in the head in the second round and the cut bled profusely for the remainder of the battle. In the sixth Frankie clouted Dado with a left hand and gave the Filipino a black eye, but that was about the only damaging punch Murray landed.

Angel De La Cruz and Johnny Norman thrilled the fans with a six-round slugfest. Norman was knocked down in the first round but arose without taking a count. He carried the fight to his opponent for the balance of the scrap and many fans thought he was entitled to the decision.

Billy Taylor lost his first fight when he "resigned" to Frankie Stetson in the fourth round at the request of his manager, Jimmy Gallagher. Taylor had ten fights previous to last night and had never been defeated or knocked down. Stetson, who has been winning consistently at National hall across the bay, was too much for Billy in the shape the latter was in and Gallagher showed good judgment by tossing a sponge into the ring in the fourth. Taylor was knocked down with a right to the chin in the first round and was wrestled down twice before the bout was stopped.

Billy was in terrible shape and was hanging on at every opportunity. Gallagher explained that Taylor was worried about his weight and took off too much, although he came in lighter than the articles called for.

Matt Callo made short work of Jimmy Stanislaus, knocking him out in the first round. Young Pancho Villa and Mickey Britton stepped four fast rounds in the curtain raiser with Villa taking the decision.

OUTGOING MAIL from Bob Shand

Mr. M. G. Callaghan,
Livermore, Calif.
Dear Mike:

Some strange stories have been coming out of the Livermore Hills and something ought to be done about it before the quail hunters sally forth, otherwise your district will get a bad name from those who drink only the real stuff.

Joe Bush, Hayward nimrod, came out of the hills one day with a story of having encountered a whole flock of baboons. They were the real thing and Joe swears that he had nothing but water in his canteen the day he saw them. According to his story he was strolling up a canyon hoping to meet a gentleman deer with forked horns, when he heard the darndest racket in some trees and there were simply dozens of baboons swinging by their tails and generally having a good time.

Then Harry Rowell, another citizen of Hayward, who says he has never disobeyed the edict of Mr. Volstead, almost got scared out of his wits in your hills when a voice told him to "beat it." Harry could locate no human being within hearing distance, but finally discovered a parrot acting as lookout for some big bucks that were browsing nearby.

Of course all this might be a conspiracy on the part of jealous residents of a neighboring town but it seems strange that two such incidents should have as their locale the Livermore hills. Maybe you might speak to John McGlinchey about it. Seems to me what you don't run in Livermore John does, and between the pair of you you might get action. Baboons and parrots—next thing we'll be hearing is that there are pink elephants and four-footed rattlesnakes.

Mike, do you remember when the Los Angeles athletic club's basketball team came to your town to play the Cowboys? I was having dinner in Malley's that afternoon when the cute little pink faced lads from the south came in. The coach ordered two soft boiled eggs for each athlete and some very weak tea. The waiter who was an ardent basketball fan, asked if that was the bunch that was going to play the Cowboys and the manager said "Yes."

"Well, then, if you're going to meet that Livermore bunch you better inhale some steaks," he advised.

After their meal the Los Angeles lads were put to bed for a rest.

The game was to start at eight o'clock and about seven-thirty a number of cowboys, right off the range, galloped into town, hitched their horses in front of the hotel and clamped down the street towards the opera house. The team was composed principally of McGlincheys. They hadn't partaken of any soft boiled eggs. They had bumped off a sheep that afternoon and had dined on mutton and beans and they had all done a hard day's riding on the range as it was branding time.

You may remember who won the basketball game and it wasn't Los Angeles.

Hoping you have as good a team this year,

Yours very truly,

Bob Shand

Former Coasters Showed Up Well in Opening Game

Joe Devine Points Out That Pirates Lost First Game to Washington and Then Won the Series.

By JOE DEVINE.
(Scout Pittsburgh Pirates)

PITTSBURGH, Oct. 6.—The first game of the big series did not turn out as I expected. The Yankees defeated us because they put up the best defense in the pinches, and Ray Kremer, who had won his last seven starts, could not pitch the ball where he wanted. I know that Ray intended to be extra careful with Babe Ruth and Lou Gehrig, and in trying to do this he probably got off stride and did not have the best control of the ball. Ruth did not give Kremer much chance to work on him and picked on the first pitch for two of his three hits.

JOE DEVINE

After the ball game some people criticised Paul Waner for trying to trap Gehrig's short fly in the first inning, but it is usually that way for a ballplayer when things do not pan out as he planned. The ball got by Waner and went for a triple while Ruth scored. Had Paul made the catch he would have retired the side and I do not think it is right to try and heap any blame on a fellow whose intentions were for the best interest of the ball club. His teammates felt that Paul did the right thing because Bob Meusel, another dangerous hitter, was following Gehrig to the plate.

WANERS HIT BALL.

When Paul Waner started hitting the ball, fans who groaned as they saw Paul let that fly get by him, were soon ready to forgive. The little rightfielder lived up to all expectations at the plate, getting three hits for a total of four bases, while Ruth got three hits for a total of three bases. Paul's kid brother Lloyd got one of the nine hits our club made off Waite Hoyt and Wilcey Moore. It was a double. Remember I said that the Waner boys would outhit Ruth and Gehrig on the series play.

George Grantham, another player who used to be out on the coast with Portland, did not have such a good day as he went to bat five times without a hit and was charged with one error in nine fielding chances, and that error came in that third inning which gave the Yankees three runs and a big lead on us. But I look for Grantham to do his share of good work before the series is at an end.

We outhit the Yankees 9 to 6, so Kremer did not pitch a bad ball game. The three walks he issued and the errors tossed in by Grantham and Earl Smith, turned the battle against us. I believe that if Kremer can come back and pitch the same ball he did yesterday, he will beat the Yankees, because we are certain to put up a better defensive game.

MILJUS WAS THERE.

It is too bad that the good pitching of John Miljus, who relieved Kremer in the sixth with no outs, went to waste. The Yanks got only one blow off him, so his work was the best showing of the opening game in my opinion.

Three former Pacific coast boys appeared in the game fore the Yankees. Bob Meusel went hitless in three times at bat and made one error that helped us. It was the only Yankee error. Tony Lazzeri at second and Mark Koenig at short cut off several hits through the sort of fielding that make a world series something out of the ordinary. They each connected for a double and Koenig scored two of the runs. It was a fairly good day for all the coasters on the two clubs.

And in closing I wish to state that the Pirates lost the opening game to the Washington Senators in the big series of 1925 and I think they can come back again this year and win out like they did before.

LAST NIGHTS FIGHT RESULTS

Johnny McCoy of Cleveland, O., won an unpopular ten-round decision over Pablo Dano, Filipino, from Manila, at National hall in San Francisco.

The fight was slow throughout, but Dano's aggressive tactics won the approval of the fans, many of wom thought he should have taken the decision. The best punch landed in the fight was a right which Dano swung to McCoy's jaw in the third. The boys weighed 114½ pounds.

Al Gracio of Portland won a four-round decision over Mickey Durano, Los Angeles lightweight.

Young Farrell, Los Angeles featherweight, knocked out Lou Janita of Columbus, O., in the first round of a scheduled four-round fight.

Clyde Headrick of Tonopah, Nev., won a four-round decision over Joe Pinto, San Francisco middleweight.

Battling Manning, New Orleans Negro welterweight, knocked out Young Firpo of San Francisco in the third round of a scheduled four-round bout.

OCEAN PARK.—Al Crips, San Francisco featherweight, decision over Bob Fernandez, Los Angeles (8).

WILMINGTON.—Ritchie King of Wilmington and Pedro Amador of Panama, lightweights, draw (10).

TACOMA.—Harry Dillon of Winnipeg, decision over Everett Strong of Omaha (6).

Del Fontaine, Winnipeg middleweight, knocked out Art Regan of Los Angeles (2).

Monk Tranas, Seattle flyweight, outpointed Harry Ketchel of Tacoma (4).

Jimmy Caponolli, Tacoma featherweight, knocked out Art Thiry of Seattle (1).

"Kid" Beachey, Tacoma welter, technically kayoed Bill Foster, also of Tacoma (2).

PARIS.—Fred Brettonnell and Emil Romerio, French welterweights, drew (10).

Pealings From Brian Bell On First Game of Series

PITTSBURGH, Oct. 6.—As the world series opened each manager in a most sportsmanlike manner expressed a hope that the better team would win. In the first game it was a case of the worst team losing. The Pirates, exhibiting a defense badly run down at the heel, beat themselves. The Yankees in winning needed the help of the Pirates. The contest resembled the first game of the season more than the opening game of a world series with baseball's best on parade.

• • •

The Pirates will not soon forget the third inning. One was out when Grantham got his feet and Koenig's slow roller tangled up, the ball finishing its course against some field boxes and Koenig on first. Ruth hit the first ball pitched safely to right. Kremer worked so carefully on Gehrig, trying to persuade him to hit a bad one.

• • •

The sun peeped through the darkness of defeat for the Pirates through the performance of John Miljus, former local sandlotter, but an able workman on major and minor league diamonds since he served his apprenticeship at Lawrenceville, a Pittsburgh suburb. Miljus relieved Kremer with none out in the sixth inning and breezed the rest of the way, baffling the Yankees consistently with a good curve ball and change of pace. He permitted but one hit, a single by Ruth, and wiped it out when he caught the big bam flat footed after he reached first, and started a successful movement for his retirement.

• • •

A total of 41,467 persons paid $182,477.59 to see the opening game. Some of them thought that they were entitled to a refund.

• • •

The hard hitting Yankees took a batting holiday for them when they made only six safeties, half of the hits being made by Babe Ruth, the homerun king. The big slugger did not choose to hit home runs but sent out three ringing singles. Two of the winner's six hits were doubles, one by Koenig paving the way for a run and the other by Lazzeri driving Kremer to cover. Lou Gehrig, Babe Ruth's companion in swat, was credited with a triple, but the credit should have gone to Paul Waner who made a single good for three bases by diving at it head first.

The Waner "twins," billed as the best brother act in baseball, ran true to form, Paul getting three of his team's nine hits and Lloyd scoring half of the runs.

The Acorn and Foothill Masonic Lodge baseball teams will tangle Sunday morning at 9 o'clock, the game to be played at the Allendale school grounds, on School street, between Thirty-fifth and Thirty-eighth avenues.

LaBarba Will Lead Freshmen In Mud Battle

STANFORD UNIVERSITY, Oct. 6.—Fidel LaBarba, flyweight boxing champion of the world who recently began studies here, has been elected to lead the freshmen forces in the annual mud battle with the sophomores.

The freshmen are of the opinion that if LaBarba is as good at slinging mud as he was at throwing moxing gloves at his ring opponents their side will win the mud battle easily.

AGGIES, S. C. BOTH SCORE

NIGHT EDITION

LOS ANGELES EVENING HERALD
AN INDEPENDENT NEWSPAPER

Reg. U. S. Patent Office. Copyright, 1927, by Evening Herald Publishing Company
The Evening Herald Grows Just Like Los Angeles

VOL. LII THREE CENTS Hotels and Trains Five Cents SATURDAY, OCTOBER 8, 1927 Hotels and Trains Five Cents THREE CENTS NO. 293

LATEST NEWS

S. C. OPENS UP IN THIRD PERIOD

The Trojans snapped out of it in the third period and made four first downs to O. A. C.'s none. Morley Drury tore loose for several long gains featured by a 27-yard runback of a punt. This put the ball in midfield, but penalties interrupted the Trojans march here. Logan intercepted a forward pass from Drury and raced to the Trojan's 42-yard line before they downed him.

U. C. L. A. DEFEATS WHITTIER, 24 TO 6

Final—U. C. L. A. 24, Whittier 6.

CANYON FIRE NEAR BEVERLY HILLS

A brush fire, which broke out in Stone canyon between Beverly Hills and the ocean, was spreading rapidly toward nearby property late today with 50 firemen attempting to control the flames. The blaze was reported to be a short distance off Beverly boulevard.

U. of C. Scores Against St. Mary's

N. Y. WINS WORLD SERIES BY BEATING PIRATES, 4-3

35,000 SEE TROJANS IN TILT WITH BEAVERS

Plastered hither, thither and yon over the landscape by a fast charging Aggie line, Southern California's Trojans barely managed to eke out a 7 to 6 lead over the fighting Oregon Aggie grid squad this afternoon at the end of the first half of their opening coast conference game at the Coliseum.

Both teams were fighting desperately during the half and the two touchdowns came as the result of breaks. Thirty-five thousand raving football fans witnessed the hot battle.

Both teams got away to a slow start in the first quarter, failing to gain much on the offensive and yielding but small yardage on the defensive.

AGGIES WARM UP

The Aggies trotted out on the field first, attired in white jerseys. They spent 15 minutes kicking, passing and warming up in all departments.

Howard Maple, star Aggie quarterback, was busy attempting field goals from the 15-yard line.

The Trojans took the field next. They were given a rousing hand by the colorful assemblage. In the preliminary game the Trojan Spartans defeated the U. S. C. freshmen, 15 to 6.

FIRST PERIOD

Moreley Drury of the Trojans won the tossup and chose to kick off, the Aggies defending the east goal. Elliott then started in place of Drury.

Elliott kicked off to Maple, who returned the ball to the 27-yard line, a return of 15 yards. Maple made two yards over left guard. It was a spin play.

Elliott made another over the same spot.

Whitlock kicked off at the 22-yard line to Saunders, who caught the ball on the 34-yard line and was downed in his tracks by Luce.

Lloyd Palmer made 13 yards around left end.

U. S. C. was penalized 5 yards on the 30 second stop rule. First down and 15 to go. Elliott made 8

(CONTINUED ON FIRST SPORT PAGE)

Again Today Herald First on World Series

The Evening Herald was first again this afternoon with the result, box score and details of the world series game.

Frantically but fruitlessly attempting to beat The Evening Herald, another Los Angeles newspaper published an incomplete box score, only a partial account of the game and enigmatical figures on the result, which left its readers floundering for the facts.

The Evening Herald extra was complete in all details and gave a full and comprehensive story of the game, with all plays and box score.

The Evening Herald score boards also were first with the news.

Babe Ruth is writing exclusively for this newspaper, giving the inside facts and gossip of the world series games.

THE EVENING HERALD FIRST WITH THE LATEST AND BEST

CRISIS NEAR IN MEX., BATTLE LOOMS

Adolfo de la Huerta, former provisional president of Mexico, today announced from his home in Hollywood that he had concluded a formal alliance with Gen. Arnulfo Gomez, southern revolutionary leader, whose troops were reported today near battle with large Calles forces.

MEXICO CITY, Oct. 8.—Federal forces were expected to establish contact with the principal rebel band commanded by General Arnulfo Gomez and Hector Almada today, and, according to government sources here, the coming 12 hours may tell the story of whether the revolution started last Sunday will be snuffed out within the week or whether it will drag along indefinitely.

A bulletin issued from presidential headquarters in Chapultepec castle last night predicted a decisive battle between federals and the rebel forces probably will get under way some time today near Perote, Vera Cruz state. Approxi-

(CONTINUED ON PAGE FOUR)

BEARS GET JUMP ON SAINTS

MEMORIAL STADIUM, BERKELEY, Oct. 8.—The Golden Bear had the advantage of a 13-point lead today at the end of the first half of play against the St. Mar's Gaels, conquerors of Stanford last Saturday.

After both teams had tried ineffective attacks during the first seven minutes of play, California pierced its way into St. Mary's territory after a punting duel. Lom of the Bear backfield then threw a forward pass to Jimmy Dougery that was good for a 33-yard gain and placed the ball on the galloping Gaels' 11-yard mark.

Lom followed up the attack with a wide sweep around right end that was good for 10 yards. With the Gaels fighting gamely to stave off a touchdown, Ralph Dougery pierced the line for the necessary yard gain. Evans failed to convert.

Football Results

Third period—Pomona 13, Cal. Tech 6.
First half—San Diego 6, Redlands 0.
First half—Stanford 14, Nevada 0.
Third period—Loyola 12, Arizona State 0
First half—California 13, St. Mary's 0.
First Half—Oregon 0, Idaho 0.
Pasadena Jr. College 18, Occidental Frosh 12.
First Hal—Occidental 28, Santa Barbara Teachers 0.
Colgate 0, Virginia Polytechnic Institute 6.
Holycross 18, Dayton 0.
Notre Dame 20, Detroit 0.
St. Johns 0, St. Marys 6.
Northwestern 13, Utah 6.
New York University 65, Alfred 0.
Purdue 19, Harvard 0.
Middlebury 12, Mass. Agri. 0.
Amhurst 14, Haverford 0.
Dartmouth 38, Allegheny 7.
Penn 14, Brown 6.
St. Francis 3, Westminster 0.
Thiel 0, Waynesburg 0.
R. I. State 26, Lowell Textile 0.
Providence 7, Norwich 7.
Georgia 14, Yale 10.
Washington and Jefferson 31, Bethany 0.
U. C. L. A. Frosh 27, Fullerton Junior College 0.
Cornell 53, Richmond 0.
Michigan 21, Michigan State 0.
Minnesota 40, Oklahoma Aggies 0.
Franklin-Marshall 13, Dickinson 8.
Temple 58, Juanita 0.
Williams 12, Vermont 0.
Lafayette 58, Rutgers 0.
Villanova 32, Lebanon Valley 7.
Syracuse 21, Johns Hopkins 6.
Wisconsin 26, Kansas 6.
Ohio State 13, Iowa 6.
Springfield 7, Union 7.
Navy 35, Drake 6.
Connecticut Aggies 13, Maine 14.
Clarkson 7, R. P. I. 0.
Indiana 0, Chicago 13.
Wabash 12, Milliken 7.
Penn State 7, Bucknell 13.
Denison 19, Case 0.
Colorado Aggies 6, Brigham U. 0.
Denver U. 7, Wyoming U. 12.
Army 21, Marquette 12.
John Carroll 7, Grove City 0.
Michigan 21, Michigan State 0.
California Freshmen 14, St. Mary's Freshmen 7.
Illinois 58, Butler 0.

FIRE RAZES $250,000 L. A. PLANT

Fire starting shortly before noon today completely destroyed the plant of the Miller Box and Lumber Co., 107 North Avenue 18 doing $250,000 damage there and partially burning eight neighboring dwellings.

The blaze started when an electrical shaving machine operated by E. Telles short circuited, throwing a spark into a pile of dry sawdust, it was stated by Detective Lieutenant George Price. The sawdust burst into flame like an explosion, it was stated.

Eight houses adjacent to the factory were partially burned and 12 more were threatened. The plant is located at the intersection of Avenue 18 with the Union Pacific tracks, near the Broadway bridge.

Three alarms turned in brought nine fire companies to the scene. Dry lumber in the plant burned like tinder and the firemen were unable to do anything but try to protect surrounding property.

The plant was almost surrounded by dwellings, the occupants of which dragged out furniture as sparks sprayed about their roofs.

The plant of the Graves Sash and Door Co., opposite the box factory on Avenue 18, was also in danger and the firemen deluged it in their endeavor to keep the flames from spreading.

Milton Metzler, manager, and L. H. Sweet, superintendent of the Miller plant, said about 90 per cent of the loss was covered by insurance.

Purdue Defeats Harvard, 19 to 0; New Back Stars

CAMBRIDGE, Mass., Oct. 8.—Playing his first college game of football before 30,000 spectators here this afternoon, W. R. Welch, a new Purdue left halfback, ran the ball and tossed it around Harvard for a 19-to-0 victory for the Lafayette, Ind., Boilermakers.

Welch scored two touchdowns and hurled a 50-yard forward pass to Hutton for another.

World Box Score

PITTSBURG	AB	R	H	O	A	E
L. Waner, cf	4	1	3	0	0	1
Barnhart, lf	5	0	1	2	0	0
P. Waner, rf	4	0	1	0	0	0
Wright, ss	4	0	1	1	6	0
Traynor, 3b	4	0	0	1	3	0
Grantham, 2b	4	0	2	0	2	0
Harris, 1b	4	0	2	13	0	0
Smith, c	3	0	0	6	0	0
xYde	0	1	0	0	0	0
Gooch, c	0	0	0	3	0	0
Hill, p	1	0	0	0	0	0
xxBrickell	1	1	0	0	0	0
Miljus, p	1	0	0	0	0	0
Totals	35	3	10	z26	11	1

zTwo out when winning run was scored.

NEW YORK	AB	R	H	O	A	E
Combs, cf	4	3	2	2	0	0
Koenig, ss	5	0	3	0	3	0
Ruth, rf	4	1	2	1	0	0
Gehrig, 1b	4	0	0	15	1	0
Meusel, lf	5	0	0	2	0	0
Lazzeri, 2b	3	0	0	4	5	1
Dugan, 3b	4	0	1	1	4	0
Collins, c	3	0	3	2	1	0
Moore, p	4	0	1	0	3	1
Totals	36	4	12	27	17	2

Yde ran for Smith in 7th.
Brickell batted for Hill in 7th.

SCORE BY INNINGS

	1	2	3	4	5	6	7	8	9	R	H	E
Pittsburg	1	0	0	0	0	0	2	0	0	3	10	1
New York	1	0	0	0	2	0	0	0	1	4	12	2

SUMMARY

Runs batted in—By Ruth 3, Wright 1, Barnhart 1, P. Waner 1. Two-base hit—Collins. Home run—Ruth. Sacrifice—L. Waner, P. Waner. Stolen base—Ruth. First base on errors—Pittsburg 2. Double plays—Lazzeri to Gehrig, Dugan to Lazzeri to Gehrig, Traynor to Wright to Harris. Left on base—Pittsburg 8, New York 11. Base on balls—Off Hill 1, off Miljus 3, off Moore 2. Struck out—By Hill 6, by Miljus 3, by Moore 2. Hits—Off Hill 9 in six innings, off Miljus 3 in two and two-thirds innings. Wild pitch—Miljus 2. Losing pitcher—Miljus. Time—2:15. Umpires—Ormsby at plate, Quigley at first, Nallin at second and Moran at third.

STANFORD 14, NEVADA 0, IN 1ST HALF

PALO ALTO, Oct. 8.—Stanford was leading Nevada 14 to 0 at the end of the first half of their football game here today.

PALO ALTO, Cal., Oct. 8.—Stanford was unable to score on Nevada during the first quarter of the game at Stanford stadium today. Coach Pop Warner started his second team with a surprise backfield consisting of Hoffman as quarterback, Frentrup and Padgett, halves, and Fleischacker at fullback. Although Stanford was unable to score, the play was all in Nevada territory.

Notre Dame Eleven Beat Detroit, 20-0

DETROIT, Oct. 8.—Notre Dame's football team today triumphed over the University of Detroit by a 20 to 0 score. The charging Notre Dame backfield time and again tore through Detroit's line for substantial gains.

YALE DEFEATED BY GEORGIA, 14 TO 10

By International News Service

YALE BOWL, NEW HAVEN, Conn., Oct. 8.—The University of Georgia with a gritty, fighting eleven defeated Yale by a score of 14 to 10, here today in game that was crowded with thrilling plays and equally dumb football. Georgia crossed Yale's coal line twice and kicked the goals from touchdown each time, while the Blue scored one touchdown, a goal from touchdown and three points on a drop-kick.

In the last two minutes of play Yale had the ball on Georgia's five-yard line and apparently had victory in its grasp as Loud hurled a forward pass to Scott over the goal line but Scott was beyond the end zone and outside the field of play so that the touchdown was denied the Blue.

CARDINAL SERIOIUSLY ILL

BELFAST, Ireland, Oct. 8.—Cardinal O'Donnell, head of the Catholic church in Ireland, was seriously ill today at Carlingford, suffering from an attack of pleurisy.

WILD PITCH IN 9TH INNING GIVES YANKS 4TH STRAIGHT GAME

YANKEE STADIUM, NEW YORK, Oct. 8.—The New York Yankees won the championship of the baseball world today. They won by defeating the Pittsburg Pirates for the fourth consecutive time, winning out, 4 to 3, in a dramatic ninth-inning rally.

A wild pitch by John Miljus, Pittsburg relief hurler, with the bases filled and two out, let Earl Combs dash home with the winning tally.

The Yankees made a clean sweep of four straight games, the first time this feat has been accomplished since the Boston Braves won four in a row from the Philadelphia Athletics in 1914.

The Pirates fought harder today than ever before in the series but that final destructive wild fling cost them all chance of gaining as much as a single victory.

RUTH HITS HOMER

Early in the game Babe Ruth put a tremendous homer into the distant right center stands, scoring Combs ahead of him. This came in the fifth inning and seemed to put the game on ice.

Wilcy Moore was working well for the Yanks but the Yank defense cracked twice in the seventh and the Pirates tied the score.

Carmen Hill, who started for Pittsburg, was not much better than any of the other pitchers Donie Bush has tried during the series.

Hill gave way to a pinch hitter in the seventh when the Pirates scored two runs.

Moore kept the Pirates' hits well scattered but was touched safely 10 times while the Yanks made 12 hits off Hill and Miljus.

RUTH PASSED

The last half of the ninth inning provided drama seldom seen in even the most exciting of world series games. Earl Combs had walked and Mark Koenig reached first on an infield hit.

With two on and none out, Babe Ruth was purposely passed, filling the bases and none out. Then and

(CONTINUED ON FIRST SPORT PAGE)

Fourth Game Play by Play

FIRST INNING

PIRATES—L. Waner beat out an infield hit to Koenig. He hit the first ball pitched and made the bag by his wonderful fleetness of foot. Barnhart was thrown out by Koenig, L. Waner taking second. P. Waner out, Dugan to Gehrig, L. Waner holding second. Wright singled to right, scoring L. Waner, and took second on the throw to the plate. Traynor hit to Dugan, who tagged Wright on the base line. ONE RUN, TWO HITS, NO ERRORS.

YANKEES—Combs hit past Grantham into right field for a single. Koenig singled to right, Combs stopping at second. Ruth singled to right, scoring Combs and sending Koenig to third. Gehrig fanned, swinging at the last one. Rain began falling. Ruth stole second. Meusel was called out on strikes. Lazzeri fanned. ONE RUN, THREE HITS, NO ERRCRS.

SECOND INNING

PIRATES—Grantham out, Dugan to Gehrig, on an attempted bunt. Harris singled past Koenig, who just managed to stop the ball but could not get it away. Smith flied to Ruth. Hill walked. L. Waner beat out a hit to Moore, filling the bases. Barnhart hit to Lazzeri, forcing L. Waner at second. NO RUNS, TWO HITS, NO ERRORS.

YANKEES—Dugan out, Wright to Harris. Collins hit into left field for

(CONTINUED ON SECOND SPORT PAGE)

HAIL THE YANKEES, CONQUERORS OF PITTSBURGH AND CHAMPIONS OF THE WIDE WIDE WORLD!

By decisively defeating the Pittsburgh Pirates, champions of the National League, the New York Yankees clinched their claim to the title of being the greatest baseball team in the world. Above are the Hugmen. From left to right (top row), GEHRIG, MEUSEL, RUTH, MOORE, PIPGRAS, COMBS, MILLER, HOYT, LAZZERI, KOENIG, SHOCKER, DURST, DOC WOODS, trainer. (Center row), SHAWKEY, GIARD, GRADOWSKI, O'LEARY, HUGGINS (himself), FLETCHER, PENNOCK, WERA, COLLINS. (Bottom row), RUETHER, DUGAN, PASCHAL, BENGOUGH, THOMAS, GAZELLA, MORE HART and EDDIE BENNETT, mascot.

SOCCER PLAYERS CAVORT AT NEPTUNE AND IDORA TODAY

EASTBAY SOCCER FANS TO SEE GOOD MATCHES TODAY

Samuels Cup Trials Start Today on Eastbay Fields as Teams Settle Down to Work; New Material Under Test on Several Outfits.

The Athens Club soccer team will swing into action again this afternoon at Idora park when it meets the rugged Scandia eleven. The game starts at 1 o'clock. The Scandia players have been showing great improvement and may figure as strong favorites in the Samuels cup competition. Following this contest the Veterans and the Sons of St. George will tangle on the same grounds. Both teams are stronger than last year.

Reeve, center for the Vets, plays the same style of kicking game as does Witschi and a battle against the goal tenders is likely. Manager Wallace of the Vets predicts a win for his team. Swan referees the first match and Currie has the second assignment.

At the Neptune stadium, the Neps will try to overcome the fast rushes of the Fruitvale team and no doubt will unless the latter let go of the ball on one time kicks. It promises to be a lively game, as both teams are speedy. The Neps forward line is greatly improving and the Fruitvale lads will have to step to stop them.

The Rangers were humiliated last week by their defeat by the Sons and are training faithfully to upset the Thistles to regain the points. They have inserted pep with their training and the fast moving combine of the Thistles will no doubt be held up. Brown will start the first match at 1 o'clock and Abrams will make the Scots behave. The Junior league Scandia and Sons teams will perform at 10 a. m. at Fruitvale grounds. The Naps and Rangers play the second game. They will play 35-minute halves.

Masonic Golfers to Play in Tourney

HEALDSBURG, Oct. 8.—Golfing members of the Masonic order from three Sonoma county cities are planning a tri-city tournament which promises interest for a hundrer lovers of the green during a portion of the winter season.

While the plans are still incomplete the first Sunday after Thanksgiving has been set as the tentative date for the opening play. The first tournament, 18 holes, is to be at the Santa Rosa Country club in charge of Hilliard Comstock and Charles Jacobs, prominent men of the county seat club.

Beardless Fan Gets Preference At Husky Gate

UNIVERSITY OF WASHINGTON, Oct. 8.—The kid who can prove that he has never had to use a razor will again free admission to the Whitman game, which will be played in Seattle, October 29. During the past few years, the combination of beards and knickers that have flourished among members of the male sex from the years of 15 to 85 has made it difficult to tell whether a boy is a man or not.

This season the short 16-year-old fellow that used to swear that he was twelve will have to shave pretty close if he wishes to get away with his story.

Penn Defeats Brown Before 35,000 Fans

FRANKLIN FIELD, PHILADELPHIA, Oct. 8.—Brown's iron men were broken for the first time in two years today, when Penn's young eleven dashed to a 14 to 6 triumph, before 35,000 spectators.

Not since Harvard stopped the Bruins two years ago has Brown tasted defeat until they crumbled before Louis Young's eleven today. Brown had won thriteen straight games during that period.

Paul Scull, Penn's dashing halfback, lifted his eleven to the victory. Playing one of the greatest games ever witnessed on Franklin Field, Scull scored two touchdowns and accounted for both extra points.

Spalding's Bookings

Smith Hdwe. Co. vs. Howard Radios, at Coast League, 2:30 p. m.; umpires, Hughes and McMurtry.

A. T. K. vs. Calatone Water Co., at Clement and Walnut, 2:30 p. m.
Ambassador Laundry vs. Rock Ridge Club, at Golden Gate Playgrounds, 3:30 p. m.
Ashland vs. Lopez Markets, at Ashland, 2:30 p. m.
A. T. K. Jrs. vs. S. F. Japanese, at Clement and Walnut, 12:30 p. m.
Berkeley Manufacturers vs 250th C. A. C., at Kenny Park, 12:30 p. m.
Brookfield Butters vs. Fruitvale Central Bank, at Eighteenth and Wood, 11:30 a. m.
Barron Tire Jrs. vs. Hopkins Pharmacy, at Eighteenth and Wood, 11:30 a. m.
Cochran & Celli vs. ——, at Roosevelt High, 11:30 a. m.
Jas. Kenny Athletic Club vs. Xavarians, at Kenny Park, 10:30 a. m.
Dolan Bros. Wrecking Co. vs. Oakland Postoffice, at San Pablo Park, 10:30 a. m.
Devereauv & Donovan vs. Zingg's Cigar Store, at Lincoln Park, 2:30 p. m.
Fruitvale De Molay vs. Valva Hardware Co., at Allendale, 11:30 a. m.
Fruitvale Outlaws vs. San Leandro Tigers, at School and Boston, 11:30 a. m.
Pullman Car Co. vs. Berkeley N. S. G. W., at Tech High, 11:30 a. m.
Imperial Sodas vs. General Petroleum, at San Pablo Park, 2:45 p. m.
McGregor Builders vs. ——, at Albany, 10:30 a. m.
Oakland Typewriter Co. vs. Oakland Billiards, at Lincoln Park, 12:00 m.
Piggly Wiggly vs. Greater Oakland Club, at Coast League, 12:00 m.
Pullman All-Stars vs. Gamble Tires, at Allendale, 3:30 p. m.
San Leandro vs. Rigney Tiles, at San Leandro, 2:30 p. m.
Smith & Dunne Tailors vs. Cranston Candy Shop, at Poplar Playgrounds, 1:30 p. m.
Telegraph Cigar Store vs. Crescent Battery Co., at Bushrod, 9:30 a. m.
Thrasher Athletic Club vs. ——, at Thrasher Park, 10:30 a. m.
West End Merchants vs. Sulmock Woodworkers, at Washington, 2:00 p. m.
Walnut Creek vs. S. P. Store Team, at Walnut Creek, 2:30 p. m.
Western Electric Co. vs Emeryville Merchants, at Roosevelt High, :30 p. m.
Woodbridge vs. Barron Tires, at Woodbridge, 2:30 p. m.
C. E. Day Coffee Co. vs. Coleman Tailors, at Tech High, 1:30 p. m.

EMERYVILLE INDUSTRIAL LEAGUE.
Johnson Washers vs. Burke Tires, at Alberger Field, 10:00 a. m.
Cozzens Motors vs. Emeryville Tires, at Mee Field, 9:30 a. m.
Pacific Manifold Book vs. Westinghouse Electric, at Mee Field, 12:00 m.
Marchants vs. Paraffine Paint Co., at Mee Field, 2:30 p. m.

TENNIS

by W. C. FULLER
Coach of Miss Helen Wills

Now that the tennis season is over so far as major events are concerned, here is something of interest to every player and follower of the game—namely, the first published list of the champions of 1927.

In the order of their importance: The Davis Cup, won by France, three matches to two. The Wightman Cup, won by the United States, five matches to two. Wimbledon, men's singles, won by Henri Cochet, France. Women's singles, Miss Helen Wills of the Berkeley tennis club. Men's doubles, W. T. Tilden and F. T. Hunter. Women's doubles, Miss Helen Wills and Miss Elizabeth Ryan, mixed doubles, Miss Ryan and Mr. Hunter.

United States national championships: Men's singles won by John Rene Lacoste, France; women's singles, Miss Helen Wills; men's doubles, Tilden and Hunter; women's doubles, Mrs. Kitty McKane Godfree and Miss Ermyntrude Harvey, England. Mixed doubles, Miss Eileen Bennett and Henri Cochet, France. Clay court, singles won by Tilden; doubles, J. F. Hennessey and Lucien Williams. National Intercollegiate: Singles, won by Wilmer Allison, University of Texas; doubles, John Van Ryn and Kenneth Appel, Princeton.

THE INDOOR CHAMP OF 1927 SEASON.

National indoor championships: Men's singles, won by Jean Borotra, France; women's singles, Mrs. Hazel Hotchkiss Wightman; men's doubles, Borotra and Brugnon, France; women's doubles, Mrs. Wightman and Mrs. Marion Zinderstein Jessup.

National Public Parks championships, formerly called National Municipal: Singles won by Theodore Drewes of St. Louis; doubles, Ralph Rice and George Jennings Jr. of Chicago.

National Veterans championships: Singles won by A. J. Cawse; doubles, William Rosenbaum and Fred C. Baggs.

National Father and Son, won by John Barton and Horace Barton, of South Dakota.

This completes the list of those in the senior classes. Winners of the junior championships are as follows:

National Junior championships, boys under 18: Singles won by Frank Shields of New York; doubles, Edward Jacobs and C. A. Smith, both of Maryland. National Junior, boys under 15: Singles won by William Jacobs of Baltimore; doubles, Frank Kready and Karl Kamrath, Pennsylvania. National Junior Girls championships: Singles won by Miss Midge Gladman, California; doubles, Miss Gladman and Miss Josephine Crookshank of the Berkeley club.

HARD COURT CHAMP AMONG THE GIRLS

Girls' National Hard Court championships: Singles won by Miss Louise McFarland; doubles, Miss Betty Fitch and Miss Margaret Smith, both of the Berkeley Tennis club.

Sectional and California state champions finish the list.

Pacific coast: Men's singles, Wm. M. Johnston; women's singles, Miss Helen Jacobs; men's doubles, Johnston and Griffin; women's doubles, Mrs. Bundy and Mrs. Dudley; mixed doubles, Miss Louise Williams and John Doeg; junior singles, Robert Seller; doubles, Joseph Coughlin and R. Fites; junior girls' singles, Miss Midge Gladman; doubles, Miss Adeline Brohm and Miss Josephine Crookshank; boys' single, Jack Cosgrove; girls' singles (under 16), Miss Evelyn Parsons; veterans' singles, I. C. Taylor.

California State: Men's singles, Bradshaw Harrison; men's doubles, Bradshaw Harrison and Sherman Lockwood; women's singles, Miss Helen Jacobs; women's doubles, Mrs. Lucy McCune Yates and Miss Marjorie Thorne; junior singles, Joseph Coughlin; doubles, Harry Plymire and Jack Cosgrove; junior girls, Miss McFarland; doubles, Miss Betty Fitch and Miss Margaret Smith; boys under 15, singles won by Jack Cosgrove; girls under 16, won by Evelyn Parsons; mixed doubles, Miss Edith Cross and M. Griffin.

The championship doubles tournament at the Berkeley club will continue today. Results of play so far follow:

Dean-Lloyd defeated Hornsberger-McCord, 6-4, 6-3; Eberson-Hatch defeated Young - Towle, 7-5, 6-4; LaCroix-Kline defeated Miller-Gilbert, default; Holmes-Holmes defeated Ross-Scheick, 6-0, 6-4; Ward-Hager defeated Hoogs-Hoogs, default; Wickson Stringham defeated Olney-Ludlow, 4-6, 8-6, 6-3; Bodinghouse-Killalee defeated Vaughn-Breckenfeld, 6-8, 6-3; Johnson - Higgins defeated Wickson-Stringham, 3-6, 6-3, 8-6; Holmes - Holmes defeated Ward-Hager, default.

Maxwell Bookings

Calatone Water Co. vs. A. T. K., at Clement and Walnut, 2:30 p. m.
Adrian A. C. vs. San Pablo Garage, at San Pablo, 2:30 p. m.
New Process Laundry vs. Johnson Dil Burners, at Bay View, 1:30 p. m.
Berkeley T. K. vs. Refining Water Softener, at San Pablo No. 2, 12:30 p. m.
Guarantee Shoe vs. Golden Gate Merchants, at Bushrod No. 1, 1:30 p. m.
J. J. Kreigs vs. Hawthorne Tigers, at Hawthorne, 10:00 a. m.
Spartan A. C. vs. Merritt A. C., at Bay View, 1:30 p. m.
Royal Roofers vs. Crew's All-Stars, at Roosevelt, 3:30 p. m.
Dalton Bros. Books vs. Italian Club, at Washington, 12:00 m.
St. Marks Tigers vs. Twenty-third Street Market, at Poplar, 11:30 a. m.
Amaral Bros. vs. Tenth Street Market, at Alvarado, 2:30 p. m.
Century A. C. vs. Kewanee Club, at Bushrod, 3:30 p. m.
Melrose Bldg. vs. Cox Cardinals, at Poplar, 3:30 p. m.
Hill Hardware vs. California Cracker, at Elmhurst, 1:30 p. m.
Goodman Clothiers vs. California Cubs, at Golden Gate, 11:30 a. m.
Goodman Clothiers vs. Piedmont Market, at Golden Gate, 1:30 p. m.
Justi Fruit vs. Alameda De Molay, at Bushrod, 11:30 a. m.
City of Albany vs. Bohemian Garage, at Albany, 2:30 p. m.
S. P. Yard Office vs. Pon Honor, at Bay View, 9:30 a. m.
St. Mary's Midgets vs. Live Oaks, at Bay View, 3:30 p. m.
Fruitvale Eagles vs. Cottrell Bros., at Fruitvale, 1:00 p. m.
Stanley Clothiers vs. Rehor Repairs, at San Pablo, 10:30 a. m.
V. O. Lawrence vs. Iberico Club, at Bushrod, 11:30 a. m.
Arcade Dancers vs. Richmond No. 192, at Richmond, 2:30 p. m.
Postoffice vs. Oakland Colored Cubs, at University, 12:00 m.
Crystal Palace vs. San Bruno, at San Bruno, 2:30 p. m.
Fontana Food Products vs. Nationals, at Recreation, 12:00 m.
Richmond All-Stars vs. Poplar Tigers, at Bay View, 9:30 a. m.
Walt Rignel Stars vs. Fruitavle W. O. W., at Bushrod, 9:30 a. m.
Vierra Billiards vs. Leslie Sale Co., at Elmhurst, 3:30 p. m.
Allendale Merchants vs. Salesian Y. M. I., at Allendale, 1:30 p. m.
Jenny Wren vs. Castro Natives, at Clubhouse, 12:00 m.

MAXWELL HDWE. SUMMER LEAGUE.
Corgiat Tires vs. National Ice and Cold Storage, at Bushrod, 1:30 p. m.
Stanley Clothiers vs. ——, at Bushrod, 3:30 p. m.

Pirate, Yank Owners Lucky To Break Even

Wild Pitch By Miljus In Ninth Cost Magnates More Than $200,000.

By EDDIE MURPHY

The wild pitch which John Miljus made in the ninth inning at New York yesterday afternoon to give the Yankees a 4 to 3 victory over the Pittsburgh Pirates and close the series with only four games played, pitched the owners of the Yankee and Pirate teams out of about $250,000. It was the first time since 1914 that a world series ended in four games and it was another tribute to the honesty of the national pastime.

Had the Pirates turned in a victory yesterday it would have meant the playing of a fifth game at New York today and advance sales indicated that a new attendance mark for a single game would be set. More than $200,000 had been collected for reservations for today's expected game and now Colonel Jacob Ruppert, president of the Yankee club, will have to keep a force of office help busy for the next few days mailing back or handing out money to those fans who paid in advance for reservations.

SIXTY THOUSAND AT GAMES.

More than 60,000 witnessed each of the two games played in New York yesterday and Friday and it was expected that many fans would be unable to buy their way into the Yankee Stadium if a game was played today.

Last year the New York Yankees and St. Louis Cardinals battled in the world series which went the full seven games and the share of the receipts for each club was $158,595.97. It is expected that the share of each club this year will run around $62,000. After all expenses are taken care of each club will be lucky to show a profit on the series.

As for the ballplayers themselves, their pocket books were not hurt the least bit by the series ending in four games, as they get a cut on the first four games only and the cut this year is likely to be the biggest in the history of world series.

Bear Cubs Defeat St. Mary's Frosh 14-7

CALIFORNIA MEMORIAL STADIUM, Oct. 8.—In a preliminary to the California-St. Mary's varsity football game, the Bear Cubs battered their way to two touchdowns to defeat the St. Mary's freshman team 14 to 7 here this afternoon. The two California scores came on straight tackle bucks and reverses, one before the game was two minutes old and the second near the middle of the last quarter. St. Mary's score came when Vincent Boyle, former Vallejo high school star, received a punt and returned it 45 yards to the line.

Max Follendorf accounted for the first California touchdown on a 9-yard reverse play at tackle, while Roger Williams dove across on the same play for 2½ yards, to score the second touchdown.

The Saint yearlings played with their backs against the wall most of the game, but their stubborn defence troubled "Brick" Mitchell's team considerably. At the end of the third quarter the Bears were held on the Saint 1-yard line by the sturdy St. Mary's line.

Nimrods Find State Game In Great Variety

Ducks, Deer, Grouse Other Lures Make Outings Real Pleasure Now.

SACRAMENTO, Oct. 10.—(AP)—If variety is the spice of life, the opening of the duck season, October 1, has added much to the joy of Calil nia nimrods. For those who took to the great open spaces during the days since duck shooting became legal, have had the cream of the land at their disposal. They will continue to enjoy theis life until October 14.

Right at present those frequenting some of the Sierra game districts, due to overlapping seasons, can certainly vary their sport to suit their needs. They can hunt deer until they tire or until they bag their limit, and then grab a shotgun and go out in search of dove or grouse.

If there is open water and ducks, these can be added. Then if the weather gets a little too warm for hunting there are speckled beauties in the mountain streams in the territory where deer, grouse and dove are to be found that can lure the anglers into the shade.

FEAST FOR KINGS.

And if a man or a few members of a party are lucky and the district right such a feast as can be spread—vension, roast duck, baked grouse, dove stew and beautiful trout, cooked to a golden brown—a feast that would make the mouth of an "office prisoner" water.

The duck season throughout the state will remain open until January 15.

Deer season, save in districts 2, 2½ and 3, which takes in those mountain counties along the Pacific coast from Mendocino south to and including Ventura and Glenn, Colusa, Lake, Yolo, Napa, Solano, Contra Costa, Alameda, Santa Clart, San Benito and part of Stanislaus, San Joauin, Merced, Madera and Fresno, will be open until October 15.

GROUSE SHOOTING.

The grouse season is open in all districts until October 14, but these birds are to be found only on the eastern mountain slopes.

The dove season is open now only in districts 4, 4½ and 4¾, these districts taking in those counties down in the southern part of the state—Mono, Inyo, San Bernardino, Los Angeles, Orange, Riverside, San Diego and Imperial—but there also are deer ranges and trout streams there as well as some ducks.

Great Net Stars Will Meet Today

LOS ANGELES, Oct. 8.—Four ranking stars of the tennis world will fight it out tomorrow in the men's and women's single championships of the Pacific southwest tournament here.

William Tilden and Francis J. Hunter will contest for masculine honors, while Molla Mallory will meet Kea Bouman, Holland, in the women's class.

Bush Managers Will Have Meet Next Tuesday

A MEETING of all managers with teams in the Spalding Winter League will be held next Tuesday evening at 7:45 o'clock at Spaldings, 1751 Broadway.

Al Erle, secretary of the league requests that all managers be present as they are to be given final instructions for the opening games which will take place next Sunday. More than sixty clubs are in the league.

Managers sending in box scores to The TRIBUNE are requested to deposit them at the Franklin street entrance on Sunday evening if possible.

Broncs May Use Reserves Against Ignatian Eleven

UNIVERSITY OF SANTA CLARA, Oct. 8.—In the possibility that the regular Bronco varsity should run up a score on their rivals in Sunday's game and lead the Ignatians by a safe margin at Kezar stadium the fans of the bay region will be treated to a performance by some of the less well known performers of the gridiron.

While Adam Walsh is not overly well blessed with reserve strength the few that form the reserves are good men. In the line he has Sidener, center, who has yet to break into a game. O'Daniels and Ahart were on the squad last year but failed to break into very many games. These two tackles tip the scales at 200 and give promise of developing.

In the backfield he has Miller and Fawley, two men who have played in some of the games this season but were not left in long enough to strut their stuff. Miller is a demon on line plunges while Fawley is good on end runs and receiving passes. Eddie Cummings and Hakkinson, quarterbacks, are also making strong bids for a regular berth. Hakkinson ran the team in fine order at Los Angeles when George Barsi, regular quarter, was taken out. He threw two passes that resulted in touchdowns besides playing a whale of a game at safety.

SAN MATEO JUNIORS WIN.

SAN MATEO, Oct. 8.—Completely outclassing the invading gridders from Bakersfield Junior college in every department of play, the San Mateo Junior college squad won a one-sided game here this afternoon by a score of 50 to 0.

Local Boxers Are Kept Busy By De Lauer

Farr to Box in the South; Wallace and Uhlan Have Matches Ahead.

By L[illegible] SHAND

Johnny Fa[illegible] ox Joey Sangor in Los A[illegible] October 18, according to [illegible] received from Manager Scotti [illegible]e Lauer last night. Scotti also has bouts lined up for other members of his stable. Here is his letter written from Cleveland, Ohio:

"Johnny Farr boxes Joey Sangor in Los Angeles October 18, and I think I will come west with him. I want to come back to Oakland shortly anyhow, as maybe Jerry Denahy and Jack Woolley want me to show them how to shoot ducks. Billy Wallace boxes Cuddy De Marco in Pittsburgh October 10, and a week later meets some good lightweight in Cleveland. Sammy Mandell still refuses $50,000 to box Wallace for the lightweight championship. Red Uhlan meets K. O. Phil Kaplan in Cleveland on the 12th and on the 17th tangles with Allentown Joe Gans. If he wins both of these matches he has been promised a bout with Dave Shade in New York."

* * *

The auditorium will probably be "dark" next Wednesday night, as Promoter Tommy Simpson had not secured a main event up to a late hour last night. Tommy tried to get Jimmy McLarnin, but the Belfast Spider, brother Sammy and Manager Charlie Foster have left Los Angeles for Chicago.

* * *

The future of the Acorn club is still shrouded in secrecy. Matchmaker Roy Stanford says he hasn't the slightest idea what his partners have in mind except that the club cannot show again at the Armory unless many improvements are made to conform to the fire ordinances.

* * *

Vic Morrison and Tiger Bob Robinson waltzed through nine rounds at El Cerrito Friday night, but they gave the fans their money's worth in the tenth, when they fought toe to toe.

Section II SPORTS NEW YORK Herald Tribune SPORTS Section II

TEN PAGES SUNDAY, OCTOBER 9, 1927 TEN PAGES

Yankees Win World Series, Gaining Fourth Successive Victory, Wild Pitch in Ninth Inning Scores Deciding Run in 4 to 3 Game; Yale and Harvard Elevens Lose---Penn Conquers Brown, 14 to 6

Georgia Wins From Yale on Passes, 14-10

Long Toss Paves Way for Deciding Points; Caldwell Stopped on 1-Yard Line in Final Minutes

Southerners Score In First 4 Minutes

Scott Makes Tying Touchdown; Field Goal Gives Elis Short Lead, 10-7

Special to the Herald Tribune

NEW HAVEN, Conn., Oct. 8.—The University of Georgia football team, playing a brilliant offensive game in the first two periods and fighting every minute to make the breaks come its way, upset Yale in the Bowl to-day, winning by 14 to 10, despite the desperate efforts of Bruce Caldwell, the Elis' halfback star, who smashed and tore his way through the Southerners' line for long gains.

Costly fumbles, bad judgment by the quarterbacks and bad breaks combined with the fighting spirit of the Southerners to bring Yale her first defeat from Georgia. For the last four years Georgia has sent a hard-fighting team to the Bowl, and each time it has provided the Elis fine opposition, but each time it has lost.

To-day, by virtue of an unexpected attack that scored a touchdown in the first four minutes of play and another in the second period, this Southern eleven outplayed Yale for these two periods and was handed the game by Yale in the final period, although the Elis completely outplayed the visitors throughout the quarter.

With the score 14 to 10 against his team as the last period opened, Tad Jones sent his first team back into the game after the second team had played an even game with the Southerners in the third period. This refreshed first team had things going its own way from the very start of the period.

McCrary Intercepts Pass

Caldwell, showing brilliance seldom seen on any gridiron, smashed the Georgia line repeatedly for long gains, and Yale put over five first downs on the first seven plays of the period, and carried the ball far into Georgia territory. Two more plays put the ball on Georgia's nine-yard line, but here, instead of depending on Caldwell, a pass was tried and it went into the hands of McCrary, an ever alert Georgia back, who played a fine game throughout.

Georgia kicked to its 43-yard line, where Yale started another rush to the goal line.

Largely through the running of Caldwell, who made gain after gain, Yale took the ball to the 7-yard line, where Duncan Cox lost this Yale opportunity by a fumble as he tried to gain through center. Following this Estes tried to kick out of danger, but his boot was short and Charlesworth took it for Yale on Georgia's 28-yard mark. On seven plays Caldwell alone carried the ball to the 1-yard line, making a gain every time, but on the eighth time the signal called for a center rush, and Caldwell was stopped by the whole Georgia team, Georgia taking the ball on downs. A third opportunity had been thrown away by what looked like bad judgment by the quarterback.

Score Is Disallowed

As the game came to an end Yale again found itself ear the leader's goal line. Georgia held the Eli backs twice and a pass was incomplete. There was less than a minute to play and Yale had the ball inside the 20-yard line for the fourth time on the quarter. As a last chance, Loud, quarterback, called for a forward pass and threw the ball, but had overrun the end zone, and so the score was not allowed.

The first two periods were the scoring periods of the game. Georgia put over its first touchdown before five minutes had elapsed, Johnson making the touchdown after taking a twenty-yard pass from Estes after Yale had held the Southerners for three downs. The extra point was added by Johnson on a placement kick.

Yale tied the score just before the close of the period. Stewart Scott, who played well for Yale at end, scoring on a long pass on which he made a brilliant catch. In the second period Yale took the lead, but only for a short time. After Yale had advanced to the Georgia 25-yard line on a steady march the Southerners held three times and then Cox scored three points for Yale on a drop-kick.

Pass Nets Fifty-eight Yards

Georgia won the game six plays later. Caldwell kicked to Johnson who ran back to the 35-yard line before Sid Quarrier could down him. A pass, Hooks to Dudley, netted fifty-eight yards on the next play, for Dudley carried the ball to Yale's 7-yard line, Hoben forcing him to step outside. McCrary made the score three plays later, and Johnson added the final point on a placement kick.

Yale played more brilliantly than the Southerners in spots, but they were guilty of seven fumbles while Georgia handled the ball perfectly. Yale made seventeen first downs to six for the winners, and ten of these came in the final quarter. In this last period Georgia did not get the ball beyond the center line.

Caldwell was the best player on the field to-day. The play of the Yale line, especially from tackle to tackle, was disappointing, and it was through this defect that Georgia was able to advance into Yale territory at the start. Captain Shivers played best for the winners, his kicking and end play being outtsanding features of the game. McCrary also played well for the Southerners.

Cox provided the longest run for the

(Continued on page four)

Purdue Routs Harvard, 19-0; Novice Stars

Ralph Welch, Sub for Wilcox, Scores Two Touchdowns and Aids in Third as Feats Astound 40,000

Youngster's Attack Smothers Crimson

Boilermakers' Backs Run Up 16 First Downs in Contest at Cambridge

Special to the Herald Tribune

CAMBRIDGE, Mass., Oct. 8.—Purdue, playing the open brand of football regarded as typical of Western teams, overwhelmed Harvard to-day, winning a one-sided game, 19 to 0. Purdue was minus its star back, Cotton Willcox, and Coach Phelan replaced the main cog of his attack with a youngster playing his first game for the Western college. Ralph Welch, nicknamed "The Pest," tore through the Harvard line ofr long gains, scoring twice and passing to a team mate for Purdue's third touchdown.

Harvard was seldom able to gain consistently against the Boilermakers, and then only through the brilliant running of Joe Crosby the Crimson eleven, with its comparatively conservative style of play, was able to collect but seven first downs, most of these barely eked out.

Backs Amass Sixteen First Downs

The Purdue backs amassed a total of sixteen first downs and the total would have been still higher if the gains per rush had not been so large.

Cross bucks, fake cross bucks, deceptive double bucks, long passes, reminiscent of Dartmouth's aerial attack of several years ago, and short flat passes, executed with speed and precision, provided the boilermakers with an attack that Harvard was unable to stop.

Welch carried the ball more than the three other men in the backfield together and rolled up a total yardage, which exceeded the total for the whole Harvard backfield. His twisting, side-step running gave the 40,000 spectators a better exhibition of ball-carrying than has been seen in the Harvard Stadium in several years.

Purdue Offensive Prevails

The Purdue offensive started with a rush at the beginning of the game and was never fully stopped during the four periods of play.

Harvard won the toss and elected to kick off. Wilson ran the ball back twelve yards to his 22-yard line. Welch, on the first play, reeled off fifteen yards around end and was followed by an eight-yard thrust through tackle by Leichtle. Welch kicked when Koransky failed to gain.

The Crimson back met stone-wall resistance and after two futile attempts to break through the line, French kicked to Welch, who eluded the Harvard ends, taking the pigskin back fifteen yards to his own 40-yard line.

Another exchange of kicks netted Purdue ten yards, placing the ball in midfield. At this point the Westerners settled down to the business of scoring. When Leichtle failed to gain on a line break Welch tossed a pass to Hutton for a ten yard gain and first down.

Advances Ball Eight Yards

Koransky drove through center for five yards, Welch took the ball, and in a sweeping end run carried the ball to the Harvard 17-yard line, and on the next play advanced the ball eight yards more, seven yards from the goal line. From here it took Welch three tries to carry the ball over. His attempted pass to score the goal after the touchdown went wild. After Purdue had kicked off the Crimson ball carriers made their initial first down of the game, on bucks by Crosby and Guarnaccia, but the gain went for naught when Wilson intercepted Guarnaccia's pass a few minutes later on Harvard's 45-yard line.

Purdue's subsequent attack was stopped on Harvard's 20-yard line when Welch's attempted pass to Hutton bounced off six or seven pairs of outstretched hands to come to rest finally in the arms of Joe Crosby.

Crosby Gains Cheer Harvard

Harvard, aided by Crosby's gains and two Purdue offsides, carired the ball to the 36-yard line. Donaghy, who had been substituted for French, got off a bad kisk which rolled out on his own 46-yard line.

Aided by a fifteen-yard penalty for holding, the Crimson team was able to win the ball on downs. Donaghy's next kick was better, but Welch returned it twenty yards, nearly to midfield. Welch and Koransky carried the ball down the field to Harvard's 40-yard line. Here Welch threw a beautiful pass to Hutton over the head of the Harvard safety man. Hutton was able to stumble the six or seven yards separating him from the goal line. Wilson kicked the goal, making the score 13 to 0, in Purdue's favor. Three plays after the next kick-off the half ended with the ball on Harvard's 30-yard line.

Harvard Opens With Attack

In the second half Harvard opened with an attack which Purdue was unable to stop before the ball had been carired from the 20-yard line to midfield. Dryer, a sub, pulled Guarnaccia's attempted pass to Burns out of the air on his own 43-yard line. Welch and Koransky, tearing off gains five or ten yards at a clip, carried the ball down the field.

The play see-sawed up and down the field with both teams exchanging stronger offense than defense, until Hook recovered Crosby's fumble on the Crimson's 13-yard line. Welch and Koransky had little trouble in scoring

(Continued on page four)

Combs Scoring the Run Which Ended the World Series in the Ninth Inning Yesterday

Herald Tribune photos—Steffen

Just after the wild pitch in the ninth inning. Combs has crossed the plate but is hidden from view by Miljus, Pirate pitcher, who ran in to cover the plate. note Jumping Joe Dugan jumping with joy

Football Results

EAST			
Penn	14	Brown	6
Purdue	19	Harvard	0
Georgia	14	Yale	10
Army	21	Marquette	12
N. Y. U.	65	Alfred	0
Columbia	28	Wesleyan	0
Syracuse	21	Johns Hopkins	6
Navy	35	Drake	6
Lafayette	56	Rutgers	0
Cornell	53	Richmond	0
Georgetown	39	Davis Elkins	0
W. and J.	31	Bethany	0
Boston U.	13	Colby	0
Holy Cross	18	Dayton	0
Bowdoin	12	New Hampshire	7
Middlebury	12	Mass. Aggies	0
Temple	58	Juniata	0
Providence	7	Norwich	7
Hobart	38	Upsala	0
Geo. Washington	27	American U.	0
St. John's, Annap.	20	Gallaudet	0
Villanova	32	Lebanon Valley	7
St. Thomas	26	St. Joseph	7
Swarthmore	6	Susquehanna	0
Bucknell	13	Penn State	7
Amherst	14	Haverford	0
Worcester Poly	14	Trinity	6
Carnegie	58	Drexel	0
New York Aggies	6	Cooper Union	0
Princeton	42	Lehigh	0
Quantico Marine	32	St. Bonaventure	0
St. Johns, Bkyn.	7	Mount St. Mary's	0
Maine	14	New York Aggies	13
Williams	12	Vermont	0
Ursinus	7	Delaware	0
West. Maryland	13	Schuylkill	0
Clarkson	7	Rensselaer	0
F. and M.	13	Rickinson	8
C. C. N. Y.	14	St. Lawrence	14
Springfield	7	Union	7
Pittsburgh	40	West Virginia	0
Dartmouth	38	Allegheny	7
Tufts	28	Bates	0
Virginia Poly	6	Colgate	0
Navy Plebes	12	Georgton Fresh	2
Niagara	34	Buffalo	0
Catholic U.	19	Loyola, Balt.	12
Rochester	18	Hamilton	0
R. I. State	26	Lowell Textile	0
WEST			
Notre Dame	20	Detroit	0
Michigan	21	Michigan State	0
Wisconsin	26	Kansas	6
Illinois	58	Butler	0
Missouri	7	Nebraska	6
Washington U.	13	Missouri Mines	0
St. Louis U.	7	Springfield Teach	0
Toledo U.	19	Hillsdale Ohio	0
Illinois Wesleyan	14	Knox	0
Coe	24	Monmouth	3
Creighton	7	North Dakota	0
Akron	19	Ashland	9
Denison	19	Case	0
Wittenberg	45	Cincinnati	0
Iowa State	26	Simpson	6
Oberlin	28	Baldwin Wallace	6
John Carroll	7	Grove City	7
St. Xavier	53	Western Reserve	7
Miami	35	Ohio Wesleyan	7
Marietta	6	Otterbein	0
Ohio U.	25	Ohio Northern	0
Muskingum	53	Kenyon	6
Haskell	15	Morningside	11
Cornell College	38	Beloit	7
S. D. State	15	Des Moines	0
N. D. Aggies	37	Valley City Teach.	0
Carleton	26	Lawrence	0
Northwestern	13	Utah	6
Ohio State	13	Iowa	6
Minnesota	40	Oklahoma Aggies	0
Chicago	13	Indiana	6
Doane	7	Still	0
Lombard	18	Kalamazoo	6
Lake Forest	6	Y. M. C. A. Col.	0
Notre Dame Res.	8	Kalamazoo Res.	0
Wooster	18	Mount Union	0
Heidelberg	26	Hiram	0
Bluffton	18	Capital	0
Wilmington	29	Findlay	6
Wabash	12	James Milliken	7
Depauw	51	Rose Poly	6
Manchester	40	Vincennes	0
Indiana Central	18	Earlham	0
SOUTH			
Georgia Tech	13	Tulane	6
Vanderbilt	53	Centre	6
Chattanooga	31	Citadel	6
Furman	27	Mercer	13
Maryville	10	Tennessee	7
Texas A. and M.	18	Sewanee	0
Alabama	0	L. S. C.	0
Spring Hill	19	S. W. La. Institute	0
Miss. A. and M.	14	Louisana Poly	0
Fort Benning	20	Milligan	8
Millsaps	13	Howard	6
Davidson	12	Wofford	2
South Carolina	13	Virginia	12
W. and L.	12	Duke	7
Arkansas	13	Baylor	6
Centenary	21	So. Methodist U.	12
La. College	39	Col. of Marshall	0
N. C. State	18	Vlemson	6
North Carolina	7	Maryland	6

Penn Springs Upset, Beating Brown, 14 to 6

Bruins Suffer First Defeat in Two Years; Paul Scull Makes All Quaker Points

By Don Skene

PHILADELPHIA, Oct. 8.—The University of Pennsylvania's fighting football team shattered the "Iron Men" of Brown by a score of 14-6 on the slippery turf of Franklin Field before a crowd of 35,000 people this afternoon. The Penn victory upset the early season dope bucket with a clattering crash and marked the first defeat of Brown's Bruins since their Harvard game of 1925.

Penn's triumph was largely the result of what might be called Sculldugery or the work of the Scull brothers, Paul and Folwell. Pittsburgh may sing of the Waner brothers, but to the happy Pennsylvania supporters to-night the two greatest brothers in the world are Paul and Folwell Scull, left halfback and left end, respectively, on the Red and Blue team.

Brother Paul had by far the more prominent role of the two to-day. All Paul managed to accomplish for Penn this afternoon was to score all fourteen points with two touchdowns and two sharp-shooting dropkicks after touchdown.

Folwell Scull Blocks Kick

Brother Folwell, who was a mighty handy young man around the field all through the game, contributed his best bit when he flashed through a crack in the line and blocked Captain Randall's attempted dropkick after Brown's touchdown in the fourth quarter. This neat bit of enterprise by brother Folwell kept Brown from tying the score at 7-all at this juncture and sent Penn out under the inspiration of a one-point lead, 7-6.

After a scoreless first half, the period of which was a conservative punting duel, Paul Scull began proving himself a ghastly death's head to the Brown warriors. Four minutes after the opening of the third period Edwards threw a forward pass which the fleet and flashy Paul, who is the shortest man on the Penn squad, grabbed out of the air and ran with for thirty yards for a touchdown. He added another point by booting a dropkick squarely between the uprights.

Brown fought back and scored on the first play of the fourth period. The Iron Men had been smothered on the three preceding plays. Then they switched their attack from the line to a forward pass, which Edwards flipped to Captain Randall. He battled his way thirty-seven yards for a touchdown. The Bruin captain failed in his golden chance to tie the score when brother Folwell swarmed in on him and messed up his attempt at a dropkick.

Long Run by Shober

Brother Paul got busy again after six minutes of play in the final period. Little Johnny Shober, Penn quarterback, who weighs 140 pounds soaking wet and carrying two suitcases, swept around Brown's left wing for twenty-eight yards. He was thrown out of bounds on the 4-yard line. Paul was called upon and he responded by darting through the Iron line for his second touchdown. He got the goal after touchdown with a nifty dropkick.

Brown was a strong favorite to win, but was unable to cope with the powerful and puzzling offensive of coach Lou Young's Penn players. Penn showed a far greater versatility of attack, riddling

(Continued on page two)

Score of Fourth Game

PITTSBURGH PIRATES

	AB	R	H	2B	3B	HR	TB	SH	SB	BB	SO	PO	A	E
L. Waner, cf	4	1	3	0	0	0	3	1	0	0	0	0	0	1
Barnhart, lf	5	0	1	0	0	0	1	0	0	0	0	2	0	0
P. Waner, rf	4	0	1	0	0	0	1	1	0	0	0	0	0	0
Wright, ss	4	0	1	0	0	0	1	0	0	0	0	1	6	0
Traynor, 3b	4	0	0	0	0	0	0	0	0	0	1	1	4	0
Grantham, 2b	4	0	2	0	0	0	2	0	0	0	0	0	2	0
Harris, 1b	4	0	2	0	0	0	2	0	0	0	0	13	0	0
Smith, c	3	0	0	0	0	0	0	0	0	0	0	6	0	0
*Yde	0	1	0	0	0	0	0	0	0	0	0	0	0	0
Gooch, c	0	0	0	0	0	0	0	0	0	1	0	3	0	0
Hill, p	1	0	0	0	0	0	0	0	0	1	0	0	0	0
†Brickell	1	1	0	0	0	0	0	0	0	0	0	0	0	0
Miljus, p	0	0	0	0	0	0	0	0	0	0	1	0	0	1
Totals	35	3	10	0	0	0	10	2	0	2	2	‡26	12	2

NEW YORK YANKEES

	AB	R	H	2B	3B	HR	TB	SH	SB	BB	SO	PO	A	E
Combs, cf	4	3	2	0	0	0	2	0	0	1	0	2	0	0
Koenig, ss	5	0	3	0	0	0	3	0	0	0	1	0	3	0
Ruth, rf	4	1	2	0	0	1	5	0	0	1	0	1	0	0
Gehrig, 1b	5	0	0	0	0	0	0	0	0	0	2	14	2	0
Meusel, lf	5	0	0	0	0	0	0	0	0	0	2	2	0	0
Lazzeri, 2b	3	0	0	0	0	0	0	0	0	1	2	5	4	1
Dugan, 3b	4	0	1	0	0	0	1	0	0	0	0	1	4	0
Collins, c	3	0	3	1	0	0	4	0	0	1	0	2	1	0
Moore, p	4	0	1	0	0	0	1	0	0	0	2	0	3	1
Totals	37	4	12	1	0	1	16	0	0	4	9	27	17	2

*Ran for Smith in seventh inning.
†Batted for Hill in seventh inning.
‡Two out when winning run was scored.

SCORE BY INNINGS

Pittsburgh	1 0 0	0 0 0	2 0 0—3
New York	1 0 0	0 2 0	0 0 1—4

Runs batted in—Ruth (3), Wright (1), Barnhart (1), P. Waner (1). Left on bases—Pittsburgh, 9; New York, 11. Double plays—Lazzeri and Gehrig; Dugan, Lazzeri and Gehrig; Traynor, Wright and Harris. Bases on balls—Off Hill, 1 (Collins); off Miljus, 3 (Lazzeri, Combs, Ruth); off Moore, 2 (Hill Gooch). Struck out—By Hill, 6 (Lazzeri, 2; Meusel, Gehrig, Moore, Koenig); by Moore, 2 (Traynor, Miljus); by Miljus, 3 (Moore Gehrig, Meusel). Hits—Off Hill, 9 in 6 innings; off Miljus, 3 in 2 2-3. Wild pitches—Miljus 2. Losing pitcher—Miljus. Umpires—Ormsby (A. L.) at the plate; Quigley (N. L.) at first; Nallin (A. L.) at second base; Moran (N. L.) at third base. Time of game—2:01.

Rochester Scores Three Touchdowns to Win, 18-0

Special to the Herald Tribune

ROCHESTER, Oct. 8.—Three touchdowns, one in each of the first three quarters, brought victory to the University of Rochester eleven here this afternoon over Hamilton, 18 to 0. Zoronow, Yeaw and Vanhorn scored the three touchdowns for the home team.

The line-up:

Pos.	Rochester (18)	Hamilton (0)
L. G.	Collame	Carpenter
L. T.	Yeaw	Carson
L. E.	Kinkaid	Wormuth
C.	Kugles	Brockway
R. E.	Longlois	Reinecke
R. T.	Dunn	Schneider
R. G.	Cloney	Scovel
Q. B.	Bleyler	Pierce
R. H. B.	Vanhorn	Chatfield
L. H. B.	Wilson	Campbell
F. B.	Zoronow	Warren

SCORE BY PERIODS

Rochester	6	6	6	0	—18
Hamilton	0	0	0	0	— 0

Touchdowns—Zoronow, Vanhorn, Yeaw. Substitutions—Rochester: Watts for Kinkaid, Steele for Watts, D. Smith for Yeaw, Colegrove for Ehaney, Minnenmayer for Colegrove, Barrett for Dunn, Hall for Longlois, McNall for Hall, Patrizio for Bleyler, Jackson for Vanhorn, P. Smith for Wilson, Buck for Zoronow. Hamilton: Jassett for Wormuth, Westerberg for Carson, Tucker for Westerberg, Westerberg for Carpenter, M. Jenks for Scoville, W. Jens for Pierce, Faller for W. Jenks, Pierce for Falley, Desermo for Campbell, Demon for Warren.

Referee—Art Powell, Buffalo. Umpire—Howie Ortner, Cornell. Linesman—J. Leipsie, Syracuse. Time of periods—Twelve minutes.

Schoolboy Football

SCHOOLBOY			
James Monroe	26	Evander Childs	12
Brooklyn Prep	26	Alex. Hamilton	0
Stuyvesant	7	C. C. N. Y. fresh.	0
Bushwick	0	St. John's	0
Bay Ridge Eve.	13	Port Jervis	0
Bordentown	18	Pingry	0
Rockaway	6	Chatham	0
Blair Academy	24	Pennington	0
Dean Academy	6	Penn Freshmen	0
Tome	26	Wash. Central	13
Princeton Prep	48	Brown Prep	0
Manlius	45	28th Infantry	0
Camden	14	Northeast (Phila.)	12
Phila. Catholic	18	Easton H. S.	6
Peddie	12	Allentown Prep	6
Norristown	6	Chester	0
Allentown	62	Lebanon	0
McKenzie	10	N. Y. M. A.	0
Lawrenceville	18	F. and M. Academy	0
Mercersburg Acad.	27	Beckley Bus. Col.	0
Montclair	6	Plainfield	6
Fairfield	32	King School	0
Stamford	26	East Patterson	0
Commerce	19	Geo. Washington	0
Flushing	20	St. Paul's	0
Yale Freshmen	6	Exeter	0
Choate	6	Suffield	0
Poly Prep	13	Montclair Acad.	0
Hockley	6	Riverdale	0
Atlantic City	6	East Orange	0
Orange	19	Belleville	6
West Orange	14	Irvington	6

Moore to Lead Williams Harriers

WILLIAMSTOWN, Mass., Oct. 8.—Terris Moore, of Haddonfield, N. J., has been elected captain of the Williams cross country team for the coming season.

Ruppert's Smile Makes Him Real Hero of Series

Colonel Chortles as Miljus's Bad Toss Robs Till of $200,000 for Fifth Game

By W. O. McGeehan

The real hero of the Yankee-Pirates World Series, which passed into history with a swiftness that upset the series cash register and scattered a few hundred thousands of dollars all over the premises, was Colonel Jacob Ruppert. The experts will be picking some athlete as the hero of this one, but it will be hard to take away the honor from the proprietor of the Yanks.

The boys in the right field bleachers will be nominating Mr. Babe Ruth and with much vociferousness because Mr. Ruth put the wallop in the last game when he drove a home run of flat and swift trajectory in among them; but the customers in those far-flung spaces were unable to see the real poignant moment in the great drama.

When Mr. Jovo Miljus heaved that last wild one, giving the game to the Yankees, a dapper gentleman seated in a box near the Yankee dug-out rose merrily and waved his hat. There was a smile on his face.

This gentleman was Colonel Jacob Ruppert, the proprietor of the Yankees. He was laughing off a couple of hundred thousand dollars for the sheer joy of seeing the Yankees take a World Series in four straight games.

Laughter Is Genuine

Those who heard the colonel laughing insist that the merriment was genuine and that the colonel was well conversant with the facts when he burst into laughter. He was well aware that in the morning his office force would be refunding the price of the tickets for the fifth game, which is not to be played.

You can rank the colonel's two hundred thousand dollar smile with Madame Somebody's hundred thousand dollar legs or somebody's hundred thousand dollar soupbone. In fact, that laugh was a bit more remarkable.

Of course, Mr. Ruth knocked off sixty home runs in the regular season and two in the world series. But, then, Mr. Ruth is an athlete, and it is natural for him to hit home runs. Colonel Jacob Ruppert, on the other hand, is a business man, and it is not easy for a business man to laugh off $200,000.

Ruth Hits Expensive Homer

Somehow, the good colonel cannot see the connection between the national pastime and the cash register. When Mr. Ruth banged out that home run yesterday, apparently banging the colonel out of his share in the gate receipts of the fifth game, the colonel was seen to rise in his chair in glee and even to wave his hat.

Yet there were financiers about who figured that at that moment the Babe, who has already cost the colonel $70,000 in the way of salary, deprived him of that much more in lawful gate receipts.

Consequently, the features of the game were Colonel Ruppert's features at those two moments, when Ruth penalized him $70,000 with a home run and when Mr. Jovo Miljus confirmed the penalty by tossing away a wild one with Tony Lazzeri at the plate.

Gives Bush Birthday Present

There are some who insist that the turning point of the game and the series came when Mr. Miljus heard that it was the birthday of his manager,

(Continued on page two)

Miljus Tosses Wildly After Fanning Two

Ruth Hits Second Homer of Series in Fifth, With Combs on Base, and His Single Scores First Run

Gehrig and Meusel Strike Out in Ninth

Errors by Lazzeri and Moore Let Pirates Tie; Wilcy Stars on Mound

By Grantland Rice

Riding the tail of a $217,000 wild pitch from the straining arm of Jovo Miljus, with two out and the bases full in the ninth inning, the Yankees mopped up Pittsburgh's Pirates for the fourth consecutive start.

They beat the Pirates, 4 to 3, as 57,909 patrons saw the most dramatic battle of the brief series thrown away at the most dramatic moment of a gray and threatening afternoon.

Jovo Miljus, Pittsburgh's relief pitcher, who had followed Carmen Hill, was on his way to herodom when the great crash came. With the score tied at 3 and 3, with the bases full and none out in the ninth, Miljus had just fanned Lou Gehrig and Bob Meusel, to the gathering thunder of an old-fashioned uproar.

He now had only Tony Lazzeri to account for, the same Lazeri who came up just t year ago with the bases full as Old Man Alexander slogged across the field to take his measure in a pinch. But Alexander was missing at the Yankee Stadium yesterday afternoon. With Lazzeri up in the crisis, Miljus unrolled a wild pitch far beyond the reach of catcher Gooch, and as the ball bounded away to the stands Earl Coombs dashed over the plate with the winning run. As Coombs turned in the winning tally to make it four in a row the Yankees tied the record of Boston's Braves against the Athletics in 1914.

Nullifies Fifth Game

This wild pitch stopped the series abruptly and shut off the golden flood of a Sunday game with $217,000 expected through the open gates. But after all it was the big battle ax of Babe Ruth that clubbed the Yankees into victory. The Babe drove across the first Yankee run in the opening inning and then in the fifth, with Wilcy Moore rolling the Pirates aback, the Babe responded once more by whaling his tenth world series home run far into the right center stands. Earl Combs was on first at the moment and there was a sausage shaped balloon swaying against the gray October sky. Ruth's wallop almost hit the balloon. It sailed up far and high in a mighty arc and when it finally fell it was many, many yards beyond the reach of any one except the spectators banked far back against the right center fence.

This was the 426th home run of Ruth's cannonading career and it would have ended the battle beyond all further argument if the Yankee defense had not buckled up in the seventh to yield Pittsburgh a pair of runs.

Ruth and Moore Heroes

The wild pitch that Miljus put through came at the big moment, but after all it was the batting of Ruth and the steady, consistent pitching of Wilcy Moore which carried the Yankees safely across to the winner's end.

It remained for this final battle to stand as the only soul-stirring, dramatic contest of the four-game series, or three days the Yankee juggernaut had rolled in Ruth and ruthless fashion across the prostrate Pirate forms. But the Pirates, with the black flag sinking from sight beneath the engulfing waves, made their stoutest stand. For the first time in the series they fought it out to the final play of the game behind the pitching of Hill and Miljus. But the combination of Ruth and Moore was beyond their reach, and if the Yankee defense had not crumbled in the seventh, where a single base hit was good enough to bring across two runs, there would have been no wild pitching epidemic at the close of the ninth.

Pittsburgh was outclassed all through the four-game spread. The weary looking Pirates were outbatted, outfielded and outpitched. They were bady outfought. They rallied in time to make their only stand in the closing act of the show, but they were doomed from the start when a staggering ball club attempted to block the road against one of the strongest teams of all time.

Only Thriller of Series

This final battle carried more high spots than the other three lumped together. In spite of a gray and threatening day nearly 60,000 fans came out to see the fourth consecutive kill and they came close to a shock. They saw the Pirates hop on Moore in the first when Lloyd Waner singled and Glenn Wright finally drove him home. They saw a startling turn in the Yankees half when Combs and Koenig singled off Carmen Hill and Ruth pumped one down the right field line for the third hit in a row as Combs pattered over. And then just as the crowd was set for a continuation of the Yankee blast Hill came back to earth and fanned Gehrig, Meusel and Lazzeri as he emerged from a hole just a trifle blacker than midnight in a storm.

For the next three innings Hill and Moore remained in a runless deadlock, suppressing every effort to break through. It was not until the fifth that Ruth had another chance. Combs had singled and Koenig had fanned as the Babe took stock of his home run output, which stood then at 425. Hill tried to work his way through, but the Babe finally caught one that suited his rugged fancy. There was apparently

(Continued on page two)

ASSOCIATED PRESS DISPATCHES

THE CLEVELAND NEWS

BULLETIN EDITION

VOL. 86.—NO. 283. Published daily and Sunday by The Cleveland Company, Cleveland, O. Entered as second-class matter at Cleveland postoffice under the act of March 3, 1879. CLEVELAND, MONDAY, OCTOBER 10, 1927. PRICE TWO CENTS

SUNDAY HERE, TALKS TO THRONGS

COURT EDICT HITS FALL

TEAPOT DOME TAKEN FROM H. F. SINCLAIR

Supreme Court Cites Liberty Bond Transfer as Fraud Evidence.

WASHINGTON, Oct. 10.—The government won a complete victory today in the supreme court in its effort to have Harry F. Sinclair's lease of the Teapot Dome naval oil reserve in Wyoming canceled.

The court, in a unanimous opinion delivered by Associate Justice Butler, held that Sinclair's lease and contract had been made by Albert B. Fall, while secretary of the interior, without authority of law and that fraud and corruption in the transaction had been proven by the evidence.

Reserve Reverts to Navy.

The decision means that the rich oil reserve, out of which Sinclair once told a senatorial committee he hoped to make $100,000,000, will revert to the navy department.

The lease was executed after President Harding signed an executive order transferring control of naval oil reserve land from the navy to the interior departments. This order was rescinded by President Coolidge after the Doheny decision.

The decision ends the civil litigation over the naval oil reserves growing out of the Senate's investigation. The government's victory today was as sweeping as it was in the Doherly case, which resulted in the cancellation of that oil magnate's lease of the Elk Hills naval reserve in California.

Hits Sinclair Companies.

The court held that the Sinclair Crude Oil Purchasing Co. and the Sinclair Pipe Line Co. which operated storage tanks, a pipe line and pumping station on the reserve, were trespassers in bad faith. They are not entitled to compensation from the court to reimburse them for their expenditures, it was held, but must go to Congress for relief.

Fall, who is to go on trial here next Monday with Sinclair on a criminal charge of conspiracy to defraud the government in connection with the leasing, was denounced in the lengthy opinion read by Justice Butler as a "faithless public officer."

Justice Butler reviewed the case in detail and mentioned alleged payment of liberty bonds to Fall by Sinclair or his representatives.

Faithless Public Officer.

"And the clandestine and unexplainable acquisition of these bonds by Fall," he said, "confirms the belief, generated by other circumstances in the case, that he was a faithless public officer. There is nothing in the record that tends to mitigate the sinister significance attaching to that enrichment."

It has been the contention of the government that $230,500 in liberty bonds found their way from Sinclair to Fall after the latter had resigned from the cabinet.

Jeweler in Clash With Police Order

Julius Eisenberg, who has fought unsuccessfully during the past two months to have a police detail removed from his E. 9th st. jewelry store and who has been arrested twice during that time, was freed in police court Monday of a third charge, resisting an officer, because of a faulty affidavit.

Detective George Franke, who had Eisenberg arrested on the third charge when, he claims, the jeweler refused to permit him to look at his pawn books, took Eisenberg into custody while he sought a flawless affidavit.

Dog Blocks Woman's Attempt at Suicide

CHICAGO, Oct. 10.—(By A. P.)—The life of a woman made despondent by ill-health and seeking release by suicide has been saved by a dog.

The animal, an English bull, whined and howled until neighbors came running to see what was the matter. They found Mrs. Arnold Fonner, 32, lying on the floor in a gas-filled room. She was revived.

WEATHER

THE NEWS BAROMETER

(Sea level)
11 a. m. 30.10

Fair tonight. Tuesday fair, with rising temperatures. Gentle to variable winds, becoming moderate to fresh southerly on Tuesday.

OHIO WEATHER—The weather forecast for Ohio today is: Fair tonight and Tuesday; rising temperature.

Deputy Inspector Sterling Is Dead of Heart Attack

CHARLES N. STERLING

Wife at Bedside as Police Veteran Passes; Rites to Be at His Home Thursday.

Deputy Police Inspector Charles N. Sterling, a member of the police department for nearly thirty-two years, died Monday at his home, 1288 W. 108th st., of a heart attack.

Sterling, who was 60, had been suffering from heart trouble for more than two years, but his death at this time was unexpected. His wife, Mrs. Mary Sterling, brought his breakfast to his bed. He appeared to be in cheerful spirits as he began his meal. A few minutes later he died as Mrs. Sterling sat beside his bed, helping him with his food.

With Sterling's death there is a vacancy in the ranks of deputy inspectors. Safety Director Barry declared that three weeks ago he had written a letter to civil service commission members, asking them to call an examination for the position Ellsworth Jeffrey, secretary of the commission, said that no such letter had been received and Barry's clerical staff could not remember sending it. Barry then declared that a duplicate would be sent immediately.

Sterling joined the police force Jan. 1, 1896. He was advanced to the rank of sergeant ten years later and to that of lieutenant in 1911. In 1914 he was assigned to the detective bureau.

Known as Fearless Worker.

As a detective, Sterling soon became known as being a tireless and fearless worker.

Police Chief Graul described him as an officer to whom "police work was not only employment but a hobby as well."

"Sterling time after time worked twelve to eighteen hours a day," Graul said, "and he has been known to go without sleep for two days at a time when he was 'hot on the trail' of a criminal."

In 1917 he was raised to the rank of a captain and less than a year later to that of deputy inspector in charge of the detective bureau.

His most outstanding work was done in the Sly-Fanner payroll robbery and murders. Within a few hours after the crime had been committed, Sterling already was on the trail of the slayers, having found a clew to their identity by searching through automobile license records.

Sterling went to Los Angeles to bring back Sam Purpera, 17, one of the murderers. In California Purpera gave Sterling a confession, which he later repudiated, naming the six other members of the murder band.

Louis Komer, "the Toledo Kid," one of the six named by Purpera, was brought back from Detroit by Sterling and George Koestle, superintendent of the bureau of criminal identification. On the boat to Detroit Sterling suffered a serious heart attack but refused to leave his work. Komer later turned state's evidence and was given a life sentence, though three pals in the murder, including Purpera, died in the electric chair.

Sterling played major roles in the capture and conviction of many other criminals notorious in the annals of Cleveland's police department, including "Johnny" Grogan and "Jiggs" Losteiner, both convicted murderers, and "Big Jim" Morton, bank robber.

Ordered to "Clean Up" Duty.

During recent years, after Sterling had been shifted from the de-

Continued on 2d Page, 2d Column

PARIS PLANE ON WAY TO BRAZIL

Frenchmen Quit Hop to U. S. for Air Mail Test to South America.

BULLETIN

BORDEAUX, France, Oct. 10.—(By A. P.)—Dieudonne Costes in the "Nungesser-Coli" passed over Poitiers about 200 miles southwest of Paris, at noon and sent a wireless message at that time that all was well, says a radio dispatch received at the Merignac airfield near here.

LE BOURGET, France, Oct. 10.—(By A. P.)—Prevented by bad weather from attempting the Paris-to-New York flight this late in the season, Dieudonne Costes and Lieutenant Le Brix turned the nose of their plane, the Nungesser-Coli, to the south today, with Buenos Aires as their ultimate destination.

They took off at 9:43 o'clock, hoping to make St. Louis, Senegal, 2,700 miles away, on the first hop, then cross the south Atlantic to Natal, on the Brazilian coast, and proceed to the Argentine capital, with one more stop, at Rio Janeiro.

Prepared for Mishap.

Their Breguet military biplane, in which Costes has made several notable long distance flights totaling 47,000 miles with various companions, rose easily.

Only 650 gallons of gasoline, about three-fourths of the plane's capacity, were taken for the first leg of the flight. The plane is driven by a single 550-horsepower Hispano-Suiza motor. All the tanks are equipped with a quick-emptying device which also seals them and converts them into buoys for the plane in case of a forced alighting at sea. The cockpit is watertight. A collapsed balloon bag is stored under part of the fuselage with a bottle of compressed air attached, to aid in floating the plane in an emergency. In addition to these precautions the airmen have a small rubber lifeboat.

Three-Day Trip, Hope.

The provisions carried include champagne, coffee, distilled water, biscuits, sandwiches, bananas and sugar. Sun helmets were taken along for use in the torrid zone. The plane's radio has a range of about 300 miles, and the call letters are FRAM.

The route of the first leg lay south to Bordeaux, across Spain to Gibraltar, Tangier and Rabat, Morocco, and thence down the coast to St. Louis.

"Paris to Buenos Aires in three days—that's what we are after," said Costes as he climbed into the cockpit. Experts agreed that, if successful, the flight would be a more valuable air feat for France than the crossing of the north Atlantic in one hop, as it would supply data for the Paris-Buenos Aires airmail, for which the Latecoere Co. has a contract.

TOY BALLOONS WRECK PLANE

Girl Killed, Youth May Die Following Crash.

BOONVILLE, Cal., Oct. 10.—(By A. P.)—A flock of toy balloons was blamed today for an airplane crash here which cost the life of Miss Thelma Farrer, 17, of Boonville, and the serious injury of the pilot and a youth who also was a passenger.

C. D. Warren of San Francisco, the pilot, declared his engine had been fouled by the balloons 350 feet in the air, causing the plane to fall.

Ralph Witherell, 21, of Ukiah, was the second passenger. He sustained injuries which probably will prove fatal. Warren was not hurt fatally.

SAYS HEAVEN IS MOSTLY MUSIC

Bishop Warns Those Who Don't Care to Sing.

CHICAGO, Oct. 10.—(By A. P.)—Bishop Edwin Holt Hughes of the Methodist Episcopal church believes that any man who gets to heaven without being able to sing is going to have a hard time of it.

Addressing the Rock River conference of the church, Bishop Hughes said: "If you don't cultivate a taste for music, you will have a miserable time for about 1,000 years after you get to heaven."

Ragtime and jazz, he said, "have had their day."

Set Pere Marquette Value at $62,705,390

WASHINGTON, Oct. 10.—(By A. P.)—A final valuation on the Pere Marquette railroad as of June 30, 1915, was fixed today by the interstate commerce commission at $62,705,390.

The corporation's book investment on that date was $87,100,296, while its outstanding capitalization at par was $108,837,176.

Last week the commission refused the Pere Marquette authority to pay a stock dividend of approximately $9,000,000 on the ground that it would increase the company's capitalization to a point not justified by its assets.

COLLECTIONS BY SLAIN PAIR ARE REVEALED

Story of How Gangsters Got $500 From Jimmy Dunn Is Revealed.

The story of how Jack Brownstein and "Young Hercules" Ernest Yorkell, "strong arm" blackmailers from Philadelphia, gathered in $500 in "life insurance fees" from Jimmy Dunn, member of Cleveland's sporting fraternity and fight manager, was told Monday as police searched the underworld for the murderers of the "insurance men."

The canny Jimmy, who has guided the destinies of a champion of the world through the hazards of the fighting ring, apparently forgot all his generalship when he met the persuasive gentleman from Philadelphia, for he went for "a ride" with them.

And it was during the ride that he was asked, rather casually, whether he'd "rather live or die?"

"Get It," He's Told.

Jimmy, who is nothing if not a fast thinker when he gets under way, was politely curious at once as to what the "insurance fee" would be—and gasped out the fact that he didn't have $500 on his person after the fatal question was popped and answered.

The "insurance" men, however, were forbearing and pressing the muzzle into the fighter's ribs as an aid to his memory of places where ready cash could be obtained, told him to hasten and get it. He did, the narrative has it.

Others who are reported to have come under the persuasive influence of Brownstein and "Young Hercules," one-time vaudeville circuit "strong man," were more fortunate.

When they invaded the institution of "Shimmie" (James) Patton, operator of a soft drink emporium in Detroit ave., near W. 28th st., they got a different answer.

"Shimmie," who was arrested in the now historic federal inquiry into the Fairview village "beer steal," didn't want to go for a ride and strong men didn't scare him worth a darn. In fact, it is reported, he went so far as to "strongarm" the "strongarm" men and threw them out bodily.

"Tommy" McGinty, well known member of the sporting fraternity, gave the insurance men an "interview," but whether Tommy is sans any of his worldly wealth as a result of the consultation over his longevity isn't being told.

Other Visits Bared.

Other visits of the pair, according to the patchwork story that is being fitted together by police, were made to Jack Dunn, operator of a soft drink parlor, W 26th st. and Detroit ave.; Billy Fergus, who has

Continued on 2d Page, 3d Column

Mrs. Corlett Flies to N. Y. in Mail Plane

Mrs. Selene Corlett, Shaker Heights clubwoman, took off for New York Monday in a National Air Transport mail plane piloted by D. C. Smith. She is the first woman to make the air mail trip to Gotham from Cleveland.

Miss Hazel Edwards, stenographer at the Chicago office of the National Air Transport, Inc., flew to Chicago from here two weeks ago. A number of friends, including City Manager Hopkins, were at the field to see Mrs. Corlett off. It is her first long flight.

Marysville School Boy Hangs Himself

MARYSVILLE, Oct. 10.—Rather than go to school, Clarence Farmer, 15, high school student, committed suicide today by hanging himself in the barn on the farm of John Crosgay, where he made his home.

News Camera Man Catches Billy Sunday in Action

"A FOOL OPENS HIS MOUTH AND IT'S ALL OFF"
BILLY SUNDAY in Action
"DON'T FALL TWICE on THE SAME BANANA PEEL"

"SOW YOUR WILD OATS BETWEEN THE AGES OF 85 and 90

Late News Bulletins

LOSES IN SUPREME COURT

WASHINGTON, Oct. 10.—(By A. P.)—The Skinner & Eddy Corporation lost in the supreme court today in its fight to compel Controller General McCarl to pass upon its claim growing out of wartime contracts with the Emergency Fleet Corporation, amounting to about $9,000,000.

MALONEY SUCCEEDS RICHARDS

PHILADELPHIA, Oct. 10.—(By A. P.)—Anthony J. Maloney of Chicago was today elected president of the Philadelphia & Reading Coal and Iron Co., the largest producing concern in the anthracite regions. He succeeds W. J. Richards, who resigned two months ago.

BANK MESSENGER ROBBED

LOS ANGELES, Cal., Oct. 10.—(By A. P.)—Five pouches of registered mail, containing mostly checks amounting to more than $100,000, were stolen from Frank F. Wilmoth, Bank of Italy messenger, by two armed robbers today.

COTTON PRICES BREAK

NEW YORK, Oct. 10.—(By A. P.)—A break of about $3.50 a bale in the New York cotton market today accompanied heavy liquidation by recent buyers, prompted by unexpected weakness in the Liverpool market and reports of favorable weather conditions over the cotton belt.

NAVY FLYER INJURED

WASHINGTON, Oct. 10.—Lieutenant E. W. Litch, U. S. N., was injured today when a torpedo plane he was piloting crashed at Anacostia naval air station here. The extent of his injuries and the cause of the crash have not been determined.

STEEL ORDERS REDUCED

NEW YORK, Oct. 10.—(By A. A.)—Unfilled orders of the United States Steel Corporation at the close of September amounted to 3,148,113 tons, a decrease of 47,924 tons compared with the month before.

SPAN NEARLY FINISHED

Will Complete Rocky River Bridge Repairs in Four Days.

Resurfacing of the Rocky River bridge will be completed in four days, James H. Rose, president of the Enterprise Construction Co. in charge of the work, announced Monday.

Paving between the car tracks is complete and work on the south side of the span was started Monday. One lane and the car tracks will be open all the time. Traffic over it Sunday was normal.

Repairs on the Lorain ave. bridge between Cleveland and Fairview village were resumed Monday. Material, lacking for several months, was delivered Sunday.

Motorists are advised to avoid the Hilliard bridge due to paving and sewer construction at the west end.

Stork Expected by Duchess of York

LONDON, Oct. 10.—(By I. N. S.)—The Duchess of York, wife of the second son of King George and Queen Mary, is expecting a second visit from the stork in November, according to The News of the World. The first child was a daughter. If the next is a son he will be in direct line of succession to the throne.

Judge Sullivan on Lawyers' Program

Appellate Judge John J. Sullivan will speak on "Separating and Use of Evidence," at a meeting of an informal conference group of the Cleveland Bar association Tuesday night at the Hotel Allerton.

INJURED IN PLUNGE

Man Falls 25 Feet Down Shaft of Elevator.

A 25-foot plunge down an elevator shaft in an office building at 730 Vincent ave. sent Carl Farshman, 26, of 1590 Ridgewood ave., Lakewood, to Lakeside hospital Monday with a broken leg and possible internal injuries.

The building was deserted when Farshman, an employee of the Independent Towel & Supply Co., arrived to make his deliveries. He opened the door of the shaft and stepped into the dimly lighted shaft, believing that the elevator was there.

Some time later Patrolman Ernest Shay, passing the building was attracted by Farshman's calls for help and went to his aid.

Navy Plane, Escort to Lindbergh, Falls

NEW ORLEANS, La., Oct. 10.—(I. N. S.)—Two naval aviators narrowly escaped injury early today when one of two planes escorting Col. Charles A. Lindbergh crashed attempt to cross the Mississippi twenty-three miles east of here.

Engine trouble forced the naval plane to land and in the aviator's attempt to cross the Mississippi, the plane crashed into the west bank and turned over. The two naval officers swam from under the overturned plane.

SPANISH ENVOY RETURNS

NEW YORK, Oct. 10.—(By A. P.)—Alejandro Padillay Bell, Spanish ambassador to the United States, had returned today from a three months' vacation in Europe.

BILLY OPENS FALL BATTLE WITH SATAN

Preaches at Euclid Avenue Baptist Temple to Noontime Crowd.

By Don Muir Strouse.

Billy Sunday drove a few more nails in the devil's coffin in Cleveland Monday.

The inimitable Billy, archenemy of Satan, launched his fall campaign against all things sinful with two meetings here Monday.

He talked to a fair portion of Cleveland's male population in the Euclid Avenue Baptist temple at noon and exhorted the males to be men. He spoke earlier in the day to employees of the Wm. Taylor Son & Co. and early shoppers at the downtown department store. He preaches again at public hall at 8 p. m. Monday.

Same Old Billy.

The mounting years have not had any great effect on Rev. William Achley Sunday and with characteristic fervor and vehemence, accompanied by his now world-famous acrobatics, Billy talked straight from the shoulder.

The meeting in the Euclid Avenue Baptist temple had all the earmarks of an old-time evangelistic campaign. Billy was there, "Ma"

Billy Sunday's Noonday Sermon for Men Only will be found on Page 16.

Sunday was there, Homer Rodeheaver, Sunday's famous song leader, was there along with the Gloria Trumpeters, a quartet of musicians.

With all these accoutrements the meeting could be nothing else but enthusiastic. The large auditorium was crowded almost to capacity when Billy mounted the rostrum and delivered his famous sermon, "Be Strong."

"Counterfeit Character."

"A fool may have a knowing look," said Billy, "but he opens his mouth and it's all off. There's too much counterfeit character. It's more common than counterfeit money," he said.

He spoke of the sterling character of the men of the Bible and called on Cleveland's men to emulate them. He cited the words of his text, the exhortation of David to Solomon, as the best advice that a father could give his son.

"Some men say that everyone must sow some wild oats. The best time to put in the first crop is between the ages of 85 and 90. By that time the desire for booze and the longing to fill two pair has turned as cold as a pair of feet inserted in the small of one's back," he thundered.

Men should set the right examples for their sons, he said.

"The devil takes many a boy by getting his father first.

"Manhood, deserving the name, must sign its own 'Declaration of Independence' and fight its own 'Revolutionary war.' If you would be master of yourself, you must learn to anticipate temptations and repel them," he declared.

Sin Like Live Wire.

"The average man," Sunday declared, "thinks he is not having a good time unless he is making a fool out of himself. Form good habits before the bad ones get control.

"Don't play with temptation or trifle with sin. Don't pick up a live wire in your bare hands," he warned.

Billy's sermon at public hall Monday night, which will be broadcast from radio station WJAY, is expected to attract a capacity audience.

In this sermon Billy is expected to attack "modernism" in religion and education, which he says is ruining the morals of America and making it a Godless country.

Sunday is appearing here under auspices of the City Mission, 801 St. Clair ave., as a feature of the mission's annual campaign. The campaign opened with a meeting in the Euclid Avenue Baptist temple Sunday afternoon.

Will Preach in Herrin.

Billy made his first appearance of the season in Buffalo Sunday. He will go from Cleveland to Akron and then to Detroit for meetings following which he will open his first campaign in the Herrin coal fields in southern Illinois.

At the meeting in the Wm. Taylor Son & Co., store, Billy told the workers "not to work for the devil and expect pay from God."

While in Cleveland Billy and "Ma" Sunday are guests of Mrs Sophia Stone Taylor, president of the Wm. Taylor Son & Co., at her home, Elmstead, in Bratenahl.

McDonald Urges Action in Lorain

COLUMBUS, O., Oct. 10.—(By A. P.)—In a secret recommendation to Governor Donahey, B. F. McDonald, state prohibition commissioner, today recommended "drastic action" by the state in law enforcement in Lorain.

The recommendation was made in writing and neither the governor nor the commissioner would make any comment.

The King and Crown Prince of Swat: Babe Ruth and Lou Gehrig of the Yankee Team, First and Second, Respectively, in Home-Run Hitting for 1927, the Babe Having Clouted Sixty, Setting Up a New Record, and Lou Having Accounted for Forty-seven, Standing at Forbes Field, Pittsburgh, Before the Opening Game of the World's Series.

(Times Wide World Photos.)

Additional Pictures of World's Series Games and Players on Pages 8, 9 and 11 of This Issue.

ST. LOUIS POST - DISPATCH

ROTOGRAVURE PICTURE SECTION

OCTOBER 7, 1928

THE PENNANT-WINNING ST. LOUIS CARDINALS

Bottomley, first base.
—Photo by Block Bros.

Douthit, center field.
—Photo by Block Bros.

Wilson, catcher.
—Photo by Block Bros.

Sherdel, pitcher.
—Photo by Block Bros.

Rhem, pitcher.
—Photo by Block Bros.

Mitchell, pitcher.
—Photo by Block Bros.

Haines, pitcher.
—Photo by Block Bros.

High, third base.
—Photo by Block Bros.

Harper, outfield.
—Photo by Block Bros.

Alexander, pitcher.
—Photo by Block Bros.

McKechnie, manager.
—Photo by Block Bros.

CHAMPIONS OF THE NATIONAL BASEBALL LEAGUE IN 1928.

Frisch, second base.
—Photo by Block Bros.

Holm, third base.
—Photo by Block Bros.

Roettger, right field.
—Photo by Block Bros.

Maranville, shortstop.
—Photo by Block Bros.

Orsatti, outfield.
—Photo by Block Bros.

Reinhardt, pitcher.
—Photo by Block Bros.

Frankhouse, pitcher.
—Photo by Block Bros.

Smith, catcher.
—Photo by Block Bros.

Thevenow, shortstop.
—Photo by Block Bros.

Johnson, pitcher.
—Photo by Block Bros.

Blades, outfield.
—Photo by Block Bros.

Haid, pitcher.
—Photo by Block Bros.

Hafey, left field.
—Photo by Block Bros.

BOX SCORE COMPLETE										
Yankees..	0	0	0	1	0	0	4	2	0—	7
Cardinals	0	0	1	1	0	0	0	0	1—	3

SPORTING FINAL ★★★★★★★

TEMPERATURES. Min., 59. Max., 73.

The Sun

Copyright, 1928, by The Sun Printing and Publishing Association.

SPORTING FINAL ★★★★★★★

United States Official Weather Forecast: Fair and cooler tonight and tomorrow. (Detailed weather report on page 23.)

VOL. XCVI.—NO. 32—DAILY. 11 NEW YORK, TUESDAY, OCTOBER 9, 1928. PRICE THREE CENTS.

YANKEES CHAMPIONS; 3 HOMERS FOR RUTH

NEW YORKERS RING UP SECOND 4-GAME VICTORY

Babe Equals Mark of 1926 With Trio of 4-Base Drives.

FIVE FOR TEAM IS NEW RECORD

Gehrig's Circuit Clout Is His 4th—Sherdel Weakens in Seventh —Hoyt's Hurling Spotty.

By JOE VILA.

SPORTSMANS PARK, St. Louis, Oct. 9.—For the second time in two years, the Yankees are world champions by virtue of winning four games in the annual series. The New York team, representing the American League, took the Cardinals of the National League into camp here this afternoon for the fourth time in as many games for the interleague title. The score was 7 to 3.

The Yankees made other world series records, principally five home runs in a single contest, which was their record this afternoon, and those home runs, three of which were knocked out of the lot by Babe Ruth, virtually settled the controversy.

The score was one to nothing against the Yanks when Ruth, in the fourth inning, found Willie Sherdel for his first tremendous wallop, which landed on the top roof of the right field stands and bounded into the street. The mighty drive tied the score but, in the last half of the inning, the Cardinals again took the lead.

The score remained two to one against the New Yorkers until Ruth, coming up first in the seventh inning, again hammered the ball high and far over the right field covered bleachers. Before Ruth hit that homer there was a fierce wrangle between Sherdel and Umpire Pfirman in which all St. Louis players and all the other umpires joined. After pitching a second strike to Ruth Sherdel, who took catcher Smith's quick return, attempted to sneak over a third strike on a fast ball. Umpire Pfirman refused to call either a ball or strike on that delivery, claiming that Sherdel was not on the slab when he made his delivery. Pfirman stood his ground and was sustained by the other umpires. Then came Ruth's second four-bagger.

Equals His 1926 Mark.

His third circuit drive was made in the eighth, the ball sailing in the same direction taken by numbers one and two, so Ruth duplicated the world series mark made by him two years ago in this park in the second game played by the Cardinals.

Gehrig followed Ruth's homer in the seventh with his fourth of the series, which was another terrific smash over the right field stands and Cedric Durst in the eighth inning lined the ball into the right field stands for a jog around the bases. The Yankees, therefore, broke the world series records for home runs by a team in a single game.

Gehrig also eclipsed Meusel's former world series mark by driving in nine runs during the four games with the Cardinals. Gehrig led with four home runs with the present series, which is another new mark.

Sherdel Wilts.

The Yankees had batted Sherdel savagely but were limited to one run—Ruth's homer—because of the sharp fielding of the Cardinals, but when Gehrig and Ruth had knocked out their four-baggers in the seventh Sherdel wilted.

The next moment Meusel got in a blazing smash for a single, whereupon Sherdel gave way to Alexander. Lazzeri doubled to left, putting Meusel on third, and both scored with no delay on a fielder's choice and a sacrifice fly that gave the Yankees four earned runs for the inning for an overpowering lead, which virtually crushed the Cardinals. Alexander yielded the home runs made by Durst and Ruth in the eighth inning.

Hoyt was touched for eleven hits and gave three bases on balls. The Cardinals first made a run in the third inning, which resulted from a lucky two-bagger by Orsatti, followed by High's bunt and Frisch's sacrifice fly.

In the fourth McKechnie's men scored their second run on errors by Koenig and Hoyt, coupled with smart base running by Maranville. Thereafter Hoyt managed to blank the St. Louis team until the ninth, when a third run resulted in the bunching of three hits.

Earl Combs, who had been kept out of the series as a result of an injured wrist, broke into today's affair as a pinch-hitter for Bengough in the seventh and helped add to the New York total by scoring Durocher with a sacrifice fly.

Ruth's wonderful hitting was topped off by a miraculous running catch as the last play of the game. The big fellow sprinted onto foul ground within a few feet of the field boxes and nabbed Frisch's twisting fly with his gloved hand. As he caught the ball he raised it above his head in triumph.

The Yankees were glad to win and they were congratulating one another in the dressing room a few minutes after leaving the field.

Manager McKechnie, manager of the Cardinals, arrived a few moments later and shook hands cordially with Huggins and all of his world champions.

After the band had played "The Star Spangled Banner" the Cardinals received encouraging cheers as they took the field, wearing brand new white uniforms.

Paschal, batting right handed, was the first Yankee to face Sherdel's left-handed delivery. Umpire Pfir-

Continued on Thirty-fifth Page.

In The Sun Today

Box Score—Fourth Game

YANKEES

	AB.	R.	H.	PO.	A.	E.	HR.	3B.	2B.	BB.	SB.	SO
Paschal, cf.	4	0	1	3	0	0	0	0	0	0	0	0
Durst, cf	1	1	1	0	0	0	1	0	0	0	0	0
Koenig, ss.	5	0	1	3	2	1	0	0	0	0	0	0
Ruth, lf.	5	3	3	2	0	0	3	0	0	0	0	0
Gehrig, 1b.	2	1	1	7	0	0	1	0	0	3	0	0
Meusel, rf.	5	1	1	0	0	0	0	0	0	0	0	2
Lazzeri, 2b.	4	1	3	2	2	0	0	0	1	0	1	0
Durocher, 2b.	1	0	0	0	0	0	0	0	0	0	0	0
Dugan, 3b	3	0	1	0	0	0	0	0	0	0	0	0
Robertson, 3b.	2	0	0	0	0	0	0	0	0	0	0	0
Bengough, c.	3	0	1	8	1	0	0	0	0	0	0	0
Collins, c.	1	0	1	2	0	0	0	0	1	0	0	0
Hoyt, p.	4	0	1	0	2	1	0	0	0	0	0	0
Combs,	0	0	0	0	0	0	0	0	0	0	0	0
Totals	40	7	15	27	7	2	5	0	2	3	1	2

CARDINALS

	AB.	R.	H.	PO.	A.	E.	HR.	3B.	2B.	BB.	SB.	SO
Orsatti cf.	5	1	2	4	0	0	0	0	1	0	0	2
High, 3b.	5	0	3	0	1	0	0	0	1	0	0	0
Frisch, 2b.	4	0	0	3	1	0	0	0	0	0	0	1
Bottomley, 1b	3	0	0	11	1	0	0	0	0	1	0	2
Hafey, lf.	3	0	0	1	0	0	0	0	0	1	0	1
Harper rf.	3	0	1	2	0	0	0	0	0	1	0	1
Smith, c.	4	0	3	3	1	0	0	0	0	0	0	0
Maranville, ss.	4	1	2	3	1	0	0	0	1	0	1	0
Sherdel, p.	3	0	0	0	0	0	0	0	0	0	0	1
Alexander, p.	0	0	0	0	3	0	0	0	0	0	0	0
Martin,	0	1	0	0	0	0	0	0	0	0	0	0
Holm,	1	0	0	0	0	0	0	0	0	0	0	0
Totals	35	3	11	27	8	0	0	0	3	3	1	8

Combs batted for Bengough in seventh.
Holm batted for Alexander in ninth.
Martin ran for Smith in ninth.

THE SUMMARY.

Sacrifice hit—Hoyt.
Sacrifice flies—Frisch, Combs.
Double play—Bottomley to Maranville.
Hits—Off Sherdel, 11 in 6 innings; off Alexander, 4 in 3 innings.
Left on bases—Yanks, 11; Cards, 9.
Umpires—Pfirman, Owens, Rigler and McGowan.

Hawthorne Results.

By Associated Press.

FIRST RACE—Purse $1,200; maidens; two-year-olds; geldings. Hawthorne course:

Horse.	Jockey.	St.	Pl.	Sh.
Calf Rober	(Hardy)	2.88	2.32	2.14
Enthusiastic	(Gevings)	—	3.88	3.66
Pokest	(Deprema)	—	—	3.50

No scratches.

SECOND RACE—Purse $1,200; claiming; two-year-olds. Hawthorne course:

Horse.	Jockey.	St.	Pl.	Sh.
Christie Flannigan	(D'pr'ma)	10.62	6.00	4.50
Moderation	(Shropshire)	—	11.34	5.98
Mekachee	(Laidley)	—	—	7.18

Scratched—Nae Breeks, Draha, Frank Keane, Marcella Agnes, Mystery Ballot, Benet.

THIRD RACE—Purse $1,200; claiming; three-year-olds and upward. Hawthorne course:

Horse.	Jockey.	St.	Pl.	Sh.
Marshall Ney	(Deprema)	4.84	2.96	2.36
Shasta Lad	(Shropshire)	—	3.26	2.78
Bramstar	(Knight)	—	—	3.60

No scratches.

FOURTH RACE—Purse $1,200; claiming; three-year-olds and upward. Mile and a sixteenth:

Horse.	Jockey.	St.	Pl.	Sh.
Grand Dad	(Warden)	3.70	2.90	2.40
Florida Gold	(Shropshire)	—	4.36	3.66
Polls	(Cavens)	—	—	3.62

No scratches.

FIFTH RACE—Purse $1,200; three-year-olds and upward. Mile and seventy yards:
No scratches.

Horse.	Jockey.	St.	Pl.	Sh.
Hiram	(Hardy)	7.70	4.60	4.48
Quick Return	(Knight)	—	11.10	7.70
Mop Up	(Shropshire)	—	—	5.90

Scratched—Platoon, Jack Savage, Lion.

SIXTH RACE—Purse $1,200; claiming; three-year-olds and upward. Mile and a sixteenth:

1—House Boy	9—Sly Polly
2—Bearing	10—Pat Field
3—By Gosh	11—Poor Boy
4—Coy	12—Turquoise
5—KnowMeGnome	13—Button
6—King Lehr	14—Princely
7—Bird Behave	15—Street Liz
8—Rainfall	

First.	Second.	Third.
12	1	3

Elderly Man Killed on Tracks.

Patrick Yanicelli, 72 years old, of 201 Oak street, Yonkers, was killed by a northbound passenger train on the Boston & Putnam Railroad track just north of the Gray Oaks station at Yonkers yesterday. His wife and several children survive.

Laurel Results.

By Associated Press.

FIRST RACE—Purse $1,300; maidens; two-year-olds; fillies. Five and a half furlongs:

Horse.	Jockey.	St.	Pl.	Sh.
Serenity	(Lang)	8.00	4.80	3.60
Jesirah	(Watters)	—	8.00	3.90
Fairy Ring	(Mergler)	—	—	2.70

Scratched—Nancy Bird.

SECOND RACE—Purse $1,200; claiming; three-year-olds and upward. Six furlongs:

Horse.	Jockey.	St.	Pl.	Sh.
Timekeeper	(O'Donnell)	6.20	4.20	3.40
Light Air	(Workman)	—	7.50	6.80
Rosinante	(Zateslo)	—	—	18.90

Scratched—Prompter, Lemnos, Fair Gold, Junetta, Mollie Elizabeth.

THIRD RACE—Purse $1,300; claiming; three-year-olds and upward. Mile and a quarter:

Horse.	Jockey.	St.	Pl.	Sh.
Leger	(Barrett)	40.50	13.70	9.70
Sonny Golden	(Fields)	—	5.20	4.60
Omrah	(Phillips)	—	—	9.50

Scratched—Northland.

FOURTH RACE—Purse $1,300; claiming; two-year-olds. Six furlongs:

Horse.	Jockey.	St.	Pl.	Sh.
Minotaur	(Pichon)	35.70	12.60	7.90
Beau Wrack	(Bejshak)	—	5.30	4.40
Jane Rinehart	(Palumbo)	—	—	11.40

Scratched—Inception.

FIFTH RACE—Purse $2,000; Severn Handicap; three-year-olds and upward. Mile and a sixteenth:

Horse	Jockey.	St.	Pl.	Sh
Boo	(Barnes)	11.40	4.10	2.70
Recreation	(Fields)	—	2.60	2.10
Gaffsman	(Pichon)	—	—	3.00

No scratches.

SIXTH RACE—Purse $1,300; claiming; three-year-olds and upward. Mile and a quarter:

Horse.	Jockey.	St.	Pl.	Sh.
Danger Signal	(Bejshak)	8.50	5.00	3.30
Daffodil	(Watters)	—	8.40	5.40
Plucky Pal	(Robson)	—	—	4.70

No scratches.

SEVENTH RACE—Purse $1,300; claiming; three-year-olds and upward. Mile and seventy yards:

Horse.	Jockey.	St.	Pl.	Sh.
William T.	(Hebert)	21.10	12.30	7.90
Burning Glass	(Fields)	—	5.40	3.90
Spanish Aster	(Watters)	—	—	4.20

Scratched—Milaria, Sun de Meur, Dear Inez.

Found Dead From Gunshot Wound.

BUTLER, N. J., Oct. 9.—Samuel Marion, 51 years old, of Bartholdi avenue, this place, was found dead yesterday beneath a tree near his home, with a shot wound in his head. A single barreled shotgun was lying near his side. Police said he had been suffering from insomnia for some time and had become despondent.

RESULTS AT JAMAICA

CHARTS ON PAGE 33.

	First	Second	Third
First Race...	Common Sense	Cowhide	Griffin
Prices....	5-1 5-2 6-5	9-2 2-1 1-1	12-1 6-1 3-1
No scratches.			
Second Race	The Beginner	Knockabout	Golden Lux
Prices	7-2 7-5 3-5	4-1 2-1 1-1	6-1 5-2 6-5
Scratched—Dumpy, Itinerant.			
Third Race...	Indian Scout	Westmount	The Tartar
Prices....	11-20 1-5 —	4-1 7-10 1-4	25-1 6-1 5-2
No scratches.			
Fourth Race	Wee Burn	Florian	Comet
Prices....	7-2 6-5 1-3	12-5 4-5 1-4	3-1 1-1 1-3
No scratches.			
Fifth Race...	Manchu	Flying Scud	Loveken
Prices....	5-1 2-1 1-1	13-5 6-5 7-10	12-1 6-1 3-1
No scratches.			
Sixth Race...	Roseomar	Nearby	Anna G.
Prices....	8-5 3-5 1-5	5-1 2-1 4-5	3-1 6-5 1-2
Scratched—Campanella, Virmer.			

BASEBALL

INTERCITY SERIES.

AT COMISKEY PARK.

										R.	H.	E.
CHICAGO (N).	6	0	0	0	6	0	1	0	0—	13	16	0
CHICAGO (A).	0	0	0	0	0	0	0	0	2—	2	7	5

Blake and Hartnett; Adkins and Berg.

PLAY BY PLAY OF THE FOURTH GAME

Yanks Knock Sherdel From Mound in Seventh.

ST. LOUIS, Mo., Oct. 9 (A. P.).—The detailed description of the fourth world series game here today between the Yankees of New York, American League champions, and the Cardinals of St. Louis, National League flag winners:

FIRST INNING.

Yankees.

Paschal up. Sherdel wound up briefly. Strike one, called. Strike two, called. This was a floater on the outside corner. Ball one, outside, low. Ball two, outside. Foul. This was a long drive into the left field stands. Smith smothered Paschal's foul behind the plate.

Koenig up. Koenig stung a single into left.

Ruth up. Ball one, wide. Strike one, called. Ball two, inside. Ruth hit into a double play. Bottomley took Ruth's grounder and touched first, then the Cardinal first baseman threw to Maranville, who tagged Koenig as he slid into the bag. No runs, one hit.

Cardinals.

Orsatti up. Foul, strike one. Strike two, called. This was a fast ball on the outside corner. Ball one, high. Ball two, outside. Ball three, outside, low. Orsatti struck out, taking a third called strike, with the wood on his shoulder.

High up. Ball one, outside. High sent up a high fly, which Ruth lost in the sun, High making two bases on the hit.

Frisch up. Strike one, called. Ball one, outside. Foul, strike two. Ball

Continued on Thirty-fifth Page.

Latonia Results.

By Associated Press.

FIRST RACE—Purse $1,200; claiming; three-year-olds and upward. Six furlongs:

Horse.	Jockey.	St.	Pl.	Sh.
Black Flyer	(Garner)	12.78	5.72	4.46
Reddy Fox	(Kern)	—	3.68	3.20
Dar Fur	(Hardy)	—	—	15.34

Scratched—Howard Lee, Lady Basil, Paton, Keeping Time, Geyser, Madam Emelie.

SECOND RACE—Purse $1,200; two-year-olds; maidens; colts and geldings. Six furlongs:

Horse.	Jockey.	St.	Pl.	Sh.
Alcman	(Garner)	5.62	2.96	2.46
Rufe McClain	(E. Pool)	—	3.14	2.78
Amsterdam	(W. Pool)	—	—	4.92

Scratched—Platoon, Jack Savage, Lion Heart, Jim McMahon, Molehill, Beechwood.

THIRD RACE—Purse $1,200; claiming; three-year-olds and upward. Six furlongs:

Horse.	Jockey.	St.	Pl.	Sh.
Critic	(Pool)	14.70	8.82	7.46
Deputy	(Meimann)	—	41.10	19.48
Merlwick	(Jones)	—	—	5.60

Scratched—St. Charles, Stoneage, Twenty One Sixty, Aspinwall Girl, Dark Angel, Storm Signal.

FOURTH RACE—Purse $1,200; claiming; three-year-olds and upward. Mile and a sixteenth:

Horse.	Jockey.	St.	Pl.	Sh.
Manzana	(Halbert)	4.66	3.44	2.62
Onup	(Garner)	—	4.60	4.50
Less K.	(Fowler)	—	—	3.62

Scratched—Provost, Polar Sea, Dolly S., Tim Gleason, Grand King, Juel Jean.

FIFTH RACE—Purse $1,200; allowances; Pauline Frederick; three-year-olds and upward. Six furlongs:

Horse.	Jockey.	St.	Pl.	Sh.
Wisdom	(Pool)	3.26	2.46	2.30
Energy	(Froggatte)	—	2.98	2.48
Dark Phantom	(Garner)	—	—	3.10

Scratched—Mino.

SIXTH RACE—Purse $1,200; allowances; two-year-olds; fillies. Six furlongs:

Horse.	Jockey.	St.	Pl.	Sh.
Nellie Custis	(Pool)	3.46	2.98	2.58
Chatter Black	(Heupel)	—	10.38	7.12
Facility	(Zucchini)	—	—	6.56

Scratched—Princess Zelda, Bessie Alix.

SEVENTH RACE—Purse $1,200; claiming; three-year-olds and upward; fillies and mares. Mile and a sixteenth:

Horse.	Jockey.	St.	Pl.	Sh.
Spotlight	(Gray)	15.66	6.02	4.64
Busy Fairy	(Kern)	—	4.14	3.06
Tangram	(Zucchini)	—	—	7.76

Scratched—Betty Bux, Night Hawk, Rocky Cliff, Dentess.

SINCLAIR DODGES PROCESS SERVERS

But Court Refuses Order to Keep Him Here for Trial.

Counsel for two former Internal Revenue agents now under indictment on a charge of accepting an alleged bribe from Harry F. Sinclair, asked Federal Judge Francis A. Winslow today to issue a mandate requiring Mr. Sinclair to remain within the jurisdiction of the court pending the trial of the two men next week.

According to United States Attorney Tuttle the men were trapped when by an arrangement between Mr. Sinclair and the Federal authorities the two agents accepted on account $10,000 of the $37,500 they demanded for saving Sinclair $250,000 on his income tax for 1925-26.

David P. Siegel, counsel for Edward F. Brown, one of the agents, explained to Judge Winslow that Mr. Sinclair "occupied a building at 45 Nassau street, which is thirty stories high, and that despite the efforts of process servers the oil magnate has not been located, nor has it been possible to exact a promise that he will be present for the trial. I believe that a mandate of this court will be necessary to keep Mr. Sinclair within its jurisdiction, rather than the intimation of the District Attorney's office that he will be available as a witness."

Mr. Siegel said that his emissaries had searched high and low for Sinclair and that he was "an elusive witness." He said that he wanted to serve notice on the Government counsel that he would stop the impending criminal trial if Sinclair was not available next week.

Assistant United States Attorney Thomas Todarelli told Judge Winslow that he did not believe it would be necessary for a court order to guarantee the appearance of the oil man. Judge Winslow thereupon directed Mr. Siegel to renew his efforts to subpœna Mr. Sinclair and intimated that the defense could not be forced to trial if he was missing from the jurisdiction of the court.

Elmer F. Andrews was indicted with Brown after he had accepted $10,000 in marked bills from Reginald Ragland, attorney for Sinclair. Both agents had been assigned to review deductions of $1,800,000 that were incorporated in the tax returns. Sinclair claimed that he had suffered losses amounting to $250,000 through his Rancocas racing stables, and a bad debt from the Selah Corporation he listed at $1,325,000. The trial of the two agents has been placed on the calendar for next Monday before Judge Thomas D. Thacher.

Fire Under Brooklyn Bridge Delays Transit Traffic

A fire occurred under the Brooklyn Bridge tower on the Brooklyn side today, destroying a painters' scaffolding and some rubbish. The flames ignited the trolley ties, delaying surface car and elevated traffic for ten minutes. The cause of the blaze was undetermined.

Five fire companies responded to an alarm, but there was little work for the firemen. Patrolman Frederick Oettinger of the bridge precinct put out the fire by pouring pails of water on it.

STATE CLOSES TESTIMONY IN CONNOLLY CASE

Buckner Adds Much Telling Evidence Against Two Defendants.

FATTENED PURSE REVEALED

Bank Accounts Show Heavily Increased Deposits Over Three-Year Period.

The case of the State of New York against Maurice Connolly and Frederick Seely, charged with conspiracy to defraud the city, was rested at 4:12 o'clock this afternoon by Emory R. Buckner, the special prosecutor. The conclusion came near the ordinary hour of adjournment of a day which had added much to the structure of evidence the prosecution has reared against the two.

After the State had rested, Max D. Steuer, counsel for Connolly, moved that the State be called upon to decide whether it would go to the jury on the count charging conspiracy to defraud, or that alleging conspiracy to obstruct justice or on that which accused the two of defrauding the city of their services. Supreme Court Justice Tompkins, presiding, reserved decision.

At the outset of the trial, in a voice too low to be heard, Steuer moved, it was learned today, to have the trial limited to one of the three counts on the grounds that the indictment charges only one conspiracy in three separate forms and not three separate conspiracies. The Judge said that the motion was premature. Today he heard the motion and was inclined to agree with Steuer. He gave Buckner permission to file a memorandum on the law at 10:30 tomorrow morning, when he will render his decision on the matter.

Trace Their Expenses.

Outstanding in the day was the evidence given by a series of witnesses that Connolly and his wife were able to spend during 1925, 1926 and 1927 a total of close to $150,000 in cash, the money going into real estate and loans. During that time Connolly was getting a salary of $15,000 a year as Borough President of Queens.

The prosecution, as its case neared the end, also gained the right, through a court decision, to treat Clifford B. Moore, consulting engineer of the borough, as a party to the conspiracy. In this connection it was able to get into the record a transcript of his bank account, showing a sharp increase in prosperity during the years in which Connolly was spending money so freely and large cash deposits during the same years.

Spent $90,000 in 1926.

The evidence on the payments of the Connollys showed that close to $90,000 of the money spent went out during 1926. In 1927 Connolly spent about $50,000 on his house in Forest Hills and in 1925 another $15,000 went out in loans. All of this money was in currency.

The Connolly disbursements made in that currency which seemed to float so freely about the borough were not recorded in Connolly's bank account. Some of the money went in loans, secured and unsecured. A part of it Mrs. Connolly paid for real estate. Most of it was ladeled out in $1,000 bills.

Almost always, as Max Steuer, Connolly's counsel, brought out carefully on cross-examination, these payments were made with no attempt at concealment. Only once was there a hint of what might be inter-

Continued on Twenty-third Page.

TYPHOON OFF JAPAN

Three Freighters in Distress; Fishing Craft Missing.

TOKIO, Oct. 9 (A. P.).—Three Japanese freighters, the Oyama Maru, the Fukel Maru and the Ibukiyama Maru, were reported today to be in distress off the east coast of Japan after a typhoon which swept the region last night.

The Fukel Maru reported that two seamen had been washed overboard and perished. The Ibukiyama Maru was en route to Japan from Gray's Harbor, Washington.

Warcraft was ordered from the Yokosuka naval station to assist the vessels.

Twenty fishing craft were missing.

FEDERAL JURY TO JOIN IN HUNT FOR POISON RUM

U. S. Attorney to Investigate Cause of Widespread Fatalities.

33 VICTIMS NOW IN MORGUE

Dry Force Begins to Show Some Interest and Asks for Information.

As deaths from poison liquor apparently reached their peak this afternoon, with thirty-three victims in the morgue, Charles H. Tuttle, United States Attorney, initiated an investigation of the alcoholic death wave. Tomorrow morning the Federal Grand Jury will start the inquiry to determine the cause of the widespread fatalities and illness and if possible to fix the responsibility.

Once the inquiry into an unprecedented situation is under way, Mr. Tuttle will move for a special Grand Jury to devote its entire time to the liquor situation which has had such appalling results. The United States Attorney said late this afternoon the inquiry should be of particular advantage to prohibition agents and to the police in their efforts to enforce the laws against liquor and crime.

Almost simultaneously with Mr. Tuttle's announcement that the Grand Jury will take charge of the death wave problem, the Federal prohibition authorities displayed interest for the first time, in the fact that thirty-three men are in the morgue because of poison liquor, and there came also an outburst of indignation from various public officials against the evil results of prohibition, and especially of the Government's practice of denaturing commercial alcohol with poisonous chemicals.

Wood Alcohol Blamed.

In the morgue, where Dr. Charles Norris, Chief Medical Examiner, and his staff of physicians were almost exhausted from many hours of labor over the autopsy tables, trying to find out what kind of poisoned liquor killed so many unfortunates along the East Side water front and in the neighborhood of the Bowery, fourteen bodies still awaited their investigation.

The autopsies on sixteen victims revealed beyond question that all had been killed by drinking wood alcohol, and while Dr. Norris and his fellow physicians were not prepared to say that this was true in all of the thirty-three cases, they were inclined to think so.

While they worked over the fourteen bodies remaining to be examined a representative of Prohibition Director Maurice Campbell appeared at the morgue and asked for Dr. Norris. This was Sylvester Brierton, a former lieutenant of the Police Department, and now confidential investigator for Director Campbell. Brierton wanted a list of the dead and their addresses, together with a list of the exact locations where their

Continued on Twenty-third Page.

Ravenna Results.

By Associated Press.

FIRST RACE—Purse $400; claiming; three-year-olds and upward. Six and a half furlongs:

Horse.	Jockey.	St.	Pl.	Sh.
Blue Agate	(Fowler)	8.20	5.00	4.00
Pennyrile	(Wallace)	—	4.40	3.40
Guy Clayton	(McQuay)	—	—	3.60

Scratched—Turnberry, Favenor, One Gold Buck, Blue Caddie, Black Monkey.

SECOND RACE—Purse $400; claiming; three-year-olds and upward; fillies and mares. About five furlongs:

Horse.	Jockey.	St.	Pl.	Sh.
Star Girl	(Guerra)	4.80	3.80	3.20
Cinch	(Madden)	—	5.00	3.60
Mally S.	(Wallace)	—	—	3.00

Scratched—Erin's Bride, Electric Storm, Rose Stark.

THIRD RACE—Purse $400; claiming; three-year-olds and upward. Six and a half furlongs:

Horse.	Jockey.	St.	Pl.	Sh.
Rimple	(Madden)	62.40	15.40	7.20
Mediator, Jr.	(Guerra)	—	8.80	4.80
Ambulance	(Kingsland)	—	—	5.20

Scratched—Pecora, Threnody, Sister Maggie, Honest Mose.

FOURTH RACE—Purse $400; claiming; three-year-olds and upward. Six and a half furlongs:

Horse.	Jockey.	St.	Pl.	Sh.
Affectionate Mary	(Wallace)	7.80	3.20	2.40
Le Maddison	(Rice)	—	2.60	2.20
Warehouseman	(Kingsland)	—	—	2.60

Scratched—Bust Buck, Vasquey, Midday, Foundation, J. B. Brown, Collar Victoria.

FIFTH RACE—Purse $400; three-year-olds and upward. Six furlongs:

Horse.	Jockey.	St.	Pl.	Sh.
Hole Card	(McCabe)	8.20	4.40	2.60
Dr. McArthur	(Kingsland)	—	3.40	2.20
Liborio	(Guerra)	—	—	2.40

Scratched—Perriquet.

SIXTH RACE—Purse $400; Barberton; three-year-olds and upward. Mile and a sixteenth:

Horse.	Jockey.	St.	Pl.	Sh.
Gus R.	(Guerra)	11.60	5.40	3.60
Sam Jowl	(Wallace)	—	5.20	3.60
Student Prince	(Fowler)	—	—	2.80

Scratched—Hardman, Capt. Stevenson.

SOMETHING NEW! THE DAILY EXAMINER NOW IN THREE SECTIONS

Telephone Classified Ads to
MEtpoltn. 4000
or bring them to any
EXAMINER OFFICE
1111 S. Broadway, 508 S. Broadway
106 S. Broadway

CHARACTER QUALITY — AMERICA FIRST! — ENTERPRISE ACCURACY

Los Angeles Examiner

AN AMERICAN PAPER FOR THE AMERICAN PEOPLE — THE GREAT NEWSPAPER OF THE GREAT SOUTHWEST

Reg. U.S. Pat. Off.

CALIFORNIA FORECASTS
Los Angeles and Vicinity—Fair Monday and Tuesday with moderate temperature.
San Francisco and Vicinity—Fair and cool Monday and Tuesday, gentle variable winds.
MEAN TEMPERATURES

LOS ANGELES	63	San Francisco	42
Boston	28	Salt Lake	28
Chicago	-6	Vancouver	33
New York	32	Winnipeg	-8

VOL. XXVI—NO. 34 C LOS ANGELES, MONDAY, JANUARY 14, 1929 Official Forecast: Fair For Complete Weather Reports See Page 14, Part I. PRICE FIVE CENTS

MRS. 'BABE' RUTH DIES IN FIRE

KEYES WILL MAKE OWN BRIBE DEFENSE PLEA; PACT FOES FIGHT ON DESPITE COOLIDGE PLEA

JACK BENNETT QUESTIONED AGAIN TODAY

'Bright Youngster' Facing Severe Grilling When Defense Continues Cross-Examination

Harold Davis May Be Next Witness Called; to Be Quizzed on Use of Office by Getzoff

By Walter Naughton

"Ladies and gentlemen of the jury——"

On hundreds of occasions during the twenty-five years he served as a prosecutor and District Attorney Asa Keyes addresed those remarks to a jury as he sought to send a man charged with a crime to the penitentiary or—in some cases—to the gallows.

In about two weeks Keyes will again repeat this time honored preface to a jury of ten women and two men. But for the first time in his life he will be pleading in his own behalf and for his own liberty and acquittal.

Dramatic Scene

The Examiner learned yesterday that the veteran prosecutor, now on trial with five other defendants on bribery and conspiracy charges before Superior Judge Edward I. Butler will plead his own case to the persons in whose hands his fate rests.

The picture, as Keyes stands there and argues his own case, is certain to bring forth as dramatic a situation as ever occurred in a Los Angeles courtroom.

The former official, who the prosecution hopes to prove received $125,000 from one man and $40,000 from another, for using his influence to aid two Julian case defendants, long has been rated a thorough, capable and convincing prosecutor.

Associate Counsel

Keyes was never given to circus tactics, a wild waving of arms, picturesque gestures, or the use of colorful or vitriolic phrases when seeking to impress a jury. Facts were his ammunition. He tried to pound facts in to his listeners, occasionally emphasizing his points by pounding one fist into the palm of the other hand as he stood before the box, talking earnestly and in moderated tones.

What Keyes' complete defense to the bribery and conspiracy charges will be is not known. But it will be entirely in evidence as he takes his place to argue to the jury. His

(Continued on Page 10, Column 1)

British Guile Scuttled Navy, Says Admiral

Fiske Declares Disarmament Pact Colossal Blunder on Part of U. S.

NEW YORK, Jan. 13.—(Universal Service.)—That America is in a situation at once ridiculous and dangerous because it has allowed itself to be "duped" and "fooled" by British diplomacy is the substance of Rear Admiral Bradley A. Fiske's article, "How British Guile Scuttled Our Navy," to be published in the February issue of Plain Talk.

REAR ADML. BRADLEY A. FISKE
"Diplomacy duped America"
—Internat'l Newsreel photo.

Calling the 1922 limitation of armament conference, widely applauded at the time, a great blunder of statesmanship, Admiral Fiske says in his "Plain Talk" article that "with the purest intentions in the world, we have allowed ourselves to be cajoled into giving up not only our naval supremacy on the sea, but also the only considerable base we had in all the world, the Philippine Islands. For let us realize frankly that our agreeing not to increase the wholly inadequate defenses of the Philippine Islands has made it not only possible but easy for Japan to capture them whenever she wishes."

PROPAGANDA'S PREY

Admiral Fiske claims the United States was inveigled into calling the limitation of armament conference by British propaganda and that we played right into the hands of English and Japanese diplomats, allowing them to come off with an advantage so great that it has been aptly termed 'Britain's greatest naval victory."

The conference was really between two parties (Great Britain and Japan, being Allies and working together), Admiral Fiske writes, and "the natural result was that the decision was to the disadvantage of the United States and to the advantage of Great Britain and Japan.

"The major parts of the decision were two in number," according to Admiral Fiske.

"One part was the voluntary

(Continued on Page 5, Cols. 4-6)

10 BELOW ZERO HITS CHICAGO; COLD KILLS 3

Twenty-two-Mile Wind Intensifies Suffering; Homeless Crowd Charity Institutions

CHICAGO, Jan. 13. — (Universal Service.)—Temperature dipped to 10 below zero in Chicago last night and will go even lower tonight.

Three persons froze to death and many others suffered from freezing.

At no time during the day did the temperature go above zero.

The cold was intensified by a twenty-two mile wind from the northwest. The fall in temperature came suddenly. At 10 o'clock Saturday night the thermometer registered 10 above zero; an hour later it was one below, and it continued to drop until 10 below was officially recorded. Unofficial readings showed 16 below zero.

After sundown tonight the temperature began falling and indications were that 12 below might be reached before dawn. Monday, however, the cold wave will be broken and the mercury is expected to go above zero by noon.

Suffering was intense. Many homes could not be properly heated and hundreds of homeless men crowded charitable institutions and police stations.

All the Central and West Central States were battling zero temperature tonight. Two cities, Devils Lake, N. D., and Duluth, Minn., reported 32 degrees below zero. Other cold places were:

Charles City, Ia., 18 below.
Minneapolis, Minn., 22 below.
Escanaba, Mich, 14 below.
Green Bay, Wis., 20 below.
White River, Ont., Canada, 40 below.

4 BELOW AT PANA, ILL.

PANA, Ill., Jan. 13.—(Universal Service.)—With the mercury 4 below zero and a heavy snow falling, Central Illinois was gripped in the severest blizzard of the winter. With the snowfall, old-fashioned sleighing of twenty-five years ago came back to its own.

15 BELOW AT ROCKFORD

ROCKFORD, Ill., Jan. 13.—(Universal Service.)—Rockford shivered today in the grip of the most severe cold of the winter. Fifteen below was the official report.

One man was found by police with his hands and arms frozen. He probably will die.

SNOW FALLS IN NEW YORK

NEW YORK, Jan. 13.—(Universal Service.) — The first snow of 1929 fell in New York today when a flurry started just after 3 p. m. As the snow began falling the strong northwest wind that had added to the cold diminished perceptibly. The only other snow of the season was in early December.

The cold wave which began Saturday night will continue tomorrow, the United States Weather Bureau predicts. However, the prediction adds that it will be fair tomorrow and the wind diminished.

Fire Traps Six Fifty Stories Above Ground

Universal Service

NEW YORK, Jan. 13.

FIVE men and a young woman were marooned for ten minutes in the observation tower of the Woolworth Building today, as flames and smoke circled them from burning wire insulation in an elevator machinery inclosure two floors below.

Edward Link, an accountant, of Sunnyside, L. I., and a member of the party in the tower, discovered the blaze. He was the first to fight his way down the spiral stairway to a clear space on the fifty-fourth floor.

There he warned Miss Phoebe Smith, saleswoman at a souvenir stand, who telephoned fire headquarters. Returning to the tower link wrapped his overcoat around Miss Margaret Shields, of Bay City, Michigan, and escorted her down the stairway. The others followed. The fire was extinguished with emergency hose.

EMIL FUCHS, ARTIST, SUICIDE

NEW YORK, Jan. 13.—(Universal Service.)—When the smoke of a revolver shot cleared away today in one of Manhattan's most luxurious studios, at No. 1 West Sixty-seventh street, the man who had painted kings and queens, the rich and the poor and achieved an international reputation as a sculptor and musician, lay dead on the carpet and the weapon clutched in his hand.

Emil Fuchs had shot himself.

To few men in the world had fame poured out her treasure so lavishly. He had modeled the figures of the world's greatest, taken the last expression of tranquil death from the face of queens with his magic pencil, portrayed the characters of financiers in Wall street and beggars in Tangiers with his facile brush, and written of the seven arts in language everyone could understand.

He left a note addressed to his sister, Renee, of the Endicott Hotel, who found the body, as he seemed to have sensed she would. It read:

"I cannot stand this agony any longer. Forgive me. EMIL."

Thus was revealed what few of his intimates knew—that he had for the past few years suffered from an intestinal cancer—and had gone about his work, despite the terrific pain it occasioned him.

23 Navy Seaplanes Flying to Panama

KEY WEST, Fla., Jan. 13.—(AP)—Twenty-three naval seaplanes of the aircraft squadron scouting fleet under the command of Lieutenant Commander Capehart arrived at Puerto Morelos, Mexico, at 1:30 o'clock this afternoon en route to the Canal Zone for maneuvers with the naval fleet, said a wireless message received here by Captain Robert W. McNeely, of the Seventh Naval District. The planes took off from Key West at 9:30 this morning.

TREATY VOTE TO BE OPPOSED, ENEMIES AGREE

Bingham Stands Firm, Insists Committee Report America's Position Under Agreement

WASHINGTON, Jan. 13.—(AP)—Renewed pressure from the White House failed today to break the deadlock in the Senate on the Kellogg anti-war treaty row and the group demanding an interpretative declaration on the pact decided late today to hold out against any agreement setting an hour to vote on its ratification.

Apparently concerned over the circulation yesterday of a "round robin petition," by those seeking an interpretative declaration of American rights under the treaty, President Coolidge last night summoned in Senator Bingham, Republican of Connecticut, who was passing the petition around.

The President made known his desire that no manner of reservation accompany American ratification of the treaty engineered by his Secretary of State. He considers a report of the foreign relations committee declaring that the treaty does not affect America's right of self-defense and does not infringe upon the Monroe Doctrine, which is asked by the petition, would be tantamount to a reservation.

BINGHAM STANDS GROUND

Senator Bingham stood his ground. He had in his pocket the "round robin petition" already bearing 24 signatures declaring for an interpretation. He insisted that a committee report, stating America's position under the treaty, could not be construed as a reservation to the pact.

Another conference of the "interpretationists" today decided to fight on, and as a result of that decision, objection will be voiced tomorrow to the proposal which Chairman Borah of the Foreign Relations committee intends to submit to limit debate on the treaty.

This decision throws the treaty into an indefinite future. Senator Borah, in charge of the pact, however, feels the responsibility is entirely on the "interpretationists." Almost to the man, this group is strongly for the cruiser construction bill which is awaiting disposition of the anti-war pact. Treaty advocates feel that the foes will be forced by their own desire for action on the cruiser bill to give in on the demand for an interpretation and are content to accept the deadlock for the present.

WANTS BOTH PASSED

But President Coolidge wants both the treaty, without reservation or interpretation, and the naval construction measure. A senatorial breakfast party, a later White

(Continued on Page 12, Column 1)

Captain Eaker Flies to Mother's Bedside

SAN ANGELO, Tex., Jan. 13.—(AP)—Capt. Ira Eaker, chief pilot of the army endurance plane Question Mark, landed at Midland, Tex., at dusk today. He flew there from San Diego, Calif., en route to Eden, forty-four miles from here, to visit his mother, Mrs. Y. Y. Eaker, near death from pneumonia. Captain Eaker immediately left for her bedside.

ANITA BALDWIN AND LENGLEN RIFT RUMORED

Tennis Star and Mother, Recent Guests at Arcadia, Found Secretly Registered at Hotel

Rumors of a rift between Suzanne Lenglen, temperamental French tennis star, and Mrs. Anita M. Baldwin, at whose Arcadia estate she has been a house guest for more than a month, took a sensational turn yesterday when Miss Lenglen and her mother were found secretly registered at the Biltmore Hotel.

Declining to open the door of her suite to reporters, Miss Lenglen, while admitting her identity, denied there had been any friction between herself and Mrs. Baldwin over the tennis star's friendship with Baldwin M. Baldwin, heir to the "Lucky" Baldwin millions.

"I have no row—it is not so," Miss Lenglen shouted through the hotel room door in answer to queries. Further than that she declined to answer. At her palatial home at Arcadia, Mrs. Baldwin could not be reached for a statement.

BALDWIN 'AT BILTMORE'

Neither could Baldwin M. Baldwin, repeatedly reported engaged to Miss Lenglen, be reached. At his rooms at the Jonathan Club, it was said that "Mr. Baldwin could be found at Room 6337, Biltmore Hotel."

The head roomclerk volunteered the information that Miss Lenglen and her mother had registered secretly at the hotel, had been assigned room 6337 and had given specific orders that they "not be disturbed." Bellboys said they understood the tennis star was planning to leave for the East immediately.

Miss Lenglen; her mother, Mrs. Baldwin, and her son, Baldwin M. Baldwin, arrived in Los Angeles December 10 last in the Baldwin private car over the Southern Pacific. They were accompanied by a retinue of servants and retainers.

(Continued on Page 3, Column 4)

Belasco, Stricken With Flu, in Bed

NEW YORK, Jan. 13.—(AP)—David Belasco, theatrical producer, is ill with influenza, it was learned today. He was taken ill Friday and since has been confined to his bed in his apartment in the Hotel Gladstone. Mr. Belasco is 69 years old. Some concern was felt among his friends, but his physician said the producer is in no great danger.

'Talkies,' in English, Make Havana Debut

HAVANA, Jan. 13.—(AP)—The "talkies" made their debut here today in what was believed to be their first appearance in Latin America. Owners of the theater were satisfied with the result, although the Spanish-speaking Cubans heard only the English of the screen.

Tragedy Reveals Her Romance With Husband's Friend

MRS. BABE RUTH
—International Newsreel photo

FATAL BLAZE BRINGS HINT OF MURDER

Woman Established in Dentist's Home Acknowledged by Home Run King as Estranged Mate

Burned Body Recovered, and Funeral Held Up for Inquiry; Yankees' Star Near Collapse

By Charles Miller
Staff Correspondent Universal Service

WATERTOWN, Mass., Jan. 13.—Helen Woodford Ruth, wife of George Herman (Babe) Ruth, the home run king in baseball, died in a mysterious fire which Friday night destroyed the home at 47 Quincy street, here, where she is alleged to have lived for nearly two years as the wife of Dr. Edward H. Kinder, wealthy dentist.

The burned body of Mrs. Ruth, unconscious, was taken from the blazing house by firemen. She died a few minutes later. Tonight ugly rumors began to raise their head that she might have died otherwise than because of the fire.

Investigation Ordered

The prosecuting attorney has ordered the funeral held up until Wednesday for a complete investigation.

The charred body of the woman, who was known as "Mr9s. Helen Kinder," positively identified by her sisters as Mrs. Babe Ruth, was tonight acknowledged by Babe himself as his wife.

Doctor Kinder was at a prize fight in Boston Friday night when the fire occurred. He collapsed when a friend, the Rev. John W. Down, got him on the telephone and told him of the tragedy. He is declared by the police to have later reported the victim of the fire as "Mrs. Kinder."

With trembling hands the big "Bambino" today held a

RUBBER FARM LURES EDISON

WEST ORANGE, N. J., Jan. 13.—(Universal Service.)—Eager for his annual winter vacation, Thomas A. Edison will leave Tuesday morning for Fort Myers, Fla. Mrs. Edison will accompany him.

Expecting to stay in the South several months, the inventor will continue the rubber experiments he started two years ago at his plantation farm in Florida, where he has been propagating rubber plants on several acres of ground.

U. S. Shipping Board Officer Dies of Flu

WASHINGTON, Jan. 13.—(Universal Service.)—Lieutenant Commander John Sitcher Woodruff, director of navigation laws and revision for the United States Shipping Board, died today in George Washington University Hospital from influenza. He will be buried Tuesday in Arlington Cemetery.

$25,000,000 DRY FUND OPPOSED

WASHINGTON, Jan. 13.—(AP)—The prospect of congressional approval of the $25,000,000 increase for prohibition enforcement voted by the Senate Appropriations Committee is dimmed by the decision of Secretary Mellon to oppose it in a letter to be transmitted tomorrow to the Senate.

The Treasury Department in disapproving the appropriation is understood to feel that the addition of $25,000,000 to the funds of the Prohibition Bureau for use in only one phase of its duties—enforcement—would not speed up the bureau's work.

ORANGE JUICE ADD TO HEIGHT

SAN FRANCISCO, Jan. 13.—More calories in the food given them at school means taller, sturdier children.

This was the conclusion of Dr. Agnes Fay Morgan, chairman of the department of household science at the University of California, who has been directing some experiments in Oakland recently, to determine what children should be fed at school.

Children given orange juice to supplement their lunches gained the most in height, while the boys and girls fed on milk and those fed on crackers gained more in weight. The children who received no extra lunch developed the least."

Kin of O. Henry Buried in Austin

AUSTIN, Tex., Jan. 13.—(AP)—Mrs. Margaret Jane Roach, 79, mother-in-law of William Sidney Porter (O. Henry), popularly thought to have influenced the writer to give up a clerkship in the Texas state land office to become an author, was buried here today beside the body of O. Henry. She died yesterday.

Kansas Inaugurates New Governor Today

TOPEKA, Kan., Jan. 13.—(AP)—Clyde M. Reed becomes Governor of Kansas tomorrow. Shortly after high noon, Governor Ben S. Paulen will turn over to his successor the reins of the state's government.

Afghan Pretender Joins Rebel Forces

MOSCOW, Jan. 13.—(AP)—Izvestia today says that Mohamed Ormor Khan, chief pretender to the throne of King Amanullah of Afgghanistan, has left secretly for the Afghan frontier to join the rebels. The newspaper's says that that King's relinquishment of westernization reforms includes permission to all ulams or priests graduated from the Divband, the supreme religious academy of India, to reside in Afghanistan.

Former U. S. Senator C. J. Faulkner Jr. Dies

MARTINSBURG, W. Va., Jan. 13.—(Universal Service.)—Former U. S. Senator Charles James Faulkner Jr., 81, Confederate veteran, died at his home here today after a brief illness. Senator Faulkner's father, a Virginia aristocrat, was once United States minister to France.

Serjeant, English Physician, 99, Dies

LONDON, Jan. 13.—(AP)—Sir David Maurice Serjeant, believed to be England's oldest physician, died today at the age of 99. He was a poet as well, and was knighted when he was 91 for his patriotic verse.

J. P. MORGAN U. S. REPARATIONS AID

WASHINGTON, Jan. 13.—Although official confirmation was lacking it was generally accepted here today that J. P. Morgan would be one of the American representatives at the forthcoming reparations conference in Paris. The other will be Owen D. Young, head of the General Electric Company, and one of the creators of the Dawes plan.

While declining to be quoted directly, it was indicated by one unusually well-informed observer here that the only thing necessary to make the appointment of Mr. Morgan complete, was the formality of public announcement.

CZARIST LEADER SLAIN IN HOME

BY EDWARD L. DEUSS
Universal Service Special Cable

MOSCOW, Jan. 13.—The famous Czarist army leader, General Shhlastchov, was assassinated last night. He was shot to death while reading by lamplight in his Moscow home, the assassins, who have not yet been identified, firing through the window.

Gen. Shlashtchov, who after the failure of the Czar's armies, became commander first of an army under General Denikin and later under General Wrangel, has been instructor in the Moscow Military Academy since 1922.

Alexander's Record

Year	Club	League	G.	W.	L.	Pct.	S.O.	B.B.	H.
1909	Galesburg a	Ill.-Mo.	24	15	8	.652	198	42	124
1910	Indianapolis b	A. A.	2						
1910	Syracuse c	N. Y. St	43	29	14	.674	204	67	215
1911	Philadelphia	N. L.	48	28	13	.683	227	129	285
1912	Philadelphia	N. L.	46	19	17	.543	195	107	289
1913	Philadelphia	N. L.	47	22	8	.733	159	75	283
1914	Philadelphia	N. L.	46	27	15	.642	214	76	327
1915	Philadelphia	N. L.	49	31	10	.756	241	64	253
1916	Philadelphia	N. L.	48	33	12	.733	167	50	323
1917	Philadelphia d	N. L.	45	30	13	.698	201	58	336
1918	Chicago	N. L.	3	2	1	.667			
1919	Chicago	N. L.	30	16	11	.593	121	38	180
1920	Chicago	N. L.	46	27	14	.659	173	69	335
1921	Chicago	N. L.	31	15	13	.536	77	33	286
1922	Chicago	N. L.	33	16	13	.552	48	34	283
1923	Chicago	N. L.	39	22	12	.647	72	30	308
1924	Chicago e	N. L.	21	12	5	.706	33	25	183
1925	Chicago	N. L.	32	15	11	.577	63	29	270
1926	Chicago-St. Louis f	N. L.	30	12	10	.545	47	31	191
1927	St. Louis	N. L.	37	21	10	.677	48	38	261
1928	St. Louis	N. L.	34	16	9	.640	59	37	262
1929	St. Louis	N. L.	21	9	7	.562	13	31	138
	Complete major league total		687	373	261	.586	2168	954	4793

World's Series Records

Year	Club	League	G.	I.P.	W.	L.	Pct.	S.O.	B.B.	H	Avg.
1915	Philadelphia	N. L.	2	18	1	1	.500	10	4	14	...
1926	St. Louis	N. L.	3	20 1-3	2	0	1.000	17	4	12	...
1928	St. Louis	N. L.	2	5	0	1	.000	2	4	10	...

New Record Set by Alexander

Places National League Mark of Games Won at 373, Passing Matty's 1916 Figures

GROVER CLEVELAND ALEXANDER
Famous pitcher, who has eclipsed record of victories hung up by the immortal Christy Mathewson.

BY HOWARD G. REYNOLDS

Grover Cleveland Alexander, harassed by illness and injuries that have hindered him from time to time, after 19 years of service as a pitcher in the National league, has at last achieved his great desire.

On Saturday, in Philadelphia, he went into the game when his team was behind and pitched a brand of ball that kept the Quakers down while his teammates were piling up the runs that put St. Louis into the winning column.

In doing so he won his 373d game, thus establishing a new record for National league games won. The old record was set by the great Christy Mathewson, who in his career placed the mark at 372.

OLD CY HAD 511 WINS

One pitching record that will probably stand for all time, unless a superman arrives, is that of Old Cy Young, who hung up a mark of 511 victories. Old Cy's feat was astonishing for he compiled his remarkable string of wins during a period of 21 years of activity with both the National and American Leagues.

It is unthinkable for anyone to believe that Alexander can ever hope to score 138 more wins before he finally decides to hang up his glove and leave the game for the younger set to carry on.

The fact that Alexander was the first to beat Mathewson's record, which has stood since 1916, shows what a task it was to turn the trick.

What is an outstanding feature of Alexander's work is that a good many of his victories were scored when he was connected with the Philadelphia Nationals, who always had a more or less banged-up organization with the lone exception of the one year when the Quaker City aggregation managed to sneak through to win the National League gonfalon.

Will Finish at St. Louis

Alexander subsequently was sent to the Chicago Cubs and from there to the St. Louis Cardinals where he will probably finish out his baseball career.

It was back in 1911 that the Philadelphia fans first glimpsed Alexander in action. He was a gangling, unheralded youngster, who was acquired for the proverbial song, yet he surprised the baseball world by coming through with 28 victories as against 13 defeats before the season came to a finish.

Alexander holds the record for scoring shutouts and in 1916, when he enjoyed his best season, he hung up a season's mark of 33 victories, among them being 16 shutouts.

Another mark, in which G. C. A. shares, is the feat of scoring four consecutive shutouts, he and Ed Reulbach sharing the honors by themselves. No other pitcher, old timer or modern, has been able to boast of such an achievement. Thirty-six scoreless innings, in four consecutive games, can be accomplished, but try and equal the mark.

For a time the popular veteran enjoyed the distinction of leading the National league pitchers in strike outs. As a matter of fact, his reign lasted six years, until Dizzy Vance, the backbone of the Brooklyn Robins, came along to mow down opposing batsmen.

It was not so long ago that talk was going around about St. Louis getting set to let Alexander out. The unconditional release or a berth in the minors stared the great moundsman in the face, but in the face of all criticism, Alexander pulled himself together and turned in a trio of victories in his last four starts.

Alexander has earned his brackets in baseball's "Hall of Fame." He may go no further than to round out the present season, but when "Old Pete" decides to chuck it, he'll have left behind him a great record, one that will indeed be difficult to surpass.

MARKSMEN BLANK HUB ELEVEN, 2-0

Both Goals Scored in First Half—Rain Slows Play

FALL RIVER, Aug. 11—The Boston football club after taking the measure of New Bedford in the opening of the American league at Fenway Park, Boston, on Saturday afternoon, fell before Fall River, 2 to 0, here this afternoon.

NEITHER CLUB EXCEPTIONAL

It was the initial league game for the marksmen, who showed better football than the Bostons. Neither club was in exceptional form, owing to the early season. A driving rainstorm not only kept the crowd down to 2200 but also slowed up play materially. Fall River got both of its goals in the initial session.

Fleming was out of the Boston lineup making it necessary to switch Nilsen to righthalf back. Sunderland, a Fall River youngster, was given an opportunity to show his wares at inside right.

Fall River had the wind for an advantage in the first half and acted accordingly. White scored in about one minute. Thirty-nine seconds later Malcolm Goldie registered the second and final goal during a scrimmage following a corner kick.

The summary:

FALL RIVER	BOSTON
Douglas, g	g, Harper
N. McAuley, rfb	rfb, McGill
Doyle, lfb	lfb, McArthur
McPherson, rhb	rhb, Adams
Caldwell, chb	chb, Nilsen
J. McAuley, lhb	lhb, Ballantyne
McNab, orf	orf, H. Burness
Gonsalves, irf	irf, Sunderland
Patenaude, cf	cf, Wall
White, ilf	ilf, J. Burness
Goldie, olf	olf, McEachran

Score—Fall River 2. Goals—White, Goldie. Officials—James Walders of Philadelphia, referee; Norse and Rose of New Bedford, linesmen. Time—45m. halves.

AT THE LUCY RECS VICTORY

Silva, crack fullback of the Newark Portuguese, is shown in the act of clearing an attack by Lucy Recs during the exhibition soccer game at Blake Field, Cambridge, yesterday afternoon. Marcedes of Newark is holding off McIntyre of Lucy Recs while Silva completes the clearance. Lucy Recs won by 4 to 1.

Lucy Recs Subdue Newark Team 4-1

Cambridge Eleven Shows Fine Form in Disposing of Far Heralded Portuguese From Jersey

BY DAVE SCOTT

The Lucy Recs soccer eleven gave another brilliant exhibition at Blake Field yesterday afternoon in trouncing the much-heralded Newark Portuguese by the score of 4 to 1, the clever Cambridge combination displaying marked all-around superiority in adding the New Jersey outfit to its list of victims.

OUTCLASS VISITORS

With the exception of a few minutes at the outset and a brief spell towards the finish, Lucy Recs clearly outclassed the Newark side in every department. The Cambridge forwards played with machine-like precision, while the home defence, in which Costa, Whalley, and Doherty were especially prominent, was well nigh unbeatable.

Some 3000 enthusiastic Portuguese followers of the sport witnessed a splendid exhibition, played at a fast pace throughout. Lusitania "B" beat Hudson Portuguese, 2 to 1, in a preliminary game.

The visitors attacked immediately after the kick-off, their forwards combining in fine style. Newark forced two corners, Costa and Shannon clearing the flag kicks. "Dobbler" Lyons brought Lucy Recs into the picture by clever footwork and McIntyre twice tested Pantland with fast low drives that the goalie just managed to save.

Dundas Opens Scoring

In end to end exchange, each team forced corners, but the respective defence proved sound against nippy vanguards. Midway through the period, Dundas opened the scoring with a grounder from 25 yards, a fast drive that Pantland misjudged. A few minutes later, the Newark goalie distinguished himself by saving a rocket shot from McIntyre and in fisting clear across from Dundas.

Lucy Recs dominated the play at this stage of the game. McIntyre headed home a Dundas centre, but the point was disallowed for the home centre fouling Rebelo prior to getting his cranium on the ball. One minute from the interval, Lyons and Foley combined to beat all opposition, the wee winger presenting Moniz with an open goal which was accepted and Lucy Recs crossed over leading by two clear goals.

Foley Adds Third Talley

Kirby replaced Macedo in the Newark intermediate line on restarting. Lucy Recs immediately attacked and Pantland luckily saved a close range shot from Dundas, the ball glancing off the goalie's arm for a fruitless corner. Ten minutes after the start of the second period poor defensive play by the visitors led to Foley adding a third tally, the wee winger walking the ball into the net following a miskick by Kirby.

O'Hara, the outstanding forward in the Newark lineup, had no luck with a great shot that Whalley managed to hold on the goal line. Although outplayed, the visitors fought gamely, O'Hara and Strong displaying pleasing footwork in their attack with Rebelo and Pacheco, prominent in an overworked defence.

Fouled Inside Penalty Area

Whalley was applauded for two saves from O'Hara, but Lucy Recs continued to enjoy the better of the exchanges and 15 minutes from time the home side increased its margin. Foley had weaved his way past all opposition and was in the act of shooting when Silva fouled him inside the penalty area. "Dobbler" Lyons, entrusted with the spot kick, registered his team's fourth marker.

With a commanding lead Lucy Recs took matters easy and the Newark side attacked in the closing stages, O'Hara obtaining a consolation tally a few seconds before the final whistle, a soft shot that rolled between Whalley's legs and over the goal line.

The summary:

LUCY RECS	NEWARK PORTUGUESE
Whalley, g	g, Pantland
Shannon, rfb	lfb, Silva
Costa, lfb	rfb, Rebelo
Corey, rhb	lhb, Macedo
Rapoza, chb	chb, Pacheco
Doherty, lhb	rhb, Eckersley
Dundas, or	ol, Fereira
Lyons, ir	il, O'Hara
McIntyre, c	c, Strong
Moniz, il	ir, Maloy
Foley, ol	or, Conn

Score—Lucy Recs 4, Newark Portuguese 1. Goals scored by—Dundas, Moniz, Foley, Lyons and O'Hara. Substitution—Kirby for Macedo. Referee—W. Andrews. Linesmen—P. Carrigan and T. White. Time—45-min. halves.

BASEBALL IN BRIEF
Told in a Nutshell

(Including games of Aug. 11, 1929)

AMERICAN LEAGUE

	R	H	E
Chicago	6	7	0
Boston	3	5	0
Cleveland	6	13	1
New York	5	8	4
Detroit	9	15	1
Philadelphia	8	12	3
Washington	7	11	0
St. Louis	5	9	0

NATIONAL LEAGUE

	R	H	E
Chicago	3	6	1
Boston	1	8	1
Brooklyn	5	9	0
Pittsburg	3	6	0
New York	6	10	1
Cincinnati	1	5	0

(Only games scheduled.)

INTERNATIONAL LEAGUE

	R	H	E
Jersey City	6	9	0
Toronto	4	7	0
(First game.)			
Toronto	3	5	2
Jersey City	1	5	0
(Second game.)			
Reading	11	18	1
Montreal	4	7	1
Newark	4	12	0
Rochester	3	7	1
(First game.)			
Rochester	7	7	0
Newark	2	4	0
(Second game.)			
Baltimore	7	13	2
Buffalo	2	6	0
(First game.)			
Buffalo	6	10	0
Baltimore	4	7	1
(Second game.)			

AMERICAN ASSOCIATION

	R	H	E
Milwaukee	11	13	1
Columbus	9	9	2
(First game.)			
Columbus	5	9	1
Milwaukee	4	9	2
(Second game.)			
Louisville	4	9	2
Minneapolis	3	9	1
(First game.)			
Louisville	6	9	2
Minneapolis	0	8	1
(Second game.)			
Kansas City	8	11	2
Toledo	4	10	2
(First game.)			
Kansas City	12	15	3
Toledo	10	16	2
(Second game.)			
St. Paul	2	6	1
Indianapolis	1	9	1
(First game.)			
Indianapolis	11	9	4
St. Paul	5	6	4
(Second: 5 innings: agreement.)			

NEW ENGLAND LEAGUE

	R	H	E
Lynn	3	6	4
Lewiston	2	5	2
Fitchburg	3	9	3
Portland	2	7	1
(First game.)			
Portland	3	5	1
Fitchburg	1	7	0
(Second game.)			

(Manchester-New Bedford: Rain.)
(Nashua-Brockton: Called in second: rain.)

EASTERN LEAGUE

	R	H	E
Albany	4	12	0
Pittsfield	3	7	2
(First game.)			
Pittsfield	3	13	1
Albany	2	8	0
(Second game.)			
Providence	5	17	1
Allentown	4	10	2
(First game.)			
Allentown	5	7	1
Providence	4	11	1
(Second game.)			

Bridgeport at New Haven: Rain.
Springfield at Hartford: Rain.

LEADING PITCHERS
(6 or More Games)

NATIONAL

	Won	Lost	P.C.
Bush, Chgo.	16	1	.941
Grimes, Pitts.	16	2	.889
Kremer, Pitts.	14	4	.778
Carlson, Chgo.	6	2	.750
Mays, N. Y.	6	2	.750
Moss, Bkln.	5	2	.714
Root, Chgo.	11	4	.733
Johnson, St. L.	9	4	.692
Lucas, Cin.	15	7	.682
Malone, Chgo.	15	8	.652
Morrison, Bkln.	9	5	.643
Haines, St. L.	12	7	.632

AMERICAN

	Won	Lost	P.C.
Zachary, N. Y.	8	0	1.000
Grove, Phila.	17	2	.895
Rommel, Phila.	8	2	.800
Earnshaw, Phila.	18	5	.783
Wells, N. Y.	9	3	.750
Yde, Det.	6	2	.750
Walberg, Phila.	15	6	.714
Ehmke, Phila.	5	2	.714
Heimach, N. Y.	10	5	.667
Pennock, N. Y.	8	4	.667
Stewart, St. L.	7	4	.636
Shores, Phila.	[illegible]	[illegible]	[illegible]

AMERICAN LEAGUE STANDING

	Won	Lost	P.C.
Philadelphia	78	31	.716
New York	65	39	.625
Cleveland	56	51	.523
St. Louis	56	52	.519
Detroit	52	55	.486
Washington	44	60	.423
Chicago	43	65	.398
BOSTON	32	73	.305

GAMES TODAY

Boston at Chicago.
Philadelphia at Detroit.
New York at Cleveland.
Washington at St. Louis.

NATIONAL LEAGUE STANDING

	Won	Lost	P.C.
Chicago	70	32	.686
Pittsburg	63	41	.606
New York	60	48	.556
St. Louis	54	53	.505
Brooklyn	46	60	.434
Cincinnati	44	61	.419
BOSTON	43	63	.406
Philadelphia	41	68	.394

GAMES TODAY

Chicago at Boston.
Cincinnati at New York.
Pittsburg at Brooklyn.
St. Louis at Philadelphia.

N. E. LEAGUE STANDING

	Won	Lost	P.C.
Manchester	22	11	.667
Lynn	22	12	.647
Lewiston	20	14	.588
New Bedford	14	14	.500
Fitchburg	16	17	.485
Brockton	14	18	.437
Nashua	13	20	.384
Portland	11	26	.297

GAMES TODAY

Lewiston at Brockton.
Manchester at New Bedford.

HAKOAH DEFEATS BRIDGEPORT, 4 TO 1

NEW YORK, Aug. 11—The new Brooklyn Hakoah Soccer Club and Bridgeport, another recent acquisition of the American Soccer league, faced each other in the second game of the double-header at Hawthorne Field today.

Outplaying their opponents early in the game and leading at the turn by 2—1, the Hakoahs registered their initial victory by the score of 4 goals to 1.

For 25 minutes there was little to choose between the rival teams. Wegner, the latest importation from Vienna, was placed in the back division by Captain Groze of Hakoah and played his position faultlessly.

The lineup:

HAKOAH	BRIDGEPORT
Joselit, g	g, McMilland
Wegner, rb	rb, Wilson
Groze, lb	lb, Watkins
Goldstein, rh	rh, Daly
Evans, ch	ch, O'Neill
Schneider, lh	lh, Nichol
Lacelo, or	or, Kelly
Braun, ir	ir, McManus
Schonfeld, c	c, Enterkin
Eisenhoffer, il	il, Cox
Pearson, ol	ol, McKenna

Score—Hakoah 4, Bridgeport 1. Goals—Pearson, Eisenhoffer, Schonfeld 2, Enterkin. Substitution—Manson for Schneider. Referee—T. Newman. Linesmen—J. Cunningham and J. Hume. Time—45m. halves.

GOLDSMITH SOLD TO CARDS BY NEWARK

NEWARK, N. J., Aug. 11 (AP)—The Newark team of the International League today announced the purchase by the St. Louis Cardinals of Harold E. Goldsmith, right hand pitcher.

Goldsmith came to the Bears from the Boston Braves in June, 1928. The purchase price was not made public.

Goldsmith will join the Cards in Philadelphia tomorrow.

MAKING HISTORY

Eddie Tolan, the Michigan flier, is said to be standing the Swedish athletic followers on their heads by his wonderful sprinting performances abroad. They claim they never saw a flier like him in spite of Uncle Sam sending the greatest collection of Yankee speedsters to the Olympic games in 1912. And the funny part of it all we still have a few at home who can make the colored runner from Steve Farrell's college step faster than ever to win.

For Other Sport News See Pages 14 and 15

Boxing Gossip

Eddie Curley of the West End will battle Pancho Villa of New Bedford at the Elm Rink in New Bedford tonight. Although Curley has scored three victories over Villa, the home boy will be the favorite to win. Curley is the only boy who has scored a win over Jake Zeramby, recent winner over Andre Routis.

• • • •

Al Rackow of Buffalo and Eddie Ciafidoni of Lynn mingle in the 10-round feature bout at Lincoln, N. H., tonight. Although Ciafidoni has won 19 out of 20 battles, Rackow is looked upon as the likely winner. The Buffalo boy recently defeated Ruby Levine and Johnny Daley, the ex-amateur star. Johnny Hanlon of Lynn and Pete Chico of the U. S. S. Florida meet in the eight-round semi-final. Three other bouts featuring New Hampshire boys will complete the card.

• • • •

Al Mello of Lowell, one of the most popular boys ever developed in New England, is starting to feel like himself again and is taking a good rest. The arm trouble that helped defeat Al in his last start is now entirely cured and the Lowell southpaw is beginning to look for action. Bobby Goldman refuses to allow Al to enter a gym and orders him to rest till at least the first of October.

• • • •

Frankie Hennessey of Fall River and Eddie Holmes of Providence, will meet in the final bout of eight rounds at Tiverton, R. I., tonight. Paddy Mullins of the navy and Battling Brosseau of Fall River, meet in the six round semi-final. Stanley Wynnerick of Lawrence meets Goodie Swartz of Cambridge in another six rounder.

• • • •

Jimmy Picardi of East Boston, who has become quite a favorite with the fans of Connecticut, is anxious to battle Gene Bianco of the North End. These boys are old rivals and would make a great main bout for the Lynn club.

• • • •

The great record being rolled up by Andy Martin, the South End featherweight has attracted the attention of Edward Foster of the Rhode Island boxing commission. Foster is also the chairman of the championship committee of the National Boxing Association and feels that the work of Martin in defeating Benny Bass, Eddie Shea and Bud Taylor, ranks Andy at the top of the featherweight division. Martin and Al Singer or Kid Chocolate would pack the Boston Garden.

• • •

Jack Sharkey is doing his training daily at Jim Toland's gymnasium and is looking much better than when he left for the South to start training for his battle with Young Stribling. Sharkey feels that Tommy Loughran is made to order for him and delights a big audience each day with his imitations of the style of the clever light-heavy champion.

• • • •

Johnny Casper, who has been making Boston his home for the last year, is anxious to meet Mike Sarkis of Lawrence in a return bout. Sarkia scored a close decision over Casper at Lawrence last week, but Johnny is certain he can reverse that verdict. Andy Callanan, also of Lawrence, is included in the defi of Casper.

• • • •

Rudy Bauer of Jamaica Plain, who has scored victories in his three professional starts, will be in great shape for his battle with Tony Firpo, at Franklin, N. H., on Thursday night. Freddy Duffy, who boxed Owen Moran and Jack Britton about 15 years ago, is training Bauer and feels certain that Jamaica Plain will have another star.

• • • •

Jim Maloney, who battles Bertazzolo, at Braves Field, next Monday night, is still looking for more sparring partners at his training camp at Marlboro. Jim is not too easy on his partners, with the result that the boys don't stick around very long.

N. Y. NATIONALS PLAY TIE WITH WANDERERS

NEW YORK, Aug. 11—A battle royal between the Brooklyn Wanderers and the New York Nationals marked the opening of the annual championship series of the American Soccer League at Hawthorne Field in Brooklyn, this afternoon. The outcome was a 3-3 tie, with the Nationals leading early in the second half and the home team coming up even 10 minutes from the end.

The Nationals presented practically the same team they have used for the past two seasons, but the Wanderers had four newcomers in their lineup. Nehadoma of Brooklyn, with two goals carried off the scoring honors and Yule accounted for Brooklyn's third. Gallagher, Leonard and Nelson sent one apiece between the uprights.

The lineup:

B'KLYN WANDERERS	N. Y. NAT'LS.
Hergert, g	g, Murdock
MacAdam, rb	lb, Donald
Crowley, lb	rb, Warden
Maguire, rh	lh, Martyn
Moore, ch	ch, Chatton
Morris, lh	rhb, Slaven
Mclure, or	ir, Carlson
Lyell, ir	or, Gallagher
Nehadoma, c	c, Nelson
Devlin, il	ol, McGhee
Yule, ol	il, Leonard

Goals, Yule, Nehadoma 2, Gallagher, Leonard, Nelson.

Referee, C. Stott. Linesmen, J. Connachin and J. Hayes. Time, 45 minute halves.

Ruffing Pitches Well But Loses

Chisox Make Most of Their 7 Blows to Conquer Carrigans 6 to 3; Rothrock Hits Homer

CHICAGO, Aug. 11—Two fine pitchers did their stuff at Comiskey Park this afternoon, with the usual inspiring effect on their supporting casts. It was a good ball game, in which Alphonse Thomas conquered Charlie Ruffing, 6 to 3.

PLAY ERRORLESS BALL

There was nothing suggestive of the misfortunes that have placed Boston in eighth place and the White Sox in seventh. Both sides played errorless ball. Thomas allowed five hits and Ruffing seven.

Among the few hits were just enough long ones to add zest to the enterprise. Jack Rothrock knocked a homer with one on, Charley Berry drove in the first run of the game with a triple, Art Shires drove in the first White Sox run with a triple, Reynolds drove in two runs with a triple and Doug Taitt drove in two with a double. What proved to be the winning run was driven home by Pitcher Thomas.

Ruffing Effective at Start

The Red Sox made their first marker with two down in the second. Todt singled and scored when Berry's smack got past Reynolds and was scored as a triple. Rhyne then flied to Taitt.

The first 11 White Sox to face Ruffing never reached first, but with two out in the fourth, Charley hit Reynolds with a pitched ball. Shires then tripled to the scoreboard in left centre and Reynolds scored the tying run. The ball was not played any too well by Rothrock, who overran the shot, but it was triple, just the same. Kamm walked and stole second; then Taitt, doubled, scoring Shires and Kamm. Reeves threw out Kerr.

The Red Sox tied the score in the sixth. Reeves walked with one out, paused while Scarritt flied to Metzler, then scored ahead of Rothrock when Jack lined one into the right field stand.

In the seventh the White Sox made three runs, their winning margin. Kerr opened with a single to left, moved to second on Berg's sacrifice bunt and scored on Thomas' single to right. Metzler walked, but Cissell popped to Regan. Reynolds tripled, scoring Thomas and Metzler. Shires was called out on strikes.

The same clubs will play tomorrow afternoon, with Faber pitching for Chicago and MacFayden for Boston. As an added feature, Jack Rothrock and Carl Reynolds, reputed to be the fastest runners in the American league, will stage a foot race for the E. S. Barnard Cup. After the sprint the two players will seek to lower the record for circling the bases.

RUFF OUT OF LUCK

CHICAGO (A)	AB	R	BH	TB	PO	A	E
Metzler, lf	4	1	1	1	4	0	0
Cissell, ss	4	0	1	2	0	3	0
Reynolds, cf	3	1	1	2	3	0	0
Shires, 1b	4	1	1	3	10	0	0
Kamm, 3b	3	1	0	0	1	1	0
Taitt, rf	4	0	1	2	1	0	0
Kerr, 2b	4	1	1	1	4	2	0
Berg, c	2	0	0	0	4	1	0
Thomas, p	3	1	1	1	0	2	0
Totals	31	6	7	12	27	9	0

BOSTON (A)	AB	R	BH	TB	PO	A	E
Reeves, 3b	1	1	0	0	1	1	0
Scarritt, lf	4	0	0	0	0	0	0
Rothrock, cf	4	1	1	4	5	0	0
Barrett, rf	4	0	1	1	3	0	0
Regan, 2b	4	0	1	1	2	1	0
Todt, 1b	3	1	1	1	6	0	0
Berry, c	3	0	1	3	6	0	0
Rhine, ss	3	0	0	0	1	4	0
Ruffing, p	3	0	0	0	0	1	0
aBigelow	1	0	0	0	0	0	0
Totals	30	3	5	10	24	7	0

Chicago ....0 0 0 3 0 0 3 0 —6
Boston ....0 1 0 0 0 2 0 0 0—3

aBatted for Berry in 9th.

Runs batted in—Shires, Taitt 2, Berry, Rothrock 2, Thomas, Reynolds 2. Home run—Rothrock. Three-base hits—Berry, Shires. Two-base hits—Taitt, Cissell, Reynolds. Sacrifices—Berg, Todt. Stolen base—Kamm. Struck out—By Thomas 5, by Ruffing 4. Base on balls—Off Ruffing 1, off Thomas 3. Left on bases—Boston 4, Chicago 5. Umpires—Dineen, Hildebrand and Ormsby. Time—1h. 34m.

HOME RUNS YESTERDAY

Ruth, Yankees	1
Gehrig, Yankees	1
Hornsby, Cubs	1
Jackson, Giants	1
Frederick, Robins	1
Hendrick, Robins	1
Bissonette, Robins	1
Rothrock, Red Sox	1
Miller, Athletics	1
Hargrave, Tigers	1
Cronin, Senators	1
Johnson, Tigers	1

LEADERS

Klein, Phillies	33
Ruth, Yankees	30
Wilson, Cubs	30
Ott, Giants	30
Gehrig, Yankees	27
Foxx, Athletics	26
Simmons, Athletics	26
Bottomley, Cardinals	25
Hornsby, Cubs	25
Hurst, Phillies	24

LEAGUE TOTALS

National	587
American	449
Grand Total	1036

HOMERS SPELL A'S DOWNFALL

Tigers Overcome Big Lead to Win in 11th

DETROIT, Aug. 11 (AP)—Detroit spotted the Athletics five runs in the first inning today and then, with the aid of timely home runs by Red Hargrave and Roy Johnson, won by 9 to 8.

Hargrave's homer came in the ninth with two on base when the Tigers were trailing by four runs. John Picus Quinn then came to the aid of George Earnshaw, but was unable to prevent the tying run, scored on Cronin's wild throw. Johnson's homer in the 11th was inside the park.

The score:

DETROIT (A)	ab	bh	po	a
Johns'n,lf,cf	7	2	7	0
Harris,2	4	1	1	4
Gehringer,2	1	0	0	0
Rice,cf,3	5	2	1	2
Heilmann,r	5	1	2	0
Alexander,1	5	1	17	[illegible]
M'Manus,3,s	5	1	1	6
Hargrave,c	5	3	4	0
Schuble,s	3	0	0	[illegible]
Fothergill,lf	2	1	0	0
Sorrell,p	0	0	0	0
Carroll,p	3	2	0	3
Whitehill,p	0	0	0	0
aYde	1	1	0	[illegible]
Totals	46	15	33	17

PHILADELPHIA (A)	ab	bh	po	a
Cronin,2	6	1	1	5
Haas,cf	4	0	3	0
Cocarane,c	6	1	6	1
Simmons,lf	6	3	[illegible]	0
Foxx,1	3	0	16	0
[illegible]	6	4	2	0
Hale,3	4	1	2	4
Boley,s	4	2	0	3
Earnshaw,p	5	0	0	3
Quinn,p	0	0	0	0
Orwoll,p	0	0	0	0
Totals	44	12	b32	16

Detroit 0 1 1 1 1 0 0 0 4 0 1—9
Phila. 5 0 1 1 0 1 0 0 0 0 0—8

aBatted for Carroll in 9th. bTwo out when winning run scored.

Runs—Johnson, Harris, Rice, Heilmann, Alexander, McManus, Hargrave, Schuble, Fothergill, Foxx 2, Miller 2, Hale 2, Cochrane, Simmons. Errors—Harris, Cronin, Cochrane. Runs batted in—Simmons, Miller 2, Boley 3, Hargrave 4, Haas, Heilmann 2, Hale, Johnson. Two-base hits—Cochrane, Simmons, Hargrave 2. Three-base hits—Boley, Rice. Home runs—Miller, Hargrave, Johnson. Stolen base—Miller. Sacrifices—Haas, Hale. Double play—Hale to Cronin to Foxx. Left on bases—Philadelphia 11, Detroit 13. Base on balls—Off Sorrell 3, off Carroll 3, off Earnshaw 8. Struck out—By Sorrell 1, by Earnshaw 5, by Whitehill 1, by Orwoll 1. Hits—Off Sorrell, 5 in 1 2-3 innings; off Carroll, 6 in 7 1-3 innings; off Whitehill, 1 in 2 innings; off Earnshaw, 11 in 8 1-3 innings; off Quinn, 3 in none (pitched to 3 batters in 9th); off Orwoll, 1 in 2 1-3 innings. Winning pitcher—Whitehill. Losing pitcher—Orwoll. Umpires—Moriarty, Giezel and VanGaflan.

PLAY BALL!

Getting ready for the season's opener at White Sox park. Moe Berg, former Princeton star, who expects to be in shape (despite his recent knee injury) to work behind the plate next Tuesday when the Cleveland Indians come to town. (By P. & A. Photos)

Spring is in the air and baseball comes once more to its place of primacy in the American world of sport. Such scenes as this will thrill the fans assembled this season at Comiskey park and Wrigley field.

Charley Root is the pitching ace who, the fans hope, will work in the first Cub game at Wrigley field a week from next Tuesday. (Daily News Photo)

Speed king of the base lines. Hazen ("Kiki") Cuyler, fleet-footed right fielder of the Cubs. (Associated Press Photo)

His eye is on another big league victory. Joe McCarthy, square - jawed manager of the Cubs, snapped in a characteristic pose. (Daily News Photo)

Hope of the White Sox. Donie Bush, now beginning his first season as manager of the Comiskey nine. Formerly he managed the Pittsburgh Pirates. (Daily News Photo)

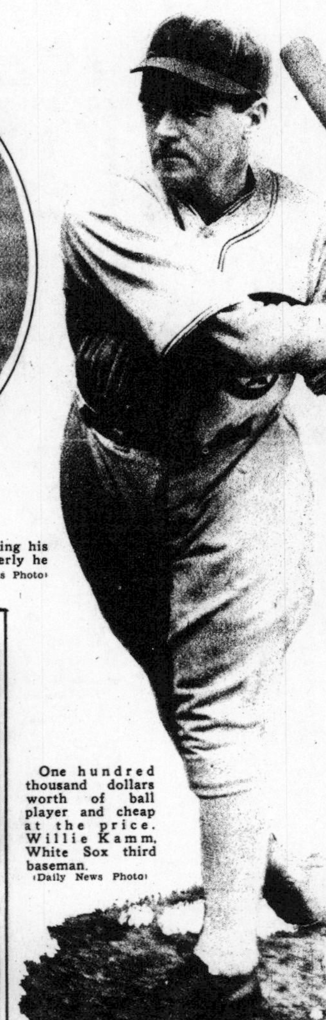

One hundred thousand dollars worth of ball player and cheap at the price. Willie Kamm, White Sox third baseman. (Daily News Photo)

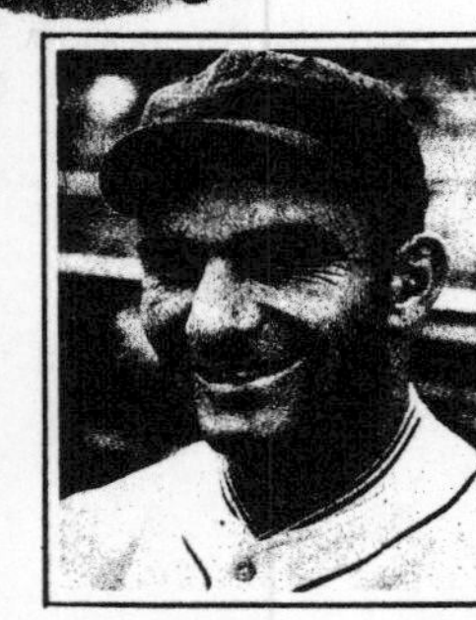

Old Reliable. Smiling Riggs Stephenson, left fielder of the Cubs, whose bat is the siege gun of "murderers' row." (Daily News Photo)

Ace of the Sox pitching staff. Alphonse ("Tommy") Thomas, who, experts say, is one of the best hurlers in the American league. (Daily News Photo)

The Rajah. Most valuable player to his team, the experts agree, is Rogers Hornsby, second baseman of the Cubs and one of the most feared batters in the league.

Stormy petrel. Hack Wilson is a battler, on the baseball diamond or anywhere else a battle is necessary. And he's one of the most popular of the Chicago Cubs. (Daily News Photo)

Captain of the Cubs. Charley Grimm, veteran first sacker of the Wrigley men. He is also a dangerous hitter.

Smead Jolley, new White Sox right fielder, whose heavy hitting is expected to help put the south siders once more in pennant-winning form.

Right—Ted Lyons of the White Sox. He is one of the American league's most effective hurlers.

Right—Gabby Hartnett is again in the game, ready to take his place behind the bat and to furnish a stream of chatter at Cubs park.

Sox fans will see him at second base. Bill Cissell, who will begin the 1930 season in a position which he seems to like better than shortstop.

ALCO-GRAVURE, INC. Chicago - New York - St. Louis - Baltimore - Cleveland - Kansas City

2 CENTS PAY NO MORE!

Chicago Daily Tribune

THE WORLD'S GREATEST NEWSPAPER

FINAL EDITION

VOLUME LXXXIX.—NO. 106 C [REG. U. S. PAT. OFFICE: COPYRIGHT 1930 BY THE CHICAGO TRIBUNE.] SATURDAY, MAY 3, 1930.—32 PAGES THIS PAPER CONSISTS OF TWO SECTIONS—SECTION ONE ** PRICE TWO CENTS IN CHICAGO AND SUBURBS ELSEWHERE THREE CENTS

PLAY FIRST NIGHT BASEBALL

10 NEW TREATY CRUISERS TO BE FIGHTING FURIES

U. S. Makes Drastic Changes in Design.

[Chicago Tribune Press Service.]

Washington, D. C., May 2.—[Special.]—The final 10 of the 18 cruisers of 8 inch gun strength allowed the United States by the London naval agreement will be far superior in armor protection and all around fighting ability to any American ships of this type, built or building, it was disclosed in administration circles today.

Construction of the first five of these vessels has been held up for several weeks, it was said, while the navy technical staffs prepared the new designs, which mark a radical departure from the plans on which construction of the first two American 10,000 ton 8 inch gun cruisers was based. Work on these ships is listed to go forward in less than a month.

Armor Increased.

Instead of being lightly protected from shell fire the new vessels are to be supplied with armor plate thick enough to protect the vital parts of the ship from 6 inch gun projectiles at normal fighting ranges. Over vital parts the armor will be from 4 to 5 inches thick, compared to 2½ inches on the two American 8 inch gun cruisers that have been completed.

The vulnerability of the Washington treaty cruisers built by the United States and other major naval powers, with the possible exception of Japan, was responsible for the decision of the navy department to depart from the first 8 inch gun cruiser plans and build vessels able to "stay in and take it."

It is considered highly possible by naval officers that this action may have a profound effect on the cruiser plans of other powers.

Old Type Described.

The first treaty cruisers were designed chiefly for speed and firing power. Protection was sacrificed to gain great gunnery strength and a long radius of action. At short ranges the armor of the Washington treaty cruisers could be punctured by the projectiles from the 6 inch gun. All the major naval powers desired better protected ships, but not being able to build all three factors into ships limited to 10,000 tons, they chose speed and armament.

Weight savings effected by the new design, with the development of lighter propelling machinery, the use of aluminum furniture and paint, and a more extensive substitution of welding for riveting, have made it possible for the United States navy to give its ships added protection without loss of speed or armament.

400 Tons Thus Saved.

Congressmen interested in naval matters estimated today that a total of 400 tons had been thus saved. This will go into added armor protection. A saving of fifteen tons was effected by the use of aluminum paint alone. Lessons in welding learned from study of the plans for Germany's 10,000 ton Ersatz Preussen have been applied to the plans for the new American cruisers.

The first two cruisers built by the United States were the Pensacola and the Salt Lake City.

These vessels, now completed, carry ten 8-inch guns, four 5-inch anti-aircraft guns, have a speed of 32.5 knots, and are armored rather lightly. The design of the next six cruisers, the last three now 75 per cent complete, was changed to increase the speed to over thirty-three knots and to increase the armor protection. One gun was abandoned and the ships are armed with nine 8-inch guns, six forward in two turrets, and three aft in one turret.

Ten to Be Latest Type.

Each of the ten last cruisers to be built will have nine 8-inch guns, eight instead of four 5-inch anti-aircraft and anti-destroyer guns, thirty-three knots plus speed, and close to five inches of armor over vital spots. Virtually the whole deck will have an armor skin of approximately four inches.

The 8 inch guns have a range of 35,000 yards, compared with 24,000 yards for the 6 inch gun. The projectile of the 8 inch gun weighs 260 pounds, compared to the 105 pounds of the 6 inch projectile. The ships also will be shorter, and according to Chairman Frederick Hale [Rep., Me]. of the senate naval affairs committee, the new design will still further widen the gap between the offensive power of the 8 inch and 6 inch gun cruiser.

JAPAN TO LAUNCH CRUISER

YOKOSUKA, Japan.—(AP)—In the presence of the Empress Nagako, presiding for the first time at such a ceremony, the 10,000 ton cruiser Takao

(Continued on page 6, column 5.)

NEWS SUMMARY of The Tribune

[And Historical Scrap Book.]
Saturday, May 3, 1930.

LOCAL.

United States seeks to confiscate two farms where stills were found; invokes 66 year old law. Page 1.

Thrush flies into court of La Salle street building and brokers' staffs try vainly to get him out. Page 1.

Attorney tells aldermen the indeterminate car permit is a perpetual franchise worth a vast sum. Page 4.

Council committee to meet on Tuesday to consider findings on fire hazards at Bridewell. Page 4.

Predict that governor's revenue amendment plan will be considered first in special session of assembly. Page 6.

First 1928 tax bills mailed; bank pays $218,877 personalty tax. Page 6.

Relief parties hurry to ravaged areas after 23 persons are killed in central states storms. Page 7.

Alta Warshawsky Shorr, suing for divorce, tells judge her husband spanked her. Page 7.

Jules K. Masse, granted immunity, tells grand jury of alleged solicitation of $10,000 for building permit. Page 8.

Property owners in Rogers Park spend thousands on seaways to guard against high lake. Page 9.

Frank McErlane and girl friend arrested for hotel spree. Page 9.

County's auto death toll for 1930 shows 23 per cent increase, coroner finds. Page 13.

Death notices, obituaries. Page 22.

WASHINGTON.

Letter recounting hard drinking of two high United States officials suppressed at senate hearing. Page 1.

United States adds more battle strength to new 8 inch gun treaty cruisers. Page 1.

Wilkins plans dash through north pole by submarine. Page 5.

Senator Norris assails Judge Parker in long speech. Page 8.

Hoover sends in budget for $10,600,000 to begin construction of Boulder dam. Page 8.

House puts lumber back on free list and votes for low sugar duty; new coalition reigns. Page 11.

Legge announces that Chamber of Commerce's opposition will not affect farm board's policies. Page 22.

FOREIGN.

French girl flyer sets new endurance mark for women by flying for nearly 36 hours. Page 2.

Distinguished Roman opera crowd sees Argentine diplomat and Italian marquis in fist fight. Page 3.

India fears new "iron hand" policy of Britain may force crisis. Page 3.

France is warned by ambassador trouble is brewing between Poland and Russia. Page 11.

DOMESTIC.

Army pilot crashes to his death on farm where he was born. Page 2.

Lindbergh back in Florida after inaugurating seven day mail service between Americans. Page 2.

Two seek congress seats from Indiana on wet tickets. Page 2.

Fire marshals blame firebug for 320 deaths in Ohio prison. Page 4.

Whalen finds Red scare, but Russians call his documents forgeries. Page 6.

SPORTS.

Bedtime baseball introduced in Western league as Des Moines beats Wichita under spotlights. Page 1.

Cubs beat Phillies, 11 to 8, in first game of eastern invasion. Page 19.

White Sox whip Yankees, 10 to 1; Clancy hits two homers, triple and single. Page 19.

Lord Derby arrives for Kentucky turf classic and starts controversy over his own name. Page 19.

Petty succeeds in rescue rôle as Pirates beat Braves, 3 to 2. Page 20.

Cleveland beats Boston, 8 to 3, for fourth straight victory. Page 21.

EDITORIALS.

Great Britain All Set for India; The Gooding Bill Resurrected; The Reviewer as Judge; Time and Some Trains Fly. Page 12.

BOOKS.

Hugh Walpole shows literary evolution in latest book, Fanny Butcher says. Page 10.

Gossip of authors in New York by Alta Mae Coleman. Page 10.

Among the weeks' new books. Page 10

FINANCE, COMMERCE.

Chicago stock prices break under bear attack. Page 23.

Stock decline is worst since last fall's collapse. Page 23.

Boost Illinois coal for wider use in Chicago district. Page 23.

Chrysler corporation earnings decline. Page 23.

Wheat trading quiet; price close unevenly. Page 26.

Want Ad index. Page 26.

Average net paid circulation of THE CHICAGO TRIBUNE March, 1930:

Daily - - - - 835,335

Sunday - - 1,191,244

BROWN THRUSH TAKES A FLYER IN LA SALLE ST.

And Busy Brokers Forget Tickers.

Six million shares of stock were sold in the exchanges yesterday. In spite of this resonant item; in spite of leagues of nations and the growing crime list; in spite of enormous enterprises and the surge of industry in La Salle street your attention this morning, neighbors, is invited to the following lines of William Morris:

"O thrush, your song is passing sweet,
But never a song that you have sung
Is half so sweet as thrushes sang
When my dear love and I were young."

Because, neighbors, a brown thrush wants to go home. If you will pursue this item far enough you will discover why it wants to go home. Now, beginning at Wacker drive, walk south in La Salle street. You will notice that on both sides of the street buildings rise to amazing heights. These heights have from time immemorial, almost, been regarded as the sides of a canyon and have been so described. But it has remained for Mister Brown Thrush to find out to his sorrow just what a canyon it is.

Down Through City's Canyon.

By the time you have walked nearly to the new Board of Trade building, gazing upwards always, you will have a crick in your neck. But you will have arrived at the State Bank building which is at 120 South La Salle street. Standing among its fellows it measures some 23 stories up. And when you get inside it you will find that it is constructed in the form of a hollow square; a hollow square 23 stories high; offices on all sides and above you as far as the eye can reach; reserving always the fact that at the top there is a patch of sky. This is Chicago sky; mostly dusty, smoky and unattractive; but yesterday clear and blue.

A Visitor from Open Spaces.

Now a brown thrush some four days ago wandered into this vertical tunnel and still is there. Which offers some sort of an explanation of why some thousands of brokers and bankers and lawyers and clerks and bookkeepers and stenographers and janitors and scrubladies and office boys and messengers and policemen and firemen and citizens have dropped all interest in 6,000,000 shares of stock sold and the tariff and the crime situation and whether a mashie is better than a niblick on a short hole; have forgotten about tonnage of the mercantile marine and whether pajamas are better than the old fashioned night shirt and where does the wind come from and who set the first clock; neighbors, all the industry and human urge that makes a day in La Salle street has stopped as cold as if Gabriel had let go a wind of his mellow horn.

Thrush Hunts Way Out.

A brown thrush has been for four days frantically trying to find its way out of that perpendicular hollow square that we have been so clumsily trying to tell you about. And the whole population of this modern office building, suddenly fused into some sort of a spiritual community, is trying to do something about it.

A brown thrush belongs in the open country. It loves to bustle among the hedges with its fellows. It loves to be up early of a summer morning, whistle a chirp or two, snap up a nice tasty bug, and enter the day's affairs with gusto. But this brown thrush in the program of accidents which makes a lifetime forged into the city and somehow turned its rudder the wrong way. Before anything could be done about it, Mister Brown Thrush found himself in a place that seemed to have no top or bottom.

Office Folk Feed Wanderer.

He was discovered after the first day He dropped on the window ledge of a broker's office and found a crumb. A stenographer saw him and gave him a few more crumbs. The next day the news of his presence was all over the building. And every window still held its offering of food, ranging from peanuts to all day suckers. Yet it wasn't food the thrush wanted. His chief desire was to get out.

But apparently the type of aviation to which Mr. Thrush has been addicted requires wide range. He could manage two or three stories on his way up and that was all. He would bang into the resisting brick wall and stop until he could manage a side spin into the nearest window ledge.

After two days the population of the building got down to business in

(Continued on page 3, column 2.)

THEY TAKE OUR MONEY BUT THEY WON'T GIVE US OUR NUMBER

ALD. SCHLAGEL FORGETS PAIN, GETS HIS MAN

Edward Schlagel, 611 Webford avenue, Des Plaines, alderman of the Third ward in that suburb, has long suffered a leg ailment which at times has required the use of crutches. But yesterday he ran up and down stairs, hurdled fences and did other fancy footwork to capture a Negro wanted by the police as a thief.

Schlagel was in the vicinity of 38th street and Indiana avenue yesterday afternoon when he was stopped by a Negro who asked him to enter a house to give assistance to a sick man. In the hallway the Negro took $2 and a diamond ring, valued at $250, from Schlagel. Then Schlagel produced his Des Plaines alderman's star, at sight of which the Negro started up the stairs, with Schlagel in pursuit.

Up two flights they went, and down two flights in the rear. Over a fence the Negro jumped, and although struck on the head by a piece of wood, thrown by the fugitive, over the fence jumped Schlagel. Another fence, and another hurdle. Down the alley they raced with Schlagel gaining, and plunged into the arms of Policemen Wellington Britton and James Hawley at 39th street and Prairie avenue. The policemen recognized the Negro as James McNirl, 3620 Michigan avenue, who has been sought in the past but never caught with the evidence.

Darkness Forces Down Boy Cross-Country Flyer

Colton, Cal., May 2.—(AP)—Forced down by darkness here tonight, Frank Goldsborough, 19 year old transcontinental flyer, had to spend the night seventy miles short of Los Angeles, where his adventurous trip will end.

THE WEATHER

SATURDAY, MAY 3, 1930.

DAYLIGHT SAVING TIME.

Sunrise, 5:43; sunset, 7:51. Moon sets at 1:37 a. m. Sunday. Uranus is a morning star. Venus, Mercury, and Jupiter are evening stars.

Chicago and vicinity—Fair Saturday; Sunday increasing cloudiness and warmer, showers by afternoon or night; gentle shifting winds Saturday, becoming southerly and increasing by Sunday.

Illinois—Fair, slightly warmer in west portion Saturday; Sunday partly cloudy, probably showers, warmer in east portion.

TRIBUNE BAROMETER.

TEMPERATURES IN CHICAGO

MAXIMUM, 4 P. M. 69
MINIMUM, 3 A. M. 58

3 a. m....58	Noon 65	8 p. m....67
4 a. m....61	1 p. m....67	9 p. m....66
5 a. m....62	2 p. m....68	10 p. m....65
6 a. m....61	3 p. m....68	Unofficial—
7 a. m....60	4 p. m....69	11 p. m....65
8 a. m....60	5 p. m....69	Midnight ..64
9 a. m....61	6 p. m....69	1 a. m....64
10 a. m....61	7 p. m....68	2 a. m....63
11 a. m....63		

For 24 hours ended at 8 p. m., May 2:
Mean temperature, 64 degrees; normal, 53; excess since Jan. 1, 315.
Precipitation, .45 of an inch; deficiency since Jan. 1, .26.
Barometer, 8 a. m., 29.75; 8 p. m., 29.93.

[Official weather table on page 22.]

U. S. Plans to Seize Farms Housing Stills

Prohibition Administrator E. C. Yellowley yesterday invoked a 66 year old revenue act in an effort to confiscate the homes and large farms of two downstate families. This action followed the raiding of an alcohol still on each of the farms.

One of the farms is a 520 acre tract near Spring Valley, Putnam county, owned by Joseph Engelhaupt, and the other consists of 208 acres near Ladd, in Bureau county, owned by Elmer Flaherty. Dry agents Wednesday night wrecked a still which they valued at $50,000 on the Engelhaupt farm, and one valued at $20,000 on the Flaherty place.

Action Without Precedent.

Legal action to confiscate the farms and all property on them was suggested by Yellowley to Walter M. Provine, United States attorney at Peoria, who immediately drew up the actions to be filed in the federal District court. Yellowley announced that this action, unprecedented in this federal circuit, was undertaken because of his belief that both Engelhaupt and Flaherty knowingly and willfully permitted the operation of the stills on their farms.

Both Engelhaupt and Flaherty will be prosecuted on charges of misprision of felony, an offense known as countenancing law violations without reporting them to authorities.

The old revenue act under which Yellowley seeks to confiscate the farms was explained by Walter Wiles, expert on prohibition and revenue law libel matters in the United States attorney's office here.

Explains Details of Laws.

"This statute, which is directed against the operation of unlicensed distilleries, is exceptionally broad," Mr. Wiles said. "Four classes of seizures may be made for such violations: First, all property used in connection with the operation of the still; second, all property found in the building, yard or inclosure where the still is found; third, all rights, titles or interests of the distiller in the building, lot or plot of ground where the still is located, and fourth, all rights, titles or interests in such property of any person who knowingly permits the operation of an unregistered still."

Mr. Wiles expressed the opinion, however, that confiscation of large farms would be a difficult proceeding. The court must rule whether a 520 acre farm can be construed as one lot or plot of ground, he said. The Supreme court has upheld the confiscation of property on lots where illicit distilleries were found, he said.

Mr. Wiles confirmed Mr. Yellowley's statement that libel actions had never before been started against farms in this federal circuit, although buildings, lots and automobiles have been confiscated.

Dry Agents in Battle.

C. Edson Smith, deputy dry enforcer, yesterday reported a gun battle between two of his agents and two supposed bootleggers in which twenty-four shots were fired. Mr. Smith said he did not believe either of the bootleggers, who escaped, was hurt.

The shooting occurred after a raid on a still in an old house near Dolton. Smith held two prisoners, William Bardinella and Mike Pedris, while Agents William Connors and Roy Timlock scouted around. An automobile drove up and the raiders announced the place had been seized.

The two men in the car opened fire, according to Smith, and the agents, first barricading themselves behind trees, did likewise. The drys shot at the automobile until it was out of sight.

Eleven permanent injunctions for dry law violations were issued yesterday by Federal Judge Wilkinson, closing a drug store, a confectionery shop, a lunch stand-poolroom, a restaurant, and several saloons.

The orders were obtained by Assistant United States Attorney La Verne Norris.

STOCKS DROP 2 TO 10 POINTS AS 6,000,000 SHARES CHANGE HANDS

New York, May 2.—[Special.]—Stock prices dropped from 2 to 10 points today in the worst decline since the crash last October and the first 6,000,000 share day of the year. The selling reached enormous proportions in the last hour, when more than 2,000,000 shares changed hands. Some of the more volatile issues were off from 10 to 18 points.

Prices were still dropping at the end of the day, although a few issues held firm at the close. Selling was in large blocks, with sales of 5,000 shares and 10,000 shares on the decline.

The break in the market followed the reduction of the New York Federal Reserve bank's rediscount rate from 3½ per cent to 3 per cent last night, which was regarded as favorable news, and the statement by President Hoover that the worst of the business depression is over. Wall street had expected the cut in the bank rate and professional profit-taking was one of the factors in the liquidation of stocks.

SUITOR SHOOTS GIRL, ENDS LIFE IN ROSE ARBOR

For eight months Albert Brown, 27 years old, salesman, had wooed Sally Kuta, 17 years old, despite the opposition of her parents.

Last night she met him by stealth a block from her parents' home, 2619 Evergreen avenue, and they strolled into Humboldt park. As they sauntered arm in arm under the rose arbor to a bench, the salesman renewed his plea. She told him she was too young and pointed out as she had done before, that her father would never consent to their marriage.

Other young couples were startled by the four shots the salesman fired as she concluded her answer. They found the girl on the bench with a bullet near her heart. Her suitor lay on the gravel walk with three bullets in his body, dead.

North avenue police took the girl in a dying condition to the Lutheran Memorial hospital.

Fifty Million Candle Power Lights Field

BY IRVING VAUGHAN.
[Chicago Tribune Press Service.]

Des Moines, Ia., May 2.—[Special.]—Some fifty million candle power of light introduced night baseball for the first time into the organized ranks of the national pastime. In the course of the introduction tonight the local Western leaguers administered a 13-6 bedtime spanking to Wichita before 10,000 patrons who came to view a novelty.

As a spectacle the introduction was impressive. There is reason to believe that for the minor leagues, which are on a starvation diet, it may be a life saver, provided there are slight improvements. And for the majors it is a matter to be considered if evil days hit the big circuits or the magnates subordinate the competitive idea to gate receipts. At present they have one eye on each.

Foul Lost in Lights.

Despite the elaborate lighting system on which a General Electric engineer labored for seven years there were noticeable defects right at the start.

In the first inning the Wichita third baseman looked up for a pop foul. The ball went into the lights shining down from a tower in that region and the fielder lost it completely.

There also were regions of darkness at the extremities of the foul lines. This, in the opinion of the engineers, may be corrected by additional light, properly focused. There also was a stratum of darkness between the light thrown by lamps directed toward the ground and those shooting their rays into the regions inhabited by high fly balls.

This meant trouble for an outfielder trying to locate a low fly sailing at about the level of the grandstand roof.

Six Towers Light Field.

The light beamed down and across the arena from six steel towers, each 90 feet in height. Two of these skeleton like structures, topped by the lamps arranged in horizontal rows, poured out their rays from behind the grandstand. Each of these towers held fourteen 1,000 watt bulbs. Behind both third and first bases were towers of 36 bulbs each. The two other towers stood back of the left and right field fences, each showing 24 beacons at respective distances of 350 and 400 feet from the plate.

The battery of 146 bulbs, each designed for a capacity of 100 watts, was given an extra voltage of 10 per cent. This meant about 190,000 watts. At local rates three hour burning would run up Owner Lee Keyser's light bill approximately $25. The entire layout cost approximately $20,000.

From a spectator's viewpoint the night club idea might be satisfactory.

Four towers of light behind the ball made it easy to follow from the stand. But there is an element of batter's eyesight involved. Put a good hitter to work a few times under artificial light and he might be ruined for hitting in daylight. That's the first thing a major star would think about if a night appearance was suggested.

DRY RAID KILLER FREED; W. C. T. U. GIVES HIM POSIES

Platteville, Wis., May 2.—(AP)—A coroner's jury tonight released Sheriff Joe Greer of Grant county from all responsibility for the death of Edward Foht, killed as officers made prohibition raids on Bishop's island in the Mississippi river April 24.

The jury found that Foht was struck by a bullet that glanced from a tree. Witnesses testified that Greer fired twice in the air to warn Foht to halt.

After the verdict of accidental death was returned the local chapter of the W. C. T. U. sent Sheriff Greer a bouquet of flowers and a congratulatory message, county officials said.

HIDE NAMES OF 2 DRINKING DRYS AT SENATE QUIZ

Suppress Telltale Stayton Letter.

[Chicago Tribune Press Service.]

Washington, D. C., May 2.—[Special.]—Statements describing two high government officials, both politically dry, as "heavy drinkers" were found in the files of the Association Against the Prohibition Amendment and suppressed today by the senate lobby committee.

Suppression of a letter written on June 20, 1928, by W. H. Stayton, chairman of the association, to the late Maj. Gen. George Barnett, left unsolved the mystery of whether a quantity of fine liquors, for which bills were found in Stayton's file, enlivened a political meeting addressed by former Senator J. W. Wadsworth Jr., or a dinner of Republican leaders shortly after the Kansas City convention to celebrate the nomination of Hoover.

Wadsworth, it appeared from his correspondence with Stayton, addressed a meeting in the University club of Baltimore on April 13, 1928, and discussed "the senate and the people" as well as "the exclusion of Smith of Illinois."

Liquor Bills Attached.

Attached to the exchange of letters arranging for the meeting were memorandums indicating the purchase of twelve bottles of champagne, four bottles of gin, two bottles of vermouth, five bottles of Scotch and three of assorted liqueurs, to a total value of $76.50.

Describing the memorandum as "a very interesting thing," Senator T. H. Caraway [Dem., Ark.], chairman of the committee, read the items into the record.

"Now, Mr. Stayton," asked Senator J. J. Blaine [Rep., Wis.], referring to Stayton's letter to Barnett, "have you any knowledge or information as to whether or not the liquor that is listed on the loose slips here which the chairman read, was served at a dinner evidently in celebration of a candidate for the presidency of the United States, just prior to June 20, 1928?"

"I have no personal knowledge, sir," answered Stayton. "I was not present at such a dinner."

"Was there such a dinner held?" asked Blaine.

"Yes," answered Stayton, "there was such a dinner held."

That Telltale Letter.

While neither Blaine nor any other member of the committee would disclose the contents of the Stayton-Barnett letter, it was learned that the chairman of a nationally known insurance company was quoted in it as having said he attended a dinner at which one high government official "drank heavily," while, of another official the letter asserted "every one knows how —— laps it up freely," and added "if you don't believe it, ask —— (a former United States senator)."

The letter, it was explained later by Caraway, was pigeonholed with the list of "wet drinking, dry voting" house members found in the files of H. H. Curran, president of the association, last week and similarly suppressed, because "of the prominence of those involved," as well as because, like the roll of congressional scofflaws, it is only remotely, if at all, connected with an investigation of lobbies.

Hoover "So Dry He Squeaks."

Digging further into Stayton's confidential correspondence, Senator Arthur Robinson [Rep., Ind.] found frequent references to and criticisms of President Hoover by the wet leader and in one case, by Representative H. H. Peavey [Rep., Wis.]. The latter, a La Follette radical, assailed the association for indorsing regular Republican candidates in Wisconsin, although some of the candidates were known as "bone drys."

"Hoover is so dry he squeaks," wrote Peavey complaining that the association was acting as a catspaw for "big business and the Republican party."

In another letter, written to Herbert L. Clarke of Philadelphia on March 19, 1929, Stayton questioned the sincerity of President Hoover as a dry and suggested that the President "believes he can get votes from the wets without espousing their cause, and that therefore, as a matter of vote getting he had better take the dry side."

Not Open to Argument.

"If he were sincerely a dry," continued the letter, "one might hope to convince him by argument or statement of facts but, as I know he is not at heart a dry, I fear I must approach the conclusion that he is a dry because of the prospective profit

PUBLIC LEDGER

VOL. CXC.—NO. 15 | Entered as second-class matter at the postoffice in Philadelphia under the Act of March 3, 1879. | PHILADELPHIA, THURSDAY MORNING, OCTOBER 9, 1930 | The Weather: Showers today. Details on Page Two. | PRICE TWO CENTS

ATHLETICS GAIN FIFTH WORLD TITLE, DEFEATING ST. LOUIS IN SIXTH GAME OF SERIES, 7-1, BEFORE 35,000 FANS

BRITTEN SPURNS ARMS DEBATE WITH PROF. HULL

Brands Swarthmore College as 'Hotbed of British Propaganda'

TEACHER IS TERMED 'RELIGIOUS PACIFIST'

Congressman Asserts Educator Couldn't Be Changed and Discussion Is Useless

Rhodes Fund Is Denied By Swarthmore Head

"Neither Swarthmore College nor any other college or university in the entire United States has ever received one cent of endowment from Cecil Rhodes or from the Rhodes trust," Frank Aydelotte, president of Swarthmore College, said last night.

"From hearing Mr. Britten's statement over the telephone, the remainder of it, it appears to me, is about as inaccurate as his reference to Mr. Rhodes.

"I think he made a wise decision not to debate with Professor Hull."

Public Ledger Bureau
Washington, Oct. 8.

Representative Britten, Illinois, today tartly declined an invitation of the Pennsylvania Committee for Total Disarmament, Philadelphia, to degate with Prof. William I. Hull, Swarthmore College, the question of immediate total disarmament for the United States.

Britten viciously attacked Prof. Hull as a "religious pacifist." He assailed Swarthmore College as "a hotbed of British propaganda and American pacifism." Long regarded as the foremost of big-navy men in Congress, Britten, who succeeded to the chairmanship of the House Naval Affairs Committee upon the death of Representative Butler, of Pennsylvania, said it would be a waste of time to debate with Prof. Hull.

Answering the invitation Mr. Britten said:

"Besides being an aggressive internationalist whose name has been on the payrolls of many so-called peace societies, Prof. Hull is a religious

Continued on Page Eight, Column Three

COURT AIDS DARROW

Ousts Prosecutor Who Bars Way to Probation for Embezzler

Chicago, Oct. 8.—(AP)—Over the objections of complainant and prosecutor, Clarence Darrow obtained probation today for a young bank teller, whose defense he undertook by request of Judge Lyle last week.

Nicholas Pace was charged with embezzlement of $1024 from his former employers. Darrow asked that the complaint be changed to petty larceny so probation could be granted at once. Prosecutor Mast refused to sign the new complaint, whereupon Judge Lyle ordered his bailiff to function in the prosecutor's place.

The youth was ordered to restore the money at $50 a month.

NEW MINISTRY FORMED

Mironescu to Present Cabinet to Rumanian King Today

Bucharest, Oct. 8.—(AP)—G. G. Mironescu, charged with forming a ministry to succeed that of Juliu Maniu, expects to submit his Cabinet list to King Carol tomorrow.

The new Government, it is said, will contain only members of the Zaranist Peasant Party. Maniu resigned Monday, after a series of disagreements with the King.

IN TODAY'S PUBLIC LEDGER

Girl, 24, Is Louisiana's New Secretary of State

MISS ALICE LE GROSJEAN

Baton Rouge, La., Oct. 8.—(AP)—Governor Long today appointed Miss Alice Le Grosjean, his private secretary, as Secretary of State, succeeding James J. Bailey, who died early this morning.

Miss Le Grosjean, who is 24 years old, becomes the first woman State official in Louisiana and is believed to be the youngest Secretary of State in the country.

TRAINER FOLLOWS PARTY LEADERS IN BOLTING PINHCOT

Two in Mackey Cabinet Due to Join Liberal Bandwagon. Vare Preparing Blast

Mayor Pays 1st Visit To Annex—to Register

Mayor Mackey entered City Hall Annex for the first time yesterday. He visited the office of the Registration Commissioners to register for the November election.

The Mayor failed to register on the first two regular registration days because he was waiting for the return of Mrs. Mackey, who was in Atlantic City, so they could register together. Last Saturday, the final registration day, Mr. Mackey was on his way to St. Louis to attend the World Series baseball game, and Mrs. Mackey registered alone.

By BERNARD HAGGARTY

The exodus of Philadelphia leaders from the camp of Gifford Pinchot, Republican nominee for Governor, continued yesterday when Councilman Henry J. Trainer, organization leader of the Third Ward, declared for the election of John M. Hemphill, Democratic-Liberal candidate.

Following the lead of Councilman Hall and State Senator Salus, members of the organization "War Board," Mr. Trainer said the anti-prohibition sentiment of his ward demanded that he support Mr. Hemphill.

It was predicted by those of the inner circle of the organization yesterday that by the end of next week or shortly thereafter from forty-two to forty-six of the ward leaders will have repudiated Mr. Pinchot's candidacy.

Resignation of any large number of leaders from the Republican City Committee is not looked for. Indeed, it is probable that Mr. Hall will be the only ward chief to quit the City Committee. John J. McKinley, Jr.,

Continued on Page Eight, Column One

REBELS TAKE BRAZIL CITY IN 48-HOUR FIGHT

Pernambuco Falls With 150 Dead and Wounded as Governor Flees

PART OF ARMY JOINS WITH LIBERAL FORCE

Provisional Regime Set Up Under Red Flag; Government Moves to Crush Rebellion

$2,000,000 Damage Done U.S. Property in Brazil

Rio de Janeiro, Oct. 8.—(AP)—A board consisting of two Government officials and two company engineers estimated that damage amounting to more than $2,000,000 was done by rioters to the property of a subsidiary of the Electric Bond and Share Company in Bahia during an alleged Communist demonstration.

Pernambuco, Brazil, Oct. 8.—(AP)—The important northern city of Pernambuco tonight was under the control of revolutionary forces which reported that the insurgent movement against the central Government had been victorious in all States north of Pernambuco.

The capture of this city, one of the largest in Brazil, followed a forty-eight-hour struggle which broke out early Saturday between revolutionary forces and part of the garrison and State military police who remained loyal to the Federal Government. Casualties in the fighting were reported at 150.

The revolution, in combination with other States in Brazil, broke out in Pernambuco at 1 A. M. Saturday. On the revolutionary side were the students, civilians and part of the army garrison, while on the Federal side were the State military police and the remainder of the army.

The revolutionists immediately took control of the arsenal and the sur-

Continued on Page Eight, Column Four

STREET SET ON FIRE

Homes Scorched as Truck's Light Ignites Gasoline Cargo

Traffic was tide up and homes on Ridge avenue near Queen lane were scorched last night when gasoline from a leaking drum caught fire on a truck and caused two other drums to explode.

The truck was driven by Roland Bonsall, of Media, who jumped to safety after stopping his vehicle when a pedestrian informed him of the blaze. The gasoline caught fire from the rear light on the truck and spread a ribbon of flames for a block along Ridge avenue. Heat from the three blazing drums scorched the houses and homeward-bound workers on trolley route 61 were delayed for nearly an hour. Firemen saved the truck.

PARACHUTES SAVE TWO

Mexico City, Oct. 8.—(AP)—Special advices from Tampico tonight stated that A. L. Connell, an American pilot, and Captain Chocoy, a Mexican, saved their lives by jumping with parachutes when their plane was wrecked near Vera Cruz. A passenger, Guillermo Gonzalez, who did not jump, was seriously injured.

Trans-Atlantic Fliers Here Today For Final Triumph of U. S. Tour

Coste and Bellonte Will Land at Navy Yard—Ceremony at Independence Hall Precedes Official Welcome at Banquet Tonight

Welcome to Philadelphia will be tendered by Mayor Mackey and an official Reception Committee to the famous French fliers, Captain Dieudonne Coste and Maurice Bellonte, when their plane, the Question Mark, conqueror of the Atlantic, alights at 4 o'clock this afternoon at the Philadelphia Navy Yard.

The visit will be the first made to Philadelphia by the French airmen, and is part of the nation-wide good-will trip begun by the fliers shortly after their Atlantic flight.

The fliers will proceed from the Navy Yard to Independence Hall in automobiles, escorted by a squad of motorcycle policemen. At 4:30 the guests will attend a ceremony staged by the Order of the Liberty Bell in the historic hall.

Following this ceremony Coste and Bellonte will be escorted to the Hotel Warwick, where they will stay during their visit in Philadelphia. At 7:30 P. M. they will attend the official reception and dinner given in their honor at the Bellevue-Stratford. Mayor Mackey will preside. Among the speakers will be Rene Weiller, French Consul to Philadelphia, and Dr. Josiah H. Penniman, provost of the University of Pennsylvania. Brief speeches by the fliers themselves are schduled.

They Bring Another Baseball Title to Philadelphia

GEORGE EARNSHAW

Ledger Photo

CONNIE MACK

Fans are still singing the praises of Connie Mack and George Earnshaw for the able manner in which they guided the Athletics to victory in the World Series. The play at the top in yesterday's final game shows Jimmy Foxx sliding into third base

HOOVER LAW GROUP DEBATES DRY ISSUE

Secret Session Takes No Action, but Wickersham Hints It Will "Speak Mind"

PROBING COST OF JUSTICE

By ROBERT B. SMITH
Public Ledger Bureau
Washington, Oct. 8

After many hours of wrangling over prohibition behind closed doors, the President's Law Enforcement Commission recessed late today without taking action, but with a hope that it would be ready to make a report to Congress in December.

George W. Wickersham, chairman of the commission and head also of the commission's Subcommittee on Prohibition Enforcement, in an interview with Washington correspondents following the session, expressed the opinion that if the commission found the Prohibition Law unenforceable it should not hesitate to say so.

Mr. Wickersham's statement caused something of a stir in view of the controversy that has raged in Congress and elsewhere over the commission's authority to go into the merits of prohibition as a national policy. As if fearful that his statement might have too much of a disturbing effect, Mr. Wickersham quickly added that the commission, as a body, had not made any decision on this phase of the problems confronting it and

Continued on Page Four, Column Three

NAVAL CUT TO SAVE $10,000,000 BY '32

Destroyer, Submarine and Personnel Reductions Included in Plan

RECRUITING TO BE CURBED

Washington, Oct. 8.—(AP)—Reductions and changes in the United States fleet which would reduce the navy personnel by 4800 men and save $3,420,000 during the present fiscal year were announced today by Admiral William V. Pratt, chief of naval operations.

The changes, to be made in accordance with the London naval treaty, will become effective immediately.

The changes involve a reduction in the number of destroyers from 109 now in operation to ninety-two, and submarines to a figure under the 52,700 tons allowed by the treaty.

The reduction in personnel will be brought about by curtailing recruiting activities from 400 to 200 a month, beginning November 1. The number of battleships and aircraft carriers will remain the same.

Admiral Halligan, assistant chief of operations, said saving in personnel, maintenance and fuel would total $10,998,949 by the end of the 1932 fiscal year.

N. J. FARM SLAYING CONFESSED BY GIRL AFTER AUTO WRECK

Prisoner, 19, Admits Firing Shots During Party—Flight Ends in Collision

After many hours of questioning by detectives, Mary McClyment, 19, formerly of South Philadelphia, yesterday confessed she fired the shot that killed Edward Nicholson, 33, of Camden, during a brawl at a party on a farm near Blackwood, N. J., Tuesday night.

The girl insisted she had intended only to frighten Nicholson, who was struggling with Joseph Van Dexter, 65, owner of the farm.

"I pulled the gun," she admitted to Camden County authorities, "but I didn't mean to shoot him. It went off. We were all drunk."

Five Held as Witnesses

She acknowledged she had a friendly feeling for Van Dexter and was afraid the younger man might injure him.

Two other girls, two men and a boy are held as witnesses. They are Catharine Carroll and Lenore Ropfel, both 17, who shared an apartment with the McClyment girl on Stevens street, Camden; Edward Sims, 16, who lives with the accused girl's mother on Williams street near Berkley, Camden; Van Dexter and Clifford Conover, a farmer, who lives near the

Continued on Page Eight, Column Three

Athletics' Pitching Best in Last 10 Years

In limiting the Cards to twelve runs in six World Series games, Mack pitchers set up a record which hasn't been matched in ten years of interleague championship contests.

Only twice in twenty-six previous World Series has the losing team been held to less than twelve runs when six games or more were necessary for a decision.

In 1918 the Chicago White Sox in losing to the Boston Sox scored only ten runs in six games and in 1920 Brooklyn was held to eight runs in seven games by the victorious Cleveland Indians.

MACK HURLS KISSES AS FANS HOWL JOY IN VICTORY PARADE

Mackey Among Multitude Roaring Acclaim at Clinching of Baseball Crown

By LOUIS R. WINTER, JR.

That was a "Yip-yip-eeeee!" game.

A long, loud, glorious howl of victory rose from Shibe Park, reverberated by radio in homes thousands of miles away, and John McGraw, the visiting New York baseball impresario, from his seat beside Gabby Street in the St. Louis dugout, saw the sage and serious Cornelius McGillicuddy throwing kisses to folks in the west stand as Eddie Collins slapped a bunch of backs.

Seven hits; seven runs; a victory; another pennant for Mr. Mack and his scintillating team. Mr. Mack has something on Alexander — not the baseball Alexander — because he can look forward to conquering more World Series contenders.

How that habit has taken hold of the lean leader of the Philadelphia Athletics, champions of 1930 for the entire world! And how the joy of winning a second World Series in two years took hold of the population of Shibe Park and spread like wildfire all over town, until the tall towers at 15th and Chestnut streets emitted snowstorms of paper scraps and a

Continued on Page Four, Column Two

SIX FACE DISBARMENT MOVE

Mississippi Candidate for Governor Among Accused Lawyers

Jackson, Miss., Oct. 8.—(AP)—The Disbarment Committee of the Mississippi Bar Association announced after a meeting here today that it had decided to start disbarment proceedings against Lester C. Franklin, chairman of the State Tax Commission and candidate for Governor, and five other attorneys.

The six are charged with reputed irregularities in the settlement of a $10,000,000 antitrust suit the State sought to bring against Warren Brothers, Boston road material firm.

EX-OFFICIAL PLEADS GUILTY

New York, Oct. 8. — (AP) — John W. Hennessey, former Public Administrator of Richmond County, pleaded guilty today to an indictment charging him with grand larceny in connection with shortages in his official accounts.

Former Congressman Convicted On Rum Charge; Argues Own Case

Obtaining Evidence of Dry-Law Violations, Not Making Liquor, Herrick Insists; Jury Is Out Only Ten Minutes

Baltimore, Oct. 8.—(AP)—Arrested while working as a $15-a-week handy man at a still in Southern Maryland, Manuel Herrick, former member of Congress from Oklahoma, was convicted today by a jury in Federal District Court of manufacture and possession of liquor.

Sentence will be imposed tomorrow, Judge Soper announced. The jury deliberated but ten minutes. Two other men were convicted with Herrick, William F. Airey, who Herrick said employed him, and Pius B. Ennels, a Negro.

Acting as his own attorney, Herrick, who is 53, read from what he described as a record book of his three weeks' career at the still, where he was arrested August 8. He maintained that he was trying to get evidence of prohibition violations, in the hope of being paid, but John P. Moore, a minor Prohibition Department official at Washington, denied that Herrick had been commissioned or promised immunity.

Attired in a neat blue suit, con-

Continued on Page Eight, Column Two

CARDS COLLECT ONLY FIVE HITS OFF EARNSHAW

Dykes, Simmons Crash Homers—A's Register 7 Runs on 7 Blows

MACK'S 'IRON MAN' NEAR MATTY'S MARK

By ED POLLOCK

Around and about the iron arm of big George Earnshaw, Connie Mack and his Athletics wove another world's championship flag for Philadelphia at Shibe Park yesterday, the fifth in history.

Thirty-five thousand spectators wildly acclaimed Earnshaw the greatest of all modern right-hand pitchers as the giant Mack moundsman once again crushed the hopes of the St. Louis Red Birds, while his teammates, regaining their power at the plate, smote seven extra-base hits to win the sixth and deciding game by the chest-swelling score of 7-1 and the most prized diadem of the diamond by four games to two.

Thus did the Athletics bring the fifth world's baseball championship to Philadelphia, enabling their beloved ledaer, the 67-year-old Connie Mack, to shatter all records for managerial success in the annual struggles for supremacy between the two major leagues.

Earnshaw, after pitching seven shutout innings in St. Louis as a vital contribution toward the conquest attained by the White Elephants Monday, came back with only a day of rest and blanked the Cards with three hits through the first eight innings.

When fatigue at last overtook him in the final frame and he could no longer propel the ball with blinding speed past the bats of the doughty

Continued on Page Sixteen, Column One

EX-SENATOR REED CHOSEN TO EULOGIZE POLITICAL FOE

Will Deliver Oration Over E. L. Morse, Veteran Missouri Leader

Excelsior Springs, Mo., Oct. 8—(AP)—E. L. Morse, veteran Republican leader of Missouri, will be buried here Sunday after a funeral oration delivered by ex-Senator James A. Reed. Morse died here today at 66 of heart disease.

Although they belonged to opposing political parties, "Liv" Morse and "Jim" Reed were friends for many years. I twas Morse's wish that Reed deliver the eulogy.

Secretary of Agriculture Hyde, when Governor of Missouri, said Morse was the "jinx" who wrecked the Lowden campaign in 1920." Morse's political star, indeed, passed its zenith with the collapse of Lowden's candidacy.

A poor boy, with little formal schooling, Morse became wealthy in a business career that paralleled the development of this health resort.

THE WEATHER

Showers and not much change in temperature is the forecast for today in Eastern Pennsylvania, New Jersey, Delaware and Maryland.

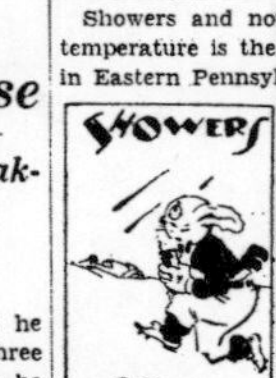

The highest temperature yesterday was 67, at 2 P. M., and the lowest was 55, at 5 A. M. The average of 61 was identical with the normal for the date and six degrees above the average temperature of the same date last year. The sun shone 6.3 hours, or 55 per cent of the day.

The warmest October 8 on record here was 84, in 1687, and the coolest was 40, in 1876.

Sunrise today is at 6:05 and sunset is at 5:31. The moon rises at 6:28 P. M. and sets at 7:53 A. M.

(Details on Page 2.)

34,000 See Cardinals Defeat Athletics, 5-1, in Fifth Game of World's Series

CARDINALS WIN, 5-1, AND NEED ONE MORE

Hallahan Subdues Athletics in Fifth Game to Give St. Louis Three Triumphs to Two.

MARTIN AGAIN THE HERO

Gets Three Hits, One a Homer, and Bats In Four Runs to the Acclaim of 34,000 Fans.

TIES RECORD FOR SERIES

Total of 12 Drives Puts Him Even With Herzog, Rice, Jackson—Clubs Meet in St. Louis Tomorrow.

By JOHN DREBINGER.

Special to The New York Times.

PHILADELPHIA, Oct. 7.—The firm of Wild Bill Hallahan and John (Pepper) Martin, comparative newcomers in the business of hoarding baseball fame, swung gayly into action again today, and by the sheer power of their combinative skill produced another amazing result in the current world's series.

For it was Wild William of the great Southwest and Martin the Magnificent who, by pooling their gifted talents and natural resources just as they had done in that memorable second game in St. Louis last week, once again led the Cardinals to a smashing victory over the Athletics in the pivotal fifth game before 34,000 of probably the most confounded baseball enthusiasts that ever packed their way into an arena.

The score was 5 to 1, and as a result of this startling turn of events the National League standard bearers once more are in front in this mad swirl for a pot of gold. Their margin now stands at three games to two, and as the entire cast in this strange sports drama sweeps back to the West tonight, the Cardinals find themselves in that highly strategic position where they need only one more triumph to crown themselves world's champions when play is resumed in St. Louis on Friday.

Defeat Bewilders Mackmen.

As for the Mackmen, quite bewildered as they happen to be at the moment, their plight is a thoroughly astounding one. The white elephant, emblematic of the power and craft that had carried the Athletics into three successive world's series, had been expected to trample over these red-breasted Cardinals with ridiculous ease.

But tonight as he is being conveyed once more to the west bank of the Mississippi he appears to be a sadly befuddled elephant and he wears a harried look. For he is now confronted with the task of winning two games in a row if ever his mentor, the venerable and sagacious Connie Mack, is to attain a life-long ambition to be the first manager in major league baseball to annex three successive world's series triumphs.

And all this came about today because Wild Bill Hallahan, the stout-hearted left-hander, who last Friday had shut out the Athletics on three hits to give the Cardinals their first victory of the series, once again showed himself capable of pitching a baseball with astonishing skill. And while he was doing this, Martin the magnificent, was hammering the stitches off it.

Hallahan Yields Nine Hits.

Hallahan was not quite as invincible today as he was in that first start, nor could this be reasonably expected, for these Mackmen were aroused and they were desperate. They pummeled Wild William for nine hits and several times had him clinging with his finger tips on the brink of disaster.

But they scored only one run and that lone tally was completely buried beneath an avalanche of brilliant deeds performed by that singular young man named Johnny Martin, who, only a few years ago, left his Oklahoma town to see the world on a dime.

This afternoon a gathering that numbered in paid attendance 32,295 and contributed $152,735 in receipts, looked on in spellbound admiration as Martin, who already had made himself a sensational hero in the first four games, now caused some three hundred baseball experts from all corners of the land to run out of superlatives.

For not since Babe Ruth blasted three home runs over the St. Louis right-field pavilion in the final game in 1928 has any one been able to put on such a one-man show in a world's series as Johnny gave today. And here is what Johnny did:

He made three hits, to give himself a total of twelve for the series to date. One of the blows was a prodigious circuit clout into the upper deck of the left-field pavilion, and he drove in four of the five Cardinal runs.

In addition to this, his third and concluding hit enabled him to tie the record for most hits in world's series competition, for, back in 1912, Buck Herzog of the Giants collected an even dozen blows, and twice later the mark was equaled, once by Joe Jackson of the White Sox in 1919 and again by Sam Rice of the Senators in 1925.

With one game still to play, and possibly another, Martin has an excellent chance to surpass the mark. Though Johnny himself stoutly asserts tonight there will be only one game, he is equally as confident that he will need only one more encounter to place his name alone on the record books for this particular line of endeavor. Certain it is the Mack pitchers haven't stopped him for a single game yet, and they never even came close to impeding his dashing progress around the bases this afternoon.

A Dour Day for Athletics.

For Connie Mack and his gallery of sympathizers the day was indeed a dour one. That gallery had confidently expected Mack, the master strategist, to manoeuvre his way to another victory that in all probability would have assured a final triumph, and it sat dumfounded when it beheld, near the end, the same master strategist floundering as hopelessly as any other baseball manager with a lost cause on his hands.

For, as all the world knows, it is a difficult feat to make good your bid when you have run out of trumps. Only a magician can do that and Connie Mack, so far as is known, has never made any pretense of being versed in the arts of legerdemain. He is, after all, only a baseball manager and so, when he began futilely to shake up his line-up in the closing innings, he was merely following the dictates of all other managers, just as your Uncle Robbie would do it in Flatbush.

He had run out of trumps when he pitched his two great mound aces, Grove and Earnshaw, on the two previous days, after both had hurled the first two games in St. Louis. So he now had no alternative but to play the fourth card of his longest suit, and he called on Waite Hoyt, the erstwhile boy wonder of Brooklyn.

Hoyt, in his day, was probably as great a pitcher in his own right as any of those appearing in the headlines of the current world's series production. Across eight brilliant seasons he was one of the mainstays of the famous staff that won six pennants and three world's championships for the late Miller Huggins and his Yankees.

Hoyt in Gallant Effort.

But though Hoyt, after being eventually cast adrift by the Yankees and later by the Tigers, displayed a promise of returning to his former greatness on being taken in tow the past season by Connie Mack, the Hoyt today was not the Hoyt of other years. He did commendably enough for five innings, in which he craftily held the Cardinals to one run, but in the sixth Johnny Martin proved one too many for him, and when Johnny pounded his homer into the stand with a comrade on base he wrote finis to Hoyt's effort.

Only once during the entire day did fortune promise to smile once more on Connie Mack. That was about two hours before game time, when a drizzling rain began to fall from a cloud-laden sky. Had it continued to rain Mack indeed would have considered himself twice blassed, for then his pitching problem would have disappeared in the knowledge that on the morrow he could come right back once more with the steel-armed Earnshaw.

But the rain soon petered out, and when, inside of another hour, the sun broke through the clouds, it shone not for Connie Mack but a flock of Cardinals, who were strangely chirping something about tormenting a white elephant until he had enough. So there remained no other avenue to provide a strategic retreat and the elephant plunged on to a beating.

There were ominous sounds almost at the very outset when Sparky Adams, leading off the Cardinal list in the first inning, cracked a sharp single to left. Sparky had sprained an ankle some ten days before the series and now was making a second valiant attempt to get into the action. He got no further than first base for he turned on the injured ankle again and Andy High, his diminutive understudy, was called upon to run for him. But Sparky's one hit did enough damage in itself, for it started the Cards on to their first tally.

Watkins hoisted a high fly to Simmons in left, but Frankie Frisch, the Fordham flash, singled brusquely to centre and Andy High's stout little legs carried him around to third.

Now came the dynamic Johnny Martin, whom Gabby Street had advanced to the No. 4 slot in the St. Louis batting order in place of Jim Bottomley, who was dropped back to No. 6, and the crowd stirred uneasily. But Johnny wasn't quite ready yet for his biggest acts of the day and so merely shot a long liner to Simmons, which gave High ample time to score after the catch.

Martin Beats Out a Bunt.

To this one-run margin Hallahan now clung tenaciously, while Hoyt as desperately strove to prevent the advantage from becoming any greater. There was trouble for Hoyt in the fourth when Martin—always it was Martin—dropped a bunt toward first base and sprinted furiously for a hit. Hafey struck out, but Bottomley, who also was stroking the ball vigorously, whistled a single into right, and in less time than it takes to write about the matter, Martin was on third.

Fortune, however, was not yet ready to forsake Hoyt. He pitched a slow ball to Wilson who lined it straight into Bishop's hands and Bottomley, who already had started at top speed for second base, was easily doubled off first to retire the side. The crowd breathed again.

But in the sixth the luck of the wheel turned and it left Hoyt, the hero of other days, with nothing but the bitter pangs of seeing a new and more luminous star bludgeon his way to the top, Frankie Frisch, who sort of keeps an even keel in maintaining a uniform standard of accomplishments in the many series in which he has performed, whipped a two-bagger down the third base line, and again came Johnny Martin and his bat.

Hoyt now called upon all his cunning as he faced this total stranger to world's series warfare, and who was now threatening to tear things apart all by himself. Waite's first pitch went slightly outside, but Johnny declined to be tempted and let it go for a ball.

Hoyt next tried a curve, a trifle low and threatening to cut the inside corner of the plate. Martin brought his bat around with tremendous force and the ball shot on a line for the upper tier of the left field pavilion. What followed is almost unbelievable, for the crowd, seemingly forgetting in whose cause Martin had hit that ball, gave him a thunderous ovation, for there is no denying that Johnny has captivated the fancy of all who have seen him play in this series.

Walberg Takes Hoyt's Place.

The game, of course, collapsed ight there, for though Hoyt managed to survive the inning without further trouble and even went to bat for himself in the latter half of the round, he was replaced by Rube Walberg in the seventh and Ed Rommel pitched the ninth.

In despair, Mack made further changes in that once impregnable line-up which had spread-eagled the field for three successive seasons in the American League. He sent Eric McNair to second base in place of Bishop, and Mule Haas was replaced by Jimmy Moore, Simmons going to centre field and Moore to left.

But it all availed nothing, for Wild Bill Hallahan was not to be denied. There was only one who was giving him any serious cause for worry. That was Al Simmons, who helped himself to three hits, one a double. But only one of these amounted to anything. That was a single that Simmons touched off in the seventh after one had been retired.

Jimmy Foxx followed with a terrific smash that caromed off Hallahan's leg for another single and Simmons dashed around to third. Then Miller topped a grounder to High, who, ignoring Simmons in his spurt for home, threw to second to force Foxx for the second out. The move proved clever enough, for though Hallahan had lost his shutout, the rally was badly broken with two out and only a runner on first. Even when Dykes followed with a single that High collared over third it yielded no further profit to the Mack cause for Williams ended the inning by popping out to Frisch.

Martin Delivers a Single.

From then on the encounter became little more than a rout, with Johnny Martin putting on his concluding number in the eighth. Watkins had drawn a pass from the left-handed Walberg and stolen second and, after Frisch had been retired on a fly, the indomitable Martin, possibly even unaware that the pitcher now opposing him was throwing left-handed instead of right-handed, plastered a single to centre field. Watkins, of course, scored, making the fourth tally that Martin's bat had propelled across the plate.

Then, just by way of demonstrating that Johnny Martin does not constitute the entire Cardinal club, even if so far he has been about 95 per cent of it, the other members of the St. Louis cast conspired to wrench one more run away from the faltering Mackmen, making this one in the ninth off Rommel.

Chick Hafey started this parting drive with a single, and after he had been forced by Bottomley, Wilson and Gelbert came along with a pair of robust one-base thumps that sent Sunny Jim over the plate.

And so tonight the world's series caravan of 1931 is wending its way westward with the same score in games prevailing as at this time a year ago. But where last Fall the Athletics rejoiced in being in possession of three victories and sat poised for the final thrust, the tables now are completely turned.

For the situation now finds the National League standard-bearers on top and if the final victory is not completely in sight a stout-hearted veteran named Burleigh Grimes is just around the corner patiently awaiting his turn to prove it.

32,295 Fans Paid $152,735 At Fifth World Series Game

STANDING OF THE CLUBS.

	Won.	Lost.	Pct.
Cardinals	3	2	.600
Athletics	2	3	.400

FIFTH GAME STATISTICS.

Attendance (paid)	32,295
Receipts	$152,735.00
Commissioner's share	22,910.25
Each club's share	32,456.16
Each league's share	32,456.16

TOTAL FOR FIVE GAMES.

Attendance (paid)	171,361
Receipts	$780,781.00
*Players' share	320,303.46
Commissioner's share	117,117.15
Each club's share	85,840.10
Each league's share	85,840.10

*Players share only in receipts of first four games.

Times Wide World Photo.

FRISCH SHAKING HANDS WITH MARTIN AFTER LATTER'S HOMER.

Official Box Score of Fifth World's Series Game.

ST. LOUIS CARDINALS.

	ab.	r.	h.	tb.	2b.	3b.	hr.	bb.	so.	sh.	sb.	po.	a.	e.
Adams, 3b	1	0	1	1	0	0	0	0	0	0	0	0	0	0
High, 3b	4	1	0	0	0	0	0	0	1	0	0	2	3	0
Watkins, rf	3	1	0	0	0	0	0	1	0	0	1	3	0	0
Frisch, 2b	4	1	2	3	1	0	0	0	0	0	0	6	1	0
Martin, cf	4	1	3	6	0	0	1	0	0	0	0	0	0	0
Hafey, lf	4	0	1	1	0	0	0	0	1	0	0	1	0	0
Bottomley, 1b	4	1	2	2	0	0	0	0	0	0	0	7	1	0
Wilson, c	4	0	2	2	0	0	0	0	0	0	0	7	0	0
Gelbert, ss	4	0	1	1	0	0	0	0	0	0	0	1	2	0
Hallahan, p	4	0	0	0	0	0	0	0	1	0	0	0	0	0
Total	36	5	12	16	1	0	1	1	3	0	1	27	7	0

PHILADELPHIA ATHLETICS.

	ab.	r.	h.	tb.	2b.	3b.	hr.	bb.	so.	sh.	sb.	po.	a.	e.
Bishop, 2b	2	0	0	0	0	0	0	0	0	0	0	3	2	0
McNair, 2b	2	0	0	0	0	0	0	0	1	0	0	1	1	0
Haas, cf	2	0	0	0	0	0	0	0	1	0	0	2	0	0
Moore, lf	2	0	1	1	0	0	0	0	0	0	0	1	0	0
Cochrane, c	4	0	1	1	0	0	0	0	0	0	0	3	2	0
Simmons, lf-cf	4	1	3	4	1	0	0	0	0	0	0	5	0	0
Foxx, 1b	3	0	2	2	0	0	0	1	0	0	0	8	1	0
Miller, rf	4	0	0	0	0	0	0	0	0	0	0	2	0	0
Dykes, 3b	4	0	1	1	0	0	0	0	0	0	0	0	1	0
Williams, ss	4	0	1	1	0	0	0	0	1	0	0	2	5	0
Hoyt, p	2	0	0	0	0	0	0	0	0	0	0	0	0	0
Walberg, p	0	0	0	0	0	0	0	0	0	0	0	0	0	0
Rommel, p	0	0	0	0	0	0	0	0	0	0	0	0	0	0
aHeving	1	0	0	0	0	0	0	0	0	0	0	0	0	0
bBoley	1	0	0	0	0	0	0	0	1	0	0	0	0	0
Total	35	1	9	10	1	0	0	1	4	0	0	27	12	0

aBatted for Walberg in eighth.
bBatted for Rommel in ninth.

SCORE BY INNINGS.

St. Louis	1	0	0	0	0	2	0	1	1	—5
Philadelphia	0	0	0	0	0	0	1	0	0	—1

Runs batted in—St. Louis: Martin 4, Gelbert 1. Philadelphia: Miller 1.

Left on bases—St. Louis 5, Philadelphia 8. Double plays—Gelbert, Bottomley and Wilson; Bishop and Foxx. Hits—Off Hoyt 7 in 6 innings, Walberg 2 in 2, Rommel 3 in 1. Struck out—By Hoyt 1, Walberg 2. Bases on balls—Off Walberg 1. Losing pitcher—Hoyt. Umpires—Klem (N. L.) at plate; Nallin (A. L.) at first base; Stark (N. L.) at second base; McGowan (A. L.) at third base. Time of game—1:56.

Ruth's Record Seems Doomed As Martin's Average Soars

Special to The New York Times.

PHILADELPHIA, Oct. 7.—Babe Ruth's record batting average of .625 for a world's series seems doomed. Martin's jumped to .667 today. Thoughtful statisticians pointed out that if sacrifice flies were being scored this year as they were in 1928, Martin's up-to-the-second average would be no less than .750.

SERIES SPOTLIGHT SHINES ON MARTIN

St. Louis Star's Every Act Is Intently Followed—Unaware He Tied Batting Record.

FRISCH COLLECTS 51ST HIT

Far Ahead in Race for Most Safe Drives, Total Series—Mackmen's Coaches Plan New Strategy.

By WILLIAM E. BRANDT.

Special to The New York Times.

PHILADELPHIA, Oct. 7.—There was a different pitching star today and a different score, but it is still a Pepper Martin world's series.

The swarthy athlete whose exploits in the first four games made him the official hero, reached new heights on all fronts today. As the teams move West tonight Pepper finds himself dominating the shifting scene as no unheralded player has succeeded in doing since 1906, when a substitute infielder, George Rohe, single handedly swung the world's championship to the Chicago White Sox by his sensational hitting.

Martin was nearly the last Red Bird to don civilian plumage and leave the Cardinals' dressing room underneath the right wing of the Shibe Park grand stand.

Fan Congratulates Him.

"Congratulations on tying the record," piped a St. Louis rooter.

"What record?"

"Twelve hits."

"Sure I got twelve hits. Is that a record?"

Informed that he had deadlocked the world's series' record for most hits, Martin replied:

"Say, thats' great. Why, maybe I'll get another bump or two out there and then that will be a new record, won't it?"

Pleased as a boy who has just found something in his Christmas stocking, Pepper jogged off to catch up with a pair of team-mates who had edged away from the group.

Martin today became a real centre of public attention for every move he made. The fans viewed with delight his observance of his two special superstitions. They buzzed when he stepped out of the batter's box after missing a swing at the ball, picked up a handful of loose gravel and tossed it into the batter's box ahead of him before resuming his batting stance.

In the eighth inning a fan tossed a veritable shower of score cards over the pavilion railing. Martin called time and held up the game about five minutes until he had picked up every last fragment of litter, for the second of his two pet hunches is to keep the outfield in back of him free from extraneous matter.

Frisch Is Far in Lead.

Frisch's two hits were his fiftieth and fifty-first in world's series competition. The Flash is far ahead of all other stars in the race for most hits, total series.

Martin's drive for the world's series base-stealing record was blocked when Cochrane shot him down in the eighth. Pepper needs two more steals to tie Jimmy Slagle's record of six, made in 1907.

With five games played, the Athletics are pretty well convinced that Martin can hit anything.

"How Martin got a homer on that curve Hoyt threw him is a mystery to all of us," said one of the Mack coaching staff after the game. "We're getting to feel that right now this fellow's weakness is a base on balls. He'll get a lot of walks from now on."

STORY OF THE GAME TOLD PLAY BY PLAY

Martin Celebrates Promotion in Batting Order by Driving In the First Score.

ADAMS AGAIN FORCED OUT

Starts Game With Single, Then Has to Retire From Contest — High, His Understudy, Tallies.

By WILLIAM E. BRANDT.

Special to The New York Times.

PHILADELPHIA, Oct. 7. — The play-by-play description of the fifth game of the world's series follows:

First Inning.

ST. LOUIS—Sparky Adams's stay in the game was brief. He cracked Hoyt's second pitch over third base for a single, but his injured leg gave way under him as he ran to first base. Andy High took over Adams's duties immediately, going to first as a pinch runner. Watkins flied to Simmons. Haas stretched out his hands as he ran for Frisch's fly to left centre pretending to be about to catch it. But his ruse failed to fool High and when Frisch's drive struck the grass for a single High was so far on his way to third that he made it safely in spite of Haas's fine throw. Frisch streaked to second, beating Dykes's relay to Bishop. Martin celebrated his promotion in the batting order by shooting a fiery liner toward the left-field stands near the foul line. Simmons caught it on the run two steps from the wall, but there was no chance to prevent High from scoring after the catch. Simmons's fast throw to third, however, made Frisch scamper back to the safety of second base. Hafey's sharp smash to deep short brought a beautiful throw from Williams to ctach Hafey at first base. One run, two hits, no errors, one left.

PHILADELPHIA—High took his stand at third base for the Cardinals. Watkins raced from back near the right-field wall to catch Bishop's high fly to short right centre. Haas fanned. Frisch ran behind the pitcher's box to get under Cochrane's pop-up. No runs, no hits, no errors, none left.

Second Inning.

ST. LOUIS—Bottomley lined a single to right. Miller and Haas converged for Wilson's high fly to short right centre, Miller making the catch. Gelbert's slow bounder to short forced Bottomley, Williams to Bishop, but Bishop's peg to first came too late to double Gelbert at first. Williams juggled Hallahan's grounder long enough to lose his chance for a play at second, but again the young shortstop's magnificent throwing arm drew cheers from the fans as he shot down Hallahan at first base. No runs, one hit, no errors, one left.

PHILADELPHIA—The crowd got its first real chance for hearty applause when Simmons crashed Hallahan's second pitch for a double against the scoreboard in right centre. High scooped up Foxx's smash, scared Simmons back to second, then threw out Foxx at first. On Miller's high bounder to Gelbert the Athletics tried their first base-running gamble of the series. Simmons turned third and headed for the plate as Gelbert made his throw to first base. This daring gesture merely served to end the inning quickly, for Gelbert's throw nipped Miller by a step and Bottomley's quick pass to Wilson landed the ball at home plate while Simmons was still three steps away. Simmons slid desperately but could not escape. It was scored as a double play, Gelbert to Bottomley to Wilson. No runs, one hit, no errors, none left.

Third Inning.

ST. LOUIS—Bishop tossed out High, then ran back into right field for Watkins's fly. Frisch flied to Haas. No runs, no hits, no errors, none left.

PHILADELPHIA — Dykes's light grounder was pocketed by Bottomley two steps from first base for an easy and unassisted put-out. Williams fouled to High. High ran in to field Hoyt's slow bounder for an easy out at first. No runs, no hits, no errors, none left.

Fourth Inning.

ST. LOUIS—Martin showed them a new trick by pushing a long bunt through the grass toward first base and tearing across the bag safely before Foxx could pick up the ball and tag him, thus recording his tenth hit of the series. Hafey struck out on a ball that nearly hit the ground. Bottomley arched a long fly down the left-field foul line which had the home fans gravely worried until it came to earth about a yard from the foul line, so that it counted only a strike instead of a two-bagger. Bottomley then lined a single to right and the Wild Horse of the Osage thundered to third, just beating Miller's quick throw. Bishop made a fine catch of Wilson's liner within inches of the ground and doubled Bottomley by a quick throw to Foxx. No runs, two hits, no errors, one left.

PHILADELPHIA — Bottomley and Frisch collided in chasing Bishop's fly out along the right-field foul line. Both fell down, but Bottomley, who backed into Frisch as he caught the ball, hung onto it. Hafey ran to the left-field foul line for Haas's long twisting liner. Cochrane hoisted a foul almost straight into the air for Wilson to catch. No runs, no hits, no errors, none left.

Fifth Inning.

ST. LOUIS—Dykes threw out Gelbert. Williams tossed out Hallahan. High lined straight at Simmons. No runs, no hits, no errors, none left.

PHILADELPHIA — Al Simmons bounced a terrific liner off Hallahan's right shin, the ball shooting to left field for a single. Hallahan got the ball over only once while giving Foxx a base on balls. Miller bunted a foul liner to Bottomley. Bottomley ran back for a fine catch of Dykes's foul. With the count three and two and both base runners in motion, Williams fanned. No runs, one hit, no errors, two left.

Sixth Inning.

ST. LOUIS—Miller had to run hard to catch Watkins's short fly. Frisch slapped a liner over third base for a two-bagger. Martin's eleventh hit of the series was the best yet. After Hoyt served one wide pitch, Martin lashed at a low curve and drove the ball into the upper tier of the left-field pavilion for the first St. Louis home run of the series, scoring Frisch ahead of him. Hafey flied to Simmons. Haas made a running catch of Bottomley's short fly to right centre. Two runs, two hits, no errors, none left.

PHILADELPHIA—Hoyt popped to Frisch. McNair batted for Bishop and fouled to Wilson on the first pitch. Moore, another right-hand hitter, batted for Haas. Moore flied easily to Watkins. No runs, no hits, no errors, none left.

Seventh Inning.

ST. LOUIS—McNair went to second base, Moore went to left field and Simmons shifted to centre, while Walberg went to the box to pitch. Wilson lined a single to left. On a hit and run play Gelbert's swing missed the ball and Wilson was out stealing, Cochrane to Williams, the first unsuccessful stealing attempt for the Cardinals in the series. Williams took Gelbert's liner on a first bounce and threw him out. Hallahan let a third strike shoot by. No runs, one hit, no errors, none left.

PHILADELPHIA — Frisch ran to second base to catch Cochrane's pop. It was his third straight pop-up. Simmons's third straight hit was a savage liner over Gelbert's head for a single to left centre. Counting his last time at bat yesterday, it was Al's fourth straight hit. Foxx bounced a liner off Hallahan's hip for a single to right. Frisch dived in an effort to head off the ball, but it rolled through the grass and Simmons reached third easily. Miller bounced to High, whose low throw to second was scooped up brilliantly by Frisch for a force-out of Foxx, Simmons scoring. Dykes bounced a single over third, High knocking down the ball but being unable to field it, Miller taking second. Frisch ran far into right centre to capture Williams's fly. One run, three hits, no errors, two left.

Eighth Inning.

ST. LOUIS—High was called out on strikes. Watkins walked. Watkins made a clean steal of second, beating Cochrane's accurate throw. Moore raced across the foul line for Frisch's long foul. Walberg got two strikes on Martin but no more. Martin singled to left for his third straight hit, scoring Watkins from second. This was Martin's twelfth hit of the series, tying the world's series record made by Buck Herzog of the Giants in 1912 and tied by Joe Jackson of the White Sox in 1919 and by Sam Rice of Washington in 1925. It was followed, however, by Pepper's first unsuccessful baseline flight of the series. He dashed for second on an attempted steal and was out, Cochrane to McNair. One run, one hit, no errors, none left.

PHILADELPHIA—Johnny Heving, substitute catcher, batted for Walberg and flied to Watkins. McNair fanned. Moore bounced the ball high in the air half way to third base. Hallahan caught it on the run, but could not stop in time to make a throw and it was scored as Philadelphia's sixth hit of the game. Cochrane's hot smash bounced off Bottomley's shoulders for another scratch hit, Moore taking second. This time Simmons failed, his easy bounder going straight to High, who had his foot on third base for a force-out as the ball nestled in his glove. No runs, two hits, no errors, two left.

Ninth Inning.

ST. LOUIS—Rommel went in to pitch for Philadelphia. Dykes deflected Hafey's liner to Williams, whose throw to Foxx apparently retired Hafey, the crowd howling when the umpire called Hafey safe. It was scored as an infield hit. Foxx made a fine pick-up of Bottomley's slow roller, throwing to Williams for a force-out of Hafey. Wilson's long single to centre sent Bottomley to third. Gelbert singled to left, scoring Bottomley and putting Wilson on second. Hallahan was cheered as he stepped up to bat and responded by hoisting a high fly to Simmons. McNair threw out High. One run, three hits, no errors, two left.

PHILADELPHIA—Foxx beat out a bunt which rolled only a dozen feet from home plate. Gelbert went behind second to get Miller's roller, tossing to Frisch for a force-out of Foxx. Dykes rolled to Frisch, forcing Miller, Frisch to Gelbert. Williams's fly dropped safely in short centre for a single in spite of Martin's flying dive. Dykes took third while Frisch retrieved the ball from centre field. Boley batted for Rommel. The game ended as his bat missed a fast ball for a third strike. No runs, two hits, no errors, two left.

Mrs. Martin Weeps for Joy As Husband Drives a Homer

PHILADELPHIA, Oct. 7 (AP).—When Pepper Martin connected for his home run today a woman in the boxes cried while the rest of the multitude rose and cheered. The woman was Mrs. Martin, wife of the series' hero. She always cries, she said, every time her now famous husband gains glory.

"He's always been a hero to me," she said. "When we were in grammar school I stood on a soap box to cheer his baseball work. Now when the crowd starts cheering him my eyes get misty. I just can't help it."

Composite Box Score of World's Series Games.

PHILADELPHIA ATHLETICS.

	G	AB	R	H	TB	2B	3B	HR	BB	SO	SB	Bat Avg	PO	A	E	TC	Fldg Avg
Bishop, 2b	5	19	2	3	3	0	0	0	1	3	0	.158	6	13	0	19	1.000
McNair, 2b	2	2	1	0	0	0	0	0	0	1	0	.000	1	1	0	2	1.000
Haas, cf	5	18	1	3	4	1	0	0	0	4	0	.167	10	0	0	10	1.000
Moore, lf	2	3	0	1	1	0	0	0	0	1	0	.333	1	0	0	1	1.000
Cochrane, c	5	16	2	3	3	0	0	0	5	2	0	.188	26	2	0	28	1.000
Simmons, lf.-cf	5	20	3	7	15	2	0	2	1	2	0	.350	17	0	0	17	1.000
Foxx, 1b	5	14	1	6	9	0	0	1	6	2	0	.428	51	2	0	53	1.000
Miller, rf	5	19	1	3	4	1	0	0	0	3	0	.158	11	0	0	11	1.000
Dykes, 3b	5	16	0	5	5	0	0	0	2	0	0	.313	2	9	0	11	1.000
Williams, ss	5	17	1	4	4	0	0	0	2	8	0	.235	6	19	0	25	1.000
Grove, p	2	6	0	0	0	0	0	0	0	4	0	.000	0	0	0	0	.000
Earnshaw, p	2	6	0	0	0	0	0	0	0	2	0	.000	1	5	0	6	1.000
Mahaffey, p	1	0	0	0	0	0	0	0	0	0	0	.000	0	1	0	1	1.000
Hoyt, p	1	2	0	0	0	0	0	0	0	0	0	.000	0	0	0	0	.000
Walberg, p	1	0	0	0	0	0	0	0	0	0	0	.000	0	0	0	0	.000
Rommel, p	1	0	0	0	0	0	0	0	0	0	0	.000	0	0	0	0	.000
*Cramer	1	1	0	0	0	0	0	0	0	0	0	.000	0	0	0	0	.000
*Heving	1	1	0	0	0	0	0	0	0	0	0	.000	0	0	0	0	.000
*Boley	1	1	0	0	0	0	0	0	0	1	0	.000	0	0	0	0	.000
Totals		161	12	35	48	4	0	3	17	33	0	.217	132	52	0	184	1.000

ST. LOUIS CARDINALS.

	G	AB	R	H	TB	2B	3B	HR	BB	SO	SB	Bat Avg	PO	A	E	TC	Fldg Avg
High, 3b	3	11	1	1	1	0	0	0	0	2	0	.091	2	5	0	7	1.000
Flowers, 3b	4	7	0	0	0	0	0	0	1	0	0	.000	3	2	0	5	1.000
Adams, 3b	2	4	0	1	1	0	0	0	0	1	0	.250	0	1	0	1	1.000
Roettger, rf	2	10	1	3	4	1	0	0	0	1	0	.300	2	0	0	2	1.000
Watkins, rf	4	11	2	2	3	1	0	0	1	1	1	.182	6	0	0	6	1.000
Frisch, 2b	5	20	2	6	8	2	0	0	1	0	1	.300	19	11	0	30	1.000
Bottomley, 1b	5	18	2	4	5	1	0	0	2	3	0	.222	38	2	1	41	.975
Hafey, lf	5	20	1	3	3	0	0	0	0	4	1	.150	7	0	0	7	1.000
Martin, cf	5	18	5	12	19	4	0	1	0	2	4	.667	8	0	0	8	1.000
Wilson, c	5	18	0	5	5	0	0	0	0	1	0	.278	37	1	1	39	.974
Gelbert, ss	5	17	0	5	6	1	0	0	0	2	0	.294	10	20	0	30	1.000
Derringer, p	2	2	0	0	0	0	0	0	0	1	0	.000	0	1	0	1	1.000
Johnson, p	2	0	0	0	0	0	0	0	0	2	0	.000	0	1	0	1	1.000
Hallahan, p	2	7	0	0	0	0	0	0	0	3	0	.000	0	0	0	0	.000
Grimes, p	1	4	0	2	2	0	0	0	0	0	0	.500	0	2	0	2	1.000
Lindsey, p	1	0	0	0	0	0	0	0	0	0	0	.000	0	0	0	0	.000
*Blades	1	1	0	0	0	0	0	0	0	1	0	.000	0	0	0	0	.000
*Mancuso	1	1	0	0	0	0	0	0	0	0	0	.000	0	0	0	0	.000
*Collins	1	1	0	0	0	0	0	0	0	1	0	.000	0	0	0	0	.000
Totals		172	14	44	57	10	0	1	5	25	7	.250	132	46	2	180	.989

*Pinch hitter.

COMPOSITE SCORE BY INNINGS.

Philadelphia	1	0	4	0	0	2	3	0	2	—12
St. Louis	3	3	0	2	0	2	1	1	2	—14

Runs batted in—Philadelphia: Simmons 5, Foxx 3, Haas 1, Dykes 1, Miller 1. St. Louis: Bottomley 2, Wilson 2, Gelbert 3, Grimes 2, Martin 5. Games won—Philadelphia 2, St. Louis 3. Pitching records—Games won: Grove 1, Earnshaw 1, Hallahan 2, Grimes 1. Games lost: Earnshaw 1, Grove 1, Hoyt 1, Derringer 1, Johnson 1. Hits—Off Grove 23 in 17 innings, Earnshaw 8 in 17, Mahaffey 1 in 1, Hoyt 7 in 6, Walberg 2 in 2, Rommell 3 in 1, Derringer 11 in 8, Johnson 9 in 7 2-3, Hallahan 12 in 18, Grimes 2 in 9, Lindsey 1 in 1 1-3. Struck out—By Grove 9, Earnshaw 13, Hoyt 1, Walberg 2, Derringer 10, Johnson 4, Hallahan 12, Grimes 5, Lindsey 2. Bases on balls—Off Grove 1, Earnshaw 2, Mahaffey 1, Walberg 1, Derringer 3, Hallahan 8, Grimes 4, Johnson 1, Lindsey 1. Earned runs—Off Grove 6, Earnshaw 2, Mahaffey 1, Hoyt 3, Walberg 1, Rommel 1, Derringer 6, Grimes 2, Johnson 3, Hallahan 1. Wild pitch—Hallahan. Sacrifices—Haas, Dykes, Gelbert. Double plays—Bishop, Williams and Foxx; Bottomley (unassisted); Frisch, Gelbert and Bottomley 2; Gelbert, Frisch and Bottomley; Gelbert, Bottomley and Wilson; Bishop and Foxx. Left on bases—Philadelphia 36, St. Louis 32.

HOW BATTING STARS FARED IN FIFTH GAME

Performances at Plate of Martin, Hafey, Bottomley, Simmons and Cochrane.

PHILADELPHIA, Oct. 7 (AP).—The batting performances of the "big five" in the fifth game of the world's series follow:

Pepper Martin.

First Inning—Flied out to Simmons, High scoring after the catch.
Fourth Inning—Beat out bunt to Foxx, went to third on Bottomley's single and was left.
Sixth Inning—Drove home run into the left field bleachers, scoring behind Frisch.
Eighth Inning—Singled to left for his twelfth hit of the series, scoring Watkins from second, then was thrown out stealing second.

Chick Hafey.

First Inning—Grounded to Williams for third out.
Fourth Inning—Struck out.
Sixth Inning—Flied out to Simmons.
Ninth Inning—Singled past third and was forced at second by Bottomley.

Jim Bottomley.

Second Inning—Singled to right and was forced at second by Gelbert.
Fourth Inning—Singled to right and was caught off first in double play on Wilson's liner to Bishop.
Sixth Inning—Flied out to Haas.
Ninth Inning—Reached first, forcing Hafey, went to third on Wilson's single and scored on Gelbert's single.

Al Simmons.

Second Inning—Doubled to scoreboard in right centre and was thrown out at plate trying to score on Miller's infield out.
Fifth Inning—Smashed a drive off Hallahan's arm into left for single and was left on second.
Seventh Inning—Singled to left, took third on Foxx's single and scored only Athletic run as Miller forced Foxx.
Eighth Inning—Hit to High, forcing Moore at third.

Mickey Cochrane.

First Inning—Popped to Frisch.
Fourth Inning—Hoisted foul to Wilson.
Seventh Inning—Popped to Frisch.
Eighth Inning—Beat out hard drive to Bottomley for single and was left on first.

Schedule of Remaining Games.

Today—Travel.
Tomorrow—at St. Louis.
Saturday—At St. Louis (if seventh game is necessary).

The series is decided on the basis of the best four out of seven games.

Games start at 1:30 P. M. (2:30 New York time.)

RUTH ARRIVES TONIGHT FOR EXHIBITIONS

Los Angeles Examiner Sports
CHARACTER · QUALITY · AMERICA FIRST · ENTERPRISE · ACCURACY
AN AMERICAN PAPER FOR THE AMERICAN PEOPLE · THE GREAT NEWSPAPER OF THE GREAT SOUTHWEST
FRIDAY, OCTOBER 16, 1931 CC · SECTION I—PAGE 17

BERGER JOINS PLAYERS FOR SUNDAY GAME

Former Angel Star in Lineup Opposed to Mighty Babe; Ticket Sale Tremendous

By John Connolly

The King of Swat, otherwise George Herman Ruth, greatest home-run hitter of all time, arrives tonight at 5:30 p. m., on the Pacific Coast Limited of the Union Pacific System. The last minute change was made known in a telegram from the Bambino from Salt Lake yesterday. Ruth was originally slated to arrive Sunday morning.

Ruth's visit here comes in the way of a mission of mercy, for beginning Sunday at Wrigley Field he will become the chief attraction in a three-game benefit series, the receipts of which will be turned over to the Marion Davies Clinic for Ailing Children of World War Veterans.

REICHOW IN CHARGE

Plans for Ruth's reception tonight are in the hands of a committee headed by Oscar Reichow, business manager of the Los Angeles club, who is assembling the players who will play with and against Babe on Sunday, Tuesday night, October 20, and Saturday night, October 31.

Accompanying Ruth is Christy Walsh, his manager. Walsh, in a wire yesterday, declared that the team captained by Bambino will be personally equipped by the King of Swat, who has secured flaming red outfits, which are likely to be the envy of the team captained by George Burns.

Wally Berger, one of the leading homerun hitters of the National League, was added to the galaxy of stars who will perform Sunday afternoon.

The Boston Brave outfielder, who formerly pastimed with the Angels, will patrol right field for the team being captained by Burns.

LINEUPS ANNOUNCED

Reichow yesterday announced the tentative lineups of both teams. He stated that it is likely that before game time other major leaguers would be added to the list. One of these is Babe Herman, Brooklyn slugger, who is playing in the Winter League here, but who may be used Sunday to appear against the Homerun King.

According to present plans, Frank Shellenback will pitch against Ruth's team Sunday, with Win Ballou twirling for the Homerun Slugger's outfit.

The advance sale of tickets took a tremendous jump yesterday, and Reichow declares that a sellout Sunday afternoon is inevitable.

"We can't miss filling the park the way reservations are pouring in," he stated. "I have never seen such a hearty response as has marked the sale of Ruth's tickets."

Yesterday, A. G. Spalding & Bros. opened the downtown ticket sale and it is expected that with Wrigley Field reservations going full blast and with Spalding's taking care of the downtown sales, the park will be filled to capacity Sunday.

Hal Rhyne, Boston American League club shortstop, will hold down his favorite spot at second base for Ruth's club.

Lillard Barred From Competing Against Trojans

Bulletin

PORTLAND, Ore., Oct. 16.—(AP)—Joe Lillard, University of Oregon negro halfback, early this morning was declared ineligible for further competition in a decision reached by faculty representatives of the Pacific Intercollegiate conference.

The decision of the faculty representatives was announced shortly after midnight when a five and a half hour meeting was adjourned.

Ground for the action, based on evidence presented by Jonathan Butler, the new conference athletic commissioner, was that Lillard had "played under an assumed name."

In a formal statement issued by Prof. W. B. Owens of Stanford University, president of the conference, no spart was specified, but the question of Lillard's eligibility arose over his having played semi-professional baseball in the Middle West. He had played with the Gilkerson Colored Giants.

Lillard is due in Los Angeles this morning with the Oregon team, which plays U. S. C. tomorrow at Olympic Stadium.

FOOTBALL SCORES

At Dallas, Mexico U., 0; Southern Methodist University Reserves, 43.

At Atchison, Kans.—Omaha University, 27; St. Benedict's College, 6.

At Raliegh: Wakeforest, 6; North Carolina State, 0.

At University, Va.: Virginia M. I. T., 18; Virginia, 3.

FISHER MISSING

NEW YORK, Oct. 15.—Fisher, quarter, may be missing when New York University plays Holy Cross on Saturday. Fisher is suffering from a shoulder injury.

CERTAIN STARTERS

ITHACA, Oct. 15.—(AP)—Viviano, Ferraro and Kline were today considered certain backfield starters for Cornell against Princeton this week end.

HOW THEY'LL LINE UP IN RUTH GAME

RUTH STARS	BURNS STARS
Statz, cf	Haney, 3b
Gazella, 3b	Summa, lf
Hill, lf	Burns, 1b
Ruth, rf	Berger, rf
Jacobs, 1b	Lee, ss
Rhyne, 2b	Stainback, cf
McIsaacs, ss	Parker, 2b
Woodaall, c	Campbell, c
Mayer, c	Bassler, c
Ballou, p	Shellenback, p

Umpires, Fanning and Chadbourne.

ATHLETICS ARE 'THROUGH'! ★ ★ ★ THAT'S BABE RUTH'S BELIEF

DENVER, Oct. 15. — (AP) — Babe Ruth says the Athletics are "through" and that 1932 will see the end of Philadelphia's domination of the American League.

Denver on a barnstorming tour, the Bambino said the New York Yankees needed only one winning pitcher to climb into the championship parade.

"Grove and Earnshaw were burned up this year," Ruth said. "They had four years taken off their baseball careers by overwork. Cochrane and Simmons are slowing up, and Bing Miller is about through."

Saying he was disappointed in the showing of the A's in the world series, Ruth added Connie Mack's team had lost its fire and dash after the second game, with the players going to the plate with their heads down.

Ruth said he expected to play two more years and retire. He said he had no intention of becoming a manager in the majors, and would devote his time to golf.

Bambino the Buster

BABE RUTH arrives tonight. He comes to Los Angeles to play a series of three exhibition games for the Marion Davies Clinic, the first of which is scheduled at Wrigley Field Sunday afternoon. The second game will be played Tuesday night and the third Saturday night, October 31. Examiner Artist Al Zinnen herewith gives you his conception of baseball's greatest home-run hitter.

GIANTS CONQUER ALL-STARS, 8-1

"Satchel" Paige proved too much for the Pirrone All Stars at White Sox Park last night and the Philadelphia Royal Giants opened the Winter League baseball race with an 8 to 1 victory. Paige gave the Stars six hits, three of which came in the fifth to give the losers their lone tally. Sam Gibson, who hurled for the Stars, was touched for eight.

Mayor Porter tossed out the first ball and a crowd of about 2000 fans turned out for the proceedings. Gordon Slade, with three hits in four attempts, starred for the Pirrone club. Paige struck out ten and proved the outstanding performer of the tussle. These clubs will meet at White Sox Park again tomorrow night.

Colt Without Name Wins at Newmarket

NEWMARKET, Eng., Oct. 15.—(AP)—W. M. G. Singer's colt without a name today won the Middle Park stakes and established himself as the probable winter book favorite for the Epsom Derby next year.

The colt, a strapping 2-year-old by Gainsborough out of Golden Hair, has won several stakes this year including the Campagne at Doncaster last month and was an odds-on choice today at 4 to 11.

Ohio State Player Has Injured Hand

COLUMBUS, Ohio, Oct. 15.—Junius Ferrall, regular Ohio State end, was in the hospital today with a broken bone in his left hand. Physicians said, however, he will be able to play with a cast in Saturday's tilt with Michigan.

WHITTIER LOSES

Monrovia High's lightweights defeated Whittier, 12-0, yesterday afternoon at Whittier.

U. S. Will Waive Entry Tax for Games Athletes

WASHINGTON, Oct. 15.—(Universal Service.)—Entry of foreign athletes competing in the Olympic Games at Los Angeles will be expedited as much as possible, Assistant Secretary of Labor R. C. White announced today. Representative Snell (Republican), New York, will sponsor legislation to waive the head tax of $8 per person which each visitor to the country must pay, and to provide for admission of the athletes on the certificates of their respective Governments.

CANADA ENTERS OLYMPIC GAMES

TORONTO, Ont., Oct. 15.—(AP)—Canada will make every effort to participate in the 1932 Olympic Games at Lake Placid and Los Angeles, it was definitely decided today, but so far the necessary funds have not been raised.

A meeting of the Canadian Olympic committee to discuss whether Canada would send athletes to the United States next year reached an affirmative conclusion and added that "the money to send such teams will be raised by Government grants, private and general subscriptions and assessments of the gate receipts of athletic meets. Various governing bodies of sports concerned will be requested to raise a percentage of the cost of sending athletes to the Olympic Games."

Lomski Gets Draw Verdict in North

TACOMA, Wash., Oct. 15.—(AP)—Leo Lomski, of Aberdeen, was held to a draw decision by George Rickard of Tacoma in the six-round main event of the boxing program here tonight. Most of the fans thought that Lomski had a distinct advantage.

Oilers Capture 4-2 Victory Over Bears

The Union Oil ice hockey team defeated the Sunfreze Bears, 4-2, last night at the Winter Garden. Nichols and Fallis were the outstanding players for the Oilers, while McLennon and Woodly featured the Bears' play.

Brabyn, Wilson in Billiard Victories

Orrin Brabyn defeated Frank Welsh, 100-71, last night at Jones' Billiard Parlor in the Southern division of the Western sectional championships. In the other match, Walter Wilson downed Thurman Jacques, 100-73.

SMITH K. O.'s WELLS

Delbert Smith knocked out Al Wells in the first round in main event last night on the Pasadena amateur card. In the semi-windup, Eddie Hoffman scored a second round kayo victory over Nick Balderrana.

BELL WINS, 12-0

Bell High Class B team defeated Jacob Riis, 12-0, yesterday afternoon at Bell. Craft scored for touchdowns for the winners.

Pasadena Board Urged to Invite Gaels for Game

PASADENA, Oct. 15.—A movement is on foot in Pasadena to urge Tournament of Roses officials to invite St. Mary's football team to represent the West in the New Year's Day Rose Bowl game if that team continues undefeated. St. Mary's would be the first nonconference contender to represent the West, if selected.

OREGON FIRST INVADER WITH NO SETBACKS

Spears' Squad Here This Morning; Make Beach Headquarters; Open Game Expected

By Maxwell Stiles

There arrives in this man's town this morning something that is even more unusual than our weather.

It is the first undefeated Oregon University football team to face an eleven representing the State of California since Andy Smith's "wonder teams" first swung supremacy's pendulum toward the South. Victories over Monmouth Normal, Idaho and Washington, the large Doctor Spears and his transcontinental tourists pay us a short visit for the purpose of meeting Southern California on the gridiron at Olympic Stadium tomorrow afternoon.

PAST VISITS MARRED

All previous Oregon visits to this state have been marred by a past. Oregon teams have come down to meet California, Stanford and St. Mary's with varying degrees of success, but in every instance these teams had been defeated by at least one Northwest rival before making the jump toward the Golden State.

But, lo, here comes the large Doctor Spears with a team whose past is as clean and lily white as a new tooth. Trojans will attempt to bore a cavity in said molar, the cavity to be as close to the goal line as possible.

The Ducks from Eugene are due to arrive on the Lark at the Glendale station at 8:45 a. m., according to latest information. They will go by bus direct to the Miramar Hotel at Santa Monica, which hostelry will be their home until after game time tomorrow. The team is scheduled to leave tomorrow evening for Grand Forks to face North Dakota University one week hence, and then will go right on to New York for a game with New York University.

Despite Oregon's 13 to 0 victory over Washington, Southern California will go into the game a favorite. The Trojans showed so much power against Washington State that their backers are willing to put up a flock of new hats that they can whip Oregon even if Oregon is as good as St. Mary's, as has been reported. Why, say, these Trojan enthusiasts, Mister Howard Jones and his gang would go right through the Gaels tomorrow if they had a chance. Maybe.

FIGURES FAVOR BOTH

Comparative scores can prove that either team ought to win. Last year Southern California walloped Washington, 32 to 0, and Oregon State, 27 to 7. Oregon State defeated Oregon and Oregon defeated

(Continued on Fourth Sport Page)

Counterfeit Ticket Ring Reported Here

Reports that the ring which was responsible for counterfeit tickets to football games at the University of California's Berkeley games this year had extended operations into Los Angeles were heard yesterday. Graduate Manager Arnold Eddy of U. S. C. urged purchasers of pasteboards for the Trojan-Oregon game here Saturday to obtain their tickets only from the U. S. C. ticket agency at Dyas' downtown store, at the Student store on the U. S. C. campus, regular ticket brokerage firms or Saturday afternoon at one of the thirty-nine booths around the Olympic Stadium.

WHAT-NOTS by Mark Kelly

CHICAGO, Oct. 15.—I was talking Cubs and King Wrigley insisted on talking Angels, so a Babelesque time was had by all.

Wrigley Has Been Too Frank

It seems that King Wrigley, the height of candor, has been a bit too frank in his interviews and Prexy Veeck, the Cub pooh-bah, has cautioned him against such candor. It isn't done in baseball. King Wrigley is much more a fan than an owner and has been approachable and affable when you sought to chatter of baseball, but sometimes blissfully unconscious of the fact that he was talking to boys who write.

When I busted into his local offices he sorta ran up his guard, feinted a lot with his left and never once came up with his right.

* * *

"Is it true?" I wanted to know, "that you are going to get rid of Wilson, Hartnett, Malone and one or two others?"

To which he replied that the Angels had finished with a profit for the year.

"And what's this talk about dissension and all that on the Cubs?" Just try to switch me, sezzi to me.

"Yes, sir, Joe Patrick has had a fairly good year despite the depression and we're busy right now trying to line up a better Angel team for next season," still on the siding, so to speak.

"And Hornsby is to stick, eh?" the old prod that struck fire.

Back to the main line came King Wrigley with a bang. His old pipe fired up on all six. "Y'dam right Hornsby sticks," sezze. "Who said he wouldn't?" and a very truculent pair of shoulders heaved forward with just a bit more menace than was necessary. I hastened to inform King Wrig-

(Continued on Fourth Sport Page)

2 CENTS PAY NO MORE!

Chicago Daily Tribune

THE WORLD'S GREATEST NEWSPAPER

FINAL EDITION

VOLUME LXXXX.—NO. 256 C [REG. U. S. PAT. OFFICE: COPYRIGHT 1931 BY THE CHICAGO TRIBUNE.] MONDAY, OCTOBER 26, 1931.—34 PAGES THIS PAPER CONSISTS OF TWO SECTIONS—SECTION ONE ** PRICE TWO CENTS IN CHICAGO AND SUBURBS ELSEWHERE THREE CENTS

CHARLES A. COMISKEY DEAD

CAPONE PRISON TRIP HINGES ON APPEAL TODAY

Al Shares Jail Cell with D'Andrea.

Al Capone spent a comfortable week-end in the county jail, and the gloom engendered by uncertainty as to his immediate future was lightened by the companionship of his faithful bodyguard, Philip D'Andrea.

D'Andrea was arrested and separated from his master two weeks ago when his fidelity led him to carry a gun into court during Capone's trial for income tax evasion, but a reunion was effected on Saturday. Capone was placed in the same cell where D'Andrea is awaiting the outcome of his contempt of court case.

Whether Capone will stay in the jail for an indefinite period or leave tonight or very soon for Leavenworth penitentiary to begin serving his eleven year sentence for tax evasion was uncertain.

Lawyers Seek a Way Out.

His lawyers, Albert Fink and Michael Ahern, were in conference last night, discussing what steps they might take today to delay his trip to prison. During the afternoon they visited their client in the jail, his only visitors of the day.

The cell where Capone received the attorneys is a large one, about twenty feet square, in the hospital ward on the fifth floor of the jail. Warden David Moneypenny said the gang chief and his bodyguard were placed there because it is more sequestered than the regular cell blocks and the possibility of commotion which their presence might cause is correspondingly diminished.

Capone was not deprived of the ordinary comforts of life. There is a shower bath and lavatory in the spacious cell and cots that afford restful sleep. All the newspapers are brought up and in addition to the regular jail fare at breakfast and supper, luncheon may be sent in by relatives or friends.

Lunch Sent In by Wife.

Capone's luncheon was sent in by his wife. It comprised kidney stew, a favorite dish, and bread and butter. D'Andrea also received his noon repast from the outside and he joined his master in the meal. The privilege of receiving luncheon from friends or relatives is not a special one, the warden explained, but is accorded to all prisoners.

For breakfast there were corn meal mush, a duffer [hard] roll, butter, and coffee; for supper, stewed apples, bread, butter, and tea. Assistant Warden Edward Nittell said that Capone greeted him with a cheery "Good morning," and ate his food with relish. During the day the gang chief read the papers, smoked many cigarets, and talked things over with D'Andrea. The music of a band which is sent out to the jail by a church organization on Sundays cheered them in the afternoon.

The gangsters' companions in the cell were four hospital prisoners, one with a broken leg, another with a lung affliction, and two who have undergone operations at the Bridewell.

Marshal Ready for Prison Trip.

Unless further orders are forthcoming from Federal Judge James H. Wilkerson, who sentenced Capone on Saturday, adding a fine of $50,000 and the costs of the trial to the penalty, United States Marshal Henry C. W. Laubenheimer is prepared to take the gang chief to prison tonight. Judge Wilkerson denied a supersedeas, which would have stayed Capone's commitment to the penitentiary, and also denied an appeal bond. But the judge instructed the marshal to wait until today before executing the writ committing the gangster to prison.

Marshal Laubenheimer said that he would superintend the removal of Capone to Leavenworth and that four extra guards would go along. The marshal and two others would sit with Capone and one guard would be stationed at each end of the car to prevent the entry of any questionable characters. A special coach would be used, the marshal said.

Two Courses Open to Attorneys.

Capone's attorneys have two courses of action before them, it was explained. They may go before Judge Wilkerson again and endeavor to convince him that a writ of error automatically acts as a supersedeas. They failed to convince him of this on Saturday.

They may go directly before the Circuit Court of Appeals and apply for a supersedeas and an appeal bond. Both are discretionary with the trial and the Appellate courts, irrespective of the writ of error, and the defense contends that the supersedeas

(Continued on page 8, column 3.)

NEWS SUMMARY of The Tribune

[And Historical Scrap Book.]

Monday, October 26, 1931.

Average daily net paid circulation of THE CHICAGO TRIBUNE September, 1931, in excess of 825,000

WILL THE NEWS OF CAPONE'S IMPRISONMENT TRAVEL AS FAR AND WIDE AS THE STORIES OF HIS EXPLOITS?

What a Chicago traveler heard in New Zealand. *What he heard in Australia.*

What he encountered in Indo-China. *What he ran up against in Java.*

What he was asked in Egypt. *What he read when he arrived home.*

5 Killed When Stunt Flyer's Plane Crashes

Alliance, Neb., Oct. 25.—(AP)—Five persons were plunged 500 feet to their death here early tonight when a Ryan monoplane lost a wing and crashed to earth.

The dead are William Dovall, Alliance, pilot of the ship; William E. Parley, Alliance; Dawes Hollibaugh, Chadron, Neb.; Henry Beem, Ashby, Neb., and W. W. Tibbetts, Alliance.

Only two persons saw the crash. They were Pilot Art Peterson and Mayor Merle Mallory of Alliance, who was flying with Peterson.

Both declared that Dovall had been stunting.

Dovall, said Peterson, appeared to be finishing a stunt maneuver when the wing of the ship collapsed. Peterson said he thought Dovall was either finishing a loop or a wing over when the ship was crippled. There was no fire. All five men were killed instantly.

Officials at the airport here said that Dovall, who was piloting a plane in the all-Nebraska air tour which visited here today and put on an air show, had borrowed the cabin plane after the four men had urged him to take them up for a few thrills.

Plane Falls on Roof; Pilot Dies.

New York, Oct. 25.—[Special.]—Harry Hall was killed today when his plane went into a power dive from a height of 1,500 feet and crashed on the roof of a house in Jersey City. Hall was one of several pilots engaged to do stunt flying at an air show staged for the benefit of the unemployed at Jersey City airport. A crowd of 8,000 persons saw the aviator take his fatal plunge.

Plane Falls in Ohio; Girl Killed.

Painsville, O., Oct. 25.—(AP)—When their plane crashed on a farm four miles north of here late today, Miss Mary Dorr, 20, East Cleveland, was killed and Raymond L. Manson, Cleveland, was critically injured. Investigators said the plane apparently attempted a forced landing.

Two Die in California Crash.

Calexico, Cal., Oct. 25.—(AP)—Harold Nichols, 38, Long Beach, and Clarence Pritchard, 27, Calexico, were killed today when the biplane they were flying dove to the earth from an altitude of 800 feet.

The airplane landed in an open field south of the municipal airport. Both had been flying for several months in this vicinity, but airport officials said neither was a licensed pilot.

Pritchard was unmarried but Nichols is survived by a widow and two children.

FATHER FREED IN KILLING TO AVENGE CHILD

(Picture on back page.)

Thomas Calabrese, 47 years old, 5424 West Congress street, was found not guilty of the charge of murdering his neighbor, James J. Hill, 54 years old, 5426 West Congress street, by a jury in the Criminal court early yesterday. Judge Rudolph F. Desort held a special session of court to receive the verdict after the jury had been out since 6 p. m. Saturday. The jury reached a verdict at 2:30 a. m., but did not return it until 9 o'clock.

Calabrese shot and killed Hill last March near their homes. He admitted the killing in his testimony, declaring he followed his victim from the latter's home after his 15 year old daughter, Rose Calabrese, told him Hill had attacked her. Calabrese asserted he fired when he thought Hill was reaching for a revolver.

The daughter supported her father's testimony. The state charged Calabrese fired deliberately. Attorney Miles J. Devine, representing Calabrese, told the jury that the "unwritten law" justified the killing.

Khartoum, Giant Captive Elephant, Dies in New York

New York, Oct. 25.—(AP)—Khartoum, 29 year old elephant, said to be the largest in captivity, died in the New York Zoölogical park today. He was taken ill suddenly Saturday night.

THE WEATHER

MONDAY, OCTOBER 26, 1931.

Sunrise, 6:16; sunset, 4:52. Moon sets at 7:26 a. m. on Tuesday. Jupiter is a morning star. Saturn is an evening star.

Chicago and vicinity—Partly cloudy to cloudy and slightly warmer Monday, followed by showers by Monday night and on Tuesday, winds becoming moderate southeasterly.

Illinois — Increasing cloudiness, slightly warmer Monday, followed by showers Monday night and Tuesday.

TRIBUNE BAROMETER.

TEMPERATURES IN CHICAGO

MAXIMUM, 2 P. M. 63
MINIMUM, 7 A. M. 49

3 a. m....54	Noon 60	8 p. m....56
4 a. m....53	1 p. m....62	9 p. m....56
5 a. m....51	2 p. m....63	Unofficial—
6 a. m....50	3 p. m....62	10 p. m....55
7 a. m....49	4 p. m....61	11 p. m....54
8 a. m....50	5 p. m....60	Midnight ..53
9 a. m....52	6 p. m....58	1 a. m....52
10 a. m....55	7 p. m....57	2 a. m....50
11 a. m....57		

For 24 hours ended 7 p. m., Oct. 25: Mean temperature, 58; normal, 50; excess since Jan. 1, 1,131 degrees; excess since Oct. 1, 142 degrees.

Precipitation, none; excess since Jan. 1, 4.02 inches; excess since Oct. 1, .13 of an inch.

Barometer, 7 a. m., 30.17; 7 p. m., 30.20.

Highest wind velocity, 18 miles an hour from the northwest at 8:48 a. m.

[Official weather table on page 31.]

One Drowned, 2 Rescued in Lake Tragedy

(Picture on back page.)

A drama was enacted on the moonlit waters of the lake within sight of the Carter Harrison crib two miles off the foot of Chicago avenue last night.

It was just after sunset when Arthur Andree, 40 years old, a plumbing contractor of 1112 Holley court, Oak Park, cranked the engine of his home built speed boat, The Skimmer, swept out of the Lincoln park lagoon and set off for an evening spin. Andree could not swim.

With him were Richard Pither, 19 years old, of 719 Ridgeland avenue, Oak Park, and Edwin Slavik, 23 years old, an insurance salesman of 732 South Elmwood avenue, Oak Park. Both were excellent swimmers.

Craft Runs Into Trouble.

The Skimmer was riding the swells about a half mile off the crib when the prow struck a white cap. The engine sputtered and died. The shock had split two seams. The craft began to ship water.

Pither and Slavik quickly donned life belts and assisted Andree to strap one on also. The boat was filling fast when Slavik, a better swimmer than Pither, decided to strike out for the crib. Just then another white cap swamped the craft.

Pither held Andree in his arms while Slavik struck out for help, but incumbered by his belt, he made slow progress. Within twenty minutes he was within hailing distance of the crib and the keeper, Andrew Sloan, heard his calls for help. The cribkeeper searched for the key to the lock which chained his own boat to the crib wharf, but it was lost, so the cribkeeper telephoned the coast guard.

Coast Guard at Scene.

Within ten minutes Acting Capt. Carl Howell and a crew from Central coast guard station were beside the crib. The keeper waved a flare in a wide arc, indicating the spot where the exhausted Slavik was swimming.

"Thank God!" Slavik murmured as they lifted him into the boat.

In the moonlit water a quarter mile away Capt. Howell saw two heads. Andree seemed lifeless as he was lifted into the boat. Pither, who had been supporting him all this time, climbed in.

Blankets and coffee restored Pither and Slavik. A crew of five worked three hours on Andree, but at 9 o'clock he was pronounced dead.

Five minutes later his wife, Marie, mother of his two children, telephoned the coast guard station. "He's gone," Capt. Howell said, and heard a clatter in the telephone, indicating she had collapsed.

FAMOUS OWNER OF WHITE SOX EXPIRES AT 72

End Comes at Eagle River, Wis.

Charles A. Comiskey, president and owner of the Chicago American league baseball club, the White Sox, died at his summer home at Eagle River, Wis., at 1:25 o'clock this morning. He was 72 years old.

Mr. Comiskey died of a heart and kidney complication which had confined him to his home for several weeks. He had been in a coma for twenty-four hours preceding his death and had been in a critical condition for the last month.

His son, Louis Comiskey, treasurer of the White Sox, the only surviving member of his immediate family, was with his father when he died. Dr. Phillip Kreuscher of Chicago, who had been attending Mr. Comiskey, returned to Chicago Saturday after it was apparent that there was no hope of his recovery.

Mr. Comiskey died in his sleep. His son was the only one with him at the time.

His son said the body probably would be brought to Chicago on Wednesday.

Last of Old League Owners.

Mr. Comiskey's death removed from baseball the last survivor of American league club owners who had developed the American league into a major baseball organization and fought through the trying days of the "baseball war" with the National league. Charles Somers of Cleveland, whose financial support made the league expansion possible, still is alive, but has been out of baseball for the last 15 years.

Mr. Comiskey had been the sole owner of the Chicago club from the day of its inception. He was the only man in the history of baseball who had risen from the ranks of the players to ownership of a major league club.

Under his leadership the White Sox developed into the most valuable baseball property in either of the two major leagues. It was estimated that the Comiskey fortune, including his baseball holdings, exceeded $3,000,000.

Retires After 1919 Series.

Comiskey had been retired from active management of his club's affairs since shortly after the world series scandal of 1919. Revelations in September, 1920, that eight of his players were involved in a plot to throw the world series to Cincinnati resulted in the expulsion of the guilty players and wrecked the greatest team Comiskey had ever assembled.

The team had won the pennant in 1917 and beaten the New York Giants of the National league for the world championship, and when Comiskey learned of his players' treachery he insisted that all of them be expelled from organized baseball for all time. After that, although he maintained his deep interest in the club's progress, he seldom appeared at the ball park and left the management of the business affairs to his son, Louis, and other officials of the club.

COMISKEY'S CAREER

Charles A. Comiskey, generally recognized as one of the men who elevated baseball to its present high plane, was born on Chicago's west side, Aug. 15, 1859. His father, John Comiskey, was born in Crosserlough, County Caven, Ireland, and migrated to Chicago, where in the city's most densely populated ward he served 11 years as an alderman.

Comiskey, at the age of 17, accepted

[Continued on page 26, column 3]

Girl Witness Against Mrs. Judd Missing

Phoenix, Ariz., Oct. 25.—[Special.]—Officers here today became alarmed over the apparent disappearance of Lucille Moore, 21 year old nurse, counted on as a key witness in the trunk murder case against Mrs. Winnie Ruth Judd, after she had been threatened over the telephone.

It was Miss Moore who informed officers that Mrs. Judd became furiously jealous when she saw J. H. Halloran, wealthy lumberman, kiss Miss Hedvig Samuelson and Mrs. Anne Le Roi, her friends, and the women Mrs. Judd is accused of slaying.

"We have become alarmed about Miss Moore," John Brinkerhoff, chief district attorney's investigator, declared. "She has not been seen since Thursday, when she voluntarily appeared for questioning and agreed to come again."

Officers said they had learned that some one called Miss Moore over the telephone after she first talked to them and told her to "keep her mouth shut." They expressed doubt that she had left town voluntarily.

WINNIE JUDD TELLS ALL

Los Angeles, Calif., Oct. 25.—[Special.]—Mrs. Winnie Ruth Judd has made a detailed, signed confession of how she murdered Miss Hedvig Samuelson and Mrs. Anne Le Roi in Phoenix, Ariz., Oct. 17, dismembered one of the bodies and then shipped them here in two trunks and a suitcase, it was learned today.

She also has given a detailed account of her movements in Los Angeles during the five days and nights she was sought after attempting to claim the trunks.

These new admissions of Mrs. Judd are contained in a letter which she wrote and signed and turned over to her husband, Dr. W. C. Judd, Santa Monica, who made it public. They supplement those in a letter she previously addressed to her husband and later tore up only to have it discovered in a department store restroom and pieced together by the police.

Ask Extradition Today.

County Prosecutor Lloyd Andrews of Phoenix, in commenting on the two letters, declared he believed he now had sufficient evidence to convict Mrs. Judd of the murders. He said that Gov. James Rolph of California would be asked to honor extradition papers tomorrow.

In her latest version of the murders Mrs. Judd sticks to her self-defense plea, repeats that the quarrel which ended in death for two of her friends was over a woman she mentions as "Miss X," that she slew the women and disposed of their bodies without the aid of an accomplice and then calmly worked the next day as if nothing had occurred and concealed the fact that she had been wounded in the hand.

Without Accomplice, She Says.

"It has been charged that I had an accomplice, either before, during or after the actual tragedy," Mrs. Judd wrote. "This is not true. I alone shot and killed both these women, who were once my friends. I did it in self-defense, and for no other reason.

"I alone disposed of the bodies. I had no help of any kind from any one.

Then Mrs. Judd expresses the fear that she may have given cause for doubting her self defense plea by attempting to conceal her crime.

"In my dazed fright," she wrote, "it seemed to me the only thing to do was to hide—hide everything and myself. I was mistaken, but that is what I did."

Tells How Quarrel Began.

Mrs. Judd wrote that she spent the night preceding the murders with Miss Samuelson and Mrs. Le Roi in their apartment and that the quarrel started the next morning.

At this point she brings in the name of J. H. Halloran, wealthy Phoenix

(Continued on page 10, column 3.)

U. S. WAR DEBT IS PERILED BY LAVAL'S PLAN

Hoover Agrees with French Premier.

The World Situation

WASHINGTON.—The Hoover-Laval conferences conclude with the understanding that revision of war debts and reparations shall go hand in hand. Page 1.

NAPLES.—Mussolini declares for a readjustment of war debts and the right of Germany to resume armament. Page 11.

RIGA.—Russia confronted with crisis following its failure to get further credits abroad. Page 14.

LONDON.—British candidates make their last appeal before general election. Page 14.

BY ARTHUR SEARS HENNING.

[Chicago Tribune Press Service.]

Washington, D. C., Oct. 25.—[Special.]—Commitments of a far reaching character—one of them opening the way to reduction, if not cancellation, of the eleven billions of war debts owed the United States—were made by President Hoover in the historic conversations with Premier Laval of France which were concluded today.

This was learned tonight following the issuance by the White House of the joint statement in which Mr. Hoover and M. Laval set forth the results of their conferences.

The statement, couched in general, frequently vague terms, is freighted with hidden meanings which only the experts in diplomatic esoterics are competent to read between the lines.

Interpretation by Expert.

Resort to such an expert who is conversant with the understandings reached by Mr. Hoover and M. Laval and knows what the veiled statements in the communique are hinting at, produces this intepretation and résumé:

1. Abandoning the policies of his predecessors and his own policy hitherto, President Hoover agrees to the linking of the allied war debts with German reparations and in the event of a reduction of reparations agrees to recommend to congress the reopening of the settlements of war debts owed the United States with a view to their eventual reduction, if not cancellation.

2. The President will make no move for an extension of the Hoover moratorium, which expires June 30, next.

3. The initiative for extension of the moratorium and revision of reparations is to be taken by Germany, which presumably will ask at an early date for the appointment of the commission of experts provided by the Young plan to examine the capacity of Germany to pay the reparations fixed by the Young committee. To this procedure M. Laval agreed.

Divorces Armaments and Debts.

4. The President abandons his project to procure a reduction of armaments as a condition precedent to reduction of war debts and accepts the French thesis that armaments can be reduced only to the extent that nations are assured of security from attack.

5. France and the United States will coöperate to maintain the gold standard and to assist other nations in maintaining or returning to that standard of exchange.

6. The raid by French banks on the gold reserve of the United States in the last six weeks has been halted by M. Laval, who also agreed that in the future there should be no withdrawals of gold from this country except after consultation between the bank of France and the Federal Reserve bank of New York.

Denies Polish Corridor Rumor.

In addition to the communique the White House issued a statement denying a published report that Mr. Hoover had proposed to M. Laval a revision of the Polish corridor provisions of the Versailles treaty.

"The President has made no suggestions of any such character," said the statement.

Although the White House conversations were concluded Friday night and the preparation of the joint statement begun yesterday morning it was not till after 5 o'clock this afternoon that it was distributed to the press.

M. Laval, accompanied by two of his advisers and by Secretary of State Henry L. Stimson, whose guest he had been over night, reached the White House at 10:30 a. m. and went into conference with the President on the phraseology of the communique.

The Frenchman examined and

'JAFSIE' TRAILS MAN WHO GOT $50,000

WEATHER

Fair Tuesday and Wednesday, probably followed by showers Wednesday night; light to moderate winds, mostly north and northeast.

High tide, 2:57 a. m.; 3:44 p. m. Sun rises, 5:15; sets, 8:08.

The American is the only Boston daily paper using Universal Service and International News Service

BOSTON EVENING AMERICAN

A HOME PAPER FOR PEOPLE WHO THINK

THE Peach METROPOLITAN

VOL. 29—No. 56 Published Daily by N. E. Newspaper Pub. Co. Entered as 2d Class Matter at Boston P. O. BOSTON, TUESDAY, MAY 24, 1932 2 CENTS ZONE PRICE 3 CENTS

RUTH TO HEAD NEW RED SOX

Today

The Party Is On
Parched Society Ladies
The Usual Dead Racketeer
Suppression Fails

—By Arthur Brisbane—

THE 1932 POLITICAL party is on.

Governor Roosevelt, who expects to be President, says national income, in the future, must be distributed differently. In good times, it is a big income, about ninety thousand million dollars, of which workers have been getting sixty thousand millions.

Talking in Atlanta to the students and faculty of Oglethorpe University, Governor Roosevelt says a large part of our trouble is due to "selfish and opportunist groups."

President Hoover, opposing great outlays for public works says: "We cannot thus squander ourselves into prosperity."

Norman Thomas, of New York, nominated for President as a Socialist, attacks corruption in both the old parties. Young members of the Socialist party paraded carrying American and red flags, singing the "Internationale."

Radicalism increases with unemployment, but the average American who believes that the red flag means blood, whereas the Socialists say it means brotherhood, still likes to see the Stars and Stripes traveling by itself.

Few agree, yet, that our system of government is permanently a failure.

Enthusiastic American women, called by reporters "society ladies," learn with surprise that Dr. Colvin, of the National Prohibition Committee, describes them as "Bacchantian maidens, parching for wine—wet women, who, like the drunkards whom their program would produce, would take pennies off the eyes of the dead for the sake of legalizing booze."

Some that have studied society women in their lairs report no signs of parching. Any genuine "society woman" has money, and anybody with money, according to reliable witnesses, can get everything from a cocktail on through sherry, hock, champagne, claret, burgundy, port and assorted liqueurs.

The president of Radcliffe College for Women, Ada L. Comstock, who never drinks but opposes prohibition, will be especially interested to learn that she is "parching for wine."

The hope of the thirsty, or "parched," was crushed to earth again yesterday when the House of Representatives, 228 to 169, defeated a proposal to legalize 2.75 per cent beer, with a tax heavy enough to bring in $500,800,000 a year and more.

Not even for $500,000,000 a year would the House abandon its ½ of 1 per cent fortress. It seems clear that the wets can THINK beer, PLAN beer, and LONG FOR beer, but they can not hope to DRINK beer for the present, without violating the law.

The usual dead racketeer incident. This time his name is Leon Goldstein, aged 19, and picked up with a bullet hole back of the ear. According to the police, he was called the "Earbender" because he bragged so much about his crimes and his willingness to murder anybody for $50.

There is nothing new in that boast. When the late New York politician, "Big Tim" Sullivan, desired the Sullivan law that deprives all except criminals of weapons, he said to this writer:

"I could have any man in New York murdered for $50."

In Turkey of late—thanks to world depression and other causes, including offences against religious prejudice, taking the veil from the faces of women, the fez from the heads of men, permitting statues and portraits that Mohammed forbade—suicides have been numerous.

Kemal Pasha's government ordered newspapers to print no suicide news for fear of encouraging the habit, and now Constantinople newspapers are all prosecuted for publishing the suicide of Kreuger, Swedish financier.

Some newspapers and public men in the United States have treated our depression as Turkey treats suicide news, thinking they can cure it by ignoring it. They cannot. Plenty of light, free discussion, ALL THE FACTS are what every situation calls for.

Mrs. Earhart Putnam, who flew across the ocean alone in less than 14 hours, going 2026 miles without a stop, a new record for women, was herself again yesterday buying things to wear in London's West End shops. Everybody praised her, and she took it quietly. Young people who "wish they had a chance," a rich father to buy them an airplane or something of that sort, will notice how Mrs. Earhart Putnam got her start.

She worked for the Telephone Co., saved her money, paid for flying lessons with her savings, broke records, and achieved fame. Nobody handed it to her ready made.

Ernest J. Lengyul, aged 19, wanted to become a flier,

Continued on Page 2, Column 8

SALE OF CLUB REPORTED TO HINGE ON THE BABE

Home Run King in New York Disclaims Knowledge of Impending Deal

By ABE KEMP

San Francisco, May 24 (US) — George Herman "Babe" Ruth will manage the Boston Red Sox of the American League in 1933.

Staid old Back Bay citizens will prick up their ears with interest and New York officials and constituents will lift their voices in fervid denials.

But nonetheless the information reaching here comes from an unimpeachable source.

The opening blast in the "Ruth for Manager" campaign will be fired shortly, if a deal now in the formative stage for the sale of the Boston franchise and holding is completed.

Interested parties, it is said, are agreeable only on the condition that Ruth can be obtained as their field leader, and have been given to understand that their man will be available next year.

"News to Me," Says Babe in New York

New York, May 24 (US)—Babe Ruth said last night that he knew nothing of a report from San Francisco that he might manage the Boston Red Sox in 1933.

"I am still the property of the Yankees," Babe said, and any rumor that there is to be any change in my status is certainly news to me."

Quinn Not Available for Comment on Story

President Bob Quinn of the Red Sox being out of town it was impossible early today to get a confirmation or denial from the Fenway prexy of the report from the Pacific Coast that Babe Ruth would manage the local American League entry next season.

John "Shono" Collins, who arrived home with the Red Sox this morning, says he knows nothing about the reported sale of the Red Sox.

"You'll have to ask Bob Quinn," said Collins, "I'm only the manager of the club."

JOS. M. CURLEY DIES IN CHELSEA

Joseph M. Curley, clerk of the Chelsea court 43 years, and the oldest clerk in point of service in the State, died today at his home, 147 Garfield ave., Chelsea, aged 56, after a short illness.

Mr. Curley, a long-time resident of Chelsea, was appointed in 1892 by Governor Russell. In 1889 he was admitted to the bar and practiced law thereafter, in addition to his court duties, specializing on probate matters.

He was past exalted ruler of the Elks and a member of the Ancient and Honorable Artillery Company and a trustee and director of Chelsea banks. He never married, and his brother, last surviving relative, was killed in a street car accident six months ago. Funeral arrangements will be announced later.

He's Coming Back Home Again

George Herman Ruth, world's slugging king and the highest salaried ball player of all time, is slated to manage the Red Sox in 1933, according to an accredited dispatch from San Francisco. Sale of the club is said to hinge on Ruth as manager.

Here's Dope on the Braves

The Braves are in first place in the National League and Boston is baseball mad as the seventh week of the season opens today.

Manager Bill McKechnie's fighting Warriors took the lead in the race by scoring a 5 to 4 victory after an uphill battle of 10 innings in the opener of a three-game series with the Brooklyn Dodgers at the Wigwam, while the Cubs were idle.

The Tribe meets the Dodgers again this afternoon, and the Chicago entry faces the world's champion Cardinals in St. Louis.

The Braves must win to be sure of retaining their lead. If they lose and the Hornsbymen whip the Cards, they'll drop back into second place, a game behind the top.

If the Braves win and the Cubs lose the standing will be:

	W.	L.	P. C.
Boston	22	11	.667
Chicago	22	13	.629

If the Braves lose and the Cubs win the standing will be:

	W.	L.	P. C.
Chicago	23	12	.657
Boston	21	12	.636

If the Braves lose and the Cubs don't play or the Cubs win and the Braves don't play the Chicagoans will regain the lead.

If both win or both lose, the Braves will stay on the top, of course.

Today's Lineup

BROOKLYN	BRAVES
Frederick, c.f	Knothe, 3b.
O'Doul, l.f.	Urbanski, s.s.
Stripp, 3b.	Berger, c.f.
Wilson, r.f.	Worthington, l.f.
Cucinello, 2b.	Schulmerich, r.f.
Wright, s.s.	Shires, 1b.
Lopez, c.	Maranville, 2b.
Kelly, 1b.	Hargrave, c.
Vance, p	Zachary, p.

Opening hour on New York Stock Market will be found on Page 2.

Fate of Two in Killing Nears Jury

WEBBER PLEA FOR SNYDER IS BEGUN

Counsel for Kiley Defendant Appeals to Save Client From the Chair

Final arguments in the Kiley murder case got under way in Middlesex Superior court today, with Atty. Abraham C. Webber pleading for the life of Herman "Red" Snyder.

Court opened an hour early in order that the case against Snyder and his co-defendant, John A. Donnellon, accused of the slaying of James M. Kiley, Somerville filling station manager, might go to the jury today.

Following the opening of court there was a short conference at the bench between Judge Hammond and counsel. Atty. Webber then began his argument.

NEGLECTED IN YOUTH

He traced the childhood of Snyder, characterizing him as a youth who was neglected in early youth by a father not mentally capable of taking care of the boy.

In the course of his argument Atty. Webber told the jury his client was not the man who killed Kiley, and that he did not have in his possession the automatic pistol which was the murder weapon.

Trial of the "scientifically solved" murder case was concluded before Judge Hammond and the jury late yesterday, after Dr. Kenneth Tillotson, an alienist, testified that in his opinion Snyder was sane and knew the difference between right and wrong.

ARGUMENTS BEGIN

Atty. Webber will be followed by Judge W. H. McDonnell, counsel for Donnellon. Asst. Dist.-Atty. Frank G. Volpe, at the conclusion of Judge McDonnell's argument, will argue for the government.

BALANCES AND RECEIPTS

Washington, May 24—Today's Treasury balance, $457,589,304. U. S. customs receipts, $12,633,381.

This Nation Needs A Prosperity Loan

—By MERRYLE STANLEY RUKEYSER—

ECONOMIC realities are no respecters of political parties or of state boundary lines.

As aggregate national, state and local public works have been declining in 1932, general business and opportunities for employment in the United States have further shrunken.

Small wonder that public men and business executives have increasingly come to a realization of the need for dealing fundamentally with the economic crisis!

* * *

ALMOST a year ago, William Randolph Hearst stressed the need of a vast prosperity loan of $5,000,000,000 for the acceleration of job creating public works. He envisaged the bond issue as a means of re-employment of the idle and as an instrument for social reconstruction.

Mr. Hearst's recommendation was consonant with the proposal of scientific economists that public works, regarded as an economic stabilizer, should be expanded in times of subnormal business and retarded in periods of boom.

The general scheme has been subsequently endorsed in a joint memorandum by 46 eminent economists, members of the faculty of the principal learned institutions in the United States.

Of late, additional leaders in and out of Congress have expressed a desire to translate the plan into workable legislation, but there has been some disposition to deal with an economic emergency in a temporizing spirit of compromise.

The Hearst newspapers warn that economic facts do not change in accordance with political expediency.

* * *

BUSINESS and employment are distinctly more subnormal than a year ago and the need is for a robust stimulant.

Congress should not be turned from a $5,000,000,000 bond issue by proposals of half measures.

The actual sale of bonds within any given period can be limited to actual need for funds to carry along work, and the emergency program can be tapered off providing business and employment return to normal while the projects are under way.

No mere tinkering with symptoms can meet the situation.

There can be no effective substitute for jobs for millions who are able and willing to perform useful work.

Before adjournment, Congress should adopt a prosperity loan as a constructive, effective means of reversing the economic trend, and restoring happier conditions.

The Problem

21 MANUFACTURING establishments, employing 500 persons, were opened in Greater Boston last month. Many others are ready to start, but how can people out of work buy their products?

The Remedy

A $5,000,000,000 bond issue by the United States to build great public works, employ several million men and start the nation back to prosperity.

WOMAN DIES IN 20-STORY FALL

New York, May 24 (AP)—Miss Helen Slater, 55, of Providence, R. I., fell to her death today from a window of her room on the 23rd floor of the Hotel Lincoln, Eighth ave. and 44th st.

The body landed on the roof of a three-story extension in the rear of the hotel. Police said she lost her balance when she went to a window to get a breath of fresh air.

Miss Slater, suffering from asthma and high blood pressure, came to New York last Saturday with a friend, Miss Jennie B. Green, of Providence, to consult a specialist.

Prince Not to Be Duke

London, May 24 (AP)—It was officially denied today that Prince George would be created Duke of Edinburgh on his 30th birthday Dec. 20, as published yesterday.

KILLING FROST IN MIDDLESEX

A killing white frost settled on Middlesex County early today, on the coldest May 24 in that section in ten years.

With Concord recording an official minimum of 29.8, and Lexington reporting an unofficial figure of 28, asparagus was frozen, corn and beans blighted and strawberry blossoms withered. Fruit trees are believed to have escaped.

One farmer reported the freezing of water in a hose left out all night and whitef rost was common on ground and roofs.

The weather man explained this condition by saying that loss of wind and radiation caused a drop in temperatures in the low places. Officially, he said, the temperature in Boston was only half a degree lower than yesterday.

'JAFSIE' WAITS WORD FROM SWINDLER

Lindbergh Negotiator in Becket, Hoping to Hear From Man He Paid $50,000

BULLETIN

North Adams, May 23 (INS)—Two New Jersey automobiles carrying men who said they were New Jersey detectives passed through here today attempting to pick up the trail of Dr. John F. Condon, who came to Becket late last evening with his friend, Walter Goodwin, of New York.

Becket, May 24—Dr. John F. "Jafsie" Condon apparently was still awaiting today the mysterious message which he said yesterday would guide his future movements.

He was still in the summer cottage of Walter Goodwin of the Bronx, New York, where with Goodwin he arrived at midday yesterday.

Dr. Condon and Goodwin arrived here after an automobile trip from his home. A large German police dog accompanied them.

The two immediately went into seclusion in Goodwin's camp.

"Jafsie" intimated that his trip to Massachusetts was made as the result of statements made last week before a grand jury, before which he appeared to give his experiences as a negotiator in the Lindbergh case. He declined to discuss the nature of the statements.

"Jafsie" sidestepped answering directly questions as to whether he came to Becket in the hope of receiving a communication from "John," the Scandinavian to whom he paid the ransom money in a New York cemetery.

His only answer was: "I certainly hope that I receiev another message from 'John.'"

He revealed that the last time he heard from "John" was on May 10, two days before the body of the Lindbergh baby was found.

Curtis, Fearing 'Vengeance of Gang,' Will Plead Guilty

Trenton, N. J., May 24 (INS)—John Hughes Curtis, Norfolk ship builder, who hoaxed Col. Lindbergh, will enter a plea of "guilty" when he is taken into court to answer for the amazing series of lies which made Col. Lindbergh and the Coast Guard spend futile weeks chasing phantom ships manned by phantom crews.

Curtis will be tried for "giving false information and obstructing justice" and Edward C. Pender, his attorney, revealed today that rathed than go through a trial Curtis will throw himself on the mercy of the court.

Pender is willing to accept a sentence of a year in jail for his client in return for the guilty plea. The maximum term is three years.

Pender said that one of the reasons why Curtis was not adverse to going to jail was because he feared underworld vengeance. Pen-

Continued on Page 2, Column 2

In Today's American

Gehrig Ties All-Time Record With Four Straight Home Runs as Yankees Win

EQUALS TWO MARKS IN 20 TO 13 VICTORY

Lou Ties Record of Four Circuit Drives in One Game as the Athletics Are Beaten.

DUPLICATES LOWE'S FEAT

He Connects in First Four Times at Bat and Nearly Makes Fifth in Ninth.

RUTH PRODUCES HIS 15TH

Total Base Marks Fall, With 50 for Yanks, 77 for Both Clubs—Victors Tie Team Homer Record.

By WILLIAM E. BRANDT.

Special to THE NEW YORK TIMES.

PHILADELPHIA, June 3.—Henry Louis Gehrig's name today took rank in baseball's archives along with Bobby Lowe and Ed Delehanty, the only other sluggers who, in more than half a century of recorded diamond battles, ever hit four home runs in one major league game.

Largely because of Gehrig's quartet of tremendous smashes the Yankees outstripped the Athletics in a run-making marathon, winning, 20 to 13, after twice losing the lead because of determined rallies by the American League champions.

Homers by Combs, Lazzeri and Ruth, the latter the Babe's fifteenth of the season, enabled the Yankees to tie the all-time record of seven homers by one club in one game, performed three times before 1900, by Detroit, New York and Pittsburgh, of the old National League, and once in modern times, by the Athletics on June 3, 1921.

Yankees Set Team Mark.

The Yanks, with their twenty-three hits, also set a new modern club-batting record for total bases, with fifty, which eclipsed the previous modern major league mark of forty-six and the American League's best total of forty-four. This achievement fell short by only five bases of the all-time record, set by Cincinnati in 1923. Both clubs' total of seventy-seven bases also set an American League mark.

Gehrig in his first four times at bat hammered the ball outside the playing area. In the first and fifth innings he sailed balls into the stands in left centre. In the fourth and seventh he fired over the right-field wall.

Saltzgaver was on base when Lou connected in the first inning, but the other three came with the bases empty. His fifth-inning homer, which made him the first man in baseball history ever to hit three homers in one game for the fourth time, came after Combs and Ruth had reached Earnshaw for drives over the right-field wall.

Lazzeri Clears Bases.

Lazzeri's drive into the left-field stands in the ninth, the last Yankee homer, came with the bases filled. In Philadelphia's half of the ninth Jimmy Foxx, the major league leader, sent his nineteenth homer of the year shooting into the left-field stands.

Cochrane had driven the ball over the right-field wall in the first inning, but the collective homer total, nine, fell one short of the major league record for both teams in a game.

The outcome of the game evened the series, two to two, but the crowd of 5,000 seemed to concentrate on encouraging Gehrig to hit a fifth homer and thus surpass a brilliant record in baseball's books.

Lou had two chances. He grounded out in the eighth, but in the ninth he pointed a terrific drive which Simmons captured only a few steps from the furthest corner of the park. A little variance to either side of its actual line of flight would have sent the ball over the fence or into the stands.

One Base Under Record.

As it was, Lou's four homers tied the all-time record of Lowe in hitting for the circuit in four successive times at bat in 1894. Only three of Delehanty's were in successive times at bat. Both Lowe and Delehanty had a single in the same game with their four homers, so that Gehrig fell one short of tying their record for total bases.

Gehrig's four made his season's total eleven, six of which have been hit against Philadelphia, four off Earnshaw and two off Mahaffey.

The defeat of the Mackmen, coupled with the Indians' double victory, dropped the Athletics to fifth place, Cleveland supplanting them in fourth.

Lazzeri's homer with the bases filled was his fifth hit of the game. He and Gehrig each drove in six runs.

The box score:

NEW YORK (A.)	ab.	r.	h.	po.	a.	e.
Combs, cf	5	2	3	3	0	0
Saltzg'er, 2b	4	1	1	3	2	0
Ruth, lf	5	2	2	3	0	1
Hoag, lf	0	1	0	1	0	0
Gehrig, 1b	6	4	4	7	0	1
Chapman, rf	5	3	2	4	0	0
Dickey, c	4	2	2	5	0	0
Lazzeri, 3b	6	3	5	0	1	0
Crosetti, ss	6	1	2	0	5	2
Allen, p	2	0	0	1	0	1
Rhodes, p	1	0	1	0	0	0
Brown, p	1	0	0	0	1	0
Gomez, p	1	1	1	0	0	0
Total	46	20	23	27	9	5

PHILADELPHIA (A.)	ab.	r.	h.	po.	a.	e.
Bishop, 2b	4	2	2	3	2	0
Cramer, cf	5	1	1	1	0	0
aRoettger	1	0	0	0	0	0
Miller, lf	0	0	0	0	0	0
Cochrane, c	5	1	1	10	2	0
bWilliams	1	0	0	0	0	0
Sim'ns, lf.cf	4	2	0	2	0	0
Foxx, 1b	3	3	2	8	0	0
Coleman, rf	6	2	2	2	1	0
McNair, ss	5	1	3	1	2	0
Dykes, 3b	4	1	1	0	1	0
Earnshaw, p	2	0	0	0	2	1
cHaas	1	0	1	0	0	0
Mahaffey, p	0	0	0	0	0	0
Walberg, p	0	0	0	0	0	0
Krausse, p	0	0	0	0	0	0
dMadjeski	1	0	0	0	0	0
Rommel, p	0	0	0	0	1	0
Total	42	13	13	27	11	1

aBatted for Cramer in eighth.
bBatted for Cochrane in ninth.
cBatted for Earnshaw in fifth.
dBatted for Krausse in eighth.

New York	2 0 0	2 3 2	3 2 6	—20
Philadelphia	2 0 0	6 0 2	0 2 1	—13

Runs batted in—Gehrig 6, Combs, Ruth, Corsetti 2, Saltzgaver, Lazzeri 6, Chapman, Dickey, Cochrane 2, Cramer 3, Coleman 3, Foxx, McNair 2.

Two-base hits—Lazzeri, McNair, Ruth, Coleman. Three-base hits—Bishop, Cramer, Chapman, Lazzeri, Foxx. Home runs—Gehrig 4, Cochrane, Combs, Ruth, Lazzeri, Foxx. Stolen base—Lazzeri. Sacrifices—Bishop, Saltzgaver. Double plays—Cochrane and McNair; Bishop and Foxx; Coleman and Cochrane. Left on bases—New York 6, Philadelphia 11. Bases on balls—Off Allen 5, Rhodes 2, Brown 1, Earnshaw 2, Walberg 1, Rommel 3. Struck out—By Allen 2, Gomez 1, Earnshaw 8, Walberg 1. Hits—Off Allen 7 in 3 2-3 innings, Rhodes 1 in 1 1-3, Brown 3 in 2, Gomez 2 in 2, Earnshaw 8 in 5, Mahaffey 6 in 1 (none out in seventh), Walberg 2 in 1, Krausse 4 in 1, Rommel 3 in 1. Wild pitch—Rhodes. Winning pitcher—Brown. Losing pitcher—Mahaffey. Umpires—Geisel, McGowan and Van Graflan. Time of game—2:55.

How Leading Batsmen Stand For Honors in Major Leagues

NATIONAL LEAGUE.

	G.	A.B.	R.	H.	PC.
P. Waner, Pittsburgh	42	172	32	69	.401
Lombardi, Cincinnati	29	106	16	41	.387
Hafey, Cincinnati	37	142	24	51	.359
Hurst, Philadelphia	45	179	33	64	.358
Ott, New York	40	149	31	53	.356

Leader a year ago—Hendrick, Cincinnati, .386.

AMERICAN LEAGUE.

	G.	A.B.	R.	H.	PC.
Foxx, Philadelphia	45	164	50	68	.415
Dickey, New York	40	157	29	58	.369
Lazzeri, New York	37	126	23	45	.357
Combs, New York	37	132	31	47	.356
Walker, Detroit	33	119	19	41	.345

Leader a year ago—Cochrane, Philadelphia, .400.

CAREER OF TERRY BEGAN IN GEORGIA

New Pilot Quit Professional Game at 19, but Returned at Urging of McGraw.

JOINED GIANTS IN 1923

Soon Displaced Kelly as First Baseman, Then Blossomed Into One of Game's Best Hitters.

Bill Terry in succeeding John McGraw as manager of the Giants replaces the man who brought him back into professional baseball after Terry had definitely quit at the age of 19.

McGraw saw Terry playing independent baseball in Memphis in 1921, had a talk with him and signed him to a contract before leaving the city. Three years later the young fellow who had decided against a baseball career on the earnest advice of his wife replaced George Kelly as the Giants' first baseman. Last year Memphis Bill was rated by many of the keenest observers of baseball as a better first baseman than Hal Chase.

Terry was born in Atlanta, Ga., Oct. 30, 1898, and became a sandlotter along with dozens of other youngsters. At 16 he was with the Atlanta club of the Southern League and Thomasville of the Georgia State League, and in 1915 was back with Atlanta, but no record of his performance is found in the record books.

Worked as Pitcher.

Later in 1915 he was a pitcher with the Newman club of the Georgia-Alabama circuit and appeared in eight games, but again the statistics are unavailable. He was still a southpaw pitcher when he joined the Shreveport club of the Texas League in 1916, but in the following year was playing the double rôle of pitcher and outfielder. His batting average then give little indication of what he was to do in the future, as he hit only .231.

But in 1922, after his all-important meeting with McGraw, he pitched and played first base for the Toledo club of the American Association and his bat began to speak with authority. In the two seasons he spent there his batting marks were .336 and .377. He ceased to be a pitcher in 1923.

Terry joined the Giants late in 1923, but appeared in only three games and came to bat only seven times, getting one hit. The following year he displaced Kelly, played in seventy-seven games and compiled an average of .239. Since then he has hit under .300 only once. That was in 1926, when he played in only ninety-eight games and performed part of his duties as an outfielder. His mark then was .289.

Batting Power Increases.

From then on his batting power and his ability as a first sacker increased steadily, until in 1930 he reached the zenith of his power by batting .401 and playing in every game of the season. Last year, with the advent of the less lively ball, his batting mark was .349, but he still has a nine-year major league mark of .342.

All ball players like Terry and all of them respect him. His announced intention of lifting some of the strict discipline that Giant players have been governed by will not change the attitude of the players toward keeping in condition.

Home-Run Hitters.

Yesterday's Homers.

Gehrig, New York Americans	4
Ruth, New York Americans	1
Lazzeri, New York Americans	1
Combs, New York Americans	1
Wilson, Brooklyn	1
Foxx, Philadelphia Americans	1
Cochrane, Philadelphia Americans	1
Goslin, St. Louis Americans	1
Campbell, St. Louis Americans	1
Ferrell, Cleveland	1
Jurges, Chicago Nationals	1
Piet, Pittsburgh	1

The Leaders.

AMERICAN LEAGUE.

Foxx, Philadelphia	19	Averill, Cleveland	9
Ruth, New York	15	Manush, Wash	8
Gehrig, New York	11	Gehringer, Detroit	8
Cochrane, Phila	10	Jolley, Boston	7
Simmons, Phila	9	Dickey, New York	6

NATIONAL LEAGUE.

Klein, Philadelphia	13	Hurst, Philadelphia	6
Collins, St. Louis	12	Lee, Philadelphia	6
Terry, New York	11	Wright, Brooklyn	5
Wilson, Brooklyn	8	Frederick, Brooklyn	5
Schulmerich, Boston	7	Moore, Chicago	5
Ott, New York	6	Worthington, Bos	5

League Totals.

American League	207
National League	162
Total	369

RECORD OF M'GRAW BRILLIANT IN SPORT

His Feat of Leading a Team to Four Pennants in a Row Is Still Unparalleled.

DEVELOPED STARS OF OLD

Mathewson, Bresnahan, McGinnity Among Them—Won Renown as Player With Famous Orioles.

By JOHN DREBINGER.

To baseball men, particularly those of the old school, John McGraw's retirement came as a stunning surprise, for while it may have been accepted that sooner or later the venerable, white-haired leader, who was 59 years old on April 7 last, would retire, it seemed difficult to believe that the man whose name has been synonymous with baseball in New York for more than a quarter of a century had finally stepped down from active leadership.

Curiously enough, McGraw's withdrawal, coming some six weeks short of thirty years from the day he first entered New York, finds the Giants in exactly the same position in which he found them, although in that long stretch he won more National League pennants than any other manager—ten in all—and became one of the most commanding and picturesque figures in the game.

It was on July 19, 1902, that McGraw, then a rather stocky, black-haired little fellow of 29, came to New York to manage the Giants, owned at the time by the late Andrew Freedman and hailed everywhere as the last-place joke of the National League.

A Member of Famous Team.

McGraw already had gained wide fame as a player and manager of the famous old Orioles, whose achievements in the days of McGraw, Wilbert Robinson and the late Hughey Jennings have become legends of the pioneer days of professional baseball. Born in Truxton, N. Y., Auril 7, 1873, McGraw made his way along the rocky trail that leads from the sand lots and was only 17 when he proudly signed his first contract with the Olean (N. Y.) club of the original New York-Pennsylvania League.

With the Baltimore Orioles McGraw became one of the greatest third basemen in the game, a powerful hitter despite a slender build, and in 1899 was appointed manager. But at the close of that year he, along with Robinson, was sold to the St. Louis National League Club.

Neither, however, relished playing in St. Louis and with that characteristic decisiveness that was later to win him national fame as a dynamic leader, McGraw, with the faithful Uncle Robbie at his heels, turned his back on the Mound City, and as they crossed the Mississippi both threw their suitcases, containing their St. Louis uniforms, overboard.

Get Baltimore Franchise.

The two then took over the Baltimore franchise in the newly organized American League. But McGraw's association with that circuit was shortlived, for, with the breaking out of a bitter war between the two major league circuits, McGraw became involved in an even more bitter controversy with Ban Johnson, founder and president of the American League, and it was as the result of this break that he came to New York, at Friedman's invitation, to manage the Giants in 1902.

The Giants at the time were in a hopelessly chaotic state. Several régimes had sought to lift the team out of the cellar without success and the patronage was in keeping with the club's ill fortunes. A tall fellow was striving to play first base. Later he became the immortal Christy Mathewson, regarded not only by McGraw, but others as well, as the greatest pitcher of all time.

By September of that first year practically every youngster on the sidewalks of New York was singing the name of John McGraw, the fiery little fellow who would jump out of his shoes at an instant's notice to protest an umpire's decision. Inside of a fortnight he had reduced the roster of the Giants from twenty-four to fourteen and when President Friedman remonstrated that he "was ruining the club," McGraw replied: "Impossible, we can finish in last place with fourteen men as easily as with four times that number."

New Team Takes Field.

The following year practically a brand new team took the field to represent the Giants. McGraw had brought Roger Bresnahan, Joe McGinnity and Dan McGann with him from the Orioles. He signed Arthur Devlin to play third base and Billy Gilbert to play second. Mathewson developed into a marvelous pitcher and then followed an unbroken string of twenty-nine years during which fortune poured into the coffers of the club until it became one of the wealthiest organizations in baseball.

In 1903 the Giants finished second and crowds jammed the Polo Grounds. The following year McGraw won his first National League pennant, repeated in 1905 and that year also engaged in the first world's series under modern rules. The Giants beat the Athletics, 4 games to 1.

No pennants came to the Giants for the next five years although McGraw's team was always in the thick of the fight, once losing on a technicality on the famous "Merkle failing to touch second" decision in 1908, while his battles with the Chicago Cubs, under the leadership of Frank Chance, contributed some of the most brilliant pages to the intensive struggles fought on the American diamond.

Club Back in the Van.

In 1911 McGraw and his Giants were back on top once more and this time they captured three straight pennants, although each year they went down to defeat in the world's series, in 1911 and 1913 to the Athletics and in 1912 the Red Sox captured the deciding game with the aid of the unfortunate "Snodgrass muff" after the Giants seemingly had the game in hand.

It was stirring episodes such as this which turned McGraw's black hair to gray and then to a snowy white, but with each reversal he came back to fight harder, and in 1917 he won another pennant, though this time he again lost a world's series. Then in 1921 he molded another famous machine which set a record that still stands unparalleled, the winning of four pennants in a row. World's series honors also came to the Giants in 1921 and 1922 when they beat the Yankees, but they lost to the Yanks in 1923 and to the Washington Senators in 1924.

That year marked McGraw's last pennant winner, though since then he always had a strong contending team in the race, twice losing after tense struggles that kept the issue in doubt until the closing week, once in 1927 and again in 1930.

As a diamond tactician and picturesque figure, McGraw probably won as much fame as through the actual results of his achievements. Many of the present rules, notably the foul-strike rule, were introduced as a curb on his ingenious tactics.

In fact, two years ago at San Antonio, McGraw, portly and white-haired, amazed a gathering of baseball writers by stepping up to the plate during batting practice and fouling off twenty-six consecutive pitches. It was because he had attained such proficiency at this in his playing days, the aim being to tire the pitcher, that the rulemakers decided to call a foul a strike up to two strikes, there having been no penalty for a foul prior to that.

It was as a developer of young players, however, that he displayed some of the most uncanny skill, and while it is true that on occasion he spent huge sums for players, some of whom he had cast adrift earlier in their career, there is little doubt he has brought forth more star youngsters than any manager in the game.

He was among the first to invade the ranks of the collegians, his success with Matty being among the first of these, and years later he lifted Frankie Frisch right out of Fordham to become one of the game's greatest second basemen.

Of his present team, practically every one of his regulars, with the exception of Critz and Hogan, whom he obtained after only one season in the majors, gained stardom entirely under McGraw's tutelage. Most prominent of these are Terry, who now succeeds him as manager; Freddy Lindstrom, Travis Jackson, Johnny Vergez and Melvin Ott, whom he signed at the age of 16 and never allowed to pass out from under his wing.

Favored Foreign Tours.

An extensive traveler and one of baseball's greatest missionaries were two more rôles that gained world-wide fame for McGraw. In 1913, after the close of the world's series between the Giants and Athletics, McGraw joined forces with Charles Comiskey, owner of the White Sox, and made a tour of the world with the Giants and Sox. The teams left San Francisco and terminated their tour in New York, visiting en route Australia, Japan, China, Egypt, Italy, France and England.

At the close of the 1924 season McGraw and Comiskey set out again with two teams, visiting England and France, and in 1929 planned to make a two-week exhibition tour of Mexico during the training season, but internal trouble in that country at the time caused him to abandon the plan. He compromised by playing a game right on the border in Laredo.

Whether McGraw has reaped the financial harvest that one might expect from his long and brilliant record is problematical. He has been known as a lavish spender and liberal to a fault with old ball players, fighters, jockeys and, in fact, all sorts of sporting men who had fallen on less prosperous days.

It is generally understood that his generosities and a few unhappy investments served to cut into his finances, though since 1919, when, with the aid of former Magistrate Francis X. McQuade, he induced Stoneham to purchase the club, he has always drawn a large salary in the dual rôle of manager and vice president.

He also was a liberal contributor to the literature of baseball, both in magazine and newspaper stories, but beyond this he rarely sought to make money outside of his direct duties with baseball.

RETIRING MANAGER AND NEW LEADER OF THE GIANTS.

Associated Press Photo.
John McGraw.

Times Wide World Photo.
Bill Terry.

M'GRAW, ILL, RESIGNS AS GIANTS' MANAGER

Continued from Page One.

charge and control of the team and will have to assume entire responsibility therefor.

"I do not intend to retire from baseball, but will continue with the Giants, not only retaining my same stock holdings but also as vice president and as general adviser and counselor in business as well as baseball matters.

"I am turning over a good team to Terry, who I believe will capably handle it.

"If at any time he wants my help, he has but to call for it. I shall be on hand at all times when needed, my health permitting.

"During my thirty years with the Giants the fans have been extremely loyal to me, for which they have my heartfelt thanks, and hope they will give Terry the same loyalty and support."

Team Congratulates Terry.

Terry, both at the clubhouse and later at his apartment, modestly accepted the congratulations of his team-mates, and as he stroked his jet-black hair he laughingly expressed the hope that it would not turn prematurely gray, a fate that usually befalls the lot of nearly all baseball managers.

"This is indeed a tremendous surprise for me," said Terry, who only three months ago became embroiled in a bitter salary dispute with his club owners, "but I intend to knuckle down to the job with everything I've got.

"I want to say that I more than appreciate the confidence that both Mr. Stoneham and Mr. McGraw have placed in me and I will do my utmost to make good. I am still as confident as ever that we have a strong team which has got off badly because of some very bad breaks, and I feel certain we are due to start climbing without further delay."

Later in the day Terry admitted he first had been approached by McGraw with the proposal to take over the team on Thursday, adding that "when I agreed and he decided to resign he looked like a man who had had a forty-pound weight lifted from his head."

Terry to Lessen Discipline.

Terry further revealed that he had certain changes in mind and that for one thing there would be a decided lessening in the strict requirements of discipline that had been in vogue during the long régime of McGraw.

"I have already talked to the players," said Terry, "and they know I am the boss. But I am going to let them relax a bit and see what they can do toward getting us out of last place. They won't have to report to the park at 10 o'clock in the morning nor get to bed at any certain hour. All I'm going to ask is that they play good ball and if they don't do that for me they're out."

Whether Terry is to receive any additional remuneration for taking over the added duties now imposed upon him was not disclosed either by President Stoneham, who declined to make any comment whatever, or by Terry himself, but the assumption is that the star first baseman very likely will receive a bonus at the end of the season, especially if he succeeds in inspiring the team to run a strong race.

For the season of 1931, following his achievement in winning the National League batting championship in 1930, Terry was understood to have received $23,000, but this Spring was asked to take a 40 per cent decrease.

Sharp Exchange of Words.

At this he rebelled, the incident at the time producing a sharp exchange of words between the star player and President Stoneham, Terry asking that he be traded to another club and Stoneham insisting that Terry would have to sign with the Giants or quit baseball.

With the training season on and McGraw acting as intermediary at a conference at New Orleans, Terry came to terms at a figure believed to be either $18,000 or $20,000.

There was considerable speculation as to whether McGraw's resignation was partly prompted by the team's poor showing since the start of this season. Its lowly position in the race is considered to have played no small part in the small attendances at the Polo Grounds.

That this hastened McGraw's decision is believed to be the case, inasmuch as the veteran pilot's ill health was making it increasingly difficult to operate his team at a time when it was dropping steadily into last place, the position it now occupies, although McGraw strove to keep in touch with his first lieutenant, Dave Bancroft.

Just why Bancroft, who has been head coach of the team for the past three seasons and commanded it on the field whenever McGraw absented himself, was not named manager also occasioned surprise, but drew no explanation from any one connected with the club.

That the start of the present season with a team that had been freely predicted to run a powerful race floundering in the second division, has been a bitter disappointment to McGraw was well known to those close to the leader whose name has been a household word wherever baseball was discussed, who has won more pennants than any other manager, whose Giant teams from 1903 have finished out of the first division only twice and whose activities as a strategist had caused him to be styled baseball's foremost "master mind" many years ago.

Forced Off the Bench.

This Spring, training his team in California, McGraw appeared confident of producing another winner, and this opinion was shared almost universally by critics, but for some inexplicable reason the team got away badly, and then a recurrence of a sinus ailment which had troubled him for several years forced McGraw off the bench.

He accompanied his team on its recent Western trip last month, but after directing the game against the Cubs in Chicago on May 10 had to remain confined in his hotel room in Pittsburgh and Cincinnati except to show a flash of all his old-time fighting spirit when he drove out to the park in Cincinnati to give Umpire Klem a piece of his mind for forcing the Giants to play through a downpour the previous day.

Whether McGraw, upon recovering his health, plans to return to active command again, maybe next Spring, was a matter on which baseball men last night appeared undecided, although those regarded closest to the veteran pilot were of the opinion that his retirement, so far as active leadership was concerned, would remain permanent.

It was cited that several times in recent years McGraw intimated a desire to retire from the taxing rigors of directing a team from the bench. He did this, in fact, so broadly in 1927 that Rogers Hornsby, acquired that Spring, was frequently mentioned as his successor and McGraw himself spoke favorably of the move. But Hornsby was traded to Boston that Winter, leaving McGraw more firmly held to his post.

The following year Stoneham announced that McGraw had signed a five-year contract, still operative, and while the salary was not mentioned it was understood to be the highest ever paid a baseball manager, estimated to be about $75,000 a year.

McGraw's Record With Giants.

NATIONAL LEAGUE RECORD.

Year.	Finished.	Year.	Finished.
1903	Second.	1918	Second.
1904	First.	1919	Second.
1905	First.	1920	Second.
1906	Second.	1921	First.
1907	Fourth.	1922	First.
1908	Second.	1923	First.
1909	Third.	1924	First.
1910	Second.	1925	Second.
1911	First.	1926	Fifth.
1912	First.	1927	Third.
1913	First.	1928	Second.
1914	Second.	1929	Third.
1915	Eighth.	1930	Third.
1916	Fourth.	1931	Second.
1917	First.		

WORLD'S SERIES RECORD.

1904—No series.
1905—Won from Athletics, 4 to 1.
1911—Lost to Athletics, 4 to 2.
1912—Lost to Red Sox, 4 to 3 (one tie).
1913—Lost to Athletics, 4 to 1.
1917—Lost to White Sox, 4 to 2.
1921—Won from Yankees, 5 to 3.
1922—Won from Yankees, 4 to 0 (one tie).
1923—Lost to Yankees, 4 to 2.
1924—Lost to Senators, 4 to 3.

Mrs. Terry, in Memphis, Is Overjoyed by News; Knows Husband Will Make Good as Manager

By The Associated Press.

MEMPHIS, Tenn., June 3.—Mrs. Bill Terry was a very, very proud young woman today when she heard of her husband's appointment as manager of the New York Giants.

"I am so glad," she said. "I know Bill will make good. I only hope that the responsibilities of his new position will not make him overtax his strength. He puts his whole soul into everything that he undertakes."

As she talked she busied herself with her packing. She and their three children are leaving tomorrow to join Terry in New York.

As much as Bill likes baseball—his wife describes him as "100 per cent baseball"—he is more devoted to his family. In fact, at Mrs. Terry's request, he gave up his baseball career and remained out of the game. It took John McGraw himself, to make him—and Mrs. Terry—give in.

He started playing baseball in Georgia, in Atlanta and at Newnan. Mrs. Terry—then Elvina Sneed—was attending a finishing school there. He was present when she received her diploma.

Not long afterward, in 1916, they were married in Memphis, where Miss Sneed made her home. That same year Terry played with the Shreveport club of the Texas League. He played again the next year, but at the end of the 1917 season Mrs. Terry persuaded him to quit and come to Memphis.

For four years Terry remained out of professional baseball, but he managed local amateur teams. Then Little Rock sought his services, but he turned the offer down.

John McGraw came to town in 1921. He talked with Terry, and before he left he had signed the hard-hitting Memphis boy.

M'GRAW IS LAUDED BY BASEBALL MEN

Leaders Hail Veteran as a Great Influence in Development of the Game.

CALLED FOREMOST MANAGER

Landis, Heydler, Mack, Hornsby and McKechnie Among Those Who Pay Him Tribute.

John J. McGraw was hailed as a great influence in the development of baseball as tributes were paid yesterday to the veteran manager who resigned his post with the Giants. Rival pilots did not hesitate to characterize him as the game's foremost manager and all agreed that his passing from active participation would be a blow to the sport.

The tributes follow:

Kenesaw M. Landis, commissioner of baseball—John J. McGraw has been a great character in the development of baseball and I am very sorry to see him go.

John A. Heydler, president of the National League—It was with great regret that I learned of the resignation of John J. McGraw. He was our foremost manager and an unquestioned asset to the game. We joined the league at practically the same time.

Joe McCarthy, manager of the Yankees—McGraw must have been pretty sick, for he is not the kind to give up baseball without a reason.

Max Carey, manager of the Robins—Baseball won't be quite the same without McGraw. Bill Terry is a great player and a good friend of mine. I hope he will trade himself to Brooklyn.

Emil Fuchs, president of the Braves—McGraw is one of my best friends. I know that he has been in ill health and that, of course, is the only reason for such a great figure leaving active baseball. I consider him the greatest manager in the game and regret more than I can express his leaving the manager's bench. Bill Terry is a fine chap and a great player and nobody could wish him more success than I.

Bill McKechnie, manager of the Braves—He was the greatest of managers. I've played with him and fought with him and I can say only what everybody else will agree to—that his connection with baseball has been one of its greatest assets. I'm sorry to see him out, but if his health has been jeopardized by staying in, I'm glad he has quit.

Burt Shotten, manager of the Phillies—They won't seem like the Giants without McGraw and I'm sorry he felt that he had to give up the job. He has been a great manager and a fighter who was always out to win from the time he first played the game. Of course the league will miss him. I'm glad to see Bill Terry take over the reins. He's a fine fellow and a great player.

Gabby Street, manager of the Cardinals—Ever since I was a kid I've looked on John J. McGraw as the greatest manager in baseball. He has always been a step ahead of everybody on the diamond during his many years in the game. I've held that opinion through my own career and I'll never change it.

Dan Howley, manager of the Reds—The greatest figure in baseball stepped off the diamond when John J. McGraw resigned as manager of the Giants. Thirty years in the headlines tell the story of his unmatched ability. The game won't look the same with McGraw out of the picture.

George Gibson, manager of the Pirates—It's a shock to me and I sincerely hope that when the details are given out it will mean that McGraw will remain actively in the game. Baseball, especially the National League, would suffer an irreparable loss were McGraw to retire from the sport he helped to make. I cannot believe he will do so. I wish Bill Terry every success, but I trust McGraw stays in the game.

Rogers Hornsby, manager of the Cubs—Baseball has lost its greatest manager, and I regret his passing from the active ranks. Having played for him, I appreciate his sincerity and interest in the sport. As a rival, I always found him fair and a good sportsman.

William E. Benswanger, president of the Pirates—I am sure the entire league will mourn the sudden resignation of John J. McGraw. He was a great force in making baseball a colorful attraction. The game will miss him.

By The Associated Press.

Clark Griffith, President of the Senators—McGraw meant as much to baseball as the game has meant to him through the years, and as old-timer to old-timer I am glad to see he will retain his connection with the club while dropping an active rôle.

Connie Mack, manager of the Athletics—All baseball will feel keenly the passing of such a man from active participation in it. To lose his brilliant mind is a blow to the game.

Kid Gleason, team-mate on the Orioles—I can't believe it. I just can't imagine him giving up the reins.

TO BOX AT WEST VIRGINIA.

Site for 1933 Championships Selected by Eastern Conference.

The Eastern Intercollegiate Boxing Conference championships will be held at the University of West Virginia next year, it has been announced by Earl R. Yeomans, president of the league and graduate manager of athletics at Temple University. It will be a two-day meet starting on March 17. Pitt, Carnegie Tech, West Virginia, Bucknell, Duquesne, Temple, and W. and J. comprise the league. Temple will defend its team championship, which it won this year.

Cain and Bowman Released.

PHILADELPHIA, June 3 (AP).—Manager Connie Mack of the Athletics announced tonight that Merritt (Sugar) Cain and Joe Bowman, rookie pitchers, had been released on option for further seasoning. Bowman will rejoin Portland and Cain will be sent to Baltimore.

Frame Enters Title Auto Race.

CHICAGO, June 3 (AP).—Freddie Frame of Los Angeles, winner of the 500-mile automobile race at Indianapolis, today entered the 100-mile national championship race at the new Roby-Chicago Speedway June 19.

BRAVES TURN BACK ROBINS IN NINTH

Worthington's Double Sends In Urbanski With the Tally Which Decides, 6 to 5.

WILSON HITS EIGHTH HOMER

Mishandling of Two Bunts Contributes to Defeat of Brooklyn, Which Drops to Fifth.

By ROSCOE McGOWEN.

Another home run by Hack Wilson, his third in two days and his eighth of the season, served only to tie the score once with the Braves yesterday and Max Carey's athletes lost a ninth-inning decision, 6 to 5, with Ben Cantwell, third Braves' hurler of the contest, getting credit for the triumph at Ebbets Field. Not more than 5,000 fans attended.

Cy Moore, who replaced Watson Clark in the sixth with the score tied at 5—all, became the losing pitcher, with errors by Mickey Finn and Bruce Caldwell in mishandling a pair of bunts contributing largely to his downfall. Red Worthington's double down the right field line brought Bill Urbanski home with the winning run.

Sets Three Down in Order.

Cantwell set down Caldwell, Sukeforth and Danny Taylor in order in Brooklyn's final turn at bat.

The defeat dropped the Flatbush flock into fifth place when a victory would have sent them into a triple tie for third with the Reds and Pirates. The Braves gained a full game on the Cubs and now are only a game and a half out of the lead.

Wilson's big blow came in the third inning, with the Braves leading, 2 to 1. McKechnie's men had scored two in the first on Maranville's single, Urbanski's triple and Worthington's single. Brooklyn got one in the second off Frankhouse on singles by Cuccinello and Slade and Lopez's long double.

Scores on Wild Pitch.

Another double by Lopez to open the fourth paved the way for two more runs, with Frederick, Finn and O'Doul contributing singles, and in the fifth, with Bruce Cunningham pitching, they counted their fifth tally, Cuccinello bringing it home on a wild pitch after his opening double and Lopez's long fly.

Clark lost the lead and retired from the game in the sixth, however, when a Boston barrage, started with consecutive doubles by Worthington and Schulmerich, and ending with another two-bagger by Cunningham, tied the score.

The box score:

BOSTON (N.)	ab.	r.	h.	po.	a.	e.
Mar'ville, 2b	3	1	2	6	1	0
Urbanski, ss	4	2	1	1	2	1
Leach, cf	4	0	1	3	0	0
Wo'th'on, lf	5	1	3	0	0	0
Schul'ich, rf	5	1	2	0	0	0
Shires, 1b	5	0	0	8	1	0
Akers, 3b	4	1	3	1	2	0
Spohrer, c	4	0	1	8	2	0
Frankh'se, p	1	0	0	0	1	0
aE. Clark	1	0	0	0	0	0
Cunnin'm, p	2	0	1	0	0	0
Cantwell, p	0	0	0	0	3	0
Total	38	6	11	27	12	1

BROOKLYN (N.)	ab.	r.	h.	po.	a.	e.
Frederick, cf	3	1	1	2	0	0
Taylor, cf	2	0	0	0	0	0
Finn, 3b	5	0	2	0	2	1
O'Doul, lf	5	0	4	0	0	0
Wilson, rf	5	1	2	1	0	0
bStripp	0	0	0	0	0	0
Rosenfeld, rf	0	0	0	0	0	0
Cuccin'lo, 2b	5	2	3	7	4	0
Slade, ss	4	0	1	4	3	0
Lopez, c	4	1	2	2	1	0
Kelly, 1b	1	0	0	7	0	0
Caldwell, 1b	1	0	0	3	0	1
W. Clark, p	1	0	0	0	1	0
W. Moore, p	1	0	0	1	1	0
cSukeforth	1	0	0	0	0	0
Total	38	5	15	27	14	2

aBatted for Frankhouse in fifth.
bRan for Wilson in eighth.
cBatted for W. Moore in ninth.

Boston	2 0 0	0 0 3	0 0 1	—6
Brooklyn	0 1 1	2 1 0	0 0 0	—5

Runs batted in—Urbanski, Worthington 2, Schulmerich, Akers, Cunningham, Lopez, Wilson, Frederick, Finn.

Two-base hits—Worthington 2, Schulmerich, Cunningham, Lopez 2, Frederick, Cuccinello. Three-base hit—Urbanski. Home run—Wilson. Sacrifices—Kelly, Lopez, Leach, Urbanski. Double plays—Slade, Cuccinello and Kelly; Akers, Maranville and Shires; Slade and Kelly. Left on bases—Boston 9, Brooklyn 14. Bases on balls—Off W. Moore 2, Frankhouse 1, Cunningham 4, Cantwell 1. Struck out—By Clark 1, Frankhouse 3, Cunningham 4. Hits—Off W. Clark 11 in 5 2-3 innings, W. Moore 3 in 3 1-3, Frankhouse 10 in 4, Cunningham 5 in 3 1-3, Cantwell 0 in 1 2-3. Wild pitch—Cunningham. Winning pitcher—Cantwell. Losing pitcher—W. Moore. Umpires—Rigler, Barr and Donnelly. Time of game—2:28.

INDIANS TRIUMPH TWICE.

Win Double Header From Tigers, 3 to 1 and 10 to 7.

DETROIT, June 3 (AP).—Cleveland took both ends of a double-header from the Detroit Tigers today, winning the first, 3 to 1, and then pounding four Detroit hurlers for a 10-to-7 victory in the nightcap.

FIRST GAME.

CLEVELAND (A.)	ab.	r.	h.	po.	a.	e.
Porter, rf	4	0	3	2	0	0
Cissell, 2b	5	0	0	0	7	0
Averill, cf	4	0	1	2	0	0
Vosmik, lf	3	0	0	2	1	0
Morgan, 1b	3	1	1	13	0	0
Sewell, c	4	0	2	4	0	1
Kamm, 3b	4	0	1	0	0	0
Montague, ss	4	1	1	1	1	0
Ferrell, p	4	1	1	1	4	0
Total	35	3	10	27	13	1

DETROIT (A.)	ab.	r.	h.	po.	a.	e.
Davis, 1b	4	0	2	14	2	0
Rogell, ss	3	1	1	2	6	0
Stone, lf	4	0	2	1	0	0
Gehringer, 2b	4	0	1	2	4	1
Walker, cf	4	0	0	2	0	0
Johnson, rf	4	0	0	0	0	0
Rich'son, 3b	3	0	2	0	4	0
Ruel, c	3	0	0	6	0	0
Bridges, p	3	0	0	0	4	0
aWhite	1	0	1	0	0	0
bAlexander	1	0	0	0	0	0
Total	34	1	9	27	20	1

aBatted for Richardson in ninth.
bBatted for Ruel in ninth.

Cleveland	0 0 0	0 2 0	0 1 0	—3
Detroit	0 0 1	0 0 0	0 0 0	—1

Runs batted in—Gehringer, Ferrell 2, Kamm. Two-base hits—Averill, Richardson, Porter. Home run—Ferrell. Sacrifice—Morgan. Double play—Gehringer, Rogell and Davis; Vosmik and Sewell; Cissel, Montague and Morgan. Left on bases—Detroit 7, Cleveland 8. Bases on balls—Off Bridges 2, Ferrell 1. Struck out—By Bridges 3, Ferrell 2. Umpires—Ormsby and Dinneen. Time of game—1:43.

SECOND GAME.

CLEVELAND (A.)	ab.	r.	h.	po.	a.	e.
Porter, rf	5	2	1	3	0	0
Cissell, 2b	5	2	1	1	1	0
Averill, cf	4	1	2	3	0	0
Vosmik, lf	5	0	0	4	0	0
Morgan, 1b	2	1	1	8	0	0
Myatt, c	4	1	1	5	0	0
Kamm, 3b	4	1	1	0	4	0
Montague, ss	5	2	2	3	3	1
Harder, p	3	1	2	0	0	0
Connally, p	0	0	0	0	0	0
Total	34	10	11	27	8	1

DETROIT (A.)	ab.	r.	h.	po.	a.	e.
Davis, 1b	5	0	1	12	0	0
Rogell, ss	5	1	3	2	4	0
Stone, lf	4	1	2	0	0	0
Gehringer, 2b	5	2	2	3	4	0
Walker, cf	5	0	2	2	0	0
Johnson, rf	5	0	2	2	0	0
Rich'son, 3b	4	0	0	1	2	0
Hayworth, c	5	1	2	2	2	0
Wyatt, p	2	0	0	1	3	0
Herring, p	0	0	0	0	0	0
Goldstein, p	1	1	1	0	0	0
Hogsett, p	1	1	1	0	0	0
aWhite	1	0	0	0	0	0
Total	43	7	13	27	15	1

aBatted for Richardson in ninth.

Cleveland	0 1 2	0 2 2	2 1 0	—10
Detroit	2 0 0	0 1 2	1 1 0	—7

Runs batted in—Averill 4, Rogell 3, Harder 3, Walker 2, Johnson 2, Myatt, Vosmik, Porter.

Two-base hits—Stone, Morgan, Walker, Goldstein, Johnson, Hogsett. Three-base hit—Averill. Stolen bases—Rogell 2, Johnson. Sacrifices—Cissell 2, Kamm. Double plays—Gehringer, Rogell and Davis; Wyatt and Davis. Left on bases—Detroit 10, Cleveland 8. Bases on balls—Off Wyatt 4, Herring 1, Goldstein 3, Connally 1. Struck out—By Wyatt 2, Harder 3, Connally 1. Hits—Off Wyatt 6 in 4 1-3 innings, Herring 3 in 2-3 (none out in sixth), Goldstein 1 in 2, Hogsett 1 in 2, Harder 12 in 6 (none out in seventh), Connally 3 in 3. Winning pitcher—Harder. Losing pitcher—Wyatt. Umpires—Dinneen and Ormsby. Time of game—2:27.

MAJOR LEAGUE BASEBALL

AMERICAN LEAGUE.

YESTERDAY'S RESULTS.

New York 20, Philadelphia 13.
Cleveland 3, Detroit 1 (1st).
Cleveland 10, Detroit 7 (2d).
St. Louis 2, Chicago 1.
(Ten innings.)
Washington at Boston, rain.

STANDING OF THE CLUBS.

	Won.	Lost.	P.C.
New York	30	13	.698
Washington	28	17	.622
Detroit	24	18	.571
Cleveland	26	20	.565
Philadelphia	25	20	.556
St. Louis	21	24	.467
Chicago	15	29	.341
Boston	7	35	.167

WHERE THEY PLAY TODAY.

New York at Philadelphia (two).
Washington at Boston (two).
Cleveland at Detroit (two).
St. Louis at Chicago.

NATIONAL LEAGUE.

YESTERDAY'S RESULTS.

Boston 6, Brooklyn 5.
Pittsburgh 6, Chicago 5.
(Eleven innings.)
Philadelphia at New York
(Two games, rain).
Cincinnati at St. Louis, rain.

STANDING OF THE CLUBS.

	Won.	Lost.	P.C.
Chicago	28	18	.609
Boston	26	19	.578
Cincinnati	24	24	.500
Pittsburgh	21	21	.500
Brooklyn	22	24	.478
St. Louis	20	24	.455
Philadelphia	20	25	.444
New York	17	23	.425

WHERE THEY PLAY TODAY.

Philadelphia at New York (two).
(First at 1:45 P. M.)
Boston at Brooklyn (two).
(First at 1:30 P. M.)
Cincinnati at St. Louis.
Chicago at Pittsburgh.

Section III SPORTS

NEW YORK Herald Tribune

SPORTS Section III

TWELVE PAGES SUNDAY, OCTOBER 2, 1932 **** TWELVE PAGES

Miss Van Wie Routs Mrs. Vare For U.S. Golf Crown, 10 and 8, 73 on First 18 Shattering Par

Chicago Star, 13 and 12 Victim in '28, Crushes Five-Time Champion in Their Third Final

Victor 8 Up at Noon, One Over Men's Par

Ex-Titleholder, Even on Drives, Bows to Deadly Spoons, Chips Unequaled in History of Tourney

By Kerr N. Petrie

SALEM, Mass., Oct. 1.—Cutting loose with a game that in its devastating power carried all the relentless sweep of a tornado, Miss Virginia Van Wie, of Chicago, crowned years of defeat and discouragement today at the Salem Country Club by overwhelming Mrs. Glenna Collett Vare, of Philadelphia, in the thirty-six-holes final of the women's national championship, 10 and 8. Four years ago at Hot Springs, Va., Mrs. Vare triumphed over Miss Van Wie by 13 and 12. The Chicago girl could not match that record in her triumph this afternoon, but she came closer to the mark than any one ever believed was humanly possible.

The game which Miss Van Wie tossed against her conqueror of former years, victor in five of these championship finals and loser in only one, has never been equaled for sheer mechanical precision and brilliance in the last round of the national championship. It is doubtful if it has ever been approximated in women's golf save perhaps in the epic match which Mrs. Vare and Miss Joyce Wethered flashed last year in the British classic.

Victor Makes One Error

Miss Van Wie this morning played a round of golf that contained one mistake. There in itself is one for the book. That single error kept her from equaling men's par for the heavily trapped, testing Salem lay-out carved from the heart of the woods. She decimated women's par completely.

With two approximations, neither too liberal, Miss Van Wie played a 73 on her march to the title, which after she had taken two final-round beatings of 13 and 12 and 6 and 5 from Mrs. Vare, she must have begun to believe was to be denied her forever. But this time a gasping, gaping gallery saw the tables completely turned. Familiar as they are with the game's eccentricities and uncertainties, they scarcely expected to see Mrs. Vare smothered as she was. Some favored this one of the finalists, some the other, but none looked for such a rout as transpired, least of all did they ever dream that anything of the kind should fall upon the shoulders of the five-time champion.

Mrs. Vare did not play up to the form of which she is capable. That must be admitted. Even so it would have taken her best, her very best, to come anything like close to stopping the Chicagoan. Mrs. Vare was 8 down at noon, an amazing position for one so skilled and experienced.

Mrs. Vare's Task Hopeless

Even the most sanguine had little hope after that of seeing Mrs. Vare shake off defeat. Miss Van Wie resumed not quite as brilliantly as she had begun in the morning, but it was not long before her relentless attack had brought her advantage to double figures.

On the second round Mrs. Vare went out in 40, two over women's par. Even with this she lost ground. The end would have come at the ninth in all probability had Miss Van Wie not found her ball down in a patch of rough following her tee shot. With an iron she endeavored to tear the ball out and send it over the pond, but the water hazard had the last word, and Mrs. Vare was enabled to continue the match after standing 10 down with 10 to play.

The concluding hole was the counterpart of many others. Miss Van Wie did not outpoint her opponent with the driver, but she made the better spoon second and the better chip. From below the plateau green she chipped a dozen feet short. Miss Van Wie had played her second to the right of the green. Her chip was four feet strong but she was not asked to try it. Missing the putt, Mrs. Vare stepped up and conceded defeat, the official margin being announced as 10 and 8, although had Miss Van Wie putted and missed the advantage would have been only 9 up. One hole at that stage made little difference either way.

Victor Over Miss Glutting

Miss Van Wie's final victory rounded out a week of consistent golf. In both medal and match play she showed her complete mastery of her clubs. The fact that she tied for the qualifying prize at 77 with Miss Maureen Orcutt removes whatever possibility there might have remained for any one's entering a claim that Miss Van Wie only came onto her game in time to catch a somewhat faltering former champion.

The Chicago girl did not play through the harder half of the draw, but in every match she played solid, consistent golf, rising to the heights whenever she happened to be facing an opponent who appeared to demand special attention.

This was particularly true of Miss Van Wie's handling of the Charlotte Glutting situation. Fired by her march to the semi-finals over such formidable opponents as Miss Mary K. Browne, Miss Bernice Wall and the British titleholder of the last two years, Miss Enid Wilson, Miss Glutting would have been difficult for any but the most expert and most experienced to subdue. Miss Van Wie handled the task perfectly.

And so today against Mrs. Vare the

(Continued on page five)

Her Perseverance Finally Is Rewarded

Miss Virginia Van Wie, of Chicago, who won the national women's golf championship yesterday by defeating Mrs. Glenna Collett Vare in the final at West Peabody, 10 and 8. Miss Van Wie had been beaten by Mrs. Vare, then Miss Glenna Collett, twice before in the final round

Equipoise Easy Victor, Adds $21,250 to Earnings

C. V. Whitney Ace, With Twenty Grand Scratched, Takes Havre de Grace Handicap by Galloping Mile and Furlong Ahead of Gallant Sir, Tred Avon

Special to the Herald Tribune

HAVRE DE GRACE, Md., Oct. 1.—Equipoise, son of Pennant, redeemed himself for his disappointing race a week ago when he ran unplaced behind Pairbypair, by galloping to easy victory in the twenty-first running of the Havre de Grace Handicap here this afternoon. It was a striking performance, and bore out the fact that when in running humor there is none to take his measure. Mrs. Payne Whitney's Twenty Grand, champion three-year-old of last season, was scratched so that the much-looked for duel between these two horses was denied the big crowd.

Equipoise, however, did not lack for competition. Thirteen of the best handicap horses in training faced the starter, but none could fully extend him through the last furlong, as he drew out to win by a comfortable margin. In spite of his doleful race recently, he went to the post favorite, around even money, and by one of those freaks of the mutuel machines he also paid even money for third. In truth, he paid slightly more to run second than to win, the mutuel prices being $4.10, $4.40 and $4.00.

Carries 128 Pounds

The race was at one mile and a furlong and the good horse ran the distance in 1:50 1-5, one-fifth of a second behind the track record. If Sonny Workman, who had the mount, had been forced to ride him out, a new track record would have been established. He carried 128 pounds, which made his performance the more praiseworthy.

The Northway Stable's Gallant Sir, Western three-year-old, finished second, while Tred Avon was three lengths back in third place. White Clover II, the English horse which won the Suburban Handicap at Belmont Park last Spring, came next, while George D. Widener's Jack High finished fifth.

Mr. and Mrs. C. V. Whitney were on hand with 20,000 others to see their good horse race to one of his most impressive victories of the year. Mr. Whitney accepted the trophy which went with the race, and was among the first to compliment Workman for his capable ride.

Equipoise earned $21,250 and so brought his earnings for the season to $104,870 and his total earnings over three seasons of racing to $264,710.

Equipoise's Tenth Victory

The son of Pennant-Swinging has won ten out of twelve starts this year, including such stakes as the Toboggan, the Metropolitan, the Stars and Stripes, the Arlington Gold Cup, the Wilson and the Whitney. He also ran second to Plucky Play in the rich Arlington Handicap, beaten a short neck. His only poor race this season came a week ago, when he behaved badly and to

(Continued on page six)

William-Mary Upsets Navy, 6-0, On End Run in Third Quarter

Middies Outrushed Throughout; Long Pass in 4th Fails in Effort to Tie

Special to the Herald Tribune

ANNAPOLIS, Md., Oct. 1.—A generously disappointed Navy contingent and some thousands of others looked on at Farragut Field this afternoon as the Naval Academy football team lost to William and Mary, 6 to 0. It was the seventh attempt for victory by the Indians, who made a strong effort last year, and their followers were elated.

The visitors clearly deserved the verdict, having the edge in first downs made, yards gained by rushing, and kicking. The Navy offense flashed rarely.

Walkup made the best showing of the Navy backs in the first half, and Chung-Hoon played well in the second, making repeated gains off tackle and passing accurately to erratic receivers.

The visitors scored in the third quarter when Becht fumbled and Halligan recovered on Navy's 30-yard line. Two plays by Palese took the ball across the goal line. One was a sprint around Navy's right end for eleven yards and the other around the other flank for nineteen. Halligan failed on the placement attempt.

Navy's great effort came in the fourth quarter, when, with the ball on William and Mary's 35-yard line, Chung-Hoon heaved a pass to the far right corner. Samuels, five yards from a score, got his arms around the ball, but it bounced off his chest.

Navy had a slight advantage at the start when Palese received Erck's punt and Halligan kicked back to Navy's 45-yard line. Chung-Hoon ran twenty yards into the visitors' territory, but Navy lost the ball when Becht missed an easy pass from Chung-Hoon.

Walkup retired in the third quarter with a bad ankle, and Harbold, center, who played well on defense, went out with the same injury in the final quarter. During the game, Baumberger, Slack, Clark and Samuels were used in the backfield, in addition to the starting group. William and Marys had several effective backs, including Palese, Slade and Lacroix.

The line-up:

Pos.	William and Mary (6)	Navy (0)
L. E.	Sorensen	Murray
L. T.	Stewart	Brooks
L. G.	Anderson	Reedy
C.	Bridges	Harbold
R. G.	Meade	Burns
R. T.	Quirk	Kane
R. E.	Halligan	Pray
Q. B.	Shade	Becht
L. H.	Palese	Chung Hoon
R. H.	Lacroix	Walkup
F. B.	Spack	Erck

SCORE BY PERIODS

Williams and Mary	0	0	6	0—6
Navy	0	0	0	0—0

Substitutions — Navy: Helleman for Brooks, Dornin for Pray, Slack for Becht, Becht for Slack, W. C. Clark for Chung Hoon, Chung Hoon for W. C. Clark, Baumberger for Chung Hoon, W. C. Clark for Baumberger, Chung Hoon for W. C. Clark, Samuels for Walkup, Waybright for Erck, Campbell for Waybright, Ruble for Burns, Dawson for Harbold. William and Mary: Yakavonas for Sorensen, Sorensen for Yakavonas, Darden for Anderson, Anderson for Darden, Darden for Anderson, Wilson for Bridges, Bridges for Wilson, Wilson for Bridges, Cholko for Shade, Smith for Palese, Giles for Lacroix, Smith for Giles, Lacroix for Smith, Worrell for Lacroix, Young for Spack.

Touchdown—Palese.

Referee—P. P. Magoffin, University of Michigan. Umpire—C. G. Eckles, Washington and Jefferson. Linesman—M. J. Thompson, Georgetown. Field Judge—E. E. Miller, Penn State. Time of quarters—15 minutes.

Bates Holds Yale to 0-0 Opening Tie

Pricher's Triple Threat Attack Twice Nearly Scores as Maine Team Outrushes Blue Line

Elis Halted at End On One-Yard Line

Belated Drive by Heim and Pony Backfield Is Futile in Short Contest

Special to the Herald Tribune

NEW HAVEN, Conn., Oct. 1.—Little Bates College of Lewiston, Me., scored a major upset in the Yale Bowl today by holding Yale's eleven to a scoreless tie. Yale's pony backfield almost saved the day in the last minutes of play, but failed after marching sixty-six yards to Bates's 1-yard line. These lightweights had first down on the Scarlet's 1-yard stripe, but time permitted only two fast plays, and Bates broke through the Blue wall to toss Charley Heim for two successive losses.

Heim, the little flash who startled Yale fans two years ago with his deeds when Albie Booth was injured, and who has not had much of a break since that time, went into the game in the final minutes and might have saved Yale had there been sufficient time. He and Clem Williamson did all the carrying for sixty yards and a penalty put the ball near the visitors' goal line.

Eleven-Minute Periods

While Yale might have scored if it had one more minute, the Eli forces, apparently confident of an overwhelming victory, had agreed upon four eleven-minute periods, cutting the game sixteen minutes short of a regulation contest. Yale was wishing for some of that wasted time tonight.

That one march was the only real threat made by the Elis. Bob Lassiter, the Blue's left halfback, was out of action because of a leg injury suffered in yesterday's practice. The backfield, without Lassiter, was comparatively helpless as far as consistent advancing was concerned, although Big Joe Crowley did more than his share. Del Marting and Eddie King, substitutes for Lassiter, failed to click.

Yale might well have been beaten and was fortunate in holding Bates to a tie for the visitors brought to the Bowl a triple threat star who menaced the Eli defense repeatedly and paved the way for a possible Bates touchdown which failed to materialize. Late in the first period Billy Pritcher, of Brooklyn, climaxed a series of fine gains by dashing sixteen yards to Yale's 15-yard line. Bates failed to make good, Stone's place kick on fourth down going wide by yards.

In the fourth period Pricher again dashed dangerously near the Yale goal line, reeling off a 38-yard run, the longest of the day, around Yale's left end, and was stopped at the Blue's 28-yard line. This threat was dashed when Joe Crowley came out of nowhere to intercept McClusky's pass which otherwise might have resulted in a touchdown.

Yale Threatens Twice

Only twice prior to the final rush did Yale appear on its way to a score and both times the Blue failed.

In the second period Yale marched 35 yards from mid-field only to lose the ball on downs when two forward passes failed, and in the third period the Blue gained three first downs in a row and appeared to have made a

(Continued on page two)

College Foot[ball]

Local

Brooklyn College	0	Arnold	0
Catholic U	47	C. C. N. Y.	0
Columbia	41	Lehigh	6
Fordham	69	Baltimore	0
Manhattan	32	St. Joseph's	2
N. Y. U.	33	Hobart	0

East

Army	13	Furman	0
Boston College	20	Loyola (Md.)	0
Boston University	13	New Hampshire	6
Bowdoin	20	Mass. State	6
Brown	19	Rhode Island	0
Bethany	0	Marietta	0
*Bluefield College	14	Campbell	0
Cornell	7	Niagara	0
Clarkson	31	Hamilton	0
Colby	19	Trinity	7
Carnegie Tech	7	Geneva	0
Colgate	27	Case	0
Cortland Tchrs	6	Mansfield Tchrs	6
Drexel	18	Westchester Tchrs.	6
Delaware	11	La Salle (Phila.)	6
Dartmouth	32	Vermont	6
Davis-Elkins	7	W. Liberty Tchrs.	6
Georgetown	26	Mt. St. Mary's	0
Harvard	66	Buffalo	0
Holy Cross	26	Providence	6
Hillsdale	31	Jackson Jr.	0
Juniata	3	Gettysburg	2
Johns Hopkins	21	Wash. College	0
Lafayette	6	Muhlenberg	0
Lowell Textile	19	St. Michael's	0
Maine	33	Conn. State	6
Morgan	38	Cheyney Tchrs	0
Montpelier Sem.	53	Norwich J. V.	0
National Farm.	27	Hartwick	0
Penn	38	F. and M.	0
Penn State	27	Lebanon Valley	0
Pittsburgh	40	West Virginia	0
Princeton	22	Amherst	0
Rochester	8	Alfred	6
Rutgers	20	P. M. C.	6
R. P. I.	7	Williams	6
*Syracuse	51	St. Lawrence	0
St. Bonaventure	39	Ithaca College	6
St. John's (Md.)	19	N. Y. Normal	6
Susquehanna	12	Moravian	7
South Carolina	7	Villanova	6
Shepherdstown	3	Shippensburg Tchrs	0
Springfield	20	E. Stroudsburg	0
Tufts	9	Middlebury	0
Upsala	35	Cooper Union	0
West Maryland	35	St. Thomas	6
Worcester Poly	0	Coast Gd. Acad.	0
W. and J.	20	W. Va. Wesleyan	0
W. and M.	6	Navy	0
Wesleyan	16	Union	6
Waynesburg	19	Slippery Rock	0
Yale	0	Bates	0

GAMES CANCELED

At Collegeville, Pa.—Haverford vs. Ursinus.

West

Aurora	0	Concordia	0
Ball State Tchrs.	26	Earlham	6
Beloit	32	Dubuque	0
Bluffton	6	Ohio Northern	6
Bowling Green	7	Mt. Union	6
*Cincinnati	22	Georgetown (Ky.)	12
Concordia	20	Moorehead Tchrs	6
*Creighton	6	Haskell	0
Dayton Reserves	13	Wilmington	6
Heidelberg	0	Findlay	0
Hope	0	Kalamazoo	0
Indiana	7	Ohio U	6
Illinois (first game)	20	Miami	7
Illinois (second game)	13	Coe	0
Iowa	31	Bradley Tech	7
Iowa State	32	Morningside	0
Iowa St. Tchrs.	14	Penn College	0
Ill. Normal	8	Dekalb Tchrs	7
Kent	6	Hiram	0
Lawrence	0	St. Norbert	0
Lake Forest	27	Northwestern Coll.	13
Lacrosse Tchrs	6	Columbia College	0
Michigan	26	Michigan State	0
Michigan B.	0	Mount Pleasant	0
Mich. Min. Tchrs.	6	Amer. Legion	0
Manchester	7	De Pauw	6
Minnesota	12	South Dakota	0

Georgia St.	40	Fort Benning	0
Hampton	19	No. Car. College	0
Hampden-Sidney	42	Bridgewater	13
Kentucky	18	Sewanee	0
Knoxville	13	Alabama A. and M.	0
Langley Field	13	Shenandoah	6
Mercer	21	Howard	6
Missouri Mines	20	Arkansas	19
Miss. College	32	Louisiana College	0
M'freesboro Tchrs	18	Tennessee Jr.	7
N. C. State	9	Richmond	0
Newberry	9	Catawba	2
Oklahoma	7	Tulsa	0
Parris Is. Mar.	19	Louisburg	7
Piedmont	19	Cullowhee Tchrs	7
Presbyterian	9	Lenoir-Rhyne	0
Rice	10	Louisiana St	8
Randolph-Macon	12	Guilford	0
*Roanoke	19	Elon	7
St. Paul	9	Shaw	0
Tennessee	33	Mississippi	0
Tennessee Tech	13	Lambuth	9
Texas Christian	55	Daniel Baker	0
Texas Mines	38	Wayland College	7
*Texas Tech	6	South Methodist	0
Tulane	26	Texas A. and M.	14
Tusculum	[illegible]	Weaver	0
Union (Ky.)	32	Louisville	6
Virginia State	7	Bluefield State	0
Vanderbilt	39	No. Carolina	[illegible]
V. P. I.	7	Georgia	6
Virginia	7	Maryland	6
Wofford	34	High Point	0

Far West

Brigham Young	38	Western State	6
Colorado	31	Colorado Mines	0
California	22	Olympic Club	6
Idaho (S. B.)	18	Ricks College	6
New Mexico Nor.	13	New Mexico Mines	0
Oregon	7	Santa Clara	0
So. Calif.	20	Wash. State	0
Stanford	27	Oregon State	0
St. Mary's	35	Nevada	0
Utah	54	Colorado College	6
Utah Aggies	26	Montana State	0
Wyoming	28	Chadron Normal	6
Washington	26	Montana	13

Freshman

Allbright '36	0	Allentown Prep	0
Bucknell '36	33	Shenandoah	0
Blair Acad	25	Penn State '36	18
California '36	63	Oneonta M. A.	0
Compton	19	So. Calif. '36	0
Exeter	14	New Hamp. '36	6
Pitt '36	9	Wyoming Sem.	0
Syracuse '36	21	Manlius	0

*Night game.

(Chick) Halsted, a Somervill[e] boy, got off punts for sixty-n[ine] and forty-four yards to keep C[...] at bay, and in the third period just inside his goal line, bo[oted the] ball far over Cliff Montgomer[y] and saw it bounce to the [...] mark before the Columbia sa[fety] picked it up. Halsted himself [made the] tackle that stopped Montgome[ry] back at the 21-yard stripe.

When Halsted was out anot[her] Jersey lad, Paul Short, a jun[ior from] Belleville, proved an able relie[f]. Their combined punting effo[rts] aged forty-two yards against [Colum]bia's thirty-six.

Columbia marched to its firs[t touch]down from the opening kick of[f, gain]ing seventy yards in fiftee[n plays.] Montgomery slithered off the [tackles] and circled the ends, Manny [Rivero] spun inside the tackles and Ed Brominski and Otto Schwartz alternated their blocking with shots at the middle of the line. A holding penalty halted the drive momentarily on Lehigh's 22-yard line but a Montgomery to Red Matal pass put the ball inside the 10-yard stripe and three plays later Rivero smashed through for the first score. Brominski place kicked the extra point and the rout was on.

Another twenty-six-yard Montgomery-Matal toss moved the ball into scoring territory just before the period ended, and one of twenty yards early in the second quarter got it down to where Montgomery could punch through for number two.

Frank Chippendale relieved Schwartz and Joe Linehan took Brominski's place at this juncture. The former's plunging and Linehan's running and pass receiving produced a third touch-

(Continued on page seven)

Yankee Home Runs Crush Cubs, 7 to 5, Ruth and Gehrig Smashing Two Apiece In Third Straight World Series Victory

Ruth Scoring the First of Two Homers Against Cubs

The Babe about to cross the plate after his first inning blow, which also scored Combs and Sewell. Those in the picture are Van Graflan, umpire, at right; Sewell, No. 21; Gehrig, No. 4, next up, and Hartnett, No. 7, Cubs catcher. Ruth hit another homer in the fifth followed by Gehrig's second, his first coming in the third inning

Associated Press telephoto

4 Drives, All Off Root, Score 6 Runs; 2 on Successive Pitches in 5th Snap Tie, Rout Hurler

Babe Cracks First With Two on Bases

Pipgras Removed in 9th, Pennock Turning Back Last Three; N. Y. Is One Game From 4th Crown

By Richards Vidmer

CHICAGO, Oct. 1.—The Cubs threw caution to the winds today and the third game of the World Series with it, the Yankees winning, 7 to 5.

Stung with the thought that too many bases on balls might have cost them the first two contests, the Cubs went out determined to pitch to the batters and make them hit, but they never realized what hitting Babe Ruth and Lou Gehrig were capable of producing.

The mighty Ruth twice drove the ball into the bleachers and out of the park for home runs and Gehrig sounded a Ruthian echo after each. Between them they drove in six runs by sheer power, and the Cubs were conquered for the third successive time.

Home Runs Silence Jeers

With a capacity crowd of 51,000 looking on, Ruth cast a spell of awe over the throng with one of his greatest World Series performances. On two other occasions in his glamorous career he has hit three home runs in the course of a single World Series game, but never with the arrogance and the supershowmanship he displayed today.

Surrounded by a hostile crowd which booed him vigorously at the start, facing the combined taunts of the Cubs, the Babe turned the jeers to cheers and silenced the sneers, leaving an awed audience staring wide-eyed through the sunshine as he lifted two balls against the blue of the skies.

The very first time he came to bat, in the opening inning, there was confidence in his manner as he stepped up to the plate. He paused to jest with the raging Cubs, pointed to the right-field bleachers and grinned.

Two men were on the bases, as Jurges had thrown Combs's grounder over Grimm's head and Sewell had walked. Charley Root stood in the box under instructions to pitch to the batters and issue no unnecessary passes. But the Cubs couldn't have done worse if that order never had been issued.

First Three Romp Across

With a step forward, a lurch of his massive shoulders and a sweep of his celebrated bat, Ruth drove the ball high into the temporary bleachers that had been erected beyond the right field fence. Upward and onward the ball flew, a white streak was outlined against the bright blue sky, and the first three Yankee runs romped home.

The crowd was in an uproar when the fifth inning started. Their Cubs at last had an even chance of winning. Root had struck out the last two men in the fourth and seemed to have the Yankees under control. The players showed a new dash as they ran out to their positions and whipped the ball about the infield.

When Sewell was retired on a grounder to shortstop, a third of another inning was safely passed. But there still were Ruth and Gehrig..

As the Babe moved toward the plate, swinging three bats over his shoulder, a concerted shout of derision broke in the stands. There was a bellowing of boos, hisses and jeers. There were cries of encouragement for the pitcher and from the Cubs' dugout came a storm of abuse leveled . . the Babe.

They Do It Again

But Ruth grinned in the face of the hostile greeting. He laughed back at the Cubs and took his plac supremely confident. A strike whistled over the plate and joyous outcries filled the air, but the Babe held up one finger as though to say: "That's only one, though. Just wait."

Two balls went by, then another strike. The stands rocked with delight. The Chicago players hurled their laughter at the great man, but Ruth held up two fingers and still grinned, the super-showman.

On the next pitch the Babe swung. There was a resounding report like the explosion of a gun. Straight for the center-field fence the ball soared on a line. Johnny Moore went racing back with some vague idea of catching it, then suddenly stopped short and stared as the ball sailed on, clearing the farthest corner of the barrier and dropping out into the street, 436 feet from home plate.

Before Ruth left the plate and started his swing around the bases he paused to laugh at the Chicago players, suddenly silent in their dugout. As he rounded first he flung a remark at Grimm, as he turned second he tossed a jest at Herman and his shoulders shook with satisfaction as he trotted on.

Hartnett; Ruffing and Dickey.

SECOND GAME

		R.	H.	E.
Chi. (N.L.)	1 0 1 0 0 0 0 0 0—2		9	0
N. Y. (A.L.)	2 0 2 0 1 0 0 0 x—5		10	1

Batteries—Warneke and Hartnett; Gomez and Dickey.

THIRD GAME

		R.	H.	E.
N. Y. (A.L.)	3 0 1 0 2 0 0 0 1—7		8	1
Chi. (N.L.)	1 0 2 1 0 0 0 0 1—5		9	4

Batteries—Pipgras, Pennock and Dickey; Root, Malone, May, Tinning and Hartnett.

STANDING OF THE CLUBS

	Won.	Lost.	Pct.
New York	3	0	1.000
Chicago	0	3	.000

SCHEDULE

Fourth game at Wrigley Field, Chicago, today at 1:30 p. m. (2:30 p. m., New York time).

Fifth game, if necessary, tomorrow at Wrigley Field.

Sixth and seventh games, if necessary, Yankee Stadium, October 5 and 6.

but never with the arrogance and the [supershowmansh]ip he displayed today. [Surrounded by] a hostile crowd which [booed him vigoro]usly at the start, fac[ing the combine]d taunts of the Cubs, [the Babe turned] the jeers to cheers [and silenced th]e sneers, leaving an [awed audience] staring wide-eyed [through the sun]shine as he lifted two [balls against the] blue of the skies. [The very first] time he came to bat, [in the opening i]nning, there was con[fidence in his m]anner as he stepped [up to the plate.] He paused to jest [with the raging] Cubs, pointed to the [right-field bleach]ers and grinned. [Two men wer]e on the bases, as [Jurges had thro]wn Combs's grounder [over Grimm's h]ead and Sewell had [walked. Charley] Root stood in the box [under instruction]s to pitch to the bat[ters and issue n]o unnecessary passes. [But the Cubs cou]ldn't have done worse [if that orde]r had been issued.

[First Thre]e Romp Across

[With a step fo]rward, a lurch of his [massive shoulder]s and a sweep of his [celebrated bat,] Ruth drove the ball [high into the tem]porary bleachers that [had been erecte]d beyond the right [field fence. Upw]ard and onward the [ball flew, a whit]e streak was outlined [against the brigh]t blue sky, and the [first three Ya]nkee runs romped [home.]

[...] only the beginning. [...] had backed Cuyler [...]atch his line drive in [...]stling line drive in [...]g, Gehrig opened the [...]er homer, his second [...]wasn't as high nor as [...] it came with nobody [...] it was just as effec[...] fear into the hearts [...]

[...]s point the thought [...]red to some of the [...]hat pitching to Ruth [...]'t such a great idea [...] took one more turn [...]

[...]e in Fourth

[...] the Cubs had tied [...]s to Herman and a [...] gave them one run [...]me run by Cuyler, a [...]son and a double by [...]m two more in the [...]le by Jurges followed [t]he tying tally across [...] fourth.

[The crowd was] in an uproar when [the fifth inning] started. Their Cubs [at last had an e]ven chance of win[ning. Root had] struck out the last [two men in the f]ourth and seemed to [have the Yankees] under control. The [players showed a] new dash as they ran [out to their pos]itions and whipped [th]e infield. [When Sewell] was retired on a [grounder to short]stop, a third of an[other inning was] safely passed. But [there still were R]uth and Gehrig.. [As the Babe mo]ved toward the plate, [swinging three ba]ts over his shoulder, [a concerted shout] of derision broke in [the stands. Ther]e was a bellowing of [boos, hisses and] jeers. There were [cries of encourage]ment for the pitcher [and from the Cu]bs' dugout came a [storm of abuse le]veled . . the Babe.

[They D]o It Again

[But Ruth grinn]ed in the face of the [hostile greeting.] He laughed back at [the Cubs and took] his plac supremely [confident. A strik]e whistled over the [plate and joyous] outcries filled the [air, but the Babe] held up one finger [as though to say]: "That's only one, [though. Just wai]t."

[Two balls went] by, then another [strike. The stan]ds rocked with de[light. The Chic]ago players hurled their laughter at the great man, but Ruth held up two fingers and still grinned, the super-showman.

On the next pitch the Babe swung. There was a resounding report like the explosion of a gun. Straight for the center-field fence the ball soared on a line. Johnny Moore went racing back with some vague idea of catching it, then suddenly stopped short and stared as the ball sailed on, clearing the farthest corner of the barrier and dropping out into the street, 436 feet from home plate.

Before Ruth left the plate and started his swing around the bases he paused to laugh at the Chicago players, suddenly silent in their dugout. As he rounded first he flung a remark at Grimm, as he turned second he tossed a jest at Herman and his shoulders shook with satisfaction as he trotted on.

The Yankee players tumbled out of

(Continued on page three)

Plane Pilot Burned to Death in Mid-Air

CHARACTER · QUALITY · AMERICA FIRST! · ENTERPRISE · ACCURACY

Los Angeles Examiner

AN AMERICAN PAPER FOR THE AMERICAN PEOPLE · THE GREAT NEWSPAPER OF THE GREAT SOUTHWEST

Reg. U.S. Pat. Off.

VOL. XXIX—NO. 297 | LOS ANGELES, MONDAY, OCTOBER 3, 1932 | Two Sections—Part One | M | PRICE FIVE CENTS

YANKEES WIN SERIES!

Today

No Drama in Depression Building Jobs, in Paris 20,000 Suicides, Yearly As Usual in Revolution

By Arthur Brisbane

(Copyright, 1932, King Features Synd., Inc.)

A West Indian hurricane struck Puerto Rico, causing great suffering with many left in want. "Immediate help" is asked, and this Government will supply it. A hurricane is dramatic, it appeals to the imagination.

Another sort of hurricane struck the United States, in 1929, and is still raging, with much suffering. But an economic hurricane is not dramatic.

Victims do not see pictures of themselves or their wrecked homes in the papers, and nothing much is done about that hurricane.

In connection with lack of employment it may interest you to know that our Government is spending two millions of dollars on a new "American chancery." The work, however, is being done in Paris, on the *Place de la Concorde*. The money will go to French workers, and to twenty French sub-contractors who say they are delighted because just now building is not active in Paris. The money contributed by American taxpayers is spent that one of our American Ambassadors, whose jobs are usually a reward for political services or cash contributions, may be housed "more worthily."

It is too bad that American stonemasons, bricklayers and carpenters can't speak French. They might go abroad and get a job with their Government.

Twenty thousand men, women and children commit suicide in this country every year. Dr. Louis L. Dublin, statistician of the Metropolitan Life Insurance Company, says more men than women commit suicide, and lack of character or mental maturity is largely responsible for self-destruction. The recent increase in suicide is not entirely due to the depression. There has been a suicide increase every year since 1925, without exception.

Lack of interest in life accounts for many suicides. About forty years ago, a New York newspaper discussed throughout one summer the question, "Is suicide a sin?" While the discussion lasted the number of suicides diminished remarkably. Those with thoughts of suicide joined the discussion and had something to make life interesting.

Bootleg whisky has increased suicide. A young woman "professional tap-dancer" fell out of a fourth-story window in New York, fracturing both legs, skull and spine. Two men explained to the policeman that there had been "an all-night drinking party."

Spain's revolution follows the usual course. Landed estates of the rich are seized, the vast holdings of dukes, counts and assorted grandees, and divided among the peasants. This was done in Russia, and the fact that moujiks own the land on which they were formerly slaves, in reality if not in name, is the chief support of the Soviet system.

French peasants got the nobles' land in exchange for worthless money. France did not let the Germans pass at Verdun, because every man in the French Army was related to some one of the millions of French land owners or himself owned land, west of Verdun.

The success of Charles the Twelfth of Sweden was based largely on the fact that his predecessor had divided the land among the people, taking it from the nobles. That gave the Swedish soldiers that went to Russia with Charles a determination to get home.

In this country actual land owners are comparatively few, and rapidly becoming fewer, with farm mortgages foreclosed by the thousands. Uncle Sam announces that he will not immediately take farms from the farmers that can't pay him what they owe. A good idea.

John Walker of 106 North Johnson street, Big Springs, Texas, would like to reply to Admiral Sims' statement that the Spanish War lasted only 114 days. More than 200,000 engaged in it. Nearly all the men have pensions costing now $119,000,000 a year. According to Admiral Sims, that is a disgrace.

John Walker says he draws a pension as a Spanish War veteran. He served in the Spanish-American War in 1898, the Philippine Insurrection in 1899, all of 1900 and up to June 3, 1901, and calls that more than 114 days.

Mr. Walker cannot understand why Admiral Sims, retired, should get a good big pension, whereas he is begrudged very small pension.

In the opinion of this writer all pensions, honorably acquired, are good for the country. They put cash where it is needed, and that's as important as scattering rain where it is needed.

Those desiring the election of Governor Roosevelt will find interesting one paragraph of a letter received from John Francis Neylan, a wise young man of San Francisco. "Roosevelt has just left California. He is one of the few political candidates who ever came to this state and did not succeed in committing political suicide."

Pope Pius ordered Catholics in Mexico to obey Mexico's religious laws, while likening persecution of

(Continued on Page 2, Columns 1-2)

NEW STORM BALKS FLOOD RESCUE WORK

Death, Horror Revealed in Wake of Tehachapi Disaster; Toll May Not Be Known for Days

Known Victims' List Grows as Workers Press Search; Tragic Details Begin to Unfold

Out of the flood-ravaged Tehachapi area there came yesterday new and horrifying word of the death and desolation left in the angry wake of the terrific cloudburst that smote the region Friday night.

Enormity of the death toll remained problematical. Terrifying in its force, but minor compared to the cataclysm which unleashed untold tons of water in what was the mountainous district's worst disaster, another storm handicapped rescue parties yesterday.

Eight bodies had been brought from the inundated section to Bakersfield mortuaries. Five other persons are known to have lost their lives. Another twenty-five are believed to have drowned.

TOLL UNDETERMINED

But because of the awful power of the giant water wall that smashed against the Tehachapi watershed and swept through the deep, rocky canyons, the complete extent of the catastrophe may not be determined for days.

The eighth body, discovered shortly before darkness fell last night, was that of an unidentified man. Every vestige of clothing had been stripped from the body, which was found in a lonely wash between Woodford-Keene and Bealville.

The receding flood waters yesterday yielded the pitifully mangled body of Mrs. Nell S. Cooper, 60-year-old telegraph operator at Caliente. The body of her 5-year-old granddaughter, Aranella Williams, still was missing. The child and her grandmother were trapped in their home when the deluge struck.

At Woodford-Keene, where the fury of the flood was centered, scenes of utter horror were revealed. It was there that A. H. Ross, engineer of a Southern Pacific freight train; Harry Moore, his brakeman; an undetermined number of transients riding the train, and a family of three perished—drowned in a roaring torrent that swept trestles, trains and houses before its fury.

EVIDENCE OF TRAGEDY

Floating in the swollen, muddy waters of Tehachapi Creek, 18 miles from Woodford-Keene, was found the crushed body of Mrs. Louise Kaad, whose husband, Peter, and their son, Peter Jr., also went to a sudden and terrible death.

Woodford-Keene lies thirteen miles north of Tehachapi. The Tehachapi Creek winds beside it and through a culvert under the Southern Pacific tracks.

Exposed to the full ferocity of

(Continued on Page 3, Column 1.)

Rudy Vallee and Wife Reunited After Row

CLEVELAND, Oct. 2.—The Vallee family—Rudy and Fay—were back in that state of marital bliss today with all thoughts of past differences forgotten.

They were together again for the first time since the crooner's youthful wife, the former Fay Webb of Santa Monica, Calif., left New York for Reno several weeks ago for the announced purpose of obtaining a divorce, only to call off her planned action when the couple reconciliated over the long distance telephone.

Couple in Auto Fall 500 Feet, Escape Death

Passing Motorists on Ridge Route Bring Aid; Pair Rescued

Carried over a 500-foot Ridge Route cliff when their auto skidded, a man and woman miraculously escaped death yesterday.

The couple were Douglas L. Phillips, 534 South Park View avenue, and Miss Alma Kincaid, 528 South Park View avenue.

The near-tragedy happened a mile south of Resorvoir Summit, when Phillips, driving, was unable to make a sharp curve in the highway.

Passing motorists saw the skid marks on the concrete and discovered the couple's plight. They notified Deputy Sheriffs Carter and Meadows of Newhall substation, who rescued Phillips and Miss Kincaid.

At Newhall Emergency Hospital, Dr. Sarah Murray reported Miss Kincaid was suffering from a fractured pelvis and cuts about the face, scalp and chest. Phillips received a fractured left arm and bruises.

Wife Fights Appeal of 'Ukulele Ike'

Attorneys for Irene L. Edwards, former wife of "Ukulele Ike" Edwards, today will move in the District Court of Appeals for a dismissal of the appeal of the film comedian from a $15,847 judgment granted her in Superior Court. Mrs. Edwards obtained the judgment on the ground that the comedian failed to keep up his payments in a property settlement.

List of Known Casualties in Big Cloudburst

Kern County Coroner W. C. Houze yesterday issued the revised list of dead and missing, based on reports from officers leading rescue work in the area devastated by the cloudburst and flood that swept the Tehachapi Friday night:

Bodies identified—Peter A. Kaad, 45, proprietor of Bear Mountain service station; his wife, Louise, and his son, Peter Jr.; Mrs. Nell Cooper, telegraph operator at Caliente.

Other bodies found: Four unidentified men, presumably itinerants riding the ill-fated Southern Pacific freight train wrecked at Woodford-Keene.

Known to be dead, still missing—A. H. Ross, 50, Southern Pacific engineer; Brakeman Harry Moore, 42; Clifford Barron, 25, Bellingham, Wash.; Aranella Williams, 5, Caliente.

Believed dead, still missing—John Tempest, 50, Caliente; twenty-five itinerants, riding freight train.

Estimated death toll, 37.

CRAFT BURSTS INTO FLAMES AND CRASHES

Student Flyer, at Controls, Leaps in Parachute, Escapes, but Injured in Landing

Accident Occurs Three Miles North of Oceanside; Ship Falls Several Hundred Feet

OCEANSIDE, Oct. 2.—Robert Sly, aviator, was burned to death late today when a plane in which he was flying with a student pilot, who was at the controls, burst into flames in midair and crashed, three miles north of here.

A. B. Swinney, the student, escaped in a parachute. He was knocked unconscious when he landed and was taken to the office of Dr. R. H. Palmateer here. His condition was believed to be serious.

FLYERS TRYING TO LAND

Swinney and Sly were believed to have flown north from the Ryan Airport at San Diego.

The ship was at an altitude of several hundred feet when it caught fire, according to witnesses, who said they believed the flyers were attempting to reach an army emergency field near here.

G.O.P. Dishing Up Old Sauce

BY ARTHUR "BUGS" BAER

The Rpeublican campaign orators are like a football team leaving a huddle. They all gallop out with the same signals.

We have read and listened to the G. O. P. campaign speakers and every one of Mrs. Brown's cows moos alike.

They dish up the same old stereotyped arguments with mimeograph sauce. It's too much like mamma sending Junior out with a list of groceries, and saying, "Now don't forget what I sent you for."

But your Democratic stumper is a hoss in a different race. He not only warbles his party platform, but he has ideas of his own. He knows that twelve years of political sawdust has the public all guffed up.

Styles change in everything. We don't see any more ventriloquists in vaudeville and we don't want to listen to their dolls in the political struggle.

We admit that the Republican soft-boiled oratory worked four years ago, but so did our pocket lighter.

Massie Case Echoes Heard in Hawaii Congress Race

HONOLULU, T. H., Oct. 2.—Victor S. K. Houston, Republican delegate to Congress, and his Democratic opponent, L. L. McCandless, wealthy 76 - year - old pioneer, emerged as nominees of their respective parties today in a bitter primary contest in which frequent references were made to the celebrated Massie case.

James Gilliland, who was in charge of prosecution at the Ala Moana trial, as the case against the five natives accused of atacking Mrs. Massie was called, was defeated in his candidacy for Mayor.

A majority of those nominated to both upper and lower House of the territorial Legislature were of white blood.

One feature of the election was the nomination of Miss Elsie Wilcox, member of a famous mainland missionary family, to the Senate. Her election was conceded, making her the first woman to sit in the Hawaiian Legislature.

The heavy vote given McCandless in the Democratic primary was hailed with delight by leaders of that party, who decalred it indicated a desire on the part of the people to send a Democrat to Congres, and was not based on an appeal to racial prejudice.

'Erbie and 'Is Playmates -:- SUDDENLY IT WAS ALL A BLANK!

'Erbie is putting on a new play entitled "She Was Happy 'Till She Met Up With Him." 'Erbie is the honest night watchman who wakes up just after the bandits have escaped with the payroll in a blue sedan. 'Erbie's playmate, Ropy, is the head bandit. Sam is the good old uncle, supposed to be very wealthy, but nobody knows what he is really worth, he has been trimmed so often. 'Erbie's playmate, Taxi, is the beautiful girl who has been waiting at the church for the past four years for a young man named "Hoover Prosperity," who is said to be just around the corner, but never shows up. Ah, well, when things get as bad as they can possibly get they usually get a little worse. Still, let's hope for the best. You remember, when Enoch Arden came home, after several years' absence, and found that his wife had made other arrangements, he didn't get discouraged. Not at all. He simply went back to where he came from and put an ad in the paper, "Single gentleman wants quiet apartment." And then there's this comforting thought, it's—

(To be continued.)

CHURCHES FACE MEXICAN DOOM

MEXICO CITY, Oct. 2.—(AP)—President Abelardo L. Rodriguez tonight issued a statement declaring that all the Roman Catholic churches in Mexico would be retired from religious use if the Catholic Church's attitude as "shown in the recent papal encyclical" should continue.

The President said that "methods filled with falsehoods" against Mexico were characteristic of the Papacy, and termed "insolent" the attitude shown in the recent encyclical issued from Vatican City.

"If the insolent, defiant attitude shown in the recent encyclical continues," President Rodriguez asserted, "I am determined that the churches shall be converted into schools and shops for the benefit of the nation's proletarian classes."

New Liner Rex Continues Journey

GIBRALTAR, Oct. 2.—The new liner Rex left here at 2 a. m. today to continue her maiden voyage to New York. Its machinery had been fully repaired and exhaustive tests made before the ship left. All was going well at last reports, and the ship was making good progress. It is expected to reach New York on Friday.

Family Sees Youth in Babcock Slaying

SAN JOSE, Oct. 2.—George Douglas Templeton Jr., 20, on trial here in Superior Court for the knife slaying of his aunt, Mrs. Lillian Babcock, wealthy Manila society woman, was visited in his cell at county jail today by his family.

Sao Paulo Rebels Give Up Unconditionally

RIO DE JANEIRO, Oct. 2.—(Universal Service.)—Sao Paulo rebels, who have been hiding out against Federal forces for the last three months, tonight surrendered unconditionally, the Government announced.

Blake Takes Paddle Board Catalina Race; 5 Hrs. 23 Min.

Battling rough and choppy seas most of the thirty-six nautical miles between Point Vicente, on the mainland, and Long Point, Catalina Island, Tom Blake crossed the channel on a paddle board yesterday in five hours and twenty-three minutes actual time.

En route he took thirty-two minutes for rest and refreshments.

Preston Peterson was second, covering the distance in six hours and twenty-nine minutes, and Wally Burton third in six hours and fifty minutes.

Blake is the Hawaiian paddle board champion and Peterson and Burton are members of the lifeguard crew of the city of Santa Monica.

The contenders were accompanied by the 40-foot cruiser Gloria H. under command of Capt. O. C. Olsen with timers and a physician aboard. They were taken to Avalon, where they were awarded prizes.

The object of the contest, according to Capt. George Watkins of the Santa Monica lifeguards, was to show the efficiency of the paddle board in life-saving work.

ANGELS, STARS SPLIT TWIN BILL

Hollywood and Los Angeles pulled down the curtain on the 1932 Pacific Coast season at Wrigley Field yesterday, splitting a doubleheader, the Stars winning the opener, 6-4, and dropping the nightcap, 6-5. The Angels won the final series, four games to three.

Harry Rubey, famous song writer, injected some comedy in the fade-out game when he relieved Ote Brannan at second base for Hollywood and amused the fans with his antics.

Young George Winchell, Angel recruit, outpitched Augie Walsh in the nightcap, while Southpaw Emil Yde of the Stars, outlasted Hal Stitzel and Ed Baecht in the first game.

Hollywood was outhit by Los Angeles in the opener, but managed to bunch their hits at opportune moments, while in the second contest, the Angels put over a three-run rally in the sixth inning on four hits to snag the verdict.

The most potent wallop of the inning was a home run by Gene Lillard, recruit third sacker. Tut Stainback also contributed a home run.

In the first game, home runs by Cleo Carlyle and Ben Franks of Hollywood were the highlights.

G.O.P. Radio League Opens Its Air Campaign Tonight

NEW YORK, Oct. 2.—The Republican Radio League opens its radio campaign tomorrow night over a hookup covering the territory from Maine to Kansas and from the northern border to the southern border state.

E. F. Hutton, New York business man, at the conclusion of his talk, will introduce William Allen White, Emporia, Kan., editor, who will speak from Chicago.

The opening program will cover a half hour. Thereafter for five nights a week until the eve of election there will be nightly fifteen-minute programs, for a total of six and one-quarter hours. Speakers will include well-known figures in political, industrial and educational life.

The program was announced by David Hinshaw, director of the radio division at Eastern headquarters of the Republican National Committee. Among the speakers this week will be: Former Attorney General Albert Ottinger, Clarance Buddington Kellandn, Herbert Kauffman, editorial writer.

CUBS BEATEN FOURTH GAME STRAIGHT BY 13 TO 6 SCORE

And as Result, Colonel Jacob Ruppert Will Have New Silk Pajamas Ripped to Shreds

52,000 Chicagoans Dazed by Deluge of Slugging; Lazzeri Gets 2 Homers; Combs One

By Damon Runyon

(Copyright, 1932, Universal Service, Inc.)

CHICAGO, Oct. 2.—Colonel Jacob Ruppert's silk pajamas will be sacrificed tonight.

His New York Yankees made a clean sweep of the World's Series of 1932 by smothering the Chicago Cubs, 13 to 6, this afternoon.

It is a ritual with the New York Yankees when they make a clean sweep of a series, to haul their dignified and fastidious multi-multi-multi-millionaire owner from his downy couch and rip his silk pajamas to shreds.

FIRST TIME IN 1927

The first time they performed this operation on Col. Jacob Ruppert was in 1927 when they won four straight from the Pittsburgh Pirates; and the Colonel, unaccustomed to having his distinguished person pawed by other than his valet's hands, thought seriously of calling the gendarmes.

The second time, in 1928, when the Yankees mopped up the St. Louis Cardinals in four straight, the Colonel submitted only after a valorous struggle.

Tonight, as the Yankees are rolling Eastward in their special train, Col. Jacob Ruppert stands prepared to emerge from his drawing room, pajama clad, the instant he hears a thunderous knock, and the subcellar voice of Babe Ruth roaring:

"Come outta there, Kernel."

BUYS NEW PAJAMAS

It is said the Colonel has even bought a new set of silk pajamas for the occasion. He feels his Yankees are entitled to tear up something after winning twelve consecutive World's Series games.

Between his silk pajamas and the briefness of the series, the colonel loses money in clean-sweep years, but he doesn't worry. Isn't beer coming back? Or is it?

Let us leave Col. Jacob Ruppert to his happy home-coming and the shedding of his slumber robes tonight, and consider the predicament of the baseball statisticians,

(Continued on First Sport Page)

Remarkable Pictures of Havoc Wrought by Cloudburst—Page 3

Weather
ARIZONA: Local thunderstorms tonight, slightly cooler in south central portion; Friday fair in west.

The Bisbee Evening Ore

"Today's News Today"

Metals
Copper quiet; electrolytic spot and future 8. Lead steady; spot New York 4.30; East St. Louis 4.05.

VOL. XIX | Registrado como articul de segunda class en la Administracion de Correos de Naco, Son., con fecha 24 de Octubre de 1930 | BISBEE, ARIZONA, THURSDAY EVENING, JULY 6, 1933 | Entered as second class matter at the postoffice at Bisbee, Arizona, under Act of Congress, March 3, 1879 | NO. 284

RUTH STARS AS A. L. WINS, 4-2

London Conference To Continue

MONETARY QUESTION EXCLUDED

Tariff Discussions Also Discarded, Steering Committee of Meet Decides

IS VICTORY FOR HULL

Brief Evening Session Ends in Triumph for Stand of American Delegation

LONDON, July 6.—(AP)—The world economic conference will continue but monetary and tariff matters will be excluded, the steering committee of the parley decided this evening.

The decision came after a furious battle and was a victory for Cordell Hull, American secretary of state, who on instruction from President Roosevelt had stoutly insisted that the conclave must continue its attempt to solve pressing world prob[illegible]

France and [illegible] members of the European gold bloc advocated formal conclusion for the major activities of the conference.

The morning session of the steering committee lasted three hours and a half but was unable to arrive at a decision. The evening session, however, was comparatively brief, ending in a triumph for the American position.

In the meantime, a drafting committee, of which Secretary Hull was a member, had been at work on a proposed program of future activities for the parley.

The conference therefore will continue in session for the discussion of economic questions, except tariffs.

The agenda for the conclave thus was substantially modified from its original form when the conference met June 12.

An official communique issued on behalf of the steering committee said:

(Continued on Page Two)

WILL ROGERS Says.

BEVERLY HILLS, July 6.—Now Europe is saying that they didn't get so sore at what Mr. Rosevelt said as they did at the way he said it. You see, diplomats have a thing they call diplomatic language. It's just lots of words, and when they are all added up they don't mean anything.

Well, on account of the President having something to say and wanting to say it, there is no diplomatic language for that. A diplomat has a hundred ways of saying nothing, but no way of saying something. Because he has never had anything, that's why they call 'em diplomats.

I have always said that a conference was held for one reason only, to give everybody a chance to get sore at everybody else. Sometimes it takes two or three conferences to scare up a war, but generally one will do it. I'll bet there was never a war between two nations that had never conferred first.

Yours,

Will Rogers

OPPORTUNITY OF BUSINESS CITED

NEW YORK, July 6. (AP)—A government spokesman bluntly warned American business today that if it fumbles the opportunity for self-government under the national recovery act "the advance of political control over private industry is inevitable."

In uncompromising words Donald A. Richberg, long-time representative of railroad labor, now general counsel of the recovery administration, said that should the industrial control plan fail it would not be a failure of government, but of the present industrial system, either proving the system fundamentally unsound or indicting its present managers of incapacity to operate it successfully.

"There is no choice presented to American business," he said, "between intelligently planned and controlled industrial operations and a return to the gold plated anarchy that masqueraded as 'rugged individualism.'

"There is only the choice presented between private and public election of the directors of industry. If the privately elected boards of directors and the privately chosen managers of industry undertake their task and fulfill their responsibility, they will end all talk of dictatorships and governmental control of business. But if they hold back and waste these precious hours, if they take counsel with prejudice and doubt, if they fumble their great opportunity, they may suddenly find that it has gone forever."

INDIAN COUNCIL BACKS COLLIER

ALBUQUERQUE, N. M., July 6. (AP) — After two days discussion with the new commissioner, the all-Pueblo council has pledged its support to the administration of John Collier.

The meeting, held at Santo Domingo and attended by Collier and representatives from 18 Pueblos in New Mexico, closed late yesterday. During the sessions the Indians talked over the problems of flood control, education and Pueblo government with Collier.

Some of the representatives were unable to agree with the Indian commissioner's new educational policy and asked that present school facilities be operated as they have been in the past. Moreover, they advocated that students from the Pueblos be given preference in the schools at Santa Fe and Albuquerque. However(a majority of the council men felt more day schols located near the Pueblos was the thing to be desired.

Collier left today for Fort Wingate, where on Friday and Saturday he will meet with the Navajo tribal council and then return to Washington.

Prominent Mining Engineer Succumbs

SAN FRANCISCO, July 6. (AP)—Frederick Worthen Bradley, 70, noted mining engineer and president of Alaska Juneau and Bunker Hill and Sullivan mining companies, died today at his summer home at Alta, (Placer county.)

Bradley, born in Nevada City, had been in mining all of his life. He was recipient of high awards from mining societies.

PLAN OF U. S. SELF SUFFICIENCY DEVELOPED BY CHIEF EXECUTIVE

America Can Make Better Domestic Progress Against Depression for Time Being by Avoiding Further International Complications, Roosevelt's Statements Indicate

WASHINGTON, July 6.—(AP)—Indiacations were seen in the capital today that President Roosevelt now believes the United States, for the time being, can make better domestic progress against the depression by avoiding further international commitments.

Some interpreters of political events claimed to have found many signs of a developing theory of American self-sufficiency. Among these, they said, were the president's attitude toward the London economic conference and United States withdrawal from the international convention for the abolition of import and export prohibitions and restrictions.

In silence' Mr. Roosevelt received announcements of the intention to adjourn the London conference. He had instructed the American delegation to work to keep it going, but it was said he felt more real and lasting results could be achieved after the rest of the world sees clearly the results of the domestic program.

His final decision not to stabilize currencies now, as gold bloc nations demanded, was no secret. The situation in the United States, it was said, remains foremost in his mind. In that domestic picture figures largely his plan for a currency based on commodity values.

Meanwhile, he was represented as believing that each nation should stabilize its own currency in relation to its own domestic purchasing power.

When that has been achieved, the

(Continued on Page Two)

BRITISH GIRL SCORES SURPRISING VICTORY OVER MISS HELEN JACOBS

WIMBLEDON, Eng., July 6 (AP)—Miss Dorothy round, second ranked British girl, scored a surprising victory over Miss Helen Jacobs, 4-6, 6-4, 6-2 in the semi-final round of the women's singles in the annual Wimbledon championships today.

The victory qualified her to meet Helen Wills Moody, defending champion, in the final round.

Miss Round, a splendid stylist but hardly considered the equal of the California girl, rallied superbly after losing the first set. Miss Jacobs defeat cost her her chance to face Mrs. Moody in the final round for the second straight year and the third time since their long rivalry started in Berkeley, Cal., years ago.

Mrs. Moody, five times champion and a favorite to win the coming final, swept through the semi-final round this morning with a straight set victory over Fraulein Hilda Krahwinkel, of Germany, 6-4, 6-3. Her past Wimbledon title victories were scored in 1927, 1928, 1929, 1930 and 1932.

Elizabeth Ryan, former Californian now living in England, and her Spanish partner, Enrique Maier, went down to defeat in the fifth round of the mixed doubles before Baroo von Cramm and Hilda Krahwinkel, German team, 6-1, 7-5.

Mrs. Moody remains in the mixed doubles competition with her veteran British Davis cup partner, George Patrick Hughes.

Ellsworth Vines, defending champion who meets Jack Crawford, of Ausralia, in the men's singles final, is the sole American male survivor.

Sanitary Engineer For Arizona Named

PHOENIX, July 6. (AP) — The state health board announced the appointment today of F. Carlyle Roberts, Jr., Tucson, as state sanitary engineer and the creation of a sanitary engineering division of the health department.

Establishment of the department and naming of an engineer is in line with the reorganization plan of the health board, Dr. George C. Truma,n superintendent of public health, said.

Roberts, a native Arizonan, took office immediately and started making inspections of sanitary conditions throughout the state.

FINANCIAL NOTES

CORN HELPS OTHER GRAINS

CHICAGO, July 6.—(AP)—Attainment of new high record prices for the season distinguished the corn market today, and helped give strength to wheat and other grains.

Continued damage to corn and other crops was reported. Conservatism in many quarters, however, was engendered by the sharp upturn of late, both wheat and corn having risen about 12 cents a bushel from last week's low.

Corn closed strong, 2 1-8@2 3-4 cents above yesterday's finish, wheat 3-8@1 14c up, oats 1-8@1-2c up and provisions unchanged to a rise of 15 cents.

COPPER STEADY

NEW YORK, July 6.—(AP)—Copper steady; electrolfytic spot and future 8 1-2. Tin easy; spot and nearby 45.87; future 46.05. Iron quiet, unchanged. Lead steady; spot New York 4.30; East St. Louis 4.15. Zinc quiet; East St. Louis spot and future 4.60. Antimony 7.00.

CALL MONEY STEAD Y

NEW YORK, July 6.(AP)—Call money steady; 1 per cent all day. Time loans steady; 60-90 days 3-4; 4-5 tons 1; 6 mos. 14 per cent. Prime commercial paper 1 12. Baners acceptances unchanged.

COTTON TRADING LESSENS

NEW YORK, July 6.—(AP)—Trading in cotton was less active today with fluctuations comparatively narrow and irregular. eYsterday's liquidation appeared to have left the market in an improved technical position, as selling was less active, and the declines brought in some covering or rebuying as well as a moderate trade demand. October contracts after selling off to 10.31 during the early trading, rallied to 10.43, with the midafternoon market quiet and steady at net advances of about 2 to 5 points.

DOLLAR GAINS IN LONDON

LONDON, July 6. (AP)—Uncertainty regarding the outlook somewhat restricted operations in the foreign exchange market today and caused irregular movements of the dollar which gained 3 3-8 cents on the day.

Opening at $4.50 as compared with the overnight price of $4.52 3-4, the dollar encountered a fair amount of buying and appreciated to $4.47 3-4 to the pound.

Later the rate weakened to $4.51 on light offerings but recovery followed bringing the closing price to $4.49 3-8.

General support was forthcoming for gold currencies which experienced further slight improvement.

INTEREST ACQUIRED

NEW YORK, July 6. (AP)—The Equity corporation, an investment trust con-

(Continued on Page Two)

MARKET IS FIRM BUT UNEVENTFUL

Pivotal Stocks Steady But Show Little Inclination to Continue Splurge

SLIGHT GAINS MADE

British Pound Sterling Sags and European Gold Currencies Fluctuate

By VICTOR EUBANK

NEW YORK, July 6. (AP)—The jigging dollar settled down to a slow waltz today and financial markets generally maintained a firm position in quiet active trading.

Pivotal stocks were steady but displayed little inclination to repeat their recent soaring movements. Pool operations were apparent in some specialties. The British pound sterling sagged a trifle in terms of dollars and most European gold currencies fluctuated in unimportant fractions.

Some of the rail shares were imbued with renewed courage by fresh news of substantial increases in traffic. Advances of 1 to 2 or more points were recorded by Pennsylvania, Santa Fe, Union Pacific, New York Central, Delaware & Hudson and Central of New Jersey. The tobaccos were also given a run with Reynolds B, Liggett & Myers B, American B and Lorillard getting up around 1 to 3. Consolidated Gas came back with a 2 point advance and American Power & Light and Public Service of New Jersey stepped up more than a point each. Oils up fractionally to 2 points included Standard of New Jersey, Houston, Pure and Socony. Douglas Aircraft, United Aircraft and Aviation Corp. showed similar gains. The alcohols and farm stocks were indifferent.

Ammunition for the carrier group was furnished by the car-loading figures of the Pennsylvania for last week

(Continued on Page Two)

Balanced Budget Is Essential to Gain Relief Says Douglas

WASHINGTON, July 6. (AP) — Lewis Douglas, director of the budget, proposed today that states be required to balance their budgets before the federal government permits them to participate in the $3,300,000,000 public works program.

The budget director, in fact, was proposing a cautious program all along the public works campaign.

To President Roosevelt he suggested elimination of many of the projects submitted to the White House for immediate construction.

Disturbed by prospect of a huge increase in indebtedness through the

(Continued on Page Two)

Bambino Hits Home Run With One On In Third

Wallop Puts American League Ahead to Stay; Frisch Also Hits For Circuit

SIX HURLERS ARE USED

A. L. Gathers Nine Blows and N. L. Eight Safeties in Bang up Encounter

COMISKEY PARK, CHICAGO, July 6.—(AP)—Babe Ruth blazed out as the star of stars once more today to smash out a home run in the third inning to give the American League All Stars their winning margin in a great 4 to 2 victory over the hand picked aces of the National League before 49,000 spectators.

As the great panorama of stars fell and shone, Ruth drove out his long distance wallop with Charley Gehringer of Detroit on base to push his mates ahead to stay as General Alvin Crowder and as Lefty Grove, relief pitchers for Vernon Gomez, kept the National batters in check except for a home run by Frankie Frisch of the St. Louis Cardinals and Lonnie Warneke, pitching star of the Chicago Cubs, who pitched well, hit a triple and scored on an infield out.

Three National League moundsmen saw action. Bill Hallahan of St. Louis, the starter, Warneke and Carl Hubbell, who yielded nine hits. Gomez, Crowder

(Continued on Page Two)

PLAY BY PLAY STORY OF BIG ALL-STAR TILT

First Inning

Martin grounde out, Cronin to Gehrig. Frisch went out the same way. Cronin made a fine running, one handed catch of Klein's short fly.

No runs, no hits, no errors, none left.

Both managers shuffled their lineups at the last minute. Jimmy Wilson went to catch for the Nationals and Pepper Martin went to third. Chapman was thrown out by Martin.

Gehringer was the first player to reach base, drawing a walk. The crowd roared as Ruth came to bat. After fedding the Bamino three straight balls, Hallahan got him with three straight strikes, the last one called. On the last strike Gehringer stole second. Gehrig was out, Terry to Hallahan, who covered first.

No runs, no hits, no errors, one left.

Second Inning

Hafey's pop fly fell safe for a single back of second. Terry hit the first pitch for a single to left, Hafey stopping at second. Berger lined to Dykes who threy to Gehrig to double Terry. Bartell struck out.

No runs, two hits, no errors, one left.

Simmons flied high to Berger. Dykes and Cronin walked. The National league infield bathered about Hallahan as McGraw waved two pitchers into action in the bull pen. Rick Ferrell flied to Klein and both runners stuck to their bases. Lefty Gomez drew first blood by slapping a hard single to short left center, scoring Dykes. Cronin stopped at second. Chapman forced Gomez, Bartell to Frisch.

One run, one hit, no errors, two left.

Third Inning

Dykes took J. Wilson's slow roller and threw him out. Hallahan got a big hand as he came to bat. Simmons made a fast dash to right center to get Bill's high one. Cronin went back on the grass to get Martin's high pop fly.

No runs, no hits, no errors, none left.

Gehringer drew another walk with a 4-1 count. Ruth, with the count one and one, hoisted one of Hallahan's slants into the lower right field grandstand seats for a home run, scoring Gehringer ahead of him. Gehrig drew still another walk and Hallahan went to the showers. Out of the bull pen strode Lonnie Warneke, pride of the Chicago Cubs pitching staff, to replace him. Hallahan had allowed three runs, two hits and five walks. Simmons hit into a lightning double play, Bartell to Frisch to Terry. Dykes singled sharply past Martin. Cronin flied to Berger. Two runs, two hits, no errors, one left.

Fourth Inning

Alvin Crowder, righthanded star of the Washington Senators, replaced Gomez on the mound for the American league. Simmons made a beautiful running catch in left center to haul down Frisch's long drive. Kelin tapped

(Continued on Page Two)

ADMINISTRATION TO HASTEN CODES

WASHINGTON, July 6.—(AP)—The administration is contemplating steps to hurry up industries which officials say have been disappointingly slow in shaping trade agreements under the national recovery law.

The situation was up for analysis and decision at a session today between President Roosevelt, Hugh S. Johnson the recovery administrator, and Secretary Roper, chairman of the cabinet advisory committee on industry.

At the rate industries are moving, officials regard it as likely that wage increases cannot become effective on a big scale before the end of summer, whereas the administration objective is to have the entire program well in operation within sixty days. Furthermore, it was definitely understood that Johnson and Roper had information to lay before the president showing that while many industries are debating what to do, individual factories have jumped in to take advantage of the expected advance in prices, by running full tilt at present low wage levels, piling up cheap stocks with the intention of making a big profit on them later.

Should this policy continue administration men see a danger that over production might again break down the painfully built upward movement.

Baseball's Dream Comes True

COMISKEY PARK, Chicago, July 6 (AP)—Baseball's dream game came true at Comiskey park today as the hand picked aces of the major leagues clashed in the first all star contest in the Great American game's history before a roaring capacity crowd of 49,000.

Not a cloud streaked the skies as the capacity throng started trooping into the park hours before game time. It was a beautiful day, crisp and just cool enough with a light breeze.

The National league stars' attired in natty uniforms with the insignia "National league" printed across their shirt fronts, arried first. The American leaguers wore travel uniforms of white.

Lonie Warneke, ace pitcher for the Cubs, drew a cheer as he beat the pack of stars to the bat bag, and started to bat out bunts. Tony Cuccinello of Brooklyn kept the others busy chasing short smashes.

Joe Cronin, young boss of the league leading Washington Senators' was the first American leaguer on the field and responded to salvos of applause by belting several long ones off Ed Rommell of the Athletics. Ben Chapman of the Yanks stole his stuff immediately by parking four successive balls into the left field bleachers as the National leaguers watched him with awe. Babe Ruth drew a big cheer, but failed to hit a ball out of the infield in five cuts. Jimmy Foxx of the A's hit three terrific drives to the upper left field grand stand seats. Babe took a squint at Jimmy's wallops and then followed suit with even longer drives to the opposite side of the field.

John McGraw, drawn out of retirement to lead the National forces' and shrewd old Connie Mack held a council of war with their stars in separate hotels and then took their time about arriving at the scene of action.

McGraw was a real fashion plate attired in a brown sack suit and straw hat. He grinned as he displayed a score card.

"Connie's got nothing on me," he beamed as he referred to the veteran Macks system of score card waving.

Joe McCarthy, manager of the world championship Yankees, sat on the American league "home club" bench ready to assist Connie in the master minding.

Bill Walker, Cardinal southpaw, tossed em up for the dazzling array of National league stars as they took their turn at batting practice. Chuck Klein of Philadelphia was the first to ram one of Bill's slants out of the park. Chick Hafey, Cincinnati's bespectacled

(Continued on Page Two)

New York Stock Exchange

BY THE ASSOCIATED PRESS

Following are high, low and closing quotations at 3:15 p. m. (E. S. T.) as received over The Associated Press-Bisbee Evening Ore leased wire and copyrighted, 1933, by the Standard Statistics Co.

	High	Low	Close		High	Low	Close		High	Low	Close
Adams Exp	13¾	12¼	13⅛	Am & For Pow	18½	17⅛	18⅛	Am Smelt & R	37½	36⅛	37¾
Affiliat Pro	9⅞	9	9⅞	Am Hide & Leath	14	13⅝	14	Am Steel Fdrs	25½	24	25¼
Air Reduct	93¾	93¼	93¾	Am Home Prod	40½	39⅛	40¼	Am Stores	47½	46½	47⅜
Alaska Jun	22⅜	20⅞	22	Am Ive	15	14¼	14⅝	Am Sug Ref	66½	64½	66
Alleghany	7½	7	7⅜	Am Internat	14¼	13⅛	14	Am Tel & Tel	132	128½	132
Al Chem & Dye	130⅞	128	130⅜	Am Loco	37¼	36½	37	Am THob	90	87	89½
Allis Ch Mfg	23⅜	21	23	Am Mach & F	20⅛	19⅜	20	Am Tob B	94¼	90¼	93¼
Amerada	41¼	39⅜	39¾	Am Pow & L	15⅞	14½	15¾	Am Wat Wks	40⅜	38	39⅜
Am Car & Fdy	35⅜	33½	35⅜	Am Rad St San	18½	17⅝	18½	Am Woolen	16½	15⅜	16⅜
Am Coml Al	42⅜	40¾	42⅜	Am Roll Mill	28	27	27¾				

(Continued on Page Two)

San Francisco Chronicle Sporting Green

EDITED BY HARRY B. SMITH

FOUNDED 1865 | CCC | SAN FRANCISCO, CAL., FRIDAY, JULY 14, 1933 | H15 | VOL. CXLII, NO. 180

DE MAGGIO HITS IN 49TH; TIES RECORD

Alice Marble Wins Way to Semifinals in Longwood Net Play

Pegler

Softies? Heck, No!

Tennis He-Man Game

Too Much Pro Spirit

Big Stars Take Orders

By WESTBROOK PEGLER

NEW YORK, July 13—I will have to admit, after all these years, that I never have become imbued with the spirit of tournament tennis.

I have witnessed many famous contests on the grass at Forest Hills and elsewhere, including the historic long one between Will Tilden, when he was at his best, and the Japanese whom the boys called Hitchy-Koo, which went on and on until everybody was late for dinner and the final result broke over into morning paper time.

It seems to be a nice game, calling for plenty of food, early and late, and something of the delicacy and skill of billiards, and the sissy implication of the technical term "love" has long since been lived down by a lot of lean, limber young athletes of exceedingly he type, who could play tennis all day, stay up all night and lick twice their weight in bartenders any time.

European Experts Shroud Game in Deep Mystery

I think that probably the writing of tennis, especially by some of the European tennis experts, is partly responsible for the mystery of the business which has defied my appreciation.

They go on with a great deal of flubdub about courage, which seems very unnecessary in connection with a game in which nobody ever has come down with so much as a black eye or a nose bleed, and when I read last week a 500-word story about the raw, red bravery of a young Australian by the name of Griffin, who had persisted in the use of a two-fisted backhand, contrary to all orthodox opinion, I just thought, "Well, now, what the heck!"

Maybe it is irregular to use both hands to the backhand and maybe the young Australian did have to stand some meddlesome advice. But he had found that he could hit a backhand better with two hands than with one.

So he did, and when he did and his method proved to be O. K. for him, you would have thought, to read about it, that he had won a war unassisted.

Two Hands Are Better Than One, Anyway

Anyway, that works in the right way in any sport but tennis. I just think the young Australian would have been very dumb to have given into his instructors and tradition if he was convinced that he couldn't hit the ball as well the right way.

Then, also, it is pretty hard to appreciate a class of players and promoters who live a lie year after year, handing down the tradition from one generation to another that a tennis player may with honor cadge, sponge, mooch and chisel his living and any pickings which he can put his hands on, but may not turn honestly pro.

Of all the hypocritical record of tennis, whose most noted amateurs have been just as determinately professional as Jack Dempsey ever was, the most disagreeable pretense was that of the young American star who recently opposed the idea of an American open tournament, including pros and amateurs, on the ground that professionalism tended to degrade the sport. This objection came from a player who had quit college because of the panic and who had at that time been playing his way around the world, living on his tennis, for more than a year.

Good Looking Tennis Gals Become Clothes Horses

Does there come along a lady player of note whose face would not scare a dog out of a boneyard, then she finds herself in receipt of much merchandise from the shopkeepers and customers of Paris.

And why? Because the big-hearted Parisian merchants are just naturally fond of her and wish to see her happy, or because, perhaps, the boys reckon to strut their merchandise on a prominent clothes horse of the tennis business.

I have heard tennis traced to royal beginnings. Athletically it is

Continued on Page 17H, Col. 3
Sporting Green

Seal Youngster Clouts 3 In Game; Equals Mark Set By Oakland Star in 1915

Los Angeles Club Wins Ball Game Behind Steady Pitching of Thomas; Kid Outfielder Will Try for New Record Tonight

By ED. R. HUGHES

WELL, FOLKS, Joe de Maggio, 18-year-old fly chaser of the Seals, was the calmest appearing person in Seals' Stadium yesterday afternoon when he stepped up in the first inning and made a hit that tied the Coast League record for hitting in consecutive games. The record was made by Jack Ness in 1915 playing for Oakland when he hit safely in 49 consecutive games.

In the first inning yesterday Young Joe lifted a fly to short center field back of second base. Arnold Statz, Jimmy Reese and Carl Dittmar all chased after the ball, but no one put a hand on it. It was a clean hit, but it was not one of the kind Joe usually makes, but that hit tied the record that had stood for 18 years.

So, just to put the crusher on all the Doubting Thomases, Young Joe stepped into the first ball pitched him in the fourth inning and belted it over the left field fence. There is no way to discount a home run when the ball is hit out of the park, so young Joe got a mighty cheer.

THREE HITS IN FOUR TRIES FOR THE DAY

And just to show that he still had something left, Joe drove a liner to right field in the eighth for a single, bringing his batting average up to .750 for the day. He went to bat four times and was thrown out by Lilliard in the sixth. The other three times he faced Fay Thomas he got hits.

Joe began his great batting streak in the second game of a double header on May 28 and during that spell he has been to bat 201 times and has made 84 hits, including 14 doubles, six three baggers and 11 home runs, including the one he made yesterday. His batting average since May 28 is .418, and his batting average for the entire season is .333.

That is a remarkable showing for a kid just breaking into professional baseball, and it is just beginning to dawn on Joe that he has done something out of the ordinary. His right hand and wrist are bound in tape because of a minor injury and he confesses that he was a bit nervous the first time he faced Fay Thomas. But he took a cut at the first ball pitched and got a hit on the Texas leaguer that fell back of second base with three Los Angeles players in pursuit.

FANS CHEER YOUNGSTER AS HE TIES RECORD

He also hit the first ball pitched him in the fourth inning and he drove it over the left-field fence with plenty of room to spare for a home run. In the sixth he hit a ground ball hard at Lilliard and was tossed out, but in the eighth, with two men out, he drove a liner to right for his third hit of the game. No wonder the fans give the boy a hand every time he goes to bat.

Los Angeles won the game easily by a score of 8 to 2. Fay Thomas did not issue a pass and he kept the ten hits well scattered, but Joe DeMaggio had no trouble hitting him.

Art McDougall started for the Seals, but was batted out of the box in the third and Lee Stine finished. He was no puzzle, either.

Jim Oglesby, first baseman of the

Continued on Page 16H, Col. 4
Sporting Green

49 DOWN ☆☆ ONE TO GO

Joe DeMaggio, youthful San Francisco outfielder, who yesterday tied the Coast League record for hitting in consecutive games. In 1915, the year Joe was born, Jack Ness of the Oakland club hit in 49 straight games. Yesterday DeMaggio singled through second base in the second inning of the 49th straight game in which he has made one or more hits. Tonight the youth will attempt to hit in his 50th game for a new record.

SEEN FROM PRESS BOX

Manager Jimmy Caveney is playing on his nerve alone because the Seals have no other third baseman. He was hit on the right elbow by a thrown ball before the game Wednesday and there is a lump as big as an egg on the elbow. Those who jeered Jimmy for his failure to throw a man out on a bunt yesterday did not know, of course, that Jimmy is so badly crippled.

* * * *

Leo Ostenberg, crippled third basemen, is not only Joe de Maggio's manager but is giving him "pep" talks before each time at bat, and he is also his social mentor, and he has told Joe it is not good form to wear a yellow shirt, especially around hotel lobbies.

* * * *

Foy Frazier, who once played with the Seals, took Charley McDaniels, a young, right-handed pitcher from Fresno to show him to Oscar Vitt of the Hollywood club. McDaniels has good speed and Hollywood may sign him.

* * * *

John T. Essick, father of Bill Essick, scout for the New York Yankees, was buried at Los Angeles last Wednesday.

Joe Coughlin Holds Place At Brookline

San Francisco Girl Scores Upset in Longwood Invitational Tourney

BROOKLINE, Mass., July 13 (AP)—The women's invitation competition, a recent addition to Brookline's historic Bowl week, held the interest

Continued on Page 16H, Col. 6
Sporting Green

Brick Morse

Rugby in 1914

BIG GAME THRILLS

By BRICK MORSE

STANFORD was quicker to grasp the details of Rugby play than was California. The red shirts won the first three Big Games under Rugby rules.

It was no easy task to switch from the one system to the other. In American football the first thing to think of after being tackled was to hang on to the ball. In Rugby, on being tackled, you must get rid of the ball.

In 1906 the players schooled in the American game hung onto the ball for dear life. They persisted in bucking the line for short gains instead of trying to start passing or dribbling rushes down the field.

It was most exasperating for the spectators who seemed more quick to grasp the system than the players themselves. By 1909, however, the boys were playing Rugby which compared with the standard established in England and Australia. St. Mary's and Santa Clara were pulling out fine Rugby teams and all of the high schools had switched to Rugby rules.

Australian Influence Helps Develop Game

Through trips to Australia and visits of foreign Rugbyites to this section progress was rapid until by 1913 we were turning out Rugby players as good as there were in the world.

Our teams could play on even terms with the best, always excepting those All-Blacks from Australia.

Those Australians were tantalizing. They trained on toddies. They smoked cigarettes on the field during rest periods. They kept the fraternity boys up most of the night before an imporant game. They did everything our trainers told us not to do. But oh my, how they could run and pass and kick when they needed points. They never seemed to tire.

We couldn't beat the All-Blacks. I remember that even after Rugby had been shuffled with the discards

Continued on Page 17H, Col. 2
Sporting Green

Ducks Beat Oakland in Slugging Bee

Triple Play by Portland in Eighth Inning Features Contest at Emeryville

PORTLAND DUCKS finally stopped the Oaks yesterday afternoon, when they put on a slugfest for a 7-to-1 victory. Art Jacobs, young Portland southpaw, twirled shutout ball until the last of the ninth, when Joe Wera connected for his fourth single to score Leroy Anton from second base.

The game was featured by a triple play pulled by the Ducks in the eighth inning. After Kintana and Mailho walked, Ben Sankey leaped into the air to spear Frenchy Uhalt's liner. He threw to Monroe, who touched second, retiring Kintana, and Monroe threw to Sheeley before Mailho could get back to the initial bag.

Plenty of fast fielding made up for the free hitting contest. Besides the triple play, there were five double plays, of which the Oaks made three.

Glen Gabler, starting pitcher for the Oaks, was driven to the showers in the fourth inning when the Ducks ran their lead up to 4 to 0. Mike Salonisen was bumped for the other three runs when four hits were bunched off him in the sixth. Wera and Joe Palmisano were the hitting stars of the day, the latter also getting four blows in as many trips to the plate.

The teams meet in their fourth game tonight at 8:15 o'clock.

PORTLAND

	AB	R	H	O	A	E
Mulligan, 3b	5	1	1	2	7	0
Monroe, 2b	5	0	0	1	5	0
Oana, cf	5	1	1	3	0	0
Sheely, 1b	3	0	1	14	0	0
Moore, rf	4	0	1	0	1	0
Berger, lf	3	1	1	0	0	0
Sankey, s	4	2	2	4	3	0
Palmisano, c	4	2	4	3	0	0
Jacobs, p	4	0	2	0	1	0
Totals	37	7	13	27	17	0

OAKLAND

	AB	R	H	O	A	E
Kintana, 2b	4	0	1	6	5	0
Mailho, cf	3	0	2	4	0	0
Uhalt, lf	4	0	1	3	0	0
Pool, rf	3	0	1	0	0	0
Anton, 1b	4	1	1	8	0	0
Reimondi, c	4	0	0	4	0	0
Wera, 3b	4	0	4	1	1	0
Deviveiros, s	4	0	1	1	7	0
Gabler, p	1	0	0	0	0	0
Salinsen, p	2	0	0	0	0	0
Scott	0	0	0	0	0	0
Totals	33	1	11	27	13	0

Scott batted for Pool in ninth.

Portland	2	0	0	2	0	3	0	0	0	—7
Hits	3	1	0	3	0	4	0	2	0	—13
Oakland	0	0	0	0	0	0	0	0	1	—1
Hits	1	1	0	1	2	2	1	1	2	—11

Runs batted in—Mulligan, Oana, Moore, Palmisano 2, Jacobs 2. Two-base hits—Sankey, Palmisano, Mailho, Uhalt. Stolen bases—Mulligan 2. Triple play—Sankey to Monroe to Sheely. Double plays—Deviveiros to Kintana to Anton 2, Jacobs to Sankey to Sheely, Kintana to Deviveiros to Anton, Mulligan to Sheely. Innings pitched—By Gabler 3 1-3. Charge defeat—To Gabler. At bat—Off Gabler 15. Hits batted—Off Gabler 7. Runs scored—Off Gabler 4. Runs responsible for—Gabler 4, Jacobs 1, Salinsen 3. Struck out—By Gabler 2, Jacobs 2, Salinsen 2. Bases on balls—Off Gabler 2, Jacobs 2. Umpires—Cady and Rue. Time of game—1h. 40m.

AMERICAN ASSOCIATION

By Associated Press

Indianapolis 0, Milwaukee 4.
Toledo 4, St. Paul 7.
Columbus 9, Minneapolis 10.
Louisville 10, Kansas City 10 (called end tenth allow Louisville catch train).

Midget Wolgast Is Beaten by Farber

NEW YORK, July 13 (AP)—Lew Farber of New York gained a disputed decision over Midget Wolgast of Philadelphia, generally recognized as flyweight champion of the world, in a 10-round non-title match at Fugazy Bowl, Coney Island, tonight.

De Maggio Hitting at .418 Clip

Batting Streak Started May 28

The batting streak of Joe de Maggio began in the second game of a double header played at Portland on Sunday, May 28, 1933, between the San Francisco Seals and Portland Beavers.

Since then the young outfielder has faced the twirling staff of every opposing club in the league with the exception of Sacramento. During this batting orgy De Maggio has faced the best pitchers in the league, including Jacobs and Boone of Portland; Haid, Caster, Page, Sewell, Herman Pillette, Radonitz, of Seattle; Sheehan, Campbell, Wetzel, Dumovich, Page, Shellenback, of Hollywood; Joiner, Salinsen, Ludolph, Gabler, Walsh, of Oakland; Babich, Ted Pillette, Cole, Osborne, Lieber, Johnson, Phebus, of Mission; Ballou, Newsom, Thomas, Ward, Hermann, of Los Angeles.

DE MAGGIO'S BATTING RECORD

	G	AB	R	H	2B	3B	HR	SH	SB	Pct
From April 4 to July 13	101	402	64	134	24	7	17	5	7	.333
From April 4 to May 28	52	201	24	50	10	1	6	2	3	.249
From May 28 to July 12	48	201	40	84	14	6	11	3	4	.418

Baer Proposes Carnera Title Charity Bout

COLORADO SPRINGS, Col., July 13 (AP)—Max Baer, heavy weight pugilist, is willing to donate his purse to charity if he can get a shot at Primo Carnera's recently won title this year, he said here today.

Baer, accompanied by his manager and trainer, interrupted his trip to Salt Lake City, where he has an exhibition bout scheduled, to spend a few hours with Spencer Penrose and C. L. Tutt.

Baer said he would later go to Hollywood to appear in a motion picture with Joan Crawford. He plans to return to Colorado Springs in the fall for an exhibition bout, and, if he lands a major fight in the West, he will train here, he said.

De Maggio to Be Honored This Evening

Mayor Angelo Rossi will take great pride at Seals' Stadium tonight in presenting to Joe de Maggio, sensational young hitter of the Seals, with a gold watch, suitably engraved to show that he has equaled the long established record for hitting in consecutive games. The watch is given by the owners of the Seals. No doubt Joe will get other presents on his "night," for a tremendous amount of interest has been created by his wonderful hitting record.

Joe is such a modest young fellow that he hardly realizes what all the "shooting" is about. He just goes up there and takes his cuts, and he is liable to establish a new Coast League record tonight. Buck Newsom, a fast ball pitcher, will try to stop him.

INTERNATIONAL LEAGUE

By Associated Press

Toronto 5, Albany 3.
Rochester 7, Baltimore 0.
Newark 7, Montreal 3.
Buffalo 17, Jersey City 6.

Fights

SEATTLE, July 13 (AP)—Tod Morgan knocked out Sailor Leo Dardeen in the sixth round of a scheduled ten-round bout at the White Center Arena tonight.

NEW HAVEN, Conn., July 13 (AP)—Frankie Petrolle, brother of Billy, lost his ten-round fight here tonight to Carmen Knapp on a decision. Petrolle scored the only knockdown of the bout in the fifth round.

Wrestling

DETROIT, July 13 (AP)—Jim Londos, tonight threw Pat O'Shocker after 44 minutes of a scheduled 90-minute match at Navin Field, Detroit's major league ball park. Londos used a body slam.

Sever Released by Mission Ball Club

LOS ANGELES, July 13 (AP)—Carl Sever, Mission shortstop, was released today. He left tonight for San Francisco, where he expects to sign with the Seals tomorrow.

Australians-English Split Davis Cup Tilts

WIMBLEDON, England, July 13 (AP)—The first skirmish in the English-Australian tennis battle for the right to go to Paris to meet the United States in the interzone Davis cup final ended all square today when the two countries divided the opening singles matches.

Jack Crawford, present king of the tennis world by reason of recent defeats of Ellsworth Vines and Henri Cochet, sent the Anzacs away to a lead with a 4-6, 6-2, 6-2, 6-3 victory over Henry W. (Bunny) Austin, but Fred Perry evened accounts for the mother country by turning back young Vivian McGrath in straight sets, 6-2, 6-4, 6-2.

With much depending on the outcome of the doubles tomorrow, Australia today named Crawford and Adrian Quist, another youngster, to oppose the veteran English internationalists, Perry and Patrick Hughes.

The surprise of today's play was not so much Crawford's victory, that was expected, but that Austin was able to take one set from the lanky Australian. Seemingly able to do no wrong, Austin played as if inspired.

That, however, was Austin's best stand, as there was no doubt as to Crawford's superiority after the first set.

Youngsters Lead in A. A. U. Trial Swims

CHICAGO, July 13 (AP)—A pair of youngsters, Jack Medica of Seattle, and Ralph Flanagan of Miami, Fla., showed the way to their older rivals today in the trials of the one-mile free style, opening event of the national A. A. U. swimming championship meet.

The Seattle youth won the first heat in 22 minutes 7 seconds. Fifteen-year-old Flanagan did likewise, covering the distance in 22:22.4.

San Francisco Chronicle Sporting Green

EDITED BY HARRY B. SMITH

FOUNDED 1865 | CCC* | SAN FRANCISCO, CAL., SATURDAY, JULY 15, 1933 | H11 | VOL. CXLII, NO. 181

DE MAGGIO HITS IN 50TH GAME, SETS RECORD

Joe Coughlin Loses Out in Longwood Bowl Tennis Tourney

Sportlight

Yanks Call on Harvard
Devens Has the Stuff
Colleges Have Helped
Collegians Aid N. Y.

By GRANTLAND RICE

(Copyright, 1933, by The North American Newspaper Alliance, Inc.)

LESS than three years ago, a young fellow named Devens decided to take a stroll.

At the moment he happened to be carrying a football. In the presence of some 60,000 spectators he strolled about 20 yards or more in the general direction of Yale's goal and put Harvard in position to win one of the hardest football games of the year.

No one in that crowd at that moment had any idea that less than three years later the Yankees would be sending out a hurry call to the same Devens to help bolster a somewhat wobbly pitching staff, with a major league pennant at stake.

There are three things, anyway, you can say about this same young Devens.

He has a cool head, a stout heart and a strong arm. He can crowd a pile of stuff on that baseball, and whether or not he is quite seasoned, he can't do much worse than several Yankee pitchers have been doing in the last few weeks.

In thinking of Devens I recall a day when young blond Arthur Clarkson, also of Harvard, yanked off his cap in the midst of a fusillade as he began increasing his speed. Maybe the fusillade blew his cap off. He was then pitching for Clarke Griffith's New York Yankees.

The Yankees seem to have the call on Harvard pitchers. After all, college pitchers have done pretty well—Mathewson of Bucknell, Plank of Gettysburg, Bender of Carlisle, Overall of California, Coombs of Colby, Coakley and Carroll of Holy Cross, Doc White of Georgetown, Rhem of Clemson, Earnshaw of Swarthmore—and maybe fifty or eighty more.

Speedy Dado Wins Verdict Over Teiken

HOLLYWOOD, July 14 (AP)—Speedy Dado, flashy Filipino bantamweight, won a decision over Joe Teiken, Korean Kewpie, in their 10 round bout here tonight. It was a spectacular fight the entire route but Teiken was unable to cope with the masterful Dado, the Filipino taking seven rounds, with three going to the Korean. Teiken went down for a three count in the first round.

Senators Win From Indians Again, 7-6

SACRAMENTO, July 14 (AP)—Seattle lost another ball game by one run tonight, as the Senators took their third in four starts, 7 to 6.

The Solons rapped George Caster hard in the early frames and finished up on him in the fifth with a four-run splurge that iced the game.

SEATTLE

	AB	R	H	O	A
Almda,rf	4	0	1	3	0
Elswrth,s	4	2	2	1	4
Welch,cf	4	0	2	3	0
Burns,1b	3	0	1	9	1
Brdbry,c	4	1	0	4	0
Wlters,lf	4	1	1	2	0
Cscrt,3b	3	1	1	1	2
Jhnsn,2b	2	0	0	1	2
Caster,p	2	1	1	0	1
Sewell,p	1	0	1	0	0
MLrny,2b	2	0	1	0	0
Bngvani	1	0	0	0	0
Totals	34	6	11	24	10

SACRAMENTO

	AB	R	H	O	A
Broja,cf	5	1	1	2	1
Backr,cf	5	0	1	0	4
Cmilli,1b	4	1	1	14	2
Stnbkr,lf	4	1	1	0	0
Lhmn,rf	4	2	2	1	0
Kmpis,2b	4	2	3	5	4
Frnch,s	3	0	1	2	8
Wirts,c	3	0	1	3	2
Noonn,p	2	0	1	0	1
House,p	0	0	0	0	1
Snders,p	1	0	1	0	1
Totals	35	7	13	27	24

McLarney batted for Johnson in the 6th.
Bongiovanni batted for Caster in the 6th.

Seattle	1	1	0	0	0	3	1	0	0	—6
Hits	3	1	1	0	0	3	0	2	1	—11
Sacramento	1	1	0	1	4	0	0	0	*	—7
Hits	1	2	1	3	4	0	1	1	*	—13

Home run—Caster. Two-base hits—Backer, Kampouris 2, Noonan, Walters. Sacrifice hits—Noonan, French. Runs batted in—Burns, Camilli, Caster, Wirts 2, Lahman, French 2, Kampouris, Walters, Coscarart, Bradbury, Bongiovanni. Double play—Backer to Kampouris to Camilli. Errors—Noonan (Sacramento 1), Burns (Seattle 1). Innings pitched—By Noonan 5 plus, Caster 5, House 1 plus. Credit victory to Noonan. Charge defeat to Caster. At bat—Off Noonan 22, Caster 24, House 2. Hits batted—Off Noonan 8, Caster 11, House none. Runs scored—Off Noonan 4, Caster 7, House 1. Runs responsible for—Noonan 5, Caster 7, House 1. Struck out—By Caster 2, Noonan 2, Sewell 2. Bases on balls—Off Noonan 2, House 1, Sanders 1. Hits by pitched balls—Wirts, Burns. Wild pitch—Sewell. Stolen bases—Boroja, Coscarart, Kampouris, Welch. Time of game—1h. 39m. Umpires—Snyder and Fanning.

Dog Scores Third Straight at Belmont

Captain Bob scored his third straight victory at Belmont last night. The McGrath pooch won from Pete Andrew and Charley's Footsteps in the featured race by hugging the rail where possible and avoiding trouble.

Pete Andrew, the choice, may have been best but he suffered interference turning for home. Wilkie Wonder, the early pacemaker, was eliminated in the same jam. An improved dog was Charley's Footsteps, which will bear tabbing from now on. Captain Bob paid $17.60.

Youthful Seal Outfielder Batting Star for Locals In Night Game at Stadium

Seal Management Presents Watch to Kid Sensation; Mayor Rossi Congratulates Hitter in Pre-Game Ceremonies

By ED. R. HUGHES

JOE DE MAGGIO, 18-year-old batting sensation of the Coast League, either has nerves of steel or he has no nerves at all, for the kid slammed out a single in the first inning of the game last night, making the fiftieth game in succession in which he has made one or more hits. That hit drove in two runs and smashed the record of forty-nine games made by Jack Ness eighteen years ago.

There was a crowd of about ten thousand out to cheer the youngster and the ceremonies before the game were enough to shake the nerve of an old campaigner, but Young Joe took it all in his stride and then made good his first time at bat.

There was Mayor Rossi to present a watch given by the owners of the Seals. Joe's mother and young sister came up with flowers as the Mayor was talking and the Mayor kissed Mother DeMaggio on the cheek, thereby making almost as big a hit as Joe did a few minutes later.

The Jolly Knights of North Beach gave a fine traveling bag and the players of the San Francisco club came through with a substantial check. Joe took all his honors calmly and as he walked to the bench with his mother on one side of him and his young sister on the other, and his arms full of flowers, there was the faint flicker of a smile on his face. No doubt the youngster was pleased, as who wouldn't be?

ANGELS SCORE THREE RUNS IN FIRST

The Seals got off to a bad start, Los Angeles scoring three runs on five hits in the first inning and it took a marvelous throw by DeMaggio from deep right field to shut them off.

He captured a fly from the bat of Dittmar and he made a line throw to the plate to retire Gudat and complete a double play that retired the side. That one play stamped Joe as a ball player of class, but there was more to come.

Naturally all eyes were on Joe when he went to bat in the first inning and he did not disappoint. Sever got a hit, Galan drew a pass and both runners moved up on Funk's out. Then up stepped Joe amid thunderous applause. He swung at the first ball pitched by Newsom and missed.

Camera men crowded up close to the plate, flashed lights, and Charley Graham, part owner of the Seals, jumped over the low railing in front of his box and ordered the camera men back.

FLASHLIGHTS BOTHER JOE IN FIRST TIME UP

Charley feared the flashlights would blind Joe and prevent his getting a hit. As the camera men moved back, Newsom pitched again and this time Joe whacked a single right over second base to score two runners, so the tension for that game at least was relieved. The boy was given a big hand for his gameness under fire.

In the third inning Joe was first man up and he popped out to Jimmy Reese. He came up again in the fifth after Funk had opened with a three-base hit. He topped the ball, sending a mean roller down near the third base line.

Newsom tried to handle it, but the ball bounced out of his hands. Had he held the ball he could not have thrown DeMaggio out at first base, for he would have had to turn clear around. But he failed to handle the ball at all, so it was scored as a hit, and rightly so.

In the seventh Joe drove a liner right into the hands of Dittmar. He came up for the last time in the ninth with two runners on and was out on a fly to Stainback.

DE MAGGIO MOST TALKED OF PLAYER ON COAST

But the kid had already done a good night's work, for he had smashed a long-standing record, and he is now the most talked of young ball player on the Pacific Coast.

What does it matter that Los Angeles won the ball game, 7 to 6? Joe DeMaggio kept his hitting streak going and there is no telling when he will be stopped, and that's the best thing that has happened to baseball in this city in the last few years.

Bill Henderson had two bad innings, the first and eighth, during which the Angels scored all their seven runs. An error by Garibaldi helped one of them to score. The other six were earned.

JOE BATS IN THREE OF SIX SEAL RUNS

Joe DeMaggio batted in three of the six runs made by the Seals. Henderson drove in one and Jerry Donovan's hit in the ninth drove in the other two. Ballou had relieved Newsom in the eighth and he

Continued on Page 13H, Col. 1

Oana Stars as Bowman Hurls Ducks to Win

Joe Bowman, Portland right-hander, won a pitching duel from Bill Ludolph to put the Portland Ducks on even terms with the Oaks in their series on the transbay diamond. The Ducks won last night's game, 2-0.

Henry Oana, former Seals player, featured the Ducks' attack. In the fifth inning he got an infield hit, advanced to third on Earl Sheely's single and scored when Moore forced Sheely at second. In the ninth Oana hit a home run over the left field fence for the only other run of the game.

Bowman was nicked for seven hits by the Oaks, and except for the eighth inning, when Emil Maihlo was caught at the plate trying to score from second on Pool's infield, the Portland pitcher was never in danger.

Earl Sheely collected three of the eight hits made by the Ducks. However, none of them helped to produce runs. Frenchy Uhalt, Oakland left fielder, made a sensational catch in the fifth to rob Joe Bowman of a double or triple.

PORTLAND

	AB	R	H	O	A	E
Mulligan, 3b	4	0	0	1	0	0
Monroe, 2b	4	0	1	2	3	0
Oana, cf	4	2	2	2	0	0
Sheely, 1b	4	0	3	7	1	0
Moore, lf	4	0	0	1	0	0
Berger, rf	3	0	0	2	0	0
Sankey, s	3	0	0	2	5	0
Palmisano, c	3	0	1	10	1	0
Bowman, p	3	0	1	0	0	0
Totals	32	2	8	27	10	0

OAKLAND

	AB	R	H	O	A	E
Kintana, 2b	4	0	1	6	2	0
Mailho, cf	3	0	1	3	0	0
Uhalt, lf	2	0	0	5	0	0
Pool, rf	4	0	1	2	0	0
Anton, 1b	4	0	2	3	1	0
Raimondi, c	4	0	1	5	2	0
Wera, 3b	4	0	0	1	1	0
Deviveros, s	4	0	1	1	3	0
Ludolph, p	3	0	0	1	0	0
Scott	1	0	0	0	0	0
Totals	33	0	7	27	9	0

Scott batted for Deviveros in ninth.

Portland	0	0	0	1	0	0	0	0	1	—2
Hits	1	0	1	2	0	0	1	1	2	—8
Oakland	0	0	0	0	0	0	0	0	0	—0
Hits	1	2	0	1	0	0	0	2	1	—7

Two-base hit—Oana. Runs batted in—Moore, Oana. Runs responsible for—Ludolph 2. Struck out—By Bowman 9, Ludolph 5. —Bases on balls—Off Bowman 3, Ludolph 1. Passed ball—Palmisano. Stolen bases—Uhalt, Monroe, Mailho 2. Double play—Wera to Kintana to Anton. Home run—Oana. Time of game—2h. Umpires—Cady, Rue.

KID HITTER HONORED ☆ ☆ DE MAGGIO ALL SMILES

Mayor Rossi (right) presenting Joe De Maggio with a watch which commemorates his new Coast League record for hitting in consecutive games. The fellow in the background with the big smile is Manager Jimmy Caveney.

Miss Marble Wins Way to Net Finals

San Francisco Boy Is Upset by Miami Youngster at Brookline

BROOKLINE, Mass., July 14 (AP)—The accurate left-handed strokings of Dick Murphy of Utica, N. Y., today enabled that Hamilton College youth to ride roughshod over G. Frederick Roll of Philadelphia into the final round of the forty-first Longwood Bowl tennis tournament, where he will engage Martin Buxby of Miami.

Murphy placed brilliantly while subduing Roll, member of the University of Pennsylvania net team, in straight sets, 6-1, 6-1, 6-2, but Buxby was forced to go overtime to conquer Joe Coughlin of San Francisco and Stanford, 6-2, 6-1, 2-6, 6-2.

Coughlin took his set by playing against Buxby's backhand, which became a bit erratic as the match wore on. The Southerner, however, refused to use it in his winning fourth set, when he ran around most of the offerings that Coughlin aimed to his left side.

COUGHLIN AND PARTNER WIN WAY TO DOUBLES FINAL

Coughlin, aided by Henry Culley of Santa Barbara, Cal., made the doubles final by upsetting Murphy and Norcross Tilney of New York in slam-bang fashion, 9-7, 6-2, 6-2, and the other title bracket was awarded to Malcolm T. Hill, Newton, and Sam Fitch, Brookline, when they wore down the Tulane team of Eddie Sutter, New Orleans, and Kendal Cram, Nashville, Tenn., in a five-set battle, after spotting the Southern youths the first two.

The scores were 7-9, 4-6, 6-1, 6-4, 6-4.

The women's final will be an all-California affair, for in today's semi-finals the top seeded Carolin Babcock of Los Angeles topped Baroness Maud Levi of New York, 6-2, 6-4, in a match that was much more one-sided than indicated by those scores.

Continued on Page 12H, Col. 6 Sporting Green

CANADIAN GOLF FINALS

VANCOUVER, B. C., July 14 (AP)—Albert (Scotty) Campbell defeated Frank Dolp, 4 and 3, in the semi-final round of the Canadian Amateur tournament here today. Ken Black, Vancouver, beat Harry Givan, Seattle, 2 and 1, in the other semi-final.

Melting Pot In Tanforan Surprise Win

By OSCAR OTIS

Everything comes to him who waits—on a racetrack. A Kentucky colt called Melting Pot proved the truth of the old adage again, if any proof were needed.

After sleeping long and snoring loudly for most of the meeting, Melting Pot was dropped into the featured 2-year-old race at Tanforan yesterday afternoon. He ran off and hid from his field, including the highly regarded Prevue and Notify.

When they opened the option pie in the counting room, it was discovered that a payoff of $15.20 per option was in order, and most any horse would be tickled with that price. Hence the victory may be said to have been a complete success from every point of view.

Racing was resumed yesterday afternoon with rather a small crowd in attendance. However, a few things happened during the day worthy of mention. The first was a bad start in the third race, in which the horses left like the Twentieth Century Limited on a holiday, in several sections.

The crowd gave vent to their displeasure in no uncertain terms. Mountain Fire eventually proved the winner, with Referee and Queen Ann the placed horses.

Perhaps the worst sufferer of it all was the "Good Major" Christensen of Pleasanton. The Good Major had seen Don't Cry as good as left at the post in the race previous, and when Dublin Hills was left absolutely flatfooted in the third, the Major watched the performance with emotions which might well be termed mixed.

Local Boys Picked On Jones Grid Team

LOS ANGELES, July 14 (AP)—Coach Howard Jones of the University of Southern California named 22 men today for his Western squad, which will meet a team coached by Dick Hanley at Soldier Field, Chicago, on the night of August 24.

The Western all-star aggregation includes:

Ends—Ray Sparling, Southern California; Dave Nesbit, Washington and Hawes Slavich, Santa Clara.

Tackles—Tay Brown and Ernie Smith, Southern California; Jack Johnson, Utah; Paul Schwegler, Washington, and Dick Tozen, California.

Guards—John Baker, Southern California; Pete Heiser, Stanford; Sam Gill, California, and William O'Brien, Washington.

Centers—Stanley Williamson of Southern California and Red Sargeant, Loyola at Los Angeles.

Jones' backfield will be composed of Gus Shaver, Morley Drury and Howard Tipton, Southern California; Hank Schaldach, California; Bill Beasley, St. Mary's; Max Krause, Gonzaga; George Sander, Washington State, and Frank Christensen, Utah.

Babe Shoots 92 in First Golf Tourney

LOS ANGELES, July 14 (AP)—Babe Didrikson, the girl athlete, competed in her first golf tournament here today and turned in a 92, which was 14 above women's par for the Rancho course.

Mrs. G. M. Midgley, former head of the women's auxiliary of the Southern California Golf Association, who played with her, predicted Miss Didrickson would be bidding for championship fame in about two years. Babe took up golf seriously a short time ago.

Baseball at a Glance

PACIFIC COAST LEAGUE

RESULTS YESTERDAY

Los Angeles 7, San Francisco 6 (night).
Portland 2, Oakland 0 (night).
Hollywood 10, Missions 0 (day).
Sacramento 7, Seattle 6 (night).

STANDING OF THE CLUBS

	Won	Lost	Pct.
Sacramento	62	41	.602
Portland	60	42	.588
Los Angeles	59	42	.584
Hollywood	58	43	.574
Oakland	47	55	.461
Missions	46	58	.442
Seattle	37	62	.374
San Francisco	38	64	.372

HOW THE SERIES STAND

Los Angeles 3, San Francisco 1.
Oakland 2, Portland 2.
Hollywood 3, Missions 1.
Sacramento 3, Seattle 1.

GAMES TODAY

Los Angeles at San Francisco.
Portland at Oakland.
Seattle at Sacramento (night).
Missions at Hollywood.

AMERICAN LEAGUE

RESULTS YESTERDAY

New York 11, St. Louis 6.
Detroit 8, Boston 3.
Philadelphia 3, Cleveland 2.
Chicago 4, Washington 0.

STANDING OF THE CLUBS

	Won	Lost	Pct.
Washington	51	29	.638
New York	52	30	.634
Philadelphia	42	40	.512
Chicago	42	41	.506
Detroit	40	44	.476
Cleveland	39	46	.459
Boston	34	47	.420
St. Louis	32	55	.368

NATIONAL LEAGUE

RESULTS YESTERDAY

Boston 4, Pittsburgh 3 (10 innings).
Philadelphia 6, Cincinnati 0.
Brooklyn 5, Chicago 3.
New York 12, St. Louis 7.

STANDING OF THE CLUBS

	Won	Lost	Pct.
New York	47	32	.595
Chicago	46	39	.541
St. Louis	43	39	.524
Pittsburgh	42	39	.519
Boston	42	41	.506
Brooklyn	36	43	.456
Philadelphia	36	45	.444
Cincinnati	35	49	.417

Jack Dempsey Says Wedding Date Not Set

SALT LAKE CITY, July 14 (AP)—Jack Dempsey, former world's heavy weight boxing champion, told newspaper reporters here today he does not know when he and Hannah Williams, musical comedy actress, will be married.

"There are no definite plans," he added.

BASEBALL'S BIG SIX

	G	AB	R	H	Pct.
Foxx, Athletics	80	297	78	111	.374
Simmons, White Sox	82	349	61	128	.367
Klein, Phillies	81	331	55	121	.366
Cronin, Senators	80	320	56	117	.366
Davis, Phillies	75	268	30	95	.355
Fullis, Phillies	81	359	55	123	.343

Bill Spaulding Gets New 5-Year Contract

LOS ANGELES, July 14 (AP)—William H. Spaulding, who came here in 1925 to give the University of California at Los Angeles its first college football victory and built the team into one of the Coast's leading elevens in seven years, was given a new five-year contract today.

Kid Swimmer Hogs Show at Chicago Meet

CHICAGO, July 14 (AP)—Ralph Flanagan, a 15-year-old "fish" from Miami, Fla., stole the show at the national amateur outdoor swimming championship today as the Detroit Athletic Club stars took the lead in the race for team honors.

Competing in the gruelling mile race in the north lagoon at the World's Fair, the husky youngster churned the waters in 21:12 1-5, to win the national title and break the former national mark of 21:27, held by Buster Crabbe of Stanford University.

The best amateur field ever assembled failed to extend the Miami aquatic star, who beat his closest rival, Jack Medica, University of Washington freshman, by 12 meters.

The Detroit A. C., with 10 points, was ahead of one of the heavy favorites, the New York A. C. Other totals were:

Greater Miami Athletic Club	5
Washington Athletic Club, Seattle	3
Los Angeles Athletic Club	3
Miami Biltmore Club	3
Illinois Athletic Club, Chicago	3
University of Michigan	1
Ohio State	6

College Conference Managers in Meeting

Graduate managers of athletics of the Pacific Coast Conference will meet at the Clift Hotel today to discuss the question of broadcasting football games over radio. All of the schools are in favor of broadcasts and the meeting today is to work out the details so sponsorships can be sold.

As some games will be broadcasted and others will not the question is quite a complicated one as the graduate managers learned when they got back home and tried to sell the idea to sponsors. So the meeting today is to clear up those details.

Baer Boxes Dempsey In Exhibition Go

SALT LAKE CITY, July 14 (AP)—Max Baer, Livermore, heavy weight title aspirant, boxed two round exhibitions with Billy Murdock of Kansas City and Ed Sheppard of Salt Lake City and one round with Jack Dempsey here tonight.

The exhibitions were special attractions on a wrestling card.

Billy Edwards won on a foul from Ira Dern. Dern was accused of striking Edwards.

Hy Sharm won by default from Joe Manning.

Al Newman tossed Pat Flanagan with a flying mare in a one-fall match.

Del Kunkel defeated Arthur Hedin, Preston, Idaho, with a flying mare in 17 minutes.

San Francisco Chronicle Sporting Green
EDITED BY HARRY B. SMITH
FOUNDED 1865 | CCC | SAN FRANCISCO, CAL., THURSDAY, JULY 27, 1933 | H11 | VOL. CXLIII, NO. 12

OAKS STOP DE MAGGIO'S HITTING RECORD

Sarah Palfrey Upsets Alice Marble in Seabright Tournament

Brick Morse

The New Gaels

'33 GRID FLASHES

By BRICK MORSE

I HAVE SAID that St. Mary's will be in midseason form for California and U. S. C., second and third games on their schedule. Through a long and intensive spring practice and the presence of many experienced players the Gaels should be in top form early in the season.

Possibly that is not the method to pursue in the chase for national championship honors. Most of the big teams believe in a gradual crescendo throughout the season.

California and Stanford have always taken other teams in stride, aiming to reach peak season just in time for the Big Game That is because the supporters of both teams demand that their team win the Big Game, even at the expense of losing other games.

Must Beat Bears, U. S. C., Say St. Mary's Fans

St. Mary's supporters demand that their team beat California, and after that U. S. C.

So Slip must bring his boys to peak form early and then try to keep them there for three months. Most observers claim that this cannot be done.

But Coach Madigan has a record list of star players. If some of his regulars go stale he will have plenty of substitutes.

St. Mary's supporters are enthusiastic about the new men. Some one will beat out Jorgenson at tackle, there are two ends better than the Canrinus boys, some one else will make Al Nichelini look slow and Wilson will be forced onto the third team.

Gael Enthusiasts Hail New Grid Performers

Experienced players like Dodson and Partee simply don't figure in the running at all.

Yes, enthusiasm is wonderful, but don't let it run away with your judgment.

Slip Madigan, too, is enthusiastic about his youngsters, but Slip knows the value of experience. When the games start we will see a full team of players on the field who know the smell of powder.

Much is also made of the size of the St. Mary's players. They start at 200 pounds and work up. Some of them weigh in at over 240 It is yet to be proven that a 200-pounder is better than a lighter man.

Eastern teams lay great stress on weight. We have seen some enormous tackles on the Eastern teams at the Shrine games, but almost without exception the Western 190-pound tackles have outplayed them.

Those Beefy Boys Aren't Impressive to Brick

No, I'm not impressed by this great show of weight, nor this great array of new material. I am impressed by the great record St. Mary's has made during the last two years, by the proven ability of their regulars and by the thorough preparation they have made for the coming season.

It will be strange if any youngster beats out either of the two Canrinus boys at end. Any team on the Coast would like to have ends like those fellows. Fred plays right and George plays left end. Both tall and rangy, 205 pounds —heavy, strong, fast and experienced.

And those tackles, Jorgenson and Gilbert, both senio... Both should be at the peak of their game They were among the best tackles on the Coast last year. Jorgenson weighs 212 and Gilbert 238. That's big.

Gerardin, at guard, is a veteran with two years of experience behind him. Slip will have to dip into his new material to find a guard to match him.

Matt Brasnyo, Commerce Hi Star, May Get Place

That should be no problem. There's Brasyno, who was great as a prep and as a frosh. He weighs 257 pounds now, and they say he's the man. We saw Eldanyan two years ago wit the Pasadena preps and thought he was one of the best prep guards we'd seen. If he has shown normal improvement I don't see how they can keep him off the team.

At center Slip has the experienced men, Yates and Danilovich, both plenty capable.

Plenty of experience in the backfield, too. Remember, that Al Nichelini played brilliantly in several games last year. He weighs over 200 and may be another Ange' Brovelli this year. There's Harris and Ahern at quarter, both of them with reputations. Hard to choose between two such brilliant quarter backs.

Plenty of Veterans on Gaels' 1933 Squad

There's George Wilson at right half. They were grooming him for all-American last year. And there's the veterans, Dodson and Partee, for fullbacks. There's experience for you right through the list.

In these days a strong list of

Continued on Page 12H, Col. 6
Sporting Green

Miss Jacobs Advances to Semifinals

San Francisco Girl Has Hand in Elimination of National Women Doubies Champs

SEABRIGHT, N. J., July 26 (AP)—A wave of surprise results, including the elimination of the defending champion in the men's division and the defeat of the women's doubles team that won the national title last year, today flavored the famous Seabright invitation tennis tournament.

Little Bryan Grant of Atlanta, Ga., accomplished the feat of removing Sidney Wood of New York from a chance to defend any longer the Seabright bowl he won last year. Grant, whose dynamic racket has been a power in Southern competition since 1927, overpowered the one-time Wimbledon champion in straight sets, 6-0, 7-5.

Two other suprises occurred among the women, with the Baroness Maud Levi of New York holding the center of attraction for the second day in a row, and little Sarah Palfrey of Brookline, Mass., taking a close second in the race for the day's honors.

VIRGINIA RICE IS ANOTHER UPSET VICTIM

Virginia Rice of Boston was the Baroness' second upset victim, losing 6-4, 10-8, and joining the third-ranked Caroline Babcock of Los Angeles in that category.

Miss Palfrey advanced by an easy 6-2, 6-0 victory over Alice Marble of San Francisco, into the semifinals, where tomorrow her hard-hitting game will come in contact with Baroness Levi's chop-stroke.

MISS JACOBS, PARTNER LOSE IN TITLE DEFENSE

Another surprise went by almost unnoticed when the team of Helen Jacobs and Miss Palfrey, national women's doubles champions, fell before the team of Josephine Cruikshank and Miss Marble. Despite the renown of the losers and their probable selection as a pair in the Wightman cup matches with the British, Miss Cruikshank and Miss Marble won easily, 6-3, 6-3.

Helen Jacobs, who is defending the women's bowl, and Josephine Cruikshank filled the semifinal bracket in the top half of the draw. Miss Jacobs, on her game for the first time this week, breezed past

Continued on Page 13H, Col. 3
Sporting Green

Baseball at a Glance

PACIFIC COAST LEAGUE

RESULTS YESTERDAY

San Francisco 4, Oakland 3 (day).
Missions 8, Seattle 7 (12 innings, twilight).
Los Angeles 9, Sacramento 3.
Hollywood 8, Portland 6.

STANDING OF THE CLUBS

	Won	Lost	Pct.
Sacramento	69	46	.600
Portland	68	46	.596
Hollywood	67	47	.588
Los Angeles	66	47	.584
Oakland	53	61	.465
Missions	48	68	.414
San Francisco	44	70	.386
Seattle	41	71	.366

HOW THE SERIES STAND

San Francisco 2, Oakland 0.
Missions 2, Seattle 0.
Los Angeles 2, Sacramento 0.
Portland 1, Hollywood 1.

GAMES TODAY

Oakland at San Francisco.
Missions at Seattle (twilight).
Sacramento at Los Angeles (night).
Hollywood at Portland (night).

AMERICAN LEAGUE

RESULTS YESTERDAY

New York 2, Boston 0 (first).
Boston 9, New York 4 (second).
Detroit 9, St. Louis 7.
Cleveland 7, Chicago 1.
Washington at Cleveland (rain).

STANDING OF THE CLUBS

	Won	Lost	Pct.
Washington	59	33	.641
New York	58	34	.630
Philadelphia	47	46	.505
Detroit	46	48	.489
Cleveland	46	50	.479
Chicago	43	50	.462
Boston	41	51	.446
St. Louis	35	63	.357

NATIONAL LEAGUE

RESULTS YESTERDAY

New York 5, Brooklyn 3 (first).
New York 4, Brooklyn 3 (second).
St. Louis 3, Cincinnati 2.
Chicago at Pittsburgh, rain.

STANDING OF THE CLUBS

	Won	Lost	Pct.
New York	55	36	.604
Chicago	53	42	.558
Pittsburgh	51	43	.543
Boston	47	45	.511
St. Louis	48	45	.516
Cincinnati	41	54	.432
Philadelphia	38	51	.427
Brooklyn	36	53	.404

DE MAGGIO STOPPED ☆☆ JOE'S LAST SWING

After hitting safely in sixty-one consecutive games to establish a new Pacific Coast League record, Joe DeMaggio's sensational batting streak was halted in the Oakland-San Francisco game here yesterday afternoon. Up five times yesterday, DeMaggio failed to get a hit off Young Ed Walsh, son of "Big Ed" Walsh of major league fame. Strangely enough, DeMaggio batted in the run that gave the Seals a 4-3 victory over the Oaks, hoisting a fly to right field in the last of the ninth inning to allow Fenton to score after the catch.
—Haas & Schreiner Photo.

Rogers Hornsby Signs As Manager of Browns

Former National League Firebrand Announces Plan to Create a Fighting Ball Club

ST. LOUIS, July 26 (AP)—Rogers Hornsby, erstwhile firebrand of the National League, today signed a contract to pilot the St. Louis Browns and immediately announced plans to create a fighting ball club and to be a playing manager.

"We'll be having them out at the ball park before long," Hornsby told President Phil Ball, shortly after signing a contract for the remainder of the present season and through 1934 and 1935.

Hornsby, who until yesterday was a member of the St. Louis Cardinals, seemed elated at his new job. The big second baseman who started his climb to baseball fame as a rookie with the Cards in 1915, and later managed the Red Birds, the Boston Braves, and the Chicago Cubs, said he planned no immediate change of players.

It was reliably reported and not denied that the Rajah's new contract gave him more authority than possessed by any other manager engaged by ball. Bill Killifer was deposed from authority last week.

Hornsby is expected to depart tomorrow or Friday night for Chicago to join his last place charges, now under the wing of Allan Sothoron, a coach under Killifer. Hornsby and Sothoron

Continued on Page 12H, Col. 8
Sporting Green

Joe Maggio Goes Hitless In 62d Game

Joe DeMaggio went to bat five times yesterday, failing to hit and thereby breaking his consecutive batting string at 61 games. This is what he did yesterday:

First Inning—Grounded out, Deviveros to Anton.

Second Inning — Grounded out, Wera to Anton.

Fourth Inning—Forced Zinn at second base, Lavagetto to Deviveros.

Seventh Inning—Flied out to Uhalt.

Ninth Inning—Flied out to Pool, allowing Fenton to score from third base after the catch with winning run.

Seal Batting Ace Fails To Get Hit Off Ed Walsh In Five Trips to Plate

San Francisco Slugger's Fly in Ninth Inning Scores Run That Beats Oakland Club, 4-3; Streak Broken After Sixty-one Games

By ED. R. HUGHES

JOE DE MAGGIO, sensational young slugger of the Seals, was stopped yesterday, but the fly ball he hit to end his hitting streak drove in the winning run for the Seals, who beat the Oaks, 4 to 3.

Ed Walsh, son of the famous Ed Walsh of the old Chicago White Sox in the days when they were called the hitless wonders, was pitching for the Oaks yesterday and he easily disposed of DeMaggio the five times the kid faced him. There was not one hard chance offered the fielders.

And no one can say that Walsh was ducking DeMaggio, for in the ninth inning, with the winning run on third base, Walsh purposely walked Jimmy Zinn, a very good hitter, to bring up DeMaggio. He did that on orders from the bench, but the important thing is that he did it, and thus put himself on the spot against DeMaggio.

Walsh put all he had on the ball, trying to make DeMaggio swing at wide curves, and finally came through with a fast one that De Maggio drove to Pool in right field. for the second out of the inning and Fenton scored after the catch with the run that won the ball game.

JOE'S RECORD LIKELY TO STAND LONG TIME

Young Joe went down gallantly, for even if he did not get a hit, he drove in the winning run, after having etsablished a record of hitting safely in 61 games in succession, a record that will probably stand for some time.

As Joe gallopped for the clubhouse after the game ended, he was pursued by a mob of excited youngsters who just wanted to get close enough to touch him and say hello. No question but that Joe DeMaggio, 18-year-old youngster from North Beach, has captured the imagination of San Francisco folks.

DeMaggio began to show the strain about a week ago and for the last five games he did not hit hard, although he got hits in every game until yesterday. He is naturally a driving hitter, but everyone was bearing down on him both on and off the field until the boy began pressing.

DE MAGGIO FAILS TO SWING WITH ABANDON

He wanted to be sure to hit the ball, so he did not swing with his natural abandon. He did hit the ball nearly every time up, but the hits were getting harder to make and the pressure was getting stronger. Naturally every one of his opponents perked up when Joe went to bat.

Yesterday Joe was moved from fourth place to the lead off position in the batting order so that he would get more chances to hit. The strategy did not work, however, for Walsh disposed of DeMaggio the five times he faced him.

In the first inning, DeMaggio was thrown out by Deviveiros on an easy chance. In the second inning Wera

Continued on Page 13H, Col. 8
Sporting Green

Luderus Released as Texas Team Manager

OKLAHOMA CITY, July 26 (AP)—Fred Luderus today was released as manager of the Oklahoma City Indians of the Texas League Luther ("Red") Harvel, hard-hitting outfielder, was named to succeed him.

Missions Win Game in 12th On Wild Pitch

SEATTLE, July 26 (AP)—Charles Lieber, Missions pitcher, raced home from third on a wild pitch in the twelfth inning tonight by George Caster, Seattle hurler, to give the visitors an 8-to-7 win for their second straight of the two games of the series.

He had got on first on a dinky roller to McLarney, at shortstop, which hopped over McLarney's head for a single, and went to third on Sherlock's grounder in the same direction, which also jumped over Ellsworth's head to go for double.

In the eleventh, the Missions had the game won with two runs batted in by Dahlgren, who singled with the bases full, but George Burns, Seattle manager, came back in the Indians' half with his twenty-fifth home run of the season with Welsh, who had singled, on first base, to knot the count.

MISSIONS	AB	R	H	O	A
Shrlck,2b	6	0	2	3	7
L.Alma,cf	6	1	1	4	1
Fribrg,3b	5	2	1	1	3
Eckhrt,rf	5	0	1	1	0
Dhlgn,1b	6	1	3	15	1
Hafey,lf	3	1	1	1	0
Mohler,s	6	2	3	5	2
Fitzptk,c	6	0	3	5	0
Osbrne,p	4	0	0	1	3
Lieber,p	1	1	1	0	1
Totals	48	8	16	36	18

SEATTLE	AB	R	H	O	A
M.Alda,rf	6	1	3	5	0
McLrny,s	7	0	2	5	7
Welsh,cf	7	2	4	4	0
Burns,1b	6	2	3	12	0
Bradbry,c	5	1	2	1	0
Bncvni,lf	5	0	1	3	0
Coscrt,3b	5	1	2	1	4
Johnsn,2b	3	0	1	4	2
Ulrich,p	3	0	0	0	2
Cox	1	0	0	0	0
Walters	1	0	0	0	0
Elswth,2b	2	0	1	1	1
Caster,p	2	0	0	0	1
Totals	53	7	19	36	17

Cox batted for Johnson in eighth.
Walters batted for Ulrich in eighth.

Missions	1	0	0	2	0	1	0	1	0	0	2	1	— 8
Hits	3	1	0	2	0	1	0	3	1	1	2	2	—16
Seattle	0	1	3	0	0	0	0	0	1	0	2	0	— 7
Hits	1	2	4	1	1	1	1	0	2	1	4	1	—19

Home runs—Coscarart, Burns. Two-base hits — Mohler, Fitzpatrick, M. Almada, Welsh, Sherlock. Sacrifice—Hafey. Runs batted in—Dahlgren, Ulrich, Bradbury, Coscarart 2, Fitzpatrick 2, Osborne, Mohler, Welsh, Burns 2. Errors—Osborne (Missions, 1), Corcarart (Seattle, 1). Innings pitched—By Ulrich 8, Osborne 10 1-3. Credit victory to Lieber. Charge defeat to Caster. At bat—Off Ulrich 33, Osborne 46. Hits batted—Off Ulrich 10, Osborne 17. Runs scored—Off Ulrich 5, Osborne 7. Runs responsible for—Osborne 7, Ulrich 3, Caster 2. Struck out—By Osborne 5. Base on balls—Off Osborne 5, Ulrich 3, Caster 3. Wild pitch—Caster. Stolen base—Mohler. Double plays—Johnson to Burns, Osborne to Mohler to Dahlgren, Ellsworth to McLarney to Burns. Passed ball—Bradbury. Time of game—2h. 55m. Umpires—Rue and Cady.

Ross Stops Farr to Defend Welter Title

KANSAS CITY, July 26 (AP)—Barney Ross, the lightweight champion, put his other and less celebrated crown, the junior welter weight title, at stake here tonight, using Johnny Farr, Cleveland, as a punching bag to win on a technical knockout in six rounds.

Dr. D. M. Nigro, physician for the Missouri State Boxing Commission, ordered the fight stopped, saying an examination disclosed Farr had a broken nose as well as a badly damaged right eye.

SOUTHERN ASSOCIATION

By Associated Press

New Orleans 5, Memphis 0.
Memphis 2, New Orleans 0.
Atlanta 3, Knoxville 2.
Little Rock at Birmingham—Postponed: wet grounds.
Nashville at Chattanooga—Postponed: rain.

Joe De Maggio Welcomes End To Bat Streak

By JOE DEMAGGIO
Sensational Young Slugger of Seals

Well, I'm glad it's over. The strain was getting a bit tough. I'll say one thing for Ed Walsh, he gave me good balls to hit yesterday, but I just couldn't get the wood on them right.

They tell me I have made a better record for hitting in successive games than any other right handed hitter in baseball. I wouldn't know about that, but anyway hitting in 61 games in succession is pretty good.

Now that the strain is lifted, I'll be in there again tomorrow trying to get my hits, and they will not all be concentrating on me so much.

I am trying to win ball games for the Seals so I am glad that the put out that ended my batting streak drove in the winning run for the Seals.

Hans Birkie Wins Nod Over Edgren

NEW YORK, July 26—Hans Birkie, German heavy weight, won a ten-round decision over Frankie Edgren of Cheyenne, Wyo., here tonight.

Birkie's big pull in the weights and his aggressiveness proved too much for the slender Edgren. It was a dull bout from the spectator's standpoint. Birkie worked at close quarters, pounding his opponent steadily about the midsection until he wore him down.

Pegler

Heartless Breadon
Sam Hires and Fires
Frisch Newest Idol
Look Out, Frankie!

By WESTBROOK PEGLER

CHICAGO, July 25—Sometimes it seems as though Sam Breadon, the St. Louis automobile dealer, who owns the town's principal ball club, the Cardinals by name, is moved no more by business considerations than by an impish desire to turn proud people upside down in his startling hirings and firings, promotions and demotions.

Mr. Breadon expresses the spirit of the howling fan who likes to see champions rise because only when they are up is it possible for them to come crashing down.

Sam has just yanked another hero off his column and put another one up there. In time, and not very long time, either, according to precedent, he will slap that one down, too, and put up still another. Unlike the common customer, however, he enjoys the privilege of making his own little kings. The customer can't set them up.

Since 1929 Mr. Breadon has named six men to the job of managing the Cardinals. This is one of the prestige jobs of the baseball business.

Sam Makes and Breaks His Kings Rapidly

Sometimes it has been a good job but generally it is just mediocre as to pay and not very good for the pride of the individual because Mr. Breadon as a king maker deals strictly in limited monarchs. He gives them the title but not much authority and, in proportion to the prominence of the position, very little money.

Frank Frisch wen to the Cardinals after the season of 1926 and in taking over the title of so many predecessors at this time he may search his own long experience in vain for some reason to take pride in the job.

It is a position that calls for humility of spirit and the man who takes it suffers less in the end if he keeps his neck bent.

Frisch was John McGraw's fair-haired prodigy from 1919, when he went from the campus of Fordham University to the polo grounds, until the summer of 1926, when McGraw drove him off the ball club. In 1924 and 1925, when Rogers Hornsby was at his best there was a famous rivalry between the boys.

Frisch was a diving, sprawling athlete who couldn't reach for the salt without diving ten yards off tackle. Whenever he handled a grounder he tried to make history and, although he covered much ground and summed up as one of the best ball players in the business on general results, the St. Louis customers said he looked great mainly because he made the easy ones look desperate.

Now Hornsby—there was a real second baseman who wasn't always flopping around in the dust, losing his cap and throwing eyelash put-

Continued on Page 13H, Col. 1
Sporting Green

Risko Takes Decision Over Tom Loughran

CHICAGO, July 26 (AP)—Tommy Loughran of Philadelphia, conceded to be the most scientific of present day heavy weights, dropped a close 10-round decision to Johnny Risko, the Cleveland rubber man, in the Mills Stadium tonight.

Floored for a count of three in the first round, Loughran came back to fight an uphill battle, but Risko was too rough and tough for him. Risko carried the battle to the Philadelphia dancing master, forcing him on the defensive. He centered his attack to Loughran's body, piling up points with hard punches with both hands.

In the first round, Risko unleashed several left hooks, one catching Loughran on the side of the head. Then a short right dropped him.

In the second and third round, Loughran found the range, and began landing left jabs to the face. In the fourth round Risko renewed his aggressive battle, mauling Loughran with body punches. The Cleveland fighter kept lunging to the head and body in the fifth and sixth rounds.

Loughran apparently had the edge in the seventh with left and rights he landed to Risko's head. From the eighth round on, however, Risko kept forcing the battle to pile up his margin.

Eddie Houghton outscored Gene Stanton in an eight-round semifinal. Davy Day knocked Any Villion out in one round.

Phils, Giants Play Pair; Hubbell Sets Record, Hurling 46 Consecutive Scoreless Innings

ED HOLLEY, MOORE TO FACE LEADERS

Shottons, Beaming With Confidence, Likely to Be Pitted Against Parmelee, Bell

By JOHN KOLBMANN

Victorious in only two starts against the New York Giants in eleven games this season, Burt Shotton's Phillies today will play a pair of contests against the Terry Terriers and there are bright gleams in the eyes of the Philadelphians.

With their combination working more smoothly than ever, the Shotton stars will have Ed Holley and Cy Moore to start the two games against the New Yorkers and feel certain that good times are in the offing.

The Phillies, home last week after the Western trip, took a trio of games from Boston's Braves, but collapsed against the Dodgers in the twin bill on Saturday and took two setbacks. In Flatbush on Sunday, with good flinging by Flint Rhem, the Phils chalked up a brilliant victory.

Today Shotton feels Holley and Moore should deliver well-pitched games. Moore was a starter and winner against the Braves and made it two victories for the series when he triumphed again in a relief role.

Cy's just coming around into the form he displayed before the season opened and that's one reason Shotton feels confident he'll deliver. Holley has been one of the most consistent performers all season.

Shotton has another problem on his hands now, with Jumbo Jim Elliott on the sidelines. Jim pulled a tendon in his back during the game with Brooklyn last Saturday and will be out of action for an indefinite period.

John Berly and Frank Pearce, while in uniform, are not yet ready to man the mound, so Shotton's mound problems increase rapidly.

New York's pacemakers, who lost ground yesterday as Carl Hubbell was beaten by the Braves after setting a National League record for runless innings, probably will have Roy Parmelee and Herman Bell as the hurlers this afternoon.

Bell's greatest triumph of the season was a shutout he scored against the Phillies, while Parmelee also held the Shottonmen to a single safety as one of his most important victories of the season.

SENATORS GET PITCHER

Washington Acquires Chapman From Rochester Club

Washington, Aug. 1.—(AP)—Seeking to strengthen their pitching staff in their drive for the American League pennant, the Washington Senators today acquired Ed Chapman, star pitcher of the Rochester, in the International League, from the St. Louis Cards.

Reports here were that Clark Griffith, owner of the Senators, paid "considerable cash" in addition to trading off Bill McAfee, relief pitcher.

Stitt Plymouth Champion

Norristown, Aug. 1.—James Stitt, 17-year-old linksman, is the new golf champion of the Plymouth Country Club. Stitt gained the club crown by beating Joe Ruby, 3 and 1, in the thirty-six-hole final. He succeeds Spencer L. Jones.

Baseball Summary

NATIONAL LEAGUE

Yesterday's Results

Phillies-Brooklyn, not scheduled.
Boston, 8; New York, 1.
Chicago, 3; Cincinnati, 1.
Pittsburgh, 9; St. Louis, 3.

Today's Schedule

Phillies vs. New York, Broad and Huntingdon streets (two games).
Brooklyn at Boston (two games).
St. Louis at Pittsburgh.
Cincinnati at Chicago.

Standing of the Teams

	W.	L.	P.C.		W.	L.	P.C.
N. York	57	38	.600	Boston	49	49	.500
Pittsbu'h	57	43	.570	Phillies	41	54	.432
Chicago	54	46	.540	Brooklyn	39	54	.429
St. Louis	52	46	.531	Cincin'ti	41	60	.406

AMERICAN LEAGUE

Yesterday's Results

St. Louis, 5; Cleveland, 2.
Chicago-Detroit—Rain.
Other clubs not scheduled.

Today's Schedule

Athletics at New York.
Boston at Washington.
Chicago at Detroit (two games).
Cleveland at St. Louis.

Standing of the Teams

	W.	L.	P.C.		W.	L.	P.C.
Wash'ton	61	35	.635	Detroit	47	51	.480
NewYork	60	36	.625	Chicago	45	52	.464
Athletics	47	49	.490	Boston	44	51	.463
Clevel'nd	49	53	.480	St.Louis	39	65	.375

NEW YORK-PENNA. LEAGUE

Yesterday's Results

Harrisburg, 6; Elmira, 4.
Reading, 6; Scranton, 5 (night game).
York, 7; Binghamton, 5 (night game).
Wilkes-Barre, Williamsport, rain.

Today's Schedule

Binghamton at York.
Elmira at Harrisburg.
Wilkes-Barre at Williamsport (two games).
Scranton at Reading.

Standing of the Teams

	W.	L.	P.C.		W.	L.	P.C.
Bing'ton	57	38	.600	Har'burg	46	52	.469
W.-Barre	51	46	.526	Elmira	42	50	.457
Reading	48	45	.516	W'msport	43	51	.457
Scranton	51	48	.515	York	43	51	.457

INTERNATIONAL LEAGUE

Yesterday's Results

Baltimore, 18; Rochester, 2.
Montreal, 11; Jersey City, 1.
Toronto, 10; Albany, 1.
Newark, 5; Buffalo, 4 (night game).

Standing of the Teams

	W.	L.	P.C.		W.	L.	P.C.
Newark	65	48	.575	Montreal	56	60	.493
Rochester	64	50	.561	Buffalo	55	63	.466
Balti'ore	64	57	.529	Albany	54	62	.466
Toronto	62	56	.525	Jer City	45	69	.395

AMERICAN ASSOCIATION

Milwaukee, 5; St. Paul, 1.
Louisville, 9; Indianapolis, 4.
Toledo, 3; Columbus, 2 (night game).
Kansas City, 5; Minneapolis, 4 (night game).

SOUTHERN ASSOCIATION

Memphis, 10; Atlanta, 9.
Chattanooga, 4; New Orleans, 1.

Shotton's Pitching Selections

ED HOLLEY

CY MOORE

JOHNSON SUSPENDS ORAL HILDEBRAND

Cleveland Manager Calls Move Disciplinary Action After Row With Pitcher

Cleveland, Aug. 1.—(AP)—An indefinite suspension of Oral Hildebrand, brilliant young right-handed pitcher of the Cleveland Indians, by Manager Walter Johnson was announced tonight by the Cleveland Plain Dealer.

Hildebrand's suspension was ordered as a disciplinary action shortly before today's game at St. Louis, when the manager and the hurler exchanged hot words in the clubhouse over a $100 fine which Johnson slapped on the player yesterday.

The Plain Dealer said Johnson did not make public the fine until after he ordered the suspension. Then he said he levied it because Hildebrand objected to being removed from the box in the midst of yesterday's wild seventh inning.

At that time Hildebrand had just forced the winning St. Louis run across the plate, by issuing a walk to Lyn Storti. Then Johnson strode from the bench to the center of the infield and waved the pitcher out.

Johnson refused Hildebrand's request to continue in the game, and the pitcher hurled the resin bag to the ground in disgust. The Plain Dealer quoted Johnson as telling him then, "That will cost you $100."

Johnson said Hildebrand could return to the team any time he announces he is ready to pitch and to restrain his temper. Hildebrand left St. Louis tonight for his home in Indianapolis and expected to present his side of the story to General Manager Billy Evans in Cleveland Thursday morning.

Veteran Baseballer Dies

Springfield, Mo., Aug. 1.—(AP)—Apparently stricken by a cerebral hemorrhage, Louis Frederick Wolter, 58, once prominent in organized baseball, died today. Wolter began his baseball career forty years ago as a second baseman with Memphis.

ST. LOUIS BROWNS BUMP INDIANS, 5-2

Gray and Hadley Twirl Hornsby's Club to Second Straight Victory

St. Louis, Aug. 1.—(AP)—Sam Gray and Bump Hadley pitched the St. Louis Browns to their second successive victory over the Cleveland Indians here today, 5 to 2.

CLEVELAND	ab	r	h	o	a	ST. LOUIS	ab	r	h	o	a
Porter,rf	5	0	1	1	0	Storti,3b	4	0	0	1	1
Ouill'er,lf	5	0	1	3	0	West,cf	4	2	2	4	0
Boss,1b	5	1	3	7	0	Reynolds,lf	5	1	3	2	0
Averill,cf	3	1	0	2	0	Ca'pbell,rf	4	1	1	2	0
Hale,2b	3	0	1	5	4	Burns,1b	4	0	2	8	1
Kamm,3b	4	0	2	1	2	Melillo,2b	2	0	0	1	3
Pytlak,c	3	0	0	2	0	Shea,c	2	0	0	6	0
Cissell,ss	1	0	0	2	2	Levey,ss	4	0	0	3	3
Burnett,ss	2	0	0	1	0	Gray,p	2	1	1	0	2
Pearson,p	2	0	0	0	2	Hadley,p	1	0	0	0	0
Brown,p	0	0	0	0	1	Totals	32	5	9	27	10
*Galatzer	1	0	0	0	0						
†Vosmik	0	0	0	0	0						
Totals	34	2	8	24	11						

*Batted for Pearson in seventh.
†Batted for Brown in ninth.

Cleveland	0	0	0	0	0	0	0	2	0	—2
St. Louis	2	1	0	0	0	0	1	0	1	x—5

Errors—Hale, 2. Runs batted in—Burns, Reynolds, Storti, Hale, Kamm, Shea, West. Two-base hits—Burns, 2; Kamm. Three-base hits—Reynolds, Gray. Home run—West. Sacrifice — Melillo. Double plays—Storti, Melillo to Burns; Cissell, Hale to Boss. Left on bases—Cleveland, 10; St. Louis, 11. Base on balls—Off Pearson, 6; Gray, 4. Struck out—By Pearson, 3; Gray, 4; Hadley, 1. Hits—Off Pearson, 7 in 6 innings; Brown, 2 in 2; Gray, 7 in 7; Hadley, 1 in 2. Wild pitch—Hadley. Winning pitcher—Gray. Losing pitcher—Pearson. Umpires—Kolls, Hildebrand and Vangraflan. Time—2:13.

RAPHAEL BEATS NICETOWN

Robertshaw Batting Star in Team's 5-4 Phila. Loop Win

Raphael, a team that floundered around in the cellar position the better part of the first half, is the real threat in the final half of the Philadelphia League race. The West Philadelphia nine proved so last night when it edged out Nicetown, the defending champion, 5-4, at 58th and Elmwood avenue.

RAPHAEL	r	h	o	a	e	NICETOWN	r	h	o	a	e
Sholly,cf	0	1	4	0	0	Walus,2b	1	2	2	2	0
Maitl'nd,3b	0	0	0	1	1	Muffler,ss	1	2	0	1	1
Holstein,1b	1	1	5	0	0	Bokeno,1b	0	1	8	0	0
Wear'ng,2b	0	0	3	3	0	M'D'ald,rf	0	0	3	0	1
Cro'pton,rf	0	1	5	1	0	Durning,cf	1	1	2	0	0
Swigler,lf	2	2	1	0	1	Linkert,lf	0	1	5	0	0
Spotts,c	0	0	5	1	0	Price,c	0	0	4	1	1
Rober'w,ss	2	2	4	3	1	L.W'ker,3b	0	1	0	3	0
M'Neill,p	0	1	0	1	0	Bailey,p	0	0	0	2	0
Totals	5	8	27	10	3	Heisler	0	0	0	0	0
						Slater	1	1	0	0	0
						Sl'ndinger	0	0	0	0	0
						Totals	4	9	24	9	3

Nicetown	0	0	0	0	0	0	1	2	1	—4
Raphael	0	2	0	2	0	0	0	1	x	—5

The Boy Who Made Good

PLAYING THE GAME

By ED POLLOCK

Copyright, 1933, by Public Ledger

"Never criticize nor dispute the decision of an umpire or referee, even though the decision is obviously wrong. We realize referees and umpires are not always right, but we believe they invariably try to render fair decisions. Among students there should be encouraged a spirit which will accept all decisions—right or wrong—with a smile, since in the long run each contestant gets his share of poor decisions. A protest against a decision is the mark of a poor sportsman, while whole-hearted acceptance is the mark of a gentleman."

A Code of Sportsmanship

C. LLOYD NEAL, faculty member, is naturally proud of the new code of sportsmanship adopted by Germantown Academy. The ideals and the idea are his. He is particularly pleased with the section of the code quoted above.

"There is entirely too much bickering by the players and booing by the spectators in school and college sports. Players argue against close decisions and the crowd boos the officials. That shouldn't be.

"I was at Hotchkiss a number of years ago and the spirit among the boys there is highly commendable. I shall never forget an experience I had there while umpiring a baseball game between student teams.

"One of the players was Johnny Hoben. You must remember him. Johnny went to Yale and became an outstanding football player. He was a great athlete and a fine gentleman.

"Johnny came sliding home in this particular game and I called him out. I noticed he looked at me over ihs shoulder as he was on the ground, but he didn't say anything. He jumped up, dusted himself off and ran over to the bench.

* * *

Passive Acceptance of Wrong Decisions

"I THOUGHT nothing of it until that evening when a friend told me I had made a terrible decision.

"'The catcher dropped the ball,' he explained.

"Of course, I hadn't seen the catcher drop the ball and I was quite put out that I hadn't. I knew then why Johnny glanced over his shoulder at me. So I looked him up and apologized.

"'Let's not talk about it,' he said. 'After all, what will it mean ten years from now?'

"That happened just ten years ago. The decision, of course, means nothing, but his attitude at that time means a great deal even ten years later.

"There was an obviously poor decision. Hoben took it and said nothing. I think that showed fine spirit, don't you?"

The philosophy was fine, particularly for a schoolboy, but at the risk of shocking Mr. Neal I said I thought the spirit was questionable.

Is it right to teach passive acceptance of decisions which are obviously wrong? Would it have been a mark of poor sportsmanship if Hoben had called the umpire's attention to the ball on the ground? I don't think so.

* * *

Friendliness Toward Rivals

HOBEN certainly would not have been less of a sportsman if he had said to the umpire:

"Ask the catcher if he dropped the ball."

It would have been fine spirit on the part of the catcher if he had admitted the error even if he had not been questioned.

Many worthy ideals are contained in the new Germantown code. The resolves never to resort to unfair tactics and never to alibi a defeat are fundamental principles of sportsmanship, and that section which aims to encourage and preserve a friendly feeling toward all rivals is highly commendable.

Regarding protests againht decisions, there are too many arguments where decisions are not wrong but merely close and the booing of officials from the stands at college and school events is deplorable. However, fan jeering fortunately is decreasing, but not at professional baseball games, where it is considered part of the sport.

I doubt if it is the intent of the Germantown faculty to glorify the student who accepts obviously wrong decisions without a word of protest.

The code is rigid, but there are always exceptions. The student who protests in a gentlemanly manner against a decision manifestly wrong is not beyond the bounds of good sportsmanship.

Foxx and Johnson Lead Attack As Macks Beat Watertown, 21-1

By AL HORWITS
Staff Correspondent Public Ledger

Watertown, N. Y., Aug. 1.—This up-State town saw its first major league team in action when the Athletics, en route to New York, stopped off here for an exhibition game this afternoon.

No matter how hard they tried to be put out, the Athletics were unsuccessful. They won by the margin of 21 to 1, but it was against their wishes.

Due to the short playing area it was agreed that all drives over the fence would be limited to two bases. A short fly ball was apt to clear the barrier and the Macks slapped easy outs for doubles. That was the reason for the big score. Otherwise there would have been less scoring.

Jimmie Foxx gave the customers a real thrill when he lifted a pitch high and far over the left-field fence. It would have cleared the bleacher wall at Shibe Park. The slugger was held to two bases, but that didn't stop the fans from having a good time.

Bobby Coombs went the route for the White Elephants. That is, all but one out. In the ninth inning, after two were down, Lefty Grove stepped to the mound and pitched to the last hitter.

Coombs gave a good exhibition and the Merchants, as the Watertown team is called, made six blows off him. One run was the product of three safeties. Foxx and Bob Johnson collected eight of the twenty-four Mack wallops, each getting four. The A's left here tonight for New York, where a three-game series will be opened tomorrow with George Earnshaw on the peak.

ATHLETICS	ab	r	h	o	a	MERCHANTS	ab	r	h	o	a
Bishop,2b	3	0	0	0	0	Percy,cf	4	0	0	3	1
M'Nair,2b	3	2	1	5	0	Carney,lf	3	0	0	1	0
Cramer,cf	3	1	2	0	0	Trap'no,lf	1	0	0	1	0
Miller,cf	4	2	1	1	0	G'ybeck,ss	4	1	2	4	2
Madjeski,c	6	3	4	9	1	G.C'man,2b	4	0	2	2	1
Foxx,1b	6	3	4	9	0	Joyner,3b	4	0	1	0	4
E.C'man,rf	6	0	1	0	0	Sixb'ry,rf	4	0	0	3	0
Johnson,lf	6	3	3	2	0	J.Cal't,c	1	0	0	5	0
Higgins,3b	6	1	2	0	4	Brett,1b	2	0	0	2	0
Willia's,ss	5	4	3	1	1	Ca'an,1b,c	3	0	0	2	0
Coombs,p	6	2	3	0	3	M'lbeck,p	2	0	0	1	1
Grove,p	0	0	0	0	0	Nicols,p	1	0	1	0	0
Tot.	54	21	24	27	9	L.O'ert,c	1	0	0	3	0
						Totals	34	1	6	27	9

Athletics	1	2	0	2	0	6	8	2	0	—21
Merchants	0	0	0	0	0	1	0	0	0	— 1

Errors—Higgins, Joyner, Brett. Two-base hits—Graybeck, Joyner, Cramer, Johnson, 2; Williams, 2; Coombs, McNair, Madjeski, Foxx, 2; Higgins. Struck out—By Meichelbeck, 2; Nicols, 3; Coombs, 9. Hits—Off Meichelbeck, 20 in 7 innings; Coombs, 6 in 9; Nicols, 4 in 2. Bases on balls—Off Meichelbeck, 1. Hit by pitcher—By Meichelbeck (McNair). Passed balls—Carman, 2.

TIGERS TO LOSE ROWE

Detroit Hurler Suffers From Shoulder Injury

Detroit, Aug. 1.—(AP)—The Detroit Tigers are going to lose the services of Lynwood (Schoolboy) Rowe, their prize-pitching find of the spring training season.

Recurrence of a shoulder injury that he suffered at Philadelphia July 15 has forced the schoolboy out of the line-up for an indefinite period that Manager Bucky Harris said might be as long as a month.

Sets Record in National League

Carl Hubbell, New York Giants' southpaw

PIRATES TROUNCE ST. LOUIS TOSSERS

Watkins, Swetonic Stage Fist Fight as Bucs Win 8th Straight, 9-3

Pittsburgh, Aug. 1. — (AP) — The Pittsburgh Pirates drew a game nearer to the league - leading New York Giants today as they defeated the St. Louis Cards, 9 to 3, for their eighth straight victory while the Giants lost to Boston. The victory put the Bucs only two and one-half games behind New York.

The game started out as a Pittsburgh swatfest when the Bucs drove Bill Walker to cover and scored five runs in the first inning, and wound up in a brief slugging match between Pitcher Steve Swetonic and George Watkins, Cards' outfielder.

The brief scrap came after Leo Durocher had been hit by a pitched ball in the seventh. Watkins made the last out of the inning and exchanged a few words with Swetonic. They squared off and started throwing punches, but other players and the umpires separated them and they both were chased from the game. Waite Hoyt finished for Swetonic, who had given only five hits up to that time.

ST. LOUIS	ab	r	h	o	a	PITTSBURGH	ab	r	h	o	a
Martin,3b	4	0	0	2	3	L.W'ner,cf	5	1	2	1	0
Watkins,rf	3	0	0	1	0	P.W'ner,rf	4	1	1	3	0
Johnson,p	0	0	0	0	0	Co'rosky,lf	5	1	2	1	0
*Slade	1	0	0	0	0	Vaugh'n,ss	5	0	1	2	4
Frisch,2b	4	1	2	3	2	Traynor,3b	5	2	1	1	4
Cra'ord,1b	3	1	1	10	1	Suhr,1b	5	2	3	11	0
Medwick,lf	4	1	2	1	0	Piet,2b	5	2	3	3	5
Orsatti,cf	3	0	1	0	0	Grace,c	2	0	2	4	0
Wilson,c	4	0	1	1	0	Swetonic,p	4	0	0	1	1
Duro'er,ss	3	0	0	4	5	Hoyt,p	0	0	0	0	0
Walker,p	0	0	0	0	0	Tot's	40	9	15	27	14
Vance,p	2	0	0	1	1						
Allen,rf	2	0	1	1	0						
Totals	33	3	8	24	12						

*Batted for Johnson in ninth.

St. Louis	0	0	0	2	0	0	0	1	0	—3
Pittsburgh	5	0	1	3	0	0	0	0	x	—9

Errors—Walker, Vance, Grace. Runs batted in—Traynor, Grace, 3; L. Waner, Orsatti, Suhr, Piet, Medwick, Wilson. Two-base hits—Piet, Medwick. Three-base hit—Suhr. Stolen bases—Piet, 2; Allen. Double plays—Traynor to Suhr; Martin, Durocher to Crawford; Piet, Vaughan to Suhr. Left on bases—St. Louis, 8; Pittsburgh, 10. Base on balls—Off Swetonic, 3; Vance, 3; Hoyt, 1. Struck out—By Vance, 1; Swetonic, 2. Hits—Off Walker, 5 in 1-3 inning; Vance, 9 in 5 2-3; Johnson, 1 in 2; Swetonic, 5 in 7; Hoyt, 3 in 2. Hit by pitcher—Swetonic (Durocher). Winning pitcher—Swetonic. Losing pitcher—Walker. Time—2:07. Umpires — McGrew, Magerkurth and Quigley.

SPHAS BOW TO CRAWFORDS

Record Throng Sees Pittsburgh Team Win Night Game, 10-1

Eddie Gottlieb's Sphas were no match for the Pittsburgh Crawfords, who handed the Hebrews a 10-to-1 trimming before one of the biggest crowds to attend a baseball game on the P. R. R. Y. M. C. A. field at 44th and Parkside avenue last night.

CRAWFORDS	ab	r	h	o	a	SPHAS	ab	r	h	o	a
Bell,cf	4	2	2	0	0	Meyers,2b	2	0	0	0	2
Russell,2b	5	2	3	2	1	Kas'an,rf	4	0	0	1	0
Char'ton,1b	4	1	0	9	1	Lieb'an,lf	1	0	0	0	0
Gibson,c	5	1	3	7	2	Sand'w,cf	4	0	0	3	1
John'n,3b	5	1	2	1	0	Vann,1b	4	0	1	11	2
Page,rf	5	1	1	7	0	Leaness,3b	4	0	0	2	2
Willia's,ss	5	0	2	0	2	Snyder,ss	4	0	0	4	4
Crutch'd,lf	5	1	0	1	0	Salt'an,c	2	0	0	4	0
Kin'nan,p	5	1	2	0	3	Sloan,p	2	1	1	1	1
Tot.	43	10	15	27	9	Saun'ers,lf	3	0	0	1	0
						Farb'n,2b	1	0	1	0	1
						Morris,p	1	0	0	0	1
						Totals	32	1	3	27	14

Crawfords	0	1	0	0	6	0	0	3	0	—10
S P H A S	0	1	0	0	0	0	0	0	0	— 1

Errors—Snyder, Sloan. Two-base hits—Sloan, Russell, Page, Kencannon, Gibson. Home run—Russell. Struck out—By Sloan, 3; Kencannon, 6; Morris, 1. Bases on balls—Off Sloan, 2; Kencannon, 3.

Runs Scored Daily In Three Leagues

AMERICAN LEAGUE

Clubs	M.	T.	W.	T.	F.	S.	S.	T'tl
St. Louis	12	5	—	—	—	—	—	17
New York	13	—	—	—	—	—	—	13
Cleveland	8	2	—	—	—	—	—	10
Washington	9	—	—	—	—	—	—	9
Athletics	—	—	—	—	—	—	—	0
Boston	—	—	—	—	—	—	—	0
Chicago	—	—	—	—	—	—	—	0
Detroit	—	—	—	—	—	—	—	0

NATIONAL LEAGUE

Clubs	M.	T.	W.	T.	F.	S.	S.	T'tl
Pittsburgh	—	9	—	—	—	—	—	9
Boston	—	3	—	—	—	—	—	3
Chicago	—	3	—	—	—	—	—	3
St. Louis	—	3	—	—	—	—	—	3
Cincinnati	—	1	—	—	—	—	—	1
New York	—	1	—	—	—	—	—	1
Brooklyn	—	—	—	—	—	—	—	0
Phillies	—	—	—	—	—	—	—	0

INTERNATIONAL LEAGUE

Clubs	M.	T.	W.	T.	F.	S.	S.	T'tl
Baltimore	2	18	—	—	—	—	—	20
Toronto	4	10	—	—	—	—	—	14
Montreal	0	11	—	—	—	—	—	11
Buffalo	7	4	—	—	—	—	—	11
Rochester	8	2	—	—	—	—	—	10
Albany	8	1	—	—	—	—	—	9
Newark	0	5	—	—	—	—	—	5
Jersey City	2	1	—	—	—	—	—	3

CUBS TOPPLE REDS AFTER 6 SETBACKS

Pat Malone Pitches Chicago to 3-1 Triumph Over Cincinnati Club

Chicago, Aug. 1.—(AP)—The Chicago Cubs broke their six-game losing streak and regained third place by defeating the Cincinnati Reds, 3 to 1, in the opening game of the series.

Pat Malone held the Reds to five hits and though his mates got only one more than that off the combined deliveries of the Frey, Benton and Stout, they bunched five in the third inning to score all their runs.

CINCINNATI	ab	r	h	o	a	CHICAGO	ab	r	h	o	a
Adams,3b	3	0	0	0	2	Koenig,3b	4	0	0	0	1
xLucas	1	0	1	0	0	W.H'an,2b	4	1	1	1	3
M'ey,2b,ss	4	1	1	0	5	Cuyler,lf	3	0	1	1	0
Hafey,cf	4	0	1	3	0	F.H'an,rf	3	0	1	2	0
Moore,lf	4	0	0	7	0	De'aree,cf	3	0	0	3	0
Bot'ley,1b	4	0	2	10	0	Ca'pbell,c	4	0	0	3	0
Rice,rf	3	0	0	1	0	Grimm,1b	3	1	1	11	3
He'sley,c	2	0	0	1	1	Jurges,ss	2	0	1	5	4
*Roettger	1	0	0	0	0	Malone,p	2	1	1	1	2
Stout,p	0	0	0	0	0	Totals	28	3	6	27	13
Bluege,ss	2	0	0	0	1						
G'tham,2b	1	0	0	0	1						
Frey,p	1	0	0	1	0						
Benton,p	1	0	0	0	0						
Manion,c	1	0	0	1	0						
Tot.	32	1	5	24	10						

xBatted for Adams in ninth.
*Batted for Hemsley in eighth.

Cincinnati	0	0	0	1	0	0	0	0	0	—1
Chicago	0	0	3	0	0	0	0	0	x	—3

Error—Jurges. Runs batted in—Moore, Cuyler, F. Herman, Malone. Two-base hits—Morrissey, F. Herman, Grimm. Stolen base—Cuyler. Sacrifices—Demaree, Malone. Double play—W. Herman, Grimm to Jurges. Left on base—Cincinnati, 4; Chicago, 6. Bases on balls—Off Benton, 2; Stout, 1. Struck out—By Stout, 1; Malone, 1. Hits—Off Frey, 4 in 2 2-3 innings; Benton, 2 in 4 1-3; Stout, 0 in 1. Losing pitcher—Frey. Umpires—Klem and Pfirman. Time, 1:43.

Leading Batters

NATIONAL LEAGUE

	G.	A.B.	R.	H.	P.C.
Klein, Phillies	95	382	63	145	.380
Davis, Phillies	89	319	32	110	.345
Piet, Pittsburgh	86	292	42	99	.339
Fullis, Phillies	94	414	63	140	.338
Terry, New York	69	258	33	86	.333
Schul'ich, Phillies	69	246	36	82	.333

Leader year ago—Hurst, Phillies, .359.

AMERICAN LEAGUE

	G.	A.B.	R.	H.	P.C.
Simmons, Chicago	97	406	66	149	.367
Foxx, Athletic..s	94	354	84	127	.359
Cronin, Wash'ton	96	383	62	133	.347
Hodapp, Boston	88	327	44	111	.339
Manush, Wash'on	97	425	77	142	.334

Leader year ago—Foxx, Athletics, .359.

BOSTON WINS, 3-1, TO HALT STREAK

Hubbell Sets New Mark for Scoreless Frames, but Braves Bump Giants

New York, Aug. 1. — (AP) — The Boston Braves put an end to Carl Hubbell's streak of consecutive scoreless innings today after the New York southpaw had created a new National League record, and defeated the league leaders, 3 to 1.

Hubbell hurled five and two-thirds scoreless frames to stretch his string to an even forty-six consecutive scoreless innings. Then, with runners on second and third, Randy Moore smacked a single that broke the streak and won the ball game for Boston.

The old National League mark was forty-four innings, established by Ed Reulbach, of the Chicago Cubs, in 1908. Walter Johnson still holds the major-league record of fifty-six consecutive scoreless innings.

Huck Betts opposed Hubbell on the hill and withstood the heat better than the Giant pitcher. He went the full route, giving only seven hits.

BOSTON	ab	r	h	o	a	NEW YORK	ab	r	h	o	a
Urbanski,ss	4	1	1	4	3	J.Moore,lf	5	3	1	6	0
Jordan,1b	4	1	1	5	0	Critz,2b	5	3	0	3	0
Berger,cf	4	0	1	3	0	¶Schum'her	0	0	0	0	0
R.Moore,rf	4	0	3	4	0	Terry,1b	5	0	2	6	0
Whitney,3b	4	0	0	2	1	Ott,rf	2	1	0	1	0
Lee,lf	4	0	0	3	0	Vergez,3b	3	0	1	0	0
Hogan,c	4	1	1	1	0	Davis,cf	4	0	1	1	0
Mar'ville,2b	3	0	0	5	4	Richard,c	2	0	0	8	0
Betts,p	3	0	0	0	1	*O'Doul	0	0	0	0	0
Totals	34	3	7	27	9	Mancuso,c	1	0	1	0	0
						Ryan,ss	4	0	1	2	7
						Hubbell,p	2	0	0	0	0
						†Peel	1	0	0	0	0
						Luque,p	0	0	0	0	1
						‡Jackson	0	0	0	0	0
						§James	0	0	0	0	0
						Totals	34	1	7	27	8

*Batted for Richards in sixth.
†Batted for Hubbell in sixth.
‡Batted for Luque in ninth.
§Ran for Jackson in ninth.
¶Ran for Critz in ninth.

Boston	0	0	0	0	0	2	1	0	0	—3
New York	0	0	0	0	0	1	0	0	0	—1

Error — Terry. Runs batted in — R. Moore, 2; Ryan, Hogan. Two-base hit—Berger. Home run—Hogan. Stolen base—Jordan. Left on base—New York, 11; Boston, 4. Bases on balls—Off Betts, 5. Struck out—By Hubbell, 6. Hits—Off Hubbell, 5 in 6 innings; Luque, 2 in 3. Losing pitcher—Hubbell. Umpires—Moran, Reardon and Powell. Time—1:53.

Independent Baseball

PHILADELPHIA LEAGUE

Raphael, 5; Nicetown, 4.

STANDING OF THE TEAMS

	W.	L.	P.C.		W.	L.	P.C.
W.-Olney	7	1	.875	Bartram	4	5	.444
Nicetown	8	3	.727	N.Phils	4	6	.400
Raphael	6	3	[illegible]	Mayfair	3	6	.333
S.Phils	4	5	.444	Col. Tur.	0	7	.000

Nicetown League—Tioga Cards, 5; P. N. A., 4.

Main Line Twilight—Narberth, 8; Cynwyd, 0. Gladwyn, 8; Ardmore A. A., 3.

West Philadelphia—Eastman, 8; Overbrook, 0.

South Philadelphia—Girard Estate, 11; Sons of Italy, 7. St. Stanislaus, 8; Quaker City, 6.

Grays Ferry League—Excel, 8; Wilmont, 5.

Northwest League—East Park, 2; Newkirk, 1.

Woodland League—Gibson, 5; St. Raphael, 1. Clearview, 1; Selmar, 0. Woodland, 14; Elmwood, 7.

South Phila. Twilight—Penrose, 4; Southwark, 2.

Delmont League—Narberth, 4; Oakmont, 3. Brookline, 20; Ardmore Maroons, 13.

Twenty-first Ward—City Line, 14; Suburban, 5. Woodvale, 9; Scholastics, 5. Manatawna, 8; Fourth Reform, 0.

North Penn Amateur—Akron, 13; Lives, 5.

Yeadon Borough—Veterans, 2; Yeadon Cubs, 2.

Starr Garden League—Casey, 6; Edmond, 3.

Wynnefield Booster—Malvern, 11; Arrows, 5.

Quaker City League—Scanlon C. C., 8; St. Mary's Angels, 7. Wissinoming, 7; Tacony Robbins, 0.

Other Games—Kirkwood, 1; Audubon B. C., 0. West Ends, 5; Goodwill Fire Company, 3. Sun Village, 5; Pike Collegians, 1. Leiperville, 8; Chester Black Sox, 1. Manoa, 9; Penn Treaty, 2. Crystal Lake, 10; Pine Hill, 5. Elmwood Grays, 13; Diamond Stars, 3. Beaumont A. C., 11; Southern Stars, 4. Bethany Presbyterian, 5; Forty-sixth Ward, 0. North City C. C., 3; Chew A. A., 1. Mayfair A. A., 8; Delanco, 3. Media A. A., 10; East Falls, 2. Mount Airy F. C., 6; North Phillies, 3. Paoli F. C., 5; Dinan A. A., 2. Richmond Pros, 2; St. Matthews, 1. St. Bartholomew C. C., 9; Olney Maroons, 2. St. Michael's C. C., 3; All-Fairmount, 1. Ed Bolden's Philadelphia Stars, 8; South Phillies, 0. Pittsburgh Crawfords, 6; Wentz-Olney, 3.

GIANTS TRIUMPH TWICE AGAINST REDS, 6-1, 2-1

Cincinnati Forces Second Battle to 11 Innings.

Cincinnati, O., Sept. 10.—(AP)—The New York Giants trounced Cincinnati, 6 to 1, in the first game of a double header today, but the Reds forced them to go 11 innings in the second before the Giants won, 2 to 1. Hal Schumacher and Ray Kolp engaged in a pitching duel in the second game.

Carl Hubbell, the Giant's star pitcher, proved a big factor in the Giants first victory when he relieved Fred Fitzsimmons in the seventh inning with the bases full and none out and set the Reds down in order.

NEW YORK.	Ab	R	H	P	A	CINCINNATI.	Ab	R	H	P	A
JoeMoore,lf	5	1	2	5	0	Adams,3b	4	0	2	2	1
Critz,2b	4	1	2	6	4	JnoMoore,lf	3	0	0	1	0
Terry,1b	5	1	2	12	0	Hafey,cf	4	0	1	5	0
Ott,rf	5	2	2	1	1	Rice,rf	3	1	1	2	0
Jackson,3b	5	0	2	1	3	Bot'ley,1b	4	0	0	11	3
Davis,cf	4	1	2	1	0	Lomb'di,c	4	0	2	0	1
Mancuso,c	3	0	1	1	0	M'sy,ss,2b	4	0	1	5	4
Ryan,ss	4	0	0	0	2	Robello,2b	2	0	0	0	4
Fitzs'm's,p	3	0	1	0	2	*Lucas	1	0	1	0	0
Hubbell,p	1	0	0	0	0	†Crouch	0	0	0	0	0
						Bluege,ss	1	0	0	1	0
						Benton,p	1	0	1	0	0
						‡Roettger	0	0	0	0	0
						Frey,p	0	0	0	0	0
	39	6	14	27	12		¶32	1	9	27	13

*Batted for Robello in seventh. †Ran for Lucas in seventh. ‡Batted for Benton in seventh. ¶Manion batted for Frey in ninth.

New York ....000 003 021—6
Cincinnati ....010 000 000—1

Error—Benton. Runs batted in—Terry, Ott, Jackson, Davis, Ryan, Morrissey. Two base hits—Terry, Ott. Stolen bases—Davis. Sacrifice—Critz. Double play—Ryan to Critiz to Terry; Terry [unassisted]; Ott to Critz. Bases on balls—Fitzsimmons, 4; Benton, 2. Struck out—Hubbell, 1. Hits—Fitzsimmons, 9 in 6 innings [none out in seventh]; Hubbell, 0 in 3; Benton, 8 in 7; Frey, 6 in 2. Winning pitcher—Fitzsimmons. Losing pitcher—Benton. Umpires—Reardon, McGrew, and Quigley. Time—1:53.

SECOND GAME.

NEW YORK.	Ab	R	H	P	A	CINCINNATI.	Ab	R	H	P	A
JoeMoore,lf	4	0	1	5	0	Adams,3b	3	0	1	1	1
Critz,2b	5	0	2	4	3	JnoMoore,lf	4	0	0	6	0
Terry,1b	4	0	0	13	2	Hafey,cf	4	0	1	1	1
Ott,rf	5	1	3	0	0	Rice,rf	5	0	1	7	0
Jackson,3b	4	0	0	1	5	Botmly,1b	5	1	2	6	0
*James	0	0	0	0	0	Lombrdi,c	4	0	2	5	2
Dressen,3b	0	0	0	0	0	Morisey,ss	4	0	1	3	4
Davis,cf	4	0	2	1	0	Robello,2b	4	0	1	4	3
Peel,cf	0	0	0	0	0	Kolp,p	4	0	0	0	1
Mancuso,c	4	0	1	3	1						
Ryan,ss	5	0	1	4	4						
Schu'her,p	5	1	1	2	3						
	†41	2	11	33	18		‡38	1	9	33	12

*Ran for Jackson in eleventh. †O'Doul batted for Davis in eleventh. ‡Lucas batted for Adams in eleventh.

New York ....001 000 000 01—2
Cincinnati ....000 010 000 00—1

Runs batted in—Terry, O'Doul, Morrissey. Two base hit—Ott. Sacrifices—Jackson, Mancuso, John Moore. Double plays—Schumacher to Terry; Ryan to Terry. Bases on balls—Schumacher, 2; Kolp, 2. Struck out—Schumacher, 3; Kolp, 3. Umpires—McGrew, Quigley and Reardon. Time—2:08.

DODGERS, PIRATES SPLIT.

Brooklyn, N. Y., Sept. 10.—(AP)—The Dodgers split their second straight double header with the Pittsburgh Pirates today, winning the second game, 3 to 2, on a ninth inning rally after the Pirates had taken the first, 2 to 1. The loss of the second game dropped the Pirates into third place, behind the Chicago Cubs.

PITTSBURGH.	Ab	R	H	P	A	BROOKLYN.	Ab	R	H	P	A
L.Waner,cf	4	0	1	3	0	Boyle,lf	4	0	2	1	0
Lind'm,lf	4	1	1	4	0	Frey,ss	4	0	1	4	2
P.Waner,rf	4	1	2	1	0	Fred'k,cf	4	0	0	3	0
Traynor,3b	4	0	0	1	0	Hutch'n,rf	4	0	0	1	0
Vaug'n,ss	2	0	0	6	2	Leslie,1b	3	1	1	13	0
Suhr,1b	4	0	0	7	3	Flowers,2b	2	0	0	2	5
Thev'w,2b	4	0	0	1	1	Stripp,3b	3	0	1	0	0
Grace,c	4	0	1	3	0	Outen,c	3	0	0	3	1
Swift,p	2	0	1	1	1	Beck,p	2	0	0	0	2
						Leonard,p	0	0	0	0	0
	32	2	6	27	7		*30	1	5	27	10

*Delmas batted for Beck in eighth.

Pittsburgh ....000 002 000—2
Brooklyn ....010 000 000—1

Errors—Vaughan, Grace [2], Swift, Trey [2]. Run batted in—Stripp. Two base hits—Swift, Frey. Stolen base—Boyle. Sacrifice—Flowers, 2. Double plays—Beck to Leslie; Vaughan to Thevenow; Suhr to Vaughan to Suhr. Bases on balls—Beck, 2; Swift, 1. Struck out—Beck, 2; Swift, 3; Leonard, 1. Hits—Beck, 6 in 8 innings; Leonard, none in 1. Hit by pitcher—Beck [Swift]. Losing pitcher—Beck. Umpires—Powell, Pfirman, and Klem. Time—1:43.

SECOND GAME.

PITTSBURGH.	Ab	R	H	P	A	BROOKLYN.	Ab	R	H	P	A
L.Waner,cf	3	0	1	1	0	Taylor,cf	4	1	1	4	1
Lind'om,lf	4	0	0	0	0	Frey,ss	3	0	0	1	3
P.Waner,rf	4	0	2	1	0	Fred'ick,rf	5	0	3	1	0
Traynor,3b	4	0	0	3	4	Wilson,lf	3	0	2	1	0
Vaug'n,ss	4	0	0	6	6	Leslie,1b	2	0	0	8	2
Suhr,1b	4	1	2	11	0	Flowers,2b	3	0	0	0	2
Thev'w,2b	4	0	2	3	4	Stripp,3b	4	1	0	3	2
Finney,c	4	0	0	0	1	Lopez,c	2	0	1	7	0
Birk'er,p	4	1	1	1	1	Mungo,p	3	0	0	2	3
Harris,p	0	0	0	0	0	‡Outen	1	1	0	0	0
	35	2	8	*26	16		†31	3	7	27	13

*Two out when winning run scored. †Boyle batted for Lopez in ninth. ‡Batted for Mungo in ninth.

Pittsburgh ....010 000 001—2
Brooklyn ....000 000 012—3

Errors—Vaughan, Finney, Leslie, Mungo. Runs batted in—Thevenow, Wilson, L. Waner, Frederick. Two base hits—Suhr, P. Waner, Frederick. Three base hit—L. Waner. Stolen base—Wilson. Sacrifice—L. Waner. Double plays—Thevenow to Vaughan to Suhr; Traynor to Suhr. Bases on balls—Mungo, 2; Birkofer, 7; Harris, 1. Struck out—Mungo, 6. Hits—Birkofer, 5 in 8 innings [none out in 9th]; Harris, 2 in 2-3. Losing pitcher—Harris. Umpires—Pfirman, Klem and Powell.

CARDINALS WIN PAIR.

St. Louis, Mo., Sept. 10.—(AP)—The St. Louis Cardinals knocked Fred Frankhouse from the mound in both games of a double header, and hammered other Boston Braves pitchers hard for two victories, 7 to 0 and 10 to 5, today. By their double victory the cardinals increased their lead over the Braves for fourth place to two and one-half games. Scores:

BOSTON.	Ab	R	H	P	A	ST. LOUIS.	Ab	R	H	P	A
Urban'i,ss	4	0	1	3	5	Martin,3b	5	2	2	0	2
Mar'n'e,2b	4	0	0	2	2	Watk's,rf	4	0	2	6	0
Gysel'n,2b	0	0	0	0	0	Frisch,2b	4	1	2	5	3
Jordan,1b	3	0	0	12	2	Medw'k,lf	4	1	0	1	0
Berger,cf	4	0	0	2	0	Collins,1b	3	1	0	8	0
Whit'y,3b	3	0	0	0	4	Allen,cf	4	0	1	2	0
Lee,lf	4	0	0	2	0	Duroc'r,ss	3	1	2	2	4
Mowry,rf	3	0	0	0	0	Wilson,c	3	1	2	3	0
Hogan,c	3	0	3	3	2	Hallah'n,p	2	0	0	0	2
Frank'e,p	1	0	0	0	0						
Zachary,p	1	0	0	0	1						
Mangum,p	1	0	0	0	2						
	31	0	4	24	18		32	7	11	27	11

Boston ....000 000 000—0
St. Louis ....000 412 00*—7

Errors—Frankhouse, Hallahan. Runs batted in—Frisch [2], Allen [2], Wilson [2], Martin. Two base hits—Martin, Wilson. Sacrifices—Watkins, Wilson. Double plays—Martin to Frisch to Collins, Maranville to Urbanski to Jordan. Bases on balls—Frankhouse, 2; Zachary, 1; Mangum, 1; Hallahan, 2. Struck out—Frankhouse, 2; Mangum, 1; Hallahan, 2. Hits—Frankhouse 5 in 3 2-3 innings; Zachary, 5 in 2; Mangum, 1 in 2 1-3. Losing pitcher—Frankhouse. Umpires—Stark, Moran, and Barr. Time—1:58.

SECOND GAME.

BOSTON.	Ab	R	H	P	A	ST. LOUIS.	Ab	R	H	P	A
Urbans'i,ss	5	2	2	3	1	Martin,3b	5	1	2	1	0
Mara'e,2b	5	0	2	0	1	Watki's,rf	5	3	4	2	0
Jordan,1b	4	2	3	4	0	Frisch,2b	5	1	2	2	2
Berger,cf	5	0	2	3	0	Medw'k,lf	5	2	4	1	0
Whit'y,3b	4	1	1	1	0	Collins,1b	4	0	0	7	1
Thom'n,rf	4	0	0	3	2	Allen,cf	3	1	1	1	0
Mowry,lf	4	0	2	1	0	Dur'her,ss	4	1	4	2	2
Spohrer,c	3	0	1	6	0	O'Farr'll,c	4	1	2	7	1
Smith,p	2	0	1	0	0	Vance,p	3	0	1	0	0
Frank'se,p	0	0	0	0	0	Carleton,p	1	0	0	1	1
Brown,p	1	0	0	0	0						
	*38	5	14	†21	4		39	10	20	24	7

*Hargrave batted for Smith in fifth.
Game called in Boston's 8th inning: darkness.

Boston ....100 022 00— 5
St. Louis ....121 114 0*—10

Errors—Maranville, O'Farrell. Runs batted in—Frisch [3], O'Farrell [2], Vance, Medwick [3], Durocher, Mowry, Spohrer, Berger, Whitney. Two base hits—Medwick, Spohrer, Berger, Martin, Frisch. Three base hit—Watkins, O'Farrell. Home run—Medwick. Stolen bases—Spohrer, Watkins, Allen, Medwick. Double plays—Maranville to Urbanski to Jordan. Bases on balls—Frankhouse, 1; Vance, 3; Struck out—Smith, 1; Frankhouse, 2; Brown, 1; Vance, 7; Carleton, 1. Hits—Smith, 12 in 4; Frankhouse, 6 in 1 1-3; Brown, 2 in 1 2-3; Vance, 11 in 5 [none out in 6th]; Carleton, 3 in 3. Passed ball—O'Farrell. Winning pitcher—Vance. Losing pitcher—Smith. Umpires—Moran, Barr and Stark. Time—2:18.

SENATORS BUNCH HITS TO DEFEAT INDIANS, 7 TO 3

Washington, D. C., Sept. 10.—(AP)—The Senators won their game with Cleveland today, 7 to 3, but saw their lead in the American league cut to 8½ games as the New York Yankees beat Detroit twice.

It was Cleveland's fifth straight defeat after a winning streak of six. Score:

CLEVELAND.	Ab	R	H	P	A	WASHINGTON.	Ab	R	H	P	A
Porter,rf	3	1	1	2	1	Myer,2b	3	2	1	2	1
Knick'r,ss	4	0	1	2	5	Goslin,rf	5	1	1	0	0
Averill,cf	4	0	3	1	0	Manush,lf	3	1	0	7	0
Hale,2b	4	0	0	3	2	Cronin,ss	4	2	2	0	3
Ferrell,lf	4	0	0	2	0	Sch'lte,cf	3	1	2	4	1
Kamm,3b											
Boss,1b											
Spencer,											
Hildeb'd											
Hudlin,p											
*Cissell											

*Batte †Burn
Clevelan Washins
Errors Manush, [2], Sci Three Double Myer to 4; Stew debrand, in 7 inr 7 1-3; B Stewart pires—M

New Yankee header Detroit

DI
Rogell,s Fox,cf Gehr'er, Walker, G'nb'g,1 Stone,lf Sch'ble, Hayw'th Fischer,

*Dolj Detroit New Y Errors inger, L berg, G Gehring Fischer, 3; Gom Owens, Time—1

DI
Rogell,ss Fox,cf G'inger, G.W'ker, G'berg,1 Stone,lf Schuble, Pasek,c Lawson, Fraser,p

*Whit Detroit New Y Errors man, G Gehrig, Three t Stolen to Geh Greenbe balls—L out—Al in 7 in —Laws

Bost pitch [Bump enable Sox to ond ga

ST
Levey,ss West,cf R'nolds, C'pbell, Burns,1 Melillo, Gullic,3 Shea,c Hadley,

*Goo Jolley St. Lou Boston Runs Melillo, Campbe Three olds. Bases c 1. Stru —Weils Losing Hildebr

ST. LOUIS.	Ab	R	H	P	A	BOSTON.	Ab	R	H	P	A
Levey,ss	5	1	0	1	0	Werber,ss	5	0	2	3	4
West,cf	5	1	3	5	0	Cooke,rf	4	0	2	1	0
Reyn'ds,lf	4	1	1	4	0	Johnson,lf	4	0	0	0	0
Camp'll,rf	5	1	2	16	0	Ferrell,c	5	0	0	8	0
Burns,1b	4	0	1	1	5	McMa's,2b	5	0	2	4	2
Melillo,2b	5	0	0	1	0	Hodapp,1b	4	0	1	11	0
Gullic,3b	3	0	0	2	0	*Leggett	0	0	0	0	0
Hemsley,c	4	0	0	1	4	Seeds,1b	0	0	0	3	1
Blae'der,p						Wal'rs,3b	5	0	0	0	2
						Welch,p	4	0	0	0	2
						Brown,p	0	0	0	0	0
						Andrews,p	0	0	0	0	0
	39	4	8	33	10		†42	0	7	33	12

*Ran for Hodapp in ninth. †Jolley batted for Andrews in eleventh.

St. Louis ....000 000 000 04—4
Boston ....000 000 000 00—0

Errors—Levey [2], Cooke, Seeds [2]. Runs batted in—Campbell, Burns. Double plays—McManus to Hodapp; Werber to Hodapp. Bases on balls—Blaeholder, 3; Welch, 4; Brown, 1; Andrews, 1. Struck out—Welch, 5; Andrews, 1. Hits—Welch, 7 in 10 2-3 innings; Brown, 1 in 0; Andrews, 0 in 1-3. Losing pitcher—Welch. Umpires—Ormsby, Hildebrand, and Dineen. Time—2:32.

FRANKIE FRISCH GETS 2,501ST HIT; JOINS LIST OF 5

Pittsburgh, Pa., Sept. 10. — (AP) — Frankie Frisch's four hits today placed him among five major league baseball players who have made more than 2,500 safeties during their careers.

Frisch has made 2,501 hits in 7,821 at bat and scored 1,365 runs in his 15 years in the National league. Only Rogers Hornsby, now managing the St. Louis Browns, Sam Rise of the Washington Senators, Rabbit Maranville of the Boston Braves and Babe Ruth have exceeded this mark. Ty Cobb holds the all time total hit record with 4,191.

West Victor, 11-7, in Negro All-Star Game

The West defeated the East, 11 to 7, yesterday at Comiskey park before a crowd of 15,000 in a game to determine sectional supremacy in Negro baseball. Willie Foster pitched all the way for the winners while his teammates pounded out 15 hits off three pitchers, Streeter, Hunter and Britt.

With the East leading, 3 to 1, as a result of Foster's wildness in the first of the fourth, the Western all-stars rallied for with three tallies in the half of the inning and never were headed thereafter. The decisive drive in this outburst was Suttles' home run into the left field seats after doubles by Wells and Davis. Score:

EAST.	Ab	R	H	P	A	WEST.	Ab	R	H	P	A
Bell,cf	5	1	0	3	0	Stearns,cf	5	1	2	2	0
Dixon,rf	4	2	1	1	0	Wells,ss	4	2	2	4	3
Charl'n,1b	3	2	0	6	0	Dairs,lf	4	2	2	5	0
Mackey,c	3	0	1	7	0	Radcl'e,3b	4	1	2	0	1
Gibson,c	2	0	1	1	0	Suttles,1b	4	2	2	8	1
Wilson,3b	3	1	2	1	1	Morney,2b	4	0	1	1	2
Johns'n,3b	1	0	1	0	1	Bankh'd,rf	4	2	1	1	0
Lundy,ss	2	0	0	1	6	Brown,c	4	0	2	6	0
Harris,lf	2	0	0	0	0	Foster,p	4	1	1	0	2
Jenkins,lf	1	0	0	1	0						
Russell,2b	3	0	0	3	2						
Streeter,p	3	0	0	0	0						
Hunter,p	0	0	0	0	0						
Britt,p	1	1	1	0	0						
	33	17	24	10			37	11	15	27	9

East ....000 320 002— 7
West ....001 303 31*—11

Errors—Harris, Gibson, Morney [3]. Sacrifices—Dixon, Gibson, Russell. Two base hits—Stearns, Wells, Davis [2], Radcliffe. Three base hit—Brown. Home run—Suttles. Stolen bases—Dixon, Charleston, Bankhead. Struck out—Foster, 5; Streeter, 4; Britt, 1. Bases on balls—Foster, 4. Double plays—Wells to Morney to Suttles. Hits—Streeter, 7 in 5 1-3 innings; Hunter, 4 in 2-3; Britt, 4 in 2-3. Hit by pitcher—Foster [2]. Losing pitcher—Hunter.

... phis, winner of the first half, took the first game today, 6 to 1, and went into the league leadership by a 3 point margin. The Pels came back to win the second, 7 to 0, and finished with a standing of .605 to .590 for Memphis.

Minor Leagues

AMERICAN ASSOCIATION.
Final Standing.

	W.	L.	Pct.		W.	L.	Pct.
Columbus	101	51	.664	Toledo	70	83	.458
Min'polis	86	67	.562	Louisville	70	83	.458
Ind'polis	82	72	.532	Milwaukee	67	87	.435
St. Paul	78	75	.510	Kas. City	57	93	.380

INTERNATIONAL LEAGUE.
Final Standing.

	W.	L.	Pct.		W.	L.	Pct.
Newark	102	62	.622	Toronto	82	85	.491
Rochester	88	77	.533	Montreal	81	84	.491
Baltimore	84	80	.512	Albany	80	84	.488
Buffalo	63	85	.494	Jersey C.	61	104	.370

SOUTHERN LEAGUE.
Final Standing.

	W.	L.	Pct.		W.	L.	Pct.
New Orlns	47	31	.603	Little Rock	37	41	.474
Memphis	45	31	.592	Birmnghm	35	39	.473
Nashville	38	32	.543	Cattanoga	35	42	.455
Knoxville	38	38	.500	Atlanta	25	47	.332

YESTERDAY'S RESULTS.
AMERICAN ASSOCIATION.
Indianapolis 4—4; Louisville, 3—5. [First game 12 innings; second game called in fifth on account of Sunday law.]
Columbus, 6; Toledo, 3.
Milwaukee, 4; St. Paul, 3.
Kansas City at Minneapolis, rain.
INTERNATIONAL LEAGUE.
Newark, 6; Baltimore, 5.
Albany, 2-2; Jersey City, 1-1.
SOUTHERN LEAGUE.
Memphis, 6-0; New Orleans, 1-7.
Atlanta, 8-0; Nashville, 6-5.
Birmingham, 5-6; Little Rock, 4-3.

In the WAKE of the NEWS

DO YOU REMEMBER 'WAY BACK WHEN:

WE came home from school we had to get out the candle molds, put the wick through the molds, pour in the candle grease, then set them out to cool for evening use [1868]?—Are En Gee.

Advertising favors from business houses were maps of your state showing the counties?—Sall of Savoy, Ill.

Living in the country when a rainstorm was brewing, mother had us put the rain barrel under the eaves trough to catch soft water for wash day?—A. A. S., Stevens Point, Wis.

* *

The country doctor arrived he had every one jumping sideways for hot water, glass, spoon, towel, etc., and sometimes a knife to spread salve on a cloth, or to mix powders which he always carried in his medicine bag?—John J. McNamara, Jackson, Miss.

Before ringing the doorbell to call on our sweetie we dusted off our shoes on the back of our pants leg and sleeked back our hair to make a good impression?—James E. Smith, Highland Park, Ill.

The One Penny candy store was located on the Newberry school grounds and at recess children hurried there to spend their pennies for spruce and white wax gums and stick candy [67 years ago]?—Mrs. I. O. Warr, Iowa City, Ia.

* *

We wore underwear made out of flour sacks and sometimes the brand of flour was easily seen!—I. M. B., Neenah, Wis.

A trip on the moving sidewalk at the World's Fair of 1893 was a high speed lark!—George E. Waugh, Grand Rapids, Mich.

"Pretty Baby" was the song hit of the season and every one was whistling it!—Tad of Old St. Joe, Mich.

THIS WAKE IS CONDUCTED BY HARVEY T. WOODRUFF. HELP! HELP!

Politicians, tophats and all, attended gangster funerals?—John L. Tapley.

In 1890 this sign was on a board on the triangle bounded by Madison, Ogden and Ashland avenues, then a vacant lot?:

If you want to get the want you want to get,
You want to get your want in the want getter;
The Chicago Tribune wants you to get your want
Because it wants you to get the want you want to get.

Chapel.

Men carried quill toothpicks in a metal case, sometimes using the case as a watch charm?—Blair L. Gilbert.

* *

We wrapped rags around the old cistern during the winter to keep it from freezing?—Grace Iris.

Tom North, now of the radio world, was piano player with "Sidetracked," which featured Joe Walters?—E. E. Meredith, Fairmont, W. Va.

We played the phonograph only on Sundays, holidays or when company came?—Mrs. John P. Morrall.

* *

All the pacifist wiseacres in 1912 insisted that a war between our Christian and civilized nations was impossible?—J. M. M.

We made small kites for the little girls, who flew them from a spool of thread as line?—John Pals.

Bootblacks put a clamp on the bottom of ladies' skirts and attached it to the top of shoes when shining shoes?—Sam C.

* *

Ice wool fascinators and crocheted pineapple lace for undies were all the go in Belvidere, Ill., 40 to 50 years ago?—Winnie Wee.

* *

Jake Schafer and Frank Ives met in a world's championship billiard match in Central Music hall, Randolph and State, in 1894?—Beverly White.

Present Garfield park was known as Central park?—R. I. P.

MINOR LEAGUES FINISH INTACT; 5 YEAR RECORD

Durham, N. C., Sept. 10.—(AP)—For the first time since 1927, the National Association of Professional Baseball leagues, which embraces all minor leagues, closes the books for the year without recording the failure of a single circuit.

Fourteen leagues played the 1933 season. Even during the years of 1928 and 1929, association officials said, several leagues went on the rocks during the summer.

Tinning and Nelson Beat Phils, 4-0, 4-2

[Continued from first sport page.]

somebody should pick up the ball, Cuyler reached first and W. Herman third. Stephenson drove a fly to center to send Herman home. Demaree's liner into the right field corner was good for three bases, Cuyler scoring. Demaree ran in with the final run of the game when Camilli flied to Klein.

Phils Threaten Twice.

One of the Phils' only two real chances to accomplish something in the way of runs came in the first inning. Fullis led off with a scratch through short and Bartell sacrificed. When Klein walked the situation became threatening, but Hurst bounced out to Camilli and Hack tossed out Davis. After that the Phils were practically helpless, except in the sixth. Fullis again opened with a scratch hit, but was forced by Bartell. Klein singled to right, putting Bartell on third. Then Hurst popped foul to Camilli and Davis boosted an easy fly into Demaree's hands.

SECOND GAME

The Phils ran into a bargain in the first inning and came into possession of one run on one hit. Nelson started his day's work by walking Fullis. Bartell followed with a single to left and was forced by Klein, which put Fullis on third. Hurst's fly to Stephenson gave Fullis ample time to scoot over the plate after the catch. In the Cubs' half Hack opened with a single and Stephenson singled with two out but Demaree was suppressed on a grounder to Bartell.

The bargain the Phils encountered in the first inning was nothing as compared to what the Cubs enjoyed in the second. Pearce handed a pass to Camilli, who stole second. Hartnett also walked. Jurges sacrificed instead of waiting to see what kind of present he'd get. A pass to Nelson filled the bases. Pearce also made plans to walk Hack, but was yanked before he could complete it. Berly took over the job with the count 3 and 1. He passed Hack, forcing Camilli to score, but the gratuity was charged against Pearce. Hartnett counted on Billy Herman's fly, and Cuyler grounded out.

Threatens to Whip Jurges.

Just before the Phils busied themselves to score the tying run in the fifth the scene was enlivened by the threat of the Phils to give Jurges a sound spanking. After Umpire Magerkurth had shooed the assembled athletes to where they belonged, play proceeded and Haslin singled to left. McLeod singled to the same spot and both advanced on Berly's sacrifice, which traveled Nelson to Hack to W Herman. Haslin scored while Nelson was throwing out Fullis. Jurges ended the inning by tossing out his pal, Bartell.

Stephenson walked to open the home sixth, and a moment later Camilli made the pass declare a dividend. After Demaree had sacrificed, the big Italian man from the coast league broke into the majors officially. He blasted one of Berly's offerings so effectively that it didn't come down until it was well back in the right field bleacher. The only other interesting thing about the inning was Jurges taking two bases on a wild throw by McLeod. Out of curiosity Bartell straddled the bag even though no play was on, but Jurges this time slid in like a gentleman.

Lon Warneke owns 16 victories against 10 defeats for the season. He'll try to add another victory today when the Cubs face the Phils in the final of the season between the two teams. The Phils probably will start Ed Holley, who was a Cub during part of the Joe McCarthy régime.

Gen. Concession of the Cub forces captured the pearl button sector yesterday in the score card war with an afternoon paper. The Cubs appeared wearing the set of numbers which button on the backs of their shirts. The afternoon paper regained ground when Ki Cuyler's buttoned on number dropped off in the second game. This revealed that his shirt had "11" sewed on the back. That number was Charley Root's, according to the park score card.

Good Pitching

PHILADELPHIA.	Ab	R	H	P	A	CHICAGO.	Ab	R	H	P	A
Fullis,cf	4	0	2	1	0	Hack,3b	4	1	3	0	4
Bartell,ss	3	0	0	3	2	W.H'an,2b	4	1	1	4	1
Klein,rf	3	0	1	2	0	Cuyler,rf	3	1	1	0	0
Hurst,1b	4	0	1	12	0	Steph'n,lf	3	0	1	1	0
Davis,c	4	0	1	4	2	Dem'ee,cf	3	1	1	4	0
Schu'ch,lf	4	0	0	2	0	Camilli,1b	3	0	0	9	2
Haslin,2b	4	0	1	0	3	Hartnett,c	3	0	0	4	0
McLe'd,3b	3	0	0	0	2	Jurges,ss	3	0	0	4	2
Rhem,p	2	0	0	0	2	Tinning,p	3	0	0	1	2
Liska,p	0	0	0	0	1						
	*32	0	6	24	12		29	4	7	27	11

*Todd batted for Rhem in seventh.

Philadelphia ....000 000 000—0
Chicago ....100 300 00*—4

Runs batted in—Hack, Stephenson, Demaree, Camilli. Three base hit—Demaree. Home run—Hack. Stolen base—Hack. Sacrifice—Bartell. Left on bases—Philadelphia, 7; Chicago, 1. Bases on balls—Tinning, 1. Struck out—Rhem, 2; Liska, 2; Tinning, 3. Hits—Rhem, 6 in 6 innings; Liska, 1 in 2. Losing pitcher—Rhem. Umpires—Magerkurth and Rigler. Time—1:19.

SECOND GAME.

PHILADELPHIA.	Ab	R	H	P	A	CHICAGO.	Ab	R	H	P	A
Fullis,cf	3	1	0	1	0	Hack,3b	3	0	1	0	2
Bartell,ss	4	0	1	3	3	W.H'r'n,2b	4	0	1	3	4
Klein,rf	4	0	0	3	0	Cuyler,rf	4	0	0	2	0
Hurst,1b	4	0	0	8	0	Steph'n,lf	3	1	2	3	0
Davis,c	4	0	1	3	2	Dem'ree,cf	3	0	0	2	0
Schul'h,lf	3	0	0	2	0	Camilli,1b	3	2	2	14	0
Haslin,2b	3	1	1	4	1	Hartnett,c	3	1	0	1	0
M'Leod,3b	3	0	1	0	5	Jurges,ss	2	0	1	2	5
Pearce,p	0	0	0	0	0	Nelson,p	2	0	0	0	5
Berly,p	1	0	0	0	2						
Ragland,p	0	0	0	0	0						
	*30	2	4	24	13		27	4	7	27	16

*McCurdy batted for Berly in 8th.

Philadelphia ....100 010 000—2
Chicago ....020 002 00*—4

Error—McLeod. Runs batted in—Fullis, Hurst, Hack, W. Herman, Camilli [2]. Two base hits—Davis, W. Herman. Home run—Camilli. Stolen base—Camilli. Sacrifice—Demaree, Jurges, Berly. Double play—Bartell to Haslin to Hurst. Left on bases—Philadelphia, 3; Chicago, 6. Bases on balls—Pearce, 4; Berly, 1; Nelson, 1. Struck out—Pearce, 1; Berly, 1; Nelson, 1. Hits—Pearce, 2 in 1 1-3 innings; Berly, 4 in 5 2-3; Ragland, 1 in 1. Losing pitcher—Berly. Umpires—Rigler and Magerkurth. Time, 1:44.

ALBIE BOOTH TO ASSIST COACH OF YALE FRESHMEN

New Haven, Conn., Sept. 10.—(AP)—Malcolm Farmer, chairman of the Yale Athletic association, announced today that Albie Booth, former three-sport star at Yale, will be assistant coach of the freshman football team this fall.

Booth, who was a member of the varsity coaching staff last season, will coach the freshman back field, taking the place left vacant by Bob Hall, who has given up coaching for his law practice.

Dr. Marvin A. Stevens, former head coach at Yale, will head the freshman coaching staff.

Wheeling Wins Opener in Middle Atlantic Series, 4-0

Wheeling, W. Va., Sept. 10.—(AP)—Behind a three-hit pitching performance by their star right hander Bud Thomas, Wheeling's Stogies today won the opening game of the Middle Atlantic league championship playoff series from Zanesville, 4 to 0.

Australian Net Players Due to Arrive Today

The Australian Davis cup team and the United States players who will oppose them in the international tennis matches at Onwentsia club, Lake Forest, tomorrow and Wednesday will begin to arrive today.

Adrian Quist and Don Turnbull of Australia will form the vanguard, being scheduled to reach Chicago early today. They will be guests of the Racquet club, 1361 North Dearborn street, and later in the day will visit A Century of Progress. The other players, Jack Crawford, the Australian captain, Vivian McGrath, his teammate, and the Americans, Wilmer Allison, Frank Shields, Lester Stoefen, Keith Gledhill, George Lott, and Frankie Parker, are due tonight or tomorrow morning.

U. S. Lineup Strengthened.

Stoefen and Shields were placed in the American lineup by Allison, playing captain, to strengthen the United States squad in view of the week's results in the national singles tournament, which ended yesterday with Fred Perry of England vanquishing Crawford. Shields replaced Ellsworth Vines and Stoefen was designated as an added starter. Both were semi-finalists in the national tournament.

Two singles and one doubles will be played each day. The first day's singles will be between Quist and Gledhill, and the 17 year old youths, McGrath and Parker, while the doubles will bring together Crawford and McGrath against Shields and Parker.

Crawford Faces Shields.

Crawford also will play on Wednesday, meeting Shields in a singles, following an opener between Turnbull and Allison. A doubles between Quist and Turnbull and Lott and Stoefen will end the events.

BEARS RUN OVER CICERO ELEVEN; CARDINALS WIN

Pro League Teams Hit 60 Point Mark.

The Chicago Bears football team overwhelmed the Vrba Cicero Pros yesterday, 60 to 0, before a crowd of 3,500 on the Morton High school gridiron in Cicero.

BEARS [60].		CICERO [0].
Hewitt	L. E.	Mazintas
Lyman	L. T.	Kasulas
Carlson	L. G.	Dini
Pearson	C	Arbar
Kopcha	R. G.	Sachs
Musso	R. T.	Ohlund
Malone	R. E.	Certik
Brumbaugh	Q B.	A. Swibas
Ronzani	L. H.	Crane
Doehring	R. H.	M. Swabas
Nagurski	F. B.	Triner

Substitutions—Bears: Karr for Hewitt; Buckler for Lyman; Engebretsen for Carlson; Kawal for Pearson; Miller for Kawal; Auer for Musso; Tackwell for Maline; Gonya for Tackwell; Corbett for Brumbaugh; Hansen for Ronzan; Nesbitt for Doehring; Sisk for Hansen; Manders for Nagurski; Bergson for Kopcha. Cicero: Silvitus for Mazintas; Thomas for Sachs; Matkovick for Ohlund; Jenista for Certik; Bajcek for A. Swibas; Campolli for Crane; Kerausch for M. Swibas; Schwartz for Kerausch; Rickenbacker for Triner.

Touchdowns—Hewitt [2], Manders [2], Sisk [2], Ronzani, Hansen, Nagurski.

Points after touchdowns—Nagurski [3], Engebretsen, Manders.

CARDINALS WIN, 65-0

The Cardinals piled up a 65 to 0 score on the Aurora Ideals at Aurora yesterday.

CARDINALS [65].		AURORA [0].
Creighton	L. E.	Stroud
Tinsley	L. T.	Barks
Kiesling	L. G.	Grozius
Moynihan	C	Balong
Blumer	R. G.	Beck
Gordon	R. T.	Ahlskog
Kassel	R. E.	Forss
Malloy	Q. B.	Johnson
Holmer	R. H.	Russell
Moe	R. H.	Lee
Ledbetter	F. B.	Colwell

Substitutions—CARDINALS—Nisbet for Creighton; Sandberg for Tinsley; Steinbach for Kiesling; McNally for Moynihan; Yarr for McNally; Broadstone for Gordon; Rogge for Kassel; Simas for Malloy; Lainhardt for Holmer; Tipton for Moe; Bennett for Tipton; Vokaty for Ledbetter; Johnson for Vokaty.

AURORA—Gee for Stroud; Davis for Gee; Lindquist for Grozius; Heagy for Ahlskog; Koentgen for Heagy; Lundtrom for Forss; Metzger for Lundstrom; Loser for Russell; Dawson for Loser; Devenny for Lee; Gusler for Devenny; O. Johnson for Colwell.

Touchdowns—Vokaty [2], Bennett [2], Johnson [2], Homer, Creighton, Nisbet, Lainhardt.

Points after touchdowns—Holmer [2], Simas [2], Nisbet.

SIMMONS, PIET BACK IN BIG SIX WITHOUT PLAYING

A general downward revision in the big six batting averages yesterday brought Al Simmons and Tony Piet into the sextet, although neither played. Heinie Manush couldn't hit in three tries and his average dropped two points to .330, putting him into a tie with Simmons for third place in the American league. None of the Phillies could do much with Chicago pitching and Wes Schulmerich slipped so far that Piet's .325 average was good for third in the National league. Chuck Klein, big six leader, lost three points as he hit only once in seven attempts against the Cubs. The standing:

	G.	Ab.	R.	H.	Pct.
Klein, Phillies	131	525	91	198	.377
Foxx, Athletics	131	504	115	184	.365
Davis, Phillies	121	434	43	148	.341
Gehrig, Yankees	135	535	126	179	.335
Manush, Senators	141	600	107	198	.330
Simmons, Wh. Sox	137	576	82	190	.330
Piet, Pirates	105	360	45	117	.325

Windy Jennings Sets New Auto Track Mark at Detroit

Detroit, Mich., Sept. 10 — (AP) — Windy Jennings, South Bend, Ind., veteran of the race tracks, set a new track record for the Veterans of Foreign Wars speedway today by winning the twenty mile feature event in 18 minutes and 34 seconds.

Castro Valley Poloist Oppose Burlingame Four Today at Beresford

Old Sea Dog Back With Big Laugh

Kicks Football Out of Column, Puts Dragoon, Waterhouse In

—By William Leiser—

Well, well, look who's back! The "Old Sea Dog" himself. Walked in yesterday afternoon and kicked every last line of football out of this column.

He was talking to himself and chuckling out loud. The California Yacht Club of Los Angeles, it seems, is still after that classic perpetual challenge cup. Has tried six times, failed six times, but isn't worried about a little thing like defeat. Sent Tommy Lee up a few weeks ago, found Lee and the Caprice unable to match the "Old Fox," Art Rousseau, who does more tricks with currents and breezes than "Pop" Warner does with reverses, and set about immediately to work out a new plot.

And now what? Why, now the southern Californians are forgetting the R's and the sixes and the small craft, and they're going after the famous 35-year-old cup with a big ship. They're challenging, in 1934, with the 81-foot, sloop-rigged Patolita, owned by John J. Mitchell and Charles Wiman.

What does that do? That places Skipper Stanley Barrows and the "Big Black Ketch," Dragoon, in line for defense of the cup the Corinthians have successfully defended for so long. And that's what tickles the "Old Sea Dog."

"Don't I know what they're in for?" says Gus Dorn, for that, if you don't know it, is the "Old Sea Dog's" name. Dorn knows. He and Dr. "Painless" Parker, with the beautiful Idalia, tried to down the picture ship all summer, tried everything in the book, and still came out, every time, second best. The "Old Sea Dog" has been the only skipper, for a long time, with the nerve to challenge the Dragoon, and the races he made were features of the big sailing season in San Francisco, but he couldn't beat the unbeatable.

Now, southern California will try, with the big Patolita, which has been almost as successful in southern waters as the Dragoon has been in the north. But the south, in avoiding Art Rousseau to get at Stanley Barrows, amuses the "Old Sea Dog." That's like walking a Ty Cobb to get at a "Babe" Ruth.

THE "OLD SEA DOG" was chortling, too, about what Glenn Waterhouse did to the international star class regatta at Long Beach. And when an old Corinthian Club sailor chortles about what a San Francisco Yacht Club skipper does, the latter must be good.

All Waterhouse did was to go south, beat the Long Beach champ, Eddie Funk, and all the rest of the skippers of the world, win the title, and bring the international regatta to San Francisco for 1934.

All the chambers of commerce in northern California couldn't have done that. It took a skipper, for, to win the right to stage the regatta, a community must present a sailor who can beat the world. This really is a world regatta, too, since entries from France, Denmark, Hawaii and everywhere else, almost invariably enter this annual international star class series.

SAILOR BY ACCIDENT.

Waterhouse once lived in the south. A friend from the east, coming to visit, wanted to sail. Waterhouse looked over a couple of little craft and finally bought a star boat.

"Why don't you race that craft?" some one asked him a year later, so he did, and suddenly became the champion of Santa Barbara.

The craft was the Three Star. Searching new fields, he loaded the Three Star on a trailer, hitched it to his car, and came to San Francisco, where he immediately became champion of these waters. He built the Three Star Two, then, for 1933, beat all of northern California and went to Long Beach to beat the world. Because he did, committees meet at the S. F. Y. C. tonight to lay preliminary plans for the world regatta next September.

THE "OLD SEA DOG" keeps talking.

"They said sailing was due for a flop this last summer," he tells. "That was before NRA, you know. And what? Why, the best competition ever. With Stanley Barrows, Art Rousseau, Myron Spaulding and Cyril Tobin (and Waterhouse) just about winning everything on the Coast.

NEW SHIPS.

"A flop!" The "Sea Dog" laughs. "Why," he tells, "George Wayland has designed four fine new yachts that are being built right now."

A 33-foot cutter rigged for B. Hasslett, a 50-foot schooner for Harry Shay, a big 60-foot schooner to be christened Mytoy for E. F. Grecian, and a 41-foot ketch-rigged craft that is being built at Calpine, 250 miles from navigable water. Frank Blagen, lumberman, is building the craft at Calpine. It will be shipped on flat car to Stockton, dropped in the water and brought, under her own power, to San Francisco, where masts, spars, sails and rigging will await. Two hours after arrival, Wayland says, the craft will be sailing.

Plans laid for a bigger fleet than ever. A more formidable list of champions than ever developed on San Francisco Bay. And a world regatta landed for 1934.

"That's how we 'flopped' in 1933," chortles the "Old Sea Dog," as he wanders out toward the china shop where he paints little pictures on cups and saucers and glasses at times when he can't sail ships.

LARGE CROWD EXPECTED FOR SECOND BATTLE

George Pope Jr. Returns to Lineup for Game; Outstanding Stars Billed on Both Sides

Scheduled to get under way at 2:30 sharp, today, the polo tilt between Castro Valley Rancho and Burlingame will attract a large crowd to the Beresford field of the San Mateo and Burlingame Polo Club, one mile south of San Mateo. A week ago today Burlingame lost to the superb malletry of its opponents.

It will be a case of "the worm turns" today, according to Lin Howard, Burlingame boss. Howard, rated with six goals, will play No. 3 post. Frank Fuller, one of the most expert backs in the nation, occupies that position. George Pope Jr., out of the tussle last week on account of a severe cold, hopes to collect a few counters from No. 2, while Bill Leib is scheduled to work forward. Leib registered three tallies Sunday.

William S. Tevis Jr., the famous horseman and pony breeder, will take his stand as captain of Castro Valley Rancho at back; Harold Anderson Jr., a sensational youngster, is up front, with Bill Gilmore and Eric Tyrrell-Martin behind him. Gilmore rang the bell six times Sunday. Martin suffered a spill at Del Monte which prevented his action last week. He reports that, while his injury still bothers, he is nevertheless confident of a good performance today. He is rated at six goals by the United States Polo Association and is a noted English player.

Officials are Irvin Keeler, polo manager of the club, and Lewis G. Carpenter, umpire of this afternoon's tangle. Positions and goal ratings appear as follows:

Castro Valley Rancho Goal Rating		Pos.	Burlingame	Goal Rating
0	H. Anderson Jr.	1	Wm. Leib	1
1	W. G. Gilmore	2	Geo. Pope Jr.	4
6	Eric Tyrrell-Martin	3	(c) L. Howard	6
4	Wm. S. Tevis Jr. (c)	4	F. Fuller	2

THREE GAMES AT FUNSTON TODAY

The Verdi Club and Langendorf Royals clash today in the feature game of the Golden Gate Valley League at Funston Field, starting at 2 o'clock.

Grissom, who pitched only one inning last Sunday, will pitch for the Verdi Club today. He will be opposed by Speed Luque, who at one time hurled for the Chicago White Sox.

On diamond No. 2 at 12 o'clock Blum Sweets tangle with the Balboa Natives. Jules Bonetti of the Blums goes against Bill Sturdevant, who won his first game in the opening round.

On diamond No. 1 Gilt Edge Market meets Evans Auto Rental. Johnny Malloy gets the assignment for the Gilt boys with Gene Belgau will be on the firing line for the opposition.

Mrs. Glendon Seeks Divorce

BARNSTABLE (Mass.), Oct. 7.—(AP)—A libel for divorce by Richard J. Glendon, crew coach at Columbia University and a resident of South Chatham, from his wife, Marie, on the grounds of cruelty was on file today in Barnstable probate court.

A short time ago Mrs. Glendon filed a petition in probate court for separate support from her husband. They have three children, two sons and a daughter.

Glendon is known in rowing circles as "Young Dick," being the son of "Old Dick" Glendon, who for nearly two decades coached Navy rowing orders.

'Battling' Levinsky In Hands of Law

PHILADELPHIA, Oct. 7.—(AP)—Barney "Battling" Levinsky, of Philadelphia, one-time American light heavyweight boxing champion, today was held in $1,500 bail for further hearing on a charge of forgery involving three checks.

Levinsky, arrested by detectives last night, said the checks were given him by two men in a business transaction, and that he believed he could locate the men. Police said the checks totaled $175.

Ohio State Eleven In Easy Triumph

COLUMBUS (Ohio), Oct. 7.—(AP)—A stalwart band of Ohio State football hopefuls ran rough shod over the Cavaliers of Virginia before a crowd of 42,000 persons today to score a 75 to 0 victory.

Look at 'Em—The Hitters of the Big Loop

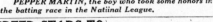

PEPPER MARTIN, the boy who took some honors in the batting race in the Natiinal League.

JIMMY FOXX, who led the American League in hitting in the season just closed.

SPEED STARS TO RACE AT S. J.

Seven auto racing events complete the speed program scheduled this afternoon at the San Jose Speedway. These include time trials, a 5-lap match race between Les Dreisbach and Al Chasteen, three 5-lap sprints, a 2-lap dash for the two fastest qualifying cars, a 30-lap main event and a 10-lap consolation race.

In addition to this card, James L. "Daredevil" Washburn will demonstrate exactly how one should ride a motorcycle at 70 miles an hour through a board wall and end up without a scratch. Manager Linn Mathewson of the San Jose Speedway, who signed Washburn, whose home is in Syracuse, New York, Wednesday isn't quite sure how the trick is done especially since the boards are half an inch thick and they don't look a bit soft.

Much interest is being displayed in the coming battle between Ralph Gregg and Jack McNamara, both of San Francisco. McNamara, a young man with more than his share of the world's goods, following his graduation from Stanford University broke into the racing game. In addition to this pair, as well as Dreisbach and Chasteen, other competitors include Herk Edwards of Watsonville, Fred Lyons, Shorty Holmes, Tom Henry, Bill Johnson of Madera, Hal Logan of Fresno, Joe Rand, Jessie Rueret, Dick Loveland, Johnny Loccoroco, Tip Bloom, R. Bartello and Joe Reese. The last four are car owners and will not nominate pilots until this morning.

Time trials start at noon today with the first race at 2 o'clock.

Promising Fighters ◊+◊ Bert Perry Departs

If Al Young continues to use boxers on his National Hall cards he is certain to develop a few promising fighters.

His opening card from an action standpoint was a huge success. There wasn't an uninteresting or dull bout on the bill.

Two boxers, inexperienced of course, who impressed me most were Ariel Vegas, a youngster from Butchertown, and Metro Sherby. Vegas, weighing 118 pounds, is just a beginner. Just the same, he seems to have the necessary qualities to elevate himself.

Sherby, in time, will graduate into the lightweight ranks. His handlers should let him take on added weight at this time. Keeping him down to 126 pounds won't do him any good. In fact, he may burn himself out in a tough fight or when he's matched with an aggressive, rough fighter.

Bert Perry, his three fighters, Jose Santa, Al Silva and Joe Zemon, are headed for New York. The wily manager left two days ago for the big town, where he departs for South America aboard the steamer American Legion on October 14. He has booked Santa and Pinto De Sa for several fights in the Argentine. His contract calls for six months of fighting, and at the expiration of the contract he will return here with several new fighters in addition to those he took with him.

The gridiron is no place for a fighter to train.

Andrew Bozzano, Olympic Club welterweight, found that out much to his sorrow last Sunday.

Bobbano, playing in a sandlot game, suffered a broken ankle, which means that he will be unable to compete for the Post street club in the coming tri-State tournament.

Spider Roache was depending upon Andy to be one of his mainstays on the squad which hopes to capture team honors.

Tiger Baby Flowers, negro featherweight, heads Ora Forman's card in San Jose Tuesday night. He is scheduled to go ten rounds with Rudy Benton. Benton is the only fighter to beat Flowers in the Garden City.

King Tut leaves tomorrow for Los Angeles, where he is booked to box hard-punching Cerefino Garcia at Hollywood on October 13.

Missouri Tigers Take Shellacking

COLUMBIA (Mo.), Oct. 7.—(AP)—The Missouri Tigers lost to the Kirksville Teachers, last year's champions of the M. I. A. A., here today, 6-26.

Arnold Embree, 160-pound quarterback from Marceline, went on a scoring spree to count 19 of the Teachers' points in the first quarter.

Harvard Over-Powers Bates Eleven, 33-0

CAMBRIDGE (Mass.), Oct. 7.—(AP)—Harvard, using only a few simple plays, today opened its football season by over-powering the light Bates team for a 33-0 victory. The Crimson regular accounted for three o fthe five touchdowns before slumping badly in the third period.

SONNENBERG TO MEET RUSSIAN

Promoter Fedderson Will Match Winner With Browning; Four Preliminary Bouts Arranged

Gus Sonnenberg and Ivan Mannagoff will have something more than the purse coming to them after their engagement on the Dreamland mat on Tuesday night.

Promoter Ernest Fedderson announces that he has Jim Browning's promise that he will meet the winner in a world's heavyweight championship bout here the week following.

The match Tuesday night is the second in which the mat giants have engaged in three weeks. Their first meeting, a splendid match to watch, resulted in a draw, each matman securing one fall.

Spectators saw som real grappling and the speed and skill of the contestants amazed them. In fact, they were on their feet many times during the tussle from thrilling attacks and holds.

Preceding the feature event, the following engagements are listed:

George Hagen vs. "Scotty" Dawlins; Dr. Freddy Meyers vs. "Indian" Jack Smith; Peo Narberes vs. "Red" O'Dell; Jack Manuel vs. Kanetaka Kitahata.

Hans Birkie Wins Over Les Kennedy

(Reprinted from Yesterday's Late Edition.)

BALTIMORE, Oct. 6.—(AP)—Hans Birkie of Germany tonight won a ten-round decision from Les Kennedy of California in the principal boxing bout here. Both are heavyweights.

WALKER, CURRO SEEK KNOCKOUT

Fred Winsor holds some kind of a record as a talkative gentleman. But there's another chap who is giving him a close run for the honors.

He is Eddie Higgins, manager of Paulie Walker. Eddie has his fighter battling Tony Curro Wednesday night in Oakland. As you probably know by this time, Curro is managed by Winsor.

"If this guy Winsor thinks he can talk his fighter into a victory against Paulie," says Higgins, "he'll have to work on a 24-hour shift.

"I'm giving Walker special instructions, and when I spend my time giving special instructions, I usually get results," declares Higgins.

Because Winsor is spreading the word that Curro will belt Walker out, Eddie says he's going to have Paulie knock Curro off in a hurry.

"Maybe that guy that Winsor has is pretty good," continues Eddie. "But he don't know how this Walker can fight. If he don't chalk up a knockout, I'll be disappointed."

Both fighters work out today in Oakland, and return to this side of the bay to finish their training Monday. Curro will box at the Royal Club, and Walker at Taussig-Ryan's.

CARNEGIE TECH TRIMS TEMPLE

PITT STADIUM, PITTSBURGH, Oct. 7.—(INS)—Old Pop Warner, grizzled gridiorn warrior, was out-Warnered by youthful Howard Harpster here this afternoon as Carnegie Tech romped over Temple University, 25 to 0. It was young Harpster's debut in the big-time coaching ranks.

Three Tech touchdowns on beautifully executed forward passes, and another on an off-tackle play spelled defeat for Temple which never seriously threatened the Tech goal line.

Score by periods:

Carnegie Tech	7	0	6	12	—25
Temple	0	0	0	0	— 0

Stanford Freshmen Drub Armstrong

PALO ALTO, Oct. 7.—Stanford University's freshmen football team had a field day at the expense of Armstrong Junior College here today and defeated the visitors, 56 to 0.

The game was played as a preliminary to the Stanford-Santa Clara encounter.

The Papooses swept down the field from the kickoff, ran up touchdowns and safeties and stopped cold every Armstrong J. C. thrust.

Nevada Youth Dies From Grid Injury

FALLON (Nev.), Oct. 7.—(AP)—In the first gridiron fatality in Nevada in many years, Howard Bradley, star halfback for the Fallon High School football team, died of a broken neck received in a game between Fallon and the University of Nevada freshmen eleven here today.

Cornell Trounces Richmond, 28 to 7

ITHACA (N. Y.), Oct. 7.—(AP)—Cornell's football forces relied on its smashing running game to defeat the University of Richmond, 28-7, before 1,200 on Schoellkopf Field here today.

CUBAN FIGHTER PLEASES FANS WITH ABILITY

Carries Hard Punch in Either Hand; Marino Should Attract Attention in Future Bouts

By Eddie Muller

Those who eyed Babe Marino as he smashed out a knockout victory over Eddie Ran Friday night were singing the praises of another fighter today who appeared on the same card.

His name is Baby Manuel. He hails from Florida and his convincing two-round knockout of Johnny Jones proved that he's a featherweight who is destined to advance in his division.

Here's two fighters, Marino and Manuel, who should be valuable attractions to local promoters. Pitted against opposition of stand-up caliber there's no reason why both of these boys can't revive some interest in the game locally, which at present is in the doldrums.

Not only is Manuel a classy performer, but he's a terrific puncher as well. With either hand he deals out plenty of punishment. In the clinches he doesn't hold, waiting for the break. He fights with hands free.

Tom Galiery, whose show was a bowling success, would do well to bring the newcomer back again, I'm sure the fans would appreciate watching a clean-cut, capable fighter in action. Manuel is all of that.

RAN LOSES TO MARINO, FIFTH

(Reprinted from Yesterday's Late Edition.)

Babe Marino, Mission's favorite fighting son, returned to the ring wars last night at Dreamland and chalked up a decisive victory in a new bid for recognition.

The stocky little Italian punched his way to a five-round technical knockout triumph over Eddie Ran, Polish slugger.

Cut over the eye and bleeding from the nose and mouth, Ran, badly battered in the fourth and fifth, was unable to answer the bell for the sixth session.

Ran gave his best, but it wasn't enough. He tried his best shots in the first three heats and when he failed to inflict any damage on the tough Marino, he was a target for hooks, uppercuts and right crosses to the jaw.

Frankie Edgren, highly touted Eastern heavyweight, proved a complete bust. He dropped a six-round decision to Kenneth Lee in the semi-final. Lee knocked Edgren down twice and then the two engaged in a clown fight after the second.

Babe Triscari lived up to advance notices by stopping Mike Luizza in two rounds.

Andy Kelleher carried too many guns for Teddy Yoscon and won a four-round decision in a fast battle.

Benny Marquez and Vincent Morris staged a thriller, with Marquez winning a well earned victory.

The program was the best staged at the Steiner Street Club since its opening under Tom Gallery.

Wyoming Held Even By Colorado College

COLORADO SPRINGS (Colo.), Oct. 7.—(AP)—Wyomings cowboys outplayed the Colorado College Tigers by a wide margin here today in a Rocky Mountain conference football game, but lacked a touchdown punch and were held to a scoreless tie.

Hampton's brilliant kicking kept the Bengals on the defensive during most of the struggle.

Chicago Trounces Cornell College

STAFF FIELD, CHICAGO, Oct. 7.—(AP)—A fast capable eleven Clark Shaughnessy a 32 to to 0 victory over Cornell College of Iowa today in his debut as a big ten conference coach.

Rugby Results

LONDON, Oct. 7.—(AP)—Today's results in the Rugby league:

Batley 2; Swinton 9.
Barrow 9; Broughton 18.
Castleford 18; Bradford Northern 7.
Huddersfield 31; Featherstone 9.
Hull 15; Wigan 11.
Keighley 16; St. Helen's 8.
Leeds 23; Hull-Kingston 20.
Oldham 18; Hunset 8.
Rochdale Hornets 22; Leigh 5.
St. Helen's Recs 6; Widnes 6.
Wakefield Trinity 4; Salford 3.
Warrington 32; Dewsbury 5.
York 29; Bramley 7.

IRISH SOCCER LEAGUE.

Coloeraine 1; Glenarm 2.
Distillery 0; Glenttoran 1.
Portadown 0; Celtic 1.
Cliftonville 2; Bangor 1.
Ballymena 2; Derry 1.
Linfield 1; Newry 0.
Ards 1; Larne 0.

RUGBY UNION.

Blackwheat 4, Old Merchant Taylors 19.
London Scottish 8, Harlequins 21.
London Welsh 5, Richmond 3.
St. Barts Hospital 3, Old Leysians 14.
Aberavon 18, Neath 8.
Bath 14 Roslyn Park 10.
Bedford 14, Mossley 5.
Bristol 3, Davenport Services 0.
Cardiff 3, Newport 6.
Coventry 5, Leicester 5.
Crosskeys 13, Penarth 6.
Gloucester 5, Northampton 0.
Headingly 5, Otley 8.
Llanelly 12, Swansea 0.
Plymouth Albion 3, Blackheath 17.
Pontypool 13, Abertillery 0.
Portsmouth Services 11, Guy's Hospital
Waterloo 21, Manchester 10.
Edinburgh Academy 15, Watsonians 5.
Glasgow Academy 5, Glasgow High School 17.

JOINER HURLS CUBS TO 5-1 WIN OVER PIRATES

Chicago Herald and Examiner Sports

XX FRIDAY, MARCH 30, 1934 TWENTY-ONE

So They Tell Me

By Warren Brown

LOS ANGELES, March 28.—I am afraid that Barney Ross, our lightweight champion, doesn't appeal to these California fight crowds.

He was tossed in here Tuesday night for ten rounds with a local named Bobby Pacho. The junior welterweight title was at stake. Ross got Referee George Blake's decision, and a well closed left eye. But that's about all he did get.

It was his first appearance in a Los Angeles ring, and he was more or less of a disappointment.

THIS PACHO is a strong sort of a fighter, much chunkier than Ross, and a fair puncher with the right hand. It was one of these that caught Barney on the left eye, early in the fight, and just about closed it. This, perhaps, was what handicapped Barney, for he showed little of the flashy boxing skill that is his, and, as a matter of fact, he had to put on a stirring finish to grab any more out of the wreakage than a draw.

I WAS WONDERING, as I sat there and watched Ross work out his battle campaign, if he isn't trying to do something that he never will be able to do, and that is to be what the boys call a "club fighter." He elected to trade swing for swing with Pacho when it wasn't necessary at all. Whenever he tried to do the boxing that he can do best he made his opponent look like the sucker that he probably was figured to be when the match was made.

IF IT WAS Barney's design to please a fight crowd he missed that by a wide margin. He didn't look like an outstanding champion, certainly, and there were many times when he didn't look like a champion at all.

He isn't a hard enough puncher to get in there and slug with some of these chunkier kids that he will encounter every now and then. But that was what he tried to do, even before the clout on the eye necessarily cramped some of his talents as a sharp-shooter.

THE FIGHT WAS not especially diverting, and I was really surprised at the number of ringsiders, among them leading lights of the film colony, who began to get up and walk out as early as the eighth round. I thought, at first, that this was a reflection on our Barney, and so my slugger, "Chuck" Klein, and I got up, and chased after the handsome screen actor, Ted Healey, and asked him why the hell everybody was walking out on our Barney.

Mr. Healey, who has a guest membership in the Rover Boys of Randolph st., wore a very pained expression.

"WE'RE NOT WALKING out on our Barney," he said. "You're a stranger here and you evidently don't know the quaint custom these galleryites have when a decision is given that doesn't please them. They throw bottles at the referee.

"That's why we're walking out. We don't mind getting hit with an occasional cabbage, carrot or even an over-ripe tomato. But bottles are too conclusive."

AS A MATTER of fact, there wasn't much demonstration when Blake raised Barney's hand.

If any bottles were thrown they hadn't landed at the time that Klein and I left the arena. The only conclusion I could draw from that was that the fight wasn't exciting enough to get any of the galleryites to a bottle throwing pitch.

I WAS MORE interested during the progress of the fight, in watching the actions of two of the Rover Boys of Randolph st., Mr. Sam Pian and Mr. Art Winch, who is a sort of Dr. Lotshaw of the fight game.

The pained expression on Mr. Pian's face was exceeded only by the pained expression on Mr. Winch's face, and that for the reason that there is more of Mr. Winch's face than there is of Mr. Pian's.

OUR BARNEY, WHO is a very nice, young lad and good to his folks, has been having a tough time out here in California trying to convince the folks that he is champion of anything.

I know he is the lightweight champion and the junor welterweight champion because I read it in the papers. But as far as the performance given in that ring the other night goes, I'm still willing to believe that it wasn't our Barney in there at all, but that gallant top sergeant in the army of the permanently unemployed, Mr. "Society Kid" Hogan.

Indeed, if it hadn't been for the workmanlike fashion in which Davy Day, another, and to me, more interesting performer, than Ross, gave in smacking down a mug in round one the evening would have been a total loss for all of us transplanted Chicagoans. As it was, I had a terrible time trying to keep Mr. Healey from tearing up his membership card in the Rover Boys of Randolph st.

HOPPE BEATS MORNINGSTAR IN CUE MEET

Takes Second Place by 400-34 Victory; Hagenlacher Retains Lead.

CUE STANDINGS.

	W.	L.	HR.	BG.	Pts.	Ins.
Hagenlacher	2	0	138	13	800	27
Hoppe	2	1	114	8	913	32
Cochran	1	1	158	13	508	31
Matsuyama	1	1	140	18	567	29
Morningstar	0	3	115	..	315	32

By Fred Proctor.

Following his debacle Wednesday night against Eric Hagenlacher, Stuttgart, Germany, Willie Hoppe of New York got back in the running for the world's 18.2 balk line title yesterday by defeating Ora Morningstar of San Diego, Cal., 400 to 34, in eight innings. Willie had two high runs of 83, while Morningstar's best cluster was 12.

The contest was the shortest in innings and elapsed time thus far, requiring only 1 hour and 24 minutes, and enabled commuters to catch the "5:15."

HOPPE GETS LEAD.

Willie started off by winning the bank and scoring 55 points in the first frame. Ora went along nicely until he failed on a short masse at the head of the table of his tenth try. The New Yorker promptly rolled up 83, ducked on a bank and Morningstar went scoreless in his half of the second.

Using the bridge on a headrail shot in the third, Hoppe failed on his fifteenth point there, but 82 in the next set him up to 234 against Morningstar's 17.

From there on it was all Hoppe, except in the sixth, where a three-cushion bank whitewashed him. The San Diego veteran followed with 12, his high run, but muffed a long table bank and failed to count thereafter while Hoppe galloped out with runs of 83 and 55.

TAKES SECOND PLACE.

The victory placed Willie in second place, with two victories and one defeat. Morningstar, losing three games thus far, was firmly intrenched in the cellar, but he never lost his friendly smile.

The score by innings:

The score by innings:

HOPPE—55, 83, 14, 82, 28, 0, 83, 55—Total, 400. Innings, 8. High run, 83.

MORNINGSTAR—9, 0, 3, 5, 5, 12, 0—Total, 34. Innings, 7. High run, 12.

Referee—Charles C. Peterson.

Delker, of Cards, Sent to Columbus

BRADENTON, Fla., March 29.—The St. Louis Cardinals were one player closer to the regular season player limit today with the sending of Eddie Delker, a utility infielder, to Columbus of the American Association.

HACK WALLOPS ONE

Hack Wilson, once mighty swatter of the Cubs, has been having his difficulties these past couple of seasons with the Brooklyn Dodgers, but hopes to regain his old slugging stride this year.

YANKEES HELD TO THREE HITS; DEFEATED, 7-2

Boston Braves' Hurlers Are Stingy as Mates Rally Near Finish.

ST. PETERSBURG, Fla., March 29.—Pounding three New York Yankee pitchers for eleven hits, the Boston Braves had little trouble in winning, 7 to 2, here today.

Betts and Mangum held the big guns of the Yanks to three hits.

		R.	H.	E.
Boston (N)	0 0 1 0 0 0 3 3 0	7	11	0
New York (A)	0 0 0 0 0 1 0 1 0	2	3	2

Batteries—Betts, Mangum and Spohrer; Macfayden, Aube, Tamulis and Dickey.

Hose Visit Lion Farm to Gain Courage

Fonseca Tries Psychology on Recruits; Lets 'Em Mingle With 'Big Cats.'

By Wayne K. Otto.

PASADENA, Cal., March 29.—In order to instill a bit of courage in the breasts of certain of his recruits, your Mr. Lew Fonseca tried a bit of psychology with the White Sox today.

He took them out to a lion farm to mingle with the big cats. In other words, to get 'em lion-hearted. Young "Frenchy" Bordagaray, the recruit from Sacramento, wanted to go right into a cage and imitate Earl Beatty, but Fonseca turned the plans on that one, Mr. Bordagaray is still swathed in bandages around the brow as a result of challenging the cement wall in center field at Los Angeles the other day.

"If that lion gets a good look at you with all those bandages, he'd start laughing. He'd know you were all softened up," Fonseca said.

SIMMONS BECOMES BRAVE.

Mr. Al Simmons, the noted slugger and leftfielder expressed a great desire to enter the cage and have his picture taken with one of the big cats.

"It would be nice for my collection. For instance, me petting a big lion! But then he might not take it in the right way. He might bite," mused Al.

"Ye-ah, you're right. If you must have a picture take one with yourself petting a bat, not a cat," observed Lew.

One of the older lions, who has been mellowed up a bit by age, looked up and down the line at Fonseca's squad and finally spied that gentleman of somber mien, Sad Samuel Jones. Whereupon his eyes became flooded with tears and he started to cry right out loud in the most improved lionesque way. Sam looked so sad

LEAVE TOUCHING SCENE.

"Come on; let's get out of here. I'll be crying myself in a few more minutes. This scene touches me strangely," snapped Fonseca.

So the boys departed, reflecting great courage once they were out of range where a playful lion might

Turn to Page 22, Column 8.

ROOKIE GOES ENTIRE ROUTE IN COAST GAME

Galan and Camilli Clout Homers for Chicago; Pittsburgh Hurler Wild.

By Warren Brown.

LOS ANGELES, March 29.—Nothing from nothing leaves nothing.

Well, not much, any how. Which is a way of explaining how Roy Joiner, the solemn lefthander, who throws a ball with 'nothing" on it, happened to go nine innings against him, though the Pittsburgh hitters collected no less than twelve hits along the route.

DOLF CAMILLI,

Clouts a homer with room to spare.

The score was 5 to 1, which may require some explanation, too, inasmuch as they were restricted to but five hits by Pitchers Lloyd Johnson and Blanton.

But first, about this Joiner, the guy who has "nothing" and sends batters away from the plate fairly daffy, as they mutter about it. For seven innings today he had the Pirates shut out, and it was not until Gussie Suhr's single turned up in the eighth inning, with Tommy Thevenow on second, that the Pirates were able to score. Suhr's hit, incidentally, was the twelfth and last that Joiner allowed.

That the Cubs were able to score five runs on five hits was accounted for partly by two home runs, one in the third inning by Augie Galan, and one in the seventh by Dolph Camilli. The other three came across in the sixth, Gabby Hartnett's single driving in one, and misplays by the Pirates permitting the other two to count.

CUYLER SAVES TROUBLE.

For two innings, during the left-handed part of the entertainment, the Cubs came closer to a run than did the Pirates. This was in the second when two passes and a single filled the bases with two outs. They were emptied when Joiner rolled to the infield for the third.

Galan's homer, which turned up at the start of the Cubs' half of the third, had room to spare when it dropped beyond the brick wall in left field.

The Pirates might have proved troublesome in the fourth, but for a swell running catch by Cuyler. Incidentally, the face of the Los Angeles hero, "Goldilocks" Stainback, must have been quite red, after Cuyler made the catch. In order to grab the baseball, "Kiki" came away over into right center and actually passed Stainback while en route.

Jurges tried to crowd his luck too far in the Cubs' half. He hit a high fly into short right field and reached second when Lavagetto dropped it. Then re decided to steal third, and did. On Jointer's tap to Johnson, Bill went for the plate, but didn't quite make it. Still he saw a lot of the country, at that.

DOUBLE-PLAY AIDS.

Joiner seemed to be heading for some suffering in the sixth, but he managed to escape. Large Poison Waner reached first on what should have been a base hit, but which the scoring, Los Angeles style, termed an error for Jurges. Then Traylor drove sharply to Jurges, and a double-play afforded temporary relief. This was followed by two singles, and then Lavagetto hit one, but directly at Jurges, for the third out.

And the Pirates went out muttering about a lucky stiff as some other six major league clubs will be doing between now and next October, when Joiner and his "nothing" are operating for the Cubs.

After being restricted to a pair of hits for five innings, the Cubs inaugurated a new deal in the sixth.

Stainback slammed past Johnson

Turn to Page 23, Column 1.

Good Work, Joiner

CUBS.

	AB.	R.	H.	PO.	A.	E.
Galan, 3b	3	1	1	2	2	0
W. Herman, 2b	3	0	0	6	3	0
Cuyler, cf	3	0	0	3	0	0
Klein, lf	3	0	0	2	1	0
Stainback, rf	4	1	1	2	0	0
Grimm, 1b	2	0	0	6	0	0
Camilli, 1b	1	1	1	3	0	0
Jurges, ss	3	1	1	2	4	1
Hartnett, c	1	1	1	1	0	0
Tate, c	1	0	0	0	0	0
Joiner, p	4	0	0	0	0	0
Totals	28	5	5	27	10	1

PIRATES.

	AB.	R.	H.	PO.	A.	E.
L. Waner, cf	4	0	1	2	0	0
Roettger, cf	2	0	0	0	0	0
Lindstrom, lf	4	0	1	0	0	0
P. Waner, rf	4	0	1	0	0	0
Traynor, 3b	3	0	1	2	0	0
Thevenow, 3b	1	1	1	0	0	0
Vaughan, ss	4	0	1	2	4	1
Suhr, 1b	4	0	3	11	0	0
Lavagetto, 2b	4	0	1	4	7	1
Veltman, c	4	0	2	3	3	0
Johnson, p	2	0	0	0	3	1
Blanton, p	0	0	0	0	0	0
Young	1	0	0	0	0	[illegible]
Totals	37	1	12	24	17	[illegible]

Pirates	0 0 0 0 0 0 0 1 0	1
CUBS	0 0 1 0 0 3 1 0 *	5

Home Runs—Galan, Camilli. Stolen Base—Jurges. Bases on Balls—Off Johnson, 7; off Blanton, 1. Struck Out—By Joiner, 1; by Johnson, 1; by Blanton, 2. Hits and Runs—Off Johnson, 4 and 4 in 6 innings. Double Plays—W. Herman to Jurges to Grimm (2); Lavagetto to Vaughan to Suhr. Umpires—Pfirman and Good.

PHILS DOWN RED SOX, 6-5

WINTERHAVEN, Fla., March 29.—Although outhit, the Philadelphia Phillies nosed out the Boston Red Sox, 6 to 5, here today.

The deciding tally was scored in the eighth. Pipgras and Pennock

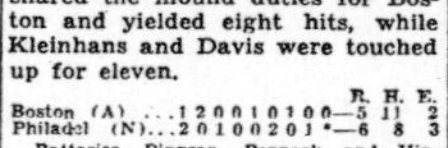

shared the mound duties for Boston and yielded eight hits, while Kleinhans and Davis were touched up for eleven.

		R.	H.	E.
Boston (A)	1 2 0 0 1 0 1 0 0	5	11	2
Philadel (N)	2 0 1 0 0 2 0 1 *	6	8	3

Batteries—Pipgras, Pennock and Hinkle, Connolly; Kleinhans, Davis and Todd, Wilson.

EXHIBITION SCORES.

Giants, 5	Brooklyn, 4
Columbus, 7	St. Louis Cards, 6
Indians, 5	New Orleans, 4
Phillies, 6	Red Sox, 5
Braves, 7	Yankees, 2
Atlanta, 9	Reds (second team), 7
Athletics, 5	Tigers, 3

Hawks Home; Drill Today for Maroons

Returning last night from Montreal, where they piled up a commanding lead over the Maroons in the first game of the Stanley Cup semi-finals, the Black Hawks "rolled in" early to get a good rest.

Strenuous days are ahead, including practice today and tomorrow and Sunday night's final battle at the Stadium. The Maroons will arrive here Saturday forenoon.

Despite Wednesday night's brisk contest at Montreal, all of the Hawks were in good shape physically. Several had minor bumps and bruises, but it requires a broken arm or leg these days to cause a team manager any concern.

SPIRITS ARE HIGH.

The players are in high spirits over their foray into the enemy's camp, while Maj. Frederic McLaughlin, president, was as happy as a boy with a pair of red-topped copper-toed boots. Many years ago the major possessed such footwear, in addition to a little red top. Hockey

Turn to Page 23, Column 1.

'Rabbit' Back in Three Months, Doctor Predicts

ST. PETERSBURG, Fla., March 29.—Walter ("Rabbit") Maranville, Boston Brave second baseman whose leg was broken during an exhibition game here yesterday, probably will be playing again in three months. Dr. Prescott Le Breton, famous surgeon who set the broken member, said today.

"Maranville's physical condition is ideal for a man of his age,"

TIGERS LOSE TO ATHLETICS, 5-3

FORT MYERS, Fla., March 29.—The Philadelphia Athletics beat the Detroit Tigers here this afternoon, 5 to 3.

Both teams collected ten hits, but the Tigers were guilty of two errors, while the A's played errorless ball.

Detroit (A)	1 0 1 0 1 0 0 0 0	3	10	2
Philadel (A)	2 0 0 1 1 0 1 0 *	5	10	0

Batteries—Bridges, Auker and Cochrane; Kennedy, Matuzak and Berry.

Dodgers Defeated by Giants, 5 to 4

ORLANDO, Fla., March 29.—The New York Giants defeated the Brooklyn Dodgers, their National League rivals, 5 to 4, here today. Schumacher, Smith and Luque worked on the mound for the world's champions. Score:

New York	0 0 0 0 0 0 3 0 2	5	9	0
Brooklyn	0 1 0 0 2 1 0 0 0	4	11	0

Batteries—Schumacher, Smith, Luque and Richards; Danning, Mungo Carroll, Page and Lopez.

Picard's 283 Takes North and South Golf

PINEHURST, N. C., March 29.—Henry Picard, young Charleston, S. C., pro, won the North and South Open Golf championship today, the first major victory of his career.

He carded a 72, one over par, on his last round for a 283 total, seven shots higher than Joe Kirkwood's record winning total last year.

Three shots behind in a triple tie for second place came George T. Dunlap Jr., national amateur champion, Harry Cooper, Chicago, and Horton Smith, also of Chicago.

Wiffy Cox of Brooklyn dropped a 69 onto the board for a final score of 289. Tommy Armour of Chicago, in the running with 214 for three rounds, had a ruinous 75 and wound up with 289.

Other final scores were: Billy Burke, Cleveland, 223-73-295; Jim Foulis, Chicago, 222-74-296; MacDonald Smith, Nashville, 221-76-297; Paul Runyan, White Plains, N. Y., 222-72-294; Bob Cruickshank, Richmond, 230-75-300; Frank Walsh, Chicago, 224-71-295; Tony Manero, Sedgefield, N. C., 223-72-295; Joe Turnesa, Elmsford, N. Y., 225-72-297, and Al Houghton, Washington, 227-75-302.

Billy Burke, Cleveland, 222-73-295; Jim Foulis, Chicago, 222-74-296; Macdonald Smith, Nashville, Tenn., 221-76-297; Wiffy Cox, Brooklyn, N. Y., 220-69-289; Tommy Armour, Chicago, 214-75-289; Bobby Cruickshank, Richmond, Va., 230-75-305.

Al Watrous, Birmingham, Mich., 219-72-291; Mike Turnesa, Elmsford, N. Y., 221-70-291; Tom Creavy, Albany, N. Y., 220-73-293; Jimmy Hines, Timberpoint, L. I., 218-76-294; John Kinder, Asbury Park, N. J., 218-71-289; Phil Perkins, Cleveland, 220-70-290; Willie Macfarlane, Tuckahoe, N. Y., 222-71-293; Denny Shute, Philadelphia, 220-74-294.

Everyday Movies Page 31

THE BOSTON HERALD

LATE CITY EDITION
BOSTON AND VICINITY—Generally fair today, tomorrow; showers tomorrow.
High water, 12:42 A. M.
Full report on page 2.

VOL. CLXXVI., NO. 11 | WEDNESDAY MORNING, JULY 11, 1934—THIRTY-TWO PAGES | ****** | TWO CENTS

A. L. STARS WIN, 9-7, AFTER HUBBELL FANS SIX IN THREE INNINGS

BOARD CONTROL OF NRA FAVORED BY GEN. JOHNSON

Has Recommended to President Naming of Governing Commission

CHANGE MAY MEAN HIS RETIREMENT

Government Must Maintain a Veto Power Over Industry, He Says

WASHINGTON, July 10 (AP)—An end to one man bossdom of industry under the blue eagle in favor of a commission control which may mean his own retirement was foreseen today by NRA'S chieftain, Hugh S. Johnson.

"I have definitely recommended to the President that NRA is not a one man job when it passes into the field of administration," Johnson told reporters.

NEED MORE BALANCING

"I think that as we move into the period of administration instead of the pioneering work of setting up codes, we need more balance in carrying out NRA. I do not think there would be any change in its underlying principle.

"As far as my recommendations are concerned, whatever is done the government must maintain a hand, a veto power. There will be no organization I'll recommend that doesn't include that principle."

In place of his own single-handed direction, Johnson has proposed to the President a board or commission. It would be non-partisan and Johnson thinks might best be composed of people experienced in NRA. He said his recommendations did not embrace the federal trade commission nor the size of the new body.

UP TO PRESIDENT

"I'd like to see it set up as soon as there is some coalescence in the diverse codes, as soon as we get the basic code out (for small industries) and a few other things done," he said. "That could be done in the next month or two."

Johnson said the question of a new set-up was entirely up to the President and that a commission could be named by executive order.

As for his own tenure in office, Johnson said:

"Don't get the idea that I'm going out because that is not the idea at all.

"I'll stay just as long as the President thinks he needs me," he added.

NOT EAGER TO BE ON BOARD

But when asked if he might serve on the commission Johnson replied with a laugh:

"If I could avoid it I'd be glad to."

Johnson, who has just returned from a week of conferences with his former business associate, Bernard Baruch in New York, said "the probability" was that he would remain in NRA until Congress meets "although I'd like to get away."

He said that a commission would not have final authority during the speaking trip he begins tomorrow but that he would confer with the agency by telephone.

In his absence, George A. Lynch, Johnson's administrative assistant, will be in charge of NRA.

"I'll be in touch every day by telephone," Johnson said. "There'll be no board running NRA."

TO SPEAK THE 12TH

"Will you speak at Waterloo, Iowa?" he was asked.

"I'll make that speech unless the President tells me not to on Thursday, the 12th," Johnson replied.

His reference was to published reports that Mr. Roosevelt had curtailed his speaking tour which originally was

(Continued on Page Five)

Today's Herald

Blaze Set by Firemen at Squantum Blankets Greater Boston in Smoke

The curtain of dense black smoke that emanated from the burning of discarded automobile tires which had been placed in a trench along the Squantum causeway at the Dennison airport caused hundreds from all parts of Boston to call newspaper offices, police and fire departments and ask if Quincy was on fire.

Firemen, usually concerned with extinguishing fires, yesterday purposely started one which was seen from almost every city and town in the metropolitan area, blanketed Dorchester, Quincy and the Old Colony boulevard with a dense, black curtain of smoke, created numberless traffic jams on the South Shore, and aroused countless persons to telephone newspaper offices and fire stations to find out what it was all about.

The smoke, much to the distress and surprise of the firemen, emanated from 500 tons of discarded automobile tires which had been placed in a trench flanking the Dennison airport and at the side of the Squantum causeway. The tires had been placed there to prevent the sand of the airport from drifting into the road. It is now desired to widen the road and as part of an ERA project the only way this could be done was to remove the tires.

When it was decided to remove by conflagration, it was also decided to call in experts on conflagrations and hence the arrival at 4 P. M. yesterday of officials from the Quincy fire department. They said it would be easy, that it would not be difficult to keep

(Continued on Page Nineteen)

OPINION ABROAD WORRIES HITLER

He Picks Friday, 13th, to Follow up Hess's Speech With Defense of Acts

REICHSTAG CALLED IN SPECIAL SESSION

By FREDERICK T. BIRCHALL
[Wireless to The Herald]

BERLIN, July 10—Adolf Hitler has called the Reichstag to hear from his own lips an account of what happened in Germany on June 30 and the week following and why his government acted as it did. It is to be another and stronger effort to allay foreign criticism, which is at present unappeased. Yesterday's London Times arriving here today was editorially sarcastic both over Hess's speech, which it characterized as being as ingenious as Marc Antony's oration over Caesar's body, and the failure to produce an official death list.

The call to the Reichstag was issued today by Hermann Goering in his capacity of president, following Hitler's sudden return to Berlin from Berchtesgaden. The restoration of the Reichstag building not having yet been completed, the Nazified German Parliament will meet in Kroll's Opera House at 8 o'clock in the evening of next Friday, the 13th. The 13th is a pregnant day in Nazi chronology. It was on Aug. 13, 1932, that Hitler, calling on Von Hindenburg, demanded and was refused that supreme power which he has since attained.

Only one item is at present on the Reichstag agenda, the declaration from the government through the chancellor. It is quite probable, however, that advantage will be taken of the meeting

(Continued on Page Seventeen)

WARNS BUDDIES AGAINST WATER

Later, Private Is Ill at Devens —'Too Much Water,' Says Doctor

FORT DEVENS, July 10—Private Bernard F. O'Meara of the 101st infantry medical detachment of the 26th division of the Massachusetts national guard in camp here, spent the early part of the day warning the men not to drink too much water. A medical officer had assigned him to that duty. During the later part of the day, another soldier was in his place, while O'Meara groaned on his bunk back at camp. "Too much water," said the doctor.

DAVIS ASSAILS BUREAUCRACY

Declares It Will Strangle Democracy in Speech Defending Capitalism

HITS BLIND BACKING OF NEW DEAL PLANS

UNIVERSITY, Va., July 10 (AP)—In a defense of the "old order," John W. Davis warned tonight against the death of representative democracy "by the slow strangulation of an engirdling bureaucracy."

If it must die, he said, "it would die a nobler death in the lightning and storm."

"Surely we have warrant to believe," the 1924 Democratic presidential candidate told the Institute of Public Affairs at the University of Virginia, "that within the framework provided by the old order, progress is still possible, reforms are still practicable and recovery is still attainable.

"In the court of reason, in the light of history, the burden of proof rests wholly on those who would persuade us to the contrary."

The New York attorney said he was speaking "neither for nor against the 'new deal' in the present use of that alluring phrase. Under that title good has been done, no doubt, which no one would wish to undo."

"And I share the general admiration evoked by the energy, promptitude and driving power shown by President Roosevelt," he continued. "On the other hand, to approve or reject any policy or group of policies in mass and without analysis is an act solely of emotion, not of reason."

Declaring that he did not wish to be regarded "as an opponent of change" and that "as a liberal I put my faith

(Continued on Page Five)

BOSTON WOMAN TO SHARE ESTATE

Inherits Half of $150,000 of Aunt, Who Kept Cash In Wisconsin Home

EAU CLAIRE, Wis., July 10 (AP)—With the exception of $5000 the $150,000 estate of Mrs. Alice Hayden will go to her niece, Mrs. William Ittman, Boston, and her son, William Ittman, the woman's will showed today.

The $5000 will go to Mrs. Hayden's sister, Mrs. Effie McLeod of Eau Claire.

GOVERNMENT QUITS IN AUSTRIA

VIENNA, July 11 (AP)—The government of Chancellor Engelbert Dollfuss resigned today to make way for a new government concentrating even greater dictatorial powers in his hands.

U. S. TAX LEVIED IN STATE DOUBLE TOTAL FOR 1933

$97,355,338 Collected as Share Toward Maintaining Government

INDIVIDUAL LEVIES JUMPED BY 20 P. C.

AAA and Liquor Assessments Account for Big Proportion of Increase

Under the ever mounting taxation system of the new deal, Massachusetts, for the fiscal year ending June 30, paid into the federal treasury $97,355,338.02, nearly twice the amount which the commonwealth was assessed the previous year toward the expense of maintaining the federal government.

The increase in the Bay State's federal tax represented a rise of but 6 per cent. in corporation taxes, which increased from $18,344,521 in 1933 to $19,444,620 this year. Individual income taxes jumped 20 per cent. from $16,825,039 in 1933 to $20,176,810.

NEW ITEMS INCLUDED

By far the preponderant portion of the huge rise was experienced in the miscellaneous tax grouping, which includes among items not taxable in 1933, the levy on liquor, the agricultural adjustment taxes and processing taxes on cotton and other commodities.

In this last category, the state paid $21,581,909, ranking first among the states of the nation in its contribution toward the subsidy by which the federal government aids the cotton grower of the South to overcome his deficits. This tax, however, is passed along to the consumer by the manufacturer.

In the general miscellaneous group of taxes, Massachusetts ranks fifth among the states. Included in this group are the gasoline tax, amusement admissions, candy and liquor levies.

A review of the figures for the nation showed the commonwealth paid federal taxes exceeding the total of the remaining five New England states by $38,574,679.

RISE OF 63 PER CENT. ELSEWHERE

The increase of almost 100 per cent. in federal taxes in Massachusetts compares somewhat strangely with a rise of approximately 63 per cent. throughout the nation.

Guy T. Helvering, commissioner of internal revenue collections at Washington, announced yesterday that collections for the nation were $2,672,318,602, compared with $1,619,839,225 for the fiscal year ending a year ago.

The increase, according to the commissioner, includes taxes collected under the agricultural adjustment act amounting to $371,225,338.60, from which source there were no collections in 1933.

While no final accounting of the disbursements has yet been made by the bureau of internal revenue, the commissioner confidently stated that the cost of collecting each $100 of revenue during the fiscal year just closed, was reduced approximately 37 per cent., compared with the previous fiscal year.

Other New England states fared in similar proportion to Massachusetts. Connecticut paid $29,124,853.38, as compared with $18,414,424.85 a year ago. Maine jumped more than 100 per cent., from $3,723,154.04 in 1933 to $7,945,784.11 this year.

The greatest increase in New England was contributed by New Hampshire, which this year paid into the federal coffers a total of $5,290,484.14, almost triple the 1933 figure of $1,790,713.93. Vermont's levy increased from $8[illegible],940.73 to $1,443,413.86.

5 STATES PAY HEAVILY

U. S. Collects More Than Half Total Taxes in Them

WASHINGTON, July 10 (AP)—In five of the 48 states—New York, North Carolina, Illinois, Pennsylvania and California—the federal government collected more than half of the $2,672,318,602 received from taxation in the fiscal year just ended.

Eleven states—Arizona, Idaho, North Dakota, South Dakota, Vermont, Wyoming, Arkansas, Mississippi, Nevada, Utah and Montana—meanwhile contributed

(Continued on Page Two)

PAST AND FUTURE OF NORTH BROOKFIELD

Jane Rooney, 11-year-old daughter of Mr. and Mrs. Francis C. Rooney, presents Connie Mack (left) and George M. Cohan with autographed gold programs as souvenirs of the big day at North Brookfield yesterday. Mack, who learned his baseball on the Common of the small town, was the guest of honor, with Cohan, the dramatic star, being the co-hero as 10,000 turned out for the festivities.

PLANS ONE TRIAL FOR 2 BANKERS

Government Moves to Bring up Mulloney and Deery Cases Sept. 11

WILL HOLD HEARING ON MOTION FRIDAY

Daniel C. Mulloney, president of the closed Federal National Bank, and John A. Deery, head of Salem Trust Company, Salem, may go to trial together Tuesday, Sept. 11, on charges of national banking law violations before Federal Judge James M. Morton, Jr., and a federal district court jury.

The department of justice, through Irving G. McCann, special assistant attorney-general, last night filed a motion requesting that both defendants be tried on that date.

A hearing will be held on this motion before Judge Morton at Fall River at 10:30 A. M. Friday. Mr. McCann, chief prosecutor of the Federal National Bank chain cases, will represent the government at the session.

This would mark the second trial of Mulloney, who was acquitted May 25 by a jury which had been out for more than 28 hours when it returned a verdict. Mulloney was tried on one indictment charging misapplication and abstraction of funds of the bank.

Mulloney and Deery are linked in one

(Continued on Page Two)

20 Horses Saved in General Alarm Fire At Gen. Peabody Stock Farm in Canton

[Special Dispatch to The Herald]

CANTON, July 11 (Wednesday)—A general alarm fire early this morning threatened the extensive stables and stock farm owned by Gen. Francis Peabody on Blue Hill street, near the Canton-Milton line.

The fire was discovered at 2:30 A. M., by a omtorist who notified the metropolitan police at Blue Hills station, who in turn notified the Canton fire department. Five minutes later a general alarm was sounded bringing all available apparatus to the scene. At 2:30 aid was asked of Milton, which sent its new high power pumper from the Milton Centre station.

The blaze started in a large hay barn recently filled. Directly in front was the large stable in which the prize stock was quartered. Stable hands and attendents aided by firemen concentrated in leading approximately 20 frightened horses to safety.

Before its purchase by Gen. Peabody, the farm was owned by J. Malcolm Forbes, and at one time was the home of the famous brood mare Nancy Hanks.

Living quarters occupied by the employes were hastily abandoned as the intense heat generated by the newly dried hay made it impossible to approach nearer than 150 feet.

The facilities of the farm include a half mile race track over which the horses are trained. The score of blooded horses, many of them prizewinners and the mainstay of the farm, were led out onto the track.

Connie Mack Returns After 51 Years For Great Reception at No. Brookfield

Tornado Ravages Area At Jacksonville, Ill.

JACKSONVILLE, Ill., July 10 (AP)—A tornado that struck this city late last night caused heavy damage. It unroofed buildings and destroyed several homes.

Owing to the debris which covered the streets, police and firemen were working slowly to rescue persons who might be trapped in the destroyed homes. Three persons were brought to the hospitals.

It was feared that the storm's severity extended to the outlying districts.

MOVIE BOYCOTT AS LAST RESORT

Fr. Sullivan Tells Plans Here—No Censorship Proposed

A program of prevention rather than censorship of immoral or indecent motion pictures is the aim of the League of Decency which expects to have an elaborate boycott system working by the end of July, the Rev. Russell M. Sullivan, S. J., of Boston College, representative of Cardinal O'Connell, explained yesterday.

"The Catholic church wants no system of censorship," he said. "It yields

(Continued on Page Six)

POLICE ROUND UP COMMON IDLERS

Take 24 in Raid Following Complaints About Loafers

Stirred by protests that Boston Common has become a hangout for loafers, the police of the Milk street station last night made a raid which resulted in the arrest of 24 men.

The police squad rounded up every individual lying on a crop of yesterday's newspapers. Indignant Bostonians had protested to City Hall because of the common's bedraggled appearance every morning.

Veteran Manager Shares Greetings of 10,000 with George M. Cohan

ATHLETICS LOSE TO HOME TEAM, 9-5

By JOHN DROHAN
[Special Dispatch to The Herald]

NORTH BROOKFIELD, July 10—History repeated itself today in this staid New England village when Connie Mack returned after 51 years absence to taste the bitterness of defeat by the North Brookfield club of the present era, the Armotreds, which thoroughly defeated his Philadelphia Athletics, 9 to 5, on "Connie Mack Day." But Connie never enjoyed a defeat so much in his life. He actually revelled in it.

The game was halted in the sixth inning, when the score was tied at four-all, so little Jane Rooney could present to Connie Mack a gold bound program commemorative of the big day, and also one to George M. Cohan. Then the local boys presented Connie's club with the licking they promised him before the game.

Little Miss Rooney said in presenting the volumes to the former local boys, "Mister Connie Mack and Mister George Cohan, I give you these books to you to show you how glad the boys and girls of North Brookfield are glad to have you here."

A prettier speech by a prettier miss

(Continued on Page Twenty-seven)

NO DRINKING AFTER ONE A. M.

License Board Ruling Applies To Consumption as Well as Sale

Not only will the sale of liquor be forbidden in the city after 1 A. M., but the drinking of it will also be forbidden in the licensed resorts after that hour, according to a ruling of the Boston licensing board, made yesterday. The board has learned a number of places in the city allow drinking after the curfew hour of 1 A. M.

The practice, according to the board, has been for patrons to stock up on a quantity of liquor at their tables just before 1 A. M., and to drink it for some time after 1 o'clock. Under the new ruling, all must be out at 1 A. M.

N. Y. SOUTHPAW GETS RUTH, FOXX, GEHRIG IN ROW

Strikes Out Simmons, Cronin and Gomez in 2d Frame To Steal Show

CROWD REACHES 55,000 15,000 TURNED AWAY

Mel Harder Saves Game, Yielding One Hit in Five Innings

By BURT WHITMAN
[Special Dispatch to The Herald]

NEW YORK, July 10—As soon as the great Carl Screw-Ball Hubbell of the Giants had finished pitching his first three no-run innings for the All-Nationals, the superior hitting of the American league all-stars asserted itself and they triumphed, 9 to 7, before a capacity crowd at the Polo Grounds this perfect mid-summer afternoon, after 15,000 late arrivals had been unable to buy tickets.

That shooting, dropping screw-ball delivery of Carl's had made history in the first inning when, with two men on and none out, Hubbell fanned three of the greatest sluggers of all time—Babe Ruth, Lou Gehrig and Jimmy Foxx.

Then he had struck out Al Simmons, Manager Joe Cronin of the American all-stars and Pitcher Lefty Vernon Gomez in the second, and had pitched a no-hit third to end his three-inning chore.

Meanwhile the stars of the National league had made four runs in those first three frames, through the medium of a home run drive into the upper field-grandstand by lead-off man, Frankie Frisch, manager of the St. Louis Cards, in the first inning, and another mighty Missouri blow, a four-bagger, far into the upper grandstand tier in left field by Outfielder Joe Medwick of the Cards, with two on base in the third.

Great had been the acclaim as Hubbell walked over the field to the Giants' club house in centre field. He had reasserted his mastery over the American league, so vividly exercised when his Giants beat the Washington Senators in the world series last fall. And he left the game, with the N. L. stars enjoying a 4 to 0 lead. Most assuredly the other stellar pitchers of his team could hold that advantage.

Yet no sooner had Carl disappeared than the great players recruited from the American league became flatly insurgent. They got to Lon Warneke of the Chicago Cubs for two runs in the fourth and then, aided and abetted by wildness on the part of Lon and of the relieving Van Mungo of Brooklyn, romped through to a six-run fifth which settled the issue.

They might be baffled by Hubbell's freaky delivery, but were not to be held cheaply by any other N. L. pitcher.

So for the second time in as many years, this great mid-summer game played by teams picked from the best in the two major leagues, has resulted in victory for the American league. The first game, played at Chicago last July, saw the American all stars win, 4 to 2, with Babe Ruth the outstanding individual. Since that first game the Giants took the world's championship by beating the Washington Senators, yet the junior league acquired much merit and a heap of satisfaction in winning this afternoon.

The Americans outhit the Nationals, 14 to 8, and the total bases for the winners were 23, to 15 for the losers. For the first time in many years the Babe failed to punctuate a gala baseball occasion in which he figured with slugging fireworks. He went to the plate four times, was called out on strikes, walked twice and rolled out to the first baseman.

The outstanding thumper for the Americans was Earl Averill of Cleveland, with a triple and a double and the honor of driving in three runs. Al Simmons of the White Sox doubled twice and singled once, drove in one run

(Continued on Page Twenty-six)

ICKES'S ADS GO TO PARTY PRESS

An Old Custom, He Explains —He Cites Letter of Albert B. Fall

WASHINGTON, July 10 (AP)—"Some newspapers have no sense of humor," said Secretary Ickes to reporters today. In ordering that general land office advertisements be placed in Democratic newspapers he said he was merely continuing a policy established by his predecessors.

He had on his desk a carbon copy of a letter by Albert B. Fall, former secretary of the interior, which suggested that newspapers "whose political principles are in harmony with the administration" be favored with advertising.

It was addressed to registrars and receivers of land offices.

Hubbell Stuns Ruth, Foxx and Gehrig With Strikeouts as Crowd Acclaims Pitching Miracle

Big 3 Foiled By Screwball With Two On

Southpaw Continues His Triumph on Mound by Fanning Simmons and Cronin in Next Inning

By Richards Vidmer

The films gave us Catherine the Great and Henry the Eighth; the stage gave us Mary Queen of Scots, but it took a baseball game to produce King Carl—the Star of Stars.

Even though his team was beaten at the Polo Grounds yesterday, Carl Hubbell held the spotlight long after he had disappeared from the view of 52,000 awed and admiring spectators.

Perhaps there were some who remembered the pitching feats of Amos Rusie among that throng. Probably several more remembered the iron arm of Joe McGinnity. There must have been hundreds who had seen the immortal Matty in his prime. But none of them ever saw such pitching as Hubbell exhibited in the three innings he worked for the National Leaguers.

It was something more than wonderful; it was magnificent. And it was more than sensational; it was unique.

Johnson's Feat Recalled

More than twenty years ago Walter Johnson, in an important game, when Washington was fighting for a pennant faced three great hitters on the Detroit team, with the bases filled in the ninth inning. And he struck out Ty Cobb, Bob Veach and Sam Crawford, one after the other, to win the game.

The story of Sir Walter's pitching on that occasion has lived through the years and several generations of baseball players, but Carl Hubbell surpassed it yesterday when he struck out three of the greatest hitters in the American League at a critical stage.

It was in the first inning when the players were tense and the vast throng was eager with expectation, waiting to see what was going to happen; and the two teams were fighting for the jump, eager to get the lead that might prove the difference between overwhelming triumph and dismal defeat.

Gehringer, of Detroit, playing second base for the American Leaguers, led off with a sharp single to center. That was the first shock tossed into the National League ranks, for it proved that Hubbell was not invincible.

Then Heine Manush, of Washington, walked. And that was the second shock. The great Hubbell, supposedly the greatest left-handed control pitcher in the game, was at least human—he could err as well as anybody else.

Situation Brings Huddle

Even Bill Terry must have had his doubts at that point. Even his own manager who has seen him in every ball game he has pitched since he came to the big leagues, an awkward, gangling prairie boy from Oklahoma, almost gave up on him. Terry came trotting in from his position at first base and asked Hubbell if he was all right. Frankie Frisch came in from second, Pie Traynor from third and Travis Jackson from short. They all huddled around the box anxiously—every man a manager for the moment.

Maybe some of them still doubted; certainly the fans did, for there were isolated cries from the packed ranks in the stands of "Take him out! Take him out before it's too late!"

But Terry asked Hubbell a question and Hubbell answered it. Terry wanted to know if Carl thought he was all right, and Carl replied that he was—not to worry. That was enough assurance for Terry and he ordered the men back to their positions. Hubbell was still his first choice to pitch.

So Gehringer was prancing around on second and Manush was dancing on first and there wasn't anybody out when Hubbell took up his task again. Those who glanced at their scorecards must have realized what a task it was, too, for the next three hitters he had to face were Babe Ruth, king of clout; Lou Gehrig, prince of punch, and Jimmy Foxx, the leading home-run hitter in the major leagues at the moment.

Scoring Seems Imminent

It seemed as though two or three runs would be driven over the plate at least, and anyone who had offered to bet that the American Leaguers wouldn't score at all would have been crushed in the stampede of eager takers—at any odds.

But Hubbell rose to his greatest heights. He hitched up his pants, took a glance at the base runners and went to work.

Four times he threw to Ruth, and the fourth pitch was the third strike. The Babe stood there as the ball cut the heart of the plate, never lifting the bat from his shoulder. He stood there even after Pfirman, the umpire, had said "You're out." But he didn't stand in an argumentative attitude, just an awed attitude.

Yet even with Ruth disposed of there was plenty of power straining toward the plate. There were still Gehrig and Foxx. And Gehrig was the first to worry about. He strode to the batter's box with confident stride. He dug his toes into the dust and set his massive shoulders.

Four times Hubbell pitched to Gehrig, and the fourth pitch was the third strike again. Gehrig made a desperate lunge at it, swinging his bat with sledgehammer force, but the ball wasn't there. And so Gehrig also went back to the bench—fanned.

Even then the danger wasn't past, for when Hubbell looked up there was Foxx at the plate; the man who has hit twenty-six home runs to date.

Goes Down Swinging

As Foxx stood there the stands of the Polo Grounds seemed to close in on him, drawing nearer and nearer to the plate. It almost seemed as though he could bunt a ball into those left-field seats where the eager, excited faces peered forth on what developed into the greatest bit of pitching ever seen on any diamond.

Four times Hubbell pitched to Foxx and three times the home run leader swung—in vain.

There was a moment of silence. The crowd was awed into a death-like stillness. And then suddenly, as the realization of what Hubbell had done struck them, a roar went up that swept across the Harlem River like thunder across the bay.

Hubbell—King Carl—the Star of Stars had fanned Ruth, Gehrig and Foxx; one after the other, on twelve pitched balls!

Nor was that the end of King Carl's reign, for he fanned Al Simmons and Joe Cronin, the first two men to face him in the next inning, making five great hitters in a row that he set down on strikes.

The battle for supremacy continued long after he had gone and eventually the American Leaguers won, but after all they didn't have to face but one Carl Hubbell, the star of stars.

Victims of Carl Hubbell's Brilliant Pitching Feat

Associated Press photos

Lou Gehrig, .371; Babe Ruth, .289, and Jimmy Foxx, .350, who struck out one right after the other with two men on bases in the first inning of all-star game

Carl Hubbell, the man who did it

Toronto Tops Newark, 4 to 3, In 11th Inning

McQuinn's Single, Scoring Schott, Enables Leafs to Rout Night-Game Jinx

By The Canadian Press

TORONTO, July 10.—Toronto finally beat its night-game jinx tonight when it defeated the Newark Bears, 4 to 3, but it took eleven innings. It was the Leafs' first victory under the lights. Until the ninth it seemed that the Bears would suffer their first shut-out of the season, but Schalk, the second man up, drew a base on balls and came home on Muller's homer that bounced off the left-field fence. Tamulis was left on third in the same frame after his triple.

Newark added one in the tenth, Hill going home from second on Glenn's single but Toronto replied with one in the same frame, Morrissey opening with a double and Boone singling him home. George McQuinn was the hero of the game, driving home Schott from second with a double after the Bears had been held hitless in their eleventh.

The score:

NEWARK (I. L.)	ab	r	h	po	a	e
Neun, 1b...	6	0	1	11	0	0
Farrell, ss..	5	0	0	4	2	0
Hill, cf....	5	1	1	5	0	0
Alex'der, lf.	4	0	2	0	0	0
Barton, rf..	3	0	1	1	0	0
Glenn, c...	4	0	2	8	1	0
Schalk, 2b..	4	1	0	3	6	0
Muller, 3b..	4	1	1	0	3	0
TAMULIS, p	5	0	2	0	3	0
Totals...	40	3	10	*32	15	0

TORONTO (I. L.)	ab	r	h	po	a	e
Moore, cf...	6	0	0	3	0	0
Morris'y, 2b	6	2	4	2	3	0
McQuinn, 1b	5	0	2	19	0	0
Boone, rf...	5	0	2	1	0	0
†Crouch....	0	0	0	0	0	0
Fitzg'ld, rf.	0	0	0	0	0	0
Howell, lf..	2	1	0	2	0	0
Rice, 3b....	4	0	0	1	3	1
Rich'son, ss	4	0	2	1	8	0
Heving, c...	5	0	0	4	1	0
SCHOTT, p.	4	1	2	0	2	0
Totals	41	4	12	33	17	1

*Two out when winning run was scored.
†Ran for Boone in tenth inning.

Newark........	000	000	002	1	0—3
Toronto........	000	200	000	1	1—4

Runs batted in—Richardson (2), Muller (2), Glenn, Boone, McQuinn. Two-base hits—McQuinn (2), Alexander, Hill, Morrissey. Three-base hit—Tamulis. Home run—Muller. Sacrifices—McQuinn, Schott. Double plays—Schott, Heving and McQuinn; McQuinn (unassisted); Richardson and Morrisey. Left on bases—Newark, 10; Toronto, 12. Struck out—By Schott, 3; by Tamulis, 6. Bases on balls—Off Schott, 6; off Tamulis, 5. Umpires—Van Graflan and Carroll. Time—2:31.

Berly, Rochester Hurler, Stops Syracuse, 5 to 1

ROCHESTER, July 10 (AP).—Rochester kept on its winning way here today with a 5-1 triumph over Syracuse in the fast time of 1 hour 34 minutes. John Berly held the Chiefs to six hits, while Bobby Coombs allowed the Red Wings nine.

Coombs made two of his team's six hits.

The score by innings:

				R.	H.	E.
Syracuse.....	000	000	010	1	6	2
Rochester....	010	130	00x	5	9	0

Batteries—Coombs and Taylor; Berly and Florence.

Tigers Win Exhibition, 3 to 2

GRAND RAPIDS, Mich., July 10 (AP).—Held in check by the excellent pitching of Earl Dietz, of Western State College, at Kalamazoo, the Detroit Tigers managed to pull an exhibition game out of the fire in the ninth inning here today, defeating the Grand Rapids All-Stars, 3 to 2.

The score by innings:

				R.	H.	E.
Detroit (A. L.).	110	000	001	3	7	2
Gr. Rapids....	010	100	000	2	9	3

Batteries—Frasier and Hayworth; Dietz and Sullivan.

Americans Beat Nationals, 9-7, In All-Star Game

(Continued from preceding page)

after he walked. Dean was still in something of a predicament until he fanned Averill. Then Lopez, the Nationals' catcher, raced out to second base and caught Cronin, who had started to steal.

Ott's Throw Nails Gehringer

This was the ball game. Ott made a fine throw to nail Gehringer trying to take two bases in the seventh, and Chapman hit a healthy triple, but was left stranded. Arky Vaughan, of the Pirates, went almost to the left-field grandstand and made a spectacular catch of a ball Averill hit in the ninth. Fred Frankhouse, of the Braves, was pitching then. It did not matter much, because Harder, working overtime, had the power of the National League restrained in the hollow of his good right hand. Even after Herman's double in the ninth, he got past Traynor and Klein when a home run would have tied the score. The game literally was not over until the last out.

It was a memorable game, played before an enthusiastic and appreciative crowd in stands strung with bunting. Mayor Fiorella H. LaGuardia was there. So was the baseball commissioner, Kenesaw M. Landis, also John A. Heydler, president of the National League, and William Harridge, head of the American League. Not in a long time has there been such an air of excitement and glamour about a ball game here.

While the American Leaguers were taking their fielding practice, the National League players gathered under the clubhouse in front of the center-field exit and there, almost unnoticed in the scheme of things, uncovered a tablet on the wall in memory of John J. McGraw. Few of the spectators were aware of this ceremony until the announcer brought it to their attention. The honor which was paid McGraw was done so unobtrusively it almost went unnoticed.

As the game progressed it became apparent that only Hubbell could quell a list of hitters like Gehringer, Manush, Ruth, Gehrig, Foxx, Simmons, Cronin, Dickey and (imagine it—hitting in the pitcher's place), Averill. There was too much power there for lesser hands to handle.

And who would have thought that Harder would step in and limit the power of the National League to one hit in five innings?

Standings in Major Leagues

WEDNESDAY, JULY 11, 1934

American League

YESTERDAY'S RESULTS

No games scheduled.

STANDING OF THE CLUBS

	New York	Detroit	Boston	Cleveland	Washington	St. Louis	Phila'phia	Chicago	Won	Lost	Percentage
New York.	—	5	5	4	8	8	8	8	46	27	.630
Detroit...	4	—	7	8	6	7	5	10	47	29	.618
Boston....	6	3	—	3	8	7	8	7	42	35	.545
Cleveland.	4	4	5	—	4	4	7	11	39	35	.527
Wash'ton.	5	4	6	6	—	6	6	6	39	38	.506
St. Louis..	2	6	3	4	5	—	5	6	31	39	.443
Phila'phia	4	4	6	4	5	4	—	3	30	45	.400
Chicago...	2	3	3	6	2	3	6	—	25	51	.329
Gms. lost.	27	29	35	35	38	39	45	51	—	—	

GAMES TODAY

New York at Cleveland.
Washington at Detroit.
Other clubs not scheduled.

National League

YESTERDAY'S RESULTS

No games scheduled.

STANDING OF THE CLUBS

	New York	Chicago	St. Louis	Pittsburgh	Boston	Brooklyn	Phila'phia	Cincinnati	Won	Lost	Percentage
New York.	—	4	4	6	9	10	8	7	48	28	.632
Chicago...	5	—	8	8	3	8	6	8	46	30	.605
St. Louis..	7	4	—	5	6	5	7	9	43	31	.581
Pit'sburgh	3	4	6	—	5	5	8	7	38	33	.535
Boston. ..	3	7	4	3	—	8	7	7	39	37	.513
Brooklyn..	4	3	3	5	4	—	7	5	31	45	.408
Phila'phia	3	4	2	3	7	6	—	5	30	47	.390
Cincinnati	3	4	4	3	3	3	4	—	24	48	.333
Gms. lost.	28	30	31	33	37	45	47	48	—	—	

GAMES TODAY

Pittsburgh at New York, 3:15 p. m.
Cincinnati at Brooklyn, 3:30 p. m.
Chicago at Boston.
St. Louis at Philadelphia.

Chocolate 7-5 Choice to Beat Hayes Tonight

Title Sanction Sought for Ebbets Field Bout; Cuban Expected to Win Verdict

By Don Skene

Kid Chocolate, the old Battling Bon-Bon of Cuba, whose picturesque punching brought him ring earnings estimated at $300,000 when the boxing business was booming a few years ago, will meet Petey Hayes, of Brooklyn, in the ten-round main event at Ebbets Field tonight. Al Weill, promoter of the show, hopes that 8,000 clients will pay $15,000 to watch the Kid's next fight on the comeback trail.

Chocolate and Hayes will weight in before the State Athletic Commission at 1 o'clock this afternoon, and after the ceremonies on the scales both contestants will ask the commissioners to consider their bout in the light of a featherweight championship match of some sort. Chocolate is expected to scale two or three pounds over the 126-pound mark, while Hayes is confident of making 126 or less.

The Cuban wants the commission to restore the featherweight title removed from him for failure to go through with a match with Freddie Miller. The Brooklyn Italian wants the commission to recognize him as official New York defender of the vacated title if he beats Chocolate this evening.

The Kid has been many places and done many things since he left his home town of Havana in 1927 with $6 cash, one suit and a one-way ticket to New York. He got a purse of $40 for his first fight at Mitchel Field, Long Island, against Eddie Enos, and a fee of $45,000 for his bout with Al Singer at the Yankee Stadium five years ago.

The Kid has had his troubles and triumphs since then, but is still in there punching. Betting odds yesterday made him a 7 to 5 favorite to out-point Hayes.

The supporting card is headed by Harry Dublinsky, of Chicago, and Jimmy Leto, of Hartford, in a ten-round semi-final that should produce some heavy hitting. The program will be completed by Lou Ambers, the Herkimer Hurricane, vs. Roger Bernard, of Flint, Mich., ten rounds; Danny London, of Coney Island, vs. Leo Dazzo, of the Bronx, six rounds, and Louis Camps vs. Tommy Mankin, four rounds.

Bouts Last Night

* * *

WRESTLING

at Fort Hamilton

Dick Shikat, 223, threw the Masked Marvel, 225, in 38:50 of the main bout to a finish.

Ted Christie, 195, California, threw John Lewandowski, 200, Trenton, N. J., in 8:15 of a scheduled thirty-minute bout.

George Hagen, 212, U. S. Marines, won the decision over Mike Romano, 210, Italy, in a thirty-minute bout.

Gene Bruce, 195, Bay Ridge, threw Mike Brenner, 196, New York, in 3:30 of a scheduled thirty-minute bout.

Mahomet Yousoff, 207, Turkey, threw George Wilchesky, 210, Poland, in 20:30 of a scheduled thirty-minute bout.

At New York Coliseum

Everett Marshall, 218, Colorado, was declared the winner over Joe (Bull) Komar, 230, Lithunia, in 7:52 of the main bout to a finish when the referee disqualified the latter for fouling.

Charlie (Buck) Weaver, 238, Oklahoma, threw Frank Jones, 204, Texas, in 10:31 1of a scheduled thirty-minute bout.

Doug Wyckoff, 215, Atlanta, threw Ghafoor Khan, 215, Turkey, in 8:45 of a scheduled thirty-minute bout.

Sid Westrich, 225, Bronx, and Joe De Vito, 215, St. Louis, wrestled thirty minutes to a draw.

Hans Steinke, 240, Germany, won the decision over Floyd Marshall, 230, Arizona, in a thirty-minute bout.

BOXING

At Coney Island Velodrome

Tony Falco, 141½, Philadephia, won the decision over Bobby Pacho, 137½, Los Angeles, in the main bout of ten rounds.

Vittorio Tamagnini, 125¼, Italian featherweight champion, won the decision over Abe Wasserman, 126¼, East Side, in the ten-round semi-final.

Ken La Salle, 142½, Los Angeles, defeated Young Firpo, 143, Philadelphia, ten rounds, decision.

Izzy Jannazzo, 142½, East Side, defeated Mickey Paul, 140½, Brooklyn, six rounds, decision.

Great Island, Aknusti Gain In Polo Tourney

Advance to Semi-Finals of Hempstead Cups; Season's Westbury Games Hit 102

By Harry Cross

WESTBURY, L. I., July 10.—The 100th game of polo's liveliest season was played at Meadow Brook this afternoon, the busy carnival of six games carrying the total to 102 contests, and the season isn't half over.

The competition has become so crowded that the playing capacity of the club's seven available fields has been taxed. Next week the club will play some of its games on the polo fields at the Phipps estate on Old Westbury Road.

The Hempstead Cups tournament went along merrily into the semi-final rounds as the Great Island team, defending champions, defeated Old Westbury, 12 to 3.

Aknusti Beats Princemere

The Old Westbury team, with the veteran Bob Bullock playing No. 3, galloped into the quarter-finals by defeating Ox Ridge in the closest contest of the day, 9 to 8. The Aknusti team, made up of the three Gerry boys and their uncle, W. Averell Harriman, downed Princemere in a close, hard-fought contest on International Field, 6 to 4, and arrived at the semi-final round. Edward Gerry, the Harvard player, picked up the shots of his teammates nicely and scored four goals. His twin brother Henry, at back, played his position well.

Many of the likely candidates for the East squad had a good workout on Belmont Field. A Hitchcock team, with the ten-goal player at No. 3; Pete Bostwick, Ebby Gerry and Cocie Rathborne, were outplayed and outridden by a side which included Laddie Sanford, Jimmy Mills, Bobby Strawbridge and Ray Guest.

Sanford Plays at No. 1

Sanford, who has been playing back all season, moved up to No. 1 and covered the forward area well as Mills, Strawbridge and Guest, playing well together, got the ball up to him often.

The three Milburns were in action again this afternoon and were going well in a practice match. Devereux Milburn and his two sons, Devereux jr. and Jack, with Averell Clark jr., defeated a side made up of C. Billups, Townsend Winmill, Dr. J. D. Richards and David Downs, 9 to 5. Jack Milburn, at No. 1, handled the passes neatly and scored five goals.

Sonny Whitney, Gerald Balding, George J. Atwell jr. and H. S. Cram teamed up in a round-robin and came out on top against the two other teams, the Blues and Reds. Whitney was hitting well, and from his No. 2 position knocked in five goals.

The quarter-final game in the Hempstead Cups will be played between Westbury and Rockaway on Thursday afternoon at 5:30. The first semi-final will be played on Saturday between Aknusti and Great Island at 5 o'clock. The other semi-final will be played Sunday afternoon at 4:30 between Burnt Mills and the winner of the Westbury-Rockaway match.

The line-ups:

Pos.	Great Island (12)	OldWestb'y (3)
No. 1	W. Ziegler	R. H. Hassler
No. 2	W. G. Reynolds	Thomas Shevlin
No. 3	C. R. Harrison	R. S. Allison
Back	J. P. Grace jr.	J. R. Fell

SCORE BY CHUKKERS

Great Island............	1	3	1	2	1	4—12
Old Westbury............	0	0	0	1	2	0— 3

Goals—Great Island: Reynolds, 5; Harrison, 3; Grace, 2; Ziegler, 1 pony. Old Westbury: Shevlin, Allison, Fell.

Referee, Gilbert Wilson. Time of chukkers, 7½ minutes each.

Post.	Westbury (9)	Ox Ridge (8)
No. 1	Alan Corey	B. Dominick
No. 2	P. Rumsey	P. Dominick
No. 3	R. Bullock	G. S. Smith
Back	Carl Crawford	G. H. Dempsey

SCORE BY CHUKKERS

Westbury............	4	1	0	2	1	1—9
Ox Ridge............	2	2	3	0	0	1—8

Goals—Westbury: Corey (3), Bullock (2), Crawford (2), by handicap (2). Ox Ridge: Dempsey (4), P. Dominick (3), Smith.

Referee—W. H. Gaylard.

Time of chukkers—7½ minutes each.

Pos.	Aknusti (6)	Princemere (4)
No. 1	E. H. Gerry	M. Field
No. 2	W. A. Harriman	C. Waring
No. 3	R. L. Gerry	J. H. Phipps
Back	H. A Gerry	F. H. Prince

SCORE BY CHUKKERS

Aknusti............	1	2	1	1	1	0—6
Princemere............	1	0	0	1	1	1—4

Goals—Aknusti: E. H. Gerry (4), Harriman (2). Princemere: Field (2), Waring, by handicap (1).

Referee—Thomas Brady.

Time of chukkers—7½ minutes each.

Pos.	Blues (8)	Whites (3)
No. 1	S. Sanford	G. H. Bostwick
No. 2	J. P. Mills	E. T. Gerry
No. 3	R. E. Strawbridge	T. Hitchcock jr.
Back	R. R. Guest	J. C. Rathborne

SCORE BY CHUKKERS

Blues............	1	1	0	2	2	2—8
Whites............	0	1	0	1	0	1—3

Goals—Blues: Sanford (5), Strawbridge (2), Guest. Whites: Bostwick (2), Hitchcock.

Referee—S. W. Pelley.

Time of chukkers—7½ minutes each.

Kammers Win Father-Son Golf With Card of 157 at Plainfield

Fenns, Runner-Ups, Trail by 11 Strokes in Jersey Golf Association's Play

Special to the Herald Tribune

PLAINFIELD, N. J., July 10.—Having won the event three times previously with his son, August F. jr., A. F. Kammer, of the Baltusrol Golf Club, paired with a younger son, Lowery, to capture the New Jersey State Golf Association's annual father-and-son championship at the Plainfield Country Club today. The Kammers put together rounds of 76 and 81 for a 157 total, eleven strokes better than the second-place pere-et-fils combination of Harrison and William B. Fenn, of Ridgewood.

The Kammers also had the low net card, but were ineligible for the award by virtue of capturing low gross and the title. Low net honors thus fell to the S. Remsen Ryders, senior and junior, of the Ridgewood Country Club, with a score of 184—38—146.

Thirty-six Teams Entered

Thirty-six teams were entered in the father-son championship. They were supplemented by four additional duos for a special eighteen-hole tournament during the afternoon round.

There was a difference of seventy years between the oldest and youngest competitors in today's event. D. H. Rowland, of Plainfield, who paired with his son, R. S. Rowland, for the morning round, is eighty years old, and H. T. Cook jr., of Springdale, who played with H. T. Cook sr. in the afternoon eighteen-hole round, is ten. The elder Rowland dropped out after the morning play, his son, R. S. Rowland, taking R. S. junior as his afternoon partner.

The elder Kammer's victory today gave him a record for the event. Heretofore he was tied among the paters, with Sheppard Homans, of Englewood, who, with his talented son, Gene, had won the championship three times.

Kammers' Play Consistent

The Kammers' card of 76 was the only better than 80 score posted during the day. The duo played alternate strokes with an amazing degree of consistency, reaching the turn in 38 and returning in a like figure.

Today's tournament was a prelude to the annual New Jersey Golf Association junior championship, which will start here tomorrow with more than fifty entered. The scores:

Thirty-six-Hole Scores

August F. and Lowrey Kammer, Baltusrol	157—16—141
S. Remsen and S. Remsen Ryder 3d, Ridgewood	184—38—146
F. E. and Fred B. Town, Essex County	178—30—148
Dr. John E. and John E. Parker jr., Essex County	169—16—153
W. S. and Gordon S. Craig, Plainfield	175—22—153
Courtland and Courtland Kelsey jr., Essex County	175—22—153
Harrison B. and William Fenn, Ridgewood	168—14—154
. Ashton and S. A. Clark jr., Ridgewood	182—28—154
Edward and Charles Whitehead, Forsgate	177—22—155
G. K. and F. D. Heyer, Braidburn	171—16—155
Dr. E. H. and E. H. Henry jr., Ridgewood	179—24—155
Wilbur Rogers and J. H. G. Rogers, Plainfield	175—18—157
Ben and Bobby Jacobson, Hollywood	183—26—157
Charles F. and Charles Brown, Essex County	196—38—158
R. E. and R. M. Crane, Echo Lake	169—10—159
J. J. and J. Story Lee, Galloping Hill	178—18—160
Louis P. and Wilbur Christenson, Montclair	176—16—160
Dr. Stephen G. and Dr. S. G. Lee jr., Essex Fells	185—24—161
Robert S. and D. Maffitt, Essex County	187—24—163
Joseph J. and Howard Carew, Baltusrol	177—14—163
Julian and John S. Harrison, Ridgewood	193—30—163
F. Miller and F. M. Fargo jr., Plainfield	186—22—164
Keith and J. Keith Clark, Ridgewood	198—32—166
Payson S. and Edward Douglas, Essex County	200—34—166
William and W. Morpath jr., Maplewood	83 withdrew
A. J. and Wilson Flohr, Canoe Brook	83 withdrew
Clifford and H. O. Norton, Baltusrol	84 withdrew
Frank and Paul Olson, Maplewood	88 withdrew
Arthur and Arthur Vreeland jr., Ridgewood	76 no cards
D. H. and D. S. Rowland, Plainfield	79 no card
H. L. and H. J. Gillespie, Shackamaxon	80 no card
J. W. and J. H. Escher, Knickerbocker	82 no card
G. W. and Donald Shannon, Braidburn	85 no card
Willard G. and Robert Wilkerson, Locust Grove	89 no card

Eighteen-Hole Scores

Dr. W. R. and Norman Tymeson, Essex County	88—16— 72
C. A. and D. W. Merrill, Essex County	90—15—.75
Horace Cook and Horace Cook jr., Springdale	88—13— 75
William H. and Oliver Rollinson, Colonia	92—13— 79
A. J. and Wilson Flohr, Canoe Brook	88— 8— 80
R. S. and R. S. Rowland jr., Plainfield	90— 7— 83
Clifford and H. O. Norton, Baltusrol	93— 9— 84
William and W. Morpeth jr., Maplewood	101—15— 86
R. T. Blauvelt and R. T. Blauvelt jr., Essex County	105—17— 88
Frank and Paul Olson, Maplewood	100—12— 88

Mrs. Vare to Captain Curtis Cup Golf Team

Mrs. Edwin H. Vare jr., the former Miss Glenna Collett, yesterday was named non-playing captain of the American Curtis Cup team, which will meet the British team in the international team golf matches at Chevy Chase, Md., September 27 and 28.

The team will be composed of Virginia Van Wie, of Chicago, United States women's champion; Maureen Orcutt, of Haworth, N. J.; Mrs. Opal S. Hill, of Kansas City; Mrs. Louis D. Cheney, of San Gabriel, Calif.; Charlotte Glutting, of West Orange, N. J.; Lucille Robinson, of Des Moines, Iowa; Mrs. Frank Goldthwaite, of Fort Worth, Tex., and Marion Miley, of Miami.

Miller Extended to Win In Bergen Tennis Play

Special to the Herald Tribune

HACKENSACK, N. J., July 10.—Three more seeded players gained their quarter-final brackets as the result of third-round matches in the Bergen County tennis championship at the Oritani Field Club here this afternoon.

Simon Miller, of New York, was pressed to defeat Ray Antignat, junior star, however. Miller is seeded third in this tournament and his play against Antignat fully justified that seeding. The youngster from Ridgewood, N. J., stroking beautifully from deep court, was effective when he came to the net, but Miller had a reply for each challenge and won, 6—3, 6—1. Antignat frequently held game points but lacked the final punch in the face of Miller's steadiness.

Davis Geller, N. Y. U. star, seeded second, made short work of Alfred Jarvis, high ranking junior star. Geller was far from impressive, but his younger opponent displayed none of the form which has carried him nearly to the top in junior ranks.

Another one-sided victory was that registered by Norman Comes, seeded fifth, over his clubmate, Charles Hallaert.

The summaries:

Third round—Simon Miller, New York, defeated Ray Antignat, Ridgewood, 6—3, 6—1; David Geller, New York, defeated Alfred Jarvis, Tenafly, 6—3, 6—2; Norman Comes, Hackensack, defeated Charles Hallaert Grantwood, 6—1, 6—1.

Stratton's 70 Sets Pace in Mass. Amateur

Par - Shattering Round Leads First Qualifying Over Brookline Course

Special to the Herald Tribune

BROOKLINE, Mass., July 10.—With a par-shattering round of 70, which equaled the competitive course record of twelve years' standing, Emery Stratton, of Sandy Burr, gained a four-stroke lead on the nearest contenders at the end of the first eighteen holes of the thirty-six-hole medal play qualifying round of the Massachusetts amateur championship today at the Country Club.

The leading scores:

E. P. Stratton, Sandy Burr	35—35—70
M. F. Heath jr., Braeburn	36—38—74
W. O. Blaney, Braeburn	35—39—74
F. H. Wright jr., Trapelo	37—37—74
J. W. Monahan, Sandy Burr	34—40—74
M. P. Merritt, Salem	41—33—74
R. W. Wilson, Charles River	36—39—75
A. V. Ellis, Country Club	37—38—75
Dave Whiteside, New Bedford	38—37—75
L. M. Grimball, Belmont Spgs.	39—37—76
J. H. Nies, United Shoe	37—39—76
Gerard Moore, Woodland	35—41—76
F. P. Hersey, Wellesley	41—35—76
William Reidy, Wachusett	38—38—76
James Dolan, Marlboro	41—36—77
R. W. Brown jr., The Country Club	39—38—77
Arthur Jorgenson, United Shoe	37—40—77
Leo Martin, Waltham	38—39—77
W. F. McPhail, Norfolk	38—39—77
J. M. Batchelder, Charles River	39—38—77
Ed Kirouac, Walpole	39—38—77
Ed Peterson, Oakley	40—37—77
Francis Doyle, Wachusett	38—39—77
Dr. V. H. Carpenter, Braeburn	39—38—77
James Gannon, Happy Valley	41—37—77
R. P. Ruggles, Stoney Brae	39—38—77
H. T. Wischusen, Bellevue	38—40—78
Don Ritchie, Charles River	37—41—78
Shirley Moulton, Tedesco	39—39—78
G. S. Reed, Belmont Spring	42—36—78
James Conroy, Wildwood	40—38—78
C. S. Reed, Thorny Lea	39—39—78
Leon K. Emerson, Stoney Rae	35—43—78

Standings in Minor Leagues

* * *

INTERNATIONAL LEAGUE

YESTERDAY'S RESULTS

Toronto, 4; Newark, 3 (11 innings, night game).
Buffalo, 8; Baltimore, 4 (night game).
Montreal, 5; Albany, 4 (night game).
Rochester, 5; Syracuse, 1.

STANDING OF THE CLUBS

	W.	L.	Pct.		W.	L.	Pct.
Newark..	55	30	.647	Montreal..	42	42	.500
Rochester.	53	35	.602	Buffalo...	37	46	.446
Toronto..	48	34	.585	Syracuse.	33	47	.413
Albany..	42	39	.519	Baltimore.	21	58	.266

GAMES TODAY

Newark at Toronto.
Baltimore at Buffalo.
Albany at Montreal.
Syracuse at Rochester.

SOUTHERN ASSOCIATION

At Atlanta (first game)—

				R.	H.	E.
Little Rock....	000	030	100	4	9	1
Atlanta.......	000	001	020	3	9	1

Batteries — Willoughby, Nachand and Whitney; Barfoot and Palmisano.

Second game—

				R.	H.	E.
Little Rock.......	000	000	1	1	4	1
Atlanta.........	030	100	x	4	2	0

Batteries—Struss, Nachand and Whitney; Jacobs and Palmisano.

At Knoxville—

				R.	H.	E
New Orleans..	210	000	010	4	8	2
Knoxville.....	400	210	00x	7	13	0

Batteries—Galehouse and Autry; Scott and Head.

At Memphis—

				R.	H.	E.
Memphis......	000	100	000	1	6	1
Nashville.....	110	000	01x	3	7	0

Batteries — Touchstone, Boward and Cuoto, Powell; Stafford and O'Malley.

At Chattanooga—

				R.	H.	E.
Birmingham...	101	000	000	2	10	3
Chattanooga..	010	030	22x	8	12	1

Batteries—Hughes and Redmond; Armbrust and Holbrook.

STANDING OF THE CLUBS

	W.	L.	Pct.		W.	L.	Pct.
Memphis...	7	3	.700	Atlanta.....	4	5	.444
Little Rock.	6	3	.667	N. Orleans..	4	6	.400
Nashville...	6	3	.667	Chattanooga	3	5	.375
Birm'gham.	4	4	.500	Knoxville...	1	6	.143

TEXAS LEAGUE

Beaumont, 1; Galveston, 0 (1st game).
Galveston, 3; Beaumont, 0 (2d game).

STANDING OF THE CLUBS

	W.	L.	Pct.		W.	L.	Pct.
*S. Antonio.	50	38	.568	*Ft. Worth..	42	43	.494
Galveston..	47	40	.540	*Dallas.....	42	46	.477
Beaumont..	47	41	.534	*Houston...	39	47	.453
*Tulsa.....	44	40	.524	*Okla. City..	35	51	.407

*Night game.

AMERICAN ASSOCIATION

At St. Paul—

				R.	H.	E.
Toledo	500	000	001	6	8	0
St. Paul....	000	001	031	5	6	5

Batteries—Sundar, Perrin, Bowler and Garbark; Thomas, Brown and Fenner.

At Minneapolis—

				R.	H.	E.
Columbus ..	000	002	001	3	10	1
Minneapolis	303	020	01x	9	12	1

Batteries—Greer, Sims and O'Dea; Petty and Hargrave.

At Milwaukee—

				R.	H.	E.
Louisville ..	100	300	000	4	10	3
Milwaukee.	100	000	010	2	6	0

Batteries—Peterson and Thompson; Polli and Rensi.

(Other clubs not scheduled)

STANDING OF THE CLUBS

	W.	L.	Pct.		W.	L.	Pct.
Ind'apolis	45	36	.556	Milw'kee.	41	42	.494
Minn'p'lis	46	37	.554	St. Paul.	39	40	.494
Columbus	42	39	.519	Kansas C	36	46	.439
Louisville	42	40	.512	Toledo ..	37	48	.435

NEW YORK-PA. LEAGUE

At Harrisburg—

				R.	H.	E.
Hazleton	000	250	200	9	15	1
Harrisburg ...	010	010	130	3	13	2

Batteries—Kerdock, Krider and Maynard; Pipgras, Lake, Heffelfinger and Maple.

At Scranton—

				R.	H.	E.
Binghamton..	200	010	333	12	13	0
Scranton	100	200	000	3	6	4

Batteries—Miller and Straub; Schesler, Shoffner, Beggs, Vandermeer and Stack.

At Reading—

				R.	H.	E.
Williamsport.	120	113	024	14	19	1
Reading	000	000	000	0	5	1

Batteries—Hearn and Baker; Simmons, Gilvary and Savino.

Elmira-Wilkes-Barre, postponed.

STANDING OF THE CLUBS

	W.	L.	Pct.		W.	L.	Pct.
Will'msport	5	1	.883	Binghamton	3	4	.429
Wilkes-B...	5	2	.714	Harrisburg..	2	3	.400
Scranton...	4	3	.571	Hazleton....	3	5	.375
Reading....	3	4	.429	Elmira.....	1	4	.200

PACIFIC COAST LEAGUE

Missions, 2; San Francisco, 1.
Oakland, 7; Sacramento, 5.

STANDING OF THE CLUBS

	W.	L.	Pct.		W.	L.	Pct.
*Hollywood.	11	3	.786	*Seattle...	8	7	.533
San Fran...	11	5	.688	Sac'mento.	6	10	.375
*L. Angeles	9	6	.600	Oakland...	5	10	.333
Missions...	9	7	.563	*Portland..	2	13	.133

*Night game.

San Francisco Chronicle Sporting Green

EDITED BY HARRY B. SMITH

FOUNDED 1865 | CCCO* | SAN FRANCISCO, CAL., SATURDAY, JULY 14, 1934 | H9 | VOL. CXLIV, NO. 180

RUTH CLOUTS 700TH HOMER, YANKEES WIN

Jack Medica Will Seek World Record in Fleishhacker Pool Today

Cold Sends Lou Gehrig Out of Game

Ruffing Hurls Steady Game as N. Y. Beats Tigers for American League Lead

DETROIT, July 13 (AP)—Babe Ruth's 700th home run, Bill Dickey's double, with two on, and Red Ruffing's steady pitching carried the Yankees back into the American League lead today, with a 4-to-2 victory over the Tigers.

The "Friday the thirteenth" jinx struck Lou Gehrig and forced the "indestructible" first baseman of the Yankees out of action in the second inning of the battle.

An acute cold in the back, gripping him suddenly as he ran for first base after hitting one of Tommy Bridges' pitches, forced Lou to abandon his efforts to play through his 1426th consecutive game. His all-time durability record remained intact, however, since he played through one full inning before retiring.

It was the third threat to Gehrig's record string of consecutive appearances in the past five weeks.

NEW YORK	AB	R	H	O	A	DETROIT	AB	R	H	O	A
Combs,cf	5	1	1	4	0	Fox,rf	5	0	0	4	1
Stgr,3,1b	4	0	0	7	1	White,cf	2	1	0	2	0
Ruth,lf	3	2	1	1	0	Goslin,lf	4	0	1	1	0
Byrd,lf	0	0	0	0	0	Ghrgr,2b	4	0	1	1	1
Ghrig,1b	1	0	1	1	0	Rogell,s	4	1	1	3	4
Rolfe,s	2	0	1	1	2	Grnbg,1b	4	0	2	8	0
Chmn,rf	3	1	1	0	0	Cochrn,c	3	0	1	8	2
Dickey,s	4	0	2	5	0	Owen,3b	3	0	0	1	0
Crst,s,3b	3	0	1	2	3	Bridges,p	3	0	0	0	2
Hffnr,2b	4	0	1	6	0	Walker	1	0	0	0	0
Rffing,p	4	0	0	0	0						
Totals	33	4	9	27	6	Totals	38	2	6	27	10

Walker batted for Bridges in 9th.

New York ... 0 0 2 0 0 0 0 0 2 0—4
Detroit ...... 0 0 1 0 0 0 0 0 1 0—2

Errors—None. Runs batted in—Ruth 2, Gehringer, Dickey 2, Greenberg. Two-base hits—Greenberg, Goslin, Dickey. Three-base hit—Greenberg. Homs run—Ruth. Stolen bases—White, Chapman, Cochrane. Double play—Fox to Gehringer. Left on bases—Detroit 8, New York 6. Base on balls—Off Bridges 4, Ruffing 4. Struck out—By Bridges 8, Ruffing 3. Wild pitch—Bridges 2. Umpires—Donnelly, McGowan, Owens. Time of game 2h. 12m.

Senators Squeeze Out Win Over Indians

CLEVELAND, July 13 (AP)—The Washington Senators choked their bases in the first inning and poked out two hits in the third inning to beat out the Indians today, 3 to 2, behind Southpaw Walter Stewart. Jonathan Stone, the Senators' right fielder, suffered a left ankle fracture in the third inning that may put him out of the lineup for the rest of the season.

WASHINGTON	AB	R	H	O	A	CLEVELAND	AB	R	H	O	A
Myer,2b	4	0	2	5	2	Seeds,rf	5	0	2	3	0
Stone,rf	2	1	2	1	0	Knkbkr,s	3	0	1	2	3
Harris,rf	2	1	0	1	1	Averill,cf	4	0	1	2	0
Mnush,lf	3	1	1	3	0	Vosmk,lf	4	0	1	2	1
Cronin,s	3	0	0	0	4	Trsky,1b	4	0	0	10	1
Trvis,3b	3	0	1	2	0	Hale,2b	4	2	4	4	3
Schlte,cf	3	0	1	4	0	Kamm,3b	4	0	1	0	3
Kress,1b	4	0	0	7	0	Pytlak,c	4	0	2	4	0
Scwell,c	4	0	0	4	1	Hldbnd,p	2	0	0	0	1
Steward	3	0	0	0	1	Holland	1	0	0	0	0
						Wngrnr,p	1	0	0	0	0
Totals	31	3	7	27	9	Totals	36	2	12	27	12

Holland batted for Hildebrand in 7th.

Washington ...2 0 1 0 0 0 0 0 0 0—3
Cleveland .....0 0 0 0 0 1 0 0 0 1—2

No errors. Runs batted in—Schulte 2, Travis, Pytlak 2. Two-base hits—Stone, Myer, Hale 2, Averill, Manush. Three-base hits—Travis. Sacrifices—Cronin. Double plays—Sewell to Myer; Kamm, Hale to Trotsky; Cronin, Myer to Kress; Gosmik to Pytlak. Left on bases—Washington 5, Cleveland 8. Bases on balls—Off Hildebrand 3, Stewart 1. Struck out—by Hildebrand 1, Garner 1 in 2 innings. Wild pitches—Stewart 2. Losing pitcher—Hildebrand. Umpires—Geisel and Moriarty. Time of game—2h. 2m.

Ferrell Aids Own Victory With Homers

ST. LOUIS, July 13 (AP)—Wesley Ferrell hit two home runs today as he pitched the Boston Red Sox to a 7-to-2 victory over the Browns in the series opener. The Browns did not score until the ninth inning. Ferrell's second homer, in the fifth inning, came with two men on base.

BOSTON	AB	R	H	O	A	ST. LOUIS	AB	R	H	O	A
						Clift,3b	5	0	1	0	1
Bishp,2b	4	1	2	3	7	West,cf	4	0	0	3	0
Werbr,3b	5	1	1	1	1	Burns,1b	4	0	1	7	0
Mrgn,1b	5	1	2	9	1	Pepper,lf	4	0	0	1	0
R.Jnsn,lf	5	0	1	3	0	Garms,rf	4	0	0	3	0
Rnlds,cf	4	0	2	1	0	Melilo,2b	4	1	2	5	2
Portr,rf	4	0	1	2	0	Hemsly,c	4	1	2	4	3
R.Ferel,c	3	1	2	3	0	Strange,s	3	0	2	4	3
Lary,s	3	1	2	4	4	Coffmn,p	1	0	0	0	0
W.Ferl,p	3	2	2	1	1	Newsm,p	1	0	0	0	2
						Andrw,p	0	0	0	0	0
Totals	36	7	15	27	14	Bejma	0	0	0	0	0
						Campbell	1	0	1	0	0
						Totals	35	2	9	27	11

Bejma batted for Newsom in eighth.
Campbell batted for Andrews in ninth.

Boston ....0 0 1 0 4 0 2 0 0—7
St. Louis......0 0 0 0 0 0 0 0 2—2

Errors—Bishop, Reynolds (Boston 2); Hemsley (St. Louis 1). Runs batted in—W. Ferrell 4, Bishop, Morgan, R. Johnson, Campbell 2. Two-base hits—R. Ferrell, Lary, Hemsley Three-base hit—Morgan. Home runs—W. Ferrell 2, Bishop. Stolen base—Werber. Sacrifices—Lary, W. Ferrell. Double plays—Strange to Melillo to Burns; Werber to Bishop to Morgan; Lary to Bishop to Morgan; Melillo to Strange to Burns. Left on bases—Boston 7, St. Louis 8. Bases on balls—Off W. Ferrell 2, Newsom 3. Struck out—By W. Ferrell 2, Coffman 1, Newsom 2. Hits—Off Coffman, 7 in 4 innings; Newsom, 7 in 4; Andrews, 1 in 1. Losing pitcher—Coffman. Umpires—Dineen and Kolls. Time of game—2h. 8m.

Yankee Is Again Yacht Victor

NEWPORT, R. I., July 13 (AP)—Yankee, Boston aspirant for the defense of the America's cup, skippered by Charles Francis Adams, former Secretary of the Navy, today preserved her record as the only candidate unbeaten by an eligible rival by gliding across the finish line 12 seconds ahead of Harold S. Vanderbilt's Rainbow.

Never Mind the Ball! ★ ★ Let's Have Some Fun!

You remember the Texas Cowboys, who, upon being introduced to football, said "never mind the ball, let's start playing!" Well, Remington Olmstead of U. C. L. A., getting tackled by Frank Piccolo during a practice rugby game at Griffith field, demonstrates the possibilities. The ball will be used, however, when these lads face H. M. S. Norfolk sailors at Pasadena tomorrow.

Verne Stewart Advances in Western Golf

OKLAHOMA CITY, July 13 (AP)—The Western amateur golf tournament late today became a battle of the South—and of youth—when Jack Westland of Chicago, a United States Walker cupper, was shorn of his title by Dave Goldman of Dallas, and veteran Chick Evans of Chicago, was checked out by Verne Stewart of Stanford and Albuquerque, N. M., in a stirring extra hole quarter final match.

Survivors besides Stewart and Goldman are Zell Eatcn of Oklahoma City, 1933 and 1934 Western medalist, and Charley Yates of Atlanta, Georgia Tech's national collegiate champion.

In the semifinals tomorrow Goldman meets Yates and Eaton plays Stewart.

Tidball, Otis in Denver Net Wins

DENVER, July 13 (AP)—The top favorite was still front-running tonight in the Colorado open tennis tourney as Jack Tidball, shock haired collegian from Los Angeles, overwhelmed Charles Carr of Hollywood in a quarter final tilt, 6-3, 6-2.

Three other contenders stayed in the sharpshooting for the title, Charles Otis, Stanford University student, defeating Mel Gallacher, Salt Lake City, 6-2, 8-6; John B. Dallas, giving Nelson McInich, Kansas City, 4-6, 6-4 lacing, and Vernon John, 18-year-old Denver flash, fighting from behind to stop Jim Quick, Dallas, 4-6, 6-1, 6-3.

Later Tidball and John got together and beat Gallacher and Fred Dixon, Provo, Utah, in a rip-and-slash doubles match by the scores of 6-4, 2-6, 6-4, 7-5.

Ladeez and Gempmun!!

Legion Colossal Today

Laaadeezz and Gempmun! Presenting the final local appearance of the greatest 16-ring kid spectacle Northern and Central California ever have seen.

The Chronicle presents for the American Legion——

THE 1934 AREA TWO BASEBALL CHAMPIONSHIP!

There's room, ladeez and gempmun, for everybody in the colossal cement amphitheater, Seals' Stadium!

Admission price is better than a thin dime or one buffalo. IT'S FREE!

And hurry, hurry, hurry, for this morning at 10 the umpires'll holler "PLAY BALL!!" and 18 performers, count 'em, ladeez and gempmun, 18 healthy, hustling lads who are the cream, absotively the cream, of Legion baseball in the Bay District will start their momentous series.

A second perfawmunse, ladeez and gempmun, tomorrow mawnin' at 9 in the same arena, but hurry, hurry, hurry. Don't miss the starter at 10 today!

On my right, ladeez and gempmun, the prides of San Francisco. Take a bow, California Post! On my left the joys of Oakland. Take your bow, Captain Bill Erwin Post, and may the best team win!

PLAY BALL!!!!!!!

Henderson Suffers Possible Fracture

SEATTLE, July 13 (AP) — Bill Henderson, Portland pitcher, who was hit on the head by a pitched ball from the arm of Bob Fitzke in a game between Seattle and the Beavers last night, was reported today as having a concussion of the brain and a possible fracture. Attending physicians said Henderson's condition was not serious, but that he would be unable to leave the hospital for some time.

Dog Track to Close After the Races Tonight

The Town and Country Club's Bayshore City greyhound meeting will celebrate a premature "farewell" tonight.

Because of strike conditions, the track will suspend its meeting with the running of tonight's program. The suspension will become effective Monday night.

The plant will be reopened when the labor situation is stabilized, according to Peter P. O'Connor, general manager.

Increasing transportation difficulties and the threat of a gasoline shortage influenced the decision to interrupt the meeting, O'Connor said.

Eleven races are on tonight's "au revoir" card, the feature bringing together eight of the track's best. Starters include Honored Officer, Frisco Play, Oswego Goer, Jollyman, Olympiad, Traffic Court, Carl Schuttle and Joe Brennan.

Honored Officer is a kennel mate of Dancing Officer, the track champion which set a course record for five-sixteenths of a mile and beat a classy field by five lengths last Thursday night.

OPERATING RESORTS

Fred Luderus, one-time National League slugger, is operating a summer resort at Three Lakes, Wis.

Night Coast League Games

	1	2	3	4	5	6	7	8	9	10	11	12	R.	H.	E.
San Francisco	1	2	2	2	0	0	0	0	1				8	11	3
Missions	0	2	0	0	0	2	0	0	0				4	3	1

Batteries—Ballou and Woodall; Daglia and Fitzpatrick.

	1	2	3	4	5	6	7	8	9	10	11	12	R.	H.	E.
Oakland	0	1	0	0	2	0	0	0							
Sacramento	0	0	0	0	1	0	0	0							

Batteries—Gregory and Wirts; Conlan and Raimondi.

	1	2	3	4	5	6	7	8	9	10	11	12	R.	H.	E.
Los Angeles	3	0	0	0	0	4	0								
Hollywood	0	0	0	0	0	0	0								

Batteries—Meola and J. Campbell; Densmore and Bassler.

	1	2	3	4	5	6	7	8	9	10	11	12	R.	H.	E.
Portland	0	1	2												
Seattle	0	0	0												

Batteries—Bryan and Cox; H. Pillette and Tobin.

Seattle Lad To Try for Tenth Mark

Nine Events on the Big Aquatic Program Sponsored by Association

Jack Medica, America's newest swimming sensation, will make a determined effort at Fleishhacker Pool this afternoon to provide swimming fans with "the big thrill." Heralded as the world's greatest middle distance and distance swimmer, he will attempt to annex his tenth world record by lowering Arne Borg's time in the 1500 meter event.

With Medica in the meet, staged under auspices of the Pacific Association of the A. A. U., will be two other champions, Al Vande Weghe, U. S. 200 meters backstrike king, and Art Highland, 100 meters free-style champion. Highland of Northwestern University and Vande Weghe, Newark, N. J., A. C., joined Medica, University of Washington flash, in San Francisco yesterday, where all three arrived fresh from new triumphs at the Chicago World's Fair.

THREE STARS ON WAY TO JAPANESE INVASION

The trio are performing at Fleishhacker while en route to Japan, where they will match their strength and speed with the Nipponese Olympic Games stars, Kusuo Kitamura, Shozo Makino and others of the Japanese mermen.

Today's meet, starting at 2:15, is a nine-event affair, with three championships and three exhibitions featuring the card. Cooperating with the Pacific Association, San Francisco Lodge, No. 3, of Elks and the Olympic Club are sponsoring one event each, according to Lincoln V. Johnson, P. A. A. swimming commissioner. The Elks will sponsor the Pacific Association junior championship 100 meters free-style swim and the Olympic Club the P. A. A. senior championship at 220 yards free style. Girls' exhibition races and the appearance of Ted Wiget, former Stanford intercollegiate champion who was dethroned by Medica, will also enhance the meet.

Medica, coached by Ray Daughters, famous tutor of Helene Madison and Olive McKean, will find his competition in the 1500 meters in the star Buster Olds of the Olympic Club, Harold Weatherbe, Y. M. C. A., and Edward Peck, unattached.

VANDE WEGHE WILL MEET LOCAL STARS

Vande Weghe, who this year won both the indoor and outdoor backstroke championship, will race Bob Walker of the "Y" and Arthur Hargrave and Frank Brissette of the Olympic Club in the 200 meter backstroke event.

Highland, who won his national 100 meters free-style championship at Chicago last week, will meet Art Lindegren, sprint swimming star of the Y. M. C. A., and Ralph Gilman of the Olympic Club.

Ten entries are included in the Pacific Association junior meters free-style event. Four are entered for the senior high diving crown and five are entered in the senior 220-yard championship event.

LOCAL JAPANESE WILL TURN OUT FOR MEET

Lincoln V. Jackson, Pacific Association swim commissioner, announced keen interest in today's meet by members of San Francisco's Japanese colony, who have made known their intentions to be out in force to "scout" the American champions before their invasion of Japan.

Fleishhacker Pool may be reached by the 12 car of the Market Street line and the L car of the municipal railway.

The program follows:

2:15 p. m., 100 meters free style (Pacific Association junior championship)—Ward Cox, Y. M. C. A.; Hirosha Shibata, Y. M. C. A.; Frank Hadley, Y. M. C. A.; Jack Hewton, Y. M. C. A.; Charles Dullea, Olympic Club; George Winberg, Olympic Club; Frank Pilling, Olympic Club; Carter Ashley, Olympic Club; Bill Myers, Elks, No. 3; Jack Reynolds, Elks, No. 3.

2:20 p. m.—Exhibition race by girls.

2:25 p. m., 200 meters back stroke—Al. Vande Weghe, U. S. champion; Bob Walker, Y. M. C. A.; Arthur Hargrave, Olympic Club; Frank Brissette, Olympic Club.

2:35 p. m., high platform diving (Pacific Association senior championship) — Ed. Throndson, Olympic Club; Al. Stariha; Roy Havner, Fairmont Hotel Swimming Club; Richard Keating, Fairmont Hotel Swimming Club.

3:00 p. m., 100 meters free style—Art Highland, U. S. champion; Art Lindegren, Y. M. C. A.; Ralph Gilman, Olympic Club.

3:05 p. m.—Comedy diving.

3:15 p. m.—Exhibition race by girls.

3:20 p. m., 1500 meters free style—Jack Medica, U. S. champion; Harold Weatherbe, Y. M. C. A.; Buster Olds, Olympic Club; Edward Peck, unattached.

3:45 p. m., 220 yards free style (Pacific Association senior championship) — Art Lindegren, Y. M. C. A.; Bob Walker, Y. M. C. A.; Jack Hewton, Y. M. C. A.; Carter Ashley, Olympic Club; Ted Wiget, Olympic Club.

World records held by Medica are: 400 meters, 4:48.2; 440 yards, 4:46.8; 500 yards, 5:26.6; 500 meters, 5:37.6; 800 meters, 10:13.3; 880 yards, 10:15.4; 1000 yards, 11:37.4; 1000 meters, 12:43.8; one mile (formerly held by Arne Borg), 20:57.8.

Davis Netmen In Shape for Big Tourney

LONDON, July 13 (AP)—The United States Davis cup team today returned to London from Felixstowe, the sea coast resort where they passed several days resting, prepared to begin practice at Wimbledon for the coming interzone final.

A heavy fog, which delayed the inbound Europa and Wilmer Allison, caused a change in the program. The first practice now is set for tomorrow, with Allison and Lester Stoefen fighting it out for the doubles berth with George M. Lott Jr. Allison was called abroad when it appeared Stoefen was faltering.

"We are all in grand condition after our holiday," said R. Norris (Dick) Williams, nonplaying captain of the team, "and eager to get back into harness. I am anxious to see how Wilmer is playing, but in any event we will not decide our lineup until we know the result of the Australia-Czechoslovakia European zone final at Praha. The result there will largely influence my selections."

Thomson Leads in Santa Monica Golf

SANTA MONICA, July 13 (AP)—Jimmy Thomson, powerful Long Beach professional, combined a fine iron game and a gentle putting touch with his booming drives today to set the pace at the end of the first 18 holes of the Santa Monica $1000 open golf tournament today, shooting a 34-32—66, five strokes under par.

Right on the heels of the Lakewood Country Club pro were Ralph Guldahl, Los Angeles, runner up to the national open title in 1933, and Cliff Strickland, assistant pro of Riverside, Cal., with 67s.

L.A. Pair Triumphs In Net Tourney

PROVIDENCE, R. I., July 13 (AP)—In the women's doubles of the State tennis tournament today, Dr. Esther Bartosh and Marianne Hunt of Los Angeles defeated Baroness Maud Levi of New York and Florence Leboutillier of Westbury, L. I., to qualify for the title bracket and the right to face Mrs. Marjorie M. Painter of Dedham, Mass., and Jane Sharp of Los Angeles in the title round.

Option Betting at N. Y. Fair Ended

SYRACUSE, N. Y., July 13 (AP)—Governor Herbert H. Lehman's orders today ended option betting at the State fair race track.

Not satisfied with merely sending telegrams to the District Attroney the Governor used the telephone to get answers.

"Governor, we'll enforce the law," the assurance was given.

No. 700

Babe Ruth's 700th home run yesterday aided the New Yankees to defeat Detroit, 4 and 2, and regain the American League lead.

Harmon Wins Two Matches In Northwest

SEATTLE, July 13 (AP)—Eliminating two Seattle youngsters, Phillip Harmon, Berkeley, and Bob Pelletreau, Pasadena, advanced to the finals in the boys' singles of the Washington State tennis tournament today.

Harmon defeated Douglas La Febvre, 6-3, 6-1, and Pelletreau downed Francis Lewis, 6-1, 6-4. The two Californians will meet tomorrow for the championship.

Mrs. Golda Meyer Gross, Berkeley, and Ann Cook, Seattle, entered the finals in the women's doubles through a default by Betty de Lacy and Irene Taylor, both of Seattle. Miss Taylor was forced to drop out on account of illness.

Baseball at a Glance

PACIFIC COAST LEAGUE

RESULTS THURSDAY NIGHT

Seattle 8, Portland 5.
Hollywood 7, Los Angeles 6.

STANDING OF THE CLUBS

	W.	L.	Pct.
Hollywood	13	4	.765
San Francisco	12	6	.667
Missions	10	8	.556
Los Angeles	10	8	.556
Seattle	10	8	.556
Oakland	6	11	.353
Sacramento	7	11	.389
Portland	3	15	.167

HOW THE SERIES STAND

San Francisco 1, Missions 2.
Oakland 2, Sacramento 1.
Seattle 2, Portland 1.
Hollywood 2, Los Angeles 1.

GAMES TODAY

San Francisco vs. Missions at San Francisco.
Sacramento at Oakland.
Portland at Seattle (night).
Los Angeles vs. Hollywood at Los Angeles (night).

NATIONAL LEAGUE

RESULTS YESTERDAY

Boston 7, Chicago 6.
Cincinnati 8, Brooklyn 6.
New York 7, Pittsburgh 6.
St. Louis at Philadelphia, rain.

STANDING OF THE CLUBS

	Won	Lost	Pct.
New York	51	29	.638
Chicago	49	31	.613
St. Louis	44	33	.571
Pittsburgh	39	36	.520
Boston	40	40	.500
Brooklyn	33	47	.413
Philadelphia	32	48	.400
Cincinnati	26	50	.342

AMERICAN LEAGUE

RESULTS YESTERDAY

Boston 7, St. Louis 2.
New York 4, Detroit 2.
Washington 3, Cleveland 2.
Philadelphia-Chicago, rain.

STANDING OF THE CLUBS

Team—	W.	L.	Pct.
New York	48	28	.632
Detroit	9	30	.620
Boston	43	35	.551
Cleveland	39	37	.513
Washington	[illegible]	39	.506
St. Louis	31	40	.437
Philadelphia	30	46	.395
Chicago	26	51	.338

O'Doul Hits Homer Again, Giants Win

'Lefty' Starts Rally in First as New York Takes 7-6 Victory Over Pirates

NEW YORK, July 13 (AP)—The Giants increased their National League lead to two full games today when they stood off a ninth inning rally to defeat the Pirates 7 to 6 in the series final.

After getting a long lead through the clouting of Joe Moore and Frank O'Doul, Freddy Fitzsimmons blew up in the ninth and gave four runs on an error by Blondy Ryan and four hits. O'Doul socked a homer with one on to climax a three-run rally against Red Lucas in the first.

PITTSBURGH	AB	R	H	O	A	NEW YORK	AB	R	H	O	A
L.Wnr,cf	5	1	0	1	0	Moore,cf	5	4	4	5	0
P.Wnr,rf	5	1	4	1	0	Critz,2b	3	2	2	3	7
Jensen,lf	5	1	1	2	0	Terry,1b	2	0	0	10	1
Vaghn,s	4	0	1	3	3	Ott,rf	4	0	1	1	0
Thnw,3b	4	0	1	3	3	O'Doul,lf	3	1	1	2	0
Suhr,1b	3	2	0	2	3	Jckson,s	4	0	1	3	5
Lvgto,2b	3	2	0	2	3	Ryan,3b	3	0	0	1	2
Grace,c	3	0	1	3	0	Mncuso,c	4	0	2	2	0
Lucas,p	1	0	1	0	1	Ftzsms,p	4	0	0	0	0
Holley,p	0	0	0	0	0	Smith,p	0	0	0	0	1
Lndstm	1	1	0	0	0	Totals	32	7	11	27	16
Chgnn,p	0	0	0	0	0						
Roetger	1	0	1	0	0						
Brkhfr,p	1	0	0	0	0						
Totals	38	6	10	24	12						

Lindstrom batted for Holley in fifth.
Roettger batted for Chagnon in seventh.

Pittsburgh ....0 0 0 0 2 0 0 0 4—6
New York ...3 0 2 1 0 1 0 0 *—7

Errors—P. Waner, Birkofer (Pittsburgh 2), Ryan (New York 1). Runs batted in—By Terry, O'Doul 2, Moore 2, Ott, L. Waner, P. Waner 2, Jensen, Vaughan 2. Two-base hits—Critz, Moore, P. Waner, Thevenow, Jensen. Home runs—O'Doul, Moore 2. Sacrifice—Terry. Double plays—Vaughan to Lavagetto to Suhr; Thevenow to Lavagetto to Suhr; Suhr to Vaughan to Suhr. Left on bases—New York 6, Pittsburgh 8. Bases on balls—Off Holley 3, Fitzsimmons 3. Struck out—By Fitzsimmons 2, Birkofer 1. Hits—Off Lucas 7 in 2 1-3, Holley 1 in 1 2-3, Chagnon 3 in 2, Birkhofer 0 in 8, Fitzsimmons 10 in 8 2-3, Smith 0 in 1-3 inning. Hit by pitcher—By Holley (Critz). Winning pitcher—Fitzsimmons. Losing pitcher—Lucas. Umpires—Reardon, Stewart and Klem. Time of game—2h. 3m.

Braves Put On Rally To Defeat Chicago

BOSTON, July 13 (AP)—The Boston Braves put on a four-run rally in the seventh today to wind up their four-game series with the Chicago Cubs with a 7-6 victory.

CHICAGO	AB	R	H	O	A	BOSTON	AB	R	H	O	A
W.Hm,2b	5	1	1	3	5	Tmpsn,rf	5	0	1	1	0
English,s	5	1	1	3	4	Jordn,1b	5	0	0	14	1
Cuylr,cf	4	1	1	2	0	Berger,cf	5	1	2	2	0
F.Hm,rf	4	1	1	2	0	H.Lee,lf	4	2	2	2	0
Stpnsn,lf	4	0	0	1	0	Wtny,s3b	3	2	2	4	1
Hrtnet,c	4	1	1	3	0	Gyslm,3b	3	0	0	1	3
Grim,1b	4	0	2	7	1	R.Moore	1	0	1	0	0
Hurst,1b	0	0	0	1	0	Cantwell	0	1	0	0	0
Hack,3b	4	1	3	2	1	Smith,p	1	0	0	0	0
W.Lee,p	3	0	0	0	1	MMns,2b	4	0	2	1	4
Tining,p	0	0	0	0	1	Sphrer,c	3	0	0	2	0
Phelps	1	0	0	0	0	Betts,p	1	0	0	0	2
Totals	38	6	10	24	13	Wrthgtn	1	1	1	0	0
						Barrett,p	1	0	0	0	1
						Urbski,s	1	0	1	0	1
						Totals	38	7	12	27	13

Phelps batted for Tinning in ninth.
Worthington batted for Betts in fifth.
R. Moore batted for Gyselmann in seventh.
Cantwell ran for R. Moore in seventh.

Chicago .....0 0 3 0 2 0 0 1 0—6
Boston ....0 2 0 0 1 0 4 0 *—7

Errors—W. Herman, Hack 2 (Chicago 3), Jordan, Gyselman (Boston 2). Runs batted in—By English 2, F. Herman 2, W. Herman, Grimm, Berger 2, McManus 2, R. Moore, Spohrer, Urbanski. Two-base hits—W. Herman, Grimm, Hack, McManus. Three-base hit—Hack. Home runs—English, F. Herman, Berger. Double plays—English to W. Herman to Grimm; Jordan to Whitney. Left on bases—Chicago 5, Boston 11. Bases on balls—Off W. Lee 2, Tinning 2. Struck out—By W. Lee 2, Barrett 1. Hits—Off W. Lee 9 in 6 1-3; Tinning 3 in 1 2-3; Betts 7 in 5; Barrett 1 in 2; Smith 2 in 2 innings. Winning pitcher—Barrett. Losing pitcher—W. Lee. Umpires—Magerkurth and Quigley. Time of game—1h. 52m.

Reds Uncork Hitting Attack; Beat Dodgers

BROOKLYN, July 13 (AP)—The Cincinnati Reds uncorked another heavy-hitting attack and defeated the Dodgers 8 to 6 today, although the Dodgers knocked Benny Frey out in the ninth.

CINCINNATI	AB	R	H	O	A	BROOKLYN	AB	R	H	O	A
Piet,3b	5	2	2	0	2	Boyle,lf	4	2	2	1	0
Slade,2b	5	1	3	3	7	L. Frey,s	3	0	0	2	4
Knig,s	5	0	1	2	3	Wilson	1	0	0	0	0
Hafey,cf	5	1	1	3	0	Stripp,s	1	0	1	1	0
Btmly,1b	5	0	0	15	1	Fdrick,rf	4	0	0	1	0
Cmsky,lf	4	1	3	1	0	Skfrth	0	0	0	0	0
Lmbrdi,c	4	0	1	0	0	Kncke,cf	4	0	1	3	0
Shlmh,rf	3	1	2	3	0	Leslie,1b	4	1	2	8	0
B. Frey,p	4	2	1	0	2	Ccnllo,3b	4	0	0	1	3
Kolp	0	0	0	0	0	Lopez,c	4	1	1	5	1
						Chpmn,2b	4	1	1	5	4
Totals	40	8	14	27	15	Zchary,p	2	0	0	0	1
						Lnrd,p	1	1	1	0	0
						Tylor	0	0	0	0	0
						Totals	36	6	9	27	13

Wilson batted for L. Frey in 7th.
Taylor batted for Leonard in 9th.
Sukeforth ran for Frederick in 9th.

Cincinnati ....1 0 0 0 2 1 3 1 0—8
Brooklyn .. ...1 1 0 0 1 0 1 0 2—6

Errors—Koenig 2, Hafey (Cincinnati 3). Stripp, Leslie (Brooklyn 2). Runs batted in—Slade 2, L. Frey, B. Frey, Lopez, Hafey, Koenig 3, Boyle, Piet, Stripp, Koenecke. Two-base hits—Leslie, Slade, Koenecke, Leonard. Three-base hits—Slade, Boyle, Schulmerich, Koenig. Home runs—Lopez, Hafey. Sacrifice—Cuccinello. Double play—Chapman and L. Frey. Left on bases—Cincinnati 6, Brooklyn 9. Base on balls—Off Frey 4, Leonard 1, Kolp 1. Struck out—By Zachary 2, Leonard 1. Hits—Off Zachary 12 in 6 1-3 innings, Leonard 2 in 2 2-3, B. Frey 9 in 8 1-3, Kolp 0 in 2-3. Wild pitches—B. Frey, Leonard. Winning pitcher—B. Frey. Losing pitcher—Zachary. Umpires—Pfirman and Moran. Time 2h 4m.

Statue of Beaten Carnera Wins Prize

PARIS, July 13 (AP)—A statue depicting Primo Carnera hanging on the ropes at Madison Square Garden bowl as he was defeated by Max Baer won the grand prix de Rome for the French sculptor Boquillon. The statue was called "The Defeated Gladiator."

Giants Split With Braves, but Hold 2½-Game Lead as Cards Also Divide; Yankees Win 2

N. Y. Wins 1st, 8-0, Drops 2d In the 11th, 4-3

Hubbell Wilts in 8th After 7-Inning Shutout; Hit Off Bowman Decides; Parmelee Yields Only 4

By Arthur E. Patterson

BOSTON, Sept. 23.—The Giants tottered but did not fall here today.

They dropped an eleven-inning decision to the Braves, 4 to 3, after Carl Hubbell had hurled no-hit, no-run ball for six sessions, but the four-hit, 8—0 beating Leroy Parmelee gave the Braves in the first game of a double-header, coupled with late news here tonight of the first Cardinal defeat in eight games, kept them two and a half games ahead in this mad National League pennant race.

What happened to Hubbell in the seventh inning this afternoon was a question asked by more than 12,000 who sat in the stands. After pitching what appeared his supreme effort in a glamorous career, he suddenly lost his spell over the Boston batters, and in a jiffy had the bases loaded on singles by Urbanski and McManus and a walk to Whitney. His downfall was not to come then, however, for in between these Boston acts Hubbell had worked in two outs, Berger's sacrifice and Lee's strike-out.

Lucky Bounce Ties Score

Hubbell, however, had little to do with the play which followed. Les Mallon, who was later to win the game with a single in the eleventh, was the next batter, and he whipped a terrific liner toward third base. The ball bounced out of Travis Jackson's glove, but Jackson, with a throw which almost defies description, rifled the ball over to Terry to beat Mellon by a step and end the troublesome inning.

For a time it appeared he might have saved the game. A single by Hogan, a pinch double by Spohrer and still another pinch single by McManus put across two Braves in the eighth. Still, Hubbell seemed to have passed the crisis when Berger sent an innocent bounder to short for what should have been a third out. Instead, the ball hopped crazily over Ryan's shoulder and the score was tied. Much to the dissent of all other press-box occupants, the official scorer called Berger's bounder an error. Ryan didn't even get a glove to it.

Bowman's Wind-Up Costly

And so, Jackson's great throw was wasted, for the even game continued only until the eleventh. By this time Joe Bowman was hurling for the Giants and doing right well. In the eleventh, however, he walked Berger, but made a fine play to force him at second on Lee's attempted sacrifice. Hughie Critz then skipped out to right field to watch Whitney's fly, and with only one out to go and a runner no further than first the Giants seemed sure of a tie, the 6:30 curfew and weather conditions, not to mention the darkness, assuring a postponement.

That official decision never had to be made, however. Bowman took an extravagant wind-up while pitching to Mallon, so Lee stole second easily. Then Bowman unleashed a wild pitch to send Lee to third, also to bring the count to three balls and two strikes. Then Mallon dropped a single over second, an unimpressive-looking blow and the only one off Bowman.

The Giants outhit Boston, 13 to 6, drew five passes, had a hit batsman, and left sixteen on base.

Two Braves Reach Third

Parmelee's shutout was his third of the year, his tenth victory and his first over the Braves this season. Only two tribal tourists set foot upon third base, and they only after two were out. In the fourth Randy Moore went to that turn on Bill Urbanski's single, but Pinkie Whitney flied to Leiber. In the eighth Les Mallon singled and Shanty Hogan walked and the former advanced a base during a fast double play on Hal Lee's pinch grounder to Jackson at third.

The Giants pecked steadily at bat, piled up twelve hits and broke up the game in the seventh after Parmelee and Ben Cantwell had progressed six innings in the throes of a 1-0 battle.

That lone tally had occurred in the first when Jackson had signaled his return to the line-up with a single, driving Moore across. Moore had walked, had gone to second on Critz's single and third on Terry's sacrifice.

Giants Get Seven in Two Innings

The Giants added three in the seventh and four in the eighth, and before the game was over Bill McKechnie had used up Fred Frankhouse, Bob Smith and Bob Brown in relief periods. After Leiber walked Mancuso sacrificed in the seventh, Ryan singled to left for the first run, and successive safeties by Moore, Critz and Terry added two more before Frankhouse retired the side. The Messrs. Moore, Critz and Terry repeated in the eighth, although this time Moore's hit was a double, the climax blow of the four-run assault which also included a single by Jackson and bases on balls to Ryan and Parmelee.

Ott was in a hitting mood but unlucky in the first game. He drove "foul homers" during one time at bat and also sent Thompson back to the far reaches of right field for two liners, both of which ended the big innings.

You figure out how the Giants felt when the scoreboard showed first a big "4" for the Reds and a moment later a bigger "4" for the Cards in their fifth inning.

The Babe Tries Mightily to Please on His Farewell Appearance

The Ruthian swing, about to be retired for all time, barely fails to produce his specialty in third inning of yesterday's first game at the Yankee Stadium. The ball went into the bleachers, but it was foul. Rick Ferrell behind the plate. The umpire is McGowan

A few of the youngsters in the crowd of 24,000 who turned out to bid farewell to baseball's idol

Cardinals Win, Then Drop 2d, As Deans Fail

Chance to Gain on Giants Lost as Reds Score, 4-3, After Yielding, 9 to 7

By The Associated Press

CINCINNATI, Sept. 23.—The St. Louis Cardinals, in dropping the second game of a double-header to the Cincinnati Reds today, remained on even terms with the league-leading Giants, who also split.

The Cards captured the first, 9 to 7, but faltered in the ninth to lose the second contest, 4 to 3.

The first game was a free-hitting affair, but in the second the Reds were able to win by scoring two runs without the aid of a hit. In the ninth of the final affair, Paul Dean walked Comorosky and then Alex Kamporis, who batted for Derringer, laid down a neat sacrifice. Dean picked it up and threw it so far over Collins's head the Comorosky scored the tying run and Kamporis went to third.

Jerome Dean relieved Paul at this point and issued passes to both Slade and Adams to fill the bases. Mark Koenig then flied to Medwick and Kamporis scampered home with the winning run. The scores:

FIRST GAME

ST. LOUIS (N. L.)	ab	r	h	po	a	e
Martin, 3b	5	1	1	1	3	0
Rothrock, rf	4	2	3	4	0	0
Frisch, 2b	4	2	3	2	3	0
Medwick, lf	5	2	1	2	1	0
Collins, 1b	5	1	4	11	1	0
Delancey, c	4	0	2	0	0	1
Davis, c	1	1	1	0	0	0
Orsatti, cf	4	0	0	2	0	0
Fullis, cf	1	0	0	0	0	0
Durocher, ss	3	0	0	5	3	0
HAL'AN, p	2	0	0	0	2	0
HAINES, p	2	0	1	0	0	0
J. DEAN, p	0	0	0	0	0	0
Totals	40	9	16	27	13	1

CINCINNATI (N. L.)	ab	r	h	po	a	e
Adams, 2b	4	0	1	9	3	0
Slade, ss	5	0	0	2	4	0
Koenig, 3b	5	0	1	0	2	0
Bottom'y, 1b	4	0	0	6	0	0
Lombardi, c	4	1	2	3	2	0
Pool, lf	4	2	2	2	0	1
Schul'ich, rf	4	2	2	0	0	0
Com'osky, cf	3	2	1	5	0	0
FREY, p	1	0	1	0	0	0
RICH'ND, p	0	0	0	0	0	0
*McCormick	1	0	1	0	0	0
JOHNS'N, p	0	0	0	0	1	0
†Kamporis	1	0	0	0	0	0
KLEIN'S, p	0	0	0	0	0	1
‡Petoskey	1	0	0	0	0	0
Totals	37	7	11	27	13	2

*Batted for Richmond in fifth inning.
†Batted for Johnson in seventh inning.
‡Batted for Kleinhans in ninth inning.

St. Louis .... 000 140 103—9
Cincinnati .... 000 040 003—7

Runs batted in—Frisch, Medwick (2), Collins (2), Delancey, Davis, Orsatti, Fullis, Adams (2), Slade, Schulmerich, Comorosky, McCormick (2). Two-base hits—Frisch, Lombardi. Three-base hits—Martin, Medwick. Sacrifices—Frisch, Adams. Double plays—Durocher, Frisch and Collins; Adams and Slade. Left on bases—St. Louis, 7; Cincinnati, 5. Bases on balls—Off Frey, 1; off Johnson, 1. Struck out—By Frey, 2; by Johnson, 1. Hits—Off Hallahan, 5 in 4 innings (none out in fifth); off Haines, 5 in 4 (none out in ninth); off J. Dean, 1 in 1; off Frey, 10 in 4 2-3; off Richmond, 0 in 1-3; off Johnson, 2 in 2; off Kleinhans, 4 in 2. Hit by pitcher—By Haines (Comorosky). Wild pitch—Johnson. Winning pitcher—Haines. Losing pitcher—Frey. Umpires—Barr, Quigley and Reardon. Time—2:17.

SECOND GAME

ST. LOUIS (N. L.)	ab	r	h	po	a	e
Martin, 3b	4	1	1	2	3	0
Rothrock, rf	3	0	3	0	0	0
Frisch, 2b	3	0	0	2	3	0
Medwick, lf	4	2	3	3	0	0
Collins, 1b	4	0	1	7	2	1
Delancey, c	3	0	0	6	2	0
Orsatti, cf	4	0	0	2	0	0
Durocher, ss	3	0	0	2	1	2
†Crawford	1	0	0	0	0	0
Whiteh'd, ss	0	0	0	0	0	0
CARL'ON, p	2	0	0	1	3	0
P. DEAN, p	2	0	0	0	0	1
J. DEAN, p	0	0	0	0	0	0
Totals	33	3	8	*25	14	4

CINCINNATI (N. L.)	ab	r	h	po	a	e
Adams, 2b	4	0	1	1	1	0
Slade, ss	4	0	2	2	4	0
Koenig, 3b	5	0	1	1	3	0
Bottom'y, 1b	3	1	1	13	1	0
Lombardi, c	4	0	1	5	0	0
Pool, lf	4	1	1	2	0	0
Schul'ich, rf	3	0	0	1	0	0
Com'osky, cf	3	1	1	2	0	0
STOUT, p	2	0	0	0	2	0
‡McCormick	1	0	0	0	0	0
DER'GER, p	0	0	0	0	1	0
§Kamporis	0	1	0	0	0	0
Totals	33	4	8	27	12	0

*One out when winning run was scored.
†Batted for Durocher in ninth inning.
‡Batted for Stout in sixth inning.
§Batted for Derringer in ninth inning.

St. Louis .... 001 100 001—3
Cincinnati .... 000 101 002—4

Runs batted in—Rothrock, Delancey, Crawford, Koenig, Lombardi. Two-base hit—Pool. Three-base hits—Martin, Medwick, Bottomley. Stolen base—Koenig. Sacrifices—Frisch, Kamporis. Left on bases—St. Louis, 6; Cincinnati, 10. Bases on balls—Off Carleton, 1; off P. Dean, 2; off J. Dean, 2; off Stout, 1; off Derringer, 1. Struck out—By Carleton, 4; by Derringer, 3. Hits—Off Carleton, 8 in 5 1-3 innings; off P. Dean, 0 in 2 2-3 (none out in ninth); off J. Dean, 0 in 1-3; off Stout, 5 in 6; off Derringer, 3 in 3. Wild pitch—Carleton. Winning pitcher—Derringer. Losing pitcher—P. Dean. Umpires—Quigley, Reardon and Barr. Time—2:03.

Giants' Box Scores

* * *

FIRST GAME

NEW YORK (N. L.)	ab	r	h	po	a	e
J. Moore, lf	4	3	2	1	0	0
Critz, 2b	5	0	3	2	6	0
Terry, 1b	3	0	3	15	0	0
Ott, rf	4	0	0	2	0	0
Jackson, 3b	5	1	2	2	4	0
Leiber, cf	3	1	0	2	0	0
Mancuso, c	4	0	0	0	0	0
Ryan, ss	3	2	1	3	3	0
PARM'E, p	3	1	1	0	4	0
Totals	34	8	12	27	17	0

BOSTON (N. L.)	ab	r	h	po	a	e
Thomp'n, rf	4	0	0	4	0	0
Jordan, 1b	4	0	0	12	0	0
Berger, cf	3	0	0	2	0	0
R. Moore, lf	4	0	1	1	0	0
Urbanski, ss	3	0	1	1	1	0
Whitney, 3b	3	0	0	0	5	0
Mallon, 2b	3	0	1	4	3	0
Hogan, c	2	0	0	2	1	0
*Fletcher	0	0	0	0	0	0
Spohrer, c	0	0	0	1	0	0
CANTW'L, p	2	0	1	0	3	0
FRANK'E, p	2	0	1	0	3	0
SMITH, p	0	0	0	0	0	0
†Lee	1	0	0	0	0	0
BROWN, p	0	0	0	0	0	0
Totals	29	0	4	27	13	0

*Ran for Hogan in eighth inning.
†Batted for Smith in eighth inning.

New York .... 100 000 340—8
Boston .... 000 000 000—0

Runs batted in—Critz (3), J. Moore (2), Terry, Jackson, Ryan. Two-base hit—J. Moore. Sacrifices—Terry, Leiber, Mancuso. Double plays—Ryan, Critz and Terry; Jackson, Critz and Terry; Whitney, Hogan and Jordan; Whitney, Mallon and Jordan. Left on bases—New York, 8; Boston, 4. Bases on balls—Off Parmelee, 2; off Cantwell, 4; off Frankhouse, 2. Struck out—By Cantwell, 1; by Brown, 1. Hits—Off Cantwell, 8 in 6 2-3 innings; off Frankhouse, 4 in 1; off Smith, 0 in 1-3; off Brown, 0 in 1. Losing pitcher—Cantwell. Umpires—Stark, Magerkurth and Pfirman. Time—1:45.

BASEBALL TODAY. Yankee Stadium, Yankees vs. Boston. Game starts 3:15 P. M. —Advt.

SECOND GAME

NEW YORK (N. L.)	ab	r	h	po	a	e
J. Moore, lf	5	0	1	2	0	0
Critz, 2b	6	1	2	2	6	0
Terry, 1b	5	0	3	13	1	0
Ott, rf	5	0	0	0	0	0
Jackson, 3b	5	0	0	3	3	0
Watkins, cf	5	1	3	4	0	0
Danning, c	5	0	1	3	0	0
Ryan, ss	3	0	2	4	2	1
HUBBE'L, p	4	1	1	0	4	0
†Leiber	1	0	0	0	0	0
BOWM'N, p	0	0	0	1	1	0
Totals	44	3	13	*32	17	1

BOSTON (N. L.)	ab	r	h	po	a	e
Thomp'n, rf	3	0	0	2	0	0
Mowry, rf	2	0	0	0	0	0
Urbanski, ss	4	1	2	2	2	2
Jordan, 1b	2	0	0	6	0	0
‡McManus	1	0	1	0	0	0
R. Moore, 1b	1	0	0	3	1	0
Berger, cf	3	0	0	4	1	0
Lee, lf	5	1	0	1	0	0
Whitney, 3b	4	0	0	4	2	1
Mallon, 2b	5	0	1	3	4	1
Hogan, c	3	0	1	4	1	0
§Fletcher	0	1	0	0	0	0
BRANDT, p	1	0	0	1	1	0
BETTS, p	1	0	0	0	3	0
Spohrer, c	2	1	1	3	0	0
Totals	37	4	6	33	15	4

*Two out when winning run was scored.
†Batted for Hubbell in ninth inning.
‡Batted for Jordan in seventh inning.
§Ran for Hogan in eighth inning.

New York .... 000 100 110 00—3
Boston .... 000 000 030 01—4

Runs batted in—Terry, Watkins, Ryan, Urbanski, Spohrer, Mallon. Two-base hit—Spohrer. Stolen base—Lee. Sacrifices—Terry, Danning, Berger, R. Moore. Double play—Betts, Urbanski and Jordan. Left on bases—New York, 16; Boston, 7. Bases on balls—Off Hubbell, 2; off Bowman, 2; off Betts, 4; off Brandt, 1. Struck out—By Hubbell, 2; by Bowman, 1; by Betts, 2; by Brandt, 3. Hits—Off Hubbell, 5 in 8 innings; off Bowman, 1 in 2 2-3; off Betts, 13 in 8; off Brandt, 0 in 3. Hit by pitcher—By Brandt (Watkins). Wild pitch—Bowman. Winning pitcher—Brandt. Losing Pitcher—Bowman. Umpires—Magerkurth, Pfirman and Stark. Time—2:27.

Dodgers Win From Phils, 7 to 2, After Losing in the 13th, 4 to 2

Leonard Takes No. 14, Giving 6 Hits; Recruit's Triple Brings Defeat in First

By Irving T. Marsh

The Dodgers and the Phillies, in the process of finishing their schedules, split a double-header in two exemplary battles of what-of-it yesterday before 15,000 at Ebbets Field. It took the Phils thirteen innings to win the first, 4 to 2, on a triple by a recruit from these precincts in his metropolitan debut. The second was called in the seventh inning on account of darkness, the Dodgers winning, 7 to 2, by virtue of a five-run onslaught in the fifth that included two homers.

Eddie Boland, of Elmhurst, L. I., a bantamweight who played with the Bushwicks the last two seasons, gave Wilson's team its victory. With the score tied at 2—all and two Phils on base, Boland slashed a triple that scored Bartell and Camilli and gave his team the two-run lead which Brooklyn could not overcome in its half of the thirteenth.

Boyle Drives Out Homer

Buzz Boyle's homer to the scoreboard in right center with Stripp on base started the sortie that gave the Dodgers their victory, and the home run to almost exactly the same spot by John McCarthy, the Dodgers' recruit first baseman, with two on base was just so much wasted effort.

Van Lingle Mungo, Brooklyn's pride speedball artist, opened the first game for the Dodgers, opposed by Phidgety Phil Collins. Mungo gave up after the tenth inning, making way for Johnny Babich. Collins was relieved in the twelfth by long Curt Davis, who was credited as the winning pitcher. Mungo, allowing ten hits during the time he worked, nevertheless kept them scattered enough to limit the Phils to two runs, but Casey Stengel refused to say why he was relieved.

The visitors tied the score at 1-all in the fourth on the combination of three singles and a long fly, and deadlocked it again at 2-all in the sixth on consecutive doubles by John Moore and Don Camilli. Brooklyn scored one in the first on two hits and an infield grounder and one in the sixth on Sam Leslie's homer over the right-field wall. Both teams then went scoreless until the thirteenth, when two bases on balls, a sacrifice and Boland's triple scored the winning runs.

Fourteenth Victory for Leonard

The second also was close until Brooklyn's fifth-inning spulrge. Philadelphia tallied one in each of the first and third, and the Dodgers counted in the second and fourth to make the score 2 all. Dutch Leonard went the route for the home team, allowing six hits for his fourteenth victory of the year, while the Dodgers hit Sylvester Johnson and Austin Moore for eight safeties, five in the fifth.

In that inning Stripp singled, Millies flied out, Leonard fanned, Boyle hit a homer. Frey singled, Koenecke singled and McCarthy lifted a four-bagger.

The Dodgers' victory yesterday was their sixty-sixth, one more than they won at the end of last season. They have six games left, two today with the Phillies, two with the Braves and two with the Giants next week end at the Polo Grounds.

The Phils wereg uided yesterday by Hans Lobert instead of Jimmy Wilson. Wilson's mother died Saturday afternoon and he rushed back to Philadelphia.

Stengel was presented with a suitcase by the Ebbets Field Section M Rooters Club in a formal ceremony in front of home plate. Not to be outdone, the Ebbets Field Section N Rooters Club rushed out with a pen-and-pencil set for the Sage of Flatbush.

The ball stopped completely dead whenever a roller was hit to the outfield. Saturday's rain started the slowing-up process and the Manhattan football game that night finished it.

Nick Tremark, the Manhattan midget, caught the fancy of the crowd and was given a great ovation after he had galloped all the way from left field to make a catch in center. He also hit the single in the second that drove in the tying run. The scores:

FIRST GAME

PHILADELPHIA (N. L.)	ab	r	h	po	a	e
G. Davis, cf	6	0	2	5	0	0
Bartell, ss	5	1	1	3	4	0
Chiozza, 2b	4	1	1	6	4	0
J. Mo're, lf, rf	6	1	3	8	0	0
Camilli, 1b	5	1	2	12	0	0
Boland, rf	6	0	3	1	0	0
Allen, lf	0	0	0	0	0	0
Walters, 3b	6	0	2	0	1	0
Holden, c	3	0	0	2	2	0
*High	0	0	0	0	0	0
Todd, c	1	0	1	2	0	0
COLLINS, p	4	0	0	0	2	0
C. DAVIS, p	1	0	0	0	0	0
Totals	47	4	15	39	13	0

BROOKLYN (N. L.)	ab	r	h	po	a	e
Boyle, rf	5	1	2	6	0	0
Frey, ss	5	0	1	6	2	0
Koenecke, cf	6	0	2	5	0	0
Leslie, 1b	5	1	4	8	1	0
†McCarthy	0	0	0	0	0	0
Cucci'llo, 2b	5	0	0	4	2	0
Fred'rick, lf	5	0	1	1	1	1
Chapman, lf	0	0	0	0	0	0
‡Bucher	1	0	0	0	0	0
Stripp, 3b	6	0	1	1	3	0
Lopez, c	4	0	1	7	2	1
MUNGO, p	4	0	0	1	1	0
BABICH, p	1	0	0	0	2	0
Totals	48	2	11	39	14	2

*Batted for Holden in ninth inning.
†Ran for Leslie in thirteenth inning.
‡Batted for Chapman in thirteenth inning.

Philadelphia .... 000 101 000 000 2—4
Brooklyn .... 100 100 000 000 0—2

Runs batted in—Boland (3), Camilli, Leslie (2). Two-base hits—J. Moore, Camilli (2), Stripp. Three-base hits—Boland. Home run—Leslie. Sacrifices—Frey, Chiozza, Cuccinello. Double plays—Cuccinello and Leslie; Babich, Frey and Leslie. Left on bases—Philadelphia, 9; Brooklyn, 11. Bases on balls—Off Mungo, 2; off Collins, 3; off Babich, 2. Struck out—By Mungo, 5; by Collins, 1; by Babich, 1; by C. Davis, 1. Hits—Off Mungo, 10 in 10 innings; off Collins, 9 in 11; off Babich, 5 in 3; off C. Davis, 2 in 2. Winning pitcher—C. Davis. Losing pitcher—Babich. Umpires—Moran and Stewart. Time—2:48.

SECOND GAME

PHILADELPHIA (N. L.)	ab	r	h	po	a	e
G. Davis, cf	4	1	1	0	0	0
Bartell, ss	3	1	1	5	3	0
Chiozza, 2b	3	0	1	0	6	0
J. Moore, lf	3	0	0	2	0	0
Camilli, 1b	3	0	0	7	0	0
Boland, rf	3	0	0	0	0	0
Walters, 3b	3	0	1	2	0	0
Todd, c	2	0	1	2	0	0
*Holden	1	0	0	0	0	0
JOHNS'N, p	2	0	0	0	0	0
A. MO'RE, p	0	0	0	0	0	0
†High	1	0	1	0	0	0
Totals	28	2	6	18	9	0

BROOKLYN (N. L.)	ab	r	h	po	a	e
Boyle, rf	2	1	1	4	0	0
Frey, ss	3	1	1	1	0	0
Koenecke, cf	3	1	1	1	0	0
M'Carthy, 1b	2	2	1	5	0	0
Bucher, 2b	3	1	2	2	3	0
Tremark, lf	2	0	1	4	0	0
Stripp, 3b	3	1	1	1	0	0
Millies, c	3	0	0	3	0	0
LEON'RD, p	2	0	0	0	2	0
Totals	23	7	8	21	5	0

*Batted for Todd in seventh inning.
†Batted for E. Moore in seventh inning.

Philadelphia .... 101 000 0—2
Brooklyn .... 010 150 x—7

Runs batted in—J. Moore, Chiozza, Tremark, Bucher, Boyle (2), McCarthy (3). Two-base hits—Chiozza, Todd, Bucher. Three-base hit—Bucher. Home runs—Boyle, McCarthy. Double plays—Bartell and Camilli; Chiozza, Bartell and Camilli (2). Left on bases—Philadelphia, 5; Brooklyn, 1. Bases on balls—Off Johnson, 2; off A. Moore, 1. Struck out—By Johnson, 1; by Leonard, 1. Hits—Off Johnson, 8 in 5 innings; off A. Moore, 0 in 1. Losing pitcher—Johnson. Umpires—Stewart and Moran. Time—1:16.

White Sox Lose Pair to Indians For 8 Straight

Averill Hits 30th Homer; Chicago Ends Home Stay With 2-1, 5-1 Reverses

By The Associated Press

CHICAGO, Sept. 23.—The Chicago White Sox closed their home season in dismal fashion, today, losing both ends of a double-header to Cleveland, 2 to 1 and 5 to 1, before 10,000, and running their losing streak to eight straight games.

Monte Pearson edged out Vernon Kennedy, recruit pitcher, in the opener for his eighteenth victory this season. Ralph Winegarner pitched steady ball in the second and was aided by Earl Averill's thirtieth homer, with two on in the seventh inning.

Averill's long blow boosted his home run bonus money to $3,000. He received $1,000 for his twenty-fifth and was to receive $400 for every one after that.

The scores:

FIRST GAME

CLEVELAND (A. L.)	ab	r	h	po	a	e
Galatzer, rf	3	1	2	1	1	0
Averill, cf	4	0	0	3	0	0
Trosky, 1b	4	0	1	13	0	0
Vosmik, lf	4	0	0	1	0	0
Hale, 2b	3	0	1	1	5	0
Kamm, 3b	4	0	0	1	2	0
Knick'er, ss	4	1	1	2	4	0
Berg, c	4	0	1	5	1	0
PEARSON, p	3	0	1	0	3	0
Totals	33	2	7	27	16	0

CHICAGO (A. L.)	ab	r	h	po	a	e
Conlan, cf	4	0	1	2	0	0
Mauldin, 3b	4	0	2	0	0	0
Simmons, lf	0	0	1	0	0	0
Bonura, 1b	4	0	2	10	1	0
*Hopkins	0	1	0	0	0	0
Appling, ss	3	0	0	3	3	0
Radcliff, rf	4	0	2	5	0	0
Hayes, 2b	3	0	0	2	3	0
†Haas	1	0	0	0	0	0
Shea, c	3	0	0	3	0	0
KEN'EDY, p	3	0	1	1	4	0
Totals	33	1	8	27	11	0

*Ran for Bonura in ninth inning.
†Batted for Hayes in ninth inning.

Cleveland .... 000 010 010—2
Chicago .... 000 000 001—1

Runs batted in—Vosmick, Berg, Radcliff. Two-base hits—Bonura, Radcliff. Stolen base—Knickerbocker. Left on bases—Cleveland, 6; Chicago, 6. Bases on balls—Off Pearson, 1; off Kennedy, 2. Struck out—By Pearson, 4; by Kennedy, 2. Wild pitch—Pearson. Passed ball—Shea. Umpires—Summers, Hildebrand and Donnelly. Time—1:40.

SECOND GAME

CLEVELAND (A. L.)	ab	r	h	po	a	e
Galatzer, rf	5	1	1	2	0	0
Averill, cf	5	1	2	2	0	0
Trosky, 1b	5	0	1	11	0	1
Vosmik, lf	4	1	0	2	0	1
Hale, 2b	4	0	1	1	4	0
Burnett, 3b	4	0	1	1	0	0
Knick'er, ss	4	1	4	3	2	0
Brenzel, c	4	1	1	5	0	0
WINE'ER, p	4	0	0	0	4	0
Totals	39	5	11	27	10	2

CHICAGO (A. L.)	ab	r	h	po	a	e
Conlan, cf	4	0	1	4	0	0
Mauldin, 3b	3	0	0	0	2	2
Simmons, lf	3	0	1	2	0	0
Bonura, 1b	3	0	0	11	0	0
Appling, ss	4	0	1	0	3	0
Radcliff, rf	4	0	1	4	0	0
Hayes, 2b	4	0	2	2	1	1
Caith'er, c	4	0	1	4	1	0
TIETJE, p	2	0	0	0	1	0
*Swanson	0	1	0	0	0	0
HEVING, p	0	0	0	0	0	0
†Haas	1	0	0	0	0	0
Totals	32	1	7	27	8	3

*Batted for Tietje in seventh inning.
†Batted for Heving in ninth inning.

Cleveland .... 000 001 400—5
Chicago .... 000 000 100—1

Runs batted in—Galatzer, Averill (3), Hale, Mauldin. Two-base hit—Simmons. Home run—Averill. Stolen base—Knickerbocker. Sacrifice—Mauldin. Double plays—Hale and Knickerbocker; Hale, Knickerbocker and Trosky. Left on bases—Cleveland, 7; Chicago, 8. Bases on balls—Off Winegarner, 3. Struck out—By Winegarner, 4; by Tietje, 2. Hits—Off Tietje, 8 in 7 innings; off Heving, 3 in 2. Losing pitcher—Tietje. Umpires—Donnelly, Hildebrand and Summers. Time—1:55.

Baby Quintana Wins Bout

HAVANA, Sept. 23 (UP).—Baby Quintana, of Panama, easily outpointed Humberto Castillo, Cuban featherweight champion, in a ten-round bout last night before 20,000 fans. Quintana weighed 117¾, Castillo 121.

Tigers, Browns Break Even as Rowe Is Beaten

Schoolboy Loses First, 4-3, Crowded Wins 2d, 2-1, but Title Is Not Clinched

By The Associated Press

ST. LOUIS, Sept. 23.—Lady Luck frowned on the Detroit Tigers today, and the New York Yankees retained their slim mathematical chance to win the American League pennant.

With a double-barreled chance to clinch the championship, the Tigers missed out both ways. They split even with the Browns when two victories would have put the Yankees out of the race, and the Yankees refused to lose either end of a double-header to Boston, which would have put Detroit "in."

The Browns beat the great Lynwood (Schoolboy) Rowe in the opener, 4 to 3, but Mickey Cochrane's pennant-hungry crew came back to win the second, 2 to 1, as General Alvin Crowder outpitched George Blaeholder.

The Tigers' even split while the Yankees were winning two reduced Detroit's lead to five and a half games. The Tigers have five more to play and New York six.

Buck Newsom limited the Tigers to four hits in the opener while the Browns were touching Rowe for eleven. Except for the second inning, when the Tigers scored all of their runs, Newsom was never in serious difficulty. Rowe, on the other hand, often found the sailing rough, but excellent support nipped several Brownie scoring threats.

The Tigers put over the run needed to win the second game in the eighth when Ray Pepper lost Goslin's long fly in the sun and it fell for a double to score Jo-Jo White, who had singled and stolen second.

The scores:

FIRST GAME

DETROIT (A. L.)	ab	r	h	po	a	e
White, cf	3	0	0	4	0	0
Cochrane, c	4	0	0	5	0	0
Gehr'ger, 2b	3	0	0	1	3	0
Green'g, 1b	3	0	0	10	1	0
Goslin, lf	3	1	0	0	1	0
Rogell, ss	4	1	1	1	3	0
Owen, 3b	4	0	1	0	2	0
Fox, rf	4	1	1	3	0	0
ROWE, p	3	0	1	0	2	0
Totals	31	3	4	24	12	0

ST. LOUIS (A. L.)	ab	r	h	po	a	e
Clift, 3b	2	3	1	1	1	1
Garms, lf	4	1	3	5	0	0
Burns, 1b	4	0	0	8	0	0
Pepper, cf	4	0	2	4	0	0
Campbell, rf	4	0	2	1	0	0
Melillo, 2b	4	0	1	0	3	0
Hemsley, c	4	0	1	6	0	0
Strange, ss	4	0	1	2	0	0
NEWSOM, p	4	0	0	0	1	0
Totals	34	4	11	27	5	1

Detroit .... 003 000 000—3
St. Louis .... 200 010 10x—4

Runs batted in—Burns (2), Campbell, Pepper, Owen, Rowe, Fox. Two-base hits—Rogell, Rowe, Campbell. Left on bases—Detroit, 5; St. Louis, 8. Bases on balls—Off Newsom, 4; off Rowe, 2. Struck out—By Newsom, 4; by Rowe, 2. Umpires—Ormsby and Kolls. Time—1:38.

SECOND GAME

DETROIT (A. L.)	ab	r	h	po	a	e
Fox, rf	5	0	2	1	0	0
White, cf	5	2	1	3	0	0
Gehr'ger, 2b	4	0	2	3	3	0
Green'g, 1b	4	0	0	9	0	1
Goslin, lf	3	0	1	1	0	0
Rogell, ss	4	0	1	5	4	0
Owen, 3b	4	0	2	2	6	0
Hayworth, c	4	0	1	3	0	0
CRO'DER, p	4	0	2	0	1	0
Totals	37	2	12	27	8	1

ST. LOUIS (A. L.)	ab	r	h	po	a	e
Clift, 3b	5	0	0	1	4	0
Garms, lf	4	0	1	1	0	0
Burns, 1b	4	0	2	8	1	0
Pepper, cf	4	0	0	3	0	0
Campbell, rf	4	1	2	1	0	0
Melillo, 2b	4	0	1	5	3	0
Hemsley, c	4	0	2	6	1	0
Strange, ss	4	0	0	1	1	0
BLAE'ER, p	3	0	1	1	1	0
*Bejma	1	0	1	0	0	0
Totals	37	1	10	27	11	0

*Batted for Blaeholder in ninth inning.

Detroit .... 100 000 010—2
St. Louis .... 000 100 000—1

Runs batted in—Greenberg, Goslin, Hemsley. Two-base hits—Garms, Goslin. Three-base hit—Campbell. Stolen bases—White, Fox. Double plays—Clift, Melillo and Burns; Rogell, Gehringer and Greenberg. Left on bases—Detroit, 9; St. Louis, 9. Base on balls—Off Blaeholder, 1. Struck out—By Crowder, 2; by Blaeholder, 3. Umpires—Kolls and Ormsby. Time—1:53.

24,430 Thunder Adieu to Ruth, Viewing Games as Mere Setting

Gomez's 3-Hit Victory, 1-0; Ruffing's 19th, 5-4, and Gehrig's Homer Incidental

By Rud Rennie

Of all the cheers set up for the Yankee athletes who defeated the Boston Red Sox, 1 to 0 and 5 to 4 in ten innings, in the Stadium yesterday, those for the Babe were loudest and longest and most repeated.

It was Ruth's farewell party and 22,973 of the 24,430 persons present paid their way into the park to see the Big Bam in action for the last time as a regular player. Others may see him today when he makes his final appearance in the Stadium in the starting line-up, but those present yesterday were bidding him hail and farewell.

By any standard of comparison, the Babe did nothing yesterday to elicit applause. It did not matter. It was the accumulated echo of 2,531 major league ball games wherein he did things that never were done before and probably never will be done again.

Gomez Gives Three Hits

Ruth, coming to the bat five times without a hit, and handling one easy fly ball in the outfield, was more stirring than the great Gomez, Charley Ruffing, Lou Gehrig, Myril Hoag, George Selkirk, Ben Chapman and Arndt Jorgens combined. These lads put the frills on a party which remained the Babe's.

Gomez, pitching the first game, shut out the Red Sox with three hits, fanned eight and chalked up his twenty-sixth victory of the season. Jorgens knocked in the winning run, the only run, with a single in the second inning.

Ruffing weathered a stormy fifth, in which the Sox made four runs in the second game, lasted ten innings and won his nineteenth victory. This is one more than he ever won in his major league career, his best effort being in 1932 when he won eighteen.

Lou Gehrig also achieved distinction, tying the score, 4 to 4, with a home run in the eighth. It was his forty-seventh homer of the year. He hit that many in 1927, when the Babe made sixty. So he tied his best home-run mark and probably will go on and set a new one for himself.

Three Homers Win Second Game

All three runs which brought the Yankees back into the second contest after they lost a one-run lead in the fifth were made by homers.

Selkirk hit one with two out in the fifth. Hoag lifted one into the right-field stands with two out in the sixth. Gehrig pumped one into the same stands with none out in the eighth, tying the score. And Chapman singled after Rolfe's double (which Almada dropped), Selkirk's perfect bunt and an intentional pass to Gehrig had filled the bases in the tenth.

All of which was interesting, but not half so thrilling as the sudden appearance of Ruth as a pinch hitter in the ninth when the score was tied.

The Babe, received like a returning hero when he took his position in right field at the start of the day, had retired in the last of the eighth inning of the first game. Four times he had come to bat and done nothing in response to the cheers and exhortations of the crowd. If good wishes could have turned into base hits, the Babe would have batted a thousand and every hit would have been a home run. Once he drove a terrific foul into the right-field stands. But eventually he popped up three times and was thrown out by the second baseman.

Hoag played right field in the second game. The Babe was on the bench. By the prodigious efforts of Selkirk, Hoag and Gehrig, the Yankees tied the score. Ruth was sent to pinch hit for Jorgens, the first man up in the ninth.

Recruits Spoil His Show

He emerged from the dugout swinging his bats. A cheer exploded in the stands. This sudden appearance of the Babe took on special significance. He might win the game and end the day in a blaze of glory, or he might strike out. In either case, it was definitely his last appearance of the day. The spotlight was all his.

The Babe, facing George Hockette, a recruit left-hander from Kansas City, smacked a line drive which Niemic, another recruit, caught after a leap. Retired by a couple of recruits, Babe walked toward the Yankee dugout. It was then that the crowd rose and really cheered, each person in his own way, applauding hurriedly, as if fearful of not giving enough before the Babe reached the dugout and disappeared.

The Babe, without a gesture, passed out of sight.

Gomez had a no-hit game until the fifth, when Solters beat out a grounder which Crosetti fumbled, and Reynolds singled to left. A double play ended this inning, the only one in which he was in difficulty. Gordon Rhodes, the Boston pitcher, made the third hit, a single to right in the sixth. Gomez walked only two men. No one reached third, and only one got as far as second.

Gehrig is the second American Leaguer to make more than 200 hits this year. His home run was his 201st hit of the season. Gehringer, of Detroit, was first to make 200 hits.

Selkirk was popular. He made a great catch and got five hits, including a home run, his first in the Stadium.

The Red Sox needed only two hits to make their four runs in the fifth. Ruffing walked three men and forced in the first and tying run. A fly let in another. Cooke's double drove in two. Cooke tripled in the fourth, but was left there when Ruffing walked Graham and fanned Leggett.

Yankees' Scores

FIRST GAME

BOSTON (A. L.)	ab	r	h	po	a	e
Niemic, 2b	3	0	0	2	4	0
*Bishop	0	0	0	0	0	0
Werber, 3b	4	0	0	3	2	0
Almada, cf	3	0	0	2	0	0
†Johnson	1	0	0	0	0	0
Solters, lf	3	0	1	2	1	0
Reynolds, rf	3	0	1	0	1	0
R. Ferrell, c	3	0	0	2	0	0
Morgan, 1b	3	0	0	9	1	0
Lary, ss	2	0	0	3	2	0
RHODES, p	3	0	1	1	1	0
Totals	28	0	3	24	12	0

NEW YORK (A. L.)	ab	r	h	po	a	e
Crosetti, ss	3	0	0	2	3	0
Rolfe, 3b	4	0	3	2	1	0
Ruth, rf	4	0	0	1	0	0
Hoag, rf	0	0	0	0	0	0
Gehrig, 1b	3	1	1	8	0	0
Selkirk, lf	4	0	2	3	0	0
Lazzeri, 2b	4	0	1	0	1	0
Chapman, cf	4	0	1	1	0	0
Jorgens, c	3	0	1	10	0	0
GOMEZ, p	3	0	1	0	3	0
Totals	32	1	10	27	8	0

*Batted for Niemic in ninth inning.
†Batted for Almada in ninth inning.

Boston .... 000 000 000—0
New York .... 010 000 00x—1

Run batted in—Jorgens. Two-base hit—Rolfe. Double plays—Lazzeri, Crosetti and Gehrig; Crosetti and Gehrig. Left on bases—New York, 9; Boston, 3. Bases on balls—Off Rhodes, 2; off Gomez, 2. Struck out—By Gomez, 8. Umpires—McGowan and Dinneen. Time—1:37.

SECOND GAME

BOSTON (A. L.)	ab	r	h	po	a	e
Bishop, 1b	4	1	1	12	2	0
Werber, 3b	3	1	1	1	2	0
Almada, cf	5	0	0	2	0	0
Cooke, lf	3	0	2	0	0	0
Graham, rf	4	0	1	2	0	0
Legett, c	4	0	0	5	2	0
Niemic, 2b	4	0	0	3	6	0
Lary, ss	3	0	1	2	3	0
HOCK'TE, p	4	1	1	1	0	0
Totals	34	4	6	*28	15	0

NEW YORK (A. L.)	ab	r	h	po	a	e
Crosetti, ss	5	0	0	1	3	0
Rolfe, 3b	4	1	1	2	4	0
Selkirk, lf	5	1	3	4	0	0
Gehrig, 1b	4	1	2	8	0	0
Lazzeri, 2b	4	1	1	6	1	0
Chapman, cf	4	0	2	1	0	0
Hoag, rf	3	1	2	3	0	0
Jorgens, c	2	0	1	5	1	0
†Ruth	1	0	0	0	0	0
Taylor, c	0	0	0	0	0	0
RUFFING, p	4	0	0	0	1	0
Totals	36	5	12	30	10	0

*One out when winning run was scored.
†Batted for Jorgens in ninth inning.

Boston .... 000 040 000 0—4
New York .... 010 011 010 1—5

Runs batted in—Jorgens, Werber, Almada, Cooke (2), Selkirk, Hoag, Gehrig, Chapman. Two-base hits—Cooke, Rolfe. Three-base hit—Cooke. Home runs—Selkirk, Hoag, Gehrig. Stolen bases—Rolfe, Cooke, Werber. Sacrifices—Hoag, Chapman. Double plays—Lary Niemic and Bishop; Werber and Bishop; Rolfe, Lazzeri and Gehrig. Left on bases—New York, 9; Boston, 7. Bases on balls—Off Ruffing, 7; off Hockette, 4. Struck out—By Ruffing, 4; by Hockette, 4. Umpires—Dinneen and McGowan. Time—2:05.

Nashville Wins and Ties Southern Title Series

NEW ORLEANS, Sept. 23 (AP).—Nashville's Volunteers bunched seven hits in the fourth and sixth innings today and defeated the New Orleans Pelicans, 4 to 0, squaring the series at two games apiece.

The score by innings:

				R.	H.	E.
Nashville	000	103	000	4	11	0
New Orleans ...	000	000	000	0	12	1

Batteries—Speece, Stafford and Crouch; Milnar, Messenger, Bryant and George, Autry.

Standings in Major Leagues

MONDAY, SEPTEMBER 24, 1934

American League

YESTERDAY'S RESULTS

New York, 1; Boston, 0 (1st).
New York, 5; Boston, 4 (2d).
Cleveland, 2; Chicago, 1 (1st, 10 ins.).
Cleveland, 5; Chicago, 1 (2d).
St. Louis, 4; Detroit, 3 (1st).
Detroit, 2; St. Louis, 1 (2d).
Washington, 2; Philadelphia, 1 (1st).
Washington, 5; Philadelphia, 5 (2d, darkness).

STANDING OF THE CLUBS

	Detroit	New York	Cleveland	Boston	Phila'phia	St. Louis	Washington	Chicago	Won	Lost	Percentage
Detroit	—	12	16	14	12	13	15	15	97	52	.651
New York	10	—	11	12	13	17	11	17	91	57	.615
Cleveland	6	11	—	15	13	14	11	12	82	67	.550
Boston	8	9	7	—	11	14	12	11	72	75	.490
Phila'phia	10	7	9	8	—	9	9	13	67	80	.456
St. Louis	7	5	6	8	12	—	14	14	66	82	.446
Wash'ton	7	8	11	8	10	8	—	13	65	81	.445
Chicago	4	5	7	10	9	7	9	—	51	95	.349
Gms. lost	52	57	67	75	80	82	81	95	—	—	

GAMES TODAY

Boston at New York, 3:15.
Washington at Philadelphia (2).
Other clubs not scheduled.

National League

YESTERDAY'S RESULTS

New York, 8; Boston, 0 (1st).
Boston, 4; New York, 3 (11 ins., 2d).
Philadelphia, 4; Brooklyn, 2 (1st).
Brooklyn, 7; Philadelphia, 2 (7 ins., darkness, 2d).
Chicago, 3; Pittsburgh, 2.
St. Louis, 9; Cincinnati, 7 (1st).
Cincinnati, 4; St. Louis, 3 (2d).

STANDING OF THE CLUBS

	New York	St. Louis	Chicago	Boston	Pittsburgh	Brooklyn	Phila'phia	Cincinnati	Won	Lost	Percentage
New York	—	9	10	15	14	14	15	16	93	56	.624
St. Louis	13	—	9	16	8	15	16	12	89	57	.610
Chicago	11	12	—	10	11	12	13	13	82	63	.566
Boston	7	5	12	—	9	15	10	15	73	72	.503
Pit'sburgh	8	12	7	11	—	6	13	15	72	72	.500
Brooklyn	6	7	8	5	16	—	11	13	66	80	.452
Phila'phia	5	6	9	8	7	9	—	10	54	87	.383
Cincinnati	6	6	8	7	7	9	9	—	52	94	.356
Gms. lost	56	57	63	72	72	80	87	94	—	—	

GAMES TODAY

Philadelphia at Brooklyn (2, first at 1:30).
St. Louis at Chicago.
Other clubs not scheduled.

DIZZY TAMES DETROIT; ROWE HURLS TODAY

Dorothy Traung Wins 19-Hole Battle to Advance in Women's Golf

San Francisco Chronicle Sporting Green
EDITED BY HARRY B. SMITH
CCC° SAN FRANCISCO, CAL., THURSDAY, OCTOBER 4, 1934 H 17

Tiger Club Routed by Own Errors

Jittery Detroits Say 'Excuse It, Please,' Plan Anew; Cards Pick Hallahan

By ALAN GOULD

DETROIT, Oct. 3 (AP)—The front-line of the Tiger defense, the iron-man infield that they heralded as the "battalion of death" crumbled and fell back today in wild disorder, spreading nothing but doom to Detroit's hopes as the rampant St. Louis Cardinals poured through gaping holes to sweeping victory in the first skirmish of the 1934 world championship baseball battle.

Five errors by this jittery Tiger infield in the first three innings, most of them the kind of mistakes that a sandlotter would have been ashamed of, enabled the National League champions to take quick command of the proceedings and then smash the remnants of Detroit's resistance with a powerhouse attack led by Joe Medwick, slugging outfielder who tied a world series record with four straight hits, including a home run.

DIZZY COASTS TO EASY WIN

The final score was 8 to 3, and the verdict overwhelmingly in favor of the clouting Cardinals as they coasted to victory behind the effective pitching of the celebrated Jerome Herman (Dizzy) Dean, king of the National League's pitchers, signalized the fact they are still riding the crest of the wave that carried them to a sensational, belated triumph in the pennant race over the New York Giants.

The mighty Dean, the tall gawky Oklahoman whose fireball had spread destruction throughout the National League and tossed fearsome reverberations into the Americans' camp, pitched his third full game victory within a six-day perod. With less than three days of rest since he blanked the Reds for the second time in the closing drive of the Cardinals to the top, Dean subdued the Tigers with a resourceful if not altogether brilliant exhibition.

MATES PILE UP INCREASING LEAD

The elder of the famous pair of pitching brothers lacked his customary control and yielded eight base hits, including a booming home run by Hank Greenberg in the eighth inning, but he was seldom in anything resembling real danger or called upon to bear down against the desultory Detroit attack. Dizzy had his "fire ball" when he needed it, however, and he was content largely to ride along behind the steadily increasing lead that his teammates piled up.

Against Alvin (General) Crowder, Fred (Firpo) Marberry and Elon (Big Chief) Hogsett, the Cardinals banged out 13 hits, capping the climax of the rout with a four-run drive in the sixth that chased Marberry from the box. This settled any lingering doubt about the outcome, as Dean himself led the onslaught with a rousing two-bagger, although the Tigers had already tossed away most of their chances in one of the most ragged exhibitions ever witnessed in a championship game.

Whatever chance the veteran

Continued on Page 18H, Col. 8

His Big Bat Throttled Tiger Roar

YESTERDAY'S BIG NOISE—Joe Medwick, St. Louis outfielder, was the big offensive charge as the Cards captured the first World Series tilt from Detroit.

FOUR STRAIGHT BINGLES—Medwick, connecting for four straight hits, one a homer, sent the Tiger hopes crashing as Dizzy Dean pitched an 8 to 3 triumph.

WIDE WORLD

Who's Dizzy?

St. Louis
National League

Player Pos.	AB	R	H	O	A	E
Martin, 3b	5	1	1	1	1	0
Rothrock, rf	4	0	2	0	0	0
Frisch, 2b	4	0	0	2	4	0
Medwick, lf	5	2	4	2	0	0
Collins, 1b	4	2	1	13	1	0
Delancey, c	5	0	1	7	1	0
Orsatti, cf	4	1	2	1	0	2
Fullis, cf	1	0	1	0	0	0
Durocher, s	5	0	0	0	4	0
J. Dean, p	5	2	1	1	2	0
Totals	42	8	13	27	13	2

Detroit
American League

Player Pos.	AB	R	H	O	A	E
White, cf	2	1	0	7	0	0
Cochrane, c	4	0	1	2	0	0
Gehringer, 2b	4	0	2	2	3	1
Greenberg, 1b	4	2	2	8	1	1
Goslin, lf	4	0	2	3	0	0
Rogell, s	4	0	1	1	4	1
Owen, 3b	4	0	0	2	1	2
Fox, rf	4	0	0	2	0	0
Crowder, p	1	0	0	0	0	0
Doljack	1	0	0	0	0	0
Marberry, p	0	0	0	0	1	0
Hogsett, p	1	0	0	0	1	0
Walker	1	0	0	0	0	0
Totals	34	3	8	27	11	5

Doljack batted for Crowder in 5th.
Walked batted for Hogsett in 9th.

St. Louis	0	2	1	0	1	4	0	0	0	—8
Detroit	0	0	1	0	0	1	0	1	0	—3

Runs batted in—Rothrock 2, Delancey 2, Medwick 2, Martin 1, Gehringer 1, Goslin 1, Greenberg 1. Two-base hits—J. Dean, Delancey. Home runs—Medwick, Greenberg. Sacrifices—Rothrock, Frisch. Double play—Delancey to Frisch. Left on bases—St. Louis 10, Detroit 6. Bases on balls—Off J. Dean 2 (White 2), Crowder 1 (Collins). Struck out—By J. Dean 6 (Rogell, Owen 2, Greenberg, White, Walker), Crowder 1 (Martin), Hogsett 1 (J. Dean). Hits—Off Crowder 6 in 5 innings, Marberry 4 in 2-3 inning, Hogsett 3 in 3 1-3 innings. Losing pitcher—Crowder. Umpires—Owen (American League), plate; Klem (National League), first base; Geisel (American League), second base; Reardon (National League), third base. Time of game—2h. 13m.

World Series Statistics

By Associated Press

STANDINGS

	W.	L.	Pct.
St. Louis (NL)	1	0	1.000
Detroit (AL)	0	1	.000

RESULTS

First game	R.	H.	E.
St. Louis (NL)	8	13	2
Detroit (AL)	3	8	5

Batteries—J. Dean and Delancey; Crowder, Marberry, Hogsett and Cochrane.

Total attendance	42,505
Gross receipts	$139,643.00
Commissioner's share	20,946.45
Players' pool	71,217.93
Each league's share	11,869.95
Each club's share	11,869.95

Caddell, Ebding Cheer Bronco Star in Vain

——By BILL MASON——
Special to The Chronicle

NAVIN FIELD, Detroit, Mich., Oct. 3—St. Mary's and Stanford rooted hard for Santa Clara at Navin Field here today. But it didn't do any good. Harry Ebding, former star for Slip Madigan, and Ernie Caddell, Stanford back, were at the ball park to cheer for Marvin Owen, Santa Clara boy. But Northern California didn't do so well. With the rest of the "Battalion of Death" Tiger infield Owen had a bad case of the jitters in the early part of the game.

One of his two errors was turned into a St. Louis run. At bat he didn't get the ball out of the infield and struck out twice. Southern California did better. Ernie Orsatti, who limped around the field until relieved by Fullis, scored the first Cardinal run. He contributed the only two errors, however, in the Cardinal defense, but his two hits offset his fielding blunders.

Jack Rothrock singled to center in the second, driving home Orsatti and Dean singled again in the eighth. So the day goes to the south. Caddell and Ebding say they will be out again tomorrow to lend Owen a helping cheer

Henry Ford and Walter P. Chrysler occupied boxes when Hank Greenberg socked one into the left field bleachers with his famous floating power swing. Mr. Chrysler smiled broadly.

'Some Pitcher,' Says Schoolboy Of Dizzy Dean

NAVIN FIELD, Detroit, Oct. 3 (AP)—Lynwood Schoolboy Rowe, who will start for Detroit in Thursday's game against the St. Louis Cardinals, has seen Dizzy Dean pitch—and thinks he's "some pitcher."

The ace of the Tigers' hurling staff didn't think that the sensational Dean had "the stuff" today, even though he had little trouble subduing the Tigers.

"He looked tired and it seemed to me he didn't have much stuff after the third inning," said Rowe. "I mean he wasn't as good today as he has been or could be.

Lutze, Savoldi On Mat Card

A consistent winner with his hammerlock and wristlocks Nick Lutze, former Venice life guard, will have the chance of trying them out on "Jumping" Joe Savoldi, drop kick and flying tackle exponent, next Tuesday night at the Dreamland Auditorium.

Lutze and Savoldi will clash in a two-hour, best two-in-three-falls match.

Lutze beat Ivan Managoff, and Bob Kruse in his two last engagements on the Dreamland mat, using the hammerlock in each instance. Savoldi drop-kicked his way to a decisive victory over Abe Kaplan;

Blower Fit To Play in Two Weeks

Medicos Pass on Star Quarterback of Bear Squad

Floyd Blower, California's most famous football sick man, will positively rejoin the Bear team on October 15, it was announced yesterday after physicians had given him a thorough going over. A complete check showed his ailment, a kidney injury, to be a temporary condition. All parental objection to Blower's playing has also been removed, California authorities announced.

Blower will begin his workouts on October 15, and may be ready for a game the following Saturday. He was considered a regular quarterback until his sickness.

Get a Divorce, Become Slugger, Says Card Star

LOS ANGELES, Oct. 3 (AP)—One way apparently of becoming a .300 hitter on a pennant-winning baseball club:

Get a divorce.

At least that's what Ernie Orsatti did. He's the Los Angeles boy who played center field today for the St. Louis Cardinals as they squared off at Detroit against the Tigers in the opening tilt of the baseball classic.

In 1933 Orsatti's batting average was .298. He smacked the old apple this year for a .301 average.

In his successful petition for a divorce from Martha O. Orsatti, it was recalled today, filed here early this year, it was declared:

"That the business of the plaintiff is of such a nature that it requires him to be in good physical and mental condition in order to properly perform his work and that the actions and course of conduct of the defendant during the married life of the parties has made him highly nervous and upset, so that he has been unable to properly perform his work."

World Series Odds Quoted By Jack Doyle

DETROIT, Oct. 3—The odds for the remainder of the world series, based on the result of the first game, are quoted as follows by Jack Doyle, nationally known betting authority:

ENTIRE SERIES
Against St. Louis—1 to 2.
Against Detroit—8 to 5.

SECOND GAME
Against St. Louis—9 to 10.
Against Detroit—9 to 10.

NEXT TWO GAMES IN SUCCESSION
Against St. Louis—2½ to 1.
Against Detroit—3 to 1.

Bets on a single game are void in the event of a tie.

Slip Madigan Banking On Reserve Strength to Defeat Bears Saturday

St. Mary's Coach Names Two Teams to Face California Squad; Proposed Strategy Similar to Last Year's Gael Plan

By PRESCOTT SULLIVAN

ST. MARY'S COLLEGE, Oct. 3—The thing that beat them last year is going to win for the Galloping Gaels next Saturday in the California Memorial Stadium.

Yes, siree. I found it out all by myself today.

Slip Madigan, the old maetsro of the Moraga Hills, is going to beat California with reserve strength.

People who saw the St. Mary's-California game of last year will never believe it, I know, but it must be true because Madigan says it's so.

As I recall it, the Gaels were leading California, 13-0, at one happy stage of last year's contest when Madigan decided that the slaughter had gone far enough and that it was time to exercise his substitutes.

Forthwith he yanked big John Yezerski, a tackle, and big Ed Gilbert, a guard, out of his line and replaced them with apprentice labor. The Bears went from there and they didn't stop until they had whipped the Gaels, 14-13.

But now Madigan is back with a similar plan of strategy and after his painful experience of last year I'm just a little bit surprised at the old maestro's behavior.

He's going to fight California not with one team, but with two of them, and if by chance one is as good as the other the plan should work out all right.

"Slip" Madigan
Repeats Strategy

On the other hand, if Madigan's

Continued on Page 20H, Col. 4

Lewis Listless, Held to Draw By Reds Barry

By HARRY B. SMITH
Chronicle Sports Editor

John Henry Lewis fought his third palooka in a row last night at the Civic Auditorium.

And the palooka, who is Reds Barry of Washington, D. C., fought a draw with the Arizona colored boy. Lewis may have had a slight shade on the rounds, but it was nothing to brag about and the crowd took Referee Toby Irwin's decision as the right sort.

The fans, who only a few months ago thought Lewis was headed for the light heavy weight championship, doubted tonight whether he could win again from Maxie Rosenbloom if they meet again. Certainly not the way Lewis was fighting last night.

The Negro's judgment of distance was absolutely lacking and his punch seemed a minus quantity. What is more, he couldn't stand off the rushes of Barry and it was Lewis who was tiring badly at the end of the 10 rounds. Barry is nothing than a willing worker, strong and capable of mixing things.

SCANTY CROWD SEES OFFERING

His short arm jolts to the body were the best punches he had. For big men they fought remarkably fast, particularly in the tenth round. The trouble with Barry seemed to be his piano legs, his open hand punching and his pawing efforts to land tellingly.

The main disappointment was in Lewis' failure to do better. Only a few weeks ago John Henry won from Norman Conrad in the same ring, but won no medals. More recently he was given a draw in Portland with young Firpo. Barry had an advantage of 22 pounds, tipping the beam at 200, as against 178 for Lewis.

The crowd was scanty. The net receipts ran to $895, so Lewis will gather in less than $225 for himself. All told, there were less than 1400 paid spectators.

The shade certainly belonged to Lewis. I handed him five rounds, with three for Barry by a shade and two even.

RAY ACTIS WINS BY TECHNICAL KAYO

Ray Actis ended the scheduled six-round semiwindup against Walter Kirkwood, from the Pop Goodwin stable in the second round with a long, looping left hook to the jaw. Kirkwood went to the mat, the rope saving him from a hard fall. As he stood up, Actis sent in another left and Referee Irwin stopped the fight.

Vincent Morris, colored 128 pounder, won by a third round technical knockout over Tony Genaro in the scheduled four-round curtain raiser. Morris scored a knockdown in the first round with a right to the head. After that the fight was onesided. Referee Toby Irwin stopped the fight when the gong sounded the end of the third round.

Bob Frazer, likewise colored, and Walter Skinner went four rounds to a draw. Frazer registered a first round knockdown, Skinner taking the count of nine.

Christy Lewis, brother of John Henry, landed a left uppercut in the first round on Curley Muniz's mouth that cut Muniz's lip and caused Irwin to stop the fight then and there. Muniz dropped from the punch and came up bleeding. That ended a fight supposed to have gone four rounds.

After Muniz went to his dressing room for treatment, it developed his jaw had been broken when Christy hit him.

S. F. Woman Star Beats Marion Lake

Virginia Van Wie Puts on Garrison Finish to Capture the Third Round Match

By BOB CAVAGNARO
Associated Press Sports Writer

PHILADELPHIA, Oct. 3 (AP)—With favored players falling on all sides, Virginia Van Wie of Chicago, the defending champion, today put on a Garrison finish to win her third-round match in the women's national golf championship and avert what would have been the most sensational upset of them all.

The Chicago holder of the championship for the past two years played the best golf she ever had to quell the onrushing Rosamond Vahey, gray-eyed Boston bridge expert and Massachusetts' State champion in 1931, one up on the 19th hole.

Two down after the 15th, Miss Van Wie on the 140-yard 16th hole with a birdie two, squared the match by taking the 17th with another birdie four and then, after halving the 18th, won the match on the first extra hole with a sub par three. It was a brilliant effort shooting the last four holes in three under perfect figures.

MISS TRAUNG AGAIN SCORES SURPRISE

Dorothy Traung, the 20-year-old San Francisco shot maker, survived the session at the expense of Marion Turpie Lake of New York, former southern champion. Mrs. Lake was

Continued on Page 20H, Col. 1

EXTRA

ASSASSINATE BALKAN KING

☆ ☆ ☆ ☆ ☆ ☆ ☆ ☆ ☆ ☆ ☆ ☆ ☆ ☆ ☆ ☆ ☆

French Minister, 2 Generals Slain in France

WEATHER
CALIFORNIA FORECASTS
San Francisco—Fair tonight and Wednesday.
Los Angeles—Fair tonight and Wednesday.
MEAN TEMPERATURES

San Francisco	67	Chicago	68
Los Angeles	74	Detroit	63
Seattle	63	Boston	59
Omaha	75	Washington	64
New York	63	Atlanta	73

NRA MEMBER U.S. WE DO OUR PART

THE CALL SAN FRANCISCO BULLETIN
AN INDEPENDENT NEWSPAPER

CALL AND POST, VOL. 136, NO. 69
THE CALL-BULLETIN, VOL. 156, NO. 69
SAN FRANCISCO, TUESDAY, OCTOBER 9, 1934
3c DAILY 75c a Month

HOME
N.Y. STOCKS
COMPLETE

RIOT AT SERIES; CARDS WIN

REPORT YUGOSLAVIA TO MOBILIZE ARMY AS KING, 3 OTHERS SLAIN

MARSEILLE, Oct. 9 (INS).—A Croatian assassin, with a pistol in each hand and a time bomb in his pocket, murdered King Alexander of Yugoslavia by design today and at the same time killed Foreign Minister Louis Barthou of France and two high military officials.

The last two victims were General Goerges of the French supreme war council and General Alexander Dimitrijivitch, marshal of the Yugoslavian court.

Admiral Berthelot, one of the highest ranking officers of the French navy, was seriously wounded.

The four deaths, comprising the worst mass assassination of leading figures in history, occurred when Kalemen Petrus, a Croat, jumped on the running board of the automobile carrying King Alexander and Barthou.

VIENAN, Oct. 9 (AP).—Unconfirmed rumors stated tonight that the Yugoslav government intends to order an immediate mobilization of its army on the Italian and Hungarian frontiers.

MARSEILLE, Oct. 9 (AP).—King Alexander of Yugoslavia and Louis Barthou, foreign minister of France, were assassinated today as the Yugoslav monarch came to France in an effort to improve Yugoslav-French relations.

The king and the minister were shot down as they rode in an automobile, receiving the cheers of the population, through the flag-bedecked streets of Marseille.

The assassin was wounded and captured, but died several hours later.

The police found five persons in the crowd, in-

Continued on Page Four, Col. Five

Fear Uprising in Yugoslav Capital

BELGRADE, Yugoslavia, Oct. 9 (AP).—Confusion gripped government offices today when news of King Alexander's assassination reached here.

Officials wept openly as telephones rang throughout the government buildings calling department leaders into conference.

Fear was expressed that the king's death might be the signal for an uprising instigated by groups, especially Crotians, which have always opposed his authoritarian rule.

Most observers seemed agreed, however, that the army, excellently organized, would be able to maintain order until a regency was arranged to exercise executive powers until Crown Prince Peter II reaches his majority.

Although unpopular, General Zivkovich is regarded as the strongest man in the country.

One Serbian official declared that Alexander's death, far from endangering the country, will have the effect of drawing various branches of the Yugoslav people together to face the dangers from without.

All members of the government closely associated with the Slav monarch were far too moved to give their opinions of the possible interna-

Continued on Page Four, Col. Two

KILLED IN FRANCE

King Alexander I of Yugoslavia, who was shot and killed today in Marseille as he arrived in France on a visit planned to cement relations between the nations.

WITNESS SAW BRUNO IN N. J.

TRENTON, N. J., Oct. 9 (AP).—An unidentified witness, who has definitely placed Bruno Richard Hauptmann, under indictment for murder in the kidnaping of Charles A. Lindbergh Jr., at the scene of the crime, has been found by New Jersey authorities, Governor A. Harry Moore disclosed today.

NEW YORK, Oct. 9 (AP.—Bruno Richard Hauptmann's shouted replies of "hey, doctor," to questions of District Attorney Samuel J. Foley brought about Colonel Charles A. Lindbergh's identification of the prisoner's voice as that of the man whom Dr. John F. Condon paid the $50,000 Lindbergh ransom.

Foley disclosed today that the identification of the voice, announced in Trenton, N. J., by Colonel H. Norman Schwarzkopf, head of the New

Continued on Page Four, Col. Four

'No Wedding Bells,' Says Esther Ralston

HOLLYWOOD, Oct. 9 (INS).—Esther Ralston, beautiful screen actress, today emphatically denied that she plans to wed Will Morgan, New York stage actor.

Miss Ralston declared "no wedding bells for me," and then pointed out that it will be some time before she receives her final divorce decree from George Webb, Hollywood film agent.

Call-Bulletin Special Features

RIOT HALTS 7TH SERIES GAME

Fans Pelt Medwick With Fruit and Buns After Alleged Spiking

DETROIT, Oct. 9.—Detroit fans broke out in a frenzied riot in the sixth inning of today's world series final, causing Judge Landis to intervene and rule Joe Medwick, Card outfielder, out of the game to avert possible injuries from the spectators.

It started when the fans thought Medwick spiked Marvin Owen while sliding into third base.

SHOWER OF FRUIT

A barrage of fruit showered the field and a crew of workmen was mustered to clear away the debris.

This barrage lasted several minutes, and just as matters seemed to subside spectator reinforcements arrived with a fresh supply of buns and hot dogs.

Then came a shower of pop bottles. Manager Mickey Cochrane rushed out to the pitcher's box, held up his hands for silence and pleaded with the Tiger fans to restore order.

The hubbub continued and finally Judge Landis went into conference with Managers Frish and Cochrane.

POLICE CALLED

Play had now been suspended for nearly fifteen minutes and a riot call had been turned in at police headquarters.

Landis decided to remove Medwick from the game to appease the irate Tiger fans. After his decision the Card players swarmed about the baseball commission, protesting his action and demanding that the game be forfeited.

Chick Fullis went out to left field in Medwick's place. The Tiger fans seemed satisfied and the game went on.

WAVES 25 FEET HIGH AT BEACH

Roaring a pagan orchestration, giant waves—foam-crested rollers 25 feet high and breaking as far as nine miles out—pounded in fury off the Golden Gate and threatened damage along the beach today.

The weird phenomenon, caused possibly by the earth shakes last week, brought thousands of spectators to watch as the rollers lashed the shore.

From the Cliff House to Fleishhacker Zoo, even at ebb-tide, the waves swept up within 50 feet of the concrete walled breakwater, strewing the beach sands with tin cans, bottles, driftwood and seaweed.

Boatswain Howard Underhill, in charge of the Golden Gate coast guard station, reported that the freak waves were the highest ever seen at this time of the year.

"They're breaking 20 to 30 feet high in about a four-mile arc known as the Potato Patch—from Fort Funston, around the San Francisco lightship, to Point Bonita," he said.

CARDS MAKE 7 RUNS IN THIRD

'Dizzy' Dean Gets Two Hits As 13 Men Bat in One Inning

NAVIN FIELD, Oct. 9 (AP).—The Cardinals staged one of the greatest rallies in world series history today to score seven runs in the third inning for Jerome Herman ("Dizzy") Dean and pile up an all but invincible lead over the battered Tigers in the seventh and deciding game of the series.

Dean got a double and a single in the inning that brought thirteen Cardinals to bat.

The Cards led, 11 to 0, in the eighth.

FIRST INNING

Cardinals—Martin fanned. Rothrock hit sharply over Rogell's head and ran to second when White handled the ball poorly. The scorer credited Rothrock with a two bagger. Frisch lifted a short fly that Rogell caught. Medwick fouled to Owen. No runs, one hit, no errors, one left.

Tigers—White grounded out, Frisch to Collins. Cochrane grounded out, Frisch to Collins. Gehringer lifted a high fly to Rothrock. No runs, no hits, no errors, none left.

SECOND INNING

Cardinals—Collins hit sharply to center for a single. Delancey grounded to Owen and the Tigers pulled a double play, Owen to Gehringer to Greenberg. Orsatti singled past Gehringer. Orsatti was thrown out trying to steal, Cochrane to Gehringer. No runs, two hits, no errors, none left.

Tigers—Goslin bounced to Collins and was out at first, Collins to Dean. Rogell bounced to Durocher, but was safe at first when Collins failed to hold the shortstop's low throw. Greenberg fanned. Owen bounced to Martin and Rogell was forced at second, Martin to Frisch. No runs, no hits, one error, one left.

THIRD INNING

Cardinals—Durocher flied to White. Dean dropped a hit in left field and stretched it to a double as Goslin handled the ball slowly. Martin hit to Greenberg and beat it out for a scratch hit. Martin stole second. Rothrock walked. Frisch hit sharply into right field for a double, scoring Dean, Martin and Rothrock. Cochrane removed Auker from the box and summoned Schoolboy Rowe. Medwick grounded out, Rogell to Greenberg. Collins singled sharply through the infield, scoring Frisch. Delancey smashed a long drive to the right field wall for a double, scoring Collins. Rowe was taken out of the box and was replaced by Elon Hogsett, the Indian southpaw. Orsatti walked. Durocher hit to right for a single and the bases were full.

Dean hit a grounder along third base line for a scratch hit, scoring Delancey and leaving the bases still full. Martin walked. Orsatti was forced over the plate with the seventh Cardinal run in the inning. Hogsett was taken out of the box. Tommy Bridges, slim right-hander who pitched the Tigers to a brilliant victory over Dizzy Dean last Sunday at St. Louis, was the fourth Detroit pitcher. Rothrock grounded to Gehringer and Martin was forced at second, Gehringer to Rogell. Seven runs, seven hits, no errors, three left.

Tigers—Fox lined to Orsatti. Bridges was thrown out by Frisch at first. White flied to Orsatti. No runs, no hits, no errors, none left.

FOURTH INNING

Cardinals—Frisch grounded sharply to Gehringer and was tossed out at first. Medwick flied to Fox. Collins dropped his third straight hit into right field for a single. Delancey bounced to Gehringer and Collins was forced at second, Gehringer to Rogell. No runs, one hit, no errors, one left.

Tigers—Cochrane popped to Frisch. Gehringer smashed a single to right. Goslin hoisted a short fly to Medwick. Rogell grounded to Frisch and Gehringer was forced at second, Frisch to Durocher. No runs, one hit, no errors, one left.

FIFTH INNING

Cardinals—Orsatti flied to Goslin. Durocher lifted another high fly to Goslin. Dean fanned. No runs, no hits, no errors, none left.

Tigers—Greenberg pumped a long single to right center. Owen flied to Rothrock. Fox hit sharply to left for a double, sending Greenberg to third. Bridges fanned. White bounced to Durocher and was thrown out at first. No runs, two hits, no errors, two left.

SIXTH INNING

Cardinals—Martin slashed a hit to left and stretched it to two bases on Goslin's poor handling of the ball. Rothrock flied to Goslin. Frisch flied to White. Medwick pumped a long hit against the right field bleachers for a triple, scoring Martin. Collins belted his fourth straight hit to center, scoring Medwick. Collins ran to second when White fumbled the ball for an error. Delancey swung and missed a third strike, but Cochrane dropped the ball and threw to Greenberg to retire the batsman. Two runs, three hits, two errors.

Tigers—Cochrane lined to Rothrock. Gehringer was thrown out on a hopper to Durocher. Goslin lifted a high foul to Collins. No runs, no hits, no errors, none left.

SEVENTH INNING

Cardinals—Orsatti lifted a long fly to W[illegible]. Durocher pounded a triple against the bleacher wall in right center. Dean bounced out, Owen to Greenberg. Martin grounded to Gehringer and Durocher scored while Pepper reached first safely on Gehringer's fumble. Rothrock hit to the bleacher barrier in left center, scoring Martin and pulling up at second for a two-base hit. Frisch flied deep to Fox. Two runs, two hits, one error, one left.

Tigers—Rogell popped to Durocher. Greenberg fanned. Owen grounded out, Frisch to Collins. No runs, no hits, no errors, none left.

EIGHTH INNING

Cardinals—Marberry went to the box for the Tigers. Fullis lashed a hit past Rogell for a single. Collins lined out to Fox. Delancey sent a hopper through the box and was thrown out at first, Gehringer to Greenberg. Orsatti walked. Durocher grounded to Rogell and Orsatti was forced at seco[illegible] Rogell to Gehringer. No ru[illegible] hit, no errors, two left.

BASEBALL

	1	2	3	4	5	6	7	8	9	R
St. Louis....	0	0	7	0	0	2	2	0	0	11
Detroit......	0	0	0	0	0	0	0	0	0	0

St. Louis	ab	r	h	po	a	e	Detroit..	ab	r	h	po	a	e
Martin 3b..	5	3	2	0	1	0	White cf...	4	0	0	3	0	1
Rothrock rf.	5	1	2	4	0	0	Cochrane c.	4	0	0	3	2	0
Frisch 2b..	5	1	1	3	5	0	Gehringer 2b	4	0	2	3	4	1
Medwick lf	4	1	1	0	0	0	Goslin lf.	4	0	0	4	0	1
Collins 1b	4	1	4	8	2	1	Rogell ss..	4	0	1	3	2	0
Delancey c.	4	1	1	4	0	0	Greenberg 1b	4	0	1	7	0	0
Orsatti cf..	3	1	1	2	0	0	Owen 3b...	4	0	0	1	2	0
Dorocher ss	5	1	2	2	3	0	Fox rf.....	3	0	2	3	0	0
J, Dean p..	5	1	2	1	0	0	Auker p....	1	0	0	0	0	0
Fullis lf...	1	0	1	1	0	0	Rowe p....	0	0	0	0	0	0
	0	0	0	0	0	0	Hogsett p..	0	0	0	0	0	0
	0	0	0	0	0	0	Bridges p..	1	0	0	0	0	0
	0	0	0	0	0	0	Crowder p.	0	0	0	0	0	0
Totals	41	11	17	27	11	1	Totals	33	0	6	27	10	3

CARDS-TIGERS—Add 8th Inn., Cont. From Below

TIGERS—Fox doubled. Walker, batting for Marberry, flied to Fullis. White fanned. Cochrane fouled to Rothrock. 0r, 1h, 0e

9TH INN.: CARDS—Crowder in box for Tigers. Dean flied to Goslin. Martin fouled to Greenberg. Rothrock fanned. 0r, 0h, 0e. TIGERS—Gehringer singled to left. Goslin forced Gehringer, Collins to Durocher. Rogell singled. Greenberg fanned. Owen grounded to Durocher and Rogell was forced, Durocher to Frisch. 0r, 2h, 0e.

JAPAN PIRATES SACK ISLE

LONDON, Oct. 9 (INS).—Thirty-five members of the crew of a Japanese ship turned Pirate, raided and sacked the British island of Haggerstone, 125 miles from Thursday Island, between Australia and New Guinea, says a dispatch in the London Daily Herald from Brisbane, Australia, today.

JUGO-SLAVIA KING, FRENCH MINISTER ASSASSINATED (DETAILS ON PAGE OF NEWS SECTION)

TODAY'S RACING RESULTS

NIGHT SPORT SPECIAL

ST. LOUIS POST-DISPATCH

The Only Evening Newspaper in St. Louis With the Associated Press News Service

PAGES 1—4B | ST. LOUIS, TUESDAY, OCTOBER 9, 1934. | PRICE 2 CENTS.

CARDINALS WIN SERIES

CROWD OF 40,902 SEES SEVENTH GAME

FRISCH HITS DOUBLE TO SCORE 3 IN 7-RUN RALLY

By a Staff Correspondent of the Post-Dispatch.

DETROIT, Oct. 9.—The seventh and deciding game of the world series attracted a crowd of 40,902 which was almost 4000 smaller than Monday's crowd. The receipts for the seventh game were $138,063.

With the usual police escort, and Dizzy Dean leading the parade wearing a tropical sun helmet, the Cardinals left Navin Field, boarding busses which carried them to their hotel downtown.

There were a few cries of "Where is Medwick?" and some fans shouted derisive words at the Cardinal outfielder involved in the controversy with Marvin Owen at third base, but for the most part the several thousand who watched the players leave were orderly.

Dean smiled and joked with the crowd which lined the corridors to the Cardinals' dressing room.

Medwick, a brown felt hat sloughed over his eyes and a topcoat muffled about his ears, was recognized by few as he left the park.

Frankie Frisch, the Fordham flash, and the fiery manager of the Cardinals, lived up to his reputation as one of the greatest "money" players in baseball.

In the third inning with the bases filled, Frankie cracked a double to right, clearing the bases. He made the smash off Elden Auker, the underhanded righthander.

The blow knocked Auker out of the box, and he was replaced by Schoolboy Rowe, who failed to finish the inning, and Elon Hogsett, Indian southpaw, was the third Detroit pitcher of the inning. It took Bridges, the fourth Tiger hurler, to stop the Redbirds and end the inning.

DEMPSEY SPURNS OFFER TO FIGHT LUIS FIRPO

WATERLOO, Ia., Oct. 9.—Casually waving aside an offer of $100,000, Jack Dempsey, former heavyweight boxing champion, told fans here that he will not go to South America to meet Luis Firpo, now attempting a comeback, in a four-round bout.

Dempsey has received an offer for that amount from South American promoters handling Firpo, whom Dempsey once knocked out after one of the greatest slugging fests of all time.

Jack, however, says, "I can make more money on these officiating tours," and, besides, with a new baby, he doesn't want to leave home for so long.

LETOURNER AND DEBAETS LEAD IN BIKE RACE

DETROIT, Oct. 9.—The veteran team of Alfred Letourner and Gerald Debaets today held the lead over a fast traveling field at the end of the thirty-fifth hour of Detroit's third international bike race.

In second place were Norman Hill and William Grimm, followed by Reggie McNamara and Dave Lands.

	Miles.	Laps.	Points.
Letourner-Debaets	668	9	129
Hill-Grimm	668	9	89
McNamara-Lands	668	9	68
Vermeersch-Boilaert	668	6	112
Martinetti-Raboli	668	6	64
Wissel-Duelberg	668	6	54
Spencer-Garrison	668	5	99
Rys-Logghe	668	5	77
Schaller-Walthour	668	5	75
Trieste-Rodman	568	5	67
Dempsery-Thomas	668	3	104
Silver-Cohen	668	0	100

Big Linemen.

Texas Christian University has another big line. Lester weighs 220, Truelson 245, Hill 260 and Groskloss

"YOU CAN'T BEAT US DEANS"

DIZZY. PAUL.

The Game, Play-by-Play

By the Associated Press.

FIRST INNING — CARDINALS Martin struck out. Rothrock doubled to center. Frisch popped to Rogell. Medwick fouled to Owen.

TIGERS—White was out, Frisch to Collins. Cochrane was out the same way. Gehringer flied to Rothrock.

SECOND — CARDINALS — Collins singled to center. De Lancey hit into a double play, Owen to Gehringer to Greenberg. Orsatti singled past Gehringer. Orsatti was out stealing, Cochrane to Gehringer.

TIGERS—Goslin grounded to Collins and was out, Collins to J. Dean. Rogell was safe when Collins dropped Durocher's throw of his grounder. Greenberg struck out. Owen forced Rogell, Martin to Frisch.

THIRD — CARDINALS — Durocher flied to White. J. Dean doubled to left. Martin beat out a hit to Greenberg, J. Dean going to third. Martin stole second. Roth- walked, filling the bases. Frisch doubled to right, scoring J. Dean, Martin and Rothrock. Auker was taken from the box and Rowe went in to pitch for the Tigers. Medwick was out, Rogell to Greenberg, Frisch going to third. Collins singled to left, scoring Frisch. De Lancey doubled to right, scoring Collins. Rowe was taken out and Hogsett became the Tigers' third pitcher. Orsatti walked. Durocher singled to right and the bases were filled. J. Dean singled along the third base line, scoring De Lancey. Martin walked, forcing in Orsatti with the seventh run of the inning. Hogsett was taken out and Bridges went in to pitch for the Tigers. Rothrock forced Martin, Gehringer to Rogell. SEVEN RUNS.

TIGERS—Fox lined to Orsatti. Bridges was out, Frisch to Collins. White flied to Orsatti.

FOURTH—CARDINALS—Frisch was out, Gehringer to Greenberg. Medwick flied to Fox. Collins singled to right for his third straight hit. De Lancey forced Collins at second, Gehringer to Rogell.

TIGERS—Cochrane popped to Frisch. Gehringer singled to right for the first hit off Dean. Goslin flied to Medwick. Rogell forced Gehringer, Frisch to Durocher.

FIFTH — CARDINALS—Orsatti flied to Goslin. Durocher also flied to Goslin. J. Dean struck out.

TIGERS—Greenberg singled to right. Owen flied to Rothrock. Fox doubled to left, sending Greenberg to third. Bridges was called out on strikes. White was out, Durocher to Collins.

SIXTH — CARDINALS — Martin singled to left and went to second when Goslin fumbled. Rothrock flied to Goslin. Frisch flied to White. Medwick tripled to right, scoring Martin. Collins singled to center for his fourth successive hit, scoring Medwick. Collins took second on the throw home. De Lancey struck out, but had to be thrown out, Cochrane to Greenberg. TWO RUNS.

TIGERS — Fullis replaced Medwick in left field for the Cardinals. Cochrane lined to Rothrock. Gehringer was out, Durocher to Collins. Goslin fouled to Collins.

SEVENTH — CARDINALS—Orsatti flied to White. Durocher tripled to right. J. Dean was out Owen to Greenberg, Durocher holding third. Martin was safe on Gehringer's fumble, Durocher scoring. Martin stole second. Rothrock doubled to left-center, scoring Martin. Frisch flied to Fox. TWO RUNS.

TIGERS—Rogell popped to Durocher. Greenberg struck out. Owen was out, Frisch to Collins.

EIGHTH — CARDINALS—Marberry went in to pitch for the Tigers. Fullis singled to center. Collins lined to Fox. De Lancey was out, Gehringer to Greenberg. Orsatti walked. Durocher forced Orsatti, Rogell to Gehringer.

TIGERS—Fox doubled to left. Walker batted for Marberry and flied to Fullis. White struck out. Cochrane fouled to Rothrock.

NINTH — CARDINALS—Crowder went in to pitch for the Tigers. He was the sixth pitcher for Detroit during the game. J. Dean flied to Goslin. Martin fouled to Greenberg. Rothrock struck out.

TIGERS—Gehringer singled to left. Goslin forced Gehringer, Collins to Durocher. Rogell singled past Frisch. Greenberg struck out. Owen forced Rogell, Durocher to Frisch.

SERIES FACTS

FINAL STANDINGS.

	W.	L.	Pct.
Cardinals	4	3	.571
Tigers	3	4	.429

RESULTS.

FIRST GAME.

Club.	R.	H.	E.
St. Louis (Nat. League)	8	13	2
Detroit (Am. League)	3	8	5

Batteries—St. Louis (National League): J. Dean and De Lancey; Detroit (American League): Crowder, Marberry, Hogsett and Cochrane.

Total attendance, 42,505.
Gross receipts, $139,643.
Commissioner's share, $20,946.45.
Player's pool, $71,217.93.
Each league's share, $11,869.95.
Each club's share, $11,869.95.

SECOND GAME.

Club.	R.	H.	E.
St. Louis (Nat. League)	2	7	3
Detroit (Am. League)	3	7	0

Batteries; St. Louis (National League—Hallahan, Walker and De Lancey. Detroit (American League)—Rowe and Cochrane.

Total attedance, 43,451.
Gross receipts, $140,827.
Commissioner's share, $21,124.05.
Players' share, $71,821.77.
Each league's share, $11,970.29.
Each club's share, $11,970.29.

THIRD GAME.

Club.	R.	H.	E.
St. Louis (Nat. League)	4	9	1
Detroit (Am. League)	1	8	2

Batteries: St. Louis—P. Dean and De Lancey; Detroit—Bridges, Hogsett and Cochrane.

Total attendance, 34,073.
Gross receipts, $148,313.
Commissioner's share, $22,246.95.
Players' share, $75,639.63.
Each league's share, $12,606.60.
Each club's share, $12,606.60.

FOURTH GAME.

St. Louis (Nat. League) 4-10-5
Detroit (Amer. League) 10-13-1

Batteries: St. Louis—Carleton, Vance, Walker, Haines, Mooney and De Lancey; Detroit—Auker and Cochrane.

Paid attendance, 37,492.
Gross receipts, $158,836.
Commissioner's share, $23,825.40.
Players' pool, $81,006.36.
Each club's share, $13,501.06.
Each league's share, $13,501.06.

FIFTH GAME.

Club.	R.	H.	E.
St. Louis Nat. League	1	7	1
Detroit (Am. League)	3	7	0

Batteries: St. Louis—J. Dean, Carleton and De Lancey; Detroit—Bridges and Cochrane.

Paid attendance, 38,536.
Gross receipts, $161,998.
Commissioner's share, $24,299.85.
Each league's share, $34,424.78.
Each club's share, $34,424.78.

SIXTH GAME.

	R.	H.	E.
St. Louis (Nat. League)	4	10	2
Detroit (Amer. League)	3	7	1

Batteries: St. Louis (Nat. League)—P. Dean and DeLancey; Detroit (Amer. League)—Rowe and Cochrane.

Paid attendance, 44,551.
Gross receipts, $143,660.00.
Commissioner's share, $21,549.00
Each league's share, $30,527.50.
Each club's share, $30,527.50.

SEVENTH GAME.

	R.	H.	E.
St. Louis (Nat. League)	11	17	1
Detroit (Amer. League)	0	6	3

Batteries: St. Louis—J. Dean and DeLancey; Detroit—Auker, Rowe, Hogsett, Bridges, Marberry, Crowder and Cochrane, Hayworth.

Paid attendance, 40,902.
Gross receipts, $138,063.00.
Commissioner's share, $20,709.45.
Each league's share, $29,338.39.
Each club's share, $29,338.39.

TOTAL SERIES STATISTICS.

Paid attendance, 281,510.
Gross receipts, $1,031,341.00.
Commissioner's share, $154,811.15.
*Players' pool, $299,785.69.
Each league's share, $144,238.57.
Each club's share, $144,238.57.
*Players' shares in first four games only.

DIZZY DEAN WINS AGAIN, 11-0; FANS, THROWING AT MEDWICK, FORCE HIS REMOVAL FROM FIELD

By J. Roy Stockton
Of the Post-Dispatch Sports Staff.

DETROIT, Oct. 9.—The Cardinals are champions of the world and Dizzy Dean and his brother Paul can have the City of St. Louis and throw the key away. Dizzy held the Detroit Tigers to six hits this afternoon, and scored his second triumph and the Dean family's fourth of the series as he shutout the American League pennant winners, 11 to 0, in the seventh and concluding game of the struggle.

It was the fifth championship competition in nine years for the St. Louis National League team and the third time the club gained the game's highest honors.

Fans' Outbreak Mars Game.

The game was marred by a disorderly outbreak in the left-field bleachers and hundreds of apples, oranges, grapefruit, bananas and milk and soda bottles twere thrown on the field in the general direction of Joe Medwick because of a display of temper by the Cardinal left fielder.

The series had been marked by rough play, and when Joe slid into third on his triple in the sixth inning, and Third Baseman Marvin Owen lunched at him with his foot when the ball was not near him. Joe thought Owen was trying to spike him. Joe angrily kicked at the third baseman with his foot and players of both teams rushed out of their dugouts. There was no further exchange of blows and the umpires quickly cleared the field and play was resumed.

But when Medwick returned to left field after the Cardinals' turn at bat the spectators in the left field sun seats greeted him with boos, jeers and showers of missiles including fruit, produce and glassware and anything else they had in their pockets or lunch baskets that could be thrown.

A dozen flunkeys tried to clear the field but as fast as they carried gunny sacks of missiles away, other missiles were tossed on the grass.

Game Delayed 20 Minutes.

After 20 minutes had elapsed and a threat over the loud speaker that the game might be forfeited to the Cardinals, had not restored order or silenced the bleacher fans, Commissioner Landis summoned Medwick, Owen and Manager Frisch to his box. He asked Owen if Medwick had been justified in his display of anger and when Owen said there was no justification Judge Landis decided the best interests of baseball demanded Medwick's ejection.

And so he ordeerd Joe out of the field, tempering his order with a statement that the action might prevent Medwick from suffering bodily harm.

Chick Fullis took Medwick's place in left field and the triumphant bleacher fans, who had accomplished what no world series or championship season crowd had ever accomplished before, greeted Fullis with a cheer and the business of completing the game was gone through without any more trouble.

Dizzy Invincible.

Dizzy was invincible as he gained the necessary fourth victory for the Redbirds. A seven-run Cardinal attack in the third inning knocked Elden Auker, Schoolboy Rowe and Elon Hogsett out of the box and gave Jerome Herman a commanding lead. But Dizzy never "eased up" as the trade describes it. He wanted a shutout to top off his year of super pitching and he got it.

There were Tiger threats, that is, threats to spoil his job of whitewashing. But Dizzy met them all like a champion. And despite a

Continued on Page 2, Column 3.

SCORE BY INNINGS

	1	2	3	4	5	6	7	8	9	[illegible]
Cardinals	0	0	7	0	0	2	2	0	0	11
Tigers	0	0	0	0	0	0	0	0	0	0

The Box Score

CARDINALS

	AB	R	H	2B	3B	HR	BB	SO	PO	A	E
MARTIN 3B	5	3	2	0	0	0	1	1	0	1	0
ROTHROCK RF	5	1	2	2	0	0	1	1	4	0	0
FRISCH 2B	5	1	1	1	0	0	0	0	3	5	0
MEDWICK LF	4	1	1	0	1	0	0	0	1	0	0
FULLIS, LF	1	0	1	0	0	0	0	0	1	0	0
COLLINS 1B	5	1	4	0	0	0	0	0	7	2	1
DeLANCEY C	5	1	1	1	0	0	0	1	5	0	0
ORSATTI CF	3	1	1	0	0	0	2	0	2	0	0
DUROCHER SS	5	1	2	0	1	0	0	0	3	4	0
J. DEAN, P	5	1	2	1	0	0	0	1	1	0	0
TOTALS	43	11	17	5	2	0	4	4	27	12	1

TIGERS

	AB	R	H	2B	3B	HR	BB	SO	PO	A	E
WHITE CF	4	0	0	0	0	0	0	1	3	0	1
COCHRANE C	4	0	0	0	0	0	0	0	2	2	0
HAYWORTH, C	0	0	0	0	0	0	0	0	1	0	0
GEHRINGER 2B	4	0	2	0	0	0	0	0	3	5	1
GOSLIN LF	4	0	0	0	0	0	0	0	3	0	1
ROGELL SS	4	0	1	0	0	0	0	0	3	2	0
GREENBERG 1B	4	0	1	0	0	0	0	3	8	0	0
OWEN 3B	4	0	0	0	0	0	0	0	1	2	0
FOX RF	3	0	2	2	0	0	0	0	3	0	0
AUKER P	0	0	0	0	0	0	0	0	0	0	0
ROWE, P	0	0	0	0	0	0	0	0	0	0	0
HOGSETT P	0	0	0	0	0	0	0	0	0	0	0
BRIDGES, P	2	0	0	0	0	0	0	1	0	0	0
MARBERRY P	0	0	0	0	0	0	0	0	0	0	0
CROWDER P	0	0	0	0	0	0	0	0	0	0	0
WALKER	1	0	0	0	0	0	0	0	0	0	0
TOTALS	34	0	6	2	0	0	0	5	27	11	2

Runs batted in—Frisch 3, Collins 2, DeLancey, J. Dean, Martin, Medwick, Rothrock. Two-base bits—Rothrock 2, J. Dean, Frisch, DeLancey, Fox, 2. Three-base hits—Medwick, Durocher. Stolen bases—Martin 2. Double plays—Owen to Gehringer to Greenberg. Pitching record—Hits off Auker, 6 in 2 1-3 innings; off Rowe 2 in 1-3 inning; off Hogsett 2 (pitched to 4 batters in third); off Bridges, 6 in 4 1-3 innings; off Marberry 1 in 1 inning. Bases on balls—off Auker 1, off Hogsett 2; off Marberry 1; off Crowder 1. Struck out—by J. Dean 5; by Auker 1; by Bridges 2. Left on bases—St. Louis 9; Detroit 4. Umpires: at the plate—Geisel (A.L.); at first base—Reardon (N. L.); at second base—Owen (A. L.) and at third base—Klem (N. L.). Time 2:19. Attendance 45,000. Losing pitcher, Auker.

Little Redbirds Lose.

By the Associated Press.

COLUMBUS, O., Oct. 9.—Toronto of the International League defeated Columbus of the American Association, 5 to 1 today, knotting the Little World Series at four games each and making necessary a ninth and deciding game.

Jimmy Callahan Buried.

Special to the Post-Dispatch.

FITCHBURG, Mass., Oct. 9.—James J. Callahan of Chicago, 60-year-old former major league baseball star and manager, was buried yesterday.

hotel Friday.

JIMMY FOXX HIT IN HEAD BY PITCHED BALL

WINNIPEG, Man., Oct. 9.—Jimmy Foxx, star first baseman of the Philadelphia Athletics, lay in a hospital here today after being struck on the left side of the head by a pitched ball during an exhibition game.

An X-ray taken last night when his condition seemed to grow worse showed no skull fracture, but it did disclose a slight fracture Foxx suffered three years ago when beaned by a fast ball, doctors said.

Foxx played with the American League All-Stars.

SEALS SELL OUTFIELDER DI MAGGIO TO NEW YORK YANKEES

Williams Ill, Ingram Frets; Cards Pose for Pictures

San Francisco Examiner Sports
Monarch of the Dailies
REG. U.S. PAT. OFF.
CCC THURSDAY SAN FRANCISCO, NOVEMBER 22, 1934 THURSDAY 23

FIVE PLAYERS COME TO S. F. IN MAJOR DEAL

Young Fly Chaser Ready for Delivery Next Fall; Big League Club Holds Option on Services

(Picture on Page 25.)

By Abe Kemp

Col. Jake Ruppert, owner of the New York Yankees, yesterday proved himself the most daring gambler in baseball when he purchased Joe Di Maggio, young outfielder of the Seals.

Ruppert paid $75,000 and gave up five ball players on the long and dangerous gamble that Di Maggio's injured knee will respond to treatment and prove sound when he reports to the Yankees in the fall of 1935.

Every major league scout in the country recommended the young Italian star prior to the fateful day he tore the ligaments in his knee in an automobile accident; after that all advised their bosses to "layoff," that is all except the Yankee scouts. They made a thorough investigation and found out to their satisfaction that Di Maggio's knee injury was not as bad as first reported.

Di Maggio did not play the last two months of the Pacific Coast League season, being advised that complete rest was the only cure.

There is no question in the minds of shrewd baseball judges that the Yankees secured one of the best outfield prospects in the minors. Di Maggio has proved himself to be a terrific hitter. He owns one of the strongest and most accurate arms in baseball; is a wonderful outfielder and much faster on his feet than he appears.

In short, the North Beach boy has every qualification And if his knee proves sound will go on to great things.

Few owners in baseball will spend money for ball players with bad legs, but evidently Ruppert thinks the gamble well worth while.

With Di Maggio in the lineup next season plus the five players coming from the Yanks the Seals will be in a position to make a determined bid for the Coast League pennant.

PEELING POTATOES.

The news of his sale came as Joe was busy peeling potatoes in the family kitchen with the spaghetti pot sizzling.

"Its hard to bélieve," said "Dead Pan," whose facial expression in all situations is minus.

"But its a fine birthday present," he added.

Joe will be twenty years old November 25.

Di Maggio broke in with the Seals the last week of the 1932 season.

He was a thin, waspy looking lad

(Continued on Page 30, Col. 4)

Sports Parade

"Sin" of Holding.
Tricks of Sports.
Spikes in Baseball.
Also in Tennis.

By Curley Grieve

Before consigning the Santa Clara-St. Mary's game to the limbo of the forgotten, I would like to discuss the little "white sin" known as holding.

A mistaken impression might have gone forth that Norm Finney, Bronco end who was penalized for holding on that disallowed touchdown play, was committing a dastardly crime.

Just to be sure there is no understanding, there has never been a football player, and particularly an end, who has not hooked an arm into a leg or clutched at a speeding ankle.

Holding is no major sin in football. With no particular reflection upon officials, it can be said in all frankness that only a small percentage of infractions in that direction are called.

* * *

How It's Done in Other Tight Games

Holding in football can be compared to a few of the tricks in other sports.

There never was a baseball player who hasn't crashed spikes first at a blocking leg or ankle, or dumped the pivot man on a double play to prevent the throw to first.

In a tight tennis game, it is not an uncommon incident for a player to smash the ball directly at the face or feet of his opponent.

Dexterous basketball players have long employed the hip to block and sock, while pocketing in quarter and half mile races, or swerving out to block a runner's path, are not unknown in track.

A baseball pitcher who hasn't heaved the pellet at a batter's ribs or head would be a fit subject for a museum.

There are "little white sins" in all sports, and if Norm Finney feels conscience-stricken he can forget the incident entirely.

* * *
* * *

Stanford, if Beaten, Still Best Bowl Bet

Victory of Stanford over Californai is tantamount to getting the Rose Bowl bid. There's no dispute there.

Defeat by the Golden Bear would throw the Cardinals into a different position. If Washington State beats Washington, it becomes the Pacific Coast Conference champion and as such unquestionably will demand recog-

(Continued on Page 30, Col. 3)

Golden Oaks Star

HARRY (TARZAN) BRITTON, novice champion at 175 pounds, will be back in action for the Golden Oaks Club of Oakland in The Examiner's Fourth Annual Golden Gloves Boxing Tournament. He is one of the three light heavies who will represent the trans-bay club.

OAKLAND RING STARS ENTER GOLDEN GLOVES

Golden Oaks Club Fighters Seek Third Straight Title in 175-Pound Class; McQuillan Best

By Eddie Muller

Will another big, hard punching battler, fighting under the colors of the Golden Oaks Club of Oakland, carry off light heavyweight honors in the Golden Gloves Fourth Annual Boxing Tournament?

That question leaves room for argument, but not in the case of Dr. O. V. Robinson, who has guided the destinies of this trans-bay organization since the club entered amateur sports competition.

For two years now, 1932 and 1933, Robinson's proteges have been supreme in the 175-pound class. And Robinson is confident that he will repeat with another kingpin again this season.

Harley Ford, a big blond youngster, with a terrific sock, waded through his opposition to capture the crown two years ago. Last year, red-headed Frankie Hammer came through with flying colors, making it two in a row for Robinson's team.

TO REPEAT?

"We'll do it again," says Robinson. "I've three boys entered at 175 and I am certain one will win the championship."

The big three are: Art McQuillan, a real slugger; Doug Carver, a punching, aggressive fighter, and Harry "Tarzan" Britton, holder of the Novice tournament title.

Of the three, McQuillan is the best bet. From the present set-up on entries, this lad will be one of the favorites. He has had plenty of experience, having taken part in four different tourneys. In the recent Labor show he took the championship, whipping George Baldwin in the finals.

Whether McQuillan wins or loses the fans are always assured of real action. He's the kind of a fighter who walks in swinging both hands in an effort to score a knockout. Futhermore, McQuillan stands up well under punishment.

Carver and Britton, according to Robinson, are greatly improved. Either one of these lads may surprise by beating out their favored stablemate by reaching the finals.

The Oakland Club is also angling for the heavyweight crown. In this class they have two entered, namely, Babe McCurdy and King Kong Lee.

Lee is a tall, lanky string-bean giant, who stands well over six feet. He gave Girard DeClerq a good battle for three rounds recently, only to be stiffened in the final heat by a right hand punch.

McCurdy will give any of the big fellows a fine tussle. He is holder of the Senior P. A. championship and went to St. Louis to take part in the Nationals earlier this year. Tough, game and rugged, McCurdy is certain to provide plenty of action.

WINS CROWN.

The other member of the squad is Gunner Froines, a middleweight. A year ago the Gunner ran second best in most events. However, he has come along in fine style, climaxing his winning streak by defeating John Dekker for the crown in the Labor tournament show.

With such a lineup of fighters Robinson will certainly have a splendid chance of grabbing some glory, regardless if his boys win or lose.

Entries close Monday, November 26. So if you want to enter don't lose any time in forwarding your blanks to Al Sandell, 830 Market street. The blanks can be secured at the following places:

Taussig and Ryan's gym, 312 Leavenworth street; Royal A. C., 541 Turk street; Al Sandell's office, 830 Market street; Duffy's and Lakeside gymnasiums in Oakland.

Tune In Tonight On Parade for Big Game Lowdown

For the "lowdown" on the Big Game—

For the latest in baseball—

Tune in at 9 o'clock tonight on the Sports Parade of the Air over KYA.

Ernie Nevers, the big blond from Stanford, and Jimmy Hole, the wise little coach from California, will discuss the contest from the "inside" out.

Don Liebendorfer of Stanford and Ken Priestley of California, publicity directors of the two schools, will argue out in public what they write about in public.

Joe Cronin, newly named manager of the Boston Red Sox, will discuss his future plans before leaving for eastern baseball meetings.

Don't forget to tune in—KYA at 9 p. m.

More Sport News on Page 30

Wraith of Stanford Campus

BIG GAME atmosphere everywhere, and wherever you find talk of Saturday's California-Stanford clash, Bobby Grayson, shown in this unusual photo, is mentioned.

ON GRAYSON'S sturdy shoulders may be heaped much of the Cards' responsibility for smashing through the Golden Bears. Grayson plays plenty of football.

Cal's Tackles Face No Soft Snap Breaking Up Stanford's Offense

By 'Dink' Templeton

Bill Ingram is wondering what will happen to Stanford's offense when a couple of stalwart tackles play in its backfield all afternoon.

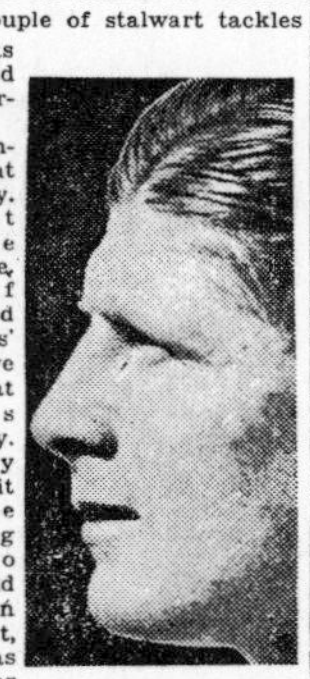

The answer to that is easy. There just won't be any offense. Several of Howard Jones' teams have proven that in days gone by. Gone by long ago it might be added. Long enough so that the old Trojan boast, "Jones has the Warner system stopped cold," is no longer anything but an unpleasant memory.

You don't hear any more about it from Howard or anyone else from the land of Troy, simply because it has been a couple of years since U. S. C. tackles were able to barge straight in at the fullback, arriving there a fraction of a second after the pass from centers, running smack into reverses, if reverses were tried; socking the fullback before he turned around after his fake, if it was a fake reverse; chasing him until he threw in desperation, if he meant a pass.

CAL CAME CLOSE.

That, in brief, was the solution to the fable reading "Jones has Warner stopped," ends alternating with the tackles at times to make it look mysterious.

California never did find it quite so simple because, after the Trojans had "ruined" Stanford's season, considerable work was done to prevent a repitition of this powerful defense against the system of reverses.

Yet Cal has come close enough, especially in the last three years, so that it would be very difficult for Big Bill to have any great respect for the Stanford offense.

He won his first game, 6 to 0. He tied his season, 0-0, the gun saving Stanford. He was beaten by a long pass, 7-3, last year after leading until the last ten minutes, when even Stanford was about to admit the Big Red Machine had shot its

(Continued on Page 30, Col. 3)

MEADOWS LONG SHOT PAYS $162

By Abe Kemp

Undercover "beetles" scampered off with all the marmalade in yesterday's highly interesting Bay Meadows activities.

It was a regular "bull" market with equine stocks soaring to the richest heights of the meeting.

The fanciest coup of the day—also the meet—was engineered in the second race, featuring pelters of dubious hue.

This sprint affair found the three-year-old maiden colt, George Renfroe, bouncing in on a holding track to the syncopated tune of $162.20.

A couple of the fourth estaters with the idea paramount of doing their Christmas shopping early selected the Renfroe colt as the medium of bringing this about, and needless to describe the state of their emotions when the golden deluge took place.

Down in the broad hinterlands of Texas, when the sharp-shooters went gunning for longshots, they invariably picked on the longshot rider, T. Sena, and it was this same Sena who had the mount on George Renfroe.

All the way down the line it was a prolific afternoon for the boys who like to speculate in outsiders.

Brown Bank started the "bull" market right at the outset when he jogged home for $48.00.

The Renfroe excitement having

(Continued on Page 26, Column 5)

Field Goal Duel May Decide California-Cards' Game Outcome

By Harry Borba

California is one field goal up on Stanford in three games played since "Navy Bill" Ingram came to Berkeley in 1931. Bill's record of Big Game achievement against the Indians is all square. California won the first one 6 to 0, tied the second 0 to 0 and Stanford won last year, 7 to 3.

Each team has had a touchdown, but the Bears have the advantage of a field goal, kicked by Arleigh Williams from the Stanford 25-yard line in the last play of the first half of the 1931 contest.

Bill Ingram declares that the "Little Champ' 'is the best field goal kicker on the Pacific Coast. He's kicked only one this year, the one that beat U. C. L. A. 3 to 0. The "Little Champ' 'is pitted against a man who has been kicking them all season, a man whom "Tiny" Thornhill might argue about with Navy Bill over championship rights.

LEADS COAST.

James "Monk" Moscrip has whistled the prolate spheroid over and through the cross bars five times this season to lead the conference as well as the coast. He has kicked 18 points after touchdown and Williams has kicked 10. Of course, the Indians have had more try-at-point opportunities than the Bears. The point is that both Arleigh and "Monk" are grand placement kickers.

And, the field goal may be a very important part of Saturday's Big Game clash in Strawberry Canyon. Yea, I know, it sounds foolish in view of Stanford's scoring record for the season as against that of the Bears; ridiculous from the Stanford record of no defeats this year against California's losses to St. Mary's, Washington and Santa Clara. Yet, one should not lose sight of the fact that this is the Big Game.

Seasonal records count no more in this collision than they do in the St. Mary's-Santa Clara battles. Last year, after California had lost two and been tied in two more and the Indians had lost only to Washington and had been tied by Northwestern, the Bears turned around held Stanford to 172 yards net from scrimmage and eight first downs against five.

Perhaps that isn't impressive but remember that Stanford was only across mid-field thrice, penetrating to California's 20, 11 and 8-yard lines to be stopped on each occasion. The Indians scored on a 55-yard

(Continued on Page 26, Column 1)

ARLEIGH HAS COLD, FAILS TO PRACTICE

No Fever, So California Coach Thinks Ace Will Be Better Today; Indians Have Laugh

By Curley Grieve

University of California's Big Game hopes received a shock yesterday afternoon when Captain Arleigh Williams failed to report for practice.

The star halfback, who will carry the major part of the Golden Bear attack, was confined to his bed with a cold.

"Navy" Bill ngram did not attempt to conceal his worry.

If no fever develops, Ingram said that Arleigh would be physically ready today.

Although fretting, Bill sent his charges through a short scrimmage and came up with the announcement that Louie Drnovich, a sophomore, "may start at guard in place of Ray Jack."

In contrast to unsettled conditions at California, with new worries striking at the most vital spot in the eleven, Stanford held "camera day."

It was the first time probably in Big Game history that the "photogs" were permitted on the field at a time when the most secret practice and longest scrimmage seemed in order.

But the Stanford practice gridiron was anything but serious. Photographers were the target for jokes as Grayson, Hamilton, Moscrip, et al, scampered over the turf to the tune of clicking shutters.

Coach C. E. "Tiny" Thornhill sat back with a beaming countenance, and answered the call himself when wanted for poses.

"Afraid of their attitude? No, those kids haven't caused me any worry yet and I don't think they will," he said. "They aren't overconfident or fat-headed. And they aren't nervous."

Thornhill added that only light practice would be in order today and tomorrow, and there would be no "hideaway" for the Cardinals.

"We will go into seclusion on the bus at 11:15 Saturday morning," he said with a laugh.

Bassi, Bronc Grid Star, Ill, Out of Columbia Game

SANTA CLARA, Nov. 21.—Dick Bassi, Bronco right guard, was confined to his bed today with a slight touch of influenza and may not be able to play in the Columbia game at Portland, Sunday, it was announced this afternoon as the Broncos resumed practice after their "Little Big Game."

Bassi picked up his cold in last Sunday's deluge.

Joe "Salty" Salatino was likewise reported suffering from a cold, while Frank Sobrero, left half back, showed a weak ankle, sprained in the second quarter of Sunday's game.

The Great Game Of Politics Page 9
U. S. debt too great—even for an anaesthetized public

THE BOSTON HERALD

VOL. CLXXVII., NO. 58 WEDNESDAY MORNING, FEBRUARY 27, 1935—TWENTY-EIGHT PAGES **** TWO CENTS

LATE CITY EDITION
CLOUDY, COLDER TODAY
Forecast for Boston and vicinity: Cloudy and colder today. Fair with slowly rising temperatures tomorrow. North and northwest winds. Full report on page 2.

RUTH JOINS BRAVES FOR THREE YEARS

Millens and Faber Defiant as Sentenced to Die April 28

DROP INSANITY PRETENSE AND CRY OUT 'CHEAT'

Counsel of Defendants Startled as Clients Vent Wrath

MOTIONS FOR NEW TRIALS REFUSED

Relatives of Prisoners Are Searched for Weapons on Entering Court

By EDWARD ALLEN

Three prisoners about to be sentenced for murder stood up in Norfolk criminal court at Dedham yesterday and threw pretense out of the window.

Doffing the identities which the defence had carefully built up, Abraham Faber and Murton and Irving Miller spoke out—the most revealing words of the whole trial. Then, Judge Nelson P. Brown sentenced them to die in the electric chair at the state prison in Charlestown April 28 for the murder of Patrolman Forbes McLeod during the robbery of the Needham Trust Company, Feb. 2, 1934.

Their elaborate insanity pleas having availed them nothing, psychiatrists and attorneys and testimony and argument and precedent and statute having availed them nothing, the three young amateurs of murder and robbery waived their final right of silence, and proceeded to show they had a sense of values, warped and twisted though it was.

Abraham Faber, whom William R. Scharton, his attorney, described as the weak tool of Murton Millen, told the court, without advice of counsel, that he had traded his confession for his life, that he had denounced his two companions in the hope of saving his own neck and that he considered he had been double-crossed by a state detective.

IRVING TALKS HALF HOUR

Irving Millen, whom George S. Harvey, counsel for the defence of the Millens, had painted as almost an imbecile with a brain hardly above that of a loyal dog, stood up and spoke for nearly a half hour. In fact, he made two speeches. He denied he was a desperado, and pointed out that few crim-

(Continued on Page Four)

AFTER NEEDHAM SLAYERS HAD BEEN SENTENCED TO CHAIR

Murton Millen (left), Irving (centre) and Abe Faber, manacled together as they left Dedham court house yesterday after being sentenced to the electric chair for the murder of a Needham policeman during a bank robbery.

Democrats Lash Curley for 'Plot' To Destroy Ward's Reputation

More Than 200 Legislators Cheer Attack at Party For Dever

HAIL SALTONSTALL AS NEXT GOVERNOR

A blistering denunciation of "Gov. Grant and Secretary Curley" for what Representative Edward P. Bacigalupo, Democrat, of the West end, termed as a "plot to destroy the reputation and character of Representative Michael J. Ward of Roxbury," was hailed by more than 200 members of the Legislature, gathered at the Copley Plaza last night to honor Atty.-Gen. Paul A. Dever and his assistants.

At the conclusion of Representative Bacigalupo's attack upon the enforced resignation of Representative Ward as assistant United States marshal, the entire assemblage, comprising for the most part Democratic members of the House and Senate, rose to its feet and cheered in a spontanious demonstration.

"Ward takes it on the chin," Representative Bacigalupo said in his capacity as master of ceremonies, "because he's no stool pigeon. Every member of the Legislature has confidence in Ward in the face of this unfair and undeserved attack on him.

"Ward has repeatedly demonstrated

(Continued on Page Six)

Cohan Says Helen Hayes, Huston Finest in U. S.

TORONTO, Feb. 26 (AP)—George M. Cohan, who by his own musical admission is "A Yankee Doodle Boy," said today he believed Walter Huston, a Canadian, to be the finest actor in America.

Cohan, appearing here in Eugene O'Neill's "Ah, Wilderness," named Helen Hayes as the best American actress.

M'CRACKEN GOES TO CAPITAL JAIL

Surrenders Voluntarily to Serve 10 Days for Contempt of Senate

WASHINGTON, Feb. 26 (AP)—Still maintaining his innocence, William P. MacCracken, Jr., assistant secretary of commerce for aeronautics in the Hoover administration, today voluntarily entered the grim District of Columbia jail to serve the 10-day sentence imposed by the Senate a year ago for contempt.

MacCracken, who is secretary of the American Bar Association, had until Saturday to petition the supreme court for reconsideration of its decision upholding the Senate's action. But he decided apparently that such a petition would only delay the jail term.

"After careful consideration I have concluded not to petition the supreme court for a rehearing of my case, and in accordance with the stipulation I entered into with the sergeant-at-arms of the Senate, I am surrendering to

(Continued on Page Four)

CAVANAGH ASKS DOG RACING BAN

Demands Curley Revoke Permits in Cambridge—Opposition Grows

CRONIN IS NAMED COMMISSION AIDE

Revocation of the license issued by the state racing commission for dog racing and pari-mutuel wagering in Cambridge, starting May 18, was demanded of Gov. Curley yesterday by State Senator Charles T. Cavanagh of that city.

"Dog racing in Cambridge would meet with an avalanche of opposition and hostility from the citizens of Cambridge, and would be a constant source of trouble and danger to the health, happiness and safety of our people," the senator wrote the Governor.

The already formidable opposition to dog racing in all four communities where licenses have thus far been granted, continued to grow yesterday. Mayor Mansfield declared he would take every legitimate means at his disposal to prevent dog racing in South Boston and the New England section of the National Association of Amusement Parks voted to lend its forces to those fighting this type of recreation.

The state racing commission probably will grant within a short time a fifth dog racing license to the Boston Garden Corporation. Officials of the corporation were in conference with the commission for several hours yesterday, explaining their plans for renovating the Garden to permit dog racing and pari-mutuel betting.

Late yesterday afternoon the commission appointed as assistant secretary Cornelius H. "Tubber" Cronin, Cambridge Latin and Boston College athlete and former Cambridge city councilman. He fills the vacancy caused by the ousting, at the insistence of Gov. Curley, of Lawrence Bresnahan last week.

Cronin officially will take up his new

(Continued on Page Six)

SENATE REBELS AWAIT ACTION OF PRESIDENT

Prevailing Wage Opponents Unyielding—Want Works Bill Brought Back

FEW LETTERS OF PROTEST RECEIVED

Leaders Fear Uprising May Spread to Other Important Measures

[Special Dispatch to The Herald]

WASHINGTON, Feb. 26—Having failed so far to incite any appreciable public reaction against those who effectively halted the $4,880,000,000 work relief plan in Congress, Senate leaders looked to President Roosevelt today for some cue as to how to proceed with the measure.

Senators against whom the reaction was intended were, if anything, more adamant. Their attitude was rendered even more unyielding when the executive council of the American Federation of Labor voted unanimously this afternoon to stand firm in the fight for the "prevailing wage" amendment, whose adoption by the Senate prompted an immediate threat of a veto by the President and caused withdrawal of the relief resolution.

SENATORS HEARTENED

The labor council's actions were reported on Capitol Hill by Senator McCarran, author of the "prevailing wage" proposal, to hearten the 44 senators, including 21 of the President's partisians, who had voted for it Thursday. Mr. McCarran, who attended the A. F. of L. meeting, reaffirmed his purpose to offer the amendment to any work relief proposal that might be laid before the Senate and expressed confidence that an even greater vote than heretofore would be piled up for it.

PWA and FERA, apparently ignoring the legislative turmoil, continued today their plans for administration of what the President hopes will be a work relief law. PWA, through its district supervisors in co-operation with county engineers, speeded up a census of potential work projects which it is said will number 90,000 by the end of this week.

The Senate leaders are expected to take their problem to the President immediately on his return here Thursday. The Senate was adjourned until Thursday after a little more than an hour of routine work this afternoon.

Senator Glass, chairman of the appropriations committee to which the

(Continued on Page Three)

'ALL THE LUCK IN THE WORLD, BABE'

(Boston Herald-Associated Press Photo)

George Herman (Babe) Ruth, centre, is shaking hands with his former boss Col. Jacob Ruppert, New York Yankees owner, in New York, just after he had agreed to affix his signature to a contract calling for his services with the Boston Braves. Judge Fuchs, with a smile, is looking on.

WILL BE PLAYER, ASST. MANAGER, 2D VICE-PRES.

Salary Is Estimated at $25,000 Plus Percentage Of Club's Profits

MAY BE CONSIDERED AS 1936 MANAGER

Intimates He Might Be Able to Play 100 Games This Season

By BURT WHITMAN

[Special Dispatch to The Herald]

NEW YORK, Feb. 26—Babe Ruth, still baseball's darling, and particularly beloved in Boston, where he got his big league start, today agreed to sign a three-year contract with the Braves as player, assistant manager and second vice-president.

The announcement of the deal which transfers from the New York Yankees to the Boston club in the rival National league the greatest drawing card baseball has known, was made here early this afternoon at a meeting of Owner Col. Jake Ruppert of the Yankees, the Babe and President Emil E. Fuchs of the Braves, with the newspaper men of the metropolis.

Ruppert handed Ruth his unconditional release from the Yankees, stated that he has obtained the necessary waivers from all other American league clubs, and forthwith was allowing Ruth to accept the position offered by the Braves.

No salary figures were mentioned, but well informed sources tonight mentioned $25,000 a year as the likely

(Continued on Page Sixteen)

Boston-Bound Freighter Feared Lost With 26 Aboard in Furious Atlantic Gale

Liner Europa and American Banker Unable to Find Stricken Vessel

SEAS MOUNTAINOUS, CAPTAINS REPORT

[Special Dispatch to The Herald]

NEW YORK, Feb. 27 (Wednesday)—With three vessels rushing to her aid through hurricane winds and battering seas, the British freighter Blairgowrie, bound for Boston, disappeared last night about 900 miles due north of the Azores and her fate remained a mystery.

After a race against time with the urgent call for immediate assistance speeding them on, despite mountainous seas, the 50,000-ton North German Lloyd liner Europa, and the diminutive American Banker of the American Merchant Lines, arrived at the freighter's position and could find no trace of her.

At 7:10 P. M. Capt. Oscar Scharf, master of the giant express liner, notified officials of the line here that he was on the way to give assistance to the Blairgowrie and the 26 weary men, who had fought hopelessly against the raging storm that has battered the eastern section of the Atlantic for four days. He said then he had 60 miles to steam before he could come alongside the Blairgowrie, already helpless with her steering apparatus gone and her holds filled with water.

TO AWAIT DAYBREAK

At 10:26 Capt. Scharf reported again. "Europa now at position at Blairgowrie, but not sighted vessel yet. Standing by until daybreak."

Station WNY, the station of the Radiomarine Corporation, which received the first messages, asked Capt. Scharf what the weather was like. He replied:

"Wind hurricane force with mountainous seas."

The American Banker, which reported earlier to its offices here and also to Radiomarine, had not mentioned reaching the freighter's position but it was assumed that she was there because she was only 30 miles away at the start. The radio company said that another vessel, Blommer Sdijk, a freighter of the Holland-American line, was also either at the position or nearby.

The American Banker, a 436-foot cargo-passenger vessel, registered at 7340 gross tons, is in command of Capt. H. L. Winslow of Canton, Mass., who is

(Continued on Page Six)

24 Tiny Stolen Boxes Contain Deadly Poison

Two dozen small but deadly boxes are in the hands of boys or men who do not know the lethal quality of the contents. They were stolen with other effects last night from the automobile of Roy Bushee, parked in the driveway of his home at 39 Charnwood road, West Somerville. Bushee immediately called police, asked them to warn the thieves that the little boxes are ant traps, containing a powerful poison paste.

POLICE ARREST 9 IN 'BOOKIE' RAIDS

2 Journal Building Offices And West End Place Taken by Surprise

Striking simultaneously on the seventh and ninth floors of the Journal building, 262 Washington street, plain clothes men from the Milk street station raided the headquarters of two alleged bookmakers, shortly before 6 o'clock last night.

Six men were arrested and horse race betting sheets, wager slips and furniture seized in both suites of offices.

A crowd of more than 500 tied-up traffic in Newspaper row for 30 minutes.

To prevent a "tip-off," the raiding officers walked up six and eight flights of stairs, avoiding the elevators.

Around the corner on Water street were three cruising cars containing 15 uniformed police, who surrounded the building after the plain clothes men had time to climb the stairs.

Confident that they have closed all of the elaborate board rooms in the city, police yesterday directed their attack at the so-called "hand bookies," who travel throughout office buildings taking bets. Late yesterday afternoon, Lt. James F. Hinchey of the special raiding squad under the supervision of Dept. Supt. James McDevitt, led a raid at 33 Norman street, West end, made three arrests and seized betting sheets.

The six arrested in the Journal building are James Lovito, 30, of 137 Chambers street, West end; Samuel Levine,

(Continued on Page Three)

200 NOW LIVING ON PITCAIRN ISLE

Descendants of British Mutineers Studied by Scientists

[Special Dispatch to The Herald]

NEW YORK, Feb. 26—Dr. H. L. Shapiro, specialist in anthropology of the American Museum of Natural History, returned today from a six months' journey of research in the South Seas which included a fortnight's stay at Pitcairn island, the historic speck of land in the South Pacific which is the site of a unique experiment in anthropology.

There is now a record population of 200 men, women and children on the island, descendants of the original band of nine English mutineers from the H. M. S. Bounty and the 12 Hahitian women who landed on the then uninhabited island in 1789 following a history making voyage, Dr. Shapiro reported.

Although they are descended from two distinct racial groups and are closely related by blood, the present generation of Pitcairn islanders are "strong, husky, above the average in stature and intelligence," Dr. Shapiro said tonight. He found them charming people, hospitable and very friendly.

OVERALLS BURN IN SCHOOL FIRE

Prompt fire fighting by three students and their two instructors confined the damage by fire in the Bigelow junior high school in Newton yesterday to the top of a worn pair of the janitor's overalls.

Ernest Sullivan, 16, of 573 Centre street, Frank Smith, 15, of 676 Centre street, and M. Parker Butts, 12, son of School Committeeman F. Marsena Butts of 303 Franklin street, were leaving from basketball practice with Guy S. Baker, physical director, and Seymour Maskell, Boston University school of education student acting as a practice teacher, when they found a corridor in the old part of the building filled with smoke.

While Baker telephoned the fire department, the others traced the blaze to the overalls and some oily rags left by a man who had been cleaning at the school. They put out the fire with extinguishers.

Today's Herald

STRONGER CHAIRS FOR COUNCILMEN

Cambridge Body Passes Order Calling on Mayor for Repairs

Among other things, the Cambridge city council last night voted for firm foundations beneath the 15 councilmen. By unanimous vote, they passed an order requesting Mayor Russell to appropriate money enough to have the council chairs repaired.

Councilman Benjamin F. Wyeth, who introduced the order, said his brother member M. Russell Cazmay, could better speak on the motion. Cazmay rose carefully to his feet, said he would like to put his chair on exhibition and feared that each time he sat it would collapse, and then cautiously retreated down to it.

The chair didn't break. Neither did the vote, which was solidly cast for repairs.

State Gets $6,000,000 ERA Grant For Next Month, Largest on Record

An ERA grant of $6,000,000 to Massachusetts for March has been made, Arthur G. Rotch, state ERA administrator, was informed yesterday. This is the largest grant in the 18 months' history of the old CWA and present ERA.

The $6,000,000 allotment represents an increase of $500,000 over that of February. Rotch had asked for $6,500,000 for March.

Rotch said there are approximately 96,000 individuals now employed on ERA projects, affecting approximately 400,000 persons, and that with the increased $500,000 for March that at least 10,000 additional persons, benefiting about 43,000 families can be put to work.

Col. Thomas F. Sullivan, Boston ERA administrator, was informed by Rotch that the March allotment for Boston would be $1,260,000, an increase of $125,000 over this month, and will give employment to about 2300 additional persons. About 14,000 are now employed on Boston ERA projects.

Maj. Roswell G. Hall, city superintendent of public buildings, announced that he had secured the Nordblom building at 14-18 Oliver street for the new Boston ERA headquarters at a rental to the city of $10,000 a year. The basement and four entire floors will be taken over. Removal from the present quarters in the old Joy street police station will start immediately.

SNOW PRECEDES NEW COLD WAVE

Two Inches Fall as Mercury Drops from 48 to 22 in Boston

With a cold wave moving eastward across the continent yesterday, the temperature dropped rapidly in Boston last night and snow began falling steadily at 11 o'clock. From a high reading of 48 degrees at noon, the mercury droped to 22 degrees at Boston.

Over the streets just made bare by the melting thaw of the previous two days, the snow spread a blanket two inches deep the first two hours of its falling. Late driving motorists were once more forced back on chains, and hundreds who had optimisdically discarded rubbers for visits to movies and theatres stepped out of the playhouses into wet snow.

Colder and cloudy weather was forecast for today by the weather man, but there was a promise that the cold snap, born of yesterday's zero temperatures in the mid-West, would last only one day. The forecast for tomorrow was for fair weather with rising temperatures.

Wealthy Will Be Asked to Increase Emergency Gifts in Face of Crisis

A drive to persuade wealthy citizens to increase their donations to the emergency campaign of 1935 by at least 10 per cent. was announced last night by William Amory Parker, chairman of the special gifts division of the campaign, as a part of round-up week. Last night contributions totaled $2,813,856.79.

Parker pointed out that a crisis faces Boston hospitals and charities, and that gifts are vitally needed from those who have given already as well as from those who have not yet made contributions to the fund.

To speed the work of the campaign many events were held yesterday. At the Exchange Club representatives of the leading chemical and fuel firms of the city met for luncheon to hear Gelston T. King, chairman of this trade division, and Paul C. Cabot, chairman of the industry and finance division, outline plans for finishing the drive. With nearly 80 per cent. of their quota secured, Mr. King urged the solicitors to reach the 100 per cent. goal within the next five days.

Visiting one of the settlement houses in the campaign to attend an Italian luncheon in behalf of the drive, Fannie Hurst, who spoke at the campaign's zero hour dinner on Monday, gratified her desire to see one of the campaign agencies in action before her return to New York. As she left on the 3 o'clock

(Continued on Page Seven)

Princeton Lightweights Conquer Penn in American Henley Feature

SPORTS
Horse Racing
ROWING—DOGS

The Philadelphia Inquirer
PUBLIC LEDGER

SPORTS
BASEBALL
FINANCIAL

PHILADELPHIA, SUNDAY MORNING, MAY 26, 1935

abcde S

MACKS LOSE, 9-6, WIN 6-1; REDS TRIP PHILLIES, 4-3

PENN OARS TRIUMPH IN ADAMS CUP RACE

LITTLE CAPTURES BRITISH AMATEUR GOLF TITLE

RED-BLUE GRABS LAST PULL FIRST TO DEFEAT NAVY

Quakers Fight Off Valiant Attempts f Middies to Forge Ahead and Keep Record Clean by Tenth of Second; President Roosevelt Follows Race and Lauds Penn Broadbacks

By ART MORROW

ANNAPOLIS, Md., May 25.—Penn's oarsmen made a brilliant final pull for victory, here today.

Churning the last half-mile of the Adams Cup classic from 34 to 41 beats per minute the Red and Blue huskies fought off repeated Navy attemps to forge ahead. Shoulder to shoulder these giants battled, but at the finish the oarsmen of Penn were the first to catch that last pull and this sweep achieved victory by the scant margin of one-tenth of a second over the Middies.

Harvard, the third boat in the race, trailed by a wide margin and was never a contender in this annual classic on the Severn. President Franklin D. Roosevelt, outstanding alumnus of the Crimson, was on hand to see the gruelling battle of oars, from the referee's boat.

Navy supporters gained some measure of solace for this defeat from the fact that the Middie Fresh and Jayvees captured both of the early races.

Brilliant Gathering

Million dollar yachts, slim, trim sailboats and expensive motor launches there were in greater color and abundance than even this historic harbor, the nation's naval capitol had ever known for an intercollegiate crew regatta.

But the two slender racing shells, each propelled by eight good oars and true, dominated the scene.

For like gayly outfitted corsairs of old, the Penn and Navy galleys came swinging down the Severn this evening to the ear-splitting tribute-shrieking whistles and thunderous roars—from all that was on the river, not to mention those who packed and hovered about the stands erected near the finish line nor those who stood on the old railroad bridge overlooking the mile and three quarters course of their race.

Bow to bow, those Penn and Navy galleys came swinging to the finish. First Penn, then the Navy seemed ahead; each pull appeared to give that crew the edge. But Penn was first to catch its last, long pull; thus ended a perfect season for the Red and Blue, and thus came Navy's first taste of defeat.

Only a dead heat would have made that finish closer. Commander W. A. Hall, judge of the finish, was forced to wig-wag his official flag faster than eye could follow in order to wave first Penn, then Navy across the invisible line.

Harvard Surprises

Harvard surprised by staying in the race, and finished a length and a half behind the pacemakers, but no one noticed the Cantabs, so close were the leaders. Harvard's time was 9 minutes 3.1 seconds, this compared to Penn's official clocking of 8.58.6 and Navy's of 8.58.7.

President Roosevelt, after following the race in Referee Charles Francis Adams' launch, waited at the boathouse for the Penn bladesmen to come in. They finally did come in with little Ernie Cane, the coxswain, stroking and with husky,

Continued on Page 5, Column 4

Annapolis Results

Adams Cup race (varsity creys), first, Penn, in 8.58.6; second, Navy, in 8.58.7; third, Harvard, in 9.3.1.

Junior varsity race—First, Navy, in 9.04.5; second, Harvard, in 9.13.1; third, Penn, in 9.15.2.

Freshman race—First, Navy, in 9.06.4; second, Harvard, in 9.13.3; third, Penn, in 9.19.8.

All races 1¾ miles

Cincinnati Raps Jorgens for Run in Seventh to Break 3-3 Tie and Defeat Phils, 4-3

CINCINNATI, Ohio, May 25.—Jimmy Wilson tried another pitcher as a starter here today and found him pretty effective, but the Phils lost just the same, 4 to 3, mainly because Ed Boland dropped an easy fly to help the Reds get two unearned runs off the pitching of the veteran Alphonse Thomas in the fifth inning.

Thomas had the Reds pretty well in check until Boland dropped that fly, but at the windup it was Orville Jorgens, not Thomas who got the black mark in the defeat column.

Jorgens took over the pitching in the last of the seventh with the score tied at 3-all and before he had a chance to get going the Reds had shoved over the winning run to make it a cheap victory for Benny Frey, Cincinnati's second pitcher.

The Phils, as is usual with them, hit without a great deal of luck. They delivered two wallops in the ninth which, if placed just a little differently, would have produced a run to extend the game, possibly would have led to a winning rally. But both smashes were line drives right at first sacker Billy Sullivan and went only for outs instead of hits for Lou Chiozza and Jhonny Moore.

Wilson was not the only manager to experiment with a pitcher here today before a slim Saturday crowd of 2085 paid admissions. The opening of the Latonia race track cut down the crowd a lot, but that had nothing to do with Dressen's choice of Southpaw Al Hollingsworth as his team's starting hurler.

Dressen believed Hollingsworth, a youngster with a lot of stuff but shaky control, had a chance to beat the Phils and for six innings he wiggled out of the holes he created for himself by issuing four passes.

But when he walked Chiozza with one out in the seventh, giving Lou a free ticket for the third straight time, and followed it up with another pass to Pinch Hitter Bucky Walters, he killed off his chances of being a winner pitcher.

Allen and Haslin followed with low line drives to the outfield for

Continued on Page 2, Column 7

Another Gone

PHILLIES

	AB.	R.	H.	O.	A.	E.
Allen, cf	5	1	2	1	0	0
Haslin, ss	4	0	1	0	1	1
Boland, rf	4	0	0	2	0	1
Camilli, 1b	3	0	0	12	1	0
Vergez, 3b	3	0	0	0	3	0
Todd, c	4	0	1	4	1	0
Watkins, lf	4	0	0	3	0	0
Chiozza, 2b	1	1	0	2	4	0
Thomas, p	2	0	0	0	2	0
A-Walters	0	1	0	0	0	0
Jorgens, p	0	0	0	0	0	0
B-J. Moore	1	0	0	0	0	0
Totals	31	3	4	24	12	2

A—Batted for Thomas in 7th.
B—Batted for Jorgens in 9th.

CINCINNATI

	AB.	R.	H.	O.	A.	E.
Myers, ss	5	1	1	2	1	1
Riggs, 3b	4	1	2	0	1	0
Goodman, rf	3	0	2	1	0	0
Sullivan, 1b	4	0	1	10	4	0
Lombardi, c	4	0	1	6	1	0
Pool, lf	4	0	0	2	0	0
Comorosky, cf	4	0	1	3	0	0
Kampouris, 2b	4	1	3	0	0	0
Hollingsworth, p	3	1	0	2	1	0
Frey, p	1	0	0	1	2	0
Totals	36	4	11	27	10	1

Phillies	0	0	0	0	0	0	3	0	0	—3
Cincinnati	0	0	0	0	3	0	1	0	x	—4

Runs batted in—Haslin 2, Boland, Myers, Goodman, Sullivan 2. Two-base hits—Haslin, Riggs, Kampouris. Three-base hit—Goodman. Stolen base—Goodman. Struck out—By Thomas 1, Jorgen 2, Hollingsworth 5. Base on balls—Off Thomas 1, Hollingsworth 6. Wild pitch—Jorgens. Pitching record—Off Thomas, 3 runs, 8 hits in 6 innings; off Jorgens, 1 run, 3 hits in 2 innings; off Hollingsworth, 3 runs, 4 hits in 6 1-3 innings; off Frey, no runs, no hits in 2 2-3 innings. Winning pitcher—Frey. Losing pitcher—Jorgens. Left on bases—Phillies, 7; Cincinnati, 9. Time of game—1.59. Umpires—Sears, Pinelli and Klem. Paid attendance 2085.

14,781 ATTEND WITH DIETRICH GRABBING FINAL

Bespectacled Hurler Gives 7 Raps in Final as Macks Pummel Hudlin and Brown for Triumph

Cascarella Yields 4 Runs in 10th Frame of Opener; Vosmik Has Six Wallops to Continue His Mad Spree

By JAMES C. ISAMINGER

Before 14,781 paid admissions, the Athletics and Cleveland divided the first double bill of the season at Shibe Park yesterday. After losing the first combat, 9 to 6, in 10 innings, the Macks snapped out of a four game losing streak by winning the second, 6 to 1.

A four-run rally in the tenth pulled the chair from under Joe Cascarella in the opening tilt. Monte Pearson was the official winning hurler but had to be relieved by Clinton Brown in the last half of the 10th and the new pitcher repulsed the Macks after they tabbed their final run.

In winning his first game of the season, Bill Dietrich held the Ohio folks to seven hits in the second struggle. The A's hammered Willis Hudlin for three runs in the first two innings and made three more off Clint Brown in the eighth.

Mack Shakes up Lineup

Declining to stand still in the face of defeat, Connie Mack gave his team a violent shakeup. He started both games with Jimmy Foxx at first base, Lou Finney in right and Charley Berry behind the bat.

After losing the first game to see his losing streak mount to four games, Connie Mack took it out on Eric McNair, his regular shortstop. He benched him and sent Lamar Newsome, rookie infielder to short for the second game and the youth clapped two singles.

Joe Vosmik, Cleveland outfielder kept up his reign of terror with the bat by making four hits in the first game and two in the second.

In the three-game series, Vosmik socked no fewer than 11 hits out of 15 times at bat for an average of .733.

Another heavy hitter in the series was Odell Hale, who had eight hits out of 13 times at bat for an average of .615.

Bob Johnson was limited to one hit in the first game, but came back with two more in the second. Jimmy Foxx also captured three hits during the day.

Past Commander Albert E. Herrmann, of George H. Dahof Post No. 153, American Legion of Central North Philadelphia, opened the poppy drive by presenting each Athletc and Cleveland player with an official Legion poppy made by disabled veterans in various hospitals.

Jimmy Dykes and his fast-going White Sox make their first appearance of the season at Shibe Park this afternoon. John Whitehead, the pitching find of 1935, will bat-

Continued on Page 2, Column 1

This Is Better

SECOND GAME

ATHLETICS

	A.B.	R.	H.	O.	A.	E.
Finney, rf	4	1	1	2	0	0
Cramer, cf	3	0	0	1	0	0
Johnson, lf	4	1	2	3	0	0
Foxx, 1b	3	1	1	10	0	0
Higgins, 3b	4	1	1	2	0	0
Newsome, ss	4	1	2	0	3	0
Warstler, 2b	4	1	1	1	5	0
Berry, c	4	0	0	8	1	0
Dietrich, p	4	0	0	0	1	0
Totals	34	6	8	27	10	0

CLEVELAND

	A.B.	R.	H.	O.	A.	E.
Knickerbocker, ss	4	0	0	2	8	0
Vosmik, lf	4	0	2	0	0	0
Averill, cf	4	0	0	2	0	0
Trosky, 1b	4	0	2	11	0	0
Hale, 3b	3	0	1	2	0	1
Galatzer, rf	4	0	0	3	0	0
Berger, 2b	4	0	1	1	2	1
Brenzel, c	2	0	0	3	0	1
Pytlak, c	1	0	0	0	0	0
Hudlin, p	2	0	0	0	1	0
C. Brown, p	0	0	0	0	0	1
a-Campbell	1	1	1	0	0	0
Totals	33	1	7	24	11	4

a-Batted for Hudlin in 8th.

Cleveland	0	0	0	0	0	0	0	1	0	—1
Athletics	2	1	0	0	0	0	0	3	x	—6

Runs batted in—Johnson 1, Higgins 1, Dietrich 1, Newsome 1, Warstler 1, Vosmik 1. Two-base hits—Hale, Foxx. Three-base hits—Johnson, Vosmik. Stolen bases—Finney, Higgins, Warstler. Double plays—Newsome, Warstler to Foxx. Left on bases—Athletics 6, Cleveland 6. Base on balls—Off Hudlin 2, Dietrich 1. Struck out—By Hudlin 3, Dietrich 7. Hits—Off Hudlin, 6 in 7 innings; C. Brown, 2 in 1. Umpires—Moriarty and Owens. Losing pitcher—Hudlin. Time of game—1.54.

Princeton Crew First - - - Penn Second - - - in Henley

Tiger lightweights kept their undefeated crew record intact in the scene above, sporting a length advantage over the University of Pennsylvania eight in the historic American Henley on the Schuylkill. Columbia sweepswingers are third, eight feet behind the Penn crew. The Lion boat showed fight at the end of the race, giving the Red and Blue a battle for second position.

Clicking Again

BABE RUTH

RUTH SMACKS THREE HOMERS BUT BRAVES LOSE TO BUC TEAM

Babe Return to Old Form as Pittsburgh Grabs Decision Before 10,000

PITTSBURGH, May 25 (A. P.).—Rising to the glorious heights of his hey-day, Babe Ruth, the Sultan of Swat, crashed out three home runs against the Pittsburgh Pirates today, but they were not enough and the Boston Braves took a 11 to 7 defeat before a crowd of 10,000 at Forbes Field.

The stands rocked with cheers for the mighty Babe as he enjoyed a field day at the expense of Pitchers Red Lucas and Guy Bush, getting a single besides the three circuit blows in four times at bat and driving in altogether six runs.

Ruth left the game amid an ovation at the end of the Braves' half of the seventh inning and after his third home run—a prodigious clout that carried clear over the right field grandstand, bounded into the street and rolled into Schenley Park. Baseball men said it was the longest drive ever made at Forbes Field.

In his first appearance at the plate, the Bambino drove the ball into the stands, scoring Urbanski ahead of him. Lucas was the victim. Again in the third, while Guy

Continued on Page 2, Column 8

THREE WORLD MARKS SET BY JESS OWENS

Great Negro Star Ties Universal Standard for Century Dash After Creating Records in Furlong, Low Hurdles and Broad Jump

ANN ARBOR, Mich., May 25 (A. P.).—Jesse Owens, spectacular Ohio State Negro, gave the most amazing demonstration of versatility in track and field history here today as he shattered three worlds' records and equalled a fourth to dominate completely the 35th annual Western Conference meet.

Michigan won its 14th team championship, but instead of a runaway as had been expected, had to battle Owens and Ohio State down to the last event for the decision. The Wolverines amassed 48 points to 43½ for the Buckeyes.

Owens climaxed his great afternoon's performance with a leap of 26 feet 8¼ inches in the broad jump, a new world mark.

Even without the astonishing leap which set him off in a class by himself as the all-time greatest broad jumper, the incomparable 21-year-old sophomore still would have turned in an almost matchless day

Breaks Nambu's Mark

Before surpassing the accepted world record of 26 feet 2⅛ inches for the jump, set by Chuhei Nambu, of Japan, in 1931, Owens tied Frank Wykoff's world 100-yard dash standard of 9.4 seconds.

After his jump he raced to spectacular world record-smashing triumphs in the 220-yard dash and the 220-yard low hurdles. Running by himself after the first few strides, he finished the furlong in 20.3 seconds. The performance was three-tenths of a second under Roland Locke's world record, shaded Locke's American mark of 20.5, and beat Ralph Metcalfe's collegiate mark of 20.4 seconds.

Apparently just as fresh as when he started his day of days, Owens completed his conquest of records by winning the low hurdles in 22.6 seconds, four-tenths of a second under the listed world standard held jointly by Charles Brookins, of Iowa, and Norman Paul, Southern California ace.

That jump, about which track fans are likely to be talking for a long time—unless Owens gives them something else to talk about soon—was just about a perfect effort.

Checked and Rechecked

He blazed down the turf runway on his first attempt with every ounce of his amazing speed, struck the taffe-off squarely and rocketed off into space. Before he landed it was apparent that he had achieved the record at which he had been shooting all season. The judges of the event withheld announcement as they checked and rechecked the leap, but the 10,000 spectators knew, when Owens started jumping up and down, that it was a record eort.

These four almost matchless vic-

Continued on Page 10, Column 8

Baseball at a Glance

AMERICAN LEAGUE

Yesterday's Results

Cleveland 9, Athletics 6 (First game.)
Athletics 6, Cleveland 1 (second game.)
New York 3, St. Louis 1 (first game.)
New York 8, St. Louis 7 (second game.)
Detroit 3, Boston 2.
Chicago 8, Washington 3.

How They Stand

	W.	L.	P.C.	G.B.
Chicago	19	10	.655	—
Cleveland	17	12	.600	2
New York	19	13	.594	1½
Detroit	17	14	.548	3
Boston	16	14	.533	3½
Washington	15	15	.500	4½
Athletics	9	19	.321	9½
St. Louis	9	21	.222	10½

Today's Games and Pitchers

St. Louis at Boston (Weiland vs. W. Ferrell)
Detroit at New York (Auker or Sullivan vs. Malone)
Chicago at Philadelphia (Whitehead vs. Blaeholder)
Cleveland at Washington (Stewart vs. Hadley)

NATIONAL LEAGUE

Yesterday's Results

Cincinnati, 4; Phillies, 3.
New York, 3; Chicago, 2.
Pittsburgh, 11; Boston, 7.
St. Louis 10; Brooklyn, 3.

How They Stand

	W.	L.	Pc.	G.B.
New York	21	9	.700	...
Brooklyn	19	14	.576	3½
St. Louis	18	14	.563	4
Chicago	16	13	.552	4½
Pittsburgh	19	17	.528	5
Cincinnati	13	16	.448	7½
Phillies	8	19	.296	11½
Boston	8	20	.286	12

Today's Games and Pitchers

Brooklyn at Chicago (Earnshaw vs. Lee)
New York at St. Louis (Castleman vs. P. Dean)
Philadelphia at Pittsburgh (Moore or Johnson vs. Blanton)
Boston at Cincinnati (Frankhouse vs. MacFayden)

Smashes Records

JESSE OWENS

FALCON CREW WINS FROM BURR RIVALS FOR FRANKLIN CUP

Henry Bugbee of Princeton Captures Blake and Reath Trophies Here

Princeton's eight-oared crew kept its undefeated record intact by defeating University of Pennsylvania 150-pounders yesterday in the feature race of the 31st annual American Henley on the Schuylkill River.

Tigers oarsmen divided honors with Northeast Catholic, scholastic crewmen who won their first major rowing event, annexing the Franklin Challenge Cup over West Catholic. The Falcon eight, third behind the Hun School and West Catholic last week in the Stotesbury Cup race, sported an eight-foot advantage over the Burrs. Hun School was not a factor, trailing in fourth place.

5000 Witness Event

More than 5000 persons lined the river banks to witness the historic classic and were hopeful for a Penn victory as Red and Blue oars flashed in the lead almost at the very beginning of the race. The Orange and Black of Princeton glistened close behind until less than half a mile remained.

Ten-good-ones altogether with George Cooke bending on his stroke

Continued on Page 5, Column 7

U. S. ACE TRIPS TWEDDELL, 1 UP IN CLOSE MATCH

By Successfully Defending Crown He Won Last Year Californian Makes Golf History

Loser Makes Gallant Rally on Late Holes After Trailing Throughout Bitterly Fought Match

ST. ANNE'S-ON-THE-SEA, England, May 25 (A. P.).—William Lawson Little, Jr., the colossus from California, fixed the mantle of golfing greatness more firmly on his shoulders today when he defeated Dr. William Tweddell, a 38-year-old British physician, one up, in 36 holes and won the British amateur golf championship for the second straight time.

Thus the burly 24-year-old San Francisco shotmaker became the first player in history to win three consecutive national amateur golf crowns and the third man ever to register a "double" in the 50 years of this championship.

During a sensational struggle which saw the husky holder of the British and American simon-pure titles three up at the end of the morning round, only to be brought back on even terms with six holes to go in the home stretch, Little played some of the grandest golf in his career. He withstood paralyzing pressure over the final, windswept passage to subdue Tweddell, the winner of the 1927 championship, who made a bold bid to restore the crown to England on the last nine holes.

Sensational Finish

Desperately needing a four on the final hole to assure victory, the American skillfully got off one of the most testing shots of the tournament, hemmed in on three sides by a gallery of almost 10,000 which had verged on riotous conduct over the prospect of witnessing Little's downfall.

Standing on the 36th tee, Little was dormie one. Tweddell, having the honor by virtue of winning the previous hole, divided the fairway with a 250-yard drive. Earlier in the day Little had been belting the ball from the tees fairly consistently about 300 yards. Down the stretch he was hard-pressed and sacrificed accuracy for distance. He sliced his drive into a swarm of spectators standing in the rough and the ball settled on a bare spot.

His fore-caddy, with a stick flying an American flag, rushed to the spot and fell on all fours, animal-like, to prevent the rampaging spectators from trampling on the ball. Little slowly ambled up to the ball and with characteristic impassiveness viewed the situation without a sign of emotion.

One hundred yards distant was the green, with two yawning traps in between. It took the marshals fully five minutes to move the crowd back to permit Little to get a free swipe at the ball. He chose a spade mashie, lobbed the pellet beautifully to clear the traps and it came to rest on the green, 28 feet from the hole. Tweddell planted his approach three feet inside of Little's.

Champion Braces

That recovery had a revitalizing effect on the champion. For the first time during the final match he smiled. He took less time than usual in lining up the putt and then rolled the ball "stone dead" for a

Continued on Page 6, Column 3

FINAL ★★

DAILY NEWS

NEW YORK'S PICTURE NEWSPAPER

Copyright 1935 by News Syndicate Co., Inc. Reg. U. S. Pat. Off.

Entered as 2nd class matter, Post Office, New York, N. Y.

The net paid circulation for May exceeded
Daily---1,575,000
Sunday-2,450,000

Vol. 16. No. 293 | 56 Pages | New York, Monday, June 3, 1935 | 2 Cents IN CITY LIMITS | 3 CENTS Elsewhere

RUTH QUITS

Story on Page 42

(NEWS photo)
Back in 1921 when Babe Ruth was a Yankee and the idol of the kids in the bleachers. He'll never play again "for a man like Fuchs," Babe says.

(NEWS photo)
Harsh words have replaced their smiles. Judge Emil Fuchs and the Bam just after the great slugger signed with Boston.

BRANDING Judge Fuchs a double-crosser, Babe Ruth yesterday announced in Boston clubhouse that he was quitting the Braves.—*Story on page 42.*

(NEWS photo)
Babe Ruth in the uniform of the Boston Braves which, he swore yesterday, he'll never put on again.

(NEWS photo)
KNOCKED GALLEY WEST.—Catcher Phelps of the Dodgers crashes heavily after being nudged by Jimmy Wilson (12) of the Phillies in exciting play yesterday. Wilson stole home after double play, aided by Stripp's bad throw to the plate. Play won game for the Phils in ninth inning, 7 to 5.—*Story on page 43.*

(NEWS photo)
WELL, WHO WON?—A disputed decision in yesterday's Yankee-Red Sox game. Gehrig, who forced Chapman at 2d, was called safe at first on this play. Neither Gehrig's foot nor ball (arrow) has reached first base yet. Yanks won, 7 to 2. Seven homers were hit.—*Story on page 42.*

Tigers Win World Series, 4 Games to 2, Beating Cubs, 4-3, on Goslin's Hit With 2 Out in 9th

Single Scores Cochrane For Detroit's First Title

BridgesConquersFrench, Getting Last 3 Chicago Batters on 10 Pitches After Hack's 3-Bagger

(Continued from page one)

ing up and took off his hat and threw it away and danced like an Indian. Cavarretta cut off the throw and put the ball in his pocket. It was not needed any more. The World Series was over and the Cubs again had finished second best for the fifth time since 1908, when Frank Chance's team beat the Tigers.

People stayed where they were for a moment, some yelling, others trying to get their breath. The Tigers pummeled Goslin and straggled off the field. And Detroit started a celebration which, judging from its gathering momentum, may go on for days.

Whistles shrieked as if for an armistice. The streets in no time were inches deep in paper. Bartenders loosened up and set out bottles. Cochrane can be President if he chooses, and Goslin can have Postmaster Farley's job. And Bridges, the dapper chap who pitched the second game and started the Tigers on their way to the title and drove them home in style by winning today—well, Bridges can have anything he wants as far as the fans are concerned.

Detroit Line-up Shifted

It was not so cold today. In fact the weather was sunny and pleasant. Cochrane changed his line-up and his batting order. Because of the left-handedness of French, he put Gerald Walker, a right-handed hitter, in center field in place of Jo-Jo White. To try to get a little power in the bottom of his batting order, he had Rogell batting seventh, and he had Herman (Flea) Clifton, a futile hitter, leading off.

With this arrangement, the Tigers scored a run in the first inning. Clifton was thrown out. But Cochrane and Gehringer hit singles and then, after Goslin popped to Jurges, Pete Fox rammed a double between Hack and third base, scoring Cochrane.

It looked at the outset as if French were in for a heavy afternoon. He was, but he handled it nobly.

With two men still on bases, after Cochrane scored, French walked Walker purposely and got Rogell to rap a grounder at him which he used to force Gehringer at the plate for the final out of the inning.

Moriarty Again

Bridges did not appear to be so fast as he was in the second game. ... Cubs tied the score in the third ...moaned over an adverse decision ... cost them a run.

...ges opened this assault with a ... to center. Bridges fanned ..., but Galan dusted a hit to ...ger's right, putting Jurges on ... Then Herman singled to right, ...g Jurges. Galan tried to take ... on the hit, but was called out ...eorge Moriarty, the American ...e umpire who attracted unwel... attention to himself when he ...hree Cub players out of a game ...icago. Klein's subsequent fly ...ould have scored Galan instead of ...g the inning.

...iarty probably was right in his ...on, but it is his hard luck that ...hould have so many close ones ...gainst the Cubs. He had another ...on, in the sixth, when he called ...k out at third while Clifton was ...king a second stab at him.

Double-Play Bid Misses

No sooner did the Cubs tie the ...ore than the Tigers untied it in the ...ourth, when Walker and Rogell sin...led, and two force plays so occupied ...he Cubs that Walker scored. He scored as the Cubs missed by inches making a double play on Bridges.

Then came a fifth inning which prompted an announcement concerning the purchase of tickets for a seventh game. With one out French got a hit. With two out Billy Herman hit a home run on a line into the left-field bleachers, making the score 3 to 2, in favor of the Cubs.

There were two out in the sixth, and the bottom of the batting order was coming up when the Tigers tied the score.

Rogell kept the inning going with a drive which rambled into the corner of left field. He was limited to two bases because some one reached out of a box and touched the ball. Then Owen, who had been to bat nineteen times without making a hit, surprised and delighted every one by getting his first and only hit of the series, a single into left field, scoring Rogell with the tying run.

Hack Drives Out Triple

From then on every pitch was a prayer, every base-runner was a menace. Still locked in a tie score the two major league champions fought through the seventh.

French turned back an attack which was about to roll right over him in the eighth. He fanned Rogell after Fox had singled and Walker had sacrificed. Then, taking no chances ... all, he walked the weak-hitting ...en purposely and fanned Bridges. So the teams rode neck and neck ...o the ninth, and put on a show ...at left people incoherent in their ...citement.

Hack, a ruddy-cheeked boy who was a bank clerk a few years ago in Sacramento, opened the inning for the Cubs with a three-base hit over Walker's head. It seemed incredible that three men could fail to bring him home. He was poised on third ready to swoop over the plate, and prolong the series.

In this nerve-wracking situation, Bridges was superb. If he did not look fast early in the game, he was fast now. He wound up as if his right arm was a steel spring and poured that ball over the plate, throwing strikes. He fanned Jurges wit hthree pitched balls. He had two strikes on French when the Cub pitcher took a half swing and rapped the ball into Bridges's hands. Tommy bluffed Hack back to third and threw swiftly to first. Two out. The people were roaring.

Bridges Doesn't Watch Finish

Bridges bore down on Galan. Strike one. Strike two. Then a wide one. Ball one. Galan lifted the next pitch to Goslin and an inning heavy with disaster was over. Bridges had made ten pitches to retire three men and leave Hack on third base.

Having staved off defeat, Bridges went into the tunnel connecting the bench with the dugout to smoke a cigarette. He did not see the Tigers winning the ball game for him.

Clifton, the first Tiger to bat in the ninth, was out on strikes. He had gone fourteen times without a hit. But then came Cochrane and Goslin with swinging bats and racing feet to win the game and the championship of the world. Goslin made only one hit in five times at bat but he picked a perfect time to make it.

The next thing Bridges knew, it was all over, and wild men in white Detroit uniforms were whooping through the tunnel. A police escort was necessary to get Cochrane and Goslin out of the park away from the joyful crowd.

Box Score of Sixth World Series Game

CHICAGO (N. L.)

	AB.	R.	H.	PO.	A.	E.
Galan, lf	5	0	1	2	0	0
Herman, 2b	4	1	3	3	4	0
Klein, rf	4	0	1	0	0	0
Hartnett, c	4	0	2	9	1	0
Demaree, cf	4	0	0	0	0	0
Cavarretta, 1b	4	0	1	8	0	0
Hack, 3b	4	0	2	0	4	0
Jurges, ss	4	1	1	3	2	0
FRENCH, p	4	1	1	1	2	0
Totals	37	3	12	*26	13	0

DETROIT (A. L.)

	AB.	R.	H.	PO.	A.	E.
Clifton, 3b	5	0	0	2	0	0
Cochrane, c	5	2	3	7	0	0
Gehringer, 2b	5	0	2	0	4	0
Goslin, lf	5	0	1	2	0	0
Fox, rf	4	0	2	3	1	1
Walker, cf	2	1	1	0	0	0
Rogell, ss	4	1	2	2	3	0
Owen, 1b	3	0	1	11	0	0
BRIDGES, p	4	0	0	0	3	0
Totals	37	4	12	27	11	1

*Two out when winning run was scored.

Chicago	0 0 1	0 2 0	0 0 0	—3
Detroit	1 0 0	1 0 1	0 0 1	—4

Runs batted in—Herman (3), Fox, Bridges, Owen, Goslin. Earned runs—Chicago, 3; Detroit, 4. Two-base hits—Fox, Gehringer, Hack, Rogell. Three-base hit—Hack. Home run—Herman. Sacrifice—Walker. Double play—Gehringer, Rogell and Owen. Left on bases—Chicago, 7; Detroit, 10. Bases on balls—Off French, 2 (Walker and Owen). Struck out—By French, 7 (Owen, Clifton (2), Cochrane, Bridges (2), Rogel); by Bridges, 7 (Hartnett, French (2), Demaree, Galan, Cavarretta, Jurges).

Umpires—Quigley (N. L.), at the plate; McGowan (A. L.), at first; Stark (N. L.), at second, and Moriarty (A. L.), at third. Time—1:57

Manager Who Scored First and Final Runs; Winning Pitcher

Herald Tribune photo—Acme

Associated Press photo

Left, Mickey Cochrane crossing the plate in the first inning on Fox's double; Walker, No. 6, is signaling Gehringer to hold third. Cochrane also scored the winning run in the ninth; right, Tommy Bridges, who pitched the deciding game for his second victory of the series

DOWN IN FRONT

By RICHARDS VIDMER

Copyright, 1935, New York Tribune Inc.

The Goose Flies High Again

DETROIT, Oct. 7.—World Series week has ended. It's all over but the shouting, and that may go on for months, for the City of Detroit was plunged into a hysterical state by an old guy named Goose Goslin this afternoon.

All the drama, romance and human interest of the whole series was brought to a triumphant climax by the Wild Goose when he singled in the ninth inning with two out. Almost instantly there was a crowd of 5,000 fans packed in front of the Tigers' dugout, into which the Goose had ducked, shouting: "Yea, Goose! Yea, Goose! Yea, Goose!" like a college crowd cheering a football hero.

Goose Goslin

For ten minutes the chant went on without a break while the broad-shouldered, baldheaded, bugle-nosed Goose sat on a stool in the Detroit dressing room sucking on a bottle of beer with grinning satisfaction.

Outside the air was filled with fluttering bits of paper, people were milling about in the streets, slapping strangers on the back. Ten thousand laughing, gurgling fanatics formed a solid mass in front of the Book Cadillac Hotel, hoping for some unknown reason that the Wild Goose would light there before the evening was over and they might catch a glimpse of him or even pluck a feather from his wing.

For the Wild Goose was bigger than the Mayor of Detroit tonight, more important than the Governor of Michigan, a greater factor in the happiness of the local citizens than Henry Ford.

He had come through in the moment of need, brought joy to their hearts and triumph to the Tigers, who won their first World Series in the history of big league baseball after striving for the honor four times in vain.

The Stage Is Set

BUT let's go back to the scene on the diamond in the ninth inning. There's where the drama took place, there's where the hero was born. Here it was the sixth game, with the Tigers needing victory for the championship and the Cubs needing victory to tie the series at three games each. The score was tied at 3-3, tied on a single by Marvin Owen, who made just one hit in all six games, but made that one when it counted.

Little Tommy Bridges, winner of the second game, was out in the box, facing the Cubs as they came up for their last turn at bat. Could he hold them? Could he?—the thought in everybody's minds at that moment suddenly was shattered as Stanley Hack tripled to center field.

A man on third and none out. The Cubs couldn't help but score. Anything—a base hit, a long fly, even a slow hit ball to the infield would bring him home and put the Cubs out in front.

Bill Jurges stepped up to the plate. Bridges pitched. He pitched again, and again. Jurges was out. He had fanned. That run, that potential winning run still was on third base. Larry French was up next. Bridges got two strikes on him. Then French pounded the ball back to the box. Bridges pounced on it, chased Hack back to third with a look and then threw to first. Two out. Next came Galan. Bridges stuck to his task. One more man to get and that run would never score. Galan swung his bat. The ball sailed toward left field. It might drop safe—safe between the infield and outfield—but no, the Wild Goose came charging in and took it on the run.

The danger was passed. Three men had been retired in a row and Hack still was on third base. But now he had his glove on and the Tigers were at bat.

French fanned Clifton, but Mickey Cochrane, leader of the Tigers, rifled a single through the infield. Gehringer—could he do it? He might have, but Cavarretta scooped up his drive down the first base line and stepped on the bag. Cochrane was on second but there were two out; two out and Goose Goslin coming to the plate.

Enter the Hero

NOW the Goose is an old guy. He has been around in the big leagues for fourteen years. He has played in four World Series before, three with Washington and last year with the Tigers. He always has been a dangerous man in a pinch, a great money player.

But French was pitching and French is left-handed. That made a difference. Goslin had looked pitiful against the left-handed Larry all afternoon. He hadn't hit a ball past the infield. He had popped up twice and grounded out the other two times. Better not to walk him and have to pitch to Fox, a right-handed swinger who had made two hits already.

There may have been just a moment of doubt as Goslin hit the first ball that came toward him a terrific blow into a right field box. Maybe it would be best to pass him after all. But if that thought occurred to Charlie Grimm, the Cubs' manager, he kept it to himself.

So they pitched to the Goose again. Just once more. But that was once too many and the series was over. The great, gray Goose hammered the ball into right field and Mickey Cochrane came racing home with the winning run.

After that the chaos broke loose. Goslin barely beat the crowds in full cry that came pouring out of the stands and bleachers to the dugout. If he ever had been caught by that thrill-dizzy throng he would have been killed—killed with kindness.

Play-by-Play Story of Last Series Game

Goslin's Single to Left in Ninth Scores Cochrane and Gives Title to Tigers

By a Staff Correspondent

DETROIT, Oct. 7.—The play-by-play account of the last game of the World Series follows:

First Inning

Cubs—Galan soht a grounder off Bridges's leg and was thrown out by Rogell. Bridges tossed out Herman. Klein fouled to Owen near the Cubs' dugout. No runs, no hits, no errors, none left.

Tigers—Hack threw out Clifton on a close play. Cochrane shot a single to left. Gehringer bounced a single to right, Cochrane going to second. Jurges took Goslin's pop. Fox doubled down the left field line, scoring Cochrane and sending Gehringer to third. Walker was passed, filling the bases. French took Rogell's grounder and forced Gehringer at the plate. One run, three hits, no errors, three left.

Second Inning

Cubs—Hartnett was called out on strikes. Fox took Demaree's fly. Cavarretta shot a hit off Owen's glove and when Fox misplayed the ball, Owen went to second. Gehringer threw out Hack. No runs, one hit, one error, one left.

Tigers—Owen fanned. Herman made a nice play behind the box to throw out Bridges. Clifton struck out. No runs, no hits, no errors, none left.

Third Inning

Cubs—Jurges singled to center. French struck out. Galan scratched a hit past Gehringer, Jurges racing to third. Herman hit to right, scoring Jurges, but Galan was out at third, Fox to Clifton. Fox backed up for Klein's long drive. One run, three hits, no errors, one left.

Tigers — Cochrane grounded to Cavarretta, who threw him out at first, French covering the bag. Gehringer doubled to short left, Galan missing a shoestring try. Goslin grounded to French and there was a run-down play between second and third on Gehringer. Gehringer slid back into second, but Goslin also was trying for that base and was tagged out as he scurried back toward first, Hack to Herman to Cavarretta. Galan took Fox's lift. No runs, one hit, no errors, one left.

Fourth Inning

Cubs—Hartnett singled through the box. Demaree was called out on strikes. Rogell took Cavarretta's fly. Gehringer tossed out Hack. No runs, one hit, no errors, one left.

Tigers—Walker singled to right. Rogell singled to left. Owen bunted and Jurges was forced at second, Hack to Jurges, Owen reaching first and Walker third on the play. Bridges grounded to third, forcing Owen, Hack to Herman, Walker scoring. Clifton forced Bridges, Jurges to Herman. One run, two hits, no errors, one left.

Fifth Inning

Cubs—Jurges flied to Fox. French singled beyond Gehringer's reach. Galan was called out on strikes. With the count at three and one, Herman hit a home run into the left field bleachers, scoring behind French. Klein singled past Gehringer. Goslin took Hartnett's fly. Two runs, three hits, no errors, one left.

Tigers—Cochrane struck out. Herman threw out Gehringer. Hartnett took Goslin's hoist in front of the plate. No runs, no hits, no errors, none left.

Sixth Inning

Cubs—Rogell made a long throw to retire Demaree. Gehringer threw out Cavarretta. Hack doubled off the scoreboard. Jurges bounded to Clifton, who tagged out Hack. The Cubs debated this decision by Umpire Moriarty. No runs, one hit, no errors, one left.

Tigers—Galan took Fox's fly. Jurges went to the boxes for Walker's lift. Rogell doubled to left, a spectator reaching out and grabbing the ball. Owen singled to left, his first hit of the series, and scored Rogell. Bridges struck out. One run, two hits, no errors, one left.

Seventh Inning

Cubs—French struck out. Owen took Galan's grounder and made the putout at first. Herman singled to left. Owen took care of Klein's grounder alone. No runs, one hit, no errors, one left.

Tigers—Jurges threw out Clifton. Cochrane singled to center. Cavarretta came in for Gehringer's pop. Herman threw out Goslin. No runs, one hit, no errors, one left.

Eighth Inning

Cubs—Hartnett singled to left. Demaree grounded into a double play, Gehringer to Rogell to Owen. Cavarretta struckt out. No runs, one hit, no errors, none left.

Tigers—Fox singled to Herman's left. Walker bunted and was out at first, Hartnett to Herman, Fox going to second on the sacrifice. Rogell went down swinging. Owen was passed intentionally. Bridges was called out on strikes. No runs, one hit, no errors, two left.

Ninth Inning

Cubs—Hack tripled to deep center. Jurges went down swinging on three pitches. After two strikes, Bridges threw French out at first, holding Hack on third. Galan flied to Goslin. No runs, one hit, no errors, one left.

Tigers—Clifton struck out. Cochrane got an infield hit on his grounder to Herman. Gehringer was out at first, Cavarretta unassisted, but Cochrane was safe at second when Cavarretta's throw hit him on the shoulder. Cochrane scored the run which ended the series on Goslin's single to left on the second pitch. One run, two hits, no errors, one left.

Billy Sunday 'Almost' Swears at Umpiring

CHICAGO, Oct. 7 (UP).—Billy Sunday, the baseball player who turned evangelist, stomped out of town today after listening to the last world series game so "het up I almost—but didn't—cuss the umpires."

Declaring war on all umpires in general, and George Moriarty in particular, the former member of the Chicago Cubs shouted that "if the Cubs had got their customary breaks and the umpires hadn't given them a bum deal Friday and Saturday, it would be all over but the shouting.

"I arranged my preaching dates so I could have the world series week off," he complained, "and I got so het up with the umpiring at the first game that I didn't dare look in on another one. I had to listen to the rest over the radio."

Goslin Nearly Loses Uniform As Admiring Fans Maul Him

By a Staff Correspondent

DETROIT, Oct. 7.—The Tigers' followers turned out in force for the sixth and what proved to be the deciding game of the World Series. It was a sunny day, not so cold, but this was a refrigerated series.

Because Larry French, a left-hander, started for the Cubs, Gerald Walker, a right-handed hitter, took Jo-Jo White's place in center field.

And it came to pass that Hank Greenberg did not have to make any decision about whether he would play on Yom Kippur, the Jewish Day of Atonement. He was out with a wrist sprained since the second game of the series.

Lindstrom's finger still bothered him, so Demaree again was in center and Klein in right.

The Detroit batting order was changed. Clifton led off; Walker batted sixth and Rogell seventh. Cochrane evidently tried to get a little power in the lower half of the line-up.

Even the schools had canceled classes so that the children could gather in the auditoriums and listen to the series over the radio.

French took Goslin's high bounce in the third and sought to trap Gehringer between second and third. Gehringer retreated to second, chased by Hack with the ball. Goslin, meanwhile, had advanced to second. So there were two men on second when Hack arrived and played eeny-meeny-miney-mo. While Hack was so engaged Goslin left and ran back toward first and almost made it. The Goose was out at first, pitcher to third to first.

Moriarity had to made a close decision on Galan, sliding into third in the third, and he had to make another on Hack ducking away from Clifton in the sixth. To make it worse, Clifton made a second stab at Hack, thinking he had missed him. Both decisions were against the Cubs.

Owen's one hit made the Cubs cautious. French walked him purposely in the eighth after Fox reached second. It was a good idea, because Bridges went out on strikes, ending the inning.

DETROIT, Oct. 7 (AP).—No sooner had Goose (Leon) Goslin smashed the winning hit, driving in Mickey Cochrane, manager, fully 25,000 fans rushed onto the field and toward the Tiger dugout. The playing field swarmed with humanity, wild and joyous.

"We want Goose! We want Goose!" they yelled.

But the Goose was too fast for them. As soon as he saw Mickey across the plate—Mickey slid across to be sure, although he had time to spare—Goose dashed from first base to the dugout. Police had a difficult time holding back the surging, wild mass. A half hour later Goslin ran across the field escorted by six policemen. He almost had his clothes ripped off by the mob.

Five policemen had to stand around the pitching mound to keep the wild crowd from ripping the rubber right out of the "hill." The playing field was littered with paper and a couple bushels of vegetables that some fans took along in case of another Joe Medwick-Marvin Owen battle.

Charlie Gehringer and Pete Fox were the chief Tigers on attack. Charlie got nine hits in twenty-four times at bat, Fox ten in twenty-six attempts. Bill Herman and Chuck Klein led the Cubs, Herman getting eight hits out of twenty-four and Klein four in eight. Herman slugged for the "circuit," getting a home run, triple, double and a single at least once during the series.

The Cubs seem to be the road back for the American League. The junior circuit hadn't won a World Series since 1932, when the Yankees beat the Cubs four straight, until today.

It was the seventh "million dollar" series, total receipts reaching $1,173,794, the largest for a six-game series. The biggest gate was $1,207,864 for the seven-game series between the St. Louis Cardinals and New York Yankees in 1926. But they didn't have the big $100,000 radio cut for the others.

George Moriarty, the umpire, got so mad at the Cubs once today that he was funny. When the Cubs protested Hack's out at third in the sixth inning Big George wheeled around, rushed over to the left of third and demonstrated how Hack had run out of line in attempting to dodge Clifton. He almost fell over showing 'em how.

Composite Score of World Series Games

By The Associated Press

Detroit Tigers (A. L.)

Player	G.	AB.	R.	H.	2B.	3B.	HR.	RBI.	B.B.	S.O.	Pct.	P.O.	A.	E.	Pct.
White, cf	5	19	3	5	0	0	0	1	5	7	.263	14	0	0	1.000
Cochrane, c	6	24	3	7	1	0	0	1	4	1	.292	32	3	1	.972
Gehringer, 2b	6	24	4	9	3	0	0	4	2	1	.375	14	23	0	1.000
Greenberg, 1b	2	6	1	1	0	0	1	2	1	0	.167	17	2	3	.864
Goslin, lf	6	22	2	6	1	0	0	3	5	0	.273	12	0	1	.923
Fox, rf	6	26	1	10	3	1	0	4	0	1	.385	8	1	1	.900
*Walker, cf	3	4	1	1	0	0	0	[illegible]	1	0	.250	0	1	0	1.000
Rogell, ss	6	24	1	7	2	0	0	1	2	5	.292	13	12	0	1.000
Owen, 3b-1b	6	20	2	1	0	0	0	1	2	3	.050	46	5	1	.981
Clifton, 3b	4	16	1	0	0	0	0	0	2	4	.000	2	9	1	.917
ROWE, p	3	8	0	2	1	0	0	0	0	1	.250	3	4	1	.875
BRIDGES, p	2	8	1	1	0	0	0	1	0	3	.125	1	5	0	1.000
AUKER, p	1	2	0	0	0	0	0	0	0	1	.000	0	2	0	1.000
HOGSETT, p	1	0	0	0	0	0	0	0	0	0	.000	1	0	0	1.000
CROWDER, p	1	3	1	1	0	0	0	1	1	0	.333	2	1	0	1.000
Totals	6	206	21	51	11	1	1	[illegible]	25	27	.248	165	70	9	.963

Chicago Cubs (N. L.)

Player	G.	AB.	R.	H.	2B.	3B.	HR.	RBI.	B.B.	S.O.	Pct.	P.O.	A.	E.	Pct.
Galan, lf	6	25	2	4	1	0	0	2	2	2	.160	12	1	1	.929
Herman, 2b	6	24	3	8	2	1	1	6	0	2	.333	15	19	1	.971
Lindst'm, cf-3b	4	15	0	3	1	0	0	0	1	1	.200	8	1	1	.900
*Klein, rf	5	12	2	4	0	0	1	2	0	2	.333	4	0	0	1.000
Hartnett, c	6	24	1	7	0	0	1	2	0	3	.292	33	6	0	1.000
Dem'ree, rf-cf	6	24	2	6	1	0	2	2	1	4	.250	8	1	0	1.000
Cavarretta, 1b	6	24	1	3	0	0	0	0	0	5	.125	58	3	1	.984
Hack, 3b-ss	6	22	2	5	1	1	0	0	2	2	.227	6	10	0	1.000
Jurges, ss	6	16	3	4	0	0	0	1	4	4	.250	16	15	1	.969
WARNEKE, p	3	5	0	1	0	0	0	0	0	0	.200	2	9	0	1.000
ROOT, p	2	0	0	0	0	0	0	0	0	0	.000	0	1	0	1.000
LEE, p	2	1	0	0	0	0	0	1	0	0	.000	1	1	0	1.000
FRENCH, p	2	4	1	1	0	0	0	0	0	2	.250	1	2	0	1.000
HENSHAW, p	1	1	0	0	0	0	0	0	0	0	.000	0	1	0	1.000
KOWALIK, p	1	2	1	1	0	0	0	0	0	0	.500	0	2	1	.666
CARLE'N, p	1	1	0	0	0	0	0	0	1	1	.000	0	2	0	1.000
*O'Dea	1	1	0	1	0	0	0	1	0	0	1.000	0	0	0	.000
*Stephenson	1	1	0	0	0	0	0	0	0	1	.000	0	0	0	.000
Totals	6	202	18	48	6	2	5	7	11	29	.238	164	74	6	.975

*Pinch hitters.

Pitching Records

Detroit Tigers

Player.	G.	C.G.	I.P.	H.	R.	ER.	B.B.	S.O.	W.P.	H.B.	W.	L.	Pct.
Bridges	2	2	18	18	6	5	4	9	0	0	2	0	1.000
Crowder	1	1	9	5	1	1	3	5	0	0	1	0	1.000
Rowe	3	2	21	19	8	6	1	14	0	0	1	2	.333
Auker	1	0	6	6	3	2	2	1	0	0	0	0	.009
Hogsett	1	0	1	0	0	0	1	0	0	1	0	0	.000

Chicago Cubs

Player.	G.	C.G.	I.P.	H.	R.	ER.	B.B.	S.O.	W.P.	H.B.	W.	L.	Pct.
Warneke	3	1	16 2-3	9	2	2	4	5	0	0	2	0	1.000
Root	2	0	2	5	4	4	1	2	0	0	0	1	.000
Lee	2	0	10 1-3	11	4	4	5	3	0	0	0	0	.000
French	2	1	10 2-3	15	5	4	2	8	0	0	0	2	.000
Carleton	1	0	7	6	2	1	7	4	0	0	0	1	.000
Henshaw	1	0	3 2-3	2	3	3	5	2	1	1	0	0	.000
Kowalik	1	0	4 1-3	3	1	1	1	1	0	1	0	0	.000

Composite Score by Innings

Detroit Tigers	5 0 1	4 0 3	1 4 2	0	1—21
Chicago Cubs	2 3 3	0 4 0	3 0 3	0	0—18

Stolen Bases—Hack, Gehringer.

Sacrifices—Lee (3), Hartnett, Lindstrom, Cavarretta, Herman, Owen, Gehringer, Walker.

Double Plays—Cochrane and Gehringer; Bridges, Rogell and Greenberg; Gehringer and Greenberg; Rogell, Gehringer and Owen (2); Gehringer, Rogell and Owen (2); Jurges, Herman and Cavarretta (2); Herman and Cavarretta; Jurges and Herman; Jurges and Cavarretta.

Left on Bases—Detroit, 51; Chicago, 38.

Passed Ball—Cochrane.

Balk—Carleton.

Umpires—Moriarty and McGowan (AL), Quigley and Stark (NL).

Times of Games—1:51, 1:30, 2:27, 2:28, 1:49, 1:57.

Just '150 Pounds of Courage,' Yelling Cochrane Calls Bridges

Goslin Mauled by Exulting Teammates; Cubs, Downcast, Praise Victors' Play

By The Associated Press

DETROIT, Oct. 7.—With blood curdling yells that rocked the rafters, the victorious Tigers charged into their dressing room after walloping the Cubs, 4 to 3, today, to cut loose in a wild hilarious celebration.

Cy Perkins, Tiger coach, led the procession. Then came big Schoolboy Rowe, Clifton, Gehringer, Goose Goslin, and the rest, all yelling, swearing and sweating. The Tigers immediately made for Goslin, whose single in the ninth scored Mickey Cochrane with the winning run. They surrounded him, pulled off his shirt and mauled and hauled him all over the place.

Cochrane, the bulldog of a man who piloted the Tigers to their first world championship, was beaming with pride. He paid a remarkable tribute to little Tommy Bridges, the Tigers' winning pitcher.

Cochrane Lauds Bridges

"A hundred and fifty pounds of courage," he yelled. "If there ever is a payoff on courage this little 150-pound pitcher is the greatest World Series hero. It was the finest exhibition of pitching I ever saw in a World Series game. In the ninth inning, after Hack had tripled, Bridges threw nine of the best curves I ever looked at to get the next three men.

"Hell—what a series. We beat a great ball club. I'm glad it's all over."

"What was your greatest thrill of the series?" Cochrane was asked.

"Crossing that plate with the winning run in the ninth," he said, as his face broke into a broad grin.

The Tiger manager, sweating and tired, dropped down on the cashier-like cage that serves as his office, and yelled for a cigarette.

Meanwhile, his players were whooping it up. They were yelling, chasing each other around the dressing room and slapping each other on the back.

In came Kenesaw Mountain Landis, gray-haired commissioner of baseball, to extend his congratulations to Cochrane. Ford Frick, president of the National League, joined him.

"I never saw a greater World Series game," was Landis's comment.

Cochrane's dad and mother, with a brother, Albert, came on from Bridgewater, Mass., their home, to witness their son's triumph and Cochrane was happy about it. Mickey plans to leave for a trip with Tris Speaker and other friends for Cody, Wyo., Wednesday, for a hunting trip and a period of forgetting about baseball, photographers and reporters.

Hartnett Joins Well Wishers

Gabby Hartnett, the Cubs' catcher, joined the crowd of well wishers congratulating Cochrane. He shook Mickey's hand warmly and said: "I hope we play you in the series next year."

Then Grimm, the Cubs' manager, came through the door to extend his congratulations.

"Thanks, Charlie," Cochrane said, gripping the Chicago leader's hand. Then Grimm told him: "It was a helluva series. It was a tough one to lose. I hope we meet up again next year."

The Cubs trooped into their dressing room weary and crushed. Grimm looked like he had lost his best friend. He was disappointed and so were his players.

"We were beaten by a grand ball club," Grimm said, "both evenly matched. It was just a question of which one would score just one more run in three games."

Big Larry French strode over to Grimm and shook his hand, remarking: "I'm sorry, Charlie," to which Grimm replied: "Sorry, hell, you pitched a helluva ball game, Larry, and it was a tough one to lose."

Billy Herman, the Cubs' sparkling second baseman, said: "The Tigers looked like a good ball club because they beat a better one."

Gabby Hartnett declared, "I'm a tough loser but we were beaten by a great ball club. I hope we can meet 'em next year."

World Series Results And Final Standing

Final Standing

	W.	L.	Pct.
Detroit (A. L.)	4	2	.667
Chicago (N. L.)	2	4	.333

Results

At Detroit (October 2)—				R.	H.	E.
Chicago	2 0 0	0 0 0	0 0 1—3		7	0
Detroit	0 0 0	0 0 0	0 0 0—0		4	3

Batteries—Warneke and Hartnett; Rowe and Cochrane.

At Detroit (October 3)—				R.	H.	E.
Chicago	0 0 0	0 1 0	2 0 0—3		6	1
Detroit	4 0 0	3 0 0	1 0 x—8		9	2

Batteries—Root, Henshaw, Kowalik and Hartnett; Bridges and Cochrane.

At Chicago (October 4)—					R.	H.	E.
Detroit	0 0 0	0 0 1	0 4 0	0 1—6		12	2
Chi	0 2 0	0 1 0	0 0 2	0 0—5		10	3

Batteries—Auker, Hogsett, Rowe and Cochrane; Lee, Warneke, French and Hartnett.

At Chicago (October 5)—				R.	H.	E.
Detroit	0 0 1	0 0 1	0 0 0—2		7	0
Chicago	0 1 0	0 0 0	0 0 0—1		5	2

Batteries—Crowder and Cochrane; Carleton, Root and Hartnett.

At Chicago (October 6)—				R.	H.	E.
Detroit	0 0 0	0 0 0	0 0 1—1		7	1
Chicago	0 0 2	0 0 0	0 1 x—3		8	0

Batteries—Rowe and Cochrane; Warneke, Lee and Hartnett.

At Detroit (October 7)				R.	H.	E.
Chicago	0 0 1	0 2 0	0 0 0—3		12	0
Detroit	1 0 0	1 0 1	0 0 1—4		12	1

Batteries—French and Hartnett; Bridges and Cochrane.

DIMAGGIO GETS 3 HITS IN N.Y. DEBUT

SEALS WIN DOUBLE HEADER FROM SACS

'OUR JOE' TAKES OVER N.Y.

Joe Blasts Triple

'Nervous at First'

DERBY HEAT OFF

Louisville Subsides

By JOHN LARDNER

Chronicle Sporting Green

EDITED BY HARRY B. SMITH AND BILL LEISER

FOUNDED 1865 MONDAY, MAY 4, 1936 CCC 21 VOL. CXLVIII, NO. 109

San Francisco Triumphs by 10-3, 10-4

PARD HERO

O'Doul's Club Takes Series, 4 to 3

By ED. R. HUGHES

The Seals finished the series with Sacramento in gallant fashion. They won Saturday afternoon, they copped two games yesterday, morning and afternoon, and they took the long end of the series, four games to three. The scores yesterday were: Seals 10, Sacramento 3, in the morning, and in the afternoon Seals 10, Sacramento 4.

The two victories were welcomed by Manager O'Doul, but, most of all, he was pleased with the pitching and hitting of Pete Daglia, a large, well-fed gentleman from Napa, who has spent the last 10 days getting in shape. Pete looks to be ready now and if he is, he will be a big help, for he can work often.

Old Pard Ballou handled the afternoon game and after the third inning he looked great, for he allowed Sacramento only two hits and no runs. The curve was breaking just right and the Old Pard kept shoving it in there, to the bewilderment of some of the young fellows on the Sacramento club.

O'DOUL SHOWS HIS CONFIDENCE IN BALLOU

Garibaldi opened the afternoon game with a single and scored on a three-bagger by Epps, so things did not look any too bright for the Old Pard right then. But Manager O'Doul had faith larger than a grain of mustard seed and even when Epps scored on an infield out, he did not disturb Old Pard.

The Seals came back with four runs in their half of the first inning and batted Andrews out of the box. Ted Norbert mopped up with a home run, to drive in two of the runs, and as Thomas followed with a single and Barath drew a pass, Andrews was banished and Lyons, a little left-hander, took his place.

Sacramento attacked Old Pard

Continued on Page 24, Col. 8

MEXICO BEATS U. S. ARMY FOUR

MEXICO CITY, May 3 (AP)—The Mexican Olympic polo team defeated the United States Army Eighth Area Corps quartet, 5 to 4, today, scoring the winning goal after a 2-minute overtime period.

PHILLY TAKES SOCCER TITLE

PHILADELPHIA, May 3 (AP)—The German-Americans, of Philadelphia, won the United States open soccer championship today by defeating the St. Louis Shamrocks, 3 to 0, in the second and final game of the national championships.

WITH A GREAT BIG BANG, Joe DiMaggio, once of our own Seals, made his bow as a baseball player in little old New York yesterday. The size of the bang Joe created can be measured only by the storm of approval scribes and fans heaped upon him after his smashing day.

DIMAGGIO COLLECTED three hits in six times at the plate and he handled his only fielding chance perfectly. A triple and two singles were his bit toward the Yankees' 14-5 victory over the St. Louis Browns and his bingles drove in one run and scored 3.

Armstrong Race Victor

Art Armstrong, San Mateo, won the 60-lap auto race on the Oakland speedway's half-mile track in 31 minutes 3 4-5 seconds yesterday.

Fred Agabashian, Berkeley, finished second and "Herk" Edwards, Watsonville, third. "Tex" Peterson Pasadena, heavy pre-race favorite, placed sixth.

Peterson, however, won the three-lap trophy dash and a 10-lap sprint race. He led the main race until he went into a spin, relinquishing his first place to Agabashian. The later whirled at the same spot several laps later and Armstrong took and held the lead to the finish.

Duane Carter, Fresno, and "Bud" Rose, Los Angeles, were winners in 10 and 15-lap events.

U. S. WALKING RECORD SET

NEW YORK, May 3 (AP)—Charles Eschenbach of the New York Athletic Club, claimed a new national record as he won the National Senior A. A. U. 30,000 meter walking championship on Staten Island today in two hours, 33 minutes. No official record for the distance is listed among national or world marks.

SO THEY'RE PERFECT?

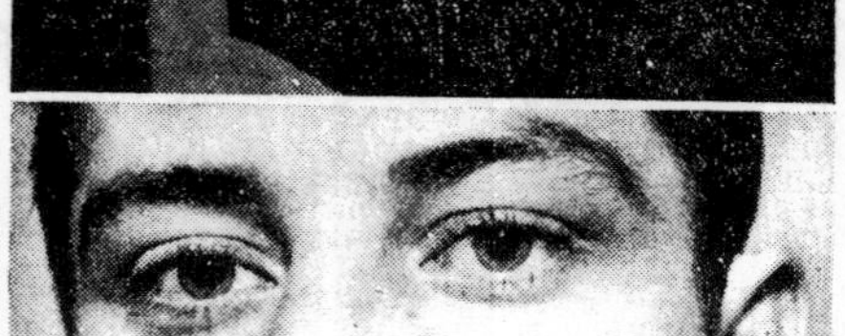

MONK MOSCRIP, Stanford end, takes a gander in the mirror at the eyes optometrists rave about. And these are the eyes, in person.

HE WANTED GLASSES

Doc Turns Down Monk

Examination Reveals Grid Star's Perfect Pair of Eyes

By WILL CONNOLLY

James Henderson Moscrip, the handsome Monk of Stanford, has a pair of eyes that are as near perfection as it is possible to get without looking like Eddie Cantor.

So Monk concluded he needed glasses.

He went to Dr. H. Gordon Smith of Palo Alto, who tends to the Stanford hypochondriacs, and suggested, maybe, please, could I have glasses for reading?

Dr. Smith, always willing to oblige, made Monk read EFTHGR on a lighted glass panel, which was easy for him, because he is a senior in college. Monk had a minor difficulty trying to pronounce it, though.

Then Dr. Smith put all kinds of testing gadgets on Monk's eyes and at length chased him out of the office.

"Get out of here! Don't be wasting my time," said Dr. Smith with some pique. "Your eyes are pips. Never in my born days have I seen such muscular coordination, such refraction, such depth of perception. You can't have glasses."

Monk was crestfallen to learn he couldn't wear cheaters and his eyes were perhaps the best Dr. Smith had ever come across. It was a great blow to discover there was nothing wrong with them.

BAD NEWS FOR MONK TO TAKE

Dr. Smith further discouraged Monk by telling him he would make a swell aviator. The ocular muscle test he passed with highest honors in his class is given student flyers before they can take a crate off the ground.

We have a prodigy in our midst. Maybe Monk's eyes are the best in the world, like Kitty Gordon's back and Claudette Colbert's legs.

I think Stanford ought to enter Mon kin the national amateur ogling tournament to afford him an opportunity to bring more glory to the old school. He might even get to Berlin and the Olympic googoo eye event, which is stern competition indeed.

Monk's eyes are either gray, sea green or tinted with brown. He isn't sure himself. But they're not blue.

The minute but sturdy muscles

Continued on Page 22, Col. 5

J. HARRINGTON OF BLUMS DIES

Joe Harrington, prominent in semi pro baseball circles of Northern California, died here yesterday. Joe was former manager of the Blum Sweets in the Golden Gate Valley League. He was son of the late Tim Harrington, one-time Fire Department lieutenant and brother of John, Bill and George Harrington. Funeral will be Wednesday from Carew and English.

FRENCH SWEEP DAVIS SERIES

PARIS, May 3 (AP)—France made a clean sweep in its Davis Cup tennis encounter with China with two singles victories today, Boussus defeating Guy Chang and Destemeau defeating Kho Sin Kie.

MONTE CARLO, May 3 (AP) — Holland clinched a berth in the second round of the European zone Davis Cup tennis competition today

LEVINSKY TO BOX RAMAGE

LOS ANGELES, May 3 (AP)—Joe Waterman, Los Angeles matchmaker, announced today he had signed Lee Ramage, San Diego heavy weight, and King Levinsky, Chicago, for a return bout at the Olympic Auditorium May 26.

2 Outboard Marks Fall

VALLEJO, May 3—Two crackups and two unofficial world records featured today's windup of the Vallejo outboard regatta.

Ernie Lewis, Windcat, an outboard, went amuck and cracked into Watson's barge after the driver had dived overboard. "Pop" Foster of the Sacramento Yacht Club rescued both.

Lou Garibaldi in his Garry III set an unofficial world's mark of 44.7 in the service runabout class while Tommy Eldridge of Oakland in his Flash set an unofficial world's mark of 50.4 in the .151 cubic inch class.

FAMILY RUNABOUT—First, E. S. Hughes, Sacramento; H. Anderson, Oakland, second; H. Brasefield, Oakland, third. Time, 47 mpd.

151 CUBIC INCH—First, Tommy Eldridge, Oakland; Bill Knight, Vallejo, second. Time, 50.4 mpd.

225 CUBIC INCH—First, Tommy Eldridge, Oakland; E. S. Hughes, Sacramento, second. Time, 44.4 mpd.

718 CUBIC INCH GOLD CUP CLASS—First, Gene Armstrong; W. H. Sheehan, second. Time, 56.4 mph.

CLASS C SERVICE RUNADOUT—First, Lou Garibaldi; Bud Kehke, second; Sid McMurtrey, all Vallejo. Time, 44.5.

CLASS C HYDROPLANE—Won, Bud Kehke, Vallejo. Time, 45.6.

OUTBOARD FREE FOR ALL—Won by Lou Garibaldi, Vallejo.

HOW DI MAG' DID IT

PLAY-BY-PLAY OF JOE

Special Story Records His Every Move at Bat, in Field

(Special to The Chronicle)

NEW YORK, May 3 — Joe DiMaggio, $25,000 slugging outfielding beauty from the San Francisco Seals made his debut with the New York Yankees today and starred with a vengeance.

Kept out of action for the first three weeks of the season by a burned foot, he took—as advertised—the field against the last-place St. Louis Browns and hit and fielded well to the delight of a sizeable section of New York's vast Italian-American element.

He, certainly not the lowly Hornsby troupe, drew 26,000 to Colonel Jake Ruppert's ball park despite intermittent showers and, spotted in third place in the batting order just ahead of the great Lou Gehrig, pounded out three hits for a total of five bases —one of his blows being a triple— in six turns at bat against four brown hurlers, drove in a run and scored three times himself to aid Joe McCarthy's charges to an easy 14 to 5 victory.

HASN'T THROWN

The youthful appearing newcomer, never off the West Coast until he trained with the Yanks at St. Petersburg this spring, comported himself like a veteran although he had but one fly to handle in his left field position and encountered no real test of his throwing prowess.

After the Browns tallied thrice in their first turn at bat with the aid of Clift's line double to DiMaggio's territory, the Browns' starting pitcher, John Knott, lasted for only one out after New York went to work on him.

Crosetti tripled and Rolfe walked. DiMaggio slapped toward third and when Knott tossed home, a runup ensued, ending in a poor throw by Knott and after Gehrig walked and Caldwell replaced Knott, Chapman's double cleared the filled bases. Chapman tallied later and the Yanks were in front, never to be headed.

In the second inning the Yankees added three more, this time DiMaggio's high fly falling for a hit in the midst of the fireworks and he subsequently scored his number two run.

OOP! FANNED

In the fourth DiMaggio struck out, but his mates added two more counters. After Lefty Gomez was batted out by the Browns in the fifth, and Caldwell went out for a pinch hitter, DiMaggio's triple to left off Hoggsett figured in another four-run scoring jamboree.

DiMaggio flied to right to start the seventh, but the Yanks added another tally in that session. With Van Atta the opposing thrower, DiMaggio once more came to bat in the eighth with two out and singled cleanly—but Gehrig fanned.

New York fandom then and there decided DiMaggio would make the grade.

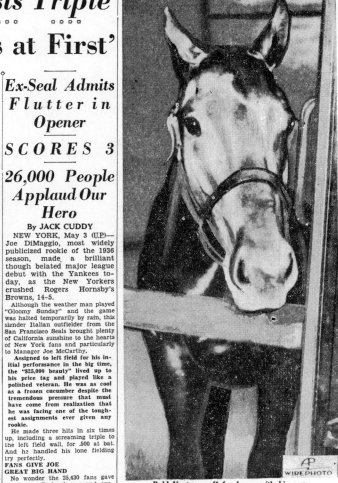

Ex-Seal Admits Flutter in Opener

SCORES 3

26,000 People Applaud Our Hero

By JACK CUDDY

NEW YORK, May 3 (U.P.)—Joe DiMaggio, most widely publicized rookie of the 1936 season, made a brilliant though belated major league debut with the Yankees today, as the New Yorkers crushed Rogers Hornsby's Browns, 14-5.

Although the weather man played "Gloomy Sunday" and the game was halted temporarily by rain, this slender Italian outfielder from the San Francisco Seals brought plenty of California sunshine to the hearts of New York fans and particularly to Manager Joe McCarthy.

Assigned to left field for his initial performance in the big time, the "$25,000 beauty" lived up to his price tag and played like a polished veteran. He was as cool as a frozen cucumber despite the tremendous pressure that must have come from realization that he was facing one of the toughest assignments ever given any rookie.

He made three hits in six times up, including a screaming triple to the left field wall, for .500 at bat. And he handled his lone fielding try perfectly.

FANS GIVE JOE GREAT BIG HAND

No wonder the 25,430 fans gave the loping fly-hawk a grand ovation in his last turn at bat, and no wonder Yankee veterans swarmed around smiling Joe in the dressing room after the game, pumping his hand and patting his back and offering congratulations.

And no wonder Marse Joe McCarthy told reporters, "Yes sir—he came through like a real money player. He lived up to my expectations. I'm certin Joe will be an important factor in our pennant drive. He'll certainly take up a lot of slack in our club."

Joe modestly disclaimed any great nervousness after the game.

"The only time I felt anything like a flutter around the heart was when I stepped up to bat for the first time," he said. "Guess that was only natural. But after I connected with the ball and got to second on

Continued on Page 24, Col. 4

SEMIPRO HAS NO-HIT GAME

MARYSVILLE, May 3 (AP)—Norman Coad, semi-pro baseball pitcher, hurled a no-hit, no-run game for the Marysville Giants as they defeated Grass Valley, 4 to 0

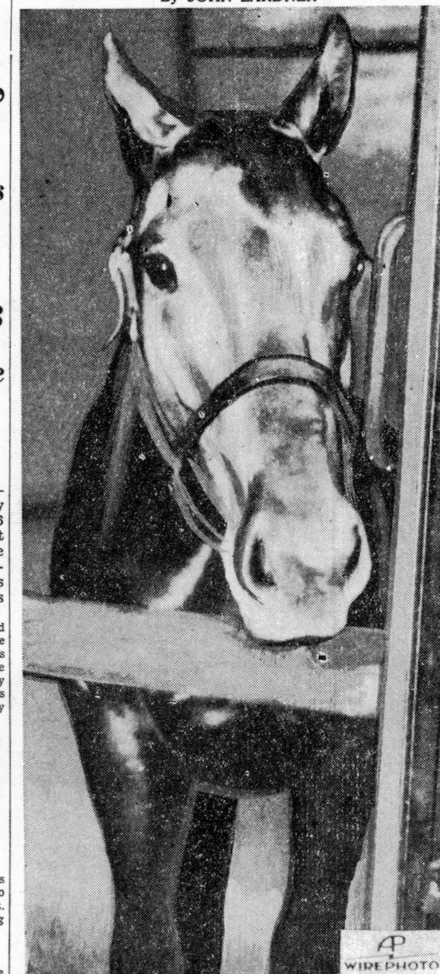

Bold Venture—off for home with big purse

Kentucky Almost Back to Normal After Big Race

By JOHN LARDNER

LOUISVILLE, Ky., May 3—They're saying that Brevity was the best horse in the Kentucky Derby, and Mr. Maxie Hirsch, who trained the winning horse, Bold Venture, does not actually deny it.

"Maybe Brevity was the best horse," said Mr. Hirsch as he swung a leg aboard the eastbound rattler. "Maybe he was. But they hung up my horse's number on the board when the race was over, and that satisfies me."

You know by this time that the sleek chestnut colt named Bold Venture won a most remarkable victory in the sixty-second edition of the Blue Grass and Julep classic. He won by the length of his barrel nose over a beast which was backed so strongly that he would have paid only eighty cents for a dollar's investment had he finished first. Brevity was supported right to the teeth. The crowd loved him. And naturally the crowd was a bit vexed by the manner in which its favorite lost.

JOHN'S IDEA

After twenty-four hours of investigation, I am prepared to give you some idea of the scenario of the race, which resulted in the suspension of three jockeys, including the winning rider. The big jam occurred soon after the start. Bold Venture, anxious to slip through the middle and toward the rail, banged hard against Granville, who promptly threw his rider, Jimmy Stout. Ira Hanford, up on Bold Venture, says he remembers this very well.

"I don't remember which horse it was we bumped against," declares Ira, better known as Babe, "but I know that when he went over I had to swing Bold Venture way to the right to avoid his heels. We lost some ground right there."

BUMPED!

Brevity, the favorite, seems to have been bumped by Mack Garner on Sangreal, though the episode was not seen clearly and Garner drew no suspension. Wayne Wright, Brevity's rider, when he conquered his bitter disappointment sufficiently to talk about it, said that the great Widener colt went almost to his knees, staggered, and lost a number of strides getting back in the race.

"And when you figure that we only lost by one stride," said Mr. Wright, "you can see what might

Continued on Page 22, Col. 7

HONUS WAGNER 'BUSH LANDIS'

WICHITA, Kas., May 3 (AP) — Honus Wagner, a former great shortstop in the National League, today was appointed national high commissioner for the National Semipro Baseball Congress.

DIMAGGIO HOMES

'Thank Youse'

JOE'S FIRST HOME RUN

Chronicle Sporting Green

EDITED BY HARRY B. SMITH AND BILL LEISER

FOUNDED 1865 SAN FRANCISCO CHRONICLE, MONDAY, MAY 11, 1936 21

32,000 ON HAND AS JOE TOURS OVER BAGS

Yanks Defeat Athletics, 7 to 2

NEW YORK, May 10 (AP)—The New York Yankees defeated the Philadelphia Athletics, 7-2, today before the second largest crowd of the season, 32,034, with Joe Di Maggio and Bill Dickey each belting a homer.

Johnny Murphy, making his first start for the Yankees, failed to go the route. He gave only four hits in the 7 2-3 innings he worked, but he passed seven and had to be relieved by Pat Malone, who retired the last four batters to give the Yankees the series, two games to one.

The Yankees took advantage of George Turbeville's wildness, mixing opportune base hits with passes and a hit batsman to roll up their run total.

DiMaggio had failed 10 consecutive trips to the plate when he hit his homer with one on in the first game. It was his only hit of the game.

Dickey's seventh homer of the year came in the fifth inning, with one on, and the Yankee's final run was scored in the next inning, when Babe Selkirk and Tony Lazzeri draw passes and Rolfe singled, to send one run home.

After holding the A's scoreless for seven innings, Murphy issued four passes in the eighth, which, together with a single by Puccinelli, gave the Athletics both their runs.

HOMER NO. 1

PHILADELPHIA	AB	H	O	A	NEW YORK	AB	H	O	A
Finney,1b	4	0	7	0	Crosetti,s	3	0	2	1
Moses,cf	3	0	2	0	Rolfe,3b	4	1	0	2
Johnson,lf	3	1	1	0	DiMaggio,lf	4	1	4	0
Pucinelli,rf	4	2	4	0	Gehrig,1b	2	0	8	1
Higgins,3b	2	0	1	0	Dickey,c	4	2	7	1
Warstler,2b	3	0	2	3	Chapman,cf	4	0	3	0
Newsome,s	3	0	1	4	Selkirk,rf	3	2	1	0
Dean	1	0	0	0	Lazzeri,2b	2	1	0	0
Peters,s	0	0	1	0	Murphy,p	3	0	2	4
Hayes,c	4	1	5	1	Malone,p	1	0	0	0
Turbville,p	2	0	1	0					
Wilshire,p	0	0	0	0	Totals	30	7	27	9
Mailho,	0	0	0	0					
Upchurch,p	0	0	0	0					
Berry	1	0	0	0					
Totals	30	4	24	9					

Mailho batted for Wilshire in eighth.
Dean batted for Newsome in eighth.
Berry batted for Upcnurch in ninth.

Philadelphia..	0	0	0	0	0	0	0	2	0	—2
New York....	2	1	0	0	3	1	0	0	*	—7

Runs—Johnson, Mailho (Philadelphia 2); Crosetti, Rolfe, DiMaggio, Gehrig, Dickey, Selkirk (New York 7). Errors—Johnson, Higgins. Runs batted in—DiMaggio 3, Lazzeri, Dickey 2, Rolfe, Puccinelli, Warstler. Home runs—DiMaggio, Dickey. Double plays—Murphy to Gehrig; Newsome to Warstler to Finey. Bases on balls—Murphy 7, Turbeville 3, Wilshire 2. Strikeouts—Murphy 4, Wilshire 2, Malone 2, Upchurch 1. Hits—Off Turbeville, 5 in 5 innings; Wilshire, 2 in 2; Murphy, 4 in 7 2-3. Hit by pitcher—By Turbeville (Gehrig, twice). Wild pitch—Turbeville. Winning pitcher—Murphy. Losing pitcher—Turbeville. Umpires—Kolls, Moriarty and Basil. Attendance, 32,034. Time of game—2h. 15m.

ALICE MARBLE TITLE WINNER

LOS ANGELES, May 10 (AP)—Bobby Riggs of Los Angeles, national junior singles champion, won the Southern California men's singles title today, defeating Chuck Carr, University of Southern California star, 6-4, 6-1, 7-5, in finals of the fiftieth annual tournament.

Alice Marble, former San Francisco player, captured the women's crown, defeating Dorothy Bundy, Los Angeles, 6-2, 6-4.

THE LAD ALL NEW YORK hopes will fill the extra large shoes of one George Herman (Babe) Ruth came through yesterday with the first home run of his young major league career.

IN THIS A. P. WIREPHOTO rushed to The Chronicle from New York, Joe DiMaggio, former Seal, steps across the plate and acknowledges applause after his first homer for the Yanks. No. 4, welcoming Joe home, is Lou Gehrig.

SEALS RAP 20 RUNS TO WIN TWICE FROM L. A.

S. F. Sluggers Stage 'Wotta' Rally

By ED. R. HUGHES

The Seals put a brilliant finish to the series with the Angels by beating them twice yesterday, 10 to 2, in the morning and 10 to 5 in the afternoon. They also won the series, four games to three.

Joe Marty put on a great display in the morning game by whacking out a triple, a double and a single in four times up and he also stole two bases. Joe is probably the most improved player in the league this year.

He got no hits in the afternoon because he was walked twice and was ordered to sacrifice another time. Harley Boss, big first baseman, has begun to hit at last, for he got two singles in the morning and a triple and a single in the afternoon. If he can continue, he will be a big help for the Seals have been shy on hitting of late.

SHEEHAN BEATS ANGELS EASILY

Kenny Sheehan beat the Angels easily in the morning, holding them to six hits, two of which were infield taps and he walked only three men. He did not try to throw the ball past the hitters as he usually does, and his slow stuff had the Angels stopped. They got to him for three hits in the fifth and scored their only two runs.

The Seals hammered Hugh Casey hard the six innings he worked, making 10 hits and scoring nine runs. They picked up the other one off Kimball, the relief man. Marty led the hitters of both clubs.

In the afternoon Ed Stutz and Salveson had a tough tussle for eight rounds, the score being 3 to 2 in favor of the Seals when Salveson was lifted for a pinch hitter and Prim, a southpaw, went to work in the eighth. He walked Holder, Rhyne singled and Marty shoved them along with a sacrifice. Nor-

Continued on Page 24, Col. 5

Gotham Sizes Up DiMaggio

NEW YORK, May 10 (AP)—Down the sport trail where we meet Joe DiMaggio, the new bambino of Yankee Stadium, whose exploits have stretched the elastic imaginations of fans like no other rookie has done in modern day baseball:

PERSONAL—Joe, somehow, reminds one of a Newfoundland puppy, big, rawboned and growing. He's 6 feet, weighs 185 and seems awkward for his carriage. Doc Painter, Yankee trainer, says Joe will need two years to fill out and that until that time he'll be highly susceptible to injuries as there is a terrific strain on his leg cords. Particularly when sliding bases.

ALSO FISHES

He doesn't go in for fancy dress despite the Italian love of color. His favorite colors are brown and gray. Next to baseball, his favorite sport is fishing. Likes to fish for striped bass in San Francisco bay with his boyhood pal, Frank Larocca, with whom he corresponds religiously. Has never played golf, but guesses the boys will have him cussing on the links soon. Likes to swim, but doesn't claim to be a Weissmuller.

A great fight fan. Favorite fighter is Heavy Weight Champion Jimmy Braddock, "because he isn't high hat." Cheered himself hoarse, however, when Tony Canzoneri, his Paisano, came back to shellack Jimmy McLarnin. Smokes cigarettes, but doesn't drink beer or liquor. A lover of Italian dishes and lonely for his place at his mother's table of sphagetti. Keeps scrapbooks with help of mother and two sisters.

Isn't hurt when writers ride him, passing it off like a veteran. Rooms with Frank Crosetti, another San Francisco Italian boy who made good with the Yankees. Gets his baseball advice from Tony Lazzeri, who coaches him carefully on each pitcher. The three have formed a "Little Italy" club on the team and get along marvelously well. Joe doesn't say it very convincingly, but he claims to be a woman hater. "I've never had a steady," says Joe, "and I don't want one. I rip up mash notes without reading them."

Just the same, girls, we have a

Continued on Page 24, Col. 1

MAJESTIC FIRST AT LONGCHAMPS

PARIS, May 10 (AP)—Majestic, owned by the Argentine sportsman, Edouardo Martinez de Hoz, won the Prix Louvesciennes, worth 15,000 francs, at Longchamps today. Mme. S. Fockans' Presbyterian was second, two lengths behind, and Rene Aumont's Massawa, third.

AS BILL LEISER SEES IT..

WESTERN SPORTSMEN DOING THINGS — MAJOR TAYLOR BEN EASTMAN TOO

A few nominations, today, of men who are doing things for Western sports. First, Major Austin C. Taylor of Vancouver, a racing man, and a racing man to whom the term "sportsman" may be applied with all the connotation that word originally was intended to imply; but, above all, a sportsman who is FOR WESTERN RACING.

It's no small boon to Coast racing, this development of the record breaker, Indian Broom, and the almost record breaker, Special Agent, at Tanforan and Bay Meadows. No, Indian Broom didn't win the Kentucky derby, but don't ever think his third was any discredit to Coast racing.

The fact that both horses were Brookmeade castoffs only argues for the acumen and sportsmanship of Major Taylor and Trainer Darrell Cannon, who took a chance and made sensations of these ponies. Major Taylor is a sportsman of the Whitney, Woodward, or Widener type, if you understand what I mean. He can't always get his special car ready and move to strips where his ponies are running, but when he can he will, and all the time he will be developing horses on Western tracks, in Western races, and

Continued on Page 23, Col. 6

Aeolians Keep Perpetual Cup

By BILL LEISER

THE CHIP off the old block was too steady, yesterday, for the first challenger sent out by the Richmond Yacht Club in quest of San Francisco's famous old Perpetual Challenge Cup.

The chip off the old block was Babe Stevens at the tiller of the Aeolian red Robin, who sailed a perfect 13 miles course while his dad, "Pop" Stevens, watched from the committee boat and almost fainted as young "Babe" hit a calm spot under Alcatraz Island.

"Why," I've struggled for two hours to get out of there," wailed "Pop" Stevens, but "Babe" didn't struggle at all. His Robin slipped on through, and when it was all over he and the three skippers he had as crew put the Robin home two minutes and 16 seconds ahead of the Skylark in command of Glen Conn.

So It Stays

And so the Perpetual Challenge Trophy, most coveted bit of sailing hardware on this coast since the year 1895, remains among the Aeolian Yacht Club collection in Alameda where it went a year ago after this same Babe Stevens, then in the Machree, defeated Myron Spaulding and the Mavis to lift the mug from its age old resting place in Corinthian vaults at Tiburon.

He comes by his sailing prowess honestly, this "Babe" Stevens, for "Pop," who wailed and worried about that calm spot yesterday, was at the tiller of the Ruby way back in 1914 when that craft went to Eureka to reclaim the old trophy

Continued on Page 23, Col. 2

HOW CUP BATTLERS STARTED (AND FINISHED)

OFF TO A LEAD with the starting gun, the Robin is shown getting an edge over the Skylark yesterday when the fight for the San Francisco perpetual cup started off Fillmore street.

MANEUVERED BY "BABE" STEVENS, of the family whose habit it is to win such events, the Robin finished just this way—in front—to keep the trophy safe on the Aeolian Club's shelf.

Portland Manager Released

PORTLAND, Or., May 10 (AP)—The Portland baseball club gave Manager Max Bishop, former Philadelphia Athletics star, his unconditional release tonight. He at once protested the severance of his contract to Judge Landis, baseball commissioner.

E. J. Schefter, president of the Portland club, said he hired Bishop as playing manager and released him because he has been ill and unable to fill the second base position.

Bill Sweeney, injured first baseman, was placed in temporary command.

DI MAGGIO'S HOMERS TIE MAJOR MARK

BUCK JOINS JOY SCHOOL

No More Gloom at Santa Clara

MIGHT SEE GAEL DEFEAT

By RALPH BELL

One ray of sunshine appears in the otherwise doleful departure of Clipper Smith from Santa Clara. The dinner in honor of the Clipper at the Greco Estate east of San Jose Tuesday night was filled with sadness, although there was every confidence that Buck Shaw will do an excellent job when he takes over his new head coaching duties in September.

It wasn't that the alumni and friends didn't believe that Shaw is capable, but Clipper Smiths aren't applying for every coaching post. There aren't so many of his cali'•r.

WON'T BE DISASTROUS SEASON, HE'S SURE

Clipper and Buck are the closest of friends, and their seven years of association at Santa Clara have been pleasant ones with nothing more serious than an occasional heated argument in the midst of the campaign as to whether they ought to play their tackles a little wider or send the ends booming in faster. But they're as different in many ways as Pop Warner and A. A. Stagg.

That's where the ray of light appeared through the clouds, for when I pinned him down L:wrence T., whom the Clipper mentions in his public utterances as "L. T.," confessed without equivocation that he was a natural optimist and that he'd join the joy school of thought when it came time to make football predictions.

He qualified almost at once, as a strict matter of fact, for before the dinner was over he had announced t' at even Clipper felt well about the 1936 Santa Clara prospects. The Clipper, Shaw quoted him, said that the Broncos "won't have such a disastrous season next Fall."

It's going to be hard to get used to listening to roseate prognostications about Santa Clara, after seven years of gloom. It will be nothing short of amazing to sit at a banquet table and hear Shaw tell of halfbacks with blistering speed and passes that can't fail, instead of the injuries that have hit the Mission campus and of the tough schedule.

It wouldn't surprise me at all if Buck would become so enthusiastic, if the opening games go well, that he'd come right out and predict a victory over St. Mary's in the Little Big Game.

Buck believes—and with a good deal of correct psychology, it seems to me, that the optimistic note may steam up his gridders more than a sorrowful mein, as long as he doesn't carry the sunshine so far that it begins to look more like the artificial glare of the incandescents instead of pure rays of light from above.

It's hard to find out just how Buck will fare in the conversational league, for he admits he has few of the Big Bertha words which endeared the Clipper to those who just can't keep away from football banquets. It was always time to listen sharply for the latest descriptive phrase of Smith's when he was introduced. You had to be keen to get his allegorical allusions.

THEY'RE ALL SO HAPPY

Buck doesn't appear greatly worried, and it may be that he has been studying public speaking secretly and ransacking the thesaurus and dictionary. If he'd only had a little more notice the Silver Fox might have prepared himself more carefully for his new work.

Of course the picture is getting so filled with joyous coaches that it may be necessary to hold 'em down a little, what with Stub Allison following his example of last year and being able to see nothing but easy victories, and Tiny Thornhill ready to call his new eleven greater than the vowers ever were. They tell me, too, that Spud Lewis is set to cheer wildly about his big list of fine reserves.

The only one you can see as a gloomy fellow now is Slip Madigan, who no doubt will heald his 1936 Gallopers as the weakest team he has had in a decade and one sure to lose most of its games. Or am I mistaken again?

Americans Win 3rd Polo Match

HURLINGHAM CLUB, LONDON, June 25.—(AP)—Firing goals through the disorganized opposition defense almost at will, America's polo forces defeated Great Britain, 15 to 9, in the third and final game of the series for the International Cup yesterday.

The game was really an exhibition, for the invaders had clinched the cup previously by beating the British, 10-5 and 8-6, in the first two matches of the series.

The Americans will remain in England for the open championship.

On Sports Spot

A tennis star and a rattlesnake share honors this evening "On the Sports Spot" at 7:45 o'clock on KLX. Edward G. "Bud" Chandler, president of the Northern California Tennis Association and one of the players in the State tennis tournament now in progress at the Berkeley Tennis Club, will be interviewed by Phil Ray concerning the tournament and the progress of his mixed doubles partner, Mrs. Helen Wills Moody.

As an added feature to the program, Bob Blake, publicity man for the wrestling industry, promises that the huge horned rattlesnake which accompanies Brother Jonathan on his mat tours, will rattle for the radio audience.

Tune in tonight — KLX — 7:45 o'clock.

JOE WALLOPS PAIR IN ONE INNING

By SID FEDER
Associated Press Sports Writer

For the youngster just breaking into the big time, Joe DiMaggio has a surprising way of grabbing off the baseball headlines from the boys who've been around.

Not only is he crowding lots of other stars out of the limelight, but to him and Slugger Lou Gehrig must go a large share of the credit for the growing conviction that the New York Yankees "murderers' row" can come pretty close to using water boys for hurlers and still coast into a pennant.

Just when "DiMag's" bat had quieted down to a level with other able, but less sensational sluggers, up he pops again with a record equalling stunt that has been done by less than ten others in the history of the game—hit two home runs in one inning.

DRIVES IN 5

In the fifth inning of yesterday's Yankee game with the White Sox, Joe let go his round trip clouts, one with two mates on base, the other with one, provided five runs in the ten-run Yankee putsch in that inning, sewing up the ball game for an 18-11 victory. This, along with the Boston Red Sox' 7-6 defeat at the hands of Tommy Bridges and the Detroit Tigers, boosted the New Yorkers' American League pace setting edge to 5½ games.

Against any other club, the White Sox'. 12 hits and 11 runs probably would have gone for a win. But not with the Yanks.

It turned out to be just another example of their power, despite mediocre pitching, for the Sox had just finished clubbing Lefty Gomez off the mound under a seven-run barrage. Pat Malone, who succeeded him, wasn't much more effective.

TIGERS SLIP

Despite their victory over the Red Sox, the Tigers slipped from fourth to fifth place, for the Cleveland Indians defeated the Athletics in both ends of a twin bill, 5-3 and 14-2, to pull up to a third place deadlock with the Senators, who found the Browns easy behind Buck Newsom's seven-hit pitching job and posted a 7-4 win. Feature of the Indians' double victory was Earl Averill's three homers.

Rain washed out warfare on three National League battlegrounds, and it remained for the Pirates and the Giants to provide all the action in splitting their doubleheaders. Carl Hubbell bested Cy Blanton in the opener, chalking up his tenth win by a 4-3 count, chiefly because the Bucs' sophomore star served a two-run home run ball to Mel Ott in the first inning. In the nightcap, big Jim Weaver finished on top 4-1 with a three-hit pitching performance.

"General" Alvin Crowder, whose sore arm and stomach ailment have cut his effectiveness this season, left the Tigers last night after asking for the rest of the season off. He'll be back next year, he hopes.

Ross Offered $40,000 To Defend Title

NEW YORK, June 25.—(AP)—Madison Square Garden yesterday telegraphed Barney Ross of Chicago an offer of $40,000 to defend his welterweight title here in August against either Jimmy McLarnin, former champion, or Tony Canzoneri, ruler of the lightweights. A reply from Ross is expected today.

HE'S MODERN SPEAR THROWER

Johnny Mottram, former Stanford I. C. A. A. A. A. javelin thrower, is shown at practice in Los Angeles. He will compete in the Olympic trials Saturday. Should Mottram ever get hungry he might be able to spear a meal, or at least a fish, with his trusty stick.—*A. P. photo.*

BENNETT LOSES COLLEGE MATCH

EVANSTON, Ill., June 25.—(U.P.)—Four seeded players led by Ernest Sutter of Tulane moved into quarter-finals of the National Intercollegiate Tennis championships today.

Sutter defeated John Law of Stanford. Vernon John, Southern California, Ben Day, Stanford, and George Stevens, Yale, all seeded, moved into the quarter-finals with him.

Four seeded players were eliminated yesterday. George Ball, Northwestern, was beaten by Ralph Minnich, Princeton; Lindsey Franklin, Texas, eliminated Russell Ball, Northwestern; Gardner Mulloy, Miami, eliminated Chuck Carr, Southern California, and Ramsey Potts, North Carolina, ousted Dick Bennett, California.

Bennett and Dick Newton, Southern California, defending champions, won their match in the doubles.

Merritt Sail Club Race Set

Skippers of the Lake Merritt Sail Club will stage the second race of this Summer's series for the Ellis Trophy next Sunday, with an even larger fleet than that which competed in last week's inaugural expected to take part.

Favorable sailing weather greeted the 13 competitors in the three divisions last Sunday. Best time was registered by Happy Days, L. Kizer's snipe class sailboat. Kizer built up a commanding lead in the seventh division with 6½ points for first place. Two boats were forced to withdraw from the race when Skimmer No. 33 lost its rudder and Alan Babcock's Bounty was eliminated after breaking the mast.

Final results of the first race, with corrected time and points awarded, follow:

DIVISION 1			
No. 33	Achor	14:17	5¼
No. 80	Allen	14:37	5
No. 37	Hall	14:58	4
Canoe	Splivalo	16:15	3
No. 33	Brown	D.N.F.	1
DIVISION 2			
Happy Days	Kizer	12:22	6¼
Sea Hag	Cleary	16:18	5
Ducky	Brophy	17:10	4
Lady Beth	Phillips	21:52	3
Dandy	Bryan	24:40	1
DIVISION 3			
Red Moon	Ellis	27:12	5¼
Lady Helen	Ayres	27:45	4
White Moon	Livingston	Dis.	

Starter—A. Babcock. Timer—P. T. Garver.

Bud Chandler Through With Singles Play

(Cont. From First Sport Page.)

whichever one he plays in the semi-finals, and will then bow to Hunt.

Oswald, a keen strategist and a remarkably astute fighter even though he hasn't as efficient strokes as some of his rivals, might upset all those calculations buy outthinking Hunt and by dogged determination. If he should get to the final he might take Senior into camp.

Oswald isn't playing the tennis he did last year, though, and it looks more like Hunt and Senior in the last match next Sunday, with the Los Angeles youth winning from the San Franciscan.

FAVOR OSBORNE

In other divisions of play Margaret Osborne should emerge as the State women's champion, if she gets by Gussie Raegener in the semis while in the lower bracket Eleanor Dawson and Mrs. Bonnie Miller Blank will stage a mighty close semi-final struggle. I wouldn't like to pick that one, but Miss Osborne ought to win from either in the final.

Eddie Alloo, after his heartbreaking defeat by Howard Blethen, 9-7, 6-0, yesterday, ought to take the junior boys title without trouble while the junior girls' championship looks like another triumph for Miss Osborne.

In mixed doubles, important because of the presence of Mrs. Helen Moody, it ought to be Mrs. Moody and Chandler against Miss Osborne and Culley for the title, which, if my dope is anywhere nearly correct, would give Osborne a chance at three crowns.

A San Diego youth, Harper Ink, who upset Larry Dee in men's singles, should breeze through to the 15-year-old title, although Dee should get another crack at him in the semi-final round.

Anne Morgan, billed for defeat in singles, should team with Eleanor Dawson to take the junior girls doubles title, giving Miss Dawson two finals.

Miss Morgan and Miss Dawson meet in the singles semi-final, with the odds favoring Miss Dawson. The winner should meet Miss Osborne after she defeats Virginia Wolfenden in the semi-finals.

DOC LONG SHOT IN MAT MATCH

In this dry and age of upsets it would not surprise the average wrestling fan to see Dr. Freddie Meyer, the wrestling medico, pin Vincent Lopez in their world heavyweight title match at the Auditorium tomorrow night.

Longer shots have come in recently. Braddock, Schmeling and a few others high in the sporting world have upset the dope bucket to emerge winners.

Lopez has not been defeated in three years of competition, while Meyer has waded through every opponent Ad Santel has signed for him.

The Mexican champ is recognized in 21 States as the undisputed titleholder, and if Meyer can throw him he will take the crown.

The medico has real wrestling ability, and since his arrival in Oakland has waited for the opportunity to meet Lopez.

The preliminaries include Brother Jonathan vs. Bill Sledge, Ed Helwig vs. Lou Thesz, Count Hugo DeCollelimo vs. Baron Ben Ginsberg and Mike Mazurki vs. Harry Jacobs.

I.A.A. Horseshoe Champs Defend

Mike Marcevich and Tom Wilson, horseshoe tossing experts from the United Register Company, will seek to withstand the efforts of some 70 Industrial Athletic Association players Saturday afternoon when they report at Mosswood Park to defend their I. A. A. championship in the annual meet.

Marcevich and Wilson, a crack team that averages around 50 per cent ringers, are expected to easily qualify for the final round in the one game 50-point, elimination team affair.

Carl Swanberg and Berg, lone team from Merco-Nordstrom, are favored to provide Marcevich and Wilson with the most competition.

Spec Stewart Gains Quarters

GLENVIEW, Ill., June 25.—(U.P.)—The 38th National intercollegiate golf tournament moved into the 36-hole quarter-final round today with the two favorites, Fred Haas Jr., of Louisiana State, and Charley Kocsis, Michigan, heavy choices to defeat their third straight goes.

Other matches today sent Verne (Spec) Stewart, Stanford, against Paul Leslie, Louisiana State.

RICHMOND CLUB HOLDS SECOND YACHT MEETING

By ALAN WARD

White sails will reflect the sunlight of upper San Francisco Bay when the Richmond Yacht Club sponsors its second annual regatta Sunday.

Starting with the diminutive snipes at 10 a. m., the regatta will continue through the afternoon, and will have in its competition the usual one-design and the percentage classes.

Regatta sponsors anticipate an enrollment of approximately 100 sailing craft in an event which has attracted the attention of all yacht clubs of the Bay area. Last season the Richmond show drew 60 entries, but considering points tallied Sunday will add to a seasonal trophy score and that similar outings held by kindred organizations earlier this year have lured gratifying numbers of boats, the Richmondites are hopeful of a record-shattering participation.

OFF POINT RICHMOND

The start and finish of each of the day's races will be off Point Richmond, assuring clear vision for devotees of the sailing sport who choose to select that vantage point for observation of the maneuvers.

The snipes will sail a windward leeward course off the point, while the larger craft will travel a route carrying them close to the San Francisco Marina.

The Dorada, winner of the recent Farallones Islands test, will be in competition, as will her arch-enemies, the Idalia and Dragoon. The Mytoy, Otter and Eloise are eligible and no doubt will be at the starting line in Division 7 when the "go" signal is flashed.

The race committee is headed by J. F. Serex and includes H. Bellus and T. Folwell.

DANCE FOLLOWS

The Richmond club will play host to competing yachtsmen at a Saturday night dance at the clubhouse. Many of the skippers, their crews and friends plan to lay over at their anchorage in Richmond Harbor Saturday evening in order to take advantage of the dance and entertainment. Shore boat service will be furnished.

☼ ☼ ☼

Advance preparations are being made by officials and members of the Aeolian Yacht Club in Alameda for the annual lightship race Sunday, July 18. Conducted under the auspices of the Yacht Racing Association of San Francisco Bay, the event will be run over a course approximately 25 miles long, to and from the lightship stationed about halfway between the Golden Gate and the Farallones.

The start will be off the Marina, and the contest will be open to all sailing yachts of the Bay, with the size minimum established at the bir. class. After all, the smaller cockleshells might come to grief in attempting to fight the waves of the temperamental old Pacific Ocean.

☼ ☼ ☼

MYTOY WINS RACE

Fred Grecian's Mytoy couldn't have been materially damaged in its recent collision with Dr. Painless Parker's Idalia in the Bay. The schooner stepped out to win the Aeolian Yacht Club annual Alameda City Trophy race, with which was combined a small-boat contest. One of 16 yachts to cross the starting line off the Alameda Mole on the first leg of the course to the marker near Pier 26, San Francisco, Grecian's craft, displayed an early supremacy and held its advantage.

Complete results of the major race, with times, follow:

Boat	Owner	El'ps'd Time	Cor'ct'd Time
Mytoy	Fred Grecian	2:37.35	2:07.39
Baby Gae	Gus Ekberg	2:48.48	2:19.50
Billiken	Com. Bill Ritter	3:06.40	2:21.52
Robin	Everett Hansen	2:45.00	2:33.27
Kestral	M. & A. Silva	2:51.38	2:39.37
Moonlight	Gerald Brady	3:02.46	2:46.19
Altair	Jack Blinn	2:54.20	2:47.22
Dodo	Archie Beckett	3:02.14	2:49.29
Dauntless	C. F. Benham	3:16.00	2:54.26
Wingding	Ed Schraeder	3:19.09	2:33.49
Sticker	Allan Hulme	3:27.31	2:41.52
White Cap		3:46.00	2:56.17

The Presto, Marijane and Tyee did not complete the route. The Marijane withdrew when she carried away her jibstay, and the other craft experienced difficulties before the distance had been completed.

In the race for the smaller craft Rip Tide took first place. Actual time was 1:43:20, and corrected time was 1:40:14. A. & A. was second, and Frisco Kid was third.

Defending Champ Beaten in North

VANCOUVER, B. C., June 25.—(AP) — Forrest Watson, Seattle, shunted Albert "Scotty" Campbell, Seattle, defending titlist, out of the Pacific Northwest Golf Association championship play yesterday, 1 up.

Pacific Northwest champion of ten years ago, Watson took a one-hole advantage on the 14th hole and held it the rest of the way against the Walker cup team member. Both men toured the course in par 71's.

DEFER SELECTIONS

DENVER, June 25. — (AP) — The Women's Transmissiissippi Golf Association deferred selection of officers and director last night until this afternoon.

PATTY FACES BEA BARRETT

DENVER, Colo., June 25.—(U.P.)—The pressure was on today as eight survivors teed off in the 10th Women's Transmississippi Golf Tourney in what promises to be one of the hardest "stretch drives" in the history of the meet, with only Marion Miley, defending champion from Lexington, Ky., a top-heavy favorite to enter the semi-final round.

Miss Miley led the field into the quarter final round of play against Mrs. James R. Arneill Jr., of Denver, who is not expected to extend the champion unless she is considerably off her game.

Patty Berg, the darling of the gallery, faced her home-town rival from Minneapolis, Beatrice Barrett, in the feature match of the day.

Mrs. Charles Newbold of Wichita, Kan., defeated Dorothy Traung of San Francisco, 3 and 2, yesterday.

In the upper bracket Phyllis Buchanan, Colorado champion who is playing on her home course, faces Mrs. R. D. Roper of Phoenix, Ariz., State champion.

Hamilton Sees New 'Dec' Mark

MILWAUKEE, June 25.—(AP)—Predicting that the Olympic record would be bettered and the world record approached, Coach Brutus Hamilton of the University of California, National chairman of the decathlon, arrived here yesterday for the American Olympic final decathlon tryouts at Marquette University, tomorrow and Saturday.

Hamilton was accompanied by three West Coast proteges—Bobby Clark, San Francisco Olympic Club, 1934-35 National champion; Runar Stone, San Francisco State, and George Mackey, California.

HE FOLLOWED THIS WITH ANOTHER

AP Wirephoto CHICAGO, June 25.—**Joe DiMaggio,** sensational New York Yankees rookie purchased from San Francisco's Seals, tied the major league record with two home runs in one inning here yesterday. He is shown crossing the plate at the end of his first circuit blow.

BEST SPORTS PAGES

Between You and Me

BY ED BANG

IT begins to look very much as if a "new order of things" for the Cleveland Indians in particular and probably major league baseball in general is close at hand.

In the past it has been the fast rule probably 99 per cent of the time that a young ball player must be put through the sprouts of class B, class A and class AA baseball, on occasions spending as many as two seasons in the latter company, before he is ready for the acid test under the big tent.

This theory has been exploded in much the same manner Max Schmeling exploded the "Brown Bomber," otherwise Joe Louis, a couple of months gone.

The credit is due none other than C. C. Slapnicka, general manager of the Indians. He fairly took the bull by the horns, to use a brand-new expression, and brought a couple of kids to the roster of the Indians and fairly knocked tradition into the proverbial cocked hat with the right of recall being conspicuous by its absence.

Weatherly and Feller Prove to Be Real Stuff

WHEN the Tribesmen lost the services of Bruce Campbell, leading batter at the time he was taken ill, Jimmy Gleeson, a New Orleans alumnus was pressed into service.

But all the while "Slap" had just one thought in mind.

That, in effect, was, "Roy Weatherly is a much better all-around player than Gleeson. Finally the day came when Jimmy departed and Roy joined up with the local baseball forces.

It isn't necessary to dwell on what Weatherly has done. He has exceeded the expectations of every last member of the Indians entourage. He has hit on a par with the best in the league, proved he is an alert and adept fielder, can throw with the best of them, has his head up every minute of the time and races around those bases just about as fast as any man in the game.

Yep, Slap was 100 per cent right on his judgment of young Weatherly, and now it looks as if he has hit the nail on the head in another youngster, Bob Feller, a kid who has yet to say hello to his eighteenth birthday anniversary.

Youngster Does Something Nobody Else Ever Did

BOB made his first major league start at League park yesterday and beat the St. Louis Browns 4-1. He allowed but five hits and struck out 15 rival batters, tying the right-handed pitching strikeout record for the league.

With a break in the eighth inning he might have tied Rube Waddell's mark of 16 set when pitching for the Browns against the Athletics July 29, 1908, and possibly Dizzy Dean's National league mark of 17, Diz fanning that many Cubs on July 30 three years ago.

However, he did something nobody before him ever did, debutted with 15 strikeouts in the big time, and that goes for pitchers anywhere from 17 to 47 years.

Some Youngsters Are Ruined in the Minors

WHEN a kid of 21 (Weatherly) can step from the Southern association into the American league and turn in the enviable job he has, there is no question in my mind but that all the insisted-upon minor league training is a delusion and a snare.

And when a youngster who is still this side of his eighteenth milestone can step on that rubber and dish out 15 strikeouts in his debut, please enlighten me if you can, just why this kid should be sent to the minors.

It is my contention he will get better nursing and handling under a wise old head like Steve O'Neill, who realizes he has a real diamond in the rough, instead of trusting his schooling and future to the tender mercies of any minor league manager.

Judging by the showing of Weatherly and Feller, it would seem that in future the big show owners and managers and scouts will pay more heed to hanging fast to kids who appear to have real class instead of trusting them to the aforementioned small time baseball pilots.

It stands to reason that the minor league bosses can't have as much behind their eyes as the 16 pilots in the two big circuits, else they would be handling clubs in the American or National.

Cleveland Has Been Fortunate With Kids

CLEVELAND has been unusually fortunate in the matter of having youngsters step from the small leagues to the local wigwam without going through the paces in the big minor loops.

Wesley Ferrell was just 21 years old when he became a regular with the Indians in 1929. He graduated from the Terre Haute club after one year of service.

Joe Vosmik had just passed his twentieth birthday when he debutted in left field as a member of Manager Roger Peckinpaugh's brigade. He had spent a year at Frederick, Md., and another at Terre Haute.

Now come Weatherly and Feller, kids who have never seen a class AA park. In fact, Roy was barely acquainted with class A company, while Feller's experience was confined to Adel, Ia., high school pitching, an insurance league and with the Rosenblums for a few minutes.

The kid stacked up as having the goods when he fanned eight members of the St. Louis Cardinals in an exhibition game here early in July. He italicized this fact yesterday.

First Start Makes Feller Major League Sensation

Misses 28-Year-Old League Record by Single Strikeout as He Fans 15 of Browns

By Ed McAuley

BASEBALL'S Hall of Immortality swung wide its hallowed gates today. Bob Feller wasn't going in. The immortals were coming out.

They were coming out to greet this 17-year-old ranch boy from the broad plains of Iowa, this boy with a dimple in his chin and magic in his long right arm.

They were coming out to hear the whistle of the greatest fast ball to reach the major leagues since Walter Johnson sent his blinder roaring down the alley.

Young Bob Feller was the talk of the baseball world today. The rugged bust of old Rube Waddell still was on its pedestal and the all-time record of Dizzy Dean still stood unequaled, but Feller held a distinction that even those masters of the national sport couldn't claim.

In his first starting assignment as a major league pitcher, Feller totaled 15 strikeouts. No right-hander in the long history of the American league has done more.

The record is held by Waddell, a southpaw. Pitching for the St. Louis Browns on July 29, 1908, Waddell sent 16 Philadelphia Athletics back to the bench on futile swings.

Yesterday—28 years later—this smooth-faced kid who hasn't even finished high school, stood on the spike-scarred mound at League park and came within one strike-out of equaling Waddell's total and within two of tying the all-time record which Dean achieved at the expense of the Chicago Cubs on July 30, 1933.

Only 9,000 See History in Making

Other pitchers have struck out 15 of the enemy. Ed Walsh of Chicago did it on that historic afternoon in 1908 when Addie Joss of Cleveland beat him, 1 to 0, with one of the four perfect games in the records of the sport.

But no pitcher, right-handed or left-handed, American league or National, did it when he was 17 years old, and in his initial start. Only 9,000 fans saw yesterday's battle, but when Feller drilled that fifteenth strikeout pitch past Lyn Lary of the St. Louis Browns to end the game, you'd have thought the stands were packed, so thundrous was the ovation.

And Feller, pushing his long, black hair out of his eyes with one hand and mopping his sweaty face with the other, walked down the dugout steps and told Manager Steve O'Neill he guessed he'd have to have more work.

"I feel a little tired," he explained. "I'm not used to going nine innings any more."

What, one hastens to inquire, will the young man do when he doesn't feel a little tired? Certainly he can't blast the atmosphere with a faster throw than that final strike on Lary.

Galehouse Warming Up As Game Starts

Feller probably is the only pitcher in history to start a game with his "successor" warming up in the bullpen. O'Neill was willing to grant a front office request that he use the boy in an effort to swell the Sunday gate, but he wasn't willing to place his prospects of second place exclusively in the untested hands of the western rookie. Dennis Galehouse was limbering his arm when the game started.

But before three innings were over, Galehouse knew he wouldn't be needed. Feller opened by fanning Lary on a pitch so fast the Brownie shortstop didn't get his bat off his shoulder.

Harland Clift looped a single to right and that apparently annoyed Feller. He stopped throwing his fast ball and started throwing his faster ball. Julius Solters and Roy Bell didn't even come close to their third strikes.

Sam West took a called third strike to open the second and, after Jim Bottomley had walked, Ollie Bejma could hit nothing but the breeze.

Retires Side on Strikes in Fifth

Feller contented himself with a single strikeout in the third and the same in the fourth. Solters and Bottomley were the victims. But in the fifth he fanned Bejma, Angelo Guiliani and Earl Caldwell in quick succession. You should have heard the customers.

The Browns got their only run—did I tell you the score was 4 to 1?—in the sixth inning, when they bunched two of their six hits, but at no time did Feller look so good. Lary opened that chapter by slashing a vicious grounder toward third base. Sammy Hale got his bare hand in front of the drive but couldn't hold it, and while Hale shook off the sting and Bill Knickerbocker did nothing, the ball lay in short left until Joe Vosmik came in to recover it.

By that time Lary was on second, one base more than he would have made had Knick been on his toes. Clift flied to Vosmik and Joe's fast throw to third made Lary decide he didn't want to advance.

No Strategy Like Feller Fast Ball

With the hard-hitting Bell at bat, Catcher Charley George and Knickerbocker went into conference with Feller. The master-minding was wasted, for Bell cracked the first pitch against the right field wall for two bases, scoring Lary. Feller then exercised a little strategy all his own. He threw the ball past West so fast that the bewildered veteran couldn't see it.

Then came the seventh, and with it Feller's outstanding bid for a place among the strong-hearted troupers of the pastime. Bottomley opened the inning with a single to center. Bejma rapped a mean hopper to Feller's left and Knickerbocker scooped it toward Roy Hughes for the forceout, but Hughes dropped the ball.

Two men on base and no one out. Guiliani fouled to Hale, then Manager Rogers Hornsby sent the slugging Ed Coleman to the plate to bat for Pitcher Caldwell.

Feller fanned Coleman, but before he completed the chore he cut loose with a wild pitch to advance both runners. This was a disturbing situation, especially since Lary, who had hit that stinging double the previous inning, was coming up. Galehouse shifted nervously in the bullpen, but before he could remove his sweater Lary was cutting viciously and vainly at a third strike.

Well, that made 14 strikeouts and over the press box crept the tension that precedes historic performance. Two innings to go—and the American league record only two strikeouts away.

But Feller couldn't fan anyone in the eighth—his only inning without a strikeout—and retired Bejma and Pinch-hitter Ray Pepper on easy chances for Trosky in the ninth.

Lary First and Last Strikeout Victim

Feller didn't know it, but there still was a chance to equal the record for right-handers. All Feller knew was that his job was almost done, he was growing tired and there was no use delaying the finish. Lary still is wondering what roared past his bat.

Feller's performance naturally dwarfed anything else that happened, but he couldn't have won unless the Indians made some runs.

Trosky took care of that assignment for his fellow-Iowan. The big first baseman got a double and three singles in four times at bat. His double in the sixth scored Hale and moved Averill to third, and Hal preceded Earl across the plate when Vosmik singled to center.

Trosky drove in the Redskins' fourth run in the next inning, scoring Hughes, who had singled.

But no one was interested in the Tribe's offensive. Nine thousand pairs of eyes were focused on a young six-footer who little more than a month ago was throwing that priceless fast ball across the sandlots.

Possibly that's where Feller really was good. On the sandlots a fellow gets used to lots of work. No danger there of growing tired—and striking out only 15 men.

Tribe Meets Senators, Returns Home Labor Day

The Indians are idle today and leave tonight for Washington, where they will open their final eastern invasion tomorrow. Thornton Lee will pitch the first game against the Senators. The Indians will not play at League park again until Labor day, when they meet the St. Louis Browns in the traditional double-header.

What's All This Fuss?

Why, It's Bob Feller, a Real Life Merriwell

Continued From Page 1

Jim Bottomley was the only Brown to fan in the fourth. Naturally, Feller was tiring under the strain. So in the fifth he struck out Bejma, Angelo Guiliani and Earl Caldwell. No one ever will do more than that, unless they change the rules . . . Sit down, Galehouse.

Galehouse sat down, glad of the chance to watch this miracle in the making. And 9,000 fans sat with him, cheering, whistlin gand clapping their hands with each successive strikeout. When he poured that fast ball past Lary for the final out of the game, they stood in stirring tribute while Feller, as cal mas if he were walking off a sandlot mound, stuck his glove in his pocket and started for the dugout.

What kind of a boy is Feller? He's justthe kind of boy you'll find in any high school classroom. He sits with those wiry fingers locked in embarrassed tension and looks atthe floor as he answers your questions.

No, no one ever taught him how to pitch.

"I just sort of picked things up myself," he tells you.

Yes, he's going back to Adel, Ia., to finish school this fall. He'd like to play basketball as he did last year, but he's a professional now.

Tired after the game? Well, just a little. He hadn't pitched nine innings since he left the sandlots.

"But I can stand lots of work," he adds quickly. "Why back home in a tournament I pitched five games in eight days."

Feller already has learned that fame can be a nuisance.

"I ducked out to a movie with Roy Weatherly last night," he said, "but the phone started ringing early this morning. I finally told the operator not to give me any more calls before noon. I thought I'd never finish shaving."

You resist the impulse to ask the youngster where he finds anything to shave on that boyish face.

You get up to leave, and Feller obviously is glad the interview is over. What can a western kid of 17 say about himself to a reporter?

But give him a round, white ball with a cover to rub and stitches to grip, and he'll make it whistle in the farthest corners of the baseball world.

Seek Cleveland For Cage League

The possibility of Cleveland's return to the ranks of organized professional basketball loomed strong again today.

With a view to enticing this city back into the fold, the Midwest Basketball Conference held its annual organization meeting at Hotel Carter over the weekend.

If Cleveland decides to join the loop, the team will wear the Rosenblum colors, and be coached by Ray Watts, Baldwin-Wallace football and basketball mentor. Home games will be played at a high school gym, probably Cathedral Latin.

The league now consists of eight teams from seven cities. Last season the Chicago Duffy Florists won the championship. Other members are Indianapolis Kautskys, Indianapolis U. S. Rubbers, Dayton Metros, Pittsburgh Y. M. H. A., Detroit Hed Aids, Toledo All-Stars and Akron Firestones.

New Hampshire Nine Wins Legion Title

MIDDLETOWN, O. (AP)—Hopes directed at the national championship, the Manchester, N. H., junior baseball squad headed for Spartansburg, S. C., today, after pocketing the regional title in American Legion tournament play here.

The Granite State boys nipped a ninth-inning rally yesterday to defeat Middletown, Buckeye State champions, 5 to 4, behind the seven-hit pitching of Wichther.

Shakespeare and Crayne to Boot

CHICAGO (AP)—Notre Dame's Bill Shakespeare and Dick Crayne of Iowa, probably will do most of the punting for the college All-Stars against the Detroit Lions Sept. 1 at Soldier field.

The former Irish star, noted for the length of his kicks, and Crayne, a long, accurate booter, have dominated a big group of star punters in practice sessions. Jay Berwanger of Chicago and Les Lindberg of Illinois also will be available if their help in needed in the kicking department.

Sttella Cracks Record

WARSAW (AP) — Stella Walsh (Walasiewicz), Polish Olympic runner from Cleveland, yesterday smashed her own listed world record for the 80 meters dash when she was timed in 9.6 seconds, two-tenths of a second under her previous mark.

Puffin Best of Class R Boats

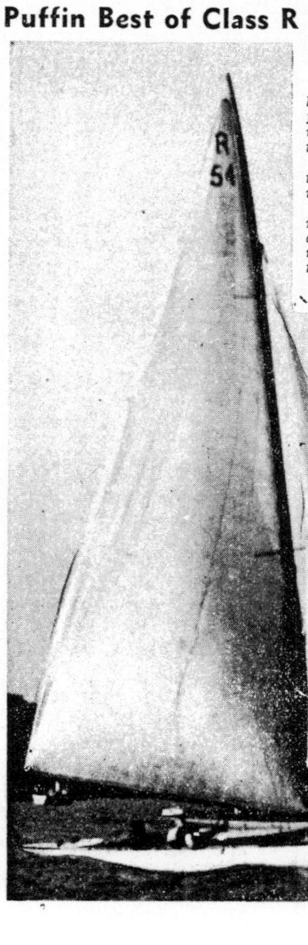

Here's Puffin, inter-lake class R champion following its race-off victory over Robin yesterday off Rocky river..

The two boats had tied at Put-in-Bay last week.

They raced over a 12-mile course yesterday and Puffin led all the way, winning by more than eight minutes.

Revelts Win Again

The Revelt's Sea Foods yesterday scored their third victory over the Madison Merchants, 11 to 2, at Madison. Howie Whale held Madison to seven hits.

Akron Nine Eliminated

WICHITA, Kan. (AP)—Elgin, Ill., eliminated Akron, O., from the national semi-pro baseball tournament, 8 to 5, here last night.

BOB FELLER [News Staff Photograph]

Meet Bob Feller

BOB FELLER is 17 years old, stands a shade under 6 feet and weighs 180 pounds.

His home is in Adel, Ia., 30 miles from Des Moines. His father is a rancher. Mother and sister Marguerite, aged seven, complete the family cheering section.

Started as shortstop on Iowa sandlot team managed by father two years ago but soon became pitcher and attracted attention of major league scouts when he fanned 18 in an amateur tournament at Dayton last summer.

Signed with New Orleans but wanted to finish high school, where he still has another year. Came to Cleveland for vacation job and pitched for Rosenblums of class A. Struck out eight of nine St. Louis Cardinals he faced in exhibition at League park July 6, and week later was bought by Indians.

Universally known as Bob, but calls himself Robert.

Perfect,' Says O'Neill, Feller Lauds George

"FELLER was perfect."

This was the tribute of Manager Steve O'Neill today as baseball fans everywhere hailed the achievement of the young Iowan who struck out 15 St. Louis Browns in his first start as an Indian.

"The kid looked like a veteran in every way," said O'Neill. "The umpires didn't even have to remind him to stay on the rubber. He was as cool as a cucumber with men on base and he was just as fast at the finish as at the start."

O'Neill said Feller's performance entitles him to the status of a regular, but the manager intends to guard carefully against overworking the youngster.

"About once a week is enough for him at this stage," said O'Neill. "His next start probably will be Sunday in Boston."

• • •

Feller says at no time did he think he had a chance to beat the American league record, which he came within a single strikeout of tying.

"I knew Dizzy Dean had fanned 17 three years ago, and I thought the American league record was the same," he said. "I wasn't nervous, but I was so anxious to make good in my first start that I just kept bearing down."

Feller seemed less inclined to talk about himself than about Charley George, rookie catcher recalled from Minneapolis less than a week ago.

"George did the best job I've ever seen," said Feller. "I was plenty wild, you know, but I had the feeling no matter where I threw that ball George would get it."

• • •

O'Neill also credited George with a good measure of Feller's success.

"Charley handled the boy just right," said O'Neill. "He kept him working deliberately and slowly, talked to him the few times he was in trouble, yet never gave him the impression that life and death depended on the next pitch."

George revealed that one of his frequent visits to the box was for the purpose of changing signals. He suspected that the Browns had caught one of the signs. Which one did they catch, Charley, the fast ball or the fast ball?

• • •

Feller gave Umpire Harry Geisel a typical Johnny Allen ogling when he disagreed with the arbiter on a ball called on Jim Bottomley in the second inning . . . Bill Knickerbocker robbed Earl Caldwell of an infield hit with a sparkling pickup and throw in the third . . . Pinch-hitter Ed Coleman had three straight balls, including a wild pitch, before Feller fanned him in the seventh.

Last-Hole Birdie Sings Title Tune for Bill

BECAUSE he was able to produce a birdie four on Lost Nation's taxing eighteenth hole yesterday, Carmen Bill, Shaw Avenue Golf school professional, today is celebrating his third city Italian-American open championship in four years.

Bill bested Joe Corsillo, Roseland pro, by two strokes in the 36-hole event. On the final tee, however, Corsillo, the defending champion, enjoyed a one-stroke lead. He needed seven blows on the final test, when his second carried over the green into a clump of bushes.

Bill played safe, short of the creek with his second, then struck his approach up for a one-putt birdie.

Bill's rounds were 73-78—151; Corsillo's 78-75—153. Nine strokes back of Corsillo, in third place, was Jim Vaden, an amateur.

In the semifinal rounds of the Italian-American amateur championship, played in conjunction with the open, Vaden eliminated Joe Carlone, 6 and 5, and Charlie Delsanter upset Bill Sasso, 4 and 3.

• • •

Defending champion Frank Metzger, a semi-finalist in last week's district amateur, advanced to the third round in the Industrial league championship yesterday by defeating Frank Demko 5 and 4 at Ridgewood. Continuing the fine golf he displayed at Kirtland, Metzger banged out a creditable 75 to win comfortably.

• • •

Maurice McCarthy and Eddie Meister had 73's, Max Matusoff 74 and Frank Pelton 76 to lead a team of six Cleveland amateurs to a 19 to 15 victory over Canton in an intercity match at Canton Brookside yesterday. Topping the Canton team were Oliver Transue and Bill Quinn of Country club. Transue shot a 74 to win three points from McCarthy, thanks to a 34 on the front nine. Quinn dropped four points to Meister, district amateur champ.

• • •

The district's women this week turn to intra-club competition. Practically every club in the district holds its women's club championship during the next seven days.

Dodgers Buy Infielder

OMAHA, Neb. (AP)—Larry Harlan, owner of the Omaha club of the Western league, today announced the sale of Second Baseman Eddie Williford to the Brooklyn Dodgers.

Save This One

Cleveland	A	H	O	A	St Louis	A	H	O	A
Hughes,2	4	1	0	1	Lary,s	4	1	3	3
Hale,3	2	0	3	1	Clift,2	2	1	2	1
Averill,cf	3	1	1	0	Solters,lf	4	0	0	0
Trosky,1	4	4	5	0	Bell,rf	4	2	1	0
Weath'rly,rf	3	0	2	0	West,cf	4	0	0	0
Vosmik,lf	4	1	1	0	Bottomley,1	3	1	7	1
George,c	4	1	15	1	Bejma,2	4	0	1	2
K'ck'b'k'r,s	4	0	0	1	Guiliani,c	4	1	8	1
Feller,p	3	1	0	0	Caldwell,p	2	0	2	3
					*Coleman	1	0	0	0
Totals	31	9	27	4	Van Atta,p	0	0	0	0
					Liebhardt,p	0	0	0	0
					†Pepper	1	0	0	0
					Totals	33	6	24	11

*Batted for Caldwell in seventh.
†Batted for Liebhardt in ninth.

Cleveland	0	0	0	0	0	3	1	0	*	—4
St. Louis	0	0	0	0	0	1	0	0	0	—1

Runs—Hughes, Hale, Averill, Trosky, Lary. Errors—Hughes, Bejma. Runs batted in—Trosky 2, Vosmik 2, Bell. Two-base hits—Lary, Bell, Trosky. Stolen base—Clift. Double play—Caldwell and Lary. Left on bases—St. Louis 9, Cleveland 7. Bases on balls—Off Caldwell 3, off Van Atta 1, off Feller 4. Struck out—By Caldwell 4, by Van Atta 1, by Feller 15. Hits—Off Caldwell, 6 in 6 innings; off Van Atta, 2 in 1 inning; off Liebhardt, 1 in 1 inning. Wild pitch—Feller. Losing pitcher—Caldwell. Umpires—Geisel, Ormsby and Basil. Time—2:20.

Home, Jesse!

Friends of Owens—
Can Catch Him Now—
Downs and Ups in Ring—

BY TOMMY TUCKER

THE good people of Cleveland missed a fine opportunity last week when they were gathering donations to send Jesse Owens' family to New York to meet the world champion athlete. The needed money could have been quickly subscribed by the simple method of auctioning off the right to throw out the first Brundage.

• • •

If you've never met Owens, here's how you'll be able to identify him during tomorrow's big celebration here. He'll be the quiet fellow some politician will be stepping in front of just at the moment a photographer is ready to make a picture.

• • •

The welcoming committee is headed by some very interesting individuals. It's obvious they are all very proud and happy to

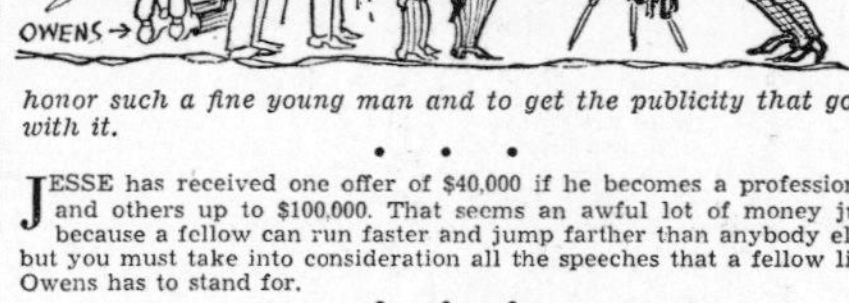

honor such a fine young man and to get the publicity that goes with it.

• • •

JESSE has received one offer of $40,000 if he becomes a professional and others up to $100,000. That seems an awful lot of money just because a fellow can run faster and jump farther than anybody else, but you must take into consideration all the speeches that a fellow like Owens has to stand for.

• • •

People have been after Owens for a long time and now he's going to let them catch up with him—if they first put the money in a bank.

• • •

I SEE that Johnny Risko still wants to fight Joe Louis and is training seriously. As soon as I find out I'll let you know whether John's training to last two rounds or three rounds.

I suppose he figures he can't do any worse than Jack Sharkey. Sharkey, too, did a lot of training but the way he was going down and up during the fight he must have done his training in an elevator.

• • •

There is real democracy in boxing. No matter if a fighter is rich or poor, if he's small or big, when he's knocked out they never count more than 10 over him.

Drinks Too Cold for Diz

ST. LOUIS (AP)—The only Cardinal pitcher who can win consistently was on the sick list today.

Dizzy Dean complained of illness and failed to show up to pitch one of yesterday's games against the Pirates.

Dr. Robert F. Hyland, Cardinal physician, said Jerome Herman had stomach pains from drinking too much cold liquid. He did not appear for Saturday's game.

The Cardinals used seven pitchers yesterday against the Bucs, and Manager Frankie Frisch scheduled Dean to pitch today "if he is well."

Cleveland Chapter Wins Catholic Slovak Title

By defeating Paramount 16 to 3 at Woodland Hills park yesterday, the Cleveland chapter captured the championship of the Catholic Slovak league. Lang and Mraz paced the victors' attack with three hits each.

BEST SPORTS PAGES

Feller American League Strikeout King

[News Staff Photograph]

"FELLER'S TAKING HIS STRETCH—"

By Ed McAuley

THE Miracle Kid is king today, on his head the crown of the fabulous Waddell, at his feet the American league's record books, tattered and obsolete.

The same dimple still digs its hole into Bob Feller's chin. The same high school desk awaits him in Adel, Ia. The same boyish grin still lights his face and the same slow blush spreads from hairline to collar when you grip his hand.

But the baseball world is gasping, telling itself over and over that it can't be true but it IS true, that it couldn't be done but it WAS done.

For Feller yesterday went out to the pitching mound at League park and did something no man in the long history of the American league ever had done before.

While Dad Bill Feller, sick of body but glowing of soul, sat smiling and speechless; while Mother Feller fought to keep back the tears of pure joy, and curly-haired Marguerite Feller squealed wtih sisterly delight, this 17-year-old boy from an Iowa farm struck out 17 members of the Philadelphia Athletics.

Way back on July 29, 1908, Rube Waddell, wearing the uniform of the St. Louis Browns, fanned 16 Philadelphians. In the 28 years since that historic afternoon some brilliant chapters have been written in baseball's pitching records. Joss, Young, Bender, Johnson, Mathewson, Alexander, Grove and Hubbell—these are a few whose deeds will never die.

But across the hallowed pages where the Big Train thundered and Matty fired his hard one, is written today the story of a boy who wasn't even born when they were kings.

Dean and Feller Share Record

Only one other big league pitcher of the thousands who have tried from the 60-foot mark since Abner Doubleday laid out his field at Cooperstown, N. Y., 100 years ago has struck out 17. That was Dizzy Dean, who set the all-time record as he fogged his St. Louis Cardinals to victory over the Chicago Cubs July 30, 1933.

But Dean was a full-grown, hard-bitten major leaguer when he set his mark. Feller has been a professional less than two months.

He never pitched so much as an inning in the minor leagues. He came unheralded from Iowa's sandlots to amaze the scouts at the national amateur tournament in Dayton last summer.

He started the present season with the Rosenblums of Cleveland's class A. Even after he joined the Indians, no one dreamed his right arm was a cannon. The first time he started his "successor" was warming up in the bull-pen.

Slapnicka Predicts 20 Strikeouts

We thought he reached the summit that day, when he struck out 15 St. Louis Browns. We thought the batters would adjust their vision to that blazing speed, would lose their instinctive fear of that murderous fast ball.

And now—

C. C. Slapnicka, business chief of the Indians, has lived for half a century. He's seen all the great ones come and go, and the years have taught him to be conservative in speech.

"Some day," said Slapnicka last night, "that kid is going out there with his control perfect and his arm a little stronger and strike out 20 men."

If he had said 27, the possible maximum in a nine-inning game, no one would have argued. You can't put a limit on a miracle.

Feller's victory was the first of two that returned the Indians to the first division, in a fourth-place tie with the Detroit Tigers. The score was 5 to 2—and the Athletics got as many runs as they got hits.

Passes Nine and Hits Batter

Chubby Dean drilled a single to center in the third and Wally Moses hit to the same spot in the seventh. Had Feller's control been as good as his speed, not a man would have passed first base.

But the Miracle Kid undeniably was wild. He walked nine and hit another. But his very wildness proved his mastery. On many of his strikeouts the count was three balls and two strikes. He had to groove the next one. The batter would dig in and swing—at a ball he couldn't even see.

Hugh Luby, Connie Mack's new second baseman, struck out three times. George Puccinelli, Bob Johnson, Frank Higgins, Frank Hayes and Randall Gumpert, the Philadelphia pitcher, each fanned twice. Lou Finney, Russ Peters, Moses and Dean saw the third one go by only once each, which made them practically heavy hitters.

Connie's Rookie Looks Good, Too

Passes to Finney and Moses in the third, followed by Dean's single, gave the A's their first run, then Moses stole home for one of the seven larceny jobs allowed by Feller's inexperience at keeping runners close to the bases.

Gumpert, meanwhile, was experiencing the misfortune of being good on a day when his opponent was great. Mack's 18-year-old right-hander gave up only seven hits, and two of the Tribe's five runs were unearned.

The Indians counted twice in the first inning on a pass to Roy Hughes, singles by Bill Knickerbocker and Hal Trosky, Earl Averill's long fly and an infield out. Passes to Knickerbocker and Averill and Peters' extremely wild throw after taking Weatherly's grounder added another pair without the aid of a hit in the third. Doubles by Hughes and Averill produced the final run in the seventh.

The second game, which might easily have been expected to be dull by comparison with the opener, was by no means an anti-climax. For the second time in five days, Trosky hit a home run with men on bases to produce the winning runs. The score was 5 to 4.

It's No. 38 For Slugging Hal

Trosky's 38th circuit smash of the season boomed over the right-center wall with Hughes and Averill on the paths in the seventh inning. Dennis Galehouse, tribal starting pitcher who had forced Billy Sullivan earlier that inning had made the rounds on singles by Hughes and Averill, so the total production of the inning was four runs. The Indians' only previous tally at the expense of Carl Fink was the fourth inning homer blasted out of the park by Geoffrey Heath, outfielder from Zanesville playing his first game as an Indian.

Galehouse pitched a good game, too. The Athletics knicked him for a run on Luby's single and Moses' double in the fourth and another on singles by Moses and Higgins, sandwiching a pass to Johnson, in the sixth.

But in the eighth, after two were out, Dean singled, Johnson walked and Higgins doubled, scoring both his mates. Manager Steve O'Neill summoned Johnny Allen from the bull-pen and the big fire-baller struck out Puccinelli to end the inning.

In the ninth he got Peters on an easy grounder to Hughes, struck out Hayes and forced Pinch-Hitter Bud Moss to foul to Billy Sullivan.

And do you know what the 6,000 customers were saying as they filed down the ramps? They were saying "Allen looked as good as Feller, didn't he?"

The great Allen, winner of 19 games and the Tribe's leading pitcher, was measured by the standard of a 17-year-old boy fresh from the sandlots!

Yet I'll bet Allen himself considered the statement a great compliment. Looking "as good as Feller" comes close enough to looking perfect.

[News Staff Photograph]

BOB, DAD, MOTHER AND SISTER MARGUERITE

Waddell's 28-Year-Old Mark Falls As Rookie Equals Dean's Record

[News Staff Photograph]

"I JUST STAYED IN THERE WINGING 'EM"

Between You and Me

BY ED BANG

I'VE been around and seen a lot of things, thrilled at this, that and the other thing in sports, and then Bob Feller happened along with 17 strikeouts.

Now mind you, in 30 years of big-time sports writing you get to rub elbows with the greatest in all lines of athletic endeavor. Consequently I have run the gantlet in baseball, football, golf, tennis, boxing, track for humans and horses, and so on down the line.

But it is with baseball I intend to deal for the moment, for the aforementioned Bob Feller is affiliated with our national pastime.

Here's a kid of 17 years—he won't be 18 for a couple months—who has set the sporting world in general, and the baseball contingent in particular, gaga by his unprecedented achievements.

You'd think a kid would rest on his laurels after striking out eight men in three innings, particularly since they were members of the crack "Gas House Gang," known otherwise as the St. Louis Cardinals.

Not Feller, though. He is made of different stuff.

Let's See What These Old Eyes of Mine Have Seen

OFFHAND let's take a glimpse into the pages of baseball history of the past and see what these old eyes of mine have seen.

I recall Neal Ball's unassisted triple play at League park, many many moons gone.

I can see Addie Joss pitching his perfect game, no-run, no-hit, no-man-reach-first effort, with Big Ed Walsh allowing but four hits in that same encounter, striking out 15 of the Naps in eight innings and losing 1-0 on his own wild pitch.

I remember Babe Ruth cracking out three home runs in a single world series game on two occasions and missing a fourth by a scant eyelash and also recall the Bambino calling his shot, so to speak, against Charley Root, Chicago Cubs' pitcher in the classic of 1932.

I have before me a mental picture of Bill Wambsganns pulling his one and only unassisted triple play in a world series game.

Doubling in brass with that effort was Elmer Smith's one and only home run with the bases full in a world series contest.

I see the Athletics counting 10 runs in a single inning, a world series record, to upset the Chicago Cubs.

I marveled the day Jimmy Foxx set up a new American league record for runs driven in in a single game at the lake front stadium.

I, but, I don't want to overlook young Bob Feller.

And They Hinted This Kid Was Flash in Pan

YOU expect elite pitching performances from experienced pitchers like the aforementioned Joss and Walsh and Christy Mathewson, Nap Rucker, Rube Waddell, Walter Johnson and Dizzy Dean, but when a seventeen-year-old lad, who still has to wrestle with geometry and the like in the classroom, turns the baseball world topsy turvy, that's something else again.

I have seen this youngster in action four times against big league clubs, against the Cardinals as already set forth, twice opposed to the St. Louis Browns and yesterday against the Philadelphia Athletics.

Frankie Frisch, boss of the "gas housers," didn't mince words in proclaiming the kid the real article after he pitched against the Cards. The same thing holds true of Dizzy Dean.

Yes, and Rogers Hornsby, manager of the Browns, waxed enthusiastic after the youngster struck out 15 of his Brownies three weeks ago yesterday.

Grover Hartley, right bower, or is he the left one, of Hornsby, went out on a limb and proclaimed the youth the greatest speedball pitcher he had ever seen after he fanned 10

Continued on Next Page

Newberry's Ready and So Are Fisher Foods

Bill Wamby gambled again, and so today Cleveland's Fisher Foods find themselves in the third round of the National Baseball federation tournament with a clean record and mounting hopes.

Wamby sent Mike Skryp to the mound Saturday, hoping to save his ace, Fred Newberry, for tougher competition. Skryp pitched excellent ball and it worked.

Yesterday Wamby elected Johnny Sviatek, recruited from the Rosenblums, for the series. Sviatek worked a smart game, blanking Toledo, 5-0. That was the bigger gamble of the two, because Toledo had looked like ready money Saturday in winning its opener by the shutout route.

So today Wamby still had Newberry, fresh and primed to toss his assortment at the Waterbury, Conn., hitters.

Arnold Kubitz, in the box for Toledo yesterday, held the Fishers to three hits, all singles, but the Foods took advantage of every break to win. Meanwhile Sviatek granted the opposition five hits and walked seven, but the Fishers, led by the alert Alex Metti, played great ball defensively to choke every Toledo threat.

Metti walked to start the Fisher half of the first inning, and went to second on Walter Pavicich's intended sacrifice. Catcher Johnny Rosetti threw wild to first trying to get Pavicich and the Fisher shortstop continued to second. Norman Schoen scored Metti with a single, and Pavicich came home on Frankie Nemeth's long fly.

Matti, Pavicich and Schoen walked in the Fishers' third, and when Nemeth hit into a double play Metti scored. Bill Drenser's single brought in Pavicich.

Schoen was hit by a pitched ball in the eighth. He went to third on Nemeth's single and came home on Drenser's fly.

That was all the scoring, and it was more than enough for the Fishers. Two double plays halted Toledo when Sviatek seemed headed for trouble.

The last three innings of the game, played at the stadium, were completed under the floodlights because of cloudy weather and early darkness.

Feller's Dad Ill

BOB FELLER, the American league's new strikeout king, was up early today to take his fathr, William Feller, to Cleveland Clinic for a thorough physical examination.

Mr. Feller has been in poor health for some time. He came to Cleveland last week, with Mrs. Feller and his seven-year-old daughter, Marguerite, to attend the Father-and-Son ceremonies Friday and Saturday. He decided to enter the clinic at the suggestion of President Alva Bradley of the Indians.

Boy, What a Feller!

FIRST GAME

Cleve.	A	H	O	A	Phila.	A	H	O	A
Hughes.2	3	1	0	2	Finney.cf	1	0	1	0
Knick'b'r.s.	2	1	0	1	Puccin'lli.rf	2	0	1	0
Averill.cf	2	1	1	0	Moses.rf-cf.	2	1	5	0
Trosky.1	4	2	5	0	Dean.1	3	1	7	0
Weath'ly.rf.	4	0	2	0	Johnson.lf.	4	0	4	0
Hale.3	4	0	0	0	Higgins.3	2	0	0	1
Heath.lf	3	1	2	0	Luby.2	4	0	0	5
George.c	4	1	17	0	Peters.s	4	0	3	1
Feller.p	4	0	0	0	Hayes.c	4	0	3	1
					Gumpert.p.	3	0	0	0
Totals	30	7	27	3	*Moss	0	0	0	0
					Totals	29	2	24	8

*Batted for Gumpert in ninth.

Cleveland	2	0	2	0	0	0	1	0	*	—5
Philadelphia	0	0	2	0	0	0	0	0	0	—2

Runs—Hughes 2, Knickerbocker 2, Averill, Finney Moses. Error—Peters. Runs batted in—Averill 2, Weatherly, Dean. Two-base hits—Hughes, Averill. Stolen bases—Finney 2, Higgins 2, Dean, Moses, Moss. Sacrifice hit—Knickerbocker. Double play—Luby to Peters to Dean. Left on bases—Cleveland 7, Philadelphia 10. Bases on balls—Off Gumpert 5, off Feller 9. Struck out—By Gumpert 2, by Feller 17. Hit by pitcher—By Feller (Moses). Wild pitch—Feller. Balk—Gumpert. Umpires—Kolls, Johnston and Owens. Time—2:03.

SECOND GAME

Cleve.	A	H	O	A	Phila.	A	H	O	A
Hughes.2	5	2	2	5	Luby.2	4	1	1	3
Knick'b'r.s.	4	1	3	5	Moses.cf	4	2	5	0
Averill.cf	4	1	2	0	Dean.1	4	2	4	4
Trosky.1	4	3	8	1	Johnson.lf.	1	0	2	0
Weath'ly.rf.	3	0	1	0	Higgins.3	4	2	2	1
Campbell.rf	1	0	1	0	Puccin'lli.rf	4	0	1	0
Hale.3	4	2	1	0	Peters.s	4	0	4	1
Heath.lf	4	3	1	0	Hayes.c	3	0	3	0
Sullivan.c.	4	1	7	0	Fink.p	3	0	2	0
Galeh'se.p.	3	0	1	0	*Moss	1	0	0	0
Allen.p	1	0	0	0	Totals	32	7	24	9
Totals	37	13	27	11					

*Batted for Fink in ninth.

Cleveland	0	0	0	1	0	0	4	0	*	—5
Philadelphia	0	0	0	1	0	1	0	2	0	—4

Runs—Hughes, Averill, Trosky, Heath, Galehouse, Luby, Moses, Dean, Johnson. Error—Puccinelli. Runs batted in—Moses, Higgins 3, Averill, Trosky 3, Heath. Two-base hits—Hughes, Trosky, Moses, Hale, Higgins. Home runs—Heath, Trosky. Double play—Hughes to Knickerbocker to Trosky 2. Left on bases—Cleveland 8, Philadelphia 5. Bases on balls—Off Galehouse 4. Struck out—By Galehouse 4, by Fink 2, by Allen 2. Hits—Off Galehouse, 7 in 7 2-3 innings; off Allen, none in 1 1-3 innings. Winning pitcher—Galehouse. Umpires—Johnson, Owens and Kolls. Time—1:59.

Bill's Clothes Reach Top

Bill's Clothes today eyed the class B sandlot championship playoff series with Chick's Blue Ribbon Grilles.

The Clothes took first division honors in the class B elimination series by walloping the Tieber Restaurants 6 to 3 at Woodland Hills park. The Chics already have qualified for the playoff through winning the percentage series.

Meanwhile the Chicks bowed to the Sunrise Beers 4 to 1 in a second division elimination series tilt. The Beers lost to the Rogers for County Commissioner team 7 to 2 in a late game yesterday.

In the class C topnotcher, Frank Meluch pitched his tenth consecutive victory for the St. Benedict team, turning back the Tom Foote Printers 6 to 2 at Gordon park.

Winning a double-header, the Euclid Beach team stayed in the class C pennant chase. They walloped the South Euclid Orioles 9 to 2 and the Track Inns 11 to 2.

The Scrub A. C. scored a run in the ninth to turn back the Goodrich Pirates in class E, 4-3.

English Defeat Scotch

The English lawn bowling team defeated the Scotch 75 to 73 at the East Cleveland Lawn Bowling club yesterday.

Heath Breaks In With Bang as Tribe Rookie

GEOFFREY HEATH, handsome six-footer from Seattle, Wash., was a full-fledged Indian today.

The debut of the former Zanesville outfielder would have been the sensation of yesterday's double-header if Bob Feller hadn't staged his record-breaking performance.

Heath, replacing the slump-ridden Joe Vosmik in left field, got only one rather apologetic single in the first game, but he smashed out a home run and two singles in the second game and missed another extra-base hit when Wally Moses leaped against the center-field wall for his terrific smash in the sixth.

GEOFFREY HEATH

Heath handled his three fielding chances in perfect style and indicated he can cover ground as well as any of the regulars. His throwing arm wasn't tested.

• • •

Heath's one mistake was hitting a foul ball in the sixth inning of the second game, just as Odell Hale slid across the plate with what should have been the tying run at that time. It was a clean steal of home, but Heath's contact with the ball sent Hale back to third. Not only was he deprived of a well-earned run, but he came within inches of being injured as Heath swung.

• • •

Did you see that white-haired gentleman hopping onto the field to join the protest of Roy Weatherly and Manager Steve O'Neill when the former was called out by Umpire Brick Owens in the sixth inning of the second game?

That was Jim Weatherly, who wasn't going to see his son deprived of a base hit if he could help it. Cooler heads prevailed and Weatherly senior returned to his seat, but Roy protested so vehemently he was tossed out of the game.

"The worst decision I've seen in all my years in the game," was the reaction of C. C. Slapnicka, the Indians' business chief. Weatherly bounded to First Baseman Chubby Dean near the edge of the grass. Dean threw to Pitcher Carl Fink, covering first, but Weatherly appeared, from the press box, to have beaten the toss by a full second.

• • •

"I just stayed in there winging 'em" was all Feller could say in description of his nation-stirring performance. "No, I wasn't aiming at the record and I'll have no particular total in mind when I pitch again. I'll just keep throwing as long as I can."

• • •

Finney was heaved off the premises by Umpire Lew Kolls for overzealous protest of a called third strike in the fifth inning of the first game. He drew a loud boo from the fans, who believed the third strike actually was his fifth. Kolls called "ball" on one that looked good from the stands, then Finney fouled another before hearing "Yer out!"

• • •

Heads-up base running by Roy Hughes turned his smash off Fink's leg in the first game into a double. Roy saw in a fraction of a second that none of the infielders was close to the caroming ball, so he kept speeding for the keystone.

Play, Boys, Play!

And No Regrets—
Little Opposition
Ho! An Impostor—

BY TOMMY TUCKER

THE boys are having their national amateur golf championship after all, I see. All thoughts of canceling the tournament as a sheer waste of time, effort and money and declaring Lawson Little champion again without the necessary slight delay occasioned by six days of play were abandoned when Little decided to become a pro.

Without Little, the tournament becomes a competition again.

• • •

Little quit as an amateur with a record of 31 consecutive victories in United States and British national amateur matches. He said he had no regrets. Neither did the other amateurs.

• • •

NO wonder the national amateur continues to interest a lot of golfers. The boys figure that sooner or later all the really good players will get too old or turn pro and then they'll have a chance to win.

• • •

The football poll:

Minnesota
Gets my vot-a!
From the poet laureate (going on nine).

• • •

FROM an A. P. dispatch describing how Fullback Jim McDonald starred in Ohio State practice, "Coach Francis A. Schmidt, as usual making no comment . . ."

Good gosh, it's an impostor. If the fellow in charge of the practice isn't saying anything it's a cinch it isn't the Francis Schmidt we know.

• • •

SOME fellow out west has come up with a suggestion to play football with teams of only six men each. I suspect it's just another scheme of the "economic royalists,"—ah, there, Franklin old boy—to cut down employment.

Scholastic Grid Program Opens With 18 Games

BY JACK CLOWSER

WILD, exulting screams of "we want a touchdown," and desperate pleading to "hold that line" will echo through the high school stands this week as 18 games usher in autumn's scholastic sports menu for the Cleveland district.

More teams than usual are getting an early start this year, a majority of those hereabouts opening either Friday or Saturday.

Two of the 1935 topnotchers, Collinwood and East, travel for games under the floodlights Friday against teams that were in the thick of contention for the mythical state championship last season.

Collinwood helps dedicate the new $85,000 stadium that will be the home of the Sandusky Blue Streaks. East High goes to engage the powerful Bulldogs of Massillon.

Old Rivalries Again

Saturday's program brings the renewal of several neighborhood rivalries, notably the Glenville-Cathedral Latin fracas at Latin field, the Lincoln at Rhodes affair, the Holy Name-West High struggle at West Tech field, and the Rocky River at Lakewood game.

John Adams, with a light team captained by Fred Hancock, pays another visit to Toledo Scott Saturday, and East Tech travels to Canton to meet McKinley high school, always one of the greatest scholastic teams in this part of the country.

Charley Blickle's West Tech team, which looms up as a Senate dark horse on the basis of material at hand, opens its season at Akron Garfield Saturday.

Berea, last year's Greater Cleveland conference champion, plays Lorain at the Steel city, and can scarcely expect to cope with the manpower of Coach E. M. McCaskey's squad.

Friday afternoon games include John Hay's visit to Shaker Heights, Garfield Heights at Bedford, Benedictine at Parma, Royalton at Strongsville, Mentor at Chagrin Falls, Orange at Bay village and Mayfield at Chester. Campbell Memorial High school meets Elyria at Elyria in a night game Friday.

Hay Pepped Up

Hay will present more than the usual amount of trouble for Shaker, which has had two seasons without defeat. Coach Bill Hall at Hay has a much heavier line than last season, and expects definite improvement in his team's play.

The schedule brings the first test for several teams under new coaches. Among them are Herb Bauer at Glenville, A. R. Skomp at Rocky River, and Clyde Newell at Collinwood.

All three have very difficult assignments. Sandusky is known to be laying for Collinwood in the hope of starting out by walloping a big city team. Latin has many experienced men to toss in against Glenville. River can't hope to match its big neighbor in power and replacements.

Bill's Qualify to Play Euclid Title Series

Bill's Clothes of the Euclid Kiwanis league qualified for the loop's championship series by defeating the Roosevelt Cafes 6 to 2 yesterday at Noble field.

Next Sunday the Clothes meet the Bliss Coals in the first game of the league title series. The Cafes won the first-half championship.

Kelly to Oppose Gamiere at Armory

Jackie Kid Kelly of Akron has been signed by Promoter Louis Wargo to replace the injured Al Weathers as the opponent of Mike Gamiere on the professional boxing program to be held in Central armory Wednesday night.

The show, headed by an all-Cleveland match between Jimmy Vaughn and Ray Sharkey, is made up of five bouts. The others are: Johnny Dobler vs. Young Gizzy, Harold Dettman vs. Al McCurdy, Jesse Levels vs. Ed Dulino.

Conley Tries Something New at Carroll

Players Get Vote but Still Must Win Jobs

BEFORE the autumn is spent you'll probably find more than one occasion for charging debits against Tom Conley in the ledger reserved for football coaches.

But right now you can take out your brightest-hued pencil and enter a large indelible mark in Tommy's credit column.

His first official act of the fall season was the stroke of a master psychologist and earned for Conley the profound respect and loyalty of the entire Blue Streak squad.

Ordinarily a new coach taking the reins of a grid squad that suffered the most disastrous season in its history the year before, surveys his material in a cursory fashion and immediately sets about realigning the personnel of his squad, arbitrarily.

Leaves It to Players

But not Conley. Before the Streaks took the field for their first practice Saturday, he put the issue squarely up to the members of the team. Working on the assumption that his players would perform to the best advantage playing in positions they enjoy playing, Conley asked each of them "Where would you like to play?"

As a result of the replies received, the new Streak mentor is altering his plans somewhat. Last spring he decided to make Captain Henry Erhardt over from a tackle into a center. But Hank expressed a preference for tackle, and a tackle he is.

The center position remains in the hands of Joe Buscher, who gained some experience at the pivot post last year. Sam Sansone, the Streaks' regular center last year, is now a guard by his own desire.

Needs Good Backs

And so it goes throughout the squad. The strange thing about the experiment is that Conley found enough men willing to play the line. The popular theory has it that most gridders must be coerced into playing the line, preferring instead the spotlight that focuses on ball-carriers.

Conley is fairly well satisfied with his forward set-up. "We'll have a good line, all right," he said, "and we'll be a pretty good club if I can find one or two good backs."

• • •

Scattered notes from the Big Four camps: Frank (Doc) Kelker, Reserve's brilliant end, is on the injured list, although he appears regularly at practice . . . A wrenched back will keep him out of action for at least two weeks . . . The status of Sherm Lyle, Case's great end last year, remains in doubt . . . You'll recall he was forced out of action with a ruptured kidney . . . The injury has responded to treatment, but still Ray Ride is not counting on him . . . "If he reports it will be a most agreable surprise," said Ride, "but we won't know for sure until he undergoes another thorough examination."

Norm Schoen won't be able to report at Baldwin-Wallace until after the Fisher Foods are through with the current N.B.F. tourney . . . And Ken Noble is still wearing a patch on his cheek, a souvenir of a baseball injury on the class A sandlots . . . Ride is worried about his halfback posts . . . He thought he was pretty well set until veterans Gordon Wagner and Don Traxler were declared ineligible.

Seven sophomores are included in the group battling for backfield jobs at Reserve . . . They are Al Litwak, Walter Reducha, Mike Rodak, Denver Johnson, John Andrews, Jim Bankert and Stan Stone . . . You'll remember the last named as the brains of Shaker's great eleven three years ago.

Johnny Wilson will play Kelker's end until the veteran returns to action, and maybe even after that, for Bill Edwards still entertains hopes of developing the colored star into a running back.

Ralph Vince lost no time in asserting his authority over the B-W linemen . . . The former Carroll coach is a driving taskmaster and had the Jacket forwards hopping at a merry clip.

THE WEATHER
Fair today; generally fair tomorrow; little change in temperature.
(Weather Details on Page 5)

ALLENTOWN MORNING CALL

Lehigh Valley's Greatest Newspaper

VOL. XCIII, NO. 94 ★ ALLENTOWN, PA., SATURDAY MORNING, OCTOBER 3, 1936

SINGLE COPY Three Cents | DAILY 12 Cents Week | DAILY & SUNDAY 15 Cents Week

Report Spanish Cabinet Officers Fleeing Country

Several Believed to Be Aboard Argentine Warship Enroute to France

General Franco Named Dictator by Insurgents

In Proclamation to People Promises Work Is Assured to All

LISBON, PORTUGAL, Oct. 2. (AP)—Several Spanish cabinet ministers were reported today in Fascist communiques to have fled to France aboard an Argentine warship.

Reports also reached here that Gen. Francisco Franco, named dictator by the insurgents, had proclaimed "a new Spain" to be ruled as a corporative state on the model of Portugal and Italy.

The reports ministry members had quit the capital emanated from insurgent headquarters at Valladolid, Spain. They said the fleeing officials had reached Alicante and were bound for Marseille, France, on the cruiser 25 de Mayo.

(Last week informed sources at Buenos Aires said President Manuel Azana of Spain had asked asylum on the Argentine man-of-war but the report was denied in Madrid.

(The reports also said Azana's wife and the wives and children of some of his ministers had been moved to Alicante under the protection of Daniel Garcia Mansilla, Argentine ambassador to Madrid, to be put aboard the 25 de Mayo.)

Gen. Franco's proclamation to the
(Continued on Page Two)

Typhoon Sweeps Toward Tokyo

Japanese Capital Expecting Full Force of Tropical Storm Today

TOKYO, Oct. 3 (Saturday). (AP)—Sixty-four persons were believed drowned today when the Japanese steamship Kashima Maru foundered in a typhoon which was sweeping on Tokyo where it was expected to strike this afternoon

The steamer was struck off the west central coast of the Korean peninsula. Eight survivors were picked up by another steamship.

The severe wind and rainstorm, moving 30 miles on hour over an area 300 miles wide, was only 130 miles southwest of this capital.

At Nagoya, about 160 miles west and slightly south of Tokyo, 8,000 houses were reported inundated as rivers overflowed.

In Yokohama and other cities along the seascoast, many homes and streets were covered by water and serious damage was done.

High seas which clashed the Yokohama harbor prevented American and other steamers from landing.

A terrific typhoon which devastated Central Japan in September, 1934, took at least 2,499 lives, official estimates showed. A total of 568 persons were listed as missing, while 8,399 were injured.

Much of the important city of Osaka was ruined in that storm, and disease spread rapidly through the stricken area.

In August of this year the worst typhoon to strike the Japanese owned Korean peninsula in recent years killed at least 1,156 persons. The government said 769 were missing, 1,183 injured, 33,254 houses demolished or washed away, and 2,500 boats sunk or destroyed.

The steamship Kashima Maru, reported to have founded off Korea, is a vessel of 9,908 gross tons with twin propellors. It was built in 1913 at Kobe, Japan.

Telegraphic News Briefs

LOS ANGELES, Oct. 2 (AP)—Elaine Barrie, exprotege of John Barrymore, was sued today for $10,000 damages as the result of an automobile accident in which Herbert Searman, 15, was injured. The accident occurred last Aug. 7. Miss Barrie's chauffeur was driving.

MONTREAL, Oct. 2 (AP)—Alfred Clark Chapin, former representative in the United States Congress for New York's second district, died here today. He was 88 years old.

MEXICO CITY, Oct. 2 (AP)—A dispatch from Tultitlan, Mexico state, today said six workers were killed in a premature explosion of dynamite used in blasting for the Levheria Dam, under construction near there.

LONDON, Oct. 2 (AP)—Jimmy Donahue's musical comedy "Trans-Atlantic Rhythm" went on tonight with Dorothy Dare in the star's role vacated by Ruth Etting after Thursday night's embattled opening. Miss Etting announced she and her husband would sail for New York Wednesday because, she said, Young Donahue, Woolworth heir and co-backer of the show with Felix Ferry, had not paid her $1,500 due salary.

LONDON, Oct. 2—(AP)—The Herald in a dispatch from Praha, Czechoslovakia, said tonight that Mme. Magda Lupescu, friend of King Carol of Rumania 'has been married to a high official of the Rumanian court." "She is now living at the palace in Bucharest," the newspaper dispatch said.

BUCHAREST, RUMANIA, Oct. 3 (Saturday) (AP)—Usually informed sources denied today that King Carol's friend, Mme. Magda Lupescu, had married.

PARIS, Oct. 2 (AP)—To be tipped or not to be tipped was a question which got Paris waiters and restaurateurs in a free-for-all fist fight today. Meeting under a strike threat, the employers rejected waiters' demands for a fixed percentage of checks instead of tips. Fists swung and the meeting broke up with employees' representatives demanding the government intervene.

Lazzeri Hits Homer With Bases Loaded

—Associated Press Photo

NEW YORK, Oct. 2.—Tony Lazzeri, Yankee second baseman, is shown scoring after hitting a home-run into the lower right field stands of the Polo Grounds in the third inning of the World's series game today when the bases were full, to give the Yankees a 7-1 lead. This was the first time this feat had been accomplished in a World's series game since 1920. Watching Lazzeri as he crosses the plate are the Yanks' batboy, Umpire Geisel and Gus Mancuso, Giant catcher.

Rival Leaders Push Activities Over Wide Front

Political Observers Ponder Smith Speech as Candidates Rest

By The Associated Press

The 1936 presidential campaign swings today into its final month with both President Roosevelt and his Republican opponent, Gov. Alf M. Landon of Kansas, enjoying a comparative calm before the final stretch to election day.

With the chief executive resting at Hyde Park before resuming his reelection campaign, and the Kansan looking forward to a college football game at Lawrence, Kas., supporters of both nevertheless pursued their activity over a broad front.

Political observers continued to ponder the effects of Al Smith's declaration that "the remedy for all the ills that we are suffering from today is the election of Alfred M. Landon."

Among party leaders and others, opinions varied.

Former President Hoover, victorious 1928 rival of the former New York governor, declared Smith had put 'country above partisanship."

Gov. James M. Curley, Democratic nominee for senator from Massachusetts, declared Smith was "a victim of circumstances," and expressed belief his declaration for the Republican nominee would "strengthen" the Democratic cause.

Landon himself described Smith as "a great Democrat and a great American.'

Democratic Chairman James A. Farley expressed the belief the Smith speech would have "no effect on the final results of the elections."

Harrison E. Spangler, executive vice chairman of the Republican National committee, declared "Smith made it clear that Mr. Roosevelt has scrapped the party of Jefferson, Jackson, Woodrow Wilson and all the great Democratic leaders."

In a nation-wide broadcast last night, Edward A. Filene, Boston mer-
(Continued on Page Two)

Say Purchasing Power Of Dollar Above 1929

NEW YORK, Oct. 2. (AP) — Wage earners in manufacturing industries find purchasing power of their average weekly earnings higher today than in 1929, while their average weekly working hours are shorte[illegible] tional Industrial Confere[illegible] statistical organization sponsored by industrial corporations, said today.

In an analysis of manufacturing statistics the board found that for the first six months of this year the average cost of living index, with average for 1929 placed at 100, was 83.7, while the average index of weekly money earnings was 86.7. This, the report said, put the index of "real" earnings at 103.6 or 3.6 per cent above the 1929 level.

Average hours worked per week were 38.4 for the six months ending June 30, compared with 48.3 in 1929.

The Call's Index

Governor Seeks To End Trouble At Reading Mill

Changes Command of State Police in Area After Brutality Is Charged

READING, PA., Oct. 2. (AP)—Governor Earle assumed the role of mediator in the Berkshire Knitting Mills strike today as picketing that lasted through two days of disorders halted for the weekend.

The Governor, at the State capitol, heard workers and plant officials tell their sides of the labor dispute at the Wyomissing factories, including charges of brutality on the part of state police from the West Reading barracks.

Three outbreaks since the strike was called yesterday morning injured more than 40 workers and two state troopers. Tear bombs were thrown and more than 100 automobiles smashed.

The Governor's first move was to send Major C. M. Wilhelm, deputy superintendent of state police, to take charge of policing in the strike area, superseding Captain Samuel W. Gearhart, commander of troop C.

Strikers charged Gearhart advised "clubbing as the only way to handle the situation."

The governor said if the charge were substantiated, Gearhart will be suspended immediately.

Attaches of the governor's office said Earle, in placing Major Wilhelm in charge of policing the strike area, instructed him to transfer Captain Gearhart to another district, pending an investigation of the charges.

Meanwhile, Luther D. Adams, president of Branch 10, American Federation of Hosiery Workers, announced picketing was suspended only until Monday morning at 5 a. m.

"We'll have our scouts around but no actual picketing," Adams said.

The Governor asked company offi-
(Continued on Page Two)

Fugmann Denies Sending Bombs

WILKES-BARRE, PA., Oct. 2. (AP)—Taking the stand in the battle to save his life, Michael Fugmann, Hanover township miner, this afternoon vigorously denied the Good Friday bomb packages were ever in his possession, that he addressed any of the packages, and swore he knew nothing of their origin or preparation.

The [illegible]man who admitted he deserted the German Imperial army in 1917 and went to Holland when the United States entered the conflict "because I knew we were licked," repudiated all charges made by the Commonwealth in nine days of testimony but was vague and forgetful when District Attorney Leon Schwartz started the cross examination in the defendant's trial for the slaying of Thomas Maloney, former labor leader.

He denied ill feelings for Thomas Maloney, Michael Gallagher, or the addressees of the four unexploded bombs, and told of his friendship for the Maloneys when he said he offered the slain labor leader a blood transfusion after he suffered the blast injuries and drove his automobile in the funeral cortege of Thomas Maloney Jr., 4, son of the former unionist.

The defendant admitted obtaining cigar boxes from Shulte cigar stores similar to those used in the bombs, but declared they had been stolen from his parked automobile the same day; denied ever seeing pieces of wood, dynamite, and other articles police said were found in his home and which experts testified corresponded with parts of the bombs; and insisted he had not been near the section of the city where the cigar bomb death packages were taken from mail boxes on Holy Thursday night, April 9.

"I had nothing to do with the bombs, so help me God," the defendant declared when turned over to District Attorney Schwartz for cross examination shortly before the calling of a recess for a night session.

Steals Pie—Jailed; Aids in Breaking Lock

CHESTER, PA., Oct. 2. (AP)—Walter Lesgo, 16, arrested yesterday on a charge of stealing a pie, worked for two hours today assisting his jailor to release him from his cell for a hearing. The cell lock jammed and several bolts and rivets on the inside and ouside of the door had to be removed.

A magistrate held Lesgo in $300 bail for the grand jury.

4000 Guardsmen Patrol Paris to Avert Civil War

Augment Police of French Capital Following Street Riots

PARIS, Oct. 2. (AP)—Four thousand guardsmen patrolled Paris boulevards tonight as the government's militant answer to Col. Francois de la Rocque's assertion "enemies of the people might unleash a civil war in France."

Some 500 leftists chanting the "Internationale" clashed with 300 of de la Rocque's followers singing the "Marseillaise" in the Trocardero sections but were quickly dispersed by police.

The guardsmen, brought to Paris to reinforce police during the parliamentary debates on devaluation, were ordered into active duty after de la Rocque defied the government of Socialist Premier Leon Blum to break up his Social party.

In a letter to Blum, de la Rocque wrote:

"We fear to see the enemies of the people whom events in Spain make still more bloodthirsty unleash a civil war in France."

Calling Communists "Moscow Fascists," de la Rocque, in the name of his party, demanded that the government take proper measures to prevent "all attempts" at an uprising.

His letter was evoked by an order from Roger Salengro, minister of the interior, for a criminal investigation to determine whether the group was an off-shoot of the disbanded "Croix de Feu"—Cross of Fire—as the leftists charge.

De la Rocque was chief of the Croix de Feu and charged by his political foes with having Fascist tendencies.

The government, which anxiously watched the devalued franc close today at 21.45 to the American dollar, devoted its energies tonight to keep the political peace of the nation.

De la Rocque, however, ordered his followers in the Social party to hold protest meetings throughout the land tonight or tomorrow against the government-ordered investigation.

Roosevelt Takes Neutral Position At World Series

Dedicates Medical Center and Breaks Ground for Queens-Manhattan Tunnel

NEW YORK, Oct. 2. (AP)—President Roosevelt interrupted his first campaign trip in the east today to become a non-partisan spectator at the second world series ball game.

He sandwiched the visit to the game between the dedication of the third largest medical center in the country at Jersey City, N. J., and a late afternoon ground-breaking for New York's $58,000,000 Queens-Manhattan tunnel, biggest non-federal project financed by the PWA.

In a short address at the huge medical center, Mr. Roosevelt gave doctors of the nation an assurance that "the federal government contemplates no action detrimental to their interests."

"The action taken in the field of health as shown by the provisions of the splendid social security act recently enacted is clear," he added. "It has provisions which are forgotten in the heat of a political campaign."

Public support is behind the social
(Continued on Page Two)

Jazz Age Dead, Say Juvenile Records

OKLAHOMA CITY, Oct. 2. (AP)—Tom Gammie of the Oklahoma Planning board looked up from a sheaf of juvenile delinquency records today and commented:

"The jazz age is dead."

Reason:

A sharp drop in the juvenile population of Oklahoma's training schools for incorrigibles.

During the period Gammie termed the 'Jazz age,"—1925 to 1930—his records showed the population of both boys' and girls' training schools jumped more than 60 per cent. In the last six years the annual increase has slumped decidedly.

To prove the demise of the jazz age, Gammie cited records of the state girls' training school for incorrigibles from 10 to 16 years old. Between 1925 and 1930 the school population gained 62.4 per cent. Since, however, the gain has been only 10.98 per cent. In the "hip flask era" the population of the boys' training school jumped up 63.2 per cent. Now the increase has dropped to only 4.5 per cent.

Gammie said boys committed to the training school also were in the 10 to 16 year old age group, as are inmates of a separate Negro training school.

Simon Lake Seeks Treasure Ship; Faces Suit for Not Paying Taxes

By GARDNER BRIDGE

NEW YORK, Oct. 2. (AP)—Faced with a foreclosure proceeding on property he owns in Connecticut, Simon Lake tonight asked permission to speed up his salvaging of a sunken treasure ship in the East River.

The 70-year-old submarine inventor, assembling equipment to explore what he believes is the submerged hulk of the British frigate Hussar, ruefully admitted that he had fallen behind on his taxes in Stratford, Conn., but explained:

"The trouble is I have been putting all the money I could get hold of into this salvage project."

He expressed hope he would find the $4,800,000 in gold and silver reputed to have been aboard the Hussar when she foundered in the treacherous waters of Hell Gate during the Revolutionary war.

In order to expedite the salvage operations, Lake said he had asked the treasury department in Washington for permission to blast his way into the silt-covered hulk.

"If they will let be blow the decks off, the job can be done very quickly," he said.

Under his arrangement with the treasury department, the Lake Submarine Salvage Corp., which is financing the project, will be permitted to retain 90 per cent of all specie recovered. Lake has a profit-sharing contract with the corporation.

The only objection to blasting, he said, is that it would destroy the ship's value as an historical relic. It had been proposed to raise it intact and exhibit it at the New York World's Fair in 1939.

To do this, however, would entail months of labor pumping the hulk free of silt.

Lake implied he did not consider it quite the sporting thing to do when the town of Stratford started court action to recover a $4,000 tax bill for the years 1922-1936.

"I have paid out more than $50,000,000 for labor in that vicinity," he said, "and I am hoping to get another business started up there soon."

During the World war the payroll at his Connecticut shipyard approximated $5,000,000, he said.

He described the property involved in the foreclosure proceeding as consisting of a house and several vacant lots which he had purchased as an investment.

He hopes to start operations in the East river within the next two weeks and continue all winter if necessary.

Yanks Break Nine World Series Records; Defeat Giants 18-4

First for Yankees

THE OFFICIAL BOX SCORE

New York (A. L.)

	Ab	R	H	O	A
Crosetti ss	5	4	3	0	1
Rolfe 3b	4	3	2	2	0
DiMaggio cf	5	2	3	6	0
Gehrig 1b	5	1	2	6	0
Dickey c	5	3	2	8	0
Selkirk rf	5	1	1	2	0
Powell lf	3	2	2	2	0
Lazzeri 2b	4	1	1	1	3
Gomez p	5	1	1	0	0
Totals	41	18	17	27	4

New York (N. L.)

	Ab	R	H	O	A
Moore lf	5	0	0	2	0
Bartell ss	3	0	1	2	2
Terry 1b	5	0	2	6	1
Leiber cf	4	0	0	7	1
Ott rf	4	0	0	4	0
Mancuso c	2	2	1	3	2
Whitehead 2b	4	0	0	2	1
Jackson 3b	4	1	1	0	2
Schumacher p	0	0	0	0	0
Smith p	0	0	0	0	0
Coffman p	0	0	0	0	1
Davis z	1	1	1	0	0
Gabler p	0	0	0	1	0
Danning zz	1	0	0	0	0
Gumbert p	0	0	0	0	0
Totals	33	4	6	27	10

z—Batted for Coffman in 4th.
zz—Batted for Gabler in 8th.

Score by innings:
New York (A.) 207 001 206—18
New York (N.) 010 300 000— 4

Error—Jackson. Runs batted in—Gehrig 3, Dickey 5, Lazzeri 5, Bartell, Terry 2, DiMaggio 2, Gomez 2, Rolfe. Two base hits—DiMaggio, Mancuso, Bartell. Home runs—Lazzeri, Dickey. Stolen base—Powell. Sacrifice—DiMaggio. Double plays — Leiber, Jackson, Bartell. Earned runs—New York (A. L.) 17; New York (N. L.) 4. Left on bases—N. Y. (AL) 6; N. Y. (NL) 9. Bases on balls—Schumacher 4 (Rolfe 2, Selkirk, Lazzeri); Smith 1 (Powell); Gomez 7 (Leiber, Mancuso 2, Schumacher, Bartell 2, Gabler); Gabler 3 (Crosetti, Dickey, Gehrig); Gumbert 1 (Powell). Strikeouts—Gomez 8 (Moore 2, Bartell, Terry, Leiber, Whitehead, Mancuso, Danning); Schumacher 1 (Gomez); Coffman 1 (Gomez); Gumbert 1 (Selkirk). Hits off—Schumacher 5 runs, 3 hits in 2 innings (none out in 3rd); Smith 3 runs, 2 hits in 1-3 inning; Coffman 1 run, 2 hits in 1 2-3 innings; Gabler 3 runs, 5 hits in 4 innings; Gumbert 6 runs, 5 hits in 1 inning. Wild pitches—Schumacher, Gomez. Umpires—Geisel, Magerkurth, Sommers and Pfirman. Time of game—2.49.

One Dead, 3 Hurt In Eviction Row

WEST CHESTER, PA., Oct. 2. (AP)—A 65-year-old man barricaded himself in a barn and blazed away with shotgun and rifle late today at neighbors who came to a constable's sale on his farm, killing one person and wounding three others.

An hour after the firing began, Police Chief Edward Darlington spied the man, Pratt Dutton, raising a rifle at a second floor window. Darlington was quicker on the bead and Dutton fell screaming, a bullet wound in his leg.

Other police and citizens who were deputized hastily rushed in on Dutton from the rear of the barn.

The man killed was Atlee Jackson, 75, of West Chester, one of about 25 persons on hand for the sale.

Lawrence Urbine, Coatesville constable who went to Dutton's small farm to levy on his effects, was shot in the thigh with birdshot. James March, West Chester, another in the group attending the sale, received birdshot wounds in the foot.

Jerry Monaghan, West Chester policeman, was wounded in the hand by a rifle bullet.

Dutton had a milk route in West Chester until three months ago. Then his small herd failed to pass a state sanitation test and the cattle were destroyed

The constable was ordered to levy on Dutton's effects to collect $75 he owed a West Chester bank.

Urbine said that as he approached Dutton the latter grabbed a rifle and a shotgun, ran into the barn and slammed the doors shut. An instant later, Dutton opened a door and blazed away at the constable.

Others in the crowd called police and in the hour's siege they fired 60 shots. During the battle, police noticed Jackson's body lying near the rear of the barn, but they did not learn just when he had fallen.

In the barn, police found two shotguns and the rifle, a full box of shotgun shells and a party-filled box of rifle cartridges.

Unemployment Insurance Law As Basis of Suit

MONTGOMERY, ALA., Oct. 2 (AP)—Federal Judge C. B. Kennamer granted the Gulf States Steel company of Gadsden, Ala., a temporary restraining order today to prevent the state from collecting $31,000 taxes due under the Alabama unemployment insurance law.

Judge Kennamer made his order contingent upon the company's placing the $31,000 in the federal depository here pending a final decision of its attack on the validity of the law.

A hearing on the company's petition for a permanent injunction against collection of the tax was set for October 9 in U. S. district court here.

Meanwhile, counsel for numerous Alabama industrial firms were preparing to become parties to the suit and thus protect their tax payments against loss in the event the law is declared unconstitutional.

The unemployment insurance tax, levied both on employe and employer, is used to provide benefits during unemployment for persons who contribute to it while employed.

The law levies one per cent on the salaries of employes, and recaptures 90 per cent of the federal unemployment insurance tax levied on employers. This latter tax ranges from one per cent on wages and salaries paid this year, to three per cent in 1928 and thereafter.

The tax falls on firms employing more than eight persons, with exemptions provided for federal, state, county and city employes, agricultural workers, sailors, and those employed in religious, charitable, educational and scientific institutions.

Yanks' Pitcher

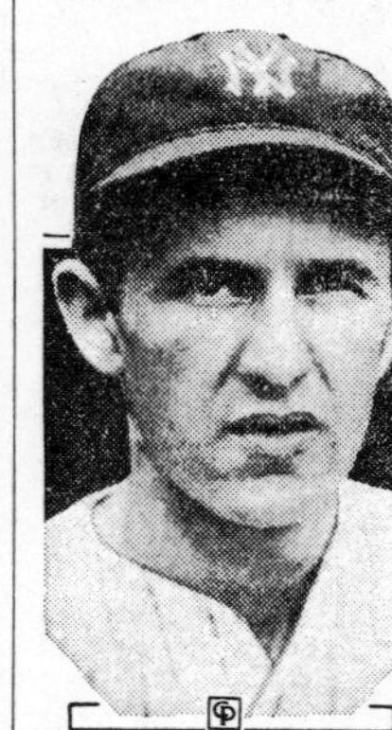

VERNON (LEFTY) GOMEZ

Series Sidelights

By SCOTTY RESTON

NEW YORK, Oct. 2. (AP)—President Roosevelt was in the stands and the reporters were enquiring about the political leanings of Vernon L. (Goofy) Gomez.

"I've been busy," said 'Goofy.' "No time for politics. Let's see, the President's a Democrat, ain't he? * * * Then I guess I'm a Democrat."

It was an embarrassing situation. Al Smith was pitching and President Roosevelt was in a nearby box. But the Yankees took care of it in a hurry. Al took a walk to the club house after pitching to only three batters.

Shortly after the game started, a lazy airplane crawled across the white clouds. It carried a long streamer which read, "Re-elect Roosevelt. Remember 1932."

"Goofy" had a great time picking up pebbles off the mound and pulling up his pants. He also had his fun before the game. The photographers made him shake hands with Hal Schumacher for 10 minutes. The two starting pitchers didn't talk at first. Then "Goofy" said, "They'll probably fine you 10 bucks for 'fraternalizing' with me."

Mayor LaGuardia went down and greeted the President. Managers McCarthy and Terry also went over and the President joked with them about the game.

Joe Moore, Giants' leadoff man, went hitless his first eight times in the series, and then hit a lightning drive into left center. But Joe DiMaggio made a great running catch of the ball to extend the hitless streak to nine.

Terry is more than leader of the Giants in name. In both series games so far he has got the first hit for the National Leaguers, and in the fourth inning, drove in two runs with a perfect lick to left center.

There was civil war in the upper left hand grandstand in the fourth inning when, with the bases full, Dick Bartell rifled one into the crowd near the foul line. Yankee fans said
(Continued on Page Two)

Producers Ditch Truck In Akron Mill War

AKRON, O., Oct. 2. (AP)—Irate producers, attempting to shut off Akron's milk supply to enforce price demands, spilled 1,000 gallons of milk from a Dayton truck, which was forced into a ditch.

Organized dairy farmers set up a cruising automobile blockade. Their representatives conferred with dealers from whom they have asked an increase of from $2.30 to $2.40 a hundred pounds for Class 1 milk.

William L. Strickland, plant manager for the Akron Pure Milk Co., asserted there would be no shortage tomorrow.

He declined to discuss how the supply was to reach the city, although Attorney Dudley Maxon, counsel for the distributors, said "if farmers halt trucks dealers will ship in milk by rail."

J. I. Shafer, president of the Milk Producers Association of Akron and vicinity, asserted the organization's membership of over 2,700 controlled 85 per cent of Akron's milk.

He reiterated, "We'll stick this out if it takes a month."

Browder Says Roosevelt, Landon Pension Enemies

NEW YORK, Oct. 2. (AP) — Earl Browder, Communist presidential candidate who was prevented from speaking from a Terre Haute, Ind., radio station this week, took to the microphone here tonight to describe Governor Alf M. Landon and Colonel Frank Knox as "the chosen candidates of the most irreconcilable enemies of old age pensions and unemployment insurance."

His reference to the Republican presidential and vice presidential candidates was contained in a speech prepared for broadcast over the NBC chain on the topic "Old Age Pensions and Unemployment Insurance."

"They represent the Liberty League, Hearst, Morgan, the Du Ponts, Mellon, the wealthy families of our land, whose central policy is to prevent the government from taxing their mounting profits and billions of capital, by so much as a single penny," Browder declared. "Landon gave a broad hint that if elected he would finance such federal relief as he could not immediately cut off, by a federal sales tax which would fall upon the whole population."

He said today "this affair in Terre Haute has won 100,000 votes for the Communist party in November."

"Neither President Roosevelt nor Governor Landon has thought it important enough to comment on the incident," Browder said.

Tony Lazzeri Hits Homer With Bases Filled

President Roosevelt Watches Records Fall

Yanks Club Their Way to Even Terms with Giants Before 43,543 Spectators — Gomez Holds Giants to 6 Hits, Strikes Out 8 but Passes 7 Men

By ALAN GOULD
Associated Press Sports Editor

NEW YORK, Oct. 2. (AP)—World Series skies cleared today in New York's baseball Civil War but there was another deluge just the same at the Polo grounds.

Instead of the rainfall it took the form of a Yankee windfall. On the diamond that was swept by showers for two previous days, the American League champions turned on a downpour of basehits that swamped the Giants by the record-smashing score of 18 to 4.

President Roosevelt, interrupting his re-election campaign to see his first world series game since 1933, was among the 43,543 fans who saw the Yankees emerge with a resounding roar from their hitting slump, batter five opposing pitchers, and coast to victory behind the erratic flinging of Vernon (Lefty) Gomez.

Clubbing their way back to even terms at one-all in the Subway Scramble for baseball's biggest money honors, the Yankees knocked Hal Schumacher from the box in the midst of a seven-run outburst in the third inning and continued a desultory attack that was climaxed in the ninth by a six-run drive off Harry Gumbert, the luckless fifth flinger for the home team.

This concluding blast in a game that dragged through two hours and 49 minutes, the longest in series history, crowned one of the greatest record-breaking sprees ever witnessed in championship competition. With an attack reminiscent of the palmiest days of Babe Ruth & Company, the stream-lined 1936 Yankees broke or tied at least nine World Series marks.

Gallant Anthony Michael Lazzeri, the veteran second sacker who was supposed to be near the end of the playing trail, contributed the biggest wallop to the record books by belting a home run with the bases full in the third inning, off the relief flinging of right-handed Dick Coffman.

Besides duplicating an achievement recorded only once before in Series annals—by Elmer Smith of Cleveland against Brooklyn in 1920—Lazzeri drove home a fifth run with a long fly, in the seventh inning, thereby wiping out a mark for runs-batted-in that he had shared himself with Babe Ruth and six other World Series batsmen.

Not even this record stood alone for long, however. Catcher Bill Dickey came through with a ninth-inning homer, with two men on, that tied him
(Continued on Page Two)

Hotelman's Body Exhumed For Second Autopsy

UNIONTOWN, PA., Oct. 2. (AP)—Attorney Charles J. Margiotti said today a second autopsy on the body of Frank C. Monaghan disclosed an additional fracture of the right jaw of the 64-year-old hotel man, whose death led to the arrest of three policemen.

Monaghan's body was exhumed today by court order upon the petition of Margiotti, and the six physicians who conducted the first autopsy examined the body again.

Physicians reported to Coroner S. A. Baltz after the first examination that Monaghan had a broken nose and jaw, 11 fractured ribs and 53 cuts and bruises, and that he suffered two hemorrhages.

Margiotti charged Monaghan was "barbarously and brutally beaten to death" in the Bertillon room of Fayette county detective headquarters in an effort to force him to confess stabbing County Detective John C. Wall Sept. 12.

The attorney general said today's examination also showed a number of small fractures on Monaghan's nose and an injury to his hand.

Margiotti expressed the belief the two fractures of the hotel man's jaw might have been caused "by one blow."

The grand jury meanwhile heard Stephen R. Haky, undertaker, and his employes. Monaghan's body was taken to his establishment from the Bertillon room.

Officials will hold a half-day's session of the grand jury tomorrow. They summoned these witnesses: Orley Jackson, night superintendent of the court house; Frank Trimble, janitor; Coroner S. A. Baltz, who filed the murder charges against the policemen, and Mrs. Z. Coraddo and U. E. Ralston.

The men charged with murder are State Troopers Anthony Sanute and Stacy Gunderman and County Detective Wilbert Minerd.

Riley's 'Baby Lizzie' Dies in Indianapolis

INDIANAPOLIS, Oct. 2 (AP)—Those who have read the works of James Whitcomb Riley, the Hoosier poet, may remember the stanza "Baby Lizzie" in "The Old Home Folks."

"Baby Lizzie with her velvet lisp,
"As though her elfin lips had caught some wisp
"Of floss between them as they strove with speech,
"Which ever seemed just in, yet out of reach.
"Though what her lips missed, her eyes could say
"With looks that made her meaning clear as day."

"Baby Lizzie" died today. She was Mrs. Mary Riley Payne, 71, the poet's sister. Before her marriage she was Mary Elizabeth Riley, youngest of the six children of Capt. R. A. and Elizabeth Marine Riley. She had been ill several years.

She was married in her early twenties to Frank Charles Payne, once an editor of the Indianapolis Journal. She was the last surviving member of the Riley family.

Jade—Mystic And Valuable Stone Of Far East

Intriguing History Of Jewel Leads Through Many Lands

By Julette S. Graf

IF we lost both limbs in the cause of Science, it would seem to us to be the ultimate example of self sacrifice. A modern mineralogist cannot be anything but incredulous when he hears the tale of the reputed discovery of jade, the mystic gem of the Orient.

According to legend, one day over 3000 years ago, an obscure Chinese student was gathering interesting pebbles and scrutinizing curious rock formations when he was suddenly amazed to observe a phoenix marvelously poised upon a rock. The singular beauty of the creature's proud position, and the fact that in China a phoenix is believed only to alight upon PRECIOUS rock, led the young scientist to approach the bird. As he did so it flew away but the youth proceeded to examine the place where it had rested. It is possible then that he respectfully uttered the equivalent for EUREKA for the stone proved to be of a quite extraordinary quality. Hurrying home he labeled his specimens JADE and without delay arranged for an audience with the reigning emperor. Indeed, he felt that he had something truly worthy to present to his august ruler.

But the eager youth was quite coolly received. It did not appear to be an auspicious day for the interview, for the emperor was clearly skeptical in regard to the newly found so-called treasure. He had not heard of Jade and clearly felt that his kingdom was as well off without it. In fact, he yawned and suggested that it might be diverting to cut off one of the scientist's legs.

Finally, after this unbelievable sacrifice, the man of science was rewarded with an appreciative listener. The emperor was fascinated by the glorious beauty of the various specimens. He sent for the court jewelers and gem cutters and a new art was created. The discoverer of jade was recompensed for his efforts by elevation to the order of Grand Master of Optimism.

Jade, although it is usually associated with China and things Chinese, is actually found for the most part in Burma. Turkestan, Siberia and New Zealand are also recognized sources of various types of the precious stone. But, in 1884, Dr. George F. Kunz, Tiffany's authority on jade and a scientific writer upon the subject, made the momentous discovery of jade on the European continent in the form of a giant boulder of nephrite in Jordansmuhl. This boulder, weighing over 4000 pounds, is now in the Museum of Natural History in New York City. A few years later Dr. Kunz discovered another Silesian deposit in Reichenstein. These two disclosures of jade in Europe settled an age-old debate between scientists who were trying to solve the question of the source of jade used in many of the earlier stone implements found on that continent.

Another motive for recent controversy has been the presence of jade relics in Mexico and Central America. Although much jade has been found in these two areas none has yet been found in its natural form and there has been speculation as to whether or not its presence is an indication of ancient contacts with the Orient.

In spite of the deposits found elsewhere, Burma continues to be the richest source of jade, with the best specimens coming from the Moguang district in Upper Burma. Dealers of Canton, Peiping and Shanghai send their representatives to the jade market annually to purchase the supply for the year's carving.

IN COLOR, specimens vary from a soapy whiteness to deep olive, or spinach green, depending upon the oxides they contain. Jadeite and nephrite are of the more pallid variety, dull and wax-like and often of an exquisite slippery-smooth texture lending itself to the creation of bowls, cups and plates. Chloromenalite, the third variety of jade is of a dark green almost black material.

The most valuable of all jade is the variety known as *fei tsui* which is emerald green. Scientists have abandoned hope of finding further deposits of this particular jade, consequently a good *fei tsui* stone brings a four figure price. Chemists attribute the brighter green shadings in some of the most valuable and admired gems to a small content of chromium. A string of 108 matched *fei tsui* beads of from six to seven carats each is reputed to be owned by the Chinese Nationalist Government and is said to be worth $200,000. Experts in jade compare a $5000 *fei tsui* necklace to a $20,000 pearl in equivalent value due to the fact that *fei tsui* jade is rapidly being bought by the collectors with no prospect of new pieces to be had when the valuable supply has been exhausted.

Imperial jade is a gem so rare as to be comparable to the most costly emeralds of a fine green. In the purchase of jade pieces it is well to bear in mind the fact that all true jade is translucent, and that there is no genuine jade without a cloudy effect through

its translucency when held to the light. The Chinese often read auspicious signs in these "jade clouds" and make their purchases because they are influenced by the supernatural meaning they have read into the opportune formations.

The name applied to jade by the Chinese is Yu, which is a

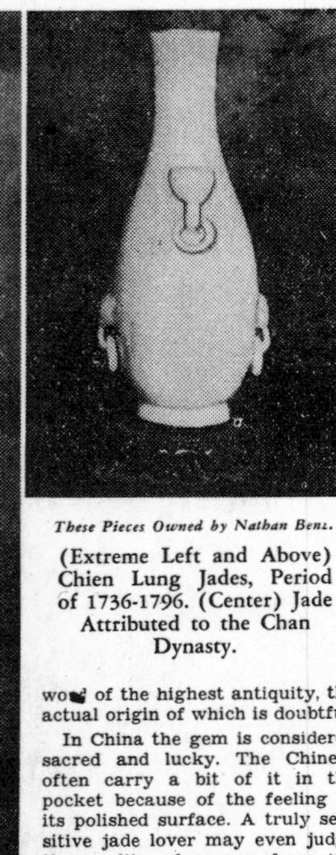

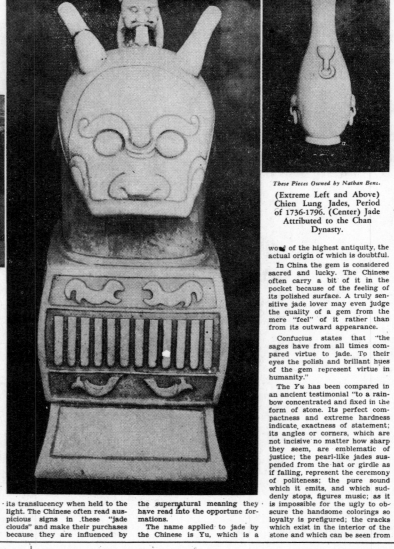

These Pieces Owned by Nathan Benz.

(Extreme Left and Above) Chien Lung Jades, Period of 1736-1796. (Center) Jade Attributed to the Chan Dynasty.

word of the highest antiquity, the actual origin of which is doubtful.

In China the gem is considered sacred and lucky. The Chinese often carry a bit of it in the pocket because of the feeling of its polished surface. A truly sensitive jade lover may even judge the quality of a gem from the mere "feel" of it rather than from its outward appearance.

Confucius states that "the sages have from all times compared virtue to jade. To their eyes the polish and brillant hues of the gem represent virtue in humanity."

The *Yu* has been compared in an ancient testimonial "to a rainbow concentrated and fixed in the form of stone. Its perfect compactness and extreme hardness indicate exactness of statement; its angles or corners, which are not incisive no matter how sharp they seem, are emblematic of justice; the pearl-like jades suspended from the hat or girdle as if falling, represent the ceremony of politeness; the pure sound which it emits, and which suddenly stops, figures music; as it is impossible for the ugly to obscure the handsome colorings so loyalty is prefigured; the cracks which exist in the interior of the stone and which can be seen from the outside are figuratively of sincerity; its irridescent lustre, similar to that of the rainbow is symbolic of the permanent; its wonderful substance extracted from the mountains or from the rivers represents the earth; when cast in a knei or chon without other embellishment it is indicative of virtue; and the high value attached to it by the whole world, without exception, is figurative of truth."

Favorite symbols used by the Chinese in jade carving are the earth symbol, a cylindrical tube handsomely embellished; the sun disc, a doughnut-like circle, flat, and representing the influence of heaven; the *tao tieh* or monster which is said to ward off evil and to represent the uncertainty in life; the sacred ox, the ceremonial knife and many others.

According to experts, America's outstanding collection today is the Herbert R. Bishop collection which is now the property of the Metropolitan Museum in New York City. It consists of 900 rare pieces. The Museum of Natural History in New York also contains some unique pieces; two jade boulders from New Zealand and one of 4170 pounds, from Siberia, also a chain and pendant carved from a single 40 pound block of jade. Owen Freeman Roberts of New York is the owner of a brilliant private collection. Nathan Benz of Santa Barbara has one of the worthwhile collections on the Pacific coast and he and his brother Phillip Benz of San Francisco have spent years in selecting and collecting priceless jades. Women owning fine jade pieces are Mrs. Christian R. Holmes, the former Betty Fleischmann, and Countess Constantini of Paris.

Mills College in Oakland, California, boasts an association known as the Friends of Far Eastern Art which has a notable collection of fine jades. The Jade Room in the Seattle Museum is devoted to Chinese and Tibetan carvings, principally emphasizing the work of the Eighteenth Century. The jades of this exhibit are most carefully and tastefully selected and jade lovers come from far and near to feast their eyes upon the delicate beauty of this particular collection. The collectors of jade are legion, they are as endless as its designs and varieties of color.

If You're Good, There's Big Money In Baseball

$10,000-A-Year Salary Paid To 18-Year-Old Bob Feller

By Bob Edgren, Jr.

FROM $75 a month to $10,000 a season . . . in one year.

That's what a ball player can do if he strikes it rich. That's what Bob Feller, 18-year-old schoolboy, has done. In fact, he nearly came into $100,000 which might have been his if a decision of Judge Landis, czar of baseball, had gone the other way.

How did Bob do it?

Two years ago he was pitching for the Farmer's Mutual Insurance team. An old ball player, Pat Donohue, saw him. Pat wrote to a couple of ball clubs. Presently, Feller was signed to a contract in which he agreed to pitch for the Fargo team for $75 a month. Although the contract was signed in June, 1935, Feller was to take over his pitching duties in 1936.

Before he ever pitched a ball for Fargo, while he was still an amateur, he went to the National Amateur Baseball Tournament at Dayton, Ohio. There he pitched a one-hit game, showing such blazing speed that he struck out 21 men.

More scouts came. They all wanted him to sign contracts. Offers got higher and higher. Suddenly someone discovered that Feller was already signed to pitch for Fargo. Feller kicked himself for signing for $75 a month, when he could have had much more, but it was too late.

As matters turned out, it didn't make any difference. His contract was assigned to New Orleans in 1936, and before he had ever pitched a ball for New Orleans, he was assigned to Cleveland.

After pitching in the big leagues for six weeks, Feller returned to Van Meter, Iowa, where 10,000 people greeted him at the railroad station. There aren't 10,000 people in Van Meter. Its population is 400. The people came from miles around. They wanted to see the boy who had set the big leagues ablaze by breaking the American League strikeout record in his first season as a raw rookie. What had Bob done? He had just struck out 17 of Connie Mack's Athletics. The record of 16 strikeouts, made by the great Rube Waddell, had stood for 28 years. And here was this 17-year-old Iowa farm boy — busting Rube's great record when he had only been in the big leagues a few weeks!

Oldtimers who hear of Feller's $10,000 salary for his first full season of big league baseball shake their heads in wonder. Why, Walter Johnson, the greatest speed ball pitcher in baseball history, was paid $1,200 for his first season. When he was at his best, he collected $7,000 for a season's work, and there wasn't a batter in the league who was sure of seeing the ball when Walter decided to put a little extra muscle behind it.

Babe Ruth, whose salary of $85,000 was tops for baseball, began his career as a great left-handed pitcher. He led the American league. And his pay check? That was $3,000!

Then there was Big Ed Walsh, one of the finest pitchers of his time. He won 40 games for the Chicago White Sox one season (something unheard of nowadays) while his salary was $3,000. At the end of that season he thought he was justified in asking for a raise. If he were pitching today, he would ask for $50,000. Big Ed thought it over a long while, and finally asked for $3,500. Comiskey turned him down coldly. Walsh held out. When the season opened, he came around to the ball park to watch the players practice. Comiskey heard about it. "Throw that guy out!" he ordered.

A little further back, in 1906, the Chicago Cubs won a pennant with a team whose combined payroll wasn't over $35,000. This season, manager Joe McCarthy of the Yankees will collect $35,000 for his services, and the salaries

(Above) Bob Feller—$10,000 in First Year. (Top) Walter Johnson—$1200 His First Year!

of the playing members of the team will of course be over and above that. Lou Gehrig alone collected more than that last season and probably will do so again. The other Yanks all have big ideas about what they want in the way of salary increases, because the New York team won a World's Series last fall in which 40 records were broken.

Are there any other rookie pitchers who collected as much as Bob Feller expects to earn in 1937? Yes. Some got more. There was Bill Breckenridge of Dartmouth, for instance. He joined the Philadelphia Athletics and was paid a bonus of $5,000 for signing his contract. The contract called for a salary of $5,000. At the end of the season, the Athletics had won the pennant, and their share of the World's Series money gave an additional $5,000 to each player. Breckenridge bought some more education with his money and now is a practicing lawyer in Oklahoma.

MAJOR league club owners nowadays confine thmselves to resisting demands for huge salary increases, but in the minor leagues, an owner must keep his eye on every item of expense.

President Sam Colacurcio of the Newark club was seated in the stands one day when Baltimore was the visiting team. Gill, one of the Baltimore outfielders, came up to bat. Gill was having one of those days when he couldn't catch the ball just right, but the pitcher couldn't put over a clean third strike. Gill must have fouled 15 balls (at $2 each) over the stands and out of the park when President Colacurcio rose from his seat and yelled: "Walk him! He's losing too many balls!"

One reason old-time baseball stars couldn't claim a high salary was that big purchase prices were almost unknown in former days, and a player couldn't go up to the business office and say: "Well, if I am worth $100,000 to this club, how about paying me $20,000 a season?" Ty Cobb and Tris Speaker, two of baseball's immortals, sold for $750 each; Rogers Hornsby cost even less. His contract price was $500.

When Babe Ruth was sold to the Yankees for $125,000 it was certain that the Yankees could never expect to pay him any small amount.

When a player becomes a hold-out—and there were about 50 of them at the start of this season—he usually hurts his chances for success during the season. He worries about his contract and misses spring training. Sometimes he even misses the first part of the baseball season. Chick Hafey of the St. Louis national leaguers was such a man. In 1931 Chick held out. He missed a lot of spring training. He missed part of the actual season. Besides, Chick had poor eyes and had to wear glasses, a big handicap in baseball. Just to show how difficult it is to predict anything in the sporting world, Chick Hafey won the batting championship of the National League that year!

JOE DIMAGGIO had such a good season with the Yankees that he demanded—and received—a salary increase. But Joe, too, was handicapped at the start of last season. His foot was injured in spring training. The Yankee trainer treated the injury with a heat lamp. The treatment was too strenuous and Joe's foot was burned. He was out of the game for the first part of the playing season, but he, too, made good.

Perhaps you think that a burn from a baking lamp isn't serious. Do you remember Dale Alexander? For four years in the American League he didn't hit less than .325; for five years before that in the minors he didn't hit below .323. He won the batting championship of the American League in 1932. Then on the morning of July 4th, 1933, he wrenched his knee slightly. Nothing to worry about; ball players often get over such things in two or three days.

The trainer of the Red Sox put Alexander's knee under the heat lamp. The leg was more or less numb from the wrench, and Alexander stayed under the lamp too long. The skin turned flaming red where the knee was burned. The burn wouldn't heal; the skin was always thin over the wound and it broke easily. It caused him to lose his batting form. He was unable to play regularly. From a batting champion he dropped to .278 and was sent to the minors. From batting champion of the American League, to Syracuse and Newark in the minor leagues—all within the space of 12 months! That's what a heat lamp burn can do.

Joe DiMaggio was fortunate that it didn't happen to him.

Yes, batting luck is a queer thing. Ed Linke, pitcher on the Washington Club, was a target for American League hitters. Jesse Hill, Ben Chapman, Oscar Melillo, Zeke Bonura, and Luke Appling bounced hard-hit baseballs off Linke's ample form in 1936. How could he take his revenge? During that time he didn't hit a single batter. But when the American League batting averages were published, Linke's revenge became apparent.

At the very top of the list of American League batters, with an average of .400, was Ed Linke. A *pitcher* leading the American League in batting!

	1	2	3	4	5	6	7	8	9	R	H	E
YANKS	0	0	0	0	0	7	0	1	★	8	7	0
GIANTS	0	0	0	0	1	0	0	0	0	1	6	2

HOME EDITION

CLOUDY

Somewhat colder; southwesterly to west winds.

High tides at 12:23 a. m. and 12:43 p. m.

See report on page 5.

DAILY RECORD

The Daily Record is supplied by International News Service and Associated Press.

BOSTON'S HOME PICTURE NEWSPAPER

Entered as second class mail matter at Boston, Mass., under the Acts of March 3, 1879.

Vol. 249, No. 85 32 Pages Boston, Thursday, October 7, 1937 ★ PRICE TWO CENTS

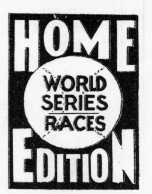

HOME WORLD SERIES RACES EDITION

YANKS WIN

TAKE FIRST GAME, 8 TO 1; KNOCK HUBBELL OUT

Story on Page 2

Yanks' Soph Slugger's Two Singles Prove Enough to Beat the N. Y. Giants!

Joe DiMaggio, slugging Yanks' fielder, shown lining out a single in the first inning of the opening game of the world series against the Giants yesterday before 60,000 fans in Yankee Stadium. In the sixth inning, with the bases loaded and none out, Joe again singled, scoring two men, to put the Yanks ahead, 2-1. Seven runs were scored in that frame, driving Carl Hubbell to the showers. International News Soundphoto.

FINAL
Suffolk Mutuels
1-2-7 $104.60
1-2-3-5-7 $163.60
7 $242.20
Three $94.80
Five $161.80
Seven $242.20

DAILY RECORD
BOSTON'S HOME PICTURE NEWSPAPER

JUNE

SUN	MON	TUE	WED	THU	FRI	SAT
			1	2	3	4
5	6	7	8	9	10	11
12	13	14	15	16	17	18
19	20	21	22	23	24	25
26	27	28	29	30		

Vol. 250, No. 174 Liberty 6390 Business and Advertising Offices Editorial Office Liberty 4000 PRICE TWO CENTS
U. S. Figures, Page 28

NO HIT AGAIN! VANDER MEER HURLS 2D IN ROW

Story on Page 27

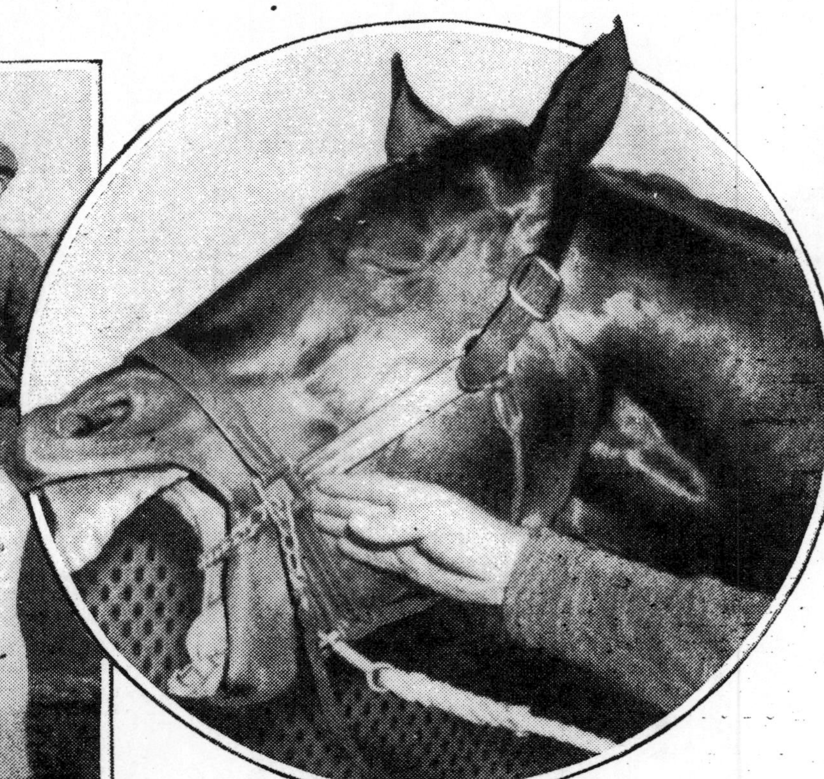

War Admiral Gives a Horse Laugh

War Admiral, Samuel G. Riddle's handicap champion, arriving at Suffolk Downs from Aqueduct for the $50,000 Massachusetts Handicap, June 29, poses for the cameraman, left, and gives a horse laugh, right, when informed his principal opposition will be Seabiscuit. The Admiral is reported in his best form. (Daily Record Photo)

Hurls Second No-Hit, No-Run

Performing what experts believed impossible, Johnny Vander Meer, Cinci Reds' rookie southpaw, pitched a no-hit, no-run game against Brooklyn Dodgers last night, his second similar performance within five days. Bees were his victims on last Saturday. Johnny is first pitcher in history of baseball to accomplish the feat. Reds won 6-0.

Another Bee Tally Choked Off at Plate

Fans had just witnessed Ray Mueller, Bees' catcher, tagged out at plate in fifth inning of yesterday's Bees-Cubs game, but hadn't figured on seeing another Bee likewise "killed off." But, here's Elbie Fletcher, local first-sacker, sliding into home for another tag-out by Catcher O'Dea of Cubs in same inning. Bees managed to score one tally in this frame. Story on Page 25. (Daily Record Photo)

SPORTS

The Detroit Free Press

FINANCE

108th Year. No. 147 — Wednesday, September 28, 1938 — Free Press Want Ads Bring Best Results

Hank Equals Foxx's 58 Homers as He Nears Record

Dean Plays Old Hero Role as Cubs Move Within Half Game

WARD TO THE WISE

By Charles P. Ward

THIS is the time of the year when the football coaches of the country spend at least two days of each week sobbing about their lot and telling the world what poor teams they have and how lucky they will be to beat the opponent of the coming Saturday. Some of the boys can become downright tearful and there are times that the lachrymose flood seems so great that the Federal Government ought to do something about it. Perhaps a scheme could be devised which would make it possible to utilize the melancholy moisture in the irrigation of the Dust Bowl and other arid areas.

Almost all football coaches are addicted to this weeping, which seems to be akin to an occupational disease. The brothers being what they are, it is quite likely that even at this late date old Amos Alonzo Stagg still is "fearing Purdue" out of sheer habit although he and his job at College of the Pacific are many versts and football schedules removed from the campus at Lafayette.

It seems strange to note that some of the most tearful sobbers of Wednesday afternoon are the most smug among the celebrants at the Saturday night victory parties. Some even will admit that they knew their club would win even while they were shedding their saltiest tears.

The attitude of the coaches somehow brings to mind the old prize fighter who almost drove a German community to distraction in the days before the United States entered the unpleasantness in Europe.

* * *

Good Burghers Kick Daylight Out of 'Allies'

THE man was a huge anthropoidal creature with bristling red hair, pale blue eyes and big, hard fists. Often gentle, he was a terror in his cups, which meant that he frequently was a terror at that stage of his career. He went about swaggering and fighting his merry wars with a maniacal laugh on his lips.

Several Saturday nights on end staid citizens were shocked to find the backslider being bounced out of various German saloons amid a great shouting and clatter of glass. And above the shouting and clatter could always be heard his bellowing laugh and his assurance that "these Germans will be the death of me yet."

Despite his assurances that he had been thoroughly trounced in each battle, the news that he was on the prowl always caused the good burghers to close their saloons and peer from the windows with apprehensive eyes pending the arrival of the police.

"How do you arouse these peaceful people to battle?" a police captain asked him one day. "Oh," he said, "I just tell them that I'm the Allies and they're the German army and let's go, and they kick the daylight out of me."

* * *

Now, Take Pugilism —Its a Direct Opposite

WHY a football coach should find it necessary to take a gloomy attitude toward his team's prospects is difficult to explain. It might be said that the melancholy

Please Turn to Page 16—*Column* 3

Dizzy Baffles Pirates Until Closing Frame

Then Bill Lee Fans Al Todd to Save Victory, 2-1

CHICAGO, Sept. 27—(A. P.)—Ol' Dizzy Dean pitched his great heart out and the Chicago Cubs smack into the thick of the National League pennant battle today.

With little else on the ball but its cover, Dean hurled the Cubs to a thrill-packed 2-to-1 victory over the league-leading Pittsburgh Pirates for a triumph which left the Cubs trailing the Bucs by only half a game, with two more games between the clubs scheduled for tomorrow and Thursday.

Diz wasn't in there at the finish. Big Bill Lee, taking the mound with two out in the ninth, retired the final Pittsburgh batsman as Diz trudged slowly to the showers. But it was Dean's victory all the way, a victory he called "the greatest of my life" and one which won him the acclaim of the 42,238 hysterical fans who jammed Wrigley Field.

Allows Just Seven Hits

Dean, in recapturing for an afternoon the glory that once was his in his St. Louis Cardinal heyday, allowed the Pirate sluggers just seven hits, their only run coming with Diz in the clubhouse. In the ninth inning, Woody Jensen scored on Lee's wild pitch, with the game ending seconds later as Lee fanned Al Todd for the final out.

Starting his first game since Aug. 20 and called on to test his ailing sore arm in a duel all-important to the Cubs' flag hopes, Dean proved his courage. He showed little "stuff," but his change of pace, mixed with the cunning of years of experience, gave the Pirates few openings.

He allowed two hits in the first inning and one in the second, then blanked the Bucs until the sixth, when they picked up another safety. They nicked him for two hits in the eighth and another in the ninth before Lee took over.

They Threaten in Eighth

The Cubs scored in the third on Rip Collins' triple to right and Bill Jurges' single. The other run came in the sixth. With one out, Frank Demaree bounced a single off Pitcher Jim Tobin's bare hand and went to third as Phil Cavarretta singled. Demaree then scored as Carl Reynolds forced Cavarretta at second.

The Pirates threatened in the eighth, which Todd opened with a single. Manush, batting for Tobin, flied out, but Lloyd Waner singled Todd to third. Paul Waner then hit to Dean, who tossed to Hartnett to get Todd. John Rizzo then flied to end the frame.

In the ninth, Arky Vaughan was hit by a pitched ball. After Suhr had popped out, Jensen pinch-hit for Young and forced Vaughan at second, Dean to Jurges. Handley doubled Jensen to third and Lee replaced Dean. A wild pitch sent Jensen home and, with the tying run on third, Lee fanned Todd to end the battle.

Galan Probably Lost

The victory, Dean's seventh as against one loss this year, cost the Cubs the services of Outfielder Augie Galan, possibly for the remainder of their five-game schedule. Sliding into second in the second inning, Galan twisted his left ankle so badly he had to be carried from the field.

Cavarretta went to right field, with Demaree moving to left, and this arrangement probably will be carried out again tomorrow, when Clay Bryant will try to make it two in a row for the Bruins. The Pirates' slab choice was Bob Klinger.

PITTSBURGH	AB	H	O	A	CHICAGO	AB	H	O	A
L.Wa'r,m	4	2	3	1	Hack,3	4	1	0	2
P.Wa'r,rf	4	0	1	0	Herman,2	3	0	4	1
Rizzo,lf	4	1	2	0	De'r'e,rf-l	4	1	2	0
Vaugh'n,s	3	1	2	2	Galan,lf	1	1	0	1
Suhr,1	4	0	9	1	Cav'etta,r	3	1	0	0
Young,2	3	0	3	7	Reyn'ds,m	3	1	6	0
†Jensen	1	0	0	0	Hartn't,c	2	0	3	0
Handley,3	4	1	4	1	Collins,1	3	1	9	1
Todd,c	4	2	0	1	Jurges,ss	3	2	2	2
Tobin,p	2	0	0	1	Dean,p	2	0	1	4
*Manush	1	0	0	0	Lee,p	0	0	0	0
Swift,p	0	0	0	0					
Totals	34	7	24	14	Totals	28	8	27	11

*Batted for Tobin in eighth.
†Batted for Young in ninth.

Pittsburgh	0	0	0	0	0	0	0	0	1	—1
Chicago	0	0	1	0	0	1	0	0	*	—2

Runs—Jensen—1; Demaree, Collins—2. Errors—Young, Jurges. Runs batted in—Reynolds, Jurges. Two-base hits—Jurges, Handley. Three-base hit—Collins. Sacrifice—Dean. Double plays—Vaughan, Young and Suhr; Young and Suhr. Left on bases—Pittsburgh 7, Chicago 5. Base on balls—Off Tobin 1. Strikeouts—By Lee 1. Hits—Off Tobin 8 in 7 innings, Swift 0 in 1, Dean 7 in 8⅔, Lee 0 in ⅓. Hit by pitcher—By Tobin (Herman); Dean (Vaughan). Wild pitch—Lee. Winning pitcher—Dean. Losing pitcher—Tobin.

Singin' Jack Doyle Knocks Self Cold

LONDON, Sept. 27—(A. P.)—Jack Doyle, handsome Irish heavyweight, neatly knocked himself out tonight in the second round of his fight with Eddie Phillips.

Letting go with a roundhouse right, the "Irish Thrush" missed his opponent, fell between the ropes, and struck his head on the edge of the ring. He still was prone on the floor outside the ropes with his feet on the press table when the referee finished the count of 10.

Doyle weighed 224 pounds, Phillips 191½.

Tonight Ends Wait for Toles

It's Do or Die in Bout with Adamick

By W. W. Edgar

Roscoe Toles, the sad-faced Negro heavyweight, gets his long-awaited chance tonight.

For more than two years he has been trailing Jimmy Adamick, the Midland Mauler, hoping to land a bout by which he could gain national prominence in the heavyweight ranks. Over that stretch of time he has issued challenge after challenge—but to no avail.

Little more than a year ago he thought he was about to get his chance. But for some reason the bout fell through and Roscoe seemed to lose all interest in the fight game. That is, he lost interest in any opponent but Adamick. He made a meeting with Jimmy his only mission in life.

Toles cared little what other heavyweights were doing. It mattered little to him who was coming along. All he wanted was a chance to meet Adamick in the ring.

Toles Has Reach, Height

That chance comes tonight in 10 rounds at Olympia and it will be a case of do or die with Roscoe.

What chance has he to realize his ambition and leave the ring a winner?

He'll take into the ring with him an advantage in reach, weight and height. Added to that, he's much the better boxer of the two.

But in the opposite corner will be a young fellow who will have the advantage in punching power and the zest to prove that he is entitled to ranking among the best heavyweights in the land.

In short, each man has the equipment to win if he gets away to a good start. Toles is not a knockerout. He can't stop a foe with one punch. But he is a damaging hitter with a good left hook. On the other hand, Adamick carries enough power in either fist to upset a foe with one punch. If Jimmy gets an opening, he may prove his mastery in short order.

Must Win Hard Way

In the other bouts on the card, Johnny Whiters engages George Richards, Toronto heavyweight, in the six-round semifinal; Lem Franklin, Chicago's Negro heavyweight, takes on Bill Allen; Jackie O'Sullivan, of Niagara Falls, meets Henry Wacker, of Chicago; Frank Egan, Windsor welterweight, swaps punches with Cleo McNeil and Steve Krusko, of Pontiac, meets Buddy Michel.

He Is Symbol of Michigan's New-Found Power

TOM HARMON, SOPHOMORE BACK WHO CARRIES WOLVERINE HOPES

In Short, It's Harmon Vs. Pingel

By Tod Rockwell

ANN ARBOR, Sept. 27—It's Tom Harmon, the sophomore symbol of Michigan's new football manpower, pitted against Johnny Pingel and the Michigan State Spartans.

For four years now, Michigan alumni and fans have pinned their hopes on some Wolverine youth, trusting that he might be the one to stop that Spartan victory parade. The meeting Saturday between these old rivals—once a warmup contest for the champions of the West—is no exception.

Ninety thousand spectators, including those thousands who will come from East Lansing and elsewhere confident of a fifth successive Spartan victory, may pack the great Michigan bowl.

In vain do the experts point out that Gene Ciolek may outshine the great Pingel Saturday. And as useless to advise that Paul Kromer, may prove capable of surpassing the feats of Harmon. Harmon is Michigan's man. He is the Wolverine yardstick of measurement against Pingel.

Does Harmon have it? That's the question on the minds of football fans, including the Spartan adherents.

Harmon, 190 pounds and six feet tall, had been clocked in :09.9 in the 100-yard dash in high school and in 1937 as a freshman at Michigan he showed vast promise as a runner, punter and a passer.

This autumn Tom Harmon continued to merit his reputation as a great football prospect. And though Kromer, Mehaffey, Christy and Meyer, other new men, also showed great promise, the interest in Harmon did not subside.

Snead Totals $17,527 with Westchester Pot

WHITE PLAINS, N. Y., Sept. 27—(A. P.)—Hitting the biggest jackpot professional golf has had in recent years Sluggin' Sam Snead today took down top money of $5,000 in the $13,500 Westchester 108-hole Open golf tournament with a score of 430 and set a new record for one-year prize winning.

The fat check brought his earnings since Jan. 1 to $17,572.83, more than double that of his closest rival. It also was more than $2,000 better than the previous mark set by Horton Smith in 1929, when he collected $15,500.

In the last two rounds, over a course that consistently baffled most of the game's greatest players, Sam showed he had everything on the ball when the pressure was on and the prize worthwhile. Tied for fourth place, four shots off the pace, at the start of the morning round, he climbed into a tie for the lead with a 71 and went around the last 18 holes in 69, one under par.

His finish and Billy Burke's start on this final day proved too much for the popular Cleveland veteran who won the 1931 National Open championship. Billy, who had slid from first place to fifth when he fizzled to a 78 this morning, improved on that by 10 strokes with a closing 68. That was good enough only for second place at 432 and $2,000.

P. G. A. Champion Paul Runyan missed an eighteen-foot putt on the home green for a 70 and Byron Nelson missed a ten-footer at the same spot for the same score, so they wound up in a third-place tie at 434 and split $1,800. Ben Hogan, Purchase, N. Y., shot a 71 and 436 for $700.

Chandler Harper, 24-year-old Virginia Open champion, fell off to a closing 75 for 437 and $600. United States Open Champion Ralph Guldahl, Metropolitan Open Champion Jimmy Hines and veteran Mike Turnesa, brother of the United States Amateur titleholder, tied at 439 and split $1,350.

Jug McSpaden, who was even with Snead at 361 going into the final round, blew up to a closing 79 for 440, $350 and tenth place.

Beyond the first 10 were such outstanding campaigners as Johnny Revolta, 442; Henry Picard and Dick Metz, 443; Vic Ghezzi and Ray Mangrum, 444; Harry Cooper, 445; Ky Laffoon, 447;

Please Turn to Page 16—*Column* 7

Americans Buy Red Wing Pair

Sorrell and Beattie Sold Outright

Detroit Red Wings have completed the outright sale of Johnny Sorrell and John (Red) Beattie, forwards, to the New York Americans, it was announced Tuesday by Manager Jack Adams. Beattie and Sorrell both finished last season with the Americans on option.

Jimmy Orlando, young defenseman who received a short trial with the Wings, also has been sold, going to the Springfield club of the International - American League. Orlando finished last season with the Pittsburgh Hornets.

Eddie Wares, rookie right winger, who was a star on the Motter-Wares-Liscombe kid line, still is the property of the New York rangers, having played here last season on option, but Adams hopes to close a deal for him with the New York club in the near future.

Bears Take Lead in I.L. Playoffs

BUFFALO, N. Y., Sept. 27—(A. P.)—The champion Newark Bears took a three-to-one lead in their final International League playoff series with Buffalo tonight by defeating the Bisons, 9-7. The Bears now need only one more victory to clinch the best-of-seven series.

											R	H	E
Newark	0	0	3	2	2	0	0	2	0	—9		10	1
Buffalo	0	0	0	3	2	1	0	1	0	—7		12	1

Haley, Page, Strincevich, Beggs and Rosar; Kowalik, Fink, Jacobs, Ash, Uhle and Savino.

St. Paul . ssumes Edge

KANSAS CITY, Sept. 27—(A. P.)—Led by Walter Judnich, who hit two home runs and two singles in four times at bat, the Blues defeated St. Paul in the fifth game of the American Association playoff finals tonight, 7 to 6. Judnich drove in five runs.

St. Paul	0	0	1	0	0	0	2	2	1	—6	12	0
Kansas City	2	0	2	0	2	0	1	0	*	—7	11	0

Frasier, Taylor, Klaerner, Brown and Silverstri, Pasek; Breuer, Makosky and Riddle.

Prep Notes

By John N. Sabo

Al Bayer, a halfback who is starting his third season on the squad, has been elected captain of Denby High School's football team. Coach Jimmy Stout announced Tuesday. Bayer also was one of the best hitters on Denby's City championship baseball team last spring.

* * *

Southwestern scrimmaged against Holy Redeemer, its next-door neighbor of the Catholic League, Tuesday, and Alex Kulik, of the Prospectors, and Bill Price, of Redeemer, carried off most of the honors. Kulik scored twice on runs of 25 and 10 yards and tossed a 15-yard pass to Steve Krukotkansky for another score. Price did most of the ground gaining for the Lions with his off tackle smashes. The boys didn't pay much attention to the score but Southwestern actually finished in front, 40 to 7.

* * *

Northwestern's reserve team will meet Wilbur Wright in a practice game Friday afternoon at Northwestern Field, the City League announced Tuesday. At the same time the Colt varsity will meet Cooley at Cooley in another contest.

* * *

There is only one boy weighing more than 200 pounds on the team which Coach Charley Leadbetter at Pershing has picked to start against Hazel Park Friday at Pershing. He is Fullback Eddie Opalewski. Eddie weighs 205. Eddie Hall, one of the best sprinters in the City League, is trying to win a halfback position on the Doughboy squad. So is Clem Goins, a quartermiler on Coach Carl Holmes' track squad.

* * *

Two former University of Detroit stars are helping Bob Tiernan with the coaching duties at U. of D. High. Cowboy Tommy Connell, captain of the 1928 U. of D. team, is working with the Cubs' first squad while Tony Skover is coaching the Cubs' bantamweight team.

* * *

Tony Michuta, the All-Catholic tackle on Catholic Central's football team, has a fourteen-year-old brother, Alphonsus, trying out for the reserve team. Alphonsus weighs 165 pounds. Tony's older brother, Johnny, was a regular tackle at Notre Dame a few years back but Tony probably will matriculate at U. of D. next fall.

Tigers Name Shea to Post of Coach

Mervyn Shea, Tiger catcher in the days of Bucky Harris, yesterday was appointed coach for the 1939 season, General Manager Jack Zeller announced. He will take the place left vacant when Del Baker was promoted to manager.

Shea

At the same time he announced Shea's appointment, Zeller announced that Bing Miller, who joined the team as a coach this season, would be re-engaged next year.

Frankie Parker Defeated Easily

LOS ANGELES, Sept. 27—(U.P.)—Frankie Parker, the one time boy wonder who appears to be slumping at the advanced age of 22, skidded out of the twelfth annual Pacific Southwest tennis championships today.

Parker was humiliated by Owen Anderson, of Los Angeles, 6-3, 6-1. Parker went down fighting before Anderson, who holds championships in England and Germany. Meanwhile, Frankjo Kukuljevic, of Yugoslavia, beat John Woodall, of Los Angeles, 6-1, 6-4, and Sidney Wood, Jr., trimmed William Reedy, strong University of Southern California sophomore, 8-6, 6-3.

Police to Escort Officials to Good-Will Golf Meet

A big turnout is anticipated Wednesday at the annual International Goodwill Golf tournament at Tam O'Shanter Golf Club. Three trophies will be at stake—for low gross among the mayors and judiciary; low gross among the police entries and low gross for the field. James (Scotty) McLinn, chairman of the affair, has announced that a police escort will meet the Canadian participants at the Detroit entrance to the tunnel at 12:30 p. m. and accompany them to the course.

Bees Reappoint Stengel to Forestall All Rumors

BOSTON, Sept. 27—(A.P.)—Reappointment of Casey Stengel as manager of the Boston Bees for 1939 was announced by General Manager Bob Quinn tonight to "forestall any rumors to the contrary."

Only 3 Clouts in Five Games Needed to Win

Tigers Collect Total of Five in Sweep of Browns' Bill

By Charles P. Ward

Only three more.

That's all the home runs Hank Greenberg needs to make in order to set a new major league record of 61.

Hank on Tuesday equalled Jimmy Foxx's mark of 58 when he banged out two homers while the Tigers were trouncing the orphaned Brownies from St. Louis in both ends of a double bill. The scores were 5 to 4 and 10 to 2.

Both of Hank's hits were made in the second game off the delivery of Bill Cox, a right-hander. The first was an inside-of-the-park affair—a line drive that got past Mel Almada in center. Big Henry had to do some fast sprinting and add to that a fancy hook slide to escape Sam Harshany's tag. But he did both and so notched up his fifty-seventh of the season.

No. 58 Is Lusty Clout

Homer No. 58, which was made in the third with Charley Gehringer on base, was a much better blow. It soared into the upper deck of the center field bleachers at a point 400 feet distant from home plate.

Hank still has five games to make three homers and beat the mark of 60 was set by Babe Ruth in 1927. Two of those five contests will be played at Briggs Stadium Wednesday and Thursday.

Greenberg's homers were two of five made by the Tigers in the two games which drew a crowd of 10,750. Charley Gehringer hit his twentieth of the season in the seventh inning of the second game, a drive into the right field pavilion with Chick Morgan and Dixie Walker on base.

Walker and Mark Christman hit homers in the first game, Christman hitting an inside-of-the-park drive past Almada in the second inning and Walker arching one into the right field pavilion in the same session. Nobody was on base when either hit was made.

Coffman Wins Easily

The Tigers had little trouble winning the second contest, getting to Cox for seven runs in the first three innings. As the result Slick Coffman, who went the route for the Tigers, was able to coast in to victory in a contest that was called at the end of the seventh on account of darkness.

Elton Walkup and Alton Benton were the opposing pitchers at the start of the first game but neither was around at the finish. The Brownies routed Benton in the sixth when they scored two runs to tie the score at four runs each, and Walkup gave way to a pinch-hitter in the seventh. His successor, Fred Johnson, was charged with the defeat when he presented the Tigers with a run in the eighth by making a bad throw to first.

Bill Rogell opened the inning by working the old-timer for a base on balls and stole second almost immediately. After Birdie Tebbetts beat out a bunt to the box, he went to third and Rogell scored when Johnson hit Birdie in the back with the ball, which then bounded into right field foul territory. That was the ball game.

A bunted single by Walker, a pass to Gehringer, a single by Greenberg and a squeeze single by Fox gave the Tigers two runs in the first inning of this contest, and homers by Christman and Walker two more in the second.

The Brownies didn't score until the fourth, when singles by Mazzera and Clift, a force play and singles by Kress and Sullivan gave them two runs.

Benton paved the way for his own downfall when he walked Clift at the start of the sixth. After Grace and Kress grounded out, Sullivan singled, scoring Clift with the Brownies' third run of the game. The fourth crossed a moment later when Sullivan stole second and moved around on a single by Heffner.

Morgan Whips Lynch

GLASGOW, Sept. 27—(A.P.)—K. O. Morgan, American bantamweight from Detroit, outpointed Benny Lynch, of Scotland, in a twelve-round bout here tonight. Lynch was deposed as bantamweight champion for failure to make the weight limit for a title fight.

Pitchers

AMERICAN LEAGUE

Boston at Philadelphia—Bagby (14-11) vs. Nelson (10-10).
Washington at New York—Krakauskas (5-5) vs. Ruffing (21-7).
Chicago at Cleveland—Lee (12-11) vs. Whitehill (9-7).
St. Louis at Detroit—Hildebrand (8-10) vs. Gill (11-9).

NATIONAL LEAGUE

Cincinnati at St. Louis—Weaver (5-3) vs. Copper (1-1).
Pittsburgh at Chicago—Klinger (12-5) vs. Bryant (19-11).
Philadelphia at Boston—T. Lanning (0-1) vs. Doll (0-0).
Only games scheduled.

The Standings

AMERICAN LEAGUE

	W	L	Pct.	*G.B.
New York	97	51	.655	..
Boston	85	60	.586	10½
Cleveland	84	63	.571	12½
DETROIT	80	69	.537	17½
Washington	73	74	.497	23½
Chicago	61	80	.433	32½
St. Louis	53	92	.366	42½
Philadelphia	52	96	.351	45

*Games behind leader.

TUESDAY'S RESULTS

DETROIT 5-10, St. Louis 4-2 (second game called end of seventh, darkness).
Boston .¹, Philadelphia 1.
Cleveland 6, Chicago 1.
New York 5, Washington 2.

WEDNESDAY'S GAMES

Washington at New York.
Boston at Philadelphia.
St. Louis at DETROIT.
Chicago at Cleveland.

NATIONAL LEAGUE

	W	L	Pct.	*G.B.
Pittsburgh	85	59	.590	..
Chicago	86	61	.585	½
New York	80	67	.544	6½
Cincinnati	78	66	.542	7
Boston	75	72	.510	11½
St. Louis	68	77	.469	17½
Brooklyn	66	79	.455	19½
Philadelphia	45	101	.308	41

*Games behind leader.

TUESDAY'S RESULTS

Boston 2-4, Philadelphia 1-1 (first game 11 innings).
Chicago 2, Pittsburgh 1.
Cincinnati 3, St. Louis 1.
New York 5-1, Brooklyn 3-5 (second game called end of sixth, darkness).

WEDNESDAY'S GAMES

Philadelphia at Boston.
Pittsburgh at Chicago.
Cincinnati at St. Louis.
Only games scheduled.

Ready for the Bell—At Last

ROSCOE TOLES

JIMMY ADAMICK

Old Connie Takes Blame Himself

By Charles P. Ward

Many a ball game and occasionally a World Series is won in the clubhouse, according to Connie Mack. And he should know for he had won and lost both in just that way. He says so himself in an article in this week's Saturday Evening Post. It was written in collaboration with Al Horwits, Philadelphia newspaperman.

Mack frankly confesses that he himself lost the 1931 World Series to the Cardinals because he became—of all things—too cocky. He failed to call a meeting before the last game with the result that the Cardinals, inspired by the daring play of Pepper Martin, won out. At least he blames himself.

"Our Athletics of 1931 were one of our good teams," says Connie, "and the boys certainly knew it. It was only natural that they would after winning two pennants and World Series in a row. Big salaries, series checks, and fees from testimonials did their softening work. The boys thought they were good and didn't have to stew and sweat and scratch for runs as of old, some of them."

Connie recalls that the A's floundered at the start of that season. Finally he called a meeting in the clubhouse, censured some of his boys in plain language and induced them to play their game. The result was a third straight pennant.

The Cardinals got the breaks in the ensuing World Series but Connie finally got his boys going,

Please Turn to Page 16—*Column* 4

2 CENTS PAY NO MORE!

Chicago Daily Tribune

THE WORLD'S GREATEST NEWSPAPER

FINAL ★ ★

VOLUME XCVII.—NO. 233 C [REG. U. S. PAT. OFFICE. COPYRIGHT 1938 BY THE CHICAGO TRIBUNE.] THURSDAY. SEPTEMBER 29. 1938.—36 PAGES THIS PAPER CONSISTS OF TWO SECTIONS—SECTION ONE PRICE TWO CENTS IN CHICAGO AND SUBURBS ELSEWHERE THREE CENTS

4 MEN DEBATE EUROPE'S FATE

British, French and Italian Chiefs to Meet Hitler Today

HARTNETT HITS HOMER IN NINTH; CUBS GO TO TOP

Beat Pirates, 6 to 5, as Night Falls.

BY EDWARD BURNS.

There was drama in Wrigley field as the Cubs won the pennant in 1929; there was more of it when they won for Charley Grimm in a late drive in 1932, and there was plenty of it when the Cubs became champions by winning twenty-one straight in 1935. But never, never, was there a game like the one Gabby Hartnett won with a homer yesterday to put his team in first place as the Pirates went down, 6 to 5, seconds before the contest was to be called a tie, on account of darkness.

The 34,465 fans would have been more than satisfied to see Gabby bust up a drab game. But that homer topped off as thrilling an afternoon as any sports carnival could produce. Mob ecstasy was choked by bitter disappointment, only to be supplanted by more ecstasy with more disappointment. Heroics nipped in the bud, opportunity hammering and not being heard. Gents thrown out at the plate. Nothing perfect, until Old Gabby rose up in the falling night and banged that homer.

He's a Hero of Heroes.

You have seen them rush out to greet a hero after he touched the plate to terminate a great contest. Well, you never saw nothin'. The mob started to gather around Gabby before he had reached first base. By the time he had rounded second he couldn't have been recognized in the mass of Cub players, frenzied fans, and excited ushers but for that red face, which shone out even in the gray shadows.

After the skipper finally had struggled to the plate things became worse. The ushers, who had fanned out to form that protective barrier around the infield, forgot their constantly rehersed pretty maneuver and rushed to save Hartnett's life. They tugged and they shoved and finally they started swinging their fists before the players could carry their boss into the safety afforded by the tunnel behind the Cub dugout. There was new hysteria after Gabby reached the catwalk which leads to the club house. But by this time the gendarmes were organized. Gabby got to the bath house without being stripped by souvenir maniacs.

Root Is the Winner.

And who was the sixth and winning pitcher? No one but old Charley Root, who, with Hartnett, forms the oldest battery in baseball. Charley tamed the Pirates in the ninth, helped out by Hartnett, who threw out Paul Waner to retire the side after Paul had presumed to try a theft of second.

There's a whole lot to tell you about things that happened before the sun went down. And sooner or later we'll settle down to the telling of it. But for the purpose of the narrative, right here we are going to jump in with the Chicago sixth, immediately after the Pirates had grabbed a 3 to 1 lead, and, most folks thought, the 1938 National league pennant.

At the start of this home sixth Gabby plucked the first leaves from his laurel wreath. He opened with a double and scored on a double by Collins. Jurges singled and O'Dea failed in a pinch rôle, but the tying run came home on a force play. This big chance to go ahead failed when Jurges was out trying to score from second on a single which he thought had gone into left field, instead of landing in Vaughan's glove in deep short.

The 3 to 3 tie prevailed through the seventh. But gloom was thicker than the gathering dusk when the Pirates, in the eighth, assaulted Vance Page, Larry French, and Bill Lee before the Cubs' third double play halted the rough-housing with two runs in.

It Looked Hopeless.

The Pirates' eighth inning was over. But the Pirates were leading, 5 to 3, and it was rapidly getting dark. Things looked terrible.

Collins, however, led off the Chicago eighth with his third hit. Bill Swift replaced Klinger and walked Jurges. Tony Lazzeri batted for Lee, failed in

[Continued on page 22, column 1]

NEWS SUMMARY

of The Tribune [And Historical Scrap Book.] Thursday, September 29, 1938.

Total average net paid circulation AUGUST, 1938 DAILY in excess of 850,000 THE CHICAGO TRIBUNE

THEY WILL NOT BE ALONE TODAY

GENTLEMEN, DO YOU REALIZE THAT WE FOUR MEN HAVE THE POWER TO STRAIGHTEN OUT MOST OF THE SERIOUS TROUBLES THAT BESET EUROPE TODAY?
FOUR POWER CONFERENCE CALLED BY HITLER THURSDAY A.M. SEPT. 29
McCUTCHEON

FOUR COLOR MAPS!

Turn to the back page for a color map of Europe as it appeared in 1914.

Tomorrow turn to the back page of your Tribune for another four color map. This one will show European boundaries after the Versailles treaty.

Kills His Wife and Their Son; Ends Own Life

A retired business executive in Clarendon Hills, a residential suburb west of Hinsdale, yesterday shot and killed his wife and their young son and then killed himself. These were the first violent deaths in the tiny village since its incorporation in 1924.

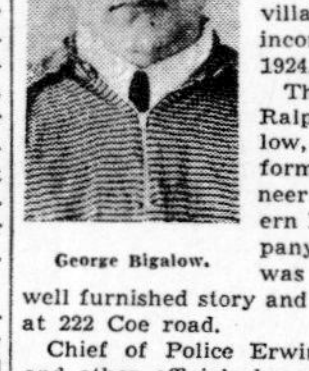

George Bigalow.

The killer was Ralph K. Bigalow, 57 years old, former sales engineer for the Western Electric company. His home was a small but well furnished story and a half house at 222 Coe road.

Chief of Police Erwin Drallmeier and other officials began an investigation, but could ascertain no motive for the tragedy. An inquest was continued until this morning.

Receives Phone Call.

At 8:30 o'clock last night Chief Drallmeier received a telephone call. An unidentified woman said she believed that a dead woman was in the Bigalow home on Coe road.

The policemen broke in the front door. Slumped on a davenport lay the body of Bigalow's son, George, 14, a freshman at the Hinsdale High school. He had been shot in the back of the head while reading the morning newspaper.

The body of Bigalow's wife, Agnes, 53, was discovered on a bed in the bedroom, covered with a sheet. Clad in a nightgown, she apparently had been shot while asleep.

Terrier Also Killed.

Chief Drallmeier searched further. On the basement floor he found Bigalow's body. Beside it lay a single barrel shotgun.

But the grisly search was not ended. The policemen discovered still a fourth shoting victim, Bagalow's pet Boston bull terier, in the breakfast room.

Police believe the deaths occurred around 7 a. m., shortly before Bigalow called a neighbor and told him not to have his son call for the Bigalow boy on the way to school.

Chief Drallmeier said that Bigalow apparently stood near a staircase leading to the second floor. With a double barreled automatic shotgun he first shot his son. Then making a right angle turn he fired into the bedroom, killing his wife.

Uses Second Gun.

After this, Chief Drallmeier said, Bigalow shot the dog, then placed the gun in the attic where it was found. Taking up the single barreled shotgun, Bigalow then went to the basement and killed himself.

Bigalow left no written explanation of his act. On a dining room table, apparently written that morning, was his will. It left his estate to a married son, Russell, of Clarendon Hills, and a daughter, Mrs. John H. Boose, wife of a La Grange undertaker.

William Lays Down 6,400 Pennies and Gets New Car

There's at least forty-four pounds of copper in William Cehak's new car. Cehak, who lives at 3749 North Leclaire avenue, laid down a sack containing 6,400 pennies as part payment when he bought the vehicle in Wheaton. Frank Dieter and John Koble, managers of the sales agency, got two mechanics to help count them. For the meticulous it may be stated that a penny weighs 48 grains and that 7,000 grains make a pound.

Maine's Governor Beats Idaho's as Spud Picker

Fort Fairfield, Me., Sept. 28.—(AP)—Gov. Lewis O. Barrows of Maine today won his five minute potato-picking duel with Gov. Barzilla W. Clark of Idaho. The match ended with Barrows having 201 pounds to his credit and Clark 197 pounds. An international picking contest saw Robert Hallett, Mars Hill, successfully retain his championship.

Britons Crash Gas Mask Lines to Get a Spare

LONDON, Sept. 28.—(AP)—Some cautious Britons, it was indicated tonight, are crashing the gas mask lines to get a spare. A home office official in a broadcast on how to take care of masks warned: "I hear people have been queuing up twice to get two masks. This is illegal."

Set to Choose Dewey for N.Y. Governor Race

BY WILLIAM FULTON.
[Chicago Tribune Press Service.]

Saratoga Springs, N. Y., Sept. 28.—[Special.]—Congressman Bruce Barton today called for a Republican victory in the November election to start business booming, to give people jobs instead of relief, to clean out corruption in government, and to prevent the Roosevelt administration from taking any "hasty action that might lead America toward war."

Barton, well known advertising executive and New York City's lone Republican representative, set the stage for the nomination by the Republican state convention tomorrow of District Attorney Thomas E. Dewey, rackets smasher, for governor.

Dewey is expected to come to the convention tomorrow night to accept in person.

Hail War on Rackets.

The delegates yelled themselves hoarse when Barton referred to Dewey's successful war on racketeers in New York City which was climaxed two weeks ago by the mistrial ruling in the conspiracy case against James J. [Jimmy] Hines, the patronage dispenser for the Roosevelt machine. The case was thrown out on a technicality by Judge Ferdinand Pecora.

"For more than five years the Democratic administration in Washington has been claiming a monopoly of virtue," asserted Barton.

Predicts Protest at Polls.

"And all that time," continued the keynoter, "as a brilliant, courageous Republican district attorney now has shown, the same Democratic party in New York City has been in partnership with gangsters, corrupting magistrates, penalizing honest policemen, and stuffing the ballot boxes with the votes of racketeers.

"Not a single Democrat in high position has denounced this iniquitous alliance. On the contrary, these high Democratic office holders have silently and gladly accepted its spirit. The people of New York have been shocked by these revelations. There will be an outpouring of indignant protest at the polls."

TWO DICTATORSHIPS MATCH WITS WITH TWO DEMOCRACIES; WAR PLANS HELD UP

May Offer Germany 'Token' Occupation of Sudetenland.

Chamberlain's Speech

The text of Prime Minister Chamberlain's speech to the house of commons will be found on page 10.

BY SAM BREWER.
[Chicago Tribune Press Service.]

HESTON AIRPORT, London, Sept. 29 [Thursday].—Prime Minister Neville Chamberlain of Great Britain departed at 8:35 a. m. this morning [1.35 a. m. Chicago time] by airplane for Munich for his third conference with Chancellor Adolf Hitler in the interest of a peaceful settlement of the dispute over the Sudeten area in Czechoslovakia. Others to be present will be Premier Benito Mussolini of Italy and Premier Edouard Daladier of France.

Cabinet ministers were among the large crowd at the airport to see Chamberlain away. Some of them brought fruit for the prime minister to eat on the way to Munich.

Keeps on Trying.

On departure the prime minister said:

"When I was a small boy I used to repeat: 'If at first you don't succeed, try, try, try again!' That's what I am doing."

Chamberlain's eleventh hour announcement yesterday of the conference followed intense diplomatic activity in London, Berlin, and Rome.

Complications were added last night, however, by a request that a Prague spokesman be permitted to attend the conference and plead Czechoslovakia's cause. The request was made by Jan Masaryk, Czechoslovak minister to London. It also was reported that an American observer would be in Munich at the time of the conference.

Speculate on Offer.

London political observers suggested that the right of an immediate token occupation of Egerland, part of the Sudeten area, might be offered Hitler at the Munich parley. They suggested that this would be contingent upon Hitler's agreement to the appointment of an international commission to arrange the delimitation of new frontiers and the transfer of populations.

If a token occupation would pave the way for a peaceful solution of the dispute it was understood that Chamberlain is prepared to support it.

Chamberlain announced the four power conference as a climax to a speech before parliament yesterday. In the speech he described the events of the last few days, during which he visited Hitler twice in an effort to find a peaceful solution to the dispute.

Delays Mobilization.

He said Hitler had postponed for twenty-four hours the general mobilization which had been planned for yesterday so representatives of the four powers could confer. The British premier received Hitler's invitation to the conference as he neared the end of his speech. He disclosed that Mussolini had persuaded Hitler to make the new move after he [Chamberlain] had sent personal pleas to Hitler and Mussolini early yesterday.

The staid house of commons went wild when the prime minister announced his news. Members cheered and shouted and threw papers into the air.

Queen Mother Mary of Great Britain, who was among the spectators in the crowded house, wept with emotion.

Ambassadors of foreign nations showed a sudden relaxation of tension in broad smiles.

Londoners Are Hysterical.

Londoners in the street went hysterical with joy. Many had gone to bed Tuesday night fearing bombing planes would be over the city before morning.

Step by step, Chamberlain had gone over the development of the crisis. From the time parliament closed last July, he worked up to midnight yesterday, taking the moves in order.

Shortly before he announced the

[Continued on page 6, column 2.]

LETTERS REVEAL PREMIER'S FIGHT TO AVERT STRIFE

LONDON, Sept. 28.—(AP)—The correspondence exchanged between Prime Minister Neville Chamberlain and Chancellor Adolf Hitler in their recent negotiations on Europe's crisis was published today as a government white paper [an official report].

It disclosed that in his first letter to Hitler, written at Godesberg last Friday, Chamberlain said he was ready to put up to the Czechoslovak government Hitler's proposal as to the areas to be ceded to the reich, so that Prague might examine the suggested provisional boundary.

Refuses to Approve Force.

Chamberlain wrote: "The difficulty I see about the proposal you put to me yesterday arises from the suggestion that the areas should in the immediate future be occupied by German troops.

"I recognize the difficulty of conducting a lengthy investigation under the existing conditions and doubtless the plan you propose would, if it were acceptable, provide an immediate easing of the tension.

"I do not think you have realized the impossibility of my agreeing to put forward any plan unless I have reason to suppose it will be considered by public opinion in my country, in France, and, indeed, in the world generally, as carrying out the principles already agreed upon in an orderly fashion and free from the threat of force."

Situation Unbearable: Hitler.

To this memorandum Hitler replied: "I have recognized gratefully that at last, after twenty years, the British government, represented by your excellency, has now decided for its part also to undertake steps to put an end to a situation which, from day to day and, indeed, from hour to hour, is becoming more unbearable.

"If formerly the behavior of the Czechoslovak government was brutal, it could only be described during recent weeks and days as madness.

"In a few weeks the number of refugees who have been driven out has risen to over 120,000. The situation, as stated above, is unbearable and now will be terminated by me.

German Rights Put First.

"I can only emphasize to your excellency that these Sudeten Germans are not coming back to the German reich by virtue of the gracious or benevolent sympathy of the other nations, but on the grounds of their own will, based on the right of the self-determination of nations and of the

[Continued on page 11, column 1.]

THE WEATHER

THURSDAY, SEPTEMBER 29, 1938.

[Central Standard Time.]

Sunrise, 5:45; sunset, 5:36. Moon sets at 9:22 p. m. Venus is the evening star. Jupiter and Saturn are night luminaries. Mars and Mercury are morning stars.

CHICAGO AND VICINITY: Fair and slightly cooler Thursday; Friday fair and warmer; moderate northeast winds Thursday.

ILLINOIS: Fair, slightly cooler in extreme northeast Thursday; Friday fair and somewhat warmer.

TRIBUNE BAROMETER.

TEMPERATURES IN CHICAGO

For 24 hours ended 2 a. m. Sept. 29:
MAXIMUM, 2 P. M. 77
MINIMUM, 3 A. M. 53

3 a. m....53	Noon 72	Unofficial—
4 a. m....53	1 p. m....75	8 p. m....68
5 a. m....53	2 p. m....77	9 p. m....67
6 a. m....53	3 p. m....76	10 p. m....66
7 a. m....54	4 p. m....76	11 p. m....66
8 a. m....57	5 p. m....73	Midnight ..65
9 a. m....62	6 p. m....69	1 a. m....65
10 a. m....66	7 p. m....68	2 a. m....65
11 a. m....69		

For 24 hours ended 6:30 p. m. Sept. 28:
Mean temperature, 64; normal, 61; deficiency for September, 3 degrees; excess since Jan. 1, 863 degrees.
Precipitation, none; excess for September, 2.38 inches; total since Jan. 1, 31.91 inches; excess since Jan. 1, 6.22 inches.
Barometer, 6:30 a. m., 30.13; 6:30 p. m., 30.08. Relative humidity, 6:30 a. m., 75; noon, 41; 6:30 p. m., 58.
Highest wind velocity, 13 miles an hour from the southwest at 10:04 a. m.

September 29, 1937:
Maximum temperature, 69; minimum, 49; mean, 59; clear; precipitation, none.

[Official weather table on page 28.]

Powers Expected to Tackle Woes of All Nations.

BULLETIN.

BRENNER PASS, Germany, Sept. 29 (Thursday).—(AP)—Premier Mussolini and Italian Foreign Minister Count Ciano arrived here by special train at 6:08 a. m. today (11:08 p. m., C. S. T. last night) on their way to the Munich four power conference.

BULLETIN.

PARIS, Sept 29 (Thursday).—(AP)—Premier Edouard Daladier left Le Bourget field by airplane at 8:45 a. m. (1:45 a. m., C. S. T.) today for the four power conference in Munich.

BULLETIN.

[Copyright: 1938: By the New York Times.]

COPENHAGEN, Denmark, Sept. 29 (Thursday).—Thirty German submarines have been sighted in the last two days on the northern coast of Jutland en route from the Baltic Sea to the North Sea.

BY SIGRID SCHULTZ.
[Chicago Tribune Press Service.]

BERLIN, Sept. 28.—The premiers of Great Britain, France, and Italy, who were allied against Germany in the world war and who believed they had vanquished her, will rush to Munich tomorrow. The statesmen will beg the new master of Germany to safeguard the peace of Europe and furthermore help him obtain the territories he claims in the name of his people.

The suggestion for an international conference was made by President Roosevelt. It was seconded most energetically by Premier Mussolini of Italy.

Asked to Delay Military Action.

Adolf Hitler was asked to postpone military action against Czechoslovakia until the conference had reached an agreement on his demand for the ceding of Sudetenland to Germany by or on Saturday.

The Fuehrer replied he would postpone it for only twenty-four hours—that by then the one time victors must have an understanding with him.

Discussion of other European problems other than the Czechoslovak-German crisis were expected to be taken up by the leaders of the four powers at the conference. Mussolini for years has been hoping to bring about a four power pact between his country, Germany, France, and England.

May Remake Europe.

It was believed that most of the troubles which have been rankling in the hearts of European statesmen for years will be studied in an attempt to find satisfactory solutions.

Diplomats indicated an effort even might be made to remake Europe so as to achieve a "lasting peace."

Nazi leaders were pleased with the sudden turn of events. They put it this way: "The humiliation Germany suffered at the hands of her victors has given her a mental strength and fierce determination that will easily match the will power of the British and French who have been able to take their vital problems more easily than the Germans have for generations."

Mussolini, in a forty-five minute talk with Hitler over the telephone, assured the Fuehrer he would support all his demands and thus force his former world war allies to come to terms with his present ally of the Rome-Berlin axis.

Germans Acclaim Hitler.

Hitler, the unknown soldier of the world war who holds the destiny of his country in his hand—and to a great extent that of Europe—kept his diplomatic triumph secret from his people until 8 o'clock tonight.

The ovations they gave him were greater and possibly more sincere than ever before. There is no doubt the overwhelming majority of the German population dislikes the thought of risking a war of any kind for the sake of the Sudeten Germans. The people have been extremely anxious as a result of the nation's vast preparations for war.

Hitler left Berlin for Munich at 8

FELLER FANS 18 FOR STRIKE-OUT RECORD

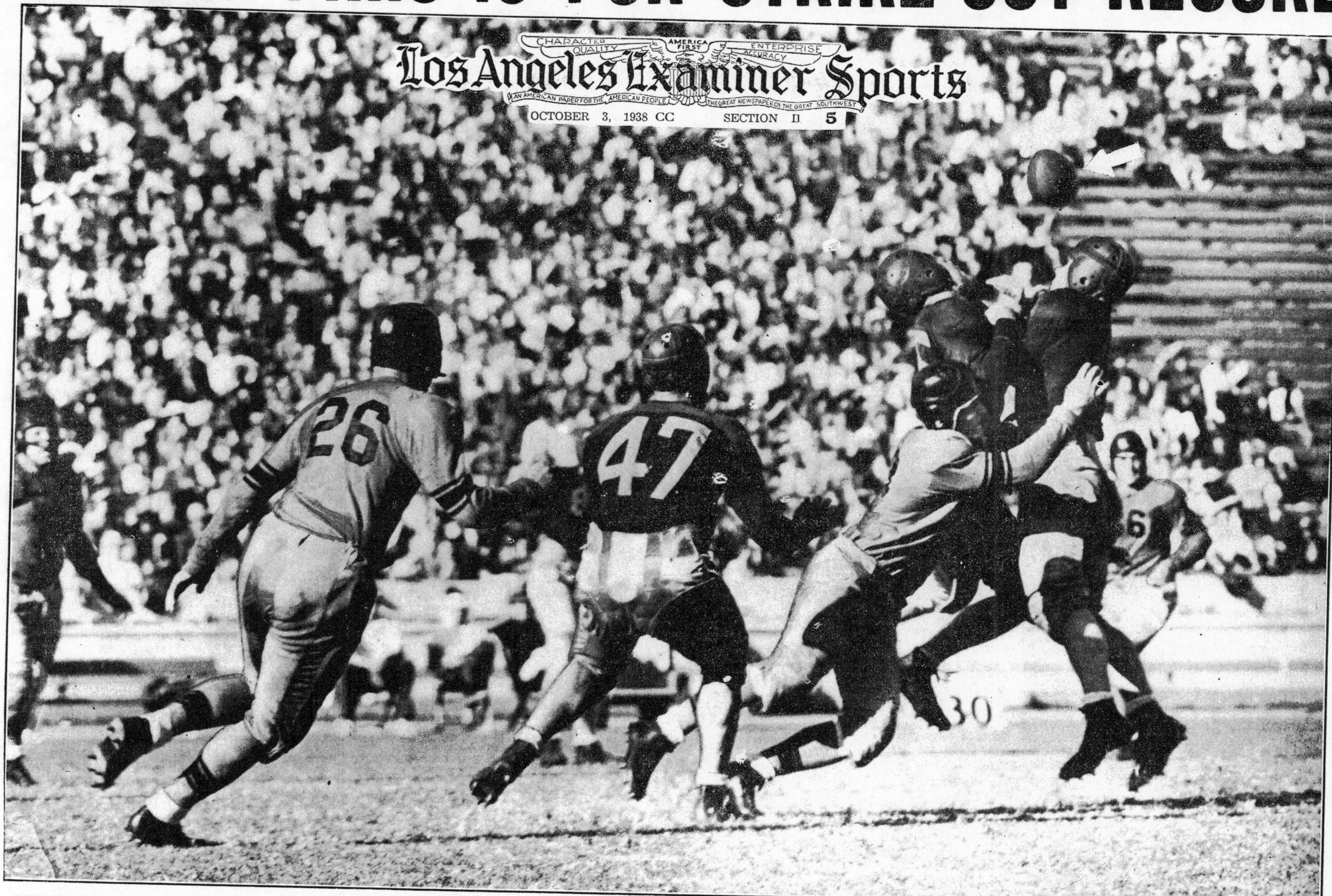

BELIEVE IT OR NOT, NUMBER 47 GOT IT!—This photograph does not look like a pass interception, exactly, but that's what it is, just the same. And furthermore, the fellow who wound up intercepting is Capt. Don McNeil, Number 47, standing here in a receptive attitude with his back to the cameraman. The play occurred in the fourth quarter of the Southern California-Oregon State game. Jim Kisselburgh, Oregon State left half, cut loose with a pass, with the scrimmage line on the Beaver 15-yard stripe. Two alert Trojans leaped in the air to slap the ball around out of reach of Quarterback Mercer (extreme right background) or End Coons (26). They fumbled and slapped, and Don McNeil finally caught the ball and held on to it. Arrow indicates the porkhide in air just prior to landing in McNeil's grasping hands.

—Los Angeles Examiner photo.

What-Nots

The Fix Is in S. F. to Fight Scribes Wrathy But Premature

—By Mark Kelly—

SAN FRANCISCO, Oct. 2.—Leave it to San Francisco to settle all of Los Angeles' problems—even when there are none—at least none of which the folks down home are aware.

This one pertains to the football problems which our Bay City friends insist has us down and grovelling. Odd to have to go 450 miles from home to get a diagnosis of illness that one has only suspected. Question of the moment which they have all the answers for deals with two football problems at Troy and Westwood, a matter of new coaches.

I had vaguely heard that the Bruins were in the market for a man to take over the reins from Bill Spaulding when the latter assumes the chair of athletic director and leaves football matters to others, but that Troy was so far along in its inquiries for a man to succeed Howard Jones comes as a surprise, but then San Francisco is as full of surprises as it is of nice people.

"And don't think you're gon-

(Continued on Page 7, Cols. 6-8)

NEVER LOST RACE

BERKELEY, Oct. 2.—Jim Werson, former California swimming captain, never lost a race in PCC competition in his favorite event, the 200-yard breaststroke.

Jones Satisfied With Troy's Play

By Gene Coughlin

Head Coach Howard Jones and his board of strategy took a look at the motion pictures of the Oregon State-Trojan game yesterday afternoon and opined that "our boys are starting to block again."

The pictures of Saturday's contest served a double purpose. They showed the mistakes and they also acted as a guide to help Jones in determining which athletes he will take back to Columbus for the Ohio State game this week end.

34 MEN IN SQUAD

The traveling squad, probably consisting of 34 men, will be named today.

Jones indicated that Jimmy Jones (no relation) will see plenty of action at right-half against Ohio State. Jones looked better on the "Pinckert reverse" than did Boyd Morgan, although the latter showed some improvement over his performance against Alabama.

With only one day's home practice this week, Jack Banta will be the prize pupil this afternoon as he starts learning the assignments for fullback and quarterback. To date he has done nothing but fullback duty—and that very well—but Jones wants to alternate him for better effect. Mickey Anderson will stick to quarterbacking.

HE'S SATISFIED

Although he wasn't chuckling, Jones was "satisfied" with the 7-0 win over a bunch of tough Beavers, defensively. He thought the score might have been larger with a better variety of plays inside the O. S. C. 20-yard line.

Anderson and Banta have recovered from leg cramps that halted them Saturday, and Peoples is ready to go again. Grenny Lansdell, who sat on the bench all afternoon, reported his leg feels fine again, which means he will start against Ohio State.

The club leaves tomorrow night at 7:45. Amby Schindler may make the trip but it's pretty certain he won't play against the Buckeyes, although he might meet Stanford later on—if his services seem necessary.

SPORTS TODAY

TENNIS

AT L. A. TENNIS CLUB—Final rounds in men's play in Pacific Southwest Tennis tourney.

BOXING

AT OLYMPIC—Weekly program of nine amateur boxing matches, starting 8:30 p. m.

WRESTLING

AT HOLLYWOOD — Weekly program of pro wrestling matches, starting at 8:30 p. m.

Japanese to Have 'Sullivan' Award

The Japanese athletic Federation is following in the footsteps of the A. A. U. by inaugurating an annual award along the precise lines of the James E. Sullivan Memorial Award. The Japanese trophy will be known as the Kishi Memorial Trophy.

Gaels Crush Bulldogs, 20-0

It was a St. Mary's show almost from the opening kickoff, with the Gaels superior on land, in the air and almost every other department.

The first period went scoreless with St. Mary's holding the edge on offense. The Gaels shoved over a touchdown in the second quarter, driving 60 yeards on straight power. Substitute left halfback Mike Klotovich went over from the one-foot line for the score.

TWO TOUCHDOWNS

After a scoreless third period, in which the Gaels again had the playing advantage, they struck twice in the final fifteen minutes for two more touchdowns.

The second tally, just after the last quarter had opened, followed recovery of the ball on Gonzaga's 13-yard line near the close of the third period. It was from a partially blocked punt and the Gaels marched over the goal on three plunges. Starting Left Halfback Heffernan went over.

A pass from Klotovich to Sub Right Half Rimassa yielded the third touchdown, the latter running 30 yards after receiving the 14-yard toss.

NEAR GOAL LINE

Gonzaga was within striking distance of the St. Mary's goal three times, twice in the opening period when it reached the 14 and 10-yard lines respectively. Late in the last quarter, the Bulldogs got down to within 17 yards of a score but the gun barked the end of the game at that point.

Greenberg Fails to Hit Homer; 2 Short of Record

FINAL MAJOR STANDINGS

National League

Club—	W.	L.	Pct.	*
Chicago	89	63	.586	....
Pittsburgh	86	64	.573	2
New York	83	67	.553	5
Cincinnati	82	68	.547	6
Boston	77	75	.507	12
St. Louis	71	80	.470	17½
Brooklyn	69	80	.463	18½
Philadelphia	45	105	.300	43

* Games behind leader.

YESTERDAYS RESULTS

New York, 3; Boston, 2.
Brooklyn, 7-7; Philadelphia, 3-2.
Cincinnati, 5; Pittsburgh, 4.
St. Louis, 7; Chicago, 5.

American League

	W.	L.	Pct.	*GBL
New York	99	53	.651	....
Boston	88	61	.591	9½
Cleveland	86	66	.566	13
Detroit	84	70	.545	16
Washington	75	76	.497	23½
Chicago	65	83	.439	32
St. Louis	55	97	.362	44
Philadelphia	53	99	.349	46

*Games behind leader.

YESTERDAY'S RESULTS

New York, 6; Boston, 1.
Washington, 5-2; Philadelphia, 2-4.
Detroit, 4-10; Cleveland, 1-8.
St. Louis, 4-0; Chicago, 3-3.

PRO FOOTBALL

Chicago Bears, 28; Philadelphia Eagles, 6.
Cleveland Rams, 21; Detroit Lions, 17.
Brooklyn Dodgers, 13; Chicago Cardinals, 0.

Tigers Trim Indians Twice

CLEVELAND, Oct. 2.—(AP)—Detroit closed its season by winning two games from the Cleveland Indians today, 4 to 1 and 10 to 8. Bob Fellers fanned 18 in the opener for a new major league record. Hank Greenberg failed to hit a homer and finished with 58, two short of Babe Ruth's mark.

Feller allowed 7 hits, walked 7 and hit one batter.

In 1936 Feller struck out 17 Philadelphia Athletics, and tied Dizzy Dean for major league honors.

Chet Laabs was the 18th victim in the ninth inning. It was also the fifth time that Laabs had fanned in the game.

(Box scores on 4th Sports Page)

American League Arbiters Named

CHICAGO, Oct. 2.—(INS)—Louis C. Koles and Cal Hubbard have been named American League umpires for the World Series between the New York Yankees and the Chicago Cubs, which opens at Wrigley Field Wednesday, William Harridge, president of the American League, announced today.

YANKEES CLIP RED SOX, 6 TO 1

BOSTON, Oct. 2.—(AP)—The world-champion New York Yankees defeated the Boston Red Sox 6 to 1 today in the last baseball game here this season. It was the Yanks' 99th win of the season which saw Joe DiMaggio belt his 32nd homer of the year with two on in the eighth.

New York	AB	H	O	A
Crosetti,ss	2	1	2	1
Knickbkr,ss	2	0	1	1
Rolfe,3b	3	1	1	1
Henrich,rf	4	1	3	0
DiMaggio,cf	3	1	4	0
Gehrig,1b	4	1	2	0
Dahlgren,1b	0	0	3	0
Dickey,c	3	1	4	1
Glenn,c	1	0	0	0
Selkirk,lf	3	0	1	0
Gordon,2b	4	1	6	2
Gomez,p	1	0	0	1
Sundra,p	3	0	0	1
Totals	33	7	27	8

Boston	AB	H	O	A
Cramer,cf	3	1	4	0
Berg,1b	1	1	3	0
Vosmk,lf,cf	4	0	1	0
Tabor,ss	4	2	1	2
Higgins,3b	3	1	1	4
Peack,lf,1b	3	1	11	0
Nonenkp,rf	4	1	0	0
Doerr,2b	4	0	5	7
DeSautels,c	4	1	1	1
Dickman,p	3	1	0	2
Harris,p	1	0	0	0
Totals	34	9	27	16

New York...... 0 1 0 0 2 0 0 3 0—6
Boston.......... 0 0 0 0 0 1 0 0 0—1

Errors—Tabor 2, Peacock.
Runs batted in—DiMaggio 3, Crosetti, Peacock. Two-base hits—Dickey, Dickman. Three-base hit—Tabor. Home run—DiMaggio. Bases on balls—Off Gomez, 2; Dickman, 3. Struck out—By Gomez, 2; Sundra, 1; Dickman, 1. Winning pitcher—Sundra. Losing pitcher—Dickman. Time—1:31.

Newark Wins, 12-4, Over Kansas City

NEWARK, N. J., Oct. 2.—(AP)—The Newark Bears of the International League clubbed four pitchers for 18 hits today to trample the Kansas City Blues of the American Association, 12 to 4, and deadlock the "Little World Series" at one victory each. Joe Beggs, going the route for the Bears, allowed nine hits.

Hopman Nabs Upset Net Victory

Agile Harry Hopman, **34-year-**old non-playing captain of **the** Australian Davis Cup team, **be**witched two-fisted John Bromwich with a crafty tennis display yesterday that defeated his pupil and placed the veteran in the final round of the Pacific Southwest men's singles championship.

The scores of the upset semi-final round match played before 3000 fans at the Los Angeles Tennis Club were 6-3, 6-3, 10-8.

The veteran Anzac rallied in all three sets to win. He captured five straight games in the first set after trailing 1-3, reeled off four straights to nab the second set and pulled himself out of a 1-5 deficit to take the third set after 18 games.

Hopman meets another teammate, Adrian Quist, who defeated Donald Budge in the other semi-final round Saturday, on the center court today.

Nancy Wynne of Australia was upset in the quarter-final round of the women's singles by Margot Lumb of England, 6-4, 3-6, 7-5. In other women's singles matches Mrs. Sarah Fabyan defeated Pauline Betz, 7-5, 6-4, and Dorothy Bundy eliminated Mrs. Bonnie Blank, 6-3, 7-5.

Mme. Rene Mathieu of France joined Margot Lumb, Dorothy Bundy and Mrs. Fabyan in the semi-final round by defeating Mrs. Harry Hopman of Australia, 6-3, 6-3.

Another of the tournament's

(Continued on Page 8, Column 8)

EXTRA

LATE NEWS

Complete BASEBALL

CHARACTER · QUALITY · AMERICA FIRST! · ENTERPRISE · ACCURACY
Los Angeles Examiner
AN AMERICAN PAPER FOR THE AMERICAN PEOPLE · THE GREAT NEWSPAPER OF THE GREAT SOUTHWEST
Reg.U.S.Pat.Off.

VOL. XXXV—NO. 303 | LOS ANGELES, MONDAY, OCTOBER 10, 1938 | P | Two Sections—Part I—FIVE CENTS

YANKS WIN SERIES!

Rolfe Is Safe After Stealing Second Base in First Inning

NEW YORK'S YANKEES made it four in a row in the World Series yesterday by taking the fourth game from the Chicago Cubs, 8 to 3. Here is one of the plays in the second inning that had some 60,000 fans on their toes. Red Rolfe, Yankee third baseman, is shown stealing second as Jurges takes the throw from first. Umpire Koll calls the play. Rolfe, by taking a long lead off first, had worried Pitcher Bill Lee, who threw to first, trying to catch him. Before First Baseman Collins could relay the ball Rolfe was safe. The Yanks by yesterday's victory became the first team ever to win the World Series three times in succession.

—Picture transmitted by International News Sound Photo System.

IN THE FIRST inning yesterday Stanley Hack, lead-off man for the Cubs, slashed a single. Billy Herman, second baseman, the next batter, then hit, forcing Hack at second base. Joe Gordon takes the throw, while Umpire Koll yanks his left arm over his shoulder.

—Picture transmitted by International News Sound Photo System.

It's All Over Now!

CHICAGO (N. L.)

	AB	R	H	O	A
Hack, 3b	5	0	2	1	0
Herman, 2b	5	0	1	1	3
Cavarretta, rf	4	1	2	1	0
Marty, cf	4	0	0	2	0
Demaree, lf	3	1	0	3	0
O'Dea, c	3	1	1	5	0
Collins, 1b	4	0	0	10	0
Jurges, ss	4	0	2	1	0
Lee, p	1	0	0	0	0
Galan	1	0	0	0	0
Root, p	0	0	0	0	0
Lazzeri	1	0	0	0	0
Page, p	0	0	0	0	1
French, p	0	0	0	0	0
Carleton, p	0	0	0	0	0
Dean, p	0	0	0	0	0
Reynolds	1	0	0	0	0
Totals	36	3	8	24	4

Galan batted for Lee in 4th.
Lazzeri batted for Root in 7th.
Reynolds batted for Dean in 9th.

NEW YORK (A. L.)

	AB	R	H	O	A
Crosetti, ss	5	0	2	6	1
Rolfe, 3b	5	0	1	0	0
Henrich, rf	4	1	1	1	0
DiMaggio, cf	4	1	1	3	0
Gehrig, 1b	4	1	1	5	2
Dickey, c	4	0	1	7	0
Hoag, lf	4	2	2	1	0
Gordon, 2b	3	2	1	2	4
Ruffing, p	3	1	1	2	3
Totals	36	8	11	27	10

Chicago (N.L.)	000	100	020	—3
New York (A.L.)	030	001	04*	—8

Errors—Jurges, Gordon.

Home runs—Henrich, O'Dea. Three-base hit—Crosetti. Two-base hits—Jurges, Cavarretta, Hoag, Crosetti. Runs batted in—Ruffing, Crosetti 4, Henrich, O'Dea 2, Hoag. Stolen bases—Rolfe, Gordon. Earned runs—Chicago (N. L.), 2; New York (A. L.), 5. Left on bases—Chicago (N. L.), 8; New York (A. L.), 6. Bases on balls—Ruffing, 2 (Demaree, O'Dea); Carleton, 2 (Gordon, Ruffing). Struck out—Ruffing, 5 (Marty 2, Lee, Collins, Galan); Lee, 2 (Crosetti, DiMaggio); Root, 1 (Rolfe). Pitching summary—Lee, 3 runs, 4 hits in 3 innings; Root, 1 run, 3 hits in 3 innings; Page, 2 runs, 2 hits in 1 1-3 innings; French, 0 runs, 0 hits in 1-3 inning; Carleton, 2 runs, 1 hit in 0 inning; Dean, 0 run, 1 hit in 1-3 inning. Wild pitches—Carleton, 2. Losing pitcher—Lee. Umpires—Hubbard (A. L.) at the plate; Moran (N. L.) first base; Kolls (A. L.) second base; Sears (N. L.) third base. Time—2:11. Attendance—59,847.

Challenger Wins First Sea Race

Defeats Canadian Champion in Fish Boat Meet

ABOARD SCHOONER GERTRUDE L. THEBAUD, OFF NAHANT, Mass., via radio telephone, Oct. 9.—(AP)—Captain Ben Pine's challenger for the international fishing trophy won the opening race of a three out of five series, defeating the Canadian champion, Captain Angus Talters' big salt bank, Bluenose. Thebaud finished the 36-mile course at 3.34:04 p. m. (Eastern Standard Time). Bluenose finished at 3.37.

Pine's challenger, the Gertrude L. Thebaud of Gloucester, and the big Lunenburger raced around an 13-mile triangle today

CUBS LOSE, 8 TO 3, IN FOURTH GAME

Yankees Take Third Consecutive World Series to Set New Record; Outclass Opponents

RUFFING WINS AGAIN

Holds Chicago to 8 Hits; Only Two of Three Runs Earned; $434,094.66 Series Purse

PLAY BY PLAY IN SPORTS SECTION

YANKEE STADIUM, NEW YORK, Oct. 9.—The New York Yankees won their third consecutive world series, a record never before equaled in baseball, when they overwhelmed the Chicago Cubs here today, 8 to 3, in the fourth game of the big series before 60,000 exultant fans. Charlie Ruffing pitched his second victory of the series, holding the Cubs to eight hits.

The Yankees, who had outclassed their luckless rivals in the first three games, more or less humiliated them before today's contest ended. Leading 4 to 3 going into the eighth inning, they scored four more times as they batted around against four Chicago pitchers. In all, six flingers tried to stave off the Yankee attack, Bill Lee, who started, lasting only three frames and losing his second decision of the series.

CROSETTI HERO

Frankie Crosetti led the winners' assault with a triple and a double, his three-bagger in the second inning driving across two runs. Tommy Henrich clouted a home run into the right field stands off Charlie Root in the sixth.

Only two of the Cubs' runs off Ruffing were earned. Ken O'Dea, young substitute catcher, pounded them across with a homer in the eighth, with Cavarretta on third. Joe Gordon's error on a thrown ball let the first Chicago run across in the fourth. Gordon made up for that by hitting a single and scoring twice. Cavarretta and Jurges each hit a double and a single off Ruffing.

RECORD PURSE

It was announced the players of the two clubs would split a purse of $434,094.66, a record for a four-game series.

Today's victory was the Yankees' eighth straight over the Chicago team in the last two

(Continued on First Sports Page)

Johnson Hurls Wings To 7-0 Victory Over Orioles

THE BALTIMORE NEWS-POST SPORTS

TUESDAY EVENING, MAY 2, 1939 21

Rodger H. Pippen Sports Editor Says:

The White Sox staged a benefit baseball game in Chicago yesterday for Monty Stratton, whose brilliant pitching career was ended suddenly last winter when his right leg was amputated after a hunting accident. That injury was fate.

Hurling for the Cubs in this game was Dizzy Dean, who "lost" his good right arm through overwork while a member of the St. Louis Cardinals. Dean's trouble was callous disregard by a manager who sacrificed a great flinger for selfish purposes. He was called upon to pitch out of turn so many times that he broke under the strain.

MONTE STRATTON

You might well say that Dizzy could have balked. True enough. Yet, unfortunately for Dean, he had all the enthusiasm and spirit of a collegian. He was willing and ready any time he was called. Dean talked a lot and boasted too much, but he was at all times a great team player.

Wearing him out may have paid dividends to Frankie Frisch, his manager. But in the end it was costly to the St. Louis club. Even though they sold him to the Cubs, sore arm and all, for a fancy figure, the Cards would have been better off financially if they had not overworked Diz and had him as the ace of their staff at this moment.

Right here in Baltimore, Harry Frank, from Walbrook, pitched his arm out helping the Birds win seven straight pennants. One week he hurled in portions of six games. In the end it doesn't pay owners or pitchers to have the hurlers go to the well too often.

The game in Chicago yesterday ended in a 4-to-1 victory for the White Sox, who blasted Dizzy Dean in the first four innings for all their runs and then held the National Leaguers in check behind the 10-hit pitching of Johnny Whitehead.

For Dean the game was bad news. After it was over the pitcher for whom the Cubs paid the St. Louis Cardinals $185,000 last year, said his arm hurt "worse than it did last year."

"There's no use kidding myself," Ol' Diz mourned, "there's still something wrong."

RALPH GULDAHL

If you enjoy seeing a master wood and long iron player in action, don't forget to be at Rodgers Forge on May 20 when Ralph Gulrahl, national open champion, comes here to play in a foursome with Johnny Flattery, Otto Greiner and Wiffy Cox.

While in Florida in February, I saw Ralph perform at Daytona Beach. With the wood, he called his shots. On one dog leg hole, he cleared a high tree fully two hundred yards from the tee. The other pros played safe.

Guldahl's success is one of the romances of the links. Only a few years ago, broke and disgusted, he gave away his clubs. Later, he made a fresh start.

Although Ralph is considered the ace golfer of today, he isn't tops in any one department. Dick Metz is credited with being golf's straightest driver. Jimmy Thompson hits the longest ball. The best mud horse is Jim Hines. And Paul Runyan is champ with the spoon.

PREAKNESS PATTER

If Charley (Flying Dutchman) Kurtsinger gets a mount in the Preakness, and it seems likely that he will, the diminutive rider will be striving to equal the record of W. Hughes, the only one to ride three winners in the Maryland Jockey Club classic. That was accomplished 'way back in 1875, 1879 and 1880.

Since then Clarence Kummer has come close with two wins, a second and a third out of nine trys. Johnny Loftus, rider of Sir Barton in the first triple crown victory, has two victories in two attempts for the perfect Preakness score. But Kummer is gone and Loftus is not riding these days.

Kurtsinger has many good races in him with an excellent opportunity to equal and, perhaps, pass the Hughes' mark.

Baseball Scores

International League

At Newark—

		R.	H.	E.
Mont....	000 310 011	6	11	3
Newark..	200 000 100	3	7	1

Batteries — Porter and Hartje; Stanceu and Holm.

At Jersey City—

		R.	H.	E.
Tor......	000 000 33000	6	9	0
Jersey C..	000 010 05001	7	11	1

Batteries—Mulligan and Klimczak; Carpenter and Padden.

At Syracuse—

		R.	H.	E.
Buffalo...	000 110 001	2	10	6
Syracuse.	103 000 00x	4	4	2

Batteries—Kline and Helf; Kleinhans and Warren.

American League

At Chicago—

		R.	H.	E.
Phila....	000 000 100	1	6	5
Chicago..	002 020 00x	4	8	1

Batteries—Parmelee and F. Hayes; Lyons and Sylvestri.

At Detroit—

		R.	H.	E.
N. York..	602 023 900	22	17	0
Detroit	000 000 200	2	7	1

Batteries—Ruffing and Dickey; Kennedy and Tebbetts.

Boston at Cleveland, postponed; cold. ..

At St. Louis—

		R.	H.	E.
Wash..	010 312 0			
St. Louis.	200 040 0			

Batteries—Deshong and Ferrell; Vanatta and Sullivan.

National League

At Boston—

		R.	H.	E.
St. Louis	010 000 001	2	5	0
Boston	000 100 000	1	6	0

Batteries — Bowman and Franks; MacFayden and Lopez.

At Philadelphia—

		R.	H.	E.
Chicago	000 010 000	1	4	2
Phila...	000 202 20x	6	11	1

Batteries—Harrell and Hartnett; Johnson and Davis.

At Brooklyn—

		R.	H.	E.
Pittsburgh	010 000 020	3	13	1
Brooklyn	020 000 000	2	3	1

Batteries—Klinger and Berres; Fitzsimmons and Todd.

At New York—

		R.	H.	E.
Cincinnati	020 100 301	7	11	1
N. York..	011 003 003	8	13	0

Batteries—Derringer and Lombardi; Gumbert and Danning.

2,130-GAME STREAK ENDED

Lou Gehrig Benches Self

Greeny Wins By Length In Second Race At Pimlico

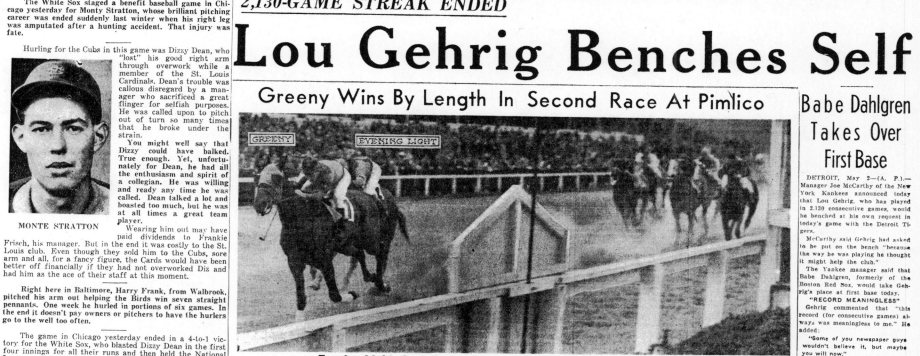

Evening Light closes fast to be sec ond with Red Glare in third position.

Adamick Ban Lifted

CHICAGO, May 2—(A. P.).—Joseph Triner, chairman of the Illinois State Athletic Commission, said today the Commission voted to lift suspension on Jimmy Adamick because he was convinced Adamick would never fight again.

Babe Dahlgren Takes Over First Base

DETROIT, May 2—(A. P.).—Manager Joe McCarthy of the New York Kankees announced today that Lou Gehrig, who has played in 2,130 consecutive games, would be benched at his own request in today's game with the Detroit Tigers.

McCarthy said Gehrig had asked to be put on the bench "because the way he was playing he thought it might help the club."

The Yankee manager said that Babe Dahlgren, formerly of the Boston Red Sox, would take Gehrig's place at first base today.

"RECORD MEANINGLESS"

Gehrig commented that "this record (for consecutive games) always was meaningless to me." He added:

"Some of you newspaper guys wouldn't believe it, but maybe you will now."

He said he made up his mind Sunday night to ask McCarthy to remove him from the line-up. He explained:

"I felt I wasn't helping the club by the way I was playing—physically, I am in wonderful condition, but I have had trouble getting started."

OUT FOR "FEW GAMES"

He said he intended to remain out of the line-up for "a few games" hoping that warmer weather would enable him to hit his stride. He said:

One thing I certainly appreciate is that, despite my slump, the fans never '*got on*' me. I want the fans in New York and elsewhere to know that I am grateful for that."

Gehrig was only slightly downhearted and was openly optimistic that he would hit his strid before the season is many weeks older.

Conclusive evidence that the "iron man" was fading came during the spring training season, and newspaper men traveling with the team regretfully predicted Gehrig's consecutive-games record probably would go by the board before midsummer.

The husky first baseman wasn't hitting, but that was expected, for he never has been a good spring hitter.

But his fielding had fallen off and he had slowed up almost to a walk. That was the real tip-off.

HOLDER OF RECORD

The thirty-five-year-old New Yorker, holder of dozens of big-league records on the offensive side of the game, batted only .295 last season, the first time he had failed to reach .300 since 1925, the year he took over Wally Pipp's duties at first base and began his remarkable endurance record.

He got away to an exceptionally bad start, and it was only by a strong finish that he got his average up that high.

In the Yankees' first eight games this season Lou had made only four hits for a .143 average.

HOLDS MANY RECORDS

Gehrig, one of the best known figures in baseball, holds numerous Major League records. Among these are:

Most consecutive games played—2,130.

Most consecutive years, 100 games or more—13.

Most years, 150 games or more—12.

Most consecutive years, 100 runs or more—13.

Most home runs with bases filled—23.

Most years, 300 or more total bases—13.

Most years, 100 runs or more driven in—13.

Double plays by first basemen—157.

Most home runs in a game—four (1932).

The "Iron Man" started his string of consecutive games in 1925.

Red Wings Down Birds, 7 To 0, As Johnson Hurls

By HUGH TRADER, JR.

ORIOLE PARK, May 2.—Cy Johnson, ace pitcher of the Rochester Red Wings, was in rare form here today and the Orioles were only able to gather three hits off his delivery and were shut out, 7 to 0.

Len Gabrielson, new first sacker of the Birds, procured from Newark, banged two of the safe blows, both to left field.

Jack Tisng, who started on the mound for the Flock and lasted six innings, gave up only five hits, but they were good for five runs. Dusty Cooke's home run with Crabtree aboard in the sixth was the big blow. Johnny Swank replaced Tising in the box in the seventh.

Immediately after the game, the Orioles will en train for Montreal where they open a 19-day trip on Thursday.

ROCHESTER	AB.	R.	H.	O.	A.	ORIOLES	AB.	R.	H.	O.	A.
Murt'h,2	3	0	0	2	0	McG'n,m	4	0	0	2	0
Gil'wr,r.	5	0	0	1	0	Corb't,2..	3	0	1	[illegible]	[illegible]
C'bt'e,m.	4	2	1	3	0	Meie,1..	4	0	0	3	0
Sturyd,1.	4	2	2	9	0	MH'w'l,l	4	0	0	1	0
Cooke,l..	4	2	3	3	0	West,c..	4	0	0	8	0
Narron,c	4	1	0	2	1	Gab'on,1	3	0	2	8	0
Marion,s	4	0	1	6	5	Lil'rd,s.	2	0	0	2	1
Stopa,3..	3	0	1	1	3	B'tl'g,3..	2	0	0	1	1
J'nson,p.	4	0	0	0	1	Tising,p.	0	0	0	0	0
						1Moore..	0	0	0	0	0
						Swank,p	0	0	0	0	0
						2Gr'm...	1	0	0	0	0
						Br'n'r,p.	0	0	0	0	0
Totals..	35	7	8	27	10	Totals..	27	0	3	27	6

1 Batted for Tising in 6th.
2 Batted for Swank in 8th.

Rochester	0 3 0 0 0 0 2 0 2 0—7
Orioles	0 0 0 0 0 0 0 0 0 0—0

Runs batted in—Marion, Stopa (2), Cooke (3). Home runs—Cooke. Stolen bases—Sturdy, Cooke. Sacrifice hit—Tising. Double plays—Marion, unassisted. Left on bases—Rochester 5; Orioles, 5. Base on balls—Off Tising, 2; off Johnson, 4; off Bruner, 1. Hits—Off Tising, 5 in 6 innings. Off Swank, 3 in 2 innings. Off Bruner, 0 in 1 inning. Struck out—By Tising, 4; by Joihnson, 2; by Swank, 2. Bruner, 1. Losing pitcher—Tising. Umpires—Swanson and Donnelly.

ROYALS, 6; BEARS, 3

MONTREAL	AB.	R.	H.	O.	A.	NEWARK	AB.	R.	H.	O.	A.
Ross,3..	4	0	0	1	3	Wuck,s	[illegible]	0	1	0	8
Deal,m..	5	2	1	2	0	Norris,s.	4	0	0	3	3
Parks,r.	4	1	1	6	0	Cr't'k,r	3	1	1	4	0
Haas,1.	5	2	3	8	0	Kel'ler,l	4	1	1	0	0
Hartje,c	4	0	2	4	1	Mills,m.	4	0	1	3	0
V'n R's,l	4	1	2	1	0	Levy,1..	3	0	1	11	0
Sankey,s	1	0	1	1	2	Kah'n,3	4	0	0	0	0
Bell,2...	3	0	1	4	3	Holm,c.	4	1	2	6	1
Porter,p	4	0	0	0	0	Stanceu,p	1	0	0	0	0
						Bed'f'ld,p.	1	0	0	0	1
						1W'hb'n.	1	0	0	0	0
						Str'ich,p	0	0	0	0	0
						2Judn'h.	1	0	0	0	0
Totals..	[illegible]	6	11	27	9	Totals..	34	3	7	27	13

1 Batted for Beddingfield in seventh.
2 Batted for Strincevich in ninth.

SCORE BY INNINGS

Montreal	0 0 0 3 1 0 0 1 1—6
Newark	2 0 0 0 0 0 1 0 0—3

Errors—Ross, Sankey, Bell, Levy. Runs batted in—Mills (2), Parks (2), Van Robays (2), Deal, Holm, Sankey. Two-base hit—Mills. Home runs—Parks, Holm, Van Robays. Stolen base—Sankey. Sacrifice—Deal. Double play—Ross to Haas. Left on base—Montreal 11; Newark, 6. Base on balls—Off Porter, 2; off Stanceu, 4; off Strincevich, 3. Struck out—By Porter, 4; by Stanceu, 2. Hits—Off Stanceu, 6 in 4 1-3 innings; off Beddingfield, 2 in 2 2-3; off Strincevich, 3 in 2. Wild pitch—Porter. Losing pitcher—Stanceu. Umpires—Schroeder, Van Graflan and Crowley.

REDMONTS CALLING

The Redmont A. C. is seeking competition with baseball teams in the 100-pound class. Address Moe Berg, 1831 Monroe street.

How The Horses Ran At Pimlico

DailyDouble {Paradise Girl / Greeny} Paid $58.20

WEATHER CLODY. TRACK GOOD.

FIRST RACE—FOUR AND ONE-HALF FURLONGS. FOR TWO-YEAR-OLDS. Maidens. Special weights. Purse $1,000. Value to winner $700, second $150, third $100, fourth $50. Went to post at 2.16. Off at 2.19½. Start good from gates. Won driving, place same. Winner ch f 2, by Balko-Parade Girl. Owned by A. G. VANDERBILT. Trained by L. McCOY. Time 23 3-5, 49, 56 1-5.

	Wt.	Post	St.	¼	Str.	Fin.	Jockeys	Odds
Paradise Girl	113	2	2	2^4	$1^{1½}$	$1^{1½}$	L. Fallon	$2.45
High Bud	115	8	3	3^h	2^2	2^h	J. Anderson	5.95
Mariyah	112	6	7	5^2	3^8	3^8	G. Seabo	45.25
Dan's Folly	112	3	5	4^h	5^2	4^2	H. Dabson	8.85
Breaking Waves	112	5	6	6½	6^8	5^h	L. Hardy	8.30
Balky Fox	115	1	1	3^1	4^1	6^3	M. Peters	2.25
Navigation	110	7	8	8	7^1	7^2	J. Reilly	14.60
Hazel W	112	4	4	$7^{1½}$	8	8	M. Berg	14.15

$2 Mutuels Paid—Paradise Girl, $6.90 straight, $4.70 place, $4.30 show. High Bud, $6.60 place, $4.60 show. Mariyah, $8.50 show. Total mutuels $35.60

Paradise Girl away nicely, was hustled along to keep up with High Bud in the early racing, stayed on the inside to draw into the lead entering the homestretch then was ridden hard to the close. High Bud showed good speed and continued willingly when caught. Mariyah bettered her position while saving ground in the late stages and finished gamely. Dan's Folly could not get to the leaders. Breaking Waves broke sluggishly and failed to enter contention. Balky Fox was never a threat. Navigation lost much ground. Hazel W was outrun.

SECOND—SIX FURLONGS. FOR THREE-YEAR-OLDS AND UP. FILLIES and mares. Claiming. Purse $1,000. Value to winner $700, second $150, third $100, fourth $50. Went to post at 2.46½. Off at 2.54. Start good from gates. Won driving, place same. Winner br f 3, by Teddy-Green Girl. Owned by CALUMET FARM. Trained by F. J. KEARNS. Time 23 2-5, 48, 1.14 4-5.

	Wt.	Post	St.	¼	½	Str.	Fin.	Jockeys	Odds
Greeny	108	7	3	1^h	$1^{1½}$	1^3	1^1	M. Berg	$5.85
Evening Light	106	4	5	3^h	2½	2^8	2^4	J. Mattison	3.35
Red Glare	108	1	4	4½	5^1	3^h	3^1	J. Reilly	15.55
Chainwick	111	10	6	$5^{1½}$	4^h	$4^{1½}$	4^h	G. Seabo	13.40
Boston Mary	122	6	1	8^1	$8^{1½}$	5½	5^1	G. Smith	10.80
Manila Bay	113	11	12	10^8	10^5	6^h	6^h	C. Grigg	87.60
Pansy's First	111	9	9	6^h	6^3	7^3	$7^{1½}$	H. Dabson	13.40
Bit By Bit	112	8	11	11	11	8^1	8^2	A. Shelhamer	3.35
Wise Sister	115	12	10	9^2	9^h	$9^{1½}$	9^3	M. Peters	17.80
Scout About	103	2	7	$7^{1½}$	7^h	10^4	10^8	F. A. Smith	23.45
Sky Hostess	116	5	8	$2^{1½}$	3^1	11	11	R. Holland	151.40
Lady Elgin	116	3	2	fell				C. Stevenson	9.55

$2 Mutuels Paid—Greeny, $13.70 straight, $6.60 place, $5.40 show. Evening Light $5.10 place, $3.30 show. Red Glare, $7.40 show. Total mutuels $41.50

Greeny drew clear, saved ground but had to be shaken up strongly to withstand Evening Light. Latter came with good energy. Red Glare continued gamely. Chainwick failed to better his position. Boston Mary suffered interference. Manila Bay was very unruly at the gate. Pansy's First was never a threat. Bit By Bit almost fell in the first furlong when unable to avoid Lady Elgin. Wise Sister had no speed. Scout About was held safe. Lady Elgin stumbled and fell.

THIRD—TWO MILES. FOR FOUR-YEAR-OLDS AND UP. MAIDENS. SPECIAL WEIGHTS. Steeplechase. Purse $1,000. Value to winner $700, second $150, third $100, fourth $50. Went to post at 3.15. Off at 3.16. Start good. Won easily, place same. Winner b g 6, by Ladkin-Mistrial. Owned by LOG CABIN STUD. Trained by E. C. BOSLEY. Time 4.12 2-5. Fifteen jumps.

	Wt.	Post	St.					Fin.	Jockeys	Odds
Angus	155	7	5	1^2	1^2	1^8	1^{20}	1^{30}	B. Ansteatt	$2.65
Irish Lancer	137½	5	7	6	$5^{1½}$	4	3	2^h	J. Novak	4.10
Loro	155	4	4	3^1	2^h	3^8	$2^{1½}$	3	G. Walker	4.65
Grumpy	141	6	6	5^3	6	5	4	4	N. Brooks	15.45
Trolight	141	3	1	4^4	4^{12}	4^{12}	2^2	fell	T. Roby	5.95
Leslie Myer	153	1	3	2^1	3^4	3^4	lost rider		J. Meehan	16.65
Calculate	155	2	2	fell					E. Roberts	4.35

$2 Mutuels Paid—Angus, $7.30 straight, $3.90 place, $2.70 show. Irish Lancer, $5.00 place, $3.80 show. Loro, $3.40 show. Total mutuels $26.10

Angus moved to the front going to the first fence, fenced nicely at all of his fences, raced reserved for a mile and a half, met a stout bid from Trolight coming to the last fence and drew out when the latter fell. Irish Lancer was badly outrun all during the running, but finished courageously to beat Loro for second. Loro raced strong for the first mile, then weakened. Grumpy lost his rider at the twelfth fence, then was remounted to finish in the time limit for fourth. Trolight saved for the first mile, gained fast when placed to a drive, reached the winner coming to the last fence, but fell. Leslie Myer raced well for a turn of the field, tired and lost rider at the eleventh jump. Calculate fell at the first fence.

FOURTH—FOUR AND ONE-HALF FURLONGS. FOR TWO-YEAR-OLD FILLIES. Allowances. Purse $1,000. Value to winner $700, second $150, third $100, fourth $50. Went to post at 3.46. Off at 3.50½. Start good from gate. Won handily, place driving. Winner b f 3, by High Quest-The Squaw. Owned by H. BRUCE. Trained by F. GARRETT. Time 23 2-5, 48 2-5, 55 2-5.

	Wt.	Post	St.	¼	Str.	Fin.	Jockeys	Odds
Ponemah	118	10	2	1^3	1^2	$1^{1½}$	M. Berg	$1.20
Ambuscade	118	7	3	2^2	2½	2^h	L. Hardy	14.30
Scorch	112	3	7	3^6	3^3	3^2	J. Anderson	4.70
aOnisac	118	8	8	8^4	5^h	4^2	G. Seabo	3.70
Flying Glee	118	9	4	3^h	$4^{1½}$	5^1	H. Dabson	17.65
aClose Quarters	107	4	9	7½	6^2	6^h	G. Martin	3.70
Be Prepared	113	5	1	6^h	7^1	7^4	L. Fallon	11.70
Polly Porter	113	6	10	9^6	9	8^2	M. Peters	38.25
Furr Buckle	112	1	5	5^h	8^2	9	A. Shelhamer	43.50
Aster Lady	112	2	6	10	pulled-up		F. A. Smith	59.45

aMrs. C. T. Grayson-T. A. Sears entry.

$2 Mutuels Paid—Ponemah, $4.40 straight, $3.10 place, $3.00 show. Ambuscade, $8.60 place, $4.40 show. Scorch, $4.40 show.

Ponemah sprinted into a long lead early, was rated while saving ground, and had speed in reserve at the close. Ambuscade followed closest to the winner from the start, was hard urged, but could not menace seriously at anytime. Scorch made up ground swiftly after the start to get into contention, and finished courageously, under punishment. Onisac swerved out at the start, settled in stride, and improved her position steadily. Flying Glee was prominent for three furlongs. Close Quarters raced greenly and could not threaten. Be Prepared broke fast, but had no speed. Polly Porter was badly outrun after breaking tardy. Furr Buckle was held safe. Aster Lady was crowded in the first sixteenth, fell back rapidly and was pulled up.

FIFTH—MILE AND SEVENTY YARDS. FOR THREE-YEAR-OLDS. CLAIMING. Purse $1,000. Value to winner $700, second $150, third $100, fourth $50. Went to post at 4.16½. Off at 4.20. Start good from gate. Won driving, place same. Winner br g 3, by Display-Prattle II. Owned and trained by C. O. FERGUSON. Time 23 3-5, 48 2-5, 1.14 3-5, 1.41 2-5, 1.46 2-5.

	Wt.	Post	St	¼	½	¾	Str.	Fin.	Jockey	Odds
Pradis	112	8	7	3^h	3^h	3½	2^h	1^h	F. A. Smith	$9.40
Tanganyika	115	4	8	8	8	7^4	4½	$2^{1½}$	A. Shelhamer	9.05
The Serf	115	2	1	2½	2^h	2^h	3^h	3^1	L. Hardy	3.35
Part One	110	7	6	6^1	5^h	$5^{1½}$	5^2	4^1	G. Seabo	4.50
Top Queen	113	6	5	7^4	$6^{1½}$	6^1	6^3	$5^{1½}$	J. Anderson	1.95
Banner Girl	108	5	4	4½	4^4	1^h	1^h	6^5	M. Berg	7.00
Soaring High	113	1	2	$1^{1½}$	1^h	4^1	7^2	7^h	O. Brown	47.90
Flag Etta	104	3	3	5^1	7^3	8	8	8	L. Machado	167.30

$2 Mutuels Paid—Pradis, $20.80 straight, $9.80 place, $6.00 show. Tanganyika, $8.10 place, $5.70 show. The Serf, $3.90 show.

Pradis going along with the leaders, and racing on the outside, rallied stoutly approaching the homestretch, bore over on The Serf when joining the pacemaker midway of the homestretch, withstood a drive gamely and was up nearing the close. Tanganyika fell far out of contention early, settled in stride and came between horses to finish with a rush on the inside of the winner. The Serf raced close up, and continued gamely after being crowded by the winner during the stretch run. Part One was taken wide from the start, and hung after making a bid at the stretch turn. Top Queen was unable to get into contention. Banner Girl was made too much use of getting to the front when she went through on the inside at the final turn. Soaring High stopped badly. Flag Etta was outrun.

SIXTH—SIX FURLONGS. FOR THREE-YEAR-OLDS. RENNERT HANDICAP. Purse $2,500 added. Value to winner $2,400, second $500, third $250, fourth $100. Went to post at 4.45½. Off at 4.48½. Start good for all but Sea Captain from gate. Won driving, place same. Winner ch c 3, by Neddie-Parade Trail. Owned by A. G. VANDERBILT. Trained by L. McCOY. Time 23 1-5, 47 2-5, 1.13 2-5.

	Wt.	Post	St.	¼	½	Str.	Fin.	Jockeys	Odds
Trailer	115	1	3	3^5	3^4	1½	1^{nn}	L. Fallon	$13.95
Sea Captain	120	5	5	5	4^h	2½	2^h	R. Donoso	1.10
Easy Mon	118	2	1	1^h	1^h	3^h	3^1	J. Anderson	2.55
Belay	116	3	4	4^h	5	$4^{1½}$	4^8	A. Shelhamer	3.15
Royal Teddy	105	4	2	$2^{1½}$	2^n	5	5	L. Machado	23.65

$2 Mutuels Paid—Trailer, $29.90 straight, $6.70 place, $2.90 show. Sea Captain, $3.30 place, $2.30 show. Easy Mon, $2.40 show.

Trailer, going sharply improved, was in close pursuit of the leaders while racing on the outside, gained a short lead midway of the homestretch and barely lasted long enough to withstand Sea Captain. Latter, practically left when he stood flat-footed at the break, reached his field on the turn, then came through on the inside in the stretch run, to finish with a bold rush. Easy Mon could not get clear after moving into a short lead and he faltered under punishment in the stretch run after blocking Royal Teddy entering the homestretch. Belay finished with good speed. Royal Teddy forced a swift pace and weakened in the stretch drive after being bumped by Easy Mon.

SEVENTH—MILE AND SEVENTY YARDS. THREE-YEAR-OLDS. CLAIMING. Purse $1,000. Value to winner $700, second 150, third $100, fourth $50. Went to post at 5.16. Off at 5.17. Start good from gate. Won easily, place driving. Winner, b g, 3, by Mowlee-Linton Nell. Owned by H. BRUCE. Trained by F. GARRETT. Time, 23 3-5, 48, 1.14, 1.40 3-5, 1.45 4-5.

	Wt.	Post	St	¼	½	¾	Str.	Fin.	Jockey	Odds
General Mowlee	109	7	2	1^h	1^1	1½	1^4	1^4	M. Berg	$2.20
Greedan	113	2	5	6^4	5^h	3^2	$2^{1½}$	2^3	M. Peters	6.35
Burner	104	6	1	$5^{1½}$	3^1	2^h	3^4	3^1	G. Seabo	9.20
Pascua	113	3	6	7½	8^1	$8^{1½}$	5^h	4^n	R. Donoso	3.35
Manymor	113	5	8	8^1	7^h	7^1	6½	5^3	A. Shelhamer	27.20
Air Eddy	106	9	4	4^h	4½	$5^{1½}$	4^h	$6^{1½}$	L. Machado	20.45
Big Ned	115	4	9	9	9	6^h	7^2	7^3	H. Dabson	4.65
Zelitone	104	8	3	2½	2^h	4^h	8^3	8^5	F. A. Smith	25.95
Sanoma	106	1	7	3^h	6^4	9	9	9	J. Mattison	39.05

$2 Mutuels Paid—General Mowlee, $6.40 straight, $4.30 place, $3.50 show. Greedan, $6.60 place, $4.20 show. Burner, $6.40 show.

General Mowlee came away without effort in the last five-sixteenths. Greedan could not reach the winner. Burner was not good enough. Pascua raced sluggishly. Manymor was always held safe. Air Eddy weakened. Big Ned raced poorly. Zelitone stopped. Sanoma showed speed for six furlongs.

EIGHTH—ONE AND ONE-SIXTEENTH MILES. FOUR-YEAR-OLDS AND UP. Fillies and mares. Claiming. Purse $1,000. Value to winner $700, second $150, third $100, fourth $50. Went to post at 5.46½. Off at 5.47½. Start good from gate. Won driving, place same. Winner br f, 4, by Philippi-Turbulent. Owned and trained by J. H. C. FORBES. Time, 24 2-5, 49 2-5, 1.15, 1.42 2-5, 1.49 4-5.

	Wt.	Post	St	¼	½	¾	Str.	Fin.	Jockey	Odds
Riotous	110	6	2	1^1	1^2	1^1	1^h	1½	P. Mills	$5.65
Last Scamp	109	10	7	6^h	7½	4^h	2^1	2^3	R. McDonald	10.60
Miss Selection	110	5	8	$10^{1½}$	8^h	6^h	3^1	3^4	H. Dabson	3.75
Squabble	117	11	9	8^h	9^1	9^1	7^3	$4^{1½}$	A. Shelhamer	2.85
Sylvia G.	117	7	5	3^n	3^h	3^1	4^n	5^h	S. Palumbo	5.45
Minna	106	2	1	$4^{1½}$	4^h	$5^{1½}$	6½	6^1	J. Mattison	75.90
Top Shell	105	4	3	$2^{1½}$	2^1	2^h	5½	7^1	G. Martin	134.45
Chilly Ebbie	105	1	4	7^1	10^8	10^{15}	$8^{1½}$	8^4	R. Placinto	81.00
Carnage	113	9	11	9^h	6^h	8^n	9^2	9^2	C. Coffman	6.60
Boeralice	105	8	6	5½	5^n	1^1	10^{20}	10^{30}	F. A. Smith	19.45
Roaming Lady	110	3	10	11	11	11	11	11	S. Connell	138.95

$2 Mutuels Paid—Riotous, $13.30 straight, $7.60 place, $4.70 show. Last Scamp, $10.10 place, $6.40 show. Miss Skeleton, $4.10 show.

Riotous outran her field to the first turn, shook off Top Shell, saved ground, and rallied to a hard drive nearing the end to withstand Last Scamp. Latter, going sharply improved, worked her way up on the outside and finished determinedly in the final drive. Miss Selection, beginning slowly, lost ground to improve her position and weakened after reaching the leaders in the last eighth. Squabble began slowly and lost a lot of ground to better her position. Sylvia G. raced well placed until reaching the final turn, then weakened under her weight. Minna tired in the last half mile. Top Shell was used up forcing the pace, and she tired. Boeralice was done early.

Chisox Whip A's, Gain Second Place

CHICAGO, May 2—(A. P.).—The Chicago White Sox climbed into second place today by defeating the Philadelphia Athletics, 4 to 1, for the Sox's fifth straight victory and their seventh ineight starts. The A's made six hits and five errors.

May Stars As Phils Defeat Cubs, 6-1

PHILADELPHIA, May 2—(A.P.). Syl Johnson pitched a four-hit ball game today to give the Phillies a 6-to-1 verdict over the Chicago Cubs. Merdrill May, Phills' rookie third baseman, connected three times in four times up for the hitting record of the game.

Dickerson Named Starter At W. Va.

Roy (Boots) Dickerson, former assistant to Marshall Cassidy at New York tracks, has been engaged as starter at the Wheeling, W. Va., track this summer. He also will do the starting at the New Orleans Fair Grounds next winter.

The Des Moines Register

DES MOINES, IOWA, TUESDAY MORNING, JUNE 13, 1939.

BASEBALL PARTY: RUTH MAKES 'COMEBACK' AS CENTENNIAL IS CELEBRATED

Sittin'In

WITH THE ATHLETES.

Landis Enforces Rule.
Hits Most Players.
Must Depend on Skill.
Webbing Outlawed.

—BY SEC TAYLOR—

THE GLOVE CONTROVERSY.

I WANTED to know what all that fuss about the gloves major league players are wearing meant so I called on Ford Frick, president of the National league.

The New York papers had been crowded with stories abusing Judge K. M. Landis, the baseball commissioner, who had issued an edict that players could not use gloves with webbing or interlaced cords or thongs between thumb and forefinger.

FORD FRICK.

Most of the criticism came from writers who were traveling with the Yankees. This was rather amusing to me because it was the Yankees who made the protest a year ago because Hank Greenberg, Detroit firstbaseman, was protecting his hand with a pad that resembled a butterfly net more than it did a glove. Hank could sweep that big basket around much as a jai-alai player does the cesta that adorns his arm.

—

WHEN I explained my mission to Frick he reached for a rulebook, turned to page 13, pointed to Rule 21 and said:

"Read that."

It read:

"The catcher may wear a leather glove or mitt of any size, shape or weight.

"The firstbaseman may wear a leather glove or mitt not more than 12 inches long from top to bottom and not more than eight inches wide across the palm, with thumb and palm connected with leather lacing of not more than four inches from thumb to palm, which lacing shall not be enlarged, extended or reinforced by any process or material whatever.

"Every other player is restricted to the use of a leather glove weighing not over 10 ounces and measuring not over 14 inches around the palm. The pitcher's glove must be uniform in color."

—

WHEN I LAID the rulebook aside Frick handed me a letter, which his secretary under his direction, had brought from a filing cabinet while I was busy studying the rule.

The letter was addressed to Frick and was from Judge Landis.

It informed Frick that he as National league president should warn all players in his organization that the rule would be strictly enforced by all umpires within a few days after receipt of the notice.

"'Shall not be enlarged, extended or reinforced' means 'Shall not be enlarged, extended or reinforced' and 'every other player is restricted to the use of a leather glove', means just that", the letter said.

In other words the firstbaseman may have single lacing but not a web between the thumb and forefinger of the glove, since an exception is made in his case, but no other player, except the catcher, who is also excepted, may have such lacing.

—

FRICK SAID that was all he knew about the matter, except that virtually all infielders and outfielders have been using gloves with a leather flap, lacing or webbing between thumb and forefinger and that the rule does not permit this.

"The rule regarding gloves was rewritten at the time the protest was made about the glove Hank Greenberg was using and was inserted in the rule-book for the first time this year," Frick explained.

He reached for a 1938 rulebook and turned to Rule 21 which read:

"The catcher or firstbaseman may wear a leather glove or mitt of any size, shape or weight. Every other player is restricted to the use of a leather glove weighing not more than 10 ounces and measuring not over 14 inches around the palm. The pitcher's glove must be uniform in color."

—

ONE OF the interesting things about the glove controversy is that while the tendency has been for firstbaseman to use larger gloves, the contrary is true insofar as catchers are concerned. Since the time of Ray Schalk, who if my memory serves me correctly, introduced the small compact catcher's mitt in place of the heavily padded, cumbersome "mattress" catchers formerly thought they needed, catchers have gradually adopted the Schalk model or a mitt similar to it, so that nowadays few, if any, use the large glove.

It looks very much like Judge Landis is going to make the players conform to the rule, whether or not they like it as individuals. They contend that the webbing or lacing between thumb and forefinger makes for more accurate fielding, which is no doubt true.

Firstbasemen contend that single lacing, permitted for them under the rules, is not sufficient. This undoubtedly is true in part.

Hereafter, players must field with more skill and can depend less on the artificial aid of the glove to handle ground balls, catch flies or stop thrown balls.

SUZANNE ILL LEADS WOMEN INTO 1ST ROUND

Mrs. Wilchinski Is Opening Foe.

TODAY'S PAIRINGS.
Championship Flight.
(9 a. m.)
UPPER BRACKET.

Suzanne Ill (Wakonda) vs. Mrs. Norman Wilchinski (Hyperion).
Lois Penn (Wakonda) vs. Mary Louise Cordingley (Hyperion).
Mrs. Henry Nollen (Wakonda) vs. Mrs. R. U. Henninger (Wakonda).
Mrs. George Whitmer (Woodside) vs. Mrs. Burton Joseph (Hyperion).

LOWER BRACKET.

Jean French (Waveland) vs. Mrs. Walter P. Davis (Wakonda).
Mrs. E. W. Buckley (Wakonda) vs. Mrs Paul Steward (Country club).
Mrs. Joe Furnas (Country club) vs. Mrs. K. D. Stone (Country club).
Mrs. Harry Herman (Hyperion) vs. Claire Wunder (Waveland).

By Bert McGrane.

With Suzanne Ill, 18-year-old June graduate of St. Joseph's academy, entrenched as medalist, contenders for the undefended Des Moines women's golf championship finished their qualifying lap at Wakonda Monday and awaited today's first-round matches.

Miss Ill, who made her first championship flight appearance in city and state competition a year ago, fired a 93 over the soft slopes of the rugged tournament course to lead the qualifying field by a three-shot margin.

Behind the young Wakonda girl on the list of leaders was Mrs. R. L. Rockholz of the Country club, a former city champion who posted a 96 for second place, then withdrew from the tournament because of an impending trip, previously planned.

One of Four.

Mrs. Rockholz was one of four former city champions in the field, all of whom made the qualifying grade. Jean French of Waveland, winner of the title in 1935, brought in a 98 to earn a third-place tie with Mrs. Henry Nollen of Wakonda, who hasn't missed a berth in the top flight in at least 11 consecutive city tournaments.

Mrs. George Whitmer, Woodside's former city champion, clinched a place midway in the championship bracket with a 102 total and Mrs. K. D. Stone of the Country club, playing only her fifth round of golf this season, totaled 104 shots.

Favorites Fail.

Although most of the women favored to finish within the first 16 succeeded, the medal test produced its jolts. Mrs. J. W. Hubbell of Wakonda, Mrs. M. I. Lutz of Hyperion and Mrs. R. F. Johnson of the Country club, all championship flight qualifiers a year ago, were squeezed out of the top group. Pat Wiseman of Hyperion, a 1937 qualifier, also fell short of the requirements.

Mrs. Joe Furnas of the Country club, semifinalist in city and state tournaments last year, racked up a qualifying 99 for fifth place in Monday's test.

Although the course was slow, the scoring average was slightly lower than was expected. Scores of 107 were needed for places in the championship although Claire Wunder of Waveland, one of three who carded 108 totals, was included in the top flight by draw, with Mrs. Pearl Barker of Hyperion and Virginia Buchanan of Wakonda being drawn into the second flight.

Plays Mrs. Wilchinski.

Important matches loom at the very outset. Miss Ill, the medalist,

Women—
Continued on Page Nine.

WIREPHOTO © (AP)

BASEBALL'S IMMORTALS—At the baseball centennial celebration in Cooperstown, N. Y., were these members of the game's hall of fame. Left to right: back row—Honus Wagner, Grover Cleveland Alexander, Tris Speaker, Napoleon Lajoie, George Sisler and Walter Johnson; front row—Eddie Collins, Babe Ruth, Connie Mack and Cy Young. Ty Cobb, eleventh living member, arrived late because of a stomach ailment.

DeCora's Left Wins Thriller From Pfantz

By Bob Price.

Levi DeCora, a Winnebago Indian lightweight armed with a left hand as relentless as a taxi meter, jabbed his way to a clean cut decision over Lyle Pfantz Monday night in the feature bout of the Des Moines Athletic club's amateur boxing session at Riverview park. The fights were witnessed by 1,800 fans.

The DeCora-Pfantz battle, a three round rematch, was a thriller all the way. The Indian couldn't have done much more damage with a bow and arrows, for his left hand was a steady stroke of lightning and carried plenty of zip. It appeared that he won all three heats. Pfantz filled the air with plenty of gloves but his elusive opponent chose to stay away and bother him with his left.

Johnny Dudley Wins.

Johnny Dudley, John Miler's protege, had too much above the ears for Bobby Callahan, Shenandoah, and was awarded a decision. Dudley jabbed beautifully and avoided getting damaged by the Irish boy's wild pitches.

Johnny Cruickshank, Grimes, Ia., a fire-and-fall-back artist, whirled three rounds with Ozzie Lewis, Des Moines Negro, and dropped a decision. The Scot was willing but was off balance both before and after tossing punches and as a result received plenty of punishment.

Other Green Victors.

Bert Smallwood, Des Moines heavyweight, was an upset knockout victim. In the first round he galloped to the center of the

Fights—
Continued on Page Eight.

Club Standings

AMERICAN LEAGUE.

	W.	L.	Pct.	Games Behind
New York	37	9	.804	....
Boston	27	17	.614	9
Cleveland	27	21	.563	11
Chicago	25	21	.543	12
Detroit	24	25	.490	14½
Philadelphia	18	30	.375	20
Washington	18	31	.367	20½
St. Louis	13	35	.271	25

Monday's Results.
Open date.
Games Today.
Open date.

NATIONAL LEAGUE.

	W.	L.	Pct.	Games Behind
Cincinnati	32	17	.653	....
St. Louis	26	21	.553	5
Brooklyn	24	22	.522	6½
Chicago	25	24	.510	7
New York	25	25	.500	7½
Pittsburgh	23	26	.469	9
Boston	20	27	.426	11
Philadelphia	17	30	.362	14

Monday's Results.
Open date.
Games Today.
Open date.

Maxie Berger Wins From Red Guggino

NEW YORK, N. Y. (AP)—Maxie Berger, Montreal, Canada, and New York, holder of the Canadian welterweight title, outpointed Carl (Red) Guggino, Hartford, Conn., in an eight-round bout before a crowd of 8,000 Monday night. Berger weighed 140¼, Guggino, 134½.

In four round bouts Paul Duke, 196, St. Louis, Mo., stopped Eddie Cooper, 185, Brooklyn, N. Y., in 1:58 of the fourth, and Ettore Penn, 142, Brooklyn, outpointed Bob Perry, 146, Pittsburgh, Penn.

WIREPHOTO © (AP)

THE JUDGE BUYS A STAMP—As part of the centennial celebration, Judge Kenesaw Mountain Landis (right), the game's high commissioner, bought a commemorative stamp from Postmaster General James A. Farley at the Cooperstown, N. Y., postoffice Monday.

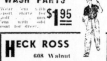

Gehrig Plays; 23,000 Watch Yankees Win

KANSAS CITY, MO. (AP)—The world champion New York Yankees defeated the little world champion Kansas City Blues Monday, 4 to 1, before 23,864 spectators.

Steve Sundra, one of the undefeated pitchers for the Yankees, held the Blues to six hits, one of them a fence-rattling triple by Clyde McCullough. The winners, their longest blow a three-bagger by Charles Keller, got nine hits off Joe Vance and Frank Makosky.

Lou Gehrig, ironman firstbaseman, returned to the Yankee lineup for the first time since May 2, when he benched himself and halted his marathon of playing in every game since 1925. Gehrig said he would leave the club here for a physical checkup at Rochester, Minn.

Joe DiMaggio went hitless in three trips to the plate, once driving a hard-hit ball to his brother, Vince, in centerfield.

Score by innings:		R.	H.	E.
New York (A)	100 010 200	4	9	1
Kansas City (AA)	001 000 000	1	6	2

Batteries: Sundra and Dickey, Rosar (4); Vance, Makosky (9) and McCullough.

BEATS WACKER

Tom Kenneally Outpoints Illinois Negro.

CHICAGO, ILL. (AP)—Tom Kenneally, 199, Chicago, outpointed Henry Wacker, 196, Taylorville, Ill., Negro, Monday night in the 10-round feature bout at Marigold gardens.

Tall Texan Gets His Reward

WIREPHOTO © (AP)

Byron Nelson (left) is shown as he received the national open championship trophy Monday from A. M. Reid (center), United States Golf association president. Craig Wood, runnerup, looks on.

Mrs. Hill's 84 Western Low In Downpour

(Scores on Page 8.)

ST. LOUIS, MO. (AP)—Mrs. Opal S. Hill, Kansas City, Mo., veteran tournament player, battled steadily through a drenching rain Monday to win medalist honors and become the favorite to take her third women's Western Open golf crown in five years.

The former Curtis cup player toured the difficult Westwood Country club course in 41-43—84, nine over par, for the qualifying round. The greens were transformed into virtual lakes during the first two hours of play.

Trailing only one stroke behind Mrs. Hill with 85's were Mrs. Helen Hicks Harb, Woodmere, N. Y., pro, and Ella Mae Williams of Chicago, one of the country's outstanding young amateurs.

Three other pre-tourney favorites were grouped at 87. They were Beatrice Barrett, Minneapolis, Minn., the defending champion; Helen Dettweiler, Washington, D. C., pro, and Alberta Neblett, New Orleans, Louisiana state champion.

The only other contenders to break 90 were Jeanne Cline, 15-year-old Bloomington, Ill., schoolgirl, 88; Shirley Ann Johnson, Chicago, 88; Goldie Bateson, Milwaukee, Wis., 88; Mrs. Bert Weil, Cincinnati, 89; Virginia Pepp, St. Louis pro, 89; and Mrs. Charles Harting, St. Louis, 89.

DRAFT GOPHER STAR.

WASHINGTON, D. C. (AP)—The Washington Redskins announced Monday they had drafted Wilbur Moore, University of Minnesota halfback.

HALL OF FAME MEMBERS AID IN CEREMONIES

Wagner's Nine 4-2 Winner.

Birthday Party

Collinses	AB.	R.	H.	O.	A.	E.
L. Waner (Pirates) cf	2	0	0	0	0	0
Thompson (Browns) cf	1	0	0	0	0	0
Herman (Cubs) 2b	4	0	0	0	0	0
Ott (Giants) lf	4	0	1	0	0	0
Greenberg (Tigers) 1b	2	1	1	9	2	0
Selkirk (Yankees) rf	2	0	0	0	0	0
T. Wright (Senators) rf	1	1	1	1	0	0
Jorgens (Yankees) c	3	0	1	4	0	0
Hack (Cubs) 3b	3	0	0	2	3	0
Travis (Senators) ss	1	0	0	0	1	0
Miller (Bees) ss	2	0	1	1	1	0
Dean (Cubs) p	0	0	0	1	2	0
Vander Meer (Reds) p	0	0	0	0	0	1
S. Johnson (Phillies) p	1	0	0	0	0	0
aShilling (Indians)	1	0	1	0	0	0
Totals	27	2	6	18	9	1
Wagners	**AB.**	**R.**	**H.**	**O.**	**A.**	**E.**
Moses (Athletics) rf	1	0	0	1	0	0
T. Moore (Cardinals) rf	1	0	0	0	0	0
Vaughan (Pirates) ss	2	1	1	3	3	1
Gehringer (Tigers) 2b	2	0	0	1	3	0
Medwick (Cardinals) lf	3	0	0	2	0	0
Berg (Red Sox) c	1	0	0	0	0	0
F. Hayes (Athletics) c	2	1	1	2	0	0
Ruel (Washington) c	0	0	0	1	0	0
Arnovich (Phillies) cf	3	0	1	2	0	0
J. Wilson (Reds) 1b	1	1	1	5	0	0
Lavagetto (Dodgers) 1b	1	0	0	2	1	0
Owen (Cardinals) 3b	1	1	1	1	1	0
Jurges (Giants) 3b	1	0	0	0	0	0
Grove (Red Sox) p	0	0	0	1	0	0
MacFayden (Bees) p	1	0	1	0	0	0
bRuth	1	0	0	0	0	0
Allen (Cleveland) p	0	0	0	0	0	0
Totals	21	4	6	21	8	1

aBatted for S. Johnson in seventh.
bBatted for MacFayden in fifth.

Score by innings:	
Collinses	000 002 0—2
Wagners	002 002 x—4

Summary—Errors, Vaughan, Vander Meer; runs batted in, Hayes, Arnovich, MacFayden, Owen, Jorgens, Hack; two base hits, Owen, MacFayden, Vaughan, Hayes, Miller; double plays, Vaughan to Gehringer to Lavagetto, Vander Meer to Jorgens to Greenberg to Jorgens; left on bases, Collinses 5, Wagners 3; bases on balls, off Vander Meer 2, Johnson 1, Allen 1; struck out, by Dean 2, MacFayden 1, Allen 2; hits, off Grove 1 in 2 innings, MacFayden 1 in 2, Allen 4 in 3, Vander Meer 3 in 1, Dean 0 in 2, Johnson 3 in 3. Umpires, Klem (NL), plate; Rommel (AL), bases. Time, 1:40.

—

By Eddie Brietz.

COOPERSTOWN, N. Y. (AP)—The first hundred years are always the hardest and Old Man Baseball took off on his second century Monday after being hailed and feted at the biggest birthday party tossed him during his 100-year rule as the No. 1 figure in American sport.

There were parades, dedications, speakings, a Babe Ruth "comeback," clam bakes, ball games and what-not for more than 11,000 people who poured into this pretty village where Abner Doubleday sat down on a hot day and invented the national pastime more than 100 years ago.

Plenty of Help.

Commissioner K. M. Landis, high priest of baseball, was there to lead the cheering. He received plenty of lusty rooting assists from a score of men whose names are found in almost every baseball bluebook ever published.

The baseball museum and hall of fame with its relics of glorious bygone days, was dedicated; so was Doubleday field, built on the actual spot where Doubleday's pioneers first trotted into action 100 years ago.

Eleven living members of the hall of fame renewed feuds and friendships and baseball as it was displayed in 1839, in the 1850's and in 1939—was reeled off by teams of schoolboys, soldiers and picked major leaguers, wearing the uniforms of the periods they represented.

"To All America."

Men who have helped make baseball history—Babe Ruth, Connie Mack, Hans Wagner, old Nap Lajoie and Walter Johnson, to name just a few—sat on the platform as Landis dedicated the hall of fame "to all America."

It was accepted by Ford C. Frick and William C. Harridge, presidents of the National and American leagues, and William C. Bramham, president of the National Association of Professional Baseball Clubs, representing the minors. John A. Heydler, former National league president, who conceived the idea of the baseball party, was a guest of honor and introduced Commissioner Landis.

Receive Bats.

Ten of the eleven living members of the hall of fame were presented with engraved bats, and a ruffle of drums and the sounding of taps answered the calling of the names of the 14 deceased members.

Ty Cobb, the old Georgia Peach of the Detroit Tigers, was delayed en route by illness and didn't arrive until after the ceremonies. But the other 10 were there from Connie Mack, the 76-year-old dean, down to Babe Ruth, the freshman of the lot.

In addition to Mack and Ruth were Honus Wagner, greatest shortstop of them all and still

Baseball—
Continued on Page Eight.

WIREPHOTO © (AP)

YOU WIN, HONUS—Honus Wagner (left) and Eddie Collins, a pair of baseball's greats, close up sides by that old familiar method at Cooperstown Monday for a game in connection with dedication of baseball's hall of fame. In addition to winning the first choice, Wagner also won the game, a seven-inning affair, 4 to 2.

2¢

DAILY NEWS

Copr. 1939 by News Syndicate Co., Inc. NEW YORK'S PICTURE NEWSPAPER Trade Mark Reg. U. S. Pat. Off.

BROOKLYN QUEENS★ LONG ISLAND

64

New York, Thursday, June 22, 1939

2 Cents IN CITY LIMITS | 3 CENTS Elsewhere

GEHRIG STRICKEN WITH INFANTILE PARALYSIS

Yanks Top Sox, 9-8; Giants Win

Stories Pages 54, 55

Audience

Lou Gehrig, the best first-baseman the Yankees ever had, tells his teammates (l. to r.) Gordon, Gomez, Dickey and Schulte, about his examination in Rochester, Minn., where his illness was diagnosed as chronic infantile paralysis.
other pic on page 1.
—Story on page 54;

(All NEWS fotos)

With the Boss

Lou, his 2130-consecutive game record now a part of baseball history, chins with Joe McCarthy after the statement of his illness was made to an unbelieving world of fans.

"To Sleep . . .

perchance to dream"—of Joe Louis. It's Tony Galento, living on borrowed time, at Summit, N. J., training camp.

British Open Golf Championship Play Begins

THE BALTIMORE NEWS-POST SPORTS
WEDNESDAY EVENING, JULY 5, 1939 21

Rodger H. Pippen
Sports Editor
Says:

As our Orioles of the diamond go from bad to worse, the supporters of the club are discussing the reasons for the poor brand of baseball being dished out at the Twenty-ninth street park.

RODGER H. PIPPEN

Is Manager Rogers Hornsby to blame? Or is it just a lousy ball club?

Some of the fans, as shown by letters to this paper, hold Hornsby responsible. They say, among other things, that—

Rogers keeps his pitchers in too long.

Rogers tries to do all the thinking for every man on the club.

Rogers antagonizes his players by his kindergarten rules about smoking in the clubhouse, etc.

Rogers destroys the initiative in his men with too many signs.

Rogers is too severe in his criticism and too sparing in his praise. A letter received this morning charges Hornsby with bawling out one of his infielders in public yesterday.

Rogers hasn't discovered that managing Class AA players is different from major league directing.

ANOTHER VIEW

Other baseball enthusiasts see the situation in an entirely different light.

These say that Hornsby is doing as well as could be expected with a bad club.

They point out that Baltimore is the only nine in organized baseball with three first basemen on the same infield, meaning Etten at first, Corbett at second and Jordan at third.

They call attention to the batting and fielding averages of the Orioles and also the fact that West, a catcher, is being used in the outfield. In conclusion, they add that figures don't lie, and the records show that the Birds really should be in the cellar.

IN NOSE DIVE

Such is the wide difference of opinion among the customers who take their sport seriously enough to get out pen and paper.

When Jack Ogden, general manager of the Orioles, announced the signing of Hornsby as leader, hearty approval was expressed in this column.

Rogers has been one of the greatest figures in baseball. In the majors he was a brilliant fielder and hitter and, in spots, a successful leader. In the language of the prizefight announcers, it appeared that Ogden had secured the best man obtainable.

When this season was two months old, Hornsby was doing a fine job with fair material. Today, with a club which looks much stronger on paper, the morale of the outfit is at its lowest ebb, the playing is pathetic and the whole situation is deplorable.

THE JUDGES

No attempt will be made to uphold or scold Hornsby. Let the customers be his judges.

I do want to be on record, however, as saying that—

Hornsby wasn't fair to the public when, for reasons best known to himself, he kept Jim Reninger on the mound yesterday until the contest became a farce. There was no excuse for that.

Hornsby, if he finds his "robot" methods are not turning the trick with the Orioles, should let his players go on their own for a while. There must be some good reason why Etten, Corbett, Lillard and so many other Orioles have been so far below their 1938 batting form.

ON PAPER

On paper, with Lillard at short, the Birds look stronger enough to finish fourth or fifth. Certainly, they are as good as Montreal, Toronto, Buffalo and Syracuse.

Red Wings, Jerseys In Close Race For Int. Loop Lead

By Associated Press.

In the kind of race they're having in the International League this season, you can't put much faith in the baseball tradition that the team that leads the pack through July 4 is bound to be the pennant-winner, but the Jersey Giants probably hope it's true.

The holiday bargain bills caught the Little Giants in the middle of a bitter battle with the Newark Bears and Rochester's second-place Red Wings in the midst of a comeback from the losing streak that cost them the lead a couple of weeks ago. The Jerseys got an even break, belting out a 5-1 victory in the second game after being blanked, 2-0, in the opener. The from Montreal, 3-2 anh 3-1. And, as a result, the Giants' lead was cut to a half game—too small for tradition or comfort.

BISONS SPLIT

The third-place Syracuse Chiefs also won a pair, whipping Baltimore's Orioles, 15- 9and 8-1, to increase their margin over Newark. Toronto and Buffalo split the other twin bill at night, the Bisons minning the first game, 4-2, and the last-place Maple Leafs the nightcap, 4-3.

Sparkling pitching performances marked the race for the lead. First it was Newark's George Washburn, who blanked eJrsey City's league leaders with three hits in a duel with Bill Harris. Then the veteran Rollie Stiles appeased 17,243 Jersey fans to some extent by giving the Bears only three blows and whiffing seven.

ROYALS LOSE TWO

Ken Raffensberger and Mike Ryba did the honors for Rochester, the former giving Montreal seven hits and the latter four, while the Red Wings collected 21 in all. Raffensberger's win was his eighth of the year.

At Buffalo it was Earl Cook, who has allowed only four runs in 21 innings since joining the Bisons, who held Toronto to four hits in the five twiligh tinnings he worked. He went out for a pinch hitter as the Bisons scored three runs in the fifth, then sewed up the decision with Joe Martin's thirteenth homer. Tom Drake also did some good flinging in the floodlight game, but poor support gave the Leafs four runs and the ball game before a man was retired in the first inning.

BABE RUTH VOICES CROWD'S FEELING

61,808 Honor Lou Gehrig

Gehrig Sobs As 61,808 Fans Honor Him

TOUCHED—Lou Gehrig is seen above overcome by his emotions, sobbing as he tried to speak to the 61,808 fans who piled into Yankee Stadium yesterday to honor him on Lou Gahrig Day. Lou was deeply moved as the multitude turned loose a demonstration unrivaled in baseball history to honor the "Iron Horse" of the game who piled up the diamond's greatest endurance record, 2,130 consecutive games, only to be forced off the field by infantile paralysis. International News Photo.

British Open Title Play Begins

ST. ANDREWS, Scotland July 5—(A. P.).—Max Faulkner, little-known English player, trimmed his game to a three-under-par 70 to lead the first group home in the opening round of the British open golf championship today, but Defending hampion Reggie Whitcombe gave the huge gallery the greatest show of his career.

ST. ANDREWS, Scotland, July 5 (I. N. S.).—Playing over a course dampened by rains yesterday and under conditions regarded as "fair," 129 golfers, including Lawson iLttle of Bretton Woods, N. H., and John Bulla of Chicago, started out today in pursuit of the British Open golf championship. A slight easterly wind blew in from the North Sea as the survivors of 36-hole qualifying play began teeing off.

Henry Cotton, the dour British professional, remained the outstanding favorite by virtue of his fine skill with every club and his long-standing experience on these links, but close behind him in the wagering were Jim Bruen, the Irish amateur, who set the qualifying pace with a pair of 69s for an aggregate of 138; Little, who tied Cotton for runner-up honors with 142; Percy Allis, another British professional, and Bulla, who were next on the qualifying list with 143s, and Reginald Whitcombe, the depending champion, next in line with a 144.

CHAMPIONSHIP PROPER

Play today opened the [illegible] ship proper over the gruelling 72-hole medal play route, [illegible] thing that has gone before thrown out along with more than 100 entrants who failed to qualify in the 36 holes played yesterday and Monday.

Little was the first of the two Americans to get away and, with his tremendous drives thrilling the gallery of Scotch experts trailing in his wake, he went to the turn in 37 one over par for the "old course," which will be the scene of all remaining competition.

PUTTING WEAK

Amateur champion of Great Britain and the United States, two years running, in 1934 and 1935, Little was on his game off the tees and approaching, but his putting continued weak today.

He played the first three holes in even par fours, then went one down to par on the fourth when he three-putted. On the sixth, he squared himself with par by sinking a 12-foot putt over a birdie three, but went down to par again on the short eighth, when he pushed his tee shot and required two to get on and two putts—one over regulation figures. He barely missed a birdie on the ninth, when he was on in two and tried gamely to hole out a six-foot putt. He took a par four, instead to start home with a 37 that was indicative of good bolf on his part.

Ice Coach Dies In Fall From Hotel

NEW YORK, July 5—(I. N. S.). Hockey players today mourned the death of Denton A. (Dinny) Mullin, thirty-nine, coach of many famous professional hockey players, who was killed in a fall or leap from a sixth floor window of a Broadway hotel.

British Open Golf Scores

ST. ANDREWS, Scotland, July 5—(A. P.). — Leading first-round scores in the British open golf championship:

Max Faulkner	70
Reggie Whitcombe	71
Len Crawley	72
Sidney Fairweather	73
Enrique Bertolino, Argentina	73
Henry Cotton	74
H. B. Rhodes	75
W. H. Green	75
F. G. Allott	75
J. H. Ballingall	73
Dan McBride	73
I. A. N. McPherson	75
Allan Dailey	75
Abe Mitchell	75
Charles Whitcombe	75

2,000 Wires Pour In To Dempsey

By EDDIE BRIETZ

NEW YORK, July 5—(A. P.).—Jack Dempsey has received nearly 2,000 wires from al' over the world since he became ill...What other sports figure—.Babe Ruth excepted—could tie that?...Don Budge, who was guaranteed $75,000 for 18 months as a pro, has passed the $55,000 mark...Lou Nova and family take off for the coast Sunday... One way to save dough: Don't bet the Giants and Yanks will renew broadcast rights next season... (Both are pretty well fed up...The bankers who own the Hippodrome will tear the joint down when the Twentieth Century moves out this month.

Lawson Little appears to be coming into his own as a medal play golfer...Another famous invalid who is doing all right, thank you, is Bill Klemm, the "old arbitrator". Billy Conn, who fights Melio Bettina in the Garden July 13, starts training in Joe Louis' old spot at Pompton Lakes this week...Remember the $800,000 Roosevelt Raseway?...It's now a two-bit parking lot.

TODAY'S GUEST STAR

Shirley Povich, Washington Post: "The suspicion is that the Nats can spot the Brooklyn Dodgers four brain concussions, a strong streak of inherent lunacy and a complete misunderstanding. of. right. and wrong and out-daffy 'em Brooklyn baseball is safe, sane and rank reactionary compared to the 1939 performances of the never-a-dull-moment Nats."

Lou Nova is picking up a few kopecks by making personal appearances with the Baer-Nova fight films in nearby small towns...He gets 25 bucks per appearance and averages three or four a day.

Two Attendance Marks Set

NEW YORK, July 5—(I. N. S.).—Two new major league attendance records were chalked up for the Fourth of July double-headers yesterday.

A total of 249,541 fans turned out for the games. The crowd of 61,808 for Lou Gehrig Day set a season's attendance record at Yankee Stadium. The 56,272 attendance at Detroit shattered all previous marks there.

The attendance figures:

AMERICAN LEAGUE	
New York	61,808
Detroit	56,272
Philadelphia	22,030
St. Louis	5,092

NATIONAL LEAGUE	
Pittsburgh	41,937
Chicago	26,409
Brooklyn	21,299
Boston	14,694

Leonard Has Formula For Trouncing Yanks

By PAT ROBINSON
International News Service Sports Writer

NEW YORK, July 5.—It is too bad for the sake of the so-called American League race that there aren't more Dutch Leonards around to pitch against the Yanks.

Dutch has a system all his own for taming the champions. He simply starts throwing a sinker around their knees at the start and keeps on throughing it there to the finish. By sticking to that system he has now beaten them three straight times, a record unmatched by any other pitcher.

He did his stuff yesterday before 61,000 cash customers who turned out to pay fitting tribute to Lou Gehrig, and he gave only six hits, including Selkirk's 13th homer, as the Senators won the opener, 3-2.

ONLY HAS ONE

Unfortunately for Bucky Harris, he had not other Leonard on tap and the Yanks walked off with the second tilt, 11-1. Sundra gave the Senators six hits and Selkirk contributed his 14th homer.

The Red Sox turned the Athletics' ball park into a shambles as they pounded out 35 hits, including seven homers, to win 17-7 and 18-12. Jim Tabor, rookie third baseman, blew himself to a homer in the first game and three more in the second.

His three homers—two of them with the bases loaded—were good for nine runs in the nightcap and tied a league mark set by Tony Lazzeri three years ago.

Buck Newsom turned in the best pitching performance of the holiday. He held the Indians to three hits as the Tigers took the first game, 4-0. Rain stopped the second contest after two innings.

MISS CHANCE TO GAIN

The White Sox took a pair from the Browns, 7-3 and 7-4. Johnny Rigney gave the Browns only four hits in the first one and Bejma's two homers helped beat the tail-enders in the second one.

The Cardinals, Giants, Cubs and Pirates all missed a fine chance to gain on the pace setting Reds but the Dodgers and Bees took advantage of their opportunities by winning doubleheaders.

The Bees ran their victory string to six straight by taking a pair from the Giants, 3-1 and 10-2. Danny MacFayden held the Giants to six hits in the opener and Milt Shoffner gave them only five in the nightcap. The Bees went on a rampage and scored eight runs in the eighth for Shoffner.

DODGERS MOVE UP

The Dodgers moved up on the heels of the Giants, Cards and Cubs by taking a pair from the Phils, 6-3 and 8-6.

The Reds outbattled the Pirates to win the first game, 7-4, but dropped the second, 4-3, as Mace Brown, making his first appearance as a starting pitcher this year, outpitched Johnny Vander Meer.

Three homers by Hank Leiber in successive times at bat failed to save the Cubs in their first game with the Cardinals. The Cubs got only six hits off the combined efforts of McGee and Cooper and the latter won his own game with a homer in the ninth to make the score, 6-4.

The Cubs won the second game, 3-2, in 10 innings although they made but four hits off the combined offerings of Paul Dean and Curt Davis. Gabby Hartnett's homer tied the score in the eighth and his understudy, Gus Mancusco, won it with a single in the tenth.

Riggs, Cooke In Semi-Finals At Wimbledon

WIMBLEDON, Eng., July 5—(I. N. S.).—Two American aces, Bobby Riggs of Chicago and Elwood Cooke of Portland, Ore., move on to Wimbledon's famous courts today in the next-to-the-last round of the annual tennis classic.

Riggs is expected to pull through his match with Ferenc Puncec, Yugoslavian entry.

The possibility of an all-American final also in the women's singles grew stronger when Alice Marble of California and Mrs. Sarah Palfrey Fabyan of Boston, moved into the semi-finals.

The California beauty swept past Jadwiga Jedrzejowska of Poland, 6—1, 6—4, and will meet Mme. Hilda Krahwinkel Sperling of Denmark on Thursday.

Mrs. Fabyan trounced Mme. Rene Mathieu of France, 6—4, 6—2, advancing to a match with England's Kay Stammers, who supplied one of the big upsets by eliminating Helen Jacobs.

Cunningham, Fenske Beaten By Rideout

LINCOLN, Neb., July 5—(I. N. S.).—Three major surprises, four new marks and eleven new champions were on the records for appraisal today following the Amateur Athletic Union's fifty-first senior track and field meet.

Some 200 athletes competed in the track carnival in Nebraska University's memorial stadium yesterday with scarcely a stellar name of American track missing from the field.

In the surprise category fell the defeat of Chuck Fenske and Glenn Cunningham by Blaine Rideout in the 1,500-meter run. Fred Wolcott's defeat by Joe Batiste in the 100-meter hurdles and Johnny Woodruff's loss to Erwin Miller in the 400-meter dash.

The 1,500-meter event was expected to develop a duel between Fenske, former Wisconsin star, and Cunningham, but instead Rideout, running in the colors of the Shore A. C., took the lead from John Munski of Missouri in the second lap and never was menaced from there to the finish. Fenske with a burst of speed drew close to Rideout near the tape, but Cunningham went way back to fourth place when he was passed near the close by Louis Zamperini, who came up fast.

GLENN CUNNINGHAM

2 Rams Accept Bids

PITTSBURGH, July 5—(A. P.).—Fordham's co-captains of 1938—Henry Jacunski, left end, and Michael A. Kochel, left guard—have accepted bids to play with the Eastern College All-Stars in New York September 7 against the New York Football Giants, Dr. John B. Sutherland, coach of the All-Stars, announced today.

'Iron Man' Is Overcome By Emotion

By SID FEDER

NEW YORK, July 5—(A. P.).—The husky figure climbed slowly up the old wooden stairs back of the Yankees' dugout, shoulders bent, right leg limping and throat torn by sobs.

This was Lo uGehrig leaving the most dramatic moment of his life. Back of him, 61,808 fans, piled on Yankee Stadium's tiered sides, cheered till the rafters shook, and out on the field a big, round-faced, flat-nosed fellow stood as tears rolled down his cheeks.

He was Babe Ruth, the one-and-only, who had just voiced for everyone who knows three strikes are out their feeling about Lou.

"C'MON, KID"

He had gone over, put one of those big arms around Gehrig's shoulders and patted Lou once or twice, trying to get him to stifle the emotion which had broken him up right out there on the ball field.

"C'mon, Kid," the Babe whispered through his tears. "C'mon, Kid, buck up now. We're all with you."

That was what everyone had been trying to say to Gehrig for an hour during all that ceremony which marked "Lou GFehrig Appreciation Day" at the Stadium yesterday. The fans had been trying to; so had his teammates—those of the current Yanks and those of the '27 World Champions—and so had the baseball writers. But there was no one who could—or should—have said it like the Bam.

OLD-TIMERS GATHER

All around them were players of the current club and those of the past generation of world beaters. They had gathered, these old-timers, from the four corners of the country to do honor to old Lou, the iron horse, who has been put back in the roundhouse by a little germ. "Beanballs" couldn't do it, nor broken bones, nor illness through the 14 years during which he chalked up sports' most amazing endurance record of 2,130 straight games in action. But this little "bug," a form of infantile paralysis, may have put a "period" on the hoss' playing career for keeps.

So the club, thanks to President Ed Barrow, put on the show for Lou yesterday before the biggest crowd of the year. And old timers unanimously agreed there has never been such a heartfelt scene on the diamond.

For Lou, a sentimental sort of fellow anyway, it was too much. Even before the speechmaking and presentations of gifts on the field, he was overcome in the clubhouse.

"There hasn't been a day since I came up that I wasn't anxious to get in uniform and out on the field," he said. "But today I wish I was anywehere but in this stadium."

VOICE BREAKS

Afterwards, on the field, he stood surrounded by gifts from the club, his teammates, the baseball writers, the Old Timers' Association of Denver, the Stadium employes and the New York Giants, and said a few words into the loud-speaker system. Several times his voice broke and a sob escaped as he announced, "Today I consider myself the luckiest man on the face of the earth."

He waved an arm at the old teammates, fellows like Ruth and Tony Lazzeri and Herb Pennock, Earl Combs, Wally Shang, Benny Bengough, Bob Shawkey, Bob Meusel, Mark Koenig, Joe Dugan, George Pipgras and the rest.

"Just look," he went on, "wouldn't you consider it a privilege to associatae yourself with such fine looking men as are standing on this ball field. Or with men like Col. Jacob Ruppert (late president of the club) or Miller Huggins (manager who died in the '20s)."

Then he stumbled, his eyes blinded by tears, back to the clubhouse. There, still the same shy retiring Gehrig, he turned to a friend and asked, "Did by speech sound silly- Did it?"

TEXAS LEAGUE

Houston, 4-2; Beaumont, 2-8.
Tulsa, 10-3; Oklahoma City, 1-1.
Fort Worth, 4-0; Dallas, 2-5.
Shreveport, 8-4; San Antonio, 2-6.

Yankees' Urge to Win Typified by DiMaggio's 'Home-Run' Single in Tenth

Slugger Swaps Another Bruise For Added Run

In Fletcher's Words, 'You Can't Lie Around, Resting,' Against Champions

By Arthur E. Patterson

CINCINNATI, Oct. 8.—The Yankees' great will to win, their daring in the face of possible injury, their urge to score more and more runs was never better exemplified than in the tenth inning today and later in the Yankee dressing room.

Joe DiMaggio singled to right, driving in the winning run, and when Ival Goodman fumbled the ball still another run went over the plate. But DiMaggio kept coming around the bases, to second on the Goodman error, to third on a throw to the plate and home when Lombardi lay outstretched, reaching for a ball he had dropped.

Fifteen minutes later, after the hilarious celebration of the fourth straight pennant, DiMaggio was lying on Doc Painter's table, sliding scars all over his thighs. The players call them "strawberries," but they aren't sweet. They're painful. But the knowledge that another slide would probably add another scrape didn't hold back DiMaggio—and there was still another bruise to be nursed tonight.

No Rest With Yankees Running

"That was one of the greatest slides I have ever seen in my life," shouted Art Fletcher after the game. "All I told Joe to do was watch the ball. You can't lie around, resting, when these Yanks are on the base paths. And let me tell you something else. No umpire ever made a greater decision than Babe Pinelli at the plate. It was on-the-spot stuff. DiMaggio slid over Lombardi's arm and then down to get the plate. Whoopee!"

Up on a truck, holding Joe McCarthy by the hair, Fletcher led the singing—first "East Side, West Side" then "The Beer Barrel Polka" and then a few hip-hip-hoorays thrown in for good measure.

"You can say for me," said Lou Gehrig, joining in the fun, "that I never saw a better finish. It was great—great—great."

Joe McCarthy, congratulated on all sides, had his hand shaken three times by Charlie Keller, the powerful rookie. On the third time he shouted:

"That's three handshakes, Charlie. What did you want me to do, kiss you?"

The manager praised the pitching of Paul Derringer and Bucky Walters.

"Any time you can beat two guys like that in the same World Series ball game you've done plenty. Walters didn't make a bad pitch all the way through the ninth."

Derringer Finds It Out, Too

Will Harridge, president of the league, pushed his way through the milling crowd to congratulate McCarthy for the fifth championship he has brought to the league. Warren Giles came in, too, and later Derringer.

"I gave them my best," said the pitcher; "we'll have another go at you fellows next year." Earlier, over in the Reds' clubhouse, he had said, "You make one mistake against them and—boom. You'd think that once they'd pop up on a bad pitch."

Lefty Gomez, who wouldn't stay in his hotel bed, but came out and listened to the game on the clubhouse radio, was beaming:

"Boy, and you think Germany took Poland in a hurry."

Your correspondent, who had given a 3-to-1 feed-box special on the Reds before the series, was chased the length of the clubhouse by the soap-laden Earle Combs. Earle fortunately isn't as fast as he used to be.

Dickey hit a fast ball for his homer, Keller a curve. Keller was complaining:

"What's the use. I hit a homer and Bill comes right along and shows me up by hitting one fifty feet further."

No Talk of Errors

The Reds were desolate. Harry Craft, removed from the game, was tightly bound in tape. He had hurt his side ten days before the close of the season and just to make matters worse added an upset stomach today. Derringer, even though out of the game, lingered until the blow-up in the tenth. Then he gave up and dressed wearily. Bucky Walters was almost in tears. He had some post-season exhibition games arranged, but gave them up in disgust.

The Reds didn't talk about Billy Myers's errors.

"We never talk about those things. I can't explain the last two innings," said McKechnie. "How can you explain, for instance, Frey almost handing the ball to Myers instead of tossing it as he has all season. Lombardi, just one of those things."

He threw up his hands in disgust. "The Yankees aren't that good," he added.

He went around the room shaking hands with each player, thanking them for their season's play, advising them on winter activities.

Simmons Ready for More

Al Simmons, inserted late and almost a hero, said he had changed his mind about not playing next year.

"The old boy can still hit 'em in the pinch. Why, in that tenth I almost had another. Keller had been playing me nearer the right-field line, but even when I hit one right on the nose, there he was."

To Frank McCormick, who played a whale of a game throughout the series, McKechnie said:

"Boy, I sure feel sorry for you. You almost had 'em."

It was Frank who made the last hit in the promising last half of the tenth.

Some one asked McKechnie about his 1940 plans. "Well, I'm not going to say anything like Hartnett did, if that's what you mean. I'm going to make two changes if I can get the man I want. That's all."

This may have been a source for relief for some of the jittery Reds, but they weren't very interested about 1940.

What they had on their minds, mostly, they kept saying over and over again;

"How did DiMaggio get around those bases." As a matter of fact, some of the Yankees are wondering about that, too."

Heavy Hitters Who Led Yankees to World Championship

Left to right, Joe DiMaggio, Bill Dickey and Charlie Keller, the siege guns of the Yankees in the last two games played in Cincinnati. All three hit homers on Saturday, Keller getting two. Yesterday Keller and Dickey hit homers off Paul Derringer and DiMaggio drove in the winning run and scored the last run himself on Red errors

Associated Press

Yankees Need Only 3 Victims In Series Play

(Continued from page seventeen)

packed his trunk last night. He has seen a bit more of the Yankees than his fellow Reds.

Hughie Critz and Mordecai Brown joined the throng of oldtimers last night. Critz saw his first major league play since leaving the Giants. "I've been reading a lot about the Yankees, but could not believe it was all true until I saw them." he remarked.

Watching the Yankees' home-run barrage during practice—they hit about twenty over the barriers and numerous other shots against them, Leo Durocher praised Paul Schreiber, the machine-like practice pitcher. "He deserves a great deal of credit for the Yankee hitting. They get more batting against him and go back to the plate feeling strong and powerful and ready for the day's job. I wish the Dodgers had one like him."

Superstitious, Oral Hildebrand refused to pose for his picture with Paul Derringer before the game. . . . The Reds watched the Yankee pre-game hitting with open-mouthed awe, but the first real swat in the ball game was McCormick's terrific shot to the center field wall, needing only four feet more to be a homer. . . . It was the Reds' first extra-base hit of the series. . . . Nothing came of it but bitter disappointment for the Ohio optimists. . . . Ruffing's arm was still stiff, he revealed before game time, so the Yankees were anxious to make it four straight.

Yankees Due This Morning

The victorious New York Yankee Baseball Club will arrive at Grand Central Terminal this morning about 9:45 in their special twelve-car train, the New York Central Railroad announced last night. Returning with the team is Mayor LaGuardia.

Registration begins today. The hours are from 5 p.m. to 10:30 p.m. daily through Friday and from 7 a.m. to 10:30 p.m. on Saturday.

Kammer and Cashel's 142 Wins Best-Ball Prize at Crestmont

Former Repeats in Guest, Member Golf; Also Takes Honors for Individuals

WEST ORANGE, N. J., Oct. 8.—Using his own ball exclusively in both rounds, A. Fred Kammer jr., of Rock Spring, former Princeton golf and hockey star, scored a clean sweep in the Crestmont Golf Club's third annual member-guest invitation tournament today for the second time in as many years.

Kammer added a sparkling 70, two under par, today to his first-round 72 and won the best-ball competition by one stroke with 142 and the individual race by six strokes. It was a remarkable single-handed achievement, considering the field was one of the strongest ever assembled in a Jersey amateur tournament.

Kammer's partner in the best-ball play was Walter Cashel. The latter found it impossible to improve on Kammer's superb brand of golf. Kammer won last year's tourney with Inspector John Brady, of Newark, getting only one-stroke assistance.

Two pairs tied for second place a stroke behind the winners. One was composed of Dick Chapman, of Greenwich, French champion and New York amateur king, and Tom Breslin, of the host club, with rounds of 73 and 70. The other was made up of Stephen Berrien, of Upper Montclair, and William Hockenjos jr., husband of the New Jersey women's champion, with 71 and 72. They were second at the halfway mark yesterday.

Willie Turnesa, 1938 national amateur champion from Briar Hills, and Ernest Minier, of Crestmont, finished seventh, four strokes behind the victors.

Kammer's Golf Spectacular

Kammer's round was unusual. Playing the back nine first, Kammer reached the turn in 38 after three-putting the eleventh and thirteenth greens. He then churned out some of the most spectacular golf of his career, scoring four birdies on the back nine for a 32. Kammer holed out a 50-yard approach shot for a birdie 4 on the first hole and canned long putts for birdies on the fifth, eighth and ninth holes.

Stuart Places Second

Mark Stuart, of Winged Foot, former Metropolitan amateur title-holder, was second in the individual event with 148, followed by Pat Mucci, of the home club, with 149. The latter beat his closest Crestmont competitor by twelve strokes.

The summaries:

(First name guest, last name member from Crestmont.)

A. F. Kammer jr., Rock Spring, and Walter Cashel	72—70—142
R. D. Chapman, Greenwich, and Tom Breslin	73—70—143
S. Berrien, Upper Montclair, and Wm. Hockenjos jr.	71—72—143
Peter Gruntal, Sunningdale, and Pat Mucci	72—72—144
Mike Cestone, Branch Brook, and James O'Connor	73—71—144
Foy W. Porter, Rock Spring, and Euene Krautter	77—68—145
Willie Turnesa, Briar Hills, and Ernest Minier	72—74—146
R. Peeney, Hopewell Valley, and Frank Courtney	74—73—147
Mark J. Stuart, Winged Foot, and Harvey Ragan	70—77—147
W. Y. Dear jr., Essex County, and William Butler	76—71—147
W. Manion, Branch Brook, and William Holmes	73—74—147
Martin Issler, Rock Spring, and George McDonough	78—70—148
Don Morano, Forest Hill, and John Quinn 1st	73—75—148
E. W. Holmberg, Forest Hill, and Jerry DeRosa	74—74—148
C. Whitehead, Plainfield, and John Poppele	74—74—148
George Voigt, Winged Foot, and Dr. John Lee	74—76—150
Philip Axt, Forest Hill, and John Hanley	77—73—150
Harold Brown, Baltusrol, and John Lindquist	76—75—151
George Currey, Essex Fells, and William Gotelli	74—77—151
Lloyd G. Beatty, Glen Ridge, and William Manion	75—76—151
John Burke, Green Meadow, and James Miller	77—76—153
William Breslin, Ridgewood, and Stanley Mason	75—78—153
John Cunniff, Branch Brook, and Robert West	78—75—153
Joseph P. Murphy, Forsgate, and Tim O'Brien	75—78—153

Leading Individual Scores

A. Fred Kammer jr., Rock Spring	72—70—142
Mark J. Stuart, Winged Foot	71—77—148
Pat Mucci, Crestmont	74—75—149
Mike Cestone, Brank Brook	76—75—151
Willie Turnesa, Briar Hills	74—77—151
Ray Peeney, Hopewell Valley	76—76—152

Baseball Writers Elect Sid Mercer as President

CINCINNATI, Oct. 8 (AP).—Sid Mercer, veteran "New York Journal-American" writer, was elected president of the Baseball Writers' Association of America at the organization's annual World Series meeting last night.

Tom Swope, "Cincinnati Post," was named vice-president, and Ken Smith, of "The New York Daily Mirror," secretary-treasurer.

Elected to the board of governors were: Ed Burns, "Chicago Tribune"; Al Horwits, "Philadelphia Ledger"; Shirley Povich, "Washington Post," and Jim Gould, "St. Louis Post-Dispatch."

The association voted a $200 gift to Henry P. Edwards, retiring secretary-treasurer.

Composite Score of 4 Games

CINCINNATI, Oct. 8 (AP).—The composite box score of the four games of the 1939 World Series between the New York Yankees and Cincinnati Reds:

New York Yankees

Player	G	AB	R	H	2B	3B	HR	RBI	BB	SO	PCT.	PO	A	E	PCT.
Crosetti, ss	4	16	2	1	0	0	0	1	2	2	.063	6	14	0	1.000
Rolfe, 3b	4	16	2	2	0	0	0	0	0	0	.125	3	8	1	.917
Keller, rf	4	16	8	7	1	1	3	6	1	2	.438	6	0	0	1.000
DiMaggio, cf	4	16	3	5	0	0	1	3	1	1	.313	11	0	0	1.000
Dickey, c	4	15	2	4	0	0	2	5	1	2	.267	27	2	0	1.000
Selkirk, lf	4	12	0	2	1	0	0	0	3	2	.167	9	0	0	1.000
Gordon, 2b	4	14	1	2	0	0	0	1	0	2	.143	7	12	0	1.000
Dahlgren, 1b	4	14	2	3	2	0	1	2	0	4	.214	41	2	0	1.000
Ruffing, p	1	3	0	1	0	0	0	0	0	1	.333	0	3	0	1.000
Pearson, p	1	2	0	0	0	0	0	0	0	1	.000	0	5	0	1.000
Gomez, p	1	1	0	0	0	0	0	0	0	1	.000	0	0	0	.000
Hadley, p	1	3	0	0	0	0	0	0	0	0	.000	1	1	1	.667
Hildebrand, p	1	1	0	0	0	0	0	0	0	1	.000	0	0	0	.000
Sundra, p	1	0	0	0	0	0	0	0	1	0	.000	0	0	0	.000
Murphy, p	1	2	0	0	0	0	0	0	0	1	.000	0	3	0	1.000
Totals	4	131	20	27	4	1	7	18	9	20	.206	111	50	2	.988

Cincinnati Reds

Player	G	AB	R	H	2B	3B	HR	RBI	BB	SO	PCT.	PO	A	E	PCT.
Werber, 3b	4	16	1	4	0	0	0	2	2	0	.250	3	5	0	1.000
Frey, 2b	4	17	0	0	0	0	0	0	1	4	.000	8	10	0	1.000
Goodman, rf	4	15	3	5	1	0	0	1	1	2	.333	10	1	1	.917
McCormick, 1b	4	15	1	6	1	0	0	1	0	1	.400	32	2	0	1.000
Lombardi, c	4	14	0	3	0	0	0	2	0	1	.214	22	1	1	.958
§Hershberger, c	3	2	0	1	0	0	0	1	0	0	.500	1	0	0	1.000
Craft, cf	4	11	0	1	0	0	0	0	0	6	.091	7	1	0	1.000
Simmons, lf	1	4	1	1	1	0	0	0	0	0	.250	3	0	0	1.000
Berger, lf-cf	4	15	0	0	0	0	0	1	0	4	.000	8	0	0	1.000
Myers, ss	4	12	2	4	0	1	0	0	2	3	.333	10	9	2	.905
Derringer, p	2	5	0	1	0	0	0	0	0	0	.200	2	0	0	1.000
Walters, p	2	3	0	0	0	0	0	0	0	0	.000	0	3	0	1.000
Thompson, p	1	1	0	1	0	0	0	0	0	0	1.000	0	0	0	.000
Grissom, p	1	0	0	0	0	0	0	0	0	0	.000	0	0	0	.000
Moore, p	1	1	0	0	0	0	0	0	0	0	.000	0	2	0	1.000
*Bordagaray	2	0	0	0	0	0	0	0	0	0	.000	0	0	0	.000
†Gamble	1	1	0	0	0	0	0	0	0	1	.000	0	0	0	.000
‡Bongiovanni	1	1	0	0	0	0	0	0	0	0	.000	0	0	0	.000
Totals	4	133	8	27	3	1	0	8	6	22	.203	106	34	4	.970

*Ran for Lombardi in eighth inning, second game, and for Lombardi in seventh inning, third game.
†Batted for Walters in ninth inning, second game.
‡Batted for Grissom in sixth inning, third game.
§Batted for Derringer in seventh inning, fourth game.

PITCHING RECORDS

New York

	G	CG	IP	H	R	ER	BB	SO	WP	HB	W	L	PCT.	ERA
Ruffing	1	1	9	4	1	1	1	4	0	0	1	0	1.000	1.00
Pearson	1	1	9	2	0	0	1	8	0	0	1	0	1.000	0.00
Hadley	1	0	8	7	2	2	3	2	0	1	1	0	1.000	2.25
Murphy	1	0	3⅓	5	1	1	0	2	0	0	1	0	1.000	2.70
Gomez	1	0	1	3	1	1	0	1	0	0	0	0	.000	9.00
Hildebrand	1	0	4	2	0	0	0	3	0	0	0	0	.000	0.00
Sundra	1	0	2⅔	4	3	0	1	2	0	0	0	0	.000	0.00

Cincinnati

	G	CG	IP	H	R	ER	BB	SO	WP	HB	W	L	PCT.	ERA
Derringer	2	1	15⅓	9	4	4	3	9	0	0	0	1	.000	2.40
Thompson	1	0	4⅔	5	7	7	4	3	1	0	0	1	.000	12.60
Walters	2	1	11	13	9	6	1	6	0	0	0	2	.000	4.91
Grissom	1	0	1⅓	0	0	0	1	0	0	0	0	0	.000	0.00
Moore	1	0	3	0	0	0	0	2	0	0	0	0	.000	0.00

COMPOSITE SCORE BY INNINGS

Cincinnati	1 2 0	1 0 0	3 1 0	0—8
New York	2 0 5	1 4 0	2 0 3	3—20

Earned runs—Cincinnati, 5; New York, 17. Stolen base—Goodman. Sacrifices—Pearson, Thompson, Rolfe, McCormick. Hit batsman—By Hadley (Lombardi). Double plays—Cincinnati, 1 (Walters, Myers and McCormick); New York, 5 (Rolfe, Gordon and Dahlgren, 2; Ruffing, Crosetti, Gordon and Dahlgren; Gordon, Crosetti and Dahlgren; Dickey and Crosetti). Left on bases—Cincinnati, 23; New York, 16. Umpires—Reardon and Pinelli (N. L.), Summers and McGowan (A. L.). Times of games—1:33, 1:27, 2:01, 2:04.

DOWN IN FRONT

By RICHARDS VIDMER

Brown Bombers of Baseball

CINCINNATI, Oct. 8.—"Break up the Yankees—they're ruining the game.

That's all that is left of the baseball season and the World Series—the annual echo which comes plaintively from the suppressed, the beaten and the persecuted. And now that the Yankees have won their fourth straight American League pennant and their fourth successive world's championship, the winter wail is certain to be longer and louder than ever.

The pitiful plea to break up the almighty Yankees is based, of course, on the premise that their swaggering superiority over all other clubs, both in their own league and the rival circuit, is ruining the national game. But it falls on deaf ears and is met simply with a smile of satisfaction.

Richards Vidmer

Those who sit in control of the Yankees have no intention of breaking up their amazing ball club. They are proud of the record which others denounce. They intend to prolong it indefinitely if money and brains will accomplish that end. Instead of breaking up the Yankees, their only thought is to improve them, though goodness knows how they could be any better and still be human.

It is a strange experience to talk baseball with any of the Yankee officials. You might imagine that in the midst of the series they would be discussing the games and singing the praises of the players. You might imagine that it would be difficult to get their conversation off the subject of Killer Keller, who hit three home runs and became just about the outstanding hero of the stampede that wrecked the Reds. Or the amazing exploits of Frank Crosetti and Joe Gordon in the field. Or Joe Di Maggio's daring base running exploits. Or the steady strength of almost the entire pitching staff.

But even in the midst of all the wonders that were being worked by the current crop of Yankees, their favorite topic was the sensational ability of the boys in the bushes—the youngsters who are headed for the biggest show in baseball though how they are going to make room for even one of them is impossible to imagine unless John Heydler's plan to play ten-man teams is adopted.

Buds in Bloom

STILL they will tell you about a first baseman named Chartak, who can hit and field and think. He broke a leg early last season, it seems, and needs one more full year in the minors. Then he will be ready to take his place with the greatest team in baseball. But they don't explain how it is possible for anybody to take the place of Babe Dahlgren, who has been playing first base this season.

And they will tell you about a shortstop named Priddy, who is just about the classiest human that ever handled a ball and who can hit with the leaders already. It seems that he is only twenty years old, however, and is staying another year in the minors at his own request, feeling that he needs just a little more experience. But what in the world can the Yankees do with a second baseman they already have, Joe Gordon, who is a fielding fiend and a home-run hitting demon?

"Well, Gordon is even a better shortstop than he is a second baseman," they smile and say.

That, of course, is ridiculous. He might be just as good a shortstop, but it is impossible to improve on what amounts to perfection. And, besides, suppose Gordon were shifted to short. What would happen to Frank Crosetti? How could any one take his place and how could even Gordon do anything that Frankie can't do?

If you ask them they will say that there is no intention of moving Gordon to shortstop, because they have one hell of a shortstop coming along in Rizzutto, another star hiding behind a minor league cloud at present. And so it goes right down the line—with a thriller-diller in every position already, the Yankees look into the future with dreamy eyes as they think of the players they have on the rise.

To the Victors

BREAK up the Yankees? Those who raise their voices to utter the annual echo of each baseball season are wasting their breath on the winter air. There isn't a chance of anybody breaking up the Yankees. In fact every effort is being bent to make them grow better and better.

The plea that the Yankees' staggering supremacy is ruining the game also has a hollow sound and is wasted on the frosty air. It is as foolish as the claim would be that Joe Louis's terrific punch is ruining the business of boxing, when every one is well aware that the greatness of the Brown Bomber lifted the pugilistic profession from a depression from which there seemed no emerging.

The greater the Yankees become, the more marked their ability to batter and beat any other ball club, the greater attraction they are. The crowds pour in to see Louis fight, even though his opponent is of practically no importance. The lure is not necessarily the prospect of a close struggle, but the assurance of seeing a champion in action who has demonstrated his right to the title.

So the crowds come to see the Yankees play, even if they are opposed by a second division club that has no chance as challengers. They come to see the closest thing to perfection that a baseball club ever has produced; a club that has no weakness and has been winning longer than any other club in the long history of the game.

Seats of the Mighty

THEY lose a game here and there in the course of the season, but so does Joe Louis drop a round now and then. But in the end both the Brown Bomber of boxing and the Brown Bombers of baseball land in same place—on top. And the more victories they put together, and the more definitely they establish their supremacy in their sphere of sports, the greater is the desire to see them in action.

So here are the Yankees as they stand today after beating the Reds in four straight games: a team that has won four American League pennants in a row; a team that has won four successive World Series, the last two without the loss of a single game; a team that won the pennant this year by a margin of seventeen games over their nearest American League rivals and has won sixteen out of nineteen World Series games from the National League champions, whoever they happened to be, in the last four series.

Break up the Yankees? Don't be silly. More power to 'em, I say.

Scots-Americans Win, 2-1

Special to the Herald Tribune

BALTIMORE, Oct. 8.—The Scots-Americans defeated the Baltimore S. C., in an American Soccer League championship fixture at Bugle Field today, 2 to 1. At halftime the two teams were deadlocked, 1 to 1. Peters and R. Brown shot a goal apiece for the Scots, while Schwanke was credited with the only tally for Baltimore.

Financial Returns of 36 World Series

The following table shows the financial end of the big series, with the winning and losing players' shares, since 1903:

Year	Game	Attendance	Largest Single Day	Receipts	Winning Players' Share	Losing Players' Share
1903	8	100,429	18,801	$50,000	Red Sox....$1,182	Pirates $1,316
1905	5	91,723	24,992	68,435	Giants 1,142	Athletics .. 832
1906	6	99,845	23,257	106,550	White Sox.. 1,874	Cubs 439
*1907	5	78,068	24,377	101,728	Cubs 2,142	Tigers 1,945
1908	5	63,232	17,760	94,975	Cubs 1,317	Tigers 870
1909	7	145,295	30,915	188,302	Pirates 1,825	Tigers 1,274
1910	5	124,222	27,371	173,930	Athletics .. 2,062	Cubs 1,375
1911	6	179,851	38,281	342,364	Athletics .. 3,564	Giants 2,436
†1912	8	252,037	36,502	490,883	Red Sox.... 4,022	Giants 2,566
1913	5	151,000	36,896	325,080	Athletics .. 3,246	Giants 2,164
1914	4	111,000	35,520	225,739	Braves 2,812	Athletics .. 2,031
1915	5	143,351	42,300	320,361	Red Sox.... 3,780	Phillies 2,520
1916	5	162,859	42,620	385,590	Red Sox.... 3,910	Robins 2,834
1917	6	186,654	33,969	425,878	White Sox. 3,669	Giants 2,442
1918	6	128,483	27,054	179,619	Red Sox.... 1,102	Cubs 671
1919	8	236,928	34,379	722,414	Reds 5,225	White Sox.. 3,254
1920	7	178,737	27,525	564,800	Indians 4,204	Robins 2,387
1921	8	269,976	36,509	900,233	Giants 5,265	Yankees ... 3,510
‡1922	5	185,947	38,551	§606,475	Giants 4,470	Yankees ... 3,225
1923	6	301,430	62,817	1,063,815	Yankees ... 6,160	Giants 4,112
1924	7	283,695	49,243	1,093,104	Senators ... 5,730	Giants 3,820
1925	7	283,830	43,810	1,182,854	Pirates 5,322	Senators .. 3,734
1926	7	328,051	63,600	1,207,864	Cardinals .. 5,584	Yankees ... 3,417
1927	4	201,105	60,695	783,217	Yankees ... 5,782	Pirates 3,985
1928	4	199,072	61,425	777,290	Yankees ... 5,813	Cardinals .. 4,181
1929	5	190,490	50,740	859,494	Athletics .. 6,003	Cubs 4,002
1930	6	212,619	39,946	953,772	Athletics .. 5,038	Cardinals .. 3,536
1931	7	231,587	39,401	1,030,723	Cardinals .. 4,484	Athletics .. 2,989
1932	4	191,988	50,709	713,377	Yankees ... 5,010	Cubs 4,244
1933	5	164,076	46,076	679,365	Giants 4,599	Senators .. 3,321
1934	7	281,510	44,451	1,031,341	Cardinals .. 5,941	Tigers 4,313
1935	6	286,672	49,350	1,073,794	Tigers 6,544	Cubs 4,198
1936	6	302,924	66,669	1,204,399	Yankees ... 6,430	Giants 4,655
1937	5	238,142	60,573	985,994	Yankees ... 6,471	Giants 4,490
1938	4	200,833	59,817	851,166	Yankees.... 5,782	Cubs 4,675
1939	4	183,849	59,791	745,329	Yankees.... 5,614	Reds...... 4,282

The underscored are the records.
*First game tie, 3—3, 12 innings. †Second game tie, 6—6, 11 innings.
‡Second game tie, 3—3, 10 innings.
§$120,551, the receipts of the second game, was given to charity.

Cubs Lose, 8-5, To White Sox In 10 Innings

Victors Tie Score in 8th After Three-Run Deficit, Forcing Sixth Contest

CHICAGO, Oct. 8 (AP).—The Chicago White Sox spotted the Cubs five runs and then defeated the National League club today, 8 to 5, in ten innings, prolonging their city championship series for at least one more game. The Cubs now have won three games and the White Sox two.

A crowd of 17,227 saw the Cubs take what appeared to be a comfortable five-run lead in the first five innings, but the White Sox came on fast late in the game, knocking the starting pitcher, Claude Passeau, out of the box and hammering Bill Lee for the winning runs.

The Sox began whittling into their rivals' lead in the sixth inning. Mike Kreevich hit a home run into the right-field stands after Joe Kuhel had reached first on Bobby Mattick's error. At this point the Cubs led, 5 to 2.

In the eighth Ollie Bejma walked and Kuhel doubled. Lee replaced Passeau on the mound and walked Kreevich, filling the bases. Bejma scored on an infield out, Eric McNair scored Kuhel with a single to right and Luke Appling scored on Larry Rosenthal's single, tying the score.

The Cubs went out in order in the eighth and ninth. In the tenth inning after two were out Gerald Walker walked and stole second and Rosenthal was purposely walked. Then Norman Schlueter crossed the Cub master minds by doubling to right center, scoring both runners. A minute later Schlueter went to third on a passed ball and scored when Lee missed a return throw from Gus Mancuso, catcher.

The two teams return to the White Sox Park for a night game Monday, with the Cubs needing one victory or the Sox two for the title.

The score:

WHITE SOX	ab	r	h	po	a	CUBS	ab	r	h	po	a
Bejma, 2b	4	1	1	3	2	Hack, 3b	5	2	2	0	0
Kuhel, 1b	5	2	2	7	0	Herman, 2b	4	0	2	0	3
Kreev'h, cf	4	1	1	6	0	Galan, lf	4	1	1	4	0
Appling, ss	5	1	1	2	2	Leiber, cf	5	0	1	3	0
McNair, 3b	5	0	1	3	3	Nichol'n, rf	4	0	1	3	0
Walker, lf	4	1	0	2	0	G. Rus'l, 1b	5	1	2	6	0
Rosen'l, rf	4	1	1	2	0	Mattick, ss	5	0	0	1	4
Tresh, c	2	0	0	4	1	Mancuso, c	4	1	2	11	0
†Marcum	1	0	0	0	0	Passeau, p	2	0	0	2	0
Schlue'r, c	1	1	1	1	0	Lee, p	1	0	0	0	1
Rigney, p	1	0	0	0	1						
*Radcliff	1	0	0	0	0						
Dietrich, p	3	0	0	0	2						
Totals	40	8	8	30	11	Totals	39	5	11	30	8

*Batted for Rigney in fifth inning.
†Batted for Tresh in eighth inning.

White Sox	000	002	030	3—8
Cubs	111	200	000	0—5

Errors—Mattick, Rosenthal Dietrich, Lee, Hack. Runs batted in—Galan (2), Mancuso, Hack, Herman, Kreevich (2), Appling, McNair, Rosenthal, Schlueter (2). Two-base hits—Herman, Kuhel, Schlueter. Home runs—Galan, Kreevich. Stolen bases—Herman, G. Russell, Walker. Sacrifices—Galan, Passeau. Left on bases—White Sox, 7; Cubs, 9. Bases on balls—Off Dietrich, 3; off Passeau, 2; off Lee, 3. Struck out—By Rigney, 2; by Dietrich, 3; by Passeau, 5; by Lee, 3. Hits—Off Rigney, 9 in 4 innings; off Dietrich, 2 in 6; off Passeau, 5 in 7; off Lee, 4 in 3. Wild pitch—Rigney. Passed balls—Tresh, Mancuso. Winning pitcher — Dietrich. Losing pitcher — Lee. Umpires—Basil, Ballanfant, Rue and Goetz. Time—2:26. Attendance—17,227.

Soccer Results

American League

Brookhattan, 2; St. Mary's Celtic, 2.
Hispano, 1; N. Y. Americans, 1.
Paterson, 4; Philadelphia Germans, 8.
Scots-Americans 2; Baltimore S. C., 1.
Irish-Americans - Baltimore Americans, postponed.
Passon-Allentown, canceled.

National League

Flatbush Wanderers, 2; Norwegian-Americans, 2.
Danish, 1; Galicia, 1.
Hatikvoh, 2; Gjoa, 0.

Metropolitan League

Red Wings, 2; Gibraltar, 3.
Segura, 7; Hatikvoh B, 1.
Celtic Circle Sport Club, 1; Cork Celtics, 1.
Armenians, 1; Building Service, 0.
Hanscom, 4; Long Island Celtics, 0.
Shell, 7; Fords United, 0.
Fort Washington, 2; Shamrock Rovers, 2.
N. Y. Hungarians, 6; Scandinavian Workers, 1.
Bronx Hungarians, Guliana, 0.
Gjoa C, 1; French, 0.
Prague C, 3; Cork Celtics B, 1.
D. Cigarettes, 3; Swedish B, 2.
Favorites, 2; Prague B, 1.
Danish B, 1; Gjoa, 1.

Metropolitan Junior League

Yorkville Juniors, 8; N. Y. Americans, 1.
Bay Ridge Hearts, 2; Swedish Juniors, 1.
Hatikvoh Juniors, 1; Gjoa Juniors, 0.

Empire State Junior League

Swedish B, 4; Danish, 0.
N. Y. Americans, 2; Norwegian-Americans, 2.
Bay Ridge Hearts B, 1; Gjoa B, 0.
Bay Ridge Hearts A, 2; Swedish A, 1.
Hatikvoh, 1; Gjoa A, 0.

Exhibition

Prague, 2; Newark Portuguese, 1.

Manhattan League

Bronx Rangers, 3; Sparta, 0.

German-American League

German-Hungarians, 6; Brooklyn Germans, 2.
Pfalzer, 10; South Germans, 0.
Eintracht, 7; Koltzman, 3.
Hoboken, 1; German-American A. C., 1.
N. Y. Germans, 1; Ridgewood, 0.
Swiss, 3; Queens, 2.
Schwaben, 5; Nassau, 1.
Minerva, 2; Hota, 4.
Newark Germans, 3; German Oaks, 1.
Elizabeth, 6; Passaic, 2.
New Brunswick, 1; Liberty Newark, 8.
Yonkers, 1; Olympic Newark, 2.
College Point, 0; Haniaten, 4.
Sparta Little Neck, 2; F. S. O., 2.

Umpire Flattened by Fan After Reds Beat Dodgers in 10th, 4-3; Indians Split Pair With A's

Magerkurth Reverses Stewart, Setting Stage for Winning Run

Baker's 'Third-Out' Fly Becomes Decisive Blow and Beggs Safeguards Lead for 9th Straight Victory; Youth Is Arrested After Battle on Field

By Robert B. Cooke

The Cincinnati Reds concluded their season's business with the Dodgers on a pleasant note yesterday, beating Brooklyn, 4 to 3, in ten innings before a resentful crowd of 6,782 fans.

As the Reds scored the winning run in the tenth with the aid of a decision by George Magerkurth, one Brooklyn follower became lost in unbridled fury. As soon as the game was over he jumped out of the stands, pounced on Magerkurth and pummeled him with several good rights and lefts before Bill Stewart and the Ebbets Field ushers could reach the scene of battle.

It was Stewart who prompted this curious ending to a ball game which carired little significance as far as the National League standings were concerned. With team mates on first and second and one out in the tenth, Frank McCormick grounded to Johnny Hudson, who tossed to Pete Coscarart on second. Coscarart, in a hurried attempt to make a double play, dropped the ball, but Stewart first ruled that a force-out had taken place at second.

The Reds objected so furiously to this decision that Stewart consulted Magerkurth, who was umpiring at third. The latter reversed Stewart's decision and every one was safe, despite some carcastic remarks by Leo Durocher, which eventually led to his dismissal before the fisticuffs later on.

Magerkurth Flattened

After Bill Baker's ensuing fly to left had pushed across the decisive run, the Dodgers were retired in order by Joe Beggs. No sooner had the last out been manufactured than Magerkurth was discovered lying flat on his back warding off the punches of his ferocious attacker. Mage got to his feet as soon as he was rescued by Stewart, however, and was able to leave the field under his own power.

The Dodgers could have saved Magerkurth all these indignities if they had received a little tighter pitching from Curt Davis in the ninth. Brooklyn was leading, 3 to 2, in this inning, but with one away, Jimmy Ripple doubled and Lew Riggs tripled, sending the game into overtime.

Cincinnati scored twice in the second when Mike McCormick singled to left with runners on second and third. The Dodgers touched Gene Thompson for a brace of tallies in the first on three walks and two inefild singles. Pete Reiser drove in Brooklyn's third run with an outfield fly in the sixth but Thompson gave way to Beggs in the ninth and so did the Dodgers.

Frank Gernano, an unemployed youth of twenty-one, who lives at 128 Thirty-third Street, Brooklyn, was arrested after the fight and taken to the 71st Precinct.

Gernano was held in $500 bail in Brooklyn-Queens afternoon court for a hearing today on a charge of simple assault.

Interest in the American League race has become so far reaching that the Ebbets Field scoreboard had no room for National League news yesterday. Even the Giant results were omitted, a fact which seemed to go unnoticed the crowd.

Lombardi's Return Uncertain

Doc Rhode, the Cincinnati trainer, said that Ernie Lombardi's ankle gave him severe pain Sunday night. "There is no break, but the ankle has swollen to about twice its usual size," said Rhode. "It's hard to tell how soon it will heal."

Mike McCormick appears to be a cinch to draw the starting assignment in center for Cincinnati in the world series. He has hit safely in the last ten games.

The Ebbets Field home attendance reached 931,421 yesterday. The Dodgers have eight more playing days at home in which to pass the million mark.

Beggs's relief job stretched his string of victories to nine in a row. He has won twelve games. With his help the Reds are now four triumphs away from their second straight pennant, no matter what the Dodgers may do.

The score:

CINCINNATI (N. L.)	ab	r	h	po	a	BROOKLYN (N. L.)	ab	r	h	po	a
Werber, 3b	5	1	1	1	3	Reiser, 3b.	5	1	3	1	1
M.McC'k,cf	5	1	2	5	1	Walker, cf	5	0	2	3	0
Good'n, rf.	4	0	2	3	0	Medwick,lf	5	0	0	3	0
F.McC'k,1b	5	0	0	10	1	Camilli, 1b	3	1	2	13	1
Ripple, lf..	4	0	1	2	0	Vosmik, rf	3	0	0	1	0
†Van'meer.	0	1	0	0	0	Franks, c.	3	0	0	6	1
Baker, c..	1	0	0	0	0	‡Phelps....	1	0	0	0	0
Wilson, c..	3	0	0	4	1	Cos'art, 2b	4	1	2	1	7
*Riggs.....	1	0	1	0	0	Hudson, ss	4	0	1	1	5
Beggs, p..	1	0	0	2	1	Davis, p..	4	0	0	1	0
Frey, 2b..	4	0	1	0	2						
Myers, ss..	3	0	0	2	5						
Thom'n, p.	3	1	1	0	1						
Arno'ch, lf	1	0	0	1	0						
Totals...	40	4	9	30	15	Totals..	37	3	10	30	15

*Batted for Wilson in ninth inning.
†Ran for Ripple in ninth inning.
‡Batted for Franks in tenth inning.

Cincinnati....... 002 000 001 1—4
Brooklyn......... 200 001 000 0—3

Error—Coscarart. Runs batted in—M. McCormick (2), Franks, Coscarart, Reiser, Riggs, Baker. Two-base hits—Werber, Frey, Goodman, Reiser, Coscarart, Ripple, M. McCormick. Three-base hits—Goodman, Camilli, Riggs. Stolen bases—Reiser, Camilli. Sacrifice—Vosmik. Double play—Beggs, Myers and F. McCormick. Left on bases—Cincinnati, 8; Brooklyn, 9. Bases on balls—Off Thompson, 4; off Davis, 2. Struck out—By Davis, 5; by Thompson, 4. Hits—Off Thompson, 9 in 8 innings; off Beggs, 1 in 2. Winning pitcher—Beggs. Umpires—Dunn, Stewart and Magerkurth. Time—2:22. Attendance—6,782.

Dodgers Hope to Meet Yankees in City Series

In a letter to Ed Barrow, president of the New York Yankees, Larry MacPhail, executive president of the Brooklyn Dodgers, yesterday challenged the Yankees to a city series in the event that they do not win the American League pennant.

"In view of the fact that the American League race may not be decided until the closing days of the season," wrote MacPhail, "I would suggest that our challenge be accepted tentatively pending the determination of the races in both leagues."

Giants Lose 8th In Row, 7-6, on Pirate Homers

Blows by DiMaggio, Van Robays and Young Offset 2 by Ott and Late Rally

By Arthur E. Patterson

Muddling through toward the end of a weary campaign, the Giants dropped their eighth straight ball game. 7 to 6, at the Polo Grounds yesterday when three Pirate homers piled up enough runs to stand off a series of rallies by Terry's tired troupers.

A single, a base on balls and Vince DiMaggio's homer scored three runs in the second. Just by way of novelty, a single, a base on balls and Maurice Van Robays's homer scored three runs in the third. Pep Young hit a solo circuit blow in the fifth and the Giants' only retaliation up to this point was Mel Ott's eighteenth and nineteenth homers.

A crowd of 1,282, if "crowd" is the correct word, yawned or heckled as they pleased. One group out in Section 33 actually hauled out a dcek of cards and, after some hunting, found a fourth for a game of bridge. It was so quiet you could hear Leo Durocher hollering over at Ebbets Field.

Klinger Stops Giants

Finally the Giants began to move and, before it was all over, it was an exciting affair, if one permits himself to become excited about the activities of the jaded Giants these days. Anyway, they finally disposed of Max Butcher, the starting pitcher, in the seventh after he had been tagged for three runs in the sixth. Against Mace Brown, his relief, they finished a one-run sortie and left two on in the seventh. Then Frankie Frisch became annoyed with it all and brought in Bob Klinger, who quelled the uprising.

It took a grand barehanded stop by Young, whose homer in the fifth proved to be the clincher, to stop Ott and the Giants in the seventh. Master Melvin had been a source of considerable disturbance until then with his two homers and a base on balls in the three-run sixth. But with the tying run at second, the winner at first and two out, Young sprinted back toward centerfield and made a stab for Ott's hopper. He came up with the ball and got his man at first. Had the ball gone through, Burgess Whitehead would have scored easily and Babe Young would have romped to third.

Lohrman Pounded

Sweet William Lohrman, who has turned a bit sour in the ripe stage of the season, was Terry's starting choice and the beaten pitcher. Van Robays put him on the toboggan with a single to center. Elbie Fletcher waited and walked and. boom! DiMaggio slapped his eighteenth homer high and deep to left. With two out in the third, Bob Elliott singled, Arkie Vaughan walked and Van Robays finished what he had started by smashing an inside-the-park homer to the Giants' bullpen, beating the Rucker-Whitehead relay with a dusty slide. Bob Carpenter came in for the fourth and struck out the first two batters. The first man up in the fifth, Young, parked his season's second homer to left, however.

Ott had been waging one-man warfare against Butcher until then. His homers in the second and fourth were hsi fifth and sixth since Sept. 11. Butcher had a three-hitter going into th esixth and seemed in no great difficulty then when he sandwiched a base on balls between two outs. But he was cautious with Ott and walked him and Hank Danning hit a two-run double against the left field wall and Tony Cuccinello scored him with his second two-bagger of the afternoon. With one away Rucker singled in the seventh and Brown replaced Butcher. He walked Whitehead, amid considerable squawking, fanned, Jo Jo Moore and was reached for a single by Babe Young. Pep Young's larceny and Klinger's pitching stopped the Giants cold.

Buster Maynard, a sturdy lad up from the Richmond Colts, worked out with the Giants and may play either third or the outfield today . . . . Pep Young's homer was No. 100 against Giant pitching and the first 100 have been the toughest. Rival homers from here in wont hurt anybody, particularly the calloused pitching staff.

The score:

PITTSBURGH (N. L.)	ab	r	h	po	a	NEW YORK (N. L.)	ab	r	h	po	a
P. Y'g, 2b	4	1	1	0	7	Rucker, cf.	5	1	1	1	0
Garms, 3b.	4	0	0	0	2	White'd,2b	3	0	0	1	1
Elliott, rf.	5	1	2	1	0	§O'Dea...	1	0	0	0	0
Vaug'n, ss	4	1	0	0	2	Moore, lf..	3	1	0	2	0
V'n R's, lf	2	2	2	1	0	N. Y'g, 1b.	4	0	1	8	1
Fl'cher, 1b	2	1	0	17	0	Ott, rf....	3	3	2	2	0
DiMag'o,cf	4	1	1	2	0	Danning, c	4	1	1	11	1
Davis, c...	4	0	1	6	0	Cucc'lo, 3b	4	0	2	1	1
Butcher, p	3	0	0	0	1	Witek, ss..	4	0	0	0	3
M. Br'n, p	0	0	0	0	0	Lohrm'n, p	1	0	0	1	0
*P. Waner.	1	0	0	0	0	Carp'ter, p	1	0	0	0	0
Klinger, p	0	0	0	0	2	†Tramback	1	0	0	0	0
						Lynn, p...	0	0	0	0	1
						‡McCarthy	1	0	0	0	0
Totals...	33	7	7	27	14	Totals....	35	6	7	27	8

*Batted for M. Brown in eighth inning.
†Batted for Carpenter in seventh inning.
‡Batted for Lynn in ninth inning.
§Batted for Whitehead in ninth inning.

Pittsburgh........... 033 010 000—7
New York............ 010 103 100—6

Errors—F. Young, N. Young. Runs batted in—DiMaggio (3). Van Robays (3), Ott (2), F. Young, Danning (2), Cuccinello, N. Young. Two-base hits—Danning, Cuccinello (2). Home runs—DiMaggio, Ott (2), Van Robays, F. Young. Sacrifice—Garms. Double play—Danning and Cuccinello. Left on bases—New York, 5; Pittsburgh, 5. Bases on balls—Off Butcher, 2; off Lohrman, 1; off Carpenter, 2; off M. Brown, 1; off Lynn, 1. Struck out—By Butcher, 2; by Lohrman, 1; by Carpenter, 6; by M. Brown, 1; by Lynn, 2; by Klinger, 1. Hits—Off Lohrman, 4 in 3 innings; off Carpenter, 2 in 4; off Lynn, 1 in 2; off Butcher, 6 in 6 1-3; off M. Brown, 1 in 2-3; off Klinger, 0 in 2. Hit by pitcher—By Lynn (F. Young). Winning pitcher—Butcher. Losing pitcher—Lohrman. Time—2:00. Umpires—Reardon, Goetz and Pinelli. Attendance—1,262.

Brooklyn Fan Fells Umpire After Tenth Inning Loss to Reds

Associated Press

With George Magerkurth on the ground Bill Stewart, fellow umpire, gets a headlock on his assailant, aided by an Ebbets Field policeman. Tom Dunn, plate umpire, is shown with his chest protector near by

Start of the melee with the Brooklyn fan about to throw Magerkurth, who is much larger. A twenty-one-year-old unemployed Brooklyn youth who gave his name as Frank Gernano, was arrested

Phils Set Back Cardinals, 3-2, Then Lose, 7-1

Double by Marty in Ninth Wins for Si Johnson, Then Hutchinson Scores

PHILADELPHIA, Sept. 16 (AP).—The lowly Phillies won their forty-sixth victory of the season, more than in any year since 1937, by beating the St. Louis Cardinals, 3 to 2, today in the first game of a double-header. They lost the second, however, 7 to 1.

Si Johnson stopped his former St. Louis clubmates with five hits in the opener. A double by Joe Marty off Mort Cooper in the ninth led to the winning run. Cooper yielded only two more hits than his mound rival.

Danny Litwhiler, the Phils' right-fielder, ran his consecutive hitting stretch to twenty-one games, belting a single in both contests.

In the second game, Ira Hutchinson, of the Cards, held the home team to six hits, while the Red Birds capitalized on three Phil errors, seven walks and eight hits.

The scores:

FIRST GAME

ST. LOUIS (N. L.)	ab	r	h	po	a	PHILA. (N. L.)	ab	r	h	po	a
Bro'n,2b,ss	4	0	1	3	4	Jumo'le, ss	4	0	0	2	3
Moore, cf.	4	0	0	0	0	Mahan, 1b	4	1	1	10	0
Slaug'r, rf.	3	0	1	4	0	Lithw'r, rf	4	0	1	1	0
Mize, 1b..	3	0	0	8	1	Marty, cf..	4	1	1	2	0
Koy, lf...	4	1	1	1	0	Rizzo, lf..	3	0	1	2	0
Or'go,3b,2b	4	0	2	3	2	May, 3b..	2	1	1	0	3
Marion, ss.	3	0	0	0	2	Schulte, 2b	3	0	1	2	0
S.Mar'n,3b	1	0	0	1	1	†Mueller...	0	0	0	0	0
Owen, c...	2	0	0	6	2	Millies, c..	2	0	0	6	0
Cooper, p..	4	1	0	0	3	‡Mazzera..	1	0	0	0	0
						Warren, c.	1	0	0	2	0
						Si Joh'n, p	3	0	1	0	2
Totals..	32	2	5	*26	15	Totals...	31	3	7	27	8

*Two out when winning run was scored.
†Batted for Millies in seventh inning.
‡Batted for Schulte in ninth inning.

St. Louis............ 001 001 000—2
Philadelphia......... 000 110 001—3

Errors—Orengo, Millies, Warren. Runs batted in—Litwhiler, Si Johnson, Warren, Mize, Orengo. Two-base hits—Mahan, May, Brown, Koy, Marty. Three-base hit—Slaughter. Stolen bases—Orengo, Owen. Sacrifices—May, Schulte. Left on bases—Philadelphia, 7; St. Louis, 7. Bases on balls—Off Si Johnson, 4; off Cooper, 3. Struck out—By Cooper, 6; by Si Johnson, 7. Umpires—Jorda, Sears and Barr. Time—1:59.

SECOND GAME

ST. LOUIS (N. L.)	ab	r	h	po	a	PHILA (N. L.)	ab	r	h	po	a
Brown, 2b.	5	1	2	2	2	Jumo'le, ss	4	0	0	2	2
Moore, cf..	4	0	1	7	0	Mahan, 1b	4	0	0	8	0
Slaug'r, rf.	3	1	1	0	0	Lithw'r, rf	4	0	1	2	0
Mize, 1b..	4	1	1	12	0	Marty, cf..	3	1	1	3	0
Koy, lf...	3	2	0	1	0	Stewart, cf	1	0	0	0	0
Orengo, 3b	5	1	2	2	1	Rizzo, lf..	2	0	1	1	1
Marion, ss.	5	0	1	1	7	Mazzera, lf	1	0	0	0	0
Owens, c..	4	0	0	2	0	May, 3b...	3	0	1	0	0
Hutch'n, p	3	1	0	0	3	File, 3b...	1	0	0	1	1
						Warren, c.	3	0	0	9	0
						Schulte, 2b	3	0	1	1	2
						Marne, 2b.	0	0	0	0	2
						Frye, p...	2	0	1	0	0
						Maste'n, p.	1	0	0	0	0
Totals..	36	7	8	27	13	Totals...	32	1	6	27	8

St. Louis............ 000 210 310—7
Philadelphia......... 000 100 000—1

Errors—Mahan, May, Schulte. Runs batted in—Brown (2), Orengo (2), Slaughter, Rizzo. Two-base hits—Moore, Orengo, Brown. Three-base hit—Marty. Double plays—Rizzo and Warren; Marion, Brown and Mize; Schulte, Jumonville and Mahan. Left on bases—Philadelphia, 5; St. Louis, 9. Bases on balls—Off Frye, 5; off Masterson, 2; off Hutchinson, 1. Struck out—By Frye, 3; by Masterson, 2; by Hutchinson, 1. Hits—Off Frye, 4 in 5 innings; off Masterson, 4 in 4. Losing pitcher—Frye. Time—1:46. Umpires—Sears, Barr and Jorda. Attendance—1,000.

Fan Finds Wife Knows Best

Earl Barnes, of Chillicothe, Mo., started to wear a brand new straw hat to a ball game. Mrs. Barnes dissuaded him by telling him dire things might happen to it. So he wore last year's hat. A foul ball knocked it off.

Yankees Suffer Worst Setback Of Season as Browns Win, 16-4

St. Louis Scores 7 in First, Hits 5 Homers; DiMaggio Poles 31st for Champions

By Rud Rennie

ST. LOUIS, Sept. 16.—Who would ever have thought that the lowly Browns could do this to the Yankees? They won a double-header yesterday and today they literally pulverized New York's staggering pennant chasers, 16 to 4.

It was the worst Yankee defeat of the year. No team had scored as many as sixteen runs against them. Fourteen, also by the Browns on July 24, had been tops. Ten runs was the most by which they had been beaten.

Today's defeat was in a class by itself, and it dropped the Yankees four games behind the league-leading Boo-Hoo Indians and three and one-half games in back of the clinging Tigers. About all the Yankees did was hang onto third place and they did this only because the fourth-place White Sox also lost.

Yankee pitching, which was what carried them on their stirring dash from fifth place up almost to the top, is the thing that has broken down in this tell-tale drive down the stretch. Marius Russo, one of the young twirlers who was so helpful, failed for the second time on this Western campaign. The Browns had four runs off him before another pitcher could be warmed up.

Gomez Hurls Hitless Inning

Vernon Gomez, making his first appearance since he finished up a game in Boston Aug. 8, was the only one of four Yankee hurlers who yielded neither hits nor runs. He worked one inning, the sixth.

Every one in the St. Louis line-up batted safely and the Browns made fifteen hits.

There were six home runs. Joe DiMaggio, conducting a one-man counter-attack for the Yankees, hit one, his thirty-first of the year, in the fourth inning. The five others were made by Brownies. Johnny Lucadello, who never had hit a homer in the majors, made two, one into the left-field bleachers and the other onto the right-field roof. Chet Laabs, Rip Radcliff and George McQuinn made the others. Lucadello drove in five runs and McQuinn four. It was murder.

And while the Browns were hammering Russo, Bump Hadley, and, eventually, Steve Sundra, making at least one homer off each, Vern Kennedy held the Yankees to six hits, two of them by DiMaggio, who clung to the batting leadership by a point.

Browns Let Loose

DiMaggio knocked in a run with a single in the first after Rolfe was hit by a pitched ball and took second on a passed ball. But that one run was all but forgotten in the blast set off by the Browns in their first turn at bat.

Russo got out Laabs, the first man up. In rapid succession Lucadello put one in the left-field bleachers, Radcliff sailed one onto the right-field roof, Hoag singled, Clift walked, McQuinn doubled, knocking in two runs and Russo was all through for the day. And so were the Yankees.

Berardino kept the rally going by poking Hadley for a single, scoring McQuinn. Swift was thrown out, but Crosetti made a bad throw with Kennedy's grounder, letting Berardino score. Laabs, up for the second time, doubled off the right-field wall, sending Kennedy home. Lucadello was thrown out by Gordon. Eleven men batted and made seven runs with six hits.

McQuinn belted Hadley for a home run with a man on base in the second. Laabs put one onto the roof for one run in the third. The Browns picked up four more in the fth, Radcliff getting a triple. Hadley was still in there, ducking base hits.

Lucadello Poles Another

After Gomez stopped the hitting in the sixth he was taken out for a pinch hitter and Sundra came along and got smacked. Laabs made his third hit and Lucadello made his second homer.

A base on balls to Selkirk, a single by Dickey and a double by Dahlgren gave the Yankees a run in the seventh, and they made their final run in the ninth after Crosetti singled and Rosar, a pinsh hitter, doubled and Clift threw away Gordon't grounder.

Tomorrow will see the final game of this sad series. If the Yankees lose it will be just too bad.

The score:

Standings in the Major Leagues

TUESDAY, SEPT. 17, 1940

National League

YESTERDAY'S RESULTS

Pittsburgh, 7; New York, 6
Cincinnati, 4; Brooklyn, 3 (10 innings)
Philadelphia, 3; St. Louis, 2 (1st)
St. Louis, 7; Philadelphia, 1 (2d)
Other clubs not scheduled.

STANDING OF THE CLUBS

	Cincinnati	Brooklyn	St. Louis	Pittsburgh	Chicago	New York	Boston	Philadelphia	Won	Lost	Percentage	Games behind
Cincinnati	—	14	10	12	16	15	12	12	91	47	.659	—
Brooklyn..	8	—	9	15	10	14	13	14	83	59	.585	10
St. Louis..	8	11	—	5	9	10	14	16	73	65	.529	18..
Pittsburgh	2	7	15	—	10	10	13	16	73	66	.525	18½
Chicago...	6	12	6	9	—	9	14	12	68	73	.482	24½
New York	7	5	11	12	10	—	11	10	66	73	.475	25½
Boston....	9	7	8	7	8	6	—	14	59	82	.418	33½
Ph'delphia	7	3	6	6	10	9	5	—	46	94	.329	46..
Games lost	47	59	65	66	73	73	82	94	—	—		

GAMES TODAY

Chicago at New York, 3:15
St. Louis at Brooklyn, 3:00
Cincinnati at Philadelphia
Pittsburgh at Boston

American League

YESTERDAY'S RESULTS

St. Louis, 16; New York, 4
Cleveland, 8; Philadelphia, 3 (1st)
Philadelphia, 3; Cleveland, 2 (2d)
Detroit, 9; Washington, 2
Boston, 6; Chicago, 2

STANDING OF THE CLUBS

	Cleveland	Detroit	New York	Chicago	Boston	St. Louis	Washington	Philadelphia	Won	Lost	Percentage	Games behind
Cleveland.	—	8	10	16	14	10	10	14	82	60	.577	—
Detroit....	8	—	14	7	11	18	15	8	81	60	.574	..½
New York.	12	8	—	9	11	13	13	11	77	63	.550	.4
Chicago...	6	13	10	—	11	10	12	16	78	65	.545	4½
Boston....	8	11	9	11	—	12	12	12	75	67	.528	7
St. Louis..	10	4	8	6	8	—	11	14	61	82	.427	21½
Wash'gton	9	6	4	10	8	11	—	12	60	81	.426	21½
Ph'delphia	7	10	8	6	4	8	8	—	51	87	.370	29
Games lost	60	60	63	65	67	82	81	87	—	—		

GAMES TODAY

New York at St. Louis
Philadelphia at Cleveland
Washington at Detroit
Other clubs not scheduled

Newsom Turns Back Senators For Tigers, 9-2

Pitcher Scores 19th Victory of Season and Detroit Narrows Lead of Indians

DETROIT, Sept. 16 (AP).—Louis (Bo-Bo) Newsom kept the Detroit Tigers charging along in the thick of the American League pennant fight today with a five-hit 9-to-2 decision over the Washington Senators. The big fellow, scoring his nineteenth triumph of the season against four defeats, kept the Senators, who had dumped the Tigers out of first place yesterday, in check throughout, easing up to allow three his and two runs in the seventh.

Thus the Tigers, breaking a two-game losing streak, climbed to within a half-game of the league-leading Cleveland Indians.

While Newsome, who had asked to be sent into the box today after being shelled from the mound by the New York Yankees Saturday, kept breezing along, his teammates hammered two of three Washington hurlers for eleven hits. One of the blows was a sixth-inning home run by Hank Greenberg, his thirty-fifth of the season and his ninth in the last dozen games, with one on base. The blow tied Hank with Jimmy Foxx, of the Red Sox for the homer leadership in the American League.

The score:

WASHINGTON (A.L.)	ab	r	h	po	a	DETROIT (A. L.)	ab	r	h	po	a
Case, cf..	4	0	0	2	0	Bartell, ss.	4	0	1	0	3
Lewis, rf.	4	1	2	4	0	McCosky,cf	4	2	2	4	0
Walker, lf.	4	0	0	3	0	Gehr'er,2b	2	2	1	2	2
Travis,3b..	4	0	1	0	4	Meyer, 2b.	0	0	0	0	0
Blood'th,2b	4	1	1	4	5	Greenb'g,lf	5	2	2	4	0
Sanford, b.	3	0	1	9	0	York, 1b..	3	1	2	10	0
Pofahl, ss..	3	0	0	1	2	Higgins,3b	3	0	0	1	3
Ferrell, c...	1	0	0	0	0	Fox, rf....	3	1	1	2	0
Early, c...	2	0	0	1	1	Tebbetts, c	4	1	1	4	0
Krakau's,p	1	0	0	0	0	Newsom, p.	4	0	1	0	0
Haynes, p.	1	0	0	0	1						
Weljab....	1	0	0	0	1						
Carrasq'l,p	0	0	0	0	1						
Totals..	32	2	5	24	14	Totals...	32	9	11	27	8

*Batted for Haynes in eighth inning.

Washington......... 000 000 200—2
Detroit.............. 024 003 00x—9

Errors—Case (2). Runs batted in—Newsom, Greenberg (3), York, Fox, Gehringer, Bloodworth, Sanford. Two-base hits—York, Bartell, Lewis, Bloodworth. Three-base hits—McCosky (2). Home run—Greenberg. Stolen base—McCosky. Sacrifice—Meyer. Double play—Travis, Bloodworth and Sanford. Left on bases—Washington, 3; Detroit, 7. Bases on balls—Off Krakauskas, 4; off Haynes, 2; off Carrasquel, 1. Struck out—By Newsom, 4. Hits—Off Krakauskas, 6 in 3 innings; off Haynes, 5 in 4; off Carrasquel, 0 in 1. Losing pitcher—Krakauskas. Umpires—McGowan, Basil and Grieve. Time—1:52. Attendance—3,911.

Probable Pitchers For Today's Games

* * *

American League

New York at St. Louis—Donald (6-3) vs. Trotter (6-5).
Washington at Detroit—Masterson (3-12) vs. Rowe (14-3).
Philadelphia at Cleveland — Marchildon (0-20) vs. Milnar (16-8).
Only games scheduled.

National League

Chicago at New York—Olsen (11-9) vs. Hubbell (11-10).
St. Louis at Brooklyn—Warneke (15-9) vs. Tamulis (8-5).
Cincinnati at Philadelphia—Vander Meer (1-0) vs. Higbe (13-17).
Pittsburgh at Boston—Lanahan (6-7) vs. Errickson (11-12).
(Won-lost records in parentheses)

Yankees' Score

* * *

NEW YORK (A. N.)	ab	r	h	po	a	ST. LOUIS (A. L.)	ab	r	h	po	a
Gordon, 2b	5	0	0	0	4	Laabs, cf..	5	3	3	7	0
Rolfe, 3b..	4	1	0	3	1	Luca'lo, 2b	5	3	3	1	3
Keller, lf..	4	0	0	5	0	Radcliff, lf	4	2	2	1	0
DiMag'o,cf	4	1	2	1	0	Hoag, rf...	5	1	1	3	0
Selkirk, rf	3	1	0	0	0	Clift, 3b..	3	1	1	0	1
Dickey, c..	4	0	1	5	0	McQ'n, 1b.	5	2	2	9	0
Dahlg'n,1b	3	0	1	9	0	Ber'no, ss.	3	1	1	1	0
Crosetti, ss	4	1	1	1	2	Strange, ss	1	0	0	1	1
Russo, p..	0	0	0	0	1	Swift, c...	5	1	1	4	1
Hadley, p.	2	0	0	0	1	Kennedy, p	5	2	1	0	1
Gomez, p..	0	0	0	0	0						
*Chartak..	1	0	0	0	0						
Sundra, p.	0	0	0	0	0						
†Rosar....	1	0	1	0	0						
Totals....	35	4	6	24	9	Totals..	41	16	15	27	7

*Batted for Gomez in seventh inning.
†Batted for Sundra in ninth inning.

New York.......... 100 100 101—4
St. Louis........... 721 040 20x—16

Errors—Crosetti (2), DiMaggio, Lucadello, Clift. Runs batted in—DiMaggio (2), Lucadello (5), Radcliff (2), McQuinn (4), Berardino, Laabs (2), Dahlgren, Gordon. Two-base hits—McQuinn, Laabs, Dahlgren, Rosar. Three-base hit—Radcliff. Home runs—Lucadello (2), Radcliff, McQuinn, Laabs, DiMaggio. Left on bases—New York, 8; St. Louis, 6. Bases on balls—Off Russo, 1; off Hadley, 2; off Gomez, 1; off Sundra, 1; off Kennedy, 3. Struck out—By Kennedy, 5; by Hadley, 2; by Gomez, 3. Hits—Off Russo, 4 in 1-3 inning; off Hadley, 9 in 4 2-3; off Gomez, 0 in 1; off Sundra, 2 in 2. Hit by pitcher—By Kennedy (Rolfe). Passed ball—Swift. Losing pitcher—Russo. Umpires—Ormsby, Summers and Quinn. Time—1:51. Attendance—1,343.

Cleveland Lead Cut to ½ Game By 3-2 Jolt After 8-3 Victory

Harder Scores as Mack Belts Four-Run Homer, but Babich Trips Leaders

CLEVELAND, Sept. 16 (AP).—Connie Mack's Athletics wound the torrid American League flag chase into a tighter knot today, snapping a nine-game losing streak to split a wash-day bargain bill with the league-leading Indians. The stand-off cost Cleveland half its one-game advantage over Detroit.

The Tribe, with Mel Harder retiring the first twenty batters in order, smashed Philadelphia in the opener, 8 to 3. Johnny Babich's six-hit twirling was too much for the Indians in the nightcap and the Athletics squeezed out a 3-to-2 triumph.

About 6,000 Cleveland Stadium customers saw the Indians unleash their war clubs on Lee (Buck) Ross, an old jinx, for an easy victory in the first game.

Heath Wallops Homer

Harder started things with a single and before the third inning was ended, seven men had scored. The dynamite blow was Ray Mack's inside-the-park homer with the bases clogged. Jeff Heath contributed another the next inning with nobody on.

Harder was headed for a perfect game until Frankie Hayes, with two men down in the seventh, smacked a single into left field. Heath might have caught it, but played the blow safe despite Cleveland's 8-to-0 advantage. With the pressure off, Harder was touched for three futile tallies in the ninth.

Babich, turning in his thirteenth triumph, was too tough in the night-cap. The clubs entered the ninth deadlocked, 2 to 2, because Harry Eisenstat, unlucky Indian southpaw, gave Sam Chapman and Hayes home-run pitches.

Chapman Scores Winning Run

Chapman led off by socking a three-and-two pitch over third base for a freak double. Ken Keltner stabbed at the slow roller, but missed it. Then Bob Johnson bounced a ball which hit Eisenstat's glove and continued into centerfield for another double, scoring Chapman with the winning run.

The scores:

FIRST GAME

PHILA. (A. L.)	ab	r	h	po	a	CLEVELAND (A. L.)	ab	r	h	po	a
Miles, cf..	4	1	1	4	0	Heath, lf..	4	2	2	0	0
Moses, rf.	4	0	1	0	0	Weath'y,cf	3	1	1	3	0
Hayes,c,1b	4	0	2	11	0	Boudr'u, ss	4	1	1	2	3
Johnson,lf	4	0	0	2	0	Peters, ss..	0	0	0	0	1
Siebert, 1b	1	0	0	3	1	Trosky, 1b.	3	1	0	13	2
Wagner, c.	3	0	0	0	1	Bell, rf...	4	0	2	2	0
McCoy, 2b	3	0	0	1	3	Keltner,3b	2	1	0	0	1
Gant'n, 3b	3	0	0	0	3	Mack, 2b..	4	1	1	2	5
F.Cha'n,ss	3	1	1	2	3	Pytlak, c..	4	0	0	4	0
Ross, p....	2	0	0	1	2	Harder, p.	4	1	2	1	2
*S. Chap'n	1	1	1	0	0						
Totals..	32	3	6	24	13	Totals..	32	8	9	27	14

*Batted for Ross in ninth inning.

Philadelphia......... 000 000 003—3
Cleveland............ 007 100 00x—8

Error—Miles. Runs batted in—Boudreau (2), Mack (4), Heath, Moses (2), Bell, Miles. Two-base hits—Boudreau, F. Chapman, Miles, Hayes. Home runs—Mack, Heath. Stolen bases—Keltner, Harder. Double plays—Harder, Trosky and Mack; Hayes and F. Chapman. Left on bases—Philadelphia, 2; Cleveland, 4. Bases on balls—Off Ross, 4. Struck out—By Ross, 3; by Harder, 4. Umpires—Moriarty, Hubbard, Rommel and Pipgras. Time—1:47.

SECOND GAME

PHILA. (A. L.)	ab	r	h	po	a	CLEVELAND (A. L.)	ab	r	h	po	a
Miles, rf..	4	0	0	3	0	Heath, lf..	4	0	0	5	0
S. Cha'n,cf	4	2	2	1	0	Weath'y,cf	4	0	1	5	1
Johnson,lf	4	0	2	3	0	Boudr'u, ss	4	1	1	2	4
Hayes, c..	4	1	2	4	0	Trosky, 1b	4	0	1	5	0
Siebert, 1b	3	0	0	12	0	Bell, rf...	3	1	2	2	0
Rubel'g,3b	4	0	1	3	3	*Grimes..	0	0	0	0	0
Davis, 2b..	3	0	0	0	4	Keltner,3b	4	0	1	1	2
Branc'o, ss	3	0	0	1	0	Mack, 2b..	4	0	0	2	3
Babich, p.	3	0	0	0	1	Hemsley, c	3	0	0	5	0
						Eisen'at, p	3	0	0	0	1
						Dobson, p..	0	0	0	0	0
Totals...	32	3	7	27	8	Totals..	33	2	6	27	11

*Ran for Bell in ninth inning.

Philadelphia......... 100 100 001—3
Cleveland............ 100 100 000—2

Errors—None. Runs batted in—S. Chapman, Trosky, Hayes, Keltner, Johnson. Two-base hits—S. Chapman, Johnson, Trosky. Three-base hits—Johnson, Keltner. Home runs—S. Chapman, Hayes. Double plays—Boudreau, Mack and Trosky; Weatherly, Boudreau and Hemsley. Left on bases—Philadelphia, 3; Cleveland, 5. Bases on balls—Off Babich, 1; off Dobson, 1. Struck out—By Babich, 4; by Eisenstat, 4. Hits—Off Eisenstat, 7 in 8 innings (none out in ninth); off Dobson, 0 in 1. Losing pitcher—Eisenstat. Umpires—Hubbard, Rommel, Pipgras and Moriarty. Time—1:34. Attendance—6,000.

Armstrong Ordered to Fight

WASHINGTON, Sept. 16 (UP).—The District of Columbia Boxing Commission today ordered Welterweight Champion Henry Armstrong to fulfill a contract for a fifteen-round title bout with Phil Furr here Sept. 23. It rejected a request by Eddie Meade, Armstrong's manager, that the bout be reduced to fourteen rounds.

DETROIT TIGERS	. . . . .	001 000 000—1 7 0
CINCINNATI REDS	. . . . .	000 000 02x—2 7 1

BISBEE + In the heart of Nature's Year Around Playground. The Copper Capital of Arizona.

The Bisbee Evening Ore

"Today's News Today"

BISBEE + Southeastern Arizona's Trade Center. Population of District 13,000. Elevation 1 mile

Vol. XXVII — BISBEE, ARIZONA. TUESDAY EVENING, OCTOBER 8, 1940 — Entered as Second Class Matter at the Postoffice at Bisbee, Arizona, Under Act of Congress, March 3, 1879 — No. 55

REDS WIN WORLD SERIES WITH 2 TO 1 TRIUMPH OVER TIGERS

BRITAIN TO REOPEN ITS BURMA ROAD IN REPLY TO TRI-POWER TREATY

Democracies Will Not Submit to Axis Threats, Prime Minister Churchill Declares in Commons Talk

By THE ASSOCIATED PRESS

LONDON, Oct. 8—Winston Churchill announced in the house of commons today that Britain would reopen the Burma war supply road to China in answer to Japan's pact with Germany and Italy and declared Japan's new allies would not be able to help her so long as the British and United States fleets "are in being."

"They will be!" the commons roared back.

It was another of the British prime minister's dramatic war reports, and he ended it with this peroration:

"Long, dark months of trial and tribulation lie before us. Not only great dangers but many more misfortunes, many shortcomings, many mistakes, many disappointments, will surely be our lot. Death and sorrow will be the companions of our journey; hardship our garment; constancy and valour our only shield."

The Prime Minister declared flatly that the three-way axis pact "binds Japan to attack the United States if the United States comes into the war," hinted it contained secret clauses and then cried defiantly:

"Neither of the branches of the English-speaking race is accustomed to react to threats of violence by submission.

"And certainly the reception of this strange and ill-balanced declaration, in the United States, has not been at all encouraging for its authors."

Aimed at Russia

Churchill also charged the tri-power pact "in a secondary degree is a point against Russia," although "primarily" aimed at the United States.

Churchill's hour-long war report made these other points, even while London's anti-aircraft guns rumbled faintly in the distance:

1. Hitler's month-old air total warfare on London and Britain's

(Continued on Page Two)

BUS STRUCK IN NAZI AIR RAID

German Planes Fly So High They Are Invisible To Pedestrians Below

By THE ASSOCIATED PRESS

LONDON, Oct. 8.—Elusive German raiders flying so high they were not visible to their victims slipped over London in four lightning raids today, dropping bombs helter skelter among streets filled with buses and pedestrians in one of the most calamitous attacks yet experienced by this bomb-wise capital.

Bombs which fell without warning blasted a bus filled with passengers into almost unrecognizable wreckage, knocked a row of nearby shops into a mass of rubble, blew out half the leaded windows from the front of a row of famous houses several hundred years old and did much other amage in many streets.

These daylight attacks followed a night-long raid in which a large west end store was wrecked, a famous west end office structure damaged, a church roof collapsed, a hospital hit, huge pieces of masonry torn from a large bank building and considerable other damage done.

(Censorship prevented more definite identification of these objectives).

The British press association described the day's four raids which came as Londoners were going to work as "murderous."

The bombs were dropped from such a height that at first pedestrians thought the explosions were anti-aircraft guns shooting.

(Continued on Page Two)

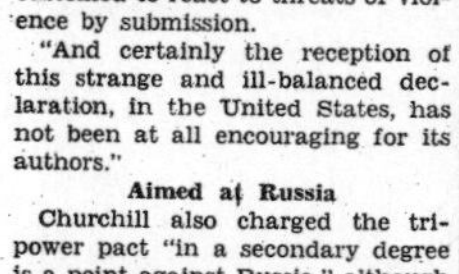

OLD BUTTERFIELD STAGE STATION AT OAKS GROVE SAN DIEGO COUNTY, Oct. 8.—Heard this yarn today and was told it was an old one but it was new to me and I hope it's new to you. An old timer here was having this corn crib robbed by a bunch of squirrels and when he would get after 'em they just hiked it up into an old hollow tree along side the corn crib.

So, one day, while they were all in the corn crib, the old timer cut the tree down, it fell with such a crash you could have heard it at Warner's Ranch, and that noise scared the squirrels.

Out of that crib they come like a shot of lightning, over to where the tree used to stand, straight as a string, the whole bunch of 'em, and hang fer a horse thief if they didn't run fifty feet straight up in the air before they found out that tree was gone!"

The first Butterfield stage in 1850 made the 282 miles from Los Angeles to Yuma in 72 hours and 20 minutes.

Mexico Is Opening Recruiting Offices

MEXICO CITY, Oct. 8. (AP)—The ministry of national defense said today that recruiting offices were being established throughout the republic as the first step toward putting Mexico's new compulsory military service law into effect.

It was expected that shortly after the first of the year enlistment of 12,000 recruits between the ages of 18 and 40 would start.

Detailed Account of Championship Game

By JUDSON BAILEY

CROSLEY FIELD, Cincinnati, Oct. 8. (AP) — The 1940 baseball season ground to a glamorous close today in the seventh and final game of the World Series with Buck Newsom of the Detroit Tigers and Paul Derringer of the Cincinnati Reds opposing each other on the mound.

The weather was ideal, warm and bright, and there was gold and glory riding on every pitch by two of the best right-handers in the major leagues this year.

The same pitchers started the opening game of the series last Wednesday and Newsom won after Derringer had been batted out in the second inning. Newsom triumphed again in the fifth game at Detroit Sunday and had a chance to become the first pitcher to earn three victories in a single series since Steve Covelskie of Cleveland did it in 1920.

Derringer came back in the fourth game of this series to win and had the advantage of two days rest to Newsom's one.

For the deciding game both teams adhered to the lineups they have used all the way except that Billy Sullivan, who generally catches Newsom, went behind the bat for Detroit instead of Birdie Tebbetts, who worked yesterday.

The veteran Jimmy Wilson again was Cincinnati's catcher.

FIRST INNING

Detroit—Bartell lined the first pitch directly at Myers. With the count two strikes and one ball, McCosky lifted a high fly to M. McCormick in deep center. After looking at one ball, Gehringer lifted a fly in short left center that looked like an almost certain hit, but Ripple came rushing in to make a great catch. No runs, no hits, no errors, none left.

Reds—Werber looked at one ball, and then lined to Greenberg deep in left. M. McCormick struck out on four pitches. With the count two strikes and one ball, Goodman grounded to Bartell and was thrown out. No runs, no hits, no errors, none left.

SECOND INNING

Tigers — After looking at one strike, Greenberg sent a sharp grounder which Myers was able to knock down but unable to throw in time to catch Greenberg and it was scored as a single. York also looked at one strike, and then topped the ball toward third base, Werber rushing in for a gloved-hand pickup and throwing to first just in time to nip the runner in a spectacular play. Campbell grounded to Derringer, who wheeled and saw Greenberg streaking for third and ran toward him setting up a trap, in which Greenberg was run down, Derringer to Myers to Werber to Joost, Campbell going to second. Higgins was thrown out, Joost to F. McCormick. No runs, one hit, no errors, one left.

Reds—F. McCormick grounded to Higgins on the grass in front of third and was thrown out. Ripple, swinging hard, struck out on five pitches. Wilson hit the first pitch on the ground into left field for a single. Wilson stole second, getting half way there before Newsom's pitch reached the catcher. After looking at two balls, Joost grounded out, Gehringer to York. No runs, one hit, no errors, one left.

THIRD INNING

Tigers—Sullivan sent a grounder along the first base line and beat F. McCormick's throw to Derringer for a single. Newsom after looking at one strike, laid down a sacrifice bunt, F. McCormick to Joost who covered first. With a one and one count, Bartell raised a high pop fly to Joost on the base path near second. McCosky walked on five pitches. With the count one and one, Gehringer sent a sharp grounder to Werber who stopped the ball but had to pick it up and threw wild to first, the ball getting past F. McCormick and Sullivan coming home before F. McCormick could throw to Wilson. The play was scored as a base hit and an error for Werber. Greenberg got the count to three and two, and then fanned on a high one inside. One run, two hits, one error, two left.

Reds—With the count one and one, Myers looped a single into short left. Derringer, attempting to bunt on the first pitch, popped directly into Newsom's glove, and Myers held first. Werber knocked the first pitch straight at Higgins who threw to Gehringer, forcing Myers at second. M. McCormick worked the count to two and two, and then struck out. No runs, one hit, no errors, one left on.

FOURTH INNING

Tigers—With the count one and one, York lifted a pop foul to Wilson in front of the Tigers' dugout. After looking at two balls, Campbell raised a high fly to Goodman. Higgins hit a hot grounder that Werber deflected against the railing in front of the left field stands and had to run down, Higgins getting a double before the ball could be retrieved. Sullivan was walked intentionally. Newsom hit a grounder that struck Higgins in the stomach as he was running toward third, making an automatic out, with Newsom getting credit for a single and Myers a putout. No runs, two, hits, no errors, two left.

Reds—With the count two and two, Goodman struck out. F. McCormick looked at one ball and then raised a high fly to McCosky in left center. After taking one strike, Ripple grounded out to York, unassisted. No runs, no hits, no errors, none left.

FIFTH INNING

Tigers—Bartell lined the first pitch to M. McCormick, who took it without moving. McCosky loked at one strike, and then flied to Goodman in right field. With the count one strike and two balls, Gehringer lifted a pop fly to Myers on the base path between second and third. No runs, no hits, no errors, none left.

Reds—With the count one strike and two balls, Wilson lined a single

(Continued on Page Two)

BERLIN IS RAIDED BY BOMBERS

German Officials Admit Attack Made on Military Goals at Capital

By THE ASSOCIATED PRESS

BERLIN, Oct. 8. — Nightlong German bombing raids on southern England were reported today by the high command, which admitted that British bombers had inflicted casualties and military damage on Berlin in a fierce exchange of air blows.

Besides subjecting this capital to the worst raid it has yet suffered, British fliers struck also at Hamburg, Germany's chief port, and Amsterdam, chief city of the Nazi-occupied Netherlands.

Informed sources said at least 15 persons were killed in Berlin and the death toll eventually might prove considerably higher.

In "rolling" attacks throughout the night, the high command reported, medium and heavy German bombs fell on traffic points, industrial centers and other targets in the London region.

"Numerous fires were started in the region of the city," it said. "Especially great fires were observed during night raids on Manchester, Liverpool and Edinburgh. Mining of British ports continued."

In Southern England, the communique declared, armament plants and "militarily important objectives" were "effectively bombed."

Yesterday's fighting, swelling again to a thunderous crescendo

(Continued on Page Two)

Nine Girls Die In Dormitory Blaze

JACKSON, Ky., Oct. 8. (AP)—Nine small girls were burned to death early today in a fire which destroyed a frame dormitory building at a mission school in a remote section of Breathitt county.

Twelve other girls and six teachers at the mission which cares for orphan children in this eastern Kentucky mountain area escaped from the second floor of the building where they were sleeping.

One of the teachers, Miss Dessie Scott, 24, was so badly burned helping rescue the children that Dr. Frank Sewell, Breathitt county health officer, said she was not expected to live.

Elected

BANKER—Members of the American Bankers Association named P. D. Houston (above) of Nashville as new A.B.A. president. He succeeds Robert Hanes of Winston-Salem, N. C.

LORD LOTHIAN NOT TO LEAVE

British Ambassador Cancels Plans to Return Home Due to Crisis

WASHINGTON, Oct. 8. (AP)—The British ambassador, Lord Lothian, asserted after a White House call today that his government had ordered him to cancel plans to return to England because "they think there may be a crisis in the Far East."

The ambassador declined to go into details of his conference with President Roosevelt, but left the clear impression they had discussed far eastern matters.

Asked how soon the British government thought a Far East crisis might develop, Lord Lothian said it might come through the reopening of the Burma Road, a supply line to China.

Prime Minister Winston Churchill announced to parliament in London today that the road, over which supplies from the outside world may move to aid China in her fight with Japan, would be opened October 17.

Lothian said he had been ordered on Sunday to fly back to England, that the trip did not look so good on Monay and that it was canceled

(Continued on Page Two)

U. S. Advises Americans in Orient To Return in Face of War Perils

WASHINGTON, Oct 8. (AP) — The government today advised American citizens in the Far East, especially women and children, to consider the advisability of returning to the United States because of disturbed conditions in that area.

State department officials said that American consuls in Japan, China and other parts of the Orient had been notified to suggest to American citizens the advisability of utilizing transportation facilities now available.

This was described as a continuation of the precautionary policy of the government regarding safety of American citizens in various parts of the world.

The advice was directed especially to women and children and men not detained by essential or urgent considerations.

American consuls were instructed to notify the state department of the number of Americans who are coming out or are considering coming out.

The state department's warning to citizens was issued almost simultaneously with Prime Minister Winston Churchill's announcement to parliament in London that the Burma Road, overland supply route to Beleaguered China, would be reopened October 17 — nine days hence.

This announcement holding the promise of renewed assistance to the country which expanding Japan long has tried to conquer followed consultations of the British with United States officials. The United States repeatedly had stated its opposition to Britain's closing of the Road last July in response to Japanese pressure.

In the face of the increasingly grave Oriental situation diplomatic activity here increased in tempo. Secretary Hull scheduled an appointment with Kensuke Horinouchi, the Japanese ambassador.

Conversations initiated weeks ago over trade relations but later broken off, were revived yesterday between the United States and Sov-

(Continued from Page One)

TWO-RUN RALLY BRINGS WINNING TALLY ACROSS IN LAST OF SEVENTH

Paul Derringer Hero of Contest As He Turns in His Second Victory; Newsom Is Losing Pitcher

CROSLEY FIELD, Cincinnati, Oct. 8—(AP)—Cincinnati's rampant Redlegs won the World Series today, four games to three, by beating the Detroit Tigers in the seventh contest, 2 to 1, before a crowd of about 25,000 thrill-crazed fans. The Reds rallied for the winning runs in the seventh inning when Big Buck Newsom, pitching for the Tigers after one day's rest, weakened to give two doubles and a fly.

It was Cincinnati's first World Series championship since 1919 when the Reds beat the Chicago White Sox.

Paul Derringer, batted out of the box in the opening game, was the winning pitcher today, as he and Newsom banged into one of the finest pitching duels the big autumn classic has ever witnessed.

Each hurler allowed seven hits, and they also finished even for the series route with two victories and one defeat.

The Detroit run was unearned, Third Baseman Bill Werber of the Reds coming up with the game's only misplay to let Sullivan across in the third inning.

The Tigers, with Newsom pitching magnificently, clung to their short lead until the last half of the seventh, when F. McCormick led off for the Reds with a resounding double against the left field wall. He scored as Jim Ripple hit the first pitch against the right field bleacher screen for another two-ply shot.

Jimmy Wilson, who had singled in his first two trips, laid down a neat sacrifice to send Ripple to third, and Myers plated him with a long fly to center.

Charley Gehringer led off the Tiger eighth with a single to right, but that was the final Detroit gesture, for Derringer tightened the clamps and got the next six in order, including pinch-hitter Earl Averill who grounded for the final out.

Newsom, back in there after his one-day rest, pitched superbly except for the fatal seventh. The big, blatant one fanned six of the Reds, and walked one — an intentional pass to big Ernie Lombardi when "Schnozzle" went in as a pinch-hitter for Joost, with Ripple on third in the seventh.

The seventh was the only frame in which the Reds could get more

(Continued on Page Two)

Box Score

CROSLEY FIELD, Cincinnati, O., Oct. 8. (AP)—Official box score of seventh World Series game:

Detroit (A.L.)—	AB	R	H	O	A
Bartell, ss	4	0	0	3	2
McCosky, cf	3	0	0	3	0
Gehringer, 2b	4	0	2	2	2
Greenberg, lf	4	0	2	1	0
York, 1b	4	0	0	6	0
Campbell, rf	3	0	0	2	0
Higgins, 3b	4	0	1	0	4
Sullivan, c	3	1	1	6	0
Newsom, p	2	0	1	1	0
xAverill	1	0	0	0	0
Totals	32	1	7	24	8

x—Batted for Newsom in 9th.

Cincinnati (N.L.)—	AB	R	H	O	A
Werber, 3b	4	0	0	1	3
M. McCormick, cf	4	0	2	3	0
Goodman ,rf	4	0	0	3	0
F. McCormick, 1b	4	1	1	7	1
Ripple, lf	3	1	1	1	0
Wilson, c	2	0	2	2	0
Wilson, c	2	0	2	2	0
Joost, 2b	2	0	0	5	1
zLombardi	0	0	0	0	0
Frey 2b	0	0	0	0	1
Myers, ss	3	0	1	5	1
Derringer, p	3	0	0	0	1
Totals	29	2	7	27	8

z—Batted for Joost in 7th.

Detroit (AL)	001 000 000—1
Cincinati (NL)	000 000 20x—2

Error—Werber.

Runs batted in—Ripple, Myers.

Two base hits—Higgins, M. McCormick, F. McCormick, Ripple.

Stolen bases—Wilson.

Sacrifices—Newsom, Wilson.

Double plays—Gehringer, Bartell and York.

Earned runs: Detroit (AL) 0; Cincinnati (NL) 2.

Left on bases—Detroit (AL) 8; Cincinati (NL) 5.

Bases on balls—Off Derringer 3 (McCosky, Sullivan, Campbell); off Newsom 1 (Lombardi).

Struck out—by Newsom 6 (M. McCormick 2, Ripple, Goodman 2, Werber); by Derringer 1 (Greenberg).

Time—1:47.

Attendance (estimated) 25,000.

George B. Landrum Claimed by Death

George B. Landrum of Johnson Addition, operator of the B. and L. Service station, died this morning at a local hospital following a heart attack yesterday afternoon.

He fell at his station after he was stricken, but attending physicians said there was no evidence of serious injuries from the fall. He was conscious most of the night but lapsed into unconsciousness early today and died about dawn.

He was the father of Lewis Landrum, engineer for the Arizona Edison company.

New Camera Will Be Used in Draft

DETROIT, Mich., Oct. 8. (AP)—A new "candid" x-ray camera which can photograph the chest and other parts of the body on a small film will be used in army physical examinations during the coming draft.

The machine developed by the General Electric X-ray corporation and announced at the annual meeting of the American public health association, reduces the picture through a special fast lens from the usual 14 inch by 17 inch full size negative to one only four inches long.

With it ten times the number of men can be examined at the same cost now required with the larger film. Photographs can be taken much more rapidly with the same exactness of detail obtained in the larger films.

20,000 NAZIS LAND IN SYRIA, SAYS LONDON

THE BALTIMORE NEWS-POST
AN INDEPENDENT NEWSPAPER
The Largest Evening Circulation in the Entire South
NIGHT
Wall St. Opening
VOL. CXXXIX.—NO. 26 Entered as second-class matter at Baltimore Postoffice. TUESDAY EVENING, JUNE 3, 1941 PRICE 3 CENTS

Gehrig, Baseball Idol, Dies

Axis Ready For U. S.---Rome

IN THE NEWS

A REPORT on general and indiscriminate vivisection made by the New England Anti-Vivisection Society says:

"Vivisection is experiment upon a living creature, human or animal, made for the demonstration, before students, of facts already known and established, or for the investigation of some theory or problem which may or may not have any relation to the treatment of human ills.

"Vivisection includes the cutting of living animals with knives, burning, roasting and freezing them to death, smothering and starving them, or in any other way maltreating them with the excuse that such action may at some future time add to the knowledge of science and of medicine and thus prove beneficial to the health of mankind. It includes the deliberate infliction of disease upon sound and wholesome creatures through inoculation with virulent matter or the feeding of unnatural substances. It ranges from procedures which are practically painless to those involving distress, exhaustion, every kind of mutilation, long-protracted agony and death.

"Since it is not the practice of laboratories to raise their own animals, the more than 400,000 dogs which Dr. William Howard Hay estimates are vivisected in the United States every year are undeniably our own strayed or stolen pets.

"WHILE in certain European countries some of the worst phases of experimentation are forbidden or curbed by law, in the United States a man may do what he likes to an animal in the name of science without fear of arrest. In many kinds of vivisection anesthesia cannot be used, such as the starvation experiments, which are common, drowning, gassing, endurance tests and the inoculations which induce virulent diseases. In cutting operations the dog struggles desperately against the ether, and is in almost every instance subjected to debarking, his jaws pried open with a long metal slab and the inserted knife severing his vocal cords. And always, unlike the human patient, he has been operated upon not for his healing and benefit but for his mutilation. The conclusions drawn from his suffering have frequently proved dangerous and sometimes fatal to the human beings he is supposed to save because of the difference between his own anatomy and reactions and theirs."

ON THE picture page of this newspaper today your columnist presents for your consideration some authoritative pictures of vivisection experiments inflicted upon *"man's best friend,"* the dog.

These pictures, assembled by the New England Anti-Vivisection Society, have not been made originally by those who desire to expose the cruelties of the experiments.

They have been made by the experimenters themselves to illustrate the experiment—to show the processes of the vivisection or to depict the result.

These pictures are not, by any means, examples of the most horrifying of the proctsses of indiscriminate vivisection.

First, because most of the experimental vivisection shuns the light and permits no illustrative record.

Second, because a great deal of it is wholly without scientific purpose and no record is made either textual or pictorial.

And third, because—as the re-

Continued on Page 4, Column 1.

'Moment For Action,' Spokesman Says After Hitler-Mussolini Talk

ROME, June 3—(U. P.).—Virginio Gayda, spokesman for Premier Mussolini, said today that Il Duce and Hitler have placed the Axis in readiness to cope with American intervention in the war and that "this is the moment for action."

Gayda declared that the Axis is prepared to launch a new phase of the war immediately and that all phases of possible United States entry into the conflict have been examined. He wrote:

"Today a new offensive must be launched. Britain cries to the United States for help. The Axis Powers can mass their reserves of military and political forces in both Europe and other parts of the world—for either defense or offense."

Gayda said that there was no doubt that Mussolini and Hitler had examined the results of the "war cycle which has just been completed and outlined plans for the new phase of the war which will commence immediately for the victorious Axis forces."

Popolo Di Roma asserted that the Brenner conference was of paramount political and diplomatic importance and that it concerned the reorganization of Europe as well as Axis war plans.

Roosevelt To Veto Farm Bill, Report

WASHINGTON, June 3—(A. P.). President Roosevelt, authoritative sources reported today, will veto the bill carrying funds for the 85 per cent. parity loan agriculture program if Congress insists on attaching an amendment fixing minimum prices for Government purchases of farm products.

Temperatures

12 Midn't,	61	6 A. M.,	59
1 A. M.,	61	7 A. M.,	61
2 A. M.,	61	8 A. M.,	65
3 A. M.,	60	9 A. M.,	66
4 A. M.,	60	10 A. M.,	68
5 A. M.,	59	11 A. M.,	70

RAF Makes 46th Raid On Berlin

LONDON, June 3—(I. N. S.).—Causing large fires, a small force of British bombers bombed Berlin for the forty-sixth time last night and early today while squadrons of other R. A. F. planes hammered industrial targets in Germany's strategic Ruhr district.

Dusseldorf, Duisberg and Ruhrort were among the objectives pounded by British planes.

(BACKGROUND NOTE: A Berlin announcement said civilians were killed and injured and buildings damaged when R. A. F. night raiders repeatedly attacked objectives in Western and Northern Germany, including Berlin. The German communique claimed three British planes were shot down.)

One German raider dropped bombs on the northeast coast this morning, causing a number of casualties, including deaths.

Shortly before dusk yesterday another raider bombed a northeast coastal district, causing slight damage. British fighters roared to the attack and the raider scampered to safety in the clouds.

British fighter planes made a sweep of Northern France and the Channel, swooping from the clouds to attack German motor transport columns, airdromes and a Nazi E-boat (motor torpedo boat).

An American pilot officer serving with the R. A. F. dived on an airdrome and "shot up" two German Messerschmitt 109s on the ground.

RACE ENTRIES, COMMENTS WILL BE FOUND ON PAGES 14-15-16

Baseball's Lou Gehrig Dies At 37

NEW YORK, June 3—(I. N. S.).—Lou Gehrig, the "Iron Man" of baseball and one of the sportsmen heroes of American youth, was dead today at thirty-seven, victim of a rare form of infantile paralysis.

The former captain and first baseman of the New York Yankees baseball team was forced to retire in 1939 because of his illness.

One of the greatest players of all time, Gehrig set an endurance record of 2,130 consecutive big league games—15 seasons of Yankee baseball with his name always in the line-up.

(Details on Sports Pages)

June Snow Climax To Soviet Spring

MOSCOW, June 3—(A. P.).—Snow fell on Central European Russia today, prolonging this section's coldest spring in more than a century. Snowfall was reported at Archangel and Leningrad as well as Moscow, where a temperature of 42.8 degrees was recorded. This was the first June snow recalled by residents.

LaGuardia Starts Defense Surveys

NEW YORK, June 3—(I. N. S.). Mayor F. H. LaGuardia flew to Boston today in the first of his series of visits to the nation's nine Army Corps areas in an attempt to "get things going" in civilian defense. The newly named director of Civilian Defense will survey the State of civilian preparedness in each area.

Father Of 33 Is Dead At 124

LIMA, Peru, June 3—(U. P.).—Fernando Ledesma, who claimed to be 124, a retired cavalry sergeant, died yesterday at the San Bartolome Military Hospital. He had survived two wives and was the father of 33 children, of whom the youngest is 48.

THE WEATHER

Cloudy, followed by light to moderate rain today and tonight. Highest temperature today around seventy degrees. Wednesday, mostly cloudy, with occasional showers and slightly warmer.

MEAN TEMPERATURES YESTERDAY

Baltimore	66	New York	66
Atlanta	82	Omaha	68
Boston	60	Portland, Me.	62
Chicago	64	Salt Lake City	62
Jacksonville	86	San Antonio	84
Los Angeles	66	Seattle	60
Miami	80	Tampa	76
New Orleans	78	Washington	70

Roosevelt Request For Right To Seize Property Hit In D. C.

By WILLIAM S. NEAL
International News Service Staff Correspondent.

WASHINGTON, June 3.—President Roosevelt's proposed bill giving him power to take over and sell any property usable for national defense—even indirectly—today jolted Congress to its depths.

Foes of the Administration's foreign policy charged it means economic dictatoriship. Thus was heatedly denied by New Deal leaders who said the measure means that nothing can stand in the way of the "all-out" defense program.

SEE THREE OBJECTIVES

Three major objectives of the bill, which the War Department sent to Congress with Mr. Roosevelt's approval and which was introduced by Senator Reynolds (Democrat) of North Carolina, chairman of the Military Affairs Committee, were seen by some informed Administration sources. They are:

1. Give the President power to halt strikes through threat of Government ownership of plants.

2. Permit seizure of Nazi-controlled corporations as the first step in a gigantic scheme of economic "defensive warfare."

3. Allow curb of production of civilian goods which compete with the defense program.

CUTS "RED TAPE"

The bill, approved also by the Navy Department and the OPM, rolls into one short measure powers now possessed under a national emergency, adds some new ones and slashes "red tape" now facing the Government in seizure of plants.

Assistant Secretary of War Patterson said in an accompanying letter to Congress it would "put teeth" into the full emergency.

Under it, the President can take over, temporarily or permanently,

Continued on Page 2, Column 7.

Reject Jap Plan For China Peace

By KINGSBURY SMITH
International News Service Staff Correspondent.

WASHINGTON, June 3.—Diplomatic quarters in Washington today believe the United States and Japan are about to enter a new period of increasingly strained relations as a result of the American Government's refusal to engage in an appeasement move with the Nippon Empire.

In the light of this situation, International News Service is able to present exclusively the current attitude of the American Government toward Japan and the reasons why it has ignored the appeasement overtures from Tokyo.

REPEATED OVERTURES

These overtures have been made repeatedly from Tokyo in the form of suggestions that Japanese Foreign Minister Yosuke Matsuoka should be invited to visit Washington to discuss a settlement of Far Eastern problems.

The American Government believes Matsuoka's idea of a satisfactory settlement of Far Eastern problems would be for the United States to cease aiding China and agree to bring pressure to bear on Gen. Issimo Chiang Kai-Shek to conclude a peace treaty with Tokyo recognizing Japan's predominance in Asia.

In return, it is thought Japan might agree to withdraw from the Axis alliance and assure the United States certain economic privileges in the Far East.

IDEA REJECTED

The idea of such a settlement with Japan has been rejected by the American Government for the following reasons:

1. Such appeasement of Japan

Continued on Page 2, Column 4.

The Baltimore News-Post today is printed in 3 Sections
Be sure you get the complete newspaper.

London Claims Nazis In Syria; French Ready For Attack By Britain

LONDON, June 3—(I. N. S.).—With hundreds of German fighting and transport planes reported at Syrian bases, the Nazi war machine was poised for a new blow against British might in the Near East today. At least 400 Nazi planes have arrived at Syrian bases, best estimates in London said, while "tourists" dispatched to the French-mandated territory to lay the groundwork for German seizure were said to number at least 20,000.

ISTANBUL, Turkey, June 3—(A. P.).—Germans in civilian clothes recently passed through Turkey to Syria with Bulgarian passports, unofficial sources asserted.

BEIRUT, Syria, June 3—(U. P.).—French officials declared today that Syria will be defended with the greatest determination and charged that British reports of German troop landings were being circulated to provide a pretext for British invasion.

Gen. Henri Dentz, High Commissioner, formally denied that any German troops have arrived in Syria and French officials asserted angrily that German troop debarkations at Latakia were "impossible."

These officials claimed that the Germans could not land troops in Syria because of British control of the seas. They pointed out that Latakia is located near Cyprus, where British sea control is particularly effective.

They warned that Syria would resist invasion from any source with all her forces.

In a formal communique, Dentz said that it was the policy of France to yield concessions to no power, including Germany, in Syria.

British Army Set To Invade Syria

LONDON, June 3—(A. P.).—Qualified observers predicted today the War Cabinet soon would declare Syria an enemy-occupied territory, opening the French-mandated wedge between Turkey and Palestine for full-scale British attack.

Reports from Turkey that the Nazis already had landed sea-borne infantry with motorized equipment at the Syrian port of Latakia, just

Continued on Page 2, Column 1.

Weygand, Petain In War Parley

VICHY, June 3—(U. P.).—Marshal Henri Philippe Petain met with his Council of Ministers today to consider the situation in Syria and the French colonies in a session described as one of the most important since France decided to seek an armistice.

A strict censorship prevailed and correspondents were unable to answer specific inquiries concerning Syria. After the Council meeting, which lasted more than two hours, a brief communique was issued. It said only that the meeting had been held.

Gen. Maxime Weygand, French commander in North Africa and specialist on Syrian problems, and Admiral Jean Francois Darlan, Vice Premier, attended.

(BACKGROUND NOTE: The dispatch made no direct mention of reports from London that the British might be planning to send forces into Syria or on Ankara reports that German motorized infantry already had landed at the Syrian port of Latakia.)

READ JAN VALTIN'S GREAT STORY 'OUT OF THE NIGHT'—PAGE 3

DiMaggio Sets All-Time Hitting Record as Yankees Win; Dodgers Triumph

HOME RUN IN FIFTH TOPS KEELER MARK

DiMaggio's Wallop Stretches His Hitting Streak to 45 Games—Old Record 44

YANKS HALT RED SOX, 8-4

Win Sixth Straight to Extend First-Place Margin Over Indians to 3 Contests

By JOHN DREBINGER

Sweeping majestically onward with a thunderous smash that soared deep into the left-field stands, Joe DiMaggio yesterday rocketed his current hitting streak beyond the all-time major league record.

For with that home-run clout, boisterously acclaimed by 8,682 sweltering fans in the sun-baked Yankee Stadium, DiMaggio the Magnificent extended his astounding string to forty-five consecutive games in which he has connected safely.

This surpasses by one the major league mark of 44 games set forty-four years ago by that famous mite of an Oriole, Wee Willie Keeler, who gained renown for his skill in "hitting them where they ain't." Yesterday DiMaggio shattered that mark by the simpler expedient of hitting one where they just couldn't get it.

Clean Sweep of Series

Jolting Joe's record-smashing blow was struck off Heber Newsome, freshman right-hander, in the fifth inning of a game which also saw the Yankees flatten the Red Sox, 8 to 4. That gave the Bronx Bombers a clean sweep of the three-game series, extended a new winning streak to six in a row and bolstered their hold on first place to three full games over the Indians.

But all this provided merely incidental music, for the crowd's attention remained riveted on the tall, dark-haired Yankee Clipper who, despite a warm and genial personality, seems to move so coldly aloof on a ball field.

The modern record of 41 games, set by George Sisler of the Browns in 1922, had already fallen by the wayside in last Sunday's double-header in Washington. Actually, there was no comparison between this new DiMaggio mark and the old record of Keeler's, for different rules prevailed in Wee Willie's day back in 1897. There was no foul strike rule hampering the hitter then so that DiMaggio, when he equalled the 44-game Keeler record on Tuesday, already seemed to have achieved a greater feat.

Makes Leaping Catch

But, in order to preclude all further argument, Joe yesterday decided to smash the last remaining record and he certainly did it in the most emphatic manner possible. He almost broke the mark the first time up when he shot a sharp liner to right center which Stanley Spence for a moment misjudged. But the Boston right fielder righted his course just in time to make a leaping catch.

A snappy pick-up and throw by Third Baseman Jim Tabor on a difficult bounding ball checked DiMaggio again in the third, but there was no stopping him in the fifth as he clubbed the ball into the left-field stand with Red Rolfe on base.

The shot came in the midst of a six-run rally which routed Newsome and enabled DiMaggio's bosom pal and roommate, Lefty Gomez, to chalk up his sixth mound victory of the year despite the fact that the heat forced Lefty to vacate in the next inning.

The DiMaggio clout was his eighteenth homer of the year, his thirteenth of the batting streak and his 100th hit of the season.

In the second inning Charlie Keller hit a homer for his No. 17 in addition to boosting his runs-batted-in total to 69, four above DiMaggio's current total.

Second Nature With DiMaggio

Hitting in streaks seems almost to be a matter of second nature with DiMaggio. His mark of 61, which he set in 1933, still stands as the record in the Pacific Coast League.

And no longer ago than last Spring he set some sort of unofficial record by connecting safely in every exhibition game he played—a total of nineteen. As the championship campaign got under way he extended this string for eight more games before Lester McCrabb of the Athletics halted Joe for his first "horse collar" of the year.

DiMaggio, in fact, remained subdued for quite a time after that, for a period going into a terrific tailspin. But on May 15 he snapped out of it and nobody has stopped him since. In all, Jolting Joe has failed to hit safely in only eleven games this year.

Much as he also likes to collect his hits, Gomez simply couldn't get up the nerve to try for a base when he came up with two out and nobody on in the fourth. So he struck out on three listless swings.

But apparently that was just a "come on" for Jack Wilson to lob one over in the fifth, with the result that Lefty banged it right into center for two runs.

A souvenir hunter almost got away with a grand coup at the close of the game when he snatched DiMaggio's cap off his head and started dashing for the nearest exit like one of football's greatest open-field runners. But the Stadium's vigilant secondary defense of special guards finally nailed the culprit some twenty yards from his goal.

Although he is supposed to be suffering from a cracked rib which has had him reported as possibly out of the All-Star game, Jimmy Foxx emerged from the dugout in the ninth to serve notice on all and sundry that old Double XX still can nudge a few by coming up with a pinch single.

Today the McCarthymen will enjoy a brief respite from the heat prior to tackling the Senators in the holiday double-header at the Stadium which starts at 1:30 o'clock tomorrow.

The box score:

BOSTON (A.)	ab.	r.	h.	po.	a.	e.
D.DiMag., cf	5	1	0	1	0	0
Finney, 1b.	5	1	2	10	1	0
Williams, lf.	3	1	1	1	0	0
Cronin, ss.	2	1	1	0	1	1
L.N'some, ss.	0	0	0	1	1	0
Spence, rf.	4	0	1	4	0	0
Tabor, 3b.	4	0	2	1	2	0
Doerr, 2b.	4	0	0	1	4	0
Pytlak, c.	4	0	0	5	1	0
H.N'some, p.	2	0	1	0	0	0
Wilson, p.	0	0	0	0	0	0
Potter, p.	1	0	0	0	0	0
aFoxx	1	0	1	0	0	0
Total	35	4	9	24	10	1

NEW YORK (A.)	ab.	r.	h.	po.	a.	e.
Sturm, 1b.	4	1	0	9	0	0
Rolfe, 3b.	3	2	2	0	4	0
Henrich, rf.	5	0	3	3	0	0
J.DiMag., cf.	5	1	1	3	0	0
Keller, lf.	4	2	2	4	0	0
Dickey, c.	3	1	0	3	0	0
Gordon, 2b.	5	1	0	2	3	0
Rizzuto, ss.	4	0	2	3	4	1
Gomez, p.	3	0	1	0	1	0
Murphy, p.	1	0	0	0	0	0
Total	37	8	11	27	12	1

aBatted for Potter in ninth.

Boston .... 0 0 0 0 0 3 1 0 0—4
New York .... 0 1 1 0 6 0 0 0 ..—8

Runs batted in—Keller, J. DiMaggio 3, Rolfe, Gomez 2, Spence 2, Tabor, Cronin.

Two-base hits—Rizzuto, Rolfe. Home runs—Keller, J. DiMaggio. Stolen base—Sturm. Double plays—Gomez, Rizzuto and Sturm; Rolfe, Gordon and Sturm. Left on bases—New York 11, Boston 7. Bases on balls—Off Gomez 2, H. Newsome 3, Wilson 1, Murphy 1, Potter 2. Struck out—By Gomez 2, H. Newsome 2, Wilson 1, Murphy 1, Potter 1. Hits—Off H. Newsome 6 in 4 1-3 innings, Wilson 1 in 2-3, Potter 4 in 3, Gomez 5 in 5 1-3, Murphy 4 in 3 2-3. Wild pitch—Gomez. Passed balls—Pytlak 2. Winning pitcher—Gomez. Losing pitcher—H. Newsome. Umpires—Rommell, Stewart, Summers and Rue. Time of game—2:22. Attendance—8,682.

AS NEW MAJOR LEAGUE BATTING MARK WAS MADE BY YANKEE STAR

Joe DiMaggio being congratulated by Red Rolfe after he hit his homer to run his consecutive hitting streak to forty-five games. Batboy Tim Sullivan also is seen.

Tiny Bonham and Tommy Henrich raise their team-mate aloft in clubhouse celebration after contest. Times Wide World

DiMaggio Streak Shows 67 Hits for 124 Bases

Although Willie Keeler compiled a greater total of hits in his string of 44 games back in 1897 than Joe DiMaggio collected in the 45 games which enabled him to surpass the old Oriole's mark yesterday, a comparison of the two records shows Jolting Joe to have excelled Keeler in the matter of total bases.

In his string of 45, DiMaggio has collected a total of 67 hits which include 12 doubles, 3 triples and 13 homers for a total of 124 bases. Against this, Keeler's record for 44 games, though Wee Willie made 82 safe blows, shows only 113 total bases. The old Oriole hit 11 doubles and 10 triples, but failed to connect for a single home run.

A comparison of Keeler's 44-game hitting streak and DiMaggio's record-smashing string of 45 follows:

	AB.	H.	2B.	3B.	H.R.	P.C.
Keeler	201	82	11	10	0	.408
DiMaggio	179	67	12	3	13	.374

ATHLETICS DEFEAT SENATORS IN TENTH

Johnson's Homer Wins, 7-6—Philadelphians Overcome Five-Run Deficit

PHILADELPHIA, July 2 (AP)—Indian Bob Johnson's home run in the tenth inning—his seventeenth of the season—gave the Athletics a 7-to-6 victory over the Senators today.

Trailing, 5 to 0, after five innings, Philadelphia pecked away at Bill Zuber for two runs in the sixth, another in the eighth and finally drove him from the hill in the ninth with a three-run outburst that deadlocked the score. George Case hit a home run in Washington's four-run fifth inning.

The box score:

WASHINGTON (A.)	ab.	r.	h.	po.	a.	e.
Archie, 3b.	5	1	2	1	1	0
Cramer, cf.	4	0	1	2	0	0
Lewis, rf.	4	0	1	3	0	0
Travis, ss.	4	2	3	3	2	0
Vernon, 1b.	5	0	2	11	0	0
Early, c.	4	1	2	4	0	0
Case, lf.	4	1	2	3	0	0
Bloodwth, 2b	4	1	1	2	6	1
Zuber, p.	4	0	0	0	1	0
Kennedy, p.	0	0	0	0	0	0
Total	38	6	14	*29	10	1

PHILADELPHIA (A.)	ab.	r.	h.	po.	a.	e.
Brancato, ss.	6	0	0	4	3	0
Miles, rf.	6	0	0	2	0	0
McCoy, 2b.	6	1	2	3	5	0
Johnson, lf.	6	2	4	2	1	0
Siebert, 1b.	5	1	0	9	0	1
S.Chapmn, cf	2	0	3	0	0	0
Wagner, c.	3	1	3	6	2	1
Suder, 3b.	5	0	1	1	4	0
Babich, p.	1	0	1	0	0	0
Hadley, p.	0	0	0	0	0	0
aMoses	1	0	1	0	0	0
bF. Chapmn	0	0	0	0	0	0
Harris, p.	1	0	1	0	1	0
cCollins	1	0	0	0	0	0
Ferrick, p.	0	0	0	0	1	0
dDean	1	0	1	0	0	0
McCrabb, p.	0	0	0	0	0	0
Total	44	7	14	30	17	2

*Two out when winning run was scored.
aBatted for Hadley in fifth.
bRan for Moses in fifth.
cBatted for Harris in eighth.
dBatted for Ferrick in ninth.

Washington .... 0 0 0 1 4 0 0 1 0 0—6
Philadelphia .... 0 0 0 0 0 2 0 1 3 1—7

Runs batted in—Case 2, Travis, Lewis, Suder, Harris, Vernon, Brancato, Wagner, Dean, Johnson.

Two-base hits—Travis 2, Early, Cramer. Three-base hit—Travis. Home runs—Case, Johnson. Stolen bases—Lewis, Archie, Bloodworth. Sacrifice—Travis. Double play—Brancato, McCoy and Siebert. Left on bases—Washington 6, Philadelphia 13. Bases on balls—Off Babich 1, Zuber 5. Struck out—By Babich 2, Harris 2, Ferrick 2, Zuber 1. Hits—Off Babich 7 in 4 2-3 innings, Harris 6 in 3, Zuber 12 in 8 1-3, McCrabb 1 in 1, Hadley 0 in 1-3, Ferrick 0 in 1, Kennedy 2 in 1 1-3. Hit by pitcher—By Babich (Early, Cramer). Wild pitch—Zuber. Winning pitcher—McCrabb. Losing pitcher—Kennedy. Umpires—Quinn, Grieve and McGowan. Time of game—2:42. Attendance—1,500.

Today's Probable Pitchers

By The Associated Press.

American League

Boston at Philadelphia—Grove (5-2) vs. Dean (2-2).
Other clubs not scheduled.

National League

Philadelphia at Boston—Hughes (5-7) vs. Javery (4-1).
Cincinnati at Pittsburgh—Pearson (1-2) vs. Lanning (2-4).
St. Louis at Chicago—Lanier (6-3) vs. Passeau (7-7).
Other clubs not scheduled.
(Figures in parentheses indicate season's won-and-lost records.)

Albany Purchases Infielder

ALBANY, July 2 (AP)—The Albany Senators of the Eastern League announced today the purchase from Riverside of the California League of Einar Willard Sorenson, 27-year-old infielder. Sorenson, a second baseman, was a member of the Cincinnati Reds farm system for several seasons.

Major League Baseball

American League

YESTERDAY'S RESULTS

New York 8, Boston 4.
Philadelphia 7, Washington 6. (ten innings).
Detroit 1, Chicago 0 (night).
Other clubs not scheduled.

STANDING OF THE CLUBS

	New York	Cleveland	Boston	Chicago	Detroit	Phila'phia	Wash'gton	St. Louis	Won	Lost	Percentage	Games Behind
N. Y.	—	7	7	5	4	4	8	10	45	26	.634	—
Cleve	3	—	6	4	6	10	7	7	43	30	.589	3
Boston	4	3	—	7	7	7	3	5	36	33	.522	8
Chicago	5	6	3	—	6	3	7	6	36	34	.514	8½
Detroit	6	4	6	5	—	8	3	5	37	36	.507	9
Phila	4	3	3	6	3	—	10	5	34	36	.486	10½
Wash	2	3	4	5	7	1	—	4	26	44	.371	18½
St. L.	2	4	4	2	3	3	6	—	24	42	.364	18½
Lost	26	30	33	34	36	36	44	42	—	—		

GAME TODAY

Boston at Philadelphia.
Other clubs not scheduled.

National League

YESTERDAY'S RESULTS

Boston 5, New York 4 (1st).
New York 6, Boston 0 (2d).
Brooklyn 9, Philadelphia 3.
Pittsburgh 8, Cincinnati 3.
Other clubs not scheduled.

STANDING OF THE CLUBS

	St. Louis	Brooklyn	New York	Cincinnati	Pittsburgh	Chicago	Boston	Phila'phia	Won	Lost	Percentage	Games Behind
St. L.	—	5	7	8	9	5	6	8	48	23	.676	—
Bklyn	6	—	6	8	5	5	7	11	48	24	.667	½
N. Y.	5	4	—	4	3	9	8	5	38	32	.543	9½
Cincin.	4	5	6	—	5	6	6	4	36	34	.514	11½
Pitts	1	3	5	3	—	6	3	8	29	34	.460	15
Chicago	2	4	3	4	4	—	6	8	31	39	.443	16½
Boston	4	2	3	3	3	5	—	6	26	40	.394	19½
Phila	1	1	2	4	5	3	4	—	20	50	.286	27½
Lost	23	24	32	34	34	39	40	50	—	—		

GAMES TODAY

Philadelphia at Boston.
Cincinnati at Pittsburgh.
St. Louis at Chicago.
Other clubs not scheduled.

Lohrman Sets Back Braves, 6 to 0, After Giants Bow, 5 to 4, in First

Terrymen's 6 in Eighth of Nightcap Break Up Mound Duel—Wittig Fails in Opener—Earley Shines in Relief Role

By LOUIS EFFRAT

Special to THE NEW YORK TIMES.

BOSTON, July 2—Where Johnny Wittig failed, Bill Lohrman met with success today. Lohrman blanked the Braves, 6—0, after the home team had gained a 5-4 decision in the first game of the double-header.

Black Bill's top-heavy margin was not realized until the eighth, when the Giants crossed the plate six times. Until then Lohrman had to pitch brilliantly and wait patiently until his mates would hand him any kind of an edge. Just as the Giants had been held to four hits in the opener, Lohrman limited the Braves to the same number, while recording his fifth victory of the campaign.

Superlative relief pitching by Tom Earley beat the Terrymen in the curtain raiser. The New Yorkers had four in and the tying run on second, when Earley replaced Dick Merriwell Errickson and faced Harry Danning, pinch hitting for Ace Adams, in the sixth.

Great Play by Sisti

There were two down at the time. Harry the Horse drove a torrid grounder just inside the third-base line, but Sibby Sisti came up with the ball and threw out the runner on a great play.

After that, Earley was in complete command. He retired the next six batters in a row. A pass to Odell Hale opened the ninth, but Bill Jurges struck out, Danning flied to left and Joe Moore bounced one behind second, and Bama Rowell came through with a brilliant force at second.

Wittig started for the Giants, but was well tagged. In the first, singles by Sisti, Buddy Hassett and Max West, plus a double by Paul Waner, made it 2—0. Then, in the fourth, the Braves made a single, a wild pitch, a pass and doubles by Sisti and Johnny Cooney count for three more. The New Yorkers got to Errickson in the sixth, but fell one run short of a tie.

Two Triples Wasted

It was a different story in the afterpiece, with both sides getting good pitching, despite wasted triples by Babe Young in the second and Hale in the fourth. The Giants batted young Lefty Art Johnson out in the eighth, breaking up the game.

After one out, Frank Demaree singled. Mel Ott hit to Hassett, whose low throw to second, trying for a double play, was scored as an error and both were safe. A single by Danning pushed home Demaree and Hale's double accounted for two more. Young dropped a single into short left, Hale stopping at third, and Johnson made way for Johnny Hutchings. Before the newcomer was able to stop the onslaught Jurges doubled and Lohrman got his second single of the game.

In the first inning of the opener Ott smashed a screaming 400-foot drive to dead center, but Cooney, who improves with age, pulled it down, even while bouncing off the concrete wall. Ottey hasn't hit many balls harder than he did this one, but it was just a time at bat.

West also hit the wall, trying to snare Jurges's first-game double. It looked serious, when Max fell, but he arose after a half minute and went right on playing. In the fifth of the nightcap, though, a sudden nose bleed forced him to retire.

Announcement that Joe DiMaggio had surpassed Wee Willie Keeler's record was made over the loud speaker and was well received here. . . . The Giants will rest tomorrow, awaiting the holiday twin bill at Ebbets Field, where Carl Hubbell and Cliff Melton will do the hurling. . . . Some of the Giants will be at Huntington, L. I., tomorrow to watch the baseball (?) game between the New York and Brooklyn scribes.

The Box Scores

FIRST GAME

NEW YORK (N.)	ab.	r.	h.	po.	a.	e.
J. Moore, lf.	5	0	1	0	0	0
Bartell, 3b.	2	0	0	2	3	0
Rucker, cf.	4	0	0	5	0	0
Ott, rf.	3	1	0	1	0	0
O'Dea, c.	2	1	0	1	0	0
Carpenter, p.	0	0	0	0	1	0
bHartnett	1	0	0	0	0	0
Brown, p.	0	0	0	0	0	0
Young, 1b.	4	1	1	8	0	0
Hale, 2b.	2	1	0	0	3	0
cWhitehead	0	0	0	0	0	0
Jurges, ss.	4	0	2	4	2	0
Wittig, p.	1	0	0	0	1	0
aOrengo	1	0	0	0	0	0
Adams, p.	0	0	0	0	0	0
Danning, c.	2	0	0	3	0	0
Total	31	4	4	24	10	0

BOSTON (N.)	ab.	r.	h.	po.	a.	e.
Sisti, 3b.	4	2	3	1	3	0
Cooney, cf.	4	0	1	5	0	0
Hassett, 1b.	4	1	2	8	0	0
West, lf.	3	0	1	4	0	0
Waner, rf.	4	0	1	1	0	0
Rowell, 2b.	3	1	1	1	2	0
Miller, ss.	3	1	0	1	2	0
Masi, c.	4	0	1	6	0	0
Errickson, p.	2	0	0	0	0	0
Earley, p.	1	0	0	0	0	0
Total	32	5	10	27	7	0

aBatted for Wittig in fifth.
bBatted for Carpenter in eighth.
cRan for Hale in ninth.

New York .... 0 0 0 0 0 4 0 0 0—4
Boston .... 2 0 0 3 0 0 0 0 ..—5

Runs batted in—Young, Jurges 3, Sisti, Cooney, West, Waner, Errickson.

Two-base hits—Young, Jurges, Sisti, Cooney, Waner. Double plays—Hale, Jurges and Young; Carpenter, Jurges and Young. Left on bases—New York 6, Boston 6. Bases on balls—Off Wittig 2, Carpenter 1, Errickson 5, Earley 1. Struck out—By Wittig 1, Carpenter 1, Brown 2, Errickson 3, Earley 2. Hits—Off Wittig 8 in 4 innings, Adams 0 in 1, Carpenter 2 in 2, Errickson 4 in 5 2-3, Early 0 in 3 1-3, Brown 0 in 1. Wild pitch—Wittig. Winning pitcher—Errickson. Losing pitcher—Wittig. Umpires—Magerkurth, Stewart and Dunn. Time of game—2:30.

SECOND GAME

NEW YORK (N.)	ab.	r.	h.	po.	a.	e.
Arnovich, lf.	5	0	1	5	0	0
Bartell, 3b.	5	0	0	1	1	0
Demaree, cf.	4	1	1	2	0	0
Ott, rf.	5	1	1	2	0	0
Danning, c	4	1	1	3	1	0
Hale, 2b.	4	1	2	2	1	0
Whiteh'd, 2b.	0	0	0	0	1	0
Young, 1b.	4	1	2	11	0	0
Jurges, ss	3	1	1	1	5	0
Lohrman, p.	4	0	2	0	1	0
Total	38	6	11	27	10	0

BOSTON (N.)	ab.	r.	h.	po.	a.	e.
Sisti, 3b	2	0	1	2	3	0
Cooney, cf	4	0	0	1	0	0
Hassett, 1b.	4	0	1	12	1	1
West, lf	2	0	0	1	0	0
E. Moore, rf.	2	0	0	0	0	0
Waner, rf, lf.	3	0	0	2	0	0
Rowell, 2b.	4	0	0	0	3	2
Miller, ss	4	0	1	4	2	0
M'tgomery, c.	2	0	1	3	1	0
Masi, c	1	0	0	1	0	0
Johnson, p.	2	0	0	1	3	0
Hutchings, p.	0	0	0	0	1	0
aRoss	1	0	0	0	0	0
Earley, p	0	0	0	0	1	0
Total	31	0	4	27	15	3

aBatted for Hutchings in eighth.

New York .... 0 0 0 0 0 0 0 6 0—6
Boston .... 0 0 0 0 0 0 0 0 0—0

Runs batted in—Danning, Hale 2, Jurges 2, Lohrman.

Three-base hits—Young, Hale. Two-base hits—Hale, Jurges. Double play—Hutchings, Miller and Hassett. Left on bases—New York 7, Boston 7. Bases on balls—Off Lohrman 3, Johnson 2. Struck out—By Lohrman 3, Johnson 2, Early 1. Hits—Off Johnson 9 in 7 1-3 innings, Hutchings 2 in 2-3, Early 0 in 1. Losing pitcher—Johnson. Umpires—Stewart, Dunn and Magerkurth. Time of game—2:04. Attendance—3,517.

MISS WORTZ GAINS FINAL

Miss Dudley Also Wins Twice in Women's College Golf

COLUMBUS, Ohio, July 2 (AP)—Miss Eddell Wortz of Fort Smith, Ark., reached the final of the first women's national intercollegiate golf championship by defeating Miss Marjorie Row of Detroit, a favorite, 3 and 2, in an eighteen-hole match today.

Miss Wortz, representing Stephens College, will meet the University of Alabama's Miss Eleanor Dudley of Chicago tomorrow. Miss Dudley beat Miss Frances Ann McCanna of Rockford, Ill., a student at St. Mary of the Woods College, Terre Haute, Ind., by 3 and 1 in the semi-finals.

In quarter-final matches Miss Row downed Miss Betty Mackemer, a Peoria, Ill., student at Rollins College, 2 and 1; Miss Wortz triumphed by 5 and 4 over Miss Betty Putnam of Oregon, Ill., a University of Arizona entry; Miss Dudley halteed Miss Martha Dakin of Lebanon, Ohio, a student at Miami (Ohio) University, 6 and 4, and Miss McCanna registered a 4-and-3 victory over Miss Alberta Little of Owensboro, Ky., a Rollins College co-ed.

Major League Leaders

BATSMEN

AMERICAN LEAGUE

	G.	AB.	R.	H.	PC.
Williams, Boston	66	222	67	89	.401
Heath, Cleveland	70	268	49	103	.384
Travis, Washington	67	269	48	98	.364
Cullenbine, St. Louis	62	199	38	72	.362
DiMaggio, New York	73	287	68	100	.348

NATIONAL LEAGUE

	G.	AB.	R.	H.	PC.
Mize, St. Louis	52	187	29	69	.369
Reiser, Brooklyn	59	228	58	81	.355
Slaughter, St. Louis	71	276	46	93	.337
Lavagetto, Brooklyn	66	232	43	74	.319
Hack, Chicago	69	264	53	84	.318

HOME-RUN HITTERS

AMERICAN LEAGUE

DiMaggio, N. Y. ...18 | Johnson, Phila. 17
Keller, New York ..17

NATIONAL LEAGUE

Ott, New York .....18 | Nicholson, Chic. 14
Camilli, Brooklyn ..15

RUNS BATTED IN

AMERICAN LEAGUE

Keller, New York ..69 | York Detroit 61
DiMaggio, N. Y. 65

NATIONAL LEAGUE

Nicholson, Chic. ....57 | Slaughter, St. L. ...50
Ott, New York ....51 | Mize, St. Louis 50
Camilli, Brooklyn ..50

BUTCHER, PIRATES, SUBDUES REDS, 8-3

Beats Cincinnati Third Time This Season as Derringer Suffers Tenth Defeat

VAN ROBAYS HITS IN 3 RUNS

Sends Across First 2 Tallies as Well as Deciding One in Game at Pittsburgh

PITTSBURGH, July 2 (AP)—Paul Derringer sustained his tenth defeat today as big Max Butcher hurled Pittsburgh to an 8-to-3 verdict, his third success over the Reds.

Maurice Van Robays sparked the Pirates to victory by driving in three runs. His fourth inning double scored two mates and his single in the sixth broke up a 3-3 tie, sending home Bobby Elliott, who had just tripled in a run.

Elbie Fletcher's double, driving in two runs in the seventh, clinched the game. Jimmy Gleeson got three of the thirteen Cincinnati safeties and counted twice.

The box score:

CINCINNATI (N.)	ab.	r.	h.	po.	a.	e.
Werber, 3b.	4	0	2	0	2	0
Waner, cf	5	0	2	2	0	0
Frey, 2b.	4	0	0	1	2	0
F.McC'k, 1b.	5	0	2	8	0	0
Gleeson, rf.	5	2	3	0	0	0
Lombardi, c.	4	1	2	4	1	0
aV'dermeer	0	0	0	0	0	0
J.Riddle, c.	0	0	0	1	0	0
cAleno	1	0	0	0	0	0
M.Mc'ck, lf.	4	0	2	5	0	0
Joost, ss	3	0	0	3	5	1
Derringer, p.	3	0	0	0	0	0
bKoy	1	0	0	0	0	0
Thompson, p.	0	0	0	0	0	0
Total	39	3	13	24	10	1

PITTSBURGH (N.)	ab.	r.	h.	po.	a.	e.
Anderson, ss.	4	1	0	2	4	0
Handley, 3b.	4	2	2	2	3	0
Fletcher, 1b.	3	1	1	8	0	0
Elliott, rf.	3	2	1	4	0	0
V.Robays, lf.	4	0	2	1	1	0
DiM'gio, cf.	4	0	1	4	0	0
Gustine, 2b.	4	1	1	3	2	0
Lopez, c	4	1	2	3	2	0
Butcher, p.	4	0	1	0	1	0
Total	34	8	11	27	13	0

aRan for Lombardi in eighth.
bBatted for Derringer in eighth.
cBatted for J. Riddle in ninth.

Cincinnati .... 0 0 0 1 0 2 0 0 0—3
Pittsburgh .... 0 0 0 2 0 2 2 2 ..—8

Runs batted in—M. McCormick, Van Robays 3, Lombardi, Joost, Elliott, Fletcher 2, Lopez.

Two-base hits—Van Robays, Gleeson, M. McCormick, Fletcher, Lopez. Three-base hits—M. McCormick, Elliott. Stolen bases—Handley, Anderson. Double play—Lombardi, Joost and F. McCormick. Left on bases—Cincinnati 12, Pittsburgh 4. Bases on balls—Off Derringer 2, Butcher 3. Struck out—By Derringer 2, Butcher 1, Thompson 1. Hits—Off Derringer 9 in 7 innings; Thompson 2 in 1. Wild pitch—Butcher. Losing pitcher — Derringer. Umpires — Conlan, Goetz and Reardon. Time of game—1:50. Attendance—1,941.

TIGERS, WITH NEWSOM, BLANK WHITE SOX, 1-0

Buck Permits 3 Hits in Night Game—Mullin Injured

CHICAGO, July 2 (AP)—Buck Newsom pitched a brilliant three-hit game tonight to five the Tigers a 1-to-0 victory over the White Sox and the rubber game of the three-game series. Detroit made only five hits off Bill Dietrich.

Detroit scored in the first inning as Pat Mullin singled, advanced on Charley Gehringer's sacrifice and raced home on Rudy York's double. Newsom fanned eight as he gained his sixth victory against eleven defeats. Dietrich was forced to retire when he was hit on the right thumb while batting in the eighth.

Mullin, Tiger outfielder, suffered what appeared to be a dislocation of the right shoulder when he collided with Dietrich at first base in the second inning.

The box score:

DETROIT (A.)	ab.	r.	h.	po.	a.	e.
Mullin, cf.	2	1	1	1	0	0
Stainback, cf	2	0	0	4	0	0
G'ringer, 2b.	2	0	0	2	1	0
Radcliff, lf.	4	0	0	1	0	0
York, 1b.	4	0	1	4	0	0
Campbell, rf.	3	0	1	2	0	0
Higgins, 3b.	3	0	0	1	1	0
Sullivan, c.	3	0	1	9	1	0
Croucher, ss.	3	0	0	3	3	0
Newsom, p.	3	0	1	0	2	0
Total	29	1	5	27	8	0

CHICAGO (A.)	ab.	r.	h.	po.	a.	e.
Kolloway, 2b	4	0	0	2	2	0
Kuhel, 1b.	3	0	0	12	2	0
L'giani, 3b.	2	0	0	0	2	0
Appling, ss.	4	0	1	1	5	0
Wright, rf.	3	0	1	3	1	0
Solters, lf.	3	0	0	1	0	0
Chapman, cf.	3	0	1	3	0	0
Tresh, c.	3	0	0	3	0	0
Dietrich, p.	2	0	0	2	1	0
aKreevich	1	0	0	0	0	0
Ross, p.	0	0	0	0	1	0
Total	28	0	3	27	14	0

aBatted for Dietrich in eighth.

Detroit .... 1 0 0 0 0 0 0 0 0—1
Chicago .... 0 0 0 0 0 0 0 0 0—0

Run batted in—York.

Two-base hits—York Chapman. Three-base hit—Campbell. Sacrifices—Gehringer, Lodigiani. Double plays—Wright and Tresh; Ross, Appling and Kuhel. Left on bases—Detroit 5, Chicago 4. Bases on balls—Off Newsom 2, Dietrich 2, Ross 1. Struck out—By Newsom 8, Dietrich 1. Hits—Off Dietrich 5 in 8 innings, Ross 0 in 1. Losing pitcher—Dietrich. Umpires—Pipgras, Hubbard, Basil and Ormsby. Time of game—2:01. Attendance—22,555.

Brooklyn Overcomes Phillies, 9-3; Kimball Is Brilliant in Victory

Relief Hurler Replaces Higbe in Fourth and Yields Only Single for Rest of Game—Dodgers Count Five Runs in First

By ARTHUR DALEY

Obviously the heat had affected the Phillies. They started against the Dodgers at Ebbets Field yesterday as though they actually were going to beat the Brooks for the second day in a row. But then they settled down to their normal stride and bowed, 9 to 3.

With this victory the Leo Durocher operatives picked up ground on the idle Cardinals and now are only a half game out of first place. However, it took some gilt-edge relief pitching by Newell Kimball to keep Philadelphia in line.

The Phils acted outrageously against Kirby Higbe, a Philadelphia alumnus, and thumped him for nine hits in three and a third innings. Yet for all of that clouting it added up to only three runs. The Phils, after all, have such a quaint way of playing baseball.

Melton Ends Frame

Then Kimball came on the scene and allowed only one pointless single the rest of the way as he scored his initial victory of the campaign. As for the Phils, they used three twirlers in the very first inning. Frank Hoerst retired one man, Boom-Boom Beck no one at all and finally Rube Melton made it three outs for the frame, not, however, until five runs had been scored.

It was Melton who went the rest of the distance. He was touched for nine hits, the Brooks getting a dozen in all. They wasted no time with Hoerst. Peewee Reese walked, Pete Reiser singled and Cookie Lavagetto strolled to fill the bases.

That brought Boom-Boom on the scene. His first contribution was to pitch four straight balls to Joe Medwick to force in one run. Dixie Walker singled to drive in two more and Jimmy Wasdell doubled for another brace of tallies. That shot finished Beck and nothing much mattered afterward.

Rest for Brooklyn Today

With yesterday's battle out of the way, the Brooks will rest on their oars today, preparatory to their double-header with the Giants at Ebbets Field tomorrow. Some of the boys will go out to Huntington today to watch the baseball writers give a demonstration of how the game should not be played in the annual outing of the scribes.

Reiser has a long way to go to catch up with Joe DiMaggio, but the brilliant little Dodger now has hit safely in fourteen successive games.

The Phils hit a futility high-spot in the third. Harry Marnie overthrew first on Wasdell's infield single and then Mickey Livingston overthrew the overthrow to right field.

Mickey Owen left the hospital yesterday, but it will be almost a week before he will be able to play. In fact, doubts were expressed that he'd be ready in time for the All-Star game on Tuesday.

Giuliani Still Missing

With Owen out, Herman Franks is the only able-bodied catcher on the squad. The mysterious Angelo Giuliani, recalled from Minneapolis and due to report two days ago, still has not put in an appearance.

Joe Vosmik didn't last long in the game. He started in right field but Left-hander Hoerst did not linger long enough for the blond to come to bat. So Walker took over and celebrated with two triples and a single.

Reese is rapidly building up a batting streak in reverse English. He has gone to bat twenty-seven straight times without a hit. His three walks yesterday amounted to a moral victory.

The Box Score

PHILADELPHIA (N)	ab.	r.	h.	po.	a.	e.
Marnie, 2b.	5	1	2	0	2	0
Litwhiler, lf.	3	1	2	2	0	0
Marty, cf.	3	0	1	3	0	0
Etten, 1b.	1	0	0	0	0	0
Benjamin, 1b., cf	4	0	1	5	1	0
Rizzo, rf.	4	0	1	3	0	0
Bragan, ss.	4	0	1	0	0	0
Livingston, c	4	1	1	7	0	1
May, 3b.	4	0	1	3	2	0
Hoerst, p.	0	0	0	1	0	0
Beck, p.	0	0	0	0	0	0
Melton, p.	3	0	0	0	0	0
aWarren	1	0	0	0	0	0
Total	36	3	10	24	5	1

BROOKLYN (N.)	ab.	r.	h.	po.	a.	e.
Reese, ss.	3	2	0	1	2	0
Herman, 2b.	5	0	0	3	3	0
Reiser, cf.	4	2	2	8	0	0
Lavag'to, 3b.	3	2	1	1	3	0
Medwick, lf.	4	2	2	2	0	0
Vosmik, rf.	0	0	0	0	0	0
Walker, rf.	4	1	3	1	0	0
Wasdell, 1b.	5	0	2	8	0	0
Franks, c.	4	0	2	3	0	0
Higbe, p.	2	0	0	0	0	0
Kimball, p.	2	0	0	0	0	0
Total	36	9	12	27	8	0

aBatted for Melton in ninth.

Philadelphia .... 2 1 0 0 0 0 0 0 0—3
Brooklyn .... 5 1 0 1 0 2 0 0 ..—9

Runs batted in—Benjamin 2, Medwick 2, Walker 5, Wasdell 2, Marnie.

Two-base hits—Wasdell, May, Franks. Three-base hits—Walker 2. Double play—Lavagetto, Herman and Wasdell. Left on bases—Philadelphia 9, Brooklyn 10. Bases on balls—Off Hoerst 2, Beck 1, Higbe 2, Kimball 1, Melton 4. Struck out—By Melton 7, Higbe 1, Kimball 2. Hits—Off Hoerst 1 in 1-3 inning, Beck 2 in 0 (pitched to three batters in 1st), Melton 9 in 7 2-3, Higbe 9 in 3 1-3, Kimball 1 in 5 2-3. Winning pitcher—Kimball. Losing pitcher—Hoerst. Umpires—Barlick, Pinelli and Ballanfant. Time of game—2:34. Attendance—2,799 paid, 5,816 boys.

NEWARK CAPTURES EIGHTH IN ROW, 8-1

Washburn, in Fine Form, Limits Syracuse to Pair of Hits

NEWARK, N. J., July 2 (AP)—George Washburn, a Yankee cast-off, limited the Chiefs to two hits today after holding them hitless until the seventh and the Bears galloped to an 8-to-1 victory, their eighth straight. The defeat was the twelfth in a row for Syracuse, which previously had won eleven in succession.

Gordy Rosen, leading off the seventh, cracked a clean single for the first hit off Washburn, who hung up his fifth victory. In the eighth Nino Bongiovanni tripled with two out and Charlie Marshall aboard on a pass to spoil Washburn's shut-out bid.

The Bears blasted Tom Sunkel to cover in the fifth and continued a 17-hit attack on three successors. All the safeties were singles. Henry Majeski and Joe Mack featured the barrage with four hits apiece and Leo Nonnenkamp had three.

George Stirnweiss of Newark collected a pair of singles to increase his batting streak to fifteen games.

The box score:

SYRACUSE (I.)	ab.	r.	h.	po.	a.	e.
B'vanni, rf.	4	0	1	2	0	0
Rosen, cf.	4	0	1	1	1	0
Storti, 3b.	3	0	0	1	3	0
Nagel, lf.	4	0	0	4	0	0
Sherlock, 2b.	3	0	0	2	3	0
Hasson, 1b.	3	0	0	7	0	0
Juelich, ss.	3	0	0	1	3	0
Marshall, c.	1	1	0	6	0	0
Sunkel, p.	1	0	0	0	0	0
Shultz, p.	1	0	0	0	0	0
Kleinhans, p.	0	0	0	0	0	0
aLongacre	1	0	0	0	0	0
Rehbein, p.	0	0	0	0	0	1
Total	28	1	2	24	10	1

NEWARK (I.)	ab.	r.	h.	po.	a.	e.
Holmes, cf.	3	0	0	0	0	0
N'enkamp, rf.	5	2	3	0	0	0
Majeski, 3b.	5	2	4	2	3	0
Kelleher, lf.	3	0	0	2	0	0
Mack, 1b.	5	2	4	13	0	0
St'weiss, 2b.	5	0	2	2	8	0
Scharein, ss.	5	1	2	2	4	0
Padden, c.	3	0	1	5	0	0
Washburn, p.	4	1	1	1	0	0
Total	38	8	17	27	15	0

aBatted for Kleinhans in eighth.

Syracuse .... 0 0 0 0 0 0 0 1 0—1
Newark .... 0 0 0 0 3 1 3 1 ..—8

Runs batted in—Mack 3, Padden, Nonnenkamp, Majeski 2, Bongiovanni, Stirnweiss. Three-base hit—Bongiovanni. Stolen bases—Stirnweiss 2, Nonnenkamp, Majeski. Sacrifice—Padden. Double plays—Storti, Sherlock and Hasson; Stirnweiss, Scharein and Mack. Left on bases; Syracuse 4, Newark 13. Bases on balls—Off Sunkel 4, Washburn 4, Shultz 2. Struck out—By Sunkel 5, Washburn 4, Kleinhaus. Hits—Off Sunkel 10 in 4 2-3 innings, Shultz 5 in 2, Kleinhans 0 in 1-3, Rehbein 2 in 1. Losing pitcher—Sunkel. Umpires—Swanson and Henline. Time of game—2:10.

Cochrane Bout Put Off a Week

MOUNT FREEDOM, N. J., July 2 (AP)—On the recommendation of State Athletic Commissioner Abe J. Greene, a ten-round bout between Freddie (Red) Cochrane of Elizabeth and Ray Napolitano of Brooklyn was postponed today from next Friday, to July 11. Greene said he felt the boxing card should not interfere with Independence Day celebrations in near-by communities.

The Des Moines Register

DES MOINES, IOWA, WEDNESDAY MORNING, JULY 9, 1941. ★★★★★

TED WILLIAMS' HOMER BEATS NATIONAL LEAGUERS, 7 TO 5

Sittin' In

WITH THE ATHLETES.

Tampa an Air Center.

Gomez Ring Prospect.

Hard-Hitting Cuban.

Short Hooks Damaging.

—BY SEC TAYLOR—

TAMPA, FLA.—Everywhere I go down here I find that a fellow by the name of Ponce de Leon and Hernando DeSoto beat me to it.

This lively city of 170,000 inhabitants, almost one-fourth of whom are of Latin extraction, is one of the spots that DeSoto found — there are more such places in Florida than there are beds in New Jersey that George Washington once slept in —in the sixteenth century when he was wandering about in search of new land and loot.

SEC TAYLOR.

But Tampa was little heard of until about 1886 when several Cuban cigar manufacturers decided on locating their factories here. Ever since many of the famous brands of Havana cigars have been made here. But even then Tampa did not become much of a city until the Panama Canal was opened and the Spanish American war came along. Then Port Tampa was used as the jumping off place to Cuba for Generals Miles and Shafter, Col. Teddy Roosevelt and his Roughriders, and for the other U. S. troops who went to little Cuba's rescue.

—

RIGHT NOW Tampa resembles a northern city in that it is businesslike, is located right next to much of Florida's best agricultural land, is a big shipping center and does not depend too much on tourist trade, as so many of the cities and towns down this way, do.

Tampa is fight-nutty these days—first because it is the center of so much federal defensive activity and second because of a young heavyweight fighter—Tommy Gomez.

It has MacDill field, a great aviation center; and training ground Drew field, which in reality is a part of MacDill field; Benjamin field, where units of the National Guard artillery are trained, a municipal airport, and the Henderson-Hillsboro airport.

At last accounts federal defense appropriations amounting to $51,000,000 had been alloted to Tampa, to say nothing of a federal monthly payroll of approximately $100,000 for the NYA, CAA, WPA, and other of the alphabetical authorities doing work here and in this vicinity.

—

TOMMY GOMEZ, the boxer, is creating a stir in spite of all the military activity. This youngster, green and inexperienced as yet, but undeniably one of the best heavyweight prospects in the country, has caught the fancy of the public, just as Johnny Paychek kept Iowa fans talking three years ago.

Gomez is a puncher and with both hands. But more than that he is fast and apparently is game as he proved in the first two rounds of his first fight when he was knocked down five times and then dropped his opponent for a technical kayo in the third. He had never fought as an amateur either.

That bout was in 1938 when he was a middleweight. Since then he fought his way through the middleweight, and light-heavyweight classes and now weighs between 181 and 185 and is meeting heavyweights.

—

HE HAS lost only one 10-round bout, a decision to Buddy Rose in one of his early starts. However, since that reverse he has scored 23 straight victories including a one-round knockout of Rose in a return engagement.

His heavyweight debut was made last year against Maynard Daniels of Washington, D. C. It is said the local boy was a bit over-awed in this bout but in spite of that won every round and took a 10-round decision.

Few of his opponents have escaped so easily since. Young Allen, Lee Silvers, Ernie Petratti, Art Sykes and Jim Bowden lasted a total of nine rounds only.

Joe Leto, who manages Gomez, makes no claims for his fighter except that he's just as promising a prospect as there is in the country and that he can punch as hard as any pugilist in the business, bar none.

But naturally there are skeptics

Sittin' In—
Continued on Page Two.

Tommy Gomez.
Has Floridans Talking.

Horatio Alger

Nationals	AB	R	H	O	A
Hack (Chi.) 3b	2	0	1	3	0
Lavagetto (Brk.) 3b	1	0	0	0	0
Moore (St. L.) lf	5	0	0	0	0
Reiser (Brk.) cf	4	0	0	6	0
Mize (St. L.) 1b	4	1	1	5	0
McCormick (Cin.) 1b	0	0	0	0	0
Nicholson (Chi.) rf	1	0	0	1	0
Elliott (Pitts.) rf	1	0	0	0	0
Slaughter (St. L.) rf	2	1	1	0	0
Vaughan (Pitts.) ss	4	2	3	1	2
Miller (Bos.) ss	0	0	0	0	1
Frey (Cin.) 2b	1	0	1	1	3
Herman (Brk.) 2b	3	0	2	3	0
Owen (Brk.) c	1	0	0	0	0
Lopez (Pitts.) c	1	0	0	3	0
Danning (N.Y.) c	1	0	0	3	0
Wyatt (Brk.) p	0	0	0	0	0
aOtt (N. Y.)	1	0	0	0	0
Derringer (Cin.) p	0	0	0	0	1
Walters (Cin.) p	1	1	1	0	0
bMedwick (Brk.)	1	0	0	0	0
Passeau (Chi.) p	1	0	0	0	0
Totals	35	5	10	26*	7
American	**AB**	**R**	**H**	**O**	**A**
Doerr (Bos.) 2b	3	0	0	0	0
Gordon (N. Y.) 2b	2	1	1	2	0
Travis (Wash.) 3b	4	1	1	1	2
J. DiMag (N. Y.) cf	4	3	1	1	0
Williams (Bos.) lf	4	1	2	3	0
Heath (Cleve.) rf	2	0	0	1	0
D. DiMag (Bos.) rf	1	0	1	1	0
Cronin (Bos.) ss	2	0	0	3	0
Boudreau (Clev.) ss	2	0	2	0	1
York (Det.) 1b	3	0	1	6	2
Foxx (Bos.) 1b	1	0	0	2	2
Dickey (N. Y.) c	3	0	1	4	2
Hayes (Phil.) c	1	0	0	2	0
Feller (Cleve.) p	0	0	0	0	1
cCullenbine (St. L.)	1	0	0	0	0
Lee (Chi.) p	1	0	0	0	1
Hudson (Wash.) p	0	0	0	0	0
dKeller (N. Y.)	1	0	0	0	0
Smith (Chi.) p	0	0	0	1	0
eKeltner (Cleve.)	1	1	1	0	0
Totals	36	7	11	27	11

*Two out when winning runs were scored.
aBatted for Wyatt in the third.
bBatted for Walters in the seventh.
cBatted for Feller in third.
dBatted for Hudson in seventh.
eBatted for Smith in ninth.

Score by innings:

National	000	001	220	—5
American	000	101	014	—7

Errors—Heath, Reiser 2, Williams, Smith.
Runs batted in—Williams 4, Moore, Boudreau, Vaughan 4, D. DiMaggio, J. DiMaggio.
Earned runs—Nationals 5, Americans 7.
Two base hits—Travis, Williams, Walters, Herman, Mize, J. DiMaggio.
Home runs—Vaughan 2, Williams.
Sacrifice hits—Hack, Lopez.
Double plays—Frey to Vaughan to Mize, York to Cronin.
Left on bases—Nationals 6, Americans 7.
Bases on balls—Off Wyatt (Williams), Walters 2 (DiMaggio, Heath), Hudson (Hack), Passeau (Travis).
Struck out—By Feller 4 (Hack, Reiser, Nicholson, Ott), Derringer 1 (Heath), Walters 2 (Cronin, Doerr), Hudson 1 (Moore), Smith 2 (Reiser, Slaughter), Passeau 3 (Keller, Williams, Foxx).
Hits—Off Feller 1 in 3 innings, Lee 4 in 3, Hudson 3 in 1, Smith 2 in 2, Wyatt 0 in 2, Derringer 2 in 2, Walters 3 in 2, Passeau 6 in 2 2-3.
Winning pitcher—Smith.
Losing pitcher—Passeau.
Umpires — Summers (AL), Jorda (NL), Grieve (AL), and Pinelli (NL).
Time—2:23.
Attendance—54,674.

Comes With Two Out in Ninth

By Judson Bailey.

DETROIT, MICH. (AP)—In the most thunderous climax in the history of baseball's big all-star spectacle, willowy Ted Williams smashed a three-run homer 90 feet high against the top of the rightfield stands in the ninth inning Tuesday to lift the American league to a 7 to 5 triumph over the National league.

The crowd of 56,674, third largest in the nine-year life of the fans' "dream game," had been dazzled earlier by brilliant pitching and by two booming home runs by Arky Vaughan which brought the National league up to the final frame with an apparently impregnable 5 to 3 advantage.

Then two singles and a walk loaded the bases with one out and there was a shrill, spontaneous outburst from the fans as Joe DiMaggio stalked to the plate. He forced a runner at second, one run scoring, and there was an obvious dramatic tenseness as Williams, slender Boston Red Sox slugger with a batting average of .405, took his place in the box and worked the count to two balls and one strike.

Umpire Lou Jorda, a National leaguer, working behind the plate the last half of the game, called in the ball and inspected it closely while Williams and Catcher Hank Danning watched. Then Jorda tossed out a new one to Pitcher Claude Passeau, the seasoned ace of the Chicago Cubs, and a moment later Williams slammed it on a vicious line against the roof top press box in rightfield 325 feet away and close to the foul marker.

Before the ball had bounced back on the field or Williams had rounded first in his trot around the bases behind Joe Gordon and DiMaggio the jubilant spectators streamed out of the stands and enveloped the retreating teams.

It was the first time an all-star game ever had been won in the ninth inning.

This was the American leaguers' sixth victory against three defeats and continued their record of never having been defeated when they were the home team.

For a while Tuesday it looked like Vaughan, Pittsburgh's former National league batting champion, and one of the stars in his teams' 4-0 triumph in last year's all-star game, might take care of this detail.

He made three hits in four times at bat and collected his home runs, each time with one aboard, on successive trips in the seventh and eighth innings. Each was a liner into the second tier of the rightfield stands.

Bob Feller and Whitlow Wyatt opened Tuesday's prize bundle with some of the finest pitching the game ever has produced.

Feller, fireball star of the Cleveland Indians, worked the first three innings for the American leaguers and never looked any more wonderful, fanning four batters and facing only the minimum of nine in his turn on the mound. He gave up the senior circuit's first safety in the third inning when weak hitting Lonnie Frey, a portsider from the Cincinnati Reds, poked a single into rightfield. But Frey was promptly caught taking too big a lead off first and was tagged out.

Wyatt, a former American leaguer, who at 32 years old is

All-Stars—
Continued on Page Three.

TED HAD 'THAT FEELIN'--SHUT HIS EYES AND--

'Nothin' Like It,' Williams Beams.

By Charles Dunkley.

DETROIT, MICH. (AP)—In stormed grinning Del Baker, manager of the triumphant American leaguers, to touch off a clubhouse celebration that all but raised the roof.

The kindly 49-year-old leader of the Detroit Tigers, immediately shouldered his way to the spot where gangling Ted Williams, hero of the game with his victorious ninth-inning homer, wearily dropped into a chair in front of his locker. The players, Coach Artie Fletcher and photographers swarmed around screaming and yelling.

Baker, shirt off, threw his arms around the happy Williams and planted a kiss on his left cheek.

"Kiss him? You're damned right I did," Baker beamed.

The gangling Williams, just 22 years old, settled his 6 foot, 3 inch frame into a chair to relax.

"Ain't it just a great feeling to bang out a home run," Williams beamed. "You're telling me. I just wanted to beat the hell out of them National leaguers. I'll bet my mother is the happiest woman in the world tonight. She must be celebrating right now out there in San Diego."

Williams said the ball he smashed off Pitcher Claude Passeau was a fast one, waist high.

"I just shut my eyes and swung," he explained.

"I had a feeling that if I got up there in the ninth I'd go for the downs. Boy, I feel great. There ain't nothing like hittin' a home run."

Williams said he had a feeling, after striking out in the eighth inning that he might connect with a homer if he had a chance to bat again. This proud youngster, currently the batting leader of the American league with an average of .405, said he'd been swinging "a little late" all afternoon and was determined to get in front of one.

Picture of Contentment.

He was dead tired, but the picture of supreme contentment. He yanked off his shoes, stretched his legs and grinned. William Harridge, president of the American league, rushed in to offer his congratulations.

Fletcher, the Yankee coach, in his excitement, pumped Williams' hand a dozen times. The players banged Williams on the head with their gloves. Then they pounded his back.

"He really hit the hell out of that ball, didn't he?" yelled Fletcher. "He certainly polished

Clubhouse—
Continued on Page Three.

Here is shown Ted Williams, Boston Red Sox outfielder, crossing the plate in the last of the ninth inning at Detroit to give the American league stars a 7 to 5 victory over the National leaguers. Williams' smash came with Joe DiMaggio and Joe Gordon on base and the American leaguers trailing, 5 to 4. DiMaggio is the player wearing No. 5. Mervyn Shea, Tiger coach, is No. 30.

AFTER THE BALL WAS OVER—Ted Williams, hero of the American league's victory over the National stars, relaxed in the dressing room of the winners and Joe DiMaggio (right) was on hand to land his teammate for the payoff blow. DiMaggio and Williams, two of the best hitters in the American loop, were on the same team for only a day, however. From now on they'll be battling each other for the American league batting title. At present Williams is hitting .405, DiMaggio .357.

McKee Nears Record

SNEAD SCORES ANOTHER 69 TO TOP GOLF FIELD

Wins P.G.A. Honors With 138.

By Russ Newland.

DENVER, COLO. (AP)—Samuel Jackson Snead roared home Tuesday to win qualifying honors of the National Professional Golfers association championship.

The former Virginia hillbilly strutted in with a par-breaking 69, identical with his first round effort on the lake and creek criss-crossed Cherry Hills course, for a 36-hole total of 138. Par for the course is 35-36—71. Slammin' Sam clipped four shots from the figures designated as standard.

He won a diamond-studded medal for the feat. For a cripple who only recently had discarded a back brace, the walloping man from Hot Springs, Ark., turned in a healthy and husky performance.

Snead snatched his latest honors in an already spectacular career with beautiful shots to the greens. Throughout his round Tuesday he never had a putt longer than eight feet.

Monday he put together nines of 33-36. With a few putting breaks Tuesday he could have knocked out a 65. He missed short ones by a hair's breadth for birdies on the first, second, fifth, tenth and eleventh holes.

Snead nosed out E. J. (Dutch) Harrison, Chicago, Ill., by one stroke. Harrison tacked up a 71 alongside a first round 68 which had enabled him to share pace-setting laurels at the halfway mark.

Harrison started as if he had the medal made to order for him. He breezed through the first nine in 34, then began scrambling on the incoming stretch. His miscues included a three-putt green, ball hit into a creek and a weak iron shot that cost him one stroke.

The other 18-hole co-leader, Harry Bassler, darkhorse from Los Altos, Cal., flopped on his first nine Tuesday for a two over par

P.G.A.—
Continued on Page Two.

Schwartz First Foe Of Medalist Today

By Bert McGrane.

Out of a fading era of Iowa golf Tuesday charged Bob McKee, an ageless contender, to manhandle Hyperion's par with a smoking 66 and take his place at the head of the field as the state's crack amateurs concluded their 36-hole qualifying test and squared away for individual combat.

Lost in the pack with an opening 77 and with his prowess all but forgotten in recent years, the 39-year-old campaigner fairly streaked down the stretch with a scorching putter, finished the lap six under par to tie the course record and won the qualifying medal with an extra stroke to spare.

As the Hyperion veteran duplicated a qualifying feat he accomplished as a kid at Grandview 25 years ago, he took over the No. 1 spot in the match play bracket and set himself for the first round battle with Harold Schwartz, a Hyperion clubmate.

Bob McKee.
Within 2 Shots of Record.

McKee's 143 total, one under par for the 36 holes, was within two strokes of the all-time state tournament qualifying record and two shots better than any rival in the current field could register.

Behind him on the list were Wayne Harrell, the Parsons college athlete who led the field through the opening lap and big Max Shelton, the telephone man from Waterloo. Harrell needed a 76 in the wake of his 69 on Monday for a 145 total, while Shelton added a 74 to his 71 of Monday.

It was McKee, a four-time state champion, who was the talk of the field as the stage was set for the eliminations that lead to the 1941 championship.

Old Bob, on the threshold of 40, turned back the golfing pages to flash all the fire of a quarter century of battle in his dash to the qualifying lead.

State Champion Johnny Jacobs meanwhile took a notch in his belt, after sharing fifth place in the

Amateur—
Continued on Page Two.

CHAMPIONSHIP FLIGHT.

First Round.

UPPER BRACKET.

Bob McKee, Des Moines (143) vs. Harold Schwartz, Des Moines (151).
Phil Donohue, Sioux City (147) vs. Bob Blackburn, Des Moines (154).
John Stoltz, Ottumwa (147) vs. Bob Hummel, Des Moines (153).
Bill Cordingley, Des Moines (149) vs. Fletcher Jones, Des Moines (154).
Wayne Harrell, Fairfield (145) vs. Wendell Robinson, Des Moines (152).
Earl Wilde, Davenport (148) vs. Earl Keim, Davenport (154).
Harold Skow, Newton (147) vs. Bob Brown, Eldora (153).
John Kraft, Oelwein (149) vs. Jerry Jerome, Des Moines (155).

LOWER BRACKET.

Max Shelton, Waterloo (145) vs. Bob Lattig, Nevada (151).
Milt Beal, Clinton (148) vs. Ira Allen, Des Moines (154).
John Jacobs, Cedar Rapids (147) vs. George Skinner, Davenport (153).
Sargio Fontanini, Des Moines (149) vs. Lou Ehlers, Davenport (155).
Dixie Smith, Waterloo (146) vs. Luti Fontanini, Des Moines (152).
Ed Updegraff, Boone (149) vs. Bob Joss, Des Moines (154).
Jack Sparks, Des Moines (147) vs. L. F. Walcott, Eldora (154).
Jack Donohue, Sioux City (150) vs. Clark Tilden, Ames (155).

The Des Moines Register

DES MOINES, IOWA, FRIDAY MORNING, JULY 18, 1941. *****

Sittin' In

WITH THE ATHLETES.

The Days of Joe Wilhoit.
White Sox Throw Series.
Prep Association Fight.
Sold to the Red Sox.

BY SEC TAYLOR

JOE DI MAGGIO was stopped Thursday night by Cleveland's Al Smith and Jim Bagby after taking a good shot at the consecutive hitting record established by Joe Wilhoit, while playing with the Wichita club of the Western league in 1919.

SEC TAYLOR.

That year, starting on June 14 and ending on Aug. 20, Wilhoit batted safely in 69 consecutive games. And Wilhoit had been a light hitter until Frank Isbel, then owner and manager of the Wichita club, took him over.

It is this mark that DiMaggio, who on July 2, this year, hit safely in the forty-fifth straight contest, to break the all time major league record held by Willie Keeler, failed to reach.

That part of the public, or at least most of it, that follows baseball was apparently "pulling" for DiMaggio to succeed, although there were quite a few who hoped it would be the young Iowan, Bob Feller, who would halt the San Francisco Italian today when he faces the Yankees.

—

DI MAGGIO'S performance had everyone the nation over talking about him. This hitting feat, together with the death of Frank Isbell early this week, brings to mind the furore among the fans when Wilhoit had his consecutive batting streak well launched, although, of course, the interest was more or less localized in the territory comprising the Western circuit.

The record, when Wilhoit started, was 45 games and was established between May 31 and July 21 by Jack Ness of the Oakland club of the Pacific Coast league.

—

TO GIVE YOU the setting for Wilhoit's phenomenal batting streak and to set the time more definitely in your mind I shall tell you a little of what was going on the day his streak was ended in a game against Tulsa, in which Elam Van Gilder, Mutt Williams and Lefty Bayne pitched the Oilers to a 5 to 2 triumph.

Van Gilder held Wilhoit hitless in three times at bat and Williams, who faced him once, gave him a pass. Bayne, who with Van Gilder later played with the St. Louis Browns for several seasons, did not oppose Wilhoit.

The Wichita lineup in those days consisted of Mule Washburn, secondbase; Art Ewoldt, shortstop; Newasha and Ham Yaryan, catchers; McBride, leftfielder; Wolf or Carl East, rightfielder. I can't recall who was the regular thirdbaseman. However, Yaryan played third the day Wilhoit was stopped.

—

ON THIS SAME day George Payne, one of the best hurlers ever in the Western loop, pitched . Des Moines team to a 9 to 5 triumph over St. Joseph at St. Joseph.

In the Des Moines lineup were Runt Marr, thirdbase; Jack Coffey, now graduate manager at Fordham university, secondbase and manager; Bob Hasbrouck, firstbase; Connolley, centerfield; Winn, rightfield; Johnny Walker, catcher; Bruce Hartford, shortstop; Faber O'Hara, a North Des Moines High boy, leftfield. Other pitchers were Boyd, Keiser, Allison and Norman.

Ewoldt had been traded to Wichita for Marr earlier in the season, the two players exchanging uniforms in the intermission between a doubleheader at the Holcomb street lot.

Names familiar to oldtime fans were in the St. Joseph lineup: Jackson, centerfield; Brubaker, thirdbase; Johnny Kelleher, shortstop; Butcher, secondbase; Walker, rightfield; Bonowitz, centerfield; Beall, firstbase; and Shestak, catcher.

—

ST. JOSEPH WAS in first place with Sioux City, Wichita, Des Moines, Tulsa, Oklahoma City, Omaha and Joplin trailing in the order named.

Chicago, Detroit, Cleveland and St. Louis were in a hot fight for the American league leadership.

The White Sox team was made up of Nemo Liebold, Eddie Collins, Buck Weaver, Joe Jackson, Happy Felsch, Chic Gandil, Swede Risberg, Ray Schalk, Eddie Cicotte, Cy Williams, Dick Kerr and several others later won the championship, threw the series to the Cincinnati Reds and cast a blot on baseball's escutcheon which has not been polished off entirely to this day.

Donie Bush, Ty Cobb, Veach, Heilmann, and Ainsmith were Detroit stars.

The Cleveland lineup was made up of Jack Graney, Chapman, Tris Speaker, Gardner, Harris, Wambsganss, Smith, and Thomas.

Jake Daubert, Heinie Groh, Roush, Greasy Neale, Sherwood Magee, Ivy Wingo, Dutch Reuther, Eller, and Fisher were starring for Cincinnati and such illustrious players as Burns, Youngs, Art Fletcher, Heinie Zimmerman, Frankie Frisch, George Kelly and Mike Gonzalez were with the Giants.

—

THE DAY Wilhoit was halted

Sittin' In—

Continued on Page Three.

Al Smith, Jim Bagby Hold Joe Hitless—

DI MAG'S STREAK ENDS AT 56

RIDDLE TAKES 11TH IN ROW; REDS WIN, 5-4

Elmer Spaces 10 New York Hits.

NEW YORK, N. Y. (AP)—Elmer Riddle, the year's pitching sensation, achieved his eleventh victory without a defeat Thursday night as the Cincinnati Reds squeezed past the New York Giants, 5 to 4. Riddle gave up 10 hits and made a faltering start, but did not allow a run after the fourth inning.

The Reds clustered seven of their nine hits for three runs in the first inning and two more in the third before Bill Lohrman gave up the Giants' hurling chore. Fiddler Bill McGee held them helpless the rest of the way, but as it turned out, their early margin was sufficient.

The first flurry came on four singles sandwiched around an error by Lohrman and the Reds'

Elmer Riddle.
Wins His Eleventh.

other scoring came on Dick Bartell's fumble of Bill Werber's grounder, a triple by Dick West and a fly by Harry Craft.

Riddle was nicked for a run in the first and two in the third. Johnny Rucker sparked both thrusts with two of his three singles and scored two runs.

But the young righthander paced himself over the remainder of the route and in the ninth inning, with the tying run on thirdbase, fanned pinchhitter Gabby Hartnett on called strikes.

Cin'nati	AB.	H.	O.	A.	N. Yk.	AB.	H.	O.	A.
Waner,rf	4	0	1	0	Rucker,cf	5	3	4	0
M.M'C.,lf	5	2	3	0	Whit'd,2b	3	1	8	2
Frey,2b	4	1	4	4	bHarnett	1	0	0	0
F.M'C.,1b	4	0	10	1	Moore,lf	4	1	2	0
W'rber,3b	4	1	1	5	Ott,rf	4	1	2	0
West,c	4	1	1	1	Danning,c	4	1	1	2
Craft,cf	4	2	4	0	Young,1b	4	0	10	0
Joost,ss	3	1	3	1	Bartell,3b	2	0	0	1
E.R'dle,p	2	1	0	3	Jurges,ss	4	3	0	4
					Lohrm'n,p	1	0	0	0
Totals	34	9	27	15	McGee,p	2	0	0	3
					aHale	0	0	0	0
					Totals	34	10	27	12

aBatted for McGee in ninth.
bBatted for Whitehead in ninth.
Score by innings:
Cincinnati ....302 000 000—5
New York ....102 100 000—4
Errors—Lohrman, Bartell.
Runs batted in—F. McCormick, Werber, Craft, Ott, West, Joost, Moore, Danning, McGee.
Threebase hit—West.
Sacrifice hits—Riddle, Whitehead, Waner, Hale.
Double play—Werber to Frey to F. McCormick.
Left on bases—New York 2, Cincinnati 7.
Bases on balls—Off Riddle 2, Lohrman 1, McGee 1.
Struck out—By Lohrman 1, Riddle 1.
Hits—Off Lohrman 7 in 2 1-3 innings, McGee 2 in 6 2-3.
Losing pitcher—Lohrman.
Umpires—Barr, Sears and Jorda.
Time—2:06.
Attendance—20,289.

High School Girls Dominat Golf Tourney

Today's Pairings.
SEMIFINAL ROUND.
Phyllis Otto (Atlantic) vs. Shirley Ramsdell (Cedar Falls).
Mrs. H. R. Staats (Davenport) vs. Ann Casey (Mason City).

By Bert McGrane.
(Staff Representative.)

DAVENPORT, IA. — The front runners of 1941 moved out of the golfing pack in the Iowa women's championship quarterfinals here Thursday and set themselves for the closing laps over the Davenport Country club hills.

Phyllis Otto, the 16-year-old high school sharpshooter from Atlantic, still held the dominating position as the title contenders rounded into the stretch with the youthful champion only one stroke away from par since the tournament opened.

Today, as the semifinal matches go into the records, another high school figure moves into the path of the title defender, with a 17-year-old Shirley Ramsdell of Cedar Falls taking her place in the closing stages of the championship for the first time.

And, advancing toward a shot at the crown from the lower bracket, Mrs. H. R. Staats of Davenport and the capable Ann Casey of Mason City await the duel that will put one of them in Saturday's 36-hole final.

Renew Rivalry.

For Mrs. Staats and Miss Casey today's engagement marks the renewal of a rivalry that started at Mason City three years ago when the Davenport woman stopped the Mason City girl in the state tournament semifinals and entered the last round of that championship.

The ultimate meeting of this pair of challengers loomed as a strong probability throughout the week. It was assured Thursday when Mrs. Staats came from behind to nose out Jean French of Des Moines and Miss Casey sent Suzanne Ill, also of Des Moines, to the sidelines.

Her Third Appearance.

Miss Casey today makes her third semifinal appearance in four years, with Mrs. Staats included in the final four twice in the same period.

Shirley Ramsdell, moving into Iowa's golfing elite for the first time, brought about the first big surprise of the tournament Thursday with her 3 and 2 conquest of Kathleen Carey, the Cedar Rapids standout.

Miss Carey, a finalist once and a semifinalist twice in three state tournament appearances, for once was stopped short of the ranking rounds by the pleasant little school girl who will be a senior at Cedar Falls High this fall.

Sets Killing Pace.

Today the same Miss Ramsdell goes up against a campaigner of 16, whose spectacular shooting has been the highlight of the week.

Miss Otto, in her stand against Jo MacRae Thursday hit a kill-

Women—

Continued on Page Three.

Littlest Dodger

This little Dodger has not yet appeared officially in the Brooklyn lineup, but he works out with the team every afternoon at Ebbets field. He's Doug Camilli, 4-year-old offspring of the Dodgers' first-baseman, Dolph.

Indians Put Blinkers on DiMag

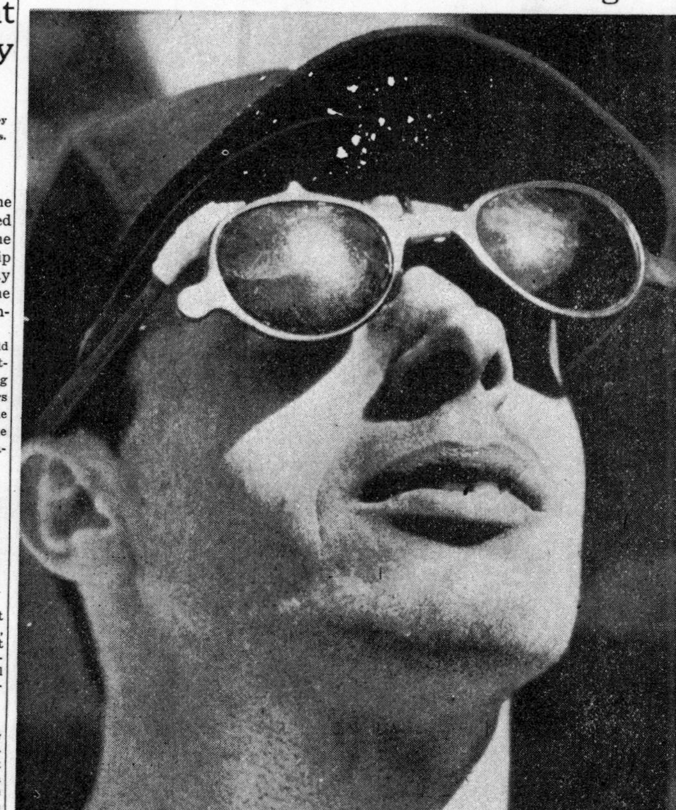

Joe DiMaggio (pictured here wearing sun glasses) went without a hit for the first time in 57 games Thursday night when he failed to bang out a safe blow off Southpaw Al Smith and Jim Bagby of the Cleveland Indians.

WILLIAMS SCARES TITLEHOLDER—

Coggy Drops 1st Set, Wins

HAINLINE OUSTS BOB SANDLER

Lord and Fletcher in Semifinals.

By Bob Price.

Well-mannered Harris Coggeshall glanced at defeat Thursday afternoon on the Birdland courts, decided he didn't like it, and then went on to beat a fighting Oklahoman, Cliff Williams, in the highlighted men's singles quarterfinal round match of the state tennis tournament.

Joining Coggeshall, the defending titlist, Thursday in the semifinal round which will be played Saturday afternoon were Dick Hainline, Rock Island, Ill., sharpshooter; Sterling Lord, Burlington, Ia., and Johnny Fletcher, who kept marching home with a 6-4, 6-4 victory over seeded Frank Brody of Des Moines.

After dropping the first set, 8-6, Coggeshall spotted the left-handed Williams from Guthrie, Okla., three games in the second set, then rallied to win, 6-4.

Battling all the way and going after every shot, Williams moved ahead in the final set. Then, with a lead, changed to soft-balling which delighted Mr. Coggeshall so much that he won in championship style although denied twice at match point. The deciding set call was 6-4.

HARRIS COGGESHALL.

Hainline, runnerup last year here and wearer of many midwest crowns simply outclassed one-armed Bob Sandler, Des Moines, in winning, 6-1, 6-3. Hainline's Saturday engagement will be with Sterling Lord, who ushered out John McNabb, Cedar Falls, Ia., blond, 6-4, 6-2, in a morning affair.

Little Ted Hainline, 14, stepped up for his share of glory Thursday when he tucked the boys singles championship under his arm after a 3-6, 7-5, 6-3 victory over Ken Johnson, Sioux City, Ia.

The women got down to brass

Tennis—

Continued on Page Two.

Club Standings

AMERICAN LEAGUE.

	W.	L.	Pct.	Games Behind
New York	56	27	.675	....
Cleveland	50	35	.588	7
Boston	45	37	.549	10½
Detroit	43	43	.500	14½
Chicago	41	42	.494	15
Philadelphia	36	45	.444	19
St. Louis	30	50	.375	24½
Washington	29	51	.367	25½

Thursday's Results.

Detroit 7, Washington 1.
New York 4, Cleveland 3.
Boston 7, Chicago 4.
St. Louis 4, Philadelphia 3.

Pitchers in Today's Games.

New York (Russo 8-5) at Cleveland (Feller 18-4).
Boston (Grove 6-3) at Chicago Rigney 7-6).
Washington (Leonard 7-11) at Detroit (Gorsica 5-5).
Philadelphia (Knott 7-7) at St. Louis (Auker 6-11).

NATIONAL LEAGUE.

	W.	L.	Pct.	Games Behind
Brooklyn	56	27	.675	...
St. Louis	53	30	.639	3
New York	43	36	.544	11
Cincinnati	44	39	.530	12
Pittsburgh	38	38	.500	14½
Chicago	37	47	.440	19½
Boston	32	47	.405	22
Philadelphia	21	60	.259	34

Thursday's Results.

Chicago 2, Philadelphia 2.
Cincinnati 5, New York 4.
Pittsburgh at Boston, rain.
Only games scheduled.

Pitchers in Today's Games.

St. Louis (White 6-3) at Brooklyn Higbe 13-6).
2—Pittsburgh (Heintzelman 5-6 and Sullivan 3-3) at Boston (Errickson 4-9 and Johnson 4-6).
Only games scheduled.

TECHNICIAN WINS INDOO.

CHICAGO, ILL. (AP)—Herbert M. Woolf's stable, which seems to take the feature races at Arlington park that aren't captured by Warren Wright's Calumet Farm stable, scored again Thursday when Technician galloped off with the Indoo purse.

TRANSPARENTI GETS DECISION

Beats Archibald in Non-Title Bout.

BALTIMORE, MD. (AP) — Lou Transparenti, 127, Baltimore featherweight, was handed a two-to-one decision Thursday night over Joey Archibald, 125¼, of Providence, R. I., recognized as featherweight champion in New York and Maryland. It was an overweight bout and Archibald's title was not at stake.

The fans obviously liked the decision. They booed Archibald in the fourth round when he came out of a crouch and dumped low to the floor and later when he appeared to have butted Transparenti in the groin.

Chalky Wright, 131, of California won a unanimous decision over Pittsburgh's Jackie Wilson, 130, after scoring a five-count knockdown in the eighth round of their 10-round semifinal.

CHANGE POLO DATE.

FT. SNELLING, MINN.—Officials of the Minneapolis Aquatennial polo tournament announced Thursday night that the championship game between Oak Brook Polo club, Chicago, Ill., and the Pierre, S. D., Polo club will be played Friday or Saturday.

Yanks 4, Tribe 3; Lead 7 Games

CLEVELAND, OHIO—The fast-stepping New York Yankees virtually knocked Cleveland out of the American league race Thursday night with their second consecutive victory over the Indians, 4 to 3, in a tight battle before 67,468 to go seven games ahead. Joe DiMaggio's hitting streak was snapped at 56 straight games as Al Smith and Jim Bagby retired him three times and walked him a fourth.

Lefty Gomez stopped the Indians with four hits and one run for eight innings, but the slim southpaw was routed by the determined Redskins in a ninth-inning rally. Fireman Johnny Murphy pitched a triple to Larry Rosenthal, batting for Ray Mack, to allow two runs but bore down to retire Pinch-hitters Clarence Campbell and Hal Trosky and Roy Weatherly to end the game.

DiMaggio's streak, started May 15 against Chicago, might have been extended but for some sharp fielding by Ken Keltner, Cleveland thirdbaseman. In the first and seventh innings he made sensational stops of hot smashes and threw out the rangy Yankee outfielder. The other time Smith pitched to DiMaggio he walked him on a three and two pitch.

Joe had his last chance in the eighth, coming to bat against Bagby with the bases filled and one out. However, he bounded to Lou Boudreau for a fast doubleplay.

After the game DiMaggio said:

"I can't say that I'm glad it's over. Of course I wanted to go on as long as I could.

"Now that the streak is over, I just want to get out there and keep helping to win ball games."

The largest crowd in night baseball history—67,468—saw two home runs, Gerry Walker getting his fourth of the season for Cleveland's first run in the fourth and Joe Gordon putting the Yanks in the lead in the seventh with his fifteenth.

The Yanks picked up eight hits, Smith being shelled out in the eighth inning rally that produced the two deciding runs. Charley Keller started the fireworks with a drive to centerfield which Weatherly misjudged and allowed to get by him for a triple. Singles by Gomez and Johnny Sturm and Red Rolfe's double did the rest of the damage.

Rolfe's single and Tommy (Baby Face) Henrich's double plated the No. 1 New York tally in the first session.

It was the eighth victory for Gomez and Smith's sixth setback.

LUMIERE SPLASHES HOME.

NEW YORK, N. Y. (AP)—After being soundly beaten in two starts this season, Lumiere, from the Chicago-owned Railroad stable of Lester Selig and Sam Laud, splashed through the mud at Empire City to win in his third race, the Pocantico purse.

★ ★ ★ ★ ★ ★ ★ ★

Stop Joe

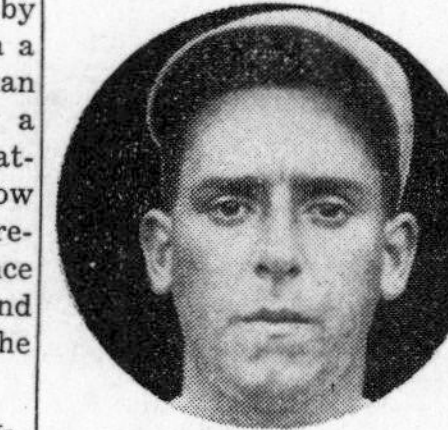

Al Smith.

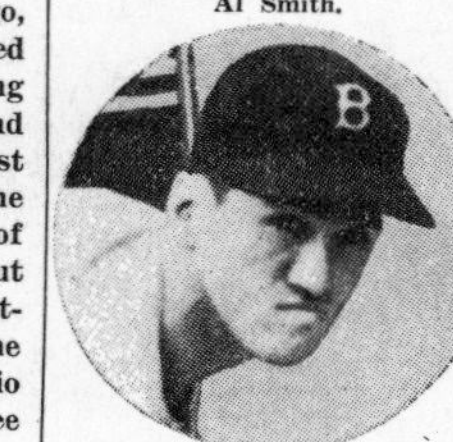

Jim Bagby.

★ ★ ★ ★ ★ ★ ★ ★

THE BOX SCORE.

N. York	AB.	H.	O.	A.	Clevel'd	AB.	H.	O.	A.
Sturm,1b	4	1	10	2	Weath'y,cf	5	1	4	0
Rolfe,3b	4	2	2	3	Keltn'r,3b	3	1	1	4
Henrich,rf	3	1	4	0	Boud'u,ss	3	0	0	2
DiM'gio,cf	3	0	2	0	Heath,rf	4	0	0	0
Gordon,2b	4	2	0	1	Walker,lf	3	2	1	0
Rosar,c	4	0	5	1	Grimes,1b	3	1	12	0
Keller,lf	3	1	0	0	Mack,2b	3	0	4	7
Rizzuto,ss	4	0	2	1	aRosenth'l	1	1	0	0
Gomez,p	4	1	2	1	Hemsley,c	3	1	5	1
Murphy,p	0	0	0	1	bTrosky	1	0	0	0
					Smith,p	3	0	0	0
Totals	33	8	27	10	Bagby,p	0	0	0	0
					cCampbell	1	0	0	0
					Totals	33	7	27	14

aBatted for Mack in ninth inning.
bBatted for Hemsley in ninth inning.
cBatted for Bagby in ninth inning.
Score by innings:
New York ....100 000 120—4
Cleveland ....000 100 002—3
Runs batted in—Henrich, Walker, Gomez, Gordon, Rolfe, Rosenthal 2.
Two-base hits—Henrich, Rolfe.
Three-base hits—Keller, Rosenthal.
Home runs—Walker, Gordon.
Sacrifice—Boudreau.
Double play—Boudreau, to Mack to Grimes.
Left on bases—New York 5, Cleveland 7.
Bases on balls—Off Smith 2, Bagby 1, Gomez 3.
Struck out—By Gomez 5, Smith 4, Bagby 1.
Hits—Off Smith 7 in 7 1-3 innings, Bagby 1 in 1 2-3, Gomez 6 in 8 (none out in ninth), Murphy 1 in 1.
Passed ball—Hemsley.
Winning pitcher—Gomez.
Losing pitcher—Smith.
Umpires—Summers, Rue and Stewart.
Time—2:03.
Attendance (actual)—67,468.

POSTPONE GRAND CIRCUIT.

OLD ORCHARD BEACH, ME. (AP)—Rain forced cancellation of Thursday's Grand Circuit races. The scheduled program will be run off today.

FINAL ★★

DAILY NEWS

Copr. 1941 by News Syndicate Co. Inc. NEW YORK'S PICTURE NEWSPAPER Trade Mark Reg. U. S. Pat. Off.

THE LARGEST CIRCULATION IN AMERICA

New York, Monday, October 6, 1941

2 Cents IN CITY LIMITS | 3 CENTS Elsewhere

YANKS WIN, 7-4

Owen's Error in 9th Loses Game

Story on Page 40.

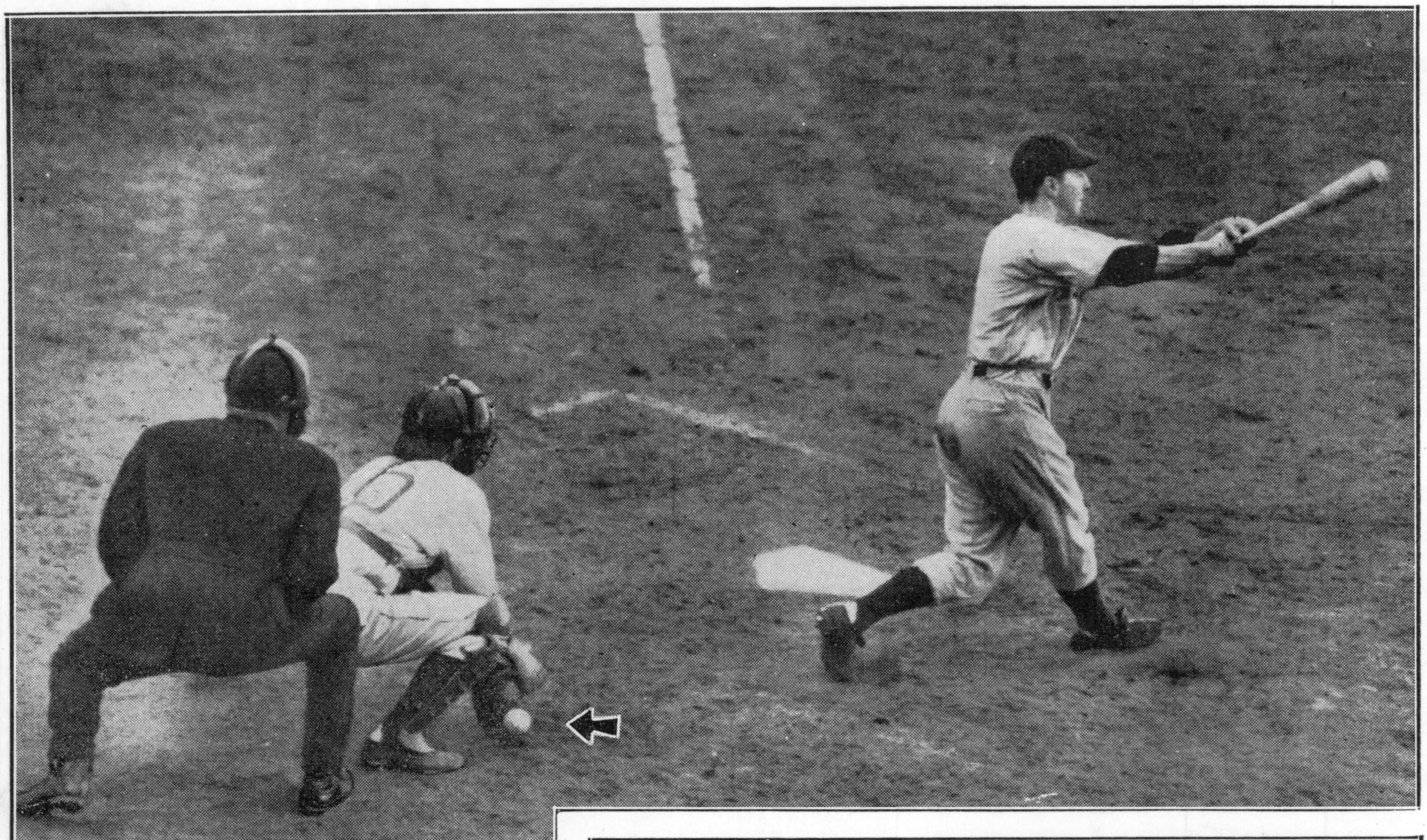

(By Associated Press)

↑THIS IS IT!→

This play, which cost the Dodgers a well-earned victory over the Yanks yesterday, will go down in baseball history as one of the game's costliest errors. As Tom Henrich swings and misses for his [⇧] third strike and what should have been the third out in the ninth, the ball gets away from Catcher Mickey Owen. Umpire Goetz' right hand is still raised for the out as Mickey, tossing off his mask, starts [⇨] after the bounding ball. Tommy hot-foots it for first, which he reached safely. Before the Dodgers could get the side out, the Bombers had scored four times to take the game, 7-4.

Turn to center fold for a 2-page foto of the dramatic climax of yesterday's game.

F.D.R. Asks Baseball Carry On as Usual

(Special to The News)

Washington, D. C., Jan. 16.—It'll be "Business as Usual" at your favorite ball-yard this Summer. President Roosevelt, the nation's No. 1 fan, today declared that he felt the national pastime should be carried on during the war and added that he hoped there would be more night games. The President's declaration was contained in a letter to Judge Kenesaw Landis, who had inquired into baseball's future because so many owners and fans were fearful that the war might blackout both night and day baseball.

The President made it clear that he was expressing only his personal opinion. But baseball men were convinced his remarks meant the majors and minors would be able to play full schedules.

READ AT CONFERENCE

Mr. Roosevelt read his letter to Judge Landis at the regular White House press conference.

"I honestly feel," The President said, "that it would be best for the country to keep baseball going. There will be fewer people unemployed and everybody will work longer hours and harder than ever before.

"And that means that they ought to have a chance for recreation and for taking their minds off their work even more than before.

"Baseball provides a recreation which does not last over two hours and a half, and which can be got for very little cost. And, incidentally, I hope that night games can be extended because it gives an opportunity to the day shift to see a game occasionally."

The President's declaration brought great sighs of relief in the

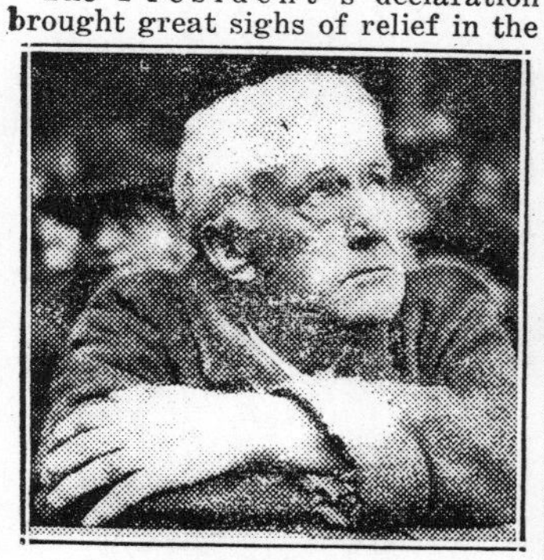

Judge Landis

baseball world which soon will be mobilizing its players for the Spring training season.

LANDIS IN FLORIDA

Judge Landis is vacationing in Florida, but his office issued the text of the letter and a statement from the high commissioner which said:

"I hope that our performance will be such to justify the President's faith."

Will Harridge, American League president, said Mr. Roosevelt had confirmed "the conviction held by all baseball men that the national pastime has a definite place in the welfare of our country, particularly during times of stress."

The President's suggestion for more night baseball was hailed by the hard-pressed second-division teams and promptly approved by the opponents of arc-light ball.

BOOST FOR NIGHT BALL

The American League already was considering calling an emergency meeting in New York Feb. 2 to discuss increasing the present limit of seven night games per park as a result of the St. Louis Browns' lament that their treasury was depleted and could only be replenished by after - dark crowds. As soon as the President's views were announced, Clark Griffith, Washington club president, said he would immediately urge lifting of the night game limit. Griff, once an arch-foe of the arc-lights, changed his chant in the last two years and has been suggesting night ball throughout the hot Summer months to increase attendance in Washington and other humid cities.

Donald L. Barnes, boss of the financially embarrassed Browns, said it was the best news he'd heard

(Continued on next page, col. 5)

"Keep Baseball Going . . ."

In a letter to Kenesaw M. Landis, high commissioner of baseball, President Roosevelt, No. 1 fan of the game, yesterday disclosed that he honestly felt it would be best for the country to keep baseball going.

Sir War Is Knighted In Hialeah Sprint

By Ray Powers

(Special Correspondent of The News)

Hialeah Park, Fla., Jan. 16.—Sir War, a handsome little son of Sir Gallahad 3d whose bids for racing fame include a sound beating by Alsab in the Walden Stakes last Fall, beat five others of his kind in the featured Tamiami sprint today after a stirring stretch drive.

The Circle M Ranch colt, choice of the 7,000 fans, came from third at the top of the home lane and under a masterful ride by Basil James, overtook the pacemaking Pig Tails in the final yards for a half length victory and a $5.60 straight mutuel.

Son Islam, with Wayne Wright in the saddle, galloped in for third money.

SIR WAR'S DEBUT

Getting away from the gate smartly, James held Sir War into a comfortable spot clear of interference until the half mark when he moved from fourth into a contending position, then went to the whip to knock off the six furlongs in 1:13 for the fast track.

It was Sir War's first appearance here after a fairly successful campaign in the East.

The most promising prospect among the two-year-olds was unveiled in the opening event when Jerry Louchheim's Kopla, made a show of the field getting home only four-fifths of a second slower than the record of :33. Alfy Robertson had the son of Okapi eased up throughout the last furlong, and went under the wire looking back at My Zaca, which took second money from Four Leaf. The popular winner paid $4.30.

WINS IN A GALLOP

Dan's Choice, stablemate of the champion Alsab, was the good thing in the second, but McCreary couldn't move him fast enough in the stretch to catch Lit Up, which lit up the boards to the tune of $36.50 straight. Ship's Run beat the favored Strolling Easy out of the show pool.

The daily double paid $144.20.

Figger It Out h d no competition in winning the fourth for the percentage players. The colt showed speed from the start and had ten lengths to the good going down the home lane but Johnny Gilbert literally walked him across the line at four. Trade Last and Back Tooth were the next in line behind the $3.40 winner.

Sam Houston, a cheap plater, upset the third sprint for $13.80, taking the lead at the three-eighth pole to outlast John Hunnicutt in the final drive.

And Tommy Atkinson, piloting outsider Sergeant Bill in the fourth, gave Jimmy Stout on Erie, a lesson in hand and boot riding to drive under for a $37.60 winner. Tommy had the Sergeant on top all the way, hugging the inside, outmaneuvering Stout with every move he made with the favorite. Theduel was clocked in 1:20 1/5 for the six and a half furlongs.

Conn McCreary, scored on the favored Navarin in the turf race, beating Ebony Boy by a nose.

Phelan Renamed Solon Head

Albany, Jan. 16 (AP). — New York's Senate received today for confirmation Gov. Lehman's reappointment of the three-member State Athletic Commission, with Brig. Gen. John J. Phelan, renamed chairman. Phelan receives $7,500 annually, while his colleagues, D. Walker Wear and William J. Brown, are paid $25 a day for time actually spent on commission work.

THE POWER HOUSE
by JIMMY POWERS

The Panicky Patseys, Jittery Joes, Fearful Freddies and Shivery Sams who were rushing about calling off football games, cancelling horse racing, abandoning golf championships and threatening to hang war crepe on everything in our sports world were unexpectedly thrown for a loss yesterday. President Roosevelt told Judge Landis the national pastime should be kept going during the war. He suggested that there be more night games because they would give day workers a chance to see an occasional contest.

Baseball can continue, and eligible baseball players can still serve their country in the Army and Navy. There are plenty of married ball players, old ball players, and young ball players with dependents to carry on.

The baseball situation was badly handled in World War 1. First off, baseball was ruled an essential industry and exempted from the first draft. A great howl went up and finally ball players were subjected to the draft, just as were football players, tennis players, golf players and any other class of athletes.

But—what the average doughboy resented was the creation of a pet class, a behind-the-lines allotment of cushy jobs for ball players. This hurt morale and if you don't think so we invite you to take a sample reading of our mail bag the past few months.

This is typical: . . . "I live in Englewood, N. J., which is 3 miles from Camp Merritt. In World War 1 there were 31 baseball players there, all in the Quartermaster Corps. They formed a team managed by George Whitted, Pirate second sacker at the time. Rube Bressler, Ben Tincup, Pickles Dilhoefer and others who slipped my mind were also there. These men were in the Quartermaster Corps 'for the duration' despite the fact that Camp Merritt was solely an embarkation camp of a minimum of 50,000 men. These men neither drilled, nor worked, and didn't even live at the camp. They lived home. Every A. M. five Dodge touring cars went to Brooklyn (for Bressler), Newark, Long Island, New York City, etc., picked up the ball players and returned to camp. They ate, changed clothes, played ball, etc., and were driven home again. They practiced at the West Side Field in Englewood and played home games there Saturday afternoons. 'Brother privates' from Camp Merritt were brought down to the field every day and worked on it to put it in shape . . . Now, I don't blame these ball players for accepting these favors. Whether they asked for them, or were ordered to take them, I don't know. I do know the average doughboy resented it. A few ball players got to France. But not many got to the front line trenches. And whether these major leaguers that I have definite knowledge of, volunteered or were drafted, or were assigned, it doesn't alter the fact that they spent their 'service' at Camp Merritt where thousands of equally able-bodied fellow privates just stopped over night en route to the battle-fields of France."—E. J. M., Englewood, N. J.

Tip: If you play the races and bet jockeys, lay off Hialeah this year. The competition is keen and the best riders are trying to make expenses. Veterans like Meade, James, Arcaro, Westrope, McCreary, Wall and Wright and an army of young ambitious apprentices are desperate. Riding will be hard and reckless. Plenty of the lads will find themselves pocketed if they try to hog it all. Meade got it the other day.

One Minute Interview:

Eddie Brannick: "Dodger fans can gloat all they want about their championship club but they forget that Brooklyn pennants have been mighty rare. The best test is to ask any ball player, including any Dodger, which club—if he had his choice between the Giant and Brooklyn payroll—he'd rather be playing with the past eight years. He'd tell you the Giants because of the higher average payroll over eight years, and those three fat World Series checks."

Nelson's 136 Paces Oakland Golf

Oakland, Calif., Jan. 16 (AP).—Byron Nelson maintained his par cracking pace today to lead the field at the half-way mark of the $5,000, 72-hole Oakland Open golf tournament with a 36-hole total of 136.

Less than half of the 140 starters had completed their second round when the Toledo, Ohio, pro checked in but there appeared little likelihood he would be displaced.

Nelson led the first round yesterday with 67, three under par for the Sequoyah Course. It gave him a one-stroke advantage.

He was out in 36 and home in 33 today. Par is 35-35.

Four players landed in a tie at 140 for the 36 holes. They were Lloyd Mangrum, Monterey Park, Calif.; Lawson Little, San Francisco; Denny Shute, Chicago and Chick Harbert, Battle Creek, Mich.

Crowd Against Him, Snead Proves Genuine Gamester in Winning P. G. A. Crown

Great Play in Stretch Whips Surprising Corpl. Turnesa

Sammy, in Washington To Join Navy, Collects $2,000 in War Coin

By GAYLE TALBOT,
Associated Press Sports Writer.

ATLANTIC CITY, June 1.—Sammy Snead, they said, never would win a national golf championship because something always seemed to happen to him in the closing stages of a tournament when the galleries were running wild and the players' hearts were in their throats.

They were wrong. Sammy held the Professional Golfers' Association championship today and had $2,000 worth of War bonds in his pocket as he left for Washington to be inducted into the Navy's physical training program.

The 30-year-old star from the hill country, after having suffered probably more major disappointments than any top-flight golfer, finally came through with a 2-and-1 victory over Corpl. Jim Turnesa in yesterday's 36-hole title match at the Seaview Club here.

It was a fighting victory, too. Sam stood three down at the halfway point. The crowd of 2,000 was pulling vociferously against his every shot and rooting for the swarthy little soldier from Fort Dix. And under those circumstances Snead went out to shoot some of the greatest home-stretch golf ever seen.

Turnesa Wins Crowd.

A triumph for Turnesa undoubtedly would have been more popular. The little guy with the nerves of steel and no business whatsoever in the final of a P. G. A. championship, had captured the fancy of everybody. The crowd had been cheering his every shot for two days as he scored upset victories over Ben Hogan and Byron Nelson, two of golfdom's greatest players. Yet Snead richly deserved his victory.

Three down through the 23d hole and with Turnesa refusing to crack, Sammy turned on the heat and blazed home. Starting on the 24th hole, he shot 433, 444, 344, 442. On the 27th hole he caught up with Turnesa, on the 28th he passed him, and from there on the scrapping corporal only could hang on.

Snead's finish would have dazed any opponent. The 35th hole, where the match ended, was typical. Sam overdrove the 213-yarder by some 60 feet and then chipped into the hole for a birdie 2.

Must Give Up Winnings.

Turnesa, 29-year-old member of the numerous Turnesa golfing clan, also earned all of the superlatives lavished on him. He "made" the tournament. Completely unheralded, the stocky, dark little fellow dropped over from his Army camp to play the finest golf of his life and completely upset the professionals' "routine." Odds of 50 to 1 could have been had against him at the start and there were no takers.

Unfortunately for Turnesa, Army regulations forbid his pocketing the $750 prize he won here, and besides, he promised to donate anything he might win to the Army Emergency Relief Fund.

So pleased were officials with the tournament they decided to hold their next championship on the same course. They don't know when that will be—probably after the war has ended—but it will be in Atlantic City.

Benning Wins Third

Benning A. C. won its third straight shutout of the season by taking a 2-0 decision over Maryland Junior Aces yesterday. The Aces got only one hit off the combined offerings of Rich and Smith.

VICTOR INVESTS IN VICTORY—Sammy Snead (seated) bought a war bond from Mrs. George Kemon after defeating Corp. Jim Turnesa in the P. G. A. finals at Atlantic City yesterday. Standing directly back of the championship trophy i s Turnesa (in uniform). —A. P. Wirephoto.

Anneke Jan, Sailed by Kanode, Surprises in Potomac Series

Scores With Lawson's Penguin Champ Far Back; Scandal, Blue Water Win Again

By MALCOLM LAMBORNE, Jr.

Favorites in two of the four classes competing in the fourth Sunday race of the Potomac River Sailing Association's spring series off Hains Point did it again yesterday as a fleet of some 25 boats drifted over a triangular course in a fitful summertime breeze.

They were Ernest Covert's Scandal in the comet class and Robert Orme's Blue Water in the Chesapeake Twenties class. Both boats beat across the finish line minutes ahead of the next boats in their class. Covert's margin was 5 minutes and 38 seconds and Orme's was 5 minutes 44 seconds.

Kanode Scores Upset.

Upset of the day was recorded in the penguin class when Walter Lawson, 1941 national penguin champion, got off to a poor and slow start and managed only a final sixth.

Don Kanode, back with the fleet after a recent illness, won in his Anneke Jan.

Exactly two minutes behind Kanode was George Dankers in his Cat's-Paw, while third place went to Wirt Gill's Skeptic. Eight penguins started for the largest single class.

Second to Covert was Clarke Daniel's Robert E. Lee, which, although starting 10 minutes late, managed to close in on the fleet. Albert Carey in Chaser was third.

Arthur Godfrey's lighting class sloop won the handicap division, on elapsed time, by the widest margin of the day. He was nearly 17 minutes ahead of H. W. Brent's Frances.

Handicap Race Shortened.

The twenties and comets sailed twice around the course, while penguins and handicappers went over the course once. The race committee on board the schooner Strombus held the latter class to one lap because of the light going.

Summaries:

20-Foot.

Blue Water (Robert Orme). Time, 1:21.50. Eight Ball (Owen Oakley), 1:27.22; Spindrift (Lynn Eldridge), 1:32.11.

Comet.

Scandal (R. E. Covert). Time, 1:31.16; Robert E. Lee (Clark Daniel), 1:37; Chaser (Albert Carey), 1:45.15; Electra (Arthur Varela).

Penguins.

Anneke Jan (Don Kanode). Time, 1:02.06; Cats Paw (George Dankers), 1:04.06; Skeptic (Wirt A. Gill), 1:05.50; Seabiscuit (Ralph Youngs), 1:07.40; Squirt (Joseph Krafft), 1:09.02; Potlatch (Walter Lawson), 1:09.50; Slug (J. J. Lewis), 1:21.30; Butch (Eric Nordholm), 1:24.15.

Handicaps.

No. 185 (Arthur Godfrey), 1:06.50; Frances (H. W. Brent), 1:23.48; Honeychile (Cooper Lightbown), 1:24.02; Rae (Steve Kotch), 1:26.11; Gypsy (F. W. Weiser), 1:43.10; Swan (Louise Kline), 1:55.16; Cymbros C. E. Meisner), 2:04.42.

Michigan Deadlocks Iowa for Midwest Diamond Title

Patterson and Scholler Of Ohio State Poison To Wolverine Nine

By the Associated Press.

CHICAGO, June 1.—Michigan fell short of wrapping up its second Big Ten baseball championship and settled in a tie for it with Iowa.

Wisconsin was dropped from the running when Minnesota captured a double-header, 3-1 and 6-1, Saturday. The Badgers can take third place this week end at Madison if they sweep the season's final two-game series from Ohio State. Both schools have six wins in ten games.

The standings:

	W.	L.	Pct.		W.	L.	Pct.
Iowa	10	2	.833	Indiana	5	7	.417
Michigan	10	2	.833	Purdue	5	7	.417
Wisconsin	6	4	.600	Minnesota	5	7	.417
Ohio State	6	4	.600	N'western	4	8	.333
Illinois	5	7	.417	Chicago	2	10	.167

Top Amateur Golfers Of District to Seek Mid-Atlantic Title

Seniors Are to Qualify Tomorrow at Manor, Others Wednesday

All the top ranking amateur golfers of Washington have entered the Middle Atlantic amateur championship, due to get under way tomorrow at the Manor Country Club with the qualifying round for the senior championship. Aspirants for the all-ages title will qualify Wednesday.

Top ranking stars include Buddy Sharkey and Charlie Malone of Indian Spring; Gene Pittman, Dr. H. L. Smith and Parker Nolan of Congressional; Ray Swearingen, Earl Skinker and Martin F. McCarthy of Columbia; Volney Burnett, the Maryland State champ, and many others.

Match play rounds in the title tourney will open Thursday. The seniors, playing for the Hinshaw Trophy, will qualify in one flight of eight, and will start match play Wednesday. Post entries will be accepted up to the first starting time in each class.

Pairings and starting times for the 71 entrants follow:

Seniors. Tuesday, 2:00 p.m.—Walter R. Tuckerman (Burning Tree), Dr. R. A. Keilty (Congressional), W. J. Peters (Manor). 2:05—John F. McCarron (Congressional), Frank G. Butler (Manor), Fay Ingalls (Hot Springs, Va.). 2:10—Dr. Noah Pomeroy (Congressional), Dr. A. T. Utz (Indian Spring), D. Paul Swope (Manor). 2:15—Bert Gamble and H. A. Neff (Manor).

Wednesday, 1:00 p.m.—Dr. H. L. Smith (Congressional), Edgar Lucas (Baltimore), Martin F. McCarthy (Columbia). 1:05—Harry G. Pitt (Manor), Gene Pittman (Congressional), John R. Miller (Prince Georges). 1:10—Parker Nolan (Congressional), Volney Burnett (Indian Spring), John O. Bergelin (Kenwood). 1:15—Dr. J. W. Nesbitt (Kenwood), R. K. Thompson (Prince Georges), Ray Swearingen (Columbia). 1:20—Joe Wilson (Kenwood), L. C. Steward, jr. (Columbia), Ralph P. Gibson (Manor). 1:25—Bill Briggs (Kenwood), Joe Barse (Columbia, H. A. Mihills (Congressional). 1:30—R. K. Benner (Kenwood), G. H. Jones (Manor), Jim Hunt (Indian Spring). 1:35—R. T. Kreuzburg (Kenwood), Clark Stoddard (Manor), E. C. Holmead (Manor). 1:40—E. B. Helkmer (Prince Georges), Lee Ritter (Manor), Dr. M. Oliveri (Indian Spring). 1:45—Frank Schrider and V. G. Myers (Kenwood), Merrill Whittlesey (Manor). 1:50—W. H. Wenzel (Kenwood), Buddy Sharkey and Sam Harvey (Indian Spring). 1:55—Jack Keele and Maury Fitzgerald (Kenwood), Billy Houghton (Bannockburn). 2:00—Charlie Malone (Indian Spring), Earl Skinker (Columbia), Dick Melvin (Kenwood). 2:05—Don Dudley (Kenwood), Robert Bowen (Indian Spring), W. A. Covert (Manor). 2:10—Charles L. Vaile (Kenwood), Eddie Ault (Indian Spring), William Young (Manor). 2:15—W. L. Jones and Chester Leakin (Manor), Jules Mercer (Indian Spring). 2:20—I. T. Donohue (Manor), Marty Gordon and Harold Gordon (Indian Spring). 2:25—C. A. Alber (Manor), Dr. J. G. Reilly (Manor), Frank Williams (Manor). 2:30—Ralph Pittman (Manor), H. G. Young and J. A. Pratt (Manor). 2:35—Buster Mrstik (Kenwood), Walter McCallum (Washington) and George F. Miller (Columbia).

Government Golfers Resume Action in Star Tournament

Two Series of Matches Scheduled This Week; Treasury Is Pressed

Government golfers take up their war clubs again this week in continuation of the matches for The Evening Star trophies, after a week with no action. Two series of matches are on the week's card, while next week the Federal linksmen get ready for the medal play individual and team championships, scheduled at Prince Georges June 15 and 16.

Hailed as a probable winner long before the series opened, Treasury's strong team is being pushed in class A, section 1, by Navy Yard, a newcomer to the tourney. Treasury has won 16 points against 13 for Navy Yard as the series moves into its final stage. In section 2, class A, the Federal Bureau of Investigation boys, with one star on the injury list, top the parade with 16½ points.

The scrap in class B, section 1, is close, with Post Office Department leading at 12½ points, against 10½ for Treasury. A missed putt or two in this section can shift the lead. But the boys in section 2 are even closer, for there Agriculture has won 13 points against 12½ for War College.

Here is the week's schedule: Tuesday—Class A, section 1, Treasury vs. Navy Yard at Bannockburn; G. P. O. vs. Labor at Woodmont. Section 2—War vs. F. H. A. at Belle Haven; F. B. I. vs. Navy at Bradley Hills.

Class B, section 1—W. P. A. vs. Mount Alto at Indian Spring; W. P. B. vs. Post Office at Army Navy. Section 2—Agriculture vs. R. F. C. at Kenwood; P. B. A. vs. Maritime.

Friday: Class A, section 1—G. A. O. vs. R. F. C. at Woodmont. Section 2—Executive Offices vs. Justice at Bradley Hills. Class B, section 1—Treasury vs. Agriculture at Army Navy. Section 2—War College vs. F. B. I. at Prince Georges.

Congressional Leads In Raising Money For Red Cross

Golf Event Nets $284; Fowler Again Champ At Washington Club

If the Red Cross gives out any pennants for hard work on fund-raising at golf courses a special award should go to the generous golfers of the Congressional Country Club and to Mrs. Inez Hyler, the Red Cross representative who worked for two days on the first tee. Those Congressional linksmen and linkswomen contributed $284 to the coffers of the humanitarian organization. It was the biggest reported "take" at any local country club in the first of three Hale America tourneys for Red Cross benefit to be held this season.

R. B. Battle won the gross award in a medal-play handicap tourney with a card of 75. G. L. Melleney won the net award with 80—15—65. Mixed foursome winners were: (Gross), Gloria Rodgers and Pat Winkler, 82; net, Jacquelyn Wood and F. E. Johnson, 87—15—72. Results in the spring handicap tourney were: First flight, G. G. Fitton defeated L. Townsend, 1 up; second flight, P. J. Crowell defeated H. Millang, 5 and 4; third flight, George K. Brobeck defeated F. T. Ronan, 2 up.

Fowler Washington Champ.

Ralph S. Fowler won his third Washington Golf and Country Club links title, defeating L. H. Whitten, 4 and 3, in a 36-hole final. Fowler, with a 71, was 3 up at the luncheon interval. Results in the other flights: Second flight, H. B. Willy defeated Al Edmonds, 2 and 1; third flight, Norman Manders defeated R. W. Westwood, 2 and 1; fourth flight, C. De Lashmutt defeated Paul Campbell, 2 and 1.

John S. Nicoll and C. L. Christie tied for the Mosby Memorial putter in a special putting event, both with 34 strokes. They will playoff later.

Four tied for the top prize in a Red Cross benefit affair at Columbia. They were C. H. Severance, 76—10—66; Jimmy Stanton, 75—9—66; E. B. Olds, 75—9—66, and Craig McKee, 71—5—66. Mr. and Mrs. Norman B. Frost won the gross award in a mixed foursome tourney with 83. Net prizes were won by Mrs. G. I. James and Robert W. McChesney, 95—25—70, and Jimmy Stanton and Mrs. W. C. Geleng, 85—13—72. E. B. Youngquist holed a 3-iron shot for an ace on the 180-yard eighth hole.

Mrs. Pray-McAleer Win.

Mrs. L. G. Pray and Earl McAleer topped a mixed foursome tourney at Manor with a card of 74—3—71, with Mr. and Mrs. Frank G. Butler next at 88—16—72. The gross award went to District women's champion, Mrs. W. R. Stokes, and Dick Meyer with 76.

Six tied for the Morris Simon Memorial Trophy at Woodmont, and will playoff later. They were Dave Frank, 89—23—66; Ed Wortman, 77—11—66; Dave Legum, 80—14—66; Sam Smith, 91—25—66; Ralph Goldsmith, 79—13—66; L. V. Freudberg, 86—18—66. In a Red Cross tourney Wortman, Legum and Goldsmith tied in class A with net 66s. In class B Frank and Freudberg tied for first, with another tie for third between Nathan Siegel, 89—22—67, and Dr. L. Shere, 86—19—67. Sam Smith won in class C with a net 66, with Dr. S. Dessoff, 93—25—68, and Leo Schlosberg, 94—26—68, tieing for second.

Ralph Goldsmith and Mrs. Milton Harris won the gross award in a mixed foursome tourney with 92. Net winners were Mr. and Mrs. A. E. Steinem, 93—18—75; Mr. and Mrs. Howard Nordlinger, 98—21—77; Mr. and Mrs. Milton Gladstein, 100—23—77.

Not Golden Enough

California's lavish Golden Gate Turf Club has closed—possibly because the gate wasn't golden enough.

THEY LURE FANS—Here are three reasons why Griffith Stadium held more than 20,000 fans yesterday, as the so-called All-Stars bowed to the Homestead Grays by an 8-1 count. At left is Cecil Travis, ex-Griffman, wearing a Camp Wheeler uniform, with Dizzy Dean, former Card and Cub in the center and the famous Satchel Paige at right. —Star Staff Photo.

Field in Federal Golf Tourney Looms as Strongest Ever

Event May Be Shifted From Prince Georges; East Potomac Announces Spring Contest

By WALTER McCALLUM.

Two weeks from today Federal golfers will descend en masse on the Prince Georges Country Club to settle their individual and team medal play championships for 1942. It may be the last year for the Federal Golf Association annual tourney, but they want to make it a good one, from President Paul Carey down. There isn't any doubt it will be a good one, for this year the class of linksmen in the Government service looms as the best ever, even during the days when Al Houghton, who organized the tourney, was the top man.

George J. Voigt, the 48-year-old veteran who at one time held every amateur title around Washington; Dick Jennings, public links champ; Cliff Spencer, former Beaver Dam pro, a little rusty as to his golf but still capable of a burst of fine scoring; John Attas, Bernie Hallock, Tommy Webb, Billy Shea, all can produce links fireworks whenever they step on any man's well manicured first tee. The coming Federal championship should be the hottest of the lengthy series.

But the boys haven't much time to enter, for entires will close with Carey at 4607 North Third street, Arlington, Va., Wednesday. The tourney, of course, is scheduled for Prince Georges June 15 and 16, but it may be changed. When the Government lads set the place and the date they didn't anticipate gasoline rationing. It may go to a spot closer to the center of the city.

Mrs. Stuart Flag Victor.

Mrs. D. E. Stuart won a women's flag tourney at Indian Spring, playing her final stroke to a point 20 yards from the pin on the nineteenth hole. Mrs. Marty Gordon was second. Perry Jones scored 87—19—68 to win a Red Cross tourney. Other winners were Ray Weisberg, 91—22—69; Harry Freas, 79—10—69, and S. B. Maize, 91—22—69.

Mrs. M. H. Shanan defeated Mrs. Charles Jorg, 4 and 2, to win the Marmion Trophy at Prince Georges, with Mrs. C. E. Purdy winning the consolation. J. A. Woodside scored a double victory, for he won the gross award in a Red Cross tourney with 76, and thumped out a prodigious tee shot to win the men's driving contest with a poke of 327 yards. Net winners were R. H. Sinclair, 81—13—68, and Jerry Burch, 77—9—68. R. W. Townsend and Charles Jorg tied in a blind bogey affair with net 77s.

Mrs. Jack Palmer won the women's driving contest, with Mrs. C. E. Purdy winning the approaching contest and Mrs. Palmer proving the best putter. Woodside hit the longest tee shot for the men, while Forrest Thompson knocked an approach shot a foot from the pin to win that class, and Doug Mattison won the putting event.

East Potomac Announces Event.

East Potomac announced a spring tourney, with qualifying to run from June 1 through June 7, and match play rounds to continue through June 30. Prizes will be awarded to the winner and runnerup in each flight.

A. L. Williams played his last stroke 20 feet from the pin on the 20th hole to win a flag tourney at Kenwood. Other winners were L. B. Sharp, Felix Altrup, Bill Briggs, Bill Wenzel, William Hardt, H. G. Thielscher and Harvey J. Cooper.

John O. Bergelin played the Kenwood course in 72 strokes to win the gross award in a Red Cross tourney, while Mrs. Betty Meckley scored 75 to win the women's gross award. Net winners were A. L. Williams, 89—26—63, and Mrs. J. M. Fetters, 102—25—78.

Amsden Scores at Argyle.

Ray Amsden, Argyle Club champ, scored a 73 with an eight-stroke handicap to win a flag tourney at his home club. Other winners were Harry Wilson, George Bond, A. B. Melzner, H. H. David, H. L. Wooten and R. L. Bedell among the men. Feminine winners were Mrs. Elsie Livingston, Mrs. V. Bose, Mrs. Billy Williams, Mrs. Helen Horner, Mrs. K. De Jong, Mrs. Evelyn Scoggins and Mrs. Virginia McFarland.

G. C. Rittenhouse scored 75—7—68 to win a Red Cross event at Bannockburn, with Tony Martino and Bill Pendergast tieing at 74 for the gross award. Ray L. Burgdorf, sr., won a blind bogey and also won low net in the Red Cross affair with 80—11—69.

Lorton Bows to Cameo

Special Dispatch to The Star.

LORTON, Va., June 1.—Cameo Furniture nine of Washington ended Lorton Blue's three-game winning streak by taking a 13-3 decision in yesterday's game here. The visitors tallied nine runs in the first inning and three more in the second for a lead Lorton never could approach.

Paige Dims All Stars As Grays Find Dean Easy at Outset

Travis Gets 1 of 4 Hits Off Colored Ace; 22,000 Storm Ball Park

Dizzy Dean's advertised appearance in yesterday's diamond duel between his All-Stars and the Washington Homestead Grays was shortlived, but Leroy (Satchelfoot) Paige, Negro baseball No. 1 twirler of all time, stayed around for five innings, much to the Stars' unfeigned embarrassment. The final count was 8-1 in the Grays' favor.

Dean was a big leaguer in name only, for the one-time Cardinal great displayed none of the speed, poise and cunning that marked his salad days in the big show. Three crackling singles, with a sacrifice and long outfield fly sandwiched between, were enough to convince old "Diz" it wasn't his day and he left the hill before the first inning was completed.

Paige, on the other hand, displayed his usual breezy form in limiting the opposition to four hits during his 5-inning stint, tossing in seven strikeouts for good measure. He was at his best in the fifth when, with one out, the Stars got two men on base. The tall colored boy cut loose with his fast one and whiffed Bud Boyle and Dick Baker to retire the side without damage.

One of the four hits gleaned from Paige's offerings was a single off the bat of Cecil Travis, former Washington infielder, who played third base for the Stars for five innings.

The Grays pounced on Relief Twirler Jim Duffey, a bulky gent, for four runs in the fifth and added two more for good measure in the seventh. Of the victors' 13 hits, two were triples by Bankhead and Harris and another a double by Gibson.

A late rush of fans for tickets threw the concourse before the gates into a state of wild confusion, necessitated an emergency call for police reserves to restore order and delayed the entrance of a couple of thousand fans so long they missed Dean entirely and saw Paige in only a couple of innings. The surge swelled the attendance to a wholly unexpected 22,000.

Two District Horses Capture Deep Run Reserve Honors

Special Dispatch to The Star.

RICHMOND, June 1.—Washington horses have two reserve championships to show for competition in yesterday's Deep Run Hunt Club meeting. Troop, owned by Mr. and Mrs. U. S. Randle, finished second in the hunter championship, while King Rock, owned by J. J. Cotter, was runnerup in the junior class.

Cornish Hills, owned by Mr. and Mrs. W. Haggin Perry of Cobham, Va., and ridden by Mrs. Perry hacked himself into the hunter title after entering the hunter preliminary half a point behind Troop. He demonstrated excellent hacking qualities and fine conformation to annex the blue, worth 2½ points to the 1½ points which went to Troop for second place. Margaret Cotter and Frost Anderson rode Troop.

The jumper award went to Egg Nog, owned and ridden by Bobby Jones of Rocky Mount, N. C., which added a second and third yesterday to his Saturday's score for a total of 12½ points. King Rock, ridden by Miss Cotter, took the reserve after a jumpoff with Mrs. K. M. Bruce's Rose Gold. Both were tied with 10 points.

Gardner Hallman of Silver Spring, Md., received a broken collarbone when his mount Smacko fell at the in-and-out in handy hunters.

Robertson's Homers Nab Twin Bill for Orioles

Special Dispatch to The Star.

Young Sherry Robertson, Clark Griffith's nephew and rookie outfielder with the Baltimore Club of the International League, is the Oriole hero today after supplying the punch giving that club both ends of yesterday's double-header over Toronto, 2-1 and 7-5.

His third-inning homer with a man on base supplied all Baltimore runs in the first game, but that was nothing to the other homer he smacked with two men on base and two out in the final frame of the second game when Toronto was leading, 5-4.

Short Will Better 47 Seconds For 440, Hoya Coach Believes

Hugh Short, Georgetown speedster who won the I. C. 4-A. quarter-mile championship in the scintillating time of 47.2 last Saturday, may compete in the N. C. A. A. championships at Lincoln, Nebr., later this month and then take a long rest, Coach Hap Hardell said today.

Al Blozis, the Hoyas' shot and discus expert, is slated to compete in the meet and probably will represent the New York A. C. in the National A. A. U. championships at New York later in the month, but he is out of school now while Short is slated to resume classwork July 7.

In praising Short for his splendid run, in which he beat Colgate's Al Diebolt in a thrilling stretch drive, Hardell called him one of the Nation's potentially greatest runners.

"He was unknown, unsung and greatly underrated by most fans," he said, "although some of the experts picked him to run second. He didn't surprise me at all because he's a determined boy, every inch a fighter."

Hardell wants Short to rest because he has been running since last September, when the Hilltoppers started cross-country, and still is growing. His coach is anxious to avoid his being burned out before he reaches his maturity because Hardell is certain Short will run under 47 seconds when he hits his peak.

OUTDOORS With BILL ACKERMAN

Frederick County Streams in Good Shape; Anglers Warned About Catoctin Parking

Frederick County trout streams were in prime condition over the week end. Some anglers complained about the levels, several inches above normal, and the consequent heavier flow. But so long as May conditions obtained in April it seems perfectly fair to have a spring flow now. And if a little thought were given the matter they would be happy about the whole thing, for those heavy rains of last week are just a little insurance against a recurrence of last fall's drouth, which already was in a fair way of being repeated.

Warned Against Parking.

Stream fishermen parking along the Foxville road as their fancy dictates in order to fish Big Hunting Creek are warned the practice must stop. The War Department, now in control of the Catoctin area, requests that the parking places provided all along the road be used. Remembering that anglers are fishing this stream on sufferance it would appear to be wise to keep stream conduct above reproach, including parking and movement along the narrow, twisting road.

We've been fishing the Poplar Island bell buoy for these many years, but it is only this week we learn the grounds are called the "Little Gooses." Why is hard to understand, for there is little to compare between the two areas unless it is the large catches made upon both. Until the last few days the best catches in the Herring Bay sector have been made the^e. Capt. Gilbert Ward, and in fact all the Ward fleet, stick to this area in spite of the longer run. It is the best midsummer grounds anywhere in the upper bay.

Bill Dear is back from his first try for sharks at Cape Charles. One 7-footer was the best he could hang, but the trout, large and plentiful, more than made up for the absence of shark. Possibly being confined to inside fishing was the reason for not hooking more, but after all it is still early.

Anglers Berth Boats.

More than a few fishermen owning their own boats are berthing in the Potomac, perhaps to save gas. They are learning first hand it is a long run down to salt water, that little can be saved that way and there i' no worthwhile fishing high up ur ss one considers the black bass in the coves on the Virginia shore. The season will open there June 15. In the Maryland creeks the season will open August 1. Fall is the time for yellow perch and pike. We'll take the bay for another two months so long as we are able to get to it.

Ancient Craft Helped In Severn Regatta By 30-Mile Gale

Comet So Solly Scores, Stardust Sails Second First Time in Years

Special Dispatch to The Star.

MILLERSVILLE, Md., June 1.—Skippers of some of the older, slower comets competing in the Indian Landing summer series of races on Round Bay of the Severn River near here could use more of the big winds which spiced yesterday's events.

The races began in calm weather, but ended with a squall and a 30-mile gale putting two of the slowest boats across the line first. So Solly, piloted by George Adamson, won the race—his second triumph in several years—and right behind was Ed Combs in the Stardust, this being the second time he has finished that high.

Winners in the other classes were: Al Geis (Aeolis) in the National one-design; Betsy Podlick (Betsy) in the Severn one-design and Peter Bartlett (Do Nut) in the penguins.

Comets—Won by So Solly (George Adamson); second, Stardust (Ed Combs); third, Betty Box (Sprigg Sands).
National one-design—Won by Aeolis (Al Geis); second, Sjovand (Rex Daniels); third, Vim (George Bartlett).
Severn one-design—Won by Betsy (Betsy Podlick); second, Crest (Gordon Schreitz); third, Zip (Tom Kauffman).
Penguins—Won by Do Nut (Peter Bartlett); second, 343 (Robert Kauffman).

Drive by Minneapolis To Third High Lights Week End in A. A.

By the Associated Press.

The close of the big holiday week end in the American Association resulted in this scramble for positions:

1. Milwaukee still in the driver's seat, although not as comfortably fixed as before.

2. Kansas City, as usual, threatening to take over the leadership, only 1½ games behind.

3. Minneapolis moving up to third place with a force that could carry it to the top if continued.

The Millers' move into a challenging position was the biggest development. They won two pitching duels with St. Paul yesterday, 2-1 and 3-1, to total up four victories out of five against the Saints this season.

Top Row of United Loft Wins 300-Mile Race

Top Row, from the United Loft, won the 300-mile race from Concord, N. C., held yesterday by the East Potomac Racing Pigeon Club.

Birds from the loft of George Gateau finished second and third.

Summaries, with name of loft and average yards per minute:

United Lost, 1,1990.05; George J. Gateau, 1,187.65; George J. Gateau, 1,186.13; Douglas & Laing, 1,185.30; Chaney & Staffel, 1,185.18; E. J. Nalley, 1,184.53; Burdette & Valdivia, 1,182.45; Carl Sterzer, 1,181.23; George Thomas, 1,180.08; William Fastnaught, 1,172.78; H. Reckeweg, 1,164.55; M. Durity, 1,163.50; Al Horan, 1,161.90; J. E. Curtin, 1,160.43; E. Gates, 1,150.85; Andrew Flaherty, 1,149.98; Alvin Dulaney, 1,148.68; John Kovach, 1,147.70; John Dougherty, 1,146.88; Mike Horan, 1,145.85; George Christy, 1,101.53; D. Moran, no report.

Gaithersburg to Face Poolesville Nine for County Loop Lead

Capturing their third consecutive victories yesterday, Gaithersburg A. C. and Poolesville set the stage for one of the Upper Montgomery County League's biggest battles next Sunday when they will collide at Gaithersburg for undisputed lead of the circuit.

Gaithersburg turned back Rockville, 7-3, while Poolesville was nosing out Germantown, 8-7, in the co-features of yesterday's card.

Gaithersburg Trojans nosed out Damascus, 2-1, in the day's closest fray, while Bethesda Barons came from behind to score 11 runs in the last three innings and drug Potomac 11-5.

Dick Kuster went the route for the Barons and also banged out a double with the bases filled in the eighth to clinch the victory.

Brewers Lose at Frederick

Special Dispatch to The Star.

FREDERICK, Md., June 1.—Pushing across a run with one out in the last inning, Frederick Hustlers defeated Heurich Brewers of Washington, 3-2, in yesterday's baseball game. The Brewers got both their markers on four hits in the sixth frame.

City Tourney Rivals Clash in Special Bowling Match

Clarendon and King Pin To Be Hosts to Boyer And Shamrock Quints

A grudge bowling battle between the Shamrocks of the Rhode Island Avenue Business Men's League and Boyer's Pharmacy of the Clarendon Major League, the aftermath of the former topping the latter by five pins to win the Class B team championship in the recent Washington City Duckpin Association tournament, promises to highlight this week's local duckpin attractions.

The first block of the six-game series will be rolled at Clarendon Wednesday night, starting at 7:30 and the final next Sunday at King Pin. The match will be a benefit for the Navy Relief Fund. Eddie Goldberg, proprietor of the Clarendon drives and Jimmy Moore, King Pin pilot, have agreed to match the donations given by the spectators at their alleys.

But before tackling the challenging Virginia outfit, the Shamrocks have another important issue to settle tomorrow, the championship of the Rhode Island Avenue loop. Deadlocked in first place with National Beer, the Shamrocks will meet the Greyhounds in the windup while the Naitonals will engage Brookland Post Office in the windup.

The Shamrocks composed of Capt. "Cap" Johnson, Ed Jeffries, Horace Tucker, Dick Townsend and Louis Rose counted 1,789 to annex the city B team title. The Boyer Pharmacy line-up will include Al Watson, captain; Carson Carlisle, Irving Bowman, Carroll Upperco and Dick Warner.

Stars Yesterday

By the Associated Press.

Joe Cronin and Lou Finney, Red Sox—Former hit three-run homer in first game and latter singled in tying and winning runs in second as Red Sox beat Senators twice.

Elden Auker, John Niggeling and Don Gutteridge, Browns—Auker and Niggeling pitched double victory over Indians with help of Gutteridge's six hits in eight times at bat.

Bill Lohrman and Willard Marshall, Giants—Former pitched four-hit ball in first game and latter hit three-run homer in second to pace double victory over Phils.

Johnny Murphy, Yankees, and Luman Harris, Athletics—Murphy checked A's in relief to save first game and Harris tossed four-hitter in nightcap to break Yanks' eight-game winning streak.

Bucky Walters and Ray Starr, Reds—Pitched their team to double triumph over Pirates on five and six hits, respectively.

Dixie Walker and Whitlow Wyatt, Dodgers—Former hit grand-slam homer in opener and latter pitched six-hitter in nightcap as Dodgers beat Braves twice.

Ted Lyons, White Sox—Pitched 10-inning victory over Tigers and collected three hits, last of which set off five-run rally in tenth.

Army Bombers Shoot Down 5 Jap Planes In Aleutians

THE WEATHER
Occasional rain ending by afternoon and followed by somewhat colder. Gentle to moderate winds. High humidity.

Read The Baltimore News-Post for complete accurate war coverage. It is the only Baltimore newspaper possessing the three great wire services—
ASSOCIATED PRESS
INTERNATIONAL NEWS SERVICE
UNITED PRESS

THE BALTIMORE NEWS-POST
AN INDEPENDENT NEWSPAPER
The Largest Evening Circulation in the Entire South

COMPLETE FINAL

VOL. CXLI.—NO. 132 | Entered as second-class matter at Baltimore Postoffice. | TUESDAY, OCTOBER 6, 1942 | PRICE 3 CENTS

CARDS BEAT YANKS, 4-2 TAKE WORLD SERIES

5 Jap Planes Bagged In Aleutians

WASHINGTON, Oct. 5—(A. P.). The Navy announced today that Army bombers operating from their new bases in the western Aleutian Islands were making almost daily raids on the Japanese at Kiska, and that last Friday they shot five enemy seaplanes.

A communique said that Thursday and Friday a large number of hits with demolition and incendiary bombs was scored on the enemy camp at Kiska and on the seaplane hangar there.

UNDER CONTINUAL FIRE

Weather conditions have permitted frequent attacks on Kiska, said the communique, and "the enemy has been under continual fire."

A photographic survey, the Navy communique added, disclosed that two cargo ships had been damaged by bombs in previous attacks, and had been beached by the Japanese.

The Navy has now reported more

Continued on Page 2, Column 3.

Dismiss Roe's Petition On 155 Votes

SALISBURY, Md., Oct. 5—(A. P.).—A petition filed by State Senator Dudley G. Roe to invalidate the 155 Democratic primary election votes in Dennis election district of Wicomico county—and thus give Roe the First District Democratic Congressional nomination—was dismissed today by Chief Judge Benjamin A. Johnson.

Roe immediately filed an appeal, which will be argued before the State Court of Appeals on Thursday morning.

Granting of Roe's petition, which he based on the assertion that ballots in Dennis district were signed with indelible pencil instead of with ink and therefore were invalid, would have given him the First District nomination by 19 votes over his opponent, Representative David J. Ward (Democrat) of Maryland.

Stalingrad Halts 12 New Nazi Attacks

MOSCOW, Oct. 5—(U. P.).—A terrific German drive, using more than 100 tanks and hundreds of planes, stormed at the narrowest parts of Stalingrad's defenses today, seeking to blast a path into the heart of the city for reinforced ground troops.

The Volga metropolis was ablaze again as German planes, determined to pulverize its remnants, unleashed new and savage atacks.

Front dispatches said the Russians' heroic resistance repelled more than 12 attacks and yielded only at one point.

NAZI LOSSES HEAVY

In the northwestern section of Stalingrad, overwhelming German forces drove the Soviets back in a factory district.

But inside the great bend of the Don River, 60 to 70 miles northwest of Stalingrad, powerful Soviet forces stabbed deeper and deeper into the German left flank, rolling over heavy German defenses.

The unslackening Russian resistance at Stalingrad was taking the heaviest casualties from the enemy's assault troops, front advices said.

According to German prisoners

Continued on Page 2, Column 7.

Report Germans Mutiny In Norway

LONDON, Oct. 5—(A. P.).—A Reuters dispatch from Stockholm quoted press reports in the Swedish capital today that 3,000 to 4,000 German soldiers had been imprisoned for a mutiny at Alta in far Northern Norway.

These reports said 17 German officers had been cashiered and 43 of the imprisoned soldiers sentenced to death by a military court at Harstad.

Allies Hold Air, Ministers Report

CANBERRA, Australia, Oct. 5—(U. P.).—War Minister F. M. Forde and Air Minister Arthur S. Drakeford reported today after a nine-day tour of New Guinea, that Allied forces had complete air superiority and Australians and Americans were working perfectly together.

Drakeford emphasized the "invaluable" assistance given by Americans.

A Double Play In The Making

In the first inning of the final World Series test at the Yankee Stadium, Jimmy Brown of the Cardinals was forced out at second on Enos Slaughter's grounder to Yankee Second Baseman Joe Gordon. Here, Yankee Shortstop Phil Rizzuto is firing the ball to first to catch Slaughter and complete a fast double play.

Tell Retreat Of Chinese In Burma

By ROBERT P. MARTIN
United Press Staff Correspondent.

SOMEWHERE IN EASTERN INDIA, Oct. 6.—The full story of the tragic retreat of valiant Chinese forces who struggled for three months and four days across razor-backed mountains from Burma and through one of the world's densest jungles, was revealed today.

Gen. Liao Yoah Siang, who led the "backward march" of his straggling units when the Japanese swept up the Burma Road and overran the entire territory, told the story at headquarters where his men are being re-equipped and trained by Americans in preparation for a counter invasion of Burma.

In the retreat the small Chinese

Continued on Page 2, Column 4.

—For Salvage Information
(1) Iron and Steel
(2) Kitchen Fats
(3) Tin Cans
Call PLaza 6877

Daily Double (Pious Display / Sollure) Paid $29.40

LAUREL CHARTS

Copyright, 1942, by Triangle Publications, Inc. (Daily Racing Form.)

TRACK FAST.

FIRST RACE—SIX FURLONGS. CHUTE. FOR TWO-YEAR-OLD MAIDENS. Claiming. Purse $1,000. Value to winner $700, second $150, third $100, fourth $50. Went to post at 2.04½. Off at 2.05. Start good from gate. Won handily, place driving. Winner br g 2, by Display-Pious. Owned by H. L. STRAUS. Trained by F. A. BONSAL. Time 22 4-5, 47 3-5, 1.14 3-5.

	Wt.	Post	St.	¼	½	Str.	Fin.	Jockeys	Odds
aPious Display	118	12	9	5½	4½	3^{8}	1^{1}½	F. Zufelt	$2.75
Good Lawyer	120	9	8	6^{2}	1^{h}	1^{h}	2^{1}	E. DeCamillis	2.20
Realman	118	1	5	7^{h}	7^{h}	5^{1}½	3^{1}	J. Wagner	66.65
Hand Me Down	118	5	3	1^{1}½	3^{2}	2^{h}	4½	D. Scocca	28.40
Mango	118	10	1	2^{1}	5^{1}	4^{h}	5^{h}	M. Fator	47.20
aJune Quest	118	2	12	8^{h}	8^{2}	8^{h}	6^{h}	R. Howell	2.75
Mare Nostrum	118	11	10	10½	10^{2}	9^{2}	7^{1}½	R. Sisto	72.90
bLa Cima Boy	118	7	2	4^{h}	2^{h}	6½	8^{2}	P. Keiper	54.55
bLord Charles	118	4	11	11^{4}	9^{1}½	7^{1}½	9^{3}	C. Rollins	54.55
Propose	118	8	7	9^{2}	11	10^{3}	10½	A. Schmidl	2.40
Alabaster	113	3	6	3^{h}	6^{1}½	11	11	L. Knapp	7.95
Missy Mary	117	6	4	12	bolted			J. Berger	31.05

aJones and Straus entry. bBrooks and La Cima Stable entry.

$2 Mutuels Paid—Pious Display, $7.50 straight, $3.40 place, $2.90 show. Good Lawyer, $3.60 place, $3.20 show. Real Man, $13.80 show. Total mutuels....$34.40

Pious Display forced to lose ground from the start, responded well when straightened away for the drive, wore down the leaders swiftly and won with something left. Good Lawyer rushed forward on the outside to reach the lead nearing the final quarter, was unable to draw clear, gave way to the winner and held on well. Realman improved his position at a saving of ground, came through the field entering the stretch and closed with a rush.

SECOND—SIX FURLONGS. CHUTE. FOR TWO-YEAR-OLDS. CLAIMING. Purse $1,500. Value to winner $1,000, second $300, third $150, fourth $50. Went to post at 2.36½. Off at once. Start good from gate. Won easily, place driving. Winner b c 2, by Soleil du Midi-Luress. Owned by H. G. BEDWELL. Trained by J. MURPHY. Time 23, 46 4-5, 1.12 4-5.

	Wt.	Post	St.	¼	½	Str.	Fin.	Jockeys	Odds
Sollure	109	2	1	1^{1}½	1^{1}½	1^{2}	1^{2}	F. Remerscheid	$3.70
Bold Dan	114	5	4	4½	3½	3½	2^{1}½	C. Rollins	7.65
His Banker	108	8	6	5^{1}	5^{1}	6^{2}	3^{h}	M. Basile	22.95
Overlin	106	7	2	2½	2½	2^{h}	4^{1}	T. Crawford	1.65
Liberty Pan	108	6	7	7^{8}	7^{3}	4^{1}	5^{8}	H. Trent	7.40
Sweet Repose	111	4	8	8	8	8	6^{3}	R. Merritt	6.65
Burgoo Maid	110	1	5	6^{h}	6^{1}	5^{h}	7^{2}½	A. Schmidl	8.25
Dr. R. Young	106	3	3	3½	4^{1}½	7½	8	J. Tammaro	83.15

$2 Mutuels Paid—Sollure, $9.40 straight, $5.20 place, $3.80 show. Bold Dan, $11.00 place, $8.40 show. His Banker, $8.90 show. Total mutuels $46.70

Sollure established a clear lead under energetic handling, responded well after drifting out entering the stretch and won with something to spare. Bold Dan going in his best form and well up from the start, finished strongly. His Banker was forced to lose ground from the start and closed with a rush. Overlin had fine speed and tired. Liberty Pan began slowly and tired after improving his position. Sweet Repose passed tiring horses in the drive. Burgoo Maid was permitted to drop back soon after the start and was eased when in close quarters in the drive. Dr. R. Young had speed.

THIRD—ABOUT TWO MILES. FOR THREE-YEAR-OLDS AND UP. CLAIMING. Steeplechase. Purse $1,000. Value to winner $700, second $150, third $100,

Continued on Page 18, Column 7.

Play-By-Play Of 5th Game

FIRST INNING

St. Louis Cardinals—

BROWN walked on four straight pitches.

MOORE went down swinging.

SLAUGHTER hit into a double play, Gordon to Rizzuto to Priddy.

No run, no hit, no error, none left.

New York Yankees—

RIZZUTO hit a home run into the left-field seats.

ROLFE went out, Brown to Hopp.

CULLENBINE grounded out to Hopp, unassisted.

DI MAGGIO flied to Moore.

One run, one hit, no error, none left.

SECOND INNING

St. Louis Cardinals—

MUSIAL popped to Rizzuto.

W. COOPER drove one over second for a single.

HOPP popped to Rizzuto.

KUROWSKI lined one into the left-field stands that was foul by a scant margin. Kurowski then popped to Gordon.

No run, one hit, no error, one left.

New York Yankees—

KELLER grounded out, Brown to Hopp.

GORDON bounced out, Marion to Hopp.

Continued on Page 18, Column 3.

Kurowski's Home Run In Ninth Inning Wins Title For Cardinals

BOX SCORE

FIFTH GAME

CARDINALS	AB.	R.	H.	O.	A.	E.	YANKEES	AB.	R.	H.	O.	A.	E.
Brown, 2b	3	0	2	3	4	2	Rizzuto, ss.	4	1	2	7	1	0
T. Moore, cf.	3	1	1	3	0	0	Rolfe, 3b.	4	1	1	1	0	0
Slaughter, rf.	4	1	2	2	0	0	Cullenbine, rf.	4	0	0	3	0	0
Musial, lf.	4	0	0	2	0	0	DiMaggio, cf.	4	0	1	3	0	0
W. Cooper, c.	4	1	2	2	1	0	Keller, lf.	4	0	1	1	0	0
Hopp, 1b	3	0	0	9	2	1	Gordon, 2b	4	0	1	2	3	0
Kurowski, 3b.	4	1	1	1	1	0	Dickey, c.	4	0	0	4	0	0
Marion, ss.	4	0	0	3	5	0	Priddy, 1b	3	0	0	6	1	1
Beazley, p.	4	0	1	2	0	1	Ruffing, p.	3	0	1	0	1	0
	0	0	0	0	0	0	1 Stainback	0	0	0	0	0	0
	0	0	0	0	0	0	2 Selkirk	1	0	0	0	0	0
	0	0	0	0	C	0		[illegible]	0	0	0	0	0
	0	0	0	0	0	0		0	0	0	0	0	0
	0	0	0	0	0	0		0	0	0	0	0	0
	0	0	0	0	0	0		C	0	0	0	0	0
Total	33	4	9	27	13	4	Total	35	2	7	27	6	1

SCORE BY INNINGS

										R.	H.	E.
Cardinals	0	0	0	1	0	1	0	0	2	4	9	4
Yankees	1	0	0	1	0	0	0	0	0	2	7	1

1 Ran for Dickey in 9th. 2 Batted for Ruffing in ninth.

Runs batted in—Rizzuto, Slaughter, DiMaggio, W. Cooper, Kurowski. Home runs—Rizzuto, Slaughter, Kurowski. Sacrifices—Moore, Hopp. Double plays—Gordon to Rizzuto to Priddy; Hopp to Marion to Brown. Left on bases—Cardinals, 5; Yankees, 6. Base on balls—Off Ruffing, 1; off Beazley, 1. Struck out—By Ruffing, 3; by Beazley, 2. Umpires—Magerkurth (N. L.); Summers (A. L.); Barr (N. L.); Hubbard (A. L.). Time, 2.25.

YANKEE STADIUM, N. Y., Oct. 5—(A. P.).—The scrapping St. Louis Cardinals won the World Series, four games to one, when they closed out the Yankees, 4 to 2, in a thrilling final battle before nearly 70,000 fans today.

Rookie George Kurowski hit a home run in the ninth inning with Walker Cooper on base to score the winning run.

With the score tied at 2-2 and one out, Kurowski pounded one of Charley Ruffing's change-of-pace pitches into the stands just inside the left-field foul line to score Cooper and wrap up the second victory of the series for Johnny Beazley, twenty-three-year-old Cardinal rookie.

GORDON SINGLES

The Yankees, still fighting, got their first two batters on base in the ninth when Joe Gordon singled to left and Bill Dickey's roller was muffed by Jimmie Brown. But the rally was choked off in a twinkling of a moment later when Catcher Cooper whipped a beautiful peg to Marion at second base and caught Gordon off.

Beazley then attended to Gerry Priddy and George Selkirk, first on

Continued on Page 18, Column 6.

WOMAN, 102, DIES

SALT LAKE CITY, Oct. 5—(A. P.).—Mrs. Anna H. Lambson, one hundred and two, who saw the United States fight and win five previous wars and is survived by three daughters and 32 grandchildren, 101 great-grandchildren and 44 great-great-grandchildren, died last night.

The Des Moines Register

Sports

DES MOINES, IOWA, WEDNESDAY MORNING, MAY 26, 1943. ★★★★★ PAGE THIRTEEN 13

Sittin' In With the Athletes

—BY SEC TAYLOR—

PAT MALONE, IRONMAN.

MANSON, IA. — The recent death of Pat Malone, naturally brought up discussions in Des Moines of some of the famous pitcher's deeds when he was serving with the Des Moines Western league club back in 1926 and of some of the other incidents in connection with the Demons of that time.

MALONE.

Out of these discussions came many controversies, since memories have a habit of playing jokes, of distorting things that are a few years' distant, and sometimes of exaggeration.

Most of the disagreement seems to have come over a doubleheader the Demons played with St. Joseph, the first game of which went nine innings, the aftermath 18 innings, with Malone pitching in both. Some assert that Pat pitched the entire 27 frames; others that he was relieved in the second encounter.

Several persons made inquiry of the writer concerning this. It was my recollection that Malone pitched only a part of the second game, but I promised to check up at the first opportunity.

—

MY OLD scorebook shows that Pat toiled on the mound for 23 innings that day, giving a total of 18 hits, four runs, four bases on balls, one hit batsman and one wild pitch. He was relieved at the start of the fifteenth inning of the second game by McClung, whose first name I have forgotten.

Des Moines won 4 to 0 and 5 to 4.

The doubleheader was played on July 25. In the first half of the twin bill Pug Griffin hit home runs over the leftfield fence with none on base in the fourth and eighth innings, providing enough scores for victory, but two others were manufactured in the seventh frame. When Dutch Wetzel walked, and took second when Bill Cissell, playing centerfield in place of Hughes, who was injured, beat out a hit, the stage was set.

Fritz Knothe's attempted sacrifice was turned into a thirdbase forceout that retired Wetzel, but Joe Sprinz sliced a triple to rightfield scoring both Cissell and Knothe. Malone then fanned and Whitey Gislason grounded out.

—

MALONE had a bit of trouble in the first, fifth and sixth innings but emerged safely each time. In the initial frame Marty Fiedler, the Saints' thirdsacker, singled and took third when Swansboro also onebased, but when Cozington whiffed, Sprinz threw out Fiedler on the latter's attempt to steal third, the double-play retiring the side.

With one away in the fifth Handley hit a fluke double to centerfield, but one of Pug Griffin's sensational throws cut him down at the plate when he tried to score on Kelly's single. The latter reached second on the throw and moved to third on an error by Sprinz, the nature of which my scorebook does not disclose. Malone passed Lisle, St. Joseph catcher, purposely and then filled the bases when he was unable to get the ball over to Swartz, the opposing pitcher, but Wallie Nufer grounded out.

Fiedler opened the sixth with a double and after Swansboro struck out, took third on Cozington's infield out. Smith was hit by a pitched ball and immediately stole second, but here Malone inserted another of his seven strikeouts with Handley the victim.

The Des Moines hurler retired the side in order after that with the aid of a sensational running catch by Cissell in the eighth inning, and looked so good in doing it that Manager John (Shano) Collins started him in the never-to-be-forgotten second game.

In that first contest the Demons garnered eight hits off Swartz. Malone gave only five.

—

PAT SHUT out the Saints in the first four frames of the afterpiece, but in the fifth they scored twice on Catcher Adams' single, Pitcher Peery's sacrifice and Nufer's homer over the leftfield boards.

However, in the home half of the same inning the Demons took a lead by scoring three times when Malone singled, Gislason tripled, Pete Brausen sacrificed, working a successful squeeze play, and Collins lofted the ball out of the park, again over the leftfield fence.

The Saints knotted the count in the next frame when Smith twobased, took third on a wild pitch, and completed the circuit while Kelly was being tossed out at first.

—

THEN CAME scoreless innings until the tenth, although the Demons threatened in the ninth after two were out. Gislason singled and reached third on a hit-and-run play when Brausen also hit safely. Here Pitcher Peery was relieved by Newton, who caused Collins to die on a long drive which Smith caught against the leftfield fence.

Cozington's single and steal of second and Handley's two-bagger against the leftfield boards gave the Saints a run that loomed large in the first of the tenth, but

Sittin' In—
Continued on Page Fourteen.

HITTERS NEED INTELLIGENCE, SISLER SAYS

Iowa Meet Delayed, Preps Get Lesson.

GAMES TODAY.

FIRST ROUND.

9 a. m.—Waterloo (East) vs. Davenport.

10:30 a. m.—Des Moines (Dowling) vs. Montour.

SEMIFINAL ROUND.

1:30 p. m.—Corwith vs. winner East Waterloo-Davenport game.

3 p. m.—Moneta vs. winner Dowling-Montour game.

—

By Sec Taylor.

(Sports Editor, The Register.)

MANSON, IA. — It takes intelligence at the plate as well as good eyes, timing and co-ordination to make a great hitter, George Sisler, famous firstbaseman of the St. Louis Browns in the days before most of his audience had been born, told coaches and players gathered here Tuesday for the Iowa state baseball tournament.

Sisler made this talk at a hurriedly organized indoor baseball clinic in the local high school when it became apparent early Tuesday that it would be impossible to play the two first-round and semifinal contests as had been planned.

Four Games Today.

The four games will be played, starting at 9 a. m. today, at the hours originally carded with East Waterloo opposing Davenport and Dowling of Des Moines meeting Montour. The winners of the foregoing contests will play Corwith and Moneta, respectively.

The delay means that the tournament's outdoor clinic, not to be confused with the indoor affair Tuesday, and the final game will be held Thursday instead of today.

★ ★ ★

"I never saw a great hitter who wasn't intelligent in a baseball way," Sisler declared. "You've got to think up there at that plate. Ty Cobb and Eddie Collins could hit inside balls to the opposite outfield because they thought and practiced until they could time the pitches perfectly.

"I've been in and around baseball for 27 or 28 years and I don't know all about it. I'm still learning. It's that kind of game.

"There's no set rule in baseball on how to make a play. There are some fundamentals of course, but no set rules on how to do this or that, for every play is different—no two just exactly alike.

"Two-thirds of the boys starting in baseball take too long a step and they take it too quickly," Sisler said in advising the boys about hitting. "TAKE A SHORT STEP RATHER THAN A LONG ONE AND YOU'LL NEVER BE OUT OF POSITION TO HIT THE BALL—and you must be in position to hit every one that comes over the plate. Always remember,

George Sisler.
"You've Got to Think."

you don't step AND hit. Instead you step TO hit. You take a different step for different pitches.

Usually Mental.

"A curve ball is not hard to hit, if you know how. If a player can't hit a curve ball, it's usually mental. He is a bit afraid of it and doesn't get in position to hit it. You've got to hesitate a little and step in a little and meet the ball over the plate, not out in front of it.

"Don't be too anxious to step but wait till you know where a pitch is going to be. Then step to get in position. Don't be a guess hitter—the pitcher can outguess you nine out of 10 times.

"Be ready to hit on every single ball that is pitched, but if you hit the first ball you're helping the pitcher. Pick a good ball, then swing.

"Many players, some of them major leaguers, handicap themselves by hitting bad balls. No pitcher can pitch if he's behind the batter, so if you swing at a first pitch, never swing at a bad one. Never swing at a bad one any time.

"Remember, also, that if you have a hitting weakness the pitchers will know it and they will work on it.

"If you hit .300 in any league you'll have to do it on balls pitched to your weakness. So don't try to cover up the weakness. It is usually due to the fact

Sisler—
Continued on Page Fourteen.

La Femme Softballer Slugs One

Josephine D'Angelo of Chicago, Ill., starts off the first drills of the All-American Girls' Softball league in Wrigley field Tuesday with a resounding smack. The catcher is Lucella MacLean of Saskatoon, Saskatchewan. Next up to bat is Margaret Stefani of Detroit, Mich. The girls above will play for South Bend, Ind., one of the four league teams, to open the season May 30.—**WIREPHOTO** (AP).

MACK EXPECTS CLOSEST A. L. RACE IN YEARS

Calls Senators Best Club Right Now.

By Jack Smith.

PHILADELPHIA, PENN. (AP)—The hottest American league race in years—one of the good old-fashioned kind with close games, underdog upsets and a finish drive calculated to make the hair tingle and the spine stand on end—was forecast Tuesday by baseball's most reluctant prognosticator.

Connie Mack, who among all the moguls is least inclined to get himself out on a limb and saw, reviewed the record of the first six weeks of the season, concluded that even his Athletics have clambered out of their decade-long doldrums and now have a pennant chance, and said:

"It looks like anybody's race to me. The teams are all pretty evenly matched and I would say that this will be the closest campaign we've had in years. Any club can win, or finish last.

"I've seen them all but Chicago, and they tell me Chicago has started to go after a bad beginning. To me, the best club in the league right now, from a playing standpoint, is Washington. They gave us such a trimming. But, of course, we weren't up to par when we played them.

Have Chance Now.

"I myself am more hopeful and optimistic for the Athletics than I have been in several years. It's been so many years that I felt we didn't have a chance against certain teams. Now I feel we can win against any team in the league."

The sage of the league, who won the last of his nine pennants in 1931, emphasized that he wasn't saying he expected to collect another this year. "I'm just saying that anything can happen," he smiled.

Better Spirit.

The 80-year-old dean gave these thumbnail sketches of his team and its leading members after six weeks of playing:

"The team has better spirit and morale than in years; everybody thinks there's a chance again. . . Russ Christopher, who won only two or three out of 20 games last year, looks like a real pitcher again. . . **JESSE FLORES IS A GREAT PITCHER** . . . Our infield, defensively, will be hard to beat. . . Irving Hall has surprised me by becoming a very good shortstop. . . Jo-Jo White is tops in centerfield. . . Thirdbaseman Ernie Mayo looks good again. . . If we're weak at all, it's in hitting, but we might improve."

"This," said Connie, his Irish eyes flashing, "is going to be a great season."

TAKES PURSE.

BOSTON, MASS. (AP)—High Name defeated eight other starters to win the mile and 70 yard Fort Heath purse at Suffolk Downs Tuesday by a half length and pay $31.40 for $2.

ARMSTRONG AND ANGOTT TO BOX

NEW YORK, N. Y. (AP)—Sammy Angott and Henry Armstrong, both former lightweight champions, Tuesday were signed for a 10-round bout in Madison Square Garden, June 11.

Angott gave up the 135-pound title last fall but after two months came out of retirement and has been designated by the National Boxing association as the man to beat for the crown. Armstrong, former holder of the featherweight, lightweight and welterweight titles, has won 19 of his 22 comeback fights, his latest being an eight-round technical knockout of Maxie Shapiro in Philadelphia Monday night.

GUARDSMEN JAR BUCS, 16-8

BALTIMORE, MD. (AP)—The Pittsburgh Pirates had a rude shock Monday when the Curtis Bay coast guard depot nine blasted out 22 safe hits to defeat the big leaguers, 16 to 8, in an exhibition game.

The Pirates managed to chalk up 18 hits on their own account, nine coming in the last three innings after the game had been salted away by the coast guardsmen. Curtis Bay had two boisterous innings, the second and fifth, during which they rammed out 13 hits good for 12 runs.

Score by innings:		R.	H.	E.
Pittsburgh (N)	100 020 410—	8	18	2
Curtis Bay C. G.	270 051 01x—	16	22	0

Batteries—Hallett, Shuman (3), Brandt (6) and Baker; Kerr, Smith (5) and Norris, Paulick (6).

Club Standings

American League.

	W.	L.	Pct.	Games Behind
Cleveland	16	11	.593	
New York	14	11	.560	1
Washington	15	13	.536	1½
Detroit	13	12	.520	2
Philadelphia	14	15	.483	3
Chicago	10	12	.455	3½
St. Louis	10	12	.455	3½
Boston	11	17	.393	5½

Tuesday's Results.

No games scheduled.

Pitchers in Today's Games.

Detroit (Newhouser 1-1) at New York (Donald 0-1).

Cleveland (Bagby 5-1) at Boston (Hughson (2-2).

Chicago (Lee 0-1) at Philadelphia (Arntzen 1-1).

Night—St. Louis (Muncrief 1-1 or Niggeling 1-1) at Washington (Pyle 3-3).

National League.

	W.	L.	Pct.	Games Behind
Brooklyn	21	9	.700	...
St. Louis	17	10	.630	2½
Boston	14	10	.583	4
Philadelphia	15	12	.556	4½
Cincinnati	12	16	.429	8
Pittsburgh	10	15	.400	8½
New York	11	18	.379	9½
Chicago	9	19	.321	11

Tuesday's Results.

No games scheduled.

Pitchers in Today's Games.

Brooklyn (Macon 3-1 at Pittsburgh (Gornicki 1-2).

New York (Lohrman 3-2) at Chicago (Derringer 1-3).

Night—Philadelphia (Gerheauser 2-2) at Cincinnati (Walters 2-3).

Night—Boston (Javery 3-1) at St. Louis (Lanier 1-2 or M. Cooper 3-2).

Few Words As Novikoff, Wilson Meet

CHICAGO, ILL. (AP)—Cub Manager Jimmy Wilson, sitting in the empty stands at Wrigley field, met his long-errant former holdout flychaser, Lou Novikoff, Tuesday in an encounter short on ceremony and equally shy on words.

WILSON.

Novikoff sauntered casually off the field, where he was working out with the injured Clyde McCullough and some 80 girl performers of the All-American Softball league, and approached the box where Wilson sat discussing the last-place status of his well-regarded Cubs.

"Hello, James," sheepishly grinned Novikoff, dripping perspiration.

"Hello, Lou," said Wilson, warmly but without excitement.

That's all there was to it right then, for Wilson at once turned to his companions in the box and steered the talk to baseball in general, the Cubs in particular, and the girl softballers.

Novikoff stood by silently, out of the conversation, apparently forgotten. Suddenly Wilson looked at him.

"Are you in shape, Lou?" he asked.

Novikoff patted his streamlined stomach affirmatively, then hesitated. "Maybe need a little batting practice," he grunted.

"You heard about Lonnie Frey of Cincinnati, didn't you?" Wilson demanded gruffly. "Got hit in the wrist during spring practice, couldn't lift a bat for days. But he's been leading the league, or darned close to it, all spring, hasn't he?"

Novikoff's face gleamed in a wide smile. He grabbed his glove, raced onto the field, and began a ferocious throwing drill with McCullough. Wilson grinned.

"He'll be in leftfield against the Giants tomorrow," he said. "What's more, one of these days our hitters will start to hit the same day our pitchers are pitching. We just haven't knit ourselves together as a ball club yet."

Once King, Hub's Star Fades

By Collie Small.

NEW YORK, N. Y. (U.P.) —The St. Louis Cardinals, nine young johnny-come-latelies you like to think couldn't have carried the old guy's glove in the days not too far gone, slammed Carl Hubbell out of the box the other day and Hub stood there with his head down, staring at a little mound of dirt he had scraped with his toe.

Almost unwillingly, it seemed, he raised his head slowly and looked out toward the rightfield bullpen where another, younger pitcher had thrown his jacket over his arm and was ambling toward the diamond to take over for old King Karl.

Then Hub squared his shoulders, hitched up his long pants and shuffled out across centerfield toward the dressing room. The big crowd had been silent, sharing his misery, but now the applause crackled and swelled and rolled at his heels. Old Hub never turned his head.

He plodded on, swinging his glove, and then he stepped through the little green door at the top of the stairs deep in centerfield. THE DOOR SWUNG SHUT ON HIS NUMBER 11 AND MAYBE IT SWUNG ON HIS NO. 11 AND MAYBE IT SWUNG SHUT ON AN ERA, TOO.

This was Hubbell, one of the very greatest. Old Crooked Arm never complained, never had an alibi. He took his turn and pitched the best he knew and usually it was the best around. Sometimes his arm slipped a little but never his heart.

Against the Cardinals, Hub was trying for his 250th major league victory. You sat there behind the plate at the Polo grounds, hoping that the next one—and then the next one—

Carl Hubbell.
His Era Ending?

would have it. But it never did and finally they got the old guy out of there.

You wanted to go around to the clubhouse and ask Hub about it, but you didn't have the heart. So you asked Mel Ott, long Hub's team-mate and now his manager, but Ott could only shake his head.

Hub probably will start again and maybe warmer weather will loosen him up, but it seems unlikely that he'll be able to do much, if anything, this year or ever again.

It's hard to see the old guy shuffle off into the twilight, growing dimmer and dimmer until suddenly he's gone. Somehow you find yourself hoping this isn't the end of the line. But then you know it is and, looking back, you suddenly realize why the folks down at Meeker, Okla., put up the big white-lettered sign that says:

"This is the home of Carl Hubbell."

SPEEDBOATS IN RIVERVIEW RACE

Riverview park will offer its first speedboat races of the season on Sunday afternoon, promising a card of eight events for the various classes of outboard powered crafts.

Bob Reichardt, manager of the park who is also a competent outboard pilot, said he expected an entry of from 12 to 15 pilots with upwards to 20 boats for his initial race card. The boats will race on the west lagoon, and admission will be free.

Joe Rynerson of Des Moines, with a new boat, was among the early entries along with Ted Ahrens, who is one of the top pilots here. A contingent of pilots is also expected from Cedar Rapids.

FINAL ★★★★

DAILY NEWS
Copr. 1944 by News Syndicate Co. Inc. NEW YORK'S PICTURE NEWSPAPER Trade Mark Reg. U. S. Pat. Off.

THE LARGEST CIRCULATION IN AMERICA

40 New York, Tuesday, October 10, 1944 2 Cents IN CITY LIMITS | 3 CENTS Elsewhere

CARDS WIN SERIES

Take 6th Game, 3-1; SO Marks Set

Stories on Page 36

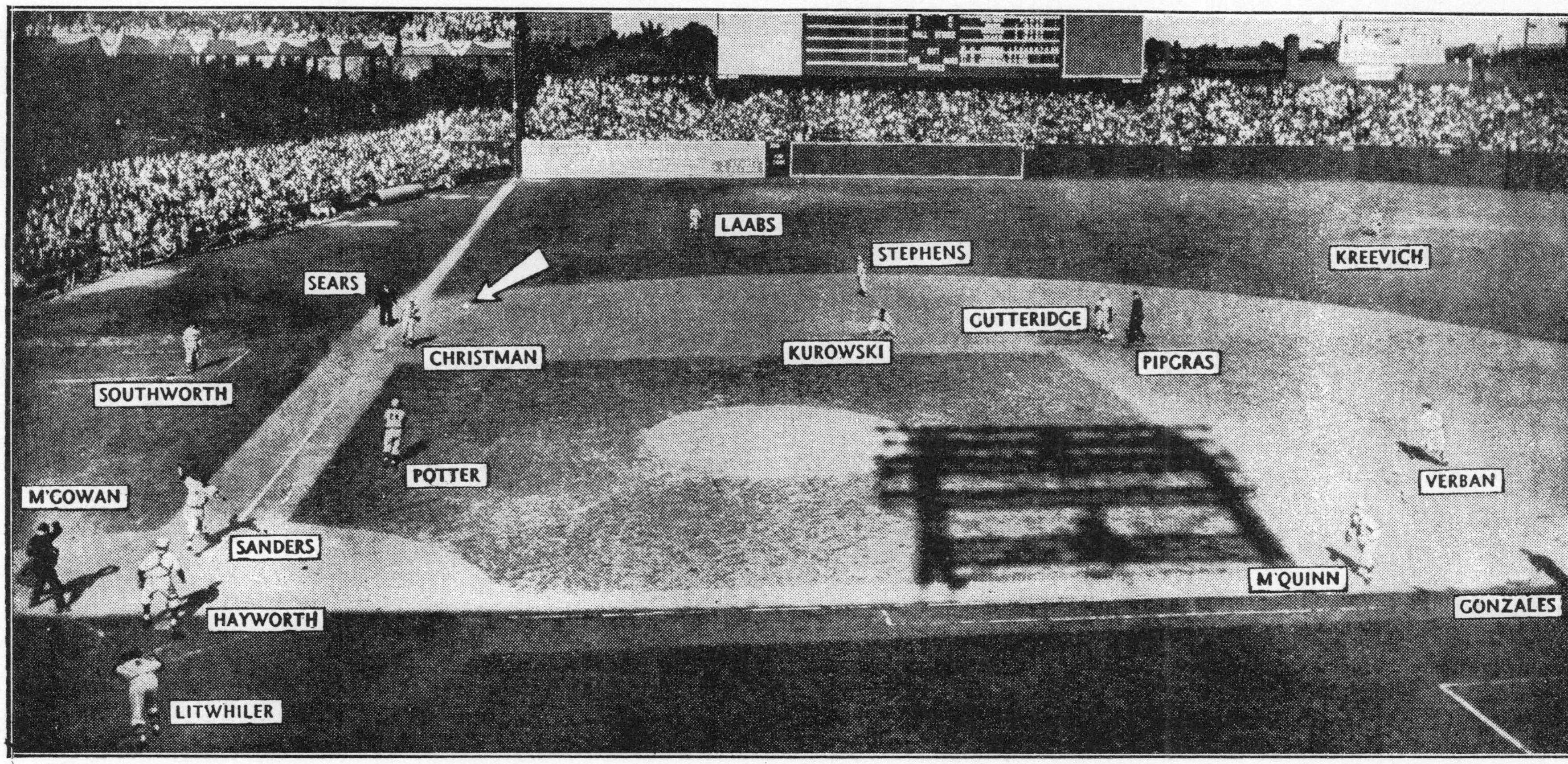

(Associated Press Wirefoto)

Sewing Up the Series. Sanders starts his slide for plate in the big fourth inning as he beats ball (arrow) on throw-in from Chet Laabs, Brownie leftfielder. Emil Verban, who hit single scoring Sanders, rounds first base while Kurowski starts retreat to second when Potter cut off throw. *—Story on page 36*

(Acme Telephotos)

↑ Last Fling... Clubhouse Capers →

Pinch-hitting for Red Hayworth, Brownie Mike Chartak [↑] goes down swinging to ring down curtain on the series. Chartak was 92d strikeout victim—a new record for a World Series. After the ball game was over [→] the Cards cut a few clubhouse capers by way of celebrating 3-1 victory. That's Johnny Hopp mussing up manager Billy Southworth.

Allies Consider Plans For Austria Occupation

Paris, May 28 (AP)—Plans to create a separate occupation zone for Austria, with Gen. Mark W. Clark as American representative on a four-power governing council at Vienna, were reported today under consideration by the Allies.

In line with the "Big Three" agreement that Austria be recreated as a separate nation, it is felt in some quarters that the country should be treated as a distinct unit for occupation purposes and given less stringent treatment and more encouragement for building up a strong government.

A Russian-sponsored government has already been set up in Vienna, but is expected to undergo some changes before being granted formal recognition.

News of Our Own Service Folk

Is Liberated

HARRY BRIZEE

A V-Mail letter from Pvt. Harry Brizee to his family brought word of his liberation by the Russians from a Nazi Prison Camp April 28. He is in New Brandenburg, Mechl, Germany and his letter was dated May 16. Private Brizee, son of Mr. and Mrs. John Brizee, 55 Maple street, was serving with the army engineers when he was reported missing November 7, 1944. He had participated in the D-Day invasion last June.

Charles C. Gaston, F/1/c, son of Mrs. Ruth J. Gaston, Ulster Park, has graduated from basic engineering school and Diesel school at Gulfport, Miss., and is now attending advanced Diesel school at General Motors Plant, Cleveland, Ohio.

ROOSA IS INSPECTOR

An Eighth Air Force Service Command Station, England—Sergeant Alton Roosa, Kingston, is a member of the air inspector's office at this large aerial repair depot where B-17 Flying Fortresses are reconditioned. As a technical inspector Sergeant Roosa is called upon to inspect all types of material—from airplanes to jeeps—to see that they are in perfect condition. One of his biggest jobs is the checking of repaired aircraft, seeing that the job of reconditioning has been properly carried out and that all technical orders have been filled. Son of Mrs. Everitt Roosa, 303 Albany avenue, Kingston, he has been overseas two years. Before entering the service, he was employed as a guard with the Hiltebrant shipyard.

TRAINS FOR DESTROYER

Donald Gordon Rice, 18, seaman, first class, U.S.N.R., of West Hurley, recently arrived at the naval training station, Norfolk, Va., to train for duties aboard a new destroyer of the Atlantic Fleet. He wears ribbons for the American Area campaign, Asiatic-Pacific Area campaign, and Philippine Liberation. Son of Mr. and Mrs. Arthur Rice of Woodstock road, West Hurley, he has a brother, Arthur, 21, a pharmacist's mate, second class, in the Navy. Before enlisting, Rice attended high school in Kingston.

IN VICTORY PARADE

Mrs. Margaret A. Whalen has received word that her son, Sgt. John E. Whalen, took part in the victory parade at Reims. Sergeant Whalen left Kingston November 17, 1942, and was stationed at Miami Beach, Fla., Hendrick's Field, Fla., and Camp Mead, Md., before going overseas. Sergeant Whalen was principal of Rosendale School when he entered the service.

Select Group Is Named for Derby Fans to Pick From

By Orlo Robertson

New York, May 28 (AP)—With less than two weeks to go before the 71st running of the Kentucky Derby the field has narrowed to where the winner is expected to come from a group of six horses.

This select half-dozen is made up of Col. E. R. Bradley's Burning Dream; Pot O'Luck from Warren Wright's Calumet Farm; Alexis of Henry Lunger's Christiana Stable; Col. C. V. Whitney's Jeep; War Jeep from Elizabeth Graham's Main Chance Farm, and John Marsch's Free For All.

A dozen or more three-year olds are expected to face the barrier at Churchill Downs June 9, but if the victor in the $75,000 added run for the roses is not one of these six the race will go down as a surprise. Wednesday's running of the mile and 70 yards of the Wood Memorial at Jamaica may further eliminate some of those now under consideration.

Bradley's hopes of winning his fifth Derby were given a big boost Saturday when Burning Dream won the mile of the Derby trial at the Downs. The time of 1:38 1/5 was not sensational, but he left behind him such talked of three-year-olds as C. C. Tanner's Best Effort, Foreign Agent from the Lookout Stock Farm, and Free For All.

Free for All, although sired by the route-running Questionnaire, showed again that his chief forte is speed and that the Derby distance of a mile and a quarter may not be to his liking.

Pot O'Luck finally gave the backers of Calumet's silks confidence by showing his staying and running ability at the Downs last Friday. Trainer Ben Jones is relying on the Son of Chance Play for his fourth Derby triumph, his third with horses carrying the Wright colors.

Alexis shapes up as the best of the three-year olds shown as Pimlico's 10 day meeting. He chalked up three straight victories, two of them at sprint distances, and on Wednesday probably will tangle with the leading New York candidates—War Jeep and Jeep.

Neither of the New Yorkers has been asked to go more than six furlongs, but War Jeep sped over the distance in 1:11 2/5 under 126 pounds Saturday while Jeep did the same distance in 1:11 3/5 under 112 pounds last Monday.

Local Trackmen Trim Arlington in Meet on Saturday

Kingston High School track squad won its third straight victory of the present season Saturday afternoon at Arlington defeating the Dutchess county squad by the score of 61½-42½. Kingston squad will travel to Monticello next Saturday to compete in a Duso meet. The sectionals will be held June 9 at Newburgh.

Saturday's meet presented one of the most unusual problems ever to confront a high school track judge. In the 440-yard run, Tom Rizzi of Kingston and Jack Smith of Arlington were neck and neck coming into the final stretch. They continued this way until they reached the finish line when Rizzi fell to the ground but across the line ahead of Smith. The first place judge, Edwin Ulrich of Arlington, picked Smith as the winner on the grounds that Rizzi did not break the tape. Miles Pollock of Kingston, second place judge, placed Smith second. However, since the rules state that the first place judges decision is final, Smith was accepted as the winner.

Gabe Szekeres, ace discus and shotput man of the Maroon and White, broke a Kingston High School record Saturday when he hurled the discus 128.9 feet. He broke his own record of 120.8 feet which he made last year.

The summary of Saturday's meet:

220 Hurdles—Lovell (A), Fitzgerald (K), Lilley (A), 29.2.
880—McCardle (K), Dolan (K), Magino (K), 2:14.
100—Whispell (K), Conlon (K), Feroe (A), 10.6.
Mile—Stahl (K), Rudick (A), Lierey (K), 4:51.5.
440—Smith (A), Rizzi (K), Lodge (K), 56.
220—Whispell (K), Riggs (A), Feroe (A), 24.1.
Shotput—Szekeres (K), Bruchholtz (K), Wisenski (K), 40 feet 4 inches.
High Jump—Rogers (A), McAlster (A), Gus Koch (K), 5 feet 9½ inches.
Broad Jump—Riggs (A), Fitzgerald (K), Kinsalla (A), 20 feet 3½ inches.
Pole Vault—Harry Koch (K), McAlster (A), Gold (A), Clark (K), tied, 10 feet 6 inches.
Discus—Szekeres (K), Bruchholz (K), Whitely (A), 128.9.
880 Relay—Arlington 2:28.2.

Marlborough Soldier Wins Boxing Tourney

With the Fifth Army, Italy—Top honors in his regiment's boxing tournament recently went to Private First Class George Gransow of Marlborough who won the middleweight title.

The bouts were held in an Apennine rest area of the 88th "Blue Devil" Infantry Division, commanded by Major General Paul W. Kendall.

For defeating all six rivals in the 165-pound class, Gransow won an eight-day pass to a Fifth Army rest center. The commanding officer of his 351st "Spearhead" Infantry Regiment, Lieut. Colonel Franklin P. Miller, also presented him with an engraved wallet.

The New Yorker holds a Purple Heart for wounds received on Mt. Grande in the Gothic Line. He also has the Combat Infantryman Badge, European Theatre Ribbon with battle star, and Good Conduct Medal. His local residence is in care of James Smith, Route 9-W, Marlborough.

PARENTS SEE PETE GRAY PLAY

Mr. and Mrs. Peter Wyshner of Nanticoke, Pa., parents of Pete Gray, one-armed St. Louis Browns outfielder, stand with their son in Yankee Stadium, New York. Watching their first major league game, Mr. and Mrs. Wyshner saw their son in action against the Yankees.

By JOE REICHLER

(Associated Press Sports Writer)

Boston may not be represented in the World Series next fall but it appeared today that the hub possesses the major leagues' two outstanding gate attractions in pitchers Dave (Boo) Ferriss of the Red Sox and Mort Cooper of the Braves.

Ferriss gained his sixth straight victory and his fourth shoutout as he limited the Chicago White Sox to one hit, a single by Tony Cuccinello, to help the Red Sox take a twin bill yesterday, 7-0 and 2-1. Emmett O'Neill turned in a two-hitter to complete the twin-triumph.

The Sox rookie righthander has drawn nearly 65,000 persons in three home appearances. In his Boston debut he lured 30,824 fans, despite the fact that the Cronin-men had dropped nine of their previous 14 games. His second home effort was witnessed by 9,-270, the largest weekday gathering at Fenway Park, and yesterday 24,547 were on hand. He promises to be an equally strong attraction on the road as attested by the 31,000 who watched him beat Dizzy Trout and the Tigers in Detroit.

Cooper paid his first dividend to the Braves on their reported $50,-000 investment by blanking Cincinnati, 4-0, in the opener of a doubleheader with the Reds, who took the nightcap, 5-0, behind the three-hit pitching of Bucky Walters. Cooper, ace righthander obtained from the St. Louis Cardinals last week, gained his third triumph without a setback by holding the Reds to four hits.

The St. Louis Browns' winning streak of nine straight over the Yankees ended when New York won both games, 10-9 in 14 innings and 3-1. The second contest was called after seven and a half innings because of darkness.

The first-place New York Giants were humbled by Pittsburgh, 16-4, in the opener of a twin bill and were behind 10-5, at the end of seven and a half innings when the nightcap was halted because of Pennsylvania's 7 p. m., Sunday law. The game will be completed today before the regular scheduled contest.

Cleveland won its fifth straight and eight of its last nine games by defeating the Philadelphia Athletics, 8-3, in the first of a scheduled doubleheader. The nightcap was called off because of rain.

The last-place Philadelphia Phillies stunned the world champion St. Louis Cardinals twice on two finely pitched games, 2-0 and 3-2. Charley Schanz and Charley Sproull each gained his first triumph, with Schanz limiting the Redbirds to two hits in the opener. The double defeat dropped the Cards into the second division.

Detroit and Washington split, Hal Newhouser winning the first for the Tigers, 3-1, for his fifth triumph and Mickey Haefner outdueling Forrest Orrell, 2-1, to give the Nats an even break. Rudy York hit his first 1945 homer for the Tigers in the first game.

The Chicago Cubs defeated Brooklyn, 6-1, in the first game and came out with a 2-2 tie in the second halted after eight innings by darkness.

Week-End Sports

By The Associated Press

West Orange, N. J.—Byron Nelson and Sammy Snead ended their 72-hole challenge golf match all even. Snead won Saturday's 36-hole medal play, 143 to 144, while Nelson took Sunday's 36-hole match play, 4 and 3.

Miami—Francisco Segura, Ecuador, won Roney Plaza Summer Tennis Tourney by beating Charles Harris, West Palm Beach, 6-4, 6-2.

New York—Aggregate of 178,-171 turf fans bet $10,006,076 at seven race tracks for biggest Saturday wagering mark in Associated Press records.

West Point, N. Y.—Army's unbeaten baseball team chalked up 14th in row by defeating Navy, 7 to 2, in traditional service clash.

San Francisco—Welker Cochran retained World's Three-Cushion Billiard Championship by beating Willie Hoppe in windup of their 90-block cross-country challenge match. Cochran had 4,819 total points, Hoppe 4,771.

Pullman, Wash.—Phil Sorboe, Tacoma High School coach, was named to succeed Orin E. "Babe" Hollingberry as head coach at Washington State College.

Philadelphia — St. Andrew's school, Middleton, Del., won Schoolboy Crew Championship in annual regatta on Schuylkill river.

Champaign, Ill.—University of Illinois won Western Conference Track and Field title, upsetting Michigan, defending champion, 65½ points to 54 1/6.

Sports Shorts

Still Wants to Run

Binghamton, N. Y., May 28 (AP)—Exterminator, 1918 Kentucky Derby winner, will be 30 years old Memorial Day and he still wants to romp.

Givan Winner

Tacoma, Wash., May 28 (AP)—Harry Givan, veteran Seattle amateur, took the 12th Annual Tacoma Open golf championship yesterday with a 68-66—134, six under par on the Allenmore course, after eight years of trying.

Pvt. Bob Hamilton, National Open champion now stationed at Fort Lewis, shot a 74-68—142 to finish in a four-way tie for seventh.

Freed of Jinx

Albany, N. Y., May 28 (AP)—Elmira's Eastern League baseball club is now freed of its jinx. The Pioneers finally won a game in their home park yesterday—the first this season—edging out Utica 6-5 in the opener of a doubleheader. The Blue Sox came back to win the nightcap 7-5 in two extra innings.

Rain caused the postponement of the Binghamton at Williamsport, Albany at Scranton and Hartford at Wilkes-Barre contests.

Explosion of a hot water heater in the clubhouse cost the Williamsport Grays the services of second baseman Frank Gallardo. Gallardo was attempting to light the heater when it exploded. He suffered burns about the eyes and was taken to a hospital. An eye specialist said he would be unable to play for 10 days, or possibly two weeks.

Cochrane Signs

New York, May 28 (AP)—Freddie (Red) Cochrane of Hillside, N. J., world welterweight champion, signed Saturday for a 10-round non-title match with Rocky Graziano of New York at Madison Square Garden June 29. Cochrane previously had agreed to fight the winner of a bout between Graziano and Al Davis which was held Friday at the Garden.

Pro Golf Society Will Hold Many Matches for Vets

West Orange, N. J., May 28 (AP)—The Professional Golfers' Association plans today to conduct matches all over the country such as the Byron Nelson-Sammy Snead affair of last week-end to get funds for its rehabilitation program for wounded servicemen.

Snead defeated Nelson by a single stroke in medal play at Fresh Meadow on Long Island Saturday with 6,000 present, but dropped the match play competition, 4 to 3, before some 1,200 well-drenched spectators at the Essex County Crounty Club Sunday.

"Our program has been in progress since 1941, but now that many of our wounded are returning from Europe and from the Pacific, we are stepping it up. Every dime we take in on these matches, and others throughout the country, goes for rehabilitation," P.G.A. President Ed Dudley asserted.

Snead spent 26 months in the Navy before a chronic back ailment brought about his discharge. He said after the match he "would be willing to play for the Rehabilitation Fund for 10 years if necessary after having seen some of our wounded veterans hobble around a pitch-and putt course on crutches."

Both Snead and Nelson spent their spare time visiting various veterans' hospitals on last winter's golf tour.

School for Coaches

Clinton, N. Y., May 28 (AP)—The football faculty for the New York State Public High School Athletic Association's coaching school at Hamilton College August 27-September 1 will be headed by Carroll C. Widdoes, coach of Ohio State's undefeated, untied 1944 grid team.

The faculty, announced Saturday, includes Ed McKeever, Cornell grid coach; Rae Crowther, University of Pennsylvania line coach, and Paul Bixler, Ohio State end coach and scout.

For Faster Service
3 Tribune Phone Numbers
SUPerior 0200 Public Information Service
SUPerior 0260 Sports Bulletin Service
SUPerior 0100 Want Ads—General Business

Chicago Daily Tribune
THE WORLD'S GREATEST NEWSPAPER

SECTION TWO
SPORTS MARKETS
Monday, Oct. 1, 1945 **** 23

TIGERS WIN FLAG ON GREENBERG'S HOMER

PACKERS DEFEAT BEARS, 31 TO 21, BEFORE 24,525

CHICAGO DRIVE FALLS SHORT IN FINAL QUARTER

Green Bay Leads at Half, 10 to 0

Shades of 1944

GREEN BAY [31]		CHICAGO [21]
Goodnight	L. E.	Smeja
Ray	L. T.	Roberts
Sorenson	L. G.	Sprinkle
C. Brock	C	Schiechl
Tinsley	R. G.	Zorich
Lipscomb	R. T.	Barbartsky
Luhn	R. E.	Berry
Craig	Q. B.	Long
Comp	L. H.	Mooney
Laws	R. H.	Mitchell
Fritsch	F. B.	Vodica

Green Bay	10	0	7	14	—31
Chicago	0	0	7	14	—21

Touchdowns—Fritsch [2], Perkins, McKay, Famiglietti [3].

Field goal—Fritsch.

Points after touchdowns—Hutson [4], Gudauskas [3].

Substitutes: Green Bay—Ends, Hutson, Mason, Mulleaneaux; tackles, Croft, Neal, McPherson; guards, Tollefson, Kuusisto, Frankowski; center, Flowers; backs, McKay, L. Brock, Perkins, Starrett.

Chicago—Ends, Kavanaugh, Morton; tackles, Artoe, Hoptowit, Ramsey, Babartsky; guards, Perez, Gudauskas, Zorich; center, Masterson; backs, Luckman, Ronzani, Gallarneau, Famiglietti, Grygo, Fordham, Margarita.

Referee—Tom Dowd. Umpire—John Kelly. Field Judge—Bill Downes. Head linesman—Sam Pecoraro.

BY EDWARD PRELL

[Chicago Tribune Press Service]

Green Bay, Wis., Sept. 30—The National Football league's oldest two-team chase is on and once again the Chicago Bears are chasing the Green Bay Packers. The old rivals raged up and down City stadium's green turf this afternoon and the Packers had to be the champions they are to win, 31 to 21.

It was almost the same story as a year ago when the Packers rushed into a 28 to 0 lead and then were almost caught. On that day, as this afternoon, the Packers recovered like a boxer who has been almost felled and went on to win, 42 to 28, the first of a series of victories which led them to the league championship.

The Packers were making their first defense of that title this afternoon and their fourth quarter sag put a strange quietness over the crowd of 24,525, most of whom were partisan.

Bears Rally in Final Quarter

It was 10 to 0 against the Bears after the first quarter. The score hadn't changed at intermission time. It was 17 to 7 at the finish of the third quarter. And with little more than three minutes of the wild battle remaining, the Bears had pulled up to 24 to 21. It was then that Packer rooters held their breath, fearful of an old-time, rousing Bear finish.

Sid Luckman was pitching and his targets were picking them out of the air with expert fingers. Then the Bears stopped. Ted Fritsch caught the ball on the Green Bay 13, battled back to his 39, then went down flat. They helped him off the field—and Fritsch had scored two of the champions' three touchdowns, plus a field goal, for 21 points.

Don Perkins replaced the injured full back. On the first play he broke to his left, went outside the Bear defenders and ran 47 yards to the Chicago 14. This was the game-breaking play, just as last year Lou Brock galloped for a touchdown in the closing minutes after the Bears had pulled up to a 28 to 28 tie.

Perkins Blasts Bears' Hopes

From the 14, Roy McKay, the Texan who was twice an All-Star, cracked thru the middle to the 2 yard line. Then they gave the ball to Perkins and he romped over the right side, standing up for the touchdown which put the game far beyond recall for the Chicagoans.

The Bears, in defeat, had their full back hero, too. He was Gary Famiglietti, who powered over for three touchdowns and added some-

[Continued on page 25, column 1]

Pro Standing

NATIONAL LEAGUE

WESTERN DIVISION

	W.	L.	T.	Pct.	TP.	OP.
Green Bay	1	0	0	1.000	31	21
Detroit	1	0	0	1.000	10	0
Cleveland	1	0	0	1.000	21	0
Chicago Bears	0	1	0	.000	21	31
Chicago Cards	0	2	0	.000	0	31

EASTERN DIVISION

	W.	L.	T.	Pct.	TP.	OP.
Boston	1	0	0	1.000	28	7
Philadelphia	0	0	0	.000	0	0
New York	0	0	0	.000	0	0
Washington	0	0	0	.000	0	0
Pittsburgh	0	1	0	.000	7	28

NATIONAL LEAGUE

Green Bay, 31; Chicago Bears, 21.

Cleveland, 21; Chicago Cardinals, 0.

EXHIBITION GAME

Washington, 21; Detroit, 14.

New York Giants, 21; Camp Lee, 0.

In the WAKE of the NEWS

BY ARCH WARD

[Chicago Tribune Press Service]

DETROIT, Mich., Sept. 30—Walter Hagen, the old golf master, is an executive in a firm distributing DDT. . . . The United States Golf association has called a meeting for Oct. 10 at which dates and sites of 1946 championship events will be set. . . . Louisiana has a new rule permitting part time coaches in high school football. . . . Doc Cramer, whose brilliant play has sparked the Detroit Tigers all season, has been in the major leagues 17 years. . . . Herbert Flam of California, the national junior tennis champion, is only 16 years old. . . . Since Mel Ott has managed the New York Giants his club has dropped three out of every four games played with the St. Louis Cardinals. . . . When the Detroit Lions were lining up their dates in Briggs stadium for 1945, General Manager Jack Zeller of the Tigers offered Fred Mandel, owner of the National Football league club, Oct. 7 for his first game. . . . "Better make it the 15th," cautioned Mandel. "I've a hunch the Tigers will be in the world series." . . . Zeller insisted he didn't think his ball club had a chance to win the pennant but yielded to Mandel. . . . If there are any postponements in the world series because of bad weather, it is possible that the Tigers still would be in Detroit on Oct. 7, still trying to get in the first three series games. . . . Charley Dunkley, the Associated Press' Chicago sports editor for more years than he cares to admit, is sporting the first goatee seen in Chicago sports writing circles since Senor Harry Neily batted out his daily columns for the American. . . . Bill Steele, who is bidding for the full back post at Northwestern university, won all-Iowa honors as a center at Davenport High school last fall.

Every club in the Pacific Coast league, regardless of its position in the pennant race, showed an increase in attendance over last season. . . . The University of Tennessee plans to increase the seating capacity of its stadium to 75,000 as soon as labor and material are available. . . . Leo Durocher's sliding scale contract with the Brooklyn Dodgers probably will net him $20,000 in attendance bonus money for the 1945 season. Zeke Bonura is back in his native New Orleans after more than four years in army service, most of it overseas. . . . When the regular season ended in the Southern association, Antonio Ordenana, Cuban short stop with Atlanta, bought a plane ticket for home, but club officials had his passport locked in the safe so he had to stick around for the play-offs. . . . Pvt. Ray Mueller, who broke the National league record for consecutive games caught with the Cincinnati Reds, still is in character. . . . Now with the Moore General Hospital nine in Asheville, N. C., Ray has worked every game this season. . . . Ty La Forest, Boston Red Sox third baseman, is Connie Mack's choice for rookie of the year.

Four-O'-Clock

I've figured out quite a few things in my time,
But it came to me with a shock
That I cannot disclose how a four-o'-clock knows
When it gets to be 4 o'clock.

I noticed them opening this evening
In a garden just down the block,
And I suddenly thought, now how do they wot
When it gets to be 4 o'clock?

Great minds have evolved the atomic bomb—
Well, here's a poser to mock:
How do you suppose the four-o'-clock knows
When it gets to be 4 o'clock?

—Jazbo of Old Dubuque

* *

It Would Seem So

According to the newspapers, cheap cuts of beef are to be unrationed after Oct. 1. Don't you think, after our long, patient wait, the government could give us more than a bum steer?—Horace.

* *

Larmer's Ledger

So that baby movie star got married. As uncle Willie says, it was bound to happen slowly but Shirley.

Made a horrible mistake last night. Mistook the grandfather's clock for scales. No wonder I weighed a quarter to nine.—Paul Larmer

* *

Eileen Gets Smart

The next man I marry must play the piano like Frankie Carle, sing like Perry Como and look like Alan Ladd. But what would a guy like that want with a droop like me?

—Eileen

* *

Famous Last Words

Extension disapproved. Report on due date of furlough.—Mazzie from Wendover

*

Holes in One

Ed Schroeder, Brookwood Country club, Addison, Ill., 14th hole, 145 yards.

Don Doring, Tam o' Shanter Country club, 11th hole, 135 yards.

Emil Johnson, Bartlett Hills Golf club, 8th hole, 175 yards.

George Adis, Glen Oaks Country club, 6th hole, yardage not given.

Dr. William Seritella, Hillside Golf course, 14th hole, 173 yards.

Edward F. Schwartzloff, Tam o' Shanter Country club, 11th hole, 135 yards.

B. Tilden and Dave Burglund, Dempster Golf club, 18th hole, 140 yards.

B. B. Jack, Flossmoor Country club, 13th hole, 110 yards.

Lou Sommerfield, Silver Lake Golf club, 8th hole, 160 yards.

Lt. W. F. Atkinson, Kokomo, Ind., Country club, 17th hole, 160 yards.

Mrs. Carl F. Ward, Pontiac Golf club, 6th hole, 140 yards.

Clashmore Mike

The Fighting Irish mascot is no more,
He cleared his final hurdle yesterday;
Peacetime athletics became such a bore.
That he made up his mind he wouldn't stay.
Ease was his one disease, and excess sleep
Had raised his weight to such an all-time high
That he could neither growl nor bark nor leap,
And so decided it was time to die.

"Hear ye! he cries to other dogs, "Beware
Of too much leisure and too many cats!
Better to live on ordinary fare,
And cut down on the starches and the sweets!
If you conserve your canine ration points
You won't contract, as I did, creampuffed joints."

—T. E. B.

* *

Pet Peeves

Mail boxes without names and doorbells that won't ring.—Art, the Messenger

Waitresses who make out my check and then turn it face down so I can't see it.—Barky of Downers

* *

Add Similes

As deflated as a successful contributor who fails to make the Wake book.—Chachee

As frustrated as a bowler with a railroad in the tenth frame.—Knute N. Newton

* *

The Wake Depends Upon Its Friends. Help! Help!

* *

Do You Remember Way Back When:

Tiny street cars were pulled up and down Wentworth av. by mules?—Mrs. Alex Skimmerhorn.

Ten Years Ago Today — Reed Kelso, captain of Indiana's football team, was injured in practice. . . . Fifty thousand were expected to see the opening game of the Cubs-Tigers world series in Detroit.

CUBS WIN, 5-3, OVER PIRATES IN FINAL GAME

Cavarretta Takes Batting Crown

Series Warmup

CHICAGO

	AB	R	H	RBI	P	A	E
Merullo, ss	5	0	2	1	3	3	0
Block, 2b	5	0	0	0	2	5	0
Lowrey, lf	3	1	1	0	2	0	0
Secory, lf	2	0	0	0	2	0	0
Cavarretta, 1b	4	1	2	1	10	0	0
Livingston, 1b	0	0	0	0	1	0	0
Pafko, cf	3	1	0	0	3	0	0
Sauer, cf	0	0	0	0	0	0	0
Nicholson, rf	4	0	0	0	1	0	0
Gillespie, rf	0	0	0	0	1	0	0
Ostrowski, 3b	4	1	2	1	1	1	1
Williams, c	3	1	1	0	1	0	0
Chipman, p	2	0	0	1	0	0	0
Erickson, p	1	0	0	0	0	1	0
	36	5	8	4	27	10	1

PITTSBURGH

	AB	R	H	RBI	P	A	E
Gionfriddo, cf	4	0	1	0	3	0	0
Barrett, rf	1	0	0	0	1	0	0
Colman, rf	4	0	0	0	2	0	0
Russell, lf	1	0	0	0	0	0	0
O'Brien, lf	3	0	1	0	3	0	0
Salkeld, c	4	1	1	0	1	0	0
Elliott, 3b	1	0	0	0	0	1	0
Barnhart, 3b	3	1	1	0	1	1	1
Dahlgren, 1b	8	1	1	1	10	0	0
Coscarart, 2b	1	0	0	0	0	1	0
Saltzgaver, 2b	3	0	2	1	1	1	0
Zak, ss	4	0	0	1	4	4	0
Gables, p	2	0	0	0	1	1	0
Rescigno, p	0	0	0	0	0	0	0
†Handley	1	0	1	0	0	0	0
	*36	3	8	3	27	9	1

*Gustine batted for Gables in eighth. †Batted for Rescigno in ninth.

Chicago	000	500	000—5
Pittsburgh	000	000	003—3

Two base hits—Gionfriddo, Cavarretta, Ostrowski [2], Dahlgren. Three base hit—Williams. Left on bases—Chicago, 7; Pittsburgh, 8. Struck out—Chipman, 1; Gables, 1. Bases on balls—Chipman, 1; Erickson, 1; Gables, 3. Hits—Off Chipman, 2 in 6 innings; Erickson, 6 in 3; Gables, 8 in 8; Rescigno, 0 in 1. Winning pitcher—Chipman. Losing pitcher—Gables. Time—1:35. Umpires—Sears, Reardon, Barr, and Dunn. Attendance—3,751.

BY EDWARD BURNS

[Chicago Tribune Press Service]

Pittsburgh, Pa., Sept. 30 — The Cubs, champions of the National

Phil Cavarretta

league in the final team standings, batting and fielding leaders of their league, and currently hailed in many quarters as favorites to win the 1945 world series, made it three straight in their final series, with the Pittsburgh Pirates, with a 5 to 3 victory today. The success was their 98th of the year, their 14th over the Pirates.

Most of the players were content to spend the chilly day as a sort of pre-world series workout, excepting Capt. Phil Cavarretta who had a chance to be nosed out of the individual batting championship.

Cavarretta Bats .3554

Cavarretta made a double and a single in four times at bat to complete his 1945 percentage at .354. Tommy Holmes of the Braves, his long time rival for the batting crown, made four hits in six times at bat tho his team was shut out by the Giants in the first game of a double header. When Cavarretta left Forbes field he didn't know whether or not he was champ, but he was aware that Holmes would have to make three hits in four times at bat to pass our Philip. But Holmes was unequal to the occasion and went hitless in two times at bat during the abbreviated second game.

Cavarretta is the first Cub to win the National league batting championship since 1912.

The Cubs will arrive in Chicago tomorrow morning at 8:40 o'clock, Chicago time, at the Union station. Later in the morning they will try on their new world series uniforms, vote on shares in the world series split, and pose for photographers in Wrigley field. At 5:40 o'clock tomorrow afternoon the champs will take off for Detroit.

Ostrowski Hits Two Doubles

In today's windup game here, Manager Grimm gave a few of his hopefuls a chance to show their stuff. Johnny Ostrowski made the best display of talent with a pair of doubles in four times at bat.

Going into the home ninth, the Cubs had a 5 to 0 shutout in hand. Bob Chipman, who accomplished the second out in the ninth inning jam in yesterday's pennant clincher, yielded two hits in six innings. Paul Erickson, who struck out Tom O'Brien with the tying run on third and the potential winning run on second, to end the clincher game, today held the Pirates to one hit in the seventh and eighth innings but the Pittsburghers fell on him for five hits and three runs in the ninth.

TIGERS' BATTERY—AND SPARK—IN TITLE GAME

Celebrating their victory in the American league championship race are members of the winning battery in the clubhouse after the Tigers defeated the Browns, 6 to 3, in St. Louis yesterday. Left to right are Hal Newhouser, credited with his 25th triumph; Virgil Trucks, who started the game; Catcher Paul Richards, and Al Benton, who pitched the last inning.

[Associated Press Wirephotos]

Hank Greenberg, Detroit left fielder, being congratulated by joyous teammates after hitting his four run homer in the ninth inning yesterday to defeat the Browns and to give the Tigers the American league pennant. John McHale (12) and Charles Hostetler (26) are among the Tigers ignoring the dark and rainy weather in St. Louis while greeting Greenberg.

PIRATES SPIKE RUMORS; SIGN FRISCH AGAIN

Pittsburgh, Pa., Sept. 30 (AP)—President William E. Benswanger of the Pittsburgh Pirates announced today that Manager Frankie Frisch had been retained for his seventh season.

Benswanger called Frisch into his office shortly before today's game and a one year contract was signed.

In six years as Pirate manager, Frisch has failed only once to land in the first division. Pittsburgh was fourth in 1940, 1941, 1943, and 1945, second in 1944 and fifth in 1942.

Major Leagues

AMERICAN LEAGUE

[FINAL STANDINGS]

	W.	L.	Pct.	G.B.
Detroit	88	65	.575	...
Washington	87	67	.565	1½
St. Louis	81	70	.537	6
New York	81	71	.533	6½
Cleveland	73	72	.503	11
CHICAGO	71	78*	.477	15
Boston	71	83	.461	17½
Philadelphia	52	98	347	.34½

YESTERDAY'S RESULTS

Detroit.............6; St. Louis.............3

[Second game canceled]

New York.......12; Boston............2

Cleveland at Chicago, both games postponed, rain.

Washington-Philadelphia not scheduled.

NATIONAL LEAGUE

[FINAL STANDINGS]

	W.	L.	Pct.	G.B.
CHICAGO	98	56	.636	....
St. Louis	95	59	.617	3
Brooklyn	87	67	.565	11
Pittsburgh	82	72	.532	16
New York	78	74	.513	19
Boston	67	85	.441	30
Cincinnati	61	93	.396	37
Philadelphia	46	108	.299	52

YESTERDAY'S RESULTS

Chicago.........5; Pittsburgh........3

New York.........1-2; Boston............0-2

[First game, 13 innings; second game, seven innings, darkness]

Brooklyn.........4; Philadelphia......1

St. Louis.........3; Cincinnati.........2

[12 innings]

Tigers Finally Cash Pennant Check Made Out in June

BY IRVING VAUGHAN

Detroit's Tigers finally cashed in yesterday on a threat they set up back in early June when they established themselves as first placers in the American league. Their lofty and profitable position, carrying with it world series rights, became official when they sheared the 1944 champion Browns in the penultimate game of the season, thus mathematically eliminating the Senators, who for more than a week have had no home because their owner leased it to the pro footballers.

The pennant clinching, which means the world series, weather permitting, will get under way in Briggs stadium next Wednesday, was Detroit's seventh. Letting it linger into the waning moments was merely following an old Tiger custom. This makes the sixth flag they tied down inside the last week of the season. In 1908, mentioned because it still stands as the league's most memorable race, they also won the pennant on the last day, Bill Donovan shutting out the White Sox.

A Series Affinity

There seems to be a strange affinity between the Tigers and Cubs, at least for world series purposes. The Cubs beat them in the series of 1907 and 1908. They beat the Cubs in the series of 1935, so this week they'll have their fourth argument with the same gang in seven pennant jobs. And it should be pointed out that the only world titles ever won by the Cubs were those 1907 and 1908 affairs with Detroit. The Tigers' lone title of that kind was the one they took at the Cubs' expense in 1935.

The Tigers, like all the others, are war born outfits, hence not up to what it took to win pennants in the pre-dictator days. Nevertheless, they topped their own league and will go into the records as full fledged champions. Maybe they deserve the titular rating more than their more capable predecessors because they had to work to win and in this case winning wasn't easy. They were dogged persistently, and the interval was always too close for comfort, but they got there by proving that staggering can be an accomplishment.

Our Sox Fade Out

During the year the first place role in the league was held by only three teams. The White Sox started off dizzily and led the pack from the opening day until May 25 except for one day in which the Yanks moved in. The Tigers jumped in front for the first time June 8 and then exchanged compliments until June 12, when Steve O'Neill's boys took over permanently except for a one day tie June 27 with the Yanks.

At least seven times since July 6 their pursuers, mostly Washington, were only a half game behind.

The Tigers' pennant climb would have been simplified if it hadn't been for further proof of that long standing contention that a two man pitching staff will invariably break in half after one heavy season. Last year Hal Newhouser won 29 and Paul Trout 27 games.

This year Newhouser continued at only a slight slower pace. Trout slowed down to a walk and in the last couple of weeks when he was greatly needed he couldn't help anybody except the opposition batters.

Cubs May Be Tough

Now with a world series coming up for the first time in three seasons of O'Neill management, the Tigers may find the National league has something tough to offer. The Cubs didn't lose much during the war. In fact most of the little they lost has been returned to them and, in addition, they skimmed off some very good, experienced minor league talent to tide them over the emergency.

The Cubs, because of Charles Grimm, the boss, also have that die for the dear old coach spirit. But these must be garnished by tight pitching and base hits.

To combat such Cub items as above, the Tigers also will have to have pitching and hitting and they were not particularly strong in either during the waning days of the race. In fact they were more futile than otherwise after Sept. 15, the day they won the double header from the contending Senators. But it is possible that the decisive pennant clinching thrust made by Hank Greenberg yesterday may prove the pick-me-up the entire outfit needed.

FOUR SENATOR HURLERS FINISH DETROIT VIGIL

Detroit, Mich., Sept. 30 (AP) — A four man Washington pitching staff, advance guard for the Senators' hoped for American league playoff with the Tigers, disbanded quickly here today when a hotel room radio provided details of Detroit's dramatic pennant clinching victory over the Browns in St. Louis.

Their last hope for a berth in the world series gone, two of the hurlers — Walter Masterson and Roger Wolff—were on a Washington bound train within an hour after the Tigers had won the flag.

The other two who had been here since this morning awaiting a chance to start warming up for the play-off—Emil [Dutch] Leonard and Mickey Haefner—planned to catch an evening train for their homes in Illinois.

DETROIT RALLY IN NINTH BEATS ST. LOUIS, 6 TO 3

Newhouser Gains 25th Victory

A. L. Clincher

DETROIT

	AB	R	H	RBI	P	A	E
Webb, ss	3	1	1	0	3	3	0
Mayo, 2b	4	0	1	1	3	3	0
Cramer, cf	5	1	1	0	2	0	0
Greenberg, lf	5	1	2	4	1	1	0
Cullenbine, rf	4	1	1	0	0	0	0
York, 1b	5	0	0	0	6	1	0
Outlaw, 3b	2	0	1	0	1	1	0
Richards, c	4	0	1	1	10	1	0
Trucks, p	2	1	0	0	1	1	0
Newhouser, p	0	0	0	0	0	0	0
*Walker	1	0	1	0	0	0	0
†Borom	0	1	0	0	0	0	0
Benton, p	0	0	0	0	0	0	0
	35	6	9	6	27	11	0

ST. LOUIS

	AB	R	H	RBI	P	A	E
Gutteridge, 2b	3	1	1	0	6	3	0
Finney, lf	2	0	2	1	1	0	0
Byrnes, cf	2	0	0	0	2	0	0
Gray, cf	1	1	0	0	2	0	0
McQuinn, 1b	4	0	1	1	5	2	0
Moore, rf	4	1	1	0	0	0	0
Stephens, ss	4	0	2	1	2	2	0
Mancuso, c	4	0	0	0	5	0	0
Schulte, 3b	4	0	0	0	3	4	0
Potter, p	3	0	1	0	1	0	0
	‡32	3	8	3	27	11	0

*Batted for Newhouser in ninth. †Benton ran for Walker in ninth. ‡Christman batted for Byrnes in sixth.

Detroit	000	011	004—6
St. Louis	100	000	110—3

Two base hits—Gutteridge, Potter, McQuinn. Home run—Greenberg. Sacrifices—Webb, Mayo. Double plays—Richards to Mayo; Outlaw to Mayo to York. Left on bases—St. Louis, 5; Detroit, 9. Bases on balls—Trucks, 2; Potter, 5; Newhouser, 1. Struck out—Trucks, 3; Potter, 4; Newhouser, 5. Hits—Trucks, 3 in 5⅓ innings; Newhouser, 4 in 2⅔ innings; Benton, 0 in 1 inning. Winning pitcher—Newhouser. Umpires—Pipgras, Berry, Rue, and Hubbard. Attendance, 5,582. Time 2:23.

St. Louis, Mo., Sept. 30 (AP)—A mighty home run by Hank Greenberg with the bases loaded in the ninth inning proved the championship punch for the Detroit Tigers today as they beat the St. Louis Browns, 6 to 3, in the first game of a concluding double header at Sportsman's park and sewed up the American league flag.

Including today's victory, the Tigers possessed an 88 to 65 won and lost record for a percentage of .575, representing the lowest average of any pennant winner in the history of the major leagues.

Never was a title won in more dramatic fashion than the one today. Premature darkness was settling over the field and a light mist was falling as big Hank stepped up with his team a run behind. He gave one of Nelson Potter's screwballs a tremendous ride into the bleachers just inside the left field foul line.

Rain Washes Out Second Game

The Tigers, the long strain of the flag race suddenly ended by Hank's big whack, raced out of their dugout in a body to meet the tall fellow as he trotted across the plate. It was Hank's 13th home run since he rejoined the club in July.

It came just in time, too, as the clubs barely had begun the second game a few minutes later when the rain, which had delayed the opener nearly an hour, started coming down in sheets and washed out any further play for the day.

25th Victory for Newhouser

Hal Newhouser was credited with the triumph, his 25th of the season against 9 defeats. He relieved Virgil Trucks in the sixth inning after the recent navy dischargee got into trouble.

Al Benton pitched the last inning for the champions and, with the aid of a double play, protected the club's lead.

It was a tense battle all the way until Hank hit the jackpot, first one club and then the other forged ahead. The Browns jumped into the lead in the first inning when Don Gutteridge and Lou Finney, first two batters to face Trucks, ganged on him for a double and a single before he could get his bearings.

Newhouser Replaces Trucks

The Tigers struck back to score one off Potter in the fifth on a walk to Trucks and successive singles by Skeeter Webb and Eddie Mayo, and they pulled ahead 2 to 1 in the sixth on a pair of walks and Catcher Paul Richards' single to left.

When Trucks weakened in the last of the sixth, yielding a double to Potter and a walk to Gutteridge, Newhouser was rushed in from the bullpen. Hal escaped damage as he struck out Milt Byrnes and caused George McQuinn to fly out to center, but the Browns got to him for the tying run in the seventh on Gene Moore's double and Vernon Stephens' single.

After the Tigers had failed to score off Potter in the eighth, even tho their first two batters singled, the Browns pushed over another run in their half on Finney's single and McQuinn's double off the screen in deep right center.

Browns Protest Decision

Things looked extremely gloomy for Manager Steve O'Neill's champions when they came up for the last time. Hub Walker batted for Newhouser and singled to center field. Webb laid down a bunt toward first, and both runners were safe when the throw to second was too late to get Walker, tho the Browns kicked hard on the decision. Red Borom went in to run for Walker.

Mayo sacrificed, moving both runners along, and then, after a mid-diamond conference, the Browns decided to pass Roger Cramer to get to Greenberg. It was a fatal mistake.

MOON MULLINS

SIX TIGERS CALLED HEROES OF SERIES

O'Neill Acclaims Newhouser, Greenberg, Cramer, Mayo Richards and Webb

PITCHING DECIDING FACTOR

Winners Parade Noisily Into Clubhouse—Grimm Consoles Borowy for Game Effort

By JAMES P. DAWSON

Special to THE NEW YORK TIMES.

CHICAGO, Oct. 10—"Well, it's all over and I'm the happiest man in the world."

That was the statement of Manager Steve O'Neill in the first full flush of the Tigers' victory over the Cubs in the seventh game of this harum-scarum world series, which ended with Detroit in possession of its second such title, both of them, incidentally, snared from the grasp of the National League's Cubs.

Right down to the last second it was a fight for the American League champions. They had to battle through seven games, in all of which anything was likely to happen and all sorts of things did, mostly funny things.

O'Neill had to fight his way through an enveloping swarm of fans to the Tigers' clubhouse, where he arrived fifteen minutes after his club had stomped in sending up a din with the victory cheer. "It was a great series to win," said the Tiger leader, when he had a chance to collect his thoughts after being manhandled by a noisy gang of photographers.

Interviewers Seize O'Neill

By main force O'Neill was dragged from the graflex operators to face a phalanx of interviewers. "It's a great thrill for me," continued O'Neill. "Coming up to the highest baseball can offer you after thirty-six years in the game almost defies description. It's a marvelous thing to be up in the majors, then go down to the minors, come back up again and win a world series. My boys did that for me.

"As baseball goes, of course, it wasn't much of a series, but it must have been great for the fans. They saw everything, including a lot of things we managers never like to see.

"If I were asked to single out one player as the standout, I honestly couldn't. I'd say about six stood out. They were Paul Richards, Hal Newhouser, Hank Greenberg, Roger Cramer, Eddie Mayo and Skeeter Webb.

"Newhouser had his stuff and he had his strength. Only once, late in the game, did I suspect his arm might be tiring. Then I had Stubby Overmire and Al Benton warming up, just in case.

"They had no pitching to stop us. I held all along pitching would decide the series and I knew I had it.

Bunt Break of Game

"The break of the game for us was Greenberg's bunt. That slap he laid down in the first inning with two men on, after Cramer's single had chased in the first run, caught the Cubs so flat-footed Hank could have beaten the throw to first if it had been necessary. They didn't know that Hank practically had to bunt because he was crippled with a bad right wrist.

"I didn't think I would start him. He hurt the wrist hitting a drive to right in the last inning of Monday's game and told me today he would start but didn't know how far he could go. I had Jimmy Outlaw all set to go in at left and had Bob Maier ready to play third.

"However, Richards solved that situation by dropping that double in left with the bases loaded and Derringer pitching. As it was, Hank took less than half a dozen full cuts at the ball through the game. He was up there waiting them out all the time."

Catcher Richards, forced out in the Cub eighth when a foul tip from Bill Nicholson's bat split the little finger on his right hand, echoed the sentiments of his leader. This was true of all the Tigers. They made their clubhouse a veritable jungle with their yells, whoops and weird shouts in an outburst of pandemonium that started as Coach Art Mills led a parade, followed by Greenberg, Overmire, Benton, Jim Tobin, Virgil Trucks and Rudy York, that grew noisier as each player raced into quarters.

Chandler Reaches Clubhouse

Commissioner Albert B. (Happy) Chandler somehow worked his way through and shivered in the face of the ear-splitting din. Ford C. Frick, National League president, almost had his overcoat torn off. Will Harridge, American League president, wisely held to the rim of the jam after seeing Frick engulfed on his way to congratulate O'Neill.

Newhouser was beside himself with joy. "I felt great out there all the time," he said. "I never felt tired. Felt about the same as always, except that my back . . ."

It is suspected the indication of tiring O'Neill thought he detected was pain from the growth on Newhouser's left shoulder blade. However, Hal would say nothing about it.

Richards, his right hand held in a Turkish towel, could laugh through his pain. "I thought at first this finger was serious," said Richards, "but it isn't much.

"For three or four innings out there Newhouser had all his stuff, but I thought he changed then, although he always held the upper hand. Hal is the kind of pitcher who must have his three days of rest to be himself.

"There were three or four pitches when he faced danger that proved his courage, one particularly in the sixth inning on Cavaretta, after Lowrey had singled. Hal came in with a change of pace ball that was a beauty."

Greenberg modestly declined to discuss his injury, but got quite a thrill out of fooling the Cub infield with that bunt.

In the quarters of the beaten Cubs the situation was, to put it conservatively, more restrained. They had the clubhouse virtually to themselves.

Irrepressible Cholly Grimm refused to be downcast, though. His first word was a placating thought for the disappointed Hank Borowy. "You gave it a good try, Hank," said Grimm to the former Yankee routed on nine pitches before he could get a man out.

"It's too late now," continued Grimm. "We were beaten by a good club, but not a better club than I have. Just pitching beat us, but these guys are still champs in my book. They gave it everything they had.

"Borowy didn't have a lot when he warmed up and I knew it, but I wanted to give it a try. I thought maybe he'd get by until he had warmed up to the job.

"There was a lot of yelling on balls and strikes at the plate. Some of the boys didn't like some of the decisions of Passarella, but umpiring didn't beat us. It was the Tigers."

Borowy Sits It Out

Borowy sat through the game on the bench. He bemoaned the fates that had deprived him of the greatness three world series victories would have brought him. "It was tough to go that way," said Hank. "With a little luck I might have made it."

Big Paul Derringer criticized himself for two things. "Walking Outlaw with the bases loaded beat us," said he. "That, and a high school curve I sent up there to Richards. Anybody could have hit that one that got away from me."

The Tigers are back in Detroit tonight, looking forward to a Chamber of Commerce dinner tomorrow night. Each player will receive a gift. The last time the Tigers were feted the gift was an automobile—and only four players showed up. The Cubs, meanwhile, will scatter to the four corners of the country.

The Detroit Tigers: They Are the Winners and New Champions of the Baseball World

Hal Newhouser (third from left) as he received the plaudits of his team-mates after his victory yesterday

Johnson of Chicago sliding safely into second in the first inning as Mayo goes high in a vain effort to take the throw in from the outfield.

Mayo scoring for Detroit in the eighth inning as Livingston attempts to get the ball which is bounding in the direction of Cullenbine.

Associated Press Wirephotos

41,590 Pay $204,177 At Final Series Game

By The Associated Press.

Final Standing of the Clubs

	W.	L.	Pct.
Detroit (A.)	4	3	.571
Chicago (N.)	3	4	.429

Seventh-Game Statistics

Paid attendance—41,590.
Gross receipts—$204,177.
Commissioner's share—$30,626.55.
Each club's share—$43,387.61.
Each league's share—$43,387.61.

Seven-Game Totals

*Paid attendance—333,457.
†Gross receipts—$1,492,454.
‡Players' share—$445,714.50.
Commissioner's share—$223,868.10.
Each club's share—$205,717.84.
Each league's share—$205,717.84.

*All-time record for world series paid attendance.

†With $100,000 received for broadcasting rights, $1,592,454 establishes all-time record for world series receipts.

‡Players participate in receipts of first four games only. They also participate in radio rights.

Grissom Discharged by Army

DENVER, Oct. 10 (AP)—Lee T. Grissom of Red Bluff, Ark., former big league baseball player, received an honorable discharge from the Army Air Forces today at Lowry Field. Before entering the service he pitched for Philadelphia, Brooklyn and Cincinnati in the National League and New York in the American.

Record of Series Games

FIRST GAME
At Detroit

					R.	H.	E.
Chicago (N. L.)	4 0 3	0 0 0	2 0 0—		9	13	0
Detroit (A. L.)	0 0 0	0 0 0	0 0 0—		0	6	0

Batteries—Borowy and Livingston; Newhouser, Benton (3), Tobin (5), Mueller (8) and Richards.

SECOND GAME
At Detroit

Chicago (N. L.)	0 0 0	1 0 0	0 0 0—	1	7	0
Detroit (A. L.)	0 0 0	0 4 0	0 0 ..—	4	7	0

Batteries—Wyse, Erickson (7) and Gillespie; Trucks and Richards.

THIRD GAME
At Detroit

Chicago (N. L.)	0 0 0	2 0 0	1 0 0—	3	8	0
Detroit (A. L.)	0 0 0	0 0 0	0 0 0—	0	1	2

Batteries—Passeau and Livingston; Overmire, Benton (7) and Swift, Richards (7).

FOURTH GAME
At Chicago

Detroit (A. L.)	0 0 0	4 0 0	0 0 0—	4	7	1
Chicago (N. L.)	0 0 0	0 0 1	0 0 0—	1	5	1

Batteries—Trout and Richards; Prim, Derringer (4), Vandenberg (6), Erickson (8) and Livingston.

FIFTH GAME
At Chicago

Detroit (A. L.)	0 0 1	0 0 4	1 0 2—	8	11	0
Chicago (N. L.)	0 0 1	0 0 0	2 0 1—	4	7	2

Batteries—Newhouser and Richards; Borowy, Vandenberg (6), Chipman (6), Derringer (7), Erickson (9) and Livingston.

SIXTH GAME
At Chicago

Detroit (A. L.)	0 1 0	0 0 0	2 4 0	0 0 0—	7	13	2
Chicago (N. L.)	0 0 0	0 4 1	2 0 0	0 0 1—	8	15	3

Batteries—Trucks, Caster (5), Bridges (6), Benton (7), Trout (8) and Richards, Swift (6); Passeau, Wyse (7), Prim (8), Borowy (9) and Livingston, Williams (10).

SEVENTH GAME
At Chicago

Detroit (A. L.)	5 1 0	0 0 0	1 2 0—	9	9	1
Chicago (N. L.)	1 0 0	1 0 0	0 1 0—	3	10	0

Batteries—Newhouser and Richards, Swift (8); Borowy, Derringer (1), Vandenberg (2), Erickson (6), Passeau (8), Wyse (9) and Livingston.

TIGERS CRUSH CUBS AND ANNEX SERIES

Continued From Page 1

for baseball, with the sun breaking only intermittently through a gray, hazy sky. However, the crowd paid little attention to it as Borowy and Newhouser, squaring off for the third time in the series, got this final encounter under way.

In their first meeting, on opening day, Borowy had triumphed with an impressive shut-out, only to bow to his southpaw rival in the fifth game here last Sunday. However, following this, the former Yankee right-hander also had to toil the last four rounds of Monday's twelve-inning thriller and the effort to appear in three successive games proved too much for him.

The Tigers lost no time demonstrating that the frail Fordham hurler had none of the effectiveness with which he had gained two victories over them. Skeeter Webb opened with a single to right and Eddie Mayo followed with a one-base shot in the same sector.

Next came a single to left by Roger Cramer and, as Webb scooted over the plate with the first tally, Grimm emerged from the Chicago dugout to lead a crestfallen Borowy off the field. The crowd gave Hank a generous hand and then greeted Derringer with an encouraging cheer as the strapping right-hander came up from the bullpen.

Lull in the Attack

It was hardly an inviting spot for Oom Paul, what with one run in, runners on first and second and still nobody out. There was a brief lull in the attack as Hank Greenberg modestly sacrificed and Roy Cullenbine received an intentional pass to fill the bases.

A cold shiver went through the gathering as Rudy York sent a towering fly down the right-field foul line that Bill Nicholson, Cub right-fielder, obviously couldn't reach. But the ball fell foul by a matter of inches and Derringer presently removed York as a threat by retiring the husky Detroit first sacker on an infield pop-up.

However, this merely delayed the inevitable. As he pitched to Jimmy Outlaw, Derringer's control suddenly strayed off the beam and he walked the Detroit third baseman on four successive balls to force in Mayo with the second run of the inning.

Before the crowd had a chance to recover from this shock, the supposedly weak-hitting Richards, so frequently removed for pinch-hitters, crossed up everyone, including Derringer, by driving a lusty double down the left-field line to send three more colleagues dashing headlong toward the plate.

For a change, no Tiger fell down on the baselines and, though Derringer now quickly erased Newhouser for the third out, the Bengals were away to a five-run lead.

It promised to be a pretty dreary afternoon for Chicago's North Side fans although, for a few fleeting moments in the lower half of the same round, it looked as though the Cubs might slice an appreciable chunk off this imposing margin.

Stan Hack, hero of Monday's stirring sixth game, received a noisy welcome, only to strike out. But Don Johnson brought the gathering up with a roar with a two-base drive into left center. On the heels of this came a fumble by Newhouser as he tried to field Peanuts Lowrey's topped ball and a loud single to right by Phil Cavarretta to score Johnson.

However, with the crowd imploring Andy Pafko to keep the rally going, Andy abruptly ended matters by grounding into a double play and the Cubs still were a long way from evening things up.

In fact, in the second the Tigers restored their five-run margin when Derringer's control again went awry to give the American Leaguers another tally with scarcely an effort on their part.

The big Kentucky rifleman had retired Webb and Mayo when Cramer came up with his second successive single and the folks then groaned in unison as Greenberg, Cullenbine and York drew three straight passes to force Cramer home.

Having accomplished this, the veteran Derringer, a world series hero himself in a happier and sunnier era, also passed out, and tall Hy Vandenberg came on to see what he could do in the rather hopeless struggle. He did all right, too, for after bringing the Tigers to a halt in this second inning without further damage, he then went on to hurl three scoreless innings before vacating for a pinch-hitter and turning the pitching chores over to Paul Erickson.

In fact, pitching at this point no longer was troubling the Cubs. Their problem now concerned itself wholly with breaking through Newhouser's southpaw pitching, and the American League's ace left-hander and 25-game winner was not giving them much encouragement.

There was an expectant note in the last half of the fourth when, with one down, Cavarretta, doughty field captain of the Cubs, singled again and Pafko this time followed with a tremendous drive down the center of the fairway that completely baffled the slow fielding, 39-year-old Cramer. The ball fell for a triple, scoring Cavarretta, and the Windy City fans again took up the chant for victory.

But Newhouser now really poured it on and neither Nicholson nor Mickey Livingston could do more than bounce the ball to the mound for successive outs to end the inning with the Cubs still four tallies in arrears.

Refuses to Give Ground

There was a Lowrey single in the sixth and a Livingston single in the seventh, followed by a wild pitch and a walk, but Newhouser again refused to give up any further ground.

To add to the discomfiture of the crowd, the Tigers came up with another tally in the seventh when Erickson walked Cullenbine who then, with two out, counted all the way from first when Richards touched off his second surprise two-bagger of the afternoon, a robust drive this time to right center.

That put the Tiger lead back to five runs, and in the eighth gave more misery for the die-hard Chicagoans. Erickson having stepped aside for a pinch-hitter in the last of the seventh, Claude Passeau, who might well have been one of the mound heroes of the series, now stepped to the rubber.

But Claude, who had hurled an epic one-hitter in the third game in Detroit, only to go out with a torn finger nail in that tempestuous sixth game Monday, had little to stop the enemy today.

He went down a run almost immediately when Webb walked and tallied on Mayo's two-bagger to left, and presently Mayo also scored on successive outs by Cramer and Greenberg.

That made the gap seven runs, but still the Cubs stubbornly fought on in the futile struggle. With one down in the last of the eighth, Lowrey tore off his second single of the afternoon and Cavarretta his third, and even though Pafko here struck out, Nicholson kept the flickering hope alive with a two-base smash into left center that drove in Lowrey.

Just before this another mishap was added to the series' long casualty list as Catcher Richards, who had been the key man of that first-inning attack, had to retire when a foul tip off Nicholson's bat broke the little finger on his right hand.

Bob Swift went behind the plate for the Detroiters and then Newhouser closed in with a burst of speed that fanned Livingston for the third out. One more Chicago single opened the last of the ninth but it proved the Cubs' last gasp and, in a few minutes, the jubilant Tigers were rushing wildly up to shower congratulations upon their ace southpaw who, coming back after his bruising first-game defeat, had pitched them into the lead in the pivotal fifth game and then had clinched the decisive seventh.

With this triumph, the American League added one more notch to its long lead over the National in world series competition. For the junior loop has now won twenty-six of these while the senior circuit has bagged only sixteen. It also marked the first time since 1935 that an American League team other than the Yankees had captured the title.

That year, too, it was the Tigers who did the trick and the Cubs also were their victims. A deep sorrow seems to be enveloping Chicago's fandom tonight.

Series Box Score

SEVENTH GAME

DETROIT TIGERS

	ab.	r.	h.	po.	a.	e.
Webb, ss	4	2	1	0	5	0
Mayo, 2b	5	2	2	2	1	0
Cramer, cf	5	2	3	2	0	0
Greenberg, lf	2	0	0	0	0	0
Mierkowicz, lf	0	0	0	0	0	0
Cullenbine, rf	2	2	0	2	0	0
York, 1b	4	0	0	8	1	0
Outlaw, 3b	4	1	1	1	2	0
Richards, c	4	0	2	9	0	0
Swift, c	1	0	0	2	0	0
Newhouser, p	4	0	0	1	2	1
Total	35	9	9	27	11	1

CHICAGO CUBS

	ab.	r.	h.	po.	a.	e.
Hack, 3b	5	0	0	1	3	0
Johnson, 2b	5	1	1	1	3	0
Lowrey, lf	4	1	2	3	0	0
Cavarretta, 1b	4	1	3	10	0	0
Pafko, cf	4	0	1	6	0	0
Nicholson, rf	4	0	1	1	0	0
Livingston, c	4	0	1	4	1	0
Hughes, ss	3	0	1	1	1	0
Borowy, p	0	0	0	0	0	0
Derringer, p	0	0	0	0	0	0
Vandenberg, p	1	0	0	0	1	0
aSauer	1	0	0	0	0	0
Erickson, p	0	0	0	0	0	0
bSecory	1	0	0	0	0	0
Passeau, p	0	0	0	0	0	0
Wyse, p	0	0	0	0	0	0
cMcCullough	1	0	0	0	0	0
Total	37	3	10	27	9	0

a Batted for Vandenberg in fifth.
b Batted for Erickson in seventh.
c Batted for Wyse in ninth.

Detroit (A. L.)...5 1 0 0 0 0 1 2 0—9
Chicago (N. L.)..1 0 0 1 0 0 0 1 0—3

Runs batted in—Cramer, Outlaw, Richards 4, Cavarretta, York, Pafko, Mayo, Greenberg, Nicholson. Two-base hits—Richards 2, Johnson, Mayo, Nicholson. Three-base hit—Pafko. Stolen bases—Outlaw, Cramer. Sacrifice—Greenberg. Double play—Webb, Mayo and York. Earned runs—Detroit 9, Chicago 3. Left on bases—Detroit 8, Chicago 8. Bases on balls—Off Derringer 5 (Cullenbine 2, Outlaw, Greenberg, York), Vandenberg 1 (Greenberg), Erickson 1 (Cullenbine), Passeau 1 (Webb), Newhouser 1 (Hughes). Struck out—By Newhouser 10 (Hack, Hughes 2, Sauer, Johnson, Pafko 2, Secory, Livingston, McCullough), Vandenberg 3 (Richards, Mayo, Cullenbine), Erickson 2 (Greenberg, York).

Pitching summary—Off Borowy 3 hits, 3 runs in 0 inning (none out in first); Derringer 2 hits, 3 runs in 1⅔ innings; Vandenberg 1 hit, 0 run in 3⅓ innings; Erickson 2 hits, 1 run in 2 innings; Passeau, 1 hit, 2 runs in 1 inning; Wyse 0 hit, 0 run in 1 inning. Wild pitch—Newhouser. Losing pitcher—Borowy.

Umpires—Passarella (A.), plate; Conlan (N.), first base; Summers (A.), second base; Jorda (N.), third base. Time of game—2:31. Attendance—41,590. Gross receipts—$204,177.

Composite Score of World Series Games

DETROIT TIGERS

	G	AB	R	H	2B	3B	HR	RBI	BB	SO	Bat Avg	PO	A	E	Fldg Avg
Webb, ss	7	27	4	5	0	0	0	1	2	1	.185	9	24	1	.971
Hoover, ss	1	3	1	1	0	0	0	1	0	0	.333	1	1	0	1.000
Mayo, 2b	7	28	4	7	1	0	0	2	3	2	.250	18	13	1	.969
Cramer, cf	7	29	7	11	0	0	0	4	1	0	.379	21	0	0	1.000
Greenberg, lf	7	23	7	7	3	0	2	7	6	5	.304	8	1	0	1.000
Mierkowicz, lf	1	0	0	0	0	0	0	0	0	0	.000	0	0	0	.000
Cullenbine, rf	7	22	5	5	2	0	0	4	8	2	.227	8	0	0	1.000
York, 1b	7	28	1	5	1	0	0	3	3	4	.179	67	8	1	.987
Outlaw, 3b	7	28	1	5	0	0	0	3	2	1	.179	5	15	0	1.000
Richards, c	7	19	0	4	2	0	0	6	4	3	.211	46	5	1	.981
Swift, c	3	4	1	1	0	0	0	0	2	0	.250	9	1	0	1.000
Newhouser, p	3	8	0	0	0	0	0	1	1	1	.000	2	6	1	.857
Benton, p	3	0	0	0	0	0	0	0	0	0	.000	0	3	0	1.000
Tobin, p	1	1	0	0	0	0	0	0	0	0	.000	0	1	0	1.000
Mueller, p	1	0	0	0	0	0	0	0	0	0	.000	0	0	0	.000
Trucks, p	2	4	0	0	0	0	0	0	1	1	.000	1	1	0	1.000
Overmire, p	1	1	0	0	0	0	0	0	0	0	.000	0	1	0	1.000
Bridges, p	1	0	0	0	0	0	0	0	0	0	.000	0	0	0	.000
Trout, p	2	6	0	1	0	0	0	0	0	0	.167	2	5	0	1.000
Caster, p	1	0	0	0	0	0	0	0	0	0	.000	0	0	0	.000
*Eaton	1	1	0	0	0	0	0	0	0	1	.000	0	0	0	.000
*Hostetler	3	3	0	0	0	0	0	0	0	0	.000	0	0	0	.000
*†Borom	2	1	0	0	0	0	0	0	0	0	.000	0	0	0	.000
*McHale	3	3	0	0	0	0	0	0	0	1	.000	0	0	0	.000
*Walker	2	2	1	1	1	0	0	0	0	0	.500	0	0	0	.000
*Maier	1	1	0	1	0	0	0	0	0	0	1.000	0	0	0	.000
Total		242	32	54	10	0	2	32	33	22	.223	197	85	5	.983

CHICAGO CUBS

	G	AB	R	H	2B	3B	HR	RBI	BB	SO	Bat Avg	PO	A	E	Fldg Avg
Hack, 3b	7	30	1	11	3	0	0	4	4	2	.367	12	13	3	.875
Johnson, 2b	7	29	4	5	2	1	0	0	0	8	.172	11	24	1	.972
Lowrey, lf	7	29	4	9	1	0	0	0	1	2	.310	21	1	0	1.000
Cavarretta, 1b	7	26	7	11	2	0	1	5	4	3	.423	71	3	0	1.000
Pafko, cf	7	28	5	6	2	1	0	2	2	5	.214	24	2	1	.963
Nicholson, rf	7	28	1	6	1	1	0	8	2	5	.214	9	0	1	.900
Livingston, c	6	22	3	8	3	0	0	4	1	1	.364	22	4	0	1.000
*Gillespie, c	3	6	0	0	0	0	0	0	0	0	.000	3	0	0	1.000
Hughes, ss	6	17	1	5	1	0	0	3	4	5	.294	13	17	0	1.000
†Merullo, ss	3	2	0	0	0	0	0	0	0	1	.000	4	2	0	1.000
†Schuster, ss	2	1	1	0	0	0	0	0	0	0	.000	1	2	0	1.000
Borowy, p	4	6	1	1	1	0	0	0	0	3	.167	1	2	0	1.000
Wyse, p	3	3	0	0	0	0	0	0	0	2	.000	0	0	0	.000
Vandenberg, p	3	1	0	0	0	0	0	0	0	0	.000	1	2	0	1.000
Erickson, p	4	0	0	0	0	0	0	0	0	0	.000	0	1	0	1.000
Derringer, p	3	0	0	0	0	0	0	0	0	0	.000	0	0	0	.000
Passeau, p	3	7	1	0	0	0	0	1	0	4	.000	1	3	0	1.000
Prim, p	2	0	0	0	0	0	0	0	0	0	.000	0	1	0	1.000
Chipman, p	1	0	0	0	0	0	0	0	0	0	.000	0	0	0	.000
*Secory	5	5	[illegible]	2	0	0	0	0	0	2	.400	0	0	0	.000
*Sauer	2	2	0	0	0	0	0	0	0	2	.000	0	0	0	.000
*Becker	3	2	0	1	0	0	0	0	1	1	.500	0	0	0	.000
*Williams, c	2	2	0	0	0	0	0	0	0	1	.000	1	1	0	1.000
†Block	1	0	0	0	0	0	0	0	0	0	.000	0	0	0	.000
*McCullough	1	1	0	0	0	0	0	0	0	1	.000	0	0	0	.000
Total		247	29	65	16	3	1	27	19	48	.263	195	78	6	.978

*Pinch hitter. †Pinch runner.

COMPOSITE SCORE BY INNINGS

Detroit ....5 2 1 4 4 4 4 6 2 0 0 0—32
Chicago ....5 0 4 4 4 2 7 1 1 0 0 1—29

PITCHING SUMMARY

	G	CG	IP	H	R	ER	BB	SO	WP	HB	W	L	PC	ERA
Trucks	2	1	13⅓	14	5	5	5	7	0	0	1	0	1.000	3.38
Newhouser	3	2	20⅔	25	14	14	4	22	1	0	2	1	.667	6.10
Trout	2	1	13⅔	9	2	1	3	9	0	0	1	1	.500	0.66
Overmire	1	0	6	4	2	2	2	2	0	0	0	1	.000	3.00
Benton	3	0	4⅔	6	1	1	0	5	0	0	0	0	.000	1.93
Tobin	1	0	3	4	2	2	1	0	0	0	0	0	.000	6.00
Bridges	1	0	1⅔	3	3	3	3	1	0	0	0	0	.000	16.20
Mueller	1	0	2	0	0	0	1	1	0	0	0	0	.000	0.00
Caster	1	0	⅔	0	0	0	0	1	0	0	0	0	.000	0.00
Passeau	3	1	16⅔	7	5	5	8	3	0	0	1	0	1.000	2.70
Borowy	4	1	18	21	8	8	6	8	0	1	2	2	.500	4.00
Wyse	3	0	7⅔	8	7	6	4	1	0	0	0	1	.000	7.04
Prim	2	0	4	4	5	4	1	1	0	0	0	1	.000	9.00
Erickson	4	0	7	8	3	3	3	5	0	1	0	0	.000	3.86
Derringer	3	0	5⅓	5	4	4	7	1	0	0	0	0	.000	6.75
Vandenberg	3	0	6	1	0	0	3	3	0	0	0	0	.000	0.00
Chipman	1	0	⅓	0	0	0	1	0	0	0	0	0	.000	0.00

Earned runs—Chicago 28, Detroit 30. Sacrifices—Lowrey, Borowy, Johnson 4, Cavarretta, Hughes, Pafko, Prim, Outlaw, Cullenbine, Greenberg. Double plays—Hughes, Johnson and Cavarretta; Johnson, Hughes and Cavarretta; Johnson, Merullo and Cavarretta; Merullo, Johnson and Cavarretta; Mayo, York, Webb and Mayo; Mayo, Webb, Richards and Webb; Mayo, Hoover and York; Webb, Mayo and York. Stolen bases—Johnson, Pafko, Cullenbine, Outlaw, Cramer. Hit by pitcher—By Borowy (Greenberg), by Erickson (Cramer). Left on bases—Chicago 50, Detroit 53. Passed balls—Richards 2, Livingston 1. Time of games—2:10, 1:47, 1:55, 2:00, 2:18, 3:28, 2:31. Umpires—Summers (A.), Jorda (N.), Passarella (A.), Conlan (N.). Attendances—First game, 54,637; second game, 53,636; third game, 55,500; fourth game, 42,923; fifth game, 43,463; sixth game, 41,708; seventh game, 41,590. Gross receipts—First game, $221,883; second game, $220,394; third game, $223,497; fourth game, $208,176; fifth game, $209,796; sixth game, $204,531; seventh game, $204,177.

SWIFT ATTACK WINS FINALE FOR DETROIT

Tigers' Five-Run First Inning Is Decisive, Play-by-Play Story of Game Shows

CHICAGO, Oct. 10 (AP)—The play-by-play description of the seventh and final game of the world series at Wrigley Field today follows:

FIRST INNING

TIGERS—With a full count, Webb slapped a single to right. Mayo clubbed the first pitch into right for a single, sending Webb to third. Cramer singled near the left-field line, scoring Webb and sending Mayo to second. That was all for Borowy, and Derringer replaced him. Greenberg sacrificed, Cavarretta unassisted. Cullenbine was purposely passed, filling the bases. York reached a full count, then popped up to Hack. Outlaw walked on four straight pitches, forcing Mayo home. Richards doubled into the left-field corner, scoring Cramer, Cullenbine and Outlaw. Newhouser rolled out, Johnson to Cavarretta. Five runs, four hits, no errors, one left.

CUBS—Hack was called out on strikes, looking at a sweeping curve. Johnson doubled to left center. Lowrey bunted and was safe on Newhouser's error, Johnson holding second. Cavarretta singled to right, scoring Johnson and sending Lowrey to third. Pafko hit into a double play, Webb to Mayo to York. One run, two hits, one error, one left.

SECOND INNING

TIGERS—Webb flied deep to Pafko. Mayo lined to Pafko. Cramer singled to right. Greenberg walked, the Cubs protesting bitterly a couple of Umpire Passarella's decisions. Cullenbine also walked, filling the bases. Derringer whipped two strikes past York and then walked him, forcing in Cramer. Vandenberg replaced Derringer. Outlaw went out, Vandenberg to Cavarretta. One run, one hit, no errors, three left.

CUBS—Nicholson fouled to Richards. Outlaw threw out Livingston. Hughes was called out on strikes. No runs, no hits, no errors, none left.

THIRD INNING

TIGERS—Richards was called out on strikes. Newhouser was an easy out, Johnson to Cavarretta. Hughes tossed out Webb. No runs, no hits, no errors, none left.

CUBS—Vandenberg flied to Cullenbine in short right. Hack went out, Outlaw to York. Webb took Johnson's hopper near second and threw him out. No runs, no hits, no errors, none left.

FOURTH INNING

TIGERS—Mayo looked at a called third strike. Cramer popped to Hughes. Greenberg walked on five pitches. Cullenbine broke his bat on a long foul, then struck out. Livingston dropped the third strike, but threw Cullenbine out at first. No runs, no hits, no errors, one left.

CUBS—Lowrey flied to Cullenbine, who made a long run to pull it down. Cavarretta singled to center. Pafko tripled over Cramer's head, scoring Cavarretta on a close play. A perfect throw-in reached the plate a step ahead of Cavarretta, but Richards dropped it. Newhouser threw out Nicholson. Livingston also went out, Newhouser to York. One run, two hits, no errors, one left.

FIFTH INNING

TIGERS—York bounced out, Hack to Cavarretta. Outlaw singled over short, then stole second. Hack threw out Richards, Outlaw holding second. Newhouser lined to Lowrey near the left-field line. No runs, one hit, no errors, one left.

CUBS—Hughes was called out on strikes. Sauer batted for Vandenberg and struck out on a change of pace. Hack went out, Webb to York. No runs, no hits, no errors, none left.

SIXTH INNING

TIGERS—Erickson was the Cubs' new pitcher. Webb flied to Pafko. Mayo flied to Lowrey close to the left center-field wall. Cramer singled to center. He stole second as Livingston dropped a pitch. Greenberg struck out. No runs, one hit, no errors, one left.

CUBS—Johnson struck out on a curve. Lowrey singled to left. Cavarretta flied to Cramer in short center. Pafko struck out. No runs, one hit, no errors, one left.

SEVENTH INNING

TIGERS—Cullenbine drew the full count and walked. York was called out on strikes. Outlaw lofted to Pafko in short center. Richards doubled to the right-field wall, scoring Cullenbine. Newhouser lined to Pafko. One run, one hit, no errors, one left.

CUBS—Nicholson was out, York to Newhouser, on a close play at first. Livingston singled to left and reached second on a wild pitch into the dirt. Hughes walked. Secory batted for Erickson and was called out on strikes. Hack forced Livingston at third, Outlaw unassisted. No runs, one hit, no errors, two left.

EIGHTH INNING

TIGERS—Passeau went to the mound for the Cubs. Webb walked. Mayo doubled down the left-field line, scoring Webb. Cramer was out, Johnson to Cavarretta, Mayo taking third. Greenberg hit a terrific liner to Lowrey in left, Mayo easily scoring after the catch. Cullenbine popped to Johnson. Two runs, one hit, no errors, none left.

CUBS—Johnson went out, Webb to York. Lowrey singled to left. Cavarretta drove a single through the box, sending Lowrey to third. Pafko struck out. A foul struck Catcher Richards on the hand and he retired to the dugout for treatment. Swift took his place for the Tigers because the little finger of Richards' right hand was broken. Nicholson doubled to center, scoring Lowrey and sending Cavarretta to third. Livingston struck

Continued on Page 19, Column 4

TOMMY HOLMES

Rickey Signs Negro Amid Complications

FIRST SQUAWK—The thing about the Jackie Robinson story today that strikes right out and hits you between the eyes is that the first Negro ever to be signed to a contract in Organized Baseball may be blocked from a bona-fide test by members of his own race.

The Kansas City Monarchs, for whom Robinson played this Summer, are preparing a formal protest to Commissioner Happy Chandler. They do not like the fact that our Mr. Branch Rickey signed their star ball player to a contract with the Montreal Royals, No. 1 farm club of the Dodgers.

Branch Rickey

Whether the Commissioner of Baseball will deem it unfair practice to sign a player under contract to a club in an established Negro league remains to be seen. If he upholds the protest, it may be years before another opportunity opens up for a Negro in Organized Baseball again.

PROSPECT—From all accounts, Robinson is an able prospect, of much greater all-around accomplishment than the average recruit to professional ball.

Georgia-born and 26 years old, Robinson is college-trained. He compiled a great all-around athletic record at U. C. L. A., specializing as a football halfback. He entered the army as a private and came out a second lieutenant. His service included 31 months overseas.

He played in the Negro league this Summer, and the three Dodger ivory hunters who scouted him rate him A-1 as a shortstop prospect. Granting that their estimate is correct, Robinson represents for his race an ideal candidate to crash through the invisible color line in what, from time to time, has been called our national pastime.

Placed with Brooklyn's farm at Montreal, he would make his debut in reasonably salubrious surroundings. There is less race prejudice on the other side of the Canadian border.

The International League, too, is distinctly a Northern circuit except for Baltimore, where the culture, if that's what you want to call it, is definitely Southern. Because Baltimore is on this side of the Potomac, it was on the winning side in the Civil War, but Maryland was one of the slave States.

In spite of all the favorable auspices, it won't be easy for Robinson. It wouldn't be easy if he had all that talent plus Paul Robeson's baritone voice.

HEADACHES—Probably, the first headache will come next Spring if Robinson reports for Spring training. That will be in Daytona Beach, Fla., and anyone who has ever traveled that far South can't help but wonder just how things can be arranged. Fundamental things, such as where Jackie will sleep and where he will eat. Not to mention what traveling accommodations they'll let him have in deepest Dixie.

Those problems would exist, perhaps to a lesser extent, after the regular season started. Should Robinson be graduated to the Dodgers, how would the club board and feed him on the road, especially in such quasi-Southern cities as St. Louis and Cincinnati?

The situation might lead to trouble with white ball players, particularly Southern ball players, but that possibility has never loomed as a bar to the Negro in baseball as much as the other social problems involved. These are not social problems peculiar to baseball, but problems that exist in the form of barriers against the Negro of greater or lesser extent everywhere in the land.

REACTION—Just what the reaction to Rickey's move will be among baseball people generally is not yet clear.

Horace Stoneham of the Giants applauded Rickey's action and said his club would scout Negro teams next season. "But we have hundreds of returning service men, and only if they fail to make the grade will we have room for new players."

In a recent statement to a committee appointed by Mayor LaGuardia to study the problem, Larry MacPhail of the Yankees, while declaring that the Negro was entitled to a better deal in baseball, said he had no intention of signing Negro players, at present.

MacPHAIL'S POINT—He took the view that signing Negroes at the present time would do the cause of Negro baseball more harm than good. He pointed out that Negro baseball is now a $2,000,000 business and Negro clubs pay salaries ranging up to $16,000 a year.

He pointed out that comparatively few good young Negro players were being developed. He feared that if Organized Baseball raided the Negro leagues and took their good young players, the Negro leagues would fold, the investments of the club owners would be lost and a lot of professional Negro ball players will lose their jobs.

The boss man of the Kansas City Monarchs seems to be thinking along the same lines.

FIGHT RESULTS

SALEM, Mass.—Joe Cellette, 139, Providence, R. I., decisioned Florent Desmarais, 139, Manchester, N. H. (10); Jackie Carroll, 127, Lawrence, knocked out Charley Celeste, 129, Boston (6); Don Goulette, 127, Lynn, stopped Johnny Bats, 136, Boston (3); Bob Haley, 154, Marblehead, stopped Sal Lupo, 150, Boston (3); Johnny Parvia, 144, Boston, decisioned Sammy Martin, 142, U. S. Navy (4).

BANGOR, Me.—Lloyd Hudson, 125, Bath, and Blond Tiger, 128, Lowell, Mass., drew (8); Bob Pooler, 142, Portland, decisioned Tiger Kid Roy, 140, Lowell, Mass. (6); Al Wooster, 138, Frankfort, knocked out Eddie George, 136, Bangor (2); Charlie Wooster, 136, Frankfort, decisioned Eddie Berry, 132, Portland (6); Mickey O'Brien, 146, Bangor, stopped Babe Querion, 146, Waterville (1).

JERSEY CITY — Dom Amoroso, 135¼, Jersey City, won an unpopular decision over Frankie Leta, 135, Irvington, N. J. (8). Police gave Referee Harry Coplin an escort as he went to the dressing room.

LOS ANGELES — Larry Bolvin, Providence, R. I., punched his way to a decision over Battling Rosando, Mexico City (6).

HARTFORD, Conn.—Pat Brady, 129, New York, stopped Mario Colon, 131, Puerto Rico (7); Bobby Polowitzer, 127, East Hartford, and Allie Minutoli, 128, New York, drew (8).

WHITE PLAINS, N. Y.—Lew Woods, 157, Detroit, used an effective left hand to stab out a decision over Coolidge Miller, 166¼, Brooklyn (8); Francisco Garcia, 119, Puerto Rico, knocked out Jimmy Jennette, 118, Lexington, Ky. (4); Freddie Yaeger, 135, Rochester, N. Y., stopped John Gebert, 134, Freeport, N. Y. (3); Al Galguet, 167, Newark, N. J., outpointed John Harvey, Port Chester, N. Y. (6); Tony Pontillo, 129, New York, outpointed Joey Dell, 127¾, New Haven, Conn. (4); Oscar Williams, 127, New York, outpointed Bennie Daniels, 129, New York (4).

BASEBALL LAUGHS

By HAROLD C. BURR

Fred Haney was a young third baseman with the Detroit Tigers and came into the Yankee Stadium in September without a single home run to his credit. He had read that morning in the papers that Babe Ruth had 49 circuit clouts.

"But in the first inning I lifted a fly ball over the low parapet in right field for my first big league four-master," said Haney. "When the Babe came jogging in to the Yankee bench at the end of the inning he had to pass third base. 'Well, you big ape,' I couldn't resist the temptation to ride him, 'I'm only 48 behind you.

"Ruth didn't say a word. But he came up in the fifth round and hit one a country mile beneath the scoreboard atop the center field bleachers. He had to pass me on his way around the bases. He didn't glance up as he rounded the bag. But I heard what he said.

"'How we stand now, kid?' he asked innocently."

Negro Ace Standout Prospect

Quakers, Rested, Set to Spring Trap On Navy Saturday

Riblett Concedes Middies' T Is Confusing But Penn Team Will Enter Fray a 14-Point Favorite

Opportunist Navy is up against its first big gridiron test Saturday when it dons its bell-bottom trousers and journeys up from Crabtown to Franklin Field, Philadelphia, to play football before an expected 73,000 turnout against a team of Quakers who are not only unbeaten, but unscored upon this Fall. Some experts contend that Penn is mightier than any embryo admiral's sword.

George Munger

"I'll beat the Army or Navy this year," brashly predicted Coach George Munger of the Pennsylvanians before the start of the pigskin parade. Munger is bedded in the hospital with the grippe and will miss Saturday's game after all.

But Hirohito, Yamashita, Tojo and a lot of other silly Japs said much the same thing after Pearl Harbor and they ended up in their own end zone without the ball.

Penn Tackles Strong

Penn State and Georgia Tech found out the past two weekends that the Middies are always on watch. It's suicide to fumble on the alert Sailors. They pounce on a loose ball like Simon Legree's bloodhounds. But Navy doesn't figure to get many such breaks against Penn's well-coached eleven.

Navy is weak at the tackles where Penn is strongest. Bo Coppedge and Chuck Kiser are the Annapolis tackles who will lock horns with the 252-pound George Savitsky and Doug Reicherbach. Navy is improving at the positions, but those same tackles must find themselves Saturday if Navy continues down the field.

"Their T is hard to stop," reports Paul Riblett, former pro Dodger, who scouted Navy in the dark at Baltimore last Saturday night in the Georgia Tech game. "It's a strong team physically and wide-awake both on the defense and offense," added Paul.

But the lights were bad at Baltimore. Even the officials had their troubles following plays. Coach Oscar Hagberg's T is still in its chrystals. Perhaps it will burst through its cocoon at Franklin Field. It certainly hasn't been any formation in Technicolor to date.

Lacked Cohesion

Navy backs have been floundering in a heavy sea, indulging in what Rip Miller calls fighting the defense, gridiron terminology for trying to do the spectacular instead of working methodically to grind out the yardage.

Munger is a wise old coach. He has been at it steadily since 1933. He missed Monday's practice for the first time in his long career, being taken down with chills Friday night, but not, however, from thinking about Navy. He has a wealth of material. Penn didn't startle the football world with its 12 to 0 win over green Dartmouth. But Munger knows how to bring his team to the peak for the game he wants to win. He has a brighter chance to make good his boast of knocking over one of the service teams by taking Navy than he has to beat Army.

Penn is in the best physical shape. It has had a two-week rest while Navy was battling an unexpectedly rugged outfit from Georgia Tech in the Second Battle of Gettysburg. Smackover Scott injured his tender ankle all over again against Tech, but insists that he will get in against Penn. Kiser has a slight sprain he's nursing. Bob Jenkins is, of course, definitely out of the Franklin Field fracas.

Duden Alert Boy

Navy's line was the heavy scorer at Baltimore and against Penn State. It scored two touchdowns and a safety at the expense of the Nittany Lions and tallied the first in the Tech game and set up the third. Dick Duden, the end converted from the backfield, scored in each game when he intercepted a forward pass and blocked a kick.

The bookies, astute gentlemen without a spark of sentiment in their hard-boiled makeup, have installed Penn favorite, with 14 Red and Blue points. Navy is gathering its latent strength to give Army a battle on the same field Dec. 1, but slowly. It's a team that will add cohesion to its power as it goes staggering along. So far, it has avoided anything approximating defeat with its heads-up football.

BURR.

'Not Worried About Robinson, He's Not With Us'—Walker

Birmingham, Ala., Oct. 24 (U.P.)—Fred (Dixie) Walker, Brooklyn Dodgers' outfielder, said today the signing of Negro shortstop Jackie Robinson by the Dodgers' Montreal club didn't worry him.

"As long as he isn't with the Dodgers," the former National League batting champion said, "I'm not worried."

Atlanta, Ga., Oct. 24 (U.P.)—Rudy York, Detroit first baseman and a native Georgian, said today he could not get excited about the signing of Jackie Robinson, a Negro, by Montreal.

"I wish him all the luck in the world and hope he makes good," York said.

Birmingham, Ala., Oct. 24 (U.P.)—Spud Davis, catcher-coach for the Pittsburgh Pirates, said today there was no need for him to worry about Montreal's signing Jackie Robinson, Negro shortstop.

"So long as the Pittsburgh club hasn't signed a Negro, there's no need for me to worry now," Davis said.

Sellout Expected For Ice Inaugural

Boston, Oct. 24 (U.P.) — The Chicago Blackhawks and the Boston Bruins open the National Hockey League season tonight before an expected sellout crowd.

The Blackhawks, strengthened by the return of many prewar stars from the services, were slight favorites. Their first line of Doug Bentley, his brother Max, and Bill Mosienko was rated as perhaps the fastest in the league. It was expected to make up for defensive weakness.

The Bruins, who also have prewar players in the lineup, were counted on to be in the game all the way.

Montreal won the regular season championship last year, but Toronto won the Stanley Cup.

LaMotta Hands Gomez First Kayo of Career

Joe LaMotta, 156½, Bronx, knocked out Indian Gomez, 163, Havana, in 2:41 of the second round of a scheduled eight-round main bout at the Park Arena last night. It was the first KO suffered by Gomez.

In the semi-final, Cleo Everett, 202¼, Jacksonville, knocked out Chris Koerkle, 187, Bayonne, at 2:30 of the first of a scheduled eight. In sixes, George Smith, 148¾, Harlem, outpointed Freddy Patterson, 149¼, and Freddie Palermo, 134½, Bronx, outpointed Oscar Lewis, 132, Newark. Bobo Boucher, 7¾, Nebraska City, stopped Steve Palko, 146, Sayerville, two rounds. Johnny King, 153, Harlem, outpointed Charley Howard, 149, Pittsburgh.

Bachelor Fete for Holman

A bachelor dinner for Nat Holman, C. C. N. Y. basketball coach, at the Town Club is scheduled for Nov. 1. Nat will be married to Ruth Jackson the next day.

Loughlin Mermen Triumph Over Tech

Mermen of Bishop Loughlin Memorial High defeated Brooklyn Tech in a swimming meet in the latter's pool yesterday, 36—22. Capt. Bill Irwin of Loughlin won two events.

50-yard freestyle—Won by Mullooley, Loughlin; Murphy, Loughlin, second; Schwartz, Tech., third. Time, 0:27.
100-yard freestyle—Won by Nugent, Loughlin; Watson, Loughlin, second; Riley, Tech., third. Time, 1:04.
100-yard breaststroke—Won by Irwin, Loughlin; Nidenberg, Tech., second; Galvin, Loughlin, third. Time, 1:16.
100 backstroke—Won by Bocy, Tech.; Delgato, Loughlin, second; Schurr, Loughlin, third. Time, 1:11.
220 freestyle—Won by Irwin, Loughlin; Simms, Tech., second; Brody, Tech., third. Time, 2:31.
150-yard medley—Won by Loughlin (Delgato, Galvin and Nugent). Time, 1:37.
200-yard freestyle relay—Won by Tech. (Volpi, Kee, Ziflagy and Treversen) Time, 1:52.

HE CRACKED IT—Jack Roosevelt Robinson of UCLA football fame, is signing contract to play shortstop for the Montreal (I. L.) farm of the Dodgers next year. It happened in Montreal. Robinson is the first Negro ever to sign in Organized Baseball.

Mancini Looks Troublesome To Welters

By HAROLD CONRAD

Lenny (Boom Boom) Mancini, who has been going through a metamorphosis from a wounded soldier to a top-notch fighter, made his second local start last night since his discharge from the army and proved that he is not only in as good physical shape as any of his contemporaries, but that he is improving. Lenny met Patsy Spataro, rugged young welterweight from the Bronx, in the eight-round Broadway Arena feature and virtually fought him into a state of exhaustion. Despite the rain, a crowd of 3,900 fans turned out for the show.

When he went into the service almost four years ago as the country's No. 1 lightweight contender, Mancini's forte was stamina. He was a ceaseless puncher who invariably wore down his opponent with a steady attack. After being wounded four times, there was much doubt as to whether he would ever be able to employ his old style again.

Several weeks ago, Mancini decisively outpointed Baby Sims, but the experts, who wanted to be sure, looked forward to the Spataro fight and "Boom-Boom" even showed an improvement over his last start. He was three and a half pounds lighter and hopes to get down to 146 pounds for his next start. He scaled 150¼ last night.

Lenny started punching at the opening bell and never stopped until the end of the fight. Patsy did some counter-punching in the second, which momentarily slowed Mancini up, but from here it was all "Boom-Boom." Ae the end of every round from the fourth, it looked as though Spataro was going to collapse, but he held on gamely and on a few occasions counterattacked.

Sid Haber of Brooklyn won a decision over Patsy Zoccano, Brooklyn, in the six-round semi-final. In other sixers, Tony Del Gatto, South Brooklyn middleweight, outpointed Freddie Lott, Newark, and Lou Perez, Puerto Rico, won over Baudelio Valencia, Mexico.

In the fours, Lou Denton, Pennsylvania middleweight, lost to Benny Davis, Port Chester, and Nate Hutchins, Elizabeth, whipped Jerry Heimowitz, Brooklyn welterweight.

Morris Reif, outstanding welterweight from Brownsville, who meets Al Davis in the Garden next month, goes to the post against Johnny Rinaldi of the Bronx in the Broadway feature Tuesday. Rinaldi is one of the few to hold a decision over Mancini.

'HAPPY TO BE FIRST TO PLAY,' SAYS JACKIE

When interviewed at the signing, Jackie Robinson said yesterday:

"Of course, I can't tell you how happy I am as the first member of my race in organized ball," Jackie said quietly. "I realize how much it means to me, to my race and to baseball. I can only add that I will do my best to come through in every manner."

Boykoff Discharge Soon Peps Indians

By PAUL GOULD

St. John's basketball stock, which skidded to a new low last week with the loss of Bill Kotsores and Ivy Summer, will make a sensational recovery in the next few weeks. Harry Boykoff, the human Empire State Building, is slated to be discharged from the army, the Brooklyn Eagle learned today, and by happy Thanksgiving will be back in Red and White—feeling anything but blue.

Harry Boykoff

The six-foot, nine-inch center is eligible for his walking papers under the same provisions of a recent War Department circular that recast Charles Trippi, the Georgia football star, into a civilian. A member of the armed forces for more than two years, ineligible for overseas duty, and surplus to the needs of the Army, Boykoff will shortly surrender his billy club and M. P. brassard for the pleasure of being guarded by the opposition for a change.

Eligible Year Ago for Release

It was in the Spring of '43 that Boykoff was inducted and assigned to limited duty. His height—long a bane to rivals on the court—proved likewise a problem for the armed forces and he was posted as a guard upstate with his home base West Point. Part of his duties involved walking post at the late President's home at Hyde Park. With the lessening emphasis on continental bases, retrenchment at West Point opened the doors to Harry's release.

Actually, Boykoff was eligible for discharge for a year, but the patriotic impulse that moved him to lie about his height and insure his enlistment was likewise the reason for his refusal to take advantage of a ruling that would have made him a student again. The regulation provided for the release of all GIs who fell "below the standards required for induction." At 6-9, Harry was a 4-F, but he did not apply for his separation.

Enlistment Episode

The story of his enlistment is one of the tingling episodes in the life of this gangling, quiet youth from Brownsvill. When he appeared at the Grand Central Palace, Harry was surveyed by an astonished medico.

"How tall are you?" he asked.

Harry hunched himself over. "Six, six and a half," he said.

The doctor understood. He looked the other way and said in a low voice,

"O. K., son, get your weight."

Six months later, Boykoff returned to Brooklyn to lead a West Point GI team against the Redmen at DeGray gym, scene of some of his phenomenal scoring achievements. He'll be doing ditto in the near future.

Corbo Dodger Prospect

Joe Corbo, who once twirled with the Kendeks of the Brooklyn Kiwanis League, has signed with the Dodgers and will report to their Thomasville, N. C., farm next Spring. Corbo is a right-handed pitcher. He won nine out of 11 Kiwanis games this past season.

ROBINSON WORTH 50 G's, K. C. OWNER SAYS

Kansas City, Mo., Oct. 24 (U.P.)—Tom Baird, co-owner of the Kansas City Monarchs, Negro professional baseball team, said today that Jackie Robinson, signed to play with the Dodgers' Montreal farm team, was worth at least $50,000.

"I talked long distance to our league president, Dr. J. B. Martin, and he will take the matter up with Commissioner Chandler as quickly as possible," Baird said.

"If players are going to be taken from the Negro League, I believe some sort of an arrangement should be worked out between the major leagues and the Negro League. We are not trying to keep any Negro ball player from the major leagues."

Marx's Goal Decides Brooklyn Tech Victory

Playing its second soccer match in 13 years, Brooklyn Tech defeated Erasmus Hall in a P. S. A. L. setto yesterday at Wingate Field, 1 to 0.

It gives the Engineers an even break in two league clashes as they bowed to Thomas Jefferson in the inaugural, 1-0. Howie Marx registered the goal in the second half

The lineup:

Pos.	Tech (1)		Erasmus (0)
G.	Knee		Hittleman
L.F.	Reinish		Sternberg
R.F.	Shapiro		Feldman
L.H.	Gilbert		Witt
C.H.	Bruskan		Faurerbach
R.H.	Larson		Schwartz
O.L.	Bayer		Salyman
O.R.	Kormen		Rosenthal
I.R.	Marx		Lubell
I.L.	Krinsky		Levine
C.F.	Volk		Smithers
Tech	0	1	1
Erasmus	0	0	0

Goal—Marx. Substitutions: Tech—Natkin, Hornens, Buongiorno, Kessler, Barnett. Referee—S. M. Galin.

Dodgers Scouted Robinson for Big-League Role

Deal Made in August —Jackie to Train in Fla. With Flock, Royals

By HAROLD C. BURR

President Branch Rickey of the Brooklyn Dodgers has broken through the color line in signing the first Negro ball player to appear in Organized Baseball in the 70 years of its life. The player who enters through the opened door is Jackie Robinson, shortstop and UCLA football star.

During the 1945 season, Robinson was a member of the Kansas City Monarchs, hitting .340. He came to the Monarchs after serving as a second lieutenant in the army. He was quietly brought to Brooklyn in August. Rickey explained what he had in mind and Jackie agreed to sign Nov. 1.

Robinson was carefully scouted by Tom Greenwade, George Sisler and Clyde Sukeforth, the Rickey bird dogs. The boy was signed yesterday to a Montreal bonus contract, the Brooklyn club's Double A International League farm. But in reality he was scouted as a major league prospect. Robinson will go to the Dodger and Montreal combined training camp at Daytona Beach, Fla., in the Spring.

Jackie previously had received a tryout at Fenway Park, Boston, by the Red Sox. Of the three Negroes tried out on that occasion, Robinson received the most favorable attention from Manager Joe Cronin. But the Red Sox made no attempt to sign him and the Dodger scouts took over and reported to Rickey that he was the best of the Negro prospects.

May Cost Club Players

"Mr. Racine and my father," Branch Jr. said, "will undoubtedly be severely criticized in some sections of the country where racial prejudice is rampant. They are not inviting trouble, but they won't avoid it if it comes. Robinson is a fine type of young man, intelligent and college-bred."

Young Rickey admitted that the move might cost the Dodgers a number of ball players.

"Some of them, particularly those who come from certain sections of the South, will steer away from a club with a Negro player on its roster. Some players now with us may even quit, but they'll be back in baseball after they work a year or two in a cotton mill."

Racine, whose Montreal team won the International League's regular-season championship, said he expected no opposition either from the league or from fans. "Negroes fought alongside whites and shared the foxhole dangers," he said, "and they should get a fair trial in baseball."

Jack Roosevelt Robinson is 26 years old. He weighs 190 pounds, stands 5 feet, 11½ inches tall.

At UCLA, Robinson received numerous nominations for All-American honors in 1940 and again in 1941. He played in the 1942 All-Star game at Soldier Field, Chicago, and went to Honolulu for another All-Star game, and took part in about a dozen pro football games in the Coast League. He went into the army as a private in April, 1942, attended Officers' Training School and was commissioned a second lieutenant in November, 1942. Early this year, he was given an inactive status.

The signing of Robinson produced a wave of wild reports. Among them was a yarn that the Dodgers had 25 other Negro prospects in mind. The Mahatma made haste to enter his denial.

Will Continue to Scout

"I haven't 25 prospects," declared Mr. Rickey. "The number I have in mind is nowhere comparable to that figure. I will continue to scout Negro talent. I know of no reason why I shouldn't go after any ball players regardless of color. If I thought it would hurt the Negro, or our players, I wouldn't have done it.

Mr. Rickey was asked about the problem of living and traveling while the Royals are on the road.

"The boy himself answered that question. 'I wouldn't want to go where I'm not welcome,' was the way he put it."

The president of the Dodgers explained why he hadn't broken ground before.

Blasts Griffith

"When I was in St. Louis Negroes were not allowed in the grandstand. Hence I could not arrange for tryouts. If I was in authority, I would have changed that. I got the idea when I came to Brooklyn after watching Negro teams play at Ebbets Field. Baseball is a game played by human beings, regardless of color, and I want to have winning baseball."

President Clark Griffith gave out a statement in Washington condemning Rickey for raiding an organized professional league. Rickey came back with a hot retort.

"The Negro leagues, as they are today constituted, are in the nature of a racket and Griffiths knows that. History will record that Mr. Griffith introduced Negro ball in the major leagues. I want to help the Negro leagues organize. I'm doing this in spite of outside interests and pressure groups who are exploiting the Negro rather than helping him."

Rickey said he had a heavy telegram reaction, mostly favorable.

Boro Leaders Support Rickey's Move

'Proper Step,' Says Mons. Campion; Dream Comes True—Wibecan

George Wibecan, one of Brooklyn's outstanding Negro leaders, was awakened from a deep slumber to be notified that the Brooklyn Dodger baseball organization had signed Jackie Robinson, a Negro shortstop.

"I was in the midst of a beautiful dream," said Mr. Wibecan, "and this great news makes me wonder if I'm still asleep.

"It's the beginning of something we hoped and dreamed would develop: that we could participate with other racial groups on an equal footing. It's in line with the trend of the times," he added.

Monsignor Raymond J. Campion, pastor of the St. Peter Claver Roman Catholic Church, whose parish includes many Negro communicants, was "delighted that Branch Rickey of the Dodgers has shown the way.

"I have always been confident that Mr. Rickey, in the best interests of baseball, would take proper steps to eliminate racial prejudice in selecting players.

Clarence Wilson, assistant district attorney, expressed his appreciation. "I am delighted that Branch Rickey has taken the first practical step in eliminating discrimination in baseball. Every Negro will be grateful to him."

Mrs. Effa Manley, who with her husband, Abe, control the Newark Eagles of the Negro National League, refused to discuss the signing of Robinson until she knows more about the circumstances.

"Robinson is the property of the Kansas City Monarchs and until I know his status in the matter, I will have to remain silent," declared Mrs. Manley.

Not Familiar With Move—Mack

Philadelphia, Oct. 24 (U.P.)—Connie Mack, veteran manager of the Athletics, was non-committal when informed of the Dodgers' action in signing Jackie Robinson for their Montreal farm club.

Mack said "I am not familiar with the move and don't know Robinson. I wouldn't care to comment."

Phillies officials were unavailable. General Manager Herb Pennock is in Miami, Fla., checking the club's training quarters.

Wichita, Kans., Oct. 24 (U.P.)—Ray Dumont, president of the National Baseball Congress, said he believed the large number of Negro performers on service teams during the war period was responsible for the admission to organized baseball of Jackie Robinson.

He noted that nearly one-half of the service teams which played in State and national semi-pro competition had one or more Negro players on their rosters.

Clubhouse Quarters Tremble as Cardinals Put On Wild Victory Celebration

JOYOUS MATES MOB HEROES OF TRIUMPH

Cards Manhandle Brecheen, Slaughter, Moore and Walker in Riotous Demonstration

DYER ELATED, HAILS CLUB

'Deserved to Win,' the Skipper Says—Cronin Is Downcast —Pesky Feels He's 'Goat'

By JAMES P. DAWSON
Special to THE NEW YORK TIMES.

ST. LOUIS, Oct. 15—What happened in the clubhouse of the triumphant Cardinals after their world series victory today almost beggars description.

It was risking life and limb to be there. The wildest scene imaginable was being enacted in the immediate flush of a victory that had been unlooked for among the majority of experts and baseball's skilled craftsmen.

A partition was shattered. Caps, gloves, shirts, towels, belts flew all over the place. Under the rumble and roar of the conquerors, their quarters vibrated and shook. Players were trampled. Commissioner Happy Chandler was trampled. So was President Ford Frick of the National League, who then was hoisted aloft on the shoulders of Slats Marion and Clyde Kluttz. President Will Harridge of the American League was elbowed and jostled.

Joe Cronin, manager of the beaten Red Sox, had to fight his way through the noisy mob to extend to a dazed-looking Eddie Dyer the traditional congratulations of the vanquished for the victor.

Victors Call for "Beer"

There were cries for "beer, a bottle of beer," for training rules were off now. Soft drinks were forgotten. The victors wanted to celebrate and were starting before doffing their uniforms. Movie lights made the place insufferably hot. Bottles were knocked from their perches. Nobody cared. This was celebration time.

It was celebration time for everybody, that is, but little Joe Garagiola, the freshman catcher who played such a prominent part in this latest Cardinal triumph. He was in the rubbing room of Doc Weaver for treatment of the injured finger on his right hand.

Enos Slaughter's ailing right arm was exposed to greater injury in the crush. Hobbling Terry Moore was mobbed. So was Harry Walker, "little brother" of Dixie.

The adulation which started for Harry Brecheen on the field, when he was raised aloft on the shoulders of his mates, was intensified when the players reached their locker room, where Brecheen escaped injury only by a miracle.

Manager Dyer was beside himself. He never stopped smiling. His arm was weary from hand-shaking. Half an hour after the game, Dyer had not yet started doffing his uniform.

"We never lost a game we had to win," said Dyer. "What a series! What a victory! I'm glad we won for myself. It justifies the confidence of a lot of fine people who had faith and thought I could manage a ball club.

"It was a marvelous victory. We beat a great ball club. But I think we deserved to win. We proved ourselves the better outfit. That's not taking anything away from the Red Sox.

"The boys deserve all the credit. They're a fine gang. It's a wonderful feeling for me to see them come out on top after a tough season. That little 'Cat.' He's great, isn't he? A grand little fellow, and what pitching courage. This is one of the happiest moments of my life. That goes for my boys, too. When you beat a good team like those Sox you've done something."

Slaughter modestly dismissed his victory run as in the nature of routine play. "I just had to run, that was all," he said. "Mike (Gonzales) gave me the green light. He was watching the ball. He knew what could be expected. And I just dug in and tore for home. I had to make it. It was the Sox's responsibility to head me off. The odds were riding with me."

Hit a Low Pitch

"I hit a low pitch that was sinking in that eighth inning," said Walker. "Say, this is the biggest thrill of my life, driving in that winning run. With Columbus in 1941 I broke up the little world series with a home run that made me feel pretty good. But that was nothing compared to this. What a game! What a finish!"

Outside, close to 1,000 fans, men and women, clogged the approach to the clubhouse, waiting to shower praise upon their baseball heroes.

About sixty feet away was a scene of desolation. It was the quarters of the beaten Sox. They were "down" after absorbing a beating in the series which most of the experts predicted they would win, some even in four or five games.

Johnny Pesky regarded himself as the "goat." He had delayed on the relay which followed Walker's game-winning hit, long enough to let Slaughter slide home with the winning run.

"I'm the goat," he said. "I never expected he'd try to score, I couldn't hear anybody hollering at me above the noise of the crowd. I gave Slaughter at least six strides with the delay. I know I could have nailed him if I had suspected he would try for the plate. I'm the 'goat.' No mistake about that."

Ted Williams could smile, but only in a flash. He felt keenly the defeat of his club, the manacles Cardinal pitching had placed on his batting power through the series. Dave (Boo) Ferriss was saddened. He wanted so much to win that decisive game.

"I felt all right. I had my stuff.

Continued on Page 38, Column 1

Plays That Helped Decide Final Game of Series as Cardinals Took World Championship

Slaughter sliding across the plate safely after running all the way from first on Walker's double with two out in the eighth inning. Catching for Boston is Partee and waiting his turn at bat is Marion. The umpire is Barlick.

Doerr is forced at second on Higgins' bunt to Kurowski. Marion, who made the play, relayed the ball to first in an attempted double play in the midst of a Red Sox ninth inning rally.

The winners are all smiles as they celebrate the victory in their clubhouse. Left to right: Slaughter, Walker, Brecheen and Manager Dyer.

Associated Press Wirephotos

CARDS TAKE SERIES, BEAT RED SOX, 4 TO 3

Continued From Page 1

dash, the inspired National League champions, with the aid of a brilliant piece of relief pitching by Harry (the Cat) Brecheen, swept to victory in the only game of the seven that had seen them move in front in the series.

Three times they had gone down to defeat as they lost the first, third and fifth encounters. Three times they had drawn even, but when they finally shot ahead they did it on an occasion which left their baffled adversaries with no rebuttal.

As for Joe Cronin and his no longer glittering Bosox, they left the field a sadly dejected and disillusioned lot. Overwhelmingly favored at the outset to win in jig time over a rival who had just come through a gruelling pennant race and an unprecedented two-game play-off, the renowned sluggers from Boston not only failed to make it short, but finished badly winded behind the eight ball. To add to their mental anxiety, they gained the added dubious distinction of becoming the first Boston club ever to lose a World Series.

Deadlock Broken in Fifth

However, they did go down fighting in as torrid a struggle as any classic has ever seen. It was a struggle that back in the fifth, with the score tied at 1-all, saw bedlam turned loose as the aroused Redbirds blasted big Dave Ferriss from the mound with a four-hit two-run attack.

That gave Murry Dickson, slick St. Louis right-hander, a 3-1 lead. Murry himself had helped spark that drive with a surprise two-bagger.

But in a turbulent eighth the Bosox surged back, routed Dickson and scored two tallies to tie as Dominic DiMaggio whacked the incoming Brecheen for a resounding double. However, this simply wasn't the Bosox' day. On the play that was to take them back into the ball game, DiMaggio pulled a muscle in his left leg and had to leave the field.

As a consequence it wasn't the flawlessly fielding "Little Professor" who was in center field when Walker hit the double that scored Slaughter from first base a few minutes later. Instead it was Leon Culberson and while the latter fielded it well enough he isn't a DiMaggio. Little Dominic might have managed it better and kept Slaughter on third.

Behind again, the American Leaguers suddenly found the door closed for good. Desperately they fought back in the ninth. Their renowned clouter, Ted Williams, had failed them badly again, going hitless in four official tries at the plate, but in this last ditch stand the still redoubtable Ruddy York singled and so did Bobby Doerr.

They even advanced a runner to third with only one out, but at that point Breechen took complete command. He had beaten the Sox in two complete games previously and was determined to win the third. He retired the next two batters and with that became the ninth hurler in world series history to win three games, the last having been Stanley Coveleskie in 1920 when he pitched the Indians to victory over the Dodgers.

Hornsby in Press Box

So to the Cardinals, most successful of all National League teams in these inter-league conflicts, went their sixth world championship against three setbacks in a twenty-year span that began in 1926 when Rogers Hornsby, who watched today's game from the press box, directed the Redbirds to their first title over the Yankees.

It also marked the Cards' fourth victory in a series requiring seven games to decide. Never have they been beaten in one of these marathon struggles.

To Dyer, who emerged from retirement last winter to accept his first major league managerial post after having spent years directing minor league clubs in the Cards' far-flung farm system, went the distinction of becoming the fifth St. Louis pilot to skipper a world series victory.

Following Hornsby's initial triumph in 1926, there was Gabby Street, whose 1931 Cardinal overthrow of the powerful Athletics was an upset comparable with the one the Redbirds achieved this year. In 1934 Frankie Frisch led the famous Gashouse Gang to victory over the Tigers, and then came Billy Southworth to win two, leading the Redbirds over the Yankees in another upset in 1942, and downing the Browns in 1944.

Pattern of 1940 Followed

Threading their way to final victory, the Cardinals followed a pattern seen only once before in world series history. That was in 1940 when the Reds, losing the first, third and fifth games to the Tigers, drew even three times and went on to win the seventh and deciding engagement for the only time they were to show in front.

It also marked the seventh time a National League club triumphed in the ten series to go to seven games. However, in total victories the American Leaguers still are far in the van, for this was only the senior loop's seventeenth title since the modern classic began in 1903 while the American League has bagged twenty-six.

Receipts today, hitting $156,379, raised the total for the seven games to $1,052,900, to make this the sixteenth million-dollar series.

The weather again was at its very finest, a brilliant autmun sun slanting through fleecy white clouds while the thermometer hovered in the temperate seventies.

And the fans, captivated by the gallant uphill struggle their Cards had made throughout the series, cut loose with a lusty cheer as Ferriss, strapping righthander and 25-game winner for the Bosox, and Dickson, the Redbirds' stout-hearted clutch pitcher, began their decisive mound struggle.

Back in Boston last Wednesday the same pair had met in the pivotal third game which Ferriss captured with a shut-out after York had floored Dickson with a three-run homer in the first inning.

There were ominous sounds at the outset. Wally Moses opened the Sox' first inning with a single and a moment later swept around to third as Johnny Pesky's bounding ball over second slipped just beyond Marty Marion's long reach and rolled into centerfield for another single.

On the heels of that followed a long fly by DiMaggio that sent Moses scampering over the plate and the Sox had one tally. They threatened more as Williams, still striving desperately to connect with one long-range blow after being held to five singles in the first six games, lifted a t[illegible]ering smash into deep center.

It was pretty much unprotected territory, for in the Card outer defenses against Thumping Ted two fielders played far to the right and only Walker remained on the left side. But Terry Moore, forgetting his years and racing with all the speed he could get out of his aging legs, caught the ball with a final lunge. Pesky, who had gone all the way to second, confident this would be a hit, had to do some tall stepping back to first.

York Lifts Infield Pop

Then the still-feared York, who had so thoroughly wrecked Dickson's otherwise fine effort in Boston, lifted a harmless infield fly and the crowd unloosed more cheers. A lone tally was all the vaunted Bosox had extracted from this inviting beginning.

There were more roars as Red Schoendienst opened the Cardinal first inning with a sharp single. When Williams momentarily fumbled, the lean Redbird streaked for second, but Ted made a quick recovery and with a fine throw nailed Schoendienst on a close play.

It proved a tough break for the St. Louisans. Though Moore popped out, Stan Musial sent a whistling drive down the left-field foul line for a double that would have scored Schoendienst easily had the latter still been on the base paths. Instead, the Cards drew a blank as Ferriss curved a strike past Enos Slaughter.

The second opened with the gathering again experiencing some uneasy moments when Doerr outgalloped an infield hit and grabbed an extra base on a wide throw to first by Whitey Kurowski. Though an infield out by Pinky Higgins advanced the runner to third, Dickson refused to give any further ground.

The plucky little right-hander, who scales 155 pounds, held Hal Wagner to a fly in short left which kept Doerr glued to third. Then he effaced Ferriss on the end of another fly ball to end this threat.

There was a great ovation for Dickson as he walked to the dugout, but scarcely had those cheers subsided before the stands again went into a turmoil as Kurowski opened the Cardinal second with a two-bagger in left center. This time the Redbirds did not miss their mark.

As Joe Garagiola went out on an infield roller to Doerr, Kurowski moved on to third. When Walker lifted a high fly to Williams in deep left Whitey streaked home with the tying run.

The cheers then were deafening enough, but the noise was scarcely a whisper compared with the din that went up in the fifth when the Redbirds exploded an offensive that sent Ferriss from the mound.

As had been the case so many times this year, the Cardinal attack began quietly enough. Walker opened with a single, but when Dyer cautiously ordered Marion to sacrifice this didn't presage an overwhelming assault. In fact, it wasn't a move many managers would have made with the pitcher the next batter.

Dickson a Hitting Pitcher

But Dickson is cast along slightly different lines. Like nearly all Cardinals, whether they be pitchers, catchers or bat boys, this slim native Missourian is a versatile ball player and an extremely dangerous hitter when a blow really means something. Hadn't he helped win a big game from the Cubs in that sizzling pennant race with a single? He certainly had, although the Sox seemed to have forgotten about it.

This time Dickson did even better. He drove a two-bagger down the left-field line and the crowd really turned it on as Walker rounded third and dashed for home to put the St. Louisans ahead.

Scarcely had the Sox recovered from this shock when Schoendienst gave them another as he larruped a single into center to drive in Dickson.

The stands were in a terrific uproar and there was no abatement when Moore followed with another single to center. That was all for Ferriss, and Joe Dobson, who had won the fifth game for the Sox with a surprisingly fine effort, left the bullpen. Joe still had a few surprises left and brought the Redbird attack to an end.

However, the Cards were two runs in front and the folks were supremely happy. To add to their enjoyment, Walker and Moore made a couple of sparkling fielding plays in the following innings.

Dark moments were still to come, though, and when they arrived in the eighth, they struck with startling swiftness. From the third through the seventh, Dickson had not allowed a hit.

But the Bosox still had a few shots left and they cut loose with them as the eighth opened. Glen Russell, hitting for Wagner, singled to center. Having met with striking success there, Cronin called on George Metkovich to bat for Dobson and drew an even better result. Metkovich hammered a double into left and the Sox had runners on second and third, with no one down.

In the twinkling of an eye the entire situation, so rosy a few moments before, had changed completely. Reluctantly Dyer waved Dickson from the mound and called up Brecheen, brilliant southpaw, who had allowed the Sox only one run in winning the second and sixth games.

There were new cheers as Brecheen fanned Moses and then retired Pesky on a short fly to Slaughter, on which Russell dared not try to score from third. But bespectacled DiMaggio slammed a double off the right-field wall, Russell and Metkovich raced across the plate and the great conflict again was in a deadlock.

Highlight of Boston Bid

This was to prove the highlight of the Bosox' bid to win a world title for Owner Tom Yawkey, who in thirteen years had spent fabulous sums to produce a winner. DiMaggio, limping badly, left the field because of his pulled muscle and Culberson ran for him. Leon did not have far to run. Williams, again utterly helpless before Cardinal pitching, fouled out to Musial.

Just before ending the inning, Ted hit a foul tip that split a finger on Catcher Garagiola's right hand, and Del Rice had to replace the injured backstop. The wounded at this point were falling left and right.

But there was no checking Slaughter, as he winged to victory in the lower half of the same round on Walker's double, the Cards' ninth hit of the day. For that matter, there was no overhauling any of the Redbirds then.

After the York and Doerr singles had opened Boston's ninth, Brecheen coolly turned back the next three on infield taps. With that, the curtain rang down on a season that at one time had threatened never to end.

The Cards, as they had so many times this year, again proved themselves to be a club which, if not one of the greatest, certainly must take rank with the most courageous. They had come through a sizzling pennant race to eliminate the Dodgers in a historic play-off, and then, after coming behind three times, overthrew a cast which, by reason of a smashing American League victory, had been looked upon as a certain world series victor.

They did it, too, with Skipper Dyer, who had never managed a major league club before. Startling things will happen in baseball and a lot of them happened this year.

Series Box Score

SEVENTH GAME

BOSTON RED SOX

	AB.	R.	H.	PO.	A.	E.
Moses, rf	4	1	1	1	0	0
Pesky, ss	4	0	1	2	1	0
DiMaggio, cf	3	0	1	0	0	0
Culberson, cf	0	0	0	0	0	0
Williams, lf	4	0	0	3	1	0
York, 1b	4	0	1	10	1	0
cCampbell	0	0	0	0	0	0
Doerr, 2b	4	0	2	3	7	0
Higgins, 3b	4	0	0	0	1	0
H. Wagner, c	2	0	0	4	0	0
aRussell	1	1	1	0	0	0
Partee, c	1	0	0	0	0	0
Ferriss, p	2	0	0	0	0	0
Dobson, p	0	0	0	0	1	0
bMetkovich	1	1	1	0	0	0
Klinger, p	0	0	0	1	0	0
Johnson, p	0	0	0	0	0	0
dMcBride	1	0	0	0	0	0
Total	35	3	8	24	12	0

ST. LOUIS CARDINALS

	AB.	R.	H.	PO.	A.	E.
Schoendienst 2b	4	0	2	2	3	0
Moore, cf	4	0	1	3	0	0
Musial, 1b	3	0	1	6	0	0
Slaughter, rf	3	1	1	4	0	0
Kurowski, 3b	4	1	1	3	1	1
Garagiola, c	3	0	0	4	0	0
Rice, c	1	0	0	0	0	0
Walker, lf	3	1	2	3	0	0
Marion, ss	2	0	0	2	1	0
Dickson, p	3	1	1	0	1	0
Brecheen, p	1	0	0	0	0	0
Total	31	4	9	27	6	1

aBatted for H. Wagner in eighth.
bBatted for Dobson in eighth.
cRan for York in ninth.
dBatted for Johnson in ninth.

Boston	1	0	0	0	0	0	0	2	0	—3
St. Louis	0	1	0	0	2	0	0	1	..	—4

Runs batted in—DiMaggio 3, Walker 2, Dickson, Schoendienst.

Two-base hits—Musial, Kurowski, Dickson, DiMaggio, Metkovich, Walker. Sacrifice—Marion. Earned runs—Boston 3, St. Louis 4. Left on bases Boston 6, St. Louis 8. Bases on Balls—Off Ferriss 1 (Musial); Dobson 2 (Slaughter, Walker); Dickson 1 (DiMaggio; Klinger 1 (Marion. Struck out—By Ferriss 2 (Slaughter, Dickson); Dickson 3 (DiMaggio, York 2); Brecheen 1 (Moses); Dobson 2 (Garagiola, Schoendienst).

Pitching summary—Off Ferriss, 7 hits, 3 runs in 4 1/3 innings; Dobson 0 hits, 0 runs in 2 2/3. Klinger 2 hits, 1 run in 2/3; Johnson 0 hits, 0 runs in 1/3; Dickson 5 hits, 3 runs in 7 (none out in 8th); Brecheen 3 hits, 0 runs in 2. Winning pitcher—Brecheen. Losing pitcher—Klinger.

Umpires—Barlick (NL), plate; Berry (AL), 1b; Ballanfant (NL), 2b; Hubbard (AL), 3b). Time of game—2:17. Attendance—36,143.

36,143 Pay $156,379 At Final Series Game

By The Associated Press.

Final Standing of Clubs

	W.	L.	Pc.
St. Louis (N)	4	3	.571
Boston (A)	3	4	.429

Seventh Game Statistics

Paid attendance—36,143.
Gross receipts—$156,379.
Commissioner's share — $23,456.85.
Each club's share—$33,230.54.
Each league's share — $33,230.54.

Seven-Game Totals

Paid attendance—250,071.
Gross receipts—$1,052,920.
*Players' share—$304,141.25.
Commissioner's share — $157,934.
Each club's share — $147,965.98.
Each league's share — $147,965.98.

*Players participate in receipts of first four games only.

Composite Score of World Series Games

BOSTON RED SOX

	G	AB	R	H	2B	3B	HR	RBI	BB	SO	Bat Avg	PO	A	E	Fldg Avg
*McBride, rf	5	12	0	2	0	0	0	1	0	1	.167	4	0	1	.800
Moses, rf	4	12	1	5	0	0	0	0	1	2	.417	5	0	0	1.000
Pesky, ss	7	30	2	7	0	0	0	0	1	3	.233	13	16	4	.879
DiMaggio, cf	7	27	2	7	3	0	0	3	2	2	.259	19	3	0	1.000
Williams, lf	7	25	2	5	0	0	0	1	5	5	.200	16	2	0	1.000
York, 1b	7	23	6	6	1	1	2	5	6	4	.261	59	4	1	.984
Doerr, 2b	6	22	1	9	1	0	1	3	2	2	.409	18	31	0	1.000
Higgins, 3b	7	24	1	5	1	0	0	2	2	0	.208	6	6	2	.857
*Russell, 3b	2	2	1	2	0	0	0	0	0	0	1.000	0	0	0	.000
H. Wagner, c	5	13	0	0	0	0	0	0	0	1	.000	20	2	0	1.000
Partee, c	5	10	1	1	0	0	0	1	1	2	.100	14	1	0	1.000
Hughson, p	3	3	0	1	0	0	0	0	1	0	.333	0	1	1	.500
Bagby, p	1	1	0	0	0	0	0	0	0	0	.000	0	1	0	1.000
Harris, p	2	3	0	1	0	0	0	0	0	1	.333	0	2	0	1.000
Zuber, p	1	0	0	0	0	0	0	0	0	0	.000	0	0	0	.000
Ferriss, p	2	6	0	0	0	0	0	0	0	1	.000	0	3	0	1.000
Brown, p	1	0	0	0	0	0	0	0	0	0	.000	0	0	0	.000
Johnson, p	3	1	0	0	0	0	0	0	0	0	.000	1	0	0	1.000
Ryba, p	1	0	0	0	0	0	0	0	0	0	.000	0	0	1	.000
Dobson, p	3	3	0	0	0	0	0	0	0	2	.000	0	2	0	1.000
Dreisewerd, p	1	0	0	0	0	0	0	0	0	0	.000	0	0	0	.000
Klinger, p	1	0	0	0	0	0	0	0	0	0	.000	1	0	0	1.000
γGutteridge, 2b	2	5	1	2	0	0	0	1	0	0	.400	0	2	0	1.000
*Culberson, rf	5	9	1	2	0	0	1	1	1	2	.222	7	0	0	1.000
*Metkovich	2	2	1	1	1	0	0	0	0	0	.500	0	0	0	.000
γCampbell	1	0	0	0	0	0	0	0	0	0	.000	0	0	0	.000
Total		233	20	56	7	1	4	18	22	28	.240	183	76	10	.963

ST. LOUIS CARDINALS

	G	AB	R	H	2B	3B	HR	RBI	BB	SO	Bat Avg	PO	A	E	Fldg Avg
Schoendienst, 2b	7	30	3	7	1	0	0	1	0	2	.233	17	21	1	.974
Moore, cf	7	27	1	4	0	0	0	2	2	6	.148	17	1	0	1.000
Musial, 1b	7	27	3	6	4	1	0	4	4	2	.222	60	2	0	1.000
Slaughter, rf	7	25	5	8	1	1	1	2	4	3	.320	20	1	0	1.000
Kurowski, 3b	7	27	5	8	3	0	0	2	0	3	.296	13	9	1	.957
Garagiola, c	5	19	2	6	2	0	0	4	0	3	.326	22	2	0	1.000
Rice, c	3	6	2	3	1	0	0	0	2	0	.500	9	1	0	1.000
Walker, lf-rf	7	17	3	7	2	0	0	6	4	2	.412	14	0	0	1.000
Dusak, lf	4	4	0	1	1	0	0	0	2	2	.250	1	1	0	1.000
Marion, ss	7	24	1	6	2	0	0	4	1	1	.250	12	22	2	.944
Pollet, p	2	4	0	0	0	0	0	0	0	1	.000	0	0	0	.000
Brecheen, p	3	8	2	1	0	0	0	1	0	1	.125	0	2	0	1.000
Dickson, p	2	5	1	2	2	0	0	1	0	1	.400	0	3	0	1.000
Munger, p	1	4	0	1	0	0	0	0	0	2	.250	1	0	0	1.000
Beazley, p	1	0	0	0	0	0	0	0	0	0	.000	0	1	0	1.000
Wilks, p	1	0	0	0	0	0	0	0	0	0	.000	0	1	0	1.000
Brazle, p	1	2	0	0	0	0	0	0	0	0	.000	0	1	0	1.000
*Sisler	2	2	0	0	0	0	0	0	0	0	.000	0	0	0	.000
*Jones	1	1	0	0	0	0	0	0	0	1	.000	0	0	0	.000
Total		232	28	60	19	2	1	27	19	30	.259	186	68	4	.984

*Pinch-hitter. γPinch-runner.

COMPOSITE SCORE BY INNINGS

Boston	5	2	0	1	0	1	4	5	1	1—20
St. Louis	0	5	7	0	5	1	1	3	6	0—28

PITCHING SUMMARY

	G	CG	IP	H	R	ER	BB	SO	HB	WP	W	L	PC	ERA
Ferriss	2	1	13 1/3	13	3	3	2	4	0	0	1	0	1.000	2.03
Johnson	3	0	3 1/3	1	1	1	2	1	0	0	1	0	1.000	2.70
Dobson	3	1	12 2/3	4	3	0	3	10	1	0	1	0	1.000	0.00
Hughson	3	0	14 1/3	14	8	5	3	8	1	0	0	1	.000	3.14
Klinger	1	0	2/3	2	1	1	1	0	0	0	0	1	.000	13.50
Harris	2	0	9 2/3	11	6	4	4	5	0	0	0	2	.000	3.72
Bagby	1	0	3	6	1	1	1	1	0	0	0	0	.000	3.00
Zuber	1	0	2	3	1	1	1	1	0	0	0	0	.000	4.50
Brown	1	0	1	4	3	3	1	0	0	0	0	0	.000	27.00
Ryba	1	0	2/3	2	1	0	1	0	0	0	0	0	.000	0.00
Dreisewerd	1	0	1/3	0	0	0	0	0	0	0	0	0	.000	0.00
Brecheen	3	2	20	14	1	1	5	11	0	0	3	0	1.000	0.45
Munger	1	1	9	9	3	1	3	2	0	0	1	0	1.000	1.00
Pollet	2	1	10 1/3	12	4	4	4	3	1	0	0	1	.000	3.48
Dickson	2	0	14	11	6	6	4	7	0	0	0	1	.000	3.50
Brazle	1	0	6 2/3	7	5	4	6	4	0	0	0	1	.000	5.40
Wilks	1	0	1	2	1	0	0	0	0	0	0	0	.000	0.00
Beazley	1	0	1	1	0	0	0	1	0	1	0	0	.000	0.00

Earned runs—Boston 16, St. Louis 19. Sacrifices—Marion 3, Moore 2, Munger, Walker, Schoendienst, H. Wagner, Dobson, DiMaggio. Double plays—Marion and Musial; DiMaggio and Pesky; Pesky, Doerr and York; Slaughter and Garagiola; Doerr, Pesky and York; Schoendienst and Musial; Pesky and Doerr; Partee and Pesky; Marion, Schoendienst and Musial; Kurowski, Schoendienst and Musial 2; Brecheen, Schoendienst, Marion and Musial. Stolen bases—Schoendienst, Musial, Slaughter, Culberson, Pesky. Passed ball—Garagiola. Left on bases—Boston 53, St. Louis 50. Times of games—2:39, 1:56, 1:54, 2:31, 2:23, 1:56, 2:17. Umpires—Ballanfant (N. L.), Hubbard (A. L.), Barlick (N. L.), Berry (A. L.). Attendances—First game, 36,218; second game, 35,815; third game, 34,500; fourth game, 35,645; fifth game, 35,982; sixth game, 35,768; seventh game, 36,143. Receipts—First game, $156,646; second game, $155,372; third game, $140,451; fourth game, $143,886; fifth game, $144,897; sixth game, $155,269; seventh game, $156,379.

Record of Series Games

FIRST GAME

											R.	H.	E.
Boston (A.)	0	1	0	0	0	0	0	0	1	1	—3	9	2
St. Louis (N.)	0	0	0	0	0	1	0	1	0	0	—2	7	0

Batteries—Hughson, Johnson (9) and H. Wagner, Partee (9); Pollett and Garagiola.

SECOND GAME

										R.	H.	E.
Boston (A.)	0	0	0	0	0	0	0	0	0	—0	4	1
St. Louis (N.)	0	0	1	0	2	0	0	0	..	—3	6	0

Batteries—Harris, Dobson (8) and Partee, H. Wagner (8); Brecheen and Rice.

THIRD GAME

										R.	H.	E.
St. Louis (N.)	0	0	0	0	0	0	0	0	0	—0	6	1
Boston (A.)	3	0	0	0	0	0	0	1	..	—4	8	0

Batteries—Dickson, Wilks (8) and Garagiola; Ferriss and H. Wagner.

FOURTH GAME

										R.	H.	E.
St. Louis (N.)	0	3	3	0	1	0	1	0	4	—12	20	1
Boston (A.)	0	0	0	1	0	0	0	2	0	—3	9	4

Batteries—Munger and Garagiola; Hughson, Bagby (3), Zuber (6), Brown (8), Ryba (9), Driesewerd (9) and H. Wagner.

FIFTH GAME

										R.	H.	E.
St. Louis (N.)	0	1	0	0	0	0	0	0	2	—3	4	1
Boston (A)	1	1	0	0	0	1	3	0	..	—6	11	3

Batteries—Pollet, Brazle (1), Beasley (8) and Garagiola; Dobson and Partee.

SIXTH GAME

										R.	H.	E.
Boston (A.)	0	0	0	0	0	0	1	0	0	—1	7	0
St. Louis (N.)	0	0	3	0	0	0	0	1	..	—4	8	0

Batteries—Harris, Hughson (3), Johnson (8) and Partee; Brecheen and Rice.

SEVENTH GAME

										R.	H.	E.
Boston (A.)	1	0	0	0	0	0	0	2	0	—3	8	0
St. Louis (N.)	0	1	0	0	2	0	0	1	..	—4	9	1

Batteries—Ferriss, Dobson (5), Klinger (8), Johnson (8) and H. Wagner, Partee (8); Dickson, Brecheen (8) and Garagiola, Rice (8).

FINAL SERIES GAME DECIDED IN EIGHTH

Double by Walker Off Klinger Sends Slaughter Home With Deciding Run for Cards

ST. LOUIS, Oct. 15 (AP)—The play-by-play description of the seventh and final game of the world series at Sportsman's Park today follows:

FIRST INNING

RED SOX — Moses singled through the middle of the diamond. Pesky smacked Dickson's first pitch for a bounding single over second base, sending Moses to third. DiMaggio flied to deep right field, Moses scoring easily after the catch. Williams flied deep to Moore. Schoendienst trotted out into short right field to catch York's pop fly. One run, two hits, no errors, one left.

CARDINALS — Schoendienst drilled a single through the hole between third and short and when Williams momentarily bobbled the ball in left field Schoendienst tried to make second but was out, Williams to Pesky. York came in on the grass to catch Moore's infield pop. Musial lined a double along the left field line. Slaughter watched a third strike breeze by. No runs, two hits, no errors, one left.

SECOND INNING

RED SOX—Doerr beat out a high bounder to Kurowski and ran to second when Kurowski's throw to first was low and bounced away from Musial. Higgins bounced out, Schoendienst to Musial, Doerr moving to third. H. Wagner raised a fly to Walker in short left. Walker raced toward the left field corner and made an over-the-shoulder catch of Ferriss' long drive. No runs, one hit, one error, one left.

CARDINALS — Kurowski doubled to left-center. Garagiola rolled out, Doerr to York, Kurowski stopping at third. Walker lined to Williams in left-center, Kurowski racing in from third after the catch. Marion bounced out, Doerr to York. One run, one hit, no errors, none left.

THIRD INNING

RED SOX—Moses fouled out to Kurowski. Schoendienst got in front of Pesky's hot grounder and easily threw him out. DiMaggio went down on strikes, looking at the third one. No runs, no hits, no errors, none left.

CARDINALS — Dickson went down swinging. Pesky swooped up Schoendienst's wicked grounder with his gloved hand and tossed to first for the out. Moore flied to Williams. No runs, no hits, no errors, none left.

FOURTH INNING

RED SOX—Walker raced into center field to make a running catch of Williams' long curving fly. York struck out. Doerr flied to Slaughter. No runs, no hits, no errors, none left.

CARDINALS — Musial walked. Pesky caught Slaughter's foul fly in left field. Kurowski flied deep to Moses. Garagiola rolled out, Doerr to York. No runs, no hits, no errors, one left.

FIFTH INNING

RED SOX—Moore made a spectacular backhand running catch of Higgins' blazing liner. H. Wagner fouled out to Kurowski. Ferriss sent a high bouncer to Dickson, who threw him out. No runs, no hits, no errors, none left.

CARDINALS — Walker singled past Pesky's outstretched glove. Marion sacrificed, York fielding his bunt along the first base line and throwing to Doerr, who covered first for the out. Dickson dumped a double over third, scoring Walker. Schoendienst smashed the first pitch on a line over second base for a single, scoring Dickson. Moore belted a single into center field, sending Schoendienst to second. Dobson went in to pitch for the Red Sox. Musial bounced out, Doerr to York, advancing both runners. Slaughter was purposely passed, filling the bases. Higgins backed up for Kurowski's bouncer and whipped to Doerr at second to force Slaughter. Two runs, four hits, no errors, three left.

SIXTH INNING

RED SOX—Moses bounced to Musial. Pesky lined to Kurowski. Dickson passed DiMaggio. Williams sent a skyscraper to right field where Slaughter made the catch. No runs, no hits, no errors, one left.

CARDINALS—Garagiola struck out. Walker walked. Doerr threw out Marion, Walker taking second. Dickson hit the first pitch to Doerr, who easily threw him out. No runs, no hits, no errors, one left.

SEVENTH INNING

RED SOX—York struck out. Doerr flied to Moore. Marion scooped up Higgins' grounder and tossed him out. No runs, no hits, no errors, none left.

CARDINALS — Schoendienst missed a three-and-two pitch. Doerr collided with Moses going after Moore's fly in short right field but held on to the ball for the out. Dobson knocked down Musial's hot smash back of the box and tossed to first for an easy out. No runs, no hits, no errors, none left.

EIGHTH INNING

RED SOX—Russell batted for H. Wagner and lined a single into center-field. Metkovich, hitting for

Continued on Page 38, Column 2

Buddy Young Weighs 3 Pro Football Offers

Illini Ace Would Earn $60,000 on 3-Year Pact

21-Year-Old Wizard Withholds Decision, Returns to School

EXCLUSIVE

BALTIMORE — Unimpeachable sources informed the AFRO on Monday that Buddy Young, Illinois backfield sensation, will sign a contract "within the next two months" to play professional football with the New York Yankees of the All-America Conference at a salary of $37,000 for two seasons, with an undisclosed cash payment, presumably $10,000, included as a bonus for signing.

By SAM LACY

CHICAGO—Claude (Buddy) Young, 21-year-old ace of the Big Nine and Rose Bowl champion Illinois eleven, is sitting on three offers to play professional football next year, instead of one as reported in the press the past few days.

The AFRO learned this on Sunday after questioning relatives and intimate friends of the 17-pound comet from Chicago's far South Side.

Buddy has not as yet accepted terms nor signed a contract with any club, but the AFRO investigation developed that he is weighing identical offers of $60,000 for three years from each of three pro clubs, the Cleveland Browns, Los Angeles Dons and New York Yankees, all of the All-American Conference.

The offers also include a bonus of $5,000 for signing.

Young could not be reached at his home, 13017 S. Evans Ave. His twin sister, Claudine, refrained from discussing the matter of Young's signing. She referred the AFRO to Robert Anderson, who as president of the Old Timers' Club is given credit for developing Buddy as an outstanding track and football athlete.

The action of Miss Young, who is known to be extremely close to her twin brother, in referring the matter to Anderson for comment, indicated that the rumor about Buddy's plan to sign with the New York Yankees was not altogether unfounded.

Has Not Signed

Anderson told the AFRO: "As far as I know, and I would know, Buddy has not committed himself to play with any professional club. At the present, he is more concerned with resuming his track career."

(Buddy was national outdoor 100-meter champion and won numerous sprint and hurdles titles prior to entering the Navy in 1944 —Ed. Note.)

Anderson explained Young's failure to return to school along with the Illinois football squad after the Rose Bowl game as due to fatigue. "Buddy was a dead tired kid," he told the AFRO, "and he made up his mind to take a few days at home to relax, regardless of the consequences. He is just 21 years old, has been going steadily hard all year and his nerves were shot to pieces complying with thousands of requests for autographs, all of which he answered with a smile."

Simmons Reveals Offer

Anderson declined to say whether or not Buddy was considering the pro offers, but admitted he had received several. "He has his future to think about, you know," was the only answer he would give in this connection.

Other reliable sources close to the crack Illini ball-carrier, however, told the AFRO it was a fact that Buddy has been approached by the three All-America Conference teams, one of which—Cleveland—already has three members of his race under contract, all-league fullback Marion Motley and all-league guard William. (Bill) Willis. and Horace Gillom, brilliant end of the 1946 University of Nevada eleven.

One of Young's intimate friends, Ozzie Simmons, ex-University of Iowa all-America halfback, revealed the amounts involved in the offers to Buddy.

MacPhail Strategy

Reached at his home, 6209 Eberhardt Ave., where Buddy had visited the previous night, Simmons said the three clubs had made the same offer, with the possibility that the Yankees, backed by the millions of Dan Topping and Larry MacPhail might try to outbid the other two.

This speculation explained why daily papers jumped to the conclusion last week that Buddy had already been signed by the New York club. It was typical MacPhail strategy to jump the gun on his competitors by premature publicity, something which always has a psychological advantage and rarely causes serious trouble.

While Buddy is married and has a child, and normally would want to be financially secure, it is a known fact that he is seeking the advice of older heads before making up his mind.

Eyes Olympic Title

Among those who have counselled him in the past is Duke Slater, another all-America from Iowa, now assistant district attorney in Des Moines.

Other persons close to Young opine that he is anxious to retain his amateur status long enough to attain the glory of an international championship in track in the Olympic Games, scheduled for London in 1948.

The $60,000 offer is equivalent to the $100,000 five-year contract signed last week by Charley Trippi, white Georgia star, to play with the Chicago Cardinals. Each would receive $20,000 a year.

Some point out, however, that there is a slight difference in the two pacts, which may work out to the advantage of Young. Under Buddy's terms, he could dicker for a better figure at the end of three years whereas Trippi would be unable to demand more money until his five years have expired. Of course, it might mean, on the other hand, that Young could be substantially cut at the close of his three-year contract.

Should he sign to play professional football, Young would no longer be eligible for college competition, but he could continue his studies without the benefit of an athletic scholarship.

Buddy to Fly to Coast for All-Star Grid Tilt

CHAMPAIGN, Ill. — Buddy Young, star of the 1947 Rose Bowl game and one of the kingpins of the champion University of Illinois eleven, will leave here Friday night for Los Angeles, Cal., to perform in Sunday's all-star football game.

The game, reportedly cosponsored by Joe Louis, will pit an all-star college eleven against a team composed of players from the Pacific Coast (pro) Football League.

Gross Honored

Pfc. William A. Gross, son of Mrs. Lucy Young, 621 Gresham Pl., N.W., recently received honors as a star tackle with the 514th Quartermaster Group Tigers, who defeated the Major Port Volunteers from Bremerhaven, 33-6, fo the Continental Base Section grid crown in Bad Nauheim, Germany.

Pvt. Gross, fromer student of Banneker Junior High, was inducted into the Army in April, 1945, and has been in the European Theater since Feb. 1946. He is assigned to the 4254th Truck Company in Munich, Germany.

FROM A TO Z

Alice Coachman, national 50-yard women's champion, and Lillie Purifoy, former national hurdles champ, are entered in the Philly Inquirer track meet in Philadelphia Friday night . . . they'll meet their traditional rivals, Stella Walsh and Nancy Cowperthwaite, both white. Coachman has beaten Walsh consistently in the 50, last year defeated her in both 50 and 100; Purifoy lost to Cowperthwaite in '46 after beating her in '45.

According to West Coast weekly writers, Bert LaBrucherie, white, UCLA head coach, says Buddy Young's sensational runs in hte Rose Bowl broke the backs of the Uclans.

Latest move of Jimmy Powers: Learning that a Brooklyn Dodger coach has predicted Jackie Robinson will give Ed Stanky a real run for the money if he's given a chance at the second-basing job of the Bums, doesn't rap the coach, Jackie or Branch Rickey as his custom . . . instead comes out immediately with: "Stanky's the most underrated ball player on the Dodgers . . ."

Jack Espey, white general manager of the Baltimore football pros, has invited AFRO readers to join the contest for naming the new All-American Conference eleven . . . Somebody ask Jesse Owens to drop me a line.

Phil Thigpen, holder of national cross-country mile title and former CIAA interscholastic mile and half-mile champion, is first of his race to be awarded a scholarship to Seton Hall and to be elected track team captain. . . Joe Louis missed this week's N.Y. Boxing Writers dinner for Mike Jacobs because he wanted to see a Los Angeles football game on the 19th and is slated to leave for his Central American tour on the 26th.

Harlem Globetrotters won their 68th pro basketball game in 70 played this year last week . . . open their 20th annual invasion of California Sunday night at Oakland. Addition of Zack Clayton to the lineup has run up the temperature of the lukewarm Washington Bears.

Visiting Mike Jacobs last week in a New York hospital, Billy Conn piped: "Maybe my showing against Joe Louis helped to put you here" . . . Jacobs's matchmaker, Nat Rogers, told Sugar Ray Robinson he didn't know when Marcel Cerdan plans to return to the U.S., when Robbie asked for a bout with the French champ in March . . . but at the same time, Lew Burston, another of Uncle Mike's lieutenants, was announcing to newsmen that Cerdan would be back in this country next month.

Philly fans are asking questions about the work of Charley Daggert, white boxing referee . . . Mayor Edward J. Kelly has asked for the 1952 Olympic Games for Chicago.

New York's Lightweight Champ Bob Montgomery has told promoters everywhere he'll be ready to defend his crown against anybody when he returns from a 6-week tour, which winds up in Hawaii in March . . . Harlemites will get a gander at Levi Jackson next fall when Yale plays Columbia at New York on October 11.

According to his aunt, Mrs. Effa Manley, owner of the Newark Eagles, Ford Anderson, only one of his race on the Loyola Catholic High (Philly) football team last year, is contemplating making application to enter Notre Dame.

The New York Cubans are seeking Tito Figueroa, the young Puerto Rican who left the Baltimore Elites last year after a fight with teammates, in exchange for Bill Anderson . . . both are pitchers . . . Baltimore hasn't said a mumbling word.

President Frank (Shag) Shaughnessy of the International League revealed last week that he instructed all league umpires to immediately wave out the game any pitcher who appeared to throw at Jackie Robinson during the 1946 campaign . . . Bernard Docusen, the young New Orleans welterweight who had to leave home before he could fight white boys, has won 14 bouts in 14 starts since arriving in New York.

Al Hoosman, promising young heavyweight of two years ago who, according to his own admission, flubbed because he couldn't stay in shape, is now under the wing of Sammy Goldman . . . New York daily writers care very little for Ray Robinson, chiefly because he's too independent for them . . . weekly writers care little for him for other reasons.

Nineteen-year-old Dolores Evans, developed along with Buddy Young in Chicago's Old Timers' Club, was buried Monday . . . had been ill eight months.

Buddy Young, who has signed his name over 5,000 times for nothing for autograph-hunters the past three months, can now sign his name just once (to a pro football contract) and get $65,000.—SAM LACY.

Va. State Ahead

PETERSBURG, Va.—Virginia State College cagers defeated Shaw University, 70-43, in a CIAA game Thursday night.

Two Shots of Josh Gibson at Height of Career

A relaxed figure at all times, Josh was caught here in a familiar pose in the Homestead Grays' dressing room. With one shoe off and a stocking dangling around his ankles, the slugging catcher takes time out to answer a question and await the click of the photographer's shutter. Death struck him down suddenly early Monday morning at the home of his mother in Pittsburgh.

Always a favorite with the youngsters, Josh is shown here signing autographs for D.C. kids shortly after he had belted out three home runs in one game in 1943, the year he hit 14 circuit blows in Griffith Stadium, more than the total number hit by white major leaguers in the Washington park during the season.

Josh Gibson Dies Suddenly Monday

Famous Homestead Grays' Catcher Was 35 Years Old

PITTSBURGH, Pa.—Death reached into the top level ranks of baseball early Monday morning and struck down Josh Gibson, slugging catcher of the Homestead Grays and one of the best known figures in the sport.

The home-run king died at 1:15 a.m., at the home of his mother, Mrs. Nancy Gibson, 2410 Strauss St., after an attack 48 hours earlier. He had been stricken Saturday morning. Gibson was 35 years of age.

The nature of the illness which felled the big, jovial receiver whom Walter Johnson once evaluated at $250,000, was not disclosed. However, it was generally known that Gibson had suffered numerous attacks in the past three years and that doctors had warned him against the extensive use of alcohol.

According to Rufus (Sonnyman) Jackson, owner of the Grays and Gibson's employer, the death of the star was "totally unexpected." Jackson told the AFRO: "I saw Josh a couple of weeks ago when he came in to talk about 1947, after he decided against going to Puerto Rico for winter baseball. He appeared to be happy and healthy. His death was totally unexpected."

Started at 15

Born in Buena Vista, Ga., Dec. 21, 1911, Gibson moved with his family to this city when he was a young boy. He first attracted attention at the age of 15, when he was playing with a group of youngsters who called themselves the North Side Red Sox.

In 1927, at the age of 16, he joined the Pittsburgh Crawfords, a sandlot team which served as the fore-runner to Gus Greenlee's famous Crawfods of later years.

Three years later, he was signed by the late Cum Posey to play with the Grays. After the 1930 and 31 seasons with the Grays, Josh went to the Crawfords to team with Satchel Paige as the greatest battery in the hisory of he game. They played together until 1936, when Gibson returned to the Gray fold.

Worth of $250,000

It was during this stay with the Crawfords and Paige that Gibson was seen in action in Florida by President Clark Griffith of the Washington Senators and his former ace, Walter Johnson. The Big Train is reputed to have told Griffith that in his opinion Gibson was "worth a quarter-million dollars."

Gibson was back with the Grays in 1937 and had been with them up to the time of his death.

Known far and wide, among his own mates and the major leaguers as well, as one of the game's longest hitters — ranking with Babe Ruth, Lou Gehrig, Ted Williams and Joe DiMaggio — Josh had his peak seasons in 1938 and 1939. During the 1938 seaosn, he hit four home runs in one game in Washington's long Griffith Stadium, and in 1943 he banged out three circuit smashes in the same park.

It was in the 1943 campaign, he knocked 14 home runs in Griffith Stadium, conquering the long leftfield which held the entire lot of white major leaguers to a total less than that.

Led NNL in 1945

In 1942, he won "the most valuable player" award playing in Mexico and duplicated the feat in Puerto Rico in 1944.

Gibson led the Negro National League with an average of .393 in 1945, and last year batted .331 for 48 games while leading the loop in home runs with 12.

Next to Paige, he was the highest paid player in either the Negro National or Negro American League, having drawn salaries of $6,000 during the seasons from 1940 to 1946. Bonuses brought his total earnings from the Grays to close to $10,000 according to President Jackson.

Josh is survived by his mother, a brother, Jerry; a sister, Mrs. Allmon; two children, Helen and Joshua Jr., twins; and an estranged wife.

Monty Signs for Pellone

DETROIT—New York Lightweight Champion Bob Montgomery signed late last week, through his manager, Joe Gramby, to box Tony Pellone, white Greenwich Village welterweight, at the Olympia here Feb. 7.

The bout will be the first of several non-title affairs booked by the Philadelphian for a six-week tour.

His Monday night bout with Eddie Giosa now history, the Bobcat will take on Pellone, whom he defeated in a previous meeting, then move on out to the coast for two more matches.

The first of these is with Joey Barnum, white, at Los Angeles, Feb. 15, and the other is with Jesse Flores, March 31, at San Francisco.

A bout in Hawaii is also on tab for the 135-pound king, probably between the Barnum and Flores engagements.

Carey 2nd In Met AAU Dash

BROOKLYN, N.Y.—Tom Carey, national 60-meter indoor champion, could do no better than second in his specialty here Saturday night as white boys for the first time in nine years swept the boards clean in the Metropolitan AAU track and field games.

Carey, Homer Gillis, Sammy Richardson, defending champion in the broad jump, Jimmy Herbert, Hartley Lewis, Fred Jones, Bob Nelson and Lawrence Ellis finished in the money in the evening's program, but none could knock down a first.

METROPOLITAN A.A.U. CHAMPIONSHIPS

BROAD JUMP—1, Irving Mondschein, NYU, 23 feet 3¼ inches (championship record; old record, 23 feet ⅛ inch, by EDDIE GORDON, 1938); 2, HOMER GILLIS, NYU, 22 feet 11¼ inches; 3, Al Boruch, St. John's, 22 feet, 6¼ inches; 4, SAMMY RICHARDSON, Pioneer Club, 21 feet 6¾ inches.

ONE-MILE RUN—1, Thomas V. Quinn, New York A.C.; 2, Edward Walsh, Manhattan; 3, William Hulse, New York A.C.; 4, LAWRENCE ELLIS, Pioneer Club. Time, 4:16.[illegible]

70-YARD HIGH HURDLES—1, Jack Morris, New York A.C.; 2, Warren Halliburton, NYU; 3, Philip Eisman, Manhattan; 4, Thomas Byrnes, Manhattan. Time, 0:09.1.

60-YARD-DASH—1, Joseph Cianciabella, Manhattan; 2, THOMAS CAREY, Pioneer Club; 3, Ira Kaplan, Grand Street Boys; 4, HARTLEY LEWIS, Grand Street Boys. Time, 0:06.4.

600-YARD RUN—1, John Quigley, Manhattan; 2, James Gilhoooley, unattached; 3, JAMES HERBERT, Grand Street Boys; 4, A. Newton Campbell, St. John's. Time, 1:13.5.

1000-YARD RUN—1, Joseph Nowicki, Fordham; 2, Bill McQuire Jr., 69th Regiment; 3, William Atkinson, Manhattan; 4, Leslie MacMitchell, New York A.C. Time, 2:15.

70-YARD LOW HURDLES—1, Warren Halliburton, NYU; 2, Tom Byrnes, Manhattan; 3, FRED JONES, Pioneer Club; 4, Jack Morris, New York A.C. Time, 0:08.3 (ties championship record).

HIGH JUMP—1, Irving Mondschein, NYU, 6 feet 3½ inches; 2, John Vislocky, New York A.C., 6 feet 2½ inches; 3, Alfred Boruch, St. Johns, 6 feet 1½ inches; 4, Triple tie among Philip Einsman, Manhattan; ROBERT NELSON, Pioneer Club, and William Eipel, New York A.C., 6 feet.

Ring Results

WASHINGTON—
Smuggy Hursey, NYC, d. Charley Hayes (w), Detroit

BALTIMORE—
Buddy Walker, Columbus, O., tko'd Odell Riley, Detroit (7).

NEW YORK—
Omelio Agramonte, Cuba, d. Teddy Randolph, NYC.

NEW HAVEN—
Willie Joyce, Gary, Ind., and Ernie Petrone (w), Phila., drew

HOLYOKE—
Bert Lytell, Fresno, Cal., d. Henry Hall, New Orleans.

ELIZABETH —
Bernard Docusen, New Orleans, d. Vinnie Rosano (w), Brooklyn

DETROIT —
Bobby McQuillar, Port Huron, d. Ace Miller, Toledo

TRENTON —
Jimmy Isler, Newark, d. Billy Lee. Hackensack, N.J.

JERSEY CITY —
Jerry Fiorello (w), Brooklyn, d. Billy Cooper, Paterson.

Heavy Champ Lauded

Sgt. Coley Wallace of Camp Kilmer, who is shown receiving the First Army boxing award from Col. John G. Murphy, executive officer of Fort Dix, is said to be a cousin of Champion Joe Louis. Sgt. Wallace, whose home address is 1504 Wood St., Jacksonville, Fla., won the First Army boxing meet lightweight crown at Fort Dix. He fought for Camp Kilmer.

Long John Files Entry

Classy Field Set for Inquirer Meet

PHILADELPHIA

Long John Woodruff, one of the stars who streaked to glory in the 1936 Olympic games, will continue his comeback attempt here Jan. 24, when he runs in the third annual Inquirer meet at Convention Hall.

Although he was famous for shorter distances and won the half-mile event in the quadrennial classic, Woodruff, ex-University of Pittsburgh flash, has entered the classy mile field which includes Frank Dixon, New York University's former intercollegiate king.

It will be one of his first important solo races since 1940. Since that time Long John has spent four years in the Army, serving in the Pacific area and attaining the rank of captain.

A teammate of Woodruff in the Olympaid, Dave Albritton, ex-Ohio State University high-jumper, has entered his specialty and will compete against an old rival, Joshua Williamson, who shared the national title with him in 1945.

Eddie Conwell, former NYU speedster, will defend the honors he won last year in the 50-yard dash. Conwell, 1944 I.C. 4-A titlist, will wear the colors of the Shore A.C.

Among the board-burners challenging the New Jersey mortician will be Wilbert Lancaster, former Central High School star who is now attending Lincoln University.

Also representing the Shore A.C. will be Elmore Harris, former Morgan State College ace, who will compete in the 1000-yard handicap and the Charles Paddock Memorial "300."

Among those running against him over the longer distance will be Roscoe Browne, ex-Lincoln half-miler, and Jim Herbert, former NYU star who has been winning track laurels since 1929.

Included among the entries in the 50-yard high hurdles competition is Norman Matlock, University of Pennsylvania timber-topper from Akron, O.

High schools from the local area have already entered teams in the mile relays. Southern won the Public High honors last year but Central will be favored to dethrone the Rams.

Levi Jackson Banquet Guest

By JOSEPH FISHER

NEW HAVEN, Conn.—A testimonial banquet and smoker, sponsored by the New Haven Branch of the National Association of Postal Employees, was given in honor of Levi Jackson, Yale's brilliant freshman fullback, last Saturday evening at the House of Hawkins, an inn.

Among the guest speakers, all of whom have seen the phantom fullback in action and had nothing but praise for him, were Norman Watts, director of the Dixwell Community Center; Patrick J. Goode, postmaster of this city; Capt. Howard O. Young, assistant chief of police, and Reggie Root, assistant football coach at Yale, who discovered the youthful star.

Root denied that there was any truth to rumors that some of the Yale players from the deep South refused to block for Levi during the past season. Many of them felt it was "an honor" to play with such a gne lad, Root declared.

Philly Boxing Drew Almost Half Million

PHILADELPHIA

Philadelphia's boxing fell just short of being a half-million dollar business in 1946, drawing $425,631.68 in gross receipts, it was revealed last week.

Figures compiled by the office of Receiver of Taxes showed that $98,131.82 of this sum was paid out in taxes, two-thirds of which went to the Federal Government.

Tough Field In '47 Bowl

DETROIT—If current averages mean anything, then the fourth annual $2,000 national singles match game championship slated for Feb. 4 through 9 on the lanes at Paradise Bowl here promises Jack Marshall, Chicago, a tough six days in defense of the title he won last February.

Marshall rolled up an average of 195 in the final 64 games to capture the top prize of $750 and tuck the championship under his wing. This record, according to close observers, will be smashed when the last ball in this year's tournament has been rolled down the lanes.

Take the Cleveland group as a striking example of what Marshall will have to face. There are 26 keglers in the Forest City with averages better than 180, with Lloyd Thomas, member of the Log Cabin five pacing the lot with 193. Close behind is Roy Strickland with 191.

Francis Grimes, who finished seventh in the tournament last year, is holding an average of 184, while Hany Payne also has 184 to his credit.

Chicago will be placing its hopes in Marshall, but there are some fellow townsmen who, according to their averages, will be strong threats for Marshall's crown. Thomas Washington, member of the Sewell team, has an average of 193 for the season, and Billie Hampton, who proved his mettle last year, has an average of 191.

Balto. Pinmen Drop D.C. Duel

WASHINGTON

A team of Baltimore bowlers dropped a special match game to a Washington lineup here on Monday night, the locals downing a total of 2312 pins to 2244 for the visitors.

High game for the night was rolled by M. Brown of the Baltimore team, who hit for 208.

Balto.				Washington			
Meyes	149	145	184	Hyson	157	148	162
Brown	152	208	131	Roy	119	191	181
Brown	142	155	151	Jones	150	133	134
Bowie	134	131	161	Exum	148	160	185
Hamilt'n	123	133	125	Coleman	124	136	184
Totals	720	772	752	Totals	698	768	846

Sports Quiz

Over 300 entrants in the Sports Quiz contest the very first day!

Take yourself a crack at the grand prize of an all-expense **trip to see Jackie Robinson play in the opening game of the 1947 baseball season,** either with Brooklyn Dodgers or Montreal Royals.

Clip this right away, print the name of the athlete pictured here in the space at the bottom and mail immediately to the Sports Quiz Editor, AFRO-AMERICAN, Balto., Md.

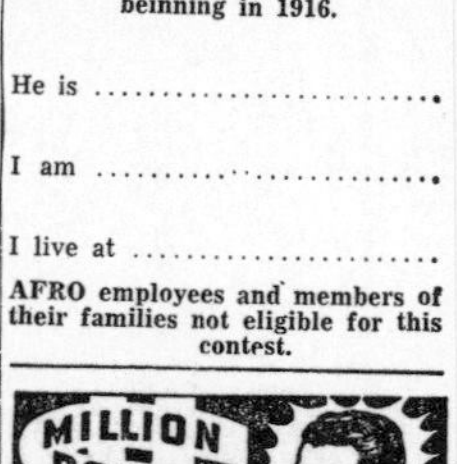

THIS GUY WAS
Born along with a twin sister, educated in Chicago, Ill., propelled into the public eye by his flying feet as a track man, taken out of school after one year in college and inducted into the U.S. Navy where he was the standout member of an otherwise all-professional football team, one of eight members of his race to perform in the Rose Bowl since its beinning in 1916.

He is ....

I am ....

I live at ....

AFRO employees and members of their families not eligible for this contest.

WINDY
Snow for the breeze along with 18 degrees.
Sun rises 7:36 a. m.; Sun sets 5:57 p. m.
DETROIT TEMPERATURES

7 a.m. 15	8 a.m. 15	9 a.m. 16
10 a.m. 17	11 a.m. 19	12 noon 20
1 p.m. 21	2 p.m. 22	3 p.m. 23
4 p.m. 23	5 p.m. 23	6 p.m. 23
7 p.m. 23	8 p.m. 22	9 p.m. 24
10 p.m. 24	11 p.m. 25	12 p.m. 25

The Detroit Free Press

MONDAY, FEBRUARY 10, 1947 — On Guard for Over a Century — Vol. 116—No. 282 — Five Cents

METRO FINAL

POWDER ROOM PLOTTERS
Women's Sanctum Becomes Their Headquarters for Mapping Important Political Strategy.

His Playing Days Over?

HANK GREENBERG—LONG A TIGER HERO
Detroit fans will find him hard to forget

HANK READY TO QUIT

Greenberg Turns Down Pirate Offer

Indicates He'll Enter New Fields

NEW YORK—(AP)—Hank Greenberg virtually closed out his brilliant baseball playing career Sunday.

Greenberg announced that he had informed the Pittsburgh Pirates that he "was considering retirement from the active playing ranks."

Although he did not say flatly that he was quitting the diamond as a player, the big, hard-hitting ace who was sold recently to Pittsburgh by the Detroit Tigers intimated as much.

He said that he did "not desire to start anew in a strange environment."

The 36-year-old veteran issued the statement at a press conference.

* * *

ABOUT THE same time, Frank McKinney, president of the Pirates, announced in Pittsburgh that Greenberg "has wavered on the matter of returning to a playing part in baseball this year as a member of the Pittsburgh club."

Both Greenberg and McKinney emphasized that money had nothing to do with the star player's long-pondered announcement.

Greenberg said that the Pirates offered him more money than he ever received in Detroit.

The first-sacker and outfielder led the American League in home runs and runs batted in four times in his 11-season Detroit career.

He received a salary of $55,000 from Detroit last year plus a $20,000 bonus when he was waived out of the junior circuit and sold to Pittsburgh for a sum believed to be $40,000.

* * *

IN HIS STATEMENT here, Greenberg said:

"This decision is not easy to make. I love the game and feel there is yet much good baseball in me as a player and executive. But after 17 years and 1,150 games in a Tiger uniform, I always expected to finish my career in Detroit.

"Since it was decided for me that this could not be, I do not desire to start anew in a strange environment."

Hank declined to elaborate on his statement or say what he intended to do. McKinney indicated that Greenberg may go outside the game.

* * *

McKINNEY SAID Greenberg had told him "that in view of several other matters which he has under consideration for his immediate future, matters having no connection whatever with baseball, he thinks it better that he should not at this time obligate himself to play baseball in 1947."

McKinney, greatly disappointed in the strange turn of

Turn to Page 14, Column 8

Blaze Kills 100 Revelers at Berlin Masked Ball

Tommies Among Dead in Fiery Trap

Many Victims Are Trampled in Panic

BY RICHARD KASISCHKE

BERLIN—(AP)—A masquerade ball became a deadly holocaust early Sunday when an estimated 100 to 150 masked merrymakers were burned or trampled to death.

A flash fire swiftly engulfed the Karlslust dance hall in the British zone of Berlin.

A mass of bodies was piled before the entrance, much as in the Cocoanut Grove fire in Boston four winters ago where 492 perished.

* * *

SURVIVORS told of women being trampled to death and of others being stripped naked as they fought vainly to reach the main exit.

The exact toll was not known when darkness forced abandonment of the search through the ruins until Monday.

A British fire control officer blamed overheated stoves.

A German civilian familiar with the structure said a short circuit was to blame because the flames first broke in the ceiling and the lights went out immediately.

* * *

IT WAS BERLIN'S worst disaster since the war.

All through the day, people milled about the ruins of the one-story structure seeking information about missing relatives.

Charred bodies, many unrecognizable, were take from the wreckage throughout the day.

At least three British soldiers were among the dead, the British Army said. Others were among the 30 severely burned who were treated in hospitals.

No American soldier had been listed as a casualty.

British authorities said about 50 British troops were among the 1,000 persons at the ball, given by the Spandau Football Club.

Those who escaped in their garish costumes ran into one of the bitterest cold waves of the winter.

* * *

MANY PAID WITH their lives in a gamble to retrieve their coats from the checkrooms, the positions of bodies showed. The British soldiers—the Karlslust was one of their favorite spots—for the most part crashed windows and escaped.

Plants Shut by Britain; Peril Grows

Power Cutoff Hits Homes in Wide Area

BY HERBERT L. MATTHEWS
New York Times Foreign Service

LONDON—The blackout of more than half of industrial England and Wales began Monday at one minute past midnight.

As a result, several million workers must remain idle, at least through this week.

National recovery and export trade will suffer for months, perhaps many months.

* * *

HOMES THAT are already very cold will become colder and more cheerless.

This, as one Labor Party MP said, is "an industrial Dunkerque."

The whole burden of pulling through is again being placed on the shoulders of the ordinary men and women of Britain.

No observer doubts that they will bear this burden, but from every side come cries of warning and anger that it must not be allowed to happen again.

From now on until reduced consumption permits sufficient restocking of coal, all industries in the Center and Northwest of England and Wales must close down except those classified as essential.

* * *

HOUSES AND SHOPS will be without electricity from 9 a. m. to noon and 2 to 4 in the afternoon. In all other regions of

Coal crisis is climax of long series of developments. For background, see Page 3.

Britain drastic reductions must be made.

(Scotland Yard announced the receipt of a telegram saying that the home of Emanuel Shinwell, fuel and power minister, would be blown up by a time bomb, the Associated Press reported. Police investigated but found no bomb.

(Shinwell has borne the brunt of criticism of the Labor Government for the fuel crisis.)

* * *

AN ACCUMULATED mass of bewilderment, resentment and acute anxiety is going to descend upon Prime Minister Clement Attlee and the Government in the House of

Picture on Back Page

Commons Monday if, as expected, he makes a statement on the crisis.

However, it is much too soon to talk of a coalition government or general election.

Meanwhile, heavy snowfalls over the week-end aggravated the transport situation. However, a thaw began to set in Sunday afternoon which may relieve the situation, although it threatens danger of flooding in many areas.

On the whole, the weather situation is still bleak. There has been no improvement in road conditions and more roads became blocked in many regions.

Plants May Get Gas Tuesday

Firm to Restore Service if Weather Permits; Snowdrifts Block Roads

The weather Monday will determine if Detroit's industrial paralysis is to continue.

Although temperatures will be slightly higher, it will still be cold, and winds which lashed the city Sunday are not expected to abate. Gusts up to 75 miles an hour were recorded.

Henry Fink, president of the Michigan Consolidated Gas Co., said service may be restored Tuesday to 60 major industrial plants which were closed Friday to conserve fuel.

* * *

THE WEATHER BUREAU forecast a high of 26 and a low of 18 for Monday. There will be snow flurries.

The driving winds Sunday piled up huge snowdrifts and blocked roads throughout Southeastern Michigan.

Traffic on some streets in Detroit was reduced to one-way. Streets in surrounding suburbs were impassable.

* * *

IN LIVINGSTON County, South Lyon was practically snowbound. Portions of Baldwin, John R., Orchard Lake and Middle Belt roads in Oakland County were closed.

At Mt. Clemens, a snowplow was stalled in four-foot drifts and two trucks sent to pull it clear also were stalled. Many Macomb County roads were blocked.

Meanwhile, more than 100,000 hourly rated workers will remain off the job Monday.

Hardest hit was Chrysler Corp., with 40,000 to 50,000 workers idled in seven plants.

* * *

THEY WERE the Dodge Main, Dodge Forge, Plymouth, Chrysler Jefferson, Chrysler Kercheval, DeSoto and Lynch Road. Office workers will report.

All plants of the Briggs Manufacturing Co., employing 16,000 hourly-rated workers, were down. Salary employees were to work.

Lincoln Division, with 2,500 idle, was the lone plant of the Ford empire to be affected.

General Motors reported 6,000 out at two Ternstedt plants, 6,000 at Chevrolet Gear & Axle and 1,200 at Chevrolet Forge.

* * *

THE HUDSON Motor Car Co., however, said all plants would operate normally. Great Lakes Steel also expected to operate.

Detroit-Michigan Stove Co. laid off 700 employees in its No. 1 plant, but continued operations in No. 2 plant, employing 150.

Timken Axle reported only 100 employees in its heat-treating department laid off.

* * *

OTHERS WITHOUT fuel gas and facing some curtailment include Budd Wheel, two plants; Bohn Aluminum, three plants; Detroit Seamless Tube, Detroit Steel Corp., Detroit Transmission, Commercial Steel Treating, Murray Corp., Packard, Cadillac, Detroit Steel Products, Kelsey-Hayes, Udylite Corp., Gemmer Manufacturing Corp., Kelvinator and Revere Copper and Brass.

The Weather Bureau held hopes that the cold wave, extending from the Dakotas to Maine and from northern Texas to Florida, would moderate slightly this week.

Hardest hit in Michigan were the Grand Rapids, Muskegon and Traverse City areas, buried beneath a 20-inch blanket. Snowplows were striving to keep trunk lanes clear.

Snow in Florida

Free Press Wire Services

ORLANDO, Fla.—Central Florida had its first snow in 29 years. Flurries were reported at Deland, 35 miles north of here. The Orlando area had sleet. Farmers battled to save their crops.

Seven Skiers Killed

ZURICH, Switzerland—(U.P.)—Seven persons were killed when an avalanche buried a group of 11 skiers near the village of Pany, in Grisons Canton.

Rubber Unions Plan Strike Vote in Week

Three Akron Firms Facing Action

AKRON—(AP)—Unions in the three major rubber concerns here have planned membership meetings and strike votes within a week, union spokesmen said.

Negotiations for a 26-cent-an-hour wage increase with the "big four" rubber firms were broken off last week at insistence of the companies.

* * *

INTERNATIONAL headquarters of the United Rubber Workers (CIO) here instructed all "big four" locals to conduct strike votes before Feb. 28.

The "big four" rubber industries included the Firestone Tire & Rubber Co., the B. F. Goodrich Co. and the Goodyear Tire & Rubber Co., all of Akron, and the U. S. Rubber Co. of Detroit and New York.

Union spokesmen said all Akron locals filed their strike notices with the National Labor Relations Board more than 30 days ago.

L. S. Buckmaster, international union president said, "we are using every resource at our command to reach an agreement without strike action, if at all possible."

N.Y. WORRIED

Foul Play Seen on Fare

NEW YORK—(AP)—New York's "battle of the subways" will begin Monday with hearings to determine whether transit fares should be raised from 5 to 10 cents.

Worried City officials, forseeing the possibility that the battle might prove bloody as well as bitter, assigned a heavy police detail and hospital catastrophe unit to the City Hall, where the hearings on the temper-trying issue will be held.

Doctors and nurses will set up a first-aid center at the scene, two ambulances will stand by and 50 husky patrolmen, five police sergeants, a captain and at least a half dozen detectives have received the task of keeping order.

Father Ends Life, but Girl Weds

CLINTON, Ia.—(AP)—Loretta Rannfeldt, 19, was married less than five hours after what Police Sgt. Cyril Robb said was the suicide death of her father, Adolph Rannfeldt, 51.

Robb said Rannfeldt, a worker in a toy factory, shot himself in the head after a quarrel with his wife, Frieda, over the marriage of his daughter, by a previous marriage, to Lester C. Pirch, 24.

Clash Upsets Chinese Rally

SHANGHAI—(U.P.)—An anti-American meeting of the Democratic League wound up in a free-for-all battle. One person was killed and 17 were injured.

The league—an organization close to the Communists—called the meeting to launch an anti-American propaganda campaign. The fight ensued when one labor faction attempted to withdraw.

Several arrests were made. Most of the injured were hit with flailing sticks and flying stones.

Britain's Bundles

LONDON—Fifteen thousand more babies were born in the first five weeks this year in 126 large cities in England and Wales, which cover about half of Britain's population, than in the same period in 1946.

Doctors Say GIs May Be Sterile Due to Military Diet

LOS ANGELES—(U.P.)—Military diet, favorite "beef" of ex-GIs, was blamed by two experts as contriubuting to temporary sterility among some former servicemen.

Addressing the Western branch of the American Society for the Study of Sterility, Drs. Gerson R. Biskind and Harry Goldblatt, of San Francisco, made the charge against the familiar Army-Navy chow.

Biskind said his experiments showed that deficiency of vitamin B complex was a contributing cause of infertility, while Goldblatt's tests blamed lack of proteins.

Relief Goods Burn

MANILA—(AP)—Approximately $250,000 in UNRRA food and clothing, intended for Philippines relief, was destroyed in a warehouse fire.

'Miracle' Child Rejoins Mother

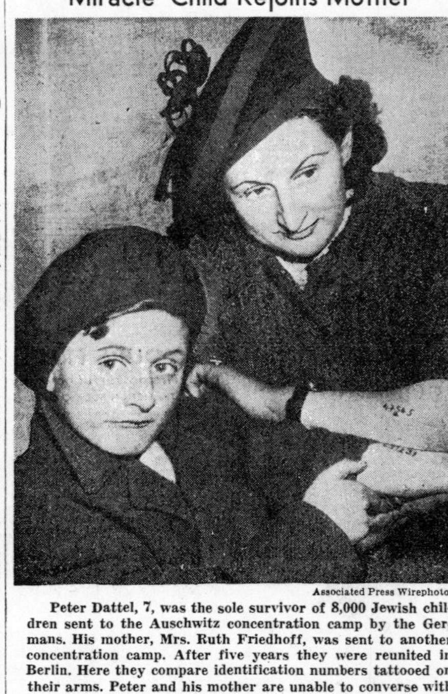

Associated Press Wirephoto

Peter Dattel, 7, was the sole survivor of 8,000 Jewish children sent to the Auschwitz concentration camp by the Germans. His mother, Mrs. Ruth Friedhoff, was sent to another concentration camp. After five years they were reunited in Berlin. Here they compare identification numbers tattooed on their arms. Peter and his mother are unable to converse with each other—he speaks only Czech and she speaks only German.

CIO Plans New Demands if Picard Is Upheld

Spokesman Says Unions May Balk at Docking for Trivial Tardiness

BY FRAN MARTIN
Free Press Labor Writer

Judge Frank A. Picard's decision throwing out the Mt. Clemens pottery workers' claims for portal-to-portal pay brought relief to industry heads and a determination among union leaders to maintain their demands.

Industry leaders looked to the Supreme Court for an early and final disposition of the case, and to Congress for clarification in the Wage and Hour Act of what constitutes a work week.

* * *

PICARD ruled that employers in industry will not be held liable for "walking and preliminary duties" which consume less than 20 to 25 minutes.

Union spokesmen said they would appeal the decision and that other suits would not be withdrawn. Nationally, the suits now total more than $5,000,000,000.

Frank E. Cooper, attorney for the Mt. Clements Pottery Co., said the decision "clearly points out" that last June's Supreme Court verdict "furnishes no basis for the many fantastic claims" made by labor in portal suits.

* * *

SPOKESMEN FOR the automotive "big three."—General Motors Corp., Ford Motor Co. and Chrysler Corp.—declined comment.

John L. Lovett, president of the Michigan Manufacturers Association, asserted: "Picard did an excellent job arriving at the facts, and deserves credit in view of the pressure put upon him from all over the country.

Frank Rising, general manager of the Automotive and Aviation Parts Manufacturers Association, said, "Picard's decision will do a

Turn to Page 2, Column 2

Flight to Save Infant Fails

Free Press-Chicago Tribune Wire

CHICAGO—Anabelle Marsh, two-and-a-half-year-old leukemia victim, died here a few hours after she was flown to Chicago from Palestine in an attempt to save her.

The child arrived on a Trans-World Airlines plane with her mother, Mrs. Adele Marsh, 28. The mother exhausted from worry and a two-week trip that included stopovers for blood transfusions at five foreign airports.

The infant received further transfusions and other medical attention, but died Sunday.

3 Robber Bands Smashed in Berlin

BERLIN—(AP)—Berlin police announced the capture of three robbery gangs having in their possession black-market booty worth thousands of dollars.

The police said the bands had burglarized scores of shops and lodging houses.

One group, which included a woman, operated with a stolen jeep.

Peace Pacts for 5 Nations Due Today

Must Be Ratified by Major Powers

PARIS—(AP)—Peace treaties will be signed Monday for Italy, Romania, Bulgaria, Hungary and Finland, all sadly disillusioned satellites of Germany in World War II.

But even the signing in the famous Clock Room of the French Foreign ministry will not finally bring peace to these vanquished states.

* * *

BEFORE THE long-debated treaties are brought into force, they must be ratified by each of the major powers—by the United States Senate, for instance—and instruments of ratification must be deposited with the Foreign Ministry here.

Italy, Romania, Hungary and Finland all lose territory in the treaties although Romania recovers Transylvania from Hungary.

A total of $1,330,000,000 reparations were asked, of which $900,000,000 was granted to Russia. The Moscow radio said that Russia had agreed to a six to eight-year postponement of Romania's reparations payments of $300,000,000.

Armed forces of all five states were reduced and all were prohibited from using atomic energy, rockets, bombers, submarines or torpedo boats.

Shooting Bares Gang Warfare by Teen-Agers

2 Boys Seized in N.Y. Street Slaying

NEW YORK—(AP)—A tale of boyland gang warfare in which teen-age boys chipped in $1 each for a gun and then used live ammunition on their rivals was unfolded in court.

Two boys were charged with homicide in the shooting of another boy.

Thomas Soto, 14, and Candido Noriega, 13, were held without bail by Magistrate Samuel Orr pending further hearing Tuesday. They are accused of shooting Early Keller, 16, in a gang battle.

* * *

KELLER DID NOT belong to a gang. He was just passing by when killed.

Soto and Noriega were members of "the Rockets" gang, they explained.

After a fight with a rival gang, "the Royals," Soto and Noriega each fired a shot from a rooftop into the street at their rivals. Keller was hit.

New Carrier Joins U.S. Fleet

PHILADELPHIA—(AP)—The 17,000-ton aircraft carrier Wright joined the United States fleet Sunday in commissioning ceremonies at the Philadelphia Naval Base.

John Nicholson Brown, assistant secretary of the Navy for air, told crewmen and guests that the ship "is a pledge that the Navy and the Navy's mission have not been forgotten with the end of hostilities."

The vessel was named for the late Wilbur Wright, aviation pioneer.

Guest Perishes in Hotel Blaze

SAN ANGELO, Tex.—(AP)—Frank Daniels, 39, was burned to death in a fire that caused $5,000 damage to the three-story, frame Plaza Hotel.

Five other persons were helped down ladders by firemen.

Firemen said the fire started in Daniels' room from a lighted cigaret.

Victim Calmly Awaits Death on Crossing

Special to the Free Press

BRIGHTON—Horrified men and women waiting at a railroad crossing here, saw a man stand calmly on the tracks until a Pere Marquette streamliner killed him Sunday.

John Corbet, 68, of 418 Maple, Brighton, was hurled nearly 400 feet, State Police said.

* * *

FRANK WARREN, of Grand Rapids, engineer of the Grand Rapids-Detroit flyer, told police he and Fireman Charles Plummer, of 649 Lincoln, Lincoln Park, saw Corbet on the tracks.

They thought he was only watching them approach, Warren said. Plummer whistled repeatedly and they tried to stop the train when Corbet did not move, he said.

Tumble on Ice May Cost an Eye

John H. Bunn, 56, may lose the sight of his left eye as the result of an injury he suffered when he slipped on ice in front of his home at 300 Chandler.

In the fall, a piece of wire pierced his eye, doctors said at Receiving Hospital.

China Air Crash Claims 11 Lives

NANKING—(U.P.)—A Chinese news agency reported that 11 persons had been killed and three injured when a Chinese Air Force transport plane made a crash landing [illegible] Chungking.

Bank notes worth $30,000,000 were destroyed in the crash.

IF CAPITAL IS WIPED OUT

Television Government Urged for Atomic War

WASHINGTON—(AP)—Senator Wiley (R., Wis.) proposed a "push-button" emergency government to function by television in case "one atomic flash" wiped out the President, his Cabinet and Congress.

The chairman of the Senate Judiciary Committee sent his suggestions to President Truman in an "open letter."

He termed Mr. Truman's own proposal for a new line of succession to the Presidency "inadequate" in an atomic age.

THE PRESIDENT asked Congress last week to make the speaker of the House next in line when there is no vice president, instead of Cabinet members.

"We know that in an atomic war it would be practically impossible for the Congress to assemble in any given spot," Wiley said. However, he asserted, television, radio and other inventions "would make an assembly possible even though legislators were separated by great distances."

"It would be vital to constantly have a legislature in session in an emergency of this kind to operate as a check and balance against any would-be dictator-minded executive," he continued.

* * *

EVEN IF ALL senators and representatives were "eliminated by an atomic attack on the Capitol," Wiley said, many states could immediately replace them through appointments by governors.

Amplifying his views in a broadcast, Wiley said there was a need "for more immediate push-button plans for the push-button warfare that will come" unless nations agreed upon an effective organization to do away with all warfare.

He noted that "there stands the Russian bear, whose official literature proclaims inevitable conflict between the Communistic and capitalistic worlds."

On Inside Pages

3 Groups Seek Teacher Salary Raises

Would Bring Pay to $4,700

Temporary Raises to End in June

CONDITIONS BAD

Committees Formed to Press for Action

A threefold fight to gain building improvements, adequate teaching personnel and salary raises for District school teachers was initiated this week as the Board of Education's bill to increase teachers' salaries was introduced in the House of Representatives by Chairman Dirksen of the House District Committee.

The bill was dropped into the hopper without changes and later referred to the District Committee which, Mr. Dirksen said, would refer it to the fiscal subcommittee for consideration.

Temporary Raise

The teachers' pay bill calls for a raise in the minimum starting salary to $2,500 and a maximum salary of $4,700. Under the 1945 teachers' pay act, which this bill would amend, the minimum was $1900 and the maximum, $3,700.

At present, however, teachers are receiving a starting salary of $2,350 and a maximum of $4,150, the result of a temporary $50 raise granted by Congress last

(Continued on Page 2, Col. 4)

WASHINGTON AFRO-AMERICAN

55th Year, No. 35 Contents of This Newspaper Copyrighted 1947 by The AFRO-AMERICAN Company WASHINGTON, D.C., APRIL 12, 1947 Entered in the Postoffice at Washington, D. C., as Second-Class Matter, under Act of March 3, 1879 28 Pages PRICE: 10c

Brooklyn Signs Jackie Robinson

A DODGER NOW—Jackie Robinson, star infielder of the Montreal Royals, whose contract purchase by the Brooklyn Dodgers was announced Thursday.

Dodgers Pick Star for Utility Position

Branch Rickey Confirms AFRO Report of Two Weeks Ago

By SAM LACY
AFRO Sports Editor

NEW YORK—"The Brooklyn Dodgers today purchased the contract of Jackie Robinson from the Montreal Royals."

With that history-making, but simple, 14-word statement here Thursday, Branch Rickey, president of the Brooklyn National League Baseball Club, announced to the world at large that there should no longer be any doubt that a colored man has qualified for organized baseball.

Robinson, whose status was uncertain up to the appearance of the Montreal Royals, here at Ebbets Field, Thursday, was not available for comment at the moment when the announcement was made by Rickey.

Jackie was at first base in the exhibition game for Montreal against his new Dodger teammates.

The Rickey statement brought to an end a long period of speculation as to whether or not the Brooklyn boss would have the temerity to place Jackie in the major leagues.

As predicted in the AFRO just two weeks ago. Robinson goes to Brooklyn as a utility infielder, capable of playing first base, second base or shortstop.

HONOR STUDENTS—These Dunbar High School students were installed recently as members of the Dunbar Honor Society, honorary scholastic club. They are, left to right, Capt. Wilbert Petty, 18, of 1625 V St., N.W.; Jacqueline Smith, 16, 417 New York Ave., N.W.; Virginia Davison, 17, 1728 First St., N.W., and Therese Thomas, 17, 57 P St., N.W.

1 Fire Damages 4 Adjacent Homes

Occupants Unharmed, Firemen Work 5 Hours

A fire of undetermined origin that was fanned by a strong wind, damaged four residences in the 1200 block of Columbia Rd., N.W., on Monday night.

Firemen reported that the blaze started in the cupola on the roof of the residence of Mrs. Katherine B. Willis at 1254 Columbia Road and spread rapidly to adjoining residences.

Other homes in the block which suffered fire and water damage or both were those of John H. Pinkard, 1256; John H. Posey, 1252 and Mrs. Marion Sellers, 1250.

Occupants Unhurt

None of the occupants of any of the houses suffered personal injury firemen reported, though the members of eight families were routed from their homes.

Fourth Battalion Chief Roy Hamback expressed the opinion that the fire started from a defective chimney or electric wiring. Since the chimneys are of brick construction however, it is thought

(Continued on Page 2, Col. 1)

Teacher Wins $300 Court Case

Paul Cooke, teacher at Miner Teachers College, is scheduled to receive about $300 in back pay this week, as the result of a decision handed down in his favor by the United States Court of Appeals.

The decision was announced on Monday, in litigation in which the District Board of Education was named defendant.

Mr. Cooke sued the board for three annual increments of $100 each, which the board had refused him on the grounds that he had forfeited his "permanent teacher" status.

Worked for Army

The board had granted him a leave of absence to teach illiterate

(Continued on Page 2 Col. 7)

Trainman's Jim Crow Effort Believed Cause of Slaying

DUNN, N.C.—Fletcher H. Melvin, 24, Baltimore Provident Hospital orderly, was shot to death, ellegedly by a white train conductor, while en route to visit relatives on Easter.

Witnesses said the youth was killed instantly by a shot through the heart fired by conductor C. A. James of Rocky Mount, N.C., after a special order had been given for all passengers to move into the jim-crow car up front.

According to Mr. and Mrs. Robert Gilmore, passengers on the crack Savannah Special of the Atlantic Coast Line Railroad, Melvin was asleep at the time the order was given and did not hear the conductor.

It was as the train neared Smithfield, a short while later that the passengers, all of whom had moved forward, learned of the tragedy.

Inquest Set

The orderly's body was removed from the train at Smithfield and turned over to the authorities there. Coroner J. O. Creech of Smithfield released the body to the Woodard Funeral Home and set a date for the inquest. Melvin's body later was transferred to the O. S. Payton Funeral Home at Dunn, N.C.

The victim's grandfather, E. H. Melvin, in Dunn, stated that the family had not received any official notification of the death, either from the railroad company or authorities at Smithfield.

Worked in Baltimore

Robert Young, white, attorney of Dunn, has been retained to represent the Melvin family in legal matters arising from the incident.

Melvin had been employed as an orderly at Provident Hospital intermittently since November, 1945, and had been given leave from his job to visit his mother, Mrs. Alice Melvin in Dunn, N.C., segregation of the races on trains

(Continued on Page 28, Col. 7)

PHYSICIANS' CASE AIRED:

Drs. Scott, Cobb Hit Hospital JC on Radio

Although three-fifths of the patients at Gallinger Hospital, a tax-supported institution, are colored, they cannot be treated there by physicians of their own race, declared Dr. Waldo Scott, in an interview over radio station WWDC, last Sunday night.

Dr. Montague Cobb said that several of the voluntary hospitals such as Children's, Providence, Casualty, Garfield and Emergency treat colored patients, but pointed out that they too, do not admit physicians who are not white to their staffs.

Dr. Cobb said this situation deprives physicians of an invaluable opportunity for professional improvement, inasmuch as they are excluded from both the staffs of the voluntary and tax-supported hospitals.

Continuing, Dr. Cobb said that in an effort to compensate for this inequity, voluntary hospitals have been erected around the country.

Growth Stymied

These, he pointed out, usually struggle contantly with financial difficulties, and at their very best are seldom equipped to offer a superior type of service.

(Continued on Page 2, Col. 2)

Howard Students Protest Food

Mass Meeting Held by 500 on Campus

DIETICIAN BLAMED

Cook, Frazier Halls' Cafe Meals Assailed

Protesting inadequate food and unsanitary conditions in cafeterias at Cook and Frazier Halls, 500 Howard University students, Tuesday, topped a spirited mass meeting with a march on the latter hall, where student leaders sought redress from Mrs. Henrietta Thayer, dietician.

The students assembled before Douglass Hall at noon, where conditions in both places were discussed pro and con, before a motion was taken to seek some remedial measures from the head dietician.

Prior to the motion, Mrs. Grant Reynolds, also a Howard dietician, asserted that the group attacked the situation in the wrong manner. The students failed to realize the high cost of food, she declared.

Conditions "Not Known"

Some action could have been taken if students' leaders had consulted Mrs. Henrietta Thayer, she said. Many of the problems the students aired were not known by the cafeteria's heads, Mrs. Reynolds concluded.

Preceded by six students bearing a corpse with an attached placard "I Ate In Frazier," the mass gathering approached Frazier Hall's cafeteria chanting their school's alma mater and "Nearer My God To Thee."

The procession halted in an orderly manner before the entrance, while a student group sought Mrs. Thayer to address the group.

Dietician Keeps Silent

Mrs. Thayer refused to speak to the students, and promised no remedial action to their charges.

(Continued on Page 6, Col. 3)

Treasurer Contradicts Theatre Head

The treasurer of the National Theatre, Percy A. Booth, 42, of 1814 M St., N.E., who is also in charge of the box office window, threw a bombshell in the National's defense Wednesday as hearing on the suits of seven ticket purchasers seeking refunds entered its fourth day in Justice Nadine Gallagher's Small Claims Court.

Mr. Booth testified that he had been given no instructions not to sell tickets to colored people.

This was contrary to the testimony made previously by the theatre's manager, Edmund Plohn, who had previously told the court he had so instructed Mr. Booth and several other employees.

Executive Testifies

Following Mr. Plohn, who had been brought back to the stand from Monday's session for cross-examintion, Cyril H. Grody of New York City, vice-president and director of the E Street Theatre Corporation, owners of the National, was put in the witness box.

Regarding the National's dis-

(Continued on Page 6, Col. 4)

Motion to Dismiss Theatre Suits Denied

Judge Gallagher Sustains 6 Cases, Reserves Decision on 7th Until Later

Attempts by National Theatre lawyers to dismiss the seven suits seeking refunds for tickets purchased for the production, "Love Goes to Press," on the night of Dec. 11, were denied by Judge Nadine Gallagher in Small Claims Court, as the trials were resumed this week.

Immediately following the judge's denial, the defense put its star witness, Edmund Plohn, manager of the National Theatre, on the stand.

Mr. Plohn made it clear that he had instructed his ticket window manager and his doorkeeper not to sell tickets to, nor admit anyone who was not white to the theatre.

Would Be Harmful

Mr. Plohn gave as reasons for the theatre's policy that "to admit colored persons would be harmful financially, and harmful to the white clientele we have bulit up over a period of years."

The seven suits were filed Jan. 30, by:

Mrs. C. Leslie Glenn, 2707 22nd St., N.W.; Mrs. Jean C. Clements, 1909 19th St., N.W.; David Lachenbruch, 635 Connecticut Ave., N.W.;

Miss Helen Mae Gould, 3501 N St., N.W.; Mrs. Helen Rice, 1837 Monroe St., N.E.; and Joseph Bierstein, 1445 Clifton St., N.W., all white.

Each had purchased tickets and tried to enter the theatre with their respective guests, some of

(Continued on Page 2, Col. 5)

Wife Claims Body of Vet Slain by Special Officer

The body of John T. Morris, 34, of the 1100 block of Rhode Island Ave., N.W., who was fatally shot by a special policeman at the Dunbar Hotel on April 4, was shipped to Gladstone, Va., where funeral rites and burial were held this week.

Scott Freed by Jury

Morris, war veteran, with one year's overseas service, was killed by Special Officer Joseph T. Scott, 59, of the 1100 block of Morse St., N.W.

Scott was absolved of blame in the killing by a coroner's jury, last Saturday, after testimony revealed that Morris threatened the officer, who had been summoned to break up a disturbance on the fifth floor of the hotel.

No weapon was found on the victim, according to police.

Mrs. Havanna Morris of Philadelphia, wife of the dead man, came to Washington, Monday, and expressed surprise that officials had held an inquest and reached a verdict in the killing without the presence of any relative at the probe.

Further Action Hinted

She assailed the hasty holding of the inquest as "unfair" and expressed the opinion that police had taken advantage of Morris, who, she declared, was ill as a result of his war service.

She indicated that she contemplated requesting further action in the case.

Prior to shipment, Morris's body lay in state at the G. Dovie Brooks Funeral Home, 12th and Florida Ave., N.W.

Besides his wife, the slain man is survived by his father, Thomas T. Morris; a sister, Mrs. Fannie Mansfield; and two brothers, James and Louis Morris.

U.S. Democracy Far Short of Goal—Mrs. Roosevelt

Admitting that democracy in the United States falls far short of what it ought to be, Mrs. Eleanor Roosevelt told an overflow audience in Andrew Rankin Memorial Chapel of Howard University, Tuesday night that Americans should practice at home what they preach abroad.

She is chairman of the Human Rights Commission of the Social and Economic Council of the United Nations.

Mrs. Roosevelt declared that the effectiveness of American representatives to the UN sessions depends to a large extent on the conviction with which they are able to present their arguments as well as the approval of American public opinion.

How We Can Help UN

American citizens, she said, can help the UN lay a foundation for peace through the wise exercise of their right to vote, electing to Congress representatives who will express the will of the people, and back up recommendations of the UN delegates.

Referring to the subject of "Human Rights in Trust Territories," Mrs. Roosevelt said that UN delegates are concerned about colonial peoples partly because of the strategic location of their homelands as well as the economic importance of mineral deposits.

In support of this, she pointed out that specific reference to the

(Continued on Page 6, Col. 1)

McDonald Attacks Wife's Petition

Earl H. McDonald, well-known sportsman, has asked District Court to dismiss the absolute divorce suit of his wife, Mrs. Hortense G. McDonald, teacher at Brookland Elementary School.

The defendant is at present at liberty, under bond, pending his appeal of a 6 to 18 months' sentence for numbers game activities.

Mrs. McDonald, who gave her address as 2807 Thirteenth St., N.E., accused Mr. McDonald, whom she described as a "chance broker," with a $5,000 per year in-

(Continued on Page 2, Col. 5)

Hit on Head With Baseball Bat in Fight, Man, 46, Dies

Hit on the head with a baseball bat during a fight on Sunday, James Smith, 46, of 90 Logan Ct., N.W., died at Casualty Hospital, on Tuesday.

Police are holding Willie Brown, 51, of 1616 Whitingham Pl., N.E., who was arraigned on the assault charge in Municipal Court, on Monday.

The coroner's office announced that an inquest into Smith's death would be held at the morgue, today (Friday).

EASTER STROLLERS—Easter Sunday in the Nation's Capital was mild and pleasant. Enjoying the spring weather were the groups shown above. Left, Charles Pettiford, Miss Sarah King, Miss Edna Moss and Oscar Blue parade in Meridian Park. Right, Lucille and Beatrice Clark of 905 Fourth St., S.E., made a pretty picture in their new straw hats and plaid coats, gifts of the Easter bunny.

ROBINSON BATTING .429 WITH DODGERS

Homer, 2 Bagger Among His 6 Hits

Ex-Montreal Star Climaxes 1st Week in Majors With 3 for 4

BOSTON—An unseasonable snowstorm caused postponement of the Brooklyn Dodger-Boston Brave baseball game, slated for Braves Field here Sunday.

NEW YORK—Jackie Robinson banged his way into a .429 batting average here last week end, collecting five hits in his last eight times at bat after being held to a lone single, a bunt, in the first two games of the season.

Held hitless as he made his major league debut with the Brooklyn Dodgers, the 1946 International League batting champion unleashed his offensive powers with a home run and single in the third game, and a double and two singles in the fourth.

His efforts were of little help to his Flatbush teammates, however, as the best they could do was finish the initial week of the campaign with a .500 average, resulting from two wins and two losses in the four games played.

Brooklyn got off to a flying start, taking two straight from the Boston Braves in her Ebbets Field home grounds, but dropped both ends of the two-game series here with the Giants.

The Dodgers captured the opening game of the season, 5-3, grabbed the second, 12-6, but lost the third and fourth, 10-4 and 4-3.

Gets 3 to 4

In the Saturday loss to the Giants here at the Polo Grounds, Jackie connected for three hits in four times at bat. Included in the trio of safeties was a slashing double to left center. Robinson checked in with one run scored.

On Friday, the former UCLA all-round star gathered a pair of safeties, one of which was a towering clout into the left field stands, good for the circuit. This was obtained off the Giants' southpaw ace, Dave Koslo, on his second trip to the plate.

He reached the Giant pitching for another safety in the eighth and later turned it into a run, the second scored by him during the afternoon.

First Hit

The Dodger first-sacker was credited with the first hit of his major league career in Boston on Thursday as his mates chalked up their second straight win of the young season over the Hub crew. It was a deft bunt in the fifth inning which he beat out with an exhibition of speedy base-running.

The second game of the series with the Braves was rained out.

Robinson was greeted with cheers as he trotted onto the field to become the first of his race to crash the major leagues on Tuesday. It marked the official opening of the National League season, and Jackie was installed at first base as the Dodgers edged the Braves, 5-3, before 25,623 typically rabid Bum fans.

Although he went through his first test without a hit, Jackie set off the game-winning rally in the seventh frame.

It was a combination of Robinson's beautifully-executed bunt and terrific speed afoot that gave him a "life" on what was meant to be a "sacrifice" play.

Jackie dropped the ball down the baseline with men on first and second, and scampered for his base.

Braves' infielder Ed Torgeson fielded the ball, but, in a frantic effort to retire the flying Robinson threw wildly to right field.

A moment later, Jackie scored all the way from first on Pete Reiser's double off the right field screen. Jackie's run broke the tie and gave the Dodgers the lead they held to the end.

25,000 Cheer Newcomer

The huge opening day throng of 25,623 expressed wholehearted approval of Jackie's presence in the lineup.

On each of four trips to the plate, one could hear pleas throughout the stands: "Come on Jackie," "We're with you, Boy;" and similar words of encouragement.

Robinson had three official times at bat for no hits, and with each failure, a groan went up from the stands as though every man, woman and child were trying as hard as he.

Beats Ball Futilely

In the fifth inning, Jackie was robbed of a hit when the Boston shortstop, Roy Culler, made a diving stop of his hard roller over second, and tossed to Bob Ryan while lying on his stomach to start a double play, with men on first and third.

In the first frame, Robinson grounded to third, in an attempt to hit past the third baseman, who was charging in in anticipation of a bunt.

In the third inning, he flied out to left field.

Jackie was kept busy before the game posing for photographers. He easily won the honor of being the most-photographed man on the field.

Cameramen posed him with Acting-Manager Clyde Sukeforth; with the infield of Ed Stanky, Pee Wee Reese and Johnny Jorgensen; and later, with Brooklyn Borough President John Cashmore, who threw out the first ball.

Witnessing the game was Elisha A. Chandler of Baltimore, winner of the AFRO Sports Quiz Contest. Before the game, Chandler had his picture taken with Jackie and received an autographed portrait of the star.

TUESDAY

BOSTON	Ab	R	H	O	A	BROOKLYN	Ab	R	H	O	A
Culler,ss	3	0	0	0	2	Stanky,2b	3	1	0	0	3
1Holmes	1	0	0	0	0	ROBN'N,1b	3	1	0	11	0
Sisti,ss	0	0	0	0	0	Schultz,1b	0	0	0	1	0
Hopp,cf	5	0	1	2	0	Reiser,cf	2	3	2	2	0
M'Cor'k,rf	4	0	3	2	0	Walker,rf	3	0	1	0	0
R.El'ott,3b	2	0	1	0	2	Tatum,rf	0	0	0	0	0
Litwh'ler,lf	3	1	0	1	0	3Vaughan	1	0	0	0	0
Rowell,lf	1	0	0	0	0	Furillo,rf	0	0	0	0	0
Torge'n,1b	4	1	0	10	1	Herm'ski,lf	4	0	1	3	0
Masi,c	3	0	0	4	0	Edwards,c	2	0	0	2	0
Ryan,2b	4	1	3	4	7	4Rackley	0	0	0	0	0
Sain,p	1	0	0	0	1	Bragan,c	1	0	0	3	0
Cooper,p	0	0	0	1	0	Jorgen'n,3b	3	0	0	0	4
2Neill	0	0	0	0	0	Reese,ss	3	0	1	3	2
Lanf'coni,p	0	0	0	0	0	Hatten,p	2	0	1	1	1
						5Stevens	1	0	0	0	0
						Gregg,p	1	0	0	1	0
						Casey,p	0	0	0	0	0
Totals	31	3	8	24	13	Totals	29	5	6	27	10

1Batted for Cooper in eighth inning.
2Batted for Culler in eighth inning.
3Batted for Hatten in sixth inning.
4Ran for Edwards in sixth inning.
5Batted for Tatum in seventh inning.

BOSTON .... 000 012 000—3
BROOKLYN ...... 000 101 30x—5

Errors—Edwards, Torgenson. Runs batted in—Edwards, Hopp, Ryan (2), Jorgenson, Reiser (2), Hermanski. Two-base hits—Resse, Reiser. Sacrifices—Sain (2), Culler, Masi, ROBINSON. Double plays—Stanky, Reese and ROBINSON; Culler, Ryan and Torgenson.

THURSDAY

BOSTON	Ab	R	H	O	A	BROOKLYN	Ab	R	H	O	A
Culler,ss	2	0	0	0	3	Stanky,2b	3	1	0	2	4
3M'Cor'ck	1	1	1	0	0	ROBN'N,1b	3	1	1	10	1
Sisti,ss	2	0	0	0	2	Reiser,cf	4	2	3	1	0
Hopp,cf	6	0	2	2	0	Furillo,cf	1	0	0	1	0
Rowell,lf	4	0	2	0	0	Walker,rf	3	2	0	0	0
R.El'ott,3b	3	0	0	1	1	Her'nski,lf	2	1	0	1	0
Neill,rf	4	0	0	2	0	Tatum,lf	1	0	0	0	0
Torge'n,1b	4	1	1	13	1	Snider,lf	2	1	1	1	0
Masi,c	5	2	2	2	2	Edwards,c	4	2	3	8	1
Ryan,2b	3	1	2	3	3	Jorg'en,3b	5	2	3	0	2
Cooper,p	0	0	0	0	0	Reese,ss	3	0	0	2	2
Karl,p	0	0	0	1	2	Higbe,p	3	0	1	1	1
1Brady	1	0	0	0	0	Taylor,p	1	0	1	0	1
G.El'ott,p	0	0	0	0	0	Casey,p	0	0	0	0	0
2Holmes	0	1	0	0	0						
Johnson,p	0	0	0	0	1						
4Her'ndez	0	0	0	0	0						
Macon,p	1	0	0	0	1						
Totals	36	6	10	24	16	Totals	35	12	13	27	12

1Flied out for Karl in fourth.
2Walked for G. Elliott in sixth.
3Singled for Culler in sixth.
4Walked for Johnson in seventh.

BOSTON .... 020 004 000— 6
BROOKLYN .... 340 302 00x—12

Errors—Torgeson, Culler, Reese. Runs batted in—Walker, Ryan (2), Hermanski, Edwards, Jorgenson (6), McCormick (2), Hopp (2), Taylor. Two-base hits—Masi, Jorgenson (2), Higbe, Ryan, Hopp, Rowell. Home run—Jorgenson. Sacrifices—Cooper, Stanky, Edwards. Double plays—Torgeson, Karl, Reese, Stankey, Robinson, Sisti, Ryan, Torgeson.

FRIDAY

BROOKLYN (N.L.)	Ab	R	H	O	A	NEW YORK (N.Y.)	Ab	R	H	O	A
Stanky,2b	3	0	0	3	3	Gearhart,cf	2	1	1	3	0
ROB'N,1b	4	2	2	8	0	4Young	1	0	0	0	0
Tatum,lf	4	0	0	2	0	White,cf	0	0	0	1	0
Walker,rf	3	1	2	1	0	Rigney,ss	4	2	2	2	6
Furillo,cf	4	1	2	2	0	Hartung,lf	3	0	0	0	0
Reese,ss	4	0	0	1	0	Mize,1b	3	1	2	15	0
Jorg'en,3b	4	0	1	0	0	Cooper,c	4	0	0	3	0
Bragan,c	3	0	0	7	1	Marshall,rf	4	1	2	1	0
Lombardi,p	1	0	0	0	0	Thomson,2b	4	3	4	1	5
1Lund	1	0	0	0	0	Lohrke,3b	3	1	1	1	3
Chandler,p	0	0	0	0	2	Koslo,p	4	1	0	0	5
2Brown	1	0	0	0	0						
Behrman,p	0	0	0	0	1						
3Edwards	1	0	0	0	0						
Totals	33	4	7	24	7	Totals	34	10	12	27	19

1Batted for Lombardin in fourth inning.
2Batted for Chandler in seventh inning.
3Batted for Behrman in ninth inning.
4Batted for Gearhart in eighth inning.

BROOKLYN .... 011 000 200— 4
NEW YORK .... 013 002 04x—10

Errors—Thomson, Bragan, Marshall, Hartung. Runs batted in—Reese, Thomson (2), ROBINSON, Rigney (6), Mize, Marshall, Walker. Two-base hits—Jorgensen, Marshall. Home runs—Thomson (2), Robinson, Rigney (2), Mize, Marshall. Sacrifice—Rigney. Double plays—Bragan and Reese; Koslo, Rigney and Mize; Lohrke and Mize.

SATURDAY

BROOKLYN	Ab	R	H	O	A	NEW YORK	Ab	R	H	O	A
Stanky,2b	4	1	1	4	2	Gearhart,cf	4	1	1	6	1
ROB'N,1b	4	1	3	4	1	Rigney,ss	5	1	2	0	1
Reiser,cf	4	1	1	5	0	Hartung,lf	4	0	0	0	0
Walker,rf	3	0	1	2	0	White,lf	0	0	0	0	0
2Rackley	0	0	0	0	0	Mize,1b	3	2	1	6	1
Furillo,lf	2	0	0	0	0	Marshall,rf	3	0	3	3	0
Her'nski,lf	3	0	0	0	0	Cooper,c	4	0	3	6	1
Edwards,c	4	0	1	7	0	Tho'son,2b	4	0	0	4	2
Jorg'sen,3b	2	0	0	1	1	Lohrke,3b	2	0	0	2	0
Reese,ss	2	0	0	1	2	Kennedy,p	1	0	1	0	1
Branca,p	2	0	0	0	1	Voiselle,p	3	0	0	0	1
Higbe,p	0	0	0	0	0						
1Snider	1	0	0	0	0						
Casey,p	0	0	0	0	0						
Totals	31	3	7	24	7	Totals	33	4	11	27	8

1Fanned for Higbe in eighth.
2 Ran for Walker in ninth.

BROOKLYN ..... 003 000 000—3
NEW YORK ..... 201 010 00x—4

Errors—None. Runs batted in—Mize (2), Walker (2), Furillo, Rigney, Cooper. Two-base hits—ROBINSON, Rigney, Cooper. Home runs—Mize, Rigney. Stolen bases—Gearhart, Jorgenson. Sacrifice—Branca. Double plays—Gearhart, Thomson; Reese, Stanky, ROBINSON.

Campy Wins Royal Clean-up Spot

THAT BUM INFIELD—Another history-making picture. It's of Jackie Robinson and his mates in the Brooklyn Dodgers' opening game infield. Left to right, it's Johnny Jorgensen, third baseman, from Folsom, Cal.; Pee Wee Reese, shortstop, from Louisville, Ky.; Ed Stanky, second baseman, from Mobile, Ala., and Jackie Robinson, first baseman, from Los Angeles, Cal.

ALL THE SAME?—Last year, Jackie Robinson launched his minor league career with a home run in his opening game. This year, he connected for the circuit in his third game. Last year, he went on to lead the International League with a .349 average. Today, he is batting .429 for four games. Picture above shows the Dodger first baseman crossing the plate after his first major league round-tripper, rapped out in the Polo Grounds, New York, on Friday. Congratulating him is teammate Tom Tatum, white outfielder.

Looking 'em Over

With SAM LACY

BALTIMORE. — A greatly changed Roy Campanella pulled a second pillow under his head and looked at the ceiling of his hotel room.

For the first time in the better-than-eight years I had known him, he appeared to be completely relaxed. This was something new for the 26-year-old Philadelphian who now rates the No. 1 slot of the Montreal Royals' catching staff.

In former years, Campanella had been the restless, devil-may-care guy who liked nothing better than being on his feet doing something, anything. Even two months ago, in Havana, the stocky little ball player found it hard to sit still long enough to finish a game of cut-throat pinochle. Idleness bored him to distraction, relaxation was something meant for someone else.

Now it is different. Now he can toss everything out of his mind at a moment's notice. Now he knows how to rest, to be quiet, to take it easy.

Had Noticed Change

Under ordinary conditions, I'd probably have been shocked by such a decided transformation. But earlier in the day I had watched him play his first game of International League ball here, catching for the Royals against the local Orioles.

I noticed then what a different catcher he was, how much he had improved over the jittery, bouncing, you-never-know-what performer he had been up to a few months ago. I noticed how cool he was under fire and how he brushed off his inability to hit as though it were a fleck of dandruff on his coat lapel.

"Say, Fellow," I began, "what's come over you? That was a nice game you caught out there today. I'm beginning to believe you're going to be all right. You know, I've been rather slow warming up to you as a catcher, but you look like you're going to make me change my mind."

"Thanks, Homey," Campy drawled sleepily, using a term he applies to just about everyone, "I kinda think I'm going to be okey, myself. I know one thing, I have improved a lot. I can feel it myself. I can actually see it.

"There are things I'm doing now, and doing naturally, that I never knew were in a catcher's book before. Like when I threw that guy out at second today when he tried to steal.

"I remember the time when I'd find myself throwing the ball to ceterfield, trying to be sure it go down there. Today, when the runner got ahead of me, I didn't get excited, I just cut loose and threw. The ball bounced down there and Campanis got his man, but it wasn't a good throw by any means.

"Many's the time I'd have been afraid to bounce a ball to second and it would have gotten away from me in my haste to catch up to the runner. I've learned to depend on my infielders a little more. But the main thing, I think, is that I don't get excited like I used to."

Mates Get Credit

I wanted to know how could he account for such a radical change in such a short time. And Campy quickly passed the credit along to his teammates.

"These guys are swell, Homey. A fellow can't help getting a hold on himself when he's with a bunch that's always pulling for him. I don't know of a single one of these guys who doesn't drop me a hint whenever he gets the chance.

"To tell you the truth, I can't put my finer on any one thing in particular, but I can say that they're a swell bunch and all of 'em are playing to win. They're really 'team' guys.

"Skipper's a good guy, too." Campanella continued referring to Manager Clay Hopper, a Mississippian by birth. "Everything Jackie said about him, I've found to be true. He hasn't shown any signs of partiality, unless it has been in my favor, and up to now working for him has been a pleasure.

Chided for his failure to hit in his first appearance in this city, where he made his record as a catcher with the Baltimore Elites, Campy laughed:

"You know, that's how I realize how much I've changed. Once upon a time, that would worry me to death almost. I'd be as evil as an old maid and I guess I'd fret until I could get out there and slam one into the stands.

"But I've learned to take all that in stride. Maybe its the soothing effect of playing with guys who make you know that whatever you do it all right, so long as you're trying.

"Whatever it is, I know I've less effort. And its so much nicer this way."

learned how to play it to the hilt and to fight just as hard with much

You guys who know Campy will see what I mean. Imagine the knock-down-drag-out little firebrand you knew two years ago, talking about something being "nice" or "nicer." Yeah, Campy's a changed man.

AFRO QUIZ WINNER GETS JACKIE'S JOHN HENRY — Elisha A. Chandler of Baltimore, winner of the AFRO sports quiz contest which carried with it an all-expense trip to NY to see Jackie Robinson in the opening game with the Brooklyn Dodgers, gets Jackie's autograph before he saw the game which the Dodgers won 5-3 on Tuesday at Ebbetts Field.

Jackie's Record

INCLUDING APRIL 20th

Batting

G	AB	R	H	2B	3B	HR	Pct.
4	14	5	6	1	0	1	.429

Fielding

G	PO	A	DP	E	Pct.
4	33	2	4	0	1.000

Campanella's Record

INCLUDING APRIL 20th

Batting

G	AB	R	H	2B	3B	HR	Pct.
2	8	1	2	0	0	0	.250

Fielding

G	PO	A	DP	E	Pct.
4	33	2	4	0	1.000

Barons In 6-4 Score Over Grays

BIRMINGHAM (ANP)—Pitcher wildness enabled the Black Barons to score two runs without a hit in the eighth inning and win, 6 to 4, from the Homestead Grays at Rickwood Field here Wednesday night.

Jimmy Newberry, who struck out 11 batters, five in a row, was hit on the head by one of relief pitcher Eugene Smith's odd pitches and had to be taken from the field. James Perry, who replaced him, retired the Grays on strikeouts in the ninth inning. Newberry was credited with the victory and William Pope charged with the loss. Grounhog Thompson, Grays' starting pitcher, left the game with his team leading 2 to 1 in the fourth.

Following the Stars

WEDNESDAY—
Phila. at BROOKLYN (Jackie)
MONTREAL (Campy) at Jersey City
THURSDAY—
Phila. at BROOKLYN (Jackie)
MONTREAL (Campy) at Jersey City
FRIDAY—
New York at BROOKLYN (Jackie)
MONTREAL (Campy) at Jersey City
SATURDAY—
New York at BROOKLYN (Jackie)
MONTREAL (Campy) at Newark
SUNDAY—
New York at BROOKLYN (Jackie)
MONTREAL (Campy) at Newark

Lincoln Ball Team Nips Scrappy Service Outfit

BAINBRIDGE, Md. — Lincoln University's baseball team eked out a 10-9 victory over Bainbridge Naval Training Station here, Friday, scoring the decisive run in the last frame.

Bob Bishop, a sophomore, one of three hurlers used by the Lions, was credited with the win. Lincoln garnered 13 hits off 4 Bainbridge pitchers, while the losers nicked Lion hurlers for 9.

The two teams will play a return game Thursday, April 24, on Lincoln's campus.

Taylor Pleased With His Chigiants' Outlook

JACKSON, Miss. (NNPA) — The Chicago American Giants broke camp here late last Saturday evening and started their trek northward, leaving for Nashville by bus.

Thoroughly satisfied with the team's showing in spring drills, "Candy Jim" Taylor, veteran manager of the Giants, said the team is the best club he has trained in the past eight years.

"The club has speed, hitting power and fielding ability, plus a good pitching staff," Taylor said, adding that "We'll be hard to beat."

Lincoln vs. Drexel

LINCOLN U., Pa. — (ANP)—Lincoln University has scheduled Drexel Institute of Technology, white, for a dual track meet on May 14 on Lincoln's campus.

New Montreal Star Lauded by Hopper

Grabs No. 1 Catcher's Berth From ex-Dodger; Gets Two Hits

SYRACUSE, N.Y. — Roy Campanella, former Baltimore Elite Giants' catching star, taking up where Jackie Robinson left off as top man of the Montreal Royals, was installed in the No. 4 slot of the batting order as the 1946 International League champions opened the season here Thursday.

The chunky little receiver, rated one of the top men in the Negro National League when he was with the Elites, responded by slapping out a pair of singles in five trips plateward as his mates edged the Chiefs, 11-10.

Kept inactive by cold weather on Saturday, Campy failed to connect in the opening game of Sunday's double-header in Baltimore but thrilled 18,502 paid customers with a smooth exhibition of catching. The Royals swept both ends of the twin-bill with the Orioles, 6-2 and 8-2.

He had an unusually busy day for a catcher, being responsible for 12 putouts, seven via strikeouts, three on high foul lofts and two on plays at the plate. In the nightcap, Campanella gave way to Mike Sandlock, former Brooklyn Dodger catcher, whom he has replaced in the favor of Manager Clay Hopper.

Hopper, speaking of his new backstopper, told the AFRO Sunday: "Roy looks like he has the goods. He has steadied down considerably back there, and the improvement he's shown in handling pitchers and throwing is amazing. There's never been any question about his hitting."

Against the Orioles, Campanella walked the first time at bat on a hitless day. He struck out in the third, and flied to left after slamming one of Southpaw Joe Pennington's slant fouls deep into the left field bleachers. In the seventh, his sharp drive near second was taken by Baltimore Shortstop Bob Repass and turned into a double-play.

THURSDAY

MONTREAL	Ab	R	H	O	A	SYRACUSE	Ab	R	H	O	A
Welaj,ss	5	0	1	3	8	Corbitt,ss	5	3	1	2	2
Woyt,3b	6	4	3	1	2	Beeler,cf	6	1	2	4	0
Naylor,cf	5	1	3	3	0	Sauer,lf	2	2	1	1	0
C'panella,c	5	1	2	2	2	Mele,rf	6	0	2	1	0
C'panis,2b	4	1	1	4	3	Rub'in 3b	5	2	2	0	4
Pless,lf	4	0	0	2	1	West,c	5	0	2	4	1
Matney,rf	1	0	1	0	0	Drews,2b	2	1	1	1	6
Whit'an,rf	3	2	1	1	0	Stokes,1b	3	0	0	13	1
Torres,1b.	5	1	1	11	0	Prend'st,p	0	0	0	0	0
Banta,p	0	0	0	0	0	Erickson,p	4	1	1	1	0
Brown,p	1	0	0	0	0	Bebber,p	0	0	0	0	0
Smolko,p	2	0	0	0	1						
1Sessi	1	1	1	0	0						
Pfund,p	0	0	0	0	0						
2Atwell	0	0	0	0	0						
Heusser,p	0	0	0	0	0						
T'ls	42	11	14	27	17	T'ls	38	10	12	27	14

1Singled for Smolko in eighth.
2Walked for Pfund in ninth.

Montreal 4 0 0 0 1 0 1 4 1—11
Syracuse 3 2 4 0 0 1 0 0 0—11

Errors — Veeler, Pluss, Campanis, Corbitt. Runs batted in—Campanella (2), Campanis, Pluss, Matney, West (2), Mele (2) (Reubeling, Erickson (2), Saurer, Naylor (2), Bessi, Woyt, Welaj. Two-base hits—Reubeling, Naylor (2). Stolen base—West.

SUNDAY

MONTREAL	Ab	R	H	O	A	ORIOLES	Ab	R	H	O	A
Weland,ss	4	2	1	0	2	Wilson,3b	3	1	0	1	4
Wyott,3b	5	1	3	1	1	C'pbell,lf	4	1	2	3	0
Naylor,cf	5	0	2	2	1	Mel'dick,cf	4	0	0	2	0
C'panella,c	3	0	0	12	1	Moss,rf	4	0	0	0	0
C'panis,2b	4	0	0	2	2	D'lgren,1b	2	0	0	10	1
Pluss,lf	2	0	0	2	0	Repass,ss	4	0	0	1	3
Matney,rf	4	1	1	4	0	Lenn,c	4	0	1	7	2
Torres,1b	4	1	2	4	1	Cihocki,2b	2	0	0	2	3
Palica,p	4	1	2	0	0	Penn'ton,p	1	0	1	0	0
						Barr'lari,p	1	0	0	0	0
						1Br'htman	1	0	0	0	0
						Gast,p	0	0	0	1	0
Totals	35	6	11	27	8	Totals	30	2	4	27	13

1Fanned for Barillari in seventh.

MONTREAL ..... 110 030 001—6
ORIOLES ...... 100 100 000—2

Errors — Dahlgren, Woyt, Welan, Moss, Cihocki. Runs batted in—Naylor (2), Campbell, Palica (2), Repass, Weland, Woyt. Three-base hits—Campbell, Torres, Lenn. Double plays—Wilson, Dahlgren; Campanis, Torres; Repass, Cihocki, Dahlgren; Naylor, Torres, Campanis, Torres.

Dixie Papers Delete Jackie's Good Playing

MIAMI, Fla. — Associated News releases dealing with the debut of Jackie Robinson, were deleted in all Florida dailies with the exception of the West Palm Beach Post.

Concerning Robinson the Post said: "Although he did not get a hit in four official times at bat, Jackie Robinson, first Negro to play in modern big league ball, signalized his official debut as a Dodger by sprinting home with the deciding run on Reiser's smash and playing perfect ball at first base.

All other papers merely emphasized the fact that Jackie had failed to connect in four times at bat.

Maid Sobs Out Tale of Bondage

RED STAR TUESDAY EDITION

WASHINGTON AFRO-AMERICAN

10¢ AND WORTH MORE!

55th Year, No. 48 Contents of This Newspaper Copyrighted 1947 by The AFRO-AMERICAN Company WASHINGTON, D.C., July 8, 1947 Entered in the Postoffice at Washington, D. C., as Second-Class Matter, under Act of March 3, 1879 16 PAGES, 8 MAGAZINE PAGES

Doby Plays With Indians

Helps Mates Win 2nd Game

Handles First Base Position Flawlessly

35,000 SEE DEBUT

Managers Promise Ex-GI 'Every Chance'

By SAM LACY
AFRO Sports Editor

CHICAGO—A shirt-sleeved crowd of 35,000 wild-eyed fans got its first glimpse of a colored player in an American League baseball game, here, Sunday, when the Cleveland Indians unveiled their rookie infielder, Larry Doby, as a starter in the nightcap of a doubleheader with the Chicago White Sox.

The 23-year-old ex-Navy veteran, and one of the top batters in the Negro National League, until his sale last week by the Newark Eagles, trotted onto the field to play first base in an infield which includes the most widely-celebrated second base combination in the junior circuit.

Doby replaced Eddie Robinson, white, former first baseman of the Baltimore Orioles, in the second game of the bill which the Indians split. He drove in one of the runs as he and his mates took the decision, 5-1, after dropping the the opener, 3-2.

Smacks Single on Second Trip

The blow was a single, acquired on his second trip to the plate in Sunday's game and his third batting appearance since joining the club the previous day.

On Saturday, the former Newark star struck out in the role of pinch-hitter. But Manager Lou Boudreau expressed little concern over this failure since Doby had just donned a uniform and was still nervous from the introductions which had taken place only a couple of hours before in the clubhouse.

Announcement of his purchase from the Eagles was made on Thursday, by Bill Veeck, president of the Indians. He was told to join the team here Saturday. He came on from Philadelphia, following completion of a July 4 double-header between the Eagles and Philly Stars.

Led Hitting in Former League

The 185-pound South Carolina-born lad batted .458 through the first half of the Negro National

(Continued on Page 13, Col. 6)

—AND NO PROBLEM—Children of both races find relief from summer heat in an ol' swimmin' hole near a village in Vermont. The colored youngsters are in the Green Mountain State under the auspices of the "Vermont Plan" to build up goodwill between the races

Jackie Stars Even Though Bums Lose

By OLLIE STEWART

NEW YORK—It took me more than 40 years to do it, but at last I have seen a major league baseball game—and Jackie Robinson in action.

Running true to form, I picked the worst day of the season to go to Ebbets Field in Brooklyn. I went on July 3, that awful day when the Giants mauled, lambasted and buried the Dodgers under a 19 to 2 score. It was murder.

A Perfect Bunt

The one bright spot of the afternoon was a perfect bunt laid down the third base line by Jackie Robinson on his third trip up to the plate.

Eddie Stanky was moved to second, and Robinson was safe at first, when Dave Koslo, Giant pitcher was unable to field the bunt in time to make a play.

20-Game Hitting Streak

This exhibition of Robinson's skill ran his hitting streak in consecutive games up to 20.

But before this happened, the well had caved in on the Dodgers. They really looked like what people call them—BUMS.

(Continued on Page 13, Col. 1)

ANTI-WESLEY MEETING FLOPS, ATTENDANCE POOR

WILBERFORCE, Ohio—A mass meeting called to win support and raise funds for the anti-Wesley faction led by Bishop Reverdy Ransom attracted only 196 of 1000 persons expected, one-third of them children.

WEALTH AND PEONAGE:

Maid Describes Event Which Led to 'Slavery'

SAN DIEGO, Calit.—Recounting her years of enslavemetn at the hands of the Alfred W. Ingallses, prominent socialites, Miss Dora Jones, their maid, broke into tears as she told a Federal court on Thursday that Mrs. Ingalls also threatened to have her committed to an insane asylum.

Now 58 years old, Miss Jones said that she had submitted to slavery since 1913 through fear of an immediate jail sentence and hell in the future because she had been intimate with Mrs. Ingall's first husband, Walter Harmon, who is now living in Washington.

As a result of that affair, Miss Jones continued, she became pregnant and was forced by Mrs. Ingalls to undergo a criminal operation. Later, she added, her employer told her that "in hell, the baby would be holding out its hands to me."

Maid, Employer Weep

Miss Jones, who has been successful in retaining her composure in spite of her 34 years of bondage, broke down when she testified that Mrs. Ingalls said that she could be placed in a mental institution as she had "the mentality of a child of 12."

Shortly after her outburst, Mrs Ingalls herself decided to weep.

Although the prosecution states that Miss Jones is still "bound psychologically," the woman already is showing the good effects of her four months of freedom.

Attired in a simple black dress with black ringlets encircling her thin face, she presents a marked contrast to the haggard woman whose curly hair was kept clipped close to the head during her years of bondage.

Calmest Person in Court

By far the calmest person in the courtroom, Miss Jones kept her eyes on Mrs. Betty M. Craydon, assistant United States attorney, instead of on the Ingallses, who smiled at her.

(Continued on Page 2, Col. 5)

138 Scholarships Awarded in Md.

20 Colleges Selected; State Outlay $16,346

BALTIMORE

One hundred thirty-eight scholarships, mostly to teachers, were awarded last week to Marylanders to study outside of the State by the State Committee on Scholarships.

The top scholarship for summer school study is $200.

New York University is the most popular school and was chosen by 52 persons. Columbia University was second with 37.

All of the scholarship recipients are working for higher degrees. The total amount awarded is $16,346.

There is every indication that the total scholarships awarded by the State of Maryland for the whole year will exceed $70,000.

Field of Education Popular

Most of the students have chosen education as the field of study.

The following is a list of scholar-

(Continued on Page 14, Col. 4)

Smuts Orders Check on Cruelty to Native Workers by Farmers

JOHANNESBURG, South Africa—Upon instructions from Prime Minister Jan Christiaan Smuts, hundreds of jeep-riding police from Pretoria and this city raided farms in the Rethal district Saturday to check on allegations of cruelty to native laborers by white farmers.

The police, working in groups of 20, took statements from the laborers and told them that farmers were not allowed to lock them in compounds like cattle. Work on many farms stopped when laborers left because of such mistreatment.

No Receiver for 'Defender' Yet; Decision Postponed

CHICAGO — Judge Robert E. Crowe of Superior Court, postponed until Aug. 11, decision on the appointment of William H. Stuart, white, as receiver of the Chicago Defender.

The receiver had been asked by James B. Cashin, chairman of the Robert A. Abbott Publishing Company and co-executor with John Sengstacke of the estate of the late Mr. Abbott, who died seven years ago. The fight between Messrs. Cashin and Sengstacke for the control of the Defender which has been going on for sometime, came to a head recently when Mr. Cashlin put in a claim for $20,000 for fees due him as a executor.

Mr. Sengstacke

When his claim was not promptly met, he charged gross mismanagement and asked for a receiver.

Once with White Daily

Stuart, who is wanted as receiver by Mr. Cashin is a former political editor of the Herald American and a one-time press agent for the late Mayor Thompson.

In fighting the appointment of a white receiver, opponents have pointed out that there is no need for one, inasmuch as the company is not an insolvent one, it does not have any serious liabilities and it was Mr. Abbott's desire to keep the corporation in the hands of the colored race, which the paper serves.

Tried to Prevent This

In connection with the last argument, they add that the founder so arranged his will as to protect the newspaper as an institu

(Continued on Page 2, Col. 3)

Suspected Slayer, Obsessed by 'Hex,' Killed in Gun Fight

NASHVILLE—Said to have been driven mad by a "hex" obsession, Robert Waddy, 47, owner of a tavern, under indictment on a murder charge, was slain by police as he shot it out with them after walking into a trap which they had laid for him the night of July 3.

Police said Waddy, the night before the fatal fight, had dynamited the combination home and filling station of Frank Tetreault, a fortune teller, in an effort to rid himself of a fancied "evil spell." Four persons were injured in the blast.

Earlier that day, police declared, Waddy had shot two women in an effort to cast off a supposed "voodoo," in which he accused them of having a hand. Having served four years in jail for killing a merchant in 1935, Waddy was out of prison on $10,000 bail, on the recent charge of slaying his wife. He was to be tried next Tuesday.

Hodge Party of 40 on Tour of Mexico

NEW YORK — Adolph Hodge, New York school teacher, and a party of 40 from seven States and the District of Columbia left June 29 on a tour of Mexico.

Before the war, Mr. Hodge conducted his tours abroad, chiefly in Europe and Africa.

Royal Welcome Assured

The party will stay in first class hotels, visit the Volcano Paracutin, and go swimming both in the Atlantic and Pacific Oceans.

Tourists sponsored by the Hodge agency always receive a royal welcome in Mexico. The party's first stop this year is the Hotel Isabel,

(Continued on Page 2, Col. 4)

Illinois Physicians Deliver Lectures at University of Ga.

ATHENS, Ga. — The University of Georgia recently invited Dr. N. O. Calloway and Dr. J. E. Bryant of Evanston, Ill., to conduct a series of lectures at the post-graduate short course given at that institution's medical school.

Dr. Calloway is an assistant professor of internal medicine at the University of Illinois Dr. Bryant is an attending physician at Provident Hospital and a member of the Chicago Institute of Tuberculosis.

Happy Harlem Children Enjoying 'Vermont Plan'

Envoys of Good Will Make Presence Felt

Many Returning for 2nd, 3rd Year; All Elated Over Natural Beauty

By STAFF CORRESPONDENT

BURLINGTON, Vt.—It was a happy, boisterous group of children who arrived in the local depot from Harlem one day last week. In charge of the party of about 80 boys and girls were Mrs. Laura B. Thomas, who was making her fourth summer visit to the Green Mountains, and Mrs. Anna Felder, who was taking the place of Mrs. Anna Newsome, unable to make the journey because of sickness.

The two women had arranged for everybody to sing "The More We Get Together" as they stepped off the train to greet their Vermont hosts, but the children were so excited that they forgot all about it and rushed pell-mell down the coach steps onto the station platform.

The youngsters were sponsored by the Abyssinian Baptist Church, the Rev Adam C. Powell Jr., pastor, and came to this State under the auspices of the "Vermont Plan," which aims to build up good will and friendship between members of the two races.

The Rev. A. Ritchie Low, a white Congregational minister of Johnson, Vt., is founder of the movement.

Youth Ambassadors

The idea is to use children as "bridges," as ambassadors of understanding; to help roll away both mists and myths, and to stress the point, whether white or black, Protestant or non-Protestant, Jew or Gentile, all are fellow Americans, sons and daughters of a common God.

This plan, simple truth, is "catching on," as is evidenced by the fact that this summer a number of other States are planning to carry out similar projects. They include Minnesota, Colorado, California, and, nearer home, Illinois and Indiana.

'So Glad to Be Back'

Waiting for the children on the platform were the hosts in whose homes they were to be entertained for two weeks.

Some boys and girls were returning for second and third visits and had no trouble finding them. The reunions were fascinating. Young tongues worked like mad. Older ones too!

"So glad to be back"; "How're Harry and Betty?" "Awfully pleased you could come"; "Did you have a nice train ride?" "It seems good to put my feet on nice soft grass again"—these were some of the greetings I overheard.

Some of the young people are on farms, others in village homes, a few in the larger places. The first batch got off the train in Bennington, the first stop in Vermont; others in Manchester, Rutland, Middlebury, Vergennes.

5 to YMCA Boys' Camp

Five boys continued on the train to South Hero, where they are to be guests at one of the largest boys' camps in the East, Camp Abnaki. It is operated by the YMCA.

This will be the third year boys have gone there. After the first visit, Camp Manager Clyde Hess was asked how the two visitors got along. There were about 200 in camp, and they were the only colored boys present.

"They got along swell," Clyde told me. "The only mistake we made was in not inviting more."

The whole camp turned up at the private railroad station and gave the young Harlemites a grand, rousing welcome. It was more than they had expected and they were very much impressed. Everyone went out of his way to be friendly to them.

Campers Become Envious

Each was put in a cabin with the white youngsters, and they quickly got acquainted. In a day or so some of the white kids in other cabins went to Mr. Hess, wanting to know why one of the lads couldn't be sent to live with them.

It wasn't fair, they pointed out, that two cabins should monopolize the boys all to themselves. Their complaint was, discrimination in reverse!

Move From Cabin to Cabin

Clyde Hess listened attentively and said he would see what he could do about it.

When he discussed it with the camp faculty, it was decided that when inspections were made each morning the two neatest cabins would be rewarded by having one of the

(Continued on Page 3, Col. 1)

COLLEGE STUDENT AT 16—After passing tests at the Fuller School with the highest grades in the institution's history, Adrian Gordon, 10, daughter of Mr. and Mrs. David Gordon of Chicago, will enter the University of Chicago this fall on a two-year $400 scholarship to the university. She writes plays and short stories, is studying music and likes to play baseball.

GOP LEADERS SORE:

Chafe Over Selection of Speakers at Rally

By RALPH MATTHEWS

WASHINGTON (AFRO National Bureau)—Republican leaders in the Capital have their mouths stuck way out to here — over the way they were ignored by speakers at the recent NAACP national conference here.

Most of the grumbling centers around the speakers who addressed the plenary sessions in which the GOP was given a verbal shellacking by one and all with no chance at rebuttal.

Leon Henderson, one of the organizers of Americans for Democratic Action, Helen Gahagan Douglas and Philip Murray laid it on thick, although the speeches were not supposed to be political, but merely expressions of the liberal point of view.

But it turned out that it was impossible to be liberal without being anti-Republican.

Strategy Challenged

The question local Republicans are asking is, "How does the NAACP expect to push its legisla-

(Continued on Page 2, Col. 1)

Rumor Says Sims May Quit AME's

PHILADELPHIA

Rumors that the Rev. David H. Sims plans to establish a church of his own gained widespread circulation here, last week, following Federal Judge George A Welsh's decision upholding the cleric's ouster as an AME bishop.

No one, however, could be pinned down on details or how far the movement had progressed. The former head of the First Episcopal District could not be reached for a statement. He was reported out of the city over the week end.

While disclaiming knowledge of

(Continued on Page 14 col. 5)

Ransom Erred, Say Cleveland Alumni

CLEVELAND, Ohio. — "The ouster of Dr. Charles H. Wesley is a serious mistake," Harold J. Barnett, president of the local Wilberforce University Alumni Association, told Bishop Reverdy C. Ransom, chairman of the university's board of trustees, in a letter on June 12.

Mr. Barnett advised Bishop Ransom then, that "your actions in removing Dr. Wesley have merely added to the confusion and the complexity of the situation at the school," and urged that he ask the board "to reconsider its action."

The local alumni president declared further that: "It seems to us that the most important problem for the board was to comply with the recommendations of the North Central Association to remedy the weaknesses pointed out by the accrediting association."

The Des Moines Register SPORTS

SATURDAY, OCTOBER 4, 1947. ★★★★ 9

Dodger Daring Squares Series with Yanks---

1 OUT FROM NO-HITTER, BEVENS BOWS, 3-2

Lavagetto's Double Ruins Hurler's Bid for Fame

Sittin' ★ ★ In ★ ★ With the Athletes

BY SEC TAYLOR

GREAT IS THE WORD FOR IT.

BROOKLYN, N. Y. — Grumblers, who criticized the baseball, or the lack of it displayed by the Yankees and Dodgers in the first three World Series games, had nothing to complain about Friday night.

Not only did they see a one-hit game by Bill Bevens, a game won on that single hit; some splendid pitching by two Brooklyn relief hurlers — Hal Gregg, who allowed only one run and four hits in seven innings, and Hugh Casey, who won the game on one pitch—three series playing records broken and another tied, and a typical Flatbush demonstration when the home team won, but also a contest punctuated with some of the finest fielding by the Yankees that one team ever put together in nine innings of play and some equally tight, though perhaps not so sensational, defensive work by the Dodgers.

George (Snuffy) Stirnweiss authored the first thriller at the expense of Pee Wee Reese in the initial inning.

Ed Stanky had teased the first of 10 passes from Bevens. Reese, who had been moved to second place in the batting order in Manager Burt Shotton's shakeup in which Jackie Robinson was dropped to third position and Carl Furillo to seventh, hit a grounder through the box and over second base.

It was a hit-and-run play, with Stanky off with the pitch. Stirnweiss darted back of the keystone bag, fielded the ball, and, apparently sensing there was not a chance for a play on Stanky, wheeled and threw out the batter at first base.

In the third inning, Robinson hit a long foul fly near the left-field box seats. Johnny Lindell made a long run, stuck out his gloved hand and speared the ball only inches from the turf and only a few feet from the railing separating boxes from field.

Next to thrill the spectators was incomparable Joe DiMaggio, not so much because of the difficulty of the catch, but because he did it with the ease and grace of the man on the flying trapeze.

Gene Hermanski laced a terrific liner over the Yankee center fielder's head and to his right. But he trotted back and gigged the ball with his padded mitt as though he were leaping into the low hanging branches of a tree to pick an apple.

He seemed to have sprained his ankle slightly in making this play, for he limped about the greensward for a few minutes before resuming play.

First Baseman George McQuinn also handled a hard grounder off Reese's bat in the seventh as if it were simply a routine stop for him.

In the eighth inning Hermanski also slammed into a Bevens pitch with a full swing. This time the resulting liner went into right field. When it seemed the drive would clash into the scoreboard for a sure double, Tommy Henrich did a leap into the azure and stifled its screams, also with his gloved flipper.

Bruce Edwards, first up in the last half of the ninth, had fanned on his three previous appearances at the chopping block. This time he lined a sizzler into left field. Lindell pushed his back

SITTIN' IN—
Continued on Page Eleven.

'HELLO, MR. CHIPS'—Manager Burt Shotton (right) greets Cookie Lavagetto with an enthusiastic hug after the latter had delivered the Dodgers from defeat in the fourth game of the World Series Friday in Ebbets Field.

★ ★ ★ ★ ★ ★ ★ ★

COOKIE JUST GRINS; BUMS LAUD LOSER

'His Curve Breaks Like Slider.'

By Ted Smits.

BROOKLYN, N. Y. (AP)—Hal Gregg was explaining in a sad, professional sort of way what it was that Bill Bevens had.

"His curve ball breaks like a slider," he was saying as he shaved. "He keeps it outside and he keeps his fast ball inside, way inside."

Harry Taylor, who put the Dodgers in quite a spot in the first inning, lay face down on a bench.

There was hardly anyone in the Dodgers dressing room because the big celebration was going to come over in the Yankee rooms when Bevens came in with a no-hitter.

The loudspeaker said Cookie Lavagetto was going to bat for Eddie Stanky.

"Yeah, I guess that's all right," someone said.

Then a roar started, growing in

DODGERS—
Continued on Page Eleven.

8 2-3 Hitless Frames

N. Y. Pitcher Also Sets Walk Record; Lombardi, Shea Go Today.

By Bill Bryson.
(Staff Writer.)

BROOKLYN, N. Y.—There was never anything like it before . . . two out in the ninth and Brooklyn's first hit of the entire ball game beat the New York Yankees, 3-2, to square the World Series Friday.

Bill Bevens was ready to step across the threshold of a personal hall of fame, the only pitcher to unfurl a no-hitter in a World Series.

Already the brawny Yankee had eclipsed by one full frame the Series mark for consecutive hitless innings.

Dodgers were on first and second, but Bevens had whistled a strike past Cookie Lavagetto, the 33-year-old spare wheel who was batting for Ed Stanky.

Ebbets Field rocked to its foundation from the stamping and yelling of 33,443 frenzied fans. The pressure was pulse-thumping, the suspense maddening.

Bevens' long right arm, weary from the extra pitching involved in allowing a record total of 10 walks, swept the vital pitch toward the plate.

Swarthy Lavagetto met it on the fat of his club. It arched against the friendly right-field fence. This time Tommy Henrich couldn't make a leaping life-saving catch as he had done the inning before.

The drive caromed off the wall which advertises the movie, "The Secret Life of Walter Mitty."

Thurber Mild.

But the public life of swarthy Harry Lavagetto was more thrilling. More heroic than anything James Thurber's shy character ever day-dreamed. The most wild-eyed, feverishly imaginative Hollywood writer would never have dared to try a script calling for such a finish.

Pinch-runners Al Gionfriddo and Ed Miksis scampered across the plate. Before Lavagetto got to second, all his mates and a big share of the box-seat customers were there to embrace him. They slapped him, they hugged him, they kissed him.

Bevens, the condemned hero, had several stays of execution as his three best friends—Henrich, Joe DiMaggio and Johnny Lindell—interceded.

Twice, Gene Hermanski was a casualty of Yankee outfielding that stirred memories of Tris Speaker and Harry Hooper and Terry Moore.

Henrich was scraping his back on the scoreboard as he jumped high for his eighth-inning stab. And, back in the fourth, DiMaggio had loped to extreme left-center for a leaping, back-handed pluck of another Hermanski wallop.

Lindell, the former Iowan who is leading the Series regulars with a .500 average, twice rescued the wildly effective Bevens.

In the third, Johnny showed the speed that once brought him the California prep hurdling record. He raced 90 feet to get in the general neighborhood of where Jackie Robinson's looping foul was descending.

It still didn't seem he had a chance. But he dived, somersaulted—and came up with the ball in his glove.

Johnny also galloped back to the fence to pull down Bruce Edwards' liner, which carried an extra-base menace, at the start of the ninth.

That made 25 Dodgers retired without a hit. The number grew to 26 when, after Carl Furillo teased Bevens for the record-fracturing walk, Spider Jorgensen lifted a puny foul to First Baseman George McQuinn.

The decibels of sound must have created a new Flatbush record (one destined to be broken a few moments later) when Pete Reiser limped out to bat for Hugh Casey, the fourth Dodger pitcher, who delivered only one ball to be-

SERIES—
Continued on Page Eleven.

★ ★ ★ ★ ★ ★ ★ ★

DAZED VICTIM SAYS PASSES SET UP LOSS

Lavagetto Hit High, Fast Pitch.

By Ralph Roden.

BROOKLYN, N. Y. (AP)—Bill Bevens' eyes were vacant of any expression as he fumbled along in changing from his uniform to street attire in the Yankee dressing room after his defeat in the fourth game of the World Series Friday.

The big right-hander, who was one out away from tossing the first no-hitter in World Series

Bill Bevens.
Stumbles on Last Step.

annals, groped for words as reporters, feeling his remorse, slowly asked questions.

Asked what kind of a ball Cookie Lavagetto of the Dodgers hit for his game-winning double in the ninth, Bevens replied:

"A high fast ball, a little on the outside."

Later Bevens shook his head when he was reminded that he set a new Series record by walking 10 batters:

"Everytime you walk some-

YANKEES—
Continued on Page Eleven.

SWEET COOKIE

N. Y. (A.L.)	AB	R	H	2B	3B	HR	O	A	E
Stirnweiss, 2b	4	1	2	0	0	0	2	1	0
Henrich, rf	5	0	1	0	0	0	2	0	0
Berra, c	4	0	0	0	0	0	6	1	1
DiMaggio, cf	2	0	0	0	0	0	2	0	0
McQuinn, 1b	4	0	1	0	0	0	7	0	0
W. Johnson, 3b	4	1	1	0	1	0	3	2	0
Lindell, lf	3	0	2	1	0	0	3	0	0
Rizzuto, ss	4	0	1	0	0	0	1	2	0
Bevens, p	3	0	0	0	0	0	0	1	0
Totals	33	2	8	1	0	0	*26	7	1

*Two out when winning run scored.

Bkl. (N.L.)	AB	R	H	2B	3B	HR	O	A	E
Stanky, 2b	1	0	0	0	0	0	2	3	0
Reese, ss	4	0	0	0	0	0	3	5	1
Robinson, 1b	4	0	0	0	0	0	11	1	0
Walker, rf	2	0	0	0	0	0	0	1	0
Hermanski, lf	4	0	0	0	0	0	2	0	0
Edwards, c	4	0	0	0	0	0	7	1	1
Furillo, cf	3	0	0	0	0	0	2	0	0
Jorgensen, 3b	2	1	0	0	0	0	0	1	1
Taylor, p	0	0	0	0	0	0	0	0	0
Gregg, p	1	0	0	0	0	0	0	1	0
Behrman, p	0	0	0	0	0	0	0	1	0
Casey, p	0	0	0	0	0	0	0	1	0
aVaughan	0	0	0	0	0	0	0	0	0
bReiser	0	0	0	0	0	0	0	0	0
cLavagetto	1	0	1	1	0	0	0	0	0
dGionfriddo	0	1	0	0	0	0	0	0	0
eMiksis	0	1	0	0	0	0	0	0	0
Totals	26	3	1	1	0	0	27	15	3

aWalked for Gregg in seventh.
bWalked for Casey in ninth.
cDoubled for Stanky in ninth.
dRan for Furillo in ninth.
eRan for Reiser in ninth.

Score by innings:

New York (A.L.) .....100 100 000—2
Brooklyn (N.L.) .....000 010 002—3

Summary—Runs batted in, DiMaggio, Lindell, Reese, Lavagetto 2; stolen bases, Rizzuto, Reese, Gionfriddo; sacrifice hits, Stanky, Bevens; double plays, Reese to Stanky to Robinson, Gregg to Reese to Robinson, Casey to Edwards to Robinson; left on bases, New York 9, Brooklyn 8.

Bases on balls, Taylor 1, Bevens 10, Gregg 3; strikeouts, Gregg 5, Bevens 5; hits, Taylor 2 (none out in first), Gregg 4 in 7, Behrman 2 in $1\frac{1}{3}$, Casey 0 in $\frac{2}{3}$; wild pitch, Bevens; winning pitcher, Casey.

Umpires, Goetz (N.L.) plate, McGowan (A.L.) 1b, Pinelli (N.L.) 2b, Rommel (A.L.) 3b, foul lines, Boyer (A.L.), Magerkurth (N.L.). Time, 2:20. Attendance, 33,443.

52,000 to See Iowa

Ready to Forgive and Forget---But Illini Look Mighty Tough.

By Tony Cordaro.
(Staff Writer.)

IOWA CITY, IA.—Fifty-two thousand jurists will give an "all is forgiven" decision this afternoon if the Iowa football team atones for its U.C.L.A. humiliation which took place eight days ago in Los Angeles.

★ ★ ★ ★ ★ ★ ★ ★

PROBABLE LINEUPS.

IOWA.		ILLINOIS.
H. Shoener 190	L. E.	183 Zatkoff
Shoaf 220 or Winslow 212	L. T.	226 Prymuski
Grothus 191	L. G.	190 Wrenn
D. Woodard 210	C.	198 Levanti
Carlson 180	R. G.	200 Siegert
Kay 215	R. T.	203 Cunz
Guzowski 193	R. E.	181 Owens
Lou King 175	Q. B.	170 Moss
Tunnell 180	L. H.	175 Dufelmeier
Kaisershot 185	R. H.	190 Eddleman
B. Smith 181	F. B.	204 Steger

Officials — Referee, Rollie Barnum (Wisconsin); umpire, Dallas Marvil (Northwestern); field judge, Dave Noble (Nebraska); headlinesman, Roy Knipschild (Chicago). Time and place —Today, 2 p. m., Iowa Stadium. Tickets—Sellout at 52,500, no tickets available.

Broadcasts — WHO, Des Moines; WSUI, Iowa City; WMT, Cedar Rapids and KSO, Des Moines (point); KXEL, Waterloo; WGN, Chicago; WJJD, Chicago; WWXL, Peoria, Ill.; TAX, Springfield, Ill.; MBD, Peoria Ill.; KSD, St. Louis, Mo.; WILL, Champaign, Ill.

The judges will be lenient if the Hawks just turn in an accountable performance against Illinois, Big Nine conference champion and Rose Bowl victor, here this afternoon.

Hawks Alert.

"The season starts today," was the cry heard on the practice field Friday afternoon. So it's evident that the Hawks have awakened from their Rip Van Winkle sleep.

All week Dr. Eddie Anderson, behind barred gates, has been experimenting with his players. The results of his tests will not be known until around 5 o'clock this afternoon.

Dr. Anderson is not promising any miracles.

"We will show an improvement over our U.C.L.A. performance," he said Friday afternoon.

There is still some doubt in Dr. Eddie's mind as to his starting lineup.

Banks Not to Start.

Earl Banks, the squatty Iowa guard, will definitely be on the bench when the kickoff takes place at 2 p. m. Ray Carlson of Fort Dodge has supplanted the Negro in the forward line.

Tony Guzowski also was promoted this week. He will start at right end ahead of Veterans Bob Phillips and Herb Shoener.

The third alteration, all on the right side of the line, will find Bill Kay, game captain, at tackle instead of Jim Cozad.

Other Starters.

Dick Woodward, center; Joe Grothus, right guard; Jim Shoaf, tackle, and Hal Shoener, will round out the front line.

No changes are contemplated in the backfield with Lou King at quarterback, Emlen Tunnell at left half, Quentin Kaiser at right half and Bob Smith at fullback.

But Dr. Anderson was still flirting with the idea of inserting hard-charging Ron Headington of Decorah at fullback and moving Smith to right half.

The Illinois forward wall is virtually the same as last year, but Buddy Young won't be around to tantalize the Hawkeye tacklers with his burst of speed.

Illini Favored.

At post time, Illinois still ranked a seven-point favorite over the Hawks. The game will be the twenty-seventh meeting between the state neighbors. The Illini

IOWA—
Continued on Page Ten.

COOKIE'S JAR—Lavagetto starts his historic pinch double on its way with two out in the ninth against the Yankees. His important jolt ended Bill Bevens' hitless string at $8\frac{2}{3}$ innings. The Dodgers squared the Series at two games each.—WIREPHOTOS (AP).

Cyclones Open Big 6 Play In Clash at Kansas Today

(Special Dispatch to The Register.)

LAWRENCE, KAN.—Iowa State's Cyclones have arrived here for their Big Six opener against Kansas today, but all Coach Abe Stuber has to insert in the favorable column is that his young squad is bubbling over with spirit.

If that isn't an advantage, then Stuber figures he holds no trump cards.

Set For Air Battle.

Stuber, the new coach who has batted .500 since coming up from Cape Girardeau Teachers in Missouri, has devoted hour after hour to the Cyclone aerial game. He feels that an air war would not be overly troublesome.

But Friday night he expressed concern about the ground attack. He has a tested backfield combination to throw against Ray Evans & Co., however, so he's one up on the Kansans on that score.

Weights Even.

Kansas holds a three-pound-per-man line average advantage, but in that backfield of Ron Norman, Webb Halbert, Vic Weber and Ray Klootwyk Stuber gets a two-pound edge, so the weights can be called even.

Bad news hit K. U.'s vulnerable center spot again Friday when Bob Drumm, who was slated to start at that post against Iowa State, entered the hospital with a kidney ailment.

"We don't know what the trouble is yet," said Team Physician Robert Jordon, but Drumm definitely is out of today's game.

Drumm's loss may force Coach

★ ★ ★ ★ ★ ★ ★ ★

PROBABLE LINEUPS.

IOWA STATE.		KANSAS.
Laun (179)	L. E.	(185) Small
Southard (196)	L. T.	(200) Ettinger
Brubaker (184)	L. G.	(184) Fambr'gh
Rust (182)	C.	(203) Monroe
And'son (180)	R. G.	(200) Crawford
Rollinger (200)	R. T.	(190) Johnson
Jensen (204)	R. E.	(183) Schnellb'r
Norman (180)	Q. B.	(175) McNutt
Halbert (183)	L. H.	(188) Evans
Weber (182)	R. H.	(168) Bertuzzi
Klootwyk (181)	F. B.	(185) Pattee

Average weight of lines—Iowa State 189, Kansas 192.

Average weight of backs—Iowa State 181, Kansas 179.

Average weight of teams—Iowa State 186, Kansas 187.

Officials—Ted O'Sullivan (Missouri), referee; John Waldorf (Missouri), umpire; Bennie Beckerman (Iowa), head linesman; Ed Ellis (Oklahoma A. and M.), field judge.

Time and place—Today, 2 p. m., Memorial Stadium, Lawrence, Kansas.

Broadcast—WOI, Ames; KMBC, Kansas City; KCKN, Kansas City; KCMO, Kansas City; KFH, Wichita; WREN, Lawrence; KWHK, Hutchinson.

George Sauer to open the battle with the injured Dick Monroe at his usual starting post. Monroe, who twisted a knee in scrimmage two nights ago, was limping along in the varsity lineup Friday.

Sauer resorted to his favorite trick of moving a former fullback into the line when he shifted Rolland Eilerts, rugged but inexperienced Hillsboro sophomore, into the hard-hit pivot spot. Eilerts, up to now a substitute end, played fullback on last year's Kansas "B" team. He lacks any type of pivot experience but is classed as a creditable linebacker and may see plenty of action.

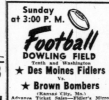

WINS LETTER AT 19.

EAST LANSING, MICH.—Warren Huey is one of the youngest athletes ever to win a major football award at Michigan State. Huey, who just turned 19, has been a regular end for the Spartans the past two seasons. He is a junior.

Music Hath Harms

New York has its Stokowski, Minneapolis has its Mitropoulos, but Brooklyn has its sym-phony (accent on the last) which entertains the fans at Ebbets Field.

THEY'RE COLD, ALL RIGHT — Huddled under a blanket in the Yankee dugout are Catcher Yogi Berra (left) and First Baseman George McQuinn, who have been playing like they have a working agreement with the Dodgers.

YANKS WIN SERIES; BEAT DODGERS, 5-2

GREGG AND SHEA ROUTED EARLY; HARRIS'S PINCH-HITTERS DELIVER

By J. Roy Stockton
Sports Editor of the Post-Dispatch.

NEW YORK, Oct. 6—Every nove that Stanley (Bucky) Iarris made this afternoon vorked like magic and his New York Yankees, overcomng an early Brooklyn lead, von the world championship y defeating Burt Shotton's Dodgers, 5 to 2, in the seventh nd final game for their eeded fourth victory.

Pinch-hitters delivered timely its and Joe Page, called from the ullpen in the fifth inning, after tarter Frank Shea had faltered nd Bill Bevens had retired for a inch-batter, hurled five brilliant nnings, retiring 13 consecutive atters before Eddie Miksis final- found his delivery for a single ith one out in the ninth. Then cooter Rizzuto, Snuffy Stirnweiss nd George McQuinn executed a ouble play on Bruce Edwards's rounder and the series was over; ne Yankees world champions for ne eleventh time.

A crowd of 71,548 witnessed the ame, bringing the total attendnce for the series to 389,763, and aking the net receipts, including dio and television rights, to the nazing total of $2,021,348.92.

While Page, making his fourth ppearance in the series, stood it as the defensive strength that revented Brooklyn from winning s first world title, pinch-batters nared the spotlight with the ard-working lefthander, who only esterday felt the sting of Dodger ats as he was knocked out of ne box.

It Turned Out Right.

Press box strategists raised eyerows in the fourth inning when Harris sent in Bobby Brown to nch-hit for Relief Pitcher Bevis.

The Yankees were only one run hind and it seemed rather imlsive to take out Bevens, who d pitched a one-hitter in the urth game, even if defeated. But Harris had the magic touch today. e called on Brown and the young edical student came through th his third pinch safety of the ries, a double to right that sent e tying run over the plate and oved a runner to third. Tommy enrich came through with anher hit before the inning ended d the Yankees were ahead. And th Page in such brilliant form at one run margin, 3 to 2, would ve been enough.

But Harris wasn't through wavg the magic wand. In the sixth ning, with two out, Phil Ruzzuto second by virtue of a safe bunt d a steal and Stirnweiss on first, a walk, Harris sent in Rookie Clark to bat for Yogi Berra. n the first pitch Clark singled center and the Yankees had nother precious run to bolster eir lead.

Final Run Off Casey.

The final Yankee run was scored ainst Old Hugh Casey, who was aking his fifth appearance in ve days, his sixth of the series. ith one out in the seventh, Bill hnson hit a towering fly that ll in deep left, beyond a circling ddie Miksis, substitute outfielder, d Aaron Robinson scored Johnn with an outfield fly.

In contrast the Dodgers couldn't anything right, except in the cond inning, when they made ur of their seven hits and both their runs. Gene Hermanski's iple, singles by Bruce Edwards d Carl Furillo and a double by hnny Jorgensen produced the o runs, but thereafter the odgers couldn't get the heavy d of their bats on the ball. Shotn sent in his pinch-hitters as ual, but they were as children in e hands of the crafty Page.

Ed Rommel, American League, npired behind the plate, with rry Goetz, National, at first se; Bill McGowan, American, at cond, and Ralph Pinelli at third. orge Magerkurth, National, and n Boyer, American, watched the ul lines.

The redhot baseball fans were t for the final and a real yell nt up as Stanky led off in the st inning.

Two Thrown Out Stealing.

Stanky took a called strike and en fouled off a pitch. Ball one s inside and Stanky hit the xt pitch for a Texas League sin- to right-center. Reese swung the first pitch but Stanky was t trying for second, Aaron Robson to Stirnweiss. Shea followed th three wide ones and Reese ung and missed the next one. ll four was far inside. Robinn took two balls and then lined Henrich, who had to reach to ke the catch. Walker took a ll and then lined into the seats right, foul by a few feet. With ly one day's rest, Shea didn't k too sharp. Walker took a ll and on the next one, Reese s out attempting to steal, Aaron binson to Stirnweiss.

Gregg's first two pitches to rnweiss, leading off in the Yane first, were wide. Snuffy took strike and then flied to Walker. nrich flied to Hermanski. Berra k a strike, two balls and then ssed a swing at an inside pitch. gi grounded to Robinson, Gregg vering first.

Four Straight Dodger Hits.

Walker opened the second with high pop foul to McQuinn. Heranski, picking on the first pitch, ed to the right field corner of e park. The ball hit a low railg and caromed out of Berra's ach and before Yogi could retrieve the ball, Hermanski was safely on his way to third with a triple, sliding under a good throw. Ball one to Edwards was a curve outside, and another just missed the outside corner. Bruce swung at a strike and missed. And a second strike was called. Edwards hit the next one down the third base line, fair by inches, for a single, scoring Hermanski. Furillo drilled a line single through the box and out to center field, Edwards stopping at second. That finished Shea and his chances to be a freshman three-time winner. Bevens took over the mound assignment. Jorgensen fouled the first pitch into the dirt and lined the next one down the right field line, foul. A ball and then Jorgensen chipped a double to right, the ball bouncing into the seats for a ground rule, two bagger. This scored Edwards, Furillo stopping at third. Gregg hit to Rizzuto and Furillo was out at the plate, Rizzuto to Aaron Robinson, Jorgensen taking third. Stanky ended the inning with a pop fly to Rizzuto.

DiMaggio started the New York second with a towering fly to center, Furillo moving back a few steps for the catch. McQuinn quickly had two strikes, but walked on four straight wide ones. Stanky ran into right field for Johnson's pop fly. Aaron Robinson walked on four straight pitches, and Rizzuto bounced a single over third, scoring McQuinn and moving Aaron Robinson to second. Jorgensen made a dive for the bounder but missed. Bevns was called out on strikes to end the frame.

Two Strikeouts.

Reese struck out to open the third. Jackie Robinson fouled trying to bunt and then lined a foul deep into the left field stand. After a ball and another foul, Jackie struck out. Walker drew a pass but Hermanski lined straight to Johnson.

Stirnweiss walked on four pitches to start the American League third, but advanced no farther than first. Henrich flied to Walker, Furillo ran back for Berra's drive in left center and DiMaggio flied to Hermanski.

Edwards, first up in the fourth, shot a grounder, too hot to handle, past Johnson, but Stirnweiss took care of the next three batters. Snuffy ran into center for Furillo's pop fly, far into right for Jorgensen's and then threw out Gregg.

McQuinn was called out on strikes as he led off for the Yankees in the fourth and after Johnson walked, Aaron Robinson took a called third strike. Rizzuto singled to left, moving Johnson to second and press box strategists questioned the wisdom of Bucky Harris's move in sending in Bobby Brown to bat for Bevens, so early in the game, and with the Dodgers only a run ahead.

Bobby Comes Through Again.

Bobby took three balls and then a strike and then made Harris's judgment look better by hitting to left for a double, scoring Johnson with the tying run and sending Rizzuto to third. The blow knocked Gregg out of the box and Hank Behrman went to the hill. Hank's first pitch to Stirnweiss was a ball outside, and a second ball in the same spot. Ball three was a foot outside and ball four far inside, Snuffy walking to fill the bases. Henrich swung at the first pitch and singled sharply to right, scoring Rizzuto, but Walker's quick throw-in stopped Brown at third. Berra lined a foul down the right field line, and then grounded to Robinson, who went to his right for the stop and threw to Behrman at first for the putout.

Joe Page, making his fourth appearance of the series, went to the hill for the Yankees as the Dodgers batted in the fifth. Joe turned back the Dodgers in order. Stanky grounded to Stirnweiss, Reese flied to Berra and Robinson's solid line drive went straight to Henrich.

Yanks Bunt, for a Change.

DiMaggio, with a three-one count, hit a long foul into the upper left field stand, and then walked, to open the New York fifth. McQuinn sacrificed, Jorgensen to Stanky. DiMaggio moved to third as Stanky was throwing out Johnson and Aaron Robinson flied to Walker in the right field corner.

Walker opened the Brooklyn sixth with a fly to DiMaggio and Eddie Miksis, batting for Hermanski, bunted and was thrown out by Johnson. Edwards sent a high fly to DiMaggio, making it another easy inning for Page.

Miksis went to left field for the Dodgers as the Yanks batted in the sixth. Rizzuto led off with a bunt toward first and when Behrman missed his grab at the ball, The Scooter was safe, credited with a single. Page was up there to sacrifice. He fouled the first strike and missed the second, but Rizzuto, in full stride, stole second, aided by an off-line throw by Edwards. Page struck out, but Behrman threw only one strike as he was walking Stirnweiss and Coach Sukeforth went to the mound and signaled to the bullpen. Joe Hatten relieved Behrman. Henrich struck out, but Al Clark batted for Berra and singled to center on the first pitch, scoring Rizzuto and moving Stirnweiss to second. Sukeforth appeared again and Rex Barney took over the pitching job. DiMaggio flied deep to Furillo to end the inning.

Shotton sent in two pinch-hitters in the seventh, but Page breezed through the inning. Furillo fouled to McQuinn and Cookie Lavagetto, batting for Jorgensen, popped to Stirnweiss. Gil Hodges batted for Barney and struck out.

Casey's Sixth Appearance.

Hugh Casey pitched and Lavagetto was at third for the Dodgers as the Yankees batted in the seventh. It was Casey's fifth appearance in the last five games and his sixth in the series. McQuinn grounded to Reese. Johnson hit a high fly to left and there was no Gionfriddo out there today. Miksis ran in circles and the ball went over his head for a triple. Aaron Robinson flied deep to Miksis and Johnson scored after the catch with the first run of the series off Fireman Casey. Rizzuto popped to Stanky.

In the Dodger eighth, Stanky flied to Clark, who had gone to right for the Yanks after batting for Berra in the sixth. Reese also flied to Clark and Jackie Robinson flied to DiMaggio, the twelfth successive batter retired by Page.

Page was cheered as he led off for the Yankees in the eighth. He grounded to Robinson, who made the play unassisted. Stirnweiss flied to Furillo, who ran in fast for the catch. Henrich flied to Miksis.

In the Brooklyn ninth, Stirnweiss threw out Walker. Miksis singled to center, but Edwards hit into a game-ending double pliay, Rizzuto to Stirnweiss to McQuinn.

SCORE BY INNINGS

	1	2	3	4	5	6	7	8	9	T.
Dodgers	0	2	0	0	0	0	0	0	0	2
Yankees	0	1	0	2	0	1	1	0	X	5

The Box Score

DODGERS

	AB	R	H	2B	3B	HR	BB	SO	PO	A	E
Stanky, 2b	4	0	1	0	0	0	0	0	3	1	0
Reese, ss	3	0	0	0	0	0	1	1	0	1	0
J. Robinson 1b	4	0	0	0	0	0	0	1	3	2	0
Walker, rf	3	0	0	0	0	0	1	0	3	0	0
Hermanski, lf	2	1	1	0	1	0	0	0	2	0	0
Miksis lf	2	0	1	0	0	0	0	0	2	0	0
Edwards, c	4	1	2	0	0	0	0	0	5	0	0
Furillo, cf	3	0	1	0	0	0	0	0	4	0	0
Jorgenson, 3b	2	0	1	1	0	0	0	0	0	1	0
Lavagetto, 3b	1	0	0	0	0	0	0	0	0	0	0
GREGG, P	2	0	0	0	0	0	0	0	1	0	0
BEHRMAN, P	0	0	0	0	0	0	0	0	1	0	0
HATTEN, P	0	0	0	0	0	0	0	0	0	0	0
BARNEY, P	0	0	0	0	0	0	0	0	0	0	0
CASEY, P	0	0	0	0	0	0	0	0	0	0	0
Hodges	1	0	0	0	0	0	0	1	0	0	0
Totals	31	2	7	1	1	0	2	3	24	5	0

Hodges, for Barney, struck out in the seventh.

YANKEES

	AB	R	H	2B	3B	HR	BB	SO	PO	A	E
Stirnweiss, 2b	2	0	0	0	0	0	3	0	5	5	0
Henrich lf	5	0	1	0	0	0	0	1	2	0	0
Berra, rf	3	0	0	0	0	0	0	0	1	0	0
Clark rf	1	0	1	0	0	0	0	0	2	0	0
DiMaggio, cf	3	0	0	0	0	0	1	0	3	0	0
McQuinn, 1b	2	1	0	0	0	0	1	0	7	0	0
W. Johnson, 3b	3	2	1	0	1	0	1	0	1	1	0
A. Robinson c	3	0	0	0	0	0	1	0	4	2	0
Rizzuto, ss	4	2	3	0	0	0	0	0	2	2	0
SHEA, P	0	0	0	0	0	0	0	0	0	0	0
BEVENS P	1	0	0	0	0	0	0	1	0	0	0
PAGE, P	2	0	0	0	0	0	0	1	0	0	0
R. Brown	1	0	1	1	0	0	0	0	0	0	0
Totals	30	5	7	1	1	0	7	3	27	10	0

Brown for Bevens, doubled in the fourth.

Runs batted in—Edwards, Jorgensen, Rizzuto, Brown, Henrich, Clark, A. Robinson. Two-base hits—Jorgensen, Brown. Three-base hits—Hermanski, Johnson. Stolen base—Rizzuto. Sacrifice—McQuinn. Double plays—Rizzuto, Stirnweiss and McQuinn. Earned runs—Brooklyn 2; New York 5. Left on bases—Brooklyn (NL) 4; New York (AL) 9. Bases on balls—Off Shea (Reese); off Gregg 4 (McQuinn, A. Robinson, Stirnweiss, Johnson); off Bevens (Walker); off Behrman 3 (Stirnweiss 2, DiMaggio). Strikeouts—By Gregg 3 (Bevens, McQuinn, A. Robinson); by Bevens 2 (Reese, J. Robinson); by Behrman (Page); by Hatten (Henrich); by Page (Hodges). Pitching summary—Shea, 2 runs, 4 hits in 1 1-3 innings; Bevens, 0 runs, 2 hits in 2 2-3 innings; Page, 0 runs, 1 hit in 5 innings; Gregg, 3 runs, 3 hits in 3 2-3 innings; Behrman, 1 run, 2 hits in 1 2-3 innings; Hatten, 0 runs, 1 hit in 1-3 inning; Barney, 0 runs, 0 hits in 1-3 inning; Casey, 1 run, 1 hit in 2 innings. Winning pitcher—Page. Losing pitcher—Gregg. Umpires—Rommel (AL) plate; Goetz (NL) 1b; McGowan (AL) 2b, Pinelli (NL) 3b; Magerkurth (NL) lf.; Boyer (AL) rf. Attendance—71,548 paid. Time—2 h 15 m.

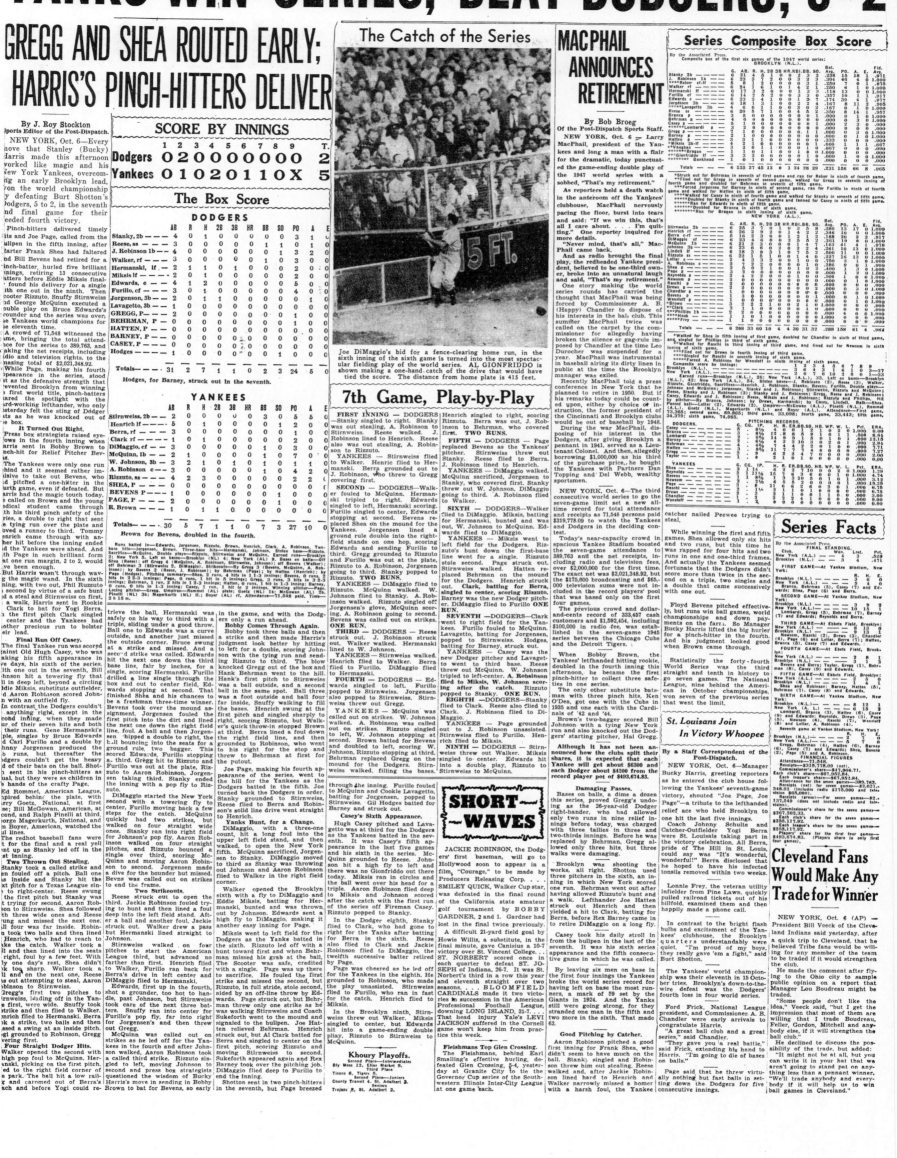

The Catch of the Series

Joe DiMaggio's bid for a fence-clearing home run, in the sixth inning of the sixth game is turned into the most spectacular fielding play of the world series. AL GIONFRIDDO is shown making a one-hand catch of the drive that would have tied the score. The distance from home plate is 415 feet.

7th Game, Play-by-Play

FIRST INNING — DODGERS —Stanky singled to right. Stanky was out stealing, A. Robinson to Stirnweiss. Reese walked. J. Robinson lined to Henrich. Reese also was out stealing, A. Robinson to Rizzuto.

YANKEES — Stirnweiss flied to Walker. Henric flied to Hermanski. Berra grounded out to J. Robinson, who threw to Gregg covering first.

SECOND — DODGERS—Walker fouled to McQuinn. Hermanski tripled to right. Edwards singled to center, scoring Hermanski. Furillo singled to center, Edwards stopping at second. Bevens replaced Shea on the mound for the Yankees. Jorgensen lined a ground rule double into the right-field stands on one hop, scoring Edwards and sending Furillo to third. Gregg grounded to Rizzuto and Furillo was out at the plate, Rizzuto to A. Robinson, Jorgensen going to third. Stanky popped to Rizzuto. **TWO RUNS.**

YANKEES — DiMaggio flied to Rizzuto. McQuinn walked. W. Johnson flied to Stanky. A. Robinson walked. Rizzuto singled off Jorgensen's glove, McQuinn scoring, A. Robinson going to second. Bevens was called out on strikes. **ONE RUN.**

THIRD — DODGERS — Reese struck out. J. Robinson struck out. Walker walked. Hermanski lined to W. Johnson.

YANKEES — Stirnweiss walked. Henrich flied to Walker. Berra flied to Furillo. DiMaggio flied to Hermanski.

FOURTH — DODGERS — Edwards singled to left. Furillo popped to Stirnweiss. Jorgensen also popped to Stirnweiss. Stirnweiss threw out Gregg.

YANKEES — McQuinn was called out on strikes. W. Johnson walked. A. Robinson was called out on strikes. Rizzuto singled to left, W. Johnson stopping at second. Brown batted for Bevens and doubled to left, scoring W. Johnson, Rizzuto stopping at third. Behrman replaced Gregg on the mound for the Dodgers. Stirnweiss walked, filling the bases. Henrich singled to right, scoring Rizzuto. Berra was out, J. Robinson to Behrman, who covered first. **TWO RUNS.**

FIFTH — DODGERS — Page replaced Bevens as the Yankees' pitcher. Stirnweiss threw out Stanky. Reese flied to Berra. J. Robinson lined to Henrich.

YANKEES — DiMaggio walked. McQuinn sacrificed, Jorgensen to Stanky, who covered first. Stanky threw out W. Johnson, DiMaggio going to third. A. Robinson flied to Walker.

SIXTH — DODGERS—Walker fouled to DiMaggio. Miksis, batting for Hermanski, bunted and was out, W. Johnson to McQuinn. Edwards flied to DiMaggio.

YANKEES — Miksis went to left field for the Dodgers. Rizzuto's bunt down the first-base line went for a single. Rizzuto stole second. Page struck out. Stirnweiss walked. Hatten replaced Behrman on the mound for the Dodgers. Henrich struck out. **Clark, batting for Berra, singled to center, scoring Rizzuto.** Barney was the new Dodger pitcher. DiMaggio flied to Furillo **ONE RUN.**

SEVENTH —DODGERS—Clark went to right field for the Yankees. Furillo fouled to McQuinn. Lavagetto, batting for Jorgensen, popped to Stirnweiss. Hodges, batting for Barney, struck out.

YANKEES — Casey was the new Dodger pitcher and Lavagetto went to third base. Reese threw out McQuinn. W. Johnson tripled to left-center. **A. Robinson flied to Miksis, W. Johnson scoring after the catch.** Rizzuto popped to Stanky. **ONE RUN.**

EIGHTH —DODGERS—Stanky flied to Clark. Reese also flied to Clark. J. Robinson flied to DiMaggio.

YANKEES — Page grounded out to J. Robinson unassisted. Stirnweiss flied to Furillo. Henrich flied to Miksis.

NINTH — DODGERS — Stirnweiss threw out Walker. Miksis singled to center. Edwards hit into a double play, Rizzuto to Stirnweiss to McQuinn.

SHORT—WAVES

JACKIE ROBINSON, the Dodgers' first baseman, will go to Hollywood soon to appear in a film, "Courage," to be made by Producers Releasing Corp. . . . SMILEY QUICK, Walker Cup star, was defeated in the final round of the California state amateur golf tournament by BOBBY GARDNER, 2 and 1. Gardner had lost in the final twice previously.

A difficult 21-yard field goal by Howie Willis, a substitute, in the final minute, gave Canisius a 10-7 victory over St. Vincent College. . . ST. NORBERT scored once in each quarter to defeat ST. JOSEPH of Indiana, 26-7. It was St. Norbert's third in a row this year and eleventh straight over two seasons. . . . BLOOMFIELD CARDINALS made it two victories in succession in the American Professional Football League, downing LONG ISLAND, 31-7. . . . That head injury Yale's LEVI JACKSON suffered in the Cornell game won't keep him from practice this week.

Fleishmans Top Glen Crossing.

The Fleishmans, behind Earl Smalling's effective hurling, defeated Glen Crossing, 5-4, yesterday at Granite City to tie the Governor Cup series of the Southwestern Illinois Inter-City League at one game each.

Khoury Playoffs.

Second Place—Intermediates
Bly Moss 12, Elias Market 9.
Third Place
Ticons 6, Tigers 5.
Second Place—Juniors
County Transit 4, St. Adalbert 3.
Seniors
Trojans 8, St. Adalbert 2.

MACPHAIL ANNOUNCES RETIREMENT

By Bob Broeg
Of the Post-Dispatch Sports Staff.

NEW YORK, Oct. 6 — Larry MacPhail, president of the Yankees and long a man with a flair for the dramatic, today punctuated the game-ending double play of the 1947 world series with a sobbed, "That's my retirement."

As reporters held a death watch in the anteroom off the Yankees' clubhouse, MacPhail nervously pacing the floor, burst into tears and said: "If we win this, that's all I care about. . . . I'm quitting." One reporter inquired for more details.

"Never mind, that's all," MacPhail came back.

And as radio brought the final play, the redheaded Yankee president, believed to be one-third owner, broke into an unnatural laugh and said, "That's my retirement."

One story making the world series rounds has carried the thought that MacPhail was being forced by Commissioner A. B. (Happy) Chandler to dispose of his interests in the ball club. This summer MacPhail twice was called on the carpet by the commissioner for allegedly having broken the silence or gag-rule imposed by Chandler at the time Leo Durocher was suspended for a year. MacPhail was instrumental in baseball airing its dirty linen in public at the time the Brooklyn manager was exiled.

Recently MacPhail told a press conference in New York that he planned to retire in 1950. But if his remarks today could be counted upon, either by choice or instruction, the former president of the Cincinnati and Brooklyn clubs would be out of baseball by 1948.

During the war MacPhail, disposing of his interest in the Dodgers, after giving Brooklyn a pennant in 1941, served as a Lieutenant Colonel. And then, allegedly borrowing $1,000,000 as his third of the purchase price, he bought the Yankees with Partners Dan Topping and Del Webb, wealthy sportsmen.

NEW YORK, Oct. 6—The third consecutive world series to go the seven-game limit set a new all-time record for total attendance and receipts as 71,548 persons paid $319,778.09 to watch the Yankees and Dodgers in the deciding contest.

Today's near-capacity crowd in spacious Yankee Stadium boosted the seven-game attendance to 389,763 and the net receipts, including radio and television fees, over $2,000,000 for the first time. The exact net was $2,021,348.92, but the $175,000 broadcasting and $65,000 television sums were not included in the record players' pool that was based only on the first four games.

The previous crowd and dollar-and-cents record of 333,457 cash customers and $1,592,454, including $100,000 in radio fee, was established in the seven-game 1945 series between the Chicago Cubs and the Detroit Tigers.

When Bobby Brown, the Yankees' letfhanded hitting rookie, doubled in the fourth inning this afternoon, he became the first pinch-hitter to collect three safeties in one series.

The only other substitute batsman with three pinch hits, Ken O'Dea, got one with the Cubs in 1935 and one each with the Cardinals of '42 and '44.

Brown's two-bagger scored Bill Johnson with a tying New York run and also knocked out the Dodgers' starting pitcher, Hal Gregg.

Although it has not been announced how the clubs split their shares, it is expected that each Yankee will get about $6300 and each Dodger about $4200 from the record player pot of $493,674.83.

Damaging Passes.

Bases on balls, a dime a dozen this series, proved Gregg's undoing as the 26-year-old Dodger right-hander, who had allowed only two runs in nine relief innings before today, was charged with three tallies in three and two-thirds innings. Before he was replaced by Behrman, Gregg allowed only three hits, but three walks were damaging.

Brooklyn was shooting the works, all right. Shotton used three pitchers in the sixth, an inning in which New York scored one run. Behrman went out after having allowed Rizzuto's bunt and a walk. Lefthander Joe Hatten struck out Henrich and then yielded a hit to Clark, batting for Berra, before Rex Barney came in to retire DiMaggio on a long fly.

Casey took his daily stroll in from the bullpen in the last of the seventh. It was his sixth series appearance and the fifth consecutive game in which he was called.

By leaving six men on base in the first four innings the Yankees broke the world series record for having left on base the most runners, a mark of 59 set by the Giants in 1924. And the Yanks still were going strong, for they stranded one man in the fifth and two more in the sixth. That made 63.

Good Pitching by Catcher.

Aaron Robinson pitched a good first inning for Frank Shea, who didn't seem to have much on the ball. Stanky singled and Robinson threw him out stealing. Reese walked and, after Jackie Robinson lined hard to Henrich and Walker narrowly missed a homer with a harsh foul, the Yankee catcher nailed Peewee trying to steal.

While winning the first and fifth games, Shea allowed only six hits and two runs, but this time he was rapped for four hits and two runs in one and one-third frames. And actually the Yankees seemed fortunate that the Dodgers didn't score more than twice in the second on a triple, two singles and a double that came successively with one out.

Floyd Bevens pitched effectively, but runs win ball games, world championships and down payments on the farm. So Manager Bucky Harris lifted the big hurler for a pinch-hitter in the fourth. And his judgment looked good when Brown came through.

Statistically the forty-fourth World Series was the third straight and tenth in history to go seven games. The National League, nine behind the American in October championships, won seven of the previous series that went the limit.

St. Louisans Join In Victory Whoopee

By a Staff Correspondent of the Post-Dispatch.

NEW YORK, Oct. 6—Manager Bucky Harris, greeting reporters as he entered the club house following the Yankees' seventh-game victory, shouted "Joe Page, Joe Page"—a tribute to the lefthanded relief ace who held Brooklyn to one hit the last five innings.

Coach Johnny Schulte and Catcher-Outfielder Yogi Berra were St. Louisais taking part in the victory celebration. All Berra, pride of The Hill in St. Louis, could say was "It's wonderful, wonderful!" Berra disclosed that he hoped to have his infected tonsils removed within two weeks.

Lonnie Frey, the veteran utility infielder from Pine Lawn, quickly pulled railroad tickets out of his billfold, examined them and then happily made a phone call.

In contrast to the bright flash bulbs and excitement of the Yankees' clubhouse, the Brooklyn quarters understandably were quiet. "I'm proud of my boys, they really gave 'em a fight," said Burt Shotton.

The Yankees' world championship was their eleventh in 15 October tries. Brooklyn's down-to-the-wire defeat was the Dodgers' fourth loss in four world series.

Ford Frick, National League president, and Commissioner A. B. Chandler were early arrivals to congratulate Harris.

"A great ball club and a great series," said Chandler.

"They gave you a real battle," said Frick, extending his hand to Harris. "I'm going to die of bases on balls."

Page said that he threw virtually nothing but fast balls in setting down the Dodgers for five consecutive innings.

Series Composite Box Score

By the Associated Press.

Composite box of the first six games of the 1947 world series:

BROOKLYN (N.L.).

	G.	AB.	R.	H.	2B	3B	HR.	RBI.	BB.	SO.	Bat. Avg.	PO.	A.	E.	Fld. Avg.
Stanky 2b	6	21	4	5	1	0	0	2	3	2	.238	15	18	1	.971
J. Robinson 1b	6	23	3	7	2	0	0	3	2	3	.304	46	4	0	1.000
****Reiser cf-lf	5	8	1	2	0	0	0	0	3	1	.250	7	0	1	.875
Walker rf	6	24	1	6	1	0	1	4	2	1	.250	6	1	0	1.000
Hermanski lf	6	17	3	2	0	0	0	1	3	3	.118	13	0	0	1.000
Furillo cf	6	14	2	5	2	0	0	3	3	0	.357	10	1	1	.917
Edwards c	6	23	2	4	1	0	0	1	3	7	.174	39	4	1	.977
Jorgensen 3b	6	18	1	3	1	0	0	2	2	4	.167	8	11	2	.905
*****Lavagetto 3b	4	6	0	1	1	0	0	3	0	2	.167	0	1	0	1.000
Reese ss	6	20	5	7	1	0	0	4	5	2	.350	8	14	1	.957
Branca p	3	5	0	0	0	0	0	0	0	1	.000	0	1	0	1.000
Behrman p	4	0	0	0	0	0	0	0	0	0	.000	0	3	0	1.000
Casey p	5	1	0	0	0	0	0	0	0	1	.000	2	3	0	.000
******Lombardi p	3	2	0	0	0	0	0	0	0	0	.000	0	0	0	.000
Gregg p	2	1	0	0	0	0	0	0	1	1	.000	0	3	0	1.000
Barney p	2	1	0	0	0	0	0	0	0	0	.000	0	1	0	1.000
Hatten p	3	3	1	1	0	0	0	0	0	0	.333	0	0	0	.000
*Miksis 2b-lf	4	2	1	0	0	0	0	0	0	1	.000	1	1	1	.667
**Vaughan	3	2	0	1	1	0	0	0	1	0	.667	0	0	0	.000
*******Bragan	1	1	0	1	1	0	0	1	0	0	1.000	0	0	0	.000
***Gionfriddo lf	3	3	2	0	0	0	0	0	1	0	.000	1	0	0	1.000
******** Bankhead	1	0	1	0	0	0	0	0	0	0	.000	0	0	0	.000
Totals	6	125	27	45	12	0	1	24	28	29	.231	156	66	8	.965

*Struck out for Behrman in seventh of first game and ran for Reiser in ninth of fourth game.
**Flied out for Gregg in seventh of second game, walked for Gregg in seventh inning of fourth game and doubled for Behrman in seventh of fifth game.
***Forced Jorgensen for Barney in ninth of second game, ran for Furillo in ninth of fourth game and walked for Hatten in sixth of fifth game.
****Walked for Casey in ninth of fourth game and walked for Stanky in seventh of fifth game.
*****Doubled for Stanky in ninth of fourth game and fanned for Casey in ninth of fifth game.
******Ran for Edwards in ninth of fifth game.
*******Doubled for Branca in sixth of sixth game.
********Ran for Bragan in sixth inning of sixth game.

NEW YORK (A.L.).

	G.	AB.	R.	H.	2B	3B	HR.	RBI.	BB.	SO.	Bat. Avg.	PO.	A.	E.	Fld. Avg.
Stirnweiss 2b	6	25	3	7	0	1	0	3	5	8	.280	13	17	0	1.000
Henrich rf	6	26	2	9	2	0	1	4	2	2	.346	10	0	0	1.000
Berra c-rf	5	16	2	3	0	0	1	2	1	2	.188	20	2	2	.917
DiMaggio cf	6	23	4	6	0	0	2	5	5	2	.261	19	0	0	1.000
McQuinn 1b	6	21	2	3	0	0	0	1	4	7	.143	41	4	1	.978
Johnson 3b	6	23	6	6	0	2	0	2	2	4	.261	10	13	0	1.000
Lindell lf	6	18	3	9	3	1	0	7	5	2	.500	11	0	0	1.000
Rizzuto ss	6	22	1	5	1	0	0	1	4	0	.227	16	13	0	1.000
Lollar c	2	4	3	3	2	0	0	1	0	0	.750	2	1	0	1.000
A. Robinson c	2	7	2	2	0	0	0	0	1	0	.286	9	0	1	.900
Shea p	2	5	0	2	1	0	0	1	0	2	.400	1	3	0	1.000
Page p	3	2	0	0	0	0	0	0	0	0	.000	1	2	0	1.000
Reynolds p	2	4	2	2	0	0	0	1	0	0	.500	1	0	0	1.000
Newsom p	2	0	0	0	0	0	0	0	0	0	.000	0	1	0	1.000
Raschi p	2	0	0	0	0	0	0	0	0	0	.000	0	0	0	.000
Drews p	2	2	0	0	0	0	0	0	0	2	.000	0	3	0	1.000
Chandler p	1	0	0	0	0	0	0	0	0	0	.000	0	0	0	.000
Bevens p	1	3	0	0	0	0	0	0	0	1	.000	0	1	0	1.000
Wensloff p	1	0	0	0	0	0	0	0	0	0	.000	0	1	0	1.000
*Brown	3	2	2	2	1	0	0	2	1	0	1.000	0	0	0	.000
**Clark	2	1	1	0	0	0	0	0	1	0	.000	0	0	0	.000
***Phillips 1b	2	2	0	0	0	0	0	0	0	0	.000	4	0	0	1.000
****Houk	1	1	0	1	0	0	0	0	0	0	1.000	0	0	0	.000
*****Frey	1	1	0	0	0	0	0	0	0	0	.000	0	0	0	.000
Totals	6	208	33	60	10	4	4	30	31	32	.288	158	61	4	.982

*Walked for Shea in fifth inning of first game, doubled for Chandler in sixth of third game, and singled for Phillips in third of sixth game.
**Walked for Raschi in third inning of third game, and lined out for Newsom in sixth inning of sixth game.
***Flied out for Drews in fourth inning of third game.
****Singled for Raschi in seventh inning of sixth game.
*****Forced A. Robinson for Wensloff in ninth inning of sixth game.

Composite score by innings:

	1	2	3	4	5	6	7	8	9	
Brooklyn (N.L.)	3	6	4	3	1	6	1	0	3	—27
New York (A.L.)	2	0	7	6	10	2	5	0	1	—33

Earned runs—Brooklyn (N.L.), 26; New York (A.L.), 33. Left on bases—Brooklyn (N.L.), 42; New York (A.L.), 54. Stolen bases—J. Robinson (2), Reese (3), Walker, Rizzuto, Gionfriddo. Sacrifices—Henrich, J. Robinson, Stanky, Bevens, Furillo. Double plays—Johnson and McQuinn; Jorgensen, Stanky and J. Robinson; Stirnweiss, Rizzuto and McQuinn; Reese, Stanky and J. Robinson (3); Stanky and J. Robinson; Gregg, Reese and J. Robinson; Casey, Edwards and J. Robinson; Reese, Miksis and J. Robinson; Rizzuto and Phillips. Hit by pitcher—By Branca, Johnson; by Drews, Hermanski; by Casey, Lindell. Balk—Shea. Passed ball—Lollar (2), Edwards (2). Umpires—McGowan (A.L.), Pinelli (N.L.), Rommel (A.L.), Goetz (N.L.), Magerkurth (N.L.) and Boyer (A.L.). Attendance—First game, 73,365; second game, 69,865; third game, 33,098; fourth game, 33,443; fifth game, 34,379; sixth game, 74,065.

PITCHING RECORDS.

DODGERS.	G.	CG.	IP.	H.	R.	ER.	BB.	SO.	HB.	WP.	W.	L.	Pct.	ERA.
Casey	5	.	8⅓	4	0	0	1	2	1	0	2	0	1.000	0.00
Branca	3	.	8⅓	12	8	8	5	9	1	0	1	1	.500	8.64
Lombardi	2	.	6⅔	14	9	9	1	5	0	1	0	1	.000	12.15
Barney	2	.	6⅓	4	2	2	10	3	0	2	0	1	.000	2.84
Behrman	4	.	4⅔	7	4	4	2	2	0	1	0	0	.000	7.71
Hatten	3	.	8⅔	11	7	7	7	4	0	0	0	0	.000	7.27
Gregg	2	.	9	6	2	2	4	7	0	0	0	0	.000	2.00
Taylor	1	.	0	2	1	0	1	0	0	0	0	0	.000	0.00

YANKEES	G.	CG.	IP.	H.	R.	ER.	BB.	SO.	HB.	WP.	W.	L.	Pct.	ERA.
Shea	2	1	14	6	2	2	7	10	0	0	2	0	1.000	1.29
Reynolds	2	1	11⅓	15	7	6	3	6	0	0	1	0	1.000	4.74
Bevens	1	1	8⅔	1	3	3	10	5	0	1	0	1	.000	3.12
Newsom	2	.	2⅓	6	5	5	2	0	0	0	0	1	.000	19.29
Page	3	.	8	11	6	6	2	6	0	2	0	1	.000	6.75
Raschi	2	.	1¼	2	1	1	0	1	0	0	0	0	.000	6.75
Drews	2	.	3	2	1	1	0	0	1	1	0	0	.000	3.00
Chandler	1	.	2	2	2	2	4	1	0	0	0	0	.000	9.00
Wensloff	1	.	2	0	0	0	0	0	0	0	0	0	.000	0.00

Series Facts

By the Associated Press.

FINAL STANDING.

Club.	Won.	Lost.	Pct.
New York (A.L.)	4	3	.529
Brooklyn (N.L.)	3	4	.471

FIRST GAME—At Yankee Stadium, New York:

	R.	H.	E.
Brooklyn (N.L.)	3	6	0
New York (A.L.)	5	4	0

Branca, Behrman (5), Casey (7) and Edwards; Shea, Page (6) and Berra.

SECOND GAME—At Yankee Stadium, New York:

	R.	H.	E.
Brooklyn (N.L.)	3	9	2
New York (A.L.)	10	15	1

Lombardi, Gregg (5), Behrman (7), Barney (7) and Edwards; Reynolds and Berra.

THIRD GAME—At Ebbets Field, Brooklyn:

	R.	H.	E.
New York (A.L.)	8	13	0
Brooklyn (N.L.)	9	13	1

Newsom, Raschi (2), Drews (3), Chandler (4), Page (6) and Lollar, Berra (7); Hatten, Branca (5), Casey (7) and Edwards.

FOURTH GAME—At Ebets Field, Brooklyn:

	R.	H.	E.
New York (A.L.)	2	8	1
Brooklyn (N.L.)	3	1	3

Bevens and Berra; Taylor, Gregg (1), Behrman (8), Casey (9) and Edwards.

FIFTH GAME—At Ebbets Field, Brooklyn:

	R.	H.	E.
New York (A.L.)	2	5	0
Brooklyn (N.L.)	1	4	1

Shea and Robinson; Barney, Hatten (5), Behrman (7), Casey (8) and Edwards.

SIXTH GAME—At Yankee Stadium, New York:

	R.	H.	E.
Brooklyn (N.L.)	8	12	1
New York (A. L.)	6	15	2

Lombardi, Branca (3), Hatten (6), Casey (9) and Edwards; Reynolds, Drews (3), Page (5), Newsom (6), Raschi (7), Wensloff (8) and Lollar, A. Robinson (4).

Seventh game at Yankee Stadium, New York:

	R.	H.	E.
Brooklyn (N.L.)	2	7	0
New York (A.L.)	5	7	0

Gregg, Behrman (4), Hatten (6), Barney (6), Casey (7) and Edwards; Shea, Bevens (2), Page (5) and A. Robinson.

FINANCIAL FIGURES

Attendance—71,548.
Receipts—$319,778.09 (net).
Commissioner's share—$47,966.71.
Each club's share—$67,952.84.
Each league's share—$67,952.84.
Attendance for the seven games—389,763.
Receipts (net) for seven games—$2,021,348.92 (includes radio $175,000 and television $65,000).
Receipts (gross)—For seven games—$2,137,549 (does not include radio and television).
Commissioner's share for the seven games—$267,202.33.
Each club's share for the seven games—$255,117.92.
Each league's share for the seven games—$255,117.92.
Players' share for the first four games—$493,674.83. (Players share in only first four games).

Cleveland Fans Would Make Any Trade for Winner

NEW YORK, Oct. 6 (AP) — President Bill Veeck of the Cleveland Indians said yesterday, after a quick trip to Cleveland, that he believed Tribe fans would be willing for any member of the team to be traded if it would strengthen the club.

He made the comment after flying to the Ohio city to sample public opinion on a report that Manager Lou Boudreau might be traded.

"Some people don't like the idea," Veeck said, "but I get the impression that most of them are willing that I trade Boudreau, Feller, Gordon, Mitchell and anybody else, if it will strengthen the ball club."

He declined to discuss the possibility of the trade, but added:

"It might not be at all, but you can write it in your hat that we aren't going to stand pat on anything less than a pennant winner. "We'll trade anybody and everybody if it will help us to win ball games in Cleveland."

At Long Last! Satchel Paige in Big League

In This Issue-Two More Pages of Pictures of D.C. Grads

(SEE PAGES 14 AND M-4)

Satchel Signed by Indians

Leroy (Satchel) Paige, famed speedball pitcher of the Kansas City Monarchs, who Wednesday was signed to pitch for the Cleveland Indians, league leading club of the American League. Paige is the second colored player on the Tribe, the other being Larry Doby, fleet-footed outfielder.

Satchel Paige to Pitch for Cleveland Indians

Famed Kansas City Monarch Hurler Signed After Personal Demonstration for Tribe

CLEVELAND—Leroy (Satchel) Paige, standout pitcher of the last 15 years, Wednesday, had a youthful dream fulfilled when he was signed by the League - leading Cleveland Indians of the American League.

Paige, reportedly 39 but generally regarded as much older, immediately joined the Indians and was in uniform when the Tribe played the Chicago White Sox Wednesday night.

Announcement of the signing of Paige, former Kansas City Monarchs hurler, was made by Manager Lou Boudreau who did not disclose whether Satchel would be used in relief roles or as a regular starter.

Fireball Pitcher

The lanky righthander, who has

(Continued on Page 7 Section 2)

Collects for Slander

Mrs. Jean Murray Smith, former assistant director of Sydenham Hospital in New York, who was awarded a substantial out-of-court settlement against a member of the hospital board and a Harlem weekly, following circulation of reports which she said caused her to be separated from her position.

THIS WEEK

The Lost Song
How Big Is a Big Job?

By RALPH MATTHEWS

You've heard about the "Lost Chord," but have you heard about the "Lost Song"? Well, here it is:

In town this week to keep a date with Cupid at the marriage license bureau came the internationally known song writer, Andy Razaf. The bride, Miss Dorothy Carpenter, an interior decorator and designer of New York.

While here, Andy took occasion to hunt through the archives of the Copyright Bureau and came up with a ditty he had written back in 1933 which has since become a big radio hit—the song, Phil Harris's "That's What I Like About the South."

Sometime ago when the number first became famous over the air and on records, Andy notified Phil Harris and his radio and record sponsors that he had written the number.

He reminded Phil that he had played it for him long before the latter became nationally famous as the band leader on the Jack Benny program.

Phil remembered enough of the number to convert it into a hit with only a few minor changes. There has been some legal bickering for sometime over royalties and by turning up the original copy this week after a two-hour search, which shows that the two numbers are practically identical, Andy will be able to collect back royalties which make his Washington honeymoon both profitable and pleasurable.

How Big's an Office?

It looks as if the Republicans who gathered in Philedalphia last

(Continued on Page 2, Col. 5)

Haitian Editor Assassinated

PORT-AU-PRINCE, Haiti—Jean Remy, director of the Government newspaper, Le Moniteur, and owner of the private newspaper, La Republique, was fatally shot, Tuesday, as he stepped from his automobile; and shortly afterward, Gerard Viau, a young student accused as his assassin, was wrested from police by a mob and killed.

The slaying of the popular publisher, allegedly by the youth, was believed not due to politics, but to a grudge nursed by Viau against Remy, occasioned by ill-feeling over the awarding of a Government scholarship, first won by him, to someone else.

Suspect Shot to Death

After the newspaper owner was

(Continued on Page 3, Col. 4)

THE CRIME OF HARRY TRUMAN - CIVIL RIGHTS

AN EDITORIAL

Seldom has America and the world seen a more disgraceful spectacle than the pre-convention gyrations of the leaders of the Democratic party, who are making fools of themselves in an attempt to draft General Eisenhower as their standard bearer in spite of his insistence that he does not want, and will not accept, the job.

There is a lot of talk about drafting the Generalissimo and some loose talk about his lack of patriotism if he refuses to "answer the call."

General Eisenhower, like everybody else, knows that this is all bunk and that there is no better way for him to show his patriotism than to refuse to be the "cat's-paw" of vicious, corrupt, selfish men whose very motives are against the best interests of the country—men who are making a wicked attempt to repudiate the man who dared to speak out for the very things promised by the platform of both political parties.

This brings us to the great question, "What is Mr. Truman's crime?" The greatest indictment that can be brought against

(Continued on Editorial Page)

WASHINGTON AFRO AMERICAN

CAPITAL EDITION

32 Pages

Entered in the Post Office of Washington, D.C., as Second-Class Matter, under Act of March 3, 1879
Contents of This Newspaper Copyrighted 1948 by The AFRO-AMERICAN Company

56th Year, No. 94 WASHINGTON, D.C., JULY 10, 1948 ★★★★★★

SCHOOL COACHES BALK

How D. C. Spent Holiday

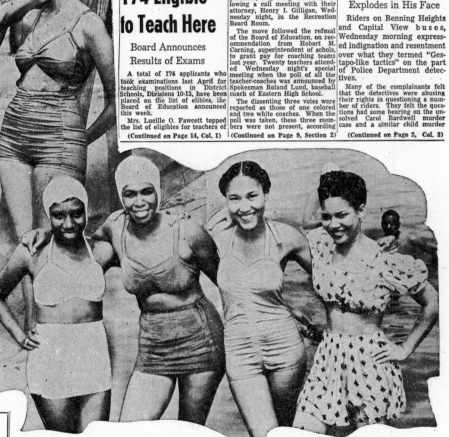

The beaches near Washington drew crowds from all over the country during the Fourth of July holiday. Those pictures taken by an AFRO photographer at Sparrows and Carrs Beaches show (above Miss Cora McCorey of 305 N. Bruce Street, Baltimore; (center) Mrs. Gertrude Myers and Claire Johnson, Harrisburg, Pa., (lower right) Miss Vivian Jackson and Miss Dorothy Johnson, Annapolis, Md., and Misses Joan and Kate Henderson of Bristol, Tenn.

(Oscar Photo.)

Vote 42-3 to Refuse Assignments in Fall

Denial of Extra Pay by School Board Blamed; Will Continue to Teach

District scholastic coaches, Division 1-13, voted 42-3 to decline all coaching activities unless compensated, beginning this fall, following a call meeting with their attorney, Henry I. Gilligan, Wednesday night, in the Recreation Board Room.

The move followed the refusal of the Board of Education, on recommendation from Hobart M. Corning, superintendent of schols, to grant pay for coaching teams last year. Twenty teachers attended Wednesday night's special meeting when the poll of all the teacher-coaches was announced by Spokesman Roland Lund, baseball coach of Eastern High School.

The dissenting three votes were reported as those of one colored and two white coaches. When the poll was taken, these three members were not present, according

(Continued on Page 9, Section 2)

174 Eligible to Teach Here

Board Announces Results of Exams

A total of 174 applicants who took examinations last April for teaching positions in District Schools, Divisions 10-13, have been placed on the list of elibles, the Board of Education announced this week.

Mrs. Lucille O. Fawcett topped the list of eligibles for teachers of

(Continued on Page 14, Col. 1)

Baffled Police Stir Protests

Try to Pin Bardwell Murder on Bus Riders

ACTION RESENTED

Barrett's Omniscience Explodes in His Face

Riders on Benning Heights and Capital View buses, Wednesday morning expressed indignation and resentment over what they termed "Gestapo-like tactics" on the part of Police Department detectives.

Many of the complainants felt that the detectives were abusing their rights in questioning a number of riders. They felt the questions had some bearing on the unsolved Carol Bardwell murder case and a similar child murder

(Continued on Page 2, Col. 3)

CALL 'ATTACK 'VICIOUS':

Officials Blast Story on Terrell Law School

Terming a story carried this week by a national weekly, which stated that 1948 Terrell Law School graduates are barred from taking the District bar examination as "vicious a piece of journalism" as he had ever read, Judge Armond W. Scott of the Municipal Court bench on Wednesday denounced the story in no uncertain terms.

Judge Scott, president of the Terrell Law School, told an AFRO reporter: "Not one of our graduates has ever been barred from taking a bar examination.

"We were advised to add three full-time professors and a dean to our faculty and to maintain a law library with at least 10,000 volumes if we wished to be accredited," he said.

"With a financial sacrifice, we have complied with the request and have filed an application for accreditation," the jurist told the AFRO.

He also remarked, "Two reporters approached me in my chambers concerning the law school as if I were a thug and in a fashion which seemed to imply

(Continued on Page 2, Col. 7)

Aid to Deceased Vets' Kin Raised

Increased compensation payments have been approved for widows, children and dependent parents of veterans who died because of service-connected causes both in war and peace, and will become effective in September of this year.

Veterans Administration officials, while making the announcement this week, urged beneficiaries not to write concerning increases, since the new benefits will be paid automatically.

New Rates Listed

The new monthly rates effective (September) with present rates in parenthesis are:

Wartime rates—Widow but no child, $75 ($60); widow with one child, $100 ($78), plus $15 ($15.60) for each additional child; no widow but one child, $58 ($30), no widow, but two children, $82 ($45.60);

No widow, but three children, $106 ($57.60), plus $20 ($12) for each additional child; one dependent parent, $60 ($54); and two dependent parents, $35 ($30) each.

Peacetime Rate Boost Large

Peacetime rates (equalling 80% of the new wartime rates)—Widow, but no child, $60 (38); widow

(Continued on Page 2, Col. 2)

Cupids Progress

Eighty - six persons, including three 16 - year - old prospective brides, a soldier and his bride - elect, and three from the States, applied to the Marriage License Bureau this week for licenses to wed.

The service man and his bride-to-be, were:

James L. Goolsby, 22, Fort Belvoir, Va., and Miss Mary M. Diggs, 27, 2015 15th St., N.W.

Those from out-of-town were:

William Matthews, 20, Chapel Oaks, Md., and Miss Pauline A. Davis, 20, 512 Second St., S.W.; Frederick N. Lee, 39, Brooklyn, N.Y., and Miss Dorothy W. Bond,

(Continued on Page 2, Col. 4)

Dr. Tate Named to UN Committee

Dr. Merze Tate, professor of history at Howard University, is one of three Americans named by the State Department to represent the United States on the United Nations Educational, Social and Cultural Organization, Howard officials have revealed.

The committee, composed of

(Continued on Page 3, Col. 1)

Lost Birth Certificate Almost Costs Bison Olympic Boxing Star's Passport

By FRED LEIGH

Norvel Lee Slated to Sail on Wednesday for London Games; Alternate on Team

A missing birth certificate almost cost Norvel Lee, Howard University heavyweight finalist, his spot on the American Olympic boxing team.

The 191-pound boxer, outpointed Coley Wallace in the semi-finals to stage the major upset of the Olympic tryouts in Boston before bowing to Jay Lambert, white, in the finals on a split decision, which won him a place as alternate on the team.

Ordered to West Point, N.Y. for final training before sailing on July 14, Lee ran into trouble when his parents in Leesburg, Va., could not locate his birth certificate in order for him to obtain his passport. A frantic trip to his home also was unsucessful and it required an affadavit from his brother, James, and others to get the necessary papers through. There is still some delay, but he expects to get approval before the sailing date.

Rises to Heights

In addition to rising to heights from the role of underdog in the elimination tourney, Lee has converted his mother who had a deep dislike for the game of fisticuffs.

"My mother has never cared for me to box, but she never did try to discourage me. Since I have gone as far as I have, she has taken an interest in boxing now," confided Lee, who pointed out that his father never did dislike the game.

A veteran of three years of Army duty, several months of which were spent in the Pacific with the 869th Engineers, Lee disclosed that he was leaving to join the Olympic team at West Point, N.Y., this week, "if I get my passport made out."

The Olympic team, including eight colored fighters, four each on the first team and the alternate squad, will sail for London, Wednesday, aboard the S.S. Ameri-

(Continued on Page 9, Section 2)

Showers May Bring Only Relief From Heat

There will be no relief from the heat again this week end in Washington the Weather Man has predicted, except possibly on Friday, when thundershowers may bring temporary relief.

The temperature for the period will average from two to three degrees above normal, he added.

Next Week!

OLLIE STEWART WRITES HIS CONCLUSIONS ABOUT EUROPE

Among Other Things He Has Found That:

- While 10 per cent of American Troops in Europe are colored, only 1 per cent of the officers are colored.
- The Army still maintains segregation in Europe, but it is doing a good job in feeding, housing and educating the soldiers.
- The soldiers in Europe are making the Army a career, and because of the American expenditure of money a lot of good jobs are open for colored civilians.
- The Only U. S. agency which excludes us from employment is ERP which has six billions to spend.

DON'T MISS THIS ARTICLE

FINAL ★★

DAILY NEWS

Copr. 1948 by News Syndicate Co. Inc. NEW YORK'S PICTURE NEWSPAPER Trade Mark Reg. U. S. Pat. Off.

5¢

Vol. 30. No. 45 New York 17, Tuesday, August 17, 1948★ 20 Pages 3 Cents IN CITY LIMITS | 4 CENTS in Suburbs | 5 CENTS Elsewhere

BABE RUTH DIES

Story on Page 3

(NEWS foto by Jackson)

King of Swat at Peak of Reign—and as He Bowed Out

The Babe in the act of sending a baseball out of the ball park which made him the greatest and most popular home run hitter in baseball history. This picture was made in the early '20s when the Yanks were called the greatest team ever assembled, with Ruth as the kingpin.

Head bowed with emotion, Ruth made his last appearance in Yankee Stadium July 13, 1948 in a farewell to fans who gathered to see his old number 3 retired from the Yank roster for all time.

(For the life story of Babe Ruth in pictures turn to centerfold.)

CLEVELAND—Cloudy, continued cool. High yesterday 64, low 38. See Page 29.

CLEVELAND PLAIN DEALER — FINAL

107TH YEAR—NO. 279 | Entered as Second Class Matter Post Office, under Act of March 3, 1879. | CLEVELAND, TUESDAY MORNING, OCTOBER 5, 1948 | 38 PAGES | FIVE CENTS

INDIANS WIN FIRST PENNANT IN 28 YEARS; BEARDEN VICTOR, 8-3

AP Wirephotos

INDIANS CARRY BEARDEN OFF FIELD. Left: Jubilant Cleveland Indians carried Pitcher Gene Bearden off the field in Fenway Park yesterday after he hurled the Indians to an 8-to-3 victory over the Red Sox to decide the American League pennant. Right: Bearden, Manager Lou Boudreau and Third Baseman Ken Keltner (left to right) were three happy Indians in the clubhouse after the game.

(More World Series Photos on Picture Page and Sports Pages.)

BOUDREAU'S 2 HOMERS LEAD 13-HIT ASSAULT THAT REPELS RED SOX

Keltner Drives Ball Over Fence With Two on to Break Tie; Rookie Southpaw, Surprise Starter, Posts 20th Victory; Tribe Heavy Favorite to Defeat Braves in Series That Starts Tomorrow

How They Finished

Club		W.	L.	Pct.	Games Behind
CLEVELAND	- - - -	97	58	626	—
Boston	- - - - - -	96	59	619	1
New York	- - - - - -	94	60	610	2½

BY HARRY JONES
Staff Correspondent

BOSTON, Oct. 4—Cleveland's beloved Indians, after all the anxious months of stress and strain and sweat in the closest race in American League history, have finally won the pennant.

They were proclaimed the champions—and deservedly so—at 3:54 this afternoon as Gene Bearden, a rookie southpaw who indelibly inscribed his name in the book of baseball immortals, pitched the final out for an 8-to-3 victory over the Boston Red Sox at Fenway Park in the winner-take-all, one-game play-off for the league's crown and world series money.

Bearden was carried off the field on the shoulders of his deliriously happy teammates, who had gained the privilege of meeting the National League's Boston Braves for the world championship by soundly thrashing the Red Sox, with whom they were tied at the close of the regular season.

But Cleveland's handsome pitcher shared the hero's role in this unprecedented play-off, first of its kind in 48 years of American League baseball, with two other performers who have been greatly responsible for bringing the first pennant in 28 years to the shores of Lake Erie.

Manager Lou Boudreau and Kenny Keltner, veterans of many losing campaigns who finally will find themselves in a world series — the lifelong dream of managers and ballplayers alike — provided Bearden with all the runs he needed to stop the feared Red Sox in their own ballyard.

Boudreau, a strong candidate for manager-of-the-year honors as well as the most valuable player award, clouted two home runs and two singles in four official times at bat, while Keltner smashed a three-run homer, a double and a single in a savage 13-hit assault on two Boston pitchers.

By reason of their fine pitching and power hitting, the Indians are now heavy favorites to win the world title by beating the Braves in the series, which starts here Wednesday. They play here again Thursday and return to Cleveland for a triumphant home-coming and games Friday, Saturday and Sunday. If need be, they will play the last two games in Boston.

(Continued on Page 26, Column 3)

ALLIES SHUN RED BID FOR BIG 4 TALKS

BY ROBERT J. MANNING

PARIS, Oct. 4 — (UP) — The United States, Great Britain and France decided tonight to reject Russia's new bid for a Big Four conference and to go ahead with their complaint to the United Nations that the Soviet blockade of Berlin is a threat to peace.

The foreign ministers of the Western Allies made their decision despite an implied Russian threat to boycott the United Nations Security Council if it takes up the Berlin crisis.

When the Security Council met to take up the Berlin charges, Russian chief delegate, Andrei Y. Vishinsky shouted, pounding the table before him:

"I insist that this item be excluded from the agenda. The Soviet Union will not be a party to such violations of the United Nations charter."

West Foreign Ministers Meet

But while the Council was meeting, Secretary of State George C. Marshall, British Foreign Secretary Ernest Bevin and French Foreign Minister Robert Schuman met separately at the French foreign office.

They formally agreed to reject Russia's proposal for a big four conference, made in a "surprise" note to the western allies Sunday night, and to adhere to their determination to conduct no further negotiations with the Soviet givernment so long as the Berlin blockade continues.

The council got bogged down in an argument over the manner in which speeches of delegates should be translated, and adjourned until 3 p. m. tomorrow without taking a vote on putting the allied complaint on its program.

United States delegate Philip Jessup and British delegate Sir Alexander Cadogan, replying to Vishinsky's threat, to walk out, made it plain that the allied charges will be pressed regardless.

Accusing Russia of repudiating the machinery of the U.N. for settling disputes, Jessup said:

(Continued on Page 8, Column 4)

Florida Hoists Storm Warnings

MIAMI, Fla., Oct. 4—(AP)—Hurricane warnings were hoisted along the Florida keys from Ley Largo to Dry Tortugas today as a tropical storm offering a threat of wind to south Florida pushed northward from the Caribbean Sea.

A hurricane alert was sounded by storm forecasters for the southern half of the Florida peninsula, south of a line extending from Tarpon Springs to Titusville.

Costly Typhoon Rakes Okinawa

TOKYO, Tuesday, Oct. 5—(AP)—A violent typhoon slashed through Okinawa yesterday, causing $10,000,000 damage, and is now heading toward populous southern Japan, the United States army reported today.

There was no mention of casualties on American-held Okinawa.

Diplomats Penned in Moscow

WASHINGTON, Oct. 4—(AP)—Russia in a new order has virtually confined American and other foreign diplomats to the city of Moscow, the State Department said today.

A set of Soviet travel restrictions putting nearly all Russia off limit to representatives of other nations was disclosed here with the explanation that Soviet censors have refused to let Moscow correspondents file the news for the last four days.

The official announcement was acompanied by hints from diplomatic authorities that some retaliatory measures are under consideration by American officials. Soviet officials in this country are as free to travel about the United States as Americans.

"Restricted to City Limits"

The new order was in a note delivered by the foreign office to the American embassy in Moscow last Thursday. It means, the State Department declared, that "to all intents and purposes members of the foreign missions are restricted to Moscow city limits."

The order supplements a 1941 regulation. It contains an expanded list of localities within or to which travel is prohibited for members of the states of foreign diplomatic missions and consulates.

Near East Program 'Conspicuous Success'

WASHINGTON, Oct. 4—(AP)—President Truman said today the American aid program designed to block Communist expansion in Greece and Turkey has been a "conspicuous success."

Greece has been enabled "to sur-

(Continued on Page 8, Column 2)

ACTRESS WALKS AGAIN

HOLLYWOOD, Cal., Oct. 4—(UP)—Film Actress Rita Johnson took her first steps today since she suffered a brain concussion Sept. 6 when struck on the head by a hair dryer in her home. The actress was unconscious for nearly three weeks.

ADD 67,500 TO COUNTY'S VOTER LIST

BY ALVIN SILVERMAN

In one of the lightest final registration days in the history of presidential election years here, an estimated 67,500 Cuyahoga County citizens visited polling places yesterday as the book was closed on registration and transfer of voters who wished to become eligible to cast ballots at the Nov. 2 election.

Although the turnout was far less than anticipated — a situation attributed to the intense interest in the Cleveland-Boston baseball game and also to the Jewish religious celebration of the new year—the deadline day registration gave the county a near-record eligibility list.

Prior to yesterday 571,171 voters had qualified, so that the total should be around 640,000. The record of 645,000 was set in 1946, while 605,188 Greater Clevelanders were eligible to vote in the last presidential year and 631,785 in 1940.

556,000 Voted in 1944

Incidentally, there is a considerable variation bettween the number of persons who can vote and those who actually bother to cast a ballot. In 1946, for example, only 427,887 voted and in 1944 approximately 556,000.

The estimate of 67,500 registrations was made early today by William A. Franz, supervisor of registration for the Board of Elections. It was based on an average of 54 registrations for the first 815 precincts reporting, but Franz said

(Continued on Page 8, Column 2)

Ticket Sale Deluged by Happy Fans

A sudden deluge of world series ticket seekers descended on the stadium yesterday after word came of an Indian victory and forced the groaning ticket distribution machinery to run after the 8 p. m. deadline, until 9:30.

Since the Indians took a day longer to clinch the pennant than was anticipated, Rudie Schaffer, ball club business manager, also extended distribution one day, as he announced windows would be open from 10 a. m. to 8 p. m. tomorrow.

Only in the early morning did crowds cramp the ticket dispensers. Lines began forming about 8 a. m. and general confusion reigned when the windows failed to open at the scheduled 10 a. m. When the gates finally opened at 11:30 some 200 persons were told to come back in the afternoon.

When the whistles blew later the stadium crew paused only for a hearty handshake and passed tickets to satisfied customers, who smilingly said: "Now that wasn't bad after all."

Dozen Tickets Misplaced

The front office had only one moment of anxiety when it was reported that a dozen tickets had been misplaced. By nightfall many had been found. The pasteboards can be claimed today by those persons who failed in the first attempt.

About .6000 out-of-town applicants poured into the ball club offices above Gate A and were handled without a hitch. Their mailed instructions—to bring their buff-colored reservation cards with certified check, cashier check or postal money order—were followed to the letter.

Today the gates will again open at 10 a. m. Greater Clevelanders who have received their mailed acknowledgments should proceed quickly to Gate A or C with their buff-colored cards—cards numbered 1 to 30,000 at Gate A and those numbered over 30,000 to Gate C.

Concerning payment, the same holds true for Clevelanders as for persons from out of town. No cash will be accepted.

(Continued on Page 7, Column 3)

Lands on Dot in Sea, 23 Survive

MIAMI, Fla., Oct. 4—(UP)—A 28-year-old pilot who belly-landed his DC-3 passenger plane on a 75-foot strip of sandy beach on a small Bahamas island in the predawn darkness today declared that his emergency landing was "just routine."

He, his 19 passengers and three fellow crew members survived the forced landing with no discomfort except a 17-hour wait for the United States Coast Guard to rescue them.

Two coast guard flying boats, racing against time and an approaching hurricane, took the 23 persons from the strip of sand on tiny Haines Key tonight and brought them 135 miles to Miami.

The downed plane, a chartered craft flying 19 Puerto Ricans back to their native land from New York City, became lost over the Atlantic at midnight last night with its fuel tanks running dry.

Pilot Richard R. Olivere said he was heading for Miami from Teterboro, N. J., to pick up another pilot, refuel and continue on to San Juan when he became aware that his plane had drifted far off its course.

"I recognized where I was when I spotted islands below," he said. "I made a pass at this beach and dropped flares. They didn't work. So I used my landing lights. The beach was just wide enough to get in."

Lieut. W. N. Durham, St. Petersburg, Fla., one of the coast guard PBM pilots who flew to the rescue, said it was a "marvelous landing."

"He came in, in pitch darkness, on a strip of beach 75 feet wide, with the sea on one side and a jagged coral ledge on the other," Durham said.

Olivere's plane slid 600 feet on its belly in the soft sand.

Wilbur L. Cross, Ex-Governor and Educator, Dead

NEW HAVEN, Conn., Tuesday, Oct. 5—(AP)—Wilbur L. Cross, 86, former four-term governor of Connecticut, died early today at his home here.

Cross, who concluded a distinguished career as an educator before entering politics with his election as governor in 1930, had been ailing for several weeks.

It was soon after Dr. Cross' retirement as dean of the Yale graduate school that he entered politics, almost by accident. Invited to a Democratic clambake, he made an unscheduled three-minute speech—an attack on prohibition.

Short as it was, that speech thrust him into the limelight and eventually won for him the Democratic nomination for governor.

He joined the Yale faculty in 1897.

Hard-Way Victory Sends City Wacky

'Love Those Indians!' Clevelanders Shout to World in Frenzied Demonstration

BY ROELIF LOVELAND

Shortly before 4 yesterday afternoon the sun trembled in his orbit and the stars shivered violently in the heavens.

The earth gave itself a couple of extra spins, and a great voice cried: "Behold, the Cleveland Indians, winners of the 1948 American League pennant."

As if in answer, the city of Cleveland, which had waited long, went completely and noisily wacky.

Cleveland let out a blast to the world at large, and Cleveland said:

"The Indians won the pennant, and they won it the hard way. They didn't float in by being rained out. They didn't end the regular season in a tie with Boston because the scrappy Detroit Tigers took it easy. They played the deciding game in the Boston park, where Boston had every advantage. They played it after traveling all night, while the Red Sox rested at home. And they didn't win by one run or two runs—they won by five runs. Love those Indians!"

Holiday in Arizona

And, believe it or not, regard for what Lou Boudreau and his lads had accomplished was not confined to Cleveland, nor yet to Ohio.

Arizona (the Indians have trained at Tucson for the last two years) will observe today as "Cleveland Pennant Day," according to an official proclamation by Acting Gov. Dan E. Garvey, as reported by the Associated Press.

And Bowman, N. D., a town of about 1,000, celebrated with horns and confetti as soon as they heard the news. They were converted to the Indians' cause by Dr. Robert L. Goulding, only former Clevelander in town, and last night were shouting: "Hey Doc, we made it!" Then they went back to tooting their horns.

Ohio's governor, Thomas J. Herbert, who served as head usher for the pennant winning Indians of 1920, wired congratulations late last night to Bill Veeck, president of the Cleveland club, and members of the team for "a great job well done."

Now go get that world series pennant for you Ohio fans, the governor added. He signed his wire: "Head usher for the Indians of years ago."

Mayor Thomas A. Burke was figuring out how he could fly to Boston for the two world series games to be played there, yet get his mayoralty chores done. Quoth His Honor: "I'm tickled to death."

Yep, Cleveland's reaction was instantaneous and of long duration.

Late last night downtown streets

(Continued on Page 7, Column 3)

Series Traffic Shift Affects Large Section

The pattern of Cleveland traffic extending over a large area of the city, but especially in the downtown district, will be changed on days when World Series games are played here, Traffic Commissioner John R. Sammon announced last night.

In the immediate downtown district on Friday, Saturday and perhaps Sunday, W. 3d Street, Lakeside Avenue, Ontario Street and St. Clair Avenue will be reserved for taxis and busses transporting people to and from the Cleveland Stadium.

Eastbound traffic using Memorial Shoreway N. W., other than that headed for the stadium, will be diverted at the W. 29th Street underpass to the Detroit-Superior Bridge.

Westbound traffic, other than that going to the games, will be diverted from Memorial Shoreway N. E. at E. 72d Street to St. Clair Avenue N. E.

At every major thoroughfare crossing E. 55th Street, police will be stationed with large arrows guiding motorists who are going to the games to Memorial Shoreway. Similar guide signs and policemen will be stationed at other strategic

(Continued on Page 7, Column 3)

Oops—Holdup Men Pick on Ex-Deputy

Two would-be holdup men last night showed considerable lack of discretion in choosing for their victim Jack Sinek, 57, a former county deputy sheriff.

Sinek, now a sales tax inspector, was accosted a few doors from his home at 3343 E. 137th Street by a pair of thugs who stepped from the bushes. He swung with one hand at a "shiny object" one man was pointing at him and with the other at the robber's companion.

Both fled down the street, outdistancing Sinek, who chased them a few hundred feet. The intended victim was a deputy sheriff under the late Fred Kohler.

WHERE TO FIND—

FIRE FOUGHT FIVE HOURS

Blaze in Candy Company on Euclid Causes $5,500 Damage

Fire that was fought for five hours last night and early today caused an estimated $5,500 damage to the Imperial Candy Co., 12213 Euclid Avenue. Flames were confined to the basement of the one-story building block that contains 10 stores.

Thick smoke from burning cardboard boxes hindered the early fighting. Members of the rescue squad equipped with emergency breathing masks worked alone until other firemen could close in.

Jubilant Tribe Met By Cheers, Tears

BY GORDON COBBLEDICK
Plain Dealer Sports Editor

BOSTON, Oct. 4 — Birdie Tebbetts topped that one, a knuckle ball that broke down and inside to him, and he bounced the ball quickly in the general direction of the shortstop position. Gene Bearden made a desperate attempt to head it off, but he could have saved the effort, for Ken Keltner came racing in and across the grass and scooped up the bounding ball and took two more steps before firing a strike to Eddie Robinson.

It was the last out and the Indians had won the championship of the American League.

Bearden turned and started to walk toward the first base dugout and the runway leading to the dressing room, but he didn't get very far. Keltner hit him from behind an instant before the jubilant Robinson swarmed all over him from the front. Lou Boudreau and Joe Gordon converged on him from their position and Jim Hegan came charging up from his.

They snatched the cap from Bearden's head and rumpled his

(Continued on Page 22, Column 7)

Tribe Cops Series in 4-3 Thriller!

San Francisco Chronicle Sporting Green
EDITED BY BILL LEISER
CCCCAAB · TUESDAY, OCT. 12, 1948 · PAGE 1 H

RELIEF HURLER HERO

Bearden Quells Desperate Rally

Boston Lapses Disastrous in Most Dramatic Battle of 1948 Classic

By BOB STEVENS, Chronicle Staff Writer

BRAVES FIELD, Boston, Oct. 11—Boston's mighty Braves, who had a season-long reputation for never beating themselves, chose the worst time possible to prove the contention in error as they bowed dramatically to the new champions of the world from Cleveland, 4-3, today to climax the 45th renewal of the greatest show on earth.

The National League pennant winners, though they went down gallantly and before the might of a better team, suffered the agony of two heartbreaking mistakes to push the highly favored Tribe from Ohio into a world series victory for the first time since 1920.

Below me now is nothing but stunned silence as the overflow crowd of 40,103 file, shuffle-like, out of this sprawling single-deck stadium that hosted its first series since the incredible Braves of 1914.

It was a long time coming to "the Land of the Bean and the Cod, where the Cabots talk only to the Lodges, and the Lodges talk only to God." And, now it's gone, the last echoes of a gutteral groan of enormous disappointment disappearing over the restless waters of the Charles river.

It could have been so different. Tommy Holmes, Back Bay's great outfielder, threw to the wrong base, and Cleveland scored. A perfect double-play ball was thrown wildly to first, dropped, and Cleveland scored—THE WINNING RUN. The battling Braves, certainly as game a gang of scrappers as ever appeared in the classic fall extravaganza, rallied, bombing starter Bob Lemon out of sight as the stadium trembled under the impact of deafening roars.

Premature Chickens

"It will be Sain, Johnny Sain, tomorrow and we will be champions of the world," screached the delirious Boston boosters as the sixth, and to be final, game of the weird 1948 series went into its last three outs.

The clouters from the Commons brought 40,000 people to their feet in the ninth when explosive Eddie Stanky faced Lefty Gene Bearden, the Van Gogh of the knuckle ball, who relieved a battered, fading Lemon in the Braves' riotous eighth inning. The situation was tense as Bearden knuckled home two balls, far off the target. The rumble of hope began to grow, to swell. A called strike, a foul, back into the screen behind the plate. Another ball, another foul, another ball. Stanky walked, and the rumble exploded.

This is it.

But, it wasn't.

Manager Billy Southworth elected to go for the tie, to place the burden of responsibility upon the capable shoulders of Holmes and young Alvin Dark to drive home the deadlocking tally. Connie Ryan was inserted to run for Stanky, the lovable brat, and Sibby Sisti was planted at the plate to swing for the great Warren Spahn, Boston's relief for gigantic Bill Voiselle.

Horrible Crash

Sibbi fouled off Bearden's first knuckler, and took a ball, high, across the whiskers. The taciturn Gene corkscrewed himself into an elaborate windup, after first checking Ryan, and threw.

The crashing of beautiful hopes may never be silenced.

Sibby moved out, toward Bearden, and offered at the letter-high pitch. Up into the air it went, maybe 20 feet, spinning, and spiraling toward the mound. Catcher Jim Hegan brushed the bewildered Sisti out of his way, gloved the ball, wheeled, and fired to first baseman Eddie Robinson. Double play.

Ryan was off with the throw and was easily cut down at the payoff end of the twin killing and the embalming of Boston dreams. He was beaten so badly he did not even bother to slide, just sort of slinking back to the dugout to pack his clothes and go home.

School was out.

I doubt one-third of the crowd saw Holmes loft harmlessly into the glove of Bob Kennedy to end the richest world series ever played. People just silently arose and slowly turned their backs to the nailing of Ryan, like it was something too horrible to look at, and shuffled out.

Cleveland, the Lou Boudreau-inspired champions of the American League, were champions of the world the moment Kennedy drew out of the sullen, humid skies of Boston that Holmes fly, and Boston had its back turned on it.

Drama in Bunches

For sheer drama, for the heights of exaltation and the depths of despair, the sixth game of the series was by far the best played. The pitchers pitched, but they did not dominate the show to such an extent that people began to hate perfection. The hitters hit and mistakes were made. It was baseball at its most dramatic, even if the Cabots and Lodges tonight are shut up on Beacon street and bawling in their champagne.

What proved to be the winning run was sort of artificially manufactured. It was unbecoming to the stature of the occasion. The Tribe from the banks of Lake Erie went into the eighth leading by 3 to 1, and had to face the artistry of Spahn, the imperturbable southpaw who worked so gallantly in relief yesterday and forced the series back to Boston for settlement.

Joe Gordon slashed a line drive

Continued on Page 2H, Col. 6

Bearden Again!

CLEVELAND (American)

	AB	R	H	O	A	E
Mitchell, lf	4	1	1	3	0	0
Kennedy, lf	1	0	0	1	0	0
Doby, rf	4	0	2	1	0	0
Boudreau, s	3	0	1	2	2	0
Gordon, 2b	4	1	1	2	3	0
Keltner, 3b	4	1	1	0	3	0
Tucker, cf	3	1	1	3	1	0
Robinson, 1b	4	0	2	13	0	0
Hegan, c	4	0	1	2	2	0
Lemon, p	3	0	0	0	3	0
Bearden, p	1	0	0	0	1	0
Totals	35	4	10	27	15	0

BOSTON (National)

	AB	R	H	O	A	E
Holmes, rf	5	1	2	1	0	0
Dark, s	4	0	1	0	1	0
Torgeson, 1b	4	1	1	5	1	0
Elliott, 3b	3	1	3	4	3	0
Rickert, lf	3	0	0	5	0	0
Conatser, cf	1	0	0	0	0	0
Salkeld, c	2	0	0	4	1	0
Masi, c	1	0	1	3	0	0
M.McCk, cf-lf	4	0	1	2	0	0
Stanky, 2b	1	0	0	3	2	0
Voiselle, p	1	0	0	0	0	0
Spahn, p	0	0	0	0	1	0
F.McCormk	1	0	0	0	0	0
Sisti	1	0	0	0	0	0
Ryan	0	0	0	0	0	0
Totals	31	3	9	27	9	0

F. McCormick grounded out for Voiselle in 7th.
Sisti popped out for Spahn in 9th.
Ryan ran for Stanky in 9th.

CLEVELAND......	001	002	010—4
BOSTON...........	000	100	020—3

Runs batted in—Boudreau, M. McCormick, Gordon, Hegan, Robinson, Conatser, Masi. Two-base hits—Mitchell, Boudreau, Torgeson, Masi. Home run—Gordon. Sacrifice—Voiselle. Left on bases—Cleveland 7, Boston 7. Bases on balls—Off Lemon 4, Voiselle 2, Bearden 1. Struck out—By Voiselle 2, Lemon 1, Spahn 4. Hits—Off Voiselle 7 in 7, Lemon 8 in 1⅓, Spahn 3 in 2, Bearden 1 in 1⅔. Hit by pitcher—Boudreau (by Voiselle). Balk—Lemon. Double plays—Tucker to Robinson, Lemon to Boudreau to Robinson, Gordon to Boudreau to Robinson, Elliott to Stanky to Torgeson, Hegan to Robinson. Winning pitcher—Lemon. Losing pitcher—Voiselle. Umpires—Summers (A), plate; Stewart (N), 1b; Grieve (A), 2b; Barr (N), 3b; foul lines, Paparella (A), Pinelli (N). Time—2h. 16m. Attendance—40,103.

PAYOFF RUN IN 1948 WORLD SERIES—KEN KELTNER RACES HOME FROM SECOND (DOTTED LINE) ON EDDIE ROBINSON'S 8TH INNING SINGLE (SOLID LINE). (AP) Wirephoto

Here's Run That Did It For Indians

HERO'S FATE—To be manhandled, but gently, and ridden off the field upon the shoulders of his teammates was the fate of yesterday's hero in the deciding game of the World Series, Relief Pitcher Gene Bearden. It was the second time in the series that the Purple Heart veteran of World War II had subdued the Boston Braves. (AP) Wirephoto

Cleveland Goes Wild

Bearden Mobbed; Boudreau Kissed Against His Will

By OSCAR FRALEY

BOSTON, Oct. 11 (U.P.)—The Cleveland Indians were a bunch of maudlin maniacs tonight and the chief target of their attention was giant Gene Bearden, the guy who got them into the series and then took them out with the championship of the baseball world.

They cheered themselves hoarse, kissed each other with almost hysterical abandon and mauled the Arkansas knuckle-ball pitcher who came out of the center field bullpen to save the big game by one run.

It was a frenzied scene in their riotous dressing room as they celebrated their triumph with tears and cheers; bone-cracking hugs and ear-splitting acclamation for themselves and the big guy.

"Yowee, we made it," roared the sweating Bearden, his brown eyes crackling with excitement. "Give me a kiss, Lou."

LOU WAS SO SHY

His target of the moment, Manager Lou Boudreau, drew hastily away.

"Aw, go away," he grinned uneasily, "that stuff is for National Leaguers."

"They don't feel like kissing over there," Bearden yelled, pointing toward the silent dressing room of the beaten Braves. "Give me a kiss, you big lug."

Joe Gordon, Kenny Keltner, Jim Hegan and Bob Lemon—the man who Bearden rescued in that perilous eighth inning when Boston tallied two runs—weren't so bashful. They fell to like women at a sewing circle and Boudreau blushed as they gathered him in.

Boudreau finally escaped from them only to be swarmed under by a horde of newspapermen and cameramen. In the midst of this malestrom, the flashbulbs popping like firecrackers, he panted:

A TEAM VICTORY

"This was a team victory all the way, and don't think these Braves weren't tough, because they really were. But I guess you'd have to say Bearden is a boy who did it. He won us the pennant in the playoff to get us into this, and now he has saved it for us. I hope Don Black was listening today, because we are glad to have him as a teammate."

Boudreau was referring to the pitcher who suffered a critical head injury just before the season ended.

Bulling their way through the mad mob came Billy Southworth, manager of the defeated Braves, and his coaches.

"We just wanted to say congratulations," Billy the Kid said heartily with a big smile which didn't reach his eyes. "You have a great team."

Dom DiMag Gets Married

WELLESLEY, Mass., Oct. 11 (U.P.)—Dominic Paul DiMaggio, bespectacled Boston Red Sox outfielder and member of one of baseball's first families, was married today to Miss Emily A. Frederick, 24-year-old Wellesley brunette.

Only a handful of relatives and close friends were present at the nuptial mass in St. Paul's (Catholic) Church and the reception that followed at the home of the bride's parents. Rev. Robert E. Lord performed the ceremony.

Guests included the bridegroom's brother, Joe DiMaggio of the New York Yankees and his parents, who came here from San Francisco.

The bride, a graduate of fashionable Dana Hall School, the Katharine Gibbs School and Emerson College, met DiMaggio in 1945 when he was serving in the Coast Guard.

Indians and Harvard in Grid Tie-Up

Stanford and Harvard have signed a home-and-home football agreement for 1949-50, Al Masters, director of athletics at Stanford, announced yesterday.

The Crimson eleven will play the Indians at Stanford on September 24 next year, and Stanford will travel to Cambridge for a game September 30, 1950. The 1949 Stanford schedule also includes Michigan at Stanford and the 1950 schedule has Army coming to the Palo Alto stadium.

This will be the first regularly-scheduled football game involving Harvard and a Pacific Coast Conference team. Harvard has played only one other PCC team, beating Oregon in the Rose Bowl on New Year's day, 1920.

The Bonanza Handicap

Triskelion Captures Feature Race on Muddy Albany Track

Never at any disadvantage on yesterday's muddy track, Mrs. Ann Peppers' Triskelion was returned the Bonanza handicap winner in the feature race at Golden Gate Fields. The four-year-old son of Heelfly, capably handled by Alan Gray, ran the mile and a sixteenth in the commendable time of 1:45 4-5 and won by a head as Biscailuz ran second and Menu third.

Triskelion assumed command soon after the start, and but for a brief period in the home stretch, was in front all the way. The Peppers horse bore out on the stretch turn and Biscailuz slipped through on the inside to take the lead. Triskelion, however, was not yet through and, responding to vigorous handling, outfinished his South American rival.

Menu was a distant third and much the best of the others in the field of seven. A casualty of the race was Boy Knight, who fell lame after about three-eighths of a mile and was pulled up.

As the public choice, Triskelion paid $6.90 for $2 in the mutuels. He next will be seen in Saturday's running of the $15,000 Forty-Niners Handicap in which some of the West's best horses will be brought together over a mile and an eighth distance.

MR. AND MRS.—Baseball's newest newlyweds, Dominic DiMaggio, Boston Red Sox star outfielder, and his bride, the former Emily A. Frederick, pose for the photographers after their marriage in Wellesley, Mass., yesterday. (AP) Wirephoto

Racing Ban Reviewed

Ruling Expected Today in Case Of Andy Coghill

A day and night session of the California Horse Racing Board in which the suspension of Andrew J. Coghill, former foreman for the stables of Robert S. Howard was reviewed ended at a late hour last evening when the testimony of an important witness was declared lacking in credibility.

Kenneth Lynch, State Attorney, upon hearing all of the evidence in the case of Coghill, said that testimony of one Robert F. Patterson, a groom, was not to be believed on three out of five counts on charges made against the defendant.

Coghill had been suspended by the board under Rules 313 and 319.

EXPECT RULING TODAY

The racing board announced before adjournment that it would hold an executive meeting this morning and it is expected that a ruling, in Coghill's favor or against, will be made then.

The groom, a sharp-eyed oldster (by his own admission) testified he went around the barn on various occasions and was on hand at just the right time to see Coghill belabor such a horse as Drumbeat with a battery, needle Fractured and Criss Cross.

However, Alfred J. Luke, attorney representing Coghill, paraded several witnesses in rebuttal, these including Jockey Ralph Zufelt and William Chew, an Arcadia farmer, who refuted Patterson's testimony.

Earlier, a hearing was granted J. R. (Red) of San Mateo on charges of violation of Rule 319. Specifically, Gregory was charged with registering a horse at Bay Meadows, Gallavant, as his own when in reality the horse was the property of Bob Howard.

Gregory testified that he had been perhaps careless and thoughtless, but certainly nothing was fraudulent in intent. He did not enter or race Gallavant.

KYNE TESTIFIES

Gregory, however, was one of his own most damaging witnesses, as his testimony differed from that given at the summer race board hearing at La Jolla during the Del Mar meeting, and it also differed from testimony given by Howard by deposition. Howard is now in Detroit.

Gregory was represented by Attorney Robert R. Ashton of Los Angeles,

Continued on Page 4H, Col. 6

AS BILL LEISER SEES IT:

Pappy Gets Roses, Needs Bowl

THE SPORTSWRITERS got cute in their Monday meeting yesterday at Press Club.

As a defense by which Nevada's Stan Heath could be stopped they presented St. Mary's Coach Joe Verducci a pair of handcuffs and a policeman's "billy."

To help the Stanford offense they gave Marchie Schwartz a picnic basket with a football in it to prevent fumbling.

Coach Lynn Waldorf of California was presented one dozen roses. Rose Bowl! Get it?

Said Waldorf of the smashing of Wisconsin: "This was our first team showing of '48, our first game in which the strength of the whole team was greater than the summation of the ability of its parts." A pretty good estimate, that.

"Our men took seriously the fact we were the last team with a chance to do something against a Big Nine foe this season, and they determined to do something about it. An indication of spirit: Before the game, Eggs Manske was warming up the passers, Wes Fry had the backs, and I was supposed to handle the linemen. I stopped for a few minutes to talk to Harry Stuhldreher. When I got down to the end of the field the linemen were already going to it, with the two who couldn't play, Hank Borghi and Bobby Dodds having taken command."

Pappy liked 160-pound Billy Main for fine blocking, Billy Montagne for great work all 'round, including touchdown scoring. "We all held our breath when he hit that goal post," said Pappy, "and boy, we were relieved when he came to the sideline on his own. It wasn't a bad injury, thank goodness."

Pappy said the loss of Fullback Bendrick hurt Wisconsin. Pappy liked the officiating of Referee Jim Cain, the former Washington halfback.

Defensive Problems

He said Oregon State's unbalanced line and its right and left side passing will pose new defensive problems for Cal. Dave Hirschler and Bobby Dodds, he expects, will be able to play for the first time in several weeks Saturday. Jacks Swaner and Jensen have developed no new injuries.

OREGON STATE'S advance man, Irving Harris, reported Coach Lon Stiner has his old favorite combination, a right halfback who passes left handed, Don Samuel, and left halfbacks who pass right-handed, Dick Gray and Ken Carpenter. Samuel and Gray call the plays.

"Stiner's new leaning to open rather than power offense will surprise you," the OSC man added. added.

"CALIFORNIA'S BLOCKING," Pappy said, "was improved, though we missed many times. Pictures show one instance in which Norm Pressley took off against Wisconsin's line backer, missed him, and did a beautiful job of bowling a surprised Jim Cullom out of the play. How Paul Keckley made 15 yards on that

STAN HEATH
For Him—Handcuffs

play I don't know. He did it all alone. Dick Erickson's faking and direction were improved."

Pappy took note of Harris' statement that, save for fumbles, Oregon State would be undefeated, and that her three top passers have a .700 average for the season. The only Oregon injury is Andy Knudsen, second fullback, who has been out for some time.

Sterling Is Tops

MARCHIE SCHWARTZ of Stanford and Len Casanova of Santa Clara agreed the Broncs' Vern Sterling is one of the greatest of guards; that his charge had a lot to do with Stanford fumbles; that Tom Payne was a most aggressive tackle and John Hock not much less so.

Casanova cited Al Martin and Billy Sheridan for generalship. When asked if he called the two touchdown plays in the second half, Cas said: "No, Sheridan called them." Cas mentioned Paul Conn for fine work in place of Hare. He though Hall Haynes kicking average, at 46 yards, noteworthy. Cas also noted the Bronco three-game winning streak the longest in his own present memory at Santa Clara.

Vern Hare has a cheek bone fracture. Casanova doesn't know if he will play the man again or not. "He has no consideration for safety. He can't do anything but play his hardest. I don't know if I should use him or not, though he has a medical OK."

Schwartz said: "We fumbled. They had men we couldn't handle. Our pass defense was bad. But, at least we didn't wilt. We were still in there at the end, and we'll get in the win column, yet."

Coach Joe Kuharich told Detroit tried to force the Dons to use a normal rather than white football in their night game. "Even the white ball can not be seen by the third line of defense," he added.

Joe opined that Detroit and Nevada would play even up, either might win, though Detroit would win if the game were played at Detroit at night. (Does that give us two teams as good as the 1941 Chicago Bears, whom Joe once thought the equal of Nevada?)

'We Have Chance'

JOE VERDUCCI reported the Gaels, after last week devoted to rest except for Thursday when there was full practice, will be at full strength, for Nevada, and that they have "a chance to win."

"The kids think they can win, and they're influencing the coaches," said Joe. "But we haven't yet been able to figure out a defense we think will work."

CONFERENCE COMMISSIONER VIC SCHMIDT said: "Washington has been a dark horse growing brighter. I think our officiating is better than last year. I can't talk about Oregon's P. E.-190 course. Yes, there is a conference rule that will now allow a newspaperman to be an official. Newspapermen asked for the rule."

MORSE SIMMS, who once coached and drove the football bus for St. Mary's of Texas, said he now executive officer for the Wig Wam and Wise Men of America, "an organization like the Spokane Round Table but chiefly concerned with high school sports. They're all wealthy men, and I spend the money for them. We pick an All-America high-school team."

Oklahoma Ags Big

SAM McKEE AND BILL COFFMAN represented the Portola Festival committee, asking for mention of the big pageant, parade, and 15 bands who will do a big show at 1 o'clock preceding the USF-Oklahoma A & M game Saturday at Kezar.

"It will compare fully with the Shrine show," said McKee.

Kuharich said this new Oklahoma team is the "same old story, big line, fast backs. Tackles run 230 pounds, ends 200, center 225. But we might beat them."

Said Carel Dotty of Pacific: "We looked like a football team for the first time. We canceled out the Willamette game and took on Portland, figuring to strengthen our schedule, so last week Portland lost to Willamette."

The Tigers gained 478 yards on the ground against San Diego, Wilbur Sites averaged 20.8 per carry.

Dannie Hill reported San Jose also looked like a football team, that 155-pound Al Cementina carried well, that Gene Mengas threw three touchdown-passes. Saturday it's Cal Poly down south.

Fight Roundup

PHILADELPHIA (UP) — Jimmy Bivins, 179½, Cleveland, dec. Johnny Flynn, 209, Rochester, N. Y. (10).

LEWISTON, Maine (UP) — Dave Andrews, 146, Lowell, Mass., dec. Earl Moore, 148, Detroit (10).

NEW YORK (UP)—Pat Brady, 132¾, The Bronx, dec. Solly Cantor, 136, Toronto (10).

HARTFORD (UP) — Frankie Vigeant, 147, Thomaston, Conn., dec. Joe DeMartino, 151, Bridgeport, Conn. (10).

NEW YORK (UP)—Tony Janiro, 151¾, Youngstown, Ohio, ko'd Ruby Kessler, 150, Brooklyn (1).

NEW HAVEN (UP)—Sandy Saddler, 128, New York, tko'd Whistlin' Willie Roach, 126, Wilmington, Del. (3).

HOLYOKE, Mass. (UP)—Ralph Zanelli, 148, Providence, dec. Ottie Graham, 147, Philadelphia (10).

CHICAGO (UP)—Sylvester Perkins, 159, Chicago, dec. Lloyd Gibson, 168, Cincinnati (10).

BALTIMORE (UP)—Leo Mattricciani, 208½, Baltimore, dec. Johnny Shkor, 216¾, Sparrows Point, Md. (10).

Casey Stengel New Yankee Pilot

San Francisco Chronicle Sporting Green
EDITED BY BILL LEISER
WEDNESDAY, OCT. 13, 1948 PAGE 1 H

CONTRACT SIGNED

Acorns' Manager Gets 2-Year Pact

Exclusive Sporting Green Report On Six-Week-Old Deal Confirmed

By **CLYDE GIRALDO**

They sold Casey Stengel up the river yesterday.

The New York Yankees signed the 58-year-old Oakland Oaks' manager to a two-year contract, salary undisclosed.

It's official!

Casey is in New York city this minute.

Instead of flying to his home in Glendale, as he told the press and friends, Stengel and Clarence L. (Brick) Laws, Oaks president, boarded a plane immediately after the Governor's Cup clincher Sunday at Emeryville.

The deal was cut and dried six weeks ago, but until recently only the Chronicle Sporting Green bared the fact.

Stengel's elevation to the most important job in baseball, handling Joe DiMaggio and the fabulous Yankees, looms as the largest in Pacific Coast League history, not excepting the sale by Dr. Charles Strub and the late George Alfred Putman of a young fellow named Willie Kamm for $125,000.

On completion of the formal signing yesterday morning in the Yankee offices at New York city, the party repaired to the 21 Club, where Del E. Webb, Casey's close friend, and Dan Topping, the Yankee owners, tossed a spread at 4:30 o'clock, New York time. And what a spread, according to telephone calls to Tee Calleri, Oaks secretary, and Harry Davis, Oaks business manager

TIPPED HAND

Early Sunday night Stengel himself tipped his hand.

"Good-by," he said to this Sporting Green representative. Usually, Stengel waved a nonchalant "See you later." This time it was "Good-by."

Next manager for the Oaks could be Lou Boudreau of the world series Indians, who doesn't see eye-to-eye with President Bill Veeck; or, perhaps, Bill Skiff, former Seattle manager, who today is trouble-shooter for the Yankees and manager of the Newark International League club late last year. Or maybe Jimmy Dykes, the ex-White Sox and Hollywood manager, who'd be a riot at Emeryville.

Stengel's signing yesterday with the Yankees came almost 25 years ago to the day when he hit a home run for the New York Giants that beat the Yankees in the world series, 1-0.

Stengel starred for John McGraw, playing right field, batting left-handed and acting left-handed to give McGraw furrowed brows with the bird cage stunt, the dipping into an outfield hole, the fights and acts imaginative.

O. K., with his world's champion-

"Mr. McGraw took we to Europe, ship team against Charley Comiskey's White Sox," Stengel oft remarked, "but sometimes I wondered if he wished he'd left me home. Not in England, though. I won the old ball game for Mr. McGraw off Red Faber. Hit a triple in the ninth inning. Sun in my eyes. Bad field. But, heck, the King and Queen were there, and I had to hit. My bride (Mrs. Edna Stengel) never saw me play. She glued her eyes on Queen Mary"

Stengel's departure from Oakland, while no surprise to Sporting Green readers, evinced polite statements from his owners.

Joe Blumenfeld made it short:

"We are sorry to lose Casey, but know he will do the job."

Laws, Oaks president, phoned this statement:

"Although we are terribly sorry to lose Casey Stengel as manager of the champion Oaks, we are happy and proud he has been chosen to manage the great New York Yankees.

"No matter how important Casey has been to the Oakland club and the fans, it would be unfair to try to influence him to reject the New York job.

"George Weiss, general manager of the Yankees, has promised the Oakland club player assistance in 1949 for its co-operation in releasing Stengel.

"The Oakland club has no one in mind to replace Stengel, and will take plenty of time to select the right man to succeed him.

"I know the Oakland fans will join me in saying, 'Best of luck, Casey'."

Stengel, the cutie, left a farewell message in the Oaks' mail box to be opened yesterday. It read, "Three of the happiest years of my baseball career have been spent in Oakland.

"I want to thank the press, the fans, city officials, owners and players of the Oakland ball club for their support. I feel their co-operation on my behalf was a major part that promoted me to this splendid position I now have."

Stengel managed Oakland in 1946, 1947 and 1948, finishing second, fourth and first, respectively.

Ironically, Stengel finished fourth in 1947 with the greatest pitching staff he ever had, including Bryan Stephens, Frank Shea and Gene Bearden. Those three wound up as big league heroes. Last season Stengel had his worst pitching staff and finished in front. That's the man.

PERSONALITY

One of the greatest personalities the Coast League has seen, from the days of the fabulous Hap Hogan, Stengel will set well in the Nation's largest city. He knows baseball and he knows people. His contacts are tremendous.

On parting Sunday night, Stengel answered the Sporting Green's query "will you send me a post card from New York?" with a grin and sharp "I know so many people I could spend 24 hours a day writing cards. But d—— right, I'll write. I love Oakland. The people out here treated me all right."

Stengel, born in Kansas City, where he studied dentistry but abandoned the profession when he found left-handed dentists aren't popular, managed Brooklyn in 1934-35-36. He sat out 1937, drawing absolutely full salary without doing a lick of work.

Wealthy in his own right, Stengel could buy a major league club, but prefers to be on the coaching lines. Stengel owns a hotel, oil wells, real estate inestimable and stocks and bonds by the jillions. The first thing he doeson opening the morn-

Continued on Page 2H, Col. 7

Pass Best OSC Bet

Cal Up Against Most Air-Minded Gang in PCC

By **IRWIN HARRIS**

(The Oregon State advance man, asked to bring Sporting Green readers up to date on the Beavers, reports as follows.)

Coach Lon Stiner will bring a pass-minded Oregon State football team to Berkeley Saturday for the Golden Bears' first Pacific Coast Conference game of the season. Althougn Pappy Waldorf's undefeated club undoubtedly will be heavily favored, the Bears probably will run into the most versatile and hardest-to-stop offense they have met this campaign.

After three games, all conference affairs, Oregon State ranks first on the Coast in passing and second in total offense. Adding the statistics from last Saturday's easy 32-6 win over Portland University, the Beavers have rolled up a net yardage of 898 on running plays and completed 42 out of 79 pass attempts for 602 yards and a nifty completion average of .532. Their total offense is 1500 yards, an average of just over 377 yards per game.

Leading the Beaver attack is the brilliant Don Samuel, triple-threat senior right halfback and a top candidate for All-Coast and All-American honors. In four games Samuel has lugged the leather 182 net yards on 26 attempts for a 7.77 average, completed 16 out of 32 aerials for 309 yards and an even .500 percentage and punted 13 times for a 36.2 average. In addition, this busy Beaver has caught five passes himself, one of them good for a touchdown.

ONLY THE BEGINNIN'

But Samuel is only one of a number of talented and experienced Orange backs. His understudy, Bob Laidlaw, sports the best ground-gaining average on the club, a 11.11 mark made on carrying the ball an even 100 yards in 9 tries. Alternating at left half are Dick Gray and Ken Carpenter, both deadeye passers and good runners. Carpenter has completed 10 out of 12 passes and has averaged 4.96 yards in running forays. Gray, third and last of the famous backfield Grays at Oregon State, connected with 13 of his first 20 aerials for 173 yards and advanced the ball 74 yards on running plays.

Starting Quarterback Rudy Ruppe, another two-year letterman, led the Nation in pass snagging last week with 14 catches good for 155 yards. In addition, he is a good blocker and a great line backer on defense. Giving him experienced help are Don Mast, another good pass catcher, and Garth Rouse, rugged defensive man. Supplying the plunging power through the line is Dick "the tank" Twenge, a two-year veteran. Twenge has averaged 4.97 yards and is fast and shifty for his 190 pounds. Ready to alternate with him is Duane Moore, also a two-stripe monogram wearer.

Oregon State still operates from Stiner's version of the single wing which he calls the "deep wing." This year the dean of the Coast Conference coaches has added a number of new wrinkles including such things as pitch-outs, flankers and man-in-motion plays. But the Beavers' bread and butter is still the famous option pass play in which the halfbacks run wide, size up the situation and then decide whether to continue running or to throw the ball.

HAS THE SETUP

For the first time since the championship club of 1941, Stiner has the ideal combination to make the play work with Samuel as the lefthanded right half and Gray and Carpenter as the righthanded pitching left halfs. All three can run or pass equally well. The three have completed 39 out of 64 throws for a neat .609 average.

The Beavers have a good solid line which is big enough, averaging around 206. Starting ends are Bud Gibbs and Bob Grove, both expert pass receivers. Experienced depth is provided by Dick Lorenz, Stan McGuire, Craig McMicken and Harry Barnes. Leading line candidate for All-Coast honors is big blonde Bill Austin, a 212-pound play wrecker, at right tackle. Backing him up is Jim Inglesby, a letter winner.

Two newcomers are taking good care of the left-tackle slot. They are Jay Simon, transfer from Marin Junior College, and Arvid Niemi, 223-pounder up from the freshman squad. Letterman Ed Carmichael is a rugged 222-pound custodian of left guard, with expert support from sophomore Jim Hanker. Tom DeSylvia, two-year veteran, has the edge at right guard, but Ron McReary, also a two-year letterman, is capable of playing the position any time. Stiner has three letter winners and a standout sophomore at center. Lettermen are Bob Krell, Jim Swarbrick and Bill Overman. The sophomore is Al Gray, brother of former Beaver All-American Bill Gray.

In its first four games Oregon State defeated Idaho, 27-12, and Portland, 32-6; tied a strong Washington eleven, 14-14, and lost to Southern California, 21-6, at Los Angeles. Had it not been for costly fumbles, the Beavers might very easily sport an undefeated rating at this time. In the first three starts, the Orange fumbled 11 times and lost the ball 7. If the Beavers can hang onto the ball, they might **show California a mighty interesting afternoon come Saturday.**

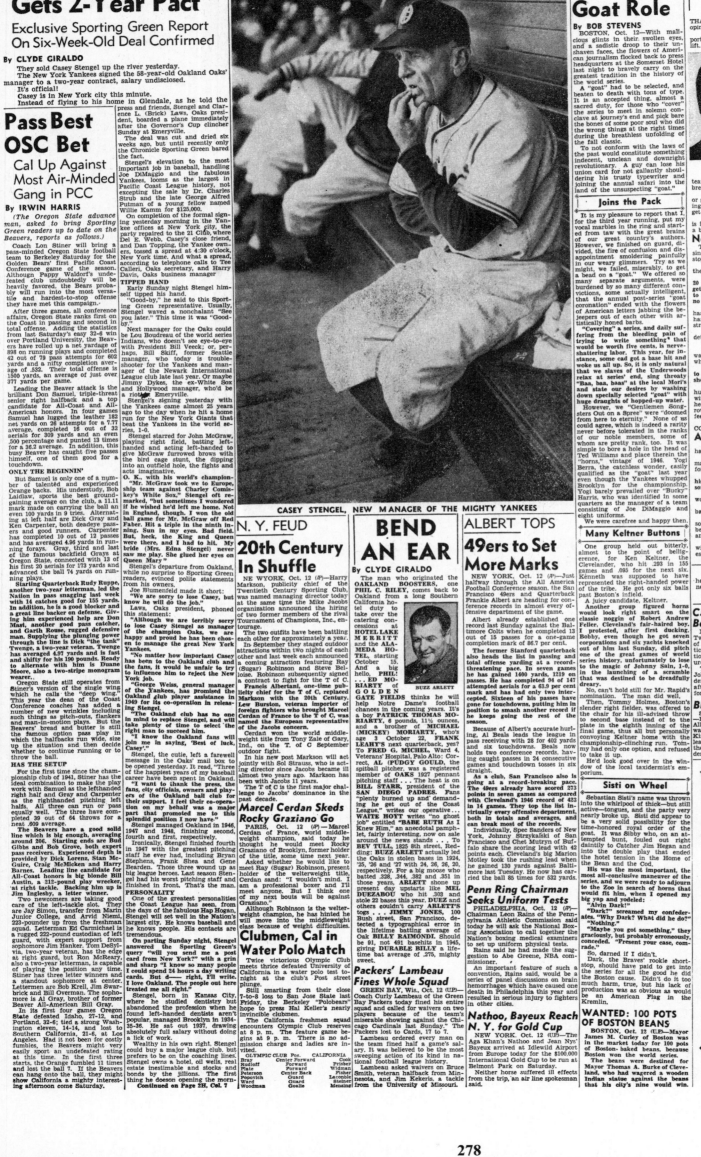

CASEY STENGEL, NEW MANAGER OF THE MIGHTY YANKEES

N. Y. FEUD

20th Century In Shuffle

NE WYORK, Oct. 12 (AP)—Harry Markson, publicity chief of the Twentieth Century Sporting Club, was named managing director today at the same time the Mike Jacobs organization announced the hiring of two former members of the rival Tournament of Champions, Inc., entourage.

The two outfits have been battling each other for approximately a year.

In September they staged outdoor attractions within two nights of each other and last week each announced a coming attraction featuring Ray (Sugar) Robinson and Steve Belloise. Robinson subsequently signed a contract to fight for the T of C.

Francis Albertani, one-time publicity chief for the T of C, replaced Markson with the 20th Century. Lew Burston, veteran importer of foreign fighters who brought Marcel Cerdan of France to the T of C, was named the European representative of the Jacobs concern.

Cerdan won the world middleweight title from Tony Zale of Gary, Ind., on the T. of C September outdoor fight.

In his new post Markson will act jointly with Sol Strauss, who is acting director since Jacobs became ill almost two years ago. Markson has been with Jacobs 11 years.

The T of C is the first major challenge to Jacobs' dominance in the past decade.

Marcel Cerdan Skeds Rocky Graziano Go

PARIS, Oct. 12 (AP)—Marcel Cerdan of France, world middleweight champion, said today he thought he would meet Rocky Graziano of Brooklyn, former holder of the title, some time next year.

Asked whether he would like to meet Ray (Sugar) Robinson, present holder of the welterweight title, Cerdan sand: "I wouldn't mind. I am a professional boxer and I'll meet anyone. But I think one of my next bouts will be against Graziano."

Although Robinson is the welterweight champion, he has hinted he will move into the middleweight class because of weight difficulties.

Clubmen, Cal in Water Polo Match

Twice victorious Olympic Club meets thrice defeated University of California in a water polo test tonight at the club's Post street plunge.

Still smarting from their close 7-to-8 loss to San Jose State last Friday, the Berkeley "Polobears" hope to press Hal Keller's nearly invincible clubmen.

The California freshmen squad encounters Olympic Club reserves at 8 p. m. The feature game begins at 9 p. m. There is no admission charge and ladies are invited.

OLYMPIC CLUB	Pos.	CALIFORNIA
Bray	Center Forward	Cook
Rudloff	Forward	Prisbey
Plate	Forward	Widman
Peterson	Center Back	Fisher
Popovich	Guard	Laconble
Ward	Guard	Steiner
Woodman	Goalie	Mensing

BEND AN EAR

By **CLYDE GIRALDO**

The man who originated the **OAKLAND BOOSTERS**, one **PHIL C. RILEY**, comes back to Oakland from a long Southern California hotel duty to take over the catering concessions at **HOTEL LAKE MERRITT** and the **ALAMEDA HOTEL**, starting October 15. And a big hello, **PHIL!** . . . **ED MORIARTY** of **GOLDEN GATE FIELDS** thinks he will help Notre Dame's football chances in the coming years. It's a boy **PATRICK THOMAS MORIARTY**, 6 pounds, 11½ ounces, and a brother of **MICHAEL (MICKEY) MORIARTY**, who's age 3 October 22, **FRANK LEAHY'S** next quarterback, yes? To **FRED G. MICHEL**, Ward 4, Veterans' Hospital, Palo Alto: Correct, **AL (PUDGY GOULD**, the spitball pitcher, was a registered member of **OAKS** 1927 pennant pitching staff . . . The heat is on **BILL STARR**, president of the **SAN DIEGO PADRES**. Fans "plenty burned up and demanding he get out of the Coast League," writes our operative . . . **WAITE HOYT** writes "no ghost job" entitled **"BABE RUTH** As I Knew Him," an anecdotal pamphlet, fairly interesting, now on sale around the news stands . . . To **BEV TULL**, 1825 8th street, Redding: **BUZZ ARLETT** actually led the Oaks in stolen bases in 1924, '25, '26 and '27 with 24, 26, 26, 20, respectively. For a big moose who batted .328, .344, .382 and .351 in those years, **ARLETT** shone up present day upstarts like **MEL DUEZABOU** who hit .303 and stole 22 bases this year. **DUEZ** and others couldn't carry **ARLETT'S** togs . . . **JIMMY JONES**, 100 Bush street, San Francisco, detected a typographical error in the lifetime batting average of Oak **BILLY RAIMONDI**. Should be 91, not 491 basehits in 1945, giving **DURABLE BILLY** a lifetime bat average of .275, mighty sweet.

BUZZ ARLETT

Packers' Lambeau Fines Whole Squad

GREEN BAY, Wis., Oct. 12 (U.P.)—Coach Curly Lambeau of the Green Bay Packers today fined his entire squad and called for waivers on two players because of the team's miserable showing against the Chicago Cardinals last Sunday." The Packers lost to Cards, 17 to 7.

Lambeau ordered every man on the team fined half a game's salary. It was believed to be the most sweeping action of its kind in national football league history.

Lambeau asked waivers on Bruce Smith, veteran halfback from Minnesota, and Jim Kekeris, a tackle from the University of Missouri.

ALBERT TOPS

49ers to Set More Marks

NEW YORK, Oct. 12 (AP)—Just halfway through the All America Football Conference season, the San Francisco 49ers and Quarterback Frankie Albert are heading for conference records in almost every offensive department of the game.

Albert already established one record last Sunday against the Baltimore Colts when he completed 13 out of 15 passes for a one-game completion mark of 86.7 per cent.

The former Stanford quarterback also heads the list in passing and total offense yarding at a record-threatening pace. In seven games he has gained 1400 yards, 1219 on passes. He has completed 94 of 147 attempted aerials for a 63.9 per cent mark and has had only two intercepted. Sixteen of his passes have gone for touchdowns, putting him in position to smash another record if he keeps going the rest of the season.

Because of Albert's accurate hurling, Al Beals leads the league in pass receiving with 28 for 402 yards and six touchdowns. Beals now holds two conference records, having caught passes in 24 consecutive games and touchdown tosses in six straight.

As a club, San Francisco also is going at a record-breaking pace. The 49ers already have scored 273 points in seven games as compared with Cleveland's 1946 record of 423 in 14 games. They top the list in virtually every offensive department, both in totals and averages, and can break most of the records.

Individually, Spec Sanders of New York, Johnny Strzykalski of San Francisco and Chet Mutryn of Buffalo share the scoring lead with 42 points each. Cleveland's big Marion Motley took the rushing lead when he gained 130 yards against Baltimore last Tuesday. He now has carried the ball 85 times for 532 yards.

Penn Ring Chairman Seeks Uniform Tests

PHILADELPHIA, Oct. 12 (AP)—Chairman Leon Rains of the Pennsylvania Athletic Commission said today he will ask the National Boxing Association to call together the Nation's boxing medical examiners to set up uniform physical tests.

Rains said he had made the suggestion to Abe Greene, NBA commissioner.

An important feature of such a convention, Rains said, would be a series of panel discussions on brain hemorrhages which have caused one death in Philadelphia this year and resulted in serious injury to fighters in other cities.

Nathoo, Bayeux Reach N. Y. for Gold Cup

NEW YORK. Oct. 12 (U.P.)—The Aga Khan's Nathoo and Jean Nys' Bayeux arrived at Idlewild Airport from Europe today for the $100,000 International Gold Cup to be run at Belmont Park on Saturday.

Neither horse suffered ill effects from the trip, an air line spokesman said.

WORLD SERIES

Al Dark Backs Into Goat Role

By **BOB STEVENS**

BOSTON, Oct. 12—With malicious glints in their swollen eyes, and a sadistic droop to their unshaven faces, the flowers of American journalism flocked back to press headquarters at the Somerset Hotel last night to bravely carry on the greatest tradition in the history of the world series.

A "goat" had to be selected, and beaten to death with tons of type. It is an accepted thing, almost a sacred duty, for those who "cover" the series to meet in solemn conclave at journey's end and pick bare the bones of some poor soul who did the wrong things at the right times during the breathless unfolding of the fall classic.

To not conform with the laws of the past would constitute something indecent, unclean and downright revolutionary. A guy can lose his union card for not gallantly shouldering his trusty typewriter and joining the annual safari into the land of the unsuspecting "goat."

Joins the Pack

It is my pleasure to report that I, for the third year running, put my vocal marbles in the ring and started from taw with the great brains of our great country's authors. However, we finished on guard, divided, the fire of confusion and disappointment smoldering painfully in our weary glimmers. Try as we might, we failed, miserably, to get a bead on a "goat." We offered so many separate arguments, were burdened by so many different convictions, some actually intelligent, that the annual post-series "goat coronation" ended with the flowers of American letters jabbing the bejeepers out of each other with artistically honed barbs.

"Covering" a series, and daily suffering from the bleeding pain of trying to write something that would be worth five cents, is nerve-shattering labor. This year, for instance, some cad got a base hit and woke us all up. So, it is only natural that we slaves of the Underwoods relax at series' end, sing throaty "Baa, baa, baas" at the local Mori's and state our desires by washing down specially selected "goat" with huge draughts of hopped-up water.

However, we "Gentlemen Songsters Out on a Spree" were "doomed from here to eternity." None of us could agree, which is indeed a rarity never before tolerated in the ranks of our noble members, some of whom are pretty rank, too. It was simple to bore a hole in the head of Ted Williams and place therein the "horns," vintage of 1946. Yogi Berra, the catchless wonder, easily qualified as the "goat" last year even though the Yankees whupped Brooklyn for the championship. Yogi barely prevailed over "Bucky" Harris, who was identified in some quarters as the manager of a team consisting of Joe DiMaggio and eight uniforms.

We were carefree and happy then.

Many Keltner Buttons

One group held out bitterly, almost to the point of belligerence, for Ken Keltner, the Clevelander, who hit .293 in 155 games and .095 for the next six. Kenneth was supposed to have represented the right-handed power of the tribe. He got only six balls past Boston's infield.

A juicy candidate, Keltner.

Another group figured horns would look right smart on the classic noggin of Robert Andrew Feller, Cleveland's fair-haired boy. I protested, after first ducking. Bobby, even though he got seven corporations and six yachts knocked out of him last Sunday, did pitch one of the great games of world series history, unfortunately to lose to the magic of Johnny Sain, 1-0, in the launching of a scramble that was destined to be dreadfully dreary.

No, can't hold still for Mr. Rapid's nomination. The man did well.

Then, Tommy Holmes, Boston's slender right fielder, was offered to the chair for his ill-advised throw to second base instead of to the plate in the eighth inning of the final game, thus all but personally convoying Keltner home with the championship-clinching run. Tommy had only one option, and refused to take it up.

He'd look good over in the window of the local taxidermist's emporium.

Sisti on Wheel

Sebastian Sisti's name was thrown into the whirlpool of thick—but still active—tongues, and the party very nearly broke up. Sisti did appear to be a very solid possibility for the time-honored royal order of the goat. It was Sibby who, on an attempted bunt, fouled out right daintily to Catcher Jim Hegan and into the double play that ended the hotel tension in the Home of the Bean and the Cod.

His was the most important, the most all-conclusive maneuver of the series, and we were ready to adjourn to the Zoo in search of horns that would fit him, when I opened my big yap and yodeled:

"Alvin Dark!"

"Dark?" screamed my confederates. "Why Dark? What did he do?"

"Nothing."

"Maybe you got something," they graciously, but probably erroneously, conceded. "Present your case, comrade."

So, darned if I didn't.

Dark, the Braves' rookie shortstop, should have paid to get into the series for all the good he did the Boston cause. Didn't do it too much harm, true, but his lack of production was as obvious as would be an American Flag in the Kremlin.

WANTED: 100 POTS OF BOSTON BEANS

BOSTON, Oct. 12 (U.P.)—Mayor James M. Curley of Boston was in the market today for 100 pots of Boston baked beans, because Boston won the world series.

The beans were destined for Mayor Thomas A. Burke of Cleveland, who had wagered a wooden Indian statue against the beans that his city's nine would win.

AS BILL LEISER SEES IT:

California Could Be Tremendous

"HOW GOOD IS CALIFORNIA? In other words, is California THAT GOOD?" a friend asks, adding, "I pay 5 cents per day for your opinion, and I want it."

California is on the verge. California showed its first real, important, impressive lift of the season against Wisconsin. It was a team lift. In fact, its greatest ground-gaining stars, Jack Jensen and Jack Swaner, showed no improvement at all. Swaner could barely run, and Jensen was no better than his first time out. Both have had no chance to practice, therefore no chance to improve.

PAPPY WALDORF

The improvement, the lift, came from the rest of the gang, just about everybody else from All-America Franz to the last-string tackles, Mulberger and Wright, showed definite upgrade inclinations.

When you get a team, as a whole, going upgrade, you may HAVE IT. It may eventually make itself THAT GOOD.

The question is how good the Bears themselves want to be, how hard they want to work being that good.

The margin between a good team and a great team is a thin line. But it's a line that few teams break through.

If the Bears happen to get the idea they're already pretty good, or good enough, they won't get much better. And they'll get the stuffing blasted out of them when they go to the Rose Bowl . . . IF they get there.

If, as seemed to be indicated Saturday, every last man of the Bears is intent on making himself a better footballer and making his team a better team, no one knows where they might wind up.

No Telling How Far Bears Could Go

They're the only chance we've had to match a top Midwestern team since before the war, and they might match it, but to do so they can't stop now.

That lift that was shown against Wisconsin must be improved as they go on against Oregon State.

Save for Wisconsin, Big 9 teams beat our Coast's top teams from 20 to 40 points, and probably could have made all scores higher. To get prepared for the best of the Big 9, California must gain the strength to beat other Coast Conference foes 40 to 60 points. That's how it is, no matter how much it hurts.

So, my friend, California is not yet THAT GOOD, but California has gained considerable ground toward being THAT GOOD, and Cal has the makings of what it takes to go there, IF the Cal men want strongly enough to do so.

Pappy Waldorf, we are sure, can tell them what to do, if it is their determination to do it.

California's potentialities are TREMENDOUS.

California, as a team, is right where one Cornelius Warmerdam was the first time in the pole vault, when he cleared 14 feet 10 inches, which was right smack under the then existing world record.

"Dutch," said his friend, Dink Templeton, "you have just begun to show what you can do in the pole vault. In another few weeks you should be going well over 15 feet."

Fifteen feet, at this time, was the "ceiling," beyond which no human pole vaulter ever was supposed to go. Warmerdam continued with serious study, hard work, and intelligent training. In a few weeks he was above 15 feet with a new world record. For three years in a row he went higher, higher, and higher, to his present record of 15 feet 8½ inches.

There's no telling how far California's Golden Bears of today COULD go.

Add Hazardous Jobs---Baseball Manager

BUCKY HARRIS, Yankee manager, was fired. He finished a long, hard season two games out of first place.

They say the "greatest of all managers," Joe McCarthy of Boston, may be dropped. He was bad enough to finish in a tie with Cleveland for first place, but the bum lost the play-off.

Manager and Player Lou Boudreau, through his personal hitting, his double plays, and his leadership, finished his American League season in first place, winning the play-off, and won the world series, too.

They tell, and not through their hats, that President Bill Veeck would like to get rid of him, too.

How good does a man have to be to deserve a manager's job in baseball?

I think I can guess what's in Veeck's mind. He has never been sold on Boudreau, well as Lou has done. He probably thinks Lou won't be so good as manager when he can't win his own games with homers and double plays.

Veeck has always had a great admiration for Eddie Stanky, now with the Braves. Once he told me Stanky would one day be the greatest manager in baseball.

He probably wants to nab Stanky, now.

EDDIE DYER, manager of the St. Louis Cards, is in a better spot. He finished six plus games out of first place, when some thought he should have won. Owner Bob Hannegan promptly signed him to a new contract. Somebody told Hannegan it was a nice thing to do.

"Why shouldn't I? He's the best manager in baseball, isn't he?"

Don't know about that, but Dyer has a nice guy to work for.

Cal Game Injuries Bench Two Badgers

MADISON, Wis., Oct. 12 (U.P.)—Two top linemen were reported out of action today as Wisconsin practiced for its important intersectional game with Yale next Saturday.

Tackle Ken Huxhold and Guard John Simcic, both sophomores, definitely will be lost to the Badgers after injuries suffered in the California tussle last Saturday.

Blanchard Marries

SAN ANTONIO, Texas, Oct. 1 (AP)—Felix (Doc) Blanchard, former All-America fullback at West Point, was married today to Miss Jody King of San Antonio. A 30-day leave from the Air Forces will give the couple a honeymoon, whose destination they classed as "secret."

Ratterman Demoted For Bills' Morale

BUFFALO, N. Y., Oct. 12 (U.P.)—A shakeup in the lineup of the Buffalo Bills of the All-America Football Conference found two players without jobs today and Quarterback George Ratterman on the bench.

Tackle Graham Armstrong and Halfback Chick Maggioli were released yesterday in the wake of the Bills' upset defeat at the hands of the New York Yankees.

Jake LaMotta Bout

NEW YORK, Oct. 12 (AP)—Robert Villemain, French middleweight boxer, has been signed to meet Jake La Motta in Madison Square Garden December 3.

HERE ARE NAT. LEAGUE STARS OF 1949 WORLD SERIES

JACKIE IN A CHARACTERISTIC POSITION

JACKIE ROBINSON

Jackie Robinson Roy Campanella Don Newcombe

OUR PUBLIC LIBRARY

San Antonio is proud of its excellent public library and of the efficient and friendly manner in which it is operated. If you have not visited the library lately, you will be surprised at its wide selections.

San Antonio Express

NO. 283—84TH YEAR SAN ANTONIO, TEXAS, MONDAY, OCTOBER 10, 1949 20 PAGES 5 CENTS

CONTINUED WARM

SAN ANTONIO AND VICINITY—Partly cloudy, continued warm and humid, gentle to moderate southerly winds; low, 75; high, 92; sunrise, 6:32; sunset, 6:10.

Official U.S. Weather Report

1 a.m....77	5 a.m....76	9 a.m....78	1 p.m....87
2 a.m....77	6 a.m....75	10 a.m....80	2 p.m....87
3 a.m....78	7 a.m....75	11 a.m....79	3 p.m....89
4 a.m....77	8 a.m....75	12 noon..85	4 p.m....90

YANKS WIN 10 TO 6 TO CAPTURE SERIES

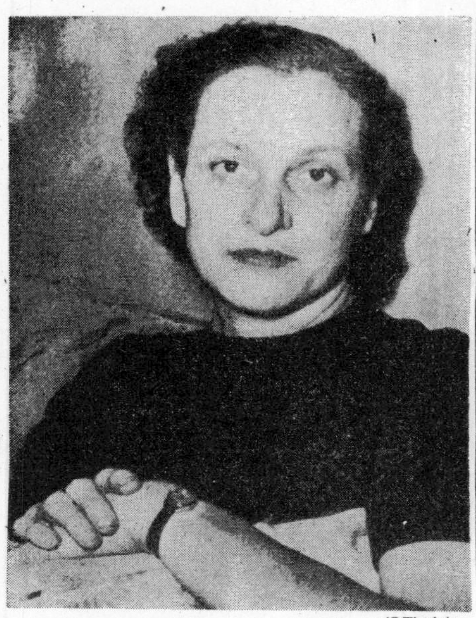

—AP Wirephoto

FACES DEPORTATION—The government has started deportation proceedings against Mrs. Antonia Sentner, 43, above, foreign-born wife of an international representative of the C.I.O. United Electrical Workers. She is charged with being a member of an organization that advocates overthrow of the United States.

Think

ALL ROADS this week lead to San Antonio. The Nation's foremost road-planners and builders are here for the five-day convention of the American Association of State Highway Officials. An honor guest and principal speaker will be Thomas H. MacDonald, who for years has headed the United States Public Roads Administration. Mr. MacDonald has been a frequent visitor and a sturdy friend to Texas. This State leads all the others, with 39,000 miles of primary, 15,000 miles of farm-to-market, road built with Federal aid. Those are also school bus and post roads.

* * *

EXPRESSWAYS through the principal cities form the opposite pole of highway-development. The 4-lane or wider urban travel-artery is a vital link in the inter-regional system. What is equally important, it is designed to relieve traffic-congestion in the population centers. As State highway officials have planned it, the cross-country system will stretch for 40,000 miles. It will serve 43 State capitals and the 183 largest cities. Construction will take 20 years and cost 11½ billion dollars.

* * *

PREVIEW of the inter-regional system will be given the visiting highway officials. They will inspect the completed section and longer stretches nearing completion on San Antonio's Expressway. Under the mercury vapor lights, that is a model highway for safe night driving. Ways to speed up super-highway and the equally important farm-to-market roads will engage the convention delegates. No doubt the gathering will put in a word for the $3,300,000 bonding proposition required to buy here Expressway rights of way. Texas' goal, pavement within a mile of every farm dwelling, is likewise due approval.

* * *

RECOGNIZING them as effective Commonwealth-builders, Texas Parade (Texas Good Roads Association magazine) bids the highway policy-makers, planners, administrators and engineers welcome to Texas. No doubt the 1949 convention will attack technological, fiscal and civic problems of far-reaching import. As Gen. Ike Ashburn, publisher of Texas Parade, emphasizes, the road-dollar is mostly a wage-earner's dollar. Thus an expanded highway program, while creating permanent economic, social and civic values, might come in handy for unemployment-relief.

* * *

GOOD ROADS bring city and suburb, farmhouse and town, North and South, Latin-American countries alike closer in travel-time. All-weather highways are incentives to both trade and tourist travel—an antidote to isolationism and provincialism. To build roads, therefore, is to build Hemispheric solidarity. This forecast by E. W. James is accordingly heartening: By next summer the Inter-American Highway should be open to the Costa Rican border. Close 300 miles in gaps, and the motorist could drive from San Antonio to Panama.

American Ship Runs Blockade Into Shanghai

BY ASSOCIATED PRESS

PUSAN, Korea, Oct. 9.—The crew of an American blockade-runner reported on arrival here Sunday that their ship got safely into Red Shanghai because a Chinese Nationalist warship surrendered to the Communists.

The Isbrandtsen liner Flying Independent and its sister ship, the Flying Clipper, were detained for a week by the Nationalists when they came out of Shanghai, but finally were released Thursday.

The Flying Independent's chief electrician, Howard Landbecker, said that when they headed into Shanghai Sept. 19, they were detained and questioned briefly by a Nationalist destroyer-escort, then allowed to proceed.

Next day, he said, the destroy-escort came up the Whangpoo under a white flag and surrendered to the Reds. He said it was learned that the crew had shot the captain and thrown his body overboard. Twenty-two others of the Nationalist crew were reported executed after the destroyer-escort was taken over by the Reds.

Czechs 'Eagerly' Learning Russian

BY ASSOCIATED PRESS

PRAGUE, Oct. 9.—Hundreds of thousands of Czechoslovaks, children and greybeards, embarked Sunday on a Communist-directed campaign to learn Russian in double quick time, with prizes for the fleetest.

Quarter-Horse Races Scheduled Oct. 26-30

SPECIAL TO SAN ANTONIO EXPRESS

EAGLE PASS, Oct. 9.—The ninth annual Eagle Pass quarter horse races will be held October 26-30, not during the Eagle Pass-Piedras Negras Centennial Oct. 12-16, centennial officials said Sunday.

Although many of the horses entered in the races will be displayed during the centennial, the actual race date remains unchanged, they explained.

Western U.S. Feels Winter Blasts Early

Danger Subsides In Snow-Hit Northwest Areas

BY ASSOCIATED PRESS

Fall had a sharp winter flavor in the Plains and Northwest Sunday. It was warm and summery in the East and South.

Alarm about hundreds of deer hunters who were caught in Saturday's heavy snow subsided Sunday. The snow, heaviest in the mountains of Idaho, Western Montana and Western Wyoming, caused one death—That of Mrs. Lois Schrechengost, 27, of Rose Lake, Idaho.

Virtually all of the blocked roads in the higher Idaho regions were reopened Saturday and Sunday. The fall of snow stopped over Idaho, but more was forecast for Monday.

It was quite cold over the Great Plains, Minnesota and Iowa, and from the Rockies westward. Butte, Mont., reported an early morning low of 15 degrees.

Snow fell Sunday in the higher regions of Utah, Colorado, and extreme eastern Nevada. At Ft. Bridger, Wyo., there was 14 inches of snow still on the ground, and depths measured over a foot in many Idaho localities, with drifts of several feet in some passes and canyons.

The flood which drowned one person in the Houston area, subsided from choked rivers and bayous as no new rains fell.

Many Houson families were going back to their homes in the southwest and northwest sections of the city Sunday. There, water stood five feet deep Saturday after a 10-inch rain. The storm fatality was that of Tony Lock, 43, who drowned in the flooding San Jacinto River 15 miles northeast of Houston Friday night.

The warm front which established an Oct. 8 record of 87 degrees at Chicago Saturday, developed in the Ohio Valley and the East Sunday. The weather bureau estimated the muggy heat would near 90 degrees in the Ohio-Kentucky-Tennessee region. The prediction for western New York was about 85, and for western Pennsylvania mid or upper 80s.

There were rain areas in the central Rockies and western Washington.

—AP Wirephoto

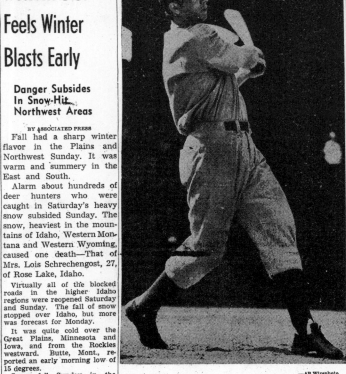

HE FINALLY HIT ONE—Joe De Di Maggio, Yank centerfielder, who has been handicapped all season by injuries and hadn't been doing so well in the world series, finally got hold of one Sunday and slammed it into the stands for a home run. It was his sixth home run in world series play.

AT HEARINGS

NAVY PRIMES GUNS FOR FINISH BATTLE

BY ASSOCIATED PRESS

WASHINGTON, Oct. 9.—The Navy brings its biggest guns to bear this week against Pentagon defense doctrines in a now-or-never battle to preserve its full sea and air power.

It marshalled before the House armed services committee such old sea dogs as Fleet Admirals W. F. (Bull) Halsey, Ernest J. King and Chester Nimitz to nail down grave contentions that the nation is being put on the wrong security track.

The committee is investigating explosive unification troubles within the armed services, and charges by Navy men that it is not getting a square deal from a "landlocked" Pentagon high command.

It was certain that Sec. of Defense Johnson and other top service chiefs will have some explaining to do before the sensation-packed hearings are over.

Crusty Chairman Carl Vinson (D.-Ga.) confirmed Sunday earlier predictions that Johnson will be called before the committee. Vinson already has proposed curbs on his powers.

And with Johnson probably will be called Air Force chiefs. They will be given a chance to answer Vinson's charges of plotting to scuttle the Navy's air arm and its carrier fleet.

Admiral Arthur W. Radford, the Navy's No. 1 airman, electrified the committee last Friday by denouncing a "cheap and easy" concept of future warfare through an "atomic blitz." He also called the Air Force's top-priority B-36 bomber a gamble with national security.

The first of a score of technical and expert witnesses—including the retired fleet admirals—comes up tomorrow to support Radford's claims in detail.

Ready to follow him are:

Lt.Comdr. E. W. Harrison, radar expert; Comdr. W. N. Leonard, jet power authority; Comdr. W. I. Martin, night fighter expert; Cofdr. A. B. Metsger, to detail naval fighter plane capabilities; Comdr. T. Tatom, on bombing accuracy, and Capt. J. H. Sides, naval authority in the hush-hush realm of guided missiles.

Big Rally Too Late For Dodgers

BY ASSOCIATED PRESS

EBBETS FIELD, BROOKLYN, Oct. 9.—The New York Yankees won their 12th world series Sunday by humbling the Brooklyn Dodgers, 10-6, in the first series contest ever finished under lights. A sellout crowd of 33,711 saw Joe Page rescue a tired Vic Raschi from a seventh-inning Dodger rally as the Yanks closed out the National Leaguers, four games to one.

The Yanks' 12th triumph in 16 series capped a brilliant season by 58-year-old Manager Casey Stengel in his first year with the club.

Under the late Miller Huggins the Yanks won the 1923, '27, '28 series. Joe McCarthy led them to victory over the National League seven times, in 1932, '36, '37, '38, '39, '41, '43. They won for Bucky Harris, also over Brooklyn, in 1947. And now Casey makes it No. 12.

The Dodgers never have won a series, losing all five. In 1916 they bowed to the Boston Red Sox, in 1920 to Cleveland and in 1941, 1947 and this fall to the Yanks.

FIRST INNING

YANKEES — Barney's first pitch to Rizzuto was low and outside. Barney followed with three more of the same to present Rizzuto with a base on balls. Jack Banta, a righthander, immediately arose to warm up in the Dodger bullpen. Henrich ignored two called balls, looked at a called strike, the first thrown by Barney, then walked when the next two pitches didn't come anywhere near the plate.

Barney, attempting to pick Rizzuto off second, fired the ball over Reese's head into center field and Rizzuto wound up at third and Henrich at second on the error. Reese managed to get his glove on the ball but could not quite hold it.

Berra went down swinging, missing one pitch that almost hit the dirt and another that was over his head.

Snider ran back to the center-field wall, 393 feet away, and made a leaping catch of DiMaggio's long smash but had no chance to head off Rizzuto who scored easily after the catch. Henrich also went to third on the out.

Brown slashed a single through the box, scoring Henrich. Woodling walked on a 3-2 pitch. Mapes worked Barney to a full count, then looked at a sharp-breaking curve for the

See YANKS, Page 3 A, Col. 2

—AP Wirephoto

ENJOYING HIMSELF—President Truman, taking a week end off, went to the Virginia home of Mr. and Mrs. Stanley Woodward, and is shown here being greeted by the couple. Woodward is chief of protcol of the State Department. The President seems unworried by failure to get his long legislative program through Congress.

Congress Nearing Recess Leaving Truman on Limb

BY ASSOCIATED PRESS

WASHINGTON, Oct. 9.—The first session of the Democratic 81st Congress headed Sunday toward early adjournment with less than half of President Truman's program written into law.

With leaders seeking a windup this week, the President could count 15 major accomplishments from the Congress he helped carry into office.

Left as unfinished business for the 1950 congressional campaign year were a number of highly controversial proposals among the 22 requests that he laid before the present session without getting final action.

Chief of these, of course, is Taft-Hartley repeal. The President got a turn down in both houses on that prime issue.

He undoubtedly will revive his request next January. Whether Congress does anything about it may depend on how some special elections to fill Senate and House vacancies turn out this year.

The House has passed a bill increasing the benefits and broadening the base of social security payments. The Senate has approved an aid to education bill. The drive will be on in January to complete action on both measures, part of the Truman program.

Senate leaders have agreed to take up them as the first order of new business in that body, the House-approved bill repealing the oleo margarine tax.

Mr. Truman undoubtedly will ask Congress again to set up a system of compulsory health insurance. That may provide the biggest fight of the second session. The request didn't get to first base in this year's meeting.

His repeated demand for action on civil rights legislation will get attention of the Senate as soon as it acts next January on the oleo tax measure.

The civil rights proposals, along with the health insurance plan, are certain to be prime issues in the 1950 campaign for control of Congress.

Sea Lion Swims Channel in 5 Hours; Being Californian, He's Used to Water

BY ASSOCIATED PRESS

DOVER, Eng., Oct. 9.—Pierre, the California sea lion, flippered across the English channel Sunday in the smashing time of just over five hours.

The newest channel swimmer made his bid for fame and radio, television and movie contracts as part of a stunt for a radio program.

Pierre, whose full name is Pierre Cilion, and whose address is California, plunged gleefully into the cold surf at Cape Gris Nez at 9:36 a.m., Greenwich mean time, and flipped onto the pebbly beach east of St. Margaret's Bay at 2:40 p.m.

Only 18 months old, Pierre thus is the youngest channel swimmer and the fastest. The swiftest crossing by man is a little over 11 hours.

In the nude, except for a tight-fitting black corset, to which was attached a long leash, Pierre started his swim after a breakfast of herring.

The 30-foot line, held by his trainer, Ross McBride, who rode in a rowboat towed by a motorboat, was to keep Pierre from wandering off toward the Bay of Biscay after more herring.

It was a loping, diving, leaping crossing. Sometimes Pierre raced ahead, apparently not noticing any tides or currents, if there were any.

At others he headed for France, and appeared to be towed backward. Then there were times when the line pointed straight down into the dark green depths. McBride said that was when he was looking for fish and perhaps finding some.

Now and then his handlers tossed out one of the 35 herring, each weighing about 15 pounds, which they had brought along, and Pierre lunched as he swam.

He seemed to think it was fun and there still was a lot of swimming in him when he reached shore. He still had energy to spare, frisked among some English spectators and took a playful nip at several.

Dauntless Reporter Delves Into Daze Of Debutantes' Daffy Designations

BY ASSOCIATED PRESS

NEW YORK, Oct. 9.—Ever wonder what debutantes talk about among themselves?

Well, the word leaked out Sunday. On the basis of the complete deb roster for 1949-50, it is possible to reconstruct a typical conversation somewhat like this:

Hello, Fifi! Did Gini tell you what Didi told her about Fifi's friend Cici?"

"No, but Gopher phoned and said Pooh was coming over. She's bringing Daze and Pebble."

The deb list, published Sunday, contains not only the names and addresses but also the nicknames of some 400 female youngsters making their bow to society.

And what nicknames do the blossoming belles acknowledge?

"Fifi" is the favorite. There's a Fifi Ford, a Fifi Harding and a Fifi Hunter. "Mimi" gets a fair play, too. Mimi Mills and Mimi Winston, for instance.

Then come Gini Turpin, Didi Bultinck, Gigi Burch and Cini Foy. Miss Foy advises that she's also known as "Poofie."

If you frequent the more fashionable tea salons, you will doubtless also be brushing elbows with:

"Poo" Pooler (not to be confused with "Pooh" Prescott), "Gopher" Hardin, "Pebble" Stone, "She" Blitz, "Sunny" Schwenk, "Corky" Cardoff, "Ido" Crabbe—

Yes, and "Bunny" Emerson, "Bootsie" Furstenberg. "Dinny" Lawrence, "Gay" Chapman, "Daze" Dyer—

We know just how you feel, Miss Dyer. We're a little dazed, too.

Williams Sets Another Mark—in Salary

$100,000-Plus Contract Fulfills Youthful Ambition

By ARTHUR SAMPSON

Ted Williams realized an ambition yesterday. He reached the goal he set for himself when he used to play sandlot baseball for ice cream cones on a playground in San Diego, Calif., only a decade and a half ago.

TEDDY DECIDES WHAT HE WANTS

When he was a youngster of 16 he decided that he wanted to become the best baseball player in the country and command the largest salary in baseball history. And following a short conference yesterday with Joe Cronin at Fenway Park Ted signed a contract which called for a higher salary than any baseball player ever received.

That it was for more than $100,000 is all that is certain. It may be either $125,000 or something in between these two figures. Neither Williams himself nor Cronin would mention the exact figure. The only thing I'm certain of after discussing the matter with both parties concerned at different intervals is that it was whatever Williams decided he wanted.

One could tell that from the smile on Ted's face and the way he talked in his dressing room at Mechanics Hall after his fly casting exhibition at the Sportsman's Show yesterday afternoon.

"There was no dickering," said Ted when asked if he had found everybody congenial during his visit to Fenway Park. "There never has been. As I've told you many times, the luckiest break I ever received in my life was that I was bought by the Red Sox.

YAWKEY BASEBALL'S MOST GENEROUS OWNER

"Throughout my career, everybody in the Red Sox organization has treated me swell. Tom Yawkey is the most generous owner in baseball. He, Eddie Collins, Joe Cronin and Joe McCarthy are the best men to work for I've ever heard of. I hope I really can repay them all some day for the way they have treated me from the very beginning right up to the present moment. I'm certainly going to do everything in my power to help them win the pennant they so deserve."

Williams, unlike the late Babe Ruth who once commanded a previously unheard of salary for his ability to smack home runs and attract fans through the turnstiles, may never amass a large fortune as a result of his high salary achievements. His contributions to Uncle Sam this year, for example, will be more than most baseball players have ever been able to make in a season.

And since he always recognizes numerous obligations in a generous fashion despite rumors and sometimes reports to the contrary, the sum he will have left for his own use following taxes and other expenses will never allow him to build a huge estate.

But the realization of this doesn't bother Williams at all. Nor does it dim the enthusiasm and satisfaction he reveals over reaching one of his many goals. "Life for me seems to be full of challenges," he told us recently. "I get a thrill out of meeting them successfully. I feel badly when I fail to conquer them."

Williams is getting a big kick out of his two daily appearances at the Sportsman's Show. His days are studded with requests on his time. He earnestly attempts to satisfy the many demands for autographs, to pose for pictures, make appearances at outside organizations and shake hands and talk with the thousands of well-wishers who flock to the show and swarm around him.

"I'll admit I didn't look forward much to leaving my outdoor life in Florida for so long," he added, "but everybody has been so nice to me during these exhibitions that I've enjoyed it.

"I've met some awfully nice people here this winter and I certainly appreciate the way everybody has treated me. My only hope now is I can have the greatest year of my career in 1950 and help bring a pennant to Boston."

Ski Conditions

U. S. WEATHER BUREAU—AP
TUESDAY, FEB. 7.
(3 P. M. Report)

MAINE
FORECAST—Fair Wednesday with temperatures well below freezing. Gentle northerly winds.
BRIDGTON—Three to 20 inches, five powder. Partly cloudy. Excellent upper; good lower.

LOWER NEW HAMPSHIRE
FORECAST—Faair Wednesday with temperatures below freezing and light variable winds.
MT. SUNAPEE—Three to six inches, two powder. Partly cloudy. None to poor upper; fair to good lower.
LACONIA-BELKNAP—Three to 10 inches, one powder. Cloudy. Poor to fair upper; fair to good lower.

UPPER NEW HAMPSHIRE
FORECAST—Same as for Maine.
CANNON MT.—Three to 10 inches, one fluffy. Partly cloudy. None upper; fair lower and slope.
JACKSON (Black Mt.)—Three to 10 inches, one powder. Partly cloudy. Fair to good upper; good to excellent lower.
JACKSON (Thorn Mt.)—Three to 15 inches, one packed powder. Partly cloudy. Fair to good.
NORTH CONWAY—Three to 15 inches, two powder. Partly cloudy. None upper; good to excellent lower.
MT. MOOSILAUKE—Eleven to 25 inches, four powder. Partly cloudy. Good to excellent.
WATERVILLE VALLEY—Seven to 25 inches, five powder. Partly cloudy. Excellent.

VERMONT
FORECAST—Same as lower New Hampshire
HOGBACK—Three to six inches, five powder. Partly cloudy. None.
DUTCH HILL—Seven to 10 inches, four powder. Partly cloudy. None.
MANCHESTER—(Big Bromley)—Two to 10 inches. One powder. Cloudy. None.
MANCHESTER (Snow Valley)—Three to 10 inches, one powder. Partly cloudy. None.
PICO PEAK—Three to 10 inches, two powder. Partly cloudy. None upper; fair to good lower.
MAD RIVER—Seven to 15 inches, one fluffy. Partly cloudy. None to poor.
MIDDLEBURY—Seven to 15 inches, five powder. Partly cloudy. Good upper; fair to god lower.

BERKSHIRES
FORECAST—Same as for Lower New Hampshire.
PITTSFIELD—Three to 10 inches, three powder. Cloudy. Good.
JIMINY PEAK—Three to six inches, three powder. Partly cloudy. Fair to good.
CHARLEMONT—Seven to 10 inches, two granular. Partly cloudy. Good to excellent.
OTIS—Seven to 10 inches, six powder. Cloudy. Good to excellent.

MASSACHUSETTS
AMESBURY—Two to three inches, one to two powder. Excellent.
ROWLEY—Four inches, one new snow. Good to excellent.

CANADA
QUEBEC CITY—(Lac Beauport)—Ten to 11 inches, two powder. Fir to good.
LAURENTIAN MTS. (Shawbridge to Mt. Tremblant)—Six to 11 inches, one to powder. Fair, smooth slopes only.

(Herald Staff Photo by Leslie Jones)

MAJORS MUST WAIT TIL MARCH 1 BUT MIT PLAYERS, refusing to wait any longer, launched spring baseball practice at Briggs Cage yesterday. Left to right, Coach Warren Berg; Amos Dixon, Norwood; Mike Johnson, Maynard; Pete Philliou, Queens, N. Y.; Cliff Rounds, Detroit, Mich.; Barney Byrne, Omaha, Neb.; Walter Brill, Pitman, N. J.; Roger Harsch, Cleveland, O., and Joe D'Annunzio, Orange, N. J.

Bruins Play Leafs In 'Must Win' Tilt On Ice at Garden

By HENRY McKENNA

After a day of preparation that was typical of teams readying for a Stanley Cup series, Boston's Bruins and Toronto's Maple Leafs square off tonight in the finale of this two-game series that is so vital to the post-season hopes and chances of the entertaining B's.

LEAFS RIDING HIGH IN RED-HOT STREAK

With 50 games behind them and time and tussles rapidly running out, the Bruins find tonight's fracas another in the "must win" category, a rugged assignment since the Leafs are riding a red-hot, late-season streak and are starting to sniff at their fourth straight Stanley Cup.

Both squads went through long sessions yesterday. The Bruins, first on the Arena ice, scrimmaged for more than 35 minutes. The Leafs followed with an hour of line work, shooting and skating with emphasis placed on speed and sniping, in sharp contrast to the Bruins' rather sluggish drill.

Presidents Conn Smythe and Weston Adams watched the practices, Smythe clad in fleece-lined flying boots and bundled in a heavy blanket. "It's been 20 years since I've been in here," remarked Smythe, "and why anybody stays up in this country when they can go to Florida is beyond me."

The Leafs watched the Bruins who, after showering, hung around to keep an eye on their rivals. Coach Hap Day gave Turk Broda (minus pads) a half-lap lead in a wild race to conclude practice and the likeable backstop still was in front when the race ended on Hap's whistle. Pudgy Turk looked like an escapee from one of the ice shows.

SCRAPING THE ICE

Eddie Sandford pulled on a Bruins' uniform and participated lightly in the scrimmage, his first real work since the night of Nov. 13 when he suffered his severe Achilles' tendon injury . . . He wore an over-sized left boot which tired his foot but otherwise he was happy to be back in action again . . . His return is indefinite.

Red Henry remains in the Bruins' net but Weston Adams feels that Jack Gelineau will be ready for the week-end series vs. Detroit and Canadiens, releasing Red for duty with Hershey . . . Adams hopes Jack will continue to make rapid progress the next few days . . . Milt Schmidt's left foot continues to bother him so Eddie Harrison will relieve him tonight with Pete Horeck getting more work on the right wing . . . Sam Bettio also will see more work tonight, alternating with Woody Dumart . . . Johnny Crawford worked yesterday and should be ready for heavier duty tonight.

Line-ups at Garden

BRUINS—g, Henry; rd, Flaman; ld, Henderson; c, Ronty; rw, Peirson; lw, Smith.
TORONTO—g, Broda; rd, Thomson; ld, Mortson; c, Kennedy; rw, Meeker; lw, Smith.
Bruins alternates—Crawford, Kryzanowski, Quackenbush, Schmidt, Creighton, Harrison, Bettio, Maloney, Dumart, Poile, Horeck.
Toronto alternates—Bentley, Klukay, Watson, Ezinicki, McCormack, Lynn, Gardner, Boesch, Juzda, Barilko, Timgren.

Face-off—8:35 P. M.

Connecticut Disavows 'Big Time' Program

STORRS, Ct., Feb. 7 (AP)—The trustees of the University of Connecticut said today they had "no intention to embark on a program of 'big time' athletics."

The announcement appeared to answer speculation which arose yesterday when it became known that Art Valpey, lately of Harvard, had been hired as head football coach.

In a "statement of intercollegiate athletic policy," the trustees asserted that "the board is determined to keep intercollegiate athletics on an amateur basis."

BU Sextet Ices Harvard, 6-4; BC Tops NU, 7-3

By JACK McCARTHY

Boston University's N. C. A. A. tournament-bound hockey team bested Harvard in a return match at the Arena last night, 6-4, before 2715 howlers.

In the second game of the double-header Boston College, on the same tourney train, defeated Northeastern in a New England League game, 7-3.

GARRITY NETS THREE FOR TERRIERS

The Terriers had to keep steam on all the way to sink the Crimson although they had a slight but sure edge in position play and skating all the way. Jack Garrity, the Cousy of college hockey, collected three goals for B. U., while bespectacled George Minot got three for Harvard.

Little Lloyd Robinson got the first B. U. goal at 8:18 of the fist period. Garrity followed at 16:13 for a 2-0 Terrier lead. Then Minot unlimbered a slap shot from 10 feet out to score twice and it was 2-2 at the end of one.

Ed Cahoon made it 3-2 B. U. at 38 seconds of the second, and Jack Martin hit an open net for 4-2. But Minot had another shot left for Harvard and 4-3. But Skinny Garrity made itt 5-3 only to have Joe Kittredge cut it to 5-4 as the period ended. Garrity scored the final goal at 4:05 of the last period.

BOSTON UNIVERSITY (6)—G. Bevins; rd. Anderson; ld. Jurgelevich; c, Cahoon; rw, Haynes; lw, J. Kelley.
HARVARD (4)—G. Chase; rd. Burke; ld. Bliss; c, Huntington; rw, Preston; lw, Timpson.
B. U. alternates—Garrity, R. Kelley, Martin, Folino, Robinson, Barnhill, Downing, Dupuis.
Harvard alternates—Di Blasio, Carman, Kittredge, Sedgewick, Minot, Abbot, Marshall.
Goals—B. U., Garrity (3), Cahoon, Robinson, Martin. Harvard—Minot (3), Kittredge. Penalties—Marshall (2), Carman, Folino.

BOSTON COLLEGE (7)—G. Maggio; rd. Delorey; ld. McCusker; c, Songin; rw, Sullivan; lw, Threadgold.
NORTHEASTERN (3)—G. Anderson; rd F. Bell; ld. Nason; c, Doherty; rw, D. Bell; lw, Tucker
B. C. alternates—Mulhern, Ceglarski, Harrington, Cleveland, Walsh
N. U. alternates—Madden, Byrne, Le Fort, Macewen, O'Brien, Shepardson.
Goals: B. C.—Harrington 2, Sullivan 2, Ceglarski 2 Mulhern; N. U.—Shannon 2, Macewen Penalties—Delorey 2, Sullivan, Le Fort, Threadgold, Tucker, McCusker, Byrne, F. Bell, Mulhern, Nason.

WEYMOUTH WINS, 65-39
At Weymouth

WEYMOUTH HIGH	G	F	Pts	HINGHAM HIGH	G	F	Pts
Sprague,rf	7	2	16	Atwood,lg	1	1	3
Cannon	4	0	8	Eaton,rg	2	1	5
Genier,lf	1	0	2	Mulcahy,c	4	5	13
Wright,c	13	2	28	Blanchon,lf	6	0	12
Healy,rg	2	2	6	Nardo,rf	3	0	6
Knight,lg	1	0	2				
Kane	1	1	3				
Totals	29	7	65	Totals	16	7	39

Williams Doesn't Play 'For Keeps' With Fishing Rod

Ted Williams, who plays "for keeps" on everything from batting average to salary on the diamond, switches to the oth er extreme when he goes fishing. He never keeps any of his catch unless someone is g oing to use it. It goes back in the water for future reference.

HIGH AVERAGE ON DEAD FISH TABOO

Fishermen who measure their success by the number of fish they kill to prove their prowess should be interested in the Red Sox star's low opinion of a high batting average of unusuable dead fish on the dock or in the creel. Like all the myriad questions asked him at the Sportsmen's Show he doesn't hold back on this one.

"Look," he says, "I like fishing—any kind of fishing—so long as I can use the lightest tackle that's sensible for whatever I'm after. But in my book the sport is catching fish, not keeping them. I catch a lot of fish, you catch a lot, the other guy catches a lot. If we all keep them when we don't need them how long do we have the fun of catching them?

"Sure, I keep a fish or two if I'm going to eat them. If I ever get a really good one I might want to have it mounted. If I'm fishing with a professional skipper who needs some fish to make out OK on his charter I'd keep them for him. But if nobody's going to use a fish I catch I put it back. I like my fishing too much."

Which seems to be plain talk that makes common sense.

SHORT CASTS SNAP SHOTS

One of the big in-town parties during show week is the 20th annual fish and game dinner at the University Club tomorrow evening . . . Fred Adams is in charge . . . A 1200-pound moose and 400-pound caribou from Newfoundland will provide steaks and stews . . . Rabbit, venison and bear are also on the menu in steak and stew form. . . . Black bean soup for a starter.

Some 500 reservations already have been received, including those of Mayor Hynes, Charles Hunt, Jeff Wilkes and Hartley Bell of Newfoundland; Martin Bovey, noted outdoor lecturer-author; Rod Gascoyne, regional director of the U. S. Fish & Wildlife Service; Fred Mitchell, former Braves manager; and many of the Sportsman's Show officials and exhibitors.

Incidentally, Ted and Jack Sharkey staged a second fly casting competition at last night's show as a sequel to their informal contest on opening day . . . The Kid again took the former heavyweight boxing champion with two out of three casts . . . Ted poked the line out 101, 100 and 106 feet for a total of 30 feet, against Sharkey's 99, 101½ and 99½ for a total of 300 feet even.

The fact that the line was landing about 10 feet beyond the end of the 60 feet long tank didn't bother Doc Wellman, the "official" judge, one little bit . . . But no fooling, those two guys really can lay out a lot of fly line.

Nelson Suggested As Coach Pro Tem

Shot for Harvard Morale; Only 15 P.C. Favor Ban

By WILL CLONEY

Latest communiques from the coaching fronts: The Harvard Corporation will take its time acting on Provost Paul Buck's football study. Inside reports from Cambridge are that football definitely will be continued although about 15 per cent. in one poll favored its demise) and that Harvard's attitude toward scholar-athletes will be humanized. . . The most unusual part of a statement attributed to Art Valpey was, "We'll be glad to get back to a co-ed atmosphere." Maybe Art plans to use the queen of the Connecticut campus as a decoy.

Not the daffiest idea in the world is the suggestion that Swede Nelson be appointed head coach for one year at Harvard. Next seaso nwill be dismal, but Swede could restore morale as well as teach some real football and win some games. Such an appointment would give the athletic committee plenty of time to choose a permanent coach. It also would give the permanent coach a chance to work with next fall's freshman squad, which will hold the key to the immediate future. Football under Swede would be fun, but it also would be football.

Myers May Take Holovak with Him

At University Heights yesterday, Denny Myers was working just as diligently as he would if he were sure he would be coaching the Eagles the next two years. He's pledged to silence about the Iowa situation, but it's common knowledge that he will go to Davenport within a week or 10 days for a final interview. Put Denny and a moving picture camera in the same room with a group of collgee officials and the sale is completed. One major problem will be to compensate Denny for any financial losses he may suffer by moving away from the lucrative radio and after-dinner speaking area. If Denny does go to Iowa, the chances are that Mike Holovak will go with him unless Mike is offered the top job at B.C. Big Ten colleges pay assistants more than most small-college head coaches receive.

UP AND DOWN THE SIDELINES: If B. C. is ruled ineligible for the N.C.A.A. hockey tournament, word is around that Holy Cross will pass up the N.C.A.A. hoop tourney and accept a bid to the national invitation affair. Officials from the Jesuit Big Four—Boston College, Holy Cross, Georgetown and Fordham—met in New York over the week-end and the subject may have been brought up. . . . Boston College apparently can regain its eligibility in the N.C.A.A. simply by completing a questionnaire, since the college is now complying with the code. It's beginning to look as if the Eagle officials prefer to make a test case as a matter of principle, however.

Tom Haggerty, the Loyola coach whose team lost to Holy Cross last week, waited until he got back to Chicago to blast Eastern officials as "homers." The two "homers" in the Holy Cross-Loyola game were John Nucatola of Bayside, L. I., and Charlie Petrino of Bridgeport, Ct. It would appear they were a long way from home. . . Walter Brown says that every dime the Garden has made in basketball in the last six years has been ploughed back into the sport. "It's tough to try to catch up with the rest of the country in basketball interest because we're so far behind the time. It's like trying to industrialize Russia in five years."

Canisius College Gives Up Football

BUFFALO, N. Y., Feb. 7 (AP)—Canisius College has decided to give up intercollegiate football, it was announced today.

The Very Rev. Raymond Schouten, S.J., president, cited heavy financial losses through the post-war years as the reason.

He also said another factor was the increasing difficulty of arranging schedules each year.

Varsity football at Canisius covered a span of 31 years, reaching its peak in 1946 when more than 35,000 witnessed the annual St. Bonaventure - Canisius game in Civic Stadium.

MOON MULLINS

THE NEBBS

Phils Win Pennant On Dick Sisler's Homer In Tenth

Three-Run Clout In Tenth Beats Dodgers, 4 To 1

BROOKLYN, Oct. 1—(AP)—Dick Sisler, son of a Hall of Fame great, clinched the National League pennant for the Philadelphia Whiz Kids today, 4-1, with a 10-inning three-run homer to back up Robin Roberts' superb pitching job against the Brooklyn Dodgers in the last game of the season.

Young Roberts, celebrating his 24th birthday a day late, throttled a bases-loaded Dodger threat in the ninth to become the Phils' first 20-game winner since 1917 in the golden days of Grover Cleveland Alexander.

The handsome $25,000 bonus baby from the Michigan State campus, turned back the Dodgers with five hits in a throbbing contest watched by a turnaway crowd of 35,073.

Pulling the Phils out of a five-game losing tailspin that threatened to cost them their first flag since 1915, Roberts came through in real championship fashion.

Thus the Dodgers, who planned to sell tickets for a post-season tie playoff, ended their dramatic "miracle finish" two games out of first place. They missed their chance for a tie on the wings of Sisler's 13th homer of the year, a curling liner over Cal Abrams' head in the lower left field seats in the 10th.

Sisler, moved to the outfield last spring when Eddie Waitkus won back his first base job, took the count to one ball and two strikes before he ripped into Don Newcombe's next pitch for the homer that meant the World Series highest cut for every delirious Phil.

They practically tore Sisler's shirt off his back as he raced to the dugout behind Eddie Waitkus and Richie Ashburn who were on base. Everybody on the bench was out to greet him, tossing caps in the air and pounding one another's backs. It seems the Phils are in favor of pennants after a 35-year wait.

It was the most dramatic baseball game since Bill Bevens lost his no-hit bid in this same park in the 1947 World Series. This was a tingler down to the final out.

Drama dripped from every pitch by Roberts in the frantic ninth when Brooklyn almost sent this sizzling race into a play-off.

Twice manager Eddie Sawyer strode from the bench to the mound to confer with his pitcher and catcher Stan Lopata following Brooklyn threats. But he stuck with him all the way in, with Jim Konstanty, baseball's best relief pitcher, straining at the leash in the bullpen.

The strapping Roberts walked Cal Abrams, his second pass of the game, to open the ninth. Pee Wee Reese, who doubled in the fourth and hit his 11th homer atop the right field fence in the sixth, singled to left. One more hit and it seemed the ball game was over.

Duke Snider came through with the hit, a single to center but little Ashburn made a perfect peg to the plate to nail Abrams trying to score all the way from second. It took a perfect throw to get him. Ashburn had it.

Still Roberts wasn't out of the woods. Sawyer came out and they decided to walk Jackie Robinson intentionally to load the bases. Konstanty was throwing hard in the bullpen but Sawyer let Robin pitch to Carl Furillo. It was the right move. He hoisted a foul pop on the first pitch. Then the Dodgers got the flyball that could have scored the winning run, one out earlier. Hodges sent Del Ennis deep near the base of the scoreboard to grab his third out hoist.

Heartened by this turn of events, the Phils dug in to big Mr. Newcombe, a 220-pound giant, for the ball game. Roberts started things himself with a single to center.

Waitkus dumped a high pop single to center that fell in front of Snider's late start. Ashburn's bunt forced Roberts at third and the Dodgers were one third out of the jam.

Then Sisler strode up looking for his fourth straight hit. He had scored the only other Phil run in the sixth when his single was backed up by more of the same from Ennis and Willie Jones.

Sisler pulled his three single to right field. He didn't pull the homer. It was a slice, by a left-handed hitter, into the left field seats maybe some 350 feet from home.

Thus the Phils averted a collapse that would have gone into the record books with the worst in baseball history—with the Pirates of 1921 and 1938, the 1934 Giants and the 1942 Dodgers. They had lost five in a row and eight of their last 10, blowing all but one game of a 7½ game lead they held the morning of Sept. 21.

Rookie Holds Braves To 3 Hits, Wins 5-1

NEW YORK, Oct. 1,— (AP) — Rookie righthander George Spencer pitched the New York Giants to a 5-1 three-hit victory over the Boston Braves today in the final game of the season. Sibby Sisti homered for Boston's lone run in the fifth inning. The Giants wrapped it up with four runs in the first inning off Warren Spahn who was gunning for his 22nd victory.

Boston	000 010 000	1	3	2
New York	400 100 00x	5	10	1

SPAHN (21-17), Cole, and Crandall; SPENCER (1-0) and Westrum, Yvars. HR—Sisti.

More than 24,000 women have been listed in Who's Who.

Pilots Phillies

EDDIE SAWYER

Eddie Sawyer, who took over as manager two years ago, led the Philadelphia Phillies to their first National League pennant in 35 years when his Whiz Kids beat Brooklyn to cop the flag yesterday. The Phils manager has banded together one of the youngest teams in baseball and has earned the respect of the entire baseball world for guiding his "bonus" pitchers and other young stars into the World Series.

Sisler Hero In Own Right

NEW YORK, Oct. 1.—(AP)—The kid who lived in the shadow of his dad emerged today in the late afternoon sunshine of Ebbets Field as a baseball hero in his own right.

Big, good-natured Dick Sisler, doggedly pursuing his own diamond career keenly aware of the belittling comparison of his own ability with that of his famous dad, George, crashed a tie-breaking, 10th-inning home run to give the Phillies their first pennant in 35 years.

Hugged and kissed and pounded by his teammates in the steam room which passed as the Phil locker room, the robust Dick had his hour of glory today, an hour probably never equalled even by his immortal father.

The Phil quarters were a bedlam. with players, coaches, officials and well-wishers jammed into one vast, writhing mass of semi-hysterical humanity. Even the sedate and usually unperturbed Eddie Sawyer, eyes suspiciously dim, embraced his boys indiscriminately.

Owner Bob Carpenter, jubilant and unrepressed, finally dropped to a seat on a trunk, his white shirt saturated and an expression of sublime ecstasy on his face as he gazed upon a scene which, for spontaneous enthusiasm, probably was unmatched in pennant-winning history.

Coaches Benny Bengough and Cy Perkins broke down and cried. Centerfielder Richie Ashburn, whose great throw to the plate to nip Cal Abrams in the ninth saved the game, kissed Sisler.

Sisler, himself, was happy beyond words.

"It's a dream," he kept saying "That's what it is. "The pitch I hit for a home run was a high, outside pitch. I was surprised he threw me that because I usually hit that kind of pitch well. Newcombe kept pitching me inside all day."

"It's the second home run I've hit off Newcombe this year," Sisler added. "Both came here and both were hit into the left field stands. "Boy, how I love Ebbets Field. I always could hit in this park."

Asked whether he thought his dad, the famous George Sisler, now a Dodger scout, would be displeased by his game-winning hit, Dick replied:

"Not dad. He must be proud as a peacock right now. Of course, he probably has mixed emotions, but I'm sure he's tickled as long as it had to end this way."

The elder Sisler, who watched the game from a box behind the Dodger dugout, said:

"How can I feel? I work for one team (Brooklyn) and my son plays for another. I can't say anything, I don't know how to feel."

Asked if he would say he felt a little happy and a little unhappy, the Dodger scout said. "that's about it."

Phils Box Score

PHILADELPHIA	AB.	R.	H.	P.	A.	E.
Waitkus, 1b.	5	1	1	18	0	0
Ashburn, cf.	5	1	0	2	1	0
Sisler, lf.	5	2	4	0	0	0
Mayo, lf.	0	0	0	1	0	0
Ennis, rf.	5	0	2	2	0	0
Jones, 3b.	5	0	1	0	3	0
Hamner, ss.	4	0	0	1	2	0
Seminick, c.	3	0	1	3	1	0
a-Caballero	0	0	0	0	0	0
Lopata, c.	0	0	0	1	0	0
Goliat, 2b.	4	0	1	1	3	0
Roberts, p.	2	0	1	1	6	0
Totals	38	4	11	30	16	0

a-Ran for Seminick 9th.

BROOKLYN	AB.	R.	H.	P.	A.	E.
Abrams, lf.	2	0	0	2	0	0
Reese, ss.	4	1	3	3	3	0
Snider, cf.	4	0	1	3	0	0
Robinson, 2b.	3	0	0	4	3	0
Furillo, rf.	4	0	0	3	0	0
Hodges, 1b.	4	0	0	9	3	0
Campanella, c.	4	0	1	2	4	0
Cox, 3b	3	0	0	1	2	0
b-Russell	1	0	0	0	0	0
Newcombe, p.	3	0	0	3	2	0
c-Brown	1	0	0	0	0	0
Totals	33	1	5	30	17	0

b-Struck out for Cox 10th.
c-Fouled out for Newcombe 10th.

Philadelphia	000 001 000 3	4
Brooklyn	000 001 000 0	1

RBI—Jones, Reese, Sisler 3. 2B—Reese—HR—Reese, Sisler. S—Roberts. DP—Reese, Robinson and Hodges; Roberts and Waitkus. Left—Philadelphia 7, Brooklyn 5. BB—Off Roberts 3, Newcombe 2. SO—By Roberts 2. Newcombe 3. Winner—Roberts (20-12) Loser—Newcombe (19-11). U—Goetz, Dascoli, Jorda and Donatelli. T—2:35. A—35,073.

Donora Dragons Take 13-0 Win Over Latrobe

DONORA, Oct. 1—Coach Jimmy Russell's Donora Dragons jolted the visiting Latrobe Wildcats here Saturday night, 13-0, to knock the losers out of the WPIAL Class AA race.

The Dragons tallied 13 points in the first quarter, and then held off Wildcots attacks to rack up their third win in four starts.

Johnny Thomas, Donora fullback, and teammate Jerry Bercik accounted for the finner's touchdowns. Thomas dashed into the end zone from the nine, with Ozzie Rands making the conversion, and Hugo Valdeserri passed to Bercik on a 33-yard play to complete the scoring.

	Donora—13	Latrobe—0
LE	Daube	Mekic
LT	Jericho	E. Smith
LG	Turkovich	Gangemi
C	Horton	Paior
RG	Ruscitti	Halua
RT	Torma	Toblas
RE	Bercik	Carpowich
Q	Perry	Caldwell
LH	Loines	Pry
RH	Watroba	Glamp
F	Thomas	Domencik

SCORE BY PERIODS

Donora	13	0	0	0	13

Touchdowns: Thomas, Bercik. Extra points—Rands (placement). Officials: Hickers, Klinzing, Wostecki.

Dartball League Season Commences

The Y. M. C. A. Church Dartball League got off to a good start with 22 of the 24 teams seeing action. Of course, the usual beginners' luck wasevident as some of the players haven't thrown darts since last Spring.

Several teams did experience consistent playing. The Broad Street Baptists, led by Scott, gatheerd 22 doubles in their first game to win it, 18 to 0. However, they were held by the Buffalo Presbyterians in the other two games to score of 5 to 4 and 7 to 4.

The following is the schedule for Tuesday:

Holy Trinity at Central Presbyterian.

Wright Chapel at Second Christian.

First Baptist at Third Presbyterian.

First United Presbyterian at St. Paul A. M. E.

Laboratory Presbyterian at Buffalo Presbyterian.

First Christian at Allison Avenue Baptist.

Broad Street Baptist at Fourth Presbyterian.

Second Presbyterian at First Methodist.

Avery Methodist at Liberty Methodist.

Jefferson Avenue Methodist at Beth Israel.

First Lutheran at Third United Presbyterian.

Trinity Episcopal at John Wesley Methodist.

STANDINGS

	W	L
Third Presbyterian	3	0
First Methodist	3	0
Broad Street Baptist	3	0
First United Presbyterian	3	0
Central Presbyterian	2	1
Allison Avenue Baptist	2	1
Avery Methodist	2	1
First Lutheran	2	1
Third United Presbyterian	2	1
John Wesley Methodist	1	2
Liberty Methodist	1	2
Fourth Presbyterian	1	2
Second Presbyterian	1	2
First Baptist	1	2
Laboratory Presbyterian	0	3
Jefferson Avenue Methodist	0	3
Buffalo Presbyterian	0	3
St. Paul A. M. E.	0	3
Second Christian	0	3

Kickers Event At Mon Valley

MONONGAHELA Oct. 1—A kickers tournament was held at Mon Valley Country Club here toray with the following results: W. H. Sharp, 82-10—72; Tess Pollock, 82-10—72; Lee Venanzi, 87-10—77; Cliff Patterson, 89-12—77; Phil Mollenauer, 98-20—78; Cubby Culbertson, 92-14—78; C. R. McConnell 86-8—78; and J. B. Eggleston, 98-20—78.

Cubs Down Cards In Eleventh, 3-2

ST. LOUIS, Oct. 1—(AP)—Former Cardinal Ron Northey pinch-singled to score Andy Pafko from third in the 11th and give the Chicago Cubs a 3 to 2 victory today. National League batting champion Stan Musial tied the game in the ninth with his 28th home run.

Musial ended the season with a .346 unofficial average.

Chicago	001 001 000 01	3	12	1
St. Louis	000 100 001 00	2	8	1

Hiller, Minner, LEONARD (5-1), Hacker and Walker, Owen; Pholsky, DUSAK (0-2), and Rice. HR—Jeffcoat, Sauer, Musial.

Mrs. Zaharias Wins Second Women's Open

WISHITA, Kas., Oct. 1—(AP)—Babe Didrickson Zaharias shot a record-equalling 291, nine strokes under par, to win her second National Womens Open Golf Championship today.

Mrs. Zaharias' 18-hole score of 70, five under par, was her second in as many days. Betsy Rawls, classy amateur from Austin, Tex., finished second with an ever par 300 on the Rolling Hills Country Club course.

Giants Defeat Browns; Steelers Ahead, 26-7

NEW YORK, Oct. 1.—(AP)—Fullback Eddie Price plunged over in the first five minutes, then great defensive play by the New York Giants frustrated the famed Cleveland Browns offensive today in the National Football League upset of the season.

The rookie fullback from Tulane rammed over from the three-yard line for the only score of the game, and the rebuilt Giants won, 6-0. The victory put New York at the top of the American Conference with a 2-0 record.

Brown Quarterback Otto Graham, perhaps the best passer in Football, never was bottled up so effectively. He failed to complete his first seven passes and had three of those intercepted by the Alert Giant defense.

New York also stopped Fullback Marion Motley on the ground. Cleveland couldn't penetrate Giant territory in the first half. The Browns made two futile drives in the last four minutes. One ended when Graham collided with Motley on a trap play and New York recovered on its eight.

It is the first time in five years the Browns, four-time champions of the dead All-America Conference, haven't scored.

At Green Bay, the surprising Packers again pulled an upset. Coach Gene Ronzani's underdogs whipped the Chicago Bears, 31-21, Throwing the National Conference into a five-way tie for first. Detroit, Green Bay, Los Angeles, the New York Yanks and the Bears all have 2-1 marks.

Green Bay trailed 7-3 at the half before breaking away for three touchdowns in the third quarter. The Packers scored twice on interceptions of Johnny Lujack passes, the first a 29-yard runback by Wally Dreyer and the second for 94 by Rebel Steiner. Then, still in the same period, Billy Grimes scooted 68 yards with a punt return.

Joe Geri passed and kicked the Pittsburgh Steelers to a 26-7 victory over the faltering Redskins at Washington.

Geri started the Steelers off with a 40-yard field goal. Later he clicked on 36 and 28-yard passes, the latter to Elbie Nickel for a touchdown.

The Lone Washington counter came on a 70-yard pass play between Harry Gilmer and Hugh Taylor. The rest of the afternoon passers Sammy Baugh and Gilmer were set on their pants by the charging Steeler line.

On the coast, the Los Angeles Rams whipped San Francisco's 49ers, 35 to 14, before 27,654. Halfback V. T. Smith raced 94 yards with the second half kickoff to snap a 14-14 tie and deal the 49ers their third straight defeat.

Pittsburgh

Left Ends — Jansante, Mehelich, Hays.
Left Tackles—Allen, Stautner, Szot.
Left Guards—Tomlinson, Nicksich.
Centers—Walsh, Sinkovitz, Balog.
Right Guards—Hughes, Hogan.
Right Tackles — Wydo, Samuelson, Wiley.
Right Ends—Nickle, McPeak, Davis.
Quarterbacks—Seabright, Gasparella, Smith.
Left Halfbacks—Gage, Geri, McWilliams, Finks.
Right Halfbacks—Nuzum, Chandnois, Hartley.
Fullbacks—Shipkey, Rogel, Hollingsworth.

Washington

Left Ends—Tayor, Berrang, D. Brown
Left Tackles—Niemi, Karras.
Left Guards—Steber, Badaczewski.
Centers—Demao, Ulinski, Quirk.
Right Guards—Siegert, Witiucki, Pepper.
Right Tackles—Hendren, Lipscomb, Houghton.
Right Ends—Tereshinski, Dale.
Quarterbacks—Baugh, Gilmer.
Left Halfbacks — Dudley, Haynes, Spaniel, Livingston.
Right Halfbacks—Dowda, Thomas, Bartos.
Fullbacks—Stout, Goode, Brazenovich, H. Brown.

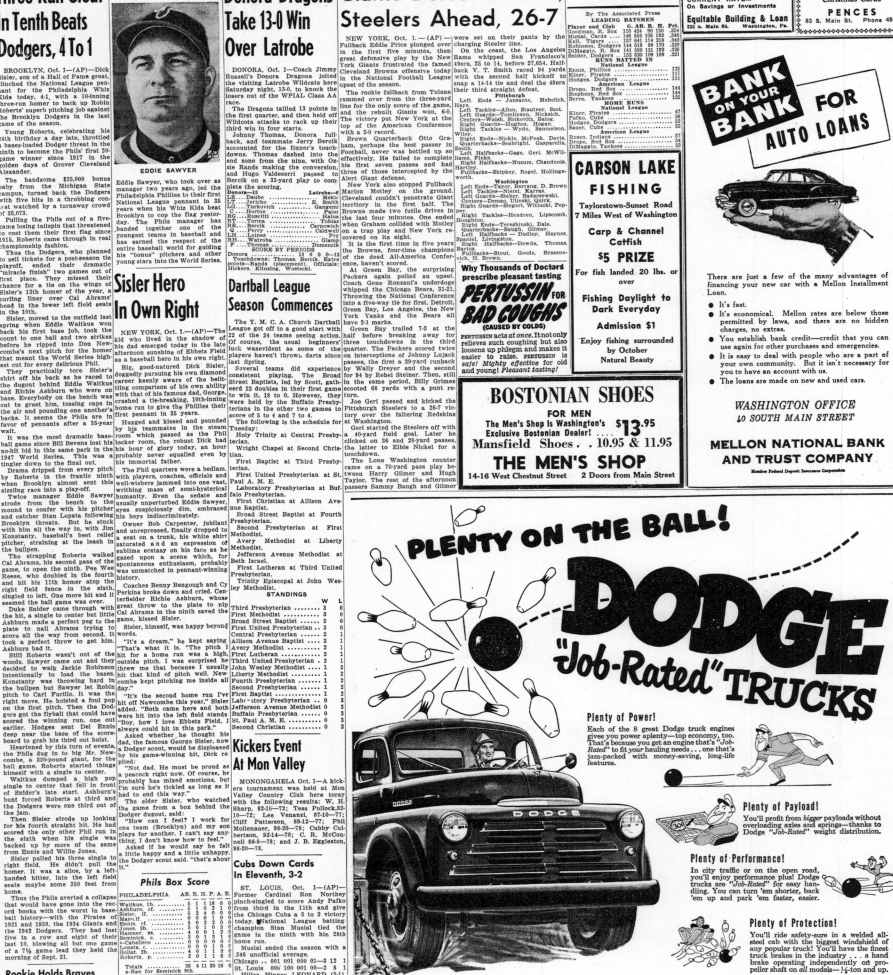

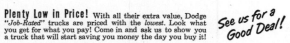

BIG SIX

By The Associated Press

LEADING BATSMEN

Player and Club	G.	AB.	R.	H.	Pct.
Goodman, R. Sox	110	424	90	150	.354
Musial, Cards	146	555	105	192	.346
Kell, Tigers	157	641	114	218	.340
Robinson, Dodgers	144	518	99	170	.328
DiMaggio, R. Sox	141	589	131	192	.326
Snider, Dodgers	152	620	109	199	.321

RUNS BATTED IN

National League

Ennis, Phillies	125
Kiner, Pirates	117
Hodges, Dodgers	111

American League

Dropo, Red Sox	144
Stephens, Red Sox	144
Berra, Yankees	125

HOME RUNS

National League

Kiner, Pirates	47
Pafko, Cubs	36
Hodges, Dodgers	32
Sauer, Cubs	32

American League

Rosen, Indians	37
Dropo, Red Sox	34
DiMaggio, Yankees	32

Korean Reds Form Lines to Meet Final Thrust by Allies

Evening Chronicle EXTRA

VOL. 131—NO. 235 Published Daily Except Sunday. ALLENTOWN, PA., THURSDAY, OCTOBER 5, 1950 Entered 2nd Class Matter March 30, 1939, Post-Office, Allentown, Pa., Act of Congress, March 5, 1879. 25c Weekly 5c Per Copy

YANKS WIN, 2-1, IN TEN INNINGS

DiMaggio Homer Decides Battle

	1	2	3	4	5	6	7	8	9	10	Totals R.	H.	E.
YANKS . .	0	1	0	0	0	0	0	0	0	1	2	10	0
PHILS . . .	0	0	0	0	1	0	0	0	0	0	1	7	0

Philadelphia—
Jolting Joe DiMaggio, the pride of the Yankees, slashed a line drive home run into the upper tier of the left field stands at Shibe park in the 10th inning of the second world Series game here today to give the New York Yankees a 2-1 victory.

The blow was surprising in view of the fact that DiMag had been held hitless up to then in the two series contests here. In four previous appearances at the plate, he had fouled out once and flied out twice, while receiving one base on balls.

32,660 in Crowd

The game, witnessed by a crowd of 32,660, was the 23rd extra-inning game in World Series history. It was the first since 1946 when the Boston Red Sox beat the St. Louis Cards in 10 innings in the opening game of that series, 3 to 2.

The homer was Joe DiMaggio's seventh in world series competition and brought to a climax a tight duel between pitchers Allie Reynolds of the Yankees and Robin Roberts of the Phillies, both of whom pitched superbly in the pinches.

The Yanks had just pulled themselves out of a hole in the bottom of the ninth, when the Phils had two on with nobody out. Gran Hamner, who had tripled earlier, smashed a double. Dick Whitman, sent in to pinch hit for Ken Silvestri, was intentionally walked. But Mike Goliat hit into a double play and ended the threat.

Then came the Yankees' turn. DiMaggio was the first man up in the 10th. He picked out a good one and that proved to be the ball game.

The Yankees threatened in the first inning when Gene Woodling and Yogi Berra singled, putting two men on with one away, but both DiMaggio and Johnny Mize, the power sluggers of the Yankees were easy outs on pops, to hold the New Yorkers scoreless. It was similar to yesterday's opening inning, when the Yanks had two on base but could not score them.

The Phils also put on a threat in the first when Richie Ashburn doubled with one away, but the gates, to home also were locked to him as Dick Sisler fanned and Del Ennis grounded out.

The Yankees drew first blood in the second inning. After two were out, Gerry Coleman received a base on balls. Allie Reynolds hit the first pitch for a single, sending Coleman to third. Then Gene Woodling beat out an infield single to Gran Hamner, Coleman scoring. That gave the Yankees a 1-0 edge.

The Phils put a man on third with one out in their half of the second when Hamner tipled, but he died there.

In the Phils third, Eddie Waitkus doubled to right with one out, but he was also stranded.

The Yanks put two on with one away in the fourth when Coleman doubled and Reynolds walked, but Roberts bore down and they were marooned.

The Phillies finally dented the scoreboard in the bottom of the fifth to tie. Mike Goliat led off with a single. Roberts tried to advance him with a bunt but popped to Reynolds instead. Eddie Waitkus hit a grounder to Coleman that took a wild hop over his head, going for a single. Ashburn then drove a long fly to left, and Goliat scored.

The sixth and seventh innings were uneventful, but the Yanks put on a rally in the eighth when Bobby Brown and Hank Bauer each singled with one away. But Gerry Coleman grounded out and then Allie Reynolds fanned.

Richie Ashburn beat out a nice bunt for a hit to lead off the Phils' eighth, but was thrown out at second on an attempted bunt. Reynolds got it and threw badly, Phil Rizzutto barely reaching it. Then Del Ennis snuffed out the threat by hitting into a double play.

The Phils had good chance in the ninth, only to see it evaporate with another Yankee double play.

The play-by-play account:

FIRST INNING

Yankees—Gene Woodling beat out an infield grounder to Hamner. It was a single. Phil Rizzuto fouled out to Andy Seminick. Yogi Berra singled to left, Woodling going to third. Joe DiMaggio popped to Goliat, the runners holding their bases. Johnny Mize fouled out easily to Seminick. No runs, two hits, no errors, two left.

Phillies—Eddie Waitkus grounded out, Coleman to Mize. Richie Ashburn doubled to right center. Dick Sisler struck out. Del Ennis grounded out, Coleman to Mize. No runs, one hit, no errors, one left.

SECOND INNING

Yankees—Bobby Brown flied out to Ashburn. Hank Bauer fouled out to Puddin' Head Jones. Gerry Coleman walked. Allie Reynolds singled to right field, sending Coleman to third. Gene Woodling made an infield single to Hamner. Reynolds went to second and Coleman scored. Rizzuto flied out to Ashburn. One run, two hits, no errors, two left.

Phillies—Willie Jones struck out. Gran Hamner tripled to center field. Seminick grounded out, Coleman to Mize, Hamner holding third. Mike Goliat flied out to DiMaggio in center. No runs, one hit, no errors, one left.

THIRD INNING

Yankees—Berra struck out. DiMaggio flied out to Goliat in short right field. Mize singled to right field. Brown flied out to Ashburn. No runs, one hit, no errors, one left.

Phillies — Roberts struck out. Waitkus doubled into right field. Ashburn fouled out to Berra. Sisler grounded out, Coleman to Mize. No runs, one hit, no errors, one left.

FOURTH INNING

Yankees—Bauer flied out to Jones. Coleman doubled to center field. Reynolds drew a base on balls. Woodling fouled out to Sisler. Rizzutto flied out to Ennis. No runs, one hit, no errors, two left.

Phillies—Ennis struck out swinging. Mize gathered in Jones's high fly. Hamner walked on four pitched balls. It was the first walk given by Reynolds. Hamner stole second. Berra made no attempt to throw him out. Seminick struck out. No runs, no hits, no errors, one left.

FIFTH INNING

Yankees—Berra popped up to Hamner. Jones caught DiMaggio's high fly. Mize struck out. No runs, no hits, no errors, none left.

Phillies—Goliat singled although Coleman made a great play. Roberts popped to Reynolds on an attempted sacrifice. Waitkus's grounder took a bad hop over Coleman's head and went for a base hit. Ashburn flied out to left, Goliat scoring. It was the first Phillie run in the series. Sisler flied out to Mize. One run, two hits, no errors, one left.

SIXTH INNING

Yankees—Brown singled to left. Waitkus took care of Bauer's popup. Waitkus also caught Coleman's popup. Reynolds struck out. No runs, one hit, no errors, one left.

Phillies—DiMaggio caught Ennis's drive in deep center field. Rizzuto took care of Jone's line drive. Hamner flied out to Coleman. No runs, no hits, no errors, none left.

SEVENTH INNING

Yankees—Woodling flied out to Sisler in left. Rizzutto was walked. Berra flies out to Ashburn in right center. DiMaggio fouled out to Waitkus. No runs, no hits, no errors, one left.

Phillies—Seminick was given a base on balls. Caballero was sent in to run for Seminick, who has an injured ankle. Goliat flied out to left, Roberts sacrificed Caballero to second with a bunt, Reynolds to Coleman, who covered first. Waitkus flied out to Joe DiMaggio in center. No runs, no hits, no errors, one left.

EIGHTH INNING

Yankees—Ken Silvestri was sent in to replace Andy Seminick as catcher for the Phils. Mize fouled out to Waitkus. Brown singled down the left field line. Bauer singled to left, sending Brown to second. Johnny Hopp was sent in to run for Bobby Brown. Coleman grounded out, Hamner to Waitkus. The base runners advanced. Reynolds struck out. No runs, two hits, no errors, two left.

Phillies—Ashburn beat out a bunt to Hopp for a hit. Sisler bunted to Reynolds, who threw out Ashburn at second. It was a high throw and Rizzuto just was able to get it in time. Ennis hit into a double play, Johnson to Coleman to Hopp. No runs, one hit, no errors, one left.

NINTH INNING

Yankees—Woodling grounded out, Goliat to Waitkus. Rizzuto grounded out, Goliat to Waitkus. Berra fouled out to Jones. No runs, no hits, no errors, none left.

Phillies—Jones flied out to Bauer in right. Hamner rapped a double to center. Dick Whitman went in to pinch hit for Ken Silvestri. He was intentionally passed. Goliat hit into a double play, Rizzuto to Coleman to Hopp. No runs, one hit, no errors, none left.

TENTH INNING

Yankees — Joe DiMaggio hit a home run. Johnson struck out. Hopp flied out to Sisler in left. Bauer grounded out, Hamner to Waitkus. One run, one hit, no errors, one left.

Phillies—Jackie Mayo batted for Roberts. Mayo walked. Waitkus sacrificed, Johnson to Coleman, Mayo advanced to second. Hopp took Ashburn's high pop foul. Mayo remained on second. Sisler struck out to end the game. No runs, no hits, no errors, one left.

Box Score

New York (AL)	Ab.	R.	H.	O.	A.
Woodling. lf	5	0	2	2	0
Rizzuto ss	4	0	0	2	1
Berra c	5	0	1	7	0
DiMaggio cf	5	1	1	3	0
Mize 1b	4	0	1	6	0
Johnson 3b	1	0	0	0	2
Brown 3b	4	0	2	0	0
Hopp 1b	1	0	0	3	0
Bauer rf	5	0	1	1	0
Coleman 2b	3	1	1	5	6
Reynolds p	3	0	1	1	2
Totals	40	2	10	30	11

Philadelphia (NL)	Ab.	R.	H.	O.	A.
Waitkus 1b	4	0	2	8	0
Ashburn cf	5	0	2	4	0
Sisler lf	5	0	0	3	0
Ennis rf	4	0	0	1	0
Jones 3b	4	0	0	3	0
Hamner ss	3	0	2	2	2
Seminick c	2	0	0	5	0
A-Caballero	0	0	0	0	0
Silvestri, c	0	0	0	1	0
B-Whitman	0	0	0	0	0
Lopata, c	0	0	0	1	0
Goliat 2b	4	1	1	2	2
Roberts p	2	0	0	0	0
C-Mayo	0	0	0	0	0
Totals	33	1	7	30	4

A-Ran for Seminick in 7th.
B-Intentionally walked for Silvestri in 9th.
C-Walked for Roberts in 10th.

E—None. RBI—Woodling, Ashburn, DiMaggio. 2B—Ashburn, Waitkus, Coleman, Hamner. 3B—Hamner. HR—DiMaggio. SB—Hamner. S—Roberts, Waitkus. DP—Johnson, Coleman and Hopp; Rizzuto, Coleman and Hopp. Left—New York (A) 11; Philadelphia (N) 8. BB—Roberts 3 (Coleman, Reynolds, Rizzuto) Reynolds 4 (Hamner, Seminick, Whitman, Mayo). SO—Reynolds 6 (Sisler 2 Jones, Roberts, Ennis, Seminick); Roberts 5 (Berra, Mize, Reynolds 2, Johnson). Winner—Reynolds; Loser—Roberts. U—Bill McGowan (AL) plate; Dusty Boggess (NL) first base; Charlie Berry (AL) second base; Jocko Conlan (NL) third base; Bill McKinley (AL) left field foul line; Al Barlick (NL) right field foul line. T—3:06. A—32,660. Receipts—$171,143.36.

WOODLING SAFE AT 3RD IN TODAY'S SERIES GAME

Gene Woodling slides back to third base safely in the first inning of today's World Series game at Shibe park after Joe DiMaggio's high pop fly to Phils' second baseman Mike Goliat. Phils' Willie Jones takes the throw while Umpire Jack Conlan makes the call. (Acme Telephoto)

U. S. Ship Strikes Mine, Sinks Off Korean Coast

Washington, (UP)—
The American minesweeper Magpie was sunk and 21 U. S. sailors are missing after the ship struck a floating mine last Sunday in Korean waters where Russian-made mines have been laid, the Navy announced today.

The Magpie was the first U. S. naval ship to be sunk in the Korean war. It was a 136-foot wooden-hulled AMS, auxiliary motor minesweeper.

It struck the mine off the Korean east coast city of Ch'uksan-Dong.

12 Survivors Rescued

Twelve survivors were picked up by a sister ship, the Merganser, and carried to the port of Pusan, Korea.

The Magpie and Merganser were engaged in minesweeping operations when the Magpie struck the mine about 5:30 p.m., Korean time.

The Magpie was the third U.S. naval vessel to strike a mine in Korean waters.

The Magpie struck the mine on her starboard side and sank about two miles offshore.

Total Casualties

Total casualties in the three mine incidents now stand at 11 killed, 24 missing and 17 injured.

Eleven enlisted men were killed and 10 injured when the American

(See SHIP—Page 4)

150,000 Allies Face Foe Over 38th Parallel

British and Australian Troops Moving Into Position For Crushing Thrust; South Koreans Resume Drive To North After Beating Off Counterattack

Tokyo, Friday, Oct. 6. (UP)—
The final battle for Korea became a race against time today, with the Communists attempting to set up a line on the west coast just north of the 38th parallel under constant air attack and the Allies massing 150,000 men for a gigantic offensive.

The start of the Allied drive to crush Communist forces throughout Korea was believed but a matter of a few days.

(The Chinese Communist radio said today that the Korean war "in its real sense has just begun." It forecast a "drawn out war of attrition perilous for foreign aggressors.")

British and Australian troops wheeled into the line today, alongside Americans and South Koreans preparing for the offensive.

As the Allies massed below the parallel, the South Korean 3rd Division resumed its northward advance along the North Korean east coast, plunging forward another 10 miles before meeting strong enemy resistance at Changjon.

Repulse Counterattack

The South Koreans repulsed a strong enemy counterattack, and then pushed forward another 5 miles beyond Changjon. They had advanced 85 miles beyond the 38th parallel and were only 45 miles from Wonsan, expected to be a Communist rallying point.

However, it appeared that the heaviest fighting would take place in the area facing the American infantrymen and marines on the route from Seoul to Pyongyang.

Maj. Gen. Earle E. Partridge's 5th Air Force summary disclosed that the Communists were attempting to regroup in prewar positions just north of the 38th parallel from Haeju on the west coast inland some 110 miles to Hwachon.

190,000 Men Available

Available to Gen. Douglas MacArthur for his all out offensive were some 190,000 allied troops, but they included divisions still engaged in mopping up operations to the south.

Lt. Gen. Walton H. Walker, 8th Army commander in Korea, sent a message of congratulations to his United Nations forces today for their heroic delaying action and the subsequent offensive which defeated the Communists in South Korea.

The South Korean campaign, he said, brought the Communists to "a condition of collapse and disintegration from which there could be no recovery."

The enemy radio at Pyongyang broadcast to the North Koreans today an admission that Communist troops were in retreat.

The enemy radio also broadcast an implied appeal to the Chinese Communists for help.

A message from North Korean Foreign minister Pak Hon Yong to Chinese Foreign Minister Chou En Lai said:

"We feel certain that the peoples of both China and Korea should make an even stronger joint effort in their strife against American imperialists."

The 5th Air Force report indi-

(See REDS—Page 4)

ICC Blames Engineer In Troop Train Crash

Washington, (UP)—
The Interstate Commerce Commission reported that the train collision which killed 33 Pennsylvania National Guardsmen Sept. 11 was caused by an engineer's failure to obey signals.

The accident, which occurred near Coshocton, Ohio, also injured 258 other passengers and 20 railroad employes.

The Pennsylvania railroad's "Spirit of St. Louis" plowed into a troop train which had stopped.

Cites "Failure"

In its report late yesterday, the ICC blamed the tragedy on "failure" of the engineer of the Spirit of St. Louis to operate "in accordance with signal indications."

The ICC said that when the Spirit of St. Louis hit the troop train it was traveling 48 miles an hour after passing two signals which required the train to slow

(See ICC—Page 4)

U.N. Activates Plan to Build Up War-Torn Korea

Lake Success, (AP)—
The United Nations moved full steam ahead today to put into effect an American-backed plan for the future of war torn Korea.

The plan, which grants tacit permission for U.N. forces to cross the 38th parallel, won 47 to 4 approval in the 60-nation political commitee last night. There were seven absentions. Only the Soviet bloc—which supported a rival resolution—voted against the proposal.

Supporters of the proposal shrugged off fears that the Chinese Communists may intervene in the Korean war because U. N. military occupation of North Korea will be necessary to enforce its decisions.

Secretary of State Dean Acheson told a news conference that any group looking to the world for recognition and for admission to the

(See U. N.—Page 4)

BOY, 7, KILLED BY TRUCK

Pottsville, Pa., (AP)—
Injuries received when he was hit by a loaded coal truck yesterday caused the death of James Matlock, 7.

Today's Chuckle

"When I get to bed at night, I always see green signals and red signals in front of my eyes."

"Did you ever see a psychiatrist?"

"No, only green signals and red signals."—Typo Graphic.

NPA Seeking Formula To Continue Flow Of Steel for Civilians

Washington, (AP)—
The National Production Authority looked today for a way to prevent military orders from disrupting the flow of steel to auto and other civilian goods producers.

It hoped that a steel industry "task force" might come up with the formula.

Both NPA and the industry fear that a flood of defense orders bearing the compulsory "DO" priority rating may be dumped on a few key steel companies which might thus be washed out of the civilian market.

The "task force" of steel executives has undertaken to draft a proposal under which no individual company would be required to accept priority orders beyond a certain percentage of its total production. The group is expected to recommend shortly a figure in the neighborhood of 20 per cent.

Any priority orders beyond that point would be steered to other companies found to be able to handle them without crippling output for civilian goods.

Along this same line, Secretary of Labor Maurice J. Tobin recommended yesterday immediate plant expansion for defense production instead of general shifting from civilian to military output.

Tobin said in a speech at Columbus, Ohio, that plant expansion and increase of manpower to handle the expanded production would allow for more rapid conversion "to

(See NPA—Page 4)

YANK FIELDERS CHASE HIT IN TODAY'S GAME

Joe DiMaggio, center fielder, and Hank Bauer, right fielder, are shown as they ran after Granny Hamner's hit against the center field wall near the 400-foot mark today at Shibe park. The ball, shown near DiMaggio's outstretched hands, was hit far enough to allow the Phillies' shortstop to reach third base standing up. (Acme Telephoto)

Stassen Makes Personal Plea To Josef Stalin

Washington, (UP)—
Harold E. Stassen's bid for a face-to-face peace talk with Josef Stalin ran into protests from two Democratic senators today, but the State Department voiced no immediate complaint.

Senators Comment

Sen. Clinton P. Anderson (D.-N.M.) commented that "initiation of any such project properly belongs with the State Department."

Sen. Elmer Thomas (D.-Okla.) said:

"Under our constitution, the President has the first, second and last word of foreign affairs. I'm sure Stalin knows that and I'm sure he will not deal with anyone except the President or someone

(See STASSEN—Page 4)

Express Train Hits Tank Car; 37 Are Injured

Erie, Pa., (UP)—
The New York Central railroad's New England States Express slammed into a derailed gasoline tank car here today setting a torch to 14 cars and injuring 37 persons.

Railroad officials said 25 persons, including three railroad employes and a rescue worker, had been treated at hospitals and 10 were detained. The Erie Red Cross said 12 other persons were treated for superficial injuries at the scene.

The train, rushing down the high-speed No. 1 track of the four track right-of-way, was passing the east-bound freight when the freight's 49th car, the tanker, derailed and

(See EXPRESS—Page 4)

Labor Throws Its Fastest Political Pitches in Ohio Drive to Beat Taft

(This is another of a series of stories dealing with the election campaigns in key states).

By ED EASTERLY

Columbus, O., (AP)—
Diligent campaigning, hot oratory and national significance are all wrapped into this year's election battle between Sen. Robert A. Taft and union leaders out to beat the man they call "Labor's No. 1 Enemy."

The Democrats as a party are striving too, of course, to keep the influential Republican senator from returning to Washington. But it is the labor-vs-Taft fight that has stirred most interest in all parts of the country.

Ferguson Defense

In the face of that, Taft's Democratic opponent in the Nov. 7 election, Joseph T. Ferguson, insists: "I'm not a labor candidate. Nobody can tell me what to do. Labor hasn't even tried it."

In reply, Taft says that the CIO's Political Action Committee is the real power behind Ferguson's campaign. He charged in a speech at Cincinnati:

"They have taken over my opponent lock, stock and barrel. They tell him what to do and say. They write his speeches for him, I think. He's kept out of certain districts and told to go into others."

Claim Statement Proved

Ferguson's statement that "nobody can tell me what to do" is proved, his friends say, by his record during 14 years as state auditor. He has cracked down on Democratic, as well as Republican, state officials when he felt they were spending the taxpayers' money too freely or unwisely.

"I have been a fearless auditor," Ferguson declares, "and I propose to be the same as senator. I'm a candidate for all the people."

These words are being digested

(See LABOR—Page 3)

PURDUE STOPS NOTRE DAME, 28-14

Yankees Win, 5-2, for Sixth Sweep

(AP Wirephoto)

ROOKIE STAR AND VETERAN MANAGER OF CHAMPIONS—Ed Ford (left), whose pitching clinched World Series for Yankees, and Casey Stengel, whose direction has brought New York club two straight world titles with the loss of a single game in 1949 and 1950 classics.

ERROR SPOILS ROOKIE FORD'S SHUTOUT JOB

Berra Poles Homer In Defeat of Phils As 68,098 Watch

By ARTHUR SAMPSON

NEW YORK, Oct. 7—The Whiz Kids were blinded by a kid with a whizzing fast ball today as they succumbed to the Yankees, 5 to 2, before a crowd of 68,098 at Yankee Stadium and bowed out of the 1950 World Series competition without winning a game.

Only a ninth inning Yankee error enabled the Phillies to escape a second coat of whitewashing in four days, this time at the hands of Ed "Whitey" Ford, a 21-year-old native of metropolitan New York. Two unearned runs scored when the young southpaw's left fielder, Gene Woodling, dropped a fly ball that should have been the final putout.

SWITCH OF PITCHERS GREETED BY BOOHS

After Woodling generously muffed Andy Seminick's loft with two out, the next batter, Mike Goliat, singled to left. With pinch hitter Stan Lopata, next up, representing the tying run, Manager Casey Stengel decided to lift the tow-headed youngster from Long Island City who had won nine out of 10 for the Yankees after he was called up from Kansas City late in mid-season.

The man who has now directed the Yankees to two straight world championship titles received a generous chorus of boohs for this decision, but the protests didn't last long.

Chief Allie Reynolds strode to the rubber and struck out Lopata wi thfour pitches. So the two gift runs were small solace to the National League champions who became the sixth team to be beaten four straight games in World Series competition by the famed Yankees.

In wrapping up the classic, the Yankees became winners of the annual series for the 13th time in 17 tries.

Their previous victims in four straight games were the Pirates in 1927, the Cardinals in 1928, the Cubs in 1932, the Cubs again in 1938 and the Reds in 1939.

INGLORIOUS COLLAPSE BY N. L. CHAMPIONS

The Phils have quite a different record. They finished their second series with just one victory in nine tries. Grover Cleveland Alexander pitched them to a 3-1 triumph over the Red Sox in the first game of the 1915 series. They dropped the next four to the Sox that year and four in a row to the Yanks this time.

The Phillies finished their season with an inglorious record of losing 12 of their last 15 starts, as complete a collapse as any league champion ever has suffered.

(Continued on Page Sixty)

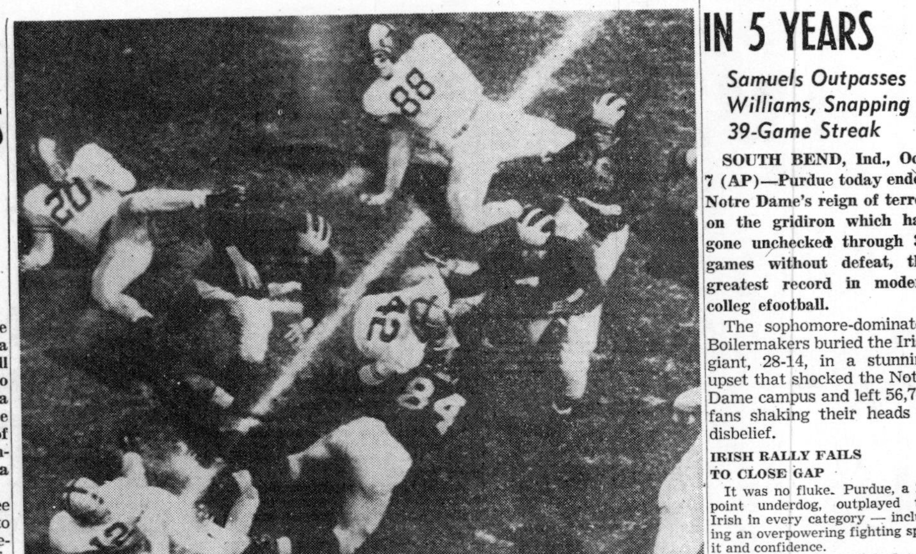

(AP Wirephoto)

THREE-YARD GAIN FOR DARTMOUTH in first period of game with Michigan at Ann Arbor as Bob Tyler (42) moves around his own right end. He is being checked by End Merritt Green (84). Other Dartmouth players are Quarterback John Clayton (20) and End John McDonald (88).

AERIALS SEAL FIRST DEFEAT IN 5 YEARS

Samuels Outpasses Williams, Snapping 39-Game Streak

SOUTH BEND, Ind., Oct. 7 (AP)—Purdue today ended Notre Dame's reign of terror on the gridiron which had gone unchecked through 39 games without defeat, the greatest record in modern colleg efootball.

The sophomore-dominated Boilermakers buried the Irish giant, 28-14, in a stunning upset that shocked the Notre Dame campus and left 56,748 fans shaking their heads in disbelief.

IRISH RALLY FAILS TO CLOSE GAP

It was no fluke. Purdue, a 20-point underdog, outplayed the Irish in every category — including an overpowering fighting spirit and confidence.

The Boilermakers lashed to a 21-0 halftime lead. Notre Dame had cut it to 21-14 by the outset of the fourth period.

But the rally, unleashed as a drizzle slicked the field, only pumped more fire into Purdue. The pent-up wrecking crew came right back to score on a 56-yard pass play, sophomore Dale Samuels to Mike Maccioli, and slam the door in Notre Dame's face.

The last time the Irish were beaten was by 39-7 by the Great Lakes naval service team on Dec. 1, 1945. Since then 37 teams went down before them.

Two others, Army with a 0-0 deadlock in 1946 and Southern California with a 14-14 standstill in 1948, came close to victory but that was all.

It was Notre Dame's first loss at home since Michigan won, 32-20, in the eighth game of the 1942 season.

ONLY FOURTH LOSS FOR LEAHY TEAM

It was only the fourth defeat a Frank Leahy-coached team has absorbed in eight seasons. His Irish have won 62 and tied five.

Leahy's pre-season plaint that Notre Dame would drop several engagements this season had been taken with a bit of salt.

But after the Irish had to go all out to shade North Carolina 14-7 in the opener a week ago, observers could see that Leahy might be right.

Purdue's victory over the nation's top-ranking team today proved it.

Notre Dame's line was ripped unmercifully, its pass attack and offense failed. The giant was thoroughly whipped.

(Continued on Page Sixty-Four)

Rockingham Mutuels

1—2—6—7 Races	$196.80
1—2—3—5—7 Races	$314.00
7 Races	$382.80
Three Races	$184.60
Five Races	$332.20
Seven Races	$382.80

B. U. Tops Duquesne, 21-7

Pavlikowski Whole Show For Terriers in Opener

By TOM MONAHAN

PITTSBURGH, Oct. 7—Billy Pavlikowski proved a snug fit for the shoes of Hary Agganis but Coach Buff Donelli was provided with plenty of fodder for criticism at Pitt Stadium this hot afternoon as Boston University opened its 1950 football season with a sputteyr albeit decisive 21-7 victory over Duquesne.

AGGANIS SEES GAME FROM BENCH

With Agganis on the B. U. bench after an all-night hitch-hike from Camp Lejune, N. C., and a disappointing crowd of 10,000 fans filling only 1-6 of this huge bowl, Pavlikowski was virtually the fhole Terrier show today.

The 21-year-old senior from neighboring Tower Hill No. 2 passed for one touchdown and set up the other B. U. scores with a display of accuracy that netted him a 60 per cent. rating for the day. In all he completed 12 out of 20 attempts for a total of 161 yards.

In addition to Pavilkowski the gathering was treated to a couple of unexpected thrills when two of the B. U. players and one Duquesne lineman were ejected from the game for engaging in fisticuffs. Bob Capuano, sophomore lineman, went out mid-way through the fourth period for chargeing Duke Fullback Leo Etler. Joe Barbagallo and Frank Betonte of Duquesne followed near the end of the game as they exchanged pleasantries.

With the exception of a 52-yard gallop by sophomore Sam Pino that set up the second B.U. score and a 37-yard jaunt by Bobby Whelan in the fading minutes of the game. The Terrier ground game was amazingly impotent.

TERRIERS INEPT ON THE GROUND

Taking away those two runs, the Terriers totaled only 81 yards against the stubborn Duquesne line.

Strange as it may seem, however, B.U. was in control of the game right from the start. The Terriers never were in real serious trouble and, thanks to Pavlikowski, they never had to worry.

After sputtering through most of the first period, Pav took charge when Jim Lyons intercepted a Blair Kramer pass at mid-field and brought it back to the Duquesne 37. Pavlikowski needed only six plays to go the rest of the distance.

(Continued on Page Sixty-Two)

Crusaders Rout Brown, 42-21, Before 20,000

By JOE LOONEY

WORCESTER, Oct. 8—Dr. Eddie Anderson got a roaring welcome back to Fitton Field this afternoon as his Holy Cross Crusaders, with Johnny Turco and Charley Maloy in the starry roles, toppled Brown University, 41-21, before a turnout of 20,000, the largest crowd to watch a football game in Worcester during the post World War II era.

Turco scored five times and Maloy threw four touchdown passes as the Crusaders' first string backfield went on a spree at the expense of the Bruins from Providence, who did all right on their own account offensively by pilinf up 14 first downs, and gaining 130 yards by rushing and 160 through the air.

CRUSADERS SCORE ON THEIR FIRST PLAY

The Crusaders struck swiftly to score on their first scrimmage play, a 51-yard pass maneuver from Maloy to Turco and capped a great offensive performance with a sixth touchdown just 40 seconds before the final whistle when Maloy hurled an 11-yard strike to Mel Massucco.

After the opening touchdown, scored a 1:56 in the first period, the Crusaders were staled until the first minute of the second sesion when Turco bolted across from the four-yard line. The first of four pass interceptions by Carmen Manganiello, who returned the ball 28 yards from his own 11 and a 57-yard jaunt by Massucco after taking a wide pitch-out from Maloy set up the scoring play.

The Crusaders stretched their margin to 21-0 in the third minute of the second period when Manganiello returned a punt 60 yards to the Brown 10, and Turco dashed into the end zone on the following play.

BEAULIEU GOES OVER FOR BROWN

Leon Beaulieu scored for Brown later in the period going over from the three-yard line to climax an eight play 30-yard drive. There was only a minute and 12 seconds remaining in the half when Beaulieu tallied yet the ball changed hands three times and time expired just as a Maloy to Turco pass clicked for 49 yards and another touchdown.

The Maloy-Turco tandem hoisted the Holy Cross lead to 34-7 by combining for another touchdown midway through the third period on a 48-yard pass and the final Crusader tally followed an attempted fourth down pass by Carl Leone of the Bruins from his own 12-yard line in the final minute of play.

(Continued on Page Sixty-Two)

(AP Wirephoto)

EASY DOES IT as the Yankees quell Phils threat with a double play in sixth inning of final series game. Phil Rizzuto (center rear) wings throw to Johnny Mize (36) to double up the training Dick Sisler (left foreground) after Sisler had grounded to Second Baseman Jerry Coleman, who tossed to Rizzuto, forcing Del Ennis (14). Umpire is Bill McGowan. Phils coach (32) is Dusty Cooke.

Lions Down Harvard, 28-7

Mrs. Coen Cheers Eagle Captain Phil

NEWPORT, R. I., Oct. 7 (AP)—The news was all bad for Capt. Philip Coen, Jr., of the Boston College football team at Oxford, Miss., this afternoon, as his team absorbed a 54 to 0 shellacking from Mississippi. But there was good news waiting here for Coen: His wife, the former Beulah Anderson of Newport, gave birth to a baby girl.

MISSISSIPPI DEALS B. C. 54-0 DEFEAT

By DAVID BLOOM

OXFORD, Mass., Oct. 7—Ole Miss reversed southern hospitality this afternoon and dealth Boston College a beating few major teams have taken. The score was 54-0.

Incredible as it seems, it might have been more. The count was 35-0 at the half and Coach Johnny Vaught retired his regulars, including John Dottley, whose battering 51-yard run near the start cracked the Eagle defense beyond repair.

There was, however, no stopping the reserves, nor any repairing of the B. C. defenses. The defeat was the second worst in Boston's history and old-timers have to go back to 1912 and a 55-0

(Continued on Page Sixty-Four)

Spoils Jordan's Debut; Belmont's Wynott Stars

By WILL CLONEY

Columbia claimed the lion's share of the glory at the Stadium yesterday by spoiling Lloyd Jordan's Harvard coaching debut, 28-7, before 15,000 hopeful spectators. The New Yorkers, happy to find somebody they could beat, scored pairs of touchdowns in the second and third periods before yielding a fourth-quarter tally to the persistent Crimson.

Only in that final quarter, when Harvard switched from winged-T to single wing formation, did the Crimson show an offensive flash. Veteran fullback John West eventually had the honor of scoring the touchdown on a four-yard smash to save Harvard from being shut out by Columbia for the first time in history.

The Lions, who had a 2-7 record last year, sent veteran Howie Hansen of West Hempstead, N.Y., ploughing over on short plunges to end two scoring marches in the second period. Vern Wynott of Belmont tallied on a three-yard cross buck at the finish of a five-play 68-yard parade at the start of the second half, and sophomore Mitch Price collaborated with the lofty Wes Bomm on a 67-yard pass play for the last Columbia touchdown toward the end of that third period.

Al Ward, a sophomore specialist on points after touchdown, pumped through all four conversions for the Lions, while Dyke

(Continued on Page Sixty-Two)

Tufts Battles Northeastern To 0-0 Draw

By TIM HORGAN

Northeastern and Tufts went at it like a couple of hungry huskies at the Tufts Oval yesterday, unraveled a panorama of goal-line stands, frantic tackles, intercepted passes, inopportune penalties, basketball ball-handling, and what not, all in a general atmosphere of blood and thunder, but came out with a scoreless tie to the audible dissatisfaction of all concerned.

There was many an explanation offered for the deadlock, but

(Continued on Page Sixty-Two)

Fourth Game Box Score

NEW YORK (A)

	ab	r	bh	tb	po	a	e
Woodling lf.	4	1	2	2	4	0	1
Rizzuto ss..	4	0	0	0	2	4	0
Berra c....	4	2	2	5	10	0	0
DiMaggio cf	3	1	2	3	1	0	0
Mize 1b....	3	0	1	1	5	1	0
Hopp 1b....	1	0	0	0	1	1	0
Brown 3b...	3	1	1	3	0	1	1
Johnson 3b.	1	0	0	0	0	0	0
Bauer rf....	3	0	0	0	1	0	0
Coleman 2b.	3	0	0	0	2	3	0
Ford p.....	3	0	0	0	1	0	0
Reynolds p..	0	0	0	0	0	0	0
..Totals	32	5	8	14	27	10	2

PHILADELPHIA (N)

	ab	r	bh	tb	po	a	e
Waitkus 1b	3	0	1	1	9	1	0
Ashburn cf..	4	0	0	0	3	0	0
Jones 3b....	4	1	2	3	0	4	0
Ennis rf....	3	0	1	1	1	0	0
Sisler lf....	4	0	0	0	2	0	0
†K. Johnson	0	1	0	0	0	0	0
Hammer ss	4	0	1	1	2	2	0
Seminick c..	4	0	0	0	3	1	0
‡Mayo......	0	0	0	0	0	0	0
Goliat 2b...	4	0	1	1	4	4	1
Miller p....	0	0	0	0	0	0	0
Konstanty p	2	0	1	1	0	1	0
*Caballero..	1	0	0	0	0	0	0
Roberts p...	0	0	0	0	0	0	0
§Lopata....	1	0	0	0	0	0	0
Totals	34	2	7	8	24	13	1

*Struck out for Konstanty in 8th.
†Ran for Sisler in 9th.
‡Ran for Seminick in 9th.
§Struck out for Roberts in 9th.

Innings	1	2	3	4	5	6	7	8	9	
PHILADELPHIA (N)	0	0	0	0	0	0	0	0	2	—2
NEW YORK	2	0	0	0	0	3	0	0	x	—5

RBI—Berra 2, DiMaggio, Brown, Bauer. 2B—Jones, DiMaggio. 3B—Brown. HR—Berra. DP—Mize and Berra; Coleman, Rizzuto and Mize. LEFT—Philadelphia (N) 7; New York (A) 4. BB—Ford 1 (Waitkus). SO—Ford 7, (Sisler, Ashburn, Goliat, Jones, Hammer 2, Caballero) Konstanty 3 (Ford 2, DiMaggio); Reynolds 1 (Lopata). HO—Miller 2 in 1-3 innings; Konstanty 5 in 6 2-3; Roberts 1 in 1; Ford 7 in 8 2-3; Reynolds 0 in 1-3. HBP—By Konstanty (DiMaggio); By Ford (Ennis). WP—Miller. Winner—Ford; Loser—Miller. U—Charlie Berry (A) Plate; Jocko Conlan (N) First Base; Bill McGowan (A) Second Base; Dusty Bogess (N) Third Bast; Bill McKinley (A) Left Field Foul Line; Al Barlick (N) Right Field Foul Line. A—68,098. T—2:05.

(Herald Staff Photo by Leslie Jones)

FIRST COLUMBIA TOUCHDOWN against Harvard yesterday came on a jet-propelled dive over the Crimson right guard by Howie Hansen (arrow) after a hand-off from Quarterback Mitch Price, shown at right with back to camera, at start of second period. Columbia won, 28-7.

ON A LATE SURGE

Kentucky Blanks Redmen Final Five Minutes to Win, 59-43, in Eastern N. C. A. A.

ST. JOHN'S AHEAD AT HALF

With the Score Tied at 43-All, Wildcats Break Away for Six Straight Baskets.

Illinois Dumps North Carolina State, 84 to 70, to Advance to Finals in Garden.

New York, March 22. (AP) — Kentucky, the No. 1 team in the country, pulled away from St. John's in the last three minutes tonight to wallop the Brooklyn Redmen, 59 to 43, in the semifinal of the Eastern N. C. A. A. basketball tourney before 14,214 at Madison Square Garden.

The victory put Kentucky in Saturday night's final against Illinois, which beat North Carolina State, 84 to 70, in the other semifinal game.

Kentucky broke the game wide open after St. John's had erased an 8-point deficit to tie the score at 43-43 with five minutes to play.

St. John's was held scoreless for the remainder of the game although it remained close until three minutes to go.

Surge By Kentucky.

At that time it was only 47-43 with St. John's very much in contention. But the situation changed abruptly when Bobby Watson, 7-foot Bill Spivey, Shelby Linville, Lucian Whitaker and Frank Ramsey broke away for six consecutive baskets.

It was an unexpected ending to a deliberately-played game that saw St. John's overcome an 8-point deficit to lead, 24-23, at half time and then again surge from behind a 42-34 score to tie it at 43-43 before Kentucky's deluge of closing baskets.

The Southeastern conference champions demonstrated a fine all-around team. Spivey, one of the tallest collegians in the game, had three personal fouls called on him in the first ten minutes of play and sat out much of the remainder of the game, but 5-foot-10 Watson, Ramsey and Linville more than took up the slack. In addition, Spivey's replacements, Roger Layne and Lou Tsioropoulos, handled themselves well.

Hits at Right Times.

Watson sank six field goals, all set shots, and all coming at opportune moments. He made three in succession in the first half that kept Kentucky ahead after the elongated Spivey was taken out. Ramsey got fifteen points on five baskets and five free throws while Linville tallied nine points, in addition to playing a great floor game.

Spivey, himself, got twelve points. Six of these came in the opening minutes and the rest in Kentucky's closing spurt that routed the Redmen.

Bob Zawoluk, St. John's star, got fifteen points on six field goals and three free throws but, at times, was completely outplayed under the net.

Illinois, ahead by eleven points at half time at 40-29, apparently was headed for defeat when the underdog Southern conference champions came from behind to lead at 66-65 with little more than five minutes left.

Illini Go On Spree.

Then unexpectedly Illinois broke the game wide open. Baskets by Don Sunderlage and Rod Fletcher put the Illini out in front at 69-68. The Big Ten champions broke loose for eleven straight points to make it 80-68.

Sunderlage, Fletcher and Ted Beach were the big guns as the lads from Champaign, Ill., turned the game into a rout. Each flung in two baskets in the Illini spurt.

Altogether Sundarlage scored twenty-one points, Fletcher nineteen and Beach seventeen. Sunderlage and Fletcher each got nine field goals. Beach rimmed eight 2-pointers.

A Spectacular Shot.

One of Fletcher's field goals was a spectacular long shot that set a tourney record of 61 feet 8 inches. The heave came as the half time buzzer went off and electrified the crowd.

This gave the Illini their 11-point intermission edge.

The wolfpack from Raleigh, N. C., was held scoreless from the field for the first five minutes of the game, but starting the second half they flipped in four field goals that turned the game into an exciting see-saw affair until the final minutes.

With Bill Kukoy and Bob Speight sparking the attack, the Southerners pulled up to 42-39. Goals by Sunderlage, Fletcher, Bob Peterson and Irv Bemoras pulled Illinois out in front at 51-43, but quick baskets by Kukoy and Speight again narrowed the gap.

Lead Changes Fast.

Finally, just before the 10-minute mark, Pete Jackmowski flipped in a basket that tied the score at 56-56. For the next six minutes the lead changed back and forth. The game was tied at 58-58, 60-60, 61-61, 63-63 before the late Illini spurt.

Kukoy tossed in 20 points for State, on seven field goals and six free throws. Speight got 17 on seven two-pointers and three conversions.

North Carolina State, which played a zone-defense to Illinois' man-for-man, was hurt by the loss of Starter Bernie Yurin. He injured his shoulder in the first two minutes of play and did not play the remainder of the tilt.

ILLINOIS—84.	G	FT	F	NORTH CAROLINA STATE—70.	G	FT	F
C. Follmer	2	2	2	Speight	7	3	2
Bemoras	3	1	2	Kukoy	7	6	2
Beach	8	1	1	Brandenburg	4	1	1
Peterson	5	0	5	Goss	3	2	3
Baumgardn'r	2	0	3	Cook	1	0	0
Fletcher	9	1	3	Yurin	0	0	0
Sunderlage	9	3	1	Norris	1	0	1
				Jack Mowski	2	0	2
				Terrill	4	0	0
Totals	38	8	17	Totals	29	12	11

Half-time—Illinois 40, North Carolina State 29.

Free throws missed—North Carolina State—Speight, Kukoy 2, Brandenburg 3, Goss, Terrill. Illinois—Peterson 2, Fletcher.

KENTUCKY	G	FT	F	ST. JOHN'S.	G	FT	F
Hagan	1	2	3	Dombrosky	1	2	4
Linville	4	1	1	McCool	0	0	0
Spivey	5	2	4	McGuire	2	1	3
Tsioropoulos	1	1	2	Mulzoff	0	0	3
Layne	1	0	2	O'Shea	0	0	0
Watson	6	0	0	Zawoluk	6	3	3
Ramsey	5	5	5	McMahon	2	3	1
Whitaker	1	0	1	Giancontieri	1	0	0
				McAndrews	0	0	0
Totals	24	11	18	McGilvary	4	2	2
				Dunn	0	0	0
				Noonan	0	0	0
				Totals	16	11	16

Half-time—St. John's 24, Kentucky 23.

Free throws missed—Kentucky, Hagan 2, Linville, Spivey, Tsioropoulous, Layne; St. Johns, Dombrosky, McGuire 3, Zawoluk 2, MacGilvary 2.

Fit of Enthusiasm Hits Dickey At Mention of Mantle's Name

Former Yankee Catching Star Is the Unexpressive Type but He Calls Rookie the Greatest Prospect He Has Seen in His Time.

LOS ANGELES, March 22. (AP)—"He's the greatest prospect Ive seen in my time, and I go back quite a ways," said Bill Dickey, the Yankees' catching coach. "I'll swear I expect to see that boy just take off and fly any time."

Dickey, who does not enthuse easily about anything or anybody, was, of course, referring to Mickey Mantle. And what he said about this 19-year-old refugee from a lead mine was only typical of what every baseball man on the coast is saying.

They say this husky Yankee kid can't miss being one of the greatest. No rookie in this writer's recollection has created the spontaneous commotion that Mantle has stirred up since portside that he walloped a near-record home run at the local Wrigley field last week end.

After watching Mickey lay down a bunt and race to first, students agree it will be very difficult ever to nail him on the second half of a double play. He did not compete in track and so never has been timed. He looks, offhand, as though he might do the hundred in about 9.8.

"No, I doubt I could do it anywhere near that fast," he demurred. "Maybe I could run it in 10.5 or 11." Several of his teammates who were within earshot broke into wide grins at that estimate.

The only question in anyone's mind is how long it will take the kid, fresh out of class C ball to learn to play the outfield the

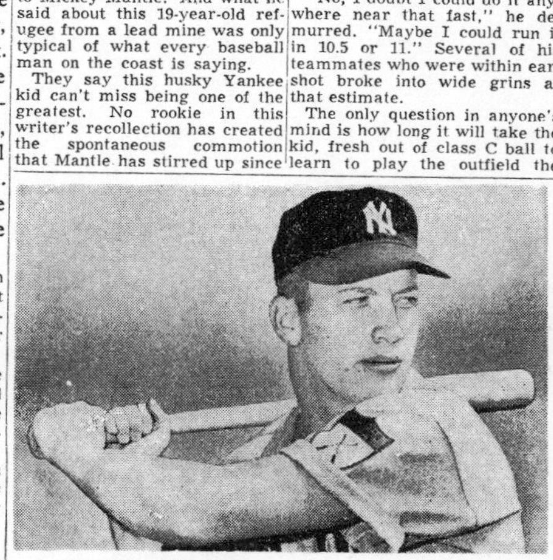

THE MANTLE BOY IS YANKEES' JOY . . . MICKEY MANTLE, THE SENSATIONAL ROOKIE WHO HAS VETERAN BASEBALL MEN TRYING TO OUTDO EACH OTHER WITH RAVE NOTICES —(Wirephoto).

he reported to the Yanks' school at Phoenix in mid-February.

"He's one of those once-in-a-lifetime boys who makes you water at the mouth just to watch him," says Manager Al Lopez of Cleveland.

Indians Agree, Too.

The Indians agree, reluctantly, that Mickey is a greater prospect than Harry (Suitcase) Simpson, their Negro rookie from San Diego who has clinched an outfield berth with his terrific hitting, fielding and running.

Manager Casey Stengel still says he'll farm Mantle out on 48-hour recall rather than let him sit on the bench a single afternoon, but it already is plain that Casey is going to have an awful problem to wrestle with when cutting down time comes.

Mickey, whose 190 pounds are stacked on a solid 5-11 frame, hits with frightful power either from left or right. He'll jolt some infielders before he's through. He is an extremely modest, quiet youngster. He finished high school at Commerce, Ok., only two years ago, and he gives the impression that all this is something of a pleasant surprise to him.

"I don't know which side I can hit better from," he says, seriously. "I'm right-handed, but it seems natural to hit from either side. I guess I've hit left-handed more, but that's because there are more right-handed pitchers."

Power from Both Sides.

Some observers believe Mickey hits with greater power right-handed, but it was from the way it must be played in the big show. It was as a shortstop that he hit .383 for Joplin in the Western association last year.

Joe Devine, the Yankees' West Coast scout who handled Mantle in the preliminary school at Phoenix, believes the kid can play big league shortstop right now, but is a little dubious about the outfield. Trouble is, the world champions have all the shortstop they need in Phil Rizzuto, and they will require a new centerfielder if Joe DiMaggio quits after this season.

Has Bone Infection.

Although a leg bone infection, chronic osteomyelitis, will prevent Mantle's serving in the army, it may never hamper his playing, says Dr. Sidney Gaynor, the Yankees' club physician and bone specialist. On the other hand, the doctor says, it might give him a spot of trouble from time to time.

The story which undoubtedly will follow Mantle through his career concerned his failure to show up at the Phoenix training camp on schedule. A wire from his worried employers elicited the information that Mickey was working in a lead mine near Joplin at $35 a week and that he didn't have money to throw away on a ticket to Phoenix. He was sent the money by return wire.

A writer asked Mickey why in the world he hadn't got in touch with the Yankees during the winter and hit them for a little advance.

"What for?" Mickey wanted to know.

BASEBALL NOTES.

The Katz team of the Ban Johnson league will work out at Forty-seventh and Woodland at 2:30 o'clock tomorrow and 12:30 o'clock Sunday, weather permitting. All signed players and any others wishing to try out please report.

The Bulldogs will work out today and tomorrow afternoon at 4:30 o'clock at Parade park, Fifteenth and Paseo. All players are urged to attend.

The Leavenworth prison team would like to schedule baseball games for the coming season. The team can play on Sundays and holidays only, between the dates of May 6 and September 30, inclusive. The games will start at 1:15 o'clock and it is requested that the visiting teams arrive not later than 12:30 o'clock. Any teams wishing to schedule such games, please contact Mr. W. E. Ary, recreation director, Leavenworth prison, Leavenworth, Kas.

PRO CAGE RESULTS.

NATIONAL ASSOCIATION PLAY-OFFS.

EASTERN DIVISION.

Syracuse 90, Philadelphia 78 (Syracuse wins series, 2-0).

WESTERN DIVISION.

Fort Wayne 83, Rochester 78 (series tied, 1-1).

YESTERDAY'S RACE RESULTS.

At Gulfstream.

1—Mon Torch (33.10, 11.50, 6.60); Bordeaux (4.20, 3.00); Bootalong (6.10).
2—Silver Plate (5.90, 3.50, 2.80); Frere Jacques (3.40, 2.80); Insultin' (6.70).
The double paid 114.80.
3—Roseada (5.10, 3.30, 2.90); Busy Indian (5.80, 4.00); I'm Sandy (6.20).
4—Japhap (81.70, 32.40, 16.50); Bold Knot (9.60, 5.70); The Prophet (4.30).
5—Bellatrix (15.40, 7.60, 5.30). How Bonnie (4.40, 3.40), Dannas Pensive (4.00).
6—Irish Game (8.10, 4.20, 2.70), Hawthorn (6.90, 2.80), Brevite (2.40).
7—Deluge (5.70, 4.10, 3.40), Blue Kay (12.60, 4.70), Ode (4.00).
8—Major Kay (8.90, 5.60, 3.50), Spider Rock (5.70, 3.20), Omen (3.40).
9—Boots Haven (67.70, 24.50, 11.10), Althor (8.00, 4.90), Intrusive (3.60).

At Oaklawn.

1—Royal Luck (24.20, 8.00, 3.60), Air Commander (7.60, 3.60), Screen Time (2.40).
2—Jess D. (6.40, 3.60, 2.80), Wild Peter (5.00, 3.60), Kindly Miss (4.20).
Daily Double—Royal Luck and Jess D. paid 80.60.
3—Justacord (5.20, 3.60, 2.80), Scalped (28.20, 9.00), Last Oscar (4.00).
4—Park Pigeon (7.20, 3.80, 2.80), Merry Tudor (3.40, 2.60), Our Snick (2.80).
5—Esta Vez (41.60, 11.00, 6.00), Memphis Bud (3.80, 3.20), Slipper Satin (5.20).
6—Pair Reno (5.40, 3.60, 2.60), Free Gift (4.60, 3.40), Gaby Haugh (3.00).
7—Old School (8.80, 4.80, 2.80), Kenayr (5.00, 3.00), Chump Trick (2.80).
8—First Tenet (8.60, 4.60, 3.60), Thunderjet (15.20, 8.20), Da Do (4.40).

At Lincoln.

1—Indian Barney (8.40, 3.20, 2.40), Halbarail (2.80, 2.20), Whiffletree (2.80).
2—Bambi Lynne (5.20, 3.80, 3.00), Dancing Gob (6.40, 4.40), Alanay (6.20).
Daily Double—Indian Barney and Bambi Lynne paid 33.00.

At Bay Meadows.

1—Star Sweep (10.70, 7.40, 5.30), Destiny Bay (32.40, 18.50), Lena (13.00).
2—In Our Time (3.00, 2.60, 2.30), Her Triumph (6.40, 4.30), Direct Win (4.40).
3—Mr. Rustom (16.50, 6.00, 4.50), Style Trend (4.70, 3.00), Fonte Gaia (5.40).
Daily Double—In Our Time and Mr. Rustom paid (43.90).
4—Sir Abbey (3.70, 2.70, 2.40), Aspiring (15.10, 6.90), Clearmont Jr. (5.10).
5—Proud Heritage (124.10, 51.90, 19.10), Rud Peddler (9.20, 5.60), Watchherspin (5.40).
6—Top Turrett (5.90, 3.40, 2.50), Irene's Angel (6.20, 4.10), End to End (3.00).
7—Top Production (14.90, 6.50, 3.30), Safe Arrival (4.10, 2.70), Contribution (2.60).
8—Interpretation (3.00, 2.40, 2.20), Sugar Sample (2.70, 2.40), Trusting (4.70).
9—Just Why (5.30, 3.00, 2.40), Song Land (2.90, 2.50), Chaldia (3.40).

DODGERS SIGN A SCOUT.

Brooklyn, March 22. (AP)—The Brooklyn Dodgers today signed A. B. (Turk) Karam of Bayonne, N. J., as a scout for the New Jersey and Southern New York areas.

KIND TO THE BLUES

Kansas City Defeats Ragged Buffalo Team, 9-2, for Second Straight Victory.

THREE PITCHERS WORK

Jones, Mitchell and Logue Are Effective, but Bisons Are Making a Late Start.

BY ERNEST MEHL.
(The Star's Sports Editor.)

Avon Park, Fla., March 22.—The Blues now have what amounts to a 2-game winning streak after their 9 to 2 triumph over the Buffalo Bisons of the International league here today.

This second exhibition game success in three starts was highlighted by the pitching efforts of three right-handed aspirants, Rex Jones, Dick Mitchell and Frank Logue. As a rebuttal against the seeming prowess of their mound work was the fact the Bisons had only gotten their spring drills under way on Monday, which could account for some of their offensive timidity.

Jones hurled four innings in which he yielded five hits and no runs; Mitchell performed in three and was touched for a tally in the seventh on a pair of singles and a balk. Three of the five hits against Jones came in the fourth but one was nullified when the author of it was thrown out stealing by Hank Foiles.

Score is Misleading.

The Blues weren't quite as robust at bat as the score would indicate. They were held to one safety in five innings and counted their five runs in the seventh on two bingles.

This round iced the affair against the weird pitching of the third Buffalo hurler, Bob Curley. Ed Barbarito started the inning with a clean single to center and Mitchell ended it by swatting into a double play.

In between these two events Kal Segrist, Chuck Wotowicz, Bob Cerv, Bob O'Neal and George Gasser were given bases on balls by a pitcher who threw at everything but the plate.

Ki Thomas, who got three hits and a walk in his five trips, singled for the other hit to score one of the five and another run came in after Jim Goff's fly to left.

Walks also pushed the Blues into their fourth inning marker. Two were out when Cerv, Foiles and Thomas strolled, Cerv scoring when the Buffalo shortstop bobbled Gasser's grounder.

Three Singles, One Run.

In the sixth, with one out, Foiles, Thomas and Gasser singled in succession for the second run. After the seventh inning deluge the boys sweetened their total with two more in the eighth. Hits by Segrist, O'Neal and Thomas and a pair of Buffalo errors figured in the scoring.

Jones, a winner at Beaumont last year and considered by the organization officials as a good competitor, walked two and struck out the same number. His fast ball was particularly effective.

Logue, who won twenty games for Muskegon last year, is a side armer with medium speed but the ball is alive and his control good. He faced only three batters in the eighth but in the ninth Barbarito made a low 2-base throwing error to start the round. As a result the Bisons picked up an unearned run as the hurler finished without permitting a hit.

Manager George Selkirk made no substitutions except in his battery. Segrist went through at short, but handled only one assist while Gasser at second had eight chances with one bobble charged against him.

NOTES OF THE GAME.

Avon Park, Fla., March 22.—Hugh Radcliffe, Bill Jankowski and Bob Keegan will pitch for the Blues tomorrow when they go to Kissimmee to meet Indianapolis. Cliff Melton, veteran left-hander, gets his first start Sunday in a game at Lake Wales with Buffalo.

Fred Speranza, young infielder who has been late in reporting because of illness, arrived in camp today. . . . This brings the number to six outfielders, six infielders, four catchers and fifteen pitchers.

Jones pitched out of trouble in the first inning by aid of a double play started by Segrist. Then he fanned the last batter, Tom Bransfield, on three pitches. . . . Ki Thomas, playing centerfield, looked at a third strike in the second.

ELECT BOWLING OFFICERS.

Macon, Mo., March 22. — The Women's City Bowling association has just elected the following officers for the coming term: President, Mrs. E. E. Sanford; vice-president, Mrs. C. W. Imlay; secretary, Mrs. Jack Devine; treasurer, Mrs. Charles Fower; sergeant-at-arms, Mrs. Paul Miller; mixed league representative, Mrs. Florence Lyman.

The Blues' Box Score.

BUFFALO.	AB.	R.	H.	O.	A.	E.
Breard, 2b	3	1	1	3	4	0
Hancock, ss	2	0	1	0	0	1
Edwards, ss	2	0	0	0	3	0
Barrett, cf	3	0	0	3	0	0
Littrell, rf	2	0	1	1	0	0
Carswell, lf	3	0	0	2	0	1
Bransfield, rf, 1b	4	0	1	8	0	0
Biasatti, 1b	2	0	1	4	1	0
Binks, rf, cf	2	0	0	0	0	0
Block, 3b	3	0	1	0	5	2
Novick, c	1	0	0	3	0	0
Valois, c	2	0	1	2	0	0
Tabacheck, c	1	1	0	0	0	0
Acker, p	1	0	0	0	0	0
Bowes, p	1	0	0	1	0	0
Curley, p	1	0	0	0	0	0
Triplett	1	0	0	0	0	0
Totals	34	2	7	27	13	4

KANSAS CITY.	AB.	R.	H.	O.	A.	E.
Barbarito, 3b	6	2	1	0	3	1
Segrist, ss	3	2	1	2	3	0
Wotowicz, lf	4	1	0	2	0	0
Cerv, rf	3	2	1	3	0	0
Foiles, c	2	1	1	3	1	0
O'Neal, c	1	1	1	2	0	0
Thomas, cf	4	0	3	3	0	0
Gasser, 2b	4	0	1	5	4	1
Goff, 1b	5	0	0	7	0	0
Jones, p	2	0	0	0	1	0
Mitchell, p	2	0	0	0	0	0
Logue, p	1	0	0	0	0	0
Totals	37	9	9	27	12	2

Triplett grounded out for Curley in ninth.

Buffalo	000	000	101	2	7	3
Kansas City	000	101	520	9	9	2

RBI—Gasser, Cerv, O'Neal 2, Thomas 2, Goff, Littrell, Edwards. DP—Segrist-Gasser-Goff; Block-Breard-Bransfield; Littrell-Breard-Bransfield. Left—Buffalo 10, Kansas City 10. BB—Jones 2, Bowes 4, Mitchell 3, Curley 5. SO—Acker 3, Mitchell 3, Bowes 1, Curley 1. HO—Acker 3, Mitchell 3, nings, off Bowes 3 in 3, Jones 5 in 4, Mitchell 2 in 3, Curley 5 in 3, Logue 0 in 2. Balks—Mitchell 2. Winner—Jones. Loser—Acker. U—Fellerski and King. Time 2:15.

QUIZ N. C. A. A. ON TV BAN.

Attorney General Asks Explanation on 1-Year Moratorium.

Oklahoma City, March 22. (AP)—The U. S. attorney general's office has asked the National Collegiate Athletic association to explain its 1-year moratorium on live televising of college football games, the Oklahoma state senate was told today.

Senator George Miskovsky, Oklahoma City, said he had been advised of the action by H. G. Morrison, assistant attorney general.

Miskovsky said Morrison had asked Dr. Hugh Willett, Los Angeles, N. C. A. A. president, for a report of its position on the television ban.

The Senate last Monday defeated a bill by Miskovsky which would have required television of University of Oklahoma games. Instead, a resolution asking a review of the problem was placed before the Senate.

Miskovsky said Morrison advised the Senate to hold up action to see if a solution can be worked out. The senator also said he has received promises from several members of the Oklahoma congressional delegation that they will help start an investigation of the television ban.

LONE EAGLE ON MAT CARD.

First Appearance in Auditorium Will Be Made April 3.

The Municipal Auditorium's wrestling patrons will get their first look at Lone Eagle, the colorful Cherokee Indian mat star, when he competes in the featured match on a 4-bout Auditorium card April 3.

Lone Eagle is a familiar wrestling personality to television audiences throughout the nation. He has appeared in numerous matches in Chicago that have been televised over WDAF-TV in recent months.

The Indian heavyweight always enters the wrestling ring wearing the full Cherokee headdress and he is accompanied by the beautiful Princess Bonita, a full-blooded Sioux from the Wisconsin Dells reservation. The princess usually retires to Lone Eagle's corner and she beats on a war drum whenever it is apparent that Eagle is in trouble during his match.

When it comes time to ply his wrestling trade the Eagle can produce for he is a capable offensive mat strategist.

HERB FLAM SEEDED No. 1.

Miami Beach, Fla., March 22. (AP)—Herbert Flam of Beverly Hills, Calif., was seeded No. 1 today in the men's singles division of the Good Neighbor tennis championships opening Monday at Flamingo Park.

EXHIBITION BASEBALL.

YESTERDAY'S RESULTS.

New York (A) 11, Sacramento (PCL) 0.
Boston (N) 11, Cincinnati (N) 10 (ten innings).
Washington (A) 6, Boston (N) 5.
St. Louis (N) 2, New York (N) 1.
Pittsburgh (N) 13, St. Louis (A) 4.
Seattle (PCL) 5, Pittsburgh B (N) 4.
Chicago (N) 8, Cleveland (A) 7 (ten innings).
Brooklyn (N) 8, Philadelphia (N) 3.

TODAY'S SCHEDULE.

Pittsburgh (N) vs. Chicago (N) at Los Angeles.
St. Louis (N) vs. Brooklyn (N) at Miami, night.
Cincinnati (N) vs. Boston (A) at Sarasota, Fla.
Boston (N) vs. Philadelphia (A) at Bradenton, Fla.
Washington (A) vs. New York (N) at St. Petersburg, Fla.
Philadelphia (N) vs. Detroit (A) at Clearwater, Fla.
St. Louis (A) vs. Chicago (A) at Pasadena, Calif.
Cleveland (A) vs. Oakland (PCL) at Oakland, Calif.
New York (A) vs. San Francisco (PCL) at San Francisco, night.

YANKS SNAP BACK

Mantle Belts Homer as New York Breaks Losing Streak by Routing Sacramento, 11-0.

CARDS TOP GIANTS, 2-1

Rice's Pinch-Hit Homer Decides the Contest—Senators Baffle the Red Sox, 6-5.

Sacramento, Calif., March 22. (AP)—Mickey Mantle, rookie outfielder, hit a home run over the left field fence today as the New York Yankees broke a 3-game exhibition losing string by walloping Sacramento, 11-0.

The youngster, who is being groomed to fill Joe DiMaggio's shoes, shared the day's limelight with another rookie, Tom Morgan, who combined with Lefty Ed Lopat to pitch a 4-hitter. Lopat permitted one hit in four innings, Morgan three in the last five.

Veterans Yogi Berra and Johnny Mize got three hits each in the Yankees' 15-hit attack.

Morgan, a 20-year-old native of El Monte, Calif., near Los Angeles, now has run up a string of thirteen scoreless innings in three exhibition appearances against Cleveland, Hollywood (P. C. L.) and the Solons. He has permitted only nine hits and has walked only two batters.

New York	205	100	111	11	15	1
Sacramento	000	000	000	0	4	3

Lopat, Morgan (5) and Barra, Silvera; Gillespie, Grubb (5) and Lakeman, Thrasher. WP—Lopat. LP—Gillespie. Homer—Mantle (N. Y.).

Fanovich Card Victim.

St. Petersburgh, Fla., March 22. (AP)—A home run by Pinch-hitter Hal Rice with one on in the third inning gave the St. Louis Cardinals a 2-1 victory over the New York Giants before a crowd of 3,423 today.

Rice connected off Southpaw Frank Fanovich, driving the ball over the right-field wall.

The Giants' lone run came in the fourth inning when Centerfielder Bobby Thomson tripled to left center and scored as Shortstop Dick Cole fumbled Bill Howerton's relay.

New York	000	100	000	1	5	1
St. Louis	002	000	00x	2	5	2

Fanovich, Bainberger (4), Bowman (7) and Westrum, Noble (8); Lanier, Poholsky (4), Mizell (7) and Garagiola. HR: St. Louis—Rice. WP—Lanier. LP—Fanovich.

Bow to Hudson, Bearden.

Sarasota, Fla., March 22. (AP)—Starter Sid Hudson and Gene Bearden held the Boston Red Sox to seven hits today as the Washington Senators gained a 6-5 decision before 2,487 fans.

Ellis Kinder, Boston pitcher, was brilliant in his first game action of the spring training season but by the time he got into the contest, the Nats had landed on Mel Parnell for a 5-run fifth inning. Washington combined five hits, an error and two walks in the splurge, adding a run off Kinder in the eighth.

Washington	000	050	010	6	9	3
Boston	100	001	201	5	7	1

Hudson, Bearden (6) and Grasso, Okrie (7); Parnell, Kinder (6) and Batts. HR: Boston—Batts. WP—Hudson. LP—Parnell.

Busy Tenth Inning.

Bradenton, Fla., March 22. (AP)—Gene Mauch's single scored Earl Torgeson with the winning run today as the Boston Braves tallied four times in the tenth inning to defeat the Cincinnati Reds, 11-10.

The Tribe's big tenth canceled out a 3-run Reds rally in their half of the same inning which featured Lloyd Merriman's 2-run inside the park homer.

Cincinnati	100	020	220	3	10	17	6
Boston	011	050	000	4	11	11	3

(Ten innings.)

Batteries—Blackwell, Blake (7), Erautt (8), Peterson (10) and Scheffing. Sain, Surkont (6), Chipman (9) and St. Claire, Cooper (7). WP—Chipman. LP—Peterson.

Dodgers Drub Phils.

Miami, March 22. (AP)—The Brooklyn Dodgers squared accounts with the Philadelphia Phillies by drubbing the National league champs, 8-3, before a crowd of 2,441 here tonight.

Rookie Jim Romano shut out the Phillies with three hits for the first six innings but the Phils scored on Clarence Podbielan in the eighth and ninth.

Jackie Robinson's 3-run homer off Russ Meyer in the third put the Dodgers out in front and they scored three more on Bob Miller in the next two innings.

				R	H	E
Philadelphia (N)	000	000	012	3	5	3
Brooklyn (N)	003	012	20x	8	9	1

Meyer, Miller (5), Trinkle (7) and Seminick; Romano, Podbielman (7) and Edwards.
Home run: Brooklyn—Robinson.
Winning pitcher—Romano; Losing pitcher—Meyer.

OTHER GAMES.

At San Bernardino, Calif.

St. L. (A.)	0 0 2	000	002	4	8	4
Pittsb'gh (N.)	0 11 0	001	01x	13	10	0

Garver, Widmar (3) and Moss; Law, Pettit (8) and McCullough. WP—Law; LP—Garver.

At Palm Springs, Fla.

Pittsburgh B (N.)	000	002	020	4	7	3
Seattle (P. C. L.)	100	100	30x	5	9	3

Muir, Walsh (6) and Reiser, Fitzgerald (6); Schanz and Montano. LP—Walsh.

AT LOS ANGELES.

Cleveland (A)	300	202	000	0	7	14	2
Chicago (N)	001	104	100	1	8	17	2

(Ten innings.)

Lemon, Olson (7) and Tebbetts; Rush, Minner (5) and Burgess. HR—Chicago: Minner (6); Baumholtz (6); Cleveland: Minosa (6). WP—Minner. LP—Olson.

Lincoln Downs Program Canceled by Snow.

Lincoln, R. I., March 22. (AP)—The racing program at Lincoln Downs was suspended after the second race today because of the snow.

About 3,500 spectators were in the stands to watch what was to have been an 8-race program.

After the first race, jockeys complained that the driving snow had blinded them most of the time.

BIG PITCHING 'IF'

Leading Contenders for Baseball Titles Rely on Key Hurlers Coming Through.

ODDS AGAINST MANY

Of the Active Chuckers, Only Twelve Have Put Together Four Years of .500.

By Oscar Fraley.

New York, April 6.(UP)—With the probable pennant contenders picked before the first pitch, the biggest question today concerning the approaching major league races was whether last season's big guns of the mound can come back effectively in 1951.

On the basis of past performance, spring training form, personnel improvements and adjustments, it is an accepted theory that there will be no great changes made in the standings. None of the bottom teams is expected to come charging out of nowhere to hit the jackpot.

Phils Need Konstanty.

And, on each of those near the top who are conceded a chance, all have pitching strength which could be a question mark. The Phillies, for instance, need another big year out of Jim Konstanty. The Cleveland Indians have to receive a fat winning effort from Bob Lemon. And so it goes for each of the teams.

Yet, of all the pitchers currently active in the majors, only twelve of them have had four seasons in a row in which they bettered the .500 mark.

Lemon is one of them. The others are Hank Borowy, Alpha Brazle, Joe Dobson, Bob Feller, Joe Hatten, Freddie Hutchinson, Max Lanier, Ed Lopat, Allie Reynolds, Warren Spahn and Paul Trout.

Notable pitchers who have not been able to tack together four winning seasons in a row include such as Hal Newhouser, who had two strings of three winning years; Johnny Sain, who won twenty or more in four of the last five years but had a 10-17 mark in 1949; Howie Pollet, Ewell Blackwell, Larry Jansen, Preacher Roe, Harry Brecheen, Virgil Trucks, Lou Brissie and Early Wynn.

Consider the case of Lemon. With Bob Feller's famed fast ball now ambling up to the plate, Lemon has become the siege gun of the Indian staff in the last three years. He was a winner the year previous, too, but with an average 11-5 mark.

But Can He Repeat?

Since then he has set the league afire with 20-14 in 1948, 22-10 in 1949 and a league-leading 23-11 last season. That's four in a row—but can he do it again?

For the pitchers who managed five such years hand running are of the legendary class. You're talking now of such immortals as Christy Mathewson, Lefty Grove and Carl Hubbell.

Lemon may be one of the greats, yet even most of the heroes in that category found a skein of better than four years impossible. Consider the case of Herb Pennock, one of the Yankee greats. He captured twenty games one year and the next season fell below .500. That, too, was the fate of Wait Hoyt and many others.

Often the best year—and this isn't said hopefully of such as Lemon and Konstanty—is followed by a bad one.

Sain in 1948 won twenty-four games. The next season he skidded to a 10-17 mark.

Lefty Gomez, back in 1934, stood the American league on its ear as he showed the way with twenty-six triumphs and a miserly 2.33 earned run average. The next season he won twelve and lost fifteen.

Certainly some of the prime pitchers of 1950 are going to fade in 1951. And that will be the main factor which decides which club wins, and which clubs lose!

APOLOGY FOR RING JOB.

Sugar Ray Robinson Attributes Poor Display to Illness.

Miami, Fla., April 6.(AP)—The winner was sad and the loser was happy after Sugar Ray Robinson's 10-round decision over Holly Mims of Washington, D. C., in Miami stadium last night.

In his dressing room after the fight, Robinson, the middleweight champion, was apologetic for "my bad showing." The bout was postponed from March 8 because of Robinson's illness and he said "I gue... hat virus had me worse than... thought. A couple of times I had him lined up but I couldn't get him."

The aggressive Mims was a contrast in cheerfulness. He came out of the bout in excellent condition and declared Robinson "never hurt me bad any time."

The crowd of 5,500, which paid a gross gate of $17,000, liked Mims because he never took a backward step from Robinson. There were scattered boos when the decision was announced, although it was unanimous.

The 23-year-old Washington fighter was required to come in over the 160-pound limit and needed several glasses of water to tip the scales at 160½.

Twelve Former Blues to Be "Home" Tuesday.

Twelve former Blues will be wearing Yankee uniforms when the world's champions play the Boston Braves at 2 o'clock Tuesday in Blues stadium. The list includes:

Pitchers — Lou Burdette, Tommy Byrne, Bob Porterfield.

Catchers — Ralph Houk, Charles Silvera.

Infielders—Gerry Coleman, Joe Collins, Johnny Mize, Phil Rizzuto, Gerry Snyder.

Outfielders — Hank Bauer, Cliff Mapes.

The Yankees arrive Tuesday morning at 8:35 o'clock from Dallas and leave at 6 o'clock for Louisville.

THE CLIPPER AND HIS REPLACEMENT?—The Yankee Clipper, Joe DiMaggio (left), smiles along with Mickey Mantle, the sensational rookie who is being touted as a possible replacement for the old pro. The two are shown talking in front of the Mission stadium dugout last night before the Yanks played San Antonio. Mantle is reported scheduled for a pre-induction draft physical at Miami, Ok., next Wednesday. The Yanks meet the Boston Braves in an exhibition at Blues stadium, Kansas City, Tuesday afternoon—(Wirephoto).

MANTLE IN A CROSSFIRE

BUT YANKEE ROOKIE IS QUIET IN DRAFT RUCKUS.

George Weiss, New York General Manager, Denies Club Made Move for Re-examination.

By Joe Trimble.
(New York News Staff Correspondent.)

San Antonio, Tex., April 6.—The Mickey Mantle muddle was the most important topic among the New York Yankees as they stopped off here yesterday for a night exhibition with the local Texas league nine.

George Weiss, business manager, stoutly maintains that no one in the Yankee organization requested a clarification of the young star's 4-F status and the chairman of the Oklahoma state selective service board insists it was the New York club, among others, who asked for a reaffirmation of the deferment ruling.

Behind the Scene Action.

It is obvious that something not wholly in the open is going on, and that Mantle, himself, is caught right in the middle. The kid, being only 19 years old and hardly ripe enough to become a national issue, is keeping quiet and merely hoping that he can remain with the Yanks. He has osteomyelitis, a disease of the leg bone a couple of inches above the left ankle. His home draft board at Miami, Ok., rejected him for the army in January because of it. Despite it he's the fastest man on the Yanks and maybe in the major leagues.

His chances of staying on with the champs probably aren't very good and, if he is called to limited service, the pennant chances of the Yanks will take quite a drop, too. With Mantle on hand a year for aging Joe DiMaggio would not have been too damaging to the club. But if the phenom is lost then the fading clipper will have to find the physical resources to play as many as 125 games—a really terrific assignment for a 36-year-old who has been brittle ever since he came to the majors in 1936.

Seen as Yank Starter.

There is no doubt that Mantle is being groomed as a regular for the start of the season and that, the draft board willing, he will be in right-field a week from Monday when the Yanks open the schedule in Washington. He is not yet officially a Yankee, by the way. Mickey was signed to a Kansas City Blues contract for $4,000 per year recently in Phoenix and handed a bonus of $5,000 to keep him reasonably happy. Comes opening day—and he still is available— the boy will get a pay rise to the minimum $5,000 a season as a major leaguer.

His fate will be decided before that, of course. He will leave the club at Kansas City next Tuesday and return to his home at Commerce, Ok., near Miami.

Weiss, in denying any faux pas on the part of the Yankee organization—and it certainly would have been one if a club official had stirred up the draft board—said today by long distance phone:

"It's ridiculous to think we had anything to do with it, I deny emphatically that any member of our organization has been in contact with the Oklahoma authorities. We didn't know anything about it until the news broke in the papers.

"We will dispatch Mantle to his draft board when he is due there, on April 11, and abide by whatever the decision is."

GRAND NATIONAL IS READY.

Aintree, England, April 6.(AP)—Artic Gold, Shagreen Freebooter and Roimond—experts tell you to forget the rest if you're trying to find the winner of tomorrow's Grand National steeplechase. Post time for the race is 9:15 in the morning, Kansas City time.

FIGHTS LAST NIGHT.

(By the Associated Press.)

Miami, Fla.—Ray (Sugar) Robinson, 159½, New York, outpointed Holly Mims, 160½, Washington, 10 (nontitle).

Brooklyn.—Henry Jordan, 147¼, Philadelphia, outpointed Bobby Lloyd, 144, Wilkes-Barre, Pa., 8.

Bangor, Me.—Hermie Freeman, 134, Bangor and Jimmy Parlin, 138, Philadelphia, drew, 10.

WILLIAMS' EYE IS KEEN

A .367 BATTING AVERAGE FOR BOSTON SLUGGER.

That's Good News to Red Sox Followers Who Worried About Star and His Injured Elbow.

(By the Associated Press.)

Folks up Boston way, especially the regular Fenway park clan, are breathing much easier these days—"The Thumper" is thumping again.

Which means, of course, Ted Williams hasn't lost his delicate batting eye.

There was some doubt about Williams's condition when spring training started. He had fractured his elbow in the All-Star game last summer and some thought it might shorten, if not end his career.

But Ted's bat has given the answer: A .367 springtime batting average, sprinkled with some of those familiar Williams home runs.

Red Sox followers welcome this news because a healthy Williams can spell pennant for the long-overdue Bostonians.

Moreover, with big Walt Dropo sidelined, the Sox can ill-afford to lose another fence-buster.

Williams, flashing his raw power, poled a tremendous 400-foot home run yesterday as the Red Sox crushed Savannah, 15 to 0. The blow came with two mates on and sent some 2,500 sally league fans home with the gratification of having seen the trigger-tempered outfielder bust one.

The $125,000 slugger also hit a single. He now has twenty-nine hits in seventy-nine at-bats, including three home runs and twenty-one R. B. I.s.

In all, the Red Sox clubbed five home runs. Dom DiMaggio hit two and Lou Boudreau and Mickey Guerra one apiece.

More important, however, was the pitching of Maurice McDermott and Paul Hinrichs, two erratic curve-ball artists. McDermott worked six innings, giving up five hits and three walks. Hinrichs, the former Yankee, also walked three and yielded three hits during his 3-inning chore.

TIME OUT!

"Whadd'ya mean he's beginning to get to you? He's been and gone!"

SEEN AS RING TONIC

TITLE BOUT HERE WOULD SPARK BOXING, PROMOTER SAYS.

Jim Downing, Who Helped Steer Layne to Big Time, Believes New York-Chicago Monopoly Is Bad.

An occasional raindrop dashed itself against the eleventh floor windows of the Continental hotel, while inside a group of sports writers and broadcasters did a highly professional job on some slices of cold ham and turkey. Conversation flowed freely and surprisingly enough most of it concerned boxing.

Pro boxing talk had become almost a dead language in Kansas City during the last year, but it underwent a sudden renaissance yesterday with the announcement that the Riverside Stadium corporation had offered Ezzard Charles a guarantee of $75,000 to defend his heavyweight boxing championship here against Rex Layne in an August bout.

A String of Attractions.

The purpose of the food and gab session was to make the formal announcement of the offer and to supply a few details about the attractions which will be offered at Riverside this summer.

For purposes of clearing the record they will include car races, rodeos and possibly night harness racing.

But yesterday boxing was the subject that held most of the attention.

One of the busiest conversationalists was Jim Downing, veteran promoter and boxing figure, who will be a co-promoter in the ring undertaking here.

Downing has been promoting boxing in Salt Lake City, Utah, for seven years and is credited with developing Layne in the pro ranks. Downing has no official tie-up with Layne or his manager, Marty Jenson, but he has helped steer the two through the ups and downs of pro boxing and they follow his advice closely on matters of promoting and match-making.

The Question of Risk.

Since Layne is in demand in New York and Chicago, it seemed appropriate to ask Downing why he wanted to risk the uncertainties of a big title fight in Kansas City, which has never had a championship bout.

Downing was ready and eager to answer.

First of all he is wrapped up in boxing as a sport and business. Downing feels that Chicago and New York have damaged boxing with a near monopoly of the best bouts.

He thinks such a venture as the one proposed here would be a big boost to pro boxing in general and would particularly be a stimulus to it in the West.

Downing of course is anxious to see Layne get a crack at the championship anywhere, but if he can choose the location he would rather have it in some place other than the eastern cities.

Faith in Drawing Power.

Downing said he was particularly impressed with the setup and plans of the Riverside Stadium corporation. He feels Kansas City has enough drawing power to support a heavyweight title fight.

"We aren't trying to buck Madison Square Garden, the Chicago stadium or anyone else," Downing said. "Myself and my associates here simply feel that it's time the West got some of the better fights, that the group in Chicago and New York shouldn't have iron-clad control of the whole business.

"Sure we'd like to see Kansas City become a pro boxing center. But that takes building and right now we'd just like to offer fans in the western part of the country their share of the good fights."

From there the talk ranged to the old time fighters and back to Layne and Charles again.

It's a different and daring promotion the stadium group is cooking up for Kansas City. Its progress should be interesting to watch.

Pacific Coast League.

	W.	L.	Pct.		W.	L.	Pct.
Portland	8	2	.800	Hollywood	5	4	.555
San Diego	7	2	.778	Seattle	3	6	.333
Los Angeles	6	3	.667	Sacramento	3	7	.300
Oakland	6	4	.600	S. Francisco	0	10	.000

YESTERDAY'S RESULTS.

	Innings	R.	H.	E.
Oakland	000 100 020	3	6	4
Sacramento	000 703 00x	10	11	0

Batteries—Harrist, Behrman (4), Tanner (4), Hittle (6), Dahle (7) and Lamanno, Cress and Hairston.

	Innings	R.	H.	E.
Los Angeles	401 100 141	12	15	0
San Diego	020 020 000	4	5	1

Batteries—Adkins and Cash; Welmaker, Clark (4), Santiago (6) and Kinaman.

	Innings	R.	H.	E.
Seattle	000 001 000	1	7	7
Hollywood	001 000 30x	4	4	2

Batteries—Grissom and Montalvo; Schallock and Sandlock.

	Innings	R.	H.	E.
Portland	000 002 220	6	10	1
San Francisco	010 001 000	2	6	3

Batteries—Adams and Rossi; Savage, Perez (8) and Orteig.

Phone your Sunday Star Want Ads today! Avoid the Saturday rush! Open until 9 p. m. Just dial HA. 1200.—Adv.

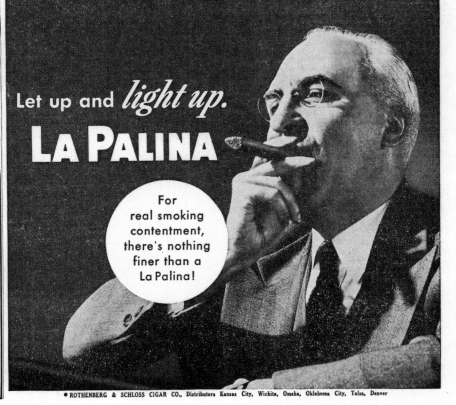

Sporting Comment

By Ernest Mehl.
(The Star's Sports Editor.)

It's the Mixture That Really Counts.

LAKE WALES, FLA., April 6.—In baseball there may be no distance so great as that between a pitcher and a thrower and the other day when the veteran Left-hander Cliff Melton hurled 2-hit ball for five innings against the Toledo Hens Manager George Selkirk gave himself up to the luxury of enjoying the performance.

It was natural then for the conversation to dwell on the craft of pitching after the dinner hour when the chairs were drawn up in front of the hotel.

"Did you ever see Herb Pennock pitch in his later years?" Selkirk asked. "He could show you what could be done with control and a controllable curve ball. He had a fair fast ball but he would use it perhaps only two or three times during a game and then he planned to strike you out with it.

"He'd start off with the wide sweeping curve, then gradually cut it down to a small hook and as a result you never knew what was coming. And then about the time you'd looked at a lot of these curves and you were all set for another one he'd throw the fast ball by you and there you'd be with the bat on your shoulder.

"What he and many others did proves one thing: no pitcher can get by with a fast ball alone unless the fast ball is doing things. I don't care if the pitcher is twice as fast as Lefty Grove was in his prime.

"Suppose, for example, you start driving a car eighty miles an hour down the highway. After a half hour the speed doesn't seem nearly as fast to you as when you started. You get accustomed to it. It's the same way when you're batting against a fast ball pitcher. After you've faced him a time or two he doesn't seem so fast and you can gauge the pitches unless he varies them.

"I never had any trouble against fast ball pitching. Fellows like Grove weren't too tough for me. But the pitchers who mixed 'em up gave me a fit. I was always off time against them."

With a Curve He Won a Long Time.

NAMES of various control experts came to mind. Johnny Schulte remembered the beet-faced Rube Benton, who hurled for so many years for the Minneapolis Millers.

Benton had no fast ball, but he possessed an educated curve which he could break so that the batter was forced to meet the ball on the bat handle. As the result Rube won game after game even after he had reached an age when he could hardly stoop to field a ball.

"There was no way possible for you to hit the ball in the air against him," Schulte said.

"I used Benton as an example to give me for one year the greatest winner I ever had," commented Johnny Neun. "I had a young left-hander by the name of Yocke at Norfolk and I convinced him that all he needed to do was master the curve to the point where it broke down across the plate. He worked with the pitch all winter and the next year won nineteen games and lost one."

Alexander Let Them Hit It.

SELKIRK returned to Grove. "What made Bob a great pitcher," he explained, "wasn't so much the fact he was fast, but that his fast ball jumped. He'd throw it at your waistline and you'd swing there, but then came the jump and all you could do was send up a fly ball. Lefty Gomez also was fast and his fast ball hopped, but he kept it low and made you hit the ball on the ground."

Then there was another perhaps greater than them all. "Look back on how Grover Alexander used to pitch," Selkirk suggested. "He depended on the batter hitting the ball. He seldom tried to strike out anybody. His theory was that it didn't make any difference how hard the ball was hit provided it could be caught.

"The Phils would go into St. Louis, where there often is a strong wind blowing in from left field and Alex would lay the fast ball down the alley for the good right-handed hitters. They'd connect and the result would be a fly ball to left field. They'd curse and accuse him of not having a thing and he'd laugh at them.

"Now, that to my mind is pitching. Throwing hard doesn't mean a thing unless you know what you're doing with the ball. The fast ball that's straight as a string is a picnic to hit against if that's all the pitcher can throw. Unless he has a change of pace or a good curve he's not going to fool anybody very long.

"You saw what happened out there today when Melton pitched. Not very fast, but the fast ball was doing something. Then the curve, the screw ball. I don't suppose he threw a half dozen fast balls, but when they were thrown the batters weren't expecting them.

"It takes kids some time to learn the truth that it isn't how hard they throw, but where they throw the ball that makes the difference between a good pitcher and a bad one. Between a pitcher and a thrower."

BAGNELL TO DIAMOND.

Philadelphia, April 6.(AP)—Francis (Reds) Bagnell, star Penn athlete and winner of the 1950 Helms foundation award as the college football player of the year, tomorrow goes after his ninth major varsity letter. Bagnell will play centerfield against Princeton in the Eastern Intercollegiate league baseball campaign opener.

NAVY ON FOOTBALL SPOT

THEY'LL NEVER FORGET ARMY UPSET, COACH SAYS.

That Buoys Hopes of Followers, but Eddie Erdelatz Believes They're Going a Bit Too Far.

Annapolis, Md., April 6.(AP)—In the spring a young football coach's dreams turn to nightmares of the fall.

Especially if you were "upset" coach of the year before as is Eddie Erdelatz at Navy.

Turning the tables on army in the last game was the best thing that happened to Erdelatz in his first year as a head football coach. Last year, that was. This year it's the worst.

Nobody will forget Navy beat undefeated Army.

High in Optimism.

"Boy, this year we're really going to roll," is Eddie's greeting from fans wherever he goes. Around the academy, too.

"They just won't close the lid on that trunk with all the clippings," is Eddie's way to describe it.

Erdelatz is trying to convince everybody, including the players, they've got to play eight teams again this season. Plus Army, as usual.

"And everybody's got the idea our schedule has been lightened. Look at it," advises Erdelatz.

The Middies still play seven of last year's nine opponents. The only one they beat, not counting Army, was Columbia. And they meet Yale and Rice instead of Southern California, one of the others they whipped, and Tulane.

How about the squad?

Not to run down the players he has, but Coach Erdelatz goes over his spring practice roster in a way to squelch that talk of "undefeated" the most rabid Navy fans are spreading.

To be sure, every position has at least one player from last year's varsity. But they weren't first stringers and there's not much behind each.

Freshman Crop Lean.

For instance, the help a coach usually looks for from among his freshmen is lacking. Out of fifty-two players spring practicing, six are freshmen. Coach Erdelatz believes three probably will stick with the varsity.

He's even brought up a couple of former 150-pound team players. And a few who didn't play football of any kind last year along with some Jay-Vees.

The Navy mentor finds himself exceptionally short on ends and defensive backs. He's got two experienced—one on each side—and the others are names he isn't yet even familiar with.

At tackle, there are three dependables. They'll be switched from left to right and offense to defense so as to give one a blow on the bench.

Navy is solid at center and guards, barring injuries, in Coach Erdelatz's mind.

Offensively, the burden will be upon two of last year's regulars, Quarterback Bob Zastrow and Frank Hauff. Outside of Fullback Freknoc, another holdover, Eddie has found little exciting among his ball carriers and none yet to fill the bill on defense in the backfield.

Section 5 | SPORTS BOATS AUTOMOBILES SHIPS—WEATHER REPORTS

The New York Times.

SPORTS SHOPPING GUIDE SITUATIONS WANTED BUSINESS OPPORTUNITIES | Section 5

S Copyright, 1951, by The New York Times Company. SUNDAY, APRIL 15, 1951. L+ S

CAMBRIDGE SCORES OVER YALE'S SHELL BY FOUR LENGTHS

First Eight-Oared Crew From Britain to Appear in U. S. Shows Brilliant Form

ELIS LOSE BEFORE 10,000

Visitors Cheered After Race on Housatonic—New Haven Men Take 2 Early Tests

By ALLISON DANZIG
Special to THE NEW YORK TIMES.

DERBY, Conn., April 14—The first appearance of an English eight-oared crew in American waters resulted in a sweeping triumph for Cambridge University over Yale today.

Off the mark with an almost unbelievable burst of speed, the British oarsmen opened up a half-length lead in the first quarter mile of the mile-and-three-quarter race over the fairly smooth Housatonic River. Rowing with faultless synchronization, whatever the rate of stroke, they widened the margin to a full boat length at a half mile and went away steadily to win by four lengths in 8:22.4. Yale was clocked in 8:36.

Some 10,000 spectators lined the Housatonic on the Derby and Shelton sides for the unprecedented unveiling of an English eight in this country—the eight that earned the history-making trip to the United States by defeating Oxford by twelve lengths on the Thames last month. If there was any feeling of disappointment over the failure of the American crew to make a close race of its first test under its new coach, Jim Rathschmidt, it was not apparent from the swelling outburst of cheers that greeted Cambridge as it shot across the finish line.

Superlatives Are Merited

As the winning shell was paddled to the boathouse the tribute increased in volume, and Old Blues of both Cambridge and Yale rushed down to the float to shower the happy, if tired, young Britons with congratulations. The superlatives that were lavished upon them were out of the ordinary and they were well merited, for this was an extraordinarily fine eight.

"The finest crew ever to row in American waters," was one appraisal.

Robert Hall, Yale's athletic director, may have been carried away with enthusiasm in so expressing himself as he bestowed tie pins to each of the Cantabrigians—gifts from the Eli oarsmen. Whether or not Cambridge is that good will be better known Thursday evening after its second and final race with Harvard, M. I. T. and Boston University on the Charles at Boston. For Harvard, with a veteran boatload, as compared with Yale's largely inexperienced eight, and the Crimson's traditional superiority, figures to put the British oarsmen to a much sterner test.

But whatever fortune awaits Cambridge on the Charles, its performance this chilly afternoon, beneath overcast skies that held the threat of rain, was up to the very highest standards of American rowing. Even so reserved a figure as Ed Leader, who boated many fine Yale crews in years past, was enraptured by the perfection of the English oarsmanship and bespoke his appreciation to Harold Rickett, Cambridge's amateur coach.

Looks Ahead to Boston

Rickett was in a happy mood over the splendid showing of his eight in this all-important international test, though his elation was tempered by consideration to the stiffer fight ahead at Boston. The London stockbroker, who rowed for Cambridge in his undergraduate days, said; "This is the biggest thrill for me, that an English crew could win in America. But we've got a job on Thursday."

The Cambridge coach said that his crew today surpassed its effort in defeating Oxford by the second biggest margin in the ninety-seven year history of that rivalry. "I deliberately did not work them up to a peak, for Oxford," he said. "We started at 35½ against Oxford, rowed at 30 thereafter until we finished at 36. I wound them up more here. We will have to wind them up still more for Thursday."

How any crew could be wound up more than Cambridge was at the start of today's race is not easy to visualize. It fairly exploded from the stake boats as the referee, Frederick Sheffield, sent the crews off, zooming away as though jet-propelled.

Every blade was in and out of the water with the precision of

Continued on Page 3, Column 3

Scottish Team Wins As 100,000 Watch

By The Associated Press.

LONDON, April 14—A brilliant Scottish team defeated England, 3—2, in the traditional international soccer match before 100,000 fans at Wembley Stadium today.

The Scots were far better than the score indicated but they wasted half a dozen scoring chances in the first half. It ended 1—1.

They added two goals in the first seven minutes of the second half and the outcome was never in doubt. England played all except the first twelve minutes of the game with only ten men.

Wilf Mannion of Middlesbrough, inside right for England, fractured his right cheekbone in a collision and had to be taken to a hospital. The rules in force here do not allow for substitutes.

PRINCETON'S CREW VICTOR OVER NAVY

Triumphs by Three Quarters of a Length—Tiger Cubs on Top, Jayvees Lose

By LINCOLN A. WERDEN
Special to THE NEW YORK TIMES.

PRINCETON, N. J., April 14—Princeton's rowing inaugural gained a warming glow under cool, grey skies today as the Tigers' varsity crew outsprinted Navy on Lake Carnegie to win by three-quarters of a length.

After gaining an edge in the first mile, the Tigers came into the decisive last quarter of the mile with an approximate lead of three-quarters. Then the beat went up in the Navy shell for a bid to cut down Princeton, but the Tiger sophomore stroke, Sam Gibbon, answered the challenge in his first varsity test.

With the encouraging shouts of Princeton enthusiasts spurring it on, the Tiger crew responded with a sprint of its own that held the margin safely and enabled Princeton to come on with its first triumph of its sixth season under Coach Delos (Dutch) Schoch.

Callow in Navy Debut

It was not the only beginning of another rowing year for Navy but it marked the debut at the Naval Academy of Coach Russell (Rusty) Callow, ex-Penn mentor, who succeeded the late Commander Buck Walsh at Annapolis.

Navy, which has been experimenting in its boatings during the last ten days, had a good looking varsity and its junior varsity succeeded in turning back Princeton in a preliminary by a three-quarters of a length. But, the major share of the day's rowing honors went to Princeton, for the Tiger freshmen set the stage with a commendable opening victory.

Princeton's varsity time was 9:23.4 to Navy's 9:25 and although a following breeze helped, the lake was calm by the time the big crews were off. The trophy at stake was the Navy-Princeton Cup donated by alumni and which the Tigers were defending.

In the rivalry thus far, the midshipmen have recorded eighteen triumphs to Princeton's nine, including today's. At the outset, Princeton moved out by a few feet in the varsity test, which was over a mile and three-quarters, as were the other races, and led by the end of the mile.

The crews had been almost even during the first phases after Navy had momentarily been ahead at the three-quarter mile.

A closing sprint by Navy staved off Princeton's bid in the junior varsity race that developed into a keen duel all the way down the

Continued on Page 3, Column 2

On and Off the Diamond as the Yankees and Dodgers Met in Brooklyn

Snider of Brooklyn out trying to steal second in the first inning. MacDougald takes Berra's throw as Umpire Berry covers the play.

Manager Casey Stengel and Joe DiMaggio talking with Mickey Mantle before the game
The New York Times (by Ernest Sisto)

YANKS TURN BACK DODGERS, 11 TO 5, AT EBBETS FIELD

Shea, Porterfield Hurl Well for Bombers Before 8,782—Mantle Plays in Right

JOHNSON WALLOPS HOMER

Connects With One On in 9th —Campanella, Snider Drive 4-Baggers for Brooks

By LOUIS EFFRAT

Slightly less than phenomenal was Mickey Mantle, the spring sensation of the Yankees—or is it Kansas City?—in his big-town debut yesterday at Ebbets Field, where Casey Stengel's champions routed the Dodgers, 11—5, before 8,782 chilled spectators.

The 19-year-old switch-hitter batted right against southpaw Preacher Roe and turned around against Carl Erskine and Bud Podbielan. Mickey's only success was at Roe's expense. He slapped the portsider's first pitch over Pee Wee Reese's head for a single. The next time he was safe on a fielder's choice. Then, in succession, he walked, fanned and popped out.

Those who had braved chills to get a first look at the most publicized rookie since Joe DiMaggio came up probably expected more. But if Mantle's first local appearance proved little, there were extenuating circumstances. The fact is that Mickey arrived at 7:30 A. M. in a plane from Kansas City. The night flight had probably tired the youngster.

Stengel had not planned to play Mantle yesterday, but a half hour before game-time Mickey asked the pilot to use him. Having watched the converted infielder hit six balls into the stands, two into the top deck, during batting practice, Stengel agreed and Mickey was sent to right field.

Average Up 6 Points

A .387 hitter when he faced Roe, Mantle saw his average rise six points, which is fair-to-middlin' punching in any league. He threw out Cal Abrams, who tried to score from second on Jackie Robinson's single to right in the sixth. Yogi Berra was waiting with the ball when Abrams slid to the plate.

All in all, therefore, it was not too bad a showing for Mickey. All the players like him and insist he cannot miss making the big league, but whether it will be this season remains a matter of conjecture.

The Yankee powers-that-be were silent regarding Mantle's immediate future. They announced that the Kansas City contracts of Infielder Gil McDougald and Pitcher Tom Morgan had been taken over by the New York club, but nothing was said concerning Mantle or Frank (Spec) Shea.

Mantle and Shea—the latter pitched the first five innings yesterday and was the winning hurler—also are signed to Kansas City contracts. Whether these two are to be moved up to the parent club is a question that Stengel, George Weiss and Dan Topping preferred to sleep on another night.

Weiss and Topping were on hand to watch the Naugatuck right-hander work for the first time in more than a week. Spec, his arm apparently all right, pulled a muscle in his side eight days ago. Except for one inning, the fourth, his performance was top-flight. Shea yielded three runs and five hits and walked only one, which is fairly good pitching against a powerful outfit like the Dodgers. Bob Porterfield, who worked the last four frames, was reached for seven hits and two runs and, on the whole, looked good, too.

Campy Hits Solo 4-Bagger

The scoring against Shea was accomplished by homers. Roy Campanella hit a solo in the second and in the fourth an infield hit by Abrams was followed by Duke Snider's drive into Bedford Avenue.

Trailing, 1—0, the Yankees came up in the third and counted three against Roe. Gene Markland singled and went all the way around on Shea's double against the railing in left. Jackie Jensen was safe at second on a high throw by Reese, Shea scoring on the overthrow. Jensen went to third on McDougald's fly to right and scored on Mantle's grounder to Rocky Bridges at third. McDougald slid under Bridges' throw to the plate.

Snider's homer tied it in the fourth, but in the sixth, Berra doubled, Johnny Mize walked and Johnny Hopp ran for him. Whereupon a single by Billy Johnson, who walloped a two-run homer in the four-run ninth, edged the Yankees in front again. An error, a

Continued on Page 2, Column 6

Sonic Takes Experimental No. 2 As Uncle Miltie Finishes Eighth

King Ranch Colt, Paying $28.80, Defeats Jumbo, a 79-1 Shot, by Half Length at Jamaica—Nullify Is Third

By JAMES ROACH

The Kentucky Derby favorite had a bad afternoon at Jamaica yesterday. So did those in the crowd of 40,351 who had pounded him down to a shade over 1 to 3 in the $27,500 Experimental Handicap No. 2.

Joseph J. Colando's Uncle Miltie, bet as if he were home free, was a toiling eighth in the field of ten 3-year-olds as first money of $18.-500 was taken by the King Ranch's Sonic, the lightweight in the line-up. Sonic, ridden by Apprentice Jack Colaneri, carried only 105 pounds to the favorite's high of 126.

It was the first stakes success for (a) the horse, and (b) the rider. Sonic was the $28.80-for-$2 third choice.

Those who had made across the board investments on the 79-to-1 outsider were the ones who cut loose with the loudest whoops when the pay-offs were posted. That outsider was Hal Price Headley's Jumbo, who led 'em into the stretch and managed to finish second, only half a length away from the winner. Jumbo paid $60.60 to place, $23.40 to show.

Third, beaten a nose by Jumbo, was the Phantom Farm's Nullify, who had swung for the stretch in seventh place, and fourth, a length

Continued on Page 4, Column 6

TIGHT RACES LOOM IN MAJOR LEAGUES

Washington, Cincinnati Games Promise to Launch Another Keen Season Tomorrow

By JOHN DREBINGER

To expect major league baseball to come up with another pair of sizzling flag races such as have characterized the past four or five campaigns, with their ties and near-ties, seems a pretty large order.

Yet that is exactly what fans and experts are confidently looking forward to as the curtain prepares to rise on another stirring season.

A terrific three-cornered pennant battle seems in prospect in the 75-year-old National League, which launches its seventy-sixth flag race this week.

Three clubs, and possibly four, are expected to fight it out for top honors as the American League launches its fifty-first pennant scramble.

Both circuits will get off to so-called "stagger starts" and after that they'll doubtless have everybody staggering.

In Washington tomorrow President Truman, beset as he is with national and international problems, nevertheless is expected to set aside his cares for a few hours as he journeys out to Griffith Stadium to toss out the first ball that will send the American League on its way with Bucky Harris' Senators playing host to the world champion Yankees.

At the same time the Reds and Pirates will get a one-day jump on the remainder of the National League field by giving Cincinnati its traditional inaugural.

On Tuesday all the clubs will see action. This will bring Casey Stengel's Bombers into the Yankee Stadium to battle their outstanding challengers, the Red Sox, while the other American League openers will see the Senators in Philadelphia in a night game, the Indians in Detroit and the White Sox in St. Louis.

In the National League, the Dodgers, with Branch Rickey gone and Chuck Dressen holding the managerial reins, will launch their pennant bid at Ebbets Field against the team that beat them out by a whisker last October, the Phillies. Leo Durocher's Giants will battle the Braves in Boston, the Cardinals

Continued on Page 2, Column 2

Giants' Three-Run Drive in Fourth Tops Indians, 4-2, to Clinch Series

Stanky's Double and Lockman's Single Pace Attack—Bowman and Spencer Excel on Mound—Irvin Extends Streak

By JOSEPH M. SHEEHAN

Carrying lightly the burden of pennant favoritism that has been thrust on them by a press box jury, the Giants yesterday celebrated their return to the Polo Grounds by beating the Cleveland Indians, 4—2, before 2,937 chilled spectators.

Their victory put the Giants out of reach of the Indians in this spring series, which ends today. It was their sixth 1951 triumph over Cleveland, which has won three games. One contest ended in a tie.

While the slugging power that has distinguished their circuitous tour up from the South was not much in evidence, Leo Durocher's hustling charges showed enough offensive opportunism to cash in on splendid pitching by two of their younger mound aspirants.

Roger Bowman, willowy 23-year-old left-hander who led the International League in strikeouts last year, worked six innings, and George Spencer, husky right-hander who was graduated from the defunct Jersey City Little Giants last year, finished the game. They had the Indians at their mercy all the way.

Although Cleveland made nine hits, as against the seven the Giants collected off Early Wynn and George Zuverink, all but two of the enemy safeties were of the scratchy variety. Had Bowman's luck been better, the Indians would have been shut out.

In a determined bid to win one of the two open berths on the nine-man mound staff Durocher plans to carry, the slender southpaw turned in an eye-catching performance.

Shooting for the corners with a whistling fast ball and a tantalizing slow curve, Bowman struck out seven, all within the first four in-

Continued on Page 2, Column 2

KROOG'S NO-HITTER DOWNS N. Y. U., 2-0

Lafayette Hurler Gains Second Shutout as Leopards Collect Twelve Blows at Easton

Special to THE NEW YORK TIMES.

EASTON, Pa., April 14—Fred Kroog, big right-hander from East Orange, N. J., hurled a no-hit game today as Lafayette blanked New York University here, 2 to 0.

Only four Violet players reached base, all on walks. Kroog struck out seven of the thirty-one batters he faced.

Maurice Meyers started for the Violet and gave up ten hits and both runs in the seven innings he was on the mound. John Kuharetz pitched the final inning and yielded two more safeties.

Today's shutout was the second for Kroog, who blanked Army with two hits in the opening game. He retired the last fifteen men in order and was given fine support as

Continued on Page 8, Column 3

COLUMBIA DEFEATS PRINCETON NINE, 4-3

Tracy, Fanning Seven, Victor on Mound as Tigers Suffer First League Setback

By JOSEPH C. NICHOLS

With right-hander Kermit Tracy contributing a fine performance on the mound, the Columbia baseball team defeated Princeton yesterday at Baker Field. Taking the lead in the fifth inning the Lions held the edge from there on to win by the score of 4 to 3.

The game was played at a brisk clip, and was witnessed by an enthusiastic gallery. When Tracy struck out the last Princeton batter the onlookers cheered him, in appreciation of the Lions' triumph over a co-champion of the Eastern Intercollegiate League. The Tigers divided the crown with Army in 1950. It was Princeton's first league defeat this season.

Tracy's pitching opponent was Harry Brightman, left-hander who yielded seven hits. Tracy was touched for only five blows and struck out seven batters while Brightman fanned four. The latter was strong at the start, though, and held the Lions hitless until the fifth.

The Tigers were sharper in the field, making only one error as against Columbia's three. The single Princeton misplay, however, was a sad one for the visitors, resulting in two runs for the Lions.

The error was committed by Catcher Willard Prior, who overthrew first base in an effort to catch a runner. The misplay took the edge off an otherwise excellent showing by the Tiger receiver, who was the hitting star of the day with three singles out of four attempts. Neither side made an extra-base hit.

Princeton was first to score, with a run in the third inning, Larry Becker reaching the plate on a sacrifice and an error. The Lions erased their rivals' advantage in the fifth, Tracy opening the inning with a single. Safe bunts by Tom Powers and Don Kimtis loaded the bases with none

Continued on Page 8, Column 2

ALICE BAUER'S 75 LEADS AT DALLAS

Betty Jameson, Patty Berg Next With 77's in Start of Weathervane Golf

By The Associated Press.

DALLAS, April 14—Alice Bauer, diminutive blonde from Midland, Tex., shot an even par 75 today to take the lead in the first 18-hole round of the $17,000, 144-hole women's cross-country Weathervane golf tournament.

Miss Bauer was the only player in a field of forty-four able to match par on the windy, dusty, 6,100-yard Lakewood Country Club course.

Tying for second place at 77 were Betty Jameson of San Antonio and Patty Berg of Minneapolis—while one stroke back was Louise Suggs of Carrollton, Ga. All four of the leaders are professionals.

Mrs. Babe Didrickson Zaharias

Continued on Page 4, Column 1

CANADIENS WIN, 3-2, TIE HOCKEY SERIES

Trip Leafs on Richard's Goal in Sudden-Death Overtime Period at Toronto

By The United Press.

TORONTO, April 14—Maurice (Rocket) Richard smashed home a goal at 2:55 of a sudden-death overtime period tonight to give the Montreal Canadiens a 3-to-2 victory over the Toronto Maple Leafs and square their Stanley Cup final play-off series at one game apiece.

A near-capacity crowd of 14,567 saw the veteran right winger, highest scorer in modern hockey history, take a long pass from Doug Harvey at the Leaf blueline and break in on the goal alone. Goalie Turk Broda of Toronto came out to block him, but the shifty Richard skated calmly around him to sink the clincher.

It was the third game-winning overtime tally of this year's Stanley Cup series for Richard. He pulled the trick twice against Detroit.

The teams now move back to Montreal, Tuesday and Thursday, for the next two clashes. Sid Smith won the first game for Toronto by the identical score, also on an overtime goal.

Ted Kennedy had tied the score for Toronto at 8:16 of the third period to force the overtime session as the Leafs overcame a 2-to-0 deficit. The goal at first was credited to Tod Sloan, but changed later by the official scorer. Rookie Paul Masnick and veteran Billy Reay had built up a lead for the Canadiens with tallies in the first and second periods.

Sid Smith was the other Leaf scorer, with Max Bentley and Kennedy assisting, shortly after Reay's second-period marker.

In winning their first game this year on Toronto ice, the Canadiens were outshot by 36—24. Referee George Gravel ruled with a tight hand, calling only six penalties, three to each team. The game threatened to get out of hand in

Continued on Page 7, Column 4

Repetoire Beats Alerted by Head In $23,025 Chesapeake at Laurel

By MICHAEL STRAUSS
Special to THE NEW YORK TIMES.

LAUREL, Md., April 14—The colt who has been having things all his own way at Laurel this season indicated he has no desire to relinquish his monopoly. At least that's the way it appeared today to a crowd of 19,073 as Repetoire, Mrs. N. A. Mikell's color-bearer raced to victory in the $23,025 Chesapeake Stakes.

Competing in a field of seven, the 3-year-old son of Happy Argo and My Hattie turned in his usual workmanlike performance. He forged to the front at the start of the mile-and-sixteenth test and remained there. Hampton Stable's Alerted and T. G. May's Whirling Bat finished behind the victor in that order.

The outcome of the event, considered as a testing block for potential triple-crown aspirants, added considerable stature to the Mikell speedster, who has proved the epitome of consistency. The victory was the third consecutive stake triumph at the Maryland oval and raised the colt's earnings during his career to $54,190.

Particularly pleased with the colt's showing was Trainer Alfred Jensen. The latter, down in the winner circle to greet Jockey Peter McLean as he brought in the star 3-year-old for the final weighing, lost little time in announcing that Repetoire, barring unforeseen accident, would make the trip to Churchill Downs for the Kentucky Derby.

In keeping with his recent successes here, Repetoire's triumph was gained by a narrow margin. He had only a head the best of it over Alerted and there were many

Continued on Page 4, Column 4

Carol Pence Breaks Own Record In Title Swim; Relay Mark Set

By The Associated Press.

HOUSTON, April 14—New American and National A. A. U. women's indoor swimming records were set today by Lafayette, Ind., Swim Club stars.

Miss Carol Pence, 21-year-old Purdue University senior, broke her own 200-yard breast stroke American record and then saw her team-mates set a new national mark in the 400-yard free style relay.

Miss Pence had a time of 2 minutes and 45 seconds in the national A. A. U. women's indoor swim meet's new 200-yard breast-stroke event, three seconds better than her American record-shattering performance of a year ago.

The Lafayette relay team, anchored brilliantly by Miss Betty Mullen, upset the favored Town Club of Chicago, the defending champion, with a 4:08.7. This took four-tenths of a second off the previous national record set in 1944 at Oakland, Calif., by the Multnomah Athletic Club of Portland, Ore., which placed third today.

Another Lafayette star, Miss Ann Moss, won the meet's new 400-yard free-style event with a time of 4:52.3. She later teamed with Miss Mullen, Miss Sheila Donahue and Miss Anna Hayes in collecting the relay championship.

The times set by Miss Pence and Miss Moss also are being accepted as A. A. U. championships in that this is the first time either race was held in a national indoor meet. Today's distances replaced the old 220 breast-stroke and 440-yard free-style events.

There were protests over the relay time being held a national record. The coach of one team

Continued on Page 8, Column 4

Yanks Blank Red Sox in First Game Before 44,860; Giants Shut Out Braves

RASCHI AND JENSEN SPARK 5-0 TRIUMPH

Yankee Ace Holds Red Sox to 6 Singles—Outfielder Gets a 2-Run Homer in Third

THEN HE DOUBLES IN SIXTH

3 Tallies Follow to Rout Wight —Bombers Honored by Many Awards Before Contest

By JOHN DREBINGER

Amid the usual pomp of a Stadium inaugural, the Yankees launched the 1951 American League season yesterday in much the same manner that they had closed the 1950 campaign last October.

They unfurled their world series banner in the snappy breeze and then, to the thunderous cheers of 44,860 paying eye witnesses, those extraordinary Bombers proceeded to take that first long stride toward another flag by convincingly drubbing those perennial spring favorites, the Red Sox.

The score of 5 to 0 scarcely begins to describe the disparity that appeared to exist between the two clubs for this important day at least.

Vic Raschi, the big wheel of Casey Stengel's mound staff, hurled the shut-out, scattering six hits, all singles, across as many innings.

Behind this effective hurling, Jackie Jensen, the blond thatched sophomore outfielder, was the surprise entry to steal the thunder of the performance. Named to play left field because Hank Bauer was sidelined with a charley horse, the bonus freshman of last year opened the scoring with a two-run homer in the third inning that sailed into the right-field stand.

Californian Doubles in Sixth

In the sixth, the husky Californian led off with a two-bagger against Southpaw Bill Wight, among the latest of Boston acquisitions the past winter. In the wake of that double came solid singles by Mickey Mantle, tagged as the rookie sensation of 1951, the venerable Joe DiMaggio and robust Yogi Berra.

The broadside, following a slight fielding miscalculation on the part of Steve O'Neill's minions, sent three tallies skipping over the plate. It routed Wight and just about completed the day's work for both sides.

Just once did the Bosox so much as offer a threatening gesture. That was right at the start and ironically the elder DiMaggio wrecked the effort.

The spectators had just settled back into their seats after a long series of presentations when Dom DiMaggio ripped one of Raschi's offerings into right-field for a single. Bill Goodman followed with a blooper into short center that appeared tagged as another single.

From deep centre, DiMaggio, J., admittedly not the nimble footed performer of old, turned back the clock as he streaked over the freshly seeded turf and snared the ball inches off the ground.

Little Professor Gets a Lesson

Since the Yankees trained on the Pacific coast this year and the Red Sox in their familiar Sarasota lair, somebody must have slightly misinformed brother Dom on just how far back brother Joe had gone in his fielding. For the little professor was virtually at second base when the Clipper made that amazing catch, so the latter almost could have walked to first base to complete the double play.

With that twin killing, which the Clipper made with the conventional toss to Johnny Mize at first, one could hear the lock on the iron door click once again on Boston hopes. Only two men had batted, but one could sense the end was written for another day, and perhaps another season, even though Ted Williams did follow resolutely with a single.

As in the past, the Tom Yawkey entry reached the Stadium loaded with additional strength. At short it had the talented Lou Boudreau and the former Cleveland skipper acquitted himself well. He got one of the six singles and, though he fumbled one ball for an inconsequential error, aided in the making of two sharp double plays.

Stephens Still in Line-up

But force of habit seems to exert an astounding influence upon a Red Sox manager, whether he be the capable O'Neill or the retired Joe McCarthy. Despite all the spring warnings that Vern Stephens, the strictly Fenway Park player, would not appear in a Boston line-up on the road and that Johnny Pesky would be the third sacker, Junior occupied the hot corner in the line-up and batted in the clean-up spot.

In that important post he got no hits, slapped into a double play and ironically in the field committed a mental slip at third that paved the way for the Yanks' decisive thrust in the sixth.

To young Jerry Coleman went the distinction of the first Yankee hit, a single to left in the third. Raschi sacrificed and a moment later Jensen, a right-handed batter, stroked a hefty shot into the right-field stand.

Coleman almost did it again for the Yanks in the fifth when he singled to right behind a pass to Bill Johnson, but a fine peg by Goodman nipped Buffalo Bill at third.

There was no checking the Bombers in the sixth, though. Following Jensen's double, also to right, Phil Rizzuto bunted.

As a bunt it wasn't up to Li'l Phil's best. It was tapped pretty hard and almost into pitcher Wight's hands. A put-out at third appeared simple, but Stephens failed to get back in time, missed the tag and the Yanks had runners on first and third.

Mantle, making his debut as a Yankee, lashed a single into left and Jensen scored. DiMaggio, J., followed with another to the same spot and Rizzuto scored. Berra slammed one into center for the third run and Wight was through.

Ellis Kinder checked the drive, gave way to a pinch-hitter and then Maurice McDermott blanked the Bombers the rest of the way.

Only two Boston runners got to second. None reached third.

In the sixth Williams drew a pass, but Rizzuto made an electrifying stop on Stephens' grounder in deep short and started a twin killing. In the eighth Goodman singled, only to be forced by Williams. After Walt Dropo had singled in the ninth the battle ended as that matchless pair, Rizzuto and Coleman, turned on one more eye-filling double play.

Pre-Game Awards Numerous

In the pre-game ceremonies, which opened with the traditional parade to the center-field flagpole behind Major Francis Sutherland's Seventh Regiment Band, prizes and awards were tossed about at home plate as if it were bank night at the lodge.

Dick Butler, deputy for the absent baseball commissioner, Albert B. Chandler, presented to all the Yankee players their individual world series emblems in the form of rings or wrist watches.

President Will Harridge of the American League bestowed upon Rizzuto the Kenesaw Mountain Landis award as the circuit's most valuable player and to the youthful Coleman went the New York Baseball Writers' Babe Ruth memorial plaque as the outstanding player in the 1950 world series.

Biggest prize of all was the three-and-a-half-foot trophy given to Mel Allen by the Sporting News as the foremost baseball broadcaster of 1950. Sporting News awards also went to Rizzuto as the year's No. 1 player and to George M. Weiss, Yankee general manager, as baseball's outstanding executive.

In the parade were Police Commissioner Thomas F. Murphy, easily recognizable as he towered above everyone else in his familiar bowler hat, and Fire Commissioner George P. Monaghan. Others to march, along with the players of both clubs, were James J. Lyons, Bronx Borough President, and the Yanks' official family, President Dan Topping, Vice President Del Webb and Weiss.

In the center-field flagpole ceremonies, Miss Lucy Monroe sang the Star Spangled Banner to the raising of the American flag, accomplished by three strong-armed young marines, after which Stengel, in a Mighty Casey solo act, raised the world series pennant all by himself.

As a reminder of last year, Eddie (Whitey) Ford, freshman star of 1950, but now a rookie in the Army, tossed out the first ball.

OPENING-DAY CEREMONIES AND A HIGHLIGHT OF YESTERDAY'S GAME AT YANKEE STADIUM

Whitey Ford, former Yankee hurler, throwing out the first ball as Managers Casey Stengel and Steve O'Neill look on.

Phil Rizzuto receiving from President William Harridge the Landis Award for being the most valuable player in the American League last year.

Jackie Jensen being congratulated by Rizzuto, the next batter, after his homer in the third inning. The umpire is Bill McGowan.

The New York Times (by Ernest Sisto)

Yankees' Box Score

BOSTON (A.)

	ab.	r.	h.	po.	a.
D.DiMag'o, cf.	3	0	2	1	0
Goodman, rf.	3	0	1	2	1
Williams, lf.	3	0	1	1	0
Stephens, 3b.	4	0	0	2	2
Dropo, 1b.	4	0	1	10	0
Doerr, 2b.	4	0	0	3	2
Boudreau, ss.	4	0	1	1	3
Rosar, c.	2	0	0	4	1
Wight, p.	2	0	0	0	2
Kinder, p.	0	0	0	0	0
aMaxwell	1	0	0	0	0
McDerm'tt, p.	0	0	0	0	1
Total	30	0	6	24	12

NEW YORK (A.)

	ab.	r.	h.	po.	a.
Jensen, lf.	4	2	2	3	0
Rizzuto, ss.	3	1	0	1	3
Mantle, rf.	4	1	1	3	0
J.DiMag'o, cf.	4	0	1	2	1
Berra, c.	2	0	1	6	0
Mize, 1b.	3	0	0	8	0
Collins, 1b.	0	0	0	1	0
Johnson, 3b.	2	0	0	1	1
Coleman, 2b.	3	1	2	2	4
Raschi, p.	2	0	0	0	1
Total	27	5	7	27	10

aBatted for Kinder in seventh.

Boston .... 0 0 0 0 0 0 0 0 0—0
New York .... 0 0 2 0 0 3 0 0 ..—5

Error—Boudreau.
Runs batted in—Jensen 2, Mantle, J DiMaggio, Berra.
Two-base hit—Jensen. Home run—Jensen. Sacrifices—Raschi, Rizzuto. Double plays—J. DiMaggio and Mize; Rizzuto, Coleman and Mize; Wight Boudreau and Dropo; Boudreau, Doerr and Dropo; Rizzuto, Coleman and Collins. Left on bases—New York 2, Boston 7. Bases on balls—Off Wight 2, Raschi 4. Struck out—By Raschi 6, Wight 1, McDermott 1. Hits—Off Wight 7 in 5 innings; McDermott 0 in 2, Kinder 0 in 1. Winning pitcher—Raschi (1—0). Losing pitcher—Wight (0—1). Umpires—McGowan, McKinley, Honochick and Soar. Time of game—2:12. Attendance—44,860.

Major League Baseball

Wednesday, April 18, 1951

American League

YESTERDAY'S RESULTS

New York 5, Boston 0.
Chicago 17, St. Louis 3.
Cleveland 2, Detroit 1.
Washington 6, Philadelphia 1 (night).

STANDING OF THE CLUBS

	New York	Chicago	Cleveland	Wash'gtn	Philadel	Boston	Detroit	St. Louis	Won	Lost	Perc'tage	Games Behind
N. Y.	—	0	0	0	0	1	0	0	1	0	1.000	—
Chic.	0	—	0	0	0	0	0	1	1	0	1.000	—
Cleve.	0	0	—	0	0	0	1	0	1	0	1.000	—
Wash.	0	0	0	—	1	0	0	0	1	0	1.000	—
Phila.	0	0	0	0	—	0	0	0	0	1	.000	1
Bost.	0	0	0	0	0	—	0	0	0	1	.000	1
Det.	0	0	0	0	0	0	—	0	0	1	.000	1
St. L.	0	0	0	0	0	0	0	—	0	1	.000	1
Lost	0	0	0	0	1	1	1	1	—	—		

TODAY'S PROBABLE PITCHERS

Boston at New York (2:30 P. M.) —Taylor (2-0) vs. Lopat (18-8).
Chicago at St. Louis (night)—Kretlow (0-2) vs. Widmar (7-15).
Cleveland at Detroit—Wynn (18-8) vs. Trout (13-5).
Washington at Philadelphia (night) —Hudson (14-14) vs. Brissie (7-19).

National League

YESTERDAY'S RESULTS

New York 4, Boston 0.
Philadelphia 5, Brooklyn 2.
Chicago 8, Cincinnati 3.
Pittsburgh 5, St. Louis 4.

STANDING OF THE CLUBS

	Pittsb'gh	New York	Chicago	Philadel	Brooklyn	Boston	St. Louis	Cincinnati	Won	Lost	Perc'tage	Games Behind
Pitts.	—	0	0	0	0	0	1	1	2	0	1.000	—
N. Y.	0	—	0	0	0	1	0	0	1	0	1.000	½
Chic.	0	0	—	0	0	0	0	1	1	0	1.000	½
Phila.	0	0	0	—	1	0	0	0	1	0	1.000	½
Bklyn.	0	0	0	0	—	0	0	0	0	1	.000	1½
Bost.	0	0	0	0	0	—	0	0	0	1	.000	1½
St. L.	0	0	0	0	0	0	—	0	0	1	.000	1½
Cinc.	0	0	0	0	0	0	0	—	0	2	.000	2
Lost	0	0	0	0	1	1	1	2	—	—		

TODAY'S PROBABLE PITCHERS

Philadelphia at Brooklyn (1:30 P. M.)—Church (8-6) vs. Roe (19-11).
New York at Boston—Maglie (18-4) vs. Sain (20-13).
Other clubs not scheduled.

(Figures in parentheses indicate last season's won-and-lost records.)

YANKS HONORED BY BRONX

500 Attend Annual Dinner—Lyons Is Toastmaster

The Yankees were the guests last night at the Hotel Concourse Plaza, Bronx, at the annual dinner tendered by the People of the Bronx. About 500 were on hand, with Borough President John J. Lyons the toastmaster.

Rabbi Henry A. Schorr of the Temple Adath Israel, the Rev. Lawrence Walsh, Fordham director of athletics; Tom Tozzi, president of the Bronx Board of Trade; Lawrence Gerosa, president of the Bronx Chamber of Commerce, and Andy Kennedy, president of the Bronx Real Estate Board, were among the speakers.

Speaking for the Yankees were President Dan Topping and Manager Casey Stengel.

Texas Aggies Aide Resigns

COLLEGE STATION, Tex., April 17 (UP)—Bill (Dog) Dawson, Texas A & M College football end coach, resigned today to take a business position.

Jansen 5-Hitter Trips Boston, 4-0, As Giants Shake Opening-Day Jinx

New York Scores One Run Against Bickford in Fourth, Two in Fifth and Another in Seventh—Braves Shackled From Start

By JAMES P. DAWSON

Special to THE NEW YORK TIMES.

BOSTON, April 17—The tradition which for some years had denied the Giants an opening-day victory was thrust aside today at Braves Field.

The club which Leo Durocher describes as the best-conditioned squad he ever took out of a spring training camp ripped an icicle-crusted lid off the season by white-washing the Boston hosts before a thoroughly chilled gathering of 6,081. The score was 4 to 0.

The victim of the jinx which had hobbled the Giants for disappointing years pitched gloriously in this triumph for Larry Jansen, slim, trim but strong-armed Oregonian, who had been humbled in three previous openings, literally stood Billy Southworth's athletes on their heads with a five-hit performance.

This opening was strictly for the television and radio addicts. The baseball fans stayed away in droves rather than run the risk of pneumonia.

Despite the handicap of chilled fingers and cooled muscles, Jansen carved a masterpiece in the Giants' first inaugural victory since 1946. The five hits he yielded were singles. An old Giant, Sid Gordon, struck two. Bob Elliott got one. So did Roy Hartsfield and Johnny Logan, successor to Buddy Kerr at short field.

Jansen struck out four and issued a single pass. He had to contend with two errors committed by overanxious Monte Irvin.

Bickford Wild at Start

Wild and unsteady at the start, Vern Bickford grew progressively more ineffective and underwent his most painful jar in the fifth when the Giants clustered four hits for two runs. The Giants collected nine blows, all of them singles and eight off Bickford, who gave seven passes through th eseventh. By that time the Giants had all their runs.

Before the battle a Marine detail marched around and across the field, the colors snapping smartly in a brisk breeze. The rich baritone of Don Dennis rang over the setting as Old Glory was flung to the breeze on the flagpole in right-center. Baron Hugo's orchestra provided the accompaniment. Mayor John B. Hynes tossed the first ball to catcher Ebba St. Claire, waiting at the plate. State Treasurer John E. Hurley, representing Gov. Paul A. Dever, watched.

Mueller Walks in Fourth

Bickford walked Henry Thompson and Irvin after getting past Eddie Stanky and Whitey Lockman in the first. He avoided any consequences then because Bobby Thomson rapped straight at Elliott for a force play.

Jansen struck the first blow off Bickford opening the third and Henry Thompson walked with two away. However, Elliott thrust aside this threat, too, by scooping up Irvin's torrid line smash.

The Box Score

NEW YORK (N.)

	ab.	r.	h.	po.	a.
Stanky, 2b.	5	0	1	2	3
Lockman, lf.	4	2	1	2	0
Thompson, 3b.	3	1	1	0	1
Irvin, 1b.	4	0	1	9	1
Thomson, cf.	5	0	1	4	0
Mueller, rf.	4	1	2	2	0
Dark, ss.	4	0	0	2	0
Westrum, c.	4	0	1	5	1
Jansen, p.	4	0	1	1	3
Totals	37	4	9	27	9

BOSTON (N.)

	ab.	r.	h.	po.	a.
Hartsf'd, 2b.	4	0	1	2	0
Jethroe, cf.	3	0	0	3	0
Torgeson, 1b.	4	0	0	0	1
Elliott, 3b.	4	0	1	3	4
Gordon, lf.	4	0	2	1	0
St. Claire, c.	4	0	0	4	1
Addis, rf.	4	0	0	3	0
Logan, ss.	3	0	1	0	2
aCooper	1	0	0	0	0
Bickford, p.	2	0	0	0	3
bMarshall	1	0	0	0	0
Donnelly, p.	0	0	0	1	0
Total	34	0	5	27	11

aFlied out for Logan in ninth. bFlied out for Bickford in seventh.

New York .... 0 0 0 1 2 0 1 0 0—4
Boston .... 0 0 0 0 0 0 0 0 0—0

Errors—Irvin 2, Jethroe.
Runs batted in—Westrum, Thomson 2, Mueller.
Stolen base—Mueller. Left on bases—New York 11, Boston 8. Bases on balls—Off Jansen 1, Bickford 5. Struck out—By Jansen 4, Bickford 3, Donnelly 1. Hits—Off Bickford 8 in 7 innings, Donnelly 1 in 2. Winning pitcher—Jansen (1—0). Losing pitcher—Bickford (0—1). Umpires—Ballanfant, Barlick and Donatelli. Time of game—2:20. Attendance—6,081.

The same Elliott robbed Bobby Thomson of a hit with a sparkling play opening the fourth, but Don Mueller walked. Mueller stole second and, after Alvin Dark had been retired, scooted home when Wes Westrum shot a single over third.

With one out in the fifth, Lockman singled and so did Henry Thompson. They advanced as Bickford threw out Irvin. Bobby Thompson almost knocked Elliott over with a single which let Lockman score. When Mueller singled, Henry Thompson loped in from third.

Starting the seventh, Lockman drew a pass. With one away, Irvin singled Lockman to third and Whitey raced home after Thomson's long fly to Gordon.

Jansen turned aside a threat in the second, which saw Gordon strike the first enemy single. He left St. Claire stranded on second after Irvin's error in the fifth. Hartsfiedl's single and the lone pass Jansen issued to Sam Jethroe saw runners on third and second with one away in the sixth, but again the Oregonian rose gloriously to the occasion. Elliott and Gordon opened the ninth with singles before Jansen got past St. Claire, Bob Addis and Walk Cooper.

Jansen bagged his fifteenth triumph over the Braves and his fourteenth shut-out as a Giant.

Pitcher Gets First Hit

Henry Thompson drew the first walk and Jansen got the first hit. Stanky was the first strikeout victim, looking at a third one in the third, so Umpire Lee Ballanfant promptly became the first object of a Giant disagreement. Mueller pilfered the first base and tore home with the first run, knocked in by Westrum.

Braves Field looked strange with a green-painted fence bereft of gaudy advertising signs and with only a cigarette ad on the wall.

The Giants and Braves looked spic and span in new, neatly pressed uniforms with the National League's seventy-fifth anniversary emblem on the left arms of the players.

CHESS DRAW RECORDED

Botvinnik, Bronstein Split Point After 33 Moves in Moscow

The fifteenth game between Mikhail Botvinnik and David Bronstein for the chess championship of the world resulted in a draw in Moscow last night, according to Soviet news sources.

Botvinnik had the white pieces in a queen's pawn opening and retained the initiative well into the middle stage. The challenger, however, met Botvinnik's every advance and held his own until, after thirty-three moves, it was agreed to halve the point.

It was the tenth draw in the series. Botvinnik has won three games and lost two for a lead of 8-7. The sixteenth game is scheduled for Friday, with eight more after that.

Chandler Pays Visit to Senate

WASHINGTON, April 17 (AP)—Baseball Commissioner A. B. Chandler visited his former colleagues on the Senate floor today Chandler, who resigned from the Senate in 1945 to take the commissionership, chatted with several Senators and listened briefly to debate.

Montreal Obtains Voiselle

MONTREAL, April 17 (UP)—General Manager Guy Moreau of the Montreal Royals announced today that former major league Pitcher Bill Voiselle had been purchased from St. Paul of the American Association. Voiselle was with the Cubs last year.

New Mexico Aggie Coach Set

ODESSA, Tex., April 17 (UP)—Football Coach Joe Coleman of Odessa High School resigned today to accept the head coaching job at New Mexico A. & M. College at Las Cruces.

INDIANS TOP TIGERS ON LEMON 2-HITTER

Triumph by 2-1 in 9th When Doby Doubles and Scores on Error by Lipon

DETROIT, April 17 (AP)—Bob Lemon of the Indians beat the Tigers, 2—1 today with a two-hit performance that thrilled 43,470 shivering opening day fans.

The clubs, battling in a chilly 37 degrees, stayed on even terms until the ninth when, with the score tied at 1-all, Detroit Shortstop Johnny Lipon bobbled an easy grounder that allowed Larry Doby to score from third.

Doby's double, the eighth and last hit off southpaw Harold Newhouser, opened the ninth. The fleet centerfielder moved to third on Bob Kennedy's sacrifice and scored while Lipon picked up and twice dropped Jim Hegan's easy grounder.

Second Baseman Jerry Priddy nicked Lemon for the two Tiger hits, a double in the third and a single in the fifth. Lemon won twenty-three and lost eleven last year.

In the first, Roberto Avila scored from second for the Indians on Luke Easter's single to center, one of the four hits Newhouser gave up in that inning. Priddy scored the Tiger run by stealing home in the third after he had doubled and moved to third on a fielder's choice.

Bill Hoeft, 18-year-old pitching standout in Detroit's spring training, said today he was being sent to the Toledo Mudhens of the American Association. Hoeft said Manager Red Rolfe advised him he would leave for the Tiger farm tonight.

The box score:

CLEVELAND (A.)

	ab.	r.	h.	po.	a.
Mitchell, lf.	4	0	0	2	0
Avila, 2b.	4	1	2	2	3
Easter, 1b.	3	0	2	4	1
Ninoso, 1b.	1	0	0	9	0
Rosen, 3b.	4	0	1	0	3
Doby, cf.	4	1	2	2	0
Kennedy, rf.	3	0	1	1	0
Boone, ss.	4	0	0	1	7
Hegan, c.	3	0	0	5	0
Lemon, p.	4	0	0	1	2
Total	34	2	8	27	15

DETROIT (A.)

	ab.	r.	h.	po.	a.
Lipon, ss.	4	0	0	0	3
Berry, 3b.	3	0	0	0	1
aMullin	1	0	0	0	0
Kolloway, 1b.	3	0	0	10	0
bKeller	1	0	0	0	0
Wertz, rf.	3	0	0	3	0
Evers, lf.	2	0	0	2	0
Groth, cf.	3	0	0	4	0
Priddy, 2b.	3	1	2	0	2
Ginsberg, c.	3	0	0	8	1
Newhouser, p.	3	0	0	0	2
Total	29	1	2	27	9

aGrounded out for Berry in ninth.
bGrounded out for Kolloway in ninth.

Cleveland .... 1 0 0 0 0 0 0 0 1—2
Detroit .... 0 0 1 0 0 0 0 0 0—1

Errors—Newhouser, Lipon.
Runs batted in—Easter.
Two-base hits—Doby, Priddy. Stolen bases—Kennedy, Priddy. Sacrifice—Kennedy. Double play—Newhouser, Ginsberg and Kolloway. Left on bases—Cleveland 7, Detroit 2. Bases on balls—Off Lemon 1, Newhouser 1. Struck out—By Lemon 2, Newhouser 6. Winning pitcher—Lemon (1—0). Losing pitcher—Newhouser—(0—1). Umpires—Passarella, Berry, Hurley and Napp. Time of game—2:16. Attendance—43,470.

POLISH ACE EN ROUTE HERE

Gerula to Play With Chicago Soccer Club for Season

LONDON, April 17 (UP)—Stanislaw Gerula, Polish amateur soccer goalkeeper, will sail for New York aboard the Queen Elizabeth today to play with the Chicago Athletic Soccer Football Club.

Gerula, 33, at present is on the squad of the Third Division South club, Leyton Orient, which he joined in 1947 after being demobilized from the Polish Army. At one time he was the Orient's regular first team goalkeeper. During the war Gerula played for Poland in international games.

He plans to stay in the United States for at least one playing season, but has made no definite plans after that.

"If I like it," Gerula said, "I hope to stay. If not, I intend to return to England."

WHITE SOX' 19 BLOWS ROUT BROWNS BY 17-3

ST. LOUIS, April 17 (AP)—Chicago's revamped White Sox pounded five pitchers for nineteen hits and ran roughshod over the Browns, 17—3, today before 5,660 fans in the opening day game at Sportsman's Park. The Browns' pitchers yielded fourteen bases on balls.

Billy Pierce went the distance and kept ten Brownie hits well scattered as the White Sox continued the mastery demonstrated by nine straight exhibition triumphs over the Browns this spring.

Nelson Fox, Chicago second baseman, tied a major league record by hitting two doubles in one inning, the eighth.

The box score:

CHICAGO (A.)

	ab.	r.	h.	po.	a.
Carr'quel, ss.	7	1	2	4	4
Baker, 3b.	4	3	2	0	0
Zarilla, rf.	6	3	3	2	0
Zernial, lf.	6	1	2	5	0
Robinson, 1b.	3	2	2	5	1
Masi, c.	4	1	1	6	0
Busby, cf.	5	1	3	3	0
Fox, 2b.	5	2	2	1	3
Pierce, p.	5	3	2	1	0
Total	45	17	19	27	8

ST. LOUIS (A.)

	ab.	r.	h.	po.	a.
Young, 2b.	5	0	3	3	1
Upton, ss.	5	0	0	3	5
Ber'dino, 3b.	4	0	2	1	2
Wood, rf.	3	1	0	3	0
Sievers, cf.	4	1	2	1	0
Lenhardt, lf.	4	0	0	3	0
Lollar, c.	3	1	2	5	0
Lutz, 1b.	4	0	1	7	2
Garver, p.	0	0	0	0	0
Kennedy, p.	2	0	0	1	1
aMarsh	1	0	0	0	0
Medlinger, p.	0	0	0	0	0
Schacht, p.	0	0	0	0	0
D. J'nson, p.	0	0	0	0	1
bMoss	1	0	0	0	0
Total	36	3	10	27	12

aFlied out for Kennedy in sixth.
bFlied out for Johnson in ninth.

Chicago .... 0 6 0 0 0 0 2 7 2—17
St. Louis .... 0 0 0 1 0 1 0 0 1— 3

Errors—Zernial, Robinson.
Runs batted in—Carrasquel 2, Robinson, Busby 3, Lollar 2 Baker, Zernial 4, Fox, Zarilla 4, Masi.
Two-base hits—Sievers, Robinson, Fox 2, Baker, Zarilla Home run—Zarilla. Double plays—Fox, Carrasquel and Robinson; Carrasquel, Fox and Robinson. Left on bases—St. Louis 8, Chicago 15. Bases on balls—Off Pierce 2, Garver 5, Kennedy 2, Medlinger 4, D. Johnson 3. Struck out—By Pierce 6, Garver 1, Kennedy 3, D. Johnson 1. Hits—Off Garver 5 in 1 2-3 innings, Kennedy 5 in 4 1-3, Medlinger 1 in 2-3, Schacht 5 in 1 D. Johnson 3 in 1 1-3. Winning pitcher—Pierce (1—0). Losing pitcher—Garver (0—1). Umpires—Hubbard, Rommell and Paparella. Time of game—2:58. Attendance—5,660.

Yanks Jolt Chisox; Mantle, Yogi Connect; DiMag Ailing

By BEN EPSTEIN

CHICAGO, May 1.—Mickey Mantle chose a sunny afternoon, in which Joe DiMaggio went to a hospital, to power his first big league homer today. And the Sweet Switcher seldom will boom a longer one, no matter how long he sticks around.

For the 19-year-old Mantle cannoned an estimated 440-foot two-runner into the extreme centerfield Comiskey Park stands today as Vic Raschi beat the White Sox, 8-3, for his third win while the Yankees were opening their initial Western trials.

DiMag showed up suffering from a crick in his neck. Unable to swing, Joe went to Mercy Hospital for X-ray. Dr. John Claridge diagnosed the condition as "nothing serious, only a muscular spasm in the neck." The doctor recommended massages and manipulation which he believed would eliminate the ailment.

The Clipper said something snapped in his neck while entering a cab in New York last Sunday. It's DiMag's second trip to an infirmary in four days. Last Saturday, at Lenox Hill, pictures of his stiff right shoulder revealed a strained ligament but he hit a homer and two singles in the afternoon.

Mantle's streaker, a right-handed shot off ex-Yankee Randy Gumpert, second of Chicago's three pitchers, was the third homer of the day. Bowing as a Soxer, Orestes Minoso drew cheers from the 14,776 by mauling a 420-foot, two-runner into the centerfield bullpen in the first. Yogi Berra arched his first round tripper of the term into the right field stands in the fifth. Yogi retired after the sock. He was hit on the right elbow by a Bob Cain pitch in the second. The injury didn't seem serious.

Although officially credited with three runs batted in, Mickey actually "drove" home five. In addition to his terrific tee shot in the sixth, and pushing home the second of two in the fourth, Mantle's two-out smash through Minoso, which was ruled an error, drilled two across in the second to tie it, 2-2. The switcher hiked his rbi total to nine, one under DiMag, and it seems as if Kansas City, which desires him, must sit back and wait for a spell.

Raschi called it a day after seven innings, during which he yielded six hits and all the Chicago runs. The temperature rose to 89 degrees, torrid for Chicago so early in the Spring and Vic probably succumbed to the heat. Tom Ferrick finished and served the Sox's last three safeties in the eighth and ninth.

In beating the lefthanded Cain, who bothered the Bombers with four defeats in 1950, the Yanks scored their eight victory over a southpaw. Rapped for six hits and five runs, Bob gave way to a pinch-hitter in the fifth. After Gumpert in the sixth and seventh, the champs scored their eighth run off lefthanded Marv Rotblatt in the eighth.

EPPIGRAMS: Dorothy Arnold, the former Mrs. Joe DiMaggio, accompanied the club to Chicago. It's rumored that the Clipper and Miss Arnold who flies to Los Angeles tomorrow, have been secretly re-married... Minoso, first Negro player on the White Sox varsity roster, got a local play on a Jackie Robinson scale. It developed into an extravaganza after Orestes bowed in with a herculean homer...Page pitched to the batters for the fourth time since his Johns Hopkins look-see. But Joe still fears to let one go ...Frank Lane explained he hung around New York over the week-end merely to avoid any possible Philadelphia leak of the big trade. Frank said Greenberg wanted to renege at the last minute but Hank had filed a confirming wire...Ex-Yankee Nick Etten visited his old mates. Out of baseball, Etten today peddles beer in Chicago... George Weiss joins club in St. Louis Thursday when, no doubt, he'll lend a hand in deciding future of four spares. Could be that he'll recall rookie left-hander Bob Weisler.

Yankees' Box Score

YANKEES	ab	r	h	o	a
Mantle, rf	4	1	1	3	0
Mapes, rf	1	0	0	1	0
Coleman, 2b	5	0	1	3	3
McDoug'ld, 3b	4	0	1	0	3
Woodling, lf	4	0	0	2	0
Berra, c	2	2	1	4	0
Silvera, c	1	0	0	2	0
Jensen, cf	4	0	0	4	0
Collins, 1b	3	2	1	7	2
Rizzuto, ss	3	2	2	1	1
Raschi, p	1	1	1	0	1
a-Mize	1	0	1	0	0
b-Martin	0	0	0	0	0
Ferrick, p	0	0	0	0	0
Totals	33	8	9	27	10

WHITE SOX	ab	r	h	o	a
Carrasquel, ss	5	0	2	0	3
Lehner, lf	4	1	1	2	0
Minoso, 3b	4	1	2	0	2
Robinson, 1b	4	0	0	13	0
Zarilla, rf	3	0	0	1	0
Busby, cf	4	0	0	2	0
Fox, 2b	4	0	0	5	4
Niarhos, c	4	1	2	4	2
Cain, p	1	0	0	0	1
c-Stewart	1	0	1	0	0
Gumpert, p	0	0	0	0	0
d-Goldsberry	1	0	0	0	0
Rotblatt, p	0	0	0	0	1
e-Baker	1	0	1	0	0
Totals	36	3	9	27	13

a-Singled for Raschi in 8th.
b-Ran for Mize in 8th.
c-Singled for Cain in 5th
d-Grounded out for Gumpert in 7th.
e-Singled for Rotblatt in 9th.

YANKEES	0	2	0	2	1	2	0	1	0	—8
WHITE SOX	2	0	0	0	1	0	0	0	0	—3

E—Minoso, Rizzuto. RBI—Minoso 2, Mantle 3, Coleman, Berra, Mize, Carrasquel. 2B—McDougald, Raschi. HR—Minoso, Berra, Mantle. SB—Coleman. Sac.—Lehner, Raschi, Rizzuto. DP—Minoso, Fox and Robinson. Left—Yankees, 5; White Sox, 8. BB—Cain, 1; Gumpert, 1; Rotblatt, 1; Raschi, 1. SO—Cain, 1; Gumpert, 1; Rotblatt, 2; Raschi, 4; Ferrick, 1. Hits—Off Cain, 6 in 5 innings; Gumpert, 2 in 2; Rotblatt, 1 in 2; Raschi, 6 in 7; Ferrick, 3 in 2. HBP—By Cain (Berra and McDougald). WP—Cain. Winner—Raschi (3-1). Loser—Cain (0-2). Umps.—Berry, Hurley, Napp and Passarella. Time—2:38.

Robby Leads NY Balloting In Play of Day

Jackie Robinson, Phil Rizzuto and Monte Irvin lead the Dodgers, Yanks and Giants in the Mirror's daily Play-of-Day race, according to figures from opening day to April 30.

Robby is the nominal leader with five mentions, followed by Rizzuto's four and Irvin's three. The Mirror will print a monthly standing of the leaders, with the winning player from each team getting a trophy at the end of the season.

Staff writers with each team are the sole judges. They daily choose a player who made the most valuable contribution to his team's cause—win, lose or tie. All players except pitchers are eligible.

(April 17-30)

Players	Club	No.
Robinson	Dodgers	5
Rizzuto	Yankees	4
Irvin	Giants	3
Mantle	Yankees	2
Jansen	Yankees	2
Westrum	Giants	2
H. Thompson	Giants	2
Thomson	Giants	2
Hartung	Giants	2
D. Thompson	Dodgers	2

INTERNATIONAL LEAGUE

YESTERDAY'S RESULTS
Montreal, 6; Rochester, 5.
Springfield at Buffalo (night).
Syracuse at Ottawa (night).
(Only games scheduled)

	W.	L.	Pct.		W.	L.	Pct.
Syracuse	7	1	.875	Baltimore	5	6	.455
Montreal	9	2	.818	Rochester	3	7	.300
Toronto	5	4	.556	Ottawa	3	7	.300
Buffalo	5	5	.500	Springfield	3	8	.273

GAMES TODAY
Toronto at Montreal.
Buffalo at Ottawa (night).
Baltimore at Rochester (night).
Springfield at Syracuse (night).

Who's Right? CCNY's Wright Or—

By DAN PARKER

Continued from Page 46

same athletic directors were following Irish's orders before the scandal—but, of course, things will be different from now on. They'll also be different insofar as the distribution of tickets is concerned. The Garden announced some weeks ago that almost half the tickets will be ear-marked for college students next season. Dr. Harry Wright, president of City College, said: "In the Garden, the best seats surrounding the court are $5, while the students get 50-cent balcony seats, when they are available. The situation is inverted. The students should get the best seats surrounding the court at 50 cents, and then let the public buy the others at $5. The game should be run for the benefit of the students; but it won't be because it's not practical for the Garden to do it that way."

It will be interesting to note how many low-priced seats are available for the student bodies after the excitement over the basketball scandal dies down and if the demand for tickets becomes brisk once more. When college basketball was first played at the Garden, the students were supposed to get preferential treatment, too. They did for a while until Uncle Nedso found he could dispose of the seats at much higher prices to non-collegiate customers. Then the college students found out where they stood—either in bed or behind a pole in the gallery.

Of course, the ideal solution of the college basketball problem in New York woud be for the colleges to organize a Metropolitan Conference as they have in such sports as baseball, track and field, rifle shooting and swimming. Then the schools would hire or even build their own arena, make their own radio and television deals and sell the film rights to games that warranted it. But the best way to scare off a New York basketball coach is to broach such a subject within his earshot. Dr. Wright of City College favors a Metropolitan Basketball Conference. Uncle Nedso Irish does not.

Baseball Summaries

NATIONAL LEAGUE

YESTERDAY'S RESULTS
Pittsburgh, 6; Brooklyn, 2.
New York, 5; Chicago, 3 (night).
Philadelphia, 6; Cincinnati, 5 (night).
St. Louis, 5; Boston, 2 (night).

	W.	L.	Pct.	GB
St. Louis	7	3	.700	—
Boston	10	6	.625	—
Brooklyn	**8**	**6**	**.571**	**1**
Philadelphia	8	6	.571	1
Pittsburgh	6	5	.545	1½
Chicago	5	6	.455	2½
Cincinnati	4	8	.333	4
New York	**4**	**12**	**.250**	**6**

GAMES TODAY
Pittsburgh at Ebbets Field, 1:30 p. m.
Chicago at Polo Grounds, 1:30 p. m.
St. Louis at Boston.
Cincinnati at Philadelphia.

AMERICAN LEAGUE

YESTERDAY'S RESULTS
New York, 8; Chicago, 3.
Philadelphia, 9; Detroit, 1 (11 inn.).
Cleveland, 7; Boston, 1 (night).
Washington at St. Louis (night).

	W.	L.	Pct.	GB
Cleveland	8	3	.727	—
Washington	7	3	.700	½
New York	**9**	**4**	**.692**	—
Boston	7	5	.583	1½
Chicago	6	5	.545	2
Detroit	3	6	.333	4
St. Louis	4	8	.333	4½
Philadelphia	2	12	.143	7½

GAMES TODAY
New York at Chicago.
Boston at Cleveland.
Philadelphia at Detroit.
Washington at St. Louis (night).

Today in Sports

BASEBALL

Polo Grounds, 155th St. and 8th Ave.—Cubs vs. Giants, 1:30 p. m. (Television, WPIX, Channel 11, 1:20 p. m.).

Ebbets Field, Bedford Ave. and Sullivan Pl., Bklyn.—Pirates vs. Dodgers, 1:30 p.m. (Television, WOR-TV, Channel 9, 1:25 p. m.).

HORSE RACING

Jamaica Race Track, Jamaica, L. I.—First race, 1:15 p. m.

Yonkers Raceway, Yonkers, N. Y.—First race, 8:40 p. m.

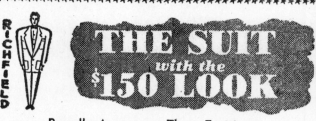

Yankees Defeat Athletics Under Stadium Lights; Giants and Dodgers Score

LOPAT OF BOMBERS TAKES 8TH IN ROW

Yanks' Southpaw Victor Over Athletics, 7-5, With Help of Reynolds in Eighth

M'DOUGALD BATTING STAR

Rookie Blasts Homer, Double and Single—Coleman Also Excels Before 30,333

By JAMES P. DAWSON

Ed Lopat, the Yankees' undefeated southpaw, won his eighth straight game at the Stadium last night, but he missed the chance to equal an American League record.

The sorrel-topped hurler failed to go the route the first time this season and needed help from Allie Reynolds to turn back the Athletics, 7-5, before a gathering of 30,333.

Until the eighth inning Lopat seemed well on the road to matching Boo Ferriss' 1945 American League mark of eight straight complete-game victories, encouraged by a 10-hit assault of his mates on four of Jimmy Dykes' pitchers. But the pressure proved too much.

Blistered for three runs in the eighth, facing loaded bases with two out and the winning run on first, Lopat was taken out and Reynolds sauntered in from the bullpen to preserve this fifth straight victory for the Yanks with a typical exhibition of air-tight pitching.

Philley Grounds Out

Reynolds got the dangerous Dave Philley on a grounder to halt the Athletics rally. Then he went right through Gus Zernial, Wally Moses and Allie Clark in the ninth. A sparkling running catch by Hank Bauer of Zernial's 400-foot smash thrilled the crowd.

With a homer, his fourth, a double and a single, Rookie Gil McDougald led the Yankee assault on Alex Kellner, Bob Hooper, Jack Kucab and Sam Zoldak.

But two singles by Jerry Coleman were key blows in this Yankee conquest. The first arrived in the third inning and sent two runs over the plate. The second opened the sixth and led to an insurance run when Joe Collins tripled.

Phil Rizzuto contributed a triple to the assault. Yogi Berra chimed in with a double, as Did Mickey Mantle. But Mantle made things difficult by missing a catch of Eddie Joost's double with the bases loaded in the eighth and hastened Lopat's recall.

The Rizzuto triple opened the assault on Kellner and became a run in the first inning when Clark, transplanted from the outfield to third, let Zernial's throw get away.

Mackmen Lead in Third

Joost's single, a pass to Ferris Fain, Philley's double, an intentional pass to Zernial and a force play gave the Athletics two and the lead in the third.

The Yanks bounced back with four in their half of the third. Kellner hit Rizzuto, yielded a double to Mantle, walked Joe DiMaggio, was smacked for a double by Berra, purposely walked Bauer, and was jarred out of the game by Coleman's two-run single.

Hooper halted the rally but gave up the McDougald homer opening the Yankee fifth. He also allowed the scratch single by Coleman, as well as Collins' triple in the sixth, which ended with the Yanks ahead b yfive runs.

In the eighth Lopat faded. Zernial tripled, Moses singled and Clark followed with a single. A pop-out by Pete Suder relieved the tension somewhat. But Ray Murray's single loaded the bases. Then Lopat braced to retire Kermit Wahl, swinging for Jack Kucab, on a foul pop. Joost doubled off Mantle's finger tips, scoring Moses and Clark and when Fain walked, filling the bases, Reynolds came along.

Including his work in the final stages of the 1950 campaign, this was Lopat's eleventh straight victory. He wound up the 1950 Yankee pennant chase with three in a row.

Jimmy Dykes still is trying for his first Stadium victory after four in reverse.

DiMaggio was robbed of his best chance for a hit in the first inning when Philley raced over to left for a glittering clutch of Joe's drive.

Berra's third-inning double stretched his hitting streak to six games. Yogi has hit safely at least once in twenty of his last twenty-two games.

Joost argued strenuously that McDougald's home was not a homer in the fifth, but Umpire Joe Paparella won his noisy debate as usual.

The box score:

PHILADELPHIA (A.)	ab	r	h	po	a
Joost, ss	5	1	2	3	3
Fain, 1b	2	1	1	8	1
Philley, cf	5	0	1	5	0
Zernial, lf	4	1	1	0	1
Moses, rf	3	1	1	2	0
Clark, 3b	5	1	1	1	2
Suder, 2b	4	0	1	1	3
Murray, c	4	0	1	3	0
Kellner, p	1	0	0	1	0
Hooper, p	1	0	0	0	0
aKlein	1	0	0	0	0
Kucab, p	0	0	0	0	0
bWahl	1	0	0	0	0
Zoldak, p	0	0	0	0	1
Total	36	5	9	24	11

NEW YORK (A.)	ab	r	h	po	a
Rizzuto, ss	4	2	1	1	4
Mantle, rf	4	1	1	1	0
McD'gald, 3b	4	1	3	0	2
DiMaggio, cf	2	1	0	2	0
Berra, c	4	1	1	4	0
Bauer, lf	1	0	0	4	0
Coleman, 2b	4	1	2	4	3
Collins, 1b	4	0	2	11	0
Lopat, p	3	0	0	0	1
Reynolds, p	1	0	0	0	0
Total	31	7	10	27	10

aSafe on error for Hooper in seventh.
bFouled out for Kucab in eighth.

Philadelphia .... 0 0 2 0 0 0 0 3 0—5
New York .... 1 0 4 0 1 1 0 0 .—7

Errors—Clark, McDougald.
Runs batted in—Philley, Moses 2, Joost 2, Mantle, Berra, Coleman 2, McDougald, Collins.
Two-base hits—Philley, Mantle, Berra, McDougald, Joost. Three-base hits—Rizzuto, Collins, Zernial. Home run—McDougald. Sacrifice—Fain. Double plays—Suder, Joost and Fain 2. Left on bases—Philadelphia 10, New York 6. Bases on balls—Off Kellner 3, Kucab 1, Lopat 5. Struck out—By Kellner 1, Hooper 1, Lopat 3. Hits—Off Kellner 6 in 2 2-3 innings, Hooper 3 in 3 1-3, Kucab 1 in 1, Zoldak 0 in 1, Lopat 9 in 7 2-3, Reynolds 0 in 1 1-3. Hit by pitcher—By Kellner (Rizzuto), Hooper (DiMaggio). Winning pitcher—Lopat (8—0). Losing pitcher—Kellner (3—2). Umpires—Napp, Hubbard, Rommel and Paparella. Time of game—2:42. Attendance—30,333.

NEW RECRUIT REPORTS TO GIANT BASEBALL CLUB

Willie Mays, 20-year-old outfielder brought up from Minneapolis of the American Association, at the team's downtown office yesterday with Manager Leo Durocher, left, and President Horace Stoneham.
Associated Press

RED SOX CONQUER SENATORS, 14 TO 2

Williams Paces 19-Hit Attack With Homer, 2 Doubles—Stobbs Yields 6 Blows

BOSTON, May 25 (UP)—Ted Williams smashed his ninth homer of the season and Chuck Stobbs won his fourth game as the Red Sox walloped the Senators tonight, 14 to 2.

Connie Marrero suffered his first defeat after five victories for Washington when the Red Sox unleashed a nineteen-hit assault powered by Williams' homer and two doubles which knocked in four runs.

Bobby Doerr was the only Red Sox player failing to hit safely—snapping an eleven-game hitting streak which the second baseman had built up.

Stobbs scattered six hits and allowed both Senator runs in the first inning, in which first-baseman Walt Dropo made two errors. Cass Michaels, who doubled in the fourth inning, was the only Senator to reach second base in the last eight innings.

Dom DiMaggio ran his batting streak to twelve games.

The box score:

WASHINGTON (A.)	ab	r	h	po	a
Yost, 3b	3	1	1	1	0
Coan, lf	4	0	0	2	1
Mele, rf	3	1	1	3	0
Vernon, 1b	3	0	1	6	0
Noren, cf	4	0	0	3	0
Michaels, 2b	4	0	1	2	1
Dente, ss	4	0	1	3	5
Guerra, c	4	0	0	4	1
Marrero, p	2	0	0	0	1
aMcCormick	1	0	1	0	0
Brown, p	0	0	0	0	1
bVerble	1	0	0	0	0
Total	33	2	6	24	10

BOSTON (A.)	ab	r	h	po	a
DiMaggio, cf	6	2	3	4	0
Goodman, rf	5	2	2	3	0
Williams, lf	5	3	3	2	0
Boudreau, ss	4	1	2	4	1
Stephens, 3b	5	0	2	1	3
Dropo, 1b	5	2	2	5	1
Doerr, 2b	2	3	0	5	1
Moss, c	5	0	3	3	0
Stobbs, p	5	1	2	0	0
Total	42	14	19	27	6

aSingled for Marrero in seventh.
bFlied out for Brown in ninth.

Washington .... 2 0 0 0 0 0 0 0 0—2
Boston .... 5 1 0 1 0 2 3 2 .—14

Errors—Dropo 2, Marrero, Stephens, Vernon. Runs batted in—Michaels, Williams 4, Boudreau 2, Dropo, Moss, Stobbs 3, Stephens 2, DiMaggio.
Two-base hits—Dropo, Michaels, Williams 2, Boudreau, Stobbs. Home run—Williams. Double plays—Doerr and Boudreau; Dropo and Boudreau; Michaels, Dente and Vernon. Left on bases—Washington 7, Boston 9. Bases on balls—Off Stobbs 3, Marrero 1, Brown 4. Struck out—By Stobbs 2, Marrero 2, Brown 2. Hits—Off Marrero 14 in 6 innings, Brown 5 in 2. Winning pitcher—Stobbs (4—1). Losing pitcher—Marrero (5—1). Umpires—Berry, Hurley and Passarella. Time of game—2:12. Attendance—21,379.

REDS HALT CARDINALS ON HOMER IN 11TH, 5-1

ST. LOUIS, May 25 (AP)—Connie Ryan whacked a grand-slam home run to the deep left centerfield seats in the eleventh inning to give the Cincinnati Reds a 5-1 victory over the St. Louis Cardinals tonight before 11,922 fans. The big blow was off Relief Pitcher Red Munger.

The score by innings:
Cincinnati—
001 000 000 04—5 8 1
St. Louis—
000 000 100 00—1 7 0

Polo Grounders Trip Phils, 8-5, With 5-Run Splurge in Eighth

Giants Blast Pitchers Church and Miller for Triumph at Shibe Park—Mays, Negro Star, Plays Centerfield

By JOHN DREBINGER
Special to THE NEW YORK TIMES.

PHILADELPHIA, May 25—Inspired by the presence of their flashy rookie star, Willie Mays, the Giants rallied for five runs in the eighth inning tonight to flatten Eddie Sawyer's Phillies, 8 to 5, before 21,082 spectators.

Actually Leo Durocher's 20-year-old Alabama Negro, imported overnight from Minneapolis, played only a minor role. He made a couple of sparkling plays in center field, but went hitless in five tries.

However, the Polo Grounders had others to carry the load on this balmy spring evening. Alvin Dark and Eddie Stanky, smarting under the sting of two glaring errors that helped the Phils to two runs in the sixth, came up with seven hits between them. Wes Westrum hit a homer, a single and walked three times, while Whitey Lockman delivered the blow in the eighth that put the Giants in front, a double with the bases full.

Miller Losing Hurler

That shot made George Spencer, relieving Jim Hearn for one inning, the winner. Bubba Church and Bob Miller were the Phils' pitchers routed in the eighth, while Konstanty was the victim of the Lockman blow that made Miller the loser.

The Phils grabbed an early lead off Hearn when, with the score 1—all in the last of the second, Granny Hamner and Mike Goliat hit homers with the bases empty. One of these the Giants got back in the fourth on Westrum's circuit clout, but in the sixth Stanky committed a two-base muff of a pop fly. Dark booted one for a two-base miscue and this, with a single by Eddie Waitkus, gave the Phils two more for a 5-2 margin.

But the Giants, after scoring one run on singles by Dark, Stanky and Lockman in the seventh, got under way in earnest in the eighth when Church walked Henry Thompson and Westrum. Miller replaced Church, got one out, but was tagged for singles by Dark and Bobby Thomson that drove in two.

Konstanty in Trouble

Then came Konstanty who, after collecting the second out, had troubles of his own. He walked Stanky, filling the bases. Lockman followed with his double to right which drove in two and Stanky scored on Del Ennis' wild throw to the infield.

That clinched it. Spencer, who had snuffed out three Phils in the seventh to receive credit for the victory, went out for a pinch hitter in the eighth and Sheldon Jones throttled the Phils the rest of the way.

Mays took a third strike on his first time up and grounded to third on the next. But in the fifth he just missed driving in Stanky with a lusty clout into deep right center which Ennis hauled down after a hard run for the third out. In the seventh the young Negro sent Dick Sisler to the left-field wall with another powerful drive for the third out with two on.

In the ninth, however, Mays had a close call when his great speed almost brought him into collision with Monty Irvin on Waitkus' smash into right center. Monty failed to hold the ball and it went for a double.

Official Family Attends

Almost the entire Giant "official family" came down from New York to take in the game. In the party were Owner Horace C. Stoneham, Chubby Feeney, the vice president, and Garry Schumacher.

Eddie Brannick, of course, also was there, but then the Giants' secretary de luxe has been there ever since the Polo Grounders came up with their first centerfield sensation, a fellow named Mike Donlin.

Mays, who flew to New York during the night and joined the club as it left Penn Station in New York this afternoon, brought several of his choice bats. During batting practice Willie brought rounds of "ah's" from the early arrivals by driving three tremendous drives into the left field stand.

It'll be Larry Jansen against Robin Roberts in the second game of the series tomorrow night.

The Box Score

NEW YORK (N.)	ab	r	h	po	a
Stanky, 2b	4	1	3	0	2
Lockman, 1b	5	0	2	11	0
Mays, cf	5	0	0	4	0
Thomp'n, 3b	3	2	0	4	3
Westrum, c	2	1	2	4	1
Irvin, rf	5	1	0	2	0
Dark, ss	5	1	4	1	3
Thomson, lf	4	2	1	1	0
Hearn, p	2	0	0	0	2
aMueller	1	0	0	0	0
Spencer, p	0	0	0	0	0
bJorgensen	1	0	0	0	0
S. Jones, p	0	0	0	0	0
Total	37	8	12	27	11

PHILADELPHIA (N.)	ab	r	h	po	a
Waitkus, 1b	5	1	4	6	0
Ashburn, cf	4	0	0	0	0
Sisler, lf	5	0	1	3	0
Ennis, rf	3	0	0	2	1
W. Jones, 3b	3	0	0	2	2
Hamner, ss	4	2	1	3	3
Seminick, c	4	0	0	5	0
Goliat, 2b	4	2	1	4	2
Church, p	3	0	1	1	0
Miller, p	0	0	0	0	0
Konstanty, p	0	0	0	1	2
cWhitman	1	0	0	0	0
Total	36	5	8	27	10

aFouled out for Hearn in seventh.
bFlied out for Spencer in eighth.
cFlied out for Konstanty in ninth.

New York .... 0 1 0 1 0 0 1 5 0—8
Philadelphia .... 1 2 0 0 0 2 0 0 0—5

Errors—Lockman 2, Stanky, Dark, Ennis, Hamner.
Runs batted in—Sisler, Hamner, Goliat, Waitkus, Dark 2, Westrum, Lockman 3, Thomson.
Two-base hits—Stanky, Lockman, Waitkus. Three-base hit—Sisler. Home runs—Hamner, Goliat, Westrum. Sacrifice—Ashburn. Double plays—Goliat, Hamner and Waitkus; Ennis and Church; Konstanty and Waitkus. Left on bases—New York 8, Philadelphia 7. Bases on balls—Off Church 4, Konstanty 2, Hearn 2. Struck out—By Church 5, Hearn 1, Jones 1. Hits—Off Hearn 7 in 6 innings, Spencer 0 in 1, Jones 1 in 2, Church 9 in 7, Miller 2 in 1-3, Konstanty 1 in 1 2-3. Winning pitcher—Spencer (2—1). Losing pitcher—Miller (1—1). Umpires—Goetz, Jorda and Dascoli. Time of game—2:52. Attendance—21,082.

WHITE SOX WIN, 6-4, FOR EIGHT STRAIGHT

Chicago Defeats Indians on Robinson, Masi Homers—Pierce Takes No. 5

CLEVELAND, May 25 (AP)—The amazing Chicago White Sox ran their victory string to eight tonight by beating the Cleveland Indians, 6 to 4. Eddie Robinson and Phil Masi clouted homers for the White Sox off Bob Lemon, who went down to his fourth straight defeat.

The White Sox, unbeaten on their present road trip, gave Southpaw Billy Pierce a 4-0 lead in the first three innings. Pierce stayed ahead all the way for his fifth triumph, although the Tribe outhit his team, 11 to 10.

The fast-moving White Sox, who haven't lost a game since Cleveland beat them in their home park May 13, left only five runners stranded, against the Indians' nine.

A three-run pinch double by Birdie Tebbetts in the sixth and a two-bagger by Al Rosen in the seventh were the only extra-base blows Pierce yielded.

Cleveland made two infield errors. First baseman Harry Simpson muffed the cut-off of Larry Doby's throw to the plate in the second, and shortstop Ray Boone muffed a throw-in by rightfielder Bob Kennedy after Orestes Minoso doubled in the seventh. On the latter play, Minoso took third. He tallied Chicago's final run when Robinson singled.

Al Zarilla started the White Sox three-run second with a double and scored Chico Carrasquel's single. Simpson's error permitted Carrasquel to tally on Lehner's single, and after Masi sacrificed Lehner came home on a single by Nelson Fox.

The box score:

CHICAGO (A.)	ab	r	h	po	a
Fox, 2b	4	0	1	3	2
Stewart, lf	4	0	0	2	0
Minoso, 3b	4	1	1	2	3
Robinson, 1b	4	1	2	7	1
Zarilla, rf	4	1	2	1	0
Busby, cf	1	0	0	0	0
Carr'quel, ss	4	1	1	4	2
Lehner, cf,rf	4	1	2	3	0
Masi, c	3	1	1	5	0
Pierce, p	4	0	0	0	0
Total	36	6	10	27	8

CLEVELAND (A.)	ab	r	h	po	a
Avila, 2b	5	0	1	0	5
Boone, ss	5	0	2	1	0
Doby, cf	4	1	2	3	0
Rosen, 3b	4	0	1	0	0
Chapman, lf	4	0	0	3	0
Kennedy, rf	4	1	1	2	0
Simpson, 1b	3	1	1	10	1
Hegan, c	4	1	2	6	0
Lemon, p	2	0	0	1	3
aTebbetts	1	0	1	0	0
bNielsen	0	0	0	0	0
Zuverink, p	0	0	0	0	0
cStirnweiss	1	0	0	0	0
Brissie, p	0	0	0	1	0
Total	37	4	11	27	9

aDoubled for Lemon in sixth.
bRan for Tebbetts in sixth.
cGrounded out for Zuverink in eighth.

Chicago .... 0 3 1 0 0 1 1 0 0—6
Cleveland .... 0 0 0 0 0 3 1 0 0—4

Errors—Simpson, Minoso, Boone.
Runs batted in—Carrasquel, Fox, Robinson 2, Masi, Tebbetts 3, Rosen.
Two-base hits—Zarilla, Tebbetts, Minoso, Rosen. Home runs—Robinson, Masi. Stolen base—Doby. Sacrifice—Masi. Double play—Carrasquel, Fox and Robinson. Left on bases—Chicago 5, Cleveland 9. Bases on balls—Off Pierce 3, Lemon 1. Struck out—By Pierce 4, Lemon 3, Zuverink 1, Brissie 1. Hits—Off Lemon 8 in 6 innings, Zuverink 2 in 2, Brissie 0 in 1. Winning pitcher—Pierce (5—2). Losing pitcher—Lemon (3—5). Umpires—McKinley, Honochick, Soar and McGowan. Time of game—2:30. Attendance—20,412.

17 SCHOOL CREWS GAIN

Jersey, Pennsylvania Eights Among the Finalists Today

PHILADELPHIA, May 25 (AP)—Scholastic crews from Pennsylvania, New Jersey and Virginia plus a lone boat from Buffalo, N. Y., made a sweep of the qualifying heats in the opening day's events of the seventeenth annual American schoolboy championships on the Schuylkill River today.

Seventeen boats won their way into tomorrow's finals.

George Washington High, Alexandria, Va., and Washington and Lee High, Arlington, Va., won their respective heats in the junior eights.

Qualifying with George Washington in the first heat were Belleville, N. J., High, and Lower Merion, Pa. Moving up in the second with Washington and Lee were Philadelphia's West Catholic and Northeast High boats.

Belleville High and Haverford (Pa.) school crews moved into the finals in the championship senior four events where eleven boats faced the starter in two heats.

Trailing Belleville in a close finish to qualify were West Catholic and St. Joseph's High, also of Philadelphia. Behind Haverford were Hun (N. J.) and Prep La Salle High of Philadelphia.

Lower Merion and St. Andrews, Middletown, Del., took heat victories in junior fours. Also qualifying were La Salle, Canisius of Buffalo, and West Catholic.

Northeast High withdrew from the championship eights, and qualifying heats in that division were cancelled. All six remaining crews were told they could start in tomorrow's final.

HAYES NINE TAKES TITLE

Beats All Hallows as Fordham Prep Upsets Mt. St. Michael

The Cardinal Hayes team won the Catholic High School Athletic Association Division 2 baseball title with the help of Fordham Prep yesterday.

Hayes defeated All Hallows, 2—1, on the losers' field, while Fordham Prep upset Mount St. Michael, 7—3, on the victors' diamond. The triumph was the eleventh in thirteen starts for Hayes.

Gene Casella of Hayes pitched and batted his team to the title. He limited All Hallows to two hits while fanning eleven, and drove in both Hayes tallies in the fifth inning.

Brooks Turn Back Braves, 4 to 3, For Roe's Sixth in Succession

Campanella Blasts Bickford for a Homer, Double and Two Singles—Reese Brilliant on Defense in Ebbets Field Game

By LOUIS EFFRAT

What if Vern Bickford of the Braves handcuffed the top three National League batters, Cal Abrams, Jackie Robinson and Pee Wee Reese, last night at Ebbets Field? What if Abrams, who had connected in every game he had started this season, finally was stopped? And what if Reese's seventeen-game hitting-streak was snapped? The Dodgers won, anyway, 4—3, making the right defensive plays at the right times for undefeated Preacher Roe.

Abrams had only one genuine chance to keep his string alive. After having walked his first four times at bat, Cal bounced an easy roller to Buddy Kerr, resulting in a seventh-inning force out. eese rapped the ball hard three times without success and Robinson failed to propel one beyond the infield.

However, offensive strength — and how!—was found in Roy Campanella's bat. The Brooklyn backstop solved Bickford for a homer, two singles and a double, crossing the plate three times as he personally accounted for half the hits yielded by the right-hander.

Reese Excels on Defense

As for the defense, the biggest pat on the back must be reserved for Reese. The little captain did not hit, but he fielded sensationally, helping Roe out of trouble three times. There were his scoop and tag to trap Sid Gordon off second in the fourth, when an attempted bunt was missed and Campanella's throw was short, and his excellent stop of Kerr's hard grounder.

But it was in the eighth, when Roe again found himself in straits, that Peewee really shone. Trailing by two runs, the Braves started a rally when Earl Torgeson opened with a double to right. Bob Elliott fouled out, but Walker Cooper smashed one toward left and it appeared a certain hit until Peewee, dashing to his right, fielded the ball and Torgeson, who could not be censured for going, was trapped and retired.

Except for these outstanding plays by Reese, Roe might not have lasted to gain his sixth straight victory. Preacher was behind most of the batters, walked a half-dozen—a lot for Roe—and gave nine hits. Three of these came in the opening round and cost the southpaw two runs.

The Box Score

BOSTON (N.)	ab	r	h	po	a
Hartsf'ld, 2b	5	0	1	4	3
Olmo, cf	5	1	1	1	0
Torgeson, 1b	2	1	2	11	0
Elliott, 3b	5	0	2	0	3
Cooper, c	4	0	0	4	0
Gordon, lf	1	0	0	2	0
Marshall, rf	4	0	1	0	0
Kerr, ss	3	0	0	2	7
aMueller	1	0	1	0	0
bJethroe	0	1	0	0	0
Bickford, p	3	0	0	0	1
cMarquez	1	0	1	0	0
Total	34	3	9	24	14

BROOKLYN (N.)	ab	r	h	po	a
Abrams, lf	1	0	0	1	0
Reese, ss	4	0	0	4	3
Robinson, 2b	3	0	0	2	4
Hodges, 1b	5	0	1	9	1
Furillo, rf	4	0	0	1	0
C'panella, c	4	3	4	3	1
Thomps'n, cf	3	1	1	4	0
Cox, 3b	4	0	1	3	4
Roe, p	4	0	1	0	3
Total	32	4	8	27	16

aSingled for Kerr in ninth.
bRan for Mueller in ninth.
cSingled for Bickford in ninth.

Boston .... 2 0 0 0 0 0 0 0 1—3
Brooklyn .... 1 2 0 0 1 0 1 0 .—4

Error—Elliott.
Runs batted in—Elliott, Cooper, Campanella, Roe 2, Cox, Hartsfield.
Two-base hits—Torgeson, Campanella. Home run—Campanella. Stolen base—Abrams. Double plays—Hartsfield, Kerr and Torgeson; Cox, Robinson and Hodges. Left on bases—Boston 10, Brooklyn 12. Bases on balls—Off Bickford 8, Roe 6. Struck out—By Bickford 4, Roe 3. Winning pitcher—Roe (6—0). Losing pitcher—Bickford (6—4). Umpires—Gore, Conlan, Robb and Stewart. Time of game—2:50. Attendance—32,309.

With one out, Luis Almo, Torgeson and Elliott singled in succession for one run. Cooper's slow roller to the mound enabled the second marker to cross before 32,309 fans.

In the second, Campanella started a rally with his third homer of the year, a blast into the lower left-field seats. Don Thompson walked and reached third when Elliott erred on Bill Cox' grounder. Don counted the tying point as Roe rolled to short.

Bloop Single for Roe

Singles by Campanella, Thompson and Cox, all in a row, made it 3—2 for Brooklyn in the fifth. Then, in the seventh, Campanella doubled, advanced on an infield out and scored on Roe's bloop single behind first.

Roe was not in the clear, however. He opened the ninth by yielding pinch singles by Ray Mueller and Luis Marquez. Sam Jethroe, running for Mueller, went to third on Marquez' hit and scored as Roy Hartsfield forced Marquez, Luis Olmo then forced Hartsfield, but a pass to Torgeson moved the potential tying run to second. A hit would have evened matters. But Reese gobbled up Elliott's grounder to deep short and flipped to Robinson for the game-ending force out.

Duke Snider, still handicapped by a thigh-injury(took batting practice, but sat this one out.

It was "Bay Shore Night" and 700 citizens of that Long Island town were present.

BROWNS TRIP TIGERS, 4-3

St. Louis Losing String Ends at 6—Widmar Victor

DETROIT, May 25 (AP)—Don Lenhardt's booming bat ended a six-game losing streak for the Browns tonight, St. Louis nipping the Detroit Tigers, 4 to 3. Pitcher Al Widmar won his third game against three losses.

The box score:

ST. LOUIS (A.)	ab	r	h	po	a
Marsh, 3b	4	1	0	2	3
Young, 2b	4	0	0	4	3
Coleman, rf	3	1	1	1	0
Wood, rf	0	0	0	0	0
Lenhardt, lf	4	1	3	4	0
Delsing, cf	4	0	0	1	0
Batts, c	4	0	1	2	1
Arft, 1b	4	0	0	9	0
Upton, ss	3	0	0	1	0
Bero, ss	[illegible]				
Widmar, p	3	0	0	0	1
Total	32	4	6	27	12

DETROIT (A.)	ab	r	h	po	a
Priddy, 2b	5	0	1	2	5
Kryhoski, 1b	5	0	1	16	0
Kell, 3b	4	0	1	1	0
Wertz, rf	4	2	2	0	0
Mullin, lf	4	1	1	1	0
Evers, cf	4	0	1	2	0
Ginsberg, c	3	0	3	4	1
Lipon, ss	3	0	1	0	4
aKeller	1	0	0	0	0
Berry, ss	0	0	0	0	0
Newhouser, p	3	0	0	1	5
bKolloway	1	0	0	0	0
White, p	0	0	0	0	1
Total	37	3	11	27	16

aGrounded out for Lipon in eighth.
bStruck out for Newhouser in eighth.

St. Louis .... 3 0 0 0 0 0 1 0 0—4
Detroit .... 0 0 0 1 0 2 0 0 0—3

Error—Batts. Runs batted in—Coleman, Lenhardt 2, Bero, Wertz 2, Lipon.
Two-base hit—Batts. Home runs—Lenhardt, Wertz 2, Bero. Sacrifice—Widmar. Double play—Widmar, Bero and Arft. Left on bases—St. Louis 6, Detroit 9. Bases on balls—Off Widmar 2, Newhouser 3. Struck out—By Widmar 3, Newhouser 2, White 1. Hits—Off Newhouser 6 in 8 innings, White 0 in 1. Hit by pitcher—By Newhouser (Upton). Wild pitch — Newhouser. Winning pitcher—Widmar (3—3). Losing pitcher—Newhouser (4—3). Umpires—Grieve, Stevens and Summers. Time of game—2:08. Attendance—25,531.

QUEENS NINE VICTOR

Kapikian Hurls 6-Hitter, Beats Brooklyn College, 10-5

Al Kapikian, a right-handed junior, pitched Queens to a 10-5 victory over Brooklyn College on the former's field yesterday. It was Kapikian's seventh triumph and he is unbeaten. He allowed six hits, struck out eleven and walked four men. Brooklyn batted last, it being a home game for the Kingsmen.

George Hall, Queens first baseman, was the batting star with three hits. He also stole four bases.

The score by innings:

		R.	H.	E.
Queens	1 2 2 2 0 0 0 3 0	10	9	3
Brooklyn	0 0 1 2 0 0 0 2 0	5	6	8

Batteries—Kapikian and Saracino. Foster, Kornhaver, Kesslin (3), Abadi (6) and Okwit, Fredlund (5).

Purdue Golfer Gains Title

EVANSTON, Ill., May 25 (AP)—Purdue's Gene Coulter won the individual title but his team had to settle for second place behind Ohio State in the thirty-second Western Conference golf championship today. Coulter shot 290 over the Northwestern University course whipped by winds in the morning and doused by a heavy downpour late this afternoon. Ohio State moved into team leadership at the 54-hole mark and held on through the final round, finishing with a five-man total of 1,528.

Governor Gets Knockdown Bill

HARTFORD, Conn., May 25 (AP)—The eight-second knockdown, now a State Athletic Commission regulation, will become law if the Governor signs a measure approved today by the Senate in concurrence with the House. It says that when a boxer is knocked down he must stay down at least until the referee's count reaches eight.

Coaching School Dates Set

HAMILTON, N. Y., May 25 (UP)—The seventh annual New York State Coaching School, sponsored by the State High School Athletic Association, will be held on the Colgate University campus Aug. 20-25, it was revealed today.

PIRATES ROUT CUBS WITH 5 IN 6TH, 10-1

Homers by Kiner, Metkovich Help Dickson Win 5-Hitter —Pafko Gets 4-Bagger

CHICAGO, May 25 (AP)—Home runs by Ralph Kiner and George Metkovich, a five-run inning and five-hit pitching by Murry Dickson today gave the Pirates a 10-1 victory over the Cubs.

Andy Pafko's ninth homer accounted for the Chicago run. Pittsburgh belted three pitchers for fourteen hits.

The Pirates knocked out Frank Hiller in their big sixth inning and continued the violence against Bob Kelly until Turk Lown retired them in order in the ninth. Metkovich drove in exactly half the Pittsburgh runs with his homer, a double and two singles.

In the second-inning, Kiner walked, took second on Gus Bell's tap in front of the plate and scored on Wally Westlake's single to left. Pafko's homer tied the score in the Cubs' half.

The deadlock was broken in the fourth when Kiner's smash fell into the left-field seats. The Bucs assumed a two-run margin in the fifth on Metkovich's windblown homer into the right-field bleachers.

The Cubs fizzled a chance when they had men on first and third with none out in the fifth.

The box score:

PITTSBURGH (N.)	ab	r	h	po	a
Castigl'ne, ss	4	2	2	2	6
Met'vitch, cf	5	1	4	5	0
Reiser, lf	5	0	1	1	0
Kiner, 1b	3	3	2	11	2
Bell, rf	5	0	0	2	0
Westlake, 3b	4	1	1	0	1
Murtaugh, 2b	4	0	1	3	2
McCull'gh, c	4	1	1	3	1
Dickson, p	4	2	2	0	3
Total	38	10	14	27	15

CHICAGO (N.)	ab	r	h	po	a
Terw'ger, 2b	4	0	1	1	4
Jackson, 3b	4	0	2	3	1
Baumh'tz, rf	3	0	0	0	1
Borkowski, rf	1	0	0	4	0
Sauer, lf	4	0	0	1	0
Pafko, cf	4	1	1	0	0
Fondy, 1b	3	0	1	11	1
Walker, c	1	0	0	1	2
aJeffcoat	0	0	0	0	0
Owen, c	2	0	0	2	1
Cusick, ss	3	0	0	2	5
Hiller, p	2	0	0	2	2
Kelly, p	0	0	0	0	1
bRamazzotti	1	0	0	0	0
Lown, p	0	0	0	0	0
Total	32	1	5	27	18

aRan for Walker in fifth.
bStruck out for Kelly in eighth.

Pittsburgh .... 0 1 0 1 1 5 0 2 0—10
Chicago .... 0 1 0 0 0 0 0 0 0— 1

Error—Jackson.
Runs batted in—Westlake, Kiner, Metkovich 5, McCullough 2, Pafko, Dickson.
Two-base hits—Kiner, Metkovich. Three-base hit—McCullough. Home runs—Pafko, Metkovich, Kiner. Double plays—Terwilliger, Cusick and Fondy; Castiglione, Murtaugh and Kiner. Left on bases—Pittsburgh 5, Chicago 6. Bases on balls—Off Hiller 2, Kelly 2, Dickson 2. Struck out—By Dickson 3, Kelly 2. Hits—Off Hiller 11 in 5 2-3 innings, Kelly 3 in 2 1-3, Lown 0 in 1. Wild pitch—Kelly. Winning pitcher—Dickson (6—3). Losing pitcher—Hiller (4—3). Umpires—Barlick, Donatelli and Ballanfant. Time of game—2:00. Attendance—8,143.

TWO HORSEMEN INJURED

Italian, Spanish Riders Hurt in Falls at Madrid Show

MADRID, May 25 (AP)—Two horsemen well known in international show circles were injured tonight in Spain's international exhibition.

Raimondo d'Inzeo, Italian lieutenant, suffered a broken collarbone in a fall from his mount, Meteore. Spanish Lieut. Col. José Navarro Morenes fell from Blason and suffered concussions of the head and chest. He was taken ot a hospital in a serious condition.

Bertrand Dubrueil, French lieutenant, won the Spanish Army Cup on Tourbillon, clearing sixteen obstacles in 1:28.1.

Major League Baseball

Saturday, May 26, 1951

American League

YESTERDAY'S GAMES

New York 7, Philadelphia 5 (night).
Chicago 6, Cleveland 4 (night).
St. Louis 4, Detroit 3 (night).
Boston 14, Washington 2 (night).

STANDING OF THE CLUBS

	New York	Chicago	Boston	Detroit	Cleveland	Wash'gtn	Philadel	St. Louis	Won	Lost	Perc'tage	Games Behind
N. Y.	—	2	2	2	4	3	5	6	24	9	.727	—
Chic.	1	—	2	3	3	5	3	3	20	9	.690	2
Bost.	2	0	—	3	2	3	5	3	18	13	.581	5
Det.	2	2	3	—	0	3	2	4	16	14	.533	6½
Cleve.	0	2	2	2	—	2	3	4	15	16	.484	8
Wash.	2	1	2	1	2	—	4	3	15	16	.484	8
Phila.	2	1	1	1	2	0	—	2	9	24	.273	15
St. L.	0	1	1	2	3	0	2	—	9	25	.265	15½
Lost	9	9	13	14	16	16	24	25	—	—		

TODAY'S PROBABLE PITCHERS

Philadelphia at New York (2 P. M.)—Martin (1-0) vs. Raschi (7-1).

Chicago at Cleveland—Holcombe (3-1) vs. Garcia (3-2).

St. Louis at Detroit—Starr (0-2) vs. Trout (2-3).

Washington at Boston — Consuegra (3-1) vs. Taylor (2-3).

National League

YESTERDAY'S GAMES

New York 8, Philadelphia 5 (night).
Brooklyn 4, Boston 3 (night).
Pittsburgh 10, Chicago 1.
Cincinnati 5, St. Louis 1 (11 innings, night).

STANDING OF THE CLUBS

	Brooklyn	St. Louis	Chicago	Boston	New York	Cincinnati	Philadel	Pittsb'gh	Won	Lost	Perc'tage	Games Behind
Bklyn.	—	2	3	3	5	4	2	2	21	13	.618	—
St. L.	2	—	3	2	2	4	4	1	18	16	.529	3
Chic.	3	2	—	4	0	2	2	4	17	16	.515	3½
Bost.	2	2	1	—	4	2	4	3	18	18	.500	4
N. Y.	1	3	3	2	—	3	3	3	18	19	.486	4½
Cinc.	1	4	1	4	1	—	2	3	16	19	.457	5½
Phila.	2	2	2	2	4	1	—	3	16	19	.457	5½
Pitts.	2	1	3	1	3	3	2	—	15	19	.441	6
Lost	13	16	16	18	19	19	19	19	—	—		

TODAY'S PROBABLE PITCHERS

Boston at Brooklyn (1:30 P. M.)—Sain (1-5) vs. Erskine (3-4) or Palica (1-2).

New York at Philadelphia (night)—Jansen (3-4) vs. Roberts (4-3).

Cincinnati at St Louis (night)—Wehmeier (1-3) vs. Lanier (2-2).

Pittsburgh at Chicago—Law (1-2) vs. Klippstein (2-1).

(Figures in parentheses indicate season's won-and-lost records.)

Batting Averages

YANKEES

	AB.	H.	PC.		AB.	H.	PC.
Brown	35	12	.343	Lopat	27	7	.259
Collins	57	19	.333	Martin	4	1	.250
Berra	122	40	.328	Morgan	9	2	.222
Coleman	107	34	.318	Raschi	20	4	.200
McDougald	63	20	.317	Byrne	5	1	.200
Bauer	48	15	.313	Shea	11	2	.182
Hopp	10	3	.300	Mapes	8	1	.125
DiMaggio	74	22	.297	Reynolds	16	1	.063
Rizzuto	120	35	.292	Ferrick	0	0	.000
Mantle	134	39	.291	Silvera	1	0	.000
Mize	55	16	.291	Sanford	2	0	.000
Jensen	87	24	.276	Houk	4	0	.000
Woodling	52	14	.269	Ostrowski	5	0	.000

Team batting, 1,116, 324, .290.

GIANTS

	AB.	H.	PC.		AB.	H.	PC.
Maguire	20	8	.400	Wilson	22	4	.182
Dark	136	45	.331	Mueller	64	12	.188
Stanky	134	40	.299	Jansen	22	2	.091
Irvin	122	34	.279	Maglie	26	2	.077
Lohrke	22	6	.273	Gettel	0	0	.000
Westrum	56	15	.268	Yvars	2	0	.000
Lockman	150	40	.267	Jones	3	0	.000
Hearn	15	4	.267	Koslo	3	0	.000
Noble	73	19	.260	Rigney	3	0	.000
Thompson	110	28	.255	Bowman	5	0	.000
Jorgensen	38	9	.237	Kennedy	5	0	.000
Thomson	140	32	.229	Spencer	9	0	.000
Hartung	30	6	.200				

Team batting—1,210, 306, .253
Last night's Giant game not included.

DODGERS

	AB.	H.	PC.		AB.	H.	PC.
Abrams	66	31	.470	Hatten	12	3	.167
Robinson	123	51	.415	Brown	25	4	.160
Reese	125	48	.384	Thompson	34	5	.147
Snider	143	43	.301	Erskine	14	2	.143
Hodges	133	40	.301	Van Cuyk	7	1	.143
Campanella	107	31	.290	H. Edwards	8	1	.125
Miksis	7	2	.286	Roe	25	3	.120
Bridges	34	9	.265	King	13	1	.077
Hermanski	50	13	.260	Bankhead	0	0	.000
Cox	94	24	.255	Haugstad	0	0	.000
Furillo	177	36	.245	Branca	2	0	.000
B. Edwards	33	8	.242	Palica	5	0	.000
Newcombe	20	4	.200				

Team batting—1,224, 360, .294.
Last night's Dodger game not included.

Major League Leaders

BATSMEN
(Based on 50 times at bat)

AMERICAN LEAGUE

	G.	AB.	R.	H.	PC.
Kryhoski, Detroit	18	67	12	26	.388
Fain, Philadelphia	32	120	14	46	.383
Busby, Chicago	26	93	18	33	.355
Fox, Chicago	29	111	19	38	.342
Minoso, Chicago	27	76	26	26	.342

NATIONAL LEAGUE

	G.	AB.	R.	H.	PC.
Abrams, Brooklyn	25	66	16	31	.470
Robinson, Brooklyn	33	123	30	51	.415
Reese, Brooklyn	34	125	21	48	.384
Elliott, Boston	32	111	22	40	.360
Sisler, Philadelphia	33	121	20	46	.357

RUNS BATTED IN

AMERICAN LEAGUE
Robinson, Chicago....29 | Zarilla, Chicago.....26
Rosen, Cleveland.....29 | Wertz, Detroit.......26
Mantle, New York.....26

NATIONAL LEAGUE
Snider, Brooklyn.....32 | Sauer, Chicago......30
Hodges, Brooklyn.....31

HOME RUN HITTERS

AMERICAN LEAGUE
Williams, Boston.....8 | Zernial, Philadelphia 7
Robinson, Chicago....7

NATIONAL LEAGUE
Hodges, Brooklyn.....14 | Kiner, Pittsburgh.....9
Westlake, Pittsburgh.13 | Pafko, Chicago........9
Snider, Brooklyn......9 | Sauer, Chicago........9

Last night's games not included.

Minor Leagues

By The Associated Press

INTERNATIONAL LEAGUE

(Night Games)

AT BUFFALO

		R.	H.	E.
Baltimore	0 1 2 2 0 0 2 0 1	8	12	0
Buffalo	2 0 0 0 0 0 1 0 0	3	6	1

Batteries—Donnelly and Anderson; Savransky, Simpson 2), Carrasquel 4), Lovenguth 9) and Landrith.

AT OTTAWA

		R.	H.	E.
Rochester	0 0 0 0 0 0 0 0 0	0	2	1
Ottawa	0 0 0 0 0 0 0 0 1	1	7	0

Batteries—Faszholz and Leblanc; Bamberger and Watlington.

AT TORONTO

		R.	H.	E.
Syracuse	0 0 4 0 0 1 0 0 0	5	8	1
Toronto	0 0 0 0 0 1 0 0 1	2	6	0

Batteries—Griffore and Baker; Bruner, Peterson (3) and Plumbo.
Other club not scheduled.

STANDING OF THE CLUBS

	W.	L.	PC.		W.	L.	PC.
Montreal	23	12	.657	Baltimore	17	20	.459
Rochester	20	15	.571	Buffalo	14	17	.452
Syracuse	19	16	.543	Toronto	14	18	.438
Ottawa	18	16	.529	Springfield	12	23	.343

EASTERN LEAGUE

(Night Games)

Hartford 7, Elmira 0.
Scranton 4, Binghamton 2.
Wilkes-Barre 5, Schenectady 3 (1st).
Wilkes-Barre 6, Schenectady 1 (2d).
Williamsport 4, Albany 1 (1st).
Williamsport 11, Albany 1 (2d).

STANDING OF THE CLUBS

	W.	L.	PC.		W.	L.	PC.
Elmira	19	11	.633	Wilkes-Barre	14	16	.467
Hartford	18	11	.621	Albany	13	15	.464
Scranton	16	14	.533	Binghamton	12	16	.429
Schenectady	16	15	.517	Williamsport	9	19	.321

[From Late Editions of Yesterday's TIMES.]

AMERICAN ASSOCIATION

(Night Games)

Columbus 3, Louisville 2.
St. Paul 8, Kansas City 4.
Toledo 15, Indianapolis 7.
Other clubs not scheduled.

STANDING OF THE CLUBS

	W.	L.	PC.		W.	L.	PC.
Milwaukee	20	11	.645	Louisville	16	19	.457
Kansas City	23	13	.639	Indianapolis	15	19	.441
Minneapolis	21	14	.600	Columbus	14	21	.400
Toledo	16	18	.471	St. Paul	10	20	.333

[From Late Editions of Yesterday's TIMES.]

SOUTHERN ASSOCIATION

(Night Game)

Nashville 7, Mobile 1.
Other clubs not scheduled.

STANDING OF THE CLUBS

	W.	L.	PC.		W.	L.	PC.
Little Rock	28	15	.651	Chattan'ga	18	20	.474
Atlanta	22	17	.564	Memphis	18	24	.429
Birm'ham	22	18	.550	N. Orleans	17	24	.415
Nashville	22	20	.524	Mobile	17	26	.395

[From Late Editions of Yesterday's TIMES.]

TEXAS LEAGUE

(Night Games)

Beaumont 3, Shreveport 1.
Fort Worth 3, Dallas 1.
Tulsa 6, Oklahoma City 3.

STANDING OF THE CLUBS

	W.	L.	PC.		W.	L.	PC.
Dallas	25	16	.610	Okla. City	20	22	.476
San Antonio	26	17	.605	Fort Worth	19	23	.452
Beaumont	24	22	.522	Shreveport	21	28	.429
Houston	22	21	.512	Tulsa	17	25	.405

PACIFIC COAST LEAGUE

(Thursday Night Games)

Hollywood 13, Los Angeles 1.
Oakland 12, San Francisco 0.
Sacramento 3, Portland 1.
San Diego 6, Seattle 3 (1st).
Seattle 6, San Diego 2 (2d).

STANDING OF THE CLUBS

	W.	L.	PC.		W.	L.	PC.
Sacramento	33	24	.579	Los Angeles	26	27	.509
Oakland	31	26	.544	Hollywood	27	29	.482
Portland	31	26	.544	San Diego	23	31	.426
Seattle	31	27	.534	San Francisco	21	35	.375

CARDS MAKE IT FOUR OUT OF FIVE UNDER MOORE

POST-DISPATCH
Sports
Edited by
J. ROY STOCKTON

PART THREE PAGES 1—4C
ST. LOUIS, MONDAY, AUGUST 20, 1951

Just a Joke, but It Might Become Serious.

OUR William Veeck is a great laugh provider for his Brownie clients. . . . But he caused a lot of tongue-wagging when he introduced a midget (regularly and duly signed to a contract) into Sunday's game. . . . The strike zone for a player so tiny was close to zero and so the doughty little mite drew a base on balls.

The crowd roared at the situation, especially when Delsing was sent in to run for him. . . . However, nothing came of it. . . . Nobody scored. . . . And there was no opportunity for the visiting club to complain.

* * *

But consider the consequences had the next man up for the Browns made a triple and scored Delsing with the run that ultimately proved to be the winning tally. . . . Worse still, suppose it was the last half of the ninth, the bases filled and the score tied. . . . If the pitcher walked the midget (which he probably could not avoid) he would force in the winning run!

A protest would be filed. . . . Organized baseball would boil over. . . . The league presidents, or the Commissioner or the executive committee would take up the matter. . . . And of couse measures would be taken to make repetition impossible of any such extra-curricular activities, designed to defeat the normal purposes of the game.

* * *

VEECK, like MacPhail and even our own Chris Von Der Ahe of long, long ago, provided interesting non-baseball entertainment for fans attending their baseball games. . . . But thus far we don't remember any attempt to put something over involving the game itself.

* * *

Tampering with baseball procedure or regulations just to create a laugh would seem to be going a little too far, say fans to whom we have talked about the situation. . . . Have fun, but not at the expense of the game itself. . . . No joke that can give the home team an original man on base, a potential run, is going to be taken lightly if repeated.

* * *

White Sox Negro Ace Rookie of the Year?

PAUL RICHARDS, White Sox manager, seems to have surrendered title hopes this year. . . . But very definitely he has done a good job in picking players. . . . One of the men he chose in a deal was Orestes Minoso, Cuban Negro, just now one of the American League's top hitters. . . . He's an infield or an outfield star as Richards may need.

If the Cleveland club should fail to win the pennant because of weak hitting, observers may conclude that it was because the Indians' front office kept Harry Simpson and let Minoso go, in a three-way deal with the Athletics and the White Sox.

* * *

In any case, Minoso vaulted from just a pretty fair hitter into one of the American League's best. . . . And you can't overlook that one. . . . A magazine labeled "Complete Baseball" already has picked Minoso as the "Rookie of the Year," in the American League. . . . He's just about that at this writing.

Orestes is in the 29-year-old division but he has been active in baseball since he was about 16. . . . In Cuba, where he made his start, he attracted the attention of scouts and soon landed with San Diego, the Indians' Farm. . . . He was brought to training camp last year and again this season. . . . He worked in both outfield and at third base. . . . And he has turned out to be a whale of a hitter and runner.

* * *

HIS batting power, if available, today would probably make the Indians a sure-shot in the A.L. pennant scramble.

* * *

And, while on the subject of the year's rookie crop, the magazine mentioned above picks Joseph Edward Presko of the Cardinals as the National League's outstanding rookie. . . . It's still early to make such a selection. . . . But if Presko hadn't suffered a muscle injury he might have been able to fully justify his choice.

* * *

The Cardinals' right-hand curvist made a fine debut and is only four years out of high school. . . . It may be that the Cards' staff really has something in this prospect. . . . And we can't think of anything the Cardinals need more than a freshman pitcher of big league stature.

* * *

Unbelievable May Add To Calumet Farm's Fame.

FROM Chicago we learn that the full brother of Citation will soon make his first start. . . . There has been some wonder that while two other Calumet Farm two-year-olds have been sent to the wars and have achieved great successes—Hail Gail and A Gleam—Unbelievable has not yet gone to the post.

However, he's eligible for the $75,000 Washington Park Futurity and as that's to be run Sept. 1 he'll need a race or two to tighten him up if he's to have a shot at that big prize. . . . Probably he can't be readied in time.

Calumet probably will have some good ones to send to the Derby next year—the best since the one-two punch of Citation and Coaltown . . . Just now it appears that the Jones boys may send Hill Gail, A Gleam and Unbelievable after all the big 3-year-old events of 1952.

* * *

The recent 3-year-old championship situation seems to have added something to Hall of Fame's title bid . . He won Saturday's American Derby in the fastest time but one in the history of the event . . . But he was pressed to win and by a little regarded horse, Abbie

Continued on Page 3, Column 4.

Al Brazle As Starter Helps Win Twin Bill

By a Staff Correspondent of the Post-Dispatch.

CINCINNATI, Aug. 20—With Brooklyn's Dodgers having lost five of their last seven games to the four eastern teams of the National League, the Cardinals are heading east today hopeful of continuing the Flatbush team's skid enough in the next 10 days to make the circuit's pennant chase a race instead of a runaway.

Of the four western teams only the Cardinals have any prospects of overhauling the Dodgers and their chances of doing so are extremely slim.

But if they can slap them down Tuesday night and Wednesday and Thursday afternoons they could make things interesting.

The Cardinals have plenty of scores to settle with the Dodgers for the way Chuck Dressen's team has manhandled them this season and now, despite the fact that they are down to seven pitchers for the time being and Country Slaughter is far from being at his physical best, they seem to be in good trim for the series at Ebbets Field.

Brazle Starts—and Finishes.

The way the Cards played in winning a double-header from the Reds yesterday, 5-4 and 5-1, before 18,636 customers, especially in the second game when Alpha Brazle made his 1951 debut as a starter, gave the band Terry Moore is directing so capably in Marty Marion's absence high hopes of getting some revenge on the Dodgers. The Cards have won four out of five under Terry.

Moore will send Gerry Staley after Tuesday night's game with Max Lanier a good bet to toe the slab in the second game and Harry Brecheen or Cliff Chambers in the third one.

Having Brazle come through with a five-hit, one walk, six-strikeout performance in his initial start of the year was a real shot in the arm for the Redbirds.

In the first eight rounds Hank Edwards was the only Red to pass first base, doing so in the second when he hit a lengthy homer into the bleachers back of right center.

Brazle appeared to be losing his grip when he walked Ted Kluszewski to start the ninth then hit Joe Adcock to make Kluszewski the second Red in the game to reach second base.

But in this spot Brazle rared back and fanned Edwards for the second time in succession and then got the game over in a hurry by causing Bob Usher to ground into a double play.

Red Schoendienst made quite a play in pivoting that final twin killing because Adock spilled him hard as he slid into the keystone sack.

Except for a shaky start (he walked three in the first three rounds and four in the first four) and Virgil Stallcup's two-run homer in the ninth Chambers matched Brazel's pitching in effectiveness.

The Cards didn't have much trouble getting five runs in each game. Nippy Jones assaulted Kenny Raffensberger and Bud Byerly ably in the first game to drive in two runs with a single off Raffy in a four-run third and another with a homer off Byerly in the fifth.

Hal in a Fox Chase.

Hal Rice, missing from the first game's lineup, hit Howard Fox for singles each of his first three times up in the nightcap and drove in a run with each of his first two.

Hal's third hit off Fox helped get another run in the fifth, this one driven in by Peanuts Lowrey.

Schoendienst singled and scored from first when Stan Musial doubled in the seventh while in the eighth Lowrey banged a triple down the right-field line and jogged home when Jones followed with a hit which bounced away from Usher for a double.

The Cards still are 16½ games behind the Dodgers and seven and a half back of the Giants, but they haven't quit trying to overtake both.

Midget Helps Veeck Do Things in a Big Way

—By a Post-Dispatch Staff Photographer.

Among many novelties introduced by Bill Veeck as the Browns observed the American League's fiftieth birthday was a midget pinch-hitter. He went to the plate as a replacement for Frank Saucier in the first inning of the second game as the 18,369 paying crowd screamed, and drew a pass. The midget, who had never played baseball, was ED GAEDEL of Chicago. He was taken out of the game immediately after walking. Behind the plate is BOB SWIFT of the Tigers and ED HURLEY is the umpire.

Lots of Frosting on Brownies' A.L. Birthday Cake, but Filling Turns Bitter With Two Defeats

By Bob Broeg

The austere American League, gravely celebrating its fiftieth anniversary this year, will reach the ripe old age of 100 before anyone other than Phineas T. Veeck, the Barnum of baseball, tops the colorful substitute for winning ball the sport-shirted showman offered yesterday at Sportsman's Park.

As frosting on the birthday cake, before and after the sub-basement Browns lost ball games to Detroit, Veeck sent into action the first midget in major league history. And like General Tom Thumb, the little person the original Barnum introduced to the crown heads of Europe a century ago, Eddie Gaedel is likely to be remembered for a long time.

Twenty-six years old, but standing just three feet seven inches low and weighing only 65 pounds, Chicago stunt man Gaedel popped out of a giant-sized paper anniversary cake, climaxing lavish between-game ceremonies, and minutes later strode up to home plate in full Brownie uniform, swinging miniature bats.

"For the Brown," droned the voice of Field Announcer Bernie Ebert, "No. One-Eighth, Eddie Gaedel, batting for Saucier."

Yes, It Was Official.

As a stunned crowd of 20,299 (18,369) came alive with laughter at the sight of the economy-sized leadoff batter, Plate Umpire Ed Hurley crooked a finger at Manager Zack Taylor, who trotted out with the legal evidence—an official American League contract signed by the midget and a carbon copy of a telegram Veeck hed sent to league headquarters, adding Gaedel to the Browns' playing roster.

Hurley nodded approval, and then it was Detroit's turn to be puzzled. As the little fellow stepped into the batter's box, Catcher Bob Swift assumed a sitting position, decided that wouldn't do and then trotted out to talk to Bob Cain, the Tigers' pitcher.

"Get outta that hole," the Detroit bench yelled at the crouched figure waiting at the plate.

Cain, deciding the strike zone offered would have been too small for even a master of control like Ol' Pete Alexander, got things over quickly—but not the ball—throwing four pitches high and wide. Gaedel threw aside his bat, ran to first base, retired for a pinch-runner and then, giving his replacement an encouraging pat, retired majestically. As the fans roared, he bowed and doffed his cap repeatedly.

Feels Like Babe Ruth.

"For a minute," the little man explained excitedly afterward, "I felt like Babe Ruth."

A Chicago White Sox fan, Gaedel returned home last night thrilled. "I never thought I'd live to see the day I'd be a major leaguer," the midget said happily.

Veeck, grinning over the success of his greatest have-fun-if-you-can't-win experiment, was disappointed only that the Browns, filling the bases after that walk, failed to score in the first inning. "I wanted to prove," he said, "that this was a practical idea, too."

The colorful character who runs the Browns pointed out that there was nothing in the baseball rules that dictated either maximum or minimum size of players, and the umpires agreed. They planned no report to league headquarters, they said. Red Rolfe, Detroit manager who made no protest because he had learned about Veeck's self-styled "secret weapon" beforehand, complained in the visitors' clubhouse later that the Brownie boss had "gone a bit too far."

"I don't blame Bill for doing all he can to get and entertain fans, but I don't think there should be anything permitted that might affect or make a joke of the game," Rolfe said mildly.

Another Defeat for Garver.

Except for the ball games, in which Detroit's Gene Bearden beat Ned Garver, 5 to 2, and then Cain triumphed over Duane Pillette, 6 to 2, there was fun throughout for the largest crowd to watch American League clubs here in more than four years.

Entering the park, spectators were given free birthday ice cream and cake from the Browns and bottle-shaped souvenir salt-

Continued on Next Page.

How They Stand

AMERICAN LEAGUE.

CLUB.	W.	L.	Pct.	Win.	Lose.	Games B'h'd.
Cleveland	74	43	.632	.636	.627	. . .
New York	73	43	.629	.632	.624	½
Boston	70	46	.603	.607	.598	3½
Chicago	64	53	.547	.551	.542	10
Detroit	55	60	.478	.483	.474	18
Washington	47	68	.409	.414	.405	26
Philadelphia	46	73	.387	.392	.383	29
BROWNS	36	79	.313	.319	.310	37

NATIONAL LEAGUE.

CLUB.	W.	L.	Pct.	Win.	Lose.	Games B'h'd.
Brooklyn	74	41	.643	.647	.638	. . . .
New York	68	51	.572	.575	.567	8
CARDS	56	56	.500	.504	.496	16½
Philadelphia	57	60	.487	.492	.483	18
Boston	54	59	.478	.482	.474	19
Cincinnati	53	63	.457	.462	.453	21½
Chicago	51	63	.447	.452	.443	22½
Pittsburgh	49	69	.415	.420	.412	26½

Yesterday's Results.

AMERICAN LEAGUE.
Detroit 5-6, Browns 2-2.
Cleveland 4-6, Chicago 0-7.
Philadelphia 15, New York 1.
Boston 8, Washington 3.

NATIONAL LEAGUE.
Cardinals 5-5, Cincinnati 4-1.
Pittsburgh 4-5, Chicago 2-4.
New York 5, Philadelphia 4.
Boston 13, Brooklyn 4.

Today's Schedule.

AMERICAN LEAGUE.
New York at Detroit (2) (5:30 and 7:30 p.m.)—Lopat (16-6) and Ostrowski (4-3) vs. Hutchinson (8-6) and Trucks (5-7).
Washington at Cleveland (7:30 p.m.)—Starr (3-7) vs. Garcia (16-8).
(Only games scheduled.)

NATIONAL LEAGUE.
Brooklyn at Boston (7:30 p.m.) — Newcombe (16-6) vs. Wilson (3-4).
(Only game scheduled.)

Tomorrow's Schedule.

AMERICAN LEAGUE.
Boston at St. Louis, 8:30 p.m.
New York at Detroit, 8:30 p.m.
Washington at Cleveland, 7:30 p.m.
Philadelphia at Chicago, 8:30 p.m.

NATIONAL LEAGUE.
Cardinals at Brooklyn, 7:30 p.m.
Pittsburgh at Boston, 7:30 p.m.
Cincinnati at New York, 12:30 p.m.
Chicago at Philadelphia, 8 p.m. (also completion of suspended game of July 22).

Saturday's Results.

AMERICAN LEAGUE.
Browns 20, Detroit 9.
New York 5, Philadelphia 1.
Cleveland 7, Chicago 0.
Boston 10, Washington 9 (night).

NATIONAL LEAGUE.
Cincinnati 1, Cardinals 0.
Brooklyn 5, Boston 3 (night).
New York 2, Philadelphia 0 (night).
Chicago 11, Pittsburgh 5.

Softball.

ST. LOUIS PARK
Girls' Game

CLUB	1	2	3	4	5	6	7	8	9		R.	H.	E.
Orphans	0	0	4	0	0	0	0	0	0	—	4	5	1
S. Gr. Mot.	0	0	0	0	1	2	0	0	0	—	3	9	2

Batteries—Woods and Mica; Price and Reinhold.

Men's Game

CLUB	1	2	3	4	5	6	7	8	9		R.	H.	E.
Poplar	0	0	0	0	0	0	1	0	0	—	1	5	4
Swift	4	0	2	0	0	0	0	0	x	—	6	6	1

Batteries—Vickers, Williams and Cope; Mueller and Borghi.

ST. LOUIS PARK—M-K-T vs. Mo-Pac, men's game; Wilmington vs. Potucek, girls' game; Terminal vs. Wabash, men's game; first game starts at 7 p.m.

OVERLAND LEGION PARK

LAST NIGHT'S RESULTS—Post 259, 5; Forest City, 4, Mock Philips, 4; Eureka, 0. Both men's games.

TONIGHT'S SCHEDULE—Tower Grove Reds vs. Jacobs Plumbers', 7:15 p.m.; I'm Inn vs. Oldani's, 9. Both men's games.

Play Begins in District Tennis Title Tourney

A field of 43 men and 15 women will begin singles play this afternoon at Triple A in the annual District Tennis Association's tournament. First matches are slated for 4 o'clock.

Robert Hill is the top-seeded male player and Mrs. Merceina Parker tops the women's division. Seeded after Hill were Frank Thompson, Bob Light and Ralph Hart. Marilyn Mueller is No. 2 seed in the women's bracket and is followed by Martha Goebel and Mary Vassely.

Men's and women's doubles will be drawn after today's play. Finals in all divisions are scheduled next Sunday.

Today's schedule:

4 p.m.—W. Roeder vs. L. Miller; F. Thompson vs. A. Holtmann; A. Siegfried vs. M. Weatherly; W. Smith vs. S. Cushing.

5 p.m.—F. Varner vs. W. Gundlach; O. S. Wall vs. R. Taylor; R. Friedman vs. G. Frumson; W. Gatlin vs. W. Heitman.

6 p.m.—P. Sparks vs. F. Keaney; L. Dorr vs. K. Oliver; G. Lund vs. W. Chaffee; L. Singer vs. R. Thias.

Tennis Doubles Final Postponed

CHESTNUT HILL, Mass., Aug. 20 (UP)—A violent thunderstorm caused a 24-hour postponement in the finals of the national doubles tennis championships today and forced Australia to wait until tomorrow to annex its third consecutive U.S. men's title.

Top-seeded Australians Frank Sedgman and Ken McGregor had been scheduled to face the No. 2 Aussie team of Mervyn Rose and Don Candy for the tandem title when the weather intervened.

Caddie Moeller Shoots 71 In Practice at Columbus

By Robert Morrison
Of the Post-Dispatch Sports Staff.

COLUMBUS, Aug. 20—Earl Moeller Jr., St. Louis caddie champion, was renewing an old acquaintance with the Ohio State U. golf course today, and it appeared to be the beginning of a beautiful friendship.

Playing with Jack Parnell, his side-kick from St. Louis, Moeller turned in a one-under-par score of 71 for his first round in the two-day practice period for the national caddie championship.

This was one of the best among the early practice rounds of 59 contestants who will open fire for the college scholarship prizes in the national tournament beginning tomorrow.

While Moeller had the benefit of previous experience here, it was the first visit for Parnell, who finished as runner-up to Earl in the St. Louis tournament sponsored by the Post-Dispatch.

Parnell Shoots a 75.

Parnell did very well here on his first time around, scoring 75. Both boys were tired from a full week of tournament play last week in St. Louis, so they wisely limited their early activity.

The 17-year-old Moeller, who has made a sweep of junior, caddie and Crystal Lake invitation titles in St. Louis this summer, seemed likely to be one of the standouts in the National.

His practice round of 71 was especially an indication. In the six years of national tournament qualifying, few have scored that well on the 7120-yard university course. The medal was won a year ago with 73-75—148. This year, however, dry weather for an extended period has made the course play shorter than usual.

That 1950 medalist, incidentally, is one of nine boys, including Moeller, who are returning for a second crack at the national title. The medal winner was Bill Curtis, Detroit.

Medalist Went 3 Rounds.

All boys returning for another shot were early victims in the 1950 National. Moeller lost in the second round, Curtis in the third.

Under a changed set-up, the tournament here has a smaller entry than that of previous years when from 76 to 100 boys competed. Now, each player must be winner or runner-up of a local tournament sponsored by a newspaper. The present plan is to increase the number of newspaper franchises next year.

But, for this tournament, there is not a sufficient number to fill a 64-place draw, so each boy who plays in tomorrow's 36-hole qualifier is certain of a match play opportunity. There will be five first-round championship flight byes.

Another change this year is the $300 scholarship put up by the Canadian P.G.A. for medalist prize. The P.G.A. of the United States offers the $1500 and $750 scholarship prizes for the winner and runner-up.

Age range in the present field is from 13 to 17 years, and the winner in Saturday's 36-hole final will have the additional prize of a flight to New York for an appearance on the "Toast of the Town" television show Sunday.

Moeller Watches Movies.

St. Louis's entries were well prepared in more ways than one. On the train ride here Saturday, they discovered that movies in the recreation car showed Cary Middlecoff in his recent All-American victory at Tan O'Shanter.

"Earl ran those movies over two or three times to watch Middlecoff's putting stroke," said Parnell.

Moeller also felt himself better equipped because the boys' home club pro, Ray Schwartz at Norwood Hills, had loaned Earl his irons. They were heavier clubs than the set Moeller had been using and Earl said they seemed to work much better.

M.A.C. Team Third In Indiana Swim Meet

The Missouri Athletic Club team took third place in the Shakamak (Ind.) State Park swimming championships with 27 points. Kenosha, Wisc., was first with 42, and the Indianapolis A.C. had 34.

The M.A.C. 300-meter relay team of Boyd Fellows, Don Clooney, and Robin Ord was first with a time of 3:39.2. Ord was second in the 100 and 200-meter events, Clooney was fourth in the 300-meter national junior individual medley and the 100- and 200-meter breast stroke events, and Fellows was fourth in the 100-meter back stroke and fifth in the 200-meter back stroke.

In the women's divisions, Helen Hughes of St. Louis Y.W.H.A. was second in the 100-, 200-, and 400-meter events.

Albert Pitches Four Touchdown Passes as San Francisco Wins

SAN FRANCISCO, Aug. 20 (UP)—The San Francisco 49ers marched for a touchdown each of the first three times they got the ball yesterday and then went on to crush the Washington Redskins, 45-14, in an exhibition game before 27,280 fans at Kezar Stadium.

With Quarterback Frankie Albert passing for four touchdowns during the game, the 49ers ran up a 28-0 lead at the halftime. It was the second shellacking of the week for the Redskins, who were whipped 58-14 last Wednesday by the Los Angeles Rams.

Washington never threatened during the first half. The Redskins got one counter in the third period after Fullback Bob Goode went 42 yards to the San Francisco 12. From there Quarterback Harry Gilmer passed into the end zone to End Hugh Taylor. Taylor also scored the other Redskin counter early in the fourth when he took a 16-yard toss from Gilmer and raced 65 yards. Bill Dudley made both conversions.

Better Late Than Never

(FIRST GAME)

CARDINALS.	AB.	R.	H.
Hemus ss	4	1	2
Sch'd'nst 2b	4	1	2
Musial lf	4	1	3
Lowrey cf	4	1	1
Jones 1b	4	1	2
Slaughter rf	4	0	0
Johnson 3b	3	0	1
D. Rice c	4	0	0
Chamb's p	4	0	0
Totals	35	5	11

CINCINNATI.	AB.	R.	H.
Adams 3b	2	1	0
Ryan 2b	3	0	0
Klusz'ki 1b	4	0	2
Adcock lf	4	0	0
Litwhiler rf	4	1	1
Usher cf	3	0	0
Stallcup ss	4	1	2
Howell c	4	0	0
Raffens'r p	0	0	0
aMeeks	1	1	1
Erautt p	0	0	0
bBlackwell	1	0	0
Byerly p	0	0	0
cMcMillan	1	0	0
Perk'wski p	0	0	0
dPramesa	1	0	0
Totals	32	4	6

aSingled for Raffensberger in third.
bStruck out for Erautt in fourth.
cPopped out for Byerly in seventh.
dGrounded out for Perskowski in ninth.

Innings.	1	2	3	4	5	6	7	8	9	
Cardinals	0	0	4	0	1	0	0	0	0	— 5
Cincinnati	1	0	1	0	0	0	0	0	2	— 4

Error—D. Rice. Runs batted in—Lowrey, Jones 3, Johnson, Adcock, Stallcup 2. (Adams scored on error by D. Rice in first). Two-base hit—Hemus. Home runs—Jones, Stallcup. Left on base—Cardinals 7, Cincinnati 5. Base on balls—Off Chambers 4, Raffensberger 1, Erautt 1, Byerly 1, Perkowski 1. Struck out—By Chambers 4, Raffensberger 2, Erautt 1, Perkowski 1. Hits and runs—Off Raffensberger 7 and 4 in 3 innings, Erautt 1 and 0 in 1, Byerly 3 and 1 in 3, Perkowski 0 and 0 in 2. Double plays—Hemus to Schonendienst to Jones; Stallcup to Kluszewski; Ryan to Stallcup to Kluszewski. Winning pitcher—Chambers (9-11). Losing pitcher—Raffensberger (12-15). Umpires—Ballanfant, Barlick, Donatelli. Time of game—2h. 32m.

(SECOND GAME)

CARDINALS.	AB.	R.	H.
Hemus ss	4	1	1
Sch'd'st 2b	5	2	2
Musial lf	3	1	1
H. Rice rf	4	0	3
aGlaviano	1	0	0
Diering rf	0	0	0
Lowrey cf	4	1	2
Jones 1b	4	0	1
Johnson 3b	4	0	0
Scheffing c	3	0	0
Brazle p	4	0	0
Totals	36	5	10

CINCINNATI.	AB.	R.	H.
Adams 3b	3	0	1
Ryan 2b	4	0	0
Klu'wski 1b	3	0	1
Adcock lf	3	0	0
Edwards rf	4	1	1
Usher cf	4	0	1
Stallcup ss	3	0	0
Howell c	3	0	1
Fox p	2	0	0
bMeeks	1	0	0
Perkowski p	0	0	0
Totals	30	1	5

aFouled out for Rice in ninth.
bFiled out for Fox in eighth.

Innings.	1	2	3	4	5	6	7	8	9	
Cardinals	1	0	1	0	1	0	1	1	0	— 5
Cincinnati	0	1	0	0	0	0	0	0	0	— 1

Error—Adams. Runs batted in—H. Rice 2, Musial, Lowrey, Jones, Edwards. Two-base hits—Schonedienst, Musial, Jones. Three-base hit—Lowrey. Home run—Edwards. Left on bases—Cardinals 8, Cincinnati 5. Bases on balls—Off Brazle 3, Fox 3, Perkowski 1. Struck out—By Brazle 6, Fox 1, Perkowski 1. Hits and runs—Off Fox 1 and 5 in 8 innings; Perowski 0 and 0 in 1. Hit by pitcher—By Brazle (Adcock). Double plays—Brazle to Schoendienst to Jones; Stallcup to Ryan to Kluszewski; Johnson to Schoendienst to Jones. Winning pitcher—Brazle (3-1). Losing pitcher—Fox (7-10). Umpires—Barlick, Donatelli and Ballanfant. Time of game—2h. 5m. Attendance—18,636.

College Drops Basketball; 'Sports Are Over-Emphasized'

DETROIT, Aug. 20 (UP)—Lawrence Tech announced today that it was dropping basketball with this season because "intercollegiate sports are too over-emphasized."

The cancellation came in the wake of basketball "fix" scandals that shocked the sports world this year. Lawrence Tech was not involved.

President E. George Lawrence said the school had cancelled its basketball schedule for the 1951-52 season.

"At a meeting of the board of control it was decided to drop the sport because the board felt that at this time intercollegiate sports are too over-emphasized throughout the country," he said.

"While the board previously supported schedules of this type, it felt that present conditions certainly indicate the need for de-emphasis," Lawrence said.

Athletic Director and Basketball Coach Dom Ridler has been asked to remain to develop "an intensified program of student activities," he said.

POST-DISPATCH Sports

Edited by J. ROY STOCKTON

Cards Swing Into One-Run Lead Without Swinging

Woodling an Old Indian Fighter, Bangs Home Run to Put Yankees Only Two Games Out of First

CLEVELAND, Aug. 25 (AP)—Gene Woodling, 29-year-old outfielder of the New York Yankees, is waging a one-man drive to prevent the Cleveland Indians from winning the 1951 American League pennant.

Woodling, a native Ohioan and one-time member of the Tribe, put the Yankees back into the thick of the fight last night as he poled a two-run two-out homer in the seventh inning off Early Wynn to lead the Bombers to a 2-0 triumph. The conquest moved the Yanks to within two games of the Indians.

Woodling's dramatic homer was his fifth decisive four-bagger against the Indians. It also was his third off Wynn, each blow coming exactly one month apart.

Look What the Guy's Done.

The little outfielder started his one-man crusade June 23 when he homered off Bob Lemon with one on in a 7-6 Yankee victory. On June 24 he beat Wynn, 5-3, with a two-run homer in the eighth. July 12 he homered off Bob Feller to account for the only run in Allie Reynold's no-hitter. Woodling ruined Wynn again July 24 when he cracked a two-run homer in a 3-2 Yankee victory.

Woodling's homer off Wynn last night was his thirteenth of the season. He also collected a single and two walks to give him a total of 15 hits in his last 20 times at bat, a .750 average.

The payoff homer, struck before 71,768 fans, largest night game crowd of the season, overshadowed some brilliant pitching by Stubby Overmire and Joe Ostrowski, obscure left-handers of the Yanks.

Overmire drew the starting assignment because Reynolds and Bob Kuzava were out with injuries. The little southpaw, entrusted with only three previous starting jobs, lasted until the fifth when he complained of a pain in his pitching arm. Ostrowski took over with runners on first and third and one out and got out of the jam.

Ostrowski singled to start the seventh inning. He moved up on a sacrifice and jogged home ahead of Woodling's smash over the right field fence. Ostrowski received credit for the victory, his sixth against three losses.

Other American League games saw the Chicago White Sox edge the Boston Red Sox, 3-2, the St. Louis Browns defeat the Athletics, 5-3, and the Washington Senators club the Detroit Tigers, 10-7.

Ed Robinson singled home Ray Coleman with Chicago's winning run against the Red Sox. Lou Kretlow limited Boston to five hits.

Mike McCormick clouted a grand-slam homer and Sam Mele and Joe Haynes homered with the bases empty to lead Washington to victory over Detroit.

In the National League, the Brooklyn Dodgers nipped the Chicago Cubs, 1-0; the New York Giants beat the Cardinals, 6-5; the Pittsburgh Pirates defeated Philadelphia, 5-1, and the Boston Braves took a twi-night doubleheader from Cincinnati, 5-1 and 2-1.

Ralph Branca blanked the Cubs on three hits and fanned 10 as Brooklyn retained its 7½-game lead over the Giants. Jackie Robinson drove in Peewee Reese with the lone run in the first inning.

Murry Dickson posted his 17th victory for the last-place Pirates in beating the Phils. Dickson allowed only two hits including a pinch-hit homer by Del Ennis in the ninth. Gus Bell smashed a grand-slam homer for the Pirates.

Warren Spahn turned in his 16th victory for Boston in the opener against Cincinnati. Sibby Sisti tripled home pitcher Chet Nichols with the payoff run in the ninth of the nightcap.

How They Stand

AMERICAN LEAGUE

Club	Won	Lost	Pct.	Win	Lose	Games Beh'd
Cleveland	78	44	.639	.642	.634	
New York	76	46	.623	.626	.618	2
Boston	72	48	.600	.603	.595	5
Chicago	66	56	.541	.545	.537	12
Detroit	57	64	.471	.475	.467	20½
Washington	49	71	.408	.413	.405	28
Philadelphia	49	75	.395	.400	.392	30
BROWNS	38	81	.319	.325	.317	38½

NATIONAL LEAGUE

Club	Won	Lost	Pct.	Win	Lose	Games Beh'd
Brooklyn	77	42	.647	.650	.642	
New York	71	51	.582	.585	.577	7½
Philadelphia	60	61	.496	.500	.492	18
Boston	58	59	.496	.500	.492	18
CARDS	57	59	.491	.496	.487	18½
Cincinnati	53	67	.442	.446	.438	24½
Chicago	51	67	.432	.437	.429	25½
Pittsburgh	50	71	.413	.418	.410	28

Yesterday's Results.

AMERICAN LEAGUE
Browns 5; Philadelphia 3.
Washington 10; Detroit 7.
Chicago 3; Boston 2.
New York 2; Cleveland 0.

NATIONAL LEAGUE
New York 6; Cardinals 5.
Pittsburgh 5; Philadelphia 1.
Brooklyn 1; Chicago 0.
Boston 5-2; Cincinnati 1-1.

Tomorrow's Schedule.

AMERICAN LEAGUE
Washington at St. Louis (2), 1:30 and 3:30 p.m.
New York at Chicago (2), 1:30 and 3:30 p.m.
Philadelphia at Detroit 2:30 p.m.
Boston at Cleveland (2), 12:30 and 2:30 p.m.

NATIONAL LEAGUE
Cardinals at Boston (2), 12:30 and 2.30 p.m.
Pittsburgh at Brooklyn (2), 1:05 and 3:00 p.m.
Chicago at New York (2), 1:05 and 3:00 p.m.
Cincinnati at Philadelphia (2), 12:30 and 2:30 p.m.

Ferguson Gridders Will Play at Night

Ferguson High School will play its home football games at night, the community's Rotary Club announced yesterday. Funds for the installation of lights, which are expected to be up in time for the team's first home game Sept. 28, will be raised at the annual Ferguson County Fair. The fair will be Sept. 5-8.

Polo Grounded

GIANTS 6, CARDINALS 5.

CARDINALS.	AB.	R.	H.	NEW YORK.	AB.	R.	H.
Hemus ss	4	0	3	Stanky 2b	3	1	1
Sch'nd'st 2b	5	0	2	Dark ss	5	1	3
Musial lf-cf	5	0	0	Mays cf	5	0	3
Westlake cf	3	0	0	Irvin lf	4	2	1
H.Rice lf	1	0	0	Thomson 3b	4	1	3
V.Jones 1b	5	0	3	Lockman 1b	5	1	2
Slaughter rf	4	0	0	Westrum c	1	0	0
Johnson 3b	4	2	2	b-Rapp	1	0	0
D.Rice c	4	1	1	Yvars c	0	0	0
a-Diering	0	1	0	Mueller rf	4	0	1
Brecheen p	2	1	0	Koslo p	3	0	0
Bokelm'nn p	0	0	0	Spencer p	0	0	0
Staley p	0	0	0	c-Rigney	1	0	0
Scheffing c	1	0	0	S.Jones p	0	0	0
				d-Williams	1	0	0
Totals	38	5	11	Totals	37	6	14

a-Ran for D. Rice in eighth.
b-Flied out for Westrum in eighth.
c-Flied out for Spencer in eighth.
d-Hit into fielder's choice for S. Jones in ninth.

Club.	1	2	3	4	5	6	7	8	9	
Cardinals	0	0	1	0	0	0	2	2	0	—5
New York	2	0	1	0	0	1	0	0	2	—6

Errors—Dark, Thomson. Runs batted in—Mays, Thomson, Johnson, Dark, Lockman 2, D. Rice, Schoendienst, Scheffing, Hemus, Williams. Home runs—Johnson, Dark, Lockman, D. Rice. Stolen base—Stanky. Sacrifice—Yvars. Double plays—Hemus-Schoendienst-Johnson-D. Rice-Schoendienst, Dark-Stanky-Lockman. Left on base—Cardinals 10, New York 14. Bases on balls—Off Brecheen 5, Koslo 2, Spencer 2, Bokelmann 1, Staley 1. Struck out—By Koslo 4, Brecheen 3, Staley 1. Hits and runs—Off Koslo, 8 and 3 in 6⅓ innings; Brecheen, 8 and 4 in 6⅔; Bokelmann, 0 and 0 in ⅓; Spencer, 2 and 2 in 1⅔; S. Jones, 1 and 0 in 1; Staley, 6 and 2 in 1⅓. Winning pitcher—S. Jones (4-9). Losing pitcher—Staley (14-13). Umpires—Dascoli, Warneke, Goetz and Jorda. Time of game—3:15. Attendance—10,559.

Mack Joins in the Fun

—By a Post-Dispatch Staff Photographer.
CONNIE MACK, grand old man of the Athletics, joined BILL VEECK briefly in the Grandstand Managers section at Sportsman's Park last night. Veeck is shown greeting Connie, who gave up managing the "A"s this year after rounding out 50 years on the job.

Giant Rookie Walks Three, Then Tosses Wild Pitch

SCORE BY INNINGS

1 2 3 4 5 6 7 8 9 T.
CARDINALS (at New York)
1 0 2
NEW YORK
0 1

Cardinals' Box Score

(2½ Innings)

CARDINALS.

	AB	R	H	O	A	E
Hemus ss	2	0	1	0	0	0
Schoend'nst 2b	1	1	0	0	0	0
Musial cf	1	1	1	2	0	0
H. Rice lf	2	0	0	0	0	0
Slaughter rf	1	1	1	1	0	0
Jones 1b	2	0	1	1	0	0
Johnson 3b	1	0	0	0	0	0
Sarni c	2	0	1	2	0	0
BRAZLE P	2	0	0	0	0	0
Totals	14	3	5	6	0	0

NEW YORK

	AB	R	H	O	A	E
Stanky 2b	1	0	0	0	1	0
Dark ss	1	0	0	1	0	0
Mays cf	1	0	0	2	0	0
Irvin lf	1	0	0	1	0	0
Thomson 3b	1	1	1	2	0	0
Lockman 1b	0	0	0	1	0	0
Westrum c	0	0	0	2	0	0
Mueller rf	1	0	0	0	0	0
CORWIN P	1	0	0	0	1	0
SPENCER P	0	0	0	0	0	0
Totals	7	1	1	9	2	0

By a Special Correspondent of the Post-Dispatch.

NEW YORK, Aug. 25 — The Cardinals, hoping to break the red-hot Giants' 12-game winning streak, scored a gift run—without swinging—in the first inning of the Redbirds' final game at the Polo Grounds today.

The starting pitchers were rookie righthander Al (4-0) Corwin of the Giants and veteran relief specialist Al (3-1) Brazle for the Redbirds. It was only Brazle's second starting assignment of the season.

In the first inning Corwin walked three batters and then uncorked a run-scoring wild pitch that gave the Cardinals a 1-0 advantage.

The game was delayed by rain in the last half of the third inning.

Attendance was estimated at 11,000.

Warneke, Goetz and Jorda were the umpires.

The game, play by play:

FIRST INNING—CARDINALS—Hemus flied to Irwin. Schoendienst walked. Musial also walked. Stanky made a nice stop of H. Rice's grounder and threw him out. Slaughter was passed intentionally, filling the bases. Schoendienst scored on a wild pitch, Musial taking third and Slaughter taking second. Jones fouled to Westrum. **ONE RUN.**

GIANTS — Stanky popped to Jones. Musial raced into right-center for Dark's long fly. Mays flied to Slaughter who made the catch against the right field wall.

SECOND — CARDINALS — Johnson popped to Thomson. Sarni singled to right. Brazle bunted and forced Sarni, Corwin to Dark. Hemus singled to right, sending Brazle to third. Schoendienst popped to Thomson.

GIANTS—Irvin flied to Musial. **Thomson hit a home run into the upper left-field stands.** It was his 24th of the season. Lockman walked. Westrum also walked. Mueller fouled to Sarni. Corwin fouled to Sarni. **ONE RUN.**

THIRD — CARDINALS—Musial hit a home run into the upper right-field stands. It was his thirtieth of the year. H. Rice flied to Mays. Slaughter singled to right. Jones doubled to right, Slaughter stopping at third. Spencer replaced Corwin on the mound for the Giants. Johnson was intentionally passed, filling the bases. **Sarni flied deep to Mays, Slaughter scoring.** Brazle fouled to Westrum. **TWO RUNS.**

EVEN STALEY CAN'T HOLD HOT GIANTS

NEW YORK, Aug. 25—The Cardinals suffered their fourth one-run defeat of five on this last eastern swing when even Gerry Staley, the old Giant-killer, couldn't hold Leo Durocher's red-hot New York Nationals yesterday.

Typifying their recent play, the Giants came from behind to score their twelfth straight victory, tallying twice off Staley in the ninth inning. The 6-5 setback dropped the Redbirds into fifth place.

With Marty Marion back in charge, the Cardinals bounced back from a 4-1 deficit, largely on the hitting of Bill Johnson, Solly Hemus, Del Rice and Red Schoendienst, to knock out nemesis Dave Koslo and forge in front in the eighth inning.

However, as successor to Harry Brecheen and Dick Bokelmann, Staley couldn't hold the Giants in the ninth. Three hits, a sacrifice and a fielder's choice enabled them to pull the game out of the fire.

The fielder's choice represented the winning run. With the bases loaded, one out, pinch-hitter Dave Williams grounded to Hemus, whose late-arriving throw to the plate grazed Bobby Thomson and Catcher Bob Scheffing couldn't hold the ball.

Army Calls Rotblatt.

CHICAGO, Aug. 25 (AP)—Marv Rotblatt, former University of Illinois pitcher, has been called for induction into the armed forces Aug. 31. Rotblatt, who pitched for the Chicago White Sox earlier in the season, may return to Memphis to hurl another game before he is called up by Uncle Sam.

Zack Lets Grandstand Managers Worry

—By Ken Gouldthorpe, Post-Dispatch Staff Photographer.
Decked out in civilian attire, his feet cocked up, smoking a pipe and leisurely reading, ZACK TAYLOR, manager of the Browns, sat in a rocking chair in a box near the dugout last night as the Grandstand Managers ran the team. It was all a Bill Veeck stunt, of course, and Taylor took the whole thing in stride.

Garver Makes Job Easy For Grandstand Managers

By John J. Archibald

The only mistake the 1100 Brownie "grandstand managers" made was choosing Ned Garver as their pitcher. After one action-filled inning that read like a chapter from a Sunday movie serial, the Browns' guest board of directors might just as well have pushed their hats back on their heads and relaxed like Zack Taylor last night, because Little Ned took over from there.

The big "Yes" and "No" signs were bobbing up and down plenty in that first inning. You could hear the wheels in 1100 baseball minds spinning like crazy as the Browns spotted the Philadelphia Athletics a three-run head start, then came back to catch them in the same frame, and go on to an eventual 5 to 3 victory.

"Steal?" read the black and white placard near the Browns' dugout. Twice the majority of the managers flashed their red "No" signs. Once they voted "Yes" and the runner, Hank Arft, was out.

A Little Slow on the Draw.

"Protest to Umpire?" That was a popular question on several occasions, but by the time the votes were tabulated it was a little late to berate the offending official. Word was relayed to Coach Johnny Berardino via a walkie-talkie set-up from grandstand to dugout, but arguments have to be spontaneous or they'd look a little silly.

League President Will Harridge didn't permit Bill Veeck to go through with his original plan of having two guest coaches on the baselines. The fans, Charles E. Hughes and Clark Mitze, were signed up and put in uniform, but Harridge ruled the stunt out on the grounds the contracts had not been approved by his office.

So Coaches Hughes and Mitze were awarded king size trophies acclaiming them as "the best coaches ever banned from the coaching lines," and sat next to Zack Taylor in a front row box.

Almost everything else went according to plan, however. The rough way in which the A's treated Garver in the first made it look like the experiment might be something short of a howling success, but that was just to keep things from being dull.

Zernial Hits 28th Homer.

Ferris Fain and Elmer Valo singled with one out, and Gus Zernial, who dotes on all Brownie pitching, hit his 28th home run of the season to make it 3-0. Hank Majeski got on through Bill Jennings's error, and when Dave Philley singled the managers were asked if another Brownie pitcher should be readied.

The answer was an overwhelming "No," and Garver, obviously touched by such a gesture, got Pete Suder to ground into a double play and was never in trouble again.

Veeck's managerial multitude hardly had to wait at all before it started pounding itself on its back again. Bobby Young, the nearest to a unanimous choice by the fans, started off an unimpressive night at bat by lining out, but Jim Delsing doubled, Sherm Lollar singled, and after Cliff Mapes struck out, Ken Wood drove in two runs with a single. Hank Arft, the managers' choice for first base and one at which they seemed particularly pleased, drove in Wood with a hit. Arft was out stealing to end the inning, but the game was 3-3.

It was Lollar who broke the tie when he hit his eighth home run into the left field seats in the third inning. Lollar also doubled in the eighth and scored on Mapes's single for the final run.

The victory was Garver's fifteenth.

* * *

Connie Mack was in the stands and openly showed his approval of Veeck's experiment. The manager of the Athletics for 50 years posed with one of the "Yes-No" signs before the game. Mack has been a consistent backer of Veeck.

* * *

One of the A's, who concealed his identity from the crowd by wearing a jacket, doused Brown-Clown Max Patkin with a bucket of ice water as he cavorted on the baselines.

* * *

Duane Pillette (5-13) will pitch against Morris Martin (8-4) in a 2:30 game with Philadelphia today.

WHO'S WHO IN BASEBALL

By the Associated Press.

NATIONAL LEAGUE.

Batting—Musial, St. Louis, .364; Robinson, Brooklyn, .343.
Runs—Kiner, Pittsburgh, 104; Hodges, Brooklyn, 97.
Runs batted in—Kiner, Pittsburgh, 91; Irvin, New York, 90.
Hits — Ashburn, Philadelphia, 171; Furillo, Brooklyn; Dark, New York; Musial, St. Louis, 159.
Doubles—Dark, New York, 32; Robinson, Brooklyn, 28.
Triples—Musial, St. Louis, 10; Bell, Pittsburgh, 9.
Home runs — Kiner, Pittsburgh, 35; Hodges, Brooklyn, 34.
Stolen bases—Jethroe, Boston, 29; Ashburn, Philadelphia, 24.
Pitching—Roe, Brooklyn, 16-2, .889; Maglie, New York, 17-5, .773.
Strikeouts—Newcombe, Brooklyn, 123; Spahn, Boston, 122.

AMERICAN LEAGUE.

Batting — Fain, Philadelphia, .333; Minoso, Chicago, .332.
Runs—Minoso, Chicago, 98; Williams, Boston, 95.
Runs batted in—Zernial, Philadelphia, 108; Williams, Boston, 107.
Hits—DiMaggio, Boston, 156; Kell, Detroit, 152.
Doubles—Noren, Washington, 31; DiMaggio, Boston, 30.
Triples — Minoso, Chicago, 13; Fox, Chicago and Coan, Washington, 8.
Home runs—Zernial, Philadelphia, 28; Williams, Boston, 26.
Stolen bases — Minoso, Chicago, 25; Busby, Chicago, 23.
Pitching — Feller, Cleveland, 20-5, .800; Morgan, New York and Kinder, Boston, 8-2, .800.
Strikeouts—Raschi, New York, 130; McDermott, Boston, 116.

Dot Kirby and Miss Doran in Women's Final

ST. PAUL, Aug. 25 (INS)—Dot Kirby, Atlanta's veteran tourney player, opposes School Teacher Claire Doran of Rocky River, O., today for the women's national amateur crown at St. Paul's Town and Country Club.

Miss Kirby reached the 36-hole championship final for the third time in 13 years of competition yesterday when she routed Grace de Moss of Corvallis, Ore., 6 and 5.

The Atlanta girl was razor sharp in her semi-final match. She needed only one putt on seven holes and used a meager total of 19 in the 13 holes played.

Miss Doran advanced to the final by ousting the sentimental favorite, 44-year-old Estelle Lawson Page of Greensboro, N.C.

Mrs. Page took the Ohioan right down to the final hole before succumbing, 2 up. The North Carolina housewife, national titleholder in 1937, came up with the best shot of the tourney when she holed a 45-foot chip for an eagle three on the ninth.

Larsen Begins Defense of His Singles Title

FOREST HILLS, N.Y., Aug. 25 (AP)—The National Tennis championships open at the West Side Club today with the men's competition a wide open affair and the women's crown already addressed to Doris Hart of Coral Gables, Fla., formerly of St. Louis.

More than 50 first-round matches are on today's schedule with Defending Champion Art Larsen of San Leandro, Calif., getting the competition underway. Larsen, rated only an outside chance of retaining his title, meets Thomas Lwyn of Scarsdale, N.Y.

The titleholder will be followed by Australia's Frank Sedgman, voted one of the players most likely to be crowned champion on Labor day. The No. 1 foreign seed plays Gil Bogley, of Warren, O.

Other top-flight players slated for first-day action include Herb Flam, runner-up last year and seeded fourth; Vic Seixas, Philadelphia youngster battling for a Davis Cup berth and three more of the challenging Australians—Ken McGregor, Mervyn Rose and Don Candy.

Flam faces what appears to be the most severe test of the seeded players. The draw has thrown him against Hal Burrows, Charlottesville (Pa.) veteran and one of the game's real stylists.

Dick Savitt, Australian and Wimbledon champion and seeded first, will not swing into action until tomorrow when he'll meet Edward Alloo of New York.

The other ranking players also will start play either tomorrow or Monday. The big event on the Sunday program is the national doubles final, brought here when it was rained out at Longwood. The match, an all-Australian affair, pits Sedgman and McGregor against Rose and Cany.

Many women's matches also are scheduled for today but none of them of special interest.

Miss Hart, Wimbledon champion who moved into the favorite's spot when Defending Champion Mrs. Margaret Osborne du Pont and Louis Brough were sidelined by injuries, meets Julia Ann Sampson of San Marino, Calif., tomorrow.

And Shirley Fry, picked as Miss Hart's most serious rival, will not start her bid until Monday.

Jim Wright First In Junior Golf Meet

Jim Wright had a 237 low gross to take the honors in the boys' first flight of the Junior Boys and Girls Medal Golf Tournament at Westborough Country Club. All entrants shot 18 holes on each of three days.

Arlo Mohlenpah and George Nuenreiter tied for low gross with 201.

In the second flight, Jim Cross had a 261 low gross and Bob Nuenrieter fired a 215 low net.

Pat Lockwood led the first flight girls with a 329 low gross, and Marlene Hoppe had a 224 net. In the second flight, Betty Marianfeld had a 358 gross and Lynn Purdum a 298 net.

Garver Managed

BROWNS 5, ATHLETICS 3.

PHILADELPHIA	AB.	R.	H.	BROWNS	AB.	R.	H.
Joost ss	5	0	0	Young 2b	4	0	0
Fain 1b	4	1	1	Delsing cf	3	1	1
Valo rf	4	1	3	Lollar c	4	3	3
Zernial lf	2	1	1	Mapes rf	4	0	1
Majeski 3b	4	0	0	Wood lf	4	1	3
Philley cf	3	0	1	Arft 1b	4	0	1
Suder 2b	4	0	0	Marsh 3b	3	0	0
Astroth c	3	0	0	Jennings ss	3	0	0
aLimmer	1	0	0	Garver p	3	0	0
Kellner p	3	0	1	Totals	32	5	9
bHitchcock	1	0	0				
Totals	34	3	7				

aPopped out for Astroth in ninth.
bGrounded out for Kellner in ninth.

Innings:	1	2	3	4	5	6	7	8	9	
Philadelphia	3	0	0	0	0	0	0	0	0	—3
Browns	3	0	1	0	0	0	0	1	x	—5

Errors—Joost, Zernial, Jennings. Runs batted in—Zernial 3, Lollar 2, Arft 2, Mapes. Two-base hits—Delsing, Wood 2; Lollar. Home runs — Zernial, Lollar. Stolen base—Valo. Double plays—Young-Jennings-Arft, Joost-Suder-Fain. Left on bases—Browns 4, Philadelphia 7. Base on balls—Off Kellner 1, Garver 3. Struck out—By Kellner 3, Garver 5. Winning pitcher—Garver (15-8). Losing pitcher—Kellner (7-13). Umpires — Summers, Grieve, Stevens. Time of game—2h. 11m. Attendance—3925.

The Scoreboard

AMERICAN LEAGUE
1 2 3 4 5 6 7 8 9 R. H. E.
NEW YORK (at Cleveland)
1 0
CLEVELAND
1
Batteries: New York—Lopat and Berry; Cleveland—Garcia and Hegan.

NATIONAL LEAGUE
1 2 3 4 5 6 7 8 9 R. H. E.
CHICAGO (at Brooklyn)
0 1 2 0 2
BROOKLYN
0 0 0 1
Batteries: Chicago—Kelly and Edwards; Brooklyn—Erskine and Campanella.

PITTSBURGH (at Philadelphia)
0 1 0 1
PHILADELPHIA
0 0 1 0
Batteries: Pittsburgh — Carlsen and Garagiola; Philadelphia—Church and Seminick.

CINCINNATI (at Boston)
0 0
BOSTON
0 0
Batteries: Cincinnati—Fox and Howell; Boston—Sair and St. Claire.

Browns, Cards Averages

Browns.

Player.	AB.	R.	H.	2b.	3b.	HR.	Rbi.	Av.
Byrne	34	7	12	2	0	1	8	.353
Garver	67	6	20	4	1	0	6	.299
Batts	193	19	57	12	1	4	21	.295
Arft	254	38	70	10	4	6	32	.276
Lollar	253	40	67	18	0	8	38	.265
Young	479	[illegible]	126	11	7	1	23	.263
Delsing	358	53	94	16	1	8	39	.263
Maguire	107	12	28	2	1	1	13	.262
Mahoney	12	3	3	0	0	0	0	.250
Taylor	47	8	11	0	0	2	4	.234
Mapes	138	18	31	6	1	4	21	.225
Marsh	32[illegible]	35	72	14	5	2	31	.224
Wood	265	32	59	17	0	11	33	.222
Widmar	28	2	5	1	0	0	3	.179
Jennings	115	9	20	6	2	0	11	.174
Sanford	22	3	3	1	0	0	0	.136
Suchecki	15	0	2	0	0	0	2	.133
Saucier	8	1	1	1	0	0	1	.125
McDonald	18	1	2	0	1	0	0	.111
Pillette	4[illegible]	3	4	0	0	0	1	.089
Paige	8	1	0	0	0	0	0	.000
	4013	478	976	171	37	65	429	.243

PITCHING RECORD.

	W.	L.		W.	L.
Garver	15	8	Pillette	5	13
Paige	2	2	Sanford	3	8
Byrne	4	7	Mahoney	1	2
McDonald	2	4	Suchecki	0	6
Widmar	4	9			

Cardinals.

Player.	AB.	R.	H.	2b.	3b.	HR.	Rbi.	Av.
Musial	437	93	159	22	10	29	86	.364
Lowrey	3[illegible]	43	95	18	5	4	33	.310
Scho'nd't	392	61	114	24	5	4	34	.291
Hemus	274	36	75	9	3	2	16	.274
Jones	277	19	76	11	0	3	39	.272
Slaughter	29[illegible]	34	79	11	3	4	34	.264
Westlake	397	56	103	12	5	20	74	.254
Rojek	20[illegible]	21	54	7	3	0	14	.267
H. Rice	144	11	37	7	0	2	24	.257
Johnson	339	37	87	15	1	9	43	.257
D. Rice	299	25	72	11	1	8	3[illegible]	.241
Chambers	50	3	12	1	0	1	5	.240
Scheffing	140	9	33	2	0	2	16	.236
Brecheen	48	4	11	2	0	1	3	.229
Boyer	17	5	4	1	0	0	2	.235
Diering	350	4	8	1	0	0	3	.229
Sarni	32	3	7	0	0	0	0	.219
Poholsky	48	1	9	1	0	0	1	.188
Glaviano	80	17	15	4	0	1	4	.188
Staley	65	3	12	1	0	0	0	.185
Munger	27	2	5	1	0	0	2	.185
Presko	37	2	6	1	0	0	1	.162
Lanier	36	2	5	0	0	0	1	.139
Brazle	20	0	1	0	0	0	0	.050
Bo'kelmann	4	0	0	0	0	0	0	.000
	4026	494	1057	173	37	78	453	.263

PITCHING RECORD.

	W.	L.		W.	L.
Brazle	3	1	Poholsky	4	11
Brecheen	8	3	Lanier	8	8
Presko	7	3	Chambers	9	11
Staley	14	13	Boyer	2	4
Munger	4	5	Bokelmann	0	2

Khoury All-Stars Win From Tricos, 2 to 1

The Khoury League All-Stars, made up of many of the outstanding high school baseball stars of the district, defeated the Tricos of southern Illinois yesterday, 2 to 1. The game was played at Sportsman's Park, prior to the Browns-Athletics contest.

John Maltagliati doubled in Bob Duncan with the winning run in the last half of the ninth. The Khoury club's other run came in the fifth when John Sabourin doubled and Sam Chetta singled. Trico tied the game in the eighth.

Major League Box Scores

PIRATES 5, PHILLIES 1.

PITTSBURGH.	AB.	R.	H.	PHILADELPHIA.	AB.	R.	H.
Castig'ne 3b	5	1	1	Caballero 2b	4	0	0
Phillips 1b	3	0	1	Ashburn cf	4	0	1
Thomas cf	5	0	1	Sisler lf	4	0	0
Kiner rf	4	1	0	Nicholson rf	3	0	0
Bell rf	5	1	4	Brown 1b	2	0	0
McCull'gh c	4	0	1	Jones 3b	3	0	0
Strickl'nd ss	4	1	1	Hamner ss	3	0	0
Cole 2b	1	0	0	Wilber c	3	0	0
Murtaugh 2b	1	0	0	Thompson p	1	0	0
Dickson p	4	1	2	aWaitkus	1	0	0
				Hansen p	0	0	0
Totals	36	5	11	bEnnis	1	1	1
				Totals	29	1	2

aFlied out for Thompson in sixth.
bHit home run for Hansen in ninth.

Innings:	1	2	3	4	5	6	7	8	9	
Pittsburgh	0	0	4	0	0	1	0	0	0	—5
Philadelphia	0	0	0	0	0	0	0	0	1	—1

Error—Brown. Runs batted in—Bell 4, (Strickland scored on double play), Ennis. Two base hits—Bell, Phillips. Home runs—Bell, Ennis. Sacrifice hit—Phillips. Double plays—Hamner to Caballero to Brown. Left on base—Pittsburgh 9, Philadelphia 2. Base on balls—Off Dickson 1, Thompson 4. Struck out—By Dickson 1, Thompson 1. Hits and runs—Off Thompson 9 and 5 in 6 innings, Hansen 2 and 0 in 3. Wild pitch—Thompson. Winning pitcher—Dickson (17-11). Losing pitcher—Thompson (3-8). Umpires—Boggess, Robb and Pinelli. Time of game—1h. 58m. Attendance—8841.

DODGERS 1, CUBS 0.

CHICAGO.	AB.	R.	H.	BROOKLYN.	AB.	R.	H.
Miksis 2b	4	0	0	Furillo rf	4	0	1
Connors 1b	3	0	0	Reese ss	4	1	2
b-Cavaretta	1	0	0	Snider cf	4	0	1
B'mholtz cf	3	0	1	Robinson 2b	4	0	2
Sauer lf	3	0	0	Hodges 1b	3	0	0
Jackson 3b	3	0	0	Camp'n'la c	3	0	1
H'rm'nski rf	3	0	0	Pafko lf	2	0	1
Edwards c	3	0	0	Cox 3b	3	0	1
Smalley ss	3	0	1	Branca p	3	0	0
Minner p	2	0	1	Totals	30	1	9
a-Burgess	1	0	0				
Totals	29	0	3				

a-Flied out for Minner in ninth.
b-Grounded out for Connors in ninth.

	1	2	3	4	5	6	7	8	9	
Chicago	0	0	0	0	0	0	0	0	0	—0
Brooklyn	1	0	0	0	0	0	0	0	x	—1

Errors—Jackson, Hermanski. Run batted in—Robinson. Two-base hits—Robinson, Reese. Double play—Smalley-Miksis-Connors. Left on base—Chicago 2, Brooklyn 6. Base on balls—Off Minner 1. Struck out—By Minner 1, Branca 10. Winning pitcher—Branca (11-5). Losing pitcher—Minner (6-13). Umpires—Conlan, Stewart and Gore. Time of game—1:57. Attendance—22,186 paid.

WHITE SOX 3, RED SOX 2.

BOSTON	AB.	R.	H.	CHICAGO	AB.	R.	H.
Pesky ss	4	0	2	Fox 2b	4	0	1
Goodman 2b	3	0	0	Coleman lf	4	1	1
Williams lf	3	0	0	Minoso 3b	2	1	1
Dropo 1b	4	0	0	E.Ro'son 1b	3	0	2
Maxwell rf	4	0	1	Zarilla rf	3	0	0
Vollmer cf	4	0	0	Busby cf	3	0	0
Hatfield 3b	4	0	1	Sheely c	3	1	1
aRobinson c	4	1	0	Car'squel ss	3	0	0
Scarb'ough p	3	1	1	Kretlow p	3	0	1
Totals	33	2	5	Totals	28	3	7

Innings:	1	2	3	4	5	6	7	8	9	
Boston	0	0	0	0	2	0	0	0	0	—2
Chicago	1	1	0	0	0	1	0	0	x	—3

Errors—E. Robinson, Carrasquel. Runs batted in—E. Robinson 2, Kretlow, Pesky. (Scarborough scored on Kretlow's wild pitch in fifth). Two-base hits—E. Robinson. Stolen bases—Minoso. Sacrifice—Minoso. Left on bases—Boston 6; Chicago 2. Bases on balls—Off Kretlow 2. Struck out—By Kretlow 5, Scarborough 4. Wild pitch—Scarborough, Kretlow. Winning pitcher—Kretlow (5-6). Losing pitcher—Scarborough (10-7). Umpires—Duffy, Hurley and Paparella. Time of game—2h. 18m. Attendance—24,281.

BRAVES 5-2, REDS 1-1.

(First Game)

CINCINNATI	AB.	R.	H.	BOSTON	AB.	R.	H.
Adams 3b2b	4	0	0	Sisti ss	4	0	1
Ryan 2b	2	0	0	Jethroe cf	3	2	1
McM'n 3b2b	1	1	1	Torgeson 1b	4	0	0
Wyrostek rf	4	0	2	Gordon 3b	3	2	1
Kl'zewski 1b	4	0	1	Cooper c	3	0	0
Adcock lf	2	0	1	Marshall rf	3	0	2
Usher cf	4	0	0	Hartsf'ld 2b	4	1	2
Stallcup ss	4	0	1	Marquez lf	3	0	1
Howell c	3	0	2	Spahn p	3	0	0
Raf'berger p	2	0	1	Totals	30	5	8
aLitwhiler	1	0	0				
Erautt p	0	0	0				
Totals	31	1	9				

aStruck out for Raffensberger in eighth.

Innings:	1	2	3	4	5	6	7	8	9	
Cincinnati	0	0	0	0	0	0	0	0	1	—1
Boston	0	1	0	0	1	0	1	2	x	—5

Error—Spahn. Runs batted in—Hartsfeild, Jethroe, Marquez, Gordon, Marshall, Usher. Two-base hits—Marquez, Gordon, Marshall. Home runs—Jethroe. Stolen bases—Gordon, Jethroe. Double plays—Hartsfeild-Sisti-Torgeson; Sisti-Hartsfield-Torgeson; Cooper-Hartsfield; McMillan-Adams-Kluszewski. Left on bases—Cincinnati 6; Boston 5. Bases on balls—Off Spahn 3, Raffensberger 3, Erautt 1. Struck out—By Spahn 6, Raffensberger 2, Erautt 1. Hits and runs — Off Raffensberger 6 and 3 in 7 innings; Erautt 2 and 2 in 1. Winning pitcher—Spahn (16-11). Losing pitcher—Raffensberger (12-16). Umpires—Donatelli, Ballanfant and Barlick. Time of game—2h. 18m.

(Second Game)

CINCINNATI	AB.	R.	H.	BOSTON	AB.	R.	H.
Adams 3b	3	0	0	Sisti ss	5	1	2
Ryan 3b	3	0	1	Jethroe cf	3	0	1
Litwhiler rf	3	0	0	Torgeson 1b	3	0	1
Kl'zewski 1b	4	0	0	Gordon 3b	3	0	0
Adcock lf	4	0	0	Marshall rf	3	0	0
Usher cf	4	1	0	St.Claire c	4	0	0
McM'lann ss	3	0	0	Addis lf	4	0	2
Howell c	3	0	0	Hartsf'ld 2b	4	0	2
Wehmeier p	3	0	3	Nichols p	4	1	0
Totals	30	1	4	Totals	33	2	9

Innings:	1	2	3	4	5	6	7	8	9	
Cincinnati	0	0	0	0	1	0	0	0	0	—1
Boston	0	0	1	0	0	0	0	0	1	—2

Error—Torgeson. Runs batted in—Gordon, Sisti, Wehmeier. Two-base hit—Sisti. Three-base hit—Sisit. Stolen base—Jethroe. Sacrifices—Adams, Gordon. Double plays — Gordon-Hartsfield-Torgeson; McMillan-Ryan. Left on bases—Cincinnati 5, Boston 9. Bases on balls—Off Nichols 2, Wehmeier 3. Struck out—By Nichols 6, Wehmeier 6. Wild pitch—Nichols. Balk—Wehmeier. Passed ball—Howell. Winning pitcher — Nichols (8-4). Losing pitcher — Wehmeier 2-8). Umpires — Ballanfant, Barlick and Donatelli. Time —2h. 19m. Attendance—8807.

YANKEES 2, INDIANS 0.

NEW YORK	AB.	R.	H.	CLEVELAND	AB.	R.	H.
Rizzuto ss	3	0	0	Mitchell lf	4	0	0
Mantle rf	4	0	1	Avila 2b	3	0	0
Bauer rf	0	0	0	Doby cf	3	0	1
Woodling lf	3	1	2	Rosen 3b	4	0	2
DiMaggio cf	5	0	1	Simpson 1b	3	0	0
Berra c	4	0	1	bChapman	1	0	0
Mize 1b	3	0	0	Kennedy rf	4	0	2
Collins 1b	0	0	0	Boone ss	4	0	1
Brown 3b	3	0	1	Hegan c	4	0	2
Coleman 2b	0	0	0	Wynn p	2	0	0
McDougald 2b-3b	3	0	0	aTebbetts	1	0	0
Overmire p	1	0	0	Brissie p	0	0	0
Ostrowski p	2	1	1	cMaddern	1	0	0
Totals	31	2	7	Totals	34	0	8

aFouled out for Wynn in seventh.
bFlied out for Simpson in ninth.
cHit into force play for Brissie in ninth.

Innings	1	2	3	4	5	6	7	8	9	
New York	0	0	0	0	0	0	2	0	0	—2
Cleveland	0	0	0	0	0	0	0	0	0	—0

Error—Avila. Runs batted in—Woodling 2. Home run—Woodling. Stolen base—Rosen. Sacrifice—Rizzuto 2. Double plays—Rizzuto-Mize, Wynn-Avila-Simpson. Left on base—New York 11, Cleveland 9. Bases on balls—Off Overmire 2, Wynn 4, Brissie 3. Struck out—By Ostrowski 1, Wynn 3, Brissie 2. Hits and runs—Off Overmire 5 and 0 in 5⅓ innings, Ostrowski 3 and 0 in 3⅔, Wynn 7 and 2 in 7; Brissie 0 and 0 in 2. Winning pitcher—Ostrowski (6-3). Losing pitcher—Wynn (14-12). Umpires—Soare, McKinley, Honochick and Hubbard. Time of game—2h 20m. Attendance—71,768.

SENATORS 10, TIGERS 7.

WASHINGTON	AB.	R.	H.	DETROIT	AB.	R.	H.
Yost 3b	3	2	3	Priddy 2b	4	2	3
Runnels ss	5	0	0	Kryhoski 1b	5	2	2
Coan lf	4	1	1	Kell 3b	5	2	2
Mele cf	5	2	3	Mullin lf	3	1	1
Vernon 1b	5	1	1	Souchock rf	4	0	2
Michaels 2b	3	2	1	dKeller	1	0	0
McC'mick rf	5	1	2	Groth cf	4	0	1
Guerra c	5	0	0	Swift c	3	0	0
Marrero p	0	0	0	bKolloway	1	0	0
aDente	1	0	0	House c	0	0	0
Haynes p	3	1	1	Berry ss	4	0	2
Ferrick p	1	0	0	Cain p	2	0	0
				Gray p	1	0	0
Totals	40	10	12	cHutchinson	1	0	0
				White p	0	0	0
				Totals	38	7	13

aFlied out for Marrero in second.
bFouled out for Swift in eighth.
cPopped out for Gray in eighth.
dStruck out for Souchock in ninth.

Innings:	1	2	3	4	5	6	7	8	9	
Washington	0	0	5	0	3	1	1	0	0	—10
Detroit	3	0	0	0	2	0	2	0	0	—7

Errors—Kryhoski, Berry. Runs batted in—Mele 2, McCormick 4, Guerra (Vernon scored on Berry's error in fifth), Vernon, Haynes, Kell 3, Souchock 2, Groth, Mullin. Home runs — McCormick, Mele, Haynes, Kell. Stolen bases—Priddy, Berry, Kell. Double plays—Michaels-Runnels-Vernon, Runnels-Michaels-Vernon, Berry-Priddy-Kryhoski. Left on base—Washington 8; Detroit 7. Base on balls—Off Marrero 2, Ferrick 1, Cain 2, Gray 3. Struck out—By Ferrick 2, Cain 1, Gray 2, White 1. Hits and runs—Off Marrero 3 and 3 in 1 inning, Haynes 8 and 4 in 5⅓, Ferrick 2 and 0 in 2⅔, Cain 8 and 7 in 4 (none out in fifth), Gray 4 and 3 in 4. White 0 and 0 in 1. Winning pitcher—Haynes (1-3). Losing pitcher—Cain (10-10). Umpires—Berry, Rommel and Napp. Time of game—2h. 18m. Attendance—2887.

Softball.

ST. LOUIS PARK.

Men's Game.

Club.	1	2	3	4	5	6	7		R.	H.	E.
Terminal	0	1	0	0	0	2	0	—	3	7	5
Mo.-Pac.	2	2	1	2	4	2	*	—	13	17	1

Batteries — Buergler, Drake and Vaughn; Frederics and Stawder.

Girls' Game.

Club.	1	2	3	4	5	6	7		R.	H.	E.
Potucek	2	0	7	5	3	0	0	—	17	16	5
Pop-Kola	3	1	1	0	0	0	0	—	5	7	8

Batteries—Sneed and Williams; Grant and Jenneman.

Men's Game.

Club.	1	2	3	4	5	6	7		R.	H.	E.
Wabash	2	0	0	0	0	0	0	—	2	4	2
M.K.N.T.	0	0	0	1	0	0	2	—	3	6	2

Batteries — Tilker and Murray; Ryan and Brown.

TONIGHT'S SCHEDULE.

ST. LOUIS PARK—Londoff vs. Kutis, men's game, 7:30 p.m.; Londoff vs. Phoenix (Ariz.) Queens, girls' game, 9.

OVERLAND LEGION PARK.

Last Night's Results.

Oldani Market 10, I'm Inn 1.

Tonight's Schedule.

Record Center vs. Tower Grove Blues, 7:30 p.m.
Post 421 vs. Lafayette K. of C., 9 p.m.

CENTRAL.

Dayton 14, Saginaw 3.
Muskegon 12, Flint 5.
Charleston 4, Grand Rapids 2.

Weather Forecast
Cloudy, windy, light rain tonight. High today upper 70s; low tonight 65. Tomorrow, clear, warm. (Full report on Page A-2.)
Midnight, 67 8 a.m. ---69 1 p.m. ---77
4 a.m. ---68 10 a.m. ---70 2 p.m. ---79
6 a.m. ---68 Noon -----75 3 p.m. ---78
Closing New York Markets, Page A-33.

The Evening Star
WITH SUNDAY MORNING EDITION

Night Final
Carrier Home Delivery
Evening and Sunday
$1.75* Per Month
Phone STerling 5000
Washington's Great Home Newspaper
*Night Final 10c Additional
An Associated Press Newspaper

99th Year. No. 277. Phone ST. 5000 WASHINGTON, D. C., THURSDAY, OCTOBER 4, 1951—SEVENTY-TWO PAGES. Home Delivery, Monthly Rates: Evening and Sunday, $1.75; Evening only, $1.30; Sunday only, 45c; Night Final, 10c Additional. 5 CENTS

GIANTS LEAD YANKEES, 5-1, IN 8TH INNING

FIRST SUCH THEFT IN 30 YEARS—Yankee Stadium, N. Y.—Monte Irwin, Giants' left fielder, sails into the plate in the first inning of the World Series opener. It was the first steal to home in a series game since 1921, also a Yankee-Giant game. Yogi Berra, Yankee catcher, has the pitch and is making a vain attempt for the putout. Bobby Thompson, who was at bat, is falling away. —AP Wirephoto.

3-Run Homer Hit By Dark; Irvin Steals Home

Error by Thompson Allows Yank Tally In Series Opener

Lineups.

GIANTS.	YANKEES.
Stanky, 2b	Mantle, rf
Dark, ss	Rizzuto, ss
Thompson, rf	Bauer, lf
Irvin, lf	DiMaggio, cf
Lockman, 1b	Berra, c
Thomson, 3b	McDougald, 3b
Mays, cf	Coleman, 2b
Westrum, c	Collins, 1b
Koslo, p	Reynolds, p

Umpires—At first, Ballanfant; at second, Paparella; at third, Barlick, in right field, Gore; in left field, Stevens; at the plate, Summers.

By Burton Hawkins
Star Staff Correspondent

NEW YORK, Oct. 4.—Al Dark's three-run homer in the sixth inning, coupled with Monte Irvin's first-inning steal of home plate, gave the New York Giants a 5-to-1 edge on the New York Yankees in their World Series opener today at Yankee Stadium.

In the eighth inning the score was Giants, 5; Yankees, 1.

Whitey Lockman's ground rule double in the first inning, scoring

Stories on yesterday's playoff game for pennant on sports pages.

Hank Thompson, gave the Giants their first run. Irvin, who had singled and advanced to third on Lockman's double, then stole home to make the count 2 to 0.

The Yanks rebounded with a run in the second, Gil McDougald scoring on Thompson's error after doubling and advancing on Gerry Coleman's single.

The Giants added three runs in the sixth when Al Dark homered, scoring Wes Westrum and Ed Stanky ahead of him.

Yanks Well-Rested.

The Yankees were fresh favorites who had worked out only briefly in the three days that the Giants and Brooklyn Dodgers staged their memorable playoff series.

Manager Casey Stengel surprised by naming Mickey Mantle, his 19-year-old rookie phenom, to lead off and play right field for the Yanks.

Mantle, a switch hitter, has not been as effective when he bats right against a southpaw pitcher like the Giants' Dave Koslo. With Mantle in the lineup, the Yanks threw only two left-handed batters against Koslo—Catcher Yogi Berra and First Baseman Joe Collins.

With Don Mueller out of action because of the ankle sprain suffered in yesterday's ninth inning, Manager Leo Durocher of the Giants had Hank Thompson in right field.

Durocher said X-rays of Mueller's ankle had not yet been returned to the club. He didn't know when he could expect Mueller in the lineup.

The series will switch to the Polo Grounds for the fourth and, if necessary, fifth games, and will return to Yankee Stadium for the sixth and seventh contests if extended that long.

The Yankees and Giants were clashing in the World Series for the sixth time, with the Giants winning in 1921, 1922 and 1936 and the Yankees winning in 1923 and 1937.

The Yankees were playing in their 18th series and held a proud record of having won 13 of the previous 17. The Giants had won 16 National League pennants but only four world championships.

FIRST INNING.

GIANTS—Rizzuto came in for Stanky's slow roller and threw him out. Dark flied to Mantle. Thompson walked. Irvin singled to right, sending Thompson to third. Lockman's smash down the left-field line bounded into the stands for a ground-rule double, scoring Thompson, Irvin stopping at third. Irvin stole home, sliding under Reynolds' high pitch to Berra. Lockman held second base. Thomson walked. Mays flied to Mantle in

(See SERIES, Page A-2.)

Reds' Attacks Slow Allies on 40-Mile Front

U. N. Flame Throwers Burn Small Wedges In Chinese Defense

By the Associated Press

UNITED STATES 8th ARMY HEADQUARTERS, Korea, Oct. 4.—Flame-throwing infantrymen from nine United Nations burned two narrow wedges in Chinese defenses on the western front today in some of the fiercest fighting of the Korean war.

But smashing Red counterattacks stopped the two-day-old

Text of Truce Note Exchange. Page A-6
Korean Truce Renewed, But Site Choice Is Unsettled. Page A-5

Allied offensive cold along much of its 40-mile front.

Gains up to 4 miles were hammered out in the two days. At other points gains were so limited the yardage was not announced.

See-saw battles ranged over all of the shrub-covered hills in the Imjin River sector northeast of Kaesong, site of the disrupted truce talks.

The Allied offensive was launched by five divisions behind one of the heaviest artillery barrages of the war. American, British, Canadian, Australian, New Zealand, Greek, Turk, South Korean and Filipino troops participated in the attack. Tanks and planes supported them.

Chinese Burned Out.

The Chinese fought so stubbornly from their deeply dug-in positions—they've been digging in since truce talks started three months ago—they had to be burned out by flame throwers or blasted by hand grenades.

Canadian troops fighting west of Yonchon, 7 miles north of the 38th Parallel, made the 4-mile advance. Fifty-seven-ton Centurion tanks supported their savage hand-to-hand attacks.

Puerto Ricans of the United States Third Division plunged a mile ahead northwest of Chorwon in the only other noteworthy United Nations advance reported Thursday. The rapid American advance apparently caught the Reds by surprise. The five-hour

(See KOREA, Page A-4.)

U. N. Ethiopians Kill 22 Communists in Bayonet Fighting

By the Associated Press

WITH UNITED STATES 7th DIVISION, Korea, Oct. 4.—Officers of the Ethiopian detachment in Korea reported today their men killed 22 Chinese Communists in bitter bayonet fighting in the Reds' former iron triangle.

The Ethiopian officers described the action as the fiercest encountered by the African troops since they were committed.

Nine Reds were killed as the Ethiopians scaled a mountain and leaped into the enemy trenches with bared bayonets.

Ambassador Returning

BRUSSELS, Oct. 4 (AP).—United States Ambassador Robert D. Murphy left Brussels today for a stay of several weeks in the United States. He plans to sail on the S. S. Liberte tomorrow.

Late Races

Garden State

FOURTH RACE—Purse, $3,000; claiming; 3-year-olds; 6 furlongs.

Apsley (Permane)	8.40	4.60	3.60
Bright Bones (Culmone)		3.60	3.00
Stag (Fernandez)			4.00

Time, 1:11.
Also ran—Wonderment, Maid Of Hearts, Let's Buz, Triumpho, Inanabout, Roz's Folly, Stag, Peter W. and King Okapi.

Belmont Park

FOURTH RACE—Purse, $4,000; allowances; 2-year-olds; 6 furlongs; Widener course.

Lady in Blue (Atkins'n)	20.60	6.50	4.20
Gun Moll (Arcaro)		4.20	3.10
Miss Pensive (Shoemaker)			5.10

Time, 1:10⅕.
Also ran—Muscidae, Risque Ma, June Time, Strings, Caucus and Ultimatum.

Rockingham

FOURTH RACE—Purse, $2,200; claiming; 4-year-olds and up; 6 furlongs.

Puffball (Davern)	7.60	4.60	3.40
Scholarship (Destasio)		4.40	3.40
Count Off (Jewell)			6.60

Time, 1:10.
Also ran—Flying Mile, Concrete, Sticker, Ula, Sulty and Tiny Admiral.

Hawthorne

By the Associated Press

FIRST RACE—Purse, $2,100; claiming; 3-year-olds and up; 6½ furlongs.

La Belle Miss (Adams)	10.60	6.20	3.80
Persiana (Bassett)		7.60	4.20
Junior Wolf (Armstrong)			3.20

Time, 1:18⅗.
Also ran—Ida A., Mother Morris, Johnny, Hi Goodie, But Definitely, Van Slam, Ranahead, Chall Amaze and My Julie.

(Earlier Results and Tomorrow's Entries, Page A-2.)

Star Program Presents Special Series Report

Star Baseball Writer Burton Hawkins tonight will give a radio report direct from New York on today's World Series game. Mr. Hawkins will speak during The Evening Star Newscast, presented from 6 to 6:15 p.m. each weekday on WMAL, The Evening Star station. Don't miss this eye-witness account of the opening game in the series.

The Forrestal Diaries

New York Speech by Wallace Stirs Furor; Truman Fires Him, Keeps Byrnes

8. Exit Henry Wallace

(On September 12, 1946, the Democrats in New York were to open their political campaign with a "beat Dewey" rally, under auspices of strongly left-liberal coloration, at which the principal speaker was to be Henry Wallace, Secretary of Commerce. Secretary of State Byrnes was at the moment in Europe. When advance copies of the Wallace speech — attacking any alliance with "British imperialism" and laying down a "soft" policy toward Russia —were circulated, it seemed to represent a complete reversal of the whole course of the Byrnes foreign policy. To make matters worse, Mr. Wallace had included the statement that the President had read and approved his speech; and when the reporters asked Mr. Truman about this on the morning of the 12th he gave them to understand both that he had read the whole speech and that he thought it in line with the policies of Mr. Byrnes.

(Mr. Forrestal entered in his dairy a memorandum by the Undersecretary of the Navy, John L. Sullivan, giving a dramatic account of what followed. At 6 that evening Mr. Sullivan, with Capt. Robert L. Dennison, then an assistant chief of naval operations, arrived at the office of Will Clayton, who was Acting Secretary of State. There they found Mr. Clayton, James W. Riddleberger of the Division of European Affairs, and other high State Department officials. Mr. Sullivan's memorandum continues):

12 September, 1946.

MEMORANDUM TO THE SECRETARY.

. . . They appeared extremely dejected and handed us a copy of a speech to be delivered this evening by Secretary Wallace at Madison Square Garden. Capt. Dennison and I read the speech and agreed with the State Department representatives that if this speech were given by Secretary Wallace with the approval of the President it would in a large part repudiate the foreign policy which this country has been trying to establish for the last year.

In response to my question, Mr. Clayton stated that the speech was to be delivered at 7 p.m. Washington time. I then inquired whether or not this speech had been submitted to the Department of State, and the reply was negative. I asked when they had gotten it and learned that at 1 this morning Riddleberger at a bridge game overheard a correspondent refer to Wallace's speech on foreign policy. Clayton advised me that the State Department's transcript of the speech had been received at 3 (presumably this means 3 p.m.) but that he was busy on an UNRRA matter and had no opportunity to read it until a few minutes before 6. I asked him if he had protested to the White House, and he answered in the negative.

I then suggested that he call the White House and see if: (a) The speech could be stopped; (b) the White House could prevail on Secretary Wallace to delete the last sentence in the second paragraph on page 5 in which Secretary Wallace stated that the President had read these words and said they represented the policy of his administration.

Wallace vs. Byrnes.

(After some telephoning in search of various presidential aides, they finally got hold of Charles G. Ross, the President's press secretary. Mr. Clayton expressed his protests; then Mr. Sullivan took the telephone):

I expressed the opinion that the President could not possibly have read this speech and approved it. Ross sent for a transcript of the press conference this afternoon and said that he was afraid the President had told the newspapermen that he had approved it. I then pointed out to Mr. Ross that if this particular sentence to which I referred was deleted from the Wallace speech the President might then be able to say, "I scanned through his speech hurriedly and the parts of it which I read were quite consistent with the foreign policy of this country and enunciated by Secretary Byrnes. Obviously, there were some parts of the speech which I did

(See FORRESTAL, Page A-3)

Wallace Statement

One of Mr. Forrestal's notes published in the fifth article of this series said that Henry A. Wallace favored giving information on the atom bomb to the Russians. Mr. Wallace has sent the following comment to the New York Herald Tribune, which is syndicating the series:

Under the front page headline of October 1, 1951, "Wallace Wants Atom Bomb Given to Russia," the New York Herald Tribune quotes the late James Forrestal as saying that Henry Wallace was "completely, everlastingly and wholeheartedly in favor of giving it (the bomb) to the Russians."

This is a lie. I branded it under oath as a lie when I testified before the House Committee on Un-American Activities on January 26, 1950. At that time I quoted from the September 24, 1945, New York Times: "The President denied firmly that Mr. Wallace had insisted that the atomic bomb be turned over to Russia."

The Forrestal lie is with respect to the September 21, 1945, cabinet meeting. Some one put out the false information to the press which appeared September 22, 1945. In my testimony under oath I say the President on his own initiative knocked this statement down and that his attitude was magnificent throughout. I also said under oath that there was a leaking liar in the cabinet and the President agreed.

Mr. Forrestal's attitude was completely different from that of Secretary Stimson and about half the cabinet took Forrestal's slant and half Stimson's. My testimony before the Committee on Un-American Activities was offered in response to questions by Congressmen Francis Case of South Dakota and John S. Wood of Georgia. This testimony is contained on pages 1092 to 1095 of the publication entitled "Hearings Regarding Shipment of Atomic Material to the Soviet Union During World War II."

Knowing the utter fairness of the Tribune I am sure that my statement will be given equal front page and headline prominence with the Forrestal statement and that the Tribune will see that my statement is made available to all papers using the syndicated material.

I do not wish to quarrel with a dead man or his widow and children. Their husband and father wished very much to see me a few months before he died, but unfortunately he was held in seclusion at the Naval Hospital shortly thereafter. Undoubtedly at that time he was trying to set his spiritual house in order. May God rest the soul of this curiously tortured man who served his country and the armed services so well in time of war.

Australia Planning to Send 1,000 More Men to Korea

By the Associated Press

CANBERRA, Australia, Oct. 4.—Prime Minister Robert G. Menzies announced today Australia will add an additional infantry battalion of 1,000 men to her Korean forces early in 1952. This will double her present groung forces fighting under the U. N. command.

In addition, Australia has one squadron of meteor jet fighters, a destroyer and an aircraft carrier in the Korean campaign.

Mr. Menzies said Australia earnestly wants a cease-fire agreement. Nevertheless, he added, if negotiations are unsuccessful, "we must continue resolutely to resist Communist aggression."

The additional battalion will lift the number of Australian servicemen in the Korea-Japan area to 6,500.

Ex-Queen Amelia Ill

PARIS, Oct. 4 (AP).—Former Queen Amelia of Portugal is very ill with heart trouble and pneumonia, her doctors said today. Amelia, 86, is the widow of King Don Carlos who was assassinated in Lisbon, January 31, 1908.

British Hold War Games

LONDON, Oct. 4 (AP).—Fifteen thousand British soldiers will converge on Wiltshire and Dorset tonight in the opening of the United Kingdom's biggest war games. Tomorrow the Royal Air Force will stage a full-scale mock atom bomb attack on Britain.

Two 'Airline Chiefs' Sputter To Landing in Police Station

Two men, each claiming to be president of an organization called World Wide Airlines, were arrested by police today on charges of disorderly conduct.

They were listed as Edward J. Daly, 31, of Teaneck, N. J., and Howard Robinson, 36, who gave his address as the Wardman Park Hotel.

The Civil Aeronautics Board said it had no registration record for either a scheduled or nonscheduled airline under the name of World Wide Airlines.

Daly, police said, also told them he lost his wallet containing between $550 and $600 while being taken to the eighth precinct station. The $25 collateral for each was posted by Robinson, who "peeled the money from a large roll of bills," the officers related.

Their occupations were listed on the arrest slips as "executive."

Two motorcycle policemen who went into the Little Tavern shop at 2628 Connecticut avenue N.W. said the men were using abusive language and complaining about the service. They urged them to be more quiet, but the men persisted, the officers said.

One of the officers grasped one of the men and the other man grasped the policeman. At that moment, several more officers who had been checking the neighborhood following a prowler report, walked into the restaurant.

Daly and Robinson surrendered meekly. They were scheduled to appear in court today.

Austin Tells Hearing That U. S. Needs Man Like Jessup in U. N.

Ambassador Labels McCarthy Accusations 'Little Picayune Things'

By L. Edgar Prina

Ambassador Warren R. Austin today gave Ambassador Philip C. Jessup resounding support in his fight for confirmation as a delegate to the United Nations in face of charges of pro-communism leveled at him.

Testifying before a Senate Foreign Relations subcommittee, which is considering Dr. Jessup's nomination, the chief of the American delegation to the U. N. referred to accusations by Senator McCarthy, Republican, of Wisconsin, on the nominee's loyalty as "these little picayune things."

Senator Fulbright, Democrat, of Arkansas asked Mr. Austin whether he ever had any reason to believe that Dr. Jessup had an "unusual affinity for Communist causes"—one of Senator McCarthy's charges.

Needs Men Like Dr. Jessup.

"Why no—everything indicates the contrary," the witness replied in a shocked voice.

Mr. Austin told the subcommittee that this Nation needs men of the "highest caliber and highest character possible," for its representatives at the U. N. General Assembly in Paris next month.

"It needs a man like Dr. Jessup and others who have the principles and policies of the United States of America part of the fiber of his being and their beings," Mr. Austin said.

Senator Fulbright, who was building a base for later questioning on Dr. Jessup's attitude toward the recognition of Communist China, asked the witness:

"Recognition doesn't connote approval of a regime in any country, does it?"

"Of course, you're right . . . recognition or non-recognition is not proof of our acceptance of the government," the Ambassador replied.

Dr. Jessup Hears Austin.

Dr. Jessup, who will take the stand later in the day, sat in the hearing room during the testimony of Mr. Austin, with whom he has served many times on U. N. business.

Declaring that "his record will speak to you rather than I," Mr. Austin took up Dr. Jessup's record in representing the United States in the U. N. It was brought out that Dr. Jessup had been confirmed unanimously by the Senate on five different occasions for high diplomatic posts.

In connection with the Indonesian dispute in 1948 and 1949, Mr. Austin said Dr. Jessup skillfully steered the course which allowed the young republic in Southeast

(See JESSUP, Page A-4.)

Gabrielson Testifies He Tried to Get Job For Ex-RFC Director

Says Stock Exchange Discussion Was Not Connected With Loan

By Robert K. Walsh

Republican National Chairman Guy G. Gabrielson disclosed to a Senate subcommittee today that he tried to get a job for former RFC Director Harvey Gunderson as president of the New York Stock Exchange last year.

Mr. Gunderson, who left RFC last October, was on the agency's Board of Directors, which in 1946 approved $18.5 million in loans to Carthage Hydrocol, Inc., of which Mr. Gabrielson is president and legal counsel.

Mr. Gabrielson could not recall the exact date or circumstances

Partial Text of Gabrielson Statement. Page A-5

of a conversation he said he had with Mr. Gunderson about the possibility of getting the stock exchange position. He insisted, however, that the talk had no connection with any dealings between Carthage Hydrocol and RFC. He explained that Mr. Gunderson was about to leave RFC and later said he had no particular desire for the New York position.

Explains RFC Dealings.

The Senate subcommittee was hearing Mr. Gabrielson at his own request to explain his connection with the $48 million company and the RFC loans it obtained long before he became national chairman in August, 1949. He declared that criticism of his recent negotiations with RFC in behalf of the company will not cause him to quit as party chairman.

"To resign as Republican Party chairman in the hope of saving my party embarrassment would have been construed as an admission of improper conduct," he said. "The alternative was to refute slander with facts, in full confidence that the people will recognize truth and reject false accusations in keeping with our traditional standards of fair play."

Mr. Gabrielson's explanation concerning Mr. Gunderson

(See RFC, Page A-5.)

Truman Says All Agencies To Aid on Price Laws

By the Associated Press

President Truman said today that every agency of the Government will co-operate to enforce meat price controls.

The President did not disclose specific agencies expected to participate in the price enforcement drive.

He replied with an emphatic no when he was asked whether the Government is going to lift controls on beef.

Kirk Meets Gromyko

MOSCOW, Oct. 4 (AP).—United States Ambassador Alan G. Kirk conferred today with Deputy Foreign Minister Andrei Gromyko at the Soviet Foreign Ministry. Mr. Kirk is leaving Moscow next week and may not return as Ambassador.

Markets at a Glance

NEW YORK (AP). — Stocks, mixed; profit taking unsettles list. Bonds, mixed; rails in demand. Cotton, lower; commission house liquidation.

CHICAGO. — Wheat, easy; trade rather light. Corn, easy; weather drys out crop. Oats, mostly easy, but December steady. Hogs, fairly active, 15 to 25 cents higher; top, $22.45. Cattle, steady to 50 cents lower.

(Late Market News, Page A-33.)

President Assails Publication Of Secret Security Information

95% Already in Print, He Says, Defending His Recent Order

By Joseph A. Fox

President Truman today vigorously defended his recent order tightening control over Government information and charged that newspapers and slick magazines had published 95 per cent of the information declared secret or otherwise classified by the military establishments.

In a lengthy news conference discussion of his controversial se-

Moody Urges Study of Security Order by Newsman Committee. Page A-25
Text of Truman Statement. Page A-10

curity order designed to prevent vital information from falling into enemy hands, the President said "considerable misrepresentation and misunderstanding" had followed the order's issuance September 24.

He defended the order in a prepared statement as "an honest effort to find the best approach to a problem that is important to the survival of the United States."

Should Withhold Material.

The President said flatly that editors and publishers should refrain from the publication of material which might disclose vital information even though it had been cleared by a Government agency.

Two hours after the news conference, however, the President's stand putting responsibility for publication directly up to newspaper and magazine officials was modified in the following statement by White House Press Secretary Joseph Short:

"The President has directed me to clarify his views on security information as follows:

"1. Every citizen, including officials and publishers, has a duty to protect our country.

May Assume It's Safe.

"2. Citizens who receive military information for publication from responsible officials qualified to judge the relationship of such information to the national security may rightfully assume it is safe to publish the information.

"3. Citizens who receive mili-

(Continued on Page A-3, Col. 1.)

Truman Violation Of Own Security Order Is Hinted

President Truman today apparently violated his own security order.

In charging that newspapers and magazines had published 95 per cent of secret or otherwise classified information, President Truman quoted a Yale University survey.

At New Haven, Conn., Yale University issued a statement saying all details of the project are confidential "by order of the Government."

U. S. Collector Paid by Agency Insuring Firms in Tax Trouble

BULLETIN

Senator Moody, Democrat, of Michigan today said Senate investigators had discovered a "number of serious irregularities in the intelligence unit of the Internal Revenue Bureau in Detroit." He did not amplify, but promised a statement later on parts of the charges that "have been nailed down" by investigators.

By Cecil Holland and George Beveridge

An Internal Revenue Bureau intelligence agent testified today that an insurance agency which sold policies to companies having tax difficulties paid $6,193.11 in 1949 and 1950 to James P. Finnegan, former St. Louis collector, and members of his family.

The agent, Rudolph H. Hartmann of the bureau's St. Louis office, detailed the payments before a House Ways and Means subcommittee investigating scandals in the Government's tax collection agency.

Two St. Louis insurance men also linked Mr. Finnegan with the insurance operation and testified they understood that he turned over lists of companies having tax troubles to the insurance agency.

The subcommittee announced at the end of the morning session that John Martin Brodsky of St. Louis will be the first witness tomorrow morning to look further into Mr. Finnegan's relation with Mr. Brodsky and what was identified as the Dudmar Insurance Agency that sold numerous policies in the last two years to St. Louis companies under tax investigation.

Mr. Hartmann told the subcommittee that the insurance agency's payments during the 1949-50 period were made to Mr. Finnegan,

(Continued on Page A-4, Col. 1.)

Irvin's Hits Make Reynolds Better Analyst Than Pitcher

By Francis Stann
Star Staff Correspondent

NEW YORK, Oct. 4.—The first Yankee-Giant World Series in 14 years opened today against a backdrop of gray, leaden skies, but with baseball enthusiasm in New York at possibly an all-time peak.

An official 65,673 spectators were in the stands of Yankee Stadium as the favored Yankees took the field against the Giants, who they defeated in the World Series of 1923, 1936 and 1937 after losing their other two series against the Polo Grounders in 1921 and 1922.

Speculators were asking $20 for reserved grandstand tickets priced at $6.

Reynolds was looking like a better analyst than a pitcher for at least half of today's game. Writing for a New York paper, Reynolds made a pre-series statement that Irvin would be a tougher hitter to fool than Willie Mays.

In his first three times at bat, Irvin singled twice and hit a triple that holled to the 457-foot mark in center field.

As the new commissioner of baseball, Ford Frick, threw out a first ball for the first time, Yankee Catcher Yogi Berra caught the pitch and returned the ball to Frick.

The first fan ejected was an unidentified male who never saw the first pitch. As the game started and Manager Leo Durocher took his place in the coaching box back of third base, the fan ran onto the field and asked for Leo's autograph. Gendarmes quickly escorted the gentleman from the premises.

Bobby Thomson's ninth-inning, game-winning, pennant-clinching home run yesterday threw a big monkey wrench in the Dodgers' plans for last night. They can-

(See STANN, Page A-2.)

Featured Reading Inside Today's Star

ROYALTY TRAINING — Princess Elizabeth's forthcoming visit here is regarded as important training for a prospective sovereign. Alvin J. Steinkopf gives an intimate glimpse of her in the second of three articles on page A-6.

CHIEF BOTTLENECK—A shortage of machine tools has become so serious this country is seeking help from two former enemies. Star Reporter Francis P. Douglas analyses the problem on page A-22.

SUCCESS FROM A SHOESTRING—With a lot of imagination and no District funds, Gallinger Hospital has created a unit giving new hope to the physically handicapped. For an account of what's being done there, see page B-1.

Guide for Readers

CITY EDITION

DAILY NEWS

Copr. 1951 by News Syndicate Co. Inc. NEW YORK'S PICTURE NEWSPAPER Trade Mark Reg. U. S. Pat. Off.

3¢

Vol. 33. No. 87 New York 17, Thursday, October 4, 1951★ 84 Main+12 Manhattan Pages 3 Cents IN CITY LIMITS | 4 CENTS In Suburbs | 5 CENTS Elsewhere

GIANTS (THOMSON, THAT IS) FACE YANKEES

Stories Page 3, 72

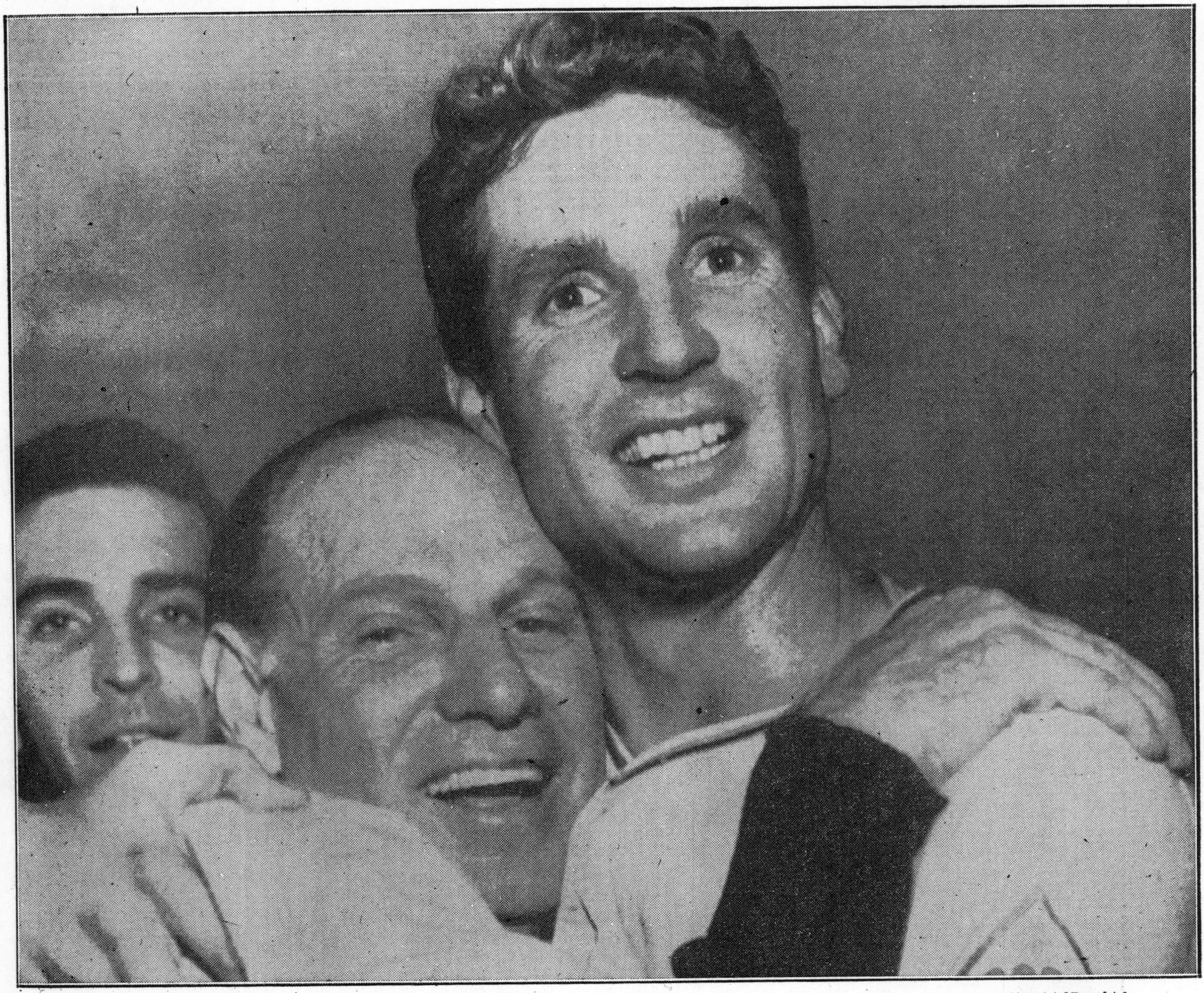

(Associated Press foto)

To the Victors Belong the Smiles. Giant manager Leo Durocher (left), who directed the greatest stretch run in baseball history, exchanges hugs and smiles with Bobby Thomson, the guy who produced playoff-payoff poke. Thomson's 3-run homer in the 9th at Polo Grounds shoved the Giants into World Series.

—Stories pages 3 and 72; other pics. centerfold, back page

CITY EDITION

DAILY NEWS

Copr. 1951 by News Syndicate Co. Inc. NEW YORK'S PICTURE NEWSPAPER Trade Mark Reg. U. S. Pat. Off.

THE LARGEST CIRCULATION IN AMERICA

84 New York 17, Thursday, October 4, 1951 3 Cents IN CITY LIMITS | 4 CENTS In Suburbs | 5 CENTS Elsewhere

GIANTS WIN NL FLAG ON THOMSON'S HR, 5-4

Story on Page 72

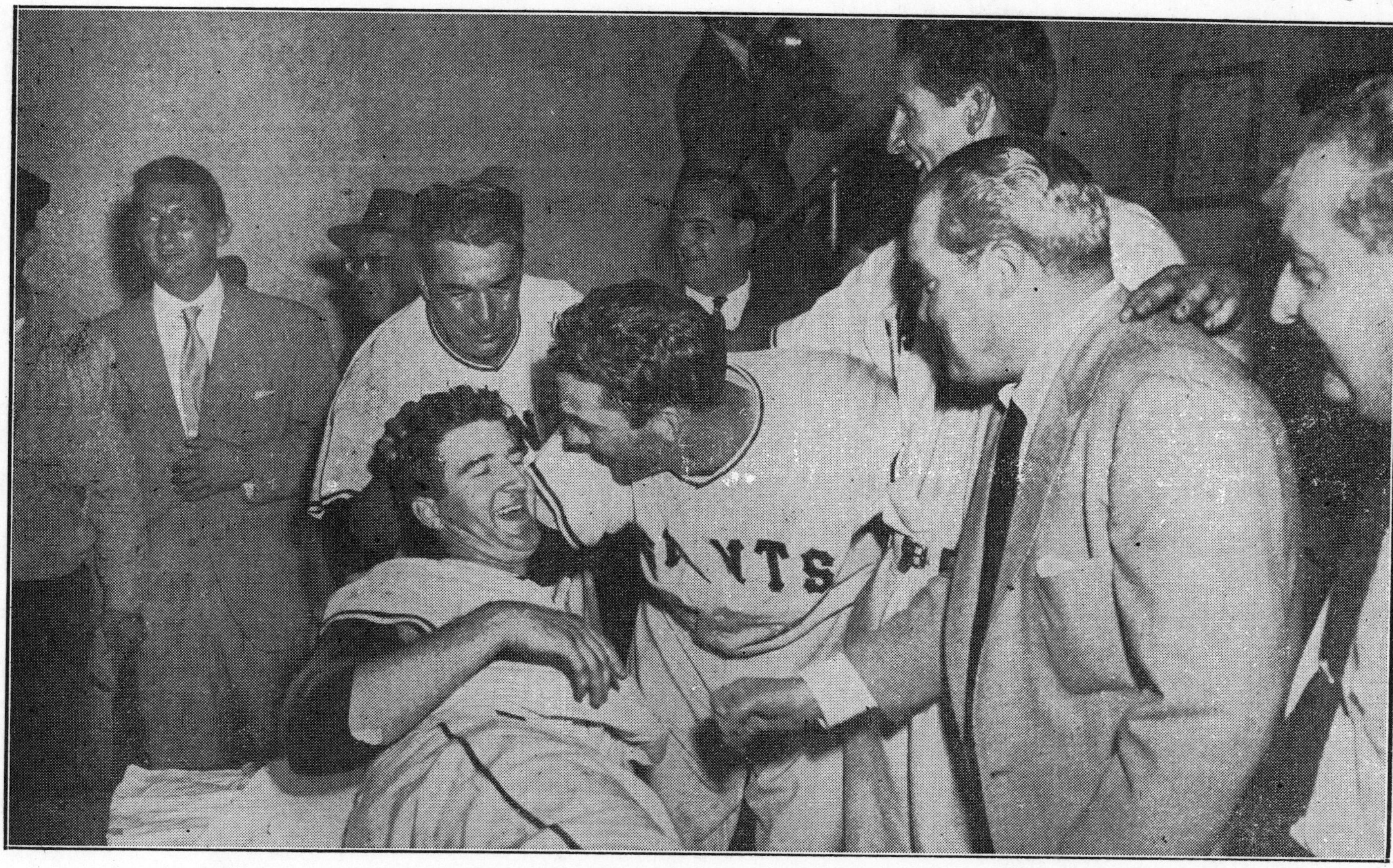

(NEWS foto by Charles Payne)

Giants' Don Mueller, who injured ankle during rally in 9th, smiles along with (l. to r.) Coach Fitzsimmons, winning pitcher Jansen, winning hitter Thomson and winning owner Stoneham in the clubhouse.

After the Ball Was Over . . . The Wall

A stunned Hodges, a dazed Robinson and a down-trodden Branca [→] leave field after Thomson's wall-clearing blast in 9th inning. *—Stories, pages 3, 72; other pics. p. 1, centerfold*

(NEWS foto by Seymour Wally)

Find Fortune in Smuggled Soviet Furs Cached Here

Story on Page 2

5¢ | U. S. Weather Forecast SOME CLOUDINESS (Details on Page 2) | **Daily Mirror** | 3c In N. Y. City 5c Elsewhere | 5¢

Vol. 28. No. 94. NEW YORK 17, N. Y., THURSDAY, OCTOBER 11, 1951 CO COMPLETE SPORTS

YANKS TAKE IT!

Bauer's 3-on Triple Ruins Giants, 4-3,

Story on Page 3

(Mirror Photo by Arthur Aidala)

IT'S THE CRUSHER Giant pitcher Koslo has just fired a 2-out, 3-2 pitch to Yank batter Bauer—and thar she goes (arrow), headed for Stadium leftfield fence and a base-clearing triple. Berra is halfway home, DiMaggio almost to third, and Mize comes into second. The three runs, in 7th inning, were just enough for Yanks to cop their third straight World Series.

(Other Photos on Page 3, Sports and Back Pages)

Dodgers' Campanella Voted National League's Most Valuable Player in 1951

VIEWS OF SPORT

By RED SMITH

Horses Are Like Providence

WHEN Dick Thomas was a four-year-old in Nebraska, he strayed away from his mother and got lost in the crowd at a harness race meeting. When they found him he was in a stall playing happily about the legs of a crazy stallion that would have kicked the brains out of any grown man within reach. "Horses," Dick Thomas says, "are like Providence. Don't they say there's a special Providence watches over women, children and drunks?"

Red Smith

Dick's grandfather was a trotting horse man. Dick's father, Henry, ran the great Hanover Shoe Farms in Pennsylvania for nine years and drove three winners of the Hambletonian, which is the Kentucky Derby, the World Series, the National Open, the heavyweight championship of trotting.

Dick rode horses bareback and he rode show horses and jumpers and rode in the terrifying Maryland Hunt Cup, a murderous course over post-and-rail fences which some authorities consider the sternest test of horse and man in America. His mother wanted him to be a veterinary and he studied for that. His Uncle Sam wanted him to be an Air Force flyer and he gave that a five-year hassel.

When it came to finding his life's work, though, where could a kid like that go except to the races with the jugheads? Where was he going to be happy except at Yonkers and Roosevelt Raceway, at Goshen and Old Orchard Beach, Me., and Reading, Pa., and What Cheer, Iowa?

You Wish They Were Shooting

TODAY, at thirty, Dick Thomas is his father's partner in a public stable. They train and drive their own horses and those sent to their barn by other owners. Henry Thomas topped all drivers at Roosevelt this year and Dick was in the running for third place but, because he frequently took animals away to race them at other tracks, he didn't have enough mounts to be officially ranked in the Long Island meeting. With a couple of weeks more to go, he's still in the running for the Yonkers championship.

"Must be kind of tame sitting up there behind a horse after five years of sitting on clouds in the Air Force," it was suggested.

His voice and his features were incredulous.

"There's no comparison," he said. "Driving takes skill. Flying a plane, any dope can do that."

"Yes, but in planes they shoot at you."

"When you're going into the turn in the middle of a pack of eight," Dick said, "you wish somebody was shooting at you instead."

McLin's First Victory

THE luncheon conversation rambled. Dick was driving in amateur races when he was fourteen, but he didn't get a mount as a professional until he was twenty. He had four years of military school in Baltimore and two years at Penn State studying to be a vet, and it was during vacation before Pearl Harbor, in August, 1941, that he enlisted as an air cadet.

"I joined up with dad when I got out." He grumbled. "He made me work with horses about three years before he'd give me a mount. Wouldn't even let me jog a horse."

He saw all three of his father's Hambletonian victories. "Dad had McLin in 1938," he said, "later named McLin Hanover. Bill Cane, you know, who runs the Hambletonian, never has had a winner of that race since he took it over. He won with Walter Dear in 1929, the year before he took charge, and since then he's sold two horses that won the race afterwards.

"Dad bought McLin from him three weeks before the Hambletonian. McLin hadn't won a race and he didn't win one until the Hambletonian. He wasn't called a maiden because dad had won one heat with him, but never a race."

"Did your father think he had a Hambletonian winner that year?"

"He did the day before the race. The day before the race he knew he had the winner."

Department of Extra Special Information

DICK hasn't driven in a Hambletonian, hasn't any immediate prospects in that direction because there are no star trotters in his charge this year.

"I'll tell you the name of the 1952 winner, though," he said. "You can put it in the paper right now. Lord of Lullwater, that horse Johnny Simpson's got. He's not the top choice now, but he will be at race time.

"I've driven Hambletonian horses, but not in that race. I used to drive Chestertown, the 1946 winner. We had two free-for-all horses in our barn, Chestertown and Dutch Harbor, and dad would drive one and I the other."

"What was your most exciting race?"

"With Dutch Harbor in the $50,000 two-mile trot. He didn't win, but he didn't figure. We finished second and dad was third with Chestertown. Next year in the same race, I drove Chestertown and dad had Dutch. I was fourth and he was fifth."

Dick grinned a little. "I get to mention that to dad," he said, "every once in a while."

Football Here and There

Two-Way Platoon Players? There Are Plenty Around

By Roger Kahn

Charlie Maloy, Holy Cross' passing attack, won the first round of his battle with a stomach ailment yesterday and returned to classes. Round two will be decided when and if the nineteen-year-old junior return to football action.

Maloy is the victim of a duodenal ulcer which surprised every one including Maloy and Holy Cross coach Eddie Anderson, an M. D., because Charlie "is not a worrier and has never seemed to be nervous."

BOB SPEARS

The ailment took him out of action after the Crusaders lost to Tulane Oct. 13 and until yesterday he was in the college infirmary.

"We're hoping," Anderson said, "that he'll be back in time for the Marquette game. He wants to get back and we'll let him dress for the Colgate game this week, but I won't let him play under any circumstances."

Without Maloy the Crusaders have been forced to rely on a ground attack and, since the ailing star is among the finest passers in the country and was the hub of the offense, they are not too happy with the arrangement.

Fed up with two platoons? Looking for ball-players who can go both ways? Stop looking. There are plenty still around who are good no matter how you play 'em. . . . A quick list of backs reveals Ollie Matson, San Francisco's All-American candidate; Bob Spears, Yale's powerful fullback; Chuck Curtis, Dartmouth's best halfback and Avatus Stone, Syracuse quarterback, as men who tackle and run with equal apiomb.

For ends there is Princeton's Frank McPhee and Colgate's Bob Kluckhohn, and the list of linemen would fill a book, or certainly a sports section.

Anyway, a good football player is still a good football player, no matter how you, or the coach, plays him.

A pair of good overlooked elevens battle at Lewisburg, Pa., Saturday when Bucknell (6—0) meets Temple (5—1) . . . It's the twenty-fifth renewal of a series and this one should be won in the line. . . . Bucknell credits its forward wall, braced by George Young, 245 pounds, and Frank Kirby, ten pounds lighter, for its success, and Temple has half a dozen tackles of over 210 pounds. . . . The Owls' only setback came at the hands of Syracuse in the season opener and since then they've beaten every one including Boston U. last week, 20 to 13.

Maine, with a perfect 3-and-0 record, has clinched the Yankee Conference title for the season. . . . The F. & M.-W. & J. football game at Lancaster, Pa., Saturday will be televised as part of category "B" in the N. C. A. A. program. "B" means "a small center with a small college and a high saturation of long time television owners." . . . Another good small college Pennsylvania football is listed at Bethlehem where Lehigh meets Muhlenberg. Lehigh's Herb Weiss will be shooting for a passing record and needs but 131 yards for a new mark.

Federal Tax on Free Sports Passes Ends

WASHINGTON, Oct. 31 (AP).—Starting tomorrow, no Federal admission tax will be collected on free passes to sporting events or places of amusement.

Also, if a person is admitted at reduced rates, he will be taxed on the cut price rather than the full admission charge as at present. The tax is one cent for each five cents of the admission charge.

Congressional tax experts said the change affects admissions to all types of events. It is part of the new tax law effective tomorrow.

Musial, Irvin, Maglie Follow Brooklyn Star

Roe Finishes in Fifth Place, Robinson Sixth in Annual Baseball Writers' Ballot

By Harold Rosenthal

Roy Campanella, the Dodgers' catcher, was named Most Valuable Player in the National League for 1951 yesterday. He won eleven of a possible twenty-four first-place votes cast by a committee of two dozen members of the Baseball Writers Association of America and finished more than fifty points ahead of Stan Musial, the Cardinals' league batting champion.

Roy Campanella, voted most valuable player in National League

Monte Irvin, whose powerful bat sparked the Giants to the National League pennant and played such an important role in the World Series against the Yankees, finished third, and his teammate, Sal Maglie, who wound up with a record of twenty-three victories and six losses, followed.

Fifth place went to Preacher Roe, the Dodgers' left-handed star, who wound up with the percentage championship of the league; sixth to Jackie Robinson, a Most Valuable Player winner two season ago; seventh to Richie Ashburn, the Phillies' all-star center fielder; eighth to Bobby Thomson, the Giants' third baseman, whose sensational homer won the third play-off game from the Dodgers and carried the Giants into the World Series; ninth to Murry Dickson, a twenty-game winning right-hander with the lowly Pirates, and tenth to Ralph Kiner, Pittsburgh's home-run champion. Last year's winner, Jim Konstanty, Phillies' relief ace, didn't so much as receive an honorable mention.

Campanella, father of five children, a cigar-smoker and an inveterate bow-tie wearer, is the second Negro to be so honored. His selection also marked the third time in the last thirteen years that the writers looked elsewhere than the pennant-winning club for the No. 1 player.

They picked a thirty-year-old roly-poly fellow liked by every one, a fellow plagued by a succession of injuries which still did not prevent him from bashing thirty-three home runs and finishing up with a .325 batting average, second only to Robinson on the Dodgers.

They also picked a fellow who served a severe apprenticeship in the Negro leagues before given his chance in organized baseball by Branch Rickey. Campanella, before he broke into the Dodger chain with Nashua in the now-defunct New England League, caught double-headers as a matter of course and on one Sunday bus-riding junket around Ohio managed to catch four games against the Indianapolis Clowns. "Nothing to it," reminisced Campanella. "I'd rather be behind the plate than sitting on the bench anyway. If I sit around I get nervous."

Campanella had to sit around more this year than any time since the Dodgers brought him up from St. Paul in June of 1948 to bolster the sagging Brooklyn club. He missed a dozen games because of injuries. The most serious stemmed from the ball which Turk Lown hit him with on the left ear during the Dodgers' final Western trip. Campanella was never the same after the injury, which kept him out for about a week.

Earlier the Dodger star was spiked on the hand, was in a violent plate collision with the Giants' Whitey Lockman, and then came up with a leg injury so bad that novocaine injections in an effort to enable him to play in the last two games of the play-off proved unsuccessful. He also slid a little too enthusiastically one day in Ebbets Field and was out for a couple of games.

Five of the eight clubs were included in the first ten, and all the first-place votes were encompassed in this group. Warren Spahn, Boston's ace left-hander, was the Braves' first man, in eleventh position; Ken Raffensberger, another left-hander, was Cincinnati's top man, in eighteenth place, and Phil Cavarretta, the Cubs' manager, tied with Hank Sauer, his left fielder, for twenty-third place, each with one vote.

Campanella's selection was kept a deep secret until just before edition time of today's morning papers to prevent possible leaks to gamblers. Last year there were reports that there were some lunatics so crazy for betting action that they actually wagered on the Most Valuable Player award in the American League with bookmakers, who had copies of the point totals tucked in their hip pockets.

Most Valuable Player Tabulation of Voting

* * *

The voting for most valuable player in the National League with points on a 14-9-8-7-6-5-4-3-2-1 basis. (First place votes in parentheses):

Player, Club	Pts.
1. Roy Campanella, Brooklyn (11)	243
2. Stan Musial, St. Louis (2)	191
3. Monte Irvin, New York (5)	166
4. Sal Maglie, New York (1)	153
5. Preacher Roe, Brooklyn (2)	138
6. Jackie Robinson, Brooklyn (1)	92
7. Richie Ashburn, Philadelphia	69
8. Bobby Thomson, New York (1)	62
9. Murry Dickson, Pittsburgh (1)	59
10. Ralph Kiner, Pittsburgh	49
11. Warren Spahn, Boston	45
12. Al Dark, New York	30
13. Robin Roberts, Philadelphia	27
14. Larry Jansen, New York	26
15. Pee Wee Reese, Brooklyn	15
16. (tie) Gil Hodges, Brooklyn	10
16. (tie) Sid Gordon, Boston	10
18. Ken Raffensberger, Cincinnati	8
19. (tie) Johnny Wyrostek, Cincinnati	6
19. (tie) Ewell Blackwell, Cincinnati	6
19. (tie) Carl Furillo, Brooklyn	6
22. Don Newcombe, Brooklyn	3
23. (tie) Phil Cavarretta, Chicago	1
23. (tie) Hank Sauer, Chicago	1

Campanella Surprised

HOUSTON, Oct. 31 (AP).—Roy Campanella, the Brooklyn Dodgers' slugging catcher, was surprised here today when informed he was named the National League's most valuable player for 1951 by the Baseball Writers Association of America poll.

"I had forgotten all about that award," he said. "After we were beaten in the play-off by the New York Giants, I just didn't think about it any more.

"I surely am happy about it now. I gave my best and I surely am grateful to the Baseball Writers Association for voting me in."

DiMaggio Retires as Player but Expects to Remain in Yankee Organization

CLIPPER GIVES HINT OF TELEVISION JOB

DiMaggio, After 13 Seasons With Yankees, Says He Is Through as a Player

NO AMBITION TO MANAGE

Decision, Made Last Spring, Laid to Age and Injuries—Mantle Due for Post

By JOHN DREBINGER

The Yankee Clipper has made his last graceful catch and taken his last cut at the ball.

Amid a fanfare without precedent in the retirement of a player, Joe DiMaggio yesterday told the Bombers and the world that he was retiring as an active performer and that nothing could ever persuade him to play again.

As newsreel cameras clicked, light bulbs flashed and photographers and reporters jammed every inch of the Yankees' Fifth Avenue suite in the Squibb Tower, the son of an Italian immigrant who rose from the wharves of San Francisco to a position of eminence and an accumulation of more than $700,000 in baseball earnings quietly revealed that he alone had made the decision.

No Longer Has 'It'

It was prompted, he said, by advancing years—he was 37 on Nov. 25—physical injuries and the conviction that as a player "I no longer have it." He said also night baseball was partly to blame and was convinced it had shortened his career by at least two years. DiMaggio started his major league career in 1936, and was with the Yankees for thirteen seasons, with three years out for Army service.

What were his future plans? These, he said, he was not prepared to reveal, but hinted that they likely would bring him into radio and television. He revealed also that for the present, at least, his plans were to remain with the Yankee organization, but in what capacity he could not say.

His new post would not be in connection with any field work or managing. Asked whether he aspired to managing the Yankees, DiMaggio replied, "That one I have answered many times. I never wanted to be a manager and never will."

Asked why he felt so strongly on this point, he answered with a wry smile, "because I had enough to do with my own troubles without worrying about the troubles of twenty-five other players."

Television Job Likely

The general belief is that part of DiMaggio's future activities will see him engaged as the Yankee television broadcaster at a salary of about $50,000. As a player he is reputed to have received $100,000 for each of the past three seasons.

Dan Topping, who was present with his co-owner Del Webb and Manager Casey Stengel, said that up to the last he had hoped to persuade DiMaggio to change his mind. But the Clipper's mind had been made up long ago.

DiMaggio said he knew last spring this would be his last year. The Clipper said he regretted having hinted at his retirement then, for he realized later his remarks had been ill-timed.

"But I knew my mind was made up, although I never mentioned it again until after the world series and then only to Topping," said DiMaggio. "He asked me to think it over a while longer and in fairness to him I decided this was the only thing to do. I never mentioned it to another soul and not even my brother Dominic knew what my decision would be today."

'What Is There to Say?'

The usually loquacious Stengel had little to say.

"What is there to say?" said Casey, "I just gave the Big Guy's glove away and it is going to the Hall of Fame, where Joe himself is certain to go. He was the greatest player I ever managed and right now I still say there isn't another centerfielder in baseball his equal."

Concerning a replacement, Stengel said the job would be "wide open," with Mickey Mantle, rookie star of the past season, receiving first call, closely followed by Jackie Jensen.

As the appointed hour of 2 P. M. arri-ed, Arthur (Red) Patterson, in charge of the ceremonies and striving to keep reporters from choking on sandwiches and stumbling over newsreel wires, issued a typed statement for DiMaggio.

"I told you fellows last spring," the statement read, "I thought this would be my last year. I only wish I could have had a better year, but even if I had hit .350, this would have been the last year for me.

"You all know I have had more than my share of physical injuries and setbacks during my career. In recent years these have been much too frequent to laugh off. When baseball is no longer fun, it's no longer a game.

"And so, I've played my last game of ball.

"Since coming to New York I've made a lot of friends and picked up a lot of advisers, but I would like to make one point clear—no one has influenced me in making this decision. It has been my problem and my decision to make.

"I feel that I have reached the stage where I can no longer produce for my ball club, my manager, my team-mates and my fans the sort of baseball their loyalty to me deserves.

"In closing, I would like to say that I feel I have been unusually privileged to play all my major league baseball for the New York Yankees.

"But it has been an even greater privilege to be able to play baseball at all. It has added much to my life. What I will remember most in days to come will be the great loyalty of the fans. They have been very good to me."

After fulfilling his obligations to the photographers and radio commentators, the Clipper drifted back to the press room, where he answered a barrage of questions.

When did he first realize he was slipping? About three years ago.

What ailments bothered him most?

"My right knee," he replied. "It kept buckling under me every little while. Also both shoulders. These have bothered me for a long time and finally retarded my swing so much I simply couldn't hit in front of the plate as I used to. Right now, though, I feel fine, and have no intention of going near a doctor. But I know I couldn't do it again on the ball field."

What were his biggest thrills in his major league career?

"Well, I guess the fifty-six game hitting streak in 1941," he said. "And then there was that series up in Boston in 1949 when, after missing the first sixty-five games because of my heel operation, I belted a couple of home runs."

In that series, the Clipper exploded four home runs in the three games, drove in nine runs and virtually wrecked the Red Sox for the rest of the campaign.

Who was the toughest pitcher he ever faced?

"When I first came up, Mel Harder. But last season," he added with a chuckle, "they all were pretty tough."

What was his greatest fielding play?

"I guess the one I made off Hank Greenberg back in 1938 or 1939, out by the flagpole in the Stadium just in front of the 461-foot mark. Don't know yet how I made it. Just stuck my glove up the last moment and there was the ball.

Failed to Get Averill

"But actually I also pulled a rock on that one," the Clipper reminisced. "Earl Averill was on first at the time and there was only one out. When I caught the ball Averill was almost to third and I should have doubled him up easily. But in the excitement I thought the catch retired the side and before I woke up Averill was back on first."

In addition to being a powerful hitter, DiMaggio displayed great fielding skill and was an excellent base runner.

Having started as a professional player with the San Francisco Seals in 1932, DiMaggio appeared in three games that season as a shortstop but the next year became an outfielder and since has not played anywhere else.

He first attracted attention in the East when, still with the Seals, he compiled a sixty-one-game hitting streak. The Yankess, then owned by the late Col. Jacob Ruppert and directed by Ed Barrow, bought DiMaggio for $25,000 for delivery in the spring of 1936. Throughout 1935 there was considerable apprehension when the youngster was believed suffering from a trick knee.

The San Francisco Club even offered to cancel the deal, but the Yanks, acting on the advice of their Coast scouts, decided to stay with it and never regretted it. For with Babe Ruth already gone from the Stadium and Lou Gehrig destined to carry on for only a few more seasons, DiMaggio was to give the Bombers still another diamond immortal who was to draw thousands through the turnstiles.

Few rookies ever had to respond to so great a ballyhoo as accompanied DiMaggio eastward in the spring of 1936. But his place in stardom was established almost from the start. Manager Joe McCarthy needed only one look to realize that he had the player of a generation.

And with the rise of DiMaggio, the Yanks rode to great triumphs. In his first four years, from 1936 through 1939, the Yanks won four pennants and world titles. In all, DiMaggio played in ten world series and nine times was with the winner. And in his final game last October, he ran his total of series games to fifty-one, one above the previous record held by Frankie Frisch.

Most impressive was his achievement in 1941, when he hit safely in fifty-six consecutive games for a major-league record. The streak began on May 15. It ended in a night game on July 17 in Cleveland and it took two great fielding plays, one by Ken Keltner, the other by Lou Boudreau, to turn the trick.

In each of his thirteen active seasons, DiMaggio was picked for the All-Star Game, but twice, in 1946 and 1951, he was sidelined because of injuries.

Starting with $8,000 in his first season and continuing until his salary reached $100,000 for each of the last three, DiMaggio received an estimated $646,250 in pay from the Yankees. World series shares raised this by $58,519.17 for an over-all total of $704,769.71. To this must be added about $250,000 received for radio and television appearances and for endorsements of products.

Despite this income, DiMaggio, when asked if he would like to loaf for a year, replied with a grim smile:

"Yes, I would like to loaf, but I'm afraid I'm not that well fixed."

Named Most Valuable

DiMaggio was named the most valuable player in the American League in 1939, 1941 and again in 1947. Three years in service kept him out of play from 1943 through 1945. He led the league in runs batted in in 1941; was twice the circuit's home-run king, with forty-six in 1937 and thirty-nine in 1948, and captured two batting crowns, his top average the .381 that won the crown in 1939.

Despite a falling off to a meager .263 average the past season for 116 games, he completed his career with a lifetime average of .325. Also, his lifetime total of home runs, 361, tops that of any active player in the game today.

Yet when asked yesterday who he considered the greatest of present-day hitters, DiMaggio replied, "Ted Wiliams. He is by far the greatest natural hitter I ever saw."

The Clipper joined the 2,000-hit group on June 20, 1950, and when he drove in five runs against the White Sox on July 29 last, he raised his RBI total to the 1,500 mark.

Small wonder Stengel ponders when and with whom he will ever plug that gap in centerfield. It was obvious, too, that Casey and the other Yanks had been hopeful to the last that the Clipper might change his mind. He undoubtedly recalled that though DiMag had gone hitless in the first three games of last October's world series, he exploded six blows in the final three, including a resounding homer.

Seldom Argued Decisions

DiMaggio rarely complained to an umpire. In striking contrast with the flamboyant Babe Ruth, the Clipper lacked utterly in glamour, yet by his quiet demeanor in time developed a fascinating hold upon the fans throughout the nation.

Shy as a rookie, his attitude developed into an aloofness that seldom relaxed except among close friends. He greeted his fellow players with a reserved cordiality but "palled" with few—for a time Lefty Gomez, later Joe Page.

DiMaggio expects to return Friday to California, where he plans to make his permanent home. Within another week or so, he said, he will be ready to reveal his future activities.

THE STAR OUTFIELDER ANNOUNCING HIS DECISION TO THE PRESS

Joe DiMaggio, center, as he talked with newsmen about his retirement at the Yankee offices yesterday. With him, left to right, are General Manager George Weiss, Manager Casey Stengel and owners Del Webb and Dan Topping. Associated Press

DiMaggio's Batting Records

MAJOR AND MINOR LEAGUES

Year. Club. League.	G.	A.B.	R.	H.	2b.	3b.	H.R.	R.B.I.	Av.
1932—San Fran., P. C. L.	3	9	2	2	1	1	0	2	.222
1933—San Fran., P. C. L.	187	762	129	259	45	13	28	169	.340
1934—San Fran., P. C. L.	101	375	58	128	18	6	12	69	.341
1935—San Fran., P. C. L.	172	679	173	270	58	18	34	154	.398
1936—New York, A. L.	138	637	132	206	44	15	29	125	.323
1937—New York, A. L.	151	621	151	215	35	15	46	167	.346
1938—New York, A. L.	145	599	129	194	32	13	32	140	.324
1939—New York, A. L.	120	462	108	176	32	6	30	126	.381
1940—New York, A. L.	132	508	93	179	28	9	31	133	.352
1941—New York, A. L.	139	541	122	193	43	11	30	125	.357
1942—New York, A. L.	154	610	123	186	29	13	21	114	.305
1943-44-45	Military Service (Army)								
1946—New York, A. L.	132	503	81	146	20	8	25	95	.290
1947—New York, A. L.	141	534	97	168	31	10	20	97	.315
1948—New York, A. L.	153	594	110	190	26	11	39	155	.320
1949—New York, A. L.	76	272	58	94	14	6	14	67	.346
1950—New York, A. L.	139	525	114	158	33	10	32	122	.301
1951—New York, A. L.	116	415	72	109	22	4	12	71	.263
Total	1,736	6,821	1,390	2,214	389	131	361	1,537	.325

WORLD SERIES

Year. Club. League.	G.	A.B.	R.	H.	2b.	3b.	H.R.	R.B.I.	Av.
1936—New York, A. L.	6	26	3	9	3	0	0	3	.346
1937—New York, A. L.	5	22	2	6	0	0	1	4	.273
1938—New York, A. L.	4	15	4	4	0	0	1	2	.267
1939—New York, A. L.	4	16	3	5	0	0	1	3	.313
1941—New York, A. L.	5	19	1	5	0	0	0	1	.263
1942—New York, A. L.	5	21	3	7	0	0	0	3	.333
1947—New York, A. L.	7	26	4	6	0	0	2	5	.231
1949—New York, A. L.	5	18	2	2	0	0	1	2	.111
1950—New York, A. L.	4	13	2	4	1	0	1	2	.308
1951—New York, A. L.	6	23	3	6	2	0	1	5	.261
Total	51	199	27	54	6	0	8	30	.271

ALL-STAR GAME

Year. League.	A.B.	R.	H.	2b.	3b.	H.R.	R.B.I.	Av.
1936—American	5	0	0	0	0	0	0	.000
1937—American	4	1	1	0	0	0	0	.250
1938—American	4	1	1	0	0	0	0	.250
1939—American	4	1	1	0	0	1	1	.250
1940—American	4	0	0	0	0	0	0	.000
1941—American	4	3	1	1	0	0	1	.250
1942—American	4	0	2	0	0	0	0	.500
1946—American	Did not play because of injury							
1947—American	3	0	1	0	0	0	0	.333
1948—American	1	0	0	0	0	0	1	.000
1949—American	4	1	2	1	0	0	3	.500
1950—American	3	0	0	0	0	0	0	.000
1951—American	Did not play because of injury							
*Total	40	7	9	2	0	1	6	.225

*Picked for thirteen All-Star squads, every active season.

Clipper's Earnings Since 1936 Placed at $704,769

Joe DiMaggio earned an estimated $704,769.71 during his major league baseball career. Here are the financial figures, including newspaper estimates of the Yankee Clipper's salary and his world series shares:

Year.	Est. Salary.	World Series Share.
1936	$8,000	$6,430.55
1937	15,000	6,471.10
1938	25,000	5,782.76
1939	27,500	5,614.26
1940	32,000	3d pl. 546.49
1941	37,500	5,943.31
1942	43,750	3,018.77
1943-45—Military Service		
1946	43,750	3d pl. 392.95
1947	43,750	5,830.03
1948	70,000	3d pl. 778.88
1949	100,000	5,526.47
1950	100,000	5,737.95
1951	100,000	6,446.09
Total	$646,250	$58,519.71

Total earnings—$704,769.71.

56-Game Batting Streak In 1941 Set New Record

Joe DiMaggio set a major league record in 1941 by batting safely in fifty-six consecutive games. The details of his streak follow:

Date Opponent	ab	r	h	2b	3b	hr	rbi
May							
15—Chicago	4	0	1	0	0	0	1
16—Chicago	4	2	2	0	1	1	1
17—Chicago	3	1	1	0	0	0	0
18—St. Louis	3	3	3	1	0	0	1
19—St. Louis	3	0	1	1	0	0	0
20—St. Louis	5	1	1	0	0	0	1
21—Detroit	5	0	2	0	0	0	1
22—Detroit	4	0	1	0	0	0	1
23—Boston	5	0	1	0	0	0	2
24—Boston	4	2	1	0	0	0	2
25—Boston	4	0	1	0	0	0	0
27—Washington	5	3	4	0	0	1	3
*28—Washington	4	1	1	0	1	0	0
29—Washington	3	1	1	0	0	0	0
30—Boston	2	1	1	0	0	0	0
30—Boston	3	0	1	1	0	0	0
June							
1—Cleveland	4	1	1	0	0	0	0
1—Cleveland	4	0	1	0	0	0	0
2—Cleveland	4	2	2	1	0	0	0
3—Detroit	4	1	1	0	0	1	1
5—Detroit	5	1	1	0	1	0	1
7—St. Louis	5	2	3	0	0	0	1
8—St. Louis	4	3	2	0	0	2	4
8—St. Louis	4	1	2	1	0	1	3
10—Chicago	5	1	1	0	0	0	0
*12—Chicago	4	1	2	0	0	1	1
14—Cleveland	2	0	1	1	0	0	1
15—Cleveland	3	1	1	0	0	1	1
16—Cleveland	5	0	1	1	0	0	0
17—Chicago	4	1	1	0	0	0	0
18—Chicago	3	0	1	0	0	0	0
19—Chicago	3	2	3	0	0	1	2
20—Detroit	5	3	4	1	0	0	1
21—Detroit	4	0	1	0	0	0	1
22—Detroit	5	1	2	1	0	1	2
24—St. Louis	4	1	1	0	0	0	0
25—St. Louis	4	1	1	0	0	1	3
26—St. Louis	4	0	1	1	0	0	1
27—Philadelphia	3	1	2	0	0	1	2
28—Philadelphia	5	1	2	1	0	0	0
29—Washington	4	1	1	1	0	0	0
29—Washington	5	1	1	0	0	0	1
July							
1—Boston	4	0	2	0	0	0	1
1—Boston	3	1	1	0	0	0	1
2—Boston	5	1	1	0	0	1	3
6—Philadelphia	5	2	4	1	0	0	2
6—Philadelphia	4	0	2	0	1	0	2
*10—St. Louis	2	0	1	0	0	0	0
11—St. Louis	5	1	4	0	0	1	2
12—St. Louis	5	1	2	1	0	0	1
13—Chicago	4	2	3	0	0	0	0
14—Chicago	3	0	1	0	0	0	0
15—Chicago	4	1	2	1	0	0	2
16—Cleveland	4	3	3	1	0	0	0
Total	223	56	91	16	4	15	55

*Night Games.
Batting average—.408.

DECISION TO RETIRE SADDENS JAPANESE

But Nation's Baseball Chief Says DiMaggio Is 'a True Sportsman' for Action

TOKYO, Wednesday, Dec. 12 (UP)—Millions of Japanese baseball fans, who made Joe DiMaggio their idol during his visits to this country, were saddened today by the news of his retirement from baseball.

Morita Fukui, commissioner of Japanese baseball, expressed the popular regret.

"It is going to be difficult for us to realize that Joe DiMaggio is no longer a ball player," said Fukui.

"His retirement is a great loss to baseball everywhere. But I want to pay tribute to DiMaggio's decision to retire when he believes a player should quit when baseball ceases to be fun to him. That is the decision of a true sportsman."

On his recent tour here, DiMaggio was followed by large crowds wherever he went and children besieged him for autographs.

Japanese fans recalled they saw the Yankee Clipper make the last home run of his active playing career when he belted a 400-foot drive into the left field stands in Tokyo's Meiji Stadium on Nov. 10.

PELLET HITS UMPIRE'S EYE

But Hubbard Bars Reports on His Condition After Mishap

ST. LOUIS, Dec. 11 (AP)—Cal Hubbard, American League umpire, who was struck in the eye by a ricocheting shot-gun pellet while on a hunting trip, tonight placed a ban on hospital reports concerning his condition.

The mishap occurred yesterday near Milan, Mo., and a hunting companion quoted a doctor as saying Hubbard stood a "50-50 or better chance" of not losing his sight in the injured eye.

Tonight a supervisor at McMillan Hospital here said only that Hubbard was "doing fine." He added that Hubbard asked further reports to the public be withheld.

James Payne of Milan, a member of the hunting party, said the accident occurred as Hubbard sat in a car. Another hunter, Willard Robinson of Pollack, Mo., fired at the ground and killed a rabbit, but a pellet glanced upward, hitting Hubbard's left eye.

Hubbard was treated at a Kirksville hospital after the accident and brought here today.

A. K. C. DELEGATES NAMED

Coleman, Craig, Myers Among 7 Elected at Meeting Here

Seven delegates to the American Kennel Club were named yesterday at the A. K. C.'s quarterly meeting at the Hotel Commodore. They included Taylor Coleman, Westport, Conn., who will represent the Longshore-Southport K. C.; Robert W. Craig, New York, the Santa Clara County K. C., and C. J. Kylie Myers, Morristown, N. J., Greater Miami Dog Club.

Others were Edwin J. Myers, Eighty,four, Pa., California Collie Clan; Melvin Schlesinger, Merriam, Kan., Heart of America K. C.; John Smietana, Hatboro, Pa., Bucks County K. C., and Charles Choads Williams, Philadelphia, Golden Gate K. C.

Sports Today

BASKETBALL

Columbia vs. Rutgers, at Columbia, Broadway and 119th Street, 8:30 P. M. (Television—Channel 9, 9:05 P. M.)

Fordham vs. New York A. C., at Fordham, Third Avenue and Fordham Road, Bronx.........8:30 P. M.

New York State Maritime College vs. Queens, at N. Y. S. M. C. gymnasium, Fort Schuyler, Bronx, 8:30 P. M.

Wagner vs. St. Johns, at Wagner, Grymes Hill, S. I.........8:30 P. M.

BOXING

Ezzard Charles vs. Joey Maxim, at San Francisco (Television—Channel 2, 10 P. M.)

HOCKEY

Rangers vs. Boston Bruins, at Madison Square Garden, Eighth Avenue and Fiftieth Street, 8:30 P. M. (Television—Channel 11, 9 P. M.)

MAXIM TO BATTLE CHARLES TONIGHT

Will Seek First Victory in Five Fights With Rival in Coast Non-Title Bout

SAN FRANCISCO, Dec. 11 (AP)—Ezzard Charles, former heavyweight champion, and Joey Maxim, light-heavyweight title-holder, renew their ring rivalry tomorrow night in a twelve-round non-title bout.

Charles won his four previous battles with Maxim.

Promoters Jimmy Murray and Lou Thomas, on the basis of advance ticket sales, predicted a gate of $100,000 for the Boys' Camp benefit event.

The fight will begin at 10 P. M. (Eastern standard time) to accommodate a nation-telecast of the fight. The television rights will add $25,000 to the total receipts.

There will be no television within 400 miles of here.

Both fighters have ended grueling training schedules, each having boxed about 150 rounds.

Maxim, who trained at near-by Santa Rosa, has shifted his headquarters to the Whitcomb Hotel to await the weigh-in and fight. His handlers reported that he was in excellent shape.

Charles was pronounced ready also. Throughout his training siege he gave every indication he would try to put the fancy-boxing Maxim away. He slugged it out with sparring mates and strove for more punching power.

Should Maxim beat Charles decisively it would lift him prominently into the heavyweight picture.

Watching the fight will be another prominent heavyweight, Rocky Marciano, who knocked out Joe Louis. Marciano will get $1,500 for refereeing one of the preliminary bouts.

STEINKRAUS RIDERS TRIUMPH IN MEXICO

MONTERREY, Mexico, Dec. 11 (AP)—A four-nation team of youngsters paced by Billy Steinkraus, Westport, Conn., won the opening jumping event of the Monterey International Horse Show tonight.

Steinkraus' team-mates were Alvaro Luciano Diaz de Toledo, Brazil; Capt. Michael J. Tubridy, Eire, and Joaquin D'Harcourt, Mexico.

The event was called the international good-will competition.

Steinkraus, Turbidy and D'Harcourt went over the long nineteen-jump course without a single fault and well within the time limit of three minutes. Toledo was charged with the team's only fault when his mount, Loveraine, refused to jump.

D'Harcourt, who will be 20 next year, won the night's individual honors. He was the only rider to complete the 600-meter (2,000-foot) course twice without fault. The other winning mounts were: Steinkraus' Black Watch, Toledo's On Fiordiose and Tubridy's Glendare.

Some 12,000 spectators saw the opening of the six-day show at the Monterrey Technological Institute Stadium.

McGovern Outpoints Tanner

LONDON, Dec. 11 (UP)—Tommy McGovern, British lightweight champion, gained a ten-round decision over Allan Tanner of Briitsh Guiana at Royal Albert Hall tonight. McGovern, leading British contender for the European title, weighed 136½ pounds, Tanner 134.

NEWCOMBE FRACTURE WAS OF LITTLE FINGER

COLONIA, N. J., Dec. 11 (UP)—Irked over "all these stories about me breaking my hand," Don Newcombe of the Dodgers declared tonight, "All I did was fracture my little finger."

The huge Negro right-hander, still waiting to hear whether or not be had been accepted for military service, snapped heatedly:

"I wish people would get things straight. Everybody's been calling to ask me about my broken hand. I didn't break my hand. I just fractured the little finger on my right hand. It happened a week ago Saturday while I was helping to move some furniture in the house."

Newcombe said the fracture wasn't "the least bit serious" and that the cast originally put on the finger already is off.

"Right now," he said, "I'm concentrating on a Mayo Clinic diet. I weigh about 234 pounds now but I expected to get down to 220."

Regarding word from Army officials, Newcombe said he had "heard nothing from them" since taking his pre-induction physical examination early last month.

36 Night Games for Athletics

PHILADELPHIA, Dec. 11 (UP)—The Athletics will play thirty-six night games in their 1952 home season which opens with the Yankees April 15, the club reported today. Four of the night games were listed as tentative. The seventy-seven-game home schedule listed nine double-headers.

DO NOT FORGET THE NEEDIEST!

OIL, STEEL STRIKES PERIL U. S.

STORY ON PAGE 2

WEATHER
CLEAR AND
LITTLE CHANGE
IN TEMPERATURE
U. S. Report, Page 38

DAILY RECORD

THE RECORD-AMERICAN HAS THE GREATEST CIRCULATION IN NEW ENGLAND

Vol. 278—No. 105 56 Pages Boston, Thursday, May 1, 1952 Entered as second class matter At Boston Postoffice ★ 5 CENTS

HOME
7 RACES

SOX WIN ON TED'S HOMER

Farewell Blast Tops Tigers 5-3

STORY ON PAGE 46

Ted Holds Hands With Mates Who Hold Hold Hands With Fans in Dramatic Farewell

Detroit Tiger players, left, and Boston Red Sox team, right, stretching across infield to grandstands, hold hands with fans in stands as Ted Williams, center, holds hands with Paraplegic Fred Wolf as band plays "Auld Lang Syne" in thrilling tableau at Fenway Park, after presentation ceremonies, during which Ted tipped cap for first time in 13-year Hub stay, before rejoining Marines. Center, l. to r., Tiger Mgr. Red Rolfe, Fire Commr. M. T. Kelleher, GI Wolf, who presented gifts to Ted for all vets in hospitals, Ted, the One and Only, Dom DiMaggio, Walt Dropo, Sox Mgr. Lou Boudreau. Many a misty-eyed fan wiped away a tear, joining in song.

(Record-American, Louie Teion) (Story, Other Pix, Pgs. 46, 58)

Sugar Asks for Another Crack at Joey's Crown

By Gene Ward

Ray Robinson's collapse in the pressure-cooking, 104-degree temperatures under the kleig arcs of Yankee Stadium posed two big questions yesterday: (1) why couldn't the championship battle have been postponed instead of being staged under intolerable conditions dangerous to the health of the participants? (2) will Sugar Ray, who flashed a winning performance before being pole-axed by heat prostration, be given another chance to complete the triple-crown?

Not a single man or woman in the steaming ball park could have helped but admire the skill and speed with which the 31-year-old,

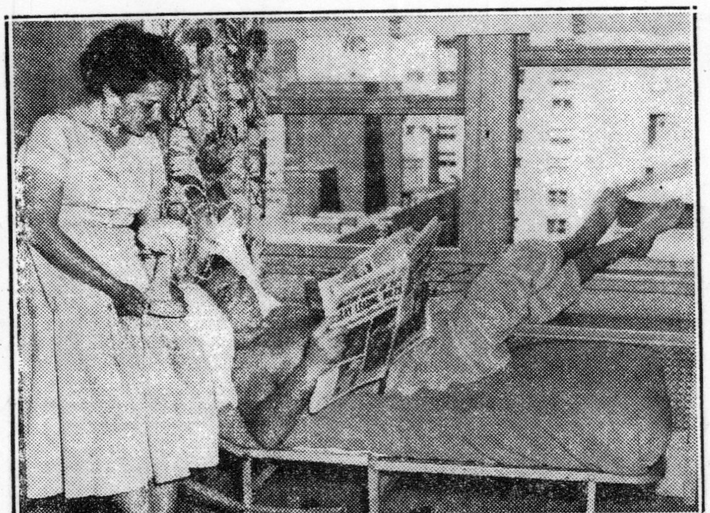

(NEWS foto by Tom Baffer)

Maxim is fan-cooled by pretty wife. Mitchie. yesterday in their hot room. They will celebrate their 10th wedding anniversary today.

Detroit-born Negro carried the fight to the heavier man. Here was a superb ringman winning his third title as only two other men in history had done—and then, suddenly, it ended and Joey Maxim, through no fault of his own, was the winner.

The Cleveland veteran yesterday proved himself a real man and a graceful winner when he said, "the guy put up a great fight and rates a return bout under normal conditions."

EARLIER IN the day, before he fled to the country for a rest, Robinson told his manager, George Gainford, that he wanted to try again, and IBC's Jim Norris promptly placed a return bout on the Maxim agenda along with proposed title-tiffs with Jake LaMotta in Detroit and Randy Turpin, either in London or New York.

In many respects Robinson gained more prestige by his unfortunate fold-up than had he gone on to win the decision. At least, he did if the reacation of the fans is any criterion, for from many lips yesterday this reporter heard, "is Sugar going to get another chance. He sure deserves it."

AND THERE WERE some experts who contended that the fight never should have been held in such a tropical heat wave, a record-busting temperature strike for a June 25 in New York.

Their claim, and it is a strong one. was that the turkish bath conditions which prevailed (104-degrees in the ring by an actual on-the-spot check) were unfair (1) to the public which paid to see a truly contested championship boxing match and (2) the participants whose abilities were handicapped and whose health was endangered.

REFEREE Ruby Goldstein had to quit after the tenth round and later given glucose injections.

Dr. Alexander Schiff, prominent New York physician, and the Commission's official attending doctor at ringside, was one of those who said that boxing in such extreme heat is dangerous, and he agreed that a postponement would have been the wiser course.

"I found Robinson's pulse to be 180 after the fight had been terminated," Dr. Schiff said, "and his skin was bone dry and extremely hot to the touch."

LIKE GOLDSTEIN, Robinson was glassy-eyed and obviously delirious as he was helped to his dressing room. Sugar yesterday told Truman Gibson of IBC that his manager had asked him. at the end of the tenth, "what's the matter with you, you're gasping."

Robinson told him, "I just want to go to sleep."

APPARENTLY, he did go to sleep on his feet as indicated by his other remarks to Gibson—"I didn't know about any change of referees until later and I don't even recall falling down." That was in the thirteenth round when he toppled after missing connections with a Sunday right.

The exhaustion was so complete that Robinson, despite his superb condition, still felt marked effects yesterday and was ordered to the country for a rest by his personal physician, Dr. Vincent Nardiello.

RAY HAD SAID some things in the dressing room which he didn't recall, either, and when told about them asked that he please be forgiven. However, he wasn't in a very forgiving mood when THE NEWS photographers asked him to let them snap a couple yesterday morning at his new home in Riverdale. Robinson refused to open the door.

As one photographer put it, "for once the public seems to be on his side, and yet Robinson refuses to co-operate."

THERE WERE those who admitted Sugar put on a whale of a show, while he lasted, but wondered how come such an experienced fighter let himself go to the point of exhaustion instead of coasting or at least pacing himself.

The doctors had the answer to that one when they said, "there is no way of telling or of knowing when heat prostration will strike." In other words, more often than not it gives little or no warning. Maxim said he knew just how Robinson felt because he, himself, had suffered heat exhaustion on three occasions.

Sugar went into the contest as a middleweight and came out a welter, while Maxim went in a heavy and came out a middleweight. Considering the post-weigh-in meal he ate, Robinson went into the ring weighing about 160 and, at his home after the fight, scaled 150.

AS FOR MAXIM, he dropped off from his ring weight of 175 to 166½ in his dressing room.

Robinson leaves for Europe on La Liberte, July 11, and will fight Albert Yvel at Tel Aviv in a benefit, Aug. 2. Maxim goes to Grossinger's tonight for a victory dinner and a tenth wedding anniversary celebration with his wife, Mitchie, then home to Cleveland on Saturday.

(Other pictures on back page)

Fight Figures

GROSS GATE—$421,615.
NET GATE—$334,082.
FEDERAL TAX—$68,201.
STATE TAX—$17,927.
ROBINSON'S GATE PURSE—$100,224.
MAXIM'S GATE PURSE—$100,224.
TV-THEATRE—Receipts to International Boxing Club, about $90,000, minus $3,700 tax.
ROBINSON'S share of Theatre-TV—$24,890.
MAXIM'S share of Theatre-TV—$24,890.
ROBINSON'S total purse—$125,114.
MAXIM'S total purse—$125,114.

Probable Pitchers

AMERICAN

Athletics, Hooper (2-7) at YANKEES, Lopat (4-4), night.
Indians, Feller (6-6) at White Sox, Pierce (7-6), night.
Senators, Marrero (6-2) at Red Sox, Hudson (5-4), night.
Tigers, Newhouser (2-2) at Browns, Cain (5-3) night.

NATIONAL

Braves, Bickford (2-7) at DODGERS, Schmitz (1-0), night.
GIANTS, Jansen (6-3) at Phillies, Simmons (5-2), night.
Cards, Mizell (2-5) at Pirates, Main (1-6), night.
Cubs, Minner (6-3) at Reds, Raffensberger (8-4), night.

How Officials Scored Maxim-Sugar

	1	2	3	4	5	6	7	8	9	10	11	12	13
Judge Aidala	R	R	R	R	R	E	R	M	R	M	R	R	M
Judge Barnes	R	R	R	R	R	M	R	R	R	M	R	R	M
Referee Goldstein	R	R	R	E	R	M	R	M	E	E			
Referee Miller											R	R	M

(Miller substituted for Goldstein as referee when latter became ill of the heat at end of 10th round.)

Girl Ball Players? Barrow Started It in Gay '90s

By Hy Turkin

Cute and curvaceous Eleanor Engle was barred earlier this week from playing professional baseball. Minor league czar George Trautman ruled that to allow her to play would be a "travesty" on the game. But the female beachhead in organized ball has long since been established, and the man behind it revealed the full story yesterday to THE NEWS.

Credit it all to 84-year-old Edward Grant Barrow builder of the Yankee empire and "executive emeritus" who has been enshrined in the Hall of Fame. At his home in suburban Rye yesterday, the beetle-browed pioneer gave the real story about "Lilly Arlington," the only woman ever to have played regular-season pro baseball.

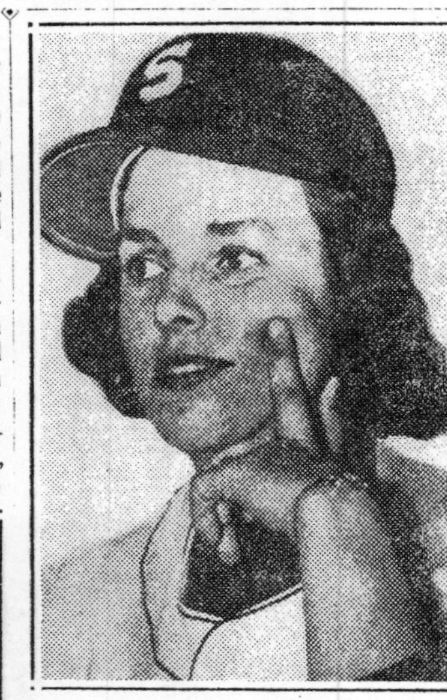

Eleanor Engle
Barred as pro.

Barrow, the brilliant baseball builder who discovered Honus Wagner and who switched Babe Ruth from pitcher to outfielder, supplied this background to the Arlington story:

"**IT WAS DURING** the Spanish-American War. Talent was scarce, and customers were scarcer. As

Ed Barrow
Started girl-player stunt.

president of the old Atlantic League, I didn't want to see any of our Class A franchises fail. So I tried all kinds of stunts to keep the fans interested.

"I played Jim Corbett at first base. I installed two other heavyweight boxing champions, John L. Sullivan and Jim Jeffries, as umpires. And when one of our scouts told me about a really good female pitcher from the mining area of Pennsylvania, I told him to bring her in for a trial.

"Elizabeth Stride was her name, but I advertised her as Lilly Arlington. Fairly nice looking. More important, she could really pitch! For four or five innings, she had plenty of stuff and control. She knew all the fundamentals of the game, having been taught by a fellow townsman, old Jake Stivetts, who pitched many years in the National League in the '90s."

THOUGH HE ADMITS it was strictly a "stunt" at the time . . . one which succeeded in hypoing the box office in league cities like Paterson, Newark, Philly, Lancaster, Norfolk, etc. . . . Barrow recalls, "Lilly had a good delivery. All the warmup actions of a good pitcher. She wasn't strong enough to pitch a full game. But she did draw the fans, and she wasn't any trouble to the other players. I signed a maid to travel around the circuit with her. She pitched about 12 league games."

Barrow succeeded in keeping the league together till the end of the year. Then he moved on to manage Toronto, Detroit and the Red Sox, winning the pennant and World Series there in '18—then into a glorious career as Yankee executive. Now he is in retirement.

THOUGH HE HAS no way of knowing whether Eleanor Engle, the lady who failed to crash the majors, is as good a player as his "Lilly Arlington" was, Barrow says he thinks commissioner Trautman may have been wrong in automatically barring women from pro baseball.

"After all," argues the wise old man of the game, "women are doing a lot more things these days than they ever did. Their golfers are breaking men's par. That Kellems woman is fighting the government taxes single-handed. And that Babe Didrikson is just a wonder. If a woman proves to be good enough for Class D ball, there ought to be a place for her."

Barrow is looking forward to his first visit of the year to Yankee Stadium, which he helped make "The Home of Champions." He has followed his old team over television (WPIX) this year but hopes to be well enough soon for a trip to the Bronx orchard. He underwent an operation earlier in the year and was hospitalized six weeks. Then he fell and broke his arm. "But I'm okay now!" he insists.

Yank Batting

	G	AB	R	H	HR	RBI	Pct.
Houk	6	1	0	1	0	0	1.000
Br'weser	11	8	6	3	0	2	.375
Collins	41	112	19	36	4	16	.321
Woodling	42	132	17	41	5	20	.311
Bauer	57	222	27	67	8	32	.302
Mantle	49	186	29	56	6	24	.301
Martin	33	121	14	36	1	8	.298
McD'gald	60	228	35	62	3	35	.272
Rizzuto	60	244	37	65	0	18	.266
Berra	51	200	38	50	14	37	.250
Noren	45	168	16	39	3	12	.232
Mize	29	69	3	16	0	11	.232
Cerv	30	71	8	16	1	7	.225
Silvera	9	23	1	5	0	3	.217
Brown	15	39	1	7	0	5	.179

ALLIE 5-6½ OVER BLACK

Story on Page 20

5 CENTS ★ FINAL

Daily Mirror

OCTOBER						
S	M	T	W	T	F	S
			1	2	3	4
5	6	7	8	9	10	11
12	13	14	15	16	17	18
19	20	21	22	23	24	25
26	27	28	29	30	31	

Vol. 29. No. 86. NEW YORK 17, N. Y., WEDNESDAY, OCTOBER 1, 1952

4c in New York City
5c Elsewhere in U.S.A.

Dodgers' Delivery Dept.

Brooklyn moundsmen line up left to right in the order of their announced appearance in the World Series classic against the Yanks, starting at Ebbets Field today. Photographed at the Stadium yesterday, they're Joe Black, Carl Erskine, Preacher Roe, Billy Loes and John Rutherford.

'LUMBERMEN' Billy Martin (left) and Mickey Mantle get the feel of their bats. Martin's hit won pennant-clinching game for Yanks.

THEY CASE THE PLACE. Walloping Dodgers Shuba (left) and Snider scan the stands.

Bombers' Takeoff Today

Yanks whip up the up-and-at-'em spirit at the Stadium for the Ebbets Field Series opener. Spurting out of the dugout are (l. to r.) Mize, Collins, Woodling, McDougald, Bauer, Rizzuto, Martin, Noren, Berra and Mantle.

(Mirror Photos by Art Sarno).

WE WUZ ATO-MIZED!

8 ★★★★★★★★ Final Edition

BROOKLYN EAGLE

1951 PULITZER PRIZE WINNER for "the most disinterested and meritorious public service."

WEATHER—Fair, cool tonight, tomorrow.

111th YEAR—No. 274—DAILY and SUNDAY (Copyright, 1952, The Brooklyn Eagle, Inc.) BROOKLYN 1, N. Y., SATURDAY, OCTOBER 4, 1952 Entered Brooklyn P. O. 2d Class Mail Matter 5 CENTS EVERYWHERE

YANKEES EVEN WORLD SERIES

Capital 'Thievery' Is Assailed by Ike

Sees Taxpayers Deeply Disturbed —He Tells of 'Sickening' Letters

Duluth, Oct. 4 (U.P.)—Dwight D. Eisenhower, campaigning into Minnesota and the Dakotas, declared today that the American taxpayers were deeply disturbed by the "sheer thievery" which had occurred in the Federal Government.

The Republican Presidential nominee left his train here for a day of plane-hopping into North and South Dakota.

Brisk Fall weather in the low 80s greeted the former General who told of receiving "saddening, sickening" mail from Americans who asked him to be sure that their tax dollars really reached the Government.

He said the nation was "disgusted" by "just sheer thievery" which he promised to correct with "a forward looking administration" instead of what he called the "inept leadership we have been having over the past seven years."

He told his Minnesota audience that he was well aware of the growth of farmer co-operatives and agreed with the action Congress had taken on taxing these co-operatives which are so numerous here in the Middle West.

He also referred to his anti-Communist speech last night at Milwaukee, saying he wanted to emphasize today that any

Continued on Page 2

CITY SUSPENDS 3 COLLEGE PROFS

Three New York City college professors — including two Brooklyn residents, one of them on the faculty of Brooklyn College — were under suspension today for refusing to answer whether or not they were Communists.

They were notified of the suspension by their college presidents, who acted under the City Charter provision which calls for dismissal of any city employe who refuses to answer questions by an investigating body on the ground of self-incrimination or agrees to answer but without waiving immunity.

The suspensions were referred to the Board of Higher Education, which will act upon them at a meeting at 5 p.m. Monday.

The three, all accused of refusing to answer questions before the Senate Internal Security Subcommittee, are:

Dr. Harry Slochower, 52, of 221 E. 18th St., associate professor of German, with a salary of $8,200, at Brooklyn College, where he has taught for 25 years, including three years at the Brooklyn branch of City College before Brooklyn College was organized.

Dr. Vera Shlakman, 43, of 195 Hicks St., assistant professor of economics at Queens College, salary $5,862, on the college faculty for 14 years.

Dr. Bernard F. Reiss, 45, of 135 Cushman Road, Scarsdale,

Continued on Page 2

HST PICTURES EISENHOWER AS 'SAD SPECTACLE'

San Francisco, Oct. 4 (U.P.)—President Truman today called Dwight D. Eisenhower the "saddest spectacle" of a man who has "betrayed himself by surrenders to narrow, selfish men and short-sighted policies."

In a double-barreled attack he said that Senator Richard M. Nixon, Eisenhower's running mate, is "not worthy to lace the shoes" of Gov. Earl Warren of California.

1,000 Plate Luncheon

The President made the statements in a campaign speech prepared for delivery by a 1,000-plate Democratic party luncheon at the Palace Hotel here.

Mr. Truman, accompanied by daughter Margaret, was in the sixth day of stumping on a two-

Continued on Page 2

Father of Schuster Suspect Cuts Throat

Felice Mazziotta, 75-year-old father of John (Chappy) Mazziotta, chief suspect in the Arnold Schuster murder, attempted suicide by slashing his throat with a razor at 2:30 a.m. today in his home at 744 39th St., Bay Ridge.

He was taken to Israel Zion Hospital and then to Kings County Hospital, where his condition was reported as critical.

A nationwide alarm is out for John Mazziotta, who disappeared last Spring after the Schuster weapon was found on a Borough Park street.

Police believe he was the "fence" who handled the murder weapon, stolen from a Brooklyn pier.

Schuster was killed last March 8 while basking in the glory of finding Willie (The Actor) Sutton, bank robber.

BELMONT PARK RESULTS

1—Tritium, 6.80-4.90-3.80; Hootsie, 5.90-3.80; Precipitate, 5.60. Off, 1:16.

2—Pennant Day, 5.60-3.20-2.60; Cup King, 4.90-3.50; Prize Ring, 4.00. Off, 1:53½.

DAILY DOUBLE PAID $21.80

3—Potpourri, 10.90-5.90-4.60; Ancient City, 8.00-5.70; Wise Market, 5.90. Off, 2:27.

—Laffango, 21.50-7.50-5.60; Invigorator, 3.90-3.50; Country Coz, 17.10 Off, 3:03½.

Eagle Staff Photo

DODGER ROOTERS COME EARLY—Here is the line which formed today at the Dodger offices at 215 Montague St. for tickets for the sixth and seventh games of the World Series. The queue formed several hours before tickets went on sale at 4 p.m.

Famed General's Daughter Held As Slayer of Mate, a Colonel

Tokyo, Oct. 4 (U.P.)—The slender brunette daughter of a famed U. S. Army general was held for "observation" today in the knife killing of her husband, Col. Aubrey D. Smith of Far East command headquarters.

A terse announcement from the headquarters of Gen. Mark Clark, Far Eastern and United Nations commander, said Smith died from knife wounds "allegedly inflicted" by his wife in their fashionable Washington Heights home.

The Far Eastern command did not identify Mrs. Smith further, but in San Antonio, Tex., the wife of retired Gen. Walter Krueger said she was their daughter, Dorothy Jane.

"Yes, it's our daughter, Dorothy," Mrs. Krueger said, "we're very broken up about it."

Krueger was assault commander for Gen. Douglas MacArthur in the southwest Pacific campaigns of World War II. He commanded the 6th Army from 1943 to 1946 and headed attacks from New Guinea to the Philippines.

Smith, 45, was chief of the plans and operations division of Clark's logistics (supply) section and a veteran of the fighting in Korea.

There were no details as to circumstances or possible motive of the knifing.

Smith died in Tokyo Army Hospital about six hours after he was wounded.

His wife, about 40, was rushed to 8,167th Station Hospital for observation. She is the mother of two, a boy and a girl, believed of high school age.

Milk Rises Up-State

Albany, Oct. 4 (U.P.)—The price of milk goes up one cent a quart tomorrow in Albany, Troy and Schenectady.

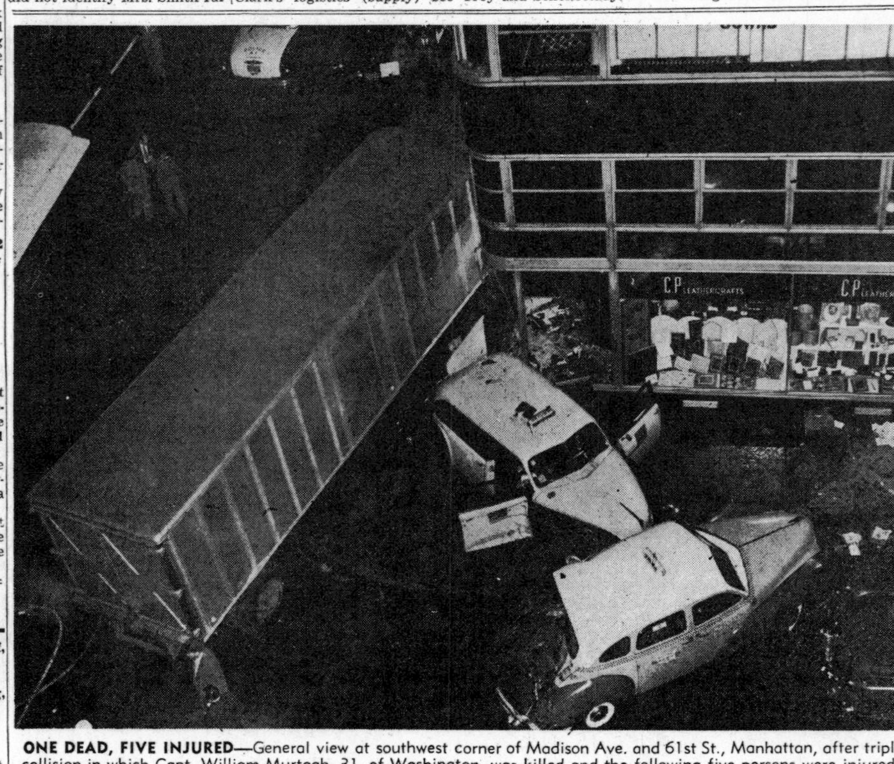

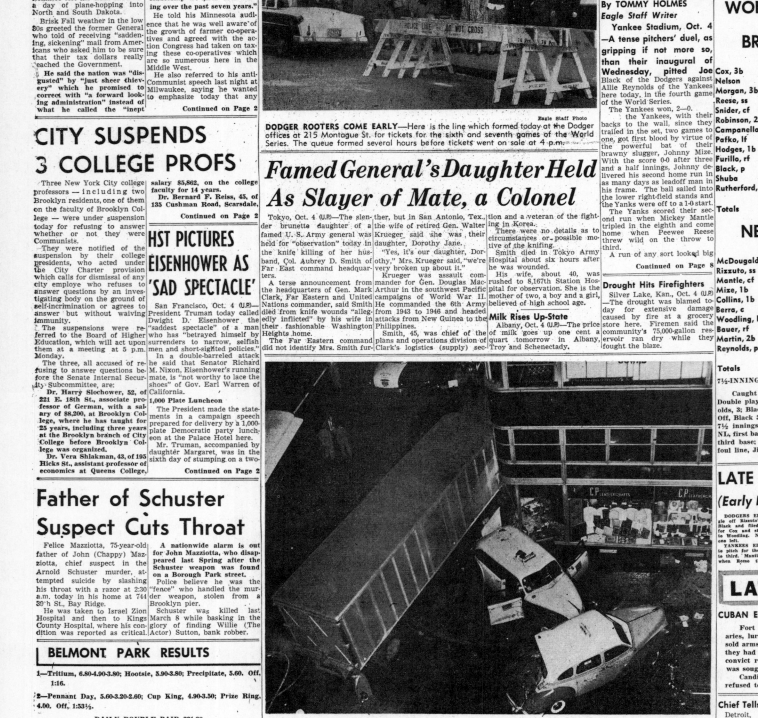

ONE DEAD, FIVE INJURED—General view at southwest corner of Madison Ave. and 61st St., Manhattan, after triple collision in which Capt. William Murtagh, 31, of Washington, was killed and the following five persons were injured: Captain Murtagh's wife, Louise, 29; his brother, Bernard, 28, and sister-in-law, of 119 7th Ave., Brooklyn, and two taxicab drivers. The injured were treated at Roosevelt Hospital. The Murtaghs were standing on the corner when the truck, driven by Benjamin Mitchell of Waterbury, swerving to avoid collision, mounted the sidewalk, collided with cabs and smashed through a store window.

Reynolds Bests Black As Dodgers Bow, 2-0

DODGERS	0	0	0	0	0	0	0	0	0—	0	4	1
YANKEES	0	0	0	1	0	0	0	1	—	2	4	1

Batteries—Black, Rutherford (8), Campanella; Reynolds, Berra.

By TOMMY HOLMES
Eagle Staff Writer

Yankee Stadium, Oct. 4 —A tense pitchers' duel, as gripping if not more so, than their inaugural of Wednesday, pitted Joe Black of the Dodgers against Allie Reynolds of the Yankees here today, in the fourth game of the World Series.

The Yankees won, 2—0.

the Yankees, with their backs to the wall, since they trailed in the set, two games to one, got first blood by virtue of the powerful bat of their brawny slugger, Johnny Mize. With the score 0-0 after three and a half innings, Johnny delivered his second home run in as many days as leadoff man in his frame. The ball sailed into the lower right-field stands and the Yanks were off to a 1-0 start.

The Yanks scored their second run when Mickey Mantle tripled in the eighth and come home when Peewee Reese threw wild on the throw to third.

A run of any sort looked big

Continued on Page 8

Drought Hits Firefighters

Silver Lake, Kan., Oct. 4 (U.P.)—The drought was blamed today for extensive damage caused by fire at a grocery store here. Firemen said the community's 75,000-gallon reservoir ran dry while they fought the blaze.

WORLD SERIES BOXSCORE

FOURTH GAME

BROOKLYN DODGERS

	ab	r	h	2b	3b	hr	rbi	o	a	e
Cox, 3b	3	0	0	0	0	0	0	2	2	0
Nelson	1	0	0	0	0	0	0	0	0	0
Morgan, 3b	0	0	0	0	0	0	0	0	1	0
Reese, ss	4	0	2	0	0	0	0	0	3	1
Snider, cf	4	0	0	0	0	0	0	5	0	0
Robinson, 2b	4	0	0	0	0	0	0	0	2	0
Campanella, c	3	0	0	0	0	0	0	4	0	0
Pafko, lf	3	0	1	0	0	0	0	2	0	0
Hodges, 1b	2	0	0	0	0	0	0	10	0	0
Furillo, rf	2	0	1	0	0	0	0	1	0	0
Black, p	1	0	0	0	0	0	0	0	2	0
Shuba	1	0	0	0	0	0	0	0	0	0
Rutherford, p	0	0	0	0	0	0	0	0	0	0
Totals	23	0	4	0	0	0	0	24	10	1

NEW YORK YANKEES

	ab	r	h	2b	3b	hr	rbi	o	a	e
McDougald, 3b	3	0	0	0	0	0	0	0	1	0
Rizzuto, ss	2	0	0	0	0	0	0	1	3	0
Mantle, cf	3	1	1	0	1	0	0	4	0	0
Mize, 1b	3	1	2	1	0	1	1	4	2	0
Collins, 1b	0	0	0	0	0	0	0	1	0	0
Berra, c	4	0	0	0	0	0	0	12	1	0
Woodling, lf	3	0	1	1	0	0	0	1	0	0
Bauer, rf	4	0	0	0	0	0	0	1	0	0
Martin, 2b	3	0	0	0	0	0	0	2	1	1
Reynolds, p	3	0	0	0	0	0	0	1	1	0
Totals	28	2	4	2	1	1	1	27	6	1

7½-INNING SUMMARY

Caught stealing by Berra—Reese. Sacrifice hit—Furillo. Double play—Rizzuto, Martin, Mize. Bases on balls—Off Reynolds, 3; Black, 5. Struck out—By Reynolds, 9; Black, 2. Hits—Off, Black 3 and 1 run in 7 innings; Reynolds, 4 and 0 runs in 7½ innings. Umpires—Bill McKinley, AL, plate; Babe Pinelli, NL, first base; Art Passarella, AL, second base; Larry Goetz, NL, third base; right field foul line, Dusty Boggess, NL; left field foul line, Jim Honochick, AL. Attendance—71,787.

LATE GAME IN DETAIL

(Early Details on Page 8)

DODGERS EIGHTH—Furillo lined a single off Rizzuto's glove. Shuba batted for Black and flied to Mantle. Nelson batted for Cox and struck out. Reese flied deep to Woodling. No runs, one hit, no errors, one left.

YANKEES EIGHTH—Rutherford went in to pitch for the Dodgers and Morgan went to third. Mantle tripled to deep center and when Reese threw over Morgan's head Mantle scored on the error. Mize walked. Collins ran for Mize. Berra lined to Furillo, Collins holding first. Woodling went out to Morgan. Bauer took a third strike. One run, one hit, one error, one left.

DODGERS NINTH—Snider flied to Mantle.

Robinson struck out.

McDougald threw out Campanella. No runs, no hits, no errors, none left.

LATE BULLETINS

CUBAN EXILES ROBBED OF $248,000 IN TEXAS

Fort Worth, Texas, Oct. 4 (U.P.)—Two exiled revolutionaries, lured to this country with promises they would be sold arms for a possible new revolution in Cuba, said today they had been robbed of $248,000. Orville Chambless, an ex-convict recently released from an Oklahoma penitentiary, was sought.

Candida de la Torres and Manuel Fernandez Madariago refused to admit they had lost the near-quarter million.

Chief Tells Detroit Cops: 'Keep Guns Fully Loaded'

Detroit, Oct. 4 (U.P.)—Police Commissiooner Donald S. Leonard ordered Detroit's police department to "load your weapons to capacity" today. Leonard issued the new order when he learned that officers had been loading only five bullets in their six-shooters since a fully loaded revolver went off accidentally 30 years ago.

"Modern guns don't do that," he said. "Six-shooters should shoot six times. Load your weapons to capacity."

THE WEATHER
Today: Fair and continued cool; moderate northwesterly winds.
Tomorrow: Fair and continued cool; moderate northwest to westerly winds.
Temperatures Yesterday: Max., 64.1; Min., 51.4.
Today's Probable Range: Max., 60; Min., 40.
Humidity at 3 p. m. Yesterday: 75%.
Expected Humidity This Afternoon: 45-55%.
Detailed Report and Map—Page 34

NEW YORK
Herald Tribune
European Edition Published Daily in Paris

Late City Edition

112th Year VOL. CXII NO. 38,678

WEDNESDAY, OCTOBER 8, 1952

230 West 41st Street, New York 36, N. Y. Telephone PEnnsylvania 6-4000

FIVE CENTS

Yankees Win 4th Series in Row; Defeat Dodgers in 7th Game, 4-2

Mantle, Woodling Wallop Home Runs

Stengel Uses 4 Pitchers; Kuzava Foils Brooklyn Attempts for Late Rally

By Roger Kahn

Every year is next year for the Yankees.

Yesterday, at Ebbets Field, Casey Stengel's proud Bombers swept past the Dodgers, 4 to 2, and retained the championship of the baseball world. The Dodgers have never held the title. It is a birthright of the Yankees, who now can boast fifteen and the last four in a row.

The bitterly earned victory gave New York the forty-ninth World Series, four games to three, after the Dodgers had won three of the first five. Never before has a Yankee team managed by Stengel been forced to scramble so hard to win and in taking the three previous series six games were the most the Bombers needed. This time they were forced to the limits of their man power and their endurance. There was a ring of greatness in the way the Yankees responded, as individuals and as a team.

Mantle Bats In Two Runs

Mickey Mantle, the twenty-year-old golden boy, was a hero because he hit a home run in the sixth inning and put the Yankees ahead, 3 to 2. Then he hit a single in the seventh that scored Gil McDougald with the final run.

Bob Kuzava, the strong left-hander, was a hero because when Stengel summoned him he responded with perfection. Kuzava became the fourth Yankee pitcher when he replaced Vic Raschi after the Dodgers had loaded the bases with one out in the seventh. He was the last pitcher the Yankees needed since he stopped Duke Snider and Jackie Robinson, ending Brooklyn's last threat to Yankee domination. The eighth and ninth innings were easy for Kuzava.

There were lesser heroes, too. Johnny Mize, who batted in the first Yankee run with a fourth-inning single, slapped away from his power; Gene Woodling, whose homer scored the second New York run in the sixth, Allie Reynolds who fought fatigue, pitched two innings and was credited with the victory. All can be proud of their effort.

33,195 Chilled Fans Sit

For Brooklyn, Pee Wee Reese, the professional, who singled home Billy Cox and tied the game in the fifth and Joe Black, who started and lost, falling under the burden of a season's weariness, were game and gallant in their failing cause.

But it was the Yankees who were the great ones yesterday—the Yankees as a team.

A crowd of 33,195 fans sat in their topcoats at Ebbets Field shivering from the chill and the tension as the battle unfolded and (Continued on page 28, column 1)

Associated Press
THE WINNER IS ON THE LEFT—Yankee Manager Casey Stengel being congratulated by Dodger Manager Charlie Dressen after Stengel's team won the seventh and final game of the Series

Florence Clock Stops After 275 Perfect Years

FLORENCE, Italy, Oct. 7 (AP).—One of the world's oldest mechanical clocks broke down today for the first time in 275 perfect years.

It was for the last time, too. Experts decided it was beyond repair, and the ancient 1677 clock of the tower of Florence's Palazzo Vecchio will be replaced with a modern one run by electricity.

Since it was built by the German craftsman Augustus Georges, the clock only stopped running once, in 1929, when it required cleaning.

Hungary Starts Purge Of 'Reactionary' Banjos

VIENNA, Oct. 7 (UP).—The Hungarian Communist newspaper Esti Budapest today branded guitars, mandolins and banjos "reactionary instruments" and said "they do not faithfully express the Hungarian national songs and melody."

Allies Retake Two Outposts In Korea Hills

ROKs Plug Breach In Bayonet Battle

Reds Fire 93,000 Rounds in 24-Hour Barrage, Their Heaviest of War

By Mac R. Johnson
From the Herald Tribune Bureau
Copyright, 1952, New York Herald Tribune Inc.

TOKYO, Wednesday, Oct. 8.—Troops of the Republic of Korea 9th Infantry Division recaptured an outpost position on White Horse Hill on the Korean central front early today. In a separate action, U. N. troops also recaptured an outpost that had been lost to the Reds on Finger Ridge.

Fighting still was heavy today at half a dozen points along the battle line, with most of it confined to the Chorwon area. White Horse Hill bore the brunt of the Communist fall offensive — although the 8th Army doesn't call it an offensive.

Heaviest Barrage of War

In the twenty-four-hour period the Communists fired their heaviest barrages of the war, some 93,000 rounds. The Communists have been stockpiling ammunition on the front despite Air Force efforts to cut railroads, blow up highway bridges and burn rolling stock and trucks. It was a record output by Red guns. The 8th Army estimated it was twice as heavy as any previous Red barrage in the twenty-eight-month-old war.

Fighting was still under way on White Horse Hill, Arrowhead Ridge, east of Kumsong, south of Pyonggang.

[The Associated Press reported from Seoul that Gen. James A. Van Fleet Wednesday said the Communists in North Korea have the strength for "sizable limited objective attacks throughout October and November." The United States 8th Army commander said, however, the Reds could not support a general attack for such a period.]

Seesaw Battle

In the action on White Horse Hill, the ROKs had beaten off one Chinese company at 7:30 p. m. yesterday, but two hours later lost the outpost to two Chinese companies in hand-to-hand fighting on the crest that lasted for fifteen minutes.

U. N. artillery and mortar fire then hammered the Red-held po- (Continued on page 4, column 4)

Road Is Paved With Gold By the Army in Korea

SEOUL, Oct. 7 (UP).—Korean "prospectors" chipped away at roads in the area of Pyongtaek today after it was discovered the highways were surfaced with gold ore.

"The gold rush is on," said an Army officer who explained how engineers had coated the roads with gold unwittingly.

The officer said the roads, built a year ago, had been surfaced by "gravel" from an abandoned slag pile. But instead of gravel, the engineers actually had used gold ore valued at $60,000.

The mistake was discovered only recently when a Korean mine owner demanded that sum for the loss of his gold. The Army was reported to have settled for $20,000.

Beria Warns 'U. S. Imperialists' Of 'Invincible' Soviet Strength

Party Congress Cheers as Secret Police Head Prophesies 'Disaster' for War Makers

By The United Press

MOSCOW, Oct. 7.—Lavrenti P. Beria, a Soviet Deputy Prime Minister, charged tonight that the United States is pushing the world's peoples "into the abyss of a world war." Mr. Beria told wildly cheering delegates to the Soviet Communist party congress here that such a war would speed up the Americans' "own collapse and their own disaster."

After Mr. Beria spoke, the congress approved a Central Committee report reviewing the last twelve years and promising that "capitalist nations" will be defeated "if they dare to attack the motherland."

World War II showed the world that Soviet strength is "invincible," Mr. Beria said.

"However," he added, "the lessons of history have not been learned by all. The American imperialists who have become opulent on two world wars are drunk with the mad idea of establishing their world domination."

He said the Americans "are again pushing peoples into the abyss of a world war although there is no doubt whatsoever that, having unleashed a war, they will but speed up their own collapse and their own disaster."

The 1,500 delegates broke into tumultuous applause at this point in Mr. Beria's speech.

Mr. Beria, who is a Politburo member, said there have been two great events in Soviet life since (Continued on page 3, column 4)

3 Magistrates' Courts Set Up On Fire Hazard

Murtagh Announces Policy; 'Bad Area' Inspections Planned Block by Block

Chief Magistrate John M. Murtagh announced yesterday that he and two other magistrates henceforth will devote themselves exclusively and "indefinitely" to fire hazard cases.

Announcement of the new policy was made by Mr. Murtagh after a conference in his office at 100 Centre St. with Frederick S. Weaver, a deputy commissioner of the Department of Housing and Buildings.

Mr. Murtagh termed his program "more than a get-tough policy" and said he would combine the imposition of substantial fines with the threat of jail sentences to insure compliance with the law. He said he would hear fire-hazard (Continued on page 41, column 7)

South Koreans Exceed G. I.s At Front by 50%

Lovett Praises Them as 'Very Good Force,' Their Fatality Rate Is Higher

By C. B. Allen

WASHINGTON, Oct. 7.—Secretary of Defense Robert A. Lovett said today that South Korean troops on the Far Eastern firing line outnumber Americans by 50 per cent, are suffering proportionately higher fatalities in battle and have generally demonstrated that they are "a very good fighting force."

He added that "we are doing all we safely can" to put still greater numbers into the defense of their homeland consistent with adequate preparatory training.

Secretary Lovett told a pentagon press conference that the combat record of the South Koreans was "a great credit to the Army's training system" under which they have been schooled. He said it has been and will continue to be the Army's policy "to employ South Korean man power as rapidly as our military leaders on the ground have decided it can be done without jeopardizing the safety of our troops or the success of our vital mission."

The secretary made no reference to the recent assertion by Gen. Dwight D. Eisenhower that South Korean troops eventually (Continued on page 4, column 6)

Eisenhower Sees Revolt In Democratic Ranks on 'Thought Control' Issue

Stevenson Says He Will Destroy Red Conspiracy 'Beyond Repair'

In Detroit Speech, He Asserts Eisenhower Joins 'Clamor' on Menace, Has No Solution

Text of Stevenson address at Detroit—Page 16.

By Raymond J. Blair

DETROIT, Oct. 7.—Gov. Adlai E. Stevenson pledged tonight that as President he would smash the Communist conspiracy in the United States "beyond repair," and he charged that while Gen. Dwight D. Eisenhower has "joined loudly" in the "clamor" about the Communist menace in Washington, he has offered "only thundering silence about a cure."

In a major address before 5,000 persons in Masonic Temple here, the Democratic Presidential nominee said Communism had its first real chance in this country when "Republicans fumbled and bungled this nation into the great depression."

The Democratic party, he said, cut off the growth of Communism in 1932 and has been dealing effectively with it ever since, long before Sen. Joseph R. McCarthy R., Wis., "suddenly appeared on the scene and began his wild and reckless campaign against the integrity of our government itself."

Gov. Stevenson asked what Gen. Eisenhower proposed to do; whether he planned to dismiss J. Edgar Hoover, the Federal Bureau of Investigation director; Gen. Walter Bedell Smith, head of the Central Intelligence Agency, and other "experienced men" whom the Governor promised he would keep on in his administration.

"I think we are entitled to ask: Is the Republican candidate seriously interested in trying to root Communists out of the government, or is he only interested in scaring the American people to get votes?" Gov. Stevenson said.

The Governor said that while (Continued on page 16, column 3)

Cites Loyalty Oath Fight at Convention

General at Portland, Ore., Warns of 'Whole-Hog' U. S. Forestry Control

Text of Eisenhower address at Portland, Ore.—Page 14

By Homer Bigart

PORTLAND, Ore., Oct. 7—Gen. Dwight D. Eisenhower today assailed the Democrats as "the party of thought control," and insisted that the Republicans opposed regimentation in political thinking. He said his "crusade" welcomed differences of opinion so long as the diverse groups supported basic American ideals.

He told a capacity crowd of 5,000 in Portland's Civic Auditorium that the Democrats tried to impose "thought control" on various party elements at the Democratic convention. Independent elements of the Democratic party were now in revolt against dictation by Administration leaders, he said.

The general returned to his attack on what he called "whole-hog" Federal government and warned that Federal agencies were seeking monopolistic control over the nation's forests.

Thousands cheered the general along a two-mile drive through downtown Portland.

Cites Agencies' Squabble

He said the national forests "should not be turned into a vehicle for Federal control of the nation's entire forest economy," and charged that two Federal agencies in Washington, the Department of the Interior and the Department of Agriculture, were squabbling over which should supervise forest lands.

"In another bureau," he said, "actual fraud and favoritism crept in. Only last summer, in your own State of Oregon, a Federal court canceled the sale of Indian timber as fraudulent and ordered its resale to the highest bidder, not to a favorite."

He accused the Administration of trying to "corrupt" the purpose of the forest and land management agencies. "Their political bosses," he said, "have departed far from the purpose laid down by that great Republican conservationist, Gifford Pinchot. They have reached out to acquire more and more private land with more and more dominating control."

Speaks at Tacoma

Earlier, at Tacoma, Wash., he told a crowd that corruption in Washington had become an international issue because it provided useful ammunition to Communists in the ideological war.

Every scandal in our government, he said, was "really a betrayal of our country."

"We just can't have it," he said.

The general warned that corruption in the American political scene gave Moscow a very effective propaganda weapon.

Reminding his listeners that (Continued on page 14, column 7)

Two-Day Total Registration Hits 1,115,249

Yesterday's Enrollment of 565,275 Puts Turnout 29% Above '48 Mark

A registration of 565,275 voters yesterday brought the city's two-day total to 1,115,249, an increase of 170,799 over the previous record for two days, established in 1944, and 246,369 higher than the two-day figure in 1948, the last presidential year.

The increase over 1948 was nearly 29 per cent.

Heavy registration on Monday, the first day, had indicated that this would be a record-shattering year, since experience has shown that the first day is almost always the lightest, and yesterday's turnout was 15,301 better than that of Monday.

Following is a table of the registration by boroughs for the first two days, as compared with that of the previous four years:

RECAPITULATION

1952	1951	1950	1949	1948
		Manhattan		
253,497	99,685	165,852	162,575	217,303
		Bronx		
221,436	75,304	127,490	126,371	174,352
		Brooklyn		
374,775	133,968	215,267	211,835	301,900
		Queens		
239,525	74,571	118,052	100,525	158,970
		Richmond		
26,016	8,564	11,945	11,371	16,355
1,115,249	392,092	638,606	612,677	868,880

Last night election officials reported long lines of registrants forming at polling places in Manhattan and the Bronx shortly after the polls opened at 5 p m. Police and other observers said the lines appeared to be heavier than in previous years.

The first-day turnout on Monday of 549,974 was 144,991, or 35 per (Continued on page 26, column 7)

Truman Says Presidency Is Civilian's Job

Calls Professional Soldiers Unfit for Post; Labels Eisenhower 'Deceitful'

Text of Truman address at Colorado Springs—Page 10

By James E. Warner

DENVER, Oct. 7. — President Truman, arriving here tonight on his whistlestop campaign, got a tumultuous welcome from a crowd of 10,000, who heard him continue his attacks on Gen. Dwight D. Eisenhower.

Mr. Truman, who spoke from the steps of Union Station, declared: "Professional generals should not be President. A man who spends all his life in the army can't possibly learn political life . . ."

He said a civilian should always head the government.

Mr. Truman quoted what he said was a statement made in 1948 by Gen. Eisenhower that a military man is not qualified for the Presidency, and got a big laugh from the crowd.

Zachary Taylor and U. S. Grant, both generals who became Presidents, were "babes in the woods" in the hands of politicians, Mr. Truman said, in commenting on the issue of government corruption.

"Political leaders never nominate generals if they think there is a chance of winning," he said. "They want the nomination for themselves."

The Republicans have nominated a general this year because they (Continued on page 10, column 3)

Shots Meant to Kill Dog In Fire Cut Him Loose

ROSSVILLE, Ga., Oct. 7 (AP).—Butch, a five-year-old hound chained under a burning house yesterday, howled helplessly as rescue efforts were blocked by flames.

A passer-by, J. B. Durham, of Chickamauga, seized a shotgun and fired at the dog's head, hoping to halt the hound's suffering.

The pellets clipped only the dog's collar, however, and Butch dashed off to a cooling brook.

Herald Tribune—United Press telephoto
EISENHOWER—The Republican nominee and his wife as they took time out in Tacoma yesterday to meet some of their relatives, Billy and Janice Causin, their grandniece and nephew

Associated Press wirephoto
STEVENSON—The Democratic nominee greeted by Gov. G. Mennen Williams of Michigan and Sen. Blair Moody (center), D., Mich., at airport in Saginaw, Mich., first stop on his new tour

Index

News Summary on Page 2

YANKEES SLIPPED US A 'MICKEY'!

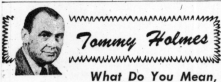

BROOKLYN EAGLE
Sports
Edited by
LOU NISS

Tommy Holmes

What Do You Mean, A Great Series?

"BY THIS MUCH"—They are calling the late, lamented World Series the greatest in years and one of the best of all time. And maybe they are right. It doesn't seem that way to this corner, but pride and prejudice may have created a jaundiced viewpoint here.

The Dodgers gave the Yankees a right fine hassle and carried the bid right down to the wire. But once again they failed to win the big one. This time their failure left a minimum target exposed to the snipers. At least, I think so, although second-guessers have fooled me before and, for all I know, every bar and grill in our town was filled last night with self-appointed managers relating how much smarter they are than Charley Dressen.

In the wild hoop-la of celebration that followed the Yankee 4-to-2 victory in the seventh game, Casey Stengel pulled away from the back-slappers long enough to pay a tribute to the Dodgers.

"I want to tell this to you," said the man who was run out of Brooklyn by the grandstand managers so many years ago and who now has four pennants and four world's championships to show for four years with the Yankees.

"Don't let anybody tell you that we didn't beat a great club," said Stengel. "And we beat 'em by just this much."

Stengel held a thumb and a forefinger about two inches apart, apparently to indicate how far Jackie Robinson's line drive to Gil McDougald needed to become an extra-base hit that might have broken the final ball game open the other way.

"They made great plays all through the series. They were greater play-makers than we were. They were slicker than we were at times at the plate and even the guys who didn't hit much never gave up. Their pitching was better than we figured it and Dressen will have some of those guys pitching even better next year.

"I won't say we were lucky," said Stengel, "but we weren't exactly unfortunate either to win this one."

BOB KUZAVA—Until the final game of the series, the Yankees never got ahead of the Dodgers. They tied it up three times after the Brooklyn bunch got ahead in games. In the final game, the Dodgers never got ahead of the Yankees. Twice they tied it up. Then they kept threatening and here the great edge the Yankees had over the Dodgers in pitching depth proved the difference.

With the front-line pitchers of both clubs worn to a frazzle, Stengel went to the bullpen and drew out Bob Kuzava, the left-hander with the fine fast ball who incidentally put out the blaze started by the Giants in the sixth and final game last year.

He brought in Kuzava with the bases filled and one out in the seventh and the Brooklyn power coming up. The big blonde fellow went to three-and-two on Snider, then made him pop up an outside fast ball to McDougald.

"I brought him in to pitch to Snider," said Stengel, "and his fast ball looked so good that I let him pitch to Robinson too. I started second-guessing myself when Robinson hit one into the stands, but I guess it worked out all right."

Indeed, it did. Robinson popped one up a mile in the center of the infield. The steady wind played tricks with the ball and that was quite a catch Billy Martin made as he dashed in on the dead run. For, with two out, everybody was running and two runs at least would have scored had the ball dropped safe.

And that was it, for Kuzava kept pumping the ball over and the Dodgers never threatened in the last two innings.

BREAK NEVER CAME—On Monday, the Dodgers brought a three-to-two edge in games to their own ancient baseball orchard. They had two chances to wrap up the championship and couldn't make it. They never cracked and they never tightened up and they never, never got a break in the last two games.

The worst damage wrought by the guardian genie of the Yankees was that trick hit Raschi caromed off the knee of Billy Loes into right field to put the Yanks ahead in the sixth game. And the big break of the series to this mind was that silly, schoolboy lapse that preceded the hit—Loes letting the ball slip out of his grasp to permit the runner to take second base and get in position to score.

But the turning point of the series came in the fourth game when Stengel made old Johnny Mize his first baseman. The oldest Yankee drove in the first run with a line single to left in the seventh game, but had to yield the hitting honors of the day to the youngest Yankee. Mickey Mantle hit a homer and a single. Mantle drove in three runs in the sixth and seventh game. One was the winning run on Monday. The others were the two winning runs yesterday.

NEW SERIES RECORDS

Sixteen World Series records were broken in the set concluded yesterday. The new marks:

INDIVIDUAL

Most total bases—Duke Snider, Dodgers, 24.
Most extra bases on long hits—Snider, Brooklyn (2-2B, 4HR), 15.
Most chances accepted, catcher Yogi Berra, Yankees, 6?.
Most putouts, catcher—Berra, Yankees, 59.
Most games without hit (regulars)—Gil Hodges, 7.

TEAM

Lowest batting percentage of club winning series—Yankees, .216.
Most times at bat, one club, total 19 series—Yankees, 3,362.
Fewest one-base hits, one club—Yankees, 33.
Fewest two-base hits, both clubs—Yankees (5) vs. Dodgers (7), 12.
Most home runs, one club—Yankees, 10.
Most home runs, both clubs—Yaunkees (10) vs. Dodgers (6), 16.
Most strikeouts, one club—Dodgers, 49.
Fewest sacrifices, one club—Yankees, 2.
Club playing most series—Yankees, 19.
Club winning most games—Yankees, 67.
Most times winner, total series—Yankees, 67.
Most times winner total series—Yankees, 15.

Eighteen records were tied, as follows:

INDIVIDUAL

Manager winning most consecutive World Series—Casey Stengel, Yankees, 4.
Most runs batted in—Snider, Dodgers, 8.
Most times at bat without a hit—Gil Hodges, Dodgers, 21.
Most home runs—Snider, Dodgers, 4.
Two home runs in a game—Snider, Dodgers, sixth game.
Most long hits—Snider, Dodgers, 6.
Most bases on balls, game—Jackie Robinson, Dodgers, fifth game, 4.
Most errors, third baseman—Gil McDougald, Yankees, 4.
Most assists, catcher—Berra, Yankees, 7.
Most errors, pitcher — Allie Reynolds, Yankees, 2.
Most games lost, pitcher—Joe Black, Dodgers, 2.
Home run by pinch-hitter—Johnny Mize, Yankees, ninth inning, third game.

TEAM

Fewest one-base hits, one club, game—Yankees, fourth game, 0.
Fewest two-base hits, one club—Yankees, 5.
Fewest three-base hits, one club—Dodgers, 0.
Most consecutive games one or more home runs—Yankees, first, second, third (2), fourth, fifth, sixth (2), seventh (2)—7.
Fewest strikeouts, one club, game—Dodgers, 0, third game.
Fewest assists, one club—Yankees, 66.

WHAT NOW, DODGER FANS?

There's No Tomorrow at Ebbets

Brooks Dress Quickly, Depart For Homes

By DAVE ANDERSON

You've been in Charley Dressen's office at Ebbets Field many times this season. But never was it like this. Never was there no tomorrow.

Most of the players, who took their defeat hard, had dressed and left and would not be seen before next Spring at Vero Beach.

Dressen was in his office, sitting on his leather couch and around him were a group of friends and reporters. Johnny Corriden, the Dodgers' scout and former coach, slumped in a chair in a corner and every now and then coaches Cookie Lavagetto, Billy Herman and Jake Pitler—whose lockers are just outside—would come in, say a few words and leave to finish dressing.

Dressen was still in his uniform, complete with cap and spikes, and he was saying "Well, tomorrow, the coaches and I are going to have a meeting right here. I'm going to give them a big sheet of yellow paper and let them write down what they think about the team. They'll do it separately and I'll do the same thing myself . . . then we'll compare 'em.

"Who was the big difference in the series? Reynolds overall, I think. Today it was Mantle and Mize but what hurts is that Mize's hit that knocked in the first run was just six inches away from Cox's glove. And he was swinging at a pitch that was past him.

Pop Fly Catch

"That catch Martin made on the pop fly when we had the bases loaded in the seventh, Collins lost it and Martin just caught it, another of those six-inch plays.

"But what hurt was the way we couldn't get those runners home from third base. We had the bases loaded twice, once with nobody out and once with one out, and we get one run out of it.

"All we needed was a fly ball and we couldn't do it. That happened about 40 times this season, too. You get the guy to third base and all your hitters have to do is hit the ball to the outfield and you got a run. But they couldn't do it."

During all this Dressen was not bitter, either at his players for failing him or at the Yankees for beating him. They were not alibis, merely explanations . . . Charley was a disappointed man but he is not a sore loser.

"Casey sure didn't take a chance with any of his pitchers today," Charley smiled. "But when he brought Kuzava in to pitch to Snider in the seventh, he went to three balls and two strikes on him before Duke popped up. Thing of it was, that pitch was just about on the plate, if it was, and Duke told me he couldn't take it, he had to swing because it was so close.

No Regrets

"But I bet if Kuzava had walked Snider, he'd of brought in Sain to pitch to the rest of my righthanded hitters."

By now, however, it was getting late and as the reporters left they shook his hand, congratulating him on his fine managerial job but their words were expressed better in a homemade sign hanging from the iron picket fence that guards the dressing rooms.

The sign said "Goodbye Dodgers. Thanks for a wonderful season that made your fans so happy. No Regrets."

JACKIE ROBINSON'S pop-up in seventh inning with bases loaded gets caught in the wind but Billy Martin comes on to make game-saving catch.

YANKEE 'PARADE' ROARS THROUGH BORO

Loud and prolonged honking of horns rubbed salt into Brooklyn wounds yesterday, immediately following the end of the game at Ebbets Field.

The Yankees, paced by Phil Rizzuto in a glistening red sports car, sped away from Flatbush preceded by two cops on motorcycles. As the entourage, in which most of the players rode by bus, sped along the main thoroughfares up Flatbush Ave. Extension to the Manhattan Bridge, the drivers sounded their horns and banners were waved from the windows.

It was a "parade" no Brooklynites had their heart in.

HURLING HELP ON WAY

Erv Palica May Rejoin Dodgers

Ervin Palica may report to the Dodgers at their Vero Beach camp in March. The pitcher wasn't due to receive his discharge from the Army until August, the month when he will have completed two full years in the service of his country.

Palica has been at Fort Dix and doing some pitching for the camp team.

"We had our chance," said Walter F. O'Malley when it was all over at Ebbets Field yesterday, "and we didn't deserve it. It's always tough to bring down the champion."

The Old Professor is going to try and make it five straight world championships.

"Quit?" growled Casey Stengel. "These are my boys. They never quit on me and I'll never quit on them. I'll be back with the Yankees next year."

Jackie Robinson is opening a department store in Harlem.

A fan interfered with Phil Rizzuto's double down the left field line in the fourth and was reprimanded by the umpires on the foul line, Art Passarella and Dusty Boggess.

The whole Dodger infield held a heavy consultation with Joe Black out on the mound before a ball was pitched.

The Yankees set a team record for World Series home runs with 10 for the seven games. The old mark was nine, set by the 1928 Yankees against the Cardinals, made in four games. The Dodgers' six homers were a record for a National League entry.

Poor Gil Hodges went hitless in all seven frays, coming to bat 21 fruitless times. Billy Sullivan of the 1906 White Sox and Red Murray of the 1911 Giants are the other regulars to go for the October horse collar.

But those were six-game Series.

It was the sixth straight setback for the N. L. which is another mark that was broken, five of 'em by the Yanks.

Coach Cookie Lavagetto, who roomed with Billy Martin when they played together on the Pacific Coast, thinks he has spotted a batting weakness in Martin.

"I can tell him now that the Series is over," said Cookie, ready to whisper his secret into the rookie's ear when they return to California.

The fences crowded Allie Reynolds at Ebbets Field.

"I like to pitch back home in Oklahoma," remarked the Yankee star who received credit for winning the final game, his fifth verdict to lead all the other hurlers still active. "We don't have any fences in my home States."

Oh well, nobody else beats the Yankees, either.

H. C. B.

BENCH BEEF COSTS IDLE BRANCA $200

Brooklyn pitcher Ralph Branca was fined $200 for being ejected from the last World Series game yesterday. Baseball Commissioner Ford Frick announced he had levied the fine, the only one of the series.

Branca did not play in the series. He was ejected from the Dodger dugout in the eighth inning by Umpire Larry Goetz for protesting too loudly from the bench when Roy Campanella struck out.

WORLD SERIES LOG

FIRST GAME

		R.	H.	E.
Yankees	0 0 1 0 0 0 0 1 0	2	6	2
Dodgers	0 1 0 0 0 2 0 1 x	4	6	0

Batteries—Reynolds, Scarborough (8) and Berra; Black and Campanella.

SECOND GAME

		R.	H.	E.
Yankees	0 0 0 1 1 5 0 0 0	7	10	0
Dodgers	0 0 1 0 0 0 0 0 0	1	3	1

Batteries—Raschi and Berra; Erskine, Loes (6), Lehman (8) and Campanella.

THIRD GAME

		R.	H.	E.
Dodgers	0 0 1 0 1 0 0 1 2	5	11	0
Yankees	0 1 0 0 0 0 0 1 1	3	6	2

Batteries—Roe and Campanella; Lopat, Gorman (9) and Berra.

FOURTH GAME

		R.	H.	E.
Dodgers	0 0 0 0 0 0 0 0 0	0	4	1
Yankees	0 0 0 1 0 0 0 1 x	2	4	1

Batteries—Black, Rutherford (8) and Campanella; Reynolds and Berra.

FIFTH GAME

		R.	H.	E.
Dodgers	0 1 0 0 3 0 1 0 0 0 1	6	10	0
Yankees	0 0 0 0 5 0 0 0 0 0 0	5	5	1

Batteries—Erskine and Campanella; Blackwell, Sain (6) and Berra.

SIXTH GAME

		R.	H.	E.
Yankees	0 0 0 0 0 0 2 1 0	3	9	0
Dodgers	0 0 0 0 0 1 0 1 0	2	8	1

Batteries—Raschi, Reynolds (8) and Berra; Loes, Roe (9) and Campanella.

SEVENTH GAME

		R.	H.	E.
Yankees	0 0 0 1 1 1 1 0 0	4	10	4
Dodgers	0 0 0 1 1 0 0 0 0	2	8	1

Batteries—Lopat, Reynolds (4), Raschi (7), Kuzava (7) and Berra; Black, Roe (6), Erskine (8) and Campanella.

DUKE COMES HOME—Duke Snider of the Dodgers comes sliding across the plate in the fourth inning on a long fly by Gil Hodges to knot the score at 1—1. George Shuba, right, waits his turn to bat. Yankees went on to win, 4—2, and take the World Series crown for fourth straight time.

Mantle Proved Self Worthy Successor To Great DiMaggio

By HAROLD C. BURR

Before the World Series started it was predicted that the Yankees would be just another ball club without the matchless Joe DiMaggio. But Mickey Mantle did just about everything Jolting Joe used to do.

His hits yesterday in the seventh game at Ebbets Field drove in the two runs responsible for the Yanks' 4-to-2 triumph that gave 'em their fourth straight world championship, with the Oklahoma 20-year-old kid the youngest champion of 'em all.

Mickey was no mouse throughout the Series. His homer in the sixth game evened the Series and he hit another off Joe Black yesterday and a long single off Preacher Roe for the tallies the Dodgers never could get back. Mantle hit .345, the same as Peewee Reese and Duke Snider, the top Brooklyn hitters.

The speedy youngster brought the all but obsolete drag bunt back into circulation, faultlessly pushing it past the pitcher on two occasions.

It was the biggest game of the year for the Yankees and they won it in their old despicably lawless fashion.

Johnny Mize, who led both squads with his .400 average, was held to a pair of singles by Black and Roe. The Big Cat was out of the game by the time Carl Erskine appeared, because Manager Casey Stengel didn't trust him to field like one. But Mize punched a hit into left field in the fourth to score the first run of the ball game.

Come Back Twice

Gene Woodling's homer in the fifth chalked up the Yankees' second tally. The Dodgers kept fighting and got those runs back one at a time, but with the advent of Bob Kuzava in the seventh, fourth Yankee hurler, they were through for the year.

Their key rounds were the fourth and the seventh. The first opening, Jackie Robinson and Roy Campanella bunted Ed Lopat right out of the ball game, filling the bases with no one out. Allie Reynolds came in and got out of it with one run on Gil Hodges' line smash to Woodling. The Flatbushers filled the bases again in the seventh with one away on Reynolds.

Kuzava retired Snider on a pop to Gil McDougald and Robinson lifted a little fly that the wind took freakishly. Billy Martin lost his cap and nearly lost the ball, too, chasing it halfway across the infield. If it had fallen safely it would have been a score with the Dodgers still batting, the greatest break in World Series history.

After that Kuzava would have set down the Dodgers in order but for an error by McDougald in the eighth. This was the second Series final for Bob, who was no great shakes on relief during the regular American League season, had saved. But his latest masterly chore was in sharp contrast to the manner in which he was slugged by the Giants last Fall when he was rescued by his outfielders.

Stengel used his three aces, Lopat, Reynolds and Raschi to stop the Dodgers and by some shrewd manipulating got away with it.

It was a great World Series, with the game battle the Dodgers put up, before going down to defeat on the tongues of everyone of the 33,195 fans. They had great defensive play by the infield in the first game and the second by their outfield in the second. Their baserunning took advantage of every Yankee slip.

They were however, up against the expected superior pitching. Black was a tired boy yesterday. The marvel is that he kept his arm hanging from his shoulder for so long.

BILLY MARTIN of Yankees is almost picked off first base on toss from Joe Black to Gil Hodges in fifth.

Broken Hearted!

YANKEES (4)

	AB	R	H	PO	A
McDougald, 3b	4	1	2	2	3
Rizzuto, ss	4	1	1	1	1
Mantle, cf	5	1	2	1	0
Mize, 1b	3	0	2	7	0
Collins, 1b	0	0	0	1	0
Berra, c	4	0	0	7	0
Woodling, lf	4	1	2	4	0
Noren, rf	2	0	0	1	0
Bauer, rf	1	0	0	0	0
Martin, 2b	4	0	1	2	4
Lopat, p	1	0	0	0	1
Reynolds, p	1	0	0	1	0
aHouk	1	0	0	0	0
Raschi, p	0	0	0	0	0
Kuzava, p	1	0	0	0	0
Totals	35	4	10	27	9

DODGERS (2)

	AB	R	H	PO	A
Cox, 3b	5	1	2	2	3
Reese, ss	4	0	1	2	2
Snider, cf	4	1	1	4	0
Robinson, 2b	4	0	1	0	4
Campanella, c	4	0	2	1	0
Hodges, 1b	4	0	0	14	0
Shuba, lf	3	0	1	1	0
cPafko	1	0	0	0	0
Holmes, lf	0	0	0	0	0
Furillo, rf	3	0	0	3	0
Black, p	2	0	0	0	0
Roe, p	0	0	0	0	0
bNelson	1	0	0	0	0
Erskine, p	0	0	0	0	0
dMorgan	1	0	0	0	0
Totals	36	2	8	27	9

aGrounded out for Reynolds in seventh.
bPopped out for Roe in seventh.
cStruck out for Shuba in eighth.
dFlied out for Erskine in ninth.

Yankees	0 0 0 1 1 1 1 0 0	4
Dodgers	0 0 0 1 1 0 0 0 0	2

Errors—McDougald 2, Reynolds, Woodling, Cox. Runs batted in—Mize, Hodges, Woodling, Reese, Mantle 2. Two-base hits—Rizzuto, Cox. Home runs—Woodling, Mantle. Sacrifice hit—Rizzuto. Double plays—Robinson-Reese-Hodges, Rizzuto-Martin-Mize. Left on bases—Yankees 8, Dodgers 9. Bases on balls—Off Black 1, Raschi 2, Erskine 1. Struck out—By Black 1, Lopat 3, Reynolds 2, Roe 1, Kuzava 2. Hits—Off Lopat 4 in 3 (pitched to three batters in fourth), Black 6 in 5⅓, Reynolds 3 in 3, Roe 3 in 1⅔, Raschi 1 in ⅓, Kuzava 0 in 2⅔, Erskine 1 in 2. Runs and earned runs—Lopat 1 and 1, Black 3 and 3, Reynolds 1 and 1, Roe 1 and 1, Raschi 0 and 0, Kuzava 0 and 0, Erskine 0 and 0. Winning pitcher — Reynolds. Losing pitcher — Black. Umpires—Goetz (N), plate; McKinley (A), 1b; Pinelli (N), 2b; Passarella (A), 3b; Boggess (N) and Honochick (A), foul lines. Time, 2:54. Attendance, 33,195.

Braves Sign Holmes To Pilot Milwaukee

Boston, Oct. 8 (U.P.)—Tommy Holmes, fired earlier this year as manager of the Boston Braves, was rehired to manage their top farm club, Milwaukee in the American Association.

News of the signing of Holmes in New York was relayed to the parent club and announced here.

Holmes replaces Bucky Walters who took over at mid-season at Milwaukee when manager Charley Grimm was called up to replace the deposed Holmes with the Braves. President Lou Perini of the Braves obtained permission to talk with Holmes at the conclusion of the World Series yesterday. Holmes had been a reserve member of the Dodgers who picked him up when the Braves dropped him.

After talking with Perini, Holmes breakfasted today with Braves general manager John Quinn and agreed to terms.

Holmes was brought in the middle of last season to replace manager Billy Southworth. The young manager had had only a brief experience managing the Braves' farm club in Hartford, Conn.

He did a better than passable job handling the Major League club but this year ran into trouble early in the season.

Perini, who always had thought highly of Holmes, reluctantly agreed to drop him and the Brooklyn resident was quickly signed by the Dodgers. He was used principally as a pinch-hitter and utility outfielder in the late innings of games, including two of the World Series tussles.

The Milwaukee post became vacant at the end of this season when Walters was transferred to the Braves as a coach.

CATCHING ON!—Dodger catcher Al Walker, center, displays manners for two Vero Beach assistants, Ann Clements, aged 8, left and her brother David, 5. (International Photo)

Highly-Touted Gomez 'Arrives' with Giants

By KEN SMITH

PHOENIX, Ariz., March 5.—It isn't often that a rookie pitcher is labeled for a big league job the first day he walks into a training camp, but this was the situation today when 25-year-old Ruben Gomez, from Puerto Rico showed up. Leo Durocher said he is counting on this lithe collegian this season. He's the most highly-touted Polo Grounds mound prospect since Larry Jansen arrived from San Francisco with a 3-6 record in 1947.

Last year Hoyt Wilhelm, with no fanfare, was the National League earned run prize.

"The Carribean is Triple A company so I have plenty of confidence that I am ready for the majors", Gomez explained. I've worked against big leaguers like Luke Easter.

"Right now I'm tired from the plane ride from Puerto Rico. I'll need five or six days to run my legs into shape. I've been pitching pretty steadily since last June but my arm isn't tired. I'll be ready for this season."

I WAS an outfielder in high school. They brought me in to pitch and I showed a natural cross fire. I've been pitching ever since. I went to the University of Puerto Rico and then played with the professionals. Later I went back to college."

Like several Cuban players of the past, Padrone Adolfo Luque and Mike Gonzales, Gomez started his career in Connecticut. He pitched for Bristol, in the Canadian Provincial League. After playing five games with Kansas City last year he brought his own release, financed by promoters in the Dominican Republic.

"I could make such more money playing in Puerto Rico," Gomez pointed out.

The Giants gave him a $5,000 bonus and signed him for $10,000. Monte Irvin and Tom Sheehan gave him a strong ok.

"I pitch a fast ball, slider and screw ball," says Ruben who has a three-year-old son. George Crowe collided with me at first base one day last year and my back ached for quite a while."

* * *

SMITH'S SPARKS—The opening lineup against Cleveland Saturday will be Williams 2b, Lockman 1b, Irvin lf, Spencer ss, Hartung rf, Thompson cf, Noble c, Adair Koslo and Picone p...The Indians intend to use a couple of southpaws. Durocher will lose no time employing the two platoon system by benching Don Mueller in favor of Hartung.

To Build Youth In Ski Resort Area

HILO, Hawaii, (UP).—Lads who never could afford to spend a winter vacation in Sun Valley or at Aspen, Colo., will get a chance to mend their broken lives in Hawaii's only ski resort area next winter.

A carefully selected group of 18 and 19-year-olds from the Mauna Loa forestry camp for delinquents on the island of Hawaii is being trained to provide rescue service, stock mountain shelters and build trails and parking areas.

It is a little known fact that on giant Mauna Loa, towering 13,680 feet above the blue Pacific, are slopes which would do credit to any mainland ski resort.

Gators in Sweep Of Bowl Rivals

GAINESVILLE, Fla. (AP).—The Florida Gators made a clean sweep in the Gator Bowl this year.

The footballers defeated Tulsa, 14-13, and the basketballers defended their championship with triumphs against Georgia, Georgia Tech and Georgia Teachers.

TIME OUT!
By JEFF KEATE

"Sure, he outclasses you . . . but that's all he's got!"

Hockey Player Dies

COLLINGWOOD, Ont., March 5 (AP).—Robert Gillies, 17-year-old defenseman of the Collingwood Greenshirts of the Ontario Hockey Association, died today some five hours after he was injured during a game. The player's head struck the boards.

Mantle in DiMag Cleanup Role in Grapefruit Opener

By BEN EPSTEIN

ST. PETERSBURG, Fla., March 5.—The step-by-step grooming of Mickey Mantle as Joe DiMaggio's replacement has reached the graduation stage. Installed as the regular centerfielder last June, the 21-year-old star inherited DiMaggio's old cleanup spot today with Casey Stengel's announcement he would bat fourth in the Yankees' first exhibition against the Cardinals Saturday.

Yogi Berra, the Bombers' No. 4 guy in most of the games down the '52 championship run, hits fifth, his favorite location in the Grapefruit League opener. Stengel, who only altered his lineup a mere 102 times last season including the World Series, hastened to add even Mickey's slotting was subject to change but hinted it was the sweet switcher's to have and to hold.

* * *

THAT CASEY visualized Mickey as his main mop-up man from scratch was brought out in a dugout talk:

"I couldn't do it last year because he was crippled and green. But he seems to be all right now."

Which, indeed he is.

What spurred Stengel to this decision apparently stemmed from Mantle's blazing batting down the stretch when he slugged .370 in the last 30 games, climaxed by a .400 mark in teh last 10 of them. Twelve of his last 16 hits went for extra bases—seven doubles, two triples and three homers. As publicist Red

Continued on Next Page

Indiana Voted Champ Quintet, Seton Hall 4th

Indiana's Big Ten powerhouse has been acclaimed the 1952-'53 national college basketball champion by an overwhelming vote of the United Press board of coaches.

The speedy, durable Hoosiers, who have clinched their conference championship and a berth in the N.C.A.A. tournament, were the No. 1 choice of 29 of the 35 leading coaches who make up the United Press rating board.

Indiana thus attracted 342 out of a posible 350 points in the final ballot of the season. Five coaches picked Coach Branch McCracken's men for second place and one for fourth.

* * *

THE WASHINGTON HUSKIES were second—57 points behind Indiana, while LaSalle was third, just five points ahead of Seton Hall. Washington had three first place votes and LaSalle one. The only other teams that attracted first place votes in the final ratings were North Carolina State (ranked eighth) and Notre Dame (ranked 13th), each polling one.

Behind fourth-place Seton Hall, which dropped from contention for the lead after suffering its first two defeats of the season this wek. Here is how the top 10 was rounded out: Kansas, Louisiana State, Oklahoma A and M, North Carolina State, Kansas State and Illinois.

Final ratings follow (with first-place votes and won-and-lost records through March 4 in parentheses):

Team.	Points.
1. Indiana (29) (18-2)	342
2. Washington (3) (25-2)	285
3. LaSalle (1) (25-2)	218
4. Seton Hall (28-2)	213
5. Kansas (14-5)	169
6. Louisiana State (21-1)	135
7. Oklahoma A&M (20-6)	126
8. North Carolina State (1) (24-5)	89
9. Kansas State (15-4)	88
10. Illinois (16-4)	83

N.L. APPROVES BRAVES SHIFT OF FRANCHISE TO MILWAUKEE

Story on Page 20

5 CENTS ★ FINAL

Daily Mirror

MARCH						
S	M	T	W	T	F	S
1	2	3	4	5	6	7
8	9	10	11	12	13	14
15	16	17	18	19	20	21
22	23	24	25	26	27	28
29	30	31				

Vol. 29. No. 231. NEW YORK 17, N. Y., THURSDAY, MARCH 19, 1953 4c in New York City. 5c Elsewhere in U.S.A.

(U. S. Army Photo via AP WIREphoto)

NEWS FOR MAYS. Willie Mays, ex-Giant outfield star, grins feebly on learning the Army had rejected his request for a dependency discharge. He was photographed at the bulletin board at Ft. Eustis, Va. He's due for discharge in May, 1954.

(Mirror Photo by Bob Gilman)

RESOLUTION for the reinstatement of football at New York University was passed by these students, who met in the chapel of the library at the University Heights campus to protest the dropping of the gridiron sport.

(AP WIREphoto)

APPROVE THE MOVE. Boston Braves President Lou Perini (right), in St. Petersburg, Fla., chats with National League representatives who okayed Braves' shift to Milwaukee. Others (l. to r.): James Gallagher, Chicago; Horace Stoneham, Giants; Bob Carpenter, Phils, and Gabe Paul, Cincy. It'll be the Milwaukee Braves!

(AP WIREphoto)

It Takes 2 to Tangle

Kansas' Allen Kelley throws out his hands to keep from falling atop Mike McCutchen of the Washington Huskies. They spill in a moment of close action at the NCAA basketball tournament semi-finals in Kansas City, Mo. McCutchen is still clutchin' the ball. Kansas won, 79-53, in upset.

Giants Divide With Dodgers; Mantle's 565-Foot Home Run Helps Yankees Win

BROOKS SCORE, 12-4, AFTER 6-3 SETBACK

Wilhelm Nips Dodgers' Rally in 9th to Save Giant Home Debut in Afternoon

MAGLIE FALTERS AT END

Hurls Hitless Ball for 6⅔ Innings—6-Run 5th Routs Hearn in Night Game

By JOHN DREBINGER

The Giants finally got around to opening the season at the Polo Grounds yesterday but in an unguarded moment they left the gates open too long. For after bringing down the Dodgers, 6 to 3, in the afternoon, a play-off of Thursday's postponement, Leo Durocher's men came a fearful cropper in the regularly scheduled night game.

Chick Dressen's champions won this one, 12 to 4, to the profound disgust of a majority in a gathering of 29,406, most of whom walked out on the chilly performance when a drizzling rain added to their general misery midway in the struggle.

A crowd of 18,307 turned out for the afternoon engagement in which the Giants deported themselves well enough as they defeated the Dodgers' latest youthful phenom, Johnny Podres. But there wasn't much they could do about young Billy Loes in the night contest, in which their own pitching went completely to pot under a sixteen-hit barrage.

A six-run outburst, with the first three riding in on a Carl Furillo homer, routed Jim Hearn in the fifth and from there on it was just a romp.

The Razor Slips

Taking the afternoon engagement was by no means a soft touch for the Giants even though Sal Maglie, a master at shaving the Flatbush Flock, had a no-hitter going for six and two-thirds innings and as late as the ninth held a commanding 6—1 lead.

For in the top half of the ninth the famed Barber's razor slipped and he almost cut himself as the aroused Brooks lashed back for four singles and two runs with only one out.

But at this point Durocher came up with a long and all too familiar move as far as the Dodgers are concerned. The Giant skipper called on his knuckleballing ace, Hoyt Wilhelm, and though there were a few more anxious moments when a pass filled the bases, the relief star of the Polo Grounds coralled the final out.

Up to this trying moment, it was pretty much all Giant. The Polo Grounders bagged three of their runs off the southpaw Podres, two riding home on a second inning circuit clout by Wes Westrum. Then, after Podres vacated for a pinch-hitter, Jim Hughes came on in the last of the eighth and was himself tagged for three more tallies. That bit of added "insurance" was to pay off handsomely a few minutes later.

Mayor Hurls a Slider

Since Giant-Dodger meetings never need any additional embellishments, the pre-game ceremonies, carried over from Thursday's rained out opener, were to the point. There was the traditional parade to the flagpole; promptly at 1:30 o'clock Mayor Impellitteri unfurled a swift slider that could win him a shutout in City Hall, and a moment later the belligerents were at it.

The first rift in the battle occurred in the second when, with two out, Daryl Spencer, making his formal bow in the championship season at the Polo Grounds, clubbed a triple to left center that cleared all of 440 feet on the fly.

Then the inexperience of youth was to take its toll. Podres, facing Westrum and with Maglie the next batter, chose not to be the least bit discreet. He laid his first pitch in there and the husky Giant backstop whacked it right over the left-field roof.

Something even more astonishing came to pass in the third when the usually flawless Peewee Reese committed misplays on two successive batters. He fumbled Al Dark's grounder, then fired wide of second on Bobby Thompson's bounder, Dark scoring all the way from first on the error.

Spencer Fumbles Grounder

In the meantime, Maglie was mowing down the Brooks. In six innings only one Dodger got on base, Spencer fumbling Don Thompson's sharp grounder in the fifth.

Two were out in the seventh when Jackie Robinson came up with the Brooks' first hit, a pop fly in short left that Monty Irvin couldn't quite reach. Monty added a wild throw-in and Jackie wound up on third. That, however, scarcely was needed as Roy Campanella followed with a mighty three-base blast into right center to score Robbie.

Two were out and only Whitey Lockman on first when throuble overtook Hughes in the Giant eighth. Don Mueller singled, Spencer doubled and one run was in. Following an intentional pass to Westrum, Maglie got an infield hit that Junior Gilliam collared back of second, only to fall asleep. For the hit not only scored Mueller but Spencer as well as the Dodgers' young second sacker nonchalantly tossed the ball to Reese standing on second.

And in the ninth those tallies suddenly became mighty handy as Gilliam opened with a single, grabbing an extra base on Spencer's wide throw to first. Resee singled and Duke Snider's fly drove in Gilliam. Robinson and Campanella singled for another run and that was where Wilhelm came on. He induced Don Thompson to slap into a force play at second, which still left runners on first and third. Then he walked Gil Hodges, filling the sacks. But a moment later the Flock breathed its last as George Shuba fouled out to Spencer back of third.

Furillo's Second Homer

The night game remained a scoreless deadlock for four innings, then blew wide open as Lockman fumbled a grounder to open the fifth. Behind that Hodges singled and Furillo sliced one into the lower right deck for his second homer of the season.

Then all sorts of things happened. Gilliam's blinding speed converted a single into a double and a moment later Junior scored from second base on a wild pitch. Snider singled, stole second and third and when Hearn walked the next two, Frank Hiller came on only to be greeted by Don Thompson's single that drove in two more.

Ruben Gomez was whacked for four more runs on five singles before George Spencer rescued him in the sixth and then George got cuffed for another pair in the eighth. It wasn't until the eighth the Giants finally bestirred themselves to grab two runs and another pair in the ninth. But by then it was all too late.

Robinson, playing third base throughout the day, came to bat nine times and got on base seven times, with five singles and two walks.

Like President Eisenhower in Washington the day before, Mayor Impelliteri sandwiched his opening pitch between speaking engagements. His toss to Westrum, which nicked the outside corner of the imaginery plate, had hardly settled in the catcher's glove before His Honor was off and running to the next stop.

The Box Scores

AFTERNOON GAME

BROOKLYN (N.)	ab.	r.	h.	po.	a.
Gilliam, 2b	4	1	1	1	2
Reese, ss	4	1	1	1	1
Snider, cf	4	0	0	1	0
Robinson, 3b	4	1	2	1	4
Campanella, c	4	0	2	3	1
Thom'n, lf, rf	4	0	0	2	0
Hodges, 1b	3	0	0	12	1
Furillo, rf	2	0	0	3	0
aShuba, lf	2	0	0	0	0
Podres, p	2	0	0	0	2
aWalker	1	0	0	0	0
Hughes, p	0	0	0	0	0
Total	34	3	6	24	11

NEW YORK (N.)	ab.	r.	h.	po.	a.
Williams, 2b	4	0	1	1	1
Dark, ss	4	1	0	1	4
Thomson, cf	3	0	1	6	0
Irvin, lf	4	0	0	1	0
Lockman, 1b	4	1	2	8	1
Mueller, rf	4	1	2	0	0
Spencer, 3b	4	2	2	3	2
Westrum, c	1	1	1	6	0
Maglie, p	3	0	1	1	1
Wilhelm, p	0	0	0	0	0
Total	31	6	10	27	9

aGrounded out for Furillo in eighth.
bStruck out for Podres in eighth.

Brooklyn .... 0 0 0 0 0 0 1 0 2—3
New York .... 0 2 1 0 0 0 0 3 .—6

Errors—Reese 2, Spencer 2, Irvin.
Runs batted in—Westrum 2, Campanella 2, Spencer, Maglie 2, Snider.
Two-base hit—Spencer. Three-base hits—Spencer, Campanella. Home run—Westrum. Sacrifice hit—Maglie. Double play—Gilliam, Reese and Hodges. Left on bases—Brooklyn 5, New York 7. Bases on balls—Off Podres 3, Hughes 2, Wilhelm 7. Struck out—By Podres 2, Maglie 5. Hits—Off Podres 7 in 7 innings, Hughes 3 in 1, Maglie 6 in 8 1-3, Wilhelm 0 in 2-3. Runs and earned runs—Off Podres 3 and 2, Hughes 3 and 3, Maglie 3 and 3. Winning pitcher—Maglie (1—0). Losing pitcher—Podres (0—1). Umpires—Boggess, Engeln, Stewart and Pinelli. Time of game—2:18. Attendance—18,307.

NIGHT GAME

BROOKLYN (N.)	ab.	r.	h.	po.	a.
Gilliam, 2b	6	2	3	4	2
Reese, ss	5	0	0	1	3
Snider, cf	5	3	2	2	0
Robinson, 3b	3	3	3	2	2
Cam'nella, c	4	0	2	5	1
D. Th'son, lf	4	1	2	3	0
Hodges, 1b	4	1	1	8	0
Furillo, rf	5	2	2	2	1
Loes, p	4	0	1	0	1
Total	40	12	16	27	10

NEW YORK (N.)	ab.	r.	h.	po.	a.
Williams, 2b	4	0	3	1	1
Dark, ss	4	0	0	0	1
Thomson, cf	4	0	0	2	0
Irvin, lf	2	0	1	3	0
Rhodes, lf	1	0	0	1	0
Lockman, 1b	4	1	2	10	1
Mueller, rf	4	1	1	2	0
D. Sp'cer, 3b	3	1	0	2	2
Westrum, c	1	0	0	5	0
Calderone, c	2	1	2	1	0
aThompson	1	0	0	0	0
Hearn, p	1	0	0	0	4
Hiller, p	0	0	0	0	0
bWilson	1	0	0	0	0
Gomez, p	0	0	0	0	1
G. Sp'cer, p	0	0	0	0	0
cGilbert	1	0	0	0	0
Lanier, p	0	0	0	0	0
dRigney	1	0	0	0	0
Total	34	4	9	27	11

aFlied out for Westrum in fifth.
bStruck out for Hiller in fifth.
cFouled out for G. Spencer in eighth.
dGrounded out for Lanier in ninth.

Brooklyn .... 0 0 0 0 6 4 0 2 0—12
New York .... 0 0 0 0 0 0 0 2 2— 4

Error—Lockman.
Runs batted in—Furillo 3, D. Thompson 3, Gilliam, Snider, Campanella 3, Williams, Dark, Calderone 2.
Two-base hits—Gilliam, Calderone. Home run—Furillo. Stolen bases—Snider 2, Robinson, Campanella. Sacrifices—Loes, Reese. Double plays—Furillo and Hodges; Reese, Gilliam and Hodges. Left on bases—Brooklyn 8, New York 5. Bases on balls—Off Loes 2, Hearn 3, G. Spencer 2. Struck out—By Loes 6, Hearn 5, G. Spencer 1. Hits—Off Hearn 6 in 4 2-3; Hiller 1 in 1-3; Gomez 5 in 2-3; G. Spencer 3 in 2 1-3; Lanier 1 in 1. Runs and earned runs—Off Loes 4 and 4, Hearn 6 and 3, Gomez 4 and 4, G. Spencer 2 and 2, Hiller 0 and 0, Lanier 0 and 0. Wild pitches—By Hearn 3. Winning pitcher—Loes (1—0). Losing pitcher—Hearn (0—1). Umpires—Engeln, Stewart, Pinelli, Boggess. Time of game—2:40. Attendance—29,406.

One Giant Out, Another Scores in Afternoon Game

Lockman of New York is picked off first base on Podres' throw to Hodges in the fourth inning

The New York Times (by Ernest Sisto)

Westrum of the Giants, scoring on his second-inning homer, is congratulated at plate by Spencer (12), who scored ahead of him, and Williams (10), who is waiting for his turn at bat.

BISHOP OF ATHLETICS CHECKS RED SOX, 5-0

PHILADELPHIA, April 17 (AP)—Rookie Charley Bishop, a surprise starter, turned back the Red Sox with a five-hit shutout and drove home a pair of runs as the Athletics won a 5-0 victory today in a game marked by the major league season's first fist fight.

Bishop struck out five and exhibited excellent control by not walking a batter.

The principals in the fight were Sammy White, Boston catcher, and Allie Clark, Philadelphia outfielder. It was a short and brief contest in which Clark landed a good right to White's jaw.

Tempers flared when White blocked Clark's attempt to tally from second on Pete Suder's single in the eighth. Jim Piersall made a great throw to the plate and White blocked the sliding Clark. There was an exchange of words and both players came up swinging.

Umpires jumped between the players and both benches emptied. The plate umpire, Charley Berry, banished White and Clark. It was White's second fight with a Philadelphia player. He and Billy Hitchcock, since traded to Detroit, exchanged punches here last year.

Eddie Joost, A's shortstop, was sidelined because of a charley horse and Joe DeMaestri replaced him.

The box score:

BOSTON (A.)	ab.	r.	h.	po.	a.
Goodman, 2b	4	0	2	4	4
Piersall, rf	4	0	1	0	1
Evers, lf	4	0	0	0	0
Gernert, 1b	3	0	0	10	0
Kell, 3b	3	0	0	1	1
White, c	3	0	1	6	0
Wilber, c	0	0	0	1	0
Umphlett, cf	3	0	1	1	0
Bolling, ss	3	0	0	1	3
McDermott, p	1	0	0	0	2
Flowers, p	1	0	0	0	0
aZarilla	1	0	0	0	0
Delock, p	0	0	0	0	0
Total	30	0	5	24	11

PHILADELPHIA (A.)	ab.	r.	h.	po.	a.
DeMaestri, ss	4	0	1	3	3
Philley, cf	4	0	1	1	0
Michaels, 2b	4	0	1	5	3
Robinson, 1b	3	0	0	9	1
Clark, rf	3	0	1	0	0
Valo, rf	0	0	0	0	0
Zernial, lf	2	2	0	3	0
Suder, 3b	4	2	3	1	3
Astroth, c	3	1	1	5	1
Bishop, p	3	0	1	0	2
Total	30	5	9	27	13

aHit into double play for Flowers in eighth.

Boston .... 0 0 0 0 0 0 0 0 0—0
Philadelphia .... 0 2 0 2 0 0 0 1 .—5

Errors—Goodman, Gernert.
Runs batted in—Bishop 2, DeMaestri, Philley.
Two-base hit—Philley. Sacrifice—Robinson. Double plays—Astroth and Michaels; Bolling, Goodman and Gernert; Kell, Goodman and Gernert; Bishop, DeMaestri and Robinson. Left on bases—Boston 3, Philadelphia 8. Bases on balls—Off McDermott 2, Flowers 1, Delock 3. Struck out—By McDermott 2, Flowers 3, Delock 1, Bishop 5. Hits—Off McDermott 7 in 4 innings, Flowers 0 in 3, Delock 2 in 1. Runs and earned runs—Off McDermott 4 and 2, Delock 1 and 1. Wild pitch—McDermott. Winning pitcher—Bishop (1—0). Losing pitcher—McDermott (0—1). Umpires—Berry, Hurley, Soar and Rommel. Time of game—2:13. Attendance—2,400.

ETCHELLS TIES FOR LEAD

Equals Star Title Series Total of Knowles, Myers Cup Winner

Special to The New York Times.

NASSAU, Bahamas, April 17—Durward Knowles of Nassau, sailing Gem III, captured the second race of the Star Class spring championships off Montagu Bay today and tied for first place on total points with E. W. (Skip) Etchells of Greenwich, Conn. Etchells finished third with Shannon in today's contest as Charles Lyons Jr., of Barnegat Bay, with Vega IV, placed second.

Robert Lippincott's Flower of Riverton, N. J., and Jack Price's Commanche of Miami shared third in the series point standing. Lippincott sailed fourth, Price ninth in the race today.

Knowles won the Myers Cup, finishing ahead of Price as George Fleitz of Los Angeles with Wench IV gained third in the three-race Star Class event. The final of the spring title competition is scheduled for tomorrow morning.

Other title race finishers included Charles Knight's Quakeress II, Riverton, N. J., eleventh; Charles Ulmer's Scylla, City Island, N. Y., fourteenth, and Andrew Lawrence's Sonata, Sea Cliff, L. I., twentieth.

REDLEGS' 3 IN 8TH STOP BRAVES, 10-9

Three Walks and Two Singles Off a Milwaukee Rookie Decide Cincinnati Game

CINCINNATI, April 17 (AP)—The Cincinnati Redlegs and the Milwaukee Braves traded hits, runs and the lead freely here today until the Redlegs shattered a 7-all deadlock with a three-run outburst in the eighth inning and then held off th Breaves in the ninth for a 10-9 triumph.

Ed Mathews belted a two-run homer for the losers while Jim Greengrass, Ted Kluszewski and Gus Bell got 4-baggers for the Redlegs. Greengrass connected with two on.

Rookie relief pitcher Bob Buhl's wildness hurt the Braves when he walked three batters in the eighth while getting only one man out on a sacrifice before Johnny Temple and Bobby Adams singled to drive in three runs. Don Liddle replaced Buhl and got Kluszewski to hit into an inning-ending double play, but the damage had been done.

The Braves blended a single, a walk and Andy Pafko's 390-foot double for two runs in the ninth inning before Joe Nuxhall got the side out. Nuxhall was the fourth and last Redleg pitcher to see action, with Frank Smith getting credit for the victory.

The Braves used three hurlers as Cincinnati came up with 10 hits against 12 for Milwaukee. Buhl was charged with the defeat.

Milwaukee made three errors, but only one—Johnny Logan's wide throw on an attempted force out at second in the second—figured in the scoring.

The box score:

MILWAUKEE (N.)	ab.	r.	h.	po.	a.
Bruton, cf	5	2	3	4	1
Logan, ss	5	2	1	2	2
Mathews, 3b	3	2	2	1	1
Gordon, lf	5	0	1	1	0
dPendleton	0	1	0	0	0
Pafko, rf	4	0	2	1	0
Adcock, 1b	5	0	1	8	1
Cooper, c	3	1	1	3	0
eSisti	0	0	0	0	0
Dittmer, 2b	4	1	1	3	3
fThorpe	1	0	0	0	0
Wilson, p	2	0	0	1	0
aKlaus	1	0	0	0	0
Buhl, p	1	0	0	0	2
Liddle, p	0	0	0	0	0
Total	39	9	12	24	10

CINCINNATI (N.)	ab.	r.	h.	po.	a.
Temple, 2b	5	0	2	4	3
Adams, 3b	5	0	1	0	3
Marshall, rf	4	1	1	2	0
Klusz'ski, 1b	4	2	1	9	0
Greengrass, lf	4	2	2	2	0
Bell, cf	3	3	2	4	0
McMillan, ss	3	0	1	2	3
Seminick, c	3	1	0	4	1
Judson, p	1	0	0	0	0
bHatton	1	0	0	0	0
Smith, p	0	0	0	0	0
cMarquis	0	1	0	0	0
Blake, p	0	0	0	0	0
Nuxhall, p	0	0	0	0	0
Total	33	10	10	27	10

aGrounded out for Wilson in sixth.
bFlied out for Judson in sixth.
cWalked for Smith in eighth.
dRan for Gordon in ninth.
eRan for Cooper in ninth.
fFlied out for Dittmer in ninth.

Milwaukee .... 2 0 2 0 0 2 1 0 2— 9
Cincinnati .... 0 2 1 0 4 0 0 3 .—10

Errors—Logan, Mathews, Adcock, Adams.
Runs batted in—Bruton, Mathews 3, Gordon, Pafko 3, Klaus, Temple 2, Adams, Kluszewski, Greengrass 3, Bell, Seminick.
Two-base hits—Gordon, Pafko. Home runs—Mathews, Kluszewski, Greengrass, Bell. Stolen base—Bruton. Sacrifice—McMillan. Double plays—Mathews, Dittmer and Adcock; Dittmer, Logan and Adcock. Left on bases—Milwaukee 8, Cincinnati 6. Bases on balls—Off Wilson 2, Buhl 3, Liddle 1, Judson 2, Smith 1, Blake 1, Nuxhall 1. Struck out—By Wilson 2, Buhl 1, Judson 1, Smith 2. Hits—Off Wilson 8 in 5 innings, Buhl 2 in 2 1-3, Liddle 0 in 2-3, Judson 8 in 6, Smith 2 in 2, Blake 1 in 0 (faced two batters), Nuxhall 1 in 1. Runs and earned runs—Off Wilson 7 and 6, Buhl 3 and 3, Judson 6 and 5, Smith 1 and 1, Blake 2 and 2. Winning pitcher—Smith (1—0). Losing pitcher—Buhl (0—1). Umpires—Warneke, Donatelli, Gorman and Conlan. Time of game—2:20. Attendance—1,295.

Pirates Purchase Pellagrini

PITTSBURGH, April 17 (UP)—The Pirates winked at their "youth movement" today by purchasing 34-year-old Eddie Pellagrini from the Cincinnati Redlegs. He will be used as a utility infielder.

Minor Leagues

[From Late Editions of Yesterday's Times.]

AMERICAN ASSOCIATION

(Night Games)

Indianapolis 3, Charleston 2.
Minneapolis 16, Kansas City 6.
Toledo 12, Columbus 6.
St. Paul at Louisville, rain.

STANDING OF THE CLUBS

	W.	L.	PC.		W.	L.	PC.
Minneapolis	2	0	1.000	Charleston	0	1	.000
Indianapolis	1	0	1.000	Columbus	0	1	.000
St. Paul	1	0	1.000	Louisville	0	1	.000
Toledo	1	0	1.000	Kansas City	0	2	.000

[From Late Editions of Yesterday's Times.]

SOUTHERN ASSOCIATION

(Night Games)

Chattanooga 12, Atlanta 0.
Little Rock 9, New Orleans 1.
Mobile 12, Memphis 7.
Birmingham at Nashville, rain.

STANDING OF THE CLUBS

	W.	L.	PC.		W.	L.	PC.
Chattanooga	4	0	1.000	New Orleans	3	3	.500
Little Rock	4	3	.571	Birmingham	2	3	.400
Atlanta	3	3	.500	Memphis	2	3	.400
Nashville	3	3	.500	Mobile	2	5	.286

[From Late Editions of Yesterday's Times.]

TEXAS LEAGUE

(Night Games)

Houston 4, Beaumont 0.
Oklahoma City 12, Fort Worth 9.
San Antonio 9, Shreveport 8.
Tulsa 5, Dallas 3.

STANDING OF THE CLUBS

	W.	L.	PC.		W.	L.	PC.
Okla. City	4	1	.800	Shreveport	4	3	.571
San Antonio	5	2	.714	Fort Worth	3	4	.429
Tulsa	4	2	.667	Dallas	1	5	.167
Beaumont	4	3	.571	Houston	1	6	.143

PACIFIC COAST LEAGUE

(Thursday Night Games)

Hollywood 5, Los Angeles 0.
Sacramento at Seattle, rain.
San Diego at Portland, rain.
San Francisco at Oakland, rain.

STANDING OF THE CLUBS

	W.	L.	PC.		W.	L.	PC.
Hollywood	12	6	.667	San Francisco	8	8	.500
Los Angeles	11	6	.647	Sacramento	7	8	.467
Seattle	10	6	.625	San Diego	4	12	.250
Portland	9	6	.600	Oakland	4	13	.235

TIGER RALLY IN 9TH HALTS INDIANS, 6-5

Batts' Triple Routing Feller Is the Key Blow—Delsing Wallops Two Homers

DETROIT, April 17 (AP)—Matt Batts, fighting for the No. 1 catching job on the Detroit Tigers, delivered a triple in the bottom of the ninth inning today to pave the Bengals to a 6-5 victory over the Cleveland Indians.

With the Tigers trailing by one run and a runner on second, Batts drove a run-scoring triple to centerfield and, moments later, his relief runner, Freddie Hatfield, skipped home with the winning tally on Owen Friend's fly ball.

Cleveland had scored once in the top of the ninth on Dale Mitchell's run-producing single. But pinch hitter Johnny Pesky walked to start the Tiger ninth. He reached second on a hit-and-run play when Indian shortstop Ray Boone dropped Catcher Jim Hegan's perfect toss.

Then Batts belted his triple and that knocked Bob Feller, the losing pitcher, from the mound.

Relief Pitcher Lou Brissie walked the next two batters to fill the bases and set up a force play at any base. But Friend, foiled the strategy by belting a long fly to center that sent Hatfield home.

Almost forgotten in the ninth inning excitement was a pair of two-run homers by the Tigers' Jim Delsing. He connected in the second and sixth innings.

Dave Madison, who replaced starter Bill Wight during the Indians' four-run rally, in the third, was the winner. It was Feller's first loss to Detroit since July 7, 1950. He had beaten the Tigers seven straight times.

The box score:

CLEVELAND (A.)	ab.	r.	h.	po.	a.
Boone, ss	3	1	0	2	6
Avila, 2b	3	1	0	2	6
Doby, cf	4	1	3	2	0
Easter, 1b	3	1	2	10	0
Glynn, 1b	0	0	0	1	1
Rosen, 3b	4	0	1	0	2
Mitchell, lf	4	0	1	3	0
Kennedy, lf	0	0	0	0	0
Simpson, rf	4	0	1	3	0
Hegan, c	4	0	1	2	2
Feller, p	1	1	0	0	1
Brissie, p	0	0	0	0	0
Total	30	5	9	*25	15

DETROIT (A.)	ab.	r.	h.	po.	a.
Kuenn, ss	4	0	2	5	3
Friend, 2b	4	0	0	5	6
Sullivan, lf	3	0	0	0	0
Dropo, 1b	4	0	0	9	1
Nieman, rf	2	2	0	2	1
Delsing, cf	3	2	2	1	0
B'gartner, 3b	3	0	0	1	3
aPesky	0	1	0	0	0
Batts, c	4	0	2	4	0
bHatfield	0	1	0	0	0
Wight, p	1	0	0	0	0
Madison, p	2	0	1	0	3
cMullin	0	0	0	0	0
dCarswell	0	0	0	0	0
Total	30	6	7	27	17

*One out when winning run was scored.
aWalked for Baumgartner in ninth.
bRan for Batts in ninth.
cAnnounced for Madison in ninth.
dWalked for Mullin in ninth.

Cleveland .... 0 0 4 0 0 0 0 0 1—5
Detroit .... 0 2 0 0 0 2 0 0 2—6

Error—Boone.
Runs batted in — Doby, Easter 2, Rosen, Mitchell, Delsing 4, Batts, Friend.
Two-base hits—Easter, Hegan, Batts. Three-base hit—Batts. Home runs—Delsing 2. Sacrifices—Feller, Glynn. Double plays—Boone, Avila and Easter; Friend, Kuenn and Dropo 2; Baumgartner, Friend and Dropo. Left on bases—Cleveland 10, Detroit 7. Bases on balls—Off Feller 6, Brissie 2, Wight 4, Madison 6. Struck out—By Feller 2, Wight 1, Madison 2. Hits—Off Feller 7 in 8 innings (none out in ninth), Brissie 0 in 1-3, Wight 3 in 2 1-3, Madison 6 in 6 2-3. Runs and earned runs—Off Feller 6 and 5, Wight 4 and 4, Madison 1 and 1. Winning pitcher—Madison (1—0). Losing pitcher—Feller (0—1). Umpires—Napp, Duffy, Grieve and Passarella. Time of game—2:51. Attendance—2,642.

BROWNS DOWN WHITE SOX

St. Louis Gets Five in Seventh for 6-to-4 Triumph

CHICAGO, April 17 (AP) — The Browns chased 36-year-old Joe Dobson in a five-run seventh to whip the White Sox today, 6—4, before 972 hardy fans who braved the gloomy 36-degree weather.

The big inning broke a 1-1 tie after the Sox scored in the fifth following Vic Wertz' first homer of the season in the top half of the frame.

The box score:

ST. LOUIS (A.)	ab.	r.	h.	po.	a.
Groth, cf	5	0	0	3	0
Young, 2b	4	0	2	3	2
Dyck, lf	3	1	0	1	0
Wertz, rf	4	2	2	4	0
Elliott, 3b	4	0	1	1	1
Sievers, 1b	4	1	2	7	1
Moss, c	4	1	2	3	1
Hunter, ss	2	0	0	4	3
Littlefield, p	3	1	0	1	1
Paige, p	1	0	0	0	2
Total	34	6	9	27	11

CHICAGO (A.)	ab.	r.	h.	po.	a.
Fox, 2b	5	0	2	3	4
Fain, 1b	5	0	1	13	0
Minoso, lf	4	1	0	1	0
Stephens, 3b	4	0	0	0	1
Rivera, cf	4	1	3	4	0
Mele, rf	4	1	1	0	0
C'rasquel, ss	4	0	3	4	8
Wilson, c	2	0	1	2	2
cBoyd	0	1	0	0	0
Dobson, p	2	0	0	0	2
Dorish, p	0	0	0	0	0
aKrsnich	0	0	0	0	0
bByrne	1	0	0	0	0
Johnson, p	0	0	0	0	1
dWright	1	0	1	0	0
Total	36	4	12	27	18

aAnnounced for Dorish in seventh.
bFlied out for Krsnich in seventh.
cWalked for Wilson in ninth.
dSingled for Johnson in ninth.

St. Louis .... 0 0 0 0 1 0 5 0 0—6
Chicago .... 0 0 0 0 1 0 1 1 1—4

Errors—Hunter, Wertz, Dobson, Carrasquel.
Runs batted in—Wertz, Elliott, Moss 2, Littlefield, Young, Dobson, Wilson, Rivera, Fox.
Two-base hits—Moss, Fain. Three-base hit—Rivera. Home run—Wertz. Sacrifice—Wilson. Double plays—Carrasquel, Fox and Fain 2; Young, Hunter and Sievers 2. Left on bases—St. Louis 4, Chicago 8. Bases on balls—Off Dobson 2, Dorish 1, Paige 2. Struck out—By Dobson 2, Littlefield 3. Hits—Off Dobson 6 in 6 1-3 innings, Dorish 2 in 2-3, Johnson 1 in 2, Littlefield 9 in 6 1-3, Paige 3 in 2 2-3. Runs and earned runs—Off Dobson 4 and 4, Dorish 2 and 1, Littlefield 2 and 2, Paige 2 and 2. Winning pitcher—Littlefield (1—0). Losing pitcher—Dobson (0—1). Umpires—Summers, Stevens, Robb and Froese. Time of game—2:28. Attendance—972.

Major League Baseball

Saturday, April 18, 1953

National League

YESTERDAY'S GAMES

New York 6, Brooklyn 3 (aft'noon).
Brooklyn 12, New York 4 (night)
Cincinnati 10, Milwaukee 9.
Philadelphia at Pittsburgh (night), rain.
Other clubs not scheduled.

STANDING OF THE CLUBS

	Brooklyn	Milwaukee	New York	Chicago	St. Louis	Cincinnati	Philadel.	Pittsb'gh	Won	Lost	Perc'tage	Games Behind
Bklyn.	—	0	1	0	0	0	0	2	3	1	.750	—
Milw.	0	—	0	0	1	1	0	0	2	1	.667	½
N. Y.	1	0	—	0	0	0	1	0	2	2	.500	1
Chic.	0	0	0	—	0	1	0	0	1	1	.500	1
St. L.	0	0	0	1	—	0	0	0	1	1	.500	1
Cinc.	0	1	0	0	0	—	0	0	1	2	.333	1½
Phila.	0	0	1	0	0	0	—	0	1	2	.333	1½
Pitts.	0	0	0	0	0	0	1	—	1	2	.333	1½
Lost	1	1	2	1	1	2	2	2	—	—		

TODAY'S PROBABLE PITCHERS

Brooklyn at New York (1:30 P. M.)—Erskine (0-0) vs. Connelly (0-0).

Chicago at Cincinnati—Rush (1-0) vs. Wehmeier (0-0).

Milwaukee at St. Louis (night)—Antonelli (0-0) vs. Miller (0-0).

Philadelphia at Pittsburgh—Konstanty (0-0) vs. Friend (0-0).

American League

YESTERDAY'S GAMES

New York 7, Washington 3.
Detroit 6, Cleveland 5.
Philadelphia 5, Boston 0.
St. Louis 6, Chicago 4.

STANDING OF THE CLUBS

	New York	Cleveland	St. Louis	Philadel.	Boston	Chicago	Detroit	Wash'gtn	Won	Lost	Perc'tage	Games Behind
N. Y.	—	0	0	1	0	0	0	2	3	1	.750	—
Cleve.	0	—	0	0	0	1	1	0	2	1	.667	½
St. L.	0	0	—	0	0	1	1	0	2	1	.667	½
Phila.	1	0	0	—	1	0	0	0	2	2	.500	1
Bost.	0	0	0	1	—	0	0	0	1	1	.500	1
Chic.	0	0	1	0	0	—	0	0	1	2	.333	1½
Det.	0	1	0	0	0	0	—	0	1	2	.333	1½
Wash.	0	0	0	0	0	0	0	—	0	2	.000	2
Lost	1	1	1	2	1	2	2	2	—	—		

TODAY'S PROBABLE PITCHERS

New York at Philadelphia—Blackwell (0-0) vs. Scheib (0-0).

Boston at Washington (night)—Freeman (0-0) vs. Masterson (0-0).

Cleveland at Chicago—Wynn (0-0) vs. Byrne (0-0).

St. Louis at Detroit (2)—Pillette (0-0) and Holloman (0-0) vs. Hoeft (0-0) and Marlowe (0-0).

(Figures in parentheses indicate season's won-and-lost records.)

Associated Press Wirephoto

MUSEUM PIECE: If Mickey Mantle didn't quite knock the cover off the ball with that 565-foot home run yesterday in Washington, he gave it a clobbering at any rate. The ball, which Mickey holds, was scuffed in two spots by the time it came to rest in the backyard of a house near Griffith Stadium.

Towering Drive by Yank Slugger Features 7-3 Defeat of Senators

Mantle's 565-Foot Homer at Capital Surpassed Only by Mighty Ruth Wallops

By LOUIS EFFRAT

Special to The New York Times.

WASHINGTON, April 17—Unless and until contrary evidence is presented, recognition for the longest ball ever hit by anyone except Babe Ruth in the history of major league baseball belongs to Mickey Mantle of the Yankees. This amazing 21-year-old athlete today walloped one over the fifty-five-foot high left-field wall at Griffith Stadium. That ball, scuffed in two spots, finally stopped in the backyard of a house, about 565 feet away from home plate.

This remarkable homer, which helped the Yankees register a 7-3 victory over the Senators, was Mickey's first of the season, but he will have to go some, as will anyone else, to match it.

Chuck Stobbs, the Nat southpaw, had just walked Yogi Berra after two out in the fifth, when Mantle strode to the plate. Batting right-handed, Mickey blasted the ball toward left center, where the base of the front bleachers wall is 391 feet from the plate. The distance to the back of the wall is sixty-nine feet more and then the back wall is fifty feet high.

Bounces Out of Sight

Atop that wall is a football scoreboard. The ball struck about five feet above the end of the wall, caromed off the right and flew out of sight. There was no telling how much farther it would have flown had the football board not been there.

Before Mantle, who had cleared the right-field roof while batting left-handed in an exhibition game at Pittsburgh last week (only Babe Ruth and Ted Beard had ever done that) had completed running out the two-run homer, Arthur Patterson of the Yankees' front-office staff was on his way to investigate the measure.

Patterson returned with the following news:

A 10-year-old lad had picked up the ball. He directed Patterson to the backyard of 434 Oakdale Street and pointed to the place where he had found it, across the street from the park. The boy, Donald Dunaway of 343 Elm Street N. W., accepted an undisclosed sum of money for the prize, which was turned over to Mantle. The Yankee was to send a substitute ball, suitably autographed to the boy.

Until today, when Mantle made it more or less easy for Lefty Ed Lopat, who worked eight innings, to gain his first triumph, no other batter had cleared the left-field wall here. Some years ago, Joe DiMaggio bounced a ball over, but Mickey's accomplishment was on the fly.

Longest Bunt as Well

Later in the contest, Mickey dragged a bunt that landed in front of second base and he outsped it for a single. Thus, in the same afternoon, it would appear, the young man from Commerce, Okla., fashioned one of the longest homers and the longest bunt on record.

Everything else that occurred in this contest was dwarfed by Mantle's round-tripper, which traveled 460 feet on the fly. There was a third-inning homer by Bill Martin, which gave the Yankees' the lead.

The Nats tied it against Lopat in the same frame on a single by Wayne Terwilliger, a sacrifice by Stobbs and Eddie Yost's single to left.

However, Hank Bauer doubled and counted on a single by Joe Collins for a 2-1 edge in the fourth then it was that Mickey connected with a fast ball and wrote diamond history. Other things happened, including Tom Gorman's appearance for the last inning, but no one appeared to be interested.

Gone With The Wind

It is true that a strong wind might have helped Mantle, but if the A. A. U. will not recognize the homer, all of baseball will.

Casey Stengel was telling before the game about the great young catching prospect the Yankees have at Kansas City. "Everyone there is raving about Elston Howard," Casey said. Howard is a Negro, who after having come out of the service last summer, played at Muskegon in the Michigan State League.

There is no connection with Stengel's mention of Howard and the fact that Berra, who fanned only a dozen times last season, already has struck out four times this year. Barring injury, it will be quite some time before anyone takes away Yogi's job.

The charley horse in Mantle's left leg did not seem to hamper the lad during batting practice. He put on an electrifying show, hitting against Whitey Ford. Bauer, too, and Jackie Jensen for the Senators smashed long drives into the bleachers.

The Box Score

NEW YORK (A.)	ab.	r.	h.	po.	a.
Martin, 2b	4	1	2	3	4
Rizzuto, ss	5	0	1	3	3
Berra, c	4	1	1	2	2
Mantle, cf	3	1	2	0	0
Bauer, rf	4	2	1	2	0
Woodling, lf	5	1	2	5	0
Collins, 1b	4	0	1	11	1
Carey, 3b	4	1	1	1	1
Lopat, p	4	0	1	0	4
Gorman, p	0	0	0	0	0
Total	37	7	12	27	15

WASHINGTON (A.)	ab.	r.	h.	po.	a.
Yost, 3b	5	0	2	1	4
Busby, cf	4	0	1	4	1
Vernon, 1b	3	0	0	13	1
Jensen, rf	4	0	0	3	0
Runnels, ss	3	1	1	0	2
Wood, lf	4	0	1	2	0
Ter'liger, 2b	4	2	3	2	5
Peden, c	4	0	1	0	1
Stobbs, p	1	0	0	2	1
aHoderlein	1	0	1	0	0
Moreno, p	0	0	0	0	0
bVerble	1	0	0	0	0
Total	34	3	10	27	15

aSingled for Stobbs in seventh.
bFlied out for Moreno in ninth.

New York .... 0 0 1 1 2 0 0 3 0—7
Washington .... 0 0 1 0 0 0 1 1 0—3

Errors—None.
Runs batted in—Martin 2, Yost, Collins, Mantle 2, Hoderlein, Carey, Woodling, Terwilliger.
Two-base hits—Bauer, Terwilliger, Woodling. Home run—Martin, Mantle. Stolen base—Mantle. Sacrifice—Stobbs. Double play—Lopat, Martin and Collins. Left on bases—New York 9, Washington 8. Bases on balls—Off Stobbs 4, Lopat 3, Moreno 2. Struck out—By Lopat 2. Hits—Off Lopat 10 in 8 innings, Stobbs 7 in 7, Gorman 0 in 1, Moreno 5 in 2. Runs and earned runs—Stobbs 4 and 4, Lopat 3 and 3, Moreno 3 and 3. Winning pitcher—Lopat (1—0). Losing pitcher—Stobbs (0—1). Umpires—Honochick, McGowan, Paparella and McKinley. Time of game—2:27. Attendance—4,206.

RUTH HIT HOMER 600 FEET

Detroit Scene of 1926 Blast—Exhibition Drive Went 587

Mickey Mantle's home run in Griffith Stadium yesterday failed by about thirty-five feet to match the homer Babe Ruth hit in Briggs Stadium at Detroit in 1926, according to The Associated Press.

Ruth's blow is considered the longest home run ever hit in a major league game. At the time, H. G. Salsinger, sports editor of The Detroit News, obtained an affidavit from several witnesses, who said the ball landed about 600 feet from home plate.

The Babe also is credited with a 587-footer in a 1919 exhibition game at Tampa, Fla., where Ken Silvestri, now with the Phillies, hit one 538 feet in 1941.

Until Mantle's blast yesterday, Ralph Kiner of the Pirates held second place in regular-season competition. He hit one about 560 feet against Cincinnati at Pittsburgh April 22, 1950.

JERSEY CITY TEAM TAKES MILE RELAY

St. Michael's High Victor in Schoolboy Phase of 7th Seton Hall Competition

By MICHAEL STRAUSS

Special to The New York Times.

NEWARK, April 17—Absent from the ranks of titleholders since 1948, New Jersey finally emerged with an eastern championship contingent this afternoon when St. Michael's High of Jersey City captured the mile relay at the seventh annual Seton Hall Relays at the Newark Schools Stadium. The triumph was the highlight of a schoolboy prelude to the big college competition tomorrow.

Sharing the honors with the New Jersey team today were two schools from New York City, Boys High and Haaren. Boys won the 880-yard relay while Haaren triumphed in the 440 by beating out New Utrecht, a rival from Brooklyn.

The victory of St. Michael's was scored over highly rated combinations from Mount St. Michael and from St. Augustine's, the national indoor champion. The Lancers from Brooklyn, though handicapped by the absence of Frank Kennedy, put up a strong showing and were in contention until the closing stages.

Maliff Is Anchor Man

The St. Michael's quartet was made up of Jack Heraut, Bill Shyne, Richard Wroblewski and Gene Maliff. Heraut found Bob Martin of St. Augustine's a worthy adversary as the race began and trailed at the completion of the first leg. But Shyne took the lead from Tierny O'Rourke of the Brooklyn team. On the third leg, the Mount's Tom Mackey took command and St. Augustine's colors were in third place. But on the final leg Maliff put on a great sprint and was five yards ahead of Bill Krebs at the finish. The time was 3:30.

Boys High, long a power in eastern schoolboy circles, took the half-mile event as expected, Roy Henry finishing with a fine burst. The time was 1:33.4. In the runner-up berth was Brooklyn Tech, followed by Bishop Loughlin and Ferris of Jersey City. Henry's teammates on the winning contingent were John Sylvester, Lowe Murray and Monzell Price.

New Utrecht and Haaren waged a keen struggle for the pace-setting role during most of the running of the 440, but the Manhattanites proved too strong. The margin at the finish was six yards, Donald Showell clinching the decision with a well-run anchor leg to complete the course in 0:44.2. Strung out behind the two leaders at the end were East New York Vocational and Abraham Lincoln of Brooklyn.

Three Records Are Set

Three new records were set in sectional competition over the mile route.

A Kearny quartet from the Hudson County division was clocked in 3:33.6; St. Cecilia of Englewood registered 3:34.7 in the New Jersey Catholic Schools competition and Tenafly posted 3:35.4 in capturing first place among Bergen County schools.

Adding to the length of the program were events for parochial, grammar and junior high school students. The youngsters went through their heats and finals in a businesslike manner and gave added support to the general feeling that New Jersey has become extremely track conscious. More than 100 schools were represented in today's competition.

The last New Jersey school to win an eastern relay title here was St. Peter's of Jersey City. The Hudson County team took the mile in 1948 with an effort of 3:33.2. Since then Loughlin, New Rochelle and Cardinal Hayes have been the champions.

THE SUMMARIES

EASTERN CHAMPIONSHIPS

440-Yard Relay—1, Haaren (Richard Habersham, Henry Burchett, George Waterman and Donald Showell); 2, New Utrecht; 3, East New York Vocational; 4, Abraham Lincoln. Time—0:44.2.

880-Yard Relay—1, Boys High (John Sylvester, Lowe Murray, Monzell Price and Roy Henry); 2, Brooklyn Technical; 3, Bishop Loughlin; 4, Ferris of Jersey City. Time—1:33.4.

One-Mile Relay—1, St. Michael's of Jersey City (Jack Heraut, William Shyne, Richard Wroblewski and Gene Maliff); 2, Mt. St. Michael; 3, St. Augustine's; 4, Boys High. Time—3:30.

SECTIONAL MILE EVENTS

Hudson County—1, Kearny (C. Rittman, W. Pfeifer, J. McLaren and J. Norton); 2, Bayonne; 3, Memorial of West New York; 4, Snyder of Jersey City. Time—3:33.6 (New record. Old record of 3:34 set by Kearny in 1952).

N. J. Catholic High Schools—1, St. Peter's of Jersey City (John Hanlon, Ted Riordan, George Bednar and Tom Costello); 2, Seton Hall; 3, St. Michael's of Jersey City; 4, St. Cecilia. Time—3:34.7 (New record. Old mark of 3:39.3 set by Seton Hall in 1951).

Central New Jersey—Trenton Central (Melvin Rose, Hy Bronner, Carl Cranmer and William McMillan); 2, Asbury Park; 3, Princeton; 4, Perth Amboy. Time—3:40.8.

Middlesex County—1, Perth Amboy (Cedric Richardson, Arthur Graham, Randolph Grant and Robert Holup); 2, New Brunswick; 3, Metuchen; 4, Highland Park. Time—3:41.

Shore Conference—1, Neptune (Don Harvey, Donald Eckart, Joseph Taylor and Michael Buchanan); 2, Long Branch; 3, Matawan; 4, Asbury Park. Time—3:45.9.

Bergen County—1, Tenafly (Hugh Cameron, Don Schive, William Davis and Arthur Mangels); 2, Englewood; 3, Lyndhurst; 4, St. Mary's of Rutherford. Time—3:35.4 (New record. Old Record of 3:37.2 set by Tenafly in 1951).

City of Newark—1, St. Benedict's (Wayne Letwink, Paul Longua, Ronald Buckingham and John Connolly); 2, West Side; 3, Weequahic; 4, East Side. Time—3:36.4.

Essex County—1, Montclair (Marvin Jones, Lowell Lockett, Peter Johnson and Aubrey Lewis); 2, Columbia; 3, Bloomfield; 4, Orange. Time—3:32.4.

Browns Sell Fannin

ST. LOUIS, April 17 (AP)—The Browns today sold Cliff Fannin, pitcher, to San Diego of the Pacific Coast League for an undisclosed amount. Fannin, who came to the Browns in 1945 from Toledo, is a 28-year-old right hander. He failed to win a game in 1952 while losing two.

Bobo Olson 3-1 Favorite To Defeat Paddy Young For U.S. Crown

Yankees Zero Browns Twice Behind Lopat And McDonald

New York, June 18—(AP)—Southpaw Edddie Lopat and righthander Jim McDonald pitched the New York Yankees to 5-0 and 3-0 shutout victories over the St. Louis Browns today as the world champions increased their huge first place margin over the Cleveland Indians to 11 games.

Lopat went all the way, scattering eight singles for his eighth triumph without a defeat in the opener of the doubleheader witnessed by 15,593 spectators. McDonald permitted just four hits but hurled only seven innings with Tom Gorman retiring the final six batters. Although Mc Donald was pitching runless ball, Yankee Manager Casey Stengel saw fit to remove him for a pinch hitter in the seventh.

Billy Martin had given the Yanks a 1-0 lead with a home run belt off Bob Cain in the sixth. The Yanks got another run in the seventh on three straight singles by Hank Bauer, Gene Woodling and Charlie Silvera to finish Cain.

With runners on first and second, one out and Satchel Paige on the mound, Stengel inserted Johnny Mize to pinch hit for McDonald. The veteran tapped back to the mound but Paige's throw to second was late to load the bases. Martin's single drove in Woodling but Paige retired the next two batters without further trouble.

(First Game)

ST. LOUIS	ab	h	o	a	NEW YORK	ab	h	o	a
Groth,cf	4	2	2	0	Martin,2b	4	2	4	2
Hunter,ss	4	1	2	2	Collins,1b	4	1	11	0
Dyck,3b	4	0	1	2	Bauer,rf	4	2	3	0
Wertz,rf	4	0	4	0	Mantle,cf	3	1	3	0
Sievers,1b	4	2	5	1	M'Doug'd,3b	4	1	0	6
Lenhardt,lf	4	0	2	0	Berra,c	3	1	2	0
Moss,c	4	1	4	0	Woodling,lf	2	0	3	0
Young,2b	3	2	3	3	Miranda,ss	4	1	1	3
Littlefield,p	1	0	1	0	Lopat,p	4	1	0	2
Stuart,p	1	0	0	0					
Totals	33	8	24	8	Totals	32	10	27	13

St. Louis .... 000 000 000—0
New York .... 001 021 10x—5

R—Martin, Bauer, Mantle, McDougald, Miranda. E—Martin. RBI—Bauer, Mantle 2, Collins, Berra. 2B—Bauer 2, McDougald, Berra, Lopat. HR—Mantle. S—Littlefield. DP—Hunter, Young and Sievers; Dyck, Young and Sievers; McDougald, Martin and Collins. Left—St. Louis 7, New York 10. BB—Littlefield 6. SO—Littlefield 4, Lopat 2. HO—Littlefield 9 in 6 1-3; Stuart 1 in 1 2-3. R and ER—Littlefield 5-5, Stuart 0-0, Lopat 0-0. HBP—by Littlefield (Berra). W—Lopat (8-0). L—Littlefield (3-6). U—Froese, Napp, Passarella, Grieve. T—2:06.

(Second Game)

ST. LOUIS	ab	h	o	a	NEW YORK	ab	h	o	a
Groth,cf	4	0	5	0	Martin,2b	4	2	0	3
Kokos,lf	4	2	2	0	Collins,1b	4	1	13	0
Sievers,1b	4	1	6	0	M'Doug'd,3b	4	0	0	1
Wertz,rf	4	1	2	0	Mantle,cf	3	1	3	0
Dyck,3b	3	0	0	2	Bauer,rf	4	1	4	2
Courtney,c	1	0	5	2	Woodling,lf	3	1	0	0
Young,2b	3	0	3	2	Silvera,c	3	1	5	0
Hunter,ss	3	0	1	2	Miranda,ss	2	1	2	6
Cain,p	1	0	0	0	McDonald,p	2	0	0	1
Paige,p	0	0	0	0	b-Mize	1	0	0	0
a-Edwards	1	0	0	0	c-Renna	0	0	0	0
Stuart,p	0	0	0	0	Gorman,p	0	0	0	1
Totals	28	4	24	8	Totals	30	8	27	14

a—Flied out for Paige in 8th.
b—Safe on fielder's choice for McDonald in 7th.
c—Ran for Mize in 7th.

St. Louis .... 000 000 000—0
New York .... 000 001 20x—3

R—Martin, Bauer, Silvera. E—None. RBI—Martin 2, Silvera. 2B—Kokos. HR—Martin. DP—Hunter, Young and Sievers; Bauer and Collins; Martin, Miranda and Collins. Left—St. Louis 4, New York 6. BB—Cain 2, Paige 1, McDonald 2. SO—Cain 3, Stuart 1, McDonald 2, Gorman 1. HO—Cain 7 in 6 (faced 3 batters in 7th); Paige 1 in 1; Stuart 0 in 1; McDonald 4 in 7; Gorman 0 in 2. R and ER—Cain 3-3, Paige 0-0, Stuart 0-0, McDonald 0-0, Gorman 0-0. HBP—by McDonald (Courtney). W—McDonald (3-2). L—Cain (1-3). U—Napp, Passarella, Grieve, Froese. T—2:09. A—15,953.

Koslo Gets First Victory As Giants Beat Redlegs 6-3

Cincinnati, June 18—(AP)—The New York Giants made it three out of four today over the Cincinnati Redlegs and gave pitcher Dave Koslo his first victory of the season. The Giants won 6-3.

The southpaw needed the help of Hoyt Wilhelm in the sixth inning, however, to get over the hump. He had lost six games. It was Wilhelm's 31st appearance this year. He allowed only one hit in the last 3 1/3 innings. It was his third appearance, too, in the series.

Jackie Collum, little left hander, was the loser for the Cincinnati club. He was blasted from the mound in the eighth when the Giants put the game on ice with two more runs to bring the total to six. Ted Kluszewski hit his 18th home run of the season for Cincinnati.

NEW YORK	ab	h	o	a	CINCINNATI	ab	h	o	a
Lockman,lf	5	0	4	0	Temple,2b	3	2	3	6
Dark,ss	5	1	3	7	b-Marshall	1	0	0	0
Thomson,cf	5	2	1	0	Bridges,2b	0	0	0	0
Irvin,rf	4	3	1	1	Adams,3b	5	0	1	2
a-Gomez	0	0	0	0	Bell,cf	5	1	2	0
Mueller,rf	0	0	0	0	Greenr's,lf	5	1	2	0
Spencer,3b	3	2	1	0	Klusze'ski,1b	4	2	9	1
Williams,2b	3	0	4	4	Borko'ski,rf	4	2	0	0
Gilbert,1b	3	1	9	0	Seminick,c	3	1	7	0
Westrum,c	2	0	2	0	McMillan,ss	4	1	2	2
Noble,c	2	1	2	0	Collum,p	3	2	0	1
Koslo,p	2	0	0	1	Smith,p	0	0	0	0
Wilhelm,p	2	0	0	0	c-Marquis	1	0	0	0
					King,p	0	0	1	0
Totals	36	10	27	13	Totals	38	12	27	12

a—Ran for Irvin in 8th.
b—Grounded out for Temple in 8th.
c—Hit into force play for Smith in 8th.

New York .... 100 300 020—6
Cincinnati .... 000 102 000—3

R—Dark, Thomson 2, Irvin, Spencer, Williams, Kluszewski, Borkowski, McMillan. E—None. RBI—Irvin 2, Spencer 2, Gilbert, Temple 2, Kluszewski. 2B—Thomson, Dark, Spencer. 3B—Spencer. HR—Kluszewski. SB—Williams, Gilbert. DP—Irvin and Gilbert; Temple, McMillan and Kluszewski. Left—New York 6, Cincinnati 10. BB—Koslo 1, Collum 1, Smith 1, Wilhelm 1. SO—Koslo 2, Collum 3, Smith 2, Wilhelm 1. HO—Koslo 11 in 5 2-3; Collum 9 in 7 (faced 3 batters in 8th); Smith 1 in 1; Wilhelm 1 in 3 1-2. R and ER—Koslo 3-3, Collum 6-6, Smith 0-0, King 0-0, Wilhelm 0-0. HBP—by Collum (Spencer). W—Koslo (1-6). L—Collum (1-2). U—Boggess, Engeln, Stewart and Pinelli. T—2:34. A—2,610.

Fights Tonight

At New York (Madison Square Garden): Paddy Young, New York, vs. Carl (Bobo) Olson, San Francisco, middles, 15 (American middleweight championship); at Eureka, Calif., Archie Whitewater, Oakland, Calif., vs. Jimmy McCoy, Eureka, welters, ten.

The Sportlight

By Grantland Rice

New York, June 19—No one can doubt any longer that Native Dancer is the horse of the year. His only challenger is Greentree's Tom Fool, another magnificent animal. But the full story of Native Dancer and Tom Fool is yet to be written through the summer and fall season on ahead when they begin to carry more and more weight. Ben Jones was raving about Whirlaway until they began to beat him by piling on poundage.

"I don't care who the horse is or what the horse is," Ben said once, "but run him often enough with an increasing weight burden and he's going to get licked."

Man o' War

Man o' War quit as a three-year-old. So did Colin. Citation made his best record during his second and third years, he won 19 of 20 starts for a total of $709,470 as a three-year-old. Citation was out of action as a four-year-old due to injuries.

Up to this point in their respective careers Citation and Native Dancer are about level. Native Dancer has yet to finish his third year and show how much weight he can carry. Colin never carried 130 pounds. Man o' War carried 130 pounds six times as a two-year-old and as high as 135 pounds and 138 pounds as a three-year-old.

He carried 138 pounds in 1920 in the Potomac Handicap at Havre de Grace. He finished with 20 victories and one second. He ran three times at bookmaker's odds of 1 to 100 as a three-year-old.

In my book the top horse of all time was Old Bones, Exterminator.

In 1922, when he was seven years old, he won six races in a row—all handicap races—from six furlongs to a mile a quarter. For those six races he carried 133, 133, 138, 133, 135 and 135 pounds. Exterminator carried from 130 to 140 pounds 33 times in various races.

Suppose they put 140 pounds on some of the horses today? It will make a big difference when Native Dancer and Jamie K. begin to pack on more and more weight.

Winfrey Knows His Horse

Bill Winfrey, who has done a marvelous job with the Dancer, expects to let him run and Bill will know better than anyone else how much of a load he wants his famous horse to carry. Ben Jones has said repeatedly that 130 pounds is enough weight to put on any horse. Others disagree. I don't know how Bill Winfrey feels about it.

Al Vanderbilt had another great horse who carried a heavy load at almost every trip. This was Discovery. There are three big tests for any thoroughbred. How fast he can move, how far he can run, how much weight he can carry. Neither Native Dancer nor Jamie K. have yet had a chance to show the weight angle, but this will come later on.

The appearance of these horses will be a big shot in the arm for summer and fall racing, provided they have a goodly share of racing luck and don't suffer an illness or injury. After all, a thoroughbred is a very delicate animal as you may recall from the last two Derby winners, Hill Gail and Dark Star.—(NANA)

Musial Bats Cards Over Brooklyn 12-4

St. Louis, June 18—(AP)—A revived Stan Musial and the home run hitting of Solly Hemus, Rip Repulski and Ray Jablonski carried the St. Louis Cardinals to an easy 12-4 victory over Brooklyn's Dodgers today to give the Redbirds a sweep of the three-game series.

The triumph moved St. Louis to within three games of the second place Brooks, who fell three games behind league-leading Milwaukee, idled by rain.

Stan The Man, deep in a batting slump, drove in four Cardinal runs, three of them on a bases-loaded double in the second inning off losing pitcher Carl Erskine. Musial also doubled in the first inning, giving him a total of four two-base hits and five RBI's in two days against the Brooks.

Hemus was the first to hit for the distance among the Cards' power threesome, slugging his seventh home run of the season with a man on base in the fourth. The swat gave St. Louis a 6-0 lead and put Erskine on the run. It was the third defeat in 11 decisions for the Brook [illegible] who usually is a toughie against [illegible] Cards.

BROOKLYN	ab	h	o	a	ST. LOUIS	ab	h	o	a
Gilliam,2b	5	2	1	3	Hemus,ss	4	2	2	4
Reese,ss	5	1	1	2	Schoen'st,2b	4	3	1	2
Snider,cf	5	2	4	0	Musial,lf	4	2	2	0
Robinson,lf	3	0	2	0	Slaughter,rf	3	0	3	0
Branca,p	0	0	0	1	Jablonski,3b	4	2	0	2
a-Walker	1	1	0	0	Castigl'ne,3b	1	1	1	0
b-Podres	0	0	0	0	Bilko,1b	4	1	9	2
Hughes,p	0	0	0	0	Repulski,cf	5	1	2	0
Hodges,1b	3	1	7	1	Rice,c	3	0	5	0
Campan'la,c	3	0	6	0	Haddix,p	2	0	1	0
Morgan,3b	3	2	1	0	White,p	1	0	1	1
Anton'lo,rf,lf	3	0	0	0					
c-Shuba,lf	1	0	0	0					
Erskine,p	1	0	1	1					
Furillo,rf	3	1	1	0					
Totals	36	10	24	8	Totals	35	12	27	11

a—Singled for Branca in 8th.
b—Ran for Walker in 8th.
c—Lined out for Antonello in 8th.

Brooklyn .... 000 030 010—4
St. Louis .... 130 210 32x—12

R—Gilliam, Podres, Morgan, Furillo, Hemus 3, Schoendienst 3, Jablonski 2, Bilko, Repulski, Rice, Haddix. E—Jablonski, Antonello. RBI—Jablonski 2, Musial 4, Hemus 2, Repulski 3, Castiglione, Gilliam 3, Morgan. 2B—Musial 2, Snider, Morgan. HR—Hemus, Gilliam, Jablonski, Repulski. DP—Hemus, Schoendienst and BILKO; Bilko, Hemus and White; Gilliam, Reese and Hodges. Left—Brooklyn 8, St. Louis 7. BB—Erskine 4, Branca 1, Hughes 1, Haddix 3. SO—Erskine 4, Branca 1, Hughes 1, Haddix 5. HO—Erskine 5 in 4; Branca 5 in 3; Hughes 2 in 1; Haddix 6 in 5 (faced one man in 6th); White 4 in 4. R and ER—Erskine 6-6, Branca 4-4, Hughes 2-2, Haddix 3-2, White 1-1. HPB—by Erskine (Haddix), Hughes (Hemus). W—Haddix (8-3). L—Erskine (5-3).

700 Boys Parade Saturday To Open PAL Baseball Play

Police Athletic League youngsters—700 of 'em—will congregate Saturday afternoon at Derby Avenue and Boulevard where they will march with a snappy fife and drum corps to Yale Field to open their baseball season.

The boys' many colored jerseys will make a colorful backdrop as they parade around the field. Then they will wait for two very important motions.

First—Mayor William C. Celentano's throwing of the first ball—then the cry "Play Ball!" which will herald another season.

After feature games Saturday afternoon, the regular season opens Sunday with four games scheduled at various parks. All games are in the 16-year old group and will start at 2 P. M.

Sunday's schedule: St,. Patrick's vs. Morris Cove at Yale Field; Johnson Cardinals vs. Westville at Waterside Park No. 1; Hill Braves vs. Jets at Kimberly Park No. 2; and St. Joseph's vs Colonial's at Rice Field No. 3.

Pratt & Read Wins

Pratt & Read of North Haven won its third straight victory in the Wallingford softball league last night at Walco Park by defeating American Cyanamid, 27-6, behind pitcher Stan Bialobrceski. Jim Dempsey with a pair of triples and two doubles led the winners at the plate.

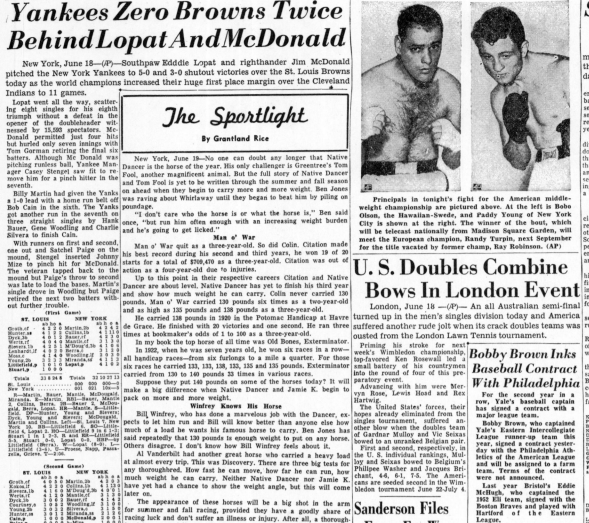

Principals in tonight's fight for the American middleweight championship are pictured above. At the left is Bobo Olson, the Hawaiian-Swede, and Paddy Young of New York City is shown at the right. The winner of the bout, which will be telecast nationally from Madison Square Garden, will meet the European champion, Randy Turpin, next September for the title vacated by former champ, Ray Robinson. (AP)

U. S. Doubles Combine Bows In London Event

London, June 18 —(AP)— An all Australian semi-final turned up in the men's singles division today and America suffered another rude jolt when its crack doubles teams was ousted from the London Lawn Tennis tournament.

Priming his stroke for next week's Wimbledon championship, top-favored Ken Rosewall led a small battery of his countrymen into the round of four of this preparatory event.

Advancing with him were Mervyn Rose, Lewis Hoad and Rex Hartwig.

The United States' forces, their hopes already eliminated from the singles tournament, suffered another blow when the doubles team of Gardnar Mulloy and Vic Seixas bowed to an unranked Belgian pair.

First and second, respectively, in the U. S. individual rankings, Mulloy and Seixas bowed to Belgium's Philipee Washer and Jacques Brichant, 4-6, 6-1, 7-5. The Americans are seeded second in the Wimbledon tournament June 22-July 4.

Sanderson Files Entry For West Haven Tourney

Albert R. Sanderson, New Haven city amateur champion, has filed entry for the first annual Town of West Haven golf championship tourney to be held Monday at the Wepawaug Country Club, Orange, it was announced yesterday by Artie Crouse, tourney director and member of the Recreation Division of the West Haven Park Department, sponsors of the event.

Sanderson, a resident of Blohm Street, is enjoying a good season as only Tuesday he was medalist at Wethersfieled Country Club in the qualifying tournament for the state amateur championship and also won the three-way play-off for the Tournament of Champions title staged by the Hartford Courant.

The event will consist of 18-holes of medal golf and there will be gross and net prizes. Entrants may tee off from 8 A. M. to 1:30 P. M. and requests for starting times should be sent to the West Haven Recreation Office. Post entries will be accepted.

Storms Seek Bookings

The Derby Storms, sponsored by the Storms Engine Company Fire Department, are seeking baseball games with teams in New Haven under the age 16 bracket. The Storms are completely uniformed and play all home games at Coon Hollow Park. Interested managers are invited to contact Joseph Bemanto Jr., 45 Fifth Street, Derby. Telephone Derby 4-7487.

Bobby Brown Inks Baseball Contract With Philadelphia

For the second year in a row, Yale's baseball captain has signed a contract with a major league team.

Bobby Brown, who captained Yale's Eastern Intercollegiate League runner-up team this year, signed a contract yesterday with the Philadelphia Athletics of the American League and will be assigned to a farm team. Terms of the contract were not announced.

Last year Bristol's Eddie McHugh, who captained the 1952 Eli team, signed with the Boston Braves and played with Hartford of the Eastern League.

He is a native of Charlotte, Mich. Brown is 21 years old, stands five feet 10 inches and weighs about 180 pounds.

Brown was an outstanding student at Yale and was elected to Phi Beta Kappa, student honorary fraternity, and to Sigma Xi, national scientific honorary society.

Middlefield Lad Gets Trial With Milwaukee Club

Middletown, June 18—(AP)—One day after his graduation from Woodrow Wilson High School here, 17-year-old Joe Jay of the Rockfall section of Middlefield left today for Milwaukee to see if the Milwaukee Braves of the National League want him to play ball for them.

Accompanying the 220-pound, six-foot, four inch athlete were his parents, Mr. and Mrs. Joseph Jay Sr., and Mr. and Mrs. John Pulley of Meriden. Pulley is a scout for the Braves hereabouts.

The Braves have promised they will take a good look at Jay.

Whether they'll look at his pitching or his hitting wasn't specified.

Jay had a 4-1 record on the mound this season for Woodrow Wilson, and he's also a power hitter.

Tags Play Tonight

The Roessler Yellow Tags will oppose Fritzie's Colored Giants tonight at 6:15 at Blake Field.

Satch Paige Stole The Show

New York, June 18—(AP)—The New York Yankees' winning string was snipped at 18 games, one short of the league record, by the St. Louis Browns a couple of nights ago, but it might have been worse. It might have been the woeful Detroit Tigers who did the snipping.

As interesting as the result, though, was the show put on by that ambulating—just barely—antique known personally in practically every whistle-stop in the country as Satchel Paige.

Now Satch didn't start the game. He didn't even win it. His presence was the result of Brownie manager Marty Marion out-hunching that renowned huncher, Casey Stengel.

It was this way. In the eighth inning the Browns were leading, 3-1, with one down in the Yankee half of the eighth. Billy Martin was on first, having singled, and the count was two balls and no strikes on Joe Collins.

Duane Pillette had been pitching fine ball for the Brownies, and he had been in much tougher spots. But Marion had a hunch. He went to the mound, and looked toward the bullpen far out in left field.

A lone figure disentangled itself from the little group out there, stepped over the low fence and headed toward the mound. It wasn't exactly a march, although there was a certain dignity in the shuffling advance.

His pants legs dangled almost to his ankles, his shirt hung on his bony shouldres like tired bunting the day after a celebration. Old Satch never was much for sartorial splendor on a ball field.

He finally made it, and the little greeting party on the mound dissolved to leave him standing there alone. He took his warmup pitches then stood back and rubbed his hands with the rosin bag. You could almost hear his mind ticking, as if he was thinking: "Well, so you want a little action, hey, boys?"

He twiched his shoulders, scratched the back of his neck, then stood there staring at Collins. Finally he was ready to pitch. His first effort was a ball, and the count was three and nothing on Collins.

Satch was unperturbed. His next was a strike, and then Collins popped out. Irv Noren was up next. Satch casually threw him three balls, then two strikes: Noren then popped out, and Satch shuffled toward the dugout.

With nobody on base at the start of the Yankee ninth, Satch gave it the works. He went into that long, slow-motion windup, and occasionally slipped a semi-blooper pitch. He got Mickey Mantle when Mickey bunted foul on a third strike. An action which bewildered Paige no little and caused him to blurt later: "Why for that boy try to that?"

Berra popped out, but Gene Woodling singled. Satch just scratched his ancient noggin, and went to work on Gil McDougald. He squawked at the umpire when what he thought was a third strike was called a ball, but finally got Gil to pop up on a three-two pitch.

That was it. Satch, his day's work over, shuffled toward the dugout like a tired laborer going home at the end of a hard day.

A remarkable gent is this ageless campaigner. No situation he might face can possibly be new to him, and he takes everything in the same easy, shuffling stride.

So the Yankees had an 18-game winning streak ended, the Brownies had a 14-game losing streak ended, Johnny Mize got his 2,000th base hit, and Whitey Ford lost his first game as a starting pitcher. Yet old Satchmo just about stole the show.

Sox Get 17 In 7th For Mark; Win 23-3

Boston, June 18—(AP)—The Boston Red Sox broke the majors' modern record for one-inning scoring by blasting three Detroit relief pitchers for 17 runs in the seventh today while overwhelming the hapless Tigers, 23-3.

The terrific scoring splurge, generated by 14 hits and six bases on balls, wiped out the 15-run mark set by the Brooklyn Dodgers last season and one shy of the all-time record set by the Chicago Cubs 70 years ago.

Gene Stephens set a modern individual record by banging out a double and two singles during his three successful batting tries in that furious frame. Sammy White and Tom Umphlett placed themselves in the record books by reaching thrice, each on two singles and a base on balls.

Dropo Homer

It is likely that baseball statisticians, given the required time for research, will discover several other new marks made as the Red Sox gorged themselves at the expense of such luckless relief flingers as Steve Gromek, Dick Weik and Earl Harrist.

George Kell, who got a double his first time up in the seventh, finally retired the Red Sox by flying out for the second time in the inning. Johnny Lipton struck out for the initial putout.

Among the 14 hits in the savage seventh was Dick Gernert's three-run homer.

During the lop-sided game, the Red Sox totaled 27 hits for a total of 32 bases and collected nine walks from the four rival flingers.

While suffering such humiliation, the Tigers managed to connect safely seven times against three Boston pitchers. Walt Dropo accounted for three hits, one his fifth homer of the season, a two-run affair.

DETROIT	ab	h	o	a	BOSTON	ab	h	o	a
Kuenn,ss	4	1	1	0	Goodman,2b	4	4	5	1
Pesky,2b	3	0	2	0	b-Lepcio,2b	1	1	3	1
Boone,3b	3	0	4	2	Piersall,rf	5	2	1	0
Nieman,rf	3	1	1	0	c-Zarilla,rf	1	1	0	0
Delsing,cf	3	1	0	0	Gernert,1b	5	2	5	2
Dropo,1b	4	3	7	0	Baker,3b	3	1	1	0
Batts,c	4	1	6	0	Kinder,p	4	2	0	3
Lund,rf	4	0	3	0	White,c	6	4	5	0
Garver,p	1	0	0	3	Stephens,lf	6	3	3	0
Gromek,p	1	0	0	1	Umphlett,cf	5	3	2	1
Weik,p	0	0	0	0	Lipon,ss	4	2	2	5
Harrist,p	0	0	0	0	Grissom,p	1	0	0	1
a-Mullin	1	0	0	0	Freeman,p	1	1	0	0
					Kell,3b	4	1	0	1
Totals	31	7	24	6	Totals	50	27	27	15

a—Flied out for Harrist in 9th.
b—Ran for Goodman in 7th.
c—Walked for Piersall in 7th.

Detroit .... 000 201 0 00—3
Boston .... 030 002 (17)1x—23

R—Boone, Delsing, Dropo, Goodman 2, Lepcio 2, Piersall, Zarilla, Gernert 2, Kinder 2, White 4, Stephens 3, Umphlett 2, Lipon 3, Kell. E—Pesky, Kuenn, Nieman 2, Boone. RBI—Lipon 3, Goodman 2, Piersall 3, Umphlett 3, Gernert 4, Stephens 3, Kinder 2, White 2, Dropo 2, Delsing. 2B—Kell, Stephens. HR—Dropo, Gernert. SB—Stephens. S—Goodman, Nieman. DP—Kell, Lepcio and Gernert. Left—Detroit 6, Boston 13. BB—Garver 2, Gromek 3, Weik 1, Harrist 3, Grissom 2, Freeman 1, Kinder 1. SO—Garver 3, Gromek 2, Harrist 1, Grissom 1, Freeman 1, Kinder 1. HO—Garver 10 in 5 1-3, Gromek 7 in 1, Weik 3 in 1-3, Harrist 7 in 1 1-3, Grissom 0 in 3, Freeman 2 in 2, Kinder 5 in 4. R and ER—Garver 5-4, Gromek 9-9, Weik 4-4, Harrist 5-5, Grissom 0-0, Freeman 2-2, Kinder 1-1. WP—Weik. W—Kinder (4-1). L—Garver (5-6). U—Hurley, Soar, Rommel, Berry. T—3:03. A—3,108.

Bob Rush Paces Chicago Cubs 8-4 Over Pittsburgh

Chicago, June 18—(AP)—Big Bob Rush, idle since June 2 with a sore arm, needed home-run assistance and the reliefing of ancient Dutch Leonard for an 8-4 Chicago Cub victory over the Pittsburgh Pirates today.

It was the third straight victory for last-place Chicago.

Shortstop Tommy Brown clouted a three-run homer in the third, his first of the season, and Hank Sauer smashed his No. 7 circuit clout in the fifth to provide Chicago's victory cushion.

PITTSBURGH	ab	h	o	a	CHICAGO	ab	h	o	a
Abrams,rf	4	1	1	0	Baumholz,cf	3	1	4	0
J.O'Brien,2b	4	1	3	2	c-Jeffcoat,cf	0	0	1	0
Cole,2b	1	0	0	1	Brown,ss	4	1	2	2
Smith,1b	3	0	8	0	Kiner,lf	3	0	0	0
Herma'ski,lf	4	0	4	0	Metko'ch,lf	0	0	0	0
O'Connell,3b	4	3	0	2	Sauer,rf	4	2	0	0
Atwell,c	4	1	2	0	Fondy,1b	4	1	9	2
Bernier,cf	3	2	5	0	Jackson,3b	4	2	2	3
E.O'Brien,ss	4	1	1	5	Garagiola,c	4	1	6	0
Hall,p	1	0	0	0	Miksis,2b	4	1	0	2
Schultz,p	1	0	0	0	Rush,p	2	1	1	3
a-Thomas	1	0	0	0	Leonard,p	0	0	2	0
Friend,p	0	0	0	0					
Dickson,p	0	0	0	0					
b-Pellagrini	1	0	0	0					
Totals	35	9	24	10	Totals	32	10	27	12

a—Popped out for Schultz in 7th.
b—Struck out for Dickson in 9th.
c—Ran for Baumholtz in 7th.

Pittsburgh .... 000 100 120—4
Chicago .... 003 410 00x—8

R—Smith, O'Connell, Atwell, Bernier, Baumholtz, Brown, Sauer 2, Fondy, Jackson, Miksis, Rush. E—Sauer, Bernier. RBI—Brown 3, Bernier 2, Jackson 2, Miksis, Rush, Sauer, Abrams, Atwell. 2B—J. O'Brien, Fondy, Atwell. 3B—Jackson. HR—Brown, Sauer. SB—Miksis. DP—E. O'Brien, J. O'Brien and Smith 2; Jackson and Fondy. Left—Pittsburgh 7, Chicago 3. BB—Hall 1, Rush 3, Friend 2. SO—Hall 1, Schultz 1, Rush 3, Leonard 1. HO—Hall 6 in 3 (pitched to three batters in 4th); Rush 5 in 6 (pitched to two batters in 7th); Schultz 3 in 3; Friend 0 in 1; Dickson 1 in 1; Leonard 4 in 3. R and ER—Hall 6-6, Schultz 2-2, Rush 2-2, Friend 0-0, Dickson 0-0, Leonard 2-2. PB—Garagiola. Balk—Rush. W—Rush (4-6). L—Hall (2-3). U—Jackowski, Gore, Ballanfant, Barlick. T—2:17.

Mendell Named To Yale Post

(Continued from Page 1)

bringing about increasing student participation in intramural sports.

Present-day Yale reflects his vision and administrative capacities of 30 years ago in more ways than one. In addition to an active intramural program which has grown during the intervening years, it was during Mr. Mendell's chairmanship that the Yale Bowl was completed, the Lapham Field House and the Cook Boat House erected, and the Yale Golf Course built.

In 1926 he was named Dean of Yale College at a time when Yale was undergoinig a tremendous physical expansion with a reorganization of the curriculum. As Dean, he worked closely with the late President James Rowland Angell in the planning and reorganization of these projects. He retired as Dean in 1937 to devote full time to teaching and research.

Among other aspects of Mr. Mendell's active career, he is known as one of the nation's leading Latin scholars.

Uncovered Manuscripts

During his lifetime he has uncovered five hitherto unknown manuscripts of works by the Latin historian Tacitus, and his Tacitus library, presented to Yale in 1932, is one of the finest in the world.

For his distinction in his several fields, and for his wide service to Yale, Mr. Mendell was the recipient of an honorary Doctor of Laws degree at Yale's recent 252nd Commencement Exercises.

President Griswold's citation read:

"As teacher and administrator at Yale and in the Navy you perfected the art of frightening professors and admirals while giving confidence to students and ensigns, but the honor and affection of the Yale family are yours."

Served In Two Wars

The reference to the Navy was to Mr. Mendell's participation in two world wars.

In 1918 he held a civilian position in France with the U. S. Army Intelligence Service for counter-espionage work and, after the Armistice, was an Assistant to the American Commission at the Paris Conference.

In World War II he was commissioned a Lieutenant Commander and later Commander in the U. S. Navy and assigned as Officer-in-charge of the Naval Air Combat Intelligence School and as Coordinator of Training at the Naval Air Station at Quonset, Rhode Island. For his war work he received the Legion of Merit.

Mr. Mandell was born in Norwood, Mass., on June 3, 1883, the son of the Rev. and Mrs. Ellis and Clara Whittlesey Mendell. He received his B.A. degree in 1904, his M.A. and Ph.D. degrees in 1905 and 1910, all from Yale.

His views on athletics are well known since he has defended the place of intercollegiate sports in a college education with as mu[ch] vigor as he has always used [in] arguing to give Latin and t[he] Classics a place in that same ed[u]cation.

"In competitive sport," he sa[id] years ago, "judgment und[er] stress, quick thinking, self-con[fi]dence against odds, cooperati[on] action, sportsmanlike respect [for] the rights of the other man a[nd] the rules of games — all these a[re] tested under expert observatio[n]. The competitions of life are d[if]ferent and often more severe, b[ut] in the laboratory of sport, the e[vi]dence is clear and the lessons a[re] lasting."

Middleweights Meet Tonight In New York

Record Boosts Hawaiian—Winner To Oppose Randy Turpin.

New York, June 18—(AP)—Carl (Bobo) Olson, a punishing boxer-puncher from Hawaii's hulu land, remained a 3 to 1 favorite today over Paddy Young, saddle-nosed New York slugger, for tomorrow's 15-round American middleweight title bout at Madison Square Garden.

Britain's Randy Turpin, claimant to the world title, has agreed to meet the winner, probably Aug 27 in New York, for the undisputed championship of the 160-pound class.

The important bout, scheduled for 9:00 P. M. (EST) will be carried on network radio (ABC) and television (NBC), the customary Friday night setup.

9,000 May Pay In

In addition to the$50,000 special TV fee, the International Boxing Club expects a crowd of 9,000 to pay some $35,000 at the gate. Each fighter gets 30 per cent of "everything," including TV, or approximately $21,000.

The Young camp, and some neutral observers, scoff at the lopsided odds. They point to Paddy's five rugged battles with rock-throwing Ernie Durando as proof he can't be hurt by Olson.

Olson, Honolulu-born but now living in San Francisco, simply predicts a decision win—also [by] body punching.

Lincoln Rams Notch 14th Of Season 7 To [4]

The Lincoln Furniture Rams w[on] their 14th game of the season la[st] night at Beaver Pond Park beati[ng] the Piccadilly Restaurant [of] Bridgeport 7 to 4. Pete Velu[...] turned in his sixth victory of t[he] campaign giving up six hits a[nd] striking out two.

Buddy Godfrey sensational p[it]cher of Bridgeport was tagged [the] hardest this year in giving up [...] hits, four of them for extra bas[es].

College Champ Moves Up In Western Gol[f]

Atlanta, June 18—(AP)—A series of lopsided matches t[o]day pushed two top professionals, an amateur veteran a[nd] a college girl newcomer into the semi-finals of the Women['s] Western Open golf championship.

Pat Lesser, the newly crowned intercollegiate champion from Seattle, continued to catch the crowd's fancy as she rolled up an 8 and 7 decision over Jean Hopkins, a much more experienced player from Cleveland.

Atlanta's Louise Suggs, the year's top money winner among the play-for-pay delegation, had almost as easy a time disposing of Major Pat Grant, the hard swinging WAC from Fort McClellan, Ala., 5 and 3.

By the same margin, Patty Berg, the stocky pro veteran from St. Andrews, Ill., knocked out Claire Doran, a Cleveland amateur, who shared medal honors over the sharply rolling Capital city course.

The nearest thing to a close test came when Dorothy Kirby, longtime Atlanta amateur, eliminated little Betty Hicks of Los Angeles, 3 and 2, with a booming birdie-three on the long 16th hole.

The lineup for tomorrow's 18-hole semi-finals is strictly a pro-amateur test with Lesser meet[ing] Suggs in the top bracket wh[ile] Berg and Kirby are paired in [the] lower half.

Bombers' Casual Acceptance of Victory Disappears After They Take 'Big One'

LOPAT LEADS CLUB IN JUBILANT SCENE

Cheers and Compliments Echo in Yanks' Dressing Room—Stengel Hails McDonald

By LOUIS EFFRAT

The casual acceptance of victory, which the Yankees displayed following their first two series victories, vanished yesterday. For the first time in the 1953 series the Bombers' dressing room presented a jubilant scene, as the players, led by Ed Lopat, whooped it up.

There were cheers for all, considerable backslapping and lots of joking. Gone was the quiet dignity that had cloaked the New York quarters after the first two triumphs. This time, perhaps realizing that they had taken the "big one" and were leading in the home stretch, the Yankees displayed their true emotions.

However, amid the bantering of the victors there was the unmistakable pride of achievement. Casey Stengel spoke glowingly about Jim McDonald's pitching. "He was great," the manager declared and no one dissented. "He kept the ball low and stopped the Dodgers from hitting the long ball until he tired in the eighth."

Turner Hails Hurler

Jim Turner, the Yankees' pitching coach, was in complete accord. "Yes, McDonald was great," he echoed.

"Do you know that he made only seventy-nine pitches in the first seven innings and did you see how he kept his pitches low?"

Admiring words for Mickey Mantle, Billy Martin, Gil McDougald and Gene Woodling were heard all over the room. There were, also, compliments for Bob Kuzava and Allie Reynolds. None in the crowded room got the impression that the Yankees were speaking in "I-told-you-so" tones, though.

Stengel, McDonald and Mantle were surrounded by interviewers. Casey conceded that his Bombers now enjoyed the big edge. "I'd have to say that, going back to our own park, we have the advantage," he declared. "McDonald's work was the big thing today. He kept the ball low and the defense behind him was splendid."

McDonald had been in trouble in the fifth, when, after one out, he had hit Junior Gilliam with a pitched ball and yielded singles to Peewee Reese and Duke Snider. At this point, with the Yankees leading, 6—2, and Jackie Robinson coming to bat, Stengel had called for time. Did he have any intention of removing McDonald then?

Went to Offer Advice

"Absolutely not!" Casey said. "I merely went to the mound to steady him and to give him some advice."

Casey did not disclose what that advice had been, but obviously it must have been sound, because Robinson popped a foul, which Yogi Berra captured, and then Roy Campanella rolled into a force out.

"Of course, I'll tell you what Casey told me," McDonald said a few minutes later. "He told me to keep the ball low. I did on the pitch to Robinson, throwing a change-up sinker.

"In fact, I was throwing the sinker most of the game. My control was pretty good and rarely did I fail to get the ball where I wanted it to go. I did get tired later, but that was after I had run out my two-bagger in the seventh. I could hardly catch my breath after that run."

The victory went to the right-hander, of course, but McDonald was sorely disappointed that he had not gone all the way. "But I guess the manager knows best," he stated. McDonald, in seven and two-thirds innings, did not walk a man.

Mantle's third-round grand-slam homer made the Oklahoma lad happy. And why not? That was the wallop that provided the biggest cushion for McDonald. Mickey said he hit a "belt-high, outside curve." However, Mickey berated himself for not having made more hits. "They were serving me good pitches all day," he said.

The homer was blasted into the upper left-field stands, although Mickey batted from the left side. It seems that Stengel had advised him to cut down on his swing and punch to the opposite field.

Reynolds Felt No Pain

Reynolds, who choked off a Brooklyn rally with only four pitches, after he had relieved Kuzava in the ninth, said his back did not pain, as he delivered four straight fast balls to Robinson, who rammed into the game-ending double play. "Perhaps I could be used again, if needed," the Chief averred. "I'll go as far as I can."

Woodling's perfect throw, erasing Gil Hodges at the plate in the second inning, was one of the key plays in the game. Woodling said he had made up his mind, before he had made the catch, that his throw would be to home. "I caught quite a few important runners at the plate during the regular season," he declared.

Alone in a corner, sat Johnny Mize. "This was my last game in Brooklyn," he said, almost in a whisper. Did that mean Big Jawn was retiring after the series? "Yes," he said. "I'm tired of carrying that lumber up there." It is pertinent to note that Mize has said this several times in past years.

Whitey Ford, who is to start today's game at the Stadium, planned a night of leisure. "I'm going to my mother-in-law's house to take things easy. I'll watch television—Martin and Lewis, Red Buttons and Jackie Gleason and Jack Benny—all the comics," he said.

When Whitey was told Chuck Dressen was to appear on a show last night, the left-hander said he did not plan to watch that one. "What's funny about Dressen?" Ford wanted to know.

Snapshots: Grand-Slam Hero, Winning Pitcher, an Out at the Plate, a Leap Against the Wall

The New York Times

Welcoming committee at the plate for Mickey Mantle, after his bases-loaded homer in third, included Yogi Berra (8), Joe Collins and Hank Bauer (9), all of whom tallied on the drive.

Gil Hodges, Dodger first baseman, being doubled at the plate by Left Fielder Gene Woodling's sharp peg to Catcher Berra on Billy Cox's fly ball in the second. The umpire is Bill Grieve.

Jim McDonald, who gained credit as the winning hurler.

Duke Snider of the Dodgers leaping against center-field wall in vain bid to grab a home run off the bat of Gene Woodling of the Yankees in opening inning of the contest at Ebbets Field.

YANKEES WIN, 11-7, FOR 3-2 SERIES EDGE

Continued From Page 1

sary for Reynolds to come in to the struggle.

For Stengel, even though he still enjoyed a four-run advantage, was taking no chances. Especially after Duke Snider had singled in the ninth with only one out. It was here the Ol' Perfessor called on the Chief to face Jackie Robinson. Reynolds, just recovering from a muscle strain in his back which he sustained in the series opener, delivered just four pitches.

The Incredible Martin

The fourth Robinson rifled along the ground just a few feet to the right of second. It looked for a moment to be good for another single that would keep the Dodger hopes alive. But that same incredible Martin, who had been torturing the life out of the good souls in Flatbush ever since this classic began, streaked over to scoop up the ball, flip it to Phil Rizzuto, who then fired it to Joe Collins at first for a double play and the struggle was over.

But the mightiest blow of all was the one that Mantle lashed into the seats in the third to cap an inning that long will remain seared in the memory of the Flatbush faithful.

With the score one-all and the youthful Podres seemingly getting along nicely, Gil Hodges 'committed a "third out" error to let in one run. Rattled, the young left-hander then hit a batsman, Hank Bauer, and walked Yogi Berra, filling the bases.

At this tense moment Dressen made a decision he doubtless will regret for many a day. He called on the unpredictable Meyer to come up from the bullpen to see what he could do about it.

Russ delivered just one pitch and Mantle who, being a switch hitter, had now shifted to the left side of the plate, put everything he had into his swing. The ball blazed a trail into the upper left tier, well down toward center. It was a tremendous blast for a left-handed batter and from there on the Dodgers kept striving and fighting back, but it was all like running uphill in sand.

Fourth Homer for Mantle

The five-run inning gave the Yanks a 6—1 lead. The homer was Mantle's fourth in world series play and second in this classic, his first having sunk the flock in the second game last Thursday.

For a time after that Meyer went fairly well and in the fifth Snider singled home the Dodgers' second tally of the day. But in the seventh the Bombers lashed into the eccentric righthander for another cluster of three, two riding in on the Martin homer. Wade was tagged for one in the eighth that Collins paced home with a double and in the ninth Black came on to get himself clubbed for a homer with the bases empty by McDougald, Gil's second of the series.

It therefore looked mighty glum for the home folks, for all that the sun was still shining and the thoughtful umpires already had ordered the lights turned on, when the Flock came to bat in the last of the eighth with the score 10—2 against them.

But, with one down, Robinson and Roy Campanella singled. Hodges fanned for the second out, but Carl Furillo singled for one tally and then Cox fetched in three more with his homer into the lower left field stand.

Here, however, the left-handed Kuzava came on to fan pinch hitter Dick Williams and though in the ninth the Dodgers were to have the satisfaction of routing this annoying southpaw, they merely ran into Reynolds, who snuffed them out with ease.

Art Krueger, one of the Pirates of that first world series fifty years ago, was the chosen survivor to toss out the first ball for this encounter and with this ceremony disposed of, the crowd settled back to sweat it out.

It was, in fact, just about as hot a day as in any series game on record, and though this time there were a few fleecy clouds, the weather for the fifth successive afternoon provided an ideal setting. Needless to say the outfielders welcomed the clouds, since it eliminated what players call a "high sky" which, oddly, adds to the difficulties of judging flies in the blinding sun.

There was a flurry in the Yankee camp just before the game when, right at the close of the Bombers' batting drill, a foul ball off Irv Noren's bat struck Mantle on the left hand. However, it proved nothing serious and that presently was to turn into a grave piece of misfortune for the Dodgers.

As Podres stepped to the mound for the first inning he brought with him no overly impressive record, since he had tossed only three complete games all season, his first in the majors. However, during the year he had faced the Yankees twice, a six inning brush back in March during the training season, then seven innings in the Mayor's Trophy benefit game on June 29, and in those thirteen innings he had not allowed the Bombers a run. It doubtless was this, more than anything else, that induced Dressen to gamble on the youngster in this all-important encounter.

Unhappily for Johnny, however, this was no longer an exhibition game and his scoreless string against the Yanks ended almost in record time.

In fact, with Stengel again brazenly naming a left-handed hitter, Woodling, to head his batting order against a southpaw pitcher, Podres had delivered only three pitches when he received his first jolt.

With the count of one strike and two balls, Woodling sent a towering fly right down the midway and, though Snider stayed right with it as far as he could go, he couldn't go any farther than the center field wall. There he made one last despairing leap, but the ball had just enough carry to clear the wall above his head.

Tied in the Second

As in the first two games the Yanks again were off to a first innning lead, although in this instance it wasn't to prove very damaging. For the margin vanished in the second, and for a time it looked as though the Flock would tear the game apart. But luck wasn't riding with the Dodgers in this round, even though an error gave them a tally.

After Campanella and Hodges had opened with singles, Furillo rapped a grounder to Rizzuto that looked like a sure-fire double play ball. But Li'l Phil's peg to second base shot by Martin for an error and, as the ball rolled into right field, Campanella lit out for home and Hodges reached third.

But that was all the Flock was to extract out of this promising start, for Cox followed with a drive that Woodling caught in left and when Hodges tried to score after the catch a perfect peg by Gene that traveled on a line into Yogi Berra's mit resulted in a double play. Ironically, Podres followed with a single to center but the rally ended when Gilliam, who had opened the Dodger first with a single, grounded to Martin for the third out.

Still, the score was tied at one-all and but for Hodges' misplay in the third it might have remained that way for a spell longer. A pass to Rizzuto started that fateful round.

McDonald sacrificed Li'l Phil to second. Woodling followed with a sharp rap to the mound which knocked Podres' glove right off his hand. That bewildered the youngster to the extent that he first picked up the glove, then the ball. But he managed to get the toss over to first for the out.

So there were two down with Rizzuto on third when Collins slapped a sharp grounder down the first base line. It looked like the third out that would have got Podres out of the inning without a tally scored against him. But Hodges let the ball skim off his glove for an error and Rizzuto counted.

What followed will ever remain a blur to Brooklyn fandom, which still hopes so fervently for that first world series title. For Podres was now palpably rattled. He hit Bauer on the arm and walked Berra, filling the bases.

Now came Meyer with the hoped for relief and Mantle with his withering blast. After that they could humanely have tossed in a towel.

This was only the fourth grand slam homer in world series history. Elmer Smith of the Indians hit the first one against another Dodger team back in 1920. The second was by the Yankees' Tony Lazzeri against the Giants at the Polo Grounds in 1936. And the next, also by the Yankees, when McDougald hit one as a rookie in 1951, also was against the Giants at the Polo Grounds.

A single by Berra preceded Martin's homer off Meyer in the seventh and on the heels of that Rizzuto singled and scored all the way from first as McDonald bashed a double down the left field foul line, to make it three for the round.

In the meantime, McDonald's work on the mound was anything but clear cut and decisive. He seemed on the verge of going out any number of times and by the time Cox's homer finally finished him in the eighth he had yielded twelve of the Dodgers' fourteen hits for the day. In fact, the Dodgers actually outslugged their rivals, 14 to 11.

But in the records McDonald's name goes with a victory in his first world series appearance. While Podres, who would at least have escaped scoreless in that harrowing third but for a misplay, was charged with the defeat.

The six homers yesterday give the present series a total of sixteen, which equals the record set by the Yanks and Dodgers in seven games last year. So one more today will crack that mark. And the six homers yesterday tied the one-game mark set by the Yanks and Cubs in 1932, with the Bombers on that occasion also coming up with the majority four.

And Martin, with a total of ten hits thus far, needs only two more to tie the record of twelve which Pepper Martin made in a seven-game series in 1931. But even if he doesn't make it, the wiry Californian already has done enough to Flatbush fans to haunt them for years to come.

Yanks 3½-1 to Win Series

The Yankees, on the strength of their victory over the Dodgers in the pivotal fifth game of the world series, last night were 3½-to-1 favorites to win their fifth straight world championship. For today's sixth game, the odds went from 5½ to 5, with the Dodgers favored, to even money.

Composite Score of World Series Games

BROOKLYN DODGERS

	G	AB	R	H	2B	3B	HR	RBI	BB	SO	Bat. Avg.	PO	A	E	Fldg. Avg.
Gilliam, 2b	5	23	4	8	3	0	2	4	0	1	.348	11	12	0	1.000
Reese, ss	5	20	0	4	0	1	0	0	4	1	.200	6	10	0	1.000
Snider, cf	5	22	2	8	3	0	1	5	1	3	.364	13	0	0	1.000
Robinson, lf	5	21	2	6	1	0	0	2	1	0	.286	5	0	0	1.000
Thompson, lf	2	0	0	0	0	0	0	0	0	0	.000	0	1	0	1.000
Campanella, c	5	18	6	5	0	0	1	1	2	1	.278	43	9	0	1.000
Hodges, 1b	5	18	3	8	0	0	1	1	3	3	.444	40	4	1	.978
Furillo, rf	5	20	3	5	1	0	0	2	1	3	.250	8	0	2	.800
Cox, 3b	5	19	3	6	3	0	1	6	1	2	.316	1	9	0	1.000
Erskine, p	2	3	0	1	0	0	0	0	0	0	.333	1	2	0	1.000
aBelardi	2	2	0	0	0	0	0	0	0	[illegible]	.000	0	0	0	.000
Hughes, p	1	1	0	0	0	0	0	0	0	1	.000	0	0	1	.000
bShuba	2	1	1	1	0	0	1	2	0	0	1.000	0	0	0	.000
Labine, p	2	1	0	0	0	0	0	0	0	0	.000	0	1	0	1.000
Wade, p	2	0	0	0	0	0	0	0	0	0	.000	0	0	0	.000
Roe, p	1	3	0	0	0	0	0	0	0	2	.000	1	1	0	1.000
cWilliams	2	2	0	1	0	0	0	0	0	1	.500	0	0	0	.000
Loes, p	1	3	0	2	0	0	0	0	0	0	.667	0	0	0	.000
Podres, p	1	1	0	1	0	0	0	0	0	0	1.000	0	1	0	1.000
Meyer, p	1	1	0	0	0	0	0	0	0	1	.000	0	1	0	1.000
Black, p	1	0	0	0	0	0	0	0	0	0	.000	0	0	0	.000
Total	5	179	24	56	11	1	7	23	13	20	.313	129	51	4	.978

NEW YORK YANKEES

	G	AB	R	H	2B	3B	HR	RBI	BB	SO	Bat. Avg.	PO	A	E	Fldg. Avg.
McDougald, 3b	5	20	2	4	0	1	2	4	1	2	.200	5	14	0	1.000
Collins, 1b	5	21	4	3	1	0	1	2	2	7	.143	44	3	0	1.000
Bauer, rf	5	20	4	5	0	1	0	1	0	4	.250	11	0	0	1.000
Berra, c	5	16	3	7	0	0	1	3	3	3	.438	26	3	0	1.000
Mantle, cf	5	20	3	4	0	0	2	7	2	8	.200	9	0	0	1.000
Woodling, lf	5	16	4	4	0	0	1	2	5	2	.250	8	1	0	1.000
Martin, 2b	5	19	5	10	0	2	2	6	1	2	.526	12	14	0	1.000
Rizzuto, ss	5	15	3	4	1	0	0	0	3	2	.267	9	17	1	.963
dBollweg	2	2	0	0	0	0	0	0	0	2	.000	0	0	0	.000
Reynolds, p	2	1	0	0	0	0	0	0	1	1	.000	0	0	0	.000
Sain, p	2	2	1	1	1	0	0	2	0	1	.500	0	0	0	.000
eNoren	2	1	0	0	0	0	0	0	1	0	.000	0	0	0	.000
Lopat, p	1	3	0	0	0	0	0	0	0	2	.000	0	2	0	1.000
Raschi, p	1	2	0	0	0	0	0	0	0	1	.000	1	1	0	1.000
fMize	2	2	0	0	0	0	0	0	0	1	.000	0	0	0	.000
Ford, p	1	0	0	0	0	0	0	0	0	0	.000	0	0	0	.000
Gorman, p	1	1	0	0	0	0	0	0	0	1	.000	1	0	0	1.000
Schallock, p	1	0	0	0	0	0	0	0	0	0	.000	0	1	0	1.000
McDonald, p	1	2	0	1	1	0	0	1	1	1	.500	3	0	0	1.000
Kuzava, p	1	1	0	0	0	0	0	0	0	1	.000	0	0	0	.000
Total	5	164	29	43	4	4	9	28	20	41	.262	129	56	1	.995

aStruck out for Erskine in second inning of first game, grounded out for Meyer in seventh inning of fifth game.

bHit homer for Hughes in sixth inning of first game, announced as batter for Wade in eighth inning of fifth game.

cSingled for Roe in ninth inning of second game, struck out for Shuba in eighth inning of fifth game.

dStruck out for Rizzuto in ninth inning of third game, struck out for Gorman in fifth inning of fourth game.

eWalked for McDougald in ninth inning of third game, popped out for Sain in seventh inning of fourth game.

fStruck out for Raschi in ninth inning of third game, flied out for Schallock in ninth inning of fourth game.

COMPOSITE SCORE BY INNINGS

Dodgers	3	1	0	3	3	6	2	5	1	—24
Yankees	6	0	5	0	4	0	5	7	2	—29

PITCHING SUMMARY

Brooklyn Dodgers

	G	CG	IP	H	R	BB	SO	HB	WP	W	L	Pct.	ER	ERA
Erskine	2	1	10	8	6	6	15	2	1	1	0	1.000	6	5.40
Hughes	1	0	4	3	1	1	3	0	0	0	0	.000	1	2.25
Labine	2	0	2⅔	5	1	0	2	0	0	0	1	.000	1	3.00
Wade	2	0	2⅓	4	4	1	2	0	0	0	0	.000	4	18.00
Roe	1	1	8	5	4	4	4	1	0	0	1	.000	4	4.50
Loes	1	0	8	8	3	2	8	0	0	1	0	1.000	3	3.38
Podres	1	0	2⅔	1	5	2	0	1	0	0	1	.000	1	3.00
Meyer	1	0	4⅓	8	4	4	5	0	0	0	0	.000	3	6.75
Black	1	0	1	1	1	0	2	0	0	0	0	.000	1	9.00
Total		2	43	43	29	20	41	4	1	2	3	.400	24	5.02

New York Yankees

	G	CG	IP	H	R	BB	SO	HB	WP	W	L	Pct.	ER	ERA
Reynolds	2	0	6	7	4	3	6	1	0	0	0	.000	4	6.00
Sain	2	0	5⅔	8	3	1	1	0	0	1	0	1.000	3	4.50
Lopat	1	1	9	9	2	4	3	0	0	1	0	1.000	2	2.00
Raschi	1	1	8	9	3	3	4	0	0	0	1	.000	3	3.38
Ford	1	0	1	3	3	1	0	0	1	0	1	.000	3	27.00
Gorman	1	0	3	4	1	0	1	0	0	0	0	.000	1	3.00
Schallock	1	0	2	2	1	1	1	0	0	0	0	.000	1	4.50
McDonald	1	0	7⅔	12	6	0	3	1	0	1	0	1.000	5	5.63
Kuzava	1	0	⅔	2	1	0	1	0	0	0	0	.000	1	13.50
Total		2	44	56	24	13	20	2	1	3	2	.600	23	4.70

Stolen bases—Martin, Hodges, Rizzuto. Sacrifices—Rizzuto, Raschi, Cox, Loes, McDonald, Bauer. Double plays—Martin, Rizzuto and Collins 2; Rizzuto, Martin and Collins; Rizzuto and Collins; Woodling and Berra. Left on bases—Brooklyn 43, New York 34. Hit by pitcher—By Reynolds (Campanella), by Roe (McDougald), by Erskine (Berra 2), by Podres (Bauer), by McDonald (Gilliam). Wild pitches—Erskine, Ford. Balk—Raschi. Umpires—Bill Stewart (N. L.), Ed Hurley (A. L.), Art Gore (N. L.), Bill Grieve (A. L.), Frank Dascoli (N. L.), Hank Soar (A. L.).

Paid attendance—First game, 69,374; second game, 66,786; third game, 35,270; fourth game, 36,775; fifth game, 36,775. Time of games—First game, 3:10; second game, 2:42; third game, 2:58; fourth game, 2.46; fifth game, 3:02.

The Box Score

FIFTH GAME

NEW YORK YANKEES

	AB.	R.	H.	PO.	A.
Woodling, lf	3	1	1	2	1
Collins, 1b	5	2	1	6	2
Bauer, rf	3	1	0	1	0
Berra, c	4	2	2	6	0
Mantle, cf	5	1	1	2	0
Martin, 2b	5	1	2	3	1
McDougald, 3b	5	1	2	0	1
Rizzuto, ss	3	2	1	4	6
McDonald, p	2	0	1	3	0
Kuvaza, p	1	0	0	0	0
Reynolds, p	0	0	0	0	0
Total	36	11	11	27	11

BROOKLYN DODGERS

	AB.	R.	H.	PO.	A.
Gilliam, 2b	4	2	2	4	3
Reese, ss	5	0	1	0	1
Snider, cf	5	0	2	3	0
Robinson, lf	5	1	1	0	0
Campanella, c	4	2	3	8	3
Hodges, 1b	4	0	2	11	1
Furillo, rf	4	1	1	0	0
Cox, 3b	4	1	1	1	4
Podres, p	1	0	1	0	1
Meyer, p	1	0	0	0	1
aBelardi	1	0	0	0	0
Wade, p	0	0	0	0	0
bShuba	0	0	0	0	0
cWilliams	1	0	0	0	0
Black, p	0	0	0	0	0
Total	39	7	14	27	14

aGrounded out for Meyer in seventh.
bAnnounced as batter for Wade in eighth.
cStruck out for Shuba in eighth.

Yankees	1 0 5 0 0 0 3 1 1—11
Dodgers	0 1 0 0 1 0 0 4 1— 7

Errors—Rizzuto, Hodges.

Runs batted in—Woodling, Mantle 4, Snider, Martin 2, McDonald, Berra, Furillo, Cox 3, McDougald, Gilliam; Campanella scored on Rizzuto's error in second; Rizzuto scored on Hodges' error in third.

Two-base hits—McDonald, Collins. Three-base hit—McDougald. Home runs—Woodling, Mantle, Martin, Cox, McDougald, Gilliam. Stolen base—Rizzuto. Sacrifices—McDonald, Bauer. Double plays—Woodling and Berra; Rizzuto and Collins; Martin, Rizzuto and Collins. Left on bases—New York 7, Brooklyn 6. Bases on balls—Off Podres 2 (Rizzuto, Berra), Meyer 4 (McDonald, Woodling 2, Rizzuto). Struck out—By Meyer 5 (McDougald, Collins, Bauer, Mantle, McDonald), Black 2 (Martin, Kuzava), McDonald 3 (Snider, Meyer, Hodges), Kuzava 1 (Williams). Hits—Off Podres 1 in 2 2-3 innings, Meyer 8 in 4 1-3, Wade 1 in 1, Black 1 in 1, McDonald 12 in 7 2-3, Kuzava 2 in 2-3, Reynolds 0 in 2-3. Runs and earned runs—Off Podres 5 and 1, Meyer 4 and 3, Wade 1 and 1, Black 1 and 1, McDonald 6 and 5, Kuzava 1 and 1, Reynolds 0 and 0. Hit by pitchers—By Podres (Bauer), by McDonald (Gilliam). Winning pitcher—McDonald. Losing pitcher—Podres.

Umpires—Grieve (A. L.) plate, Stewart (N. L.) first base, Hurley (A. L.) second base, Gore (N. L.) third base, Soar (A. L.) left field, Dascoli (N. L.) right field. Time of game—3:02. Paid attendance—36,775.

'TRYING TOO HARD,' M'DONALD STATES

Pitcher Disappointed at Not Finishing, But Pleased at Gaining Series Victory

By JIM McDONALD
As Told to The United Press.

I would have given anything in the world to finish yesterday's game but I simply ran out of gas.

My downfall came about because I was trying too hard. That might sound funny to the average fan but any big league pitcher will know what I mean by that.

The blow that finished me—Billy Cox' three-run homer with two out in the eighth—was my own fault. I tried to put too much on that fast ball and as a result I "overthrew" the ball. It came up to Cox real fat and he put it away.

Started to Get Tired

Frankly, I was starting to get a litle tired when Cox sent me on my way. But I'm not griping. We won the ball game and that's the important thing.

But you have no idea how rotten I felt when I had to come out of there. Before the game, I promised myself I'd win this one if I never did anything else in my life. Being around at the finish would have given me the greatest satisfaction I've ever had. As it turned out, though, this is still the biggest kick I've ever gotten out of baseball.

Remember, it wasn't so long ago that I was pitching for the St. Louis Browns and I never dreamed of working in a world series.

I know a lot of people won't believe me but the truth of the matter is that I wasn't the least bit nervous when Casey Stengel told me I was going to start the game. I'm not the nervous type but I'll tell you if there's anything that will make you a little tense, it's pitching in a world series game.

Snider Most Feared

Oddly enough, it wasn't Cox whom I feared the most. The guy I pitched most carefully to was Duke Snider. I remembered what he had done in the other games.

Even when Jackie Robinson, Roy Campanella and Carl Furillo clipped me for those singles before Cox' homer, I thought I'd get out of the inning all right. But then Cox came through with their first extra base hit of the game and it was all over for me.

I have two bid consolations, though. First of all, I know I did my best and secondly, we won.

I guess I can't ask for much more. A fellow can't be a hog, you know.

SCORE? DIAL ME 7-1212

Phone Service Keeps Up With World Series Contests

The New York Telephone Company, MEridian 7-1212, is covering the world series between the Dodgers and the Yankees by giving the inning-by-inning scores along with its time signals.

The scores are given three times a minute by a special operator who receives bulletins by leased wire direct from the ball park. Final scores are announced after every game until 6:30 P. M. If there is a postponement because of the weather, it will be disclosed by this service.

Please do not call THE NEW YORK TIMES for world series information. This request is made to prevent impairment of other services of THE NEW YORK TIMES.

TWO HOMER RECORDS TIED

6 in Game Matches '32 Mark, Total Equals '52 Standard

The six home runs hit in yesterday's game between the Yankees and Dodgers tied two world series' records, one for most homers in a game set by the Cubs and Yankees on Oct. 1, 1932, and the other for most homers in a series, sixteen, set by the two rivals last year.

The Yankees have the edge, having belted nine to the Dodgers' seven. The Brooklyn home run hitters were Junior Gilliam 2, Gil Hodges, George Shuba, Roy Campanella, Duke Snider and Billy Cox.

For the Yankees they were Billy Martin, Mickey Mantle and Gil McDougald, two each; Yogi Berra, Joe Collins and Gene Woodling.

World Series Schedule

Today—At Yankee Stadium, 1 P. M.

Tomorrow—At Yankee Stadium, 1 P. M. (if necessary).

In event of a postponement, game will be held over until played on field where originally scheduled.

Your privilege of voting in the election of Nov. 3 will be lost unless you register at the voting place in your election district this week. Registration books will be opened from 3:30 P. M. to 10:30 P. M. Monday through Friday and from 7 A. M. to 10:30 P. M. on Saturday.

Mantle Slam Rocks Brooklyn, 11-7

Reynolds Stops Flock in 9th; 6 HRs Set 1-Game Series Mark

By GUS STEIGER

The big guns, supposedly on the side of the Dodgers, must have been misplaced Sunday for it was the Yankees who accounted for the heavy fire in the free-hitting fifth contest of the 1953 World Series. The American

SMASH OPENING: Gene Woodling, nominated as lead-off man by Casey Stengel Sunday, crosses plate after slamming Podres for first inning homer. Joe Collins congratulates Gene as Ump Bill Grieve stands by. (Mirror Photo)

Leaguers assaulted four Flatbush hurlers for 11 blows that produced 27 total bases to ease the way to an 11-7 triumph at Ebbets Field and a three-two lead in games that placed Manager Casey Stengel and his Yankees one victory away from their fifth consecutive World's Championship.

Included in the New York attack were a pair of doubles, a triple and four lusty homers in chronological order, by Gene Woodling, Mickey Mantle, Billy Martin and Gil McDougald, who also belted a three-bagger.

The quartet of four-baggers accounted for eight of the Yankee tallies. The biggest of these was that by Mantle, who crowned a five-run third inning with the fourth grand-slam of Series history to provide Jim McDonald a substantial lead.

* * *

THIS WAS the third Series slam by a Yankee, for Tony Lazzeri in 1936 and McDougald in 1951 had accounted for two of thee blows, with Elmer Smith delivering the first in 1920, wherein the chastened Dodgers also were the victims.

It was the second homer of the current title event for both Mantle and Martin as these young worthies had collaborated in such fashion to encompass the defeat of Preacher Roe in the second game.

Now the Series shifts back to the Yankee Stadium with the defending champions in the driver's seat and in position to end the exercises with another win Monday. The Dodgers, who began the Sabbath on even terms and with such bright prospects of ending Yankee domination, now are in a desperate situation and will come back with their ace, Carl Erskine, in their effort to win today and carry the event into a seventh and deciding contest.

THE DODGERS actually outhit the Yankees, 14-11, but the Bombers got a worthy game out of McDonald, credited with the victory, although Bob Kuzava, who appeared ahead of normal Series schedule and Allie Reynolds got into the affair before it was over. In his two previous Series showings, Kusava didn't [illegible]ow up until the seventh game. [illegible]nald, however, served [illegible]y until Billy Cox came

Statistics!

NEW YORK (AL)	3	2	.600
BROOKLYN (NL)	2	3	.400

REMAINING SCHEDULE:

Sixth Game at Yankee Stadium, Monday, Oct. 5; Seventh game (if necessary), at Yankee Stadium, Tuesday, Oct. 6.

FINANCIAL FIGURES
FIFTH GAME

Attendance (paid), 36,775.
Receipts (net), $214,394.33.
Commissioner's share, $32,159.15.

(FIVE-GAME FIGURES)

Attendance (paid), 244,981.
Receipts (net), $1,407,221.00.
Players pool (first 4 games only) $691,341.61.
Commissioner's share, $211,083.15.
Clubs' and league's share $587,796.24.

through with a three-run homer to finish off a four-run eighth.

This also finished McDonald, but his club was far in front when he left.

Junior Gilliam belted Kuzava for another four-bagger in the ninth and to subdue the Brooks for the day Stengel brought in Reynolds to serve a double-play ball to Jackie Robinson.

Manager Charley Dressen did not have his thinking cap properly adjusted Sunday. He took a flyer to begin with by starting John Podres, who marked his 21st birthday last Wednesday. Only pitcher younger than the rookie southpaw to start a series game was Joe Bush of the Athletics in 1913.

PODRES LACKED control and

Continued on Next Page

ALL YOURS: Charley Dressen hands youthful Johnny Podres ball along with some last minute instructions before fifth Series conflict at Ebbets Field Sunday. Charley kept his pitching selection mum over night and rookie southpaw was in nature of surprise starter, getting call over veteran Russ Meyer. (Mirror Photo)

Cholly Playing Last Ace Again-Erskine!

By KEN SMITH

Ever since Rube Marquard, Sherrod Smith and Jake Pfeffer were thumped by the Red Sox in 1916, the Dodgers have been searching for a pitching staff that can win a World Series and Charley Dressen was down to his last ace again, Carl Erskine, as the Big Tent was pitched again in the Stadium Monday (today).

Casey Stengel, with his 3-2 lead, was in a position to gamble on Whitey Ford transforming himself into a Dr. Jekyl Monday after his Mr. Hyde one-inning performance of last Saturday, same as Erskine had done on Friday. Vic Raschi gets ready for game 7, if necessary, and Ed Lopat also looms handy.

THE AMERICAN LEAGUERS sit pretty at six or six and one-half to five favorites in Game 6 and 2-1 to cop the Series. Once more, the Brooks are on the brink of defeat because they ran short of pitchers when John Podres and Russ Meyer failed, while the Yankees came up with a surprise winner, Jim McDonald, supported by Bob Kuzava, and Allie Reynolds under the late afternoon lights.

But Series history is dotted with stars like Erskine, who have shouldered most of the responsibility, on undermanned staffs and Erskine has the stuff to do it. Seven years ago, Harry Brecheen won three games. Dizzy and Paul Dean each won three in 1934.

A year ago at this time, the Yankees trailed Brooklyn, 3-2 and copped the last two as

MICKEY MANTLE

Raschi and Reynolds came back. Brooklyn has a good chance of doing the same with Erskine and Bill Loes.

Nine times teams have been in the same predicament as Brooklyn Monday when the loss of one game meant goodbye to the Series, and swept through to win. The Cards turned this trick three times, the Yankees twice and the Reds, Giants, Pirates and Red Sox each once.

Junior Gilliam's ninth-inning homer was the sixth of the game, tying the record set by the 1932 Yankees and Cubs. It brought the 1953 total to 16, tying last year's record set by the Dodgers and Yankees.

Sunday's 47 total bases were more than any two clubs ever amassed in a Series game.

Snider, Robinson, Berra, Martin and other sluggers flailed away at the fences in practice oblivious to the pitching plotting which dominated Sunday's pregame dugout sceen.

Charley Dressen used Russ Meyer as a decoy, keeping the veteran on the bench instead of letting him roam the outfield with the other twirlers not expected to get into the game. Although it became known early that Podres had been tapped for the starting assignment, the

Continued on Page 40

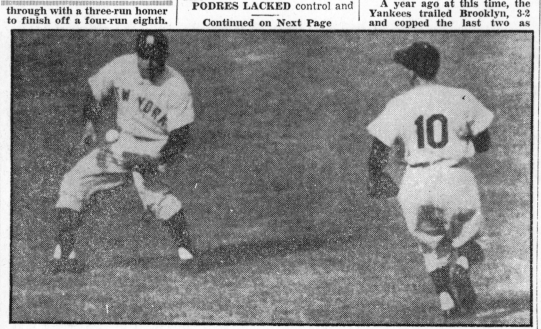

BROOKLYN BLOOPER: Woodling fields Junior Gilliam's Texas League single in opening frame at Ebbets Field as Phil Rizzuto (10) pulls up after futile pursuit. Ball dropped between oWodling and Rizzuto. (Mirror Photo)

THE WEATHER
Today: Cloudy and cool, with rain; tonight some rain becoming windy.
Tomorrow: Mostly fair, windy and cool.
Temperatures Yesterday: Max., 66.2; Min., 5?
Today's Probable Range: Max., 58; Min., 50.
Humidity at 3 p. m. Yesterday: 70%.
Expected Humidity This Afternoon: 70-80%.
Detailed Report, Map—Page 31

NEW YORK Herald Tribune

European Edition Published Daily in Paris

Late City Edition

113th Year VOL. CXIII NO. 39,041 | 230 West 41st Street, New York 36, N. Y. Telephone PEnnsylvania 6-4000 | TUESDAY, OCTOBER 6, 1953 | FIVE CENTS

Yanks Win

Ted Kell

No hard feelings in Brooklyn—Chuck Dressen, Dodgers' manager, lighting a cigar for Billy Martin in the Yankee dressing room yesterday after Martin's single had won the title for the Yankees and Casey Stengel, who looks on.

Red Smith's Column

Martin's Hit in 9th Wins Yanks 5th Series in Row

The New York Yankees yesterday won their fifth straight World Series—an unprecedented feat—by defeating the Brooklyn Dodgers, 4 to 3, at the Yankee Stadium on Billy Martin's single in the ninth inning. Here is the account of the game as seen by Red Smith.

By Red Smith

The morgue doors yawned yesterday, snapped shut, then swung open again, and as they carted the remains away a man in the press box gazed thoughtfully at the knot of Yankee baseball players at first base tossing Billy Martin aloft like a beanbag. "You wouldn't think," said Mike Lee, the man in the press box, "that they could—get so mercenary over a lousy $2,000."

The fiftieth World Series was over and this time the Dodgers really and truly was dead, beaten 4 to 3, in the sixth and final game after Carl Furillo had snatched them to temporary safety when they were only four strikes away from destruction.

In a florid finish that stretched dramatic license to the breaking point, Furillo saved the Dodgers from routine defeat by tying the score in the ninth inning with a two-run homer with one out and a count of three balls, two strikes on the scoreboard. Then Martin lowered the boom.

The gray and chilly day, suitable for funerals, had thickened into grayer, chillier twilight and some of the Yankee Stadium crowd of 62,370 had departed when Martin walked to the plate in the rusty glow of the floodlights. Hank Bauer was on second base, Mickey Mantle on first and Yogi Berra had been retired. Clem Labine, Brooklyn's best pitcher, threw once for a called strike.

He threw another and Martin slapped a ground single over second base into centerfield. Duke Snider fielded the ball but didn't trouble to throw as Bauer went ripping home with the winning run.

Billy the Kid

The Dodgers trudged to their dugout behind third base, looking over their shoulders toward first, where the Yankees were spanking Martin. It was a sight worth at least a backward glance. Never again, perhaps, will it be possible to look on a baseball team that has just won the championship of the world for a fifth consecutive year. It never was possible before, never in any age.

Martin's single was a mercenary stroke, worth something like $2,000 to each Yankee, this being the approximate difference between winner's and loser's shares. On the holy pages of the record books—and these are sacred writings to a ball player—it represents a good deal more, for the blow broke a noteworthy World Series record.

It was Martin's twelfth hit of the six games. Nobody ever made more, even in an eight-game series, and nobody ever made so many in six. Twelve hits had stood as a record since

Continued on page 26, column 3

Denied Reappointment

Stockholder in Raceway Loses Nassau County Job

Irving Bergman, Nassau County labor consultant and son-in-law of Benjamin Feinberg, Public Service Commission chairman, failed of re-appointment to the job yesterday, after he admitted owning shares in the Nassau Trotting Association.

Mr. Bergman, whose name was up for re-appointment with a salary raise from $5,500 to $7,500 a year, was dropped from the list at a meeting of the Nassau County Board of Supervisors, at Mineola, L. I., becoming the first political casualty of the widening harness racing probes.

A. Holly Patterson, County Executive, said in announcing the action, "The board feels that his interest in the raceway might possibly impair his service to the county." The Nassau Trotting Association jointly operates Roosevelt Raceway at Westbury, L. I., with the Old Country Trotting Association.

In another phase of the raceway investigations, Atwood C. Wolf, vice-president and executive secretary of Yonkers Raceway, was questioned for four hours yesterday as the first witness in District Attorney

Continued on page 21, column 1

Wicks Won't Quit; Hits At Wagner

By Walter Arm

Acting Lt. Gov. Arthur H. Wicks rejected yesterday the demands of Democratic party leaders that he resign because he visited Joseph S. Fay, convicted labor extortionist, at Sing Sing prison.

The Kingston Republican, who is also Senate Majority Leader, sent a telegram to Robert F. Wagner jr., Democratic candidate for Mayor, saying: "I shall not resign any position I now hold." Mr. Wicks charged that Democratic administrations had "coddled labor racketeers" and had allowed them to gain control of labor unions.

Assails Wagner

Sen. Wicks called Mr. Wagner's demand that he resign "impertinent" and remarked sarcastically: "Your career in the Assembly and every other public office you have ever held marks you as a real flop."

Mr. Wagner had called for Mr. Wicks' resignation after publication Friday of Fay's prison-visiting list which showed that among eighty-eight persons who called on Fay in his cell were Mr. Wicks, former State Supreme Court Justice William F. Bleakley, State Sen. William F. Condon and Mayor John V. Kenney of Jersey City.

Richard H. Balch, Democratic State Chairman, also called for Mr. Wicks' resignation and said the Acting Lieutenant Governor had "destroyed the faith of the people in him."

Mr. Wagner—just before he received Sen. Wicks' telegram—called upon Gov. Thomas E. Dewey to convene a special session of the State Legislature "receive and prosecute impeach-

Continued on page 12, column 1

Clark Declares P. W.s Will Remain Anti-Red

By Mac R. Johnson
From the Herald Tribune Bureau

TOKYO, Tuesday, Oct. 6.—Gen. Mark W. Clark, United Nations Commander, today took the Neutral Nations Repatriation Commission to task for failing to uphold the principle of freedom of choice of prisoners in its custody.

"It appears that decisions and activities of the commission to date have been predicated upon an assumption that prisoners in your custody actually desire repatriation," Gen. Clark said in an 1,800-word letter to Lt. Gen. K. S. Thimayya, Indian chairman of the commission.

Gen. Clark, on the eve of relinquishing his command to Gen. John E. Hull, wrote Gen. Thimayya that this was especially difficult to understand in view of "strong opposition Korean and Chinese anti-Communist prisoners have demonstrated individually and collectively even to the physical presence of Communist representatives.

"It would seem that the commission has not taken full cognizance of the fact that Korean and Chinese prisoners made their choice many months ago and that in the absence of force or coercion the vast majority will adhere to that decision," Gen. Clark said.

He left no doubt that the U. N. command was displeased with the manner in which the N. N. R. C. was operating and with India's "neutral" leadership of the commission as its chairman.

Gen. Clark said he appreciated the administrative difficul-

Continued on page 29, column 5

Registration Starts in City With Turnout of 259,630

The first day of registration for the Nov. 3 election, in which the Mayoralty is the principal office at stake, brought out a total of 259,630 voters yesterday. The total was almost 30,000 below that of the number who registered on the first day for the last regular Mayoralty election, in 1949, and almost 300,000 below the first day for last year's Presidential election.

The relatively light turnout was attributed in part to the weather and also to the fact that what turned out to be the last game of the World Series was in progress.

The registration is to entitle voters to cast their ballots for Mayor, President of the City Council, Controller, presidents of the five boroughs, and other offices.

A recapitulation of the registration by boroughs follows:

RECAPITULATION

	1953	1952	1951	1950	1949
Manhattan	65,197	126938	49,545	78,251	77,666
Bronx	52,353	111,778	37,660	59,866	59,324
Brooklyn	86,127	181,889	66,915	97,755	99,139
Queens	50,203	116,067	35,318	53,499	46,573
Richmond	5,750	13,601	3,941	5,268	5,464
	259,630	550,273	193,379	294,639	288,166

Polling places opened at 3:30 p. m. and closed at 10:30. They will maintain the same hours throughout the week until Saturday, when they will open at 7 a. m. and close at 10:30 p. m. Any one who fails to register by Saturday night will not be eligible to vote this year.

Candidates were the center of attraction yesterday as they appeared to register. The Republican candidate for Mayor, Harold

Continued on page 10, column 3

Still a Handy Guy at 54

Sande Is 3d in 1st Race Since 1932

Don Rice

Earl Sande in his silks again (left) and booting home Honest Bread to finish third in the third race yesterday at Belmont Park.

By Ed Sinclair

Earl Sande, the track idol of the Golden Age in sports and one of the greatest jockeys of all time, began his riding comeback at the age of fifty-four yesterday and the atmosphere at Belmont Park had all the flavor of the Roaring '20s.

While 18,228 unashamedly sentimental patrons shouted and clapped encouragement after backing his long-shot assignment down to 7 to 1 on the board, the balding, gray-haired little champion of yesteryear brought his first mount in twenty-one years home third in the third race.

Aboard Mrs. Ethel D. Jacobs' Honest Bread, a nervous three-year-old gelding which had raced only once before, Sande came out of a starting gate for the first time in his life and gave Mrs. Drinkhouse's

Continued on page 29, column 1

Dock Strike Enjoined Ten Days By Taft Law, Full Return in Doubt

Associated Press wirephoto

Chief Justice Warren donning his robe for first time yesterday with the aid of P. H. Marshall, attendant.

I.L.A. Boycott Set on A.F.L. Piers, Ships

By Walter Hamshar

The International Longshoremen's Association was ordered last night in a Taft-Hartley law injunction to call off for at least ten days the five-day strike that has paralyzed New York and eleven other Atlantic Coast ports.

Judge Edward Weinfeld ordered the union's 50,000 East Coast membership to return to work in a temporary restraining order issued in United States District Court here on the application of United States Attorney J. Edward Lumbard and of Warren Burger, Assistant United States Attorney, who had flown from Washington at the order of President Eisenhower.

Expires Oct. 15

Judge Weinfeld issued a temporary order which expires Oct. 15 to give the I. L. A. and waterfront employers an opportunity to argue against extension of the injunction for the full eighty-day period provided by the labor law as a cooling-off period. He set hearings for next Tuesday in his court.

I. L. A. officials accepted the court's action quietly when deputy Federal marshals served them with injunction papers at the Hotel Governor Clinton, where they had met all day in strike meetings. They promised that their membership would be instructed to obey the court's order at once.

The extent of a return-to-work movement today, however, was uncertain. The same officials had warned earlier the day that I. L. A. longshoremen will not work on the same piers and ships with members of the A. F. L. longshoremen's union that was formed after the I. L. A. was ousted from the national labor organization two weeks ago as being dominated by racketeers and gangsters.

May Shut Big Piers

Should the I. L. A. members carry out this threat, large segments of the Brooklyn and Manhattan waterfronts will remain closed despite the injunctions, since members of both organizations work on many piers.

Patrick J. Connolly, I. L. A. executive vice-president and leader of the strike, said the membership would probably be unable to answer the back-to-work order before the 7 o'clock shift tonight or tomorrow morning's shape-up, because of "confusion." "I will order them

Continued on page 31, column 1

Warren Sworn as Chief Justice

By Don Irwin

WASHINGTON, Oct. 5.—Earl Warren took his place as fourteenth Chief Justice of the United States at 12:06 p. m. today after a simple ceremony that opened the fall term of the Supreme Court. Forty minutes later, he was conferring with his eight colleagues on the important and controversial issues before them. The sixty-two-year-old former Governor of California ascended to the place on the high bench left vacant by the death on Sept. 8 of Chief

Continued on page 23, column 4

Turkey Defeats Poland For U. N. Council Seat

By John Molleson

UNITED NATIONS, N. Y., Oct. 5.—All sixty of the United Nations members had to vote eight times by secret ballot today before Turkey, backed by the United States, defeated Poland, the Soviet candidate, for a coveted two-year term on the Security Council.

Only one ballot was required to elect Brazil and New Zealand, filling two of the three impending vacancies in the Council. The delegates had to file down the aisles of the General Assembly hall seven more times to the ballot box before Turkey also attained the necessary forty votes to win, a two-thirds majority of the sixty nations voting. Another contender for the third seat was the Philippines, backed by a group of Asian-African states.

Before the balloting began, Andrei Y. Vishinsky, of Russia, launched into what might have become a nominating speech for Poland. But he barely had time to warm up when Mme. Vijaya Lakshmi Pandit, the Assembly President, interrupted and told him that the Assembly rules did not permit nominations.

The Soviet diplomat continued to speak briefly, but his remarks in Russian were not translated and he took his seat. The President's desk has an electric switch which can cut off a speaker from the simultaneous translators when a speaker is ruled out of order.

On the first ballot Brazil had 56 votes, New Zealand 48, Turkey 32, Poland 18, Philippines 17, Czechoslovakia 2, Ecuador 2 and Mexico 1. Brazil and New Zealand were easily elected by this count, and interest turned to the race among the next three highest candidates.

Poland's strength on each of the eight ballots was fairly consistent—running as high as 23 votes on the fourth ballot, dropping to

Continued on page 6, column 3

Girl, 4, Dies In Refrigerator

GRAND HAVEN, Mich., Oct. 5 (AP).—Four-year-old Pamela Pfishner became another victim of an old refrigerator today when she and a playmate crawled into the small box and were trapped. Her death was the sixteenth such tragedy in the United States and Canada in less than two months.

Rescuers revived her playmate, Lila Mae Carpenter, but Pamela was dead when Lila Mae's mother, Mrs. Robert Carpenter, opened the box and found the children.

Mrs. Carpenter said she called for the children at 12:30 p. m. but neither answered. She looked in the icebox at 1 o'clock and found the girls. A small hole had been punched in the back, but it was not enough to provide air for both children.

It was only three weeks ago that Lila Mae had escaped death in the icebox when she crawled in and the door closed. Her mother found her in time.

Liner Diverted in Strike

Boat Trains Going to Meet The Queen Mary at Halifax

Passengers scheduled to sail for Europe on the Queen Mary tomorrow will board the first boat trains in many years at Grand Central Terminal tonight to meet the Cunard liner at Halifax, where she was diverted because of the longshoremen's walkout here.

The Queen Mary arrived at the Canadian port at 7:30 a. m. yesterday. New York-bound passengers boarded trains that will arrive at Grand Central tomorrow.

Four special boat trains with sleeping accommodations will leave Grand Central tonight at half-hour intervals beginning at 6:30 to take more than 1,000 Europe-bound passengers on the thirty-eight-hour trip to Halifax. The Queen Mary, which used the Port of Halifax regularly during World War II, is scheduled to sail from there at 4:30 p. m. Thursday.

First of the special trains will arrive in Halifax at 9:45 a. m. Thursday, with the other sections arriving at hourly intervals thereafter. The cost of Pullman fare and all meals on the train will be paid by Cunard, so there will be no additional expense for passengers.

Hopeful that peace would be restored to the waterfront today, American Export Lines rescheduled the postponed sailing of the liner Constitution for late this afternoon from Pier 84, Hudson River and 44th St.

The Cunard liner Mauretania docked here without tugs at 4:30 p. m. yesterday at Pier 90, Hudson River and 50th St., with Cunard personnel assisting 1,027 passengers with their luggage.

The Britannic, which was diverted by Cunard to Halifax where she discharged New York-bound passengers, was on her way here after all yesterday when the line decided to have the Britannic, as well as the Mauretania, sail from here Thursday for European ports as scheduled.

INDEX

KANSAS
THE GREATEST MILERS OF ALL TIME, RUNNING THEIR WORLD RECORD TIMES, WOULD HAVE FINISHED THIS FAR BEHIND
WES SANTEE
LAST SATURDAY, WHEN THE KANSAS STRINGBEAN RAN THE 2ND FASTEST MILE IN HISTORY...
...HE GOES AFTER BANNISTER'S WORLD RECORD TONIGHT IN THE COMPTON RELAYS...

Thompson Slams 3

CHARACTER · QUALITY · AMERICA FIRST · ENTERPRISE · ACCURACY
Examiner Sports
AN AMERICAN PAPER FOR THE AMERICAN PEOPLE · THE GREAT NEWSPAPER OF THE GREAT SOUTHWEST
Section Four FRIDAY, JUNE 4, 1954 CCC

Vincent X. Flaherty—

Tennis & Crumpet Club Stages Big Net Program | Odds Against Ex-Jail Athlete Making Good

America's fanciest tennis tournament gets underway tomorrow when a unique organization known as the Tennis and Crumpet Club puts on its annual show for the benefit of the John Tracy Clinic.

The Tennis and Crumpet Club, headed by the Examiner's Carter Ludlow, has been functioning for eight years. Each year its 300 members get together to stage a tournament for a worthy charity, selecting a different charity annually.

DAN REEVES

The John Tracy Clinic, for whose benefit this year's tournament is being staged, was founded to help deaf children. It has performed a wonderful service to the community for the past 12 years.

The main portion of the tournament is to be held at the Beverly Wilshire Hotel, starting tomorrow afternoon at 1 o'clock. The rest of the tournament will be played on private courts at members' homes in Beverly Hills, Bel Air and Brentwood.

From a standpoint of sheer glamour there just isn't anything like the Tennis and Crumpet Club tournament. The affair is loaded with motion picture stars, blue-bookers and tennis stars.

Mrs. Howard Tullis is the tournament chairman. Frank Feltrop, the Beverly Wilshire professional, is the tournament manager. Among those who are donating trophies are Dan Reeves and Fred Levy, major stockholders of the Los Angeles Rams; Ray Hommes, Leslie Kelley, Thomas Bert and Mrs. Cosmo Bellew.

Among those lending their private tennis courts to the cause are: Dr. and Mrs. Omar Fareed, Robert Stack, B. B. Robinson and Mr. and Mrs. Arnold Kirkeby, Leonard Firestone, Paul Henry, Glenn Austin, Roger Converse, William Gargaro, John McNabb, Jack Warner, John McConaty, Roy Scott, the Beverly Hills tennis Club and the Brentwood Country Club.

Among the motion picture people who will be in the tourney are Dinah Shore, Howard Duff, Jack Warner, Mona Freeman, Robert Stack, Walter Pidgeon, Marie Windsor and Marguerite Chapman.

Feltrop said yesterday the tournament should net at least $5000 for the Tracy Clinic.

★ ★ ★

The signing of Billy Joe Moore, a 24-year-old convict, by the New York Yankees, brings to mind the brief and ill-starred career of the late "Alabama" Pitts, who took a fling at pro football and big league baseball during the '30s.

Pitt, a Sing Sing graduate, was the most publicized unknown ever to crash either sport. No rookie ever was a lustier gate attraction. But Pitt's star was dimmed in short order.

Pitt, a halfback, was the Red Grange of prison football. But he was something less than mediocre when he joined the Philadelphia Eagles.

In prison baseball Pitt was sensational. But when Connie Mack gave him a chance to play with the Philadelphia Athletics, Pitt found himself completely out of his class. He disappeared from the scene as quickly as he arrived, but without fanfare.

A couple of years later he was knifed to death as the result of a quarrel.

However, Billy Joe Moore's record in prison baseball displays an arresting array of figures. Any man who can smack 46 homers in 67 games in any kind of baseball is worthy of consideration. His .390 batting average demonstrates his possibilities, too.

At the age of 24 Moore should be just coming into his own as a baseball player. Still and all, there is a world of difference between the kind of baseball they play behind cold prison walls and the brand Billy Joe will run up against on the outside.

★ ★ ★

Americans consider ours the greatest sports-loving nation in the world. But if you read an account of the Derby at Epsom Downs the other day and spotted the attendance you might have found cause for wonderment.

According to the stories, 250,000 racing fans saw Never Say Die, the Kentucky thoroughbred, romp away with the British classic. That's a tremendous crowd, all right, but it is nothing unusual in England.

In England they draw as many as 175,000 people for football. Over here our biggest throngs hardly ever go beyond 100,000 people.

(Continued on Page 5, Cols. 2-3)

Giant Star Ties Record, Bats in Eight

ST. LOUIS, June 3.—(AP)—Hank Thompson blasted out three home runs and Willie Mays two to lead the New York Giants to a 13-8 victory tonight over the St. Louis Cardinals.

Thompson's three home runs in his first three times at bat tied the modern National League record for consecutive homers in a single game.

He also had a single and drove in a total of eight runs.

Thompson's home runs—all to the right field pavilion—were off the pitching of Gerald Staley. He was purposely walked on his fourth trip to the plate, thus losing a chance to set a new league mark.

TWO HOMERS

May's two homers to the left field bleachers were good for five runs and ran his home run mark for the season to 16. This put him into a tie with Hank Sauer of the Chicago Cubs for the lead in that department.

Marv Grissom came into the game in the fourth inning and suppressed a Cardinal attack that had routed Sal Maglie and Bob McCall. Grissom was credited with his third victory against one defeat.

The loss was charged to Joe Presko, the second of three Cardinal pitchers.

Strangely, Thompson previously had not hit a home run since May 18 and Staley was the pitcher on that occasion, too. Thompson's home-run splurge tonight ran his home run total for the season to nine.

The count was tied at 7-7 when Mays blasted his first home run, in the seventh off Presko, and scored behind Alvin Dark and Thompson, who had walked.

N. Y.	AB	H	O	A	St. Louis	AB	H	O	A
Lckmn,1b	4	0	8	1	Moon,cf	5	3	1	0
Dark,ss	4	4	1	3	Shdnst,2b	4	2	4	2
Tmpsn,3b	4	4	2	1	Musial,rf	4	2	3	0
Irvin,lf	5	0	1	0	Jblnski,3b	5	3	1	4
Mueller,rf	5	2	0	0	Alston,1b	5	0	10	0
Mays,cf	5	3	2	0	Repiski,lf	5	0	4	0
Katt,c	4	0	9	0	Gramas,ss	3	0	1	3
Willms,2b	5	1	4	3	Hemus,ss	1	0	0	1
Maglie,p	1	0	0	0	Sarni,c	5	3	3	1
McCall,p	1	0	0	0	Staley,p	1	0	0	0
Grissom,p	3	0	0	2	Burgess	1	0	0	0
					Presko,p	0	0	0	0
					Frazier	0	0	0	0
					Haddix	0	0	0	0
					Brazle,p	0	0	0	1
					Lowrey	1	0	0	0
Totals	41	14	27	10	Totals	40	13	27	12

Burgess grounded out for Staley in 5th.
Hemus walked for Grammas in 7th.
Frazier walked for Presko in 7th.
Haddix ran for Frazier in 7th.
Lowrey struck out for Brazle in 9th.

New York	203 020 312—13
St. Louis	240 100 010— 8

E—Grammas, Maglie. RBI—Thompson 8, Mays 5, Schoendienst, Musial 3, Moon 2, Jablonski 2. 2B—Sarni 2, Moon, Mays, Dark 2. 3B—Schoendienst 2. HR—Thompson 3, Musial, Mays 2. SH—Schoendienst. LOB—New York 5, St. Louis 13. BB—Maglie 1, McCall 1, Grissom 5, Staley 2, Presko 2. SO—Maglie 2, McCall 2, Grissom 5, Presko 1. HO—Maglie 5 in 1⅔, McCall 3 in 1⅔, Grissom 5 in 5⅔, Staley 6 in 5, Presko 4 in 2, Brazle 4 in 2. R-ER—Maglie 6-6, McCall 1-1, Grissom 1-1, Staley 7-6, Presko 3-3, Brazle 3-3. W—Grissom (3-1). L—Presko (3-3). U—Stewart, Pinelli, Boggess. T—2:59. A—

Coast League

	W.	L.	Pct.	*GBL
HOLLYWOOD	37	22	.627	...
San Francisco	32	28	.533	5½
Oakland	31	30	.508	7
San Diego	30	30	.500	7½
Seattle	29	29	.500	7½
Sacramento	29	31	.483	8½
LOS ANGELES	27	31	.466	9½
Portland	22	36	.379	14½

YESTERDAY'S RESULTS

HOLLYWOOD, 4; Sacramento, 1.
San Francisco, 3; Portland, 1.
San Diego, 4; Oakland, 3.
LOS ANGELES at Seattle, rain.

TODAY'S GAMES, PITCHERS

Sacramento (Daley 2-0) at HOLLYWOOD (Queen 11-1), Gilmore Field, 8:15 p. m.
LOS ANGELES (McLish 6-4 and Hatten 7-6) at Seattle (Bearden 4-7 and Widmar 4-4).
Oakland, (Ferrarese 5-6) at San Diego (Erautt 6-5).
Portland (Alexander 2-4) at San Francisco (Holcombe 3-4).

AMERICAN LEAGUE

	W.	L.	Pct.	*GBL
Cleveland	29	14	.674	....
Chicago	29	16	.644	1
New York	27	18	.600	3
Detroit	21	19	.525	6½
Washington	19	24	.442	10
Boston	14	23	.378	12
Philadelphia	16	28	.364	13½
Baltimore	15	28	.349	14

YESTERDAY'S RESULTS

New York, 2; Cleveland, 1.
Chicago, 9; Boston, 6.
Philadelphia, 6; Baltimore, 2.
Washington, 4; Detroit, 3.

TODAY'S GAMES, PITCHERS

Cleveland at New York—Wynn (6-2) vs. Ford (2-4).
Chicago at Boston—Keegan (7-1) vs. Nixon (3-3).
Detroit at Washington—Gray (1-2) vs. Porterfield (6-3).
Baltimore at Philadelphia — Pillette (3-5) or Tulley (4-5) vs. Van Brabant (0-1).

NATIONAL LEAGUE

	W.	L.	Pct.	*GBL
Brooklyn	25	18	.581	...
Milwaukee	23	18	.561	1
New York	24	19	.558	1
Philadelphia	23	19	.548	1½
St. Louis	23	22	.511	3
Cincinnati	21	22	.488	4
Chicago	20	22	.476	4½
Pittsburgh	14	33	.298	13

*Games behind leader.

YESTERDAY'S RESULTS

New York, 13; St. Louis, 8.
Other games, rain.

TODAY'S GAMES, PITCHERS

New York at Cincinnati (night)—Gomez (4-3) vs. Podbielan (3-1).
Pittsburgh at Milwaukee (night)—Surkont (4-5) vs. Nichols (4-4).
Brooklyn at Chicago—Erskine (5-4) vs. Rush (4-3).
Philadelphia at St. Louis (night)—Roberts (7-4) vs. Haddix (7-3).

Trentonian, 8 Picks Run Out

By Maurice Bernard

The form players pitched a shutout yesterday at Hollywood Park as all of the eight favorites were raced into submission, including the Calumet Farm's promising 2-year-old, Trentonian, backed down to 70 cents on the dollar for the $16,525 Westchester stakes.

Running in his first stake after scoring two impressive overnight wins, Trentonian met up with a colt he couldn't handle up and had to settle for second money.

Back Hoe, a double winner in Florida last winter, coming out for his first Hollywood Park appearance, dashed to a $41.30 upset with Ray York riding him hard through the stretch to hold Trentonian safe by a length and one quarter. R. C. Ellsworth's Swaps was third.

One of the two fillies in the field of seven starters, Mrs. Gordon Guiberson's Fly Past, finished fourth in a fine performance after almost getting left at the post.

Back Hoe was clocked in 58 seconds flat for the five furlongs, second fastest time of the season for the short sprint.

It was York's third stake triumph of the season, following his scores aboard Miz Clementine and Is Proud. He had the race won after running down the quick-breaking Modern World, ridden by Bill Shoemaker. Trentonian made up much ground from fifth place on the backstretch, but he wasn't getting to the winner.

Joseph Tomlinson, a Canadian sportsman who bought Back Hoe for $3200 at the Keeneland yearling sales last year, flew in today to see his colt perform and was surprised that he should be so neglected in the betting after the speed he displayed in Florida and in local workouts.

SHOEMAKER BLANK

He is in the construction business and named Back Hoe after a big shovel that scoops up the dirt backwards.

This was the first time during the 13-day meeting the favorites were shut out and Shoemaker also drew his first blank.

The Alberta Ranches' champion filly from England, Sixpence II, looked good winning her first start on American soil, leading Heather Khal and Real Hope from wire to wire to score in 1:10 4-5 for the six furlongs with William Steed aboard.

She paid $22.80 for winning tickets and this was the only surprising thing about the race, for everybody on the track knew she could run. She was undefeated in five starts abroad.

Her Irish groom expressed amazement that she should be quoted at 10-1 on the board, saying that if this race was being run in England or Ireland she would be odds-on.

Replied Jockey Steed: "The filly was even money and I was 9-1."

But Steed gave Sixpence II a real smooth ride, withstanding repeated challenges for the full distance, and got her home safely by a half length. You don't see many of those foreign horses breaking out of the gate with the speed of Sixpence and going on to win that way first time out.

Steed is riding second string

(Continued on Page 4, Col. 7)

HOME AND FAMILY—Former Middleweight Boxing Champion Jake LaMotta, who announced his retirement from ring Wednesday, displays four good reasons for quitting—his family: Wife Vickie; Jack, 7; Christie, 2, and Joe, 5½.
—Associated Press wirephoto.

Ram Tackle Dahms Quits

SAN DIEGO, June 3.—Tom Dahms, first-string tackle for the Los Angeles Rams, said today he expects to quit football this fall to take a job as an assistant coach at San Diego High School.

Ram spokesmen entertain hopes that Dahms will change his mind.

If he leaves, Los Angeles will have only one veteran tackle left — Charley Toogood.

Of the other three veterans, Frank Fuller is in military service, Bob Fry expects to be called and Len Teeuws has been traded to the Chicago Cardinals.

Dahms will be transferred from Horace Mann Junior High, where he has been teaching this spring, to the San Diego High School physical education department, Frank Tait of the city schools personnel department said.

Livingston Named Scholtz Winner

Ronnie Livingston, UCLA's great basketball and net star, was named the Orville Scholtz Sportsmanship trophy winner last night at the annual tennis banquet at the Westwood Hills University.

Dick Doss and Jim Read were named co-captains of the 1955 squad and Coach J. D. Morgan selected Livingston, Doss, Read and Bob Perry to go to the NCAA meet in Seattle, June 21-26.

Santee Bids Tonight in Mile Event

By Melvin Durslag

Wes Santee, the young Kansas foot racer who has been fighting a ceaseless battle lately with some of the world's most honored watches, steps out at the Compton Invitational tonight for another whirl at the four-minute mile.

Wesley will do this at the Compton College stadium, where the mile run has been billed the feature of this year's Invitational, which will be televised from 8:30 to 10 p. m. over KTTV, Channel 11.

It is Santee's rather prejudiced view that he will run the distance tonight in time ranging from 4:00 to 4:01. He bases this opinion on two factors:

(1) On his clocking of 4:01.3, the second fastest mile in history, which he posted at Mission, Kan., last week, and (2) on his self-appraisal as the greatest two-legged racer of all time.

Either reason, he feels, is grounds enough for a mile roughly in the neighborhood of four minutes tonight.

Queried in Lawrence, Kan., shortly before departure on how he feels he would do in a race against England's Roger Bannister, Santee replied:

"If you hooked Bannister onto the Twentieth Century Limited, he couldn't beat Santee."

While you might say that Wes is foot racing's answer to Art Aragon, the fact remains that the guy is a fine runner; the best American miler, in fact, ever.

In catching a clocking of 4:01.3 last week, a time exceeded only by Bannister's 3:59.4 last month, Santee turned his quarters in 58 seconds, 62.2, 61.8 and 59.3.

He feels he can knock a full second from his second lap which, if possible, would bring him down to 4:00.3 at Compton.

HITS PRIMARY OPPOSITION

Santee's opposition will come primarily from a Swedish civil servant named Ingvar Ericsson, who slides down the pole with the boys in a Stockholm fire house.

Ericsson whipped the field at the Coliseum Relays two weeks ago, but pulled up unexpectedly short of breath in 4:13.1. He says he has benefited from the race and will shorten his time noticeably in his race against Santee.

Russ Bonham of Whittier, Marty Montgomery of USC, Walt Boehm of the Olympic Club and Billy Tidwell of Fort Ord will round out the field.

Apart from the mile run, the Compton management has booked a rather interesting supporting card which will include the following:

(a) A 440 involving Jim Lea, J. W. Mashburn and George Rhoden.

(b) An 880 involving Mal Whitfield, Jim Terrill and Bobby Seaman.

(c) A two-mile struggle between Fred Wilt and Horace Ashenfelter.

(d) A 100-yard dash between

(Continued on Page 5, Col. 4)

Lausse TV Ring Choice

NEW YORK, June 3.—(AP)—Eduardo (KO) Lausse, Argentina's hope for a world boxing title, aims for his 17th straight victory tomorrow night when he faces veteran middleweight Joe Rindone of Boston in Madison Square Garden.

The belting, 26-year-old Gaucho is a 1-4 favorite to keep his streak alive in the 10-rounder. The bout will start at 7 p. m. (PDT), and will be broadcast and telecast coast to coast. (KNBH, 4, and KABC will air the fight in Los Angeles).

Yanks Nip Tribe in Thriller, 2-1

NEW YORK, June 3.—(AP)—Joe Collins' eighth inning home run and a brilliant ninth inning defensive stand gave the New York Yankees a thrilling 2-1 victory over the Cleveland Indians today.

Collins' homer, his second of the season, broke up a 1-1 pitching duel between Cleveland's Bob Lemon and New York's Ed Lopat but it took some sensational fielding by Left Fielder Irv Noren and Shortstop Phil Rizzuto in the ninth to stop the Indians.

After Rudy Regalado had opened the Tribe's ninth with a single, George Strickland followed with a liner to left field but Noren, charging in head-on, made a spectacular tumbling catch for his second great play of the game.

RIZZUTO DIVES FOR BALL

In the seventh, he had raced far back to deep left to take away an extra base hit from Jim Hegan with a backhanded grab.

The Indians weren't through yet. Hegan singled moving Dave Pope, running for Regalado, to second. Dale Mitchell, batting for Lemon, rapped a sharp grounder through the box that was headed for centerfield. But Rizzuto dived headlong, snared the ball in the webbing of his glove and flipped it in time to force Hegan at second while Pope stopped at third. Jerry Coleman ended the game with a neat stop of Al Smith's bouncing ball near second to force Mitchell.

The Indians outhit the Yanks, 11 to four, but, as usual, couldn't hit Lopat in the pinches. The wily southpaw did not walk a batter and permitted only one extra base hit, Lemon's two-out double in the fourth, as he racked up his sixth triumph against a lone defeat. Nine Indians were stranded on the basepaths.

Cleveland	A	H	O	A	New York	A	H	O	A
Smith,lf	5	0	3	0	Rizzuto,ss	3	0	4	2
Avila, 2b	4	0	1	3	Collins, 1b	3	1	11	0
Doby, cf	4	2	2	0	Mantle, cf	4	1	1	0
Rosen, 1b	4	1	12	0	Berra, c	4	1	5	0
Philley,rf	4	1	2	0	Slaughter	4	0	0	0
Regalado	4	1	1	1	Noren, lf	3	1	3	0
Pope	0	0	0	0	Coleman	3	0	2	2
Strickland	4	2	1	4	Carey, 3b	1	0	0	1
Hegan, c	4	2	2	0	McDougald	2	0	1	3
Lemon, p	3	2	0	3	Lopat, p	3	0	0	2
Mitchell	1	0	0	0					
Totals	37	11	24	11	Totals	30	4	27	10

Pope ran for Regalado in 9th.
Mitchell hit into force play for Lemon in 9th.

Cleveland	010 000 000— 1
New York	000 100 01x— 2

E—Doby, Strickland, Rosen, Coleman. RBI—Lemon, Noren, Collins. 2b—Lemon. HR—Collins. DP—Rizzuoto and Collins; McDougald and Collins. Left—Cleveland 9, New York 6. BB—Lemon 2. SO—Lemon 1, Lopat 5. R-ER—Lemon 2-2; Lopat 1-1. W—Lopat (6-1). L—Lemon (7-2). U—Hurley, Grieve, Umont, Berry. T—2:06. A—15,141.

Lions Okay College Rules for Chi All-Star Tussle

DETROIT, June 3.—(AP)—The Detroit Lions, who have been feuding with sponsors of the all-star football game over rules of substitution, today said they are willing to abide by the complete set of collegiate rules.

In a press statement, Edwin J. Anderson, president of the world champion Lions, said "as world champions for the second straight year we now feel we can serve the best interests of football by adhering to the 1953 collegiate rule book for this year's game."

"If the best interests of this great game will be served," Anderson continued, "and if Commissioner Bert Bell agrees to our new stand, then we shall recommend the complete use of collegiate rules for the all-star game August 13 in Soldier Field in Chicago."

In Philadelphia, Bell said he will ask the Chicago Tribune Charities to allow the game to be played under the complete set of college rules.

Bell said, "The Detroit Lions football club has wired me requesting that they be allowed to meet the College All-Stars . . . under the complete set of college rules.

"I congratulate the Detroit Lions and their head coach, Buddy Parker, for making this request. It is the mark of a true champion. They have placed the game itself above all other considerations.

"I, therefore, will ask the Chicago Tribune Charities that this year's game be played under the complete set of college rules."

'Mays' Catch One of Best I Ever Saw--Di Maggio'

By Joe Di Maggio

NEW YORK, Sept. 30. — All summer long out on the Coast I wondered how the Giants managed to stay on top in the National League. Yesterday at the Polo Grounds I found out.

JOE DI MAGGIO

Leo Durocher has a club with great fighting spirit, a good bench and Willie Mays. Cleveland had a corking chance to win the game in the eighth with men on first and second, nobody out and the score tied at 2 to 2. Nothing came of this chance because Mays made one of the finest catches I ever saw. And I'm something of an expert on World Series catches because in 1947 little Al Gionfriddo of the Dodgers went practically out of the Yankee Stadium to take a home run away from me.

Dusty Rhodes' homer in the tenth with two on which won the game 5 to 2 for the Giants was typical of the way Dusty and the club have been going all year. Rhodes had an average of .333 as a pinch hitter and the home run he hit yesterday wasn't his first as a pinch hitter. And I am pretty sure that it will not be his last.

The wind played a big part in the game. It was blowing across the field from left to right all day, particularly strong in the later innings. It carried a home run away from Al Dark in the ninth and in the eighth Jim Hegan, the Cleveland catcher, hit one to left which seemed certain to carry to the seats until the wind held it up.

This same wind which took homers away from Dark and Hegan gave Rhodes his game-buster, blowing the ball just over the parapet of the lower right field stands, fair by about five feet. Dave Pope, who had relieved Dave Philley in right for Cleveland, played Rhodes' ball perfectly and was under it all the way until the wind nudged it to the stands. He made a desperate leap but the ball was just out of his reach.

THE NEWS SPORTS

Another victim of the wind was Monte Irvin, although his mishap when the wind blew a ball out of his hands for a two-base error had no bearing on the outcome.

Both Sal Maglie and Bob Lemon had a little trouble with their control at the start but Bob settled down to do a wonderful pitching job. His slider was far more effective in the late innings. Of the nine Giant hits only two were made after the fourth. Marvin Grissom did an excellent job in relief. His screwball was particularly good against left-handed pinch hitters, getting Pope and Bill Glynn on strikes.

All this year and indeed in other years when I was playing with the Yankees, the Indians have been a great late inning club. You had to watch them carefully from the seventh on. Yesterday Clevelanc held to the same pattern, putting Maglie on the ropes in the seventh. Sal walker Larry Doby and then Al Rosen smashed a terrific shot at Dark which the Giant shortstop knocked down with his bare hand.

With men on first and second, Leo Durocher lifted Maglie and put in a left-hander, Don Liddle, to pitch against the left-handed Vic Wertz who had tripled home two in the first and singled in each of his next two tries. This time Wertz really unloaded. The ball took off for the green screen in front of the right center bleachers, about 450 feet from the plate. Mays raced with the ball, never took his eyes off it once and caught it only a few feet from the bleacher wall.

As remarkable as the ground Willie had to cover to make the catch—and he just did get to the ball—was the judgment he showed in not letting the fence scare him off. One of the most difficult plays for an outfielder to make is to go at top speed to the fence for the ball. Mays turned his back to the plate and just ran. He and the ball reached the edge of the wall at the same time. And he wasted no time hustling the ball back to the infield, either.

Remember that any time you see an outfielder go against the fence for a catch, you've seen something special. If they played baseball on open prairies, anybody who could run could make a catch.

After Mays made his great catch, Durocher took out Liddle and called on Grissom. Sitting right behind home plate, I could see both his screwball breaking sharply and his curve breaking nicely and he was getting the ball where he wanted it. He was a revelation to me. When I saw him working for Detroit, he was just a run of the mine pitcher, barely getting by. I had heard about how valuable he had been to the Giants this year and after looking at him I could see why.

In fact, after looking at the Giants, I could see how they've won the National League pennant. I also could see why they won the world series opener. And it never hurts to win the opener.

(Copyright, 1954, Mirror Enterprise Co.)

By Bud Spencer
THE NEWS SPORTS EDITOR

Say Hey Kid Makes Most Unnatural Catch

NEW YORK, Sept. 30.—It will go down in the box scores that a 10th inning pinch-hit home run by Dusty Rhodes won the opening game of this richest World Series, but the hero of the New York Giants' ding-dong victory was Willie (The Wonder) Mays.

WILLIE MAYS

For there wasn't going to be any 10th inning if the Say Hey Kid didn't pull off one of his super-special acts in the eighth inning. Willie, who just does what comes natural, made one of the most unnatural catches in World Series history. It was right out of Ringling Bros. Mays went to the deepest fence to pull down Vic Wertz' 450-foot drive that was labeled a three-base-hit from the very start.

There were two men on at the time, and Mays' wonderful effort either so inspired Giant reliefer Marv Grissom or so dumbfounded the Cleveland Indians that the Giants got out of a peck of trouble without a run.

In the dressing room after the exciting denoument, reporters crowded around Willie. Groping for a question that would pinpoint the catch-as-catch-can talking Mays on the greatness of the catch, a reporter asked: "Willie, did you ever think you could make that catch?"

Willie gave it studied thought for a moment.

"Not at first, I didn't."

"When did you then?"

"When my feet tells me I am."

"When did they tell you?"

"When they get me to the wall ahead of the ball, and the ball drops in my glove."

"Just as simple as that, Willie?"

"Yes sir, simple as long as my feet gets me there."

* * *

Make It Simple Game

As has been noted for the entire season, baseball—the way Willie The Wonder plays it—is a remarkably simple game.

It is said that Leo Durocher, the dandy little manager of the Giants, never leaves a hunch unused, and aside from Willie's perfectly wonderful sprint—and—gymnastics feat, the game was won by a pair of Durocher's hunches. Durocher's ouija board seems to respond with amazing accuracy in times of crisis. That's when he is the most psychic.

He removed Sal Maglie, the unshaven barber, in the eighth after a walk and Al Rosen's infield bingle that Al Dark knocked down bare-handed. Little Don Liddle, a leftie, served up that 480-footer to Vic Wertz, who had batted in the Indians' two runs in the opening inning.

That was enough for Durocher to quit thinking, and reach for the hunch bag. Granted a reprieve on the Mays catch, Durocher wasted no time in waving in his established fireman, Marv Grissom, who put out the fire.

Before the game Durocher had elected to start Monte Irvin in left field. Leo explained that after sleeping on it he went for Irvin rather than Rhodes.

"I'd rather have Rhodes on the bench in case I need him in a jam," he explained.

* * *

Short Hit, Big Payoff

Obviously it wasn't strawberry jam. Actually Rhodes' drive into the short corner of the right field stands was a two-bit hit. But it was a $100,000 baby for results; that is if the Giants win the series.

Bob Lemon, who won 23 games for the Tribe, was not at his loveliest best all afternoon, and he made a mistake in throwing to Rhodes.

Rhodes is a pull hitter who likes fast balls, but doesn't relish a low curve any too well. Lemon, who was having trouble with his control all afternoon, broke off a curve that was waist high in the slot and Rhodes pulled it into the shortest corner. One of those things. An easy out in most parks but Dave Pope and Bobby Avila had to lean against the fence and watch the winning blow ricochet off the hand of a screaming Giant fan.

It was actually not an overly exciting game most of the way. But Willie the Wonder set off the fire and things got real exciting after that. It was no shining day for the mighty men of swat—Mays, Avila, Doby, Mueller and Rosen. Their bats, except for here and there, were rather demure, but Vic Wertz almost did it alone.

* * *

Came Up From Orioles

The amiable Dutchman, who was rescued in June from the lowly Orioles, belted that two-run triple in the first, came up with two more singles and a double after that.

And then, of course, there was one of those Ruthian swats that Mays just caught with his feet. That's the way Willie said it, didn't he?

For sure this is a different World Series. The Yanks aren't in it. And so Lucy Monroe didn't sing the national anthem. That wasn't Lucy's voice changing. It was Perry Como, and crooner Como got the biggest hand of the day up to Rhodes' homer. What did Como lead the league in?

Pinch-Hit Homer First to Decide A Series Game

NEW YORK, Sept. 30.—Dusty Rhodes' 10th-inning, pinch-hit home run yesterday was the first of its kind which decided a world series game.

Three other pinch homers have been hit in series games—but all were delivered in a losing cause.

They were Yogi Berra, Yankees, 1947; Johnny Mize, Yankees, 1952, and George Shuba, Dodgers, 1953.

Buckeyes Drill On Cal Plays

COLUMBUS, O., Sept. 30. — Ohio State's varsity scrimmaged against California plays in preparation for Saturday's game here.

The offensive scrimmage was short, with the third and fourth stringers getting in an extra half hour, but coach Woody Hayes held a long defensive workout. The Buckeye passing fizzled at first but then improved as quarterbacks John Borton and David Leggett combined to complete all but one of 11 tries.

Tribe Homer Lifts Curtain on 2nd Tilt

Smith Hits 1st Antonelli Pitch

Cleveland Jumps Into Early Lead

By Bud Spencer
News Sports Editor

POLO GROUNDS, New York, Sept. 30.—Outfielder Al Smith's homerun on southpaw Johnny Antonelli's first pitch of the gave gave Cleveland a 1-0 lead over the Giants after three innings of their second game in the World Series.

Cleveland took command on the very first pitch of the game when Antonelli grooved a fast ball that Smith crashed into the leftfield stands for the first Indian homerun of the series. Flychaser Irvin didn't even bother to run for the ball when he heard the crack of the bat.

Out Of Trouble

Antonelli retired the next two Indians, but then walked Rosen and Wertz. Westlake followed by ripping a single through the box, but the Giants' southpaw was saved a run because the ailing-legged Rosen was held at third. Mays threw a strike to the plate that would have caught Rosen by a mile. With the bases loaded, Antonelli retired Strickland on a popup to Lockman.

Hegan led off the Tribe second inning by greeting Antonelli's first pitch for a double down the leftfield line. Wynn's sacrifice bunt moved Hegan to third. But Smith, who had homered the previous inning, struck out swinging and Avila fouled out to Thompson.

Wertz punctuated the Tribe's third frame with his fifth hit of the series, a blooper off the tip of the bat. Antonelli walked Westlake, but Strickland grounded to shortstop to retire the side and the Indians had stranded six men in the first third of the game.

Gem by Thompson

An electrifying play by third baseman Thompson helped Antonelli in the fourth after the young southpaw walked Smith with two outs. Avila drove a terrific ground smash that Thompson speared with a full-length dive to his left. The third baseman leaped to his feet to force the speedy Smith with a fine throw to second base.

—United Press Telephoto

GOT IT—Willie Mays turned in the most spectacular defensive play of the game yesterday when he raced back only several feet away from the right center field wall to rob Vic Wertz of at least a triple. Here he has just completed the catch with his back to the playing field. The robbery occurred in the eighth inning.

—United Press Photo

GIANT HEROES—Dusty Rhodes, whose three-run homer gave the Giants a 5-2 victory over Cleveland in the first game of the World Series, cracks a weak smile as Willie Mays tips Dusty's hat for the photographer. Mays contributed a tremendous catch on Vic Wertz' mighty clout to keep Giants in the game.

—United Press Telephoto

BLEACHER VIEW—Here's how bleacher fans witnessed Willie Mays' great catch on Vic Wertz' long drive deep in centerfield.

Leo, Boss Agreed on Next Season

By United Press Sports Wire

NEW YORK, Sept. 30. — Arm in arm, toasting their big World Series victory, big boss Horace Stoneham and Giant Manager Leo Durocher, made it plain today they would operate together next year despite reports to the contrary.

Stoneham said he had heard the reports and was getting a little tired of them.

"Listen—I still sign the pay checks in this outfit and I'm going to keep right on doing them for Leo," he said. "He signed a two year contract and it has a year to go. That's all there is to it and anybody who says otherwise doesn't know what they're talking about."

Two years ago, after the Giants failed to defend the National League championship they won ir 1951, Durocher and Stoneham had a show-down. Leo had received offers from Hollywood, where his wife, Laraine Day, is an established star, and he was listening. Stoneham told him then to forget about either the Hollywood offers—or the Giants.

Last year there were differences again when Stoneham thought Leo lost interest and let his club flounder.

Rhodes Brought Them Down Out Of the Clouds

By United Press Sports Wire

HAVANA, Cuba, Sept. 30.—Dusty Rhodes' game-winning world series home run yesterday came as a blessing to crewmen in a transport plane high over the Gulf of Mexico.

They were acting as a relay for the "live" transmission of the first game of the series to a cuban television network and had been in the air four hours and 20 minutes when Rhodes settled the issue in the 10th inning.

Who Was 1st Hero? Here's Vote for Mays

Hard to Pick Against Rhodes, but Writer Strings Along With Willie

By Dan Daniel
Scripps-Howard Staff Writer

NEW YORK, Sept. 30.—Quite often the comparative evaluation of heroic achievements in World Series presents considerable difficulty. The opening game of the current classic developed a striking example of this not unpleasant dilemma.

With two runners on base and one out in the 10th inning, James (Dusty) Rhodes came out of the Giant dugout to bat for Monte Irvin. He blew Bob Lemon's first pitch into the right field stands, beating the Indians by 5 to 2.

Now let us turn back to the eighth inning, and a thoroughly amazing, I might even say preposterous, catch by Willie Mays.

Stage Is Set

Now after Larry Doby had walked and Al Rosen had singled, Vic Wertz, a lefthanded batter, who had delivered a triple and two singles, appeared at the plate.

Leo Durocher lost no time in rushing the southpaw Don Liddle to the relief of Sal Maglie. This strategic maneuver offered scarcely any impediment to Wertz, who crashed a pitch to the concrete wall in front of the right center bleachers.

At the crack of the bat, the fleet Willie Mays began to run. He turned his back to the diamond, and kept right on running until, just as the ball was about to carom off the barrier and ruin the Giants, Willie grabbed it.

The Indians lost the game then and there.

He Casts His Vote

Who, then, was the hero of the game? Rhodes, with his conclusive, devastating blow? Or Mays, with his catch? Before the jury goes out to create more confusion, let me cast my vote, emphatically and irrevocably, for Mays and the greatest fielding exploit it has been my privilege to witness in many years of World Series reporting.

In allocating the honors of the 10-inning thriller to a player who caught a ball rather than to the one who contrived the climactic homer, I have no intention of joining the demeaners of Rhodes' exploit.

Rhodes Homer Barely Cleared Wall in Outfield

By United Press Sports Wire

NEW YORK, Sept. 30.—Dusty Rhodes' game-winning blow, which gave the Giants a 5-2, 10-inning victory over the Indians in the World Series opener, is known jokingly around the National League as a Polo Grounds "Chinese" homer.

The right field foul pole in the Giant's home park is only 257 feet from home plate. The wall is 11 feet high.

Rhodes' homer barely cleared the wall about six or seven feet in fair territory. A fan tried to catch the ball but succeeded only in deflecting it back onto the playing field.

There were many spectators who thought at first that the ball might be called a ground-rule double because the fan had reached over the wall to grab the ball.

Numerous television fans also were bewildered because the ball was ruled a home run after bouncing back on the field.

First Game Box Score

CLEVELAND (A)

	AB	R	H	O	A
Smith, lf	4	1	1	1	0
Avila, 2b	5	1	1	2	3
Doby, cf	3	0	1	3	0
Rosen, 3b	5	0	1	1	3
Wertz, 1b	5	0	4	11	1
dRegalado	0	0	0	0	0
Grasso, c	0	0	0	1	0
Philley, rf	3	0	0	0	0
aMajeski	0	0	0	0	0
bMitchell	0	0	0	0	0
Strickland, ss	3	0	0	2	3
Dente, ss	0	0	0	0	0
cPope, rf	1	0	0	0	0
Hegan, c	4	0	0	6	1
eGlynn, 1b	1	0	0	0	0
Lemon, p	4	0	0	1	1
TOTALS	38	2	8	28	12

NEW YORK (N)

	AB	R	H	O	A
Lockman, 1b	5	1	1	9	0
Dark, ss	4	0	2	3	2
Mueller, rf	5	1	2	2	0
Mays, cf	3	1	0	2	0
Thompson, 3b	3	1	1	3	3
Irvin, lf	3	0	0	5	0
fRhodes	1	1	1	0	0
Williams, 2b	4	0	0	1	1
Westrum, c	4	0	2	5	0
Maglie, p	3	0	0	0	2
Liddle, p	0	0	0	0	0
Grissom, p	1	0	0	0	0
Totals	36	5	9	30	8

a—Announced for Philley in 8th.
b—Walked for Majeski in 8th.
c—Called out on strikes for Strickland in 8th.
d—Ran for Wertz in 10th.
f—Hit home run for Irvin in 10th.

Cleveland (A) .... 200 000 000 0—2
New York (N) .... 002 000 000 3—5

E—Mueller 2, Irvin. RBI—Wertz 2, Mueller, Thompson, Rhodes 3. 2B—Wertz. 3B—Wertz. HR—Rhodes. SB—Mays. S—Irvin, Dente. LOB—Cleveland 13, New York 9. BB—Lemon 5, Maglie 2, Grissom 3. SO—Maglie 2, Lemon 6, Grissom 2. HO—Maglie 7-7 (pitched to two batters in 8th), Liddle 0-⅓, Grissom 1-2⅔. R-ER—Maglie 2-2, Liddle 0-0, Lemon 5-5, Grissom 0-0. WP—Lemon. HBP—Maglie (Smith). W—Grissom. L—Lemon. U—Barlick (N), plate; Berry (A), 1B; Conlan (N), 2B; Stevens (A), 3B; Warneke (N), left field; Napp (A), right field. T—3:11. A—52,751.

Illinois Rooters Happy as Eliot Gives Bates Nod at Right Half

No Relief for Stanford in Injury Shelving Woodson That Forces Switch in Illini Backs

By Bucky Walter

Soph Abe Woodson, Illinois' starting right halfback in the Penn State opener, is hobbled by a leg injury and is scheduled for only limited duty against Stanford this Saturday.

But the Injuns have no reason to sigh in relief.

Woodson's absence at the Palo Alto kickoff merely forces a lineup switch that Grandstand Quarterbacks wanted Illini Coach Ray Eliot to make regardless of the sophomore's absence through injury.

Now Mickey Bates, J. C. Caroline's halfback running mate last season, will return to duty at right half. From this arrangement, Bates tallied 11 touchdowns to lead the Illini in scoring.

Eliot's strategy was to convert the chunky, 200-pound Bates to fullback because he carries sock as a blocker. But Illini rooters groaned that Bates carried the mail only three times in the 14-12 Penn State defeat and advanced the ball but four yards. Such a terrible waste, moaned Eliot's second guessers.

Illini Arrive Tonight

Anyhow, Bob Wiman, 195-pound letterman end-converted-to-fullback, will start against the Stanfords. Wiman played some against Penn State behind Bates.

The Illini squad of 38 will arrive tonight at 7:40 via United Airlines charter flight and bed at Rickey's Studio Inn, Palo Alto, Eliot will introduce his Big Ten gridders to Stanford Stadium's turf in an afternoon workout tomorrow.

In a telephonic gabfest with the Illinois coach, Publicist Chuck Flynn learned that the quarterback assignment will go to Em Lindbeck, junior letterman. Early this week, Flynn felt that Soph Hiles Stout would take over because of his superior passing skill.

Stress Ground Attack

However, the Illini are noted for their infantry attack. The invaders moved the bal 230 yards on the ground against Penn State and only 77 by air, with a 1953 background of 2481 yards rushing and only 724 passing.

Flynn reported that Eliot is concerned by lack of depth at guards, although the two starters, Jan Smid (196) and Walt Vernasco (197), are highly regarded senior lettermen.

"Bucky Tate, a topgrade senior, has an ankle injury and will see only limited duty," explained Flynn. "Paul Furimsky and George Walsh both have hurt legs and won't make the trip. We're digging deeply for two inexperienced sophomores, Ralph Nelson at right guard and Vito Iovino at the left post."

Baseball Ballad

* * *

Dusty Does It

By Berton Braley

The home run hitters weren't hitting them strong enough, the long-ball hitters weren't gettin' much "lenth," for nobody's wallops were high and long enough, 'till Dusty dusted one in the tenth.

Yes, Dusty Rhodes, of the battling Giants, stepped up to bat in the "pinch" or "clutch," and with precision and skill and science, delivered the homer they needed much.

* * *

HE PROVED the Giant team's greatest "strenth" when Dusty dusted one in the tenth. Up to that time it was mostly pitching, and hitting rallies were pretty few, for hitters didn't seem to be hitching onto the stuff that the twirlers threw—and the score for ages was two to two.

The amazing Mays wasn't real amazing, for he didn't garner a single hit, his red hot bat was far from blazing, but his fielding cheered up the fans a bit—for the Indian, Wertz, cracked a wallop bound, apparently, for Long Island sound, but Willie chased it for half a mile, and grabbed it in truly amazin' style.

* * *

ON THE Cleveland team it was Wertz who starred (or that's the viewpoint of this here bard) for, except for Mays' amazing catch of his almost-homer, throughout the match Wertz was so dependable that he got a hit every time at bat.

Lemon's pitching was something splendid, and that's a tribute you can't refuse, he pitched all through 'til the game was ended—for Bob 'twas a darn tough game to lose.

But Dusty Rhodes was the glamor boy—Dusty Rhodes was the starry actor, Dusty's beautiful right-seats fly was the chief event and the winning factor. Oh that was a wall of "lenth" and "strenth" when Dusty dusted one in the tenth.

Race Driver Killed

OKLAHOMA CITY, Sept. 30.—Stan Calloway, Miami, Fla., race driver, was killed when his racing car crashed into a guard rail and overturned at the Oklahoma State Fair yesterday.

WEATHER

CLOUDY
U. S. Report, Page 2
★

DAILY RECORD

Vol. 283—No. 79 52 Pages Boston, Thursday, Sept. 30, 1954 Entered as Second Class Matter at Boston Postoffice 5 CENTS

THE RECORD HAS THE LARGEST CIRCULATION IN NEW ENGLAND

SUNRISE EDITION

PINCH HOMER PACES 5-2 GIANT WIN

Antonelli, Wynn Hurl 2nd Game

STORY ON BACK PAGE

Shortest Homer

That's what Cleveland Mgr. Al Lopez called this 270-ft. belt by Jim "Dusty" Rhodes, Giants' pinch-hitter, which gave Giants 5-2 victory in first World Series game. Dave Pope vainly leaps for the ball. (AP Wirephoto)

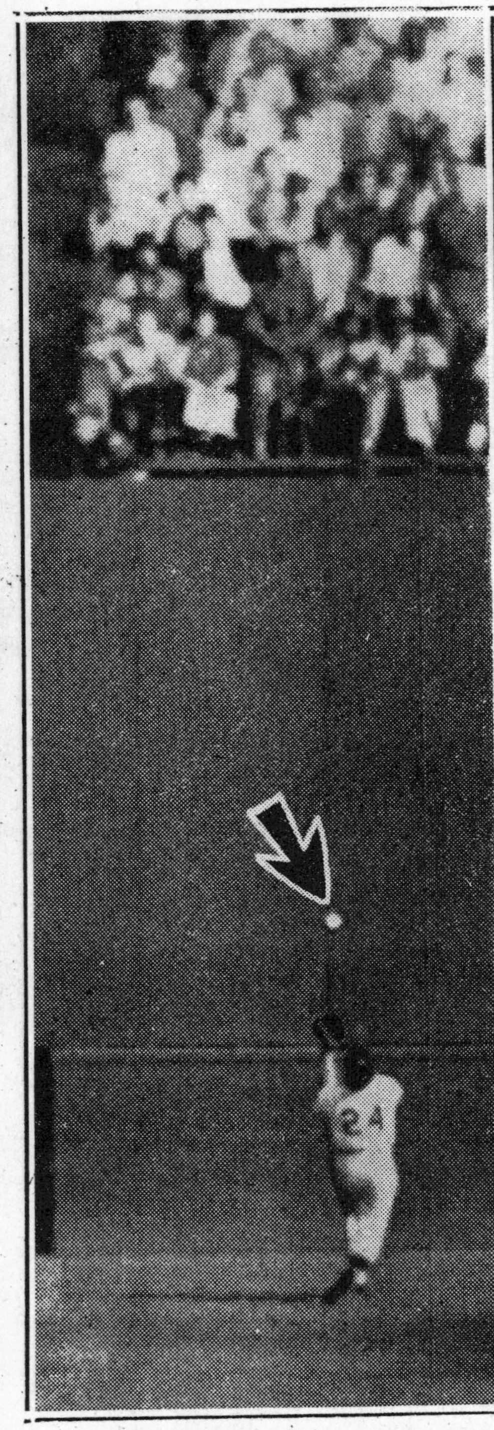

Longest Out—Lopez, in after-game interview, said this was the "longest out" as Willie Mays, running full tilt and back to the plate, snagged 450 ft drive of Vic Wertz, with two men on base, to end eighth inning. (AP Wirephoto)

The Top of the News

Wynn vs. Antonelli
The Indians will come back with Early Wynn against Johnny Antonelli of the Giants today after losing the World Series opener 5-2. —Back Page

Warn of Killer
Parents of slain Stephen Goldberg, 4½, warn Springfield killer will strike again if not caught. —Page 3

Boy Beheaded
Headless body of missing Iowa boy found in pasture. Salesman taken into custody. —Page 2

$19,897 Missing
Probers are trying to trace a shortage of $19,897 in state accounts. A woman is under suspicion. —Page 3

France Yielding
U. S. and Britain bring France near agreement to rearm Germany. —Page 2

Blumenthal Plea
Dist. Atty. Lane agrees to Ronnie Blumenthal second degree murder plea. —Page 5

Candidate Fired On
Missouri man's eye injured by flying glass from auto hit by bullet. —Page 4

Hits Gen. Bradley
Gen. Van Fleet testified before Senate board of mistakes by Gen. Bradley and Gen. Collins. —Page 4

Pleads for Gun
Chicago father pleads for cop's gun to shoot driver who killed his son. —Page 5

ANOTHER FOOTBALL WEEKLY PAYOFF--$550 IN PRIZES

TURN TO PAGE 40

Sunday Mirror FINAL ★★
Vol. 23. NEW YORK 17, N. Y., SUNDAY, OCTOBER 3, 1954 No. 39.

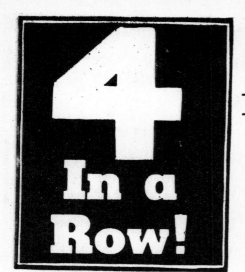

4 In a Row!

Sweep Series, 7-4

G-I-A-N-T-S World Champs!

Stories on Page 58; other photos on Center Fold, Page 58 and Back Page

(AP WIREphoto)

Who's on bass? Wonderful Willie Mays and pitcher Paul Giel (right) team up for a victory song in the shower after the World Champion Giants washed out the Cleveland Indians in a four-game Series cleanup.

MARILYN DIVORCES JOE

He Didn't Talk for 10 Days, Says Star

—International News Photo

MARILYN MONROE SIGNS THE DIVORCE PAPERS
The Marriage Lasted Nine Months—The Divorce Took 15 Minutes

(Other Photos A-14)

By DICK O'CONNOR

Testimony that she had expected "love and warmth" but was treated with "coldness and indifference"—including 10-day stretches of the silent treatment when she displeased him—won a divorce for Film Star Marilyn Monroe from Joe DiMaggio today.

She soaked a little white handkerchief with tears as she told how the ex-baseball star's chilly moods drove her to despair.

In Santa Monica's Superior Court before Judge Orlando H. Rhodes and a jammed courtroom, the wiggly little blonde wept as she told her story under guidance of Attorney Jerry Geisler. She testified:

"I hoped to have out of my marriage love, warmth, affection and understanding. But the relationship turned out to be one of coldness and indifference.

WOULDN'T SPEAK

"My husband would get into moods when he wouldn't speak to me for periods of sometimes 10 days. If I would ask him what the trouble was,

(Continued on Page 5, Col. 3)

Sixth Jury Seated at Trial

Dr. Sheppard Family Barred From Talking

(For Dorothy Kilgallen story see page A-5, and Burris Jenkins Pen Sketches see page A-14).

CLEVELAND, Oct. 27 (AP)—The state—for the second time—approved a final jury today to try Dr. Samuel H. Sheppard for murder. But the defense removed another juror. The defense had just one challenge or automatic dismissal left when the trial adjourned for the day.

By JACK LOTTO

CLEVELAND, Oct. 27 (INS)—The family of Dr. Samuel Sheppard was barred today from talking to the accused wife-slayer in the courtroom as a sixth full jury was tentatively seated.

The osteopath's brother, Dr. Stephen Sheppard, angrily described the ruling by Sheriff Joseph Sweeney as "asinine."

Sheriff Sweeney said he ordered the family to keep behind the railing separating the visitors from the court floor because "that's the rule around here."

Before the sheriff acted today, the family of the babyfaced defendant had congregated around him during re-

(Continued on Page 4, Col. 1)

Woman Falls Ten Floors to Death

Mrs. Thelma Silbert, 28, leaped or fell to her death from the tenth story of the Bay Cities Building in Santa Monica today, landing on the roof of an adjoining two-story building. She was dead on arrival at Santa Monica Hospital, where her husband was taken to identify the body.

Wants Europe Secure, Then Might Talk

Ike Spurns Red Meet

By MARVIN L. ARROWSMITH

WASHINGTON, Oct. 27 (AP)—President Eisenhower spoke out today against any meeting of the Western Powers with Russia at this time, but left the way open for a conference later.

The President stated his position at a news conference in which he also said that in his opinion there is better reason today to hope for lasting peace than there has been in the past.

He did not pin that view directly to the new agreements for Western European defense with West Germany in the lineup, but related it to that development along with others in the past two years.

He was specific, however, in saying it is his opinion this is not the time for any meeting of the United States Great Britain and France with the Soviet Union.

SEEKS SECURITY

He added that whenever this government has reason to believe the Russians are sincere about wanting to build an en-

(Continued on Page 4, Col. 2-3)

LOS ANGELES EVENING
HERALD EXPRESS
International News Service Associated Press, United Press Dow-Jones

8 STAR LATEST SPORTS

VOL. LXXXIV Three Sections Section A 1243 Trenton St., L. A. 54 Phone RI. 4141 WEDNESDAY, OCTOBER 27, 1954 10 CENTS NO. 184

Wife of Golfer Von Elm Dead in Poison Mystery

Latest Sports

RACE RESULTS

AT HOLLYWOOD PARK

1 Dickie Frost 8.80,5.90,4.00; Sue C. 48.00,13.60; Kaynover D. 16.50
2 P. Pointer 24.80,5.60,3.00; Dot Collingwood 2.80,2.10; H. Tass 2.60

Daily double paid $99.50.

THIRD—One mile, Class CC Trot. Purse $1500:

DIANA VOLO	9.40	3.10	2.80
VICTORY LYNN		2.60	2.40
PRONTO GIRL			2.90

Scratched—Belle Prone and Grand Star Volo.

AT TANFORAN

1 Big Success 65.90, 23.80, 10.70; Femur 5.00, 3.60; Albert L. 3.50
2 Marsh's Turk 4.10,3.00,2.50; Catchie's L. 9.80,5.00; Verli McC 4.70

(For Hollypark and Tanforan selections and other races, see sport pages.)

Larson Before Smog Quiz Jury

Director to Tell His Side of 'Black Thursday'

Gordon P. Larson today was called before the County Grand Jury which is investigating complaints of official laxity in the enforcement of anti-smog laws.

Larson, who yesterday was retained as the director of the Air Pollution Control District by the County Board of Supervisors, was kept waiting while the jury secretly quizzed County Counsel Harold W. Kennedy and Dr. Francis Pottenger jr. of the Los Angeles County Medical Association.

Jurors were reported eager to hear Larson's side of his "Black Thursday" controversy with Mayor Norris Poulson.

The Mayor has restified that Larson on "Black Thursday" had asked him to "stand by prepared to issue an emergency proclamation" in the face of an impending smog disaster.

Larson has denied it.

It was indicated that the jury may end its session today with a vote on whether testimony has shown dereliction of duty in smog law enforcement by officials.

Kennedy would make no statement after the jurors questioned him for more than an hour. He said that they had instructed him not to talk about his secret testimony.

The supervisors, after reject-

(Continued on Page 4, Col. 5)

Trash Fires 4 to 7 P. M. Start Nov. 10

The City Council today adopted an emergency ordinance changing the hours of trash burning in backyard incinerators to from 4 to 7 p. m., from the present 6 to 10 a. m., hours.

Mayor Norris Poulson was expected to sign it in a day or so. It will go into effect Nov. 10 for a 90-day test period.

Councilman Harold Henry, who introduced the measure, said that the Nov. 10 date would give other cities and areas in the County opportunities to provide for afternoon trash burning in a move to cut down morning smog.

Backyard incinerators, Henry said, would make less smoke if the fire is started at the top instead of the bottom of the rubbish pile.

The Council also accepted an invitation from the oil industry to inspect the refinery district Nov. 19.

2 Here Win Rich Prizes In Irish Sweepstakes

Two Los Angeles area persons hit the jackpot in the Irish Sweepstakes today, winning $56,000 and $28,000 respectively.

Mrs. Marie Urban, employe of a Hollywood film processing plant and wife of a retired mailman, won $56,000 on a ticket she bought on a trip to her home town, Pettigo, Ireland, last June on the horse Queen's Britches.

The other winner, getting $28,000, was Mark M. Meyers, of 5203 Inadale avenue, who held a ticket on the horse Marshal Ney.

Mrs. Urban was away from her home at 13389 Dronfield, San Fernando, when news arrived of the $56,000 windfall today, but her husband, Michael, said:

"My wife has been investing money, up to $5 a week, every week for years in pools of one kind or another, but she never won anything before."

Asked what they would do with the money, after taxes are paid, he said:

"I haven't had a chance to talk it over with my wife yet, but we've always been poor and we're not going to break out in a rash of new cars."

Meyers also was away from home and his wife declared:

"We don't want to talk about it."

MRS. MARY VON ELM
Found Dead in Mystery

ROY FORD
Quizzed in Death

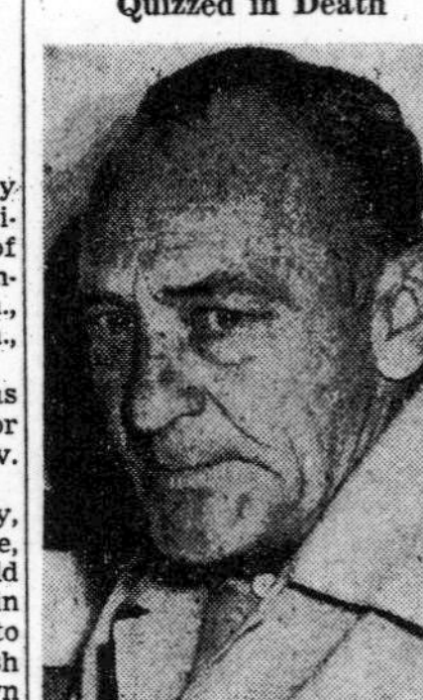

—Herald-Express Photo

GEORGE VON ELM
'I Believe Roy'

Smog-Free And Balmy

(For Nation's Weather Map and Temperatures See Page B-10)

Desert and sea breezes united today to give Los Angeles a smog-free day, with a top temperature of 81, and visibility that fluctuated from 70 miles at 7 a. m., to 40 miles this afternoon.

Blue skies, smogless days and cool nights may bless the area for the next two or three days and give smog-struck citizens a chance to inhale pure fresh air of the pre-smog era variety.

Weather forecast: "Clear tonight and Thursday. High fire danger in foothill sections. Low surface haze."

The lowest temperature today was 54 degrees at 5:47 a. m.

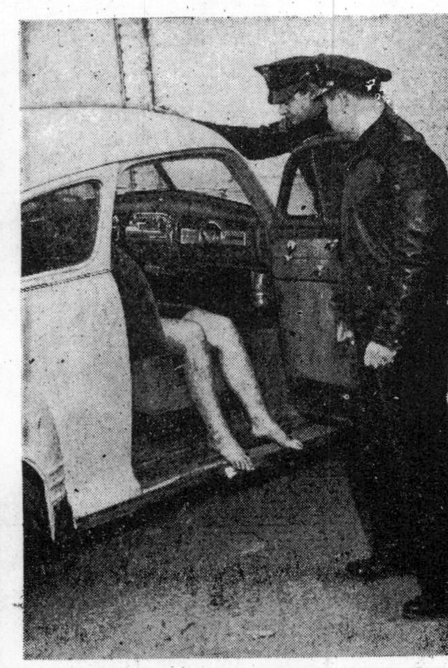

EX-GOLF CHAMP'S WIFE DEAD IN CAR
Police View Mrs. George Von Elm Mystery Death Scene

Top Golfer's Wife Dies in Car Mystery

Mrs. Mary Von Elm, 47, wife of former golf champion George Von Elm, was found dead in a poison mystery today.

Her body was found in her car parked in the rear of a Valley restaurant, and police booked her 29-year-old companion on suspicion of homicide.

Roy Ford, the young auto salesman regarded by the Von Elms "just like our own son"—according to the ex-golfer—told officers he knocked a bottle of insect poison away from Mrs. Von Elm's lips but "it was too late." He lived with them at 10750 Magnolia avenue. Officers said evidence indicated a romantic interlude preceded the death.

Dr. Frederick F. Newbarr, county autopsy surgeon, said his examination showed that Mrs. Von Elm had died of nicotine poisoning, bearing out Ford's story. Nicotine was an ingredient of the insectide which, according to Ford, she swallowed in a pre-dawn fit of despondency.

In a preliminary examination of the body, Dr. Newbarr reported that he found a deep

(Continued on Page 6, Col. 1)

Radio Firm Sues Note-Holders For $4,650,000

Charging a group of note-holders took over a $2,500,000 radio business and ruined it, Quality Radio, Inc., today filed suit in Superior Court for $4,650,000 damages against R. F. Jensen, A. E. Whitworth, and over 100 other defendants.

The radio firm explained it financed its business by borrowing money from the note-holders on sales contracts. The note-holders were paid interest and principal but had no rights of participation in the ownership or management of the firm, the suit added.

Specials In Herald Today

In addition to your regular favorites, you will want to read these special features in today's Herald and Express.

ELECTION FORECAST—For Wm. K. Hutchinson, INS writer's view of election scene, see Page A-2.

WHAT FOLKS THINK — Will residents leave Los Angeles because of the smog? Page B-11.

ODD JOBS—Bridal Gowns By the Hour is big business.

PRO AND CON — Arguments for and against state propositions on the November 2 Ballot. Page B-6.

Special Features

Bobbin' Around—

Reichle 'Steals' Heil From Sanders

—By Bob Hunter—

I remember how happy Red Sanders was when Billy Heil of Glendale City College wheeled into Westwood and asked for desk space. Heil was considered one of the good football catches of the season.

Now I note that Art Reichle, the Bruin baseball coach, has kidnaped Billy and has him playing third base on probably the best UCLA nine in history.

RED SANDERS

Reichle tells me Heil is an old pro, although I surmise Sanders has had a few of those on his teams through the years, too.

What Reichle means is that Billy is a veteran-type player, certainly a rarity on a college club.

"He's a real leader," the UCLA coach told me. "There are some fellows who can say no more than five words, and yet lead a team. That's Heil.

"Billy is terrific to coach, has a fine attitude, lots of power and hits when we need 'em."

Although Billy is the Silent Shoe type, the 5-10, 188-pounder does like to talk baseball, and I've sort of gathered he likes this sport be'ter than football.

W..ich is what I started out to say in the first place. It looks as though an athlete finally has been proselyted by a fellow coach.

Heil started in American Legion baseball with Glendale Post 127, then played for Glendale High and later Glendale City College.

Defensively Billy is a fine fielder and strong thrower, but Bruin fans will tell you he's the greatest hitter they-have ever had; that he really can wallop a curve ball, already having slammed a couple of homers with the bases loaded.

Best in UCLA History

No matter where the Bruins finish the season, they already have the winningest team in UCLA history, with the ace pitcher being 152-pound Don Nichols, a transfer from East Los Angeles Jaysee.

Another star is Daryl Westerfield, and a fine fireman is Tom O'Donnell. A couple of other good ones in the unusually deep pitching staff are ex-outfielder Johnny White and ex-basketballer Carroll Adams.

But Heil seems to be the prize package, although Reichle may never be around if and when the Bruins run up the pennant on their flagpole.

Both Sanders and Casey Stengel, from whose very backyard the Bruin coach kidnaped Heil, are gunning for Reichle.

They want to string him up to the nearest tree as a common horseshide thief.

* * *

In town for a few days with his charming bride was Elmer Frey, the Mobile home executive who promoted the Winnie Roach channel swim here last summer.

Winnie didn't do so well, but Elmer did.

He now is president of Marshfield Homes, Incorporated, a product Frey says is a "quality home on wheels."

Winnie was housed in one of these lavish layouts before her Catalina try, and it was obvious before too long she should never have left it.

Not Disenchanted

Frey, however, is not disenchanted with channel swimmers, but says for the next one he'll have the first 10-foot wide mobile home ever constructed in which the challenger can take up residence.

He calls these "Tenwide Homes," and they're constructed more for permanent residences.

In fact, he just installed two of these mobile mansions in a Palm Springs park operated by Bing Crosby, Barbara Stanwyck, Phil Harris, Jack Benny and Alice Faye.

Each street in the unique village is named after a star, and in front of Benny's home on wheels is a parking meter.

Frey asked Harris what it was for.

"For Benny's old age retirement fund," was the answer.

Frey, incidentally, represents one of the great success stories of American business.

He built his first mobile home in a hay loft, for a cost of $800, when he received his discharge from the service a few years ago.

Now he's the president of a million dollar firm.

Bosox Win Pair for AL Lead

BOSTON, April 17.—(AP)—The fast-starting Boston Red Sox moved into undisputed possession of first place in the American League today, sweeping a marathon doubleheader from winless Baltimore, 14-5 and 12-9, in the rain and cold at Fenway Park.

Boston Catcher Sammy White's two-run, tie-breaking double in the eighth inning off Reliever Don Johnson was the big blow in the hectic nightcap, which was played under lights from the fourth inning on.

Only about 4000 of the original 15,345 fans were still on hand for the windup of six hours, 17 minutes of heavy-hitting and at times, very sloppy baseball. Boston's record now is 5-1 with four victories over the Orioles.

Baltimore, which has lost all five of its starts, pulled into a 9-9 tie in the top of the eighth when Shortstop Billy Klaus of Boston threw wild past first base, permitting Pinch Runner Chuck Diering to score.

Then Boston got to Johnson, who succeeded Starter Lou Kretlow in the fifth, for three runs in the eighth. Faye Throneberry led off with a single. Catcher Hal Smith threw wild past first on Jackie Jensen's bunt to set the stage for White's payoff double. Johnson got the next two men, then Skinny Brown, fifth and winning Red Sox pitcher, scored White with a single.

(FIRST GAME)

Baltmre.	AB	H	O	A	Boston	AB	H	O	A
Cox,ss-2b	4	2	1	2	Gdman,2b	4	2	2	0
Pyburn,3b	1	0	1	0	Klaus,ss	0	0	0	1
Kenndy,rf	5	1	2	0	Piersall,cf	3	1	5	1
Evers,cf	5	1	1	1	Thrnbry,lf	3	2	2	0
Wooding,lf	4	0	1	0	Jensen,rf	4	3	2	0
Coan,lf	0	0	0	0	White,c	5	2	5	0
Stphns,3b	1	0	0	1	Aggns,1b	4	2	8	1
Mirnda,ss	2	1	1	2	Lepcio,3b	5	2	2	3
Trndos,1b	4	0	10	0	Frnd,ss-2b	5	3	2	1
Smith,c	4	3	5	1	Sullivan,p	4	1	0	1
Young,2b	3	1	2	3					
Rogovin,p	1	0	0	0					
Alxndr,p	0	0	0	0					
Moss	1	0	0	0					
McDnld,p	0	0	0	1					
Miller,p	0	0	0	0					
Abrams	1	0	0	0					
Colemn,p	0	0	0	1					
Ferrarse,p	0	0	0	0					
Totals	37	10	24	12	Totals	35	17	27	10

Moss grounded into force play for Alexander in 4th.
Abrams popped out for Miller in 6th.
Waitkus singled for Ferrarese in 9th.
Klhus ran for Goodman in 7th.

Baltimore	201 020 000— 5
Boston	032 404 10x—14

E—Jensen, Miranda, Friend. RBI—Evers, 2; Cox, Miranda, 2; Jensen, 4; Sullivan, 2; Thorneberry, 3; Agganis, White, 3; Piersall. 3B—Sullivan, Piersall, Jensen. HR—Evers, Jensen, Cox, Thorneberry, White. SH—Piersall. SF—Piersall. DP—Cox, Young and Triandos; Miranda and Triandos; Young and Triandos. LOB—Baltimore, 7; Boston, 7. BB—McDonald, 3; Miller, 1; Coleman, 1; Ferrarese, 3; Sullivan, 1. SO—Alexander, 1; McDonald, 1; Ferrarese, 2; Sullivan, 5. HO—Rogovin, 7 in 2 (faced 3 batters in 3rd); Alexander, 1 in 1; McDonald, 3 in 1; Miller, 0 in 1; Coleman, 3 in ⅓; Ferrarese, 3 in 2⅔. R-ER—Gogovin, 5-5; McDonald, 4-0; Coleman, 4-4; Ferrarese, 1-1; Sullivan, 5-3. HBP—By Sullivan (Stephens). W—Sullivan (2-0). L—Rogovin 0-1). U—Berry, McKinley, Flaherty, Chylak. T—2:39.

SECOND GAME

Baltimore	AB	H	O	A	Boston	AB	H	O	A
Cox,3b	5	3	2	0	Goodmn,2b	3	0	1	3
Abrams,cf	5	1	3	0	Piersall,cf	4	0	2	0
Coan,lf	2	1	0	0	Thrnbry,lf	5	2	2	0
Evers,lf	2	1	1	0	Jensen,rf	4	2	1	1
Wooding,rf	5	1	2	0	White,c	5	3	8	0
Moss,c	3	1	6	0	Agganis,1b	5	2	9	0
Diering	0	0	0	0	Lepcio,3b	5	2	2	4
Smith,c	0	0	0	0	Friend,ss	3	0	1	3
Triands,1b	5	3	4	1	Hatton	0	0	0	0
Marsh,ss	0	0	0	1	Brown,p	1	1	0	0
Young,2b	4	1	3	1	Kmmerer,p	0	0	0	0
Miranda,ss	2	0	2	2	Kiely,p	2	1	0	0
Waitks,1b	1	0	1	0	Freeman,p	0	0	0	0
Kretlow,p	3	0	0	1	Stephens	0	0	0	0
Johnson,p	1	0	0	1	Susce,p	0	0	0	0
Leppert	1	0	0	0	Klaus,ss	1	0	1	0
Totals	39	12	24	7	Totals	38	13	27	11

Evers walked for Coan in 4th.
Diering ran for Moss in 8th.
Marsh ran for Triandos in 8th.
Waitkus grounded out for Miranda in 8th.
Leppert fanned for Johnson in 9th.
Stephens walked for Freeman in 6th.
Hatton walked for Friend in 7th.
Klaus walked for Susce in 7th.

Baltimore	310 004 010— 9
Boston	000 430 23x—12

E—Triandos, Agganis 2, Miranda, Klaus, Smith. RBI—Woodling 3, Triandos 2, Abrams, Moss, Young, Agganis 2, Lepcio 2, Throneberry, White 4, Klaus, Goodman, Brown. 2B—Coan, Woodling, Cox 2, Throneberry, Jensen, Lepcio, White. HR—Lepcio. S—Young, Jensen. SF—Goodman. DP—Lepcio, Friend and Agganis. Left—Baltimore, 11; Boston, 9. BB—Kretlow, 1; Johnson, 4; Kemmerer, 1; Kiely, 4; Freeman, 1; Brown, 1. SO—Kretlow, 4; Johnson, 2; Kemmerer, 3; Kiely, 3; Freeman, 1; Brown, 1. HO—Kretlow, 8 in 4⅓; Johnson, 5 in 3⅔; Kemmerer, 8 in 2⅔; Kiely, 2 in 2⅓ (faced 4 batters in 6th); Freeman, 1 in 1; Susce, 0 in 1; Brown, 1 in 2. R-ER—Kretlow, 7-7; Johnson, 5-3; Kemmerer, 4-4; Kiely, 4-3; Freeman, 0-0; Susce, 0-0; Brown, 1-1. WP—Kretlow. PB—White. W—Brown (1-0). L—Johnson (0-1). U—McKinley, Flaherty, Chylak, Berry. T—3:38. A—15,345.

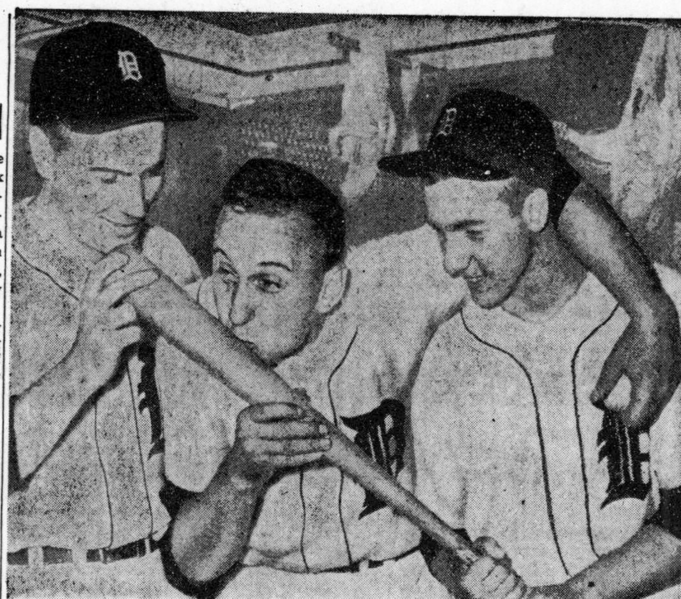

BIG GUNS—Steve Gromek, Detroit hurler, kisses bat of Al Kaline (right) who hit three homers, two of them in one inning. Catcher House (left) also homered.

—Associated Press wirephoto.

Detroit's Kaline Hits Three Homers

DETROIT, April 17.—(AP)—Young Al Kaline hammered three home runs, two of them in the sixth inning, to tie a major league record—and lead the Detroit Tigers to a 16-0 romp over the hapless Kansas City A's today.

The 20-year-old outfielder, who hit only four home runs last season, also collected a bloop single to knock in six runs.

The four hits boosted Kaline's early season batting average to .560. He has 14 hits in 25 times at bat.

Kaline, who added 15 pounds to his slender frame during the winter, started his rampage in the third inning, driving a two-run homer into the leftfield seats off starter John Gray.

Kaline connected twice as the Tigers scored nine times in the sixth inning. He drove an inning-opening homer off Bob Spicer and then closed out the rally with a two-run blast off Bob Trice. Both drives sailed into the left field seats.

Kaline was the 13th major league player to hit two home runs in one inning. The last to do it was Sid Gordon, who cracked two for the New York Giants in the second game of a doubleheader July 31, 1949.

The 6-foot- Kaline was the first Tiger in history to turn the feat.

His slugging led a 15-hit attack against five Kansas City pitchers and send the A's to their fourth defeat in five starts.

Steve Gromek, veteran 34-year-old righthander, went all the way for the second time this season in beating the A's. He gave up seven hits to post his first shutout.

Shortstop Harvey Kuenn of the Tigers collected a single and three doubles to knock in three runs. Catcher Frank House batted home four runs with a sacrifice fly and a three-run homer. House also had a single.

Kaline missed a perfect day at the plate when he popped to shortstop in the eighth inning.

Kn. City	AB	H	O	A	Detroit	AB	H	O	A
Jacobs,2b	4	1	0	1	Kuenn,ss	6	4	0	2
Valo,rf	3	1	2	0	Hatfld,2b	5	1	5	2
Finigan,3b	3	1	0	2	Kaline,rf	5	4	2	0
Bevan,3b	1	0	1	0	Fain,1b	4	0	6	0
Zernial,lf	3	0	2	0	Boone,3b	5	2	2	2
Stewart,lf	1	0	0	0	Delsing,lf	3	0	2	0
W.Wlsn,cf	4	0	4	0	Tuttle,cf	4	1	3	0
Power,1b	3	0	9	0	House,c	3	2	7	1
Kryhki,1b	1	1	1	0	Gromek,p	4	1	0	0
Littrell,ss	4	1	1	2					
Astroth,c	2	0	2	1					
Robertsn,c	0	0	2	0					
Gray,p	1	1	0	0					
Bishop,p	0	0	0	0					
Bollweg	1	0	0	0					
Spicer,p	0	0	0	0					
Wheat,p	0	0	0	0					
Trice,p	1	1	0	2					
Totals	32	7	24	8	Totals	39	15	27	7

Bollweg popped out for Bishop in 5th.

Kansas City	000 000 000— 0
Detroit	002 419 00x—16

E—Littrell. RBI—Kaline 6, House 4, Kuenn 3, Tuttle 2, Hatfield. 2B—Valo, Kuenn 3. HR—Kaline 3, House. SB—Tuttle. SF—House. LOB—Kansas City, 7; Detroit, 9. BB—Gray 5, Bishop 1, Spicer 2, Trice 1, Gromek 1. SO—Gray 3, Trice 2, Gromek 5. HO—Gray 4 in 3⅓, Bishop 1 in ⅔, Spicer 5 in 1 (faced 4 batters in 6th), Wheat 3 in 0 (faced 4 batters in 6th), Trice 2 in 3. R & ER—Gray 6-6, Spicer 5-5, Wheat 4-3, Trice 1-1. HBP—By Gromek (Astroth). W—Gromek (2-0). L—Gray (0-1). U—Rommel, Paparella, Honochick, Umont. T—2:40. A—16,662.

First Fiddle, Sumiki Take Yacht Races

William Negaard sailed his yacht Sumiki to win the Red Harris trophy race, one of the two special events sailed in Los Angeles Harbor yesterday, under the sponsorship of the Cabrillo Beach Yacht Club.

In the order named, the other arbitrary Handicap class yachts to finish were Kelem, Dave Commons; Marilyn, Howard Ritchie; Patience, Harry Blacher.

The second event, the Point Fermin race for PC class sloops, was won by Hillyard Brown's First Fiddle. As listed, the next three finishers were Leilani, Bill Evans; Six Bits, Richard MacDonald; Panacea, Dr. George W. Campbell.

M'Shain to Face Bolo

Great Bolo and Danny McShain will fight as well as wrestle at the Hollywood Legion Stadium tonight.

McShain says he will take the hooded mask off Bolo and reveal his real identity. Bolo says that if McShain attempts to unmask him he will floor McShain.

TONIGHT'S CARD

Great Bolo vs. Danny McShain, two falls out of three, one hour.
Sandor Szabo vs. Big Ed Gardenia, two falls out of three, 45 minutes.
Jack Ellena vs. Pedro Martinez, one fall, 15 minutes.
Johnny Demchuk vs. Gory Guerrero, one fall, 15 minutes.

Redlegs Option Fisher to Seals

CINCINNATI, April 17.—(AP)—The Cincinnati Redlegs tonight optioned Pitcher Tom Acker to Nashville of the Southern Association, and Pitcher Maurice Fisher to San Francisco of the Coast League. Both may be recalled on 24 hours notice.

BRAVES, REDLEGS EACH WIN

CINCINNATI, April 17.—(AP)—Ted Kluszewski singled with two out in the ninth inning to give his Cincinnati Redlegs their first victory of the 1955 National League season, a 6-5 triumph over the Milwaukee Braves in the second game of a doubleheader today.

The Braves plastered the Reds with their fifth straight setback, a 10-1 affair, in the first game.

FIRST GAME

Milw'kee	AB	H	O	A	Cincinn.	AB	H	O	A
Bruton,cf	6	4	7	0	Temple,2b	4	1	1	1
Aaron,rf	5	1	1	0	M'Milln,ss	5	1	4	4
Pafko,rf	1	0	0	0	Bell,cf	4	1	1	0
Mthws,3b	2	1	1	2	Kluszk,1b	2	1	8	0
Thomsn,lf	4	1	1	0	Jablki,3b	4	1	1	1
Tanner,lf	0	0	0	0	Grngras,lf	3	0	2	0
Adcock,1b	3	1	7	0	Seminck,c	4	1	7	0
Logan,ss	5	2	2	5	Post,rf	4	3	3	0
Dittmr,2b	5	2	2	2	Fowler,p	0	0	0	2
Crandall,c	5	2	6	0	Borkowski	1	0	0	0
Spahn,p	5	0	0	0	Minarcin,p	1	0	0	0
					Adams	1	0	0	0
					Hooper,p	0	0	0	0
					Harmon	1	0	0	0
Totals	41	14	27	9	Totals	34	9	27	8

Tanner ran for Thomson in 8th.
Borkowski fouled out for Fowler in 2nd.
Adams flied out for Minarcin in 6th.
Harmon grounded out for Hooper in 9th.

Milwaukee	400 102 030—10
Cincinnati	000 010 000— 1

E—McMillan. RBI—Bruton 3, Logan 3, Aaron, Thomson 2, Kluszewski, Dittmer. 2B—Bruton, Mathews, Aaron, Post, Temple. HR—Bruton, Logan. SF—Thomson, Kluszewski. DP—Logan-Dittmer-Adcock. LOB—Milwaukee, 10; Cincinnati, 10. BB—Fowler 2, Minarcin 2, Hooper 1, Spahn 3. SO—Fowler 1, Minarcin 3, Hooper 1, Spahn 2. HO—Fowler 2 in 2, Minarcin 7 in 4, Hooper 5 in 3. R & ER—Fowler 4-4, Minarcin 3-3, Hooper 3-3, Spahn 1-1. W—Spahn (2-0). L—Fowler (0-2).

SECOND GAME

Milwke.	AB	H	O	A	Cinn.	AB	H	O	A
Bruton,cf	5	2	4	1	Temple,2b	3	1	4	5
Aaron,rf	5	1	0	0	Gorbous,lf	4	3	3	0
Mthws,3b	5	2	1	2	Bell,cf	5	1	4	0
Thomsn,lf	3	0	2	0	Kluzski,1b	4	2	10	2
Adcock,1b	4	4	6	1	Jblnski,3b	4	0	0	2
Logan,ss	2	1	5	2	Bailey,c	4	1	3	1
Dittmr,2b	4	0	1	1	Post,rf	4	1	2	1
Crandal,c	2	0	7	0	M'Milln,ss	2	0	1	2
Crone,p	2	1	0	0	Thurman	1	0	0	0
Gorin,p	0	0	0	0	Bridges,ss	0	0	0	0
Vargas,p	0	0	0	0	Staley,p	3	0	0	2
Crowe	1	0	0	0					
Nichols,p	0	0	0	2					
Tanner	1	0	0	0					
Jolly,p	0	0	0	1					
Totals	34	11	26	10	Totals	34	9	27	15

Crowe grounded out for Vargas in 6th.
Tanner grounded out for Nichols in 8th.
Thurman grounded out for McMillan in 8th.

Milwaukee	003 001 100—5
Cincinnati	000 500 001—6

E—Jablonski, Gorbous. RBI—Adcock, 2; Thomson, Aaron, Crandall, Gorbous, 2; Kluszewski, 2; Bailey, Post. 2B—Adcock, 2; Gorbous. HR—Aaron, Kluszewski, Bailey, Post. SH—Logan. SF—Crandall. DP—Staley, Bailey and Kluszewski; McMillan, Temple and Kluszewski; Bailey and Temple. Left—Milwaukee, 7; Cincinnati, 8. BB—Crone, 1; Gorin, 3; Staley, 3; Nichols, 1; Jolly, 1. SO—Crone, 3; Vargas, 1; Jolly, 2; Staley, 1. HO—Crone, 5 in 3⅓; Vargas, 0 in 1⅓; Nicholas, 1 in 2; Jolly, 2 in 2. R-ER—Crone, 3-3; Gorin, 2-2; Vargas, 0-0; Nichols, 0-0; Staley, 5-2; Jolly, 1-1. W—Staley (1-1). L—Jolly (0-1). U—Dascoli, Warneke, Secory, Goetz.

U. S. Table Netters Win

UTRECHT, Netherlands, April 17.—(AP)—The United States' men's table tennis team remained undefeated today after the fifth round of play for the Swaythling Cup.

But Uncle Sam's girls dropped their second match in five starts to fall farther behind in the competition for the Corbillon Cup.

Indians Split With Chisox

CHICAGO, April 17.—(AP)—Bob Lemon of the Cleveland Indians and Jack Harshman of the Chicago White Sox tossed a pair of five-hitters today as the two teams split a doubleheader, with the Sox taking the opener, 3-1, and Cleveland the nightcap, 4-2.

Unlike Harshman who had himself in trouble several times because of wildness, Lemon turned the Sox back in fashion with the exception of a leadoff home run by Chico Carrasquel in the fourth and a shaky seventh which netted the Sox one run.

Vic Wertz provided Cleveland's winning margin with a two-run homer in the top of the sixth. The Indians could have made Lemon's task much easier if it hadn't been for some poor base running.

Virgil Trucks started the second game for the Sox and was in trouble constantly until he got knocked out in the seventh inning.

MUFF CHANCE

Cleveland muffed a chance to score in the second inning. Ralph Kiner doubled after Al Rosen had singled with nobody out, only to have Rosen out at the plate trying to score.

In the fourth, Kiner walked with one out. After Wertz had flied to center, George Strickland doubled, but Kiner was trapped between home and third and run down to retire the side.

George Kell opened the ninth with a single only to have Jim Rivera, who has now gone hitless in 17 official trips, ground into a double play. Lemon then walked Walt Dropo and Bob Nieman and served a run-scoring single to Sherman Lollar.

Nieman paved the way for Chicago's victory as he hammered his third home run of the season to open the seventh inning and break a 1-1 tie.

The Indians scored their only run in the third inning of the first game on a double by rookie catcher Hank Foiles and a single by Al Smith.

Harshman walked four batters and gave up four of Cleveland's five hits in the first five innings and was pulled out of trouble twice on double plays. However, he settled down after that.

Cleveland	AB	H	O	A	Chicago	AB	H	O	A
Smith,rf	4	2	3	0	Carsqul,ss	3	0	0	7
Avila,2b	4	1	4	1	Fox,2b	4	2	3	5
Doby,cf	3	0	1	0	Minoso,lf	4	1	0	0
Rosen,3b	3	0	3	0	Kell,3b	3	0	0	0
Kiner,lf	2	0	2	0	River,cf-rf	3	0	2	0
Wertz,1b	4	0	10	1	Dropo,1b	3	1	12	0
Strickld,ss	4	0	1	3	Nieman,rf	3	2	3	0
Foiles,c	3	1	3	0	Courtney,c	1	0	1	0
Houtemn,p	2	1	0	2	Lollar,c	3	1	6	2
Mossi,p	0	0	0	0	McGhee,cf	1	0	0	0
Majeski	1	0	0	0	Harshm,p	1	0	0	0
Totals	30	5	24	10	Totals	29	7	27	14

McGhee ran for Lollar in 7th.
Majeski grounded out for Mossi in 9th.

Cleveland	001 000 000—1
Chicago	001 000 20x—3

E—Wertz, Carrasquel. RBI—Smith, Minoso, Nieman, Fox. 2B—Foiles, Minoso. 3B—Fox. HR—Nieman. SH—Houtteman, Harshman, Rivera. DP—Carrasquel-Fox-Dropo 2, Strickland-Avila-Wertz. LOB—Cleveland, 8; Chicago, 8. BB—Harshman 5, Houtteman 4. SO—Harshman 7, Houtteman 3. HO—Houtteman 7 in 7⅓, Mossi 0 in ⅔. R & ER—Houtteman 3-3, Harshman 1-1, Mossi 0-0. W—Harshman (1-0). L—Houtteman (0-1). U—Summers, Hurley, Soar and Runge. T—2:26.

SECOND GAME

Cleveland	AB	H	O	A	Chicago	AB	H	O	A
Smith,rf	5	0	0	0	Crsquel,ss	4	1	3	6
Avila,2b	3	1	1	3	Fox,2b	4	0	2	5
Doby,cf	3	1	2	0	Minoso,lf	4	1	3	1
Rosen,3b	4	1	0	2	Kell,3b	4	1	0	1
Kiner,lf	3	2	2	0	Rivera,cf	4	0	3	1
Wertz,1b	2	1	10	0	Dropo,1b	3	0	10	1
Altobili,1b	1	0	4	0	Nieman,rf	1	0	1	1
Strickld,ss	4	1	2	5	Lollar,c	3	2	4	1
Hegan,c	4	0	6	0	McGhee	0	0	0	0
Lemon,p	3	2	0	3	Courtney,c	0	0	1	0
					Trucks,p	2	0	0	1
					Martin,p	0	0	0	1
					Donovan,p	1	0	0	0
Totals	32	9	27	13	Totals	30	5	27	19

McGhee ran for Lollar in 7th.
Donovan struck out for Martin in 7th.

Cleveland	000 012 100—4
Chicago	000 100 100—2

E—Fox.
RBI—Carrasquel, Wertz 2, Doby 2, Lollar. 2B—Kiner, Strickland. HR—Carras-Doby 2, Lollar. 2B—Kiner. HR—Carrasquel, Wertz. SF—Doby. DP—Avila and Wertz; Lemon to Strickland to Altobelli. LOB—Cleveland 6, Chicago 4. BB—Trucks 3, Lemon 3. SO—Trucks 3, Lemon 5, Donovan 1. HO—Trucks 9 in 6⅓. Martin 0 in ⅔, Donovan 0 in 2. R and ER—Trucks 4-4, Martin 0-0, Donovan 0-0, Lemon 2-2. HBP—By Trucks (Wertz). W—Lemon (2-0). L—Trucks (0-2). U—Hurley, Soar, Runge, Summers. T—2:21. A—32,314.

Underwater Diver Injured

Bill Troy, who was seeking to set a new endurance underwater record at the Sportsmen's Show last night, was taken to Santa Monica Community Hospital after his air lines became jammed. His condition was not announced immediately.

Red Devils Nip Braves, 22-20

The Brooklyn Red Devils downed the Los Angeles Braves, 22-20, before 3600 Roller Derby fans at the Olympic last night to take an 8-7 series lead with five games to go.

Cards, Cubs Divide Bill; Jackson Hot

ST. LOUIS, April 17.—(AP)—Rookie Larry Jackson broke into the major leagues with a four-hit pitching job today as the St. Louis Cardinals backed his hurling with a 10-run first inning for a 14-1 nightcap victory over the Chicago Cubs after dropping the doubleheader opener in the ninth, 6-5.

The 23-year-old righthander had a no-hitter going until the seventh inning of the second game when Gene Baker singled and the Cubs got two other hits that frame. Jackson walked only one and struck out three.

DOUBLE PLAY

Scoring their 10 runs on eight of their 17 hits, the Cardinals sent 14 men to bat in the first inning against southpaw Harry Perkowski and young righthander Hy Cohen.

Only one man had reached base against Jackson until the seventh and that came on an error by first baseman Stan Musial but the runner was rubbed out by a double play to end the first inning.

Wally Moon, who wound up with four hits, including an inside-the-park homer, singled in the first. A hit by Red Schoendienst and walk to Stan Musial, filled the bases. Rip Repulski hammered a three-run double.

FIRST GAME

Chicago	AB	H	O	A	St. Louis	AB	H	O	A
Merrimn,cf	5	2	3	0	Moon,cf	5	1	0	0
Baker,3b	3	1	2	5	Schdst,2b	5	2	2	5
Bamhtz,rf	5	3	4	0	Msal,1b-rf	5	0	10	0
Sauer,lf	3	0	0	0	Repulski,lf	4	1	4	0
Lary	0	0	0	0	Elliott,rf	4	4	1	0
Miksis,3b	0	0	0	0	Alston,1b	0	0	2	0
Jacksn,3b	2	0	0	1	Boyer,3b	4	2	1	1
Morgan,3b	1	0	0	0	D.Rice,c	4	1	3	1
Cooper	0	0	0	0	Gramas,ss	1	0	4	3
Church	0	0	0	0	G.Jones,p	3	0	0	1
Fanning,c	0	0	0	0	Smith,p	1	0	0	0
Banks,ss	5	1	5	4	LaPalme,p	0	0	0	0
Fondy,1b	4	2	11	2	Tiefnuer,p	0	0	0	0
Chiti,c	1	0	0	1					
Speake	1	1	0	0					
E.Tappe,c	0	0	2	1					
King,lf	0	0	0	0					
Minner,p	2	0	0	0					
T.Tappe	1	0	0	0					
Davis,p	0	0	0	0					
Totals	33	10	27	14	Totals	36	11	27	11

Speake singled for Chiti in 7th.
T. Tappe fouled out for Minner in 7th.
King walked for E. Tappe in 9th.
Lary ran for Sauer in 9th.
Cooper was intentionally walked for Morgan in 9th.
Church ran for Cooper in 9th.

Chicago	100 000 302—6
St. Louis	002 101 010—5

E—Minner, Merriman. RBI—Jackson, Speake, Baker, Baumholtz 2, Merriman, Schoendienst, Boyer 2, D. Rice. 2B—Baker, Fondy, Boyer, D. Rice. 3B—Baumholtz, Merriman. S—Davis. SF—Baker. DP—Fondy-Banks-Fondy, Baker-Banks-Fondy, Schoendienst-Grammas-Musial, Schoendienst-Musial. LOB—Chicago, 9; St. Louis, 7. BB—Minner 2, Davis 1, G. Jones 3, Smith 2, La Palme 1. SO—Minner 1, Davis 2, G. Jones 2. HO—Minner 8 in 6, Davis 3 in 3, G. Jones 8 in 6⅔, Smith 2 in 2, La Palme 0 in 0 (faced one batter in 9th), Tiefenauer 0 in ⅓. R & ER—Minner 4-2, Davis 1-1, G. Jones 4-4, Smith 2-2, La Palmes 0-0. HBP—By Smith (Sauer). WP—Minner, La Palme. W—Davis (1-0). L—Smith (1-1). U—Dixon, Conlan, Gore, Donatelli. T—2:48.

SECOND GAME

Chicago	AB	H	O	A	St. Louis	AB	H	O	A
Merrmn,cf	4	0	1	0	Moon,cf	5	4	3	0
Baker,2b	4	1	4	0	Schdnst,2b	4	1	1	5
Bmhlotz,rf	1	0	1	0	Stphsn,2b	0	0	1	1
King,rf	3	0	1	0	Musial,1b	4	3	11	1
Sauer,lf	1	0	0	0	Alston,1b	0	0	2	0
Bolger,lf	3	1	3	0	Repulski,lf	5	1	1	0
Banks,ss	4	1	1	2	Elliott,rf	4	3	1	0
Morgan,3b	3	1	2	2	Boyer,3b	5	2	1	2
Fondy,1b	3	0	7	0	D.Rice,c	4	2	3	0
Chiti,c	3	0	4	2	Gramms,ss	5	0	2	4
Prkwski,p	0	0	0	0	L.Jacksn,p	4	1	1	1
Cohen,p	1	0	0	1					
T.Tappe	1	0	0	0					
Thorpe,p	0	0	0	1					
Totals	31	4	24	8	Totals	40	17	27	14

T. Tappe grounded out for Cohen in 8th.
Stephenson ran for Schoendienst in 7th.
Alston ran for Musial in 7th.

Chicago	000 000 100—1
St. Louis	(10)00 002 20x—14

E—Musial, Morgan 2, Bolger. RBI—Repulski 4, Boyer, D. Rice 2, Moon 2, Musial 2, Morgan. 2B—Repulski, Boyer, D. Rice. 3B—Musial. HR—Moon. DP—Schoendienst, Grammas and Musial. Left—Chicago 4, St. Louis 7. BB—Perkowski 1, Cohen 3, L. Jackson 1. SO—Cohen 2, L. Jackson 3. HO—Perkowski 5 in 0 (faced 6 batters in 1st), Cohen 12 in 7, Thorpe 0 in 1. R-ER—Perkowski 6-6, Cohen 8-6, Thorpe 0-0, L. Jackson 1-1. HBP—By Cohen (Elliott). Winner—Jackson (1-0). Loser—Perkowski (0-1). U—Conlan, Gore, Donatelli, Dixon. T—2:01. A—26,730.

Senators' Homers Crush Yankees

WASHINGTON, April 17.—(AP)—Ed Lopat, long-time Washington nemesis, was shelled for two-run homers by Mickey Vernon and Roy Sievers today as the Senators defeated the New York Yankees, 7-3.

Johnny Schmitz, the winner, and Spec Shea restricted the Yankees to eight hits, three of them infield taps. Shea relieved Schmitz with two out in the ninth when the Yankees threatened.

The Yankees produced a run in the second inning after Bill Skowron singled and came around as the result of errors by Eddie Yost and Pete Runnels.

The Senators erupted for four runs in the fourth inning. Jim Busby singled and Vernon slammed a home run into the Washington bullpen. Sievers singled and Yost tripled to center.

Yost scored after Runnels flied to Bob Cerv in leftfield.

Tom Umphlett was safe in the fifth inning when Shortstop Phil Rizzuto fumbled his grounder and when Rizzuto threw wild past first for another error, Umphlett continued to second. Vernon's single scored him and Sievers then belted a home run into the leftfield bleachers.

The Yankees scored a run in the eighth on Hank Bauer's single and Yogi Berra's double. They added a run with two out in the ninth when Enos Slaughter was hit by a pitched ball and Bauer singled. Shea replaced Schmitz at that point and tossed out Andy Carey.

* * *

New York	AB	H	O	A	Wshngtn	AB	H	O	A
Bauer,rf	5	3	3	0	Umphltt,rf	4	2	3	1
Carey,3b	5	2	1	4	Busby,cf	4	1	2	0
Mantle,cf	2	0	3	0	Vernon,1b	3	2	14	2
Berra,c	4	1	2	0	Sievers,lf	4	2	1	0
Skwron,1b	4	1	10	0	Yost,3b	3	1	1	3
Cerv,lf	4	1	3	0	Fitzgerld,c	4	0	2	1
Colemn,2b	4	0	1	2	Runnels,2b	2	0	0	1
Rizzuto,ss	1	0	1	2	Kline,ss	4	0	2	2
Howard	1	0	0	0	Schmitz,p	3	1	2	5
Hunter,ss	0	0	0	0	Shea,p	0	0	0	1
Slaughter	0	0	0	0					
Lopat,p	1	0	0	1					
Larsen,p	1	0	0	2					
Kucks,p	0	0	0	0					
Robinson	0	0	0	0					
Totals	[illegible]	[illegible]	24	11	Totals	31	9	27	16

Howa.. flied out for Rizzuto in 7th.
Slaugh.er walked for Hunter in 9th.
Robinson hit by pitcher for Kucks in 9th.

New York	000 100 011—3
Washington	000 430 00x—7

E—Berra, Yost, Runnels, Rizzuto 2. RBI—Coleman, Vernon 3, Yost, Runnels, Sievers 2, Berra, Bauer. 2B—Berra. 3B—Yost. HR—Vernon, Sievers. DP—Schmitz and Vernon, 2; Umphlett, Fitzgerald and Yost; Larsen, Rizzuto and Skowron. SF—Runnels. LOB—New York, 8; Washington, 4. BB—Schmitz, 5; Lopat, 1; Larsen, 2. SO—Schmitz, 2; Lopat, 1; Larsen, 1. HO—Lopat, 7 in 5; Larsen, 2 in 2; Kucks, 0 in 1; Schmitz, 8 in 8⅔; Shea, 0 in ⅓. R-ER—Lopat, 7-4; Schmitz, 3-2. HBP—By Schmitz (Robinson). W—Schmitz, 1-0. L—Lopat, 0-1. U—Napp, Rice, Grieve, Stevens. T—2:11. A—11,062.

Sherman in Net Victory

Bob Sherman of Temple City, a crisp and deadly volleyer, wore down the steady southpaw slants of Bill Parks to capture the men's singles title of the seventh annual West Hollywood tennis tournament yesterday at Plummer Park.

Sherman, serving and smashing solidly, cashed in on his strong backhand volley to down Parks, 6-4, 7-5. Sherman scored the only service break in the first set in the ninth game, then held his delivery to win.

In the second set, service was broken nine times in 11 games before Sherman held for only the second time to take the stanza, 7-5. He had led at 5-4 and 40-15 and again at 6-5 and 40-15, but lost a total of seven match points, all on errors at the net. However, he punched home on the eighth match point with a beautiful spinning backhand volley down the line.

Joan Johnson rallied to take the women's singles in a baseline duel with Marilyn Joseph, 4-6, 6-3, 6-2.

Men's Doubles — Duane-Gomer-Roger Skinner def. Tom Freiberg-Jim McDaniels, 4-6, 7-5, 6-4.

Mixed Doubles—Jeri Shepard-Leonard Platt def. Joan Johnson-Runar Ohls, 11-9, 6-4.

Lowry, Fiore Set

TOLEDO, Ohio, April 17.—(AP)—Promoter Sid Goldberg announced today that he has signed Pat Lowry, Toledo welterweight, and Carmine Fiore of Brooklyn for a 10-round main event Tuesday, May 10, at the Sports Arena.

Myers Wins Kern Regatta

BAKERSFIELD, April 17.—Before 35,000 spectators at Hart Park Lake near here, three 1954 winners repeated their triumphs, as a spectacular spill marked the opening Western inboard regatta of 1955.

The win-again boys of the fourth annual Kern county regatta were hydroplane drivers Bud Myers of Hollywood; Marion Beaver, Parker, Ariz., and Ernie Bender, Fresno.

The spill was furnished by Carl Maginn of Glendale and his co-pilot, Don Oakley, in the Cracker Boy runabout, Hot Ice, number one boat of the nation in the class.

Maginn, who will defend his national title May 30 in Long Beach, went in favored but lost the first heat by a squeak to Bakersfield's Earl John.

In the second five-lapper, trying to beat his arch-rival from Van Nuys, Bob Patterson, with Hot Cinders, into the first turn, Maginn wing-dinged.

Neither was seriously injured, but Patterson won class honors on points. Winners in other competing classes:

48-Cu. In. Hydroplane—Fat Pants III, Vernon Dallman Jr., Daly City, 800 points. 136-Cu. In.—Jerky, Bob Boehm, Healdsburg, 700. 225-Cu. In.—King Pin II, George King, Fresno, 800. B Racing Runabouts—Lil' Bee, Ernest Rose, Patterson, 800.

Seven Pin Qualifying Days Left

Only seven days remained to qualify for the championship finals today as the fifth and final $2625 weekly sweepstakes opened in the sixth annual Los Angeles Examiner's $20,000 Men's Singles Bowling Classic.

Daylight saving time starts next Sunday, so actually the time before the 2 a. m. deadline to qualifying on April 25, is even shorter—by an hour anyway.

Participation in the Examiner Classic is open to all bowlers with a league average that can be verified and the field for the finals is determined on the basis of those entrants with the eight-high series in each class at the 10 tournament sites.

The only requirements, other than an average, call for a $3 entry fee for each three-game series as well as an official coupon obtained from the sports section of the daily Examiner.

All competition is staged in five classes, without handicap, with fifth week awards distributed equally to all classes. These include $150 for the high series, $100 for the high game and $75 for the second high game, plus $20 for the high series in each class at the 10 pin plants.

Examiner Classic classes are: 154 and under (D), 155-164 (C), 165-175 (B), 176-187 (A) and 188 and over (O).

There is no limit on the number of times an individual may enter and a bowler can sign up at any time to bowl on any pair of lanes desired.

Advanced reservations are being accepted now for late evening squads throughout the week as well as for the closing hours leading up to the deadline on Friday, Saturday and Sunday.

The rush to qualify—or for bowlers trying to improve their scores—will be tremendous. Make certain you don't get shut out. Call these numbers now to insure yourself an opportunity for fame and fortune:

Boulevard Bowl (Long Beach 6-3990); Good Old Luxor (ADams 2-7408); Jackson Recreation (CItrus 2-8876); Mar-Lin-Do Lanes (THornwall 8-1600); Paradise Bowl (ORchard 1-3677); San Gabriel Lanes (ATlantic 6-3177); Southeast Bowling Center (KImball 6266); Trojan Bowl (REpublic 4-1105); Virginia Bowl (Long Beach 616-460) or Vogue Bowl (TRinity 1101).

Chicago Daily Tribune

Wednesday, August 3, 1955 F**

Sports / Finance

PART 3 WANT ADS

YANKS WIN IN 10TH; SOX BEAT BOSTON, 2-1

In the WAKE of the NEWS

BY DAVID CONDON

MEL OTT, who never did time in the minor leagues, was among those buttonholing Rogers Hornsby, who served less than two seasons' apprenticeship before graduating to baseball's big time, in Wrigley field Monday to ask about the Rajah's job as director of Mayor Daley's Chicago Youth commission. . . . "The mayor telephoned this morning and said to get to his office for pictures, 'cause I had the job I'd outlined to him," said Hornsby. "You know, I'd rather do this than manage a major club. I'm working with kids. Kids who play baseball won't have time for trouble." . . . "I guess," Hornsby added reluctantly, "this commission even will teach kids that football and basketball stuff." . . . Harry Creighton, the TV announcer, asked how many softball players Hornsby hoped to teach. . . . "Softball players?" snorted Hornsby. "We're gonna teach baseball, America's No. 1 sport! You and those other radio fellows come out and I'll teach you to second guess like experts." . . . "I'll be out when you start teaching golf," said Creighton. . . . "Never played golf in my life," declared Hornsby, "but I'll bet a steak I can hit a golf ball farther than you can. I can hit a golf ball farther than you and Jack Brickhouse together. I'll hit it the first pitch, too!"

David Condon

Ott said that New Orleans had an excellent boys' baseball program. . . . "We'll have a good one," promised Hornsby. "We aren't tryin' to make the young fellows major leaguers. Just to get them interested in sports. I'll start with throwing; that's the most important. So many kids have played that silly softball they throw a whole handful of ball. We'll teach 'em to throw with two fingers and the thumb. If a baseball player can't throw, what good if he's the world's best fielder? Watch these kids today. They throw off their back foot. With pitchers, we'll teach 'em how to stand on the mound, and how to hold runners on base. We'll teach the kids how to swing a bat, and how to follow the ball so they can hit."

While the Rajah, perhaps greatest of all right hand hitters, whispered with Ott, whose 511 home runs as a New York Giant represent the National league life record, a writer recalled Mel's signing with John McGraw. . . . Mel was 16, and a catcher. . . . McGraw asked him: "You ever play the outfield?" . . . "Sure," said Ott, "back when I was a kid." Conversation switched to the White Sox, and the writer ventured: "The Sox certainly made it rough for Chuck Dressen in Washington. He couldn't mastermind much there." . . . Mention of Chuck's masterminding recalled a year when Dressen coached the National league in the All-Star game. . . . The players asked about signals. . . . "Don't worry," said Dressen, "I'll give ya the signals." . . . "Fine, but what signals?" asked an All-Star. . . . "I'll just give each of ya the signals your own club uses," pronounced Dressen, baseball's most renowned signal-swiper. . . . There was a lull, and you could overhear Ott boosting New Orleans' baseball program to Hornsby. . . . When Mel had gone, Hornsby said: "Chicago'll have a better program than New Orleans." . . . That's typical of Rogers Hornsby. . . . Second best is not good enough. . . . He always has been impatient with anything less than perfection. . . . This may have hampered him as a manager, but it put him in the Hall of Fame as a player. . . . It's nice to see Rogers Hornsby back in a baseball uniform, where he belongs.

Today's Worst Jokes

My girl loaned me her wrist watch to wear but I'm going to give it back. She's been telling her friends that her watch is on the bum.
—Jack Herbert

My brother is so lazy his self-winding watch has to keep him going.
—The Old Sourdough

I was feeling sorry for a scavenger's horse stumbling along in a shower today when I suddenly remembered it was accustomed to the rein. —Harry Steele.

* *

Fringe Benefits

I thought I should have
Presentable feet,
So I got a shine
From a boy on the street;
The cost? Two bits!
That was pretty rough,
But I guess he charged extra
For shining my cuff.
—Arch the Archer

* *

Sudden Thought

I'd rather owe my success to my wife than to owe my wife to my success.—Stephen Napierala.

* *

Don't Be Nasty

If the Cubs drop much deeper in the National league, they're going to interfere with the Moon Mullins comic strip.
—Ray Crikota

* *

Famous Last Words

We're just good friends.—Park Forest Tom.

A Wife's Lament

**He has a hobby all his own,
Much to my disgust;
He sits all day in a corner,
Collecting dust!**
—Carice Williams

* *

Two Cents Worth

The Earl of Urbana says: "Nowadays a postoffice is the only place where you still can get your 'two cents worth.'" I am paying 3 cents for that two cents worth and so is he. —Gee Kay

* *

Boom!

A friend of mine, who had a job of polishing a large cannon, is out of work. He was working inside the muzzle when it was shot off, so he was fired.
—Dan of the Fed.

**The Wake Depends Help!
Upon Its Friends Help!**

Ten Years Ago Today—Phil Cavarretta hit a home run, four doubles, and a single in eight times at bat as the Cubs extended their winning streak to 15 by beating Cincinnati, 11 to 5 and 9 to 1.

Banks Ties Grand Slam Record

HEBERT'S 65 TOPS PROS IN TAM TRIALS

Gadja 2d with 66; 23 Crack Par

BY CHARLES BARTLETT

In the gloaming of Aug. 4, 1954, Lionel Hebert, a young golf professional from Erie, Pa., by way of Lafayette, La., was one of 29 players lined up on the first tee of the Tam O'Shanter Country club.

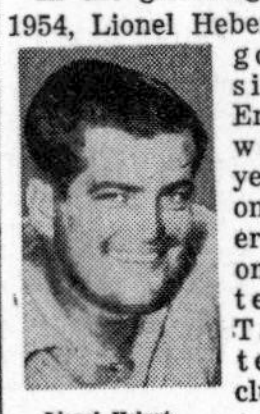

Lionel Hebert

This platoon all had shot par 72 to tie for last place in the qualifying round for last year's All-American championship. Now they met in a sudden death duel for the last 17 berths in the main event cast.

Seventeen of them got par fours at the extra hole. Lionel was one of the fortunate gents who slipped into the first of George S. May's big shows in this back gate fashion.

Comes in with 65

Shortly after 1 o'clock of yesterday's sticky afternoon, the same Lionel Hebert strolled off Tam's 18th green with a ticket that admits him thru the front door of the 1955 All-American tourneys, opening at Tam tomorrow.

Hebert's ducat was embellished with a sparkling 32—33—65, seven under Tam's 6,915 yard par of 36—36—72 and only two above Lloyd Mangrum's course record of 63. It shone with five birdies and an eagle and was dimmed by only a single bogey.

Hebert's card:

Par-out	453	444	435—36	
Hebert	332	444	534—32	
Par-in	534	445	344—36	72
Hebert	424	444	344—33	65

Hebert played Tam's first three holes in eight strokes. He had a three footer for his first birdie. After a drive and a 3 iron had left him in a trap off the 495 yard second, Lionel up and blasted from the sand into the cup from 25 feet. An 8 iron and a 20 foot putt deuced the 160 yard third.

End Qualifying Today

The 27 year old Lionel, younger brother of the more celebrated Jay, shot his round in the men's professional qualifying quiz, which opened with a test of 150 players yesterday. Another 150 will be examined today. The low 72 scorers for the two day trial will earn places in the tournament proper, a 72 hole medal battle opening at 6 a. m. tomorrow and continuing thru Sunday.

The All-American tournaments, which offer $31,350 in cash and merchandise to four fields—men's and women's professionals and amateurs—form the first section of May's triple header. He will present his second international cup series between eight United States men pros and as many foreigners next Tuesday and Wednesday.

World Meet Opens Aug. 11

On Thursday, Aug. 11, May's world championship event will begin, with the men pro winner due to receive $106,000 and the feminine professional victor $5,000 after the final round of Aug. 14.

Almost matching Hebert's swift pace was bespectacled Bob Gadja, Detroit veteran, who mixed up a 33—33—66 on

[Continued on page 3, col. 2]

32d Homer Helps to Beat Pirates, 12-4

1 for the Books!

PITTSBURGH

	AB	R	H	RBI	P	A	E
E. O'Brien, cf.	4	1	1	0	3	0	0
Freese, 3b.	4	1	1	0	0	1	0
Lynch, rf.	2	1	1	1	4	0	0
Long, 1b.	3	1	1	1	5	1	0
Atwell, c.	4	0	1	2	6	0	0
Peterson, c.	0	0	0	0	0	0	0
Thomas, lf.	4	0	0	0	1	0	1
J. O'Brien, 2b	4	0	1	0	0	2	0
Groat, ss.	4	0	0	0	5	1	0
Law, p.	1	0	1	0	0	1	0
Littlefield, p.	1	0	0	0	0	0	1
Pepper, p.	0	0	0	0	0	0	0
a-Saffell	1	0	1	0	0	0	0
Martin, p.	0	0	0	0	0	0	0
	32	4	8	4	24	6	2

a-Singled for Pepper in 7th.

CHICAGO

	AB	R	H	RBI	P	A	E
Fondy, 1b.	4	1	0	0	12	2	0
Baker, 2b.	4	3	2	0	3	4	0
Baumholtz, lf	4	0	1	1	0	0	0
Banks, ss.	5	2	3	5	3	6	0
King, rf.	4	1	0	0	0	0	0
Jackson, 3b.	5	3	2	0	1	1	0
Miksis, cf.	4	1	2	1	3	0	0
Chiti, c.	3	0	2	2	3	0	0
Rush, p.	3	1	1	3	2	3	0
	36	12	13	12	27	16	0

Pittsburgh	300	010	000— 4
Chicago	120	062	10x—12

Sacrifices—Chiti, Fondy, Baker. Two base hits—Atwell, Baker [2], Law, J. O'Brien. Three base hit—Lynch. Home run—Banks. Stolen bases—Freese, Baker. Double plays—Banks to Baker; Banks to Baker to Fondy; Long to Groat; Baker to Banks to Fondy. Left on bases—Pittsburgh, 4; Chicago, 9. Struck out—Rush, 2; Law, 1; Littlefield, 4; Pepper, 1. Bases on balls—Rush, 3; Littlefield, 1; Pepper, 3; Martin, 2. Hits—Law, 5 in 1⅓ innings; Littlefield, 2 in 3; Pepper, 3 in 1⅔; Martin, 3 in 2. Runs and earned runs—Rush, 4-4; Law, 3-3; Littlefield, 6-3; Pepper, 2-2; Martin, 1-1. Hit by pitcher—Littlefield [King]. Winning pitcher—Rush [7-8]. Losing pitcher—Littlefield [4-9]. Time—2:40. Umpires—Dickson, Gore, Donatelli, and Conlan. Attendance—4,788.

BY IRVING VAUGHAN

The Cubs solved the Pirate problem yesterday and the solution proved so simple that Stan Hack's athletes wandered off wondering why they hadn't thought of it before dropping five straight to the perennial eighth placers.

Principal ingredients were Ernie Bank's fourth grand slam home run of the year, tying the major league record, and the pitching performance of Bob Rush, who went the route for the first time since June 26. Together with several other pleasant occurrences, these heroics produced a 12 to 4 triumph before 4,788 in Wrigley field.

It was the nifty shortstop's 32d homer of the year and with a single, enabled him to boost his runs batted in total to 79.

6 Runs in 5th Inning

Banks pounded his grand slam into Waveland av. in the fifth,

[United Press Photo]

Dick Groat, Pittsburgh Pirate shortstop, leaps to catch relay throw from Eddie O'Brien as Gene Baker of Cubs slides safely into second base in first inning.

which was quite an inning in other ways, too. Six runs scored to wipe out a Pirate lead, 12 batters stepped to the plate before the melee subsided. Rush batted twice, walking on both occasions. And the Pirate perpetrated two errors.

Rush started poorly, yielding three runs and dodging dismissal because Banks speared a line drive for a double play. The Cubs tied it by knocking out Vern Law in the second. That brought Dick Littlefield into action and he, along with Laurin Pepper from Mississippi, were the sufferers in the giddy fifth. Later Pepper yielded two runs and, still

[Continued on page 5, col. 3]

JOINING BASEBALL'S SELECT CIRCLE

[TRIBUNE Photos]

Ernie Banks, Cub shortstop, who yesterday hit his fourth grand slam homer of the season to equal major league record held by 10 others, pictured above. It also was his 32d home run of the year. He needs seven more home runs to equal the major league record for shortstops.

Fourth Bases-Filled Homer Puts Banks Among Elite

BY IRVING VAUGHAN

That fellow Ernie Banks who handles the shortstop chores and wields a highly respected bat for the Cubs, must have some record breaking feats in mind.

As a major league sofomore, on a full season basis, he has already equalled or gone beyond some club and league marks.

The 24 year old graduate of the Kansas City Monarchs is aiming to knock out the major league mark of 39 home runs by a shortstop. It was set by Vern Stephens with the Red Sox in 1949. Banks has 32 now, with 46 more games to play.

Joins Select Group

Yesterday when he knocked the ball out of the park with the bases loaded, he crowded in among a batch of 10 other fellows who have hit four grand slam homers in one season. The last to join that group was Ray Boone of the Tigers on Aug. 12, 1953.

The others and the clubs they were with at the time were Frank Schulte, Cubs; Babe Ruth, Boston Red Sox; Lou Gehrig, New York Yankees; Rudy York, Detroit Tigers; Vince DiMaggio, Philadelphia Phillies; Tom Henrich, Yankees; Ralph Kiner, Pittsburgh Pirates; Sid Gordon, Boston Braves, and Al Rosen, Cleveland, Indians.

Hits Fast Ball

"That pitch Ernie hit over the fence was a fast ball, a little above the belt and slightly inside," Manager Stan Hack said after the game. "But he's not particularly partial to that. I've seen him do the same with other types of pitches. He can connect with curves—and change of pace doesn't bother him.

"The key to his power is wrist action. When we first got him, his wiry build didn't lead us to expect a slugger. He'd been batting sixth before that and he was in a good streak, so we made the change. He's really come thru for us."

That's His Job

"Ernie has a nice, even disposition. When he hits a homer he acts as tho he's just doing his job. To see him come back to the bench you couldn't tell whether he'd struck out or put one over the fence.

"About 10 days ago I moved him up to the cleanup spot.

Banks' first four run homer was hit on May 11 against Russ Meyer of the Dodgers. On May 29 Lew Burdette of the Braves became a grand slam victim. On July 17 he did it against Ron Negray of the Phillies.

The Pirates aren't exactly unaccustomed to grand slam happenings such as Ernie Banks perpetrated in the fifth. It was the fourth against them in their last eight games.

Major Leagues

NATIONAL LEAGUE

	W.	L.	Pct.	G. B.
Brooklyn	72	33	.686	....
MILWAUKEE	58	46	.558	13½
New York	56	50	.528	16½
Philadelphia	53	57	.482	21½
CHICAGO	51	57	.472	22½
Cincinnati	49	56	.467	23
St. Louis	45	56	.446	25
Pittsburgh	39	68	.364	34

YESTERDAY'S RESULTS

Chicago, 12; Pittsburgh, 4.
New York, 3; St. Louis, 0.
Cincinnati, 2-4; Philadelphia, 0-0.
Milwaukee, 5; Brooklyn, 3.

GAMES TODAY

Pitts. at Chgo. [2]. *New York at St. L.
*Phila. at Cinci. *Bklyn. at Milw.
*Night game.

AMERICAN LEAGUE

	W.	L.	Pct.	G. B.
CHICAGO	63	39	.618	....
New York	63	41	.606	1
Cleveland	62	42	.596	2
Boston	60	44	.577	4
Detroit	56	47	.544	7½
Kansas City	43	61	.413	21
Washington	35	68	.340	28½
Baltimore	31	71	.304	32

LAST NIGHT'S RESULTS

Baltimore, 5; Kansas City, 1.
Chicago, 2; Boston, 1.
New York, 2; Cleveland, 1 [10 innings].
Detroit, 13; Washington, 10.

GAMES TODAY

Chicago at Boston. Cleveland at N. Y.
*Detroit at Wash. †K. C. at Balt.
*Night game. †Twilight and night games.

YANKEES WHIP INDIANS, 2 TO 1

Collins Clouts Tying, Winning Homers

(Picture on back page)

New York, Aug. 2 (AP)—Joe Collins belted his second home run of the game with one out in the 10th inning tonight, breaking up a 1 to 1 tie and giving New York a 2 to 1 victory over Cleveland while lifting the Yankees out of a second place tie with the Indians in the blistering American league race.

Collins' first shot, boomed into the lower right field seats, pulled the Yanks into a 1 to 1 tie with the Indians in the first inning. Cleveland scored in the top of the first when Al Smith led off with a triple and came home on Bobby Avila's sacrifice fly.

Byrne Now 10-2

Early Wynn, losing his sixth in 19 decisions, yielded nine hits. Byrne, the 35 year old lefty who now has won 10 while losing only two for the Yanks, yielded seven hits.

The Cleveland right hander closed the door on the Yanks in the eighth after a 3-2 pitch to Collins went for a ball, setting off some verbal fireworks among Wynn, Catcher Jim Hegan and Umpire Bill Grieve.

Cleveland Coach Mel Harder and Manager Al Lopez took up

[Continued on page 5, col. 2]

HOWELL HALTS UPRISING IN NINTH INNING

Brilliant Defense Helps Johnson

Yowl for Howell

CHICAGO

	AB	R	H	RBI	P	A	E
Minoso, lf.	4	0	1	1	3	0	0
Fox, 2b.	4	0	1	0	2	3	0
Kell, 3b.	4	0	0	0	0	0	0
Dropo, 1b.	4	0	2	0	7	0	0
Rivera, rf.	3	1	1	1	1	0	0
Lollar, c.	4	0	0	0	6	1	0
Busby, cf.	4	1	1	0	4	1	0
Carrasquel, ss.	2	0	1	0	4	5	0
Johnson, p.	3	0	0	0	0	0	0
Martin, p.	0	0	0	0	0	0	0
Howell, p.	0	0	0	0	0	0	0
	32	2	7	2	27	10	0

BOSTON

	AB	R	H	RBI	P	A	E
Goodman, 2b.	4	0	2	0	1	1	0
Joost, 2b	1	0	0	0	0	0	0
Klaus, ss.	4	0	1	0	1	$1	0
Williams, lf.	3	0	2	0	5	0	0
Jensen, rf	4	0	0	0	1	0	0
Zauchin, 1b.	3	0	0	0	9	0	0
White, c	4	0	0	0	5	1	0
Hatton, 3b	3	0	0	0	0	3	0
Piersall, cf	3	1	1	0	3	0	0
Brewer, p	2	0	0	0	2	3	0
a-Stephens	0	0	0	0	0	0	0
Kinder, p.	0	0	0	0	0	1	0
b-Throneberry	1	0	1	1	0	0	0
	32	1	7	1	27	10	0

a-Walked for Brewer in 7th; b-Tripled for Kinder in 9th.

Chicago	001	100	000—2
Boston	000	000	001—1

Sacrifice—Rivera. Two base hits—Williams, Fox. Three base hit—Throneberry. Home run—Rivera. Double plays—Busby to Fox; Lollar to Fox to Lollar; Brewer to Goodman. Left on bases—Chicago, 5; Boston, 9. Struck out—Brewer, 4; Kinder, 1; Johnson, 4. Base on balls—Brewer, 1; Johnson, 5. Hits—Brewer, 5 in 7 innings; Kinder, 2 in 2; Johnson, 6 in 8⅔; Martin, 1 in 0 [pitched to 1 in 9th]; Howell, 0 in ⅓. Runs and earned runs—Brewer, 2-2; Kinder, 0-0; Johnson, 1-1; Martin, 0-0; Howell, 0-0. Winning pitcher—Johnson [4-1]. Losing pitcher—Brewer [8-9]. Time—2:45. Umpires—Summers, Hurley, Soar, and Runge. Attendance—35,455.

BY EDWARD PRELL

[Chicago Tribune Press Service]

Boston, Aug. 2—The White Sox leaped their biggest hurdle in Boston tonight in the same old way, complete with chills and thrills, when they certified a 2 to 1 victory in the ninth inning.

In this profitable night, the White Sox remained a game ahead of the second place New York Yankees while increasing their advantage over Cleveland to a pair of games and over the Red Sox to four.

35,455 Watch Thriller

The largest paying crowd of the season in this now one-team baseball town, and a wild one at that, 35,455, had a few moments of pleasurable anticipation that the Red Sox were going to pull another one out.

Connie Johnson, who last week pitched the Chicago Sox into first place by whipping the Yankees, 3 to 2, had a 2 to 0 shutout going into the ninth. It had been provided with singles in the third inning off Tom Brewer by Jim Busby, Chico Carrasquel, and Minnie Minoso, and Jungle Jim Rivera's home run in the fourth inning off the same gent.

MINNIE TALKS

Minnie Minoso tries to put finger on reason for batting slump. Story on page 4.

Piersall Raises Boston Hopes

That lead was ample as Johnson, tho wilder than usual, kept at bay all but three Red Sox hitters, a trio of left handers. Ted Williams and Billy Goodman had two hits each, and Billy Klaus one as Connie came into the final inning for the kill.

The first two Red Sox were easy outs, but Jimmy Piersall scratched a single off George Kell's glove. Faye Throneberry, a left handed batter, came up to hit for Ellis Kinder, who had replaced Brewer after the seventh.

Johnson, who had walked

[Continued on page 4, col. 7]

DON'T LET IT HAPPEN TO YOU!

He came home without All-Star tickets. Be smart. Be safe. Order today from All-Star Ticket Manager, Tribune Tower, Chicago 11. Make check or money order payable to Chicago Tribune Charities, Inc., and inclose self-addressed envelope and 35 cents for mailing and handling.

In the Loop, you can pick up tickets for the annual football classic—All-Stars vs. Cleveland Browns, Soldiers' field, Aug. 12—at Tribune Public Service offices, 33 W. Madison st. and in lobby of The Tribune Tower, 9 a. m. to 5 p. m. Prices:

~~$10~~ $7 $5.50 $4
$2.75 $1.50 $1

MOON MULLINS

The World Series: The Scenes and the Players

New York Yankees

Yankee Stadium: First two games of the series will be played here. The home of the Bronx Bombers seats 67,000.

Top Hurlers: Bob Turley, Whitey Ford and Don Larsen (left to right).

Manager: Casey Stengel.

Byrne Sturdivant Grim Kucks Morgan

Robinson Cerv Mantle Bauer Noren

Carey Silvera Howard Berra Coleman

Collins Martin Skowron Rizzuto McDougald

Brooklyn Dodgers

Spooner Amoros Shuba Roebuck Koufax Meyer

Loes Robinson Craig Walker Erskine Bessent

Rhody's pride: Clem Labine, North Smithfield

Gilliam Reese Newcombe

Zimmer Podres Hoak

Ebbets Field: The Dodgers' home field seats 32,111. Third, fourth and fifth games will be played here.

Manager: Walter Alston

Top hitters: From left, Carl Furillo, Gil Hodges, Roy Campanella and Duke Snider.

Camera Sides With Ump . . .

Says Robbie Was Safe in Steal Of Homeplate in Series Opener

DODGERS' ROBINSON RACES BALL TO PLATE IN EIGHTH INNING, THEN SLIDES UNDER CATCHER BERRA'S GLOVE. BATTER IS FRANK KELLERT; ARBITER IS BILL SUMMERS. NOTE ESPECIALLY PICTURE AT LEFT CENTER.

—Associated Press Wirephoto

KUCKS TAKES NAP AND SNIDER HITS

Yank Pitcher's Failure to Cover First Forces Stengel to Change Strategy

By WILL GRIMSLEY

BROOKLYN, Oct. 1 (AP)—Young Johnny Kucks said he "froze" temporarily when he failed to cover first base today in the fifth inning on Peewee Reese's hot infield hit, and the blunder probably cost the New York Yankees the fourth World Series game, won by the Brooklyn Dodgers, 8-5.

"If Reese is out we planned to walk Duke Snider, the next man up," said Manager Casey Stengel. "As it was, we had to pitch to him and so they get three runs."

After Kucks' momentary "blackout," Snider hit a prodigious drive into a Bedford Avenue parking lot, scoring three runs which tied the series at two games each.

Kucks himself was distraught and near tears after his mistake.

Kucks Is Baffled

"I don't know what happened to me," the young righthander said. "I've never done anything like that before in my life.

"I thought Reese's hit was going through the hole between first and second. I know I should have started for first anyway but somehow I didn't. Then I saw Collins (first baseman Joe Collins) backhand the ball. I started again but for some reason I hesitated too long again.

"I feel terrible about it. It was a horrible mistake and to think it had to happen in the World Series."

Reese's ball was hit sharply to Collins, who made a great stab and then, seeing Kucks hesitating, dashed madly toward the base, and tossed to Kucks too late.

"I ran like the devil, but I couldn't make it," said Collins.

Snider Tees Off

The play came in the fifth with Junior Gilliam on base via a walk and with the score 4-3 in favor of the Dodgers.

Snider, the next man up, teed off on the longest home run of the series for three runs and a 7-3 lead.

Stengel was charitable to Kucks, saying Brooklyn may have won the game anyhow on its lusty hitting, but he added:

"One of the rules of baseball is for the pitcher to cover first base in such situations. He doesn't need to think, just move."

Stengel said the Yankees had had bad luck with pitchers' fielding in the first two games.

Turley Slipped, Too

"Turley (Bob Turley, third-game starter) failed to field Johnny Podres' bunt in the second inning yesterday and it filled the bases. Before we're through, they have four runs."

Stengel was asked if he was discouraged now that the series has been levelled.

"We're just back where we started," the gravel - voiced Yanks' pilot said. "We're not worried."

Someone surmised that Brooklyn is a mighty tough ball club at Ebbets Field.

"We can be tough in this ball park, too," Stengel said, "that is, if we can just start getting that long ball again. They got the long ball today. We didn't, except for Gil McDougald's home run. We got to hit to give our pitchers some breathing room."

He said he would pitch Bob Grim tomorrow and follow with his lefthanders, Whitey Ford and Tommy Byrne, at the Stadium, if necessary.

The Yankee manager said he would check with ailing Mickey Mantle before deciding whether to play him again in the outfield tomorrow.

"We've just got five legs out there but we're fielding all right," he added, failing to take too much note of Mantle's failure to get Roy Campanella's long double in the fifth.

Fair Weather for Series Today

NEW YORK, Oct. 1 (AP)—It'll be mostly fair with little change in temperature for the fifth game of the World Series tomorrow at Ebbets Field the weather bureau said today.

Holy Cross' Air Attack Topples Dartmouth, 29-21

HANOVER, N.H., Oct. 1 (AP)—Holy Cross beat Dartmouth at its own aerial game in a 29-21 football victory today, but was kept in turmoil to the finish as the Indians scored all three touchdowns in the final period.

Quarterbacks Jack Stephans and Billy Smithers passed for two touchdowns each for the speedier, alert Crusaders who took a 23-0 lead in the second period.

However, Coach Bob Blackman's game Indians finally unleashed the full fury of their passing attack late in the contest paced by Bill Beagle and Mike Brown, son of the Cleveland Browns' coach.

Holy Cross	0	23	0	6—29
Dartmouth	0	0	0	21—21

3 HOMERS 7 R.B.I.'s

AP Wirephoto

"Bang! Bang! Bang! Went the Dodgers. Brooklyn home run power generated six runs as the Dodgers defeated the Yankees, 8 to 5, at Ebbets Field to square the World Series at two games apiece. Roy Campanella (left) homered with the sacks empty. Duke Snider (center) connected with two on base and Gil Hodges (right) with one on for a total of six runs batted in. Hodges, with three hits, also batted in a run with a single. The heavy artillerymen of Flatbush drove in 345 runs and blasted 101 homers in the Brooks' pennant rush.

* * *

BUMS' HOMERS TIE SERIES; YOUNGSTERS DUE TO HURL

(Continued From First Page)

between the mound and second base and Furillo beat a throw made by Billy Martin, who had raced over to scoop up the ball.

Wind Helps Homer

Hodges, a right-handed hitter who generally pulls the ball, then put the Dodgers ahead with a home run over the scoreboard in right center, a drive given some assistance by the breeze.

The Dodgers carried their 4-3 advantage into the last of the fifth and then wrapped things up nicely with three more runs on Snider's tremendous poke over the right field fence. The breeze didn't help that one.

Larsen started the inning off by walking Junior Gilliam on four balls in succession. His first two offerings to Pee Wee Reese were also balls, Gilliam stealing second as the second pitch was in the dirt.

Casey Walks, Larsen Leaves

Manager Casey Stengel of the Yankees walked out to the mound at this point and called for Kucks, who had pitched two scoreless innings against the Dodgers yesterday. He wasn't as fortunate today.

Reese hit a sharp grounder to Joe Collins' right. The Yankee first baseman fielded the ball cleanly, but Kucks failed to cover the bag quickly enough and Reese arrived there first, credited with a single.

Snider, up next, leaned heavily into a letter-high fast ball and sent it sailing toward Bedford Avenue, outside the park. It was his seventh home run in World Series competition, a new National League record.

McDougald Connects

The Dodgers hit three home runs to the Yankees' one. In the first round, Gil McDougald selected a fat 3-1 pitch offered by Erskine and deposited it in the stands in left center. It was his fifth World Series homer.

Collins led off with a walk in the second inning, advanced to second on Elston Howard's fine sacrifice and took third as Martin grounded out. He scored on a line drive single to left center by Phil Rizzuto.

The Dodgers scored in the third on a hit-and-run double by Gilliam, a shot down the third base line, no more than a foot inside the bag. Sandy Amoros, who had walked, scored all the way from first on the hit.

Erskine, who struck out 14 Yankees in a World Series game in 1953, did not finish the fourth. He was replaced by young Don Bessent after Yogi Berra led off with a single to center and Collins again drew a walk.

Berra was forced at third by another bunt by Howard, but Martin, with the hit-and-run on, blooped a broken-bat single to right, scoring Collins, who had stolen third just one pitch earlier.

Double Play Ends Rally

A double play brought this rally to an abrupt close. Rizzuto bounced to Jackie Robinson, who moved a few steps to his left before spearing the ball. Gilliam made an exceptionally quick relay at second base.

After the Dodgers went ahead, 4-3, on the homers by Campy and Hodges, the Yankees tried another rally. Singles by Irv Noren and Mickey Mantle and a walk to Berra loaded the bases with two out.

Bessent was removed here for Labine, who induced Collins to tap into a force at second base.

Labine improved as the game progressed. The Yankees scored two runs on three hits off him in the sixth, but he denied them a hit in the last three rounds. Rizzuto, who walked, was the only man to get on base.

Robinson Gets Single

Howard greeted Labine in the sixth with a single to left. Martin then hit an ordinary 370-foot fly to dead center, but Snider misjudged the ball and it sailed over his head for a double, scoring Howard.

With one out, Martin scored as Eddie Robinson, pinch hitting for Kucks, looped a single to right. Labine was in danger of being removed here but he got Noren and McDougald on flies to Snider in deep center.

Two inninng later, Snyder made the fielding play of the day. Racing in fast, he plucked Pinch Hitter Bill Skowron's fly a foot off the ground and was loudly applauded by the partisian Brooklyn crowd.

The Dodgers got their last run off Southpaw Gary (Rip) Coleman, third Yankee pitcher. Campanella, Furillo and Hodges hit successive singles in the seventh, Campy scoring on Hodges' line drive to center.

Tom Morgan replaced Coleman and got the side out without more damage. Tom Sturdivant blanked the Dodgers in the eighth.

UCLA Romps in PCC Grid Opener, 55-0

PULLMAN, Wash., Oct. 1 (AP)—The UCLA Bruins, with every back a hero, opened defense of their Pacific Coast Conference football title today with a massive 55-0 thumping of Washington State.

It was the Cougars' worst beating in 33 years and strengthened the Bruins' hold on their No. 7 spot in The Associated Press poll.

UCLA .... 7 21 14 13—55

UCLA scoring—Touchdowns: Davenport 2 (3, plunge; 1, plunge); Brown 2 (5 run; 6, run); Decker (21, pass from Bradley); Peters (9, run); Hollaway 2 (60, run; 3, pass from McDougall). Conversions: Brown 4, Hermann, Bradley, McDougall.

Yanks Behind 8-5 Ball

NEW YORK	AB	R	H	O	A	E
Noren, cf	5	0	1	3	0	0
McDougald, 3b	5	1	1	1	1	0
Mantle, rf	5	0	1	2	0	0
Berra, c	3	0	1	4	1	0
Collins, 1b	2	2	0	11	1	0
Howard, lf	3	1	1	0	0	0
Martin, 2b	4	1	2	1	3	0
Rizzuto, ss	3	0	1	2	2	0
Larsen, p	2	0	0	0	1	0
Kucks, p	0	0	0	0	1	0
a-E. Robinson	1	0	1	0	0	0
b-Carroll	0	0	0	0	0	0
R. Coleman, p	0	0	0	0	0	0
Morgan, p	0	0	0	0	0	0
c-Skowron	1	0	0	0	0	0
Sturdivant, p	0	0	0	0	0	0
Totals	**34**	**5**	**9**	**24**	**10**	**0**

BROOKLYN	AB	R	H	O	A	E
Gilliam, 2b	4	1	2	1	4	0
Reese, ss	4	1	2	1	2	0
Snider, cf	4	1	1	6	0	0
Campanella, c	5	2	3	4	0	0
Furillo, rf	5	1	2	1	0	0
Hodges, 1b	4	1	3	11	0	0
J. Robinson, 3b	4	0	0	1	2	0
Amoros, lf	3	1	1	2	0	0
Erskine, p	1	0	0	0	1	0
Bessent, p	1	0	0	0	1	0
Labine, p	2	0	0	0	2	0
Totals	**37**	**8**	**14**	**27**	**12**	**0**

a-Singled for Kucks in 6th.
r-Ran for E. Robinson in 6th.
c-Flied out for Morgan in 8th.

New York (A)	110	102	000—5
Brooklyn (N)	001	330	10x—8

E—None. RBI—McDougald, Rizzuto, Gilliam, Martin 2, Campanella, Hodges 3, Snider 3. E. Robinson. 2B—Gilliam, Campanella, Martin. HR—McDougald, Campanella, Hodges, Snider. SB—Rizzuto, Collins, Gilliam. S—Howard, Reese. DP—J. Robinson, Gilliam and Hodges. Left—New York 7, Brooklyn 9. BB—Erskine 2 (Collins 2), Bessent 1 (Berra), Labine 1 (Rizuto), Larsen 2 (Amoros, Gilliam), Sturdivant 1 (Snider). SO—Erskine 3 (Noren, Mantle 2), Bessent 1 (McDougald), Larsen 2 (Furillo, Bessent), Kucks 1 (Furillo), R. Coleman 1 (Labine). HO—Erskine 3 in 3 (faced two batters in 4th), Bessent 3 in 1⅔, Larsen 5 in 4 (faced one batter in 5th), Kucks 3 in 1, R. Coleman 5 in 1 (faced three batters in 7th), Morgan 0 in 1, Sturdivant 1 in 1, Labine 3 in 4⅓. R-ER—Erskine 3-3, Bessent 0-0, Larsen 5-5, Kucks 2-2, R. Coleman 1-1, Morgan 0-0, Sturdivant 0-0, Labine 2-2. W—Labine. L—Larsen. U—Dascoli (N.) plate, Summers (A.) first base, Ballanfant (N.) second base, Honochick (A.) third base, Donatelli (N.) left field, Flaherty (A.) right field. T—2:57. A—36,242.

NY Pilot Ready for 'Bum' Rush

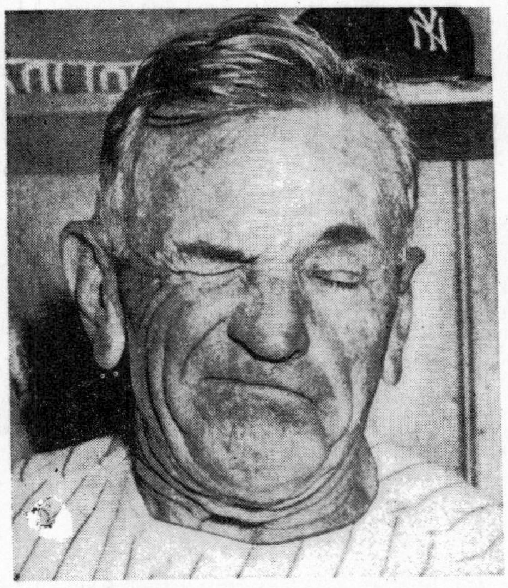

GAY CASEY — After yesterday's Series-evening New York victory it was no trick at all for Manager Casey Stengel to wink in manner of real confidence.
—International News soundphoto.

THE BIG BLAST—Bill (Moose) Skowron races to first as his home run goes into rightfield bleachers to climax Yankees' five-run first inning yesterday against Dodgers. Ahead of Skowron are Hank Bauer (nearing second) and Yogi Berra (nearing third). Homer ended Karl Spooner, Dodger pitcher, and brought in Russ Meyer, who checked the Yankees remainder of game. Yankees won, 5-1, to even Series at three games apiece. Teams battle in their final game today.
—International News soundphoto.

TUMBLE TIME—New York's Billy Martin spills over Gil Hodges, Brooklyn first baseman, as latter attempts to prevent double play in second inning yesterday. Hodges' antics were in vain as Martin got throw away in time to double Jackie Robinson at 1st.
—International News soundphoto.

Three for Three—at Home, Sweet, Home

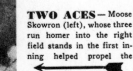

TWO ACES—Moose Skowron (left), whose three run homer into the right field stands in the first inning helped propel the Yanks into a Series tie, and Ed (Whitey) Ford, who set Brooklyn down with four hits, congratulate each other in dressing room.
—International News soundphoto.

GOIN' FOR TWO—After forcing out Yankee Billy Martin at second, Shortstop Peewee Reese tries for double play at first on Yogi Berra, but Reese's toss was late to catch Berra in seventh inning action. Teams set Series record for double plays, pulling off 18 twin killings—11 for the Dodgers and 7 for Yankees.
—International News soundphoto.

WEATHER TODAY
Showers
High, 75; Low, 64
Yesterday
High, 78; Low 61

THE INDIANAPOLIS STAR

"Where the spirit of the Lord is, there is Liberty"—II Cor. 3-17

TODAY'S CHUCKLE
Desperate maiden: "I want a husband of the LS/MFT type: Long, Short, Medium, Fat, or Thin.

VOL. 53. NO. 122 ★★★★ WEDNESDAY MORNING, OCTOBER 5, 1955

Delivered by Carrier (daily only): 35c per week
5c in Marion County; 7c elsewhere in Indiana.

BUMS ARE CHAMPS-AT LAST

Suit Perils Vital Sewage Expansion

Delay Seen As Menace To Health

The "health and welfare" of every citizen in metropolitan Indianapolis may be imperiled through court action halting vitally needed expansion of the city's sewage system.

Clarence T. Drayer, president of the Board of Sanitary Commissioners, said an injunction suit filed Monday has stopped the $22,570,000 expansion program which included such needed improvements as:

1 Garbage and trash incinerators to eliminate the overpowering stench on the South Side.

2 Construction of the Belmont interceptor sewer to handle the ever-increasing flow of sewage into the City Sanitation Plant.

3 Extension of other interceptor lines to provide health facilities to newly annexed areas and to encourage other big industries to move to Indianapolis.

"It is unthinkable that anyone of our citizens devoted to the betterment of Indianapolis and the community which we serve would be so shortsighted as to file a suit impairing the health and welfare of the entire community," Drayer declared.

THE CRIPPLING suit was filed Monday in Superior Court, Room 4, by Bruce Short, former secretary and Democratic member of the Indiana Toll Road Commission.

The sanitary board already has purchased some $3,000,000 worth of incinerators and it planned under a recent bond issue to construct buildings to house them.

Unless the injunction suit is settled soon, the incinerators will be delivered only to lie out in the weather and rust, Drayer pointed out.

"As a result of this suit, it will be impossible to alleviate the conditions which have made life almost unbearable for people on the South Side and along White River," he added.

THE INCINERATORS would help eliminate the odorous lagoons at the city sanitation

Turn to Page 13, Column 4

The Weather

Joe Crow Says: One Indianapolis hotel announces the purchase of two beds seven-feet long. No doubt the officials realize the basketball season is almost upon us.

Indianapolis—Mild and occasional rain today. Mild and showers tomorrow.

John Lewis Suffers Mild Heart Attack

Washington (INS) — The physician attending John L. Lewis, who is in a local hospital, said yesterday he had suffered a "slight heart attack," but is in "very good shape."

Dr. John Minor did not describe the nature of the attack. Asked, however, whether the United Mine Workers' chief had been stricken by a coronary thrombosis, he replied: "He has had a slight damage to his coronary circulation."

Minor said Lewis' attack was not comparable in severity to that suffered by President Eisenhower. He declared that the famed labor leader, who is 75 years old, should be able to go home "by the end of this week." Lewis has been in the hospital 11 days.

Feuding Bared In Probe Of Traffic Toll

By AL G. McCORD

The Legislative Traffic Study Commission, which met last night to consider mounting highway traffic slaughter, rebuked Traffic Safety Director Joseph L. Lingo for failing to disclose friction between his office and the State Police.

State Representative Phillip C. Johnson of Mooresville, chairman of the commission, said the success of the traffic safety program rests on complete co-operation of all state agencies.

'It is evident that something is wrong when our traffic death rate soars as it has in Indiana this year," Johnson said. "This is a matter of life and death for the people. It is too vital to permit it to fail through a lack of co-operation or friction between officials."

Johnson said another emergency meeting will be called, possibly within two weeks, to question state officials responsible for highway safety to determine what has gone wrong.

TO BE SUMMONED will be State Police Superintendent Frank A. Jessup, Commissioner of Motor Vehicles Morris J. Carter, Chairman Virgil W. Smith of the Highway Commission and Lingo.

Lingo appeared at the meeting last night, held at Johnson's home in Mooresville.

He was questioned regarding reports of friction with the State Poice and admitted there had been disagreements, Johnson said.

"He was criticized for not bringing this to our attention

Turn to Page 13, Column 5

Happy Dodgers 'Mob' World Series Heroes

Dodgers' Johnny Podres yells happily as he is grabbed by Catcher Roy Campanella after getting the final out against the New York Yankees in Yankee Stadium in New York yesterday to give his team its first World Series title (left). It was Johnny's second victory of the series. Third Baseman Don Hoak is racing over to get in on the celebration. (Right) Walter O'Malley (left), Dodgers' boss lets out a howl as he grabs Manager Walter Alston in the dressing room after the victory with a score of 2 to 0. The Dodgers had made seven previous tries for the title. (AP Wirephoto)

Stun Yanks, 2-0, In Thrill-Packed Windup To Series

By BOB CONSIDINE

New York (INS)—Please don't refer to Dem Bums as Bums again. Ever!

They won the first World Series of their long and abused lives yesterday behind the almost miraculous pitching of Johnny Podres. When only absolute perfection would suffice, Podres shut out the Yankees 2-0 in this the seventh, last and greatest game of the annual baseball classic.

Brooklyn made baseball history in the stadium where so many previous hopes were crushed to earth. Never before had a team which lost the first two games of a seven-game series rallied to win the game's most coveted laurel.

THE SLENDER DODGER southpaw poisoned the perennial world champions with a mixture of whistling speed, crazy-breaking screwballs, crackling curves and a slow that waddled up to the plate like a paper sack of wind. He literally broke their bats, though they hit him safely eight tense times, and figuratively he broke their backs.

The sorcery of the man reached its summit in the eighth when with the tying runs at first and third, and only one out, Podres rid himself of two of the finest clutch hitters in baseball history, Yogi Berra and Hank Bauer. It was a moment of triumph and disaster that made the palms of your hands perspire.

It took one of the most memorable fielding plays in World Series history to give Podres his second victory of the post-season play and the now happily deranged Dodgers their first championship in eight tries dating back to 1916. Here's what happened:

In the Yankee sixth, Podres walked Billy Martin and the Yankee fans in the crowd of 62,465 set up the caterwaul that means "here we go!" Their joy knew little restraint a moment later when Gil McDougald, up there to sacrifice, made his third base line bunt so perfect that he easily beat Podres' throw.

INTO THIS torment of tension stepped Yogi Berra, the most consistent and most feared hitter in the series.

Yogi is a man composed entirely of muscle—a short, squat, unnerving type at the plate. Podres studied him like a Mississippi riverboat gambler inspecting a poacher. Then Podres began dealing. First it was something that spit and thrashed about like a loose live wire, then something straight and around the speed of sound, then (with the same motion) something that forgot gravity and loafed into Roy Campanella's glove like a sock of mush.

At last Yogi took a shine to one. He swung late and hit a ball high against the perfect blue sky and straight as a string down the third base line.

A dusky Cuban named Sandy Amoros, who had just been put in left field as a defensive measure, was playing Yogi far over toward center field, as a left fielder in command of his senses must play a good left-handed hitter who pulls the ball. But here was Yogi hitting completely opposite from his normal manner.

AMOROS TOOK off in des-

Turn to Page 28, Column 3

Truck-Train Crash Kills 5, Injures 2

West Newton, Pa. (AP)—A runaway lumber truck smashed into a moving freight train in this small town yesterday, derailing several freight cars which catapaulted against two buildings. The truck driver and four persons in the building were killed.

Rolling with terrifying speed down a half-mile hill, the truck knocked the second car of a long Baltimore & Ohio Railroad freight off the rails.

EIGHT other cars piled up on both sides of the track, hitting the Casale Fruit Store on one side and the Fries Hardware and Electric Store on the other.

"It was an awful crash—it sent chills right through you," said a woman a half block away.

The truck was ground to a pulp under the wreckage. Engineer William McManus of Connellsville, Pa., said he saw the truck speeding at his train

Turn to Page 12, Column 2

Alas, Da Bums Is Kings!

Bedlam Explodes Over Flatbush As Dodgers Take 'Woild Serious'

Flatbush Avenue, Brooklyn (INS) — At 2:44 p.m. (CDT) yesterday, the New York borough of Brooklyn exploded.

That was the moment the ball slid into Gil Hodges' mitt for the final out at Yankee Stadium. The Dodgers were champs for the first time.

From the east end of the Brooklyn Bridge, up along the Gowanus Canal and on into "Greenpernt," the shout went up:

"Da bums is kings . . . whadda woild serious!"

Bedlam was never like this, and the ashes haven't settled yet.

Every auto horn in the borough began blasting, factory sirens started to shrill and the voices of the delirious multitudes became screams. The sound must have carried far across the Hudson River into Newark.

THEY LOCKED UP shop, boarded up the glass fronts and went on a baseball binge —all 3,000,000 of them.

Men and women danced in the streets. Respectable housewives threw their arms around the nearest male and kissed like so many Marilyn Monroes.

Dodger rooters throughout the other New York boroughs went almost as crazy over the first Dodger World Series triumph.

Telephones were jammed as every fan in Brooklyn called every other fan. Offices stopped work. Factories gave up as the workers went out into the streets to snake-dance.

From the windows of Brooklyn's staid board of education and courts buildings, torn-up telephone books, wastebaskets of paper and shredded newspapers, poured into the streets.

IN THE MIDST of the bedlam along Lovington Street, an old man with a long white beard and a portable radio leaned on his cane and said:

"I never thought I'd live so long!"

A fan named Joe Flanders shouted "This is next year," and Cabbie Irving Davidoff predicted the series win would mean the end of Brooklyn gang wars and juvenile delinquency.

As two chartered busses brought the Dodgers back to their Ebbets Field dressing rooms, a police escort led the procession.

Around the Brooklyn field where the Dodgers won three straight, four cars cruised bearing huge signs: "Podres for President . . . We're in."

In the crowd at the dressing room entrance stood Mrs. Mildred Silverman and her 10-year-old son, Elliott, waiting for autographs.

"Daddy's just going to have to wait for supper tonight," she announced.

Anywhere in Brooklyn last night, it was "moider" to mention "Joisey" — or any place else as a home for the Dodgers. Outside a corner bar along howling Flatbush, one Dodger partisan summed it up:

"Yesterday dey was da Bums. Today dey's kings. And dey's stayin' right here in Flatbush fer good."

Ike Signs Record Batch Of Official Documents

Denver (AP)—President Eisenhower continued to make satisfactory progress toward recovery throughout yesterday and signed half a dozen more official documents, the most since his heart attack.

One of the papers on which the chief executive put his name in a 10-minute business conference with his top assistant, Sherman Adams, releases $500,000 of disaster relief funds which the Agriculture Department will use for conservation measures in the hurricane and flood-damaged states of Connecticut, Massachusetts and North Carolina.

Three of the signatures were on commissions for Federal positions and one was on a letter accepting the resignation Jack K. McFall as ambassador to Finland.

LIKE THE PRESIDENT himself, McFall has a heart condition and that was the reason for turning in his resignation.

The final signature was a technical action on a letter to Governor Shivers of Texas legalizing drought disaster allocations to the state.

Shivers was notified of the allocations by telegram Sept. 19, before the President became ill. His signature on a letter was needed to make them legal.

EISENHOWER still is in the period of danger from his heart attack but with the hospital charts showing two nights of good rest in a row, the last tinges of concern over the President's Sunday night weari-

Turn to Page 13, Column 4

Soviet Softening Boomerangs

Hungarians Flock Back To Church

This is the fifth of a series of dispatches from Eugene C. Pulliam, publisher of The Indianapolis Star and The Indianapolis News, on a writing tour of Europe.

By EUGENE C. PULLIAM

Budapest, Hungary — Startling evidence that the Good Lord works in mysterious ways to proclaim His gospel and to give hope and comfort to His followers can be seen on any Sunday anywhere in Hungary where there is a church.

In keeping with the new Soviet line of "sweetness and light" the Communist high command in Hungary revised its policy of persecution of priests and pastors. A program of so-called co-operation between state and church was inaugurated. Instead of being scolded and threatened for believing in God and attending church, people now are urged to go to mass and to church.

Pulliam

The response of the people to this new policy has astounded even the most devout priests and pastors. Never has Hungary witnessed such a revival of church attendance. Every church is packed for every service. So great has the interest been that in all the larger Catholic churches and Reformed churches of Budapest three and in some instances four services are held each Sunday.

OF COURSE there always is a catch in any program the Soviets institute in behalf of the people. In this case it was a requirement that priests and pastors should read each Sunday a short "sermon" extolling the Communist philosophy.

That was the price demanded for permitting normal church services and activities.

Not a few Catholic priests and Reformed church pastors have publicly embraced communism and these "favored ones" are being loudly exploited by Communist propaganda chiefs. Some of the "joiners" have excused their conduct on the grounds that it is better to have the churches open and functioning even with a sprinkling of Communist poison than to have no religious services at all. Others of the "joiners" profess to being sincerely converted to communism as a way of life and religion. Obviously the "joiners" are very popular with government officials but the great rank and file of the people distrust and hate them.

POPE PIUS XII has been greatly disturbed by this new development in Hungary. Just last week he issued a strong statement on the Hungarian situation in which he said there can be no compromise between the Christian faith and Communist materialism. Hungarians, both Catholic and Protestant, were overjoyed when they learned via the grapevine of the Pope's pronouncement.

The unmolested opportunity to attend mass and services has given the people a much needed morale boost. They now have a place where they can see and talk to each other in safety. They have had a chance to renew and re-confirm their faith. In short the new "religious" policy of the Communists has boomeranged tremendously in favor of the Christian Lord. The unprecedented church attendance of these last months has served as a warning to the Communists. They will hardly dare again to use force in regimenting religious worship.

Incidentally Cardinal Mindszenty still is under house arrest, the Communist press and Bishop G. Bromley Oxnam to the contrary notwithstanding.

INSIDE TODAY'S STAR

Popular Greek Premier Papagos Dies At 71 Of Heart Exhaustion

Athens, Greece (AP) — Greece's Premier Marshal Alexander Papagos, victor over Mussolini's legions in World War II and the Communists in postwar battles, died last night. He was 71.

The Greek warrior-politician suffered a lung hemorrhage and died of heart exhaustion.

He had been ailing for months but his death now had been unexpected.

THE FIRST PERSON to be notified of his death was Foreign Minister Stephan Stepanopoulos. Earlier yesterday Papagos signed papers nominating Stephanopoulos as a provisional premier during his illness.

King Paul and Queen Frederika also were notified and drove immediately to Papagos' house.

The funeral will be held Friday.

PAPAGOS HAD been confined since January to his Ekali residence with gastric troubles that stemmed from his term in a World War II Nazi prison camp.

A photgraph of him published last July showed a spent man with sunken checks. The first picture of him to be put out in months, it shocked Greeks.

Papagos was chief of the army general staff when Mussolini launched his invasion of Greece Oct. 28, 1940. Dictator John Metaxas promptly appointed Papagos commander of all armed forces. Only sudden German blows from Yugoslavia and Bulgaria by Hitler's panzer divisions in the spring of 1941 put an end to six months of Greek victories.

(AP Wirephoto)

MARSHAL PAPAGOS
Premier And War Hero

TEN YEARS LATER Papagos took command of the war against the Communist guerrillas in the northern mountains of Greece. The struggle had been going on for three years. Papagos, grand chamberlain to the royal court at the time, agreed to take command on condition that he be given dictatorial powers and the authority to keep politicians at home in Athens. In six months — with U.S. aid—the war was over.

Papagos became a living legend. The marshal then became head of the conservative Greek Rally Party. In the nation's 1951 elections, Papagos' faction returned the largest number of deputies of any party in Parliament but did not win a majority.

But with new elections in 1952 his rally gained the greatest majority in the Greek Parliament since World War II.

HIS DEATH is expected to set off a wide open struggle for power in Greece.

As a popular hero as a military leader, Papagos held a unique position in Greek public life. He stood apart from party politics. His government was made up of a "rally" of various political elements held together by his personal stature and prestige.

In Washington, American officials were distressed to hear of his death, realizing the political contesting for power which in their view is bound to result.

Daily Mirror

NEW YORK 17, N. Y.,

TUESDAY, OCTOBER 9, 1956

Vol. 33. No. 94

Weather: Fair CO· 4c in N.Y.C. 5c Within 800 mi 10c Elsewhere

5 CENTS ★★★ FINAL

Larseny In The Bronx!

DON WINS PERFECT GAME

No-Hits Brooks 2 to 0

PASSPORT TO HALL OF FAME In a frenzy of joy, Yanks' Yogi Berra hurls himself on hurler Don Larsen seconds after Don retired the last Dodger to win 2-0 victory—and go into record books as first pitcher in World Series history to hurl a perfect game!

(Mirror Photo by Art Abfier)

... Stories on Page 20

YANKEES TAKE SERIES ON 9-0 WIN

Kucks' 3-Hit Job Backed By 4 Homers

Berra, Skowron, Howard Account for All Runs; Newcombe Routed Early

BROOKLYN (AP)—The New York Yankees overwhelmed the Dodgers and Don Newcombe with a record-breaking home run assault today and won the World Series, four games to three, with a 9-0 victory.

Yogi Berra hit two homers and Bill Skowron smashed a grand slam homer to back up superb 3-hit pitching by 23-year-old Johnny Kucks.

The Yankees thus duplicated Brooklyn's 1955 feat of winning a seven - game series after losing the first two games. It was the Yanks' 17th World Series victory in 22 attempts since 1923 and their sixth in seven series against Brooklyn.

The Dodgers took the first two games in Ebbets Field. The Yanks won the next three in their stadium and then Brooklyn squared the series yesterday in their home park. Today's game was the first break - through by the visiting team.

Berra, who clubbed a bases-loaded homer off Newcombe in the second game, hit over the right field wall the first two times he came to bat against Newk today, each time with a man on base. After that he was intentionally passed twice and one of those walks set up Skowron's bases-full blow off Roger Craig, the third Dodger pitcher. Elston Howard belted the other Yankee homer, with Newcombe as the victim.

The seven - game series drew a paid attendance of 345,903 with 33,782 fans watching the final game. The net receipts for the series were $2,183,353.59.

The four Yankee homers set a series record of 12 by one club in a series, breaking the mark of ten set by the 1952 Yanks, and Berra, with ten runs batted in during the Series, smashed another record.

FIRST INNING

YANKEES — Hank Bauer singled into center. He stole second. Billy Martin struck out. Mantle struck out. Yogi Berra hit a home run over the rightfield fence, Bauer scoring ahead of him. Bill Skowron struck out. Two runs, two hits, no errors, none left on base.

DODGERS — Jim Gilliam grounded out to Skowron, at first. PeeWee Reese walked. Duke Snider singled on the first pitch, sending Gilliam to second. Jackie Robinson hit into a double play, Kucks to Martin to Collins. No runs, one hit, no errors, one left on base.

SECOND INNING

YANKEES — Elston Howard grounded out, Reese to Hodges. Gil McDougald lined out to Gilliam. Andy Carey walked. Johnny Kucks forced Carey at second, Newcombe to Reese. No runs, no hits, no errors, one left on base.

DODGERS — Gil Hodges grounded out, Carey to Collins. Sandy Amoros grounded out, Martin to Collins. Carl Furillo grounded out, Martin to Collins. No runs, no hits, no errors, none left on base.

THIRD INNING

YANKEES — Bauer bunted to Gilliam at second and was thrown out to Hodges. Martin singled into center. Mantle struck out for the second time. Berra hit his second home run over the rightfield fence, scoring Martin. Skowron popped out to Gilliam. Two runs, two hits, no errors, none left on base.

DODGERS — Roy Campanella grounded out, Martin to Skowron. Don Newcombe grounded out, Kucks to Skowron. Gilliam flied out to Howard in left. No runs, no hits, no errors, none left on base.

FOURTH INNING

YANKEES — Howard hit a home run over the rightfield wall. It was the end for Newcombe and Don Bessent went in to relieve him. McDougald flied out to Gilliam at second. Carey grounded to PeeWee .Reese, but Reese muffed it for an error and Carey was safe at first. Kucks sacrifice bunted Carey to second, being thrown out Hodges to Gilliam. Bauer grounded out, Gilliam to Hodges. One run, one hit, one error, one left on base.

DODGERS—Reese led off with a walk. He was forced at second on a grounder, Skowron to McDougald. Robinson tried a surprise bunt, but popped to Kucks. Hodges grounded out, Martin to Skowron. No runs, no hits, no errors, none left on base.

FIFTH INNING

YANKEES — Martin grounded out, Robinson to Hodges. Mantle doubled into centerfield. Berra was deliberately walked. Skowron popped to Martin. Howard forces Berra at second, Hodges to Reese. No runs, one hit, no errors, two left on base.

DODGERS — Amoros flied out to Howard in left. Furillo grounded out, Carey to Skowron. Campanella grounded out, McDougald to Skowron. No runs, no hits, no errors, none left on base.

SIXTH INNING

YANKEES — McDougald singled into leftfield. Carey grounded out, Reese to Hodges, with McDougald going to second. Kucks struck out. Bauer fouled out to Hodges. No runs, one hit, no errors, one left on base.

DODGERS — Dale Mitchell went in to pinch hit for Bessent. He grounded out, McDougald to Skowron. Gilliam lined out to Martin. Reese popped out to McDougald. No runs, no hits, no errors, none left on base.

SEVENTH INNING

YANKEES — Roger Craig went in to pitch for the Dodgers. Martin singled into center. Mantle walked. A wild pitch enabled Martin and Mantle to advance a base. Berra was deliberately walked. Skowron hit a home run into the leftfield stands, scoring the three runners ahead of him. Howard doubled against the centerfield wall. McDougald popped out to Hodges. Carey struck out. Kucks grounded out, Reese to Hodges. Four runs, three hits, no errors, one left on base.

DODGERS—Snider flied out to Carey at third. Robinson was walked. Hodges lined out to McDougald at short, and Robinson was thrown out before he could get back to first for a double play. No runs, no hits, no errors, none left on base.

EIGHTH INNING

YANKEES — Bauer flied out to Snider in center. Martin struck out. Mantle struck out. No runs, no hits, no errors, none left on base.

DODGERS — Amoros grounded out to Skowron. Furillo got the Dodgers' second hit, a single to center. Campanella popped out to Carey. Rube Walker went into pinch hit for Roebuck. He grounded out, Martin to Skowron. No runs, one hit, no errors, one left on base.

NINTH INNING

YANKEES — Carl Erskine went in to pitch for Brooklyn. Berra lined out to Gilliam. Skowron grounded out, Reese to Hodges. Howard grounded out, Reese to Hodges. No runs, no hits, no errors, none left on base.

DODGERS — Gilliam grounded out to Skowron. Reese tried to bunt but the ball went foul into the air and was snatched by Berra for the out. Snider rifled a single into center. Robinson struck out, but had to be thrown out when Berra let the third strike get away, Berra to Skowron. No runs, one hit, no errors, one left on base.

Stingy With Hits

Johnny Kucks

New Tropical Storm Raging in Caribbean

MIAMI (UP)—An Air Force plane left Bermuda today to investigate a new tropical disturbance kicking up high winds in the Windward Islands well over 2,000 miles from Florida.

The area was located in a weather bureau bulletin Tuesday night about 1,250 miles east-southeast of San Juan, P.R., at latitude 15.5 north, longitude 48.0 west. The disturbance was moving slowly west - northwest.

Today's Chuckle

A bartender was wiping off the bar one day when a drunk staggered in and slumped over the bar.

"Say, can you tell me who runs Alcoholics Anonymous around here?" he asked.

"Why, do you want to join?" the bartender asked.

"Nope," said the drunk, "I want to resign."

The World Champion Yankees

The New York Yankees' baseball team which today won the symbol emblematic of universal supremacy on the diamond—the World Series—is pictured above. Members of the team, left to right, are: Front row—Ed Ford, Billy Martin, Bill Hunter, Tom Carroll, Coach Bill Dickey, Coach Frank Crosetti, Manager Casey Stengel, Coach Jim Turner, Yogi Berra, Irv Noren, Charlie Silvera, Gil McDougald. Second row—Trainer Gus Mauch, Enos Slaughter, Bob Cerv, Jerry Coleman, Bill Skowron, Elston Howard, Bob Turley, Sonny Dixon, George Wilson, Rip Coleman, Don Larsen. Third row—Tom Sturdivant, Norm Siebern, Andy Carey, Tommy Byrne, Bob Grim, Mickey Mantle, Hank Bauer, Mickey McDermott, Tom Morgan, Johnny Kucks and Joe Collins. Bat boys are Eddie Carr and Bill Loperfido. (AP)

Evening Chronicle EXTRA

VOL. 137—NO. 240 ALLENTOWN, PA., WEDNESDAY, OCTOBER 10, 1956 Telephone HE 3-4241 Entered 2nd Class Matter Post Office, Allentown, Pa. 5c Per Copy

Today's Box Score

Brooklyn (AP)—The official box score of the seventh game of the 1956 World Series:

NEW YORK (A)	Ab	R	H	O	A
Bauer, RF	5	1	1	0	0
Martin, 2B	5	2	2	2	6
Mantle, CF	4	1	1	0	0
Berra, C	3	3	2	1	1
Skowron, 1B	5	1	1	16	1
Howard, LF	5	1	2	2	0
McDougald, LF	4	0	1	3	3
Carey, 3B	3	0	0	2	2
Kucks, P	3	0	0	1	2
Totals	37	9	10	27	15

BROOKLYN (N)	Ab	R	H	O	A
Gilliam, 2B	4	0	0	6	2
Reese, SS	2	0	0	2	5
Snider, CF	4	0	2	1	0
Robinson, 3B	3	0	0	0	1
Hodges, 1B	3	0	0	10	2
Amoros, LF	3	0	0	0	0
Furillo, RF	3	0	1	0	0
Campanella, C	3	0	0	8	0
Newcombe, P	1	0	0	0	1
Bessent, P	0	0	0	0	0
a—Mitchell	1	0	0	0	0
Craig, P	0	0	0	0	0
Roebuck, P	0	0	0	0	0
b—Walker	1	0	0	0	0
Erskine, P	0	0	0	0	0
Totals	28	0	3	27	11

a—Grounded out for Bessent in 6th.
b—Grounded out for Roebuck in 8th.

E—Reese. RBI—Berra 4, Howard, Skowron 4. 2B—Mantle, Howard. HR—Berra 2, Howard, Skowron. SB—Bauer. S—Kucks. DP—Kucks, Martin and Skowron; McDougald and Skowron. Left—New York (A) 6, Brooklyn (N) 4. BB—Newcombe 1 (Carey), Bessent 1 (Berra), Craig 2 (Mantle, Berra), Kucks 3 (Reese 2, Robinson). SO—Newcombe 4 (Martin, Mantle 2, Skowron), Bessent 1 (Kucks), Roebuck 3 (Carey, Martin, Mantle), Kucks 1 (Robinson). HO—Newcombe 5 in 3 (faced one batter in 4th), Bessent 2 in 3, Craig 3 in 0 (faced five batters in 7th), Roebuck 0 in 2, Erskine 0 in 1. R-ER—Newcombe 5-5, Bessent 0-0, Craig 4-4, Roebuck 0-0, Erskine 0-0, Kucks 0-0. WP—Craig. W—Kucks. L—Newcombe.

Pitcher Johnny Kucks, of the Yankees, charges across the third base foul line to grab a foul pop off the bat of Dodger Jackie Robinson in the fourth inning of today's World Series game. Third baseman Andy Carey charges in to give a hand. Robinson fouled out attempting a surprise bunt. (AP)

BULLETIN

WASHINGTON (UP) — The Supreme Court today ordered a new trial for Pennsylvania Communist Leader Steve Nelson and four co-defendants.

Demos Hold Slight Lead In Alaska

JUNEAU, Alaska (AP)—Democrats moved into a commanding lead today in mounting returns from Alaska's general election.

Overcoming an early trend toward the Republican side in the first returns from conservative southeast Alaska, the Democrats moved overnight into this dominant position.:

They led for all six of the territory-wide offices at stake, although by narrow margins in some cases. They led for 18 seats in the Territorial House of Representatives while Republicans were ahead only for three.

In contrast, Republicans were ahead for five out of seven Territorial Senate seats on which enough votes had been tallied to establish a trend. One of them, however, was by only a one-vote margin.

The swing in favor of the Democrats came largely on big blocks of votes from the populous Anchorage and Fairbanks districts, although it was at Fairbanks that three of the five Re-

(See ALASKA—Page 4)

Food Prices Hit 6-Month Low Point

NEW YORK (UP) — Continued declines in meat prices last week dropped the Dun & Bradstreet wholesale food index to a six month low, the agency reported today.

D&B set the index for the week ended Oct. 9 at $5.97, the lowest figure in the books since April 10, when it stood at $5.96. The index was measured at $6.00 the previous week and $6.11 in the comparable week of 1955. Percentage wise, the indicator shows a 2.3 per cent decline from the similar week last year.

The new price represents a cumulative decline of 11 cents over the past two weeks.

Restless Jury Quieted

INDEPENDENCE, Mo. (AP) — Circuit Judge John R. James noticed the jury in his courtroom was restless.

He broke into the damage suit proceedings with this statement: "Gentlemen, I know you were called away from the television before the game ended. I have just been told that Brooklyn won, 1 to 0, in 10 innings."

Where To Find It

	1 2 3	4 5 6	7 8 9	R.	H.	E.
YANKS	202	100	400	9	10	0
DODGERS	000	000	000	0	3	1

Berra Blasts Two in a Row

Yankee Yogi Berra sticks out a hand to receive congratulations of the batboy as he scores on his first inning homer in today's World Series game. Plate umpire is Dusty Boggess. Yogi followed up his smash with another round tripper his next time at bat. Both times there was a man on base, giving the Yanks a 4-0 lead. (AP)

With the Presidential Candidates

PITTSBURGH (UP)—Buoyed by an enthusiastic reception given President Eisenhower in this Democratic stronghold, state Republican leaders rallied today to keep Pennsylvania's 32 electoral votes in the November elections under the Eisenhower-Nixon banner.

His opponent, Adlai Stevenson, was campaigning in Oregon and Washington today.

GOP leaders declared the cheering throngs which greeted Mr. Eisenhower in Pittsburgh Tuesday night overshadlowed the turnouts drawn the previous night by former President Harry S. Truman, who campaigned two days in the district in behalf of Democratic presidential candidate Adlai E. Stevenson.

A standing room only crowd of 11,000 jammed Hunt Armory to cheer the President during his nationwide radio and television address. An additional 4,000 listened to loudspeakers installed outside the hall. And police estimated more than 100,000 persons got a glimpse of the President during his trip from the airport here to the Armory.

Waving banners proclaiming victory for the Eisenhower team in November, the audience roared its approval when the President urged the return to the Senate of Sen. James H. Duff. Mr. Eisenhower termed Duff, who is battling Democrat Joseph S. Clark Jr. for re-election, "one of the stalwarts who has assisted the administration straight through."

Mr. Eisenhower also urged support for all other state GOP candidates, including Congressmen James G. Fulton and Robert H. Corbett and congressional candidate Herbert Morrison of Scottdale, Westmoreland County.

Duff, who introduced the President, proclaimed Mr. Eisenhower "the most beloved man who has been President of the United States in our lifetimes."

Earlier, thousands jammed the Golden Triangle and overflowed from sidewalks to the streets as the President's motorcade wound its way to the Penn-Sheraton Hotel from Greater Pittsburgh Airport, where the President arrived at 4 p.m. EDT.

Ticker tape and torn paper fluttered down on the motorcade from windows of office buildings lining

'Joe Smith's' Check Bounces

HUNTINGTON, W.Va. (AP) —Police hereabouts are looking for "Joe Smith."

The address he affixed to a $38.25 check that bounced proved to be a vacant lot.

Inquiry of Huntington's six bonafide Joe Smiths developed that all were respectable burgers and that none of them had anything to do with the phony check that was cashed by a grocer.

HYLAND FLING

By DICK HYLAND

When two married people develop widely divergent ideas, beliefs and habits, the courts agree that it is a good thing that they do not attempt to live together. Only trouble will be had if they do.

The Pacific Coast Conference is no different. It is made up of people. And what people!

Take, for instance, the subject of scholarship. The northern colleges accept athletes who could not get onto a major California university campus except for a brief visit.

The California colleges have high academic standards and standings. After seeing the prep school records of a few now at college in the great State of Oregon, I wonder if it has any academic standard at all.

There is a 9.8s 100-yard sprinter who is also a hurdler and potentially great football end or halfback. He is a senior at Dorsey High School in Los Angeles right now. He says he is headed for Oregon State with "a four-year scholarship."

This fellow is taking one pip of a set of courses to prepare himself for higher education. They are, to be exact: shopwork, senior (year) problems, boys personnel, choir, senior English and track and field!

You would think, wouldn't you, that university professors and presidents who deem it a heinous crime that an athlete receive $10 per week to level out sectional differences in living costs would also be concerned with the academic standards and standings of their universities?

Official releases to the press at the last PCC meeting strongly suggested that this was so, that at long last something **HAD BEEN DONE** about the spread in academic standards within the conference.

At least, the PCC spokesmen permitted reporters to believe and print that PCC standards had been raised to the point where prep school athletes had to have a 2.5 (C plus) average upon graduation in order to enroll and compete for a PCC school.

There was no refutation of those printed reports, no clarifications, either from the universities or Commissioner Victor O. Schmidt's office.

In brief, the public was led to believe that the profs and prexies, high-minded youth leaders and educators, had finally become as concerned with their own academic standards as with a $10 bill.

Haw! What fools we mortals be! Those profs and prexies just let us THINK that; and we will raise no moral question on such action at this time.

Actually, the PCC merely agreed upon that 2.5 average proposal as a "matter of principle." This is like being against sin.

They did NOTHING to implement the proposal, to make it into a rule that would apply to all nine conference universities equally — and WORK.

Instead, the bumbling, righteous-appearing profs appointed another "committee" to "study" the matter and report back, circa 1960! Such a thing needs study? If the past is criterion of the future, such committee reports are ignored, anyway, by the PCC. They are stalls, time gainers.

How the regents, trustees and academic senates of the University of California at Los Angeles and Berkeley, the University of Southern California and Leland Stanford Junior University can accept dictation from universities with such scholarship standards, is beyond my understanding.

As for LIVING with 'em—Judge, please, sir, we just gotta have a divorce or sumbody's gonna get hurt!

EFFECT OF MAJOR MOVE ON PCL TO BE PROBED

WASHINGTON, June 13 (UP) The House Judiciary Committee intends to investigate the possible impact of the proposed transfer of the Brooklyn Dodgers and New York Giants to the West Coast on Pacific Coast League teams, Rep. Don Magnuson (D) Wash., said today.

Magnuson said Committee Chairman Emanuel Celler (D) N.Y., planned to look into problems concerning the PCL's future in hearings scheduled to begin June 17.

"Congressman Celler believes that the fate of the PCL is closely bound up with the plans of the major leagues to begin operations in Los Angeles and San Francisco."

Magnuson said Celler intended to "explore every facet of the antitrust and monopoly aspects of professional baseball."

Ted Williams Smacks Three Homers in 9-3 Bosox Win

CLEVELAND, June 13 (UP) Ted Williams became the first player in American League history to hit three homers in one game twice in one season today when his booming bat powered the Boston Red Sox to a 9-3 victory over the Cleveland Indians.

Williams, who hit three homers against the Chicago White Sox on May 8, walloped his first two today off Cleveland Starter Early Wynn and tagged his third in the ninth inning off Bob Lemon. The three home runs gave the 38-year-old Boston slugger 17 for the season, one less than major league Pacesetter Mickey Mantle of the New York Yankees.

Williams' first home run came in the second with two on, and his next two were solo blasts, giving him five RBIs.

Ralph Kiner did it in the National League in 1947, and Johnny Mize did it twice, in 1938 and 1940.

All of Williams' home runs today were well hit over the fence in right center and two went more than 400 feet.

Despite a bad leg Tom Brewer went all the way for his seventh victory.

Boston	AB	H	O	A	Cleveland	AB	H	O	A
Piersall,cf	4	2	2	0	Smith,3b	5	2	0	2
Klaus,ss	5	1	1	4	Avila,2b	2	0	0	0
Williams,lf	5	3	1	0	Kuhn,2b	3	1	1	1
Stephens,lf	0	0	0	0	Wertz,1b	3	1	6	0
Vernon,1b	2	1	9	0	Robinson,1b	1	1	4	0
Zauchin,1b	2	0	3	1	Colavito,rf	3	0	2	0
Jensen,rf	4	1	2	0	Woodling,lf	2	1	1	0
Malzone,3b	4	3	0	2	Raines,lf	2	0	0	0
Mauch,2b	4	1	3	5	Maris,cf	4	0	3	0
White,c	5	0	5	1	Carrasquel,ss	2	0	3	6
Brewer,p	4	1	1	1	Naragon,c	1	0	4	0
					Nixon,c	2	0	3	0
					Wynn,p-L	2	0	0	1
					Aguirre,p	1	0	0	0
					Lemon,p	0	0	0	0
					Busby	1	0	0	0
Totals	39	13	27	14	Totals	34	6	27	10

Kuhn grounded out for Avila in 5th.
Zauchin filed out for Vernon in 7th.
Busby struck out for Lemon in 9th.

SCORE BY INNINGS

Boston ....013 040 001—9
Cleveland ....100 000 020—3

E—Mauch, Zauchin. RBI—Williams, 5; Malzone, 3; Colavito, Mauch, Kuhn, Raines. 2B—Malzone, Smith. HR—Williams, 3; Malzone. SF—Mauch. DP—Mauch to Klaus to Vernon. LOB—Boston, 8; Cleveland, 8. BB—Off Brewer, 4; Wynn, 4. SO—By Brewer, 4; Wynn, 4; Aguirre, 2; Lemon, 1. Hits—Off Wynn, 7 in 4⅓; Aguirre, 3 in 3⅔; Lemon, 3 in 1. R and ER—Wynn, 8-8; Lemon, 1-1; Brewer, 3-2. WP—Aguirre. Winner—Brewer (7-5). Loser—Wynn (7-7). Umpires—Chylak, Summers, Honochick, Flaherty. Time—2h. 38m. Attendance—4719.

HOLLYWOOD WINS

Continued from First Page

second, Causion's fifth, Stevens' 10th and Daniels' third.

Loser George Bamberger (7-4) yielded all but Bennie's blast, which came off Gordon Sundin.

Hall Triples

Hollywood twisted the knife when Bill Hall, who has six RBIs for the series, tripled with two men on off Dick Marlowe in the fourth frame to close out the scoring.

Causion and Jacobs extended their hitting streaks to eight straight games. However, Causion dropped three points to .333 in his fight to retain the league leadership.

The loop's winningest pitcher with an 8-2 record, Daniels hurled Hollywood's third successive complete game.

In other words, it was a great night for the statisticians at Gilmore Field. Attendance was 3560.

The Bull Pen

Erv Palica (6-4) faces Hollywood's Hugh Pepper (0-1) in tonight's Family Night fracas . . . Ez O'Donnell, a 20-game winner for Hollywood when he was the PCL Rookie of the Year in 1953, has been sent outright to Columbus (International). A relief specialist the last several seasons, the popular O'Donnell compiled a 43-26 record during his tenure with the Twinks . . . The Mounties miss the power stick of their injured outfielder, Joe Frazier.

Umpire Mel Steiner, who was working the Angel-Padre series at San Diego with another crew, switched with Einar Sorenson at Gilmore last night so that Mel could be close to home for a visit by the stork to the Steiner manse, expected momentarily . . . Since we revealed that Hollywood is willing to deal a top twirler for a top hitter, the club has had several nibbles and the front office is hopeful of working something out . . . Irv Kaze is busy cooking up a special pre-game program for Father's Day.

Vancouver	AB	H	O	A	Hollywood	AB	H	O	A
Peterson,ss	4	2	0	4	Jacobs,2b	5	3	1	8
Jorgensen,2b	4	0	0	2	Duhem,lf	5	1	1	0
Marshall,1b	4	1	12	1	Causion,cf	5	1	3	0
Segrist,3b	4	1	1	3	Stevens,1b	4	1	13	2
Powis,rf	4	0	1	0	Pettit,rf	2	0	2	0
Green,cf	4	2	2	0	Hall,c	3	2	4	0
White,c	4	1	1	0	Rodriguez,3b	4	1	0	2
Friend,lf	2	0	6	0	Smith,ss	4	1	1	2
B'berger,p-L	1	0	0	0	Daniels,p	4	2	2	1
Sundin,p	0	0	0	0					
Frazier	1	0	0	0					
Marlowe,p	1	0	1	1					
Totals	33	7	24	11	Totals	36	12	27	15

Frazier grounded out for Sundin in 4th.

SCORE BY INNINGS

Vancouver ....110 000 000—2
Hollywood ....205 200 00x—9

Pitcher—	IP	AB	R	H	ER	BB	SO
Bamberger ...	2⅓	14	4	7	6	2	0
Sudin	⅔	3	3	1	1	0	0
Marlowe	5	19	2	4	2	2	1
Daniels	9	33	2	7	2	1	4

E—Smith. LOB—Vancouver, 5; Hollywood, 7. 2B—Jacobs, Peterson, Rodriguez. 3B—Hall. HR—Peterson, Duhem, Causion, Stevens, Daniels. RBI—Peterson, Duhem, 2; Causion, Stevens, Daniels, 3; Hall, 2. DP—Smith to Jacobs to Stevens. Winner—Daniels (8-2). Loser—Bamberger (7-4). Time—2h. 12m. Umpires—Sorensen, Mutart and Ashford. Attendance—3560.

Angels' Herb Olson Fined $25 for Tantrum

Catcher Herb Olson was fined $25 yesterday by Manager Cly Bryant of the Angels for a display of temper last Friday night at Seattle after Olson had been replaced by a pinch hitter.

Called on the carpet by General Manager Bill Heymans, Olson admitted the tantrum and said that "I was really mad at myself because I've been in a slump."

Herb Score to Wed

CLEVELAND, O., June 13 (UP)—Pitcher Herb Score and his fiancee, Nancy McNamara, 20, announced today they will marry July 10.

Leading Seals Stifle Solons

SACRAMENTO, June 13 (AP)—R. W. Smith went all the way tonight for the San Francisco Seals and southpawed a 4-1 decision for the league leaders over the Sacramento Solons.

San Fran.	AB	H	O	A	Sacramento	AB	H	O	A
Pearson,rf	4	1	4	0	Wilson,2b	4	0	1	2
Hatton,3b	3	1	2	1	Righetti,ss	4	2	1	3
Keough,cf	3	1	0	0	Gr'ngrass,rf	3	1	2	0
Aspr'mnte,2b	4	0	5	5	Jones,1b	4	1	8	1
Renna,lf	4	0	1	0	Westlake,lf	4	1	2	0
Kellert,1b	4	0	12	1	Bright,3b	4	1	1	3
Malmberg,ss	4	1	1	4	Heist,cf	4	0	3	0
Sadowski,c	4	0	1	0	Barragan,c	3	1	8	0
Smith,p	4	1	1	3	Fracchia,p-L	0	0	1	1
					Coen,p	1	0	0	0
					Heron	1	1	0	0
					Watkins,p	0	0	0	0
Totals	34	5	27	14	Totals	32	8	27	10

Heron homered for Coen in 8th.

SCORE BY INNINGS

San Francisco ....130 000 000—4
Sacramento ....000 000 010—1

E—Malmberg, Jones, Bright, 2. RBI—Keough, Malmberg, Smith, Hatton, Heron. 2B—Righetti. HR—Keough, Heron. SH—Coen, Hatton. DP—Aspromonte to Malmberg to Kellert; Smith to Aspromonte to Jones; Aspromonte to Kellert. LOB—San Francisco, 6; Sacramento, 7. BB—Smith, 2; Coen, 2. SO—Smith, 1; Coen, 6; Watkins, 1. Hits—Off Fracchia, 4 in 1⅔ innings; Coen, 1 in 6⅓; Watkins, 0 in 1. R and ER—Smith, 1-1; Fracchia, 4-1; Coen, 0-0; Watkins, 0-0. WP—Smith. Winner—Smith (4-5). Loser—Fracchia (0-2). Umpires — Pelekoudas, Yuhase and Nenezich. Time—2h. 23m. Attendance—3385.

3 Homers Pace Giant Victory Over Cubs, 7-4

NEW YORK, June 13 (AP)—Home runs by Whitey Lockman, Ray Jablonski and Red Schoendienst paced a 10-hit attack today as New York downed Chicago 7-4 for a sweep of the three-game series.

Chicago	AB	H	O	A	New York	AB	H	O	A
Morgan,2b	5	2	5	1	Lock'n,1b-lf	3	1	6	2
Speake,1b	2	1	7	1	Schoend't,2b	4	3	2	4
Banks,3b	4	0	1	1	Mays,cf	3	2	2	0
Moryn,rf	4	0	2	0	Jablonski,3b	3	1	0	1
Bolger,lf	4	2	1	0	Harris,1b	1	0	4	0
Walls,cf	4	1	0	0	Mueller,rf	4	0	4	0
Neeman,c	4	0	6	1	Spencer,ss	4	0	0	3
Wise,ss	3	1	2	1	Virgil,lf-3b	3	1	1	1
Tanner	1	0	0	0	Thomas,c	4	1	7	0
Hillman,p-L	0	0	0	1	Burnside,p	1	0	1	0
Brosnan,p	3	2	0	0	Davis,p-W	1	1	0	1
Long	1	0	0	0	Grissom,p	0	0	0	0
Totals	35	9	24	6	Totals	31	10	27	12

Tanner popped out for Wise in 9th.
Long struck out for Brosnan in 9th.

SCORE BY INNINGS

Chicago ....003 000 010—4
New York ....150 100 00x—7

E—Harris. RBI—Mays, Thomas, Lockman, 2; Jablonski, 2; Schoendienst, Moryn, Bolger, (Morgan scored on Burnside's balk in 3rd). (Moryn scored while Walls batted into double play in 8th). 2B—Morgan, Thomas, Brosnan. HR—Lockman, Jablonski, Schoendienst. S—Burnside. DP—Spencer to Schoendienst to Lockman; Speake to Wise; Spencer to Schoendienst to Harris. LOB—Chicago, 6; New York, 4. BB—Off Hillman, 2; Brosnan, 1; Burnside, 2. SO—By Brosnan, 3; Burnside, 2; Davis, 2; Grissom, 2. Hits—Off Hillman, 5 in 1⅓; Brosnan, 5 in 6⅔; Burnside, 7 in 3⅓; Davis, 2 in 3⅔; Grissom, 0 in 2. R and ER—Hillman, 5-5; Brosnan, 2-2; Burnside, 3-3; Davis, 1-0; Grissom, 0-0. Winner—Davis (1-1). Loser—Hillman (0-3). Umpires — Landes, Dascoli, Secory. Time—2h. 24m. Attendance—1875.

REDLEGS KNOCKED OUT OF FIRST, 3-2

PITTSBURGH, June 13 (UP) Gene Baker drove in Bill Mazeroski with a sacrifice fly in the ninth inning today to give the Pittsburgh Pirates a 3-2 victory over Cincinnati and knock the Redlegs out of first place in the National League.

The victory gave the Pirates a sweep of their four-game series here with Cincinnati.

The Redleg runs came on two 400-foot home runs by Don Hoak in the second and fifth innings.

Cincinnati	AB	H	O	A	Pittsburgh	AB	H	O	A
Temple,2b	3	0	5	2	Clemente,rf	4	0	5	0
Post,rf	3	0	2	0	Baker,ss	4	1	0	3
Bell,cf	4	1	4	0	Fondy,1b	4	3	12	0
Robinson,lf	4	1	3	0	Thomas,lf	3	1	1	0
Klusz'ski,1b	4	1	7	1	Virdon,cf	4	1	1	0
Whisenant	0	0	0	0	Freese,3b	2	0	0	2
Crowe,1b	0	0	0	0	Mazeroski,2b	4	2	0	3
Bailey,c	4	0	0	1	Rand,c	3	1	8	0
Hoak,3b	4	2	3	3	P.Smith	1	1	0	0
Grammas,ss	3	1	2	6	Friend,p	3	1	0	1
Jeffcoat,p	3	0	0	1	Skinner	1	0	0	0
Totals	32	6	26	14	Totals	33	11	27	9

Two out when winning run scored.
Whisenant ran for Kluszewski in 9th.
P. Smith singled for Rand in 9th.
Skinner hit into force play for Friend in 9th.

SCORE BY INNINGS

Cincinnati ....001 010 000—2
Pittsburgh ....011 000 001—3

RBI—Hoak, 2; Rand, Thomas, Baker. 2B—Baker, Thomas, Friend. HR—Hoak, 2. SH—Temple, Thomas, Baker (f). LOB—Cincinnati, 5; Pittsburgh, 9. BB—Off Jeffcoat, 2; Friend, 1. SO—Friend, 7. R and ER—Jeffcoat, 3-3; Friend, 2-2. HB—Freese (Jeffcoat). Winner—Friend (4-7). Loser—Jeffcoat (5-3). Umpires—Gorman, Dixon, Boggess. Time—2h. 26m. Attendance—7346.

Tank Younger Signs for '57

Paul (Tank) Younger has signed his 1957 Los Angeles Ram contract, General Manager Pete Rozelle revealed yesterday. It will be Younger's ninth season with Los Angeles.

A work horse in the backfield, Tank packed the ball 586 times during his eight-year career, an average of 74 times a season, for an average gain of 4.9 yards and a total of 174 points.

July 21, 1957

This Week MAGAZINE

The Pittsburgh Press

Tex and Jinx plunge into a hot controversy:

Are American Wives Spoiled?...page 7

Mickey Mantle: He'll never break Babe Ruth's record — says Duke Snider... page 10

Sports NEW YORK Herald Tribune Sports

Section Three WEDNESDAY, OCTOBER 9, 1957 Section Three

It's Official—Dodgers Go to Los Angeles

Mantle Lost to Yankees for Rest of Series

RED SMITH

The Man Who Saved Baseball

THIS savior of baseball is a large lump of meat who will be twenty-six years old next Sunday. He is a taciturn young man with broad shoulders and rather heavy features, and the World Series heroics of Charles Dillon Stengel, the inventor of baseball, had been virtually forgotten before he was born in Texarkana, Tex. His name is Eddie Mathews and he became the redeemer of the national pastime the other day by hitting a ball with a stick, just once.

Red Smith

It was the fourth day of competition for the championship of the earth and Sputnik I. After 111 years in the gazeteer of American cities and five seasons in the National League, Milwaukee was at last represented in a World Series. At the moment, Milwaukee was wondering whether it had been worth all the excitement and trouble, the wistful dreaming and burning disappointments.

In the first game in New York the Braves had stood frozen at the plate while Whitey Ford pitched the Yankees to a routine victory. If the darlings of the dairylands had lost the second game and arrived home two down for the first World Series show in Wisconsin history, they'd have found the purling Kinnickinnic clogged with bodies.

So Lew Burdette spat on his hands and went to work. Thanks to him, the teams were all square when services opened in Milwaukee County Stadium. The Braves responded to the occasion like idols graven in cheese. The Yankees romped through what may have been the dreariest game of fifty-four World Series. Desolation spread like undulant fever across the midland pastures. Holstein heifers hung their heads.

Life Begins in the Tenth

IF THE Yankees had trampled the opposition in the fourth game, it might have destroyed baseball in the state. And the Yankees were showing symptoms of doing just that in the tenth inning. Trailing by three runs with only one pitch to go, they had tied the score in the ninth and gone ahead, 5 to 4, in the tenth. Nippy Jones walked up to the plate, and although none of the witnesses realized it then, that was a ray of hope which glistened in the high polish of his shoes. In a matter of moments the score was tied again, Johnny Logan was on second base and Mathews was at bat. It was then Mathews swung his stick. As his winning smash cleared the fence in right, cows capered in the fields, silos swayed, beer foamed in the vats and limp, dispirited pretzels drew rigidly erect. The game of the people belonged once more to the people who have supported it in a style to which it never was accustomed.

Mathews had saved the sport. Yesterday Burdette put a spit-and-polish gloss on it. Today services are resumed in the Bronx with Milwaukee needing only one more victory, and everybody is delighted. Everybody, that is, except where the Yankees are regarded as somebody.

The Public Pulse

EVER since the Boston Braves struck gold among the cheddar mines, fans in New York and New Caledonia, Ypsilanti and Yokohama, have been saying, "I wish Milwaukee could win a pennant. The fans up there deserve it."

Even if one doesn't agree that a customer who buys a ticket in Milwaukee is automatically entitled to receive greater value than the fellow who pays full price in Washington, it was high time for the Eastern monopoly on success to be broken. Those repetitious charades involving the Yankees and the Dodgers were getting downright monotonous.

Getting the show on the road revived baseball interest outside the metropolitan area, or at least produced visible evidence of interest that has existed too long unnoticed. In the tiny hamlet of Sturtevant, Wis. for example, there must have been 2,000 people gathered along the right-of-way to see the Yankees' train go through to Milwaukee.

It recalled a time, too long past, when teams barnstorming home from spring training would be met by crowds like this in other Sturtevants throughout the South and Southwest. Unfortunately this crowd was disappointed because plans were changed en route and the players didn't get off there to board buses for their quarters at near-by Brown's Lake. Going right on for a workout in Milwaukee was the sensible and proper thing, but baseball's public relations would have been served if somebody in the Yankee party had given Sturtevant warning of the change in schedule.

Ah, There, Dale Carnegie

IT WAS also unfortunate that on arrival in Milwaukee the Yankees had no time for the brief welcome arranged at the station, and "unfortunate" is hardly adequate for the unidentified character who described that small gesture of hospitality as "bush league."

To be sure, there is an unsophisticated quality about the partisan enthusiasm in a territory still new to the major leagues. After five years the Braves are still a new toy, treasured with an undisguised affection whose lack of restraint seems juvenile to visitors jaded by old customs. Sometimes Milwaukee newspapers are annoying to those accustomed to a more objective detachment.

It is real enthusiasm, however, and a precious thing for baseball. Those who sneer at it do baseball a disservice. In this case, they also do New York and the Yankees a disservice. In almost every American city there is a certain community resentment of New York, just because New York is bigger. Everywhere there are Yankee haters, merely because the Yankees have everything and most people are have-nots.

Sentiment naturally inclines toward the humble striver, and there is widespread rejoicing when the lordly get their come-uppance. As the lordly Yankees may do within forty-eight hours.

Five Shifts Since 1953 Redraw Baseball Map

The major league's baseball map has been altered more in the last five years than in the previous half century.

The transfer of the Dodgers from Brooklyn to Los Angeles marks the fifth franchise shift since 1953. Los Angeles, San Francisco and Kansas City are new to major league baseball. Baltimore and Milwaukee formerly held American League franchises.

Here's how the baseball map has changed:

March 18, 1953—National League, in an unprecedented move, approved shift of Boston Braves' franchise to Milwaukee.

Sept. 29, 1953—American League approved sale and transfer of St. Louis Browns to Baltimore.

Nov. 8, 1954—American League approved sale and transfer of Philadelphia Athletics to Kansas City.

Aug. 19, 1957—New York Giants announced transfer of club to San Francisco after receiving approval from National League on May 28.

Oct. 8, 1957—Brooklyn Dodgers announced transfer to Los Angeles, following National League's May 28 approval.

Mickey Has Torn Tendon In Shoulder

Turley Vs. Buhl For Sixth Game

By Harold Rosenthal

Hope for help from Mickey Mantle, who had figured to be the key player in the World Series, virtually vanished for the Yankees on the eve of the sixth game. The Yankee slugging star, who missed the fifth game in Milwaukee Monday, will not only be absent from today's lineup when the fall classic resumes at Yankee Stadium, but is ticketed for a seat on the bench for the seventh game—if there is a seventh game.

The Yankees got the bad news on Mantle yesterday during a day of idleness, and no one had to spell it out for them. It was apparent in the manner in which he was unable to slip his undershirt over his head without help after undergoing diathermy while the rest of the team sat around and read fan mail.

Earlier, Mantle had submitted to X-ray examination which had proved negative. He had been examined by Dr. Sidney Gaynor, the Yankee team physician, and the word from Dr Gaynor was not optimistic.

Long Time to Heal

"He says it's bad," advised Mickey. "It's a torn tendon and the doc says it takes a long time to heal."

Actually it is the supraspinatus tendon in the right shoulder which is involved. It affects both his hitting and throwing. He came out for a defensive outfielder in the tenth inning of the fourth game in Milwaukee and hasn't gone back since except as a pinch-runner in the fifth game in which Lew Burdette shut out the Yankees.

Chances are slim that the Yankees will see Burdette again this year, but Casey Stengel was still talking about him yesterday noon when the wet conditions at the Stadium prevented both his club and the Braves from working out.

"Their two pitchers have been very good," he offered (Burdette and Warren Spahn). "They've been pitching out of holes and with men on bases. We got more hits than they have but we don't get the runs.

"Burdette knows how to pitch to lefthanders and Spahn knows how to pitch to righthanders and they got three or four pitches, all down around here." Stengel cracked his kneecap sharply with the edge of his palm.

Stengel said that the Braves pitching he was looking at in this Series was better than anything he had seen in the various Series with the Dodgers. "That open date helps," he offered, "but these men are good.

"They got other good men. That Aaron. What's he hitting? (.421). We've been trying to keep him from bothering us but we ain't had much luck.

"That leftfielder (Covington)

Continued on page 2, column 5

Yankees 7 to 5 To Win Today

Although they are only one game from total defeat the Yankees are 6½-7½ to win the sixth contest of the World Series this afternoon. This means that you receive 6½ to 5 if you like the Braves, but must give 7½ to 5 if you prefer the Yankees. In man-to-man betting this becomes a straight 7 to 5 on the New Yorkers.

The Yankees have been favored in every game except the third, which was a pick-'em proposition.

Probable Line-Up For Today

Milwaukee (N)	New York (A)
Mantilla 2b	Bauer rf
Logan ss	Kubek cf
Mathews 3b	McDougald ss
Aaron cf	Berra c
Torre 1b	Slaughter lf
Covington lf	Simpson 1b
Hazle rf	Lumpe 3b
Rice c	Coleman 2b
Buhl p	Turley p

Umpires—Conlan (N), plate; McKinley (A), first base; Donatelli (N), second base; Paparella (A), third base; Chylak (A), rightfield; Secory (N), leftfield.

Herald Tribune photo by Don Rice

THE BIG NEWS—Newsmen eagerly reach for statement handed out by Red Patterson announcing that the Dodgers are moving to Los Angeles in 1958. The statement was telephoned to Patterson by his boss, Walter O'Malley.

Favored Neji Wins 'Chase At Belmont

Independence 2d In Grand National

By Bill Lauder Jr.

Mrs. Ogden Phipps' Neji, making a comeback this year after having gone lame a year ago August, yesterday won the fifty-seventh running of the $32,250 Grand National Steeplechase Handicap at Belmont Park and took a long stride toward regaining the title of steeplechase horse of the year. Burdened by the crushing weight of 168 pounds, Neji came from well back in the race of about three miles and a furlong and won by six lengths.

Neji was boss of the steeplechasers in 1955, when he won the Grand National under 163 pounds. Last year Montpelier's Shipboard won the Grand National and was named jumper of the year, but Neji was on the sidelines at the time. The last time these two met was in the Temple Gwathmey, which followed the Grand National in 1955 and Neji won as Shipboard fell each time. Yesterday Shipboard picked up 163 pounds in an attempt to repeat last year's victory and finished fourth.

Mrs. Michael Walsh's Independence was second, six lengths back of Neji and a length and three-quarters in front of Brookmeade Stable's His Boots, which won this race in 1949 and 1953 and which was a neck in front of Shipboard yesterday. The only other starter, Arcadia Stable's Caste, an entry mate with Neji, set all the pace until the twelfth of the sixteen jumps and then lost his rider, Scott Riles. The boy was only shaken up.

The Neji entry was favored by the crowd of 15,486 and paid only $3.60. It was Neji's third race of the year and his second victory. It was the twelfth victory for his trainer, Mike Smithwick, making him the leader of all trainers at the meeting, flat or jump.

Independence, His Boots, Neji and Shipboard, in that order, followed Caste's early pace. That alignment held until Caste

Continued on page 4, column 1

Greater Love Hath No Fan

SUMMIT, N. J., Oct. 8 (AP).—Mrs. Naomi Gage, an ardent Yankee baseball fan, plans a supreme sacrifice in order to watch her team on on TV tomorrow in the World Series.

For one year Mrs. Gage has treasured a ticket to tomorrow's matinee performance of the Broadway hit musical, My Fair Lady.

She is giving up the ticket in preference to a chair in front of her TV set.

A fan since her school days, Mrs. Gage never missed a Yankee game on TV or radio.

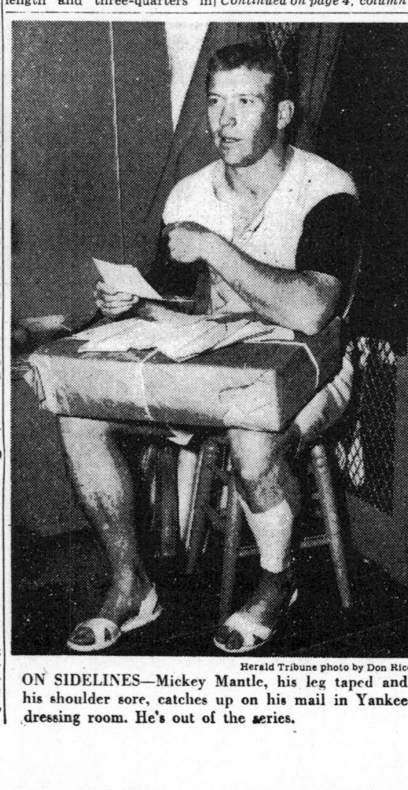

Herald Tribune photo by Don Rice

ON SIDELINES—Mickey Mantle, his leg taped and his shoulder sore, catches up on his mail in Yankee dressing room. He's out of the series.

Notre Dame to Give Army 1st Key Test

By Jesse Abramson

WEST POINT, Oct. 8.—Red Blaik leafed through his mail today and from its contents it was like old times before an Army-Notre Dame game.

"Notre Dame will tear your guts out," read one missive signed "Subway Alumni," and "Death to all Cadets" said another.

"I get a laugh out of them," said Blaik. "My correspondence for the Notre Dame game hasn't changed much."

This sort of thing helped cause the break. Though time has healed it, at least to the extent of an occasional series, starting with the big renewal in Philadelphia's Municipal Stadium before a crowd of 100,000 Saturday, there are other changes noted in the barracks and in the competitive size-up.

Though some Cadets have put together some displays on the barracks walls, it's nothing like the old days when the Notre Dame game had come to mean more to the team and corps than the Navy finale.

One of Key Games

There's evidence the Cadets will take this game in emotional stride, keenly desirous of winning it, as Blaik is, because Saturday's test and the following Pitt game will be the key to Army's season.

For the "darn near amazing" development of his team, Blaik singled out some vital cogs besides the regular holdovers of last year—Jim Kernan, the fiery leader at Center; Stan Slater, tremendous blocking guard, and Dave Bourland, quarterback.

Bourland, shunted aside while Blaik made his quarterback experiments the last two years, has come from "way in the woods." The 185-pound Texas from El Paso has completed 11 of 18 passes, but his sharper passing is only a small part of his value. He runs the team with new authority and confidence, he runs the options and because he's a blocker too, Blaik can throw four blockers ahead of his halfback sweeps. The strength to the outside is the one department where Army has made its greatest strides since last year.

The other backs who make it go are Bob Anderson, a sophomore; Pete Dawkins, a converted quarterback, and Bin Barta, at fullback. Sophomore Steve Waldrop, Gil Roesler and Harry Walters, who shares fullback time with Bart, give Blaik a strong second unit.

Scrimmage in Rain

Anderson, who was knocked dizzy last Saturday, and Waldrop, who damaged a leg, will both be ready, it was noted as the squad went through a rain-soaked scrimmage. Blaik will have the same starting line-up he had last week. For the first time in four years Army hasn't lost a key back in its early games.

Some other reasons why Army has come "faster" than Blaik

Continued on page 3, column 2

Welsh Women Win In Hockey Again

The women's Welsh field hockey touring team scored its third straight victory of its 23-game tour of the United States with an 11-to-0 rout of a New York Field Hockey Association squad at Hunter College's Bronx campus yesterday.

Center Rita Jones scored four times as the victors tallied eight goals in the second half.

Cardinals Retain Hutchinson Aids

ST. LOUIS, Oct. 8 (AP).—The St. Louis Cardinals announced today they are keeping intact the coaching staff of Sam Hack, Al Hollingsworth and Terry Moore that helped guide the club to a second-place finish the year.

Manager Fred Hutchinson had been signed earlier.

"We think the combination of Hutch an dhis coaches did a remarkable job this past season," said Frank Lane, general manager. "We're happy that they have all agreed to terms for next year."

New York Loses 2d N. L. Club

Wagner Hopes To Attract One

By Tommy Holmes

The Dodgers yesterday took the irrevocable step from Ebbets Field to Los Angeles. Less than twenty-four hours after the City Council of the sprawling California metropolis had approved a controversial offer for the Brooklyn baseball franchise, stockholders and directors of the ball club unanimously voted to move.

Together with the formal announcement just a week ago that the Giants would quit the Polo Grounds for San Francisco, the Dodger action constitutes the abandonment of New York by the 81-year-old National League.

Although long expected, the definite Dodger decision to go West triggered flurries of official statements.

Wagner Has a Plan

At City Hall, Mayor Wagner again declared his intention to appoint a group of citizens within the next few days "to help us get another National League club."

The Mayor refused to discuss a question whether the city would seriously consider a municipal stadium in Flushing Meadows, Queens, as an inducement to attract another team, but added, "Naturally, they must have some place to play."

At Borough Hall, Brooklyn, Borough President John Cashmore said. "I have personally done everything I could to keep the Dodgers in Brooklyn, but I couldn't do it alone."

He said he would "leave nothing undone to have National League baseball continued in Brooklyn. It is important to the economic life of the borough."

But baseball men regarded the prospect of a National League return to this city in the foreseeable future as bleak, indeed.

O'Malley's Statement

The announcement came from Walter O'Malley, president of the Dodgers, and was followed by a statement from Warren Giles, president of the National League. Neither was present at the World Series press headquarters at the Waldorf-Astoria to preside over the liquidation of National League baseball here.

Arthur E. Patterson, O'Malley's executive assistant, passed out typewritten copies of O'Malley's statement, which simply read: "In view of the action of the Los Angeles City Council yesterday and in accordance with the resolution of the National League made Oct. 1, the stockholders and directors of the Brooklyn baseball club have today met and unanimously agreed that the necessary steps be taken to

Continued on page 2, column 4

750,000 Greet Braves

Stories, Picture on Page 3

In 50s
Fair and a little warmer Friday. High in the 50's. Weather map appears on Page 2.

MILWAUKEE SENTINEL
Wisconsin's Dynamic Newspaper

What a Line
Hauls in a catch every time. The Person-to-Person Want Ad line, one line, one week, one dollar, try one!

40 PAGES—2 PARTS ★ ★ ★ ★ ★ ★ FINAL | FRIDAY, OCTOBER 11, 1957 | TELEPHONE BR. 6-3900 | SEVEN CENTS

HAIL TO OUR BRAVES

Best in the World!

Burdette Wins 3rd Game, 2nd Shutout

By RED THISTED
Sentinel Staff Writer

NEW YORK, Oct. 10 — The Braves became the professional baseball champions of the world here Thursday afternoon.

They swamped the defending Yankee titleholders 5-0 and the long search for baseball's golden fleece was at an end.

This was a spit and polish job from beginning to end by all of the Braves and particularly Lew Burdette, who shut out the cocky champs for the second time in three days and became the first starting pitcher to win three World Series games in one set since Stan Coveleski did it to Brooklyn for Cleveland in 1920.

There was drama, soul-thrilling drama from the first pitch to the last one, which saw Eddie Mathews make a spectacular backhanded stab with the bases filled and rush to third for a forceout, the biggest putout of the season.

Eddie Mathews Comes Through

Then there was Mathews' two-run double in the decisive fourth which provided Burdette with all of the runs he was destined to require and to make Don (Perfect Game) Larsen the loser.

It wasn't a two-man story of Burdette and Mathews, although the record books will proclaim as much. It was strictly a team triumph as it has been all year and certainly not to be overlooked were the contributions of Henry Aaron, Bob Hazle and Del Crandall, in particular.

Aaron, Hazle and Crandall all had two hits apiece and Del provided a big moment in the eighth when he lofted a Tommy Byrne pitch into the distant left field stands, his first Series home run.

Braves Get Aid From Kubek

The Braves put all of their eggs in one basket this day, the four-run fourth, and then fought a beautiful delaying action the rest of the afternoon to spear the pot of gold at the end of the rainbow.

They had considerable help in this inning, unwitting assistance, of course, from Milwaukee's 20-year-old youngster, Tony Kubek, who threw badly on a certain double play ball which would have enabled Larsen to escape the inning unscathed.

Hazle singled with one out, his first hit of the Series. When Johnny Logan grounded to Kubek, young Tony fired high and wide to Jerry Coleman at second, permitting Hazle to slide in safely, and Johnny beat Coleman's throw to first although the Yankees disputed the decision there.

Mathews accepted a couple of strikes looking for the ball he wanted, got it and doubled down the right field line, Hazle scoring easily and the hatless Logan just beating the peg to the plate.

2 MORE SCORE

Bobby Shantz relieved at this juncture, a not particularly shrewd move by Casey Stengel with the righthanded hitting Aaron at the plate, and it cost

(Turn to Page 4, Col. 2, Part. 2.)

BRAVES OWNER LOU PERINI HUGGING LEW BURDETTE. AND YOU KNOW WHY!

Associated Press Wirephoto.

BUSHED!

City Dances in Streets!

By KEN GERMANSON

Mighty Mathews stepped off third base at 1:54 p.m. Thursday and a million hearts skipped a beat.

The Milwaukee Braves were World Champions!

There was a brief moment when everyone looked as if they didn't believe it.

Then, they were sure. And they didn't waste any time in making sure everyone else knew—this is the Baseball Capital of the World.

These best fans in baseball triggered the biggest celebration Milwaukee has had since V-J day in 1945.

Within a half hour, police found things getting out of control along W. Wisconsin Av. and sent for reinforcements from outlying districts. Day-shift police were ordered to work overtime and late-shift men told to report in early.

But police officers still smiled and early in the celebration their orders still carried weight.

Shortly before that dramatic third Yankee out in the last of the ninth, Wisconsin Avenue was virtually empty. A few women shoppers, a police officer and an occasional Braves souvenir seller were the only ones in sight.

CELEBRATION ON

Then that Wonderful Man, Lew Burdette, got that last fearful Yankee to ground out to Mathews—and the celebration was on.

Fans poured slowly, almost uneasily out of stores and office buildings. They wore smiles and their grins grew wider as they looked at one another.

A horn started honking — and then downtown Milwaukee was engulfed with honking horns.

Soon the downtown was engulfed with people. Hugging and cheering and shaking hands and waving and yelling, they were having just a wonderful time.

For a while pedestrians observed walk signs and cars remained in orderly lines.

Then, youths burst forth, blocking off Wisconsin Av. at N. 5th St.

A taxicab was caught in the midst of the onrush. At least 15 youths piled atop the cab, crushing in its top and hood. The cabbie, Miss Dorothy Markiewicz, 2030 S. 58th St., may have at first been enjoying the celebration. But she had tears in her eyes as Sgt. Harold Breitlow cleared the way for her to drive from the mob.

BLOCK OFF AVENUE

Police blocked off W. Wisconsin Av. from N. 6th St. to the river and then were forced to extend that to N. 8th St. Buses were allowed through to make normal stops.

Armed with flags and man-sized Braves taken from decorated utility poles, the celebrants, predominantly youths, began parading informally up and down the avenue.

Leading the way were two youths, Richard Lofton, 1133 N. 24th Pl., and Jack Higgins, 1129 N. 24th Pl., both Marquette students, who carried signs reading:

"Burdette for President."

"Mathews for Vice President."

What a ticket! They'd win for sure and the celebrants cheered loudly as the two youths danced wildly down the avenue.

"Happy Braves Day," was the salutation between fans in front of the Schroeder Hotel.

POSE FOR CAMERAS

Spying out-of-town cameramen atop the hotel's marquee, the mobs took joy in performing for the cameras.

Somebody yelled "World Champs" and a roar went up from the crowd as the celebrants waved for the cameras.

A middleaged man in a busi-

(Please Turn to Page 5, Col. 4)

Lonely Mary Burdette Sees Lew's Title Triumph on TV

By ROSA TUSA

The shouts of millions echoed the praises of Lew Burdette Thursday, but for the girl he left behind, it was a lonely afternoon.

"I hollered all by myself," pretty Mary Burdette, wife of the World Series hero, said.

There were no cheers to keep her company in the living room of the Burdette home on S. 96th St. as she watched the final game on TV with this reporter. Asian flu had pitched a mean curve bringing her 6-year-old son, Lewis Kent, down with the illness and causing her to miss the second trip to New York.

MOTHER RECENTLY

Her new baby, Mary Lou was born Sept. 24 at St. Mary's Hospital the day after the pennant clincher, so she missed the first New York trip.

"I was afraid to leave the children. Although I had a girl to help with Lewis, I thought if she handled the baby, Mary Lou might get Asian flu too. And then my 3-year-old, Madge, developed the stomach flu," she said.

"I haven't had a chance to enjoy it," Mary, who was feeling sick herself on Thursday said. It's been one thing after another in the Burdette household since the series began.

DIDN'T TELL LEW

"I missed the first game of the series on TV because of Midgie. She ran into some bushes chasing a ball and got a thorn in her eye. I was at the hospital with her while the first game was on."

But when Lew called her

(Turn to Page A, Col. 6)

Today's Chuckle

The average woman has a smaller stock of words than the average man, but the turnover is greater.

INDEX

EXTRA

LOS ANGELES EVENING HERALD EXPRESS

International News Service Associated Press United Press Dow-Jones

8 STAR LATEST SPORTS

VOL. LXXXVII | Four Sections Section A | 1111 S. Broadway, 54 | TUESDAY, JANUARY 28, 1958 | Phone RI. 8-4141 | 8-R | NO. 264

CAMPANELLA, STAR OF DODGERS, BREAKS NECK

—International News Soundphoto

MRS. CAMPANELLA SEES CAR IN WHICH HUSBAND CRASHED
Wife of Famous Baseball Player Examines the Wreckage of Family Car; He Was Trapped Just Inside That Door for 30 Minutes

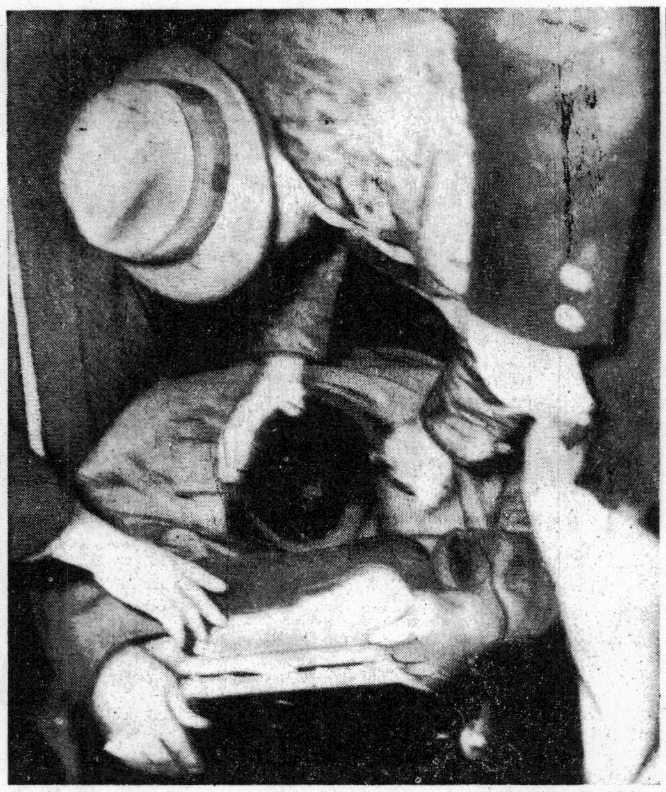

—International News Soundphoto

CAMPANELLA LIES FACE DOWN ON STRETCHER AFTER CRASH
Attendants Prepare to Put Him in Ambulance; His Car Skidded and Crashed Into a Pole as He Returned Home From TV Appearance

Catcher in Auto Crash Has Surgery; May Play Again

(From Wires of UP, AP, INS)

GLEN COVE, N. Y., Jan 28—Roy Campanella of the Los Angeles Dodgers, three times voted the National League's most valuable player, broke his neck today in an automobile accident and doctors said his condition was critical.

A subsequent operation was termed successful and was expected to halt paralysis which had seized him from the chest down.

Dr. Robert W. Sengstaken, neuro-surgeon who headed a team of seven doctors performing the 4-hour and 20-minute operation, gave the report. He said he did not rule out the possibility of Campanella playing baseball again for the Dodgers.

However, the doctor said the main thing now is to help him recover. The physician said it was too early to say when Campanella might be up and around but it might be six weeks.

The doctor said the catcher and home-run slugger received a fracture-dislocation of two cervical vertebrae, the 5th and 6th. He said that if the injury had occurred to the 3rd and 4th vertebrae Campanella would be dead.

The doctor explained that the fracture-dislocation depressed the spinal cord, and this pressure caused paralysis.

TO LOSE PARALYSIS

Relief of the pressure by the operation, he said, should enable Campanella to lose the paralysis gradually.

Dr. Sengstaken said he expected the catcher, who has been plagued throughout his career by injuries and ailments, to recover to a normal state of health but that he might have to wear a neck brace for a while after leaving the hospital.

The doctor said the operation took a long time because the 215-pound Campanella has a thick, muscular neck.

Dodger president, Walter O'Malley, was at the hospital nad saw the player following the operation. O'Malley said he was conscious. O'Malley added that he spoke to Campanella, but did not report whether the patient made any reply.

ON CRITICAL LIST—

Despite the announced success of the operation, Campanella was kept on the critical list after he came out of the operating room at 1 p. m.

(Cont. on Page D-1, Col. 7-8)

Shocks Teammates

Sparkplug Lost to Dodgers

The Los Angeles Dodgers was a team without its key man today, shocked to the core by the serious injury of their fiery catcher, Roy Campanella, in a Glen Cove, N. Y. automobile crash.

Campanella, three times voted the National League's "Most Valuable Player," was a sparkplug of the entire team, the man who inspired great pitching feats from Dodger hurlers, and in general pepped up the entire morale of the squad.

Dodger front office personnel in L. A. couldn't find words to express their sorrow.

When informed that "Campy" had suffered a broken neck, Arthur Patterson, vice president in charge of public relations, moaned:

"I had no idea it was that serious. I just hope and pray Roy will be alright."

Campanella's teammates

(Continued on Page D-1, Col. 4)

Caltech 'Space Ball' in Jupiter

30-Pound Science Sphere Developed at S. Cal. Lab.

When the Army's mighty Jupiter-C missile ts off from its Cape Canaveral, Fla., launching pa. —probably tomorrow—it will carry a 30-pound bit of Southland genius into space.

The rockets, which will carry the "moon" into outer space and "into orbit," were developed at the Caltech JPL.

A giant space-tracking camera designed and built by Boller & Chivens, in South Pasadena, will monitor the orbitting "moon" from a site in New Mexico, where the first of 12 such photographic devices has been stationed.

This was disclosed here today, when a spokesman for Caltech's Jet Propulsion Laboratoriesat Devil's Gate Dam, near Pasadena, admitted:

"When the Army puts up a satellite, it will be the JPL satellite—but, of course, the date is secret."

Persistent rumors, based on the fact the Jupiter-C is poised and ready for firing at the Florida launching site, were that the firing would be some time tomorrow.

CALTECH OFFICIALS

Supporting these rumors is the fact that Dr. William Pickering, head of the laboratory, and other top-ranking Caltech officials were

(Continued on Page 5, Col. 4)

L. A. Gets High of 71

(Tides, U. S. Weather, A-16)

The mercury soared to a warm 71 degrees here today after Monday's high 68 following the 1.97-inch rainstorm.

The Weather Bureau reported little chance of rain before the end of the week.

Jet Crashes on Desert, 2 Die

BARSTOW, Calif., Jan. 28 (UP) — A military twin jet bomber with two persons aboard crashed and burned shortly after noon today seven miles northwest of here.

First reports said both crewmen were killed, one dying as he sought to parachute from the plane as it hurtled to earth.

Army Jupiter Set

AF Thor Missile Launched

CAPE CANAVERAL, Fla., Jan. 28 (UP)—The air force test-fired its own version of a potential satellite launching vehicle—a Thor 1,500-mile range rocket—today.

In Washington, the defense department said the Thor "flew its prescribed course and landed in the preselected impact area."

Similar language has been used at the Pentagon to describe successful flights of new missiles.

Although the Thor is listed as a 1,500-mile missile, one that was test-flown last Oct. 24 went 2300 nautical miles, which is 2645 statue miles.

NINTH TEST

Today's was the ninth attempted test of the intermediate range missile. The first Thor test was made one year and one day ago. Of the previous eight launchings, four were officially described as definitely successful.

As the Thor thundered aloft at 3:16½, EST, a huge Army Jupiter-C stood poised on its launching pad, ready for an effort to propel its 30-pound satellite into space possibly tomorrow or the next day.

Nearby also was the Navy Vanguard satellite rocket, now partially dismantled, but

(Continued on Page 5, Col. 2)

Baby-Sat to Buy Narcotics

L. A. Girl, 15, Fights 'Dope Pills' Death

Misplaced confidence in the youth who assertedly traded her dope for baby sitting profits almost cost the life of a 15-year-old high school freshman early today.

In critical condition at Harbor General Hospital is Carolyn June Studie, of 14730 Cerise ave., Gardena.

Capt. Dick Brooks of the sheriff's narcotics detail said the girl gulped 15 or 20 capsules of a powerful depressant in the belief that she was taking a stimulant "for kicks."

The dope, said Brooks, had been unwittingly misrepresented by 16-year-old Clarence Edward Legg.

Booked on suspicion of violating the State Narcotics Act, young Legg implicated two associates who allegedly supplied him with the "caps."

Also booked on dope charges were Rudolfo Fernandez, 19, of 908½ Bayview st., and Adolph Trinidad, 22, of 1325 E. Mauretania st., both of Wilmington.

According to Legg's story, blurted out to Sheriff's Deputies B. J. Hatfield and Barton

(Continued on Page 4, Col. 3)

Herald-Express Special Features

Your Income Tax-No. 7

Deductions: The expenses you can deduct from your income to lower your tax.

Story on Page B-3

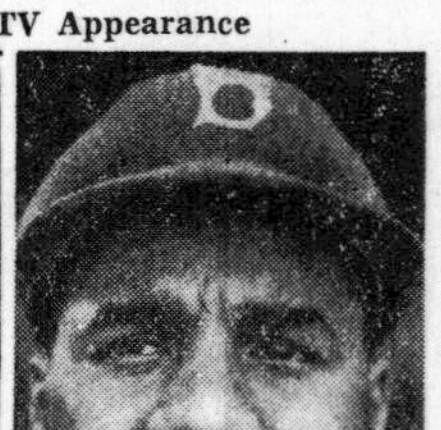

ROY CAMPANELLA
Doctors Refuse to Say His Career Is Ended

Quake Shakes 4-State Area In Middle West

ST. LOUIS, Jan. 28 (UP)—A fairly strong earthquake, the second of two, shook a four-state area last night, the St. Louis University geophysics center reported today.

Dr. Ross Heinrich said the seismograph registered the quake of 4.5 magnitude and indicated it was centered 110 miles southeast of St. Louis in the vicinity of Grand Tower, Ill.

There were no reports of damage.

Tremors also were felt at Paducah, Ky., Cairo, Ill., Caruthersville, Mo., and northwest Tennessee.

Race Results

AT SANTA ANITA

1 Lady Noon 3.90, 2.70, 2.40; Moneen 4.60, 3.50; B. Lily 5.90
2 WarTorch 73,50,28.00,10.10;Gallapade 7.60,4.10;Troj.Rey 3.00
3 Chris S. 13.50, 8.10, 3.20; Uncus 6.90, 3.70; Initiate 2.50
FOURTH—1 1-16th miles, 3 yrs., opt. clmg. Purse $5000:

Scratched—Mobilize.

(For tomorrow's Santa Anita race selections and other races, see sport pages.)

MUSIAL GETS 3000TH HIT IN CARDS' GAME AT CHICAGO

Stan Cracks Double In Pinch; Walls Is Batting Star for Cubs

By Bob Broeg
Of the Post-Dispatch Staff.

CHICAGO, May 13 — Stan Musial, held outof the starting lineup, doubled as a pinch-hitter for the Cardinals in the sixth inning this afternoon for the 3000th hit of his colorful National League career.

With one away in the sixth inning, Musial batted for Pitcher Sam Jones and drove in Gene Green, who also had doubled, with the Cardinals' second run of the game. The Redbirds were trying for their sixth straight victory.

Lee Walls had a hand in three runs for the Cubs. He doubled in the first inning and scored on a sacrifice fly, smashed his tenth homer of the season in the third and drove in another mate with a sacrifice fly in the fifth.

Moe Drabowsky was the Chicago pitcher.

Musial became only the eighth major leaguer to reach the historic 3000-hit milestone.

The seven players to achieve 3000 hits previously were Ty Cobb, who leads with 4191; Tris Speaker, 3515; Honus Wagner, 3403; Eddie Collins, 3311; Napoleon Lajoie, 3251; Paul Waner, 3152 and Adrian (Cap) Anson, 3081.

By reaching this milestone of high-level batting consistency and durability at the beginning of his sixteenth full major league season, Musial made it earlier in his career than any other 3000-hit played. Cobb, who played 24 years in the big leagues, got No. 3000 late in his sixteenth season, 1921.

Attendance in beautiful weather was about 5000.

Umpires were Donatelli, Crawford, V. Smith and Dascoli.

FIRST INNING — CARDINALS—Schofield ground out to T. Taylor. Blasingame flied to Moryn. Cunningham walked. Noren singled to left, Cunningham stopping at second. Moon tapped to Drabowsky.

CUBS—Schofield threw out T. Taylor. Walls doubled down to left field line. Walls took third on a wild pitch. Walls scored on Banks's sacrifice fly deep to Green. Moryn struck one. **ONE RUN.**

SECOND — CARDINALS — Boyer singled to left. Green hit into a double play, Banks to T. Taylor to Long. H. Smith doubled over Moryn's head. Jones was called out on strikes.

CUBS—Long lined to Moon. S. Taylor singled to right. Thomson was called out on strikes. Goryl lined to Noren.

THIRD — CARDINALS — Schofield walked. Blasingame grounded to Banks, whose throw to second base dropped by T. Taylor for an error and both runners were safe. Moryn dropped Cunningham's short fly for an error, filling the bases. Noren singled to left, scoring Schofield and leaving bases loaded. Moon popped to Goryl. Boyer was called out on strikes. Green lined to Thomson. **ONE RUN.**

CUBS — Drabowsky struck out. Boyer threw out T. Taylor. **Walls hit a home run over the left-field wall, his tenth of the season.** Blanks struck out. **ONE RUN.**

FOURTH — CARDINALS—H. Smith flied to Walls. So did Jones. Schofield walked. Blasingame fouled to S. Taylor.

CUBS — Blasingame threw out Moryn. Long struck out. S. Taylor flied to Moon.

FIFTH — CARDINALS — Drabowski threw out Cunningham. Noren was hit on the right arm by a pitched ball. Moon flied to Thomson. Boyer fouled to Long.

CUBS—Thomson walked on four pitches. Goryl singled off Schofield's glove to deep short. Drabowsky popped a bunt to Boyer. T. Taylor beat out a slow roller past the mound, filling the bases. Walls's sacrifice fly to Moon scored Thomson. Jones threw out Banks. **ONE RUN.**

SIXTH — CARDINALS — Green doubled to right. Banks threw out H. Smith, Green holding second. **Musial batted for Jones and doubled to the left field corner, scoring Green. Third Base Umpire Frank Dascoli halted play to present Musial with the ball that represented his 3000th hit. The crowd stood and applauded and cheered as Manager Fred Hutchinson went on to the field and shook Musial's hand at second base. Photographers hurried on the diamond and took pictures of the manager congratulating the player.** Surprisingly Barnes, ran for Musial, who talked to his wife in a box near the dugout, before returning to bench. Schofield walked. Blasingame singled to left for his first hit at 16 times at bat and scored Barnes with the tying run, Schofield reaching third and Blasingame second on the throw to the plate.

Cunningham was passed intentionally, filling the bases. Noren forced Cunningham, T. Taylor to Banks, Schofield scoring and Blasingame taking third. Moon doubled to deep right, scoring Blasingame, but Noren was out at the plate, Walls to T. Taylor to S. Taylor. **FOUR RUNS.**

SCORE BY INNINGS

CARDINALS (At Chicago)
001004
CHICAGO
101010

Cardinals' Box Score

CARDINALS

	AB.	R.	H.	RBI.	E.
Schofield s s	1	2	0	0	0
Blasingame 2 b	4	1	1	1	0
Cunning'm r f	2	0	0	0	0
Noren l f	3	0	2	2	0
Moon c f	4	0	1	1	0
Boyer 3 b	3	0	1	0	0
Green rf	3	1	1	0	0
H.Smith c	3	0	1	0	0
Jones p	2	0	0	0	0
Musial	1	0	1	1	0
Barnes	0	1	0	0	0
Totals	26	5	8	5	0

CHICAGO

	AB.	R.	H.	RBI.	E.
T.Taylor 2 b	3	0	1	0	0
Walls r f	2	2	2	2	0
Banks s s	2	0	0	1	0
Moryn l f	2	0	0	0	1
Long 1 b	2	0	0	0	0
S.Taylor c	2	0	1	0	1
Thomson cf	1	1	0	0	0
Goryl 3 b	2	0	1	0	0
Drabowsky p	2	0	0	0	0
Totals	18	3	4	3	2

Pinson Is Sent To Seattle by Cincinnati Club

NEW YORK, May 13 (UP)—It was back to the minors today for Vada Pinson, the major leagues' outstanding rookie during the spring training season.

The Cincinnati Redlegs optioned the 19-year-old outfielder to Seattle of the Pacific Coast League subject to 24-hour recall after his batting average nose-dived to .194.

Pinson, who played Class C ball last year, belted the ball at better than a .350 clip this spring and impressed Manager Birdie Tebbetts so much with his speed that he won a starting spot in the Redlegs' lineup on opening day.

"He's so fast," Tebbetts said, "that he will run away from his mistakes."

Pinson hit a grand-slam home run April 18 to give the Redlegs a 4-1 victory over the Pirates, but those were the only runs he batted in.

"He's a potentially great ball player," Tebbetts said yesterday, "and I'm sure he'll be back with us."

In Detroit, the Tigers purchased right-handed pitcher George Susce Jr. from the Red Sox and optioned veteran reliever George Spencer to Charleston of the American Association. Susce compiled an 18-14 record with Boston in three seasons, winning seven games and losing three last season. Spencer, formerly with the New York Giants, came up from Charleston earlier this season and had a 1-0 record in relief with the Tigers.

Other major league clubs also began paring down in anticipation of Thursday's deadline for the 25-player limit.

The San Francisco Giants optioned Pitcher Paul Giel to Phoenix of the Pacific Coast League on 24-hour recall. Giel, a former football star with Minnesota, spent two seasons in the Army and returned to the Giants last year. Manager Bill Rigney said the 25-year-old righthander needs more steady work. The Giants are still three players over the limit.

The Baltimore Orioles asked waivers on veteran infielder-outfielder Eddie Miksis for the purpose of giving him his unconditional release. Miksis was claimed from the Cardinals on waivers last year and was hitless in two times at bat this season. The Orioles also recalled 19-year-old southpaw Ron Moeller from Vancouver of the Pacific Coast League where he had won his first three starts. Baltimore is now down to the required 25-player limit. The Orioles sent Pitcher Jerry Walker to Knoxville.

The Los Angeles Dodgers announced the release of three pitchers and an outfielder. The pitchers released were Jackie Collum, who was sold outright to the Dodgers farm club at Montreal; Ron Negray, also sold outright to the St. Paul farm club, and Larry Sherry, optioned to the Dodger Pacific Coast League farm at Spokane. Rookie Outfielder Don Demeter was sent on 24-hour option to St. Paul.

Bobby Joe Mason's Injuries Not Serious

PEORIA, Ill., May 13 (UP)—Bobby Joe Mason, a Bradley University athlete, was released from St. Francis Hospital here late Monday, where he had been treated for injuries received in an automobile accident.

Mason, whose home is at Centralia, was hospitalized after a car which he was driving was involved in a collision in downtown Peoria Saturday.

Stretz Has Cataract, Doctor Reports

MILWAUKEE, Wis., May 13 (INS)—The Wisconsin State Athletic Commission reports that Hans Stretz, former middleweight and light heavyweight champion of Germany is suffering from a serious eye ailment.

Dr. Irwin Gaynon, commission physician, said yesterday that a physical examination showed Stretz's right eye is impaired by a cataract.

The doctor added that Stretz, scheduled to fight Orville Pitts in Milwaukee May 19, was not in condition to box.

The Man's Day Out With the Boys

—United Press Telephoto.

These five Chicago boys all are the same age—13—and it's their lucky year. They were asked to pose with the Cardinals star STAN MUSIAL at Wrigley Field, and the request obviously was met with pleasure, on both sides of the wall. The boys in front are, from the left, BILL TRIPPE, GLEN NORLING and JIM MARTIN. In back are, from the left, MARK McGUIRE and DAVE TRIPPE.

Newcomer Has Ace, St. Clair Golfers Win

A hole-in-one by a 13-stroke handicap player provided an unusual touch to the Eastern Missouri P.G.A. pro-women's golf tournament won by the St. Clair Country Club team yesterday at Westborough.

Mrs. John Leonard, wife of a Scott Air Base civilian worker recently transferred from Arlington, Va., got the ace on the 183-yard No. 9 hole. Her driver shot carried within 20 yards of the pin and rolled into the cup. It was her first ace in seven years of golfing.

Mrs. Leonard was a member of Pro Monk Watkins's Air Base team.

Pro Clark Morse and his St. Clair team of Doris Phillips, Barbara Beuckman and Pat Fischer won the best-ball tournament with a score of 60. Morse had excellent help from Miss Phillips, a three-handicap player whose gross score was 73.

Tim O'Connell, St. Ann's Golf club, was low pro with a net score of 68. He had a three-stroke handicap. Don Clarkson of Glen Echo and Frank Keller of Westborough each shot a gross score of 69.

Results.

Clarke Morse, St. Clair (37-35—72); Miss Doris Phillips, Miss Barbara Beuckman, Miss Pat Fischer. Best ball: 30-30—60.

Richard Craden, St. Louis C.C. (37-35—72); Mrs. Lucian Fouke, Miss Carol Culver. B.B.: 31-30—61.

Bob Green, Triple A (75—3—72); Mrs. C. Gould, Mrs. C. Gilpen, Mrs. B. Felo. B.B.: 28-33—61.

Jim Cockburn, Westwood (x); Mrs. K. Samuel, Mrs. Harry Esserman, Mrs. Alfred Goldman. B.B.: 30-32—62.

Frank Keller, Westborough (32-37—69); Mrs. D. Reid, Mrs. T. Picreaux, Mrs. J. McCarran. B.B.: 32-30—62.

Ross Hart, Glen Echo (75—4—71); Miss Mae Cella, Mrs. D. Folley, Mrs. A. Devereux. B.B.: 31-32—63.

Jim Fogertey, Sunset (74—2—72); Mrs. H. Lutz, Mrs. J. Peterson, Mrs. V. Lillard. B.B.—32-31—63.

Tony Henschel, Westborough (35-37—72); Mrs. T. Briell, Mrs. W. Parshall, Mrs. E. Wilson. B.B.—32-32—64.

A. L. (Monk) Watkins, Scott Air Base (80—2—78); Mrs. A. L. Watkins, Mrs. Lee Rath, Mrs. John Leonard. B.B.: 29-35—64.

Ed Johnson, Meadow Brook (35-35—70); Mrs. J. Goldstein, Mrs. S. Handelman, Mrs. H. Eder. B.B.: 31-33—64.

Phil Hewitt, Sunset (76—2—74); Mrs. W. Wotawa, Mrs. Al Grosch, Mrs. J. DeBasio. B.B.: 30-34—64.

Roger Pedigo, Westwood (33-36—69); Mrs. I. Landy, Mrs. M. H. Meyerhard, Mrs. S. Katz. B.B.: 31-33—64.

Carl Gleson, Westborough (38-41—79); Mrs. Schmidt, Mrs. White, Mrs. E. House. B.B.: 30-34—64.

Milan Marusic, Algonquin (x); Mrs. R. Savage, Mrs. G. Metcalfe, Mrs. K. White. B.B.: 31-33—64.

Gene Webb, Norwood (x); Mrs. A. Simmons, Mrs. J. Hill, Mrs. W. Sutton. B.B.: 32-33—65.

Don Clarkson, Glen Echo (32-37—69; Mrs. C. Schoelhamer, Mrs. A. Diederich, Mrs. J. Strong. B.B.: 31-34—65.

Lou Miller, Lockhaven (81—3—78); Mrs. N. K. McBrien, Mrs. G. Bassford, Mrs. A. G. Goveiga. B.B.: 33-32—65.

Ken Sample, Meadow Brook (78—3—75); Mrs. J. Jablonow, Mrs. J. Goldstein, Mrs. B. Blum. B.B.: 32-33—65.

Walter Ambo, Ambo Golf Tee (73—3—73); Mrs. T. Ferguson, Mrs. R. Pommer, Mrs. Frank Bush. B.B.: 31-34—65.

Nick Riviezzo, Norwood (38-44—82; Mrs. B. Vollmer, Mrs. F. O'Rourke, Mrs. M. Connelly. B.B.: 32-34—66.

Ken Burnett, Algonquin (73—2—71); Mrs. J. B. Miller, Mrs. R. Metcalf, Mrs. E. Dumont. B.B.: 34-32—66.

Howard Popham, Sunset of Edwardsville (37-38—75); Mrs. B. Oesterle, Mrs. M. Maddox, Mrs. L. Daniel. B.B.: 34-32—66.

Winton Dryden, Greenbriar (x); Mrs. M. Wainwright, Mrs. K. Itschner, Mrs. J. Wright. B.B.: 33-34—67.

Ben Richter, Bellerive (73—2—71); Mrs. P. E. Johanson, Mrs. R. E. Burns, Mrs. A. W. Meyer. B.B.: 33-34—67.

Fred Kolb, Triple A (x); Mrs. R. Scott, Mrs. A. Fleischer, Mrs. C. Arendes. B.B.: 34-33—67.

Henry Christman, University City (36-39—75); Mrs. D. Siegel, Mrs. D. Drake, Mrs. Heuchan. B.B.: 33-35—68.

Frank Fogertey, Greenbriar (x); Mrs. J. Loveridge, Mrs. Keith Kepley, Mrs. J. Keller. B.B.: 34-34—68.

Fred Clarkson, Glen Echo (81—3—78); Miss Susan Driscoll, Mrs. C. Howard, Mrs. James R. Medart. B.B.: 32-36—68.

Gene Rolfe, Norwood (38-36—74); Mrs. H. Anderson, Mrs. J. Meador, Mrs. C. Yost. B.B.: 34-34—68.

Bob Riley, Forest Park (x); Mrs. R. Diefenbach, Mrs. Coba Street, Miss Marcella Rose. B.B.: 34-35—69.

Harold Basinsk, Greenbriar (85—5—80); Mrs. E. Marx, Mrs. E. Storz, Mrs. R. Cameron. B.B.: 38-34—72.

Note (x) Pro did not turn in own score.

Newcombe's Brother Fined.

NEWARK, N.J., May 13 (AP)—The brother of Los Angeles Dodgers Pitcher Don Newcombe has been fined $200 for punching a policeman. Harold Newcombe, 30, had pleaded innocent to a charge of assaulting Patrolman Edward Coates at the tavern he operates for his brother. Chief Magistrate Nicholas Castellano found Newcombe guilty of the charge yesterday.

Paine Again Victor in Relief, 6-4

By Bob Broeg
Of the Post-Dispatch Staff.

CHICAGO, May 13 — The emphasis on brawn has not put brains completely out of business in baseball, Phillips Stephen Paine demonstrated yesterday to the glee of his Cardinal comrades and to the consternation of the Cubs, especially Walt (Moose) Moryn.

The Redbirds' fifth straight victory and their sixth in succession over their Chicago nemesis was a 6-4 triumph that delighted the players and, more important, served to lift the Cards out of the cellar for the first time.

Yesterday's verdict went to St. Louis because the Cubs continued to treat the ball as though it was radioactive, committing four errors, and, in addition, Redbird pinch-hitters came through as nobly in windy Wrigley Field here as they had in Sunday's dandy double victory at Busch Stadium.

Primarily, though, the Cardinals won because they got superb relief pitching from Paine, only recently acquired on waivers from Milwaukee, and from Larry Jackson, the staff leader who had become an ineffectual follower.

On the strength of three game-saving performances against the Cubs the last four days, Jackson now seems ready to take charge, either as a starter, if Manager Fred Hutchinson desires, or a relief specialist. For that matter, as he proved in the past, the Idaho athlete could do both in limited amounts.

A Question of Need.

Whether Jackson will be needed most on the front line or as the club's best bet to choke off an enemy rally will depend on basic needs. If Paine pitches as effectively as on most occasions this four-week-old season, Jackson might be able to return to the starting staff.

There's no attempt here to make miracle-remedy claims for Paine, a 27-year-old Rhode Island righthander who fits the tall, dark and handsome cliche. Regardless of how much pitching Milwaukee had and still has, there's always room for a good pitcher, especially one with the knack of coming out of the bullpen in a tight situation. Therefore, Paine still is suspect.

So far, however, he has done what has been asked of him and, as he demonstrated yesterday, even more. He picked up his second victory within 24 hours, allowing only three hits in four-plus innings. And it might be interesting to note that in fractions of five assorted seasons, Fearless Phil now has a 7-0 record in the majors.

The Fearless is not merely an alliterative adjective when used here. James (The Ripper) Collins, Gas House Gang first baseman and now a sporting goods representative here, remembered Paine's attitude when Rip managed Hartford in the Eastern League for the Braves in 1950.

Gas-House Touch.

"I had this guy I wasn't counting on at all," recalled Collins. "All he had, it seemed, was pretty good control. Just before cutdown date when we were taking a real trimming, I put him in. He immediately hit three straight batters, broke one fella's arm, and I went out to the mound.

"'Look,' I said, 'The one thing you can do is get the ball over. You're not afraid of these guys, are you?'"

"H——, no," Collins quoted Paine as saying. "This club has just been murdering our pitching, and I decided to do something about it."

Paine's hardboiled reaction touched a soft—or should it be hard?—spot in the old Gashouser's heart. Phil stayed with Hartford to begin his climb as a tender-aged specialist of the toe-plate profession.

Eight years and 57 trips to major league mounds later, Paine yesterday baffled the Cubs with a sidearmed sinker he consistently kept low. And he showed that smart baseball didn't die with the dead ball.

Paine's Trap.

With the Cardinals overcoming a three-run deficit to take a 6-4 lead, thanks largely to Chicago errors and timely pinch blows by Gene Green and Alvin Dark, Paine blanked the Cubs from the fifth into the eighth when slugger Moryn got their first hit off him, a double. The Moose held second as Dale Long hit back to the pitcher.

With Sammy Taylor up, Paine casually called Catcher Hal Smith to the mound and told him, "Instead of using a stretch motion, I'm going into my full windup. I'll shorten it at the top and speed up, though. We might catch Moryn breaking. And if we don't, I'll still be able to get more on the ball."

Apparently ignoring the runner, Paine turned his back toward second base, wound halfway, cut the ball loose and Moryn, certain he had an easy base to steal, took the bait and broke for third. He was an easy out, ending the inning.

That's not all, either. To begin the ninth, Taylor smashed a line base hit off Paine's leg and Bobby Thomson also singled before Jackson rushed in to save a game that, except for Fearless Phil Paine's baseball shrewdness, might have been gone before Fire Chief Jackson answered the alarm.

How They Stand

NATIONAL LEAGUE

	W.	L.	Pct.	G.B.
Milwaukee	15	7	.682	...
San Fr'nc'co	16	9	.640	½
Pittsburgh	15	9	.625	1
Chicago	13	13	.500	4
Cincinnati	9	11	.450	5
Philadelphia	9	15	.375	7
CARDINALS	8	14	.364	7
Los Angeles	9	16	.360	7½

AMERICAN LEAGUE

	W.	L.	Pct.	G.B.
New York	13	5	.722	...
Washington	13	9	.591	2
Baltimore	11	9	.550	3
Detroit	12	12	.500	4
Kansas City	9	10	.474	4½
Cleveland	11	13	.458	5
Boston	10	15	.400	6½
Chicago	7	13	.350	7

Today's Schedule.

NATIONAL LEAGUE

San Francisco (McCormick 2-0) at Los Angeles (Newcombe 0-2), 3:30 p.m.

Milwaukee (Buhl 4-1) at Philadelphia (Roberts 1-4), 7 p.m.

Cincinnati (Lawrence 2-1) at Pittsburgh (Kline 3-2), 7:15 p.m.

AMERICAN LEAGUE

Baltimore (Johnson 1-2) at New York (Larsen 2-0), 7 p.m.

Boston (Smith 1-0) at Washington (Ramos 2-1), 7:05 p.m.

Cleveland (Grant 3-1) at Detroit (Lary 2-2), 8:15 p.m.

Chicago (Wynn 2-2) at Kansas City (Burnette 1-0), 9 p.m.

Yesterday's Results.

NATIONAL LEAGUE

Cardinals 6, Chicago 4.

San Francisco 12, Los Angeles 3 (night).

(Only games scheduled.)

AMERICAN LEAGUE

Washington 5, Boston 4.

Kansas City 2, Chicago 1 (11 innings).

(Only games scheduled.)

Tomorrow's Schedule.

NATIONAL LEAGUE

San Francisco at St. Louis, 8 p.m.
Los Angeles at Chicago.
Milwaukee at Philadelphia.
Cincinnati at Pittsburgh.

AMERICAN LEAGUE

Baltimore at New York.
Cleveland at Detroit.
Boston at Washington.
Chicago at Kansas City.

Feeling No Paine

CARDINALS

	AB.	R.	H.	Rbi.	E.
Scofield ss	5	0	0	0	0
Blasingame 2b	5	0	0	0	0
Musial 1b	4	0	1	0	0
Cunningham rf	4	1	3	0	0
Flood cf	0	0	0	0	0
Moon cf-rf	5	1	1	0	0
Noren lf	3	1	2	1	0
Boyer 3b	1	2	0	0	0
Paine p	1	0	0	0	0
Jackson p	0	0	0	0	0
H. Smith c	5	1	1	1	0
Barnes p	1	0	0	0	0
aGreen	1	0	1	2	0
Mabe p	0	0	0	0	0
bDark 3b	2	0	1	1	0
Totals	37	6	10	5	0

CHICAGO

	AB.	R.	H.	Rbi.	E.
T. Taylor 2b	2	2	1	0	1
dTanner	1	0	0	0	0
Adams 3b	0	0	0	0	0
hErnaga	1	0	0	0	0
Walls rf	4	0	1	1	1
Banks ss	3	1	1	2	1
Moryn lf	4	0	1	0	0
Long 1b	3	0	0	0	0
S. Taylor c	4	0	1	0	0
pNeeman	0	0	0	0	0
Thomson cf	4	0	1	0	0
Goryl 3b	3	1	1	0	1
Hobbie p	1	0	0	1	0
Freeman p	0	0	0	0	0
cP. Smith	1	0	0	0	0
Nichols p	0	0	0	0	0
gBolger	1	0	0	0	0
Totals	32	4	7	4	4

A—Doubled for Barnes in fourth; B—Singled for Mabe in fifth; C—Struck out for Freeman in seventh; D—Grounded out for T. Taylor in seventh; E—Ran for Cunningham in eighth; F—Ran for S. Taylor in ninth; G—Called out on strikes for Nichols in ninth; H—Hit into force play for Adams in ninth.

Innings	1	2	3	4	5	6	7	8	9	T.
Cardinals	0	0	0	2	4	0	0	0	0	6
Chicago	1	0	2	1	0	0	0	0	0	4

DP—T. Taylor, Banks and Long. Left—Cardinals 11, Chicago 6. 2B—Musial, Cunningham, Moryn. 3B—Goryl. HR—Banks. SB—T. Taylor. S—Boyer. SF—Hobbie.

Pitching	IP.	H.	R.	ER.	BB.	WO.
Barnes	3	3	3	3	3	3
Mabe	1	1	1	1	0	0
Paine (W. 2-0)	4	3	0	0	1	1
Jackson	1	0	0	0	0	1
Habbie (L. 2-3)	4⅓	6	5	4	4	1
Freeman	2⅔	2	1	0	2	0
Nichols	2	2	0	0	0	0

(Paine pitched to 2 batters in ninth.

U—Dascoli, Donatelli, Crawford and Smith. T—2h, 19m. A—5083.

Champions Lose in Playground Bowling

Harrison No. 1, the defending champion, was eliminated in the Playground Mothers bowling tournament on the Sports Bowl lanes. Laurene Ingerson rolled 544, but the team totaled only 1796.

Advancing to the semifinals were Mallinckrodt No. 5 with 1958; Central No. 3 with 1848; Baden No. 1 with 1916 and Mallinckrodt No. 7 with 1816. Other teams eliminated were Dewey No. 2, Baden No. 4, and Mallinckrodt No. 6.

Semifinals will be rolled Friday.

925-Average Team Needed for Classic

There is an opening for a team in one or both divisions of the Classic League for the next bowling season. To qualify a club must have an average of 925 or better.

The Classic League voted to return to Floriss Lanes on Tuesday nights and to Sports Bowl on Thursdays for 1958-59. A team wishing to enter the circuit need not compete in both divisions. Any captain interested may contact Joe Walsh, league secretary, at CH 1-2313.

POST-DISPATCH Sports
Edited by J. ROY STOCKTON

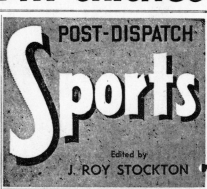

Meadowbrook Player Leads Grandmothers' Golf With Net 77

Mrs Harry Meyer of Meadowbrook today had a net score of 77 on a gross tally of 115 to win the Grandmothers' golf tournament at Norwood Hills Country Club.

Scores:

Player	Score.	Hdcp.	Net.
Mrs. Harry Meyer, Meadowbrook	115	38	77
Mrs. Clay M. Zinser, Algonquin	112	33	79
Mrs. Elmer R. Ohl, Edwardsville	98	16	82
Mrs. V. H. Laager, Algonquin	108	27	81
Mrs. W. L. Clinton, Norwood	127	38	89
Mrs. Charles Harris, Norwood	107	20	87
Mrs. A. F. Koedding, Norwood	105	15	90
Mrs. Marsh P. Duke, Norwood	119	25	94
Mrs. C. W. Emons, Lockhaven	120	26	94
Mrs. H. G. Wickenhauser, Lockhaven	98	13	85
Mrs. Pearl Obrock, Triple A	116	22	94
Mrs. Leroy Dietschy, Lockhaven	117	28	89
Mrs. Etta Wickenhauser, Lockhaven	123	22	101
Mrs. Clyde Metcalfe, Algonquin	131	28	103
Mrs. Oscar Schmidt, Edwardsville	106	20	86
Mrs. Elsie Gorin, Normandie	117	25	92
Mrs. Ralph Kalish, Westwood	115	24	91
Mrs. C. S. Reynolds, Norwood	111	23	88
Mrs. Art Shipherd, Norwrood	115	28	87
Mrs. J. Dreitlein, Norwood	121	28	93
Mrs. B. E. Schiffman, Norwood	110	27	83
Mrs. M. Feinstein, Meadowbrook	122	36	86
Mrs. Wilfred Eilers, Edwardsville	127	24	103
Mrs. D. W. Helman, Meadowbrook	116	31	85
Mrs. Myron Goldberg, Triple A	125	38	87
Mrs. Robert Mayer, Westwood	107	19	88
Mrs. E. Guy Myover, Greenbriar	101	18	84
Mrs. John R. Wright, Greenbriar	103	16	87
Mrs. George C. Robbins, Greenbriar	127	33	94
Mrs. A. U. Simmons, Norwood	99	9	94
Mrs. J. R. Medart, Glen Echo	93	11	82
Mrs. C. W. Newport, Triple A	119	26	93
Mrs. William Gaterman, Norwood	111	30	81
Mrs. F. C. Catanzare, Norwood	122	38	84
Mrs. M. Meyerhardt, Westwood	98	15	88
Mrs. Alvin Saeks, Meadowbrook	112	22	[illegible]
Mrs. George Metcalfe, Algonquin	98	20	78
Mrs. Jack Adler, Triple A	106	18	88
Mrs. Emil Lasker, Westwood	113	26	87
Mrs. Alfred Vernaus, Westwood	108	26	82
Mrs. C. W. Fawcett, Norwood	109	19	90
Mrs. L. L. Held, Norwood	127	31	96
Mrs. A. M. Schieler, Norwood	140	38	102

Martinez Starts Work For Bout With Akins

GROSSINGER, N.Y., May 13 (UP) — Vince Martinez of Paterson, N.J., today began his boxing preparations for his June 6 welterweight title bout against Virgil Akins by sparring six rounds.

Martinez went three rounds with Ike Jenkins of New York and three with Red Raines of Stamford, Conn.

Martinez did five miles of road work today. He said he would box six more rounds Wednesday. He will meet Akins for the vacant welterweight crown at St. Louis.

Northern League

Duluth-Superior 9, Fargo-Moorhead 6.
[illegible] 10, Aberdeen 5.
Eau Claire 9, Minot 4.
[illegible] Forks, postponed, high winds and dust.

Tigers Beat A's, 9-5, Near 5th

See Page 33

HUMID

Cloudy, warm, showers. Low 62-66, high 82-86.

Map and Details on Page 3

HOURLY TEMPERATURES

12 noon	72	5 p.m.	76	10 p.m.	70
1 p.m.	76	6 p.m.	71	11 p.m.	70
2 p.m.	77	7 p.m.	75	12 mid.	69
3 p.m.	77	8 p.m.	73	1 a.m.	69
4 p.m.	75	9 p.m.	71	2 a.m.	68

The Detroit Free Press

METRO FINAL ★ BLUE STREAK

WEDNESDAY, MAY 27, 1959 — On Guard for 128 Years — Vol. 129—No. 23 — 40 Pages — Seven Cents

GREATEST NO-HITTER ENDS IN 2-0 DEFEAT

HIGHWAY TRAGEDIES

'Stopping The Wheels Of Death'

Injury of Roy Campanella Brings Home Safety Point

Once again as the Memorial Day weekend approaches, the nation can expect a repeat of a traffic massacre that will leave hundreds dead across the country. And once again highway safety experts declare that these deaths need not occur, but, knowing motorists, they are prepared for the worst. Here, in this special three-part series on "Stopping the Wheels of Death," a writer takes a close look at highway slaughter and hopes desperately you will not be among the weekend casualty list.

BY HERBERT KAMM
Free Press Special Writer

On Jan. 28, 1958, a car traveling about 30 miles an hour crashed into a telephone pole and doomed baseball star Roy Campanella to the life of an invalid.

Almost a year later—Jan. 19, 1959—a car traveling at 40 miles an hour collided with a 3,300-pound trailer, and the same Roy Campanella escaped without a scratch.

Of the two accidents, the second was by far the more violent terms of impact.

Campanella's tragic experience is by no means unique. Accidents which killed 37,000 and injured 1,350,000 last year contain many parallels.

A man can walk away from the wreckage of a major crash, but lose his life or be permanently crippled in what seems like a minor accident. Why?

* * *

THERE IS no pat answer. ...st safety and auto experts ...it, in fact, that their ... is much more complex ...day than it was 10 or 20 years ago.

While the number of fatalities has been dropping, the number of injuries has grown alarmingly.

There is almost universal agreement, however, on one point: Now that the chances of surviving an auto accident are better than ever before, more ways and means must be devised to protect its occupants against injury.

The Campanella case illustrates that challenge better than any other in recent years.

John O. Moore, who heads the Cornell University Auto Crash Research Center, says Campanella most likely would have escaped that first accident unscathed or with minor injuries had he been wearing a safety belt.

* * *

IN AN ANALYSIS of that mishap, crash researchers determined that Campanella,

Turn to Page 10, Column 6

Smiles

Cuba Digs For Gold

Free Press Wire Services

Cuba's revolutionary regime is considering a tax on each name, each adjective and each picture appearing on the society pages of newspapers, El Mundo reported Tuesday.

●

Dry Run

British rain makers reported that since they started tests on Salisbury Plain in September 1955 the area has had less rain than in previous years.

Chrysler Revamps Sales Setup

Chrysler Corp. Tuesday announced establishment of a new sales structure in a tightening and realignment of its retail operations.

Combination of the Plymouth and De Soto sales into a single unit was the major change in the announcement by Byron J. Nichols, vice president of automotive sales.

A new Sales Division Group has been set up, Nichols said, headed by Edward C. Quinn, vice president and general manager of Chrysler Motors Corp. (Chrysler's sales organization).

* * *

QUINN'S NEW group, taking over next Monday, will be divided into three individual sales divisions:

Chrysler - Imperial, under Clair E. Briggs; Dodge car and Dodge truck, under M. C. Patterson; and Plymouth-De Soto, under Harry E. Chesebrough, formerly Plymouth division manager.

These divisions, and the sales organization for Chrysler's French-made Simca, will report directly to Quinn.

Each sales divisions will be directly responsible for all field-sales activities in its line, Nichols said.

Each division will handle its own distribution, product planning, advertising, sales promotion, market analysis, field

Turn to Page 2, Column 6

Wedding Bells

NEW YORK—(UPI)—The engagement of Hope Aldrich Rockefeller, great-granddaughter of the late John D. Rockefeller, Sr., to John Spencer was announced Tuesday. She is a niece of New York Gov. Nelson A. Rockefeller.

On the Inside . . .

State Bares 'Slavery' in Job Deals

Employment Broker Gets Third of Pay

An employment broker was charged Tuesday with holding destitute workers in bondage and then denying them unemployment compensation after they tried—and failed—to find work.

The charge was made against Manpower, Inc., 1336 Cass, by Charles Rubinoff, a referee for the Michigan Employment Commission.

Rubinoff said Manpower bound workers to an indefinite contract and then collected one-third of their pay for referring them to temporary jobs.

He said Manpower applicants are required to sign a contract stating:

"I will not accept permanent employment from any customer of Manpower, Inc., for whom I have worked until three months have elapsed after last assignment to the customer."

* * *

HIS INDICTMENT of Manpower was contained in Rubinoff's ruling on an unemployment compensation claim made by Howard F. Gerst, 44, of 28 Temple.

Gerst was forced on welfare when Manpower successfully blocked his claim for $285 in unemployment compensation, Rubinoff said.

Actually, Gerst was entitled to $267 of the sum, the referee ruled.

Gerst's attorney, Cass Jaros, said the ruling also qualifies Gerst for an estimated $300 in future payments, most of which will go in refunds to the Detroit Welfare Department.

* * *

MANPOWER, INC., registered with the State of Michigan as an "employer," refers dozens of men daily to temporary labor jobs in the Detroit area.

In Gerst's case, Rubinoff said, Manpower collected $1.42 an hour for his services and gave Gerst $1 of it. Manpower pre-

Turn to Page 9, Column 3

John Foster Dulles Leaves His Home for the Last Time

Pair Loot Truck of $164,450

DENVER —(AP)— While a woman watched in astonishment, a man looted an armored truck of $164,450 in currency Tuesday and escaped with a male partner in a green-and-white auto.

It was the second largest cash haul in the history of the Denver area. In 1922 armed men ambushed a Federal Reserve truck in front of the Denver mint and got away with $200,000.

* * *

TUESDAY'S THEFT was in the drive-in area of the Jefferson County Bank, just west of Denver.

The thief opened the locked truck door with a key and tossed four canvas sacks holding the money to his confederate. Then they drove out past tellers sitting at drive-in windows and vanished.

The getaway car was found

Turn to Page 7, Column 1

Thousands Pay Homage To Dulles at Cathedral

WASHINGTON —(UPI)— A seemingly endless line of officials and private citizens filed slowly past the flag-draped bier of John Foster Dulles Tuesday in silent tribute to the man who fought so hard for world peace.

Mourning rites for the former Secretary of State began officially at noon in Washington's towering National Cathedral. Dulles will lie in state there until the funeral services at 2 p.m. (1 p.m., Detroit time) Wednesday.

Burial will be in Arlington National Cemetery.

(Two Detroit television stations will show the services. WWJ-TV(4) will carry the rites, taped, from 3:30 p.m. to 4 p.m. (Detroit time) and WJBK-TV(2) will show it, also taped, from 3:30 p.m. to 4:30 p.m.)

As foreign dignitaries converged on the capital for the funeral, the body was removed from the Dulles home and taken by hearse to the cathedral. Riding slowly behind were members of the family, except for Mrs. Dulles, who remained at home to rest for her most trying day.

* * *

BY MIDAFTERNOON the line of people was moving past the bier at the rate of 800 an hour. It was planned to keep the chapel open until noon Wednesday.

An honor guard of servicemen bore the coffin into the cathedral's vaulted Bethlehem Chapel—through a doorway inscribed: "The Way of Peace"—and placed it on a bier in the center of the room.

The Rev. Roswell Barnes, of New York, United States secretary of the World Council of Churches and an old friend of Dulles, conducted a brief ceremony that included a prayer and the First Psalm.

* * *

THE ROOM was heady with the scent of flowers banked around the massive stone walls. Among the floral pieces was a wreath of white carnations in the form of a cross from President and Mrs. Eisenhower.

The President and First Lady will lead the mourners at the funeral services and the Arlington burial. They will be joined by diplomatic leaders from all parts of the world.

Big Four To Bargain In Secret

Free Press Wire Services

GENEVA — The Big Four foreign ministers agreed Tuesday to start secret bargaining on Berlin and a summit meeting when they resume their conference here Friday.

Then they flew off to Washington for the funeral of John Foster Dulles.

Christian A. Herter of the United States, Britain's Selwyn Lloyd and France's Maurice Couve de Murville thundered out of Geneva in the glistening Constellation of Gen. Lauris Norstad, NATO commander in Europe.

Russia's Andrei Gromyko left two hours earlier in a tourist-class flight via London for the Washington rites.

He had asked Herter about a ride to Washington in the Constellation but there was only one seat available and Gromyko wanted to take along several aides.

But Gromyko accepted an invitation to ride back from Washington to Geneva on Herter's plane.

* * *

BEFORE THE ministers met Tuesday, Gromyko and Lloyd hammered out an East-West agreement for secret negotiations to begin Friday.

The decision on secret diplomacy came after 12 sessions of stalemated debate on the big issues.

The secret talks will pivot around more limited objectives—a stopgap agreement on the explosive Berlin crisis and an agreement for a summit parley.

The agreement came just the day before Premier Nikita Khrushchev's original ultimatum for the Allies to get out of West Berlin was to expire.

In Berlin, Communist and Western spokesman agreed the May 27 Soviet deadline will pass without incident.

Haddix Perfect for 12 Innings

Braves' Only Hit Ruins Feat in 13th

How Adcock Ruined It in 13th—Page 33.

Free Press Wire Services

MILWAUKEE — Pittsburgh left-hander Harvey Haddix pitched 12 perfect innings Tuesday night — the longest no-hit performance in history—then lost, 2 to 0, in the 13th to the Milwaukee Braves.

The end came on an error, an intentional walk and a rule-book double by Joe Adcock—the Braves' only hit.

Haddix retired the first 36 men in order before Don Hoak's throwing error permitted Felix Mantilla to reach base leading off the 13th inning.

After Ed Mathews sacrificed, Haddix intentionally passed Hank Aaron, but the strategy backfired when Adcock sent a long drive into the stands.

* * *

ADCOCK AT first was credited with a home run. But he was declared out, and given only a double, when he passed Aaron between second and third.

The jubilant Aaron had cut across the diamond without touching third. His run was permitted to count, however, after he was sent back by his mates to touch third and home. Adcock's run was nullified.

It was a heart-breaking climax for Haddix, who became the first pitcher in history to carry a perfect performance past nine innings.

He did salvage, however, the longest no-hitter in major league history.

National League President Warren Giles said he believed the final score of the game would be changed by official ruling to 1-0 rather than 2-0.

Giles said he could make "no official ruling" until he studies reports on the game, but expressed the opinion that only the number of runs sufficient

Turn to Page 35, Column 2

Philip's All Wet

★ ★ ★ ★ ★ ★

Press Raps Duke for Squirt Scene

LONDON —(AP)— A British newspaper advised Prince Philip Tuesday that squirting water on people who can't squirt back is second-rate humor.

The British press usually handles the royal family with kid gloves. But in a front-page editorial headed "Not So Funny," the Evening Star really let the Queen's husband have it.

The squirting incident occurred Monday at the annual Chelsea Flower Show. The victims were two photographers of the British Press Association, Walter Lockyear and Mark Seymour. They carried passes from Buckingham Palace and, as the Star remarked, represented "the press of the world."

* * *

A SPRINKLING system had been demonstrated to Philip. He was still standing by the control panel when the two cameramen moved into position to take a picture of Queen Elizabeth II.

Then, the Star said, "the Duke said to the two men operating the control panel of the sprinkler: "If I press this will I get those two photographers?' The men said 'yes.'

Fun for Philip

"The Duke then pressed the button and Lockyear and Seymour were drenched with the water, which came up from concealed sprays in the ground.

"Their clothes were soaked, their cameras were also drenched, and it was 10 to 15 minutes before they could dry their apparatus to take pictures.

"The Duke asked Lockyear, 'did you get wet?' Lockyear replied sarcastically, 'Oh, no, not much.'

"Both men were in fact, very wet, very embarrassed and very annoyed."

Philip has demonstrated many times in the past that he often regards news photographers as invaders of the royal privacy. Twice he has threatened to withdraw from racing in the annual Cowes Regatta unless they kept their distance.

Other members of the royal family take the popping flash bulbs in stride.

Reds Plan to Ring Italy with Missiles

MOSCOW —(AP)— Soviet Premier Nikita Khrushchev Tuesday threatened to set up missile bases in Communist Albania if the United States puts rocket bases in Greece and Italy.

He said Soviet rockets, both medium range and short range, could cover both countries from Albania.

The Soviet leader spoke in Albania where he is visiting with a party of Russian military and defense officials.

Albania is the only Soviet satellite on the Mediterranean.

Mentioned frequently as a potential Soviet submarine base, it has a common frontier with Greece and is not a long shot from Italy.

* * *

"IF THE GOVERNMENTS of Italy and Greece permit the Americans to set up rocket bases on their territory then it is possible we will be forced to arrange with the government of the Peoples' Republic of Albania to set up something

Turn to Page 2, Column 3

Raul Castro Plane Missing

HAVANA—(AP)—Fidel Castro's firebrand younger brother, Raul, was missing Tuesday night on a flight in a light plane over south central Cuba.

Raul Castro, who succeeded his brother as commander in chief of the revolutionary armed forces, had taken off at 12:30 p.m. (Detroit time) with a pilot and three aides in search of a helicopter in which Maj. Luis Diaz Lanz, commander of the revolutionary air force, had crashed. Diaz was found unhurt.

The presidential palace announced at 10:45 p.m. that Raul's plane was missing. The plane had fuel for only one hour of flight.

Record Fifth Straight Homer Rocky's Target for Tonight

Cleveland Press
SPORTS
Bob August . . . Sports Editor
THURSDAY, JUNE 11, 1959 PAGE 59

By BEN FLIEGER
Press Sports Writer

BALTIMORE—Rocky Colavito, newest haloed hero in baseball's record book, will make the most important trip of his career to home plate here tonight.

When the Rock steps up to face the Orioles' Milt Pappas shortly after 8 o'clock he will be swinging to make hitting history — to become the first player to ever to hit five home runs in consecutive times at bat.

"I'm going to bunt," kidded Colavito, a cheek-splitting grin on his boyish face, a wink in his eye as he relaxed on a locker stool last night at Memorial Stadium.

It was his first smile of that size in almost a month. And he was entitled. His four mighty homers that ended a sour slump also put him in on a level reached by only two other sluggers since the first major league was organized in 1876.

Only Bobby Lowe (Boston, National League, May 30, 1894) and Lou Gehrig of the Yankees (June 3, 1932) ever socked four consecutively. Just five others have hit four in a single game. And this list of the distinguished does not include Babe Ruth or Ted Williams or Joe DiMaggio, Colavito's boyhood idol.

"Bobby Lowe? 1894? Well, I don't know him," admitted Rocky between sips on a cooling brew in the steaming clubhouse.

"But Gehrig, gosh, I'm proud to be up with Lou. He was one of my first heroes in those days in the Bronx. I guess it was because my brother Vito was a first baseman and loved Gehrig.

"What'll I be thinking up there tomorrow night? Well, I'm just going to be swinging for a base hit. That's all I was trying for on the last one. But I'd be lying if I said I didn't know a homer would tie the record.

That was a long, soaring blow into the left field bleachers with one out in the ninth off Ernie Johnson, who hadn't given up a homer in 30 previous innings this season.

"A fast ball," remembered Rock, "thrown up high. Were all the homer pitches the same? No sirree. All different, in fact.

"The first one (off starter Jerry Walker in the third inning after Rocky had walked in the first) was a low slider or maybe a curve. No. 2 (off Arnold Portocarrero in the fifth) a slider, up and inside. No. 3 (off Portocarrero again in the sixth) a fast ball down and out over the plate. The first one I hit pretty good but the last three were best."

The first second and fourth went into the high-walled stands which curve sharply from the foul pole, 309 feet away, to form a deep left field. The third sock was a rocket to left center. It carried over a temporary fence, much like the one in Cleveland Stadium.

To indicate the depth of Colavito's slump before the barrage in the Indians' 11-7 victory, his four homers were as many as he had hit in 90 previous at-bats covering 24 games back to May 16. Over this stretch, his average was .211.

"I'm going to call my wife right away," promised the handsome Italian, thinking of this. "I know she was listening. She always shares my misery when I'm not hitting, so I want her also to share my joy."

Also sharing his joy were Baltimore fans who just innings before were making him miserable. They heckled loud and often. At the start one even sprayed him with beer when he caught a fly near the stands.

"I was mad and ready to challenge him," said Colavito. "But I'll say this for the guy, after the last homer, he stood up and waved to me."

As Rocky sat by the locker, teammates, one by one, broke through the thin ring of reporters to add congratulations.

Between handshakes Colavito held his refreshment in one hand. The ball from the final out was fondled in the other. "No one better try taking this," he warned with a fake snarl.

Rock's Socks

Four sweeps of his bat last night and Rocky Colavito bombed his way out of that hitting slump in super-spectacular fashion with consecutive home runs in third, fifth, sixth and ninth innings and a total of six RBI's as the Indians outslugged the Orioles, 11-8, in Baltimore's spacious Memorial Stadium. Only two other players, Bobby Lowe (Boston Braves, 1894) and Lou Gehrig (Yankees, 1932) have hit four consecutive homers in the history of major league ball. Five other players have clouted four out of the park, but not consecutively, in a single game. They are Ed Delehanty (Philadelphia Phils, 1896), Chuck Klein (Phils, 1936), ex-Indian Pat Seerey (White Sox, 1948), Gil Hodges (Brooklyn Dodgers, 1950) and Joe Adcock (Milwaukee Braves, 1954). Colavito tied the American League record for total bases (16) in one game and his season total of 18 homers puts him only one shy of league leader Harmon Killebrew of Washington.

Frank Gibbons

Gordon Should Quit Panning His Players

Perhaps just as important as Rocky Colavito's magnificent mauling last night was the hitting of Minnie Minoso and Billy Martin. Important, that is, in what the Indians will be next week.

Frank Lane has been kicking the notion around in his fertile mind that Minoso is over the hill. Joe Gordon, whose second basing and slugging standards are very high, has given Martin a bad rating.

Old Minnie provided the Indians with the opening blast off in what must be rated as a very, very important game, by hitting a first-inning home run with two on. Martin, who has been hitting well for the past week, contributed a solo home run later on.

I didn't think Colavito was in danger of being traded before he hit four home runs in the Baltimore park last night, which must be put down as the greatest slugging feat in history.

Memorial Stadium in Baltimore is an all-sports park which was not built with home runs in mind. You've got to earn them there, and Colavito did just that. He drove in six runs which, temporarily, should silence those critics who are saying he never hits when it matters. The Indians won by three runs, so Rocky's contributions were very important.

In this strange baseball season, I haven't joined the throng in criticizing Gordon for his handling of pitchers and his lineup juggling, but I have been distressed over his fingering of individual ball players.

Gordon has been sharply critical of Martin, a dead-end kid type who is not a great ball player, but who is the best we have at second base. As a matter of fact, he batted Ray Webster for Martin in the seventh inning last night, which was rubbing it in.

I don't blame Gordon for getting upset over things that go wrong in ball games. As a matter of fact, when I heard

Tuesday night's game on the radio at home, I almost did a jacknife dive off the patio when Jim Grant threw wild to first base after walking two men, setting up three runs.

I do blame Gordon, however, for putting men such as Grant and Martin on the spot in the public eye. I'm certain they, and all of the Indians, are doing the best they can, and you can't ask for more of any man, whether he is a ball player or a sports writer. Gordon threatened Grant with banishment to San Diego if he didn't do better. If I were handled the same way, I would have to be sent out to Siberia for seasoning.

Gordon, like all of us, is bitter over the failure of the Indians to grasp a fat opportunity to dominate the American League. They had the chance and now it is gone and they must do it the hard way.

It's too bad, but that's the way it is and Gordon isn't improving matters when he relieves his frustration by abusing his players in public. A ball player is no different than any other workman. If he can't do the job you get rid of him, but you don't kick his teeth in before you do.

When we got Martin, I thought it was pretty well established that we had no illusions about his greatness. We felt that he would improve the team around second base, and I believe he has. I don't expect him to be another Larry Lajoie, or even another Gordon.

Minoso got three hits last night and that could have the effect of soothing Lane. I would hate to see Minnie leave for a second time, because I still have a vivid recollection of the first.

We were in St. Louis when they made the announcement that Minoso was going to the White Sox and we were going to get Lou Brissie. I hated to see Minnie leave then, and I would hate to see him leave now.

Baseball Roundup:

Chicago Can Thank Tribe

The Chicago White Sox can thank the Indians—present and past—for holding undisputed possession of first place in the American League today.

While the Indians were troucing Baltimore, which had been tied with Chicago, former Tribesmen were playing a big part in the White Sox's 4-1 victory over the Washington Senators last night.

Early Wynn, a former Indian, pitched a five-hitter and struck out seven Washington batters in registering his eighth victory against four defeats for the season.

The White Sox gave him all the margin he needed by scoring two runs off Hal Woodeshick, an ex-Indian, in the first inning. A hit batsman, a triple by Al Smith, another ex-Indian, and an error by Washington catcher Hal Naragon, still another ex-Indian, did the trick.

Yanks Roll On

The Yankees scored their 11th victory in 13 games by beating the Athletics, 6-4; the Tigers remained in a fourth-place tie with the Yanks by outlasting the Red Sox in a slugging bee, 10-9; the Giants climbed to within a game of the National League lead with an 11-7 decision over the Pirates as the Cardinals topped the Braves, 5-2; the Dodgers nipped the Phillies, 2-1 and the Reds clipped the Cubs, 6-4.

Elston Howard's two-run double sparked a four-run seventh-inning rally that gave the Yankees their triumph over the A's.

Winner Art Ditmar and loser Bud Daley were tied at 2-2 in the seventh when the Yanks loaded the bases. A passed ball by Catcher Frank House allowed the tie-breaking run to score and Howard followed with his double for two more.

Tigers Rally

Detroit trailed Boston, 6-3, until it came up with five runs in the seventh. Rookie Larry Osborne then homered in the eighth and Al Kaline drove in what proved to be the winning run with his fourth hit of the game.

Ike Delock, the Red Sox starter, and Gary Geiger also hit homers.

Willie Kirkland drove in three runs for the Giants on three hits, including his eighth homer, and Orlando Cepeda also helped sink the Pirates by accounting for two more runs with a single and his 14th homer.

Sam Jones notched his seventh victory although Stu Miller had to bail him out when Pittsburgh rallied for five runs in the seventh.

Bill White of the Cardinals boosted his average to .342 with three hits and Lindy McDaniel turned in a fine piece of relief pitching against the league-leading Braves. McDaniel blanked the Braves after the sixth inning.

Gene Conley, who hadn't beaten the Dodgers since 1957, held them to four hits and picked up his third triumph in pitching the Phils to their victory.

San Fran Five on Orient Tour

SAN FRANCISCO—(UPI)—The University of San Francisco basketball team, accompanied by Coach Phil Woolpert, will leave tomorrow for a month-long tour of the Orient.

The Dons will play 17 games in the Philippines and also play in Hong Kong and Tokyo.

Rock 'Em Rocky!

INDIANS	ab	r	h	rbi	Orioles	ab	r	h	rbi
Held,ss	5	1	1	0	Pearson,cf	3	1	2	0
Power,1b	4	1	0	0	Pilarcik,rf	5	1	1	2
Francona,cf	5	2	2	1	Woodling,lf	5	1	3	1
Colavito,rf	4	5	4	6	Triandos,c	2	0	1	1
Minoso,lf	5	1	3	3	Ginsberg,c	1	1	0	0
Jones,3b	3	0	0	0	Hale,1b	3	0	0	0
Strickland,3b	2	0	1	0	Zuverink,p	0	0	0	0
Brown,c	4	0	1	0	†Boyd	1	0	0	0
Martin,2b	3	1	1	1	Johnson,p	0	0	0	0
*Webster,2b	1	0	0	0	‡Nieman	1	1	1	0
Bell,p	3	0	0	0	Klaus,3b	5	0	2	4
Garcia,p	1	0	0	0	Carrasquel,ss	5	0	0	0
					Gardner,2b	4	1	1	0
Totals	40	11	13	11	Walker,p	1	1	1	0
					Portoc'rero,p	1	0	0	0
					Lockman,1b	1	1	0	0
					Totals	38	8	12	8

*Popped out for Martin in seventh.
†Flied out for Zuverink in seventh.
‡Doubled for Johnson in ninth.

INDIANS	312	013	001—11
ORIOLES	120	000	401— 8

PUTOUTS and ASSISTS: INDIANS 27-6, Orioles 27-9.
LEFT ON BASES: INDIANS 5, Orioles 8.
TWO-BASE HITS: Brown, Held, Francona, Klaus, Nieman.
HOME RUNS: Minoso, Martin, Colavito 4.
STOLEN BASE: Minoso.
SACRIFICE FLY: Triandos.

PITCHING	IP	H	R	ER	BB	SO
Walker (L, 4-3)	2⅓	4	6	6	2	1
Portocarrero	3⅓	7	4	4	1	3
Zuverink	1⅓	0	0	0	0	0
Johnson	2	2	1	1	0	0
Bell (W, 5-5)	6⅓	8	7	7	4	3
Garcia	2⅔	3	1	1	0	3

UMPIRES: Summers, McKinley, Chylak, Soar.
TIME: 2:54.
ATTENDANCE: 15,833.

THUNDER BOLT is what they call terrible-tempered Tommy Bolt, who is the defending champion in the U. S. Open which starts today at Winged Foot, Mamaroneck, N. Y. Here Bolt seems about to break one of his clubs. Actually, he is limbering up, preparing to get started. (UPI Photo)

U. S. Open Cry: "Watch Hogan"

By JACK CLOWSER
Press Sports Writer

MAMARONECK, N. Y. — Watch out for "The Hawk."

For approximately 20 years, during the Ben Hogan era of golf, that phrase has been a familiar warning at major tournaments. As the 59th United States Open championship began here today, the cry was being raised again—apparently with good reason.

The circuit pros gave him his nickname long ago. Partly, it was because he seemed always to be hovering above the field, ready to make his killing swoop just when someone else was wrapping up a victory. Partly it was because Hogan's slit-like eyes looked keen as the bird of prey's.

Jay Hebert, who has played five complete tuneup rounds with Hogan here at Winged Foot, was strongly affirmative about it at dinner last night.

He's Consistent

"I've never seen Ben hitting so many great golf shots so consistently," said the handsome Louisiana circuit pro. "I'm telling you, he isn't hitting that 'inside-out' shot any more. Remember, though he won at Oakmont in '53, he almost lost control of half a dozen shots like that—a pronounced fade.

"Not any more. He's hitting everything right on the sweet spot. In fact, he sometimes gives indications of going back to his early days, when he had a slight hook.

"You know he got away from that, with the well-founded theory that the fade shot is easier to control. But now, he's gunning practically everything along the closeline," Hebert concluded.

I told Hogan about Hebert's observations. The tiny crinkles around "The Hawk's" eyes narrowed in his inimitable grin.

Not Worried

"I sure hope he's right," chuckled Hogan. "People have started to say I'm worrying about my record being broken on this course. But that idea doesn't bother me a bit. Of course, I'd like to break it myself, but I don't think the scoring will be quite that low."

Hogan's U. S. Open record is 276, at Los Angeles Riviera in 1948. That was the year before the auto accident that nearly cost Ben his life. Four times in all, this biggest of all golf championships has gone to him. There are thousands who, for sentiment's sake, would like to see the great master make it a record five times.

No one ever has done that, not even Bob Jones.

Coe Has 65

The idea that any of these 150 players can average four 69's for 276 is remote. But former U. S. Amateur Champion Charley Coe posted 33-32—65 yesterday, and Gene Littler carded 34-32—66. Those were the best of all practice rounds since Winged Foot was dropped to par 70 for the big one.

Minnie, Martin Join Swing Spree

By BEN FLIEGER, *Press Sports Writer*

BALTIMORE—This Oriole series continues to be an explosive one for the Indians.

Twenty-four hours after Joe Gordon blew up over another apathetic Tribe performance the team itself exploded last night to blast the Birds out of first place, 11-8.

Whether it was Gordon's produce-or-depart ultimatum or simply the law of averages that says men with bats in their fists must hit sooner or later, the Indians finally have statistical reason to believe their slump is over.

Thought It Was Over

Gordon, in a moment of premature elation following Sunday's split with New York, thought the end had come.

Camp followers weren't so easily convinced. Two of the seven runs in the opening victory were unearned, another was forced home by a bases-loaded walk and three more resulted from a homer by emergency substitute Tito Francona.

Last night was different. The 11 tallies, top Tribe total since May 16 when the Red Sox were belted, 12-6, came in an awesome way:

Six home runs (four by Colavito in one of baseball's greatest individual power shows), three doubles and 13 hits for 34 total bases.

Trade Bait Belts

It may be coincidence, too, that the biggest belters—Colavito and Minnie Minoso, who had a homer and two singles—were the main bait in recent trade talks by Frank Lane. Colavito, who homered himself off the market last night, was the key in a proposed seven-man swap with Boston.

Minoso still is being sought by Chicago's Bill Veeck, who had his emissary, Hank Greenberg, sitting with Lane through the victory.

Jim Landis of the White Sox and Carroll Hardy are believed to be new names in the bartering sessions.

Other Cleveland homer last night was by Billy Martin, who now has seven. A big total for the little man, who has done well in all ways recently.

Garcia Saves Bell

Doubles were by Woodie Held, Francona and Dick Brown.

The Indians picked an appropriate time to break loose with their bats since the Orioles scored far above their quota. Six Tribe runs in the first three innings got Gary Bell past a shaky start. But following four good middle innings Bell was charged with the last four Baltimore runs before Mike Garcia rescued him in the seventh.

Preppers Win Swim Honors

Lyman Narten of the University School placed in four events on the All-America Prep School swimming team.

The unbeaten U. S. team placed six swimmers on the honor squad. Besides Narten, they were John Woodworth, John AuWerter, Pete Hodges, Don Lintz and Pete Steck.

The Kind of Moments That Make Heroes (and Zeros)

—Herald-Express Photo by Cliff Brown

Wow! What a chance for pinch-hitter Carl Furillo to be the big hero again! It's the last half of the eighth inning. Sox leading, 1-0. Dodgers have the bases loaded. Only one out. Just a single or a long fly to the outfield would bring in the tying run, maybe also the winning run. But what does Furillo do? He pops out to Phillips. Zimmer also flied out.

Most Critical Catch Of the World Series

—Associated Press Wirephoto

Here's the sensational—and certainly most critical—catch of the World Series so far. White Sox Jim Rivera, running full speed, snares Charley Neal's long belt near the fence about 390 feet from home plate. If he had missed it, Dodgers on second third would have scored and probably won the game. Great catch ended the seventh inning.

—Herald-Express Photo

After the game, Jim Rivera shows how the ball plopped into his glove during series-saving catch in seventh inning. Note the black socks (arrow) which Chicagoans wore for the first time in a series since the 1919 scandal.

Hodges Barrels Into Third

—United Press International Telephoto

Gil Hodges comes barreling into third base in the fourth inning after socking triple to centerfield. Jim Landis's throw is accurate (arrow) but too late for Bubba Phillips to get Hodges. Gil never got home.

Double Play, But Winning Run Scores

—United Press International Telephoto

Nellie Fox scoots toward home as White Sox catcher Sherm Lollar hits a hot grounder down to Charley Neal in the fourth inning. Neal forced Landis at second and got Lollar at first, for a double play, but Fox's run won the game.

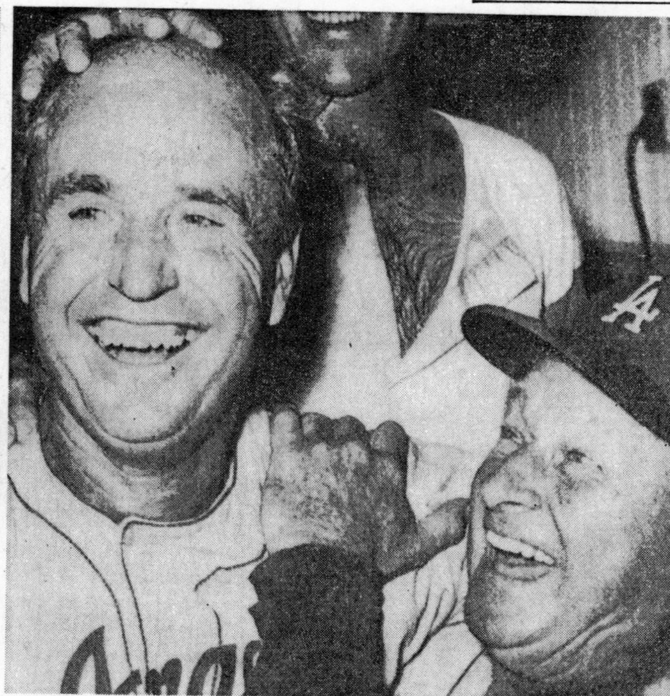

MOST HAPPY DODGERS — It was nothing but celebration for the Los Angeles Dodgers in Chicago Thursday after they had grabbed off their first World Baseball Championship. At left, Winning Pitcher Larry Sherry, who twice beat the White Sox, holds up the ball which was in play when he got Lou Aparicio to fly out to Wally Moon for the final out in the crucial series game. At right, is part of the wild celebration that took place in the Dodgers dressing room. Walt Alston, left, Dodger manager, and Coach Chuck Dressen whoop it up with the other Dodgers. Dressen was ejected from the game after a heated discussion with the umpires but had the last laugh as this photo shows. The man massaging Alston's pate was not identified. [AP Photofax.]

Bums Gay, Sox Sad In Dressing Rooms

CHICAGO [AP] — The Dodgers were happy and the Sox weren't sad.

That was the summation of the two dressing rooms Thursday after the Los Angeles Dodgers had defeated the Chicago White Sox 9-3 to take the 1959 World Series four games to two.

Dodger utility man Don Zimmer shouted "so the Coliseum got 'em" in reference to White Sox remarks of having to play in a makeshift park in Los Angeles.

But the White Sox weren't taking him up on it. For them, the long, tense season was over and they were looking for a rest.

White Sox and major league officials pushed their way into the Dodger dressing room to offer congratulations to Manager Walt Alston. And Alston was smiling from ear to ear.

"This victory seems bigger to me right now than the 1955 championship over New York in seven games," said Alston. "This was a better team effort. It was the hardest working team I've ever had. I can't single out any player as our key man. But I'll say I've never seen a kid so young so good as Larry Sherry."

Sherry, the 24-year-old relief ace, was swarmed under by well-wishers and newsmen. "I had good luck, they were swinging at my pitches, I just wanted to get the batters out," were Sherry's routine answers to routine questions.

Coach Chuck Dressen, who was ejected from the game in the fourth inning after a hassle with Umpire Ed Hurley, said:

"We beat those White Sox at their own game. We outran them, and Lord knows we sure outhit them. We were very satisfactory. We just played better."

After shaking off the effects of having lost, the White Sox settled down and went about their business of getting home for the winter.

Manager Al Lopez called the loss "one of those things. We lost the ones we should have won. This one we were never in. We had our chances in the series, but just didn't make it."

Team members went around shaking hands with each other and wishing each other "a good winter."

Meredith Leads SMU Against Missouri Tonight

By The Associated Press

Don Meredith, Southern Methodist's highly touted quarterback, is supposed to come into his own tonight when the Mustangs face Missouri at Dallas. The inter-sectional game kicks off a rip-roaring college football weekend.

Just why Southwest football observers feel that Meredith isn't up to his usual par is hard to understand. SMU has a 1-1 record, scoring five touchdowns. Meredith has been involved in four. He has thrown three touchdown passes and scored one on a short run.

Coach Dan Devine of Missouri isn't commenting on a Meredith "surge" for he has already felt the sting of Penn State's Richie Lucas, who completed 10 of 11 in handing the Tigers their only loss, 19-8.

Other top games tonight find West Virginia at Boston University, Detroit at Tulane and Oregon at San Jose State.

Saturday the fur flies — and in large gobs in Knoxville, Tenn., Lafayette, Ind., and back again in Dallas' Cotton Bowl.

Georgia Tech and Tennessee meet in Knoxville in a battle of defenses that promises to rock the Southeastern Conference. The winner can draw a bead on Louisiana State's SEC title, though only the Vols play LSU.

Ninth-ranked Wisconsin travels to Lafayette to meet Purdue [No. 7] to see if it can live up to its pick to be the Big Ten's champ and Rose Bowl Participant.

In Dallas Oklahoma comes to meet fourth-ranked Texas. Coach Bud Wilkinson's Sooners are 1-1 but on the upgrade following the disasterous 45-13 opening loss to Northwestern. The game is being televised regionally in the Southwest.

Top-ranked Louisiana State [3-0] plays Miami [Fla.], whose Hurricane's have emerged with a solid defense. Second - ranked Northwestern plays Minnesota, with the Wildcats also eyeing a Big Ten title after beating Iowa last week.

Fifth-ranked Mississippi pits its 3-0 record against SEC neighbor Vanderbilt, a two-touchdown underdog. The other member of the Associated Press' top ten in action is tenth-ranked Iowa, who plays Michigan State in a game that is regionally televised in the Big Ten area.

The season's first bowl game—the Oyster Bowl, at Norfolk, Va.—pits power - packed Syracuse, with its second - ranked [415.5 yards per game] offense and top-rated defense [48.0] against Navy, who will get only limited service from top ground-gainer Joe Bellino.

Penn travels to Princeton for a good shot at the Ivy League title and Penn State matches passes with Army at West Point in the East's top games. Florida State is at Virginia Tech for the South's regionally televised game.

Lanier Poets Polish Defense

Coach Cotton Harrison and his Lanier Senior High School Poets, finding themselves with a weekend off, continued today to prepare for next week's outing.

Their opponent then, on Oct. 17 at Porter Stadium, will be the Red Jackets of Jordan High of Columbus.

Despite the fact that the Poets will sit this week out, Harrison and his assistants have had their young charges scrimmaging and working out every day.

Harrison said he is putting his emphasis on defense at present and that he and his coaching staff have been trying out several new men in the defensive set-up.

Included among the defensive newcomers getting try-outs are Buddy Chase, as a line-backer, Bari Vickers and Bert Maxwell, defensive sidebacks; and Johnny McArthur, defensive end.

Harrison said he was pleased with the Lanier drills Thursday, following an early-week letdown Monday and Tuesday.

Sgt. Thomas Wins Horseshoe Honors

ROBINS AIR FORCE BASE — Throwing ringers with about the same consistency that he rolls strikes on the bowling alleys, Sgt. Eric Thomas made a clean sweep of the Robins Air Force Base horseshoe pitching honors by winning the singles and sharing the doubles crown.

The top average bowler on the base last year, Thomas routed A-1C Joe Leverett for the solo crown, and then helped Sgt. Don Spears to outlast the 14th AF team of Bob Leichliter and Frank Moore to win the doubles.

The veteran 1926th AACS athlete got off to a slow start in the singles but came back strong to win the four straight games from the SEAACS hopeful.

Pro Cage Scores

By The Associated Press

Philadelphia 122, St. Louis 104.
Boston 123, Minneapolis 97.
Cincinnati 118, Detroit 90.

Series Victory Was Alston's Top Triumph

CHICAGO [AP] — You could never tell it by the calm manner in which he was accepting congratulations and by the serious, almost solemn look on his round face that the happiest man in the Dodgers' dressing room was Walter Alston.

The Dodgers' World Series success, capping their pennant victory, was in many ways a personal triumph for this kindly, good-natured, shy, Ohioan who, after six seasons of big league managing, finally has convinced his hard-bitten critics that he is highly capable leader.

"From a personal standpoint, this would have to be my greatest triumph, at least the most satisfying," he said slowly, choosing every word. "Winning the World Series with the Dodgers back in 1955 gave me a big thrill. At the time it was the greatest. After all, it was only my second year of managing, and it was the first world championship ever won by Brooklyn.

"But the Dodgers of '55 were a great team. They were, more or less, expected to win. We won 20 of our first 22 games and won the pennant by some 13½ games. I don't want to take anything away from either of the teams but I think this team has given me a greater kick.

"After all, it wasn't expected to win. It started off slowly and gradually got better. This was a team job, pure and simple."

Alston's six year reign with the Dodgers, except for one year, has been a highly successful but not necessarily a happy one. Each year, it seems, rumors persisted that he was on the verge of being replaced as manager—first by Leo Durocher, then by Charlie Dressen and finally, by Pee Wee Reese.

True or not, Alston went about his work quietly rebuilding a team that had finished seventh into a pennant contender.

Veeck Sights In On Next Season

CHICAGO [AP] — The phone rang in the Comiskey Park club room shortly after the Dodgers had rapped the White Sox 9-3 to take the World Series.

Owner Bill Veeck of the Sox answered.

After a pause, Veeck exclaimed: "YOU lost a lot of money on this game? What about me?

"Who am I? I'm Veeck and nobody wanted to see a seventh game more than me.

"No, don't be sorry. Now we got something to shoot for next year."

And so it went.

"I think Al Lopez did the best job of managing I've ever seen," said sport-shirt Bill. "We went a lot further than I thought we could this season.

"We simply hit disaster in the series. We were beat. They just belted us out for the count in the last game.

"I think we can beat any team in baseball, if we can keep the ball in the park. But they were hitting it over our outfielders' heads."

Veeck said he anticipated a lively trading season because of the new rule that eliminates waivers for a three-week period in November. This means a club in one league can deal directly with a club in another league.

"We're not going to stand still," he said. "We hope to trade as much as we can."

Manager Lopez, recently signed to boss the Sox again in 1960 for between $50,000 and $60,000, seemed more intent on congratulating the umpires and Dodger Manager Walt Alston than trying to alibi to writers.

CHISOX FALL 9-3 IN SIXTH GAME

Los Angeles Dodgers Win Series To Capture World Championship

CHICAGO [AP]—The Los Angeles Dodgers are the world champions of baseball today.

They beat the Chicago White Sox 9-3 Thursday in the sixth game of the World Series — and they did it in Chicago's Comiskey Park.

The Dodgers' victory, behind right-hander Larry Sherry, smashed the hopes of the White Sox, which had soared when the Chicago team scored a 1-0 come-back triumph Tuesday in the Los Angeles Coliseum, returning the Series to their home ground.

The Dodgers got rid of the best in the way of pitching the Sox had to offer, chasing burly Early Wynn early and sending Dick Donovan off in close pursuit.

It was only the second world championship in 10 tries for the Dodgers, their first since shifting to Los Angeles from Brooklyn two years ago.

Both championship teams have been managed by Walt Alston, who has led the Dodgers to three pennants in his six years.

This could be the richest of all series when the record $892,365.04 player pool is split up. A full winner's share should be worth at least $10,000 a man to the Dodgers possibly $11,000. The Sox should get from $7,000 to $7,500 each, which would be a record for a losing share.

Whether the Dodgers will top the record $11,147.90 pocketed by each of the New York Giants in 1954 depends on the number of shares they vote among themselves. The number of winning and losing shares won't be released until next week by Commissioner Ford Frick.

This Dodger victory, making them the first ever to rocket from seventh place one year to the world championship the next, is the National League's fourth in six years over the American. The AL still leads in the over-all standings, however, 35-21.

The Dodgers, whose two defeats were shutouts, started rumbling against Wynn in the third in the finale when Duke Snider sent a 400-foot home run into the lower left-center-field seats with a man on.

Wynn, the first game winner at 11-0, got as far as the fourth inning in his third start of the series. The big right-hander showed quick signs of wildness. He gave way when Dodger southpaw Johnny Podres walloped an RBI double to center.

That brought in right - hander Donovan, whose brilliant relief performance in Los Angeles had saved the fifth game for the Sox. This time, he gave up a walk to Junior Gilliam, a two-run double by Charlie Neal and a two-run homer by Wally Moon.

That made it a six-run inning, the Dodgers' largest ever in a series, and led to a string of six Sox pitchers. No. 5 was Billy Pierce, the experienced little southpaw.

There is no doubting the big man of the series. At 24, Sherry proved a cool, careful right-handed reliever. He was in on each of the Dodgers' four victories.

The 6-2, 200-pounder, the same kid who won the opening game of the National League pennant playoff for the Dodgers, put down what was left of White Sox hopes after the big Los Angeles fourth. Over 5 2-3 innings he hurled four-hit, shutout ball for his second victory.

Sherry saved the second game, won by Podres 4-3 at Comiskey Park, and the third game, won by Don Drysdale 3-1 in the Coliseum opener. Then he won the fourth game, 5-4 in relief at the Coliseum.

In all, he worked 12 2-3 innings in the four games, giving up eight hits and just one run while walking but two and striking out five in the series — first ever without a complete game pitcher on either club.

The Sox, a tight defensive club that made the most of its opportunities to win its first pennant in 40 years, were unsettled by the Coliseum, where the white-shirted, three-game crowd of 277,550 provided a poor background for fielders and hitters alike.

But Manager Al Lopez figured the best way to say what beat his Sox was "Sherry and Neal. They were the difference."

Neal, the thin thumper who plays second base, led both clubs with 10 hits and batted .370. He won the second game with two home runs.

LOS ANGELES	AB	R	H	BI	O	A
Gilliam 3b	4	1	0	0	0	2
Neal 2b	5	1	3	2	4	4
Moon lf	4	2	1	2	3	0
Snider cf-rf	3	1	1	2	2	0
eEssegian	1	1	1	1	0	0
Fairly rf	0	0	0	0	0	0
Hodges 1b	5	0	1	0	10	0
Larker rf	1	0	1	0	0	0
aDemeter cf	3	1	1	0	4	0
Roseboro c	4	0	0	0	2	0
Wills ss	4	1	1	1	2	3
Podres p	2	1	1	1	0	1
Sherry p	2	0	2	0	0	2
Totals	38	9	13	9	27	12

CHICAGO	Ab	R	H	Bi	O	A
Aparicio, ss	5	0	1	0	1	2
Fox, 2b	4	0	1	0	2	2
Landis, cf	3	1	1	0	2	0
Lollah, c	3	1	0	0	5	2
Kluszewski, 1b	4	1	2	3	10	0
Smith, lf	2	0	0	0	2	0
Phillips, eb-rf	4	0	1	0	3	1
McAnany, rf	1	0	0	0	1	0
bGoldman, 3b	3	0	0	0	0	1
Wynn, p	1	0	0	0	0	1
Donovan, p	0	0	0	0	0	0
Lown, p	0	0	0	0	0	0
cTorgeson	0	0	0	0	0	0
Staley, p	0	0	0	0	1	0
dRomano	1	0	0	0	0	0
Pierce, p	0	0	0	0	0	0
Moore, p	0	0	0	0	0	0
fCash	1	0	0	0	0	0
TOTALS	32	3	6	3	27	9

a—Ran for Larker in 4th.
b—Struck out for McAnany in 4th.
c—Walked for Lown in 4th.
d—Grounded out for Staley in 7th.
e—Homered for Snider in 9th.
f—Flied out for Moore in 9th.

Los Angeles	002	600	001—9
Chicago	000	300	000—3

E—Aparicio. DP—Podres, Neal and Hodges. LOB—Los Angeles [7], Chicago [7]. 2B—Podres, Neal, Fox, Kluszewski. HR—Snider, Moon, Kluszewski, Essegian. S—Roeboro.

	IP	H	R	ER
Wynn [L]	3⅓	5	5	5
x-Donovan	0	2	3	3
Lown	⅔	1	0	0
Staley	3	2	0	0
Pierce	1	2	0	0
Moore	1	1	1	1
Podre	3⅔	2	3	3
Sherry [W]	3⅓	4	0	0

x—Faced 3 batters in 4th.

BB—Wynn 3, Snider, Larker, Moon, Donovan 1, Gilliam, Podres 3, Smith 2, Lollar, Sherry 1, Torgeson. S—Wynn 2, Gilliam, Neal, Pierce 1, Moon, Moore 1, Demeter, Podres 1, Wynn, Sherry 1, Goodman. HBP-By Podres, Landis. U—Dascoli [N] plate, Hurley [A], first base, Secory [N], second base, Summers [A], third base, Rice [A], left field, Dixon, [N], right field. T—2:33. A—47,653.

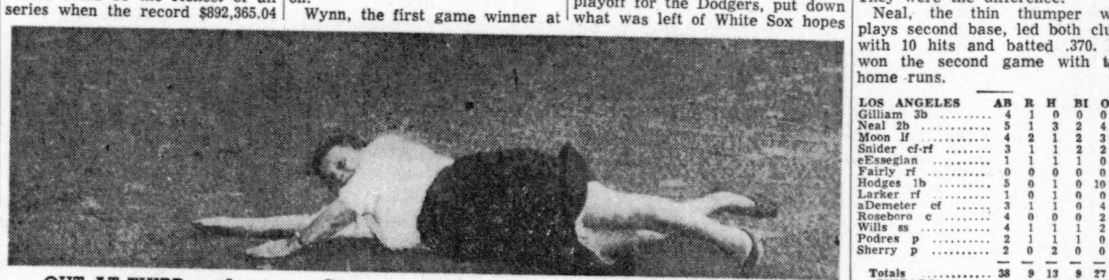

OUT AT THIRD — Antoinette Green provided amusement for early World Series fans with an unscheduled base-running performance at Comiskey Park Thursday. Here she slides wide of third base in a headfirst try. Police officers made the final out of the performance as they escorted the fun-loving White Sox fan off the field. Oh, yes. The White Sox came on the field shortly thereafter and were downed by the Los Angeles Dodgers, 9-3. [AP Photofax.]

Final Facts and Figures for Series

By The Associated Press

	W.	L.	Pct.
Los Angeles [NL]	4	2	.667
Chicago [AL]	2	4	.333

First Game at Chicago, Oct. 1

Los Angeles	000 000 000— 0	8 3
Chicago	207 200 00x—11	11 0

Craig, Churn [3], Labine [4], Koufax [5], Klippstein [7] and Roseboro; Wynn, Staley [8] and Lollar. W—Wynn. L—Craig.

Home runs—Chicago, Kluszewski 2.

Second Game at Chicago, Lct. 2

Los Angeles	000 010 300—4	9 1
Chicago	200 000 010—3	8 0

Podres, Sherry [7] and Roseboro; Shaw, Lown [7] and Lollar. W—Podres. L—Shaw.

Home runs—Los Angeles, Neal 2, Essegian.

Third Game at Los Angeles, Oct. 4

Chicago	000 000 010—1	12 0
Los Angeles	000 000 21x—3	5 0

Donovan, Staley [7] and Lollar; Drysdale, Sherry [8] and Roseboro. W—Drysdale. L—Donovan.

Fourth Game at Los Angeles, Oct. 5

Chicago	000 000 400—4	10 3
Los Angeles	004 000 01x—5	9 0

Wynn, Lown [3], Pierce [4], Staley [7] and Lollar; Craig, Sherry [8] and Roseboro. W—Sherry. L—Staley.

Home runs — Chicago, Lollar. Los Angeles, Hodges.

Fifth Game at Los Angeles, Oct. 6

Chicago	000 100 000—1	5 0
Los Angeles	000 000 000—0	9 0

Shaw, Pierce [8], Donovan [8] and Lollar; Koufax, Williams [8] and Roseboro, Pignatano [8]. W—Shaw. L—Koufax.

Sixth Game at Chicago, Oct. 8

Los Angeles	002 600 001—9	13 0
Chicago	000 300 000—3	6 1

Podres, Sherry [4] and Roseboro; Wynn, Donovan [4], Lown [4], Staley [5], Pierce [8], Moore [9] and Lollar. W—Sherry. L — Wynn.

Home runs—Los Angeles, Snider, Moon, Essegian. Chicago, Kluszewski.

Financial Figures
Sixth Game

Attendance—47,653
Total receipts—$324,463.32
Commissioner's share — $48,669.50
National League share — $68,948.45
American League share — $68,948.45
Los Angeles club's share—$68,948.46
Chicago club's share—$68,948.46

Six-Game Final Totals

Attendance—420,784
Total receipts—$2,626,973.44
Commissioner's share — $394,046.00
Player's share—$892,365.04
National League share — $335,140.59
American League share—$335,140.58
Los Angeles club's share—$335,140.61
Chicago Club's share — $335,140.62

Virus Strikes Miami Gridders

MIAMI [UPI] — Intestinal virus has struck 19 players of the University of Miami football team which will play Louisiana State Saturday night at Baton Rouge, it was revealed today.

"What a break," moaned Coach Andy Gustafson. "It' not enough that we're playing the number one team of the nation Saturday—but almost half of the squad has to get sick."

Gustafson had to call off a full scale practice Thursday. His team worked out in shorts.

Trainer Dave Wike declined to name all of the players affected, but said halfbacks Mike Harrison, Ron Fritzche, Jim Bruno and John Ellis, guard Joe Stanley, and tackle Vic Savoca had been sick.

Savoca, a 225-pound sophomore starter, missed Thursday's drill.

"Except for Savoca none are very sick right now," Wike said, "but they're still weak and uncomfortable."

College Grid Scores

By The Associated Press

Youngstown 6, Baldwin Wallace 0.

St. Thomas [Minn.] 37, Augusburg 0.

Milton Gross
On Page 77

New York Post Sports

Pigskin Prophet
On Page 71

 NEW YORK, THURSDAY, OCTOBER 13, 1960

Pirates Take It All On Mazeroski's HR

By IKE GELLIS
New York Post Sports Editor

Forbes Field, Pittsburgh, Oct. 13—The Pirates came from behind here today to beat the Yankees and bring Pittsburgh its first world championship in 35 years.

The score was 10-9.

Law set the Yankees down without difficulty in the first inning. Richardson lined to Groat. Kubek popped to Mazeroski and Maris fouled to Hoak.

Nelson, starting the game in place of Stuart, made his manager look like a genius with a two-run homer in the first. Turley got past the first two Pirate hitters without damage as Virdon flied to Berra and Groat popped to Kubek. But then Skinner walked and Nelson sent a smash into the right field stands. It was only the Pirates' second home run of the Series. Clemente popped to Richardson to end the frame.

The Yankees went down quietly again in the second. Mantle flied to Virdon. Hoak made a diving stop of Berra's smash and threw him out. Skowron grounded to short.

Burgess opened the Pirates' second inning with a single to right. Stengel didn't wait. He came out to the mound and signaled for Stafford to come in. Stafford walked Hoak. Mazeroski bunted down the third base line and when Stafford's throw to first was too late the bases were loaded with nobody out. Then Stafford took Law's high bouncer and threw to Blanchard to begin a pitcher-to-catcher-to-first double play. But Virdon singled to right to score Hoak and Mazeroski. Groat then grounded to Boyer to end the inning.

In the third inning Law made a nice backhand grab of Blanchard's bouncer and threw him out. Boyer popped to Mazeroski but Lopez batted for Stafford and got the Yankees' first hit of the game, a single to left. But Richardson flied gently to Skinner.

Schantz came in to pitch the third for the Yankees and got the Pirates out without damage in the inning. Skinner grounded out. Nelson walked but Clemente hit into a double play. Richardson to Kubek to Skowron.

Law continued to hold off the Yankees in the fourth. Kubek popped to short. Maris flied to Clemente. Mantle singled to right for the Yanks' second hit but Berra flied to Clemente.

In the bottom half Schantz set the Pirates down in order for the first time. Richardson threw out Burgess and Hoak and Kubek took Mazeroski's pop.

Skowron Homers

Skowron opened the fifth inning with a home run into the right field stands, his second of the Series. But Blanchard flied to Virdon, Boyer lined to Mazeroski and Schantz popped to Nelson.

Schantz stopped the Bucs again in the fifth. Law grounded out to Boyer. Virdon grounded to Richardson and Groat lined back to the box.

Law finally ran into trouble in the sixth. He gave up a single to Richardson to open the inning and then walked Kubek.

YOGI BERRA

Face was brought in from the bullpen. He got Maris on a foul pop to Hoak but Mantle singled through the middle to score Richardson. Berra then belted a three-run homer into the right field stands to put the Yankees ahead for the first time in the game. Skowron fouled to Hoak. Blanchard grounded to Nelson.

Shantz Stops Bucs

In the Pirate half Skinner flied to Mantle, Nelson grounded to Skowron and Clemente grounded to Shantz.

In the seventh Boyer flied to Virdon. Shantz singled and was forced at second on Richardson's grounder to Hoak. Kubek lined to Clemente.

Burgess opened the Pirate seventh with a single. But Hoak lined to Berra and Mazeroski hit into a double play, Kubek to Richardson to Skowron.

With two out in the eighth the Yankees added two more runs. Berra walked and Skowron got an infield single. Blanchard singled to right scoring Berra and Boyer followed with a double, scoring Skowron.

SEVENTH GAME

YANKEES..000 014 022–9 13 1
PIRATES...220 000 051–10 11 0

Turley, Stafford (2), Shantz (3), Coates (8), Terry (8) & Blanchard; Law, Face (6), Friend (9), Haddix (9) & Burgess, Smith (8).

YANKEES	AB	R	H	2B	3B	HR	RBI	PO	A	E
Richardson, 2b	5	2	2	0	0	0	0	2	5	0
Kubek, ss	3	1	0	0	0	0	0	3	2	0
DeMaestri, ss	0	0	0	0	0	0	0	0	0	0
Maris, rf	5	0	0	0	0	0	0	2	0	1
Mantle, cf	5	1	3	0	0	0	2	0	0	0
Berra, lf	4	2	1	0	0	1	4	3	0	0
Skowron, 1b	5	2	2	0	0	1	1	10	2	0
Blanchard, c	4	0	1	0	0	0	1	1	1	0
Boyer, 3b, ss	4	0	1	1	0	0	1	0	3	0
Turley, p	0	0	0	0	0	0	0	0	0	0
Stafford, p	0	0	0	0	0	0	0	0	1	0
Shantz, p	3	0	1	0	0	0	0	3	1	0
Coates, p	0	0	0	0	0	0	0	0	0	0
Terry, p	0	0	0	0	0	0	0	0	0	0
Lopez	1	0	1	0	0	0	0	0	0	0
Long	1	0	1	0	0	0	0	0	0	0
McDougald, 3b	0	1	0	0	0	0	0	0	0	0
Totals	40	9	13	1	0	2	9	*24	15	1

*None out when winning run was scored.

PIRATES	AB	R	H	2B	3B	HR	RBI	PO	A	E
Virdon, cf	4	1	2	0	0	0	2	3	0	0
Groat, ss	4	1	1	0	0	0	1	3	2	0
Skinner, lf	2	1	0	0	0	0	0	1	0	0
Nelson, 1b	3	1	1	0	0	1	2	7	0	0
Clemente, rf	4	1	1	0	0	0	1	4	0	0
Burgess, c	3	0	2	0	0	0	0	0	0	0
Smith, c	1	1	1	0	0	1	3	1	0	0
Hoak, 3b	3	1	0	0	0	0	0	3	2	0
Mazeroski, 2b	4	2	2	0	0	1	1	5	0	0
Law, p	2	0	0	0	0	0	0	0	1	0
Face, p	0	0	0	0	0	0	0	0	1	0
Friend, p	0	0	0	0	0	0	0	0	0	0
Haddix, p	0	0	0	0	0	0	0	0	0	0
Christopher	0	0	0	0	0	0	0	0	0	0
Cimoli	1	1	1	0	0	0	0	0	0	0
Totals	31	10	11	0	0	3	10	27	6	0

Lopez singled for Stafford in 3d. Christopher ran for Burgess in 7th.

7-Inning Summary

Left on Bases—Yankees 3, Pirates 1.

Base on Balls—Off Turley 1, Stafford 1, Shantz 1, Law 1.

Double Plays—Stafford-Blanchard-Skowron; Richardson-Kubek-Skowron; Kubek-Richardson-Skowron.

Hits—Off Turley 2, Stafford 2, Shantz 1, Law 4, Face 3.

More About Yogi

Pittsburgh, Oct. 13 (AP)—Manager Danny Murtaugh of Pittsburgh and catcher Yogi Berra of New York sat on the Pirates' bench before yesterday's sixth World Series game chatting on things in general.

Up walked Frank Slocum, an aide to Baseball Commissioner Ford Frick. "Want to hear a good story about Yogi?" he asked Murtaugh.

"Sure," said Murtaugh.

So Slocum continued:

"During World War II, Yogi walked into the Yankees' dressing room wearing a sailor's uniform.

" 'Who's that?' inquired one of the Yankees.

"That's Yogi Berra. He's a catcher in our farm system," said one Yankee.

"Hell," replied another. "He doesn't even look like a sailor."

Belmont Park Results

FIRST—7 furlongs; off 1:30:

Bireme (Solomone)	9.00	4.10	3.00
Scarlet Slipper (Ycaza)		4.80	3.30
B. Hunt (Valenzuela)			7.00

SCRATCHED—Some Tune, Battle Empress, Frank's Lass, Matins, Miss Murlogg, Sabena II.

SECOND—7 furlongs; off 2:00:

Slight Error (Broussard)	18.10	9.80	6.60
Heliotide (Holborn)		4.50	3.10
Lady Salonga (Yother)			4.10

SCRATCHED—Sunny Gem, Bebby's Beau, Breeze Home, Don't Miss Nuthin, Letmeatum, Scope.

DAILY DOUBLE (4 & 2) PAID $183.70.

THIRD—1⅞ miles; off 2:30:

Greek Brother (McDonald)	9.70	4.00	2.80
Nizam's Pet (Smithwick)		2.90	2.20
Cool Warrior (Deveau)			3.10

WINNER SELECTED BY TRACKMAN

Garden State Results

By the Associated Press

FIRST—6 furlongs; off 1:36:

Trojan Khan (Blum)	9.60	4.20	3.20
Overton Miss (Corle)		3.00	2.60
Blue Noble (Choquette)			5.00

SECOND—1 3-16 miles; off 2:07½:

Double Flight II (Cutshaw)	20.00	8.20	6.20
Mon Key Do (Monacelli)		4.60	3.80
Eto General (Corle)			6.40

Daily Double paid $125.60.

Narragansetts Results

By the Associated Press

FIRST—6 furlongs; off 1:42:

Solar Heat (Bradley)	10.20	3.20	2.60
Miss Sheila (Sorensen)		2,80	2.20
Jeddah Chant (Manganello)			2.60

SECOND—6 furlongs; off 2:09:

Hillinvari (Skuse)	4.40	2.80	2.60
Dizzy Gamble (Spinale)		3.20	2.80
Lucky Chucky (Manganello)			4.80

Daily double paid $25.00.

THIRD—6 furlongs; off 2:38:

Fraganza (Landers)	58.80	13.80	5.00
Rock Road (DeSpirito)		4.00	2.80
Mack's Star (Sorensen)			3.60

Today's Homers

Berra, Yankees, two on.
Skowron, Yankees, none on.
Nelson, Pirates, one on.
Smith, Pirates, two on

The Pittsburgh Press

VOL. 77, No. 113 | THURSDAY, OCTOBER 13, 1960 | WEATHER—Warm. | 76 Pages—5 Cents

WORLD SERIES FINAL

PIRATES WORLD CHAMPS

Final Game Box

NEW YORK

	AB	R	H	RBI
RICHARDSON, 2b	5	2	2	0
KUBEK, ss	3	1	0	0
DeMAESTRI, ss	0	0	0	0
LONG	1	0	1	0
McDOUGALD	0	1	0	0
MARIS, rf	5	0	0	0
MANTLE, cf	5	1	3	2
BERRA, lf	4	2	1	4
SKOWRON, 1b	5	2	2	1
BLANCHARD, c	4	0	1	1
BOYER, 3b	4	0	1	1
TURLEY, p	0	0	0	0
STAFFORD, p	0	0	0	0
LOPEZ	1	0	1	0
SHANTZ, p	3	0	1	0
COATES, p	0	0	0	0
TERRY, p	0	0	0	0
TOTALS	40	9	13	9

PITTSBURGH

	AB	R	H	RBI
VIRDON, cf	4	1	2	2
GROAT, ss	4	1	1	1
SKINNER, lf	2	1	0	0
NELSON, 1b	3	1	1	2
CLEMENTE, rf	4	1	1	1
BURGESS, c	3	0	2	0
CHRISTOPHER	0	0	0	0
SMITH, c	1	1	1	3
HOAK, 3b	3	1	0	0
MAZEROSKI, 2b	4	2	2	1
LAW, p	2	0	0	0
FACE, p	0	0	0	0
CIMOLI	1	1	1	0
FRIEND, p	0	0	0	0
HADDIX, p	0	0	0	0
TOTALS	31	10	11	10

Score By Innings

YANKEES	000	014	022	9
PIRATES	220	000	051	10

Pitching

	IP	H	R	ER	BB	SO
TURLEY	1	2	2	2	1	0
STAFFORD	1	2	2	2	1	0
SHANTZ	5	4	3	3	1	0
COATES	⅔	2	2	2	0	0
TERRY	⅓	1	1	1	0	0
LAW	5	4	3	3	1	0
FACE	3	6	4	4	1	0
FRIEND, p	0	2	2	2	0	0
HADDIX	1	1	0	0	0	0

Turley faced one batter in 2nd.
Law faced two batters in 6th.
Shantz faced three batters in 8th.
Friend faced two batters in 9th.
Lopez singled for Stafford in 3rd.
Christopher ran for Burgess in 7th.
Cimoli singled for Face in 8th.
Long singled for DeMaestri in the 9th.
McDougald ran for Long in 9th.

E—Maris.

DP—Stafford to Blanchard to Skowron; Richardson to Kubek to Skowron; Kubek to Richardson to Skowron.

LOB—New York 6; Pittsburgh 1.

2B—Boyer.

HR—Nelson, Skowron, Berra, Smith, Mazeroski.

S—Skinner.

A—36,683.

U—Plate, Jackowski (NL); first base, Chylak (AL); second base, Boggess (NL); third base, Stevens (AL); foul lines, Landes (NL) and Honochick (AL).

Press Backs Nixon-Lodge

The Press today endorses Richard M. Nixon and his running mate, Henry Cabot Lodge, as the team to lead the United States in the '60s.

The Press explains its reasons for the selection of Mr. Nixon as the most qualified man to cope with the threat of war, the march of communism and the domestic problems of the nation in an editorial, "Our Choice For President," on—

PAGE 24

Bucs' Rocky Nelson runs into dugout after blasting two-run, first-inning home run.

Cops Don't Kid With Truants

Roundup Time At Forbes Field

City police were ordered today to round up all school-age youngsters who mingle with the World Series crowd in Oakland, and check them for truancy.

"Too many kids have been playing hooky around here," grumbled Inspector Vincent Dixon, in charge of the Series detail at Forbes Field.

He instructed his men to run all urchins into Oakland stations, where principals will be telephoned. If the students are AWOL, they will be returned to school or to their homes—whichever is more convenient.

* * *

Heartened by yesterday's largest World Series attendance, Oakland parking lots had jacked their rates up by $1 today, their last chance for a killing before the fanfare folds.

* * *

Police said they expect dancing in the streets in Oakland if the Pirates win—so two special 100-man details have been assigned to "guard" the celebration.

Officials said street demonstrations will be permitted if the Pirates manage to pull the Series out of the fire.

Confused? So's Frick

Baseball Commissioner Ford Frick is just as mystified by this topsy-turvy World Series as the most devoted Pirate fan.

"I can't recall a Series so confusing to the fans," Mr. Frick said today before the start of the final and decisive game at Forbes Field.

"When the Yanks hit—look out. But when they don't, they can be taken," he observed.

On Inside Pages

Press Telephones

Want-Ads —COurt 1-4900
Other Depts.—COurt 1-7200

Play-By-Play Detail Of 7th Series Game

Following is a play-by-play description of the seventh game of the World Series between the Pirates and Yankees today at Forbes Field:

FIRST INNING

YANKEES—Richardson lined to Groat. Kubek popped to Mazeroski on the edge of the right-field grass. Maris fouled to Hoak between third and the plate.

PIRATES—Virdon flied to Berra in deep left-center. Groat popped to Kubek in short left. Skinner walked on a 3-2 pitch. Nelson lined a 2-1 pitch over the screen into the lower deck in right field for a home run, Skinner scoring ahead of him. Clemente popped to Richardson in short right. Two runs. One hit.

SECOND INNING

YANKEES—Mantle lined to Virdon in deep right-center. Hoak dove to grab Berra's shot into the hole at short and, scrambling to his knees, threw him out. Groat threw out Skowron on a bounder to short.

PIRATES—Burgess lined a single down the right-field line. Stafford replaced Turley on the mound for New York. Hoak walked on four pitches. Mazeroski bunted along the third-base line and beat Stafford's throw to Richardson, covering first, for a hit, loading the bases. Stengel went to the mound to talk to Stafford, but made no change. Law tapped back to the mound and the Yankees turned it into a double play, Stafford to Blanchard to Skowron. Virdon lined a single to right-center, driving in Hoak and Mazeroski, and when Maris bobbled the ball, Virdon raced to second. Boyer threw out Groat. Two runs. Three hits. One error. One left.

THIRD INNING

YANKEES—Law leaped for Blanchard's high bounder and threw him out. Boyer flied to Mazeroski in short center. Lopez batted for Stafford and lined a single between Hoak and Groat, the Yankees' first hit. Richardson flied to Skinner. One hit. One left.

PIRATES—Shantz was the new Yankee pitcher. Skinner grounded out, Skowron to Shantz, covering first. Nelson walked. Clemente hit into a double play, Richardson to Kubek to Skowron.

FOURTH INNING

YANKEES—Kubek popped to Groat. Maris lined deep to Clemente. Mantle tapped a single into right field. Clemente made a running one-handed catch of Berra's line drive down the right-field line. One hit. One left.

PIRATES—Burgess grounded out, Richardson to Skowron. Richardson also threw out Hoak. Kubek took Mazeroski's fly in short left.

FIFTH INNING

YANKEES—Skowron hit a towering shot to the opposite field over the screen into the lower deck in right for a home run, his second of the Series. Blanchard flied to Virdon in shallow center. Face began to warm up for the Pirates. Boyer lined to Mazeroski. Nelson moved in and took Shantz' pop-up in front of the mound. One run. One hit.

PIRATES—Law, after drilling a shot barely foul as it left the park in left, grounded out, Boyer to Skowron. Richardson threw out Virdon. Groat lined to Shantz.

SIXTH INNING

YANKEES — Richardson dropped a line single into center. Face and Haddix loosened up in the Pirate bullpen. Kubek worked the count to 3-2 and then walked. Murtaugh went to the mound, talked to Law, then called for Face. The crowd gave Law a standing ovation as he departed. Maris fouled out to Hoak behind third. Mantle, hitting the first pitch, rapped a single up the middle, scoring Richardson and chasing Kubek to third. Berra lifted a long, high blast down the right-field line and into the stands for his first homer of the Series, scoring Kubek and Mantle ahead of him. Skowron fouled to Hoak. Blanchard grounded out to Nelson. Four runs. Three hits.

PIRATES—Skinner flied to Maris. Nelson grounded out, Skowron to Shantz, covering first. Terry and Coates warmed up in the Yankee bullpen. Shantz fielded Clemente's dribbler and threw him out.

SEVENTH INNING

YANKEES—Virdon raced into left-center to take Boyer's fly. Shantz bounced a single over Hoak's head into left field. Richardson bounced to Hoak, who fired to Mazeroski, forcing Shantz. Kubek lined to Clemente. One hit. One left.

PIRATES — Burgess drilled a single through the box into center. Christopher ran for Burgess. Terry and Coates began to throw hard in the Yankee bullpen. Hoak took three balls, a called strike, bunted foul and lined to Berra down the left-field line. Mazeroski bounced into a double play, Kubek to Richardson to Skowron. One hit.

EIGHTH INNING

YANKEES—Smith went behind the plate for the Pirates. Face grabbed Maris' grounder near the mound and threw him out. Groat leaped and nailed Mantle's liner. Berra walked. Hoak, after waiting for Skowron's high bounder to come down, threw to second too late to force Berra. It was ruled an infield hit. Blanchard looped a single into right, driving in Berra and sending Skowron to third. Boyer lined the first pitch for a double into the left-field corner, scoring Skowron with Blanchard stopping at third. Shantz, with the count 3-2, flied to Clemente. Two runs. Three hits. Two left.

PIRATES—Cimoli batted for Face and, with the count 2-2, dropped a single in front of Maris in right. Virdon's hard grounder took a bad hop and struck Kubek in the neck. Cimoli was safe at second and Virdon reached first on the hit. The ball knocked down the Yankee shortstop and he left the game, being replaced by DeMaestri. Groat shot a single through the hole into left, scoring Cimoli with Virdon stopping at second. Stengel lifted Shantz, bringing in Coates. Skinner placed a perfect sacrifice bunt down the third-base line, Boyer throwing him out at first as both runners advanced. Nelson flied to Maris in medium right, Virdon bluffing a run to the plate then retreating. Clemente, with two strikes on him, hit a dribbler toward Skowron and beat the play to first for a hit, Virdon scoring and Groat taking third. With the count 2-2, Smith drove Coates' pitch over the 406-foot mark in left-center into Schenley Park for a home run, scoring Groat and Clemente ahead of him. Terry replaced Coates for the Yankees. Hoak flied to Berra. Five runs. Five hits.

NINTH INNING

YANKEES—Friend went to the mound for the Pirates. Richardson dropped a single to short left.

Long batted for DeMaestri and lined a single to right.
single to right. Murtaugh replaced Friend with Haddix.

With first and second occupied, Maris fouled to Simth. Mantle singled to right, scoring Richardson, Long going to third. McDougald ran for Long.

Berra hit a one-hopper to Nelson who stagged first but missed Mantle sliding back as McDougald scored. Skowron forced Mantle, Hoak to Mazeroski. Two runs. Three hits. One left.

PIRATES—McDougald went to third and Boyer moved to second for the Yankees.

Mazeroski homered over the left-field wall.

Long Distance Strategy Tips

Baseball fans from Tallahassee to Tacoma called Forbes Field yesterday with hot tips on game strategy for the opposing managers down on the field.

The Pirate telephone operators patiently explained that "we're sorry, but both Mr. Murtaugh and Mr. Stengel are busy right now."

Tension Gripped Faithful Fans

Berra's Homer Came As Shocker

By DAVID KELLY

Starting with the Yanks at bat in the sixth inning, the word for Pirate fans at Forbes Field was **TENSION.**

In that blurry kind of way—like the signs you see.

As the Yanks faced Vern Law and then Elroy Face, the turning of the tide produced a slowly developing state of shock that left Pirate followers in a momentary stupor.

With the Pirates leading 4-1 and the home rooters somewhat confident, there was only mild dismay when Bobby Richardson (the villain) of the Yankees singled. Then Tony Kubek walked and Manager Danny Murtaugh ambled out of the dugout and waved to the bullpen.

As Roy Face came to the mound the crowd applauded, and when Vernon Law left the mound the crowd gave him a standing ovation.

Roger Maris popped to short, causing some relief, but Mickey Mantle got a scratch single and the moans began again.

Yogi Berra poled the ball down the right-field line, and when it dropped for a home run a tremendous groan went up and the fans slumped in their seats in shock.

Then the tense waiting among the 36,683 began as they sat back to pull for the Buccos to fight from behind.

The TENSION mounted through the eighth inning when the Pirates scored five runs and went ahead 9 to 7.

Smile A Day

"Doctor, my wife has dislocated her jaw. If you're out this way next week or the week after, you might drop in."

Skowron can't reach single to right by Smokey Burgess in 2nd inning.

Bucs Win 10-9 On Homer By Mazeroski

By LESTER J. BIEDERMAN

Hail to the Pittsburgh Pirates, Champions of the World.

A ninth-inning home run by Mazeroski gave the Pnrates a 10-9 victory over the New York Yankees today, the second four-bagger in the game's late innings.

Mazeroski's homer came after the Yankees had rallied for two runs to tie the score, 9-9, in the ninth.

A tremendous eight-inning three-run homer by Catcher Hal Smbith, a clutch hitter for the Pirates all year had the Pirates ahead of the New York Yankees at Forbes Field today in the seventh and deciding game of the World Series.

Smith's homer, a towering blast that sailed into Schenley Park over the 406-foot sign in left field, climaxed a five-run rally.

A crowd of 36,683 went wild.

It was an uphill battle for the Pirates all the way.

Disparaged throughout the Series for their kitten-hitting, the Pirates exploded hurriedly today in one of their rare, but vigorous, displays of power.

After Bob Skinner walked in the first inning, Rocky Nelson, a journeyman first baseman who had watched most of the Series from the dugout, boomed a towering drive that cleared the screen in right field to give the Pirates a 2-0 lead.

It was the first time the Pirate fans had seen their heroes ahead in Pittsburgh since the opening game of the Series. It was also the first Pirate homer since Second Baseman Bill Mazeroski tagged a ball over the scoreboard in the opening game.

The Bucs added two more runs in the second. Reverting to type, they painstaking extruded the runs after kayoing Bob Turley, Yankees starter, on a lone single by Smoky Burgess.

Twenty-two-year-old Bill Stafford, a rookie who had been called up from Richmond only two months ago, relieved Turley and walked Don Hoak. Bill Mazeroski, bunting, beat the throw at first to load the bases with nobody out.

Here Manager Casey Stengel walked out to the mound to encourage his young pitcher. It was an effective visit, for Stafford forced Law to tap feebly to the mound. A double-play erased Burgess at the plate and Law at first.

But it didn't extinguish the rally. Bill Virdon, who has been a conspicuously valuable chattel in the Series, ripped a single to left center that drove home Hoak and Mazeroski and gave Law a comfortable 4-0 cushion.

But a trace of the Yankee power, which had been minimized by Law's pitching in two earlier Series appearances, expressed itself to open the fifth inning as Bill Skowron, a notorious opposite-field hitter, blasted a shot into the lower deck in right field for the Yankees' first run.

In the sixth the inevitable occurred.

After Bobby Richardson lined a single into center and Tony Kubek walked, Manager Danny Murtaugh made his first appearance on the mound. He was as decisive as Stengel had been, calling unhesitatingly for Face to put out the blaze.

He was not as successful, however. Face, who had stopped the Yankee powerhouse twice earlier in the Series, gave up a single to Mickey Mantle that scored Richardson. Then came the sky-high blast that Berra dumped into the right field stands, scoring Kubek and Mantle.

Berra's three-run homer, the Yankees' 10th of the Series, put New York ahead, 5-4.

Yankee pitching—eclipsed heretofore by the fence-rattling din of Yankee hits—started to dominate the game, just as it did when another southpaw, Whitey Ford twice stilled the Pirate bats.

The crowd suddenly came to life again in the seventh inning as Burgess drilled a base hit through the box and out into center field. Hope soared as Schantz threw three straight balls to Hoak, before he lined to Berra down the left field line.

But they dipped again as Mazeroski bounced into a double play to end the inning.

After retiring Roger Maris and Mantle in the eighth, Face ran into trouble again as Berra out-waited him for a walk. Skowron followed with a high bounder to Hoak which wouldn't come down in time to make the play at second.

Here, Johnny Blanchard, playing for the injured Elston Howard, blasted a single to right that scored Berra. Cletis Boyer followed with a double to left, sending Skowron home with a 7-4 lead before Shantz ended the inning with a fly to Clemente.

The Pirates, refusing to wilt under the pressure, came charging right back at the Yankees in the eight as Gino Cimoli, batting for Face, dropped a single into right field.

Virdon then blasted a grounder that bounced off Shortstop Tony Kubek's neck for a hit. After Dick Groat blasted a single that scored Cimoli, Bob Coates replaced Shantz for the Yankees.

That's when the Yankee bubble burst.

Bob Skinner laid down a perfect bunt, advancing Virdon and Groat. But when Nelson flied to Maris, there were two outs on the Pirates.

Roberto Clemente kept the rally alive with a dribbler to Skowron that scored Virdon and sent Groat to third.

Then, with a 2-2 count, Smith unloaded his game-winning blast.

Even in the face of the Pirates' 9-7 lead, the Yankees persisted. Singles by Richardson, Dale Long and Mantle scored a run to make it 9-8, with McDougald, running for Long, on third and Mantle on first.

Here, as Murtaugh gambled with Bob Friend and Harvey Haddix in the ninth, Berra hit a homer to Nelson who taged first but missed Mantle sliding back.

McDougald scored on the play to tie the score **9-9, before** Skowron forced Mantle to end the inning.

MARGARET SULLAVAN'S DAUGHTER A SUICIDE

See Page 4

WEATHER
Fair, in the upper 60s.
Tomorrow: Mostly fair, in the low 60s.
FROM THE WEATHER BUREAU

New York Post

©1960 New York Post Corporation
Re-entered as 2nd class matter Nov. 22, 1949, at the Post Office at New York under Act of March 3, 1879.

TWO SECTIONS 76 PAGES | NEW YORK, TUESDAY, OCTOBER 18, 1960 | Volume 159 No. 284 | 10 Cents

BLUE ★★★★ FINAL

STENGEL FIRED

Post Photo by Calvacca

"I Was Told That My Services Would No Longer Be Required"

By LEONARD KOPPETT

Casey Stengel was fired by the Yankees today.

Casey told reporters:

"I was told that my services would no longer be required. Mr. Webb listens to Mr. Topping and that is that. They have the same opinion regarding the age that a man should be retired."

Stengel was referring to Del Webb and Dan Topping, owners of the Yankees.

The 70-year-old Stengel made his announcement at a press conference today at the Savoy Hilton.

Stengel spoke with unconcealed bitterness.

"My contract runs until November," he said. "After that I won't stay here and handicap this ball club."

Asked if he would have come back if the club wanted him to, Stengel said:

"I would demand two or three things be changed first and there would have to be a discussion. I would want to know exactly where I stood with the new people and the reorganization going on."

He implied that there was to be a whole change in management and that General Manager George Weiss was on his way out, too. Weiss is 65.

Another press conference has been called for Thursday, possibly to name Stengel's successor. Or to announce the official retirement of Weiss? Ralph Houk, present first base coach, is expected to get Casey's job.

Topping said that Stengel was released because of

Continued on Back Page

Spahn's Second No-Hitter Ices Down Giants, 1 to 0

Warren Spahn . . . picks up his 2d no-hitter against Giants.

MILWAUKEE (AP) — Milwaukee's southpaw great Warren Spahn pitched the second no-hitter of his career for Victory No. 290 Friday night as the Braves took a 1-0 decision from the San Francisco Giants.

Spahn, who was 40 just last Sunday, walked only two men in dazzling the Giants and becoming the second oldest ever to pitch a no-hitter. The immortal-Cy Young pitched his third and last no-hitter at the age of 41 in 1908.

The Braves' run was unearned. It came in the first inning on singles by Frank Bolling and Hank Aaron around a passed ball. That was all Spahnie needed in outpitching right-hander Sam Jones.

Spahn, the all-time National League shutout king among left-handers, boosted his career total to 52 while moving the Braves into first place, replacing he Giants.

In winnings his second decision against one defeat this season, Spahn struck out five. He needed flashy fielding help on only a couple of occasions. In the sixth inning, shortstop Roy McMillan went to his left for a grounder, momentarily bobbled the ball, but fired to first in time to get Jose Pagan.

Spahn also helped himself with some neat fielding. In the fourth inning, rookie Chuck Hiller walked on four pitches and became the first San Francisco base runner. But he was promptly erased as Spahn got dangerous Harvey Kuenn to hit back to the mound, starting a double play.

Spahn, the last to pitch a no-hitter in the majors, against Philadelphia last Sept. 16, suffered a momentary lapse of control again at the outset of the fifth inning. He walked Willie McCovey on four pitches. But he then forced Orlando Cepeda to rap back to the mound—and Spahn once again started a double play.

Spahn needed only five pitches to retire the Giants in the eighth inning. Then he went to the mound in the ninth with the big zero showing for San Francisco on the scoreboard in right center.

Ed Bailey, acquired by the Giants from Cincinnati Thursday, ran the count to 2-2 before striking out on Spahn's ninth pitch for the first out in the final inning.

Then Spahn came up with the play of the game to preserve his no-hitter. Matty Alou, batting for Pagan, dragged a bunt down the first base line. But Spahn got over to the ball in time to nail the speedy rookie.

Spahn then got pinch-hitter Joe Amalfitano to ground out to McMillan to end the game.

The weather was similar to that on the night last September when Spahn reached one of the few goals which had eluded him by no-hitting the Phils. The temperature at game time Friday night was 4 degrees and fell steadily throughout the 2-hour and 16-minute game.

Jones, who had won two straight this season, struck out 10—seven in the first three innings—and finished with a 5-hitter. He walked five, two intentionally.

It was only the fifth time the Giatns have been hitless since the turn of the century. The last time was in 1956, when Carl Erskine of the then Brooklyn Dodgers did it when the Giants were a New York bunch.

SAN FRANCISCO	ab	r	h	bi	MILWAUKEE	ab	r	h	bi
Hiller 2b	2	0	0	0	McMillan ss	3	0	0	0
Kuenn 3b	3	0	0	0	Bolling 2b	3	1	2	0
Mays cf	3	0	0	0	Mathews 3b	3	0	0	0
McCovey 1b	2	0	0	0	Aaron rf	3	0	1	1
Cepeda lf	3	0	0	0	Roach lf	4	0	1	0
F. Alou rf	3	0	0	0	Spangler lf	0	0	0	0
Bailey c	3	0	0	0	Adcock 1b	3	0	1	0
Pagan ss	2	0	0	0	Lau c	2	0	0	0
Alou	1	0	0	0	DeMerit rf	4	0	0	0
bAm'fit'no	1	0	0	0	Spahn p	4	0	0	0
Jones p	2	0	0	0					
Totals	25	0	0	0	Totals	29	1	5	1

a—Grounded out for Pagan in 9th; b—Grounded out for Jones in 9th.

San Francisco	000 000 000—0
Milwaukee	100 000 00x—1

E—McCovey, Lau. PO-A—San Francisco 24-2. Milwaukee 27-11. DP—Spahn, McMillan and Adcock 2. LOB—San Francisco 0. Milwaukee 1. S—McMillan.

	IP	H	R	ER	BB	SO
Jones (L. 2-1)	8	5	1	0	5	10
Spahn (W. 2-1)	9	0	0	0	2	5

HBP—By Jones (Bolling). PB—Bailey 2. U—Donatelli, Burkhart, Pelckoudas, Forman, Conlan. T—2:16. A—8,518.

Race Track Mishap

WINCHESTER, Va. (AP) — James F. Edwards, 50, owner of Waterford race track in Newell, W. Va., suffered a broken back when kicked by a horse Friday.

Hyndman, Chapman In Finals

PINEHURST, N.C. (AP) — Bill Hyndman, stylish 45-year-old Huntingdon Valley, Pa., veteran, knocked in a 7-foot birdie putt on the third extra hole Friday to win a spine-tingling semifinals match from defending champion Charlie Smith in the North and South Amateur golf tournament.

Dick Chapman of Palm Beach, Fla., who won here in 1958, won three holes in a row starting at the 13th to eliminate Gobby Ware of Augusta, Ga., 2 and 1.

Hyndman and Chapman meet Saturday over the 36-hole distance for the champion.

Hyndman, an insurance executive and twice a Walker Cup player, was runner-up in 1956 and four times since 1953 has lost in the semifinals.

Chapman, who is 50, has won amateur championships of the United States, Britain, Canada and France and also has played in Walker Cup competition.

Aggies SMU 10th Loss, 8 to 0

COLLEGE STATION, Texas (AP)—Bob Collins tamed the SMU Mustangs on four singles here Friday afternoon, and Texas AM romped to an 8-0 Southwest Conference baseball victory.

The lanky Dallas right-hander was never in trouble as the Aggies collected their fourth league triumph in nine starts. Southern Mehtodist is 0-10.

Two of SMU's hits were collected by losing pitcher Joe Miller and his successor, Soug Thompson who relieved in the fifth. Three of the blows were fround hits to the outfield.

While Collins provided the pitching, striking out six and walking a like number, teammates Terry Cobb, Clifford Davis and Ray Hall furnished the power.

They collected eight of the 10 A M hits, with Cobb going 4-for-4, and Davis and Hall both 2-for-4. Davis hit a 2-run homer in the fourth. Cobb has now hit safely 13 of his last 29 times at bat.

The teams complete their 2-game series with a 2 p.m. contest Saturday.

UT Netters Stop SMU

Texas turned back SMU's bid for the Southwest Conference tennis lead Friday afternoon at the SMU courts, winning three of the four close matches for a 5-1 decision.

In two of its losses, SMU needed only one game to win, but the Longhorns stormed back on both occasions. SMU's record in SWC play is now 20 victories and 10 losses while the Longhorns, with two matches to go, have lost only twice.

Friday's results:

Mac White (UT) def. Willie Wolff, 4-6, 8-6, 6-4; Tom Howorth (SMU) def. Neil Unterscher, 7-5, 6-4; Jack Kamrath (UT) def. Bill Ingram, 6-1, 6-4; John Heath (UT) def. Mike Amis, 5-7, 6-3, 6-4; Kamrath-Heath def. Ingram-Lee Como, 6-1, 6-2; White-Unterscher def. Wolff-Howorth, 3-6, 8-6, 6-4.

Spring Tilt Set at NTS

DENTON, Texas (Sp.)—North Texas State's annual Green-White intrasquad game will be played Saturday night at Fouts Field with the opening kickoff at 7:30.

There will be no admission charge and the public is invited.

The spring training feature was switched from Friday night. Backfield Coach Fred McCain will direct the Whites and Line Coach Herb Ferrill will have charge of the Green team.

Ferrill's Green unit has the edge in experienced linemen with such returning lettermen as tackles Bill Kirbie and Gerry Hawkins, center Herbert Schulze, and Mike Pirkle and guard Frank Lawlis.

The Whites will counter with a veteran backfield headed by fullback Arthur Perkins and halfbacks Billy Christle and Chuck Holloway. McCain will also have the three lettermen quarterbacks—Ray Williamson, Merle Boyd and Kenneth Burkhalter.

Jesuit Splits At Houston

HOUSTON, Texas (Sp.)—Jesuit split its opening games in the Texas Catholic Interscholastic League baseball tournament Friday.

St. Thomas of Houston, the accepted favorite, blanked Jesuit, 6-0, in late afternoon game after Jesuit had beat Corpus Christi Academy by the same score earlier in the day.

Jesuit next will meet Central Catholic of San Antonio Saturday morning in the double elimination tournament.

First Game

Corpus Christi	000 000 0—0	4	1
Jesuit	013 110 x—6	13	0

Nemec and Hort; Black and Murphy.

Second Game

St. Thomas	001 212 0—6	9	2
Jesuit	000 000 0—0	5	2

Golazinski and Pizzitola; Davies and Murphy.

Austin Defeats St. Thomas, 5-4

Sherman, Texas (Sp.) — Austin College baseball team rapped out a 5-4 win over St. Thomas University of Houston Friday afternoon in the first of a two-game series.

Cory Adams, Austin second baseman, drove in three runs to pace the Kangaroos.

The Kangaroos will meet St. Thomas again at 1:30 p.m. Saturday in the season finale.

St. Thomas	002 000 200—4	9
Austin	010 004 00x—5	5

Bogan and Lojo; Sebesta and Williams.

★

PLANE STOPS ATLANTA CLUB MISSES GAME

ATLANTA (AP) — A new wrinkle in baseball postponements turned up in the Southern Association Friday when plane engine trouble grounded the Atlanta Crackers, who had hoped to open a series Friday night at Shreveport, La.

The Crackers, Class AA farm of the Los Angeles Dodgers, got as far as Birmingham when the trouble developed. They returned to Atlanta where mechanics were still tinkering with the balky engine hours later.

TRINITY CLUB

Caygle Takes First in Shoot

E. E. Caygle, an Air Force Technical Sergeant from Lackland Air Force Base, Texas, scored 1070 x 1200 to take first place in the preliminary match Friday of the 35th Annual Southwestern Smallbore Tournament.

The 3-day meet, being held at the Trinity Rifle Club off Highway 114 on Luna Road, saw a dark horse in the form of a teen-age Kemah, Texas, youth. Robert Schleyer, shoot a score of 1023 x 1200 to place second.

This preliminary match, called a position match, consisted of 120 shots, 40 standing, 40 kneeling and 40 prone with iron sights at 50 meters under International Shooting Union rules.

Other trophy winners included Capt. Donald Lockstrom, Lackland AFB, 997; Edward M. Hairfield, Fort Bliss, 979; and H. M. Soule, League City, Texas, 976.

Two and 4-man team matches are scheduled Saturday, followed Sunday by four matches, including 40 shots prone at 100 yards, Dewar Sights; 40 shots at 50 yards prone; and 40 shots at 50 meters, prone, any sights.

NBA Bars Players in Fix Scandal

NEW YORK (AP)—None of the players involved in the new college basketball game-fixing scandal will be permitted to play in the National Basketball Association, NBA president Maurice Podoloff said Friday night.

"I believe if we take any of these boys in we'd be lowering the high standards we have set for our players," said Podoloff. "If we allowed any of these boys to play we would be failing the youth of our country."

The statement by Podoloff was a reiteration of the stand he and the NBA took after the scandals of 1951, when drafted players who had been out for a year or more—including All-Americas Ralph Beard and Alex Groza of the Indianapolis Olympians.

The Olympians were disbanded with the unaffected players going to other teams.

Of those so far listed as admitting accepting bribes in the current scandal, three were draft choices in the NBA. Jack Egan of St. Joseph's (Pa.) was the third draft pick of the Philadelphia Warriors; Egan's teammate, 6-8 Vince Kempton, was a draft pick of the New York Knickerbockers and Jerry Graves of Mississippi State, second high scorer in the Southeastern Conference, was a draft pick of the new Chicago team in the NBA.

Rain Postpones UT, Baylor Game

WACO, Texas (AP) — A hard rain fell Friday just as the Texas Longhorns and Baylor Bears were about to take the field for the first game of their vital Southwest Conference baseball series and washed out the contest.

BASEBALL CALENDAR

AMERICAN ASSOCIATION

(Through Thursday)

Team—	W	L	Pct.	G.B.
Louisville	7	5	.583	...
Denver	6	5	.545	½
Dallas-Ft. Worth	6	6	.500	1
Indianapolis	6	6	.500	1
Houston	6	7	.462	1½
Omaha	5	7	.417	2

THURSDAY'S RESULTS

Houston 6, Dallas-Fort Worth 1.
Denver 8, Louisville 7.
Indianapolis at Omaha, ppd., rain.

FRIDAY'S SCHEDULE

Indianapolis (John Tsitouris, 0-2) at Omaha (Nels Chittum, 1-1).
Dallas-Fort Worth (Hugh Pepper, 2-0) at Houston (Jim Proctor, 0-2).
Denver at Louisville (2).

AMERICAN LEAGUE

(Through Thursday)

	W	L	Pct.	G.B.
Minnesota	9	3	.750	..
Detroit	8	3	.727	½
New York	7	4	.636	1½
Boston	6	5	.545	2½
Cleveland	7	6	.538	2½
Chicago	5	5	.500	3
Baltimore	5	7	.417	4
Kansas City	3	6	.333	4½
Washington	4	8	.333	5
Los Angeles	1	8	.111	6½

FRIDAY RESULTS

Cleveland at New York, rain.
Boston at Detroit, rain.
All night games.

SUNDAY GAMES

Minnesota (Kralick 1-0) at Los Angeles (McBride 0-2).
Cleveland (Perry 2-0) at New York (Turley 2-1).
Baltimore (Pappas 0-2) at Washington (Hobaugh 0-0).
Boston (Brewer 2-0) at Detroit (Bary 3-0).
Chicago (Score 0-0 or Shaw 1-0) at Kansas City (Walker 0-1).

NATIONAL LEAGUE

(Through Thursday)

	W	L	Pct.	G.B.
San Francisco	8	5	.615	...
Pittsburg	7	5	.583	½
Milwaukee	5	4	.556	1
Chicago	7	6	.538	1
Los Angeles	8	7	.533	1
St. Louis	6	7	.462	2
Cincinnati	5	8	.385	3
Philadelphia	4	8	.333	3½

FRIDAY RESULTS

Los Angeles at Chicago, cold weather.
Pittsburgh at Cincinnati, cold weather.
Milwaukee 1, San Francisco 0.
All night games.

SATURDAY GAMES

Pittsburgh (Law 0-3) at Cincinnati (Jay 0-2), night.
Philadelphia (Mahaffey 1-1) at St. Louis (Sadecki 1-0), night.
San Francisco (Marichal 0-1) at Milwaukee (Buhl 0-1).
Los Angeles (Koufax 1-1) at Chicago (Ellsworth 0-1).

SOUTHERN ASSOCIATION

(Through Thursday)

Team—	W	L	Pct.	Team—	W	L	Pct.
Chttnooga	13	6	.684	Ltl Rck	9	8	.529
Atlanta	11	6	.647	Nashville	7	9	.438
Brmnghm	10	8	.556	Macon	6	12	.333
Shrvprt	11	9	.550	Mobile	5	14	.263

THURSDAY'S RESULTS

Birmingham 8, Little Rock 3.
Macon 8, Shreveport 6.
Mobile 3, Chattanooga 1.
Atlanta 9, Nashville 5.

TEXAS LEAGUE

(Through Thursday)

Team—	W	L	Pct.	Team—	W	L	Pct.
San Antonio	9	5	.643	Tulsa	6	7	.462
Amarillo	8	5	.615	Ri Grnd Vlly	5	8	.384
Austin	8	6	.571	Victoria	4	9	.307

THURSDAY'S RESULTS

San Antonio 6, Victoria 5 (12 innings).
Austin 8, Amarillo 7.
Rio Grande Valley 3, Tulsa 2.

INTERNATIONAL LEAGUE

Team—	W	L	Pct.	Team—	W	L	Pct.
Columbus	5	1	.833	San Juan	5	5	.500
Toronto	5	2	.714	Buffalo	3	4	.429
Richmond	6	4	.600	Rochester	3	6	.333
Jersey City	3	2	.600	Syracuse	1	7	.125

FRIDAY RESULTS

Buffalo 8, Richmond 4.
Rochester 1, San Juan 0.
Syracuse at Jersey iCty, rain.
Toronto at Columbus, cold weather.

CORNELIUS, WRIGHT

Titleholders In Tie

AUGUSTA, Ga. (AP) — Kathy Cornelius fired four birdies on the back nine Friday and surged into a tie with Mickey Wright for the lead at the halfway point of the $6,500 Titleholders golf tournament.

Mrs. Cornelius of Phoenix, Ariz., shot a one-over-par 73 for a 36-hole total of 147. Miss Wright, who led the tournament after the opening round with a 72, slipped to 75 when she bogied three holes on the back nine. Only an eagle-2 on No. 8 saved the San Diego, Calif., blonde from losing the top spot altogether.

The best round of the day was shot by Betty Jameson of San Antonio, Texas. Her blazing putter rarely missed and she whipped par by one stroke for a 71, moving into third place at 149.

Louise Suggs of Atlanta, who said her play was spotty, came in with a 74 for 150 and a fourth-place tie with veteran Patty Berg of St. Andrews, Ill. Miss Berg had a 75.

Barbara McIntire of Lake Park, Fla., took over the amateur lead with 159.

THE LEADERS

Mickey Wright	72-75—147
Kathy Cornelius	74-73—147
Betty Jameson	78-71—149
Patty Berg	75-75—150
Louise Suggs	76-74—150
Beverly Hanson	80-72—152
Kathy Whitworth	77-75—152
Beth Stone	77-75—152
Marlene Bauer Hagge	76-77—153
Shirley Englehorn	76-78—154
Betsy Rawls	77-72—159
Ruth Jessen	79-75—154
Murle MacKenzie	78-77—155
Mary Lena Faulk	79-76—155
Jo Ann Prentice	75-81—156
Marilynn Smith	80-76—156
Carol Mann	78-78—156
Barbara Romack	81-75—156
Wanda Sanches	79-78—157
Barbara Green	76-82—158

Navarro Defeats Panola, 4 to 3

CARTHAGE, Texas (Sp.) — Panola Junior College stroked its way into a first-place tie with Navarro in the Zone 2 Texas Junior College baseball race Friday with a 4-3 victory.

Panola and Navarro now own identical 5-1 records, with one game left to play. Both will face Blinn in the windup.

Navarro	000 003 000—3	3	3
Panola	000 004 00x—4	6	2

Jenkins, Hill (7) and Dawson; Wooley and Bounds.

Lots of Points

When Green Bay's Paul Hornung scored 176 National Football League points in 1960 he set a new league record.

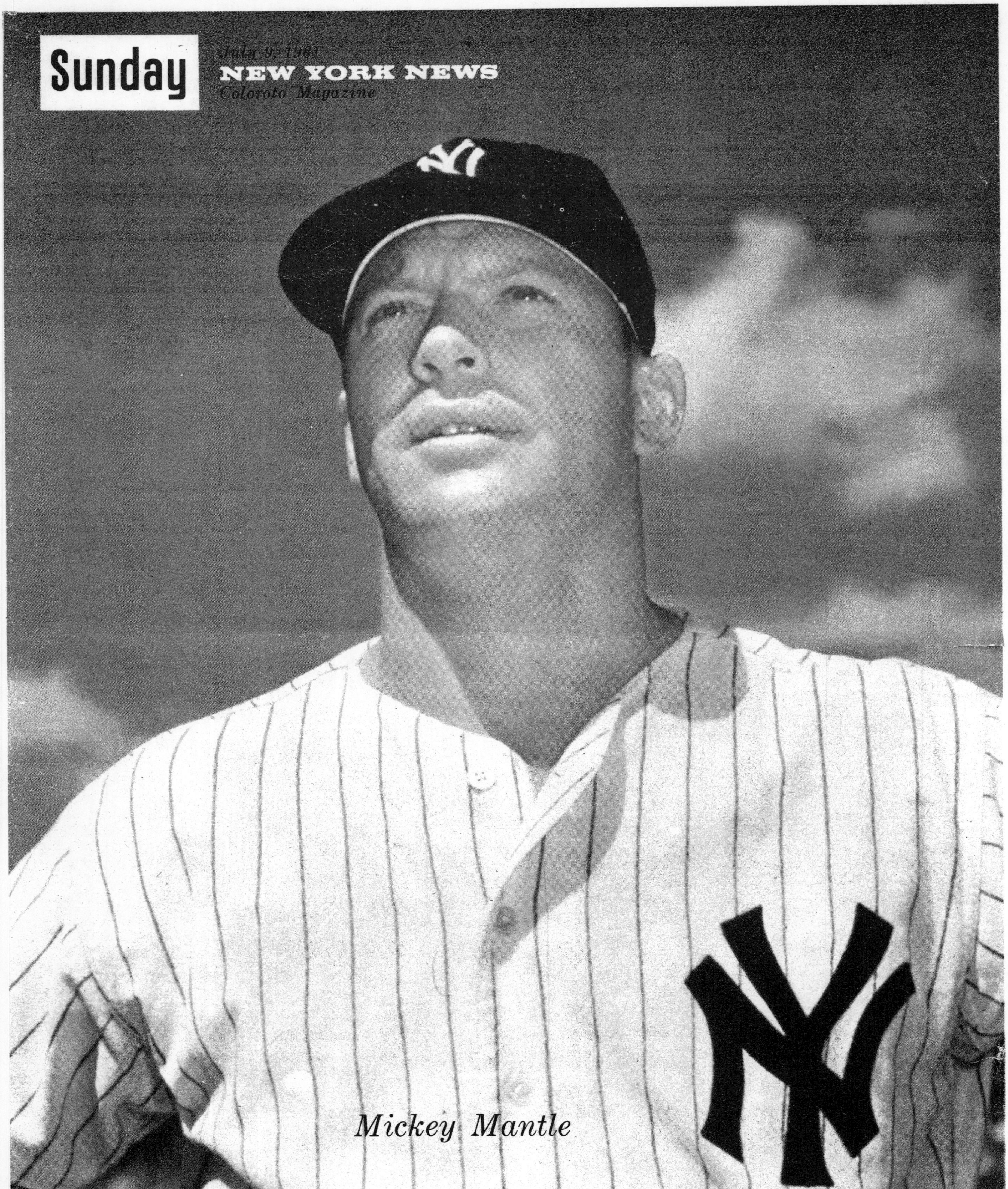
Sunday
July 9, 1961
NEW YORK NEWS
Coloroto Magazine
Mickey Mantle

THE PLAIN DEALER

NEWS OF SPORTS
Classified Ads, Comics
and Picture Page

MARIS CLOUTS NO. 60 TO TIE RUTH

Reds Win National League Flag

Pennant First in 21 Seasons

CHICAGO (AP)—The Cincinnati Reds are the new champions of the National League.

Their 6-3 victory over the Chicago Cubs yesterday, coupled with Los Angeles' 8-0 loss to Pittsburgh last night gave the Reds their first flag in 21 years.

Two-run homers by Frank Robinson and Jerry Lynch brought the Reds an uphill victory over the Cubs and assured them of a title tie.

Several hours later—after the Reds had arrived in Cincinnati to celebrate the event — the lame duck world champion Pirates upended the Dodgers to end the pennant race.

Yesterday's action left the Reds four games ahead with three to play.

Lynch's pinch hit drive in the eighth inning broke a 3-3 tie brought about by Robinson's game-tying drive in the seventh inning. Winning pitcher Jim Brosnan, working in relief, singled home an insurance run in the ninth.

28 Behind Last Year

The Reds, who finished sixth last season 28 games behind the Pirates, fell behind, 3-0, in the early innings. But as has been their custom this season, they fought back.

Cub starter Bob Anderson seemed well on the way toward maintaining Chicago's season-long jinx over the Reds, who trailed the Cubs 12-9 entering the final meeting between the teams.

Anderson held the Reds to one hit before catcher John Edwards led off the sixth with his second home run since his first major league start here June 28. In that game, Edwards hit his first homer.

The Reds tied it 3-3 in the seventh when Gordy Coleman walked and Frank Robinson followed with his 37th homer of the season.

Pinson Starts Rally

Two were out in the Cincinnati eighth when Vada Pinson singled to right and Lynch, who makes a specialty of homering against the Cubs, jolted a 3-1 count over the right field wall.

Robinson's leadoff two-bagger and Brosnan's single with two out, shoved across the sixth Red run in the ninth.

It was the 10th victory against 3 defeats for fireman Brosnan, who appeared in his 52nd game.

BOX SCORE ON PAGE 33

Cincy Flag Winners

Year	Manager	Won	Lost	G.A.
1919	Pat Moran	96	44	9
1939	Bill McKechnie	97	57	4½
1940	Bill McKechnie	100	53	12
*1961	Fred Hutchinson	92	59	4½

*Has 3 games left to play.

One-Hitter Blasts LA's Last Hopes

PITTSBURGH (AP)—Pittsburgh knocked Los Angeles out of National League contention last night with an 8-0 victory behind Joe Gibbon's one-hit pitching.

Gibbon's performance came in the second game of a twi-night doubleheader after Los Angeles won the first game, 5-3.

The lone hit off Gibbon, now 12-10, came in the sixth when pinch hitter Bob Aspromonte singled to left.

The Pirates actually won the nightcap with a five-run splurge in the third that kayoed the Dodgers starting pitcher, Don Drysdale.

BOX SCORES ON PAGE 32

Nats Win Battle of Homers, 3-2

LOS ANGELES (AP) — Gene Green hit a tie-breaking home run in the ninth inning last night to give the Washington Senators a 3-2 victory over the Los Angeles Angels before only 1,835.

Pinch hitter Ted Kluszewski tied the score for the Angels in the eighth with his 15th homer.

Benny Daniels of Washington held the Angels hitless for 5⅔ innings before Eddie Yost homered.

		R.	H.	E.
Washington	000 200 001—3	5	0
Los Angeles	000 001 010—2	4	2

Batteries—Daniels and Dailey; Bowsfield and Rodgers. W—Daniels (11-11). L—Bowsfield (10-8).
Home runs—Washington, Johnson (6), Green (18); Los Angeles, Yost (3), Kluszewski (15).

Landing of Jay and Freese Put Reds in Flag Race

By HAROLD HARRISON

CINCINNATI (AP)—Somewhere back in the hills or underbrush there may be a man, woman or child who publicly, before the season opened, picked the Cincinnati Reds to win the 1961 National League pennant.

If there be such a person, he or she should come forth and be honored.

Even though they were passed over so lightly in pre-season doping, the Reds are the champions—for the first time since 1940.

As a matter of fact, the Associated Press poll of sports writers prior to the start of the season failed to turn up a single vote for the Reds to finish either first, second or third and only eight writers figured them to finish as high as fourth.

They generally were relegated to sixth place.

Hold Lead 103 Days

But they spent virtually the whole season convincing skeptics they were headed for the pennant. They held undisputed first place eight different times for a total of 103 days.

The Reds finished a lowly sixth last season, 28 games behind the pennant-winning Pittsburgh Pirates.

The Reds were almost forgotten in late April when they lost eight straight and dropped to a seventh place tie. But on April 30; they caught fire, surged to nine consecutive victories, and by May 10 they had climbed to third place.

The turning point came the last two days of May when the Reds swept four on the West Coast, two at San Francisco and two at Los Angeles.

After June 16, there came a 43-day first place run by the Reds, whose six-game margin on July 16 was the largest by any leader for the season.

However, the favored Dodgers moved back in front July 29.

On Aug. 16, Cincinnati moved into first and it has been there ever since.

Hutch Hedges

Manager Fred Hutchinson hedges a bit now. He says he began thinking his team had a chance when it swept a four-game exhibition series with Milwaukee at the end of spring training.

What happened to provide this amazing rags-to-riches performance?

There were trades that clicked, young pitchers who achieved maturity and poise, astute and patient managing by Hutchinson and his aides, good hitting when pitchers slumped and good pitching when hitters slumped.

Last winter new general man-

Continued on Page 33, Col. 3

CHEERED FOR 60TH. Roger Maris heads for the dugout second time after hitting 60th home run. Maris had entered the dugout, but was summoned back out by the fans' applause.

AP Wirephoto

Guns for High In Four Games

BY JOE REICHLER

NEW YORK (AP)—Roger Maris blasted his 60th home run of the season last night to equal Babe Ruth's top mark set 34 years ago, but it came four games too late for Maris to receive official credit for a tie within a 154-game limit.

Maris connected with a 2-2 pitch by Baltimore right-hander Jack Fisher and sent it into the upper right field stands in the third inning. It came in the Yanks' 158th game of the season, excluding one tie.

Commissioner Ford Frick had set 154 team decisions as the limit for Maris to tie or surpass Ruth's 1927 record. He does become only the second player in major league history to reach the magic 60-mark. Frick has ruled that Maris' record will go down in the record books as a standard for a 162-game schedule.

His homer also helped the Yanks beat the Orioles, 3-2, with Ronnie Sheldon winning in relief of Bud Daley.

Served Homer to Ted

The 22-year-old, 6-2 Fisher also served up Ted Williams his 521st career home run last year. After he hit it on Sept. 20, 1960, Williams promptly retired.

Maris fouled off the first two pitches to fall behind Fisher, 0 and 2. Then he took two balls and fouled one into the dirt before connecting. The ball appeared to strike a concrete step and rebound back onto the field.

Maris raced around the bases, jogged into the dugout where Yogi Berra was the first to meet him. Roger was mobbed by his teammates. The fans gave him a standing ovation and Maris came out of the dugout to tip his hat, then ducked back in.

Maris has four more games remaining on the expanded American League program in which to surpass Ruth's total. The Yankees meet the Orioles again today, are idle tomorrow, then close out the 162-game schedule with a three-game set with Boston.

Maris' 60th came against the same team that gave up No. 59 last Wednesday at Baltimore.

The ball, after hitting in the upper stands, about two feet fair, onto the playing field and was retrieved by Baltimore right fielder Earl Robinson, who tossed it in to umpire Ed Hurley. Hurley presented it to Maris.

The 60th was only the third homer for Maris off Baltimore pitching this season, and his second against the Orioles at Yankee Stadium, where Ruth hit his 60th the next to last day of the 1927 season.

In his first time at bat against Fisher, Maris took two pitches inside for balls, then grounded a single back through the middle into center field for a single.

The 27-year-old left-handed hitting outfielder from Fargo,

Continued on Page 32, Col. 4

Maris' Magic 60

BALL PARKS AT	TOTAL	OPPOSING CLUBS Club	Total
Baltimore	1	Baltimore	3
Boston	4	Boston	6
Chicago	5	Chicago	13
Cleveland	5	Cleveland	8
Detroit	5	Detroit	8
Kansas City	5	Kansas City	4
Los Angeles	2	Los Angeles	4
Minnesota	1	Minnesota	4
New York	29	Washington	9
Washington	4	Total	60
Total	60		

Home Run Puts Lynch on Bench

CHICAGO (AP) — Jerry Lynch's game-winning home run for Cincinnati against the Cubs yesterday put Lynch back on the bench as a utility player for the rest of the season.

The reason Lynch is going back to the bench is that he has five pinch home runs this season and Cincinnati manager Fred Hutchinson is going to give Lynch a shot at the record of six.

Major Leagues

AMERICAN LEAGUE

Club	W	L	Pct.	*GB
†New York	106	52	671	..
Detroit	97	61	614	9
Baltimore	92	67	579	14½
Chicago	86	73	541	20½
CLEVELAND	76	80	487	29
Boston	75	83	475	31
Minnesota	69	86	445	35½
Los Angeles	66	90	421	39
Kansas City	60	97	382	45½
Washington	59	97	378	46

*Games behind leader
†Clinched pennant

YESTERDAY

CLEVELAND 7, Minnesota 3
Chicago 7-5, Boston 5-7
New York 3, Baltimore 2, night
Kansas City 8, Detroit 5
Washington 3, Los Angeles 2, night

TODAY

CLEVELAND at Minnesota, 3:30 p.m.—Perry (10-16) vs. Schroll (3-3)
Baltimore at New York, 2 p.m.—Barber (17-12) vs. Stafford (13-8)
Chicago at Boston, 2 p.m.—Horlen (1-2) vs. Brewer (3-2)
Detroit at Kansas City, 10 p.m.—Lary (22-9) vs. Walker (8-13)
Washington at Los Angeles, 11 p.m.—Daniels (10-11) vs. Grba (10-13)

TOMORROW

CLEVELAND at Minnesota
Washington at Los Angeles, night
Only games

NATIONAL LEAGUE

Club	W	L	Pct.	*GB
†Cincinnati	92	59	609	...
Los Angeles	87	63	580	4½
San Francisco	83	66	557	8
Milwaukee	81	70	536	11
St. Louis	78	73	517	14
Pittsburgh	72	77	483	19
Chicago	62	89	411	30
Philadelphia	46	104	307	45½

*Games behind leader
†Clinched pennant

YESTERDAY

Cincinnati 6, Chicago 3
Los Angeles 5-0, Pittsburgh 3-8, twi-night
Milwaukee 9, St. Louis 2
Only games

TODAY

St. Louis at Chicago, 2:30 p.m.—Simmons (9-10) vs. Cardwell (14-13)
Los Angeles at Philadelphia, 8:05 p.m.—Koufax (18-12) vs. Owens (4-10)
San Francisco at Pittsburgh, 8:15 p.m.—Loes (6-5) or O'Dell (6-5) vs. Sturdivant (5-2)
Only games

TOMORROW NIGHT

Los Angeles at Philadelphia
San Francisco at Pittsburgh
Only games

Bell Wins No. 12; Guessing on New Tribe Pilot Grows

By BOB DOLGAN
Staff Correspondent

MINNEAPOLIS — Gary Bell, a strong pitcher for the past month, won his 12th game for the Indians yesterday, beating the Minnesota Twins, 7-3 but most topical comment around the park concerned the identity of next year's tribe manager.

General Manager Gabe Paul will make his managerial choice known in Los Angeles this weekend and if it isn't Mel McGaha, a new course record for secrecy will have been established.

Two doubts linger regarding McGaha's candidacy—(1) He swears nobody has asked him if he wants the job and (2) if it is McGaha why wasn't he named while the tribe was at home last week, where maximum publicity would have been gained?

It's McGaha, Says Dykes

The possibility exists that Paul is going to give everyone a shock by picking a man whose name hasn't even been considered.

Charley Dressen's name was kicked around here yesterday, but Dykes says he's sure McGaha is the next pilot.

While these thoughts were running through everyone's head yesterday Bell threw a 10-hitter and stranded 10 Twins on the bases.

He lost a shutout in the eighth inning when Zorro Versalles smacked a homer with two on.

The tribe whacked 14 hits, including three by Bell, got a run in the first on John Romano's RBI single and two more in the second, when Lennie Green dropped Jim Piersall's short fly with the bases full, after Bell had singled in a run off Jack Kralick (13-11).

Kralick grew tough after this and froze the score through the sixth. But the tribe got another in the seventh off rookie Lee Stange, when Woodie Held

Continued on Page 33, Col. 1

Runs Batted In

AMERICAN		NATIONAL	
Maris, N. Y.	141	Cepeda, S. F.	140
Gentile, Balt.	138	Robinson, Cinn.	123
Colavito, Dtt.	136	Aaron, Milw.	120
Mantle, N. Y.	128	Mays, S. F.	119
Cash, Detroit	127	Stuart, Pitts.	111

The Sport Trail

by JAMES · E · DOYLE

Sixty for Roger!

So Roger Maris finally hit that magic number—60 in the Yank's 158th game of the season—and now the members of his cheering section and the Babe Ruth loyalists will really go to it in the longest and loudest sports argument since that other Battle of the Long Count . . . The second Tunney-Dempsey fight.

* * *

Gosh, what a load of Stove League fuel:
The Rajah-and-Bambino duel!

— Egg Shelley.

He's a Porky Sort

In case anybody is wondering how such a glib galloping horse as Oink rated a name that sounds like a pig's grunt, the explanation is that he was sired by To Market . . . Yup, his name is out of Mother Goose, in a roundabout way.

A Huff-Hampered Brown

The Browns' Jim Brown has had enough
And more than that of guys named Huff.

—Lank Fellow.

* * *

As no big-league football addict needs to be told, Big Jim has been stopped all too frequently by the New York Giants' line-backing stalwart, Sam Huff . . . And the other night, while driving on Euclid Avenue, he was stopped by Patrolman Clarence Huff and pinched for failing to have a driver's license on his person . . . So don't mention that name of Huff to Jim unless you wish to turn him huffy as all get-out.

They Need a Cure, Yet?

The Cincy fans have swollen heads,
Thanks to their pennant-winning Reds.
But for that swelling—this is sure—
The Yanks will come up with a cure.

—Noah Balm of Mt. Gilead.

Rough Break at Northfield

Gone with the wind and the tornado warnings of early Monday night was the Northfield management's hope for a crowd of some 7,000 customers and a stylishly stout handle at the tote windows . . . For it was a no-admission night out there, with all the free-gated patrons eligible to take part in a drawing for a handsome gas chariot . . . But 4,399 brave citizens showed up, despite the wind and the oft-repeated tip that a tornado might be approaching.

Man Off Carry Back

They say he's training not too well, so
I can't bet Carry Back 'gainst Kelso.

—Man o' Warrensville.

* * *

Three-year-old Carry Back and four-year-old Kelso will be meeting for the first time—and for the Horse of the Year title—in the $100,000-added Woodward Stakes at Belmont Saturday . . . And since he hasn't been nearly as sharp as usual in his practice spins, it appears that Clevelander Jack Price's priceless colt won't have to carry the added weight of the favorite players' money.

Plain Dealing

Loughran Revealed Fascinating Background of Boxing During Kefauver Hearings

By GORDON COBBLEDICK
Plain Dealer Sports Editor

GORDON COBBLEDICK

It has long seemed to me that, in a time when the world is in danger of disappearing in a mushroom-shaped cloud of smoke, a United States senator could occupy himself more usefully than by messing around with the sports business in its various aspects.

I have not, therefore, been numbered among the warmest admirers of Estes Kefauver, as busy a little messer-arounder as ever stuck his fingers into such frivolous matters as baseball, football and boxing.

And yet I am indebted to the gentleman from Tennessee for a voluminous and thoroughly fascinating report of hearings conducted by him on "a bill to curb monopolistic control of professional boxing, to establish within the department of justice the office of the national boxing commissioner, and for other purposes."

There was the day, back in June, when the senator's subcommittee had Tommy Loughran on the stand and elicited from him the opinion that the fight game was healthier in the years immediately before, during and immediately after his reign as light heavyweight champion because—and get this, I beg of you— it was largely controlled by bootleggers.

Bootleggers liked to own fighters, Tommy said, for the same reason that "a fellow wants a race horse or another fellow a baseball team."

Says Bootleggers Didn't Need Money

"They weren't interested in the thing from a financial standpoint," he went on. "They wanted the thing. Money meant nothing to them because they were making so much money from liquor, and they didn't get into it with that idea in mind."

Later, the old champ noted, came repeal and the end of the bootlegging industry, whereupon the gambling element took over.

"They," he charged, "were interested in the money. It was a different thing from what had happened back in the 20s. In those days they wanted a fighter because of their pride in the ownership of a fighter. But this other crowd is entirely different. It is going to be very injurious and harmful for everybody in the boxing game."

In response to questions by subcommittee counsel, Loughran said it was his opinion that a fighter, to get ahead, was obliged to align himself with the criminal element.

He also paid his respects to the present-day fighters who, after they've won a title, put it into cold storage. Counsel, now functioning as a fight fan rather than an inquisitor, observed that Loughran had fought the very tough Harry Greb twice within 15 days and expressed wonder that it was possible.

Loughran Defended Title Often

Tommy said that was nothing, really. At one stage of his career as champion, he had defended the title twice in three weeks—at Madison Square Garden and at Ebbets Field. And Greb boxed Tommy Gibbons in the Garden one Friday night and earned $75,000 for his efforts, then fought Jimmy Dines the next evening for $350. Things were, indeed, different in those days.

A highlight of Loughran's testimony was his report of a bout at the Racket Club in Washington for the entertainment of the delegates to a peace conference following World War I. The referee was a dignified Englishman who so angered the usually affable youngster that he exploded with, "One more word out of you and I'll belt you right on the chin."

Later he was sought out in his dressing room by Sen. David Walsh of Massachusetts, who asked if he knew the referee's identity. Tommy didn't.

"That," said Sen. Walsh, "was Lord Balfour. Boy, I'd have given $5,000 if you'd hit him."

"Maybe he isn't out of the building yet," said Tommy. "Maybe I can still catch him."

It was clear that Loughran, unlike the bootleggers, was interested in money.

Ex-Browns Set Dallas Pace

By CHUCK HEATON

Members of the Cleveland Browns alumni association are pretty well scattered over the National Football League.

BILL HOWTON

FRANK CLARKE

Two of them—Frank Clarke and Billy Howton—will be returning to the Stadium Sunday afternoon as important members of the Dallas Cowboys. Both have been prime targets for the passes of Eddie LeBaron and Don Meredith who have had Browns before being drafted by Dallas when the team was formed last season. Possessed of fine speed, he also seems to have developed the ability both back.

Clarke, a Colorado graduate, spent three seasons with the to get loose and to come out of the pack with the football.

Frank, who still makes Cleveland his off-season home, plays the same flanking backfield spot as Ray Renfro. As the Cowboys scored 48 points in their first two victories to lead the league, he grabbed nine passes for 156 yards and one touchdown.

The six-foot, one-inch back has put on a little weight. He now tips the scales at 215, but still can outrun most safety men, according to Dallas sources.

Continued on Page 32, Col. 2

Cincy Blows Top as Redlegs Win

CINCINNATI (AP) — The heart of Cincinnati's downtown area last night erupted into a seething, howling mass of humanity as the Reds captured their first National League pennant since 1941.

The crowd began building up in the two-block long Government and Fountain Squares late in the afternoon as the Reds clinched at least a tie for the pennant by beating the Chicago Cubs.

It was jammed with people by the time the Pittsburgh Pirates beat Los Angeles in the finale of a twi-night doubleheader to make the Cincinnati victory a certainty.

Thousands greeted the Reds at Greater Cincinnati airport as they came home from Chicago.

FINAL ★★★★ 5¢

WEATHER: Cloudy, high in the 70s.

New York Mirror

Vol. 37, No. 86 MONDAY, OCTOBER 2, 1961 Q

61 FOR ROG

Souvenir Home-Run Edition

SEE SPECIAL 4-PAGE SECTION IN CENTER; PAGES 1, 3, BACK PAGE, SPORTS PAGES AND CENTERFOLD.

History at the Stadium! After blasting record-making 61st homer, Roger Maris is shown the ball—worth $5,000—by Sal Durante who caught it.

(Mirror Photo by Anthony Bernato)

$2,410 Waiting! Mail Post Position Claims Now!

STORY ON PAGE 5

THE PLAIN DEALER

CLEVELAND, THURSDAY MORNING, OCTOBER 5, 1961

FORD'S 27 ZERO INNINGS NEAR MARK

ALL YANKEES NEEDED. Wally Post of the Reds has eyes glued on high fly hit by Yanks' Elston Howard, but before the right-fielder could flag it down, the ball dropped one foot out of his reach into the first row of seats at Yankee Stadium yesterday for a home run. It came in fourth inning. AP Wirephoto

Yank Aims at Ruth's Series Record of 29⅔

By TED SMITS

NEW YORK (AP)—This is the year for the attack on the records of the mighty Babe Ruth. But the man who threatened the Babe yesterday did it with his stout left arm and not with his bat.

Whitey Ford, ace of the New York Yankee pitching staff, spun his third consecutive World Series shutout which adds up to 27 scoreless innings—and in the words of Manager Ralph Houk it "was as nice a one as he has pitched all year."

"I did it with a sinker, a fast ball, a slider, and some curves," Ford said. "I didn't have a good change of pace."

Ruth's record, back when he pitched for the Boston Red Sox in the 1916 and 1918 World Series, is 29 2-3 scoreless innings. Ford will get a solid chance to beat this when the Series moves to Cincinnati this weekend.

Maris Is Hitless

Roger Maris, who came within one home run of tying Ruth's 154-game record total of 60, but wound up with 61 in the American League's expanded 1961 162-game schedule, went hitless in four at bats. He never hit a ball out of the infield and struck out once.

But Ford, all grins and his blond hair rumpled from sweat, was the center of attraction in the Yankees' dressing room.

"Someone told me about Ruth's pitching record before the game," he said. "But it wasn't on my mind. All I wanted to do was win."

Off in the office where once the gravel-voiced Casey Stengel held forth in fractured English Houk leaned back with a broad grin on his face, puffed a cigar, and gave out rounded, grammatical sentences.

Boyer Stars at Third

"It's always good to win the first one," he said. "Ford's the guy who did it, and of course those homers (by Moose Skowron and Elston Howard) helped.

"And you'd have to say Clete Boyer played a lot of third. That was a heck of a play he made on Dick Gernert in the eighth."

Boyer trapped a terrific smash and, on his knees, threw to first to catch Gernert.

"He made four plays as good as that this year," said Houk.

Houk was asked about Mickey Mantle, his slugging outfielder who was sidelined with a hip infection.

Terry Hurls Today

"It's a day-to-day proposition," said Houk. "I'm doubtful if he can play Thursday, but fairly optimistic that he can play in Cincinnati.

"Ralph Terry is the pitcher today. I would assume that if they pitch Joey Jay, John Blanchard will play right field."

Continued on Page 50, Col. 6

Yanks Are Now Favored 4 to 1

LAS VEGAS, Nev. (AP) — New odds favoring New York to win the World Series are 4-1. Yesterday the Yankees were favored 2½-1.

Odds are 8½-5 for New York to take its second contest in a row.

The odds against New York winning in 4 straight games are 3½-1.

Post Stab for Homer Foot Short

By HAROLD HARRISON

NEW YORK (AP) — "That's what you would call a good, clean incision."

That was Cincinnati Manager Fred Hutchinson's description of the New York Yankees' 2-0 victory over the Reds yesterday in the opener of the 1961 World Series.

"There's not a helluva lot you can say about that game," the grim-faced Hutchinson said in the subdued Redleg club house.

"You have to give Mr. (Whitey) Ford a lot of credit. He pitched a fine game but our kid (Jim O'Toole) did, too. The only thing he (O'Toole) could have done was shut them out."

Post Just Misses

The Yankees' first run off O'Toole was Elston Howard's homer in the fourth which barely dropped into the right field seats.

It appeared for a bit that Cincinnati right fielder Wally Post might have made a catch, if he might have gotten a glove on the ball.

Post said, however, his stab for the ball was about a foot short. The ball dropped into the first row of seats.

"I thought I had a chance for it," Post said, "but it kept drifting away."

Post explained he was playing Howard a bit toward right center.

"He hits a lot to right center and he has a lot of power there," Post added.

Praises Boyer

Hutchinson merely shook his head and said, "I don't know" when he was asked if he believed the faster Frank Robinson might have made the catch. Robinson usually plays in right field but was shifted to left yesterday.

Hutchinson also had some praise for Clete Boyer, the Yankees' third baseman, who made two brilliant stops to rob the Reds of hits.

"Our scouting reports said he was better than his brother and I said I'd have to see it," Hutchinson declared. "Well, I saw it. But his brother makes those stops too."

Boyer's brother is Ken Boyer of the St. Louis Cardinals.

Just Got Careless

O'Toole, who had a 19-9 record this year in the regular season, said Howard "didn't get good wood" on his homer. About the one hit by Bill Skowron, O'Tcole said, "I just got careless."

Continued on Page 50, Col. 6

ROBBING THE REDS. Clete Boyer, Yankee third baseman, makes two brilliant stops against the Reds. Above, he dives to his right and stabs Gene Freese's hot grounder in second inning. Below, he spears Dick Gernert's smash in eighth inning. Both times, he throws out batter at first base. AP Wirephoto

* * *

Reds Can't Blast Ball Past Boyer

By JOE REICHLER

NEW YORK (AP)—They came to see the M & M boys but they left singing the praises of Clete Boyer.

The cheers of the 62,397 were not the only thing ringing in the New York Yankee third baseman's ears yesterday. His head still throbbing and his lip swollen from a collision with Cincinnati's Wally Post in the fifth inning, Boyer called his sensational eighth inning play on pinch hitter Dick Gernert his best ever.

"I've made a lot of good plays," said the 24-year-old brother of St. Louis Cardinal star Ken Boyer, "but this was my best ever. I thought the one I made on Romano (Cleveland's John Romano) earlier this year was my best. But I had to go farther for this one. I didn't believe it when I saw the ball in the glove. It gave me my biggest thrill."

Makes Great Stop

Whitey Ford was bidding for his third consecutive World Series shutout and had two out in the eighth. Gernert, batting for losing pitcher Jim O'Toole, drove a hard smash headed for the hole between third and short. Boyer flung himself at the ball and gloved the ball. Then, from a kneeling position, he threw a strike to first baseman Bill Skowron.

It was his second outstanding play of the game. In the second inning, Boyer made a sprawling stop of Gene Freese's hard drive, this time to his right, and as in the eighth, got his man with a throw from a kneeling position.

In the fifth, Post singled. Two outs later with Post on second base, Darrell Johnson bounced to Boyer who elected to make the tag on the incharging runner instead of throwing to first base. Post made a football-type arm and shouldeer block as he came barging down the line. Boyer, although knocked back several feet, held the ball, and trotted into the dugout.

Has Headache

In the club house, Boyer said his head still hurt from the collision. He also displayed a bruised lip and felt his head gingerly, feeling around for a sore spot.

"I've had a headache since the fifth inning," he said ruefully. "I think he hit me with his shoulder on the lip. He hit me pretty good. I was waiting for him. I wasn't going to back off.

"No hard feelings, except in my head. He was just playing the game. I would have done the same thing."

Fair and Cool for Game Today

NEW YORK (AP) — The Weather Bureau forecast a mostly fair, cool day for today's second game of the World Series.

Winds are expected to be brisk, at 15 to 20 miles an hour from the northwest and high temperature about 60.

Plain Dealing

World Series Scribes Ignore 'M' on Typewriters After Ford Mows Down Reds

By GORDON COBBLEDICK
Plain Dealer Sports Editor

GORDON COBBLEDICK

NEW YORK — This is one a man can write without an "M" on his typewriter. With Mickey Mantle out of action and with Roger Maris failing to hit the ball out of the infield in four tries, the story of the first game of the 1961 World Series can be told in four names —Ford, Howard, Skowron and Boyer.

The rest of the 62,000-odd in attendance at the Yankee Stadium, including the Cincinnati Reds, could as profitably gone to the movies on a chill, unpleasant day.

Whitey Ford was magnificent in holding the Reds to two hits.

Boyer Makes Pair of Diving Stops

Boyer, the Yankee third baseman, made two incredible diving stops of hard-hit grounders—the only balls the Reds hit solidly in the whole game.

Skowron and Howard hit solo home runs to give the Yanks the margin of their 2-to-0 victory.

In recording his eighth World Series triumph against four defeats, Ford was so completely in command that those two homers would have been all he needed even if, by special dispensation of the commissioner, second base had been the pay station for the National League champions.

Wally Post got that far on an infield out after leading off in the fifth with a single, his team's second and last hit. The other two Reds who became base runners—Ed Kasko on a single in the first inning and Frank Robinson by a walk in the seventh—perished on first base.

Skowron Drives Ball 400 Feet

Skowron's homer, stroked with one out in the sixth, was a mighty blast that carried deep into the stands in left, a good 400 feet from the plate.

Howard's, on the other hand, was of the sort that ought to be marked in the box score by an asterisk signifying that it was a typical Yankee Stadium right field home run. It carried barely 310 feet, barely eluded the clutching hand of Wally Post and barely cleared the 3-foot-high wall.

Boyer showed why the Yankees regard him as the best defensive third baseman in the game. In the second inning he dived to his right, came up with Gene Freese's bid for a double and threw out the frustrated Redleg with plenty to spare. In the eighth, by way of proving his ambidexterity, he dived to his left for Dick Gernert's smash and fired a perfect throw to first while on his knees.

It would heighten the dramatic impact of the story if it could be written that Boyer's play saved, or contributed substantially to the saving of, the game.

Reds Didn't Have Chance Against Ford

But all the evidence indicates that its only effect was to give Ford a two-hit shutout instead of a four-hit shutout. It was impossible for an onlooker to escape the impression that the Reds could have gone on swinging at the stocky southpaw's stuff until curfew time without producing a run.

This was Ford's third consecutive shutout in World Series competition, following as it did the two coats of whitewash he applied to the Pittsburgh Pirates in the Yankees' losing cause a year ago. And now the shade of Babe Ruth is fidgeting anxiously in whatever Valhalla it occupies. With his cherished home run record already broken by Roger Maris (with, to be sure, an asterisk), the prospect that Ford will shatter his record of 29 and two-thirds consecutive scoreless innings of World Series pitching has taken frightening form.

The probability is that Ford will pitch again in the fourth game of this set in Cincinnati Sunday, and if he blanks the Reds for three innings he'll have set a new standard.

To bet against it would be, on the basis of his performance yesterday, as well as that of his opponents, comparable to wagering that the sun won't rise tomorrow morning.

Can't Run or Swing, Mick Out

NEW YORK (AP) — "I know I won't be able to play Thursday either," said Mickey Mantle, after watching yesterday's World Series opener from the sidelines. "I can't swing left-handed . . . I can't throw and I can't run."

The New York Yankee slugger sat out the first game, still hobbled by the after effects of minor surgery for an abscess on his right hip.

Roger Maris, the other half of the M and M boys, did nothing to distinguish himself. The man who hit 61 home runs during the regular season went hitless in four times at bat against left-hander Jim O'Toole. He popped up in the first, struck out in the third, grounded out in the fifth and fouled out to the catcher in the seventh.

No Pressure

"I didn't do anything," admitted Maris after the game, "but I feel great. I don't feel any pressure at all. Even a World Series is like a rest after what I went through this season.

"I picked the right time to go 0 for 4, anyway," he added. "The time to go hitless is when you win."

Despite his inability to fathom O'Toole's breaking stuff, Maris didn't appear too impressed by the pitching of the Reds' left-hander.

"He's the same as any other pitcher," Roger said. "He's not overpowering. He's more of a stuff pitcher. He keeps mixing them up—a little inside, a little outside. I expected him to be faster. Pizarro and Mossi (Juan Pizarro of Chicago and Don Mossi of Detroit) throw harder.

Wastes Fast Ball

"O'Toole wastes his fast ball, throws a lot of breaking stuff and pitches to spots, with the idea of making you go for bad pitches.

"You've got to give him credit. He faced a lineup with a lot of power and pitched well."

Mantle wasn't sure when he'd be back in the lineup, but said:

"I know I won't be able to play Thursday. I can swing right-handed, but I can't swing left-handed. I can't throw and I can't run either."

The hip injury of the switch hitting center fielder is on the right side. If he were playing today, he would bat left-handed against the right-handed pitching of Joey Jay.

"I hope I can get into the Series," Mantle said. "But I have no idea right now when I'll be able to play. It's a day to day proposition."

Mickey said he wasn't particularly upset about not playing.

"As long as we keep on winning," he said, "I'm satisfied."

The Sport Trail

By JAMES E. DOYLE

Reds Blinded by Whitey

Once more the mighty Whitey Ford
Was sharper than old Bluebeard's sword.
And so the Reds were kalsomined—
Or Whitey-washed—all swinging blind.

—Lank Fellow.

* * *

Ford strikes have been called all over the country this week. . . . And perhaps the Reds would have been smart to walk out, too, when that first bell rang at Yankee Stadium yesterday.

Perfect Fits

Those nine horsecollars looked real good
On Cincy's hapless heroes,
Just as slick Whitey thought they would.
Great guy for throwing zeroes!

—Egg Shelley.

* * *

Greatest guy for throwing successive World Series shutouts, indeed, since the youthful Babe Ruth of the Boston Red Sox, whose record of twenty-nine and two-third scoreless innings is more than likely to be another record wrecked when Whitey bears down on it in Cincinnati.

* * *

But maybe the Reds will call a Ford strike yet.

Another Sharp Lefty

The N. L. champs' young Jim O'Toole
Hung in there like a cool man, cool.
He had the Yankees well in hand,
Save when two wallops reached the stand.

* * *

And the first of those homers—Elston Howard's—was strictly Chinese, as they say, just dropping out of the reach of Right Fielder Wally Post, who should have gloved it.

* * *

But Moose Skowron's was an old-style Yankee blast . . . Over the wall and far away.

Tops With the Stops

Boy, oh, Boyer! What a whiz
Out there at third that Boyer is!

—Yankee Frankovic.

* * *

Simply grand larceny—those two Boyer stops of Red hot shots tagged as surefire hits . . . Or, if you prefer, fielding gems of purest ray serene.

* * *

But nary a Red could reach third to tell Clete Boyer he should be jailed for those thefts.

* * *

Whitey Ford made sure of that.

Sellers Rides 8 Straight Winners to Share Record

ATLANTIC CITY, N. J. (AP) —Johnny Sellers, the nation's leading jockey, equalled an American record by extending his winning streak to eight at Atlantic City.

After winning the last three races Tuesday, Sellers brought home the winners of the first five yesterday.

This duplicated Howard Craig's feat of riding the last six winners at Waterford Park, W.Va., July 2, 1951, and the first two on the next day's program.

It was the best performance since Danny Weiler won six in a row at ThistleDown last Aug. 12.

Sellers, who rocketed into prominence this year as the regular jockey of Carry Back—the Kentucky Derby and Preakness winner—is a 24-year-old native of Los Angeles.

He began his string Tuesday by winning with Fleet Sailor ($4.20), Terrorize $5, and Part Time Indian ($4.80.)

Yesterday he started out in the opener with Swifty Bill ($13.20), and completed a $43.40 daily double in the second race with Our Jennifer ($11.). Then he won with Johnny Blue ($7.60), Elmo's Ethel ($7.60), and Miss Tradition ($7.80).

The Atlantic City meeting closed yesterday, and Sellers equalled the all-time record here of 69 winners set by Joe Culmone in 1950.

Dial for Score

Folks who don't have radios or TV sets handy can keep up on the World Series action by using Dial-A-Program. You simply call SW 1-1200 for the information.

Ceiling Zero for Ford

Cincinnati (N)	AB	R	H	BI	O	A
Blasingame 2b	3	0	0	0	3	2
dLynch	1	0	0	0	0	0
Kasko ss	4	0	1	0	3	3
Pinson cf	4	0	0	0	4	0
Robinson lf	2	0	0	0	0	0
Post rf	3	0	1	0	2	0
Freese 3b	3	0	0	0	1	0
Coleman 1b	3	0	0	0	7	0
D. Johnson c	2	0	0	0	3	1
aCardenas	1	0	0	0	0	0
Zimmerman c	0	0	0	0	1	0
O'Toole p	2	0	0	0	0	0
bGernert	1	0	0	0	0	0
Brosnan p	0	0	0	0	0	0
Totals	29	0	2	0	24	6

New York (A)	AB	R	H	BI	O	A
Richardson 2b	4	0	3	0	1	4
Kubek ss	3	0	0	0	2	3
Maris cf-rf	4	0	0	0	2	0
Howard c	4	1	1	1	6	0
Skowron 1b	3	1	1	1	3	0
Berra lf	2	0	0	0	1	0
Lopez rf	2	0	0	0	0	0
cBlanchard	1	0	0	0	0	0
Reed cf	0	0	0	0	0	0
Boyer 3b	3	0	1	0	2	5
Ford p	3	0	0	0	0	1
Totals	29	2	7	2	27	13

a—Struck out for D. Johnson in 8th.
b—Grounded out for O'Toole in 8th.
c—Popped out for Lopez in 8th.
d—Popped out for Blasingame in 9th.

New York A .... 000 101 00x—2

E—None. DP—D. Johnson, Kasko and Coleman. LOB—Cincinnati N 3, New York A 8. HR—Howard, Skowron.

PITCHERS RECORDS

	IP	H	R	ER
O'Toole (L)	7	6	2	2
Brosnan	1	0	0	0
Ford (W)	9	2	0	0

B—O'Toole 4, Kubek, Skowron, Berra, Lopez, Bosnan 1, Ford 1, Robinson. SO—O'Toole 2, Maris, Lopez, Brosnan 1, Skowron; Ford 6, Blasingame 2, Robinson 2, O'Toole, Cardenas. U—Runge (A) plate, Conlan (N) first base, Umont (A) second base, Donatelli (N) third base, Crawford (N) left field, Steward (A) right field. T—2:11. A—62,397.

Toronto Lands Patterson Bout

TORONTO (AP)—Floyd Patterson will defend his world heavyweight championship against Tom McNeeley here on Dec. 4—all because they could not agree on a referee in Boston.

Originally, the bout was set for Boston on Nov. 13, but was called off because the Massachusetts boxing commission refused to go along with Patterson's request for an out-of-state referee.

Promoter Tom Bolan made the announcement that the Patterson-McNeeley bout would be held here in the 15,000-seat Maple Leaf Gardens.

Freshman Football

Benedictine 24, Patrick Henry 0
Chanel 6, St. Joseph 6 (tie)
Cathedral Latin 14, Collinwood 0

THE PLAIN DEALER

News of Sports, Financial, Amusements General News

CLEVELAND, MONDAY MORNING, OCTOBER 9, 1961

YANKS WIN, 7-0; SEEK TITLE TODAY

Mitchell Scores 3, Browns Roll

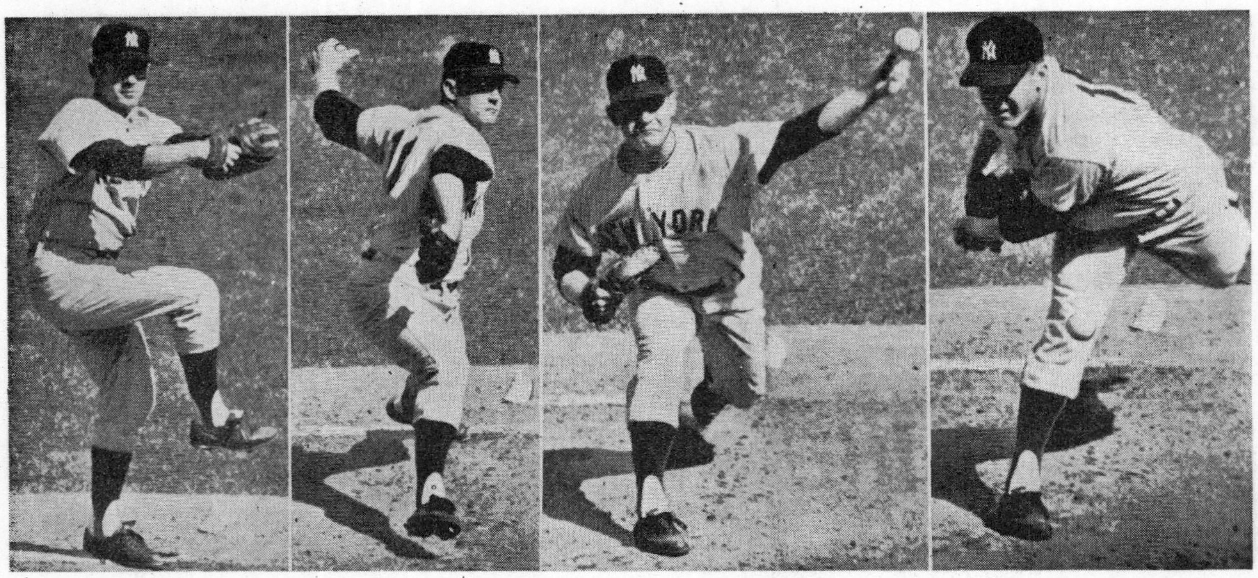

WHITEY FORD CUTS LOOSE AS HE BREAKS BABE RUTH'S SCORELESS INNING RECORD

AP Wirephoto

Ford Smashes Ruth's Series Zero Record

By BOB DOLGAN
Staff Correspondent

CINCINNATI — The National League champion Cincinnati Redlegs died yesterday, 7-0. Cause of demise was acute paralysis at the plate, induced by five-hit pitching by Yankees' White Ford and Jim Coates.

Attendant complications included cerebral hemorrhages on the part of Redleg Manager Fred Hutchinson, who ordered three men walked intentionally, whereupon suceeding batters proceeded to whack the tar out of the ball. Hutch's brainstorms led to five runs.

Early symptoms of the Reds' illness were suspect fielding by Second Baseman Elio Chacon and Centerfielder Vada Pinson. Pinson fumbled one grounder and threw to the wrong base on two other occasions.

Chacon, who can make an adventure out of fielding a simple grounder, bungled two double play balls in third inning. Neither turned out to be important, but gave indications of serious internal problems.

Friends and relatives of the deceased may pay respects today at Crosley Field where the fifth game of the World Series will be played. Funeral services will, in all probability, be held immediately following the contest, during which Yankee Ralph Terry will oppose Joey Jay.

Yanks Now 10-1

LAS VEGAS, Nev. (AP) — The New York Yankees now are prohibitive 10-1 favorites to take the world series and 3-2 favorites to win today.

The Yanks took a 3-1 series lead and need only one more triumph to wrap up another world title. The way the Reds played yesterday it seems they are a cinch to do it.

Ford's Mark May Stand

Ford and Coates were the chief executioners before a packed house of 32,589, and Ford set a series record that may stand for a long, long time.

The sharp left-hander threw shutout ball for five innings before leaving with a sore foot (he fouled a ball off his instep) and ran his streak of scoreless innings in series competition to 32, breaking Babe Ruth's record of 29⅔ innings, set in the 1916 and '18 tournaments, when Babe was a young pitcher with the Boston Red Sox.

Incidentally, this has been a horrible year for Ruth. In one season his home run record and series pitching record have been broken, records that had withstood the test of years and years.

Cheers From Press Box

When Ford cracked the mark after whitewashing the Reds in the third inning, his pressbox friends stood up and broke into spontaneous applause.

This was Ford's second victory of the current festival and in each case Lefty Jim O'Toole was his victim. Ford pitched two shutouts last year against the Pittsburgh Pirates, another in the opener last Wednesday at Yankee Stadium.

He now has nine series victories, two more than any other pitcher.

Coates kept the hook on the Reds after Ford took a shower. Whitey gave Chacon a lead-off single in the sixth and manager Ralph Houk immediately pulled him, with the score 4-0.

Coates fired one-hit ball the rest of the way.

Bobby Richardson, the Yankees' banjo-strumming second baseman, was one of the pallbearers also, belting two singles and a double and losing a fourth hit when Chacon made a leaping stab of a liner.

Richardson is the biggest hitter in the series as he was last year when he set slugging records. The little guy came into the festival with three hits in his last 33 regular season appearances. So far in the classic he has eight hits in 17 trips, an average of .471.

Here are the gory details. In the fourth, Roger Maris walked and went to third on a hit to

Continued on Page 35, Column 3

'Skins Routed by Long Runs, 31-7

By CHUCK HEATON

Bobby Mitchell returned to the Browns' lineup just in the nick of time.

The slippery halfback, restricted to punt-return duties a week ago, exploded for three touchdowns as Paul Brown's team defeated the Washington Redskins, 31-7, yesterday before 46,186 fans on a bright, pleasant afternoon at the Stadium.

This third straight victory left the Browns in a four-way tie with the New York Giants, Dallas Cowboys and Philadelphia Eagles for first place in the National Football League's eastern division.

Moving into the lake front bowl next Sunday afternoon will be the Green Bay Packers. They are defending champions in the western conference and also have a 3-1 mark after routing Baltimore 45-7, yesterday.

Mitchell's eruption was overdue. He had opened the season with two costly fumbles against Philadelphia. Then he was kayoed and sidelined early against the St. Louis Cardinals.

That gave Tom Watkins his chance. The rookie performed so well that he remained in there last week as the Browns turned back Dallas.

Brown decided to use Watkins and Mitchell as messengers part of the time against Washington. This provided for Bobby just the opportunity he needed.

He struck early in the second quarter on a 52-yard pass after an exasperating first period for Cleveland. Lou Groza's 34-yard field goal was the only score of that session. Twice the Browns lost the ball on fourth-down tries deep in Redskin territory.

Dave Lloyd blocked a field goal attempt of John Aveni from 41 yards out to give the home club the ball on its own 36 and set the stage for Mitchell's first burst.

Three plays made it first down on the Cleveland 48 and Brown called for the long toss to Bobby. Milt Plum's pass was a trifle overthrown but Mitchell, arms completely extended and running at top speed, pulled in the ball around the 20.

Bobby stumbled the next 15, finally seemed to be caught by Jim Kerr, rookie defensive back from Penn State, about the four but rolled into the end zone.

Continued on Page 35, Column 3

Statistics

	Browns	Redskins
Total first downs	13	15
First downs rushing	4	2
First downs passing	8	12
First downs by penalty	1	1
Total yards gained (net)	285	245
Yds. gained rushing (net)	91	44
Yds. gained passing (net)	194	201
Passes attempted	27	29
Passes completed	17	15
Yards lost attempting to pass	7	30
Passes intercepted by	2	0
Yards interceptions returned	61	0
Number of punts	4	5
Average distance	45	41
Punts returned	4	1
Yards punts returned	89	10
Kickoffs returned	1	6
Yards kickoffs returned	25	155
Penalties	5	3
Yards penalized	45	26
Fumbles	0	0
Fumbles lost	0	0
Number of rushing plays	27	24
Average gain per rush	3.3	1.9
Total offensive plays (includes plays attempting to pass)	55	59
Average gain per try	5.1	4.1

Packers Rip Colts on 33 by Hornung

GREEN BAY, Wis. (AP) — Green Bay's great Paul Hornung touched off apersonal 33-point scoring spree with a 54-yard touchdown jaunt and the Packers went on to rout the Baltimore Colts 45-7 yesterday in a National Football League showdown.

Hornung, who set an NFL record by scoring 176 point a year ago, tallied four touchdowns booted a 38-yard field goal and kicked six extra points as the Packers registered their third straight triumph since being upset by Detroit in the season's opener.

Green Bay's stingy defense, which has allowed only 34 points in four outings, smothered Baltimore's vaunted passing attack triggered by Johnny Unitas. The Packers intercepted five Unitas passes and one by Lamar McHan, the Colts' No. 2 quarterback.

Continued on Page 38, Column 5

Bobby Is Praised by Brown

By CHUCK HEATON

Bobby Mitchell was just as much a man of distinction the past two weeks at League Park practice sessions as during yesterday's romping against Washington at the Stadium.

That's the opinion of Paul Brown and he expressed it to the players in a brief talk in the dressing room immediately after the Browns victory over the Redskins.

"When some fellows are removed from the starting lineup they get moody and sour," said the coach. "That was'nt the case with Bobby.

"He not only worked harder than ever and remained in good spirits but also kept right on helping Tom Watkins. When you can do that it's the sign of a real man. I'm proud of him."

It was Watkins, the rookie runner from Iowa State who temporarily took over the starting job at left half—and shared it yesterday.

Gets Game Ball

Mitchell was presented with a game ball by the players and so was Dave Lloyd who operated in his usual slashing fashion as middle line backer.

Continued on Page 38, Column 5

★ ★ ★

Plain Dealing—

By GORDON COBBLEDICK
Plain Dealer Sports Editor

GORDON COBBLEDICK

CINCINNATI—A widely held belief that the National is the tougher of the two major leagues is being shot full of holes in this battle for the championship of the baseball world.

No American League team in the season recently ended looked as feeble against the Yankees as have Cincinnati's ragamuffin Reds. Nor did any American League batsman of stature appear as helpless against Yankee pitching as have the big guns of the National League champions.

Yankee pitching, excepting only Whitey Ford and his loyal deputy, Luis Arroyo, is admittedly the weak point of an otherwise mighty team—a team that in all other departments compares favorably with the great Yankees of the Ruth-Gehrig and the DiMaggio-Keller-Henrich eras.

But Yankee pitching has so effectively handcuffed the Reds' heavy hitters in the current world series as to make the Ruffing-Gomez and the Reynolds-Raschi-Lopat combinations look like minor leaguers.

Since American League opponents have proved that it isn't that good, the only possible alternative belief is that the Reds are incredibly bad.

Reds' Big Four Batting Average is .104

In the championship season, Cincinnati's offensive Big Four, consisting of Frank Robinson, Vada Pinson, Gene Freese and Gordon Coleman, compiled a collective batting average of .308 and batted in a total of 385 runs, an average of 96 per man.

In five games against the Yankees the same quartet is batting .104, and the mark is that high only because Coleman, the big kid who grew to maturity in the Cleveland Indians' farm system, is hitting a relatively robust .250. Robinson's avreage is .077, Pinson's .071 and Freese's a cool zero. Coleman has batted in two runs and Robinson one. Neither Pinson nor Freese has come close.

Because they have failed so dismally, it seems likely now that this will be the shortest World Series since the New York Giants whomped the Indians in four straight in 1954. It may be that an investigation by the Ohio legislature is in order.

Since the tragic debacle of 1954, five World Series have

Reds Futility at Bat Blasts Belief That National League Is the Strongest

gone the limit of seven games and one has taken six, but only a sharp reversal of form this afternoon can keep the present one from ending in five.

It's up to Joey Jay, the only Cincinnati pitcher ever to defeat the Yankees in a game that counted, to repeat today, and he must be wondering what he's going to use in lieu of runs.

Little Chance Ford Will Go Again This Year

Yesterday his mates suffered their second shutout defeat as Ford inscribed his name in indelible ink in the record book by completing a string of 32 consecutive scoreless innings in world series competition, wiping out Babe Ruth's 43-year-old record of 29.

Ford's string is still unbroken, but there is next to no chance that he will have the opportunity to extend it this year.

Only if the Reds rally and send the series into a seventh game for a decision will he pitch again.

Thus it comes about that two of Ruth's long-standing records have falled in the space of eight days. It was just a week ago yesterday, in the last game of the American League season, that Roger Maris hit his 61st home run, bettering by one the mark set by the Babe in 1927.

Another Ruthian standard remains, but probably only because Mickey Mantle has played parts of only two games in the current series. Ruth hit 15 home runs in world series play. Mantle has 14, but may not get another chance this year to boost his total. A few days ago his crippled condition looked like an important factor in the match with the Reds. But now—who needs him?

Victor's Share $8,000

CINCINNATI (AP) — Yesterday's fourth World Series game was the last one in which the players have a share of the receipts.

The total player pool came to $645,928.28, of which 70%, or $452,149.80, will be divided between the two Series clubs. The other 30% is spread among the second, third and fourth place clubs in each league.

The winning pool will be $271,289.88, the losers $180,859.92. On the unofficial basis of 34 shares a team each winner would get about $8,000 and each loser about $5,200.

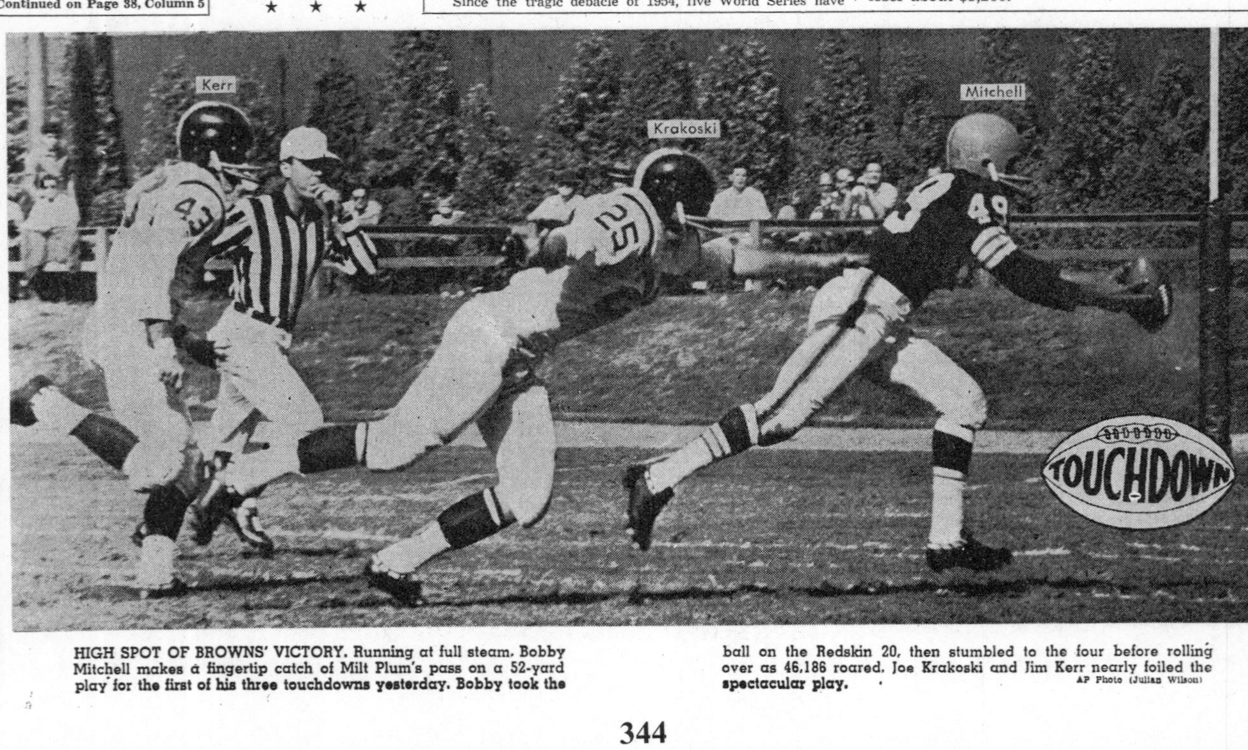

HIGH SPOT OF BROWNS' VICTORY. Running at full steam, Bobby Mitchell makes a fingertip catch of Milt Plum's pass on a 52-yard play for the first of his three touchdowns yesterday. Bobby took the ball on the Redskin 20, then stumbled to the four before rolling over as 46,186 roared. Joe Krakoski and Jim Kerr nearly foiled the spectacular play.

AP Photo (Julian Wilson)

Pro Football

National League

EASTERN DIVISION

	W	L	T	Pct.	Pts.	OP
CLEVELAND	3	1	0	.750	96	58
Dallas	3	1	0	.750	87	56
Philadelphia	3	1	0	.750	89	73
New York	3	1	0	.750	75	65
St. Louis	2	2	0	.500	77	81
Pittsburgh	0	4	0	.000	68	89
Washington	0	4	0	.000	38	104

WESTERN DIVISION

	W	L	T	Pct.	Pts.	OP
San Francisco	3	1	0	.750	129	33
Green Bay	3	1	0	.750	112	34
Detroit	2	2	0	.500	50	108
Baltimore	2	2	0	.500	83	118
Chicago	2	2	0	.500	65	95
Minnesota	1	3	0	.250	77	96
Los Angeles	1	3	0	.250	65	97

YESTERDAY

CLEVELAND 31, Washington 7
New York 24, St. Louis 9
Philadelphia 21, Pittsburgh 16
Dallas 28, Minnesota 0
Green Bay 45, Baltimore 7
Chicago 31, Detroit 17
San Francisco 35, Los Angeles 0

NEXT SUNDAY

Green Bay at CLEVELAND
New York at Dallas
Philadelphia at St. Louis
Washington at Pittsburgh
Los Angeles at Detroit
San Francisco at Minnesota
Baltimore at Chicago

American League

EASTERN DIVISION

Team	W	L	T	Pct.	Pts.	OP
New York	3	1	0	.750	124	119
Boston	2	3	0	.400	145	134
Buffalo	2	3	0	.400	105	107
Houston	1	3	0	.250	112	82

WESTERN DIVISION

Team	W	L	T	Pct.	Pts.	OP
San Diego	5	0	0	1.000	161	72
Dallas	3	1	0	.750	97	94
Oakland	1	3	0	.250	67	160
Denver	1	4	0	.200	98	142

SATURDAY'S RESULT

San Diego 38, Boston 27

YESTERDAY'S RESULTS

Dallas 19, Denver 12
Buffalo 22, Houston 12

NEXT FRIDAY

Houston at Boston

NEXT SUNDAY

San Diego at New York, Oakland at Denver, Dallas at Buffalo

Don't Feel Kings Out Of Picture

By THE ASSOCIATED PRESS

Wichita hasn't won a game and the other Missouri Valley Conference teams have yet to lose, but don't be surprised if the Shockers bounce back for their third straight football title.

The Kansans, nipped 21-20 by Louisville in the last quarter, gave way in the closing minutes against another tough foe Saturday night and Arizona State won 21-10. The Sun Devils moved ahead on an 83-yard pass play and scored again on a pass interception with 15 seconds left.

TULSA, Cincinnati and North Texas State all stand 1-0 but each runs into major opposition Saturday which should put their title chances in much better focus.

Bobby Smith ran 31 and 11 yards for second half touchdowns, pacing North Texas to a 19-6 victory over Texas Western. Memphis State, which smashed North Texas 41-0 a year ago, plays the Eagles at Denton in a night game. Memphis lost to highly-ranked Mississippi 21-7, but likely will have too much talent for North Texas.

GLENN DOBBS sends his rebuilt Tulsa team, 39-0 winner a week ago over hapless Hardin-Simmons, against Arkansas, defending co-champion of the Southwest Conference. The Razorbacks manhandled Oklahoma State 34-7.

Cincinnati gave Chuck Studley an opening 13-0 victory over Dayton in a game broken open by sophomore Errol Prisby's 45-yard scoring run. But the Bearcats play this Saturday at Indiana, 21-0 winner over Kansas State.

Wichita will play a night game at home against Hardin-Simmons, which has lost 24 in a row. The Wheatshockers should have little trouble.

Wills Still Feels He Broke Record

ST. LOUIS — (AP) — Maury Wills headed back to Los Angeles Sunday with satisfaction and a base—his 97th stolen base of the season.

The Dodger shortstop finished "right on schedeule" as far as he was concerned in his race to break Ty Cobb's single season mark of 96 stolen bases.

WILLS SWIPED SECOND base twice once in the third inning and again in the seventh—against the St. Louis Cardinals at Busch Stadium.

The thefts gave him 97 for 156 games played to a decision by the Dodgers.

However baseball commissioner Ford Frick ruled earlier that Wills had to break the record in 154 decisions, the same as Cobb, although Cobb had 156 games because of two ties. Cobb stole one base in each of the tie replays.

Although Wills' performance didn't officially break Cobb's record, set in 1915, it was enough to satisfy Wills.

"As far as I'm concerned, I was right on schedule," said Wills. "He (Cobb) did it in 156 games and what's good enough for Cobb is good enough for me."

Wills actually did better than Cobb. The Dodger switch hitter, who had 194 hits and a .298 average after Sunday's contest, has been caught stealing only 12 times. Cobb was thrown out 39 times in a season he hit .369 with 208 hits.

WILLS' LAST BASE was the easiest of all to get. The Cardinals made him a present of it before his last time at bat in the ninth inning.

In a short ceremony at home plate, field announcer Charlie Jones presented Wills with second base, saying, "Since you stole so many bases, you won't have to steal this one. We're giving it to you."

AP Photo

MAURY WILLS . . . He can keep this one.

Oiler Duo Goes Wild Against SD

By THE ASSOCIATED PRESS

The Houston Oilers are back in stride in the American Football league Monday, and it's mainly because of the ground work done by Charlie Tolar and Billy Cannon.

And ground work thed did—the hard way against a defensive line reputed to be the league's best.

This blockbusting pair rolled for 212 yards Sunday as the Champion Oilers blitzed the San Diego Chargers 42-17, making a shambles of the defensive line on Ron Nery, Earl Faison, Bill Hudson and Ernie Wright.

THIS CLUB record — making performance came after the Oilers had been held to only 69 yards rushing in a 34-21 lacing a week ago by Boston, which had people wondering if perhaps the two-time champions weren't running out of gas.

Houston's triumph put it in a three-way tie for first place in the eastern division with Boston, which won Friday night, and New York, which handed Buffalo its third straight loss, 17-6 Saturday night. All are 2-1.

Dallas' 26-16 victory over Oakland put the Texans atop the Western Division with a 2-0 mark, while San Diego is 1-2, Denver 2-1 and Oakland 0-2.

TOLAR HAS been the Oilers' big gun on the ground so far this season, and added 142 yards in 18 carries to the 144 he had gained in the first two games. Cannon, last year's ground-gaining champ got 70 in 12 tries for a three-game total of 214. Sunday because of a muscle Sunday because o fa muscle spasm.

Lavorante Now 50-50

LOS ANGELES — (AP) — A neurosurgeon says stricken Argentine heavyweight Alejandro Lavorante has slightly better than a 50-50 chance of living.

Doctors removed a piece of bone from the prize fighter's skull Sunday to ease the pressure of his swelling brain. It was the third operation performed on the boxer since his knockout loss to unheralded Johnny Riggins Friday night.

AFTER THE three-hour operation yesterday, Dr. J. DeWitt Fox said the 212-pound, 6-foot-4 fighter is "far from out of danger."

"But he responds with boxer-like motions of the arms to painful stimuli, like pinches," said Dr. Fox. He said it would be two days before he could predict Lavorante's future.

Early Saturday Fox performed a four-hour brain operation. On Saturday night doctors made a tiny incision in Alejandro's throat and inserted a tube so he could breathe.

DR. FOX said Lavorante's brain swelling may take two weeks to subside. The piece of bone cut from the skull will be replaced later, he said.

The hospital listed Lavorante, 25, in serious condition rather than critical because his blood pressure and temperature were improving.

Yanks Need One Victory

By THE ASSOCIATED PRESS

The proud New York Yankees, who hate to be accused of backing in—which is just what they are doing — have clinched at least a tie for the American League pennant and can wrap it all up Tuesday night by beating the last place Washington Senators.

The Yankees all but nailed down their 27th championship in 42 years, 12th in 14 and second in two years under manager Ralph Houk, by defeating the Chicago White Sox 5-1 in 10 innings Sunday.

MINNESOTA vanquished Baltimore 9-2 but all the second place Twins accomplished was to avoid mathematical elimination. Trailing by 4½ games, the best they can do is force a post-season playoff provided they win their remaining four games while the Yankees lose all five they have left.

That's like asking one of our astronauts to journey to the moon in a swim suit.

Los Angeles' third place Angels were mathematically eliminated from the race, dropping an 11-5 decision to Cleveland for their eighth loss in the last 10 games. Detroit defeated Kansas City 3-1. Rain forced the postponement of the Red Sox-Senators game scheduled in Washington. The game has been re-scheduled for Boston as part of a Sept. 29 double-header.

IN THE National League, San Francisco trimmed Los Angeles' first place lead to three games, defeating Houston 10-3 after the St. Louis Cardinals had walloped the Dodgers 12-2. Cincinnati defeated Philadelphia 4-2 in 10 innings, Milwaukee thrashed Pittsburgh 10-3 and New York nipped Chicago 3-1.

The Yankees ruined Early Wynn's bid to become the American League's first 300-game winner since Lefty Grove reached that total two decades ago. The 42-year-old White Sox right-hander battled the Yankees through 10 innings before suffering his 14th loss in 21 decisions.

Right-hander Bill Stafford took a 1-0 lead into the ninth when the Whtie Sox tied the score on successive doubles by Joe Cunningham and Floyd Robinson. The Yankees, however, raked Wynn for four runs, all after two out, in the 10th. Hector Lopez broke the tie with a single and Ellie Howard iced the victory with a two-run homer, his 21st.

The Twins scored eight runs in the last two innings to overcome a 2-1 Baltimore lead. Harmon Killebrew hit a three-run homer in the eighth to snap a 2-2 tie. It was Killebrew's 45th homer and gave him 120 runs batted in. Both figures are tops in the league.

DETROIT southpaw Hank Aguirre pitched a six-hitter against the Athletics and lowered his league leading earned run average to 2.24. Tiger shortstop Dick McAuliffe paved the way for Aguirre's 15th triumph of the season with a bases-loaded single which drove in what proved to be the winning runs.

Detroit (3)	ab	r	h	rbi	Kansas City (1)	ab	r	h	rbi
Fer'dez,ss	4	0	0	0	D' Gr'co,cf	3	0	2	0
Bruton,cf	4	1	1	0	Cimoli,rf	4	0	0	0
Kaline,rf	5	1	2	0	Lumpe,2b	4	1	1	0
Colavito,lf	2	0	0	0	Siebern,1b	4	0	0	0
Cash,1b	3	1	0	0	Charles,3b	4	0	2	1
McA'fe,2b	4	0	1	2	Kern,lf	4	0	1	0
Boros,3b	3	0	0	0	Causey,ss	4	0	0	0
Brown,c	2	0	0	0	Sullivan,c	2	0	0	0
a-Wertz	1	0	0	0	Bryan,c	1	0	0	0
Roarke,c	0	0	0	0	Pfister,p	2	0	0	0
Aguirre,p	3	0	0	0	b-Alusik	1	0	0	0
					Wyatt,p	0	0	0	0
Totals	31	3	4	2	Totals	33	1	6	1

A—Popped out for Brown in 8th; B—Grounded out for Pfister in 8th.

Detroit	200 000 010—3
Kansas City	000 100 000—1

E—Charles, McAuliffe, Bryan. PO-A—Detroit 27-8, Kansas City 27-7. LOB—Detroit 9, Kansas City 6.

SB—Cash, Bruton. S—Aguirre.

	IP	H	R	ER	BB	SO
Aguirre (W, 15-8)	9	6	1	0	1	2
Pfister (L, 4-14)	8	4	3	2	6	4
Wyatt	1	0	0	0	1	2

U—Drummond, Napp, Schwarts, Stevens. T—2:09. A—7,561.

Spain Leads All Jalopies

Leon Spain dominated the next-to-last jalopy racing program of the season Sunday at Shawnee Speedway. He won the trophy dash, a heat race and the feature.

The final session of the season will be next Sunday afternoon.

Trophy Dash—Leon Spain.
First Heat—1. Chet Paul; 2. Terry Broyles; 3. Harold Adkins.
Second Heat—1. Dave Peavler; 2. Red Andrews. 3. Garry Hastings.
Third Heat—1. Spain; 2. Lou Hoppe; 3. Johnny Green.
Consolation — 1. Don Garst; 2. Dale Rogers; 3. Bud Lebrand.
B Main—1. Peavler; 2. Rogers; 3. Paul; 4. Rockey Meyers; 5. Peanuts; 6. Francis Baker.
A Main—1. Spain; 2. Hoppe; 3. Ken Theis; 4. Green; 5. Andrews; 6. Earl Reaves.
Mechanics Race—Bob Lux.

Form Chart

NATIONAL LEAGUE

	W	L	Pct.	GB		W	L	Pct.	GB
L.A.	100	56	.641	..	S.L.	80	76	.513	20
S.F.	57	59	.622	3	Phil.	79	78	.503	21½
Cin.	95	63	.601	6	Hous.	61	93	.396	38
Pitts.	90	66	.577	10	Chic.	57	100	.363	43½
Milw.	83	74	.529	17½	N.Y.	39	116	.252	69½

RESULTS SUNDAY
Milwaukee 10, Pittsburgh 3.
Cincinnati 4, Philadelphia 2 (10 innings).
New York 2, Chicago 1.
St. Louis 12, Los Angeles 2.
San Francisco 10, Houston 3.
GAMES MONDAY
No games scheduled.

AMERICAN LEAGUE

	W	L	Pct.	GB		W	L	Pct.	GB
N Y	92	65	.586	..	Bal.	75	80	.487	15½
Minn.	88	70	.557	4½	Cleve.	76	81	.484	16
L A	84	72	.538	7½	Boston	74	82	.474	17½
Chcg.	83	74	.529	9	K C	70	86	.449	21½
Det.	81	75	.519	10½	Wash.	59	98	.376	33

RESULTS SUNDAY
New York 5, Chicago 1 (10 innings).
Minnesota 9, Baltimore 2.
Detroit 3, Kansas City 1.
Cleveland 11, Los Angeles 5.
Boston at Washington, postponed, rain.
GAMES MONDAY
Kansas City (Rakow 13-16) at Baltimore (Fisher 7-8) 6 p.m.
Only game scheduled.

INTERNATIONAL LEAGUE

RESULTS SUNDAY
Atlanta at Jacksonville, ppd, rain (Best-of-Seven series tied, 3-3).

Fight Results

BESCIA, Italy—Giuliano Nervino, 146, outpointed Charley Douglas, 145, New York, 8.

BOSTON—Bob Fosmire, 146, Revere, Mass., outpointed Gaspar Ortega, 148, Mexico, 10.

NL Leaders

BATTING (based on 375 or more at bats) — T. Davis, Los Angeles and Robinson, Cincinnati, .343; Musial, St. Louis, 3.27; H. Aaron, Milwaukee, .325; White, St. Louis, .324.

RUNS — Robinson, Cincinnati ,132; H. Aaron, Milwaukee and Mays, San Francisco, 124; Wills, Los Angeles, 123; T. Davis, Los Angeles, 114.

RUNS BATTED IN—T. Davis, Los Angeles, 147; Robinson, Cincinnati and Mays, San Francisco, 134; H. Aaron, Milwaukee, 122; Howard, Los Angeles, 110.

HITS — T. Davis, Los Angeles, 216; Robinson, Cincinnati, 205; Wills, Los Angeles, 194; Groat, Pittsburgh and White, St. Louis, 192.

TRIPLES—W. Davis, Los Angeles, Callison, Philadelphia and Virdon, Pittsburgh, 10; six tied with 9.

HOME RUNS — Mays, San Francisco, 46; H. Aaron, Milwaukee, 43; Robinson, Cincinnati, 39; Banks, Chicago, 36; Thomas, New York, 33.

STOLEN BASES — Wills, Los Angeles, 97; W. Davis, Los Angeles, 31; Javier, St. Louis, 26; Pinson, Cincinnati, 22; Taylor, Philadelphia, 20.

PITCHING (based on 15 or more decisions)—Purkey, Cincinnati, 22-5, .815; Sanford, San Francisco, 22-7, .759; Drysdale, Los Angeles, 25-8, .758; Koufax, Los Angeles and Pierce, San Francisco, 14-6, .700.

Sunday's Stars

BATTING—Hector Lopez, Yankees—Hit a two-out, single in 10th inning to snap a 1-1 tie and lead the Yankees to a 5-1 victory over the Chicago White Sox, assuring New York of at least a tie for the American League pennant.

PITCHING—Hank Aguirre, Tigers—Assured himself of the American League earned run title, pitching a six-hitter for a 3-1 triumph over the Kansas City Athletics. He has an ERA mark of 2.24, far ahead of his nearest rival.

AL Leaders

BATTING — (based on 375 or more at bats) — Runnels, Boston, .328; Hinton, Washington, .311; Robinson, Chicago, .309; Lumpe, Kansas City, .306; Robinson, Baltimore and Siebern and Jimenez, Kansas City, .303.

RUNS — Pearson, Los Angeles, 111; Siebern, Kansas City, 109; Allison, Minnesota, 100; Yastrzemski, Boston, 97; Richardson, New York, 96.

RUNS BATTED IN — Killebrew, Minnesota 120; Siebern, Kansas City, 111; Colavito ,Detroit, 109; Wagner, Los Angeles, 106; Robinson, Chicago and L. Thomas, Los Angeles, 101.

HITS — Richardson, New York, 202; Lumpe, Kansas City, 193; Robinson, Baltimore and Yastrzemski, Boston, 186; Runnels, Boston, 183.

TRIPLES — Cimoli, Kansas City, 15; Clinton, Boston, 10; Bressoud, Boston, Robinson, Chicago and Lumpe, Kansas City, 9.

HOME RUNS — Killebrew, Minnesota, 45; Cash, Detroit, 38; Wagner, Los Angeles, 37; Colavito, Detroit, 36; Gentile, Baltimore, 33.

STOLEN BASES — Aparicio, Chicago, 30; Hinton, Washington, 27; Wood, Detroit, 24; Charles and Howser, Kansas City, 19.

PITCHING (based on 15 or more decisions) — Stigman, Minnesota, 12-5, .706; Donovan, Cleveland, 20-9, .690; McBride, Los Angeles, 11-5, .688; Herbert, Chicago and Bunning, Detroit, 18-9, .667.

Senior Erdelatz Dies

SAN RAFAEL, Calif.—(AP)—Joseph Erdelatz, father of former Navy football coach Eddie Erdelatz, died Sunday at the San Rafael Medical Center after a lengthy illness.

Missouri Player Stays in Hospital

BERKELEY, Calif.—(AP) Missouri end Don Wainwright will remain in Cowell Hospital here for about a week after suffering a cerebral concussion in Saturday's Missouri-California football game.

A Missouri spokesman reported Sunday that the 200-pound senior from Kirkwood, Mo., was in satisfactory condition and had regained consciousness. He was kicked in the head accidentally by a teammate.

Pro Football Form Chart

NFL STANDINGS

EASTERN CONFERENCE

	W	L	T	Pct.	Pts.	Op.
Washington	1	0	1	1.000	52	51
St. Louis	1	1	0	.500	27	38
Cleveland	1	1	0	.500	33	24
New York	1	1	0	.500	36	30
Pittsburgh	1	1	0	.500	37	73
Dallas	0	1	1	.000	63	65
Philadelphia	0	2	0	.000	34	56
WESTERN CONFERENCE						
Detroit	2	0	0	1.000	90	31
Green Bay	2	0	0	1.000	51	7
Baltimore	2	0	0	1.000	64	34
Chicago	2	0	0	1.000	57	37
Los Angeles	0	2	0	.000	50	57
San Francisco	0	2	0	.000	38	75
Minnesota	0	2	0	.000	14	68

RESULTS SUNDAY
New York 29, Philadelphia 13.
Baltimore 34, Minnesota 7.
Pittsburgh 30, Dallas 28.
Green Bay 17, St. Louis 0.
Detroit 45, San Francisco 24.
Washington 17, Cleveland 16.
Chicago 27, Los Angeles 23.
GAMES NEXT SUNDAY
Cleveland at Philadelphia.
Chicago at Green Bay.
Dallas at Los Angeles .
Detroit at Baltimore.
Minnesota at San Francisco.
New York at Pittsburgh.
St. Louis at Washington.

AFL STANDINGS

EASTERN DIVISION

	W	L	T	Pct.	Pts.	Op.
Boston	2	1	0	.667	103	79
New York	2	1	0	.667	59	63
Houston	2	1	0	.667	91	74
Buffalo	0	3	0	.000	49	68
WESTERN DIVISION						
Dallas	2	0	0	1.000	68	44
Denver	2	1	0	.667	69	82
San Diego	1	2	0	.333	78	86
Oakland	0	2	0	.000	33	54

RESULTS FRIDAY
Boston 41, Denver 16.
RESULTS SATURDAY
New York 17, Buffalo 6.
RESULTS SUNDAY
Houston 42, San Diego 17.
Dallas 26, Oakland 16.
CAMES NEXT SUNDAY
San Diego at Oakland.
Denver at New York.
Buffalo at Dallas.
Only games scheduled.

Pauline Resident Tops Grid Picks

Charles W. Yenkey of Pauline was the winner of Ray Beers' first weekly football guessing contest. Yenkey, like several other contestants, missed on two games. One was a tie. He won by coming closest on K-State's total yardage against Indiana.

Because he mailed in his ballot, Yenkey will receive $25 in merchandise from Ray Beers. Had he delivered the ballot to the store he would have received $50 in merchandise.

GIANTS WIN!

Fair

BAY AREA—Fair through Thursday, but low cloudiness near coast Thursday morning. Highs 66-72. Westerly winds.

News Call Bulletin

San Francisco's Evening Newspaper

Vol. 4, No. 47 | Phone EX 7-5700 | WEDNESDAY, OCTOBER 3, 1962 | Price 10c

9 STAR FINAL SPORTS PICTORIAL

COMPLETE N. Y. STOCKS

Spaceman Lands; 6 Orbits

Giants Win 6-4 in Ninth

By JAMES K. McGEE

LOS ANGELES—A last-ditch, four-run rally in the ninth inning enabled the San Francisco Giants to defeat Los Angeles, 6-4, Wednesday to win the National League pennant and earn the right to take on the New York Yankees Thursday noon in the first game of the World Series at Candlestick Park.

Down, 4-2, and apparently headed for defeat in the ninth, the Giants started their winning rally when Matty Alou, batting for Don Larsen, singled.

After Harvey Kuenn forced Matty at second, Willie McCovey, batting for Hiller, walked as did Felipe Alou to load the bags.

Mays then singled off pitcher Ed Roebuck's glove to score M. Alou and make the count 4-3. Out came Dodger pitcher Ed Roebuck and in came Stan Williams with the bags loaded.

ORLANDO Cepeda then greeted Williams with a long sacrifice fly to score Ernie Bowman ,running for McCovey for a 4-4 ballgame. Williams then was intentionally walked to again load the bases and Williams walked Jim Davenport to force in F. Alou with the go-ahead run.

The Giants added their final tally when Larry Burright fumbled Pagan's grounder.

The win went to Don Larsen, who pitched only the eighth inning. He was relieved by Billy Pierce in the ninth and Pierce retired the only three men to face him, pinchhitter Lee Walls lining to Mays for the final out.

The Giants had a 2-1 lead in the sixth, but Tommy Davis followed Duke Snider's single with a two run homer over the left-center-field fence to give the Dodgers their 3-2 lead.

Maury Wills scored Los Angeles fourth run on a single, two stolen bases and Ed Bailey's throwing error in the seventh.

Box Score Play-by-Play On Page 50

Crop Prices Up

WASHINGTON (UPI) — Prices of farm crops have averaged about 3 pct. above 1961, the Agriculture Dept. said Wednesday.

LATEST BULLETINS

TROOP WITHDRAWAL SOON—MAYBE

WASHINGTON (AP)—Atty. Gen. Robert Kennedy said Wednesday he hopes federal troops can be withdrawn soon from Mississippi, but added that no time for such a move has been set.

"DAISY" STORM NEAR PUERTO RICO

MIAMI (UPI) — Tropical storm Daisy boosted its power to 55 miles an hour winds and hovered north of Puerto Rico on an uncertain course. But it did obligingly move out of the path of Astronaut Walter Schirra.

VEGAS 'FACIAL' TRIAL NEAR JURY

LAS VEGAS (UPI)—The federal court trial of Madame Cora Galenti Smith on charges of using the mails to defraud, in connection with her facial rejuvenation establishments, was near the jury Wednesday.

BABY CROP FALLS BEHIND AGAIN IN JULY

WASHINGTON (AP) — There were an estimated 366,000 babies born in the U. S. during July—2.1 pct. fewer than in the corresponding month in 1961, the Public Health Service reported. This was the sixth month this year to show a decline.

CALIFORNIA PROPERTY VALUATION RISES

SACRAMENTO (AP) — The value of tax exempt property in California rose 2 pct. to $1.6 billion in 1962, the Board of Equalization said Wednesday. The value of non-exempt property rose 6 pct.

Phone EXbrook 7-5700 for Home Delivery

NY Blast Kills 20; 70 Injured

By UPI and AP

NEW YORK—A basement boiler exploded and was hurled through an upper Manhattan office building Wednesday like a cannonball, collapsing walls and ceilings on scores of young women.

At least 20 were killed and others were trapped in the wreckage.

Police Commissioner Michael Murphy estimated the number of dead—most of them young women working in the New York Telephone Co. training and accounting building.

MORE THAN 60 persons were injured.

The block-square two-story building in upper Manhattan's Inwood section did not appear heavily damaged from the outside, but, inside, rescuers found a jumble of wreckage.

Nearly three hours after the noon blast firemen and police wearing gas masks were still seeking persons trapped in the basement debris.

ABOUT 500 persons were in the building at Broadway and 213th st. when the explosion occurred. Many had just been seated in the cafeteria for lunch.

New York City Building Commissioner Harold Birns said the one-ton iron basement boiler exploded and was "propelled by a tremendous force beyond comprehension."

It blasted through the boiler room wall and up through the first floor, through the cafeteria and a records room.

HUGE CHUNKS of the first floor ceiling collapsed on the women employes, many in training for their first jobs.

"Girls were lying all over the floor covered with blood," said Dorothy Murphy, 19, one of those who escaped.

"I was at a table in the cafeteria with my girl friends," said Mrs. Rosemary Meade, 32, of Garnersville, N. Y., a phone company employe.

A PIXY? NO—ASTRONAUT WALLY SCHIRRA
He gives the eye to nearby teammates
—United Press International Telephoto

Football Ban At Ole Miss?

OXFORD, Miss. (AP)—The Justice Dept. disclosed Wednesday the possibility that the University of Mississippi homecoming football game Saturday may be called off.

The game to be played against Houston University is expected to bring between 20,000 and 30,000 persons to Oxford.

Edwin Guthman, spokesman for the Justice Dept., said:

"We must make an assessment. There has been a major disturbance here, two people killed, and numerous others injured.

"We expect to have an announcement tonight or tomorrow."

RIOTS BROKE OUT Sunday when James H. Meredith, a Negro, was installed in a university dormitory.

Related Stories on Page 11

While the situation on the campus apears quiet, there have been nightly disturbances. The campus is heavily patroled by federal troops.

Between 35 and 50 students gathered in front of Baxter Hall, set fire to an effigy of Meredith and exploded fireworks.

Armed soldiers scattered the crowd quickly. There were no arrests.

Soldiers arrested 14 persons at roadblocks during the night, including two students. All were released.

Nearly 4000 troops left the campus, but 8000 remained.

A Justice Dept. spokesman said an "awful lot of ammunition" and other weapons were confiscated, including a .22 caliber rifle and a shotgun.

ATTENDANCE at the university dropped after the enrollment of Meredith.

University chancellor J. D. Williams appealed to the students to return.

The 29-year-old Meredith spent his second day as a student Tuesday, accompanied to classes by federal marshals. There were no demonstrations.

Inside Today's News Call Bulletin

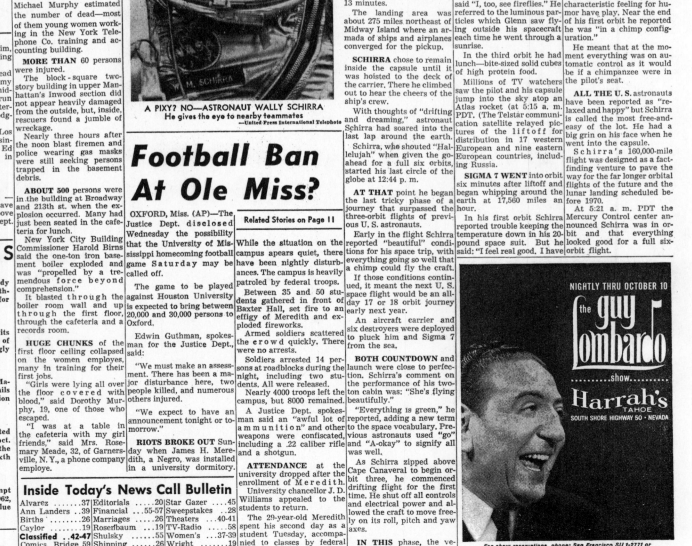

By United Press International and Associated Press

ABOARD USS KEARSARGE—Astronaut Walter M. Schirra Jr. flashed around the earth six times Wednesday, splashed down in a bullseye mid-Pacific landing and was picked up safely to cap America's longest and highest space flight.

"Beautiful . . . beautiful . . . beautiful" were the words of sailors aboard the Kearsarge as the capsule floated down dead ahead of the big carrier.

They echoed Schirra's own words as he whirled through space in the Sigma 7 on a trip that went smoothly from start to finish and ended in the water just two minutes later than the scheduled time.

He was taken aboard at 3:09 p. m. PDT.

The 39-year-old Navy commander blasted off from Cape Canaveral at 5:15 a. m. PDT and splashed down at 2:28 p. m. PDT after a U. S. record flight of 9 hours and 13 minutes.

The landing area was about 275 miles northeast of Midway Island where an armada of ships and airplanes converged for the pickup.

SCHIRRA chose to remain inside the capsule until it was hoisted to the deck of the carrier. There he climbed out to hear the cheers of the ship's crew.

With thoughts of "drifting and dreaming," astronaut Schirra had soared into the last lap around the earth.

Schirra, who shouted "Hallelujah" when given the go-ahead for a full six orbits, started his last circle of the globe at 12:44 p. m.

AT THAT point he began the last tricky phase of a journey that surpassed the three-orbit flights of previous U. S. astronauts.

Early in the flight Schirra reported "beautiful" conditions for his space trip, with everything going so well that a chimp could fly the craft.

If those conditions continued, it meant the next U. S. space flight would be an all-day 17 or 18 orbit journey early next year.

An aircraft carrier and six destroyers were deployed to pluck him and Sigma 7 from the sea.

BOTH COUNTDOWN and launch were close to perfection. Schirra's comment on the performance of his two-ton cabin was: "She's flying beautifully."

"Everything is green," he reported, adding a new term to the space vocabulary. Previous astronauts used "go" and "A-okay" to signify all was well.

As Schirra zipped above Cape Canaveral to begin orbit three, he commenced drifting flight for the first time. He shut off all controls and electrical power and allowed the craft to move freely on its roll, pitch and yaw axes.

IN THIS phase, the vehicle rotates slowly, making about one revolution every 30 minutes if control is not re-established by the pilot.

In drifting flight, the capsule does not float far off course because it is flying an orbital path determined by the laws of nature, much like a bullet fired by a rifle.

Purpose of the drifting is to conserve control fuel and electrical power.

In a discussion with astronaut Glenn, monitoring the flight at the Point Arguello, Cal., tracking station, Schirra said "I, too, see fireflies." He referred to the luminous particles which Glenn saw flying outside his spacecraft each time he went through a sunrise.

In the third orbit he had lunch—bite-sized solid cubes of high protein food.

Millions of TV watchers saw the pilot and his capsule jump into the sky atop an Atlas rocket (at 5:15 a. m. PDT. (The Telstar communication satellite relayed pictures of the liftoff for distribution in 17 western European and nine eastern European countries, including Russia.

SIGMA 7 WENT into orbit six minutes after liftoff and began whipping around the earth at 17,560 miles an hour.

In his first orbit Schirra reported trouble keeping the temperature down in his 20-pound space suit. But he said: "I feel real good. I have beads of perspiration on my lips but that's about all."

AT 55 MINUTES after liftoff he tilted his cabin steeply for one of the major experiments of the flight.

This was to see whether he could observe a high-intensity flare fired from Woomera, Australia. Because of weather conditions, Schirra said the flare looked like "a block of light" rather than a bright point.

Schirra kept his chatter to ground stations at a minimum but occasionally let his characteristic feeling for humor have play. Near the end of his first orbit he reported he was "in a chimp configuration."

He meant that at the moment everything was on automatic control as it would be if a chimpanzee were in the pilot's seat.

ALL THE U. S. astronauts have been reported as "relaxed and happy" but Schirra is called the most free-and-easy of the lot. He had a big grin on his face when he went into the capsule.

Schirra's 160,000-mile flight was designed as a fact-finding venture to pave the way for the far longer orbital flights of the future and the lunar landing scheduled before 1970.

At 5:21 a. m. PDT the Mercury Control center announced Schirra was in orbit and that everything looked good for a full six-orbit flight.

Related Stories on Pages 2, 3

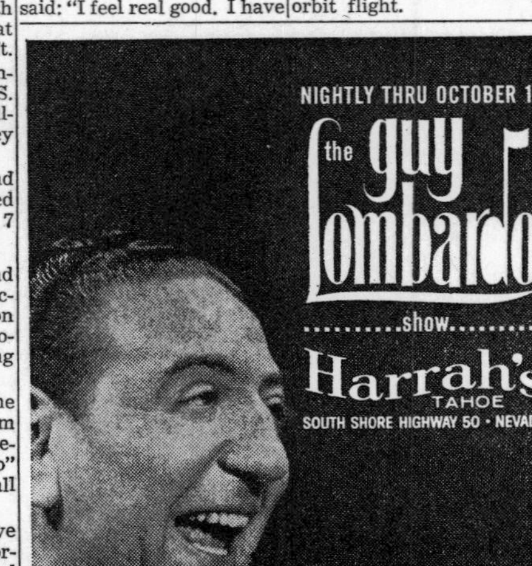

Koufax Changes Series Tempo and Odds

Yanks Want Second Shot At Southpaw

By MERRELL WHITTLESEY
Star Staff Writer

NEW YORK, Oct. 3.—Sandy Koufax picked up the tempo of this World Series in one magnificent afternoon's work, and millions of television viewers across the Nation—and even the Yankees — are looking forward to seeing him again.

The Dodgers' 5-2 triumph in the opener yesterday in Yankee Stadium put an extra burden on Al Downing, the 22-year-old southpaw who drew the task of trying to get the Yankees even against Johnny Podres in the second game.

The Yankees know that if Downing should be unequal to the assignment they would face the heaviest comeback odds in their long series history. That would send them to the West Coast with an 0-2 record and the knowledge that Koufax will be ready to start again in game No. 4 Sunday in Dodger Stadium.

Shift in Odds

The odds on the eventual outcome of the series were turned around by Koufax's great performance. The Yankees went into the best-of-seven playoff as 3-to-2 favorites, but this morning the odds favored the Dodgers, 11 to 10.

The 27-year-old Brooklyn-born Koufax, who has averaged more strikeouts per game than any pitcher in major league history, set a World Series mark of 15 when he fanned Pinch-hitter Harry Bright for the final out.

The ovation that the 69,000 gave the lefthander might have been the greatest for a visiting player in Yankee Stadium.

Elston Howard's line single to right with two out in the fifth broke up Koufax's bid for a perfect game. He lost his shutout with two away in the eighth when Tom Tresh laced a home run to left with Tony Kubek on base.

The Yankees were respectful but not downcast losers.

"Give the guy credit," Manager Ralph Houk said. "He pitched a helluva ball game, but we'll be seeing him again, maybe twice more.

"Koufax beat a great pitcher today," Houk said of his own Whitey Ford. "Whitey had an off day, a bad inning, but he'll be back."

Except for the pitchers, no lineup changes were planned today on either side. And the Yankees will use the same batting order when they face Koufax on Sunday.

"Why shouldn't we?" Houk said. "We've been shut out before. We got two runs off this guy. All of our men who struck out today want another crack at him."

Twelve of Koufax's strikeout victims swung at the third strike, with Tresh twice looking at the third one and Mickey Mantle caught looking once. Kubek looked the worst. He made two feeble swings at third strikes the two times he struck out and then ran to the dugout.

Mantle was the only Yankee who openly showed frustration. That was after a popout with two on base in the sixth, after Koufax walked Bobby Richardson and Tresh in succession. Mickey slammed down his helmet and threw a couple of gloves when he returned to the dugout.

Roseboro Surprises

The Dodgers' winning runs came from a completely unexpected source, John Roseboro, the 30-year-old catcher who inherited the position after Roy Campanella's tragic accident.

Roseboro, who had two singles in 21 times at bat in the 1959 World Series, arched an approximate 315-foot homer into the rightfield seats in the second inning with Dick Tracewski and Bill Skowron on base. It was Roseboro's first homer of the year off a left-handed pitcher.

Skowron, with two run-scoring singles, took away the sting of a miserable season in one afternoon. Skowron's first hit drove in Frank Howard, who opened the Dodgers' big inning with a line-drive, 460-foot double to centerfield that was easily the hardest-hit ball of the day.

With Maury Wills going 0-for-5 in the leadoff spot and the Dodgers with a 4-0 lead after 1½ innings, they didn't tip their hand on their famed speed. Tommy Davis stole second in the seventh after his third straight single, but it was meaningless.

Koufax, Ford, ex-Dodger Stan Williams and ex-Senator Steve Hamilton combined to break a series strikeout record with 25. Ford fanned four in five innings, Williams five in a strong three innings of relief and Hamilton fanned Koufax in the ninth. The Yankee pitchers fanned 10, but that was completely overshadowed by Koufax's superb effort.

Koufax, a modest, obliging bachelor, struck out the first five and fanned nine of the first 11 batters he faced with his fast ball, curve and an occasional changeup.

Three Hits in Fifth

Elston Howard, Joe Pepitone and Clete Boyer singled in succession in the fifth, but the Yankees didn't score because Tracewski got a glove on Boyer's hit and saved a run. Hector Lopez batted for Ford and fanned with the bases loaded.

Sandy found his second wind, as he said later, after walking Richardson and Tresh in the sixth. Walt Alston made his only visit to the mound in the eighth when Koufax walked Mantle after Tresh's homer.

Koufax, whose wildness prevented him from earlier fame, apparently regards a walk as a greater sin than giving up a homer.

"I knew how to pitch for years before I became a good pitcher," he said in the clubhouse. "But what's the good of knowing how if you are not able?"

Both teams planned to leave immediately after today's game in separate charter planes for Los Angeles, where the series resumes Saturday after an open date tomorrow. It will be Don Drysdale against Jim Bouton on Saturday, with Ron Fairly, Wally Moon and Ken McMullen probable replacements for the Dodgers against a righthander. The Yankee lineup will remain the same.

Carl Erskine (right) seems just as happy as Sandy Koufax after the Dodgers' lefthander struck out 15 Yankees in yesterday's World Series opener at Yankee Stadium to break Erskine's series record. Ten years ago to the day, Erskine a former Dodger, fanned 14 Yanks in a series game. Koufax whiffed Harry Bright for the final out.—AP Wirephoto.

DODGERS, 5; YANKEES, 2

NEW YORK, Oct. 3 (AP).—The box score of the first game of the 1963 World Series:

LOS ANGELES (N)

	AB	R	H	BI	O	A
Wills ss	5	0	0	0	2	0
Gilliam 3b	4	0	1	0	1	1
W. Davis cf	3	1	0	0	1	0
T. Davis lf	4	0	3	0	0	0
F. Howard rf	4	1	1	0	0	0
Fairly rf	0	0	0	0	0	0
Showron 1b	3	1	2	2	3	0
Tracewski 2b	4	1	1	0	2	2
Roseboro c	4	1	1	3	18	0
Koufax p	4	0	0	0	0	1
Totals	35	5	9	5	27	4

NEW YORK (A)

	AB	R	H	BI	O	A
Kubek ss	4	1	1	0	1	5
Richardson 2b	3	0	0	0	2	2
Tresh lf	3	1	1	2	0	0
Mantle cf	3	0	0	0	1	0
Maris rf	4	0	0	0	2	0
E. Howard c	4	0	1	0	11	0
Pepitone 1b	4	0	2	0	8	0
Boyer 3b	4	0	1	0	1	2
Ford p	1	0	0	0	1	2
aLopez	1	0	0	0	0	0
Williams p	0	0	0	0	0	0
bLinz	1	0	0	0	0	0
Hamilton p	0	0	0	0	0	0
cBright	1	0	0	0	0	0
Totals	33	2	6	2	27	11

a—Struck out for Ford in 5th. b—Struck out for Williams in 8th. c—Struck out for Hamilton in 9th.

Los Angeles (N)	041 000 000—5
New York (A)	000 000 020—2

E—None. LOB—Los Angeles (N) 6, New York (A) 7.

2B—F. Howard. HR—Roseboro, Tresh. SB—T. Davis. S—W. Davis.

	IP	H	R	ER
Koufax (W)	9	6	2	2
Ford (L)	5	8	5	5
Williams	3	1	0	0
Hamilton	1	0	0	0

BB—Koufax 3 (Richardson, Tresh, Mantle), Ford 2 (Gilliam, Skowron). SO—Koufax 15 (Kubek 2, Richardson 3, Tresh 2, Mantle 2, Maris, Pepitone, Lopez, E. Howard, Linz, Bright); Ford 4 (Wills 2, W. Davis, Roseboro); Williams 5 (Gilliam, W. Davis, F. Howard, Skowron, Roseboro); Hamilton 1 (Koufax). U—Paparella (A) plate, Gorman (N) First base, Napp (A) Second base, Crawford (N) Third base, Venzon (N) Leftfield, Rice (A) Rightfield. T—2:09. A—69,000.

WIN, LOSE OR DRAW

Erskine Thinks Sandy Could Whiff 18 or 20

By FRANCIS STANN

NEW YORK, OCT. 3.—Round one of the Sandy Koufax-Whitey Ford debate wasn't even close. The Dodger flame-thrower is all the Yankees had been led to believe, a sort of Rube Waddell and Bob Feller rolled into one. By the third inning a slender insurance man from Indiana shrugged in resignation.

"I knew he had my record beat when he struck out his fifth hitter," Carl Erskine said as he visited the Dodger clubhouse. Ten years ago to the day—October 2, 1953—Erskine fanned 14 Yankees in a 3-2 victory for the Dodgers, who were Brooklyn-based in those times.

Not many of the clubhouse journalists recognized Erskine when a path was beaten for him to Koufax's locker. But the new hero, the man whose whiff of pinch-hitter Harry Bright for the last out of the game broke the record, looked and sounded apologetic as he met Erskine.

Sandy was a kid of 17 when Carl, who pitched right-handed, performed his feat. A Brooklyn kid who, oddly, didn't hang around old Ebbets Field and worship the old Flatbushers. Koufax had been more of a basketball buff.

* * * *

"I HAD NO BUSINESS striking out 14 Yankees," Erskine said after congratulating the Dodger southpaw. "I wasn't that good a pitcher. I was sharp that day but this guy is great four out of five times, apparently. The only thing that surprised me was that he didn't strike out more. Maybe 18 or 20."

For four innings Koufax looked like the greatest pitcher who ever lived. Ten of the first 13 Yankees to face him went down swinging, or looked at his smoke, and it didn't matter whether they batted right or left.

Koufax had struck out Kubek, Richardson, Tresh, Mantle and Maris, the power of the New York batting order, the first two times each batted. It wasn't a question, as Carl Erskine commented afterward, of breaking the mark but by how big a margin.

There even were visions of a second perfect game, a la Don Larsen, only more spectacular. Or at least a no-hitter.

* * * *

ONLY THE STRIKEOUT goal did Koufax achieve, but it sufficed. Sandy is an extremely rough customer and an hour later the Yankees, talking in their clubhouse, still were trying to evaluate him.

"What I don't understand," Clete Boyer said, "is how he lost those five games during the season." Koufax was 25-5 in the National League.

"When I hit against him in that league," Dale Long remembered, "he was just a wild kid thrower. Now he throws a fast ball like Feller, and a curve that's at least as good as Feller's, and he gets everything over the plate."

Only Rookie Joe Peptione hit Koufax twice, pulling two singles to right. "Best curve I ever saw from a lefthander," Pepitone said. "He's a lefthanded (Camilo) Pascual with that curve, only faster." Pepitone was shooting marbles when Feller was breaking off *his* jug.

* * * *

FRANK HOWARD IS 6-7 and 255 pounds. He handles his bat like a swizzle stick. The Dodger rightfielder is so strong that he can compensate for a noticeable hitch in his swing.

Howard hit Ford with a 460-foot "rope" to the centerfield wall in the second inning. John Roseboro, the catcher who hadn't homered all year against a southpaw pitcher, ruined Whitey with his down-the-line homer in the same inning.

These blasts were of more heroic proportions than Moose Skowron's, but don't overlook the ex-Yankee who is platooning at first base for Los Angeles. His first single drove in the first run of the series, and a second hit wrapped up the Dodger scoring.

Ralph Houk's pre-game words in the dugout were to be remembered later.

* * * *

THE YANKEE MANAGER was asked if he feared Skowron, whom he traded for Pitcher Stan Williams. "You know Moose," said Houk. "He's streaky. If he's hitting, he'll hurt you."

As a secondary hero, Skowron also was holding court. "Whitey made a couple mistakes pitching to me," Moose said.

"I wouldn't know what kind of pitches I hit. Never do when I'm hitting."

Skowron is supposed to be all done. He hit .203 despite late-season improvement.

"I had a blankety-blank year," Moose confessed, "but the Dodgers have been wonderful. Front office and the players. The other day I pick up a paper and see where I'm going to play when Ford and Downing pitch.

"I can't do nothing about that lousy year, but maybe I can have a good series. You get to be a 10-year man, you want one more good series real bad. I owe a lot to Marv Breeding."

Marv Breeding? "Yeah," Moose said. "He joined the club and watched me being so lousy and said, 'Why don't you hit like you did in the American League? You're holding the bat too low.' I didn't realize it and the Dodgers don't know how I used to hit."

"And you owe it to Marv Breeding?" asked a man, doubtfully.

"Yeah, Marv."

The man turned away. "I wonder," he muttered, "who the hell Marv Breeding is."

Of such stuff is history made.

New NBA Boss Hits Auerbach With $500 Fine

EAST ORANGE, N. J., Oct. 3 (AP).—The new president of the National Basketball Association has made a lasting impression on Red Auerbach—right in the wallet.

The fiery coach of the world champion Boston Celtics was socked with a $500 fine by league President Walter Kennedy yesterday for "conduct contrary to NBA rules."

It was the biggest sum ever plastered on the oft-fined coach and stemmed from a dispute with Referee Mendy Rudolph during Tuesday night's exhibition game between Boston and the New York Knickerbockers at Oceanside, N. Y.

Auerbach was assessed the heavy penalty after Rudolph called two technical fouls against him and ordered him to leave the floor. Auerbach refused to leave and was slapped with a third technical. He later pulled his team off the court for several minutes.

The fuss started, Auerbach said, when a Boston player missed a shot and rookie official Manny Sokolofsky ruled against the Celtics. Auerbach called a timeout and went onto the floor to talk with Rudolph.

Sports on Air

Television

Baseball

World Series, Los Angeles vs. New York, WRC-4, 1 p.m.

Radio

Baseball

World Series, Los Angeles vs. New York, WRC, 1 p.m.

Holloran's Return 'Frees' Drummond

By DICK SLAY
Star Staff Writer

George Washington will be missing three players for its home opener tomorrow night against The Citadel at D. C. Stadium, but one of them will not be Mike Holloran.

Holloran, sophomore understudy to Dick Drummond at tailback, returned to practice yesterday after missing more than a week with an ankle infection. Considering his period of inactivity, the former Gonzaga flash ran rather well as Coach Jim Camp worked to sharpen GW's running attack and kicking game.

Meanwhile, Quarterback Tom Branch's injured back was placed in a cast, and Tackle John Zier and End George Ferguson—both reserves—also were declared out of tomorrow's game. Zier has mononucleosis and joined Branch as a GWU Hospital patient. Ferguson is suffering from a virus.

Changes Plans

The return of Holloran prompted Camp to change his plans for Drummond, who has been GW's best defensive back in the two games so far this season but has gained only 35 yards in 14 carries.

Camp said yesterday he will alternate Holloran and Jody Glass as Drummond's replacement on defense and save Dick for offense whenever the substitution rules allow.

As the defensive left wing, Holloran and Glass will have the assignment of keeping an eye on The Citadel's dangerous lonesome end, Vince Petno, and also helping protect against the Bulldogs' strong-side rushes. The visitors use an unbalanced line, most often strong to the right side, or GW's left.

MIKE HOLLORAN
Soph Back Recovers

Ready for Old Format

Although Drummond has been outstanding on defense at left wing, Holloran and Glass have the agility to do almost as well, Camp figures. More important, Camp will have his All-Southern Conference halfback in fresh condition to carry the football.

Employed about 95 per cent of the time in 1961 and '62 as an offensive specialist, Drummond averaged 64 yards a game from scrimmage. The last time GW played The Citadel, two years ago in Charleston, S. C., Dick ran for 129 and the Colonials won, 17-13.

After losses to Virginia Military and Furman, Camp obviously is ready to return to the old format.

HOME ★★★

SUNDAY NEWS

NEW YORK'S PICTURE NEWSPAPER®

MORE THAN TWICE THE CIRCULATION OF ANY OTHER PAPER IN AMERICA

40 New York 17, N.Y., Sunday, October 6, 1963 3 Sections | MAIN, MAGAZINE, COMICS

YANKEES	000 000 000	- 0	3	0
DODGERS	100 000 00X	- 1	4	1

BOUTON, Reniff (8) and E. Howard; DRYSDALE and Roseboro.

LA'S DRYSDALE, 1-0

Story on page 36

(Associated Press Wirefoto)

Dolph Camilli (l.) a member of Dodger team that lost to Yanks in '41 series, chats with son, Doug, and Leo Durocher at Dodger Stadium prior to yesterday's game. Doug is catcher for 1963 NL champs.

West Coast Edition

Glum Ralph Houk [⟵] ponders Yankee strategy for third clash with LA. Ralph went with right-hander Jim Bouton in attempt to stave off Dodger runaway of World Series.

(UPI Telefoto)

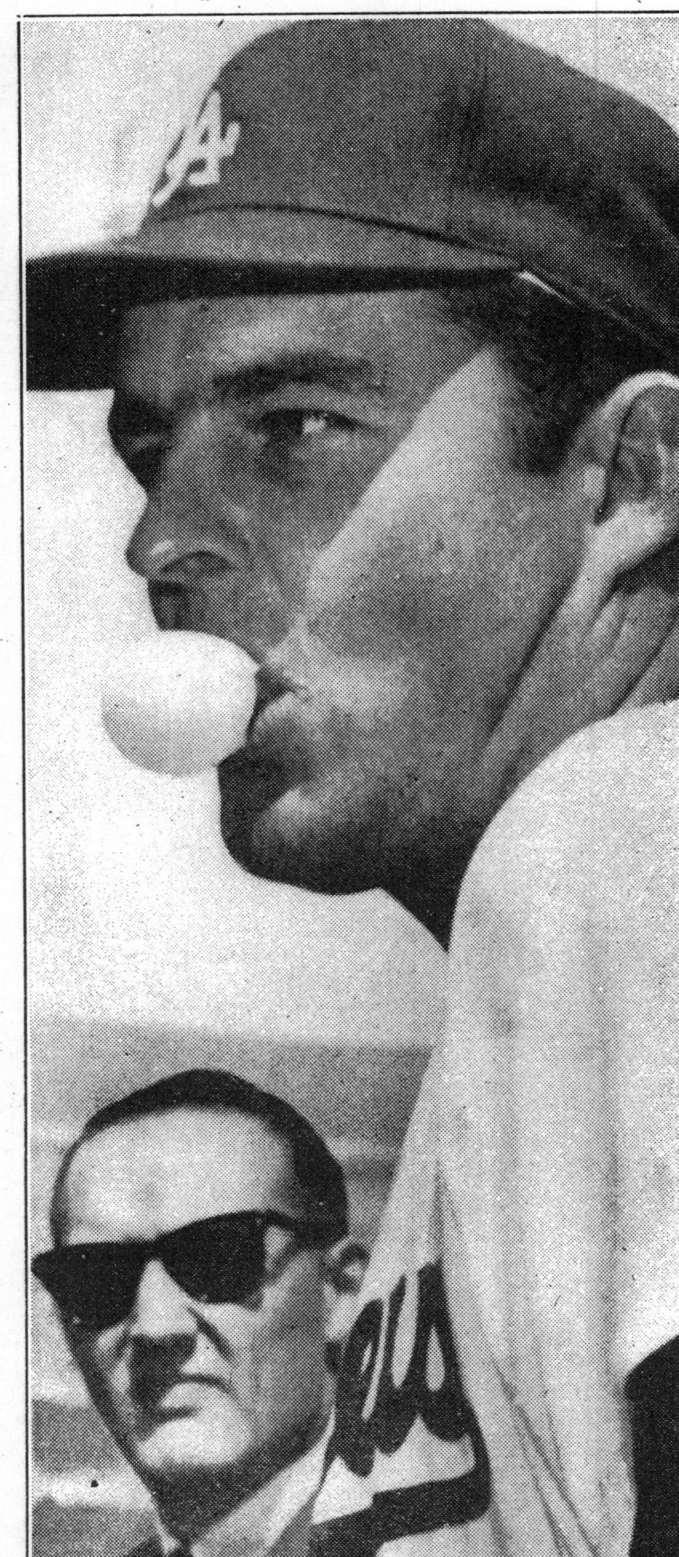

(UPI Telefoto)

Dodger hurler Don Drysdale hopes to blow 'em past Yanks.

"All the News That's Fit to Print"

The New York Times.

CITY EDITION

U. S. Weather Bureau Report (Page 52) forecasts:
Sunny and warm today.
Partly cloudy tomorrow.
Temp. range: 84—55; yesterday: 81—52.

VOL. CXIII....No. 38,607. NEW YORK, MONDAY, OCTOBER 7, 1963. M TEN CENTS

DODGERS WIN, 2-1, SWEEPING SERIES AGAINST YANKEES

Koufax Triumphs Again as New York Loses Four in Row for First Time

FORD YIELDS TWO HITS

Pepitone's Error Is Costly—Frank Howard and Mantle Hit Homers

By JOHN DREBINGER
Special to The New York Times

LOS ANGELES, Oct. 6—The Los Angeles Dodgers brought the long reign of the high and mighty New York Yankees to a dramatic end today.

Behind another superb pitching effort by their brilliant left-hander, Sandy Koufax, the Dodgers downed the perennial American League champions, 2—1. That gave Walter Alston's National League champions a stunning four-game sweep of the World Series before a deliriously happy crowd of 55,912.

The Yankees' indomitable Whitey Ford, fighting desperately to keep the Bombers alive, pitched perhaps an even greater game than his adversary, who had defeated him so easily in the first game. Whitey allowed only two hits to six by Koufax.

Ball Eludes Pepitone

But in the seventh inning, minutes after Mickey Mantle had hit a homer that matched a tremendous clout by Frank Howard in the fifth and made the score 1—1, a ghastly error by the usually flawlessly fielding Yanks plunged the Bombers to their most humiliating World Series defeat in more than 40 years.

Junior Gilliam, first up for the Dodgers in the seventh, bounced a "Baltimore chop" off the plate and down the third-base line. For a moment it appeared that the ball might sail over Cletis Boyer's head.

But the Yanks' classy third baseman made a leaping catch of the ball and fired it like a bullet across the infield to first base. The ball, still traveling like a bullet, went right through Joe Pepitone, the crack young first baseman, for an error. It appeared that in the last instant Pepitone had lost sight of the ball in the glaring sun.

Before the ball could be retrieved in a corner of right field, the fleet-footed Gilliam had raced to third base. Willie Davis followed with a towering fly deep in center field, where it was caught by Mantle, who with this play was to see all of his noble effort undone.

Gilliam Scores

Mickey fired the ball faultlessly toward the plate, but there was no chance of heading off Gilliam as he went winging home on the sacrifice fly.

Once again in front, Koufax, who in last Wednesday's opener had set a World Series record of 15 strike-outs, refused to let the lead slip away again.

There were some more tense moments in the ninth, when Bobby Richardson led off the Yanks' last desperate bid with a single. Koufax fanned Tom Tresh and Mantle to bring his total of strike-outs for this game to eight.

But the victory still wasn't nailed down. Elston Howard grounded to Maury Wills, whose

Continued on Page 38, Column 7

To the Victor—And Again It's Koufax—Go His Teammates' Cheers

Associated Press
Sandy Koufax whoops after the last putout

United Press International Telephoto
And his fellow Dodgers cover him with congratulations on beating Yanks

WAGNER DERIDES GOVERNOR'S TRIPS

Urges Rockefeller to 'Stay Home' and Stop His 'Hot Pursuit' of Presidency

Special to The New York Times

TROY, N. Y., Oct. 6—Mayor Wagner advised Governor Rockefeller yesterday to "stay home" and "stop wasting his time" pursuing the Presidency.

In a speech prepared for a Democratic audience here, Mr. Wagner poked fun at the Governor's travels abroad and to other states, and offered this "man-to-man" counsel to Mr. Rockefeller:

"Come back home and tend to the urgent business of your office."

Declaring that state and city governments were struggling with many pressing problems, the Mayor said that when "we knock at the door with our entreaties, the Governor is not at home."

Warming to his subject, the Mayor advised Mr. Rockefeller to forget about running for the Presidency because President Kennedy would "soundly and overwhelmingly" defeat him or any other Republican candidate next year.

Inspiration Needed

While Governor Rockefeller presses his "hot pursuit" of the Presidential nomination, Mr. Wagner told the annual Rensselaer County Democratic dinner, "he is neglecting our problems, the problems of the people of the state of New York."

"These problems," the Mayor went on, "call for all the energy, all the inspiration and and all of the leadership of which the Governor of this state — no matter what his name might be —is capable."

The Mayor said the state and its localities faced urgent prob-

Continued on Page 25, Column 5

Merchants Ignoring Fair-Sabbath Law; Open All Weekend

By PHILIP BENJAMIN

The city's Fair-Sabbath Law became effective over the weekend, but it had about as much effect on Lower East Side stores as Prohibition had on speakeasies.

The Fair-Sabbath Law, signed by Mayor Wagner last Monday, permits small, family-operated businesses to stay open on Sundays if the owners observe another Sabbath. The new law, it appears, was more honored in the breach than in the observance.

The Jewish Sabbath is from sundown Friday to sundown Saturday. A weekend tour of Orchard St., Rivington St. and other shopping streets on the Lower East Side showed that virtually all stores—novelty shops, toy shops, shoe shops, clothing shops—were open both Saturday and Sunday.

The same was true of one area of the Williamsburg section of Brooklyn. But in another area of Williamsburg—the neighborhood of the ultra-Orthodox Hasidic sect of Jews—almost every store was closed Saturday and open Sunday.

On the Lower East Side yesterday, it was like a carnival. The narrow sidewalks of Orchard St. were jammed with people; in front of the stores, Spanish-speaking clerks were enticing strollers to come in and look around. In recent years this area of the Lower

Continued on Page 25, Column 3

HOUSE WILL VOTE ON RIGHTS PANEL

Expects to Complete Action Today on Bill Extending Commission a Year

Special to The New York Times

WASHINGTON, Oct. 6 — Congress is expected to complete action tomorrow on a stop-gap bill to keep the Civil Rights Commission alive another year.

The measure, passed by the Senate, comes before the House of Representatives under a suspension of the rules. That procedure limits debate to 40 minutes, bars amendments and requires a two-thirds vote for the bill's passage.

The commission, created in 1957, is due to expire Nov. 30. Many key staff members have already resigned.

The year's extension is designed to continue the commission until Congress makes a longer-term decision on its future.

A provision making the commission permanent and broadening its duties is part of the omnibus civil rights bill before the House Judiciary Committee.

The committee begins work Tuesday on the rights measure, which was approved last week by a subcommittee. It will be a tricky job to produce a bill that can win majority support in the full committee and on the House floor.

Four points of view are at

Continued on Page 16, Column 5

Violence in Saigon Renews U.S. Debate On Vietnam Policy

By MAX FRANKEL
Special to The New York Times

WASHINGTON, Oct. 6 — Violence in South Vietnam has rekindled the Washington policy debate that President Kennedy tried to dampen last week. It is expected to bring new demands that the United States apply strong pressure to change the policies and personnel of the Saigon Government.

The issues that have long divided the Administration were suddenly reopened by the fiery suicide yesterday of a sixth Buddhist monk in Saigon, and by the beating of three American newsmen by South Vietnamese plainclothes policemen.

"We're right back where we started from," one official here remarked today. "The same arguments are going to flare all over town, and this time you have more Congressmen in the act and Mrs. Nhu all over television."

The official meant that Mr. Kennedy would again be bombarded by conflicting advice from Americans handling the war against Communist guerrillas in South Vietnam — advice that would have him either ignore the political turmoil in Saigon and press the military campaign, or finally decide that the war cannot be won without political changes.

The official's reference to new legislative interest was demonstrated by expressions of shock

Continued on Page 2, Column 1

SUPREME COURT CONVENES TODAY FOR CRUCIAL TERM

Decisions on Apportionment and Race Curbs Expected to Have Wide Impact

By ANTHONY LEWIS
Special to The New York Times

WASHINGTON, Oct. 6—The Supreme Court convenes tomorrow in a new term that promises to produce further significant change at the frontiers of the law.

Reapportionment, race relations and freedom of speech and press are among the subjects of national importance to be considered. There are no signs of any ebb in the controversy that has surrounded the Court in recent years.

If custom is followed, tomorrow's opening session will be routine. The Justices will file in to the marble courtroom, some lawyers will be admitted to the Supreme Court bar, and then the Court will recess.

In conferences during the rest of the week the Justices will consider hundreds of applications for review that have piled up during the summer. Many will be disposed of when the Court issues its first list of orders a week from tomorrow.

Sit-In Cases First

Oral arguments will also begin a week from tomorrow. At the head of the argument list are five cases arising from the sit-in demonstrations for racial equality that have swept the country in the last two years.

The five cases pose, ultimately, the most sensitive issue: does the Constitution permit a state to prosecute individuals for demanding service without racial discrimination at privately owned lunch counters, restaurants and similar facilities?

This issue, of course, is intimately involved in the civil rights debate now shaping up in Congress. The Kennedy Administration has asked for legislation prohibiting racial discrimination in places of public accommodation.

Congressional approval of the Administration draft would ease the burden of the Court. On the other hand, Congress would be free of the problem if the Court were to hold that the Constitution forbids state enforcement of segregation at public accommodations.

The constitutional issue is most difficult. In the past the Court has held that the 14th Amendment's ban on racial discrimination applies only to action by the states and their officials, not to purely private discrimination.

The five cases to be argued come from Maryland, South Carolina and Florida. Student demonstrators were convicted for trespass after refusing to leave segregated lunch counters or, in two Maryland cases, an amusement park and a restaurant.

Lawyers for the students

Continued on Page 24, Column 5

Rickover Charges Poor Workmanship Delays Submarines

Special to The New York Times

WASHINGTON, Oct. 6—Vice Adm. Hyman G. Rickover disclosed today that the completion of some atomic submarines was being held up because of poor workmanship by industrial contractors.

He linked the poor quality of work by Government contractors to industrial managers "more interested in getting new contracts than in seeing to it that the things they have already contracted for are done well."

"Right today," he said, "we are holding up atomic submarines because the equipment was not made in accordance with drawings and wasn't inspected properly."

He said the equipment would have to be repaired in the submarines at the cost of considerable time and money.

He declined to say, however, how many submarines were delayed in construction or which Government con-

Continued on Page 19, Column 1

SOVIET INDICATES 18% CROP DECLINE

Moscow Presses for a 75% Expansion in Fertilizer Output Within 2 Years

Special to The New York Times

MOSCOW, Oct. 6—An official Soviet source indicated today that grain supplies available to the Government from domestic production this year would be as much as 18 per cent below the 1962 level.

This disclosure, by a commentator of Tass, the official press agency, was the first to be made publicly by an official source on the extent of the Soviet crop failure.

The gravity of the agricultural situation was underscored by two other developments today.

All morning newspapers printed on their front pages an open letter of the Communist party's Central Committee and the Soviet Government. The letter called on workers in the chemical fertilizer industry to do their utmost to fulfill the ambitious plans for expanding production by 75 per cent in the next two years.

2,500 Workers Mobilized

On a more immediate level, 25,000 citizens and all available trucks were mobilized today in Moscow to stock the city's warehouses with potatoes, cabbages and other vegetables for the winter. The Sunday work was necessitated by a backlog of loaded freight cars in rail yards.

The disclosure of the 18 per cent decline in the grain harvest, which has not yet been publicized in the Soviet Press, was contained in an English-language report prepared for foreign subscribers by Ivan Artemov, economic commentator for Tass.

In the report, designed to rebut speculation in the foreign press regarding the gravity of the grain situation, Mr. Artemov wrote: "Incidentally procurement (by the Government from the farms) will be approximately on the level of 1959 and 1960."

Procurements in those years

Continued on Page 9, Column 1

SOVIET HINTS PLAN FOR A NATO FLEET IMPERILS ACCORDS

Gromyko Links a Pact to Bar Spread of Nuclear Arms to West's Naval Project

BONN'S ROLE IS FEARED

U.S. Is Reported to Believe Atlantic Force Would Limit Weapons Dissemination

By SYDNEY GRUSON
Special to The New York Times

LONDON, Oct. 6 — The Soviet Union appears to have made the abandonment of the proposed multinational nuclear-armed fleet a condition for further major steps toward relaxing East-West tension.

Soviet objections to the fleet were raised again by Andrei A. Gromyko, the Soviet Foreign Minister, during his talks in New York last week with the Earl of Home, Britain's Foreign Secretary, and Secretary of State Dean Rusk, according to reliable diplomatic sources.

Mr. Gromyko Specifically linked the abandonment of the projected fleet of atomic-armed surface ships manned by International crews from North Atlantic Treaty Organization nations with the possibility of agreement to prevent the dissemination of nuclear weapons and knowledge, the sources said.

The Soviet Foreign Minister apparently rejected the argument that the fleet, if it is established, would not change the nuclear situation between East and West.

[In another area of East-West negotiations, Secretary of the Treasury Douglas Dillon supported in Washington the idea of selling wheat to the Soviet bloc, The Associated Press reported. He said such sales would be valuable in helping to solve the United States deficit of payments.]

Concern on West Germany

The Russians have made it clear in other talks with Western diplomats that they are concerned over West Germany's possible role in the proposed nuclear-armed fleet.

The United States is reported to have argued that West Germany's participation would reduce rather than increase the danger of the Germans' getting independent control of nuclear weapons.

The proposal, originated by the United States, would establish a fleet of 25 ships armed with 200 Polaris medium-range ballistic missiles. Each ship's

Continued on Page 8, Column 3

DOMINICANS URGE JUNTA TO RESIGN

Citizens Demand a Return to Constitutional Rule

By HENRY RAYMONT
Special to The New York Times

SANTO DOMINGO, Dominican Republic, Oct. 6—Lawyers and politicians demanded today that the military-backed civilian junta ruling the Dominican Republic resign to permit the restoration of constitutional government.

The three junta leaders were asked to reconvene both legislative chambers and let Congress determine the future of the country.

Congress was dissolved after the bloodless military coup d'état that deposed Juan D. Bosch as President on Sept. 25.

Protests against the civilian junta, which took over the reins of government from the armed forces 36 hours after the coup, appeared today in pamphlets and newspaper advertisements.

A member of the Cabinet dismissed the protests as "a movement started by the Communists."

Mr. Bosch, in his first ad-

Continued on Page 14, Column 4

Costikyan Calls for an Overhaul Of 'Archaic' Voter Registration

Edward N. Costikyan, the leader of Manhattan's Democratic organization, called yesterday for a drastic overhaul of the state's "archaic" voter-registration system.

Mr. Costikyan was particularly critical of the requirements that persons go to assigned places to register and pass a literacy test in English. He charged that the rules discouraged many persons from taking part in elections.

"It's very hard for a person who is working for a living and getting paid a low wage to take off a day or a half a day, or two days to go take a literacy test in Brooklyn and then to come back and then go down on another day to get registered," Mr. Costikyan said.

In contrast, Mr. Costikyan noted, California permits deputized political workers "to set up card tables on the street corner" for voter registration.

"It's time," he asserted on a WABC television program, "that we faced up to this and started to put our whole electoral system into the 20th century."

This year's five-day registration period begins today. Under the system of permanent personal registration in the city, and all suburban counties except Rockland, those who are already registered and who voted last year or in 1961 are not required to reregister unless they have moved since they last voted.

New York's "archaic and primitive" registration system was designed to prevent fraudulent voting, Mr. Costikyan said, but he charged that it constituted the "biggest fraud of all" because it deprived

Continued on Page 56, Column 1

The New York Times (by Ernest Sisto)
FIRST DAY UNDER NEW LAW: Shoppers examining wares yesterday on Lower East Side. A new law signed last week permits stores to stay open Sunday if owner observes another Sabbath. Some confusion has arisen over the law.

Toll in Haiti is 400; Storm Lashes Cuba

By The Associated Press

MIAMI, Oct. 6—A tropical hurricane, having caused more than 400 deaths in Haiti, lay stalled today just south of the Cuban coast. It was battering Cuba for the third straight day.

The Haitian Embassy in Washington reported that 400 dead had been counted. With roads to many towns blocked by floods and landslides, the survey had not yet been completed.

The Cuban radio reported severe flooding and heavy crop and property damage in the eastern area. But it made no mention of deaths and injuries. Two men were reported missing.

For nearly two days the hur-

Continued on Page 21, Column 1

NEWS INDEX

NATIONAL LEAGUERS BEAT AMERICAN, 7-4

EVENING TRIBUNE

Evening Tribune-Established 1895 San Diego Daily Journal-Established 1944 San Diego Sun-Established 1881

Phone 234-7111 4 PARTS — 48 PAGES SAN DIEGO, CALIF., TUESDAY, JULY 7, 1964 10 CENTS

THERE SHE GOES — Philadelphia's Johnny Callison watches ball head for right-field wall in New York's Shea Stadium for three-run home run, giving N[illegible] victory in today's All Star game. (AP Photo)

Callison Blast In 9th Inning Sinks Losers

Mays' Steal Sets Up Winning Rally Against Radatz

NEW YORK (UPI)—Johnny Callison hit a three-run home run with two out in the ninth inning today to give the National League a 7-4 victory over the American League in the 35th major league All-Star Game.

The hit brought a crowd of 50,850 in Shea Stadium to its feet and enabled the National League to tie the 31-year-old series.

The seventh victory in the last eight games by the Nationals evened the series at 17-17-1.

Williams Puts NL Ahead

The Nationals had moved off to an early 3-1 lead with the aid of homers by Billy Williams and Ken Boyer. They fell behind in the seventh inning and for two innings seemed helpless before the pitching of Dick (Monster) Radatz.

Coming in after a sacrifice fly by Jim Fregosi had scored Elston Howard with a run to put the Americans ahead, 4-3, in the seventh, Radatz struck out four of the first five men he faced.

Willie Mays walked to open the ninth inning and stole second for his sixth steal in All-Star competition, [illegible] Cepeda then punch for a single.

Throw Misses Mark

Mays took a wide turn at third and Joe Pepitone, who had fielded the ball in short right, made a hurried throw to the plate which bounded over Howard's mitt. Mays scored and Cepeda went to second on the error.

Radatz got Boyer to pop to third, walked Johnny Edwards intentionally and struck out pinch-hitter Hank Aaron.

That left it up to Callison, Philadelphia outfielder. He hit Radatz' first pitch into the right-field stands above the 341-foot sign.

Marichal is Winner

Although Mays scored on Pepitone's error, Callison's homer made all four runs in the ninth inning earned and also dealt Radatz the defeat.

Juan Marichal of the San Francisco Giants, who pitched a perfect top half of the ninth, received credit for the victory.

The loss was a bitter blow to the Americans, who had battled back from a 3-1 deficit to take a 4-3 lead.

Fregosi Scores First

The Americans scored an unearned run against Don Drysdale in the first inning on Fregosi's game - opening single, a passed ball by Joe Torre and Harmon Killebrew's single to left field.

The National League scored in the fourth on the home runs by Williams and Boyer.

Brooks Robinson of Baltimore put the Americans back into the lead in the fifth inning with a two-run triple, scoring Mickey Mantle and Killebrew.

Lead Dissipates

The lead was short-lived, however, as Roberto Clemente of Pittsburgh singled in the bottom of the fifth and scored on a double by Dick Groat.

Fregosi's sacrifice fly scoring Howard put the AL back on top in the seventh.

Play-by-play, B-6

3 Escondidoans Die in Car Crash

Two Pinned In Wreckage Off Highway

Fourth Victim Survives Accident In North County

EVENING TRIBUNE Dispatch

RANCHO SANTA FE — Three Escondido youths were killed today and a fourth injured when their car ran off [illegible]

Theodore Copeland, 20, of 2251 Bear Valley Road.

Gary Forill, 18, of 126 E. 15th Ave.

Robert Churchill Jr., 19, of 961 W. 11th Ave.

In serious condition at Palomar Memorial Hospital with a broken wrist and breastbone and a back injury was John R. Allen, 21, of 1157 Elmwood Drive, Escondido.

Boy Finds Wreckage

The youths' crumpled car was found at 5:30 a.m. off El Monte-Video near Lago Lindo by a newspaperboy.

California Highway Patrolmen said the car was southbound on El Montevideo, probably about 3 a.m., when it missed a curve, plunged down a bank and hit the tree at 50 miles an hour.

The engine was pushed back into the passenger compartment. Copeland, the driver, was pinned behind the wheel, officers said. Forill's body was crumpled under the dashboard. It took patrolmen an hour to extract the bodies.

Coroner Tells View

Deputy Coroner R. W. Ricker said the three youths had been dead several hours when they were found. Witnesses in Rancho Santa Fe saw the car about 2:30 a.m., Ricker said.

FINAL EDITION

COMPLETE FINANCIAL

Rocky Wants Broad Planks In Platform

Back Rights Act, Remain in U.N., Ex-Candidate Says

By RALPH BENNETT
EVENING TRIBUNE Political Writer

SAN FRANCISCO — Gov. Nelson A. Rockefeller of New [illegible] transforming the Republican party into "a narrow, doctrinaire instrument of extremism."

Rockefeller appeared before the Platform Committee of the Republican National Convention.

He set forth in a seven-page statement his views on what the platform should contain.

Rockefeller's statement included many of the positions he took earlier this year when he campaigned in California against Sen. Barry Goldwater, R-Ariz.

Goldwater won California's 86 delegates in the June 2 presidential primary election.

Rockefeller called for platform planks as follows:

First — Affirming the constitutionality of the Civil Rights Act and pledging "other affirmative steps" toward equal opportunity for all Americans.

Second — A sound federal fiscal policy, aimed at a balanced budget and opposing any effort to eliminate the graduated features of the income tax.

Third — Pledging continued support to the present contributory Social Security system and opposing efforts to making it voluntary.

Fourth— Supporting a program for hospital and nursing home insurance for the elderly under Social Security.

Fifth—Standing for "a calm considered and expeditious execution of firm, clear foreign policy"—offering a leadership that "will neither yield to aggression nor react rashly to threats or frustrations, particularly in this age of nuclear weaponry."

Sixth — Declaring that the United States should remain in the United Nations and that the United Nations remain in the United States.

"We must not permit the Republican party to be trans-

(Continued Next Page, Col. 5)

MIRAMAR JET CRASHES AT POWAY; PILOT OK

A jet trainer plane from Miramar Naval Air Station [illegible] this afternoon.

Navy officials said the pilot ejected and was returned to Miramar. He was not immediately identified.

The disabled plane hit a barn, killing a horse, knocked down power lines and started a brush fire.

Navy officials sent crash and fire equipment from the Kearny Mesa air station, a few miles from the crash scene near Midland Avenue and Community Road. Fire rigs also were sent from area state Division of Forestry units.

The plane missed one home by only 40 feet.

Anti-Birch Stand Goal of Scranton

EVENING TRIBUNE Dispatch

SAN FRANCISCO — Gov. William W. Scranton of Pennsylvania thinks the Republican platform should specifically disapprove of the John Birch Society.

He said so in a letter to Rep. Melvin R. Laird, chairman of the Platform Committee of the Republican National Convention.

Text Made Public

Text of the letter was made public late yesterday by the governor's convention headquarters here.

The convention starts next Monday. Meanwhile, the Platform Committee started hearings last night.

Laird earlier asked Scranton to submit his views on platform planks.

Responding, Scranton said there is broad agreement among Republicans on most platform subjects. "Therefore, I will concentrate the following remarks on a few subjects," he said.

'Condemnation' Requested

On "extremism," Scranton said:

"I feel that the platform should contain an outright condemnation of extremist groups of both the left and the right and that it should name the John Birch Society as an organization of which the Republican party specifically disapproves."

Barry Backer Talks

Scranton is the candidate of forces seeking to stop the presidential nomination of Sen. Barry Goldwater, R-Ariz., at the convention.

A Goldwater supporter on

(Continued Next Page, Col. 4)

TRAFFIC SLAUGHTER 128

Chula Vista	3	Imperial Beach	0
Coronado	3	La Mesa	2
Del Mar	0	National City	3
El Cajon	5	Oceanside	12
Vista	3	San Marcos	2
Carlsbad	0	Escondido	2

In San Diego 49

In rural areas 44

County traffic deaths by this date last year, 107.

14 Climbers Die in France

CHAMONIX, France (AP) — A summer avalanche on Aiguille Verte Peak in the Mont Blanc Range today swept 14 Alpinists to a snowy death.

Among them was Charles Bozon, world special slalom ski champion in 1962.

All the victims were experienced mountain climbers. Four were professors from the French National School for High Mountains which trains and licenses mountain gudes. Nine were students at the school. Bozon had joined the group for his pleasure.

Slide 9,000 Feet Up

The avalanche occurred at an altitude of about 9,000 feet at a place called the Couloir Coururier.

Rescuers found all 14 climbers dead from suffocation. The bodies had to be dug out of deep snowdrifts. They were flown down to Chamonix by helicopter.

Bozon, 31, a native of Chamonix, was often called France's greatest skier. He had been skiing since the age of 3, racing since he was 9 and a member of French national ski teams more than a decade.

Games Hopes Hit

He was unable to take part in the Winter Olympic Games at Innsbruck, Austria, earlier this year because he had been suspended by the International Ski Federation on charges of professionalism.

During a trip to the United States and Canada last year he took part in a race organized by professionals. Although he gave back prize money he won, the federation suspended him for one year.

The group was going up the 12,000 - foot Aiguille Verte peak when caught by the avalanche.

U.N. Will Occupy Cyprus Peace Line

NICOSIA, Cyprus (UPI) — United Nations troops received orders today to take over a demilitarized zone slicing through Nicosia in a bid to restore peace to the island.

The troops will have full rights to search, arrest and disarm Cypriots in the strip under a plan approved by U.N. Secretary General Thant and announced by Galo Plaza of Ecuador, top U.N. civilian on the island.

He said the move was "our first major breakthrough."

Plaza also announced he is leaving Cyprus July 7 and will not be replaced as Thant's personal representative here.

Plaza said he received approval from Thant this morning for the United Nations to take over "exclusive rights to patrol, search, arrest, detain and disarm" persons in the planned "free zone."

The zone, he said would extend 100 yards on each side of the existing "green line"—the cease fire line where fighting halted inside the city last January.

Greek Cypriot President Makarios has agreed that Greek Cypriots will withdraw the 100 yards on their side and will not erect new fortifications, Plaza said.

He said the withdrawal will take place "very imminently," even if the Turkish Cypriots decline to withdraw on their side.

Main reason for Turkish Cypriot reluctance to withdrawn he said, was the desire to know who would control the "free zone." He said that with Thant's approval for the United Nations to do so, "I believe we shall now obtain Turkish Cypriot agreement also."

Taylor Arrives In Viet Nam

SAIGON (AP) — U.S. Ambassador Maxwell D. Taylor arrived in South Viet Nam today, declaring that the war programs already under way are sound but need "vigorous implementation and execution."

"I am sure that in the months to come we will see that vigorous implementation," Taylor said at Saigon Airport as more than 100 police and security agents stood guard.

"I have no illusions about the tasks that face your country in the days ahead," Taylor told the Vietnamese. "The fight against tyranny and injustice is never easy; the road to success is always long. But your brothers in the Free World stand with you, and together — with determination, patience and resourcefulness — I know we shall prevail."

Taylor, former chairman of the U.S. Joint Chiefs of Staff, was greeted by his deputy ambassador, U. Alexis Johnson; Lt. Gen. William C. Westmoreland, commander of U.S. forces in Viet Nam, and Vietnamese protocol officials.

3 Surviving Quads Reported as Fair

KIRBY MUXLOE, England (UPI)—Three surviving quads born six weeks prematurely Sunday to Mrs. Patricia White, 33, were reported in fair condition today in a hospital incubator.

The smallest of the four, a three-pound girl named Theresa, died yesterday. The other three, Clinton, Katrina and John, all weigh less than four pounds. The father, John White, 36, is a machinst.

Russians Report Crime Rate Drop

MOSCOW (AP)—Soviet law enforcers today reported a steep drop in the crime rate in the Soviet Union.

Pravda said the plenum of the supreme court had disclosed that convictions in 1963 were down 16.4 per cent from 1962. The report gave no breakdown on crime statistics but said the crime rate in 1962 was the lowest in the Soviet Union in 30 years.

WEATHER

Forecast — Generally clear tomorrow throughout the county. Coastal low clouds expected night and early morning. San Diego high tomorrow 75; low tonight 62. High yesterday 72, low today 61. Details Page A-9.

CHUCKLE

It is now the season for the flies to come around to make screen tests.

TABLES, A-20-23

Stocks Edge To Record

NEW YORK (AP)—The stock market edged up to another high today but it was hard going.

The Dow Jones industrial average closed up .70 at 844.94.

Trading was active.

Steels led a brisk advance in midafternoon that attracted a following among other groups. But the momentum faded near the close and many issues finished below their best levels of the day.

Gains by steels were shaved in the profit taking flurry.

American Telephone again reached 75, the new high set yesterday, but eased back and finished unchanged for the day.

Volume expanded to 5.25 million shares, compared with 5.07 million yesterday.

Of 1,376 issues traded, 605 advanced and 513 declined. There were 103 1964 highs and 9 lows.

'LOST' COMET RETURNS TO SAN DIEGO'S SKY

Tomita-Gerber-Honda, the "lost" comet, has been found.

It hadn't actually been lost, just made invisible by the bright rays of the sun.

The comet was last seen Thursday morning as it moved into the area of the sun.

It can be seen in the west now, just above the horizon, in the evening, said Rudolph Lippert, professor of astronomy at the University of San Diego College for Women.

The comet is moving east toward Regulus, brightest star in the constellation Leo. The comet has a magnitude (brightness) of 3.5.

The comet is traveling rapidly, Lippert said, but an observer must watch it for about an hour before its progress across the sky can be discerned.

TODAY'S EVENING TRIBUNE

All Cards Are Wild— And St. Louis Is, Too

By MAURY ALLEN
New York Post Correspondent

St. Louis, Oct. 16—There was a smell of stale beer in the Yankee clubhouse and the running shower water crashed against the thin floors.

Just 12 steps up a staircase, the World champion St. Louis Cardinals stood barefoot in trays of ice, gurgled champagne, blew kisses through a clubhouse window to pretty girls downstairs and cavorted like giddy children in a soggy sandpile.

"What the hell," said Ken Boyer, "it *is* our first."

"I was nine years old," said Clete Boyer, "when the Cards won in 1946. I remember the radio announcers saying how wonderful it was to see that championship flag waving in the wind. We tried hard to win. Now they have it. This town will appreciate it."

They found St. Louis resting along the Mississippi River 200 years ago and legend will recall yesterday as its finest day since.

The Cardinals beat the Yankees 7-5, in the seventh game of the World Series behind the gritty pitching of Bob Gibson on two days rest and a charging elan the Gashouse Gang would have claimed was gone.

That's All

Bobby Richardson popped to Dal Maxvill for the last out and a thousand fans raced on the field to hug and kiss and maul their heroes.

The Cardinals raced into their clubhouse and the corks flew off the champagne and the beer cans rattled against the lockers and the television men pushed their cameras against the combatants.

"Thanks for being here," said manager Johnny Keane, "this is where the action is."

"All my life," said Curt Flood, "I thought about this moment. Do you know what it means to be the champions of the world? You are at the upper echelon of your profession. There are no better. We won the big bag of money and beat the Yankees. It's the most wonderful thing to ever happen to me. I'm king of the mountain."

Flood stared glassy-eyed into the mad whirl in the room and shook his head from side to side, over and over and over again.

"There are no words," he said, "there are no words. You just have to live through it."

Somebody asked about next year.

"Next year," said Flood, "that's a lifetime away."

It is often the spear carriers of baseball who celebrate the triumph with the greatest glee. Next year may never come for them. With the Cards it was Bob Uecker, a catcher who never catches because Tim McCarver, the fine 23-year-old receiver, never rests.

"I'm on a damn championship team, man, do you know what that is? I'm going out tonight and throw up in every bar in St. Louis."

Uecker rubbed his face with shaving cream, threw champagne on his own head and beat his breast.

"I am the greatest," he said.

Perfection

Gerry Buchek, infield spare, splashed into the ice-filled trays with his bare foot and did a soft shoe.

"I hit a thousand in a World Series (one for one)," he said, "and we won."

Dick Groat, the old pro of the Cardinals had won in 1960 with the Pirates but conceded this was even better. Now, there was satisfaction.

"Joe Brown (Pirate general manager) traded me over here because he said I was washed up. Now I'm on a championship team two years later. I think I'll send him a telegram."

Groat turned to his Pirate teammate of 1960, Bob Skinner, and togther they reveled in the moment.

"Dear Joe," said Groat. "Hi. Signed Groat and Skinner."

Outside the Cardinal clubhouse a huge crowd of fans had gathered and they stared up at the clubhouse door, waved banners and shouted their hoorays.

"We want Boyer. We want Boyer. We want Boyer," they chanted.

McCarver appeared in the doorway to tell his wife to meet him at Stan Musial's because that's where the party would be.

"On to Musial's," the kids shouted, "On to Musial's."

Just then Musial, the Card vice president, came out of the clubhouse and took their cheers.

He laughed and waved and pointed back to the clubhouse. "They won it," he said, "not me."

The Hero

The fellow who really won it was standing in a knot of reporters with an empty champagne bottle cradled under his left armpit and the bottle neck held firm in his right hand.

He was Bob Gibson, the pitcher who had beaten the Yankees twice in four days.

Gibson had given up a three run homer to Mickey Mantle and single homers in the ninth to Clete Boyer and Phil Linz.

"I threw as hard as I could," said Gigson. "I wasn't saving anything."

Gibson set a World Series record for total strikeouts (31) with nine yesterday and never once showed signs of letting up.

"In the end when they hit those home runs," he said, "I was trying to get the ball over."

"He threw as hard at the end," said Tom Tresh, "as he had anytime all Series. He's a fine pitcher."

Gibson walked into manager Johnny Keane's crowded office and Keane shook his pitcher's hand.

"You got it," said Keane, tapping his heart, "right here."

Mel Stottlemyre, also coming back on two days rest, had matched Gibson until the fourth inning. Three singles, an error by Phil Linz on a questionable throw to first and a double steal by the Cards gave them a 3-0 lead.

"When that happened," said Gibson, "I knew I had to go hard."

Berra hit for Stottlemyre and Al Downing threw four pitches in the fifth inning. Lou Brock hit one 450 feet for a home run. Bill White lined the next to right field for a single. Ken Boyer took a wild ball and hit the next one up against the fence for a double.

Roland Sheldon came in and the Cards got two more on a grounder and a sacrifice and led 6-0.

Mantle's homer, lefthanded to left field, made it 6-3 and Ken Boyer's second Series homer made it 7-3. The two ninth inning homers ended the scoring.

Richardson, who set a Series record with 13 hits, then popped out to end it.

"If he got on," said Keane, "I would have taken him out. I didn't want him to pitch to Maris."

Gibson's magnificent performance earned him the white Corvette from Sport Magazine and a huge kiss from Roger Craig, who might have started.

"You," said Craig to Gibson, "are my hero."

It was three hours after the game now three Cards lay sprawled on a foot locker, their toes touching the tray of ice, their eyes closed and their hands holding empty champagne bottles.

In the Yankee clubhouse three beer cans sat in a pyramid on a foot locker. The shower was still running. A clubhouse boy scratched his broom against the floor.

Facts and Figures

	W	L	Pct.
St. Louis (NL)	4	3	.571
New York (AL)	3	4	.429

FIRST GAME

New York	030	010	010—5	12	2
St. Louis	110	004	03x—9	12	0

FORD, Downing (6), Sheldon (8), Mikkelsen (8) and Howard; SADECKI, Schultz (7) and McCarver.

SECOND GAME

New York	000	101	204—8	12	0
St. Louis	001	000	011—3	7	0

STOTTLEMYRE and Howard; GIBSON, Schultz (9), Richardson (9), Craig (9) and McCarver.

THIRD GAME

St. Louis	000	010	000—1	6	0
New York	010	000	001—2	5	2

Simmons, SCHULTZ (9) and McCarver; BOUTON and Howard.

FOURTH GAME

St. Louis	000	004	000—4	6	1
New York	300	000	000—3	6	1

Sadecki, CRAIG (1), Taylor (6) and McCarver; DOWNING, Mikkelsen (7), Terry (8) and Howard.

FIFTH GAME

St. Louis	000	020	000	3—5	10	1
New York	000	000	002	0—2	6	2

GIBSON and McCarver; Stottlemyre, Reniff (8), MIKKELSEN (8) and Howard.

SIXTH GAME

New York	000	012	050—8	10	0
St. Louis	100	000	011—3	10	1

BOUTON, Hamilton (9) and Howard; SIMMONS, Taylor (7), Schultz (8), Richardson (8), Humphreys (9) and McCarver.

FINANCIAL FIGURES

SEVENTH GAME

New York	000	003	002—5	9	2
St. Louis	000	330	10x—7	10	1

GIBSON and McCarver; STOTTLEMYRE, Downing (5), Sheldon (5), Hamilton (7), Mikkelsen (8) and Howard.

SEVENTH GAME

Attendance—30,346.
Net receipts—$198,420,95.
Commissioner's share—$29,763.14.
Yankees' share—$42,164.45.
Cardinals' share—$42,164.45.
American League's share—$42,164.45.
National League's share—$42,164.46.

SEVEN-GAME TOTALS

Attendance—321,807.
Net recipts—$2,243,187.96.
Commissioner's share—$334,478.21.
Players' share—$696,520.15.
Yankees' share—$302,547.40.
Cardinals' share—$302,547.40.
American League's share—$302,547.40.
National League's share—$302,547.40.

Cicada Runs 4th In Racing Return

Cicada, top money-winning mare of all time, returned to the wars at Garden State Park yesterday after a 14-month layoff and finished fourth in a six-furlong dash.

The Meadow Stable mare carried a light 110 pounds and was ridden by Willie Shoemaker. Cicada trailed the field in the early going but made up considerable ground in the late stages.

SPEAKING OUT

Houk Shaking Up the Yanks?

MILTON GROSS

The blow that struck the Yankees as they lost the World Series to the Cardinals is only the first which may fall on Yogi Berra's shaky crew before they play baseball again next spring.

Many are thinking this is the beginning of the end for the Yankee dynasty as we've known it. That is not necessarily true. There is too much solid talent here for it to finish this way, but despite immediate denials by general manager Ralph Houk, there is reason to believe that if the Yankees have not been broken up they will be shaken up during the fall and winter.

"We really haven't thought about it," said Houk in the dismal quiet of the dressing room after Cardinal hitting, pitching and base running and sloppy Yankee defensive play and weak relief pitching produced St. Louis' 7-5 victory in the seventh game yesterday. "This is still a pretty good club."

HOUK

It isn't, really, even if it was good enough to win the AL flag with the help of Pedro Ramos' relief work that wasn't available for the Series. For one thing, Whitey Ford may have to face surgery and the end of his pitching career because of a circulatory blockage in his left shoulder. For another, Mickey Mantle, despite his three Series home runs, has defied legs that no longer obey. For a third, there is too much excess baggage being carried on the roster. There isn't much down on the farm for the Yankees to replace the parts that can't contribute and all of it means that Houk may be forced to enter the trading market in earnest to rebuild for the greater glory of CBS.

Never, in fact, in recent memory must so many Yankees be so uncertain that they will be in spring training next February when the roll is called.

Perhaps the tell on the whole thing is that Bobby Richardson, who may be the most solid player on the roster, finally got around to confessing yesterday that until a week ago his mind was made up to retire.

"Something came up within the past week," he said, "that made me decide to play for one more year only. Betsy (Mrs. Richardson) and I talked it over and made the decision. I've four little children and I've been away from my family too much. I told the front office long ago that I was getting out."

* * *

Richardson wouldn't say what the "something" was, but it could have been Houk's promise that Bobby's next and last contract would be too profitable to bypass. Ralph appreciates how badly the Yanks need Bobby. Besides, Houk is extremely close to the second baseman, who broke a Series record for hits with 13, while messing up several key plays in the field. When Richardson was at Denver while Houk was managing there, Bobby asked for time off to get married.

The Denver front office refused the permission. Houk overruled his bosses and told Bobby to go ahead.

Mantle, of course, can still swing a bat, but he has difficulty running and in the field he is a hazard whether going for a ball or throwing one.

Some have even suggested that Mick, in pain most of the year although playing more than he anticipated he would be able to play, may retire. This is ridiculous. He can't afford to.

"I got to keep playing," Mantle said after he hit the 18th Series homer of his career off MVP Bob Gibson, who won Sport Magazine's Corvette for his two Series victories and record-breaking 31 strikeouts. "I don't know what I could do when I quit."

Ford has become a tremendous question mark. He may have to undergo the same kind of vascular surgery that recently had Jack Sanford of the Giants on the operating table for nine hours. When Whitey finally broke down yesterday and admitted that he's had no pulse in his left wrist since pitching the Series opener last week, the first thing the veteran southpaw asked was, "Will Sanford be able to pitch again?" Nobody knows about Jack and nobody knows about Ford.

* * *

Other Yankees, for a variety of reasons, must judge themselves suspect and in danger.

Clete Boyer, for instance, has the feeling that he's being measured for trade bait because of his weak hitting during much of the year. The Yankees can maneuver at third, with Phil Linz playing there. Joe Pepitone, who hot-dogged it through much of the Series after being cold through much of the season, is not in front office favor.

Consequently it comes down to an off-season when the once lordly Yanks, pressured at the gate by the Mets and in bad odor with the press because of the reluctance of some players to make themselves available for interviews, will have to scuffle like ordinary mortals.

Pitchers Jim Bouton and Mel Stottlemyre emerge as the team's two most valuables, but the rest of the pitching staff is burdened by such as Bill Stafford, Hal Reniff and Stan Williams, who have become liabilities. Ralph Terry is said to be ticketed for Cleveland, in delayed payment for Ramos, and Al Downing, who has been stricken by gopheritis, has to be rejuvenated.

Pride did not go before the fall, but what comes after may become the most frantic juggling act in show biz history. It could make owner Dan Topping the wisest man in the entertainment and capital gains field for selling out to that unblinking red eye, which could develop a nervous tic if the government allows the deal to stand.

★★★★ FINAL

DAILY NEWS

NEW YORK'S PICTURE NEWSPAPER ®

MORE THAN TWICE THE CIRCULATION OF ANY OTHER PAPER IN AMERICA

64 New York, N.Y. 10017, Tuesday, November 17, 1964

BERRA TO JOIN METS TODAY

Story on page 56

(Associated Press foto)

Can't Keep Good Man Down

A jubilant Joe Lynch is held up by his Georgetown University teammates at Van Cortlandt Park, Bronx, after Lynch copped the University Division Championship in 56th IC4A cross-country meet yesterday. Lynch led Hoyas to win over Notre Dame. *Story p. 56*

(UPI foto)

Is He a MET-iculous Person?

Former Yank manager Yogi Berra watches John Fiorendino wipe lane in Yogi's Clifton, N.J., bowling alley. It was reported yesterday that Berra will sign a two-year, $80,000 contract with the Mets today.

←Roger Lodges A Nod

British and Empire heavyweight champ Henry Cooper (left) sticks left jab to head of Roger Rischer, Oakland, Calif., during their 10-round London bout. Rischer outboxed Britain's best en route to 25th win in 35 bouts.

—Stories on page 56

(UPI Cablefoto)

Redskins in Twin Bill?

Bob Addie . . .

THE REDSKINS are being sought as opponents for the Minnesota Vikings in next year's football doubleheader in Cleveland. Art Modell, young owner of the Browns, wants to get the Baltimore Colts to play Cleveland. Modell said the other day that he was sure of a sellout every year but he wanted to keep the doubleheader fresh and appealing. The four football doubleheaders in Cleveland have drawn 327,755 people. When Modell first broached the idea, everybody thought he was crazy. The New York Giants, meanwhile, are trying to get the Browns for their annual exhibition game in the Yale Bowl.

Addie

In New York the other day I encountered Carlos Ortiz, the deposed lightweight champion who is getting a return bout with Ismael Laguna, the boy who beat him. Ortiz said the fight will be held sometime in November in San Juan, Puerto Rico, where Ortiz was born. However, he was brought to New York City as a baby, was educated there and also served eight years in the Army as a sergeant. "I tried to help the people in Puerto Rico by donating a part of my purse in a fight there," he related. "It was an outright gift and the money is to help build a playground for underprivileged children. The sad thing is that there is so much red tape."

In Milwaukee, where the people are angry with the Braves, the club has drawn just over 500,000 admissions. Nobody is mad at the Senators but that's about what they've drawn, too.

DANNY O'CONNELL, who was the first player signed by the Washington expansion club in December of 1960, was a Yankee Stadium visitor the other day when the Senators were there. He had his young son with him and the boy asked: "Why do they keep that big screen in front of the pitcher in batting practice?" O'Connell explained: "That screen is there so the Yankees won't hurt their own players." And then he added: "But the way some of those Yankees have been pitching maybe they ought to take the screen down."

On the day Johnny Keane was rehired as the Yankee manager, southpaw Steve Hamilton announced solemnly that he might quit next year. "It all depends," said Hamilton, who has a wry sense of humor. "I am holding out for a cushion to sit on when I'm in the bullpen. If I don't get it, I may have to quit."

Pedro Ramos, the Yankee relief specialist, hinted he may ask to become a starter again next year. "It all depends on what kind of salary I get," Ramos explained. "If the Yankees appreciate my services in the bullpen, and give me a raise, I'll stay as a reliever. But if I don't get paid for it, I'm going to insist on becoming a starter again."

RAMOS, A CUBAN refugee who now lives in Miami, said Hurricane Betsy caused considerable damage to his house. Ramos still is trying to get his mother and father from behind Cuba's bearded curtain. He has petitioned several legislators and hopes to see Sen. George Smathers (D-Fla.) when the Yankees come to Washington.

When the New York Jets put John Huarte on the taxi squad, there was surprisingly little protest. Apparently, Huarte hurt his own chances by becoming a "loner." He didn't seem to mix well with his teammates. The Jets paid $200,000 for Huarte and $400,000 for Joe Namath, who seems to be a better mixer. The Jets have cashed in on all the bonus money publicity and at last count had over 37,000 season tickets sold.

BILLY ROBERTSON, director of stadium operations for the Twins, represented them in the New York meeting called by Commissioner Ford Frick of all teams which have a chance to get into the World Series. "I hope," Robertson said pessimistically, "this trip is not in vain. The pressure really is beginning to build up but we still think we're going to win it."

The Yankees expect an absolute sellout Sept. 18 but the attraction won't be the Detroit Tigers. Mickey Mantle is being given a "day" for the first time and the demand for tickets has been phenomenal. Mantle is turning over all the cash proceeds to the Mickey Mantle Foundation for Hodgkins Disease research.

Sports columnist Shirley Povich is on vacation.

Firemen Honor Kline

Nats Again Seek No. 63 As Angels Visit Tonight

By Bob Addie

Washington Post Staff Writer

Still seeking that elusive 63d victory, the Senators try again at D.C. Stadium tonight against an old team with a new label—the California Angels. Pete Richert gets the call for the Nats and he will be the top winner on the staff if he can post his 13th.

The Nats return home with a four-game losing streak. The reason they want that 63d victory so badly is that it will make this year's entry the best of the five clubs that have represented Washington since expansion in 1961.

Manager Gil Hodges and the rest of the Senators will join in a celebration for ace reliever Ron Kline, who broke the old club record of 64 appearances established by Fred Marberry in 1926. Kline has appeared in 68 games this season and, of course, every time he pitches he adds to his own mark.

There should be considerable fun before the game, because Kline is being honored by the District of Columbia Fire Department as "the fireman of the century." Kline will be presented with an authentic fireman's helmet. The Nats will issue paper (firemen's) hats to the first 7500 persons who come through the gate.

All firemen and volunteer firemen in the Washington area will be admitted free and all will be entitled to bring one guest.

Since June 28, the Nats have compiled a 34-35 record — eminently respectable. Starting tonight, they will get more help. Officially added to the roster will be pitchers Joe Coleman and Jim Hannan, outfielder-first baseman Brant Alyea, catchers Jim French and Paul Casanova, infielder Frank Coggins and outfielder Fred Valentine.

The Senators yesterday called up the 18-year-old Coleman, the righthanded pitcher who received a $75,000 bonus in the free-agent draft in June. Coleman pitched for Burlington and had a 2-10 record with an earned run average of 4.56.

At the same time the Senators purchased catcher French, 24, from their Hawaii farm club. French spent most of the season with York, Pa., in the Eastern League.

Both players are expected to report in time for the game with the Angels tonight.

Koufax Hurls Perfect Game

L. A. Lefty 1st to Pitch 4 No-Hitters

LOS ANGELES, Sept. 9 (AP)—Sandy Koufax of the Los Angeles Dodgers pitched a perfect game tonight in a 1-0 victory over the Chicago Cubs and became the first pitcher in baseball history to throw four no-hitters.

Outpitching Bob Hendley in a brilliant duel of lefthanders, Koufax marked off his fourth no-hitter in consecutive years and surpassed the record for multiple no-hitters he shared with Bob Feller, Cy Young and Larry Corcoran.

Only One Hit in Game

Hendley, who allowed only one hit, was reached for a run in the fifth inning, when the Dodgers scored without a hit. Lou Johnson walked to open the inning, was sacrificed to second, stole third and raced home when catcher Chris Krug threw wild.

That was enough for the Dodgers, who remained one-half game back of first-place San Francisco in the tight National League pennant race.

Johnson Doubles

The only hit off Henley—and the only hit of the game—was Johnson's bloop double to right field with two out in the seventh inning.

Koufax, a 29-year-old fireballer whose career was in jeopardy because of circulatory ailment in his pitching hand, achieved a baseball plateau no other hurler ever reached as he set 27 Cubs down in order.

Koufax also struck out 14, lifting his major league-leading total to 332, as he posted the eighth perfect game in modern history and only the third in National League annals. Jim Bunning of Philadelphia pitched one last year against the New York Mets.

Feller Threw Three

Feller, the longtime Cleveland ace, pitched no-hitters in 1940, 1946 and 1951 and was the only modern pitcher besides Koufax to have as many as three no-hitters.

Corcoran pitched three pre-1900 no-hitters for the Cubs, in 1880, 1882 and 1884. Young pitched his first no-hitter for Cleveland, which was then in the National League, in 1897, and pitched no-hitters for Boston of the American League in 1904 and 1908.

Koufax, in bringing his record to 22-7, was overpowering with his assortment of fast balls and breaking stuff, striking out the last six batters he faced.

In the eighth he faced two of the Cubs' hardest hitting players, third baseman Ron Santo and Ernie Banks. He struck out both, then ended the inning by fanning Byron Browne, rookie left fielder.

Then, in the ninth as the tension mounted for a crowd of 29,139, Koufax fired a third strike past the Cubs' young catcher, Krug. Pinch-hitter Joey Amalfitano also went down swinging—on three pitches.

Then it was up to pinch-hitter Harvey Kuenn, former American League batting champion, who also went down swinging.

Koufax also closed in on another of baseball's most spectacular achievements, Feller's all-time strikeout record of

See KOUFAX, D2, Col. 5

Giants Win On 4-Hitter By Marichal

SAN FRANCISCO, Sept. 9 (AP)—Righthander Juan Marichal made his first start in Candlestick Park today since his Aug. 22 battle with John Roseboro and pitched the National League-leading San Francisco Giants to a 4-0 triumph over Houston.

Marichal notched his 21st victory and his tenth shutout, limiting the Astros to four hits, only two out of the infield.

The Giants won their sixth straight, jumping into a two-run lead in the second inning on a walk to Willie McCovey, a triple by Len Gabrielson and Tom Haller's sacrifice fly.

Haller whacked his 12th homer in the fifth. The Giants added another run in that inning when Dick Schofield doubled and came all the way around as Jesus Alou beat out a hit to deep short.

HOUSTON	ab	r	h	bi	SAN FRANCISCO	ab	r	h	bi
Maye lf	4	0	0	0	Schofield ss	4	1	1	0
Morgan 2b	4	0	0	0	J.Alou rf	4	0	1	1
Wynn cf	3	0	1	0	Mays cf	3	0	0	0
Bond 1b	4	0	1	0	Hend'son cf	1	0	0	0
Aspro'te 3b	3	0	0	0	McCovey 1b	2	1	1	0
Staub rf	3	0	1	0	Hart 3b	3	0	0	0
Brand c	1	0	0	0	G'br'ls'n lf	3	1	1	1
Adlesh c	2	0	1	0	Haller c	2	1	1	2
Kasko ss	3	0	0	0	Lanier 2b	3	0	0	0
Bruce p	2	0	0	0	Marichal p	3	0	0	0
Gentile ph	1	0	0	0					
Totals	30	0	4	0	Totals	28	4	5	4

Houston	000 000 000—0
San Francisco	020 020 00x—4

Errors—None. DP—San Francisco 1. LOB—Houston 4, San Francisco 2.
2B—Schofield, Wynn. 3B—Gabrielson. HR—Haller (12). SB—Wynn. SF—Haller.

ASTROS PITCHING

	IP	H	R	ER	BB	SO
Bruce L, 9-18	7	5	4	4	1	4
Raymond	1	0	0	0	0	2

GIANTS PITCHING

	IP	H	R	ER	BB	SO
Marichal W, 21-10	9	4	0	0	1	5

WP—Bruce 2. T—1:55. A—20,076.

The Washington Post Sports

SECTION D FRIDAY, SEPTEMBER 10, 1965 ...R1 D1

OUTDOORS
FINANCIAL
COMICS

United Press International

GIANT TRY — San Francisco shortstop Dick Schofield makes a gallant stop of a grounder by Walt Bond of Houston. Schofield threw to second baseman Hal Lanier (not shown) whose relay to first was too late to retire Bond. Giants won, 4-0.

Ralston Upset By Drysdale In Five Sets

FOREST HILLS, N.Y., Sept. 9 (AP)—South African Cliff Drysdale knocked America's top player, Dennis Ralston, into possible retirement with a stirring five-set quarterfinal victory today and left Arthur Ashe as the lone U.S. hope in the National Tennis Championships.

In a touch-and-go battle that lasted 2½ hours and that saw each player blow match points, Drysdale upset the fuming, third-seeded Ralston, 2—6, 3—6, 7—5, 6—3, 8—6.

Shortly afterward, another American hopeful, giant-killer Charlie Pasarell of Puerto Rico, went down before the tricky, change-of-pace shots of Mexico's Rafael Osuna, 1—6, 6—3, 6—3, 7—5. Osuna broke Pasarell at love in the 12th game of the fourth set after Pasarell had staved off two match points in the ninth.

The 24-year-old Drysdale, seeded eighth, and Osuna, No. 6, meet in one of Saturday's semifinals with the other bracket to be decided Friday.

In those matches, Roy Emerson of Australia, top-seeded and rated the world's best amateur, plays Ashe, 22-year-old Davis Cupper from Los Angeles, and Manuel Santana of Spain takes on Antonio Palafox, the other half of Mexico's Davis Cup team.

Ralston, a disappointment in the recent Davis Cup interzone matches in Spain, was glum and unsure of his future after blowing a two-set lead.

Asked if he would return here next year, Ralston said, "I don't know." He has talked of quitting big time tennis to return to his studies at the University of Southern California.

Ralston, once the bad boy of the game who had undergone a reform, reverted to type in the match with Drysdale.

He threw his racket against

See TENNIS, D3, Col. 3

Kaat Wins 15th

Twins Blast Chisox, Lead by Seven Games

See Picture, Page D2

CHICAGO, Sept. 9 (AP)—The Minnesota Twins scored four runs in the first two innings today and then coasted to a 10-4 victory over the second-place Chicago White Sox, building their American League lead to seven games.

In taking the final two games of the season between the teams, the Twins all but knocked the White Sox out of the race. Chicago is only one-half game ahead of third-place Baltimore.

The Twins unloaded 15 hits off Joe Horlen, Bob Locker, Eddie Fisher and Greg Bollo.

Tony Oliva's sacrifice fly accounted for one run in the first inning and the Twins scored three more in the second, when they collected five singles. Hits by Rich Rollins and Zoilo Versalles and Jerry Kindall's sacrifice fly brought in the runs.

The Twins picked up two unearned runs in the sixth off Locker and then blasted Fisher for two more in the seventh on doubles by Sandy Valdespino and Oliva and Earl Battey's single.

Jim Kaat, now 15-10 for the season and 4-0 over the White Sox, had a perfect game through the first four innings.

He walked John Romano to start the fifth and then Moose Skowron singled to right.

MINNESOTA	ab	r	h	bi	CHICAGO	ab	r	h	bi
V'rsalles ss	5	1	2	1	Buford 2b	4	0	1	1
V'ld'pino lf	4	1	3	0	Robinson rf	4	0	1	1
Oliva rf	4	1	1	2	Cater lf	4	0	0	0
Mincher 1b	4	0	0	0	Romano c	3	1	0	0
Battey c	4	1	2	1	Skowron 1b	4	0	2	0
Zim'man c	0	1	0	0	Ward 3b	4	0	0	0
Hall cf	5	2	3	2	Hansen ss	4	2	1	1
Rollins 3b	5	2	2	1	Berry cf	4	0	1	0
Kindall 2b	2	1	0	1	Horlen p	0	0	0	0
Kaat p	3	0	2	0	Locker p	1	0	0	0
Wo'h'gt'n p	1	0	0	0	Hicks ph	1	1	1	0
					Freese ph	0	0	0	0
					Burgess ph	1	0	1	1
					Staehle ph	1	0	1	0
Totals	37	10	15	8	Totals	35	4	9	4

Minnesota	130 002 202—10
Chicago	000 011 101— 4

E—Versalles, Buford. DP—Chicago 1. LOB—Minnesota 6, Chicago 7.
2B—Kaat, Valdespino, Oliva, Hicks. HR—Hall (20). SB—Hall. S—Valdespino, Mincher. SF—Oliva, Kindall, Robinson, Buford.

TWINS PITCHING

	IP	H	R	ER	BB	SO
Kaat W, 15-10	6 2-3	5	3	3	1	3
W'thi'gt'n	2 1-3	4	1	1	0	3

WHITE SOX PITCHING

	IP	H	R	ER	BB	SO
Horlen L, 12-12	1 2-3	6	4	4	0	0
Locker	4 1-3	4	2	0	1	2
Fisher	1	4	2	2	0	1
Bollo	2	1	2	2	1	2

WP—Horlen. T—2:46. A—5,786.

Majors Standings

AMERICAN LEAGUE

	W.	L.	Pct.	G.B.
Minnesota	89	54	.620	....
Chicago	82	61	.573	7
Baltimore	80	60	.571	7½
Cleveland	77	63	.550	10½
Detroit	78	64	.549	10½
New York	69	75	.479	20½
California	66	77	.465	23
Washington	62	80	.437	26½
Boston	56	87	.392	33
Kansas City	51	89	.364	36½

THURSDAY RESULTS

Minnesota 10, Chicago 4
California 7, Kansas City 2
Only games scheduled

FRIDAY GAMES

California (Brunet 8-10) at Washington (Richert 12-10), 8:05 p.m.
Kansas City (Sheldon 7-7 and Hunter 6-6) at Baltimore (Pappas 12-7 and J. Miller 6-3), 2 games, twi-night.
Minnesota (Perry 9-6) at Boston (Lonborg 9-15), night.
Detroit (Lolich 11-8) at Cleveland (Siebert 14-6), night.
New York (Stottlemyre 16-8) at Chicago (Peters 9-11), night.

WEDNESDAY NIGHT RESULTS

New York, 6, Washington 5
Baltimore 2-0, Detroit 0-5
Minnesota 3, Chicago 2
Boston 5, Cleveland 3.
Los Angeles 5, Kansas City 3

NATIONAL LEAGUE

	W.	L.	Pct.	Pct.
San Francisco	79	59	.572	....
Los Angeles	80	61	.567	½
Cincinnati	80	61	567	½
Milwaukee	77	62	.554	2½
Pittsburgh	77	66	.538	4½
Philadelphia	71	68	.511	8½
St. Louis	70	71	.496	10½
Chicago	65	77	.458	16
Houston	60	81	.426	20½
New York	45	98	.317	36½

THURSDAY RESULTS

San Francisco 4, Houston 0
Cincinnati 3, New York 2
Los Angeles 1, Chicago 0
Phila. at Milwaukee, ppd.
Only games scheduled

FRIDAY GAMES

Milwaukee (Blasingame 16-9) at New York (Fisher 8-19), night.
St. Louis (Gibson 17-10) at Philadelphia (Short 16-9), night.
Cincinnati (Jay 9-6) at Pittsburgh (Veale 15-10), night.
Houston (Roberts 9-8) at Los Angeles (Drysdale 18-12), night.
Chicago (Ellsworth 13-13) at San Francisco (Herbel 9-7), night.

WEDNESDAY NIGHT RESULTS

Philadelphia 6, Milwaukee 5
Cincinnati 11, New York 2
Pittsburgh 2, St. Louis 1

Guard Courts Lions

Karras Refuses To Join Redskins

By Dave Brady

Washington Post Staff Writer

CANTON, Ohio, Sept. 9—Ted Karras said today he is not going to report to the Redskins.

Karras, eight-year veteran guard, was dealt to Washington Tuesday by the Chicago Bears in exchange for guard George Seals, who had walked out of the Redskin training camp a week before.

"I have a real estate business here," Karras said on the telephone from his home in Gary, Ind. "I have bought a new home and my wife is expecting another child shortly. I am in a bad position to move now. I am 31 years old and I have to think of my future.

May Change Mind

"The only solution I see to this situation would be for me to play at Detroit. That is closer to my home and my brother, Alex, of course, plays defensive tackle for the Lions. I have been told that the Lions do not need a guard, but if I cannot play for them I will retire, even though it will leave me in a hole financially."

Coach Bill McPeak said today he is hopeful of convincing Karras to play for the Redskins after Ted gets over the shock of being traded. Friends of Karras say his real estate business is not quite booming and that he may change his mind about playing before the teams cut their rosters to 40 players by next Tuesday.

"There is no rush," McPeak said. "We would not be able to use Ted by Sunday anyhow. He would not know our plays in time."

Geographical Problem

The Redskins play the Lions in an exhibition game here Sunday and McPeak is hopeful of making a deal with them.

Karras said, "I have deep respect for Bill McPeak. He is a fine man. I knew him in Pittsburgh. I would love to play for the Redskins.

"They have a good team and I know fellows playing for McPeak, who are happy. It is only a matter of geography. I am hurt if I am not traded to the Lions.

"I was not prepared for a trade. It would be different if I were a rookie, but I am 31, not 21. I have always played regularly with every team I have been with. I have never sat on the bench.

"I think the owners are often unfair in these things. George Halas, our coach at Chicago, telephoned me and told me I had better join the Redskins. He said the Lions do not want me. I suspect Halas got together with Bill Ford, the owner of the Lions.

"I have talked to McPeak twice and told him about wanting to join the Lions but he pointed out that the Lions reject . . .

See REDSKINS, D3, Col. 1

Seedborg, Jacobs Put on Taxi Squad

CANTON, Ohio, Sept. 9 The Redskins put kicker John Seedborg and rookie quarterback John Jacobs, both from Arizona State, on the taxi squad today when other clubs did not claim them off the waiver list.

It was Seedborg's second try for the team. He played with Joliet in the United League last season after being put on waivers by the Redskins.

Bob Jencks, obtained in a deal with the Chicago Bears last spring, has won the place-kicking job and split end Pat Richter will do the punting again.

Seedborg does both.

Jacobs was dropped by the Dallas Cowboys last month before the Redskins acquired him as a free agent.

GILLIAM, 3B

WILLS, SS

GRANT, P

VERSALLES, SS

VALDESPINO, LF

DAVIS, CF

New York Post Sports

112 NEW YORK, WEDNESDAY, OCTOBER 6, 1965

Dodgers Choice In Opener, Too

OLIVA, RF

By MAURY ALLEN
New York Post Correspondent

Minneapolis, Oct. 6—All the experts who have conceded the 62d World Series to the Dodgers retire to the sidelines this afternoon and allow the players to settle it on the field.

FAIRLY, RF

"We're not conceding a thing," said Sam Mele, the grey 48-year-old manager of the Twins. "You win or lose on the field."

"We're in fine shape," said Walter Alston, the dean of baseball managers. "It should be a good series."

Jim(Mudcat) Grant, 30-year-old righthander from Lacoochee,

James A. Wechsler on the World Series. See Page 54.

Fla., starts for the American League champions against Don Drysdale, 29-year-old Dodger righthand ace.

Oddsmakers favor the Dodgers at 6½-7½ (7-5 man to man) to win the series with Drysdale favored even 6 (11-10 man to man) for the first game.

Regulars Start

Sandy Koufax will skip the first game today in deference to the Jewish holiday but will be ready for the second game tomorrow against Jim Kaat, the tall Twins lefthander.

The game will be seen and heard at 3 P.M. New York time on Ch. 4.

Both teams will present their regular starting lineups for the opening game. The Dodgers

DRYSDALE, P

probably will play the same eight men every day while the Twins will platoon two outfielders.

The visiting Dodgers, the most famous patty-cake players in the world, will have four switch hitters in the lineup against Grant.

The entire switch-hitting infield of Maury Wills, Jim Gilliam, Jim Lefebvre and Wes Parker will be batting left handed against the right-hander.

The Twins starter used to be a hard thrower but this season, under the teaching of Johnny Sain, Grant has become a curve balling pitcher.

Wills will lead off for the Dodgers followed by Gilliam, who is an expert at taking pitches long enough for Wills to run.

Willie Davis bats third and Ron Fairly is the cleanup hitter in the Dodger attack.

Lou Johnson, the surprising rookie, Lefebvre, Parker, Johnny Roseboro and Drysdale complete the linup. Drysdale has been the Dodgers best pinch hitter down the stretch and is the team's only .300 hitter with seven home runs and 19 runs

The teams will have their aces leading off in both cases. Zoilo Versalles a candidate for American League Most Valuable Player, starts the Twins linup. Like Wills he can run. Unlike Wills he can also hit the ball over the fence.

Against Drysdale, Sandy Valdespino will be in left field followed by Tony Oliva, the batting champion and Harmon Killebrew, who looks, acts and talks like a cleanup hitter.

Jimmie Hall, the lefthanded hitting centerfielder, will bat fifth with Don Michner sixth, Earl Battey seventh and Frank Quilici eighth.

Grant isn't in Drysdale's class as a hitter. He batted .155.

A capacity crowd of more than 40,000 is expected for the opening game at Bloomington's Metropolitan Stadium.

Clear weather with temperatures in the 50's are forecast.

The only players with World Series experience on the Twins are Earl Battey, who never played but was on the 1959 White Sox and Johnny Klippstein who was with the 1959 Dodgers.

All the preliminaries are over now and the battle begins on the field.

"That," said Mele," is the only place it counts.

KILLEBREW, 3B

JOHNSON, LF

HALL, CF

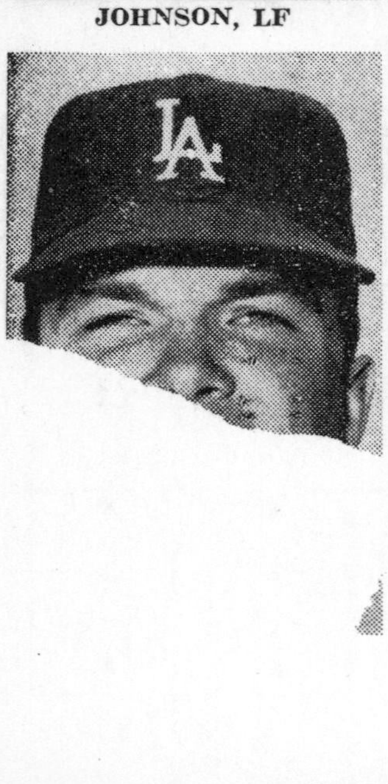

BATTEY, C

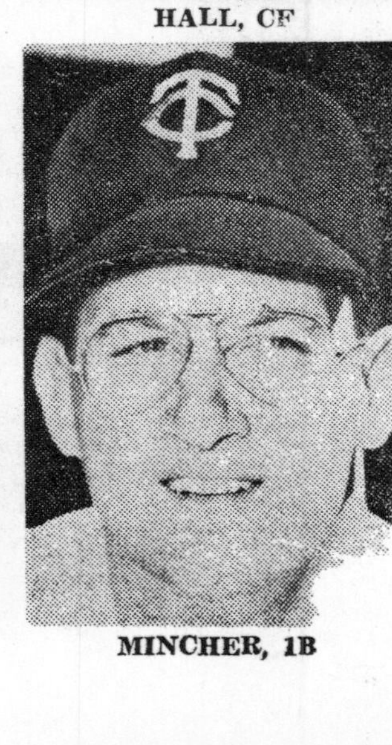

MINCHER, 1B

GETS 93.3% OF VOTE; NAMED RED SOX VEEP

Ted Sweeps Into Hall of Fame

THE KID'S IN—Former Red Sox slugger, Ted Williams, is all smiles as he faces battery of photographers after he was named to baseball's Hall of Fame. He also huddled with Hose VP Dick O'Connell after it was announced Williams would also become a vice-president in the organization.
(Associated Press Photo) (Record American Photo, Dick Thomson)

By LARRY CLAFLIN and JOE CASHMAN

He didn't make it unanimously, but Ted Williams came very close to it Thursday when he was named to baseball's Hall of Fame by a whopping 93.3 per cent of the votes cast by the members of the Baseball Writers Association of America. The expected announcement was made at Fenway Park with Ted present. At the same time, the Red Sox announced Williams will assume more duties with the Sox in the future and that he has been named a Vice President of the club.

CANDIDATE	NUMBER OF VOTES	%
1. TED WILLIAMS	282	93.3%
2. CHARLES H RUFFING	208	68.8%
3. ROY CAMPANELLA	197	65.2%
4. JOE MEDWICK	187	61.9%
5. LOU BOUDREAU	115	38.0%
6. AL LOPEZ	109	36.0%
7. ENOS SLAUGHTER	100	33.1%
8. HAROLD REESE	95	31.4%
9. MARTY MARION	86	28.4%

TED WILLIAMS AUTOGRAPHS HALL OF FAME BALLOT

Williams was the only player elected. Pitching great Red Ruffing finished second, 18 short of the 226 votes necessary for election. Third was Roy Campanella and in fourth place was Ducky Medwick.

Nobody else was close to being elected.

A total of 320 writers—all with at least 10 years membership in the writers group—voted. Williams was named on 282 of the ballots. It was the greatest number of votes ever cast for one man, but Bob Feller received a greater percentage (94) of the vote when he went in four years ago.

Williams, last of the .400 hitters, was obviously pleased with his huge vote, but he was on the verge of the unemotional as he talked with the press on the Fenway roof.

"I can't begin to tell you how pleased I am to have been elected to the Hall of Fame," Ted began. "I have always known how lucky I was to have been connected with the Boston Red Sox and Tom Yawkey.

"I have also known how lucky I am to have been able to play in such a rabid baseball town as Boston. Boston fans are the best."

"This is a wonderful day for me," Williams added. "I can't think of anything a ball player would want more."

Williams expressed sympathy for Ruffing and others who did not make the grade.

"Red Ruffing won more than 270 games, and he missed three years because of the war," Ted said. "He would have been a cinch 300-game winner otherwise. Medwick was the greatest right handed hitter I ever saw in the National League except for Hornsby. Campanella was a great catcher.

"I'm sorry those guys won't be with me at Cooperstown."

Williams will be formally inducted next July 25 at ceremonies in that quaint village in upper New York State. (If you plan to attend you better start making hotel reservations right now.)

Williams will become the 103rd person to be elevated to baseball's shrine. He is the 40th person elected by the writers. Sixty-three others were named by old-timers committees.

A disappointment in the election was the fact that Casey Stengel was ignored. Stengel is not eligible until 1970 because of the peculiarities of the voting. However, the baseball writers went on unanimous record in December, asking the Hall of Fame to waive the rules and allow Stengel to be admitted, immediately.

Williams was in good humor during his hour-long press conference. He made frequent reference to his celebrated feuds with the press, but tempered his remarks by saying:

"Many of the feuds were

Turn to Page 63, Col. 1

Two Full Pages of Photos of Highlights of Ted Williams Career in Center Fold

Bruins Nip Hawks, 4-3

By D. LEO MONAHAN

Rookie goalie Bernard Parent was slated to start last night's game for the Bruins, but he came down with a stomach ailment and gave way to veteran Eddie Johnston, who won the unenviable job of facing Chicago's highscoring Bobby Hull.

Final Score: Bruins 4, Chicago 3.

Hull had six previous goals vs. Boston, a team with just two ties in seven previous meetings with the first-place Black Hawks.

FIRST PERIOD

Ed Westfall once again was shadowing Hull, who had one weak shot on his first shift. Green flattened Hodge with an elbow, but it went unpenalized. Moments later, at 5:01, Tom Williams, playing on a checking line vs. Hull, put the B's in front at 8:04 with his 10th goal.

Wharram swooped down on a loose puck and parked his 15th goal low to a far corner at 11:37 to equalize for the Hawks. Then Hull scored his 37th goal on a power play at 12:36.

Martin converted Marotte's rebound at 14:13 to give the B's a 2-2 standoff for the period.

Score: Bruins 2, Chicago 2.

SECOND PERIOD

Ashley called a chintzy hooking penalty vs. Williams at 1:45 and five seconds later Mohns his 12th goal.

Stapleton was penalized at 8:32 and Dillabough at 17:00 but neither team scored.

Score: Chicago 3, Bruins 2.

THIRD PERIOD

Nesterenko drew an interference penalty at 2:44 and Hull broke away briefly from Westfall to put a testing chance on Johnston.

McKenzie scored at 9:03 on a Boivin assist to tie the score.

B's center Forbes Kenney—

Turn to Page 61, Col. 3

Orioles Win 2, Move Into First

BALTIMORE (AP) — The streaking Baltimore Orioles night on Boog Powell's two-run homer in the sixth inning after scoring an 8-7 victory in a suspended game with a four-run rally in the eighth and took over first place in the American League.

The Orioles, who have won 10 of their last 12, moved one game ahead of Cleveland, which had its game with New Yorkrk rained out.

Dick Nen's homer, following Paul Casanova's double, gave Washington a 2-0 lead in the second inning of the regulation game.

Baltimore tied it 2-2 in the fourth on two walks and singles by Powell and Curt Blefary. Powell then hit his homer off loser Diego Segui with two out in the sixth.

WASHINGTON	ab	r	h	bi	BALTIMORE	ab	r	h	bi
Valentine rf	5	1	3	3	Snyder cf	5	1	2	2
Saverine 3b	5	0	0	0	Blefary lf	5	0	2	0
Lock cf	3	2	1	1	Watt p	0	0	0	0
FHoward lf	5	1	1	1	FRobinsn rf	4	2	2	0
McMulln 1b	3	0	0	1	BRobinsn 3b	4	1	2	0
King ph	1	0	0	0	Powell 1b	4	1	2	2
Hamlin 2b	3	1	2	0	DJohnson ss	4	0	1	2
Camilli c	4	1	2	0	Adair 2b	4	1	3	0
Brinkmn ss	3	0	2	1	Carreon c	3	1	1	1
Nen 1b	0	0	0	0	Barber p	1	0	0	0
Hannan p	2	1	1	0	Brabendr p	2	0	0	0
BChance ph	1	0	0	0	Bowens lf	1	1	1	1
Bosman p	1	0	0	0					
Cox p	0	0	0	0					
Total	36	7	12	7	Total	37	8	16	8

Washington ...... 005 000 011—7
Baltimore .... 300 010 04x—8

E—D.Johnson, Lock. DP—Washington 3, Baltimore 1. LOB—Washington 7, Baltimore 7. 2B—D.Johnson, Hamlin, Fr.Robinson, Carreon. 3B—F.Howard, Valentine. HR—Valentine (5), Snyder (2), Lock (7). SF—McMullen.

	IP	H	R	ER	BB	SO
Hannan	5	10	4	4	2	5
Bosman (L, 1-3)	2 1-3	5	4	4	0	1
Cox	2-3	1	0	0	0	0
Barber	2 2-3	6	5	5	3	3
Brabender (W, 1-1)	5 1-3	5	1	1	1	8
Watt	1	1	1	1	0	1

WP—Hannan. PB—Carreon (2). T—2:54.

WASHINGTON	ab	r	h	bi	BALTIMORE	ab	r	h	bi
Valentine rf	3	0	0	0	Aparicio ss	4	0	1	0
Hamlin 2b	4	0	0	0	Snyder cf	3	1	0	0
Lock cf	3	0	0	0	FRobinsn rf	3	2	1	0
FHoward lf	4	0	2	0	BRobinsn 3b	4	0	0	0
McMulln 3b	4	0	1	0	Powell 1b	3	1	3	3
Casanova c	4	1	1	0	Blefary lf	3	0	1	1
Nen 1b	4	1	1	2	Blair lf	0	0	0	0
Brinkmn ss	4	0	0	0	DJohnson 2b	2	0	0	0
Segui p	2	0	0	0	Etchebrn c	3	0	0	0
Camilli ph	1	0	1	0	McNally p	2	0	0	0
Lines p	0	0	0	0	SMiller p	0	0	0	0
King ph	1	0	0						
Total	34	2	6	2	Total	27	4	6	4

Washington ...... 020 000 000—2
Baltimore .... 000 202 00x—4

E—McMullen. DP—Washington 2. LOB—Washington 7, Baltimore 3. 2B—Casanova, F.Howard, Camilli. HR—Nen (3), PowellS—McNally.

	IP	H	R	ER	BB	SO
Segui (L, 2-5)	6	6	4	4	2	3
Lines	2	0	0	0	1	0
McNally (W, 5-2)	7 1-3	6	2	2	2	11
S.Miller	1 2-3	0	0	0	0	1

WP—McNally, Segui. T—2:36. A—6,318.

Dave McNally, who struck out 11 including seven of nine during one stretch, was the winner for Baltimore, but he needed relief help fro Stu Miller in the eighth.

Washington led 5-4 when play was resumed in the sixth inning of the suspended game which had been halted by a city curfew Wednesday night.

Fred Valentine, who had socked a two-run homer during a five-run Washington rally in the third inning Wednesday, singled home another run in the eighth to make it 6-4.

But Baltimore tied it 6-6 on an infield single by Jerry Adair, a double by Camilo Carreon and a pinch single by Sam Bowens. Russ Snyder then smacked his second homer of the year off loser Dick Bosman. Don Lock homered for Washington in the ninth.

Gene Brabender, who hurled 2 1-3 innings in relief Wednesday, continued on the mound and went three more innings before Bowens batted for him. Brabender struck out eighth over the two nigts and scored his first major league victory.

Tigers 9, Bosox 1

DETROIT (AP) — Norm Cash, Don Demeter and Bill Freehan hammered home runs that backed up Dave Wickersham's five-hit pitching and led the Detroit Tigers to their fifth straight victory, 9-1, over the Boston Red Sox Thursday.

Cash's 3-run homer in the fourth and Demeter's two-run shot in the sixth highlighted the Tiger offense that was aided by 10 bases on balls off five Boston pitchers.

BOSTON	ab	r	h	bi	DETROIT	ab	r	h	bi
Petrocelli 3b	3	1	1	0	MAuliffe ss	2	2	1	1
Thomas 3b	1	0	0	0	Lumpe 2b	2	0	2	1
Gosger cf	2	0	1	0	Trcewski 2b	3	1	1	0
Ystrmski lf	4	0	1	0	Cash 1b	4	2	1	4
Conigliaro rf	4	0	1	0	Kaline cf	2	0	0	0
Foy ss	4	0	0	0	Demeter cf	2	1	1	2
Scott 1b	4	0	0	0	Northrup rf	5	0	1	0
Jones 2b	4	0	0	0	WHorton lf	3	1	0	0
Tillman c	3	0	0	0	Freehan c	4	1	2	1
Santiago p	2	0	1	0	Wert 3b	2	1	1	0
Stephnsn p	0	0	0	0	Wood 3b	1	0	1	0
Sanders p	0	0	0	0	Wickshm p	5	0	0	0
Brandon p	0	0	0	0					
Christphr ph	1	0	0	0					
Osinski p	0	0	0	0					
Total	32	1	5	0	Total	35	9	11	9

Boston .... 100 000 000—1
Detroit .... 110 312 01x—9

E—McAuliffe. DP—Detroit 1. LOB—Boston 7, Detroit 12. HR—Cash (9), Demeter (4), Freehan (6).

	IP	H	R	ER	BB	SO
Santiago (L, 4-3)	3 2-3	7	5	5	3	2
Stephenson	1	1	1	1	3	2
Sanders	2-3	1	2	2	4	2
Brandon	2-3	0	0	0	0	0
Osinski	2	2	1	1	0	1
Wickshm (W, 2-0)	9	5	1	0	3	6

WP—Wickersham. T—2:48. A—6,507.

Astros Bow To Giants In 11, 3 to 1

HOUSTON (AP) — Jim Davenport's 11th inning double drove in two runs and gave San Francisco a 3-1 victory over Houston Thursday night.

Willie McCovey opened the Giants' 11th with a single against Jim Owens, Houston's third pitcher. After Jim Hart walked intentionally.

Then Davenport doubled to left, scoring McCovey and Haller with the tie-breaking runs.

Jim Gentile and Rusty Staub clipped Giants' starter Ron Herbel for Houston's first inning run.

Card Homers Win

PITTSBURGH (AP) — Jerry Buchek and Phil Gagliane each cracked two-run homers as the St. Louis Cardinals defeated Pittsburgh 4-2 Thursday night and tagged rookie Pirate southpaw Woody Fryman with his first defeat.

The homers were the first this season for the Cardinal infielders. Buchek hit his in the second after Mike Shannon singled off Fryman.

ST. LOUIS	ab	r	h	bi	PITTSBURGH	ab	r	h	bi
Brock lf	4	1	1	0	Alley ss	4	1	1	0
Gagliano 3b	4	1	2	2	Mota cf	3	0	0	0
Flood cf	4	0	0	0	Clemente rf	4	1	3	1
Cepeda 1b	4	0	1	0	Paglaroni c	4	0	0	1
Shannon rf	4	1	2	0	Clndenon 1b	4	0	2	0
Buchek 2b	3	1	2	2	Mazroski 2b	4	0	0	0
Corrales c	4	0	0	0	Bailey 3b	4	0	1	0
Maxvill ss	4	0	0	0	Stargell lf	3	0	0	0
AJackson p	3	0	0	0	Fryman p	2	0	1	0
					Pagan ph	1	0	0	
					McBean p	0	0	0	0
Total	34	4	8	4	Total	33	2	8	2

St.Louis .... 020 002 000—4
Pittsburgh .... 000 001 010—2

DP—Pittsburgh 1. LOB—St.Louis 4, Pittsburgh 5. 2B—Shannon. HR—Buchek (1), Gagliano (1), Clemente (8). S—Mota.

	IP	H	R	ER	BB	SO
A.Jackson (W, 5-4)	9	8	2	2		0
Fryman (L, 4-1)	7	7	4	4	1	5
McBean	2	1	0	0	0	2

T—1:58. A—11,232.

Braves Knock Mets

NEW YORK (AP) — Mack Jones' three-run homer highlighted Atlanta's five-run first inning and led the Braves past the New York Mets 8-4 Thursday night for their sixth straight victory.

ATLANTA	ab	r	h	bi	NEW YORK	ab	r	h	bi
Mathews 3b	4	1	1	0	Hunt 2b	5	1	2	0
Woodwrd ss	4	1	0	0	Luplow rf	1	2	0	0
Aaron rf	3	2	1	0	CJones cf	5	0	1	1
FAlou lf	5	1	3	2	Boyer 3b	3	1	1	3
MJones cf	3	1	1	4	Kranpool lf	4	0	1	0
Torre 1b	5	0	2	0	Stuart 1b	3	0	0	0
Carty c	4	2	4	1	Grote c	2	0	0	0
Millan 2b	5	0	1	1	Hiller ph	1	0	1	0
Cloninger p	4	0	0	0	Eilers p	0	0	0	0
					McMilln ss	3	0	0	0
					Stephnsn c	1	0	0	0
					Hamilton p	0	0	0	0
					Arrigo p	0	0	0	0
					Lewis ph	1	0	0	0
					Hepler p	1	0	0	0
					Swoboda ph	1	0	0	0
					Selma p	0	0	0	0
					Bressoud ss	1	0	0	0
Total	37	8	13	8	Total	32	4	6	4

Atlanta .... 510 001 100—8
New York .... 200 020 000—4

E—Kranepool, Carty, Torre. DP—Atlanta 1. LOB—Atlanta 9, New York 10. 2B—Torre. 3B—Mathews. HR—M.Jones (7), Boyer (5), Carty (1). SB—Millan. SF—Boyer, M.Jones.

	IP	H	R	ER	BB	SO
Cloninger (W, 5-6)	9	6	4	4	8	7
Hamilton (L, 4-6)	1	5	5	5	1	0
Arrigo	1	1	1	1	1	0
Hepler	4	2	1	1	0	2
Selma	2	3	1	1	2	0
Eilers	1	2	0	0	2	1

WP—Hamilton, Cloninger (3). T—2:52. A—13,356.

Met Pitcher Sports Dislocated Finger

NEW YORK (AP) — New York Met pitcher Gerry Arrigo was forced to leave Thursday night's game against Atlanta when he suffered a possible dislocation and fracture of the little finger on his left hand.

Arrigo deflected a ball hit by Felipe Alou in the second inning. It struck his left hand and bounced to Ron Hunt, who made the putout.

Cincy Nips Phillies

PHILADELPHIA (AP) — Joey Jay pitched a six-hitter and Leo Cardenas drove in the only run with an eighth inning single as Cincinnati edged Philadelphia 1-0 Thursday night.

Jay and Phillie starter Bob Buhl were locked in a scoreless duel until the eighth. Then with two out, the Reds scored their run.

CINCINNATI	ab	r	h	bi	PHILADELPHIA	ab	r	h	bi
Harper rf	5	0	2	0	Rojas 2b	4	0	0	0
Rose 2b	5	0	0	0	Callison rf	4	0	2	0
Pinson cf	4	0	1	0	Allen lf	3	0	0	0
DJohnson lf	4	0	0	0	Wine ss	0	0	0	0
Perez 1b	4	0	1	0	White 1b	4	0	1	0
Simpson rf	0	1	0	0	Gonzalez cf	3	0	0	0
Helms 3b	4	0	4	0	Groat ss	4	0	0	0
Ruiz 3b	0	0	0	0	Dalrmple c	2	0	1	0
Cardenas ss	4	0	1	1	Linz 3b	2	0	0	0
Edwards c	2	0	1	0	Clemens lf	1	0	1	0
Jay p	3	0	0	0	Buhl p	2	0	0	0
					Knowles p	0	0	0	0
					Kuenn ph	1	0	0	0
					Fox p	0	0	0	0
Total	35	1	10	1	Total	30	0	5	0

Cincinnati .... 000 000 010—1
Philadelphia .... 000 000 000—0

E—D.Johnson. DP—Cincinnati 2, Philadelphia 1. LOB—Cincinnati 10, Philadelphia 6. 2B—Harper, Helms. 3B—Callison. SB—Allen, Gonzalez. S—Jay.

	IP	H	R	ER	BB	SO
Jay (W, 6-2)	9	5	0	0	2	5
Buhl (L, 1-4)	7 2-3	10	1	1	2	3
Knowles	1-3	0	0	0	0	1
Fox	1	0	0	0	0	0

HBP—By Jay (Gonzalez). T—2:40. A—13,566.

Munch Dead at 75

PHILADELPHIA (AP) — Jacob (Jake) Munch, who played with the Philadelphia Phillies and the old Philadelphia Athletics, died Wednesday at his suburban Lansdowne home. He was 75.

Pitchers Battle In Little League

CLEARFIELD, Pa. (AP) — A little league team in Clearfield may be tough to match.

Madera of the Moshannon Valley Little League scored 49 runs in a six-inning game. It beat Janesville 49-1.

The winner scored 35 runs in the last three innings, including 15 in the fourth. Madera also had 33 hits.

Dodgers Clip Spurs, 2 to 1

The Dallas-Fort Worth Spurs blew chances in the eighth and ninth and dropped the finale of their three-game series to Albuquerque 2-1 Thursday night.

The Dodgers, blanked by Ron Law and Len Church after the third, survived two late rallies.

Jesse White's single and Gene Etter's triple to right center gave the Spurs their only run in the eighth.

Tom Hillary and John Felsky, the first two men up in the ninth, singled but the Spurs refused to sacrifice and pinch hit too late, wasting their opportunity.

Tom Hutton increased his league-leading runs-batted-in total to 49. He drove home the first Dodger run with a sacrifice fly in the first and singled home the other one in the third.

Mets Recall Pitcher From Jacksonville

NEW YORK (AP)—Dick Rusteck, a left-handed pitcher with a 6-1 won-lost record at Jacksonville in the International League, was recalled by the New York Mets Thursday and will join the club in time to pitch Friday night against Cincinnati.

RACING FEATURES

DELAWARE PARK—1. Admiral Tudor ($16.80 $7, $4.60); 2. Besito ($4, $3.40); 3. Al's Runner ($4.80).

MONMOUTH PARK—1. In Zeal ($3.60, $2.80, $2.60); 2. Customs Officer ($5, $3.60); 3. Jeannie's Ruler ($3).

AQUEDUCT—1. Lake Delaware ($3.40, $3, $2.20); 2. Free Romance ($5.80, $2.60); 3. Farmers Lot ($2.40).

SUFFOLK DOWNS—1. Beamingly Yours ($3.20, $2.40, $2.20); 2. Unfair Play ($10.60, $4); 3. Fungo ($4).

ARLINGTON PARK—1. Jungle Boy ($6.40, $3, $2.40); 2. Fleet Fella ($2.60, $2.20); 3. Craft Step ($2.60).

Twins Unload on A's, 9-4

Minnesota's 5 HR's in Inning Sets AL Mark

ST. PAUL-MINNEAPOLIS (AP) — The Minnesota Twins smashed a record tying five home runs in the seventh inning Thursday, riding the late explosion to a 9-4 victory over Kansas City.

The Twins just missed breaking the major league record for most home runs in an inning when Jimmie Hall came within about two feet of clearing the fence after Harmon Killebrew had crashed the fifth homer of the frame.

Minnesota trailed 4-3 going into the big inning after Killebrew's two-run homer in the sixth inning had pulled the Twins back into contention.

Pinch hitter Rich Rollins started the barrage, connecting off A's starter Jim (Catfish) Hunter after Earl Battey walked. That put the Twins ahead 5-4.

Zoilo Versalles followed with another homer, finishing Hunter and bringing on Paul Lindblad.

Sandy Valdespino went out, but Tony Oliva tagged Lindblad for the third homer of the rally. Then Don Mincher followed Oliva with the fourth.

John Wyatt replaced Lindblad and was greeted by Killebrew's second homer of the game. Hall then narrowly missed.

The five homers in one inning was an American League record. Three National League teams have accomplished the feat, the last time by San Francisco on Aug. 23, 1961.

Ironically, it was against the Athletics in 1964 when the Twins tied the American League record for consecutive homers with four.

Oliva's homer was his 14th, tying him for the league lead.

The A's got four runs off Twins starter Camilo Pascual in the first inning, three of them on Larry Stahl's two-out triple. Minnesota got one run back in the fifth when Bob Allison doubled.

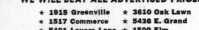

KANSAS CITY	ab	r	h	bi	MINNESOTA	ab	r	h	bi
Cmpneris ss	4	0	2	0	Versalles ss	5	1	2	1
Nossek cf	4	1	1	0	Valdspino lf	4	0	0	0
Hershbgr rf	3	1	1	0	Oliva cf	4	1	2	1
Cater 3b	3	1	0	0	Mincher 1b	4	2	2	1
Harrelson 1b	1	0	0	0	Killebrew 3b	4	2	3	3
Stone 1b	3	0	0	0	JHall rf	4	0	1	0
Stahl lf	4	1	1	3	Battey c	3	1	0	0
DGreen 2b	4	0	1	1	BAllen 2b	4	1	1	0
Roof c	4	0	1	0	Pascual p	0	0	0	0
Hunter p	3	0	0	0	Siebler p	0	0	0	0
Lindblad p	0	0	0	0	Allison ph	1	0	1	1
Wyatt p	0	0	0	0	Cimino p	0	0	0	0
Tartabull ph	1	0	0	0	Rollins ph	1	1	1	2
					Worthgtn p	1	0	0	0
Total	34	4	7	4	Total	35	9	13	9

Kansas City ..... 400 000 000—4
Minnesota .... 000 012 60x—9

E—Stone. DP—Kansas City 3. LOB—Kansas City 5, Minnesota 5. 2B—Allison, J.Hall. 3B—Stahl. HR—Killebrew 2 (11), Rollins (2), Versalles (5), Oliva (14), Mincher (6). SB—Campaneris.

	IP	H	R	ER	BB	SO
Hunter (L, 4-5)	6 1-3	9	6	6	3	0
Lindblad	1-3	2	2	2	0	0
Wyatt	1 1-3	2	1	1	0	3
Pascual	2-3	3	4	4	1	1
Siebler	4 1-3	3	0	0	0	2
Cimino (W, 1-1)	2	1	0	0	0	2
Worthington	2	0	0	0	1	2

T—2:28. A—9,621.

NY Signs Infielder

NEW YORK (AP) — The New York Yankees signed Walter Manuel, a 22-year-old shortstop from Perth Amboy, N.J., and Lafayette College, Thursday.

The Series Sweep Put a Head on It

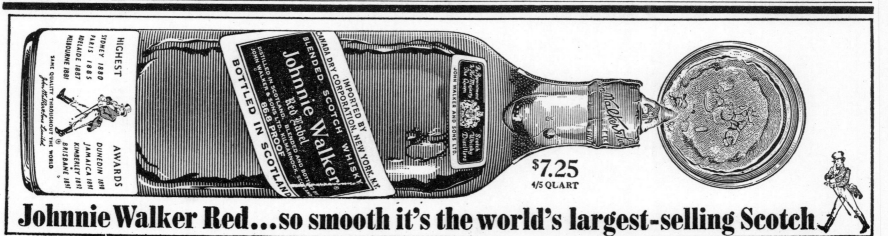

Associated Press Wirephoto

Victory celebration has Hank Bauer in a lather as he happily embraces his fourth-game winning pitcher, Dave McNally.

By VIC ZIEGEL
New York Post Correspondent

Baltimore, Oct. 10—There were two baseballs wrapped in tin foil on Hank Bauer's desk. And a picture of Hank Bauer. And another photo of that remarkably ugly face. And a telegram asking the Baltimore manager to please win the Series in no more than four games. And an open bottle of the sponsor's beer.

"Give Hank a cold beer," somebody yelled

"I got one," Bauer said.

"Is one enough?"

"No," boomed the manager of the team that had just ended the World Series as quickly as possible.

Bauer likes to sit in his swivel chair after a game, answer questions in a growling mumble (or maybe a mumbling growl), thumb through the pages of the little black book he keeps on the Baltimore pitchers and sip from a can of beer.

Yesterday afternoon, after "The biggest thrill I ever had," Bauer was standing up, giving answers at something close to a shout, trying very hard to grab at his beer and smiling. Yes, the face like a clenched fist was wide open and smiling.

"They want me on TV," Bauer said. He walked out of his office, into the Oriole clubhouse, past the platform that held the television camera and onto the interviewing platform.

After a few minutes, Bauer stepped away from the microphone, jumped to the clubhouse floor and walked to another corner of the room.

Somebody put a can of beer in his right hand and Bauer, his other hand shoved into a back pocket, tried to talk about the last baseball game of the year.

"I was all right until they walked Wills in the ninth . . . then I think if they had loaded the bases I would have taken McNally out . . ."

'Hank," said a man pulling at Bauer's sleeve, "the Vice President's here. Talk to him."

Bauer turned quickly and started back toward the television cameras. "Hank, I wonder . . ."

"No, No," Bauer said, pushing away a radio microphone, "the Vice President's here."

The manager was stopped by a wall of photographers, pushed through, put his can of beer into a photographer's hand, said "hold this for me," and busted out of the crowd to stand next to Vice President Humphrey.

"Congratulations, champ," Humphrey said. "Great show."

Bauer thanked the Vice President, they shook hands, smiled at the cameras and carried on a very small conversation.

A little while later—after fighting his way through the clubhouse—Bauer stood near his desk and answered questions from the second wave of reporters.

There was a noise at the door and Walter Alston, followed by a half-dozen photographers, walked in Bauer's office.

The two managers grabbed hands, made a few more pictures and Alston said "Congratulations, boy, damn you, I hope you have to come to my clubhouse next year."

When Alston left, Bauer went behind his desk, sat in his swivel chair and drank from a fresh bottle of beer.

The phone rang and Bauer answered it. "Hello, call back later," he said.

"Hank," a photographer yelled, "how about one more picture? smile, now."

"No sweat," Bauer said.

He smiled.

The Bird Bath

By a Staff Correspondent

Baltimore, Oct. 10—Woodie Held and Vic Roznovsky were sitting on the top shelf of Held's locker, their feet dangling about five feet off the ground.

Held was drinking beer, Roznovsky eating a sandwich. And Boog Powell—trying very hard to celebrate the World Series romp—was standing on a trunk opposite the locker. There was a bucket of water in his hand.

"One . . ." said Powell, swinging the bucket.

"No . . . no . . ." Held pleaded.

"Two . . . "

"Don't do it," Held hollered. "No . . . no . . . "

"Three," Powell screamed and Held went "aaaaaaaah" and Rosnovsky stuck the sandwich in his mouth and the water hit.

"Heh, heh," Powell laughed. "Heh, heh, heh."

* * *

Gene Brabender, Baltimore's curly-haired relief pitcher, was drinking his Series beer from a quart bottle.

"You got to get with it," Brabender said. "I mean, get with it!"

Brabender came to the Orioles this year when he was drafted from the Dodgers. He had just finished two years in the Army.

"One year ago at this time I was wearing my MP uniform and sitting in a shack in the boondocks. I've gone from the Army to the Orioles to winning a pennant and winning a World Series. How's that?"

* * *

"I'm not drinking," said second baseman Dave Johnson. "After we clinched the pennant in Kansas City, I got so sick I like to die. I decided no drinking when we win this one."

And if the Orioles had lost? "Well . . ."

The last out of the World Series was Lou Johnson's fly ball to Baltimore centerfielder Paul Blair. It came with runners on first and second.

"I was afraid," Dave Johnson admitted. "Johnson's been hitting good all Series and McNally was tired. I was hoping he would hit the ball to me."

The soft fly started up and McNally turned around to watch Blair make the final play.

"I just couldn't wait for that damn ball to come down" the pitcher said.

"It seemed like it took an hour."

It seemed like it took five days. ZIEGEL.

Astros Get Angel Reliever

Houston, Oct. 10 (AP)—The Astros have obtained relief pitcher Howie Reed of the Angels' Seattle farm club.

Facts and Figures

	W	L	Pct.
Baltimore	4	0	1.000
Los Angeles	0	4	.000

FIRST GAME

		R	H	E
Baltimore	310 100 000	5	9	0
Los Angeles	011 000 000	2	3	0

McNally, DRABOWSKY (3) and Etchebarren; DRYSDALE, Moeller (3), Miller (5), Perranoski (8) and Roseboro.

HOME RUNS—Baltimore: F. Robinson, B. Robinson. Los Angeles: Lefebvre.

SECOND GAME

		R	H	E
Baltimore	000 031 020	6	8	0
Los Angeles	000 000 000	0	4	6

PALMER and Etchebarren; KOUFAX, Perranoski (7), Regan (8), Brewer (9) and Roseboro.

THIRD GAME

		R	H	E
Los Angeles	000 000 000	0	6	0
Baltimore	000 010 00x	1	3	0

OSTEEN, Regan (8) and Roseboro; BUNKER and Etchebarren.

HOME RUN—Baltimore: Blair.

FOURTH GAME

		R	H	E
Los Angeles	000 000 000	0	4	0
Baltimore	000 100 00x	1	4	0

DRYSDALE and Roseboro. McNALLY and Etchebarren.

HOME RUN—Baltimore: F. Robinson.

FINANCIAL FACTS (FOURTH GAME)

Attendance—54,458.
Net receipts—$466,253.02.
Commissioner's share—$69,937.95.
Players' share—$237,789.04.
Dodgers' share—$39,631.51.
Orioles' share—$39,631.50.
National League's share—$39,631.51.
American League's share—$39,631.51

FOUR GAME TOTAL

Attendance—220,791.
Net Receipts—$2,047,142.46.
Commissioner's share—$307,071.37.
Players' share—$1,044,042.65.
Dodgers' share—$174,007.12.
Orioles' share—$174,007.10.
National League's share—$174,007.11.
American League's share—$174,004.11.

Four-Game Box Score

DODGERS

	g	ab	r	h	2b	3b	hr	rbi	bb	so	*b.av.	po	a	e	*f.av.
Wills, ss	4	13	0	1	0	0	0	0	0	3	.077	12	15	0	1.000
W. Davis, cf	4	16	0	1	0	0	0	0	0	4	.063	6	0	3	.667
L. Johnson, rf	4	15	1	4	1	0	0	0	1	1	.267	9	0	0	1.000
e-T. Davis, lf	4	8	0	2	0	0	0	0	1	1	.250	3	0	0	1.000
Lefebvre, 2b	4	12	1	2	0	0	1	1	3	4	.167	10	10	0	1.000
Parker, 1b	4	13	0	3	2	0	0	0	1	3	.231	31	2	0	1.000
Gilliam, 3b	2	6	0	0	0	0	0	1	2	0	.000	3	4	1	.875
Roseboro, c	4	14	0	1	0	0	0	0	0	3	.071	22	2	0	1.000
Kennedy, 3b	2	5	0	1	0	0	0	0	0	0	.200	0	3	0	1.000
Drysdale, p	2	2	0	0	0	0	0	0	0	1	.000	0	3	0	1.000
a-Stuart	2	2	0	0	0	0	0	0	0	1	.000	0	0	0	.000
Moeller, p	1	0	0	0	0	0	0	0	0	0	.000	0	0	0	.000
b-Barbieri	1	1	0	0	0	0	0	0	0	1	.000	0	0	0	.000
R. Miller, p	1	0	0	0	0	0	0	0	0	0	.000	0	1	0	1.000
c-Covington	1	1	0	0	0	0	0	0	0	1	.000	0	0	0	.000
Perranoski, p	2	0	0	0	0	0	0	0	0	0	.000	0	2	1	.667
d-Fairly, rf	3	7	0	1	0	0	0	0	2	4	.071	5	0	1	.833
Koufax, p	1	2	0	0	0	0	0	0	0	0	.000	0	1	0	1.000
Regan, p	2	0	0	0	0	0	0	0	0	0	.000	0	1	0	1.000
Brewer, p	1	0	0	0	0	0	0	0	0	0	.000	0	0	0	.000
Osteen, p	1	2	0	0	0	0	0	0	0	1	.000	1	0	0	1.000
f-Ferrara	1	1	0	1	0	0	0	0	0	0	1.000	0	0	0	.000
g-Oliver	1	0	0	0	0	0	0	0	0	0	.000	0	0	0	.000
Totals	4	120	2	17	3	0	0	2	13	28	.142	102	44	6	.961

ORIOLES

	g	ab	r	h	2b	3b	hr	rbi	bb	so	*b.av.	po	a	e	*f.av.
Aparicio, ss	4	16	0	4	1	0	0	2	0	0	.250	9	8	0	1.000
Snyder, cf	3	6	1	1	0	0	0	1	2	0	.167	2	0	0	1.000
F. Robinson, rf	4	14	4	4	0	1	2	3	2	3	.286	6	0	0	1.000
B. Robinson, 3b	4	14	2	3	0	0	1	1	1	0	.214	4	6	0	1.000
Powell, 1b	4	14	1	5	1	0	0	1	0	1	.357	27	1	0	1.000
Blefary, lf	4	13	0	1	0	0	0	0	2	3	.077	7	0	0	1.000
Blair, cf	4	6	2	1	0	0	1	1	1	0	.167	9	0	0	1.000
D. Johnson, 2b	4	14	1	4	1	0	0	1	0	1	.286	12	12	0	1.000
Etchebarren, c	4	12	2	1	0	0	0	0	2	4	.083	32	1	0	1.000
McNally, p	2	3	0	0	0	0	0	0	0	1	.000	0	0	0	.000
Drabowsky, p	1	2	0	0	0	0	0	0	1	1	.000	0	0	0	.000
Palmer, p	1	4	0	0	0	0	0	0	0	2	.000	0	2	0	1.000
Bunker, p	1	2	0	0	0	0	0	0	0	1	.000	0	3	0	1.000
Totals	4	120	13	24	3	1	4	10	11	17	.200	108	33	0	1.000

a-Flied out for Drysdale in 2d inning of first game; Struck out for Kennedy in 9th inning of fourth game. b-Struck out for Moeller in 4th inning of first game. c-Struck out for R. Miller in 7th inning of first game. d-Struck out for Perranoski in 9th inning of first game. e-Singled for Regan in 8th inning of first game. Singled for Osteen in 8th inning of third game. f-Singled for Drysdale in 9th inning of fourth game. g-Ran for Ferrara in 9th inning of fourth game.

DODGERS PITCHING

	G	CG	IP	H	R	BB	SO	HBP	WP	W	L	Pct.	ER	ERA
Drysdale	2	1	10	8	5	3	6	0	0	0	2	.000	5	4.50
Moeller	1	0	2	1	1	1	0	0	0	0	0	.000	1	4.50
R. Miller	1	0	3	2	0	2	1	0	0	0	0	.000	0	0.00
Perranoski	2	0	3⅓	4	2	1	2	0	0	0	0	.000	2	6.00
Koufax	1	0	6	6	4	2	2	0	0	0	1	.000	1	1.50
Regan	2	0	1⅔	0	0	1	2	0	1	0	0	.000	0	0.00
Brewer	1	0	1	0	1	0	1	0	0	0	0	.000	0	0.00
Osteen	1	0	7	3	0	1	3	0	0	0	1	.000	1	1.29
Totals	4	1	34	24	13	11	17	0	1	0	4	.000	10	2.65

ORIOLES PITCHING

	G	CG	IP	H	R	BB	SO	HBP	WP	W	L	Pct.	ER	ERA
McNally	2	1	11⅓	6	2	7	5	0	0	1	0	1.000	2	1.64
Drabowsky	1	0	6⅔	1	0	2	11	0	0	1	0	1.000	0	0.00
Palmer	1	1	9	4	0	3	6	0	1	1	0	1.000	0	0.00
Bunker	1	1	9	6	0	1	6	0	0	1	0	1.000	0	0.00
Totals	4	3	36	17	2	13	28	0	1	4	0	1.000	2	0.50

Shoutouts—Palmer, Bunker, McNally.

*World Series Batting & Fielding Averages

Composite score by innings:

LOS ANGELES	0	1	1	0	0	0	0	0	0	2
BALTIMORE	3	1	0	2	4	1	0	2	0	13

SB—Wills. S—McNally, Powell, Wills. DP—Dodgers 4 (Gilliam, Roseboro and Parker; Wills, Lefebvre and Parker; Lefebvre, Wills and Parker 2); Orioles 4 (Aparicio, D. Johnson and Powell 2; B. Robinson, D. Johnson and Powell; Etchebarren and D. Johnson). LOB—Dodgers 24, Orioles 18. U—Jackowski (N), Chylak (A), Pelekoudas (N), Rice (A), Steiner (N), Drummond (A). T—2:56 (first game), 2:26 (second game), 1:55 (third game), 1:45 (fourth game). A—55,941 (first game), 55,947 (second game), 54,445 (third game), 54,458 (fourth game).

N. L. WINS ON PEREZ'S HOME RUN IN 15TH

'I Knew I Hit It Good', Beams Perez

A Record Game, Homer by Homer

Manager Walter Alston (right) of National league beaming while teammates congratulate Richie Allen following his home run in second inning of All-Star game in Anaheim yesterday. [UPI Telephoto]

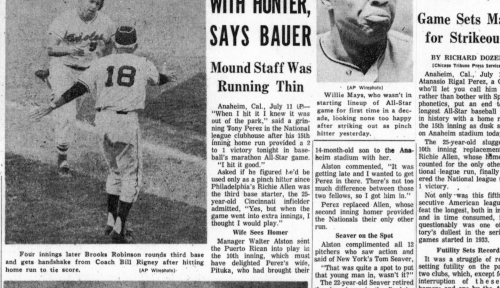

Four innings later Brooks Robinson rounds third base and gets handshake from Coach Bill Rigney after hitting home run to tie score. [AP Wirephoto]

HAD TO STAY WITH HUNTER, SAYS BAUER

Mound Staff Was Running Thin

Anaheim, Cal., July 11 (AP)—"When I hit it I knew it was out of the park," said a grinning Tony Perez in the National league clubhouse after his 15th inning home run provided a 2 to 1 victory tonight in baseball's marathon All-Star game.

"I hit it good."

Asked if he figured he'd be used only as a pinch hitter since Philadelphia's Richie Allen was the third base starter, the 25-year-old Cincinnati infielder admitted, "Yes, but when the game went into extra innings, I thought I would play."

Wife Sees Homer

Manager Walter Alston sent the Puerto Rican into play in the 10th inning, which must have delighted Perez's wife, Pituka, who had brought their 14-month-old son to the Anaheim stadium with her.

Alston commented, "It was getting late and I wanted to get Perez in there. There's not too much difference between those two fellows, so I got him in."

Perez replaced Allen, whose second inning homer provided the Nationals their only other run.

Seaver on the Spot

Alston complimented all 12 pitchers who saw action and said of New York's Tom Seaver,

"That was quite a spot to put that young man in, wasn't it?"

The 22-year-old Seaver retired the Americans in the final inning, striking out Ken Berry to end the game.

"This was possibly over-all the best pitching in any All-Star game I've seen. You'd have a hard time picking the best one today."

"I guess they just got some good pitching thrown at them," was Manager Hank

[Continued on page 2, col. 4]

Weary Willie

[AP Wirephoto]

Willie Mays, who wasn't in starting lineup of All-Star game for first time in a decade, looking none too happy after striking out as pinch hitter yesterday.

TAKES FIFTH IN ROW FROM AMERICAN, 2-1

Game Sets Mark for Strikeouts

BY RICHARD DOZER
[Chicago Tribune Press Service]

Anaheim, Cal., July 11 — Atanasio Rigal Perez, a Cuban who'll let you call him Tony rather than bother with Spanish phonetics, put an end to the longest All-Star baseball game in history with a home run in the 15th inning as dusk settled on Anaheim stadium today.

The 25-year-old slugger, a 10th inning replacement for Richie Allen, whose homer accounted for the only other National league run, finally powered the National league to a 2 1 victory.

Not only was this fifth consecutive American league defeat the longest, both in innings and in time consumed, it unquestionably was one of history's dullest in the series of games started in 1933.

Futility Sets Record

It was a struggle of record-setting futility on the part of two clubs, which, except for the interruption of these two homers and one by the American league's Brooks Robinson, was strictly in the control of a dozen of baseball's best pitchers.

Seven moundsmen worked for the victorious Nationals, with Don Drysdale winning the first All-Star decision of his career. Drysdale, the only Dodger to get into this 38th All-Star clas-

[Continued on page 2, col. 1]

Trio of Strong Linemen Boost All-Star Variety

BY ROY DAMER

Center George Goeddeke of Notre Dame, End Dave Williams of Washington, and Tackle Dave Rowe of Penn State will contribute a variety of skills to the College All-Star squad which will battle the Green Bay Packers in Soldiers' field three weeks from Friday night.

Goeddeke is one of the best and most colorful of Notre Dame's offensive linemen in recent years. He kept his head shaved and often was referred to as "Mr. Clean."

George is the young man who was rushed from the Irish locker room shortly before the North Carolina game in 1965 with an attack of appendicitis. As he was leaving he quipped to Coach Ara Parseghian that he would be back for the second half.

Quick Recovery

An appendectomy prevented that, of course, but Goeddeke made an amazing recovery and two weeks later went all the way on offense as Notre Dame played a scoreless tie against Miami.

The 6-3, 235-pound Goeddeke was an excellent center for two years on outstanding teams.

DAVE WILLIAMS . . . deceptive

"His blocking ranks with the best and his spirit and desire are all that any coach could ask," says Parseghian.

Goeddeke is used to being in the center of things, even off the gridiron. "I have six brothers and four sisters at home," he explains, "and I have to say that I was kind of used to having a lot of activity going on around me. I had to be

[Continued on page 2, col. 8]

9 RACE TODAY IN HYDE PARK

54th Renewal Goes at Arlington

BY THOMAS RIVERA

The heroes of the future will contest one of Illinois' oldest stakes today when a field of nine 2-year-old colts and geldings goes to the post in the $27,000 Hyde Park at Arlington Park.

The six-furlong race, first run at the old Washington Park track at 61st street and Cottage Grove in 1884, will be up for its 54th renewal in a colorful history which saw such exceptional thorobreds as Misty Isle, Alsab, Bewitch, Greek Game, Ridan, and Jet Traffic posted as victors. Verano won the inaugural running.

Today's race marks the first time this season the juveniles will be asked to go more than 5½ furlongs in stakes competition as they continue the campaign toward the seven furlongs of the $367,000 Arlington-Washington Futurity on Sept. 9.

All Carry 113 Pounds

All nine entered will carry equal weight of 113 pounds with the trio of Perfect Plus, Gin-Rob, and Nash Co K. meriting special attention off their performances so far this season.

Perfect Plus, a son of Nashua, will be running for his new owner, Harvey Peltier, for the first time since the New Orleans lawyer purchased him for $150,000.

The chestnut colt, out of a Greek Ship mare, has finished in the money in seven of his eight starts with two victories in that string, including a 3½-length triumph in a speedy 1:04 2/5 for 5½ furlongs on a sloppy track in his last race.

Calvin Stone rode Perfect Plus for Trainer Arnold Winick in that allowance event and the two will put the horse on the track again today for the last time before John Meaux, Pel-

[Continued on page 4, col. 4]

President for a Day

Anaheim, Cal. July 11 (UPI)—The manager of Anaheim's Grand hotel must have had a premonition that Tony Perez was going to be named the All-Star game's most valuable player today.

When the Cincinnati Reds third baseman checked in yesterday with his wife and son, the manager found that a room had not been reserved for the Perez family.

So the hotel official promptly made up for it by moving them into the $58-a-day Presidential suite.

Peréz not only earned the room but also the most valuable player award as he hit a fast ball by Jim Hunter into the left field stands to put a merciful end to the longest All-Star game on record in the 15th inning. That homer gave the National league its 2 to 1 victory.

Tony Perez sprints for home in front of glum American league bench after hitting winning homer in 15th inning. [UPI Photo]

Pinch Hitter Mickey Mantle of Yankees striking out on fast ball thrown by Ferguson Jenkins of Cubs in fifth inning. Jenkins tied All-Star record with six strikeouts in three innings. [UPI Telephoto]

All-Stars Give Striking Performance

NATIONAL LEAGUE

	AB	R	H	RBI	P	A	E
Brock, Cards, lf	2	0	0	0	1	0	0
Mays, Giants, cf	4	0	0	0	3	0	0
Clemente, Pir., rf	6	0	1	0	6	0	0
Aaron, Braves, cf-lf	6	0	1	0	2	0	0
Cepeda, Cards, 1b	6	0	0	0	6	0	0
Allen, Phils, 3b	4	1	1	1	0	2	0
Perez, Reds, 3b	2	1	1	1	0	3	0
Torre, Braves, c	2	0	0	0	4	1	0
Haller, Giants, c	1	0	0	0	7	0	0
e-Banks, Cubs	1	0	1	0	0	0	0
McCarver, Cards, c	2	0	2	0	7	1	0
Mazeroski, Pir., 2b	4	0	0	0	7	1	0
Drysdale, Dod., p	0	0	0	0	0	0	0
Seaver, Mets, p	0	0	0	0	0	0	0
Alley, Pirates, ss	5	0	0	0	1	3	0
Marichal, Giants, p	1	0	0	0	0	0	0
Jenkins, Cubs, p	1	0	0	0	0	0	0
Gibson, Cards, p	0	0	0	0	0	1	0
d-Wynn, Astros	1	0	1	0	0	0	0
Short, Phils, p	0	0	0	0	0	1	0
g-Staub, Astros	1	0	1	0	0	0	0
Cuellar, Astros, p	0	0	0	0	0	0	0
Rose, Reds, 2b	1	0	0	0	1	0	0
	h-51	2	9	2	45	13	0

AMERICAN LEAGUE

	AB	R	H	RBI	P	A	E
Robins'n, Or., 3b	6	1	1	1	0	6	0
Carew, Twins, 2b	3	0	0	0	2	3	0
McAuliffe, Tig., 2b	3	0	0	0	3	2	0
Oliva, Twins, cf	6	0	2	0	4	0	0
Killebrew, Tws, lb	6	0	0	0	15	1	0
Conigliaro, R.S. rf	6	0	0	0	4	0	0
Yastr'ski, R.S., lf	4	0	3	0	2	0	0
Freehan, Tig. c	5	0	0	0	13	0	0
Petro'li, R. S., ss	1	0	0	0	0	1	0
McGloth., Ang., p	0	0	0	0	0	0	0
Peters, W. Sox, p	0	0	0	0	0	1	0
b-Mincher, Ang.	1	0	1	0	0	0	0
c-Agee, W. Sox	0	0	0	0	0	0	0
Downing, Yank., p	0	0	0	0	0	0	0
f-Alvis, Ind.	1	0	0	0	0	0	0
Hunter, A's, p	1	0	0	0	0	0	0
Chance, Ang., p	0	0	0	0	0	0	0
Fregosi, Ang., ss	4	0	1	0	2	3	0
	a-49	1	8	1	45	16	0

a—Mantle, Yankees, was called out on strikes for McGlothin in fifth, and Berry, White Sox, struck out for Hunter in 15th.
b—Singled for Peters in eighth.
c—Ran for Mincher in eighth.
d—Singled for Gibson in ninth.
e—Singled for Haller in 10th.
f—Safe on fielder's choice for Downing in 10th.
g—Singled for Short in 11th.
h—Helms, Reds, hit into double play for Drysdale in 15th.

National League	010	000	000	000	001—2
American League	000	001	000	000	000—1

Double plays—Robinson to Carew to Killebrew [Cepeda]; McAuliffe to Killebrew [Helms]. Left on bases—National, 5; American, 7.

Two base hits—Yastrzemski, McCarver. Home runs—Allen, Robinson, Perez. Stolen base—Aaron. Sacrifices—Fregosi, Freehan, Mazeroski. Pitching summary:

NATIONAL LEAGUE

	IP	H	R	ER
Marichal	3	1	0	0
Jenkins	3	3	1	1
Gibson	2	2	0	0
Short	2	0	0	0
Cuellar	2	1	0	0
Drysdale	2	1	0	0
Seaver	1	0	0	0

AMERICAN LEAGUE

	IP	H	R	ER
Chance	3	2	1	1
McGlothlin	2	1	0	0
Peters	3	0	0	0
Downing	2	2	0	0
Hunter	5	4	1	1

Bases on balls—National: Short 1 [Yastrzemski]; Seaver 1 [Yastrzemski]. American: none.

Strikeouts—National: Marichal 3 [Oliva, Yastrzemski, Freehan]; Jenkins 6 [Killebrew, Conigliaro, Mantle, Fregosi, Carew, Oliva]; Gibson 2 [Conigliaro, Freehan]; Short 1 [Fregosi]; Cuellar 2 [Robinson, Oliva]; Drysdale 2 [Hunter, Killebrew]; Seaver 1 [Berry]. American: Chance 1 [Clemente]; McGlothlin 2 [Allen, Alley]; Peters 4 [Mays, Clemente, Cepeda, Allen]; Downing 2 [Clemente, Allen]; Hunter 4 Alley 2, Clemente, Perez].

Winning pitcher—Drysdale. Losing pitcher—Hunter. Time—3:41. Attendance—46,039.

Umpires—Runge [A. L.], plate; Secory [N. L.], 1b; Dimuro [A. L.], 2b; Burkhary [N. L.], 3b; Ashford [A. L.], l. f. line, and Pelekoudas [N. L.], r. f line

In the Wake of the News . . . . By David Condon

HANK STRAM, boss man of the Kansas City Chiefs and the last coach to lose to the Green Bay Packers [in the Super bowl] is drooling about the talent available the College All-Star squad that duels the world champs in Soldiers' field on Aug. 4. Says Hank: "The All-Stars' defensive squad is absolutely awesome. On offense, you start with two great quarterbacks—Steve Spurrier and Bob Griese—fortified by some running backs that can spring a scoring bomb from any distance. The All-Stars have the talent. Their chances of success depend upon how well they use it. To have a chance against the Packers, you must execute without a single mistake."

Hank Stram . . . eyes talent

Personal to Buddy Hackett, who did such a tremendous job as toastmaster at the National Football League Players' association awards dinner in the Conrad Hilton: The president of the San Francisco 49ers, who flew here for the hoedown, is Lou Spadia—not Lou Spadina, the name the script writers gave you. But otherwise, thanks for a memorable evening.

Bob Culp, who has been director of sports information at Western Michigan university for 11 years, has become business manager of athletics for the Broncos. His publicity post has been taken by Hal Bateman, a newspaper man. . . . The death of Mrs. Warren [Olive] Brown, wife of the famous sports columnist, has saddened friends everywhere. Olive was generous, kind, charitable, and, always, a friend. The Notre Dame gang, this observer included, never will forget the meals she arranged for the college chums of sons Bill, Pete, and Roger. . . . Doesn't the change of ownership in the Balmoral race track in Crete mean that the quarter horses finally will be exposed to pari-mutuel bettors in this state? . . . They asked Tom Landry, coach of football's Dallas Cowboys, if he'd ever seen anyone faster than his ace pass receiver, Bob Hayes. "Yes," said Landry. "Buckpasser."

THE MOTHER OF DR. BILL McCOLL, former Bear end, passed away recently in San Diego. Dr. Bill, who was a medical missionary—treating lepers—in Korea after leaving the Bears, now is a surgeon in Covina, Cal. . . . Max Patkin, the baseball clown, sends notice that so far this year he already has traveled 30,000 miles along the barnstorming circuit. . . . Rev. John Lefko, new president of the St. Joseph's college Calumet campus, will be feted at a reception at the school in East Chicago this afternoon. . . . Bobby Hull, the Black Hawks' hockey ace, has written a book without benefit of ghost, and the publishers are enthused. . . . Tom Sakal, Minnesota's football captain, warns: "We are going to surprise a lot of people this fall. The potential is there for a good team. We have a lot more experience, a lot more depth, and we are a lot bigger." . . . Voters in Dallas will be asked—next month—to approve bond issues that would include vast improvements to the Cotton bowl. One feature of the improvements would be more parking; 10,000 additional spaces. . . . Ernie Ladd of the American Football league [he's now with the Houston Oilers] was the main target of autograph seekers when he appeared on the Verne Gagne wrestling show in International Amphitheater last Friday. Ernie confesses that he earns near $35,000 a year in the rassling racket—and he accepts dates only between football seasons. . . . Incidentally, the Amphitheater folks scored big when they turned over their concessions to Pat O'Malley's Canteen corporation. . . . Frank McNamara, the former "singing sergeant" of the Chicago police department, still wields a mean golf stick at the age of 69. Frank, long one of Chicago's top amateur golfers, climaxed a comeback by winning the recent Police Sergeants' tournament. He was president of the Police Sergeants' association until retirement at 63. . . . Pitcher Juan Marichal of the San Francisco Giants would be just as happy if he never had to pitch in Houston's Astrodome. "The air conditioning causes me to get pains in the neck, and that bothers my control," says Juan.

HOW TOUGH ARE things in college football? Bill Dooley, new coach at North Carolina, used the university's daily to advertise for a punter! . . . Lefty O'Doul, the former baseball great, is a victim of arthritis and concedes that he must abandon his second favorite sport, golf. Says Lefty: "There comes a time in every baseball player's life when he must hang up his spikes. I knew the time had arrived when I finally quit baseball. Now the time has come for me to hang up golf spikes." . . . O'Doul, 70 last March 4, had a lifetime major league batting average of .349. . . . The St. Louis Browns' Fans club of Chicago recently feted Sherman Lollar and Bill Hunter, former Brownies who now coach with the Baltimore Orioles. . . . Some of our nation's new soccer teams are becoming f-r-a-n-t-i-c, financially. . . . Quick quote from Pappy Waldorf, the former Northwestern football coach who now is talent scout for the San Francisco 49ers: "A good quarterback is money in the bank." . . . Whatever happened to all those hippies with their Cubs' pennants?

Larmer's Ledger

Always ask questions before you sound off.

I can do without parents who give you free tickets to their kid's recital.

I never pay attention to a woman's final decision. It never agrees with the one that follows.—Paul Larmer.

Ten Years Ago Today—Don Bowden of California, America's only 4 minute miler [3:58.7], won the 800-meter run in 1:49.2 and the 200-meter dash in 21.7 at a track meet in Finland.

MOON MULLINS
THANK YOU FOR HIRING ME, MR. VIGGERS!!
YES, YES-- WELCOME TO THE WONDERFUL WORLD OF ICE CREAM.
VIGGERS ICE CREAM
YUM!
7/12
NOW GO OUT AND SELL VIGGERS ICE CREAM VIGOROUSLY!
MY GOSH, HE'S GOT COLD FINGERS...
10¢
WELL, AFTER ALL, HE'S BEEN IN THE ICE CREAM BUSINESS 37 YEARS.
FERD JOHNSON
© 1967 by News Syndicate Co. Inc. World Rights Reserved

BOSTON HERALD TRAVELER

THE WEATHER — SUNNY, WARMER (PAGE 2) MONDAY, OCTOBER 2, 1967 HA 6-3000 TEN CENTS

Pennant Is Ours!

FRONT ROW . . . left to right: Tony Conigliaro, Carl Yastrzemski, Jerry Adair, Sal Maglie, pitching coach; Bobby Doerr, coach; Mgr. Dick Williams, Eddie Popowski, coach; Al Lakeman, bullpen coach; Reggie Smith, George Scott, Tom Dowd, traveling secretary, and Buddy LeRoux, trainer.
MIDDLE ROW . . . left to right Keith Rosenfeld, bat boy; Rico Petrocelli, Joe Foy, Mike Andrews, Ken Harrelson, Elston Howard, Mike Ryan, George Thomas, Dalton Jones, Jose Tartabull, Norm Siebern, Jimmy Jackson, bat boy; equipment managers Vince Orlando and Don Fitzpatrick.
BACK ROW . . . left to right: Jose Santiago, Gary Bell, Dave Morehead, Jerry Stephenson, Jim Lonborg, Darrell Brandon, Sparky Lyle, John Wyatt, Dan Osinski, Lee Stange, Bill Landis.

More on the Red Sox

Kenmore Square Surrenders to Jubilant Crowd Page 3

PLUS Two Pages of Photos and These Stories beginning on Page 21:

Lonborg Goes "On Road" to Solve Hex by Bill Liston

Tom Yawkey's Tears Sweeter Than Wine by Tim Horgan

Boston Goes on a Baseball Bender by Al Hirshberg

Twins Expect Sun Tomorrow—Maybe by Jack McCarthy

All of Boston Goes Wild Over Those Fabulous Sox

By HENRY McKENNA

Hail our Cinderella Red Sox, newly crowned American League champions of 1967!

Twenty-one years of frustration, defeat and despair ended on a screaming note of wild excitement Sunday at Fenway Park where the Red Sox, behind Jim Lonborg's capable pitching and Carl Yastrzemski's brilliant hitting, rallied to defeat the Minnesota Twins, 5-3.

That outcome, before 35,770 wildly applauding fans, coupled with Detroit's loss to California in the second game of their doubleheader some four hours later, gave the Hose the championship for the first time since 1946 and turned loose the flow of champagne in their dressing room.

This almost unbelievable triumph by a team which moved from ninth to first in one brief season under their freshman manager, Dick Williams, 38, means that the World Series will open Wednesday at Fenway Park against the National League titlist, the St. Louis Cardinals, the same team which downed the Red Sox in a seven-game series back in 1946.

(Continued on Page Twenty-four)

A LOVE AFFAIR!

By GEORGE FORSYTHE

Boston is a city in love.

The object of its affections—naturally—is a group of wonderful guys who have acted as though they were working in cahoots with Dr. Paul Dudley White.

The Boston Red Sox have made heart attacks their specialty. But never have so many hearts been tried as on Sunday afternoon when the Sox proved they are destiny's special children.

Around Fenway Park you could find the floor plans

(Continued on Page Seven)

SANTIAGO TO OPEN

The stage is set for Boston's first World Series since 1948, starting Wednesday at Fenway Park and continuing there Thursday before switching to St. Louis.

Jose Santiago, a 6-foot-2, 185-pound right-hander who was born in Juana Diaz, Puerto Rico, 27 years ago, is the likely choice of Red Sox manager Dick Williams to pitch the opener. He will be opposed by Bob Gibson, strapping right-hander of the Cardinals who has come back strong from a broken leg suffered when he was struck by a line drive.

(Continued on Page Twenty-four)

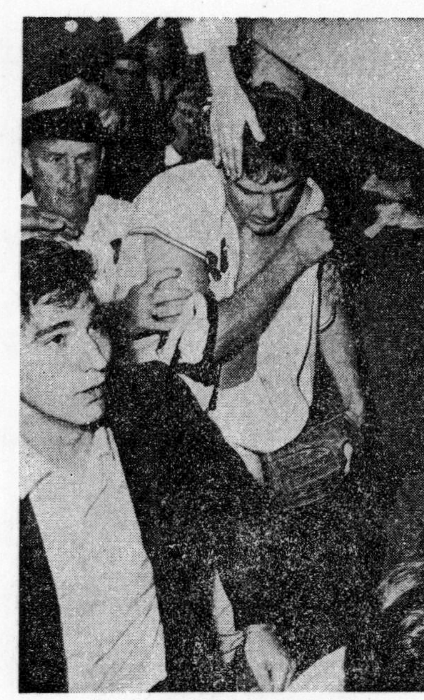

(Herald Traveler Staff Photo by Rocco Paoletta)

BESIEGED by fans and escorted by Boston policeman, Red Sox pitcher Jim Lonborg makes his way into clubhouse following his spectacularly-pitched 5-3 victory over Minnesota Twins which clinched the pennant for Sox.

Tigers' Score in; Yaz Let Out Yell

By LOU CONNELLY

They waited and waited.

It seemed like an eternity for these Red Sox players listening to the reports from Detroit. They had already gone berserk after beating the Twins in the afternoon, but when the Tigers' Dick McAuliffe bounced into a game ending double play, it set off utter madness.

Carl Yastrzemski, sitting quietly in shorts, a Red Sox jacket and white sneakers, was the first to leap into a yell, and then for a full 10 minutes all was lost in an unbelievable champagne shower.

"We won the pennant!" Joy Foy kept screaming over and over.

"Mr. Rigney, I thank you for stopping that Detroit juggernaut," a weeping Manager Dick

(Continued on Page Twenty-seven)

Try Puzzle 2 For Big Prizes

By PAUL GIGUERE

How did you make out Sunday with Puzzle No. 1 of the Boston Herald Traveler's great $40,175 "Know Your Newspaper Contest?"

(Continued on Page Nineteen)

It's a Great Town for Baseball

By JIMMY BRESLIN

The day started with the street in front of the ballpark blocked off and everybody was standing in the street and pushing to get inside and see the Red Sox win the American League pennant. The thieves, which this town always has held in great esteem, were at work in the crowd. They were pushing people off balance and then snatching at their tickets or dipping fingers into pockets where wallets could be. Every now and then a woman would let out a squall, but this was only because some legitimate man was pinching her. A thief doesn't do things like this when he is at work. A thief steals.

In the middle of the crowd there was this old,

(Continued on Page Three)

The FINAL Standings

	Won	Lost	Pct.	Behind
BOSTON	92	70	.568	—
Detroit	91	71	.562	1
Minnesota	91	71	.562	1
Chicago	89	73	.549	3
California	84	77	.522	7½
Baltimore	76	85	.472	15½
Washington	76	85	.472	15½
Cleveland	75	87	.463	17
New York	72	90	.444	20
Kansas City	62	99	.385	29½

The Revolution That Shook the World

Russia 50 Years After Is 'a Promise Unfulfilled'

The Russian revolution shook the world in 1917 and the shock waves are still spreading. To mark the 50th anniversary of this gigantic social upheaval, The Herald Traveler begins publication [illegible] morning of a penetrating and authoritative series of articles on all aspects of life in the Soviet Union today.

The articles, gathered and written over a two-year period by experts and specialists of The New York Times, reflect a rare degree of cooperation by the Soviet Government. The result, after thousands of miles of travel and hundreds of unrestricted interviews, is a fascinating document. Its important revelations will give you an insight into the past and future of the people and country that inherited the revolution that shook the world.

By HARRISON E. SALISBURY

(Copyright New York Times News Service)

"We were one of the most backward of nations and now we are one of the most advanced."

Sitting in his Kremlin office with the summer sun glancing through the window, Anastas I. Mikoyan, member of the Central Committee of the Communist Party for 44 years, thus summed up Bolshevik rule in Russia.

PROBABLY NO ONE in Moscow was in a better position to assess the 50 Bolshevik years that will be celebrated Nov. 7 than Mikoyan, dapper and sparkling-eyed despite his 71 years. No one has stood so close so long to the fulcrum of Soviet power as Mikoyan—first as one of the young men from the Caucasus brought up to Moscow in 1926 by Stalin and later, after Stalin's death, as the right-hand man of Nikita S. Khrushchev.

Born the son of a poor Armenian village carpenter, educated in the Ar-

(Continued on Page Eighteen)

INDEX

Gibson Halts Bosox As Cards Win Series, 7-2

(Continued From Page 1)

right-hander, working with three days rest after Sunday's shutout, had a no-hitter going until Scott opened the fifth with a triple off the wall in center. Scott came all the way home to score when Julian Javier's relay throw sailed past third base into the Cards' dugout.

Second Run

Boston picked up another mean-nothing run in the eighth on a double by Rico Petrocelli, a wild pitch and pinch hitter Norm Siebern's force out.

Manager Red Schoendienst went out to talk with Gibson in the seventh when he went 2-1 on Ken Harrelson after Carl Yastrzemski walked. Pitching coach Billy Muffett went to the mound in the eigth after the wild pitch to pinch hitter Dalton Jones. Red made the stroll again in the ninth after Yaz opened with a single. Gibson obviously pleaded to stay and got permission.

The next man, Harrelson, grounded into a double play and Gibson struck out Scott.

As a reward for his three wins, Gibson was named the winner of the sports car annually give to the outstanding player of the Series by Sport Magazine.

It was a brilliant comeback for Gibson who was out of action from July 15 to Sept. 6 with a broken leg and barely regained his sharpness in time for the Series.

The Series triumph, the Cards' fourth in a row, meant about $8,900 to each St. Louis player. Each of the losing Red Sox will get about $5,606 but they already had enough glory for their spectacular rise from ninth place in 1966 to the pennant in 1967 on the final day of the season.

If it was a day of wild excitement for the Red Birds, it was a cloudy, cool afternoon of heartbreak for Lonborg, the handsome Stanford graduate who had pitched so magnificently in winning his first two starts.

Trying to bounce back without sufficient rest, Gentleman Jim was bombed by the Cards and was left in there to take a rough going over in the sixth when Javier's three-run homer drove the final nails in the Red Sox's coffin.

Fought Mightily

The Red Sox fought mightily in an effort to become the fourth club ever to overcome a 3-1 deficit in games but Gibson was just too much for them.

The hand writing was on the wall for Lonborg, who had a perfect game going for 6 1-3 innings and a no-hitter for 7 2-3 innings in this same park a week ago. But Roger Maris, a hitting star for the Cards, singled in the first and Javier, another big swinger for the Cards, singled in the second.

Little Dal Maxvill, a good field, no-hit shortstop, hammered a 400-foot triple off the center field wall opening the third. After Gibson lined out to Joe Foy and Brock popped up, Curt Flood singled to center, scoring Maxvill. Maris followed with his second single and Flood scored when Lonborg uncorked a wild pitch to Cepeda.

Guarding a 2-0 lead, Gibson took matters into his own hands in the fifth when he slugged a 380-foot homer high off the green wall in center field, just to the right of the yellow line that separates doubles from home runs.

Then Brock, the speed bullet, put on his show. Lou singled to left and stole second on the second pitch to Flood. Brock also also stole third on the fourth ball to Flood, tying the record for two steals in an inning, held by four others including Babe Ruth in 1921. Maris' sacrifice fly knocked in Brock for a 4-0 lead.

Lonborg obviously was struggling but he was left into take another beating in the sixth when Tim McCarver doubled on a ball that right fielder Harrelson dove for but couldn't hold as he rolled over on the grass.

Said Grand

Mike Shannon got a life on an error by Foy and Javier iced it with a 350-foot homer into the screen atop the Green Monster left field wall.

Despite the 7-0 deficit, Manager Dick Williams left Lonborg in the game to complete the sixth inning.

Williams sent up Jose Tartabull to bat for Lonborg in the last of the sixth and then got two perfect innings of relief ball from Jose Santiago.

Dave Morehead walked the bases full in the ninth but the Red Sox escaped without further scoring by using Dan Osinski and finally 19-year-old Ken Brett to put down the rally.

Right to the bitter end, Yastrzemski was in there swinging that big bat. He opened the ninth with a single that gave him a .400 Series but Harrelson's double play and Scott's strikeout ended it.

The stolen base record that Brock erased had been held jointly by Jim Slagle of the 1907 Chicago Cubs and Honus Wagner of the 1909 Pittsburgh Pirates. The two thefts in the fifth tied the old mark and his steal of second base in the ninth set a new standard of seven for a series.

As a foreboding of things to come, a black cloud of smoke curled over the left field wall right after Maxvill unloaded his triple in the third. The fire in a freight car soon was under control but the Cards already had pushed Lonborg and the Red Sox beyond the point of no return.

Given Raise

Gibson had won the outstanding player award in 1964 when he lost his first start to the New York Yankees but came back to win his next two, including the seventh with only two days of rest. He struck out 31 in that series and wound up with 26 in this one in a performance that has to earn him a healthy raise from owner Gussie Busch.

The victory cut the American League's over-all Series edge to 38-26 and boosted the Cards' Series mark to 8-3, the last four in succession in 1944, 1946, 1964 and 1967. The Red Sox, losing their second series to three wins, had not been in one since they lost to the Cards in 1946.

Although Gibson was one short of the Series record of six victories held jointly by Lefty Gomez and Ruffing, his five complete games equalled Ruffing's Yankee feats in 1937, 1938, 1939 and 1941.

Williams told his Red Sox to hold their heads high as he spoke in the clubhouse after the game. "You have nothing to be ashamed of," he said.

AP Wirephoto

BOB GIBSON LETS GO WITH FINAL PITCH
Cards Whipped Bosox, 7-2, To Win World Series

THE BOX

St. Louis (N)	ab	r	h	bi	Boston (A)	ab	r	h	bi
Brock lf	4	1	2	0	Foy 3b	3	0	0	0
Flood cf	3	1	1	1	Morehd p	0	0	0	0
Maris rf	3	0	2	1	Osinski p	0	0	0	0
Cepeda 1b	5	0	0	0	Brett p	0	0	0	0
MCarver c	5	1	1	0	Andws 2b	3	0	0	0
Shanon 3b	4	1	0	0	Ystzmski lf	3	0	1	0
Javier 2b	4	1	2	3	Harlson rf	4	0	0	0
Maxvill ss	4	1	1	0	Scott b1	4	1	1	0
Gibson p	4	1	1	1	RSmith cf	3	0	0	0
					Petcelli ss	3	1	1	0
					Howard c	2	0	0	0
					bJones 3b	0	0	0	0
					Lonborg p	1	0	0	0
					aTatbul ph	1	0	0	0
					Santiago p	0	0	0	0
					cSiebern ph	1	0	0	1
					RGibson c	0	0	0	0
Totals	36	7	10	6	Totals	28	2	3	1

St. Louis (N)	002 023 000—7
Bostn (A)	000 010 010—2

E—Javier, Foy. DP—Maxvill, Javier, and Cepeda. LOB—St. Louis 7, Boston 3. SB—Brock 3. S—Andrews. SF—Maris.

2B—McCarver, Brock, Petrocelli. 3B—Maxvill, Scott. HR—B.Gibson, Javier.

	IP	H	R	ER	BB	SO
B.Gibson (W)	9	3	2	2	3	10
Lonborg (L)	6	10	7	6	1	1
Santiago	2	0	0	0	0	0
Morehead	1-3	0	0	0	3	1
Osinksi	1-3	0	0	0	0	0
Brett	1-3	0	0	0	0	0

SP—Lonborg, Gibson.

T—2:23. A—35,188.

U—Stevens (A) Plate, Barlick (N) First Base, Umont (A) Second Base, Donatelli (N) Third Base, Runge (A) Left Field, Pryor (N) Right Field.

Yarbrough Demolishes Car In Racing Practice Mishap

CHARLOTTE, N. C. (AP) — One of Ford's big entries in the National 500-mile stock car race was wiped out Thursday when front row starter Lee Roy Yarbrough demolished his car in a spectacular practice accident.

The accident left the 26-year-old Yarbrough uninjured, but it also nearly took from Sunday's $100,800 fall classic Ford's other front row starter, Cale Yarborough, who had won the pole Wednesday with a record-breaking 154.872 miles per hour.

Yarbrough, who had qualified No. 2 at 154.639 m.p.h., blew an engine in the 1.5-mile Charlotte Motor Speedway's second turn. The shock of the engine blowing set off the automatic fire extinguisher in the car, blinding the driver temporarily, and the speeding Ford crashed into the steel retaining wall.

The impact was so great that the car broke in two, the engine and front end of the racer flying in one direction, the cockpit and rear section in another.

Yarborough, in the Glenn Wood Ford, was running close behind Yarbrough at high speed when the accident occurred. Yarborough managed to get through the smoke and debris without damage to his car.

"I don't know how I did it," said Yarborough, "but here I am. Right now, I'd say I'm the luckiest person alive."

Yarbrough was checked over at the infield hospital and released. He will be available for relief driving in the Ford teams effort to put an end to Plymouth ace Richard Petty's 10-race winning streak.

With Yarbrough's car out of the field, Wednesday's other nine qualifiers moved up a notch in the starting order, putting three - time Indianapolis winner A. J. Foyt into the front row beside Yarborough. Foyt is the unofficial captain of Sunday's Ford's team effort.

Petty moved up from his original sixth place start to fifth place. Ironically, it will be Petty's third fifth place start in as many races. And the 30-year-old winner of $126,000 this year won both of the other events.

Ten more drivers qualified for the 44 - car starting field Thursday, including another Ford ace, Mario Andretti. The Nazareth, Pa., star earned 17th position. His four - lap average speed was 149.615 m.p.h. It is his first start at Charlotte.

The day's top qualifier was James Hylton, who won 10th position in a Dodge at 151.770 m.p.h. Plymouth's Jim Paschal had the next best time at 151.610.

Other qualifiers, in 12th through 19th positions, were Gordon Johncock in a Murcury, 151.610; Donnie Allison, Ford, 151.493; Bobby Allison, Dodge, 151.175; Bobby Isaac, Dodge, 150.533; Whitey Gerkin, Ford, 150.000; Andretti; Curtis Turner, Chevelle, 149.109; and Bud Moore, Dodge, 148.474.

Another Jacket On Injured List

ATLANTA (AP)—Coach Bud Carson said Thursday his Georgia Tech Yellow Jackets will be in their worst condition of the season Saturday for a regionally televised football game with Tennessee at Knoxville.

"I can't imagine a team being in worse condition," Carson said after learning that a fourth starter, sophomore linebacker Mike Bradley, would miss the game because of injuries.

Three other regulars—quarterback Kim King, defensive end Tommy Carlisle and flanker Percy Helmer—already were on the injured list.

Greyhounds Eye Big Fray Tonight

By TOMMY DESSELLE
Telegraph Sports Writer

The Jones County Greyhounds, with a surprising record of 2-3-1, clash tonight in Gray with the Ft. Valley Green Wave, 5-2, in an important Region 2-B West contest.

Jones County head Coach Albert Radford, who coached Ft. Valley last year, inherited a club that lost 16 lettermen and has only three seniors back and is relying mainly on juniors and sophomores to carry the load.

Radford made some personnel changes after the first two ball games and the results have been pleasing. After losing to Wilkinson County and Putnam County, the Greyhounds tied Monticello, 6-6, and beat Vienna, 35-20, and Hawkinsville, 12-7. However, they were whipped last week by a strong Mary Persons team and need to bounce back.

The Greyhounds are a balanced ball club that tries to mix running and passing. Radford said John Childs, 172-pound senior end, and Joe Barnes, 161-pound junior guard, are the two blockers that make the running attack go.

The backfield has Rick Childs at quarterback, Gary Faulkner and Muriel Brackin at halfbacks and Donald Greene at fullback. Greene is a good runner and helps the running attack go with his blocking.

This will be homecoming for Jones County and the winner of the game will take the lead in the region standings.

Ft. Valley also enters the game on a losing note, having bowed to Manchester, 30-7, last week. However, the Green Wave have a terrific offensive attack that has rolled over Terrell County, 35-12, Vienna, 62-7, Randolph County, 32-13, Cochran, 21-7, and Macon County, 49-27.

The Wave presents a balanced attack led by quarterback Tom Cleveland, halfbacks Bobby Lane and Warren Young and fullback Bob Hardeman or Philip Rigdon.

Head coach Norman Faircloth said, "We have a senior ball club but most of the boys who are playing did not play last year and we are not as experienced as most senior clubs.

"However, our team has given good effort and played good all year and played their best all round game at Cochran." He went on to say, "Ft. Valley played good against Manchester and with a couple of breaks might have pulled it out."

Lane is the leading scorer and tackles Charles Clark and Bucky Duke along with guards Al Pearson and Tommy Smissin and center Buddy Reddick are responsible for opening holes.

YOUNG IDEAS

By DICK YOUNG

Anytime you have conclusions and disjointed action within an organization, such as there is in baseball concerning whether or not games shall be played over the weekend of mourning, it is an indication of weakness at the top.

Two months ago, when Martin Luther King was shot to death, baseball teams were in the late stages of their exhibition schedules. Some clubs announced immediately that they were calling off exhibition games that Sunday. Some clubs said they would play, and this led to at least one visiting club saying it wouldn't put a team on the field if the game was scheduled to go on. The game eventually was called off.

This Commissioner Always Asks First

Meanwhile, the commissioner of baseball was running around as if his head had been cut off. That is not as catastrophic as if his

IF YOU DON'T WANT TO PLAY, DON'T PLAY! SEE IF I CARE!
COMMISSIONER
·G·

phone had been cut off. He was calling up all the club owners, not to tell them what to do, but to ask them.

On the basis of his calls to the owners, and to some civic leaders, decisions were made. Not one decision; decisions. They were made on the basis of individual needs and circumstances. They were made, not out of any great compassion for Dr. King or for his family, or for what he stood for, but out of fear. If the commissioner was assured that a ball game could be played without provoking a racial demonstration, it was not cancelled. This was the motivating factor, and let us not kid ourselves, let us not pretend.

Then came the most astonishing ruling of all. Tuesday was to be the day of Dr. King's funeral, and Tuesday was opening day of the season for most ball clubs. It was decided that teams in the East and Midwest, who would be playing during the funeral, should postpone the game. It was decided that teams in California, who would be opening at an hour when the funeral had concluded, would play. It was as though someone was standing by the side of the bier with a stopwatch and a starter's gun.

This is the portrait of a commissioner trying to please everyone. He does not wish to offend an owner, not a single owner, nor does he wish to offend the public. So, he rationalizes, rather than make strong decisions. In most cases, the club owners make decisions for him, and in some cases players have been making them.

Still Hasn't Profited by His Mistake

Now, Commissioner Eckert has had two months to make the same equivocating mistake. The tragic murder of Robert Kennedy again plunges the nation into mourning, and required that similar decisions be made by sports leaders.

I feel strongly that each man recognizes his own grief: each man mourns in his own way, and if he is truly moved, and his day's movements are dictated, then he gets up an hour earlier and goes to church and prays, or prays in his own corner, in his own solitude. I can recognize that certain institutions require policy-making judgments and baseball evidently is one of these.

Then it is up to the commissioner of baseball, leader of the game, to make the decision, make it strong, make it quick, make it absolute. There were two choices. Robert Kennedy's funeral was set for Saturday. The President of the United States proclaimed Sunday a national day of mourning.

The commissioner could issue a decree. All baseball games for Saturday are cancelled. Or, he could have said, all games for Sunday are cancelled. Eiher way. It would have been baseball's uniform observance, baseball's mark of respect, and it would have been observed, I'm sure, without question, without challenge.

Instead, the commissioner equivocated. He consulted several club owners, not all, who had gathered in New York for draft meetings. Some had bat days on Saturday and wanted to save them. They preferred to give up Sunday. Some had bat days on Sunday, and would prefer to give up Saturday. "There were tremendous pressures from both sides," one owner told me.

A man is subjected to pressure when it is recognized he submits to pressure. The stronger the man the less the pressure.

Strength of Leadership Is Missing

The strength, the leadership, required of the office of commissioner of baseball, was not there again. He said that games scheduled on Saturday afternoon should be pushed back to Saturday night so as not to conflict with the funeral hours That's the same preposterous stopwatch concept as last time. But this time he got caught between ticks because the ceremony was long delayed until after the games had started. The commissioner also said that games would be played on Sunday.

The announcements by the Yankees and the Senators that they would not play at all on Saturday were their decisions, not the commissioner's. There followed word from Boston and Baltimore that they would not play on Sunday. The Mets' players voted not to play on one date, and left it up to the host club to decide. Horace Stoneham

NOW, DON'T ANYBODY GO LOSING THEIR HEADS!
YIPES! WHAT HAPPENED TO MY PHONE?
·G·

then cancelled out Saturday. The Players' Association wired the commissioner expressing resentment over his failure to set aside one day for all clubs.

I have funny, old-fashioned notions that students should not run universities, inmates should not run asylums, and ballplayers should not tell owners when they will or will not play. Twice, in recent months, ball players have felt impelled to make ultimatums. When that happens, the commissioner looks bad. When that happens, baseball looks bad. It would not happen with strong leadership.

Don Passes Johnson's 56

Los Angeles, June 8 (AP)—Don Drysdale of the Dodgers shattered a 55-year-old record when he carried a streak of scoreless innings pitched past Walter Johnson's record of 56 in the third inning of tonight's game against the Philadelphia Phillies.

Drysdale had hurled six straight shutouts—54 scoreless innings—breaking the major league mark of five consecutive shutouts set by Doc White in 1904 and the NL mark of 46 1-3 consecutive scoreless innings established by Carl Hubbell in 1933.

THE BIG righthander tied Johnson's major league mark of 56 innings by blanking the Phillies in the first and second innings tonight and then broke the record when he recorded the first out in the third.

Johnson's record was set on a combination of starts and relief appearances. Drysdale has pieced his string together in seven starts beginning May 14, when he blanked the Cubs, 1-0.

After that, it was 1-0 against Houston, May 18; 2-0 against St. Louis, May 22; 5-0 against Houston, May 26; 3-0 against San Francisco, May 31, and 5-0 against Pittsburgh, June 4.

THE LAST remaining member of the team that moved west from Brooklyn in 1958, Drysdale is the dean of the Dodger players, although not yet 32 years old.

He had won 190 games for the Dodgers in 12 big-league seasons before 1968. His seven victories this season gave him 197 for his career and made him the winningest pitcher in club history. Dazzy Vance, a Hall of Famer, also had 190 victories for the Dodgers.

Dodgers vs. Phillies

PHILS, FIRST: Rojas flied to Davis. Briggs walked. Versalles made a backhand stop of Gonzales' grounder and threw to Popovich, forcing Briggs. Callison flied to Davis.

No runs, no hits, no errors, one left.

DODGERS, FIRST: Parker singled. Davis forced Parker. Rojas to Pena. Gabrielson struck out. Davis stole second. Haller was purposely walked. Boyer singled, scoring Davis. Haller advanced to third. Fairly flied to Gonzalez.

One run, two hits, no errors, two left.

PHILS, SECOND: White grounded to Parker. Popovich threw out Taylor. Dalrymple struck out.

Nothing across.

Don Drysdale
Record-breaker

U.S. Clinches on Doubles Win

Charlotte, N.C., June 8 (AP)—The U.S. won the Davis Cup American Zone tennis finals tonight by taking the doubles after it opened with two victories over Ecuador in the singles last night.

Clark Graebner and Bob Lutz employed booming services and aggressive net game to thoroughly dominate Pancho Guzman and Miguel Olvera of Ecuador, 6-3, 6-2, 7-5.

TOMORROW afternoon's two singles matches at the Coliseum will be a formality.

For the second night in a row, the smaller Latin Americans failed to break the U.S. service.

The 6-foot-2 Graebner and 6-foot-1 Lutz broke Olvera's service in the fourth game of the first set and breezed for an easy victory. They broke Olvera's service in games 3 and 7 in the second set, and in the 11th game of the final set.

LAST NIGHT, Olvera, a 5-foot-3, 125-pounder, was beaten by Graebner, and Guzman lost to Arthur Ashe.

The doubles victory completed revenge for the U.S. team, which was defeated by Ecuador last year in Guayaquil.

Graebner was on the losing U.S. doubles team last year, along with Marty Riessen.

The U.S. team will face the European zone winner in the next round of Davis Cup competition.

Rosewall Defeats Laver For French Open Title

Paris, June 8 (UPI)—Australian Ken Rosewall crushed fellow Aussie Rod Laver, 6-3, 6-1, 2-6, 6-2, in the men's singles finals of the French Open Championships today.

Rosewall intimidated his opponent from the start. He hardly made a mistake in the first two sets. He broke Laver's service in the ninth game to take the first set.

ROSEWALL GAVE his opponent little space, but at the same time was always ready for an opening at the net. The dominance of Laver continued in the second set while Rosewall went to five-love by taking seven games in succession.

Having won the second set, 6-1, Rosewall threatened an overwhelming victory when he broke Laver's service at 2-1. At this point Laver made a desperate effort and his pressure tactics coincided with Rosewall tiring. The upshot was five games in a row for Laver, giving him the third set, 6-2.

Rosewall reasserted his earlier dominance and with two service breaks went to three-love in the fourth set. Laver rallied by breaking Rosewall's service in the next game but could not stop Rosewall.

THE FRENCH-British pro combination of Francoise Durr and Ann Hayden Jones were surprise victors in the women's doubles finals, when they beat Rosemary Casals of San Francisco and Billie Jean King by 7-5, 4-6, 6-4.

Hill (66) Leads Snead By 3; Crampton 7 Back

Indianapolis, June 8 (AP)—Mike Hill led a par-busting charge with a six-under 66 today and captured the third-round lead in the $100,000 Speedway Open golf tournament.

The 29-year-old pro from Jackson, Mich., playing in his second PGA tourney, has a 10-under-par 206 for 54 holes.

SAM SNEAD, who shot 69 for 209, is second. Billy Casper, the PGA's leading-money winner this year, and 58-year-old Dutch Harrison also shot 69s for 210 totals.

Bruce Crampton, leader the first two rounds, shot 75 and slipped to 213.

Hill, who flunked the PGA's school twice before passing, missed the cut by a stroke in the Memphis Open two weeks ago and failed to qualify for the Atlanta Classic last week.

HE OPENED this tournament with 71 and shot 69 yesterday before tying the tournament record with his 66.

Hill made four birdies on the front nine and two on the backside. Although his tee-to-green game was tremendous, he missed at least three possible birdies on the back nine.

Hill finished with a birdie on the par 5,555-yard 18th hole.

THE 56-YEAR-OLD SNEAD matched par on the front nine. But he birdied three holes for a 3-under-par 33 on the back nine.

Crampton, who went in with a two-stroke lead, started with a bogey and was unable to pull his game together.

Whitworth, Mann 141s Share Bluegrass Lead

Louisville, Ky. June 8 (AP)—The reliables, Kathy Whitworth and Carol Mann, each played sub-par golf today to move into the lead after two rounds in the Women's PGA Bluegrass Invitational Golf Tournament.

Miss Whitworth, who had a first round 73, shot a four-under-par 68 for a 36-hole total of 141, one under par. Miss Mann improved her opening round 71 by one stroke today for her 141 total.

Bonallack Downs Carr, Takes British Amateur

Troon, Scotland, June 8 (UPI)—Mike Bonallack of England gave his Walker Cup captain, Joe Carr, a golf lesson today in scoring an easy 7 and 6 victory which gave the Englishman his third British Amateur championship.

Bonallack, who twice previously lost to Carr in the Amateur, thus became only the fourth man in the 83-year history of the prestigeous tournament to score three wins. The others were Carr, John Ball and Harold Hilton.

Bonallack's victory margin was the biggest since Carr himself won in 1960, beating Bob Cochran, 8 and 7, at Royal Portrush.

Associated Press Wirephoto

Putt-ing it Away

Mike Hill receives applause from spectator after sinking birdie putt on seventh hole.

FINAL ★★★★

DAILY NEWS

NEW YORK'S PICTURE NEWSPAPER ®

MORE THAN TWICE THE CIRCULATION OF ANY OTHER PAPER IN AMERICA

72 New York, N.Y. 10017, Wednesday, October 2, 1968

World Series Showdown:

McLAIN VS. GIBSON

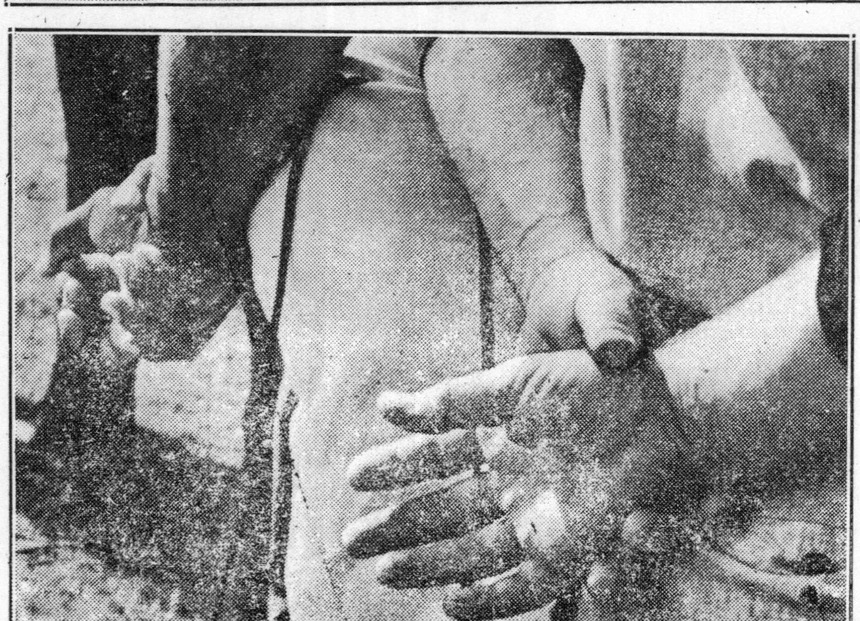

Associated Press Wirephotos

Today, It's in Their Hands

The pitchers of the year—Tiger Dennis McLain (left) and Cardinal Bob Gibson—stand side-by-side at Busch Stadium, St. Louis. Today, they'll be facing each other there as the 65th World Series begins at 2 p.m. In their big hands (←) rest the fortunes of their teammates. Literally. The difference between a winning and losing player's Series share is between $3,000-$4,000. Neither was born when the 1934 Gas House Gang of St. Louis and the Tigers last met in the most flamboyant World Series in memory. Let's see what's in store for 1968.

—*Story on page 64*

FINAL ★★★★

DAILY NEWS

NEW YORK'S PICTURE NEWSPAPER ®

MORE THAN TWICE THE CIRCULATION OF ANY OTHER PAPER IN AMERICA

136

New York, N.Y. 10017, Thursday, October 3, 1968

GIBSON'S HIGH CARD

Strikes Out Record 17 Tigers, 4-0

Associated Press Wirephoto

Bob Gibson almost falls off mound as he zaps record-breaking strike to Norm Cash in ninth of Series opener at St. Louis. Cash swung—but hit nothing but air—and Gibson had his 16th strikeout of day. It was a 4-0 victory. *—Stories page 116; other pictures centerfold*

Gibson: 'I Wasn't Even Trying for Strikeouts'

By BOB GIBSON

St. Louis, Oct. 2—When the game was over and I walked into the clubhouse, Butch Yatkeman, our clubhouse man, told me I had a long distance telephone call from Vice President Humphrey.

The vice president said he had watched the game on television and he wanted to call and congratulate me on the game I pitched. He asked me how my family was and he said, "I'm with you all the way."

I guess we talked for about five minutes.

He remembered the few times we had met. Once in Boston and last year at a dinner in the White House that President Johnson had given for the premier of Japan. I was invited to the dinner and I talked with the vice president at that time. He and I were the only ones wearing blue shirts with our tuxedos and he commented on that.

"YOU AND I ARE the only ones around here to dress with any class," he said.

Naturally, I'm happy about breaking the World Series record for strikeouts in a game, but believe me, the record is not the important thing. Winning is. I'd rather have the victory without the record than the record without the victory. Having both makes it nicer.

I didn't even know about the record. I couldn't imagine what all the shouting was about. Then I happened to turn around and look at the scoreboard. I saw something about 16 strikeouts and a World Series record and I knew what all the shouting was about. When I got Willie Horton for my 17th strikeout I was happy because the game was over.

I NEVER TRY FOR strikeouts and I wasn't trying for them today. The thing about strikeouts is that when you're getting a lot of them, naturally, you're throwing a lot of pitches. I'd rather get a man out with one pitch and save my strength. Today I threw 144 pitches. That's a lot of pitches, but I didn't feel tired anytime during the game or after

(Continued on page 117)

The American Paper for Americans

Chicago Tribune

THE WORLD'S GREATEST NEWSPAPER

SPORTS ★★★★ FINAL

122d YEAR—No. 285

FRIDAY, OCTOBER 11, 1968

84 PAGES, 4 SECTIONS 10c

TIGER ROAR ROCKS DETROIT

Gun Bill Sent to LBJ

IT PROHIBITS INTERSTATE MAIL SALES

Ammunition Also Covered

BY RUSSELL FREEBURG

[Chicago Tribune Press Service]

Washington, Oct. 10—The House passed and sent to the White House today legislation that would prohibit the interstate mail order sale of rifles, shotguns, and ammunition.

The vote was 160 to 129. Passage came with little opposition as the House moved impatiently toward adjournment.

Rep. Emanuel Celler [D., N. Y.], chairman of the House judiciary committee, called the bill one of the most controversial in House history.

Battling against the bill to the end was Rep. Clark MacGregor [R., Minn.], who objected to the ban on the mail order sale of ammunition. He called the measure "hypocritical on its face."

Opponents Charge Sellout

The final compromise legislation was a combination of the stronger points of differing bills passed earlier by the House and the Senate. House opponents

Rep. Clark MacGregor

charged that they had been sold down the river.

Under the legislation, which takes effect Dec. 16, an over-the-counter gun purchaser would have to be resident of the state or, if laws of both states permit, of an adjacent state; would have to be 21 years old to buy hand guns and 18 to buy rifles or shotguns, and would have to have a record clear of felony and drug addiction convictions. The purchaser would have to be mentally competent.

Must Keep Records

Dealers are required to keep records of all sales under the new law, which President Johnson is expected to sign.

The measure also regulates the sale of firearms by mail within a state by providing for filing of an affidavit of eligibility by the purchaser and a seven day waiting period.

Ammunition sales would generally be restricted to the types of ammunition fitting guns which the purchaser would be eligible to buy.

The bill permits the Pentagon to supply surplus weapons and ammunition to marksmanship clubs.

The legislation also provides for imprisonment of at least five years for a second or subsequent offense of possessing a gun during a federal felony.

LBJ Appoints Davis Envoy to Guatemala

[Chicago Tribune Press Service]

Washington, Oct. 10—President Johnson today announced his appointment of Nathaniel Davis, 43, a career foreign service officer, as ambassador to Guatemala. Davis will succeed John G. Mein, the American ambassador assassinated in Guatemala City by suspected left-wing terrorists Aug. 28.

Winds May Bar Apollo Flight Today

By FRED FARRAR

[Chicago Tribune Press Service]

Cape Kennedy, Fla., Oct. 10—The possibility of rain and high winds poses a threat to tomorrow morning's scheduled launching of the Apollo spacecraft, National Aeronautics and Space administration officials said today.

They said, however, that they hope the weather will cooperate and that the flight, the first manned test of the three-man spacecraft designed to put Americans on the moon before the end of next year, will go off as scheduled at 10 a. m. [Chicago time].

Test Rocket Systems

The latest weather forecast calls for a slight chance of showers and winds of 10 knots, below the danger level, but NASA officials will be keeping an apprehensive eye on the weather.

The final countdown began at 1:45 p. m. today as power was applied briefly to the Saturn 1B rocket which will put the astronauts into orbit around the earth for a flight that could last as long as 11 days.

The purpose of the power test was to make another complete check of the rocket's electrical and control systems.

The wind problem, which threatens to mar what up to now has been an almost perfect countdown, is a serious one because the rocket is subject to being blown over in the first few seconds when it is slowly rising off the launch pad.

Must Abort Over Water

NASA officials said that winds of up to 27 knots can be tolerated if they are coming from the west. If from the east, the limit is 18 knots.

If the winds exceed the imposed limits, the launch will be postponed 24 hours, officials said.

The officials said high winds from the east could cause the space capsule to come down on land instead of water if the astronauts are forced to trigger their emergency abort system. The system uses rockets attached to the spacecraft to take it up and away from the Saturn 1B in the event of trouble.

Only minor problems have turned up so far in the countdown. The latest was an apparent malfunction in a system

[Continued on page 2, col. 5]

ALL IN A POINT OF VIEW

Democrats in House Pushing Senate Vote on TV Debates

BY WILLIAM KLING

[From Tribune Wire Services]

Washington, Oct. 10—House Democrats threatened tonight to block final adjournment of Congress unless the Senate clears the way for three-way Presidential campaign debates on nation-wide television.

Sen. Dirksen [R., Ill.], the minority leader, earlier today foiled Vice President Humphrey's bid for the debates with his Republican opponent, Richard M. Nixon, and George C. Wallace, third party Presidential candidate.

Dems Back Down

Senate Democrats, faced with a shortage of votes because many of their number were campaigning for reelection in their home states, backed down when Dirksen threatened "to use every weapon at my command" to scuttle suspension of equal time provisions of the federal communications act.

"They know they can stop it,

THE DEBATE AS A 'PSEUDO-EVENT'

See the editorial on page 20

and they know I know they can stop it," said Sen. John O. Pastore [D., R. I.], Senate floor manager of the bill which was passed by the House yesterday after Democrats outlasted a marathon Republican "filibuster."

In an effort to revive the bill, Rep. James G. O'Hara [D., Mich.], co-chairman of Congressmen for Humphrey, said he may lead Democrats in a "sit-out" to prevent sine die adjournment of the House.

Could Prevent Quorum

O'Hara said the tactic, which could deprive the House of a quorum needed to consider an adjournment resolution expected tomorrow, would give Senate Democrats leverage to force a vote on the bill.

About 50 Democratic congressmen already have agreed to go along with the strategy, O'Hara said, and House Speaker John McCormack [D., Mass.] has been informed of it "but he's not part of it."

Final decision on whether to pursue the strategy will be made tomorrow, O'Hara said, after he confers with officials of the Democratic national committee and key Humphrey supporters in the Senate.

Eager to Adjourn

With only four weeks left before the Nov. 5 election, Congress is eager to end its session so that members may campaign in their home districts. O'Hara said he hopes a "sit-out" would force the Senate to pass the bill rather than stay in session.

After blasts at Humphrey and Wallace by G.O.P. senators, Sen. Mike Mansfield [D., Mont.], the majority leader, indefinitely postponed consideration of the bill, asserting that he was acting in "the best interest of all concerned."

Earlier, Mansfield said the Senate, which had hoped to adjourn tomorrow or Saturday, probably will have to meet next week because of a tie-up over funds for the Alliance for Progress and possible action yet this session on the nuclear nonproliferation treaty. He said he will announce tomorrow whether the Johnson administration has decided to press for an immediate Senate vote on the treaty.

"Have Enough Votes"

Pastore said, in a floor speech, that the Republicans "have enough troops here . . . to call 'live' quorum calls or extend debate" on the equal time suspension, which would have permitted television and radio networks to broadcast Humphrey - Nixon - Wallace debates without granting an equal amount of air time to minor Presidential candidates.

Humphrey, with polls indicating trouble for his Democratic campaign for the White House, has challenged Nixon to debates. The Republican nominee, while contending he is willing to meet Humphrey alone, has refused to engage in debates that include Wallace, a third-party candidate for the Presidency.

Sen. Hugh Scott [R. Pa.] defended Nixon's position, asserting that inclusion of Wallace in the debates "would give recognition to the most blatant of demagogs, to the most irresponsible candidate for President in our lifetime, to a racist and a bigot, to a man who appeals to hatred and class warfare."

Scott said Wallace would use

[Continued on page 6, col. 4]

Find Priest from City Living a Double Life

BY JOHN MACLEAN

A Roman Catholic priest who grew up in Chicago was accused yesterday of living a double life—one as a priest, the other as a highly paid business executive with tax problems.

The priest, who heads a boys' orphanage near Los Angeles, was said by federal government officials to be living part time in a $75,000 home in Palm Springs.

The government charged he failed to declare personal income of nearly $120,000 over a three-year period.

Called "Dedicated Boy"

The Rev. Robert Nikliborc, 37, was described by his family here as "a quiet dedicated boy who was always wanting to do things for others."

United States Atty. Matt Byrne, of Los Angeles, said the Rev. Mr. Nikliborc was charged with failing to report personal income for 1963 thru 1965, and arraignment was set for Oct. 31.

Byrne said Nikliborc made the money as president of an electronics firm under the assumed name of Robert Drew Rand.

Neighbors near the Palm Springs home said Rand had been a quiet neighbor, who was seldom seen.

Raised in Poverty

Nikliboc's family said he was ordained here after growing up in poverty on the south side.

"His father died when he was 17 and he worked as a bookkeeper to help support his mother and seven brothers and sisters," said an aunt of the priest, Mrs. John Nikliborc, who lives at 5719 S. Sacramento av.

"He was a wonderful priest," the woman said. Two other brothers, Francis and Edward, also became priests, and one

[Continued on page 2, col. 7]

ROBERT TAYLOR, ACTOR, IMPROVES AFTER SURGERY

Santa Monica, Cal., Oct. 10 (UPI)—Robert Taylor, the actor, 57, was reported "doing very well" today in the intensive care unit of St. John's hospital, where he underwent surgery for removal of his right lung.

Following the operation last Tuesday, doctors discovered "some small tumors" in the removed lung, a hospital spokesman said. However, it has not been determined if the tumors were cancerous.

Doctors predicted that the star of the television series, The Detectives, would be able to return home within two weeks.

30,000 FANS JAM AIRPORT, HALT FLIGHTS

But Team Lands at Willow Run

(Pictures on back page)

[From Tribune Wire Service]

Detroit, Oct. 10—The nation's fifth largest city erupted into a horn-tooting, traffic-stopping, paper-throwing celebration tonight after the Detroit Tigers won the world series.

The team won its third straight series game today and toppled the St. Louis Cardinals four games to three, bringing the title back to Detroit for the first time since 1945.

Air raid sirens wailed, horns blared, and church bells pealed. Office workers jammed downtown streets, and secretaries became flower children, passing out posies to passers-by along with hugs and kisses.

Tons of paper and ticker tape fluttered to the ground from office windows.

Airport Shut Down

Detroit Metropolitan airport was closed down after 30,000 jubilant fans poured onto the grounds to await the triumphant return of the Tigers. The Tigers' plane, en route from St. Louis, was diverted to Willow Run airport.

Thousands of fans began crowding Metropolitan airport shortly after 3 p. m. [Chicago time] when the Tigers clinched the championship. An hour and a half later, they began breaking thru barricades and were blocking several of the runways at the huge airport.

All air traffic to and from the airport was halted.

A group of Wayne county sheriff's officers were huddled in a hangar working out plans on how to manage the crowd when the plane arrived. Then they were informed the airport was being closed.

"It's too late to handle them now," the officer said.

Go to Other Airports

About 1,000 persons, hearing all flights at Metropolitan had been canceled, went to Willow Run and met the triumphant team.

Another thousand showed up at Bishop airport at Flint and in a jubilant mood refused to leave after repeated denials by airport officials that the Tigers had chosen their city, 60 miles northwest of Detroit, for the return to Michigan.

Eventually the airport greeters trickled home or joined the tens of thousands roaming the streets of downtown Detroit. The team was hauled to Tiger stadium in buses and was forced to wait inside until traffic outside cleared.

The buses carrying the team were recognized even tho an evasive path was followed from the suburban air field to Tiger stadium, a few blocks from the center of town.

Fans Recognize Team

Fans recognized the team and beat on the sides of the buses trying to catch the eyes of their heroes.

"I was going to go home, but since the baggage wasn't going to be taken to Tiger stadium until tomorrow I'm glad because I wouldn't miss this for the world," said Dick Tracewski, a reserve infielder, from a bus.

"Gibson is Human" was one sign read by the Tigers as they passed thru suburban Dearborn. It referred to pitcher Bob Gibson of the Cardinals, the losing pitcher today. The Tigers approved.

"Look at all those people," said Mayo Smith, team manager. "They're even coming out of the bars."

[AP Wirephoto]

Happy Winners

Winning pitcher Mickey Lolich is lifted off his feet by Detroit catcher Bill Freehan after final out of world series, won by Tigers, 4 to 1, in seventh game.

The Editor's DIGEST of the News

Friday, October 11, 1968

NATIONAL

House of Representatives passes and sends gun bill to President Johnson. Page 1

House Democrats threaten to block adjournment of Congress unless Senate clears way for three-way Presidential campaign debates on TV. Page 1

All is ready for first manned Apollo space test, but officials say high winds may force postponement. Page 1

President Johnson says he will not make another nomination for chief justice. Page 3

Federal court jury in Baltimore finds nine war protestors, accused of destroying draft records, guilty after only one hour and 25 minutes of deliberation. Page 5

President Johnson blasts Richard M. Nixon, as representative of "do-nothing, standpat politics." Page 7

Richard M. Nixon confers with former Gov. William Scranton of Pennsylvania. Page 8

Vice President Humphrey draws a large crowd in Wall street. Page 10

Sen. Muskie gives his net worth as $106,468. Page 10

THE WEATHER

FRIDAY, OCTOBER 11, 1968

CHICAGO AND VICINITY: Sunny and warmer today; high, in upper 60s; fair and not so cool tonight; low, mid 40s; south to southwest winds 10 to 18 m. p. h. Tomorrow: Partly sunny and warmer.

NORTHERN ILLINOIS: Fair and warmer today and tonight; high, 66 to 72; low, 42 to 50. Tomorrow: Partly sunny and mild.

WEATHERMAN'S RECORD

His forecast for yesterday was: Fair; cool; high, in mid 50s; low, upper 30s.

HOURLY TEMPERATURES

7 a. m.	‡42	4 p. m.	63	11 p. m.	49
8 a. m.	43	4:30	†64	Midnight	48
9 a. m.	48	5 p. m.	63	1 a. m.	48
10 a. m.	52	6 p. m.	60	2 a. m.	*47
11 a. m.	55	7 p. m.	56	3 a. m.	*47
Noon	55	8 p. m.	53	4 a. m.	*46
1 p. m.	59	9 p. m.	52	5 a. m.	*44
2 p. m.	62	10 p. m.	50	6 a. m.	*43
3 p. m.	63				

*Estimated. †High. ‡Low.

THE MOON

Full	Last Qu.	Waning	New	Waxing	First Qu.
Oct.6	Oct.14	Oct.15-20	Oct.21	Oct.22-27	Oct.28

Sunrise, 6:58. Sunset, 6:16. Moonrise, 8:53 p. m. Morning stars: Saturn, Mars, and Jupiter. Evening stars: Venus and Saturn.

For 24 hours ended 1 a. m., Oct. 11:

Mean temperature, 53 degrees; normal, 58; month's deficiency, 38; year's deficiency, 190.

Relative humidity, 7 a. m., 86 per cent; 1 p. m., 49; 7 p. m., 51.

Precipitation, move; month's total, .31 inch; October normal, 2.78 inches; year's total, 21.07 inches; deficiency thru Sept. 30, 5.54 inches.

Highest wind velocity, 22 m. p. h. at 10:57 a. m. from west.

Barometer, 7 a. m., 30.15; 7 p. m., 30.18.

[Map and other reports on page 18]

Features

CARTOONS

LOCAL

Students walk out of meeting with authorities at Harrison High school. Page 2

Two prominent Negroes disagree over student walkouts in city schools. Page 2

Robert Potenzo, 21, son of north suburban gambling czar Rocco [The Parrot] Potenzo, and two other men are arrested by Skokie police in connection with the sale of marijuana to juveniles. Page 22

City building department suspends the permit privileges of firm that cooperated with police in arrest of building inspector. Sec. 1A, p. 2

INTERNATIONAL

Britain's Conservative party demands severe limits on entry of colored immigrants. Page 14

American troops guarding Saigon follow Viet Cong defector to two huge communist ammunition caches and then unearth two others. Page 22

SPORTS

Detroit goes beserk as Tigers win series. Page 1

Avery Brundage is reelected Olympic chief. Sec. 3, p. 1

FINANCIAL

Stock market closes with fairly sharp loss. Sec. 3, p. 7

I. B. M. reports nine-month income up 30.9%. Sec. 3, p. 7

EDITORIALS

The Debate as a 'Pseudo-Event'; The Noose Tightens on Czechoslovakia; Causes of Student Disorders; Certifying Teachers. Page [illegible]

Mantle, Saying He Can No Longer Hit 'When I Need To,' Gives Up Baseball

SLUGGER RETIRES WITH 536 HOMERS

Finishes 3d to Ruth, Mays —'There's No Use Trying,' Yankee Star Declares

Continued From Page 1

he said, and then had a long talk with Burke at breakfast this morning.

"I really hadn't made up my mind," Mantle said, "but I think I was just kidding myself. I told Ralph how I felt and he said if he was me he'd make up his mind as fast as possible. I'm really glad I decided to do it."

In recent years it had seemed the Yankees needed Mantle for his ability and his appeal at the gate as much as he needd his $100,000 salary. But business has improved for both of them.

A victim of several bad investments in his early years, Mantle recently became involved in Mickey Mantle's Country Cookin', a Southern-style resttaurant chain, and Mickey Mantle's Clothing Store, both based in Dallas.

"I've got to appear at the opening of each franchise," Mantle said today. "We've opened 45 of them so far and if we sell 100 more this year, that's one every three days."

Things have improved in the Bronx, also. The Yankees finished fifth last year after having been out of the first division for three years.

"We've got some good players who had terrible years and should come back," Mantle said, "and we've got some good young players like Roy White and Bill Robinson. It may be another year before the Yankees win the pennant, but I think they'll be back again."

He Becomes Dispensable

The Yankees have also come up with some fine young prospects like Jerry Kenney, Bobby Murcer and Tony Solaita this spring. The urgency for dragging one more year out of Mantle has been dissipated.

What will Mantle's future be with the club?

"We've simply not had the time to formulate the relationship," Burke said, "so we'll leave it as a continuing relationship. Mickey is part of our family."

Mantle and his wife, Merlyn, plan to stay in town for two weeks "because we packed a lot of clothes," Mantle said. Mantle's oldest son, Mickey Jr., is attending the Riverside Military Academy near here and Mantle insisted on delaying the announcement until he had seen Mickey Jr. play center field for the school team this morning.

A Star Is Born

"He lost," Mantle reported, "but he made one of the greatest catches I've ever seen."

He said he would spend tomorrow with his son, who has a weekend pass.

"I'll probably go to the ball park on Monday, but I'm not going to put on a uniform again," he said. "I'll probably sit around and talk to the guys.

"I don't know how I'll feel not playing ball. I've been playing ball for 20 years and I'll probably miss it like crazy. But Mike told me I have a job with the Yankees any time I want it. I'm not going to say I never want to be a manager, because Ted Williams said that nine years ago and now he's managing.

"I don't know how my four boys feel about it, but my wife has been after me to quit for three years. I know she's happy."

Highlights From Mickey Mantle's Baseball Career: Superlatives Seemed to Be a Permanent Part of All His Accomplishments

Associated Press

In 1963, against the Athletics, he hit stand at Yankee Stadium 117 feet above right field, 500 from the plate, the closest anyone came to driving a homer out of that park.

MAGIC-MESSAGE
MANTLE IN
2165TH GAME
A YANKEE
RECORD

In 1967 he broke Lou Gehrig's mark for games played

The New York Times

With Michael Burke after hitting 500th homer that year

Associated Press

The 300th home run of his major league career came in 1960, year the Bombers were American League champions.

Mantle's Road to Fame: 18 Years of Pain, Struggle and Frustration

Special to The New York Times

FORT LAUDERDALE, March 1—The retirement of a player as great as Mickey Mantle should inspire only a recitation of great deeds and enjoyable moments, yet his story must include frustration and unfulfillment along with the glory. Mantle never enjoyed his 18 years in New York the way many other stars have enjoyed their careers and injuries and personal struggles were equally responsible.

For many years he seemed on the verge of becoming a happy, healthy star—he was certainly a hero to millions of fans—but injuries and temper delayed that process. Then in the closing years, after he had achieved many great things on the field and developed a relative maturity to appreciate them, he was cheered every time he poked his head out of the dugout.

However, Mantle understood that the cheers were for him as a descending star and he had never wished to be the central figure in a tragic-opera situation. When fans in Houston gave him a standing ovation last summer after he had struck out in the All-Star Game, he talked of being "tired" and retiring. The one glorious year of being whole and happy had never quite come.

The intermingling of pain and joy began in Mantle's first season in the major leagues. Born in Spavinaw, Okla., on Oct. 20, 1931, he needed only two years in the minor leagues before joining the Yankees in 1951—a powerful, fleet young man who could not miss being a star if a boyhood case of osteomyelitis, a bone disease, remained arrested.

From World Series to Hospital

That first season saw him twist his right knee on a drain pipe while playing right field in the second game of the World Series. For the rest of the Series he was in the hospital—in the bed next to his father, who was suffering from Hodgkins disease, which would eventually kill him.

The records show that Mantle's best years were in 1956-57, when the Yankees won pennants as usual and he was twice voted Most Valuable Player. He batted .353 in 1956, hit 52 home runs and drove in 130 runs, leading the league in all three categories, the so-called "triple crown." In 1957, he batted .365 with 34 homers and 94 runs batted in. When the Giants took Willie Mays to San Francisco after 1957,

Associated Press

Injuries plagued him. In 1963 he broke a a foot while chasing a ball in Baltimore.

Willie Mays to San Francisco afte Mantle was clearly New York's biggest sports hero.

But Mantle never was at home in New York, preferring to settle in Dallas with his wife and four sons and rent homes or live in hotels during the season. And even in the best of summers, New York was not his scene. The fans saw him heave his batting helmet in disgust when he struck out and he heard as many boos as cheers.

"Me and the fans really had a go-around those first couple of years," he recalled recently. "I didn't like them and they didn't like me. But it's gotten better since then."

"When fans did approach Mantle, he often did not seem to know how to react. Whereas many stars would chat with their fans—while trotting toward the sanctuary of the clubhouse—Mantle would often would bolt frozen-faced through them, occasionally scattering youngsters like the halfback he wished he had been. And Mantle's reaction to the press was inconsistent and occasionally rude, although he was a funny and loyal friend to his teammates, who liked and respected him.

After the first decade, Mantle began to cope with many things, running bases, playing center field and swinging the bat with a new understanding, coupling wisdom with his physical skills.

"It seemed like I was finally getting the hang of it," he once said.

Hard Luck Continues Its Course

Then the injuries struck again. He tried to play the 1961 World Series with an abscess on his right buttock that oozed blood through his uniform, visible to players and fans. In 1962 he pulled a right-thigh muscle while running to first base and fell to the ground "as if he had been shot," as one reporter described it. Mantle recovered in a month from the hamstring, but he had bruised his left knee in the fall and he wound up playing only 123 games that year. Yet the Yankees won the pennant and he was voted Most Valuable Player for the third time.

The games diminished to 65 in 1963 as he broke his foot when his spikes caught in a wire fence in Baltimore. He also had knee cartilage removed in the offseason.

By 1964 it was commonly accepted by players and fans that Mantle was playing mostly on courage. Players saw him pull himself up stairways using his powerful arms to supplement his wobbly knees, and they marveled that he could play at all.

"Every time he misses, he grunts in pain," one opposing catcher said. "You think he's going to fall down."

In 1965, as the Kankees fell from first to sixth place, Mantle suffered back and neck spasms, shoulder and elbow aches and he pulled his left hamstring and missed 21 games. He had a chip removed from his right shoulder before the 1966 season, yet he insisted on opening the season in left field—to minimize his throwing. He later strained a hamstring and bruised his left hand.

By 1967, Mantle moved to first base and played in 144 games, suffering only minor aches. His average fell to .245 and

Associated Press

The 1967 season saw Mantle, an outfielder, playing a new spot: first baseman.

his pride was hurt, but he did not quit.

"I need the money," he sometimes said, laughing as if it were a joke. But friends whispered that he needed his $100,000 salary because of poor investments, so he played on. Last year he appeared in 144 games again, this time batting only .237.

Ae he grew older, Mantle became extremely popular with the New York fans and he had always been adulated by fans in other cities. Last year many clubs asked if they could honor Mantle on the Yankees' final appearance in their town, just in case it was his final performance. Mantle usually said he did not want a fuss made over him and he refused the honors. He still will be honored many times, of course, but as a retired hero rather than as a future hero or a declining one, two roles he never thoroughly enjoyed.

NAVY TEAM FIRST IN 4-MAN BOBSLED

Lamey Pilots Unit to Victory in Diamond Trophy Race

LAKE PLACID, N. Y., March 1 (AP)—A United States Navy team, headed by Paul Lamey, won the four-man international Diamond Trophy bobsled race today at the nearby Mount Van Hoevenberg course.

The Navy team covered the 1,500-meter course in a total time of 4 minutes 25.50 seconds for four heats.

Bob Huscher was the brakeman on the Navy sled.

Second-place went to a team representing the Lake Placid Bobsled Club. The driver was Bob Said and Phil Duprey was the brakeman.

The total time for the Lake Placid club was 4:26.50.

In third place was another Lake Placid Bobsled Club entry, driven by Harry Peterson with Paul King the brakeman.

The third-place finisher in last weekend's four-man world championships, Les Fenner, piloted his Hurricane Bobsled Club entry to fourth place in today's competition.

In fifth-place was an Adirondack Bobsled Club team headed by Fred Fortune, who guided his United States sled to fourth place in the world event.

The remaining teams in the Diamond Trophy races, in the order of their finishes, were the Lake Placid Bobsled Club, piloted by Mike Hollrock; the Canadian Bobsled Club, led by Hans Gehrig and the Saranac Lake Bobsled Club, under the guidance of Harley Webb.

The two-man international Diamond Trophy races were scheduled for tomorrow. The field includes 14 United States teams and two Canadian entries.

Reprinted from yesterday's late editions.

Poland Six Beats Rumania

LJUBLJANA, Yugoslavia, Feb. 28 (AP) — Poland defeated Rumania, 4-2, and Norway tied Austria, 3-3, in Group B matches of the world amateur ice hockey championships today.

N.H.L. SEALS SOLD FOR $4.5-MILLION

Whitey Ford Listed in New Ownership Syndicate

Special to The New York Times

OAKLAND, Calif., March 1—The Oakland Seals of the National Hockey League were sold today for in excess of $4.5-million to Trans-National Communications, whose ownership roster includes, Whitey Ford, the former New York Yankee pitcher, Dick Lynch and Pat Summerall, former New York Giant football stars.

The purchase price was reported to be for 80 per cent of the stock. The other 20 per cent was retained bv Sevmour H. Knox 3d and his brother, Northrup, of Buffalo.

Immediately after the announcement of the sale, the National Hockey League said its Board of Governors would meet to act on the deal later this month.

William Creasy, former producer for the Columbia Broadcasting System until he joined T.N.C. last January, was named the Seals' president.

"In my first act as president of the Seals," said Creasy during the news conference, "I can state with equivocation that we intend to operate right here in Oakland. We have no doubt that the Bay area will respond to the National Hockey League."

The Seals, the poores record in the league last season but currently in second place in the West Division, have been the weak financial link in the expansion of the N.H.L. two years ago.

Two weeks ago, the N.H.L., in a decision that infuriated interests from Vancouver, British Columbia, and disappointed Buffalo, refused to permit the Seals to move their franchise.

The Knox brothers are believed to be holding on to their interest in the Seals in hopes that further expansion would bring a team to Buffalo.

Vancouver, seeking the Oakland franchise, guaranteed the N.H.L. an average attendance of 12,000 a game. The league dismissed the move because of added travel costs and the fact that the Los Angeles Kings would lose a natural rival.

193 Juveniles Nominated For 1971 Jersey Futurity

The 1971 New Jersey Futurity has closed with 193 nominations. The $17,500-added, six-furlong event will be run in the fall of 1971 at Garden State Park.

Garden State will be the new home of the futurity, for 2-year-olds foaled in New Jersey, starting in 1971. The race was first run at Monmouth Park in 1957 and will remain on the seashore oval's schedule through 1970.

It is being switched to Garden State at the request of the Thoroughbred Breeders Association of New Jersey and will replace the New Jersey Breeders Stakes on the stakes calendar.

Speed-Skating Marks Fall

INZELL, Germany, March 1 (UPI)—Two world records fell and another was tied today in international speed-skating competition. Ivar Eriksen of Norway broke his 1,000-meter record by eight-tenths of a second with a time of 1 minute 19.5 seconds. Kees Verkerk of The Netherlands was time in 7:13.2 for the 5,000-meter race, and Kelichi Suzuki of Japan equaled the 00-5meter record of 39.2 seconds.

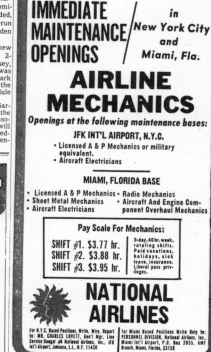

In 18 Years With the Yankees, He Enjoyed Fame, Endured Frustration

United Press International

As a young rookie in 1951. His best years were '56, 57 and '62, when he was voted the league's most valuable player.

The New York Times

Between '61 and '65, injuries hurt his performance. His strong swing became more and more a visibly painful act.

Mets Down, 8-6; Up 3-0, on Jones' HR

By Red Foley

On a day when the nation pushed its clocks ahead, the Mets, showing a marvelous sense of timing, yesterday

(Second Game)

CHICAGO	*b.av.	ab.	r.	h.	tb.	rbi.	po.	a.	e.
Kessinger, ss	.296	4	0	1	1	0	1	6	0
Beckert, 2b	.253	4	0	0	0	0	3	4	0
Williams, lf	.292	4	0	2	2	0	1	0	1
Santo, 3b	.174	3	0	0	0	0	3	2	0
Banks, 1b	.303	4	0	2	3	0	10	0	0
Hundley, c	.268	2	0	0	0	0	4	0	0
Spangler, rf	.333	2	0	0	0	0	1	0	0
a-Hickman, rf	.125	2	0	0	0	0	0	0	0
Phillips, cf	.167	2	0	1	1	0	2	0	0
Nye, p	.000	3	0	0	0	0	0	0	0
Team	.248								
Totals		30	0	6	7	0	25	12	1

*Including yesterday's second game.
a-Struck out for Spangler in 7th.
b-Struck out for Weis in 8th.
‡One out when winning runs scored.

METS	*b.av.	ab.	r.	h.	tb.	rbi.	po.	a.	e.
Gaspar, cf	.224	4	1	1	1	0	2	0	0
Boswell, 2b	.276	3	1	0	0	0	3	2	1
Charles, 3b	.147	4	0	0	0	0	0	2	0
Jones, lf	.443	4	1	2	5	3	3	0	0
Swoboda, rf	.326	3	0	0	0	0	4	0	0
Grote, c	.235	3	0	1	2	0	6	2	0
Kranepool, 1b	.294	2	0	0	0	0	5	1	0
Weis, ss	.000	2	0	0	0	0	1	2	0
b-Agee	.190	1	0	0	0	0	0	0	0
Garrett, ss	.267	0	0	0	0	0	0	0	0
McAndrew, p	.200	1	0	0	0	0	3	0	0
MCGraw, p	.000	1	0	0	0	0	0	0	0
Team	.240								
Totals		28	3	‡	8	3	27	10	1

Chicago	000	000	000	—0
METS	000	000	003	—3

Earned runs—Chicago 0; Mets 2. Left on bases—Chicago 7; Mets 3. Two-base hits—Grote, Banks. Home run—Jones. Caught stealing-by—Grote (Phillips). Sacrifice—Hundley. Double plays—Chicago 2 (Beckert-Mets 2 (Weis-Kranepool; Grote-Boswell). Kessinger-Banks; Kessinger-Beckert- Banks) Bases on balls-off—Nye 3 (Kranepool, M'Andrew, Boswell); M'Andrew 2 (Santo, Phillips); McGraw 1 (Hundley). Struck out by—Nye 3 (Charles, Kranepool, Agee); McGraw 6 (Santo 2, Hickman, Phillips Nye,,Kessinger). Hits off—Nye 4 and 3 runs (2 earned) in 8⅓ inns.; McAndrew 3 and 0 (0) in 5 (faced 2 in 6th); McGraw 3 and 0 (0) in 1. Passed ball—Grote. Winning Pitcher—McGraw (2-0). Losing Pitcher—Nye (0-2). Time 2:28. Umpires—Harvey, Dezelan, Crawford, Pelekoudas. Attendance: 37,437.

split a Shea twinner with the Cubs in which they gáve 37,437 customers a look at the dismal past and then a peek into the glorious future.

Cleon Jones is mobbed by Mets after game-winning homer.

First Game

CHICAGO (8) at METS (6)

CHICAGO	ab	r	h	rbi
Kessinger, ss	3	3	2	0
Beckert, 2b	5	0	2	0
Williams, lf	5	1	0	1
Santo, 3b	5	0	1	2
Banks, 1b	5	1	2	1
Hundley, c	3	2	1	2
Spangler, rf	3	0	1	1
Young, cf	2	0	0	0
Jimenez, ph	1	0	0	0
Phillips, cf	0	0	0	0
Selma, p	2	1	1	0
Aguirre, p	0	0	0	0
Smith, ph	1	0	0	0
Abernathy, p	0	0	0	0
Oliver, ph	1	0	0	0
Regan, p	1	0	0	0
Totals	37	8	10	7

METS	ab	r	h	rbi
Gasper, cf	4	1	1	0
Garrett, ss	5	1	1	0
Boswell, 2b'	4	2	2	0
Jones, lf	5	2	3	3
Kranepool, 1b	4	0	1	1
Swoboda, rf	3	0	2	2
Martin, c	4	0	0	0
Collins, 3b	4	0	1	0
Gentry, p	1	0	0	0
Otis, ph	1	0	0	0
Koonce, p	1	0	1	0
Seaver, p	0	0	0	0
Totals	36	6	12	6

Chicago	002	010	014	—8
METS	300	030	000	—6

E—Boswell DP—Mets 1. LOB—Chicago 10, Mets 7. 2B—Gaspar, Santo, Jones, Spangler. HR—Hundley (3). S—Gentry. SF—Swoboda.

	IP	H	R	ER	BB	SO
Selma	4	8	6	6	2	2
Aguirre	1	0	0	0	0	0
Abernathy	2	2	0	0	0	2
Regan (W—4-0)	2	2	0	0	0	3
Gentry	6	6	3	3	3	3
Koonce (L—0-2)	2⅔	4	5	1	4	0
Seaver	⅓	0	0	0	1	1

Cleon Jones, who spans both eras, introduced the faithful to their promised land when he busted a two-on homer in the ninth for the 3-0 triumph that followed the four-run final frame giveaway that blew the 8-6 opener.

JONES' FIFTH hit of the long matinee, the one that hoisted his league-leading average to .443, came on a 1-0 delivery by luckless lefty Rich Nye. Rod Gaspar and Ken Boswell, on via gifts of one kind or another, preceded Cloutin' Cleon across to fracture what had been a scoreless pitching duel.

Gaspar, replacing slump-shackled Amos Otis in center, was aboard when Billy Williams turned his inning-leading liner into a two-base muff. Boswell, one of the goats of the opener, was then purposely passed. After Ed Charles bunted foul and then popped to Ron Santo, Jones jolted his game winner over the boards in left-center.

Among the more ecstatic Mets to mob Jones at the plate was Tug McGraw. The lefty, who did a snazzy job of rescuing starter Jim McAndrew in the sixth, finally found a home—in the Mets' bullpen. And this time city zoning laws won't prevent it. You may remember that Tug originally wanted to park his two-room trailer at Shea, but the statutes prohibited it.

BUT AFTER HIS dandy three-hit, six-whiff showing, an effort he wasn't actually prepared to perform, Gil Hodges will probably see to it that Mac gets all the comforts of home now. The skipper can't get the law changed, but he can see to it that Tug gets preferential treatment during working hours.

McGraw was lolling in the pen when McAndrew, who'd been matching zips with Nye for five, broke a blister on the middle finger of his right hand. Tug took a brief warmup and then proclaimed himself ready. The Cubs had runners on second and third, none out and a full count on Glen Beckert.

MAC'S FIRST pitch was a comebacker, the runners holding. He then got Williams on a short loft to Jones and fanned Santo to keep the quoits on the scoreboard. After Williams led the ninth with a single, Tug again fanned Santo and got a bonus when Jerry Grote's bullet nailed Williams going to second. Ernie Banks then doubled, and after Randy Hundley, one of Chi's first-game heores, was purposely passed, he got Jim Hickman on a pop to center.

The lidlifter, the one that reminded long-suffering Met fans of how it used to be, was blown on sour relief and botched fielding. The Mets had bopped former teammate Dick Selma, making his Cub debut, for three in the first before disposing of him with three more in the fifth.

IN BETWEEN, the visitors nibbled at starter Gary Gentry. They'd managed to square it, 3-3, in the fifth, but when Selma blew in the Mets' half they had to do it all over again. Cal Koonce relieved the tiring Gentry in the seventh and a walk, plus Al Spangler's double, cut the Cub deficit to two after eight.

A leadoff pass to Don Kessinger opened the fateful finale. Beckert's advancing grounder gave the Mets one out, but when Boswell booted Williams' roller, the visitors had runners at the corners. Santo then high-hopped to Kevin Collins. The kid, trying for Williams and perhaps the game-ending twin kill, heaved the forcing toss past Boswell as Kessinger scored.

Ernie Banks promptly singled Koonce's first pitch into right for the knotter. Hundley then followed with a loft into the visitors' bullpen, that gave batterymate Phil Regan his fourth win in seven relief appearances.

Something Old, Something New... by Stark

..BALL TWO!
TRY AGAIN, BUSH!
10
...SOME SAY THEY EVEN LIVENED UP THE BALL...
...AND WE ALL KNOW THEY MADE LIFE MISERABLE FOR THE MICKEY ROONEYS OF THE PITCHING TRADE...
WHERE AT'S TH' PLATE ?
...BY LOWERING THE MOUND...
OH, SURE, THEY CHANGED THE STRIKE ZONE...
GIMME FIVE, I'M BABE RUTH!
...ALL INNOVATIONS TO MAKE THE GRAND OL' GAME NEW AND EXCITING...
...THAT'S ALL WELL AND GOOD, I SUPPOSE, BUT, FOR MY MONEY, ALL BASEBALL NEEDS IS A COUPLE MORE SUPER STARS LIKE OLD Willie MAYS
...NEARING HIS 600TH HOME RUN !

National League

YESTERDAY

Chicago 8, METS 6 (1st).
METS 3, Chicago 0 (2d).
Philadelphia 1, St. Louis 0.
Montreal 4, Pittsburgh 2.
San Francisco 8, Houston 5 (1st).
San Francisco 4, Houston 3 (2d game).
Los Angeles 10, Atlanta 0.
San Diego 5, Cincinnati 2 (1st).
San Diego 10, Cincinnati 9 (2d, 13 inn.).

EASTERN DIVISION

	W.	L.	Pct.	G.B.
Chicago	14	6	.700	—
Pittsburgh	12	6	.667	1
Philadelphia	7	9	.438	5
METS	7	11	.389	6
St. Louis	7	11	.389	6
Montreal	7	11	.389	6

WESTERN DIVISION

	W.	L.	Pct.	G.B.
Los Angeles	12	6	.667	—
San Francisco	12	6	.667	—
Atlanta	11	7	.611	1
Cincinnati	8	9	.471	3½
San Diego	9	11	.450	4
Houston	4	17	.190	9½

TODAY

Cincinnati, Nolan (1-2) at San Francisco, Perry (3-2).
Chicago, Holtzman (2-1) at Philadelphia, Wise (2-1) night.
St. Louis, Carlton (1-2) at Pittsburgh, Moose (2-0) night.
Houston, Dierker (2-2) at Atlanta, Stone (3-0) night.
Only games scheduled.

American League

YESTERDAY

Baltimore 6, YANKEES 0 (1st).
Baltimore 10, YANKEES 5 (2d).
Detroit 7, Boston 3.
Washington 6, Cleveland 5.
California 6, Kansas City 2.
Minnesota 4, Chicago 3 (8.)
Oakland 13, Seattle 5.

EASTERN DIVISION

	W.	L.	Pct.	G.B.
Baltimore	15	7	.682	—
Boston	10	7	.588	2½
YANKEES	10	8	.556	3
Detroit	9	8	.529	3½
Washington	10	10	.500	4
Cleveland	1	15	.063	11

WESTERN DIVISION

	W.	L.	Pct.	G.B.
Minnesota	10	7	.588	—
Oakland	10	8	.556	½
Chicago	8	7	.533	1
Kansas City	8	8	.500	1½
California	6	8	.429	2½
Seattle	6	10	.375	3½

TODAY

Boston, Jarvis (1-0) at YANKEES, Peterson (2-2) night.
Baltimore, McNally (3-0) at Cleveland, Tiant (0-4) night.
California, McGlothlin (1-1) at Seattle, Pattin (2-1) night.
Kansas City, Hedlund (1-0) at Minnesota, Hall (1-1) night.
Washington, Pascual (0-2) at Detroit, Wilson (1-2) night.

Durocher, Baseball's Liperace Without Candelabra

By Lynn Hudson

They may never call him Mr. Baseball but that's okay because they should probably call him Mr. Show Business. That's what all of it is to Leo Durocher—show business.

The Cubs were on a four-game losing streak as they prepared to open the weekend series here with the Mets. But was Leo Durocher worried? Not on your manicure. He was sitting there in the manager's room of the Cubs' Shea Stadium clubhouse telling the boys about his appearance on the Dean Martin show.

"When was that filmed?" someone asked.

Sports Special

"Back in February," said the Lip, who used to threaten to quit the National Pastime about every other year with the boast that he could be making twice as much in show business.

"He's so funny!" Leo says of pal Dean. "When we finished the show, he and the producer and his wife were guests of mine in Acapulco for about 10 days. I rent this house down there. So one day Dean says, 'I've been your guest long enough. Today, we're goin' out.'

"Well, we're sittin' there in this restaurant at two o'clock in the afternoon and Dean says, 'Armando, bring me a vodka.' So I tell him, 'It's not the cocktail hour yet. And Dean just says, 'Well, it's dark in my stomach.' "

They all roar, of course. The reporters and TV men and club functionaries. This is Leo the Raconteur in action. The sort of stuff that has made him an eligible "guest personality" ever since he was a hit on the old Fred Allen radio show back in the early '40s.

Leo and Fred would do comedy skits on baseball and once Leo sang: "When I was a lad, my eyes were so weak/That I became an umpire in the National Leak"—to a tune from H.M.S. Pinafore.

Now Leo doesn't have to threaten to quit baseball and go into show business.

The contract he signed with the Cubs this year is said to be substantially above the 65 thousand he made in 1968. And John Holland, the Cub GM, said at the time the only reason there is a contract at all is that baseball law required it.

"Leo knows he can manage the Cubs as long as he wants to," Holland said.

It beats getting fired twice a week by Larry MacPhail.

As for managing as long as he wants to, there may be a team from Red China in the National League before Leo quits.

Now the talk turned to baseball, and Leo the Actor took over. The stories were mostly about umpires. And Leo, still trim in his snugly-tailored Cub uniform and looking maybe only a little over two-thirds of his 62 years, got up and acted out all the parts.

The stories are about umpires who are losing their eyesight, or umpires who insist on literal interpretations of minor rules to the point of absurdity, or umpires whom Leo has told off or stepped out of line with and not been thumbed out.

They are told in a language that is Durocher — which means a wealth of four-letter words.

He was less voluble when pressed about specifics. Are this year's Cubs "his kind of ballclub," as he once said of the '54 Giants?

"Any kind of club that wins is my kind of club."

Can this club win?

"I don't know yet."

How about the lowered pitching mound? Has it affected his staff?

"If a guy can't pitch, he can't pitch if he's throwing off a cliff. Sure, there's more hitting this year, but the mound doesn't have anything to do with it."

They used to say of Humphrey Bogart that he was an all right guy until about two o'clock in the morning when he'd been drinking: Then he would start thinking he was Humphrey Bogart.

Leo doesn't need the booze. He turns into Leo Durocher, 1930's tough guy, at the drop of an anecdote—jawing, gesticulating, mimicking—and loving every minute of being the center of attention.

Raconteur, con man, umpire baiter, actor, tough guy—Leo Durocher is a big part of the diminishing color that's left in baseball. And the way things are going, they'd better hope he doesn't start threatening again to go into show business.

NEWS photo by Frank Hurley

Lip Loses Another Squawk.

Carew Steals Home, Right Past Cobb

Second baseman Red Carew of the Twins broke the AL record for steals of home in a season last night and tied the major league mark of seven set in 1946 by Brooklyn's Pete Reiser as Minnesota swept a doubleheader from the White Sox, 9-8 and 6-3.

Carew, seven for seven in steals of home this year, broke the AL mark of six set in 1915 by Ty Cobb of Detroit and tied in 1917 by Robert Roth of Cleveland.

Carew stole home in the second inning of the first game when Chicago catcher Don Pavletich couldn't hold on to Gerry Nyman's pitch as Carew slid across the plate.

The theft was part of a triple steal by the Twins. Harmon Killebrew, who was on second, stole his fifth base this season—a personal high. Charlie Manuel, who was on first, stole his first base of the season.

You couldn't blame Chicago pitchers if they saw Minnesota runners stealing bases in their sleep after the twinkletoed Twins wound up swiping eight bases in nine tries in the doubleheader. Carew, Cesar Tovar and Killebrew each had two stolen bases. Carew also stole second in the eighth inning of the opener and scored what turned out to be the winning run on Rich Reese's single.

"To me it's more of a thrill to steal home than to hit one out," said Carew, who has 15 stolen bases in 17 tries.

Billy Martin said, "We go on certain pitches. We didn't have anything on the White Sox. We watch where the infielders are playing, what the count is and several other things.

"We weren't trying to embarrass them. We were trying to score runs and the steals turned out to help win the game."

The White Sox pounded out 17 hits in the opener against Minnesota's 11 and came back for nine hits in the nightcap to Minnesota's eight. But the Twins stretched their winning streak to eight (17 in their last 19 outings).

"We don't expect winning streaks," said Martin. "They just come and we're happy when they're here."

The Twins started out by giving the White Sox a dose of power and then switching quickly to finesse. Reese started the fireworks with a three-run homer in the first inning of the opener — and he drove in two later runs with another homer and a single.

Then, in the second, after Chicago scored twice in the top of the inning, Tovar singled and stole second. Pitcher Tom Hall popped a single to right, sending Tovar to third, and Ted Uhlaender beat out a bunt for a run. Carew forced Uhlaender and Reese struck out but Killebrew walked and so did Charlie Manuel, forcing in a run and making it 5-2.

Rally in Ninth

Carew then swiped home on the front end of a triple steal.

Ron Hansen and Carlos May belted solo homers for the Sox.

The Twins ran their winning streak to eight in a row as Uhlaender drove in three runs with as many singles in the second game. The lumbering Killebrew stole second in the fifth inning and Tovar and Frank Quilici did it in the seventh.

Two-run homers by Dick Green, Rick Monday and Sal Bando powered Oakland past Seattle 6-1 and Lew Krausse limited the losers to four hits, including Don Mincher's solo homer. The setback stretched the Pilots' losing streak to seven games.

Brooks Robinson singled with two out in the ninth inning to break a tie and win the nightcap for Baltimore, 6-5, after Stan Williams had retired Curt Motton and pinch-hitter Frank Robinson with the bases loaded. Motten hit a two-run homer for the Orioles and Tony Horton belted a pair of solo shots for the Indians.

Ken Suarez and Chuck Hinton each drove in a pair of runs as Cleveland took a 6-0 lead in the opener, but Mike Paul had to put down a ninth-inning rally for a 6-4 Indians' victory. Frank Robinson hit his 21st homer.

Detroit's Mickey Lolich and Washington's Dick Bosman were locked in a scoreless battle until Willie Horton doubled in three unearned runs with two out in the eighth inning to give the Tigers a 3-0 win. Lolich scattered four singles and struck out nine, getting slugging Frank Howard three times.

Andy Messersmith stopped Kansas City 4-2 on six hits and doubled in a run as the Angels made it three straight and tied their longest 1969 winning streak, set during the first week of the season. Loser Jim Rooker homered for the Royals, his third in two games. Messersmith fanned 10, most by an Angel hurler this year.

Major League Standings

AMERICAN LEAGUE

Eastern Division

	W	L	Pct.	GB
Balt.	64	28	.696	—
Boston	51	42	.548	13½
Det.	48	40	.545	14
Wash.	50	46	.521	16
N. Y.	43	51	.457	22
Cleve.	37	55	.402	27

Western Division

	W	L	Pct.	GB
Minn.	56	35	.615	—
Oak.	49	38	.563	5
K. C.	39	53	.424	17½
Seattle	38	52	.422	17½
Chi.	38	53	.418	18
Calif.	35	55	.398	20½

NATIONAL LEAGUE

Eastern Division

	W	L	Pct.	GB
Chi.	57	36	.613	—
N. Y.	51	37	.580	3½
St. L.	48	46	.511	9½
Pitts.	45	47	.498	11½
Phila.	38	51	.427	17
Mont'l	28	63	.308	28

Western Division

	W	L	Pct.	GB
L. A.	52	38	.578	—
Atlan.	52	41	.559	1½
S. F.	51	41	.554	2
Cinn.	47	39	.547	3
H'ston	47	47	.500	7
S. D'go	32	62	.340	22

HOW THEY DID IT	Baltimore	Boston	California	Chicago	Cleveland	Detroit	Kansas City	Minnesota	New York	Oakland	Seattle	Washington
Baltimore	—	7	3	4	7	7	5	4	9	5	3	10
Boston	5	—	5	3	10	7	5	4	5	1	3	3
California	1	1	—	5	3	2	8	4	1	2	5	3
Chicago	2	3	5	—	5	2	2	2	1	5	8	3
Cleveland	3	4	3	1	—	4	4	3	7	3	3	2
Detroit	4	4	5	3	6	—	3	3	8	3	4	5
Kansas City	1	1	5	5	2	1	—	6	2	5	7	4
Minnesota	2	2	10	10	2	1	6	—	6	8	7	2
New York	4	5	5	5	4	6	4	1	—	2	2	5
Oakland	0	4	6	6	2	2	9	4	3	—	5	4
Seattle	2	2	6	6	3	2	5	0	4	3	—	5
Washington	4	9	2	5	11	6	2	4	5	1	1	—

HOW THEY DID IT	Atlanta	Chicago	Cincinnati	Houston	Los Angeles	Montreal	New York	Philadelphia	Pittsburgh	St. Louis	San Diego	S. Francisco
Atlanta	—	1	8	9	7	3	3	3	4	3	4	7
Chicago	5	—	3	3	3	8	7	8	6	6	6	2
Cincinnati	4	2	—	4	5	4	1	4	4	3	9	7
Houston	3	2	4	—	4	5	4	4	2	4	8	7
Los Angeles	7	2	5	9	—	5	2	3	5	2	9	3
Montreal	1	6	2	0	1	—	3	5	3	4	2	1
New York	2	7	3	2	4	6	—	6	5	8	4	4
Philadelphia	2	2	1	1	3	6	5	—	7	6	3	2
Pittsburgh	3	6	0	5	0	10	4	5	—	5	4	3
St. Louis	3	5	3	2	4	7	6	6	6	—	3	3
San Diego	4	1	5	6	2	4	1	3	1	3	—	2
S Francisco	7	2	5	6	5	5	1	4	4	2	10	—

(For today's games see pitching form)

RESULTS LAST NIGHT

Boston 6, **New York** 2.
Cleveland 6, Baltimore 4 (1st, twl.).
Baltimore 6, Cleveland 5 (2d).
Detroit 3, Washington 0.
Minnesota 9, Chicago 8 (1st, twi.).
Minnesota 6, Chicago 3 (2d).
California 4, Kansas City 2.
Oakland 6, Seattle 1.

TOMORROW NIGHT

Washington at **New York.**
Oakland at California.
Minnesota at Seattle (2, twi.).
Kansas City at Chicago.
Detroit at Cleveland.
Baltimore at Boston.

RESULTS YESTERDAY

New York 9, Chicago 5.
St. Louis 5, Philadelphia 0 (N).
Pittsburgh 8, Montreal 7 (N).
Cincinnati 10, Atlanta 7 (N).
Los Angeles 3, Houston 2 (N).
San Francisco 4, San Diego 3.

TOMORROW NIGHT

New York at Montreal.
Chicago at Philadelphia.
St. Louis at Pittsburgh.
San Diego at Atlanta (2, twi.).
Houston at Cincinnati.
Los Angeles at San Francisco.

Anything for Peace

The Miracle Mets did it again—and with Abdullah looking out the window of the Astrodome. Poor Abs. He bet on the Astros last night and dropped 13 bananas while his sentimental favorites upset the Cubs. Abs is now minus $83.

Tonight two units on the Braves.

Club	Pitcher	1969 Record	1969 vs. Club	Lifetime vs. Club
Red Sox	Lonborg (R)	6—3	0—0	8—5
Yanks (8:00)	Peterson (L)	9—11	1—0	2—1
Tigers	Dobson (R)	4—7	0—1	0—4
	or Wilson (R)	7—7	0—1	14—7
Senators (7:30)	Hannan (R)	3—5	0—0	2—1
Indians	Paul (L)	1—7	0—0	1—0
Orioles (8:00)	McNally (L)	13—0	0—0	12—7
White Sox	Horlen (R)	6—10	0—2	10—14
Twins (9:00)	Kaat (L)	9—6	0—0	22—11
	or Miller (R)	2—2	1—0	1—1
A's	Hunter (R)	7—7	0—0	0—0
Seat. Pilots (11:00)	Pattin (R)	7—8	0—1	0—2
Dodgers	Singer (R)	12—7	1—1	3—4
Giants (4:00)	Herbel (R)	4—1	0—0	4—1
Braves	Niekro (R)	14—7	3—0	5—4
Reds (8:05)	Merritt (L)	8—3	0—0	0—0
Pirates	Bunning (R)	8—6	0—0	0—0
Mont. Expos (8:05)	Reed (R)	4—2	0—1	0—1
Phils	Wise (R)	6—7	0—0	1—6
Cards (9:00)	Washburn (R)	3—7	0—0	5—2

OFFICIAL LINE

Red Sox-Yanks pick 'em; Tigers 5½-6½ over Senators; Orioles 2 runs over Indians; Twins 8-9 over White Sox; A's 7-8 over Pilots.

Dodgers even-6 over Giants; Braves-Reds pick 'em; Pirates 7½-8½ over Expos; Cards 8-9 over Phils.

Gross On Webster: P. 106

New York Post Sports

Merchant On Giants: P. 104

112 NEW YORK, TUESDAY, SEPTEMBER 23, 1969

Seaver: Easy As 3...2...1

By MAURY ALLEN

Pennant fever? Spell it Koosman and Seaver.

Three is the number and then comes the magic. Three Met wins or three Cub losses or two from Column A and one from Column B and the Mets become the one, the only, the original team to win the Eastern Division championship of the National League.

The Tom and Jerry Show was up again last night. Tom Seaver won his 24th game, the major league high, with a spirited 3-1 victory over the Cardinals. Jerry Koosman won his 16th the day before. Tom and Jerry have won 16 of their last 17 as the Mets have made Leo Durocher a sick joke.

It's time to stop worrying about the division, you nervous Nellies, and start sweating out the pennant. Will the Mets win it?

"No comment," said Seaver. "Me and Leo."

Seaver had his best put-on grin going last night and his fastball. He was good on the field and around the table where writers gather every four days to hear his description of his latest win.

Pretty Pitching

"I threw 116 pitches," said Seaver, "and 82 were strikes."

Only guided missiles have better control than Seaver, baseball's complete pitcher, complete pitcher, complete athlete and next commissioner.

The nice thing about Seaver and all of the young and old Mets is the grace, charm and opise they are winning with. They are nice guys. They are finishing first. They are generous.

Seaver has a lock on the National League Cy Young Award and could win the MVP. He's pushing another guy.

"No. 20 is the MVP," he said. "He's made the difference in this club. I told everybody that in spring training. I'm a great believer in the kid who tries."

Seaver was sold on No. 20 —Tommie Agee—last May when Agee went oh-for-34 and kept busting his butt on the ball-field.

"Every time he went on the field he gave 100 per cent, not just as a player, but a man. You can't fool the people at Shea," Seaver said. "When he got a ground-single, they gave him a standing ovation. I gave him one, too, on the bench. It almost brought tears to your eyes."

Nelson Briles wrestled Seaver scoreless through the first five innings. Then in the Met sixth, Seaver's MVP lined a single to left. It bounced off Lou Brock and Agee was on second. A passed ball and he was on third.

Shamsky Delivers

Art Shamsky, who had foregone batting practice to wait for sundown and the end of Yom Kippur, lined a soft single to left for the run.

"I tried to hit the ball hard," said Shamsky, "but my back's been bothering me in cold weather, so it came out soft."

Singles in the seventh by Jerry Grote, Bud Harrelson, Seaver and Agee's force gave the Mets their last two runs. Seaver lost his shutout on Julian Javier's double and Vic Davalillo's single.

And now the number is three. Magic number? Uhh, uhh, just the number of weeks to go in the long-running Tom and Jerry Show.

Belmont Scratches

3—Wedel, Woofee, Alamo Lancer, Onion John, Silver Finger, Wheat Crop.
5—Mile Roulettee.
7—Fairfleet, Monticello, Sir Omni.
9—Cerisier, Golden Skein, Miss Sparks, Speedy Minstrel, Ticket Wicket, Tudor Blue 2d.

Clear and fast. Post 1:30 p.m.

Say Hey!

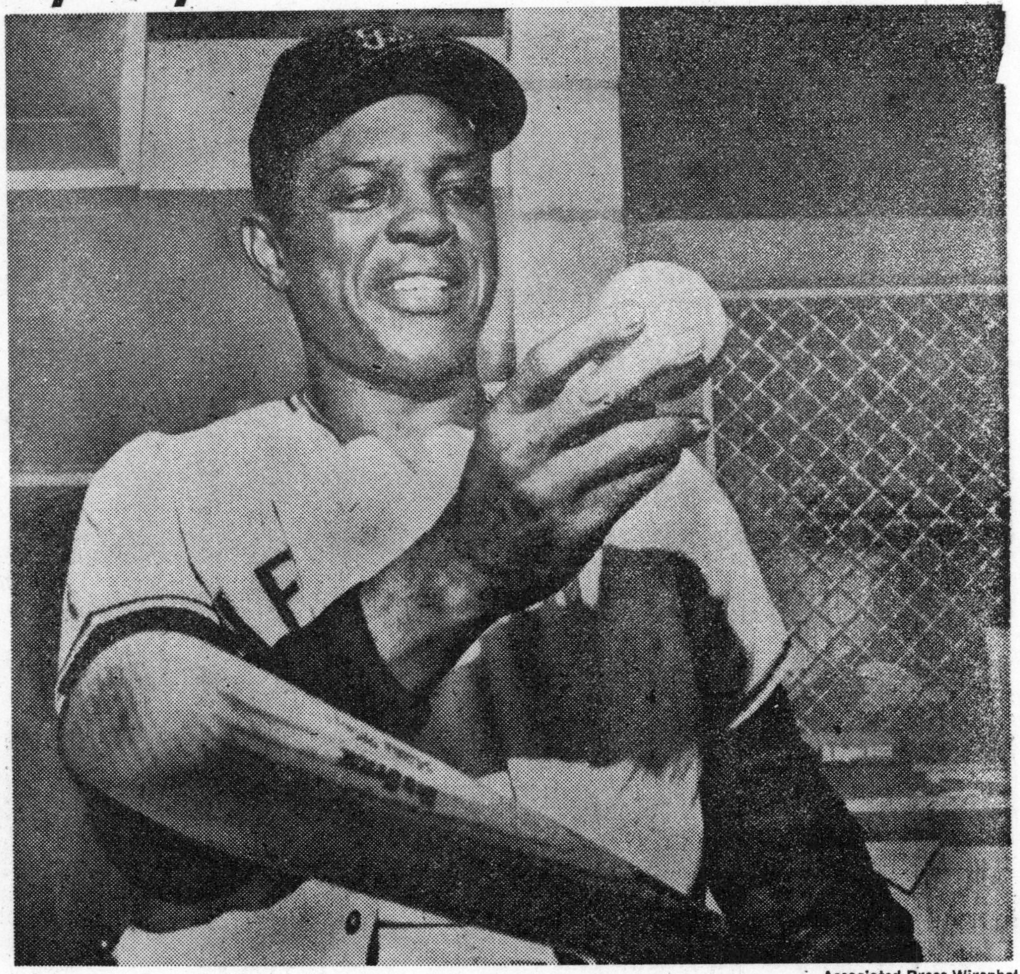

Associated Press Wirephot

Willie Mays displays the bat and ball that figured in home run No. 600.

600 Eases Pressure on Willie

SAN DIEGO (AP) — Willie Mays says he thrives on pressure, but he felt relieved to have some of it lifted from his back here when he became the second major leaguer ever to hit 600 home runs.

"The pressure was building up; I had been trying too hard to hit home runs," said the 38-year-old wonder after he clouted No. 600 as a pinch-hitter last night with one on in the seventh inning to give San Francisco a 4-2 victory over San Diego.

"The big thing is that it won the game," said Mays after keeping the Giants a half game ahead of Atlanta in the National League's frantic Western Diivsion race.

The Braves beat the Astros 5-3. The Reds, who took the Dodgers 2-1, are third, four games back, while Los Angeles is 4½ out.

"The person I'm happy for," he said, "is Frank Torre."

Torre, the former Milwaukee first baseman, represents the Adirondack Bat Co. and has been following Mays and the Giants around for several weeks, waiting for Willie to hit No. 600. The milestone smash earned Mays a $12,500 sports car and one share of stock for each foot the homer traveled.

The blast off Padre rookie righthander Mike Corkins was estimated to have traveled 390 feet. It followed an infield hit by Ron Hunt and obliterated a 2-2 tie.

A small crowd of 4779 gave Mays a standing ovation and the entire San Francisco bench was waiting at home plate as Willie rounded the bases on a gimpy knee injured several weeks ago in a home plate collision with Chicago catcher Randy Hundley.

"It was a thrill to see all my teammates waiting at home plate. That's something you don't see very often," Mays said.

"I'm happy for Torre because now he can go back to his family. He's waited so long for me to hit 600 that he was afraid his family might forget him.

It was on Sept. 15 that Mays hit No. 599, off Atlanta righthander Pat Jarvis, and the pressure of waiting for No. 600 was like the pressure he felt in 1966 when he was striving for the National League record of 512.

"After I hit 599 I knew I'd hit 600," he said grinning, "but I was beginning to wonder when. That's the way it was with No. 512. I waited eight or nine days to get it."

It's a homer he remembers well.

"It was off Claude Osteen of the Dodgers at Candlestick," he said.

Mays also remembers his first big league homer and so does Bill Rigney, a former teammate and big league manager who now is a Giants broa caster.

"He hit his first one o Warren Spahn in 1951," Rigne said, "and it went over the roo at the Polo Grounds."

Mays, slowed by age and i juries, doesn't even consider th possibility of catching the al time home run leader, Bab Ruth, who hit 714 roundtrippers Ruth was the only other bi leaguer ever to hit as man as 600.

"I don't know how much long er I can go," said Mays, "bu I know I'll hit some more home runs if I can stay healthy That's been my trouble. I wa out of the lineup for a coupl of weeks and I had trouble getting my timing back."

"Yes, but you've hit the bal as well the last couple of week as you have in several years,' said teammate Jim Davenport

Mays has 10 hits in his las 27 at bats and has driven in seven runs in his last eight games. He says he thrives on the kind of excitement the Giants and Braves are generating in their run to the Western Division wire.

"I love pressure," he said, "because it doesn't bother me. I love to be in a situation where

Continued on Page 108

A Proud Record

Year-by-year rundown of Willie Mays' 600 home runs:

1951	New York	20
1952	New York	4
1953	New York	Military Svc.
1954	New York	41
1955	New York	51
1956	New York	36
1957	New York	35
1958	San Francisco	29
1959	San Francisco	34
1960	San Francisco	29
1961	San Francisco	40
1962	San Francisco	x-49
1963	San Francisco	38
1964	San Francisco	x-47
1965	San Francisco	x-52
1966	San Francisco	37
1967	San Francisco	22
1968	San Francisco	23
1969	San Francisco	13

x-Led league.

★

DAILY NEWS

NEW YORK'S PICTURE NEWSPAPER ®

10¢

Vol. 51. No. 98 Copr. 1969 News Syndicate Co. Inc. New York, N.Y. 10017, Friday, October 17, 1969★ WEAHTER: Fair, breezy, very cool.

WORLD CHAMPS!

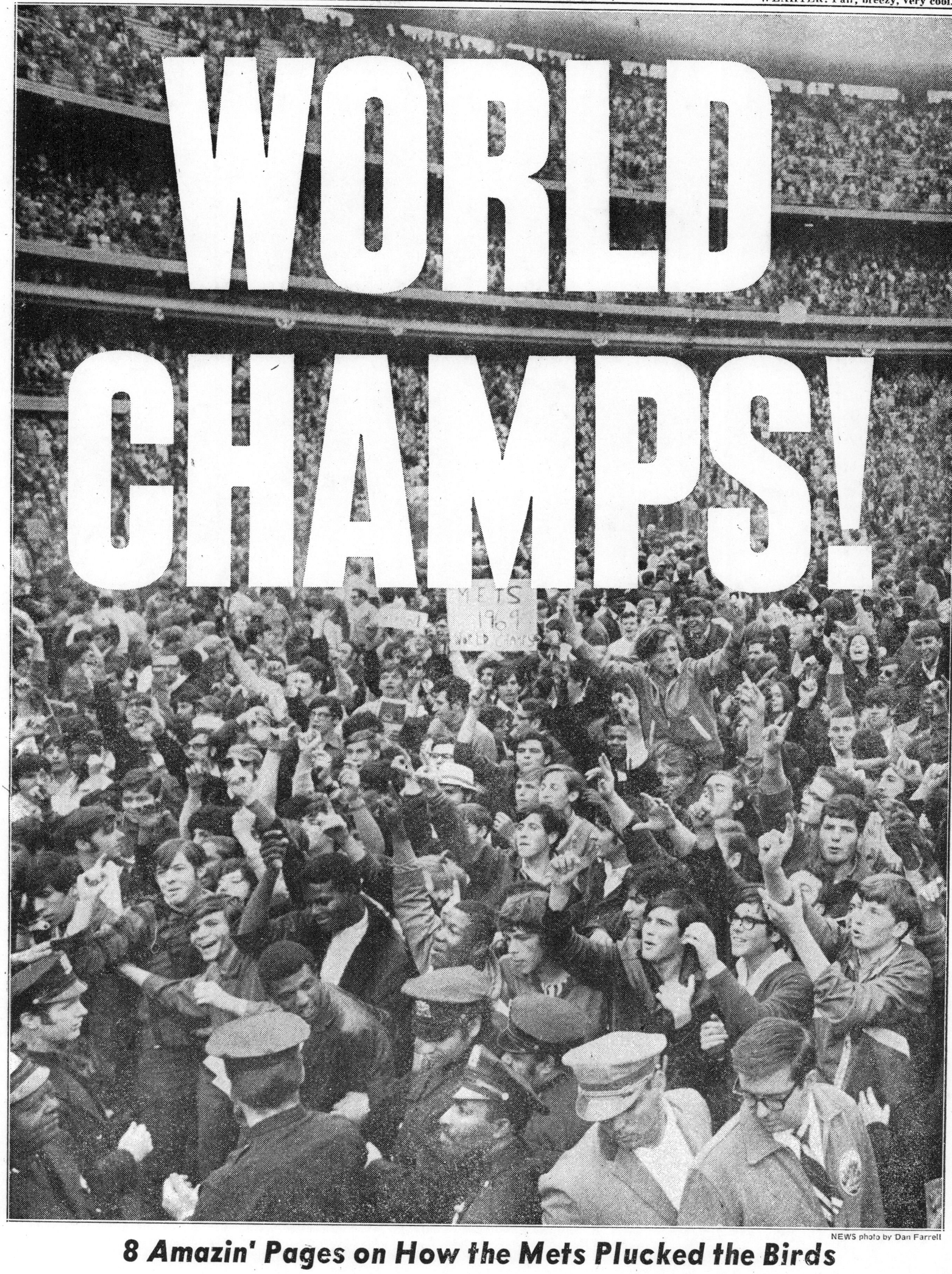

NEWS photo by Dan Farrell

8 Amazin' Pages on How the Mets Plucked the Birds

FINAL ★★★★

DAILY NEWS
NEW YORK'S PICTURE NEWSPAPER ®

MORE THAN TWICE THE CIRCULATION OF ANY OTHER PAPER IN AMERICA

80 New York, N.Y. 10017, Monday, May 18, 1970

AARON JOINS 3,000-HIT CLUB

Associated Press Wirephoto

Hitting a Milestone. Hank Aaron completes follow-through after stroking his 3,000th career hit in second game of twinbill in Cincinnati yesterday. Held hitless in opener, the Atlanta, star became ninth man in history to reach plateau—and first to have hit at least 500 homers as well. His 3001st hit? A homer, natch: ***—Story on page 66***

Birdies Sing Bye-Bye Red Machine

Dazed Dave Liked Hitting; Robbys Star

Baltimore (AP) — Dave McNally didn't know where he was, Frank Robinson returned from the twilight zone, and Brooks Robinson . . . played brilliantly again.

McNally confessed to "not knowing what was going on" while rounding the bases after hitting a grand slam homer in Baltimore's 9-3 victory over the Cincinnati Reds yesterday as the Orioles took a 3-0 lead in the World Series.

"I WAS IN A bit of a daze," said the left-hander who won 24 games during the regular season.

McNally said he didn't recall what his teammates said to him when he returned to the dugout after hitting his second series homer in two years and the second grand slam of his career.

"I don't remember what I said, either," McNally said. "I was just yelling, I think."

"I liked my hitting better than my pitching. I wasn't getting my slow curve over the plate, so I stuck mostly with my fast ball and slider. And the support was great. Brooks had another fabulous day."

Brooks Robinson, who was called the difference between the two teams by Cincinnati Manager Sparky Anderson even before game No. 3, helped quash the Reds again.

He made two spectacular plays, one a diving catch of a Johnny Bench liner in the sixth inning—which led to a standing ovation by the home crowd the next time he came to bat.

"I was fortunate on the liner," Robinson said, "because the ball sort of curved back toward me as I dove to the left. It is just a reflex action—sometimes you catch it and sometimes you don't."

The third baseman, who 10 times has been voted the best at his position in the American League, said when he talks salary, "they never say anything about my field. They just want to know how I hit."

IN THE 1970 series, Robinson has four hits and four runs batted in. His homer won the opener, 4-3, and yesterday he had two doubles and two RBI off Tony Cloninger.

Asked if his arm felt weak now that the season was nearing an end, Robinson said, "nothing about me feels weak right now."

Frank Robinson, hitless in nine trips at Cincinnati, broke out of his slump with two singles and a home run over the center field fence, driving in one run and scoring twice.

Involved in a third-person dispute with Anderson over his playing ability at age 35, Robinson refused comment on what the Reds' manager has described as a misunderstanding.

Asked why he didn't bring in a right-hander to face Frank in the second game, Anderson was quoted as saying he didn't think Robinson could handle young left-hander Don Gullett "in the twilight of his career."

Robinson struck back with a few choice comments of his own after being told of the alleged remark. Anderson later contended he had been talking about the twilight shadows in Cincinnati's Riverfront Stadium.

Asked about the "twilight" yesterday Robinson said merely, "No comment." It was an unusual response from the outspoken outfielder.

"The fact that I had some hits," Robinson added, however, "doesn't prove anything to me. I know I'm not on the downside yet. I can't hit like I did when I was 26. I was a swinger then and, I mean on the field."

"BUT I CAN do more with the bat now, so I think I'm a better over-all hitter. I can go to right field maybe 75 per cent of the time when I have to. When I was 26, I couldn't throw the ball out there."

Both Robinsons said the Orioles had come into the American League playoffs and World Series better prepared this year than in 1969 when the New York Mets won the World Series.

"We relaxed a little bit too much last year," Frank said. "We took too many days off and then failed to reach a peak before the end of the regular season."

Asked if the Orioles—winners of 17 straight—expected to return to Cincinnati for game No. 6, Robinson replied: "We didn't expect to go back to Cincinnati when we left Sunday."

Baltimore manager Earl Weaver made a couple of lineup changes yesterday, inserting catcher Andy Etchbarren and moving shortstop Mark Belanger to the no. 2 spot, but Weaver said he didn't expect the moves to produce nine runs.

"Day-to-day during the season we've been changing our lineup," he said. "I'd guess Sunday was the only time, or one of the few times, that we went with the same lineup two days in a row."

World Series 3-Game Composite Box Score

CINCINNATI REDS

	G	AB	R	H	2B	3B	HR	RBI	SO	BB	Pct.	PO	A	E	Pct.
Rose, rf	3	11	0	2	0	0	0	1	0	2	.182	10	0	0	1.000
Tolan, cf	3	12	4	3	1	0	1	1	0	1	.250	2	0	0	1.000
Perez, 3b	3	10	1	1	0	0	0	0	2	2	.100	0	8	0	1.000
Bench, c	3	11	1	2	0	0	1	2	1	1	.182	22	2	0	1.000
May, 1b	3	11	3	4	1	0	1	4	1	1	.364	29	2	0	1.000
Carbo, lf	2	3	0	0	0	0	0	0	0	2	.000	2	0	0	1.000
McRae, lf	2	8	1	4	1	0	0	1	1	0	.500	1	1	0	1.000
Helms, 2b	3	12	1	2	0	0	0	0	0	0	.167	8	7	0	1.000
Woodward, ss	3	5	0	1	0	0	0	0	0	0	.200	4	5	0	1.000
Cline, ph	3	3	0	1	0	0	0	0.	0	0	.333	0	0	0	.000
Chaney, ss	2	0	0	0	0	0	0	0	0	0	.000	0	1	0	1.000
Concepcion, ss	1	3	0	1	0	0	0	2	0	0	.333	0	2	0	1.000
Stewart, ph	2	2	0	0	0	0	0	0	1	0	.000	0	0	0	.000
Nolan, p	1	2	0	0	0	0	0	0	0	0	.000	0	0	0	.000
Carroll, p	2	0	0	0	0	0	0	0	0	0	.000	0	0	0	.000
Bravo, ph	2	1	0	0	0	0	0	0	1	0	.000	0	0	0	.000
McGlothlin, p	1	2	0	0	0	0	0	0	1	0	.000	0	0	0	.000
Wilcox, p	1	0	0	0	0	0	0	0	0	0	.000	0	0	0	.000
Gullett, p	2	0	0	0	0	0	0	0	0	0	.000	0	0	0	.000
Cloninger, p	1	2	0	0	0	0	0	0	1	0	.000	0	0	0	.000
Granger, p	1	0	0	0	0	0	0	0	0	0	.000	0	1	0	1.000
Totals	3	98	11	21	3	0	3	11	9	9	.214	78	29	0	1.000

BALTIMORE ORIOLES

	G	AB	R	H	2B	3B	HR	RBI	SO	BB	Pct.	PO	A	E	Pct.
Buford, lf	3	11	3	4	0	0	1	1	0	2	.364	5	0	0	1.000
Blair, cf	3	12	3	6	1	0	0	2	1	1	.500	13	0	1	.929
Powell, 1b	3	9	4	3	0	0	2	4	1	4	.333	23	2	0	1.000
F. Robinson, rf	3	13	2	3	0	0	1	1	2	0	.231	5	0	0	1.000
B. Robinson, 3b	3	12	3	4	2	0	1	4	1	0	.333	7	12	1	.950
Hendricks, c	2	7	1	2	1	0	1	3	2	1	.286	7	1	1	.889
Johnson, 2b	3	8	1	2	1	0	0	0	1	4	.250	11	5	0	1.000
Belanger, ss	3	11	0	1	0	0	0	0	2	1	.091	4	9	1	.929
Etchebarren, c	1	4	0	0	0	0	0	0	2	0	.000	5	0	1	.833
Palmer, p	1	4	0	0	0	0	0	0	2	0	.000	0	0	0	.000
Richert, p	1	0	0	0	0	0	0	0	0	0	.000	0	0	0	.000
Cuellar, p	1	1	0	0	0	0	0	0	1	0	.000	0	0	0	.000
Phoebus, p	1	0	0	0	0	0	0	0	0	0	.000	0	0	0	.000
Salmon, ph	1	1	1	1	0	0	0	0	0	0	1.000	0	0	0	.000
Drabowsky, p	1	1	0	0	0	0	0	0	1	0	.000	1	0	0	1.000
Lopez, p	1	0	0	0	0	0	0	0	0	0	.000	0	0	0	.000
Hall, p	1	1	0	0	0	0	0	0	1	0	.000	0	0	0	.000
McNally, p	1	4	1	1	0	0	1	4	2	0	.250	0	1	0	1.000
Totals	3	99	19	27	5	0	7	19	19	13	.273	81	30	5	.957

x-Rose safe on catcher's interference in 5th inning of 1st game.

Composite score by innings:

Cincinnati (National)	4	1	3	0	0	1	2	0	0	— 11
Baltimore (American)	2	0	1	3	7	4	2	0	0	— 19

DP—Cincinnati 4, Baltimore 2. LOB—Cincinnati 19, Baltimore 15. S—Nolan, Bravo. SF—Concepcion. SB—Tolan. Save—Richert, Hall. U—Burkhart (NL, Flaherty (AL), Venzon (NL), Stewart (AL). CF—Williams (NL), Ashford (AL). T—2:24 (1st game), 2:26 (2d game), 2:09 (3d game). A—51,531 (1st game), 51,531 (2d game), 51,773 (3d game).

PITCHING SUMMARY

Cincinnati

	G	CG	IP	H	R	BB	SO	HB	WP	W	L	PCT.	ER	ERA
Nolan	1	0	6⅔	5	4	1	7	0	0	0	1	.000	4	5.40
Carroll	2	0	4⅔	3	0	2	5	0	0	0	0	.000	0	0.00
McGlothlin	1	0	4⅓	6	4	2	2	0	0	0	0	.000	4	8.30
Wilcox	1	0	⅓	3	2	0	0	0	0	0	1	.000	2	54.00
Gullett	2	0	4	2	1	4	1	0	0	0	0	.000	1	2.25
Cloninger	1	0	5⅓	6	5	3	3	0	0	0	1	.000	5	8.44
Granger	1	0	⅔	2	3	1	1	0	0	0	0	.000	3	40.50
Totals	3	0	26	27	19	13	19	0	0	0	3	.000	19	6.58

Baltimore

	G	CG	IP	H	R	BB	SO	HB	WP	W	L	PCT.	ER	ERA
Palmer	1	0	8⅔	5	3	5	2	0	1	1	0	1.000	3	3.12
Richert	1	0	⅓	0	0	0	0	0	0	0	0	.000	0	0.00
Cuellar	1	0	2⅓	4	4	1	1	0	0	0	0	.000	1	3.86
Phoebus	1	0	1⅔	1	0	0	0	0	0	1	0	1.000	0	0.00
Drabowsky	1	0	2⅓	2	1	1	1	0	0	0	0	.000	1	3.86
Lopez	1	0	⅓	0	0	0	0	0	0	0	0	.000	0	0.00
Hall	1	0	2⅓	0	0	0	0	0	0	0	0	.000	0	0.00
McNally	1	1	9	9	3	2	5	0	0	1	0	1.000	3	3.00
Totals	3	1	27	21	1	1	9	9	0	1	3	1.000	8	2.67

GRAND 'OLE DAVE—Baltimore's Dave McNally trots rather unbelievably and very happily across home plate yesterday after swatting a grand slam homer off Cincinnati's Wayne Granger. Frank Robinson, Dave Johnson and Paul Blair greet McNally, whose hit put the victorious Orioles ahead 8-1. (UPI Telephoto)

'KNEW IT WAS OUT'

Slam Shadows Pitching For Orioles' McNally

Baltimore (AP) — If you think Baltimore's Dave McNally was surprised when he became the first pitcher in the 61-year history of the World Series to hit a bases loaded home run, you should have seen a 7-year-old boy behind the Orioles' dugout.

The youngster was McNally's son, Jeff. After his dad blasted a pitch into the left field seats for four runs in the sixth inning, the boy commented: "When he (McNally) came up, I thought there was no way he could hit a home run."

The 27-year-old McNally was more excited about his grand slam than about his nine-hit pitching that helped Baltimore to a 9-3 victory yesterday and a 3-0 lead in the best-of-seven game series.

"I KNEW IT was going out the moment I hit it," said the 190-pound left-hander. "My ears were ringing from the crowd as I was going around the bases. I wasn't thinking. I was just excited."

The count was two balls, two strikes on McNally when Cincinnati reliever Wayne Granger tried to get a fast ball down on the right-hand hitting pitcher. Reds' catcher Johnny Bench said the ball kept rising and McNally, a high ball hitter, slammed it out of the park to wrap up the game for the Orioles.

McNally, a native of Billings, Mont., said he wasn't concerned with the great reputation the National League champions have built beating left-handers. The Reds won 33 and lost 8 against southpaws during the regular season. Only five went the route against the power packed right-hand hitting lineup.

"I knew they were great against left-handers, but I wasn't concerned," McNally said. "I can't throw right handed, so I did the best I can."

His best was to allow nine singles, giving up a second-inning run and two in the eighth after the Orioles led, 8-1.

McNally said he won without his best stuff.

"I COULDN'T get my curve ball over and junked it after five innings," he noted. "I went with my fast ball and slider, moving them in and out on the hitters."

Baltimore catcher Andy Etchebarren agreed that it wasn't one of McNally's better days.

"He didn't have real good stuff," said the catcher. "His curve ball didn't have that hard rotation, so we stayed away from it after the early innings. It shows what kind of pitcher he is that he stays with 'em even without his best stuff. He has great determination and is a great competitor."

Baltimore Manager Earl Weaver said he felt McNally mixed his pitches well, but that he has seen the left-hander with better stuff.

"He had a pretty good fast ball and slider. I've seen him with a lot better curve though," said Weaver.

CAMERA 'BENCHED'

John Unhappy After 'Thefts'

Baltimore (UPI) — Johnny Bench wasn't in any mood for pictures whether they were rated GP, R, X or anything else.

So the 22-year-old Cincinnati catcher did something about it.

He took off his shirt, placed it squarely over the lens of a portable TV camera and kept it there to the complete consternation of the camerman.

THE CAMERAMAN was 6-feet-4 and Bench is only 6-feet-1 but the TV man wasn't about to press the point, especially since he and his assistant had pushed themselves to the head of a line of newsmen waiting outside the beaten Reds' clubhouse.

"I'm only trying to do my job," the cameraman protested.

"Yeah, I know," Bench said, still keeping his shirt over the lens. "Why don't you go over to the other side and get your pictures? You'll get a lot more happy ones over there. We've just lost our third game, you know."

Inside the solemn Reds' quarters, Bench said he asked the TV man what he was doing outside the clubhouse but had received an answer he didn't consider satisfactory.

"I just couldn't see the educational value of film like that," said the Cincinnati catcher.

Bench twice was robbed of base hits in yesterday's 9-3 victory by the Orioles, and both times it was Brooks Robinson, the Baltimore third baseman, who took hits away from him.

Robinson grabbed his hot liner with a man on in the first inning and then made an utterly fantastic catch on Bench again in the sixth when he left his feet, stretched his body parallel with the ground and snared the ball with his gloved hand.

When Robinson came up in the bottom of the sixth, and the Reds were making a pitching change, Bench said to the Baltimore third baseman:

"I'm gonna hit the next one over your head."

"Okay," laughed the always amiable Robinson.

Sparky Anderson, the Reds' manager, tried to sound some words of hope and encouragement in his private quarters but the effort came hard, terribly hard.

"SOMETHING'S gotta change," he said. "Things have happened so far that nobody would ever believe. I'm not taking a single thing away from them, but everything they do turns out right and everything we do turns out wrong. I just don't believe it can keep going on that way.

"One thing I feel now. If we beat 'em tomorrow with (Gary) Nolan, I feel we'll go all the way. I honestly feel that way."

Pete Rose, the Reds' captain and team leader, sat on a table in the middle of the clubhouse and bit into a potato chip rather dispiritedly. Relief pitcher Clay Carroll sat a few feet away and was doing the same thing.

"You know, me and Johnny Bench got an automobile distributorship," Rose said. "If we knew Robinson wanted a car so badly we'd have given him one before this thing started. I've never seen anything like him in my life."

The car Rose meant was the one that annually is awarded the outstanding World Series performer by Sport Magazine.

"He's got it locked up," Rose said.

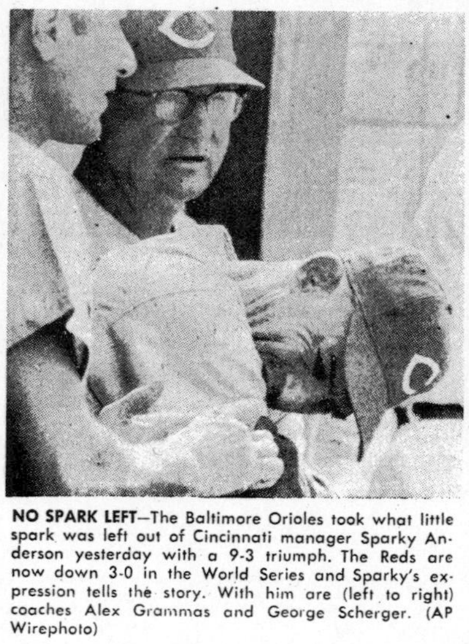

NO SPARK LEFT—The Baltimore Orioles took what little spark was left out of Cincinnati manager Sparky Anderson yesterday with a 9-3 triumph. The Reds are now down 3-0 in the World Series and Sparky's expression tells the story. With him are (left to right) coaches Alex Grammas and George Scherger. (AP Wirephoto)

Pro Basketball

NATIONAL ASSOCIATION

New York 114, Boston 107.
Chicago 111, San Diego 96.

Baltimore Leads 3-0 After 9-3 Demolition

Baltimore (UPI) — The charging Baltimore Orioles parlayed another sensational game by Brooks Robinson and Dave McNally's grand slam homer—the first by a pitcher in World Series competition — into a 9-3 rout yesterday over the dazed Cincinnati Reds and a 3-0 lead in the series.

The Orioles, who've now reeled off 17 consecutive victories since their last loss on Sept. 19, can close out their second four-game series sweep in the last five years with a victory today.

Righthanders Jim Palmer of Baltimore and Gary Nolan, the rivals in the opening game of the series, will oppose each other again today. Palmer was the 4-3 victor and Nolan the loser in the opener.

BALTIMORE'S FIRST two victories were close but this time the Reds never were in the game. The 51,773 Oriole partisans — a crowd slightly short of capacity — roared at the play of Brooks Robinson, McNally, Frank Robinson, who snapped out of an 0-9 slump with three hits including a homer, Paul Blair, who had three hits, and Don Buford, who hit a solo homer.

But the standing ovations were saved for Brooks and McNally.

After each game in which Brooks makes a standout play, Manager Earl Weaver always says, "watch tomorrow and he'll make another one"—and sure enough, he does.

Brooks made one sensational play with a dive to his right on Johnny Bench's liner in the sixth, added several merely superb ones in the first four innings and had two doubles—driving in the Orioles' first two runs off Tony Cloninger in the first inning.

Brooks' first double and the solo homers by Frank Robinson in the third and Buford in the fifth made it 4-1.

Cloninger was then routed in the sixth inning and Wayne Granger, the Reds' ace reliever, came out of the bullpen and served up the grand slam to McNally on a 2-2 pitch that made it 8-1.

McNally, who hit a grand slam during the regular season, also had a homer in last year's Series when the Orioles hit only three homers while losing to the New York Mets in five games. This year the Orioles have seven homers in three games and their power has been a key difference.

McNALLY'S SLAM was the 12th in World Series competition. Jim Northrup of Detroit hit the last one in the sixth game of the 1968 Series.

Ironically, McNally — who was working with eight days off — didn't have his best stuff and was touched for nine hits while going the route. None of the Orioles' three starters — Jim Palmer, Mike Cuellar and McNally — have been at their sharpest, but it hasn't mattered because the Oriole hitters have been teeing off on the crippled Reds' pitching staff.

Red Nightmare

CINCINNATI	ab	r	h	bi
Rose,rf	5	0	2	1
Tolan,cf	4	0	1	0
Perez,3	3	0	0	0
Bench,c	4	0	0	0
LMay,1	3	1	1	0
McRae,lf	4	1	2	0
Helms,2	4	1	1	0
Concepcn,ss	3	0	1	2
Cloninger,p	2	0	0	0
Granger,p	0	0	0	0
Woodwrd,ph	1	0	1	0
Gullet,p	0	0	0	0
Cline,ph	1	0	0	0
Total	31	9	10	9

BALTIMORE	ab	r	h	bi
Buford,lf	3	2	1	1
Belanger,ss	4	0	0	0
JPowell,1	3	1	0	0
FRobinsn,rf	4	2	3	1
Blair,cf	3	1	3	1
BRobinsn,3	4	1	2	2
DJohnson,2	2	1	0	0
Etchebrn,c	4	0	0	0
McNally,p	4	1	1	4
TOTAL	34	3	9	3

Cincinnati	010	000	200—3
Baltimore	201	014	10x—9

E—Etchebarren. DP—Cincinnati 1, Baltimore 1. LOB—Cincinnati 7, Baltimore 3. 2B—B. Robinson 2, Blair. HR—F. Robinson (1), Buford (1), McNally (1). SF—Concepcion.

	IP	H	R	ER	BB	SO
Cloninger (L, 0-1)	5⅓	6	5	5	3	3
Granger	⅔	2	3	3	1	1
Gullet	2	2	1	1	1	0
McNally (W, 1-0)	9	9	3	3	2	5

T—2:09. A—51,773.

Cloninger, who hasn't completed a game all season, got the nod for the Reds. He had a lot of heart but not much stuff. In fact, he barely survived the first inning.

Buford walked on four pitches to lead off the Orioles' first and after the next two batters were retired, Frank Robinson sent him to third with a hit-and-run single for his first hit of the Series. It's bound to be said that Frank was charged up by Manager Sparky Anderson's quote — which the Cincinnati manager has denied — that Frank's in the "twilight of his career." But, it could be just that Frank was overdue.

Cloninger then walked Blair on a 3-2 pitch and Brooks Robinson followed with his two-run double that brought the cheering Orioles' fans out of their seats.

Cloninger then struggled into the sixth — giving up the third-inning homer to Frank and the fifth inning blast to Buford. When Blair hit a one-out single in the sixth, Anderson decided to bring on Granger, his best short relief man who hasn't seen work in this Series.

Granger gave up a double to Brooks and then walked Dave Johnson intentionally to load the bases.

Granger struck out Andy Etchebarren and seemed out of the jam since McNally had struck out in his first two appearances. But the Oriole pitcher pulled a 2-2 pitch into the left field seats.

THE GAME WAS over then, although Blair doubled in an insurance run in the seventh off Don Gullett and the Reds touched McNally for a pair of runs in the top of that inning on Dave Concepcion's sacrifice fly and Pete Rose's run-scoring single.

McNally managed to survive early in the game when it was still close—mainly because the Reds kept hitting the ball at Brooks at thind.

Another Picture, Page 46

Rose led off the game with a single on the first pitch and Bobby Tolan laid down a bunt that would have rolled foul on Cincinnati's Astro Turf but hit a clump of real dirt down the third base line at Memorial Stadium and stayed fair.

It looked like Cincinnati had a real rally going with runners on first and second with none out and Perez and Bench coming up. But Perez hit a hard grounder right at Brooks, who stepped on third and fired to first for the double play. Bench then hit a line shot—but right at Brooks for the first out.

Brooks, who personally accounted for five of the first 10 outs, also threw out runners in the second and fourth innings. But he saved his "ooooooooohhhhhhhh play"—that's the reaction from the crowd—for the sixth.

He'd already shown the Cincinnati fans and national TV how he goes to his right when he robbed Lee Mays of doubles in each of the first two games. But he saved a display of how he goes to his left for the home fans.

Bench hit a line shot towards left field with two out in the sixth and Brooks took one step and dived. He caught the ball inches off the ground and held on to it as he slammed into the dirt.

The score still was 4-1 at the time but Brooks' play just seemed to seal the victory — although McNally's slam made it official in the last of the inning.

CINCINNATI'S first run in the second came on a single by Concepcion, who had two of the Reds' three RBIs, with two out but McNally struck out Cloninger to end the rally.

It was the second World Series victory for McNally, who won the clincher in the sweep of the Dodgers in 1966.

Mike Price Makes New York Knicks

New York (UPI) — Mike Price, a former Indianapolis Tech High School basketball star, survived the last cut of the New York Knickerbockers of the National Basketball Association to earn a spot as a reserve guard.

Price was one of three rookies to make the 12-man squad. He was the Knicks No. 1 draft choice from the University of Illinois.

The other rookies who survived included Milt Williams, a reserve guard, and Ed Mast, center.

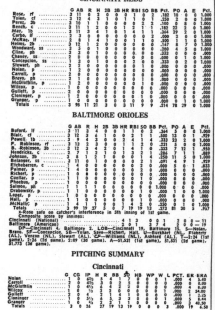

Skidding Bosox Swept By Oakland, 6-5, 7-5

Boston, Aug. 10 (UPI)—Reggie Jackson drove in three runs to insure a 7-5 Oakland victory tonight and give the Athletics a doubleheader sweep over the Red Sox after a ninth-inning single by Gene Tenace had given the A's a 6-5 day-game victory.

Jackson drilled a two-run double off Ray Culp to key an Oakland rally in the fifth and hit a homer, his 20th, with the bases empty in the seventh as the Red Sox lost for the fifth time in six games.

Oakland pitcher John Odom gained his eighth win in 15 decisions with relief help from Jim Grant as Sal Bando and Dave Duncan each hit solo homers for the Athletics.

MIKE FIORE hit a pinch two-run homer in the night game as Culp suffered his 10th loss against 15 wins.

Oakland had protested the opener before Tenace gave the Athletics the win with a single in the ninth. His hit off reliever Al Lyle came after a pair of walks with Roland Fingers getting the victory for two innings of scoreless relief.

A's manager Dick Williams was ejected by umpire Jim Odom during a dispute over a Reggie Smith double down the first base line that tied the day game in the seventh.

Odom pointed to foul territory on the hit but admitted later he had lost his sense of direction and that the hit was fair.

Tommy Davis drove in three first-game runs, two with his second homer while Dick Green also homered for Oakland and Joe Lahoud hit a two-run homer and Smith a solo homer for Boston.

(First Game)

OAKLAND (6) at BOSTON (5)

	ab	r	h	rbi		ab	r	h	rbi
Camp'ris,ss	5	1	2	0	Griffin,2b	4	1	1	0
Rudi,lf	5	1	2	1	Aparicio,ss	5	1	1	0
Jackson,rf	3	0	0	0	Smith,cf	5	0	2	2
Davis,1b	5	2	2	3	Ystrmski,lf	3	1	3	1
Hegan,1b	0	0	0	0	Scott,1b	4	0	0	0
Bando,3b	3	0	3	0	Lahoud,rf	4	1	2	2
Tenace,c	4	0	1	1	Kennedy,3b	3	0	0	0
Hendrick,cf	4	0	1	0	Josephsn,c	3	0	0	0
Green,2b	4	1	2	1	Peters,p	1	0	1	0
Hunter,p	3	1	1	0	Tatum,p	1	0	0	0
Epstein,ph	1	0	0	0	Fiore,ph	1	1	1	0
Fingers,p	0	0	0	0	Tiant,p	0	0	0	0
					Petrocelli,ph	1	0	0	0
					Lyle,p	0	0	0	0
Totals	37	6	14	6	Totals	35	5	11	5

Oakland	102	101	001—6
Boston	002	002	100—5

DP—Oakland 1, Boston 3. LOB—Oakland 9, Boston 7. 2B—Yastrzemski, Smith. 3B—Rudi. HR—Davis (2), Green (11), Lahoud (11). SB—Campaneris, Jackson. S—Griffin, Kennedy.

	IP	H	R	ER	BB	SO
Hunter	7	10	5	5	1	2
Fingers (W—3-6)	2	1	0	0	1	1
Peters	4⅓	10	4	4	1	2
Tatum	2⅔	3	1	1	0	0
Tiant	1	0	0	0	0	0
Lyle (L—4-4)	1	1	1	1	2	0

HBP—by Peters (Bando, Tenace). WP—Tatum. T.-2:38. A.-24,202.

(Second Game)

OAKLAND (7) at BOSTON (5)

	ab	r	h	rbi		ab	r	h	rbi
Campanris,ss	4	1	1	2	Griffin,2b	5	0	0	0
Rudi,lf	5	1	1	0	Kennedy,ss	5	0	1	0
Jackson,rf	4	1	2	3	Smith,cf	5	1	4	1
Epstein,1b	2	0	0	0	Yastrzski,lf	5	1	1	0
Hegan,1b	1	0	0	0	Petrocelli,3b	3	1	0	0
Bando,3b	5	1	1	1	Scott,1b	4	0	2	0
Hendrick,cf	4	1	1	0	Lahoud,rf	3	0	0	0
Duncan,c	4	1	1	1	Montgmry,c	2	1	1	2
Brown,2b	4	1	2	0	Culp,p	2	0	0	0
Odom,p	3	0	2	0	Fiore,ph	1	1	1	2
Grant,p	0	0	0	0	Lee,p	0	0	0	0
					Peters,ph	1	0	0	0
					Moret,p	0	0	0	0
Totals	36	7	11	7	Totals	0	0	0	0

Oakland	000	131	110—7
Boston	010	102	001—5

E—Odon, Kennedy. DP—Oakland 2, Boston 1. LOB—Oakland 7, Boston 8. 2—Brown, Jackson, Scott. HRS—Bando (18), Fiore (1), Jackson, (20), Duncan (23) Smith (24). S—Grant. SF—Canpanaris.

	IP	H	R	ER	BB	SO
Odom (W-8—7)	5⅔	7	4	4	4	5
Grant	3⅓	3	1	1	0	3
Culp (L-13—10)	6	8	5	4	2	4
Lee	2	3	2	2	1	0
Moret	1	0	0	0	0	1

Save—Grant (1st). T—2:41. A—30,004.

Killebrew Hits 500th Homer

Minneapolis, Aug. 10 (AP)—Harmon Killebrew of the Twins blasted his 500th major league homer—only the 10th man in history to do so—in the first inning of the Twins' game against Baltimore tonight.

The 35-year-old slugger, now in his 18th season in the majors, clouted a one-ball pitch by Mike Cuellar 385 feet into the left-field pavilion for only his 13th of the season and first since July 25.

HIS PRESENT output is the lowest since the 17 he slammed in 1968, when an injury in the All-Star game sidelined him for much of the season.

The momentous blast put him 11 behind the late Mel Ott and the Cubs' Ernie Banks, and 12 behind the retired Eddie Mathews.

The Killer, as the 5-foot-11, 215-pound powerhouse is appropriately known, entered the home run derby on June 24, 1955—his second year in the majors—with a shot off Billy Hoeft of the Tigers.

His top minor league homer output was 29 with Chattanooga in 1957.

Two years later he was back in the majors to stay, bombing 42. It was the first of his eight 40-plus homer seasons, including a peak of 49 in 1964 and 1969 and 48 in 1962.

HE REACHED No. 100 on June 16, 1961, against Early Wynn of the White Sox and No. 200 on July 19, 1963 against Jim Duckworth of the Senators, the league's new franchise which began play in Washington when the old one shifted to Minnesota at the start of the 1961 season.

No. 300 came against Bob Friend of the Yankees on May 21, 1966 and No. 400 was off Chicago's Gary Peters on April 27, 1969.

Among his personal records, he has led the league in homers five times and tied for it twice.

He started on the long trek toward No. 600 with another round-tripper in the sixth, No. 501 of his career and his 14th of the year, also off Cuellar, a two-run bomb 396' into the left field stands.

KILLEBREW HIT more than 40 home runs in eight of his previous 12 seasons as a regular, reaching the 49 mark in 1964 and again in 1969.

Before the 1969 season, there were some who thought Killebrew was finished. He ruptured a hamstring muscle in the All-Star Game at Houston in 1968 and hit only 17 home runs.

But his performance the next year sparked the Twins to the West Division pennant in the American League and he was named the Most Valuable Player.

"HE'S CERTAINLY kept us going through the years," said Griffith. "He's been the big attraction of the Twins. We can't forget what Tony Oliva means to the club. But the crowds are home run conscious. That's what mon certainly has given them the fans like to see. And Harwhat they want."

Off the field, Killebrew is greatly admired.

"He's the all-American," said Griffith. "He's a gentleman in every sense. He's a family man, he's religious . . . a great man."

Miller a Buc

San Diego, Aug. 10 (UPI)—The Padres traded relief pitcher Bob Miller to the Pirates today as the Bucs shored to make a final drive for the pennant.

San Diego received cash and two players who are to be named Monday after they clear waivers. The Padres already had secured waivers on Miller, 32, who was signed as a free agent May 11 after being released by the Cubs. Miller was 7-3 with the Padres and was regarded as their most effective reliever. He appeared in two games with the Cubs with no record. He is to join Pittsburgh tomorrow.

Pirates Win Series; Redskins Take 5

Clemente, Pagan Help Blass Top Orioles, 2-1

By George Winot Jr.
Washington Post Staff Writer

BALTIMORE, Oct. 17—Steve Blass strong-armed the Pittsburgh Pirates to the world baseball championship today by dethroning the Baltimore Orioles on a four-hit masterpiece.

By a 2-1 score, the seventh game of the World Series went to the underdog Bucs, a team apparently out of title contention after losing the first two Series games.

The remarkable Roberto Clemente, with a fourth-inning homer, his 12th World Series hit, and Jose Pagan, with a run-scoring double, presented Blass with all the runs he needed to subdue the club that has captured the last three American League pennants.

It was Blass who pitched the Pirates to their first victory, a 5-1, three-hitter in Pittsburgh Tuesday. Today, he was working on a two-hit shutout going into the home half of the eighth inning.

Cuellar Tagged

The Pirates had just score their second run, on Willie Stagell's single and Pagan's two-bagger, both off loser Mike Cuellar, in the top half of the eighth.

The crowd of 47,291 (some 6,000 under Memorial Stadium capacity) roared for a rally and the Orioles answered the call to arms.

Ellie Hendricks grounded a single to left center and Mark Belanger dropped a soft liner into an open space behind second. Pinch-hitter Tom Shopay shoved the runners ahead with a sacrifice.

So the Orioles had the tying runs in scoring position, one out. Don Buford's grounder to first base scored Hendricks and now the tying run was on third.

Belanger Expires

Belanger expired there as Dave Johnson grounded to shortstop Jack Hernandez, positioned perfectly, to the right of his normal position. Hermandez's throw to Bob Robertson, waiting at first base, was true and in time.

Baltimore sent the heart of its order—Boog Powell, Frank Robinson and Merv Rettenmund—at Blass in the ninth inning. They were no match for the fast balls and hard sliders that jumped out of the pitcher's right hand.

Powell topped a ball to the second baseman, Robinson popped to short, completing his fourth consecutive hitless game, and Rettenmund grounded out to Hernandez, who had smartly positioned himself near second base.

That out touched off much jumping and shouting on the part of the Pirates, who were celebrating their first championship since 1960.

Weaver Lauds Blass

Afterward, Baltimore manager Earl Weaver lauded Blass as "Mr. World Series. As great as Clemente was, Blass was greater and he made the difference."

Blass, a 15-game winner who was knocked out twice by San Francisco in the National League playoffs, walked only two men both in early innings, and struck out five.

Two times before the eighth inning the Orioles had runners in scoring position against Blass.In the second he forced Belanger to roll into a double play with runners on first and second bases; in the fifth he retired Belanger and Cuellar following Hendricks' double.

Clemente hit his homer to the right of the 390-foot sign in left center after Cuellar had retired the first 11 batters. Like Blass, the Baltimore hurler held his opponents to two hits through seven innings.

Stargell Singles

Stragell's single, which Belanger nicked with his glove, led off the eighth inning. Then Pagan, who starts only against lefthanders and was a hitting hero for the San Francisco Giants in the 1962 World Series, drilled a hit-and-run double into left center.

Rettenmund bobbled the ball as it bounced back from the fence, and that lost for the Orioles whatever chance they had of catching Stargell at the plate.

Then, Blass secured the championship for his team.

PITTSBURGH

	AB	R	H	2b	3b	Hr	Bi
Cash, 2b	4	0	0	0	0	0	0
Clines, cf	4	0	0	0	0	0	0
Clemente, rf	4	1	1	0	0	1	1
Robertson, 1b	4	0	1	0	0	0	0
Sanguillen, c	4	0	2	0	0	0	0
Stargell, lf	4	1	1	0	0	0	0
Pagan, 3b	3	0	1	1	0	0	1
Hernandez, ss	3	0	0	0	0	0	0
Blass, p	3	0	0	0	0	0	0
Totals	33	2	6	1	0	1	2

BALTIMORE

	AB	R	H	2b	3b	Hr	Bi
Buford, lf	3	0	1	0	0	0	1
Johnson, 2b	4	0	0	0	0	0	0
Powell, 1b	4	0	0	0	0	0	0
F. Robinson, rf	4	0	0	0	0	0	0
Rettenmund, cf	4	0	0	0	0	0	0
B. Robinson, 3b	2	0	0	0	0	0	0
Hendricks, c	3	1	2	1	0	0	0
Belanger, ss	3	0	1	0	0	0	0
Cuellar, p	2	0	0	0	0	0	0
Shopay, ph	0	0	0	0	0	0	0
Dobson, p	0	0	0	0	0	0	0
McNally, p	0	0	0	0	0	0	0
Totals	27	1	4	1	0	0	1

Pittsburgh	000	100	010	—2
Baltimore	000	000	010	—1

E—B. Robertson. DP—Pittsburgh 1. LOB—Pittsburgh 4, Baltimore 4. TB—Hendricks, Pagan. HR—Clemente (2). S—Shopay.

PIRATES' PITCHING

	IP	H	R	ER	BB	SO
Blass (W, 2-0)	9	4	1	1	2	5

ORIOLES' PITCHING

	IP	H	R	ER	BB	SO
Cuellar (L, 0-2)	8	4	2	2	0	6
P. Dobson	⅔	2	0	0	0	1
McNally	⅓	0	0	0	0	0

T—2:10. A—47,291.

This Morning...

With Shirley Povich

BALTIMORE, Oct. 17—Back in 1960, scouts of the Pittsburgh Pirates, as if given divine instructions, went down to the land of Canaan (Conn.) and signed a young schoolboy pitcher named Steve Blass, and today for the Pirates it came up milk and honey in the 1971 World Series, plus paychecks of at least $18,000 for each man, because Steve Blass was here, pitching another beaut against the Orioles.

Povich

He's the same chap who turned the whole Series around Tuesday by winning the third game, succoring the twice-floored Pirates. Today, if Blass didn't quite match the elegance of that three-hit pitching job, he made everything supremely conclusive for the Pirates with a four-hitter amidst all the pressures of the decisive seventh game.

For the second time in the Series, Blass was again proving he could lick one of Baltimore's four 20-game winners, Mike Cuellar. It was a near thing, with the final score a squeaky 2-1, because Cuellar, too, was magnificent. Like Blass, he had a sly curve ball and a good fast one and a change of pace, plus his screw ball, and after seven innings, Cuellar, like Blass, was pitching a two-hitter.

But, unlike Blass, Cuellar didn't have a Clemente going for him. In the fourth, Roberto Clemente, as he often does, hit one out of the park to set Blass up in a 1-0 lead. And that proved to be the difference, with the two teams matching each other's one-run eighth innings.

THE LAST CRUEL frustration for the Orioles came with the game-ending out, which evolved from what appeared to be a Baltimore hit that would put the tying run on base. But shortstop Jack Hernandez, stationing himself brightly behind second base in the special shift the Pirates used against Merve Rettenmund, grabbed off the ground ball that was headed toward center field and had an easy play.

It set off an on-field celebration by the Pirates among themselves, and they embraced and kissed each other, indiscriminately, before cutting out for the dugout to avoid the flood of fans onto the field. Blass led the sprint to safety, his cap lost, his shirttail flying and his upraised arms showing his happiness.

At the outset of today's game, Secretary of State William Rogers was tapped for the throw-out-the-first-ball role. He performed the ceremony, and it was an episode that evoked a rare unanimity among Rogers-watchers on both sides of the Suez Canal. Both the Arabs and Israelis agreed that Rogers threw a curve.

BALTIMORE MANAGER Earl Weaver called time in the first inning with Boog Powell at bat. He complained to umpire Nestor Chylak that Blass was not obeying the pitching rules, that Blass' right foot was not in contact with the pitching rubber when he was delivering the pitch. Blass scoffed at the whole idea, but umpire Chylak nevertheless took pains to go to the mound and show the Pirates' pitcher how it must be done.

Inevitably, there were cynics among the crowd who suspected that Weaver was merely attempting to psyche Blass or provoke him to temper. But those who know Weaver best would not agree to this, and hasten to point out to the dum-dums who are quick to think evil of all persons that the Orioles' manager is merely a strict constructionist who wants enforcement of both the letter and the spirit of the rules, and in fact has possibilities as a Nixon nomination for the high court.

Blass was completely unaffected by Weaver's gambit, if it was a gambit, although after the fifth inning Weaver tried the same stuff again. But by this time, Blass' game plan was being revealed. It was the simple blueprint that called for shutting out the Orioles while waiting for Clemente to hit a home run, which he did on Cuellar's last pitch to him in the fourth.

BLASS ALSO DEALT personally with Don Buford, the pesky Orioles who got on base the first two times up, with a walk and a hit. After Buford singled with one out in the third, Blass made a deceptive little motion that taught Buford not to take too big a lead off first against right-handed pitchers, and picked him off cleanly. It went into the books as "Buford caught stealing," but it was a clean trap by Blass, who baited the Oriole into going.

The useful second run of the Pirates was scored in the eighth on Jose Pagan's two-bagger off the left-center wall. There were some carpers who said center fielder Rettenmund bobbled the rebound a bit, and others who said Boog Powell shouldn't have cut off the relay to the plate. But all of this fault finding with the Orioles could have been avoided by Willie Stargell, who scored from first on Pagan's hit. Among the 47,291 plus in the park, only Stargell, who stopped almost too long at second base, was unaware that the ball was hit too deep to be catchable.

The Orioles finally put two hits together in the eighth and came up with one futile run, which scored on an infield out. If Blass was to buckle under the pressure, the time appeared ripe when he took his skimpy one-run lead into the last of the ninth against the power and the glory of the Baltimore batting order, Boog Powell, Frank Robinson and Merv Rettenmund, any of whom could tie the game up with one swipe. None of 'em got on base, none of 'em got the ball out of the infield, against the imperturbable Blass, to whom this game, and this day, belonged.

By Richard Darcey—The Washington Post

HABIT FORMING — Redskin linebacker Jack Pardee picks off a pass thrown by the Cardinals' Pete Beathard at the St. Louis 40 in the third period. It was the second of three interceptions by Pardee as Redskins won yesterday, 20-0.

Manning Engineers Surprise

Aggressive Saints Upend Stumbling Cowboys, 24-14

NEW ORLEANS, Oct. 17 (AP)—The New Orleans Saints, capitalizing on three interceptions and three fumble recoveries, upset the Dallas Cowboys, 24-14, today.

Dave Kopay, playing his first game for the Saints, recovered Cliff Harris' fumbled punt reception on the Dallas three-yard line with less than two minutes to play, and quarterback Archie Manning scored an insurance touchdown three plays later to preserve the upset.

The loss, was the Cowboy's second in five games and dropped Dallas two games behind Washington in the NFC Eastern Division.

New Orleans took a 17-0 halftime lead on a 29-yard pass from Manning to Tony Baker, a 36-yard field goal by Charlie Durkee and Manning's 13-yard run.

Durkee's field goal was set up by Dallas Howell's 60-yard interception return, and Manning's 13-yard touchdown run came on the second play after Al Dodd returned a Cowboy field goal attempt 77 yards to the Dallas 15.

New Orleans' swarming defense harrassed quarterback Craig Morton in the first half, but it appeared Roger Staubach might rally the Cowboys in the second half. Staubach hit Gloster Richardson with a 41-yard scoring pass in the third quarter and Bob Hayes with a 16-yard scoring pass in the final period.

The Cowboys were empty-handed after thier **first eight** possessions, giving up the ball twice on interceptions, once on a fumble, five times by punting and again on Mike Clark's short 50-yard field goal attempt which led to Dodd's runback.

Dallas dominated the third period behind Staubach's passing and scrambling, but did not score its second touchdown until two minutes into the fourth quarter.

STATISTICS

	Dallas	New Orleans
First downs	20	10
Rushing yardage	96	104
Passing yardage	204	49
Return yardage	18	142
Passes	17-34-3	6-15-1
Punts	5-49	7-42
Fumbles lost	0	1
Yards penalized	58	63

Dallas	0	0	7	7—14
New Orleans	7	10	0	7—24

New Orleans—Baker (29, pass from Manning); Burkee (kick).
New Orleans—Durkee (36, field goal).
New Orleans—Manning (13, run); Durkee (kick).
Dallas—Richardson (41, pass from Staubach); Clark (kick).
Dallas—Hayes (16, pass from Staubach); Clark (kick).
New Orleans—Manning (2, run); Durkee (kick).
Attendance—83,088.

Individual Leaders

RUSHING: New Orleans—Manning 7-52, Baker 12-35, Ford 10-19, Granger 2-2; Dallas—Thomas 16-58, Garrison 11-19, Staubach 2-12.
PASSING: New Orleans—Manning 6-15-1, 83 yards; Dallas—Morton 10-24-2, 113 yards; Staubach 7-10-1, 117 yards.
RECEIVING: New Orleans—Abramowics 2-36, Baker 1-29, Dodd 2-28; Dallas—Garrison 3-54, Hayes 3-30, Truax 2-38, Alworth 5-40, Ditka 2-23, Richardson 1-41.

Chiefs-Steelers On TV Tonight

PRO FOOTBALL

7:30 p.m.—St. Louis at Washington (replay), WDCA-TV Channel 20.

9 p.m.—Pittsburgh at Kansas City, WMAL-TV, Channel 7.

Defense Stuns St. Louis, 20-0

By Dave Brady
Washington Post Staff Writer

Jack Pardee ran as far with three interceptions yesterday—25 yards—as the St. Louis Cardinals gained rushing and, when the Redskins opened the dressing room to the media, the blackboard message read: "On to Kansas City."

After Larry Brown gained 150 yards in defense of his National Football League rushing title and quarterback Bill Kilmer ran three yards for the touchdown that sealed the Cardinals' fate, 20-0, playoff talk was conspicuously absent as the Redskins won their first five games for the first time in 31 years.

Coach George Allen strove mightily to avoid rash optimism about the long-range future but did permit himself a reference to Camelot. For the first time this season, a platform with a folding chair was set up for Allen's meeting with his growing number of inquisitors.

"I feel like I am sitting on a throne," he said, as he remarked that yesterday's outcome proved the Redskins' first two victories over the Cardinals within eight weeks were not flukes.

Upset News Awaited

Like the curious among the sellout crowd of 53,041 in RFK Stadium, Allen was eager for confirmation of the prospect that New Orleans was about to upset Dallas and drop the Cowboys two games behind the Redskins. The Saints did so.

There was additional cause for joy about the Eastern Division race when two other chasers of the Redskins, the New York Giants and Philadelphia Eagles, also lost.

The Redskins will catch the Chiefs coming off tonight's game in Kansas City against the Pittsburgh Steelers. The Redskins then play the Saints and Eagles at RFK and the Bears at Chicago before confronting the Cowboys here.

The Redskins duplicated in part their 27-17 regular-season opener over the Cardinals, once more intercepting four passes and recovering three St. Louis fumbles. For the fifth consecutive game, the opponent's starting quarterback was driven to the sidelines.

Attack Rejuvenated

The Cardinals were shut out for the first time since Nov. 16, 1969, when the Detroit Lions did it, also 20-0. Yesterday the Redskins limited the deep, St. Louis running game to one first down rushing.

Kilmer injected oxygen into an attack that sputtered last week as he rolled up 349 yards of total offensive yesterday. Brown hammered out his 150 yards in 25 carries for a six-yard average, including a 23-yard burst to set up the second of Curt Knight's two field goals.

Charley Harraway carried 12 times for 40 yards, including a one-yard plunge for a score in the 10-point first quarter during which the Red-

See REDSKINS, D5, Col. 4

Redskins Accepted By Selves

By Kenneth Turan
Washington Post Staff Writer

The hardest thing the Washington Redskins had to deal with after yesterday's fifth consecutive victory was the hard time other people have in accepting them as legitimate winners.

"I think a lot of people are envious of the Redskins being so successful," said defensive tackle Diron Talbert, just about the last man left in an almost-empty locker room.

"We're not lucky, we've worked our butts off, I've worked harder than I ever did in Los Angeles. We've got 22 new faces out of 40, we put in a new defense, the coaches have been at it until midnight. Now we're 5-0 and hell, I'm proud of it."

Quarterback Bill Kilmer was similarly querulous when he said, "Anytime someone tells you you're not good you've got to go out and prove it every week.

"St. Louis should have been high as a kite, but we took it to them, we played one hell of a football game, that 's the essence of it. Now you've got to say we're a pretty good football team, one of the top 10 teams, and they weren't saying that last week."

"A lot of people had written us off, Jimmy the Greek wrote us off," said Talbert. "I like to hear that stuff, it helps us a hell of a lot. We had to find out how good a team we were,

See TURAN, D5, Col. 3

The Scoring

R.Opp.

First quarter

3-0—Curt Knight, 16-yard field goal on fourth play after Norm Thompson of Cardinals fumbled runback of opening kickoff and Terry Hermeling of Redskins recovered on St. Louis 14. Time 1:22.

10-0—Charley Harraway, one-yard plunge, capping 15-play, 72-yard drive that used up 6 minutes 59 seconds, including three penalties against Redskins and two against Cardinals. Bill Kilmer's 23-yard pass to Charley Taylor in end zone was nullified by motion penalty against Roy Jefferson. Big plays: Kilmer's passes, 21 yards to Mack Alston and 17 to Taylor and Jefferson's 13-yard end-around run to St. Louis 5. Knight PAT. Time 10:46.

Third quarter

13-0—Knight, 11-yard field goal, following Jack Pardee's second of three interceptions, at St. Louis 38. Big play: Larry Brown's 23-yard run to 11. Time 9:33.

Fourth Quarter

20-0—Kilmer, three-yard run, capping 49-yard march. Big plays: Kilmer's 10-yard pass to Boyd Dowler and 38-yard pass to Jefferson to St. Louis two-yard line. Knight PAT. Time 4:43.

Statistics

	St. Louis	Washington
First downs	11	21
Rushing yardage	25	229
Passing yardage	180	120
Return yardage	8	27
Passes	15-30-4	9-17-1
Punts	5-41	4-43
Fumbles lost	3	1
Yards penalized	30	60

Attendance—53,041.

RUSHING

St. Louis

	Att.	Net Yds.	Long	TD
Shivers	6	11	7	0
Edwards	5	9	4	0
Lane	3	5	2	0

Washington

	Att.	Net Yds.	Long	TD
Brown	25	150	29	0
Harraway	12	40	19	1
Jefferson	1	13	13	0
Mason	5	11	13	0
Hull	2	8	6	0
Wyche	1	4	4	0
Kilmer	1	3	3	1

PASSING

St. Louis

	Att.	Comp.	Yds.	TD	Int.
Beathard	22	12	142	0	3
Hart	8	3	38	0	1

Washington

	Att.	Comp.	Yds.	TD	Int.
Kilmer	17	9	126	0	1

RECEIVING

	No.	Yds.	Long	TD
Gilliam	4	54	19	0
Shivers	4	26	10	0
Gray	3	67	40	0
Lane	2	14	16	0
Ja. Smith	1	16	16	0
Edwards	1	3	3	0.

Washington

	No.	Yds.	Long	TD
Jefferson	4	62	38	0
Taylor	3	33	17	0
Alston	1	21	21	0
Dowler	1	10	10	0

Associated Press

THROWN FOR LOSS—The World Series featured a number of plays that looked more like football blocks. On this one, Baltimore's Don Buford, left, and Pirates' Dave Cash go flying after Cash tagged Buford out in third inning. Buford was picked off first and tried in vain to reach second. Pirates won, 2-1, and took Series.

Cards Nip Cubs, 2-1, In 16 Innings

CHICAGO — (UPI) — Ted Simmons led off the 16th inning with a bloop double, his fourth hit of the game, and Ted Sizemore drove him in with a single to give the St. Louis Cardinals a 2-1 victory over the Chicago Cubs Saturday.

Bill Stein followed Simmons' double with his third sacrifice of the game an with the infield drawn in, Sizemore lined a single to left against losing pitcherTom Phoebus.

The Cubs scored first on a double by Ron Santo and a single by Glenn Beckert in the fourth and the Cards tied it in the seventh on a home run by Jose Cruz.

BILL HANDS, Chicago starter, had allowed only one hit before the homer by Cruz. Hands pitched the first nine innings for the Cubs, limiting St. Louis to five hits and Rick Wise pitched the first 11 for St. Louis, scattering nine hits. Rich Folkers hurled the final two and one-third innings for St. Louis to gain the victory.

St. Louis	ab r h bi	Chicago	ab r h bi
Brock lf	7 0 3 0	Kessinger ss	7 0 0 0
Tyson 2b	2 0 0 0	Cardenal rf	8 0 1 0
Carbo ph	1 0 0 0	Williams lf	6 0 2 0
Crosby ss	3 0 2 0	Hickman 1b	7 0 1 0
Cruz rf	6 1 1 1	Santo 3b	4 1 1 0
Torre 1b	7 0 0 0	Tyrone pr	0 0 0 0
Simmons c	7 1 4 0	Fanzone 3b	2 0 0 0
Reitz 3b	1 0 0 0	Monday cf	3 0 1 0
Stein 3b	3 0 1 0	Aker p	0 0 0 0
Roque cf	6 0 0 0	North ph	1 0 0 0
Kelleher ss	3 0 1 0	Bonham p	0 0 0 0
Sizemore 2b	2 0 1 1	Gura p	1 0 0 0
Wise p	4 0 0 0	Popovich ph	1 0 1 0
Melendez ph	1 0 0 0	Phoebus p	0 0 0 0
Segui p	0 0 0 0	Beckert 2b	7 0 2 1
Jutze ph	1 0 0 0	Hundley c	6 0 1 0
Bare p	0 0 0 0	Hands p	3 0 1 0
Folkers p	1 0 0 0	Hiser cf	3 0 1 0
Totals	55 2 13 2	Totals	59 1 12 1

St. Louis 000 000 100 000 000 1—2
Chicago 000 100 000 000 000 0—1

E-Hickman, Beckert, Torre. DP-St. Louis 1, Chicago 1. LOB-St. Louis 13, Chicago 17.
2B-Santo, Williams 2, Simmons. 3B-Stein. HR-Cruz (2). S-Stein 3, Roque, Kessinger, Crosby.

	IP	H	R	ER	BB	SO
Wise	11	9	1	1	3	5
Segui	2	0	0	0	2	3
Bare	2-3	2	0	0	0	1
Folkers W 1-0	2 1-3	1	0	0	1	2
Hands	9	5	1	1	0	6
Aker	2	2	0	0	1	0
Bonham	2-3	1	0	0	1	1
Gura	3 1-3	3	0	0	1	4
Phoebus L 3-4	1	2	1	1	0	1

WP-Wise. T-4:49. A-12,388.

Giants Trip Braves, 3-1

SAN FRANCISCO — (UPI). Solo home runs by Bobby Bonds and Garry Maddox powered the San Francisco Giants to a 3-1 victory over the Atlanta Braves Saturday.

The Giants by winning, also clinched the season series over the Braves with their 10th win in 17 meetings.

Atlanta	ab r h bi	San Francisco	ab r h bi
Garr lf	5 0 2 0	Bonds rf	3 2 1 1
Jackson ss	5 0 1 0	Fuentes 2b	3 0 2 0
Evans 3b	4 0 1 0	Speier ss	3 0 1 0
Williams c	4 0 0 0	Kingman 3b	3 0 0 1
Baker cf	4 0 2 0	Rader c	3 0 0 0
Breazeal 1b	4 0 0 0	Matthews lf	3 0 0 0
Lum rf	4 1 1 0	Maddox cf	4 1 2 1
Blanks 2b	3 0 2 0	Thomssn 1b	3 0 1 0
McQueen p	2 0 0 0	Barr p	3 0 0 0
Aaron ph	1 0 1 1		
Jarvis p	0 0 0 0		
Brown ph	1 0 0 0		
Totals	37 1 10 1	Totals	28 3 7 3

Atlanta 000 001 000—1
San Francisco 001 100 10x—3

E-Williams. DP-Atlanta 2. LOB-Atlanta 11, San Francisco 8.
2B-Baker 2, Evans, Fuentes. HR-Bonds (25), Maddox (12). SF-Kingman.

	ip	h	r	er	bb	so
McQueen L 0-5	5	6	2	1	4	1
Jarvis	3	1	1	1	2	2
Barr W 8-10	9	10	1	1	2	4

WP-Jarvis. T—2:20. A—4,238.

TIGERS . . .

Continued from Page 1D

double play to score one run and followed Kaline's home run with his fourth of the season to drive in the final Detroit run. Cash hit into a force play with the bases loaded in the fourth for the other Tigers' run.

Milwaukee	ab r h bi	Detroit	ab r h bi
Theobald 2b	5 0 0 0	McAuliffe 2b	3 1 1 0
ERodriguz c	5 0 1 0	TTaylor 2b	2 2 2 0
May cf	5 1 2 0	Kaline rf	5 2 4 2
Scott 1b	5 1 2 1	Sims c	4 1 2 1
Briggs lf	3 1 0 0	Cash 1b	3 2 1 3
Brett pr	0 1 0 0	Horton lf	3 1 0 0
Linzy p	0 0 0 0	Stanley cf	1 1 1 0
Lahoud lf	2 0 1 1	Northrup lf	5 1 2 2
Ferraro 3b	4 0 3 1	ARodrigz 3b	5 0 1 1
Auerbach ss	4 0 1 1	Brinkman ss	5 1 1 3
Lockwood p	0 0 0 0	Coleman p	3 1 1 0
Colborn p	0 0 0 0	GBrown ph	1 0 0 0
Reynolds ph	1 0 0 0	Seelbach p	0 0 0 0
Ryerson p	0 0 0 0		
O'Brien ph	1 0 0 0		
Stephensn p	0 0 0 0		
Davis ph	1 0 0 0		
Sanders p	0 0 0 0		
OBrown rf	1 0 1 0		
Totals	37 4 11 4	Totals	40 13 16 12

Milwaukee 010 001 020—4
Detroit 600 101 05x-13

E-TTaylor. DP-Milwaukee 1, Detroit 2. LOB-Milwaukee 9, Detroit 7.
2B-Kaline, TTaylor. HR-Brinkman (6), Scott (20), Kaline (8), Sims (4). SB-Scott.

	IP	H	R	ER	BB	SO
Lockwood L 7-15	2-3	5	6	6	1	1
Colborn	1-3	0	0	0	0	1
Ryerson	3	3	1	1	2	1
Stephenson	2	2	1	1	0	1
Sanders	1	0	0	0	0	0
Linzy	1	6	5	5	1	1
Coleman W 19-13	8	8	4	2	3	5
Seelbach	1	3	0	0	0	0

Save-Seelbach (13). WP-Stephenson 2. T-2:51. A-24,538.

HITS HIS 3000th—Pirates right fielder Roberto Clemete swings at pitch that became his 3000th, making him one of 11 players in the major leagues to hit that number or more. It came in the fourth inning off Mets pitcher Jon Matlack, in game played in Pittsburgh Saturday afternoon. It was a double to center field.

—AP Wirephoto.

Expos Top Phils, 8-4, After, 3-0, Setback

MONTREAL — (UPI) — Rookie lefthander Balro Moore, with relief help in the ninth inning from Mike Marshall, won his ninth game of the year and helped his own cause by driving in two runs in the second game of a doubleheader Saturday as the Montreal Expos defeated the Phillies, 8-4, after Philadelphia won the opener, 3-0, on Barry Lersch's two-hitter.

Moore, who has lost eight games, gave up nine hits while walking seven and striking out ten before Marshall came on to pick up his 18th save.

In the fourth inning of the nightcap, the Expos scored their first runs after 32 innings as they took 3-1 lead.

In the seventh inning, Moore walked with the bases-loaded to force in another run. Jim Fairey doubled in the seventh to drive in two more Montreal runs.

IN THE OPENER, the Phillies scored their first run in the fourth inning when Bob Boone singled, advanced to second when Lersch walked and scored on Denny Doyle's single to center.

The Phillies scored their other two runs in the seventh when Doyle singled to left, Larry Bowa walked, sending Doyle to second. Doyle then stole third and scored on a Willie Montanez' single. Bowa then scored on Greg Luzinski's single.

Philadelphia	ab r h bi	Montreal	ab r h bi
Doyle 2b	5 1 2 1	Hunt 2b	3 0 2 0
Bowa ss	4 1 0 0	Fairey rf	4 0 0 0
Montanez 1b	4 0 2 1	Singleton lf	4 0 0 0
Reed rf	1 0 0 0	Breeden 1b	3 0 0 0
Luzinski lf	5 0 2 1	McCarver c	3 0 0 0
Huton 1b	2 0 0 0	Woods cf	3 0 0 0
BRobinsn cf	3 0 1 0	Foli ss	0 0 0 0
Money 3b	4 0 1 0	Laboy 3b	3 0 0 0
Boone c	4 1 1 0	Torres ss	2 0 0 0
Lersch p	3 0 0 0	Day cf	1 0 0 0
		Torrez p	2 0 0 0
		Fairly ph	1 0 0 0
Totals	35 3 9 3	Totals	29 0 2 0

Philadelphia 000 010 200—3
Montreal 000 000 000—0

LOB-Philadelphia 10, Montreal 3.
2B-Montanez. SB-Doyle.

	IP	H	R	ER	BB	SO
Lersch W 3-6	9	2	0	0	0	6
Torrez L 16-12	9	9	3	3	5	4

HBP-Hunt (by Lersch).
T-1:52.

2nd game

Philadelphia	ab r h bi	Montreal	ab r h bi
Harmon ss	4 1 2 0	Hunt 2b	3 0 0 0
Money 3b	2 0 0 0	McCarver c	5 2 2 2
Koegel 3b	1 1 0 0	Singleton lf	5 2 2 0
Luzinski lf	4 1 1 1	Fairly 1b	4 2 2 1
Lis 1b	3 0 1 1	Fairey rf	4 1 3 2
Freed rf	4 0 0 0	Day cf	4 1 1 1
BRobinsn cf	5 1 3 1	Foli ss	3 0 0 0
Schmidt 2b	4 0 1 0	Laboy 3b	2 0 0 0
Ryan c	2 0 0 0	Moore p	3 0 0 2
Nash p	2 0 0 0		
Scarce p	0 0 0 0		
Johnson ph	1 0 1 0		
Doyle pr	0 0 0 0		
Brandon p	0 0 0 0		
Boone ph	1 0 0 0		
Selma p	0 0 0 0		
Totals	33 4 9 3	Totals	33 8 10 8

Philadelphia 001 001 002—4
Montreal 000 400 31x—8

E-Fairey, Schmidt. DP-Montreal 1. LOB-Philadelphia 12, Montreal 10.
2B-Harmon, Luzinski, Singleton 2, BRobinson. HR-McCarver (7). S-Money, Foli, Fairey.

	IP	H	R	ER	BB	SO
Nash L 1-9	3 1-3	4	4	4	2	0
Scarce	2-3	2	0	0	1	0
Brandon	3	2	3	1	3	3
Selma	1	2	1	1	0	0
Moore W 9-8	8 2-3	9	4	4	7	10
Marshall	1-3	0	0	0	0	0

Save-Marshall (18). HBP-by Nash (Hunt), by Moore (Schmidt).
A-7,262. T-2:34.

Towson State Blanked by R-M, 30-0

Tim Rzepkowski of Randolph-Macon scored three touchdowns during a five-minute span of the first half and led the unbeaten Yellow Jackets to a 30-0 victory over Towson State Saturday.

Rzepkowski tallied on a 14-yard pass from quarterback Bob Sesco with 1:01 left in the first quarter to put Randolph-Macon on top 10-0.

Only 57 seconds into the second period, Rzepkowski rambled 60 yards to score, and a little over three minutes later went over from one yard out.

LATE IN the game, reserve split end Larry Wallace scored on a 61-yard pass from secondstring quarterback Jay Tingle. Wallace also booted a 27-yard field goal and three extra points.

The first touchdown for Randolph-Macon, now 3-0, ws set up on a blocked punt by Lucky Jones, and a recovery funble by Randy Scott led to the third TD.

Brindisi Shines In Eagles' Win

Rick Brindisi ran for one touchdown and threw for another Saturday night to lead the Baltimore Eagles to a come-from-behind, 14-12, conquest of the Waynesboro, Pa. Tigers at Brooklyn Park.

Brindisi scored the first Eagle TD on a one-yard keeper. Then, with the Tigers leading 12-7, the quarterback pass to Jim Augustowsky for a 36-yard TD that lifted Baltimore to its third win of the season.

Waynesboro	0	6	6	0—12
Baltimore	0	7	7	0—14

W—Toms 44 pass from Webb (kick failed).
B—Brindisi 1 run (Martin kick).
W—Webb 2 run (kick failed.)
B—Augustowsky 36 pass from Brindisi (Martin kick).

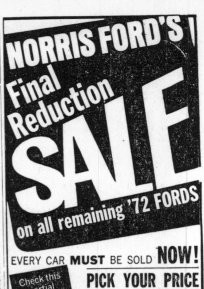

Dodgers Trim Reds, 4-2, On Osteen's Hit

CINCINNATI — (UPI) — Pitcher Claude Osteen doubled home two runs with two out in the 10th inning to give the Los Angeles Dodgers a 4-2 victory over the Cincinnati Reds Saturday afternoon.

The victory was the 19th against 11 losses for Osteen, who also singled home Willie Crawford in the eighth inning to tie the score at 2-2.

RON CEY touched off the Dodger 10th inning rally with a single and was replaced by pinch-runner Maury Wills. Two outs later, Bill Russell moved Willis to second with an infield hit. Osteen's game-winning double off loser Pedro Borbon followed.

The veteran Dodger lefty gave up six hits, three off the bat of Pete Rose who boosted his average to 295.

Los Angeles	ab r h bi	Cincinnati	ab r h bi
Lopes 2b	5 1 1 0	Rose lf	5 1 3 0
Buckner rf	4 0 0 1	Morgan 2b	5 1 2 1
Davis cf	4 0 0 0	Tolan cf	5 0 1 1
Paciorek 1b	4 0 1 0	Bench c	2 0 0 0
Cey 3b	4 p 2 0	Perez 1b	3 0 0 0
Wills 3b	0 1 0 0	Foster pr	0 0 0 0
Crawford lf	4 1 1 0	Hague 1b	0 0 0 0
Ferguson c	2 0 0 0	McRae rf	3 0 0 0
Mota ph	1 0 0 0	Geronimo rf	0 0 0 0
Yaeger c	1 0 0 0	Menke 3b	3 0 0 0
Russell ss	4 1 1 0	Concepcn ss	4 0 0 0
Osteen p	4 0 2 3	Simpson p	2 0 0 0
		Javier ph	1 0 0 0
		Borbon p	0 0 0 0
		Uhlaendr ph	1 0 0 0
Totals	37 4 8 4	Totals	34 2 6 2

Los Angeles 100 000 010 2—4
Cincinnati 000 200 000 0—2

DP-Cincinnati 1. LOB-Los Angeles 3, Cincinnati 7.
2B-Lopes, Paciorek, Osteen, Rose 2. 3B-Morgan. S-Geronimo.

	IP	H	R	ER	BB	SO
Osteen W 19-11	10	6	2	2	4	8
Simpson	8	5	2	2	0	2
Borbon L 8-3	2	3	2	2	0	0

WP-Simpson. T-2:26. A-20,080.

Wolverines Rip Tulane

ANN ARBOR, Mich. — (UPI) — Junior fullback Ed Shuttlesworth rushed for 151 yards and three touchdowns along the way Saturday in a 41-7 Michigan triumph over Tulane.

Clemente's 3,000th Hit Keys Bucs Win

PITTSBURGH — (UPI) — Roberto Clemente's 3,000th major league hit triggered a three-run fourth inning ralley as the Pirates beat the New York Mets 5-0 Saturday behind the two-hit pitching of Dock Ellis and Bob Johnson.

Clemente's double to left center field ranks him with 10 other players in the 3,000 hit class, two of whom are still active — Willie Mays and Hank Aaron. The others were Ty Cobb, Stan Musial, Cap Anson, Tris Speaker, Nap Lajoie, Ed Collins, Paul Waner and Honus Wagner.

JON MATLACK gave up the double to Clemente and suffered his 10th loss against 14 Richie Zisk walked, Manny wins when, with one out, Sanguillen singled for the first run and Jackie Hernandez lofted a two-out, two-run triple to deep center. Matlack had pitched 28 and 1-3 successive scoreless inning against the Pirates.

Third baseman's Wayne Garret's error on Sanguillen's grounder gave Pittsburgh two more runs in the sixth after Matlack had walked Willie Stargell and Zisk.

Ellis picked up his 15th win in 22 decisions, allowing only one hit and fanning five in six innings, before Johnson went the last three innings giving the other hit.

New York	ab r h bi	Pittsburgh	ab r h bi
Garrett 3b	4 0 0 0	Goggin 2b	4 0 2 0
Boswell 2b	4 0 1 0	Stennett cf	4 0 0 0
Milner lf	3 0 0 0	Clemente rf	2 1 1 0
Staub rf	3 0 0 0	Mazursk ph	1 0 0 0
Rauch p	0 0 0 0	Davalillo rf	1 0 0 0
Marshall ph	1 0 0 0	Stargell 1b	3 1 1 0
Kranepol 1b	3 0 1 0	Zisk lf	1 2 0 0
Fregosi ss	3 0 0 0	Sanguillen c	3 1 1 1
Schneck cf	3 0 0 0	Pagan 3b	3 0 0 0
Dyer c	2 0 0 0	JHernndz ss	3 0 1 2
Nolan c	1 0 0 0	Ellis p	2 0 0 0
Matlack p	2 0 0 0	Clines ph	1 0 0 0
Hahn rf	0 0 0 0	Johnson p	0 0 0 0
Totals	29 0 2 0	Totals	28 5 6 3

New York 000 000 000—0
Pittsburgh 000 302 00x—5

E-Garrett. DP-New York 3. LOB-New York 5, Pittsburgh 4.
2B-Clemente. 3B-JHernandez.

	IP	H	R	ER	BB	SO
Matlack L 14-10	6	5	5	3	5	5
Rauch	2	1	0	0	0	1
Ellis W 15-7	6	1	0	0	2	5
Johnson	3	1	0	0	1	1

Save-Johnson 3. PB-Dyer, Nolan. T-2:10. A-13,117.

Playoff Schedule

NEW YORK—(AP)—Here is the schedule for baseball's championship series in both the National and American Leagues:

National League

Sat., Oct. 7—Cincinnati at Pittsburgh, 1 p.m., EDT
Sun., Oct. 8—Cincinnati at Pittsburgh, 1 p.m., EDT
Mon., Oct. 9—Pittsburgh at Cincinnati, [illegible] EDT
Tues., Oct. 10—Pittsburgh at Cincinnati, 3 p.m., EDT, if necessary
Wed., Oct. 11—Pittsburgh at Cincinnati, 3 p.m., EDT, if necessary

American League

Sat., Oct. 7—East Division winner at Oakland, 4 p.m., EDT
Sun., Oct. 8—East Division winner at Oakland, 4 p.m., EDT
Mon., Oct. 9—Travel
Tues., Oct. 10—Oakland at East Division winner, 1:30 EDT
Wed., Oct. 11—Oakland at East Division winner, if necessary, 1:30 EDT
Thurs., Oct. 12—Oakland at East Division winner, if necessary, 1:30 EDT

Buckeyes Bounce Tar Heels, 29-14

COLUMBUS, Ohio — (AP) — Archie Griffin, a hometown freshman tailback carrying the ball for the first time in college, broke loose for an Ohio State-record 239 rushing yards Saturday, leading the fifth-ranked Buckeyes to a 29-14 victory over North Carolina.

The Black Neighborhoods

Today: South Jamaica • Series by Joel Dreyfuss Continues on Page 37

WEATHER
Chance of rain, 60s.
Tonight: Cloudy, 45.
Tomorrow: Sunny, 55.
Fair on Thursday.
SUNSET: 6:03
SUNRISE TOMORROW: 7:18

New York Post

FOUNDED 1801. THE OLDEST CONTINUOUSLY PUBLISHED DAILY IN THE UNITED STATES.

Vol. 171 No. 289 | NEW YORK, TUESDAY, OCTOBER 24, 1972 | 15 Cents

CITY LATE
OVER THE COUNTER.

JACKIE ROBINSON IS DEAD AT 51

Bust 2 More Cops in Probe

By Jerry Capeci and Irving Lieberman

Police from Brooklyn District Attorney Gold's office arrested two detectives today amid indications that they were linked to the prosecutor's crackdown on organized crime.

The two detectives were assigned to the district in which a reputed mob headquarters raided by Gold last week was located.

The raid followed a lengthy wiretap of a trailer, which Gold called a headquarters for mobsters. He issued 677 subpenas for persons seen in and around the trailer.

The action followed the suspension last week of Lieut. Meyer Rubenstein, assigned to the precinct in which the trailer was located.

Rubenstein, a 30-year veteran of the force, was accused of tipping off mob leaders about the wiretaps. He faces a departmental hearing today (**See Page 2**).

The two detectives nabbed today were Ralph Caccia, and John Cuomo, both assigned to the 12th Detective District Robbery Squad. They were suspended from the force early today for "conduct unbecoming an officer and prejudicial to the . . . department."

Gold refused to say if the action against the two was directly linked to his underworld investigation. But he called a news conference later in the day to explain the criminal charges on which they were booked at his office.

A week ago yesterday, more than 1200 cops under Gold's command fanned out to serve grand jury subpenas on alleged mob members and others spotted during the lengthy stakeout and wiretapping of the trailer, in an auto junkyard at 5702 Av. D.

By Carl Pelleck

Hall of Fame baseball great Jackie Robinson — the first black man to play in the major leagues —died early today of an apparent heart attack after he fell ill suddenly at his Stamford, Conn., home.

JACKIE ROBINSON as he was presented with an award for columns in The Post supporting civil rights in 1960.

Robinson, 51, died at 7:10 a.m. apparently enroute to Stamford Hospital where he was being rushed.

Police said they received a call from Robinson's wife at 6:26 a.m. saying her husband had become very ill and asked for an ambulance.

The first policemen who rushed to the house administered oxygen until an ambulance arrived and then rushed him, apparently unconscious, to the hospital.

Hospital officials said the baseball star—who had taken courageous stands on many social issues—was dead on arrival at the emergency ward.

Robinson has achieved greatness and immortal fame as the first baseman for the Brooklyn Dodgers when "Dem Bums" were still at Brooklyn's Ebbets Field and the pride of all New York.

He spent ten years with the Dodgers during which the team won six pennants.

Prior to the opening of the World Series last week, Robinson was honored by Baseball Commissioner Bowie Kuhn for his fight against drug addiction. His son, killed in a car crash, was a reformed addict.

Most recently Robinson was involved in major undertaking to build biracial housing with one of the first large developments slated for Brooklyn Bedford Stuyvesant ghetto.

Robinson joined the Dodgers in 1947 and his illustrious career never waned until he retired as a player in 1957 and then went into many other things including politics.

Once he opened the baseball world to blacks other minorities slowly ebbed their way in until today when the game is quite heavily represented by all ethnic groups.

Robinson cut a place in the game by starting out as Rookie of the Year in 1947 and then two years later copping the Most Valuable Player Award.

"I think I've been much more aggressive since I left baseball," Robinson told a reporter 10 years after he left the game.

But if that was true he had done much outside of the diamond where he had compiled a .311 lifetime batting average.

Ryan Breaks Koufax SO Record

Rigney Out Of A's Booth

Oakland, Sept. 27 (AP)— Bill Rigney, former major league manager, was fired from his job as a member of the Oakland A's broadcast crew Wednesday.

Rigney previously had managed the San Francisco Giants, California Angels and Minnesota Twins.

Dobson 9-Hits Brewers, 2-0

Milwaukee, Sept. 27 (AP) — Pitcher Pat Dobson scattered nine and the Yankees clinched a fourth-place tie in the American League East by defeating the Brewers, 2-0, Thursday night.

The Yanks scored the only run they needed in the second inning

YANKEES

	*b.av.	ab.	r.	h.	tb.	rbi.	po.	a.	e.
White,lf	.245	4	0	1	1	0	3	0	0
Hegan,1b	.241	3	0	1	1	0	10	0	0
Munson,c	.301	4	0	1	1	0	4	1	0
Murcer,cf	.301	4	0	0	0	0	2	0	0
Sims,dh	.244	4	1	1	1	0	—	—	—
Nettles,3b	.235	4	0	2	3	1	0	4	0
Velez,rf	.176	4	0	1	2	0	5	0	0
Lanier,2b	.200	4	0	0	0	0	1	3	0
Stanley,ss	.288	3	1	1	1	0	2	0	0
Dobson,p	—	—	—	—	—	—	0	1	0
Team	.261								
Totals		34	0	8	10	1	27	9	0

MILWAUKEE

	*b.av.	ab.	r.	h.	tb.	rbi.	po.	a.	e.
Garcia,2b	.248	4	0	0	0	0	1	4	1
Money,3b	.286	4	0	1	1	0	2	0	0
Scott,1b	.301	4	0	1	1	0	7	1	0
May,cf	.305	4	0	1	1	0	2	0	0
Briggs,lf	.246	4	0	1	1	0	2	0	0
a-Thomas	.199	0	0	0	0	0	0	0	0
Porter,c	.257	4	0	2	2	0	8	0	0
Lahoud,dh	.209	4	0	1	1	0	—	—	—
Howard,rf	.269	4	0	1	1	0	3	0	0
Johnson,ss	.214	3	0	1	1	0	2	2	0
Slaton,p	—	—	—	—	—	—	0	1	0
Team	.256								
Totals		35	0	9	9	0	27	8	1

*Including last night's game.
a-Ran for Porter in 9th.

YANKEES .... 011 000 000—2
Milwaukee .... 000 000 000—0

Earned runs—Yankees 1, Milwaukee 0. Left on bases—Yankees 6, Milwaukee 6. Two-base hits—Nettles, Velez. Caught stealing—by Munson (May). Sacrifice—Hegan. Struck out—by Dobson 4 (Garcia, Howard, Briggs 2); Slaton 7 (Velez 2, Lanier 2, Munson, White, Stanley). Wild pitch—Slaton. Winning Pitcher—Dobson (9-8). Losing Pitcher—Slaton (13-15). Time—2:18. Umpires—Honochick, Barnett, McCoy, Odom. Attendance—5,130.

when newly acquired Duke Sims singled off loser Jim Slaton and raced all the way home on a long double by Graig Nettles.

New York made it 2-0 in the third as Fred Stanley opened with a single and came around on an error by Pedro Garcia, a sacrifice and a wild pitch.

Dobson walked none and pitched out of bases-loaded jams in the eighth and ninth innings.

NL Boxscores

PHILADELPHIA (3) at PITTSBURGH (2)

Philadelphia	ab	r	h	rbi
Grabrkewtz,2b	4	1	0	0
Hutton,ph	1	0	0	0
Culver,p	0	0	0	0
Wallace,p	0	0	0	0
Unser,cf	5	1	2	2
Anderson,rf	0	0	0	0
Montanez,1b	6	0	1	0
Luzinski,lf	6	1	1	0
BRobinson,cf	4	0	1	0
Boone,c	6	0	4	0
Schmidt,3b	5	0	0	0
Bowa,ss	5	0	1	0
Lersch,p	3	0	1	0
Rogodznski,ph	1	0	0	0
Diorio,p	0	0	0	0
Scarce,p	0	0	0	0
C.Robinson,2b	1	0	0	0
Totals	47	3	11	2

Pittsburgh	ab	r	h	rbi
Cash,2b	6	1	1	0
Clines,cf	5	0	1	0
Oliver,1b	6	1	2	2
Stargell,lf	5	0	0	0
Hebner,1b	5	0	2	0
Zisk,rf	4	0	1	0
Augustine,rf	1	0	0	0
Sanguillen,c	4	0	0	0
Maxvill,ss	2	0	0	0
Parker,ph	1	0	1	0
JHernandez,ss	1	0	0	0
Robertson,ph	0	0	0	0
Zachary,p	0	0	0	0
Kison,p	2	0	0	0
RHernandez,p	0	0	0	0
May,ph	1	0	0	0
Giusti,p	0	0	0	0
Gonzales,ph	1	0	0	0
Johnson,p	0	0	0	0
Foor,p	0	0	0	0
Alley,ss	1	0	0	0
Totals	46	2	8	2

Philadelphia 200 000 000 000 1—3
Pittsburgh 200 000 000 000 0—2

DP—Philadelphia 1. LOB—Philadelphia 11, Pittsburgh 7. 2B—Cash, Unser, Zisk. HR—Unser (11), Oliver (20). SB—Bowa. S—B.Robinson.

	IP	H	R	ER	BB	SO
Lersch	8	4	2	2	0	2
Diorio	⅔	0	0	0	0	0
Scarce	2⅓	3	0	0	1	0
Culver (W—7-5)	1⅔	1	0	0	1	1
Wallace	⅓	0	0	0	0	0
Kison	6⅔	4	2	2	4	4
R.Hernandez	1⅓	1	0	0	0	0
Giusti	2	2	0	0	0	2
Johnson	1⅔	2	0	0	0	2
Foor	⅓	0	0	0	1	0
Zachary (L—0-1)	1	2	1	1	0	1

Save—Wallace (1). WP—Zachary. T—3:33. A—11,577.

CHICAGO (0) at ST. LOUIS (2)

Chicago	ab	r	h	rbi
Monday,cf	3	0	0	0
Kessinger,ss	3	0	0	0
Williams,lf	3	0	0	0
Santo,3b	3	0	0	0
Cardenal,rf	3	0	0	0
Marquez,1b	3	0	0	0
Rosello,2b	2	0	0	0
Beckert,ph	1	0	0	0
Rudolph,c	2	0	1	0
Lacock,ph	1	0	0	0
Houton,p	2	0	0	0
Paul,p	0	0	0	0
Garrett,ph	1	0	0	0
Totals	27	0	1	0

St. Louis	ab	r	h	rbi
Brock,lf	4	1	1	2
Sizemore,2b	4	0	2	0
McBride,cf	4	0	1	0
Simmons,c	4	0	1	0
McCarver,1b	4	0	0	0
J.Cruz,rf	3	0	1	0
Reitz,3b	3	0	1	0
Tyson,ss	2	1	1	0
Cleveland,p	2	0	0	0
Totals	30	2	8	2

Chicago .... 000 000 000—0
St. Louis .... 000 002 00x—2

DP—St. Louis 1. LOB—Chicago 0, St. Louis 6. HR—Brock (7). SB—Sizemore. S—Cleveland.

	IP	H	R	ER	BB	SO
Heuton (L, 14-16)	7⅔	8	2	2	1	6
Paul	⅓	0	0	0	0	0
Cleveland (W, 14-10)	9	1	0	0	0	3

WP—Heuton. T—1:40. A—13,014.

Anaheim, Calif., Sept. 27 (UPI)—Nolan Ryan of the California Angels broke Sandy Koufax's major league single-season strikeout record of 382 Thursday night by fanning Rich Reese of the Minnesota Twins in the 11th inning.

The Angels won the game, 5-4, Ryan ending with 16 trikeouts.

Ryan, 26, went into the game needing 15 strikeouts to equal the record set by Koufax for the Los Angeles Dodgers in 1965. He tied the mark by striking out Steve Brye in the eighth inning and set the record by striking out Reese on a 0-2 pitch to end the top of the 11th.

Ryan, expected to pitch Sunday against the Twins if he didn't get the record in this start, got off to a quick start on his record-breaking night by striking out three Twins in the first inning, although he allowed three runs on three hits and a pair of walks. He fanned two men in the second, one in the third, struck out the side in the fourth, added two more in the fifth and moved to within two of a record by striking out three in the seventh.

The hard-throwing right-hander from Alvin, Tex., also broke Koufax' two-season strikeout mark of 699, set in 1965-66, when he fanned American League batting champion Rod Carew for his first out in the second inning, giving

Nolan Ryan
700 in two seasons

him a total of 700 for his two seasons as an Angel.

Pinch-hitter Richie Scheinblum's one-out double over centerfielder Steve Brye's head scored Tom McCraw wtih the winning run in the 11th.

Tigers Beat Orioles 5-2

Baltimore Sept. 27 (UPI) — Dick Sharon's three-run double backed Joe Coleman's 23d victory as the Tigers halted the Orioles' six-game winning streak, 5-2, Thursday night.

Coleman defeated the Orioles for the fifth time while six-hitting the Eastern Division champs. Sharon's two-bagger in the fourth inning erased a 1-0 Baltimore lead and ruined the first major league start by rookie pitcher of Wayne Garland.

Singles by Ron Cash, Mickey Stanley and a walk to Gates Brown preceded Sharon's two-out double to rightfield. Cash and Bill Freehan notched RBI singles in the seventh and eighth innings.

Brooks Robinson scored Baltimore's first run in the second inning when he singled, went to third on an outfield error and scored on a wild pitch.

Chisox, 3-2, in 10th

Chicago, Sept. 27 (AP)—Buddy Bradford's solo home run in the bottom of the 10th inning lifted the Chicago White Sox to a 3-2 triumph over the Kansas City Royals Thursday.

Bradford led off the Chicago half of the inning with his eighth homer. Hal McRae had delivered Jim Wohlford in the Royals' sixth with the run that tied the game 2-2.

Wohlford, who tripled before Frank Ortenzo singled him home in the first inning, beat out a topped roller, took second on Kurt Bevacqua's single and went to third on a fielder's choice before McRae drove him home for the tying run in the sixth.

AL Boxscores

DETROIT (5) at BALTIMORE (2)

Detroit	ab	r	h	rbi
Knox,2b	4	0	0	0
R. Cash,lf	4	1	2	1
Northrup,lf	1	0	0	0
Stanley,cf	5	0	2	0
N. Cash,1b	5	1	1	0
G.Brown,dh	2	2	0	0
Sharon,rf	3	0	1	3
Freehan,c	3	1	1	1
Rodriguez,3b	4	0	0	0
Brinkman,ss	3	0	0	0
Coleman,p	0	0	0	0
Totals	34	5	7	5

Baltimore	ab	r	h	rbi
Bumbry,lf	3	0	1	0
Coggins,cf	4	0	1	0
Baylor,1b	4	0	0	0
Fuller,rf	4	0	0	0
Robinson,3b	4	2	2	0
Crowley,dh	4	0	2	1
Grich,2b	1	0	0	0
Baker,2b	3	0	0	0
Belanger,ss	3	0	0	0
Powell,ph	1	0	0	0
Robles,c	2	0	0	0
Totals	33	2	6	1

Detroit .... 000 003 110—5
Baltimore .... 010 000 001—2

E—Baker, R. Cash, N. Cash. DP—Detroit 1. LOB—Detroit 8, Baltimore 6. 2B—Crowley, Sharon. 3B—Robinson. SB—Belanger.

	IP	H	R	ER	BB	SO
Coleman (W, 23-15)	9	6	2	1	2	[illegible]
Garland (L, 0-1)	7	6	4	3	3	3
Reynolds	2	1	1	1	3	3

KANSAS CITY (2) at CHICAGO (3)

Kansas City	ab	r	h	rbi
Patek,ss	5	0	0	0
Wohlford,lf	4	2	2	0
Bevqua,3b	4	0	1	0
Kirkpatrick,cf	4	0	0	0
Ortenzio,1b	4	0	1	1
McRae,dh	4	0	2	1
Reichardt,rf	4	0	0	0
Floyd,2b	4	0	1	0
Martinez,c	4	0	1	0
Fitsmorris,p	0	0	0	0
Totals	37	2	8	2

Chicago	ab	r	h	rbi
Kelly,rf	3	0	1	0
Bradford,rf	2	1	1	1
Sharp,cf	4	1	[illegible]	0
Hairston,lf	4	0	1	0
Melton,3b	4	0	1	1
C. May,dh	3	1	[illegible]	0
Orta,2b	4	0	0	0
Ewing,1b	4	0	1	1
Dent,ss	4	0	0	0
Brinkman,c	4	0	0	0
Kaat,p	0	0	0	0
Totals	36	3	9	3

Kansas City .... 100 001 000 0—2
Chicago .... 100 100 000 1—3

DP—Chicago 1. LOB—Kansas City 5, Chicago 7. 2B—McRae. 3B—Wolhford. HR—Bradford (8).

	IP	H	R	ER	BB	SO
Fitzmorris (L, 8-3)	9	9	3	3	1	4
Kaat (W, 15-13)	10	8	2	2	0	4

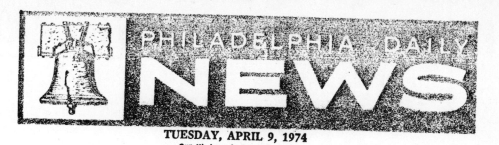

Tonight
Windy, Cold

Tomorrow
Partly Sunny, Cold

Details on Page 2

PHILADELPHIA DAILY NEWS

TUESDAY, APRIL 9, 1974
Our 8th Issue In Our 50th Year

4★

10c Sports

So Long, Babe

Stan Hochman Reports from Atlanta–Back Page

Unifax

Hank Aaron hugs his mother, Mrs. Herbert Aaron, as teammate holds ball Hank used to hit record-breaking 715th homer.

FINAL ★★★

DAILY NEWS
NEW YORK'S PICTURE NEWSPAPER ®

MORE THAN TWICE THE CIRCULATION OF ANY OTHER PAPER IN AMERICA

92 New York, N.Y. 10017, Wednesday, October 16, 1974

A's TOP DODGERS, 3-2

Oakland Takes 2-1 Series Lead

Associated Press Wirephotos

Gunning For Tiebreaker

Three members of the Oakland A's pitching staff, Vida Blue, Catfish Hunter and John "Blue Moon" Odom, watch with more than passing interest as their teammates whale ball in batting practice before last night's World Series clash in Oakland. Hunter started for the A's and was opposed by ex-Yankee Al Downing who started for Dodgers. At left, opposing managers Alvin Dark (left) and Walt Alston confer on ground rules. Chief ground rule: win the game to go up two games to one in Series. *—Stories p. 78*

NBA Sizeups: It All Centers Around the Pivotmen — See Page 88

A's Defeat Dodgers, 3-2, to Win Third Straight World Series

Bill North of the A's sailing into second base on a successful steal as off-target peg from Steve Yeager skipped into right-center field. Tom Gorman is the umpire.

Associated Press

Ray Fosse of the A's stroking a Don Sutton pitch for a home run in the second inning at Oakland last night.

Rudi's Homer in 7th Snaps 2-2 Deadlock

Continued From Page 1, Col. 3

any mistakes that could not be salvaged by late theatrics, and the theatrics were supplied chiefly by Joe Rudi in the seventh inning when he broke a 2-2 tie with a resounding home run off Mike Marshall, who was pitching in his 113th game of the year.

In an era of workhorse relief pitching, Marshall was working for the fifth time in a five-game match. But Oakland produced an iron man of its own: Rollie Fingers, the man with the Svengali mustache, who appeared 76 times during the six-month regular season and four times in the Series. The 29-year-old Ohioan worked the final two innings tonight, protected the lead provided by Rudi and then was voted the most valuable player on the scene.

So for the third October in a row, champagne flowed in the often tumultuous clubhouse of Charles O. Finley's ball team, including some that Reggie Jackson poured over the head of the commissioner of baseball, Bowie Kuhn, on national television.

Some of the best men on the Oakland team were still demanding to be traded from Finley's heavy-handed grip. The best pitched, Jim (Catfish) Hunter, was still pursuing a grievance claim for half his $100,000 salary and his outright release. And there was reminders of the customary bickering in a season that was enlivened y a fistfight or two and by the best record in recent times: four Western Division titles in a row, three American League pennants in a row and three world championships.

There was even a flashback to some of the rowdyism of recent years by the fans in other cities. It broke out in the seventh inning, just before Rudi struck his winning home run, and not long after Vida Blue and Don Sutton had been replaced as the starting pitchers. But when it subsided, the A's charged ahead and won with their usual flourishes.

They also won by the usual score of 3-2, which proved the final score in four of the five games played since last Saturday — the first two in Los Angeles and the last three in Oakland in California's first World Series. And when Fingers retired the Dodgers in order in the ninth, the A's fans tumbled onto the gras and littered it with debris while manager Alvin Dark surveyed the situation and said:

"I know a lot of people aren't going to understand this, but I say: Glory to God. I've leaned on him all through this season, and I'll continue to do so."

If the A's felt any nervousness about their date with history, because of their strange behavior on such occasions in the past, they didn't betray it. Nor did Manager Alvin Dark, who took over the Oakland team this season after Dick Williams made an "abdication speech" on national television moments after the A's had defeated the Mets in last year's Series.

In fact, the A's seemed unimpressed by events as ever, and they wasted no time treating Blue to a lead after he had retired the first three Dodger batters. Bert Campaneris led the charge as Oakland's first battery by lining a single to left field. Then Bill North twisted a double-play grounder to Bill Russell at shortstop, but the Dodgers didn't put enough zip into it and settled for the force-out at second base.

They lived to regret it when North promptly stole second and continued on to third after Steve Yeager's throw carried wide of the bag into right-center field. Then Sal Bando, with only one single in 13 times at bat in the Series, fetched the run home with a sacrifice fly to Bill Buckner in left field.

For a while it looked as though the A's were not only relaxed but also greedy. Reggie Jackson drew a base on balls; Joe Rudi rammed a single through the middle of the infield to center, and Sutton was surrounded by more trouble than he'd seen during his eight innings against Oakland last Sunday. But he survived it when Claudell Washington lifted a fly to right field for the final out.

In the second inning, Sutton pitched one strike to Fosse, who had only one single in 11 times at bat. Then the 27-year-old catcher from Ohio drove a high home run into the seats in left field. That made it 2-0, Oakland, and it guaranteed that Fosse would be remembered this season for something more than the neck injury he had suffered while breaking up a locker-room fight between Jackson and North.

After that, Sutton retired 11 of the next 12 batters—but they were the last 12 he faced because he was lifted for a pinch hitter in the top of the sixth with the A's still nursing their two-run lead.

They didn't nurse it for long, though. The pinch-hitter, Tom Paciorek, drilled the first pitch he saw into left-center and it skipped to the wall for a double. Dave Lopes walked and Buckner, trying to get both runners into scoring position, duly bunted and did just that.

Now it was up to the fat part of the Los Angeles batting order—Wynn, the No. 3 hitter, and Steve Garvey, the No. 4. They produced, too, starting with a sacrifice fly to deep left field by Wynn for one run and ending with a single to left by Garvey for another. And for Garvey, the batting star of the Series, the hit was his eighth in 20 trips to the plate.

United Press International

Vida Blue winding up for first pitch of the game.

Associated Press

Davey Lopes being tagged out at second by Bert Campaneris on an attempted steal in the third inning last night.

A.A.U. Sets New Rules On Travel

By NEIL AMDUR

Special to The New York Times

WASHINGTON, Oct. 17—The Amateur Athletic Union approved legislation today to suspend any American track and field athlete who violates travel-permit moratoriums before national championships and international meets.

The new regulation, which carries a one-year suspension from all A.A.U. and international meets, is the strongest attempt yet by the organization to cut down on under-the-table expense payments to American competitors by meet promoters, particularly in Europe.

Countries that violate the moratorium, the A.A.U., said, would be declared off limits to American athletes for one year.

Under terms of the moratorium, an athlete may not receive a travel permit to compete abroad 10 days before the A.A.U. outdoor championships or five days before an international meet if he has had the opportunity to be selected for a national team.

The suspension threat was one of several important policy revisions that emerged from discussions and meetings at the week-long 87th annual A.A.U. convention at the Shoreham Americana Hotel. Other revisions included the following:

¶Top American athletes will have their transportation and expenses paid to the 1976 United States Olympic track and field trials, according to Dr. Leroy T. Walker, the new men's coach.

¶Approval was given for the first joint men's and women's Olympic trials in track and field for 1976.

¶The 1975 women's outdoor track and field championships will be held in White Plains and the men's meet in Eugene, Ore.

A.A.U. officials are negotiating for the first dual track meet against East Germany

Continued on Page 52, Column 7

Dave Anderson

The Kid in Left Field for the A's

Sports of The Times

OAKLAND, Calif., Oct. 17—When the Oakland A's discovered Claudell Washington two years ago, he was playing in nearby Berkeley for a sandlot team.

"What were you hitting?" he was asked last night.

"Close to .700 when I left," he replied casually.

He sounded as unimpressed with that average as might be expected for a 20-year-old rookie who was hitting .750, with three singles in four at-bats, when the World Series resumed tonight. He has the look of one of baseball's next great hitters. He also has the poise. As a teen-ager he was unknown and undrafted until an A's scout, Jim Guinn, Berkeley policeman, recommended that he be signed. Now he's unflappable. When he was inserted as the left fielder for last night's fourth game, Joe Rudi was transferred to first base and Gene Tenace was benched. Tenace naturally was annoyed, but Claudell wasn't apologetic.

"I feel I'm a good ballplayer myself," he said quietly. "I feel I can do the job, too."

He did, with two singles and also an intentional walk, loading the bases, that he resented.

"With runners on second and third," he explained. "I wanted to hit in that situation."

The Hit Off Gaylord Perry

Good hitters always do. Typical of that breed, he's proud rather than awed at competing in the World Series atmosphere. "I feel," he says, "like I've been up here 10 to 15 years." He's really been up here only 15 weeks. He was promoted from the A's farm club at Birmingham, Ala., in the Southern League in early July when he was batting .362 with 55 runs batted in and 11 homers. In one of his first games, he singled to drive in the A's winning run in a 10th-inning triumph over the Cleveland Indians that spoiled Gaylord Perry's opportunity for his 16th consecutive victory.

United Press International

Claudell Washington: poised and self-confident

"That's when I knew," he says now, "that I'd be here for good."

He hit .285 for the A's, with 15 runs batted in. He didn't hit any homers but he will. He's a muscular 6-footer who weighs 195 pounds, with most of his strength in a wide, firm neck and shoulders. Throughout baseball history, the great hitters arrived in the major leagues at a tender age. Great pitchers often mature late, as Sandy Koufax did. But the great hitters are great young hitters, such as Henry Aaron, Willie Mays, Ted Williams, Stan Musial and Joe DiMaggio.

"You're either a hitter," Williams once said, "or you're not."

Caudell Washington is a hitter. He just turned 20 on Aug. 31.

"He reminds me of a young Carl Yastrzemski," says Reggie Jackson, "because he hits the ball the other way. He's a left-handed hitter who hits the ball to left field. If he stays like he is, he'll hit .330 or .340 but if he tries to hit home runs, he'll hit .290 with 30 or 40 homers. He's got power. I had a home-run hitting contest with him in batting practice in Detroit one day. He hit one up on the right-field roof. I had to hit one up there, too. I didn't want to lose my throne."

Jackson may be converted into a first baseman next season in order to establish Washington as the A's right fielder.

"The thinking," says John Claiborne, the A's administrative assistant, "would be to move Tenace to catcher. Or if we kept Ray Fosse as the catcher, Tenace would be the designated hitter."

Claiborne was the A's executive who signed Washington on the recommendation of Jim Guinn after the June, 1972, draft.

"Jim Guinn told me," Claiborne recalls, "that he had this kid he'd like to sign. It was three days after the draft and I naturally wondered if the kid was so good, why hadn't Jim told me about him before the draft or why hadn't anybody else drafted him."

Watching the '73 Series

The main reason was that Washington hadn't played schoolboy baseball at Berkeley High.

"I didn't want to play baseball there because I preferred basketball and track. I was a high jumper," he recalled. "In junior high, I'd been a pitcher and I started our team's first give games. Nobody cared whether I hurt my arm or not, so I quit the team. I didn't want to go through that in high school. I did play for the Berkeley team in the Connie Mack League, and that's where the A's found me. My manager, Jim McCray, had played minor league baseball with Jim Guinn, the A's scout. I think the Orioles, the Mets and the Pirates looked at me, but nothing ever came of it."

The oldest of six children, he was working in a lawn-sprinkler factory when the A's signed him for a $3,000 bonus.

"I put that money in the bank," he says. "I don't care about home runs. I just want to be a .300 hitter, spend 10 or 15 years in the major leagues and make a lot of money."

His contract is for $17,500 now, but a World Series victory means about $28,000 in bonus money, including playoffs.

"I went to the last game of the World Series when the A's won it last year," Claudell Washington remembered. "Somebody gave me a ticket. I got in late and there were no seats left. I stood around in the bleachers."

He stood around in this World Series, too. In left field.

'New' Knicks Open by Spoiling Jazz Debut, 89-74

The New York Times

Bill Bradley of the Knicks defending against Ollie Johnson of the Jazz at the Garden last night.

By SAM GOLDAPER

The only resemblance between the Knicks of old and the Knicks who defeated the New Orleans Jazz, 89-74, last night in their National Basketball Association opener, was in the concept of defense.

Missing at Madison Square Garden were many familiar faces, the offense of old, especially with Walt Frazier sidelined with the flu, the style of play and the usual big crowd.

The attendance was announced as 15,833, but only because there are more than 13,000 season ticket-holders. Many of them passed up the opener.

But the defense was more than enough to carry the Knicks through a poor shooting night against an expansion team that was weakened because four of its best big men were back in New Orleans nursing injuries.

Without them the Knicks, who do not often outrebound teams, even in the good old days, won the battle of the boards.

John Gianelli, the Knicks center, operating against the aging and slow-moving Walt Bellamy and Toby Kimball, grabbed a career high of 18 rebounds, 14 off the defensive boards.

"Our defense was real good, said Phil Jackson, who scored 17 points, but hit only 5 of 13 floor shots." We pressured them into continuous turnovers [33]. But our offense was awful, we had so many open shots and missed them, I felt gunshy out there."

The only Knick on target was Earl Monroe, who scored a game high of 20 points. In a 7½-minute span from late in the second quarter into the third period, he collected 14 of New York's 19 points.

The Knicks' defense forced the Jazz into bad shooting and constant misplays. The Jazz shot only 36 per cent.

Red Holzman, the Knicks' coach, realizing that if his team is to have a respectable season while rebuilding it must win on defense, said he was pleased with the over-all defensive performance. He was especially happy with the job Dennis Bell and Henry Bibby did in limiting Pete Maravich, the league's second best scorer last season to 4 baskets in 16 shots.

When Maravich was asked about the poor shooting night, he said: "How can I concentrate on basketball at this time." He was alluding to the suicide death of his mother last week.

Holzman called a practice session for today to get his team ready for tomorrow night's game against the Philadelphia 76ers at the Garden.

"There are lot of things we are doing wrong offensively," he said. "Our offense has not been good. Some of us are doing things correctly in the gymnasium, but not in game situations. We need a lot of work."

Gene Shue, the Philadelphia coach, who was scouting the game, said: "If anybody expects the Knicks to be what they were, it's unrealistic. You can't lose as much as they have and not get into a rebuilding situation."

When someone asked him how he liked his new player, referring to Monroe, who is expected to be traded to the 76ers for the rights to George McGinnis of the Indiana Pacers, Shue smiled and when pressed said, "It's a deal, but not necessarily as reported."

The original deal was that Philadelphia, which has the rights to McGinnis, would give them up to the Knicks. In return Philadelphia would receive Monroe and cash, and the Knicks would get Fred Carter. It is now reported that the Knicks have sweetened the pot for the 76ers with the addition of Mel Davis.

Box score on Page 52.

FINAL ★★★★

DAILY NEWS

NEW YORK'S PICTURE NEWSPAPER®

15¢

Vol. 57. No. 83 New York, N.Y. 10017, Tuesday, September 30, 1975★ Partly sunny, 56-72. Details p. 71

CASEY STENGEL DIES AT 85

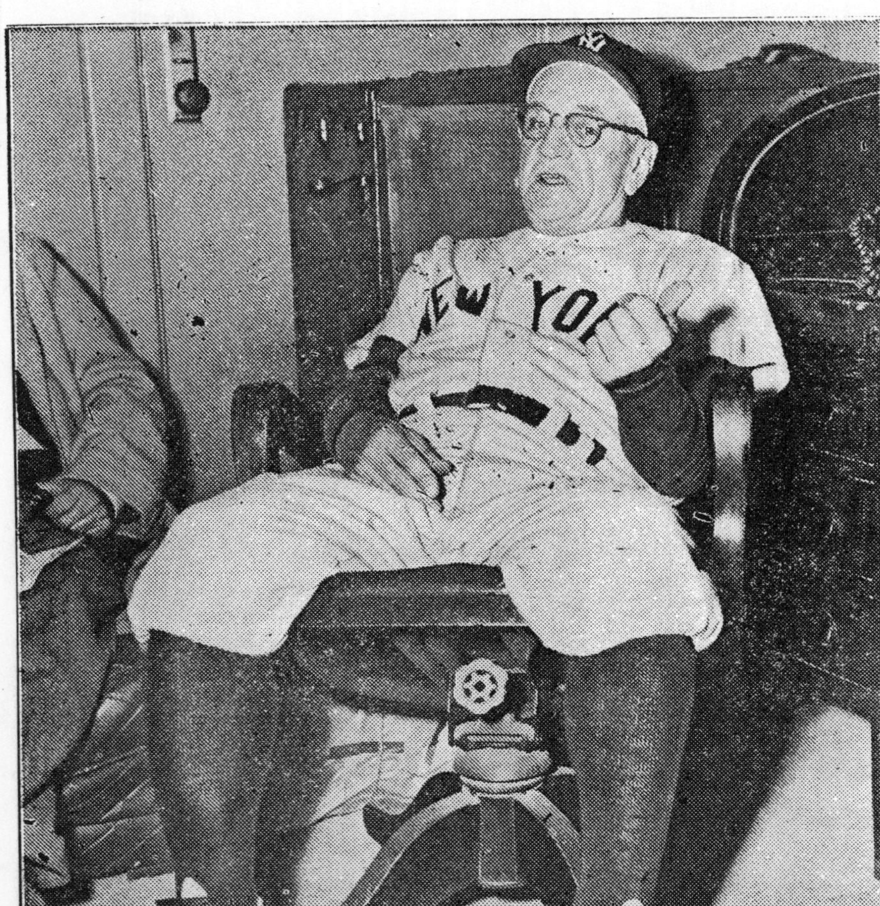

No. 37 Is Retired. In his last days as Yankee manager, Casey Stengel, who died early today, tells reporters in October 1960, that Whitey Ford will start third game of World Series with Pittsburgh. Ford won it, 10-0, but Yanks lost series, 4-3. Stengel was "retired" after season. In 1962 Casey began a new career as manager of the hapless Mets. Photo right, he tries to keep his cool as Metsies begin another disastrous season at the old Polo Grounds. *—Story on page 5; other pictures centerfold*

Report Patty a Willing Rebel

Stories on page 3

An ecstatic Carlton Fisk leaped on home plate with both feet following his dramatic, game-winning homer in the 12th inning which tied the Series. —Staff Photo

Bostonians view greatest ballgame in history of city

By WILL GRIMSLEY
AP Special Correspondent

BOSTON (AP) —It was like V-J day. Men went berserk. Women cried. Tykes bolted from the hands of their parents and got lost in the yelling-stampeding crowd.

There had never been a game like it in staid, old Boston— maybe never in a World Series—and New Englanders let their hair down in style.

The Red Sox had come back from the edge of Death Valley to beat the Cincinnati Reds in a 12-inning thriller and carry baseball's championship into tonight's seventh and deciding game.

It has to be an anticlimax.

"Tell you the truth, goose pimples were popping up all over me and chills were running down my back," said Bernie Carbo, who came off bench to stroke the eighth inning three-run homer that tied the game at 6-6.

"When I went to left field, I got the greatest ovation I've ever had—or ever will have. It really moved me."

CARLTON FISK, whose towering shot against the left-field foul pole in the 12th inning clinched the game, said he was worried that the crowd might envelop him before he made the four-base circuit.

"This is a great crowd and I knew they would go sky high and swarm out on the field," he said. "I made sure to touch everything that was white. I didn't want to miss a base."

Carbo and Fisk shared hero's honors and the adulation of the crowd with the old man and the kid.

For seven innings, 34-year-old Luis Tiant, who had won two of the earlier games, pitched his gizzard out—only to be recalled from the mound after dealing a home run to Cesar Geronimo in the top of the eighth, giving the Reds a 6-3 lead.

The wad of tobacco and bubble gum in his jaw having gone sour and the sweat of frustration dripping down his Fu Manchu mustache, old Luis lumbered to the dugout with his head down and his shoulders sagging.

"LUIS, LUIS, LUIS!" came the thundering chant from the crowd of 35,205, recalling similar salutes to Muhammad Ali at Zaire and Manila. Everybody stood.

"Loo-ey for President," read one huge sign which was carried from one end of the stadium to the other.

"You're still a hero," someone said to the hulking Cuban pitcher after he had showered and donned a blue flowered shirt.

"I'm no hero—I'm just me," the old man said modestly.

A similar cheer went up when the kid, Fred Lynn, the 23-year-old rookie centerfielder, smashed a home run in the first inning, giving Boston a 3-0 lead.

An hour and a half later cheers turned to stunned silence when the same Lynn went slamming into the wall at the 379-foot marker while trying to run down Ken Griffey's long blast.

He lay there for seeming minutes, unmoving. The crowd's alarm turned to near panic until Manager Darrell Johnson and the team trainer brought the young outfielder to his feet.

"He insisted on staying in," Johnson said afterward. "I let my players decide such things."

"No, I didn't hurt my head—I took a hard blow on my hip," Lynn said. "I didn't have any feeling for a long time. I felt paralyzed. But this went away. I wanted to stay in."

He was on base with a single and scored one of the three runs off Carbo's eighth-inning homer.

"I heard the crowd screaming as I ran around the bases," Carbo said. "What a thrill it was."

"A SUPER GAME, what can you say about it?" said Carl Yastrzemski, Red Sox captain and veteran of the 1967 losing seven-game series against the St. Louis Cardinals.

In the Red Sox dressing room, Bill Lee, who faces Cincinnati's Don Gullett in tonight's showdown, was asked how he enjoyed the game.

"I didn't see it," he said. "I was back in a room reading about black holes—the ultimate source of cosmic energy."

Bernie Carbo (left) and Carlton Fisk, two of the Red Sox heroes, celebrated in their dressing room after the game Tuesday night, won by Boston 7-6 in 12 innings.

Fisk picked best spot

By MILTON RICHMAN

BOSTON (UPI) — Maybe you remember how Roy Campanella always said you had to have some little boy in you to play professional baseball and nobody goes along with him more on that than another big kid by the name of Carlton Fisk.

You should've heard him go back to his boyhood in the Boston Red Sox dressing quarters early this morning after the majority of interviewers had gone, most of the pictures of him had been taken and what he done out there on the field more than an hour before finally started to sink in.

Johnny Bench, over in the losing clubhouse, had put it best about Carlton Fisk.

"He did what every single one of us wanted to do," said the Cincinnati catcher. "He hit the home run that won the ball game. If you were a ballplayer and ever wanted to pick the perfect spot, you couldn't ask for a better one unless maybe it would be in the seventh game."

Carlton Fisk decided not to wait that long.

He stepped up there leading off the last of the 12th inning, took the first pitch for a ball off reliever Pat Darcy, then ripped the second one high off the left field foul pole for a home run that brought the Red Sox a 7-6 storybook victory and squared the World Series at three games apiece.

Fisk had a hunch he was going to hit safely. Before leaving the Red Sox dugout, he said to Freddie Lynn, the next batter, "when I hit one off the wall, I want you to drive me in."

That was perfectly all right with Freddie Lynn. He wasn't about to argue.

Fisk then stepped in against Darcy, a stringy right-hander out of Troy, Ohio, and when he hit a sinker that was down and in on him, the ball took off quickly and began veering inside out toward the foul pole up against the left field wall.

The strapping 27-year-old Red Sox catcher wasn't sure whether the ball would wind up fair or foul, so instead of starting to run, which he should have done, he stood there stock still watching the ball, which he shouldn't have.

"Don't go foul! Don't go foul!" he hollered, as if that could possibly influence which way the ball would go.

Eventually, Fisk started down the first base line, sideways, so he could still keep an eye on the ball, and after taking a couple of hipperty-hops, he saw the ball had stayed fair whereupon he threw both hands in the air in a gesture of unrestrained joy.

Now he was back in the clubhouse talking about his emotions immediately after he realized he had hit the home run that had tied the Series and brought the whole business right down to tonight's seventh game.

"When you're a kid, you dream about being Ted Williams or Mickey Mantle and hitting a home run to win an All-Star game or one like this," said Fisk.

"You only dream about it. You never expect it to happen. When you think about what happened out there tonight, it's like something out of a story book. The pressure . . . playing against the best club in the National League . . . 12 innings . . . I mean, it's almost too good to be true."

Carlton Fisk's career with the Red Sox has been one fraught with misfortune.

He missed the first 17 games last year due to a groin injury and after returning to the lineup, he looked as if he was going to have a great year when his knee was torn up in a home plate collision on June 28.

Trying to come back after his knee operation this spring, Fisk broke his arm in an exhibition game and was out until June 23. When he came back from that, he suffered a split finger but still contributed substantially to the Red Sox pennant victory with his .331 average and fine work behind the plate.

Generally acknowledged to be the No. 1 catcher in the American League, Carlton Fisk has had to take the leavings after Johnny Bench in this series. Everybody says Bench and Fisk are 1-2, but everybody knows who's No. 1.

"I think Johnny Bench is an excellent catcher. He does things his way and I do them mine," said the Red Sox receiver after squaring the series.

Last night nobody did things any better than Carlton Fisk.

Even Johnny Bench would have to concede that, and he did.

—AP Wirephoto

Sparky Anderson and his catcher Johnny Bench conferred a lot Tuesday as the Reds used eight pitchers in the game.

Sparky still has ace, but chips now even

Jim Murray
L. A. Times Columnist

BOSTON— If there's anything I can't stand, it's an act that doesn't know when to get off.

Now, they're starting to take two days to play these things. Help!

The famous wall of Boston finally got into this World Series. At half past midnight on October 22nd of a game that started October 21st.

This World Series is like a guy with a lampshade on his head who thinks he's the life of the party and everybody wishes he'd go home. We may have to turn off the electricity on this thing, throw its clothes out in the street or locking it out of its room.

It was a great game but I wish they'd finish them on the same day they started. This is like the second longest and wettest World Series in history but it isn't going till it gets kicked out.

The hit that won it was a home run. It says here. As home runs go, Babe Ruth would throw it back.

The trouble with the Red Sox is, they don't know how to take a 10-count.

BUT, THE THING IS, it's an axiom in sports when you have your opponent on the ropes, you don't clinch with him. You throw your Sunday punch. When you have a ribbon clerk who is down to his lunch money, you raise him, you don't fold your hand or say "I pass." You don't punt when it's your ball on the 10-yard line.

You don't hand over the dice when you're hot.

But Sparky Anderson had the Red Sox down 3 games to 2 Tuesday night and he had a well-rested ace in Don Gullett who was so fast the last outing the Red Sox couldn't even hear the pitches clearly.

It was time to play the ace, go for the killer instinct, run the ribbon clerks out.

Sparky started a pitcher that only five pitchers in the history of baseball had given up more home runs. Before the first inning was over, he had tied them. Gary Nolan threw his eighth career World Series home run. In only 26 innings of World Series pitching, that is a mark which should inspire awe. That is major league gophering. It took Whitey Ford 11 World Series and 146 innings to set it. Only Don Newcombe did it in three World Series and he had Yogi Berra to help him.

It was like Dempsey letting Tunney get away in 1927. Don Gullett could very possibly have steered this game in the hangar for Cincinnati. Instead, when Sparky Anderson found out Boston's venerable Luis Tiant didn't have it on this balmy evening, he had only a collection of short relief men. It's why the horns are blowing all over this town at 2 o'clock in the morning, why they may be blowing again tomorrow morning at this same time.

WHEN YOUR OPPONENT is down to his last ace, his last knockdown, you move in, you don't pass or say "I'll sit this one out and see what happens." When you have your enemy in your gunsights, you take your best shot. When you have a bridgehead, you don't retreat. When you have an advantage, you force the issue. You raise. You fade. You turn the screws. You don't play for the next inning, the next game, the next war. You don't clinch, vamp, fold the hand. You never give him a second chance.

You don't spot the Red Sox three runs in the first inning unless you're the 1927 Yankees when it doesn't matter whom you pitch. In a World Series, you hit a man when he's down. You stamp on his fingers when he's clinging to the edge of the precipice.

You slam the cage on a lion, right? Well, Sparky let him out for air. And the next thing you knew, He was the one in the cage.

Anderson saved his ace, Don Gullett. But he may have let the hand get away that he could have trumped. He led with a deuce.

It was one of the greatest games ever played. For that, we can thank Sparky Anderson. He had the Red Sox ready to fold. And he didn't bet his hand. He had them ready to go down for the count. And he threw a lot of fancy footwork at them. He had them ready to sink for the third time. And he didn't pull the trigger. He had a chance to finish a game in one day. To say nothing of a World Series.

He may play his ace in the last game. And it may be enough. But the Red Sox are coming to the table with as many chips as he has now. But the horns may be blowing in Boston Wednesday night (or Thursday morning), too, because a guy didn't turn over his hole card before his opponent drew three-of-a-kind. Because Sparky's ante wasn't high enough. It looks from here as if the Red Sox may call his ace now — and say "Ha!" you should have called me when I was bluffing with Tiant. And he didn't have a thing."

Joe Morgan Drives in Winning Run off Red Sox Pitcher Jim Burton

AP Photo

Big Red Machine Captures Series

BOSTON (AP) — For several years, the Cincinnati Reds have been thinking like world champions . . . and almost playing that way. Now they've finally got the hardware to prove their supremacy.

After a fistful of agonizing frustrations, the Reds took care of that matter Wednesday night by beating the Boston Red Sox 4-3 in the finale of the exquisite 1975 World Series.

"We went to the Series in 1972 and thought we were the best team and were beaten by the Oakland A's and then we lost in the playoffs to the New York Mets in 1973 and thought we were the best then," said Joe Morgan, who got the game-winning hit with two outs in the ninth inning Wednesday night.

"Until we prove it on the field, we're nothing," Morgan added. "Now I can go home and say, 'We're the best.'"

The dramatic victory, won in Hollywood style on Morgan's single, not only gave the peppery second baseman a flag to wave but did wonders for Manager Sparky Anderson's psyche.

Before winning the tense seventh game in the hostile atmosphere of Boston's colorful old Fenway Park, Anderson had been discredited for not winning big games. His failures went back to the 1970 World Series, when the Big Red Machine was steamrolled by the Baltimore Orioles in five games.

Then, after running away with the National League pennant in 1972, the Reds and their supposed superiority were deflated by the A's in seven games. In 1973, the Reds won the NL's West Division but were taken in the playoffs by the upstart Mets.

"We always believed we were the best team," said Morgan, "even if we didn't win the championships."

Rose MVP

BOSTON (AP) — Pete Rose, the Cincinnati third baseman whose 10 hits were the most in the 1975 World Series, was voted Most Valuable Player of the classic here Wednesday night.

Rose drove in the tying run in the Reds' 4-3 victory over Boston and was voted the honor.

He receives a car from Sport Magazine.

Anderson had an explanation of sorts for the Reds' past failures. "The true test of a great club is what they do over a 162-game season," he said, "not what happens in a short five-game or seven-game series. In a short series, only luck prevails."

For a change, Lady Luck had a kiss rather than a slap in the face for the Reds.

The Boston Red Sox, in the championship round for the first time since 1967, were truly a Cinderella team. In preseason prognostications, the Red Sox were not even picked by most to win the East Division, let alone the American League pennant.

But at the end, the Red Sox were there, thanks to the best crop of rookies in recent major league seasons. Fred Lynn and Jim Rice led the Boston charge through the East. And the Red Sox raised even more eyebrows when they took three straight games from the three-time defending world champion A's in the AL playoffs.

With their awesome record behind them, the Reds had every right to play the

See BOSTON, 2C

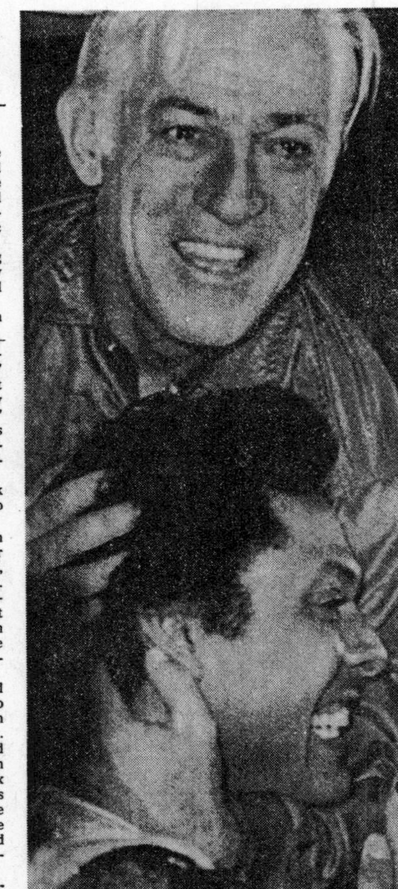

AP Photo

Joy: Sparky Anderson, Tony Perez

What Now for Csonka? Shula Thinks About It

MIAMI (AP) — Fullback Larry Csonka, out of a job when the World Football League folded Wednesday, says he'd like to rejoin his old National Football League team, the Miami Dolphins.

"I still want to play some football, but the league just fell out from under us," Csonka said in a telephone interview from emphis, Tenn., where he and former Dolphins Paul Warfield and Jim Kiick spent half a season playing for the WFL's Memphis Southmen.

"I intend to talk to Miami, and I've said many times that I'd prefer to play under (Dolphin Coach) Don Shula if I played anywhere again this year."

But Csonka, 29, said he would have to consider his contractual obligations, taken on when he and his two teammates signed a much-publicized $3.7 million package deal with Southmen owner John Bassett.

"We're just not sure right now where we stand," said Csonka, a former All-Pro NFL star who for seven years spearheaded the Dolphin offensive attack with bruising runs.

Saying he has received about half the money provided for by his WFL contract, Csonka said, "Practically, I just can't throw the rest of the money I'm due out the window. It would be an ignorant thing as far as my future is concerned to jump off the deep end real quick.

"I qve to go over a lot of legalities very thoroughly, like c r i s s-crossing contracts. I wouldn't want to jeopardize anything in my Memphis contract that might have legal implications with Bassett."

Although the three ex-Dolphins, now free agents as far as the NFL is concerned, signed personal services contracts with Memphis, those contracts were binding only as long as the WFL existed.

"It would be nice to think that everything could be peaches and cream," Csonka said. "But, unfortunately, pro sports is no longer peaches and cream. It's lawyers and complications that were beyond my belief when I started to play football."

Csonka noted that the Dolphins, 4-1 and tied with Buffalo for the American Football Conference's eastern division lead, seem to be getting along very well without him. Fullbacks Don Nottingham and Norm Bulaich have combined for 483 yards and nine touchdowns.

But Shula Wednesday expressed interest in talking to Csonka before an NFL-imposed Tuesday deadline in signing any players left out in the cold by the WFL.

"There's no question of Csonka's value to our team and of his contributions in the past," Shula said while praising the play of the Dolphins' current two fullbacks.

But Shula appeared lukewarm to the idea of rehiring Warfield, a veteran All-Pro wide receiver, and Kiick, used last year as a reserve running back by Miami.

"From all I've been given to understand, Warfield was considering retirement. Kiick's part in our offense has been filled very satisfactorily by Larry Seiple," Shula said.

While Kiick, 29, Wednesday expressed a hope that he would be able to continue his football career, Warfield, 32, said his f u t u r e plans were "incomplete."

WFL Non-Future Under Scrutiny

NEW YORK (UPI) — Upton Bell says the World Football League ran out of time. Dave Stringer says it ran out of fans. Chris Hemmeter says it ran out of money.

Wednesday the WFL shut down for the second and final time with the announcement by Hemmeter, the league president, that the board of governors has decided to terminate operations.

Hemmeter said two of the 10 teams, Birmingham and Memphis, would apply for admission to the National Football League.

Hemmeter said that it would two more years and $25 to $40 million to make the WFL a success.

"The governors have determined that this enormous capital expenditure in light of an unstable economy in our nation, continuing inflation, no assurance of national television revenues and a softening market for new leagues in professional sports was an unwise investment."

NFL Commissioner Pete Rozelle said his league member teams are free to sign any of the former WFL players— provided they are free of any contractual obligations — before Oct. 28.

The prize players of the league appear to be in limbo, however, because of John Bassett's decision to seek admission for his Memphis Southmen into the NFL. Bassett has personal service contracts with Larry Csonka, Paul Warfield and Jim Kiick—whom Don Shula would dearly like back with his Miami Dolphins.

"San Antonio is not the cause of the demise of the WFL," said Wings' governor Norm Bevan.

Bevan said San Antonio voted with Memphis, Charlotte and Jacksonville to keep the league alive, but failed by a 6-4 vote.

Said Charlotte Hornets President Bell, "We just ran out of time."

Born To Bite

Bulldog Henderson Followed His Dad's Lead

Georgia's Johnny Henderson

By MELITA EASTERS
News Correspondent

Johnny Henderson was born a bulldog. His father, Billy, played football and baseball for the University of Georgia from 1946 to 1950.

The fact that his father was a former University of Georgia standout had a lot to do with Henderson's decision to sign with the Georgia team, but it was not the only deciding factor. "It's something I always wanted to do," said the younger Henderson. "It was my decision entirely, Dad didn't pressure me."

Henderson has started every game this season as a defensive halfback. At 6-foot-0 and 185 pounds, Henderson often plays against much bigger men.

"The fact that they're bigger than you is not something you worry about," he said. "You've got 10 other guys on your side to help out."

Henderson's high school career was spent on the other side of the hall — as quarterback for the Mount De Sales High School team coached by Mike Garvin, assisted by his father. He also played basketball and caught for the baseball team. He made both the all-state football and baseball teams three years straight.

Coaching his son, was a real joy and pleasure, according to the elder Henderson. "I expected more and demanded more of Johnny," the elder Henderson said. "His teammates were often upset with me for pushing him so hard, but I didn't mind them being angry with me."

The feelings of the team about the coach-son relationship were probably best stated one day after a particularly long and extremely tough practice. One of Henderson's teammates said, "We think we've got it bad, but, Johnny has to go home with it."

According to Henderson, his father is one of his greatest fans and still offers advice on improving his game. "When I'm down, its really great to talk to him," the younger Henderson said.

Talking to his father is quite easy these days since the family now resides in Athens where Billy Henderson is head coach at Clarke Central High School. It's nice to have his family so near, according to Johnny. "I can take my laundry home and when I get tired of dormitory food I can go home to eat," he said.

Henderson did not play college baseball last year, but plans to this year. He is very proud of being drafted by the Chicago Cubs his senior year. Although he would prefer to play professional football, he feels that because of his size it is more realistic to aim for a professional career in baseball.

"Inexperience at this stage is the only factor not working in Johnny's favor," said Defensive Coordinator Erskine Russell. "His experience as a quarterback gives him a good idea of what the other team is doing. He has good speed and all the physical attributes necessary to be a good player."

The decision to use Henderson on the defensive team was not an easy one to make, according to Russell. The fact that we had two established quarter-

See HENDERSON ,3C

Tiger Win Lucky?

Tech Players Give Views on Auburn Upset

By AL JENNINGS
News Sports Correspondent

ATLANTA — Why the Georgia Tech Yellow Jackets lost to the Auburn Tigers last Saturday still remains a question.

Opinions vary from person to person. Reasons range from a "super Auburn performance," and lucky upset" to a "non-effort" by Tech. Reasons come from professionals to amateurs.

But, what about the football players opinions?

Yellow Jacket halfback Bruce Yeager of Elyria, Ohio, said, "We couldn't afford to give them the breaks that we did. They capitalized on our mistakes."

Defensive end Freeman Colbert of Warner Robins commented, "I think our defensive effort just fell a little short. Like the roughing the punter penalty I caused. I was sure I could block that one."

"Auburn had a real tough front four and it was a physical game," said fullback Tony Head, who scored three touchdowns. "But, we'll be alright."

All Yellow Jackets did not feel that Auburn played well or that Tech played that badly. Reserve quarterback Rudy Allen, of Columbus said, "I feel that our loss was due to the four fumbles and the injuries, but for the most part, our inability to compose ourselves and play inspired football."

Allen, who substituted Saturday for only five plays, said that despite the detrimental efforts and the fumbles, the situation was not one which could not have been overcome.

"The statistics show that we are primarily a rushing offense," he said quietly, "and any team which runs the ball as much as we do, should expect and should cope with fumbles."

Discounting the fluke theory, Allen said that any team would have defeated Tech, whose fourth quarter play he termed "unbelievable."

"It was hard to accept the fact that our offense was as ineffective as it was in the final minutes," he said.

After scoring twice in the third quarter, the Yellow Jackets lost their sting. Fumbles by quarterback Danny Myers and fullback Tony Head set up Auburn's final scores. And if Tech was not fumbling, they were in a punting situation.

"Our showing for the game was even indicated in Harper's (Brown) punting. He was leading the nation before, but I'm sure that his average dropped," said Allen.

Allen, who managed to complete a 10-yard pass despite onrushing Tigers, added that Tech's passing was also ineffective partly due to Auburn's newly-inspired pass rush and "mental errors" by the Yellow Jacket offense.

"Our offense seldom calls for a pass," he said, "but when the situation called for a pass, we couldn't come up with the completion."

Allen added that the offensive lineman, who was called for crossing the scrimmage line, nullifying Tech's last hope for a comeback, could easily have "gotten crossed up" because running

See ALLEN, 3C

Tech's Rudy Allen

FINAL ★★★★

DAILY NEWS

NEW YORK'S PICTURE NEWSPAPER®

LARGEST CIRCULATION OF ANY PAPER IN AMERICA

84

New York, N.Y. 10017, Friday, April 16, 1976

OPENER A SMASH HIT

Yankees Like Bombers of Old, 11-4

News photo by Anthony Casale

A Return to the Thrilling Days...

Bob Shawkey (←) who was on the mound when Yankee Stadium opened April 23, 1923, returned yesterday to do the honors for the new stadium. An enthusiastic crowd of 52,613, who cheered the procession of former players, fighters and others who had helped make the old stadium memorable, stayed to watch a typical Yankee victory. The league-leaders climbed on Minnesota pitching for 14 hits and there were two big innings to awe the faithful. Rudy May started, Dick Tidow got win. —*Stories p. 3, 72; other pics centerfold*

News photo by Dan Farrell

Yanks' Willie Randolph leaps high at second but Munson's throw goes into center and Twins' Rod Carew slides into second safely in third inning.

METS WIN, 10-8; ISLES, 5-3

Stories on Page 73

Mets Triumph, 5-4, on a Wild Pitch; Tigers' Fidrych Stops Yankees, 5-1

United Press International

Chris Evert defeating Olga Morozova in women's singles play at Wimbledon yesterday

Miss Evert Easily in Semifinal

By FRED TUPPER

Special to The New York Times

WIMBLEDON, England, June 28—If anything is predictable, it's women's tennis.

In the All-England championships today, top-seeded Chris Evert won from Olga Morozova, 6-3, 6-0, without strain. She has lost a mere 10 games in reaching the semifinals.

Second-seeded Evonne Goolagong was pushed by the vastly improved serve-and-volley game of Rosie Casals, but won, 7-5, 6-3.

Third-seeded Virginia Wade hit much too hard for Kerry Reid of Australia, triumphing by 6-4,6-2. And in the only tussle that had the crowd in an uproar, blonde Sue Barker was serving for the match against fourth-seeded Martina Navratilova when she suddenly tightened, legs going light and concentration waning. She was a victim of the English disease of being overwhelmed at doing well at Wimbledon, a malady associated with Miss Wade for 15 frustrating years.

"I was not expected to win, but I knew I could win," said the 20-year-old champion of West Germany and France.

The mirage vanished in the shimmering heat of the No. 1 court somewhere in the middle of the third set. Miss Barker was at 4-1, going like an express train; Miss Navratilova was too heavy and too slow, seemingly resigned to the beating that she was getting.

Martina had won the first set, 6-3, and lost the next, 3-6, as Miss Barker, with the most versatile forehand in women's tennis, hit winners that streamed by her. The only thing Martina could do was to keep the ball in play and pray that Miss Barker would collapse under the pressure.

"I wasn't moving to the ball," said Miss Barker. "I was so busy trying to concentrate."

So that 4-1 lead went glimmering, but Sue was still there at 5-3 and serving at

Continued on Page 39, Column 1

Rookie Hurls 7-Hitter for 8-1 Record

By THOMAS ROGERS

Special to The New York Times

DETROIT, June 28—The Yankees got their first look at Mark Steven Fidrych the 21-year-old right-handed rookie sensation tonight. And the hard-hitting Yankees had to be impressed.

The fidgety, 6-foot-3-inch bundle of nerves fed the Yankees a diet of on-target fastballs that enabled the Detroit Tigers to top the Yankees, 5-1, in the opener of a three-game series before a jubilant crowd of 47,855 at Tiger Stadium and a national television audience.

Fidrych, called "The Bird" by Detroit fans for his habit of flopping around the mound and his constant chattering to himself, allowed seven hits and only one was damaging. It was Elrod Hendrick's third homer of the season, a shot into the lower right-field stands.

As well as winning for the eighth time in nine decisions and pitching his eighth complete game, he also stopped the 20-game hitting streak of Mickey Rivers. The Yankee center fielder grounded out four times.

Another streak broken was New York's string of five victories. The loss cost them a game of their American League East lead over the Cleveland Indians, who

Continued on Page 38, Column 5

United Press International

Mets' Tom Seaver looks disconsolately at the ball as Manager Joe Frazier signals to the bullpen for a relief pitcher. Seaver pitched seven innings and allowed three runs.

Run in Eighth Tops Cards at Shea

By MURRAY CHASS

Overcoming a late St. Louis Rally and freakish windstorm, the Mets gained their fifth straight victory last night, edging the Cardinals, 5-4, on the bounce of a baseball.

Al Hrabosky, the Mad Hunfans and enrages others, threw the bouncing ball and Ted Simmons couldn't follow it well enough. It became a wild pitch and it gave the Mets the winning run in the eighth inning.

The Cardinals and the windstorm struck suddenly, at about the same time. But John Milner led off the eighth with a single but was out trying to steal second. Dave Kingman, who earlier hit his 26th home run, followed with a single and Hrabosky relieved Bill Greif.

Joe Torre batted for Ed Kranepool and singled Kingman to third. Mike Vail batted for Del Unser but struck out. That brought up Wayne Garrett, and Hrabosky bounced the first pitch in the dirt and it scooted between Simmons' legs to the backstop. Kingman romped home and all that was left was for Bob Apodaca to retire three Cardinals in the ninth inning.

The Cardinals overcame the Mets' 4-1 lead with a sudden late-inning effort.

Neither Did Lockwood

Tom Seaver had been cruising with seeming certainty toward his ninth victory, allowing just two hits in six innings. However, Lou Brock opened the seventh with a bloop single to left and Ted Simmons and Willie Crawford followed with line singles that brought Brock home.

Ron Fairly then rapped a one-bouncer to first, which Ed Kranepool fielded cleanly but which Seaver didn't catch cleanly when Kranepool threw it to him at first. That gave St. Louis its third run of the game and runners at first and third with no one out.

That also gave the manager, Joe Frazier, reason to remove Seaver and bring in Skip Lockwood. As Lockwood entered the game, a windstorm suddenly invaded the hot, muggy evening and whipped dirt and papers around the field. It was a bizarre scene as flying dirt enveloped the players and papers flew out of the stands behind first base and swirled their way onto the grass in the left-field corner.

The windstorm didn't ease up the rest of the inning and neither did Lockwood. Throwing only 12 pitches, he struck out Hector Cruz, Mike Tyson and Jerry Mumphrey in lightning-like order and the Mets emerged from the inning with a shaky one-run lead.

Minutes later, the lead evaporated altogether as Lockwood failed to match his initial effort.

With one out in the eighth, Don Kessinger walked and with two out, Simmons sin-

Continued on Page 38, Column 1

Big Red Sox Shuffle Pays Off

By AL HARVIN

In an attempt to snap his team's prolonged batting slump and stem its slide downward in the Eastern Division race, Manager Darrell Johnson made sweeping lineup changes for the Boston Red Sox's opener of a three-game home series against the Baltimore Orioles last night.

And it worked.

Butch Hobson, a rookie third baseman called up from the minors earlier in the day, was the most welcome change. He smacked a two-run inside-the-park homer in the sixth inning, leading the Sox to a 12-8 slugfest victory. The clout broke an 8-8 tie.

It was the third major league game for Hobson, a right-handed batter who hit .306 with 22 home runs and 67 runs batted in for Boston's Triple A Rhode Island farm club. His drive to left-center was just out of reach of Paul Blair. Hobson made a belly slide to beat the relay to the plate. Cecil Cooper scored head of him.

Besides calling up Hobson, Johnson replaced Rick Burleson at short with Steve Dillard, another rookie; put Cooper at first and moved Carl Yastrzemski to left in place of Jim Rice, who was made the designated hitter. His other moves were to put Bobby Darwin in right and shift Rico Petrocelli, the seasoned third baseman, to second.

That left only Fred Lynn, the center fielder and Carlton Fisk, the catcher, unchanged.

"We've got to try to put some runs on the board," said Johnson. His team had scored just 26 in their previous 10 games. "Our biggest problem lately has been our offense.

Baseball Roundup

I'm just putting the best nine offensive players on the field. It doesn't necessarily mean it will be the same next week. We've got a lot of hitters who have been trying too hard, trying to do everything all by themselves.

Johnson also made a pitching innovation of sorts by using Ferguson Jenkins in relief for the last four innings. It was the first relief appearance since 1970 for Jenkins, he got into the mood of things by striking out eight men to gain his sixth victory against eight defeats.

AMERICAN LEAGUE

Indians 5, Brewers 3

AT CLEVELAND — John Lowenstein and George Hendrick each slammed a home hun and Jim Bibby pitched 6 2/3 innings of two-hit relief to help send Milwaukee to its fifth straight and the ninth in its last 1 games. For the surging Indians, it was the 13th victory in their last 19 games. After spotting the Brewers a 2-0 lead in the first, Cleveland came back Lowenstein's first homer of the season. Don Money's run-scoring triple chased the Indian starter, Don Hood, and brought on Bibby. The big right-hander gave up only a leadoff single in the third to Henry Aaron and a two-out single to George Scott in the

Continued on Page 38, Column 2

Soviet Woman Sets 1,500 Mark of 3:56

MOSCOW, June 28 (Reuters)—Tatyana Kazankina of the Soviet Union became the first woman to break the four-minute barrier for the 1,500-meter run today. She ran the metric mile in 3 minutes 56 seconds in a pre-Olympic competition.

Her time cut more than five seconds off the listed world mark of 4:01.4 set by her compatriot, Ludmila Bragina, at the 1972 Olympics in Munich.

Raisa Katyukova, second in today's race, also beat the previous world record by clocking 3:59.8. Miss Bragina finished third in 4:02.6.

Breedlove: The Quest For Speed Burns Out

By JACKIE LAPIN

Four hundred . . . 500 . . . 600 miles per hour. Only one barrier remained unchallenged by Craig Breedlove, the world's fastest man on wheels—the speed of sound.

"It was my moment of truth," recalled Breedlove the other day. He was sitting in his bachelor pad at Manhattan Beach, Calif., a long distance from the Bonneville Salt Flats in Utah, where he had set his records.

"I had to admit to myself I didn't have what it took," he said. "I just knew I had to stop. Emotionally, I couldn't cope with the fear and pressure any longer. I had crashed going 620 miles per hour on the Flats and that shook me awake.

"'What am I doing?' I asked myself. "I had lost 20 good friends in 20 years of racing. At 600 miles per hour, one tiny mistake can end your life. I was in debt almost $30,000. I'd spent every cent I'd made in racing. It was time to decide who was running the show, me or my insatiable ego?"

Many people thought Breedlove was crazy. Looking back, he tended to agree with them.

At the age of 38, Breedlove is finding himself at peace for the first time in his life. In 1973 he sold his tools, leased his garage and went to work selling real estate.

Instead of designing jet-powered cars, he has turned his creative talents full-time to renovating two old beach cottages. He uses redwood and cedar and beautifully crafted mirrors of his own making.

"I've always been artistic," he says. "I never really wanted to race cars in the beginning. That was an accident because I couldn't get a

Continued on Page 39, Column 3

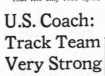

United Press International

Craig Breedlove in 1965

Dave Anderson

O. Is for ? and Other Baseball Trivia

What does the O. in Charles O. Finley stand for? No, not Owner, as so many like to think. It stands for Oscar.

In the years to come, that will be among the trivia questions inspired by the Oakland A's owner. At the moment Charles O. Finley is too controversial to be trivial. Also too stubborn. For once he had most people on his side when Commissioner Bowie Kuhn nullified the transfers of Vida Blue, Joe Rudi and Rollie Fingers for $3.5 million. But by refusing to use those players for more than a week,

Sports of The Times

Charles O. Finley managed to turn most people against him. Perhaps the O. should stand for Obstinate. But as a respite from the complications of the Finley Sales, the time for serious trivia has arrived in a paperback, "Who was Harry Steinfeldt? and Other Baseball Trivia Questions" (Playboy Press $1.50). The author, Bert Randolph Sugar, has assembled everything you wanted to know about baseball but were afraid to look up. It includes:

Q. Who was the only pitcher to lead his league in earned-run average and not pitch a shutout?

A. Dave Koslo of the New York Giants in 1949, with a 2.50 earned-run average despite an 11-14 won-lost record.

Q. What candidate received the most votes in a Hall of Fame election.

A. Sandy Koufax—344 in the 1972 balloting.

Benched for a Midget

Q. Who was the St. Louis Browns' player for whom Bill Veeck's midget, Eddie Gaedel, pinch hit?

A. Frank Saucier.

Q. Who played in at least 150 games the most consecutive seasons?

A. Nellie Fox, 11 seasons. Lou Gehrig played in 149 games in 1935.

Q. Who played in the most major-league games before he was 20 years old?

A. Robin Yount, the current shortstop of the Milwaukee Brewers, 243 games. Mel Ott was in 241 games.

Q. Who had the longest career under one major-league manager?

A. Don Drysdale, 14 seasons under Walter Alston of the Dodgers in Los Angeles and Brooklyn.

Q. Who was the only player to pinch hit for Ted Williams?

A. Carroll Hardy in the final week of the 1960 season when Williams's retirement had been announced.

Q. What modern player hit the fewest home runs in over 2,000 times at bat in the majors?

A. Floyd Baker, an infielder with five teams over 13 seasons, hit one homer in 2,280 times at bat.

Q. Who has broken up the most no-hitters?

A. Cesar Tovar spoiled five with the only hit in games pitched by Catfish Hunter, Dave McNally, Mike Cuellar, Dick Bosman and Barry Moore.

Q. Who hit the most career home runs at Yankee Stadium?

A. Mickey Mantle with 266; Babe Ruth hit 259 there and another 85 at the Polo Grounds when the Yankees played there.

Q. Who hit into the most triple plays?

A. Brooks Robinson, four.

Q. What was the only year that produced a triple-crown winner in each league?

A. 1933—Jimmie Foxx and Chuck Klein.

Q. Who were the four men to get 200 hits in a season and not hit .300 that year?

A. Lou Brock, Maury Wills, Matty Alou and Jo-Jo Moore.

Q. Who was the only player to hit a home run in each of his first two times at bat in the majors?

A. Bob Neiman for the St. Louis Browns in 1951.

Q. Who were the youngest and oldest pitchers to throw no-hitters?

A. Vida Blue at 21 years 3 months; Cy Young at 41 years 3 months.

Q. Who permitted the most bases on balls in organized baseball?

A. Louis Bobo) Newsom, with 2,630—1,732 in the majors and 898 in the minors.

Q. Who was the only pitcher to win 20 games before he was 20 years old?

A. Jake Weimer of the 1903 Chicago Cubs won 21 games at age 19.

The Best Fielding DiMaggio

Q. Who were the only pitchers taken out in the eighth inning while pitching no-hitters?

A. Clay Kirby of the San Diego Padres in 1970 and Don Wilson of the Houston Astros in 1974.

Q. Who was the only pitcher to win 200 games without having a 20-game season?

A. Milt Pappas won 244 games but never won more than 17 games in any one season.

Q. Which of the DiMaggio brothers had the highest career fielding average?

A. Vince with .981, to .978 for both Joe and Dom.

Q. How many grand-slam homers have been hit in All-Star games?

A. None.

Q. How many Heisman Trophy winners have played in the majors?

A. One, Vic Janowicz of Ohio State and the Pittsburgh Pirates.

Q. How many double plays did the Tinker-to-Evers-to Chance combination make in four World Series?

A. One.

Q. Who was Harry Steinfeldt?

A. The third baseman in the Tinker-to-Evers-to-Chance infield for the Chicago Cubs.

U.S. Coach: Track Team Very Strong

By FRANK LITSKY

Special to The New York Times

EUGENE, Ore., June 28—Let's say you are the coach of the United States men's Olympic track team. How would you like to go to the Montreal Olympics next month with a team that includes such world record-holders as Steve Williams, Dan Ripley, Terry Albritton and Jim Bolding; such 1972 Olympic medalists as Tom Hill and Ralph Mann; such present and past national champions as Marty Liquori, Reggie Jones, Maurice Peoples, Tom McLean, Randy Smith and Tom Woods, and a Pan American Games champion and Ronnie Ray?

If you are Dr. Leroy Walker, coach of the American men at Montreal, you already have reconciled yourself to their absence. For all those athletes, almost everyone a potential Olympic medalist, failed to qualify for the United States team in nine-day trials that ended yesterday.

Some were hurt and some performed poorly. It was do or die because, as American Olympic officials like to say, the team picked itself. The first three men and first three women in most events made the team.

"The men's team is very strong, very capable," said Walker. "There are some very pleasant surprises. If we are up to maximum performance, we will come off very well."

How well? How many gold medals?

"It's difficult to say," said Walker. "When you get to the finals, there are such fine

Continued on Page 38, C...

Max Nichols

NCAA ACTION UNFAIR TO 'U'

NEW YORK — There is a basic unfairness in yesterday's NCAA action to place all University of Minnesota men's intercollegiate athletics on probation.

Numerous athletes who had no part in any wrongdoing must pay the price for the alleged actions of three basketball players and the defense of those three by the Assembly Committee on Intercollegiate Athletics.

The university was placed on probation because the assembly committee refused to declare Mike Thompson, David Winey and Phil Saunders ineligible.

The NCAA's method of enforcing its rules in such "defiance" cases is to punish all athletes in a program. That is consistent with past NCAA policy.

But it is clearly unfair that the football team, hockey team, baseball team, wrestlers, swimmers and others must be banned from post-season competition because of a basketball program.

The university is a member of the NCAA and should abide by the rules, and the rules must be enforced. But if the policy of enforcing the rules is unfair, the policy should be changed.

LOOK FOR the New York Yankees to get better, probably with the addition of Reggie Jackson, Baltimore slugging outfielder who is now a free agent.

George Steinbrenner, Yankee owner, made it clear last night he will spend whatever money it takes to improve the Yanks from an American League pennant-winning baseball team to a world champion.

Steinbrenner

"I said when I bought the club in 1973 we would win a pennant in three years, and we did," said Steinbrenner. "Whatever it takes to win the World Series, we're going to get and do."

THAT KIND OF AGGRESSIVE talk and action would do wonders for the Twins. But Calvin Griffith, Twin president, has given no indication so far that he will make the aggressive move needed to get the Twins a left-handed starting pitcher and make them a contender.

I'M NOT CONVINCED the Cincinnati Reds rank with baseball's best all-time teams, even though they beat the Yanks four straight. The Reds weren't really tested by the Yankees, who made fundamental mistakes on defense and in base running.

Last night the Reds made a few mistakes of their own. Pete Rose blundered into a rundown between second base and third base, and there were errors on easy plays by Joe Morgan at second base and Dave Concepcion at shortstop.

The Reds are a great club in scoring runs. They can score with power, as Johnny Bench did last night with two home runs, and with speed and hitting to various fields. But their pitching is mediocre. If they are as good as manager Sparky Anderson says, they will be back in the Series a time or two.

THE 15 TWIN PLAYERS to be protected from the draft to stock expansion teams in Seattle and Toronto have been determined by Griffith. He can't release the names because of an American League ruling, but it is easy to pick the first 13.

They are catcher Butch Wynegar, infielders Rod Carew, Bobby Randall, Roy Smalley and Mike Cubbage; outfielders Larry Hisle, Lyman Bostock and Dan Ford, and pitchers Dave Goltz, Pete Redfern, Bill Singer, Tom Johnson and Tom Burmeier.

The other two probably come from outfielder Steve Braun, and pitchers Jim Hughes and Steve Luebber.

There has been some consideration of not protecting Braun. He signed a 1976 contract, but he could become a free agent again next year. The thinking is that expansion clubs might not want to risk the $175,000 draft price on a player who might leave a year later.

IF YOU'RE WONDERING why television can influence the scheduling of night baseball in the World Series, the answer is money.

Baseball will receive $92 million over a four-year period from 1976 through 1979 for the network televising of about 50 games a year, including the Series, the All-Star games, 26 Saturday games and 16 Monday night games.

The higher the ratings, the more money television can charge for commercials, the more baseball can get in the future. Sunday night's game had 65 million viewers — 14 million or 49 percent more than a Sunday afternoon Series telecast a year ago. Money talks.

Bench: '*My biggest game*'

By CHAN KEITH
Minneapolis Star Staff Writer

NEW YORK—When Johnny Bench was a six-year-old in Binger, Okla., his dad raked the dirt near their house, pushed around some sand, painted a few lines and set some bases in place.

That was Johnny Bench's formal introduction to baseball, a game that he's gripped by the throat ever since.

"That's the first field I ever played on," Bench proudly announces. "A few years ago they put in some seats, did some work on it and named it Johnny Bench Field. Now they play Little League games there.

"I still go back there. I'm proud of that field."

All of Binger, and all of Oklahoma, and all of Cincinnati, are proud of Johnny Bench, too . . . even before last night . . . but especially after last night. Bench hit two home runs to power the Reds 7-2 win and 4-0 World Series sweep of the Yankees.

It was an impressive show, even for a guy who's twice been the National League's Most Valuable Player and who was named this Series' outstanding player. It was, in fact, the pinnacle of the All-Star catcher's brilliant career.

"This was the best game I've ever had," he said, "because it meant so much, because of the magnitude of this event."

TWO YEARS AGO a tumor was removed from the right side of Bench's chest. He was quick to heal but slow to regain the greatness that had so distinguished his first years in baseball. The bad habits he developed last year while favoring his right side carried into the current season. Severance of a marriage that lasted less than a year didn't help, either.

This past season, Bench hit only 16 home runs, drove in only 74 runs and posted a lightweight .234 average.

"The only thing I did consistently all year was make outs," he said. "I came to the point where I concerned myself more with handling the pitchers than driving in runs. We had lots of other guys doing that. I guess I was just riding the crest of their success.

"Well, about three or four weeks ago that changed. I've tried 14 different ways to get my hitting stroke back. But I've had trouble getting my hands started and I've had trouble keeping my right shoulder in. Then I stumbled onto something that felt good and I've stayed with it.

"There was a time when I wasn't sure I'd ever find the solution. But I was prepared to accept that. Look, things aren't always going to be great. None of us remain the same forever. I'm sure your wives will concur.

"BUT I feel like those concerns are behind me for the moment."

The Yankees would be sure to agree. Ditto the Philadelphia Phillies.

In the National League playoffs, won by the Reds 3-games-0, Bench had just two hits but both were home runs, the last coming in the ninth inning of the third game to tie the score at 6-6.

His second home run, last night, also came in the ninth inning. It was a three-run bolt that turned a 3-2 thriller into a 6-2 romp. For the Series, Bench had eight hits, six runs batted in, two home runs, one triple, one double and a .533 average.

"I hadn't done it for the club all year," he said. "It was my time to help."

Associated Press

CINCINNATI'S SLUGGING CATCHER JOHNNY BENCH SOCKS SECOND HOME RUN OF NIGHT
Second homer comes off Yankee relief pitcher Dick Tidrow in ninth inning as Reds sweep Series

Munson sees red on Sparky's remarks

By CHAN KEITH
Minneapolis Star Staff Writer

NEW YORK — For five agaonizing minutes, the seemingly innocent words of Sparky Anderson singed the disbelieving ears of Thurman Munson.

"In a book I'm writing," said Anderson, occuped with the audience before him and apparently unaware of Munson standing behind him, "I talk about how God must have come down and touched Johnny Bench's mother. He must have said 'Mrs. Bench, I'm going to make you the mother of the greatest catcher that ever was.

"WHEN JOHN Bench is right," rambled Anderson, moments after his Reds had swept to their second straight World Series title with a 7-2, fourth game win over the Yankees, "there's none better . . . Thurman Munson is a great hitter, one of the best we've seen . . . but you should never put anyone in a position to be compared with Bench. Why embarrass the other guy. No one compares with Bench."

A few moments passed before Anderson finished his oratory. He

MUNSON
Turn to Page 12B

Probation could cost 'U' bowl bid

By BOB FOWLER
Minneapolis Star Staff Writer

It appears the University of Minnesota's football team will confront two opponents tomorrow at Memorial Stadium. The Gophers will oppose Iowa and Apathy.

Of the two, the latter may be the more difficult foe.

APATHY BECAME a problem yesterday when the National Collegiate Athletic Association announced it had placed Minnesota's entire men's intercollegiate athletic program on indefinite probation for failing to declare three basketball players ineligible for rules violations.

In other words, until a court reverses that ruling, or until the NCAA changes its decision, or until the school complies with the NCAA's order, the football team can't participate in a post-season game.

And there is no doubt members of this year's team have been thinking about such a post-season event since the first day of practice. Their plan has been to finish at least third in the Big Ten with a 9-2 or 8-3 record and accept an invitation to a bowl game.

NOW IT'S Goodbye Pasadena. So Long Miami. Adios New Orleans, Dallas and Phoenix.

Can the Gophers overcome what must be considered a mental defeat to concentrate on Iowa?

All university officials were under a gag rule until a press conference this morning at which the school's position was to be detailed. Apparently officials have decided to fight the NCAA in the courts.

Gopher coach Cal Stoll said he told his team of the impending sanctions after practice Monday. He said, "If you win your last five games, you'll still go to a bowl game."

Later he added, "I've been led to understand that this restriction won't effect our team this season. But I'm not certain of that."

What he means is that, if the team continues winning—it takes a 5-1 record into the Iowa game—and receives a bowl bit, it will accept.

It could be allowed to participate under the temporary injunction the university was expected to obtain against the NCAA on behalf of all other teams. The school's argument is that the NCAA can't penalize other teams and athletes for illegalities committed in basketball.

The legalities of the situation seem confusing and, at best, cheerless for the Gophers. Still Stoll has selected the only course open to him—he's retaining his optimism, saying:

"This won't have any effect on the play of our team."

If not, the Gophers still may have problems in retaining the bronze pig trophy called Floyd of Rosedale. As the Minnesota coach put it, "Iowa isn't a bad team."

The Hawkeyes have a 2-4 record, the victories coming over Penn State and Syracuse, prompting Stoll to say, "Any team that can beat those two must be respected."

Also, Iowa ranks second in the conference to top-ranked Michigan in defense.

"I worry about any team that plays good defense," the coach added. "Iowa is very good at stopping straight ahead plays and that's what we do offensively."

Offensively, Iowa Coach Bob Commings said, "It's no secret, we're going to have to throw the ball."

Yet the Hawkeyes are 9th in passing.

"Our quarterback, Butch Caldwell, has his confidence down now, but if he completes a few he can regain it quickly," Commings said. "He has the potential to become a very exciting player."

"So does Dennis Mosley," Stoll said. "He's a 9.5-second sprinter who scored on a 74-yard run last week. If he gets loose, we don't have anyone who can catch him."

Minnesota quarterback Tony Dungy, meanwhile, will be attempting to break several school career records.

He needs 87 yards to move ahead of athletic director Paul Giel's 4,117 yards in total offense. He needs five pass completions to surpass Craig Curry's 226 (1969-71) and must pick up 100 yards passing to top Curry's total of 3,060.

In talking about Iowa's five straight losses to Minnesota, Commings said he was optimistic because, "We've got to accentuate the positive, we've been negative too long here."

Stoll is trying to accentuate the positive, too. Indeed, perhaps Norman Vincent Peale should be coaching in this game.

The harried Gopher coach was asked if his team would be thinking ahead to next week's game at Michigan instead of concentrating on the Hawkeyes.

"No way," he answered.

Especially now.

'U' puck champs take NCAA verdict calmly

By JIMMY BYRNE
Minneapolis Star Staff Writer

Coach Herb Brooks has taken a University of Minnesota hockey team to the National Collegiate Athletic Association tournament for the last three years. The Gophers have won the title twice, including last season.

Yesterday's ruling by the NCAA that the entire Gopher men's athletic program was in non-compliance means the university would be kept from a chance to repeat as champions.

Gopher coach Herb Brooks told his squad of the NCAA decision last night.

"I told the squad to play each game as if nothing happened and to try to finish as high as they can in the Western Collegiate Hockey Association and then shoot for the playoffs. I told them not to be disturbed.

"The players reacted very calmly.

"I told them also that we have to have faith in the actions of our president (C. Peter Magrath), our Senate Committee on athletics, and the lawyers that things will work out for the best. We just have to wait and see what happens."

The Gophers open their home season today at 7:30 p.m. in the first of a two-game series at Williams Arena against St. Louis University. The second game is tomorrow at 7:30 p.m. Sellout crowds of more than 7,500 are expected for both contests.

Minnesota beat University of Minnesota-Duluth 9-5 in the Gophers only other game. Minnesota left winger Ken Yackel Jr. scored four goals in that exhibition game.

"Ken got one goal in the first period and just kept going," said Brooks. "He was hot."

THIS IS Yackel's third Gopher season. He played one season with the St. Paul Vulcans of the Midwest Junior League.

"I have only scored four goals in one game once before," said Yackel the former South St. Paul prep star. "That was when I was with the Vulcans and it was in a game against Thunder Bay."

Yackel's four goals is more than half as many as he scored last season. He made seven in 42 games for the 1976 NCAA champions. He had 15 assists. Two years ago Ken played 19 games and had one goal and one assist.

In the UMD game Yackel played on a revamped first line which had Mark Lambert at center for Tom Vannelli and Tom Gorance at right wing. Vannelli is still favoring an injured knee and Gorance has been held out of practice this week with a back injury. Both are now ready.

GOPHER TALES: Three of the freshmen to be watched in the series are Eric Strobel of Rochester, Rob McClanahan of Mounds View and Steve Christoff of Richfield . . . The trio has impressed Brooks very much . . .

Minnesota defeated St. Louis University four times last season, twice at Williams Arena 4-3 and 6-3, and twice at St. Louis, 7-4 and 7-5 . . .

VIKES EXPECTED TO SIGN GRIM

The Minnesota Vikings were expected today to sign wide receiver Bob Grim to a contract.

Grim, who played with Minnesota from 1967 to 1972 when he was traded to New York as part of the deal which brought back quarterback Fran Tarkenton, had a one-game tryout with the Vikings yesterday.

Grim was drafted in the second round by the Vikings in 1967. He missed the 1968 season with a knee injury. In his four Viking seasons he caught 84 passes for 1,241 yards and nine touchdowns.

The Giants traded him to Chicago last year where he caught 28 passes for 374 yards and two TDs. The Bears placed him on waivers in September.

Baylor

Garland

Campbell

Grich

Matthews

Jackson

Fingers

Rudy

Bando

Tenance

Gullett

With stars leading the way

Baseball sends young men east

By AL MARI
Staff Writer

NEW YORK — Alright now, everybody get together, follow the bouncing ball and sing:

"By the sea, by the sea, by the beautiful sea. You and me, you and me, oh how happy we'll be..."

Nobody is quite sure how happy 23 major league baseball teams will be within the next week or so, but after Thursday's "slave auction," (also called the Free Agent Negotiation Selections by major league baseball) was conducted at a midtown hotel, the certainty is that the next move is East ... towards the sea.

After the cream of the crop ... baseball's glamourpuss free agents ... were selected by the American and National League teams, the first phase was settled. The next phase will be settled when the teams trek to the Providence, R.I. Hospital Trust Building to negotiate with Jerry Kapstein, the agent who controls 10 of the superstars who have played out their option and seek employment elsewhere.

Kapstein and his brother Daniel will be talking to the general managers and owners of the 12 teams teams who have put in their claim for Joe Rudi, Gene Tenace, Bert Campaneris, Rollie Fingers, Don Baylor, Bobby Grich, Wayne Garland, Doyle Alexander, David Cash and Don Gullett.

"The players and the owners voted for this and we are just playing by the rules," Kapstein said. "It's the American way, isn't it? The players who produce the most get paid the most. I'll start talking to the clubs during the next few days in Providence."

The draft, unprecedented in baseball history, came about when the teams and the Major League Players' Association agreed to let players who had not signed a contract with their current (1976) team be placed on a kind of "Pay-me-and-I'm yours" basis. Each of the 24 players available were bidded for by all the teams, with the stipulation that the first 12 clubs that put in a claim would preclude others from drafting him. On Thursday, the prime candidates (drafted by 12 teams) were Baylor, Rudi, Gary Matthews, Tenace, Gullett, Bill Campbell, Garland, Fingers, Grich, Sal Bando and Campaneris. Six are ... sorry, were, Oakland A's.

"If I were an athlete I'd get all I could too," sputtered A's owner Charles O. Finley. "Because of the stupidity in baseball and in all sports, this stuff can't continue. The average club just can't come up with enough money and compete in the bidding. I wouldn't say I've been raped by this ... I'd say I've been royally raped. The draft! Hah! I think it's horsebleep."

Other owners were not quite as flamboyant or outspoken as Charlie O. They realize the process has just begun, and the numbers game (spelled $$$$$$$) is just beginning.

Reggie Jackson, who said a few hours after the draft that he was "considering" buying a baseball team of his own, is not represented by Kapstein, nor are Matthews, Bando and Campbell, all sure of commanding a figure in the millions for their services for the team that dickers best and comes along with the greenbacks. The rules, as set up, allow a team to sign only two of the players they draft, so that still leads to trade speculations, depending on what players the team signs, and for how much.

But the "filet mignon" players are still represented by Kapstein, who expects most of his stock to be signed "in the next four or five days."

"Providence," he concluded, "is a nice city. There are enough hotel rooms for the people I'll be doing business with. And we'll be doing business starting tomorrow."

"Tomorrow?" said Yankee president Gabe Paul. "I'll be glad to sit down with him right now."

But the Atlantic Ocean is so much more attractive than the Hudson River. So follow the bouncing ball, everybody, and remember the famous words: "By the sea, by the sea..."

NEW YORK (AP) — The team-by-team selections in Thursday's major league baseball re-entry draft:

Atlanta Braves

Gary Matthews, Don Gullett, Reggie Jackson, Richie Hebner.

Baltimore Orioles

Joe Rudi, Gene Tenace, Don Baylor, Don Gullett, Rollie Fingers, Sal Bando, Dave Cash, Richie Hebner, Bert Campaneris, Billy Smith.

Boston Red Sox

Bill Campbell, Bobby Grich, Rollie Fingers, Joe Rudi, Don Gullett, Dave Cash, Doyle Alexander, Bert Campaneris, Billy Smith.

California Angels

Joe Rudi, Don Baylor, Gene Tenace, Gary Matthews, Bill Campbell, Reggie Jackson, Bobby Grich, Bert Campaneris, Doyle Alexander.

Chicago Cubs

Gene Tenace, Bill Campbell, Don Baylor, Wayne Garland.

Chicago White Sox

Joe Rudi, Don Baylor, Gene Tenace, Wayne Garland, Don Gullett, Bill Campbell, Dave Cash, Sal Bando, Richie Hebner, Doyla Alexander, Bert Campaneris, Billy Smith, Steve Stone, Reggie Jackson, Tito Fuentes, Tim Nordbrook, Eric Soderholm, Royle Stillman.

Cincinnati

None.

Cleveland Indians

Wayne Garland, Don Baylor, Gene Tenace, Don Gullett, Gary Matthews, Doyle Alexander, Sal Bando, Bert Campaneris, Steve Stone, Paul Dade.

Detroit Tigers

Bobby Grich, Dave Cash, Wayne Garland, Bill Campbell, Rollie Fingers, Doyle Alexander, Sal Bando, Tito Fuentes, Steve Stone.

Houston Astros

Gary Matthews, Gene Tenace, Bill Campbell.

Kansas City Royals

Gene Tenace, Bill Campbell, Don Baylor, Wayne Garland, Bobby Grich, Rollie Fingers, Sal Bando, Dave Cash, Billy Smith, Tim Nordbrook.

Los Angeles Dodgers

Don Gullett, Reggie Jackson, Bill Campbell, Joe Rudi, Wayne Garland, Rollie Fingers, Doyle Alexander, Dave Cash.

Milwaukee Brewers

Sal Bando, Gene Tenace, Don Baylor, Joe Rudi, Gary Matthews, Wayne Garland, Bobby Grich, Dave Cash.

Minnesota Twins

Sal Bando, Wayne Garland, Dave Cash, Don Baylor, Gary Matthews, Doyle Alexander, Bert Campaneris.

Montreal Expos

Reggie Jackson, Gary Matthews, Dave Cash, Bill Campbell, Bobby Grich, Rollie Fingers, Bert Campaneris, Doyle Alexander.

New York Mets

Gary Matthews, Joe Rudi, Bobby Grich, Don Baylor, Don Gullett, Reggie Jackson, Sal Bando, Bert Campaneris.

New York Yankees

Bobby Grich, Don Baylor, Don Gullett, Gary Matthews, Wayne Garland, Reggie Jackson, Bert Campaneris, Dave Cash, Billy Smith.

Oakland A's

Bobby Grich, Gary Matthews, Bill Campbell, Wayne Garland, Don Gullett, Dave Cash, Richie Hebner, Doyle Alexander, Reggie Jackson, Royle Stillman, Billy Smith, Steve Stone, Tito Fuentes, Eric Soderholm, Tim Nordbrook, Paul Dade.

Philadelphia Phillies

Joe Rudi, Gene Tenace, Don Baylor, Bill Campbell, Don Gullett, Rollie Fingers, Richie Hebner, Bert Campaneris, Reggie Jackson, Tito Fuentes.

Pittsburgh Pirates

Joe Rudi, Gene Tenace, Sal Bando, Gary Matthews, Don Gullett, Rollie Fingers, Doyle Alexander, Reggie Jackson, Tito Fuentes, Royle Stillman.

St. Louis Cardinals

Bill Campbell, Rollie Fingers, Joe Rudi, Bobby Grich, Don Gullett, Sal Bando.

San Diego Padres

Joe Rudi, Bobby Grich, Gene Tenace, Gary Matthews, Rollie Fingers, Reggie Jackson, Sal Bando.

San Francisco Giants

Rollie Fingers, Joe Rudi, Gene Tenace, Wayne Garland, Bobby Grich, Sal Bando, Reggie Jackson, Dave Cash, Doyle Alexander, Richie Hebner, Tito Fuentes, Billy Smith.

Texas Rangers

Don Baylor, Bert Campaneris, Sal Bando, Wayne Garland, Doyle Alexander, Rollie Fingers, Richie Hebner, Steve Stone, Eric Soderholm, Tim Nordbrook, Billy Smith.

Reds use option and others follow

NEW YORK — The World Champion Cincinnati Reds stuck by their guns.

They said they wouldn't draft any of the 24 players who have played out their options, and they didn't. All the Reds did was exercise the right they have to draft a player currently on their roster ... lefty Don Gullett.

All of the other major league teams which participated in the Free Agent draft on Thursday in New York also exercised their option, e.g., the Yanks with Doyle Alexander, the Baltimore Orioles with infielder Bobby Grich, outfielder Reggie Jackson and pitcher Wayne Garland, and the Minnesota Twins with Bill Campbell ...

Even the Oakland A's, after choosing 12 players up for grabs, used the clause in the agreement that allowed them to select five of their six unhappy players ... Joe Rudi, Sal Bando, Bert Campaneris, Don Baylor and Rollie Fingers.

But the surprise of the day was the Yanks, in not selecting the rights to negotiate with Rudi, probably the best clutch hitter in the American League, and a natural for Yankee Stadium with his array of line drives. The Yanks selected, in order, Grich, Baylor, Gullett, Matthews, Garland, Jackson, Campaneris, Dave Cash and Billy Smith.

Their across-the-river rivals, the New York Mets, drafted the rights to negotiate with Matthews, Rudi, Grich, Baylor, Gullett, Jackson, Bando and Campaneris.

"Rudi is a fine player," said Yankee president Gabe Paul, "but he is not in our pattern, which is speed. Grich might be slow, although I don't think he is — but he falls into a different pattern. He is an infielder. Rudi might have a godd arm, but weak arms in our outfield didn't beat us in the World Series. A lack of hitting beat us. Add one guy who can run like Baylor to our team and that will make a hell of a difference.

"When we saw the drafting pattern unfold, we knew Reggie would be around by the time we had another selection, (the Yanks drafted 24th and last.) But by the time we were ready to select Rudi, he was gone."

Rudi was drafted by six teams on the first round alone while Jackson, the first pick of the draft by the Montreal Expos, had that lone claim on him. It seemed obvious the Yanks were not going to draft Rudi. Jerry Kapstein, his agent, said:

"I've already had talks with a lot of clubs, and I will say the Yanks have been very honorable to this point. I more or less knew who would be drafted by the various teams on the first round. Was Rudi on the Yanks' list? I'd rather not comment on that."

"The order we drafted in," added Yankee principal owner George Steinbrenner, "is not necessarily the order we'll go after. Maybe our third or fourth pick is the key man. There's a lot of strategy involved in the draft. I'd say Grich is one of our top guys, for our needs.

"I know the Kapstein brothers, and they are excellent people to deal with. As for Doyle (Alexander) I don't know if we'll be able to meet his demands. The main competition as I see it, for Grich, will come from Boston. As for Baltimore, they watched us like hawks. They took notes on every move we made. And the Mets? They drafted right along with us, didn't they?"

Almost, but not quite. Met general manager Joe McDonald and chairman of the board M. Donald Grant made no secret of the fact that Matthews, an all-around star for the San Francisco Giants, would be their prime objective.

"Rather than look for a righty or a lefty," McDonald said, "we are looking for the complete ball player who can help our club the most. If signing two of the players is realistic, we'll try and sign both, whoever they might be. The important thing is that we have to keep our own players happy, as well as the fans."

"Maybe," added Grant, "there will be a lot of money spent this time. It's a first. But nobody is going to spend money like this continually, and we have no intentions of going crazy."

—AL MARI

Arnsparger back for a N.Y. visit

By DON MARKUS
Staff Writer

HEMPSTEAD — The magic carpet on which Bill Arnsparger rode up to New York a little over two years ago made its return trip this week.

"It's what I wanted to do," Arnsparger said from Miami."I could have sat out until next Oct. 26 (a year from the day he was fired by the Giants) but I couldn't do that."

Arnsparger, after being let go by the Giants, came back to the Dolphins in the capacity which he left, as the team's defensive coordinator. On Sunday, he will make a quickie visit to New York when the Dolphins (4-4) take on the Jets (2-6) at Shea.

"I had to catch up with what they were doing," Arnsparger said of his first few days back home. "Nothing ever stays the same."

Surely, it didn't take Arnsparger long to catch up with the Dolphins. In the team's first seven games, the once-feared defense gave up 150 points — the same number they surrendered during the entire 1973 season. That was when Arns was the defensive genius, inventor of the 53 and the Dolphins were Super Bowl champions for the second straight year.

In his first game back, the Dolphins gave up only a John Smith field goal in a 10-3 victory over New England. The Patriots had been averaging 28 points a game. After the game, several Dolphins commented about the good psychological effect Arns had coming back. "I heard of guys winning for their coach," said linebacker Nick Buoniconti, "but never for an assistant."

Bunniconti has been a great help to the Dolphins defense, where Don Shula and his assistants had been playing the game "Who's Healthy This Week." Three defensive starters along with split end Howard Twilley have been knocked out with knee injuries.

"He's having a helluva year," said Lou Holtz of the veteran linebacker. "He's playing just like a rookie but without the rookie mistakes."

Holtz has been a wonder himself in re-arranging the starting lineups because of all the injuries. I'm glad we won because they say you have more injuries when you lose," he said. "The trainer is even out today."

Trainer Jeff Snedeker is listed as probable for Sunday and he doesn't even count on a team which has no less than 15 men trying to heal. Running backs Ed Marinaro and Steve Davis are definitely out, as is Jerome Barkum. Joe Namath is again questionable with a sore right knee and Richard Todd will make his second start. The rookie from Alabama had a less than auspicious debut last week up in Buffalo, throwing six-for-20 and one TD pass to David Knight. The Jets won, 19-14.Holtz has made a practice of never making his decisions at night."I never make decisions at night," said Holtz. "The only one I ever made at night was when I decided to get married ... and I wouldn't want to ruin a perfect one-for-one.

Minneapolis Tribune
Sports
1C..
Wednesday
October 19
1977

United Press International Photos

Reggie Jackson unloaded for his first of three World Series-clinching homers Tuesday, left. And when the 8-4 victory over the Dodgers was complete, Yankees pitcher Mike Torrez jumped in glee over catcher Thurman Munson.

Yanks are Series champions

Jackson smacks three home runs as Dodgers fall 8-4 in sixth game

By M. Howard Gelfand
Staff Writer

New York, N.Y.
The New York Yankees captured their 21st World Series championship Tuesday with an 8-4 victory over Los Angeles that assured baseball fans of a winter's worth of fireside conversation.

After a summer of debate over whether Yankees owner George Steinbrenner had foolishly attempted to purchase the championship, his most expensive acquisition — Reggie Jackson — dominated the sixth and final game of the series by hitting three home runs, driving in five runs and scoring four times. Only Babe Ruth before Jackson had hit three home runs in a World Series game.

"Nothing can top this," Jackson said afterward. "Who is gonna hit three home runs and clinch the World Series?" He laughed and shook his head as if in disbelief. "I mean, I'm not," he added.

Coupled with two previous homers, three RBIs and six runs in the series, Jackson's performance established him as the hero of the Yankees' surprising performance. His role was even more dramatic because it triumphantly ended a year in which Jackson's ego was depicted as a corrupting force in a team that needed no more talent.

And Jackson knew that he and Steinbrenner had achieved sudden vindication. "I'm happy for Steinbrenner," Jackson said. "That man had his neck stuck out farther than me. If I had been a bust, he would have even been more of a bust."

Steinbrenner had paid Jackson about $3 million for five years, and he had insisted that Jackson bat in the clean-up slot. From the start, Jackson's penchant for publicity had caused tension, and as the series unfolded, the tensions were exacerbated by the crush of publicity. But the Yankees only played better.

The question as the day began was whether the Yankees could survive the sudden absence of any new controversy. Not only had no one demanded to be traded in the past 24 hours, but old tensions were in danger of being calmed.

Manager Billy Martin, balancing precariously all year between employment and unemployment, had been given a bonus and expression of faith by Steinbrenner before the game.

The bonus, said Jackson, "was planned perfectly, because it was needed. The timing was perfect."

But it was Jackson whose timing best approached perfection. With the Dodgers leading 3-2 in the fourth inning and Thurman Munson on first, Jackson lined a homer to right field off Burt Hooton. Hooton, who had dazzled the Yankees with his dipping knuckle-curve in Game 2, couldn't put the pitch across the plate last night, and Jackson was the last batter he faced.

With the Yankees seemingly lulled into a New York version of complacency, the Dodgers had taken a 2-0 lead in the first inning. With two outs, Reggie Smith reached first on an error by shortstop Bucky Dent, who was unable to make a difficult backhand play. A walk to Ron Cey and a triple by Steve Garvey produced the runs off Mike Torrez.

The Yankees tied it in the second on a walk to Jackson and a long homer by Chris Chambliss. By then it was apparent that Hooton was having trouble directing his knuckle-curve. Chambliss, waiting for the fast ball, hit it 400 feet even though it was no higher than his knees when it crossed the plate.

Series continued on page 4C

Yanks' victory ends in violent Saturnalia

By M. Howard Gelfand
Staff Writer

New York, N.Y.
The night ended with a curious tableau: The fans destroying the field, each other and themselves in celebration. The field had as much garbage on it as the streets outside the stadium, and large chunks of turf had been torn away to expose the dirt below.

The police made a few random stabs with their nightsticks, but all they could do was beat an occasional fan senseless.

The violence was all of a random nature; even Reggie Jackson, who owned the night, had been the target of firecrackers as he stood in right field.

It was the kind of self-destruction that characterized the year for the Yankees, and it would not end even with glory. Right to the end, the Yankees sounded like victims of each other's talent and wealth.

On the surface, it should not have been that way. Ed Figueroa, the latest Yank to yearn for freedom, was back in uniform instead of in Puerto Rico. Manager Billy Martin had been given a new Continental and $30,000 to buy gas for it. The

Yankees continued on page 4C

Goodrum tackles guard job

Charles Goodrum

By Allan Holbert
Staff Writer

His lodge brothers in the Loyal and Protective Order of the Vikings Offensive Linemen call him "Goody."

Even if his name wasn't Charles Goodrum they might call him Goody anyway, because he usually says "my goodness" in situations where his less mellow fellows probably would use a harsher expletive. And right now his nickname might have something to do with the way he has been playing.

The Vikings' left guard once got so down on himself and the game when he had to play tackle that he almost quit. But now he is considered by his coaches to be one of the most improved players on the team.

And there are those — Chicago's defensive linemen included, perhaps — who feel that the entire Vikings' offensive line is vastly improved over last year's model, although wet fields may have hidden that improvement until Sunday.

"This team has developed further in terms of its offensive scheme than any since I've been here," Goodrum said. "But as far as displaying a good offense, we didn't have a good track to do it on until Sunday.

"One reason is Ed White. When you have a talent like that playing backup and trying to get your job, everyone is going to play better. He's capable of starting any time. Having him there motivates all of us. He came in for me when I got my knee kicked in Tampa and I experienced a miraculous recovery just watching him," Goodrum said.

John Michels, the offensive line coach, feels that the dry field was just one factor contributing to the Vikings' impressive running game (4.7 yards per carry) Sunday.

"We just happened to meet a defense that was to our liking," Mi-

Goodrum continued on page 4C

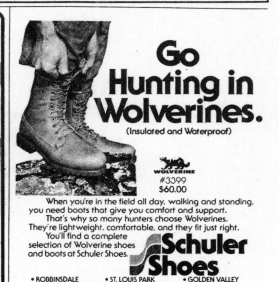

Metro/SPORTS

LATE CITY

Tuesday, Oct. 3, 1978

Yankees Beat Red Sox for Title

Continued From Page 1

"I remember the feeling in 1948, when we won with Cleveland," said Manager Bob Lemon, "and this is the way it was."

The Yankee clubhouse—packed tighter than Times Square on New Year's Eve—exploded in a strong show of emotion for this very professional team.

"It's great, said Lemon. "They earned it."

They certainly did, beating the Red Sox in their home park with a left-hander. This left-hander was Ron Guidry, who collected his 25th victory against three losses.

"I went as far as I could," said Guidry. "I started getting stiff. That's when I came out."

The Red Sox, who had battled up hill all the way since falling from a 14-game first-place lead on July 19, got off in front.

Carl Yastrzemski, the grand old man of the Red Sox, homered off Guidry in the second for a 1-0 lead. Then a sixth-inning double by Rick Burleson, a sacrifice and Jim Rice's R.B.I. single made it 2-0. The Fenway crowd of 32,925 was going wild with anticipation.

In the seventh Torrez, the $2.5-million free-agent ex-Yankee, cracked under the strain.

Chris Chambliss singled, Roy White singled. After Jim Spencer flied out for Brian Doyle, Lemon had no pinch hitter for Dent. So Dent batted. First he fouled one off his ankle. Then he hit one fair off the screen for a 3-2 lead. A walk to Rivers, a stolen base and Thurman Munson's double made it 4-2.

Reggie Jackson hit his 27th homer of the season in the eighth for a 5-2 lead.

Then Boston battled back against Rich (Goose) Gossage. It was close but no cigar.

The Red Sox got two in the eighth off Gossage on a double by Jerry Remy and singles by Yastrzemski, Carlton Fisk and Fred Lynn.

The ninth was the season in miniature, the Red Sox good but not good enough, the Yankees always a little better when they had to be.

With one out Burleson walked and Remy singled. Rice hit a long fly and Burleson was on third with the tying run.

Then the 39-year-old Yastrzemski popped out easily to Graig Nettles and the Yankees were the Eastern champions.

It had to be the worst kind of news for the Kansas City Royals.

The Yankees' Bucky Dent returning to the dugout after he smacked a home run against the Red Sox. AP photo

Intrigue Spiced a Playoff 30 Years Ago

BOSTON, Oct. 2 — For many years, Johnny Orlando was an all-purpose fellow in the clubhouse of the Boston Red Sox whose duties included spying on the opposition. On Oct. 4, 1948, the Indians outfoxed the Boston superspy. This was not a factor in their playoff victory that day, but it didn't hurt either.

Bob Lemon was a member of the Indians that year, and he recalled the incident before leading his new team, the Yankees, against the Red Sox in the first such playoff since division play began in 1969.

"The game was on Monday," Lemon said. "Bob Feller had been beaten by Hal Newhouser of Detroit on Sunday. Gene Bearden had pitched on Saturday. I had pitched on Friday. The question was, Who would pitch in Boston?' "

Bearden was a left-hander with a knuckleball. He had the best earned-run average in the American League, 2.43, and was a 20-game winner. Lemon was also a 20-game winner. Feller, who had won 19, was still considered the best pitcher in baseball.

"Lou Boudreau [the Cleveland player-manager] came to us after the Sunday loss and said Bearden would be the pitcher," Lemon went on. "He told us to keep it quiet so he could confuse Boston."

The Indians took the overnight train to Boston,

Maury Allen

arrived at 8:30 in the morning, checked into the Kenmore Hotel for a couple of hours' rest and then took cabs to the ball park.

"When we got there," said Lemon, "Boudreau had put baseballs into the shoes [the standard sign for a starting pitcher] of Bearden, Feller and me. Orlando came snooping around the clubhouse, looked into the shoes and almost collapsed."

Minutes before game time Boudreau finally allowed the Red Sox to see his lineup card, at home plate. "Bearden, P," was marked clearly on the card.

Bearden was never much of a pitcher after that, because hitters began laying off his knuckleball and crushing his fastball. This day he was shaky all game.

"He only gave up five hits, but he also walked five, and a dozen line drives were caught," Lemon said.

The Indians went after 37-year-old Denny Galehouse, who had volunteered for the assignment when other Boston pitchers ducked it, with a vengeance. Boudreau had four hits, including two homers. Ken Keltner hit a three-run homer. Larry Doby had two doubles. The Indians collected 13 hits and won, 8-3.

"I was on the team," said the Yankee president, Al Rosen. "I was up for a cup of coffee at the end of the season. Since it was considered a regular-season game, I was eligible."

Rosen didn't get into the game, but he did get a big scare.

"A lot of players pulled my leg and told me I was starting," he said. "They said Keltner was hurt and I would be in it. I was a wreck until I saw the lineup card."

WEATHER TODAY
Partly Sunny
High, 86; Low, 67
Yesterday
High, 80; Low, 66

THE INDIANAPOLIS STAR

"Where the Spirit of the Lord is, there is Liberty"—II Cor. 3:17

TODAY'S CHUCKLE
These days a person's take-home pay can hardly survive the trip.

VOLUME 77, No. 59 | FRIDAY, AUGUST 3, 1979 | ☆ ☆ ☆ ☆ | CARRIER DELIVERED 85c PER WK. MOTOR DELIVERED 90c PER WK. Single Copy 20c

N.Y. Yankees' Thurman Munson Killed

By UPI And AP

Akron, Ohio — New York Yankees catcher Thurman Munson, the first member of the club ever to win the Rookie of the Year and Most Valuable Player awards, was killed Thursday in the crash of a private plane at Akron-Canton Regional Airport. He was 32.

Don Rawlings, a Federal Aviation Administration official, said the crash took place at 3:02 p.m. EST. Munson was killed while he was practicing landing and two other passengers were injured. The twin-engine Cessna Citation burst into flames when it hit the ground 1,000 feet short of the runway.

The injured were identified as David Hall, 32, and Jerry Anderson, 31, both of Canton. Hall was in fair condition with

More Pictures, Page 60

second-degree burns on his arms, hands and face. Anderson also was listed in fair condition.

HALL, THE co-pilot, was taken to the burn unit at Akron Children's Hospital. Anderson, a friend of Munson's, was taken to Timken Mercy Hospital in Canton.

Munson recently purchased the plane and had his uniform number, 15, painted on its side. He was in Wichita, Kan., during the All-Star break to receive his certification to fly the plane.

Summit County (Ohio) Sheriff's deputy Jeff Kashburn, one of the first officials at the scene, said he saw the two survivors running from the crash site and he tried to reach the plane. "I tried but I couldn't come closer than 30 feet because of the intensity of the flames. The body was burned beyond recognition."

The Yankees had a day off Thursday after playing in Chicago and Munson decided to spend the day in his hometown of Canton.

The director of the Akron airport called Yankee owner George Steinbrenner in his New York office and told him of Munson's death.

STEINBRENNER called as many of the Yankee players as possible and Manager Billy Martin "cried like a baby" when told of Munson's death, according to a club spokesman.

Munson married Diane Dominick in September 1968, and the couple had three children — Tracy Lynn, 9, Kelly, 8, and Michael, 4.

Munson won the Rookie of the Year award in 1970 and the Most Valuable Player award in 1976. He batted more than .300 in five of his nine full seasons with the Yankees and was the American League's third leading hitter in 1975 with a career high .318.

He also set a World Series record in 1976 for the highest average by a player on a losing team, .529.

Considered among the best catchers in baseball and one of the most consistent hitters in the game, Munson batted more than .300 for three consecutive seasons before dropping to .297 last year, an average that ranked ninth in the American League. Munson, known for his tremendous intensity, ranked among the top clutch hitters in the game with eight game-winning hits last season and a .303 average with men on base.

HE ALSO APPEARED in 13 games as a right fielder last year and this week was moved to first base after complaining of pain in his knees.

Last season Munson played with bad knees, was hit in the head by a pitched ball and was struck in the throat by a foul ball, but still appeared in 154 games as the Yankees won their third straight pennant and second straight world championship. He had off-season surgery on his right shoulder.

Munson, a former All-America catcher at Kent State, was the Yankees' No. 1 draft pick in 1968. He reached the majors after only 99 minor league games, winning the Gold Glove award as the top fielding catcher in the American League in 1973, 1974 and 1975. In 1971 he tied a club record with only one error for the season.

This season Munson appeared in 97 games and was batting .288.

MUNSON IS THE second New York athlete killed in the last six weeks. Troy Archer, a defensive tackle for the pro football New York Giants, was killed in

See MUNSON Page 10

(AP Photo)
THURMAN MUNSON
Was Practicing Landing

'TALKING' THROUGH WEST EUROPE NATIONS

U.S. Confirms PLO 'Contacts'

By UNITED PRESS INTERNATIONAL

The United States and Palestine Liberation Organization confirmed Thursday that they are engaged in indirect negotiations through West European countries — contacts angrily condemned by Israel as appeasement to Saudi Arab oil producers.

"The United States and the PLO have started indirect negotiations through other parties, particularly Western European countries," Talal Naji, a member of the PLO executive committee, told the Qatari News Agency in Amman, Jordan.

State Department spokesman Tom Reston said Thursday the United States was "working with other countries working on an agenda" for the Aug. 23 U.N. debate on Palestinian rights, postponed last week amid indications the PLO might be willing to modify its hard-line demands.

ON TUESDAY, Hodding Carter III — Reston's boss — referred to the same U.N. debate, and said, "We are in touch with a number of other countries and they have contact with the PLO."

The New York Times reported Thursday that high Carter administration officials believe Saudi Arabia and other Arab oil states might begin exerting pressure on world oil consumers unless noticeable progress is made on Palestinian autonomy in the next 10 weeks.

Israel reacted to the reports of a shift in U.S. policy toward the PLO with anger. Israeli sources said their cabinet would discuss at its next meeting Sunday "the change in the U.S. policy toward the PLO, which contradicts American commitments made to Israel."

Although both the United States and the PLO confirmed their mutual contacts, neither side would discuss which West European nations were involved, or give any details of the negotiations.

AT THE HEART of the dispute are U.S. attempts to work out language for a U.N. resolution on the Palestinian issue that would be acceptable to the PLO and would also include provisions of U.N. Resolution 242, the basis of all Mideast peace efforts since the 1967 Arab-Israeli war.

Resolution 242 called on all sides to agree to live in peace within "secure and recognized boundaries" and on Israel to "withdraw from lands" occupied in the 1967 war.

The PLO has rejected Resolution 242, partly because it refers to Palestinians only as refugees. The guerrillas insist on having their own sovereign state, a demand which, in turn, has been repeatedly rejected by Israel.

Yehiel Kadishai, one of Prime Minister Menachem Begin's top aides, said the Israeli reaction to a change in U.S. policy would be "sharp and harsh. The credibility of the United States has been shattered. Commitments given are not being adhered to."

ASKED ABOUT motivations behind the U.S. initiative, Kadishai said, "Nowadays, when oil is the main commodity, the whole world is yielding to the Arabs. There's no doubt about it."

For their part, the Palestinians publicly adhered to their former demands.

In his interview with the Qatari agency, Naji said, "The Palestinian stand in any negotiations . . . are based on the recognition of the national Palestinian rights and particularly their right of self-determination and establishing their independent state."

Help Is On The Way!

Sullivan, Vigo Disaster Funds Asked; Levee Bursts, Flooding 25,000 Acres

By TIM McDONOUGH

Gov. Otis R. Bowen Thursday declared flood-ravaged Sullivan and Vigo counties disaster areas and sent a request to President Carter to make them available for federal disaster relief funds.

A similar declaration could be made after a survey is made of the damage caused Thursday morning when a Wabash River levee burst, spilling flood waters onto 25,000 acres of corn and soybeans in eastern Posey and Gibson counties in the vicinity of Griffin.

Meanwhile, flood warnings remain in effect on the lower White River and the East Fork of the White.

Partially sunny skies and air drier than it has been for 11 days helped dry other flooded areas of the state including English and Marengo where cleanup work continued in the wake of heavy flooding there last week.

FAIR SKIES are forecast for today in Indiana but there is a 30 percent chance of showers and thundershowers tonight and Saturday.

Included in Bowen's request for funds was Vermillion County which already had been declared a disaster area by Mr. Carter but is eligible only for compensation to individuals.

Bowen's request would expand that to include money for replacement of public facilities.

The request was made after a new evaluation of the area by state Civil Defense workers, according to the governor's executive assistant, William J. Watt. He said the flood damage in the areas was greater than at first thought.

WATT SAID that the damage to public facilities in Sullivan County was in excess of $200,000, in Vermillion in excess of $160,000, and in Vigo more than $575,000.

Watt also estimated agricultural damage at $7.1 million for Sullivan, $4.8 million for Vermillion, and $400,000 for Vigo. In addition, he said there was flood damage to about 80 homes in Sullivan County.

President Carter earlier declared 10 counties in southern and southwestern Indiana eligible for federal disaster funds.

Watt said civil defense workers were forced to abandon sandbagging operations along the Wabash River in Posey County Thursday morning when it became apparent a levee constructed there would not hold the rising waters. Only about seven or eight houses were in danger from the ever-widening Wabash River in the Griffin area.

ONE VOLUNTEER suffered a heart attack late Wednesday while helping place sandbags on the Griffin area levee. The volunteer, Robert Riggs, 36, of near Owensville, was listed in critical condition in Gibson County Hospital at Princeton. Another 10,000 acres to the north of Griffin in the Crawleyville area of Gibson County are in danger from

See FLOOD Page 6

AMENDMENTS 'UNACCEPTABLE'

House-Senate Committee Named To Work On Fuel-Rationing Bill

Washington (AP) — Congress abandoned on Thursday the attempt to send President Carter a standby gasoline-rationing bill before the congressional August recess.

Instead, a House-Senate conference committee was named to work out a compromise. Leaders said that they hoped it could go to the President's desk in September.

THE CONFERENCE was named after the Senate formally rejected, by voice vote, a rationing bill approved by the House on Wednesday night.

The legislation would give the President authority to ration gasoline and take other fuel-saving steps during major fuel shortages. But the House saddled the bill with a number of weakening amendments.

Senate Majority Leader Robert C. Byrd said the House had "emasculated" the bill. He claimed there was no way House and Senate differences could be resolved without sending the bill to conference.

And Sen. Bennett Johnston (D-La.), who will be one of the Senate negotiators on the bill, said, "We had to weigh symbolism against practicality." He indicated practicality prevailed.

At the White House, presidential spokesman Jody Powell also called the House-passed bill unacceptable.

He expressed hope that the objectionable parts could be smoothed out in conference.

What exactly does the adminstration object to in the bill?

"I DON'T HAVE time to list them all," Powell said.

Generalizing, he said the bill had many "ill-advised, unenforceable amendments."

"The one that's brought over from the House has been riddled with loopholes," said the Senate Energy Committee chairman, Henry M. Jackson (D-Wash.), of the House-passed bill.

Byrd urged the House and Senate negotiators on the bill to "get together during the recess and try to work out this thing."

But other congressional leaders said they didn't expect formal conference sessions actually to begin until early September — although they said staff sessions to develop ground rules on the bill were likely during August.

Byrd also dismissed the symbolic importance of producing a bill, saying "symbolism is not the issue. There is no gain in passing a plan for the purpose of symbolism if the plan isn't going to work."

AND HE SAID the White House shouldn't be critical of Congress for not getting the measure out before its August recess — noting that when the House rejected Mr. Carter's original plan in May, the President refused to propose a new one.

"The President should have sent another plan up to the Hill rather than simply washing his hands and saying I challenge you to come up with something," Byrd said.

White House and congressional energy specialists met most of the day trying to devise a strategy for rushing a compromise bill through Congress before the beginning of the four-week August recess.

But they gave up in mid-afternoon after realizing it couldn't be done — especially in light of House Speaker Thomas P. O'Neill's assertion that he intended to stick to his plan to recess the House at 7 p.m. EST.

Senate leaders said that one of the House amendments they object to the most is one allowing businesses to ignore the 78-degree national thermostat-setting requirement if they can save an equiva-

See RATION Page 6

BODY IDENTIFIED

Boyfriend Quizzed In Divorcee's Murder

By LISA G. BAIRD

Police Thursday night continued questioning a man believed to be a boyfriend of slain Rita Jane Ridge, 29, 219 Rockshire Road, whose body was dragged from the swollen waters of Fall Creek Tuesday morning.

She had been strangled and her hands were tied behind her back with a length of electric cord.

The man, whose identity was withheld, had been under interrogation by detectives since 2 p.m. Thursday.

Late Thursday, police were administering a lie detector test to the 29-year-old man. He had turned himself in at police headquarters about noon Thursday after he learned he was wanted for questioning.

Investigators revealed Friday morning that the man showed deception on certain questions, but declined to elaborate.

Detectives said the man lived about four blocks from Mrs. Ridge, divorced wife of Dr. Fredrick R. Ridge Jr., a family practice physician at Corydon who is in the process of moving his practice to Linton.

MRS. RIDGE'S identity was established early Thursday after her car, a 1977 gold Cutlass, was found abandoned

See MURDER Page 6

Affirmative Action Rules Show Ex-Cong Could Get Job Priority

North American Newspaper Alliance

Washington — Former Vietcong soldiers could get priority over non-minority U.S. citizens for jobs, training and government loans under revised federal affirmative-action guidelines, according to the U.S. Department of Labor.

"The revised guidelines require private employers who hold government contracts of ten thousand dollars or more to give preference to resident aliens from Latin America, Africa, Asia and the Pacific Islands," said Deputy Director Richard Devine of the Office of Federal Contract Compliance Programs at the Labor Department.

"We don't make the laws, we just enforce them," Devine added.

THE SITUATION came to public attention after Rep. Harold Sawyer (R-Mich.) complained on the House floor that significant numbers of former Vietcong soldiers are among the thousands of Vietnamese boat people entering the United States as refugees.

Sawyer said he learned of the presence of former Vietcong soldiers among the fleeing boat people after reading a London Observer story that was reprinted in the Washington Star.

"It makes no sense for an affirmative-action program designed to correct past discrimination against U.S. minorities to also give preference to citizens of other countries just because they happen to fall into recognized minority groups and hold 'green cards' allowing them to work in this country," Sawyer said in an interview.

"THIS MEANS that a former Marine with a Purple Heart and a Silver Star for service in the Vietnam War has to get

See CONG Page 6

The Weather

Joe Crow Says:

The Senate decided that the gasoline rationing bill the House sent them wasn't rational.

Indianapolis — Partly sunny today; high, 86. Chance of showers and thunderstorms tonight; low, 67. Chance of showers and thunderstorms again Saturday; high 86.

Indiana — Partly sunny and warmer today; highs, 85-89. Chance of showers and thunderstorms tonight; lows, 64-69. Chance of showers and thunderstorms again Saturday; highs, 84-89.

CRIME ALERT

If You See A Crime
Committed Or Spot
Suspicious Activity
Call This Number
911

Inside Today's Star

News Summary On Page 3

Star Telephone Numbers

Circulation	633-9211
Main Office	633-1240
Want Ads	633-1212
Scores After 4:30 p.m.	633-1200

Today's Prayer

Thank You, gracious Lord, for this moment of prayer, bringing to us a peace and strength to cope with whatever this day may bring. In Your name we pray. Amen.

DIDN'T SELL QUOTA OF CANDY

Dad Testifies On Children's Little League Bar

By WILLIAM E. ANDERSON

A father of two Little League ballplayers testified Thursday in Superior Court his children were not permitted to participate in games this season because they were unable to sell their quota of candy.

Charles W. Ponsler, a chauffeur for the Perry Township Fire Department, told Judge Michael T. Dugan his children, Carole Ponsler, 13, and Paul Ponsler, 10, were barred from playing in the Edgewood Athletic Association Inc. Little League because they sold only 38 bars of candy instead of the 96 bars he said the league required for membership in the league.

Ponsler filed a suit in May against the association and its president, David Conley, seeking $20,000 in damages.

THURSDAY, DURING opening arguments of the trial, Challoner Morse McBride, attorney for the Ponslers, was chastised by Dugan for "editorializing" for her remarks of "innocent children who have been the victim of mercenary adults who victimized them."

Dugan told Mrs. McBride to state her case without editorials.

Mrs. Bride then recited events that led to the two children not being able to play baseball this season after she said the father attempted to do hauling to pay their part of the funding.

"But the children were damaged mentally and physically and lost a summer that never can be relived. They just wanted to play baseball, but now we have a case of a $29 price tag for the abuse of the children," she said.

Jerry Miller, attorney for the athletic association, denied the accusation during his opening remarks and said testimony will reveal that the league did everything possible to rectify the problem.

PONSLER TESTIFIED he was told of

See LITTLE Page 6

POST SPORTS

THURSDAY, SEPTEMBER 13, 1979 25 CENTS

YAZ JOINS THE CLUB

Ty Cobb	4191	Willie Mays	3283
Henry Aaron	3771	Nap Lajoie	3251
Stan Musial	3630	Paul Waner	3152
Tris Speaker	3515	Cap Anson	3041
Honus Wagner	3430	Lou Brock	3017
Pete Rose	3339	Al Kaline	3007
Eddie Collins	3311	R. Clemente	3000

Carl Yastrzemski 3000

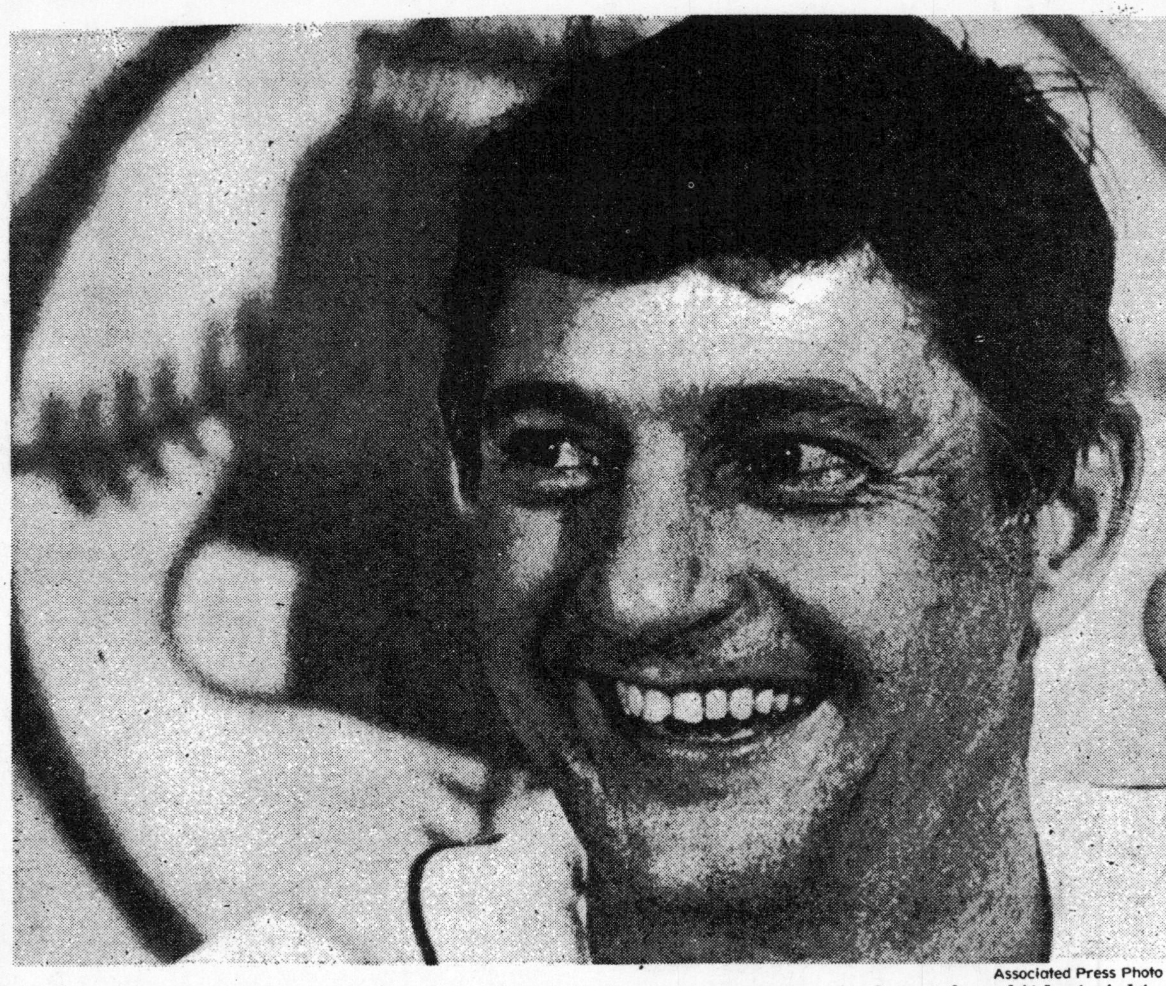

Associated Press Photo

Carl Yastrzemski unwinds in the clubhouse after picking up his 3000th major league base hit last night.

3000!

'I wanted to get that hit for those people in the seats.'

By MIKE MARLEY

BOSTON — The summer is officially over in this city. It ended in glorious fashion at 9:39 last night when Carl Yastrzemski hit a ground ball past Willie Randolph and into rightfield at Fenway Park.

Yaz, New England's 40-year-old demi-god, finally put himself in the record book, 13 trips to the plate after he collected hit No. 2999 Sunday. He became the 15th major leaguer to get 3000 hits and the first American Leaguer to have both 3000 hits and 400 home runs.

The Red Sox beat the Yankees 9-2 last night, but it was Yaz who kept the Fenway Faithful on the edge of their seats. Batting third, he walked on four straight pitches against Catfish Hunter in the first inning. Hunter retired him on a fly to the rightfield warning track in the third. The media mob that has followed Yaz for days started thinking it would go one more night when he grounded out to first base in the fourth.

But Yaz got two chances against reliever Jim Beattie, a Dartmouth grad from South Portland, Me., and he made the best of the second.

Leading off the sixth with the Red Sox ahead 8-1, Yaz went out on a routine 4-3 play. But in the eighth, on the 15th pitch he saw, this son of a Southampton, L.I., potato farmer was able to knock the ball into right.

There were two out and none on and Boston led 8-2 when Yastrzemski came up for the fifth time. He connected on Beattie's first delivery, and the ball went past Randolph cleanly, the way Yaz had said two weeks ago he wanted his historic hit to come. The place went wild.

The game was delayed for an on-the-field ceremony, and a choked-up Yaz joked with the fans about how long it took him to get No. 3000.

"I know one thing — the last hit was the hardest of the 3000," he said. "I really enjoyed all the standing ovations you gave me in the last couple of days. I really don't know what to say. I want to thank all the guys. I'd like to thank Don Zimmer (heavy boos). And I'd like to thank Haywood Sullivan and Buddy LeRoux (more booing), Mrs. Yawkey and my family."

When the commotion had subsided, Yaz attended a press conference in a room under the leftfield stands. Here the Boston pols got in on the act. Someone handed out a message from Mayor Kevin White proclaiming today "Carl Yastrzemski Day" in the city and someone else handed out a

Continued on Page 78

- **Reds lengthen lead: P. 79**
- **Pacers cut Meyers: P. 79**
- **College grid preview: P. 74**

Pops brings home bacon for Pirates

Associated Press

Willie Stargell deplaned in Pittsburgh early this morning toting a trophy fit for a World Series hero

By BOB FOWLER
Minneapolis Star Staff Writer

BALTIMORE—Willie Stargell put on quite a show Wednesday night. First, he played as if he had discovered the Fountain of Youth. Then, he talked as if the water was intoxicating.

Few players have had such spectacular performances in the World Series, especially in the seventh game. And few have been so quotable when baseball's showcase affair ended.

Stargell, the 38-year-old captain and father figure of the Pittsburgh Pirates, was the event's Most Valuable Player on the field and off it. He alone made the 1979 World Series a memorable tournament.

He had four hits in Game 7, including a decisive two-run homer, in the Pirates' 4-1 victory over Baltimore. He had a .400 batting average against the American League's best pitching staff, knocked in seven runs and set a Series record with seven extra-base hits (four doubles, three homers).

And when the television cameras had been turned off, when President Carter had left the stadium after offering his congratulations, Willie Stargell laughed and cried and sipped some wine.

He also talked . . . and talked . . . and talked . . . and . . . .

"This equals my biggest thrill in baseball," Pittsburgh's all-time leader in homers and RBIs said. "My biggest thrill until now came in 1959 when I signed to play pro ball. I got a $1,500 bonus and $175 a month. That was big money in those days."

Those were the days when Stargell was being groomed to become the left-handed hitting equal of the famed Roberto Clemente. Even Baltimore Manager Earl Weaver could recall them fondly after suffering defeat.

"I was managing our team in the Arizona Instructional League in 1960," he said. "We played the Pirates' team and we thought we could get Willie out with low pitches.

"Our pitcher, Johnny Ellen, threw one low and he hit it over the fence. He threw one at the waist and Willie hit that out, too. He threw one high and that was a home run.

"I told Ellen to pitch him higher. He threw one about cap high and Stargell hit a line drive that almost knocked my pitcher's head off. Ellen looked at me and shouted, 'Was that high enough?' "

While those may have been days in the sun, these are the days of wine and roses for Stargell. Not only is he Pittsburgh's senior citizen, he is the man who holds The Family (it was his nickname) together.

"Our family hasn't been overrated," he said. "It's not fair to criticize that nickname, unless you've seen what we've been through all year.

"I don't have the words to describe the closeness on this team. We overcame, we scratched, we crawled. We have a lot to be proud of.

"We made 'We Are Family' (Sister Sledge's disco hit) our theme song. But we weren't trying to be sassy, or fancy. It just seemed to typify our club.

"We had whites, blacks, Latins, you name it. We had 25 guys united in achieving a common goal.

"I'm proud to be the MVP. I don't know what kind of award I'll receive (a new sports car), but it should be divided among our coaches, manager, clubhouse men and players. We needed all of them to win."

Stargell was standing on a platform in a large room filled with newsmen. He spoke into a microphone while squinting because camera lights were shining in his eyes. He still had on his gold-and-black Pirate uniform and there was a white towel draped around his neck. He was holding a bottle of wine (California white) in his right hand.

Suddenly, a woman broke out of the crowd and rushed the stage. She hugged Stargell and they embraced for about a minute. Then she sat in a nearby chair and wiped her eyes.

"This is my sister, Sandra, and I think she knows what I'm feeling at this moment," he said.

Then he started to sob and he held the towel to his face for several seconds.

"Look at me up here acting just like a big old dummy," he said.

"You had a helluva Series, man," shouted a Baltimore fan who had sneaked into the room wearing an Oriole cap.

And the newsmen in the room applauded.

They had seen what Stargell had done throughout the seven-game series. His team had trailed 3-1 after four contests, but he wouldn't let his teammates concede to the Orioles.

He never lost his cool. He never tried to become a cheerleader. He kept his composure and his dignity and he influenced those around him.

Second baseman Phil Garner, a MVP candidate because he managed at least one hit in every game, said: "No better man could have won the award. Every time we needed a lift, he came through for us. And he never changed whether we won or lost."

The best example of that occurred in the eighth inning when the Orioles were delighting their fans with an apparent miraculous finish.

This contest was played in 65 degrees—the event's best conditions—and Oriole fans were ready for a parade when Rich Dauer homered off Jim Bibby to start the third.

The Pirates had managed only three hits off lefthander Scott McGregor until Bill Robinson grounded a single to left with one out in the sixth. Two of those hits had been by Stargell, a bloop single to left and a bloop double in the same spot.

Now he stepped to the plate, went though his pre-pitch bat gyrations and hit McGregor's slider into the right-field seats.

"I was lucky on the first two hits, I just

Pirates
Turn to Page 16B

Stargell watched long drive. . .

. . . clear Ken Singleton's glove for game-winning home run

Richfield survives battle of hitters

By BOB SCHRANCK
Minneapolis Star Staff Writer

A towel draped around his body, Scott Schuveiller leaned against the locker room wall. He shook his head to clear the cobwebs.

"I'm still a little dizzy," he apologized. "That was the toughest team we faced. They've got some big guys who know how to hit."

And a hitting game it was. On both sides. It was played with the intensity of a state championship game because that was what it represented to both teams.

And when the gun sounded, Richfield, led by the play of Schuveiller, was a 14-6 victor over Burnsville Wednesday. Although there is one more game in the regular season, the triumph advanced the Spartans to the 1979 Class AA playoffs as Richfield clinched the Lake Conference South Division championship.

Richfield has been the team of the big break all season. It comes on the slashing drive of Schuveiller, or the strong tackling of linebackers Kirk Budde and Steve Garskel, or on a punt high and strong.

Burnsville added another dimension with some moments of over-eagerness that brought fumbles and penalties that ultimately torpedoed the hopes of the team.

"We told the team championship games come in lots of different packages," said Burnsville Coach Dick Hanson. "At the Met (where Burnsville won the first Class A title in 1972), at St. Peter, at Rosemount. We told them this was our state championship game.

"You get opportunities like this very seldom. You have to seize them immediately."

Richfield turned out to be the opportunistic team. After an early exchange of fumbles, Richfield had the field position. Quarterback Tim Thomas sneaked the final yard and kicked the extra point to give Richfield a 7-0 first-quarter lead.

Burnsville was right back in the game when Rick Jurchisin slid off tackle for the final 11 yards, bringing his team within a point after the extra point was missed.

Richfield's insurance touchdown, which was never really enough points to make the coaches comfortable, came with 5:58 left in the first half. The key play in the 61-yard drive was a 39-yard run by Schuveiller to Burnsville's 15-yard line.

Three plays later, (fourth-and-three at the 8), Richfield Coach Dick Walker sent in *the* play. With Schuveiller decoying the defense, Brian Ammann swung into the middle to take the ball for a touchdown.

"Brian made a heck of a catch," said Walker. "It was a slant pass against the grain. You better hit it or she's intercepted. They were keying on Schuveiller so we had him flare out. He draws a few with him."

* * *

A 70-yard touchdown pass with less than two minutes to play provided the winning margin for Edina West's 14-7 victory over Bloomington Jefferson.

Ed Chapman, on the receiving end of the aerial bomb launched by quarterback Scott Housh, crossed the goal line with just 1:36 left on the clock. Doug Bailey scored a two-point conversion on a pitchout from Housh. Housh put the Cougars in the game with a second-quarter touchdown pass to Scott Wales, but that extra-point effort failed.

Toronto turns off Stars again

By DAN STONEKING
The Star's Sports Editor

TORONTO—The Minnesota North Stars will not go undefeated this hockey season, but then you probably knew that.

Coach Glen Sonmor said he did.

"I never expected we could win them all," Sonmor joked after the Toronto Maple Leafs beat Minnesota 6-2 Wednesday night.

The defeat ended the best getaway—three victories—the North Stars have had in 13 National Hockey League seasons. If you want to throw in the last six exhibition games (Minnesota won five and tied one), it was the first loss in nearly a month, and neither management nor labor were enamored with the feeling.

Sonmor doesn't often show emotion after a loss. And while he wasn't kicking water coolers or throwing chairs or locking reporters out of the locker room, he was disappointed in the digits glowing on the Maple Garden scoreboard.

General Manager Lou Nanne put it this way: "Toronto was horse-bleep, and we were worse."

What Nanne was saying was that the Leafs demonstrated something less than midseason form.

"We aren't any super team," said Sonmor. "We are a very good team if we play up to our potential. But when we play without any zip, when we aren't aggressive, we are just an ordinary squad. I thought the second period was the worst we have played in a long time."

Perhaps it was the worst since March 31, when the North Stars were bombed here 7-1 and the Leafs rapped in four goals in the middle 20 minutes.

Wednesday night, Toronto only got three, from Dan Maloney, Dave "Tiger" Williams and Lanny Mc-

Stars
Turn to Page 18B

The Philadelphia Inquirer

SPORTS FINAL

Vol. 303, No. 114 ©1980, The Philadelphia Inquirer Wednesday, October 22, 1980 20 CENTS

Champions!

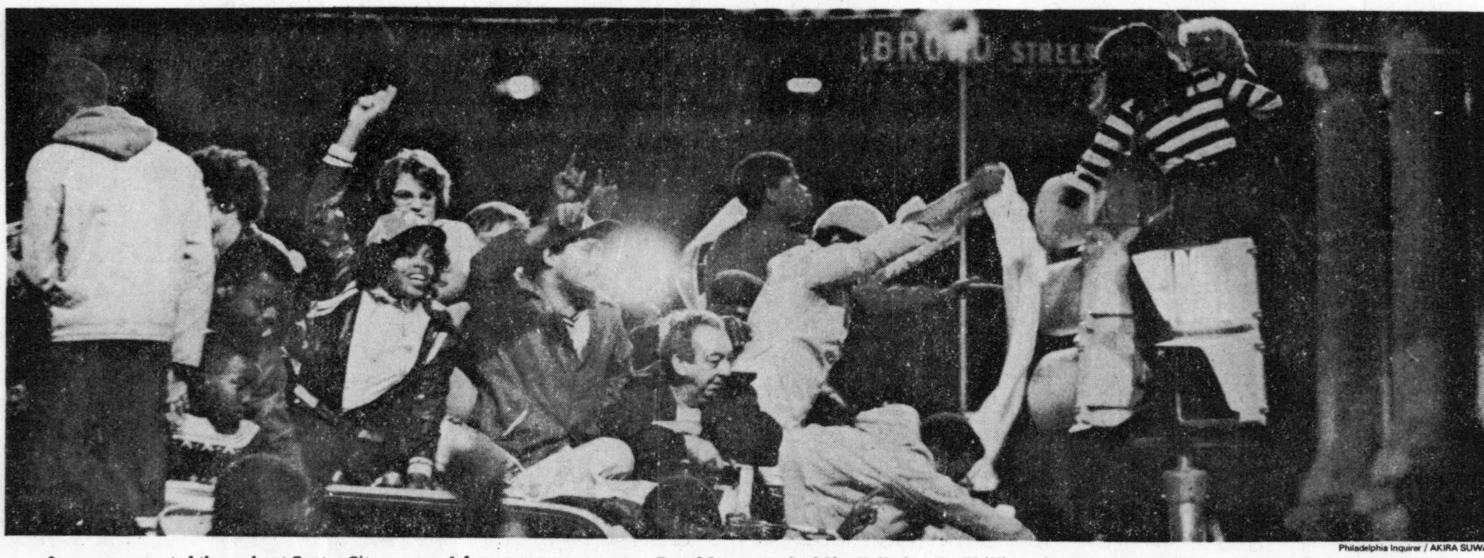

Philadelphia Inquirer / AKIRA SUWA

In a scene repeated throughout Center City, scores of fans swarm over a car on Broad Street south of City Hall after the Phillies' victory; six pages of game coverage in Sports, Section E

Phils Win Series; City Goes Wild

Del. plant explodes; 5 die, 30 hurt

By Joyce Gemperlein, Dominic Sama and Sharon Sexton
Special to The Inquirer

NEW CASTLE, Del. — Five persons were killed and at least 30 were injured last night in an explosion and fire that ripped through the Amoco Chemical Corp. plant on U.S. Route 9 here, forcing 500 families in a 1½-mile radius to evacuate and shattering windows in New Jersey communities across the Delaware River.

State police and a spokesman for the chemical company said all of the 35 workers on the plant's night shift have been accounted for. But local fire officials said that as many as a dozen employees were unaccounted for and were possibly buried in the blazing plastics plant.

The fire was so intense and the possibility of additional explosions so likely that only one fire company entered the plant to search for survivors.

As of midnight, hundreds of firefighters, who had come from four states, were unable to enter the plant, which they expected to burn throughout the night.

Early this morning Kent Carson, manager of employee relations at the plant, said that the fire was under control and that the probable source of the fire was propylene contained in six storage tanks. The six tanks have a combined capacity of 1 million pounds of propylene.

"We do not feel there is any imminent danger to the residents of this area," Carson said in an early morning interview.

Two huge tanks holding natural gas were hosed down with water and firefighters laid hoses to shoot water into the plant without entering it.

The cause of the explosion was not known. The fire, which began after the 6:30 p.m. explosion and two smaller blasts, caused scattered brush fires in the nearby fields of Dobbinsville, Washington Park and Gratham Lane, New Castle neighborhoods where many chemical plants are located.

The Washington Park development was filled with homes with windows blown out, some with window air conditioners hanging by cords, and, as Frances Mathewson described it,

(See EXPLOSION on 9-A)

Philadelphia Inquirer / CHUCK ISAACS

After the victory, joyous teammates hoist Mike Schmidt, the Series' Most Valuable Player

Finally, a win in 97th year

By Donald Kimelman
Inquirer Staff Writer

Tens of thousands of long-suffering Philadelphians took to the streets last night for a raucous, tumultuous, horn-blowing, firecracker-exploding celebration of the Phillies' World Series victory — the first in the team's 97-year history.

However, the celebration was marred by the shooting death of a man, 22, who was fatally wounded by a shot fired on Wallace Street near Broad Street.

The identity of man, who was shot about 2:10 a.m. from a group of about 40 males as they ran east on Wallace, was not immediately known, police said. He died about 2:35 a.m. at Hahnemann Hospital.

Police also reported numerous incidents of robbery, minor assaults and looting. In general, however, celebrants were peaceful, although exuberant.

In the river wards and the Far Northeast, in South Philadelphia and around City Hall, people poured out of houses and taverns and into the streets the moment the last out was recorded in the Phillies' dramatic 4-1 victory over the Kansas City Royals in the sixth and deciding game of the Series.

Celebrants jumped on tops of cars and hung on, waving wildly, as the cars, with horns blaring, traveled in long processions up and down the city's main streets.

Thousands blocked intersections,

(See CELEBRATION on 11-A A)

Firefighters can only watch 'damn inferno'

By Robert J. Rosenthal
Inquirer Staff Writer

NEW CASTLE, Del. — At 11:40 last night, a muffled boom, one of a series of many explosions that racked the Amoco Chemical Corp. plant here through the evening, rolled across the marshlands surrounding the plant.

Flames from the fire illuminated the sky but a dark acrid cloud of smoke blotted out a nearly full moon.

Half a mile from the plant, dozens of firefighters stood around drinking coffee and talking in small groups. A few minutes earlier, the men had cheered as word of the Phillies victory came over the police and fire radios.

The firefighters, some of whom

(See SCENE on 9-A)

THE LONG STRIKE of teachers in the Chester-Upland district is over. This student looks happy about it. Page 1-F.

Weather & Index

SUNNY TODAY and a high in the low 60s. Full weather report, Page 7-F.

BINGO numbers are on Page 5-B.

Sweet vindication

The wine was delicious . . . the victory, more so

By Bill Lyon
Inquirer Staff Writer

It was a weird, eerie Phillies clubhouse, part asylum, part library.

There was chaos and the obligatory champagne shampoos. And there was also subdued quiet.

Steve Carlton, the winner of the game that made The Team That Wouldn't Die champions of baseball at last, retreated as always to the trainers room. It is strictly off-limits. No one tried to crash his private inner sanctum.

Through the glass in the doors, Carlton could be seen, in his private refuge, swigging from a magnum. The label could not be read, but it was not the Great Western brand that was being sprayed and hosed out in the clubhouse. Perhaps it was a selection from his own private stock, which is reputed to be impressive.

Once, Carlton came to the door, peered out to survey the madness outside, and then returned to a rubdown table to sit and sip.

Phillies filed in individually to join him. Some stayed. Nino Espinosa. Ramon Aviles, who pressed an ice bag to his right eye. Larry Christensen, who reached out a plastic glass, which Carlton filled.

Dickie Noles barged in, embraced Carlton, and started to douse him with champagne, but Carlton backed off, smiled firmly but gently, and shook his head no. Noles grinned, shrugged, settled for another hug, and came back out, looking for something a bit more raucous.

Watching Carlton was rather like watching an emperor of some banana republic hunkered down in comfort while the streets outside explode.

Tug McGraw, the emotional antithesis to Carlton, fire to his ice, broke through and entered the trainer's room. He stood there, like a high-strung thoroughbred waiting to be shod, while they strapped an immense ice bag to his left elbow, then trussed the whole wing up in a sling.

"It's gonna stay right there the

(See LOCKER ROOM on 11-A-C)

For the victors, there's a parade today

Rain or shine, Philadelphia today will celebrate the Phillies' first World Series championship with a parade through Center City and South Philadelphia and festivities at JFK Stadium.

The parade will begin at 11:30 a.m. at 18th and Market Streets and move east to City Hall, around City Hall to Broad Street and then south to the stadium, where the official ceremony will begin at 1 p.m. There will be no charge for admission to the 103,000-seat stadium, which will open at 9 a.m. to accommodate the fans.

Late Racing

Los Angeles Times

Morning Final

Circulation: 1,036,522 Daily / 1,290,194 Sunday

Thursday, October 29, 1981

MF/184 pages / Copyright 1981, Los Angeles Times / Daily 25¢

Dodgers Rout N.Y., Win Series

Reagan Wins AWACS Fight

By RUDY ABRAMSON, *Times Staff Writer*

WASHINGTON—By a vote of 52 to 48, the Senate on Wednesday cleared the way for the controversial $8.5-billion AWACS sale to Saudi Arabia, handing President Reagan a come-from-behind victory in his first major foreign policy showdown with Congress.

Ending a fierce struggle that had gone on for months, the vote turned back a bid by opponents of the sale to veto an agreement concluded between the Reagan Administration and the Saudi government last February.

Four senators who had opposed the sale—Sen. Slade Gorton (R-Wash.), Sen. William S. Cohen (R-Me.), Sen. Mark Andrews (R-N.D.) and Sen. Edward Zorinsky (D-Neb.)—switched sides during the final debate, two of them on the roll-call vote, to give the President his victory.

Until this week, the Senate had appeared certain to veto the transaction and block a presidential arms sale for the first time in history

Breakdown by Party

However, the President carried the day when 41 Republicans, 10 Democrats and Independent Harry F. Byrd of Virginia voted to kill a resolution that would have disapproved the sale. Voting for the resolution were 36 Democrats and 12 Republicans. California's senators split on the issue, with Republican S. I. Hayakawa supporting the President and Democrat Alan Cranston opposing him.

The House voted, 301 to 111, two weeks ago to disapprove the sale, but both houses of Congress must reject proposed arms sales before they are dead.

The White House managed to reverse the votes of several opposing Republican senators and save the agreement Wednesday by sending Congress a five-page letter of assurances regarding sale of the five airborne warning and control system planes to the Saudis. The letter went beyond the language of the official agreement itself.

In recent days, the President had given top priority to personal appeals to senators, arguing that defeat of the sale would gravely undermine his foreign policy leadership. He waged his campaign into the last hours of Senate consideration.

Opponents of the sale maintained to the end that it would accelerate the arms race in the volatile Middle East, undermine the security of Israel and jeopardize the security of sophisticated military technology by putting it into the hands of a potentially unstable government in Saudi Arabia.

Minutes after the vote, the President took the first step in what is expected to be a concerted effort to reassure Israel that the present relationship between the two countries will remain the keystone of U.S. Middle East policy.

Please see AWACS, Page 6

Text of Reagan letter, Page 11. Other stories, Pages 7, 9 and 10.

Wage Concessions

Steelmaker, Union Going Through Mill

By BARRY SIEGEL, *Times Staff Writer*

CANTON, Ohio—When the Timken Co. announced earlier this year it was considering building a $500-million steel mill here that would provide 1,000 new jobs, it seemed a godsend for this depressed industrial area.

There was just one hitch.

The Timken Co. wanted the sort of contract concessions from the United Steelworkers that a number of other unions have recently been granting recession-strained companies in an effort to retain jobs and keep plants open.

The company said the concessions were needed to make the project economically feasible and competitive in the world market. Without them, Timken might build the plant on alternative sites in Kentucky or Tennessee. County and state officials there were eagerly offering everything from tax breaks to new roads.

A Second Hitch

So, after negotiations, union leaders here endorsed the concession package and offered it to the rank-and-file workers.

Then came a second hitch.

On Oct. 11, workers startled Timken, government and union leaders by voting narrowly to reject the concessions. Distracted by warm fall weather and a Cleveland Browns-Pittsburgh Steelers football game on television, 83% of the 9,000 union members eligible did not even bother to vote.

The union rejection has left this city of 95,000 in an uproar.

Community leaders, letter writers and local newspaper editorials have described the vote with expressions such as "disbelief," "amazed," "hard to understand," "self-destructive" and "selfish tunnel vision."

The steelworkers have not been very happy either.

Workers have threatened periodically to burn down union leaders' houses if they negotiated concessions, according to some sources within the union. Union officials shake their heads and acknowledge

Please see UNION, Page 16

SUSAN HENDLER / Los Angeles Times

Dodger players rejoice over winning the World Series by beating Yankees, 9-2, in sixth game in New York. From left are Derrel Thomas, Steve Howe, Steve Yeager and Steve Garvey.

Comeback Trail Led to 4th Title

Pedro Guerrero drove in five runs with a home run, triple and single and the Dodgers climaxed a remarkable series of playoff comebacks Wednesday night by routing the New York Yankess, 9-2, to win the 78th World Series at Yankee Stadium.

It was the fourth straight victory for the Dodgers after they had dropped the first two games at Yankee Stadium. Previously, they had come from an 0-2 deficit to beat the Houston Astros, 3-2, in the National League West divisional playoffs and had overcome Montreal, 3-2, after trailing 1-2 in the NL championship playoffs.

The result was an exact reversal of the 1978 World Series when the Yankees lost the first two games at Dodger Stadium, then won the next four.

The victory gave Los Angeles its fourth world championship and its first since 1965 when they beat the Minnesota Twins. Previously they won championships in 1959 over the Chicago White Sox and in 1963 over the Yankees.

Frustrated Since 1965

They had been frustrated since 1965, however, losing to the Baltimore Orioles in 1966, the Oakland A's in 1974 and the Yankees in 1977 and 1978.

"It feels just like I anticipated," said Dodger manager Tom Lasorda. "I'm the happiest man in the world. We're bringing the championship back to Los Angeles where ít belongs.

"These guys gave me a lifetime of thrills in one year."

Said Guerrero, who was voted a share of the Most Valuable Player award with Ron Cey and Steve Yeager: "I feel so happy. I thank God for making this dream come true. I always dream of playing the Yankees in the World Series and winning. I'm having trouble believing it really happened. It feels so good."

Cey, whose participation in the game had been doubtful because of the effects of his beaning by Rich Gossage on Sunday, started at third base and got two hits in three trips, scoring a run and driving in one, before taking himself out of the lineup in the sixth inning.

"I felt OK at the beginning but then I got a little queasy," Cey said. "I may have tried to do too much. I'm glad it's over."

Steinbrenner Apologizes

Yankee owner George Steinbrenner, bitter over his team's collapse, issued this statement: "I want to sincerely apologize to the people of New York and to the fans of the New York Yankees everywhere for the performance of the Yankee team in the World Series."

Burt Hooton was the winning pitcher, going 5⅓ innings and allowing five hits and both New York runs. Steve Howe came on in relief, giving up only two hits and no runs in 3⅔ innings.

Victory parade Friday, Part II, Page 1. Game details in Sports Section.

Last-Minute Letter Sews Up Vote in Senate

By GEORGE SKELTON and PAUL HOUSTON, *Times Staff Writers*

WASHINGTON—A last-minute letter from President Reagan spelling out guarantees to keep AWACS radar surveillance planes from being used against Israel or falling into enemy hands was the final maneuver that sewed up the President's dramatic victory in the Senate on Wednesday.

But what really spelled victory for the White House was a combination of Reagan charm and old-fashioned pressure politics—a combination Reagan has used several times before in such legislative fights.

As Reagan is fond of saying, he first tries to help legislators "see the light." And if they don't, he says, "we make them feel the heat."

One of those who felt the heat was Sen. David Pryor (D-Ark.). Called to the White House for a private meeting, Pryor held out and voted against Reagan in the end but said, "The President's lobbying effort was as strong as train smoke, as they say back home."

Voted Against, Then For

Another Democrat who got the treatment, Sen. Edward Zorinsky of Nebraska, had previously voted against the sale of AWACS and other military equipment to Saudi Arabia when the deal came up in the Senate Foreign Relations Committee. But after his session with Reagan on Wednesday, Zorinsky went back to the Senate and voted for the sale.

"Sure I feel pressured," the senator told reporters.

Zorinsky said he was lobbied intensely by "everyone who's got a vested interest (in the deal) economically, both in the state of Ne-

Please see STRATEGY, Page 8

Millions Walk Off Jobs in 1-Hour Polish Strike

By DAN FISHER *Times Staff Writer*

WARSAW—Millions of Polish workers walked peacefully off the job for an hour Wednesday in what both Solidarity union chief Lech Walesa and Premier Wojciech Jaruzelski said they hoped would be the last such nationwide strike in Poland.

Walesa, who appeared at Warsaw's Rosa Luxembourg light-bulb factory for the national protest, said: "I want this to be the last strike of this kind. We should find more effective protests that would help us."

A few hours later, Jaruzelski—who is also the head of Poland's Communist Party, the country's defense minister and a general in the army—opened a meeting of the party's policy-setting Central Committee by calling on the union to stop such walkouts "in the name of the highest good, in the name of the salvation of the nation."

Despite an intense government propaganda campaign over the last several days and dire warnings to cancel the protest, the strike went off without incident. Solidarity had called the walkout to protest food shortages, government economic policies and alleged harassment of union activists.

Solidarity officials described the strike as an unqualified success that, they claimed, was supported by 75% to 90% of all Polish workers—not just Solidarity members—depending on their location.

Jaruzelski, however, told the Central Committee that "this time the strike did not have total support. For the first time, on such a scale and with such clarity, a stand against the strike was taken" by a number of organizations, including the pro-government trade unions.

Polish television reported Wednesday night that almost one-third of the workers at the Luxembourg light bulb plant where Walesa spoke, refused to support the strike.

The walkout was only the second of its kind since Solidarity was born more than 14 months ago in the shipyards of the port city of Gdansk. The union staged a four-hour national warning strike on March 27 to protest the beatings of three of its members in Bydgoszcz.

Wednesday's protest halted all municipal transportation in cities

Please see POLES, Page 14

Attorney Sues

Store Pays for Rude Cashier

By MARK GLADSTONE, *Times Staff Writer*

Torrance attorney Donald B. Brown was angry enough when a market checker was rude and suspicious over his $25 check, but he became really furious when his complaint to the store chain brought a response he calls "insulting and humiliating."

Brown filed a $150,000 suit against Alpha Beta and the checker on charges of slander and intentional infliction of emotional distress. He contended it was time someone stood up for courtesy and good manners on the part of those serving the public.

Superior Court Judge Thomas Fredericks agreed with him and, after a brief non-jury trial, ruled in his favor. Brown was awarded a judgment of $500, plus court costs.

Please see RUDE, Page 21

AWACS Struggle Carries a Price, However

Victory Bolsters Reagan's Hand at Home, Abroad

By JACK NELSON, *Times Washington Bureau Chief*

WASHINGTON—President Reagan's stunning victory in the Senate on the sale of AWACS radar aircraft to Saudi Arabia should strengthen his hand at home and abroad, even though he achieved it at some political cost.

At home, the victory bolstered Reagan's image as a strong leader by demonstrating once again his mastery of the legislative process and his determination to keep a promise, even when he faces what seems to be almost insurmountable opposition.

Abroad, the victory should shore up U.S. relations with Saudi Arabia and strengthen pro-Western elements in the Saudi ruling family, who favor the continued high levels of oil production that are important for the U.S. economy as well as its security.

But Administration officials recognize that in the end they may have to pay for their victory. A White House aide, suggesting that the wounds inflicted at home and abroad might be a long time healing, said, "A win is better than a loss, but there is blood all over the floor."

In forcing the issue on the sale despite heavy opposition, the Administration rolled over some Republicans as well as Democrats in the Senate and antagonized the American Jewish community, which fought the deal to the bitter end.

A leading Jewish lobbyist in Washington, who declined to be identified, said he expects the Jewish community to react bitterly against Reagan, but added, "A lot

Please see REAGAN, Page 12

INDEX

The Weather

Variable clouds today and fair Friday. Highs today, 68 and Friday 72 to 76; lows 52 to 56. High Wednesday, 72; low, 60. High Oct. 28 last year, 82; low, 56. Record high Oct. 28, 94 in 1931; record low, 45 in 1903.

Complete weather details and smog forecast in Part II, Page 8.

Soviet Sub Runs Aground Near Swedish Naval Base

STOCKHOLM (AP)—A 250-foot Soviet submarine with a crew of 54 ran aground and became stuck in shallow water in a secret zone near a Swedish naval base, authorities said Wednesday.

Sweden lodged a strong protest with the Soviet Union over violation of Swedish territorial waters and refused Kremlin requests to let the Soviets tow the sub free.

Authorities said that Warsaw Pact units equipped for submarine salvage apparently were heading toward the area 300 miles south of Stockholm where the submarine ran aground Tuesday night. They said Swedish naval reinforcements were on their way to ward them off.

The sub was aground in the Karlskrona Archipelago, which juts into the Baltic Sea. The captain, identified only as Gushin, blamed "navigational error due to faulty radar and bad weather," officials said.

But Jan-Ake Berg, spokesman for the Swedish chief of staff, discounted the possibility of navigational failure. He said, "You only have to look at the nautical charts to realize that it is virtually impossible. To get that far inside the archipelago requires very careful navigation."

Swedish Foreign Minister Ola Ullsten said the government found the captain's plea unacceptable and demanded an explanation from the Soviets, who frequently hold maneuvers in the Baltic and call it the "Sea of Peace."

"When we were alerted that a sub had been sighted so far inside Swedish waters, we were very skeptical," Lennart Forsman, navy commander, said. "We thought it very unlikely that a submarine managed to get that far into Swedish waters, which are very unsuitable for navigation in submerged position."

The sub was identified belonging to the "Whisky" class, a non-

Please see SUB, Page 12

Souvenir Edition ST. LOUIS POST-DISPATCH Souvenir Edition

St. Louis Cardinals: World Champions '82

THE season of '82! It has been a year to remember for the St. Louis Cardinals — and for the fans who followed them on the path to their ninth world championship, a feat unprecedented among National League teams.

Here, in a special section, is that season in capsule form, from the first pitch on opening day to the final out of the World Series.

After it was all over, pandemonium. "We Win," screams the scoreboard. At left, the acrobatic Ozzie Smith avoids a runner. Below, Darrell Porter, Most Valuable Player of the Series.

Above, Bruce Sutter, the winner in relief in Game 2.

Left, a playful George Hendrick chides his opponents while on second base. Above, Joaquin Andujar and his winning form.

Photos by Wayne Crosslin and J. B. Forbes
Of the Post-Dispatch Staff

POST
SPORTS

MONDAY, JULY 25, 1983 30 CENTS

Today's results at Belmont

FIRST—7 fur; cl; Off: 1:00

G1a-Creme DFt(Crd)	5.20	3.20	2.60
B3-Dancer Melody(Thb)		3.80	2.60
I8-Raise Buck(Douglas)			4.00

a-coupled with Milliard
Scr: Counselor George, Firstee, Delta Leader, Sweet Steal, Reverse Decision

SECOND—6 fur; mdn; Off: 1:31

D5-Nutmeg(Clytn)	11.20	6.00	3.20
J9-Elevator Shoe(Sntgt)		4.20	2.80
K10-Foolsh Clover(Cdr)			3.00

Scratched: Swift Gal
QUINELLA PAID $27.80
DAILY DOUBLE PAID $62.40

THIRD—1⅛ mi(ch); cl; Off: 2:02

C2-Letter Lucy(Dgls)	4.40	3.00	2.40
D3-Lederhosen(Mrphy)		4.40	3.20
E4-Stretch Dancer(Beit)			4.80

Scratched: The Mangler, Hot Words
EXACTA PAID $17.80

It's Keystone tomorrow: Page 44

De-bat-gate furor

Billy Martin watches as umpire Tim McClelland holds aloft George Brett's bat with illegal pine tar after he made the out call which sends an inflamed Brett out of the dugout . . .

Yankees win as umpires nullify Brett HR

By BOB KLAPISCH

IN ONE lockerroom there was slick Billy Martin, victorious and smug. Down the hall, there was helpless George Brett, defeated and furious. Only minutes before, he and the Royals had been deprived of winning a game because of one bat, one rule, and, ultimately, one inch.

The circus that ended in a 4-3 win for the Yanks yesterday at the Stadium began after Brett had clocked a 400-foot home run off Goose Gossage with two out in the ninth to give the Royals a 5-4

Continued on Page 50

Post Photos by Nury Hernandez

. . . and onto the field for wild confrontation with umps as the Royals' third baseman's two-run ninth-inning home run was disallowed and Yanks were awarded 4-3 win.

McNeil had surgery on right knee in April

By PETER FINNEY Jr.

THE JETS today announced that Freeman McNeil, the league's leading rusher last year, underwent an arthroscopic examination in April on his right knee to probe for partially-torn cartilage.

The examination was disclosed today by coach Joe Walton, who will hold McNeil and Joe Klecko out of all morning workouts during training camp so that they can lift weights to strengthen their legs. Both players will work out with the rest of the team in the afternoons.

Walton informed reporters of McNeil's examination during his regular interview session. Klecko's surgery and rehabilitation already were widely known.

"Freeman in April had a scope on his knee," Walton said. "The rehabilitation wasn't as good as we had hoped."

Walton said McNeil's leg strength, as measured by the Cybex machine, showed that the running back was "a litte behind getting his strength back."

"Rather than have (McNeil and Klecko) take the pounding of two-a-days, they'll do some weight work in the morning," Walton said.

"(Freeman) could practice. I just made the decision that I don't think either one needs

Continued on Page 50

Reds mow down Seaver, Mets — ALLEN: P. 52 —

Cardinals' Allen blanks Dodgers: P. 51

THE WARHEAD FACTORY
Living with the bomb
Second in a six-part series — Page 4

DAILY NEWS
NEW YORK'S PICTURE NEWSPAPER®
★★★★ 30¢ Monday, October 17, 1983 Chance of late showers. 65-70. Almanac p. 66

ORIOLES FLY AWAY WITH SERIES

See back page and centerfold

AP

Oriole catcher Rick Dempsey and pitcher Scott McGregor after Series win.

Another Marine killed in Beirut

Page 2

'Good Samaritan' held in murder

Page 3

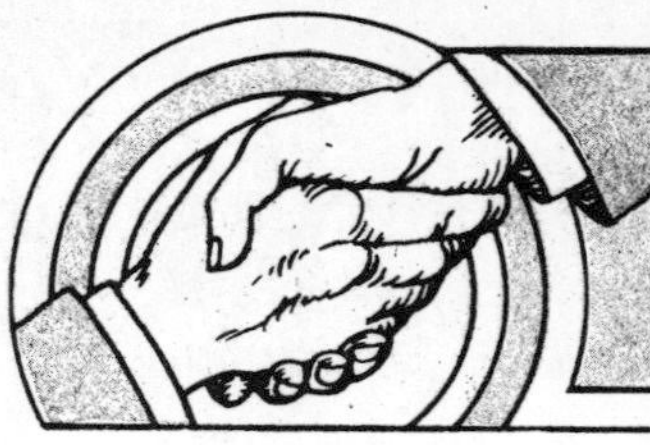

The Ford-UAW deal

— Story, Page 3A

A 2d Front Page on 3A today

foggy, showers
High 69, low 55
Mostly cloudy Tuesday
Details on Page 2A

Detroit Free Press

Volume 154, Number 164 · ON GUARD FOR 153 YEARS · Monday, October 15, 1984

monday
20¢
metro final

Gr-r-reat!

Free Press Photo by MARY SCHROEDER

The culmination of an incredible season, the high point of a still-young career: Kirk Gibson after his second home run Sunday.

Fans go wild over Tigers

By MARTIN F. KOHN
Free Press Staff Writer

Five or so ounces of cork wound in twine and wrapped in sewn white leather settled into the glove of a man named Larry Herndon, and the baseball season of 1984 settled into the massive mitt of History.

The Tigers, the come-from-ahead ball club from the coming-from-behind town, won the World Series, beating the San Diego Padres 8-4 before Vice-President George Bush and a home crowd of 51,901 who hollered themselves hoarse and waved themselves silly and, years from now, can show their ticket stubs to their grandchildren and say they were there.

the roar of '84

- *Game story and special Series Report. Section F.*
- *More pictures. Page 12F.*
- *Talbert's Tiger diary. 7E.*
- *Series Sidelights. 1E.*

Playing no favorites, President Reagan telephoned both locker rooms after the game to congratulate the players.

For Detroit, for Michigan, for the Midwest, for everybody who has been with the Tigers in spirit, the victory was a moment to cherish in a season to savor.

Starting in the Tigers locker room and spreading out in immeasurable waves wherever fans of the home team gathered, it was "cel-e-brate good times, come on!" and dancing in the streets.

BUT IT wasn't all fun. At least four police cars were damaged at Michigan and Trumbull; another was set afire and destroyed, and a private car also was set afire.

Emergency Medical Services ambulances had trouble reaching at least one accident victim, police said.

Souvenir vendors near the stadium had their remaining wares stolen.

Many bottles were thrown at police officers. No serious injuries had been reported within the first couple of hours after the game.

For the most part, though, just as it happened 16 years ago, when the Tigers last won the Series, hearts swelled and spirits lifted. Banished for the moment were thoughts of crime and unemployment, recession and soup kitchens. The Tigers were world champions, and all things good suddenly had become possible, or even likely.

See **WORLD SERIES**, Page 15A

The naturals win in maverick way

Mike Downey

They won it, just the way everybody in Detroit thought they would.

They won it, in a way nobody thought they could.

They won it on a sacrifice fly ... *to second base.*

They won it on a pinch-hit, bases-loaded pop-up ... *by Rusty Kuntz.*

They won it on a wild run for the money by Kirk Gibson, who tagged up and scored on a ball that might not have gone 25 feet onto the outfield grass.

They did it with two Gibson home runs, one of which opened the scoring, one of which closed it.

They won it.

The World Series.

THE DETROIT Tigers became the undisputed best team in baseball Sunday, beating the San Diego Padres, 8-4, for their fourth world championship since joining the American League in 1901. When Willie Hernandez got Tony Gwynn on a short fly to left field for the final out, the crowd of 51,901 stormed onto the Tiger Stadium field, as did thousands of non-paying customers outside the park who didn't want to be left out.

They couldn't restrain themselves. The Tigers had won it.

They won it with Gibson tying into a Mark Thurmond pitch in the first inning and sending it halfway to Hamtramck. The two-run homer landed in the upper deck in right-center.

They won it because another San Diego pitcher failed to last beyond the first inning. Thurmond threw only 15 pitches and faced only six batters.

They won it even though the Padres put together a rally that knocked out Dan Petry and tied the game at 3-all.

See **DOWNEY**, Page 15A

Pete Rose in 1964

Pete Rose—The Collector's Edition

Pete Rose in 1985

THE CINCINNATI ENQUIRER

FINAL EDITION/NEWSSTAND PRICE 35¢ THURSDAY, SEPTEMBER 12, 1985 A GANNETT NEWSPAPER

4,192: Pete Singles Past Ty Cobb

Tim Sullivan

Numbers Don't Tell Full Story

Now that Pete Rose has the record we have anticipated so long, it should be remembered that he never needed it.

It is the milestone of his baseball career, not the measure. It is his landmark, not his legacy.

No, anyone who would appraise Pete Rose would be wrong to do so by the numbers. For he is not so much a ballplayer as he is an emotion, an attitude, a symbol. "Pete Rose," Commissioner Peter Ueberroth said, "*is* baseball."

He is, at least, what baseball ought to be. In our time, perhaps in all time, no one has played this boy's game so boyishly.

He perfected the head-first slide and has turned even the inning-ending putout at first base into a stylish celebration. The wonder of Pete Rose is that baseball has no drudgery for him. If he is a hot dog, it is because he plays the game with so much relish.

"He should bypass the Hall of Fame," Steve Garvey says, "and go straight to the Smithsonian."

HE IS, in short, an original. Four thousand, one hundred and ninety-two hits no better define Pete Rose than five acts define Hamlet. In both cases, the play's the thing.

Rose's pages in the record books, to borrow a line he once used for his paycheck, could be piled so high that a show dog couldn't jump over them. Yet future generations could not fully appreciate him without film: the All-Star collision with Ray Fosse, the playoff bout with Bud Harrelson, the autumn evening in 1975 when he turned to Carlton Fisk and said, "Ain't it great just to be playing a game like this."

Just as easily, though, the footage could come from lesser contests, for Pete Rose views *every* game with glee—the arctic nights in San Francisco, the Saharan afternoons in St. Louis, the twi-night doubleheaders of long-lost pennant races.

"I live for baseball," he says.

THE RECORD he reached Wednesday is merely the measure of that devotion. It represents 23 seasons of fighting fatigue and ignoring aches, of wanting things a little more and a lot longer than the next guy.

It does not mean he is the greatest hitter of all-time. It does not even mean he is the greatest hitter of his own time. "It will mean," Rose says simply, "that I'm the guy with the most hits."

This does not diminish the accomplishment; rather it makes it all the more extraordinary. It is a triumph of desire over talent, of endurance over opportunity.

It is Cinderella landing the prince, Galahad locating the Grail. It is justice served and romance rewarded.

It is exactly what Pete Rose deserves.

Tim Sullivan is sports columnist for The Enquirer.

The Cincinnati Enquirer/Annalisa Kraft

PETE ROSE hits an Eric Show pitch for a single to left-center field Wednesday night to become baseball's all-time hit leader.

Memory Will Last Forever

BY HOWARD WILKINSON
The Cincinnati Enquirer

When Pete Rose hit the magic 4,192nd hit Wednesday, he made 47,237 memories that will last just as many lifetimes.

You could see it in the eyes of Tina McGary, sitting behind home plate in the blue seats and wishing she could run out to first base and kiss the 44-year-old ballplayer. It was the same player she watched play high school ball at Western Hills a quarter of a century ago.

It was in the eyes, too, of 11-year-old Brad McGinniss of Chillicothe. He strained to see over the heads of the grown-ups in front of him for the sight he'll be able to describe to his children's children some day when he's old and gray.

He'll tell of a cool September evening when a ballplayer named Rose stepped to the plate, took the count to 2-1, and lofted a ball into left center field that seemed to hang in the crisp air forever before coming down with a bounce on the Riverfront AstroTurf.

When it did, it let loose magic.

WAVE AFTER wave of cheers rocked the perfect circle of a stadium, from the box seats behind home plate to the highest reaches of the red.

Flashbulbs exploded; fireworks shot into the air; his teammates surged onto the field to congratulate the man who, in a short year, has brought them from nothing to something special, indeed.

"I don't think I'll ever feel this way again," said Esther Peterson of Dayton, standing behind the blue seats on the left-field line, tears rolling down her cheeks.

"He's the fans' player. I feel like we're part of everything he does. And this is the greatest thing he's ever done."

After six minutes of bedlam, the cheers had just begun to subside when Rose's son, Petey, dressed as always in his No. 14 uniform, came onto the field and hugged his dad at first base.

The sight just set the crowd off again.

"HE IS what baseball is all about," said Greg Maone of Ironton, watching from the green seats on the third base line. "He did it all on his own. He showed us what hard work and determination could bring."

7th-Inning Triple Adds No. 4,193

BY GREG HOARD
The Cincinnati Enquirer

Pete Rose tried but could never quite capture the words. He could never describe what it meant to him to pass Ty Cobb.

But Wednesday night he showed us. He stood at first base and cried.

At 8:01 p.m., Pete Rose slapped a 2-and-1 pitch from Eric Show into left-center field for the 4,192nd hit of his career.

Then the wave of affection took over.

At first, Rose tried to hold back the tears. He tried to take all of it in stride: the screams, the handshakes, the congratulations from his teammates and the San Diego Padres, the cheers from 47,237 fans that went on for seven minutes.

But this was too big, too much. It had taken too long, and it had taken more effort than anyone would ever realize.

Rose could not handle this alone. When he could no longer fight the tears, he turned to Tommy Helms, the Reds' first base coach and a friend for years. He clutched Helms around the neck and shoulders and sobbed.

"I don't know what to do," he told Helms.

Helms replied: "That's OK, Boss. You're Number One. You deserve it all."

"I WAS awful lonely standing out there at first base," Rose said later, during a ceremony after the Reds' 2-0 victory. "I can't describe what was going through my mind, what was going through my stomach . . .

"I wish everyone in baseball could go through what I went through tonight at first base. I was all right until I looked up in the air. I looked up in the air and I saw my dad and Ty Cobb. That took care of me."

With Rose sobbing, Helms turned and motioned toward the dugout. Rose's son, Petey, came to his father's side, and the scene was repeated.

This hit was one for the heart, as well as the record book.

It didn't take long. It happened only 11 minutes after the game began, on Rose's first trip to the plate.

Eddie Milner, the lead-off hitter, was out on an infield pop-up. Rose went to the batter's box with the same determined look he has worn since 1963, his rookie season.

Show's first pitch was a fastball, and Rose let it go for a ball. Rose fouled the next pitch back for a strike. Rose took the third pitch, a slider, for another ball.

With each pitch, the standing-room-only crowd stood taller, craning their necks for a better look. At 8:01, they saw.

THE HIT was like many others in Rose's career. It left the bat on a line, headed for the alley between left and center field. Carmelo Martinez gave chase from left field and Kevin McReynolds from center, but to no avail. This was Rose's "Big Knock," the record breaker.

Fireworks exploded. Rose's teammates left the dugout en masse. Two of his oldest friends, Tony Perez and Davey Concepcion, hoisted him on their shoulders. Marge Schott, the Reds' president, was led to field. And a red Corvette, specifically designed for Rose and this moment, was driven onto the field. It's license plate said, "PR 4192."

After the game, President Reagan telephoned with congratulations: "Is this Pete Rose, alias Charlie Hustle?" And Schott presented Rose with a silver punch bowl, a silver tray and 12 silver cups.

"I'm not smart enough," Rose said, "to come up with the words to show my appreciation for the fans."

Not long ago, Rose described the hit as something "that will affect me years from now, I'm talking about way down the road."

SOUVENIR EDITION

EXTRA **THE KANSAS CITY STAR.** EXTRA

Monday, October 28, 1985, World Series Special, 20 Pages 50c

THIS ONE'S FOR YOU!

The championship ending to the 1985 season left the Royals jumping for joy. (staff photos by Jim McTaggart and Patrick Sullivan)

It was a glorious, crazy season for Miracle Royals

By Joe McGuff
sports editor

COMMENT

For better or worse, there is a time in human affairs when events assume a momentum of their own and overwhelm any attempt to control them. Perhaps that is the only rational way to explain the team that took its place in history Sunday night as the Miracle Royals.

No matter how long baseball is played in Kansas City, there never will be another season like the season of '85.

Those who were eyewitnesses to it will tell their children and their grandchildren about the light-hitting team that kept making comeback after comeback and then won the seventh game of the World Series with an 11-0 walloping of the Cardinals, who were favored in the Series by slightly more than 2-1.

The Cardinals led the National League in hitting, but they were limited to 13 runs by the Royals and batted only .185, the lowest average ever for a seven-game Series. The team known as the running Redbirds stole only two bases while the Royals were stealing nine.

"It's amazing," Cardinal Manager Whitey Herzog said. "I know they've got good pitching, but if they were that good, they would have won 130 games in a weak division."

There is reason to wonder if any team ever again will win a World Series the way the Royals did. To say they won the hard way is to hopelessly understate the case. What the Royals did was the equivalent of winning the Tour de France without touching the handlebars, or climbing Mount Everest without a rope.

The Royals' success can be explained in part by their superb pitching, but pitching alone cannot account for a team coming back from 3-1 deficits and winning both the American League Championship Series and the World Series. Pitching alone does not explain how the Royals became the first team in history to lose the first two games of the World Series at home and come back to win.

"You have to throw intangibles in," Manager Dick Howser said Sunday night. "You can't deny that now. It we got beat tonight, intangibles wouldn't have meant a hill of beans, but now that we've won, you can talk about it.

"How can you explain the look in a player's eyes? I can't explain it. I call it a fighter pilot's look. It's not in awe. It's not saying, 'Oh, gee, we're in the World Series.' I've seen it for a long time on this team."

Anyone who has followed sports is aware that real-life fairy stories sometimes have unhappy endings, but from the time Darryl Motley drove a two-run homer deep into the left-field seats in the second inning, the blue-clad fans in Royals Stadium became true believers. This was the Royals' year, and nothing was going to stop them.

John Tudor, who had won two Series games for the Cardinals and shut out the Royals in game four, struggled from the outset in his matchup with Bret Saberhagen. This pairing of 20-game winners was expected to produce a great pitching duel, but the fastball, the change-up and the surgical control Tudor exhibited in pitching his shutout were missing.

Tudor was a man trying to survive on guts and instinct.

"I felt good before the game, but I didn't make the pitches I had to make," Tudor said. "There's no way to change it unless you've got some kind of time machine."

Sometimes pitchers will be off early in a game and then find themselves, but things grew worse for Tudor when the Royals scored three runs in the third. A walk, a checked-swing single by Brett, a double steal and a walk to Frank White filled the bases. Tudor walked Jim Sundberg and was gone.

Bill Campbell relieved him and gave up a two-run single to Steve Balboni.

The Royals scored six runs in a tumultuous fifth, and with Saberhagen methodically cutting down the Cardinals, it was obvious that the Royals had only to run four more innings off the scoreboard, and Kansas City could start celebrating its first World Series championship.

The World Series was not the only thing that got away from the Cardinals in the fifth. The Cardinals also lost their composure, and both Herzog and pitcher Joaquin Andujar were ejected by plate umpire Don Denkinger even though the score was 10-0 at the time.

When Denkinger called a 2-2 pitch to Sundberg a ball, Andujar argued vigorously. Herzog came out to save his pitcher and wound up getting ejected himself after arguing with Denkinger.

Andujar threw ball four to Sundberg, started toward the plate and was ejected after a brief exchange with Denkinger. Andujar had to be restrained by his teammates and was partly carried from the field.

The frustration with Denkinger was principally a carryover from Saturday night when he called Jorge Orta safe on a play at first at the beginning of the Royals' half of the ninth, and they went on to score twice and defeated St. Louis 2-1.

"I'm not ashamed of what happened," Herzog said. "The

See McGuff, pg. 17, col. 1

RACING ★ ★ ★ ★ FINAL

METS SPECIAL EDITION

DAILY NEWS

35¢ NEW YORK'S PICTURE NEWSPAPER® Thursday, October 16, 1986

CHAMPS

GENE KAPPOCK/DAILY NEWS

JUBILANT METS toss Len Dykstra in the air after edging the Astros, 7-6, in 16 innings yesterday in Houston to win the team's third pennant.

IT'S A WRAP
8-page special section and more in Sports

WORLD SERIES: RED SOX VS. METS

SERIES LINE

Red Sox Barrett nears World Series hit mark

Boston second baseman Marty Barrett has 22 hits in the post-season playoffs, breaking Thurman Munson's major league record of 19 set in 1976.

Barrett said he's surprised by his production.

"Even if someone like Wade Boggs did it, it would be hard to believe," Barrett said. "I'm a .280 hitter, not a .350 hitter, so if I hit .280 in the post season, that would mean about 14 hits."

Barrett's 12 hits in the World Series are one short of the seven-game record held by New York Yankees second baseman Bobby Richardson (1964) and St. Louis Cardinals outfielder Lou Brock (1967).

LATE NIGHT CALLERS: California Angels designated hitter Reggie Jackson called Boston manager John McNamara after the Red Sox' tough, 10-inning loss in Game 6.

"He said, 'Tough loss,'" said McNamara, who managed Jackson with the California Angels in 1983.

Jackson also spoke with Don Baylor and Bill Buckner of the Red Sox.

Said Baylor: "He told me just don't let the guys get down. It's easy at that point just to sit back and not take it to them. We're not going to sit back and be a spectator."

McNamara said he didn't sleep after the Game 6 loss, but he didn't agonize over any moves he did or did not make.

"No second-guesses," he said. "I did exactly what I wanted to do."

McNamara's son Mike, a lieutenant in the Marine Corps, screened his calls.

McNamara said he had two hostile callers, but his son Mike "could handle it, he's in the Marines."

WORST NIGHTMARE: Boston relief pitcher Bob Stanley, who threw the wild pitch to Mookie Wilson that allowed the New York Mets to tie Game 6, said he has never been so depressed over a loss.

"I walked off the mound, and it was very depressing," Stanley said. "I have always dreamed of being on the mound to throw the pitch that ends the World Series."

Stanley's sinker goes down and away from left-handed batters. "But this one stayed inside and got away from me," Stanley said.

Mets pitcher Ron Darling, who watched Stanley's pitch on television from the trainer's room, said: "Everyone now says they called the wild pitch, "but Roger (McDowell) said just before the pitch, 'I bet he will throw a wild pitch,' and he did."

HIGH PRESSURE CENTER: The Mets were down to their last strike three times in dramatic Game 6.

Gary Carter had two strikes on him before he singled to keep the 10th inning alive. Ray Knight had an 0-2 count on him before he singled home Carter, and Mookie Wilson fouled off two pitches before Bob Stanley's wild pitch sent the tying run home.

"I've heard that concentration is the ability to think of nothing," Knight said. "That's how I felt. I was just trying to make contact. But I was really numb, like a trance. All you can do is let your eyes guide you."

BETTER THAN 1951?: The Mets surprised even themselves with their comeback in the 10th inning of Game 6.

"This one ranks right up there with Bobby Thomson," said Keith Hernandez, who wasn't born when Thomson hit his three-run home run in the ninth inning of a playoff against the Brooklyn Dodgers, giving the New York Giants the 1951 National League pennant. "This was sweet. Incredible. I don't care how we did it."

KNIGHT'S DESIRE: Knight, whose contract expires at the end of the season, said he wants a two-year contract.

Knight, 34, hit .298 this season with 11 home runs and 76 runs batted in.

The Mets have several options at third, including switch-hitter Howard Johnson, rookie Kevin Mitchell and left-handed hitting prospect Dave Magadan, who received a few late-season at-bats.

AROUND THE HORN: The Mets, who scored three times in the 10th Saturday, are the first team to to win a World Series game when it trailed by more than one run in extra innings. ... Mets rightfielder Darryl Strawberry has left 13 runners stranded in the first six Series games. The Red Sox left 63 runners on base in the first six games.

Contributing: Kevin Allen, Mel Antonen, Rod Beaton, Hal Bodley, Ken Picking and Tom Weir.

Series finally generates some excitement

BASEBALL

BY HAL BODLEY

NEW YORK — Baseball's season of '86 was headed for oblivion when along came the playoffs. The games were dramatic and exciting and had everybody talking.

The 83rd World Series was headed in the same direction as the regular season when Boston and New York squared off Saturday night for the sixth game.

After two innings, the Red Sox led a 2-0 lead, flame-thrower Roger Clemens was mowing the Mets down and champagne was wheeled into the Boston clubhouse. Boston's first World Series title since 1918 was seven innings away.

It didn't happen. In the greatest comeback in Series history, New York scored three times with two out in the 10th inning and won 6-5.

The Series is even at three games. Sunday's rainout cooled New York's momentum, but Boston faces an almost impossible task coming back from such a shocking setback. This World Series might be another ghost of past failures and frustrations.

The Red Sox were within one strike of the title and it got away.

Saturday night's four-hour, two-minute marathon will be talked about for years. It will go down in baseball lore with Bobby Thomson's 1951 homer that gave the New York Giants the NL pennant — and all the other unbelievable comebacks.

Fans will say it was a great game. It wasn't, far from it. Poor play and suspect managerial decisions paved the way for the final outcome.

Until the Mets scored their three runs — Boston had broken a 3-3 tie with two in the top of the 10th — Red Sox manager John McNamara was getting away with murder. In the end, one of his decisions cost him.

Ahead 3-2 in the eighth inning, Boston loaded the bases against reliever Roger McDowell. When Mets manager Davey Johnson called on left-handed reliever Jesse Orosco to pitch to gimpy-footed left-handed batter Bill Buckner, McNamara could have used Don Baylor as a pinch-hitter. Instead, he let Buckner bat and the first baseman flied out on Orosco's first pitch.

Later, it would be Buckner's error on Mookie Wilson's grounder in the 10th that allowed the winning run to score.

Johnson prefers to have either McDowell or Orosco as his closers. Saturday night, Orosco pitched to just one batter and was out of the game. Johnson let Lee Mazzilli bat for Orosco in the eighth. In his defense, Mazzilli did get a hit and scored the tying run.

In the ninth inning, tied 3-3, the Mets could have won had the manager ordered Howard Johnson to bunt — he was batting for rookie Kelvin Elster — with runners on first and second and nobody out. Johnson showed bunt on the first pitch, but the sign was taken off and the batter struck out. Mazzilli followed with a fly to deep left field that would have scored a runner from third base.

"I didn't like how he went after the first pitch," said Johnson. "My choice was to let a rookie bunt (Elster) or put up a good hitter who could bunt. It was a decision I rehashed over and over in my mind."

McNamara was soundly criticized for letting Buckner, who is having trouble moving around first because of his ailing ankles, remain in the game.

"Most of the times when I do that, I pinch run for him (Buckner)," said McNamara. "We didn't have to tonight and he has very good hands."

With two down and runners on first and second and the count 0-2, Ray Knight singled home the Mets' first 10th-inning run with a single to center. With Wilson batting and reliever Bob Stanley piching, the count went 2-2. Stanley threw a wild pitch, allowing Kevin Mitchell to score from third.

On a 3-2 pitch, Wilson hit his grounder to first that went through Buckner's legs and the Mets had ruined Boston's dream.

"I saw the ball well," said Buckner. "It bounced and bounced and then it didn't bounce. It just skipped. I can't remember the last time I missed a ball like that."

Game 7 starting pitchers

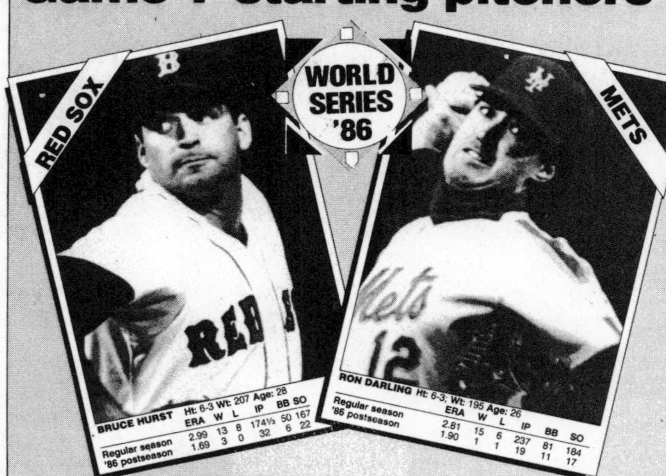

Bruce Hurst at a glance

The Red Sox' big left-hander is starting his third World Series game. In the opener he pitched eight innings of shutout ball for the victory. In Game 5, he threw a complete game, striking out six while scattering 10 hits in a 4-2 victory. Hurst mixes a fastball with a sweeping curveball to set up his outpitch, a devastating forkball. He has not lost in this postseason. Career record: 55-54. Born: St. George, Utah. College: attended Dixie College (Utah). Selected by the Boston in the 1st round of 1976 free-agent draft.

Ron Darling at a glance

Darling will be rested and ready for his third start of the World Series. He has been outstanding in his first two starts, losing a Game 1 start 1-0 on one unearned run in seven innings of work. Darling threw seven innings of four-hit ball in a 7-1 Game 4 win. He had some control problems in that start, walking six. Darling throws a good fastball with movement and a split-fingered pitch that acts as a hard slider. He occasionally throws a slider or curve. "He has been very effective against us," said Boston manager John McNamara. "It will help him to get the extra rest, but our hitters have a better idea of what they expect to see."

'Oil Can' has that empty feeling after hearing the bad news

By Ken Picking
USA TODAY

NEW YORK — Dennis "Oil Can" Boyd, concerned about rumors he would not start Game 7 of the World Series tonight, rushed to Boston Red Sox manager John McNamara ascending the escalator at the Grand Hyatt Sunday night.

Boyd, his nervousness building, stood looking McNamara in the eye. The Can's chin dropped to his narrow chest. He took three steps backwards to lean against a lobby pillar.

The tears squirted out. Boyd wiped his eyes and tried to pull down the brim of his cap.

McNamara, who Boyd says has been like a father to him this season, gripped his pitcher by the shoulders.

"It hurts so bad, but what can I do?," Boyd told USA TODAY. He will be replaced by Bruce Hurst, the Red Sox' best pitcher in the postseason.

"Bruce is on a roll, and Mac thinks the Mets have a better left-handed lineup (which would have faced Boyd).

"It's just that it was my turn, and after all I've been through ... I'm sorry, but my sensitivities are going to show through every time."

After McNamara broke the news to Boyd, the pitcher paced the lobby, requesting friends and autograph seekers to leave him alone.

Finally pitcher Al Nipper, Boyd's friend the longest of any teammate, put his arm around Boyd and walked him to the second-floor.

"Nip cooled me down; talked sense to me," said Boyd, who had reacted strongly when he was not chosen for the All-Star Game earlier this season.

"This hurts more (than not going to the All-Star Game) because I was so psyched to pitch the one game that means everything. Mac said I'd be the first out of the bullpen, but I really don't know if the intensity will be there. How'd they expect me to feel after this?

"I'll fool them this time. I'm not going to do nothing. I'm going to take this like a man. What else can I do?"

Before McNamara told Boyd that Game 7 would go to Hurst, Boyd said: "That (being scratched) is pretty much the writing on the wall. If they don't believe in me now, why would they want me back?"

But when McNamara spoke with him, Boyd said the manager told him: "'You'll be on my staff (in 1987).' That made me feel a little better, but I don't know really what to think. I hurt too much to think."

WORLD SERIES SCHEDULE

Game 1: Saturday, Oct. 17
Boston 1, N.Y. Mets 0

Game 2: Sunday, Oct. 18
Boston 9, N.Y. Mets 3

Game 3: Tuesday
N.Y. Mets 7, Boston 1

Game 4: Wednesday
N.Y. Mets 6, Boston 2

Game 5: Thursday
Boston 4, N.Y. Mets 2

Game 6: Saturday
N.Y. Mets 6, Boston 5 (10)

Game 7: Sunday
Boston at N.Y. Mets, ppd., rain
Series tied 3-3

Game 7: Monday
Boston at N.Y. Mets
TV: 8; First pitch: 8:10
Radio: 7:55

All times Eastern and p.m.

SERIES ODDS

The New York Mets are favored (8½:5 with Hurst pitching, 2:1 with Boyd pitching) to win tonight's Game 7, according to USA TODAY oddsmaker Danny Sheridan.

GAME 7 PROBABLE STARTING LINEUPS

BOSTON RED SOX (Through Game 6)	NEW YORK METS (Through Game 6)
3B — Wade Boggs (.296)	CF — Len Dykstra (.280)
2B — Marty Barrett (.480)	2B — Tim Teufel (.571)
1B — Bill Buckner (.143)	1B — Keith Hernandez (.227)
LF — Jim Rice (.304)	C — Gary Carter (.320)
RF — Dwight Evans (.273)	RF — Darryl Strawberry (.200)
C — Rich Gedman (.192)	3B — Ray Knight (.316)
CF — Dave Henderson (.435)	LF — Mookie Wilson (.261)
SS — Spike Owen (.353)	SS — Rafael Santana (.235)
P — Bruce Hurst (2-0)	P — Ron Darling (1-1)

AMERICA'S MARATHON/CHICAGO

Kristiansen runs off in huff after dispute

By Karen Allen
USA TODAY

CHICAGO — America's Marathon did not end Sunday as race director Bob Bright and Ingrid Kristiansen had hoped — with her becoming the first woman to run a sub-2 hour, 20 minute marathon.

Instead it ended angrily.

Kristiansen says she will not return to Chicago as long as he is associated with the race.

Bright says that's just as well, because the people who manage Kristiansen — International Management Group — are making her greedy.

The trouble was over a little — or in this case not-so-little — Mazda logo Kristiansen wanted to wear on her shirt. It was larger than most endorsements athletes wear — about 10 inches across and 4 inches high.

Bright, faced with complaints from Nissan, which contributed equipment, television sponsorship and money to the marathon, asked that the logo be reduced.

Kristiansen at first refused, and a compromise (a 6x1½-inch logo) wasn't reached until 11 p.m. Saturday.

Kristiansen said she didn't think the controversy affected her performance.

But Bright wasn't so sure.

"It seems to me that when the focus of running for an athlete becomes money, performance suffers," he said.

Bright was angry because in addition to the $40,000 Kristiansen won for her first-place finish, she also got a $40,000 appearance fee and "travel and accommodations for an entourage of seven."

During the negotiations, Bright became so angry he offered to give Kristiansen the appearance fee "for not showing up."

"I had to take a stand," Bright said. "All we wanted was the thing reduced to tasteful size. You can't have someone on your payroll becoming a billboard. It's a little like the NFL being upset about Jim McMahon and his adidas headband."

Ironically, Bright's biggest ally in the logo feud was Fred Lebow, director of next week's New York City Marathon — Bright's biggest competitor for top marathoners and the man who stands to gain the most if Kristiansen deserts Chicago.

"We agree on something for the first — and probably the last — time in our lives," Lebow said.

Lebow will likely take a stiffer bargaining line with Kristiansen if he knows he has no competition from Bright.

"We all want the good athletes," Lebow said. "But the races are bigger. New York will always be there, Boston will always be there, Chicago will always be there. Athletes come and go. Their careers are short. There is always someone new coming on the scene."

By Charlie Bennett, AP

TO THE VICTORS: Japan's Toshihiko Seko, left, and Norway's Ingrid Kristiansen savor their victories at Chicago.

Rodgers' unique remedy enables him to finish 11th

By Debbie Becker
USA TODAY

CHICAGO — Forget conventional medicine. Food and water was all Bill Rodgers needed to shake the flu and finish 11th in America's Marathon/Chicago Sunday.

Rodgers' 2:15:31 finish made him the top U.S. male finisher. .

"I ran 3 miles Saturday and was seeing lights," said Rodgers, 38. "My throat was tight, I couldn't breathe. I didn't take any medication. My wife Gail brought me spaghetti and chocolate-chip cookies, and I drank lots of water."

Debbie Raunig of Missoula, Mont., was the top U.S. female finisher, fourth in 2:31:28.

8,173 finish the race

Of the more than 12,000 runners that began the race, 8,173 finished.

Among the more notable dropouts was Lisa Weidenbach of Battle Creek, Mich. Weidenbach, whose best marathon time is 2:31:31, dropped out at 20 miles.

Rono makes debut

Henry Rono, 34, one of the top distance runners of his generation, finished 26th at 2:19:12 in his marathon debut. Rono has been away from international competition since 1982.

How the race was won

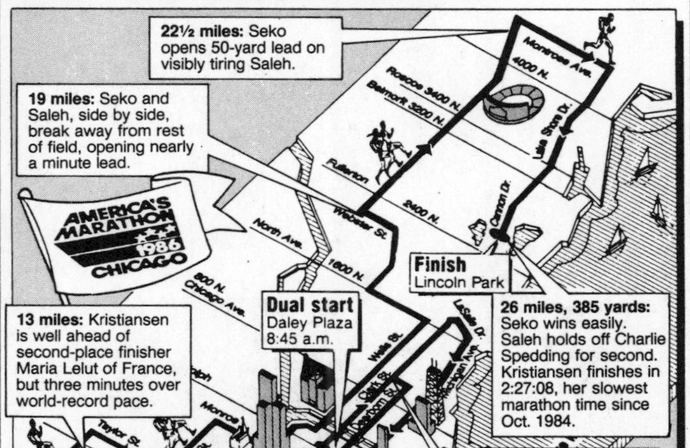

Source: America's Marathon/Chicago

By John Sherlock, USA TODAY

RACING ★ ★ ★ ★ FINAL

Mets sweep Phillies

Pepe, P. 47

DAILY NEWS Sports

Monday, June 22, 1987

starts on Page 46

Bosox batter Tewks

Madden, P. 48

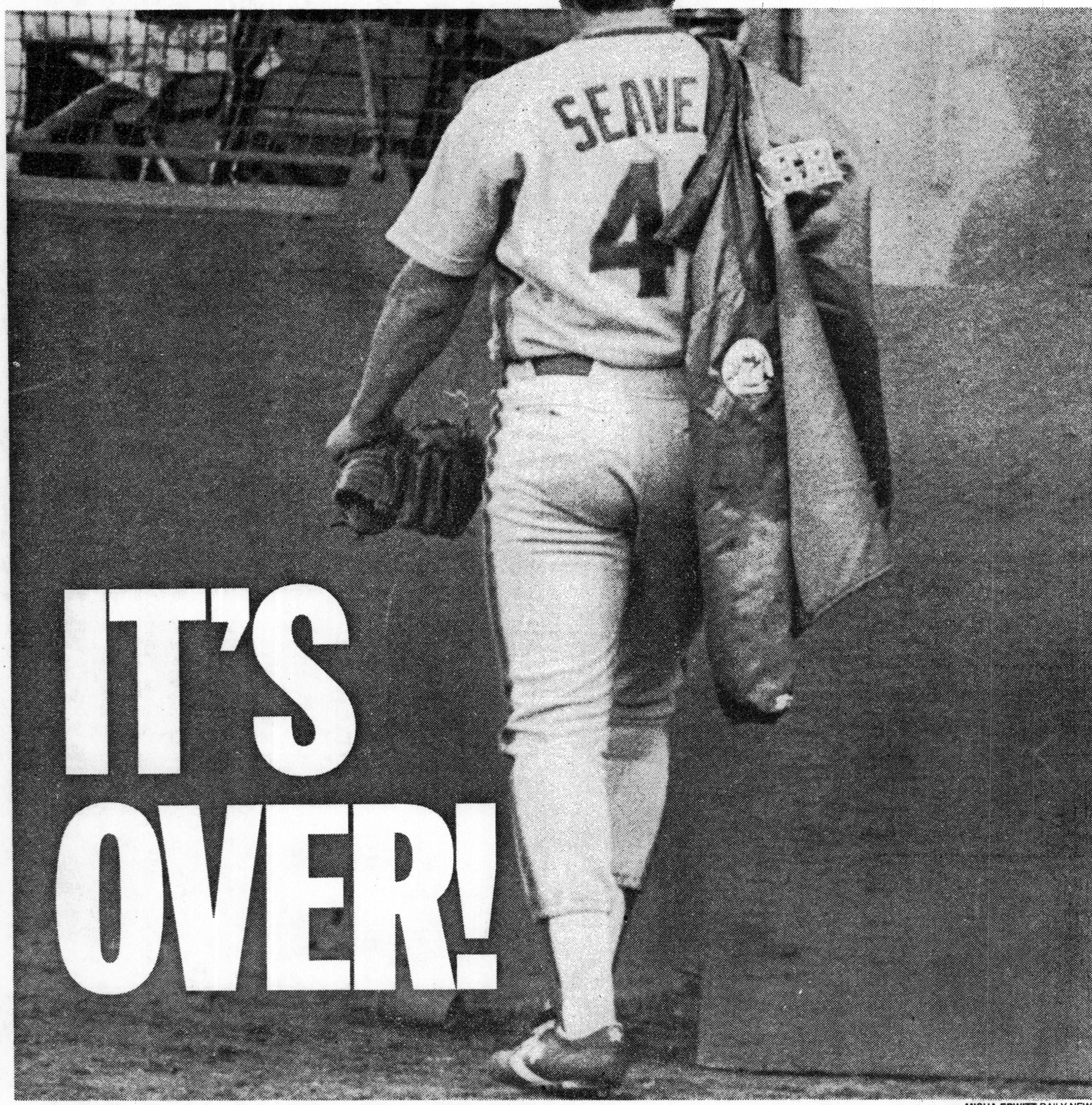

IT'S OVER!

MISHA ERWITT DAILY NEWS

He said he would know when it was time to hang 'em up. It's time. Tom Seaver, unable to impress himself in a comeback bid with the Mets, will announce today that he is quitting. **Phil Pepe, Page 46**

Simpson wins Open

Page 49

Mr. Bill going?

Page 51

4 * RFS 06/22/87 MON

1987 World Series

11 pages on the Series in News and Sports

Star Tribune

MONDAY/October 26/1987

NEWSPAPER OF THE TWIN CITIES

MINNEAPOLIS EDITION

35¢

TODAY'S NEWS STARTS ON 3A

■ Voters to decide on electing school board members by districts/**3A**

Magic!

Twins make Minnesota No. 1

Staff Photo by Bruce Bisping

Arms waved and towels twirled on the Metrodome infield after the Twins recorded the final out in their 4-2 victory over the St. Louis Cardinals in the seventh game of the 1987 World Series Sunday night. Jubilant fans turned downtown Minneapolis into a virtual parking lot.

FOUNDED IN 1801 BY ALEXANDER HAMILTON

NEW YORK POST

SPORTS FINAL

FRIDAY, JUNE 24, 1988 / Sunny, upper 70s today; partly cloudy, mid 60s tonight / Details, Page 2

35¢ in New York City **50¢** elsewhere

BYE, BYE, BYE, BYE, BYE!

Downfall begins when Billy benches Reggie Jackson. Then, on July 24, 1978, he tearfully resigns on balcony of hotel room.

NEW YORK POST FINAL
Rose going for record at Shea: Back Page
Billy Martin on way out
Hint Bob Lemon to be replacement
The heat fells 17 aged: Rome's owner fled in '77
Tonelli pleads

George brings Billy back on June 18, 1979. He finishes fourth, but punches a marshmallow salesman Oct. 25, and is canned.

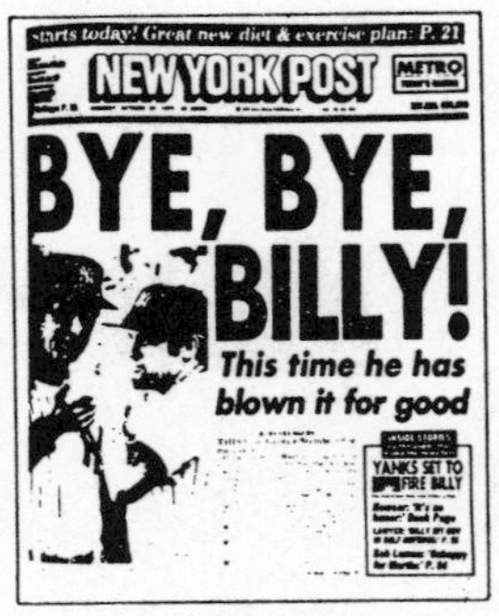
Starts today! Great new diet & exercise plan: P. 21
NEW YORK POST METRO
BYE, BYE, BILLY!
This time he has blown it for good
YANKS SET TO FIRE BILLY

He's cleaned up his act. May 25, 1983, he clashes with bar patron. On June 14, he smashes a urinal with a bat. Dec. 16, he's fired.

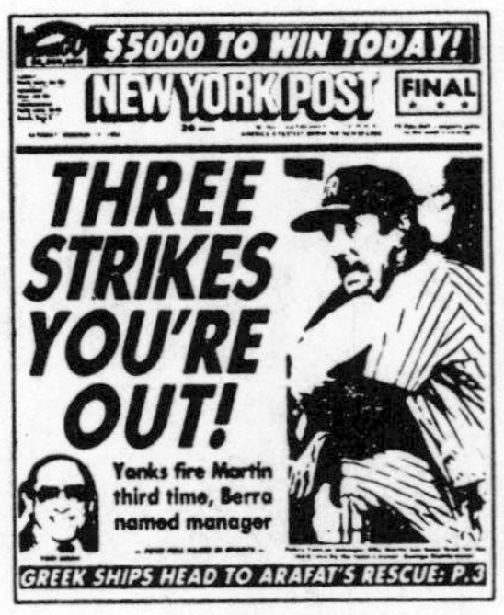
$5000 TO WIN TODAY!
NEW YORK POST FINAL
THREE STRIKES YOU'RE OUT!
Yanks fire Martin third time, Berra named manager
GREEK SHIPS HEAD TO ARAFAT'S RESCUE: P. 3

Billy takes over again. On Sept. 20, 1985, he shoves a bar patron. Next night, pitcher Ed Whitson breaks Billy's arm in brawl. He's fired again.

NEW YORK POST SPORTS Extra
Sweet Lou takes helm as Billy IV bites dust
PIZZOLATO, WAITZ WIN MARATHON: P. 3
"Light my Lucky."

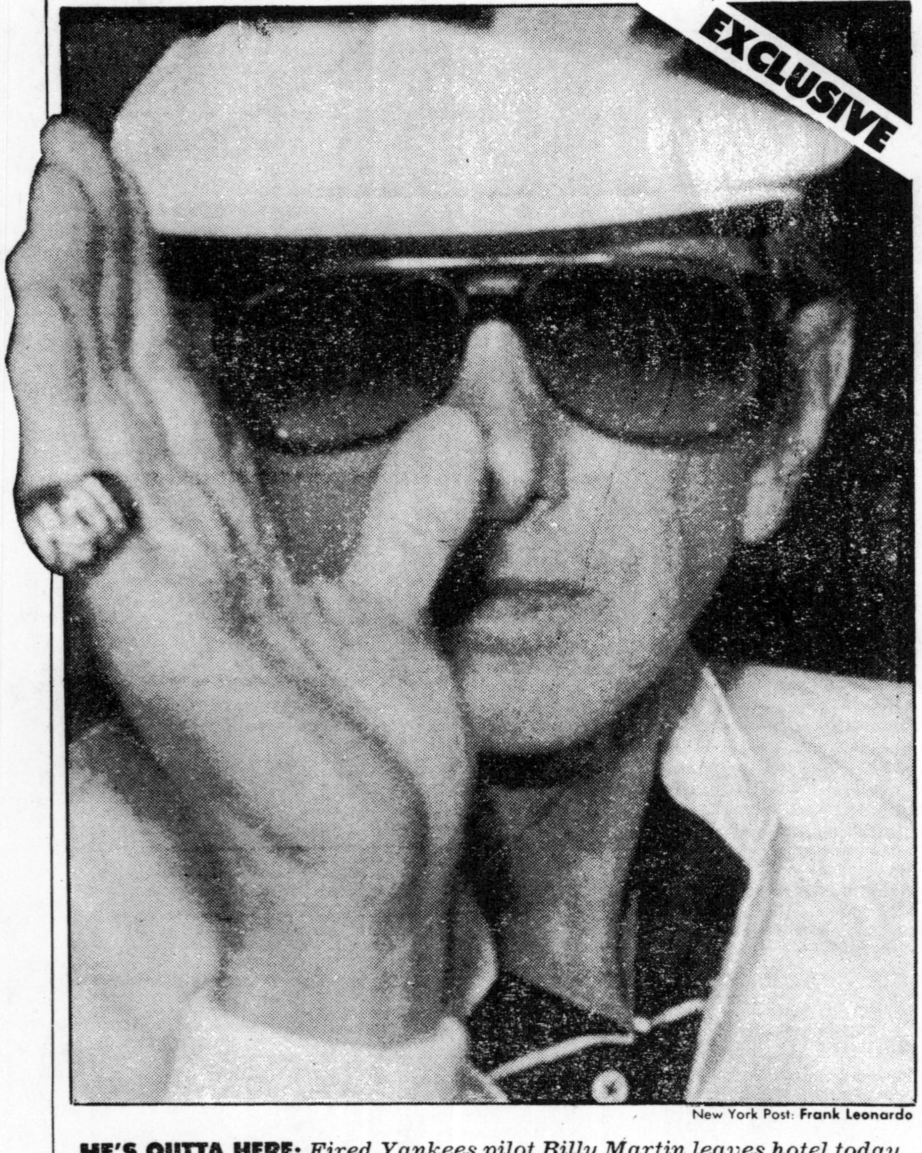
New York Post: **Frank Leonardo**

HE'S OUTTA HERE: *Fired Yankees pilot Billy Martin leaves hotel today.*

EXCLUSIVE

BILLY TAKES THE FIFTH

5-TIME LOSER

Billy's gone again & Lou Piniella's back — coverage starts Page 7 & Back Page

VALLEY EDITION
Los Angeles Times
Sunday, October 16, 1988

SPORTS

THE WORLD SERIES
OAKLAND ATHLETICS vs. LOS ANGELES DODGERS

Gibson's Shot in the Dark Stuns A's

Jim Murray

It Could Happen Only in Hollywood

Well, you can believe that if you want to.

As for me, I know a Warner Bros. movie when I see one. I've been around this town long enough to spot a hokey movie script.

I mean, this is Rambo IV, right? That was Sylvester Stallone that came out of the dugout in the 9th inning of Game 1 of the 1988 World Series. That wasn't a real player?

Believe this one and you'll think Superman is a documentary.

The country's never going to buy it. This is the thing Hollywood does best. But it never happens in real life. In real life, the hero pops up in this situation. In an Italian movie, he dies. He doesn't hit a last-minute home run with 2 outs and 2 strikes and the best relief pitcher in baseball throwing. This is John Wayne saving the fort stuff. Errol Flynn taking the Burma Road.

A guy who can hardly walk, hits a ball where he doesn't have to. A few minutes before he's sitting in a tub of ice like a broken-down racehorse.

Kirk Gibson is the biggest bargain since Alaska. He should be on crutches—or at least a cane. He wasn't even introduced to the World Series crowd in the pregame ceremonies. He wasn't even in the dugout till the game got dramatic. Some people were surprised he was in uniform. Some were surprised he was upright.

The odds against his hitting a home run in this situation were about the odds of winning a lottery. The manager was just milking the situation, trying to keep the crowd from walking out early. No one seriously expected a guy with two unhinged knees to get a hit, never mind *the* hit.

Here was the situation: the Oakland Athletics who are less a team than a packet of mastodons, baseball's answer to a massed artillery attack, had the game all but won, ahead by 1 with 2 out, 1 on.

Somehow, a quartet of Dodger pitchers had held this mass of muscle to 4 measly runs. The Dodgers had somehow pasted together 3. They got 2 of them when Mickey (Himself) Hatcher who

Please see MURRAY, Page 8

JOE KENNEDY / Los Angeles Times

Kirk Gibson raises his arms and lets out a roar as he hobbles toward second base after hitting the game-winning homer for the Dodgers in the ninth inning of Game 1 of the World Series.

His Pinch Homer Wins Game 1 for Dodgers, 5-4

By SAM McMANIS,
Times Staff Writer

If Kirk Gibson really is the embodiment of these incredibly resilient Dodgers, then this had to be the ultimate example of the unbridled spirit and resolve of this team.

There were the Dodgers, one out away from a 4-3 loss to the Oakland Athletics in Game 1 of the World Series Saturday night at Dodger Stadium, when Gibson came lurching out of the dugout with a bat and the Dodgers' hopes in his hands.

With Mike Davis on base after a two-out walk, Gibson, who did not start because of a sprained ligament in his right knee and lingering soreness from a strained left hamstring, gingerly stepped to the plate to face A's ace Dennis Eckersley, who led the major leagues in saves this season.

Burrowing his feet into the batter's box, Gibson somehow managed to work Eckersley to a full count, with Davis taking second on a stolen base.

Then, with a quick turn of his hips and a snap of his wrists, Gibson sent Eckersley's pitch over the right-field fence to complete an exhilarating 5-4 comeback victory by the Dodgers before a crowd of 55,983 that simply would not stop cheering, even after the Dodger players had left the field.

RESULTS, SCHEDULE

Game 1	Dodgers 5, Athletics 4	
Date	**Site**	**Time**
Tonight	Dodger Stadium	5:30 p.m.
Tues.	Oakland	5:30 p.m.
Weds.	Oakland	5:30 p.m.
Thur.*	Oakland	5:30 p.m.
Sat.*	Dodger Stadium	2:30 p.m.
Oct. 23*	Dodger Stadium	5:30 p.m.

* If necessary. All times Pacific.

■ **TV:** Ch. 4, 36, 39.

■ **Tonight's Starters:** Storm Davis (16-7) vs. Orel Hershiser (23-8)

"It was a great moment," Gibson said. "I felt fortunate to be in there and be a part of it. It was a classic, good for the fans to see and people around in all the nations."

In the wake of his global embarrassment, Eckersley could only shake his head and recall what had gone wrong when his 3-and-2 slider slid directly onto Gibson's bat.

"It was a terrible pitch," Eckersley said. "I've got to live with it."

As dramatic and unexpected as Gibson's home run was, the consummate moment of what probably will be remembered as a World Series classic was the sight of Gibson lugging that battered body

Please see DODGERS, Page 7

Mike Downey

Though He Can Hardly Stand, Gibson Delivers

Before Kirk Gibson came to bat, with two Detroit teammates on base, one final time in what turned out to be the final game of the 1984 World Series, he noticed the San Diego Padres engaged in an animated discussion on the pitching mound. They looked unhappy.

Goose Gossage, it turned out, was trying to talk his manager, Dick Williams, into letting him pitch to Gibson instead of walking him intentionally. Williams, who already had seen Gibson belt one home run in this game, shook his head from side to side. He looked as though he would rather eat the rosin bag than pitch to Gibson.

Gibby strolled from the on-deck circle to the dugout.

"Hey," he yelled down to Tiger Manager Sparky Anderson. "Ten bucks says they pitch to me."

Sparky called.

"Ten bucks say they don't," he said.

They did.

The score immediately transformed from 5-4 to 8-4. The final game of the World Series belonged to the Tigers, with Gibson homering twice and scoring another run by tagging up and racing home on a sacrifice fly—that was caught by the second baseman.

Let's face it, the man thrives on this stuff.

Please see DOWNEY, Page 8

THE BATTLE FOR NO. 1 IN COLLEGE FOOTBALL

Irish Knock Miami Off Its Perch, 31-30

By RICHARD HOFFER,
Times Staff Writer

SOUTH BEND, Ind.—Great football games, those rare occasions when the play actually corresponds to the importance, do not simply pass into legend. Not even at Notre Dame, where everything seems to be instant lore. But when you add controversy, an upset and bad feelings and mix in national championship ingredients (the weather was sensational, too), you definitely have another chapter in the game's Big Book of History.

Saturday's game, in which top-

Please see IRISH, Page 15

United Press International

Pat Terrell returns an interception for an Irish score.

UCLA Stops Cal, 38-21, Aims for Top

By JERRY CROWE,
Times Staff Writer

BERKELEY—UCLA, which has been ranked No. 2 since it beat Nebraska in the second week of the season, staked its claim to No. 1 Saturday with another workmanlike dissection of an outclassed opponent, a 38-21 victory over California before a crowd of 58,000 at Memorial Stadium.

Since top-ranked Miami, the defending national champion, lost at Notre Dame, 31-30, the Bruins await what they believe will be their rightful ascension to the top of the polls this week.

Please see UCLA, Page 13

United Press International

UCLA's Paul Richardson celebrates his touchdown catch.

Huskies Fail on 2-Pointer, and USC Wins

By MAL FLORENCE,
Times Staff Writer

USC remained unbeaten Saturday by barely withstanding a pro-type passing performance by Washington quarterback Cary Conklin.

The Trojans won, 28-27, at the Coliseum as the Huskies elected to go for a 2-point conversion that failed with only 1:39 remaining in the game.

Conklin, who completed 15 of 19 passes for 239 yards and 3 touchdowns in the second half, underthrew his receiver, tailback Vince Weathersby, on the 2-point

Please see USC, Page 12

STEVE DYKES / Los Angeles Times

USC's Scott Lockwood breaks loose for 41 yards.

SATURDAY'S COLLEGE FOOTBALL

5. Florida State ..45 **East Carolina ..21** Please see Page 11	**Georgia Tech ..34** **8. South Carolina ..0** Please see Page 11	**11. Clemson ......49** **Duke ....17** Please see Page 11	**14. Wyoming .....55** **New Mexico ....7** Please see Page 14
7. Nebraska .....63 **10. Oklahoma St. ..42** Please see Page 15	**9. Oklahoma ....70** **Kansas State ..24** Please see Page 15	**12. Auburn ....42** **Akron ....0** Please see Page 11	**15. Michigan .....17** **Iowa ....17** Please see Page 10

INSIDE

■ White Sets Record

Russell White of Crespi High becomes the state's all-time scoring leader in the Celts' win over Alemany.

Please see Page 22.

LOS ANGELES

Herald Examiner

Friday
October 21, 1988

Final news

Weather
Hazy sunshine/A2

25 cents

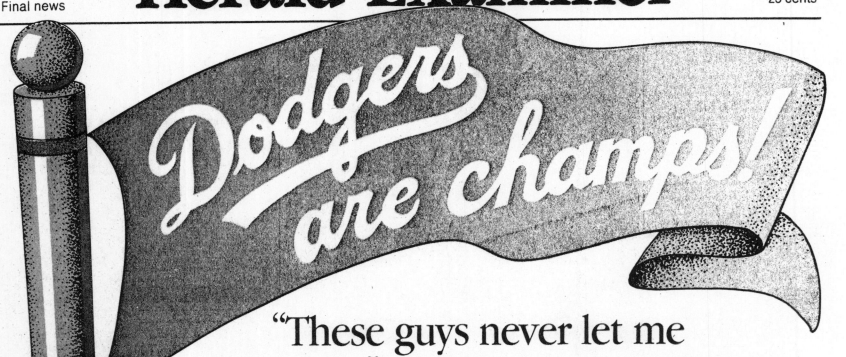

Dodgers are champs!

"These guys never let me down" — Tommy Lasorda

Bulldog and underdogs do it

It was the only game in town

By Andy Furillo
Herald Examiner staff writer

From Mickey Hatcher's first-inning home run to Orel Hershiser's strikeout of Tony Phillips for the final out, it was a victory that the Dodger faithful throughout Los Angeles shared in and exulted over.

In their homes and workplaces, at bars and in shopping malls, Dodger fans parked themselves in front of the television early in anticipation of the club's first World Series championship in seven years.

But television couldn't do the trick for Larry Crino, 31, who runs a Round Table Pizza franchise in Tarzana. He hopped on a plane yesterday at 4:20 p.m. for Oakland, where he personally witnessed the Dodgers' 5-2 championship-clinching win.

It was the 84th Dodger game Crino attended this year, including three Series contests, four league championship tilts against the Mets and seven trips to San Francisco to see his team play the Giants. He was not disappointed.

"When you win in the manner the Dodgers have won, you feel that any obstacle can be overcome." Crino said in a telephone

Fans, A-14 ▶

THE FULL STORY

- ▶ **The upset:** L.A. ranks with all-time oddsbusters. **A-14**
- ▶ **The game:** Ken Gurnick has the final play-by-play. **C-1**
- ▶ **Melvin Durslag** looks at the A's false advertising. **C-1**
- ▶ **Doug Krikorian** on the impossible dream team. **C-8**
- ▶ **Roger Brigham** on how Bulldog took bite out of A's. **C-8**

Paul Chinn/Herald Examiner

Head and shoulders above: Jubilant Dodgers mob Orel Hershiser after strikeout that won series.

By Roger Brigham
Herald Examiner staff writer

OAKLAND — The Dodgers, who began their Improbable Dream five days earlier with a swing and a prayer, last night ended it with a fling and a snare.

Yes, one final fling from the right arm of Dodgers ace Orel Hershiser, and one last snare by the mitt of catcher Rick Dempsey of the last strike by the swinging bat of Tony Phillips, and the Dodgers were once again World Champions.

Sherlock Holmes once observed to his friend, Dr. Watson, that if one eliminates the impossible, whatever is left, however improbable, is the truth.

The truth last night was that since it was impossible for the slumping Oakland offense to overcome unbeatable Orel, who'd pitched complete-game shutouts his last two postseason starts and allowed only three earned runs in his previous 92⅔ innings, the Dodgers were destined to become the most improbable World Series champions since the invention of the horsehide.

The baseball record book will show that last night's 5-2 victory gave the Dodgers the 1988 World Series championship, four games to one, over their American

Dodgers, A-14 ▶

INSIDE

Loose talk of Bush

A top Dukakis aide quits after commenting on widespread rumors of Bush adultery. **A-3**

Comics relief

We're conducting a serious reader poll on our comics. Cast your ballot today. **B-7**

NOLAN K-LIMBS TO TOP OF BASEBALL WORLD

By LYLE SPENCER

ARLINGTON, Tex. — Call it Mount Ryan, and don't expect anyone to ever make the climb again.

Nolan Ryan, baseball's all-time strikeout genius, scaled his greatest peak last night, reaching 5,000 Ks with a fifth-inning wasting of Rickey Henderson. He went on to notch seven more in a 13-K effort before, characteristic of his bittersweet career, falling victim to Bob Welch and the A's 2-0.

"You're excited by what you accomplish," Ryan said, summing up, "but disappointed you didn't get the win. I saw Steve Carlton strike out 19 against the Mets and get beat 2-1 when Ron Swoboda hit two home runs."

He was more nervous than usual coming into this rendezvous with history. How nervous was the 42-year-old Ranger legend?

"I drove past the ballpark and had to turn around and come back," he said, grinning. "That shows where my mind was."

After blowing a 3-2 fastball clocked at 96 mph past Henderson, low and on the outside corner, Ryan took a step off the mound to collect his thoughts. Then he turned and raised his cap to the roaring Arlington Stadium crowd that included commissioner A. Bartlett Giamatti and waited for catcher Chad Kreuter and the rest of the Rangers to come congratulate him.

"You never really know how to act in those situations," Ryan said. "If I could have asked for the way I wanted No. 5,000, it would have been on a fastball."

In the seven-pitch sequence against Henderson, Ryan threw three fastballs at 95 mph and another at 94 before turning it up a notch for the big one.

"I was looking fastball all the way, and he got me," Rickey said. "I'm not embarrassed or anything. He's the kind of pitcher every hitter admires, because he comes right at you. That's all you can ask for."

Never one to be outdone, Henderson also lifted his cap to the crowd on his way into the Oakland dugout, thrusting both arms outward.

"It was an honor for me to be part of it," Henderson said. "When I came up, I asked the ump [Larry Young] if I could take the ball out if I struck out and congratulate Nolan with it. But the catcher decided he wanted to do that, so I got left out of it."

It was the second time the Man of Steal had gone down hacking, and it was also the second time Ryan had got up to to 96 — an astonishing feat for a man in his 23d major league season.

With his next K — Ron Hassey, two hitters later, following an RBI double by Jose Canseco — Ryan established the all-time Rangers' season record with 226.

With 13 last night and 232 for the year, he leads the AL comfortably over runner-up Roger Clemens, with 167. Mark Langston is second overall with 185.

Overthrowing early in 95-degree heat before settling down and finding his rhythm, Ryan was jolted by Rickey, who crushed a leadoff double

A Canseco punchout was Ryan's first and only K of the first inning. It was the first time the game's young muscleman had hooked up with The Express, and Ryan put him away not with his heat but with an off-speed curve.

Ryan put away Dave Henderson on a 3-2 fastball leading off the second and used the curve again to make Tony Phillips victim No. 3. The A's scored in the third on Walt Weiss' leadoff double and successive singles by Carney Lansford and Canseco, but the crowd had eyes only for Ks — and Ryan gave them a pair, burying Rickey on a 3-2 fastball and then catching Hassey looking at a 1-2 fastball.

"I feel it's a possibility that someone will do it again," Ryan said of 5,000. "It'll have to be someone who combines longetivity, staying healthy and the stuff it takes."

Ryan's stuff, at 42, is still the right stuff. There's never been anyone like this guy.

Associated Press

FIVE GRAND: *Nolan Ryan fires patented fastball last night in Arlington against Athletics en route to notching 5,000th career strikeout. Ryan became first player ever to reach plateau when he fanned ex-Yankee Rickey Henderson in fifth inning.*

Ryan's 1st K victim unwittingly gains fame

DECATUR, Ga. (AP) — Former Braves pitcher Pat Jarvis, now a sheriff in suburban Atlanta, was Nolan Ryan's first strikeout victim in the major leagues — but didn't think much about it.

Ryan, 42 and now with the Rangers, went into last night's appearance against the Athletics only six strikeouts shy of 5,000 — a mark no major-league pitcher has ever approached.

The 48-year-old Jarvis, sheriff of DeKalb County for the last 13 years, pitched in the major leagues for eight years, with Atlanta and Montreal. Jarvis, who had a .121 lifetime average as a hitter, doesn't recall that time at bat on Sept. 11, 1966, against the hard-throwing Ryan.

"I really don't remember," Jarvis said this week. "I've been getting calls from all over the coontry, and I tell everyone the same thing: I can't remember."

Jarvis, called up from Class AAA Richmond by the parent Braves in September 1966, batted 22 times that season, but didn't get a hit that year.

He unwittingly became a part of baseball history when he struck out against the then-19-year-old Ryan.

"Everybody knew of him, but he was so wild no one wanted to dig in on this guy," Jarvis said. "I'm sure I was standing way in back of the box and giving him the whole plate."

Ryan, who also was recalled from the minors late in the 1966 season, by the Mets, pitched only three innings that season, but struck out six batters. He spent 1967 in the minor leagues before returning to the majors in 1968.

"I didn't know from Adam's housecat who Nolan Ryan was," Jarvis said. "But I'll be associated with him any day of the week."

Jarvis was not aware of his part in baseball history until Ryan, then with the Astros, broke Walter Johnson's all-time strikeout record six years ago.

"Somebody had to have started it," Jarvis said. "Pat Jarvis might as well have."

A's Welch wins war

ARLINGTON, Tex. — Nolan Ryan got his 5,000th strikeout, and then seven more, but it was another hard-throwing right-hander who won the game last night before 42,869 fans, the second largest Ranger crowd ever.

Oakland's Bob Welch, with an inning of relief from Dennis Eckersley, dispatched the Rangers 2-0. Welch, extending his scoreless string to 16 innings, allowed only five hits and struck out nine to take just a dash of the lustre off Ryan's historic occasion.

"Nolan Ryan was my hero when I was a kid," said Michigan native Welch, who ran his record to 14-7. "I copied his windup and everything. Here, watch."

Welch then launched into a Ryan impersonation that was letter-perfect.

"I just wish I could've hit against him," Welch said. "That would've been great. I might have gotten punched out, but I'd have had some hacks."

HOMETOWN HERO HELPS BIRDS BURN BREWERS PAGE 57

SPECIAL REPORT: THE ROSE LEGACY

THE CINCINNATI KID

CHARLIE HUSTLE: A CAREER IN PICTURES

PAGE 1C

BONUS SECTIONS INSIDE

DINING GUIDE

PLUS: PULL-AND-SAVE CINCINNATI GUIDE

SCRIPPS HOWARD

The Cincinnati Post

Final | THURSDAY, AUGUST 24, 1989 | 35 Cents

ROSE IS OUT!

'I made some mistakes'

By Al Salvato
Post staff reporter

Vowing to return someday to the game he loves, an emotionally wracked Pete Rose today ended his 30-year professional baseball career with a lifetime suspension, an apology to fans and a denial that he bet on ball games.

"I made some mistakes, and I am being punished for those mistakes," Rose said, clenching his hands and pausing a moment to compose himself. "As you can imagine, this is a sad day."

At separate press conferences today, Rose and Major League Baseball Commissioner A. Bartlett Giamatti announced that Rose is suspended from baseball for life but can apply for reinstatement within a year. However, Giamatti said there is no guarantee that reinstatement will ever be granted.

The suspension agreement sidesteps the major issue in the case — whether Rose bet on professional baseball and his team, the Cincinnati Reds — and an issue that for months has pitted the baseball legend against the freshman commissioner.

"Nothing in this agreement shall be deemed either an admission or a denial by Peter Edward Rose of the allegation that he bet on any Major League Baseball game," the agreement says.

Rather, Rose and Giamatti agreed that the baseball legend was being suspended for misconduct as allowed by a catch-all clause in the game's rule book.

At a press/conference in New York, however, Giamatti said he has concluded Rose had bet on baseball and on the Reds.

At Riverfront Stadium, Rose — flanked by three of his lawyers — continued to deny the betting accusations by former friends and was baffled by the commissioner's assertions.

"Regardless of what the commissioner said, I did not bet on baseball. I did not bet on the Reds," Rose insisted. "It's something I told the commissioner in February, and it's something I've said to you (the media) for four months."

Rose said that he is not an habitual gambler and will not undergo rehabilitation for a

Please see MISTAKES, 7A

Pete Rose: An era ends

DALE A. DUNAWAY/The Cincinnati Post

A solemn Pete Rose told the media today: "As you can imagine this is a very sad day."

The Rose case unravels

Today's Post includes three full pages of Pete Rose coverage, including a look at Rose's career, in photos, on Page 1C.

You'll also find inside:

■ **Rose** faces a whole new ballgame: A profile of Rose the man and Rose the baseball man.................................. **Page 4A.**

■ **The quotable** Pete Rose: "They can take me out of the game. But they can't take the game out of me."........... **Page 4A.**

■ **Rose hawked memorabilia** on a cable TV station Wednesday night as word spread of his suspension................. **Page 4A.**

■ **Today's trial** of Tommy Gioiosa, ex-Rose housemate, could yield even more revelations................................ **Page 4A.**

■ **Baseball** players and baseball followers tell what they think of today's compromise.. **Page 4A.**

■ **One of Rose's** accusers says he's disappointed the Reds manager didn't admit that he bet on baseball............... **Page 4A.**

■ **Baseball's A. Bartlett Giamatti** today notched his pistol with the name of a baseball legend.............................. **Page 5A.**

■ **Pete Rose's** troubles and what they might mean for his chances for the Hall of Fame.. **Page 5A.**

■ **A chronology:** Gambling story refused to die despite denials.. **Page 5A.**

■ **Rose's career** at a glance — the highs and the lows for the Reds manager.. **Page 5A.**

■ **Fans are split** over whether the Reds manager got what he deserved.. **Page 6A.**

■ **Highlights** from the settlement and from Giamatti press briefing.. **Page 7A.**

■ **Even to the end,** Rose sold his soul. Commentary by Post columnist Paul Daugherty.. **Page 1B.**

ROBERT DICKERSON/The Cincinnati Post

The man who dethroned Rose

Throughout baseball's investigation of Pete Rose, Commissioner A. Bartlett Giamatti has maintained he's not out to get Cincinnati's hometown hero. Page 5A.

Pete banished, but vows return

By Randy Ludlow
Post staff reporter

NEW YORK — Today, Pete Rose left the game that has been his life.

Baseball Commissioner A. Bartlett Giamatti suspended the baseball legend for life.

As of today, Giamatti said, Rose is "no longer employed or employable by baseball. He is ineligible."

However, Giamatti said, Rose can apply to the baseball commissioner for reinstatement in one year. But, Giamatti emphasized, there is no guarantee that application will be granted.

Rose, at a Cincinnati press conference today, promised to apply for reinstatement in exactly one year and continued to deny he bet on baseball.

Giamatti, at his press conference in New York City, said he personally is convinced that Rose did bet on baseball, but said he has an "open mind" about the manager's possible reinstatement. However, under the agreement signed by Rose and baseball, Rose is permanently ineligible to participate in any aspect of the game, the commissioner said.

Giamatti said Rose agreed not to contest the decision suspending him for life or the procedures used by the commissioner's office in ruling on any petition he may file seeking reinstatement.

The agreement between Rose and Giamatti, signed Wednes-

Please see ROSE, 7A

The penalty

■ **Pete Rose** today was declared "permanently ineligible" to play baseball by Commissioner A. Bartlett Giamatti.

■ **Rose can,** in accordance with Major League Baseball rules, apply for reinstatement after one year.

■ **Should he apply** for reinstatement, Rose agreed not to challenge the commissioner's decision on the application.

■ **All parties** involved formally agree that Rose neither admits nor denies that he bet on any Major League Baseball game.

Reds keeping quiet on Rose replacement

By Jerry Crasnick
Post staff reporter

Tommy Helms, the man considered by many to be Pete Rose's logical successor as Cincinnati Reds manager, still was in the dark about his prospects this morning.

Helms watched Rose's farewell press conference on television, but said he has had no contact with Reds general manager Murray Cook since Tuesday.

"Nobody's called me about anything," Helms said. "I haven't given it much thought, I'm just so damn sad about Pete. When you work with a guy this long . . . It's just a sad thing.

"All I know is what I read in the paper. I really don't know what they'll do. Why worry about something you can't control?"

Cook was unavailable for comment this morning.

Team spokesman Jim Ferguson said an announcement on the new manager is forthcoming but would give no specifics. "There's no timetable," Ferguson said.

The Reds have two options: go outside the organization, or choose one of their coaches, most likely Helms or Dave Bristol, to manage the final 35 games.

One player, outfielder Paul O'Neill, expressed support for the second option.

"I don't see any reason to bring in anybody," O'Neill said. "We've got guys who have been

Please see MANAGER, 6A

Inside The Post

4 sections, 102 pages		Living	1C-9C
Ann Landers	3C	Local News	10A,11A
Business	11B,12B	Lottery	11A
Classified	10C-16C	Races	4B
Comics	8C	Sports	1B-10B
Deaths	11A,10C	Stocks	12C
Editorial	16A,17A	Television	9C
Entertainment	6C,7C	Weather	2C

Weather: Tonight and Friday cloudy, with chance of showers or thunderstorms. Low 68. High 84. Details, Page 2C.

Weatherline.............241-1010

Sportsline................651-1515

The news inside today

■ **Colombia's drug** traffickers today declared war on the government in retaliation for a crackdown on the drug trade. The headquarters of two political parties were bombed and two politicians' homes were set on fire...................... **Page 2A.**

■ **Solidarity journalist** Tadeusz Mazowiecki won overwhelming approval today to become the East bloc's first non-communist prime minister, ending 45 years of communist control of Poland's government.......................... **Page 2A.**

■ **In another** act of East bloc defiance, more than a million people linked hands in the three Baltic republics of the U.S.S.R. to show support for self rule........................ **Page 2A.**

■ **A new poll** shows Americans want "tradition-shattering changes" in their schools.. **Page 12A.**

■ **Seattle is** rated the top city in the U.S. in Money magazine's latest poll. Cincinnati slips to No. 55..... **Page 14A.**

■ **The spacecraft** Voyager 2 began its final approach to the planet Neptune today.. **Page 18A.**

MELVIN GRIER/The Cincinnati Post

Prep preview

The high school football season kicks off Friday night and The Post takes a look at the coaches, the players and the schools in a special prep preview inside today's sports section.

One new wrinkle: A new league, the Queen City Conference, which combines teams from the Eastern Metro League, Cross County Conference and Western Metro Conference.

Elder's Panthers, shown practicing at left, were 10-2 last year and finished No. 1 in The Post's final coaches poll.

Please see stories, Pages 1B, 6B-10B.

Quake puts Series on hold

Game 3 at Candlestick postponed

By Mark Vancil
Staff Writer

San Francisco, Calif.
For approximately 15 seconds Tuesday night, with more than 60,000 people crammed into Candlestick Park and the height of rush hour traffic in motion, the San Andreas Fault erupted.

The earthquake exploded concrete floors in Candlestick's upper deck and sents tremors through virtually the entire state.

Baseball Commissioner Fay Vincent called off Tuesday's World Series Game 3 and said he would decide early today whether the Oakland Athletics and San Francisco Giants would be able to resume the Series this evening after he receives a report on the structural inspection of the stadium.

Although the damage to Candlestick won't be known until today, the possiblity of another game being played before Thursday was unlikely.

"We haven't had an opportunity to access the damage," said Jorge Costa, director of stadium operations. "We'll do an evaluation tomorrow. It will take 24 hours. . . . We will not jeopordize 62,000 people."

Vincent, composed and surrounded by stunned league officials, acknowledge cracks and falling debris in and around Candlestick.

"There is damage," said Vincent. "We know there are cracks."

Oakland Coliseum, just eight miles away, is in an area that sustained damage at least as severe and maybe worse as the Candlestick Park area.

At Candlestick, the motion, which started as a slow shake a built into a frenzied ripple, swung light standards and the entire building itself. An elevated press box, at the upper most point of the Stadium, rocked hard nearly unhinging television sets positioned for reporters.

Phone lines immediately went down and the stadium's electricity soon followed. The stadium clocks locked at 5:05 p.m. and an eerie, fear-induced cheer rose from the stadium. With electricity coming and going, a voice came across the public address system calling for calm and urging fans to leave the upper deck.

Outside the stadium the Bay Area had turned into a disaster site. Information poured in immediately and pockets of fans, most shaken and their faces blank of emotion, listened to radios and portable televisions sets. Slowly, but with an unmistakable purpose, they moved toward the parking lots.

Todd DeVelbiss, 73, stood near the center field upper deck, still shaken,

World Series continued on page 7C

Associated Press

Oakland players watched fans leave the Candlestick Park grandstand during Tuesday's earthquake, left, and A's pitcher Storm Davis (14), right, took a baby from the arms of an unidentified woman in the stands.

Stars win, equal their best start

By Tony Moton
Staff Writer

Uniondale, N.Y.
The North Stars were well aware of what the New York Islanders could do against them entering Tuesday night's game at Nassau Coliseum. It was two weeks ago that the Islanders almost rebounded from a four-goal deficit to nearly beat the Stars at Met Center.

"We said, 'Hey, what did they do last time?' " Stars coach Pierre Page said. "It looked like a replica for a while. But I think we kept our composure."

Composure isn't the only thing the Stars kept last night before 10,230 fans. After taking another four-goal lead against the Islanders, they went on to a 6-3 victory to remain unbeaten in six games.

The Stars got two goals apiece from Neal Broten and Mike Gartner, a record-setting five assists from defenseman Larry Murphy and three power-play goals in improving to 5-0-1 as the NHL's only unbeaten team. The mark ties the Stars' best start, which came in the 1982-83 season.

"It feels good," Page said. "I know a lot of the guys were saying they weren't paying attention to being undefeated, but they are paying attention to the next game. People warned us about being cocky, they didn't come in cocky and I didn't see any cockiness tonight."

The Stars built a 6-2 lead with a dominating four-goal second period, capped by Dave Gagner's power-play goal with one second left. "Those penalties killed us," Islanders coach Al Arbour said. "I hope they (his players) learned a lesson."

Shooting Stars

With Tuesday night's 6-3 victory over the Islanders, the North Stars tied the team record for fastest start. Below is a chart of the Stars' best starts after six games, their final regular-season record and how they placed in the division:

	After 6 games	Finish	Place
1989-90/	5-0-1	?	?
1982-83/	5-0-1	40-24-16	2nd
1980-81/	4-1-1	35-28-17	3rd
1971-72/	4-1-1	37-29-12	2nd
1986-87/	3-2-1	30-40-10	5th
1981-82/	3-2-1	37-23-20	1st
1979-80/	3-2-1	36-28-16	3rd

In the opener Oct. 5, the Stars took a 6-2 lead early in the third period before holding on to win. This time, the Islanders only got a goal by Gerald Diduck at 2:53 of the third period after falling behind by four goals.

The Islanders (2-3-1) were 2-0-1 in their last three games, taking a 3-0 lead in all three. "We had to be sharp because this team was blowing people away early in the game," Page said.

Center Pat LaFontaine's fourth goal of the season gave the Islanders a 1-0 lead 6:52 into the game for their only lead. The Stars, who haven't trailed at the end of a period this season, then took a 2-1 lead on goals by Gartner and Broten. In the second period, left wing Brian Bellows scored his seventh goal for a 3-1 lead at 3:40. Islanders left wing David Volek made it 3-2 at 8:35, but Gartner, Broten and Gagner scored again to secure the victory.

Murphy's five assists set a team rec-

North Stars continued on page 7C

Staff Photo by Brian Peterson

All eyes were skyward following a leaping Timberwolf at the Metrodome shoot-around that preceded the team's first exhibition game tonight.

Show time arrives for Wolves as Lakers visit for exhibition

By Jerry Zgoda
Staff Writer

The Timberwolves, minus holdouts Rick Mahorn, Tyrone Corbin and Steve Johnson, have practiced together 22 times in the past 12 days, but they only know two things about tonight's exhibition opener against the Los Angeles Lakers at the Metrodome.

"We know we're going to play hard and we know we will play together," forward/center/guard Scott Roth said.

But just how good, or bad, will they be? "As for talent level, I don't think we have any idea where we're at yet," forward Brad Lohaus said.

They will know much more by 9:30 tonight. The Lakers are, well, the Lakers. Magic Johnson. James Worthy. Byron Scott. A.C. Green. Mychal Thompson. They have reached the NBA finals the past three seasons, winning the title twice. Their dominance is not limited only to the post-season: The Lakers won their first five exhibition games this season by nearly 21 points a game, including a 117-75 romp over the New Jersey

Timberwolves continued on page 5C

Nelson gets wish in joining Chargers

By Robert Sansevere
Staff Writer

Darrin Nelson had two wishes granted Tuesday. He was 1) traded to a West Coast team that 2) plays its home games on a grass field.

The Dallas Cowboys traded Nelson to the San Diego Chargers for a 1990 fifth-round draft choice that was sent to the Vikings. The Vikings, in return, shipped to the Cowboys a 1990 sixth-round draft choice and a 1991 second-round selection that was one of the six conditional picks tied to the Herschel Walker deal between Dallas and the Vikings.

"I get to go home and play on grass," said Nelson, who grew up in Los Angeles. "I may not be going to one of the top teams, but the Chargers are playing well. I have to take off my hat to the Cowboys. They bent over backwards to find the area I like. I'm real pleased with them."

Benevolence wasn't the only reason the Cowboys traded Nelson on the NFL's final day of trading until Feb. 5. They also picked up an additional draft pick — that sixth-round selection from the Vikings in 1990. The Vikings also benefitted by getting a better pick in that draft.

If the Vikings hadn't received some sort of compensation, it's unlikely Nelson would have been traded to the Chargers or any other team. The Cowboys would have forfeited the conditional second-round pick in 1991 without the Vikings' cooperation. It took that fifth-round draft pick that originated in San Diego for them to cooperate.

When the Vikings traded Nelson, cornerback Issiac Holt, linebackers

Nelson continued on page 5C

Bay Area residents learn to cope after the earthquake — *See Local*

SUNDAY TRIBUNE

Final ★★★★

WINNING LOTTO NUMBERS, PAGE A-7

Oakland, California | Sunday, October 29, 1989 | $1.00

THE WORLD SERIES

OAKLAND 9, SAN FRANCISCO 6

GAME 4

World Champs!

Heavy-hitting Athletics score sweep in earthquake-interrupted Series; Stewart is MVP

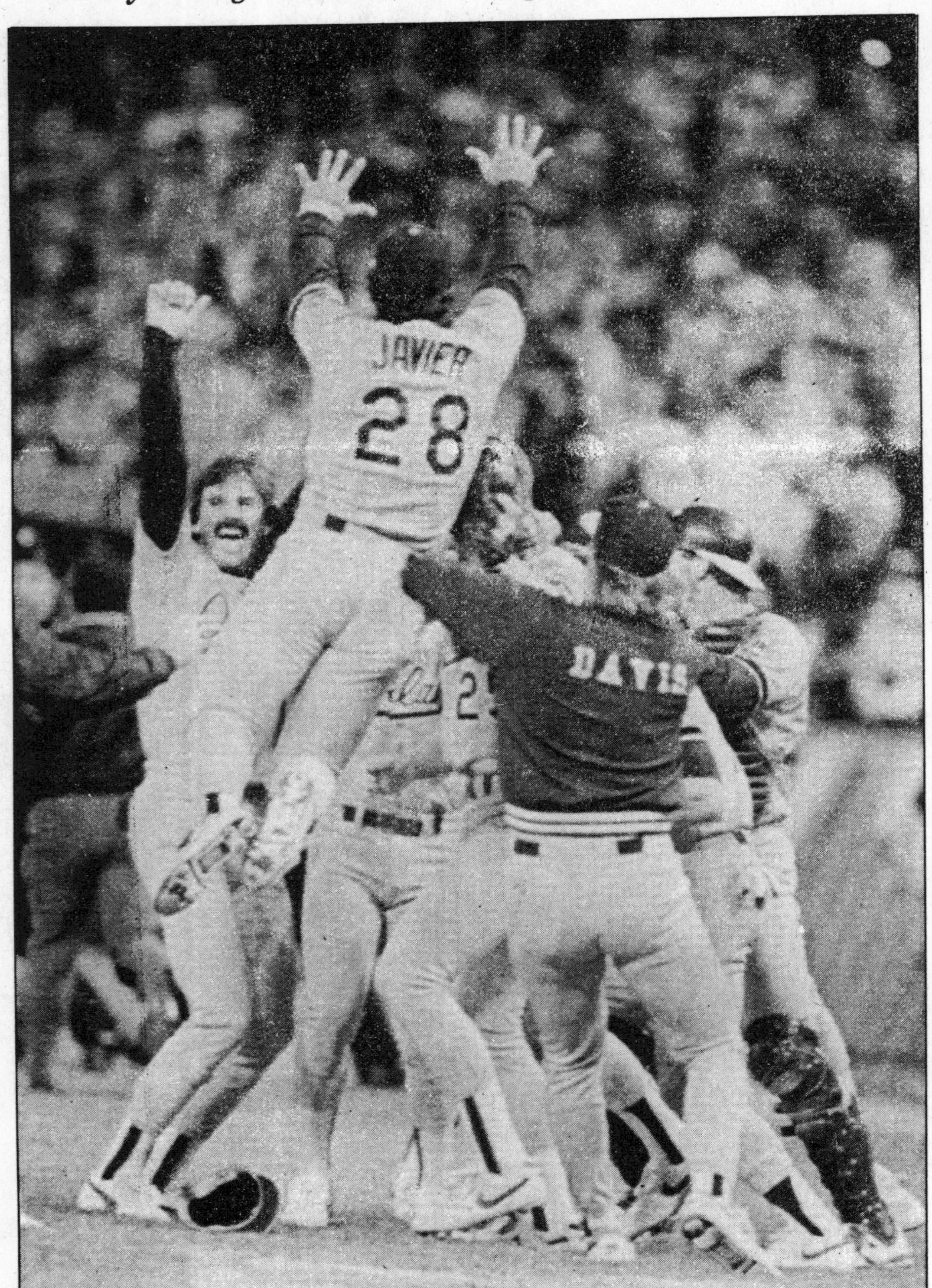

The Associated Press

Jumpin' and hollerin' Oakland A's teammates meet Dennis Eckersley, facing camera at left, after last out against San Francisco Giants.

By Michael Collier
The Tribune

SAN FRANCISCO — The 1989 World Series, an all-Oakland affair through the first three games, exploded with sheer excitement last night and nearly gave fans of the San Francisco Giants a glimmer of life.

But in the end, the Athletics fought off a fierce comeback to win 9-6, sweep the Series and capture their first world championship since 1974.

MVP Dave Stewart

The final victory was truly sweet for Oakland — the final out came on a brilliant pickup by second baseman Tony Phillips, who flipped to Dennis Eckersley as the pitcher stretched his foot onto first.

That's where the green and yellow began a leaping, dancing celebration, which they and their fans took well into a night lengthened by an hour because of the switch back to standard time.

The four-game sweep, delayed by the earthquake for 10 days after two games had been already played, marks the first time a team has won four straight World Series games since the "Big Red Machine" Cincinnati Reds in 1976.

The A's were truly a machine themselves, turning power, speed and pitching into a memorable revenge of their loss to the Los Angeles Dodgers in last year's series.

And it was the pitching of Dave Stewart, the workhorse hurler who won Games 1 and 3, that earned the Oakland native the Series' Most Valuable Player award.

Stewart, flanked by his mother Nathalie in a postgame interview, called the moment "a bright spot" for the entire Bay Area in the wake of the deadly temblor.

For the Giants and their faithful fans, who made up most of the crowd of 62,032 last night, the loss brought disappointment and pain.

"Pain, pain, pain. It's the only word to describe it," said Chris Lennen of Redwood City. "I guess we can only look to next year."

But for A's booster Sherry Stevens, there was nothing but glee.

"It feels great because we're number one," she said, waving a broom in joy.

And so ends a historic series, the longest ever played because of the quake delay and the first ever between the two Bay Area clubs.

The finale of the series was a real roller-coaster of a game, from Rickey Henderson's leadoff home run

See A'S, Page A-3

A's victory provides respite for earthquake homeless

By Howard Levine
The Tribune

The A's World Series sweep brought wild cheers all over Oakland, but two groups of fans had different reasons for celebrating.

Revelers watching the game on the big screen at the Kings X bar in Oakland found the victory especially sweet after the disappointing loss last year in World Series at the hands of the Los Angeles Dodgers.

But at the Red Cross emergency shelter at Laney College, fans who huddled around portable televisions savored the victory because of the respite, at least for a short time, from the tragedy of the recent earthquake.

"As long as I'm watching the game in front of me, and the A's are winning, I don't remember that I'm here," said Eddie Franklin.

Franklin, 35, was evacuated from his home in the shadow of the Cypress Structure after the collapse of the freeway.

"The Series couldn't have happened at a better time," he said.

While most of the people at the shelter

See LIFT, Page A-3

INSIDE

Big win, quake make some A's fans root for the Giants
Page A-2

Giants fans react to a dream swept away
Page A-3

The A's dominated the Giants with perfection, says Dave Newhouse
Page D-1

Get bash-by-bash coverage of the A's championship win
Page D-1

RACING ★ ★ ★ ★ FINAL

B'KLYN BOY, 3, HURLED TO DEATH

Story on page 4

DAILY NEWS

35¢

NEW YORK'S PICTURE NEWSPAPER®

Monday, July 2, 1990

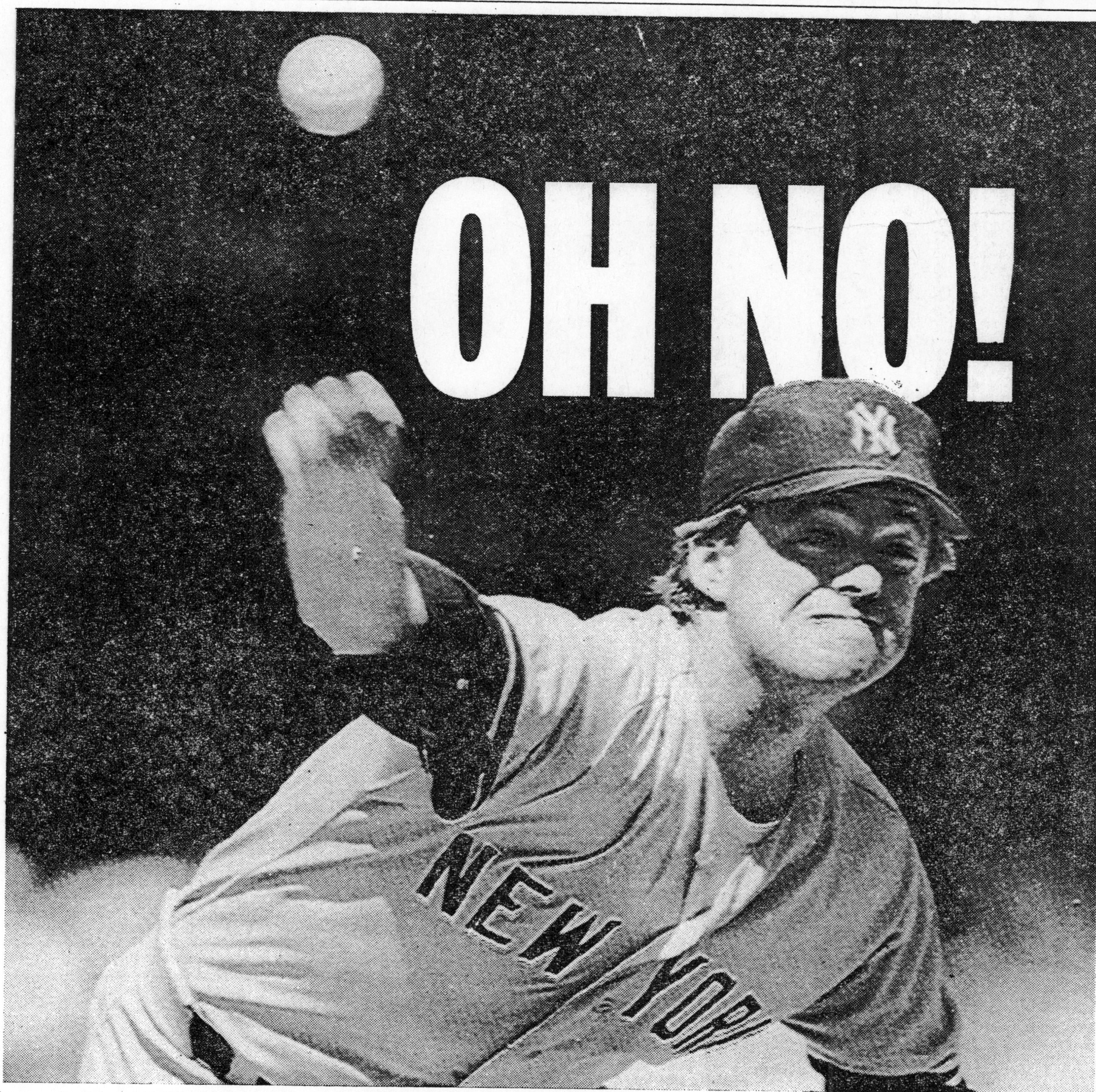

AP

ANDY WAS DANDY, BUT . . .

A grimly determined Yankee pitcher Andy Hawkins mows down another hitter yesterday in Chicago. He allowed no hits in the entire game. But walks and errors let Chisox waltz, 4-0. Hard Luck Hawkins is second man ever to pitch complete game no-hitter — and lose. **Stories in Sports**

Sports Day

Wednesday, August 1, 1990 · ©1990, The Dallas Morning News · The Dallas Morning News · ... A · Section B

RYAN WINS 300

Vincent adds to penalty

Steinbrenner gets what he asks for

Associated Press

NEW YORK — Commissioner Fay Vincent indicated Tuesday he had planned only to suspend George Steinbrenner, but the New York Yankees owner inexplicably asked for what amounted to a lifetime ban.

Vincent also suggested the penalty he planned to impose was for a fixed term and was less severe than the punishment Steinbrenner agreed to after 11 hours of negotiations Monday.

A baseball official, speaking on the condition that he not be identified, said the length of the suspension would have been two years plus three years' probation.

"I have to say to you I found some aspects of yesterday strange and I still find them strange this morning," Vincent said.

Steinbrenner agreed to give up control of the team and resign as general partner by Aug. 20.

On other fronts, the United States Olympic Committee will consider beleaguered George Steinbrenner's continued role with the organization at a USOC executive committee meeting on Aug. 22, USOC president Bob Helmick said Tuesday. Steinbrenner has been active in U.S. Olympic affairs as one of three USOC vice presidents.

Also, Gov. Mario Cuomo's chief economic development adviser said Tuesday that New York state would likely go ahead with an attempt to buy the Yankees, if Steinbrenner decides to sell. Cuomo aide Vincent Tese said he didn't think any such sale was imminent, but that New York would be ready to move if conditions changed.

As the baseball world still reacted to Steinbrenner's departure, the commissioner placed the Yankees under American League supervision for the next five years.

Steinbrenner, meantime, confirmed he wants his 33-year-old son Hank to take over the day-to-day operations of the Yankees. The move, already cleared by Vincent, must still be approved by the team's limited partners and major league clubs.

"I think it's time to turn that over to the young blood in the family," said Steinbrenner, who was punished

Please see STEINBRENNER Page 5B.

The Dallas Morning News: Ken Geiger

Nolan Ryan reacts to walking the Brewers' Jim Gantner in the second inning of Tuesday's game in Milwaukee. Ryan went 7⅔ innings for his 300th victory.

Rangers survive shaky 8th, 11-3

By Tim Cowlishaw
Staff Writer of The Dallas Morning News

RYAN AT A GLANCE

Pitches	IP	H	R	ER	BB	SO	HR
146	7⅔	6	2	1	2	8	0

Pitch count by inning

First	17	Fifth	18
Second	24	Sixth	12
Third	13	Seventh	20
Fourth	17	Eighth	25

■ Related stories 15-17B
■ Update, box score 15B

MILWAUKEE — The support Nolan Ryan needed arrived in the form of a four-run fifth inning. The support he didn't need showed up in a two error-eighth by Julio Franco.

Still, the Rangers escaped serious trouble in the eighth and Franco made amends with a grand slam in the ninth as Texas crushed Milwaukee, 11-3, putting Ryan into the history books one more time. He became the majors' 20th pitcher to reach 300 victories, and it apparently came to the delight of the paid County Stadium crowd of 51,533 as Ryan received ovations throughout, the loudest and longest coming when he departed the game two outs into the eighth inning.

The Rangers took a 5-1 lead into the eighth before Paul Molitor opened with a single to left. Robin Yount followed with a potential double-play grounder near the bag, but Franco let it slip through his legs. After Gary Sheffield popped to short, Dave Parker hit another ground ball that scooted past Franco for an error, cutting Texas' lead to 5-2.

Ryan got Greg Vaughn to pop up before Jim Gantner singled to left to cut the lead to 5-3, ending Ryan's night at 146 pitches. Reliever Brad Arnsberg, who saved Monday's game, got Mike Felder to fly out to end the inning.

The lead grew much more comfortable in the top of ninth when Franco sent his third career grand slam into the left-field seats.

For four innings, the Rangers fired blanks against Chris Bosio. Twelve men up, 12 down. In the fifth, trailing, 1-0, following Yount's RBI-triple, the Rangers opened fire with four hits, the biggest one a two-out, two-run double by Jeff Huson that staked Ryan to a three-run lead.

Ruben Sierra led off the fifth with a single to center, and Harold Baines lined Bosio's next pitch for a base hit to right, putting the go-ahead run on first. Incaviglia drew

Please see FRANCO on Page 15B.

Rangers nervous over ailing Witt, Russell

By Gerry Fraley
Staff Writer of The Dallas Morning News

MILWAUKEE — The Rangers' concerns over ailing pitchers Jeff Russell and Bobby Witt eased only slightly Tuesday.

An examination found tendon inflammation the cause of pain in Witt's right elbow. The status of his next start, scheduled for Saturday against Toronto, is uncertain.

Russell, on an injury-rehabilitation assignment with Class A Charlotte, had renewed problems with his right elbow during a brief throwing session. If the pain persists Wednesday, Russell wants to be re-examined by Dr. James Andrews, who performed elbow surgery in May.

"We might be in a little bind for pitching," general manager Tom Grieve said. "We'll have to see how these guys respond."

Russell, making his first game appearance since May 28, pulled himself after only three pitches

Please see WITT on Page 15B.

NOLAN RYAN
SPECIAL SECTION

EXPRESSLY RYAN
in honor of 300

Thursday, *The Dallas Morning News* will publish a special section commemorating Nolan Ryan's 300th victory. Among the features: pitching lines and results from each major league appearance; a look at the 20 members of the 300 club; a color graphic examining his delivery; and remembrances from people important to him throughout his career.

Landry's QB succession left indelible impression

Meredith, Staubach, White won in different ways

By Sam Blair
Staff Writer of The Dallas Morning News

TOM LANDRY'S
HALL OF FAME
JOURNEY

■ *Tom Landry, who will be inducted into the Pro Football Hall of Fame on Saturday in Canton, Ohio, coached the Cowboys for 29 years. Three quarterbacks — Don Meredith, Roger Staubach and Danny White — started almost 75 percent of the games coached by Landry. Staubach had the most success, but all three had their moments.*

Don Meredith had some fun and some fame in those early years with the Cowboys, but he never figured he was Tom Landry's dream quarterback.

"If Tom were going to create a quarterback, it would be Roger Staubach," Meredith said years after his retirement as a player. "Roger is the ideal quarterback for Tom, for the Cowboys, for the system. His character, the way he plays, the intensity with which he plays . . . he really does an excellent job."

Meredith offered his assessment in the summer of 1978, for him an ideal time for reflection and perspective. Nine years had passed since he suddenly quit as the Cowboys' No. 1 quarterback at 31. By retiring, Dandy Don unknowingly created a greater opportunity for a rookie backup, a newly discharged Navy lieutenant starting his pro football career four years late.

When he hung up his silver helmet, Meredith figured four-year veteran Craig Morton would be the main man in the Cowboys' offense for years to come. It was a popular opinion at the time, but not one privately shared by Staubach. Ultimately, Staubach was in, Morton was out and the

Please see LANDRY'S on Page 6B.

SWC, Big Eight to meet soon to plot next steps

Talks expected to center on possible merger, alliance

By Steve Richardson
Staff Writer of The Dallas Morning News

■ SMU reaction 13B
■ SWC coaches react 13B

A meeting of Southwest Conference and Big Eight Conference officials could occur as early as this week about a possible merger or playing alliance involving the leagues.

SWC president James Vick said he knew there was an interest by the Big Eight in learning more about a possible merger and/or playing alliance with the SWC, which will be down to eight schools in 1991-92 after Arkansas' expected announcement that it will join the Southeastern Conference.

"They (Big Eight officials) are interested in some of the alternatives, but I don't know which ones," Vick said.

"But whether there will be a decision to do anything, I don't know. Whether it's a scheduling alliance, a TV-playing agreement or some sort of playing alliance I

Please see SWC on Page 13B.

Sherrod

Jimmy Johnson says the worst mistake he made last year was listening too much to other people.

Page 6B

Horse racing

A 1,000-acre tract in southwest Dallas has been selected as a prospective site for a racetrack.

Page 1A

No PGA protest

A civil rights group cancels protest at the PGA after the all-white host club admits a black as an honorary member.

Page 9B

BASEBALL

AMERICAN

Texas	11
at Milwaukee	3
at Boston	7
Chicago	2
at New York	10
Detroit	4
Kansas City	8
at Cleveland	4
at Baltimore	6
Toronto	4
California	13
at Minn.	2

NATIONAL

at San Fran.	3
Houston	2
St. Louis	4
at Phila.	2
Pittsburgh	9
at Chicago	1
at Montreal	7
New York 4	

THE WORLD CHAMPS
REDS
1990

THE KENTUCKY ENQUIRER

K

AN EDITION OF THE CINCINNATI ENQUIRER/Single-copy price $1.25

OCTOBER 21, 1990 SUNDAY A GANNETT NEWSPAPER

Jose Rijo retired 20 consecutive hitters before leaving the game in the ninth inning.

SWEEP!

The Cincinnati Enquirer/Michael E. Keating

Billy Hatcher is hit on the wrist by a Dave Stewart pitch in the first inning. Hatcher had to leave the game in the second inning.

Oakland can't touch Rijo, 2-1

BY JACK BRENNAN
The Cincinnati Enquirer

OAKLAND, Calif. — OK, so they weren't the Big Red Machine. But no Big Red Machine team ever won the World Series any more efficiently than the 1990 Reds.

Underdogs turned executioners, manager Lou Piniella's team completed a four-game sweep of the once-heralded Oakland A's here Saturday.

They took the clinching game in fitting style, appearing to toy with the A's before dispatching them, 2-1. They did it without big Series guns Billy Hatcher and Eric Davis, both of whom left the game early with injuries.

Hal Morris drove in the winning run with a sacrifice fly in the eighth inning, scoring Herm Winningham.

After Todd Benzinger caught a foul fly from Carney Lansford for the final out, the on-field celebration began. Chris Sabo, who had sarcastically asked reporters if they wanted him to jump up and down after Game 3, was seen jumping up and down.

The Reds became the fifth World Series winners in franchise history, joining the clubs of 1919, 1940, 1975 and 1976. The franchise now has won nine World Series games in a row.

"The way we played, we deserved to win it all," said manager Lou Piniella. "We were aggressive and unselfish. Oakland had a great season, but somebody's got to win and somebody's got to lose.

"After playing well all season and winning wire-to-wire and then having a very exciting NL Championship Series with Pittsburgh, we truly felt we would do well.

"We had to score runs off their starting pitchers and have our starting pitchers get us to the bullpen, and both of those things happened."

Jose Rijo, the starter for Cincinnati, was named Most Valuable Player of the Series.

"I don't think I deserved it," he said. "I think we all deserved it."

As for his pitching, he said "I don't think I've ever had a better slider or better control."

Oakland took a 1-0 lead in the first inning against Rijo, then saw its offense go comatose again as Rijo went on to throw a two-hitter for 8⅓ innings.

The Reds didn't put the tying and winning runs on the board until the eighth inning, but that surely just made it hurt all the more for the vanquished favorites. Though clinging to the lead for most of the game, the A's continued all the while to let the Reds look like the better team.

Cincinnati manufactured all varieties of scoring opportunities in the third through seventh innings. Though losing pitcher

(Please see GAME 4, Page 6)

2:00 2-MINUTE DRILL

BASEBALL — Page C-4.

American League				National League			
Texas	3	Detroit	6	Atlanta	5	Montreal	9
Toronto	0	K.C.	4	St.L.	4 (10)	L.A.	3
Milwaukee	10	Baltimore	2	Chicago	11	Phila.	4
Chi.	9 (19)	Seattle	1	Houston	8	San Fran.	1
Oakland	7	Cleve. at		Pittsburgh	6	San Diego	8
New York	4	Cal., late		Cincinnati	4	New York	7
Minnesota	1						
Boston	0						

NBA PLAYOFFS — Page C-8.

Eastern Conference
Boston 112,
Indiana 105

Western Conference
San Antonio at
Golden State, late

STANLEY CUP PLAYOFFS — Page C-8.

Boston 6, Pittsburgh 3

PLAY IT AGAIN: For the Milwaukee Brewers and Chicago White Sox, a nine-inning game just isn't enough. The two teams went 19 innings Wednesday, the longest game in the American League since the two teams played a 25-inning game in 1984. **Willie Randolph** finally decided the issue with a two-out single that drove in **Jim Gantner**. The White Sox led 5-0 at one point and went in front 9-6 in the 15th. However, the Brewers came up with three runs in the bottom of the inning off former Ranger **Charlie Hough** and **Brian Drahman** to prolong the game. **Game details, Page C-4.**

TOP TICKETS

TODAY

■ **GOLF:** GTE Byron Nelson Classic first round, TPC at Four Seasons Resort and Club, Las Colinas. Radio updates: KRLD-AM 1080 and WBAP-AM 820.

■ **NBA:** Playoff doubleheader: Detroit at Atlanta and Phoenix at Utah, 7 p.m. TV: TNT. Radio: KAAM-AM 1310 (Phoenix-Utah game only, 9 p.m.).

DRESS CODE: A school district in Boca Raton, Fla., has tried to ban all clothes with the logo of the Los Angeles Raiders or the Los Angeles Kings to head off the spread of gangs at a junior high. NFL spokesman **Greg Aiello** said the league was aware that black-and-silver logos of the two Los Angeles teams are favored by many gangs and has initiated a program aimed at discouraging gang violence. Most students defied the ban Wednesday.

TIME FOR A CHANGE: Even though the Miami Heat showed steady improvement in the win column its first three season, **Ron Rothstein** resigned Wednesday as coach, citing the emotional toll of coaching an expansion team. Rothstein was offered a new contract during the season, but he turned it down. Despite winning 24 games this season, the Heat had the NBA's second worst record behind Denver.

SCHEDULING CONFLICT: Houston became a leading candidate to be the host city for the 1995 Super Bowl when New Orleans withdrew its bid because of scheduling conflicts with two conventions that have tied up 9,000 hotel rooms. The NFL requires bidding cities to assure that 36,000 rooms will be reserved for two weekends at the end of January and the beginning of February. If the NFL maintains its request to reserve two dates, New Orleans, which has been the host for seven Super Bowls, would not be in a position to bid for the game until 2001. Miami and Tampa, Fla., also are being considered for the 1995 game, which will be awarded during league meetings May 21-22 in Minneapolis.

RULING UPHELD: The Oregon Court of Appeals upheld an $11.1 million damage award against the Bike Athletic Co. and Kendall Research Center, the designer and maker of the "Air Power" helmet. The damages were award to **Richard Austria**, who was left permanently disabled when a player's knee smashed into his helmet. Austria was found to have severe brain swelling and blood accumulation, a condition known as hematoma, which required surgery. The Court of Appeals ruled "that a properly designed helmet would have greatly reduced the likelihood of a hematoma and that defendant's helmet was not adequately designed to reduce that likelihood."

THE LATEST LINE

Home team in bold

NBA PLAYOFFS
Today's games

Favorite	Odds	Underdog
Atlanta	1½	Detroit
Portland	4	**Seattle**
Utah	4	Phoenix

Saturday's game

Favorite	Odds	Underdog
Chicago	9	Philadelphia

WLAF
Saturday's games

Favorite	Odds	Underdog
Barcelona	13	Birmingham
Frankfurt	2½	**Orlando**
Sacramento	8	Montreal

Sunday's game

New York	11	**Raleigh**

Monday's game

London	6½	**San Antonio**

STANLEY CUP PLAYOFFS
Today's game

Favorite	Goals	Underdog	Goals
Edmonton	-1½	Minnesota	+1

You would give 1½ goals to bet on the favorite or receive one goal for betting on the underdog.

Baseball odds, Page C-4.

No. 7: No-hit magic

Louis DeLuca/Dallas Times Herald

Nolan Ryan, his seventh no-hitter in hand, tips his hat to the standing ovation at Arlington Stadium.

Legendary Ryan adds another gem

By Kurt Iverson
OF THE TIMES HERALD STAFF

ARLINGTON — Having already achieved 5,000 strikeouts and 300 victories, Nolan Ryan was ready for a relaxing 1991, free from undue public and media attention.

He simply forgot about No. 7 — a figure he didn't dare contemplate. He made it a number they can add to his Hall of Fame plaque after the historic seventh no-hitter he threw for a 3-0 victory over the Toronto Blue Jays Wednesday night.

"I think that this one is the most rewarding because it was in front of these hometown fans who have supported me since I have been here," Ryan said.

So much for obscurity. The 33,439 Arlington Stadium fans were on their feet chanting "No-lan, No-lan" by the end of the seventh inning when Ryan recorded his 13th strikeout on his way to 16, including striking out Roberto Alomar to end the game. A crowd gathered outside the stadium gates as fans tried to buy their way into a non-sellout that quickly became a late standing-room-only affair.

The Rangers defense cooperated by staying alert between the strikeouts, and the offense provided Ryan all the backing he would need with an early spanking of Toronto's Jimmy Key, one of the hottest starters in the American League. Key came to Texas with a 4-0 record and 1.86

Please see **RANGERS, C-2**

Ryan makes the appreciation mutual

SKIP BAYLESS

ARLINGTON — By the seventh inning, lines had formed again outside Arlington Stadium. Tickets were being sold again. The game wasn't televised locally, so these people were keeping up by radio. When Nolan pitches, you listen.

When this incredible 44-year-old human takes the mound, it's always possible.

And he was doing it again. Was it possible? He wasn't just no-hitting the Toronto Blue Jays, he was no-hoping them. He was overpowering and overmatching the best-hitting team in the American League. He was making the Blue Jays swing foolishly late at rising fastballs and haplessly early at off-speed curves. Is it conceivable? Nolan Ryan was more overpowering — at age 44 — than he had ever been.

So an announced crowd of 33,439 was growing in the eighth and ninth. Ryan had pitched six no-hitters, but never one at Arlington Stadium. A line of headlights stretched back down the stadium access roads. People wanted to see it happen. People at least wanted to be in the parking lot.

After all, we've suffered enough around here. We had paid in anguish and humiliation during the Brad Corbett and Eddie Chiles regimes. We had covered our eyes through flop after phenom flop, from David Clyde to Nelson Norman to George Wright to Dave Hostetler to Edwin Correa. Bad Rangers starts have been topped only by worse Rangers finishes. With this franchise, hope always has sprung infernal.

Oh, have Rangers fans earned what happened Wednesday night between 9:55 and 10:04. If only the stadium could have held several million of them. By the bottom of the ninth, it appeared to be screaming-room-only — completely full.

By the way, this was happening on Arlington Appreciation Night. Yes, free bleacher tickets had been distributed among Arlington residents who voted in a tax that will help build a new stadi-

Please see **BAYLESS, C-6**

Henderson is king of thieves

By Ross Newhan
LOS ANGELES TIMES

OAKLAND, Calif. — The dream, as Rickey Henderson called his improbable goal of becoming the greatest base stealer ever, was born when a counselor at Oakland's Technical High promised to pay a quarter for every one he stole there. But it was Bobbie Henderson who sent her son out

Please see **RICKEY, C-2**

Mature TPC to produce high scores in Nelson

By Bill Nichols
OF THE TIMES HERALD STAFF

IRVING — Thick rough. Fast greens. High scores.

No, it's not the U.S. Open.

But the players at the GTE Byron Nelson Classic are talking about the fierce course conditions at the TPC Four Seasons at Las Colinas in a major way.

Tom Watson, a winner of five British Opens, two Masters, one U.S. Open and four Nelsons, says "Par will be a good score. If we get the usual Texas winds, this may be the highest winning score all year. Mark my words."

Ray Floyd, a winner of 21 tour events, including the Open, the Masters and the Nelson, says, "You've got a golf course that's really set up for championship play."

Dallas' Lanny Wadkins, the tour's leading money winner, said the greens were the "best I've seen outside of Augusta," and Ben Crenshaw said the greens were "the best we've seen this year."

No need to check your compass. Today's first round is on the

Please see **NELSON, C-3**

BYRON NELSON Classic

Today-Sunday
TV: WFAA – Channel 8
Saturday: 1:30 – 3:30 p.m.
Sunday: 3 – 5 p.m.
Radio: KRLD – AM 1080

■ O'Meara bags pro-am when clubs arrive late. **Page C-3.**

■ Results, pairings, **Page C-3.**

MacLeod apparently gets job at Notre Dame

By Marvin Wamble and Mike McAllister
OF THE TIMES HERALD STAFF

Former Mavericks coach John MacLeod is the new Notre Dame basketball coach, former Fighting Irish assistants John Shumate and Danny Nee said Wednesday.

"I was informed today around 2 p.m. that [Notre Dame] has hired John MacLeod," said Shumate, a Notre Dame assistant for the two seasons before his appointment June 30, 1988, as SMU coach.

"I think John MacLeod is going to get it," said Nee, who spent four years at Notre Dame and just completed his fifth season as coach at Nebraska.

MacLeod, hired as interim coach of the New York Knicks Dec. 3, coached the Mavericks for two seasons. Though the Mavs fired him Nov. 29, 1990, he continued to live in Dallas. Sources told the Times Herald that Notre Dame's announcement on MacLeod would be

Please see **MACLEOD, C-3**

Rangers saved the Goose and he's saving games

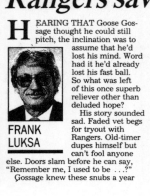

FRANK LUKSA

HEARING THAT Goose Gossage thought he could still pitch, the inclination was to assume that he'd lost his mind. Word had it he'd already lost his fast ball. So what was left of this once superb reliever other than deluded hope?

His story sounded sad. Faded vet begs for tryout with Rangers. Old-timer dupes himself but can't fool anyone else. Doors slam before he can say, "Remember me, I used to be . . .?"

Gossage knew these snubs a year ago. He couldn't get to first base and nowhere close to the mound with a major league team on the continent.

"I called teams while the lockout was going on," he said Wednesday. "I told them I'd go to spring training as a minor-leaguer. If they didn't like what they saw, they had nothing to lose.

"I was willing to do anything. But I couldn't get a response. It was just, 'No.' "

Finding domestic dugouts closed, Gossage pitched in Japan. So sorry but numbers there suggest he laid a dried squid. He went 2-3 with a 4.40 ERA — stats that hinted of career twilight in the Land of the Rising Sun.

If anyone in the States paid slight attention, Gossage knew what they were saying. Yep, ol' Goose wears a Fu Man Chu and pitches like Charlie Chan. He never read the Oriental proverb that says, "Man who throws baseballs hit into neighbors rice paddy should retire and raise eels."

To which Goose honked: "When you get knocked around at 21, they say, 'Oh, he just doesn't know how to pitch.' Get knocked around at 39 and they say, 'He's over the hill.' "

Gossage hadn't been knocked around in previous seasons as much as shuffled about and cuffed a bit. He was with the Cubs in '88. With the Giants and Yankees in '89. Then on to pleasant oblivion in Fukuoka.

Gossage traveled a lot but wasn't getting anywhere. At this rate, he was en route to nowhere except a rocking chair. He'd had a dust-up with Cubs manager Don Zimmer after going 4-4 with 13 saves: "Frankly, I don't know a pitcher who gets along with Zimmer."

He'd felt isolated with the Giants after figuring that general manager Al Rosen, a former Yankees boss, signed him over objections of manager Roger Craig who's a best pal of Zimmer: "Roger never welcomed me. Craig was cold as he could be."

He'd felt unwelcome returning to the Yankees under Dallas Green: "I heard him say, 'What do we want with a guy who's been released twice?' " Then forgotten after Green

Please see **LUSKA, C-2**

14 pages on the Series in News and Sports

1991 World Series

Star Tribune

METRO EDITION

■ For Page 1A and the start of today's paper, turn the page

MONDAY/October 28/1991

NEWSPAPER OF THE TWIN CITIES

Y 35¢

Twincredible!

One for the storybooks

Staff Photo by Jeff Wheeler

Dan Gladden was mobbed by teammates as he touched home plate in the 10th inning at the Metrodome Sunday night, scoring the only run of a 1-0 Minnesota victory over Atlanta in Game 7 of the World Series. Jack Morris, at left, pitched all 10 innings and was named the Series' most valuable player.

THE GLOBE AND MAIL
SPORTWEEK

© 1992 The Globe and Mail ■ Monday, October 26, 1992 ■ Section D

TOP OF THE WORLD

Jays ready to reap rewards after white-knuckle victory over Braves

BY NEIL A. CAMPBELL
Sport Reporter

ATLANTA — By yesterday morning, the grey baseball uniforms and blue caps had given way to suits and dark glasses for the Toronto Blue Jays. They filed out of the Nikko Hotel into bright Sunday morning sunshine, the dark glasses a much-needed buffer for eyes still red from a night of celebrating Canada's first World Series win.

The Blue Jays' 4-3 victory over the Atlanta Braves on Saturday was an epic. It is sure to rank alongside Canada's 1972 hockey victory over the Soviet Union as one of the great sporting moments in Canadian history.

Saturday's was the sixth game of the Series. The Jays had won three of the previous five and they desperately wanted to avoid a winner-take-all seventh game on Atlanta soil.

The Jays held a slight lead for most of the game, enough to fuel their fans' optimism but nowhere near enough to cure their white-knuckle tension. As they recalled yesterday morning, Jay players and executives felt that unbearable tension, too.

Pat Gillick, the team's executive vice-president, remembered the bottom of the ninth inning, when the Jays had a 2-1 lead and two Braves were out. "I thought we were going to win it right there, we were one strike away. I'm usually pretty calm at a game but when they tied the game at that point, at the point where I was so sure we'd won, I was a little squeamish."

By the 11th inning, when the Jays scored two runs to take a 4-2 lead, first baseman John Olerud's "stomach had had a real workout turning up and down. When they began to come back at us again, when they scored a run to make it 4-3," Olerud said as he checked out of the hotel, "we started really wondering if it was meant to be for us."

The game ended at 50 minutes past midnight with Blue Jay players running on the field and leaping on top of Joe Carter, who made the final out. The 50,000 Braves fans who had stayed to the bitter end chanted for their team to return to the field for a final salute, but the losing players simply headed to the showers.

Braves owner Ted Turner and his wife, Jane Fonda, dejectedly walked to their Chevy Suburban, parked in a tunnel under the stadium. They piled in and, with Turner at the wheel, quickly drove through the tunnel and out of the stadium.

The blank look on the faces of Turner and Fonda as they drove away shows that baseball is more than a business. The Braves, who are promoted as America's Team, are a programming staple for Turner Broadcasting Systems. In an era of enormous baseball payrolls, the Braves will be one of only a few teams to show a profit this season.

But money was obviously the farthest thing for Turner's mind and it was also farthest from the minds of Peter Widdrington and Paul Beeston, the Jays' main policy makers.

"One of the things the World Series has done," said Beeston, the Jay president and chief executive officer, "is take our focus off what we like to think is our business acumen and put us back into the state where we're fans again. We're caught up in it. no one has thought of the money yet.

"We're not measuring our goals this year in terms of dollar signs. It's measured in wins and losses, and we won the American League East, we won the American League and now we've won the World Series. It's a complete year."

While everyone connected with the Jays wanted the team to clinch the World Series in front of the home fans at the SkyDome on Thursday — the Braves won that game, 7-2, to stay alive — the team benefited financially from the sixth game.

A large percentage of ticket revenue from baseball postseason games goes into a pool that is divided among players from teams that finished either first, second or third in their division. More than $14.5-million (U.S.) is in the kitty for 1992 and as World Series winners, each Jay will receive more than $100,000.

But the players' kitty is closed after the first four games of a World Series. And the participating teams, which each earned about $160,000 for the first four games of this World Series, stood to collect about $550,000 for any games beyond that point. As a result, the Blue Jay organization raked in close to $2-million from its first World Series appearance.

"We'll make money this year, helped by the last 10 days," said Widdrington, the Jays' chairman of the board. "It's unfortunate you're left in a position where you'd like to see the World Series go six or seven games because you only make [significant] money out of the last three. But that's the way it is.

"In all honesty, if we could have ended that thing in Toronto, we would have taken it gladly."

The Jays' travelling party arrived in Toronto yesterday afternoon and everyone will assemble in the downtown area of the city today for a parade that will end up at the SkyDome. "We're going to enjoy this together, players and fans," Carter said. "The Prime Minister of Canada, Dave Winfield, got the SkyDome fans pumped up the second part of the year and we know they'll be pumped for the parade. It's going to be some great day for Canada."

Beyond the parade, there are decisions for the Jays to make. Their major-league player payroll this year was close to $48-million, and if they were to re-sign all the players whose contracts have expired — Carter, Jimmy Key, Tom Henke and David Cone to name a few — it would rocket beyond $50-million.

"First of all," Widdrington said, "You enjoy this for a while. There's no sense in doing these things unless you take time out to enjoy them. But not for very long. You have to get right back at it and start making your moves for the next season. You just can't relax. You don't want to."

Police expect hundreds of thousands of people to greet the Toronto Blue Jays during a victory parade this afternoon, and they are warning that the city's downtown core will be virtually shut down from 7 a.m.

The parade for the World Series champions is scheduled to begin at 1 p.m. at the Royal York Hotel and end up at the SkyDome, where the first 40,000 people will be admitted free. Stadium gates open at 10 a.m., but if the attendance at Saturday's telecast of Game Six is any indication, lineups will form much earlier.

Even yesterday, when Toronto players did nothing but return to the SkyDome to pick up their cars, several hundred fans had staked out the stadium and its parking garage, cheering wildly and hoping for autographs.

The Ontario weather office reports that today is expected to be cool, windy and cloudy, with a slight chance of rain.

Police also advise people to take public transit to work today. GO Transit will provide free transportation to the celebration on certain trains.

— Scott Feschuk

President George Bush yesterday congratulated the Toronto Blue Jays for winning the World Series and invited them to the White House to celebrate their victory.

Bush called manager Cito Gaston from Air Force One as he flew to Montana fcr a campaign stop and told him "America is proud of you." Bush had made no secret of the fact that he was an Atlanta Braves fan, showing off his tomahawk chop on the campaign trail.

The President watched the sixth game Saturday night, the Blue Jays' 4-3, 11-inning victory.

Toronto Blue Jay Joe Carter, arm raised, is mobbed by teammates after getting the final out in the World Series. *(RUSTY KENNEDY/Associated Press)*

It doesn't get any better than this

MARTY YORK

ATLANTA

HEART-WRENCHING, it was. Nerve-racking. Gut-turning.

Your stress level took a pounding, no doubt. Your nails and your cuticles may not be quite as lengthy or as healthy as they were eight days ago.

But, gosh, it was a wonderful week.

It must be savoured. It must be treasured. It must be ensconced in your memory banks as an extraordinary World Series, not only for the millions of Canadians who crammed aboard the Toronto Blue Jays' bandwagon, but for anyone anywhere who gives a hoot about the ineffable sport of baseball.

Fact is, it doesn't get any better than this.

And the most electrifying spectacle of the Series happened to be saved for last — a drama-filled, 11th-inning triumph for the Jays at The Chop Shop on Saturday night.

All four of the Toronto victories over the Atlanta Braves in this six-game Series were recorded by one run, which meant that success came neither easy nor without excessive tension for the Jays and their boosters.

But guess what?

The consensus among the baseball intelligentsia here during the weekend was that there will be more of the same for you and your nerves next season because the hunches are that, barring an owners' lockout of the players, the Jays will be right back in the World Series in 1993.

The suspicions are that, now that their choke tags have been removed from their necks, the Jays possess enough poise, character, postseason experience and, chiefly, enough talent to become the first team since the 1977 and 1978 New York Yankees to garner two consecutive championships.

Please see GASTON — A19

TUESDAY
1892 101 YEARS
Rain, Some Snow
High 46

THE DENVER POST

April 6, 1993
Voice of the Rocky Mountain Empire
★ Final Edition / 25 cents
35 cents in Designated Areas

NCAA CHAMPIONS

The Associated Press / Ed Reinke
Eric Montross in closing seconds. North Carolina's Tar Heels take the 1993 NCAA championship with a 77-71 win over the Michigan Wolverines in New Orleans.
SPORTS, 1, 3D

INSIDE THE POST

CLINTON READY TO COMPROMISE
The White House signals that it is prepared to compromise on its jobs bill as Senate Democrats and Republicans hunted for a way to end their standoff. **STORY, 2A**

LONG, BLOODY YEAR

Associated Press
Refugees from the Muslim town of Srebrenica sit in camp in Bosnia-Herzegovina.
Marking the first anniversary of a war that has shattered their lives, residents of Bosnia struggle to survive amid the ruins.
SPECIAL REPORT, 2A

CONNOR AVENUE
The street that Denver Post sports writer Dick Connor knew so well, a stretch of West 17th Avenue, will now bear his name.
DENVER & THE WEST, 1B

INMATE FOUND DEAD
A 19-year-old man serving a four-year sentence for menacing is found dead in his cell bunk at the trouble-plagued state prison at Limon. **DENVER & THE WEST, 1B**

FINAL CHAPTER?
At 61, Mike Nichols has embarked on what he terms the final chapter of his directing and producing career. **LIVING, 1E**

WEATHER

Today: Rain. Some wet snow. High: 46; low: 32
Tomorrow: High: 46; low: 30
Yesterday: High: 65; low: 37
Thursday: High: 52; low: 34
Complete weather report, 8B
Weatherline® — 337-2500

TO CALL THE POST

Main number	820-1010
News	820-1201
Outside Metro Area	1-800-336-7678
Classified	825-2525
Outside Metro Area	1-800-525-9502
TDD for the deaf	820-1050

FOR HOME DELIVERY

Home Delivery	832-3232
Outside Metro Area	1-800-543-5543

RECYCLE THIS PAPER
There is more recycled paper in The Denver Post than any other Colorado newspaper.

Big leagues, Big Apple

Colorado Rockies' second baseman Eric Young waits for the first pitch — thrown by the Mets' Dwight Gooden — of the first regular-season game for the new expansion team. The Post has the game at New York's Shea Stadium covered, from start to finish — and then some:

- **FIRST AND FOREMOST:** Cut away the hype and history and it was just another game./ **1D**
- **NO SECONDS:** Dwight Gooden finishes what he started./ **6D**
- **THIRD STRIKE:** Not everyone reveled in game./ **9A**
- **STOPPED SHORT:** Coalition gets warm welcome./ **1C**
- **PITCHER PANIC:** Pitcher David Nied let it get to him./ **1D**
- **THE CATCH(ER):** 'To swing or not to swing' for Andres Galarraga./ **7D**
- **NOT RIGHT:** Manager Don Baylor 'was expecting to win.'/ **6D**
- **WHAT'S LEFT:** Expect plenty of traffic woes Friday./ **8A**
- **FRONT AND CENTER:** Colorado bigwigs in the stands./ **9A**

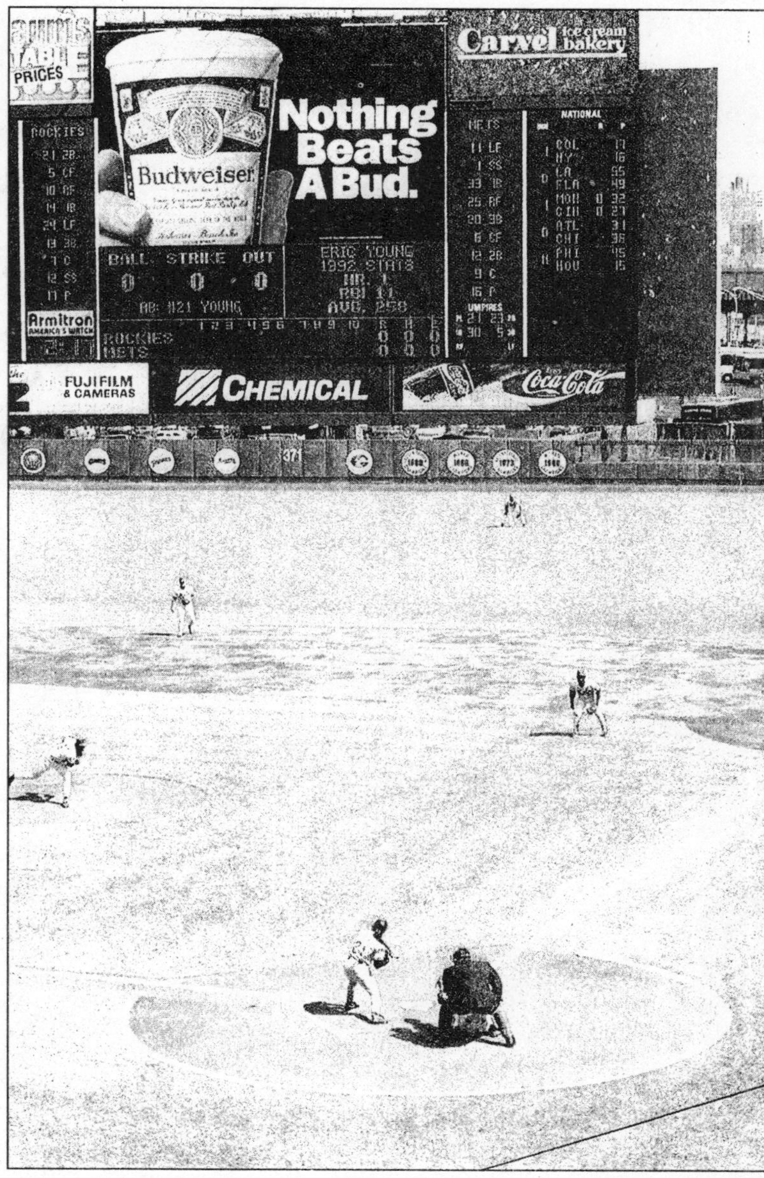

Special to The Denver Post
Damian Strohmeyer

Even big 0 can't take Rockies' magic away

NEW YORK — The world will little note, nor long remember, what happened here yesterday, but the Colorado Rockies never can forget what they did here. They got a life.

You can't win 'em all, though.

Alas, the Rockies can't win 162 games this year.

How about 161-1?

Maybe not.

When New York Mets pitcher-hitter-runner-physician Dwight Gooden crossed home plate in the fourth inning yesterday with the first run, the Colorado Rockies were history.

The Purple Rox lost in their coming-out party 3-0.

(Historically, the Rockies have problems scoring runs.)

"Before we came in here, we had no history. Now we have one," Rockies' official historian Don Baylor said. "It was a great

WOODY PAIGE

day all around, except I expected to win."

In a historical retrospective, the Colorado Rockies actually lost a double-header around the core of Appleville over an 18-hour span.

Before the New Colorado Rockies fell to the New York Mets at Shea Stadium yesterday afternoon, the Old Colorado Rockies were beaten the previous night by the Pittsburgh Penguins, 5-2 at the Meadowlands Arena.

The original Rockies, who have been on an extended road trip for years since their last home game in Denver and are performing under the pseudonym New Jersey Devils, dropped a few games their first season, too.

The old Rockies play with a puck in hockey's National League, instead of baseball's National League.

These Rockies never have heard of *those* Rockies, though. The Old Rockies are lost in history, and the New Rockies found their history yesterday.

At least, it wasn't a no-hitter.

At least, it wasn't a blowout.

At least, the Rockies weren't embarrassing in the field.

At least, Amy Fisher didn't throw out the first ball.

At least, yesterday's road opener and the surrounding hysteria are over — until Friday's home opener.

On an affable, spring-like afternoon in Flushing Meadows, with appropriate pomp and ceremony and excitement and exhilaration, the Rockies, as shiny silver soldiers, marched into baseball.

Later the Rockies' first expansion draft pick/poster boy/starting pitcher/losing pitcher/intern, David Nied, said: "It's uncharacteristic of me to walk six batters,

Please see **PAIGE** on 8A

Old-time Mets fans rule

Perseverance pays off with best seats in the stands

behind THE seams
An outsider's look at big-league baseball

By Alan Gottlieb
Denver Post Staff Writer

NEW YORK — Cops in uniform were hard at work at noon yesterday, keeping a growing and restless crowd from charging the still-shuttered gates of Shea Stadium.

But then 68-year-old Kal Liepper came along, smiling a crooked smile and calling each officer by name, and the the cops parted like the Red Sea and let Liepper through.

That's what life's like when you're a native New Yorker and have had season tickets to the Mets since the team was born in 1962. Liepper commands a dozen seats directly behind the visitors' dugout, which means he and his party had a better view of the Colorado Rockies during yesterday's game than anyone in the place — including Rockies' owner Jerry McMorris.

Dozens of Colorado business and media bigwigs were in evidence at the game yesterday — deposed Greater Denver Chamber of Commerce honcho Dick Fleming, longtime Denver Bears owner Dick Howsam, all the Rockies front office brass, as well as major team sponsors and the ownership group, represented by various Coorses and Monforts and Bentons and McMorrises. They all flew in together Sunday on a charter flight, and yesterday they were decked out in Rockies regalia and close enough to the dugout so players could hear their cheers. But none of them had a seat as good as Liepper's.

"Listen, over the years I've found housing for a lot of the players, I've sold them condos in Florida, I even lived with Willie Mays for awhile in Florida," said Liepper,

Please see **FANS** on 9A

Elitch's delays move until '95

Local financing tough to find

By Steve Raabe and Mark Eddy
Denver Post Staff Writers

Elitch Gardens will delay the proposed opening of its new Central Platte Valley amusement park for one year as it makes a final attempt to pull the project's financing together.

The $94 million development could open by spring 1995 if a loan package is successfully negotiated. But Elitch President Sandy Gurtler warned that the project will die if a financing agreement is not reached this year.

"We're going to give this one more shot," Gurtler said yesterday. "If it doesn't work, then it won't happen. I don't think any of us have the stamina or the fire to try it again."

The Denver landmark was to have moved from its 102-year-old northwest Denver location to 68 acres in the Platte Valley in time for a 1994 open-

Please see **ELITCH** on 10A

Denver Post file photo
WILD RIDE: Elitch Gardens' customers for years have thrilled to the Denver amusement park's roller-coaster ride.

TCI to upgrade wiring systems

Denver Post Staff and Wire Reports

Denver-based Tele-Communications Inc., the nation's largest cable television company, next week will unveil plans to take the lead in creating a nationwide information "superhighway" by rewiring its cable systems with 7,000 miles of high-capacity, fiber-optic lines.

About 300 TCI systems, including suburban and urban Denver systems in Colorado, will be upgraded to fiber wires from existing copper lines within the next four years, a company source said.

The multibillion-dollar program, which sources say will be revealed publicly next Monday, will lay the foundation for a host of futuristic telecommunications services that TCI and

- **CHANNELS:** Calls about service problems swamp cable-operator TCI./**1C**

other cable companies have been hoping to offer as they gear up to compete with the nation's phone companies.

The fiber-optic network will eventually enable TCI to deliver hundreds of TV channels, "video-on-demand" programming and interactive shopping services, and to transmit computer data and phone conversations. TCI expects to start offering 500-plus channel service nationally next year.

Steve Doughty, manager of TCI of Colorado, said next

Please see **CABLE** on 5A

DAVE WINFIELD GETS 3,000!

Staff Photo by Brian Peterson

September 16, 1993, vs. Oakland at the Metrodome

Dave Winfield bounced a single to left field in the ninth inning Thursday night against Oakland to reach one of baseball's most magnificent milestones. Winfield became only the 19th player to collect 3,000 hits.

StarTribune

WORLD SERIES

G. Paul Burnett/The New York Times

Todd Stottlemyre being thrown out on third base Wednesday night after a single by Roberto Alomar. Stottlemyre scraped his chin on the bag.

G. Paul Burnett/The New York Times

Phillies' Lenny Dýkstra hitting a two-run home run in the fifth inning. He hit his first two-run home run in the second inning.

Associated Press

Blue Jay outfielder Rǐckey Henderson scoring the winning run on a triple by Devon White during the eighth inning on Wednesday.

15-14, 15-14, 15-14 15-14, 15-14, 15-14

By JACK CURRY

Special to The New York Times

PHILADELPHIA, Oct. 21 — Never before had a World Series game taken so long to complete. Never before had so many runs been scored in a World Series game. Never before had a losing team scored 14 runs. Never before had so many emotional twists and turns been packed into one stadium on one drizzly, foggy night. Never before. Maybe never again.

The strange and charming fourth game of the 90th World Series between the Blue Jays and the Phillies left one Toronto pitcher, Todd Stottlemyre, bloody after he tried to run the bases; left the entire Philadelphia team bloodied after its closer disintegrated; left Lenny Dykstra groping for words to explain what happened after his virtuoso offensive performance was denied, and also left Toronto one victory from its second straight championship. The Jays won, 15-14, but not before several stunning, game-turning events were packed into 4 hours 14 minutes of sometimes radiant, sometimes rancid, baseball.

STRIKING BACK The Phillies have been called the Broad Street Bellies, but they were bullies after the Jays scored three runs off Tommy Greene in the first inning. Patient bullies. Dykstra walked against Stottlemyre, three more batters walked and then Milt Thompson, the super sub, smoked a triple to center field that Devon White could not corral as three runs scored to give the Phillies a 4-3 lead. A silent warning was issued at Veterans Stadium. Venture to the concession stands at your own risk. The risk was the chance of missing splendid action. Forget the hot dog. Where's Lenny?

DUDE, PART I: Dykstra provided more to chew on in the bottom of the second inning by poking a two-run homer to put the Phillies ahead, 6-3. The slugfest was now in session. "It was," said Toronto's Joe Carter, "like a slow-pitch softball game out there."

NO FUSS, NO MUSS: How talented are the Jays? So talented that some of their lesser-known superstars countered Dykstra's power show with run-scoring singles in the third in drilling Greene for four more runs and sending him to dry land along with Stottlemyre. Pat Borders and Tony Fernandez delivered one each and White knocked in two as the Jays regained the lead by one run. But stay tuned.

SERIES SHOCKER: The Phillies are retired 1-2-3 in bottom of third and the Jays are retired 1-2-3 in the top of the fourth. What great pitching!

DUDE AGAIN: Who else? Dykstra doubled in the fourth and then scored on Mariano Duncan's single that made it 7-7. Somewhere in Connecticut, David Letterman was probably cursing CBS for letting another lengthy baseball game erase his 11:35 P.M. start time.

DAVE, DARREN AND DYKSTRA: What was supposed to be the winning rally started with a bunt single by a power hitter. Dave Hollins, struggling with 2 hits in 12 at-bats, told reporters he would not try to test new third baseman Paul Molitor by bunting. He did. It worked. Darren Daulton followed with a two-run homer to snap a 7-7 tie, the pesky Thompson whacked a two-run double and Dykstra (ho-hum) clubbed another two-run homer. The Phillies led by 12-7 and they were dancing on Broad Street.

MITCH ADVENTURE: It got crazier in the eighth. The teams had traded a couple of runs and the Phillies started the inning with Larry Andersen on the mound and a 14-9 lead. Andersen allowed one unearned run and was then replaced by Williams with runners perched on second and third. Defying his post-season strategy, Jim Fregosi, the Phillies' manager, did not insert Kim Batiste at third base for defensive reasons because he wanted Hollins's bat in the lineup. Would it have mattered? Batiste had already made two errors in the post-season and the Astroturf was slick, but. . . . What did matter is that Williams gave up a run-scoring single to Fernandez, a two-out, two-run single to Rickey Henderson to chop the score to 14-13 and a two-run triple to White. Veterans Stadium suddenly grew quiet. It had been wet and wild. Now it was just wet. "I stink," Williams said. "There is no other way to put it." No one argued.

RELIEF WARD: Dykstra had one last opportunity to be a hero, as if two homers, a double and four runs scored were not heroic enough. But he struck out looking at a Duane Ward pitch in the eighth. Dykstra did not like the call, but he did not moan. He pulled off his batting gloves and trudged to center field. What Dykstra did not want to contemplate became a reality when Ward zipped through the ninth, 1-2-3, pitching like a closer is supposed to and exactly how Williams did not. "It kept going along like it was going to be a 'Nightmare on Elm Street,'" Ward said. "We tried to turn the water faucet off. We tried to get out of here. We finally did after about four and a half hours."

CLOSE THAT COFFIN: While the respectful Jays politely explained how they were not supposed to nick Williams and how thrilling it was to be part of such a memorable game, the Philadelphia clubhouse resembled a funeral home. "Everyone knows we let it get away," Dykstra said. "It doesn't take a baseball genius to figure that one out."

GAME 4

Blue Jays 15, Phillies 14

Toronto	AB	R	H	BI	BB	SO	Avg.
RHenderson lf	5	2	2	2	1	1	.333
White cf	5	2	3	4	1	1	.412
RAlomar 2b	6	1	2	1	0	1	.444
Carter rf	6	2	3	0	0	0	.353
Olerud 1b	4	2	1	0	2	0	.300
Molitor 3b	4	2	1	1	1	0	.467
Griffin 3b	0	0	0	0	0	0	---
TFernandez ss	6	2	3	5	0	1	.467
Borders c	4	1	1	1	1	0	.188
Stottlemyre p	0	0	0	0	1	0	---
a-Butler ph	1	1	0	0	0	0	.000
ALeiter p	1	0	1	0	0	0	1.000
Castillo p	1	0	0	0	0	1	.000
d-Sprague ph	1	0	0	0	0	1	.077
Timlin p	0	0	0	0	0	0	---
DWard p	0	0	0	0	0	0	---
Totals	44	15	17	14	7	6	

Philadelphia	AB	R	H	BI	BB	SO	Avg.
Dykstra cf	5	4	3	4	1	1	.389
Duncan 2b	6	1	3	1	0	0	.450
Kruk 1b	5	0	0	0	1	2	.412
DHollins 3b	4	3	2	0	2	0	.267
Daulton c	3	2	1	3	1	1	.200
Eisenreich rf	4	2	1	1	1	0	.235
MThompson lf	5	1	3	5	0	0	.500
Stocker ss	4	0	0	0	1	1	.214
TGreene p	1	1	1	0	0	0	1.000
Mason p	1	0	0	0	0	0	.000
b-RJordan ph	1	0	0	0	0	0	.200
West p	0	0	0	0	0	0	---
c-Chamberlain ph	1	0	0	0	0	1	.000
Andersen p	0	0	0	0	0	0	---
MtWilliams p	0	0	0	0	0	0	---
e-Morandini ph	1	0	0	0	0	1	.000
Thigpen p	0	0	0	0	0	0	---
Totals	41	14	14	14	7	7	

Toronto	304 002 060—15	17	0
Philadelphia	420 151 100—14	14	1

a-grounded into fielder's choice for Stottlemyre in the 3rd. b-grounded out for Mason in the 5th. c-struck out for West in the 6th. d-struck out for Castillo in the 8th. e-struck out for MtWilliams in the 8th. **E**—DHollins (1). **LOB**—Toronto 10, Philadelphia 8. **2B**—RHenderson (2), White (3), Carter (1), ALeiter (1), Dykstra (1), DHollins (1), MThompson (1). **3B**—White (2), MThompson (1). **HR**—Dykstra (2) off Stottlemyre, Dykstra (3) off ALeiter, Daulton (1) off ALeiter. **RBI**—RHenderson 2 (2), White 4 (7), RAlomar (5), Molitor (5), TFernandez 5 (9), Borders (1), Dykstra 4 (5), Duncan (2), Daulton 3 (4), Eisenreich (6), MThompson 5 (6). **SB**—RHenderson (1), White (1), Dykstra (2), Duncan (2). **Runners left in scoring position**—Toronto 8 (RHenderson, RAlomar 3, TFernandez, Borders 3); Philadelphia 5 (Kruk, MThompson 2, Stocker, Chamberlain). **Runners moved up**—Olerud, TFernandez, Butler.

Toronto	IP	H	R	ER	BB	SO	NP	ERA
Stottlemyre	2	3	6	6	4	1	53	27.00
ALeiter	2⅔	8	6	6	0	1	52	10.13
Castillo W, 1-0	2⅓	3	2	2	3	1	54	8.10
Timlin	⅔	0	0	0	0	2	8	0.00
DWard S, 2	1⅓	0	0	0	0	2	14	2.45
Philadelphia	**IP**	**H**	**R**	**ER**	**BB**	**SO**	**NP**	**ERA**
TGreene	2⅓	7	7	7	4	1	66	27.00
Mason	2⅔	2	0	0	1	2	38	1.69
West	1	3	2	2	0	0	19	27.00
Andersen	1⅓	1	3	1	1	2	26	9.00
MtWilliams L, 0-1	⅔	3	3	3	1	1	20	11.57
Thigpen	1	1	0	0	0	0	17	0.00

Inherited runners-scored—Castillo 1-0, Mason 2-2, MtWilliams 2-2. **HBP**—by Castillo (Daulton), by West (Molitor). **Umpires**—Home, Williams; First, McClelland; Second, DeMuth; Third, Phillips; Left, Runge; Right, Johnson. **T**—4:14. **A**—62,731.

HOW THE RUNS SCORED

Blue Jays First: Henderson doubled to center. White walked. Alomar fouled out to left fielder Thompson. Carter singled to third, Henderson to third, White to second. Olerud popped out to first baseman Kruk. Molitor walked, Henderson scored, White to third, Carter to second. Fernandez singled to right, White and Carter scored, Molitor to third. Borders lined out to left fielder Thompson.
3 runs, 3 hits, 0 errors, 2 left on.
Blue Jays 3, Phillies 0

Phillies First: Dykstra walked. Duncan flied out to right fielder Carter. Dykstra stole second. Kruk struck out. Hollins walked. Daulton walked, Dykstra to third, Hollins to second. Eisenreich walked, Dykstra scored, Hollins to third, Daulton to second. Thompson tripled to center, Hollins, Daulton and Eisenreich scored. Stocker grounded out to first baseman Olerud.
4 runs, 1 hit, 0 errors, 1 left on.
Phillies 4, Blue Jays 3

Phillies Second: Greene singled to center. Dykstra homered down the right field line on 0-1 count, Greene and Dykstra scored. Duncan flied out to center fielder White. Kruk grounded out to second baseman Alomar. Hollins popped out to catcher Borders.
2 runs, 2 hits, 0 errors, 0 left on.
Phillies 6, Blue Jays 3

Blue Jays Third: Carter popped out to second baseman Duncan. Olerud walked. Molitor singled to right center, Olerud to third. Fernandez singled to right, Olerud scored, Molitor to third. Borders singled to left, Molitor scored, Fernandez to second. Butler pinch hit for Stottlemyre. Mason relieved Greene. Butler grounded into fielder's choice, first baseman Kruk to shortstop Stocker, Fernandez to third, Borders forced at second. Henderson walked, Butler to second. White singled to right, Fernandez and Butler scored, Henderson to second. Henderson stole third. White stole second. Alomar struck out.
4 runs, 4 hits, 0 errors, 2 left on.
Blue Jays 7, Phillies 6

Phillies Fourth: Stocker popped out to shortstop Fernandez. Mason lined out to center fielder White. Dykstra doubled to right center. Duncan singled to center, Dykstra scored. Kruk lined out to right fielder Carter.
1 run, 2 hits, 0 errors, 1 left on.
Phillies 7, Blue Jays 7

Phillies Fifth: Hollins singled to third. Daulton homered down the right field line on 1-1 count, Hollins and Daulton scored. Eisenreich singled to second. Thompson doubled down the left field line, Eisenreich scored. Stocker grounded out to third baseman Molitor. Jordan, pinch hitting for Mason, grounded out to shortstop Fernandez. Dykstra homered to right on 1-0 count, Thompson and Dykstra scored. Duncan singled to center. Castillo relieved Leiter, Duncan stole second. Kruk grounded out to second baseman Alomar.
5 runs, 6 hits, 0 errors, 1 left on.
Phillies 12, Blue Jays 7

Blue Jays Sixth: West pitching. White doubled down the left field line. Alomar singled to center, White scored. Carter flied out to right fielder Eisenreich. Olerud singled to left, Alomar to third. Molitor hit by pitch, Olerud to second. Fernandez grounded out to second baseman Duncan, Alomar scored, Olerud to third, Molitor to second. Borders flied out to right fielder Eisenreich.
2 runs, 3 hits, 0 errors, 2 left on.
Phillies 12, Blue Jays 9

Phillies Sixth: Hollins doubled to center. Daulton flied out to left fielder Henderson. Eisenreich popped out to catcher Borders. Thompson singled to second, Hollins scored. Stocker walked, Thompson to second. Chamberlain, pinch hitting for West, struck out.
1 run, 2 hits, 0 errors, 2 left on.
Phillies 13, Blue Jays 9

Phillies Seventh: Dykstra grounded out to second baseman Alomar. Duncan singled to shortstop. Kruk walked, Duncan to second. Hollins walked, Duncan to third, Kruk to second. Daulton hit by pitch, Duncan scored, Kruk to third, Hollins to second. Eisenreich popped out to shortstop Fernandez. Thompson grounded into fielder's choice, second baseman Alomar to shortstop Fernandez, Daulton forced at second.
1 run, 1 hit, 0 errors, 3 left on.
Phillies 14, Blue Jays 9

Blue Jays Eighth: Alomar grounded out to third baseman Hollins. Carter singled to right center. Olerud walked, Carter to second. Molitor safe at second on third baseman Hollins' fielding error, Carter scored, Olerud to third. Mt.Williams relieved Andersen. Fernandez singled to left, Olerud scored, Molitor to third. Borders walked, Fernandez to second. Sprague, pinch hitting for Castillo, struck out. Henderson singled to center, Molitor and Fernandez scored, Borders to second. White tripled to center, Borders and Henderson scored. Alomar grounded out to third baseman Hollins.
6 runs, 4 hits, 1 error, 1 left on.
Blue Jays 15, Phillies 14.

SportsPeople

BOXING

Tyson Tells Newspaper He May Settle in Africa

MIKE TYSON, the former world heavyweight champion who has been in prison since last year on a rape conviction, has said he may settle in Africa to escape racism against blacks in the United States.

"Maybe I should consider settling there since America has become an asylum, especially for blacks," he told The Herald newspaper in Harare, Zimbabwe.

Speaking from inside the Indiana prison where he is serving a six-year sentence for rape, Tyson, 27, said that white Americans hate successful blacks like himself, **MICHAEL JORDAN** and the pop superstar **MICHAEL JACKSON**.

"Michael Jackson, that great philanthropist who has done so much for children, is now being typecast as a child molester," Tyson said. "Isn't that preposterous?" Tyson was alluding to charges leveled against Jackson by a teen-aged boy. "Look at what they have done to me. I am rich and powerful. Suddenly, I have become a rapist." (AP)

FOOTBALL

Dickerson Is Finished

ERIC DICKERSON, the National Football League's second-leading career rusher, has decided to retire. "I know I'm not going to play again; I mean that's obvious," Dickerson said from his California home Wednesday night.

"It's still tough to say the word 'retirement,' but I'm a realistic guy. I'm a great believer that everything happens for a reason, and this is something I've been thinking about anyway. My mother's been telling me for years to get out, so now she'll be happy."

The Atlanta Falcons said they placed Dickerson, 33, on the league's reserve-retired list to create a roster spot for the free-agent cornerback **LEMUEL STINSON**. Dickerson has suffered from a bulging disk this season. (AP)

Mayes Retires Again

RUEBEN MAYES's second retirement from the N.F.L. will apparently be his last. Mayes, 30, announced he was retiring for good Wednesday after Seattle Coach **TOM FLORES** decided to put him on the Seahawks' injured reserve list. (AP)

HOCKEY

The Brothers Gretzky

BRENT GRETZKY couldn't look his brother in the eyes. "I was too nervous," the Tampa Bay rookie said Wednesday night, describing the first face-off of his pro career against his older brother and nine-time National Hockey League most valuable player **WAYNE**.

"The second time I got him with a stick, and the third time, I think he knew what I was going to do," Brent said. "After that, I was able to look at him."

Wayne won most of the personal matchups and contributed a goal and two assists to help the Los Angeles Kings to a 4-3 victory before a crowd of 21,536 at the Thunderdome in St. Petersburg, Fla.

"I tried my best," the younger Gretzky said. "We are on different levels, and Wayne is supreme."

"He wanted to win. I wanted to win," Wayne said. (AP)

BASEBALL

Abbott Is Honored

Making it to the majors as a one-handed pitcher was an impressive enough achievement, but it was the no-hitter he threw against Cleveland on Sept. 4 that apparently clinched **JIM ABBOTT**'s selection to receive the Freedom Forum's Free Spirit Award at a dinner at the New York Public Library last night.

JOHN C. QUINN, the deputy chairman of the international organization, said the Yankee's no-hitter was "the clearest and most compelling statement that ever could be made about the potential of the disabled to 'mainstream' into America."

TENNIS

54 Years of Talent

The next American teen-aged tennis phenomenon, 13-year-old **VENUS WILLIAMS**, will team up with the evergreen phenom, 41-year-old **JIMMY CONNORS**, tomorrow night in Baltimore for the First National Bank Tennis Festival. The event is sponsored by the tennis player **PAM SHRIVER** to assist children's charities in her hometown.

Venus and her 12-year-old sister, **SERENA**, will play the baseball players **CAL** and **BILLY RIPKEN** in doubles, and Venus and Connors will later face Shriver and **JIM COURIER** in a mixed doubles exhibition at the Baltimore Arena.

Sponsors Are Skate Issue

Special to The New York Times

DALLAS, Oct. 21 — The continuing marriage between Olympic sports and corporate sponsorships has led to an awkward relationship in the world of figure skating.

This week's Skate America, the only international skating competition in the United States and an important prelude to the 1994 Winter Olympics in Lillehammer, Norway, is sponsored by Sudafed, the cold relief medicine that contains stimulant properties and is thus contained on the International Olympic Committee's list of banned substances. Another related development that raised some eyebrows was the unveiling of Korbel Champagne Cellars as a figure-skating sponsor in the United States. This comes at a time of increased debate about the propriety of supporting athletic endeavors on the flow of alcohol.

According to Jerry Lace, executive director of the United States Figure Skating Association, as costs rise, corporate sponsorships have become a necessity. "Who is going to pay for these programs?" Lace said. "What do we do, not send teams to certain events? Program availability would be limited without sponsors. These programs provide far more in opportunities than in downside."

THE GLOBE AND MAIL

SPORTWEEK

Monday, October 25, 1993

Section D

ANOTHER IN A SERIES

UNBRIDLED JOY

MVP at peace amid the din

BY LARRY MILLSON
Sport Reporter
Toronto

THE first sounds Paul Molitor heard were those of the fireworks, and that was when he reached home plate after a joyous trip from first base.

"Then, as we began kind of a bedlam scene, the high-pitched sound of screaming set in," the most valuable player of the World Series said. "It's amazing that that last 180 feet you're really not taking in all the noise."

It had all happened so quickly. As Molitor said, "It wasn't like we were 5-1 and cruising."

No, that situation had evaporated when the Philadelphia Phillies scored five runs in the seventh inning. So the Toronto Blue Jays came to bat in the bottom of the ninth down 6-5.

Rickey Henderson drew a leadoff walk and Devon White flied out. Then Molitor stung a 1-1 pitch from Mitch Williams so hard for a single that Henderson progressed no farther than second. It was Molitor's third hit of the game, following a first-inning triple and a fifth-inning homer, and it made him 12-for-24 for the Series with eight runs batted in.

Five pitches later, Joe Carter lined his historic home run over the left-field fence on a 2-2 count and the frenzy began.

"Those few minutes, you just start off saying, 'Man, I can't believe that's a home run,' " said Molitor, who came home with his 10th run of the six-game Series. " 'I can't believe the game's over. I can't believe we're world champs.'

"Then, all of a sudden, it starts to sink in. This is what I'm here for. You get taken over by emotion. I'm not ashamed or embarrassed about it happening."

Molitor had a right to be emotional. He is 37 and just had completed his 16th major-league season — in which he was one of the best players in the game. When manager Cito Gaston talked about repeating as Series champions, he wanted it for players such as Molitor.

"When I was hugging Molitor out there, he had tears in his eyes and I did, too," Gaston said.

"There's a lot of feeling in a very short time," Molitor said. "The days and the weeks and the months of this off-season are going to get deeper and deeper in appreciation. But now I'm very peaceful with it."

His only other chance at a World Series championship was in 1982, when the Milwaukee Brewers led 3-2 but lost in seven games to the St. Louis Cardinals.

Long forgotten by this time was the wailing of so many Blue Jay fans last December when the club signed Molitor as a free agent, and that meant Toronto would not re-sign Dave Winfield.

Winfield had a terrific season with the Jays, batting .290 with 26 homers and 108 RBIs, but had a so-so post-season — .250 with two homers and three RBIs in the American League Championship Series and .227 with three RBIs in the World Series. But two of Winfield's Series RBIs came on a game-winning, 11th-inning double in the sixth game at Atlanta against the Braves.

Please see MOLITOR — Page D2

FRED LUM, ROGER HALLETT/The Globe and Mail

Toronto's Joe Carter won the hearts of teammates and a nation Saturday night when he hit the ninth-inning homer that gave the Jays an 8-6 win over the Philadelphia Phillies. The reward was unveiled in the rafters of the SkyDome yesterday: World Series Champs.

THE FAN

Sequel's script unbelievable

BY KIRK MAKIN
The Globe and Mail

JOE Carter choked.

Fortunately, the 35 Toronto Blue Jays piled atop his prone body had the good grace to roll off and allow him to breathe before that chronic Pepsodent grin became a death mask.

The jumping, heaving pile of Jay flesh after Carter's game-winning homer certainly served one purpose. It buried any deluded thoughts that the Jays had become jaded about winning.

Were it a script, this season would be rejected as impossibly hackneyed.

Fan loyalty somehow survived a November of cold, mercenary roster moves. By spring training, fans remained moderately ruffled by the exit of team heroes.

Suddenly, Tony Fernandez returned and blossomed. Rickey Henderson, a walking Hall of Fame exhibit, arrived to do what he does best — riling and running.

By playoff time, the lineup was breathtaking. Henderson, Molitor, Carter, Alomar, Morris, Stewart — all on one team? And behind them — White, Olerud, Guzman, Ward. It was almost obscene.

The pennant race became a season-long cliffhanger and both playoffs were exquisitely matched affairs that mercifully spared us the blood-curdling excitement of a Game Seven.

No wonder Americans revile the Jays. You almost could see the cartoon thought-bubbles over the heads of the CBS boys after the Jays won: "Oh, God, how are we going to explain this a second time back home?"

You'll get used to it, friends. Just as we got used to losing the Stanley Cup to traditional hockey hotbeds such as Pittsburgh.

Personally, I will be blessed with a joyous memory all my own to treasure when the details of Game Six begin to fade. In fact, I suppose it was the ultimate fan moment.

Caught taking illicit home videotape of the festivities on the field, my moving appeal to the home-town loyalties of an officious security twerp and a Metro Toronto cop fell on deaf ears.

Their steely grip on my arms, I was thrown out of the SkyDome in front of 20,000 revellers. Bad boy, go home.

In the end, the enormity of Carter's winning home run may be equalled one day. But it will not be surpassed. Nor will the supreme justice of teary-eyed Paul Molitor — Mr. Baseball — winning his first World Series and the most-valuable-player award at 37.

And, when the inevitable, painful jettisoning of players starts again this winter, we only can hope the result will be so divine.

CHANGES

Roster shakeup due at SkyDome

BY NEIL A. CAMPBELL
Sport Reporter
Toronto

CHAMPAGNE dripped from Mark Eichhorn as he related what is likely to be his final memory as a relief pitcher with the Toronto Blue Jays. At least a quarter of the Jays' World Series roster will be somewhere else next year and Eichhorn, whose $700,000 salary is not in line with his value to the team, is a leading candidate.

"We're sitting in our perch in the bullpen and we see Joe [Carter] swing at a pitch in the dirt," Eichhorn said. "I was a little nervous so I said 'Geez, Joe, don't swing at a pitch like that from a guy like Mitch Williams.' Mike Timlin tells me to calm down. So I said 'all right then, go ahead and swing at the next pitch for a three-run dinger.'

"Next thing I know the ball's coming right at us and we've won the game."

Eichhorn and his teammates doused each other with beer and champagne Saturday night. Yesterday, they attended a private party at the SkyDome and then took part in the victory parade.

Now, many will leave and not return. Just as Dave Winfield, David Cone, Candy Maldonado, Jimmy Key, Tom Henke and Manuel Lee left last year's World Series-winning team, expect Tony Fernandez, Rickey Henderson, Jack Morris, Alfredo Griffin and Eichhorn to not be invited back now that their contracts have expired. There's also a strong possibility that several players will be traded, perhaps Todd Stottlemyre and Pat Borders.

"The sad part is losing anybody at all," said Ed Sprague, whose splendid season at third base and modest salary ($200,000 this season) guarantee his return. "When you play together for six months, day in and day out, that's something special."

The Jays were accused last winter of being somewhat callous in dumping players. Many hasty decision were made about players' status, some because of time constraints. "We learned our lesson last year," Gord Ash, the team's assistant general manager, said. "We're going to savour this and then do our business later in the week."

Still, changes are necessary. Winning a second consecutive World Series cost the Jays $50-million (U.S.) in player salaries. The end of baseball's four-year television contract with CBS will mean a revenue shortfall of about $7-million (U.S.) per club. So Ash and his boss, executive vice-president Pat Gillick, want the salary tab back to $43-million or so.

Say goodbye first to Morris, who missed the playoffs and World Series because of an arm injury. Morris, 37, earned $5.5-million this season. The Jays can pay him a similar amount for 1994 or buy him out for $1-million. He will be bought out.

Henderson, acquired by the Jays in a trade July 31, earned $3.25-million this season. His contract has expired and he is free to deal with any team. Toronto native Rob Butler can take his place for $150,000 or so. "The payroll's too high here but other than that I'd love to be back," he said. He knows he won't, though.

Please see ROSTER — Page D2

NATIONAL

BEER COMMERCIAL FALLOUT

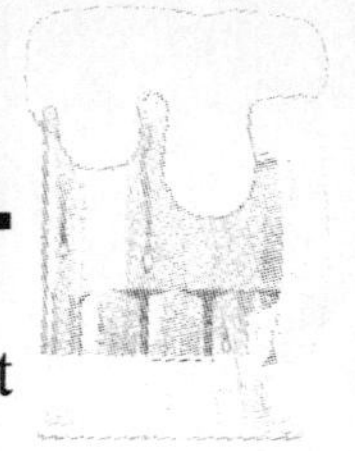

Research finds impact on youth — A12

STATE

SCHOOL TAX CHANGE

Thompson takes aim at Democrat's initial plan — B1

SPORTS

THE BUCKS SLIDE ON

Players are surprised at 14-34 record after loss to the Bulls

Friday
February 11, 1994

THE JOURNAL

Latest • •
Edition — III

Child care in state faulted

Children found to be at risk in 38 of 39 facilities examined in US report

By FRANK A. AUKOFER
Journal Washington bureau

Washington, D.C. — Federal and state officials, in unannounced inspections of 39 child care facilities in Wisconsin, found 755 violations of state regulations, according to a government report made public here Friday.

Among them were such things as fire hazards, toxic substances where children could get to them, exposed light sockets and electrical wiring and firewood stacked against a wood-burning stove.

"Children receiving care at 38 of the 39 facilities we inspected were, to varying degrees, at risk of exposure to health and safety hazards," the report said.

The report was discussed in testimony before a House subcommittee Friday by June Gibbs Brown, inspector general of the Health and Human Services Department. She testified at a hearing on the quality and availability of child care.

Please see **Trade** *page* **15**

'The Kid' retires

MILWAUKEE BREWERS LEGEND ROBIN YOUNT celebrates his 3,000th hit with his teammates in 1992.

Journal photo by Tom Lynn

Yount caps stellar career

By BOB BERGHAUS
Journal sports reporter

Pride in his own performance had as much as anything to do with Robin Yount retiring from baseball after a 20-year career with the Milwaukee Brewers.

In a setting of familiarity and of simple elegance, Yount officially announced the end of his career in the Brewers' clubhouse, sitting at a table in front of his locker stall and a variety of poster-size pictures that helped capture part of his amazing career, which began in 1974 as an 18-year-old shortstop.

Typically a man of few words, Yount didn't change his style this day.

"I'm here to announce my retirement from major-league baseball," he said. "There's not going to be any emotional speeches or tears or anything. I think I'm going to wait to get home to do that."

He said their were many factors that went into his decision to forgo an option to play this season for $3.2

Please see **Brewers** *page* **16**

Associated Press photo

ROBIN YOUNT REFLECTS ON HIS RETIREMENT at a news conference Friday at County Stadium.

No. 19 gave us years of thrills

By TOM FLAHERTY
Journal sports reporter

It's etched in the mind of every major-leaguer.

A screaming line drive or a bloop over the infield. That first hit.

They all remember.

Except Robin Yount.

"No, I really don't," Yount said 2,999 hits after that first one.

"Somebody asked me that a couple days ago. He told me. I guess it was a single to right off Dave McNally.

"I may be wrong. If what the guy told me was bad information, then I got it wrong."

The information was right. Yount got his first hit in the major leagues off the Baltimore pitcher on April 12, 1974.

There were many more hits over his 20-year career, some of the biggest hits in the Milwaukee Brewers' 25-year history.

Please see **Yount** *page* **9**

Homeowners

Snow, ice increase work for roofers

By JO SANDIN
of The Journal staff

As residential rooftops begin to groan under the thickest ice and snow in recent winters, professional roofers offered this advice to homeowners across the state:

Shovel the driveway. Shovel the sidewalk. But *don't* shovel the roof.

ON A3

■ *Storm spreads misery from South to East*

"For safety reasons, I wouldn't recommend that anybody get up on their roof to remove ice and snow," said John Millen, the third generation of his family to operate the roofing business that has been a part of Milwaukee's North Side for 101 years. "Even for a professional roofer, it's a matter for caution."

A spot check of roofing com-

Please see **Snow** *page* **14**

From rookie . . .

Journal file photo

ROBIN YOUNT, shown in his rookie season, was a first-round pick in the 1973 amateur draft.

On A9: *Photo highlights of Yount's career.*
On C1: *How the '94 Brewers shape up.*
On C4: *Yount's colleagues remember 'The Kid.'*
Sunday: *A 2-page keepsake poster featuring original artwork highlighting Yount's career.*
Monday: *A second 2-page keepsake poster, including Yount's stats and Topps baseball cards.*

. . . to finale

Journal photo by Karen A. Sherlock

YOUNT WAVES TO FANS AFTER HIS LAST GAME AT MILWAUKEE COUNTY STADIUM in 1993. Yount, the sole remaining player from the 1982 World Series team, played 20 years for the Brewers.

Boy's promising life slides suddenly into adult court

By MARY CAROLE McCAULEY
of The Journal staff

He had a summer job he loved, was on the honor roll at a suburban high school and hoped to study electronics at the Milwaukee School of Engineering.

There were piano lessons, a trip to Disneyland, family excursions for ice skating and picking strawberries. He learned how to grow flowers, joined the Boy Scouts and baked birthday cakes for his mother.

So what was he doing with a gun?

That's the question that Children's Court Judge Christopher Foley grappled with Thursday when he ordered that the 16-year-old boy's case be transferred to adult court in the slaying of Christine Schweiger.

"This is the most despicable

Please see **Youth** *page* **14**

INSIDE

WEATHER

TONIGHT: Becoming cloudy; lows near 20.
SATURDAY: Snow; highs 25-30.
SUNDAY: Partly cloudy; low 20s.
Details on B2.

7 31544 10500 4

Japan, US fail to break impasse

Important trade talks break down as leaders hold their first summit

From Journal wire reports

Washington, D.C. — President Clinton and Japanese Prime Minister Morihiro Hosokawa held their first face-to-face meeting Friday with trade relations between their nations at the brink of collapse.

Hosokawa's limousine arrived at the White House in an ice storm that shut down most of the federal government. The two leaders began their meeting shortly before noon.

US Trade Representative Mickey Kantor and Japanese Foreign Minister Tsutomu Hata met early Friday morning in a last-minute effort to reach a trade agreement before the summit. The three-hour session broke up at about 4 a.m. EST with no breakthrough, a spokeswoman for Kantor told Bloomberg Business News.

Jiro Okayama, a spokesman for the Japanese delegation, disputed the US characterization that the talks had broken down, but he said that at the present time no further sessions between Kantor and Hata were scheduled.

The meeting at the White House on Friday was intended to herald a new US-Japan economic partnership. But on the eve of the summit, the two leaders who came to office promising reform

Please see **Day Care** *page* **15**

SPORTS ★ ★ ★ ★ FINAL

DAILY NEWS

50¢ NEW YORK'S HOMETOWN NEWSPAPER Monday, August 14, 1995

28-PAGE COMMEMORATIVE SPECIAL WRAPS MAIN NEWS

THE MICK

1931-1995

'A big part of the whole baseball world has passed away... '

– Buck Showalter

DAILY NEWS PHOTO

SPORTS ★ ★ ★ ★ FINAL

SENT PACKIN'

Senate committee votes to expel Packwood PAGE 5

FUHRMAN TAKES THE FIFTH

SEE STORY PAGE 7

DAILY NEWS

50¢ NEW YORK'S HOMETOWN NEWSPAPER Thursday, September 7, 1995

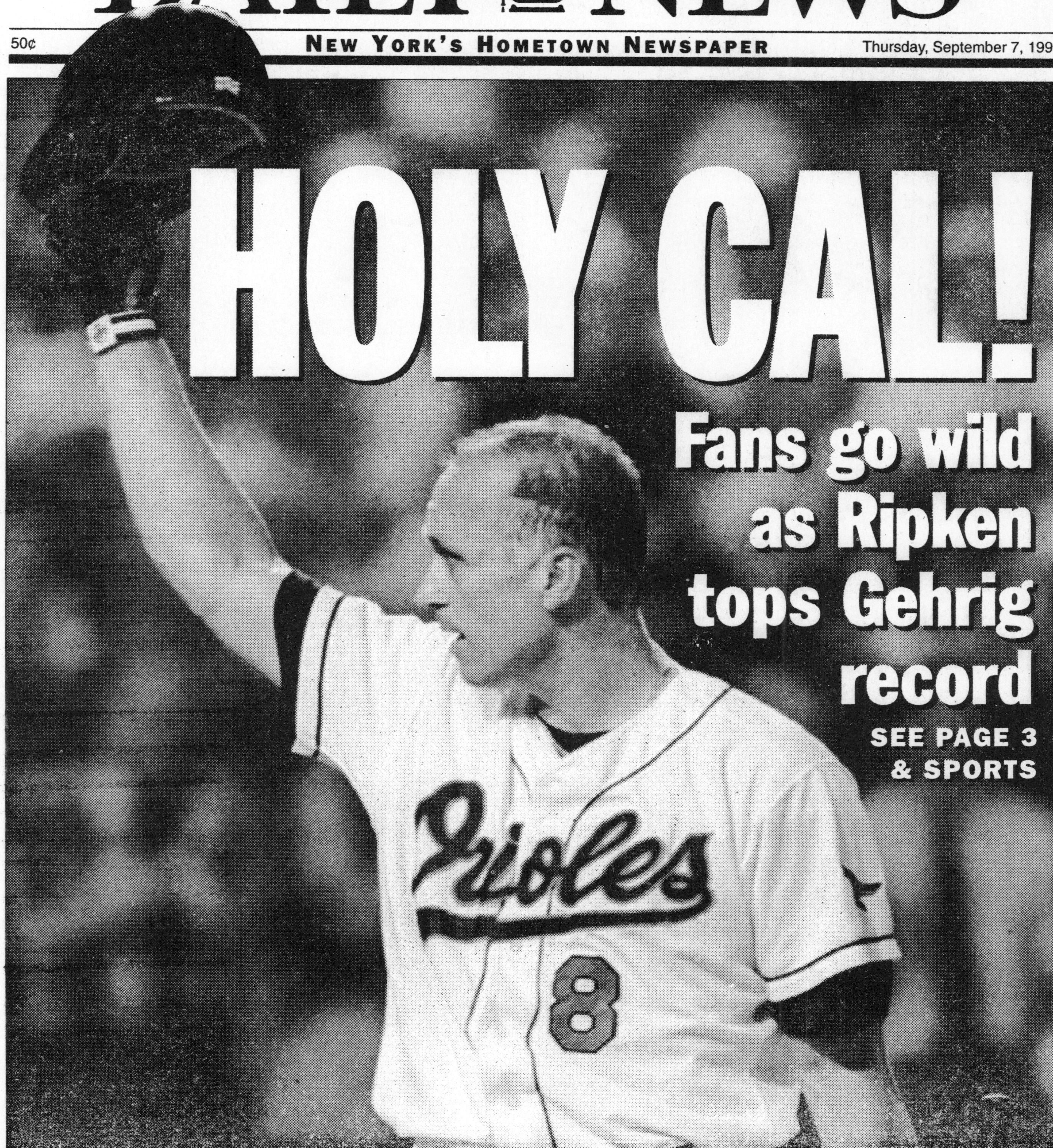

HOLY CAL!

Fans go wild as Ripken tops Gehrig record

SEE PAGE 3 & SPORTS

"All the News
That's Fit to Print"

The New York Times

Late Edition
New York: **Today,** brisk, becoming mostly cloudy. High 57. **Tonight,** clearing, chilly. Low 43. **Tomorrow,** clouds arriving. High 58. **Yesterday,** high 68, low 59. Details are on page 42.

VOL.CXLV . . . No. 50,229 | NEW YORK, SUNDAY, OCTOBER 29, 1995 | $2.50

Srebrenica: The Days of Slaughter

Luc Delahaye/Magnum

THE AGONY A Muslim woman from the Bosnian town of Srebrenica cried out after arriving at a refugee camp in July.

BBC

THE VICTIMS Bosnian Serbs guarded captured Muslim men after the fall of Srebrenica. The scene was photographed by a Serbian television cameraman and later broadcast on the BBC.

The following article is by ***Stephen Engelberg*** *and* ***Tim Weiner*** *with further reporting from* ***Raymond Bonner*** *in Bosnia and* ***Jane Perlez*** *in Serbia.*

WASHINGTON, Oct. 28 — On the afternoon of July 10, soldiers of the Bosnian Serb army began storming Srebrenica, a city of refuge created by the United Nations, where more than 40,000 people sought shelter from war. A United Nations officer in the town hunched over his computer and tapped out a desperate plea to his leaders in Geneva:

"Urgent urgent urgent. B.S.A. is entering the town of Srebrenica. Will someone stop this immediately and save these people. Thousands of them are gathering around the hospital. Please help."

Nobody did. As the Western alliance stood by, the eastern Bosnian city was overrun. What followed in the towns and fields around

MASSACRE IN BOSNIA

A special report.

Srebrenica is described by Western officials and human rights groups as the worst war crime in Europe since World War II: the summary killing of perhaps 6,000 people.

As recounted by the few Muslims who survived, the killing was chillingly methodical, part mass slaughter, part blood sport.

The Muslim men were herded by the thousands into trucks, delivered to killing sites near the Drina River, lined up four by four and shot. One survivor, 17-year-old Nezad Avdic, recalled in an interview this week that as he lay wounded among the dead Muslims, a Serbian soldier surveyed the stony, moonlit field piled with bodies and merrily declared: "That was a good hunt. There were a lot of rabbits here."

Serbian civilians interviewed this week in the villages around Srebrenica confirmed for the first time the mass killings carried out in their midst.

They pointed out the schools that were used as holding pens for the doomed Muslims — including

Continued on Page 14, Column 1

Barton Silverman/The New York Times

Braves Win the World Series

The Atlanta Braves defeated the Cleveland Indians, 1-0, behind Tom Glavine's eight innings of one-hit pitching. The victory gave Atlanta its first major sports championship ever. Articles, SportsSunday, section 8. (Some copies went to press before the game ended.)

PRESIDENT WARNS CONGRESS TO DROP SOME BUDGET CUTS

VETO THREAT IS RENEWED

Clinton Says He Will Not Talk or Compromise on Health, Education or Pollution

By TODD S. PURDUM

WASHINGTON, Oct. 28 — Hours after the Senate approved a sweeping budget bill, President Clinton today made his strongest warning yet to the Republican Congress, saying not only that he would veto the bill but also that "there is nothing for us to talk about" until money is restored for health, education and the environment.

By a vote of 52 to 47 shortly after midnight, the Senate approved the huge revenue and spending measure, which would cut taxes by $245 billion over seven years, sharply curb the growth of outlays for Medicare and Medicaid and turn over to the states broad new responsibility for caring for the poor.

Negotiators must now reconcile it, probably late next month, with a similar bill approved in the House by a vote of 227 to 203.

During a session of almost 15 hours beginning on Friday morning, the Senate adopted a number of proposals, demanded by moderate Republicans, that veered away from the more conservative House version.

But the President insisted today that he had no intention of negotiating a compromise until the Republicans moved his way, even if they tried to force his hand by refusing to extend the Government's borrowing authority so it could keep paying its bills during a stalemate — a threat Mr. Clinton called "blackmail tactics."

"Hear this: Before or after a veto, I am not prepared to discuss the destruction of Medicare and Medicaid, the gutting of our commitment to education, the ravaging of our environment, or raising taxes on working people," Mr. Clinton said in his weekly radio address. "So I say to the Republican leaders: Back off your cuts in these vital areas. Until you do, there is nothing for us to talk about."

In the Republican response, Speaker Newt Gingrich warned Mr. Clinton to "think twice about vetoing the balanced budget and jeopardizing long-overdue revolutionary change" and said the President "promises to be a roadblock." The Senate majority leader, Bob Dole of Kansas, added, "America cannot afford to continue on this destructive course."

This morning's vote sets the stage for a new round of wrangling between Capitol Hill and the Administration that White House aides acknowledge could well result in a series of vetoes, not only of the budget package passed this week but also of some of the individual appropriations bills that accompany it, and a virtual stalemate through the end of the year. They say that is a risk Mr. Clinton is prepared to take to preserve what he can of his priorities and build a record for his re-election

Continued on Page 30, Column 1

With Millions and Billions, G.O.P. Budget Takes Shape

By ROBERT PEAR

WASHINGTON, Oct. 28 — As debate on Federal budget policy lurched forward on the Senate floor on Friday night, a member of the Republican leadership scribbled a new row of figures into the legislation, sending an additional $50 million of Medicaid money to Vermont. The new figures put the final touch on a last-minute change to the bill, one of many that clinched its passage early this morning in a milestone Republican victory.

But the deal, which had taken shape in corridors and cloakrooms just off the Senate floor, involved states far larger than Vermont and sums far greater than $50 million. Texas, for instance, with two Republican Senators, gained $5.2 billion as a result of changes in the legislation's Medicaid formula. California, with two Democratic Senators, lost $4.2 billion.

The three days of debate that led up to the vote had been full of lofty oratory. In the big budget-balancing bill, Republicans saw the dawning of a new, fiscally responsible era; Democrats delivered predictions of doom.

But the hours just before the 52-to-47 vote this morning were dominated by classic senatorial logrolling, presided over by that master of legislative maneuvers, Bob Dole of Kansas, the majority leader.

On the floor, Democrats said the Republicans were buying votes with their disbursement of increases in Medicaid money to a handful of states, some represented by two Republican senators, at the expense of other states.

But the chairman of the Senate Finance Committee, William V. Roth Jr., the Delaware Republican who served as Mr. Dole's deputy in the negotiations, denied that today. "Every time you have a formula or allocation," Mr. Roth said, "there are always complaints." Even after the last-minute changes, he said, the Medicaid programs of 45 states would fare better under the Senate's budget bill than under the version passed on Thursday by the House.

Some evidence in support of Mr. Roth's position could be found in the way the late Medicaid alterations treated the New York region. While New York State lost a seven-year total of $246 million, a modest sum compared with the seven-year allocation of $98.1 billion by the Finance Committee, New Jersey, with two Democratic Senators, gained $781 million, for a total of $21.6 billion. And the allocation for Connecticut, which also has two Democratic Senators, rose by $1.2 billion, or 12.8 percent, to $10.6 billion.

Mr. Dole, who on an extraordinari-

Continued on Page 30, Column 4

At Shaken-Up Javits Center, Costs Stay Sky-High

By RANDY KENNEDY

Nearly four months after the Pataki administration announced major labor changes intended to purge organized crime from the Jacob K. Javits Convention Center and reduce the cost of doing business there, many exhibitors say their bills have remained exorbitant, and in some cases have risen slightly.

While the ultimate goal of bringing down costs has not been met, the exhibitors and center officials say that some operations have been transformed, from the elimination of payoffs down to the disappearance of folding chairs along the loading docks on 12th Avenue. "In the old days, you'd find dozens of guys who were on the job, parked in those chairs all the way down the line," said Robert E. Boyle, who became president and chief executive of the center in April.

But while the changes may have rooted out featherbedding and long-entrenched acts of corruption, the cost of participating in trade shows at the Javits Center still surpasses that of other convention halls across the country, say officials at more than two dozen companies that have taken part in five large shows since the shake-up in July. The exhibitors have seen no decrease in their bills for major services, like freight handling, electrical work and the construction of booths where they display their wares. Nearly all the exhibitors interviewed said they were frustrated that their expectations about costs had been raised unrealistically.

"Somebody may be saving money but it doesn't seem to be filtering down to us yet," said Rob Blair, marketing director for Optex (U.S.A.), a California security systems manufacturer that participated in the International Security Conference Expo East in September. He said that his freight delivery charges went up more than $150, to $2,756, and that he was still required to hire an electrician for a one-hour minimum, at more than $50, just to plug in an extension cord.

When the changes were made, Gov. George E. Pataki said exhibitors would save up to 40 percent because of simplified union rules and fewer laborers doing more work, although he did not specify how

Continued on Page 39, Column 1

Medicines From Afar Raise Safety Concerns

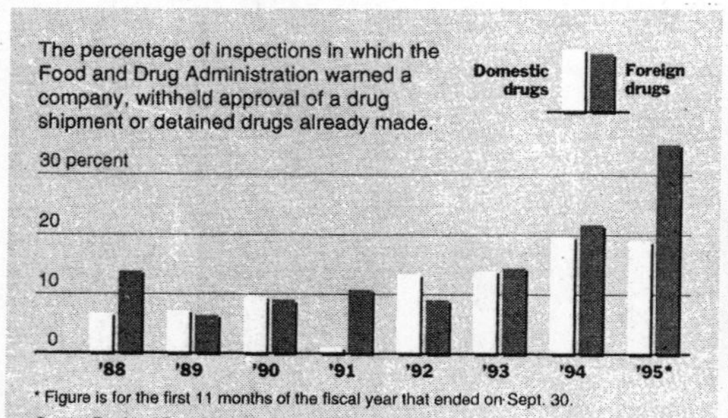

The New York Times

By CHRISTOPHER DREW

WASHINGTON, Oct. 28 — As the American medical system rushes to control costs, imports of discount drugs and their ingredients are rising. And that is causing concern about how well foreign manufacturers meet American standards aimed at preventing toxic contamination and poor quality.

Over the last three years the Food and Drug Administration has doubled the number of its inspections at foreign plants, and it has been rejecting or detaining more products. In the last year alone, the agency has found serious manufacturing deficiencies, from contaminated water supplies to lax quality controls, in 35 percent of its overseas inspections, in countries as varied as Switzerland and China, compared with 19 percent at domestic plants.

But policing this far-flung trade is daunting, given the barriers of language and distance. Interviews and a review of dozens of F.D.A. documents raise questions about whether the agency, known as a tough regulator at home, will be able to keep defective drugs from slipping through.

Top F.D.A. officials and other drug experts say they are confident that nearly all imported products reaching consumers are safe and effective, and that there is little chance an individual will receive tainted drugs. But concern is rising as pharmaceutical companies, under pressure to help control medical costs, increasingly look to lower-priced suppliers

DRUG IMPORTS: Rx NEEDED

A special report.

abroad. And more foreign pharmaceutical companies have begun to sell finished drugs in the huge United States market.

The safety concerns are "a legitimate worry," said William F. Haddad, chairman of Mir Pharmaceutical Inc. in Brewster, N.Y., and the head of the international committee of the Generic Pharmaceutical Industry Association. "I'm not so sure F.D.A. has the manpower. The trade is expanding quicker than their ability to respond to it."

Ronald G. Chesemore, the F.D.A.'s associate commissioner for regulatory affairs, said top agency officials felt that "we've done a tremendous job of beefing up the foreign inspection program" and that American consumers remained safe. The agency has increased the number of foreign companies inspected to 325 this year, from 156 in the 1992 fiscal year, and it is training agents better and increasing the length of the inspections, he said.

But James G. Phillips, a former special assistant to the F.D.A. Commissioner, David A. Kessler, who examined the program before he left the agency a year ago, said, "This thing is like a ticking time bomb that could explode at any time."

An episode at one Canadian plant illustrates the problems. In 1991, an

Continued on Page 32, Column 3

INSIDE

An Energetic Secessionist

Quebec votes on independence tomorrow, and the tenor of Lucien Bouchard's secessionist campaign and of support for his Bloc Québécois is growing raucous. Page 22.

Breast Implant Verdict

For the first time, a jury found the Dow Chemical Company solely liable in a woman's claim of health problems caused by silicone breast implants. Page 33.

Cigar Rides Again

Cigar won the Breeders' Cup Classic at Belmont Park to cap an unbeaten season and clinch the Horse of the Year title. SportsSunday, Section 8.

TODAY'S SECTIONS

* *In New York City and the metropolitan region.*
(† Elsewhere, auto pages are in section 3.)
§ In most parts of New York City.
¶ In Long Island, Westchester, Connecticut and central and northern New Jersey.

1
2
3
A Reminder
Standard time resumed at 2 A.M. today. Clocks were set back one hour.

REMEMBERING

Kirby

34

For more than a decade, fans of the Minnesota Twins laughed and cried with Kirby Puckett. His playing days are over, but his legacy to his sport, his state, his team and his followers lives on as we look back over his memorable career.

Star Tribune

SOUVENIR SECTION

Friday, September 6 · 1996

4 STAR ★ ★ ★ ★ FINAL

DAILY NEWS

$1.50 http://www.mostnewyork.com **NEW YORK'S HOMETOWN NEWSPAPER** Sunday, October 27, 1996

TOP OF THE WORLD!

GERALD HERBERT DAILY NEWS

It's high-fives all around as Paul O'Neill scores the first of three runs in the third inning, and the Yankees hold off the Braves, 3-2, to win the World Series in six games.

PAGES 2-6 & SPORTS

BIG BLUE SQUEAKS PAST LOWLY BENGALS PAGES 76-72, 62

NEW YORK POST
Monday Sports Special
28 Pages
OCTOBER 27, 1997 R

Comeback puts Marlins on top of the World

WALDSTEIN, SHERMAN, KEEGAN, KING
PAGES 81-78

Edgar Renteria greets Moises Alou at home after Marlin scored game-tying run against Indians in ninth inning last night in Miami. Marlins went on to capture their first World Series, 3-2, on Renteria's bases-loaded single in 11th.

Mark McGwire breaks Roger Maris' home run record — 16 pages of coverage in the A, B and Sports sections.

62 ST. LOUIS POST-DISPATCH

Vol. 120, No. 252 ©1998 WEDNESDAY, SEPTEMBER 9, 1998 6 ★★★★★ ●● 50¢

JUBILATION

KEVIN MANNING / POST-DISPATCH

A home run trot to remember: Mark McGwire hails first base coach Dave McKay. The facts: fourth inning, first pitch, 341 feet (his shortest homer of the year.) The pitcher: Steve Trachsel. Final score: Cards 6, Cubs 3.

For Mark McGwire, it was the culmination of a season-long quest. For the fans of St. Louis, it was the thrill of a lifetime.

BY MIKE EISENBATH
Of the Post-Dispatch

Mark McGwire reached baseball immortality Tuesday night with a line-drive home run at Busch Stadium that shone the spotlight on St. Louis and rejuvenated the national pastime.

McGwire hit his 62nd home run of the season, breaking Roger Maris' single-season standard of 61 home runs — the most hallowed record in baseball.

Maris' record stood for nearly 37 years until 8:18 p.m. Tuesday, Sept. 8, on a balmy evening graced by a nearly full moon. The Chicago Cubs were up 2-0 in the fourth inning when McGwire lashed Cubs pitcher Steve Trachsel's first pitch on a line to left field. The ball began to sink as it neared the eight-foot fence, making over by less than than two feet. It was his shortest home run of the season but touched off the most electric, emotional celebration that possibly could be mustered in the best baseball town in America. The Cardinals went on to beat the Cubs, 6-3.

"Yesterday," McGwire said afterward, "doing what I did for my father, hitting my 61st home run on his 61st birthday, I thought what a perfect way to end the home stand, by hitting my 62nd home run for the city of St. Louis and all the great fans. I really and truly wanted to do it here.

"Thank you, St. Louis."

McGwire trotted around the bases with the glee of a 10-year-old, the deliberate manner of a man wanting to savor each step, the

See McGwire, Page A11

POST-DISPATCH WEATHERBIRD ®

http://www.stlnet.com

IN OTHER NEWS

Alan Greenspan propelled the stock market to its biggest point gain ever Tuesday, as the Dow Jones Industrial Average soared 381 points. **A3**

The governor of Maryland, a Democrat, refused to share the stage with President Bill Clinton, who spoke at a school to promote his education plan. **A3**

THE SCENE OUTSIDE

Outside the stadium, most of the fans went on faith. When the lucky ones with tickets inside erupted in a roar, they started screaming, too.

PAGE A14

FRINGE BENEFITS

McGwire's feats have added $50 million to $60 million in economic benefits to the region this year.

PAGE A16

THE ANTICIPATION

McGwire mania spread as old fans joined new fans in holding their collective breath in anticipation of baseball history.

PAGE A16

COMMENTARY

Gerald Early of Washington University and others pay tribute to Mark McGwire's virtuosity.

PAGE B7

0 09189 21100 9

50 YEARS
Chicago Sun-Times
35¢
Chicago/Suburbs
50¢ Elsewhere
RAIN Pages 2, 51
MONDAY, SEPTEMBER 14, 1998
Late Sports Final

Emmys honor TV stars
Page 37

Lisa Kudrow

Great Car GIVEAWAY!
Buick Century finalists list
Page 23

Sosa slams 62

AL PODGORSKI/SUN-TIMES
Sammy Sosa and his teammates celebrate his 62nd home run in the ninth inning at Wrigley Field on Sunday.

Cubs slugger ties McGwire's record

BY DAVE VAN DYCK
STAFF REPORTER

The Cubs' Sammy Sosa swung his way into baseball history Sunday, becoming only the second player to hit more than 61 home runs in a season—but also the second this season.

Sosa launched two majestic homers over the storied walls of Wrigley Field, joining the Cardinals' Mark McGwire with 62 home runs.

After being in St. Louis for McGwire's 62nd on Tuesday, Sosa had this message for McGwire on Sunday: "I wish you could be with me today, but I know you're watching me. . . . This is for you. I love you."

And with that, Sosa gave his signature gesture, kissing the tips of his first two fingers and pointing toward the television cameras.

McGwire went 0-for-2 Sunday against Houston and left after the fourth inning because of minor back spasms. McGwire said he left a telephone message for Sosa congratulating him on tying him for

Turn to Page 3

INSIDE
■ Complete coverage of historic homer
In Sports

George Wallace dies at 79
Page 26

Hyde favors House hearings

BY LYNN SWEET
SUN-TIMES WASHINGTON BUREAU

WASHINGTON—As President Clinton's top lawyers went on the offensive Sunday to head off an impeachment inquiry, House Judiciary Committee Chairman Henry Hyde said he personally believes hearings are warranted.

"I must say I do, but I want to hear from everyone on the committee," Hyde, the Illinois Republican whose committee is in charge of the case, told the Associated Press.

Congress returns to work today after members had the weekend to absorb the lurid details of Independent Counsel Kenneth Starr's report that concludes there may be 11 grounds for impeachment in the wake of Clinton's intimate relationship with Monica Lewinsky.

"It may be an abuse of power if it happened, but it's not an impeachable offense," said David Kendall, Clinton's personal attorney, on ABC's "This

Turn to next page

What should happen to Clinton? Editorial, Page 33.

Sun-Times 2 Poll
Ryan holds on to wide lead over Poshard
Page 8

ST. LOUIS POST-DISPATCH

Vol. 120, No. 271 ©1998 MONDAY, SEPTEMBER 28, 1998 3 ★★★★★ ● 50¢

70

DILIP VISHWANAT / POST-DISPATCH

Mark McGwire heads home on No. 70. "I'm a perfect example of a player who has dealt with so much adversity ... but working hard and climbing that mountain and reaching my peak."

Mighty McGwire dazzles right up to the end

BY MIKE EISENBATH
Of the Post-Dispatch

Mark McGwire brought a tall tale to life Sunday afternoon at Busch Stadium.

He hit his 70th home run.

Go ahead. Laugh. Laugh the giddy laugh of disbelief, of absurdity, of sheer joy. Men, whether they are named Babe Ruth or Roger Maris or Roy Hobbs, don't hit 70 home runs in one baseball season. It didn't make sense until Sunday, when the big, red-headed first baseman in a Cardinals uniform swatted *two home runs* on a day that made sense only in cheap novels, bad movies and this most wonderful of baseball seasons.

In the Cardinals' final game of the year, on a hot and muggy Fan Appreciation Day, the ballpark turned into a carnival.

"I can't believe I did it," McGwire said. "Can you?"

See McGwire, Page A6

THE FANS

As McGwire's season comes to an end, some fans are preparing for the letdown from the home run race and learning to accept Cardinal-free television for the fall.

PAGE B13

AROUND TOWN

From department store dressing rooms to police stations to truck stops, busy St. Louisans tried to stay in tune to the game throughout the day.

PAGE A8

NO. 70 PAGE

Look on the back of Sports for the latest collector's page.

BERGER'S BITS

Jerry Berger made it to both the Rams' and Cardinals' games and rubbed elbows with lots of fans, including Cuba Gooding Jr. and Bill Bidwill.

PAGE A7

Weather

Today: Chance of storms. High 86. Low 70.

Tuesday: Partly cloudy. High 87.

Other weather, Page C8.

Obituaries, C5
Movies, E7
Classified, D1
Editorials, C6

IN OTHER NEWS

Hurricane Georges threatens the Gulf Coast Page A4

Kohl is defeated in German elections Page A5

0 09189 21100 9

RACING ★ ★ ★ ★ FINAL

DAILY NEWS

50¢ www.nydailynews.com **NEW YORK'S HOMETOWN NEWSPAPER** Thursday, October 22, 1998

CHAMPS!

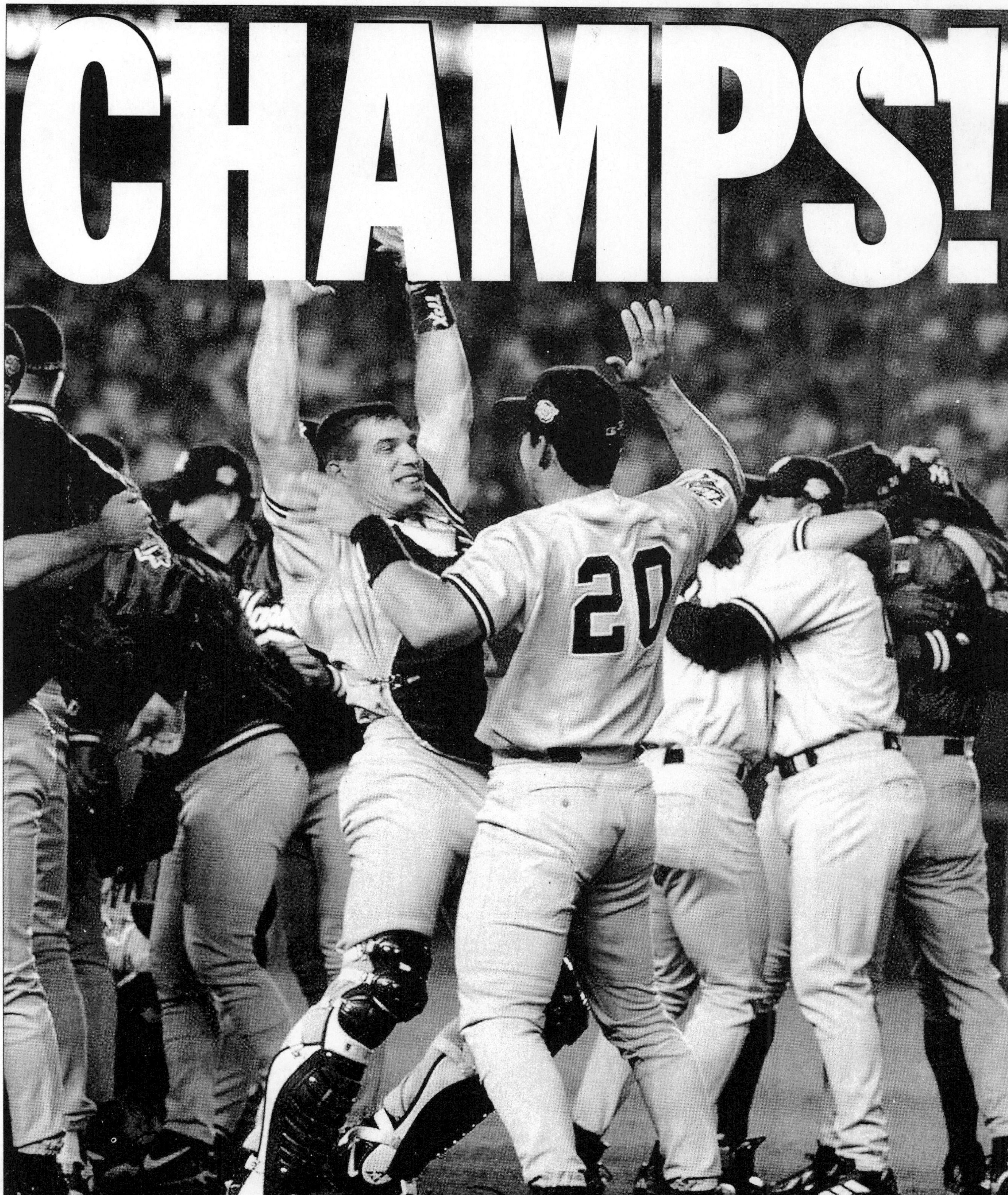

KEITH TORRIE DAILY NEWS

YANKEES SWEEP SAN DIEGO PADRES

4 STAR ★★★★ FINAL

SPECIAL SOUVENIR SECTION WRAPS MAIN NEWSPAPER

DAILY NEWS

50¢ www.nydailynews.com NEW YORK'S HOMETOWN NEWSPAPER Tuesday, March 9, 1999

FAREWELL YANKEE CLIPPER

JOE DIMAGGIO 1914-1999

32-PAGE SPECIAL SECTION WRAPS MAIN NEWS

The New York Times

THOMAS GEORGE
Sports of The Times

He's Made It, And Yet More Needs Doing

CANTON, Ohio

OZZIE NEWSOME was born in Muscle Shoals, Ala., in 1956, early enough to pick cotton as a youth and to watch everyone nearby tend his own garden and harvest his own food. Back then in Muscle Shoals, any type of work at the local Ford plant was the dream job.

"You get a job at Ford," Newsome said, "and you've made it."

Newsome did. While playing football for Bear Bryant at Alabama during the fall of 1974 through 1977, Newsome would work summers at Ford back home.

"I worked with hot metal, lava, in a big bin," he said. "I worked with the lava to make molds for pistons. I had to make sure the bins didn't overflow. I did it for a while and then they got concerned about me doing that type of work with my hands, so then I moved on to other things there."

• • •

Even then, all could see that Newsome possessed magnificent hands. Special ones. Newsome knew it, too, and so did Bryant, because he always said of Newsome, "He can catch a BB in the dark."

Let alone footballs.

And catch them he did, in big games at Alabama and then in big ones in the National Football League. Newsome would play 13 Cleveland Browns seasons, catch more passes (662) than any other tight end in pro football history, grab passes in 150 consecutive games, play in 198 professional games and become a Browns team captain in a career that ended in 1990. At 6 feet 2 inches and 225 pounds, he helped reinvent the position by showing how tight ends could not only block but could also catch the ball frequently and as a deep threat.

Associated Press
Ozzie Newsome

Today Newsome — along with Eric Dickerson, Tom Mack, Billy Shaw and Lawrence Taylor — will become enshrined here at the Pro Football Hall of Fame.

You get into this place and you've made it.

This week of ceremonies leading to today's induction has allowed Newsome to reflect on his sacrifice, how he emerged from the pack, and to remember teammates and family. He is the third of five children. His brothers, Willie and Thomas, will be here today, and so will his sisters, Gloria and Sheila, and his wife, Gloria, and his 7-year-old son, Thomas. His mother, Ethel, 76, will be present. That means a lot to Newsome.

And so does his new challenge, building the Baltimore Ravens into champions. Newsome is the Ravens' vice president for player personnel, an encompassing and powerful job. Newsome and Bobby Grier of the New England Patriots are the only two African-Americans with such complete authority in N.F.L. club personnel matters.

In a league where nearly 70 percent of the players are African-American, only Newsome and Grier have been granted this opportunity. More programs are in place around the league to improve the numbers of African-American executives, but only when men of sterling vision and scope like Art Modell and Robert K. Kraft, owners of the Ravens and the Patriots, respectively, make the move, take the risk, give African-Americans a shot, will the numbers improve.

Thus, Newsome knows that though he has made it, he is still being evaluated.

"I've been evaluated all of my life, even though now my job is one of constant evaluation," he said. "There are blacks out there, former players and others, willing to climb their way up. A lot of people, owners included, are looking to see how I do. I am being compared closely with my peers."

And that is fine with Newsome. There are more sacrifices to make, more challenges to emerge from the pack.

• • •

Newsome was appointed to his current job by Modell when the Cleveland Browns moved to Baltimore in 1996. Now that the new Browns begin play against the Dallas Cowboys in the Hall of Fame preseason game here on Monday night, the resentment in this area of the old team's moving is beginning to fade. Newsome expects cheers from the slew of Browns fans attending today's ceremonies. He also expects boos.

"I grew up as a Cleveland Brown," he said, "and when I left with Art, I could understand the fans' passion. But the people should know that I'll always be No. 82 and a Cleveland Brown. No matter how many boos are there, my mom will be there, and that is what matters most to me. Now that is a lady who knows something about sacrifice. I am the product of a lot of prayers that lady has made for me."

Ozzie Newsome has made it — for now.

But there is more to mold.

Another Day, Another Milestone

With a Single, Gwynn Reaches Elite Circle of 3,000 Hits

Associated Press
San Diego's Tony Gwynn following the flight of the ball on his 3,000th hit, which came on a line single in the first inning off the Expos' Dan Smith last night.

The Pride of San Diego

Last night Tony Gwynn made baseball history by becoming only the 22d player to record 3,000 hits.

THE MILESTONE HITS		
No. 1	July 19, 1982	*vs. Philadelphia's Sid Monge*
No. 1,000	April 22, 1988	*vs. Houston's Nolan Ryan*
No. 2,000	Aug. 6, 1993	*vs. Colorado's Bruce Ruffin*
No. 2,500	Sept. 14, 1996	*vs. Cincinnati's Hector Carrasco*
No. 3,000	Aug. 6, 1999	*vs. Montreal's Dan Smith*

FAVORITE TARGETS	
Greg Maddux	**35**
Rick Mahler	**33**
Tom Browning	**31**
Tom Glavine	**28**

CONSECUTIVE .300 SEASONS	
Ty Cobb (1906-28)	**23**
Honus Wagner (1897-1913)	**17**
Stan Musial ('42-58)	**16**
Gwynn ('83-98)	**16**

CAREER BATTING TITLES	
1. Cobb (1907-15, 17-19)	**12**
2. Wagner (1900, '03-04, '06-09, '11)	**8**
3. Gwynn ('84, 87-89, 94-97)	**8**

By MURRAY CHASS

In what seems to be baseball's nightly milestone, Tony Gwynn of the San Diego Padres took his long expected place among the game's great hitters last night, stroking the 3,000th hit of his career at Olympic Stadium in Montreal. He was the 22d player to reach the 3,000 plateau and the first to do it outside the United States.

Gwynn's first-inning line single against Dan Smith, the Expos' rookie right-hander, ended what little suspense was left after he hit No. 2,999 on Thursday night in St. Louis. That hit came in the same game in which Mark McGwire became the 16th player to hit 500 home runs.

Never before had two hitters attained the 500 home run and 3,000 hit milestones in such proximity. In 1970, Ernie Banks slugged his 500th home run on May 12, and five days later Hank Aaron collected his 3,000th hit. Two months after that Willie Mays joined Aaron and, at the time, eight other players in the 3,000 circle.

"I just want to get it done," Gwynn had said in St. Louis after Thursday night's game. "I just want to get a hit. It's down to one little hit. One hit. Chinker, blooper, line drive, just one hit."

But Gwynn went well beyond the hit he wanted. He collected four hits and left the game in the eighth inning with a career total of 3,003.

Waiting to join Gwynn was Wade Boggs, but he did not get any of the three hits he needed in Tampa Bay's 4-2 victory over Cleveland, failing in four times at bat. The careers of Gwynn and Boggs have paralleled each other. Both first played in the major leagues in 1982, and both have won multiple batting championships, eight in the National League for Gwynn, five in the American League for Boggs.

Gwynn, whose physique belies his talent as a hitter, would have made

Continued on Page D2

Reuters
Tony Gwynn acknowledging the reception from the small, but appreciative crowd in Montreal.

ON BASEBALL/Murray Chass

Win or Lose, Valentine Is Always Carrying a Burden

Years and years from now, fans of the 1999 Mets will tell their grandchildren the tale of how, 55 games and three fired coaches into the season, Bobby Valentine declared to the world, "In the next 55 games, if we're not better, I shouldn't be the manager."

That story was related to Davey Johnson last night, and when he was told that the Mets had run up a 39-15 record since the Valentine declaration, he said, "Those three new coaches must really be something."

Johnson, who has had experience losing a job as manager, was at Shea Stadium with his woefully underachieving Los Angeles Dodgers, just in time to complete Valentine's 55-game cycle. A victory for the Mets would even make their manager a prophet in his own time.

"Someone said, 'Do you want to win eight in a row?' " Valentine said, recalling that agonizing night exactly two months earlier, when the Mets had just lost eight in a row. "I said, no, I'd rather have a sustained run; something like 40 and 15 would be good."

Thirty-nine and 15 had been terrific for the Mets. The run had catapulted them from 27-28, in third place, six games out of the lead, to 66-43, in first place, one and a half games ahead of the perennial champion Atlanta Braves.

Chang W. Lee/The New York Times
Bobby Valentine before last night's game. The Mets' second 55 games have been much better than their first 55, though Valentine is focusing on their final 52.

"I was confident that they'd play better," Valentine said last night. "That's why I said it. I'm really proud of them, the way they've come together. It's a good team right now."

Steve Phillips is the man who made necessary the news conference at which Valentine issued his declaration. As the general manager, Phillips had fired half of the manager's coaching staff, including the two coaches with whom he was the closest.

At the time Valentine uttered his 55-game remark, some listeners suspected he did it before Phillips could suggest that the manager's job was on the line. Last night Phillips took no credit for the timetable.

"It's not my line of demarcation," he said. "He threw it out there. It does not have any special significance to me. I like where we are today. We responded to the challenges of the season and to adversity.

Continued on Page D3

BASEBALL
Pettitte does not clear waivers, meaning no trade.
PAGE D3

PRO FOOTBALL
Kickers' footballs to be kept under lock and key.
PAGE D6

PRO BASKETBALL
Knicks bring John Wallace back to New York.
PAGE D6

ON THE WEB
Late coverage and scores are available from The New York Times on the Web:
www.nytimes.com/sports

The New York Times

Sunday, August 8, 1999

SportsSunday

L Section 8

It's Boggs's Turn to Reach 3,000 Hits, With a (Gasp) Home Run

By MURRAY CHASS

For his milestone of the moment, Wade Boggs decided to be different. On the previous two nights, Mark McGwire had slugged his 500th home run and Tony Gwynn had lashed his 3,000th hit. Boggs followed with his 3,000th hit last night, but he did not attain that elite circle routinely.

After putting himself in position by stroking singles in the third and fourth innings, Boggs cracked a home run in the Tampa Bay Devil Rays' sixth inning at Tropicana Field in St. Petersburg, Fla., becoming the 23d player to reach 3,000 but the first to get there with a home run.

There had been 16 singles, five doubles and one triple as 3,000th hits, but no home run before the 41-year-old Boggs connected against Chris Haney, a journeyman left-hander, who had entered the game for the Cleveland Indians at the start of the inning. When the ball landed in the right-field stands, it was only Boggs's second home run of the season and the 118th of his career.

As he joyously rounded the bases, Boggs pointed skyward in a tribute to his late mother, pointed skyward again a few steps before he reached home plate, then got down on his knees and kissed the plate as he completed his historic 360-foot trot.

His feat completed an incredible three-night run for major league baseball. Never before had its players achieved these legendary numbers on consecutive nights. In 1970, the only previous season in which three players attained those plateaus, Ernie Banks hit his 500th home run on May 12, Hank Aaron rapped his 3,000th hit on May 17 and Willie Mays chipped in with his 3,000th hit on July 18. In the only other comparable coincidental occurrence, Rod Carew stroked his 3,000th hit and Tom Seaver pitched his 300th victory on

Continued on Page 6

3,000 Club Grows

Wade Boggs recorded three hits yesterday and became the 23d player in major league history to reach 3,000.

THE MILESTONE HITS	
No. 1 *vs. Chicago's Rich Dotson*	April 26, 1982
No. 1,000 *vs. Seattle's Scott Bankhead*	April 30, 1987
No. 2,000 *vs. California's Mark Langston*	May 17, 1992
No. 2,500 *vs. Oakland's Don Wengert*	Aug. 23, 1995
No. 3,000 *vs. Cleveland's Chris Haney*	Aug. 7, 1999

200-HIT SEASONS	
Pete Rose	10
Ty Cobb	9
Lou Gehrig	8
Willie Keeler	8
Paul Waner	8
Wade Boggs *(Tied with Charlie Gehringer and Rogers Hornsby)*	**7**

CONSECUTIVE BATTING TITLES	
Ty Cobb (1907-15)	9
Rogers Hornsby ('20-25)	6
Wade Boggs ('85-88)	**4**
Tony Gwynn ('94-97)	4
Rod Carew ('72-75)	4

Associated Press

Wade Boggs's home run off Chris Haney was his 3,000th hit.

Hard Feelings Linger After Yanks Brawl With Mariners

By BUSTER OLNEY

SEATTLE, Aug. 7 — The Yankees and Seattle engaged in a game so hideously long and dull Friday night that fans began streaming out of Safeco Field in the fifth inning. Those who remained witnessed a nasty ninth-inning brawl that created a binge of ill will.

Some teammates in the Yankees' clubhouse were annoyed with Jason Grimsley, whose actions served as the spark for the fight. Joe Girardi, his forehead bruised, said he would never forget how Seattle's Frank Rodriguez tried to hurt him. Manager Joe Torre chastised the way the home-plate umpire, Gary Cederstrom, handled the moments preceding the fracas. And Chad Curtis and Derek Jeter apparently have an issue to sort out — something Curtis wanted to settle in the clubhouse afterward, in full view of reporters.

"It's just part of baseball — it's been a part of baseball since Ty Cobb," said Chili Davis, who was among those most heavily involved in the shoving and pushing and tackling in the ninth inning.

After a 3-run homer and a hit batsman, a routine game gets emotional.

Bernie Williams said, "It was like a war zone out there."

It had been an eminently forgettable game before the craziness at the end, both sides seemingly resigned to the fact that the Yankees were on the way to an 11-8 victory. Paul O'Neill, Williams and Scott Brosius all banged homers in the first inning. Orlando Hernández, however, made the shortest start of his major league career. Plagued by control problems, he allowed three hits, three walks and three runs before a perplexed Torre removed him after a third of an inning. Even so, the Yankees rolled along toward their 66th victory. The first four and one-half innings required 2 hours 28 minutes, and by the sixth inning, players from both teams were often swinging at the first pitch, in an unspoken collaboration to end the game.

But a couple of Seattle runners reached base against Grimsley in the bottom of the eighth, and Alex Rodriguez slammed a three-run homer, closing the Yankees' lead to three runs. Grimsley's next pitch sailed over the head of Edgar Martinez, and was followed by a fastball into Martinez's side.

Grimsley insisted later that he had not thrown at Martinez intentionally — "I have too much respect for a hitter like Edgar Martinez," he said — but if he had not done it on purpose, he was at least guilty of terrible timing. "They started it," said Lou Piniella, the Seattle manager. "It was blatant. I thought the first pitch at Edgar maybe got away from Grimsley, but the second was obvious."

Cederstrom ejected Grimsley, a decision Torre understood completely; all he asked Cederstrom was how much time Mariano Rivera would have to warm up. Torre, too, was unhappy with Grimsley, convinced until a later conversation with Grimsley that the pitcher had hit Martinez intentionally.

Before the eighth inning ended, Torre was

Continued on Page 3

THE CLASS OF '99

ERIC DICKERSON	TOM MACK	OZZIE NEWSOME	BILLY SHAW	LAWRENCE TAYLOR
Running Back	*Guard*	*Tight End*	*Guard*	*Linebacker*
Rams (1983-87), Colts ('87-91), Raiders ('92), Falcons ('93)	Rams (1966-78)	Browns (1978-90)	Bills (1961-69)	Giants (1981-93)

Taylor's New Home: 'Place Where Legends Live'

Lawrence Taylor was embraced literally by his son, T. J., and figuratively by hundreds of Giants fans yesterday at the Hall of Fame induction ceremonies.

Photographs by Associated Press

No. 56 for Giants Becomes No. 199 In the Hall of Fame

By THOMAS GEORGE

CANTON, Ohio, Aug. 7 — Lawrence Taylor stood near the steps of the Pro Football Hall of Fame today and talked about being knocked down and about getting up, about honor, class, friendship and family. He talked about football. Giants football.

His son, Lawrence Jr., had presented him as a member of the Class of '99 — Taylor said those moments almost made him cry — and they stood together onstage in a long embrace, whispering into each other's ears an exchange meant only for father and son. A memory for both that will last a lifetime.

So it went for Taylor and for each of the inductees, an overflow of emotion and memories that will last forever, and bronze busts in their likeness placed in the Hall to last as long. Taylor, Eric Dickerson, Tom Mack, Ozzie Newsome and Billy Shaw pushed the number in the Hall of Fame to 199.

Taylor was the last among the five to be inducted, No. 199, and thus the last entrant of the 1900's. His number and name in the hearts of Giants fans, though, will always be No. 56 and L. T.

More than 300 Giants fans were here today, including the team owner Wellington Mara, who was inducted into the Hall last year. Giants fans filled an entire section in the upper tier of the crowd and were loud and bold in their blue and white.

"L. T.! L. T.! L. T.!" they chanted, all day long.

Taylor noticed.

"I was a little nervous before I came out," Taylor said, "but then I saw all that Giants stuff through the glass door and I knew I was in Giants territory. I think back; how did I get here?"

Others wondered, too. There was no denying his impact in pro football, a fearless linebacker who rushed the passer and pursued ballcarriers with venom and power and then delivered punishing tackles. Taylor was the key cog in two Giants Super Bowl championships, in 1987 and 1991. But his selection to the Hall was controversial to some because of his off-field problems since he retired from the Giants in 1993, including drug arrests and his admission of cocaine addiction.

Some Hall of Fame voters, all of whom are news media representatives, said he did not belong because his personal life had tarnished the game. Taylor criticized those voters, asking who they were to judge him. Because of that backdrop, many arrived today wondering what Taylor might say. There were fears that he might lash out and make a spectacle out of what was supposed to be a special day for all involved.

There was none of that.

"I do understand the game and how this is an honor," Taylor said.

He was humble. He was reflective. He talked about one of his teammates, a peer at linebacker, Harry Carson, who was in the crowd. Taylor and Carson "had some

Continued on Page 9

HARVEY ARATON

What is; what could have been: McGwire, Strawberry.

PAGE 3

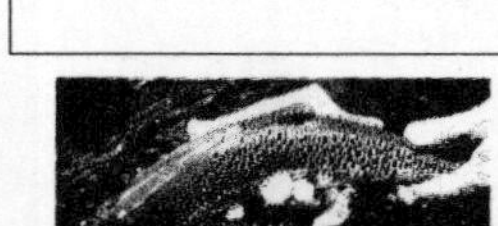

OUTDOORS

The best little trout town in the world (amenities not included).

PAGE 13

GEORGE VECSEY

When is it gamesmanship, and when is it cheating?

PAGE 13

ON THE WEB

Late coverage and scores are available from The New York Times on the Web:

www.nytimes.com/sports

The New York Times
Sunday, September 19, 1999
SportsSunday
L Section 8

Need a Hit? Ordóñez's Slam Lifts the Mets

Chang W. Lee/The New York Times

The Mets' Masato Yoshii pitched superbly last night, allowing one run on five hits in seven innings. He also knocked in two runs with this fifth-inning single.

Yoshii in Control as Braves' Lead Shrinks

By JUDY BATTISTA

Surely Bobby Valentine was looking down his bench last night, wondering who would replace the offense that was missing with Mike Piazza sitting in the clubhouse with a bag of ice on his swollen catching hand. Surely, Valentine's eyes skipped over Rey Ordóñez.

PHILLIES	1
METS	11

Ordóñez is the flashy member of the Mets' magnificent infield — sliding and tumbling to make one spectacular stop after another — but he has been less than eye-catching at the plate. He was batting .249 with 53 runs batted in entering the game. The biggest pop he has had this season was the one he took from Luis Lopez in a fight on the team bus.

But last night, with the Mets struggling for offense to support a superb pitching effort by Masato Yoshii, it was the diminutive shortstop who provided it. Ordóñez hit his first career grand slam — it was also his first home run of the season — and had three other hits in his five at-bats in leading the Mets to an 11-1 pummeling of the Phillies. Ordóñez's four runs batted in were a career high.

With Atlanta's loss to Montreal — the crowd at Shea cheered when the final score was posted — the Mets are again just one game back in the National League East, and they start a three-game series in Atlanta on Tuesday night. Cincinnati beat Pittsburgh to remain three games back in the wild-card race.

Ordóñez hit just one home run in each of his previous three seasons and all, like this one, came in September. But it is hard to imagine that the others were as dramatic. The Mets were leading by 6-1 when Ordóñez came to the plate in the sixth, but the Mets — who had looked half asleep in losing the first game of the series to the lowly Phillies — were clamoring for more than a cushion. They wanted an entire sofa of padding for this victory.

Yoshii had done all he could to insure the victory. Before last night's game, Valentine said that fans who have occasionally booed Piazza this season are "brain dead." You wonder what he now thinks about those who once hooted Yoshii off the mound.

They were probably the same people standing and roaring "Yos-hii! Yos-hii!" last night, as the once-scorned member of the Mets' rotation — his pitches had deteriorated so much that he was sent to the bullpen for almost two weeks — hit a two-run single in the fifth inning. The hit was a major boost for his outing, in which he allowed one run on five hits in seven innings.

Yoshii has been the Mets' best pitcher in the last

Continued on Page 3

BEANBALL DRAW, YANKEE LOSS

Omar Vizquel and Derek Jeter were the latest to be hit by pitches as Cleveland beat the Yankees, 5-4. Page 3.

It's 60 Times 2: Sosa Becomes First to Complete The Double Feat

By BILL DEDMAN

CHICAGO, Sept. 18 — As the Chicago Cubs took their places in the field for the seventh inning this afternoon at Wrigley Field, they were a one-man team When Sammy Sosa jogged out to right field, his teammates stayed in the dugout, allowing him the entire spotlight as the fans chanted, "Sammy! Sammy!"

Sosa had just become the first player in major league history to hit 60 home runs twice, leading off the bottom of the sixth with a blast to center field. He hit 66 last season. Only three other major league players have ever reached 60: Mark McGwire, who hit 70 last year; Roger Maris, who hit 61 in 1961; and Babe Ruth, who hit 60 in 1927.

And now Sosa has done it twice.

"Nobody was thinking I would have an opportunity, Mark and I, to do this again," Sosa said after the Cubs' 7-4 loss in 14 innings.

He added, "It made me proud of myself; of all the players to play this game, I'm the first to do it."

McGwire may yet get to 60 home runs again this season; he has 56 with 13 games to play. The feat was nearly accomplished another time by Ruth (59 in 1921) and by McGwire (58 in 1997).

Sosa's 60th came after he had gone seven games and 33 at-bats without a homer. He hit it on a 2-2 pitch, a split-finger fastball on the outside corner from Jason Bere, a 28-year-old right-hander for the Milwaukee Brewers. It landed an estimated 400 feet away, a line drive into the wire basket just beyond the brick and ivy in center field.

Sosa hopped in exultation as soon as he hit the ball and as he rounded first base he pointed to the heavens

Continued on Page 2

Reuters

Sammy Sosa watching his 60th home run of the season, a sixth-inning shot off Jason Bere.

Is There Some Vinny in Him?

Mirer Succeeds Testaverde as the Jets' Leader

By GERALD ESKENAZI

First of all, his name is pronounced Meyer — not Myra, or Myrer.

Second, Rick Mirer, who replaces the injured Vinny Testaverde as the Jets' quarterback tonight against the Bills at Buffalo, is no mini-Vinny.

The temptation is great for fans and members of the news media who cover the Jets — even for Coach Bill Parcells — to present the careers of the two quarterbacks as mirror images of each other.

"The situation is not unlike what happened to Vinny," Parcells told Mirer last month after obtaining him from the Green Bay Packers for an undetermined draft choice.

Parcells meant the up-and-mostly down career Mirer has had in the pros following high draft-pick status, record-breaking college years and schoolboy hero status. But Mirer is no Testaverde yet. Testaverde has led a National Football League team superbly through a near-championship season; Mirer has not.

For Parcells and the Jets, the unthinkable happened when Testaverde's season ended last Sunday against the Patriots with a torn Achilles' tendon. Now Mirer, who hasn't started since he was with the Bears two years ago, takes over. Despite his lack of accomplishment, he will start for a team that is better than any he has played for. Now, the deck no longer is stacked against him.

With the Packers last season, Mirer was a backup who never got into a game. He started three games for Chicago in 1997, which followed four seasons with Seattle. The Seahawks and Bears teams he actually played for had a combined record of 28-52. His career touchdowns total 41, his interceptions 64. He has never played

Continued on Page 9

The pressure is on Rick Mirer, playbook in hand, who thinks he will fit in well with the Jets' offense.

Barton Silverman/The New York Times

Penn State Wins On 79-Yard Pass With 1:41 to Play

By CHARLIE NOBLES

MIAMI, Sept. 18 — As Chafie Fields lined up for the play that ultimately would determine Penn State's fate today, the wide receiver made eye contact with quarterback Kevin Thompson.

"That's all it took — we knew it'd work," Fields said of his improbable 79-yard touchdown catch with 1 minute 41 seconds left that helped propel the Nittany Lions to a 27-23 victory over the University of Miami before 74,427 at the Orange Bowl.

PENN STATE	27
MIAMI	23

"I stay in coaching for games like this," Penn State's Joe Paterno said.

On the play, called a streak because Fields sprinted as far and as fast into the secondary as possible, Fields caught the ball over his right shoulder near the left sideline. He first wriggled free of cornerback Michael Rumph, then 15 yards later eluded the diving safety Edward Reed.

"I just stood there thinking, 'I can't believe this -- this is almost like a fairy tale,' " said Penn State offensive tackle John Blick, who quickly joined in the end-zone celebration.

It was Fields's second touchdown of the game. At the end of the first quarter, he caught a 49-yarder from the backup quarterback Rashard Casey.

Fields's catch came just when it appeared that Penn State would become Miami's latest victim at the Orange Bowl.

Through much of the second half, the visitors received a jolting idea of how Miami had been able to fashion 58 straight home victories, a National Colle-

Continued on Page 7

COLLEGE FOOTBALL

Michigan State	**23**	Central Mich.	16	Wisconsin	12
Notre Dame	13	**Purdue**	**58**	**Cincinnati**	**17**
So. Mississippi	13	**Louisiana Tech**	**29**	N.C. State	11
Nebraska	**20**	Alabama	28	**Florida State**	**42**

GOLF

The U.S. tries to reclaim pride in Ryder Cup.

PAGE 4

PRO FOOTBALL

Senate inquiry could shed light on drug policy.

PAGE 9

ON THE WEB

Late coverage and scores are available from The New York Times on the Web:

www.nytimes.com/sports

SPORTS ★ ★ ★ ★ FINAL

20-PAGE SERIES SPECIAL

DAILY NEWS

50¢ www.nydailynews.com NEW YORK'S HOMETOWN NEWSPAPER Thursday, October 28, 1999

TEAM OF THE CENTURY

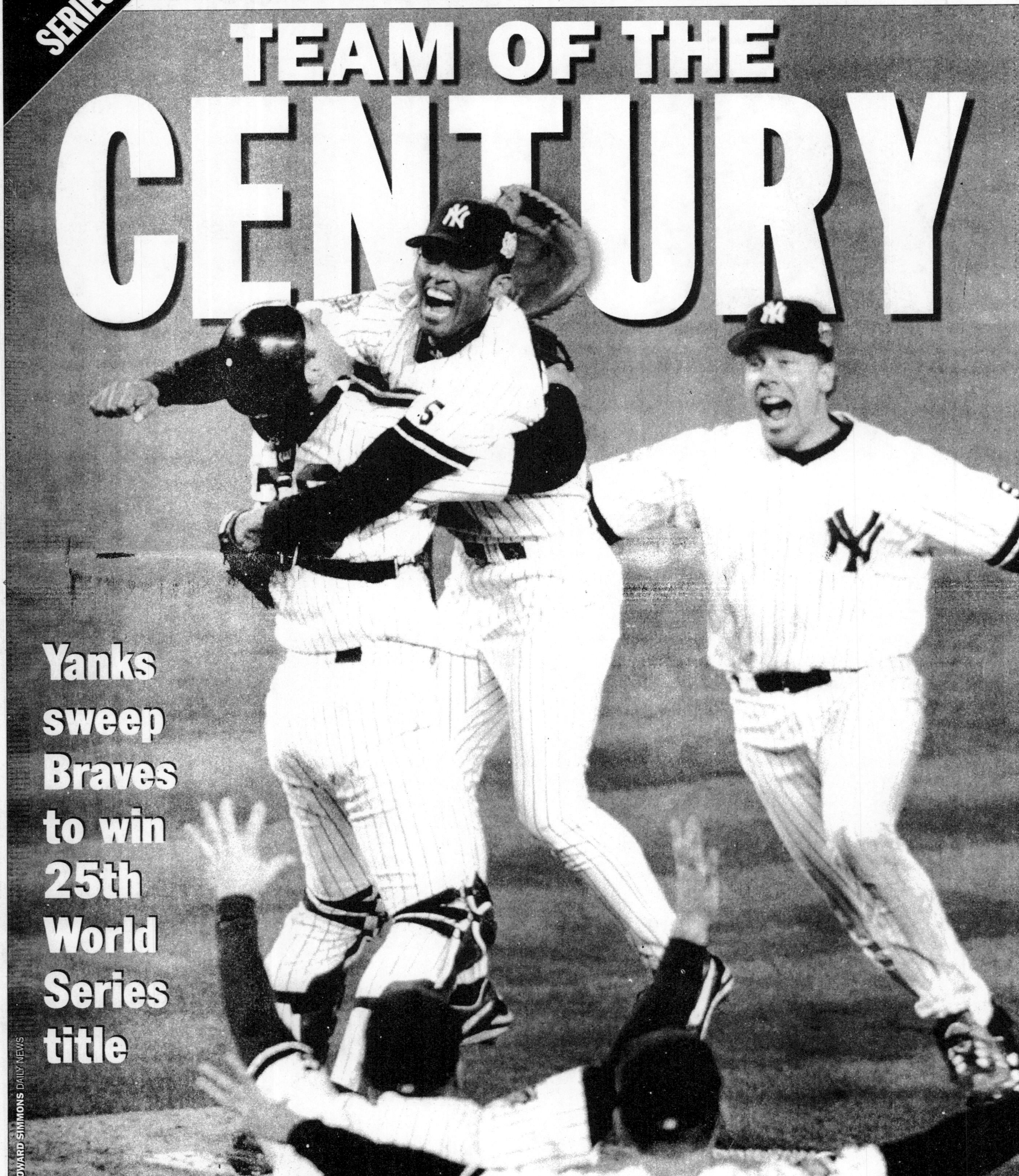

Yanks sweep Braves to win 25th World Series title

HOWARD SIMMONS DAILY NEWS

DAILY NEWS

0 26832 10001 5 03444